£55-25 pub

£42-50.

UNIVERSAL

PRONOUNCING DICTIONARY

OF

BIOGRAPHY

AND

MYTHOLOGY.

BY J. THOMAS, A.M., M.D.,

AUTHOR OF

THE SYSTEM OF PRONUNCIATION IN "LIPPINCOTT'S PRONOUNCING GAZETTEER OF THE WORLD,"
AND OF THE PRONOUNCING VOCABULARIES OF BIOGRAPHICAL AND GEOGRAPHICAL
NAMES IN "WEBSTER'S UNABRIDGED DICTIONARY."

VOL. I.

PHILADELPHIA:

J. B. LIPPINCOTT AND CO.

1870.

Entered according to Act of Congress, in the year 1870, by

J. B. LIPPINCOTT & CO.,

In the Clerk's Office of the District Court of the United States for the
Eastern District of Pennsylvania.

**Library of Congress
Cataloging in Publication Data**

Thomas, Joseph, 1811-1891.
    Universal pronouncing dictionary of biography
and mythology.

    Reprint of the 1870-71 ed. published by Lippin-
cott, Philadelphia.
    1. Biography. 2. Mythology--Dictionaries.
I. Title.
CT103.T46   1976   920'.02   79-167222
ISBN 0-8103-4221-9

PREFACE.

THE plan of the present work differs in several important respects from that of any other biographical dictionary which has yet been offered to the public. In its preparation the aim has been to produce a convenient and complete book of reference, both for Mythology and Biography,—one which in all essential respects should, if possible, be fully equal to the best biographical dictionaries in the language, and include, in addition, succinct notices of all the more important subjects of the Norse and Hindoo, as well as of Classic, Mythology, with THE CORRECT PRONUNCIATION of the various names. In order to accomplish these objects, and at the same time confine the work within reasonable limits, great attention has been given to the condensation as well as to the proper selection of the different articles. That the work, moreover, may combine, as far as practicable, completeness with brevity, to the more important notices have been added ample bibliographical references,* indicating to the reader the sources whence he can obtain the fullest information respecting any person in whom he may chance to feel a particular interest.

Among the peculiar features of the present work, that of the pronunciation of the names may justly claim the first place, both on account of its intrinsic importance, and because (so far as we are aware) this is the first time that anything of the kind has ever been attempted in any work on general biography.

The utility of such a feature (if thoroughly carried out) would seem to be too obvious to require any argument. Its great importance, however, can only be fully appreciated by those who—like teachers or public speakers—have learned by large experience the exceeding inconvenience arising from the want of a standard for the pronunciation of modern names.

In pronouncing modern proper names there are only three courses which can by any possibility be pursued: 1st. To blunder over or pronounce them at random, like a barbarian who should attempt to speak a language of which he knows nothing ; 2dly. To endeavour to pronounce all names, foreign as well as English, according to the principles of our own language, giving each letter its proper English sound ; or, lastly, To adopt the system of pronunciation now generally recognized by the more highly educated classes not only in England and America, but also in Germany and most other parts of Europe—that is, to pronounce all names, as nearly as possible, as they are pronounced by the well-educated people of the different countries to which such names belong, with the exception of those very few celebrated names, such as CALVIN, CERVANTES, GALILEO, LUTHER, NAPOLEON, PETRARCH, etc., which may be said to have acquired an established English pronunciation.

Respecting the first method—if method it can be called—we need not waste our own or the reader's time in pointing out its absurdity. As to the second, although at the first glance it may have an appearance of plausibility, we shall find, if we scan it attentively, that for all practical purposes it is little, if any, better than the first. A few examples will suffice to show the utter absurdity of attempting to pronounce foreign names according to the

---

* The only exceptions to this statement, of any consequence, will be found under the notices of living persons, of whom, generally speaking, there are either no published biographies or else such only as are very defective and unsatisfactory.

English sounds of the letters.* How, for example, should we pronounce the name of the celebrated German poet HEINE, according to such a system? Should the *ei* be sounded like *ee*, as in the English words *seize, ceiling*, etc.? or like long *a*, as in *vein, weight, inveigh?* or like long *i*, as in *height, sleight*, etc.? Should HEINE then be pronounced *heen, hān*, or *hīn?* or should we sound the final *e*, and make it *hee'ne, hā'ne*, or *hī'ne?* Or take, if you choose, another name, equally well or better known—that of SCHILLER. Now, the proper English sound of *sch* is *sk*, as in *school, scholar, schooner*, etc. We have no genuine English word in which *sch* has the sound of *sh*,† although we have some, as *schism, schismatic*, etc., in which it sounds like simple *s*. Yet would any one in his senses seriously advocate pronouncing the name of Germany's most popular poet either as *Skil'ler* or *Sil'ler ?* Innumerable instances, moreover, occur, in which it is very difficult, if not impossible, to pronounce the names of other countries according to the English sounds of the letters, as BJÖRNSON, CZAJKOWSKI, etc., although there is not the slightest difficulty in pronouncing them according to the sounds of the languages to which they belong. A multitude of instances also occur in which the English mode of pronouncing, though not difficult, would be far less euphonious than the native pronunciation. CAGLIARI (kȧl'yȧ-ree) and BORGOGNONE, (boR-gŏn-yo'nȧ,) two distinguished painters of Italy, and CARVALHO, (kaR-vȧl'yo,) a Portuguese bibliographer, may serve as examples. Another insuperable difficulty in the way of pronouncing many foreign names according to the sounds of our own tongue arises from the fact that in some languages the same sound is often represented by different letters. Thus, *oe* and *ö* in German are sounded precisely alike; hence, GOETHE and GÖTHE should clearly have the same pronunciation. Again, the Spanish *j* and *x* are, in sound, exactly equivalent to each other : therefore, CARAVAJAL and CARAVAXAL should be pronounced exactly alike. So also the Portuguese *ch* and *x*, having the same sound (that of our *sh*), were formerly often interchanged, as in the names XAVES or CHAVES,‡ XINGU or CHINGU, XOA or CHOA, (written in English, SHOA, etc.) Innumerable examples of this kind might be adduced. It must be obvious, even to the least intelligent mind, that the attempt to pronounce names so differently written according to the English sounds of the letters would lead to endless confusion.

The only rational course then left for us is to adopt the third method noticed above, and to pronounce modern names, as nearly as possible, as they are pronounced by the inhabitants of the respective countries to which such names belong. It is admitted that cases not unfrequently occur in which it is impossible to convey, with any great degree of precision, the pronunciation of foreign sounds by means of English letters; but something is undoubtedly gained by such an approximation to the true sound as would enable one more readily to understand, and to be understood by, those who are familiar with names as spoken in their proper tongue. Nor are the obstacles in the way of acquiring such a pronunciation nearly so great, even for the ordinary English scholar, as at first sight might appear. Take, for example, the various names which occur in the histories and biographies of modern Italy. In all the countless thousands of those names (whether of persons or places) there is not a single vowel or consonant sound which has not its exact equivalent, or something very near it, in our own language; and, consequently, not one which, *if properly explained*, an Englishman or American could not pronounce with ease. Though, to one unacquainted with the language, many of the names may have, when written, an uncouth and even formidable appearance, there is nothing uncouth or formidable in the sounds which they represent. Again, in the fifty thousand or more names of Spain and Spanish America there is only one sound (that of *j* or *x*) which presents any real difficulty to the English

---

* The celebrated Charles James Fox is said to have favoured such a system. It is probable, however, that he merely proposed to Anglicize the pronunciation of well-known foreign names somewhat more generally than is customary. He could hardly have intended to apply the principles of English pronunciation to *all* foreign names, without exception.

† All words of this kind, as *schist, schorl*, are clearly of foreign origin, and of *recent introduction* into our language.

‡ In old books instances of this kind are very frequent, but at present the Spaniards nearly always use *j*, (not *x*,) the Portuguese, *ch*, (not *x*,) except in a few words and names of foreign origin, and the Germans, *ö*, (not *oe*.) But, as the English and French still very frequently employ *x* for *j* in writing Spanish, so they generally make use of *oe* instead of *ö* in writing German names.

speaker, and this corresponds almost exactly to the sound of the German *ch* in such words as *ach*, *nach*, *doch*, etc. For those, therefore, who may have already acquired the elements of German pronunciation even this difficulty would be wholly removed. The names of Portugal or Portuguese America (Brazil) are scarcely more formidable than those of Italy. There is, indeed, only one sound * (that of *m* or *ão*) unknown to our language, and this is by no means difficult to acquire. So that by learning two foreign sounds an Englishman or American will be enabled, if the pronunciation be properly marked, to pronounce, with tolerable correctness, all the myriads of names belonging to Italy, Portugal, Spain, Brazil, and Spanish America. With regard to French, the case is, we admit, very different; but, as an offset to the inherent difficulties of this language, we have the fact that it is more universally studied than any other; so that if one is really desirous of mastering its peculiar sounds he will at least be pretty sure to find near at hand every needful aid for doing so.

Persons who view the different European languages separately are apt to regard the mastering of the difficult sounds in all as a far more formidable task than it really is. They forget that a large proportion of the most difficult sounds are common to several different languages. For example, the French and Dutch *u* is equivalent to the German and Hungarian *ü*, and to the Danish, Norwegian, and Swedish *y*. Here it will be seen that the same sound (and that one of the most difficult for an Englishman to acquire) occurs in seven different languages. Again, the German *ö* or *oe* is found in Hungarian, Danish, Norwegian, and Swedish, and nearly corresponds to one of the most difficult of the French and Dutch sounds, that of *eu* in the Dutch words *breuk*, *reuk*, or in the French *leur*, *peur*, etc. The German *ch*, as already remarked, corresponds almost exactly to the Spanish *j* or *x*, and is essentially the same as the modern Greek *χ*, the Russian *x*, the Polish, Scottish, and Welsh *ch*, and the Dutch *g*.†

The acquisition of ten or twelve new sounds, which might be learned by persons of ordinary aptitude in a few hours, would enable any one who can read correctly the pronunciation of English words, as marked in Walker's, Webster's, or Worcester's Dictionary, to pronounce with tolerable correctness all the names of Portugal, Spain, Italy, France, Belgium, Holland, Germany, Denmark, Norway, and (we might perhaps add) of Sweden, Russia, and Hungary.

In another part of the work will be given a full and particular explanation of the system of orthoëpy which has been adopted, and of the method pursued in order to insure the greatest attainable accuracy. It may, however, be proper to say here, that the author, fully sensible that the value of this most important feature (the pronunciation of the names) must depend almost entirely on the thoroughness and accuracy with which it is carried out, has spared neither time, labour, nor expense in order to render it as perfect as possible. Particular attention has been given to what may be termed the five principal languages of Continental Europe—namely, the Italian, French, German, Spanish, and Russian. In regard to the French especially, this being by far the most important of all, both on account of its being so widely spoken, and on account of the inherent difficulty of the sounds to be represented, the utmost pains have been taken not only to ascertain the correct pronunciation, but to mark it so fully and clearly that any intelligent person who has once acquired the elementary sounds of the language, and made himself acquainted with our system of notation, may pronounce with facility and with tolerable accuracy whatever name he may have occasion to speak. As already observed, the Italian, Spanish, and Portuguese names are comparatively easy for the English or American learner. Those of Germany are not very formidable, for although the German vowel sounds are more difficult than the Italian, the similarity of accent that exists between the German and our own tongue is an important help to us in acquiring the correct German pronunciation. Of the five languages above named, the Russian is undoubtedly the most difficult; but in overcoming the essential diffi-

---

* There are one or two other sounds, such as the diphthongs *ou* and *ei*, (or *ey*,) which, though having no exact equivalent in English, yet differ so slightly from some of our sounds, and, we may add, are so easy to acquire, that for practical purposes they may be said to form no exception to the above statement.

† The same sound occurs in Arabic and Persian, besides many other languages.

culties of the language, the author has had the assistance of some of the best Russian scholars in Europe; and he has reason to hope that the pronunciation of the Russian names contained in this work will be found not only generally correct in regard to the accent, (perhaps the most important point of all,) but sufficiently accurate in other respects for all practical purposes.

As the Russian Empire unites Asia with Europe, so the language of Russia may be said to form, in one sense, the connecting link between the Oriental and European tongues. The names belonging to the other languages of Europe are all written either with Roman letters, or in characters, like the German and modern Greek, which can readily be converted into corresponding Roman letters; and the mode of writing such names is, with very few exceptions, the same in all the various European languages; for example, MAZZINI, the name of the renowned Italian patriot, is not only the Italian, but the English, French, German, Dutch, Danish, Swedish, and Spanish name of the same person; in like manner, the name of the celebrated French philosopher, DESCARTES, will be found to be invariably written with the same letters in all the modern languages of Western and Southern Europe; so also the name of SCHILLER, the illustrious German poet, is spelled alike in Italian, French, Spanish, German, etc.; for though in the last-named language it is usually (but by no means universally) written in German characters, (Schiller,) yet as these exactly correspond to the Roman letters usually employed in spelling the name, the difference is only apparent, not essential. Russian names, on the contrary—as they (like all Oriental names) are neither written in Roman letters nor in characters which can be converted into corresponding Roman letters— are spelled ACCORDING TO THE SOUND, the writers of the different nations seeking to indicate the pronunciation of the name in the manner which to them seems most proper. Thus the name of one of the most distinguished Russian poets is written in English DERZHAVIN, in French DERJAVINE, and in German DERSCHAWIN, each spelling being intended to represent the sound of the name according to the different languages; so likewise the name of another celebrated Russian poet is written in English POOSHKIN or PUSHKIN, in French POUCHKINE or POUCHEKINE, and in German PUSCHKIN; each of these different modes being intended to represent exactly the same pronunciation. It is curious to observe that the Russians adopt precisely the same rule in writing foreign names; that is, they spell them (with a few exceptions) according to the sound, without attempting to follow the letters of the original spelling; thus, they would write *Bordo* for Bordeaux, *Dzhonson** for Johnson, *Davoo* for DAVOUST, *Roosso* for ROUSSEAU, *Chimaroza*† for CIMAROSA, *Chartoriskee‡* for CZARTORYSKI, etc.; in the same manner as a Frenchman might write *Ouachintonn* for WASHINGTON, (as Volney§ actually does,) *Chéquespir* for SHAKESPEARE, and so on. (See "Reiff's Russian Grammar," pp. 167, 168.)

There is perhaps no branch of pronunciation attended with so many difficulties as that of Oriental names. One great source of perplexity arises from there being in our language no uniform and established system for writing such names. French and German writers, for the most part, adhere pretty strictly to the rule referred to above—that is, they try to represent as nearly as possible the sound of the name in their own language. The French write the name of the celebrated Mongol conqueror of the thirteenth century, DJENGUIS, or DJENGUYZ. The Germans write it DSCHENGIS; and both give the sound of the name, as nearly as it can be done, in their own tongue. The French have no other way of representing the sound of our *j* (a very common sound in the Oriental languages) than by *Dj* or *Dg*. The Germans represent the same sound in the best way they can, but very imperfectly, by *Dsch*. In the second syllable of the above name the French use *u* after *g*, to make this consonant hard before *e*, *i*, or *y*. If the *u* were omitted, the *g* (being before *e*) must necessarily, according to

---

* They have no single letter to represent our *j*, but one which is exactly equivalent to our *zh*.

† They represent the sound of our *ch* by a single character, Ч.

‡ As we are unable to give the Russian letters, we give the nearest equivalent.

§ See Volney's "Tableau du Climat et du Sol des États-Unis d'Amérique," (2 vols., Paris, 1803,) where the reader will also find WAYNE spelled *Ouayne;* WILLIAMS written *Ouilliams;* RUSH, (Dr.,) *Roche;* GREEN BRIER, *Grîne-braïar;* WORCESTER, *Ouorcester*, etc.

rules of the French tongue, have the sound of their *j* or our *zh*. But in German, as *g* is always hard, they need use only the simplest form, (*gis.*) The sound of the name, however. is represented much more simply and more perfectly in English by Jengis or Jengiz. Again : the name of a celebrated Sultan of Syria and Egypt is written in French, Nour-ed-Din Mahmoud, in German, Nur-ed-Din-Mahmud, and would be written in English, Noor-ed-Deen-Mahmood. It should be observed that the French make no attempt to conform to the German spelling, nor the Germans to the French ; but both nations adhere very generally to the principles of their respective languages. Unfortunately, a large majority of English writers, instead of conforming to a rule which has the double merit of being (in most instances) simple and easy for the writer and perfectly intelligible to the reader, by sometimes writing in the French and sometimes in the German or Italian mode, and not very unfre-quently combining the two in the same name, have involved the department of Oriental names in a confusion which is most perplexing to all, and is absolutely inextricable to those who have not made it the subject of long and laborious study.*

Even if the mode of writing Oriental names according to the French and German letters were equally intelligible to ordinary readers as the English mode, there would still be one paramount argument in favour of the last—viz. : the letters of our language are capable of conveniently expressing or representing a greater variety of sounds than those of any other European tongue. There is no sound much used either in Oriental or Russian names which we cannot express as well as the French ; while there are several which we can express much better than they ; and there are sounds perfectly familiar to our tongue which they cannot express at all. Take, for example, the sound of our *j*, (which, as already intimated, is of very frequent occurrence in Asiatic names :) what we express by a single letter is indicated less perfectly in their language by two—*dj*. So also the sound of our *ch*, one of continual occur-rence both in the names of Asia and of Eastern Europe, is indicated in French by three letters instead of our two, as *Tchandra* for Chandra, etc. It may be remarked that this sound, as well as that of *j*, is one of the most common and familiar to the English tongue, while both are foreign to the French language, since neither of them is to be found in any genuine French word. Again : our *w* expresses a sound (common in the Oriental languages) which is not nearly so neatly nor so well expressed by the French *ou*. This defect in their language is so obvious that some eminent French writers (Pauthier, for example, in his works on China) often make use of *w* when they wish to represent the sound of our *w* at the begin-ning of a name ; *e.g.*, Wen Wang—not Ouen Ouang, as the strictly French mode of writing would require. Lastly, there are sounds expressed in our language with perfect ease which they cannot represent at all ; among them are the sounds of the Greek *θ* (th) and *δ*, (th ;) the first of these is of frequent occurrence, not only in modern Greek, but in Spanish names.

With respect to the German language, there is, if we mistake not, but one frequently-occurring sound in Oriental names (that of *kh*, indicated in German by *ch*) which can be better represented in German than in English, while there are many which can not only be more conveniently expressed in English, but much more correctly than in German. Thus, the Germans employ four letters (*dsch*) to indicate the sound of our *j*, and after all represent it most imperfectly, as in the example of Dschengis, (Jengis,) noticed above. Their four letters, *tsch*, do not represent correctly the sound of our *ch*, nor does their *sch* convey even a tolerable idea of our *zh*, (the sound of *s* in *pleasure* or *occasion*.) Like the French, they have no letter or combination of letters equivalent to our *w*, nor can they in any manner represent the sound of the modern Greek *θ* or *δ*.

One mode of writing Oriental names, which has been recommended by several eminent scholars, is to employ English consonants in conjunction with German or Italian vowels, marked with certain accents in order to show their quantity or quality. Thus, *a* without the accent represents the Italian *a* either short or obscure, *á* or *â* denotes the long Italian *a*, as in

---

* One great cause of this confusion undoubtedly arises from the fact that many English writers, in attempting to translate works from the German and French, fail to translate the names. But such an omission could scarcely occur if there was any generally-recognized system of writing such names.

father, often approaching the sound of *a* in *fall; e* as in *met* or *her; é* or *è* as in *fête* or *there; i* as in *pin; î* or *i* as in *marine; o* nearly as in *opinion; ó* or *ô* as in *hope; u* as in *push* or *pull; ú* or *ú* like *oo* in *moon.* This method has the merit of combining brevity with precision, and is well adapted to publications designed chiefly for the use of scholars; but there are serious, if not insuperable, objections to its general employment in English works intended for popular perusal. While such works are printed under the immediate superintendence of some competent linguist, they may, perhaps, answer every needful purpose; but as soon as they get into general and popular use, and require to be reprinted, the accents, as all experience proves, will be dropped either through carelessness on the part of the printer, or, what is more likely to occur, from a want of the proper kind of type. And let it be remembered that the omission of the proper accent in such a case is equivalent to the omission of a letter, with this great disadvantage, that the former error would be much less likely to attract attention, and would therefore be less readily corrected.

Those accustomed to the study of languages can scarcely conceive the difficulty which the unlearned experience in attempting to pronounce for the first time the letters of a foreign tongue. Readers of this class would be almost sure to miscall such names as NUREDDIN or NOUREDDIN, ABDUL MEJID or ABDOUL MEDJID, and a multitude of others, while they could pronounce them without the slightest difficulty if written according to the English sounds of the letters—NOOR-ED-DEEN, ABDOOL MEJEED, etc. We admit that there are many names which, in order to give a correct idea of their pronunciation, would require some additional explanation besides merely writing them with English letters. But in a realm where the intricacies are so perplexing and the obstacles so formidable as often to bewilder and discourage the most intelligent, it is certainly no unworthy or useless task to attempt to do all that can be done to smooth and straighten the paths and to remove every unnecessary obstruction.

The rule adopted in the present work has been to give various spellings of every celebrated Oriental name, whenever these spellings appeared to be sanctioned by any good authority; the biographical notice being given under the English spelling, which is placed first in order.* Thus, in the name above cited, the English NOOR-ED-DEEN MAHMOOD is given first, to which are added the French NOUREDDIN (or NOUR-ED-DYN) MAHMOUD, and the German NUREDDIN MAHMUD. So, also, the notice of the great Mongol conqueror, referred to above, is given under the English spelling JENGIS, this being followed not only by the French and German forms, (DJENGUIZ and DSCHENGIS,) but by many others, it being the rare fortune of this famous name to be written by respectable authorities in no fewer than TWENTY different modes. In the proper alphabetical place of each of these different spellings will be found a reference to that form of the name under which the biographical notice is given. The only exceptions to the rule above indicated are those very few names which appear to have acquired by universal (or almost universal) usage an established form common to the different European languages; as AVICENNA, (changed from *Ibn-Seenâ,*) AVENZOAR, (*Ibn-Zohr,*) AVERROES, (*Ibn-Roshd,*) ELMACIN, (*El-Makeen* or *El-Makîn,*) SALADIN, (*Sala-ed-Deen* or *Sala-eddîn,*) SOLYMAN, (of Turkey, *Sooleymân,*) etc.

The confusion which prevails in regard to the spelling of Oriental names is not, however, the only cause of the difficulties with which this subject is surrounded. The character of the Oriental languages, so different in many respects from those with which we are most familiar, renders it often exceedingly difficult to indicate the pronunciation in a manner satisfactory to the English reader. In order that he might, as far as possible, enjoy every needful facility and aid in encountering the difficulties in question, the author deemed it necessary that he

---

* The only exception to this rule of any importance will be found in Mythological and other names from the Sanscrit, which, like the Greek and Latin, may be regarded as a dead language; the names occurring in it, written according to the system established by Sir William Jones, (see page vii., near the bottom,) are pronounced according to the *spelling* rather than the (modern) *sound* of the letters. At the same time, the modern Hindoo pronunciation, when this appears to differ essentially from the pronunciation first given, has usually been added. For illustration, see the articles on AGNI, BRAHMA, GARUDA, etc.

should have some knowledge of those tongues besides what books alone could furnish. He accordingly spent nearly two years in the East in studying the rudiments of several Asiatic languages, (with particular reference to their pronunciation,) including the Arabic, Persian, Sanscrit, and Hindostanee. The time and labour thus bestowed, he feels persuaded, have not been spent in vain. He has, in consequence of this preparation, not only been enabled to proceed with a surer step in representing the pronunciation of Asiatic and African names, but he has also in many instances, by referring to the name as written in Arabic or Sanscrit, been enabled to correct errors of greater or less importance in the prevalent European spellings of Oriental names.

Respecting the bibliographical references, it may be proper to remark that they are intended not so much to indicate the materials from which the preceding notice has been prepared, as to point out to the reader the sources whence he can obtain fuller information. The works referred to will be found generally, but not always, to contain all the materials used in the composition of the article to which the references are appended. Occasionally an isolated fact or circumstance of minor importance, but yet of sufficient interest to make it worth stating, may have been obtained from some source deemed good authority, to which, nevertheless, our plan, requiring the utmost condensation, would not admit of a special reference. Many of our facts, moreover, have been taken from the " Biographie Universelle," the " Nouvelle Biographie Générale," BROCKHAUS's " Conversations-Lexikon," or other similar works, when the article from which it is taken was too brief to make it worth while to refer to it particularly. As a general rule, it has not been deemed expedient to make a special reference to works like the above, unless the notice referred to extended to a page or more. This rule would, of course, preclude a reference in nearly all cases in which the subject of our notice is of minor importance. It would, however, be an error to infer that the omission of all references is intended as any indication of mediocrity in the subjects of our articles, more especially in regard to living characters, since, as has been already intimated, the materials for the biographies of living persons, however distinguished, are often extremely meagre and defective. Nor would it be just to conclude that in all cases the length of the different notices is designed to be a measure of the relative importance of the individuals noticed, since he who has written many passable works may perhaps require a longer notice than he who has produced a single work of superior merit. Other things being equal, the man of action will almost of necessity occupy much more space than the man of thought, although the latter may have perhaps far juster claims upon the esteem and gratitude of mankind, and his glory may be as much more permanent as it is less dazzling, and less fitted to win the admiration of the unthinking and fickle multitude.

It may be observed also that considerably less space, relatively speaking, has generally been allotted to living persons than to those who are deceased ; not merely because it is often much more difficult to obtain the necessary information in regard to the living, but more especially because it behooves us to speak with great circumspection, whether in the way of praise or censure, of those whose earthly career is still unfinished, and whose future conduct may possibly redeem the errors or throw discredit on the virtues of their past life.*

The subjects of the Hindoo and Norse Mythologies have been treated somewhat more fully in proportion to their relative importance than those of Classic Mythology, for the simple reason that while one can find almost everywhere excellent works relating to the last, there exists scarcely any book of convenient reference to which the ordinary reader can have recourse in order to satisfy his curiosity respecting the two former.

With respect to the relative length of the various articles there will of course be considerable diversity of opinion among different readers, according to their respective pursuits and habits of thought. We are not, however, without hopes that the majority of candid

---

* Voltaire has well remarked : " On doit des égards aux vivants ; on ne doit aux morts que la vérité"—(" We owe consideration to the living ; to the dead we owe only truth.") This consideration for the living was, indeed, formerly deemed so important that, until the last half century, all works of reference of this kind systematically excluded the biographies of living persons, however illustrious ; thus rejecting the very class in which perhaps a large majority of readers feel the deepest interest.

I

critics will admit that on the whole the space allotted to each notice has been apportioned with a fair measure of justice and impartiality. Those who are familiar with works of this kind cannot fail to have remarked that certain principles of perspective, so to speak, prevail in history and biography as well as in the arts of design. No French historian or biographer would treat the events or the actors of English history with the same fulness or minuteness that an English writer would naturally employ in describing the same occurrences or persons. The same general remark, *mutatis mutandis*, will apply with equal truth to English, German, or Italian writers of history and biography. As events are magnified in importance by nearness of place, they are in like manner modified by nearness of time. Although the author of the present work has felt himself justified in following principles so universally recognized, and has accordingly given a greater prominence to the distinguished men of his own country, and to those of recent times, than to individuals equally eminent among other nations or living in a remote age, it has been his earnest aim not to allow this liberty to degenerate into license. In regard to this and all similar questions respecting which there are no clearly defined rules or authoritative precedents by which his course could be surely guided, he feels that he may safely rely on the candour and intelligence of his critics, since those whose opinion is most to be valued or feared will be most capable of appreciating the inherent difficulties as well as the extraordinary labour involved in the preparation of such a work.

To the following works on general biography we have been under especial obligations in the preparation of this Dictionary :

1. MICHAUD'S "Biographie Universelle," of which the first edition, (the publication of which was begun in Paris in 1810,) with the supplement, has extended to nearly ninety volumes 8vo, and has included among its contributors many of the most distinguished names in French literature and science; *e.g.*, those of BIOT, CUVIER, DE SACY, GUIZOT, SISMONDI, Madame DE STAËL, VILLEMAIN, etc.

2. The "Nouvelle Biographie Générale," edited by Dr. J. C. F. HOEFER, and published at Paris by Messrs. F. DIDOT Frères in forty-six volumes 8vo, (1857–1866.) This is one of the most valuable works on general biography to be found in any language. That portion embracing the first twelve letters of the alphabet (*i.e.*, from A to M, inclusive) exceeds in completeness every other publication of the kind of which we have any knowledge. If inferior to the "Biographie Universelle" in the length and fulness of many of the memoirs, it greatly surpasses that work in the number of its biographical notices; and it possesses two important additional recommendations—first, of including the living as well as the dead, and, secondly, of giving the reader valuable bibliographic information under almost every article.

3. BROCKHAUS'S "Conversations-Lexikon," in 16 volumes large 8vo, (Leipsic, 1851–1855,) which is especially full in regard to the distinguished men of the present century, and particularly those of Germany; also the annual continuation of that work, entitled "Jahrbuch zum Conversations-Lexikon."

4. PIERER'S "Universal-Lexikon," in 19 volumes, fourth (last) edition, greatly enlarged, (Altenburg, 1857–1865.)

5. VAPEREAU'S "Dictionnaire des Contemporains," (1858 *et seq.*,) important for the information it gives respecting living persons.

6. ERSCH und GRUBER, "Allgemeine Encyclopädie der Wissenschaften und Künste," 145 vols. 4to, (Leipsic, 1818–1869.) This great work has numbered among its contributors several of the most eminent literary and scientific men of Germany.

Nor must we omit to notice, among the important works of general reference, the "Critical Dictionary of English Literature and British and American Authors," by S. AUSTIN ALLIBONE, to be completed in three volumes imperial 8vo, of which two volumes (1858–1870, pp. 2326) have already appeared; and the "Dictionary of the United States Congress and the General Government, compiled as a Book of Reference for the American People," by CHARLES LANMAN, (6th edition, 1869.)

As this Dictionary of Biography and Mythology, comprising, as it does, distinguished individuals of all ages and countries, must of necessity be extremely brief in regard to a large majority of the notices, and especially those of persons belonging to foreign countries, and as our plan does not admit of special bibliographical references, except under the more important articles, it may not be without use to refer the reader to the following works on NATIONAL biography:

In relation to the distinguished men of Denmark, Norway, etc., see KRAFT og NYERUP, "Almindeligt Litteraturlexicon for Danmark, Norge og Island," (Copenhagen, 2 vols. 4to, 1820;) and T. H. ERSLEW, "Almindeligt Forfatter-Lexicon fra 1814 til nær værende Tid," (Copenhagen, 3 vols. 8vo, 1843–1853,) with a supplement extending to 1864, (2 vols.)

For Holland.—See A. J. VAN DER AA, "Biographisch Woordenboek der Nederlanden," (2 vols., 1852–1855.)

For Italy.—G. M. MAZZUCHELLI, "Gli Scrittori d' Italia, cioe Notizie storiche e critiche intorno alle Vite e agli Scritti dei Letterati Italiani," (6 vols., 1753–1763; a work of great merit, but unfortunately not extending beyond the first two letters of the alphabet;) E. DE TIPALDO, "Biografia degli Italiani illustri nelle Scienze, Lettere ed Arte del Secolo XVIII. e de' Contemporanei," (10 vols. 8vo, 1835–1847;) G. TIRABOSCHI "Storia della Letteratura Italiana," (20 vols. 8vo, 1805–1813.)

For Portugal.—D. BARBOSA MACHADO, "Bibliotheca Lusitana na qual se comprehende a Noticia dos Authores Portuguezes e das Obras que compuserão," (4 vols. fol., 1741–1759.)

For Spain.—N. ANTONIO, "Bibliotheca Hispana sive Hispanorum qui usquam unquamve seu Latina seu populari, seu alia quavis Lingua scripto aliquid consignaverunt, Notitia," (2 vols. fol., 1672,) and "Bibliotheca Hispana Nova," (2 vols. fol., 1783–1788.) To which may be added CEAN-BERMUDEZ' "Diccionario Historico de los mas ilustres Professores de las bellas Artes en España," (6 vols. small 8vo, 1800.)

For Sweden.—GEORG GEZELIUS, "Försök til et biographiskt Lexicon öfver namnkunnige och lärde Svenska Män" (3 vols. 8vo, 1776–1778,) and supplement, (2 vols. 8vo, 1780;) and a more recent work, of great value, (edited chiefly by W. F. Palmblad,) entitled "Biographiskt Lexicon öfver namnkunnige Svenska Män," extending to 23 vols. 8vo; the publication of which was begun at Upsal in 1835, and was afterwards continued at Oerebro, (1856;) and a sequel to the same, in 5 vols. (Oerebro, 1857–1864.)

We cannot conclude without expressing our grateful acknowledgments to our numerous friends, both in this city and in other parts of the United States, not merely for valuable information of various kinds, but still more for the generous words of encouragement which we have received from them during our long and arduous labours. We feel confident that this general expression of our gratitude will be more acceptable to most of them than a more particular and open acknowledgment of their disinterested kindness.

But there are those whose claims are so important that justice to the public, if not to them and to ourselves, demands a more explicit statement of the nature of our obligations. To Mr. William Jacobs, our almost constant collaborator for more than ten years, our acknowledgments are pre-eminently due for his conscientious fidelity, no less than for his untiring diligence and well-directed research, to which must be ascribed in no small measure whatever of accuracy or thoroughness our work may possess. To his pen we owe not only a multitude of the minor notices, but no inconsiderable number of the more important articles, among which may be mentioned those on CICERO, MILTON, NEWTON, LA FAYETTE, HAMILTON, (Alexander,) and NAPOLEON III.

Justice and gratitude alike require that we should acknowledge our great obligations to Professor Edward H. Magill,* of Swarthmore College, for ascertaining, during his recent visit to Europe, the correct pronunciation of a multitude of difficult or doubtful names in the French, Italian, and Russian languages. He performed this important task not merely with the ability of a skilful linguist, but with a conscientious thoroughness and accuracy which can

---

* Known to the public as the author of a series of excellent elementary books on the French language.

only be fully appreciated by those who know by experience the peculiar difficulties attending researches of this kind.

We gladly avail ourselves of this opportunity to express our heartfelt thanks to the Rev. Charles P. Krauth, D.D., for many important favours, the value of which has been trebly enhanced by the spirit of truest kindness and generosity in which they have been bestowed. To cite one example out of many, he has placed at our entire disposal the contents of a library which, for the number of its volumes, and more especially for the rarity of many of its books, is surpassed by few, if any, private libraries in the United States.

Nor must we omit to mention our important obligations to Daniel B. Smith, of Germantown, to whose friendly sympathy and encouragement, enjoyed through a series of years, no less than to his judicious suggestions and valuable counsel, which his extensive and varied learning so eminently qualifies him to impart, we are more deeply indebted than any words of ours can express.

To Mr. James S. Lippincott, of Haddonfield, so well known through his important contributions to climatology and other kindred branches of science, our warmest thanks are due for much accurate and valuable information relating to a great variety of subjects.

Justice requires that we should not withhold the acknowledgment of our great obligations to Mr. Joseph McCreery, our accomplished proof-reader, to whose intelligence and judgment as a critic we are scarcely less indebted than to the remarkable fidelity and accuracy with which he habitually performs the duties of his office.

Nor can we omit the expression of our heartfelt gratitude to Mr. Rudolf Blankenburg for the aid he has rendered us in regard to the pronunciation of German names, and for other important assistance in the prosecution of our arduous labours.

With sincere pleasure we embrace this opportunity to express our cordial thanks to Mr. Lloyd P. Smith, the librarian of the Philadelphia Library, to whose extensive knowledge of books, as well as to his unfailing courtesy and kindness in aiding our researches, we are under especial obligations.

We should do injustice to our own feelings did we not acknowledge our great indebtedness to Mr. William A. Wheeler, of Boston, for a variety of interesting information in regard to the pronunciation of difficult or doubtful names, to which his rare skill in questions of orthoëpy has added a double value.

Nor can we withhold the acknowledgment of our heartfelt obligations to the Trustees and Superintendent of the Boston Public Library, for their liberality in affording us every possible facility for availing ourselves of the rich literary treasures of an institution, no less remarkable for the endless variety and value of its works, than for the liberal and enlightened spirit which presides over its administration.

J. THOMAS.

PHILADELPHIA, June, 1870.

INTRODUCTION.

We have already in our Preface spoken in general terms of the system of pronunciation and orthography adopted in the present work.   It is proposed in this introductory portion to offer, in support of the plan that we have thought proper to pursue, some additional arguments and observations, which will be followed by an explanation of the general principles of pronunciation of each of the more important European and Asiatic languages.

It is interesting to observe that the practice of nearly all our distinguished poets, but more particularly of those of the present century, goes to support the system of pronunciation which we have adopted; that is, they almost invariably follow the native accentuation of proper names,—even where this is very irregular,—except in the case of those few well-known names which have acquired an established English pronunciation, as CAL-VIN, CORTEZ, KOSCIUSKO, etc. As the principles of geographical pronunciation are precisely the same as those of the names of persons, and as geographical names very often form a part either of the surnames or titles of distinguished men, we may without impropriety cite, in order to prove our position, either the names of places or of persons occurring in the works of the poets. It is indeed the more necessary that we should be allowed the liberty of doing so, since names of *irregular* accentuation are, comparatively speaking, of rare occurrence. We have spoken particularly of *accentuation*, because, in a large majority of cases, that is all that can be determined from the usage of the poets. It is scarcely necessary to remind the classical reader that the misaccentuation of Latin or Greek names is justly considered an inexcusable fault in an educated poet. We will endeavour to show that our best poets are not less punctilious in the pronunciation of modern names. That they should accentuate correctly such names as GRANADA, BOLOGNA, RAVENNA, etc. is nothing surprising, since the easiest and most natural accentuation is also the correct one ; but that they should be scrupulously exact in the pronunciation of names in which the accent is placed irregularly, is more remarkable. It may be affirmed without fear of contradiction that in all the poetry of BYRON, MOORE, ROGERS, SOUTHEY, SCOTT—and, we may perhaps add, of any other distinguished poet of the present century—scarcely a solitary instance can be pointed out of the misaccentuation of a name of which the poet had any opportunity of knowing the correct pronunciation.*

True, SCOTT says "Panáma ;" but, at the time when he wrote, very few persons, even in the United States, were acquainted with the correct accentuation of that name. Some of our old poets also mispronounced Niagara. GOLDSMITH says,

> "Where wild Oswego spreads her swamps around,
> And NIAGÁRA stuns with thund'ring sound."†
> *The Traveller.*

But this is to be explained simply by the fact that he had no means of learning the true pronunciation, and therefore he accentuated the name in the manner which appeared to him the most easy or most natural. It is worthy of remark that the only English poet of note who had an opportunity of ascertaining the true pronunciation of the name of the great cataract is the only one (so far as we are aware) who has pronounced that name correctly. We have heard it asserted that MOORE also, using a "poet's license," has placed the accent on the penultima ; but any one, we feel sure, who will read his verse attentively, will see that he always gives the correct pronunciation.   The name occurs several times in his poems, but the following passage shows his accentuation so clearly as to leave no room for doubt or equivocation :

> "I could fancy almost he and I were a pair
> Of unhappy young lovers, who thus, side by side,
> Were taking, instead of rope, pistol, or *dagger, a*
> Desperate dash down the falls of *Niagara.*"
> *Fudge Family in Paris*, Letter V.

The following are a few examples illustrating the usage of eminent English poets respecting foreign names of irregular accentuation :

> "Lerma 'the generous,' AV'ILA ' the proud.' "
> ROGERS: *Voyage of Columbus.*

> "So acted to the life, as Maurice might
> And SPÍNOLA have blushéd at the sight."
> BEN JONSON: *Underwoods,*
> (vol. viii. p. 427 of Gifford's edition, London, 1816.)

MILÁNO or MILÁN,) TYR'OL, (Ger. TYRÓL,) etc. HANOVER, which might be pronounced with the native accentuation (HANÓVER) without the slightest offence to the genius of our tongue, (for we have a multitude of words similar in accent, as *devotion, promoter,* etc.,) has become irrecoverably HAN'OVER. Thus, also, we pronounce ANDALU'SIA, (in Spanish, ANDALUCÍA,) AR'AGON, (in Spanish, ARA-GŌN',) etc.

† Many persons suppose that Niagara corresponds in accentuation with the old Indian name : but this, we have reason to believe, is an error: the Indians pronounce the name very much as the French pronounce it,—Ne'ä'gä'rä'.

* The only exception to this rule, if we mistake not, occurs in French names, which, as the accent rests equally (or nearly so) on all the syllables, cannot readily be adjusted to the metre of English verse, in which case the poet usually places the accent according to the general rule of English pronunciation,—that is, on the penultima or antepenultima, very rarely on the last syllable.   In the pronunciation of foreign names that have become thoroughly anglicized, it is interesting to observe the tendency of our language to throw the accent as far as possible from the termination: *e.g.* MIL'AN, (It.

5

" And strangers were received by thee,
Of Córdova the chivalry."

BYRON: *Translation of a Spanish Ballad
on the Conquest of Alhama.*

" The regal seat
Of Abdalazis, ancient Córdoba."

" Till they saw
The temples and the towers of Córdoba
Shining majestic in the light of eve."

SOUTHEY: *Roderick,* book v.

" How quick they carved their victims, and how well,
Let Saxony, let injured Génoa tell."

MOORE.

" Remember the moment when Prévesa fell,
The shrieks of the conquered, the conquerors' yell."

BYRON: *Childe Harold,* canto ii.

" Unseen is Yánina, though not remote."

Childe Harold, canto ii.

There is, perhaps, no class of names whose accentuation seems more foreign to an English ear than those ending in *ia* with the accent on the penultima. Yet even in such cases the poets conform to the native pronunciation :

" Sustained by thoughts like these, from morn till eve
He journeyed, and drew near Levría's walls."

SOUTHEY: *Roderick,* book iii.

" And now appear, as on a phosphor sea,
Numberless barks from Mil'an, from Pavía."

ROGERS: *Italy,* Part i., vii.

Among the principal languages of continental Europe, the German, in its accent and in the metre of its verse, has perhaps the nearest affinity to the English ; and it is worthy of remark that precisely the same general usage prevails with respect to foreign names in German poetry as in that of our own tongue. Any one may satisfy himself of the correctness of this statement if he will consult the poems of Schiller, who seems to have had occasion to use foreign names far more frequently than almost any other German poet. In his drama of " Don Carlos," MADRID occurs nearly twenty times, and *always* with the accent on the last syllable. This one fact (even were there no other) may show how sparingly the " poetical license," so often alluded to, is used by perhaps the most careless in versification of all the great poets of Germany. MIRANDOLA (a town in Italy) occurs twice, and in both instances has the accent on the antepenultima :

" Zwei edle Häuser in Mirándola."
" Eilt nach Mirándola der Trunkene."

Act i. Scene 3.

This is the more remarkable because MIRANDOLA is an exception to the general rule of Italian pronunciation, which places the accent on the penultima of words ending in a vowel.

The name of the famous Princess of EBOLI occurs a great number of times, and invariably with the correct accentuation,—that is, with the accent on the antepenultima, although this is contrary to the general rule both of Spanish and Italian pronunciation. The following lines will suffice to show Schiller's accentuation :

" Ich hoffe meine Eb'oli denkt anders."

" Prinzessin Eb'oli, sie haben uns
Noch nicht gesagt ob Gómez hoffen darf."

" Wir wollen wissen, ob er lieben kann,
Und Liebe kann verdienen,—Eb'oli?"

Don Carlos, Act i. Scene 3.

" Der Fürstin Eb'oli die Hand zu reichen."

Act ii. Scene 8.

" Das lang' entbehrte Glück verschafft, der Fürstin
Von Eb'oli mich wiederum zu nähern."

Act ii. Scene 11.

If our poet is not equally correct in regard to ALCALÁ, (a small town of Spain,) it was owing, doubtless, either to the difficulty of making such a name " lie smooth in rhyme," or to his being ignorant of its true accentuation. The latter is by no means improbable, inasmuch as the Spanish language is far less studied by the generality of European scholars than the Italian. That it was not the result of carelessness is shown by the fact that ALCALA is *always pronounced* in the poem *in the same manner, and according to the general rule of Spanish accentuation ;* that is, with the accent on the penultima. It may be remarked, however, that Schiller places the accent on the last syllable of PARIS, SAINT-DENIS, and SAINT-QUENTIN,*—in all of which he differs from the English and conforms to the French accentuation. (See " Remarks on the French Accent," page 13.)

But perhaps the most remarkable illustration of this tendency to adopt the native pronunciation of foreign names is found in his drama of " Mary Stuart ;" where the poet, with the obvious intention of obliging his countrymen to pronounce the English names correctly, invariably in his verse spells LEICESTER " LESTER," although in the explanatory (prose) parts of the play he as invariably writes it " LEICESTER," as we do in English. For the same reason, doubtless, he writes BOLEYN " BOULEN," that his countrymen might pronounce the name *Boo'len,* nearly as it is spoken in England. Had he written it BOLEYN, the Germans might have placed the accent on the last syllable, as we often hear it pronounced in the United States.

The *accentuation* of names occurring in poetry, as already intimated, can readily be determined by the metre ; but the manner in which the poets pronounced the letters of a foreign name cannot be so easily ascertained, since it can be known only when the name ends a line in rhyme ; and even then it is often extremely uncertain, as they appear to consider themselves entitled, in such cases, to much greater license than in the accentuation of words. Thus, we often see associated, in rhyme, words which correspond very imperfectly in sound, as *enemy* and *lie, mourn* and *burn,* etc. Nevertheless, by comparing a number of passages, especially of those poets who are most remarkable for the correctness of their rhymes, we shall often be enabled to ascertain the true pronunciation of a word or name.

Now, it will be found that the system which we have adopted is supported by the practice of the poets in this respect also. In other words, it will be found that, while *foreign names that are very commonly used* in our language *have an English pronunciation, those not very well known are generally pronounced with the foreign sound of the letters,* as will be seen from the following passages :

" ' 'Tis *Jacqueline !* 'tis *Jacqueline !'*
Her little brother laughing cried ;
' I know her by her kirtle *green,*
She comes along the mountain side.' "

" Not now to while an hour *away,*
Gone to the falls in *Valombré.*"

" De Courcy, lord of *Argentière !*

. . . .

Thy thirst for vengeance sought the *snare.*"—ROGERS.

* The two former names occur in " The Maid of Orleans," (" Die Jungfrau von Orleans,") the last in " Don Carlos."

" Winding between Alpine trees,
Spiry and dark around their house of *prayer*,
Below the icy bed of bright *Argentière.*"—WORDSWORTH.

" This circumstance may serve to give a notion
Of the high talents of this new *Vauban :**
But the town-ditch below was deep as ocean,
The rampart higher than you'd wish to *hang.*"—BYRON.

" For many an age remember'd *long*
Shall live the towers of *Hougomont**
And fields of Waterloo."—SCOTT.

On the other hand, we shall find the poets pronounce foreign names of some celebrity with the English sound of the letters, as may be seen from these and similar examples :

" Oh, never talk again to me
Of northern climes and British *ladies ;*
It has not been your lot to see,
Like me, the lovely girl of *Cadiz.*"—BYRON.

" And Courtenay's pride and Percy's fame
Blazed broader yet in after-*years*,
At Cressy red and fell *Poitiers.*"—SCOTT.

" So the shaft
Of victory mounts high, and blood is quaff'd
In fields that rival Cressy and *Poictiers*,—
Pride to be wash'd away by bitter *tears.*"—WORDSWORTH.

Not unfrequently the poets will be found to give the correct pronunciation of names even when this differs essentially from the popular usage. Thus, Halleck says,

" Born in a camp, its watchfires bright
Alone illumed my cradle-bed,
And I had borne with wild delight
My banner where BOLI'VAR led."—*Magdalen.*

The pronunciation of the name of COKE, the celebrated lawyer and statesman, is almost always given correctly (kōōk) by the poets, although this does not correspond with the usual spelling.† In proof of this we may, out of a multitude of examples, cite the following :

" May he
Be by his father in his study *took*
At Shakespeare's plays instead of my Lord *Coke.*"
See "A Poetical Revenge," in COWLEY'S *Miscellanies.*

" And said she must consult her *books*,
The lover's Fletas, Bractons, *Cokes.*"
SWIFT : *Cadenus and Vanessa.*

" Also observe that, like the great Lord *Coke*,
(See Littleton,) whene'er I have expressed
Opinions two which at first sight may *look*
Twin opposites, the second is the best."
BYRON : *Don Juan*, canto xv. stanza lxxxvii.

The name of Bolingbroke is almost always pronounced correctly (Bolingbrōōk) by the poets. The following example, out of several occurring in the same poem, may serve as an illustration :

" What hope have you that ever *Bolingbroke*
Will live a subject that hath tried his fate?
Or what good reconcilement can you *look*,
When he must always fear and you must hate ?"
DANIEL : *History of the Civil War*, book ii. stanza xxxv.

* In these names the letter *n* is similar in sound to *ng*. The rhymes, however, are not perfect : the *o* in the last syllable of *Hougomont* should be sounded like *o* in *won't*, but the final *t* is silent. The final syllable of *Vauban* sounds almost like *bŏng.*

† We say *usual* spelling, because in Coke's own time it was not unfrequently written *Cook.* " In the reigns of Elizabeth and James I., Sir Edward's name was frequently spelt Cook. Lady Hatton, his second wife, who would not assume it, adopted this spelling in writing to him, and *according to this spelling it has invariably been pronounced.*" (See LORD CAMPBELL'S " Lives of the Chief Justices," vol. i. chap. vii.)

There is one difficulty in carrying out the system of foreign pronunciation adopted by us, which it may be proper to notice here, viz., that of drawing the lines between foreign names which *are*, and those which *are not*, well known. With respect to the more obvious in each division there cannot be the slightest hesitation ; but the two classes meet and pass into each other by imperceptible gradations, so that sometimes the question whether they should be pronounced according to the foreign or the English mode can be settled only by arbitrary decision. In these doubtful instances we have spared no pains to ascertain the prevailing practice of the best speakers, as well as the usage of the poets : when these have been found unsatisfactory, nothing has remained for us but to decide according to the best of our ability. We have in these cases usually given both pronunciations, placing that first which, in our judgment, is to be preferred.

In those cases where it is impossible to express accurately the sounds of other languages by English letters, we have endeavoured to employ a mode of indicating those sounds which, if it does not afford any effectual assistance to the mere English scholar, may at least be in no danger of embarrassing or leading him astray. Thus, we have represented the sound of the German *ch* by K, distinguished by being a small capital. Perhaps a strongly aspirated *h*—which might be indicated by *hh* —would convey a nearer idea of the German sound ; but it seems less eligible than the other mode, both because persons might differ in the pronunciation of it or perhaps be at a loss to pronounce it at all, and because the established mode of anglicizing the German *ch* seems to be to change its sound to that of *k*, as in the instances BLUCHER,‡ BLUMENBACH, METTERNICH, etc. The Scottish and Dutch sounds of *ch*, so similar to the German, when anglicized, assume invariably, if we mistake not, the sound of *k*. The ordinary mode of pronouncing the Greek χ tends to the same result. We have not, however, represented the sound of the German *g*, *at the end of a syllable*, in the same manner as the *ch*, though it has nearly the same sound, because it is not customary to anglicize it by the sound of *k*, except in a few instances.§ Were the pronunciation of such a word as *berg* represented by *ber*K, the effect would be to lead the English scholar to pronounce it differently from the ordinary mode, while he would be in no respect nearer the German than those who pronounce the word according to the English sound of the letters. Another consideration may, perhaps, be allowed to have some weight, viz., that though the more approved mode of German pronunciation requires that *g*, when it does not begin a word, should be pronounced nearly like *ch*, yet in some parts of Germany it is pronounced in every case like *g* hard in English. In a similar manner, and for similar reasons, we have usually represented the German *w* by a

‡ Although in America we very frequently hear this name pronounced *Blu'tcher* by intelligent speakers, the *ch* should unquestionably be hard, as is indicated by the following passage from Moore's " Fudge Family in Paris :"

" A fine sallow sublime sort of Werter-faced man,
With mustachios that gave (what we read of so oft)
The dear Corsair expression, half savage, half soft ;
As hyenas in love may be fancied to *look*, *or*
A something between Abelard and old *Blucher.*"

§ DANTZIC or DANTZICK, (German, *Danzig*,) LEIPSIC or LEIPSICK, (German, *Leipzig*,) SLESWICK, (German, *Schleswig* ; Danish, *Slesvig*,) are the only examples that we now recollect.

ŵ, and not by a *v*, though this is nearer the sound of the German letter.

With regard to French names, however, a different plan has been pursued, both because it is less easy, so to speak, to anglicize the French letters, and because, from the circumstance of this being far more studied than any other foreign language, it is much more usual for English or American speakers to adopt all the peculiar sounds in pronouncing French words or names.

ARABIC.

I.

The Arabic belongs to what is called the Semitic* family of languages, and is nearly related to the Hebrew, which it resembles not only in its general grammatical structure, but also in the form of many of its individual words. Of all the Semitic family it is by far the richest in its literature and the most copious in its vocabulary. Like the Hebrew, it is written from right to left. It belongs to the class referred to in the Preface (p. vi.) as "neither written in Roman letters nor in characters which can be converted into corresponding Roman letters;" it is therefore customary for Europeans in giving Arabic words or names to spell them *according to the sound*, the writers of the different nations seeking to indicate the pronunciation in the manner which to them seems most proper. In order to be able to point out more clearly the causes of the diversity which prevails among European writers respecting the manner of representing the sounds of the Arabic tongue, and for other reasons, we have deemed it proper to present to the reader a table of the Arabic characters, accompanied by such explanations as seemed necessary for our purpose.

The Arabic alphabet consists of twenty-eight letters, as follows:

	UNCON-NECTED.	FINAL CON-NECTED.	MEDIAL.	INITIAL.	NAME.	POWER.
1.	اٗ†	ا	ا	ا	alif,	a.
2.	ب	ب	ب	ب	bâ,	b.
3.	ت	ت	ت	ت	tâ.	t.
4.	ث	ث	ث	ث	thâ.	th.
5.	ج	ج	ج	ج	jeem or jîm.	j.
6.	ح	ح	ح	ح	Hâ.	H.
7.	خ	خ	خ	خ	khâ.	kh.
8.	د†	د	د	د	dâl.	d.
9.	ذ†	ذ	ذ	ذ	dhâl.	dh.
10.	ر†	ر	ر	ر	râ.	r.
11.	ز†	ز	ز	ز	zâ.	z.
12.	س	س	س	س	seen or sîn,	s.
13.	ش	ش	ش	ش	sheen or shîn,	sh.
14.	ص	ص	ص	ص	sâd,	s or ss.
15.	ض	ض	ض	ض	dsâd,	ds or dh.
16.	ط	ط	ط	ط	tâ,	t.
17.	ظ	ظ	ظ	ظ	dza.	dz or dh.

	UNCON-NECTED.	FINAL CON-NECTED.	MEDIAL.	INITIAL.	NAME.	POWER.
18.	ع	ع	ع	ع	ain, (ä′in or in,)	‡
19.	غ	غ	غ	غ	ghain, (gä′in or Gín,)	‡
20.	ف	ف	ف	ف	fâ,	f.
21.	ق	ق	ق	ق	ḳâf,	ḳ.
22.	ك	ك	ك§	ك	kâf,	k.
23.	ل	ل	ل	ل	lâm,	l.
24.	م	م	م	م	meem or mîm,	m.
25.	ن	ن	ن	ن	noon or nûn,	n.
26.	و	و	و	و	waw,	w.
27.	ه	ه	ه	ه	hâ,	h.
28.	ي	ي	ي	ي	yâ,	y.

In the Persian, (and Hindostanee,) besides the foregoing, the following four additional characters are used:

UNCONNECTED.	FINAL CONNECTED.	MEDIAL.	INITIAL.	POWER.
پ	پ	پ	پ	p.
چ	چ	چ	چ	ch.
ژ	ژ	ژ	ژ	zh.
گ‖	گ	گ	گ	g.

(See Section XIV.)

1. ا at the beginning of a word is sounded variously, according to the vowel-points placed upon it, (see 31 of this section;) in the middle of a word it is sounded as a long *a*, as in باب (*bâb*,) a gate.

2. ب sounds like *b* in English.

3. ت has the sound of the Spanish *t*. (See XIX. 17.)

4. ث sounds like our *th* in *thin*, or the Spanish *z*. ☞In Persian and Hindostanee it has the sound of *s*.

5. ج is usually pronounced like the English *j*, though in some dialects it has the sound of *g* hard.

6. ح sounds nearly like the Spanish *j* or *x*, (see XIX. 9,) but it is formed lower in the throat.

7. خ sounds like the German *ch* in *ach*, *doch*, etc. It is commonly represented in the French and English languages by *kh*, and in the German by *ch*.

8. د nearly resembles the English *d* in sound, but, in pronouncing it, the tip of the tongue is placed against the teeth. It bears the same relation to our *d* that the Spanish *t* does to our *t*.

9. ذ has no exact equivalent in any European language, though it nearly resembles the sound of our *th* in *thy*. It is often represented by *dh*, and sometimes by *ds*, *dhs*, or simple *d*. ☞ In Persian and Hindostanee it takes the sound of *z*.

10. ر sounds like the French or Italian *r*, or like *rr* in the English word *terror*.

11. ز has the sound of our *z*.

12. س sounds like our *s* in *this*.

13. ش is like the English *sh*.

14. ص sounds nearly like the English sharp *s*; but,

---

* *I.e.* Shemitic,—a term derived from Shem, the son of Noah.

† The letters thus marked ought never, according to the rules of Arabic orthography, to be connected with those that follow them.

‡ These letters have in sound nothing like them in English. (See 18 and 19 of this section.)

§ Written, also, ك   ‖ Written, also, گ

in pronouncing it, the teeth are not brought so nearly into contact. It is often represented by ss, or by ç.

15. ض has no equivalent in any European language. It is variously represented by dz, dh, dd, and ds. ☞ This letter, in Persian and Hindostanee, takes the sound of z.

16. ط is in sound nearly like the English t, but is pronounced somewhat harder. It is variously represented by t, tt, and th.*

17. ظ has a sound somewhat similar to ض. It cannot be indicated by any English letter or combination of letters; it is, however, usually represented by dh or dth. ☞ It is pronounced like z in Persian and Hindostanee.

18. ع has no exact equivalent in any European tongue. It nearly corresponds to the Hebrew ע. In the hiatus produced in uttering â—â in quick succession, we make a sound very similar to the Arabic ain, but the latter is formed lower in the throat.

19. غ has no equivalent in English. It bears nearly the same relation to hard g that kh (к) does to k. It is sometimes represented by g, but more frequently by gh, at least by French and English Orientalists.

20. ف has the sound of our f.

21. ق is similar to our k, but is formed lower in the throat. There seems to be a sort of aspirate mixed with the sound of k. It is sometimes represented by ḳ, (with a dot under it,) and sometimes by q.

22. ك in sound is exactly like our k.

23. ل is like the English l.

24. م is pronounced like our m.

25. ن is in sound like the English n.

26. و, as a vowel, is equivalent to ōō or û; as a consonant, it sounds like the English w or v.

27. ه sounds like our h; when final, it is nearly silent.

28. ي, as a vowel, sounds like ee or î, in which case a kasra is implied or expressed; as a consonant, like y. In the middle of a word the sound of ي may be doubled by means of the tashdeed, which, in writing, is often omitted. Preceded by fatha, (see below,) this letter assumes the sound of our long î, and is represented by ai.

29. All the foregoing characters are regarded by Arab grammarians as consonants. ا has been compared to the soft breathing (spiritus lenis) of the Greeks; ع is a similar breathing, though the place of its formation is lower in the throat.

30. The true vowels are three. They are called—1. Fat'ha, (a ;†) 2. Kas'ra, (i, sometimes ĕ;) and 3. Dhamma,‡ (oo or u.§) Fatha is written thus—over the consonant to which it belongs; kasra is placed beneath its consonant, thus ⸗; dhamma (which is in fact a minute و) is written over its consonant, thus ــٔ. These vowels are always joined to the consonant which in pronunciation precedes them: thus, in قَلَم, (kălăm,) a "reed" or "pen," the first fatha is considered to belong to the kâf, over which it is placed, the second to the lâm, (not to

the meem which comes after it;) and so in all similar cases: it follows that no vowel can stand by itself.‖ Hence, if we wish to write an initial short fatha, it must be associated either with alif or ain, as أَحَد, (ăhăd,) a "unit," عَفُو, (ăfû,) "forgiveness." If we would write a short initial kasra or dhamma, we must begin the word in the same manner: e.g. اِبْن, (ĭb'n,) a "son," عِبَاد, (ĭbâd,) "servants," أُف, (uf or ōōf,) "fie!" عُبُور, (ubûr or ōōbōōr,) a "passage" or "crossing."

31. As a general rule, if any one of the simple vowels is joined to an ordinary consonant, or to an initial alif or ain, it is short, as will be seen from the previous examples; but if in any syllable not initial they are joined with any of the (so-called) consonants (alif, ain, waw, etc.) to which they naturally correspond, they become long: for example, fatha with alif or ain gives us the sound of â, as بَاب, (bâb,) a "gate," بَعْد, (bâd or bâ-ad,) "after:" so kasra with yâ gives the sound of î, (or ee,) as سِين, (seen or sîn,) the name of the letter س; so also dhamma with waw gives the sound of û or ōō, as نُون, (nûn or nōōn,) the name of the letter ن. It should be observed that the fatha or dhamma is not written on the alif or waw, nor the kasra under the yâ, but is joined to the previous consonant, the semi-consonants coming after, for the sole purpose, it would seem, of prolonging the vowel.¶ In order to indicate the sound of â at the beginning of a word, it is usual to place a circumflex over the alif,—thus, آ. The initial long i (î or ee) is represented by اِ, and long u (û or ōō) by اُ.

32. The vowels are not usually written in Arabic manuscripts, and they are scarcely needed by the native Arabs who already know the language; but they are of great utility to foreigners in learning Arabic. The same may be said of the jăzm or jĕzm, (ٜ,) a mark placed upon a consonant to show that it has no vowel following it, as أَزْرَك, (ăzrăk, "blue," which without the jazm might be pronounced ăzârăk,) and the tashdeed or tashdîd, (ّ,) placed on a consonant to show that it must be doubled in pronunciation; as مُحَمَّد, (Mohammed.)

33. It is proper to observe that when the Arabic article al or el is followed by certain letters it changes its sound to that of the letter following: thus, el-Deen becomes el-Deen; el-Dowlah, ed-Dowlah; al-Rahman or el-Rahman, ar-Rahman or er-Rahman; al-Temeemee, at-Temeemee; and so on. (See XIII. 4.)

REMARKS ON ARABIC PRONUNCIATION.

When any of the long vowels (see 31 of this section) occur in the final syllable of a word or name ending in a consonant, that syllable always takes the accent according to the common European signification of this term.

Some eminent grammarians lay it down as a rule that the accent in Arabic never falls on the last syllable; but this rule proceeds on the supposition that the final syllable is short. Or, if it be meant to apply to all syllables, long as well as short, the term "accent" cannot be understood in the sense in which it is used by most European

---

* In such cases th is not intended to indicate a sound like that of the English th or the Greek θ, but rather a sound similar to that of the Hindoo th. (See XVIII. 6.)

† Often represented by e, and sometimes (in English) by u short. (See IX. 3, and XIII. 3.)

‡ Pronounced by the Persians zam'ma.

§ Often represented by o, as in the case of Mohammed, (see 32 of this section.)

‖ It may be remarked as an apparent exception to this rule that Ibn, "son," is often written simply بن (bn;) but this is usually to be considered as an abbreviation for ابن, though ben or bin is not unfrequently used instead of the longer form ibn.

¶ The long vowels in Arabic are to be pronounced very full and long,—particularly the long a, which is not only longer but sensibly broader than our a in far. (See XIV. 4.)

9

nations. In support of our position, we may cite, as a practical argument of great force, the fact that when an Arabic word ending in a consonant, preceded by a long vowel, is adopted into any European language, it takes the accent on the final syllable: thus, *Wâdy-al-Kebír* becomes in Spanish *Guadalquivír*, *Al-Mansoor* becomes *Almansór*, and so on. Nor can it be said that this ultimate accent is due to the tendency of the Spanish language to throw the accent on the last syllable; for *Almodovar*, derived from the Arabic *Al-Modhofer*, (which, like Al-Mansoor, signifies "the Victorious,") is in its Spanish form accentuated precisely as in the Arabic,—that is, on the penultima. If an Englishman who should hear a native Arab pronounce the word *kebír*, "great," or *kethír*, "much," should be told, by one who had any knowledge of the subject, that the first and not the last syllable was accentuated, he could come to no other conclusion than that in the mind of the speaker *accent* had a totally different meaning from what it has in English and in most other European tongues. In Hammer-Purgstall's great work on the literature of the Arabs, he translates into German verse many thousand lines from the Arabian poets, and he invariably, if we are not mistaken, places the accent on a long final syllable ending in a consonant. In illustration and support of this statement, we may select, from a multitude of the same general character, the following passage. A witty Arabian poet had been found half drunk by one of the caliph's police-officers in a tippling-house. The officer questioned the offender, as he had been instructed to do,—"Who art thou, and what is thy religion?" The poet's answer, rendered into German, is as follows:

> "Ich glaube was glauben die Beni Abbás
> Und was ist besiegelt mit Thon auf Papier;
> Wenn ich getrunken ein fröliches Glas,
> Und wenn es im Kopfe rumóret bei mir,
> So sei die geringste der Sorgen dir das."*

See "Literaturgeschichte der Araber," vol. iii. p. 462.

If there were any Arabic words, ending in a long final syllable, that might be considered doubtful, it would be those which, like Abbás, have a double consonant in the penultima; and yet nothing can be clearer than that the accent is placed on the final syllable only, in the foregoing verse. Mansur, (Mansoor,) though having also two consonants after the penultimate vowel, is pronounced by Hammer-Purgstall in the same manner. The reader, by referring to the above work, will find a multitude of similar examples, among others BAGDAD, with the accent on the last syllable, (see vol. iii. p. 440,) to which testimony we may add that of one of the most learned and accurate of our English poets. Southey in his "Thalaba" says,

> "The old man answered, To BAGDAD I go."
>
> "Stands not BAGDAD
> Near to the site of ancient Babylon?"
>
> "At length BAGDAD appeared,
> The city of his search."

---

* The following is a nearly literal translation: "I believe whatever the Beni Abbás [then the reigning family of caliphs] believe, and whatever is sealed with wax upon paper, [that is, whatever is generally recognized and established.] If I have drunk a cheerful glass, and if it causes some confusion in my head, let that be the least of thy cares."

CHINESE.
II.

As it would be out of the question in a work like the present to attempt to give a minute and systematic exposition of the principles of Chinese pronunciation, varying greatly as they do in different provinces and among different classes of the community, we shall content ourselves with merely offering a few brief observations, for the purpose of explaining the more obvious differences in the mode of representing Chinese names among the nations of the West.

1. One of the remarkable peculiarities of the Chinese tongue is the perpetual occurrence of nasal sounds. It was through the Portuguese, who, among all the nations of Europe, were the first to become intimately acquainted with China and the Chinese, that the forms of celebrated Chinese names first became familiar to Europeans. It so happened that the Portuguese language abounded in the same class of nasal sounds; and in representing these sounds in Chinese names according to the principles of their own language the Portuguese missionaries adopted a spelling which would necessarily convey an erroneous idea of the pronunciation to the great majority of Europeans. Thus, they wrote for the name of the great northern capital of China, *Pequim* or *Pequin*, and for that of the southern capital, *Nanquim* or *Nanquin*, the Portuguese pronunciation of which would be nearly pȧ′keeɴ′ or pȧ′keeng′, and nȧɴ′keeɴ′ or nȧng′keeng′. The Spaniards, then the leading nation in the world, having conquered Macao and the other Portuguese possessions in the far East, adopted, with little or no change, the Portuguese spellings, giving to them their own pronunciation, which they introduced among the other nations of Europe. The result was that, until very recently, PEKING was often written *Pekin*, and was generally pronounced in Europe pȧ-keen′ or pe-kin′; and NANKING, commonly written *Nankin*, was called nan′keen′.† TONQUIN (pronounced almost tong′king′ by the Chinese) still retains its Spanish pronunciation, ton-keen′; and CANTON (in Chinese *Quantong*) has in English and in most other European tongues completely dropped the nasal termination and taken the sound of *n* pure. In like manner we are to explain the fact that the names CONFUCIUS and MENCIUS, by which the two great Chinese philosophers (KONG-FOO-TSE and MENG-TSE) are generally known in Europe, have no trace of that nasal sound which is so distinct an element in those names as spoken by the Chinese.

2. Several consonant sounds which are found in all, or nearly all, European tongues, are wanting in most of the Chinese dialects, viz., *b*, *d*, *g*, (hard,) *r*, *v*, and *z*. It being a principle or law of this language that every individual word must be a monosyllable, ending either in a pure vowel or a nasal, it often causes strange transformations when an attempt is made to introduce words or names from other nations: thus, the Hindoo *Booddha* is changed into *Fo*, the initial *B* being necessarily replaced by a Chinese consonant, and the monosyllable which is substituted for the original dissyllable drops the terminal consonant, according to the usage of the language.

On account of the difficulty and uncertainty attending the pronunciation of Chinese names, resulting from the

---

† As is shown by the common English name of a kind of cloth manufactured there.

great diversity of dialects in that country, to attempt any great exactness or nicety in representing that pronunciation would clearly be a work of supererogation. We have deemed it sufficient to give the names according to the usage of the best European writers, taking care only, when there is occasion to do so, to render the French, Portuguese, or German spellings into their nearest English equivalents. ☞ Respecting the diversity of forms caused by writing Oriental names in different languages, see Preface, (pp. vi.–viii.,) and Section XIII., on the Oriental Languages, in this Introduction.

DANISH.
III.

1. *A* usually has a sound between that in the English word *far* and that in *fat*. It may be represented by **ã**. When it ends a syllable it is usually longer than when followed by a vowel in the same syllable : thus, *fader* ("father") is pronounced fã′der, nearly like the English *father*. *Aa* is commonly pronounced nearly like our *aw*, (or *au*.)

2. *E*, at the end of an accented syllable, usually has a sound like that of *i* in *pin*, (see XX., 3 ;) in other cases it is sometimes like *e* in *met*, and sometimes like *e* in *battery*.

3. *I* is like *ee*, or like *i* in *pin*. *Ii* is like our *ee*.

4. *O* is like the English *o*.

5. *U* is like *oo*.

6. *Y* is equivalent to the French *u* or *ü*.

7. *Ae* sounds like *a* in *fate*.

8. *Ie* sounds like *ee* in English.

9. *Oe* or *ö* is the same as in German.

10. The consonants *b, c, f, h, k, l, m, n, p, q, s, t, x, z* are like the English.

11. *D*, at the beginning of a word, is like the English *d ;* between two vowels, or at the end of a syllable in which it follows a vowel, it sounds nearly like *th* in *this*, (*th*.) When preceded by *l, n,* or *r,* more particularly when it occurs at the end of a word, it is almost or quite silent, as in Abil*d*gard.

12. *G* is always hard ; at the end of a word it is sounded very slightly, so as to resemble *h : e.g.* AALBORG is pronounced nearly *ol′bor′h*.

13. *J* is like the English *y,* (consonant.)

14. *R* is similar to the German.

15. *V* is usually like the English ; but *av* sounds like *öw,* (or *ou* in *our :*) *plov* (a "plough") is pronounced *plöw*.

16. *W* has a sound similar to that of our *v* or the German *w*. It is sometimes interchangeable with *v*.

DUTCH.
IV.

1. The vowels *a, e, i, o,* and *u* are similar to the French.

2. *Y* is like long *i* in English, as in *nigh*.

Obs. *Ij* is often made use of instead of *y* : thus, OVERYSSEL (the old spelling) is now commonly written *Overijssel*.

3. *Aa* is **ã** long, (**ã**.)

4. *Ae* is equivalent to **ãã** or **ã**.

5. *Ee* (equivalent to *e* long) sounds like our *a* in *fate*.

6. *Ei* or *ey* is like the German *ei,* or our long *i,* (ī.)

7. *Ie* sounds like *ee* in English.

8. *Oe* sounds like *oo*.

9. *Oo* is always pronounced like *o* long in English, or like *oo* in *door*.

10. *Ui* or *uy* is similar to *oi* in English, or *eu* in German. It appears, however, that formerly the Dutch *ui* had a different sound, somewhat resembling a lengthened *ü*. (See H. FRIJLINK, " Woordenboek voor vreemde Eigennamen," p. 31, Amsterdam, 1858.)

11. The consonants *b, c, f, h, k, l, m, n, p, q, r, s, t, x,* and *z* are similar to the English.

12. *D*, at the end of a word, is like *t ;* in other cases it is the same as in English.

13. *G* resembles in sound a strongly aspirated *h,* or the German *ch*.

14. *J* is equivalent to the English *y,* (consonant.)

15. *V*, at the beginning of a word or name, usually sounds nearly like *f :* or, to speak more exactly, it has a sound intermediate between that of the German *v* (*f*) and our *v*.

16. *W* is somewhat like the German, but softer ; in other words, it has a sound between that of our *w* and the German *w*. In the word *Nieuw,* (" new,") followed by a consonant, as NIEUWPOORT, (written also NIEUPOORT,) it is silent.

17. *Ch* is similar to the German *ch*.

18. *Sch,* however, has not, as in German, the sound of the English *sh,* but the pure sound of *s,* followed by the guttural *ch,* resembling *sk* in English.

☞ The FLEMISH is so closely allied to the Dutch that it may be regarded as essentially the same language. It differs, however, somewhat in the spelling of words. According to the modern Dutch orthography, *aa* is generally substituted for *ae,* and *ij* for *y*. In Flemish both of these old forms are still retained.

FRENCH.
V.

1. *A*, in French, has two sounds : the short, as in *ami, la bal,* etc., is intermediate between **ã** (as in the English word *far*) and **ã**, (as in *fat :*) this sound in the present work is represented by **ã**. The second or long sound is like that in our word *far ;* it occurs in the *a* circumflexed (â) and *a* followed by a silent *s,* as in *pas,* which should be pronounced as if written pâ. This sound is represented by **ã**.

2. *E* has four sounds : (1) *close,* like *a* in the English word *fate, e.g.* in *été,* (represented in this work by à ;) (2 and 3) *open,** the second è, nearly as in *met,* but more prolonged, *e.g.* in *procès,* (represented by ê or à ;) the third ê (*e* circumflexed) is like the preceding, but still more open and more prolonged, *e.g.* in *tête;* it is represented by **ê** ; (4) *obscure,* as in *battery, e.g.* in *retour, devrait.*†

3. *I* has two sounds : the first nearly as in the English word *fig,* in *il, ami ;* the second like *ie* in *field,* or *ee, e.g.* in *gît, pie,* etc.

4. *O* has three sounds : (1) nearly as in *robe, e.g.* in *trône,* (represented by ō ;) (2) as in *rob, e.g.* in *parole;* (3) as in *lord, e.g.* in *corps*. The second and third are both represented by *o* without any mark.

5. The sound of the French *u* has no equivalent in English. It may be said to be intermediate between *ee*

---

* In pronouncing this sound the mouth must be freely opened, —whence the name.

† The *e* in these and similar cases is often scarcely sounded at all, and appears to pass imperceptibly into *e* mute ; *retour* and *devrait* may be pronounced r′toor and d′vrà. It should, however, be observed that in reading poetry, as well as in the graver style of public speaking, the unaccented *e,* even when it forms the terminal letter of such words as *tête, parle,* etc., nearly always makes a distinct and separate syllable. (See 18 of this section.)

and *oo*. This is one of the most difficult sounds in the language, but may readily be produced if the speaker, after placing his lips in the position proper for sounding our *oo*, attempts, *without moving his lips*, to utter the sound of *ee*. In the present work it is represented by the German *ü*.

Obs. *U*, before *n* nasal, has its second English sound nearly, *un* being pronounced almost like *üN*.

6. *Y* is similar to the French *i*. In the middle of a word *y* is usually equivalent to *ii*, as in *fuyard*, fü-e′yăR′, (pronounced in French, *fui-iar*.)

7. *Ai* and *ay* are like *è*, (represented by ą̆.)

Obs. When *ai* forms the termination of verbs, as in *j'ai*, ("I have,") *je parlai*, ("I spoke,") *je parlerai*, ("I shall speak,") it has the sound of *é*, or *a* in *fate*. Some authorities say that while *aie*, *ais*, and *aye* are to be sounded as *è*, *ai*, *ay*, *ei*, and *ey* terminal (that is, when not followed by *e* or *s* mute) should be pronounced as *é*, (ı̆ ;) but to this general rule there appear to be many exceptions.*

8. *Au* is like *ō*.

9. *Ei* and *ey* are like *è*, (see 7 of this Section; Observation.)

10. *Eu* is nearly similar to the English *u* in *tub*, but the sound is somewhat closer and more prolonged, nearly resembling that of *u* in *fur*. It is similar to the German *ö*, but is rather more open.

Obs. *Eu*, in the different parts of the verb *avoir*, "to have," always has the sound of simple *u*.

11. *Ie* is like *ee* in English, or *i*.

12. *Oi* usually sounds like wă : *e.g. moi* is pronounced mwă or *mwŏh*.

Obs. *Oi* was formerly used in the termination of the French verbs, *e.g. avois, avoit, avoient*; also in the final syllable of many adjectives,

---

* There is not only considerable diversity among the different French authorities in regard to the pronunciation of words or names with these terminations, but scarcely any one writer appears to be consistent with himself in this respect. In Boyer's "French Dictionary," with the pronunciation according to the Abbé Tardy, (Boston, 1822,) *Bey* (a Turkish governor) is pronounced bı̆, (or bé:) but all words ending in *ai*, as *balai, délai, essai, gai, geai, lai, Mai, quai, vrai*, are pronounced with the open sound of *e*, (ı̆ or ą̆ ;) the *ai* of *balai, gai, geai, lai, Mai*, and *quai* is sounded like the English *e* in *met*, but in *délai, essai*, and *vrai*, like *e* in *there*. In the Dictionary of Fleming and Tibbins, (American edition, Philadelphia, 1843,) *ai* in *gai, Mai*, and *quai* has the sound of *e*, close ą̆, (or é,) but *balai, délai, essai, lai*, and *vrai* are pronounced in precisely the same manner as in the preceding work. In Spiers and Surenne's Dictionary (American edition, 1852) *gai* has the sound of *e* close, (ą̆ or é:) but *balai, Mai*, and all other words (not verbs) of this termination are pronounced with the sound of open *e. Bey*, as in Boyer and Fleming and Tibbins, is pronounced bı̆, (or bé:) but *dey*, a word similar in its origin and general character, has the open sound of *e*, (dè.) *Ay* and *ey*, when forming the termination of proper names, are in Spiers and Surenne's Dictionary invariably represented in pronunciation by è, with the single exception of *Solway*. See, also, "Surenne's French Pronouncing Dictionary,"(American edition, from the Edinburgh edition of 1840,) in which is given the pronunciation of a great many proper names ending in *ay* and *ey*, and never with the sound of *e* close, (é,) except in the solitary instance of *Solway*, just noticed. Mr. Bescherelle, perhaps the highest modern authority in regard to the pronunciation as well as the definition of French words, does not speak very definitely in regard to the sound of *ai* or *ay* terminal; but, under the letter *E*, he says *ey* has its middle sound ("*son moyen* ou *demi-ouvert*") in *bey, dey, Hervey, Ney, Volney*, etc., (see "Dictionnaire National," vol. i., pp. 1049 and 1050.) In consideration of the general tendency of the preceding writers, and supported by the high authority last named, we have adopted the general rule to make the *e* open in the final syllables of all names of this class. At the same time, those who are anxious to be accurate in their pronunciation should take care to make the sound of *ai*, *ay*, and *ey*, terminal, less open and less full than in the final syllables *aie, aye, ais, eys*, etc.

---

as *Polonois*, "Polish," and *Lyonnois*, "belonging to Lyons." The *oi* in these words—which are now usually written *avais, avait, avaient, Polonais, Lyonnais*—sounds like *ai*, (or *è*.)

13. *Ou* sounds like *oo* in English.

14. *B, c,† d, f, k, p, t, v*, and *z* are the same as in English.

15. *G*, before *a, o*, and *u*, is hard, as in the English word *gap* ; before *e, i*, and *y* it is soft, having the sound of *zh*, or of *s* in the English word *pleasure. Gu* sounds like *g* hard : thus, *gué, guide*, are pronounced gă̆, ḡĕd or ḡeed.

16. *H* is never pronounced in French so forcibly as in English. Some of the best French authorities, indeed, say that the *h* should never be sounded at all in French words or names ; the only difference they would make between the (so-called) aspirated and unaspirated initial *h* is, that before the latter the *a* or unaccented *e* in such particles as *la, le*, etc. is dropped, as *l'herbe*, (pronounced lą̆Rb,) "the grass ;" *l'homme*, (lom,) "the man ;" while before the former it is retained, as *la halle*, (pronounced lă̆ ă̆l,) "the market ;" *le hamac*, (lĕh ă̆′mă̆k′,) "the hammock," etc.

17. *J* sounds like soft *g* in French, or *zh* in English.

18. *L* has usually the same sound as in English ; but when it ends a word, being preceded by *i*, or when *ll* follows *i* in any situation, it usually has what is called its *liquid* sound. This may be said to answer nearly to the sound of *lli* in *million*, the sound of *l* in such cases being blended with that of *y*, (consonant :) *e.g. papillon* is pronounced pă̆′pĕl′yŏN′; CHANTILLY, shŏN′tĕl′ye′, etc. It should, however, be observed that at present, according to the general practice of the more polite French speakers, the sound of *l* in such words is in ordinary conversation scarcely heard at all, so that their pronunciation may rather be indicated thus,—pă̆′pe′yŏN′, shŏN′te′ye′; but in the higher style of speaking, and in public discourses, the *l* in such cases is, according to the best usage, distinctly pronounced.

19. *M* and *n*, when followed by a vowel, or when double, have the same sound as in English ; but when at the end of a word, (not immediately followed by another word beginning with a vowel,) or when followed by another consonant in the middle of a word, they have what is termed the *nasal* sound, which somewhat resembles that of *ng* in *long, pang*, etc., but is softer :‡ thus, *m* and *n* are nasal in such words as co*M*parer, co*N*te*N*te, but have their natural sound in such as *commune, connu. Bon*, ("good,") before a consonant or standing by itself, would be pronounced bŏN ; but if followed immediately by a vowel, as in the phrase *bon ami*, ("good friend,") the final *n* is sounded distinctly, as *nn* would be in the same position. The pronoun *sien*, when not followed by a vowel, is pronounced nearly se-ă̆N′ ; but when it takes the feminine termination the *n*, being doubled, has the same sound as in English, so that *sienne* is pronounced *se-ĕn′*.

20. *M* or *n* nasal, when preceded by *e*, causes this vowel to assume the broad sound of *a* : thus, *dents, sens*, are pronounced like the French words *dans* and *sans*, almost as if written in English dŏN and sŏN.

---

† *C* with a cedilla, (ç) before *a, o*, and *u*, sounds like *s* : thus, *ça, ço, çu* are pronounced like *sa, so, su*.

‡ In uttering this sound, care should be taken not to press the back part of the tongue against the palate, as is done in pronouncing the English *ng*.

21. *In, im, ain, aim, ein, oin,* and *en, preceded immediately by i,* when nasal, have a sound nearly resembling that of *ang* in the English word *pang.* In such cases, *in, im, ain, aim, ein,* and *en* are pronounced alike ǎN ; the *o* in *oin* has the sound of our *w,* so that *loin* and *soin* are pronounced almost lwǎN, swǎN.

22. In *om* and *on* nasal, the *o* has nearly the sound of ǒ as in *won't.*

OBS. The French nasal sound is represented in the present work by N or M, distinguished as a small capital: *e.g.* CHAUMONT, shō'-mǒN'.

23. *Q* or *qu,* in French, always sounds like *k: e.g. quel* is pronounced *kěl ; qui, ke.*

OBS. *Q,* in *French* words, (except when terminal, as in *coq* and *cinq,*) is always followed by *u,* though it is often employed without this letter in writing certain foreign names.

24. *R* is like the English, but is trilled more strongly, especially when it precedes another consonant, or stands at the end of a word, as in *veRtu, puniR* : in similar cases the English *r* is but very slightly sounded. This sound is represented by a small capital R.

25. *S,* when single and between two vowels, sounds like *z:* in other cases it is the same as in English.

26. *X* generally has the same sound as in English, but is sometimes sounded like *s,—e.g.* in *six,* pronounced sěss, and *Bruxelles,* (Brussels,) pronounced brü'sěl',—and occasionally like *z,* as in *dixième,* de'ze-ặm'.

27. *Ch* is like *sh* in English ; *th* is always like *t.*

28. *Gn* (the same as in Italian) has a sound which blends that of *n* and *y,* (consonant,) or, in other words, is equivalent to the sound of *ni* in *minion.* Thus, AVIGNON is pronounced ǎ'věn'yòN'.

OBS. This sound is represented in Spanish by *ñ,* and bears the same relation to *n* that the liquid *l* (ĺ) does to the ordinary *l.* In Hungarian it is expressed by *ny,* and in Portuguese by *nh.*

When it occurs in the middle of a word, we have represented it by *n* and *y,* as in the example above given ; but when it stands at the end of a word, as it cannot then be expressed by any letter or combination of letters in English, it has been indicated by the Spanish *ñ:* accordingly, the French pronunciation of such names as COLOGNE and BOULOGNE is thus given :—ko'loñ', boo'loñ'.

SILENT LETTERS.

29. The vowel *e* at the end of a word, when not marked with an accent, is invariably mute : *e.g.* in *parle, contente,** etc.

30. The French consonants, when occurring at the end of a word, are generally not pronounced, unless they are immediately followed by a word beginning with a vowel : *e.g.* in *content,* (pronounced còn'tòN',) and *dents,* (dòN.) If, however, they are followed by a mute *e* or any other vowel, they must always be articulated : *e.g.* in *con-tenve, denvé,* etc.

OBS. 1. The letters *c, f, l,* and *r* are, when final, very often pronounced, (the two former almost always:) *e.g.* in *avec, neuf, il,* and *punir.*

OBS. 2. The French articulate the final consonants in almost all foreign and classical names: *e.g.* in AMSTERDAM, (*m* not nasal,) VÉNUS, etc.

REMARKS ON THE FRENCH ACCENT.

It may be observed that the French language has no accent, in the sense in which we employ this term. The

* The particles *le, ne,* and the pronouns *je, me, te,* etc., are perhaps, strictly speaking, exceptions ; but though the *e* in these words is not always absolutely mute, it is very often so : thus, the sentence *vous me trouverez le même* is pronounced in rapid conversation *voom troov ràl mem,* the vowel in *me* and *ne* being entirely suppressed, and the consonants attached to the preceding words.

marks, called *accents,* that are placed over the different vowels, serve only to indicate some particular sound of these letters, and not that peculiar impulse of the voice which characterizes an accented syllable in the English and most other European tongues. Thus, the accent over the *e* in *parlé* serves to show that this vowel has its first French sound, and at the same time distinguishes it from *parle,* another form of the same verb, in which the *e* is mute. The circumflex imparts to the vowel over which it is placed a longer and deeper sound than ordinary : *e.g.* in *hâte, tempête, gîte,* and *apôtre.*

It is commonly said that the French pronounce all the syllables of a word with an equal stress of voice, but that they *seem* to an English ear to accentuate the last, because in our language the universal tendency is to throw the accent towards the beginning of the word. Others, on the contrary, maintain that in pronouncing words of a number of syllables the voice of a native French speaker almost invariably rises and dwells on the last, and that this peculiar terminal intonation is very analogous, and nearly equivalent, to our accent. This last opinion appears to us to be not without a real foundation. But, however the question may be settled, the fact that the English who have learned the pronunciation of names from hearing them spoken by the French themselves, almost invariably throw the accent on the final syllable, furnishes, in our judgment, sufficient grounds for establishing a general rule on this subject. Accordingly, in the present work we have, with very few exceptions, placed the principal accent on the last syllable of French names ; at the same time, it has been thought proper to mark the others with secondary accents, in order to prevent them from being pronounced too slightly or indistinctly, as is usually the case with unaccented syllables in English. The pronunciation of ORLÉANS, for example, has been thus given :—OR'lâ'òN'.

OBS. Particular care, however, should be taken not to break such names into as many isolated sounds as there are different syllables, but, while pronouncing these syllables with a stress of voice nearly equal, to let each glide smoothly into that which follows it. It may be observed that the French, in uttering short sentences, usually make the different words run into each other, as if they were parts of the same word.

GERMAN.
VI.

1. *A,* in German, usually sounds as in the English word *far,* though sometimes approximating the *a* in *fat.*

2. *E,* when long, sounds like *a* in *fate ;* when short, like *e* in *met :* frequently, however, it has an obscure sound, like *e* in *bitter, paper,* etc. It should have this obscure sound whenever it ends an unaccented syllable, (as in *Goethe,*) or when it precedes *l, n,* or *r* in an unaccented syllable, (as in *Schlegel, Bunsen, Schiller.*)

3. *I* long sounds like *i* in *marine,* (or *ee* in English ;) *i* short, like *i* in *pit.*

4. *O* long sounds like *o* in *no ; o* short, nearly like *o* in *on.*

5. *U* long is like *oo* in *moon ; u* short, like *oo* in *good.*

6. *Y* sounds like the German *i.*

7. *Ae,* or *ä,* is similar to the German *e,* or to the English *a* in *fate* or *e* in *met.*

8. *Ie* is equivalent to *i* long, (or *ee* in English.)

9. *Oe,* or *ö,* nearly resembles the *eu* in French, but has no parallel sound in English : the sound in our lan-

guage nearest to it is that of *e* in *her*, or *u* in *fur :* the German poets often rhyme it with with *e*, (ĕ or ā.)

10. *Ue*, or *ü*, is like the French *u*.

11. *Ai* is similar in sound to *ei*, but somewhat broader. (See 14 of this section.)

12. *Au* is equivalent to the English *ou* in *our*.

13. *äu* and *eu* resemble in sound the English *oi*, as in *oil*.

14. *Ei* and *ey* have the sound of our *i* in *mine*, *as pronounced by the Americans*, (the English draw the corners of the mouth farther back.)

Obs. It may be observed that *ai* and *au*, in German, as well as in several other languages, are *proper* diphthongs, the vowels preserving their distinct and proper sound : thus, *ai* is equivalent to ā'e, and *au* to ā'oo, in English.

15. The consonants *f, k, l, m, n, p, q, t,* and *x* are pronounced as in English.

16. *B* and *d*, at the beginning of a word, have the same sound as in English ; at the end of a word, *b* is pronounced like *p*, and *d* like *t*.

17. *C*, before *a, o,* and *u,* sounds like *k ;* before *e, i,* and *y,* like *ts*.

18. *Ch* has a sound unknown to our language, which can be learned from an oral instructor only. It somewhat resembles that of our *h*, with a strong aspiration : after *a, o,* and *u,* it is guttural ; for example, in the word *ach*.* When it follows *e, i, ä, ö, ü, äu,* or *eu,* it seems to be sounded more in the palate or roof of the mouth, as in *ich, euch,* etc. We have represented this sound in the present work by κ, distinguished as a small capital.

Obs. *Ch*, before *s radical*, (*i.e.* forming a part of the root of the word,) has the sound of *k : e.g. Ochs* is pronounced *oks ; Sachsen,* sāk'sen, etc.

19. *G*, at the beginning of a word, sounds as in the English word *get*. In other situations it is usually pronounced nearly like the German *ch*, in which cases it is represented by G small capital. In some German dialects, however, it is sounded in all cases nearly like *g* hard in English : *gg* is usually sounded nearly like *k*.

20. *H* is pronounced only when it begins a word.

Obs. 1. When *g* and *h* occur in the middle of a compound word, they have the same sound as when they are initial, provided they begin any part which is a complete word in itself: thus, in the participle *gegeben,* ("given,") the latter *g* has the same sound as the former, because it begins the verb *geben,* (to "give,") from which that participle is derived. It is sounded in like manner in *aufgeben,* (to "give up,") *vergeben,* (to "forgive,") etc. *H,* in similar instances, is pronounced: *e.g.* in *gehabt, aufhalten,* etc.

Obs. 2. *G* and *h,* occurring after a vowel, lengthen its sound : *e.g.* in *Tag, Zahl, Floh,* pronounced tāāG, tsāāl, flō, etc. A silent *h* has the same effect though occurring before a vowel, as *Thal,* (pronounced tāāl,) *That,* (tāāt,) and so on. (See Remarks on the German Pronunciation, at the end of this section.)

21. *J* has the sound of the English *y,* (consonant.)

22. *Q* is only used before *u,* and sounds as in the English word *quit*.

23. *R* is pronounced like *rr* in the English word *terror,* but somewhat more strongly. (See V., 24.)

Obs. Care should be taken to pronounce the *r* in German distinctly and forcibly. In such words as *Berg* and *Werth,* the learner should be particularly on his guard against allowing the *e* to become like short *u,* as in similar words in English. The *e,* in such cases, should have the same sound as in our word *merit,* so that *Berg*

---

* Those who have no opportunity of acquiring this sound from a German might perhaps learn it from a Scotchman, as the Scottish *ch* is essentially the same with the German, though pronounced somewhat more strongly.

should be pronounced almost as if written *bairG,* (not *bürG ;*) *Werth* as *wairt,* (not *würt,*) but somewhat shorter.

24. *S,* at the beginning of a word, or between two vowels, is like *z ;* in other cases it is sharp, as in *this. Ss* is always sharp.

25. *Sch* sounds like the English *sh ; sz,* like *ss*.

26. *Th* is pronounced like *t,* as in most other languages.

27. *V* sounds like *f* in English, except when between two vowels ; it is then pronounced somewhat softer, approximating the sound our *v*.

28. *W* resembles our *v,* but in pronouncing it the upper teeth should not be allowed to touch the lower lip, as is done in uttering the English *v*. This sound is indicated by a *w* marked thus, ŵ.

29. *Z* and *tz* sound like *ts*.

REMARKS ON THE GERMAN ACCENT AND PRONUNCIATION.

No general rule can be given for the accent of German words or names : it may be remarked, however, that the penultimate accent occurs much less frequently than in the Spanish or the Italian language. The German accent is in all respects very similar to the English, differing widely from the Spanish and entirely from the French. It is proper to observe, however, that the secondary accent on compound German words or names is more distinctly marked than it would be in English in the same situation : thus, the English say Pe'ters-burg, with scarcely any appreciable accent on the last syllable, while the Germans say Pe'ters-burg', (pā'tẹrs-bŏŏRG',) the last accent being distinctly marked, though decidedly less than the first.

It is a rule in German that an accented vowel ending a syllable is long, as in *ā'ber,* (ā'bẹr,) "but," *ge'ben,* (gā'bẹn,) to "give," *Vā'ter,* (fā'tẹr,) "father," *lo'ben,* (to "praise.") The vowel is considered to end the syllable when followed by a single consonant in the middle of a word, in which case the consonant always goes to the following vowel, as in the instances above cited ; but, if the vowel is followed by a consonant in the same syllable, it is generally short, as in *fal'len,* (to "fall,") *Mut'ter,* ("mother,") etc. But to this last remark there are several exceptions. In declinable words ending in a single consonant, whether monosyllables or dissyllables, with the accent on the *ultima,* the syllable on which the stress of the voice is laid is long, as *Blūt,* ("blood,") *gūt,* ("good,") *Grāf,* ("count,") *Eugēn,* ("Eugene,") and so on. This exception may be said to follow almost as a matter of course from the first part of the foregoing rule ; for if the vowel in such words as *Graf* was short, then in the genitive and dative *(Grafes, Grafe)* it must also be short, thus violating the rule referred to, or else be the cause of a very objectionable and inconvenient irregularity, by making in the same word the nominative and accusative short and the genitive and dative long. The letters *g* and *h* have the effect of making long the vowel which precedes them. (See 20 of this section, Observation 2.)

GREEK, (MODERN.)
VII.

1. A *a* (alpha) is like *a* in *far*.

2. E *ε* (epsilon) is like *a* in *fate*.

3. H *η* (ēta) is like *ee* in English.

4. Ι ι (iōta) is like *e* in *me* or *i* in *pin.*

5. Ο ο (omicron) is like *o* in English.

6. Υ υ (upsīlon) is nearly like the French *u*, (or *ü.*)

7. Ω ω (ōmĕga) is like *o* in English, there being no difference between this and *omicron* in prose ; in poetry ω is longer.

8. Αι is like *a* in *fate.*

9. Eι and oι sound like *ee* in English.

10. Ου is like our *oo.*

11. Β β (bēta) is like *v* in English.*

12. Γ γ (gamma) is like *g* hard, as in *get.*

13. Δ δ (delta) is like *th* in *this*, (†h.)

14. Ζ ζ (zēta) is like the English *z.*

15. Θ θ (thēta) is like *th* in *thin.*

16. Κ κ (kappa) is like *k.*

17. Λ λ (lambda) is like *l.*

18. Μ μ (mu) is like *m.*

19. Ν ν (nu) is like *n.*

20. Ξ ξ (xi) is like *x.*

21. Π π (pi) is usually like the English *p;* but after μ (m) it is like *b: e.g.* ἔμπορος is pronounced *em'bo-ros.**

22. Ρ ρ (rho) is similar to the German *r.*

23. Σ σ ς (sigma) is like the English *s.*

24. Τ τ (tau) is usually like the English *t;* after ν, (n,) however, it is sounded like *d: e.g.* ἐντὸς is pronounced *en-dos'.*

25. Υ υ, (*consonant,*) when before a vowel or the liquids *l, m, n, r,* is like our *v: e.g.* ἀνερύω is pronounced âv-à-rü'o, αὐλὸς, âv-los', αἴριον, âv're-on ; in other cases it is like *f: e.g.* Λευκαδία (Leucadia) is pronounced lef-kâ-thee'â.

26. Φ φ (phi) is equivalent to our *f.*

27. Χ χ (chi) is similar to *ch* in German.

28. Ψ ψ (psi) is like *ps* in English.

HEBREW.
VIII.

As in the case of classical names we have not attempted to give the ancient Latin or Greek pronunciation, so we have never aimed to give the ancient Hebrew pronunciation of Scripture names. Nevertheless, that such of our readers as may happen to be ignorant of Hebrew may be furnished with a key to the Hebrew forms of these names, as well as for purposes of comparison with other languages, we have thought it necessary to present the following table, exhibiting the form and power of the Hebrew letters :

ANCIENT HEBREW ALPHABET.

	NAME.	POWER.
1. א	â'lef	a
2. ב	bêth or bāth	v, b
3. ג	gîmel or ḡee'mel	g
4. ד	dâ'leth	d or dh
5. ה	hê or hā	h
6. ו	vâv or vauv	v
7. ז	zâ'yin	z
8. ח	Hêth or Hāth	H (like the Arabic ح)
9. ט	têt or tāt	t
10. י	yōdh	y

* As the modern Greeks have no letter corresponding to our *b*, in order to represent this letter in words or names from other languages they employ μπ: as Μπάσρα, BASRA or BASSORA, Μπάμπω, BABO, etc.

	NAME.	POWER.
11. כ or ך†	kaf	kh, k
12. ל	lâ'medh	l
13. מ	mêm or mām	m
14. נ or ן†	nûn or noon	n
15. ס	sâ'mek	s
16. ע	â'yin	a (like the Arabic ع)
17. פ	pê or pā	ph, p (nearly equivalent to the Arabic ﻒ)
18. צ	tsâ'dā	ts
19. ק	kōf	ḳ (like the Arabic ﻖ)
20. ר	rêsh or rāsh	r
21. ש	shîn or sheen	sh, s
22. ת	tâv	th, t (nearly equivalent to the Arabic ﺚ)

HINDOSTANEE.
IX.

1. Hindostanee is the name given to the language formed by the interfusion of the native Hindoo dialects with the Persian, which was introduced into India chiefly by the conquering Mongols under Bâber and his successors. It was called Hindostanee or Hindustani (hin-dus-tân'ee) because it originated in Hindostan,‡ which is still its principal seat, although the language is extensively spoken not only throughout the whole of India proper, but also in Afghanistan and Beloochistan. It is also frequently called Oordoo or Urdû, (ŏŏr'dŏŏ',) or [the "language of the] camp," because it was in the camp or army that the intermixture of the Persian with the Hindoo languages first took place. In writing Hindostanee, the Persian alphabet, with some slight modifications, is commonly employed, though the Nâgaree (Nâgari) is not unfrequently made use of. (See Sections XIII. and XVIII.)

2. The pronunciation of the Hindostanee nearly corresponds in all essential points with the Persian ; perhaps the only differences of any importance are in the sound of the short ă Nâgaree, which, following the Sanscrit pronunciation of that vowel, is usually like our short *u*, as in *but*, the nasal *n*, (seldom found in Persian,) in the sounds of *kh, gh, th, dh,* etc., and in those of the lingual (or cerebral) *d, t,* and *r.* (See Section XVIII. for the mode of distinguishing, as well as for the pronunciation of, these letters.)

3. Care should be taken not to apply the pronunciation of India to Persian and Arabic names of persons who have never had anything to do with India. While it may not be improper to pronounce the name of the great Akbar—ŭk'ber,—for, though an Arabic name, it was doubtless so called by a large majority of his subjects,— it would be inexcusable for an Englishman (except when tâlking with Hindoos) to pronounce the name of the Arabian prophet Mo-hŭm'mŭd or Mŏŏ-hŭm'mŭd, as it is nearly always called by the natives of India. (See Table on page 18.)

OBS. There is a remarkable general analogy, both in their history and in their composition, between the Hindostanee and the English

† These characters are called *terminal,* being used only at the end of a word or name.

‡ It may be remarked that HINDOSTAN or HINDOOSTAN, (the "country of the Hindoos,") in its strict and original signification, was applied only to India north of the Vindhya Mountains. The application of the name to the entire peninsula is comparatively recent.

languages. In both tongues the staple (if we may use the term) was furnished by the native dialects of the country, while the higher style of speech, and particularly the language of the court, was for a long time that of the conquerors,—Norman-French or Persian; and, even after the amalgamation of the language of the conquerors and that of the conquered had taken place to a great extent, it was in both countries regarded as a mark of rank and high breeding to introduce into conversation and into written composition as large an admixture of the former as possible. The analogy may be extended still further: as the Norman-French was not the original language of the Normans, so the Persian was not the original language of the Mongol conquerors of India, but derived from one of the countries which they had subdued and in which they had established themselves.

HUNGARIAN.

X.

1. *A*, unaccented, is like *o* in *not;* with an accent, (*á*,) it sounds as *a* in *far*, and is always long: thus, *Aba Uj-vár*, the name of a town, is pronounced ŏb'ŏh oo'e-vảʀ.

2. *E*, unaccented, is like *e* in *met;* with an accent, (*é*,) it has a sound intermediate between *e* in *met* and *i* in *pit*, but more prolonged.

3. *I*, and *y* when a vowel, sound like *e* in *me*, or *i* in *fig*.

4. *O*, without an accent, is the same as in English; when accented, (*ó*,) it has a longer and deeper sound.

5. *U*, without an accent, is like *oo* in English; with the accent, (*ú*,) its sound is fuller and deeper.

6. *Oe* or *ö*, and *ue* or *ü*, are the same as in German.

7. The consonants *b*, *d*, *f*, *h*, *k*, *l*, *m*, *n*, *p*, *t*, *v*, *z*, are like the English.

8. *C* is not used without being joined with some other consonant; *cs* is sounded like *ch* in English; *cz*, like *ts*.

9. *G*, except when followed by *j* or *y*, is always hard, as in the English word *get*. *Gh* sounds like a simple *g*.

10. *J* is usually like *e* in English; *uj* is pronounced *oo-e*. *Dj* and *gj* are equivalent to *dy* and *gy*, and *tj* to *ty*. (See 16, 17, and 20 of this Section.)

11. *R* is like the German; in other words, it is to be trilled more strongly than the English.

12. *S* is like the English *sh*.

13. *Sz* is like *s* sharp, or *ss*.

14. *Ts* is equivalent to *cs*, (or *ch* in English.)

15. *Tz* is like *cz*, (or *ts* in English.)

16. *Y*, in Hungarian, is nearly always a consonant. When it follows *d*, *g*, *l*, *n*, and *t*, it seems to be blended with these letters, so as to form but one consonant sound.

17. *Dy* and *gy* are alike. *Magyar* is pronounced mŏd'-yŏr.

18. *Ly* is like *l* in Spanish, or *lli* in the English word *million*. *Vásárhely* is pronounced in three syllables,—vả'shảʀ-hĕl.

19. *Ny* is like the Spanish *ñ*, or *ni* in *minion*. *Mártony* is pronounced in two syllables,—mảⁿ'toñ.

20. *Ty* approximates the sound of our *ch*, bearing the same relation to *t* that *dy* does to *d*.

21. *Zs* is sounded like the French *j*, or *zh* in English.

Obs. In Hungarian, the accent usually falls on the first syllable.

ITALIAN.

XI.

1. *A*, in Italian, is like the English *a* in *far*, though its sound varies somewhat in different situations.*

2. *E* has two sounds: (1.) *close*, like *a* in *fate;* (2.) *open*, like *e* in *met*.

3. *I* is like *e* in *me*, or *i* in *fig*.

4. *O* has two sounds: (1.) *close*, as in *note;* (2.) *open*, similar to *o* in *not*, but rather broader.

5. *U* is like *oo* in English.

6. *Ai* and *au*, in Italian, are *proper* diphthongs. (See VI. 14, Observation.) Accordingly, CAIRO is to be pronounced kī'ro, AUSA, ŏw'sả, etc.

7. The consonants *b*, *d*, *f*, *l*, *m*, *n*, *p*, *q*, *s*, *t*, and *v* are similar to the English.

Obs. *K*, *w*, *x*, and *y* are not used by the Italians, except in spelling foreign names.

8. *C* and *cc*, before *a*, *o*, and *u*, are sounded like *k;* before *e*, *i*, and *y*, like *ch* or *tsh*.

Obs. *Cc* should be pronounced more strongly than a single *c*. This remark will apply to all double letters in Italian, as well as in most other languages.

9. As *c*, when immediately before *a*, *o*, or *u*, is never pronounced like *ch*, in order to express this sound in such cases, the vowel *i* is inserted: thus, *cia*, *cio*, *ciu*, are pronounced *chả*, *cho*, *choo*. (See table at the end of this Section.)

10. *Ch* is employed to express the sound of *k* before *e* and *i*.

11. *G*, before *a*, *o*, and *u*, is hard, as in the English word *get;* before *e*, *i*, and *y*, it sounds like the English *j: gia*, *gio*, *giu*, are pronounced *jả*, *jo*, *joo*. (See table at the end of this Section.)

12. *Gh* is used to express the sound of hard *g*, before *e* and *i*.

13. *Gli* has the sound of the liquid *l*, (*l*,) or of *lli* in *million:* thus, BOGLIO is pronounced bŏl'yo.

14. *Gn* has the same sound as in French; in other words, it is like the Spanish *ñ: e.g.* BOLOGNA is pronounced bo-lŏn'yả.

15. *H* is never sounded in Italian.

16. *J*, at the beginning of a syllable, is like the English *y*, (consonant;) at the end of a word it is equivalent to *ii*, (in Italian.)

17. *R* resembles the French, but is trilled somewhat more strongly. (See V. 24.)

18. *Sc*, before *e* and *i*, is like the English *sh : e.g.* SCIO is pronounced *shee'o*.

19. *Z* commonly has the sound of *dz* in English; *zz* is generally pronounced like *ts*. But to both these rules there are a number of exceptions. (See Monti's Italian Grammar, p. 4 and pp. 206–208.)

The following table will perhaps enable the reader more readily to understand the mode in which *c* and *ch*, *g* and *gh*, are employed by the Italians:

ca	is pronounced		kả.	ga	is pronounced		gả.
che	"	"	kả.	ghe	"	"	gả.
chi	"	"	ke.	ghi	"	"	ge.
co	"	"	ko.	go	"	"	go.
cu	"	"	koo.	gu	"	"	goo.
cia	"	"	chả.	gia	"	"	jả.
ce	"	"	che.	ge	"	"	jĭ.
ci	"	"	che.	gi	"	"	je.
cio	"	"	cho.	gio	"	"	jo.
ciu	"	"	choo.	giu	"	"	joo.

Obs. In Italian, the accent of words ending in a vowel is usually on the penultima; but to this general rule there are many exceptions.

---

* There are a number of niceties in Italian pronunciation, which, however interesting to a thorough linguist, cannot properly be noticed in a work like the present. The difficulty of giving a brief and at the same time a satisfactory exposition of the principles of this language is increased by the existence of different dialects in different parts of Italy. It has been deemed sufficient, in this synopsis, merely to explain those principles of pronunciation which appear to be recognized by the Italians generally.

NORWEGIAN.

XII.

As a written language, the Norwegian may be said to be identical with the Danish, since not only the grammar, but, with very few exceptions, the words, of both, are precisely the same. In pronunciation, however, the Norwegians differ widely from the Danes, while these, again, differ considerably among themselves. Under Section III. we have given the elements of Danish pronunciation as the language is spoken by the educated classes in Copenhagen. The principal points of difference between this and the Norwegian appear to be the following: (1.) *d* in the latter tongue always has its proper sound, while in the Danish it is often pronounced like the English *th*: (2.) *g* at the end of a word, in Norwegian, is usually sounded distinctly as *g* hard in English; (3.) *e* at the end of a word always retains its distinct sound; (4.) *ou* is like the Dutch and English *ou*, (*ŏw*.)

ORIENTAL LANGUAGES.

XIII.

1. Under this general term we include all those languages which are neither written in Roman letters nor in characters that can readily be converted into corresponding Roman letters. (See Preface, p. vi.) In this sense it would embrace not merely the Asiatic languages, to which the term "Oriental" is commonly limited, but also the Russian, which may in one sense be said to form the connecting link between the Asiatic and European tongues. It is proposed under this head to offer some remarks and explanations respecting the causes of the perplexity and confusion in which the whole subject of Oriental orthography seems at first sight so hopelessly involved. By a reference to what has been said on the different sounds of the Arabic tongue, (see Section I.,) it will readily be seen that, from the different modes employed to represent with Roman letters the sounds of many of the Arabic characters, an almost endless diversity may, or rather must, result in regard to the spelling of names in which those characters occur. The confusion is not a little increased by the fact that the same character has a different power according as it is employed by Arabian, Persian, or Indian writers.

2. As an illustration of the foregoing remarks, we may take غَيْبَال, an Oriental surname, signifying a "redresser of wrongs." In this name each of the four letters may be represented in two or more different ways: 1. the غ may be represented either by *g* or *gh*; 2. the ی may be represented by *y*, *i*, or (supposing it to be doubled) by *iy*, and (in English) by *ey* or *e*; 3. the ﺍ by *â*, *a*, and (in English) *au*; 4. the ﺙ may be represented by *th* or *s*, (or *ss*.) The name may then be written (without impropriety) by European writers in the following modes: First, as an Arabic name, in which the ﺙ retains its proper sound: Ghiyâth, Giyâth, Gheâth, Geâth, Ghiyauth, Giyauth, Gheauth, and Geauth. Secondly, as a Persian or Hindostanee name, in which the ﺙ is represented by a sharp *s* or *ss*: Ghiyâs, Giyâs, Gheâs, Geâs, Ghiaus, Giaus, Gheaus,* and Geaus. These sixteen spellings are not all the modes which might legitimately be used to represent the above name of four Arabic letters, but they are, perhaps, amply sufficient to illustrate what has been said above.

3. Another source of perplexity in regard to names of

---

* So written by Sir John Malcolm.

Arabic origin is the difference which obtains in the pronunciation of the fatha, (short *a*.) In Western Asia it often approaches very nearly the sound of *e* in met, (as in يَمَن Yemen, (yĕm'ęn,) the name of Arabia Felix,) while in some of the eastern parts of Persia the fatha is pronounced nearly like â, and in India it is sounded like our short *u*, (as in *tub*.) Accordingly, in Eastern Persia they say yăm'ăn, and in India yŭm'ŭn, for Arabia Felix.

4. The pronunciation of the Arabic article is of itself often the cause of much perplexity,—first, by the frequent change of the *l* to correspond with the sound of the initial letter of the following word, (see I. 33,) and, secondly, by the change of the *vowel*, which is variously sounded, commonly as *al* or *el*, often as *ool*, and sometimes as *ŭl*. Hence we have *Abd-el-Malek, Abd-al-Malek, Abd-ool-Malek,* (written also *Abd-ul-Malek* or *Abd-oul-Malik;*) *Abd-al-Rahman, Abd-el-Rahman, Abdar-Rahman, Abderrahman, Abdurrahman,* or *Abdourrahman.*

As it would be wholly out of the question for us in every instance to give all the different spellings of Oriental names,—and we have not attempted to do so, except in the case of a very few of great celebrity, (such as Jengis Khan,)—we have thought it might be useful to give the following table, by glancing at which the reader will perhaps acquire a greater practical facility in identifying names which at first sight may appear wholly different from each other, than he could by a more elaborate or more scientific explanation of the causes of such diversity. At the same time, that he may, if he desires to do so, clearly understand the principles which lie at the bottom of all this apparent confusion, we shall refer by numbers (indicated by figures included in a parenthesis) to the explanations and remarks made when speaking of the Arabic alphabet, (see Section I.,) where also we have pointed out the chief differences between the power of the letters in that tongue and in the Persian and Hindostanee.

TABLE OF CELEBRATED ORIENTAL NAMES WRITTEN VARIOUSLY.

Aboo-Bekr,[1] Abu-Becr, Aboubecre, Abu-Bakr, (30,)†
Abou- (or Abu-) Beker (or -Bekr,) Ebubekr, Uboo-Bekr or Ub'oo-Bukr,‡ (or -Buk'ker.)

Aboo- (Abou- or Abu-) Tâlib, (or -Tâleb,) Ebu-Thalib, Ub'oo-Tâ'leb.§

Adhad-ed-Daulah,[2] Adadoddaulah, Azad-ed-Daulah, (or -Dowlah,) (15,)‡ Uz'ud-ud-Dow'lah.§

Adherbijan, Aderbijan, Azerbaijan, (9.)†

---

[1] The "father of the virgin," (*i.e.* of Ayeshah.)
[2] The "arm (or defender) of the state."

† The use of the numerals in parenthesis will be clearly seen from the following examples. Under Aboo-Bekr we find 30. By a reference to this number in Section I., (note †,) we find that fatha is sounded sometimes like ă, sometimes like ĕ, and sometimes like ŭ; hence the variations of *Bakr*, *Bekr*, and *Bukr* or *Bukker*. Under Adherbijan we are referred to 9 in Section I., where we find that while the ﺫ, as an Arabic letter, is commonly represented by *dh* or *d*, it has in Persian the sound of *z*: and so on.

‡ Major Price, in his "Mahommedan History," (London, 1811,) writes the name Abû-Bukker,—somewhat inconsistently, since the first part of the name (Abû) is written with the Italian or German vowels, while the second (Bukker) is written in the English mode,—a mode, moreover, which no Englishman would be likely to use who had not acquired his pronunciation of the name in India. A worse inconsistency is found in Major Stewart's spelling of the name of Hoomayoon, (Houmaioon,) in which the first and second parts of the name are French, and the third English. He should either have written it Houmaioun or Houmayoun, or else Hoomayoon.

§ So generally pronounced in India.

Adh-Dhahabee,[1] (or -Dhahabî,) (9,) Al-Dzahabî, Uz-Zŭ′hŭbee,* (30.)

Akbar,[2] Akber, Ekber, Uk′bŭr,* (sometimes improperly written Akhbar and Ackbar.)

Alee,[3] Alî, Aly, (or Ally,) Ul′ee.*

Al-kâhir-Billah,[4] Al-Qahir-† (or Qaher-) Billah, (21.)

Bâber, Bâbar, or Baubur.

Bayazeed, Bayezeed, Bayazid; Bajasid, (German;) sometimes corrupted into Bajazet.

Fereedoon, Feridoun, Feridûn, Fureedoon; written also Pheridun or Pheridoun.

Firdousee, Firdausi, Ferdouçy, Firdousi, Firdusi, Ferdosi. (For the signification of this name, see FIRDOUSEE, in the body of the work.)

Hassan,[5] Haçan, (14,) Hussun.‡

Hoolâkoo, Houlakou, Hulaku or Hoolâgoo, Houlagou, Hulagu.

Hoomâyoon,[6] Houmayoun, Humayûn or Humayoon, Houmaioon.

Isfendiyâr, Asfandiyar, Isfundear.‡

Jehân- (or Jahân-) Geer,[7] Djehan-Ghyr, Djahan-Guire, Dschehan- (or Dschahan-) Gir.

Kai-Kâoos, Kai-Kaous, Kai-Kaus, Key-Kawuss.

Kereem,* (or Kareem,) Kerîm, Karîm, Carim, Kurreem.‡

Khadîjah, (or Khadeejah,) Chadidsha or Khadidschah, Khadidjah or Khadidja, Kadijah.

Khaled, Chaled, Caled.

Khaleel, Chalil, Khulleel.‡

Lokmân, Locman, Loqman, (21,) Lockmaun.

Mahmood-Abool-Kâsim- (or Kasem-) Yemeen-ed-Dow-lah,[9] Mahmoud-Abul-Kaçem-Yemîn-eddaulah, Mahmûd-Abûl-Kassim-Jemin-eddaulah.

Mansoor,[10] (Al,) Mansour or Mançour, (14,) Mansûr, Munsoor.‡

Meerzâ,[11] Mîrza, Mirsa, (German.)

Moâweeyah, Moawiah, Moawiyah, Moawije and Muawijjah, (German,) Moâveah, Mauweiah, (in Latin, Moawias.)

Modhafar,[12] Modhofar, Mozaffer, Mozuffur, Muzuffer, Moozuffur,‡ (17.)

Mohammed,[13] Mahomed, Mahomet, Muhammed, Mehemet, Moohummud,* (moō-hŭm′mŭd.)

Nâdir Shâh,[14] Nadir (or Nader) Chah, Nadir Schah, Nauder Shah.

Nâsir-ed-Deen,[15] Nassireddyn, Nâçireddîn, (14,) Nasser-u-deen, Nausser-ud-deen.

Nizâmee, Nizami, Nisami, Nidhami, (17.)

Noor-ed-Deen[16] or Nour-ed-Din, Nour-u-deen, Noureddyn, Nureddin.

[1] "The golden."   [2] The "great," or "greatest."
[3] "High," "eminent," "noble."   [4] "Victorious through God."
[5] "Beautiful," "handsome," "good."
[6] "Fortunate," "blessed."   [7] "Conqueror of the world."
[8] "Bountiful," "generous," "merciful."
[9] Yemeen-ed-Dowlah signifies "right hand of the state (or empire.")
[10] "The victorious."
[11] *I.e. Meer-Zâd*, or *Ameer-Zâd*, "son of a prince."
[12] "Victorious."   [13] "Praised."
[14] "Wonderful king."   [15] "Defender of the faith."
[16] "Light of the faith."

* Sometimes so written and so pronounced by the English in India. (See Section IX. 3.)

† Sir G. Wilkinson writes the name of the celebrated capital of Egypt (Cairo) *Qahera.*

‡ So written by Sir John Malcolm, and so pronounced in India.

18

Nousheerwân, Noushirwân, Nauschirwan or Naouchirwan, Nuschirwan. (See KHOSROO, in the body of this work.)

Omeyyah, Ommeyah, Ommaiah, Umeyyah, Omâee; (in German,) Omajjah, Omijjah, or Umaijjah.

Othmân, Osman, Otman, (or Ottoman.)

Rōōstam, Rōōstum, Roustam, Roustem, Rustam, Rustem.

Shah-Alam[17] (or -Aulum,) Chah-Alam (or -Alem,) Schah-Alam.

Shah-Jehân[18] (or -Jahan,) Chah-Djehan, Schah-Dschehan or Schah-Dschahan.

Sooleymân, Suleiman, Solyman, Soliman, Souleyman.

Soovórof, Souvorof, Suworow, Suwarow, Suwarrow, Souvarof, Suvaroff, Suvorow.

Taimoor or Teemoor, Timour, Taïmour, Taimur or Timur, Tamerlane.[19]

Yakoob, Yacoob, Yakoub, Yacoub, Yakûb; Jakub, (German.)

Yazeed or Yezeed, Yazid or Yezid; Jezid, (Dutch;) Jasid or Jesid, (German.)

Yoozuf, Yoosōōf, Youzouf or Youzef, Iouzef; Jusuf or Jusef, (German.)

The following table of names of a certain kind, classified according to their spelling, in the four principal European languages, will, it is believed, furnish a key to many of the difficulties which the reader is likely to meet with in works on Oriental history or biography:

ENGLISH.	FRENCH.	GERMAN.	ITALIAN.
Chengiz,	Tchenguiz,	Tschengis,	Cenghis.
Chenghiz,	Tchenghis,	Tschingis,	Cinghis.
Chenghis,	Tchenguis,		
Chingiz,	Tchinguiz.		
Chingis,	Tchinguis.		
Chinghis,	Tchinghis.		
Jengis,§	Djenguiz,	Dschengis,	Genghis.
Jengiz,	Djenguyz.		
Jenghis,	Djenguis.		

The first of the above spellings are based on the supposition that the initial consonant in the Mongol name had the sound of our *ch*; while those below (Jengis, etc.) rest on the supposition that the initial letter had the sound of *j*. On this question the best Oriental authorities are not agreed. It very probably had a sound somewhat differing from either.

ENGLISH.	FRENCH.	GERMAN.	ITALIAN.
Jaafar,	Djafar,	Dschafar,	Giafar.
Jafar,	Djafer,	Dschafer,	Giaffar.
Jafer,	Djaafar,	Dschaafar,	Giaafar, etc.
Jamsheed	Djamchid,	Dschamschid,	Giamscid.
or	Djamchyd,	Dschemschid.	
Jemsheed,	Djemchid,		
	Djemchyd,		
	Djamschid, etc.‖		

[17] "King of the world," or "king of the universe."
[18] "King of the world."
[19] A corruption of *Taimoor-leng* or *Timur-lenk,—i.e.* "Taimoor the lame"

§ Gibbon, the historian, writes the name *Zingis.*

‖ It is extremely common for French writers, in spelling Oriental or Russian names, to use *sch* instead of *ch*, which is more strictly French. It has not been deemed necessary to present in the table every possible form, such as Djamschyd, Djemschyd, Dgemchid, Dgemchyd, etc., although these would be perfectly legitimate French spellings.

ENGLISH.	FRENCH.	GERMAN.	ITALIAN.
Jahan Geer,*	Djahanguir,*	Dschahangir,*	Giahanghir.
Jehan Geer	Djahanguyr,	Dschehangir,	Gehanghir.
or	Djehanguir,		
Jehangeer,	Djehanguyr,		
	Djahanguire, etc.		
Khadijah,	Khadidja,	Chadidscha,	Cadigia.
Khadeejah.			
Meerza,	Mirza,	Mirsa or Mirza,	Mirsa or Mirza.
Nizâmee,	Nizami,	Nisami,	Nisami.
Noor-ed-Deen,*	Noureddin,*	Nureddin,*	Nureddin.
Noor-ud-deen,	Noureddyn.		
Shah-Jahân,	Chah-Djahan,	Schah-Dschahan,Sciah Giahan.	
Shah-Jehân,	Chah-Djehan,	Schah-Dschehan, Sciach Giacan.	
Shah-Jehaun.			
Yazeed	Yazid,	Jasid,	Jasid.
or	Yasid,	Jesid,	Jesid.
Yezeed,	Iazid,		
	Yezid,		
	Iesid.		
Yoosuf	Youzouf,	Jussuf (or	Jusuf.
or	Youzef,	Jusuf,)	Jusef.
Yoozoof,	Youseph,	Jusef,	
Yoozef,	Iouzef, etc.,	Juseph.	
Zeid or Zeyd,	Zeïd,	Seid or Seyd.	
Zhookofski	Joukofski,	Schukowski,	
or	Joukovski,	Schukovski,	Sciucofschi.
Zhookofskee,	Joucofski,	Schukofski,	Sciucovschi.
	Zhoukofski.†	Shukowski.	

Any number of instances might be cited in which respectable English writers use in the same work, and, it may be, in the same sentence, the English, French, and German orthography indiscriminately, as Aboo, Abou, or Abu, Abool-Kausim, Aboul-Kâssim, Abul-Kâssim, Arghoun, Feridoon, etc. etc. This is unquestionably a serious defect in any work, as in most cases the reader must be wholly at a loss to determine what sound the writer intends to convey; yet the universal prevalence of this practice, and the absence of any settled orthography in regard to Oriental names, may be justly urged as some extenuation. But there is another very common fault, which in our view is far more objectionable,—that of combining French and English or English and German orthography in the same name: as, Abou-Yusoof, (in which the second syllable is French, the third German, and the fourth English,) Abou-Aly-Sumjoovee, (in which the first part is French, and the second and third English,) Aboushirwan, Aboul-Kausim, (in both of which the second syllable is French, and the third English,) Abulfiradge, (Aboolfaraj,) (in which the second syllable is German, and the fourth French,) Nour-u-deen-Mahmood, (in which the first syllable is French, and all the rest English.)

All the examples last cited, and most of the others, are taken from Sir John Malcolm's "History of Persia,"

a work of decided merit, whose author was not wanting either in the learning or judgment required to produce a work essentially free from the above defects, had his attention been directed to the great importance of consistency and uniformity in writings of this kind.

PERSIAN.
XIV.

1. The modern Persian is a mixed product formed by the union of words derived from the different Aryan dialects of ancient Persia with the Arabic, which was introduced into the language by the Mohammedan conquerors of the country. The mixture of these heterogeneous elements may be aptly compared to that of oil and water. As in such a mixture we see portions or masses of each ingredient in contact, but not combined or assimilated with each other, so in modern Persian we often find the Aryan and Semitic elements thrown together side by side, without the slightest attempt to assimilate or combine them into a harmonious whole. We constantly meet with scraps of pure Arabic—not merely phrases, but even whole sentences—introduced bodily into a passage of which all. the rest is Persian, both in etymology and grammatical construction.‡

2. The Persian alphabet includes, along with the twenty-eight Arabic letters, these four additional ones : پ, (p,) ژ, (zh,) چ, (ch,) and گ, (g.) The following characters have, in Persian, a totally different power from that given them in the Arabic alphabet, viz.: ذ, ض, and ظ, which are pronounced like z, and ث, which takes the sound of s. This diversity of sound, as might naturally be expected, often causes much confusion, because European writers are apt to spell the name according to the language with which they happen to be most familiar: thus, one who is familiar with Arabic and but little acquainted with Persian, as pronounced by the natives of that country, will write *Adherbijan, Modhafer* or *Modhofar*, while those who have learned the pronunciation of these names in Persia or India will write *Azerbijan, Mozafer* or *Mozaffer.*

3. The Persian has also two vowel-sounds unknown to the Arabic,—namely, *é* and *ô*. These sounds of *yâ* and *waw* are usually distinguished from the common Arabic sounds of the same letters (namely, *i* or *ee* and *û* or *oo*) by the Arabic epithet *Mâjhool* or *Majhûl*, (signifying "unknown,") or *Ajemee, (Ajemî,) (i.e.* "Persian,") while the ordinary sound is designated by the term *Ma'roof, (Ma'rûf,)* that is, "known" or "familiar."

4. It may be observed that the long *a (â)* in Persian is considerably broader than the long *a* in Arabic or in Sanscrit, though the pronunciation varies somewhat in different provinces. In the city of Shirâz (where it is claimed that the best Persian is spoken) the sound of *â* is scarcely, if at all, less broad than in the English words *awe, fall,* etc.

---

* It may be proper to observe that compound names, like the above, (as Jahangeer or Djahanguir, Noureddin or Nureddin, etc., may be written as one word or divided into their separate parts, according to the option of the writer. Thus, we may write Jahangeer or Jahan-Geer, Djahanguir or Djahan-Guir; Nooreddeen, Noor-ed-Deen, Noureddin, (or Noureddyn,) Naur-ed-Din, Nour-Eddin, or Nour-Eddyn: etc. etc. We have, however, in giving the English spellings, generally preferred to divide the names into their separate parts, which appears to accord with the general usage of our language in regard to compound words of modern origin.

† It may be remarked that French writers sometimes, though rarely, use *zh* instead of *j* in order to represent the sound of the Russian Ж. The Germans often employ *sh* (*s* in German being usually equivalent to our *z*) for the same purpose.

‡ Sir William Jones, in the Preface to his "Persian Grammar," gives a very striking illustration of the difference between the crude mixture of different ingredients composing the modern Persian, and the more thoroughly assimilated elements of our own tongue, by the following parallel sentences. The first, exhibiting the structure of the English language, is from Middleton's "Life of Cicero," (vol. iii. p. 351:) "The true law is right reason conformable to the nature of things: which calls us to duty by commanding, deters us from sin by forbidding." The composition of the Persian is similar to the following: "The true *lex* is *recta ratio* conformable *naturæ*, which by commanding *vocet ad officium*, by forbidding *à fraude deterreat.*"

POLISH.
XV.

1. *A* sounds as *a* in the English word *far.*

2. *E*, without an accent, like *e* in *met ;* with an accent, (*é,*) like *a* in *fate.*

3. *I* as in *marine.*

4. *O*, unaccented, as in *note ;* with an accent, like *oo* in *good,* or *ōŏ.*

5. *U* is like *oo* in *moon.*

6. *Y* resembles *e* in *me*, but is more guttural, being similar to *i* in *pin.*

7. *A* sounds nearly like *on* in French, (òN ;) *e* is *in* in French, (or âN.)

8. The consonants *b, d, f, g,* (always hard,) *h, k, m, n, p, s,* (always sharp,) *t* and *z,* are essentially the same as in English.

9. *C* in all cases, even before *a* or *o,* sounds like *ts* in English ; *cz* is equivalent to our *ch ; ch* is like the German *ch.*

10. *J* is like the German, being equivalent to *y* consonant.

11. *L* (without any mark) is similar to our *l,* but softer ; *ł* is very hard, somewhat resembling the *ll* of the Welsh.

12. *R* is like the German.

13. *W* is similar to the German, resembling our *v.*

14. *N*, with an accent over it, (*ń,*) sounds like the Spanish *ñ.*

15. *S*, marked in a similar manner, (*ś,*) has a sound blending that of *s* and *y* consonant. *Sć* has a sound which cannot be given in English : its nearest approximation in our language is *sts.*

16. *Sz* is equivalent to *sh* in English.

17. *Z*, with a point over it, (*ż,*) is like the French *j,* or *zh* in English.

18. *Z*, with an accent, (*ź,*) is somewhat similar to the above, but has no equivalent in our language.

Obs. 1. The accent in Polish words or names of more than one syllable is nearly always on the penultima.

Obs. 2. The sounds of the letters in Slavonian, Bohemian, and Illyrian correspond, with slight exceptions, to those of the Polish language.

PORTUGUESE.
XVI.

1. The vowels *a, e, i, o, u,* and *y,* and the diphthongs *ai, ay, au,** are essentially the same as in Spanish.

2. *Ao* and *am* are pronounced almost *ŏwN.*

3. The consonants *b, d, f, l, m, n, p, s, t, v,* and *z* are similar to the English.

4. *C* is the same as in French, differing from the English only by sometimes having the *cedilla.*

5. *Ch* is the same as in French, or, in other words, is like our *sh.*

6. *G* and *j* are the same as in French. (See V. 15 and 17.)

7. *H*, in Portuguese, is always silent. When, however, it follows *l* or *n,* it renders these letters *liquid :* thus, *filho* ("son") is pronounced feel'yoo or fèl'yo ; *senhora,* ("lady,") sàn-yo'rà, etc.

8. *M* frequently, and *n* sometimes, has a nasal sound. *Sam,* like *são,* is pronounced almost *souN ; alem* or *alen* sounds like â-lêN'.

9. *Qu* is pronounced as in French, the *u* in this case not being sounded.

10. *R* is like the French. (See V. 24.)

11. *X* is sounded like *ch* in Portuguese, or *sh* in English.

Obs. In Portuguese the general rules of accentuation are similar to those in the Spanish language. (See XIX. Obs. 1.)

RUSSIAN.
XVII.

The Russian is the most important of all the Slavic family of languages, not merely on account of its being the tongue of one of the most powerful and most populous empires in the world, but it is probably not inferior, viewed simply as a vehicle of expression, to any other member of that family, if we take into consideration all the qualities which go to form a good language, such as softness, flexibility, variety, richness, and force. Although some of its consonants—Щ, for example—seem sufficiently harsh to an English ear, it is much softer than the Polish, and is mostly free from that concourse of consonants† which makes the latter tongue so formidable to foreigners.

The power of the greater number of the Russian letters is perhaps sufficiently explained in the table on the opposite page. The following, however, require some additional explanation :

1. Г sounds usually nearly like our hard *g,* but is somewhat more guttural, as if an aspirate were mingled with the other sound. Occasionally it is pronounced like *k,* and not unfrequently, when at the end of words, like the German *ch.* It also has sometimes nearly the sound of our *h ;* and, as the Russians have no other letter to represent *h* in foreign names, they use Г for this purpose. Thus, they would write *Kopengagen* for *Copenhagen.*

2. E, though generally possessing the pronunciation indicated in the table, (à or yà,) in some cases takes the sound of yo or e-o ; it is then usual to mark it thus, ё, as несёте, "you carry," (pronounced něs-yo'tě or něs-e-o'tě.)

Obs. 1. The omission of this mark sometimes leads to important errors: thus, *Feodor,* ("Theodore,") always in three syllables, is not unfrequently written and pronounced by foreigners *Fedor.*

Obs. 2. The varying sound of *e* (à or yà) will explain why certain names beginning with this vowel are written sometimes with an initial *E* and sometimes with *Y,* as *Ekaterinoslaf* or *Yekaterinoslaf, Elisavetgrad* or *Yelisavetgrad,* etc.

3. К is usually sounded as in English, but in certain positions it takes the sound of *kh,* (or the German *ch.*)

4. Л has usually the same sound as the English *l,* but when followed by the hard semi-vowel Ъ, or by the vowels *a, o, y,* (*oo,*) it is similar to the Polish *ł.*

5. The hard semi-vowel Ъ imparts to the preceding consonant a strong harsh sound, as if it were doubled. When preceded by в (*v*) it changes the sound of this consonant into that of *f* or *ff ;* as, орловъ, pronounced or-loff'. Following ж, it changes the sound of this letter into *sh ;* as, ножъ, pronounced—nosh. In like manner, when it follows д, it changes its sound to *t ;* and so on.

6. The soft semi-vowel ь usually imparts a soft or liquid sound to the preceding consonant. Thus, стань is pronounced almost stâñ ; столъ, stol, etc.

7. The semi-vowel й is placed after vowels with which it coalesces, forming but one syllable ; as, дай pronounced dä-ĭ or dī ; пей, pà-e or pā, etc.

---

* *Ei* and *ey* are almost the same as in Spanish, but have a sound sometimes approaching that of the English long *i.*

† As occurs, for example, in such Polish names as the following : *Brzesc, Przemysl, Skrzenbski,* etc. etc.

The Russian alphabet consists of thirty-six letters, as follows :

	Power	Name as pronounced in English.			Power.	Name as pronounced in English.
1. А а	â	â		19. Т т ш	t	tâ
2. Б б	b	bâ		20. У у	oo	oo
3. В в	v	vâ		21. Ф ф	f	êf
4. Г г	g or *gh*	ghâ		22. Х х	к (like the German *ch*)	kâ
5. Д д	a	dâ		23. Ц ц	ts	tsâ
6. Е е	â or yâ	yâ		24. Ч ч	ch or tch (equivalent to the Persian ﺥ)	châ
7. Ж ж	zh	zhâ		25. Ш ш	sh	shâ
8. З з	z	zâ		26. Щ щ	sh-tsh	sh'tchâ
9. И и	è, ï, yè	yè		27. Ъ ъ	*e* mute (making the preceding consonant hard)	yâʀ
10. I i	è or ï	è		28. Ы ы	è or wè	yâr-we
11. К к	k	kâ		29. Ь ь	y, nearly mute	yâ'rï
12. Л л	l	êl		30. Ѣ ѣ	yâ or â	yâ'tў or yâ'tï
13. М м	m	êm		31. Э э	ê	ê
14. Н н	n	ên		32. Ю ю	û (yoo) or ü	yoo
15. О о	o	ò		33. Я я	yâ or yê	yâ
16. П п	p	pâ		34. Ѳ ѳ	f	fê-tâ'
17. Р р	r	êʀ		35. Ѵ ѵ	è, ï	ee'zhêt-sâ
18. С с	s	êss		36. Й й	y, nearly mute, (like a half-uttered ï.)	è or ï

SANSCRIT.

XVIII.

1. The Sanscrit* (*i.e.* the "elaborate" or "perfect" language) was the language used by the more highly cultivated portion of the ancient Aryan inhabitants of India, (see Arya in the body of this work,) and is still the learned language of their descendants, the modern Hindoos.† It is regarded as the oldest of the Indo-European tongues. The character in which it is written is called Nâgarî‡ or Dêvanâgarî, (pronounced dâ'vạ nâ'gạ-ree',) and, like most other alphabets of the Indo-European family, it is written from left to right. The Nâgarî, (or Nâgaree,) considered simply as a phonetic system, is perhaps the most perfect of human alphabets. It not only has a separate letter for every one of its elementary sounds, but it is also remarkable for its ad-

mirable classification of these sounds. It consists of fifty letters, of which fourteen are vowels and thirty-six consonants, besides various compound characters, which may be said to be merely abbreviated modes of writing two or three consonants together.

2. The vowels are

अ	ă§	ऊ	û (or ōō)	ऋ	ê
आ or आ	â	ऋ	rï	or	ai (*i.e.* â'e)
इ	ï	ॠ	rî (or ree)	ओ	ï ô
ई	î (or ee)	ऌ	lï	औ	ï au (or ôu)
उ	u (or ōō)	ॡ	lî (or lee)		

Obs. It will be seen that most of the Sanscrit vowels have two forms: the first is used at the beginning of a clause or sentence, the other occurs in other positions, particularly in the middle of a word.

3. The consonants are as follows :

क	k	ख	kh	ग	g	घ	gh	ङ	ng
च	ch	छ	chh	ज	j	झ	jh	ञ	ñ
ट	ṭ	ठ	ṭh	ड	ḍ	ढ	ḍh	ण	ṇ
त	t	थ	th	द	d	ध	dh	न	n
प	p	फ	ph	ब	b	भ	bh	म	m
य	y	र	r	ल	l	व	v	ं	ṁ
श	sh	ष	ṣh	स	s	ह	h	़	ḥ‖

---

* Written also *Sanskrit* and *Sungskrit.* The term is derived from the Sanscrit particle *săm*, nearly equivalent to the Latin *con*, "together," (and, like it, often used as an intensive,) and *kṛĭtă*, "made" or "done." It signifies "made or done thoroughly," and, hence, "elaborate," "complete," "perfect."

† It may be said to bear nearly the same relation to the modern Hindoo dialects that the Latin bears to the dialects of modern Italy.

‡ Nâgarî [from *Nagara*, a "city"] signifies "of the city," and, hence, "refined" or "cultivated." Dêva, (nearly related to the Latin *Deus* and *Divus*,) a Sanscrit word, denoting a "god" or "deity," was often applied as a term of honour to the Brahmans. (See "Institutes of Manu," ix. 317, 319.) Dêvanâgarî would appear, then, to signify the "cultivated (written) language of the gods, (or Brahmans,") the use of it having originally been for the most part, if not exclusively, confined to the priestly caste.

§ The pronunciation of अ, in modern India, is like that of our short *u* in *but*. It should be observed that ऋ and ऌ do not involve any sound of *i*, but are similar to our *r* and *l*.

‖ To these may be added ऋ, (ऌ) occurring only in the Vedas.

4. The vowels are divided into

Short, अ इ उ ऋ लृ

Long, आ ई ऊ ॠ लॄ

5. The Sanscrit letters may be classified as follows:

	VOWELS.	SEMI-VOWELS.	NASALS.	MUTES.	SIBI-LANTS.	ASPIRA-TION, ETC.
Gutturals,	अ आ		ङ	क ख ग घ		ह
Palatals,	इ ई	य	ञ	च छ ज झ	श	
Linguals,	ऋ ॠ	र	ण	ट ठ ड ढ	ष	:
Dentals,	लृ लॄ	ल	न	त थ द ध	स	.
Labials,	उ ऊ	व	म	प फ ब भ		

6. The only Sanscrit sounds of frequent occurrence which present any serious difficulty to the European learner are the combinations of the mutes *k, g, ch, j, ṭ, ḍ, t, d, p,* and *b* with *h*, making *kh*, (ख,) *gh*, (घ,) *ṭh*, (ठ,) and so on. It is important to observe that ख has a totally different sound from the Arabic or Persian ﺥ, (equivalent to the German *ch ;*) and ठ or थ is pronounced quite differently from the Arabic ﺙ, or our *th.* The sound of *kh, gh, th, dh, ph,* and *bh,* in Sanscrit as well as in the modern Hindoo dialects, may be said to resemble that produced in such English phrases as "bake-house," "stag-horn," "hot-house," "bid him," "stop him," etc., when these words are pronounced quickly and yet very distinctly; with this important difference, however, that the Indian mute and *h* are to be uttered with a single impulse of the voice, and never divided into separate syllables.

7. The dental *t* (त) and *d,* (द,) in Sanscrit, have essentially the same sound as the Arabic ﺕ and ﺩ, (see Section I. 4 and 8;) but the lingual (cerebral) *t* (ट) and *d* (ड) have no equivalent either in Arabic or Persian. They somewhat resemble the English *t* and *d,* but are formed by reverting the end of the tongue far back into the dome of the mouth: hence the name of *cerebrals* sometimes given to them.* The Hindostanee *r* (ड़) is pronounced in a similar manner. (See 8 of this Section.)

8. It may be observed that in the modern dialects of India, including Hindostanee, we have, in addition to the lingual and dental sounds of *t* and *d,* a lingual (or cerebral) *r,* (not found in Sanscrit.) The Sanscrit घोट (ghôṭâ,) a "horse," becomes in Hindostanee ghôṛa; गरुड, (Găruḍă,) the vâhăn of Vishnu, takes the modern form of găruṛ, (pronounced gŭr'ŏŏṛ.) In writing Hindostanee with the Nâgarî alphabet, this lingual *r* is represented by ड with a dot beneath, thus, ड़, while in the ordinary (Persian) alphabet it is indicated thus, ؇ or ڑ. The lingual *t* and *d* in the modern Nâgarî are written precisely as in Sanscrit; but in the common alphabet they are distinguished from ﺕ and ﺩ either by having four dots, as ﺕ, ﺩ, or by a stroke placed above, ﻁ, ﺩ.

9. In writing Sanscrit, अ *(ă)* is never expressed after a consonant, but it is implied after every consonant unless this be followed by another vowel or by the rest-sign: thus, कमल, (kml,) "lotus," is to be read kămălă; but if the final consonant has the rest sign, it does not take the *ă* after it, as मरुत्, (mărut,) "wind."

(For a fuller and more systematic exposition of the elements, etc. of the Sanscrit language, the reader is referred to the very able article entitled "Sanscrit," by Professor Whitney, in the "New American Cyclopædia.")

* They are called in Sanscrit "mûrdhanya," (from *mûrdhan,* the "head,") because they seem to be pronounced more nearly in the centre of the head than any other class of letters.

22

SPANISH.

XIX.

1. The Spanish *a* sounds as in the English word *far ; e,* like *a* in *ale ; i,* like *e* in *mete ; o,* as in English ; *u,* like *oo ;* and *y,* (when a vowel,) like the Spanish *i.*

2. *Ai* and *ay* are like long *i* in English. *Au* sounds like *ou* in *our.* (See XVII. 13, Obs.) *Ei* and *ey* are pronounced ā′e.

3. The consonants *f, l,* (single,) *m, n, p, s, t,* and *v* are pronounced nearly as in English.

4. *B,* at the beginning of a word, sounds as in English ; but when between two vowels its sound somewhat resembles that of *v,* with this difference,—*v* is pronounced with the upper teeth placed against the under lip, while the sound of the Spanish *b* is formed by bringing the lips loosely or feebly into contact. This sound seems to be between that of *b* and the English *w.* It is represented by ʙ or v.

5. *C,* before *a, o,* and *u,* is pronounced as in English ; before *e* and *i,* it has the sound of *th* in the word *thin.* In the Catalan dialect it is the same as in English.

6. *Ch* has the same sound as in English, except in the dialect of Catalonia, where it is pronounced like *k.*

7. *D,* at the beginning of a word, is sounded nearly as in English, but is pronounced with the tip of the tongue against the upper teeth, while in pronouncing the English *d* the tongue is made to touch the roof of the mouth. At the end of a syllable, or between two vowels, *d,* in Spanish, sounds like the English *th* in *this,* but is somewhat softer. This sound is usually represented in the present work by a small capital ᴅ.

8. *G,* before *a, o,* and *u,* is hard, as in English.

9. *G* before *e* and *i,* and *j* before every vowel, are pronounced like a strong guttural *h,* similar to the German *ch* in *ach.* This sound is indicated by ʜ, distinguished as a small capital.

10. *Gua* and *guo* sound somewhat like gwâ, gwo, but the *g* is so soft that it is scarcely perceived; so that in these cases the sound of *gu* seems to approximate very nearly to that of the English *w. Gu,* before *e* and *i,* is usually sounded like *g* hard : thus, GUIANA is pronounced ge-â′nâ. When, however, the *u* is marked with a diæresis, thus, *güi,* these two letters have the same sound as when before *a* or *o,* and consequently *güi* is pronounced gwe or we. (See table at the end of this Section.)

11. *H,* in Spanish, is never pronounced, except in words beginning with *hue,* and then very slightly.

12. *J:* for this letter, see 9 and 18 of this Section.

13. *Ll* (now sometimes written l) has a sound which combines that of *l* and *y* consonant, and is similar to the liquid *l* in French : *e.g. villa* or *vil̃a* is pronounced veel′yâ ; *Llerena,* lâ-rā′nâ or lyâ-rā′nâ.

14. *N,* in similar manner, unites the sounds of *n* and *y,* and is like *gn* in French : thus, *peña* is pronounced pên′yâ or pân′yâ.

15. *Q,* in Spanish, is always followed by *u. Qu,* before *a* and *o,* is sounded as in English, or, in other words, is equivalent to *kw ;* before *e* and *i,* it is pronounced like *k,* unless the *u* be marked with a diæresis, in which case it is like *kw.* (See table at the end of this Section.)

16. *R* is similar to the French, but is trilled more strongly. (See V. 24.)

17. *T* is to be pronounced by putting the tip of the tongue against the upper teeth.

18. *X* is usually sounded like the Spanish *j*, which letter, according to the present mode of spelling, has been generally substituted for it: thus, instead of the old spelling XIMENES, XUCAR, etc., we now often see in Spanish works JIMENES, JUCAR, etc. *X*, before a consonant, or before a vowel marked with this sign, ^, is sounded as in English: Examples,—*Exterior, Exâminar.*

19. *Y*, at the beginning of Spanish words, is usually a semi-consonant, as initial *y* is for the most part in English words.

20. *Z* is to be pronounced like *th* in *thin*.

The following table may serve to show more clearly the manner in which *c, g, j, q, x,* and *z* are used in Spanish.

ca	is pronounced	kȧ.	cua or qua is pronounced quȧ.		
que	"	"	kȧ.	cue or qüe "	"	quȧ.
qui	"	"	ke.	cui or qüi "	"	que.
co	"	"	ko.	cuo or quo "	"	quo.
cu	"	"	koo.		
ga	is pronounced	gȧ.	gua is pronounced gwȧ or wȧ.		
gue	"	"	gȧ.	güe "	"	gwȧ or wȧ.
gui	"	"	ḡe.	gui "	"	gwe or we.
go	"	"	go.	guo "	"	gwo or wo.
gu	"	"	goo.		
ja or xa	is pronounced	нȧ.	za	is pronounced	thȧ.
je, xe, or ge	"	"	нȧ.	ze or ce	"	"	thȧ.
ji, xi, or gi	"	"	нe.	zi or ci	"	"	the.
jo or xo	"	"	нo.	zo	"	"	tho.
ju or xu	"	"	нoo.	zu	"	"	thoo.

OBS. 1. Spanish words or names ending in a consonant have the accent almost always on the last syllable; those ending in a vowel are generally accentuated on the penultima. If a word or name be an exception to either of these rules, in correctly-printed Spanish works the accent is usually marked; as, CÓRDOVA, ALCALÁ, JÚCAR, CÁCERES. It should be observed that the *s* in the *plural* does not change the accent: hence *casas,* "houses," though ending in a consonant, has the penultimate accent as well as the singular *casa,* a "house."

OBS. 2. The Spanish accent, though resembling the German and Italian, is much less distinctly marked than the accent of those languages,—so much so, that it is sometimes difficult for an English ear to determine positively which is the accentuated syllable. In this respect it may be said to approximate very nearly to the French.

OBS. 3. The Spanish language as spoken in Mexico and South America differs in some points materially from the true Spanish.

Thus, *z,* and *c* before *e* and *i,* instead of having the sound of *th,* are generally pronounced like *s.* Among the uneducated classes *ll* is universally sounded like *y:* thus, *gallo* is pronounced almost gȧ′yo.

SWEDISH.

XX.

1. The vowels *a* and *i,* and the diphthongs *ä* and *ö,* are similar to the German.

2. Å sounds like the English *o.* Luleå is pronounced loo′lĬ-ō; Torneå, tor′nĭ-o, etc.

3. *E,* when accentuated, has almost the sound of our short *i* prolonged, represented in this work by *ĭĭ.*

4. *O,* at the end of a syllable, is like our *oo;* in other cases, like *o* in *not.*

5. *U,* in Swedish, is a very difficult sound for foreigners to acquire; it seems remotely to resemble the French *u,* and to blend (very obscurely) the sounds of the English *ĭ* or *ĕ* and *oo.* It has been represented in the present work by *oo,* this sound being the nearest to it of any in our language.

6. *Y* is the same as in Danish, or, in other words, is similar to the French *u.*

7. The Swedish consonants are, for the most part, pronounced like the English, with the exception of *j* and *g,* (before *e, i, ä, ö,* and *ü,*) which are nearly equivalent to *y* consonant, (*g,* before *a, o,* and *u,* is hard, as in English,) and of *z,* which commonly sounds like *s,* or else like the English *z.*

8. *Ch* initial (except when immediately followed by *r*) is sounded like the English *ch* in *child;* in the middle or at the end of a word it takes the sound of *k. Kj* sounds like the English *ch* in *child:* thus, *Kjöping* (written, also, simply *Köping*) is pronounced chö′ping. *C,* (as in English,) before *a, o,* and *u,* is like *k;* before *e, i,* and *y,* like *s. Qv* or *qu* is like *qu* in English.

9. *St,* followed by *j,* has the sound of our *sh:* hence *Stjerna* is pronounced shêʀ′nȧ. *K* before *e* sometimes takes the sound of our *ch:* thus, *Kellgren* is pronounced chel′gren.

EXPLANATIONS.

SIGNS, ETC. RELATING TO ORTHOEPY.

1. ā sounds as *a* in *fate.*

2. ă denotes the sound of *a* in *fare* or *e* in *there.* It is used to indicate the sound of the long open *e* before *r* in cases where it would be objectionable to employ *ai.* It has not been deemed proper to use exactly the same letters (without any distinctive mark) in the pronunciation as in the spelling of a name; because if the same letters were used for both, and the reader should happen to miscall the name as ordinarily written, he would perhaps be equally liable to miscall the pronunciation. While, therefore, the pronunciation of MOLIÈRE may very properly be represented by mo′le-aiʀ′, it would, for the reason just given, be improper to represent that of BEAUCAIRE by bō′kaiʀ′, instead of which we write bō′kăʀ′.

3. ȧ is essentially the same as ā, but less prolonged.*

4. ȧ is nearly like the preceding, but more open. It is used to represent a sound very similar to that of *e* in *met,* (ĕ,) but somewhat longer. (See Introduction, V. 7, note.)

5. ä sounds like *a* in *far* or *father.*

6. ă (the short sound of ä) has a sound between ȧ and ä; it is shorter than the former, and somewhat more open than the latter.

7. ā (the long sound of ä) indicates a sound longer than ä; in the pronunciation of Oriental names it approximates ä very nearly.

been deemed preferable in certain cases, particularly in the pronunciation of French names, in order to guard against a drawling sound.

For a similar reason, *e,* in marking French pronunciation, has been preferred to *ee,* even when under the full accent.

It may be remarked that long *a,* (ā,) as pronounced in English, is a sort of diphthong, almost ā-e. In pronouncing foreign languages, this diphthongal sound should be carefully avoided; the sound of ȧ should be pure, without any, even the slightest, sound of *e* after it.

* The vowels ȧ, ė, and ȯ, though very similar to ā, ē, (or *ee,*) ō, have

8. ă has the sound of *a* in *fall*.

9. â (or ǎ) sounds as *a* in *fat, pang*, etc.

10. â denotes the long *a* in Oriental names; it is also sometimes used in English names to indicate the sound of *a* in *fall, halt*, etc. : *e.g.* Dâl′tọn.

11. ạ is obscure, as in the first and last syllables of *America*.

12. ē is like *ee;* the latter (ee) is mostly used in this work.

13. ê is like the preceding, but less prolonged.*

14. ĕ (or ě) sounds as *e* in *met, pen*, etc.

15. ê̤ has essentially the same sound as the preceding, but is more open and more prolonged. (See V. 2.)

16. ẹ is obscure, as in *berth, her, rider*.

17. ī indicates the long sound of *i* in English, as in *pine, triangle*, etc.

18. ĭ or ĩ sounds as *i* in *pin, pit*, etc.

19. ị is obscure, as in *fir*.

20. ō sounds as *o* in *note, home*, etc.

21. ô is like the preceding, but less prolonged.*

22. ŏ (or ǒ) sounds as *o* in *not*.

23. o͞o (or ŭ) has the sound of *u* in *bull, pull*, etc., or of *oo* in *good*.

24. o͞o sounds as *u* in *rule*, or *oo* in *moon, noon*, etc.

25. ö has a sound similar to the French *eu*. It has no equivalent in English. (VI. 9.†)

26. ọ is obscure, as in *Boston, terror*, etc.

27. ü indicates the sound of the French *u*. It has no equivalent in our language. (V. 5, VI. 10.†)

28. ŭ̈ is the short sound of the preceding.

29. U (small capital) indicates the sound of the French *eu*, almost like that of our *u* in *fur;* it resembles the sound of the German *ö*. (V. 10, VI. 9.†)

30. ủ denotes the sound of o͞o, (very short.)

31. B (small capital) approximates *v* in sound.

32. D (small capital) indicates a sound nearly like *th*, (as in *this*.) (XIX. 7.†)

33. G and K (small capitals) indicate the sound of the German *ch*, or one similar to it.

34. H (small capital) has a sound nearly like the preceding. It resembles a guttural and strongly-aspirated *h*. (I. 6, and XIX. 9.†)

35. *h* Italic is used to represent the *undetermined* sound of the so-called aspirated *h*. (See V. 16.)

36. I (*l* liquid) is pronounced like *lli* in *million ;* it blends the sounds of *l* and *y* consonant. (XIX. 13.†)

37. ñ in like manner blends the sounds of *n* and *y* consonant. (XIX. 14.†)

38. M and N (small capitals) denote the nasal sound in French. (V. 19.†)

39. R (small capital) is to be strongly trilled ; it resembles the sound of *rr* in *terror*.

40. ş is used to denote the sound of a very soft *z*.

41. ŵ indicates a sound similar to our *v*. (VI. 28.†)

42. *ai* or *ay* (unless otherwise marked) is to be sounded like *a* in *fate*.

43. *au* and *aw* have the sound of *a* in *fall*.

44. *ey* at the end of an unaccented syllable (in English names) is to be sounded like *e* or short *i*.

45. ĕe has the same sound as *ee* in *been* or *i* in the first syllable of *spirit*.

46. ĩi indicates a sound similar to the preceding, but longer ; it is, in fact, the sound of short *i* (as in *pin*) prolonged. (XX. 3.†)

47. ŏw or *ou* sounds as in *now* or *our*.

☞ Ꮐ, (capital,) like ḡ, denotes the sound of *g* hard, as in *get, give*, etc.

☞ Ꮹ, (capital,) like ġ, denotes the sound of *j* or soft *g*, as in *gentle*.

☞ This mark ‿ indicates that the vowels joined by it are to be pronounced almost in one syllable, as BERTHIER, bĕr′te-à′.

---

* See note * on preceding page.

† These refer to the principles of pronunciation, as explained in the Introduction. The Roman numerals have reference to the section, the figures to the sound of the particular letter.

☞ When a name occurs several times, it has not been deemed necessary to pronounce it more than once ; in which case the reader should look for the very first occurrence of the name, where the pronunciation will be given. If a name having the same spelling occurs in several different languages, it will be pronounced but once for each of the different languages ; that is, the first time that it occurs in that particular language.

☞ It may be observed, in regard to the arrangement of the names in the present work, that if the ordinary names are spelled differently they are given in strict alphabetical order, without the slightest reference to the Christian or first names, (which are always placed in a parenthesis and in a different kind of type :) but if a number of names occur spelled in precisely the same manner, they follow the order of the Christian names. Thus, Smith, (CHARLES,) is given before Smith, (JOHN, ROBERT, or WILLIAM.) If it should happen that both the ordinary name and Christian name of two or more different persons are exactly alike, then the precedence is determined by the priority of date: *e. g.* Smith, (WILLIAM,) of the seventeenth century is given before Smith, (WILLIAM,) of the eighteenth century ; and so on.

☞ When the same name belongs to a great number of princes or sovereigns, those of antiquity are given first ; among modern rulers, emperors are placed before kings, and these before inferior personages, princes or dukes. Emperors or kings having the same name are usually given in the alphabetical order of the names of the countries which they rule : thus, the emperors of Austria precede the emperors of Russia, and the kings of England are given before those of France, Italy, or Spain.

☞ When a date in parenthesis is placed immediately after the title of a work, it always has reference to the time of publication, which may be, and not unfrequently is, long after the death of the author.

☞ In marking the pronunciation in the present work, our aim has been not to embarrass the reader with unnecessary marks or signs. Thus, in giving the pronunciation of the Italian name CIARPI, we have simply written chär′pee, which gives the pronunciation of this name as perfectly as chĭk′pĕ could do ; because, in English, *a*, immediately followed by *r* and another consonant, always takes its second, or Italian sound, and *ee* usually represents the sound of the Italian *i* quite as well as ē or è could do. For a similar reason, in such names as ANTONELLI, pronounced än-to-nel′lee, we have not thought it necessary to place any marks on the *e* in the penultimate syllable, as the English reader would be sure to pronounce the *e* with its short sound in this position when followed by two consonants of the same kind. In all cases, however, when it seemed possible that the omission of the diacritical mark might give rise to doubt or error, such sign has been added, since practical utility has been deemed of more importance than the mere appearance of consistency. Thus, *es* in modern names, even when under the full accent, has been marked short,—for example, in VALDES, väl-dĕs′,—because, in accordance with the usual Latin pronunciation, the *e* in such positions is commonly made long, as in SOCRATES.

ABBREVIATIONS.

Fr., French.	It., Italian.	Port., Portuguese.	Sp., Spanish.
Ger., German.	Lat., Latin.	Pron., Pronunciation.	Sw., Swedish.
Gr., Greek.	Myth., Mythology.	Russ., Russian.	Turk., Turkish.

A

PRONOUNCING DICTIONARY

OF

BIOGRAPHY AND MYTHOLOGY.

A.

Aa, van der, vän der ä, (CHRISTIAN KAREL HENDRIK,) a Dutch scholar, divine, and writer on natural science, born at Zwolle in 1718; died in 1793.

Aa, van der, (CHRISTIAN PIETER ROBIDÉ,) a poet, born at Amsterdam in 1791, was a grandson of the preceding. Died in 1851.

Aa, van der, (DIEDERIK,) a Dutch painter, born at the Hague in 1731. His works are commended for grace and other merits. Died in 1809.

Aa, van der, (JAN,) a Dutch biographer of the present age. He published an excellent "Biographical Dictionary of the Netherlands," ("Biographisch Woordenboek der Nederlanden.")

Aa, van der, (PIETER,) a Dutch lawyer and writer on jurisprudence, born at Louvain. The date of his birth is unknown. He published a "Commentary on the Rights of Creditors," ("De Privilegiis Creditorum Commentarium," 1560.) Died in 1594.

Aa, van der, (PIETER,) a learned bookseller of Leyden, flourished in the latter half of the seventeenth and the beginning of the eighteenth century. Died about 1730.

Aacs. See ACS.

Aagaard, au'goRd, (CHRISTIAN,) written also **Aagard,** a Danish writer of Latin poetry, born at Viborg in 1616. Died in 1664.

See ROSTGAARD, "Deliciæ Poetarum Danorum;" MOLLER, "Cimbria literata."

Aagaard or **Aagard,** (NIELS, neels,) a Danish poet, born at Viborg in 1612, was probably a brother of the preceding. He was professor of eloquence at Soröe. He wrote several Latin poems and critical essays, among which is "Prolusions on Tacitus." Died in 1657.

Aagesen, (SVEND,) svênd au'gêh-sen, [in Latin, SUE'NO AGGO'NIS FIL'IUS,] regarded as the earliest Danish historian, flourished in the latter part of the twelfth century. He wrote a history of Denmark, extending from about A.D. 300 to 1187.

See "Nouvelle Biographie Générale."

Aali. See ALEE.

Aalst. See AELST.

Aare, van der, vän der ä'reh, (DIEDERIK or DIRCK,) Bishop of Utrecht, and also a powerful temporal lord, flourished in the latter part of the twelfth century. Died in 1212.

See WAGENAAR's "Vaderlandsche Historie."

Aaron, ä'ron, [Heb. אהרון; Gr. Ἀαρών,] the first of the high-priests of the Israelites, was the eldest son of Amram, who was the grandson of Levi. He is supposed to have been born about 1600 B.C.; but on this point the different authorities are not agreed. When Moses was called by Heaven to deliver his countrymen from the tyranny of Egypt, Aaron was commissioned to assist him as his spokesman. He died at the age of one hundred and twenty-three, and was succeeded in the priesthood by his son Eleazar. (See Exodus iv. 14 et seq.; also Numbers, particularly chap. xx. 23–29.)

Aaron, (HARISCHON, hä're-shōn, or ARISCON,) a rabbi of the Caraites, practised medicine at Constantinople in the thirteenth century, and wrote a commentary on the Pentateuch.

Aaron, [It. ARONNE, ä-ron'nä,] (PIETRO,) a monk, born at Florence about 1480, was a canon of Rimini. He published several treatises on music, (1516–45.)

Aaron of Alexandria, a physician who lived in the first half of the seventh century. He wrote a medical work, in which the small-pox is first mentioned.

Aa'ron-Ben-Ash'er, a Jewish rabbi of the eleventh century, wrote a "Treatise on Hebrew Accents," (1517.)

Aaron-Ben-Jo'seph-Sa'son, a Jewish rabbi and writer, lived at Thessalonica about 1600.

Aaron-Ben-Sam'uel, a Jewish writer of the seventeenth century. His chief work is "The House of Aaron," (Frankfort, 1690,) which is said to be a very useful book for biblical students.

Aaron-Margalitha, (-maR-gä-lee'tä,) a Polish professor and rabbi, born in 1665. He was converted to the Protestant faith at Leyden, and wrote a number of theological treatises. Died about 1725.

Aaron-Raschid. See HAROUN-AL-RASCHID.

Aarschot or **Aerschot,** äR'sKot, (PHILIPPE de Croi—dęh krwä,) DUKE OF, a Flemish general who served under Charles V., and afterwards, when the troubles broke out in the Low Countries, espoused the cause of Philip II. of Spain. Died in 1595.

See MOTLEY, "Rise of the Dutch Republic," vols. i. and iii.

Aarsens, van, vän äR'sens, (CORNELIS,) Lord of Spyck, (spīk,) a statesman of Holland, born at Antwerp in 1543. He was many years *griffier* ("recorder" or "registrar") to the States-General, and died at an advanced age.

Aarsens, van, (FRANS or FRANCISCUS,) a distinguished Dutch diplomatist, son of the preceding, was born at the Hague in 1572. His talents, address, and unscrupulousness won the admiration of Cardinal Richelieu, who ranked him with the most consummate politicians of the age. The unjust death of Barneveldt is ascribed partly to his intrigues. Died in 1641.

See AUBERY, "Mémoires pour servir à l'Histoire de Hollande;" MOTLEY, "History of the United Netherlands," vol. iii.

Aarsens, van, (FRANS,) a grandson of the preceding, wrote a work called "Voyage en Espagne," (1666.) He was drowned at sea in 1659.

Aartgens, äRt'gens, or **Aertgen,** äRt'gen, a Dutch painter, called also ARTHUS CLAESSOON, (ar'tus kläs-sōn',) born at Leyden in 1498. He worked with success in his native city. Died in 1564.

Aartsbergen, äRts'bêR'gen, (ALEXANDER van der Capellen,—vän der kä-pel'len,) an eminent Dutch statesman, who was born about 1600, and died in 1656. According to G. Vossius, he was a man of rare talents and incredible industry.

Aartsen, (PIETER.) See AERTSEN.

Aascov, au'skov, (URBAN BRUUN,) a Danish physician, who served in the navy about 1770.

Aba, öb'öh, called also **Samuel,** of a noble Magyar

ã, ē, ī, ō, ū, ȳ, *long;* ă, ĕ, ĭ, ŏ, ŭ, ў, *short;* ạ, ẹ, ị, ọ, *obscure;* fär, fâll, fät; mêt; nŏt; gŏŏd; mōōn;
€ as *k;* ç as *s;* ğ *hard;* ġ as *j;* G, H, K, *guttural;* N, *nasal;* R, *trilled;* š as z; th as in *this.* (☞See Explanations, p. 23.)

family, became King of Hungary in 1041, as successor to Peter, whom a revolution had compelled to fly the country. His injustice and cruelty at length irritated the Hungarians, who entreated the assistance of the emperor Henry III. In 1044 a battle was fought on the Raab, in which Aba was defeated and slain, and Peter was restored to the throne of Hungary.

Abacco, â-bâk′ko, (ANTONIO,) an Italian architect of the sixteenth century, a pupil of San Gallo. He published a work on architecture in 1558.

Abacco, (or **Abaco,**) **dall′,** dâl-lâ-bâk′ko, (PAOLO,) a Florentine mathematician and poet, who flourished about the middle of the fourteenth century.

Abad. See ABBAD.

Abad I., II., and **III.,** (Sultans of Seville.) See ABBAD.

Abadia, â-Bâ-dee′â, (FRANCISCO XAVIER — Hâ-ve-air′,) a Spanish general, born at Valencia in 1774. Died about 1830.

Abad y Queypeo, â-bâd′ e kâ-pâ′o, (MANUEL,) a Spanish bishop, born in Asturias about 1775. He was imprisoned about 1815 for hostility to the Inquisition, and was released in 1824. Died after 1824.

Abælardus. See ABELARD.

Abailard. See ABELARD.

Abâka Khan, â-bâ′kâ kân, son of Hoolâkoo, (Hû-lâkû,) and grandson of Jengis Khan, succeeded his father on the Persian throne A.D. 1264. He was a just and enlightened ruler. He curbed the soldiery, who had been so licentious under his father, and established order and justice throughout his dominions. Died about 1280.

Abamonti, â-bâ-mon′tee, or **Abbamonte,** âb-bâ-mon′tâ, (GIUSEPPE,) a Neapolitan statesman, born about 1759. He became secretary-general of the Cisalpine Republic in 1798, and a member of the executive commission at Naples. After the king was restored in 1799, he removed to Milan, and acted as secretary-general until 1805. Died in 1818.

Abancourt, d′, dâ′bôN′kooR′, (CHARLES XAVIER JOSEPH Franqueville—frôNk′vèl′,) one of the ministers of Louis XVI., and nephew of Calonne. He was massacred at Versailles on the 9th of September, 1792.

Abancourt, d′, (FRANÇOIS JEAN Villemain— vèl′-mâN′,) a French dramatist, born in Paris in 1745. Died in 1803.

Abano, di, de â-bâ′no, or **Apo′no,** (PIETRO,) [in Latin, PE′TRUS APO′NUS or PE′TRUS DE APO′NO,] a learned physician and astrologer, born at Abano, near Padua, in 1250. He was appointed professor of medicine in the University of Padua about 1303, and died about 1316. He wrote a work entitled "Conciliator Differentiarum Philosophorum et præcipue Medicorum," the object of which was to reconcile the various opinions held by the different philosophical and medical schools; from which he has been surnamed *Conciliator,* "Reconciler." Another of his works, entitled "On Poisons and their Treatment," ("De Venenis eorumque Remediis,") though much celebrated, shows him to have possessed more learning than originality or cautious observation.

See MAZZUCHELLI, "Raccolta d'Opuscoli Scientifici e Filologici," 1741; ÉLOY, "Dictionnaire de la Médecine," article APONO.

A-ban′tĭ-das, ['Aβαντίδας,] a tyrant of Sicyon, (one of the small states of Greece,) who obtained the supreme power about 264 B.C. He was afterwards assassinated.

Abarbanel. See ABRABANEL.

Abarca, â-baR′kâ, (JOAQUIN,) a Spanish prelate, born in Aragon in 1780, became Bishop of Leon. He was a chief of the Carlist party in the civil war which began about 1833. Died in 1844.

Abarca, de, dâ â-baR′kâ, (Doña MARIA,) a Spanish amateur portrait-painter. She died about 1660.

Abarca, de, dâ â-baR′kâ, (PEDRO,) a Spanish historian, born in 1619. He belonged to the society of Jesuits, and was for many years professor of theology in the University of Salamanca. Died about 1690. His chief work, "The Kings of Aragon," ("Los Reyes de Aragon,") appeared in 1684.

Abascal, â-bâs-kâl′, (JOSÉ FERNANDO,) a Spanish commander, born at Oviedo in 1743. At 19 he entered the army, and in 1804 was appointed Viceroy of Peru. Through his abilities and indefatigable exertions, not

only were the Peruvians preserved in a state of subjection to Spain while other parts of South America were in open insurrection, but the Spanish arms gained many advantages over the insurgents of Buenos Ayres and Chili. In 1816 he was superseded in the government by General Pezuela, and returned to Spain, where he died in 1821.

See W. B. STEVENSON, "Twenty Years' Residence in South America."

Abati, â-bâ′tee, (ANTONIO,) an Italian poet, born at Gubbio in 1614. He was governor of several cities in the papal dominions. Died in 1667.

Abati, degli, dâl′yee â-bâ′tee, a Florentine family known in history chiefly through the treachery of one of its members, BOCCO DEGLI ABATI. During a battle between the Guelphs (the party of the Florentines) and the Ghibelines, (1260,) he cut off the hand of Jacopo del Vacca, who carried the Florentine standard, which consequently fell, and caused the defeat of his countrymen. For this crime Dante assigns him a place in the ninth or lowest circle of hell. See "Inferno," canto xxxii.

Abatini, â-bâ-tee′nee, (GUIDO UBALDO,) an Italian fresco-painter, born about 1600, worked in Rome, and died in 1656.

Abauzit, â′bō′ze′, (FIRMIN,) a justly celebrated philosopher and mathematician, born at Uzès, in France, in 1679. When he was two years old his father died, and on the revocation of the edict of Nantes his mother, being a Protestant, was obliged to seek a refuge in some foreign country. Her two sons were sent to Geneva, where Firmin soon distinguished himself by his rapid progress in almost every branch of learning and science. The fame of Abauzit does not rest so much on his publications as on the opinion entertained of him by his contemporaries. He not only enjoyed the respect of the greatest writers and philosophers of France, but received the most flattering testimonials of regard from other countries. Sir Isaac Newton esteemed him highly, and, after having once made his acquaintance, kept up a constant correspondence with him. Died at Geneva in 1767.

See SABATIER DE CASTRES, "Les Trois Siècles de la Littérature Française;" J. J. ROUSSEAU, "Œuvres;" SENEBIER, "Histoire littéraire de Genève," tome iii.; BÉRENGER, "Éloge d'Abauzit."

Abba Arica, âb′bâ â-ree′kâ, [Heb. אבא אריכא,] commonly known by the name of RAV, (רב,) a learned Jewish rabbi, native of Babylon, flourished in the early part of the third century. He died 243 A.D.

Abbâd (or **Abâd,**) âb′bâd′, **I.,** (called also ABOO-L-KASIM (or ABOUL-CACEM) MOHAMMED, â′bōōl kâ′sĭm mo-hâm′med,) the founder of the Abbadite (or Abadite) dynasty of Seville, became sovereign of that city about 1023, and died 1042 A.D.

Abbâd (or **Abâd) II., Aboo-Amroo,** (Abû-Am-rû,) âb′bâd′ â′bōō âm′rōō, the second sultan of Seville, succeeded his father, Aboo-l-Kâsim, (Abû′l-Kâsim,) about 1042, aged 26 years. He was an able and successful general, and was well versed in the learning and science of the times. In splendour and luxury he rivalled the most powerful sovereigns of the East; but all his glory was stained by his sanguinary cruelty. He used to keep, it is said, in a private apartment, the skulls of all the chiefs and princes who had fallen into his hands, and paved the alleys of his gardens with those of inferior rank. He died in 1069.

Abbâd (or **Abâd) III.,** Moorish King of Seville, born in 1039, was a son of Abbâd II. He was a brave and prudent ruler, and patronized arts and learning. He was deposed by Yoosuf, (Yûsuf,) King of Morocco, in 1091, and died in 1095.

Abbadie, â′bâ′de′, (JACQUES,) a distinguished Protestant divine, born in Béarn, in the south of France, in 1658. His "Treatise on the Truth of the Christian Religion" ("Traité de la Vérité de la Religion Chrétienne," 2 vols., 1684) was received with great favour both by Catholics and Protestants, and still enjoys a high reputation. He was the author of several other works of less note. He preached for some time in London, and afterwards became Dean of Killaloe, Ireland. Died in London in 1727.

See NICÉRON, "Mémoires," and "Biographia Britannica."

Abbadie, d′, dâ′bâ′de′, (ANTOINE and ARNOULD

MICHEL,) two brothers of Irish origin, but citizens of France. They made some scientific researches in Abyssinia, where they passed about five years,—1840-45.

Abbamonte. See ABAMONTI.

Abbâs I., or **Shah Abbâs,** shâh âb'bâs', (*i.e.* "King Abbâs,") surnamed the Great, King of Persia, was born in 1557. His father, Mohammed Meerzâ, whose want of capacity rendered him unpopular, was deposed by the discontented nobles, and Shah Abbâs succeeded to the throne at the age of twenty-five. He exhibited an energy and wisdom which commanded the respect alike of his subjects and of his enemies. After having healed the dissensions and curbed the lawlessness which had prevailed among his nobles, he marched against the Turks, who, with an army of 100,000 men, were then ravaging the Persian provinces on the north. The army of Abbâs consisted of scarcely more than 60,000 men ; but it had been disciplined under the direction of two English gentlemen, Sir Anthony and Sir Robert Shirley, and was provided with an efficient artillery. In August, 1605, a battle was fought, in which the Turks suffered a total defeat. The Persian king recovered all his lost provinces, and was not molested by the Turks during the remainder of his reign. He died in 1627.

See MALCOLM, " History of Persia," 1829 ; "Travels of the Brothers Shirley," 1825.

Abbâs II., Shah of Persia, born about 1631, succeeded his father Sûfi, or Sophy, in 1641. He possessed some good qualities, and was noted for his liberal treatment of the Christians and other foreigners in his dominions. Died in 1666.

Abbâs III., King of Persia, born in 1731, was the last king of the dynasty of Sophys. He was a son of Shah Tamâsp, who was dethroned by Nâdir Shah. Died in childhood in 1736.

Abbâs, or more fully **Abbâs-Ibn-Abd-il-Moottalib,** (or **-Mottalib,**) âb'bâs' îb'n âbd-il-moot'tâ-lib, written also **Abbâs-Ben-Abdel-Mottâlib,** a paternal uncle of Mohammed, born at Mecca about 566 A.D., was the ancestor of the dynasty of Abbassides. He fought against Mohammed at the battle of Bedr, but afterwards was converted to the cause of that prophet, to whom he rendered important services. (See MOHAMMED.) Died in 652 A.D.

See CAUSSIN DE PERCEVAL, " Essai sur l'Histoire des Arabes."

Abbâs, âb'bâs', (PASHA,) Viceroy of Egypt, born at Yedda, Arabia, in 1813, was a grandson of Mehemet Ali. He succeeded his uncle Ibrâheem in November, 1848. Died in 1854.

Abbâs-Meerzâ, (-Mîrzâ,) âb'bâs' meer'zâ', son of Fatah Alee Shah, King of Persia, was born about 1785. He was distinguished for his zealous and enlightened efforts to introduce into his own country the arts, sciences, and military tactics of Europe. He died in 1833.

Abbassah, âb-bâs'sâ, a pasha of Erzeroom, distinguished first for his successful rebellion against the sultan Amurâth (Muṛâd) IV., and afterwards for his great favour and influence with that monarch. At last, however, he fell a victim to the suspicions of his sovereign, and was executed in 1634.

Abbassides or **Abbasides,** ab-bǎs'sīdz, singular, ABBASSIDE, ab-bǎs'sīd, [Fr. pron. ǎ'bǎ'sèd' ; Ger. ABBASSIDEN, ǎb-bǎs-see'den ; Lat. ABBAS'IDÆ ; called by the Arabs BENEE (BENÎ) ABBÂS, *i.e.* "sons or descendants of Abbâs,"] the name of the most illustrious dynasty of caliphs. They traced their genealogy to Abbâs the uncle of Mohammed, and reigned at Damascus and afterwards at Bagdâd from 749 to 1258 A.D. See ABOO-L-ABBAS-ABDALLAH.

Abbate, âb-bâ'tâ, or **Abate,** â-bâ'tâ, (ANDREA,) a Neapolitan painter of natural history and inanimate objects. Died in 1732.

Abbate, âb-bâ'tâ, **Abbati** or **Abati,** â-bâ'tee, (NICHOLAS, or NICCOLO,) a celebrated Italian painter, born at Modena about 1512. Although his productions rank him with the greatest Italian masters, very little is known of the circumstances of his life. He died in Paris in 1571. Among his works were frescos at Fontainebleau. His oil pictures are very scarce.

See VEDRIANI, " Vite dei Pittori Modenesi."

Abbate or **Abatî,** (PIETRO PAOLO,) a brother of

Niccolò, noticed above, was a skilful painter of battles and horses, at Modena. Died about 1580.

Abbate, dell', dĕl-lâb-bâ'tâ, (GIOVANNI,) an Italian painter and modeller, worked at Modena. Died in 1557.

Abba-Thulle, âb'bâ t'hul'lee, a king of the Pelew Islands, who hospitably entertained the crew of the English ship Antelope, wrecked on an island of that group in 1783. Struck with admiration on witnessing for the first time the effect of fire-arms, he prevailed on Captain Wilson, commander of the Antelope, to assist him in his contests with the neighbouring islanders. The allied forces, armed with "thunder and lightning," easily subdued their enemies, destitute of these novel and terrific implements of war. When his English friends were about to return to their native country, the king intrusted to their care his son Lee Boo, that he might visit Europe.

See KEATE's "Account of the Pelew Islands, from the Journal of Captain Wilson."

Abbati, âb-bâ'tee, or **Abbatio,** âb-bâ'te-o, (BALDI ANGELO,) commonly called ABBA'TIUS, a physician and naturalist, who flourished about the middle of the sixteenth century.

Abbatini, âb-bâ-tee'nee, (ANTONIO MARIA,) an Italian composer of music, who flourished in the first half of the seventeenth century. Died about 1675.

Abbatucci, âb-bâ-toot'chee, (CARLO, or CHARLES,) a Corsican general, born in 1771, was a son of Giacomo Pietro. He gained the rank of general of division by his conduct at the passage of the Lech in 1796. He was killed at Huningue in 1796.

Abbatucci, (JACQUES PIERRE, or GIACOMO PIETRO,) a Corsican, who was a lieutenant under General Paoli, and after various changes of fortune was raised to the rank of a general of division in the French army. Born 1726, died 1812.

See JACOBI, " Histoire de la Corse ;" " Nouvelle Biographie Générale."

Abbatucci, (JACQUES PIERRE CHARLES,) a French lawyer, born in Corsica in 1791, was a grandson of Carlo A., noticed above. He was elected to the Constituent Assembly in 1848, and became a partisan of Louis Napoleon, who appointed him minister of justice about 1852. Died in 1857.

Abbeville, d', dâb'vêl', (PÈRE (paiR) CLAUDE,) a Capuchin, who wrote a history of the French mission to the island of Maranham, on the coast of Brazil, entitled " Histoire de la Mission des Pères Capucins en l'Isle de Maragnan." He gives an interesting account of the character and customs of the natives of that island and the neighbouring continent. The mission alluded to was undertaken in 1612.

Abbiati, âb-be-â'tee, (FILIPPO,) an excellent Italian painter, born at Milan in 1640. He painted both in oil and fresco with great facility. Among his best works is a fresco of " John the Baptist preaching in the wilderness." Died at Milan in 1715.

Abbiati, (GIUSEPPE,) an Italian painter and engraver, flourished at Milan about 1700.

Abbon, â'bòn', [in Latin, AB'BO CER'NUUS, "Abbon the bent or bowed down,"] a learned French monk, who flourished about 900. He wrote a Latin poem on the siege of Paris by the Northmen, (A.D. 885-6.)

Abbon of Fleury, [in Latin, AB'BO FLORIACEN'SIS,] an eminent ecclesiastic of the tenth century, born near Orleans in France. He was one of the most learned men of his age, and after he was elected Abbot of Fleury showed himself a patron of learning. He died in 1004.

Abbondanti, âb-bon-dân'tee, (ANTONIO,) sometimes called ABUNDAN'TIUS OF IMOLA, (ee'mo-lâ,) an Italian historian and poet, lived about 1625. He wrote an account of the war in the Low Countries, 1559-1609.

Ab'bọt, (ABIEL,) an American divine, born at Andover, Massachusetts, in 1770. He died in 1828, on his return from Cuba, which he had visited on account of his health. A posthumous volume of letters written while in that island, evinces strong powers of observation and considerable talent for description.

Abbot, (BENJAMIN,) LL.D., an American teacher, born about 1763, was for half a century the principal of Phillips Academy, at Exeter, New Hampshire. He numbered among his pupils Daniel Webster, Edward

€ as *k*; ç as *s*; g *hard*; g as *j*; G, H, K, *guttural*; N, *nasal*; R, *trilled*; s as *z*; th as in *this*. (☞See Explanations, p. 23.)

Everett, Jared Sparks, George Bancroft, and John G. Palfrey. Died in 1849.

Ab'bọt, (CHARLES,) LORD COLCHESTER, a British statesman, born at Abingdon in 1757, was educated at Oxford, and was called to the bar about 1784. He was elected to Parliament in 1795, showed himself a warm supporter of Pitt, and distinguished himself by his talents for business and his public spirit. He was the mover of the bill which in 1800 authorized the first census of the population of Great Britain ever taken. In 1801 he became chief secretary for Ireland. He was speaker of the House of Commons from February, 1802, until May, 1817, when he resigned on account of ill health, and was raised to the peerage as Baron Colchester. He had performed his duties as speaker to the general satisfaction. He died in 1829, leaving two sons.

See "Gentleman's Magazine" for May, 1829; "Annual Obituary," 1830.

Abbot, (GEORGE,) an English prelate, born at Guildford, Surrey, in 1562. He studied at Oxford, took orders in 1583, became a very popular preacher, and was employed in the translation of the Bible authorized by King James in 1604. He was one of eight divines who translated the Four Gospels and the book of Acts. In 1609 he obtained the see of Lichfield, from which he was translated to the see of London in 1610. He was appointed Archbishop of Canterbury in January, 1611. He was a zealous Calvinist, both before and after his high promotion. In the latter part of his life he favoured the popular party, but his influence in the church and state was ruined by the ascendency of Laud, who had long been his rival and adversary. Among his works is a "Brief Description of the Whole World," (1634.) Died in 1633.

See WILLIAM RUSSELL, "Life of George Abbot," 1777; GARDINER, "History of England from 1603 to 1616."

Abbot, (GEORGE,) a nephew of Archbishop Abbot, was born about 1602. He fought against the royalists in the civil war. He published "The Book of Job Paraphrased," (1640.) Died in 1648.

Abbot, (LEMUEL,) an English portrait-painter, born about 1760, worked in London, and was well patronized. Most of his portraits are considered to be excellent likenesses. Among his works are portraits of the poet Cowper and Lord Nelson. Died in 1803.

Abbot, (Sir MAURICE or MORRIS,) a distinguished merchant of London, was the youngest brother of Archbishop Abbot. He was appointed one of the council for settling the colony of Virginia in 1624, and became governor or chairman of the East India Company in 1633. Died in 1640.

Abbot, (ROBERT,) a learned divine, born at Guildford in 1560, was a brother of Archbishop Abbot. He was a popular preacher, a chaplain to James I., and King's professor of divinity at Oxford. In 1615 he became Bishop of Salisbury. He was a strenuous opponent of Laud's opinions and church policy. Among his works is a "Defence of the Royal Supremacy," in Latin, (1619.) He was esteemed a man of more profound learning than the archbishop. Died in 1617.

See "Biographia Britannica;" WOOD, "Athenæ Oxonienses."

Abbot, (ROBERT,) an English Puritan divine, became vicar of Cranbrook, Kent, and minister of Southwick in Hampshire. He published, besides other works, "The Trial of our Church-Forsakers," (1639.) Died about 1655.

Abbot, (SAMUEL,) born at Wilton, New Hampshire, in 1786; died in 1839. He invented a process of extracting starch from the potato.

Ab'bọtt, (CHARLES,) LORD TENTERDEN, an eminent English judge, was born at Canterbury in 1762, and studied at Oxford. He was admitted to the bar in 1795, and in 1802 published a "Treatise on the Law of Merchant Ships and Seamen," which has since been regarded in England and the United States as the standard work on maritime law. He became a judge in the Court of Common Pleas in 1816. Lord Ellenborough having resigned his position as Lord Chief Justice of the King's Bench in 1818, Mr. Abbott succeeded him, and in 1827 was raised to the peerage, with the title of Lord Tenterden. He died in November, 1832. He was a firm adherent of the Tory party. His judicial merits were of a very high order. According to some, he excelled

Lord Mansfield in industry and learning, and equalled him in acuteness of perception and power of reasoning.

See LORD CAMPBELL, "Lives of the Chief Justices," vol. iii.; FOSS, "The Judges of England," vol. ix.; also a criticism on Lord Tenterden's professional character, by BROUGHAM, in the "Edinburgh Review," vol. lxix. p. 14.

Abbott, (Rev. JACOB,) a popular American author, born at Hallowell, Maine, in 1803. He graduated at Bowdoin College in 1820. Few writers have given to the public a greater number of volumes. Among them may be mentioned "The Young Christian;" "The Corner-Stone;" "A Series of Histories of Celebrated Sovereigns;" "The Rollo Books," 28 vols.; "Harper's Story-Books," 36 vols., etc. etc. Mr. Abbott has addressed himself principally to the young, with whom his works have been exceedingly popular. Nearly all his books have been republished in England, and some, it is said, have been translated into various European and Asiatic languages.

Abbott, (JOHN S. C.,) an American author, brother of the Rev. Jacob Abbott, was born at Brunswick, Maine, in 1805. He graduated at Bowdoin College in 1825, studied divinity at the Theological Seminary in Andover, Mass., and was subsequently minister in Worcester and Roxbury. Among his principal works may be named the "Mother at Home," (1833;) "Histories of Marie Antoinette, Josephine, Madame Roland, Cortez," etc., forming a series in six vols.; "History of Napoleon Bonaparte," 2 vols. 8vo; "History of the French Revolution," and "History of the Civil War in America," 2 vols. 8vo, 1863–66. Most of his books have obtained an extensive circulation. He is a pleasing and animated writer, but as a historian he is scarcely to be relied on. His "History" of Napoleon, in particular, is perhaps the most remarkable example of indiscriminate and extravagant eulogy ever given to the world under the august name of History. He has recently published a "History of Napoleon III., Emperor of the French," (1868,) which is said to possess the merits and demerits of the preceding work.

Abbt, âpt, (THOMAS,) an eminent German writer, born at Ulm in 1738. He studied at the University of Halle, and in 1761 was appointed professor of mathematics in the University of Rinteln. Here he wrote his two most celebrated works, "On Merit," ("Vom Verdienste," 1765,) and "On Dying for one's Native Country," ("Ueber den Tod für's Vaterland," 1761.) He was afterwards invited by Count William of Lippe-Schauenburg to his court at Bückeburg, where he died in 1766. Like Lessing, he exerted himself to improve and refine the German language, and had he lived longer his name would undoubtedly have become one of the most distinguished in his country's literature.

See NICOLAÏ, "Ehrengedächtniss des Herrn Thomas Abbt," 1767; WOLF, "Encyklopaedie der Deutschen National-Literatur;" MEUSEL, "Dictionnaire des Littérateurs d'Allemagne."

ABD, an Arabic word signifying "servant," and forming the prefix in many names; as ABD-ALLAH, (ABDALLAH,) the "servant of God."

Abd-al-Kâdir. See ABD-EL-KADER.

Abdallah, âb-dâl'lah, (almost âb-dŭl'lah.) or **Abdullah,** âb-dool'lah, the last shereef (sherif) or prince of the Wahabites, was born about 1740. Having been captured by Ibrâheem (Ibrâhîm) Pasha, he was executed in 1818.

Abdallah, (or **Abd-Allah,**) **Abû-l-Abbâs.** See ABOO-L-ABBAS-ABDALLAH.

Abdallah- (or **Abdullah-) Ibn-Abd-il-Moottalib,** (-ib'n âb'dil mo͞ot'tâ-lib,) the father of the prophet Mohammed, is said to have been distinguished for his virtue and personal beauty. Died about 570 A.D.

See ABDALLAH-BEN-ABDELMOTTALIB, in the "Nouvelle Biographie Générale."

Abdallah-Ibn-Al-Aftas, (-âl-âf'tas,) the founder of the dynasty of Benee Al-Aftas, was born at Mequinez in Africa about 1004. He possessed eminent military talents, and was surnamed Al-Mansoor, or "the victorious." He died about 1060.

Abdallah-Ibn-Balkeen, (or **-Balkîn,** -bâl-keen',) the fourth and last sultan of Granada; dethroned (A.D. 1090) by Yoosuf, whom he had invited from Africa to assist him against Alphonso I. of Castile. He was a brave and enlightened monarch. He was a patron of science, and wrote a learned and valuable commentary on the Koran.

Abdallah-Ibn-Koteyba, (**-Coteyba.**) See IBN-KOTEYBA.

Abdallah-Ibn-Mohammed, (-ĭb'n mo-hăm′med,) the seventh sultan of Córdova of the dynasty of Omeyyah, ascended the throne in 888, and died in 912. He was a poet and a patron of literature.

Abdallah- (or **Abdullah-**) **Ibnool-Fara-dhee,** (-Ib-nul-Faradhî, ĭb′nōōl fä′rä-dhee,) a Mohammedan historian, born at Córdova in 962. He was killed at the taking of his native city by Suleymân, 1013.

Abdallah- (or **Abdullah-**) **Ibnool-Hijâree,** (-Ib-nul-Hijârî, ĭb′nōōl he-jä′ree,) a celebrated Mohammedan historian, born in the territory of Guadalajara in 1105. He was the author of a valuable and voluminous history of Spain, most of which is lost. He died about 1195.

Abdallah-Ibn-Sa'd (-sâd or -sä′d) was one of the earliest converts to the Mohammedan faith, and was employed by the prophet to write down his pretended revelations. He was afterwards appointed governor of Egypt, under the caliph Othmân, about the year 646. On the death of the caliph, in 656, he was deposed; but the year of his death is unknown.

Abdallah-Ibn-Yaseen, (or **-Yâsîn,**) -yä′seen′, the founder of the dynasty of the Almoravides, was born at Nafees, a little town in North Africa. He began his career as a zealous teacher of religion, about the year 1041. His followers were called ALMORABITŌŌN, "men devoted to the service of God," (whence the European name ALMORAVIDES.) At first he contented himself with forcibly converting the pagan tribes of the Berbers to Mohammedanism, but finally aspired to the entire subjugation of Africa and the overthrow of the ruling dynasty of Zenatah. After entire success had crowned his undertaking, although he exercised all the functions of royalty, he never assumed the titles, but contented himself with the name of Fakîh, (fä-keeh′,) or "Theologian." He died in 1059. His successors ruled over the greater part of North Africa and Spain for nearly a century.

Abdallah-Ibn- (or **Ben-**) **Zobeyr,** (or **-Zobair,**) -zo-bār′, surnamed **Aboo-Beker** or **Abû-Bekr,** ä′bōō bek′ĕr, Caliph of Mecca, was born in 622. He maintained his independence against the Omeyyah dynasty from 680 till 692, when he was conquered and slain by Abdel-Malek-Ibn-Merwân.

See ABDALLAH-BEN-ZOBAIR, in the "Nouvelle Biographie Générale."

Abdallatif or **Abdallatiphus.** See ABD-EL-LATEEF.

Abdalmalek or **Abd-al-Malik.** See ABD-EL-MALEK.

Ab-da-lon′y̆-mus or **Ab-do-lon′ĭ-mus,** a Sidonian, raised by Alexander the Great from the occupation of a gardener to the throne. He was descended from the kings of Sidon.

Abdalrahman. See ABD-ER-RAHMAN.

Abdal-Wahab. See ABD-EL-WAHAB.

Ab′das, [Gr. Ἀβδας,] Bishop of Susa, in Persia, offended the Guebers, or fire-worshippers, by burning one of their temples, for which he was put to death in 430 A.D.

Abdelaziz, âb′del-ä-zeez′, or **Abdu-l-azîz,** âb′dōō-lä-zeez′, (Anglicized pron. ab-dą-lä′ziz,*) written also **Ab-dalazis** and **Abdelasis,** the son of Moosa, (Mûsa,) was the third governor of Spain after its conquest by the Arabs. He was assassinated in 716, at the instigation of the caliph, against whom he had revolted.

Abdelaziz or **Abdulaziz,** (Abul-Hassan, ä′bool hăs′sän,) the first sultan of Valencia, was grandson of the famous Al-Mansoor. He adorned his capital with magnificent gardens and buildings. Died about 1060.

Abd-el-Bâkî, (or **-Backi.**) See BÂKEE.

Abd-el-Hakk, âbd el hâk, (**Ibn-Ghaleeb** or **-Gha-lîb,** ĭb'n gä-leeb′,) a Mohammedan divine and poet, born in the province of Granada in 1088. He wrote a voluminous commentary on the Koran, which was highly esteemed by the Spanish Moslems. Died 1152.

Abd-el-Kâder, âbd'el-kä′dĕr, (**Ibn-Mehi-ed-Deen,**

ĭb'n mêh′hĭ-ęd-deen′,) (see remarks on Oriental names, in the Introduction,) one of the most remarkable men of whom history makes mention, was born near Mascara, Algeria, about 1807. His father, Mehi-ed-Deen, was ą Maraboot (Marabout) or religious noble of great influence. Having become distinguished for his piety and talents, Abd-el-Kâder was chosen emir of the Arab tribes in Algeria soon after that region was invaded by the French in 1830. He attacked Orân in 1832, but, after the most determined and repeated assaults, was repulsed by the French artillery, and in 1834 concluded a treaty with the French general, who recognized him as Emir of Mascara and Orân. In 1835 he defeated a French army at Macta. After the victory of General Bugeaud at Sikka, 1836, the war was suspended by a treaty, (1837.) Hostilities were renewed in 1839 by the Arabs, who were stimulated against the infidel invaders by fanaticism as well as patriotism. In the long contest which ensued against a power immeasurably superior to his own, Abd-el-Kâder displayed remarkable energy, skill, presence of mind, and fertility of resources, combined with administrative talents of the highest order; but he was finally compelled to surrender, in December, 1847, which he did on condition that he should be sent to Alexandria or St. Jean-d'Acre. By a flagrant violation of public faith, he was sent tó France, and detained as a captive until about the end of 1852, when he was released by the order of Louis Napoleon. He has since resided chiefly at Brussa and Damascus.

While Abd-el-Kâder was imprisoned in France, General Daumas, who had charge of him, wrote to one of his friends, "You are going to see the illustrious prisoner of the château of Pau. . . . You have known Abd-el-Kâder in his prosperity, at a time when, so to speak, all Algeria acknowledged his rule. Well, you will find him greater and more extraordinary in his adversity than he was in his prosperity." In 1860, when all the Christian population of Syria was threatened with massacre, Abd-el-Kâder protected, with sleepless vigilance and at the imminent peril of his own life, many thousands of both sexes until the danger was past.

Abd-el-Kâder excelled in all martial exercises. As an equestrian he was unrivalled, even among a people whose warriors may be said to live on horseback. His quickness of intellect and his memory were extraordinary. At the age of fourteen he already knew the Koran by heart. His literary attainments would have conferred distinction even upon one who had devoted his whole life to peaceful and uninterrupted study. In addition to his other accomplishments, he was endowed with a graceful and spirit-stirring eloquence.

See "Life of Abd-el-Kâder," written from his own dictation, and compiled from other authentic sources, by COLONEL CHURCHILL, London, 1867; also the "Nouvelle Biographie Générale."

Abd-el-Kâder-Ghilânee, (**-Ghilânî,**) âbd′el-kä′dęr ge-lä′nee or ge-lä′nee, an eminent Persian doctor of the Soofee (Sûfi) sect, flourished about the middle of the twelfth century. Like the orthodox Mohammedans, the Scofees believe in one eternal God; but their views of a future state are more spiritual than those taught by the Koran. Abd-el-Kâder wrote various works on the doctrines of the Soofees, some of which are still extant. Died at Bagdâd in 1165.

Abd-el-Kadir. See ABD-EL-KADER.

Abd-el-Lateef or **Abdellatif,** âb′del-lä-teef′, or **Abdullattif,** âb′dōōl-lä-teef′, an eminent Arabian historian and physician, born at Bagdâd in 1162. He wrote an important work on the history, antiquities, and geography of Egypt, of which De Sacy published a French version entitled "Relation de l'Égypte," (1810.)

See WÜSTENFELD, "Geschichte der Arabischen Aerzte;" "Nouvelle Biographie Générale."

Abd-el-Malek or **-Malik,*** âb′del-mä′lek or -mâl′ek, (**Ibn-Habeeb** or **-Habîb,** ĭb'n hâ-beeb′,) a famous Mohammedan historian and divine, born at Córdova in 801; died 853.

Abd-el-Malek,* (**Ibn-Koreyb**—ko-rāb′,) generally

---

* It should be observed that the Arabic words Malek (mȧ′l′ek) (writ ten also Melek, mĕl′ek) and Mâlek (mä′lek) differ in signification as well as pronunciation: the former signifies "king," the latter "master" or "possessor."

є as *k;* ç as *s;* ḡ *hard;* ġ as *j;* G, H, K, *guttural;* N, *nasal;* R, *trilled;* s̄ as *z;* ŧh as in *this.* (☞ See Explanations, p. 23.)

called ALASMAEE, (ALASMA'Î,) âl-âs'mâ-ee', a celebrated Mohammedan doctor, born at Bassöra about 740. He possessed an extraordinary memory, and is said to have known by heart above 16,000 poems. Haroun-al-Raschid, hearing of the fame of Alasmaee, invited him to his court and chose him as his own instructor. He died at Bagdâd about 821. The famous romance of Antar has been ascribed to him.

Abd-el-Mâlek or **Abd-ul-Mâlik**,* âbd'ool-mâ'lik, a sultan of Western Africa, was born at Fez about 1500. When his dominions were invaded by Sebastian, King of Portugal, he made vigorous preparations for defence, and, though labouring under severe disease, accompanied his army, in a litter, to the field of battle, (August, 1578.) The Moors were victorious, and Sebastian was taken and put to death ; but Abd-el-Mâlik died of exhaustion during the contest, and Mohammed, his nephew, whom he had dethroned, and at whose instigation the Portuguese king had begun the war, was drowned in his flight. This battle has been called " the battle of the three kings."

Abd-el-Malek,* (**Ibn-Merwân** — mer'wân',) the fifth caliph of the house of Omeyyah, ascended the throne in 685. He distinguished himself as a warrior while quelling several formidable rebellions in his dominions ; he was brave, just, and strict in the observance of all the duties of his religion, and was moreover a patron of learning and the useful arts. Died in 705, aged sixty years.

See WEIL, " Geschichte der Chalifen," vol. i. chap. ix.

Abd-el-Melek. See ABD-EL-MALEK.

Abd-el-Moomen, (-**Moumen** or -**Mûmen**,) âbd'el-moo'men, written also **Abdul-Mûmen**, the second prince or sultan of the line of Almohades, in Africa, was born in the province of Tlemsen, about 1100. On the death of Al-Mahdee, (Al-Mahdî,) founder of the new dynasty, he managed to get himself elected successor to the throne, in 1130. His reign was constantly occupied with wars, in which he was for the most part eminently successful. Having subdued all his enemies in Western Africa, he was preparing to cross into Spain, that he might put a stop to the victorious career of Alphonso VIII., when he was attacked by the disease of which he died, in 1163. He assumed the title of caliph, which his successors retained.

See ABD-EL-MOUMEN, in the " Nouvelle Biographie Générale."

Abd-el-Moottalib, (or -**Muttalib**,) âbd'el-moot'-tâ-lib,† written also **Abd-el-Mottalib** and **Abdol-Motalleb**, a rich citizen of Mecca, born in 497 A.D., was the son of Hâshem and grandfather of the prophet Mohammed. He is said to have dug at Mecca, in obedience to a command given him in a vision, the famous well of Zemzem, which was destined to supply pilgrims with water through all succeeding ages. Died in 579.

See ABD-EL-MOTTALIB, in the " Nouvelle Biographie Générale ;" SPRENGER, " Life of Mohammad."

Abdel-Mumen. See ABD-EL-MOOMEN.

Abd-el-Wahâb,âbd'el-wâ-Hâb', or**Abdul-Wahâb**, âb'dool-wâ-hâb', the founder of the sect of the Wahabites, (Wahâbees or Wahâbys,) was born in the Arabian province of Nejd in 1691. He did not, as has been asserted, promulgate the doctrines of a new religion. He saw, as he believed, that the primitive Mohammedan faith had become totally corrupted, and his efforts were directed towards introducing a thorough reformation. He acknowledged the Koran and the traditionary law, the " Soönnah," (or " Sunnah,") to be the foundation of religion ; but the opinions even of the greatest commentators were not, he maintained, to be received implicitly. He complained that many of the Mohammedan professors bestowed upon the prophet and the saints honours which were equivalent to adoration. He held and proclaimed that before God all men were equal, and

that it was a sin to pray to departed saints or to honour their relics more than those of ordinary persons. The Wahabites, wherever they had the power to do so, destroyed the domes and ornamental tombs : even the cupola over the birthplace of Mohammed, at Mecca, and his tomb at Medina, were demolished. Abd-el-Wahâb died in 1787.

See BURCKHARDT, " Materials for a History of the Wahabys," London, 1830 ; " Voyages d'Ali-Bey," Paris, 1814 ; NIEBUHR, " Reisebeschreibung nach Arabien," etc.

Abd-er-Rahman, âbd'er-RÂH'mân,* (or **Abd-ur-Rahman,** âb'dooR-RÂH'mân,) I., written also **Abdar-rahman**, (the " servant of the Merciful," that is, of God,) the founder of the Omeyyah dynasty of sultans in Spain, in opposition to the caliphs of the new line, (the Abbassides.) He wrested Moslem Spain from the government of the caliph in 756, and died in 788 A.D.

See AL-MAKKARI, " History of the Mohammedan Dynasties in Spain."

Abd-er-Rahman II.,the fourth sultan of Córdova of the Omeyyah dynasty, ascended the throne in 822 A.D. He was an able warrior, was eminent for his moderation, justice, and humanity, and was a distinguished patron of learning. Died in 852 A.D.

Abd-er-Rahman III.,surnamed AN-NÂSIR-LIDEEN-ILLAH or -LIDÎNILLAH, ân-nâ'sir-lę-dee'nil'lâh, (*i.e.* "the defender of the religion of God,") the eighth sultan and first caliph of Córdova, began to reign in 912, and by his talents and energy raised the Mohammedan empire in Spain to the highest pinnacle of glory. He was distinguished both as a warrior and as a patron of learning and the arts. One of his palaces near Córdova was decorated with unequalled magnificence ; the audience-room, in particular, was adorned with golden images of the most exquisite workmanship, and the roof was covered with pure gold. After a reign of nearly fifty years, An-Nâsir died in 961, at the age of 73. An-Nâsir-Lideen-Illah was also the name of one of the caliphs of the Abbasside dynasty, as well as of several other Mohammedan princes.

See AL-MAKKARI, " History of the Mohammedan Dynasties in Spain," translated into English by GAYANGOS, London, 1840-43; CONDE, " Histoire de la Domination des Arabes ;" CASIRI, " Bibliotheca Arabico-Hispana."

Abd-er-Rahman, Sultan or Emperor of Morocco, born in 1778, succeeded his uncle Muley Soliman in 1823. He became the ally of Abd-el-Kâder in the war against the French, who defeated his army at Isly in 1844.

Abd-er-Rahman-Alghâfekee, (or -**Alghâfekî**,) âl-Gâ'fĕ-kee', a Moslem governor of Spain, invaded Gaul at the head of eighty thousand men, and having ravaged Aquitaine, encountered the French army under Charles Martel near Tours, in October, 732 A.D. After a severe and prolonged contest, the Christians gained a complete victory, which saved Europe from the Mohammedan yoke and put an effectual check to the conquests of the Saracens of Spain. Abd-er-Rahman himself was left dead on the field of battle.

See " Nouvelle Biographie Générale."

Abd-er-Rahman, (**Ibn-Khaldoon** or -**Khaldûn**.) See IBN-KHALDOON.

Abd-er-Razzâk, âbd'er-RÂz-zâk', or **Abdurrazzâk**, âb'dooR-RÂz-zâk', the founder of a small empire in Eastern Persia, about 1336, which lasted only till the conquest of Tamerlane in 1381.

Abd-er-Razzâk, or **Abd-er-Rezzâk**, (**Kamâl-ed-Deen** or **Kemâl-ed-Dîn**, kạ-mâl' ed-deen',) a Persian traveller and historian, born at Herât in 1413 ; died about 1475. He wrote an interesting history of the descendants of Tamerlane.

Abdias, âb-dee'âs, (**Ben-Shalom**—shâ'lom,) a Jewish rabbi of the seventh century, went to Arabia to dispute with Mohammed, who is said to have converted him.

* See note on last column of preceding page.
† There is some discrepancy in regard to the accentuation of this name : some writers give *Abd-el-Mutâlib*, (or -Motâlib ;) but the best authorities make the penultima short. HAMMER-PURGSTALL (Literaturgeschichte der Araber, vol. i. p. 384) spells it *Abdol-Moththalib*, (*i.e.* -Moththâlib, for he uniformly places an accent on the long syllables :) it should also be observed that he employs *th* (in German) for *t* hard. Pocock, in his Latin version of Abulpharagius, writes the name with *ll*, *Abdol-Motallab* or -*Motalleb* ; but in the Arabic text the penultima is short. (See " Historia Dynastiarum," Oxford, 1663.)

* Most European writers accentuate this name on the last syllable, ABD-ER-RAHMÂN ; but we have preferred to follow Hammer-Purgstall, who invariably gives it with the *ultima* short—ABDERRAHMĂN, (ab-der-răh'măn.) So far as we have had an opportunity of consulting the Arabic texts of the Mohammedan writers, they have nearly always confirmed the practice of that eminent Orientalist. Both forms are undoubtedly correct ; but that given above is sanctioned by the best Arabic usage.

ā, ē, ī, ō, ū, ȳ, *long;* à, è, ò, same, less prolonged; ă, ĕ, ĭ, ŏ, ŭ, ў, *short;* ạ, ę, į, ǫ, *obscure;* fär, fâll, fât; mĕt; nŏt; gōōd; mōⁿn;

Abdol-Malik. See ABD-EL-MALEK.
Abdol-Moththalib. See ABD-EL-MOOTTALIB.
Abdolonimus. See ABDALONYMUS.

Abd-ool- (Abdul- or **Abdoul-) Hamid,** (or **-Hamet,**) âb′dōōl- hä′mid,(or hä′met,) Sultan of Turkey, born in 1725, was a son of Ahmed III. He succeeded his brother Mustapha III. in 1774. Having been defeated by the Russians, he obtained a short peace by the treaty of Kootchook-Kainarji in July, 1774. He was again involved in war against Russia, and lost a battle at Oczakow, in 1788. Died in 1789.

See VON HAMMER, "Histoire de l'Empire Ottoman."

Abd-ool-Mejeed, Abdoul-Medjîd, or **Abdul-Mejîd,** âb′dōōl-me-jeed′, an eminent Mohammedan poet, vizier to Aboo-Mohammed, the last king of Badajoz. He died about 1125.

Abd-ool-Mejeed, Abdul-Mejîd, or **Abdoul-Medjîd,** âb′dōōl-mê-jeed′,[Ger. spelling, ABDUL MEDSCHID,] Sultan of Turkey, born in 1823, was the eldest son of Mahmood II., whom he succeeded July 1, 1839. He found Turkey at war against Mehemet Ali of Egypt, whose victorious army was marching towards his capital. From this danger he was saved by the intervention of the great European powers in 1840. He pursued the course of reform commenced by his father, which was resisted by a fanatical party among his subjects, and exhibited a spirit of tolerance towards Christians. About the end of 1853 he was involved in a war with Russia, in which France and England were the allies of Abd-ōōl-Mejeed. (See NICHOLAS I.) He died in June, 1861, and was succeeded by his brother Abd-ōōl-Azeez, (Abdul-Aziz.)

See ABDOUL MEDJID, in the "Nouvelle Biographie Générale."

Abdor-Rahman. See ABD-ER-RAHMAN.
Abdoul-Melek. See ABD-EL-MALEK.
Abdulaziz. See ABDELAZIZ.
Abdul-Kadir. See ABD-EL-KADER.
Abdul-Malik. See ABD-EL-MALEK.
Abdul-Mûmen. See ABD-EL-MOOMEN.
Abdurrahman. See ABD-ER-RAHMAN.

Ab′dÿ, (MI′RA SMITH,) an English authoress, born in London about 1818, was a niece of Horace and James Smith. She married a Rev. Mr. Abdy, of London. She has written agreeable verses and tales, some of which appeared in various annuals. Perhaps her most important work is her "Appeal on Behalf of Governesses." Died in July, 1867.

A′Bec′ket, (GILBERT ABBOT,) a witty and humorous English writer, born in London in 1810 or 1811. He was admitted to the bar in 1841. He contributed to the London "Times" and "Punch." Among his works are "The Comic Blackstone," (1844–46,) and "The Comic History of England," (1848.) Died in 1856.

A Becket, (THOMAS.) See BECKET.

A-bed′ne-go′, called also **Az-a-rī′ah,** one of the three Hebrew captives whom Nebuchadnezzar, King of Babylon, ordered to be thrown into his fiery furnace. (See Daniel i. 7 ; ii. 49 ; iii. 10, etc.)

A-beel′, (DAVID,) an American missionary, born at New Brunswick, New Jersey, in 1804. He published "A Journal of a Residence in China, 1829–33." Died in 1846.

Abegg, â′bĕk, (BRUNO Erhard—êR′haRt,) a German lawyer, born at Elbing in 1803. Died in Berlin in 1848.

Abegg, (JULIUS FRIEDRICH HEINRICH,) a German jurist, born at Erlangen in 1796. He became professor of law at Breslau in 1826, and published many legal works.

Abeille, â′bȧl′, [Fr. pron. ä′bȧl′ or ä′bȧ′yĕ,] (GASPARD,) a mediocre French lyric and tragic poet, born in Provence in 1648. He was educated for the church, and received the title of "Abbé." In 1704 he was elected a member of the French Academy. Died in 1718.

Abeille, â′bȧl′, (LOUIS,) a German pianist and composer, born at Baireuth about 1765. He produced several successful operas, etc. Died in 1832.

See FÉTIS, "Biographie Universelle des Musiciens."

Abeille, (LOUIS PAUL,) a French writer and agriculturist, born at Toulon in 1719. He was for several

years inspector-general of the manufactures of France. Died in 1807.

Abeille, (SCIPION,) a French surgeon and poet, was a brother of Gaspard, noticed above. He wrote in verse a "Description of the Bones," ("Histoire des Os," 1685.) Died in 1697.

Abeken, âb′ęh-kęn, (BERNHARD RUDOLPH,) a German writer, born at Osnabrück in 1780. He was employed by Schiller as tutor to his children, and was afterwards professor in the College of Osnabrück. Among his works are "Studies on the Divina Commedia of Dante," (1826,) and a valuable contribution to the biography of Cicero, "Cicero in seinen Briefen," (1835,) of which an English version was published in 1854.

A′bel, [in Hebrew הֶבֶל,] the second son of Adam and Eve. He is regarded as the first martyr, and the first of mankind who suffered physical death, having been murdered by Cain, his brother. (See Genesis iv., and Hebrews xi. 4 ; also Matthew xxiii. 35.)

Abel, [Dan. pron. ä′bêl,] a king of Denmark, second son of Waldemar II. He secretly instigated the murder of his brother, Erik VI., and was elected king in his stead in 1250. He was killed, while endeavouring to suppress a rebellion of the Frisians, in 1252.

Abel, ä′bȩl, (CASPAR,) a German writer and antiquary, born in 1676 ; died 1763.

Abel, ä′bel, (CLARKE,) an English surgeon and naturalist, born about 1780. He accompanied Lord Amherst to China in 1816 as naturalist of the expedition, and published a "Narrative of a Journey in the Interior of China," (1818,) which has been highly commended. He was afterwards surgeon-in-chief to the governor-general of India, and died in 1826.

See "Gentleman's Magazine," Dec. 1827.

Abel, (FRIEDRICH GOTTFRIED,) a German physician, born in 1714, was a son of Caspar, noticed above. Died in 1794.

Abel, (JOSEPH,) a distinguished historical painter, born near Linz, on the Danube, in 1768. He passed six years, 1802–8, in Rome, where he painted "Prometheus Bound" and designs from the Iliad. He afterwards worked in Vienna, and produced, besides many portraits, some historical pictures, among which is a "Flight into Egypt." Died in Vienna in 1818.

Abel, (KARL FRIEDRICH,) a German musician, born at Köthen in 1725. In 1763 he removed to London, where for many years he enjoyed the highest popularity ; but, owing to the fickleness of the public taste, his concerts ceased at last to attract any attention. He died in 1787. He is noted as having been the teacher of Cramer.

Abel, ä′bêl, (NIELS HENRIK,) a distinguished mathematician, born at Findö, in Norway, in 1802. He studied at the University of Christiania ; and afterwards, by the aid of a pension from the government, travelled through Germany, Italy, Switzerland, and France. He returned to his native country in 1827, and died in 1829. The special object of Abel's scientific labours was the theory of elliptic functions. The celebrated Legendre spoke with astonishment of his discoveries, and evidently regarded his mathematical talents as of the most original and highest order.

See BROCKHAUS, "Conversations-Lexikon ;" "Nouvelle Biographie Générale."

Abel, von, fon ä′bȩl, (JAKOB FRIEDRICH,) a German philosopher, born in Würtemberg in 1751, was professor of philosophy at Tübingen. He wrote, besides other works, "Collection and Explanation of the Remarkable Phenomena of Human Life," ("Sammlung und Erklärung merkwürdiger Erscheinungen aus dem menschlichen Leben," 3 vols., 1790.) Died in 1829.

Abel, von, (KARL,) a Bavarian statesman, born at Wetzlar in 1788. He became minister of the interior in 1838, and the chief of the absolutist or ultramontane party. By the influence of Lola Montes he was driven from power in February, 1847.

Abel-De-Pujol. See PUJOL.
Abel Rémusat. See RÉMUSAT.

Abela, â-bā′lä, (GIOVANNI FRANCESCO,) a Maltese, of noble family, who in the early part of the seventeenth

century wrote a valuable work entitled "Malta Illus-
trated, with its Antiquities, and other Information,"
(" Malta illustrata con le sue Antichità ed altre Notizie.")
Born in 1582 ; died in 1655.

Ab′ę-lard′ (PIERRE) or **Abailard**, [Fr. pron. ä′bȧ̇′-
läR′; in Latin, PE′TRUS ABÆLAR′DUS,] a celebrated
French philosopher and logician, was born near Nantes
in 1079. After having studied Latin, Greek, and Hebrew, he visited Paris, where he became the pupil of
William de Champeaux, the most skilful dialectician of
the age. But the pupil soon surpassed his master, and
often challenged him to public disputations, so common in the eleventh and twelfth centuries. He is said
to have been so elated by his frequent triumphs that not
only his master but his fellow-students were disgusted
with his vanity. About 1101 he retired from Paris and set
up a school at Melun, whither crowds of pupils repaired
to hear his instructions. Not long after, he returned to
Paris, where, both as teacher and disputant, he was soon
without a rival. When he was about thirty-four years
old, Abelard turned his attention to divinity, and went
to Laon to study under Anselme. His brilliant reputation, joined to his vanity and arrogance, raised up
against him bitter enemies, whose persecution compelled
him to leave the town. He then reopened a school in
Paris, and his fame became greater than ever before.
His well-known and unfortunate amour with his pupil
Heloise need not be related here. Suffice it to say that
it left his defenceless against the malice of those enemies whom his former triumphs and arrogance had provoked. The remainder of his life was little else than a
succession of persecutions. His errors and his afflictions appear to have at last taught him simplicity and
humility. He died in 1142, at the priory of St. Marcel,
near Châlons, whither he had gone for his health. His
remains were, at her request, given up to Heloise, and
buried at the oratory of the Paraclete, which he had
founded, and where she was then prioress. Twenty
years afterwards, she was interred in the same tomb.

Abelard left many writings, nearly all dialectical or
theological, except his "Letters to Heloise," (" Epistolæ
Petri Abælardi et Heloisæ,") and the "History of [his]
Misfortunes," (" Historia Calamitatum.")

"Abelard's reputation," says the "Foreign Quarterly
Review" for January, 1846, "was higher than that of any
living man. . . . It is from his connection with Heloise
that Abelard has descended to posterity ; his own claims
are slight, and have been greatly overrated. . . . He
discovers nothing ; he improves nothing. He can only
dazzle and confuse."

"Abelard," observes Hallam, "was almost the first who
awakened mankind, in the age of darkness, to a sympathy with intellectual excellence. His bold theories, not
the less attractive, perhaps, for treading upon the bounds
of heresy, his imprudent vanity that scorned the regularly acquired reputation of older men, allured a multitude of disciples who would never have listened to an
ordinary teacher. . . . But the whole of Abelard's
life was the shipwreck of genius ; and of genius both
the source of his own calamities and unserviceable to
posterity." (" Middle Ages," vol. iv. p. 377.)

See COUSIN′s " Introduction to the Works of Abelard," 1836 ; BER-
INGTON, " History of Abelard and Heloise," 1787 ; J. HUGHES, " Life
of Abelard," 1751 ; BERINGTON, " History of the Middle Ages," 1814 ;
BRUCKER, " History of Philosophy," 1766 ; DOM GERVAISE, " Vie
d'Abelard," 1720 ; FESSLER, " Abälard and Heloise," 2 vols., 1806 ;
SCHLOSSER, " Abälard und Dulcin," 1807 ; FEUERBACH, " Abälard
und Heloise," 1834 ; O. GUIZOT, " Essai sur la Vie et les Écrits
d'Abailard et de Héloïse," 1839 ; CH. DE RÉMUSAT, " Abelard," 2
vols., 1845 ; FLEURY, " Histoire de l'Église," 1751 ; BERNARDUS,
(Saint,) " Epistolæ ;" also articles in the " Westminster Review," vol.
xxxii., and the " Foreign Quarterly," vol. xxxvi.

Abelin, ä′bęh′lȧn′, or **Abeling,** ä′bęh-ling, (JOHANN
PHILIPP,) a German historian, born at Strasburg, assumed in some of his works the name of JOHANN LUD-
WIG GOTTFRIED, (GOTHOFREDUS.) He published many
works, among which are the first and second volumes of
the "Theatrum Europæum," a valuable record of contemporary history, which was continued to the twenty-
first volume, and a description of the West Indies, (" Historia Antipodum," 1655.) Died about 1646.

See JÖCHER, " Allgemeines Gelehrten-Lexikon."

Abell, ä′bel or ȧ-bĕl′, (JOHN,) an English singer and

performer on the lute, was attached to the chapel of
Charles II. He was banished as a papist in 1688.
Died after 1700.

Abelli or **Abelly,** ä′bȧ̇′le′, (ANTOINE,) an eminent
French ecclesiastic, born in Paris in 1527. He was confessor to Catherine de Medicis. He is supposed to have
died about 1600.

Abelli or **Abelly,** (LOUIS,) a French ecclesiastic,
born in Paris in 1603. He was made Bishop of Rodez
in 1664, and died in 1691. He wrote numerous theological works.

Aben- (or **Ebn-**) **Beitar,** ä′bĕn-bȧ̇-e-taR′ or -bī-taR′,
(**Abdal′lah-Ibn-** (ĭb′n) **Ah′med,**) an Arabian botanist, born near Malaga ; died in 1248.

Abencerage, ạ-bĕn′se-rȧj′, [Sp. pron. ä-Bĕn-thä-rä′-
Hȧ̇,] plural, **Abencerages** or **Abencerrages,** (a Spanish corruption of the Arabic BENÎ SERRÂJ, *i.e.* the " Sons
of Serrâj,") the name of a noble Moorish family in the
kingdom of Granada, originally from Córdova. Several
members of this family acted prominent parts in the period which preceded the conquest of Granada by the
Spaniards. There was a deadly feud between the Abencerages and the Zegris.

Abendana, ä-bĕn-dä′nä, (JACOB,) a Spanish Jew,
who lived in London, and wrote commentaries on the
Scriptures. Died in 1685.

Abendroth, ä′bęnt-rōt′, (AMADEUS AUGUST,) a German lawyer, born at Hamburg in 1767. He became
mayor of that city in 1810, and burgomaster in 1831.
Died in 1842.

Aben- (ä′bĕn) **Ez′ra,** a Spanish Jew, born at Toledo
in 1119. As a commentator on the Scriptures he stands
in the foremost rank. He excelled in almost every
branch of science ; he was an eminent astronomer, mathematician, physician, linguist, and poet. He is supposed
to have died in 1194.

Aben-Humeya, ä′bĕn-hoo-mä′yä, the last king of
Granada, born about 1520. He was of Spanish origin,
and was chosen king by the Moors who had revolted
against Philip II. He was captured and strangled in 1568.

Abenpace. See AVENPACE.

Abercrombie, ab′ęr-krŭm-be, (JAMES,) D.D., an eloquent and learned clergyman of the Episcopal Church
in Philadelphia, born in 1758 ; died in 1841.

Abercrombie, (JAMES,) a major-general in the British army in America, where he arrived and took command of the troops at Albany in 1756. The French
having obtained possession of the lakes, Abercrombie in
1758 was intrusted by Pitt with a force of 50,000 men to
recover the places which had been lost. On the 8th of
July he attacked Ticonderoga at the head of 15,000
troops, but was repulsed by Montcalm with great loss.
He was shortly after superseded by Lord Amherst.

Abercrombie, (JOHN,) an eminent Scottish physician,
born at Aberdeen in 1781. Having graduated as an
M.D. in 1803, he settled in Edinburgh, and rose to the
highest rank in his profession. His reputation was
widely extended by his writings, among which are
"Pathological and Practical Researches on Diseases of
the Brain and Spinal Cord," (1828,) "Inquiries concerning the Intellectual Powers of Man, and the Investigation of Truth," (1830,) and "The Philosophy of the Moral
Feelings," (1833.) Referring to his work on the intellectual powers, the "Quarterly Review" observes, "His descriptions of the mental phenomena are clear and precise, and his reasonings perspicuous and sound. . . .
The style of the work merits equal praise. It is simple and unambitious, without being devoid of ornament
or power." (" London Quarterly" for July, 1831.) He
was chosen lord rector of Marischal College, Aberdeen, in 1835. Died in November, 1844.

See CHAMBERS, " Biographical Dictionary of Eminent Scotsmen,"
vol. v.

Abercromby, ab′ęr-krŭm-be, (ALEXANDER,) a Scottish judge, the youngest brother of Sir Ralph Abercromby,
was born in 1745. In 1792 (on the death of Lord Hailes)
he became a judge in the court of justiciary. Died in
1795. He wrote several interesting papers for "The
Mirror" and "The Lounger," two literary periodicals
edited by Mackenzie.

See CHAMBERS, " Biographical Dictionary of Eminent Scotsmen."

ā, ē, ī, ō, ū, ȳ, *long;* ȧ, ė, ȯ, *same, less prolonged;* ă, ĕ, ĭ, ŏ, ŭ, ў, *short;* ạ, ę, į, ǫ, *obscure;* fär, fȧll, fȧt; mĕt; nŏt; gŏŏd; mō̄n;

Abercromby, (DAVID,) a Scottish physician, who flourished in the latter half of the seventeenth century. Besides four short treatises on medicine, he wrote several works on other subjects. His "Fur Academicus" ("Academical Thief") shows him to have been a man of wit and learning. The time of his birth and that of his death are unknown.

Abercromby, (JAMES,) BARON DUNFERMLINE, a British peer, a son of Sir Ralph, noticed below, was born in 1776. He entered Parliament about 1812, voted with the Whigs, and acquired distinction as a debater. He was speaker of the House of Commons from 1835 to 1839, in which year he resigned and passed into the House of Lords as Baron Dunfermline. Died in 1858.

Abercromby, (JOHN,) a horticultural writer, born near Edinburgh in 1726. His first work, entitled "Every Man his own Gardener," had a great sale ; and he afterwards published a number of others, among which may be mentioned "The British Fruit Gardener" and "The Gardener's Daily Assistant." Died in 1806.

Abercromby, (Sir JOHN,) the second son of Sir Ralph, served under him in Egypt, and obtained the rank of general. Having been appointed governor of Madras, he took Mauritius from the French in 1810. He died, it is supposed, in 1817.

Abercromby, (PATRICK,) M.D., the author of a work entitled "Martial Achievements of the Scots Nation," (2 vols., 1711-15,) was born at Forfar in 1656, and is supposed to have died about the year 1720. Although his work has enjoyed a considerable reputation, it possesses little merit.

Abercromby, (Sir RALPH,) a distinguished military commander, was born in Clackmannanshire, Scotland, in 1734. He entered the University of Edinburgh in 1752, and in 1754 was sent by his father to Leipsic to study civil law. But, as he manifested a decided preference for the military profession, his father yielded to his wishes and permitted him to join the army. In 1773 he was elected member of Parliament. He does not, however, appear to have particularly distinguished himself in any way till the breaking out of the war with France in 1793. In 1795 he was created Knight of the Bath. In the unfortunate campaigns in Holland under the Duke of York in 1793-5, and especially in that of 1799, he did everything that a subordinate officer could do. The bravery and military skill which he evinced won for him universal respect, and every one was satisfied that had he commanded in chief the results would have been very different. Abercromby was appointed commander-in-chief of the expedition against Egypt, which set out in 1800 and reached its destination in 1801. A few days after the landing of the troops near Alexandria, the British camp was suddenly attacked by all the French troops in that country. The assailants were bravely repulsed, but during the action the British commander received a wound in the thigh, of which he died a few days after. As an officer, Sir Ralph Abercromby was distinguished by talents of a high order, and still more by a humane and generous regard for the welfare of his soldiers. Though perfectly reckless in exposing himself, he was extremely careful never to expose those under his command to any unnecessary danger. As a man, he was distinguished for benevolence, superiority to prejudice, and a high sense of honour. Sir Ralph Abercromby had four sons : the first Lord Abercromby ; Sir John Abercromby, who served with credit under his father in Egypt, and afterwards rose to the rank of a general ; Lord Dunfermline ; and Alexander, a lieutenant-colonel in the army.

See "Memoir of Sir Ralph Abercromby," by LORD DUNFERMLINE; CHAMBERS, "Biographical Dictionary of Eminent Scotsmen ;" WILSON, "History of the British Expedition to Egypt."

Abercromby, (Sir ROBERT,) a British general, was a younger brother of Sir Ralph. He became governor of Bombay in 1789, and commander-in-chief in India in 1792. After a successful campaign against the Rohillas, he returned to England in 1797, and was elected to Parliament. Died about 1827.

Ab-er-deen', (GEORGE HAMILTON GORDON,) EARL OF, a British statesman, born in 1784, inherited the earldom (in the Scottish peerage) from his grandfather, who died in 1802. He was elected one of the Scottish representative peers about 1807, identified himself with the Tory party, and was sent on a diplomatic mission to Vienna in 1813. In 1814 he became Viscount Gordon in the peerage of the United Kingdom. He was secretary of state for foreign affairs, in the cabinet of Wellington, from 1828 until November, 1830, when his party went out of power. In September, 1841, Sir Robert Peel appointed him to the same office, which he retained until the triumph of the Whig party, in July, 1846. His foreign policy was pacific.

After the death of Peel, (1850,) the Earl of Aberdeen was regarded as the head of the Peelite party. On the defeat of Lord Derby, in December, 1852, he became prime minister, and formed his cabinet by a coalition of Conservatives and Whigs or Liberals. In spite of his efforts to maintain peace, Great Britain "drifted into war" against Russia, in 1854. He lost popularity by his moderation towards Russia, and was censured for remissness in the prosecution of the war. Having been defeated in the House of Commons about February 1, 1855, he resigned his office, and was succeeded by Lord Palmerston. Died in December, 1860. He had been twice married, and left a son, who was styled Lord Haddo.

See "Gentleman's Magazine" for February, 1861.

Aberli, ä'bĕr-lee, (JOHANN LUDWIG,) a Swiss landscape-painter and engraver, born at Winterthur in 1723. His landscapes of Swiss scenery, engraved and coloured, were much admired, and found many imitators. Died at Berne in 1786.

Abernethy, ab'er-ne-the, (JOHN,) an eminent dissenting divine, born at Coleraine, in Ireland, in 1680. He took the degree of M.A. at the College of Glasgow, and afterwards studied divinity in Edinburgh. Upon finishing his course he returned to Ireland, and at length became the pastor of a Presbyterian congregation at Antrim. Some new views which he subsequently adopted, on the right of private judgment in matters of faith, together with the spirit of independence which he manifested with respect to the authority of the synod, caused at last a schism in the church. In 1730 he became the pastor of an independent congregation, in addressing whom he carefully avoided all appeals to the affections, maintaining that nothing else was requisite than merely to convince the reason. Hence his followers were termed Rational Dissenters. Abernethy died in 1740.

See DUCHAL, "Life of Abernethy," prefixed to his Sermons; "Biographia Britannica."

Abernethy, (JOHN,) a celebrated English surgeon and physiologist, born in London in 1764, was a pupil of John Hunter. He was a grandson of John Abernethy, noticed above. In 1786 he became assistant-surgeon of St. Bartholomew's Hospital, London, and on the death of Sir C. Blick he succeeded him as chief surgeon in that institution. He lectured on anatomy and surgery, and acquired immense popularity as a teacher. He published, in 1809, an able work "On the Constitutional Origin and Treatment of Local Diseases," in which he propounded doctrines which have made a great change in the science of surgery. He is said to have been the first surgeon who performed the ligature of the carotid artery and the external iliac artery. Many amusing anecdotes are related of him, exhibiting that singular mixture of shrewd sense, wit, and eccentricity for which he was so remarkable. A gouty rich man having consulted him received for answer, "Live on sixpence a day, and earn it." In domestic relations he is said to have been amiable. He married Ann Threlfall in 1800. Died at Enfield in April, 1831.

See GEORGE MACILWAIN. "Memoirs of J. Abernethy," 1853 CHAMBERS, "Biographical Dictionary of Eminent Scotsmen."

Abert, ä'bĕrt, (JOHN J.,) an American engineer, born in Maryland in 1790. He was appointed major of topographical engineers in 1814, and colonel of the same in 1838. He was at the head of the corps of topographical engineers for about thirty years. Died in January, 1863.

Abesch, ä'bĕsh, (ANNA BARBARA,) a famous Swiss painter on glass. Died about 1750.

Ab'gar-us, [Gr. Ἄβγαρος,] written also **Abagarus,**

ĕ as ĕ; ç as s; ğ hard; ğ as j; G, H, K, guttural; N, nasal; R, trilled; ş as z; th as in this. (☞ See Explanations, p. 23.)

3

Agbarus, and **Augarus,** a name common to several kings of Edessa in Mesopotamia.

Ab-i´a-thar, [in Hebrew, אביתר,] a high-priest of the Jews, and one of the chief counsellors of King David. (See I. Samuel xxii., xxiii., and xxx.; II. Samuel viii. and xx.; I. Kings ii. and iv.)

Abicht, ä´bikt, (JOHANN GEORG,) a German author and divine, born in Schwarzburg-Rudolstadt in 1672. He wrote several works on the Hebrew language and antiquities, and also on theology. Died in 1740.

Abicot. See HABICOT.

Abidenus. See ABYDENUS.

Ab´i-gail, [Heb. אביגיל,] a Hebrew matron, who was married first to Nabal, and secondly to King David. (See I. Samuel xxv.)

A-bi´jah or **A-bi´a,** [in Hebrew, אביה,] a name common to several Israelites, among whom may be named a son of Jeroboam and a son of the prophet Samuel.

Ab-i´jam [Heb. אבים] or **Abijah,** King of Judah, was a son of Rehoboam, whom he succeeded on the throne. After a reign of three years, he died about 955 B.C. (I. Kings xv. 1–8; II. Chronicles xiii.)

Abildgaard, ä´bild-gord´,(NICHOLAS,) a distinguished Danish historical painter, born in Copenhagen in 1744. In 1772 he visited Italy, where he spent five years. He was afterwards appointed professor of painting in the Academy of Copenhagen. Died about 1806. He is considered by many as the best painter that Denmark has produced. Among his works are a "Socrates," and the "Creation of the World, after Orpheus."

See ERSCH and GRUBER. "Allgemeine Encyklopaedie;" NAGLER, "Neues Allgemeines Künstler-Lexikon."

Abildgaard, (PETER CHRISTIAN,) an able Danish physician and naturalist, born at Copenhagen about 1740, was, according to Malte-Brun, a brother of the preceding. He wrote many treatises on medicine, zoology, etc., and gave a description of the *Megatherium* at the same time as Cuvier, (1796.) He was secretary of the Academy of Sciences, and founder of the Veterinary School of Copenhagen. Died about 1808.

See "Biographie Universelle;" "Historia brevis Regii Instituti Veterinarii," etc., Copenhagen, 1788; CUVIER, "Sur les Ossements Fossiles."

Abildgaard, (SÖ´REN,) a Danish naturalist, born between 1720 and 1730. He wrote two works on topographical mineralogy, one of which is entitled "Physico-Mineralogical Description of the Promontory of Möen," ("Physik-mineralogisk Beskrivelse over Möens Klint," 1781.) Died in 1791.

See ERSCH, "Handbuch der Deutschen Literatur."

Abilfedæ. See ABOOLFEDA.

A-bim´e-lech, [Heb. אבימלך,] an illegitimate son of Gideon, chosen king by the men of Shechem after he had slain all his brothers except Jotham. Afterwards, while attempting to take Thebez, he was mortally wounded with a stone thrown from the top of the citadel by a woman; upon which his armour-bearer, at his request, ran him through the body with a sword, lest it should be said that he had been slain by a woman. (See Judges ix.) Two kings of Gerar, named Abimelech, are mentioned in the book of Genesis, (chaps. xx. and xxvi.)

Ab´in-ger, (Lord,) an English lawyer, whose proper name was JAMES SCARLETT, was born in Jamaica about 1769. Having been educated in England, he was called to the bar in 1791, and obtained great success as a pleader. He was appointed attorney-general in 1827, and became an adherent of the Tory party. In 1834 he was appointed chief baron of the exchequer, and raised to the peerage as Baron Abinger. He is said to have been almost unrivalled in the tact and address with which he operated on the minds of juries. Died in 1844, leaving several sons.

See "Gentleman's Magazine" for June, 1844; FOSS, "The Judges of England," vol. ix.

Ab´ing-ton, (FRANCES,) a celebrated English actress, born about the year 1731. She excelled in every department of comedy, and was for a long time without a rival. Her taste in dress was greatly admired. Her talents and elegant manners procured her admittance into society of the highest rank; but, as a woman, her character was marred with those moral blemishes so common in persons of her profession. She died in 1815.

Abington, (THOMAS and WILLIAM.) See HABINGTON.

Abisbal, ä-bès-bäl´, (HENRY O'DONNELL,) COUNT, a Spanish general of Irish descent, who greatly distinguished himself in resisting the French invasion in 1809–10. He afterwards acted a conspicuous part in the political as well as military affairs of Spain until his death, in 1834.

A-bish´a-i, [Heb. אבישי,] one of the three sons of Zeruiah, sister of King David, in whose army he was a leader. See II. Samuel xxiii. 18; also I. Samuel xxvi. 6–9.

Ablancourt, d´, dä´blôn´koor´, (NICOLAS **Perrot**—pă´ro´,) an eminent French translator, born at Châlons-sur-Marne in 1606. He produced translations of Tacitus, Thucydides, Cæsar, and Lucian, which were received with favour; but they are not faithful, and are now neglected. He was admitted into the French Academy in 1637. Colbert proposed him as historiographer in 1662, but Louis XIV. rejected him because he was a Protestant. Died in 1664.

Ab-la´vi-us, a Roman historian, cited by Jornandes in his History of the Goths. The age in which he lived is unknown.

Ableitner, äb´lit-ner, (JOHANN,) a Bavarian sculptor, who flourished in the early part of the seventeenth century.

Ablesimof or **Ablecimof,** ä-blès´e-mof´, (ALEXANDER,) an officer in the Russian army, who became distinguished as a dramatist. Among his works is a successful national comic opera entitled "The Miller," (1779,) which is considered a faithful picture of Russian manners. Died at Moscow in 1784.

Ab´ner or **Abiner,** [Heb. אבנר or אבינר,] the son of Ner, was captain of the host of Saul, King of Israel. After the death of Saul, in consequence of an affront offered him by Ishbosheth, Abner sought to transfer the whole kingdom to David. But Joab, exasperated because Abner had killed his brother Asahel in battle, and perhaps jealous of the influence which he might acquire with David, called him aside under pretence of speaking with him privately, and treacherously slew him.

Ab´ney, (Sir THOMAS,) M.P., Lord Mayor of London, born in 1639. He rendered important services to William III. Died in 1722.

Abondio, ä-bon´de-o, (ALESSANDRO,) a Florentine painter, was a pupil of Michael Angelo. He worked in Germany, and died at Prague. He had a son of the same name, who lived at Munich and was no less distinguished as a painter than his father.

AB´OO, ABOU, or *ABÛ,* an Arabic word signifying "father," forming a prefix to many Oriental names, as ABOO-BEKR, (which see,) the "father of the virgin."

Aboo- (Abû- or **Abou-) Abdillah,** ä´boo äb-dil´-läh, the Sheeite, the chief actor in the revolution which established the dynasty of the Fatimites on the throne of Egypt. He was born at Sanaa about 865. By his preaching and by his arms he induced a great part of the Mohammedans in Africa to join the new sect and to recognize the claims of Obeydallah, the first sultan of the Fatimite line. But having afterwards been detected in a conspiracy against his sovereign, whom he had raised to the throne, he was put to death in 911.

Aboo- (Abû- or **Abou-) Abdillah-Mohammed,** surnamed AL-MAHDEE or AL-MAHDÎ, (*i.e.* "director" or "ruler,") founder of the sect and dynasty of the Almohades, (Almowahedûn,) was born in the province of Soos, in Morocco, about the year 1087. Like many other leaders of Mohammedan sects, he began with preaching and ended with the sword. He died in 1130, leaving to Abd-el-Moomen the prosecution of his plans of reform and conquest.

Aboo-Amroo-Al-Owzâee, (Abû-Amrû-Alau-zâî,) ä´boo äm´roo äl-ŏw-zä´ee, a famous Mohammedan doctor, who was born at Baalbek about 706 and died about 774 A.D.

Aboo- (Abû- or **Abou-) Bahr-Sefwân,** ä´boo´-bäh´r sef´wän´, a distinguished Moslem poet and historian, born at Murcia, in Spain, about the year 1106. Besides many other valuable works, he wrote a biographical dictionary of eminent contemporary authors. He died about 1182.

Aboo-Bekr, (Abû-Beker, Abû-Bekr, or Abou-Bekr,) ä′bōō bek′ẹr, or ä-boo′bêk-ẹr, written also **Abu-Bakr, Abu-Bacr,** and **Aboubecre,** the first of Mohammed's successors, was born in 571 A.D. He belonged to the celebrated tribe of Koreish, and was one of the first and most zealous of the converts to Islâm. His original name was ABD-EL-KAABA, (äbd-el-kä′bä ;) but after the prophet Mohammed had married his virgin daughter Ayeshah, he was called ABOO-BEKR, the "Father of the Virgin." He was elected to the throne in 632, and died in 634, after a reign of two years and three months. Aboo-Bekr is admitted by all to have been a pious and humble man, and a mild, generous, and excellent prince. He was succeeded by Omăr.

See GIBBON, "Decline and Fall of the Roman Empire," chap. l. ; IRVING, "Mahomet and his Successors ;" WEIL, "Geschichte der Chalifen," vol. i. chap. i. For a notice of the character of Aboo-Bekr, see SPRENGER'S "Life of Mohammad," p. 170 *et seq.*

Aboo- (Abû- or Abou-) **Bekr-al-Mahree,** (Almahrî,) ä′bōō bek′ẹr äl-mäu′ree′, the vizier of Almutamed, Sultan of Seville, was born about 1030. He appears to have been an able minister, but, having incurred the suspicion of his sovereign, he was put to death in 1084. He was regarded as one of the first poets of his age.

Aboo-Bekr (Abû-Beker) **-Ibn-Tofail,** (Ib′n to-fil′,) an eminent Arabian philosopher, born at Guadix, in Spain. He wrote a philosophical romance entitled "Hai-Ibn-Yokdhân," (or "Hayyi-Ibn-Yokttân,") which was translated into Latin by Pocock and published in 1671, and into English by Simon Ockley, (London, 1708.) Died at Morocco in 1186.

See AL-MAKKARI, "History of the Mohammedan Dynasties in Spain," translated by GAYANGOS, vol. i. pp. 335-6.

Aboo- (Abû- or Abou-) **Farâs,** ä′bōō fä-räs′, a distinguished Arabian poet, born in 932. He was cousin to Seyf-ed-Dowlah, (Seyfu-d-daulah,) Sultan of Aleppo, at whose court he lived. A Mohammedan writer calls him "the pearl of his time, and the sun of his age, in learning, talent, generosity, glory, eloquence, horsemanship, and bravery." He was killed in a skirmish in 968.

Aboo- (or Abou-) **Hâmid-Alghazâlee,** (Abû-Hâmid-Al-ghazâlî or Alghazzâlî,) ä′bōō hä′mid äl-gä-zä′lee, a distinguished doctor, born at Toos, (Tûs,) in Khorassân, about 1058. He spent a part of his time in travelling ; but much the greater portion appears to have been passed in seclusion and wholly devoted to philosophy and divinity. He is said to have been a man of sound judgment and immense learning. From his rare attainments as a divine, he was called ZEYN-ED-DEEN, "the ornament of religion." Died at Bagdâd in 1111.

Aboo-Haneefah. See HANEEFAH.

Aboo- (Abû- or Abou-) **Hayyân,** ä′bōō hī′yân′, surnamed ATHEER-ED-DEEN, (ATHÎR-UD-DÎN,) "the glory of religion," a distinguished Arabian author, born in the province of Jaen, in Spain, in 1256. When very young, he visited several towns in Andalusia, where he supported himself by transcribing books and lecturing on the Koran. He afterwards went to Egypt, and was appointed a professor and lecturer on the Koran in one of the colleges of that country. He died in Cairo in 1344. He was called "the prince of his age in the science of grammar." Besides numerous other important works, he wrote a "History of the Turkish Race," and a voluminous commentary on the Koran.

Aboo- (Abû- or Abou-) **Ishâk,** (-is-hâk′,) an Arabian geographer, who lived about the beginning of the tenth century. The place of his birth is unknown.

Aboo- (Abû- or Abou-) **Ishâk-Al-Hos′ree′,** (or Al-Hosrî,) a noted poet, born near Kairwan in Africa ; died in 1061.

Aboo-Jaafar, (or -Jafar.) See MANSOOR, AL.

Aboo-l- (Abû-l-) **Abbâs-Abdallah,** ä′bōō′ äb′bâs′ äb-dâl′lâh, surnamed As-SEFFÂH (äs-sêf′fâh′,) *i.e.* "the shedder of blood," the twenty-second caliph of the East, and the first of the dynasty of the Abbassides, was born at Damascus about 720 A.D. He was a descendant of Abbâs, the uncle of Mohammed. His family had

always, during the usurpation of the house of Omey yah, considered themselves the rightful heirs to the caliphate ; at length, during the reign of Merwân II., the standard of revolt was raised in Khorassân. Upon hearing this, Merwân caused Ibrâheem, the brother of Aboo-l-Abbâs-Abdallah, the representative of the line of Abbâs, to be seized and put to death. His brothers, Aboo-l-Abbâs and Aboo-Jaafar, being then, absent from Damascus, fled to Koofah, (Kûfah,) where the former was proclaimed caliph by the people, (A.D. 749.) Merwân, having advanced against the rebels with an army, was defeated, and fled to Damascus, and thence to Egypt, where he was overtaken and slain. It is estimated that more than one hundred of the Omeyyah family fell victims to the vengeance of the new caliph. As-Seffâh died in 754. Notwithstanding his severity against the enemies of his family, he is represented by some historians as a liberal, benevolent, and able prince. He was esteemed the handsomest man of his time.

See WEIL, "Geschichte der Chalifen," vol. ii. chap. i.; D'HERBELOT, "Bibliothèque Orientale."

Aboo-l-ala, (Abû-l-'ala,) ä′bōōl′ ä′lä, a famous Arabian poet, born in Syria about 970. When only four years old, he lost his sight from the small-pox. He used to call himself "the doubly-imprisoned captive," alluding to his blindness and the voluntary seclusion in which he devoted himself to study. He soon won so great a reputation that his house was filled with students, who came to him from different countries. Died in 1057.

Abool-Cacem. See ABOO-L-KASIM.

Aboolfaraj, (Abû-l-faraj,) ä′bōōl′ fär′âj, (or -fär′aj,) an eminent Arabian author and compiler, a descendant of Merwân II., born at Ispahan in 897. His works are numerous and very valuable. Died at Bagdâd in 967.

Aboolfaraj, (Abu-l- (or Aboul-) **faraj,**) [written in French ABOULFARADGE, ä′bōōl′ fä′râj ; Latin, ABULFARA′GIUS or ABULPHARA′GIUS ; called also BARHE-BRÆ′US,] GREGORIUS, an eminent historical writer, born in Armenia in 1226. At the age of twenty he was ordained Bishop of Guba by Ignatius, the patriarch of the Jacobite Christians. About 1266 he was chosen Primate of the Jacobites, which position he held till his death in 1286. His entire life was devoted to literature, —principally history, in which he left works of great value. He wrote in Arabic and Syriac. His talents and virtues gained for him the esteem of Mohammedans as well as Christians.

See ABOULFARADGE, in the "Nouvelle Biographie Générale."

Aboolfaraj (Abu- (or Abou-) l-faraj) OF RONAH, a distinguished Persian poet, born in the first half of the eleventh century. He lived at the court of Ibrâheem of Ghiznee, (Gazna.) He died, it is supposed, about 1090.

Aboolfazl, (Abû-l-fazl or Aboul-Fazl,) ä′bōōl′fâz′l, (commonly pronounced in India ŭb′ōōl-fŭz′l,) the enlightened minister and historiographer of Akbăr, the greatest of the Mogul emperors. The date of his birth is unknown. In 1572 he was raised to the office of prime minister, which he held for about twenty-eight years. He was waylaid and assassinated about the year 1600, leaving behind him the justly-won reputation of an excellent historian, and of a wise, virtuous, and truly great man. His works are numerous and extremely valuable. Among them we may mention the "Akbar Namah," a minute history of the times of Akbăr ; "Ayeen Akbari," (or "Ayin-i-Akbari,") "Institutes of Akbar ;" and a posthumous work entitled "Muktōōbat," (or "Maktûbat,") the "writings," or "letters," including Aboolfazl's own correspondence.

See ABOULFAZL, in the "Nouvelle Biographie Générale."

Aboolfeda, (Abû-l-fedâ* or Aboulfeda,) ä′bōōl′ fêd′ä or ä-bōōl′fê-dä′, a prince and warrior, and one of the most celebrated of the Arabian authors, was born at Damascus about 1273. He was a direct descendant from Aiyoob, (Aiyûb,) the founder of the Aiyoobite dynasty in Egypt. His family had possessed the throne of Ha-

* It may be proper to observe that the Latin name ABULFEDA forms the genitive very irregularly—ABILFEDÆ. This peculiarity is owing to the fact that the *Abû* in the first part of the name has in Arabic *Abî* for its genitive. In like manner, we say (in the nominative) Abû Tâlib ; but Ibn Abî Tâlib, the "son of Abû Tâlib," the chnnge of û (oo) to î (ee) being necessary to mark the genitive case.

mah, but the fief which they held having been declared extinct by Nâsir, (or An-Nâsir-Ibn-Kalâun,) Sultan of Syria and Egypt, Aboolfedâ was deprived of his inheritance. Upon this he entered the service of the sultan, and was with him in all his wars against the Tartars. Afterwards, as an acknowledgment of his eminent services, the sultan conferred upon him the title of Prince of Hamah. He remained in undisturbed possession of his newly-acquired dignity until his death in 1331. All the Moslem writers agree in representing Aboolfedâ as a man of the greatest talents; he was as much distinguished for skill and courage in the field as for wisdom. and prudence in the divân. In spite of the cares of his government, he devoted much of his attention to the cultivation of literature. He has left valuable works on history, geography, and medicine. His work entitled "The Description of the Countries" is considered to be the best and most complete Arabic geography which exists. His great history, called "An Abridgment of the History of Mankind," is a work of vast erudition. Besides containing a history of the Mohammedans from the birth of the prophet down to the date of the work itself, (1328,) it furnishes much information respecting Arabia before the time of Mohammed, the ancient Persian dynasties, the Copts, the Hindoos, etc.

See "Nouvelle Biographie Générale;" ERSCH und GRUBER, "Allgemeine Encyklopaedie."

Aboo-l-Hassan or **Abû-l- (Aboul-) hassan,** å′bōōl′ hås′san, an Arabian astronomer, who flourished in Morocco in the beginning of the thirteenth century.

Aboo-l-Hassan, (or **Abû-l- (Aboul-) hassan,**) written also **Aboul-Haçan,** a Samaritan, who embraced the Mohammedan religion and repaired to the court of the King of Damascus, by whom he was appointed vizier about the year 1231. Accompanying an expedition into Egypt, he was taken prisoner and put to death in 1251.

Aboo-l-Hassan or **Aboul-Haçan,** (Alee (or Alî) **Ibn Omar,** å′lee ïb′n o′mar,) an Arabian astronomer of Morocco, lived about the year 1200. He wrote a valuable treatise on philosophical instruments, which was translated into French by Sedillot.

Aboo-l-Kâsim, Abû-l-kâsim, or **Aboul-cacem,** å′bōōl′ kå′sim, [in Latin, ALBUCA′SIS or ABULCA′SIS,] the most celebrated of all the Arabian writers on surgery. Scarcely anything is known of his life; he is supposed to have practised medicine in Córdova in the latter part of the eleventh and the beginning of the twelfth century, and to have died about 1110. His principal work, which treats of anatomy, physiology, the practice of medicine, and surgery, is one of extraordinary value. That portion which is devoted to surgery has been pronounced the best treatise on this subject that has come down to us from antiquity. It is especially interesting and valuable to those who desire to trace the gradual progress of the surgical art in its various departments.

See WÜSTENFELD, "Geschichte der Arabischen Aerzte;" SPRENGEL, "History of Medicine."

Aboo-l-Kâsim, (Abû-l-kâsim or Abou-l-cacem,) a distinguished Mohammedan theologian and poet, born in the province of Valencia, Spain, about 1143. He visited several foreign countries, and finally settled in Cairo, where he was appointed to a professorship. He died in 1194. He wrote several works on the Koran, which are highly esteemed.

Aboo-l-Kâsim or **Aboul-Cacem,** a Turkish general, lived about 1050. He took Nicæa, and advanced towards Constantinople, but was repulsed by Taticius, and put to death by the Shah of Persia.

Aboo-l-Kâsim-Mansoor. See FIRDOUSEE.

Aboo-l-Khatâr or **Abû- (Aboul-) Khattâr,** å′bōōl′ kåt′tår′, a governor of Spain under the caliphs. He was a native of Arabia, and was sent by the Viceroy of Africa to quiet the contending factions by which Spain was at that time distracted. He arrived in Córdova in 743 A.D. At first he was entirely successful, but at length a rebellion broke out, which he was unable to quell; and he was finally slain by the conquering party.

Aboo-l-Maalee or **Abûl- (Aboul-) Maalî,** å′bōōl′ mâ′a-lee, a learned Persian who flourished in the reign of Bahram Shah, of Ghiznee, between 1118 and 1152.

Aboo-l-Mahânes or **Abûl- (Aboul-) mahânî,**

å′bōōl′ mä-hä′nee, an Arabian astronomer, who lived at the court of Al-Mâmoon, the seventh caliph of the Abbassides, between 813 and 833.

Aboo-l-Wafâ or **Abûl- (Aboul-) Wafâ,** å′bōōl′ wä′fä′, a distinguished mathematician and astronomer, born in Khorassân about 940; died in 998. He was employed at Bagdâd, with other eminent astronomers, to correct the astronomical tables of Aboo-l-Mahânee.

Aboo-l-Waleed or **Abûl- (Aboul-) Walîd,** å′bōōl′ wä-leed′, a famous Mohammedan divine, born at Beja, in Portugal, about 1012. His talents and learning attracted the notice of Al-Mōōtamed, King of Seville, by whom he was appointed chief justice, which position he held till his death, in 1081.

Aboo-l-Waleed or **Abûl- (Aboul-) Walîd,** a distinguished Moslem divine and historian, born at Aleppo about the year 1400; died 1478.

Aboo-l-Waleed- (or **Abûl- (Aboul-) Walîd-) Ibn-Jehwar**—ïb′n-jêh′wår or -jêh′war, the second sultan of Córdova of the Jehwar dynasty, whose capital was treacherously wrested from him by Al-Mōōtamed King of Seville, about the year 1045; the latter having with a large army entered Aboo-l-Waleed's kingdom with the professed object of assisting him against Al Mâmoon, King of Toledo. Aboo-l-Waleed died, or was killed, soon after.

Abool-Waleed-Mohammed-Ibn-Roshd. See AVERROËS.

Aboo-Mansoor, (Abû-Mansûr or Abou-Mansour,) å′bōō mån′sōōR′, a distinguished astronomer, born at Mecca in 855. He lived at the court of the caliph Al-Mâmoon, who appointed him president of an academy of astronomers at Bagdâd, and committed to his superintendence the building of two observatories. The time of his death is unknown.

Aboo- (Abû- or Abou-) **Merwân** or **Merouan,** å′bōō meR′wân′, a distinguished Mohammedan divine, born at Seville about 1170. He was for several years chief justice of his native city. Having made a pilgrimage to Mecca, he died at Cairo, on his return, in 1237.

Aboo- (Abû- or Abou-) **Mos'lem,** (or -Muslim,) a general, who contributed greatly to the overthrow of the Omeyyah dynasty and the establishment of that of the Abbassides, was born about 720 A.D. Neither his fidelity nor the greatness of his merits availed him against the jealous cruelty of a sovereign whom he had raised to the throne. Aboo-Jaafar had employed him in quelling some formidable rebellions which threatened to dismember the empire. But, when his services were no longer needed, the caliph, having invited him, with every mark of friendship, to visit him in his palace at Roomeeyeh, (Rûmiyyah,) caused Aboo-Moslem to be basely assassinated, in 755. Although Aboo-Moslem's character was undoubtedly stained with many crimes, he appears to have been always faithful to his sovereign.

See WEIL, "Geschichte der Chalifen," vol. i. chap. xvii., and vol. ii. chaps. i. and ii.

Aboo- (Abû- or Abou-) **Nowâs**—no-wâss′, an Arabian poet, born about 744, and died about 810 A.D.

Aboo- (Abû- or Abou-) **Obeyd**—o′bâd′ or -o bïd′, a noted Mohammedan geographer and historian, born in Spain about 1040. He was vizier to Mohammed, King of Almería. Died about 1095.

Aboo- (Abû- or Abou-) **Obeydah**—o-bâ′dah, a celebrated Mohammedan general, who commanded under the caliphs Aboo-Bekr and Omâr. He died of the plague, at Damascus, in 639.

Aboo-Reehân or **Abû- (Abou-) Rîhân,** written also **Abou-Ryhan,** å′bōō ree′hân′, a distinguished Arabian astronomer, born about 970; died in 1038. He was employed on several embassies by Al-Mâmoon, (Mâmûn,) Sultan of Kharasm.

Aboo-Saeed or **Abû- (Aboul-) Saîd,** å′bōō sâ-eed′, the ninth of the Persian kings of the race of Jengis Khan, ascended the throne in 1317. He was a weak prince, being ruled first by his favourite, the emir Choobân, and afterwards by his wife, the daughter of that nobleman. He died in 1335, at the age of thirty.

Aboo-Saeed-Meerza, (Abû-Saîd-Mîrzâ or Abou Saïd Mîrzâ,) å′bōō sâ-eed′ meer′zâ, a prince of the Moguls, born about 1427, was a descendant of Tamerlane.

ï, e, ï, ō, ü, ÿ, *long;* å, ė, ò, same, less prolonged; ă, ĕ, ĭ, ŏ, ŭ, ÿ, *short;* a, ę, i, o, *obscure;* fär, fåll, fåt; mët; nŏt; gōōd; mōōn;

Having invaded Irâk and Azerbaijân, he was taken prisoner and put to death in 1469.

Aboo- (Abû- or Abou-) Sahl-Isa, â'boo sâhl is'â, (or ee'sạ,) an eminent Christian physician of Khorassân, tutor to the famous Avicenna, (Ibn-Seenâ.) He lived in the early part of the eleventh century.

Aboo-Salat or **Abû- (Abou-)s-Salat,** â'boo sâl'ât, (or sâl'ạt,) a Spanish physician, astronomer, and poet, born in 1068 ; died in 1134.

Aboo- (Abou- or Abû-) Sofiân, (Sophiân or Sophyân,) â'boo so-fe-ân', a chief among the Koreish, who distinguished himself by his obstinate hostility to the claims of Mohammed. After all resistance was vain, he reluctantly acknowledged the divine mission of the prophet. Aboo-Sofiân was the father of the caliph Moâwceyeh, the founder of the Omeyyah dynasty at Damascus. (See MOHAMMED.)

Aboo-Tâhir or **Abû- (Abou-) Tâhir,** â'boo tâ'hir, the chief of a sect called Karmatians, who, with a comparatively small number of followers, took and plundered Koofah, (Kûfah,) Mecca, and several other cities of Asia, and at length, in 931, was bold enough to advance, with only 500 horse, to within a short distance of Bagdâd. He suddenly attacked, defeated, and took prisoner Abissâj, (â'be-sâj',) whom, at the head of 30,000 men, the caliph had sent against him. Died in 943. Bahrein, on the Persian Gulf, was the capital of his dominions.

Aboo-Tâlib, (or -Tâleb,) Abû-Tâlib, or **Abou-Talib, (or -Thaleb,)** â'boo tâ'lib, written also **Ebû-Thâlib,** an uncle of Mohammed, and the father of Alee, (Ali,) who married the prophet's only daughter, Fâtimah. He belonged to the illustrious tribe of Koreish, and flourished in the latter half of the sixth and beginning of the seventh century. Died about 620 A.D. (See MOHAMMED.)

**Aboo- (Abû- or Abou-) Tâlib, (pronounced by the Hindoos ûb'oo tâ'lib,) a native of India, born at Lucknow in 1752. For a number of years he was employed by the East India Company in various offices, civil and military. At length, in 1800, he visited England, where he was received with the most flattering attentions by the royal family and many of the nobility. He returned to India through France, Italy, Turkey, and Persia. He wrote a very interesting journal of his travels, a translation of which into English has been published. Died in 1806.

Aboo- (Abû- or Abou-) Temâm—tẹ-mâm', a famous Arabian poet, born in Syria about 805 A.D. He spent the first years of his life in Damascus in the service of a tailor. He afterwards repaired to Bagdâd, where he was munificently patronized by the caliph and the officers of his court. Died in 845.

Aboo-Yakoob-Yoosuf, Abû-Ya'kûb-Yûsuf, or **Abou-Yakoub-Yousouf, (or -Yousef,)** â'boo yâ'koob' yoo'soof, (or yoo'sûf,) the third sultan of Africa and Spain of the Almohade dynasty, succeeded his father, Abd-el-Moomen, in 1163. In 1184 he was mortally wounded before the walls of Santarem, a fortress of Portugal, in the possession of the Christians, which he had besieged with a large army. Aboo-Yakoob was a mild and enlightened sovereign, and a patron of learning.

Aboo-Yoosuf, Abû-Yûsuf, or **Abou-Yousef,** an eminent Moslem divine, born at Koofah (Kûfah) about 731 A.D. In consequence of his great talents and legal knowledge, he was appointed chief judge of Bagdâd, an office which he held till his death, in 798. In the latter part of his life he was the subject of the famous Haroun al-Raschid.

Aboo-Yoosuf-Yakoob, Abû-Yûsuf-Ya'kûb, or **Abou-Yousouf-Yakoub,** â'boo yoo'soof yâ'koob', surnamed ALMANSOOR, (AL-MANSÛR,) "The Victorious," the fourth sultan of Africa and Spain of the Almohade dynasty, was born at Morocco in 1160. He succeeded his father Aboo-Yakoob-Yoosuf, who fell at the siege of Santarem, in 1184. Having established himself on his throne, and put down several rebellions in his African dominions, he determined to cross the Straits of Gibraltar and avenge the death of his father. He made, in all, three expeditions into the Spanish peninsula : in the first (1189) he took captive, of both sexes, 40,000 persons, whom he led into Africa and settled at Rabatt,

near Salé ; in the second (1190) he reduced the fortress of Torres and the town of Silves in Portugal ; in the third (1195) he defeated the Christians under Alphonso III., in a great battle near Valencia ; after which he took Calatrava, Guadalajara, Madrid, Alcalá, and Salamanca He died at Morocco in 1198, leaving behind him the character of an able and enlightened prince. He has been pronounced the greatest and best of the Almohade sultans.

Aboubecre. See ABOO-BEKR.

Abou-Bekr. See ABOO-BEKR.

Abou-l-Cacem, (or **Kâsim.)** See ABOO-L-KASIM.

Abou-l-Casim-Mansour. See FIRDOUSEE.

Aboulfaradge. See ABOOLFARAJ.

Aboul-Haçan. See ABOO-L-HASSAN.

About, â'boo', (EDMOND FRANÇOIS VALENTIN,) a successful and pithy French writer, born at Dieuze (in Meurthe) in 1828. Having passed some time at Athens, he published, in 1855, a work on modern Greece, "La Grèce contemporaine," which is said to be remarkable for the best qualities of a truly French style. His romance entitled "Tolla" (1855) is also much admired. He has written several novels, among which are "The King of the Mountains," (1856,) and "Germaine," (1857,) and a remarkable political work on the "Roman Question," (about 1860,) which shows a decided sympathy for the liberal cause.

Abou-Tahir. See ABOO-TAHIR.

Abou-Taleb, (or-Thaleb.) See ABOO-TALIB.

Abou-Yousouf. See ABOO-YOOSUF.

Aboville, d', dâ'bo'vèl', (FRANÇOIS MARIE,) COMTE, a French general, born at Brest in 1730. He served with distinction as colonel at Yorktown, Virginia, where he directed the artillery, (1781,) became a general about 1790, and opposed Dumouriez at the time of his defection, 1793. Under the régime of Bonaparte he was inspector-general of artillery, and senator. Died in 1817.

Abrabanel, â-BRÂ'BÄ-nèl', [Span. pron. almost âv-RÄ'-vä-nêl',] written also **Abarbanel** and **Abrabaniel,** (ISAAC,) the most illustrious of all the Spanish rabbis, was born in Lisbon in 1437. His family, which was supposed to be descended from King David, had dwelt in Spain from a very early period. The parents of Abrabanel were rich, and no expense was spared in his education. Endowed with extraordinary quickness of intellect and great powers of application, he soon made himself master of all the learning of that time, and was particularly distinguished for his thorough acquaintance with the Holy Scriptures and the writings of the rabbis. His great abilities attracted the attention of Alphonso V. of Portugal, who frequently consulted him on the most important affairs. On the death of this king, in 1481, his son, John II., yielding to the bigoted spirit of that age, banished Abrabanel from his presence and forced him to seek refuge in Spain. Here he was at first received with great favour by Ferdinand and Isabella ; but in 1492 a decree was promulgated by which all the Jews were banished from the Spanish dominions and their property confiscated. Abrabanel fled at first to Naples ; he afterwards resided for a short time in several of the Italian cities, and at last died in Venice in 1508. His works consist of commentaries on various parts of the Scriptures. They are considered by the best judges to display not only the greatest learning, but powers almost unrivalled in this species of writing.

See ANTONIO, "Bibliotheca Hispana ;" LE LONG, "Bibliotheca Sacra ;" J. H. MAI, "Dissertatio de Vita et Scriptis Abrabanielis," 1708.

Ab-ra-dâ'tạs, a king of Susa, who at first fought on the side of the Assyrians, but afterwards attached himself to Cyrus the Great, King of Persia. He fell in the war which Cyrus waged against Crœsus.

See XENOPHON's "Cyropædia," book v.

Abraham, â'brạ-ham, [Heb. אברהם,] or **Abram** â'brạm, one of the most eminent of the Hebrew patriarchs, was born at Ur, a city of Chaldea, about 2000 years (it is supposed) before the Christian era. "Abraham" signifies the "father of a numerous people," and "Abram" "exalted father." In consequence of his exemplary obedience and trust in God, he has been honoured with the title of "father of the faithful." He died at or near Hebron, aged 175 years. (See Genesis xi.–xxv.)

---

e as ẽ; ç as s; g̃ hard; g̃ s j; G, H, K, guttural; N, nasal; R, trilled; s as z; th as in this. (☞ See Explanations, p. 23.)

Abraham-a-Sancta-Clara — â-sânk′tä klä′rä, an Augustine friar, regarded as the greatest popular preacher of Germany during the seventeenth century, was born in Suabia, in 1642. His proper name was ULRIC MEGERLE, (mä′ger-lä). He studied philosophy and theology in the Augustine convent at Vienna. In 1662 he entered holy orders, and took the degree of doctor of divinity ; in 1669 the emperor Leopold appointed him preacher to the imperial court at Vienna, which office he continued to hold for many years. He died in 1709, leaving many religious works.

See LONGFELLOW, "Poets and Poetry of Europe;" "Oesterreichisches Biographisches Lexikon," Vienna, 1851.

Abraham-Bar-Chasdai-Hallevi—baR-Hâs′dī′hal′-leh-vee′, a Jewish rabbi, born at Barcelona, Spain, lived in the last half of the twelfth century. He wrote "The Book of the Soul," and other works.

Abraham-Ben-Chanania-Jagel (or **-Jaghel**)— kä-nä-nee′ä yä′gel, an Italian rabbi, was born near the close of the sixteenth century. He wrote a work entitled "The Book of Good Doctrine," a catechism on the articles of the Jewish faith, which is much celebrated. He embraced Christianity about the beginning of the seventeenth century, and was baptized by the name of Camillus Jaghel. The exact time of his death is unknown.

Abraham-Ben-Dior—de′ōR′, (The Levite,) a famous rabbi, born at Toledo, in Spain, in the early part of the twelfth century. He is said to have been a personal friend of Maimonides, who speaks of him with great respect. He is supposed to have suffered death on account of his religion about the year 1180.

Abraham-Ben-Haja (-hä′yä) or **-Chaja**, (-Kä′yä,) a Spanish rabbi, wrote a treatise "On Nativities," and one entitled the "Globe of the World," ("Sphæra Mundi," 1546.) Died in 1105.

Abraham-Ben-Isaac-Zahalon—zä-hạ-lōn′, a distinguished Spanish rabbi, who lived in the sixteenth century. He was an excellent lawyer, an eminent astronomer, and also a poet. He was banished from Spain with the other Jews, and took refuge in Italy.

Abraham-di- (or **de-**) **Balmis**—de bäl′mès, a celebrated Italian rabbi and physician, born at Lecce in the latter part of the fifteenth century. Died about 1522.

Abraham-Zacuth (or **-Zacut**, -zä-kōōt′) or **-Zacutho**—zä-koo′to, [Span. pron. thä-koot′ or thä-koo′to,] a Spanish rabbi and astronomer, born at Salamanca near the middle of the fifteenth century. He was one of the Jews banished from Spain in 1492. On leaving his native country he went to Portugal, where he was kindly received by King Emmanuel and appointed astronomer and chronographer royal. The date of his death is unknown.

Abram, ä′bRŏN′, (NICHOLAS,) a learned French Jesuit, born near Charmes, in 1589. In 1636 he became professor of theology in the University of Pont-à-Mousson. Died in 1655.

Abranches, de, dä â-bRän′shès, (ALVARO,) a Portuguese noble, who took a prominent part in the revolution which occurred in 1640, and which resulted in the expulsion of the Spaniards from Portugal.

Abrantes, â-bRän′tès, fourth MARQUIS OF, a Portuguese nobleman, born in 1784. He occupies a prominent place in the political history of his country from 1807 to 1824, when, in consequence of the part which he took in the murder of the Marquis of Loulé, he was banished from Portugal. He went first to Italy, and thence to England, where he died in 1827.

Abrantes, DUKE OF. See JUNOT.

Abresch, ä′brĕsh, (FRIEDRICH LUDWIG,) a learned German author, born at Hesse-Homburg in 1699. He studied at the University of Utrecht. His parents had designed him for the Church, but his own inclinations led him to devote himself wholly to classical literature. Among his works are "Notes on Æschylus and Thucydides." He was rector of the College of Middelburg, 1725-41. Died in 1782.

Abreu, d', dä′bRĕ-oo, (ALEXIS,) a distinguished Portuguese physician, born about 1570. In 1606 he was appointed consulting physician to Philip III. of Spain. Died in 1630.

Abreu y Bertodano, de, dà ä′bRĕ-oo è bĕR-to-dä′no, (FELIX JOSÉ,) a Spanish knight, (caballero,) son of the Marquis de Regalia, born about 1720. He devoted himself to the study of international law, and published, in 1746, a "Treatise on Maritime Prizes," (Tratado juridico-politico sobre Presas de Mar,") which attracted considerable attention. From 1755 to 1760 he was envoy extraordinary to the court of St. James. The year of his death is unknown.

Abreu y Bertodano, de, (JOSÉ ANTONIO,) a Spanish writer on international law, was brother to the preceding. Died in 1775.

Abrial, ä′bRe-äl′, (JOSEPH ANDRÉ,) a French advocate, born in 1750, at Annonay, was educated in the College of Louis-le-Grand, at Paris. He was sent in 1800 to Naples, in order to organize a republican government, in which work he manifested great ability. During the whole of his administration, his mildness and moderation won for him the affection of the Neapolitans. He was made senator, and received the title of count, under Napoleon, but was nevertheless one of the first to vote for his dethronement in 1814. He was afterwards created a peer by Louis XVIII. Died in 1828.

Abriani, â-bRe-ä′nee, (PAOLO,) an Italian poet, born at Vicenza in 1607. He was employed as professor or teacher in Genoa, Verona, and Padua. Among his works are a volume of sonnets, "Canzoni," etc., and a poetical version of Horace's "Art of Poetry," (1663.) Died at Venice in 1699.

Abril, â-bReel′, almost â-vReel′, [in Latin, APRI′LIS,] (PEDRO SIMON,) a Spanish grammarian, who is supposed to have died near the close of the sixteenth century. He was the author of a number of books, some of which are in Spanish, and some in Latin.

Abruzzi, â-bRoot′see, a landscape-painter, who lived in Rome towards the close of the last century.

Abruzzo, â-bRoot′so, (BALDASSARE,) a Sicilian philosopher and civilian, born about 1600 ; died in 1665.

Ab′sạ-lọm, [Heb. אבשלום,] the third son of David, was born in Hebron after his father ascended the throne. Possessed of winning manners and an exceedingly handsome person, he became very popular throughout the land of Israel, and at length sought openly to dethrone his father. In the battle which was subsequently fought, Absalom was slain by Joab, although King David had expressly commanded that the life of his son should be spared. The rebellion of Absalom is supposed to have occurred in 1036 B.C. (See II. Samuel xiii.-xviii.)

Absalon, âb′sä-lon′, called also **Axel**, a descendant of Slagus, was born in Iceland in 1128. He studied in Paris, and in 1178 was appointed to the archbishopric of Lund, in Scania, which office he held till his death in 1201. Absalon was undoubtedly one of the greatest men of his age ; he was a wise counsellor to his king, a brave general, and a generous patron of learning.

See ESTRUP, "Absalon considéré comme héros, homme d'État et évêque," 1856.

Abschatz, äp′shâts, (HANS **Assmann**—äss′mân,) BARON OF, a poet and statesman, born in Silesia in 1646. He studied jurisprudence at the Universities of Strasburg and Leyden. In 1675 he was appointed governor of the principality of Liegnitz, and afterwards was Silesian ambassador at the court of Vienna. Died in 1699. He is ranked among the principal German poets of the seventeenth century. Many hymns of his composition are still sung in the Protestant churches.

Abshoven. See APSHOVEN.

Abstemio, âb-stä′me-o, or **Astemio**, [Lat. ABSTE′MIUS,] (GIAMPIETRO,) an eminent teacher, who lived in Friuli about the middle of the sixteenth century. His school was attended by young men of the first Italian families.

Ab-stē′mĭ-us Lau-ren′tĭ-us, (lau-rĕn′shẹ-ụs,) [It. ASTEMIO, âs-tä′me-o,] an Italian writer, who was born at Macerata in the latter half of the fifteenth century. Besides several works on grammar and criticism, and one on geography, he wrote, in Latin, a book of Fables, which at one time enjoyed considerable popularity.

Ab-sȳr′tus or **Apsyr′tus**, [Gr. Ἄψυρτος; Fr. AB

ă, ē, ĭ, ō, ū, ȳ, *long;* à, è, ò, *same, less prolonged;* ă, ĕ, ĭ, ŏ, ŭ, ў, *short;* ạ, ẹ, ị, ọ, *obscure;* fär, fãll, fât; mêt; nŏt; gōŏd; mōōn;

SYRTE, ăb'sèRt',] a son of Æetes, King of Colchis, was a brother of Medea, who took him with her when she fled with Jason. When she was pursued by her father, she killed her brother and scattered his severed limbs along the road, in order to retard the pursuit.

ABU, ABÛ, or *ABÚ,* a prefix to many Arabian names. See ABOO.

Abu-Bakr, (or -**Bacr.**) See ABOO-BEKR.

Abubeker or **Abubekr.** See ABOO-BEKR.

A-bu'ça-ra, [Gr. 'Αβουκαρά,] (THEODORUS,) a Christian theological writer, who lived in the eighth century. Of the circumstances of his life little or nothing is known. He wrote a great number of works, mostly in Greek, though a few are in Arabic.

Ab-u-dac'nus, (JOSEPH,) a native of Cairo, who, about the year 1600, was a teacher of Arabic at Oxford. Besides some grammatical treatises on Hebrew, he wrote a "History of the Copts," ("Historia Jacobitarum seu Coptorum in Ægypto Libya," etc.)

See WOOD, "Athenæ Oxonienses."

Abulfaragius. See ABOOLFARAJ.

Abul-Faraj, (or **Farage.**) See ABOOLFARAJ.

Abulfeda. See ABOOLFEDA.

Abul-Kâsim or **Abû-l-Kâsim.** See ABOO-L-KASIM.

Abu-l-Kâsim-Mansur. See FIRDOUSEE.

Abulola. See ABOO-L-ALA.

Abulpharagius. See ABOOLFARAJ.

Abûl-Walîd-Ibn-Roshd. See AVERROËS.

Abundance, d', dâ'büN'dôNss', (JEAN,) a French poet and satirist, who flourished in the early part of the sixteenth century. Nothing is known of his life; the name is supposed by some to be fictitious. One of his works is entitled "The Great and Marvellous Acts of Nobody," ("Les Grands et Merveilleux Faits de Nemo.")

Ab-ȳ-de'nus, ['Αβυδηνός,] a Greek historian, who wrote a work on Assyria, very valuable, so far as can be judged from the few fragments which remain. Of his life nothing is known.

Acace. The French spelling of ACACIUS, which see.

A-ca'ci-us, a-kā'she-us, [Gr. 'Ακάκιος; Fr. ACACE, ầ'kầss',] a bishop of Cæsare'a, who succeeded Eusebius in 339 A.D. Died about 366.

Acacius, a philosopher and rhetorician of Cæsarea, contemporary with the preceding.

Acacius, a bishop of Beroë, who lived in the fourth and fifth centuries.

Acacius, a bishop of Amida, in Mesopotamia, who ransomed 7000 Persians that had been taken prisoners by the Romans, about the beginning of the fifth century.

Acacius, a patriarch of Constantinople, to which dignity he was appointed in 471 A.D. He was ambitious and crafty, and aimed to raise the church of Constantinople above all other Eastern churches. Died in 489.

Ac-a-de'mus ['Ακάδημος] or **Hec-a-de'mus,** an Athenian, who disclosed, it is said, to Castor and Pollux the place where their sister Helen was secreted. The garden or grove called *Academia,* in which Plato founded his school of philosophy, is supposed to have been named in honour of Academus.

Acamapichtli, â-kâ-mâ-pĕtch'tlee, the first king of Tenochtitlan or Mexico, was elected to the throne, according to the Mexican annalists, in the year 1352. His authority extended only to the Aztecs inhabiting the island on which Tenochtitlan was built. Under his reign the Aztecs increased in fame, stone edifices were built, and canals were constructed. Died in 1389.

Ac'a-mas, ['Ακάμας,] a son of Theseus and Phædra, is said to have been sent with Diomede to Troy to demand the surrender of Helen. According to Virgil, he was one of the band enclosed in the wooden horse.

Açarq, d', dâ'sâRk', a French critic and grammarian, who was born in 1720 and died in 1795.

A-cas'tus, [Gr. 'Ακαστος; Fr. ACASTE, ầ'kầst',] a son of Pelias, King of Iolcus, was one of the Argonautæ. He married Astydami'a, who, by false accusations, produced an enmity between Acastus and Peleus.

Ac'ça, a learned bishop of Hexham, a contemporary and friend of the celebrated Bede. Died in 740 A.D.

Ac'ca Lauren'tia (lau-rĕn'she-a) or **Larentia,** lâ-

rĕn'she-a, the wife of the shepherd Faustulus, is said to have been the nurse of Romulus and Remus. According to one tradition, she was a courtesan who was renowned for her beauty, and who bequeathed a large sum of money to the Roman people in the time of Ancus Martius.

Accama, âk'kâ-mâ, (BERNARD,) a Dutch historical and portrait painter, born in Friesland. Died in 1756.

Accarigi, âk-kâ-ree'jee, or **Accarisi,** âk-kâ-ree'see, [Lat. ACCARIS'IUS,] (FRANCESCO,) a distinguished professor of civil law, born at Ancona about 1550. He taught successively in the Universities of Sienna, Parma, and Pisa. Died at Pisa in 1622.

Accarrigi, (JACOPO,) a native of Bologna, who was professor of rhetoric in the University of Mantua. Died in 1654.

Accarisio, âk-kâ-ree'se-o,(ALBERTO,) an Italian, born at Cento, near Ferrara, in the early part of the sixteenth century, was the author of an Italian grammar of some celebrity.

Acciajuoli or **Acciaioli,** ât-châ-yo'lee, (DONATO,) a distinguished Italian scholar, born at Florence in 1428, wrote commentaries on the ethics and politics of Aristotle. Died in 1478.

Acciajuoli or **Acciaioli,** (FILIPPO,) a dramatic writer and composer, born at Rome in 1637; died in 1700.

Acciajuoli or **Acciaioli,** (NICCOLÒ or NICHOLAS,) an eminent statesman, born at Florence about 1310. He was for many years the chief adviser of Joanna, Queen of Naples, to whom he was recommended by his talents, eloquence, and fine personal appearance. Died in 1366.

Acciajuoli or **Acciaioli,** (RENIER,) a' Florentine, who obtained possession of Athens and Corinth about 1364, and was styled Duke of Athens.

See GIBBON, "Decline and Fall of the Roman Empire."

Acciajuoli or **Acciaioli,** (ZENOBIO,) a classical scholar, born at Florence in 1461, became librarian of the Vatican and a friend of Politian. He translated Eusebius and Theodoret into Latin, and wrote Latin verses, which were praised by Giraldi and other critics. Died in 1519.

Acciajuoli-Salvetti, ât-châ-yo'lee sâl-vet'tee,(MADDALENA,) an Italian poetess of Florence, wrote "Rime Toscane," and other works. Died in 1610.

Accioli, ât-cho'lee, (JUAN de Cerqueira y Silva— dâ sĕR-kā'e-râ e se'vâ,) a Brazilian historian, born about the end of the eighteenth century. Among his works is "Historical and Political Memoirs of the Province of Bahia," (6 vols., 1835 and the years following.)

Accius, ak'she-us, or **Attius,** at'she-us, (LUCIUS,) a celebrated Roman tragic poet, born about 170 B.C. None of his dramas have come down to us entire; but the numerous fragments which remain justify the admiration with which the ancients regarded him. The date of his death is unknown.

See SELLARS, "Roman Poets of the Republic," chap. v.

Accius, (TITUS,) a Roman orator, born at Pisaurum, (now Pesaro,) in Umbria. He lived about 70 years B.C.

Accolti, âk-kol'tee, (BENEDETTO, or BENEDICT,) an Italian writer, born at Arezzo in 1415. He was doctor and professor of law at Florence; in 1459 he was made chancellor of the republic, which office he held till his death in 1466. He wrote a Latin history of the conquest of Palestine by Godfrey of Bouillon, from which Tasso derived the materials of his great poem.

Accolti, âk-kol'tee, (BENEDETTO,) an Italian cardinal, born at Florence in 1497, was a grandson of the preceding, and a son of Michele Accolti. He became a cardinal in 1527, after which he was sometimes called Cardinal de Ravenna. He was an elegant Latin poet, in the opinion of such judges as Vida and Sadoleto, and was also a patron of learning. Died in 1549.

See AUBERY, "Histoire des Cardinaux."

Accolti, (BERNARDO,) a noted Italian poet and improvisatore, who lived at the court of Leo X., was a son of the historian Benedetto, and uncle of the preceding. Whenever he recited his verses in public, great crowds flocked to hear him. Died about 1535.

Accolti, (FRANCESCO,) a distinguished Italian lawyer, (better known as **Areti'nus** or **Aretino,** â-râ-tee'no,) a name assumed by several members of his family,) born at Arezzo about 1418, was a brother of Benedetto the historian. In 1440 he was made professor of law at Bologna, and in 1479 was appointed senior professor of law at Pisa, which position he held till his death, about 1485. Besides a number of works of a strictly professional character, he wrote several essays in general literature, including translations from the ancient authors.

See MAZZUCHELLI, "Scrittori d'Italia."

' **Accolti,** (PIETRO,) Cardinal, son of Benedetto the historian, was born at Florence in 1455. He held for some time the professorship of law in the University of Pisa; afterwards, in 1511, he was made Cardinal of St. Eusebius. He has generally been called, though incorrectly, Cardinal of Ancona : it is under this title that he is said to have had the principal share in preparing the bull against Luther, in 1520. It is certain that he possessed great influence at the court of Leo X. Died in 1549.

See MAZZUCHELLI, "Scrittori d'Italia."

Accolti, (PIETRO, the younger,) grandson of Cardinal Benedetto, lived in the early part of the seventeenth century. He lectured on canon law at Pisa.

Accoramboni, âk-ko-râm-bo'nee, (FABIO,) an Italian lawyer, born in 1502. In 1523, or soon after, he was appointed professor of civil law in the University of Pisa, and afterwards, about 1527, became professor of canon law at Rome. Died in 1559.

Accoramboni, (FELIX,) an Italian philosopher and physician, a grandson of Geronimo, noticed below, lived about 1600. He wrote commentaries on Aristotle and Galen.

Accoramboni, (GIROLAMO,) an eminent Italian physician, born about 1467, at Gubbio, in the duchy of Urbino. He was professor of medicine at Perugia, and afterwards at Rome. Leo X. chose him as his own physician. Died in 1537.

Accoramboni, (VIRGINIA,) an Italian poetess, was the wife of Francesco Peretti, a nephew of Pope Sixtus V. She was murdered by Luigi Orsini in 1585.

See ADRY, "Vie de V. Accoramboni," 1807.

Accorso, âk-koR'so, [Fr. ACCURSE, ä'kürss',] (BUO-NO, boo-o'no,) written also **Buonaccorso,** [Lat. Bo'NUS ACCUR'SIUS,] a celebrated classical scholar and rhetorician, native of Pisa, lived in the latter half of the fifteenth century. He wrote commentaries on the writings of Cæsar and other Latin classics.

Accorso, (or Accursio, âk-kooR'se-o,) (MARIAN-GELO,) an Italian writer and critic, who lived at Rome in the time of Leo X.

Accum, âk'kŭm or âk'kйm, (FRIEDRICH,) a German chemist, born at Bückeburg in 1769. He emigrated to London in 1793, and became professor of chemistry there about 1802. He published an excellent "Practical Treatise on Gas Light," (1815,) which contributed greatly to promote the use of gas for illumination of cities. Among his other works are, "On the Adulteration of Food," (1822,) and "Essay on Chemical Reagents," (London, 1816.) Died in Berlin in 1838.

Accurse. See ACCORSO and ACCURSIUS.

Accursii, ak-kur'she-ī, (CERVOT'TUS,) second son of Accursius, noticed below, born about 1240 ; died in 1287.

Accursii, ak-kur'she-ī, or **Accursius,** ak-kur'she-us, (FRANCISCUS,) or **Accorso,** (FRANCESCO,) the son of Accursius mentioned below, was born at Bologna in 1225. He was for several years a counsellor to Edward I. of England, and afterwards a professor of law at Bologna, where he died in 1293.

Accursii, (WILHELMUS,) a third son of Accursius, mentioned below, born in 1246, obtained several ecclesiastical preferments, and was for some time in the service of the pope. Died about 1310.

Accursius, ak-kur'she-us, (the Latinized form of Accorso,) [Fr. ACCURSE, ä'kürss',] an Italian lawyer, whose Christian name is supposed to have been FRANCESCO, was born in or near Florence about 1182. He was for many years a teacher of law in Bologna. His "Glossa," i.e. a collection of *glossæ*, or notes, made by different commentators on Justinian, is very celebrated. Died in 1260.

Acebedo, ä-thä-Bä'DO, (Don MANUEL,) a Spanish historical painter, born at Madrid in 1744, and died in 1800.

A-çer'bas, or **Sichæus,** si-kee'us, a Tyrian priest, who married Dido and was murdered by her brother Pygmalion. Servius gives Sicharbas or Sicharbes for Sichæus.

Acerbi, ä-chĕR'bee, (ENRICO,) an Italian surgeon, born at Castano, near Milan, in 1785. Died in 1827.

Acerbi, (GIUSEPPE,) an Italian traveller, born near Mantua in 1773. He performed, in 1799, a journey through Lapland to Cape North, and published a narrative of that journey in English, (1802.) In 1816 he founded, at Milan, the "Biblioteca Italiana," a periodical of some merit. Died in 1846.

Acernus. See KLONOWICZ.

Aç'e-sas [Gr. Ἀκεσᾶς] or **Aceseus,** as'e-sûs, [Ἀκεσεύς,] a celebrated embroiderer or weaver of remote antiquity, was born in Cyprus. The time in which he lived is unknown.

Acesius, a-see'she-us, [Ἀκέσιος,] a bishop of Constantinople, who flourished in the early part of the fourth century.

A-çes'tor, [Ἀκέστωρ,] a sculptor of Gnossus, or Cnosus, in Crete, lived about 430 B.C.

Acevedo or **Azevedo,** ä-thä-vä'DO, (FELIX AL-VAREZ,) a brave Spanish officer, born in the province of Leon, was one of the chiefs of the popular party in the revolution of 1820. Having gained a victory near the Minho, he was shot in March, 1820, by some royalists whom he had approached with friendly overtures. The Junta ordered that his name should be retained in the army list as if he were alive.

Acevedo, de, dä ä-thä-vä'DO, (ALONZO MARIA,) an advocate in the royal council at Madrid, and doctor of canon law in the University of Salamanca, flourished from about 1760 to 1770. Died about 1775.

Acevedo, de, (CRISTOBAL,) an eminent Spanish historical painter, born at Murcia. He studied with B. Carducci, at Madrid, about 1590, after which he worked in Murcia. He excelled in design and in grandeur of expression.

See CEAN-BERMUDEZ, "Diccionario Historico."

Ach, (JOHANN VAN.) See ACHEN.

Achæmenes, a-kem'e-nêz, [Gr. Ἀχαιμένης,] the father of a line of Persian kings, named from him ACHÆMENIDÆ, (ak-e-men'I-dē.) He is supposed to have been the great-grandfather of Cyrus the Great.

Achæmenidæ. See ACHÆMENES.

Achæus, a-kee'us, [Gr. Ἀχαιός ; Fr. ACHÉE, ä'shä',] the mythical ancestor of the Achæans, was said to be a son of Xuthus, a grandson of Helen, and a brother of Ion.

Achæus, a Greek dramatic writer, born at Eretria, 484 B.C. He wrote several tragedies, but succeeded best in the satiric drama. Only a few fragments of his works remain.

Achæus, a cousin of Antiochus III., by whom he was appointed governor of Asia Minor. Having rebelled against his sovereign, he was taken and put to death, 214 B.C.

Achaintre, ä'shäNtr', (NICOLAS LOUIS,) a French philologer, born in Paris in 1771, became a schoolteacher. He was patronized by Firmin Didot, and produced good editions, with notes, of Horace, (1806,) Juvenal, (1810,) and Persius, (1812.) Died about 1830.

Achard, ä'shäR', (ANTOINE,) a Swiss Protestant minister, born at Geneva in 1696, was an eloquent preacher. He settled in Berlin in 1724, received the title of privy counsellor, and was admitted into the Royal Academy of Berlin in 1743. Two volumes of his sermons were published, (1774.) Died in 1772.

Achard, ä'shäR', (CLAUDE FRANÇOIS,) a French writer, born at Marseilles in 1758. Among his works are a "Description of Provence," (1787,) and "Elements of Bibliography," (3 vols., 1807.) Died in 1809.

Achard, (FRANZ KARL,) a distinguished German chemist, son of Antoine Achard, born at Berlin in 1753. He was elected, in 1776, a member of the Royal Academy of Sciences at Berlin. The extraction of sugar from the beet-root appears to have engaged his especial

---

ā, ē, ī, ō, ū, ȳ, *long;* à, ė, ò, same, less prolonged ; ă, ĕ, ĭ, ŏ, ŭ, ў, *short;* a, e, i, o, *obscure;* fär, fäll, fät; mĕt; nŏt; gōŏd, mōōn;

attention; and his essays on the subject contributed much towards the introduction of this manufacture into France. Among his works is "Lectures on Experimental Philosophy," (4 vols., 1792.) Died in 1821.

Achard, (LOUIS AMÉDÉE EUGÈNE,) a French writer of fiction, born at Marseilles in 1814. He removed to Paris about 1838, and wrote for several journals, among which was the "Charivari." His romance "La Belle Rose" (5 vols., 1847) obtained success.

Achards, de la Baume des, d'lä bōm dǎ-zä'shäR', (ÉLÉAZAR FRANÇOIS,) a French bishop, born at Avignon in 1679. He is commended for acts of charity during the prevalence of the plague at Marseilles in 1721. Died in Cochin in 1741.

Acharius, ä-kä're-ŭs, (ERIK,) a distinguished botanist and physician, born at Gefle, in Sweden, in 1757. He studied at Upsal, under the celebrated Linnæus. As a botanist, his attention seems to have been chiefly directed to cryptogamous plants, and especially to lichens. He published "Lichenographia Universalis," (1810.) Died in 1819.

See "Biographiskt Lexicon öfver namnkunnige Svenska Män," Upsala and Oerebro, 1835-1856.

A-ehā'tēš, [Fr. ACHATE, ǎ'shǎt',]* a friend of Æneas, whose fidelity was so exemplary that "Fidus Achates" became a proverb. (See VIRGIL, "Æneid," lib. i. 188 and 312.)

Achates, ä-kä'tās, (LEONARDUS,) one of the early printers, who carried the art from Germany into Italy. He flourished in the latter half of the fifteenth century.

Achelom. See ANTIQUUS.

A-eh-e-lo'us, [Ἀχελῷος,] a river-god of Greek mythology, was a son of Oce'anus. The poets relate that he had the assurance to compete with Hercules as a suitor of Dejanira, and was defeated by that hero in a combat.

Achen or **Aachen, van**, vån ä'ken, (JOHANN,) written also **Acken, Fanachen**, and **Janachen**, an eminent German painter of history and portraits, born at Cologne in 1552. He was employed at Munich by the Elector of Bavaria, and afterwards at Prague by the emperors Rudolph and Matthias. Died at Prague about 1620. He was reputed the richest artist of his time.

See DESCAMPS, "Vies des Peintres Flamands," etc.

Achenbach, ä'ken-bäk', (ANDREAS,) a German painter, of the Dusseldorf school, born at Cassel in 1815. He excels in landscapes and marine views. He obtained a medal of the first class at Paris in 1855, when he exhibited "High Tide at Ostend;" a "Moonlight Scene," etc.

Achenbach, (OSWALD,) a brother of the preceding, and like him distinguished as a painter of landscapes, was born at Dusseldorf in 1827.

Achenwall, ä'ken-wäl, (GOTTFRIED,) an eminent writer on statistics, born at Elbing, in Prussia, in 1719. He may almost be said to have created the science of statistics, called by him, in German, Staatswissenschaft, (in Latin, "Scientia Statistica,") *i.e.* "the science or information relating to States." He appears to have included in the terms above cited all those facts of which a knowledge is necessary to thorough statesmanship. Accordingly, in his lectures he treated of the laws of nations and history, as well as of statistics in the present acceptation of the word. He first taught in the University of Marburg; but in 1748 he was employed at Göttingen, where he continued till his death, in 1772.

Acherley, ak'er-le, (ROGER,) an English lawyer and political writer, who lived in the early part of the eighteenth century. He wrote a work on the Britannic Constitution, and another on Free Parliaments.

Acheron. See PLUTO.

Achéry, d', dä'shä're', (JEAN LUC,) a learned French Benedictine monk, born at St. Quentin in 1609. His most important work is a collection of rare documents, entitled a "Gleaning [Spicilegium] of certain old Writers who have been buried in the Libraries of France," (13 vols., 1653-77.) Died in 1685.

A-ehil'las, [Gr. Ἀχίλλᾶς,] an Egyptian general, who, on the death of Ptolemy Auletes, was appointed regent

of Egypt and guardian to Ptolemy XIII. and his sister Cleopatra. He was afterwards put to death by Arsinoë, sister of Ptolemy.

Achilles, a-kil'lēz,[Gr.Ἀχιλλεύς; Fr. ACHILLE, ä'shêl', It. ACHILLE, ä-kèl'là,] a celebrated Grecian warrior, the hero of Homer's Iliad, was the son of Peleus, King of Thessaly, and the sea-nymph Thetis : hence he is often called PELI'DES. The poets feigned that his mother dipped him into the river Styx to render him invulnerable, and that he was vulnerable only in the heel by which she held him. He led to the siege of Troy a band of Myrmidones in fifty ships, and performed great exploits; but he quarrelled with Agamemnon before the end of the war, and withdrew from the contest. To avenge the death of Patroclus, he again took arms, and slew Hector. He was at last killed by Paris, (or, as some say, by Apollo,) who shot him in the heel.

See "Iliad," *passim*, and "Odyssey," xxiv. 36.

Achilles, [Ger. pron. ä-kil'lès,] (ALEXANDER,) a Prussian nobleman, whom Ladislaus, King of Poland, sent on an embassy to Persia. Born in 1584; died in 1675.

Achilles Tatius, a-kil'lēz tā'she-us,) [Ἀχιλλεὺς Τάτιος,] a Greek poet and romance-writer, who is supposed to have lived in the fourth or fifth century. This writer, or another of the same name, is the author of an astronomical work called the "Sphere."

Achillini, ä-kèl-lee'nee, [Lat. ACHILLI'NUS,] (ALESSANDRO,) a celebrated physician and philosopher, born at Bologna in 1463. He studied at Paris, and in 1485 began to teach in his native town. In 1506 he was appointed professor of philosophy and medicine at Padua ; but three years after, in consequence of a war, he returned to Bologna, where he died in 1512. He left several works on anatomy, and some philosophical treatises.

Achillini, (CLAUDIO,) [Lat. CLAU'DIUS ACHILLI'NUS,] born at Bologna in 1574, was professor of law successively in the Universities of Bologna, Ferrara, and Parma. He wrote poems in the inflated style which was prevalent in his time. He was a grandson of Giovanni Filoteo. Died in 1640.

Achillini, (GIOVANNI FILOTEO,) a poet and antiquary, brother of Alexander the physician, was born at Bologna in 1466, and died in 1538.

Achish, ä'kish, a king of Gath, to whom David fled from Saul. (See I. Samuel xxi. 10.)

Achitophel, (a-kit'o-fel.) See AHITHOPHEL.

Achmet. See AHMED.

Achmet Geduc. See AHMED KEDÜK.

Achrelius, ä-kree'le-ŭs, (DANIEL,) a professor at the University of Abo, wrote a book against the Copernican system, in the latter part of the seventeenth century.

See "Biographiskt Lexicon öfver namnkunnige Svenska Män," Upsala, 1835.

Achterveldt, äk'ter-vèlt', (JACOB,) a Dutch painter, who died in 1704.

Achtschelling, äkt'sKèl-ling, (LUCAS,) a skilful landscape-painter, who lived at Brussels towards the close of the seventeenth century. He was a close imitator of nature.

Acidalius, as-se-dä'le-us or ät-se-dä'le-us, (VA'LENS,) a German classical scholar, born at Wittstock, in Brandenburg, in 1567 ; died in 1595. His commentaries on Velleius Paterculus, Quintus Curtius, and other Latin authors, exhibit much critical acumen.

See LEUSCHNER, "De V. Acidalii Vita, Moribus et Scriptis," 1757.

Acier, ä'se-ā', (MICHEL VICTOR,) a French sculptor, born at Versailles in 1736 ; died in 1799.

A-çil'ī-us Gla'brī-o, (MANIUS,) a Roman general, who became consul in 191 B.C., and commanded the army sent against Antiochus of Syria, whom he defeated at Thermopylæ. He also subdued the Bœotians and Ætolians. A golden statue of Acilius Glabrio was the first of that material seen in Italy.

Aç-in-dy'nus, [Ἀκίνδυνος,] (GREGORIUS,) a Greek monk and polemical writer, who lived at Constantinople during the fourteenth century.

Acinelli, ä-che-nel'lee, a Genoese historian, who flourished about the middle of the eighteenth century. He wrote a "History of Genoa," (1745-47.)

* Chaucer writes the name *Achate*. (See the "House of Fame.")

Ack, âk, (JOHN,) a distinguished painter on glass, who flourished at Brussels about 1550.

Acken, (JAN VAN.) See ACHEN.

Ac'ker-mann, [Ger. pron. âk'ker-mân',] (CONRAD,) a celebrated German comedian, born in 1710; died in 1771.

Ackermann, (JACOB,) an eminent German physiologist, born near Mentz in 1765. He was professor of botany and afterwards of anatomy in the University of Mentz. In 1804 he was appointed to the chair of anatomy at Jena, and in 1805 to the same position in Heidelberg, which he held till his death, in 1813.

Ackermann, (JOHANN CHRISTIAN GOTTLIEB,) a physician and distinguished classical scholar and critic, was born in Upper Saxony in 1756. He studied at Jena in 1771, and subsequently at Göttingen, under the celebrated Heyne. Some years after, he was appointed professor of pathology and therapeutics in the University of Altorf, where he died in 1801. Among his various works the lives of Hippocrates, Galen, and other Greek physicians deserve particular mention.

Ackermann, (RUDOLPH,) a German artist and dealer in prints, was born in Saxony in 1764. He settled in London, where he prospered as a print-seller, and established an extensive repository of arts, which had a European reputation. He published coloured engravings and lithographs, and an annual or series of annuals entitled "The Forget-me-not." He is said to have been the first who introduced lithography as a fine art into England. According to Jerdan, he published the first annual in England. Died in 1834.

See "Autobiography of William Jerdan," vol. iv. chap. xiii.

Ac'land, (HENRY WENTWORTH,) M.D., F.R.S., a distinguished English physician, born in 1815, graduated as M.D. at Oxford in 1848. In 1860 he accompanied the Prince of Wales to America as his medical attendant.

Acland, (Lady HARRIET,) wife of Major Acland, who served with distinction in the British army under Burgoyne. She accompanied her husband in the campaigns of 1776-7, of which she wrote a narrative. Her husband was seriously wounded and taken prisoner in October, 1777. She died in 1815.

Açôka. See ASHOKA.

Acoluth, â'ko-loot', [Lat. ACOLU'THUS,] (ANDREAS,) a distinguished Oriental scholar, born in Silesia in 1654, was a member of the Academy of Sciences at Berlin. Died in 1704.

Acoluth, (JOHANN,) a German theologian, born in Silesia in 1628. Died in 1689.

Acominatus. See NICETAS.

Aconce. See ACONZIO.

Aconz Köver, â'konts kö'ver, (STEPHEN,) a distinguished Armenian writer, born in Transylvania in 1740. His ancestors had removed from Armenia, in Asia, in 1330. He was chosen, in 1800, abbot of the convent of St. Lazarus at Venice, regarded as the great centre of Armenian learning. Died in 1824.

Aconzio, â-kon'ze-o, (GIACOMO, or JAMES,) [Lat. JACO'BUS ACON'TIUS, (a-kon'she-us;) Fr. ACONCE, â'kônss',] a distinguished writer, born at Trent about 1500. Having relinquished the Catholic and embraced the Protestant faith, he left his native country about 1557, and, passing through Switzerland, went to England, where it is supposed that he died about 1565. He wrote a book entitled "Stratagems of Satan," (1565,) which has enjoyed great celebrity. His work on the Best Method of Acquiring Knowledge, evinces an acute understanding; and all his writings show him to have been a man of learning and literary taste.

Ac'o-ris, [Gr. 'Ακωρις,] a king of Egypt, who flourished about 380 B.C. He made war, though with little success, against Artaxerxes Mnemon, King of Persia.

Acosta, â-kos'tâ, (CHRISTOVÃO, or CHRISTOPHER,) a Portuguese naturalist, who visited India to procure drugs, and afterwards practised medicine at Burgos. He wrote a "Treatise on the Drugs and Plants of the East Indies," (1578.) Died about 1580.

Acosta, (GABRIEL,) a professor of theology at Coimbra, Portugal, wrote commentaries on the Scriptures. Died in 1616.

Acosta, (JOAQUIN,) a native of South America, a colonel of engineers in the service of New Granada, published a "Historical Compendium of the Discovery and Settlement of New Granada," (1848,) with a good map of that country.

Acosta, â-kos'tâ, or **d'Acosta,** dâ-kos'tâ, (JOSÉ,) a Spanish Jesuit and writer, born at Medina del Campo about 1539. He went to South America as a missionary in 1571, returned in 1588, and published a work entitled "Natural and Moral History of the Indies," ("Historia Natural y Moral de las Indias," 1590,) which was much esteemed, and translated into several languages. He became rector of the University at Salamanca, where he died in 1600.

Acosta, (URIEL,) a Portuguese, who was educated as a Christian, converted to Judaism, and afterwards excommunicated by the Jews in consequence of his having written against the Mosaic Scriptures and the immortality of the soul. He killed himself in 1640, or, according to some accounts, in 1647.

See his Autobiography, Leipsic, 1847; JELLINEK, "Acostas Leben," 1847.

Acquapendente. See FABRICIUS or FABRIZIO, GERONIMO.

Acquaviva, âk-kwâ-vee'vâ, a noble family of Naples that has produced a number of distinguished commanders, statesmen, and men of learning. Its representative has for several generations borne the title of Duke of Atri.

Acquaviva, (ANDREA MATTEO,) Duke of Atri, â'tree, a Neapolitan, born about 1460, was a munificent patron of learning. Died in 1528.

Acquino, âk-kwee'no, a Piedmontese chronicler, who lived about the beginning of the sixteenth century.

Acquisti, âk-kwès'tee or âk-kwis'tee, (LUIGI,) an Italian sculptor, born at Forlì in 1744; died in 1824. He worked at Rome and Milan. A group of "Venus pacifying Mars" is considered his master-piece.

Ac'ra-gas, [Gr. 'Ακράγας,] a celebrated engraver or chaser in silver, supposed to have lived in the fifth century B.C.

Acrel, â'krel, (OLOF,) an eminent Swedish surgeon, born near Stockholm in 1717. Having spent some time in Paris in observing the practice of the most distinguished surgeons of that city, he entered the French army in 1743; but, after serving in two campaigns, he retired on account of ill health. He died at Stockholm in 1807, leaving several surgical works.

See "Biographiskt Lexicon öfver namnkunnige Svenska Män."

Acrisius, a-krish'e-us, [Gr. 'Ακρίσιος,] a son of Abas, King of Argos, and the father of Danaë, whom he confined, it is said, in a brazen tower or other prison, because an oracle had declared that she would bear a son who should kill her father. He was killed accidentally by Perseus, the son of Danaë by Jupiter. (See DANAË.)

A'cron, [Gr. 'Ακρων,] a celebrated physician of Agrigentum, (now Girgenti,) in Sicily, who lived in the fifth century B.C.

A'cron Hel-e'nĭ-us, a Roman grammarian, who wrote a commentary on Horace. The age in which he lived is unknown.

A-cro'nĭ-us or **Acron,** â-krōn', (JAN, or JOHN,) a Dutch physician, born in 1520. Died at Bâle in 1563.

A-crop-o-li'ta, [Gr. 'Ακροπολίτης,] (CONSTANTINE,) a Byzantine writer, lived between 1250 and 1300. He was a son of George, below noticed.

Acropolita, (GEORGE,) a celebrated Byzantine historian, born at Constantinople in 1220. He was highly esteemed by the emperors Ducas (to whom he was related) and Michael Palæologus, and held the office of chancellor (logotheta) at the Byzantine court. He was, moreover, employed on several important embassies. His greatest work is a history of the Byzantine Empire from the capture of Constantinople by the Latins in 1204 down to 1260, when Michael Palæologus again took possession of the city. Died in 1282.

See GIBBON, "History of the Decline and Fall of the Roman Empire," chap. lxii.

A-crot'a-tus, ['Ακρότατος,] King of Sparta, was the son of Areus, whom he succeeded about 265 B.C. Before his accession he distinguished himself by the defence of Sparta against Pyrrhus in 272. After a reign of

ā, ē, ī, ō, ū, ȳ, *long;* à, ĕ,ŏ, same, less prolonged; ă, ĕ, ĭ, ŏ, ŭ, ў, *short;* ạ, ẹ, ị, ọ, *obscure;* fâr, fâll, fât; mêt; nŏt; gŏŏd; mōŏn;

one year, he was killed in battle against Aristodemus of Megalopolis.

See PLUTARCH, "Life of Pyrrhus."

Acs or **Aacs**, åtch, (MICHAEL,) a Hungarian philosopher, born at St. Martin in 1631. Died in 1708.

Acs or **Aacs**, (MICHAEL,) a theologian, born at Raab in 1672, was a son of the preceding. Died in 1711.

Actæon, ak-tee'on, [Gr. Ἀκταίων; Fr. ACTÉON, äk'tå'ȯN',] in the Greek mythology, a hunter, who was a son of Aristæus and Autonoë, a daughter of Cadmus. He was changed into a stag by Diana and torn to pieces by his own hounds, because he had seen that goddess bathing.

Ac-tis'ạ-nēs, [Gr. Ἀκτισάνης,] an ancient king of Ethiopia, who is said to have conquered Egypt before the time of the Trojan war.

Ac'ton, [Fr. pron. åk'tȯN',] (JOSEPH,) an officer of Irish descent, born at Besançon, France, in 1737. He entered the navy of Tuscany, became a captain, and afterwards passed into the service of the King of Naples. The favour of the queen, and his own intrigues, procured his promotion to the office of minister of the marine. He was prime minister from 1784 to 1798. His policy was implacably hostile to the French. Died about 1810.

See COLLETTA, "Storia del Regno di Napoli."

Ac'tor, [Gr. Ἀκτωρ,] a son of Deion, (or, as some say, of Myrmidon,) was the husband of Ægina, and grandfather of Patroclus, who was called Actor'ides.

Ac-tu-ā'rĭ-us, [Ἀκτουάριος,] (JOHN,) a Greek physician and medical writer, who flourished about the end of the thirteenth century.

A-cu'le-o, (CAIUS,) a Roman knight and distinguished lawyer, who married an aunt of Cicero the orator.

A-cu'me-nus, [Ἀκουμενός,] an Athenian physician, and friend of Socrates, lived in the fifth century B.C.

Acuña, de, å-koon'yå, (ANTONIO,) Bishop of Zamora, Spain, distinguished for his martial exploits in the insurrection of Castile in 1520. He was strangled in prison in 1526.

Acuña, de, (CRISTOVAL,) a Spanish Jesuit, born at Burgos in 1597, wrote an interesting narrative of the voyage of exploration of the river Amazon in 1639-41. His work is entitled "New Discovery of the Great River of the Amazons," ("Nuevo Descubrimiento del gran Rio de las Amazonas.") Died about 1680.

Acuña, de, (HERNANDO,) a distinguished Spanish soldier and poet, born about 1500, was a friend of Garcilasso de la Vega. His sonnets and eclogues were much admired. Died in 1580.

Acuña, de, (Don PEDRO BRAVO,) a Spanish governor of the Philippine Islands, distinguished as a warrior and naval commander. His principal exploit was the reconquest of the Moluccas from the Dutch in 1606. He died the same year, at Manilla.

A-cu-sĭ-lā'us, [Ἀκουσίλαος,] a Greek historian, supposed to have flourished about 530 B.C.

A'dạ, a Carian princess, who succeeded her husband on the throne of Caria in 344 B.C. When Alexander conquered Asia Minor, he appointed her to the satrapy of Caria.

Ada, å'då, a countess of Holland, deprived of her patrimonial estate by William of Friesland. She is supposed to have died about the year 1218.

A'dạ, (Bar-Ahaba or -Ahavah,) a celebrated rabbi, regarded as the greatest of all the Jewish astronomers, was born at Babylon, A.D. 183. He is said to have lived to the age of 170 years.

Adadurof, å-då-doo'rof, (BASIL,) a Russian savant, born at St. Petersburg in 1709, was preceptor to Catherine II. He wrote some scientific works. Died in 1780.

Adæus [Ἀδαῖος] or **Addæus**, [Ἀδδαῖος,] ad-dee'us, a Greek poet, native of Macedonia, flourished, it is supposed, about 320 B.C.

A-dair', (JAMES,) a trader and resident among the Chickasaw and other neighbouring tribes of Indians, published in 1775 a "History of the American Indians," in which he endeavours to establish their descent from the Israelites.

A-dair', (JAMES,) an eminent English lawyer, and member of Parliament. He was recorder of London about 1780, or after that date. Died in 1798.

A-dair', (JAMES MAKIT'TRICK,) a Scottish physician, born in 1728, died in 1802. He spent many years of his life in the West Indies. Besides a number of medical essays, he wrote a pamphlet against the abolition of the slave-trade.

A-dair', (JOHN,) an American general and senator, born in South Carolina in 1757. He served in the wars against the frontier Indians in 1791-2-3, was a senator in Congress from Kentucky, 1805-6, and in 1814 distinguished himself in command of the Kentucky troops at the battle of New Orleans. From 1820 to 1824 he was Governor of Kentucky, and from 1831 to 1833 a representative in Congress. Died in 1840.

Adair, (JOHN,) F.R.S., a noted Scottish hydrographer, who lived in the seventeenth and eighteenth centuries. He is the author of a work entitled "Description of the Sea-coast and Islands of Scotland, Large and Exact Maps for the Use of Seamen."

Adair, (Sir ROBERT,) an able English diplomatist, born in London in 1763. He entered Parliament about 1802 as a friend of Fox, and was sent on an embassy to Vienna in 1806. In 1808, although not identified in politics with the ministry, he was appointed on a special mission to the Ottoman Porte. He was ambassador at that court from 1809 until 1811. In 1831 he was sent by Earl Grey on a special mission to the court of Belgium, and in 1835 retired from public service with the rank of privy counsellor. Died in 1855, aged about 92.

See "Gentleman's Magazine" for Nov. 1855.

Adalard. See ADALHARD.

Adalbero, å-dål-bā'ro, or **Adalberon**, å'dål'bęh-rȯN', Archbishop of Rheims, flourished in the latter half of the tenth century. He officiated at the coronation of Hugh Capet in 987, and died in 988.

Adalbero, a bishop of Laon in the time of Louis the last of the Carlovingians, and Hugh Capet.

Ad'ạl-bert, [Fr. pron. å'dål'baiR'; Lat. ADALBER'-TUS,] written also **Al'debert** or **Aldeber'tus**, a French bishop of great popularity, who lived about the middle of the eighth century. He pretended, it is said, to work miracles, and to be possessed of all knowledge. He was deposed from his bishopric for heresy, and imprisoned, about 775 A.D.

Ad'ạl-bęrt, [Ger. pron. å'dål-bĕRt',] an archbishop of Bremen, born, it is supposed, about 1000 A.D. He was descended from the emperor Otho II., and became a favourite of Henry IV. Died in 1072.

Ad'ạl-bęrt (**Adalberto**, å-dål-bĕr'to) **I.**, son of Boniface, Count of Lucca, assumed the title of Marquis of Tuscany. His son Adalbert (or Adalberto) II. succeeded him, with the titles of duke and marquis. Died about 888.

Ad'ạl-bęrt or **Adalber'tus**, Bishop of Prague, called the "Apostle of the Prussians," commonly known as Saint Adalbert, was born in 939. He was killed in 997.

Ad'ạl-bęrt, an eminent prelate who lived in the time of Henry V., Emperor of Germany, by whom he was made Archbishop of Mentz. When Henry was excommunicated by the pope, in 1112, Adalbert was one of the first to turn against him, and became at length his irreconcilable enemy; and on his death, in 1125, had sufficient influence to prevent his nephew, Frederick of Suabia, from being elected emperor. He died in 1137.

Adalbert, å'dål-bĕRt', (HEINRICH WILHELM,) a Prussian prince, cousin-german of Frederick William IV., born in Berlin in 1811. He entered the army in his youth, and made a voyage to Brazil, of which he wrote a narrative: "Passages from my Travelling Diary," ("Aus meinem Reisetagbuch," 1842.) He obtained command of the Prussian navy about 1850.

Adalbertus. See ADALBERT.

Adalhard, ad'ạ-lard', [Lat. ADALAR'DUS,] an abbot and eminent preacher, allied to the family of Charles Martel, born about 753. He stood in high favour at the court of Charlemagne, who employed him on several important missions. Died in 826.

A-da'lo-äl'dus, a king of the Lombards, son of Agilulfus and Theudelinda, was born at Mu'tina (Mod'ena) about 602 A.D. He is said to have been poisoned by some of his subjects whom his tyranny had exasperated.

Ad'am, [Heb. אָדָם, *i.e.* "man,"] the first man, (see Genesis i., ii., and iii.,) is commonly supposed to have been created a little more than 4000 years before the Christian era; though according to the computation of some writers, his date should be placed much earlier.

Adam, ä'dôN', (ADOLPHE CHARLES,) a popular composer, born in Paris in 1803, was a son of Jean Louis, noticed below. He composed with extreme facility. In 1844 he was chosen a member of the Institute. Among his works are operas entitled "Le Châlet," (1834,) and "Le Postillon de Lonjumeau," (1836.) Died in 1856.

Adam, ä'dåm, (ALBRECHT,) a German painter of battles, was born at Nordlingen in 1786. He entered the service of Eugene, Viceroy of Italy, whom he accompanied in the Russian campaign of 1812. Among his works is "The Battle of the Moskwa," (1835.) Died in 1862.

Ad'am, (ALEXANDER,) an eminent teacher and grammarian, born in 1741 in Murrayshire, Scotland. In 1768 he became rector of the Edinburgh high school, which, under his able management, acquired a reputation almost unequalled among institutions of its kind. He published his "Principles of Latin and English Grammar" in 1772, and in 1791 his "Roman Antiquities." Both of these works, until within a few years, have been extensively used in many schools in the United States as well as in Great Britain. His "Roman Antiquities," (1791,) considered the most creditable of all his works, immediately established his reputation as a sound and thorough scholar. In 1794 appeared his "Summary of Geography and History, both Ancient and Modern," which afterwards passed through several editions. Besides the foregoing, and a little book entitled "Classical Biography," he published a compendious Latin dictionary, ("Lexicon Linguæ Latinæ Compendiarium,") abridged from a much larger work, of the same kind, which was never finished. He died in 1809.

See ALEXANDER HENDERSON, "Life of A. Adam," 1810; CHAMBERS, "Biographical Dictionary of Eminent Scotsmen;" and SIR WALTER SCOTT'S "Autobiography," which contains some interesting particulars illustrating Dr. Adam's character, both as a teacher and as a man.

Adam, (DANIEL,) a German historian, born at Prague in 1546. Died in 1599.

Adam, ä'dôN', (FRANÇOIS GASPARD,) a French sculptor, born at Nancy in 1710, was a brother of Lambert Sigisbert, noticed below. He worked in Paris and Berlin. Died in 1759.

Adam, ä'dåm, (GEORG,) a German landscape-painter, of Nuremberg, born about 1783 ; died in 1823.

Adam, (JACOB,) a German engraver, lived in Vienna about 1800. He engraved plates for the "Bilder-Bibel" of Vienna.

Adam, (JACQUES,) a French writer, born at Vendôme in 1663 ; died in 1735. He was one of the translators of De Thou's Universal History, (16 vols., 1734,) and was a member of the French Academy.

Ad'am, (JAMES,) an architect, was a brother and partner of Robert, noticed below. Died in 1794.

Adam, (JEAN LOUIS,) a French composer and pianist, born in the department of the Lower Rhine about 1760. He had great success as professor of music in Paris, and published a "Méthode de Piano," (1802,) which was very popular. Died in 1848.

Adam, (JEAN VICTOR,) a French painter and lithographer, born at Paris in 1801. He painted several battle-pieces for the gallery of Versailles, and produced many lithographs, among which are the "Promenades and Environs of Paris."

Adam, (LAMBERT SIGISBERT,) a distinguished French sculptor, born at Nancy in 1700. When only twenty-three years of age, he obtained the first prize in the Academy at Paris. He executed several groups for the royal gardens at Versailles and Choisy. In 1744 he was appointed professor in the Royal Academy of Paris. His works were less remarkable for their conception than for their finished execution, and are deficient in the simplicity of antique art. Died in 1759.

Adam, ä'dåm, (MELCHIOR,) an eminent German biographer, born in Silesia in the latter part of the six-

teenth century, and died in 1622. He wrote the lives of many eminent men, both Germans and foreigners, who lived between 1500 and 1618. He was rector of the College of Heidelberg. One of his works is entitled "Lives of German Philosophers," (" Vitæ Germanorum Philosophorum," 4 vols., 1615–20.)

Adam, (NICOLAS,) a French grammarian and translator, born in Paris in 1716. Died in 1792.

Adam, (NICOLAS SÉBASTIEN,) a younger brother of Lambert Adam the sculptor, whom he surpassed in all the higher qualities of the art, was born at Nancy in 1705. His two greatest works are his "Prometheus Chained," and his "Monument of the Queen of Poland." He was professor of sculpture in the Academy of Paris. Died in 1778.

Adam, (ROBERT,) an architect, born at Edinburgh in 1728, and died in 1792. He and his brother James erected a number of mansions for the nobility, and public edifices in different parts of England. His style, though strikingly novel at the time of its introduction, has the great defect of excessive and minute decoration ; and his works generally are deficient in unity of composition.

See CHAMBERS, "Biographical Dictionary of Eminent Scotsmen."

Adam, (Rev. ROBERT,) a Scottish writer, born at Udney about 1770, published "The Religious World Displayed." Died in 1826.

Adam, (Rev. THOMAS,) born at Leeds in 1701, and died in 1784. He wrote numerous works of a religious character, of which his "Private Thoughts on Religion" (published in 1786) is probably the best-known.

Adam, (Right Hon. WILLIAM,) a British lawyer, born in Scotland in 1751, was a nephew of Robert Adam the architect. He was chosen a member of Parliament in 1774, fought a duel with Charles James Fox in 1779, and was one of the managers appointed by the Commons to conduct the impeachment of Warren Hastings in 1788. He was sworn of the privy council in 1815, and presided over the Scottish jury court for the trial of civil causes from 1816 until his death in 1839. His son John became Governor-General of India, and died in 1820. Another son, Charles, obtained the rank of admiral.

See LOCKHART, "Life of Scott."

Adam-Billaut, ä'dôN' be'yō', commonly styled MAÎTRE ADAM, mêt'R ä'dôN', (*i.e.* "Master Adam,") a French poet, and a joiner by trade, sometimes called THE JOINER OF NEVERS. He was patronized by the great Condé, and pensioned by Richelieu. Died in 1662.

Adam of Brem'en, [Lat. ADA'MUS BREMEN'SIS,] an ecclesiastical author, who flourished in the latter part of the eleventh century. He wrote a history of the efforts to extend Christianity from the time of Charlemagne to that of Henry IV.

Adam de la Halle—deh'lä-häl', surnamed LE BOSSU D'ARRAS, leh bo'sü' dä'räss', (*i.e.* "The Hunchback of Arras,") a French poet of the thirteenth century. He wrote a piece called "The Play of the Shepherd and Shepherdess," (" Le Jeu du Berger et de la Bergère,") which is regarded as the earliest specimen of the modern drama.

Adam de Marisco. See ADAMUS MARISCUS.

Adamannus or **Adamanus.** See ADOMNAN.

Adamanteo, ä-dä-män-tä'o, an Italian mathematician and Orientalist. Died in 1581.

Adamantius, ad-a-man'she-us, ['Αδαμάντιος,] the author of a treatise in Greek on physiognomy, is supposed to have lived about the beginning of the fifth century after Christ.

Adami, ä-dä'mee, (ADAM,) a German ecclesiastic, statesman, and historian, born at Mühlheim about 1600. He was chosen by the prelates of Würtemberg to represent them in the congress which met in 1643 to negotiate the peace of Westphalia ; and afterwards wrote an excellent and impartial history of those negotiations, "Arcana Pacis Westphalicæ," (published in 1698.) Died in 1663.

Adami, ä-dä'mee, (ANTONIO FILIPPO,) an Italian poet and prose-writer, born at Florence about 1720. Died in 1761.

Adami, (LIONARDO,) an Italian author and excellent classical scholar, born in Tuscany in 1690. He wrote a history of ancient Arcadia, (1716.) Died in 1719.

Adami, â-dä′mee,· (TOBIAS,) a writer born in Saxony in 1581, first introduced the works of Campanella to the notice of the philosophers of Germany. Died in 1643.

Adami-da-Bolsena, â-dä′mee dä bol-sä′nä, (AN-DREA,) an Italian musician, born at Rome in 1663, published a work called "Observations for the Regulation of the Choir of Singers in the Pontifical Chapel," ("Osservazioni per ben regolare il Coro dei Cantori della Capella Pontificia," 1711.) Died in 1742.

Adamino, â-dä-mee′no, an Italian sculptor, who lived in the eleventh century.

Adamnan or **Adamnanus.** See ADOMNAN.

Ad′ams, (ABIGAIL,) the daughter of the Rev. William Smith, was born at Weymouth, Massachusetts, in 1744. She was married in 1764 to John Adams, afterwards President of the United States, and died in 1818. Her "Letters" are interesting and valuable for the hints which they furnish of the manners of her country at the period in which she lived, and for her original and graphic notices of European society.

Adams, (AMOS,) an American divine, born in 1727. He published several sermons, two of which, giving a "Concise Historical View, etc., of New England," were republished in London. Died in 1775.

Adams, (CHARLES BAKER,) an American naturalist, born at Dorchester, Massachusetts, in 1814. He graduated at Amherst College, became, in 1838, professor of chemistry and natural history in Middlebury College, Vermont, and afterwards of chemistry and zoology at Amherst. He assisted Professor Hitchcock in his geological survey of New York, and as State geologist was engaged for several years in a survey of Vermont. He published "Contributions to Conchology," and other works. Died in 1853.

Adams, (CHARLES FRANCIS,) an American diplomatist, the son of John Quincy Adams, was born in Boston on the 18th of August, 1807. He passed his childhood mostly in St. Petersburg and London, graduated at Harvard College in 1825, studied law, and was admitted to the bar in 1828. He served for five years in the legislature of Massachusetts. He was nominated at Buffalo, in August, 1848, for the office of Vice-President by the convention of Free-Soilers which nominated Martin Van Buren for the Presidency.

He published the "Life and Works of John Adams," (10 vols., 1850–56.) In 1858 he was elected to Congress as a Republican by the voters of the third district of Massachusetts. He was re-elected in 1860, and was appointed minister to England in the spring of 1861. He encountered the most bitter social hostility in England, but he maintained the rights of his country, and acquitted himself with credit in the difficult and important controversies that arose during the great rebellion. Among the principal subjects of his negotiations was the damage inflicted on the American mercantile marine by piratical war-steamers built in England and depending for success on British aid and sympathy.

"No ambassador in recent times," says the "London Spectator" of Feb. 8, 1868, "has ever had to fill a position, not merely so delicate and difficult, but so trying to the equanimity of him who held it through the rapid and extreme changes of fortune in the State of which he has been the mouth-piece. . . . Mr. Adams must have entered on his diplomatic task with a just sense of soreness, which, but for his great self-command and even self-forgetfulness, might have resulted after the most lamentable fashion." He resigned about February, 1868. "It has been the good fortune of Mr. Adams," says the "London Illustrated News" of February 15, 1868, "to have exercised the grandest qualities of true statesmanship just where and when they were of priceless value, and to have exercised them with complete success."

Adams, (GEORGE,) an English optician and scientific writer, distinguished as a maker of mathematical instruments and globes. Among his works are a "Treatise on the Construction and Use of Globes," (1766,) and an "Essay on the Microscope," (1771.) Died in London, 1786.

His ₅son GEORGE, born about 1750, was also an optician. He published an "Essay on Vision," (1789,) and "Astronomical and Geometrical Essays," (1789, often reprinted.) Died in 1795.

Adams, (HANNAH,) one of the earliest female writers of America, born at Medfield, Massachusetts, in 1755. She was the author of a "View of Religious Opinions," (1784,) "History of New England," (1799,) "Evidences of Christianity," (1801,) "History of the Jews," (1812,) and of several other works. She numbered among her friends the Abbé Grégoire and other distinguished persons. Died in 1832.

Adams, (ISAAC,) of Boston, inventor of the Adams printing-press, was born near the commencement of the present century. His printing-presses are now in general use in all parts of the United States, and in the principal cities have nearly or quite superseded every other.

Adams, (JASPER,) D.D., an American divine, born at Medway, Massachusetts, in 1793. He graduated at Brown University in 1815, and soon after became professor of mathematics in that institution. He was subsequently president of Charleston College, South Carolina. Died in 1841.

Adams, (JOHN,) an Englishman, who lived in the seventeenth century. He published "Index Villaris ; or, An Alphabetical Table of all the Cities, Market Towns, Parishes, etc., in England and Wales," (1680,) which has been pronounced the best work of its kind.

See GOUGH, "British Topography."

Adams, (JOHN,) an eminent preacher, born in London in 1662, was chaplain to William III. and to Queen Anne. He obtained a prebend at Canterbury, which he exchanged in 1708 for a stall in the royal chapel at Windsor. He left a treatise on suicide, and several sermons. Died in 1719 or 1720.

Adams, (JOHN,) an American divine and poet, born in 1704. Died at Cambridge, Massachusetts, in 1740.

Adams, (JOHN,) an eminent American statesman, the second President of the United States, was born in Braintree, Massachusetts, about ten miles from Boston, on the 19th of October, 1735, O. S. He was the eldest son of John Adams, a farmer, and Susanna Boylston. He graduated at Harvard College in 1755, and, while he was preparing himself for the profession of the law, taught school at Worcester for two years or more. In choosing a profession he was at first inclined to be a minister of the gospel ; but he found he could not assent to the orthodox creed in the doctrine of election and reprobation. "His disgust at the doctrines of Calvinism," says John Quincy Adams, "was perhaps riveted by the opinions which he found disseminated in the social circle into which he had been introduced." He studied law, and was admitted to the bar in 1758, and afterwards resided with his father at Braintree for several years.

"For the profession of the law," says his grandson, "John Adams had been pre-eminently gifted with the endowments of nature ; a sound constitution of body, a clear and sonorous voice, a quick conception, a discriminating judgment, and a ready elocution."

Among the intimate friends of his youth was Jonathan Sewall, an eloquent lawyer. In 1761 his patriotic zeal was inflamed by the argument of James Otis (which he heard) on the subject of writs of assistance. Alluding to the time and place of that plea, John Adams said, "American independence was then and there born." He married, in 1764, Abigail Smith, (a grand-daughter of Colonel John Quincy,) a woman of excellent character and superior talents. The passage of the stamp act in 1765 was the occasion of his first active participation in political affairs. At a meeting of the citizens of Braintree he offered resolutions or instructions addressed to the legislature, which were approved, and were adopted by forty other towns in Massachusetts. He published, in 1765, an "Essay on Canon and Feudal Law."

The same year, Jeremiah Gridley, James Otis, and John Adams were employed by the people of Boston as their counsel to support an important memorial, addressed to the governor and council, praying that the courts of law, which had been closed, might be reopened. In order to induce him to join the Tory party, he was offered in 1763 the place of advocate-general, which he declined. He removed from Braintree to Boston in 1768, and soon obtained an extensive practice.

He had now become distinguished as one of the most prominent and intrepid advocates of the popular cause; yet he was also disposed to act the part of a moderator and to counteract the violent excesses of the patriots. He acted as counsel for the defence in the trial of the soldiers who, when attacked by a mob in Boston in March, 1770, had fired and killed several persons. In this case he firmly resisted the storm of popular excitement and the violence of party spirit. He was elected a member of the general court (*i.e.* the legislature) in 1770. "It was not as a politician," says Charles Francis Adams, "but as a lawyer, that John Adams was first drawn into public life." He became the chief legal adviser of the patriots. The destruction of the tea in the harbour of Boston, December, 1773, opened the active drama of the Revolution by a resort to physical force.

Mr. Adams was one of the five delegates sent by Massachusetts to the first continental Congress, which met at Philadelphia in September, 1774. To his friend Sewall, who urged him not to engage in the perilous enterprise of revolution, he replied, "The die is now cast; I have passed the Rubicon. Sink or swim, live or die, survive or perish with my country, is my unalterable determination." In Congress he found a fitting arena for the exercise of those great talents, both for business and debate, which ultimately raised him to the leadership of that body. His diary and letters give a graphic account of the proceedings of that assembly.

During the winter of 1774-75 he wrote, under the signature of *Novanglus*, a series of able essays in defence of the rights of the colonists. These first appeared in a journal of Boston, and may be found in the fourth volume of his collected works. After the battle of Lexington, (April, 1775,) which made many converts to the cause of independence, he returned to Congress. The majority of the members, however, were still disposed to temporize, and adopted another petition to the king, which Mr. Adams opposed. He was more successful in his efforts to induce the Congress to provide for the defence of the colonies. It appears that he was the first to propose George Washington as commander-in-chief of the army. He was again elected to the Federal Congress for one year, and went to Philadelphia in February, 1776. In a letter dated March 23, 1776, he wrote, "All our misfortunes arise from the reluctance of the southern colonies to republican government." He procured, in May, the passage in Congress of a resolution that the colonies should assume the duty of self-government. On the 7th of June a resolution was moved by Richard Henry Lee, and seconded by Mr. Adams, that these colonies "are and of right ought to be free and independent States." On the 11th of June, Thomas Jefferson, John Adams, Benjamin Franklin, Roger Sherman, and Robert R. Livingston were appointed a committee to prepare a declaration of independence. This measure was opposed by a strong party, of which John Dickinson was the leader and spokesman. In reply to him, Mr. Adams made, about July 2, a memorable speech, in reference to which Jefferson said, "John Adams was the ablest advocate and champion of independence on the floor of the house." "He was the colossus of that Congress. Not graceful, not eloquent, not always fluent in his public addresses, he yet came out with a power of thought and expression which moved his hearers from their seats."

On the 3d of July he wrote to his wife, "The second day of July,* 1776, will be the most memorable epoch in the history of America. I am apt to believe that it will be celebrated by succeeding generations as the great anniversary festival."

Mr. Adams was the president, or chairman, of the board of war appointed in June, 1776. He was also chairman of twenty-five committees in Congress. He was appointed commissioner to France in November, 1777, and arrived in Paris in April, 1778, to learn that a treaty between France and the United States had already been concluded. He returned to the United States in July, 1779, and in the ensuing autumn served in the convention which formed a new constitution for Massachusetts. Before this business was finished, Mr. Adams was appointed minister to negotiate a treaty of peace and commerce with Great Britain. He embarked in November, 1779, but did not reach Paris until February, 1780. Having changed his base of operations to Amsterdam, in July, he was authorized in January, 1781, to act as minister to Holland. The difficulty of his position was increased by the intrigues and duplicity of the French minister, De Vergennes, who induced Congress to revoke Mr. Adams's powers to negotiate a treaty of commerce. Adams, Franklin, Jay, and Laurens, who had been appointed joint commissioners, negotiated with Great Britain a treaty, the preliminary articles of which were signed November 30, 1782. He was minister at London from May, 1785, until the spring of 1788, during which period he published a "Defence of the American Constitutions." When, in 1789, Washington was inaugurated as President of the United States, Adams became Vice-President. As an advocate of the Federal constitution he was identified with the Federalist party, by which he was again elected Vice-President in 1792. In the first Congress he gave no less than twenty casting votes, all on points of importance in the organic laws, and thus rendered an efficient support to the policy of Washington. When the French Revolution divided the Americans into two parties, Mr. Adams joined the Anti-Gallican party.

In 1796, John Adams and Thomas Pinckney were nominated by the Federalists for the offices of President and Vice-President. The Republican candidate for the Presidency was Thomas Jefferson. Mr. Adams wrote to his wife, under date of January 20, 1796, "I am heir-apparent, you know, and a succession is soon to take place." His friends assert that General Hamilton, who was the favourite leader of the Federal party, used his influence to elect Pinckney to the Presidency. The result of the canvass was that Adams received seventy-one electoral votes and became President, while Jefferson received sixty-eight votes and became Vice-President. As President, Adams retained the cabinet ministers appointed by Washington, viz., Timothy Pickering, Oliver Wolcott, James McHenry, Joseph Habersham, and Charles Lee. With the first two of these secretaries, however, he had no cordial relations. In the war between France and England he maintained neutrality; but the French Directory provoked the enmity of the Americans by the violation of their maritime rights, and by the expulsion of the envoys, Marshall and Pinckney, from France. In 1798 the government of the United States organized a new army, of which General Washington was appointed commander-in-chief. For the post of second in command Washington preferred Hamilton, whom the President regarded with ill will or distrust; but the general-in-chief procured the appointment of Hamilton by a "menace of resignation." In February, 1799, without consulting his cabinet, Adams nominated a Mr. Van Murray as minister to the French Republic. This act, which Charles Francis Adams says was "the most noted event of Mr. Adams's administration," gave great offence to many of his own party, although the result, by averting a war with France, was probably advantageous to the country. His unpopularity was increased by the alien and sedition laws, the latter of which made the mere expression of opinions or public men and measures a penal offence. In May, 1800, he removed Mr. Pickering from the office of secretary of state, and appointed John Marshall in his stead.

In the presidential election of 1800 he was again the Federal candidate, and received sixty-five electoral votes, but was defeated by Thomas Jefferson, who received seventy-three votes. In March, 1801, he retired from public life, and sank into neglect, covered with obloquy by both of the great political parties. A reaction of public sentiment, however, gradually took place in his favour, and his faults—which, indeed, were of a kind to impair his popularity rather than his usefulness—were almost lost sight of, after he had withdrawn from political life, in the remembrance of his many and inestimable public services.

---

* The day on which the resolution in favour of independence was passed: the Declaration of Independence, with its various amendments, was not agreed to until the 4th, and then only after a long and vehement debate.

ā, ē, ī, ō, ū, ȳ, *long;* ă, ĕ, ŏ, same, less prolonged; ă, ĕ, ĭ, ŏ, ŭ, ў, *short;* ạ, ẹ, ị, ọ, *obscure;* fär, fäll, fät; mēt; nŏt; gōōd; mōōn;

He began to write an Autobiography, which he never finished. Having lived to see his son, John Quincy, elected President of the United States, he died at Quincy on the 4th of July, 1826. By a remarkable coincidence, Thomas Jefferson died on the same day. The character of John Adams as drawn by Jefferson before these distinguished men had become rivals for the suffrages of the American people, is probably very near the truth. He says, writing from Paris, "A seven months' intimacy with him here, and as many weeks in London, have given me opportunities of studying him closely. He is vain, irritable, and a bad calculator of the force and probable effect of the motives which govern men. *This is all the ill which can possibly be said of him.* He is profound in his views and accurate in his judgment, except where knowledge of the world is necessary to form a judgment."—*Letter to Madison,* dated January 30, 1787.

See "The Life and Works of John Adams," edited by his grandson, CHARLES FRANCIS ADAMS, 10 vols. 8vo, 1850-56; BANCROFT, "History of the United States;" HILDRETH, "History of the United States;" "Quarterly Review" for December, 1841; "New York Review" for January, 1842; "North American Review" for October, 1850; JARED SPARKS, "Diplomatic Correspondence of the American Revolution."

Adams, (JOHN,) a British sailor, was one of the mutinous crew of the "Bounty," who, in 1789, sent their commander, Bligh, adrift in a boat, and established themselves in Pitcairn's Island. After some of his comrades had been killed by the natives, he became religious, trained his children in habits of strict morality, and was regarded as the patriarch of the colony. His proper name is said to have been Alexander Smith. Died in 1829. An account of this colony was published in a "Voyage to the Pacific," etc., by Captain Beechey, who visited it in 1825; also by Rev. É. Murray, (1853.) Lord Byron has made the history of this colony the subject of a poem in four cantos, entitled "The Island."

See, also, SIR JOHN BARROW, "History of the Mutiny of the Bounty."

Adams, (JOHN COUCH,) an eminent English astronomer, born in Cornwall about 1817, was educated at Cambridge. He shares with Leverrier the honour of the discovery of the planet Neptune, although he was anticipated by that astronomer in the publication of the discovery. He began his researches into the causes of the irregularities in the motion of Uranus as early as 1843, and communicated the results to Professor Airy in 1845. In November, 1846, he made public his "Explanation of the Observed Irregularities in the Motion of Uranus." He received the Copley medal in 1848, was chosen a fellow of the Royal Society in 1849, and President of the Astronomical Society in 1851. He was appointed professor of astronomy at Cambridge in 1858.

Adams, (JOHN QUINCY,) an American statesman, orator, and diplomatist, the sixth President of the United States, was born in Braintree, Massachusetts, on the 11th of July, 1767. He was the eldest son of President John Adams, above noticed. He enjoyed peculiar and rare advantages for education. In childhood he was instructed by his mother, a grand-daughter of Colonel John Quincy, and a woman of superior talents. In 1778, when only eleven years old, he accompanied his father to France, attended a school in Paris, and returned home in August, 1779. Having been taken again to Europe by his father in 1780, he pursued his studies at the University of Leyden, where he learned Latin and Greek. In July, 1781, at the age of fourteen, he was appointed private secretary to Francis Dana, minister to Russia. He remained at St. Petersburg until October, 1782, after which he resumed his studies at the Hague, and was present at the signing of the definitive treaty of peace in Paris, September 3, 1783. Having passed some months with his father in London, he returned to the United States to complete his education, entered Harvard College in 1786, and graduated in 1788.

He studied law with the celebrated Theophilus Parsons, of Newburyport, was admitted to the bar in 1791, and began to practise in Boston. In 1791 he published in the "Boston Centinel," under the signature of *Publicola,* a series of able essays, in which he exposed the fallacies and vagaries of the French political reformers.

These papers attracted much attention in Europe as well as in the United States.

Under the signature of *Marcellus* he wrote, in 1793, several articles, in which he argued that the United States should observe strict neutrality in the war between the French and the British. "To him," says Mr. Seward, "it is believed, belongs the honour of first publicly advocating this line of policy, which afterwards became a settled principle of the American government." These writings having commended him to the favour of General Washington, he was appointed minister to Holland in May, 1794. He married, in July, 1797, Louisa Catherine Johnson, a daughter of Joshua Johnson, of Maryland, who was then American consul at London. In a letter dated February 20, 1797, Washington wrote to the elder Adams, "I give it as my decided opinion that Mr. Adams is the most valuable public character we have abroad," and he advised the President-elect not to withhold promotion from him because he was his son. John Quincy Adams was accordingly appointed minister to Berlin, in 1797. He translated Wieland's "Oberon" into English, and published an account of his travels in Silesia, which he visited in 1800. He succeeded in negotiating a treaty of amity and commerce with the Prussian government, and was recalled about February, 1801.

He was elected a senator of the United States by the Federalists of Massachusetts, for the term beginning March, 1803. In 1805 he was appointed professor of rhetoric and belles-lettres at Harvard College, and accepted that office on condition that he should be permitted to attend to his senatorial duties while Congress was in session. His lectures at Harvard were much admired, and were published in 1810. In 1805 he endeavoured to procure the passage of a law to levy a duty on the importation of slaves. He offended his political friends, the Federalists, by supporting Jefferson's embargo act, which was passed in December, 1807, and thus became connected with the Democratic party. The legislature of Massachusetts elected another person to take the place of Mr. Adams, who resigned his seat in March, 1808, declining to serve for the remainder of the term, rather than obey the instructions of the Federalists, who were then the dominant party in his State. He subsequently gave far deeper offence by charging some of the Federal leaders with a plot to dissolve the Union and establish an independent northern confederacy. This accusation was doubtless one of the principal causes of the hostility and distrust which were long felt towards New England, not only in the Southern, but also in the Middle and Western States.

While a member of the Senate, Mr. Adams had distinguished himself as an able and eloquent public speaker, as well as an accomplished scholar. In March, 1809, he was appointed by President Madison minister to Russia. During his residence in that country he was nominated an associate justice of the supreme court of the United States, and confirmed February, 1811; but he declined the appointment. His influence and diplomatic services at St. Petersburg laid the foundation of those amicable relations which have ever since been maintained between Russia and the United States. In 1813, Adams, Clay, Gallatin, and Russell were appointed commissioners to negotiate a treaty of peace with Great Britain. They met the British diplomatists at Ghent, and, after a protracted negotiation of six months, signed a treaty of peace on the 24th of December, 1814.

In the spring of 1815, Adams was appointed minister to the court of St. James, where he remained until he was selected by Mr. Monroe for the office of secretary of state in 1817. In his long and successful career as a diplomatist he had justified the confidence of Washington, who, in 1797, had predicted that Mr. Adams would "prove himself to be the ablest of all our diplomatic corps." He entered upon his duties as secretary of state in September, 1817, and performed them with a fidelity and success which obtained the approbation of the country. He defended General Jackson's conduct in Florida, when the other members of the cabinet censured him for transcending his orders.

According to Mr. Seward, "Mr. Adams deserved and received a high share of credit" for negotiating, in

1819, with Spain, a treaty which was very advantageous to the United States.

In 1824, Adams, Jackson, Crawford, and Clay were candidates for the Presidency; all Democrats, and professing substantially the same political creed. Mr. Adams, who was supported by the Eastern States and New York, received eighty-four electoral votes; General Jackson, ninety-nine; Mr. Crawford, forty-one; and Mr. Clay, thirty-seven. Neither of the candidates having received a majority in the electoral colleges, the election devolved on the House of Representatives. Aided by the influence of Henry Clay, Mr. Adams received the votes of thirteen States, and was elected.

He appointed Mr. Clay secretary of state, Richard Rush secretary of the treasury, James Barbour secretary of war, Samuel L. Southard secretary of the navy, and William Wirt attorney-general. The friends of Jackson were indignant, and accused Adams and Clay of obtaining their success by "bargain and corruption." Although Mr. Crawford wrote to Mr. Clay, after the election, "I approved of your vote when it was given, and should have voted as you did between Jackson and Adams," yet the friends of Crawford formed a coalition with the Jacksonians to oppose the new administration. Mr. Adams favoured internal improvements, and the protection of domestic manufactures. It ought to be remembered to his honour that he refused to remove competent men from office merely because they were his political opponents. In the latter part of his Presidential term the opposition had a majority in both houses of Congress, and assailed the President with unscrupulous and bitter hostility. At the election of 1828 he received eighty-three electoral votes, and was defeated by General Jackson, who received one hundred and seventy-eight votes. His defeat was probably promoted by the charge of corrupt collusion with Mr. Clay in 1825, although that charge appears to have been wholly destitute of foundation. On the 4th of March, 1829, he retired to his estate at Quincy.

In 1830 the public were greatly surprised by the election of Mr. Adams to Congress, in which he took his seat in December, 1831. He continued to represent his native district in that body for seventeen years, during which he was constantly at his post, and surpassed nearly all the members in close application to business and in the power of endurance. "In every respect," says Seward, "he was a model legislator." He usually acted with the Whigs, but kept himself free from the trammels of party. His most memorable service in Congress was his defence of the right of petition, and his inflexible resistance to the encroachments of the slave power. In 1836 the opponents of slavery began to send to Congress petitions for the abolition of slavery, which were presented by Mr. Adams. The House of Representatives adopted a rule that no petition relating to slavery should be read, printed, or debated. "With unwavering firmness," says Seward, "against a bitter and unscrupulous opposition, exasperated to the highest pitch by his pertinacity—amidst a perfect tempest of vituperation and abuse—he persevered in presenting these petitions, one by one, to the amount sometimes of two hundred in a day—demanding the action of the house on each separate petition." His opponents once made a motion to punish him by a vote of censure for presenting a petition from slaves; but they were baffled in their object when the fact was announced that the said petitioners prayed that slavery should NOT be abolished.

On the 21st of February, 1848, while in his seat in the Capitol, he was struck with paralysis. He died on the 23d of that month; his last words were, "This is the last of earth! I AM CONTENT!"

In the latter part of his career he was popularly known by the title of "the Old Man Eloquent." He kept a copious diary of his public life, and was a voluminous writer of prose and verse. Many of his orations, poems, and discourses have been published. In religion he was, like his father, a Unitarian.

See WILLIAM H. SEWARD, "Life of John Quincy Adams," 1849; JOSIAH QUINCY, "Memoir of the Life of John Quincy Adams," 1858; HILDRETH, "History of the United States," vol. vi. (or vol. iii., Second Series.)

Adams, (JOSEPH,) a physician and medical writer, born in 1756. He practised in London from 1805 till his death in 1818. His principal work is entitled "Observations on Morbid Poisons," (1796.) He was an enthusiastic admirer of Hunter, and appears to have adopted, too implicitly, most of the views of that eminent physiologist.

Adams, (NEHEMIAH,) D.D., an American divine, born at Salem, Massachusetts, in 1806. He graduated at Harvard University in 1826. For many years he has been pastor of the Essex Street Congregational Church, Boston. Among his various publications may be mentioned "Remarks on the Unitarian Belief;" "Friends of Christ in the New Testament;" "Life of John Eliot;" and "South Side View of Slavery," (1854,) which has been severely criticised by the free-soil press of the country.

Adams, (RICHARD,) an English non-conformist minister, born in Cheshire, graduated in 1644. He was ejected from a living in Bread street, London, in 1662. Died near the close of the seventeenth century.

Adams, (SAMUEL,) an eminent American patriot and orator, born in Boston on the 27th of September, 1722, was a second-cousin of President John Adams. He graduated at Harvard College in 1740. A few years afterwards, on taking the degree of master of arts, he chose for his thesis the question, "Whether it be lawful to resist the supreme magistrate if the commonwealth cannot otherwise be preserved?" of which he maintained the affirmative. In early life he applied himself to mercantile business, in which he was not successful. He afterwards served as collector of taxes in Boston. Having gained distinction as a political writer, he was elected a member of the general assembly of Massachusetts in 1765. He continued to represent Boston in that assembly for nine years, and by his courage, talents, and energy acquired great influence. Before the Revolution he was a zealous opponent of the policy of the British ministers, and an advocate of independence. John Adams, in his diary, written in 1765, after some notice of James Otis and others, says, "Adams, I believe, has the most thorough understanding of liberty and her resources in the temper and character of the people, though not in the law and constitution, as well as the most habitual radical love of it, of any of them."

He was elected a member of the continental Congress in 1774, and was one of the two popular leaders excepted from the general pardon offered by the British government in June, 1775. As a member of Congress, in which he continued about eight years, he rendered important services, and signed the Declaration of Independence. Mr. Adams took part in the formation of the constitution of Massachusetts, adopted in 1780, served afterwards as a senator of that State, and was a member of the convention which ratified the Federal constitution in 1788. In national politics he favoured the Republican or Jeffersonian party. He was lieutenant-governor from 1789 to 1794, and in 1795 succeeded John Hancock as Governor of Massachusetts. Having been several times re-elected, he served as Governor until 1797, and then retired from public life. He had married young, and had an only son, whom he survived. In religion he was a strict Calvinist. An oration on the independence of his country, which he delivered in Philadelphia in August, 1776, has been published. He died in Boston, on the 2d of October, 1803. Respecting his merits as a speaker and writer, John Adams remarks that in his works may be found "specimens of a nervous simplicity of reasoning and eloquence that have never been rivalled in America."

See "Life and Public Services of Samuel Adams," by WILLIAM V. WELLS, 3 vols. 8vo, Boston, 1865: see also the "Encyclopædia Americana;" GOODRICH, "Lives of the Signers to the Declaration of Independence;" SANDERSON, "Biography of the Signers to the Declaration of Independence;" BANCROFT, "History of the United States," vol. v. chaps. x. and xix.; HILDRETH, "History of the United States," vol. ii.

Adams, (Sir THOMAS,) an English royalist, noted for munificence, born in Shropshire in 1586. He was lord mayor of London in 1645. Died in 1667.

Adams, (THOMAS,) an English dissenting minister, who was rejected for non-conformity about 1662. He wrote a work called "Protestant Union." Died in 1670.

Adams, (WILLIAM,) an English navigator, born in

Kent about 1575. He entered the Dutch navy as pilot, and passed some time in Japan, where he is said to have rendered important services to the commerce of the Dutch and English. Died in 1621.

Adams, (Rev. WILLIAM,) distinguished as the friend of Dr. Johnson, was born in 1707, and died in 1789. Besides some smaller pieces, he published "An Answer to Mr. Hume's Essay on Miracles," (1752,) which attracted considerable attention.

Adams, (WILLIAM,) an English divine and writer, born in 1814. He held the position of vicar of St. Peters, Oxford. Among his works are "The Shadow of the Cross," (1842, 8th edition, 1849,) and "Distant Hills," (4th edition, 1847.) Died in 1848.

Ad'am-son, (HENRY,) a Scottish poet, who lived in the early part of the seventeenth century. He was a nephew of Archbishop Adamson. Died in 1639.

See CHAMBERS, "Biographical Dictionary of Eminent Scotsmen."

Adamson, (JOHN,) an English author, born in 1787. He published a "Memoir of Camoens," (1820,) and "History, Antiquities, and Literature of Portugal," (2 vols., 1842-46.) Died in 1855.

Adamson, (PATRICK,) an eminent Scottish prelate and writer, born at Perth in 1536. He embraced the cause of the Reformation on its gaining the ascendency, and in 1564 published a poem "On the Superstitious Follies of the Papists," ("De Papistarum Superstitiosis Ineptiis.") In 1576, through the influence of Morton, the regent, he was raised to the archbishopric of St. Andrews. From this time to the end of his life he was engaged in an almost incessant struggle with the Presbyterian party, who were growing every day more powerful, and who at last succeeded in deposing him, not only from the primacy, but from all his functions as a minister. He died in 1592, in great indigence. Besides the poem already mentioned, he wrote translations of the book of Job, of the Apocalypse, and other parts of the Bible, in Latin verse.

See CALDERWOOD, "History of the Church of Scotland ;" CHAMBERS, "Biographical Dictionary of Eminent Scotsmen ;" SPOTTSWOOD, "History of the Church of Scotland."

A-dā'mus Ma-ris'cus or **Ad'am de Maris'co,** a learned monk, and teacher of theology at Oxford, born about the end of the twelfth century. Roger Bacon, who was his contemporary, speaks of him as an eminent mathematician. He died about 1260.

A-dā'mus Mu-re-mu-then'sis (or **Murimuthensis**) or **Adam de Murimuth, Murimouth,** or **Murymouth,** an English chronicler, who wrote a "Chronicle or History of his Own Time," extending from 1303 to 1337. He appears to have been employed on several important missions ; in 1323 he was ambassador from Edward II. (of England) to the pope and the King of Sicily.

Ada'mus Sco'tus, (i.e. "Adam the Scotchman,") a learned bishop, who lived in the twelfth century, chiefly remarkable as the author of a curious dialogue between the Soul and Reason. Of the events of his life little or nothing is known.

Adanson, ǎ'dôn'sôN', (MICHEL,) an eminent French naturalist, born at Aix in 1727. His family were of Scottish extraction, and had been exiled from their country on account of their devotion to the house of Stuart. He was distinguished at school for his great application, and won many of the prizes while at the College of Plessis. In 1748 he visited Senegal, in Africa, where he remained five years, and in spite of burning suns and drenching rains he collected, by unremitting labour, an immense number of new plants and animals, as well as objects of commerce, clothes, utensils, and implements of war peculiar to the inhabitants ; made exact maps of the countries through which he travelled ; prepared grammars and vocabularies of the different nations of that region, and kept an exact register of meteorological observations. After his return to France, he published, in 1757, his "Natural History of Senegal," ("Histoire Naturelle du Sénégal,") and in 1763, his "Families of Plants," ("Familles des Plantes.") In these, and all his other works, he strenuously opposed the artificial system of Linnæus ; but the influence and popularity of the Swedish naturalist were so great as

not only to resist uninjured all the efforts of his talented and powerful assailant, but to throw for a time even Adanson's extraordinary merits into the shade. Though on the publication of the "Natural History of Senegal" he was elected member of the Royal Academy of Sciences of Paris, and fellow of the Royal Society of London, yet he passed a considerable portion of his after-life in obscurity and extreme indigence ; but he was finally maintained by a pension from the French government. He died in 1806. In addition to the works already mentioned, Adanson contributed many valuable papers to the Mémoires of the Royal Academy of Sciences ; and also prepared an immense work entitled "Universal Order of Nature," ("Ordre Universel de la Nature,")—a sort of encyclopædia of natural science,—which has never been published. He read, in 1761, before the Academy of Sciences, a very interesting notice (accompanied by an accurate botanical description) of the baobab-tree, which was afterwards named, in honour of the illustrious botanist, Adansonia. As a naturalist, Adanson is not unworthy to be the rival of Linnæus ; in the estimation of Cuvier, indeed, he ought to rank far above the illustrious Swede. His eulogy was composed by Cuvier, who represents his character as noble, but eccentric.

See CUVIER, "Éloge d'Adanson," 1819 ; LEJOYAND, "Notice sur la Vie et les Travaux de M. Adanson," 8vo, 1808 ; "Observations sur feu M. Adanson," by his nephew, M. ADANSON ; "Nouvelle Biographie Générale."

Adashef, â-dä-shěf', or **Adashev,** written also **Adaschew,** (ALEXIS,) an eminent Russian statesman, who was the minister and favourite of Ivan IV. from 1547 to 1560. His administration was distinguished for its justice, humanity, and enlightened policy. Having incurred the displeasure of his sovereign, he died, in prison, at Dorpat, in 1561.

See KARAMZIN, "History of the Russian Empire."

Adashef or **Adashev,** (DANIEL,) a brother of the preceding, greatly distinguished himself by a successful expedition which he commanded against the Crim Tartars in 1559. Two years after, he was beheaded by the order of his capricious and ungrateful sovereign.

Addemeeree or **Addemirî,** ăd-děh-mee'ree, written also **Al-Damiri,** surnamed KEMÂL-ED-DEEN, (or -ED-DÎN,) kě-mâl' ed-deen', ("Perfection of the Faith,") a distinguished Arabian naturalist, born in Egypt about 1350. He wrote on history and biography as well as natural science. The best-known of his works is "The Lives of Living Creatures." Died about 1405.

Ad'ding-ton, (ANTHONY,) an English physician, who was the confidential friend and adviser of Lord Chatham, was educated at Oxford, where he took the degree of master of arts in 1740, and that of doctor of medicine in 1744. He practised at Reading, and died in 1790.

Addington, (HENRY,) afterwards LORD SIDMOUTH, son of the preceding, was born in 1756, and educated with Pitt, the son of Lord Chatham. He soon distinguished himself in the political world ; in 1789 he was chosen speaker of the House of Commons, and in 1801, on the resignation of Pitt, to whom he had ever shown himself an unfaltering friend, he succeeded that great statesman as chancellor of the exchequer and first lord of the treasury. The opposition of his enemies obliged him to leave his station in May, 1804 : the king then conferred upon him the title of Lord Viscount Sidmouth. He became home secretary in 1812, and retired from public life in 1822. Died in 1844.

See "Life and Correspondence of the Hon. Henry Addington," by PELLEW, 1847.

Addington, (STEPHEN,) D.D., a dissenting minister, born at Northampton, England, about 1730, and died in 1796. He wrote, besides other religious works, a life of the Apostle Paul.

See WILSON's "Dissenting Churches."

Ad'di-son, (ALEXANDER,) an American lawyer and judge, distinguished for his learning and eloquence, was born in 1759. Died at Pittsburg in 1807.

Ad'dison, (G. H.,) an Englishman, born in 1793 ; was a youth of high promise when he died, in India, in 1815, leaving a work called "Indian Reminiscences," (1837.)

Addison, (JOSEPH,) an English author, pre-eminent as an essayist, humorist, and moralist, was born at Mil-

ε as k; ç as s; ġ hard; ġ as j; G, H, K, guttural; N, nasal; R, trilled; ṡ as z; th as in this. (☞See Explanations, p. 23.)

4

ston, near Amesbury, in Wiltshire, on the 1st of May, 1672. He was a son of the Rev. Lancelot Addison. He attended school at the Charter House, from which, about the age of fifteen, he passed to Queen's College, Oxford, with a stock of classical learning that would have done honour to a master of arts. In 1689 he removed to Magdalen College, where he remained about ten years. He acquired at college a high reputation as a writer of Latin verse, in which he probably excelled all his contemporaries. His first English composition was a piece of complimentary verse addressed, in 1694, to Dryden, who appears to have been pleased with this tribute, and became a friend of the author. Addison wrote the critical preface which Dryden prefixed to his version of the "Georgics," (1697.)

His friends destined him for the church, to which his opinions and habits of thought were well adapted. Before he had decided in relation to the choice of a profession, he formed an acquaintance with Charles Montagu, the eminent Whig financier, to whom he dedicated an elegant Latin poem on the peace of Ryswick, (1697.) He was persuaded by Montagu to decline the clerical profession and to devote himself to the service of the state. The course of his life was determined in 1699, when he received an annual pension of £300, and set out on a tour to France and Italy, partly with the design to qualify himself for diplomacy by the study of the French language. At Paris he met with Boileau, who complimented him highly on his Latin poetry. He passed many months in the chief cities of Italy, and addressed to his friend Montagu, now Lord Halifax, a "Letter from Italy," in verse, (1701,) which was greatly admired. In consequence of the death of King William and the removal of his Whig friends from office, Addison was deprived of his pension in 1702. He returned to England about the end of 1703.

One morning he was surprised to receive, in the garret which he occupied in the Haymarket, a visit from Mr. Boyle, chancellor of the exchequer, who, on behalf of the chief minister, Godolphin, requested him to write a poem on the battle of Blenheim, (1704.) The result of this visit was "The Campaign," which was received with immense applause by the public, and procured for the author a commissionership as an earnest of greater favours. He published an interesting "Narrative of his Travels in Italy," which, before it was reprinted, sold for five times the original price. His next work was the opera "Rosamond;" which failed on the stage through the fault of the music, but was completely successful as a publication.

In 1705 Addison was appointed under-secretary of state, through the influence of Halifax and Somers, who had formed a coalition with Godolphin and Marlborough. He was elected to Parliament in 1708, and on one occasion rose to speak, but could not overcome his diffidence, and made no further effort to become a debater. His literary talents and character, however, rendered him one of the main pillars of the Whig party, for at that time public opinion was influenced more by the pen than by the tongue. "When these things are duly considered," says Macaulay, "it will not be thought strange that Addison should have climbed higher in the state than any other Englishman has ever, by means merely of literary talents, been able to climb."

He was chief secretary to Lord Wharton, Lord-Lieutenant of Ireland, in 1709, with a salary of about £2000. In this year his friend Steele began to issue "The Tatler," which afforded to Addison an opportunity to display his genius in a new department of literature. His graceful style, his genial spirit, his excellent invention and inimitable humour rendered The Tatler, and its successor "The Spectator," extremely popular. The Spectator was issued daily from March 1, 1711, until December 6, 1712, and was revived in 1714 as a tri-weekly paper. Addison wrote about three-sevenths of The Spectator, the success of which was such as no similar work has ever obtained. The circulation of it amounted to nearly four thousand copies. For some particular papers, it is said, the demand was so great that not less than twenty thousand copies were required. These essays exerted a great and salutary influence on society. "He not only

made the proper use of wit himself," says Dr. Johnson, "but taught it to others. . . . He has dissipated the prejudice that had long connected gaiety with vice, and easiness of manners with laxity of principles. He has restored virtue to its dignity, and taught innocence not to be ashamed. This is an elevation of literary character, 'above all Greek, above all Roman fame,'" Although the Whigs were defeated in the general election of 1710, Addison was so popular that he was returned to Parliament without a contest. On this occasion Swift writes, "I believe if he had a mind to be king, he would hardly be refused."

In 1713 he produced his tragedy of "Cato," which was greeted with "thunders of unanimous applause," and obtained more celebrity among his contemporaries than any other of his works; but this favourable estimate has not been confirmed by the suffrages of a later age. On the death of Queen Anne, August, 1714, he was appointed secretary to the regency or lords justices. Soon after that date he again became chief secretary to the Lord-Lieutenant of Ireland. He exchanged this office for a seat at the board of trade in 1715, and began to publish "The Freeholder," his best political work. After a long courtship, he married, in 1716, the Countess-dowager of Warwick, who, according to Johnson, "thought herself entitled to treat with very little ceremony the tutor of her son." He became one of the two principal secretaries of state in the new ministry formed in the spring of 1717, but remained in office only eleven months. His retirement is attributed to ill health and inefficiency as a public speaker.

He died on the 17th of June, 1719, leaving no child but a daughter, and was buried in Westminster Abbey. Shortly before his death he said to his step-son, Lord Warwick, "I have sent for you in order that you might see in what peace a Christian can die!"

The two gravest faults charged against him are his habit of drinking wine, and his insidious enmity to Pope. The former has, in all probability, been much exaggerated, and the latter is said to have been fully and distinctly disproved. It appears, indeed, to have never had any better foundation than Pope's morbid suspicion. (See POPE, ALEXANDER.)

Addison's colloquial powers are extolled by several authors. Lady Mary Montagu said that "she had known all the wits, and that Addison was the best company in the world." "Addison's conversation," says Pope, "had something in it more charming than I have found in any other man. But this was only when familiar: before strangers, or perhaps a single stranger, he preserved his dignity by a stiff silence." "His humanity," says Macaulay, "is without a parallel in literary history. The highest proof of human virtue is to possess boundless power without abusing it. No kind of power is more formidable than the power of making men ridiculous; and that power Addison possessed in boundless measure. But it would be difficult, if not impossible, to find, in all the volumes which he has left us, a single taunt which can be called ungenerous or unkind. . . . The numerous fictions, generally original, often wild and grotesque, but always graceful and happy, which are found in his essays, fully entitle him to the rank of a great poet,—a rank to which his metrical compositions give him no claim. As an observer of life, of manners, of all the shades of human character, he stands in the first class."

See JOHNSON, "Lives of the English Poets;" MACAULAY, "Essays," article Addison; STEELE, "Memoirs of the Life and Writings of J. Addison," 1724; DES MAIZEAUX, "Vie de J. Addison;" LUCY AIKIN, "Life of Joseph Addison," 1843; ELWIN, "Life of Addison," 1857; "Biographia Britannica;" VILLEMAIN, "Cours de Littérature."

Addison, (Rev. LANCELOT,) father of the preceding, was born in Westmoreland in 1632, and educated at Queen's College, Oxford. He passed seven years at Tangier as chaplain to the garrison, and, after his return, published "West Barbary, or a Short Narrative of the Revolutions of the Kingdoms of Fez and Morocco," (1671,) which attracted considerable attention both in England and foreign countries. He became a royal chaplain about 1670, Dean of Lichfield in 1683, and Archdeacon of Coventry in 1684. Among his writings are several religious treatises, and a work on "The Present State of the Jews, (more particularly relating to those in Barbary,") (1675.) He died in 1703, leaving three sons:— Joseph; Gulston, who died Governor of Madras; and Lancelot, who was eminent as a classical scholar.

See WOOD, "Athenæ Oxonienses."

Adel, ä'del, or **Adils,** ä'dils, one of the early kings of Sweden, whose history is lost in fable. He is supposed to have lived in the fifth or sixth century.

Adelaar. See ADELER.

Adelaide, ăd'êl-ād, [Ger. ADELHEID, ä'dĕl-hīt',] an empress of Germany, daughter of Rudolph II., and wife of Otho I., (surnamed the Great,) was born in 931. After the death of the emperor, her husband, she governed the empire with great ability during the early part of the reign of her son, Otho II. She was afterwards regent during a part of the minority of Otho III. She died in 999, universally beloved, and is regarded as a saint, though her name does not appear in the Roman calendar.

Adelaide, ad'ę-lād, [Fr. ADÉLAÏDE, ä'dä'lä'ĕd',] (MADAME,) the eldest daughter of Louis XV., was born in 1732, at Versailles. On the breaking out of the revolution, she, with her sister, Madame Victoire, left their native country for Italy. She died at Trieste in 1800.

Adelaide, ad'ę-lād, Queen of England, born in 1792, was a daughter of the Duke of Saxe-Meiningen, and was married, in 1818, to the Duke of Clarence, who became William IV. Died in 1849.

See DORAN, "Life of Queen Adelaide."

Adélaïde, ä'dä'lä'ĕd', (EUGÈNE LOUISE,) a French princess, born in Paris in 1777, was a sister of King Louis Philippe. She was an exile from 1792 until 1814. In 1830 she urged Louis Philippe, with whom she had much influence, to accept the crown. Died in 1847.

Adelais, (ăd'lā' or ä'dęh-lā') OF LOUVAIN, the daughter of Godfrey, Duke of Brabant, and the second queen of Henry I. of England, was born about 1103, and married in 1121. Her beauty was celebrated under the designation of "The Fair Maid of Brabant." After the death of Henry I. she married William de Albini, an English nobleman, and died in 1151.

Ad'el-ard or **Athelard,** a king of the West Saxons, who ascended the throne in 727, and died in 740.

Adelard OF BATH, [Lat. ADELAR'DUS BATHONIEN'-SIS,] a student of natural science, who lived in England in the early part of the twelfth century. He wrote a book entitled "Concerning the Natures of Things," ("De Naturis Rerum,") and made a translation of Euclid from the Arabic into Latin, at a time when this work was almost unknown in Western Europe.

Adelbert. See ADALBERT.

Ad'el-bold, [Lat. ADELBOL'DUS, ADELBAL'DUS, or ATHELBAL'DUS,] a bishop of Utrecht, who flourished in the early part of the eleventh century. He was distinguished for his piety, and was a great patron of learning and the arts. Died in 1027.

Adelburner, ä'dęl-bōōr'nęr, or **Adelbulner,** ä'dęl-bōōl'nęr, (MICHAEL,) a German mathematician, born at Nuremberg in 1702, became professor at Altdorf in 1743. He published an astronomical journal, called "Commercium Astronomicum," (1735-40,) which had great success. Died in 1779.

See MONTUCLA, "Histoire des Mathématiques."

Adelcrantz or **Adelkrantz,** ä'dęl-krȧnts', the name of two Swedish architects, father and son. The latter, CHARLES FREDERICK, who was the more eminent, was born at Stockholm in 1716, and died in 1796.

Adeler, ä'dĕl-ęr, also written **Adelaar,** (CORD or CONRAD SIVERTSEN,) a famous admiral, born in Norway in 1622. He entered the service of Venice in his youth, and obtained command of a fleet. In 1654 he gained a signal victory over the Turkish fleet, and killed with his own hand the admiral Ibrâheem Pasha. The King of Denmark recalled him in 1663, and gave him the command of his navy. Adeler was appointed grand admiral in 1675, and died the same year.

Ad'el-frid, a Saxon king, was slain in battle in 617.

Ad-el-ği'sus, called also **A'del-chis,** the only son of Desiderius, King of the Longobards. Though a brave

prince, he was defeated, with his father, by Charlemagne, in 773; after which he fled to Constantinople. Little else is known respecting him.

Adelgisus, a prince of Beneventum, (now Benevento,) who lived in the ninth century. He was murdered by his own relations in 878.

Adelgreiff, ä'dęl-grīf', (JOHANN ALBRECHT,) a notorious fanatic of the seventeenth century. He claimed to represent God on earth. He was beheaded at Königsberg in 1636.

Ad'ęl-man, (or ä'dĕl-mȧn',) an ecclesiastical writer, who lived about the middle of the eleventh century, was Bishop of Brescia.

Adelon, ăd'lôn', (NICOLAS PHILIBERT,) a French physician and writer, born at Dijon about 1780. He was a favourite pupil of Chaussier, with whom he co-operated in the first volumes of the "Biographie Universelle." In 1823-24 he published a "Treatise on the Physiology of Man," (4 vols.) He obtained the chair of legal medicine in Paris in 1826, and continued to occupy it so late as 1858. Died in July, 1862.

Adelstan. See ATHELSTAN.

Adelung, ä'dęh-lōōng, (FRIEDRICH,) a German philologist, born at Stettin in 1768, was a nephew of Johann Christoph, noticed below. He removed to St. Petersburg, where he became preceptor to the grand duke Nicholas, (afterwards emperor,) and a counsellor of state. Among his works are "The Relations between the Sanscrit and Russian Languages," (1815,) and an "Essay on the Sanscrit Literature and Language," (1830.) Died at St. Petersburg in 1843.

See GRETSCH, "Histoire de la Littérature Russe."

Adelung or **Adlung,** ä'dlōōng, (JACOB,) an organist and writer on music, born near Erfurt, in Germany, in 1699; died in 1762.

Adelung, (JOHANN CHRISTOPH,) a distinguished philologist and lexicographer, born near Anklam, in Pomerania, in 1732. He commenced the study of theology at the University of Halle, but his tastes led him to general literature and philology, to which, from about the year 1761, he appears to have devoted all his time and thoughts. He wrote several historical works, which, however, have attracted but little attention. That on which his fame principally rests is his "Attempt at a Complete Grammatico-Critical Dictionary of the German Language," ("Versuch eines vollständigen Grammatisch-Kritischen Wörterbuches der Hochdeutschen Mundart.") This great German work has been compared to the great English dictionary of Dr. Johnson; but Adelung's is superior to Johnson's in its definitions, and in all that relates to etymology. His dictionary attracted great attention in Germany; and, as a reward for the important service he had rendered to German literature, he was appointed, by the Elector of Saxony, chief librarian of the public library of Dresden, with the title of Hofrath, ("court-counsellor,") an office which he held until his death. Among the defects, however, of Adelung's dictionary may be named: 1st, an excessive partiality for the dialect of Upper Saxony, which caused him to reject words used in other parts of Germany; 2dly, his fastidious rejection of all new words not sanctioned by what he considered good authority. Besides writing a German grammar, and several other books illustrating his own tongue, he commenced a great work, entitled "Mithridates, oder Allgemeine Sprachen-Kunde," a general treatise on language, which was finished, after his death, by J. S. Vater. Died in 1806.

See EFSCH und GRUBER, "Allgemeine Encyklopaedie;" "Nouvelle Biographie Générale."

Adelwalch, ad'el-wŏlk, a king of Sussex, who was slain in battle in 686.

Ad'e-mar' [Lat. ADEMA'RUS] or **Aymar,** ā'mȧr', a French historical writer, who flourished in the early part of the eleventh century.

Ad-e-ma'rus, a courtier of Otho III., Emperor of Germany, by whom he was appointed Duke of Spoletum (Spoleto) and Marquis of Camerino, about the end of the tenth century.

Adenez or **Adenes,** ăd'nā' or ä'dęh-nä', sometimes written **Adans,** surnamed LE ROI, (lęh rwä,) a celebrated minstrel, born in Brabant about 1240. He was first patronized by Henry III., Duke of Brabant, and afterwards by Philip the Bold, King of France. The time of his death is unknown.

Adeodat. See DIEUDONNÉ.

Adeodato, ä-dä-o-dä′to, an Italian sculptor, who lived in the twelfth century.

Ader, ä′dair′, (GUILLAUME,) a physician and medical writer, who lived at Toulouse, in France, about the beginning of the seventeenth century.

Adet, ä′dŏ′, (PIERRE AUGUSTE,) a French politician and chemist, born at Nevers in 1763. He was sent, in 1795, as minister to the United States, but resigned or suspended his office in 1797, on account of an alleged violation of neutrality. Having returned to France, he became, in 1809, a member of the legislative body. He published "Elements of Chemistry," (1804.) Died in 1832.

Adgillus (ad-jil′lus) **I.** and **II.,** two dukes of Friesland, who lived in the latter part of the seventh and the beginning of the eighth century.

Adhad-ed-Daulah, (or **-Eddoulat.**) See AZAD-UD-DOWLAH.

Adh-dhahebee or **Adh-dhahebî,** äD-Dä′hĕh-bee′, (almost äth-thä′hĕh-bee′,) written also **Al-Dzahabi,** surnamed SHEMS-ED-DEEN, (*i.e.* the "Sun of Religion,") an eminent Arabian writer and lawyer, born at Damascus about 1274. He was raised to the high office of Mufti of Damascus. Died about 1347. His principal work is a chronological history of all the Moslem nations from the creation down to his own time.

Adh-dhobbee (Adh-dhobbî) or **Ad-dobbee,** äD-Dŏb′bee′ or äth-thŏb′bee′, a native of Córdova, who wrote a valuable history of the Spanish Arabs. He flourished about the beginning of the thirteenth century.

Adhemar, ä′dĕh-maR′, written also **Azemars,** (WILLIAM,) a Provençal poet of the twelfth century, who is said to have loved the Countess of Die so passionately that, on hearing she was about to be married to the Count of Embrun, he fell desperately ill, and, having sent for her, expired in her presence. This so affected her that she abandoned all thoughts of marriage, and died of grief a few years afterwards.

Adhemar de Monteil, ad′ĕh-mar′ dĕh mon-tāl′, [Fr. pron. ăd′mäR′dĕh mŏN′tăl′ or mŏN′tặ′yĕ,] an ecclesiastic, statesman, and warrior, who lived in the fourteenth century. He was appointed Bishop of Metz in 1327, and died in 1361. He had the reputation of a spirited and magnificent prince.

Ad-her′bal, [Gr. Ἀτάρβας,] a Carthaginian commander during the first Punic war, who gained a great victory over the Roman fleet 249 B.C.

Adherbal, the son of Micipsa, King of Numidia. On the death of his father (B.C. 118) he shared the kingdom with his brother Hiempsal and his cousin Jugurtha, by whom he was slain, 112 B.C. (See JUGURTHA.)

Adi-Buddha, (or **-Booddha.**) See BOODDHA.

Adil-Shah-Yoosuf, (or **-Yûsuf,**) ä′dĭl-shäh yoo′sŏŏf, a son of the Turkish sultan Amurâth II., whom, on the death of this monarch in 1451, his mother contrived to secrete from the executioners sent by his brother, Mohammed II., for the purpose of destroying him, and caused him to be privately conveyed to Persia, whence he afterwards fled to Hindostan. Here he entered the service of Mohammed Shah, (II.,) King of the Dekkan, and gradually rose to the highest military offices in the state. On the death of Mohammed Shah, an attempt was made by a corrupt faction at court to destroy Yoosuf; but he withdrew to Bejapoor, (of which province he had been appointed governor,) where his military fame and his high character for liberality and justice soon drew to his standard multitudes of the best and bravest of the land. Though at first he acted uniformly on the defensive, he at length (about 1500) established an empire on the ruin of his enemies. He had previously, in 1489, assumed the title of royalty. He died about 1510. His posterity continued to reign at Bejapoor till 1689, when their capital was taken by Aurungzebe, and Sikandar, the last of the Adil-Shah dynasty, was made prisoner by the conqueror.

Ad-ï-man′tus, ['Αδείμαντος,] the commander of the Corinthian ships during the invasion of Greece by Xerxes,

480 B.C. He appears to have been destitute alike of skill and bravery.

Adimantus is also the name of an Athenian general who was defeated and taken prisoner by Lysander at Ægospotami, 405 B.C.

Adimantus, a Manichæan writer, who is supposed to have lived in the fourth century.

Adimari, ä-de-mä′ree, a noted, though not noble, Florentine family, who hold a considerable place in the history of Italy in the middle ages.

Adimari, (ALESSANDRO,) a classical scholar and poet, born at Florence about 1580, made a translation of Pindar into Italian verse. Died in 1649.

Adimari, (LUDOVICO,) born at Naples in 1644; died at Florence in 1708. He was professor of Tuscan in the Academy of Florence, and wrote, in Italian, satiric poetry which is much admired by some.

Aditi, ad′ï-tï, [common Hindoo pron. ŭd′ï-tï,] the wife of Kasyapa, and the mother of the gods. She is sometimes styled, for greater distinction, the "mother of Indra." She is supposed to personify the earth.

See MOOR, "Hindu Pantheon."

Aditya, ä′dït-yạ, [in the English plural, ÂDITYAS,] the name given to twelve Hindoo deities, sons of Aditi. They are said to represent the sun in each of the different months of the year. Among the Adityas the principal are Varuna, Surya, Indra, Yama, and Vishnu, who, in his fifth Avatar, was born as the son of Kasyapa and Aditi.

See MOOR, "Hindu Pantheon."

Adler, (CASPAR.) See AQUILA.

Adler, äd′lẹr, (GEORG CHRISTIAN,) a theological writer and eminent teacher, born in Silesia in 1674. He founded a school at Königsberg, which afterwards became a gymnasium, being now called the "Collegium Fredericianum." Died in 1741.

Adler, (GEORG CHRISTIAN,) son of the preceding, was born in 1734. He was chief pastor of a Lutheran congregation at Altona, and died in 1804. Besides other works of the same kind, he wrote one on the topography of the city of Rome, (1781.)

Adler, (GEORG J.,) a philologist, born at Leipsic, in Germany, in 1821. He came to the United States in 1833, graduated at the University of New York in 1844, and from 1846 to 1854 was professor of the German language in that institution. He is the author of several German and Latin school manuals, and of an excellent German and English dictionary. Died in New York in August, 1868.

Adler, äd′lẹr, (JACOB GEORG,) a Danish Orientalist, born at Arnis, in Sleswick, in 1755, became professor of theology at Copenhagen in 1788. Among his works is one on the Cufic writings or inscriptions, ("Musæum Cuficum Borgianum," 2 vols., 1782–92.) Died in 1805.

Adler, (PHILIPP,) the first who carried the art of etching to any degree of excellence, was born in Nuremberg in 1484. The date of his death is unknown. He engraved many of the works of Albert Dürer.

Adlerbeth, äd′lẹr-bêt′, (GUDMUND GORAN,) a translator and Swedish poet, born at Jönköping in 1751. In 1778 he was appointed antiquary and private secretary to Gustavus III., whom he accompanied on a tour to Rome. He was afterwards made councillor of the state, and baron, besides receiving numerous other honours. Died in 1818. He was a voluminous writer; among his works are many operas and tragedies, constructed on the plan of the French school. He translated the works of Virgil, Horace, and the Metamorphoses of Ovid.

Adlerfeld or **Adlerfelt,** äd′lẹr-fĕlt′, (GUSTAF,) a Swedish historical writer, born near Stockholm in 1671. He was appointed by Charles XII. *hof-junkare,* or gentleman of the court, and afterwards accompanied the king on several of his campaigns, of which he wrote a regular journal until his death. He was killed by a cannon-ball in the famous battle of Pultowa, (or Poltava,) July 8, 1709.

Adlerfeld, (PEHR, or PETER,) a brother of the preceding, born at Stockholm in 1680. He was made a colonel in the Swedish army in 1712, and in 1720 was raised to the rank of a baron, and made a member of the Riksråd, "Council of the Kingdom." He was killed, in

1743, while defending his native city against the insurgent Dalecarlians.

Adlerscreutz, ăd'lĕʀs-kʀoits', (BARON,) a Swedish general, was the leader of the party which dethroned Gustavus IV. in 1809.

Adlersparre, ăd'lẹr-spâr'rạ, (GEORG,) COUNT OF, a Swedish general and writer, born in 1760. He acted a prominent part in the conspiracy or revolt which dethroned Gustavus IV. in 1809. Died in 1837.

Adlung. See ADELUNG.

Adlzreiter, ăd'ẹlts-rī'tẹr or ăd'lts'rī'tẹr, (JOHANN,) a lawyer and statesman, born at Rosenheim, in Bavaria, in 1596. He became vice-chancellor and privy counsellor to Maximilian, Elector of Bavaria. Died in 1662. He furnished important materials to the history of Bavaria, by Fervaux, which was published under his name.

Ad-me′tus, [Gr. Ἄδμητος; Fr. ADMÈTE, ăd'mȧt',] a son of Pheres, King of Pheræ in Thessaly, succeeded his father on the throne. Apollo, who had been banished from Olympus for one year, tended the herds of Admetus during that period. Admetus became a suitor for Alcestis, the daughter of Pelias, who promised her to him on condition that he would come in a chariot drawn by a lion and a wild boar. With the help of Apollo he fulfilled that condition, and married Alcestis. (See ALCESTIS.)

Admiral, L′, lăd'me'răl', (JEAN,) a French portrait-painter in miniature, born in Normandy in 1698. Died in 1773.

Ado, ä'do, SAINT, born about 800, in the territory of Gâtinois, in the north of Gaul, became Archbishop of Vienne in 860, and died in 875. He wrote a work purporting to be a chronicle of events from the creation to the year 874.

Adoaldus. See ADALOALDUS.

Adolf, ä'dolf, a German sculptor, who lived in the beginning of the sixteenth century.

Adolf, (JOSEPH FRANZ,) a German painter, who died about 1750. He excelled in painting horses.

Adolfi, ä-dol'fee, (CIRO,) an Italian painter, born at Bergamo in 1683; died in 1758. As an artist he was much superior to his brother Giacomo.

Adolfi, (GIACOMO,) a brother of the preceding, also a painter, was born in 1682; died in 1741.

Adolphe, (of Cleves, Guelders, etc.) See ADOLPHUS.

Adolphi, ä-dol'fee, (CHRISTIAN MICHAEL,) a German physician, professor of medicine at Leipsic, born in 1676; died in 1753.

Adolphi, (CIRO.) See ADOLFI.

A-dol′phus, [Fr. ADOLPHE, ă'dolf',] son of Arnold, the sixth Duke of Guelderland, born in 1438. He was in constant disputes with his father from his earliest years, and at length, in 1465, suddenly seized and imprisoned him, and then extorted from him a formal act of abdication. But he was afterwards compelled by John I., Duke of Cleves, and Charles the Bold, of Burgundy, to release him and restore to him all his possessions. Adolphus, in turn, was seized and kept in confinement for several years, during which time his father died. Having at length, on the death of Charles the Bold, been released, he was soon after killed, while besieging Tournay, in 1477.

Adolphus (or **Adolph**) **I.,** Duke of Holstein and Sleswick, son of Frederick I., King of Denmark, was born in 1526. He was distinguished as a soldier, and was the founder of several hospitals and flourishing public schools. Died in 1586, after a rule of forty-two years.

Adolphus (or **Adolph**) **I.,** Count of Holstein, one of the most remarkable men of his time, flourished in the early part of the twelfth century. Little is known respecting him, except that he was distinguished both as a statesman and a warrior, and contributed greatly to the diffusion of Christianity among the Wendi, a neighbouring nation of Slavonian origin. Died in 1131.

Adolphus (**Adolph**) **II.,** a son of the preceding, succeeded his father while still very young. Though at first unsuccessful in his campaign against Magnus, Duke of Sleswick, and in his war with Henry the Proud, Duke of Saxony, he soon recovered himself, and afterwards eclipsed even the glory of his father. He completely subdued the Wendi, and, by planting colonies in the territories which they had occupied, thoroughly Germanized the country. To those colonies the towns of Lubeck and Eutin owe their origin. He gained several victories over Canute, Prince of the Danes. In 1164, however, while engaged in the siege of Demmin, in Pomerania, he was, through treachery, suddenly attacked and slain, after an administration of thirty-three years.

Adolphus (**Adolph**) **III.,** Count of Holstein, was a son of Adolphus II., whom he succeeded. Although a valiant soldier, he appears to have been far inferior to his father in justice and wisdom. Having sided with Waldemar, Bishop of Sleswick, in his contest with Canute, King of Denmark, in 1200, Adolphus lost nearly all his possessions, and died soon after.

Adolphus (**Adolph**) **IV.,** son of the preceding, recovered Holstein from Waldemar, King of Denmark, whom he defeated in a great battle near Eutin. In 1238 he entered a monastery, where he passed the remaining fourteen years of his life as an humble friar.

Adolphus [Fr. ADOLPHE, ă'dolf'] **II.,** Duke of Cleves, was born in 1371. He was almost constantly engaged in wars, chiefly with his brother Gerard, Duke of Mark. He died in 1448, leaving behind him a high reputation for piety and justice, as well as for bravery and enterprise as a soldier.

Adolphus (**Adolph**) **VIII.,** Duke of Sleswick, was the son of Gerard, Count of Holstein. His father having died when he was but three years old, he received his education at the court of the emperor Sigismund. In 1440 Christopher, King of Denmark, conferred Sleswick upon Adolphus as a fief. When Christopher died, in 1448, the crown of Denmark was offered him, but he declined it. He died in 1459, leaving a high character for wisdom and justice.

Adolphus, (FREDERICK,) a king of Sweden, born in 1710, was descended from the royal line of Vasa. He was elected to the Swedish throne in 1743. The royal authority, however, was at this period almost entirely overborne by the council of the states; and, after having been continually thwarted in his wishes by that body, Frederick Adolphus at length, in 1769, tendered the resignation of his crown. Upon this the council made some trifling concessions, and he remained a nominal king till his death, in 1771.

Adolphus (or **Adolph**) **II.,** (JOHN, or JOHANN,) Duke of Saxe-Weissenfels, sprung from a collateral branch of the electoral (now royal) line of Saxony, was born in 1685. He early distinguished himself by his bravery and military skill. In 1704 he was made a lieutenant-general in the Hessian service, and in 1710, Augustus, Elector of Saxony, appointed him one of the generals of his forces then engaged against Charles XII. of Sweden. His two older brothers having died, Adolphus became Duke of Saxe-Weissenfels in 1736. In 1744 he took an active part against Frederick II. of Prussia; but, exhausted by the fatigues and hardships through which he had passed, he soon after retired to his duchy, where he died in 1746.

Adolphus (**Adolph**) OF NASSAU [in Latin, ADOL'-PHUS NASSOVIEN'SIS] was elected, in 1292, successor to Rudolph, Emperor of Germany. Though possessed of considerable military talents, by his falsehood and brutality he soon became very unpopular, and in 1298 was deposed by an assembly of the electors. He refused, however, to relinquish his power. But in a battle fought soon after (in 1298) between him and Albert his successor, Adolphus was slain, fighting desperately.

See J. P. WAGNER, "Vita Adolphi Nassoviensis," 1775-80: J. G. LEUCHS, "Adolph der Nassauer, Kaiser und König der Deutschen," 1798.

A-dol′phus, (JOHN,) an English lawyer and historian, born about 1770. He practised in the criminal courts of London, and had a high reputation as an eloquent advocate. His chief work is a "History of England, from the Accession of George III.," (7 vols., 1805-45,) which displays considerable research and learning. Among his other works we may name "Biographical Memoirs of the French Revolution," (4 vols., 1799.) He gained great credit by his able defence of Thistlewood, charged with treason, in 1820. Died in 1845.

Ad′om-nan′ or **Ad′am-nan′,** [Lat. ADOMNA'NUS

or ADAMNA′NUS,] also written **Adaman′nus**, an abbot of the monastery of Iona, born about 624. According to some writers, he was a native of Ireland ; according to others, of Scotland. He was a contemporary and friend of King Alfred of Northumbria. He is the author of a "Life of St. Columba," a curious work, which throws interesting light upon the political and social condition of that period.

Ad-o-ni′jah, [Heb. אֲדֹנִיָּה‎,] a son of King David and Haggith, who, near the close of his father's reign, aspired to the succession in opposition to the claims of Solomon. He was afterwards put to death by the order of Solomon, 1030 B.C., it is supposed. (See I. Kings i. 5 ; ii. 13.)

A-do′nis, [Gr. Ἄδωνις,] a son of Cin′yras, King of Cyprus, represented by the poets as a youth of exquisite beauty. He was passionately fond of hunting, and, notwithstanding the anxious admonitions of Venus, by whom he was greatly beloved, he exposed himself daily in the chase, and at last was killed by a boar which he had wounded. From his blood sprang the anemone, a beautiful flower. Venus was inconsolable at his loss ; but she obtained at last from Proserpine that Adonis should spend six months of every year with her on earth, and the other six in Hades. Adonis or Adonai (*i.e.* "Lord") was an Oriental title sometimes given to the sun, as the "lord of day :" the preceding fable, therefore, is supposed to allude to the periodical return of summer and winter. Hence the expressions " Beautiful as Adonis" and " Beautiful as day"* (in French, " Beau comme le jour") may be considered as equivalent to each other.

Adorni, â-dor′nee, (CATERINA or CATHERINA Fieschi—fe-ĕs′kee,) an Italian poetess, born at Genoa in 1447, wrote on religious subjects. Died in 1510.

See CATTANEO MARBATTO, " Vita de Catherina Adorni."

Adorno, â-dor′no, (in the plural, **Adorni**, â-dor′nee,) an influential Genoese family, from which, between 1360 and 1530, no fewer than six doges of Genoa were chosen. They held, however, a precarious authority, being ever and anon driven from the city according as the opposing faction (the Fregosi) chanced for the moment to prevail.

Adorno, (ANTONIO,) a doge of Genoa, elected in 1384, is said to have been an enlightened and liberal statesman. Died in 1397.

Adorno, (FRANCESCO,) an eminent Italian Jesuit, born about 1530, was the author of several theological works. Died in 1586.

Adorno, (PROSPER or PROS′PERO,) was elected Doge of Genoa in 1461, but was soon expelled from the city by Paul Fregoso. He was restored to power in 1477, and defeated the Duke of Milan in battle in 1478, soon after which he was driven out by a sedition. Died at Naples in 1486.

See VARESE, " Storia della Republica di Genova."

A-drain′, (ROBERT,) LL.D., a distinguished mathematician, born in Ireland in 1775. Having emigrated to America, he became successively professor of mathematics and natural philosophy in Rutgers College, New Brunswick, and Columbia College, New York, and subsequently professor of mathematics in the University of Pennsylvania. He edited Hutton's Mathematics. Died at New Brunswick, New Jersey, in 1843.

A-dras′tus, [Gr. Ἄδραστος; Fr. ADRASTE, ȧ′dRȧst′,] a king of Argos, contemporary with Theseus. He was the leader of a celebrated expedition against Thebes, the object of which was to restore Polynices to the throne of that state. This expedition, which was called the war of the " Seven against Thebes," was not successful. All of the Seven, except Adrastus, were killed at Thebes. The war of the Seven against Thebes was a favourite subject of ancient epic and tragic poets.

Adrastus, [Ἄδραστος,] a Greek, who wrote a commentary on the works of Aristotle, and a treatise on music, which is extant. Nothing is known of his life ; it is supposed that he lived in the first or second century.

Adrets, des, dȧ′zȧ′dRȧ′, (FRANÇOIS **Beaumont**—bō′mǒN′,) BARON, usually called simply **Des Adrets**,

---

* " For he was *beautiful as day*
When day was beautiful to me
As to young eagles being free."
BYRON's *Prisoner of Chillon.*

a celebrated French nobleman, born in 1513, became a leader of the Huguenots in 1562, out of resentment to the Duke of Guise. He was distinguished for great military talents, the boldness and celerity of his movements, and for the most atrocious cruelty. In 1567 he joined the Catholic party ; but soon after, incurring their suspicions, he was thrown into prison. Though released in 1571, he never regained his influence, but, distrusted and abhorred by all, died in 1587.

See GUI-ALLARD, " Vie du Baron Des Adrets," 1675.

Adria, ä′dre-ä, (GIOVANNI GIACOMO,) an eminent Italian physician, born at Mazara, in Sicily, about the beginning of the fifteenth century. The emperor Charles V. made him his own physician, ennobled him, and appointed him *proto-medicus* of Sicily. Died in 1560.

Adriaens, ä′dre-äns′, (LUCAS,) a Flemish painter, who lived in the latter half of the fifteenth century.

Adriaensen, ä′dre-än′sen, (ALEXANDER,) a Flemish painter, born at Antwerp about 1620. He painted flowers, fruit, vases, etc., with exquisite skill.

See DESCAMPS, " Vies des Peintres Flamands."

Adriaensen, (CORNELIS,) a popular Catholic preacher and Franciscan friar, born at Dordrecht (Dort) about 1520. The Protestants, to whom he was extremely obnoxious, charged him with the most scandalous conduct, —whether justly or not cannot now be determined. Died in 1581.

See VOET, " Historia von Bruder Cornelis, etc.," 1613.

Adrian, ä′dre-an, [Gr. Ἀδριανός; Lat. ADRIA′NUS,] a Greek writer of the fifth century, who wrote an introduction to the Scriptures.

A′drian [Ἀδριανός] or **Ha′drian** OF TYRE, a Greek sophist of the second century, studied eloquence at Athens under Herodes Atticus, whom he succeeded in his school. His reputation was so high that he was invited to Rome by Marcus Aurelius. He died at Rome during the reign of Commodus, whom he served as secretary.

Adrian or **Adrianus**, (Emperor.) See HADRIAN.

A′dri-an or **Hā′drĭ-an**,[Lat. ADRIA′NUS or HADRIA′-NUS,] a native of Africa, who was made abbot of the monastery of St. Peter, at Canterbury, about 670. According to Bede, he was a man of great learning, both theological and secular.

Adrian [Lat. ADRIA′NUS ; It. ADRIANO, ä-dre-ä′no ; Fr. ADRIEN, ȧ′dre-äN′] **I.**, son of Theodore, of a distinguished Roman family, was elected pope in 772. When Desiderius, King of the Longobards, had taken several towns belonging to the papal see, and was proceeding to Rome, Adrian threatened him with excommunication,—the first instance on record of such a threat to a sovereign prince. He was, however, indebted to Charlemagne for protection against the Longobard king. In the reign of this pontiff (A.D. 787) was held at Nicæa, (Nice,) in Bithynia, the seventh œcumenical council, which recognized and restored the worship of images. In 794 Charlemagne assembled at Frankfort-on-the-Main a general council of the West, which justified the use of images in churches, but condemned their worship,—a limitation disapproved by the pope, though countenanced by the King of the Franks. Adrian appears to have been an able and liberal prince. During his pontificate Rome enjoyed a degree of peace and prosperity to which she had long been a stranger. He built, or repaired, at his own expense, several public edifices ; he was also very liberal towards the poor. Died in 795.

See PANVINIO, " Vite dei Pontefici."

Adrian II., a native of Rome, succeeded Nicholas I. in the popedom in 867, and died in 872.

Adrian III., a native of Rome, succeeded Marinus as pope in 884, and died in 885.

Adrian IV. (NICHOLAS BREAKSPERE) was born about the end of the eleventh century, near Saint Albans, in England. Having gone to France to seek his fortune, he was made abbot of a monastery near Avignon in 1137. But the canons, displeased with his strict discipline, brought charges against his character, which obliged him to repair to Rome. The pope, Eugenius III., having examined the matter, not only acquitted Nicholas entirely, but was so pleased with him that he kept him about his person, and in 1146 appointed him Cardinal-Bishop of

---

ā, ē, ī, ō, ū, ȳ, *long;* ȧ, ė, ȯ, same, less prolonged; ă, ĕ, ĭ, ŏ, ŭ, ў, *short;* ạ, ẹ, ị, ọ, *obscure;* fär, fȧll, fȧt; mēt; nŏt; gōōd; mōōn·

Albano. After the death of Anastasius IV., in 1154, he was ráised to the holy see by the name of Adrian IV. He was a man of acknowledged talents, but his exalted views of papal supremacy involved him in serious differences with the emperor Frederick, (of Suabia,) which, still unsettled at his death, led to an open rupture during the pontificate of his successor, Alexander III. Adrian IV. died in 1159. He was the only Englishman ever raised to the papal chair.

Adrian V., a native of Genoa, was elected to the Roman see in 1276, and died the same year.

Adrian VI., a native of Utrecht, was raised to the papal see on the death of Leo X., in 1521. He had formerly been preceptor to the emperor Charles V., by whom he was greatly esteemed. He was a sincere and upright man, and saw with profound sorrow the scandalous abuses which then prevailed in the Catholic churches. He justly attributed the formidable progress of Protestantism to the sins of the Catholics, particularly to those of the higher clergy. He undertook and accomplished several important reforms ; which, however, rendered him extremely unpopular. When he died, (A.D. 1523,) the people of Rome, especially those about the court, expressed the most indecent joy.

See MORING, "Life of Adrian VI.," 1536 ; GASPAR BURMANN, "Analecta Historica de Hadriano VI.," 1727 ; L. E. ROSCH, "Jets over Paus Adriaan VI.," 1836.

A'drian de Cas-tel'lo or **Adriano di Castello,** â-dRe-â'no de kâs-tel'lo, a native of Tuscany, who was agent for English affairs at the court of Rome, and was afterwards appointed Bishop of Hereford, whence he was translated to the bishopric of Bath and Wells. He was made cardinal by Pope Alexander VI. Wolsey succeeded him as Bishop of Bath and Wells in 1518. He wrote Latin poems, and "On True Philosophy," ("De Vera Philosophia,") which was frequently printed. Died about 1520.

A'drĭ-an, [Russ. pron. â-dre-ân',] the last primate or patriarch of Russia, died in 1702, after which the office of patriarch was suppressed by Peter the Great.

Adrian, â'dRe-ân, (JOHANN VALENTIN,) a German littérateur, born at Klingenberg, on the Main, in 1793. He became professor of modern languages at Giessen in 1823. Among his works is one called "Pictures of England," ("Bilder aus England," 2 vols., 1828.)

Adriani, â-dRe-â'nee, (JOHN BAPTIST, or GIOVANNI BATTISTA,) an Italian historian, born at Florence in 1513. He was appointed, in 1549, professor of eloquence in the University of Florence, which office he held till his death in 1579. He wrote a "History of his own Times," ("Istoria de' suoi Tempi," 1583,) which is much esteemed.

Adriani, (MARCELLO,) a son of John Baptist Adriani, whom he succeeded as professor of eloquence. Died in 1604, aged about 70.

Adriani, (MARCELLO VIRGILIO,) the father of John Baptist Adriani. He was born at Florence in 1464, and became professor of belles-lettres ; in 1498 he was made chancellor of the republic. He made a good Latin version of Dioscorides' "De Materia Medica." Died in 1521.

Adriano, (Pope.) See ADRIAN.

Adriano (â-dRe-â'no) THE FRIAR, a Spanish historical painter, who was born at Cordova, and died there in 1630. He was a pupil of Cespedes, and painted a Magdalen, which Palomino pronounced equal to Titian in style.

Adriansen, â-dRe-ân'sen, (ALEXANDER,) a Flemish painter of fish, born about 1625.

Adrichomia, â-dre-ko'me-â, (CORNELIA,) a nun of the order of St. Augustine, in the sixteenth century, who versified the Psalms of David, and composed other sacred poems.

Ad-rĭ-cho'mĭ-us, (CHRISTIANUS,) a writer, born at Delft, in Holland, in 1533. Being a Catholic priest, he was driven from his native country on the overthrow of the authority of Spain, and died at Cologne in 1585. He left a work on the geography of the Holy Land, entitled "Theatrum Terræ Sanctæ," (1593.) He also wrote, under the name of Christianus Crucius, a "Life of Christ."

Adrien, the French of ADRIAN, which see.

Adry, ǎ'dRe', (JEAN F.,) a French writer, born near Auxerre in 1749. He was professor of rhetoric at Troyes, and afterwards received a pension from the government. He wrote several biographical works, besides making various compilations, translations, etc. Died in 1818.

Adryan, â-drĭ-ân', (ALBIN,) a Polish poet, born about 1490. Died at Cracow about 1540.

Ad'so, Az'o, or **As'so,**[Fr. ADSON, ǎd'sòN',] a French monk, born about 910 A.D. He wrote the lives of several saints.

Aduarte, â-DOO-aR'tâ, almost âd-wâR'tâ, (DIEGO,) a Spanish historian, born at Saragossa about 1570. He was a missionary to the Philippine Islands, and in 1632 was made Prior of Manilla, where he died in 1637. He has left a very interesting account of his missionary labours, and of the dangers and sufferings which he and the other Spanish missionaries encountered in consequence of their efforts to introduce Christianity into Cambodia ; he also wrote a history of the martyrdom of the Christian converts in Japan, and several other works.

Advenier-Fontenille, ǎd'veh-ne-â' fòNt'nèl' or fòNt'-ne'yĕ, a French captain of engineers. who wrote an opera and other works. Born at Paris in 1773 ; died in 1827.

Adventius, ad-ven'she-us, a bishop of Metz, who flourished in the latter half of the ninth century.

Æacides, ē-ass'e-dèz, [Gr. Αἰακίδης,] the father of Pyrrhus, King of Epirus, was killed in battle 313 B.C.

Æacus, ee'a-kus, [Gr. Αἴακος ; Fr. ÉAQUE, ǎ'ǎk',] (Myth.,) a son of Jupiter and Ægina, reigned in the island of Ægina. He was the father of Telamon and Peleus. He was renowned for justice and piety, and after his death became one of the judges of Hades.

Æantides, ē-an'te-dèz, [Αἰαντίδης,] a Greek poet, lived at Alexandria about 300 B.C.

Ædesius, ē-dee'she-us, [Gr. Αἰδέσιος,] a New-Platonist, native of Cappadocia, lived in the time of Constantine the Great. He was a disciple of the celebrated Iamblichus. Some of the most distinguished men of the subsequent age were taught by him ; among others, the emperor Julian.

Æetes, ē-ee'tèz, or **Æeta,** ē-ee'tạ, [Gr. Αἰήτης ; Fr. ÉÈTE, ǎ'èt' or ǎ'ǎt',] a fabulous king of Colchis, regarded as a son of Helios and Perseis, and the father of Medea and Absyrtus. He was renowned as the possessor of the golden fleece, the object of the Argonautic expedition.

Ægæon, ē-jee'on, [Gr. Αἰγαίων ; Fr. ÉGÉON, ǎ'zhâ'òN',] a monster said to have a hundred arms. (See BRIAREUS.)

Ægeus, ee'jūs, [Gr. Αἰγεύς ; Fr. ÉGÉE, ǎ'zhâ',] a king of Athens, was a son or adopted son of Pandi'on, and was the father of Theseus. According to tradition, he drowned himself in the Ægean Sea.

Ægidius-a-Columna. See COLONNA, EGIDIO.

Ægidius, ē-jid'e-us, (PETRUS,) OF ANTWERP, born in 1490, travelled in Asia and Africa, and wrote a "Description of Thrace," etc. Died in 1555.

Ægid'ius Corbolien'sis, a medical writer, and physician to Philip Augustus, King of France. lived about the end of the twelfth century. He wrote several medical treatises in Latin verse, which show him to have been a man of information and considerable poetical skill.

Ægid'ius Leodien'sis, or **Giles of Liège,** a monk and historical writer, lived between 1200 and 1250.

Ægidius Romanus. See COLONNA, EGIDIO.

Ægidius OF VITERBO [Lat. ÆGID'IUS VITERBIEN'SIS] was born near Viterbo in 1470. He was made cardinal in 1517, and died in 1532. He was regarded as one of the most eminent scholars and the best pulpit-orator of that age.

Ægimus, ej'I-mus, or **Ægimius,** ē-jim'e-us, [Αἴγιμος or Αἰγίμιος,] a Greek physician, who is supposed to have lived before the time of Hippocrates. He is said to have been the first who wrote particularly on the pulse.

Ægineta. See PAULUS ÆGINETA.

Æginhard. See EGINHARD.

Ægisthus, ē-jis'thus, [Gr. Αἴγισθος ; Fr. ÉGISTHE, ǎ'-zhèst',] in classic mythology was regarded as a son of Thyestes and Pelopea. The latter was a daughter of Thyestes. He was adopted as a son by Atreus, and in the absence of Agamemnon seduced Clytemnestra. He was an accomplice in the murder of Agamemnon, and was killed by Orestes.

Ægyptus, ē-jip′tus, [Gr. Αἴγυπτος; Fr. ÉGYPTUS, à′zhěp′tüs′,] a son of Belus, and a brother of Danaus. He inherited Arabia from his father, and obtained by conquest the country which derived from him the name of Egypt. The poets feigned that he had fifty sons, who were about to marry the fifty daughters of Danaus, but were murdered by them. (See DANAIDES.)

Ælfred. See ALFRED.

Ælfric or **Ælfricus.** See ALFRIC.

Ælian, ee′le-an, [Lat. ÆLIANUS, ē-le-ā′nus ; Gr. Αἰλιανός; Fr. ÉLIEN, à′le′ǎN′,] (CLAUDIUS,) a native of Præneste in Italy, lived in the early part of the third century. Although an Italian by birth, he ranks among the purest Greek writers. He is the author of a work entitled "Various History," made up chiefly of extracts from other authors, and of a history of animals, which, though written in a clear and agreeable style, is full of absurd stories.

Ælian or **Æ-lĭ-ā′nus Tac′tĭ-cus,** [Αἰλιανός Τακτικός,] a Greek writer, who flourished about the middle of the second century. He wrote a work on the military tactics of the Greeks, whence his surname "Tacticus."

Ælianus Meccius—mek′she-us, a Roman physician, who lived in the second century. He is mentioned by Galen with high commendation.

Ælius, ee′le-us, (SEXTUS PÆTUS CATUS,) an eminent Roman jurist, became consul in 536 A.U.C. A portion of the Roman law was named after him the Ælian law.

Ælius Donatus. See DONATUS.

Ælius Gallus. See GALLUS.

Ælius Marcianus. See MARCIANUS.

Æ′lius Pro-mo′tus, [Gr. Αἴλιος Προμῶτος,] a physician of Alexandria, who wrote several medical works in the Greek language. His date is uncertain. Most critics suppose that he lived before the Christian era.

Ælnoth, el′noth, a monk, who was born in England in the eleventh century, and removed to Denmark about 1085. He wrote a life of Saint Canute the Martyr.

Aelst or **Aalst, van,** văn ălst, (EVERT,) a distinguished Dutch painter, born at Delft in 1602. He painted principally inanimate objects, as dead game, vessels of gold and silver, etc. Died in 1658.

Aelst, van, (WILLEM,) a nephew of the preceding, by whom he was instructed, was born at Delft in 1620. He excelled in the same department of art as his uncle. He also represented fruits and flowers with exquisite skill. Died in 1679.

Æmilia, ē-mil′e-a, (JULIANA,) [Ger. pron. yoo-le-ä′nä à-mee′le-ä,] a countess of Schwarzburg-Rudolstadt, born in 1637. She married Count Albert Anton in 1665, and died in 1706. She was eminent for her benevolence and piety, and wrote a number of religious poems and hymns.

Æmilia Tertia, ē-mil′e-a ter′she-a, a daughter of Paulus Æmilius, and wife of Scipio Africanus the elder, a Roman matron, distinguished for her prudence and conjugal affection. Cornelia, the mother of the Gracchi, was her daughter.

Æmilianus, ē-mil-e-ā′nus, [Fr. ÉMILIEN, à′me′le′-ǎN′,] a Roman prefect of Egypt, put to death for rebellion, by order of the emperor Gallienus.

Æmilianus, (MARCUS JULIUS ÆMILIUS,) a native of Mauritania, born about 208 A.D. He was governor of Pannonia and Mœsia under the emperor Gallus. His soldiers having proclaimed him emperor, Gallus marched against him, but was murdered by his own men, who went over to Æmilianus. The reign of the latter, however, lasted but four months. He, in his turn, was killed by his own soldiers, at Spoletum, in 254 A.D.

Æmilius, ē-mil′e-us, or **Æmilianus,** ē-mil-e-ā′nus, a Christian martyr, put to death by Huneric, King of the Vandals, in 484 A.D.

Æmilius, (ANTONIUS,) a professor of history and a friend of Descartes, was born at Aix-la-Chapelle in 1589. He wrote Latin verses. Died in 1660.

Æmilia Macer. See MACER.

Æmilius, (MAMER′CUS,) a Roman, who was three times dictator. His first dictatorship was in 437 B.C.

Æmilius (PAULUS or PAULLUS) **I.,** a Roman consul and able general, who fell bravely at the battle of Cannæ, 216 B.C.

Æmilius (PAULUS or PAULLUS) **II.** See PAULUS.

Æmilius, (PAULUS,) an Italian historian. See EMILIO.

Æneæ, à-nā′à, (HENRICUS,) a Dutch mathematician and physicist, born in Friesland in 1743, became a member of the committee of the marine. He wrote a "Treatise on Hydrostatics," and other works. Died in 1810.

Æneas, ē-nee′as, [Gr. Αἰνείας; Fr. ÉNÉE, à′nà′,] the hero of Virgil's great poem, (the "Æneid,") was, according to tradition, the son of Anchises, a Trojan prince, and the goddess Venus. In the various accounts given of his life it is impossible to distinguish the fabulous from the historical. Some writers relate that he went to Thrace, and died there ; but, according to the more popular tradition, which is followed by Virgil, Æneas, after the destruction of Troy, came to Italy, married Lavinia the daughter of Latinus, King of Latium, and prepared the foundation of the Roman empire. He had a son, Ascanius or Iulus, to whom the Julian family of Rome traced their origin.

Æneas Gazæus—ga-zee′us, (so named from Gaza, where he was born,) a Platonic philosopher, who embraced Christianity in the latter half of the fifth century. He wrote a book called "Theophrastus," in which the Platonic and Christian doctrines are strangely blended.

Æneas Sylvius. See PIUS II.

Æneas Tacticus, [ὁ Τακτικός,] a Greek writer on military tactics, lived, it is supposed, 350 B.C.

Ænesidemus, ē-nĕs′e-dee′mus, [Gr. Αἰνησίδημος,] a skeptical philosopher, native of Gnossus, (or Cnossus,) in Crete, is supposed to have lived in the first century.

Ænobarbus. See AHENOBARBUS.

Æolus, ee′o-lus, [Gr. Αἴολος; Fr. ÉOLE, à′ol′,] in the Greek mythology, the god or ruler of the winds. He is said to have reigned in the Æolian Islands, and to have enjoyed the favour of Juno. For a vivid description of the country of the winds, and their prison, constructed of high mountains, whence they could issue only on the permission of Æolus, see Virgil's Æneid, book i. 51-63.

Æolus, a mythical personage, said to have been a son of Helen, a brother of Dorus, and the father of Cretheus, Athamas, and Sisyphus. He was supposed to be the founder of the Æolic branch of the Greek nation.

Æpinus, ē-pī′nus, (FRANZ MARIA ULRIC THEODOR,) a German natural philosopher and eminent electrician, born at Rostock in 1724. His proper name was HOCH. Having settled in Saint Petersburg in 1757, he became a member of the Academy of Sciences of that city, and professor of physics. He possessed great sagacity as an experimenter, discovered the electric properties of tourmaline, and is justly regarded, says Biot, as the inventor of the electrical condenser and electrophorus. His principal work is an attempt to establish a new theory of electricity, etc., entitled "Tentamen Theoriæ Electricitatis et Magnetismi," (1759.) In this he endeavoured to subject the phenomena of electricity to mathematical analysis. He contributed many memoirs to the academy above named. Died at Dorpat in 1802.

See "Mémoires de l'Académie de Berlin," 1756.

Æ-pi′nus, (JOHN,) [in German, HUCH or HOECK,] an eminent Protestant divine, born at Brandenburg in 1499, was a disciple of Luther. He became minister of a church in Hamburg in 1529, and was the most influential theologian in the North of Germany. In 1538 he signed the Articles of Schmalkalden. He wrote several polemical works. Died in 1553.

See ARNOLD GREVIUS, "Memoria Æpini," 1736.

A-e′rĭ-us, [Gr. 'Αέριος,] a native of Pontus, who lived in the fourth century. He was the founder of a heretical sect called Aerians. He opposed offering prayers for the dead, the keeping of Easter, and some other prevailing customs of the church.

Aerope, a-ēr′o-pe, [Gr. 'Αερόπη ; Fr. ÉROPE, à′rop′, or AÉROPE, ä′à′rop′,] a daughter of Crateus, King of Crete, was married to Plisthenes, and afterwards to

---

Atreus. She was the mother of Agamemnon and Menelaus.

Aerschot, DUKE OF. See AARSCHOT.

Aersens. See AARSENS.

Aertsen, ărt'sẹn, (PETER,) surnamed LUNGO, ("long,") an eminent historical painter, born at Amsterdam in 1519; died in 1573.

Aertsz, ărts, (RICHARD,) a Dutch historical painter, born at Wyck, in North Holland, in 1482, worked at Antwerp, and died in 1577.

Æschines, ês'ke-nêz, [Gr. Αἰσχίνης; Fr. ESCHINE, ês'-shěn',] a celebrated orator, and rival of Demosthenes, born at Athens about 389 B.C. He first became distinguished as a soldier in the battle of Mantinea, (362 B.C.,) and won the approbation of his general, Phocion, in that of Tamynæ, (350 B.C.) He began his political career as a violent opposer of Philip of Macedon; but, after his embassy to the Macedonian court, a change took place, and he afterwards opposed a war with the king as zealously as he had urged it before. This was either the cause or the pretext of a quarrel between him and Demosthenes, who charged Æschines with preferring Macedonian gold to the interests of his country. The contest which followed between the rival orators is one of the most remarkable in history, and it gave birth to perhaps the finest specimens of rhetorical genius and skill that are to be found in the literature of any nation. At length Demosthenes triumphed: Æschines went into exile, (330 B.C.,) and afterwards opened a school of rhetoric at Rhodes, where he taught with great applause. Died 314 B.C.

See LIBANIUS, "Vita Æschinis;" NORBERG, "Programmata ii. de Æschine Oratore," 1792; STECHOW, "De Æschinis Oratoris Vita," 1841; GROTE, "History of Greece," vol. xii. chap. xcv.; HIERON. WOLF, "Vita Demosthenis et Æschinis," 1572; W. F. PALMBLAD, "Æschines Atheniensium ad Philippum Regem Legatus," 1836; article "Æschines," by PASSOW, in ERSCH and GRUBER's "Allgemeine Encyklopaedie;" PLUTARCH, "Demosthenes," also "Vitæ Decem Oratorum."

Æschines surnamed SOCRAT'ICUS, a disciple of Socrates, by whom he was highly esteemed. He lived about 360 B.C.

Æschrion, ês'kre-on, [Gr. Αἰσχρίων,] a physician, native of Pergamus, and preceptor of Galen. He lived in the early part of the second century.

Æschylus, ês'ke-lus, [Gr. Αἰσχύλος; Fr. ESCHYLE, ês'shěl',] the first of the three great tragic poets of Greece, was born at Eleusis, in Attica, 525 B.C. He distinguished himself at the battle of Marathon, 490 B.C., and ever after regarded this as the most glorious event of his life. He gained his first prize in tragedy 484 B.C. Having in 468 B.C. been defeated by Sophocles in the first trial of this young poet, he left his native country and went to Syracuse, in Sicily, where he was held in great regard by King Hiero. He afterwards returned to Athens. The manner of his death, which took place 456 B.C., was extraordinary. An eagle soaring above him dropped a tortoise on the bald head of the poet, and killed him. Æschylus is said to have written seventy tragedies, besides a number of satiric dramas, and to have gained thirteen prizes. Seven of his tragedies are extant, viz., "Prometheus Bound;" "The Seven against Thebes;" "The Persians;" "The Female Suppliants;" "Agamemnon;" "Choephoræ;" and "Eumenides."

According to Macaulay, Æschylus was a great lyric poet, rather than a great dramatist. "Considered as plays," he remarks, "his works are absurd; considered as choruses, they are above all praise. . . . But if we forget the characters and think only of the poetry, we shall admit that it has never been surpassed in energy and magnificence." (See article on Milton in the "Edinburgh Review," 1825.)

Speaking of the spirit of Æschylus' poetry, another critic remarks, "If ever there was a poet filled with a deep sense of the sacred nature of his calling as the teacher of religion, and of all virtue as therewith connected, Æschylus was he. And this it is which—to all such as have studied him earnestly—gives a character to his poetry nothing less than awful." (See article entitled "Modern Criticism on Æschylus," in the "Quarterly Review" of October, 1839.)

See PETERSEN, "De Æschyli Vita et Fabulis," 1814; AHRENS,

"Ueber Æschylus," 1832; R.H.KLAUSEN, "Theologumena Æschyli Tragici," 1829; F. JACOBS, "Ueber den Charakter des Æschylus;" ROCHEFORT, "Sur la Vie d'Eschyle," 1785; FRENSDORFF, "Études sur Eschyle," 1847; K. O. MÜLLER, "History of the Literature of Ancient Greece;" EDWARD R. LANGE, "Programma de Æschylo Poeta," 1832.

Æsculapius, ês-ku-lā'pe-us, [Gr. Ἀσκληπιός, (Asklēpios); Fr. ESCULAPE, ês'kü'lăp',] (Myth.,) the god of medicine, supposed to have been the son of Apollo and Coronis. He is said to have raised men from the dead, so that Jupiter, fearing lest the realms of Pluto should become depopulated, struck him with thunder. After his death he was translated to heaven. He is usually represented as a venerable old man with a flowing beard. Hygieia (i.e. "Health") is said to have been a daughter of Æsculapius.

Æsir, ā'sịr, [Icelandic pron. ī'sịr,] sometimes incorrectly written **Asir, Asar,** or **Aser,** [the Norse plural of As, âs, or ASA, ä'sạ, a word of doubtful etymology, but not improbably related to the Sanscrit ăs, to "be," and applied to the gods as "beings" par excellence. ☞The German plural of As is ASEN, ä'zẹn; the English plural ASAS or ASES is sometimes used,] the name of the principal or ruling gods in the Norse mythology. They may be said to be the representatives of life, order, and progress, in contrast to the Jötuns, who typify, under various forms, confusion, desolation, and death. (See JÖTUNS, and VANIR.) Among the Æsir are generally reckoned twelve gods, viz., Odin, Thor, Balder, Niörd, (or Njörd,) Frey, (or Freyr,) Tyr, Bragi, Heimdall,Vidar, Vali, Ullur, and Forseti; and the same number of goddesses, Frigga, Freyia,(called also Van'adis,) Iduna, Eira, Saga, Fulla, Siöfn, (or Siona,) Lofn, (or Lovna,) Vara, (or Vör,) Hlin, Gefione, and Syn, (or Synia.)

The dwelling-place of the Æsir is called Asgard, (i.e. the "Asa court, ward, or garden.") It is represented as a vast fortress, sufficiently capacious to contain the mansions of all the gods and goddesses, as well as the field or plain of Ida, the assembling-place of the gods. It is Heimdall's special office to keep watch that the giants (Jötuns) do not approach Asgard unperceived. Odin also is said to have a lofty throne in Asgard, whence his eye surveys all the regions of the world. (See ODIN.)

For a more particular account of the Æsir, see separate articles in this work; also, THORPE's "Northern Mythology," vol. i., MALLET's "Northern Antiquities," vol. ii., and PETERSEN's "Nordisk Mythologi."

Æson, ee'sọn, [Gr. Αἴσων; Fr. ÉSON, ä'zöN',] (Myth.,) a son of Cretheus, king of Iolchos in Thessaly, and the father of Jason. He was deprived of the kingdom by his half-brother Pelias.

Æsop, ee'sọp, [Gr. Αἴσωπος; Lat. Æso'pus; Fr. ÉSOPE, ä'zop',] the celebrated fabulist, was born about 619, died 564 B.C. He is supposed to have been a Phrygian. He was the slave of Iadmon the Samian, who set him free as a reward for his wit and pleasantry. The Athenians erected a statue in honour of him. The fables of Æsop are among the very earliest compositions of this kind, and probably have never been surpassed for point and brevity, as well as for the practical good sense which they display. It should, however, be remembered that in most of the popular collections of fables which go under Æsop's name a large proportion are spurious, and perhaps all have been more or less modified by the translator or compiler. Phædrus says,

"Æsopo ingentem statuam posuere Attici,
Servumque collocarunt æterna in basi
Patere honoris scirent ut cunctis viam."[*]

See SUIDAS, "Æsopus;" BACHET DE MÉZIRIAC, "Vie d'Ésope," 1632; MANOEL MENDES, "Vida y Fabulas de Esopo," 1603; BENI LEV, "Dissertatio in Æsopi Fabulas;" A WESTERMANN, "Vita Æsopi," 1845; "Æsopi Leben und auserlesene Fabeln," Nuremberg, 1747; M. PLANUDES, "Vita Æsopi," 1505; CLINTON, "Fasti Hellenici," vol. i.

Æsopus, ē-so'pus, (CLODIUS,) the most eminent tragic actor of Rome, was a friend of Cicero, who speaks of him as an old man in 55 B.C. At this date he made his last appearance on the stage. He was grave, dignified, and impassioned, but less versatile and graceful than Roscius, his contemporary. He is styled gravis Æsopus by Horace.

* "The Athenians erected a great statue to Æsop, and placed [him who was] a slave on an eternal pedestal, that [men] might know that the road to glory was open to all."

Æthelred. See ETHELRED.

Ætherius, ē-_thee'_re-us, [Αἰθέριος,] a Greek architect, who flourished about 500 A.D., and built an edifice, called "Calchis," at Constantinople.

Æthicus or **Ethicus,** eth'e-kus, the supposed author of an ancient "Cosmography" of uncertain date, written in barbarous Latin, consisting of three treatises on Geography, one of which is by some ascribed to Julius Honorius, and another is found in Orosius, forming the second chapter of his history. In some MSS. he is surnamed _Ister,_ a native of Istria.

Æthra, ee'thrą, [Gr. Αἴθρα; Fr. ÉTHRA, ā'trĂ',] (Myth.,) a daughter of Pittheus, was a wife of Ægeus, and the mother of Theseus. She was taken as a captive to Sparta by Castor and Pollux, and became a servant of Helen.

Aetion, a-ee'te-on, ['Αετίων,] an eminent Greek painter of antiquity, who is supposed to have lived in the early part of the second century. His most celebrated work was a painting of the marriage of Alexander the Great and Roxana, which, it is said, exhibited the most exquisite skill.

Aetius, a-ee'she-us, sometimes improperly written **Ætius,** a Roman general, born near the end of the fourth century. For many years he successfully defended Gaul against the encroachments of the barbarians. In 451, when Attila the Hun had besieged and was on the point of taking Orleans, the approach of the combined armies of Aetius and Theodoric obliged him to raise the siege ; and, these generals having followed the Huns in their retreat to the plains of Châlons, a great but indecisive battle was fought, in which 300,000 men are said to have been slain. Soon after, Attila retreated beyond the Rhine. But the emperor Valentinian, having become jealous of the fame and influence of Aetius, slew him with his own hand in 454. The emperor, it is said, asked a Roman if he had done well in killing Aetius. He replied, "I do not know ; but I think you have cut off your right hand with your left."

See GIBBON, "Decline and Fall of the Roman Empire ;" JORNANDES, "De Rebus Geticis."

Aetius, a-ee'she-us, written also, but incorrectly, **Ætius,** ['Αέτιος,] a Greek physician, who is supposed to have lived at Amida about the end of the fifth century. He wrote a work on medicine, divided into sixteen books, which is extant, and possesses great merit.

Aetius surnamed THE ATHEIST, a heresiarch of the fourth century, who favoured the doctrine of the Arians, and taught fatalism. He wrote a work in defence of his doctrines, and had a number of followers, called Aetians.

Aettenkover or **Ättenkover,** et'ten-ko'ver, (JOSEPH ANTON,) a German historian, wrote a "History of the Dukes of Bavaria." Died at Munich in 1775.

Afer, ā'fer, (DOMITIUS,) a distinguished Roman orator, who flourished in the reigns of the emperors Tiberius and Caligula. He was born at Nîmes, (Nemausus,) in Gaul, 15 B.C., and died 60 A.D. He was the preceptor of Quintilian, (by whom his oratory was highly extolled,) and was made consul by Caligula.

Afesa, ā-fā'så, (PIETRO,) an eminent Italian painter, who flourished about the middle of the seventeenth century. He was born in Basilicata, a province of Naples.

Affaitati, åf-fī-tä'tee, (FORTUNIO,) an Italian of the sixteenth century, who wrote a work on astronomy and natural philosophy, (1549.) He was drowned in the Thames, England, about 1550.

Affelman, åf'fel-mån, (JOHANN,) a German theologian, born at Soest in 1588, was professor at Rostock, where he died in 1624.

Affichard, l', lå'fe'shĂr', (THOMAS,) a French dramatist and romance-writer, born in 1698 ; died in 1753.

Afflitto, åf-flèt'to, (GIOVANNI MARIA,) a Neapolitan monk, who wrote a "Treatise on Fortifications." Died in 1673.

Afflitto, d', dåf-flèt'to, (EUSTACHIO,) an Italian Dominican, wrote "Memoirs of the Writers of the Kingdom of Naples," ("Memorie degli Scrittori del Regno di Napoli,") 2 vols., 1792, (unfinished.) Died in 1709.

Afflitto, d', (MATTEO,) [in Latin, MATTHÆ'US DE AFFLIC'TIS,] an eminent Italian lawyer, was born in

Naples in 1448. He became professor of civil and canon law in the University of Naples in 1469. He wrote a number of works, all on the subject of law. Died in 1524.

Affo, åf'fo, (IRENEO,) an Italian historian, philologist, and antiquary, born at Busseto, in the duchy of Parma, in 1741 ; died about 1800. His works are very numerous : they relate chiefly to the antiquities and history, both literary and political, of his native country, Parma. He is regarded as one of the most eminent Italian critics and philologists that the last century produced.

Affonso. See ALFONSO.

Affre, åfr, (DENIS AUGUSTE,) Archbishop of Paris, born at Saint-Rome-de-Tarn in 1793. He was appointed canon titular and vicar-general at Paris in 1834. Having become Archbishop of Paris in 1840, he distinguished himself by his virtues. During the insurrection of June, 1848, he made a noble effort to arrest the carnage. The troops having at his request suspended their fire, he advanced towards the insurgents, preceded by M. Albert, who wore the dress of a workman and carried a green branch. He began to address the insurgents, who, hearing the report of a gun, and suspecting treachery, opened a fire on the Garde Mobile, and he was mortally wounded. He left, besides several religious works, an "Essay on the Egyptian Hieroglyphics," (1834.)

See ABBÉ CRUICE, "Vie de Denis Auguste Affre," 1849; DENIS E. AFFRE, "Biographie de D. A. Affre," 1848 ; E. GOURDON, "Biographie authentique de l'Archevêque de Paris, D. A. Affre," 1848.

Affrikan, åf-fre-kån', (a corruption of **Africanus,**) the name by which Chaucer designates SCIPIO AFRICANUS the elder. (See the "Assembly of Foules.")

Affry, ă'fRe', (LOUIS,) of a Swiss family, was born at Versailles in 1713. In 1755 he was sent as French minister to the Hague. He afterwards became colonel of the Swiss guards under Louis XVI. In 1792 he was imprisoned by the revolutionists ; on being released, he retired to Switzerland. Died in 1798.

Affry, (LOUIS AUGUSTE PHILIPPE,) COUNT, a son of the preceding, was born at Friburg in 1743. He was a lieutenant-general in the French army; but after the massacre of 1792, in which he lost a brother, he retired to Friburg. He afterwards became _Landamann_ or chief of the Helvetic Confederacy, as established in 1803. Died in 1810.

Afhacker, åf'håk'er, (GILES,) a Dutch theologian, born at Vreeswyk, lived about 1600.

A-frā'nĭ-us, (LUCIUS,) a Roman comic poet and orator, who flourished about 100 B.C. Scarcely anything of his writings has been preserved.

A-frā'nĭ-us or **Afra'nius Ne'pos,** (LUCIUS,) an adherent of Cneius Pompey, was killed in Africa by the soldiers of Cæsar, 46 B.C.

Afrasiâb, ā-frä-se-åb', a semi-fabulous king of ancient Persia, who, though born in Tartary, (Turân,) claimed to be a direct descendant of the famous Fereedoon, (Feridûn.) He is said, with an army of Tartars, to have invaded Persia, which he conquered after an obstinate resistance and for many years ruled with a rod of iron. The people, exasperated by his tyranny, rose in rebellion, and, headed by Zâl, (the father of Rõõstum,) drove out Afrasiâb and restored the lawful line of Persian kings to the throne. Afrasiâb is supposed to have lived about 1000 years before the Christian era.

Africanus. See SCIPIO AFRICANUS.

Africanus, Leo. See LEO, (JOHN.)

Af-rĭ-cā'nus, (SEXTUS CÆCILIUS,) a Roman jurist, who is supposed to have lived in the second century.

Africanus, (SEXTUS JULIUS,) [Fr. SEXTE JULES AFRICAIN, sĕxt zhül ă'fRe'kăN',] a Christian writer, who lived in the early part of the third century. He was a man of extensive learning, and wrote a history of the world from the creation to the year 221 A.D. He fixes the date of the creation 5499 years B.C., and the birth of Christ three years earlier than the ordinary computation. The era thus fixed is known as the historical era, or that of the Alexandrian historians. He is supposed to have died in 232 A.D.

Af-ze'lĭ-us, [Sw. pron. åf-tsī'le-ùs,] (ADAM,) a Swedish botanist, born in 1750. He was a pupil of Linnæus. Having visited England in 1789, he was appointed botanist to the Sierra Leone Company. In 1792 he left

ā, ē, ī, ō, ū, ȳ, _long;_ ă, ĕ, ĭ, ŏ, ŭ, ў, _short;_ ą, ę, į, ǫ, _obscure;_ fär, fåll, fåt; mēt; nŏt; gŏŏd; mŏŏn;

London for Africa, and returned in 1794 with collections of plants from the regions which he visited. In 1812 he became professor of dietetics and materia medica in the University of Upsal, an office which he held till his death in 1836. Most of the writings of Afzelius are in the form of papers contributed to different scientific periodicals.

Afzelius, (ARVID AUGUST,) a Swedish historical writer, born in 1785. Among his works is "Legendary History of the Swedish People," ("Svenska Folkets Sagohäfder," 1839–43.)

Afzelius, (JOHAN,) a Swedish chemist, born in 1753, was a brother of Adam, noticed above. He became professor of chemistry at Upsal. Died in 1837.

Ag′a-bus, a Christian prophet in the time of the apostles. (See Acts xi. 28, and xxi. 10.)

Ag-a-me′dēs ['Αγαμήδης] and **Trophonius,** two ancient architects of Greece, who are supposed to have lived in the time of Homer. See TROPHONIUS.

Ag-a-mem′non, ['Αγαμέμνων,] the son of Atreus, King of Mycenæ, and brother of Menelaus, was appointed generalissimo of the Greek forces during the Trojan war. On his return to his native country, Argolis, after the destruction of Troy, he was murdered by his wife Clytemnestra and her paramour Ægisthus, who had possessed the kingdom in his absence. He was the father of Orestes, Electra, and Iphigeni′a. He and his brother Menelaus were often called ATRI′DÆ.
See HOMER's "Iliad;" ÆSCHYLUS, "Agamemnon."

Aga- (or **Agha-**) **Mohammed,** ä′gä mo-hâm′med, the founder of the present dynasty of Persia, was born in 1734. He was an artful as well as a warlike prince. Commencing his career about 1780, he overran in a few years a large part of Persia, also Georgia and Khorassân. He was assassinated in 1797.

Aganduru, ä-gän-doo′roo, or **Aganduro,** ä-gän-doo′ro, (RODRIGO MAURICIO,) a Spanish missionary, who laboured in Japan about 1640. He wrote a "History of the Moluccas and Philippine Islands."

Ag-a-pe′tus, [Gr. 'Αγαπητός; Fr. AGAPET, ä′gä′pĕ′,] a deacon of the principal church of Constantinople, lived in the sixth century. He is the author of a work addressed to the emperor Justinian in 527, containing many excellent precepts, religious, moral, and political.

Agapetus I., an archdeacon of Rome, who was elevated to the Roman see in 535. Died at Constantinople in 536.

Agapetus II. was raised to the Roman see in 946. He is supposed to have died about 955.

Agar. See HAGAR.

Agar, ä′gär′, or **d'Agar,** dä′gär′, (JACQUES,) a native of Paris, born in 1640. He became court painter and chamberlain to Christian V., King of Denmark, and died at Copenhagen in 1716.

Agar, ä′gär′, (JEAN ANTOINE MICHEL,) Count of Mosbourg, a French administrator, born near Cahors in 1771. He was chosen a member of the legislative body in 1804, and became minister of finances to Murat, Duke of Berg, in 1806. Murat having ascended the throne of Naples, Agar administered the finances of that kingdom with success from 1809 to 1815. He was elected to the French Chamber of Deputies in 1830, and became a peer of France in 1837. Died in 1844.

Agar, ä-gär′, (PEDRO,) a Spanish officer, born in America, was one of the three members of the regency chosen in 1808 by the Cortes after the abdication of Charles IV. His conduct was prudent and moderate. He was banished by the absolutists in 1814. On the revolution of 1820 he became president of the Junta of Galicia. He resigned in July of that year. Died about 1840.

Agarde or **Agard,** ä-gard′, (ARTHUR,) an eminent English archivist and antiquary, born at Foston about 1540, became one of the deputy chamberlains in the Exchequer in 1570. He contributed several treatises to the Society of Antiquaries, which were published by Hearne. Died in 1615.
See HEARNE, "Curious Discourses."

Agardh, ä′gard, (KARL ADOLPH,) a Swedish naturalist, was born at Bastad, or Bostad, in Scania, in 1785. He became professor of botany and rural economy at Lund about 1812, and was ordained a priest in 1816.

Besides several works on theology and economy, he published many remarkable treatises on botany, among which we notice "Species of Sea-weeds," ("Species Algarum," 1820–28,) "Systematic Arrangement of Seaweeds," ("Systema Algarum," 1824,) and a "Manual of Botany," (2 vols., 1830–31.) He was appointed Bishop of Karlstad in 1834. Died in October, 1862.
See "Biographiskt Lexicon öfver namnkunnige Svenska Man."

A-gā′sĭ-as, [Gr. 'Αγασίας,] a sculptor of Ephesus, who is supposed to have lived about 400 B.C. He was the author of a statue called the Fighting Gladiator, a fine specimen of ancient art, discovered at Antium (where the Apollo Belvidere was also found) in the beginning of the seventeenth century.

Agassiz, ä′gä′see′ or ą-gas′sĭz, (LOUIS,) a Swiss naturalist of great eminence, was born in the parish of Motier, near the lake of Neufchâtel, in 1807. His father was a Protestant divine. Young Agassiz studied the medical sciences at Zurich, Heidelberg, and Munich, where he graduated about 1830. In 1827 he was selected by Martius to describe the species of fishes which Spix had brought from Brazil, and on which he produced an able work in Latin, (1829–31.) He had previously, during the college vacations, visited many parts of Europe to study the fossil and fresh-water fishes. In 1832 or '33 he was appointed professor of natural history or zoology at Neufchâtel. He published a "Natural History of the Fresh-Water Fishes of Central Europe," (1839,) and "Researches on Fossil Fishes," (14 livraisons, or 5 vols., with 311 plates, 1832–42,) a work of high order, in which he made important changes in classification.

The Transactions of the British Association, the "Annales des Sciences Naturelles," and other journals, contain many contributions from Agassiz on fossil fishes and on geology. He propounded some new and remarkable ideas on geology and the agency of glaciers, in his capital work entitled "Études sur les Glaciers," (1840,) and in his "Système Glacière," (1847.)

In 1846 he visited the United States on a scientific mission, and about the end of 1847 was induced to accept the professorship of zoology and geology at Harvard University, Cambridge. About 1854 he declined the offer of a chair of natural history in the University of Edinburgh. He has delivered several courses of lectures in Boston, and has given a decided impulse to the study of his favourite sciences in the New World. M. Agassiz favours the theory that the human race is not descended from a single pair, and discredits that of organic development, or metamorphosis, which was maintained by Lamarck and others. In 1865 he went to Brazil with a corps of assistants, and explored the Lower Amazon and its tributaries with reference to natural history, geology, etc. It is stated that he discovered more than 1800 new species of fishes in that region.

Among his other works are a "Monography of Living and Fossil Echinodermata,"(1838–42,) "Outlines of Comparative Physiology," (1848,) "Principles of Zoology," in conjunction with Dr. A. A. Gould, (2d edition, 1851,) "Contributions to the Natural History of the United States," to be completed in ten volumes, quarto, of which the first two were published in 1857; and a "Journey in Brazil," (1868.) Mr. Agassiz became in 1868 a non-resident professor at the Cornell University at Ithaca, New York.

"In the operation of his [Agassiz's] mind," says one of the ablest of American critics, "there is no predominance of any single power, but the intellectual action of what we feel to be a powerful nature. When he observes, his whole mind enters into the act of observation ; just as, when he reasons, his whole mind enters into the act of reasoning. . . . He is not merely a scientific thinker ; he is a scientific force ; and no small portion of the immense influence he exerts is due to the energy, intensity, and geniality which distinguish the nature of the man. In personal intercourse he inspires as well as informs, communicates not only knowledge, but the love of knowledge. . . . He is at once one of the most dominating and one of the most sympathetic of men, having the qualities of leader and companion combined in singular harmony." (See WHIPPLE's "Character and Characteristic Men," Boston, 1866.)

Ag'a-tha, SAINT, [Fr. SAINTE-AGATHE, sån'tä'gåt',] a virgin martyr of Sicily in the middle of the third century. She was put to death by Quintianus, Proconsul of Sicily, in 251.

See Mrs. JAMESON, "Sacred and Legendary Art;" TILLEMONT, "Mémoires ecclés astiques," etc.

Ag-a-than'ge-lus, an Armenian historian, lived about 320 A.D., and was secretary to King Tiridates.

Ag-a-thar'chi-des ['Αγαθαρχίδης] or **Ag-a-thar'-chus,** a Greek writer and grammarian, born at Cnidos, lived about 130 B.C. He was guardian to the young king of Egypt, probably Ptolemy Soter II., who became king 117 B.C.

Ag-a-thar'chus, [Gr. Αγάθαρχος; Fr. AGATHARQUE, ä'gä'täRk',] a Greek painter, who lived about 480 B.C., is considered as the first artist who applied the laws of perspective in painting. Vitruvius says that he made a scene for Æschylus at Athens. From the context it is inferred that a painted perspective scene is signified.

Agatharchus, a Greek painter, born at Samos, lived about 420 B.C. He was patronized by Alcibiades, who once confined him in his house until he had painted certain pictures which he had ordered. Plutarch states that he boasted of his facility and rapidity in the presence of Zeuxis, who reproved him by a simple remark that he (Zeuxis) painted slowly.

Agatharque. See AGATHARCHUS.

Agathe. See AGATHA.

Ag-a-them'e-rus, [Gr.'Αγαθήμερος; Fr. AGATHÉMÈRE, ä'gä'tà'maiʀ',] the author of a small work on geography in Greek, is supposed to have lived about 200 A.D.

A-ga'thi-as, ['Αγαθίας,] surnamed ASIANUS, a-she-ā'-nus, a Greek historian and poet, born at Myrina, in Asia Minor, in the early part of the sixth century. He studied at Alexandria, and afterwards settled at Constantinople, where he died about 580. He commenced a history of his own time, but left it unfinished. His history and some of his epigrams are extant; his other poems are lost.

Ag-a-thi'nus, ['Αγάθινος,] an eminent Greek physician, born at Sparta, lived in the latter half of the first century. He was a pupil of Athenæus, from whose doctrines, however, he dissented in many points, and founded a school or sect of his own.

Agatho. See AGATHON.

Agathocle. See AGATHOCLES.

A-gath-o-cle'a, [Gr. 'Αγαθόκλεια; Fr. AGATHOCLÉE, ä'gä'to'klå',] a mistress of Ptolemy Philopator, who, with her brother Agathocles, obtained an absolute ascendency over that king. After his death, which for a time was kept secret, Agathocles ruled in the name of the young prince; but his tyranny became so intolerable that the people rose in revolt, and killed him, his sister, and also his mother Œnanthe, who had been the first, if not the principal, instigator of his crimes.

A-gath'o-cles, [Gr. 'Αγαθοκλῆς; Fr. AGATHOCLE, ä'gä'tok'l',] a tyrant of Syracuse, who reigned from 317 to 289 B.C. Born at Thermi, in Sicily, he learned the trade of a potter. Being distinguished, however, for bodily strength and beauty, he was raised to the military rank of chiliarch. He afterwards married a rich widow, and became in consequence one of the wealthiest of the Syracusans. As an officer he was not only brave and fertile in resources, but he was distinguished for readiness and boldness as an orator. In 317 B.C. he caused all the men of note opposed to him in Syracuse to be massacred, and became ·tyrant of the city. The subsequent career of Agathocles is marked with a variety of fortune, in which the boldness, cruelty, and treachery of his character are conspicuous. His death, as related by Diodorus Siculus, is remarkable. His grandson Archagathus, aspiring to the succession, corrupted a favourite of his grandfather, named Mænon, who gave him a poisoned toothpick, by which his mouth became incurably gangrened. Being speechless, he was placed on a funeral pile and burnt while still alive, (289 B.C.,) in his seventy-second year.

See R. PERRINCHIEF, "The Sicilian Tyrant; or, The Life of Agathocles," London, 8vo, 1661; DIODORUS SICULUS, "History."

Agath'ocles OF CYZ'ICUS,·a Greek historian, lived probably about 100 or 150 B.C. He wrote a "History of Cyzicus," which is lost.

Agathocles OF EGYPT. See AGATHOCLEA.

Agathodæmon, ag'a-tho-dee'mon, [Gr. 'Αγαθοδαί-μων,] OF ALEXANDRIA, an ancient geographer and map-maker of an uncertain date. He probably lived after 200 A.D.

Ag'a-thon or **Ag'a-tho,** ['Αγάθων,] an eminent Greek tragic poet, born at Athens about 450 B.C., was a contemporary and friend of Plato and Euripides. He gained the prize in tragedy at a public festival in 417 B.C. His works are praised by Plato and Aristotle. He was rather fond of antithesis and sophistical subtleties. Only a few fragments of his works remain. Died about 400 B.C.

See BENTLEY, "Dissertation on the Epistles of Euripides."

Agathon, a monk, native of Sicily, was raised to the Roman see in 679, and died in 681 A.D.

Agay, d', dä'gå', (FRANÇOIS MARIE Bruno—brü'no',) COUNT, a French jurist, born at Besançon in 1722. Died in 1805.

Agazzari, ä-gåt-så'ree, (AGOSTINO,) an Italian musician, native of Sienna. Died about 1640.

A-gel'a-das, ['Αγελάδας,] a Grecian sculptor, who lived at Argos about 500 B.C. He was the master of Phidias.

Agelet, äzh'lå', or **d'Agelet,** däzh'lå', (JOSEPH Le Paute—lĕh pōt,) a French astronomer, born in 1751. He became professor of mathematics in the École Militaire in 1777. He accompanied La Pérouse on his voyage of discovery in 1785, and perished with him in 1788. (See LA PÉROUSE.)

Agelli, â-jel'lee, [Lat. AGEL'LIUS,] (ANTONIO,) a distinguished Italian commentator, born at Sorrento in 1532. He was made Bishop of Acerno in 1593, and died in 1608. He wrote a commentary on the Psalms, the Lamentations of Jeremiah, and many other parts of Scripture.

Agellio, â-jel'le-o, (GIUSEPPE,) an Italian painter, born at Sorrento. He worked at Rome in the early part of the seventeenth century, and excelled in landscapes. He assisted Roncalli and other artists in the figures and the landscapes of their paintings.

Agellius. See GELLIUS, AULUS.

Ag'el-noth, [Lat. AGELNO'THUS,] also called **Eth'-el-noth,** an archbishop of Canterbury, who lived in the early part of the eleventh century, and died in 1038. He was one of the principal advisers of the Danish king Canute.

See HOOK, "Lives of the Archbishops of Canterbury," vol. iii. chap. iii.

A-ge'nor, [Gr. 'Αγήνωρ; Fr. AGÉNOR, ä'zhå'noʀ',] a fabulous king of Phœnicia, regarded as a son of Neptune, a brother of Belus, and the father of Cadmus, Phœnix, Phineus, and Europa.

Agenor, a brave Trojan warrior, was a son of Antenor. According to Homer, he wounded Achilles, and was rescued from him by Apollo.

Ager, ä'zhå', [in Latin, AGE'RIUS,] (NICOLAS,) a French botanist, born in Alsace in 1568, wrote a treatise "On Vegetable Life," ("De Anima Vegetiva," 1629.) Died in 1634.

Ag-e-san'der, [Gr. 'Αγήσανδρος; Fr. AGÉSANDRE, ä'zhå'zòNdʀ',] a sculptor of Rhodes, mentioned by Pliny as one of the three artists who executed a group of Laocoon and his sons, which was in the palace of Titus at Rome. This same group, there is reason to believe, is now in the Vatican. It was accidentally discovered in 1506. The time of Agesander is unknown; some suppose him to have been contemporary with the earlier Roman emperors.

Agesias. See HEGESIAS.

A-ges'i-cles, a king of Sparta, who lived about 600 B.C.

A-ges-i-la'us [Gr. 'Αγησίλαος; Fr. AGÉSILAS, ä'zhå'-ze'lås'] I., a king of Sparta, who lived in the ninth century B.C. He was contemporary with Lycurgus.

Agesilaus II., one of the most distinguished of the Spartan kings, was a son of Archidamus. He ascended the throne at the death of his brother Agis in 398 B.C., and reigned thirty-seven years in the most eventful period in the history of Sparta. In the second year of his reign he commanded an expedition into Persia, in which, by his generosity and courtesy, as well as by his success as a general, he won over to his cause many of the subjects of Artaxerxes. He even contemplated the conquest of the Persian empire; but the accomplishment of this great scheme was prevented by a hostile confederacy of the Greeks at home. He was summoned home by the Ephori about 394 B.C. In the subsequent contest between the Spartans on the one side, and the Argives, Thebans, Athenians, and Corinthians on the other, Agesilaus, if not always successful, at least fully justified the high opinion which his countrymen entertained of his statesmanship and military skill. His vigilance and energy saved the city of Sparta, which was menaced by Epaminondas in 362. He was not present at the battle of Leuctra, where the Spartans were defeated in 371. He died about 361 B.C., being more than eighty years old.

See "Life of Agesilaus," by PLUTARCH, who compares him with Pompey; XENOPHON, "Agesilaus" and "Hellenica;" CORNELIUS NEPOS, "Agesilaus;" GROTE, "History of Greece," vol. ix. chaps. lxxiii.–lxxiv.; THIRLWALL, "History of Greece;" CAUER, "Questionum de Fontibus ad Agesilai Historiam pertinentibus," Pars I., Breslau, 1847.

Ag̃-e-sip′o-lis, [᾽Αγησίπολις,] a Spartan king, who ascended the throne as colleague of Agesilaus in 394. Died in 380 B.C.
There were several other kings of this name.

Agezio or **Agesio,** ä-gā′ze-o, (THADDEUS,) a Bohemian, born at Prague in 1525, wrote on physiognomy.

Ag′gas or **Au′gus,** (ROBERT,) an English landscape-painter, who lived in the reign of Charles I. Died in 1679, aged about 60.

Aggée. See HAGGAI.

Aggenus Urbicus, ad-jee′nus ur′be-kus, a Latin writer on agriculture, who probably lived in the time of the emperor Vespasian.

Agha-Mohammed. See AGA-MOHAMMED.

Agier, ä′zhe-ā′, (PIERRE JEAN,) a French judge, born in Paris in 1748. He was president of the revolutionary tribunal in 1795, when Fouquier-Tinville and his accomplices were condemned to death, and became vice-president of the tribunal of appeal in Paris in 1802. He published, besides several legal works, a new version of the Hebrew Prophets, (11 vols., 1820–23.) Died in 1823.

Agila, aj′e-la, or **Agilan,** aj-e-lan′, a Gothic king of Spain, who began to reign in 549, and was murdered in 554 A.D.

Agiles, d′, dä′zhèl′ or dä′zhe′lès′, (RAYMOND,) Canon of Puy, followed the Count of Toulouse to Palestine, and wrote a "History of the Crusade of 1095."

Ag̃-ĭ-lul′fus or **Agilul′phus,** [Fr. AGILULPHE, ä′zhe′-lülf′,] a Longobard duke of Turin, who became King of the Longobards, in 590, by marrying Theudelinda, the widow of King Autaris or Autarich. Through her influence he embraced the Catholic faith, and induced many of his nobles to do the same. He died in 616 A.D. From the reign of Agilulfus may be dated the commencement of civilization among the Longobards.

Agincourt. See D'AGINCOURT.

Agis, ā′jis, [᾽Αγις.] There were four kings of Sparta of this name. The first began to reign about 1060 B.C. The second became king 427 B.C., and reigned twenty-eight years, during a great part of the Peloponnesian war. He defeated the Athenians and their allies in a great battle at Mantinea, about 414 B.C. He died in 399 B.C. Agis III. ascended the throne in 338 and died 331 B.C., being contemporary with Alexander the Great. Agis IV. began to reign 244 B.C. He attempted to restore the ancient Spartan discipline, and the simplicity of manners which had prevailed under the earlier Spartan kings; but the nation was too deeply sunk in effeminacy and corruption. Agis became a martyr to his virtuous ambition. He was condemned by the Ephori for an attempt to subvert the laws of his country, and was strangled 240 B.C. He met his death with a heroism worthy of the glorious cause in which he had been engaged.

See PLUTARCH, "Life of Agis;" THIRLWALL, "History of Greece," vol. viii. chap. lxii.; BARRAU, "Histoire d'Agis IV, Roi de Lacédémone," 8vo, 1817.

A′g̃ĭ-us (or **Agio,** ä′jo) **de Solda′nis,** dà sol-dä′-nèss, (PIETRO,) an Italian antiquary, born in the isle of Gozzo. Died in 1760.

Aglaia. See CHARITES.

Ag-lā′o-phon, [᾽Αγλαοφῶν,] a painter, native of Thasos, (a Grecian island,) supposed to have lived about 500 B.C. He was the father of Polygnotus the painter.

Aglaophon, a Greek painter, supposed to have been a descendant of the preceding, lived about 416 B.C. He painted a picture of Alcibiades.

Agliata, äl-yä′tä, (GIOVANNI,) a distinguished Sicilian lawyer, born at Palermo, held several high offices under the government. Died in 1675.

Aglietti, äl-yet′tee, (FRANCESCO,) an Italian physician, born in 1757. Died in 1836.

See ZANNINI, "Biografia di F. Aglietti," Padua, 1836.

Ag′lĭ-on-bў̃, (JOHN,) an English divine, born in Cumberland about 1568. He was chaplain to Queen Elizabeth, and one of the translators of the New Testament for the English Bible authorized by James I. Died in 1610.

Agnani, di, de än-yä′nee, (GIOVANNI,) an Italian jurist, born about 1390, was professor of law at Bologna. Died in 1457.

Agneaux. See AIGNEAUX.

Agnelli, än-yel′lee, (GIUSEPPE,) an Italian Jesuit, who wrote several theological works. Born in 1621; died in 1706.

Agnelli, (JACOB, or JACOPO,) an eminent Italian Jesuit, born at Ferrara in 1701. He was professor of eloquence, and afterwards of medicine, in the University of Ferrara. He wrote a number of poems, some of which possess great merit. He died in 1798, aged more than ninety-six years.

Agnello, än-yel′lo, (ANDREA,) or **Ag-nel′lus,** (ANDREAS,) an abbot of Ravenna in the latter half of the ninth century, wrote a history or chronicle of Ravenna. His work is valuable as illustrating an important portion of ecclesiastical and civil history.

Agnen, än′yŏn′, (JEROME,) a Dutch painter, born at Bois-le-Duc about the middle of the fifteenth century. He worked in Spain. Died in 1530.

Agnes, ag′nèz, [Ger. pron. äg′nĕs,] a German empress, who, after the death of her husband, Henry III., was regent during the minority of her son, Henry IV. She died in 1057.

Agnes OF AUSTRIA, the daughter of Albert I., Duke of Austria, (afterwards King of Germany,) was remarkable for the atrocious cruelty with which she revenged the death of her father, murdered in 1308. Many persons were put to a death of torture on mere suspicion, and a multitude of persons, innocent in all probability, were beheaded by her order. She died in 1364.

Agnes, ag′nĕz, SAINT, a Roman virgin of noble family, who, according to the legend, suffered martyrdom under Diocletian in 303 A.D., when only thirteen years of age.

See Mrs. JAMESON, "Sacred and Legendary Art;" BAILLET, "Vies des Saints;" J. A. MARTIGNY, "Notice Historique, etc. sur le Culte de Sainte Agnès."

Agnes (ag′nĕz or än′yĕs′) **de Méranie,** dĕh mâ′rā′ne′, Queen of France, was married to Philippe Auguste in 1196. The censure of the church, because he had divorced Ingelburge to marry Agnes, induced the king to discard the latter. Died in 1201.

Agnes Sorel. See SOREL.

Agnesi, än-yā′see, (MARIA Gaetana—gä-à-tä′nä,) an Italian lady of wonderful intellectual powers and acquirements, born at Milan in 1718. When she was only twenty years of age, she was able to discourse in a great number of different languages on abstruse questions of mathematics and philosophy. Her Latin is said to have been remarkably pure and correct. She published, in 1748, her "Instituzioni Analitiche," ("Analytical Institutions,") a treatise on algebra, including the differential and integral calculus, and displaying wonderful knowledge as well as judgment. "We cannot," says a recent critic, "take leave of a work which does so much honour to female genius, without earnestly recommending the perusal of it to those who believe that great talents are bestowed by nature exclusively on men." (See review of Maria G. Agnesi's "Analytical Institutions" in the "Edinburgh Review" for January, 1804.) In 1750, during the illness of her father, (who was professor in the University of Bologna,) she supplied his place. Shortly after this she retired to a nunnery, where she spent the remainder of her life, and died in 1799.

See PAOLO FRISI, "Elogio Storico di M. Agnesi;" BIANCA MILESI-MOJON, "Vita di Mar.a Gaetana Agnesi," 1836.

Agnesi, (MARIA THERESA,) a composer of operas, born at Milan about 1724, was a sister of the preceding.

Ag'new, (Sir ANDREW,) M.P., a noted Scottish Sabbatarian, born in Wigtonshire in 1793; died in 1849.

See DR. MCCRIE's "Life of Sir Andrew Agnew."

Agnew, (JAMES,) a brigadier-general in the British army in the American Revolution, was killed at the battle of Germantown in October, 1777.

Agnĭ, ag'nĭ, or **Ag'nis,**[common Hindoo pron. ŭg'nĭ or ŭg'nis; etymologically allied to the Latin *ignis*,] the name of the Hindoo god of fire. He is sometimes represented in pictures with two faces, three legs, and seven arms, and is usually painted of a deep-red colour. His two faces are supposed to symbolize fire in its two characters—beneficent (or creative) and destructive. His seven arms have been conjectured to indicate the seven prismatic colours. Agni has been called the Hindoo Vulcan; but he does not appear anywhere as an artificer, like the Vulcan of classic mythology, his most prominent characters being those of a purifier and of a bearer of incense to heaven, becoming thus a mediator between men on earth and the gods above.

See MOOR, "Hindu Pantheon;" KÖPPEN, "Religion des Buddha," p. 5; SIR W. JONES on "The Gods of Greece, Italy, and India," in "Asiatic Researches," vol. i. p. 264.

Ag-nod'ĭ-çe ['Αγνοδίκη,] an Athenian woman, who, disguised in the dress of a man, studied medicine under Herophilus, and practised with success, in the third century B.C. She devoted herself chiefly to midwifery.

Ágnolo, d', dän'yo-lo, (BACCIO, bät'cho,) an eminent Italian architect and sculptor in wood, was born at Florence in 1460. He was the first who adorned the windows of mansions and palaces with frontons, or frontispieces. Among his chief works are the Palazzo Bartolini, (Florence,) and the Villa Borgherini, near Florence. Died in 1543.

See VASARI, "Lives of the Painters and Sculptors."

Agnolo, d', (GABRIELE,) a Neapolitan architect, who designed the Gravina Palace, and the church of Santa Maria, at Naples. Died in 1510.

Agnolo, d', (GIULIANO,) a son of the preceding, who followed the profession of his father, both as sculptor and architect. Died in 1555.

Ag-non'ĭ-dēs, [Gr. Ἀγνωνίδης; Fr. AGNONIDE, ăn'yo'-nēd',] an Athenian orator, who induced the Athenians to put Phocion to death. For this he was afterwards, in his turn, condemned to die.

Ag'o-bard', SAINT, [Fr. pron. săn'tả'go'bảR',) an archbishop of Lyons in the ninth century, took part with the sons of Louis le Débonnaire against their father, for which he was deposed in 835. He was, however, restored to his see about 838, on the reconciliation of Louis and his sons. He died in 840.

See C. B. HUNDESHAGEN, "De Vita et Scriptis Agobardi," 1831.

Agocchi, â-gok'kee, or **Agucchio,** â-gook'ke-o, (GIOVANNI BATTISTA,) a learned Italian ecclesiastic, born at Bologna in 1570. About 1624, Pope Urban VIII. appointed him his nuncio to Venice, with the title of Archbishop of Amasia. Died in 1632.

Ag-o-rac'rĭ-tus, [Gr. Ἀγοράκριτος; Fr. AGORACRITE, ă'go'rẳ'krēt',] a famous sculptor, native of Paros, lived in the fifth century B.C. He was a pupil of Phidias.

Agosti, â-gos'tee, (GIULIO,) an Italian dramatic poet, born at Reggio in the latter part of the seventeenth century. Died young in 1704.

Agostini, â-gos-tee'nee, (LIONARDO,) an Italian antiquary, born at Sienna, went to Rome about 1623, and was appointed by Alexander VII. pontifical antiquary. He published an enlarged edition of Filippo Paruta's work on the medals of Sicily, (1649,) and another work, of great merit, on antique gems, "Antique Gems Delineated," (" Le Gemme antiche figurate," 1636 and 1657.)

Agostini, (MIGUEL.) See AGUSTI.

Agostini, degli, dầl'yee â-gos-tee'nee, (GIOVANNI,) a learned Italian monk, born at Venice about 1700. He wrote "Historical and Critical Notices of the Lives and Works of Venetian Authors," 2 vols., 1754, which is said to be a valuable work. Died about 1755.

Agostini, degli, (NICCOLÒ,) a mediocre Italian poet, born at Venice, flourished in the first half of the sixteenth century. He translated Ovid's "Metamorphoses," (1522,) and wrote a continuation of Bojardo's "Orlando Innamorato," (1538.)

Agostino (â-gos-tee'no) and **Agnolo,** ân'yo-lo, of Sienna, sculptors and architects, born about 1265, were brothers, and always worked together. Among their works were the Palazzo de' Novi, the church of St. Francesco at Sienna, and the tomb of Bishop Guido at Arezzo, which was designed by Giotto. Died about 1350.

See VASARI, "Lives of the Painters," etc.

Agostino surnamed VENEZIANO, vả-nêt-se-â'no, or the "Venetian," a celebrated Italian engraver, also called **Augusti'nus de Mu'sis,** and in French **Augustin,** (o'güs'tăN',) was born about 1490. He was a pupil of Marcantonio Raimondi, for whom he worked in Rome. He engraved several works after Raphael and Giulio Romano. Some of his works are dated 1536.

See VASARI, "Lives of the Painters," etc.

Agostino, sometimes called **Agostino dalle Prospettive**—dâl'là pRo-spêt-tee'vầ, (which may be translated "Perspective Agostino,") an Italian painter, who flourished in the first half of the sixteenth century. He was distinguished for his skill in perspective.

Agostino, (PAOLO,) an eminent Italian musician of the seventeenth century, was chapel-master of St. Peter's, Rome. Died about 1660.

Agoub, â'goōb', (JOSEPH,) a native of Cairo, in Egypt, born in 1795. His parents removed to France when he was about seven years old. In 1820, or soon after, he was appointed professor of Arabic at Paris, but, having been deprived of this situation in 1831, he died the next year, it is said, of a broken heart.

Agoult, â'goo', (CHARLES CONSTANCE CÉSAR LOUP JOSEPH,) born at Grenoble in 1747, became Bishop of Pamiers in 1787. He took part in political affairs, and was one of the friends of Louis XVI. whom that king consulted just before his flight to Varennes. He published several works on finance. Died in Paris in 1824.

Agoult, (WILLIAM,) a French poet of the twelfth century. He was a gentleman of the household of Alfonso X., King of Castile, and has been styled the chief and father of troubadours. Died in 1181.

Agoult, d', dả'goo', (MARIE de Flavigny — dẹh flẳ'vẻn'ye',) COUNTESS, a French authoress, who assumed the name of Daniel Stern, was born at Frankfort-on-the-Main about 1800. She was married to Count d'Agoult in 1827. She has written several successful novels, among which is "Nelida," (1845;) and a "History of the Revolution of 1848," (2 vols., 1851.)

Agrain, d', dả'gRăN', (EUSTACHE,) a French warrior, who went to Palestine in the first crusade with Raymond of Toulouse, and became Viceroy of Jerusalem. He was called "The Sword and Shield of Palestine."

Agrate, â-grả'tầ, (MARCO Ferrerio—fêr-rã're-o,) an Italian sculptor, lived about the year 1500.

Agreda, de, dẳ â-grả'Dẳ, (MARIA,) a Spanish abbess, born in 1602. She wrote a "Life of the Virgin Mary," which Bossuet censured as indecent. Died in 1665.

Agresti, â-grês'tee, (LIVIO,) an eminent Italian painter, who died about 1580. He was a native of Forlì. He painted frescos at Rome and Forlì. Vasari extols the grandeur of his style.

Agricola, â-grik'o-lả, (CHRISTOPH LUDWIG,) an eminent German landscape-painter, born at Augsburg (or, according to some authorities, at Ratisbon) in 1667. He worked for a long time in Naples, and painted several views of Southern Italy. Died at Augsburg in 1719.

A-gric'o-lạ, (CNÆUS JULIUS,) a distinguished Roman general, born at Forum Julii, (Fréjus,) a Roman colony in Gaul, A.D. 37. In 62 he married at Rome a lady of high rank, and the next year went as quæstor to Asia, under the proconsul Salvius Titianus, where he distinguished himself by his strict integrity. In 73, Vespasian (whose cause Agricola had early espoused) made him a patrician, and appointed him governor of Aquitania, which position he held for nearly three years. In 77 he was chosen consul, and not long after was made

---

ā, ē, ī, ō, ū, ȳ, *long;* ả, ẻ, ỏ, same, less prolonged; ă, ĕ, ĭ, ŏ, ŭ, y̆, *short;* ạ, ẹ, ị, ọ, *obscure;* fär, fȧll, fȧt; mêt; nȯt; gōōd; mōōn;

Governor of Britain, where he subdued the Ordovices in North Wales, and conquered the island of Mona, (Anglesea.) He adopted a wise and generous policy towards the Britons, encouraging them to embrace the Roman customs and dress and to instruct their children in the Latin language. He afterwards crossed the Tweed, and carried his arms (80 A.D.) as far as the Frith of Tay, and erected a chain of fortresses from the Clyde to the Frith of Forth. He was soon after recalled by the emperor Domitian, and retired into private life, whither, however, the admiration of the people followed him. He died in 93, not without a general suspicion of his having been poisoned through the jealousy of Domitian. Agricola was the father-in-law of the historian Tacitus. (See TACITUS.)

See TACITUS, "J. Agricolæ Vita;" DION CASSIUS, "History of Rome;" HELD, "Commentatio de C. J. Agricolæ Vita quæ vulgo Cornelio Tacito assignatur," Schweidnitz, 1845.

A-gric′o-la, (FRANCIS,) a German theologian, born at Lunen, wrote against the Reformation. Died in 1621.

Agricola, (GEORG,) an eminent mineralogist and physician, whose proper name was BAUER, was born at Glauchau, in Saxony, about 1490. He became well versed in metallurgy and the art of mining. "He was the first mineralogist," says Cuvier, "who appeared after the *renaissance* of the sciences in Europe. He was to mineralogy what Conrad Gesner was to zoology." His principal works are, "Concerning Ores, (or Mines,)" ("De Re Metallica," 1546,) and "On the Origin and Causes of Subterranean Things," ("De Ortu et Causis Subterraneorum,") both written in elegant Latin. Died in 1555.

See A. D. RICHTER, "Vita Georgii Agricolæ," 1755; M. ADAM, "Vitæ Medicorum Germanorum;" BAYLE, "Historical and Critical Dictionary;" ERSCH and GRUBER, "Allgemeine Encyklopædie."

Agricola, (GEORG ANDREAS,) a German physician, born at Ratisbon in 1672. He pretended to have discovered a method by which the growth of plants might be greatly accelerated, and published in 1717 a useful work on the culture and propagation of plants. Died about 1738.

Agricola, (JOHAN′NES AMMO′NIUS,) a German physician, who was one of the best commentators on Hippocrates and Galen. He became professor of Greek at Ingolstadt, where he died about 1570.

Agricola, (JOHANN FRIEDRICH,) a German musician and composer, born in Altenburg in 1720. He composed "Achilles," an opera. Died at Berlin in 1774.

Agricola, (JOHN, or JOHANN,) was originally called JOHN **Schneider** (shnī′der) or **Schnit′ter**; but, according to the usage of that time, he changed his name into Agricola. Born at Eisleben, in Prussian Saxony, in 1492, he studied at Wittenberg, where he formed an intimate friendship with Luther. But from being one of that great reformer's most active supporters, he afterwards became a bitter opponent. Agricola asserted that obedience to the Mosaic law was not necessary for a Christian,—that nothing was required but penitence and faith; while Luther maintained the necessity of obeying the Ten Commandments. The followers of Agricola were styled Antinomians, ("opposers of the law.") He died in 1566. Besides writing a great number of theological works, he made a valuable collection of German proverbs, to which he added a commentary, with numerous illustrations.

See UNGER, "Dissertatio de Johanne Agricola," 1732; B. KORDES, "J. Agricola aus Eisleben," 1817; DE THOU, "Histoire," book v.; ERSCH and GRUBER, "Allgemeine Encyklopaedie."

Agricola, (MARTIN,) an eminent musician, born in Silesia about 1486; died in 1556.

Agricola, â-grik′o-lâ, (MICHAEL,) an early Swedish reformer of the sixteenth century, who translated the New Testament into the Finnish tongue. Died in 1577.

Agricola, (RUDOLPH,) an eminent Dutch scholar, born near Groningen, in Friesland, in 1443. In 1476 he went to Italy, where he studied Greek, and afterwards excited the admiration of the Italians (who had previously regarded the Germans as barbarians) by his various accomplishments. In 1482 he became professor at Heidelberg, where he died in 1485. He was highly eulogized by Erasmus. His influence contributed greatly to diffuse a taste for Grecian literature among the Germans.

"He was," says Guizot, ("Biographie Universelle,") "a good painter, a good writer, a good poet, and a learned philologer." His greatest work is "De Inventione Dialectica."

See PHILIP MELANCHTHON, "Orationes II., prior de Vita Rud. Agricolæ," etc., 1539; T. F. TRESLING, "Vita et Merita Rud. Agricolæ," 1830; ERSCH und GRUBER, "Allgemeine Encyklopaedie;" JÖCHER, "Allgemeines Gelehrten-Lexikon."

A-grip′pa, an ancient skeptical philosopher, mentioned by Diogenes Laertius as author of a treatise called "Five Reasons for Doubt."

Agrippa, KING. See HEROD AGRIPPA.

Agrippa, â-grėp′pâ, (CAMILLO,) an Italian architect, born at Milan, flourished in the latter half of the sixteenth century.

Agrippa, â-grip′pâ, (HENRY CORNELIUS,) a German physician, theologian, and astrologer, who acquired celebrity by his varied learning, superior talents, and supposed skill in alchemy and occult philosophy, was born at Cologne in 1486. He was extolled by some as an ornament of his age, and denounced by others as an impostor and a heretic. In his youth he served several campaigns in the Imperial army with distinction. His success in the various pursuits which he followed in many countries of Europe was hindered by his quarrelsome or satirical temper. After he had lectured on theology at Cologne, Pisa, Turin, and Pavia, and practised medicine in France, he received, in 1529, invitations from Henry VIII. of England, and from other sovereigns. He accepted that of Margaret of Austria, regent of the Low Countries; but she died in 1530. He died poor, at Grenoble, in 1535, leaving, besides other works, one "On the Vanity of the Sciences," in Latin, (1527,) which has been translated into English and several other languages. Hallam calls him "a meteor of philosophy."

See H. MORLEY, "Life of Agrippa," 1856; "Agrippæana oder H. C. Agrippas Leben," 1722; "Retrospective Review," vol. xiv. (1826.)

A-grip′pa, (MAR′CUS VIPSA′NIUS,) a distinguished Roman commander and statesman, born 63 B.C. His family was obscure, but a friendship was early formed between him and Octavius, (afterwards Augustus Cæsar,) and his fortunes became inseparably associated with those of the future emperor. To the skill and wisdom of Agrippa, Augustus owed much of his continued success; especially his victory at Actium, which gave him the empire of the world. After the death of Marcellus, in 23 B.C., Agrippa married his widow, Julia, the daughter of the emperor, by whom he had three sons, two of whom were adopted by Augustus, (see CAIUS CÆSAR,) and two daughters. He died 12 B.C., in the fifty-first year of his age. Agrippa and Mæcenas were the chief ministers or advisers of Augustus, and the former was for some time regarded as his destined successor.

See G. C. GEBAUER, "Dissertatio de M. V. Agrippa," 1717; P. FRANDSEN, "Marc. Vipsanius Agrippa: historische Untersuchung über dessen Leben und Wirken," 1836; LIVY, "Epitome;" TACITUS, "Annales."

Agrippa, (MENE′NIUS,) a Roman consul, who gained a victory over the Sabines in 503 B.C., and afterwards quelled a sedition of the plebeians by relating to them the well-known fable of the belly and the members.

Agrip′pa Post′umus, a posthumous son of M. Vipsanius Agrippa, put to death by Tiberius, 14 A.D.

Ag-rip-pī′na [Fr. AGRIPPINE, ăˈgre′pĕn′] I., a daughter of M. Vipsanius Agrippa and Julia, was married to Cæsar Germanicus, the nephew of the emperor Tiberius. She was the mother of the emperor Caligula. She died, it is supposed, about 31 A.D.

See ELIZABETH HAMILTON, "Memoirs of the Life of Agrippina," 1800; C. BURKHARD, "Agrippina des M. V. Agrippa Tochter," 1846.

Agrippina II., or **Agrippina Augusta,** a daughter of the preceding, and mother of the emperor Nero by her first husband, Domitius. She was a woman of abandoned principles and remorseless cruelty. She married her father's brother, the emperor Claudius, and afterwards poisoned him. After a life of almost uninterrupted crime, she was put to death (A.D. 60) by the order of her son Nero.

See C. H. GRAUN, "Dissertatio de Agrippina Neronis Matre," 1681; F. F. WALBRAT, "Agrippina Gemahlin des Claudius Stifterin von Cöln," 1800; TACITUS, "Annales."

Aguado, â-gwä′do, (A. Maria,) a financier and millionaire, born at Seville, Spain, in 1784. He became à banker of Paris. Died in 1842.

Aguado, de, dà â-gwä′do, (Francisco,) a learned and pious Spanish Jesuit, born near Madrid in 1572; died in 1654, leaving many religious works.

Agucchio. See Agocchi.

Agüero, de, dà à-gwä′ro, (Benedicto Manuel,) a distinguished Spanish painter, born at Madrid in 1626; died in 1670. He excelled in landscapes and battle-pieces.

Aguesseau, d′, dä′gà′sō′, (Henri François,) (written by himself **Daguesseau,**) a celebrated French chancellor, orator, and legislator, was born at Limoges, November 27, 1668. He passes for the most learned lawyer that France ever produced, and is called the father of French forensic eloquence. In 1691 he was appointed by Louis XIV. one of the advocates-royal. He became procureur-général to the Parliament in 1700, and chancellor of France in 1717. Before the latter date he had resolutely defended the liberties of the Gallican Church against the aggressions of the papal power in the case of the bull *Unigenitus,* (1713.) He was banished from court in 1718 for his opposition to the financial system of Law, but was restored to his high functions in 1720, after the ruinous collapse of that system. A contest for precedency between D'Aguesseau and Cardinal Dubois resulted in the removal of the former from office in 1722. He was again appointed chancellor in 1737, and kept the seals until 1750, when he resigned on account of his great age. Died in Paris in February, 1751. His works, consisting chiefly of forensic arguments, official papers, and treatises on law, were published in thirteen volumes, (1759–89.) His legislative reforms constitute perhaps his greatest claim to the remembrance of posterity.

See St. Simon's "Memoirs;" Antoine Thomas, "Éloge de H. F. d'Aguesseau," 1760; "Histoire de la Vie et des Ouvrages de D'Aguesseau," 2 vols., 1835; "Discours sur la Vie et la Mort de M. D'Aguesseau," by his son; Bourlet de Vauxcelles, "Éloge de D'Aguesseau," 1760; Morlhon, "Éloge du Chancelier D'Aguesseau," 1760; Boinvilliers, "Éloge du Chancelier D'Aguesseau," 1848; Boullée, "Histoire de la Vie du Chancelier D'Aguesseau," 1849.

Aguesseau, d′, (Henri C. Jean Baptiste,) Count, born at Fresnes in 1746, was a grandson of the chancellor. He became a member of the French Academy in 1789, and a senator in 1805. Died in 1826.

Aguiar, â-ge-ar′, (Tomas,) a Spanish portrait-painter of the seventeenth century.

Aguila, d′, dä′ge-lä, (C.F.E.H.,) an officer of engineers, who travelled extensively between 1770 and 1774. He appears to have been a native of Spain. He wrote, in French, a "History of the Reign of Gustavus III. of Sweden," (1803.) Died in 1815.

Aguila, del, del â′ge-lä, (Miguel,) a Spanish painter, whose works are said to be in the style of Murillo. Died at Seville in 1736.

Aguilar, â-ge-lar′, (Grace,) a Jewish authoress, of Spanish extraction, born at Hackney, near London, in 1816. She wrote "The Magic Wreath," in verse, and a number of prose works, among which are "Women of Israel," "Home Scenes and Heart Studies," and "Home Influence: a Tale." Died at Frankfort in 1847.

Aguilera, de, dà â-ge-lā′rà, (Diego,) a Spanish historical painter, who was born at Toledo, and lived in the latter part of the sixteenth century.

Aguillon, â′ge-yôn′, (François,) a learned Jesuit, born at Brussels in 1566; died in 1617. He wrote a work on optics, (1613.)

Aguirre, de, dà â-gêr′rà, (José Saenz—sä-ênth′,) a learned Spanish ecclesiastic, born in 1630, was made cardinal in 1686 by Pope Innocent XI. Died in 1699. He wrote several works on theology.

Agujari, â-goo-yä′ree, (Lucretia,) a popular singer and performer, who flourished in the latter half of the eighteenth century. Died at Parma in 1783.

Agusti, â-goos′tee, written also **Agustin,** â-goos-teen′, or **Agostini,** â-gos-tee′nee, (Miguel,) a Spanish agriculturist, born at Bañolas, in the sixteenth century, was prior of the order of St. John at Perpignan. He wrote a useful and popular work called "The Book of the Secrets of Agriculture," (1617.)

Agylæus, aj-e-lee′us or â-ge-lä′us, [Fr. Agylée, â′zhe′lâ′,] (Hendrik,) a Dutch jurist, born at Bois-le-Duc about 1533, was noted as a Greek scholar. Died in 1595.

Ahab, ā′hab, [Heb. אחאב,] an idolatrous king of Israel, who reigned from 931 to 909 B.C. He was slain in battle in a war against Benhadad, King of Syria. (See I. Kings xvi.–xxii.)

A-has-u-e′rus, or, more correctly, **Ahhasverosh** or **Akhasverosh,** [Heb. אחשורש,] a Hebrew name applied in the Scriptures to various Persian and Median kings. It is in all probability derived from the ancient Persian word *Khshvershe,* (the Xerxes of the Greeks, and corresponding to the Sanscrit Kshätră,) which signifies "king" or "lion-king."

The Ahasuerus mentioned in the book of Esther is generally believed to be Artaxerxes Longimanus, (in modern Persian, Ardashîr Darâz-dăst,) who reigned from 464 to 425 B.C. (See Artaxerxes.)

Ahaz, ā′haz, or **Achaz,** ā′kaz, [Heb. אחז,] a son of Jotham, King of Judah, succeeded his father about 741 and died 725 B.C. He distinguished himself above all his predecessors by his abominable idolatry, even sacrificing his own children to Moloch. (See II. Kings xvi., and II. Chronicles xxviii.)

Ahaziah, â-hạ-zī′ạ, [Heb. אחזיה,] King of Israel, the son and successor of Ahab. He reigned two years, from 909 to 907 B.C. (See I. Kings xxii.; II. Kings i.) Also, a son of Jehoram, King of Judah. He succeeded his father about 896 B.C., and after a reign of one year was slain by Jehu. (See II. Chronicles xxii. 1–10; II. Kings viii. 25–29.)

A-hen′o-bar′bus, in the plural **A-hen′o-bar′bi,** a name given to a branch or division of the Domitian family of Rome. It signifies "having red or coloured beard," and is said to have originated as follows. When Castor and Pollux, on their return from the battle of Lake Regillus, announced to Lucius Domitius the victory of his countrymen, he did not believe them; whereupon they stroked his hair and beard, which were instantly changed from black to red. The most distinguished of this name are the following:

Ahenobarbus, (Cneius Domitius,) a consul, 122 B.C., who gained a victory over the Allobroges and Arverni, nations in the south of Gaul.

Ahenobarbus, (Cneius Domitius,) a son of Lucius Domitius, noticed below. In the civil wars he joined the party of Brutus and Cassius, but after the battle of Philippi he attached himself first to Antony and afterwards to Octavius. He died a few days after the battle of Actium, 31 B.C.

Ahenobarbus, (Cneius Domitius,) a grandson of the preceding, distinguished for his profligacy and ferocity. He married Agrippina, by whom he became the father of the emperor Nero.

Ahenobarbus, (Lucius Domitius,) a Roman general, who married a sister of Cato Uticensis. He became prætor in 58 and consul in 54 B.C. He opposed Cæsar and Pompey during their coalition. In the civil war that ensued, he was appointed by the Senate to succeed Cæsar in Farther Gaul in the year 49. He was, it is said, the only leader of the senatorial party who showed energy when Cæsar invaded Italy. He was, however, on account of the defection of his army, compelled to surrender at Corfinium. He was killed in 48 B.C. at Pharsalia, where he commanded a wing of Pompey's army.

See Cæsar, "De Bello Civili;" Suetonius, "Life of Cæsar;" Dion Cassius, "History of Rome."

A-hī′jah, [Heb. אחיה,] a prophet who lived in the reigns of Solomon and Rehoboam. (See I. Kings xi., xii.; I. Chronicles xxvi. 20; II. Chronicles ix. 29.)

Ahimelech, a-him′e-lek, a priest, the son of Ahitub, slain by the command of Saul. (See I. Samuel xxi., xxii.)

A-hith′o-phel or **A-chit′o-phel,** a Hebrew courtier, a counsellor of King David, whose cause he deserted and became an adherent of Absalom in his rebellion. (See II. Samuel xv. 12, xvi. and xvii.)

Ahle, â′leh, (Johann Georg,) a German musician and composer, born at Mühlhausen in 1650; died in 1701.

ā, ē, ī, ō, ū, y̆, *long;* à, è, ò, same, less prolonged; ă, ĕ, ĭ, ŏ, ŭ, y̆, *short;* ạ, ẹ, ị, ọ, *obscure;* fär, fâll, fât; mêt; nŏt; gŏŏd; mōōn;

Ahle, (Johann Rudolph,) a German organist, born at Mühlhausen in 1625 ; died in 1673. He was the father of the preceding.

Ahlee or **Ahli,** ăh'le', surnamed Shirâzee or Sheerâzee, (Shirâzî,) she-râ'zee, from the place of his birth, a celebrated Persian poet, born at Shirâz about the middle of the fifteenth century ; died about 1535.

Ahlwardt, ăl'wăRt, (Christian Wilhelm,) an eminent German linguist, born at Greifswalde in 1760. In 1818 he was appointed professor of ancient literature in the university of his native town, where he died in 1830. He translated into German portions of many of the most celebrated poems in the ancient as well as in the different modern languages. He made, moreover, a complete translation of the poems of Ossian.

Ahlwardt, (Peter,) born at Greifswalde in 1710. Though the son of a shoemaker, by diligence he made great progress in learning, and in 1752 was appointed professor of logic and metaphysics in the University of Greifswalde. Died in 1791.

Ahmed (ăh'med) or **Achmet** (ăk'met) **I.,** a son of Mahomet III., born in 1590. He succeeded his father on the Ottoman throne in 1603, and died in 1617.

Ahmed or **Achmet II.,** born in 1643, was the son of Sultan Ibrâheem, (Ibrâhîm.) He began to reign in 1691. His army was defeated with great loss by the Austrians, at Slankament, in the same year. He was a feeble ruler, and his reign was disastrous in various respects. He died in 1695, and was succeeded by Mustafa II.

Ahmed or **Achmet III.,** son of Mahomet IV., born in 1673, was raised to the Ottoman throne in consequence of a revolt of the Janissaries in 1703. Though unfortunate in his war with Austria and Venice, his reign was, on the whole, not inglorious. The Turkish name was respected abroad, while learning and the arts of peace flourished at home. Yet Ahmed was deposed by the rebellious Janissaries in 1730, and died in 1739.

Ahmed or **Achmet IV.,** or **Abd-ool-** (Abdul-) **Hâmid,** ăb'dool-hă'mid, was born in 1725, and succeeded the sultan Mustafa III. in 1773. His reign is memorable for two disastrous wars with Russia, in which Turkey lost the Crimea, a considerable portion of Circassia, and some other territories, besides a number of. important fortresses. Died in 1789.

See Hammer, "Geschichte des Osmanischen Reichs."

Ahmed Pasha, surnamed the Traitor, a Turkish commander, who, in the reign of Solyman I., captured the island of Rhodes, defended by the Knights of St. John. Afterwards offended because the sultan did not make him grand vizier, he raised the standard of revolt in Egypt, and caused himself to be proclaimed sultan in 1524 ; but, though successful at first, he was soon after taken and put to death.

Ahmed the Renegade, grand vizier to the sultan Solyman the Great, was a native of Grätz, in Styria. He was educated a Christian, but, having been taken prisoner by the Turks, he embraced the Mohammedan faith, rose to distinction at the Ottoman court, and married the grand-daughter of the sultan. Died in 1580.

Ahmed-al-Kastâlee, (al-Kastâlî,) -âl-kăs-tă'lee, a distinguished Arabian poet, born in Spain in 958 ; died about 1030.

Ahmed-al-Makkarî, (or **Mekkarî.**) See Makkaree.

Ahmed An-Nahhâs—ăn-năh-hăs', a distinguished Arabian grammarian and philologist, who was drowned in the Nile about 950. He was a native of Egypt.

Ahmed-ar-Râzî. See Ahmed-er-Razee.

Ahmed-er-Râzee, (el-Râzî,) -er-râ'zee, a native of Córdova, lived in the tenth century. He was the author of a voluminous work on the geography and history of Spain. Another **Ahmed-er-Râzee,** distinguished as Ibn- (or Ben-) Faris, (fâ'ris,) *i.e.* "son of Fâris," wrote an Arabic dictionary and a work on biography. Died in 985.

Ahmed-Ibn (or **-Ben**) **-Arab-Shah,**[*] (-Ib'n ă'răb-shâh',) an Arabian historian of the fifteenth century, was

the author of a "History of Tamerlane," which was translated into Latin by Manger and into French by Vattier. Died in 1450.

Ahmed-Ibn-Faraj—făr'ăj, a distinguished Arabian poet and historian, native of Spain, died about 970.

Ahmed-Ibn-Hanbal. See Ibn-Hanbal.

Ahmed-Ibn-Tooloon. See Tooloon.

Ah'med-Kedük—ke-dük', written also **Achmet-Geduc,** a celebrated Turkish commander, who was grand vizier of Mahomet II. from 1473 to 1477. During this period he conquered the Crimea, and took the towns of Kaffa and Azof, (or Tana.) Under Bayazeed (Bajazet) II., the son and successor of Mahomet II., Ahmed-Kedük greatly distinguished himself. He quelled a formidable rebellion headed by Prince Jem, a brother of the sultan, and conquered Kazim Bey, the last of the Caramanian princes. But, having by his arrogance deeply offended Bayazeed, he was put to death in 1482.

Ahmed Khan Abdâlee (Abdâlî) or **Abdâllee**—kăn âb-dâ'lee, a celebrated conqueror, the founder of the Doorânee (or Durrânî) dynasty in Afghanistan. He commenced his military career in the service of the famous Nâdir Shah, by whom when a child he had been taken prisoner. After the death of that monarch, he succeeded in getting possession of a large convoy of treasure on its way from India to Nâdir's camp, and by this means laid the foundation of a powerful kingdom. He was crowned at Candahar in 1747, and died in 1773. In the intermediate period he had extended his sway over the eastern part of Persia, the whole of Afghanistan, and a large portion of India.

See Elphinstone's "Caubul ;" Malcolm's "History of Persia."

Ahmed- (or **Achmet-**) **Resmi-Effendi,** ăh'med res'mee ĕf-fĕn'dee, a Turkish historian and diplomatist, who signed the treaty of Kainarji. He wrote a "History of the War between the Turks and Russians," (1768–74.) Died about 1788.

Ahmed (or **Ahmad**) **Shah,** (of Afghanistan.) See Ahmed Khan Abdalee.

Ahmed Shah—shâh, succeeded his grandfather, Muzaffar Shah, on the throne of Guzerat, in 1411. He founded Ahmedâbâd, (*i.e.* "city of Ahmed,") and made it his capital. Died in 1443.

Ahmed Shah Walee Bâhmanee,[*] **(Bâhmanî,)** —wâ'lee bâh'mă-nee', the ninth king of the Bahmanee dynasty in the Dekkan. He succeeded his brother Firoz in 1422, and died in 1435.

Ahrens, ä'rĕns, (Heinrich,) a German jurist, born in Hanover in 1808. He was professor of philosophy at Brussels from 1839 to 1848, after which he obtained a chair at Grätz. His "Course of Natural Law" (Paris, 1838) has been often reprinted, and translated into several languages.

Ahriman. See Ormuzd.

Ahroon, (Ahrûn,) âh'roon', or **Aaron,** a Christian priest of Alexandria, lived in the early part of the seventh century. He composed a voluminous medical work, of which some extracts only are extant.

Aibek-Azad-ed-Deen, (-ed-Dîn,) ă'e-bĕk (or ī'bek) ă'zad ed-deen', the first Egyptian sultan of the dynasty of Mamelukes. He began to reign in 1254, and was assassinated, through the jealousy of his wife, in 1257.

Aicardo, ī-kaR'do, (Giovanni,) an Italian architect, born in Piedmont, worked in Genoa. Among his works is the aqueduct which supplies Genoa with water. Died in 1650.

Aicher, ī'kĕr, (Otto,) a German antiquary and historian, born in 1628, lived at Salzburg, and died in 1705. He wrote a work on epitaphs, entitled "Theatrum Funebre," (1675,) and many treatises on points of ancient history.

Aichspalt, īk'spâlt, (Peter,) an archbishop of Mentz, born about 1250. Died in 1320.

Aidan or **Ædan,** ă'dan, Saint, a pious monk of Iona, who was employed about 635 A.D. by Oswald, King of Northumbria, to instruct his subjects in the Christian religion. He is considered as the first of the line of bishops now styled Bishops of Durham.

See Hook, "Lives of the Archbishops of Canterbury," vol.i. chap. ii.

---

[*] This name is incorrectly given *Ahmed-Ibn-Arabsham* in the 'Nouvelle Biographie Générale."

[*] Pronounced in India, ŭh'mŭd shăh wŭl'ee băh'mŭn-ee.

꜀ as *k;* ç as *s;* g̃ *hard;* g̃ as *j;* G, H, K, *guttural;* N, *nasal;* R, *trilled;* s̃ as *z;* th as in *this.* (☞ See Explanations, p. 23.)

5

Aidan, ā′dan, King of Scotland, began to reign about 578 A.D. Died in 606.

Aidoneus. See PLUTO.

Aignan, ȧn′yôN′, (ÉTIENNE,) an able French transla or and political writer, born at Beaugency-sur-Loire in 1773. He produced a translation of the Iliad in verse, which is one of the best in the French language. In 1814 he was chosen a member of the French Academy in place of Bernardin de Saint Pierre. After the restoration of 1815, he entered the ranks of the liberal opposition as a publicist. His work entitled "The Condition (*État*) of the Protestants in France" (1818) is highly commended for the sentiments and style. Died in 1824.

Aigneaux or **Aignaux,** ȧn′yō′, (ROBERT and ANTOINE,) two brothers, born at Vire, in Normandy, in the sixteenth century, translated Virgil into French verse. Their work appeared in 1582, and in that age enjoyed a high reputation.

Aiguani, ī-gwä′nee, a Carmelite friar of the fourteenth century, was a respectable sculptor, and afterwards became Cardinal of Bologna. Died in 1400.

Aiguebère, ȧg′baiR′, (JOHN Dumas—dü′mä′,) a French dramatic writer, born at Toulouse in 1692. He studied at Paris, where he formed a friendship with Voltaire which lasted through life. He was a counsellor of the Parliament of Toulouse, the duties of which office he performed with equal zeal and integrity. Died in 1755.

Aiguillon, d′, dȧ′ge′yôN′ or dȧ′gèl′yôN′, (ARMAND VIGNEROT (or VIGNEROD) DUPLESSIS RICHELIEU,) är′-môN′ vèn′yeh-ro′ dü′plȧ′sè, rèsh′le-uh′,) DUC, born in 1720, is said to have been a great-grand-nephew of Cardinal Richelieu. He was prime minister of France during the last three years of the reign of Louis XV. He was chiefly indebted for his promotion at court to the favour of Madame du Barry, mistress of the king. His administration was highly disgraceful to France; for, though an accomplished courtier, he was destitute of all the great and solid qualities necessary to form a statesman. During his ministry the partition of Poland took place; yet he knew nothing of this nefarious project till it was already accomplished. On the accession of Louis XVI., Aiguillon was removed from office, and died in 1788.

See "Mémoires du Duc d'Aiguillon;" LACRETELLE, "Histoire du Dix-huitième Siècle."

Aiguillon, d′, (ARMAND DE VIGNEROT DUPLESSIS RICHELIEU,) DUC, a son of the preceding. He warmly supported the popular cause in the States-General of 1789, and was the second of the *noblesse* to renounce his privileges in the session of August 4. He superseded Custine in the command of one of the armies, early in 1792, but was proscribed by the dominant party in August of that year. He escaped by flight, and died in 1800.

See THIERS, "History of the French Revolution."

Aiguillon, d′, (MARIE MADELEINE DE VIGNEROT or VIGNEROD,) DUCHESSE, a niece of Cardinal Richelieu, born about 1610. She founded several charitable institutions. Died in 1675.

Aiken, ā′ken, (WILLIAM,) born in Charleston, South Carolina, in 1806, graduated at the College of South Carolina in 1825, served sessions in the State Legislature, and was chosen Governor of his native State in 1844. In 1850 the Democratic party elected him a representative to Congress, of which he continued a member till 1857. In the memorable contest for the speakership, 1855-6, he came within one vote of being elected to that office. Among Southern statesmen he has distinguished himself by his moderation and good sense.

Aikin, (ANNA LÆTITIA.) See BARBAULD.

Aikin, ā′kin, (ARTHUR,) a son of Dr. John Aikin, noticed below, was born about 1780, and gained distinction as a scientific writer. He was editor of the "Annual Review," (1803-08,) and was for many years secretary of the Society of Arts. His principal works are a "Manual of Mineralogy," (1814,) and a "Dictionary of Chemistry and Mineralogy." Died in 1854.

Aikin, (EDMUND,) an English architect, born at Warrington in 1780, was a brother of the preceding. Died in 1820.

Aikin, (JOHN,) M.D., an eminent miscellaneous writer, born in Leicestershire, England, in 1747. Besides a number of essays and papers, scientific and literary, he published an instructive and popular work, entitled "Evenings at Home," (1792-95,) in which he was assisted by his sister, Mrs. Barbauld. His greatest work was his "General Biography," a biographical dictionary, extending to ten closely-printed quarto volumes : it was completed in 1815. In 1816 he published his "Annals of the Reign of George III.," in 2 vols. 8vo; and in 1820, his "Select Works of the British Poets," with biographical and critical prefaces. He died in 1822.

Aikin, (LUCY,) a daughter of the preceding, born in 1781. She published, among other works, a "Memoir" of her father, in 2 vols. 8vo, (1823,) and a "Life of Joseph Addison," (1843.) Died in 1864.

Aikman, āk′man, (WILLIAM,) a Scottish portrait-painter, born in Aberdeenshire in 1682. He studied in Rome, returned to Scotland in 1712, and settled in London in 1723, after which he painted portraits of many eminent persons. He was a friend and patron of the poet Thomson, who was introduced by him to Sir Robert Walpole, and who wrote verses to the memory of Aikman. Died in 1731.

See WALPOLE, "Anecdotes of Painting," etc.

Aillaud, ä′yō′, (PIERRE Toussaint—too′sâN′,) a French poet, born at Montpellier in 1759, became an abbé and a professor at Montauban. Among his works are "L'Égyptiade," a heroic poem, (1802); and "Le Nouveau Lutrin," (1815,) an imitation of Boileau's "Lutrin." Died in 1826.

Ailly or **Ailli,** äl′ye′ or ä′ye′, (PETER OF,) an eminent French ecclesiastic, born at Compiègne, in Picardy, in 1350. In 1389 he was made chancellor of the University of Paris; in 1395, Archbishop of Cambray; and in 1411 he was elevated to the dignity of cardinal. He presided at one of the sessions of the famous Council of Constance, in which John Huss was condemned to the stake. Yet he was a reformer, and confessed and boldly denounced the abuses and impurities of the church. He died about 1420.

See DINAUX, "Notice historique sur P. D'Ailly," 1824.

Ailred, āl′red, a religious and historical writer of the twelfth century, and abbot of the monastery of Rievaulx, in Yorkshire.

Aimar Rivault. .See RIVAULT.

Aimé (ȧ′mä′) **de Varenne.** See AIMON DE VARENNE.

Aimeric, ā′mer-ik or êm′rèk′, written also **Haimeric,** a native of France, chosen Patriarch of Antioch in 1142; died in 1187.

Aimeric de Pegulha—dȧ pȧ-gool′yä, or **Aimeri de Peguilain,** ȧ′meh-re′ deh peh-ge′läN′, a troubadour of the thirteenth century, wrote a number of popular poems and songs. Died about 1260.

Aimeric OF JERUSALEM. See AMAURY.

Aimerich, ī-mȧ-rèk′, (MATEO,) a Spanish Jesuit of great learning, born in Catalonia in 1715, became professor of philosophy and divinity. He was noted for the elegance of his Latin style. Among his works is "Novum Lexicon Historicum et Criticum Antiquæ Romanæ Literaturæ," ("A New Historical and Critical Lexicon of Ancient Roman Literature," 1787.) Died at Ferrara in 1799.

Aimery. See AMAURY.

Aimoin, ȧ′moin′, [Fr. pron. ȧm′wâN′; Lat. AIMOI′-NUS,] a French monk and writer, who flourished in the latter part of the tenth century. Died in 1008.

Aimon. See AYMON.

Aimon de Varenne, ȧ′môN′ deh vȧ′rên′, a French poet, who lived in the thirteenth century.

Ainmüller, īn′mül′ler, (MAXIMILIAN EMANUEL,) a German painter, born at Munich in 1807, is called the restorer of the art of painting on glass in Germany. Among his works are the glass windows of Nôtre Dame de Bon Secours, Munich. He has also a fair reputation as an oil-painter.

Ainslie, änz′le, (GEORGE ROBERT,) born at Edinburgh in 1766, was appointed Governor of Dominica in 1813, but soon after retired, having obtained the rank of lieutenant-general. Died in 1839. He was a distinguished numismatologist, and published "Illustrations of the Anglo-French Coinage," (1830.)

Ainslie, (HEW,) a poet, born in Scotland in 1792, emigrated to America in 1822. He is author of "Pilgrimage to the Land of Burns;" and of "Scottish Songs, Ballads, and Poems," (1855.)

Ainslie, (Sir ROBERT,) born in Scotland about 1730, was knighted and sent as English ambassador to the Ottoman Porte in 1755. While in Constantinople, he made an extensive collection of coins and other curiosities. Died in 1812.

Ainsworth, ānz'wọrth, (HENRY,) one of the leaders of the English Independents in the sixteenth century, and a distinguished controversial writer. He was banished from England, with others of his sect, in 1593, and settled in Amsterdam, where he became the pastor of a church. Died about 1622. His "Annotations" on the five books of Moses, the Psalms, and the Song of Solomon, is a work of great merit.

See NEAL's "History of the Puritans;" BROOK's "Lives of the Puritans."

Ainsworth, (ROBERT,) a writer, teacher, and eminent classical scholar, born near Manchester, England, in 1660; died in 1743. He is principally known as the author of an excellent Latin Dictionary, (1736,) which is still extensively used.

Ainsworth, (WILLIAM FRANCIS,) an English geologist, physician, and traveller, born at Exeter in 1807. He went with the expedition of Colonel Chesney to the Euphrates in 1835, and afterwards, as agent of the Bible Society and Geographical Society, was sent to explore the river Halys and visit the Christians of Koordistan. He has published "Researches in Assyria," and "Travels and Researches in Asia Minor, Mesopotamia, Chaldea, etc.," (2 vols., 1842.)

Ainsworth, (WILLIAM HARRISON,) a cousin of the preceding, an English novelist, born at Manchester in 1805. He produced in 1834 "Rookwood," which had great success. His popularity with a certain class was maintained by his "Jack Sheppard," (1839.) He has been censured for choosing robbers as the heroes of these novels. Among his other works are "The Tower of London," and "The Admirable Crichton." He is, or was recently, proprietor of the "New Monthly Magazine." "With a great regard for Ainsworth," says an English critic, "and a full sense of the talent and research which he brings to bear upon every subject which he touches, we must say, we like not this gallows school of literature." (See article on "Ainsworth and Jack Sheppard" in "Fraser's Magazine" for February, 1840.)

Airault. See AYRAULT.

Airay, ā're, (CHRISTOPHER,) an English clergyman, born in Westmoreland about the beginning of the seventeenth century. He wrote on logic. Died in 1670.

Airay, (HENRY,) an English Puritan, born in Westmoreland in 1560, became provost of Queen's College, Oxford, and vice-chancellor of the university, about 1606. He wrote "A Treatise against Bowing at the Name of Jesus," and several other works. Died in 1616.

Aird, ârd, (THOMAS,) a Scottish poet, for some time editor of the "Dumfries Herald," born in Roxburghshire about 1802. He published in 1846 a volume of poems, which are commended. He has also written some prose works, among which is "Religious Characteristics."

Airey, ā're, (Sir RICHARD,) a British officer, born in 1803, served in the Crimean war, 1854-55, as quartermaster-general. He became lieutenant-general in 1862.

Airy, ā're, (GEORGE BID'DELL,) an English astronomer, born at Alnwick, Northumberland, in 1801, was educated at Trinity College, Cambridge, of which he was elected a Fellow in 1824. He became Lucasian professor of mathematics at Cambridge in 1826, and Plumian professor of astronomy in 1828. In 1835 he was appointed astronomer royal and director of the Observatory at Greenwich, the efficiency of which he increased by improved methods and new instruments. He was elected in 1836 a Fellow of the Royal Society, from which he has received the Copley and Royal medals. He published in 1846 an important "Abridgment of the Planet-

ary and Lunar Observations from 1750 to 1830." Among his works are the articles "Figure of the Earth," and "Tides and Waves," in the "Encyclopædia Metropolitana," and the article "Gravitation," in the "Penny Cyclopædia."

Aischah. See AYESHAH.

Aissé, ä'sä', (MADEMOISELLE,) a fair Circassian, born about 1694, was brought to France by Count de Ferriol in 1698. She was educated by Madame de Tencin. Her letters were published, with notes by Voltaire, (1787.) Died in 1733.

Aitken, āt'ken, (JOHN,) M.D., a Scottish physician and medical writer, who died in 1790.

Ait'kin, (ROBERT,) for many years a printer and publisher in Philadelphia, was born in Great Britain in 1734, and came to America in 1769. He died in 1802. To him is generally attributed the authorship of an "Inquiry into the Principles of a Commercial System for the United States."

Aiton, ā'ton, (JOHN,) D.D., a British writer of the present era, was minister of Dolphinton, county of Lanark, Scotland. He published "The Lands of the Messiah, Mohammed, and the Pope, as visited in 1851," (1852.)

Aiton, (WILLIAM,) an eminent Scottish botanist, born near Hamilton in 1731. He was selected in 1759 by George III. to establish and arrange a botanic garden at Kew. In 1783 he became superintendent of the pleasure- and kitchen-gardens of the king. He published a descriptive catalogue of the plants cultivated in the botanic garden, entitled "Hortus Kewensis," (3 vols., 1789,) which Lowndes calls an excellent work. Died in 1793.

Ai'ton, (WILLIAM TOWNSEND,) a landscape-gardener, born in 1766, was a son of the preceding, whom he succeeded as superintendent at Kew. Died in 1849.

Aitsingerus or **Aytsingerus**, īt-sin'jer-us, (MICHAEL,) otherwise called MICHAEL **von Eytzing**—fon īt'sing, an Austrian chronologist and historian, born about 1535; died about 1600.

Aitzema, van, vän īt-zā'mä, (FOPPE, fop'peh,) a Dutch diplomatist, born in Friesland in 1586. Died at Vienna in 1637.

Aitzema, van, (LEO,) a Dutch historian, born at Doccum in 1600; died in 1669. He wrote a valuable history of Holland, extending from 1621 to 1668, (15 vols., 1657-71.)

Aiyoob. Aiyûb, or **Aiyoub.** See JOB.

Aiyoob- (**Aiyûb-** or **Ayyûb-**) (**Ibn-Shâdi** or **-Shâdhi,**) i'yoob' Ib'n shä'dee, [written in French AIOUB (or AYOUB) EBN (or BEN) SCHADI, and EÏOUB BEN CHÂDY,] surnamed NEJM-ED-DEEN or NEDJM-ED-DÎN, nĕjm-ed-deen', (the "star of religion,") was born in Armenia, or Western Persia, in the early part of the twelfth century. His son, the famous Salah-ed-Dîn or Saladin, having become the vizier of the Egyptian caliph Al-Adhed, invited his father to Egypt. Aiyoob was received with the highest honour by the caliph, as well as by Saladin, who offered to resign his position in favour of his father. But the latter refused to accept it, and died in retirement in 1173. The dynasty founded by Saladin is called, from the name of his father, that of the Aiyoobites.

See D'HERBELOT, "Bibliothèque Orientale;" QUATREMÈRE, "Histoire des Sultans Mamelouks d'Égypte;" also, the "Biographical Dictionary" of IBN-KHALLIKÂN.

Aiyoobites or **Aiyubites**, i'yoob'īts, written also **Ayyubites**, **Aioubites**, and **Eïoubites**, [called in Arabic AIYOO'BIA and BENEE (or BENÎ) AIYOOB, bĕn'ee' i'yoob', i.e. the "sons of Aiyoob,"] a name applied to the successors of Saladin, who founded the Aiyoobite dynasties of Egypt, Damascus, etc. (See preceding article.)

Ajala or **Axala**, de, dä ä-Hä'lä, (MARTIN PEREZ,) a Spanish prelate, born in 1504, became Archbishop of Valencia. He wrote "Apostolic Traditions," (1562.) Died in 1566.

Ajax, ā'jax, [Gr. Aîaς,] the name of two Grecian heroes who fought in the Trojan war.

Ajax, the son of Telamon, [in Latin, A'JAX TELAMO'-NIUS,] was King of Salamis. He was often called "the Great," on account of his great stature, in which he exceeded all the other Greeks. He was also distinguished for his valour and beauty. He contended with Ulysses for the armour of Achilles without success, became mad in consequence of this defeat, and killed himself.

See the "Iliad;" SOPHOCLES, "Ajax;" HYGINUS, "Fabulæ."

Ajax, son of Oïleus, was King of Locris, and was called the "Lesser Ajax," to distinguish him from the son of Telamon. Next to Achilles, he was the swiftest-footed of the Greeks. He perished while returning from Troy, through the wrath of Minerva and Neptune, whom he had offended by his impiety.

Ajello, ä-yel'lo, (SEBASTIANO,) a Neapolitan medical writer, who flourished about 1575.

Ajescha. See AYESHAH.

Akakia, ä'kä'ke'ä', written also **Acacia,** (MARTIN,) an eminent French physician of the sixteenth century; died in 1551. His real name was SANS-MALICE, ("without malice,") which, according to the usage of those times, he changed into the Greek AKAKIA, having the same signification. He translated portions of Galen's works, to which he added commentaries that show him to have been a man of judgment and a close observer of facts. He left a son of the same name, who became a professor of surgery, and second physician to Henry III. Died in 1588.

Akbar or **Akber,** äk'ber,* [usually pronounced by the Hindoos ŭk'ber,] (written also **Acbar, Ackbar, Ekber,**) **Mohammed,** surnamed JALÂL-ED-DEEN, (or DJELÂL-ED-DÎN,) jä-lâl' ed-deen', the "glory of the faith," the greatest and best of all the Mogul emperors, was born at Amerkote, in the valley of the Indus, the 14th of October, 1542. He appears to have been, like Alfred the Great, one of those thoroughly accomplished sovereigns of whom history presents us with so few examples. His father Humâyoon had been driven from his capital by his rebellious subjects: so that Akbar was born in exile. The young prince grew up amid privations and dangers. He early distinguished himself by his courage and magnanimity. The victory which restored Humâyoon to the throne of his father, after his long banishment, was due in a great measure to the heroic example of young Akbar, then only about fourteen years of age. But, although he displayed on various occasions the most splendid abilities as a general, his military achievements form the least part of the glory of his reign. He was not only a brave and able commander, but a far-seeing statesman and a humane, magnanimous, and enlightened ruler. He treated all his subjects, whether Mohammedans, Christians, Jews, or Hindoos, with strict and impartial justice, so that he received and deserved the title of Jŭg'ät Gŏŏrŏŏ, the "protector or guardian of mankind;" and he furnishes perhaps the only example in which an Oriental sovereign has really merited such an appellation. If he had any fault as a ruler, it was, perhaps, too great a lenity towards his enemies. It is related that in the early part of his reign, when he had not yet completed his sixteenth year, he had defeated and taken prisoner a brave but most troublesome leader of a rebellious faction. The captive, covered with wounds, was brought into the presence of the young emperor. Akbar's vizier, who also held the office of tutor or governor, exhorted him to take away with his own hands the life of his dangerous foe. But, though on the field of battle he had no superior, he had not the nerve to kill in cold blood a defenceless captive. He drew his sword, but, scarcely touching with it his victim, he burst into tears. The vizier regarded the young prince with a look of stern disapprobation, and then with his own sabre struck off the head of his prisoner.

Akbar earnestly sought to lighten as far as practicable the taxes and imposts of his subjects. With a view to regulate the imposts according to a just scale,

* This is sometimes erroneously accentuated on the last syllable— Akbár; but the name is nothing more than the comparative and superlative degree of the Arabic adjective *Keheer* or *Kebîr*, ("great,") and should be pronounced, as every Arabic scholar knows, äk'bär. It signifies "greater" *or* "superior;" also "greatest;" hence as a surname it nearly corresponds to the Latin *Maximus*, which was given as a surname to the greatest of the Fabii. "Allah Akbar," the battle-cry of the Moslems, is often incorrectly rendered "God is great;" it properly signifies "God is greatest," or superior to every other power: hence Gibbon translates it "God is victorious."

he caused to be taken a complete survey or census of his whole empire, with minute statistical details in regard to the extent or area of the different provinces and their various productions. The book treating of these particulars, called *Ayeen Akbery*, ("Institutes of Akbar,") enjoys a great celebrity, and is probably without a parallel in Oriental history. Among his other regulations, Akbar established throughout his vast dominions posts, (called by the Hindoos Dâk Chowkee,) to convey either ordinary letters or the expresses of the government. According to Ferishtah, he never during his reign had less than five thousand elephants, (probably the greatest number ever possessed by any Indian sovereign;) he had also twelve thousand stable-horses, and nearly one thousand hunting leopards. Akbar died in 1605, after a reign of fifty-one years, during which he had enlarged his dominions by the conquest of Bengal and the greater part of the Dekkan. With him died, it would seem, all the magnanimity which had hitherto distinguished the race of Bâber. He was succeeded by his son Selim, better known by the proud title of Jehângeer, or the "Conqueror of the World."

See FERISHTA, "History of the Mahomedan Power in India," translated by BRIGGS, vol. ii.; ELPHINSTONE, "History of India;" MILL, "History of British India," 1841; ABOOL-FAZL, "Akbar Namah;" "Memoirs of Humayoon," translated into English by STEWART; RICKARDS, "India," 2 vols., 1821.

Akemoff. See AKIMOFF.

Aken, van, vän ä'ken, (JAN or JEAN,) a Dutch or Flemish artist, distinguished as a painter and still more as an engraver, lived in the first half of the seventeenth century.

Aken, van, (JOSEPH,) a painter of Antwerp, born about 1710, excelled in his representations of draperies and embroidery. He came to England, where he died about 1750.

Akenside, ä'ken-sīd, (MARK,) an eminent English didactic poet, born at Newcastle-on-Tyne in 1721, was the son of a butcher. His parents were dissenters. His mother's name was Mary Lumsden. He studied at the University of Edinburgh, devoting his chief attention to medical sciences, and took his degree of M.D. at Leyden in 1744. On this occasion he wrote an able Latin thesis on the origin and growth of the human fœtus, and attacked some prevalent theories on that subject which have since been supplanted. He had begun to write verse at an early age. His principal poem, "The Pleasures of the Imagination," in blank verse, appeared in 1744, and had a great success.

"It has undoubtedly a just claim to very particular notice," says Dr. Johnson, "as an example of great felicity of genius and uncommon amplitude of acquisitions, of a young mind stored with images and much exercised in combining and comparing them. . . . In the general fabrication of his lines he is perhaps superior to any other writer of blank verse; his flow is smooth and his pauses are musical, but the concatenation of his verses is commonly too long continued, and the full close does not recur with sufficient frequency." Addison's essays on the Pleasures of the Imagination formed the groundwork of this poem.

Akenside published a volume of odes in 1745. In 1748 he became a resident of London, where he practised medicine with moderate success until his death. He was appointed a physician to St. Thomas's Hospital, and one of the physicians to the queen about 1760. Besides the works above named, he wrote several short poems and medical treatises, including a treatise on Dysentery, (1764,) in elegant Latin, which, says Johnson, "entitled him to the same height of place among the scholars as he possessed before among the wits." Died in 1770.

See JOHNSON, "Lives of the Poets;" BUCKE, "Life, Writings, and Genius of Akenside," 1832; KIPPIS, "Biographia Britannica;" CAMPBELL, "Specimens of the English Poets."

Akerblad, ä'ker-blâd, (JOHAN DAVID,) a distinguished Orientalist and antiquary, born in Sweden in 1760. Having been attached to the Swedish embassy at Constantinople, he visited Jerusalem in 1792, and the Troad (*i.e.* the plain on which ancient Troy was situated) in 1797. He was the first who attempted with any success

ä, ē, ī, ō, ū, ȳ, *long;* à, è, ò, same, less prolonged; ă, ĕ, ĭ, ŏ, ŭ, ў, *short;* a, e, i, o, *obscure;* fär, fåll, fåt; mêt; nŏt; gŏŏd; mo͞on,

to decipher the cursive or demotic writing of the ancient Egyptians. His chief work is a "Letter on the Egyptian Inscription of Rosetta," (1802.) Died in 1819.

See CHAMPOLLION, "Grammaire Égyptienne;" "Biographie Universelle," (Supplement.)

Akerel, ä′kẹr-el, (FREDRICK,) a Swedish engraver, born at Södermannland in 1748. Died in 1804.

Akerhielm, o′kẹr-hyêlm′, (ANNA,) a learned Swedish lady, born in 1642. Died in 1698.

Akermann, ä′kẹr-män, (ANDERS,) a Swedish engraver, born at Upsal in 1718. Died in 1778.

Akers, ä′kẹrz, (BENJAMIN PAUL,) an American sculptor, born at Saccarappa, in Maine, in 1825. He passed several years at Rome, whither he went in 1855. Among his works are busts of Edward Everett and Henry W. Longfellow, and a head of Milton. Died in Philadelphia in May, 1861.

See TUCKERMAN, "Book of the Artists," New York, 1867.

Akersbot, ä′kẹrs-bot, (WILLEM,) a Dutch painter and engraver, lived at Haarlem in the first half of the seventeenth century.

Akiba, ä-kee′bä, (Ben Joseph,) a famous Jewish rabbi, born in the first year of the Christian era. Having joined the false Messiah Bar-Cokeba, (A.D. 120,) he was taken prisoner and put to a cruel death by the Romans, after a life of one hundred and twenty years.

Akimoff, Akimov, or **Akimow,** ä-ke-mof′, written also **Akemov,** (IVAN,) an eminent Russian painter, born in 1754; died in 1814.

Akoui. See AKWEI.

Ak-Shems-ed-Deen, (or **-ed-Dîn,**) äk-shêms-ẹd-deen′, (i.e. the "White (or bright) Sun of the Faith,") a Turkish sheikh, famous for his prophecies, born in Syria in 1389; died about 1472. When the troops of Mahomet II., after having besieged Constantinople, had become discouraged with the obstinate resistance of the Greeks, Ak-Shems-ed-Deen is said to have predicted truly the day and hour in which the city would be taken.

Akwei, ä-kwä′e, (or **Akoui,** ä-kwee′,) a distinguished Chinese general and prime minister during the reign of Këen-Loong, (or -Loung,) which lasted from 1736 to 1796.

AL, äl or ạl, the Arabic definite article, forming a prefix to a multitude of Oriental names : as, AL-ADEL, a surname signifying "the Just;" AL-AMEEN (-AMÎN,) "the Trustworthy;" AL-MANSOOR, "the Victorious," etc. It should be observed that the l in this particle is often changed so as to correspond to the initial consonant of the following word: as, AD-DEMEEREE for AL-DEMEEREE, (-DEMÎRÍ,) AN-NÂSIR for AL-NÂSIR, AR-RASHEED for AL-RASHEED, (-RASCHÎD,) AS-SEFFÂH for AL-SEFFÂH, (or -SAFFÂH.) The a in al has an obscure sound, and is sometimes pronounced nearly like ŏŏl, at other times like ŭl or ẹl, varying according to the different dialects. (See remarks on Oriental names in the Introduction to this work.)

Al-ạ-bas′tẹr, (WILLIAM,) an English writer, born in Suffolk in 1567; died in 1640. He was chaplain to the Earl of Essex in his expedition to Cadiz in 1596. He is chiefly known as the author of a Latin tragedy entitled "Roxana," said to be to a great extent a mere translation from an Italian drama by Groto. The poet Spenser expressed great admiration for his poetry.

See FULLER, "Worthies of England;" WOOD, "Fasti Oxonienses," in "Athenæ Oxonienses;" ADDISON, "Spectator," No. 221.

Alacoque, ä′lä′kok′, (MARGUERITE,) a French nun, born in 1647; died in 1690. As a reward for her eminent piety, she was, it is said, gifted with prophecy, and foretold correctly the time of her own death.

Alâ-ed-Deen,(or **Alâ-ed-Dîn,**) ä-lä′ẹd-deen′, written also **Aladdin,** a younger son of Osmân the founder of the Ottoman Empire, was a distinguished statesman of the fourteenth century, and first organized the band called Janissaries, (i.e. Yeñi-Sheri, yà′nee-shä′ree, or the "new troops.") In 1370, Alâ-ed-Deen, at the head of his new soldiers, gained a great victory over the emperor Andronicus, and took Nicæa, the bulwark of the Greek Empire in Asia.

See VON HAMMER, "Geschichte des Osmanischen Reichs;" MARSIGLI, "Stato militare dell' Imperio Ottomano."

Alagon, d′, dä′lä′gòN′, (LOUIS,) a French nobleman put to death in 1605 for having entered into a plot for delivering Marseilles into the hands of the Spaniards.

Alahmar, ä-läH′mar, (Ibn (Ib'n) Moham′med,) the first king of Granada, built the Alhambra. Died in 1237.

Alaimo. See ALAYMO.

Alaimo, ä-lī′mo, a Sicilian nobleman, who took a part in the famous conspiracy called the Sicilian Vespers in 1282. Afterwards, in 1287, he was drowned by the order of the King of Sicily.

Alain, ä′läN′, or **Alan,** ä′lòN′, [Lat. ALA′NUS,] a bishop of Auxerre (France) in the twelfth century, who wrote a life of Saint Bernard. Died about 1185.

Alain, (JOHN.) See ALAN.

Alain Chartier. See CHARTIER.

Alain de Lille, ä′läN′ dẹh lêl, [in Latin, ALA′NUS DE IN′SULIS,] a French ecclesiastic, surnamed THE UNIVERSAL DOCTOR, was reputed one of the most learned men of the twelfth century. He died about the year 1200, leaving numerous works, some of which are in verse.

Alaleona,* ä-lä-lä-o′nä, (GIUSEPPE,) an Italian lawyer and littérateur, born at Macerata in 1670; died in 1749.

Alaman, ä-lä-mân′, (LUCAS,) a Mexican politician, born in the eighteenth century. He was appointed minister of foreign affairs (1853) by Santa Anna. His policy was reactionary and despotic. Died in 1855.

Alaman, d′, dä′lä′mòN′, (SICARD,) the chief minister and favourite of Raymond VII. of Toulouse. Died in 1275.

Alamanni. See ALEMANNI.

Alamanno. See ALEMANNI.

Alameen, (Alamîn,) ä-lä-meen′, (Mohammed,) a son of Haroon-ar-Rasheed, (Haroun-al-Raschîd,) whom he succeeded in the caliphate in 809. Having disregarded his father's injunctions that he should give the command of the army to his brother Al-Mamoon and continue him in the government of Khorassân, he was, after a short and troubled reign, besieged in his own capital, and slain while on his way to surrender himself to his victorious brother, in 813.

Al-Ameer′ or **Al-Amir,** äl-ä-meer′, a Saracen, who assumed the title of caliph in the ninth century, and ravaged some parts of the Greek Empire.

Alamos, ä′lä-mòs, (BALTAZAR,) a Spanish writer, who lived in the latter part of the sixteenth and beginning of the seventeenth century, was born at Medina del Campo. He is the author of an accurate Spanish translation of Tacitus, (1614.)

Alamundar, äl-ä-moon-dar′,(?) a Saracen prince, who invaded Palestine in 509 A.D., and, it is said, was converted by the anchorites.

Alan, CARDINAL. See ALLEN, (WILLIAM.)

Alan (äl′ạn) OF LYNN, an English theologian and monk, born at Lynn. Died about 1420.

Alan OF TEWKESBURY, an English monk of the twelfth century, wrote a Life of Thomas à Becket. Died in 1201.

Alan, ä′lân, or **Alanus,** ä-lä′nŭs, (JOHANN,) a Danish writer and professor of philosophy, was born at Ala about 1565. Died in 1631.

Aland. See FORTESCUE, (Sir JOHN.)

Al′ạn-sọn, (EDWARD,) an English surgeon, born in Lancashire in 1747. He practised in Liverpool, made improvements in the method of amputation, and wrote "Practical Observations upon Amputation," (1779.) Died in 1823.

Alarcon, ä-laR-kōn′, (FERNAN MARTINEZ de Cevallos—dä thä-väl′yòs,) the founder of the noble house of Alarcon, fought against the Moors in Spain in the twelfth century.

Alarcon, de, dä ä-laR-kōn′, (Don ANTONIO Suarez —swä′rêth,) a Spanish historian, born about 1636, was a son of the Marquis of Trocifal. Died about 1663.

Alarcon, de, (Don FERNANDO,) called El Señor Alarcon, a famous Spanish general, born about 1466, to whose custody Francis I. was committed after the

* The "Nouvelle Biographie Générale" spells this name Alalcona; but this is doubtless a misprint. Compare MAZZUCHELLI, "Scrittori d'Italia."

c as k; ç as s; g hard; g as j; G, H, K, guttural; N, nasal; R, trilled; s as z; th as in this. (☞See Explanations, p. 23.)

battle of Pavia, 1525. He had a high reputation for honour and bravery. To him was intrusted the custody of the captive pope Clement VII. in 1527. Died in 1540.

See ANTONIO SUAREZ DE ALARCON, "Comentarios de los hechos del Señor Alarcon," 1665.

Alarcon, de, (HERNANDO,) a Spanish navigator, of whom little is known. He was sent in 1540 to explore the coast of California, of which he made an accurate survey. He was the first who ascertained that Lower California was not an island, but a peninsula.

See D. DE MOFRAS, "Explorations des Territoires de l'Orégon, des Californies, etc."

Alarcon y Mendoza, de, dà à-laR-kōn' e mĕn-do'-thâ, (Don JUAN RUIZ—roo-eeth',) an excellent Spanish dramatic poet, born in the province of Mexico about the end of the sixteenth century. He removed to Spain about 1622, and attained eminence as a lawyer. A volume of his dramas was published in 1628, and another in 1634. Among his works are "Las Paredes oyen," ("Walls have Ears ;") "El Examen de Maridos," ("Trial of Husbands ;") and "La Verdad sospechosa," ("Suspicious Truth,") which was the original of Corneille's "Menteur." His moral tone is highly commended; his versification is easy and harmonious. His other principal merits are a faithful delineation of Spanish manners, and a nervous expression of noble sentiments.

See A. DE PUIBUSQUE, "Histoire comparée des Littératures Espagnoles et Françaises ;" N. ANTONIO, "Bibliotheca Hispana."

Alard, ä'lâRt or ä'lăR', written also **Adelard,** a Dutch ecclesiastic, born at Amsterdam in 1490, was the author of several controversial works.

Alard, (FRANCIS,) a theologian, born at Brussels in the sixteenth century. He was converted to Protestantism by reading a work by Luther. Having been denounced to the Inquisition by his own mother, it was determined to poison him, in order to save his relatives from the shame of a public execution. The poison did not take effect; and he afterwards escaped from prison, and died in Holstein in 1578.

See a Life of F. Alard, by his grandson Lambert, in "Dänische Bibliothek," vi. ; and NICHOLAS ALARD, "Decas Alardorum Scriptis Clarorum."

Alard, ä'lâRt, (LAMBERT,) a German writer, a son of Wilhelm, noticed below, born in Holstein in 1602, was the author of a treatise "On the Music of the Ancients," in Latin, and a history of Holstein, entitled "Nordalbingia," etc., (1628.) Died in 1672.

Alard, ä'lâR', (MARIE JOSEPH LOUIS,) a French medical writer, born at Toulouse in 1779. Died in Paris in 1850.

Alard, ä'lâRt, (NICHOLAS,) a German biographer, born at Tönningen in 1683, wrote "Decas Alardorum Scriptis Clarorum," (1721.) Died in 1756.

Alard, (WILHELM, or WILLIAM,) a son of Francis, above named, was born in 1572, and became pastor at Crempe, in Holstein. He wrote many religious works, and Latin poetry which was much admired. Died in 1645.

A-lar'dus, (surnamed ÆMSTELREDA'MUS, from the place of his birth,) a distinguished scholar and rhetorician, born in Amsterdam towards the end of the fifteenth century ; died about 1541.

Al'ar-ic, [Lat. ALARI'CUS,] a famous conqueror, King of the Visigoths, was born about 350 A.D. He served for some time in the army of the emperor Theodosius, who died in 393. Having been offended by Arcadius, he invaded the Eastern Empire with a large army in 396. He captured Corinth and other cities, and ravaged the country, but was checked by Stilicho, (or Stilicon,) and concluded a treaty with the ministers of Arcadius, who admitted him again into his service, with the rank of general. In 402 he invaded Italy, where he was defeated by Stilicho at Pollentia, and was compelled to withdraw from Italy. After the death of Stilicho, Alaric renewed, in 408, the invasion of Italy, where the feeble Honorius offered little resistance. He advanced to the gates of Rome, then the most magnificent city of the world, the citizens of which induced him to spare it by the payment of five thousand pounds of gold and thirty thousand pounds of silver. He soon after withdrew his army into Tuscany. Negotiations ensued between Ala-

ric and Honorius; but the latter foolishly rejected the reasonable terms offered by the victorious Goth, who captured Rome in 410 and delivered it up to pillage for six days. The churches and public buildings, however, were spared. Alaric marched southward, with a design to conquer Sicily, and died at Cosenza in 410.

See JORNANDES, "De Rebus Geticis ;" SOZOMEN, "Historia ;" GIBBON, "Decline and Fall of the Roman Empire ;" CLAUDIAN, "De Bello Getico."

Alaric II., a king of the Visigoths, who succeeded his father Euric in 484 A.D. He was killed in battle by the hand of Clovis, King of the Franks, in 507. The reign of Alaric II. was distinguished by the formation of a body of laws known as the "Breviarium Alaricianum," i.e. "Compilation or Abridgment of Alaric."

Alary, ä'lâ're', (GEORGE,) a French missionary, born in 1731 ; died in 1817. He preached in the Burmese Empire, and afterwards in China, making many converts. He returned to his native country about 1772.

Alary, (JEAN,) a French poet, born at Toulouse in the sixteenth century. He wrote, besides other poems, "Virtue Triumphant over Fortune," (1622,) and a prose work called "Abrégé des longues Études," ("Abridgment of Long Studies.")

Alary, (PIERRE JOSEPH,) a French academician, born in Paris in 1689. He was sub-preceptor to Louis XV., and was admitted into the French Academy in 1723. His Letters to Bolingbroke were published. Died in 1770.

See BOLINGBROKE'S "Letters."

A Lasco, Alasco, or **Alasko,** ä-lâs'ko, (JOHN,) a Polish Protestant theologian, born in 1499. He avowed his conversion to the doctrines of the Reformation after he had become Bishop of Vesprim in 1529. He preached some years at Emden, and in the reign of Edward VI. went to London, where he had charge of a congregation, On the accession of Mary (1553) he was compelled to leave England, and returned to Germany. He wrote several works on theology. Died in Poland in 1560.

See J. F. BERTRAM, "Gründlicher Bericht von Johann Alasco," 3 vols., 1733.

Al-Asharee, (Al-Asharî,) âl-âsh'â-ree', an Arabian doctor, born at Basrah about 860 A.D. He was the founder of a Mohammedan sect called Asharites. Died about 940.

Alasko. See ALASCO.

Alasmai. See ABDEL-MALEK-IBN-KOREYB.

Alatino, ä-lä-tee'no, (MOSES,) a Jewish physician, born at Spoleto, Italy ; lived about 1600. He translated into Latin Galen's treatise on Hippocrates' work entitled "De Aere Locis et Aquis." (See HIPPOCRATES.)

Alaudanus. See ALLOUETTE.

Alaux, ä'lo', (JEAN,) a French historical painter, born at Bordeaux in 1786. He was patronized by Louis Philippe, and became a member of the Institute.

Alava, d', dä'lä-vä, (MIGUEL RICARDO,) a Spanish general, born at Vittoria in 1771. He fought against the French in the Peninsular war, became aide-de-camp to Wellington, and obtained the rank of general of brigade about 1813. In May, 1822, he was chosen President of the Cortes, and in the next month fought for the Constitution and the Cortes against the insurgents. His party having been subdued by French intervention, he went into exile in 1823. He returned to Spain after the death of Ferdinand, and was sent as ambassador to London in 1834. Died in 1843.

Alava Esquivel, d', dä'lä-vä ĕs-ke-vĕl', (DIEGO,) a Spanish prelate, born at Vittoria. He was successively Bishop of Astorga, of Avila, and of Córdova, and wrote a work on Councils, "De Consiliis Universalibus," (published in 1582.) Died in 1562.

Alava y Navarete, de, dà ä'lä-vä e nä-vä-rä'tä, (Don IGNACIO MARIA,) a Spanish admiral, born at Vittoria. He entered the navy in 1766, and became rear-admiral in 1787. In 1794 he set out on a voyage of circumnavigation, during which he rectified many errors in the charts of the South Sea. He was second in command of the Spanish fleet at Trafalgar, (1805,) where he was wounded. In 1817 he was raised to the rank of high-admiral. Died the same year.

See CLARK'S "Life of Nelson."

Alawy, ä-lä'wee, a Persian physician, born at Shirâz in 1669, was patronized by Aurungzebe. Died in 1749.

Alaymo, Alaimo, pronounced alike â-lī′mo, or **Alcaimo,** âl-kī′mo, (MARCO ANTONIO,) an Italian physician, born in Sicily in 1590. He practised at Palermo, and was regarded as the first physician of his time in Sicily. Among his works is one called " Diadecticon," giving an account of different medicinal substances, (1637.) Died in 1662.

Alba. See ALVA.

Alba, d′, (MACHINO.) See MACHINO D′ALBA.

Albacini, âl-bâ-chee′nee, (CARLO,) a Roman sculptor who flourished in the latter part of the eighteenth century. He was much employed in the restoration of antique statues. He was living in 1807.

Alban, aul′ban, SAINT, the first person put to death in England for embracing the Christian faith. He suffered martyrdom in the time of Diocletian, about 285 A.D. The monastery of Saint Albans was founded, in honour of him, in the eighth century.

Albane. See ALBANI, (FRANCESCO.)

Albaneze, âl′bâ′nâz′, or **Albanese,** âl-bâ-nā′sà, a noted Italian singer, who lived in Paris. He died in 1800.

Albani, âl-bâ′nee, (ALESSANDRO,) [Lat. ALEXAN′-DER ALBA′NUS,] a nephew of Pope Clement XI., born at Urbino in 1692, was made cardinal in 1721. He was a liberal patron of learning and the arts. He made a very valuable collection of statues and other works of art. Died in 1779.

See STROCCHI, " De Vita Alex. Albani Cardinalis," 1790.

Albani, (ANNIBALE,) CARDINAL, born at Urbino in 1682, wrote " Memoirs of the City of Urbino," (1724.) Died about 1750.

Albani, (FRANCESCO,) [in French, L′ALBANE, lâl′-bân′,] a distinguished Italian painter, born at Bologna in 1578, was a pupil of Denis Calvart and of Ludovico Caracci. He painted mostly in Bologna and Rome; in the latter city he executed some large frescos. His best works are small oil-pictures, treating of subjects from ancient poetry and mythology, and are highly finished. In the opinion of Mengs, his studies of women surpass those of all other painters. He excelled also in rural prospects. He reproduced in many of his works " Venus Sleeping," " Diana Bathing," and similar subjects. Among his master-pieces are " The Four Elements," " The Toilet of Venus," a " Noli-me-Tangere," and an Annunciation. He had a family of twelve children, who, as well as his wife, were remarkable for their beauty, and served him as models for his angels, Venuses, and Cupids. The sculptors Algardi and Fiammingo, it is said, likewise studied Albani's children as models. Died at Bologna in 1660.

See MALVASIA, " Felsina Pittrice;" PASSERI, " Vite de′ Pittori;" HEINECKEN, " Dictionnaire des Artistes."

Albani, (GIOVANNI BATTISTA,) an Italian landscape-painter, was a brother of the preceding. Died in 1668.

Albani, (GIOVANNI FRANCESCO.) See CLEMENT XI.

Albani, (GIOVANNI FRANCESCO,) a nephew of the cardinal Alessandro Albani, born at Urbino in 1720, and made cardinal in 1747. Died in 1809.

Albani, (GIUSEPPE,) an Italian nobleman, born at Rome in 1750, became cardinal in 1801, and died in 1834.

Albano. See ALBANI, (FRANCESCO.)

Albano, âl-bâ′no, (GIOVANNI GIROLAMO,) [Lat. JO-HAN′NES HIERON′YMUS ALBA′NUS,] an eminent Italian lawyer, born at Bergamo in 1504, made cardinal in 1570, and died in 1591.

Albans, Saint, sent aul′banz, (JOHN OF,) a physician, philosopher, and theologian, born near Saint Albans, in England. In 1198 he became chief physician to Philip II. of France; in 1228 he joined the Dominican order, and died about the middle of the thirteenth century.

Albans, Saint, (DUCHESS OF,) an English actress, whose maiden name was **Mellon,** was married first to the rich banker Coutts, and again to the Duke of Saint Albans. Died in 1837.

Albany, âl′ba-ne, (LOUISA,) COUNTESS OF, a daughter of Prince Stolberg-Gedern, was born in 1753. She was married in 1772 to the Pretender Charles Stuart, a grandson of James II., from whom she was separated in 1780. Soon after the death of her husband (1788) she was privately married to the poet Alfieri, and settled at Florence. (See ALFIERI.) He ascribed to her influence much of his success as an author. Died in 1824.

Albarelli, âl-bâ-rel′lee,(JACOPO,) a Venetian sculptor. born about 1570; died in 1620.

Albaspinus. See AUBESPINE.

Al-ba-teg′nĭ-us, the Latin name of **Albatenee, (Albatenî,)** âl-bâ-tā′nee, or **Albatînî,** âl-bâ-tee′nee, a celebrated Arabian astronomer, who died at Bagdâd in 929. He made an abridgment of the Almagest of Ptolemy, with a commentary, and wrote other valuable works.

Albe, d′, DUC. See ALVA, DUKE OF.

Al-Beidawi, (or -Beidhawi.) See BEIDAWEE.

Albeladory or **Al-Beladori,** (an Arabian historian.) See BELÂDORI.

Al′be-marle, (ARNOLD van Kep′pel,) EARL OF, a Dutch gentleman, born in Guelderland in 1669. He became a favourite courtier and attendant of William, Prince of Orange, whom he accompanied to England in 1688. " Courage, loyalty, and secrecy were common between him and Portland," says Macaulay. He was created Earl of Albemarle and Master of the Robes by William III., and was a rival of the Duke of Portland. He served as general in the war against Louis XIV., (1702–12.) Died in 1718.

See MACAULAY's " History of England," vol. v.

Albemarle, DUKE OF. See MONK.

Albenas, d′, dâlb′nâ′, or dâl′beh-nâ′, (JEAN JOSEPH,) VICOMTE, a French military officer and writer, born near Nîmes in 1760; died in 1824.

Albenas, d′, (JEAN Poldo—pol′do′,) a French antiquary, born at Nîmes in 1512, was a Protestant. He wrote a work on the antiquities of Nîmes, (1560.) Died in 1565.

Alber, âl′ber, [Lat. AL′BERUS,] (ERASMUS,) a learned German poet and witty satirist, who was an intimate friend of Luther, and a zealous Protestant. He was born at Sprendlingen, a village of Hesse-Darmstadt, but the date of his birth is unknown. He was employed as teacher or preacher at Stade, Magdeburg, and other places. He wrote, besides satires against the Roman Catholics, many sacred songs or hymns, abounding in original ideas. Died in 1553.

See J. J. KÖRBER, " Beitrag zu der Lebensbeschreibung Erasmi Alberi."

Albergati, âl-bêr-gâ′tee, (FABIO,) an Italian political writer, born at Bologna. Died about 1605.

Albergati, (NICCOLÒ,) an Italian, born at Bologna in 1375, was made cardinal in 1426, and died in 1443.

Albergati-Capacelli, d′, dâl-bêr-gâ′tee kâ-pâ-chel′-lee, (FRANCESCO,) an Italian marquis, senator of Bologna, born in 1728, devoted himself to theatrical representations and became a consummate actor. He also composed several comedies and farces. Died in 1804.

Albergoni, âl-bêr-go′nee, an Italian preacher and learned theologian, born at Milan in the latter part of the sixteenth century; died in 1636.

Albergotti, âl-bêr-got′tee, (FRANCESCO,) an Italian lawyer, born at Arezzo in 1304; died in 1376.

Alberi, âl′bà-ree, (EUGENIO,) an Italian writer, born at Padua in 1817. He published a Life of Catherine de Médicis, (1838,) and a work, " De′ Lavori di G. Galilei," (1843.)

Alberic I. and II. See ALBERICUS I. and II.

Alberic, âl′bà′rèk′, a Benedictine monk, afterwards a bishop, born at Beauvais in 1080. In 1140 he convoked at Antioch a council which deposed the patriarch Rodolphus, (or Rudolphus.) Died in 1147.

Albéric (âl′bà′rèk′) OF TROIS FONTAINES, (tRwâ fôn′tàn′,) a French chronicler of the thirteenth century.

Alberici, âl-bà-ree′chee, or **Albrizzi,** âl-brèt′see, (ENRICO,) an Italian painter of Bergamo, born in 1714; died in 1775.

Alberico de Rosciate, âl-bà-ree′ko dà ro-shâ′tà, an eminent Italian lawyer, born near Bergamo about the beginning of the fourteenth century. Died in 1354.

Al-be-rī′cus or **Alberico** (âl-bà-ree′ko) [Fr. AL-BÉRIC, âl′bà′rèk′] **I.,** a count of Tusculum, and consul of Rome in the tenth century.

Albericus II., a son of the preceding, married the

daughter of Hugo, King of Italy, and governed Rome with full authority from 936 till his death in 954.

Al'be-ro I. and II., the name of two bishop-princes of Liege in the twelfth century.

Alberoni, âl-bà-ro'nee, (GIULIO,) an Italian, born near Piacenza in 1664. Having been appointed agent of the Duke of Parma at the court of Madrid, he won the favour of Philip V., obtained a cardinal's hat, and was made prime minister of Spain about 1716. Aiming to restore to that country the power she had possessed under Philip II., Alberoni, as little restrained by sound judgment as by principle or the laws of nations, without any declaration of war, surprised and captured Cagliari and other towns of Sardinia then belonging to the Emperor of Germany. All Europe cried out against this violation of the rights of nations, and the ambitious cardinal was, in consequence, deprived of his office, in 1719, and banished from Spain. He retired to Italy, where he died in 1792.

See ROUSSET DE MISSY, "Vie d'Alberoni," 1719; G. MOORE, "Life of Cardinal Alberoni," 1806.

Albers, âl'bers, (HEINRICH PHILIPP,) a German physician, born at Hameln in 1768; died in 1830.

Albers, (JOHANN ABRAHAM,) a distinguished German physician, born at Bremen in 1772. He first introduced among his countrymen a knowledge of the doctrines of Broussais and the discoveries of Laennec. Died in 1821.

Albers, (JOHANN FRIEDRICH HERMANN,) a German physician, born at Dorsten, near Wesel, in 1805. He became professor of medicine at Bonn in 1831. Among his works is a "Manual of General Pathology," (2 vols., 1842–44.)

Albert, âl'bert, [Ger. ALBRECHT, âl'brĕkt,] I., Duke of Austria, son of Rudolph of Habsburg, was born in 1248, and elected Emperor of Germany in 1298, in the place of Adolphus of Nassau, who had been deposed. He was distinguished for his avarice, cruelty, and for an all-grasping and unprincipled ambition. In 1308 a conspiracy of the nobles was formed against him, and he was killed by his own nephew, John surnamed the Parricide.

See PEZZL, "Oesterreichische Biographie;" J. C. PFISTER, "Geschichte der Teutschen."

Albert (Albrecht) II., (or THE LAME,) Duke of Austria, was a younger son of the preceding. He was born in 1298, began to reign in 1330, and died in 1358.

Albert III., Duke of Austria, a son of Albert the Lame, born in 1348, died in 1395. He was a distinguished patron of the arts and sciences.

See ERSCH and GRUBER, "Allgemeine Encyklopaedie;" LUDEN, "Histoire de l'Allemagne."

Albert (Albrecht) IV., Duke of Austria, born in 1377, succeeded his father, Albert III., in 1395. He was a nephew of Sigismund, King of Hungary, and of Wenceslaus of Bohemia, each of whom appointed Albert his successor. Died in 1404.

See ERSCH und GRUBER, "Allgemeine Encyklopaedie."

Albert (Albrecht) V., Duke of Austria, son of Albert IV., was born in 1397, and succeeded his father in 1404. He distinguished himself by his activity against the Hussites, over whom he gained several victories. In 1435 he drove the Turks from Hungary; and on the death of Sigismund, his father-in-law, the Hungarians chose Albert for their king. In 1438 he was elected Emperor, and thus became Albert II. of Germany. He died in 1439.

See WENK, "Historia Alberti II.," 1740; HORMAYR, "Oesterreichischer Plutarch;" ERSCH und GRUBER, "Allgemeine Encyklopaedie."

Albert (Albrecht) VI., Duke of Austria, surnamed THE PRODIGAL, born in 1418, was a son of Ernest. The dominions of Ernest were divided, in 1438, between Albert and his brother Frederick III., Emperor of Germany. Died in 1463.

Albert, (Albrecht,) Archduke of Austria, a son of the emperor Maximilian II., was born in 1559. He was appointed Governor of the Low Countries by Philip II. in 1596, and married Isabella, (Elizabeth,) a daughter of that king. In an attempt to conquer the Dutch, he

was defeated by Maurice at Nieuport, in 1600. He took Ostend, after a memorable siege of three years, in 1604. The war was suspended in 1609 by a truce of twelve years. Died in 1621.

See LE MIRE, "Vita Alberti Pii," 1622; CHARLES DUBOIS, "Histoire d'Albert et d'Isabelle," 1847; DE THOU, "Histoire."

Albert or Albrecht, (FRIEDRICH RUDOLPH,) ARCHDUKE, an Austrian prince and general, son of the Archduke Charles, the famous commander against Napoleon, was born in 1817. He fought under Radetzky at Novara in 1849, and was appointed Governor of Hungary in 1851. Having obtained command of the southern army, he defeated the Italians at Custozza, about the 1st of July, 1856, soon after which he succeeded Benedek as commander-in-chief.

Albert (Albrecht) I. of Baireuth, surnamed ALCIBIADES, born in 1522, was a son of Casimir, Margrave of Brandenburg. He was a man of dissolute habits. He was defeated in 1553 by the Elector Moritz of Saxony, and his allies. Died in 1555.

Albert (Albrecht) I. of Bavaria, son of the emperor Lewis (Ludwig) V., succeeded to the territory of Lower Bavaria in 1349; died in 1404.

Albert (Albrecht) IV. of Bavaria, surnamed THE WISE, succeeded to the government in 1463, and, turning all his attention to the consolidation and organization of his estates, contributed greatly to the rank and influence which Bavaria has since attained among the powers of Europe. Died in 1508.

Albert (Albrecht) V. of Bavaria, surnamed THE MAGNANIMOUS, succeeded his father, William IV., in 1550. He was a distinguished patron of learning and the arts. Died in 1579, aged about fifty.

Albert I., Margrave of Brandenburg, surnamed THE BEAR, was born about 1106. He is called the founder of the house of Brandenburg. Died about 1170.

Albert II., Margrave of Brandenburg, succeeded his brother, Otho II., in 1206. Died in 1221.

Albert III., Margrave of Brandenburg, surnamed ACHILLES, and ULYSSES, on account of his bravery and wisdom, born in 1414, was renowned for martial exploits. He was a son of Frederick I. He commanded the army of the emperor, in 1471, against the Duke of Bavaria. Died in 1486.

Albert (Albrecht) of Brandenburg, a grandson of the preceding, and first Duke of Prussia, was born in 1490. In 1511 he was elected Grand Master of the Teutonic Order, who held Prussia proper as a fief of the King of Poland. In 1525 he abandoned the vows of his order, became a Protestant, and received Prussia as a hereditary fief of the crown of Poland. Thus the dominion of the Teutonic Knights was brought to an end. Died in 1568.

Albert, (Albrecht,) Duke of Brunswick, called THE GREAT, born in 1236, was a son of Duke Otho. He was an energetic and warlike prince. Died in 1279.

Albert, (Albrecht,) Archbishop of Magdeburg, waged war against the emperor Otho, and promoted the election of Frederick II. in 1212. Died about 1232.

Albert, (Albrecht,) an archbishop of Magdeburg and Mentz, the son of John Cicero, Elector of Brandenburg, was born in 1489. He was elected Archbishop of Magdeburg in 1513, Archbishop and Prince Elector of Mentz in 1514, and raised to the dignity of cardinal in 1518. Died in 1545. He was a patron of literature, and possessed popular manners, but was unfitted by his want of energy and courage to contend with the storms which prevailed in Germany at the time of the Reformation.

Albert (Albrecht) of Mecklenburg, a son of Albrecht, Duke of Mecklenburg, was chosen King of Sweden in 1363. He waged war against Margaret, Queen of Denmark, who gained a decisive victory in 1388 and deprived him of the crown. Died in 1412.

Albert, (Albrecht,) Archbishop of Mentz in the twelfth century, was a turbulent politician, and an enemy of the emperor Henry V. Died in 1137.

Albert (Albrecht) I., Duke and Elector of Saxony, began to reign in 1212. He accompanied the emperor Frederick II. in a crusade against the Saracens in 1228. Died in 1260.

Albert (Albrecht) II. of Saxony, was a son of the

preceding. He contributed to the election of three emperors, Rudolph I., Adolph, and Albert I. Died about 1300.

Albert (Albrecht) III. succeeded his brother Rudolph as Elector of Saxony in 1418. Died in 1422.

Albert, äl'baiR', a French revolutionist, whose proper name is ALEXANDRE MARTIN, was born in Oise about 1815, and became a mechanic. In 1840 he founded a journal called "L'Atelier," ("The Workshop.") He was a member of the provisional government formed in February, 1848, and of the Constituent Assembly which met in May of that year. For his alleged complicity in a sedition of May 15, 1848, he was sentenced to deportation.

Albert THE BLESSED, Patriarch of Jerusalem, born in the diocese of Parma about 1150, was the legislator of the order of the Carmelites, (or White Friars.) He was chosen Patriarch of Jerusalem in 1204, and assassinated at Acre in 1214.

Albert, (CHARLES.) See CHARLES ALBERT.
Albert OF COLOGNE. See ALBERTUS MAGNUS.
Albert, (ERASMUS.) See ALBER.
Albert LE GRAND. See ALBERTUS MAGNUS.
Albert THE GREAT. See ALBERTUS MAGNUS.
Albert (Albrecht) VON HALBERSTADT, (fon häl'ber-stät',) a German poet or minnesinger, wrote about 1210-20.

Albert, äl'bĕRt, (HEINRICH,) a German lyric poet and musician, born at Lobenstein, Saxony, in 1604. He produced sacred and secular airs and songs which are highly esteemed. He was organist of the cathedral of Königsberg from 1631 till his death. Died in 1668.

Albert, (MICHAEL and SALOMON.) See ALBERTI.

Albert, (PRINCE,) or, more fully, **Albert Francis Augustus Charles Emmanuel**, Prince of Saxe-Coburg-Gotha and Consort of Queen Victoria of Great Britain, was born near Coburg in August, 1819. He was the second son of Duke Ernest I. He visited England in 1838, and was married to Victoria in February, 1840. In 1842 he was elected Chancellor of the University of Cambridge. He obtained the rank of field-marshal in the British army and colonel of the Grenadier Guards. While maintaining a proper reserve and neutrality with respect to political parties, he acquired a great influence in the public councils, and merited the confidence of the queen by his discretion and other qualifications which rendered him her best adviser. He was the efficient chairman of the Council of the Great Exhibition of 1851, and in 1859 was chosen president of the British Association for the Advancement of Science. Prince Albert was interested in the promotion of the fine arts, of agriculture, and, we may add, of every benevolent enterprise. By the manner in which he passed through the somewhat peculiar trials of his exceptional position, in which there were no safe precedents to guide him, he won the general approbation of the British people. Died on the 14th of December, 1861. His death was regarded as an irreparable loss, not merely to the queen, but to the nation of which he had been king in all but the name.

See "Early Years of His Royal Highness the Prince Consort," 1867.

Albert OF STADE. See ALBERTUS STADENSIS.
Albert OF SWEDEN. See ALBRECHT OF MECKLENBURG.
Albert, d', (CHARLES.) See LUYNES, DUC DE.
Albert, d', däl'baiR', (LOUIS JOSEPH,) Prince of Grünberghen or Grimbergen, born in 1672, was a grandson of Constable de Luynes. He entered the service of the emperor Charles VII. He published "The Dream of Alcibiades," (1735.) Died in 1758.

Albert, d', däl'baiR', (PAUL,) born in 1703, was made Archbishop of Sens in 1753, and Cardinal of Luynes in 1756. Died in 1788. He was distinguished for his liberality of mind and for his high moral character.

Albert d'Ailly. See CHAULNES, DUC DE.
Albert Dürer. See DÜRER.
Albert Edward, Prince of Wales, the eldest son of Prince Albert, noticed above, and Queen Victoria, and heir apparent to the British crown, was born on the 9th of November, 1841. Besides being Prince of Wales, he

is Prince of Saxe-Coburg-Gotha, Duke of Cornwall and Rothesay, and Baron Renfrew. In 1860 he visited the United States, where he was received with flattering demonstrations of popular favour. In the winter of 1861-2 he set out on a tour to Syria, Palestine, Egypt, etc. He married, in March, 1863, the Princess Alexandra of Denmark, and has a son, Albert Edward, born in January, 1864.

Albertano da Brescia, äl-bĕR-tä'no dä bRĕsh'yä, an Italian writer, who was magistrate of Brescia in the early part of the thirteenth century.

Albertazzo, Marquis of Este. See ESTE.

Alberti, äl-bĕR'tee, (ARISTOTILE,) called also **Ridolfo Fioravanti**, re-dol'fo fe-o-rä-vän'tee, an architect and engineer, born at Bologna, was one of the greatest mechanicians of the fifteenth century.

Alberti, (BENEDETTO,) a Florentine chief of the popular party in the revolution which occurred at Florence in 1379-80. He was exiled in 1387.

Alberti, (CHERUBINO,) a brother of Giovanni, noticed below, a painter and noted engraver, was born in 1552. Died in 1615.

Alberti, (DURANTE,) an Italian painter, born at Borgo San Sepolcro in 1538. He worked in Rome, where he painted in fresco and oil. Died in 1613.

Alberti, (FILIPPO,) an Italian poet, born at Perugia in 1548, was a friend of Tasso. Died in 1612.

Alberti, äl-bĕR'tee, (GEORG WILHELM,) a German Protestant minister, born at Thundern, in Hanover, in 1723. He published "Letters on the State of Religion and Science in Great Britain," (1752-54,) which are commended by Guizot in the "Biographie Universelle." Died in 1758.

See ERSCH und GRUBER, "Allgemeine Encyklopaedie."

Alberti, (GIOVANNI,) an Italian painter, born at Borgo San Sepolcro in 1558, was a brother of Cherubino. He was unrivalled in his age for foreshortenings of the figure, and excelled in perspective and landscape. He painted frescos in the Vatican for Clement VIII. Died in 1601.

Alberti, (JOHANN,) a German jurist and Orientalist of the sixteenth century, born at Widmannstadt. He was appointed Chancellor of Austria by Ferdinand I., and published an "Epitome of the Koran," with critical notes, (1543.) Died in 1559.

Alberti, (JOHANN,) a Dutch theologian and profound scholar, was born at Assen in 1698. He became professor of theology at Leyden in 1740. He was well versed in Greek literature, and had a high reputation as a critic. His greatest merit consists in his labours to perfect the Lexicon of Hesychius, of which he published an excellent edition, 2 vols., 1746-66. Died in 1762.

Alberti, (JOHANN GUSTAV WILHELM,) a German manufacturer, born at Hamburg in 1757. He invented, about 1817, a machine for spinning linen. Died in 1837.

Alberti, (LEANDRO,) a learned Italian friar, born at Bologna in 1479. He wrote, besides other works, a "History of Bologna," (1541-43,) and a "Description of all Italy," (1550.) Died in 1552.

Alberti, (LEON BATTISTA,) an eminent Italian architect and philosopher, born of a noble family, at Genoa, (or, as some writers say, at Florence,) in 1404. He was also a poet and a painter, and highly distinguished by his general learning and personal character. He succeeded to the direction of several works which Brunelleschi left unfinished at Florence, where he completed the Pitti Palace and was one of the restorers of the classic style. The church of St. Francis at Rimini is called his master-piece. He also gained a high reputation as a writer on art, by his "Treatise on Architecture" (" De Re Ædificatoria," 1485) and treatises on painting (1540) and sculpture. Died in 1472.

See G. B. NICCOLINI, "Elogio di L. B. Alberti," 1819; MILIZIA, "Vite degli Architetti ;" TIRABOSCHI, "Storia della Letteratura Italiana ;" QUATREMÈRE DE QUINCY, "Histoire des plus célèbres Architectes."

Alberti (äl-bĕR'tee) or **Albert**, (MICHAEL,) a learned German physician and medical writer, born at Nuremberg in 1682. In 1716 he was appointed professor of medicine, and in 1719 professor of philosophy, in the University of Halle. Died in 1757.

Alberti, (ROMANO,) an Italian painter and writer on art, born at Borgo San Sepolcro, lived about 1600.

Alberti, (SALOMON,) an eminent German physician and anatomist, born at Naumburg in 1540, was appointed professor of anatomy and philosophy in the University of Wittenberg in 1576, and died in 1600. His writings and discoveries entitle him to a high rank among modern anatomists.

Alberti, (VALENTIN,) a German theologian, born in Silesia in 1635, became professor of theology at Leipsic. He wrote many polemical works on questions of theology. His "Compendium of the Law of Nature" ("Compendium Juris Naturæ," 1673) was written in opposition to a work of Puffendorf; it has often been reprinted. Died in 1697.

Alberti di Villanova, âl-bĕR'tee de vĕl-lâ-no'vâ, (FRANCESCO,) an Italian, born at Nice in 1731, known as the author of several popular dictionaries. His 'Dictionnaire Italien-Français et Français-Italien" had a high reputation, and has passed through a number of editions. Died in 1800.

Albertinelli, âl-bĕR-te-nĕl'lee, (MARIOTTO,) an eminent Florentine painter, born about 1475, imitated and equalled Fra Bartolommeo. He painted religious subjects at Florence and Rome. "The Visitation of Elizabeth to the Virgin" is his master-piece. Innocenzio da Imola was his pupil. Died about 1520.

See VASARI, "Lives of the Painters."

Albertini, âl-bĕR-tee'nee, or **Alberti,** âl-bĕR'tee, (ANNIBALE,) an Italian medical writer, lived about 1600, and wrote "On Diseases of the Heart," ("De Affectionibus Cordis," 1618.)

Albertini, [Lat. ALBERTI'NUS,] (FRANCESCO,) an Italian priest and antiquary, born at Florence in the fifteenth century. His chief work is one on the Antiquities of Rome, entitled "On the Wonders of Ancient and Modern Rome," ("De Mirabilibus novæ et veteris Urbis Romæ," 1505.)

Albertini, (GIORGIO FRANCESCO,) an Italian theological writer, born in Istria in 1732. He became professor of theology in the University of Padua. Died in 1810.

Albertini, (IPPOLITO FRANCESCO,) an eminent Italian physician, born at Crevalcore in 1662. He studied under Malpighi, whom he succeeded as professor of medicine in the University of Bologna. Died in 1738, leaving a valuable essay on diseases of the heart.

Albertini, (PAOLO,) an Italian priest, writer, and political agent, born at Venice about 1430. Died in 1475.

Albertini, von, fon âl-bĕR-tee'nee, (JOHANN BAPTIST,) an eminent Moravian minister, born at Neuwied, on the Rhine, in Germany, in 1769. He wrote hymns which display much poetical talent. He was a man of extensive acquirements and most estimable character. His sermons are remarkable for beautiful simplicity of style. He was made a bishop in 1814. Died near Herrnhut in 1831.

Al-ber-ti'nus, (ÆGID'IUS,) a German satirist, born at Deventer, in Holland, in 1560; died in 1620. He is remarkable for having written in the German tongue at a time when Latin was almost universally employed by the learned men of Germany. His works were very popular in his time.

Albertolli, âl-bĕR-tol'lee, (FERDINANDO,) an Italian architect, was a nephew of Giocondo, whom he succeeded at the Academy of Milan. Died in 1846.

Albertolli, (GIACOMO,) an Italian architect, born in 1761, became professor of civil architecture in the University of Padua. Died in 1805.

Albertolli, (GIOCONDO,) a distinguished Italian architect, born in 1742, was appointed professor of decorative architecture at Milan about 1775. Died in 1840.

Albertrandy, âl-bĕR-trân'de, (JOHN CHRISTIAN,) an eminent Polish historian, linguist, and numismatist, born at Warsaw in 1731. He became librarian to King Stanislaus, who appointed him Bishop of Zenopolis. Among his works are "Roman Antiquities explained by Medals," (3 vols., 1805-08,) and a "History of Poland during the Last Three Centuries." Died in 1808.

Albertsen, âl'bĕrt-sĕn, (HAMILTON HENDRIK,) a Danish writer of Latin poetry, born at Copenhagen in 1592. Died in Egypt about 1630.

Albertucci de' Borselli, âl-bĕR-toot'chee dâ boR-sel'lee, (GIROLAMO,) an Italian preacher and chronicler, born at Bologna about 1432. Died in 1497.

Albertus, âl-bĕR'tùs, a German painter and engraver, born in Saxony. Died about 1680.

Alber'tus Mag'nus, [Fr. ALBERT LE GRAND,âl'baiR' lĕh gRôN,] (*i.e.* "Albert the Great,") a celebrated schoolman and philosopher, born at Lauingen, in Bavaria, about 1200, was sometimes called **Albert de Bollstadt** (bol'stât) and **Alber'tus Gro'tus.** He occupies the first rank among the philosophers and theologians of the middle ages. He became a Dominican friar in his youth, and, after lecturing on theology for three years at Paris, was chosen provincial of his order in 1254. During a long period he gave public lectures at Cologne. He was appointed Bishop of Ratisbon in 1260, but about 1263 he resigned that office, which he had never solicited. He died in 1280. As a man, he was remarkable for an enthusiastic love of knowledge, for modesty, and for a noble and disinterested spirit. He left a great number of works, which treat of logic, theology, physics, and metaphysics. Thomas Aquinas was his disciple.

See RUDOLPHUS NOVIOMAGENSIS, "De Vita Alberti Magni," 1499; RAFFAELE BADI, "Ristretto della prodigiosa Vita del Alberto Magno," 1680-88; PETRUS DE PRUSSIA, "Vita Alberti Magni;" ECHARD, "Scriptores Ordinis Prædicatorum;" GAUSLINUS, "Synopsis Vitæ Alberti Magni," 1630; LUDWIG CHOULANT, "Albertus Magnus."

Al-ber'tus Sta̢-den'sis, an abbot of Stade, Hanover, in the thirteenth century, known as the author of the "Chronicon Alberti," (*i.e.* "Chronicle of Albertus,") containing an account of many events which occurred in the north of Germany in the middle ages down to 1256.

Alberus. See ALBER.

Albi, âl'be', (HENRI,) a French Jesuit, born in Provence in 1590. He wrote biographical notices of several religious persons. Died in 1659.

Albicante, âl-be-kân'tâ, (GIOVANNI ALBERTO,) a mediocre Milanese poet, who flourished about the middle of the sixteenth century.

Al-bi'cus, (SIGISMUNDUS,) or **Albicus** OF PRAGUE, called also **Al'bic** or **Albik** and **Albicius,** al-bish'e̢-us, a distinguished physician, born in Moravia in the latter part of the fourteenth century. He taught medicine at Prague for many years, and was physician to Wenceslaus IV., King of Bohemia, by whom in 1409 he was made Archbishop of Prague. He held this office only about four years. Died in 1427.

Albignac, 'd', dâl'bĕn'yȃk', (LOUIS ALEXANDRE,) BARON, a French military officer, born in Gascony in 1739. He served in Hindostan previous to the peace of 1783, and afterwards commanded the tenth division under the French Directory. He retired from service in 1798, and died in 1820.

Albignac, d', (PHILIPPE FRANÇOIS MAURICE,) COUNT, a French royalist general, born at Milhaud in 1775; died in 1824.

Albin, aul'bin, (ELEAZAR,) an English artist and painter in water-colours, published in 1731 a "Natural History of Birds," with 205 fine coloured plates; also a work on English Insects, in Latin, (1731,) and the same in English in 1749, with 100 copper-plates, coloured. The figures were correctly drawn from the life by himself.

Albina, âl-bee'nâ, (GIUSEPPE,) an Italian painter, sculptor, and architect, lived at Palermo, and died in 1611.

Albini, âl-bee'nee, (ALESSANDRO,) a distinguished Italian painter, born at Bologna in 1568, was a pupil and coadjutor of the Caracci. Among his works is a "Prometheus bringing Fire from Heaven." Died in 1646.

Albini, âl-bee'nee, (FRANZ JOSEPH,) a distinguished German lawyer and statesman, born at Saint Goar, in Rhenish Prussia, in 1748. His great fame as a jurist introduced him to the notice of the emperor Joseph II., who conceived a warm affection for him and gave him a place in the imperial cabinet. After the death of the emperor, in 1790, Albini was invited to the court of the Elector of Mentz, (Mayence,) and soon after was placed at the head of the government. From 1792 to the death of the elector in 1802, his prince allowed him to manage everything; and he proved himself worthy of the trust

---

ā, ē, ī, ō, ū, ȳ, *long;* ă, ĕ, ĭ, ŏ, ŭ, ў, *short;* a̢, e̢, i̢, o̢, *obscure;* fär, fȧll, fât; mĕt; nŏt; gŏŏd; mōŏn;

He not only showed distinguished ability in the management of all civil affairs, but also on a number of occasions evinced military talents of a high order. Died in 1816.

Albini, de, dä äl-bee'nee, (WILLIAM,) Earl of Arundel, the son of a Norman baron who followed William the Conqueror to England. He married Adelais, queen-dowager of Henry I., by whom he obtained the castle of Arundel and other estates. He took an active part in those troublous times, and died in 1176, during the reign of Henry II.

Albino, äl-bee'no, (GIOVANNI,) [Lat. JOAN'NES ALBI'NUS,] a Neapolitan statesman and historian, who lived towards the close of the fifteenth century. He was a counsellor to Ferdinand of Aragon, who appears to have consulted him in military as well as in civil affairs. He wrote a history of the events of his own time.

Al-bi-no-vā'nus, (CAIUS PEDO,) a Latin poet of the Augustan age, was a friend of Ovid, who addressed to him one of his "Epistolæ ex Ponto," ("Letters from Pontus.") He is said to have excelled in epic poetry, and is supposed to have written an epic poem on the exploits of Germanicus, which is lost. There is extant a beautiful elegy on the death of Drusus, which is ascribed to Albinovanus.

Al-bi'nus, [Gr. Ἀλβῖνος,] a Platonic philosopher, who lived at Smyrna about 150 A.D., was one of the teachers of Galen. He wrote an "Introduction to the Dialogues of Plato," which is extant.

See FABRICIUS, "Bibliotheca Græca."

Albi'nus, a Roman procurator of Judea in the time of Nero. He succeeded Portius Festus.

Al-bi'nus, [Ger. pron. äl-bee'nûs,] (ADRIAN,) a German professor of law, born at Lauban in 1513, was a friend of Luther. Died in 1590.

Albinus, (BERNARD,) a German physician, born at Dessau in 1653, was appointed professor of medicine in the University of Frankfort-on-the-Oder in 1681, and in 1702 to the chair of anatomy at Leyden. Died in 1721.

Albinus, (BERNARD SIEGFRIED,) an eminent German anatomist and physician, son of the preceding, was born at Frankfort-on-the-Oder in 1696 or 1697. He was educated at Leyden, and on the death of his father in 1721 was unanimously chosen professor of anatomy and surgery in the university. In 1745 he became professor of therapeutics, and held this office till his death in 1770. As an anatomist he was distinguished for the accuracy of his observations and the clearness and fulness of his descriptions. Almost all his works are on anatomy. His excellent "History of the Muscles of Man" ("Historia Musculorum Hominis," 1734) is highly praised by Haller.

See BOERHAAVE, "Oratio de Vita et Obitu B. Albini," 1721; HALLER, "Bibliotheca Anatomica."

Albinus, (CHRISTIAN BERNARD,) a brother of the preceding, was born near the close of the seventeenth century. He became professor of anatomy at Utrecht, where he died in 1752.

Al-bi'nus, (CLODIUS,) a native of Adrumetum, in Africa, became Roman governor of Gaul about 180 A.D., and defeated the Frisian tribes beyond the Rhine. Prompted by jealousy, the emperor Severus endeavoured to remove him by assassination; but, this proving unsuccessful, the two leaders met in battle near Lyons. Albinus was defeated and slain in 197. He appears to have been at one time associated with Severus in the empire; at all events, he reigned three years in Gaul and Britain, with the title of Cæsar.

Albinus Flaccus. See ALCUIN.

Albinus, (FRIEDRICH BERNARD,) born at Leyden in 1715, was a brother of Bernard Siegfried, whom he succeeded as professor of anatomy in 1745. His chief work is a physiological treatise "On the Nature of Man," ("De Natura Hominis," 1775.) Died in 1778.

Albinus, (JOHANN GEORG,) a German poet, born at Naumburg, was a son of an inferior poet of the same name, (1624–79.) The son wrote in German a number of popular idyls and hymns, a volume of which was published in 1686. He was living in 1714.

See J. B. LIEBLER, "Nachrichten von J. G. Albinus Leben," 1728.

Albinus, (or **Weiss,** wīss,) (PETRUS, or PETER,) a learned German writer and historian, who was born in

Saxony and lived in the latter half of the sixteenth century. Died at Dresden in 1598.

Al'bĭ-on, [Gr. Ἀλβίων or Ἀλεβίων,] a fabulous giant, regarded as a son of Neptune. He and his brother Bergion attacked Hercules near the Rhone, and were killed by that hero.

Albisson, äl'be'sôn', (JEAN,) a French lawyer and politician, born at Montpellier in 1732, was made tribune in 1802. He assisted in the preparation of several portions of Napoleon's celebrated Code. Died in 1810.

Albitte, äl'bět', (ANTOINE LOUIS,) a French Jacobin, member of the Legislative Assembly in 1791, distinguished for his violence and cruelty. He was a leader of the desperate revolt of May 20, 1795, against the Convention. For this he was condemned to death, but succeeded in concealing himself till the danger was over. He perished in the retreat from Russia in 1812, after he had served some years as sub-inspector of reviews.

Albizzi, äl-bit'see or äl-bět'see, a Florentine family which occupies a considerable place in the history of Florence during the thirteenth and fourteenth centuries. The most worthy of notice are PIETRO, RINALDO, and TOMMASO ALBIZZI, noticed below.

Albizzi, [Lat. ALBICIUS, äl-bish'e-us,] (BARTOLOMMEO,) an Italian friar, born in Tuscany, was the author of a work called "Conformities of the Life of Saint Francis with that of Jesus Christ." Erasmus Alber published in 1542 a refutation of this work, entitled "The Barefooted Monk's Jester and Alcoran," with a preface by Luther. Died in 1401.

Albizzi, (PIETRO,) the leader of the Guelph party at Florence, was put to death in 1379 by the Ghibelines.

Albizzi, (RINALDO,) a son of Tommaso, noticed below, born towards the close of the fourteenth century. He became involved in an unsuccessful contest with the family of the Medici, and died in exile at Ancona in 1452.

Albizzi, (TOMMASO,) born in 1347, was a nephew of Pietro and father of Rinaldo. He was chief magistrate of the republic from 1382 to 1417, which is accounted the most glorious period in the history of Florence. Died in 1417.

Albo, äl'bo, (JOSEPH, or JOSÉ,) an eminent Spanish rabbi, born at Soria in the latter part of the fourteenth century. He wrote a very able work in defence of his religion, entitled "The Foundations of the Jewish Faith." Died in 1428.

Al'boin, [Lat. ALBOI'NUS,] the son of Alduin, became King of the Longobards on the death of his father, about 553. Alduin had defeated the Gepidæ, who occupied the countries corresponding with the modern provinces of Slavonia and Servia. Alboin nearly exterminated that nation, killed Cunimund, their king, and compelled his daughter Rosamund to become his wife. He next (about 570) turned his arms against the northern provinces of Italy, and, conquering everything in his course, excepting Mantua and Padua, advanced as far as Spoletum, (or Spoleto.) In 573, Alboin, after drinking deeply at a banquet at Verona, ordered a cup, which he had made out of the skull of Cunimund, to be brought, and invited his wife Rosamund to drink out of it. This outrage roused her to deadly vengeance. She conspired with two of his officers, and they killed the king when he was sunk in his afternoon sleep.

See GIBBON, "History of the Decline and Fall of the Roman Empire," chap. xlv.; MURATORI, "Annali d'Italia."

Albon, (JACQUES.) See SAINT-ANDRÉ.

Albon, d', däl'bôn', (CLAUDE CAMILLE FRANÇOIS,) a French *littérateur*, born at Lyons in 1753. He wrote a discourse on the "History, Government, Arts, etc. of some Nations of Europe," (4 vols.) Died in 1788.

Alboni, äl-bo'nee, (MARIETTA,) a celebrated Italian singer, born at Cesena in 1824, was a pupil of Rossini. She made her *début* at Milan in 1841, with a success which was repeated, or surpassed, at Vienna and Saint Petersburg. In 1847 her performances excited great enthusiasm in London and Paris, and a few years later she visited the United States. Her voice is a contralto of great purity, compass, and flexibility. "There never existed a voice more bewitching," says M. Bousquet, "whose tone was more limpid and sweet, whose sonо

є as *k*; ç as *s*; ḡ *hard*; ġ as *j*; G, H, K, *guttural*; N, *nasal*; R, *trilled*; š as *z*; ŧh as in *this*. (☞ See Explanations, p. 23.)

rousness was more homogeneous in its different registers." She was married to the Marquis de Pepoli.

See "Nouvelle Biographie Générale."

Alboni, (PAOLO,) a distinguished landscape-painter of Bologna. He worked in Vienna from 1710 to 1722, and afterwards at Bologna. Died in 1730.

Al-Borâk or **Al-Burâk.** See BORAK.

Alboresi, âl-bo-râ′see, (GIACOMO,) an Italian painter of architecture, born at Bologna in 1632. He painted (with M. Pasio) the west façade of the cathedral of Florence. Died in 1677.

Albornotius. See ALBORNOZ, (GIL ALVAREZ CARILLO DE.)

Albornoz, âl-boR-nòth′, (DIEGO FELIPE,) a Spanish historian, lived about 1650, and published "Castilla Politica y Cristiana," 1666.)

Albornoz, de, dà âl-boR-nòth′, [Lat. ALBORNO′TIUS,] (GIL ALVAREZ CARILLO,) or simply Ægidius de Albornoz, a noble Spaniard, born at Cuenca about the beginning of the fourteenth century. He was chaplain and counsellor to Alfonso XI. of Castile, who raised him to the archbishopric of Toledo. After the accession of Pedro the Cruel to the throne, Albornoz, having incurred his displeasure, fled to Avignon to Pope Clement VI., by whom he was made cardinal. Innocent VI., Clement's successor, subsequently appointed him his legate, in which capacity Albornoz showed great wisdom as well as military skill, and in a few years recovered a multitude of Italian towns which had become disaffected or openly rebellious to the Papal see. He died in 1367.

See MURATORI, "Annali d'Italia;" STEPHANO, "Vita del Cardinale Albornoz;" SEPULVEDA, "De Vita et Rebus gestis G. Albornotii."

Albosius, âl-bo′she-us, or **Aillebout,** ȧl′boo′ or ȧ′ye-boo′, (JEAN,) a French physician, born at Autun, published in 1587 a description of a remarkable monstrosity, (a petrified embryo,) entitled "Portentosum Lithopædium sive Embryon petrifactum."

Albrand, âl′bRòN′, (FORTUNÉ,) a French Orientalist, born about 1795, planted a colony in Madagascar. Died in 1827.

Albrecht OF AUSTRIA. See ALBERT.

Albrecht OF BAVARIA. See ALBERT.

Albrecht OF MECKLENBURG. See ALBERT.

Albrecht, (ACHILLES.) See ALBERT.

Albrecht, âl′bRĕkt, (BALTHASAR AUGUSTIN,) a German painter, born at Berg, near Munich, in 1687. Died at Munich in 1765.

Albrecht, (JOHANN LORENZ,) a German musician and composer, born near Mühlhausen in 1732. Died in 1773.

Albrecht, (JOHANN SEBASTIAN,) a German naturalist and writer, born in 1695, lived at Coburg.

Albrecht, (JOHANN WILHELM,) a German physician, born at Erfurt in 1703, became professor of medicine in his native town in 1729, and professor of anatomy, surgery, and botany in the University of Göttingen in 1734. Died in 1736.

Albrecht, (SOPHIE,) a German poetess, born in 1757 at Erfurt, where her father, J. P. Baumer, was professor of medicine and philosophy. She was married at the age of fourteen, and died in 1837. Her poems are lyric and dramatic; they display deep feeling and considerable poetic power.

Albrecht, (WILHELM,) a German agriculturist, born in 1786, was a pupil of Thaer. In 1820 he was appointed director of an experimental school of agriculture founded at Idstein in Nassau, and afterwards removed to Geisberg near Wiesbaden. He wrote, or edited, "The Annals of the Agricultural Society of Nassau," (15 vols.,) and had a high reputation as a teacher. Died in 1848.

Albrecht, (WILHELM EDUARD,) a German legist, born at Elbing in 1800, was professor of German law at Göttingen from 1829 to 1837. He became professor of law at Leipsic in 1840.

Albrechtsberger, âl′bRĕkts-bĕRG′ĕr, (JOHANN GEORG,) a distinguished German musician, born near Vienna in 1736; died in 1809. The celebrated Beethoven was one of his pupils.

Albret, âl′bRȧ′, (CHARLES OF,) [Fr. CHARLES D'ALBRET, shȧRl dȧl′bRȧ′,] a cousin-german of Charles VI.,

appointed Constable of France in 1402. He commanded the French army at the disastrous battle of Agincourt, in which he was defeated and slain, in 1415.

Albret, (HENRY OF.) See HENRY II. OF NAVARRE.

Albret, (JEANNE OF.) See JEANNE OF NAVARRE.

Albrici, âl-bRee′chee, (VINCENZO,) an Italian composer and organist, who flourished in the latter part of the seventeenth century. He spent some time at the court of Christina, Queen of Sweden.

Albrion, de, dà âl-bRe-ōn′, (DOMINGO,) a Spanish sculptor, lived between 1550 and 1600. His works are praised by Ponz.

Albrizzi. See ALBERICI.

Albrizzi, âl-bRĕt′see or âl-bRit′see, (ISABELLA **Teotoki**—tà-o-to′kee,) a daughter of Count Teotoki, was born at Corfu about 1770. She was married to a Venetian nobleman; and her house in Venice became a place of resort for persons of distinction, both natives and foreigners. She was distinguished for her learning, wit, and taste, and not less for her domestic virtues. She wrote several works of merit. Died in 1835.

Albucasis. See ABOO-L-KASIM.

Albufera, DUKE OF. See SUCHET.

Albumazar, âl-boo-mã′zar, (a corruption of **Aboo-Mashar,**) a celebrated Arabian astronomer, born at Bulkh (or Balkh) about 780 A.D. He died in 885, aged above one hundred years.

Albuquerque, de, dà âl-boo-kĕR′kà or âl′boo-kĕRk′, (ALFONSO,) [Port. AFFONSO D'ALBOQUERQUE, âf-fon′so dâl-bo-kĕR′kà,] surnamed THE GREAT, and THE PORTUGUESE MARS, a famous Portuguese commander, was born of a branch of the royal family, near Alhandra, in 1453. He commanded a squadron in the fleet which in 1506 was sent to India under Tristan da Cunha, and carried a secret commission by virtue of which he should supersede Francisco de Almeida as governor or viceroy of the Indies. On his way he took Ormuz, then a great emporium; but he was soon forced to evacuate that place, in consequence of the defection or insubordination of some officers of his squadron. He arrived in India in 1508. In 1510 he captured the rich city of Goa, and in 1511 performed a brilliant exploit in the conquest of Malacca. He entered the Red Sea in 1513 with the first European fleet that ever navigated its waters, and afterwards obtained permanent possession of Ormuz. He raised the affairs of the Portuguese in India to the highest state of prosperity. Having, however, been superseded in the government of India, he died near Goa in 1515. (See ALMEIDA.) His son wrote a history of his campaigns, entitled "Comentarios do grande Affonso d'Alboquerque," Lisbon, 1557.

See, also, A. THEVET, "Vie des Hommes illustres;" LAFITAU, "Histoire des Decouvertes, etc. des Portugais;" BARROS, "Decada Segunda;" FARIA Y SOUZA, "Asia Portugueza;" "Nouvelle Biographie Générale."

Albuquerque, de, (BRAS AFFONSO,) a son of the preceding, was born at Alhandra in 1500. He obtained command of a ship of war, and was afterwards "Veedor" or manager of the royal patrimony. He was noted for his integrity. He wrote a narrative of his father's exploits, (1557.) Died in 1580.

Albuquerque, de, (DUARTE COELHO, doo-aR′tà ko-ĕl′yo,) Marquis of Basto, served as a general in the war against the Dutch in Brazil, 1620–39, and wrote an account of that war, (1654.) Died at Madrid in 1658.

Albuquerque, de, dà âl-boo-kĕR′kà, (JUAN ALFONSO,) the tutor, and afterwards minister and favourite, of Pedro the Cruel, of Castile, was the unprincipled agent of that monarch's perfidy and cruelty; but, having at last incurred his displeasure, he was banished from court. Died in 1354.

Albuquerque, de, (MATEO,) a Portuguese general, who was appointed, in 1628, governor of the province of Pernambuco, which he defended against the Dutch. He was recalled to Portugal in 1635, after which he commanded a division in the war against the Spaniards, and gained an important victory at Campo Mayor in 1644. Died in 1646.

See SOUTHEY's "History of Brazil."

Albutius, âl-bu′she-us, (CAIUS SILAS,) a Roman ora-

ā, ē, ī, ō, ū, ȳ, *long;* ȧ, ė, ȯ, same, less prolonged; ă, ĕ, ĭ, ŏ, ŭ, ў, *short;* ạ, ẹ, ị, ọ, *obscure;* fär, fȧll, fȧt; mĕt; nŏt; gōōd; mōōn;

tor, born in Cisalpine Gaul. He lived in the time of the emperor Augustus.

Albutius or **Albucius**, (Titus,) a Roman, who lived about 100 B.C., distinguished by his devotion to the doctrines of Epicurus.

Alcaçoba, âl-kâ-so′bâ, or **Alcazova**, a Portuguese navigator in the service of Charles V. of Germany. He was murdered in a mutiny in 1535.

Al-ça-di′nus or **Alcadino**, âl-kâ-dee′no, a Syracusan physician, who attended the emperors Henry VI. and Frederick II. He lived about the beginning of the thirteenth century.

Alcæus, âl-see′us, [Gr. Ἀλκαῖος; Fr. ALCÉE, ἅl′sâ′,] a celebrated Greek lyric poet, a native of Mitylene, in Lesbos, flourished about 600 B.C. He wrote in the Æolic dialect, and is said to have invented the metre called Alcaic. His odes were characterized by strong passion and enthusiasm; they were admired and imitated by Horace. Among the nine lyric poets of the Alexandrian canon, Alcæus occupied the second* or, according to some writers, the first place. Quintilian expressed the opinion that he was often equal to Homer. Nothing remains of his productions except a number of small fragments. Some of his poems were addressed to Sappho, his contemporary. In the contest between the nobles and the people of Lesbos, he fought and wrote for the former.

See BODE, "Geschichte der lyrischen Dichtkunst der Hellenen," and "ALKAIOS," in ERSCH und GRUBER's "Allgemeine Encyklopaedie."

Alcæus, a comic poet, a native of Mitylene, contended in 388 B.C. with Aristophanes for the prize which the latter gained by his "Plutus."

Alcæus OF MESSENE, author of a number of epigrams in the Greek Anthology, lived about 210 B.C. He wrote epigrams against Philip III. of Macedonia.

Alcaforada, âl-kâ-fo-râ′dâ, (MARIANNA,) a Portuguese nun, who, about 1662, conceived a passion for a French marquis (De Chamilly) who is noticed in this work. Her letters to him were published in a French version, ("Lettres Portugaises," 1669,) and were much admired. He did not return her affection, and appears to have published them to gratify his vanity.

Alcaforado, âl-kâ-fo-râ′do, (FRANCISCO,) a Portuguese who took part in the expedition which discovered Madeira in 1420 and wrote a narrative of the discovery.

Alcalá, âl-kâ-lâ′, (Don **Parafan de Rivera**—pâ-râ-fân′ dâ re-vâ′râ,) DUKE OF, born in 1508, was Viceroy of Naples under Philip II. Died in 1571.

Alcalá y Herrera, de, dâ âl-kâ-lâ′ e êr-râ′râ, (ALFONSO,) a Spanish poet and novelist, who lived in the early part of the sixteenth century. He wrote a novel called "The Two Suns of Toledo," (1641,) in which the letter *a* was not used.

Al-cam′e-nēs, [Gr. Ἀλκαμένης; Fr. ALCAMÈNE, ἅl′-kâ′mân′,] one of the most distinguished sculptors of antiquity, was a native of Athens, and flourished in the fifth century B.C. According to Pausanias, he was living in 400 B.C. He was a pupil of Phidias. His most celebrated work was a statue of Venus, (now lost,) known as "Venus of the Gardens." He is considered to have been second to no Greek sculptor of his age except Phidias.

Alcamo, d′, dâl′kâ-mo, (CIULLO,) a Sicilian, who lived near the close of the twelfth century; supposed to be the earliest writer of Italian poetry.

Alcantara, de, dâ âl-kân′tâ-râ, (DIEGO,) a Spanish architect, employed by Philip II. Died in 1587.

Alcantara, de, (San PEDRO,) a Spanish zealot, who founded a monastic order in the sixteenth century. He was born at Alcántara in 1499. Died in 1562. His penitential austerities were almost incredible. For nearly forty years, it is said, his daily allowance of sleep was less than two hours.

Al-cath′o-us, a son of Pelops, married the daughter of the King of Megara, and afterwards became himself king of that city.

Alcazar or **Alcaçar**, âl-kâ′thaR or âl-kâ′sar, (ANDRES,) an eminent Spanish surgeon, who lived in the latter part of the sixteenth century. He was professor of surgery in the University of Salamanca. His most important work was a treatise on syphilis.

* The FIRST place being accorded to ALCMAN, (which see.)

Alcazar, de, dâ âl-kâ′thaR, (BALTAZAR,) a Spanish poet, who lived at Seville about 1600. He composed many "redondillas," and was highly commended by Cervantes in his "Canto de Caliope."

See LONGFELLOW's "Poets and Poetry of Europe."

Alcazar, de, written also **Alcasar**, (LUIS,) a Spanish Jesuit, born at Seville in 1554. He wrote on the Apocalypse. Died in 1613.

Alcazova. See ALCAÇOBA.

Alcedo, de, dâ âl-sâ′DO, (ANTONIO,) a native of Spanish America, published at Madrid in 1786 a valuable work on the geography of America, "Diccionario Geografico-historico de las Indias Occidentales ò America," (5 vols.) Scarcely anything is known of his life.

Alcée. See ALCÆUS.

Al-çĕs′tis, [Gr. Ἀλκηστις or Ἀλκέστη; Fr. ALCESTE, ἅl′sĕst′,] the daughter of Pelias and wife of Admetus, King of Thessaly, is fabled to have prevented the death of her husband by offering to die for him. Tradition adds that she was rescued from the realms of death by Hercules. The story of her heroic devotion forms the subject of one of the best tragedies of Euripides.

Al′çe-tas [Gr. Ἀλκέτας] I., King of Epirus, was an ally of the Athenians. He reigned about 375 B.C.

Al′cetas II., King of Epirus, was a grandson of Alcetas I. He was killed by his own subjects, and was succeeded by Pyrrhus.

Al′cetas, a brother of Perdiccas, the favourite of Alexander the Great. After the death of his brother, 321 B.C., he killed himself, to avoid falling into the hands of Antigonus. (See PERDICCAS.)

Alchabitius, al-kâ-bish′e-us, [Arab. ABDALAZEEZ or ABDALAZÍZ,] an Arabian astrologer, who lived at Aleppo about the middle of the tenth century.

Alchfred. See ALFRED.

Al-chin′dus or **Al-kin′dus**, [Arab. AL-KIN′DEE or ALKINDI,] a noted Arabian astrologer, physician, and writer, born about the end of the eighth century. He lived at the court of Al-Mamoon, Caliph of Bagdâd. He wrote many works, in one of which he pretended to explain the action of medicines by the principles of mathematics and music.

Alciati, âl-châ′tee, [Fr. ALCIAT, ἅl′se-â′,] (ANDREA,) a celebrated lawyer of Milan, born in 1492. He became professor of law in the University of Avignon in 1518, and afterwards filled the same chair in Bourges, (1528 to 1532,) and subsequently in Bologna, Pavia, and Ferrara. He died at Pavia in 1550. Though possessed of popular and brilliant talents, he was far from being a profound jurist. He left "Commentaries on the Digest," and many other legal works.

"Alciati," says Hallam, "was the first who taught the lawyers to write with purity and elegance. Erasmus has applied to him the eulogy of Cicero on Scævola, that he was the most jurisprudent of orators and the most eloquent of lawyers." (See "Introduction to the Literature of Europe.")

See "Vita Alciati," prefixed to his "Emblemata," published by CLAUDE MIGNAULT in 1581; MAZZUCHELLI, "Scrittori d'Italia."

Alciàti, (FRANCESCO,) a nephew of the preceding, and tutor to the celebrated Saint Carlo Borromeo, born in 1522, was made cardinal in 1565. Died in 1580.

Alciati, (GIOVANNI PAOLO,) an Italian Protestant of the sixteenth century, who was accused, or at least strongly suspected, of heresy by Calvin and other reformers, in consequence of which he retired to Dantzic, where he died about 1570.

Alciati, (TERENZIO,) a learned Jesuit, born at Rome in 1570. He taught divinity for seventeen years in the Jesuits' College at Rome, and wrote several works on theology. Died in 1651.

Alcibiades, âl-se-bī′a-dêz, written also **Alkibi′ades**, [Gr. Ἀλκιβιάδης; Fr. ALCIBIADE, ἅl′se′be′ἅd′; Ger. ALCIBIADES, âlt-se-bee′â-dês,] a celebrated Athenian, son of Cleinias, was born about 450 B.C. He seemed to combine all the gifts of nature and of fortune. He was descended from the noblest families and inherited one of the largest estates of Athens. He possessed remarkable personal beauty, and an intellect of wonderful strength and versatility. The ward of Pericles, and the favourite pupil and companion of Socrates, he enjoyed unequalled opportunities for cultivating his talents to the highest degree. Yet all these advantages were rendered futile or pernicious by his fickleness and want of virtue. He was elected one of the board of generals in 419 B.C., and became the leader of the democratic party. Through his intrigues and counsels, the Athenians were involved in a war with Sparta and Syracuse, 414 B.C. About the time he was to sail for Sicily with the fleet, (in the command of which Nicias was associated with him,) he was accused of an act of sacrilege which had been recently committed, and was afterwards condemned in his absence. Upon this he joined the enemies of his country, and by his counsels contributed powerfully, though indirectly, to the destruction of the Athenian army in Sicily in 413. (See NICIAS.) Having quarrelled with the Spartans, he was recalled by the fickle populace of Athens in 411, and was again intrusted with the command of the fleet. Under his conduct the Athenians gained several signal victories, at Cynossema and Abydos in 411 B.C., at Cyzicus in 410; and in the two following years they acquired Chalcedon and Byzantium. But subsequently he made an unsuccessful attempt on the island of Andros, and soon after his lieutenant in his absence was defeated at Notium, near Ephesus. He was superseded in the command of the fleet, and retired into Thrace, for he thought it unsafe to return to Athens. After the fall of Athens and the establishment of the rule of the thirty tyrants, he withdrew into Asia, where he was honourably received by the satrap Pharnabazos. Not long after, the house in which he slept was attacked at night by a body of men, who set it on fire, and when he rushed out, sword in hand, dispatched him with darts and arrows, 404 B.C. It is not known whether this deed was done at the instigation of his public or his private enemies.

See his life in PLUTARCH; GROTE, "History of Greece," vol. viii. chaps. lxii. to lxiv., also lxvi.; THIRLWALL, "History of Greece;" A. G. MEISSNER, "Alcibiades," 4 vols., 1785-88; J. H. JOANIN, "Histoire d'Alcibiades," 1819; HERTZBERG, "Alkibiades der Staatsmann und Feldherr," Halle, 1853; W. VISCHER, "Alcibiades und Lysandros," 1845; XENOPHON, "Hellenica;" THUCYDIDES, "History."

Al-çid′a-mas, [᾽Αλκιδάμας,] a Greek rhetorician, who lived about 400 B.C. He was a native of Elæa, in Asia Minor.

Alcides. See HERCULES.

Al-çī′dēs, [Gr. ᾽Αλκείδης; Fr. ALCIDE, ȧl′sěd′,] a name of Hercules, supposed to have been derived from the Greek ἀλκή, (alkē,) "strength."

Al-çim′a-ehus, [᾽Αλκίμαχος,] a Greek painter, supposed to have lived in the time of Alexander the Great.

Alcime. See ALCIMUS.

Al-çim′e-nēs, [᾽Αλκιμένης,] a Greek comic poet, who is supposed to have lived at Athens about 500 B.C.

Al′çī-mus, [Gr. ᾽Αλκιμος; Fr. ALCIME, ȧl′sėm′,] (called also **Ja-çī′mus** [Gr. ᾽Ιάκειμος] or **Jo′a-chim**,) a Jewish high-priest, contemporary with Judas Maccabæus. He apostatized and joined Demetrius.

See I. Maccabees vii., ix.

Al′çī-mus A-le′thĭ-us, a Latin writer and rhetorician of the fourth century. He lived in Burdigala, (Bordeaux.)

Al-çin′o-us, [Gr. ᾽Αλκίνοος,] a king of the Phæacians, whose beautiful gardens, described by Homer in the Odyssey, have afforded a favourite theme for other poets. He reigned in the island of Scheria, (now Corfu.)

Alcinous, a Greek philosopher, who wrote an introduction to the philosophy of Plato. He is supposed to have flourished in the time of the early Roman emperors.

Alcionio, (PIETRO.) See ALCYONIUS.

Al′çī-phrǫn, [᾽Αλκίφρων,] a Greek epistolary writer, supposed to have lived about 200 A.D. His works are interesting as exhibiting a picture of the domestic life of that period. The number of his letters is above seventy. His language is elegant and purely Attic.

Alcmæon, ȧlk-mee′on, [Gr. ᾽Αλκμαίων; Fr. ALCMÉON, ȧlk′mȧ′ŏN′,] a son of Amphiaraus and Eriphyle, renowned as the leader of the Epigoni in their successful expedition against Thebes.

Alcmæ′on, [Gr. ᾽Αλκμαίων,] a natural philosopher, native of Crotona, lived in the sixth century B.C., and was a pupil of Pythagoras. He is said to have been the first who dissected animals in order to study anatomy.

Alcmæon, (the lyric poet.) See ALCMAN.

Alcmæonidæ, ȧlk-me-on′ĭ-dē, [Gr. ᾽Αλκμαιωνίδαι,] one of the most distinguished of the noble families of Athens.

Alcman, ȧlk′man, [Gr. ᾽Αλκμάν,] called **Alcmæ′on** [᾽Αλκμαίων] by the later Greek writers, the chief lyric poet of Sparta, flourished about 650 B.C. He was originally a Lydian slave, born at Sardis, and was emancipated in his youth and nationalized by the Spartans. He wrote Parthenia, pæans, bridal hymns, and other poems, which were highly prized by the ancients. Some beautiful fragments of his works are extant. He was considered by some ancient writers the inventor of erotic poetry. To Alcman was assigned the first place in the canon of lyric poets, by the Alexandrian grammarians.

See SCHOELL, "Histoire de la Littérature Grecque."

Alcmene, ȧlk-mee′ne, or **Alc-me′na**, [Gr. ᾽Αλκμήνη; Fr. ALCMÈNE, ȧlk′mȧn′,] the daughter of Electryon, King of Mycenæ, and wife of Amphitryon. She bore Hercules to Jupiter, who, it is said, in the absence of her husband, deceived her by assuming the form of Amphitryon.

Alcock or **Alcok**, aul′kok, (JOHN,) a native of Yorkshire, England, was sent as ambassador by Edward IV. to John II. of Castile, and afterwards became successively Bishop of Rochester, of Worcester, and of Ely. He was also tutor to Prince Edward of Wales, and president of his council. He held the chancellorship a short time under both Edward IV. and Henry VIII. Died in 1500. He was a patron of learning, and founded Jesus College, Cambridge.

Alcock, (JOHN,) an English musical composer, born in London in 1715. Died in 1806.

Alcock, (THOMAS,) an English surgeon, born in 1784; died in 1833.

Al′con [᾽Αλκων] or **Al′co**, a Greek statuary of unknown epoch, noted for having made an iron statue of Hercules.

Alcott, aul′kot, (AMOS BRONSON,) an American writer on education, born in Wolcott, Connecticut, in 1799.

Alcott, (WILLIAM A.,) M.D., an American reformer and educational writer, born in Wolcott, Connecticut, in 1798. He studied medicine at New Haven; but, after following the profession for a few years, united with William C. Woodbridge in the preparation of his school geographies and atlases, and in editing the "Annals of Education," etc. He has since laboured zealously in the cause of educational reforms, and lectured extensively on the best modes of instruction, hygiene, physiology, etc. Besides editing and contributing to various journals, he has published many volumes on educational and kindred subjects. Some of his works have enjoyed a great popularity, especially "The House I Live in;" "The Young Man's Guide;" "The Young Woman's Guide;" "The Young Mother;" "The Young Housekeeper," etc.

Alcuin, ȧl′kwin, or **Al′cwin**, an English prelate, who passes for the most learned man of his age, and whose full name was **Flac′cus Albi′nus Alcui′nus**, was born at York about 735 A.D. About 780 he accepted an invitation to the court of Charlemagne, with whom he lived thenceforth on terms of intimate friendship. The court of that monarch, it is said, became a school of which Alcuin was the head. According to some writers, he founded schools at Aix-la-Chapelle and Paris. He was appointed in 796 abbot of St. Martin at Tours, where he died in 804. He left many epistles, poems, and theological works, which are among the best specimens of mediæval Latinity. A life of Alcuin, by Professor F. Lorenz, of Halle, has been translated into English, (1837.)

See also BÄHR, "Geschichte der Römischen Literatur;" "Biographia Britannica Literaria," 1842.

Alcyone, (ȧl-sī′o-ne) or **Hal-çy′o-ne**, [Gr. ᾽Αλκυόνη,] (Myth.,) a daughter of Æolus, who became the wife of Ceyx. They were remarkable for their mutual and devoted love. Ceyx having perished in a storm at sea, Alcyone, overcome by grief and despair, threw herself into the waves. To reward their conjugal devotion, the

ā, ē, ī, ō, ū, ȳ, *long;* ȧ, ė, ȯ, same, less prolonged; ă, ĕ, ĭ, ŏ, ŭ, ў, *short;* ạ, ẹ, ị, ọ, *obscure;* fär, fȧll, fȧt; mēt; nŏt; gŏŏd; mōŏn;

gods transformed them into kingfishers. The sea, as ancient writers tell us, is always calm and the weather delightful during the period in which these birds build their nests and hatch their young: hence the origin of the expression "halcyon days," signifying those of peace and happiness.

Al-çў-o'nĭ-us or **Al-çĭ-o'nĭ-us,** (PETRUS,) [It. AL-CIONIO, âl-cho'ne-o, PIETRO,] a distinguished Italian scholar, was born at Venice about 1490. He translated into elegant Latin several works of Aristotle, and became professor of Greek at Florence about 1521. His most celebrated work is "Medices Legatus de Exsilio," (1522,) a dissertation on Exile. He was erroneously suspected of having taken the finest passages of this work from Cicero's lost treatise on Glory. He died in Rome in 1527.

See MAZZUCHELLI, "Scrittori d'Italia;" PAOLO GIOVIO, "Elogia Virorum illustrium," Bâle, 1677.

Al-Damiri. See ADDEMEEREE.

Alday, aul'de, (JOHN,) an English translator, of whom little is known. He translated a popular French work by Boaistuau, (or Boistuau,) entitled "The Theatre of the World," ("Theatrum Mundi," 1581.)

Alde, van, vân âl'deh, (HENDRIK,) a Dutch painter and engraver, lived at Amsterdam about 1650.

Aldebert. See ADALBERT.

Aldegati, âl-dà-gä'tee, (MARCO or MARCANTONIO,) an Italian poet, born at Mantua, lived in the latter part of the fifteenth century.

Aldegonde, SAINT. See MARNIX, (PHILIP VAN.)

Aldegrever, âl'deh-grà'ver, or **Aldegraef,** âl'deh-grêf', (HEINRICH,) an eminent German painter and engraver, born at Soest, Westphalia, in 1502, was a pupil of Albert Dürer, whose style he closely imitated. He left a great number of engravings, mostly from his own designs. They are finely executed in the Gothic style. Among his plates are "Susanna and the Elders;" "The Labours of Hercules;" and portraits of Luther and Melanchthon. His paintings are not numerous. Died about 1562.

Aldeguela, de, dà âl-dà-gä'là, (JOSEF or JOSÉ MARTIN,) a Spanish architect, born in 1730; died in 1802.

Al-Demiri. See ADDEMEEREE.

Alden, aul'den, (JOHN,) one of the first settlers of Plymouth, Massachusetts, came over in the Mayflower in 1620. He was a magistrate in that colony for more than fifty years. He forms one of the principal characters in Longfellow's poem on "Miles Standish's Courtship." Died in 1687, aged about eighty-nine.

Alden, (TIMOTHY,) an American clergyman, born in Massachusetts in 1771, was the founder and first president of Alleghany College, Meadville, Pennsylvania. He published a collection of epitaphs and inscriptions, in 5 vols. Died in 1839.

Alderete, de, dà âl-dà-rā'tà, or **Aldrete,** âl-drā'tà, (BERNARDO,) a learned Spanish writer and priest, born at Málaga about 1550. He was distinguished for his knowledge of Hebrew, Arabic, and Greek, and was reputed one of the best Spanish writers of his time. Among his works is "The Origin and Principles of the Castilian Language," (1606,) which, says Gayangos, is the best on that subject. The date of his death is unknown.

Alderete, de, (DIEGO GRACIAN,) a Spanish Hellenist of the sixteenth century, was employed as private secretary by Charles V. and by Philip II., at whose court he enjoyed great favour. He made good Spanish versions of Xenophon, (1552,) Thucydides, (1554,) and other Greek writers. He died at an advanced age about 1590.

Alderete, de, (JOSÉ,) a younger brother of Bernardo, noticed above, was rector of the College of Granada, and author of a treatise "De Religiosa Disciplina tuenda," (1615.) Died in 1616, aged about fifty-six.

See N. ANTONIO, "Bibliotheca Hispana Nova."

Alderoti, âl-dà-ro'tee, (TADDEO,) a celebrated physician, and a friend of Dante, was born at Florence in 1215. Died in 1295.

See VILLANI, "Vie d'Alderoti."

Alderson, aul'der-son, (JOHN,) M.D., a distinguished English physician, born in Suffolk in 1758, practised in Hull. Died in 1829.

Aldhelm, âld'hêlm, SAINT, a distinguished Saxon ecclesiastic, born about the middle of the seventh century. He was made Bishop of Sherborn in 705, and died in 709.

Aldigieri. See ALTICHERIO.

Aldini, âl-dee'nee, (ANTONIO,) COUNT, an Italian statesman, born at Bologna in 1756, was a nephew of Galvani. Having become a political friend of Bonaparte, he was chosen president of the Council of State of the Cisalpine Republic, and in 1805 secretary of state in the kingdom of Italy. He continued to live at Milan after it passed into the power of Austria. Died in 1826.

Aldini, (GIOVANNI,) a distinguished natural philosopher, nephew of the celebrated Galvani, and brother of the preceding, was born at Bologna in 1762. In 1798 he was appointed professor of physics in the university of his native city. In 1807 he became a member of the council of state at Milan, and Knight of the Iron Crown. Died in 1834. He has left essays on galvanism, steam, the hydraulic lever, and other subjects.

See TIPALDO, "Biografia degli Italiani illustri."

Aldini, (TOBIA,) an Italian botanist of Cesena, wrote a "Description of the Garden of Cardinal Farnese at Rome," (1625.)

Aldobrandini, âl-do-brân-dee'nee, (CINZIO,) a nephew of Pope Clement VIII., born at Sinigaglia, became cardinal in 1593. He was a friend of Tasso, who dedicated to him his "Jerusalem Delivered," ("Gerusalemme Liberata.")

Aldobrandini, (SILVESTRO,) a learned Italian jurist, born in 1499. He was for some years professor of law at Pisa. Died in 1558. His son Ippolito became pope in 1592. (See CLEMENT VIII.) He had a son, Giovanni, and two grandsons, Pietro and Cinzio, (noticed above,) who became cardinals.

Aldobrandini, (TOMMASO,) a son of Silvestro, born at Rome about 1540, was a brother of Clement VIII. He produced a translation of Diogenes Laertius, (1594.) He died in the prime of life.

Aldobrandino, âl-do-brân-dee'no, (called FIOREN-TINO, or the "Florentine,") an Italian physician, practised at Sienna, and died at Florence in 1327.

Aldo Manuzio. See MANUTIUS.

Aldred, âl'dred or âl'dred, surnamed THE GLOSSER, [Lat. GLOSSA'TOR,] an Anglo-Saxon writer, author of the "Book of Durham," lived about 800 A.D.

Aldred, âl'dred, [Lat. ALDRE'DUS, called also AL-RE'DUS and EALRE'DUS,] an archbishop of York in the eleventh century. He enjoyed high favour with Edward the Confessor. In 1066 William the Conqueror was crowned by him. Died in 1069.

Aldrete. See ALDERETE.

Aldric, âl'drik, [Lat. ALDRI'CUS,] SAINT, was born in France about 800. He was elected to the bishopric of Le Mans in 832, in which office he acquired the highest character for wisdom and sanctity. Died about 856.

Aldrich, auld'ritch or auld'rij, (HENRY,) D.D., an eminent English scholar and divine, born at Westminster in 1647, was educated at Oxford. He became a tutor of the college of Christ Church, and edited several Greek classics. In the reign of James II. he was one of the most able defenders of the Protestant cause. He was appointed dean of Christ Church, Oxford, in 1689. He possessed great skill in music, and composed numerous services and anthems which are used in the English cathedrals. His "Compendium of the Art of Logic" ("Artis Logicæ Compendium") was extensively used in England until the publication of Whately's "Elements of Logic" in 1826.

See MACAULAY'S "History of England," vol. iii. ch. xiv.; HAWKINS'S "History of Music."

Aldrich, auld'ritch, (JAMES,) an American poet and journalist, born in Suffolk county, New York, in 1810. He at first engaged in mercantile pursuits, but subsequently devoted himself entirely to literature. Died in 1856. He edited several popular periodicals, and was author of numerous poems.

See GRISWOLD'S "Poets and Poetry of America."

Aldrich or **Aldridge,** auld'rij, (ROBERT,) born in Buckinghamshire, England, became Bishop of Carlisle in 1537, and died in 1555.

ɕ as *k;* ç as *s;* ḡ *hard;* ġ as *j;* G, H, K, *guttural;* N, *nasal;* R, *trilled;* s̄ as *z;* th as in *this.* (☞See Explanations, p. 23.)

Aldrich, (THOMAS BAILEY,) an American poet, and assistant editor of the "New York Home Journal," was born at Portsmouth, New Hampshire, in 1836. He is author of "Miscellaneous Poems," "The Course of True Love Never Did Run Smooth," etc.

Aldridge, auld'rĭj, (IRA,) a negro tragedian, born near Baltimore, in Maryland, about 1810. He early exhibited uncommon powers of mind, acquiring knowledge with great facility, and learning, among other things, to speak the German language. Having attracted the notice of Kean, the eminent tragedian, he accompanied him, as an attendant, to Europe, and at Belfast appeared on the stage in the character of Othello to Kean's Iago. He subsequently rose to distinction as an actor, personating with great success a wide range of characters, both in Great Britain and on the continent. Particular honours were conferred on him by the King of Prussia and the Emperor of Austria, and in 1857 the King of Sweden invited him to visit Stockholm. Died in 1867.

See "Leben und Künstlerlaufbahn des Negers I. Aldrige," Berlin, 1852.

Aldrighetti, ål-dRo-ġet′tee, an Italian physician and medical writer, born at Padua in 1573; died in 1631.

Aldringer, ålt′ring-ẹr, or **Altringer,** (JOHANN,) an officer in the Thirty Years' War, was born in the duchy of Luxemburg, of an obscure family. From a common soldier in the Imperial (Austrian) army, he rose gradually to the highest rank, and after the death of Tilly, in 1632, was made field-marshal. He was killed while defending the bridge of Landshut against the Swedes in 1634.

Aldrovande. See ALDROVANDUS.

Aldrovandi. See ALDROVANDUS.

Aldrovandini, ål-dRo-vån-dee′nee, a family of artists who lived in Bologna in the seventeenth and eighteenth centuries. The most celebrated were the following:

Aldrovandini, (POMPEO AGOSTINO,) born in 1677, died in 1739. Like the others of his family, he was distinguished as an architectural and decorative painter. He painted in oil and fresco, in Vienna, Dresden, and Italy.

Aldrovandini, (TOMMASO,) a painter of Bologna, born in 1653, was a cousin of the preceding. Died in 1736.

Al-dro-van′dus, [Fr. ALDROVANDE, ål′dRo′vŏnd′; It. ALDROVANDI, ål-dRo-vån′dee,] (ULYSSES,) a great Italian naturalist, born of a noble family, at Bologna, about 1524. Having studied botany, medicine, and other sciences, he graduated in medicine in 1553, and obtained the chair of natural history at Bologna in 1560. He pursued his favourite studies with unremitting zeal, and spent his fortune in collecting specimens and procuring engravings by the best artists. The result of his labours is a "Natural History," in 13 volumes, of which four appeared during his life. He published three volumes on Birds, 1599-1603, and one volume on Insects, 1602. The other volumes were edited by various persons. His works are praised for their completeness, but are deficient in scientific arrangement and condensation. "The book of Aldrovandus," says Cuvier, "can only be regarded as an enormous compilation, without taste or genius: the plan and materials of it are in a great measure borrowed from Gesner. Died at Bologna in 1607. Buffon praises the method of Aldrovandus and his fidelity of description.

See FANTUZZI, "Memorie della Vita d'Ulisse Aldrovandi," 1774; HALLER, "Bibliotheca Botanica;" JÖCHER, "Allgemeines Gelehrten-Lexikon."

Alduin, åld′win, [Lat. ALDUI′NUS or ALDOVI′NUS,] written also **Aud′win, Aud′oin,** and sometimes **Hieldui′nus,** the first king of the second dynasty of Longobards or Lombards, reigned about the middle of the sixth century. The emperor Justinian made an alliance with him, and gave him Pannonia, (now the southwestern part of Hungary,) and the Longobard king sent him in return 5000 mercenaries to fight in the imperial army. (See ALBOIN.)

Alduinus. See ALDUIN.

Aldus Manutius. See MANUTIUS.

Ale, å′lẹh, (EGIDIUS,) a Flemish painter, who was born at Liege, and worked at Rome. Died in 1689.

Aleander and **Aléandre.** See ALEANDRO.

Aleandro, â-là-ân′dro, [Lat. ALEAN′DER; Fr. ALÉANDRE, ᾱ′là′ŏNdR′,] (GIROLAMO,) a distinguished Italian scholar, born near Friuli in 1480, was reputed one of the most learned men of his time. He became professor of belles-lettres in the University of Paris in 1508, and librarian of the Vatican in 1519. In 1520 he was sent by Pope Leo X. as nuncio to Germany, to oppose the doctrines of Luther, against whom he showed a violent hostility. He was the *rédacteur* of the edict against Luther which the emperor and diet adopted. In 1525 he was taken prisoner at Pavia with Francis I., whom he had accompanied as nuncio. He was made a cardinal in 1538, and died in 1542, leaving an unfinished work on holding councils, ("De Concilio habendo.")

See D'AUBIGNÉ, "History of the Reformation;" MAZZUCHELLI, "Scrittori d'Italia;" A. VICTORELLI, "Vie d'Aléandre," in a collection of lives of Pontiffs, published at Rome in 1630, 2 vols.

Aleandro, (GIROLAMO the younger,) a very learned Italian poet and antiquary, born in Friuli in 1574, was a grand-nephew of the preceding. He was remarkable for the precocity of his intellect, and composed, at the age of sixteen, seven beautiful odes, called "The Tears of Penitence," ("Le Lagrime di Penitenza.") He was for about twenty years secretary to Cardinal Bandini, at Rome. He was also for some time secretary to Pope Urban VIII. Among his works are "Penitential Psalms," (in Latin. 1593,) and an antiquarian treatise entitled "Antiquæ Tabulæ Marmoreæ," etc., (1616.) Died in 1629.

See MAZZUCHELLI, "Scrittori d'Italia;" GASPARO DE SIMEONI, "In morte di G. Aleandro orazione," 1636.

Aléaume, ᾱ′là′ōm′, (LOUIS,) a French *littérateur,* born in 1525, died in 1596. He wrote Latin verses.

Alecto. See EUMENIDES.

Alee or **Alî,** â′lee, or **Ali-Ibn-Abi-Tâlib,** â′lee ĭb′n â′bee tâ′lib, (*i.e.* "Alee the son of Aboo-Tâlib:" see note to ABOOLFEDA, on page 35,) surnamed THE LION OF GOD, an Arabian caliph, born at Mecca about 600 A.D., was a cousin-german of the prophet Mohammed. He was one of the first to embrace the new faith, which he afterwards defended with unequalled zeal and valour. He married Fâtimah, a daughter of Mohammed. Upon the death of the prophet in 632, Alee and Aboo-Bekr were rival candidates for the succession, which the latter obtained. This contest was the origin of the great schism between the Soönnites (orthodox) and Sheeites, the latter of whom were partisans of Alee. On the death of Othmân in 655, Alee became caliph; but he was obliged to maintain his cause in battle against Moâweeyeh, a powerful rival. Three fanatics conspired to assassinate both of these rivals in order to end the war, and Alee was killed by one of them in 660 A.D. He left a son, Hassan, who became caliph. Alee is a popular hero, especially with the Persians, who belong to the sect of Sheeites. He is also celebrated as an author of maxims and sentences.

See IRVING, "Mahomet and his Successors," vol. ii.; WEIL, "Geschichte der Chalifen," vol. i. chap. iv.; OCKLEY, "History of the Saracens;" ELMACIN, "Historia Saracenica;" D'HERBELOT, "Bibliothèque Orientale;" NOËL DES VERGERS, "Histoire de l'Arabie," 1846.

Alee or **Alî,** (Abool-Hassan, â′bool′ hâs′san,) King of Granada, ascended the throne in 1466. He renewed the war against Ferdinand and Isabella in 1481, and was defeated at Alhama. In 1482 his subjects revolted, and proclaimed his son Boabdil, or Aboo-Abdillah, king. Alee died soon after that date.

Alee, Ali, or **Aali,** â′lee, a Turkish historian, who wrote a history of the Ottoman Empire. Died in 1597.

Alee- (or **Alî-**) **ar-Ridhâ,** â′lee ạr-rĭd′â, a descendant of Alee the son-in-law of Mohammed, born in 758 A.D., was considered one of the legitimate successors of the prophet. He married a daughter of the caliph Al-Mamoon. Died in 819.

Alee Beg, (of Poland.) See ALI BEG.

Alee-Bestâmee or **Ali-Bestâmi,** â′lee bês-tâ′mee, a famous sheikh and learned Mohammedan writer, born at Herât in 1400. He came to Turkey in 1443, and resided at the court of the sultan Mahomet II. He wrote on ethics, grammar, philosophy, etc. Died in 1470.

Alee (or **Ali**) **Bey,** â′lee bā, or **Alee Beg,** a Mam-

ā, ē, ī, ō, ū, ȳ, *long;* ă, ĕ, ŏ, same, less prolonged; ă, ĕ, ĭ, ŏ, ŭ, ў, *short;* ạ, ẹ, ị, ọ, *obscure;* fär, fåll, fåt; mĕt; nŏt; gŏŏd; mŏŏn;

eluke chief, was born in 1728, on or near Mount Caucasus. Having been taken to Cairo when a child, he was sold to an officer of the Janissaries, who adopted and, educated him. He soon distinguished himself by his courage and ability. Having at length got possession of the chief power in Egypt in 1768, he aimed to make it an independent kingdom. In 1770 he attempted to conquer Palestine and Syria from the Turks, which led to a long contest, in which Alee was at length slain in 1776.

Alee-Chor-lee'lee, (or **Ali-Chorlîli,**) sometimes written **-Chourlouli,** a vizier of Sultan Ahmed III. during the time that Charles XII. of Sweden was in Turkey in 1709–10. He was an enemy of Charles XII. Died in 1711, aged about forty.

Alee-Ibn-Hammood, or **Ali-Ibn-Hammoud,** (or **-Hammûd,**) ä'lee îb'n hăm-mōōd', the founder of the dynasty of Hammood'ites in Spain. He defeated in battle and killed Suleimân, an aspirant to the throne. Died in 1017.

Alee-Ibnool-Abbâs, or **Ali-Ibnu-l-Abbâs,** ä'lee ib'nōōl âb'bâs', (often called **Haly Abbâs,**) a celebrated Arabian physician, who was probably a native of Persia, and died about 994. Little is known of the events of his life. His work, commonly known as "Royal Book," ("Liber Regius,") is considered by some as the best or most complete treatise on medicine which has come down to us from ancient times.

Alee- (or **Ali-**) **Ibn-Rodhwân,** ä'lee îb'n rōd'wân', (often called **Haly Rodoân,**) a noted Arabian physician, born near Cairo in Egypt, flourished in the early part of the eleventh century.

Alee-Ibn-Saeed, (or **Ali-Ibn-Saîd,**) ä'lee îb'n sä'eed', a distinguished Mohammedan geographer and historian, born at Granada in 1214; died about 1286.

Alee- (or **Ali-**) **Ibn-Yoonas,** (-**Yûnas** or -**Younis,**) ä'lee îb'n yoo'nąs, surnamed Al'ōōl Has'san, an eminent Arabian astronomer, born at Cairo. He was author of astronomical tables, which were considered the best in the language. Died in 1008.

Alee- (or **Ali-**) **Ibn-** (**Ben-**) **Yoosuf,** (or -**Yûsuf,**) ä'lee îb'n yoo'sōōf, a sultan of Africa and Spain of the Almoravide dynasty, began to reign in 1107. He waged war against the Christian princes of Spain, who captured a number of his cities. Died in 1142–3.

A'lee-Koo'jee, [Ger. spelling, Ali Kudschi,] an Ottoman astronomer, who lived at Constantinople. Died in 1474.

Alee-Koolee- (or **Ali-Kuli-**) **Khân,** ä'lee koo'lee kǎn, a nephew of the famous Nâdir Shâh of Persia, succeeded that monarch in 1747. He was dethroned and deprived of sight in 1748.

A'lee-Mo-ez-zeen', (**Ali-Moezzîn** or -**Muezzîn,**) Kapudan Pasha under Sultan Selim I., was defeated and killed in the great naval battle of Lepanto, (1571,) where he commanded the Turkish fleet.

Alee- (**Ali-**) **Mustafa-Ben-Ahmed,** ä'lee mōōs'tä-fä ben âH'med, an excellent Turkish historian and indifferent poet, born at Gallipoli in 1542. His chief work is a universal history, called "Mine of Information." Died in 1599.

Alee-Sheer-Ameer, or **Ali-Shîr-Amîr,** ä'lee' sheer ä-meer', a Persian poet and statesman, born about 1440. He became vizier or prime minister of Sultan Husain of Persia about 1470. He has been styled the Mæcenas of his age and country, and had a high reputation as a poet. Died about 1500.

Alee-Welee-Zade, or **Ali-Weli-Zade,** ä'lee wel'ee zä'deh, surnamed Arslân, ars-lân', (i.e. the "Lion,") and commonly called **Alee** (or **Ali**) **Pasha,** was born at Tepaleen, or Tepalen, in Albania, about 1750. He began his career as a robber. At one time, when he was in a state of extreme destitution, after having sold his sword to avoid starvation, he accidentally discovered, partially buried in the earth, a large iron box filled with gold. With this he levied two thousand Albanian soldiers. From this time forward fortune seemed to smile upon almost all his enterprises. He possessed extraordinary courage, shrewdness, and strength of mind, and well knew how to take advantage of the weakness of the Porte, and of the troubles in which it was involved with the surrounding nations. In return for his services in the war against

Austria and Russia, the sultan appointed him Pasha of Trikala in 1787. Soon after, by intrigue, bribery, and force, he caused himself to be declared Pasha of Yánina, (Janina,) by which title he is generally known. He subsequently rose, step by step, to be the most powerful subordinate prince (subject he could scarcely be called) in the Ottoman Empire. In the wars which convulsed Europe after the breaking out of the French Revolution, Alee Pasha took part now with this power and now with that, as it suited his interest. Though the Porte had abundant reason to distrust and fear him, its weakness obliged it to temporize. At length, in 1820, the Sultan Mahmoud II., who had too much pride and energy to endure any longer the greatness and independent spirit of Alee, sent against him a powerful army; and, though the Pasha of Yánina strove to avail himself of the aid of the Greeks, who were then beginning to assert their independence, he lost one fortress after another, and was at last entrapped by the craft of Khurshid Pasha, the commander of the sultan's forces. Hassan Pasha was dispatched for Alee's head. No sooner had he announced his errand than Alee, seizing his pistols, rose with the fury of a lion, broke with one shot the thigh of his opponent, and with two others killed two of Hassan's lieutenants, but was shot dead himself the same moment. This occurred in February, 1822.

See Malte-Brun, "Tableau historique et politique de la Vie d'Ali Pacha;" Beauchamp, "Histoire du fameux Ali Pacha," 1822; Davenport, "Life of Ali Pasha," 1837; article on Ali Pacha in the "North American Review," January, 1824; Pouqueville, "Mémoire sur la Vie et la Puissance d'Ali Pacha;" Vaudoncourt, "Memoirs on the Ionian Islands, including the Life of Ali Pacha."

Alefeld, ä'leh-fĕlt', (Georg Ludwig,) a German physician and writer, born at Giessen in 1732, became professor of medicine and physics at that place in 1758, and died in 1774.

Alegambe, ä'leh-gŏmb' or ä'leh-gâm'beh, (Philip,) a learned Flemish Jesuit, born at Brussels in 1592. He became superior of the house of the Jesuits at Rome, where he died in 1652. He was the principal author of an excellent work entitled "Library of the Writers of the Society of Jesus," ("Bibliotheca Scriptorum Societatis Jesu," 1643,) devoted to the biography and bibliography of Jesuit writers.

Alègre, d', dä'lågR', (Yves or Ives, èv,) Baron, a celebrated French captain, who served in Italy in the time of Charles VIII. and Louis XII., from 1495 to 1512, when he fell at the head of his victorious troops in the battle of Ravenna.

Alègre, d', (Yves,) Marquis, a distinguished French general in the time of Louis XIV. He became marshal of France in 1724. Died in 1733, aged about eighty.

Alejandro, the Spanish for Alexander, which see.

Alekseief or **Alexejev,** ä-lĕx-ä'-yĕf, (Feodor Yakovlevitch,) a Russian architectural painter, born in 1755. He excelled in perspective, and in a skilful selection of the point of view from which his pictures were drawn. Died in 1821.

Alemagna, di, dĕ ä-lä-mân'yä, (Giusto,) [Lat. Jus'tus de Alema'nia,] an eminent artist, probably of German origin, painted at Genoa about 1450.

Al'e-man, [Fr. pron. ăl'mŏN',] (Louis,) a distinguished French ecclesiastic, born in 1390, was made cardinal in 1426. For his resolute defence of the authority of the councils in opposition to the despotism of the Papal see, Eugenius IV. issued a bull depriving him of all his ecclesiastical dignities; but these were restored by Nicholas V., the successor of Eugenius. Aleman died in 1452.

Aleman, ä-lä-mân', (Mateo,) a Spanish writer of the time of Philip II., born at Seville about the middle of the sixteenth century. He was the author of a celebrated novel, "Guzman de Alfarache," (gooth-mân' dä âl-fä-rä'chä,) (1599,) which was translated into many languages; and of a few other works of less importance. Aleman is said to have been a man of sterling integrity as well as of great wit and judgment. He was employed twenty years by the king in the department of finances.

Alemand, ä'l'mŏN', (Louis Augustin,) a French writer, born at Grenoble in 1653. He practised law and medicine at Grenoble, and displayed both judgment and

ɛ as *k*; ç as *s*; ḡ *hard*; ğ as *j*; G, H, K, *guttural*; N, *nasal*; R, *trilled*; š as *z*; ᵺh as in *this*. (☞See Explanations, p. 23.)

6

erudition in his works, among which is a collection of critical remarks on the history of words, called "New Observations, or Civil War of the French respecting Language," ("Nouvelles Observations, ou Guerre Civile des Français sur la Langue," 1688.) Died in 1728.

Alemann, ä'lẹh-mân', (CONRAD,) a German writer, born at Magdeburg in 1309. Died in 1398.

Alemanni, ä-lä-mân'nee, sometimes written **Alamanno,** ä-lä-mân'no, (ANTONIO,) a Florentine poet, who flourished about 1500. He is cited for the purity of his style in the "Vocabulario della Crusca."

Alemanni, (GIOVANNI BATTISTA,) a son of Luigi, the celebrated poet noticed below, born in 1519, became a privy counsellor of Francis I., and, in 1558, Bishop of Mascon, (Mâcon.) He wrote several sonnets and letters. Died in 1581.

Alemanni, written also **Alamanni,** ä-lä-mân'nee, (LUIGI,) an eminent Italian poet, born at Florence in 1495. He removed to Paris about 1530, and passed many years at the court of Francis I., in whom he found a liberal patron, and by whom he was sent as ambassador to Charles V. in 1544. He was also patronized by Henry II. His chief work is an excellent didactic poem on agriculture, "La Coltivazione," (1546,) which, says Ginguené, "abounds in elegant imitations of Virgil's Georgics, and in true and poetical descriptions of the rural beauties of Italy and France." He was author of numerous sonnets, epigrams, elegies, satires, etc. Died at Amboise in 1556.

See MAZZUCHELLI, "Scrittori d'Italia;" TIRABOSCHI, "Storia della Letteratura Italiana;" LONGFELLOW, "Poets and Poetry of Europe."

Alemanni, (LUIGI,) a grand-nephew of the poet of that name, was born at Florence in 1558. He was a good classical scholar, and author of several short Latin poems. Died in 1603.

Alemanni, (NICCOLÒ,) an antiquary of Greek origin, born at Ancona in 1583. He became a priest, and was for some time professor of Greek in Rome. In 1614 he was appointed librarian of the Vatican. He published, besides other works, the ninth book of the history of Procopius, with a Latin version and notes. Died in 1626.

Alemans, ä'l'môN', a miniature-painter of rare merit, resided at Brussels in the early part of the eighteenth century. His works were in great demand, and commanded very high prices.

Alembek, ä'lẹm-bêk', (LOUIS VALERIAN,) a Polish poet, born at Leopol about 1620. Died about 1690.

Alembert, d', dä'lôN'baiR', (JEAN le Rond—lẹh rôN,) an eminent French geometer and philosopher, born in Paris on the 16th of November, 1717, was an illegitimate son of M. Destouches-Canon, a commissary of artillery, and Madame de Tencin, an authoress. Having been found exposed in the street, he was placed by the police in the care of a glazier's wife, named Rousseau, by whom he was brought up. A few days after his birth his parents settled upon him an annuity of 1200 livres. It is said that after his remarkable talents became known his mother discovered herself to him, but he replied, "Je ne connais qu'une mère, c'est la vitrière," ("I know but one mother—the glazier's wife.") He was educated in the Collége Mazarin, which he entered in 1730. After he left college he studied mathematics and law, and continued to reside with his foster-mother for many years.

Having written a "Memoir on the Integral Calculus," he was elected to the Academy of Sciences in 1741. He published, in 1743, a celebrated "Treatise on Dynamics," containing an important principle which will always be known by the name of D'Alembert, and which initiated a revolution in physico-mathematical sciences. The principle in question amounts simply to this, that every force applied to a system must produce its entire effect somewhere, if not at the point of application, then somewhere else. In other words, there is *an absolute equality at all times between the entire amount of force applied and the sum total of the effects produced:* thus, one portion of the force may be spent in neutralizing an antagonistic force,—for example, in overcoming the momentum which a body may have already acquired; another portion,

in overcoming the resistance caused by friction; a third, in imparting motion in a new direction. D'Alembert's work "On the General Theory of the Winds" gained a prize of the Academy of Berlin in 1746. He declined, in 1752, the invitation of Frederick II. of Prussia, who offered him the presidency of the Royal Academy with a liberal pension, but he accepted an unconditional pension of 1200 francs from that monarch in 1754. From this time until his death a constant epistolary correspondence was maintained between him and Frederick.

D'Alembert was elected to the French Academy in 1754, and received a pension of 1200 francs from Louis XV. in 1756. He declined, in 1762, an urgent invitation from Catherine II. of Russia to come to her court and direct the education of her son for a salary of 100,000 francs.

About 1764 he became attached to the accomplished Mademoiselle de l'Espinasse, who lived with him twelve years, but rendered him unhappy by her growing indifference to him and her partiality to another. (See ESPINASSE.) D'Alembert was for a time joint editor with Diderot of the famous "Encyclopédie," (commenced about 1750,) for which he wrote many mathematical articles, and an introductory discourse that was highly commended as a model of accurate thinking and elegant composition. (See DIDEROT.) For many years he was on terms of great intimacy with Voltaire, to whom he was as superior in justness of thought as he was inferior in wit and brilliancy. D'Alembert was a skeptic in the true sense of the word, (*i.e.* a "doubter" or "inquirer,") but not a scoffer or blasphemer, as he has been commonly represented. We find in his published works no attacks on the Christian religion; although he did not conceal his hostility to Roman Catholicism.

In 1772 he was chosen secretary of the French Academy. He wrote "Éloges" of the members of that institution who died between 1700 and 1772. Among his numerous works are "Researches on Various Important Points of the System of the Universe," (3 vols., 1754–56;) "Mélanges of Literature and Philosophy," (5 vols. ;) and "Éléments of Philosophy," (1759.) He was a member of all the prominent learned societies of Europe. Died in Paris on the 29th of October, 1783.

Lacroix, in the "Biographie Universelle," expresses the opinion that D'Alembert should be ranked as high as any contemporary geometer, when we consider the difficulties he overcame, the intrinsic value of the methods which he invented, and the ingenuity (*finesse*) of his ideas.

"His literary works," says Lacroix, "constantly directed to the perfection of reason and the propagation of correct ideas, were highly appreciated by all men of sense, (*bons esprits*.) All of them are remarkable for a pure diction, a neat style, and strong or pithy thought." His character presents many amiable traits, among which are candour, modesty, and beneficence.

See "Éloge de D'Alembert," par CONDORCET; a notice in the first volume of the edition of his literary and philosophical works published by J. B. BASTIEN, Paris, 18 vols., 1805; and the notice prefixed to an edition of his works by BOSSANGE, 5 vols., 1821; N. ROSEN VON ROSENSTEIN, "Lefnadsbeskrifning öfver J. L. d'Alembert," Stockholm, 8vo, 1787; "Biographie Universelle."

Alen, van, vän ä'lẹn, (or **van O'lẹn,**) (JOHN, or JAN,) a Dutch painter, born in 1631, imitated Melchior Hondekoeter. Died at Amsterdam in 1698.

Alencé, dä'lôN'sâ', (JOACHIM,) a French astronomer and physicist, born in Paris. Died in 1707.

Alençon, ạ-len'sọn or ä'lôN'sôN', COUNTS, and afterwards DUKES OF, a distinguished line of French nobles in the middle ages.

Alençon, (CHARLES DE Valois—vȧl'wä',) COUNT OF, a brother of Philippe de Valois, King of France. He was killed at the battle of Crécy in 1346.

Alençon, (CHARLES,) DUKE OF, a grandson of Jean, who died in 1476, was born in 1489. He married a sister of Francis I. The loss of the battle of Pavia was attributed to him. He is said to have died of shame for his misconduct in that action. Died in 1525.

Alençon, (FRANÇOIS,) DUKE OF, afterwards Duke of Anjou, the youngest son of Henry II. of France and

Catherine de Médicis, born in 1554; died in 1584. He was awkwardly made, was disfigured by the small-pox, and, to crown all, was of a cowardly and malignant disposition. Although he acted a conspicuous part in the wars and intrigues of his time, he accomplished nothing useful or great. He paid court to Queen Elizabeth of England, and his proposals were very favourably received by her, but the marriage was broken off on account of his being a Catholic.

See DE THOU, "Historia sui Temporis;" SIMONDE DE SISMONDI, "Histoire des Français;" SULLY, "Mémoires;" MOTLEY, "Rise of the Dutch Republic," vol. iii. ; FROUDE, "Reign of Elizabeth."

Alençon, (JEAN,) first DUKE OF, a French nobleman, born in 1385. He was killed at the battle of Agincourt in 1415.

Alençon, (JEAN,) fourth DUKE OF, a French nobleman in the reigns of Charles VII. and Louis XI., noted for his turbulent ambition. Died in prison about 1474.

Aleni, â-lā'nee, or **Alenio,** â-lā'ne-o, (GIULIO,) a learned Italian Jesuit and missionary, born at Brescia. He visited China in 1610, and preached with great success; he caused several churches to be erected, and made many converts. Died in China in 1649. He wrote a number of works in the Chinese language.

Aleni, (TOMMASO,) an Italian historical painter, born at Cremona in 1500. Died about 1560.

Aleotti, â-là-ot'tee, (GIAMBATTISTA,) an Italian engineer and architect, born near Ferrara in 1546; died in 1636. His chief work is the theatre of Parma.

Aler, â'ler, (PAUL,) a German Jesuit, born in Luxemburg in 1656, passed many years as a teacher at Cologne. He wrote several Latin dramas, and published a popular school-book called "Gradus ad Parnassum," of which it is said he was not the author. Died in 1727.

Ales, Aless, or **Alesse,** â-less', [Lat. ALESIUS, a-lee'-she-us,] (ALEXANDER,) an eminent Scottish divine, born in Edinburgh in 1500. His family name was ALANE. He was driven into exile about 1530 by persecution for religion, and became a pupil of Melanchthon, with whom he formed an intimate and lasting friendship. He was professor of theology at Leipsic from 1543 until 1565. He wrote commentaries on several books of Scripture, and some polemical works. Died at Leipsic in 1565.

See CHAMBERS, "Biographical Dictionary of Eminent Scotsmen;" MACKENZIE, "Lives of Scotch Writers."

Alès, â'lês', (PIERRE ALEXANDRE,) Vicomte de Corbet, a French writer, born in Touraine in 1715. His chief work is "On the Origin of Evil," (2 vols., 1758.) Died about 1770.

Alesio, â-lā'se-o, (MATTEO PIETRO; more properly MATTEO Lecce—lêt'chà,) a painter and engraver, born at Rome, was a pupil of Michael Angelo. He worked at Seville. His fresco of Saint Christopher in that city is highly praised. He returned to Italy, and died in 1600.

Alesius. See ALES, (ALEXANDER.)

Alessandri, â-lês-sân'dree, (ALESSANDRO,) [in Latin, ALEXAN'DER AB ALEXAN'DRO,] an Italian writer and jurist, born at Naples about 1460; died in 1523. He left a work on philology, called "Dies Geniales," (1522,) often reprinted. It is on the model of the "Attic Nights" of Aulus Gellius.

Alessandri, â-lês-sân'dree, (FELICE,) an Italian composer of operas, born at Rome in 1742. Died about 1810.

Alessandri, (INNOCENTE,) an Italian engraver of Venice, born about 1742.

Alessandrini, â-lês-sân-dree'nee, (GIULIO,) an Italian medical writer, born at Trent in 1506. Died in 1590.

Alessandro, the Italian for ALEXANDER, which see.

Alessandro, â-lês-sân'dro, and **Ju'li-o,** (or **Giuglio,** jool'yo,) two Italian fresco-painters, who are supposed to have been pupils of Raphael, (or, according to some writers, of Giovanni da Udine,) and appear to have been partners. They worked for Charles V. in Spain, and decorated the Alhambra. Died about 1530.

Alessi, â-lês'see, (GALEAZZO, gâ-là-àt'so,) an eminent Italian architect, born at Perugia in 1500, was an intimate friend of Michael Angelo. Having adorned his native city with several palazzi, (palaces,) he was called to Genoa in 1552, to design the Carignano Church. He

was architect of the Grimaldi Palace, and of other grand palaces of Genoa. Died in 1572.

See Q. DE QUINCY, "Histoire des plus célèbres Architectes; MILIZIA, "Vite de' più celebri Architetti."

Alessio Piemontese, â-lês'se-o pe-à-mon-tā'sà. [Lat. ALEX'IS PEDEMONTA'NUS,] a physician of the sixteenth century, who dealt in secret remedies. Stung by remorse at the death of a person who, as he supposed might have been saved if he had communicated his knowledge to the attending surgeon, he resolved to make known to the world all his remedies, and published a curious book called "The Secrets of Alexis of Piedmont."

Al'e-vas or **Aleu'as,** ['Αλεύας,] an ancient Greek statuary, who worked in bronze. He is mentioned by Pliny.

Al-ex-am'e-nus, ['Αλεξαμενός,] a native of Teos, was, according to Aristotle, the first Greek who wrote dialogues in the Socratic style.

Al-ex-an'der ['Αλέξανδρος] **I.,** King of Macedonia, a son of Amyntas I., began to reign about 500 B.C. He was obliged to join his forces with the army of Persian invaders in 480.

Alexander II., King of Macedonia, was a son of Amyntas II., whom he succeeded about 370 B.C. He was assassinated in 367.

Alexander [Gr. 'Αλέξανδρος; Lat. ALEXAN'DER; Fr. ALEXANDRE, â'lĕk'sôndR';* It. ALESSANDRO, â-lês-sân'-dro; Sp. ALEJANDRO, â-lâ-Hân'dro; Persian and Turkish, ISKAN'DER and SIKAN'DER] surnamed THE GREAT, the first in order of time of the four most celebrated commanders of whom history makes mention,† and the third Macedonian king of his name, was born at Pella, 356 B.C. He was the son of Philip and Olympias, being descended on his father's side from the ancient royal line of Macedonia, and on his mother's from the kings of Epirus, who boasted their descent from Achilles. When Alexander was about fourteen years of age, his father sent for Aristotle, that he might become the tutor of the young prince. Under this illustrious master, the greatest intellect of that or, perhaps, of any age, Alexander rapidly advanced in knowledge of every kind, and developed mental powers of the highest order. Unhappily, his descent from Achilles, and the flattery of the courtiers around him, gave his mind an early bias towards war, and the ambition to be a great conqueror became the ruling passion of his soul. The Iliad was his favourite book; and it is said that he had a copy of that poem which he regularly placed under his pillow at night along with his sword. He seemed fitted to excel in every department of knowledge, as well as in every manly and martial exercise. He showed himself he was unequalled; and when the famous steed Bucephalus was brought to Pella, the Macedonian capital, as none of the grooms or nobles could manage him, Philip, displeased, ordered the animal to be sent back whence he came; but the young prince begged to be allowed to try his skill. His wish was at first regarded as the thoughtless expression of youthful folly; but, when he earnestly insisted, the king asked what forfeit he would be willing to pay in case he failed. "The price of the horse," said Alexander.‡ He had observed that Bucephalus was excited by his own shadow. He therefore turned the horse's head towards the sun, and, at the same time using every means to soothe him, he soon succeeded in bringing him under complete control. The king was so delighted with his son's success that he is said to have wept for joy, telling him he must seek for another kingdom, for Macedonia was too small for him. He had such confidence in Alexander's abilities, that when he set out on an expedition against Byzantium he left the young prince, then only sixteen years old, as regent of the kingdom during his absence. According to Plutarch, Philip was delighted to hear the Macedonians call his son "king," while he him-

* Chaucer has *Alexandre* and *Alisaunder,* the latter being evidently derived from the Italian, but not improbably through an old French form.
† Alexander, Hannibal, Cæsar, and Napoleon.
‡ The price of Bucephalus, says Pliny, in his "Natural History," was sixteen talents,—probably more than twenty thousand dollars of our money.

є as *k;* ç as *s;* ğ *hard;* ğ as *j;* G, H, K, *guttural;* N, *nasal;* R, *trilled;* ŝ as *z;* ᵗh as in *this.* (☞ See Explanations, p. 23.)

self received the title of "general" only. When but eighteen years of age, Alexander greatly distinguished himself in the battle of Chærone'a, and the victory which Philip won on that memorable field was due in a great measure to his son's courage and valour. On the death of his father, (336 B.C.,) Alexander, who was not yet twenty years old, succeeded to the throne. Several of the Grecian states which had been subjugated by Philip, deemed this a favourable opportunity for regaining their independence. Alexander's energy and promptitude, however, disconcerted all their measures, and even those who had been most active submitted to his power without a struggle. But soon after, while he was engaged in subduing the Triballi and other barbarous nations in the east of Europe, a report having been circulated that he was dead, the Thebans revolted a second time. But the young king advanced into Bœotia by rapid strides, and was soon at their gates. The city was taken by storm, the houses levelled to the ground, and all the citizens who had escaped massacre in the assault were sold into slavery—the posterity of the poet Pindar, and the families of those who had opposed the revolt, alone excepted. The other states of Greece, intimidated by this terrible example, were fain to accept Alexander as their ruler. In a general assembly held not long after, at Corinth, he was chosen generalissimo of all the Grecian forces destined for the expedition against Persia. In the spring of 334 B.C. he passed over into Asia Minor with an army of not more than 35,000 men, including the cavalry, which scarcely amounted to 5000. He first engaged the Persians at the river Grani'cus, where they endeavoured to prevent his passage. Although the Macedonians fought at a great disadvantage, being attacked by the Persians while they were still in the river, they soon put their enemies to flight. He afterwards advanced to Gordium, where was the famous Gordian knot. He had been told that the fates had decreed the empire of the world to him who should untie the knot. He tried therefore for some time; but, finding all his efforts to be vain, he at last drew his sword and cut the knot, declaring that this was the only way to untie it. In 333 B.C., having received reinforcements from Macedonia, he advanced to meet Darius, who had assembled an army·of about 600,000 men. The opposing forces met at Issus. The Persians were defeated with terrible slaughter. Darius himself escaped from the battle, but his mother, his wife, and two daughters were taken by the conqueror, who treated them with the greatest kindness and consideration. The booty which fell into the hands of the Macedonians after their victory at Issus was immense. Before proceeding farther, Alexander deemed it wisest to reduce the maritime states. Most of the other towns and cities submitted at once to his power; but Tyre offered a most determined resistance. After a siege of seven months, during which the Tyrians defended the place with equal skill and obstinacy, the city was taken, 332 B.C. The glory of this achievement, however, was stained by the cruelty of the conqueror towards the inhabitants, of whom several thousands were mercilessly slaughtered, and the remainder, amounting to thirty thousand, sold into slavery. As he proceeded southward, all the towns opened their gates except Gaza, which experienced a fate similar to that of Tyre. Alexander then marched into Egypt, where he was received by the people, who were weary of the Persian domination, as a liberator. Here he founded a city called, after his own name, Alexandria. He afterwards visited the temple of Jupiter Ammon on an oasis in the desert of Libya, in the hope, as some say, that the god would acknowledge him as his son. This acknowledgment having been made through the priest of the temple, Alexander returned to Egypt, and, not long after, marched against Darius, who had collected another army of more than a million men, with 40,000 cavalry. The Macedonians had only about 40,000 foot-soldiers and 7000 horsemen. The armies met at Gaugamela, near Arbela, 331 B.C. The Persians were routed with immense slaughter. Soon after Babylon and Susa opened their gates to the conqueror. Persepolis, the capital of the empire, defended by Ariobarzanes, was taken after a slight resistance. Alexander was now the undisputed master of Persia; but his successes appear to have turned his brain. Having persuaded himself that he was a god, he thought that he owed no obedience to laws which were made for mortals only. While at Persepolis, he is said, in a drunken revel, at the instigation of the courtesan Thais, to have set fire, with his own hand, to the magnificent residence of the Persian kings, then one of the wonders of the world. In 330 B.C., having learned that Darius was collecting another army in Media, Alexander set out in pursuit of him. The Persian king fled towards Bactria; but before he reached its confines he was murdered by Bessus, the satrap of that country, who aspired to the throne of Persia. The conqueror came up just as Darius was breathing his last. The dying king, covered with wounds, lay extended on a chariot. At this sad spectacle Alexander could not restrain his tears. He caused the body of Darius to be conveyed to Persepolis and interred in the tombs of the Persian kings. He then marched in pursuit of Bessus, who, having at last fallen into his hands, was put to death, as Plutarch informs us, in the following manner. He was attached by his limbs to two trees, which had been bent towards each other for this purpose, and, on their being allowed to recoil, his body was torn asunder. Alexander had carried his victorious arms to the northward beyond the Jaxartes. He afterwards subdued Sogdiana. Oxyartes, a Bactrian prince, had, for the sake of security, placed his wife and daughters in a fortress built upon a lofty rock. Alexander took it, and was so deeply smitten with the beauty of Roxana, one of the daughters, that he married her. After his conquest of Persia there were formed against his life two conspiracies, in the first of which Philotas, the son of Parmenio, was implicated, and which led to the death both of son and father, (see PARMENIO;) the second, of which Hermolaus was the chief instigator, involved Callisthenes, the pupil, and, according to some, the nephew, according to others the cousin, of Aristotle, and several of the royal pages. All the conspirators were put to death, except Callisthenes, who was mutilated and afterwards killed; though some say he destroyed himself by poison.

In 327 B.C. Alexander invaded India, a country of which until that time even the name was scarcely known to the Greeks. Having crossed the Indus, he formed an alliance with Taxiles, one of the kings of that region, who is said to have brought him, in addition to a large body of troops, one hundred and thirty elephants. He appears to have met with little opposition until he arrived at the banks of the Hydaspes, (Jhylum.) Here his advance was resisted by a king named Porus, at the head of a great army, with a large number of elephants. After a hard-fought and bloody battle, Alexander was victorious. He took Porus prisoner, but afterwards he restored him to his kingdom and treated him with the highest consideration. His favourite horse Bucephalus had been severely wounded in the battle, so that he died soon after. On the spot where he was buried Alexander founded a town, which he called, in honour of him, Bucephala. He afterwards advanced, subduing many cities in his course, as far as the Hyphasis, (Gharra,) when his soldiers refused to go any farther. His commands and entreaties were equally unavailing, and he was under the necessity of returning. · Having previously given orders that a fleet should be built on the Hydaspes, they immediately embarked upon that river, continuing their course down the Indus to the sea. Committing his fleet to Nearchus, he proceeded by land to Susa. In his march he encountered incredible hardships, and a large number of his men perished from hunger and thirst. At Susa, where he rested for some time, he married, as his second wife, the daughter of Darius: and to all those Macedonians (amounting, it is said, to 9000 or 10,000) who married Persian women he gave presents. His object was to unite the two nations as intimately as possible. Soon after, his friend Hephæstion died, for whose loss he was for a long time inconsolable. As he was forming vast projects for the improvement of his empire, and for the subjugation of the surrounding nations, he died at Babylon, 323 B.C., in his thirty-third year.

In the extent of his conquests, and in the splendour

of his exploits, Alexander may be said to have surpassed all other military heroes. He overran and subdued the greater part of the world known to the ancients, almost as quickly as the same could have been explored by an active and enterprising traveller. Even now, after the lapse of twenty-two hundred years, his name is still "familiar as household words" in most of the countries that he conquered. It may not be irrelevant to state— in order to show what a deep impression the arms and policy of Alexander had made upon the mind of the Persian nation—that Firdousee, (Firdausi,) in his great historic poem, the "Shah Nameh," written about the year 1000 A.D., speaks of Alexander (Iskander) as the greatest of heroes; but, following probably the traditions of his country, the poet represents him as the son of a Persian king who had married a Macedonian princess, and, while she was on a visit to her father in Macedon, Alexander was born. This is equivalent to an acknowledgment, on the part of the Persians, that they considered his glory too great not to be appropriated at least in part by themselves. Although it must be admitted that Alexander owed more to fortune than any other of the great conquerors mentioned in history, it can scarcely be questioned that his military talents were of the very highest order. Many of his views of public policy were liberal and enlightened; and his ideas respecting the greatness and dignity that became a king were very different from those of an ordinary or vulgar sovereign. Undoubtedly, much of what was greatest and noblest in his character was due to the instructions of his illustrious teacher Aristotle; but it is certainly no small praise that the royal pupil was, at least in the early part of his career, before his brain had been turned by his unparalleled successes, every way worthy of such a teacher. He appears to have regarded him with an affectionate reverence such as he felt for no other human being, not even his father. And if these sentiments were afterwards somewhat changed by the folly or crime of Aristotle's relative Callisthenes, they were never wholly extinguished. There was in Alexander's nature a generosity and magnanimity rare even among men most distinguished for greatness of soul. His treatment of the family of Darius, and his generous conduct towards Porus, have already been spoken of. We may cite another example of his magnanimity, related by Plutarch and some other writers. A letter from Parmenio, one of his ablest and most trusted officers, informed Alexander, when he was once lying very ill, that his physician Philip had been bribed by Darius, with presents of immense value and the promise of his daughter in marriage, to take him off by poison. As Philip entered the chamber with a cup of medicine for his royal patient, Alexander drew the letter from under his pillow and gave it to him to read, while he himself, without the slightest hesitation, drank off the medicine prepared for him. The result fully justified the trust with which Philip's character had inspired him, and which his countenance then confirmed. Although the strength of his intellect and of his will was most extraordinary, unhappily that of his passions was still greater. Accordingly, we behold him, after the conquest of Persia, so elated as eagerly to accept the adulation which his flatterers offered to him as to a god, and yet surrendering himself up at one time to the most insane paroxysms of anger, at another to the most passionate and uncontrollable grief. In a fit of rage he slew his friend and foster-brother Clitus, who had once saved his life, after which he became a prey to sorrow and remorse no less violent than his anger had been, so that had he not been restrained by his friends he would probably have killed himself. Pope, in his "Temple of Fame," appropriately calls him

"The youth who all things but himself subdued."

See PLUTARCH's "Lives;" ARRIAN's "History of Alexander's Expedition;" "Life of Alexander," by QUINTUS CURTIUS; "Bibliotheca" of DIODORUS SICULUS." books xvii.-xx.; SAINTE-CROIX, "Examen critique des anciens Historiens d'Alexandre le Grand," 1775; DROYSEN, "Geschichte Alexanders des Grossen," 1833: WILLIAMS, "Life and Actions of Alexander the Great," 1829; THIRLWALL, "History of Greece;" VALERIUS, "Historia Alexandri Magni," 1589; LEHMANN, "Historia Magni Alexandri," 1667; KOSSIN, "L'Eroismo ponderato nella Vita di Alessandro il Grande," 2 vols., 1716; FONSECA-REBELO, "Historia abreviada de Alexandro Magro,"

1753; LINGUET, "Histoire du Siècle d'Alexandre le Grand," 1762 DE BURY, "Vie d'Alexandre le Grand," 1760; G. SCHLEGEL, "Einleitung zu einer Alexandropädie oder über die Jugendjahre Alexander des Grossen," 1775; GUSTAV PFIZER, "Geschichte Alexanders des Grossen," 1845; IGNAZ A. FESSLER, "Alexander der Eroberer,' 1797; C. MATTHIAS, "Historia Alexandri Magni," 1645; F. AU GUSTI, "Riflessioni critiche sopra il Carattere e le Gesta d'Alessandro etc.," 1764.

Alexander IV., a son of Alexander the Great and Roxana, was born in 323 B.C., after his father's death. He was saluted as king by the army at Babylon, and was under the guardianship of successive regents, Perdiccas, Antipater, and Polysperchon. About 316 he fell into the power of Cassander, who put him and Roxana to death in 310 B.C.

Alexander V. of Macedonia, was the third son of Cassander. He disputed with his brother Antipater for the royal power, and was put to death by Demetrius Poliorcetes in 294 B.C.

Alexander I., King of Epirus, was a son of Neoptolemus, and brother of Olympias, who was the mother of Alexander the Great. He was killed in a war against the Lucanians about 330 B.C.

Alexander II. of Epirus, succeeded his father Pyrrhus in 272 B.C. He waged war against Demetrius of Macedon. Died about 242 B.C.

Alexander, tyrant of Pheræ in Thessaly, usurped the throne in 369 B.C., and was notorious for cruelty. He was compelled by Epaminondas to give up Pelopidas, whom he had taken prisoner in 367. In 364 he was defeated by the Thebans under Pelopidas, who fell in the action. He was killed by conspirators in 359 B.C.

Alexander I. of Egypt, was a son of Ptolemy Evergetes II. He reigned jointly with his mother Cleopatra eighteen years, from 107 to 89 B.C. He was dethroned and killed in battle soon after the latter date. His son Alexander reigned a few weeks in 81 B.C., and was killed by his own subjects in the same year.

Alexander I., surnamed BA'LAS, King of Syria, pretended to be the son of Antiochus Epiphanes. He began to reign in 150 B.C., after he had defeated Demetrius Soter in battle, and after the Roman Senate had issued a decree in his favour. The kingdom was invaded in 148 by an army raised by Demetrius II., and by another under Ptolemy of Egypt, who gained a decisive victory over Alexander in 147. He fled into Arabia, where he was killed in 146 B.C. His surname of Balas is supposed to signify "Lord."

See JOSEPHUS, "History of the Jews."

Alexander II., otherwise called **Alexander Zabi'nas**, (or Zebina, i.e. "a purchased slave,") was a pretender, who, being favoured or instigated by Ptolemy Physcon of Egypt, obtained the throne of Syria in 128 B.C., after he had defeated Demetrius II. Refusing to pay tribute, he provoked the hostility of Ptolemy, by whom he was defeated and put to death in 122 B.C.

Alexander, a grandson of Alexander Jannæus, and a son of Aristobu'lus II. He raised an army in 57 B.C. and entered Judea, then occupied by the Romans. He made himself master of that country in 56, but was defeated by Gabinius about the end of that year. He was put to death by Q. M. Scipio in 49 B.C.

Alexander OF ÆGÆ, (ee'jē,) a Peripatetic philosopher, instructor of the Roman emperor Nero.

Alexander OF APHRODISIAS. See ALEXANDER EXEGETES.

Alexander surnamed ÆTOLUS, (ē-to'lus,) from his birthplace, Ætolia, a Greek poet, who lived in the third century B.C. He was regarded as one of the Pleias of tragic poets.

Alexander surnamed EXEGE'TES, (i.e. the "Expounder,") a celebrated philosopher and commentator on Aristotle, flourished in the early part of the third century. He was a native of Aphrodisias, in Caria, Asia Minor.

Alexander JANNÆUS, (jan-nee'us,) a son of John Hyrcanus, succeeded his brother Aristobu'lus as King of Judea in 105 B.C. The enmity of the Pharisees against him caused a rebellion, which raged several years, and was suppressed with much cruelty in 86 B.C. Died in 78 B.C.

See article by GESENIUS in ERSCH und GRUBER's "Allgemeine Encyklopaedie."

ϵ as k; ς as s; $\underline{g}$ hard; $\dot{g}$ as j; G, H, K, *guttural*; N, *nasal*; R, *trilled*; $\bar{s}$ as z; th as in *this*.   (☞See Explanations, p. 23.)

Alexan'der MYN'DIUS, a Greek writer and naturalist, lived probably in the second century B.C.

Alexan'der NUME'NIUS, a Greek rhetorician of the second century, wrote a book on the "Figures of Rhetoric," which is extant.

Alexan'der PELOP'LATON, a Greek orator, who was secretary to Antoninus Pius about 150 A.D.

Alexan'der PHILALE'THES, [Φιλαλήθης,] a Greek physician, who was the head of a celebrated medical school in Phrygia. He is mentioned by Strabo as his contemporary, and by Galen. His works are not extant.

Alexan'der TRALLIA'NUS, [Gr. ὁ Τραλλιανός; Fr. ALEXANDRE DE TRALLES, ȧ'lĕk'sŏNdR' dęh tRȧl',] a Greek medical writer of great merit, was born at Tralles, in Lydia, and lived in the sixth century. He settled in Rome, and attained great distinction in his profession. It is supposed that he was a Christian. His great work is entitled "Twelve Books on Medicine," (Βιβλία Ἰατρικὰ δυοκαίδεκα.) He is considered one of the best Greek physicians after Hippocrates. His style is clear and elegant. His works have often been printed.

See E. MILWARD, "Trallianus Revivescens," 1734; FREIND, "History of Physic."

Alexander, a bishop of Jerusalem, who was persecuted under the emperor Septimius Severus. He was translated from the see of Cappadocia to that of Jerusalem, where he founded a library. Died in prison about 250 A.D.

Alexander, Patriarch of Alexandria from 312 to 325 A.D., is noted as the first orthodox theologian who took a prominent part in the Arian controversy. He wrote many epistles against Arianism. He attended the Council of Nice in 325, and died in 326 A.D. (See ATHANASIUS.)

Alexander, Emperor of Constantinople, born about 870 A.D., was a son of Basilius. He succeeded his brother Leo the Philosopher in 911, and disgraced himself by his debaucheries. Died in 912.

Alexander I., POPE, became Bishop of Rome in 108 A.D.; died in 117. He is said to have been the first to introduce the use of holy water in the service of the church.

Alexander II., named originally **Anselmo Badagio**, (bȧ-dä'jo,) was elected pope in 1061; died in 1073, and was succeeded by Gregory VII.

Alexander III. (previously Cardinal ROLANDO **Ranuccio Bandinelli**—rä-noo'cho bȧn-de-nel'lee) was raised to the papal chair in 1159; died in 1181, and was succeeded by Lucius III. He was distinguished for his learning and great abilities.

See "Vita Alexandri III.," by the CARDINAL OF ARAGON; MURATORI, "Annali d'Italia;" G. F. LOREDANO, "Vita di Alessandro III.," 1672.

Alexander IV. (RINALDO **di Anagni**—de ȧ-nȧn'yee) became pope in 1254; died in 1261, and was succeeded by Urban IV.

Alexander V. (PIETRO **Filargo**—fe-laR'go) became pope in 1409; died in 1410. His successor was John XXIII.

Alexander VI. (RODRIGO **Lenzuoli Borgia**—lĕn-zoo-o'lee boR'jä) was born at Valencia, Spain, about 1430. He first studied law, and distinguished himself as an advocate, but afterwards embraced the military profession. When he was only twenty-five, his uncle, Calixtus III., was raised to the papal see. This circumstance directed his ambition towards the church. He was made cardinal through the influence of his uncle in 1456, and at length, in 1492, was elected pope as successor to Innocent VIII. He was distinguished, both while he was a cardinal and after he became pontiff, for his profligacy, inhumanity, and unscrupulous ambition. Alexander's illegitimate son, the infamous Cesare Borgia, was made cardinal soon after his father's accession to the papal throne. (See BORGIA.) He died in August, 1503, and was succeeded by Pius III. It has been asserted by several historians that Alexander VI. died from the effects of a poison which he and his son Borgia had designed for certain of their guests at a banquet, but which, by mistake, was taken by the pope himself. The "Nouvelle Biographie Générale," in an elaborate article,

endorses this accusation. It has, however, been discredited by several historical critics, on the ground that the evidence is insufficient. But, whatever judgment we may form on this question, it can scarcely be denied that the reign of Alexander VI. constitutes the blackest and most infamous page in the history of modern times.

See GORDON, "Lives of Alexander VI. and Cæsar Borgia," 1729; MURCHARD, "Specimen Historiæ Arcanæ seu Anecdota de Vita Alexandri VI.," 1697; PANVINIO, "Vite dei Pontefici;" ÉTIENNE MICHEL MASSE, "Histoire du Pape Alexandre VI," 1830; F. DE LA FONTAINE, "Le Pape Alexandre VI," 1844; TOMASI, "Vita di Cesare Borgia."

Alexander VII. (FABIO **Chigi**—kee'jee) was born at Sienna in 1599, and chosen pope in 1655, on the death of Innocent X. He is noted for his zealous and successful efforts to improve and embellish the city of Rome. He died in May, 1667, and was succeeded by Clement IX.

See BAGATTA, "Vita di Alessandro VII.;" BOTTA, "Storia d'Italia;" N. N. SFORZA PALLAVICINO, "Della Vita di Alessandro VII.," 2 vols., 1840.

Alexander VIII. (named originally PIETRO **Ottoboni**—ot-to-bo'nee) was born at Venice in 1610. He succeeded Innocent XI. in 1689. He aided the Venetians in war against the Turks. Died in 1691. His successor was Innocent XII.

See ARTAUD DE MONTOR, "Vies des souverains Pontifes."

Alexander I., King of Scotland, was a younger son of Malcolm Canmore. He succeeded his brother Edgar in 1107, and married a natural daughter of Henry I. of England. He died in 1124, and left the throne to his brother, David I.

See BURTON, "History of Scotland," vol. i. chap. xi. and vol. ii. chap. xii.

Alexander II. of Scotland, born in 1198, succeeded his father William the Lion in 1214. He fought against King John of England, as an ally of the revolted barons, and after the end of the war married a sister of Henry III. He is represented as a wise and able ruler. Died in 1249, and was succeeded by his son.

See BURTON, "History of Scotland," vol. ii. chap. xiv.

Alexander III. of Scotland, a son of the preceding, was born in 1241, and began to reign in 1249. His nuptials were celebrated with Margaret, the daughter of Henry III. of England, in 1251. His long reign was prosperous and peaceful, with the exception of an unsuccessful invasion of Scotland by Haco, King of Norway, with a large army, in 1263. Alexander fell with his horse over a precipice, and was killed by the fall, in 1286. He left no surviving children, and was succeeded by his infant grand-daughter Margaret.

See BURTON, "History of Scotland," vol. ii. chap. xv. ; TYTLER, "History of Scotland;" WYNTOWN, "Chronicle of Scotland."

Alexander JAGELLON—yȧ-ğel'lon, King of Poland and Grand Duke of Lithuania, born in 1461, was a son of Casimir IV. of Poland. He became king at the death of his brother John Albert in 1501. He waged war with little success against the Grand Duke Ivan of Russia. In his reign the laws of Poland were reduced to a code by John Laski. Died in 1506.

Alexander-NEVSKY—nev'ske, (*i.e.* "of the Neva,") sometimes written -NEVSKOI and -NEWSKOJ, a brave Russian prince, born in 1219, was a son of Yaroslav (Jaroslaw) II. He is said to have gained, in 1240, a great victory over the Swedes on the river Neva, whence his surname. He succeeded his father as grand duke in 1245. Died in 1263. He is venerated as a saint by the Russians.

Alexander I., (or, more fully, **Alexander-Pavlovitch**—pȧv'lo-vitch', *i.e.* "Alexander the son of Paul,") Emperor of Russia, the son of Paul and Maria Feodorovna, daughter of Prince Eugene of Würtemberg, was born at Saint Petersburg in 1777. The care of his education was taken from his father by Catherine II., his grandmother, who herself wrote tales for the amusement and instruction of the young prince. Catherine died in 1796, having named, it is said, Alexander as her successor in a will which was destroyed by Paul. In 1801 Paul was assassinated; but there is no sufficient ground for believing that Alexander in any way, directly or indirectly, sanctioned this crime, although he appears

ā, ē, ī, ō, ū, ȳ, *long;* ȧ, ė, ȯ, same, less prolonged; ă, ĕ, ĭ, ŏ, ŭ, ў, *short :* ą, ę, į, ǫ, *obscure;* fär, fȧll, fȧt; mȇt; nȏt; gŏŏd; mōōn;

to have consented to the dethronement of his father. The chief defect of his character in the early part of his life was the yielding too passively to the advice of the corrupt courtiers about him, and the want of reliance on his own judgment and on the dictates of his own noble nature. This may perhaps account for the inconsistencies which appear in his conduct in different parts of his life. He does not seem to have exhibited any striking indications of that greatness of mind which was afterwards so conspicuous, till about the time of the French invasion in 1812. Our limits necessarily compel us to pass over the military movements and those other acts of his reign which are found in every history of that eventful period. Suffice it to say that as his firmness and wisdom had led to the overthrow of Napoleon in 1813, so, after that event, his magnanimity preserved the city of Paris from the fury of the Russian soldiers, liberated one hundred and fifty thousand French prisoners of war confined in Russia, and sought to obtain for his fallen foe the most liberal terms compatible with what he deemed the safety of Europe. It was, in fact, through his influence that Bonaparte was allowed an independent sovereignty in Elba and the command of a portion of his former guard. On Alexander's return to Russia he granted an absolute pardon to all his subjects who had taken part against him in the late war. When it was proposed to erect a monument to commemorate his exploits, he peremptorily declined the honour, adding, "May a monument be erected to me in your hearts, as it is to you in mine." He gave unremitting attention to the internal improvement of his empire. Reform was introduced into every department, military and civil. In the army, the soldier was subjected to the restraints not merely of discipline, but also of humanity. Persecution on account of religion was first abolished in Russia under his reign. He entered Paris with the army of the Allies in July, 1815, and in September of that year he concluded with the Emperor of Austria and the King of Prussia a treaty called the Holy Alliance, which, although ostensibly formed to promote religion, peace, and justice, proved to be a bulwark against the progress of liberal principles. He died without issue, at Taganrog, on the 1st of December, 1825, and was succeeded by his brother Nicholas.

In reviewing the life and character of Alexander I. of Russia, we are obliged to confess that although his nature was on the whole kind and generous, and most of the acts of his reign were prompted by the spirit of justice and humanity, the cause of freedom owes little or nothing to his influence. It may be that he, like so many others, received such an impression from the excesses of the French Revolution that he came to believe that the people could not safely be trusted with any portion of liberty. In the latter part of his life especially, his mind sharing, perhaps, in his bodily infirmities, he regarded with morbid apprehension every public manifestation which looked towards the slightest enlargement of the privileges and powers of the people, and his attention was chiefly devoted to suppressing liberal movements not only in Poland, but also in Italy, Spain, Portugal, and Germany.

See HENRY EVANS LLOYD, "Alexander I., Emperor of Russia," 1826; SIR WALTER SCOTT, "Life of Napoleon Bonaparte;" ALISON, "History of Europe;" HEINRICH STORCH, "Russland unter Alexander I.," 8 vols., 1803-06; J. D. F. RUMPF, "Alexander I. Kaiser von Russland," 1814; COUSIN D'AVALLON, "Vie privée, politique et militaire d'Alexandre I," 1826; CARL F. LEIDENFROST, "Abriss einer Lebens Alexanders I.," 1826; ADRIEN EGRON, "Vie d'Alexandre I de Russie," 1826; ALPHONSE RABBE, "Histoire d'Alexandre I," etc., 1826; CARL MORGENSTERN, "Zum Gedaechtnisse Alexanders I.," 1827; E. W. C. VOIGT, "Alexander I.," 1830.

Alexander II, surnamed NICOLAEVITCH, nẹ-ko-lä'e-vitch, (*i.e.* "son of Nicholas,") Emperor of Russia, the eldest son of Nicholas I., was born on the 29th of April, 1818. His mother, Alexandra Feodorovna, was a sister of Frederick William IV. of Prussia. He married, in 1841, a daughter of Louis II., Grand Duke of Hesse-Darmstadt, who, on joining the Greek Church, adopted the name of Marie Alexandrovna. On the death of Nicholas, March 2, 1855, he ascended the throne, in the midst of a war between Russia on one side, and France, England, Turkey, and Sardinia on the other. He retained in office the ministers of his father, and pro-

claimed his intention to pursue the policy of his predecessor. The war was prosecuted with vigour even after the capture of Sebastopol, September, 1855. Conferences for the negotiation of peace, opened in Paris in March, 1856, resulted in a treaty by which neither party gained any important advantages.

Since the restoration of peace he has ordered several reforms in the administration, and has acquired the reputation of being more moderate and liberal than his father. Among the important measures of his reign is the gradual emancipation of more than twenty millions of serfs, which was decreed in March, 1861.

A letter which he addressed to the government of the United States in 1861, on the subject of the great rebellion, was received as an indication of a most friendly feeling on the part of Russia towards this country, which was doubly welcome on account of the doubtful or hostile attitude assumed by some of the other leading European powers.

Alexan'der ALEN'SIS, (*i.e.* "of Hales,") a renowned English theologian, styled the "Irrefragable Doctor." His chief work is a "System of Theology," ("Summa Theologiæ,") written by order of Pope Innocent IV. Died in 1245.

Alexander [Fr. ALEXANDRE, ả'lêk'sôɴdR'] OF BER'-NAY', afterwards ALEXANDER OF PARIS, a French poet of the twelfth century, born at the village of Bernay, in Normandy. He was the author (or one of the authors) of a poem on the exploits of Alexander the Great, in verses of twelve syllables, a measure which has ever since been termed "Alexandrine."

Alexander OF CANTERBURY, an English abbot and writer, who was noted for his assertion of the rights or interests of King John against the pope. Died about 1220.

Alexan'der ESSEBIEN'SIS, (*i.e.* "of Ashby,") an English monk, who wrote historical and theological works in the first part of the thirteenth century.

Alexan'der INSULA'NUS, a monk and chronicler of Westphalia, flourished about 1210.

Alexander, Bishop of Lincoln, born at Blois, was surnamed THE MAGNIFICENT. He rebuilt Lincoln Cathedral. Died in 1147.

Alexan'der OF VILLE DIEU, (vėl de̱-uh',) a grammarian of the thirteenth century. He taught in Paris, and composed a book of grammar in verse, which was long in general use as a school-book.

Alexan'der, (ARCHIBALD,) D.D., an eminent American divine, born in Rockbridge county, Virginia, in 1772. His grandfather, of Scottish descent, came from Ireland to Pennsylvania in 1736, and, after a residence of about two years, removed to Virginia. His father was a farmer. Archibald received his classical education at the academy of the Rev. William Graham, with whom he also studied theology. He was licensed to preach in 1791, and for several years devoted himself to itinerant labours, in which he acquired great fluency as a speaker. In 1796 he succeeded the Rev. Dr. John Blair Smith as president of Hampden-Sidney College, Virginia. He became pastor of the Pine Street Presbyterian Church of Philadelphia in 1807. On the organization of the Theological Seminary at Princeton in 1812, Dr. Alexander was unanimously chosen the first professor, with the sole charge of the several branches of a theological education. As the number of students increased, other professors were called to his assistance, which enabled him to direct his attention more particularly to the department of pastoral and polemic theology, in promoting which and the general interests of the institution he continued to labour with great zeal and success till his death in 1851. Dr. Alexander's powers, both for pulpit oratory and polemic disquisition, were extraordinary; and in all the relations of life he possessed rare excellencies. Few persons who have commenced authorship at so late a period in life have written so much. With the exception of some occasional sermons and contributions to periodicals, he had published nothing till the appearance of his "Outlines of the Evidences of Christianity," in his fifty-second year,—a work which has been translated into various foreign languages and is a text-book of high authority in several colleges. This was followed by his "Treatise on the Canon of the Scriptures;" "Christian Experience;" "History of African Colonization;" "History of the Israelites;" "Bible Dictionary;" "Counsels from the Aged to the Young;" besides many other works which our limits will not permit us to mention. His "Outlines of Moral Science," published in 1852, (after his decease,) says the "Westminster Review," "is a calm, clear stream of abstract reasoning flowing from a thoughtful, well-instructed mind, without any parade of logic, but with an intuitive simplicity and directness which give an almost axiomatic force." Dr. Alexander married in 1802 Janetta Waddell, daughter of the celebrated blind preacher mentioned by Wirt in his "British Spy." He left five sons and one daughter. Of the former, three were ministers.

See "Life of Dr. Archibald Alexander," by his son, JAMES W. ALEXANDER, New York, 1852; SPRAGUE's "Annals of the American Pulpit," vol. iii.

Alexander, (CALEB,) D.D., an American clergyman, was born at Northfield, Massachusetts, and graduated at Yale College in 1777. He afterwards settled at Onondaga Hollow, New York, where he died in 1828. He was the author of a Latin Grammar, (1794,) an English Grammar, and an Essay on the Deity of Jesus Christ, (1796.)

Alexander, (Sir JAMES EDWARD,) a British officer and writer, born in Scotland in 1803. He was employed about 1835 in an exploration of Africa, and commanded a regiment at Sebastopol in 1855. Among his works are "An Expedition into Southern Africa," "Travels through Russia and the Crimea," and a "Life of the Duke of Wellington."

Alexander, (JAMES WADDELL,) D.D., an American divine, eldest son of Dr. Archibald Alexander, was born in Louisa county, Virginia, in 1804. He graduated at Princeton in 1820, and, after studying theology, was for some time tutor in that institution. He commenced his labours as a minister in Charlotte county, Virginia, about 1826; subsequently removed to Trenton, New Jersey; and, from 1830 to 1833, edited "The Presbyterian," published in Philadelphia. He filled the chair of rhetoric and belles-lettres in the College of New Jersey (Princeton) until 1844, when he became pastor of the Duane Street Presbyterian Church, New York. From 1849 to 1851 he was professor of ecclesiastical history and church government in the Princeton Theological Seminary, and, for the remainder of his life, minister of the Presbyterian church in Fifth Avenue, New York. Dr. Alexander was a ripe scholar and vigorous writer. Among his works may be mentioned above thirty juvenile books written for the American Sunday-School Union; "Life of Dr. Archibald Alexander," 8vo, pp. 700; "American Mechanic's and Working-Man's Companion," 2 vols.; "Gift to the Afflicted;" besides numerous sermons, essays, etc. For many years he was one of the principal contributors to the "Princeton Review." Died at Virginia Springs, July, 1859.

See "Forty Years' Familiar Letters of James W. Alexander," by JOHN HALL, D.D.

Alexander, (JOSEPH ADDISON,) D.D., a distinguished theologian and Oriental scholar, third son of Dr. Archibald Alexander, was born in Philadelphia in 1809. At the age of twelve he commenced the study of Arabic, and before entering college had made considerable progress in the Persian and Hebrew. After graduating at Princeton in 1826, he continued his studies under private tutors, and from 1830 to 1833 was adjunct professor of ancient languages and literature in the College of New Jersey. In 1838 he became professor of biblical criticism and ecclesiastical history in the Princeton Theological Seminary, and in 1852 was transferred to the chair of biblical and ecclesiastical history. This position he occupied till his death, (1859.) In the extent and accuracy of his learning Dr. Alexander had few superiors in America; and several of his works have had a great success. His "Commentary on the Prophecies of Isaiah," (8vo, pp. 968,) republished in Scotland, Dr. Eadie, of Glasgow, pronounces "among the best commentaries on Isaiah of any age or language." His "Psalms Translated and Explained," in

three volumes, which appeared in 1850, reached a sale of ten thousand copies in four years. In 1851 he gave to the public his "Essays on the Primitive Church Offices." He was one of the principal contributors to the "Princeton Review." At the time of his decease he was engaged, with Dr. Hodge, in the preparation of a commentary on the New Testament.

See "Life of J. A. Alexander," by the REV. HENRY C. ALEXANDER, New York, 1870.

Alexander, (NATHANIEL,) born in 1756, was elected Governor of North Carolina in 1806; died in 1808.

Alexander, (NOËL.) See ALEXANDRE.

Alexander, (STEPHEN,) LL.D., an American astronomer, was born at Schenectady, New York, in 1806. He graduated at Union College in 1824, entered Princeton Theological Seminary in 1832, and in 1834 was appointed adjunct professor of mathematics in the College of New Jersey. In 1840 the professorship of astronomy was created and assigned to him, and on the death of Dr. Albert D. Dod, in 1845, he succeeded him as professor of mathematics. Since 1854 he has filled the chairs of mechanics and astronomy. He has published numerous papers on astronomy, mathematics, etc., some of which have attracted the attention of eminent astronomers both at home and abroad. Among these may be mentioned one on the "Physical Phenomena attendant upon Solar Eclipses;" "Fundamental Principles of Mathematics;" "On the Origin of the Forms and the Present Condition of some of the Clusters of Stars," etc. In 1860 he conducted an astronomical expedition sent out to the coast of Labrador by the United States government for the purpose of making observations on the solar eclipse of July 18 of that year.

Alexander, (THOMAS,) Earl of Selkirk, a British writer on politics, etc., planted a colony in Canada. Died in 1820.

Aïexander, (WILLIAM,) Earl of Stirling, a Scottish poet and courtier, born, it is supposed, about 1580. He produced in 1604 tragedies entitled "Julius Cæsar" and "Crœsus;" and "Parænesis to the Prince," a didactic poem. His long didactic poem of "Doomesday" appeared in 1614. These works were greatly admired by his contemporaries, but are now obsolete. He received from James I., by charter, in 1621, the territory of Nova Scotia, which he afterwards sold to the French. He was appointed secretary of state for Scotland in 1626, and received the title of Earl of Stirling in 1633. Died in 1640.

See CHAMBERS, "Biographical Dictionary of Eminent Scotsmen;" "Biographia Britannica."

Alexander, (WILLIAM,) (generally known in American history as LORD STIRLING,) a major-general in the American army of the Revolution, was born in 1726 in New York, of which his father, a Scotchman, was for many years the provincial secretary. He served as an officer in the war with the French and Indians, and at its close went to Scotland, where he spent a large portion of his fortune in an unsuccessful attempt to establish his claim to the estates and earldom of Stirling, of which many believed him the rightful heir. He early and warmly espoused the patriotic cause in the war of the Revolution, and, before the arrival of Washington from Boston, captured with a small fleet of boats a British transport in the harbour of New York. He led the attack in the battle of Long Island, in which he displayed the most determined courage, but was finally compelled to surrender, after securing the safe retreat of a large part of his detachment. On being exchanged, he at once resumed his command under Washington, fought with him at Brandywine, and especially distinguished himself at Germantown and Monmouth. In the last of these engagements he commanded the left wing of the American army. Through his fidelity, Washington was made acquainted with the intrigues and cabals of General Conway in 1777. Besides his military achievements, General Alexander won an honourable distinction as a mathematician and astronomer. Died at Albany in 1783.

See WILLIAM A. DUER, "Life of William Alexander, Earl of Stirling," New York, 1847.

Alexander, (WILLIAM,) an English artist, born at

Maidstone in 1768. He accompanied Lord Macartney as draughtsman on his embassy to China in 1792, and published "Views of Chinese Scenery," etc. Died in 1816.

Alexander, (WILLIAM,) a British medical writer, practised in London. Died in 1783.

Alexander, (WILLIAM LINDSAY,) D.D., a Scottish writer on theology, born at Leith in 1808. He became pastor of a church in Edinburgh. He is author of numerous works, among which are "The Connection and Harmony of the Old and New Testaments," (1841,) and "Memoirs of Ralph Wardlaw," (1856.)

Alexander ab Alexandro. See ALESSANDRI.

Alexander, (Ben-Moses-Ethu′san or -Ethuzan— êt-hoo′zạn,) a German rabbi, born at Fulda, lived about 1710, and wrote a History of the Jews, (1719.)

Alexander Farnese. See FARNESE.

Alexander de Medici. See MEDICI.

Alexander Polyhistor. See POLYHISTOR.

Alexander Severus. See SEVERUS.

Al-ex-an′drạ, a daughter of Hyrcanus, was the mother of Mariamne, the wife of Herod the Great. She conspired against Herod, and was put to death in 28 B.C.

Alexandre, the French of ALEXANDER, which see.

Alexandre, ǎ′lĕk′sǒNdR′, (CHARLES,) a philologist, born in Paris in 1797. Among his works is a "Greek-and-French Dictionary," ("Dictionnaire Grec-Français.")

Alexandre, (Dom JACQUES,) a French Benedictine, born at Orléans in 1653. He wrote a "Treatise on Tides," (1726,) and a valuable "General Treatise on Clocks," (1734.) Died in 1734.

Alexandre, (NICOLAS,) a French monk and medical writer, born in Paris in 1654, published a "Botanical Dictionary," (1716.) Died in 1728.

Alexandre, (NOËL,) a French Jansenist theologian, born at Rouen in 1639. He published, besides other works, "Dogmatic and Moral Theology," ("Theologia Dogmatica et Moralis," 10 vols., 1694.) Died in 1724.

See NICÉRON, "Mémoires."

Alexandre-Sévère. See SEVERUS.

Al-ex-an-dri′nus or Alexandrini, ä-lĕk-sȧn-dRee′-nee, (JULIUS,) a medical writer, physician to the emperors Frederick II., Maximilian, and Rudolph II., was born at Trent in 1506; died in 1590. He translated and commented on several of Galen's works.

Al-ex-ī′nus [Gr. 'Αλεξῖνος] OF ELIS, a disciple of Eubulides, lived about 350 B.C., and distinguished himself as a logician. He attacked Aristotle and Zeno the Stoic, and was nicknamed ELENXI′NUS, ("the fault-finder.")

Al-ex′is, ['Άλεξις,] a Greek comic poet, an uncle of the poet Menander, was born at Thurium, and flourished between 350 and 290 B.C. He removed to Attica in his youth. He excelled in the delineation of the characters of Parasites, belonged to the middle school of the Attic comedy, and was a very prolific writer. Only small fragments of his works are extant.

See A. MEINEKE, "Historia Critica Comicorum Græcorum."

Alexis, a Greek sculptor, who is mentioned by Pliny as a pupil of Polycletus, and of whom nothing more is known. He is supposed by some to have been identical with the Alexis whom Pausanias mentions as the father of Cantharus.

Alexis, ȧ′lĕk′se′, (GUILLAUME,) a French Benedictine, who lived in the latter part of the fifteenth century. He wrote in verse and prose several works, among which is "Le Grand Blason de Faulces Amours," ("The Great Blazon of False Loves," 1493.)

Al-ex′is or Al-ex′ī-us I., (Com-ne′nus,) [Gr. 'Αλεξις or 'Αλέξιος Κομνηνός,] an emperor of Constantinople, born about 1048. He was of high birth, and became general of the Byzantine armies, in which capacity he showed considerable military skill. About 1080 he was proclaimed emperor by his soldiers, in opposition to Nicephorus, who, on the approach of the troops of Alexis, left his throne for a monastery. It was during the reign of Alexis that the first crusade to Jerusalem took place. He died in 1118, and was succeeded by his son John. As a ruler he was more distinguished for craft and intrigue than for any higher qualities.

See ANNA COMNENA, "Alexias;" GIBBON, "Decline and Fall of the Roman Empire," chaps. xlviii., lvi., lviii., lix.; MILL, "History of the Crusades."

Alexis or Alexius II., (Comne′nus,) Emperor of Constantinople, a son of Manuel, was born about 1168, and became emperor in 1180. He was deposed and strangled by Androni′cus in 1183.

Alexis or Alexius III., (An′ge-lus,) was a brother of Isaac Angelus, Emperor of Constantinople, whose throne he usurped in 1195. An army of crusaders, whose destination was Palestine, besieged Constantinople in 1203, ostensibly to restore Alexis, son of Isaac, to the throne. (See DANDOLO.) Alexis III. fled on the capture of the city, and died in exile in 1210.

Alexis or Alexius IV., (Angelus,) a son of Isaac Angelus, reigned a few months. He was put to death in 1204 by Alexis Ducas.

Alexis or Alexius V., (Du′cas,) surnamed MURZU′PHLUS, usurped the throne in 1204. The Latin chiefs who commanded the crusaders, having resolved to partition the Empire of the East, took Constantinople by assault in 1204. Alexis escaped, but was arrested in the Morea, was tried for the murder of Alexis IV., and was executed in the same year. He was succeeded by Baldwin I.

See GIBBON, "History of the Decline and Fall of the Roman Empire."

Alex′is or Alex′ius Comne′nus is also the name of several emperors who reigned at Trebizond (Trapezus) in the thirteenth, fourteenth, and fifteenth centuries. They were of the same family as the Alexis Comnenus noticed above.

Al-ex′is or Alexei (ȧ-lĕk-sā′e) **Michaelovitch or Mikhaylovitch**—me-KĪ′lo-vitch, Czar of Muscovy, born in 1629 or 1630, succeeded his father Michael in 1645. He introduced many improvements, particularly with respect to the administration of the laws. He also succeeded in transferring from Poland to Russia the allegiance of the Cossacks who were attached to the Greek Church. He may, indeed, be said to have prepared the way for the great undertakings of his son Peter. (See PETER I. of Russia.) Died in 1676, and was succeeded by his son Feodor.

Alexis, a monk, who became Patriarch of Constantinople in 1025. In 1042 he crowned the emperor Constantine Monomachus. Died in 1043.

Alexis of Samos, a Greek historian, the author of a "History of Samos," which is mentioned by Athenæus. The period in which he lived is not known.

Alexis Pedemontanus. See ALESSIO PIEMONTESE.

Alexis Petrovitch or Petrowitsch, (pȧ-tRo′vitch,) written also **Petrowitz,** a Russian prince, born in 1690, was a son of Peter the Great and his first wife Eudokia. He is said to have been a studious youth, averse to martial pursuits and hostile to the innovations of his father. While Peter was absent on one of his long European tours in 1716, Alexis retired furtively to Vienna and Naples, for refuge from the dreaded ire of the Czar. This strange proceeding, which perhaps was as wise as any course that was open to him in the circumstances, was treated as a crime by his father. Having been induced to return, Alexis was compelled to renounce his claim to the throne, and was condemned to death on a charge of meditated rebellion, in 1718. He was found dead in prison a few days after his sentence was pronounced. There are very strong reasons for believing that he was poisoned by order of the Czar. He left a son, Peter, who became Czar in 1727.

See VOLTAIRE, "Histoire de Russie;" LÉVESQUE, "Histoire de Russie;" Sir JOHN BARROW, "Life of Peter the Great," in the "Family Library;" VON HALEM, "Leben Peters des Grossen;" ERSCH und GRUBER, "Allgemeine Encyklopædie."

Alexis del Arco. See ARCO, (ALONSO DEL.)

Aleyn, ȧl′en, (CHARLES,) an English poet, who once had considerable reputation, born, it is supposed, about 1590, was educated at Cambridge, and became tutor to Sir Edward Sherburne. His principal poems are "The Battles of Cressy and Poitiers," (1632,) and a "History of Henry VII., etc.," (1638.) Died about 1640.

See WINSTANLEY, "Lives of the Poets," 1687.

Alfani, ȧl-fä′nee, (DOMENICO DI PARIS,) an eminent Italian painter, born at Perugia about 1483, was a pupil of Pietro Perugino. Among his works are a "Virgin Mary" and a "Saint John." Died about 1540.

ē as k; ç as s; ğ hard; ḡ as j; G, H, K, guttural; N, nasal; R, trilled; s̄ as z; ᵵh as in this. (☞See Explanations, p. 23.)

Alfani, (ORAZIO DI PARIS,) an able artist, a son of the preceding, born at Perugia about 1510. He imitated the manner of Raphael with success, and painted both in oil and fresco. Among his chief works are several Madonnas. Died in 1583.

See LANZI, "History of Painting in Italy."

Alfar. See ELVES.

Al-fa-rā′bĭ-us, [Arab. ALFARÂBEE or ALFARÂBÎ, ăl-fă-ră′bee,] the Latin name of a distinguished Arabian philosopher who lived at Damascus in the tenth century. He is said to have understood seventy different languages. Besides other works on various sciences, he wrote several treatises on the philosophy of Aristotle.

Alfarazdâk, ăl-fă′răz-dăk′, an eminent Arabian poet of the seventh century.

Alfaro, ăl-fă′ro, (FRANCISCO,) a Spanish silversmith and artist, who flourished at Seville towards the close of the sixteenth century. His representations on silver were designed and executed with great taste.

Alfaro y Gomez, de, dà ăl-fă′ro e go′mĕth, (JUAN,) a Spanish painter of high reputation, born at Córdova in 1640, was a pupil of Castillo and Velasquez. He worked at Madrid, and excelled in portraits, in which he imitated the style of Velasquez. Among his best works is an "Incarnation," at Córdova, and a portrait of Calderon the poet. He was a brilliant colorist. Died in 1680.

See BERMUDEZ, "Diccionario Historico," etc.

Alfâth, ăl-fât′, or **Alfatah,** ăl-fă′tă, a distinguished Arabian philologist, born at Seville, in Spain, near the close of the eleventh century. He was put to death at Morocco in 1135. He wrote a book containing biographical notices of various Arabian poets, with specimens of their poetry.

Alfen, ăl′fĕn, (JOHAN EUSEBIUS,) a Danish miniature-painter, worked in Vienna. Died in 1770.

Al-fe′nus Vā′rus, an eminent Roman jurist, and a pupil of Servius Sulpicius, lived in the last half of the first century B.C. He wrote forty books of Digesta, extracts from which are to be found in the Digest of Justinian. He is often quoted by other jurists. A passage in Horace Sat. i. 3, v. 130 is supposed to refer to this Alfenus.

Alferghânee, (**Alferghânî,**) ăl-fĕr-Gâ′nee, written also **Alferghânee, Alfergany,** and **Alferganus,** sometimes called **Al-frą-gan′,** an Arabian astronomer of the ninth century, was born in Sogdiana. He wrote a work entitled "Elements of Astronomy," which has been translated into Latin.

Alfez, ăl-fĕz′, or **Alphesi,** ăl-fĕz′ee or ăl-fă′zee, (ISAAC **Berabbi**—bę-răb′be,) a rabbi and eminent Jewish writer, born near Fez, in Africa, about 1013. Died in Spain in 1103. His chief work is an abridgment of the Talmud, called the "Lesser Talmud."

Alfheim. See ELVES.

Alfieri, ăl-fe-ā′ree, (BENEDETTO,) COUNT, an Italian architect, born in Rome in 1700, was an uncle of the great poet Alfieri, who, in his own memoirs, speaks of him as a very worthy man. He designed the Royal Opera-House of Turin, one of the noblest structures of the kind in Italy, and was patronized by the king, Charles Emmanuel. Among his other works are the façade of Saint Peter's Church at Geneva, and the church at Carignano. Died at Turin in 1767.

Alfieri, (VITTORIO,) the most celebrated Italian poet of his age, was born of a noble family at Asti, in Piedmont, on the 17th of January, 1749. He inherited an ample fortune from his father, who died while Vittorio was an infant, and was sent to the Accademia or College of Turin, in which he received such an education as those wholly incompetent to teach could impart. He left school about the age of fifteen, and indulged his passion for travel and reckless dissipation. He visited Paris, passed over to England, and sojourned in Holland. From a second tour through Germany, Sweden, Russia, etc., he returned to Turin in 1772. He once went to England on purpose to purchase horses, of which he was very fond. The success of his first drama, "Cleopatra," which was performed at Turin in 1775, appears to have produced a change in his mode of life, which

was thenceforth devoted to study and to dramatic composition.

In the course of the seven ensuing years he composed fourteen tragedies, among which are "Filippo II.," "Virginia," "Orestes," "Mary Stuart," "Octavia," "Merope," and "Saul," (1782.) The first and the last of these are considered his master-pieces. His dramas are simple in design, noble in sentiment, sententious in style, and pervaded by intense passion. About 1778 Alfieri became acquainted with the Countess of Albany, (wife of the Pretender, Charles Edward Stuart,) who inspired his wayward heart with a lasting passion. (See ALBANY, COUNTESS OF.) It is supposed that he was privately married to her after the death of her husband in 1788. He resided some years in France, and invested a large sum of money in French stocks, which he lost when he fled from the outrages of the Revolution in 1792. He then became a resident of Florence, and about the age of forty-six commenced the study of Greek, in which he made good progress. He translated some of the plays of Æschylus, Sophocles, and Euripides.

Among the other works of Alfieri are an "Essay on Tyranny," a translation of Sallust, a number of sonnets and epigrams, and five odes on the American Revolution. He died at Florence on the 8th of October, 1803. Notwithstanding his faults, he was a man of public spirit, a sincere patriot, and an ardent lover of liberty. A monument, designed by Canova, was erected to him by the Countess of Albany in Santa Croce, Florence, between the tombs of Michael Angelo and Machiavel. "He rarely speaks to the heart," says Ginguené, "but he is eloquent and nervous in intense passions ; he possesses grandeur, and in his ideas, as well as in his style, aspires always to the sublime. . . . His dialogue is often a model of precision and dramatic argumentation." "The aim of his works," says Madame de Staël, "is so noble, the sentiments which the author expresses accord so well with his personal conduct, that his tragedies ought always to be praised as actions, even when they may be criticised as literary works." (*Corinne.*) "A parallel between Alfieri and Cowper," says Macaulay, (in his article on Byron, in the "Edinburgh Review," 1831,) "may at first sight seem as unpromising as that which a loyal Presbyterian minister is said to have drawn in 1745 between George the Second and Enoch. . . . But though the private lives of these remarkable men present scarcely any points of resemblance, their literary lives bear a close analogy to each other. They both found poetry in its lowest state of degradation, feeble, artificial, and altogether nerveless. They both possessed precisely the talents which fitted them for the task of raising it from that deep abasement. . . . They had not in a very high degree the creative power, but they had great vigour of thought, great warmth of feeling, and, what was above all things important, a manliness of taste which approached to roughness."

See his Autobiography entitled "Vita di Vittorio Alfieri scritta da Esso," translated into English by C. E. LESTER ; "Vita di Vittorio Alfieri," Milan, 1823 ; SERAFICO GRASSI, "Dissertazione in lode di Vittorio Alfieri," 1819 ; ANTONIO ZEZON, "Biografia di Vittorio Alfieri," 1835 ; LONGFELLOW, "Poets and Poetry of Europe ;" VILLEMAIN, "Cours de Littérature ;" A. BUCCELLINI, "Elogio de Vittorio Alfieri," 1811 ; R. SOUTHEY, article on the Life and Writings of Alfieri, in the "Quarterly Review" for January, 1816.

Alfon, ăl-fòn′, (JUAN,) a Spanish painter, born at Toledo, lived about 1418.

Alfonse, ăl′fòNs′, (JEAN,) a French navigator of the sixteenth century, was a native of Saintonge, whence his surname LE SAINTONGEOIS, (lęh săN′tòN′zhwā′.) He made several voyages of discovery in the South Seas, an account of which was published in 1559, entitled "Voyages Adventureux du Capitaine Jean Alfonse."

Al-fon′so I., surnamed EL BATALLADOR, ĕl bă-tâl-yă-dōR′, (*i.e.* the "battler" or "warrior,") King of Aragon and Navarre, ascended the throne in 1104. He fell in battle in 1134. He had, it is said, previously defeated the Mohammedans in thirty-nine successive conflicts, and taken from them a much greater extent of territory than he had inherited from his ancestors. He was succeeded by his brother, Ramiro II.

Alfonso II. of Aragon, a grandson of Ramiro II., born in 1152, became king in 1163. He inherited Bar-

ā, ē, ī, ō, ū, ȳ, *long;* à, ė, ȯ, same, less prolonged; ă, ĕ, ĭ, ŏ, ŭ, y̆, *short;* ą, ę, į, ǫ, *obscure;* fär, fåll, fät; mĕt; nŏt; gōōd; mᴏ̄ōn;

celona from his father, Raymond V., and extended his dominions at the expense of the Mussulmans. Died in 1196, leaving the throne to his son, Pedro II.

Alfonso III. of Aragon, born about 1265, was a son of Pedro III., whom he succeeded in 1285. The Cortes asserted their privileges with success in this reign, and set bounds to the royal prerogative. He died in 1291, and was succeeded by his brother, Jaime II.

Alfonso IV. of Aragon, a son of Jaime II., began to reign in 1327. He waged a war against the Genoese, who invaded his kingdom, but were repulsed. Died in 1336, and was succeeded by his son, Pedro IV.

See ZURITA, "Annales de Aragon."

Alfonso V. OF ARAGON. See ALFONSO I. OF NAPLES.

Alfonso I., King of Asturias, ascended the throne in 739 A.D. He gained many victories over the Moslems, and took from them a multitude of towns and fortresses. From his zeal for religion, evinced in building churches and founding monasteries, etc., he received the surname of EL CATÓLICO, ("the Catholic.") Died in 756.

Alfonso II. of Asturias, surnamed EL CASTO, ("the Chaste,") succeeded to the throne in 791 A.D. He was distinguished for his successful wars against the Mohammedans. He died in 842, after a prosperous reign of more than fifty years.

Alfonso III. of Asturias and Leon, surnamed EL MAGNO, ("the Great,") succeeded his father Ordoño in 866 A.D. He greatly extended his dominions by conquests from the Mohammedans. Died in 910, leaving the throne to his son Garcia.

Alfonso I. of Castile, (or **Alfonso VI.** of Leon,) surnamed EL BRAVO, (êl brä'vo, ("the Brave,") a son of Fernando I., ascended the throne of Leon in 1065. On the death of his brother, Sancho II. of Castile, in 1073, Galicia, Asturias, Castile, etc. were added to his sway. He acquired great renown in his wars against the Moors. His reign may be considered as the dawn of Christian prosperity in modern Spain. Died in 1109, aged seventy-nine.

Alfonso II. of Castile, (called **Alfonso VII.** of Leon by some historians, who count Alfonso I. of Castile as VI. of Leon,) named also **Alfonso Raymond,** a grandson of the preceding, ascended the throne in 1126. He was very successful in his wars with the Mohammedans, and removed the frontiers of Castile from the Tagus to the Sierra Morena Mountains. In 1135 he assumed the imperial title, and is accordingly sometimes styled "the Emperor." Died in 1157, leaving Castile to his son Sancho, and Leon to his son Fernando. The written language of Spain is supposed to date from about the beginning of the reign of Alfonso VII., and the oldest Spanish document of which the date is known is one given by Alfonso VII. to the city of Avilés, in Asturias, in confirmation of certain privileges previously granted.

See TICKNOR'S "Spanish Literature," vol. i. chap. ii.

Alfonso VIII. of Castile, called by some **Alfonso III.,** surnamed EL NOBLE, (êl no'Blä, ("the Noble,") succeeded to the throne in 1158, when he was only three years old. After he became of age he was almost constantly engaged in war with the Mohammedans. In 1195 he sustained a severe defeat from the arms of Aboo-Yoosuf-Yakoob; but in 1212, with the kings of Aragon and Navarre, he gained a great victory over the Almohade sultan Mohammed An-Nâsir, at the head of 600,000 men. Tne loss of the Mohammedans, as estimated by their own writers, was not less than 160,000. Alfonso died in 1214, and was succeeded by his son, Enrique I.

Alfonso XI. of Castile, a son of Fernando IV., succeeded to the throne in 1312, when he was only a year old. In 1333, aided by Alfonso IV. of Portugal, whose daughter he had married, he turned his arms against the Moors, and in 1340 gained a great victory over the sultan Abool-Hassan (or Alboacen) under the walls of Tarifa, then besieged by the Mohammedan forces. He died in 1350, respected even by his enemies. The Moorish king of Granada is said to have exclaimed, when he heard of Alfonso's death, "We have lost the best king in the world,—one who knew how to honour

the worthy, whether friend or foe." He was succeeded by his son, Pedro the Cruel.

See MARIANA, "Historia general de España."

Alfonso I., II., and **III.** OF LEON. See ALFONSO OF ASTURIAS.

Alfonso IV. of Leon and Asturias, surnamed THE MONK, succeeded his uncle Fruela in 924. He abdicated in favour of his brother Ramiro about 930, and became a monk. Died about 932.

Alfonso V., King of Leon, born in 994, succeeded his father, Bermudo II., in 999. His reign was prosperous, and his armies gained several victories over the Moors. He was killed at the siege of Viseu in 1028, and was succeeded by his son, Bermudo III.

Alfonso VI. OF LEON. See ALFONSO I. OF CASTILE.

Alfonso VII. OF LEON. See ALFONSO II. OF CASTILE.

Alfonso IX., King of Leon, succeeded his father Fernando II. in 1158. He waged war against Alfonso of Castile, and afterwards married his daughter. Died in 1230, leaving a son Fernando, who was King of Castile and Leon.

Alfonso X., King of Leon and Castile, surnamed EL SABIO, êl sä'Be-o, ("the Wise,") born in 1226, was a son of Fernando III., whom he succeeded in 1252. He had a high reputation for learning and eloquence, and was distinguished for the patronage he extended to science and literature; but he was not a successful or popular ruler. His reign was disturbed by civil wars, one of which was instigated by his second son, Sancho, about 1281. The situation of Alfonso was so desperate that he solicited aid from the Moors. Spain owes to him an excellent code of laws, a translation of the Bible into Castilian, the restoration of the University of Salamanca, and the first use of the Castilian language in public affairs. Europe is indebted to him for the valuable astronomical tables called Alphonsine Tables. Died in 1284.

See TICKNOR, "History of Spanish Literature," vol. i. chap. iii.; LONGFELLOW, "Poets and Poetry of Europe;" CONDE, "Historia de la Dominacion de los Arabes en España;" MARIANA, "Historia general de España;" MARQUIS DE MONDEJAR, "Memorias historicas del Rey Don Alfonso el Sabio."

Alfonso I. of Naples, Sicily, and Aragon, born in 1385, succeeded his father Fernando I. on the throne of Aragon in 1416. He had been adopted as the heir of Queen Joanna of Naples, and in 1442, seven years after the death of that princess, and after encountering much opposition, he obtained possession of the whole Neapolitan kingdom. Died in 1458. He was a man of learning, and a liberal patron of literature and science. His son Ferdinand became King of Naples.

See FACIO, "Fatti d'Alfonso d'Aragona."

Alfonso II., King of Naples, born in 1448, was a son of Ferdinand I. He defeated the Florentines at Poggio in 1479, and the Turks at Otranto in 1481. He ascended the throne in January, 1494, and rendered himself odious by his cruelty and avarice. Alarmed at the approach of Charles VIII. of France with an army, he abdicated in favour of his son Ferdinand in January, 1495, and died about the end of that year.

See GIANNONE, "Storia del Regno di Napoli."

Alfonso I., [Port. AFFONSO,] or, more fully, **Dom Affonso Enriques,** dòn âf-fon'so ên-ree'kês, the founder of the Portuguese monarchy, son of Henry of Besançon, Count of Toulouse, was born in 1094. He inherited the title of Count of Portugal from his father, who had received it from Alfonso I. of Castile, his father-in-law. Enriques was yet a child when his father died, and Portugal was for a long time under the rule, or rather misrule, of his mother Theresa ; but in 1128 he took the supreme authority into his own hands. Alfonso VIII. (or more properly III.) of Castile, having supported the claims of Theresa, Enriques met him in the field, defeated him, and established the entire independence of Portugal. He did not, however, take the title of king till 1139 when, at the head of about 13,000 Portuguese, he completely routed, at Ourique, the combined army of the Mohammedans, amounting, it is said, to 200,000 men, and made prisoners the five kings by whom this mighty host was led. In 1146 he took Santarem from the Moors by assault, and in the same year, or early in the next, reduced Lisbon, after a siege of more than five months. He turned his arms successively against the other towns and fortresses in possession of the Mohammedans, and in 1158 became undisputed possessor of his kingdom. Died in 1185, aged ninety. He left a son, who became King Sancho I.

See MARIANA, "Historia de España;" SCHAEFFER, "Histoire du Portugal."

Alfonso (or **Affonso**) **II.** of Portugal, a son of Sancho I., was born in 1185, and began to reign in 1211. His kingdom was placed under an interdict by the pope because he taxed the property of the clergy. Alfonso was thus reduced to submission. He died in 1223, leaving the throne to his son, Sancho II.

Alfonso (**Affonso**) **III.**, a son of the preceding, born in 1210, succeeded his brother Sancho II. in 1248. His reign was rather prosperous, though he was once excommunicated by the pope. He died in 1279, and was succeeded by his son Denis, (Diniz.)

Alfonso (**Affonso**) **IV.** of Portugal, surnamed THE BRAVE, a son of Denis, was born in 1290, and began to reign in 1325. Among the remarkable events of his reign was the rebellion of his son Dom Pedro, whose motive was revenge for the murder of Iñes de Castro, to which the king had consented. He died in 1357, leaving the throne to his son, Pedro I.

Alfonso (**Affonso**) **V.** of Portugal, a son of Duarte, was born in 1432, and became king in 1438, under the regency of his mother. He conducted a large armament against Africa in 1458, and captured Tangier. Having invaded Castile, he was defeated by Ferdinand of Aragon in 1476. He died in 1481, and was succeeded by his son João II.

See MARIANA, "Historia de España."

Alfonso (**Affonso**) **VI.** of Portugal, a son of John IV., was born in 1643, and became king in 1656. His imbecility or vices having rendered him unpopular, he was forced to abdicate in 1667 in favour of his brother Dom Pedro, and was banished to Terceira. He was confined in the castle of Cintra in 1675, and died in 1683.

Alfonso I. of Este, Duke of Ferrara, born in 1476, began to reign in 1505. He commanded the Papal troops in the war of the League of Cambrai, 1509. In 1512 he fought against the Pope, Julius II., at Ravenna. He married the famous Lucretia Borgia. Died in 1534.

Alfonso, (the Navigator.) See ALPHONSE.

Alfonso, ál-fon′so, (PEDRO,) a Spanish Jew, who was born in Aragon in 1062, and was converted to Christianity. He wrote after his conversion, besides other works, one called "Clerical Discipline," ("Disciplina Clericalis,") which was much esteemed. Died about 1140.

Alfonso OF CARTAGENA, (or DE CARTAGENA, dâ kaR-tâ-Hâ′nâ,) [Lat. ALPHON′SUS A SANC′TA-MARI′A,] a celebrated Spanish historian, born at Carthagena (or Cartagena) in 1396, became Bishop of Burgos. He wrote a "History of Spain," from the earliest ages down to his own time, and other works. Died in 1456.

Alfonso de Cartagena. See ALFONSO OF CARTHAGENA.

Alfonso Lopez de Corella, (lo′pĕth dâ ko-rĕl′yâ,) a Spanish physician, born in Navarre, wrote numerous medical works, dated 1546-82.

Alfonso de Palencia, (de pâ-lĕn′she-a,) [Sp. pron. âl-fon′so dâ pâ-lĕn′the-â; Lat. ALPHON′SUS PALENTI′-NUS,] a distinguished Spanish historian, born at Palencia, in Old Castile, in 1423. He was royal historiographer to Queen Isabella of Castile. The precise time of his death is unknown. He was alive in 1492. He wrote in Latin a history of the reign of Isabella, and a chronicle of Henry IV.

See PRESCOTT, "Ferdinand and Isabella," vol. i. part i.

Alfonso Tostado. See ALPHONSUS ABULENSIS.

Alford, awl′fǫrd, (HENRY,) D.D., commonly known as DEAN ALFORD, an English poet and divine, born in London in 1810, was educated at Trinity College, Cambridge. He became vicar of Wymeswold, Leicestershire, in 1835, Hulsean Lecturer at Cambridge in 1841, incumbent of Quebec Street Chapel, London, in 1853, and Dean of Canterbury about 1856. He pub-

lished in 1835 "The School of the Heart, and other Poems," (2 vols.,) which are commended. "The present volumes," says the "Edinburgh Review," "appear to us to be a beginning of great promise. . . . Extracts so much longer than we are in the habit of making, are a sufficient proof of our sense of the talent displayed in these poems." (Critique on "The School of the Heart, and other Poems," January, 1836.) His reputation as a divine is founded on an excellent edition of the Greek New Testament in four or more volumes, 1841-61. He has also published a small volume entitled "The Queen's English," (2d edition, 1864,) which has attracted much attention.

Alford, (MICHAEL,) an English Jesuit and writer, born in London in 1587; died at Saint Omer, in France, in 1651. He wrote "Britannia Illustrata," (1641,) treating of the ecclesiastical history of Britain.

Alfragan. See ALFERGHANEE.

Alfrago, âl-frâ′go, (ANDREA,) an Italian physician, wrote a history of Arabian physicians, etc. Died at Padua in 1520.

Alfred, âl′fred, written also ÆEl′fred, El′fred, and **Alured,** i.e. **Alvred,** [Lat. ÆLFRE′DUS,] surnamed THE GREAT, King of the West Saxons in England, was born in 848 or 849. He was the son of King Æthelwulf and Osburga, (or Osberga,) the daughter of a Gothic nobleman. On the death of his brother Æthelred, in 871, Alfred became king. At this period the country was in the most deplorable condition. The Danes had overrun a great portion of England, and many of the bravest Saxons had fallen in vain attempts to resist their pagan invaders. King Ethelred himself had died of a wound received in this unequal conflict. Alfred was fain to procure peace on almost any terms, and at last agreed to pay the Danes a sum of money on condition that they would leave his dominions. But they broke their oaths, and, attacking him by night, destroyed all his cavalry. All the means of resistance being lost, Alfred for a time laid aside the ensigns of royalty and concealed himself in the family of a poor herdsman. Having at length been discovered by some of his nobles, he gradually, but secretly, collected a considerable force, with which he occasionally made inroads into the territory occupied by the Danes, and thus procured the means of subsisting himself and his army. About this time Odun, Earl of Devon, sallied from his castle, defeated the besiegers, slew Ubbo, one of the principal leaders, and took the Danish standard. Upon this, Alfred resolved to attack the main army of his enemies, which he routed with great slaughter at Eddington in 878, and soon after obliged the survivors to surrender at discretion. The Danish king, Godrun, (or Guthrun,) embraced the Christian religion, Alfred standing as his godfather; and a considerable tract of country was allotted to the converted Danes. Alfred now directed his earnest efforts towards the fortifying and internal improvement of his kingdom. He caused a number of ships to be built, and may be said to have laid the foundation of the British navy. He repaired the old dilapidated fortresses, and erected new ones wherever they were needed. He exerted himself, moreover, to establish an efficient police and a thorough administration of justice within his dominions. He was not, however, as has frequently been stated, the author of the trial by jury. It was his highest glory that he did so much for his country's literature and the intellectual improvement of his people. He not only established schools in all the principal towns, but he began himself, it is said, to learn Latin at the age of thirty-nine, and afterwards translated a number of works from that language into his native tongue. In 894 the Northmen again invaded England, with a fleet of three hundred ships; but they were defeated by Alfred, and those who escaped the sword were either taken captive and executed as pirates or chased from the kingdom. Alfred died in 901.

Alfred the Great presents to us one of the most perfect characters to be found on the page of history. He was, to use the language of a recent author, "a saint without superstition, a scholar without ostentation, a warrior all whose wars were fought in defence of his country, a conqueror whose hands were never stained by cruelty, a

---

ā, ē, ī, ō, ū, ȳ, *long;* ă, ĕ, ĭ, ŏ, ŭ, ў, *short;* a, ẹ, ị, ǫ, *obscure;* fär, fäll, fât; mêt; nŏt; gōͦd; mōͦn;

prince never cast down by adversity, never lifted up to insolence in the day of triumph." (See Freeman's "Norman Conquest," vol. i. chap. ii.; also, Hume's character of Alfred in his "History of England," vol. i. chap. ii.)

See J. A. GILES, "Life and Times of Alfred the Great," 1854; SPELMAN, "Life of Alfred," 1709; A. BICKNELL, "Life of Alfred," 1777; STOLBERG, "Leben Alfreds des Grossen," 1815; ASSER, "Life of Alfred," ("De Aelfredi Rebus gestis," 1571:) RICHARD PAULLI, "König Alfred und seine Stelle in der Geschichte Englands," London, 1851, translated into English by THOMAS WRIGHT, 1852.

Alfred, a son of the Saxon king Ethelred II., and Emma. He attempted to obtain the throne in 1042, but failed, and lost his life.

Alfred, surnamed AN'GLICUS (or the "Englishman") and THE PHILOSOPHER, wrote some scientific works,— one, "On the Motion of the Heart," ("De Cordis Motu.") A part of his life was passed in England; but the place of his nativity is unknown. Died about 1270.

Alfred or **Alured** OF BEVERLEY, an English historian, born about 1100, became a priest. He left a Latin History of Britain, which is supposed to be an abridgment of the work of Geoffrey of Monmouth.

Alfred OF MALMESBURY, an English monk and writer, became Bishop of Crediton about 990.

Alfred, (ERNEST ALBERT,) Duke of Edinburgh, the second son of Victoria, Queen of England, was born in 1844. He entered the navy in 1858, and made voyages to various countries. In 1862 he declined the throne of Greece, which had been offered to him. He was shot at and wounded by an assassin in Australia in 1868.

Alfred and **A-bi'ram,** two German architects, born in Bavaria, lived in the ninth century. They built the imperial palace of Ratisbon.

Alfric, ăl'frik, written also **Ælfric** and **Elfric,** [Lat. ALFRI'CUS, ÆLFRI'CUS, or ELFRI'CUS,] surnamed ABBAS, (the "Abbot,") and GRAMMATICUS, (the "Grammarian,") a celebrated Anglo-Saxon writer, who flourished in the latter half of the tenth century. Of his life nothing certain is known. It is supposed that he became Archbishop of Canterbury in 995. Among his works are numerous homilies.

Alfric or **Ælfric,** Archbishop of York, an Anglo-Saxon writer, who is by some identified with the famous writer Alfric surnamed Grammaticus, above noticed. Died in 1051.

Algardi, ăl-gaʀ'dee, (ALESSANDRO,) a celebrated Italian sculptor and architect, born at Bologna about 1600. His birth is variously dated at 1588, 1593, and 1602. He studied design with the Caracci, became a pupil of Cesare Conventi, and went to Rome about 1625. He was architect of the Villa Panfili or Pamphili, and of the façade of the church of St. Ignatius, Rome. His master-piece in sculpture is a colossal bas-relief* in the church of Saint Peter's, representing Saint Leo forbidding Attila to enter Rome, (1640.) This is said to be the largest bas-relief in the world. Among his works are statues of Saint Philip de Neri and Innocent X. He is regarded by some critics as the greatest sculptor of his age. Died in 1654.

See PASSERI, "Vite de' Pittori," etc.; MILIZIA, "Vite degli Architetti."

Algarotti, ăl-gă-rot'tee, (FRANCESCO,) COUNT, a distinguished Italian writer and connoisseur, born at Venice in 1712. He was not only well versed in many languages and sciences, but possessed decided skill in the art of design, and wrote verses with facility. In 1733 he produced popular dialogues on Optics, entitled "Optics for Ladies," ("Neutonianismo per le Dame,") which were translated into several languages. Invited by Frederick the Great, he went to Berlin about 1740, and passed many years at that court as a friend of the king, who gave him the title of count. This friendship continued until the death of Algarotti. He corresponded with Voltaire and many other eminent authors. Besides essays on various subjects, he wrote "Letters on Painting," which display good taste and judgment. He died at Pisa in March, 1764.

See D. MICHELESSI, "Memorie intorno alla vita del Conte F. Algarotti," 1770, and French version of the same, 1772; FABRONI,

* Some authorities call Algardi's great work an *alto-relievo*; we have followed the "Nouvelle Biographie Générale."

"Vitæ Italorum doctrina excellentium;" and VOLTAIRE, "Correspondance Générale."

Algazi, ăl-gă'zee, (**Solomon Ben Abraham,**) a voluminous Jewish writer, born in the Levant. Died in 1683.

Algazzali, Algazali, or **Alghazzali.** See ABOO-HAMID-ALGHAZALEE.

Alger, ăl'jĕr, [Fr. pron. ăl'zhaiʀ'; Lat. AL'GERUS,] an ecclesiastical writer, who died about the middle of the twelfth century. He was a native of Liège.

Alger, ăl'jĕr, (WILLIAM ROUNSEVILLE,) an American writer, born in Freetown, Massachusetts, in 1823. He is author of "Symbolic History of the Cross of Christ;" "Oriental Poetry;" "History of the Doctrine of a Future Life, as it has Prevailed in all Nations and Ages," (1862,) to which was contributed a very complete bibliography of the subject, by Ezra Abbot, assistant librarian at Harvard University; and various other works. Mr. Alger has furnished numerous contributions to the "Christian Examiner" and other periodicals.

Alghâfikee or **Alghâfikî,** ăl-Gă'fe-kee', an eminent physician, who lived in Mohammedan Spain in the twelfth century. Died about 1164.

Alghisi, ăl-ġee'see, sometimes written Algisi, (FRANCESCO,) an Italian musical composer, born at Brescia in 1666. He composed two operas, one of which, called "Il Trionfo della Continenza," ("The Triumph of Continence,") had a great success. Died in 1733.

Alghisi, (GALASSO,) an Italian architect of the sixteenth century, born at Carpi. He published a splendid work on fortifications, ("Della Fortificazione," 1570.)

Alghisi, (TOMMASO,) a distinguished Italian surgeon, born at Florence in 1669. He particularly excelled in lithotomy, on which he wrote an able treatise, (1707.) Died in 1713.

Algrin, ăl'gRăN', (JEAN,) a French theologian, who became Archbishop of Besançon. Died in 1237.

Alhakem or **Al-Hakem** (ăl-hăk'em) I., Sultan of Córdova, began to reign in 796 A.D. He waged war against Alfonso of Asturias and the Franks, and suppressed with great cruelty a rebellion in Córdova. Died in 822.

Alhakem II., Sultan and Caliph of Córdova, succeeded his father Abd-er-Rahman III. in 961. He was a pacific and enlightened sovereign, and was celebrated as a patron of literature and science. His reign has been called the golden age of Arabian literature. He collected a great library, and expended vast sums in the erection of colleges, mosques, hospitals, etc. He died in 976, aged sixty-three, and was succeeded by his son Hishâm (or Heschâm) II.

Al-Hakem-Ibn-Attâ, ăl-hă'kem ĭb'n ăt'tă', commonly called **Al-Mo-ken'na,** (-Mo-can'na or -Mukanna,** mŏŏ-kăn'na,) or "the veiled one," a famous impostor, who arose in the time of Aboo-Jaafar Al-Mansoor, the second caliph of the Abbasside dynasty. He first made his appearance as a legislator and prophet at Merv or Meru, the capital of Khorassân, in 774 A.D. About 780 the caliph Mahdee (Mahdi) sent an army that besieged the impostor in his principal fortress. When Al-Hakem found that there was no chance of escape, he administered, it is said, a mortal poison to those about his person, and afterwards burned their bodies to ashes, so that no vestige might be left; and, the better to impress posterity with the idea of his divine character, he plunged into a large caldron filled with a liquid so powerful and penetrating that no part of his body remained unconsumed. The truth appears to have been, that he burned himself in the castle in which he was, so that no trace of him remained except ashes. This story forms the basis of Moore's poem entitled "Mokanna, or the Veiled Prophet of Khorassan."

See WEIL, "Geschichte der Chalifen," vol. ii. chap. iii.; D'HERBELOT, "Bibliothèque Orientale;" ABULPHARAGIUS, "Historia Dynastiarum;" ABULFEDA, "Annales Moslemici."

Alhazan or **Alhazen,** written also **Alhacen** and **Alhasan,** ăl-hăz'an, an Arabian philosopher and mathematician, native of Bassŏra, celebrated as the author of a treatise on optics, of great merit. Died at Cairo about 1038.

Al-Homaydee or **Al-Homaydî,** ăl-ho-mī'dee', a distingui:hed Arabian writer, born at Majorca in 1029. Among his works is a valuable biography of the distinguished Moslems of Spain. Died at Bagdâd about 1095.

Alhoy, ä'lwä', (LOUIS,) a French *littérateur*, born at Angers in 1755, succeeded Abbé Sicard as Director of the Institution for Deaf-Mutes in 1797. He wrote "Les Hospices," a poem. Died in 1826.

Ali. See ALEE.

Ali, (PACHA.) See ALEE-WELEE-ZADE.

Aliamet, ä'le-ä'mä' or äl'yä'mä', (FRANÇOIS GERMAIN,) a French engraver, born at Abbeville in 1734, was a brother of Jacques, noticed below, to whom he was inferior in skill. He worked some years in London, and engraved historical works after the Italian masters.

Aliamet, (JACQUES,) a skilful French engraver, born at Abbeville in 1727; died in Paris in 1788. He excelled in landscapes and sea-pieces. His engravings, after Vernet, are much admired.

Alibaud, ä'le'bō', (LOUIS,) a French fanatic, born at Nîmes in 1810. He attempted to assassinate Louis Philippe with a pistol in June, 1836, and was guillotined in July of the same year.

Ali Beg, ä'lee bĕg, a native of Poland, was captured in childhood by Tartars, who sold him to a Turk. He became dragoman to the sultan, and translated the Bible into the Turkish language. Died in 1675.

Alibert, ä'le'baiR', (JEAN LOUIS,) an eminent French physician, born in Aveyron in 1766. He became one of the chief physicians of the Hospital Saint Louis, Paris, in 1801, and professor of medicine in 1802. In 1814 he was appointed consulting physician to Louis XVIII., and a few years later was made first physician-in-ordinary. He gave special attention to diseases of the skin, on which he wrote a work of much merit, called "Description of Diseases of the Skin," ("Description des Maladies de la Peau," 1806-25.) He was author of other medical works, written in an elegant style. Died in 1837.

See QUÉRARD, "La France Littéraire."

Aliberti, ä-le-bĕR'tee, (GIANCARLO,) an Italian frescopainter, born at Asti, in Piedmont, in 1680; died about 1740. His chief works were executed at his native city.

Ali Bey, ä'lee bā, the assumed name of **Domingo Badia y Leblich,** do-ming'go bä-dee'ä e lä-blĕk', a Spanish traveller and projector, born in Biscay in 1766. He travelled in the disguise of a Mussulman, and published "Travels in Asia and Africa, 1803-1807," (3 vols., 1814.) Died in 1818.

See the "Quarterly Review" for July, 1816.

Alibrandi, ä-le-bRän'dee, (FRANCESCO,) an Italian Jesuit and casuist, born at Messina. Died in 1711.

Alibrandi, (GIROLAMO,) a distinguished painter, called "the Raphael of Messina," where he was born in 1470. His manner resembled that of Leonardo da Vinci, with whom he studied. Died of the plague in 1524. His master-piece is a "Purification of the Virgin."

See LANZI, "History of Painting in Italy."

Alidosi, ä-le-do'see, (GIOVANNI NICCOLÒ PASQUALE,) an antiquary of Bologna. Died about 1630.

Alighieri. See DANTE.

Alignan, ä'lĕn'yôN', **Benedict of,** [Fr. BÉNOÎT D'ALIGNAN, beh-nwä' dä'lĕn'yôN',] a French Benedictine monk, who was elected Bishop of Marseilles in 1229. Died in 1268.

Aligre, ä'lĕgR', (ÉTIENNE FRANÇOIS,) born about 1726, became president of the Parliament of Paris in 1768, which office he held for twenty years. Died in exile in 1798.

Ali, Hyder. See HYDER ALEE.

Al-I-men'tus, (LUCIUS CINCIUS,) a Roman historian of merit, became tribune of the people in 214 B.C., and prætor in 210. He received with the province of Sicily the command of two legions which had been defeated at Cannæ and were afterwards condemned to serve in Sicily. Some time after 208 he was taken prisoner by Hannibal, who appears to have treated him with great respect. He wrote, in Greek, a history of Rome from the foundation of the city to his own time, and other works, on law, grammar, etc. His diligence and erudition are commended by Livy. Only fragments of his works are extant.

See NIEBUHR, "History of Rome;" AULUS GELLIUS, xvi.; VOSS, "De Historicis Latinis."

Alinard, äl'e-nard' or ä'le'näR', written also **Halinard,** a learned French prelate, born in Burgundy about 990, became Archbishop of Lyons in 1046. Died in 1052.

A-lip'I-us, a friend of Saint Augustine, was an eminent lawyer. Having been baptized by Saint Ambrose in 387 A.D., he became Bishop of Tagaste. Died about 428.

Aliprandi, ä-le-prän'dee, (BUONAMENTE,) an Italian poet, native of Mantua. He wrote a history of Mantua and other cities of Italy, a work of little merit. Died in 1414.

Alisaunder, one of the modes in which Chaucer writes the name of ALEXANDER the Great.

Al'I-son, (ALEXANDER,) a British writer, born in Scotland about 1812. He published, besides other works, "The Philosophy and History of Civilization," (1860,) and is about to publish, it is said, "The Church and the World Reconciled."

Alison, (Rev. ARCHIBALD,) a Scottish writer, born in Edinburgh in 1757. He took orders in the Anglican Church in 1784, and married the same year a daughter of the well-known Dr. John Gregory of Edinburgh. He became curate of Kenley, Shropshire, in 1790, and vicar of Ercall in 1794. In 1790 he published "Essays on the Nature and Principles of Taste," a popular work, which Lord Jeffrey made the subject of a laudatory article in the "Edinburgh Review" in 1811. He became senior minister of the Episcopal Chapel, Cowgate, Edinburgh, in 1800. Two volumes of his sermons were published.

"We do not know any sermons," says the "Edinburgh Review" for September, 1814, "so pleasing, or so likely both to be popular and to do good to those who are pleased with them. All the feelings are generous and gentle—all the sentiments liberal—and all the general views just and ennobling." Died in 1839.

See CHAMBERS, "Biographical Dictionary of Eminent Scotsmen," Supplement, vol. v.; "Gentleman's Magazine," September, 1839.

Alison, (Sir ARCHIBALD,) a historian, a son of the preceding, was born at Kenley, Shropshire, in December, 1792. He was educated in Edinburgh, studied law, and was called to the Scottish bar in 1814. In 1828 he was chosen sheriff of Lanarkshire. He gained distinction by his "Principles of Criminal Law," (1832.) His most important work is a "History of Europe from the Commencement of the French Revolution to the Restoration of the Bourbons, 1815," (1st vol., 1839,) which has been eminently successful. The ninth edition was published in 1853-55, 12 vols. "It is upon the whole," says the "Edinburgh Review" for October, 1842, "a valuable addition to European literature, evidently compiled with the utmost care: its narration, so far as we can judge, is not perverted by the slightest partiality. . . . Its merits are minuteness and honesty—qualities which may well excuse a faulty style, gross political prejudices, and a fondness for exaggerated and frothy declamation." He published in 1847 "The Life of John, Duke of Marlborough," (3d edition, 1855,) and in 1852-57 a continuation of his "History of Europe" to the year 1852, (6 vols.) The latter work is not so able nor so popular as his first history. He was created a baronet in 1852. His political sympathies were ultraconservative. He was the author of several other works, among which are "Essays, Political, Historical, etc.," (3 vols., 1850,) originally published in "Blackwood's Magazine." Died near Glasgow in May, 1867.

See a review of his History in "Blackwood's Magazine" for July, 1840.

Alison, (WILLIAM PULTENEY,) an eminent physician and physiologist, son of the Rev. Archibald Alison, born in Edinburgh in 1790. He became professor of medical jurisprudence at Edinburgh in 1820, and was appointed professor of the institutes of medicine in 1828. In 1830 he published "First Lines of Physiology." He became professor of the practice of medicine in the University of Edinburgh in 1832, and published "Outlines of Physiology and Pathology" in 1833. He received the title of "First Physician to the Queen for Scotland." Died in Edinburgh in 1859.

Alix, ä'lĕss', or **Alice,** äl'iss, (called by the older writers **Adela, Ada,** and **Ala,**) a daughter of Theobald, (Thibaud le Grand,) Count of Champagne, was married to Louis VII., King of France, in 1160; died in 1206. Her son became King Philippe Auguste.

Alix, ä′lèss′, (MATTHIEU FRANÇOIS,) a French physician, born in Paris in 1738. He was professor of anatomy at Fulda, and wrote a work of merit, entitled "Surgical Observations," ("Observata Chirurgica," 1774–78.) Died at Brückenau in 1782.

Alix, (PIERRE,) a French priest, born at Dôle in 1600, became a canon at Besançon. He defended against the pope, in several tracts, the rights of his chapter in regard to the election of archbishops. Died in 1676.

Alix, (P. M.,) a French engraver, born 1752; died 1809.

Al-Jannabi or **Al-Jannabius.** See JANNÂBEE.

Al-Kâder-Billah, âl-kä′dir bil′lä, (i.e. "mighty by the grace of God,") a caliph of the house of Abbâs, born at Bagdâd about 947, succeeded to the throne in 991; died in 1031 or 1032. He received and protected at his court Firdousee, (Firdausi,) the celebrated Persian poet, who fled from the anger of Mahmood of Gazna.

Al-Kâhir-Billah, âl-kä′hir bil′lä, (i.e. "victorious by the grace of God,") a caliph of the house of Abbâs, who ascended the throne in 929. His tyranny and cruelty rendered him an object of execration, and caused his dethronement after a reign of rather more than a year.

Alkaios. See ALCÆUS.

Al-Kâsim-Ibn-Hammood, (-Hammûd,) âl-kä′-sim ĭb'n hâm′mood′, a sultan of Córdova, dethroned by his nephew Yahya in 1024.

Al-Kâyim, âl-kä′yim or âl-kī′yim, a caliph of the house of Abbâs, succeeded his father Al-Kâder-Billah about 1031. Died in 1073.

Alkemade, van, vän âl-keh-mä′deh,(KORNELIS,) a Dutch antiquary, born in 1654. He was first commissioner of import and export duties at Rotterdam. He published, besides other works, a curious treatise on old Dutch customs in civil life, entitled "Nederlandsche Displechtigheden," (3 vols., 1732.) Died in 1737.

Al-Khazrejee or **Al-Khazrejî,** âl-kăz′reh-jee′, an excellent historian of Mohammedan Spain, supposed to have lived about the end of the twelfth century.

Alkhowarezmi,âl-kŏw-ä-rez′mee,an Arabian mathematician, lived about 810–830 A.D. He was librarian to Al-Mamoon at Bagdâd.

Alkibiades. See ALCIBIADES.

Alkindi, Alkindus, or **Alkendi.** See ALCHINDUS.

Alkman. See ALCMAN.

Alkmar or **Alkmaar, van,** vän âlk-mär′, (HENRY, or HINREK,) a Low-German poet, who lived in the latter half of the fifteenth century, was the author or first translator of a celebrated poem and satire, "Reynard the Fox," which he published in Low German at Lübeck in 1498. In the preface he states that he translated it from the Walsch (supposed to be the Walloon) and the French, and that he was a schoolmaster and teacher of virtue in the service of the Duke of Lorraine. The original is lost, if it ever existed. The poem of Alkmar is one of the most popular in the language, and has been translated into several other languages. Goethe produced a modern German version of it in hexameters, which has been splendidly illustrated by Kaulbach.

See J. GRIMM, "Die Sage von Reinhart Vos," 1834.

Allacci. See ALLATIUS.

Allainval, ä′lăn′vâl′, (LÉONOR JEAN CHRISTINE Soulas—soo′lâs′) a French dramatic poet, born at Chartres about 1700; died in 1753. Although he assumed the title of abbé, he never entered holy orders. Among his best works is "L'École des Bourgeois," (1728,) a comedy which is praised by La Harpe.

Allais, ä′lä′, (DENYS Vairasse—vä′răss′,) a French writer of the seventeenth century, born in Languedoc, was known as the author of a political romance called the "History of the Sevarambians," ("Histoire des Sévarambes," 1677.)

Al'lam, (ANDREW,) a learned English antiquary, born near Oxford in 1655. He entered holy orders in 1680. He assisted Wood in the "Athenæ Oxonienses," and began a "History of English Cathedrals," the completion of which was prevented by his death in 1685.

Allamand, ä′lä′mŏN′, (JEAN NICOLAS SÉBASTIEN,) a philosopher and naturalist, born at Lausanne, in Switzerland, in 1713. In 1749 he became professor of philosophy, and afterwards of natural history, in the University of Leyden, both of which chairs he held with credit till his death in 1787. He was the first to explain the phenomena of the Leyden jar, and rendered an important service to the public by the publication of the Historical Dictionary of his friend Prosper Marchand, (1758–9,) which the latter left in manuscript. The writing was so minute that he was obliged to use a powerful microscope to decipher it.

Allan, âl′lan, (DAVID,) a Scottish historical painter, sometimes called "the Scotch Hogarth," was born at Alloa in 1744. He went to Rome in 1764, and gained there a gold medal for his picture of a Corinthian maiden drawing her lover's profile on the wall by the shadow, which is esteemed his master-piece. He settled in Edinburgh about 1780, and increased his reputation by illustrations of Allan Ramsay's "Gentle Shepherd." He owes the name of the Scotch Hogarth to his humorous designs of the Roman Carnival. Died in 1796.

See CHAMBERS, "Biographical Dictionary of Eminent Scotsmen;" CUNNINGHAM, "Lives of Painters, Sculptors," etc.

Allan, âl′lan, (GEORGE,) an English attorney and antiquary, who resided at Darlington, was a zealous student of national antiquities. He contributed to Hutchinson's "History and Antiquities of Durham," and published, besides other works, a "Life of Bishop Trevor," (1776.) Died in 1800.

See NICHOLS, "Literary Anecdotes," etc.

Allan, (ROBERT,) a Scottish lyric poet, born at Kilbarchan in 1774, was a weaver. He produced a volume of poems in 1836. Having emigrated to the United States, he died at New York in 1841.

Allan, (THOMAS.) See ALLEN.

Allan, (THOMAS,) F.R.S., a Scottish mineralogist, born in Edinburgh in 1777. He formed a collection of about seven thousand specimens of minerals, said to be the finest collection in Scotland. His knowledge of mineralogy was extensive and accurate. He wrote the article Diamond for the "Encyclopædia Britannica," and a work on Mineralogical Nomenclature. Died in 1833.

Allan, (Sir WILLIAM,) an eminent British historical painter, born in Edinburgh in 1782. He studied in the Royal Academy of London, worked some years in Saint Petersburg, visited Circassia and Turkey, and returned to Scotland in 1814. His large picture of the "Circassian Captives" was purchased for 1000 guineas by Sir Walter Scott and ninety-nine other subscribers. He afterwards painted subjects of Scottish history, among which are the "Parting of Charles Stuart and Flora Macdonald," and "The Murder of Regent Murray." He was elected academician of the Royal Academy, London, in 1835, and succeeded Wilkie in 1840 as her Majesty's limner for Scotland. From 1838 until his death he was president of the Scottish Royal Academy. Among his chief works are two pictures of the "Battle of Waterloo." Died in 1850.

See CHAMBERS, "Biographical Dictionary of Eminent Scotsmen," vol. v.; "Encyclopædia Britannica."

Allard, ä′lȧR′, (GUI,) a French writer, noted for his works on the history and genealogy of Dauphiné. Born at Grenoble about 1645; died in 1715.

Allard, (JEAN FRANÇOIS,) a French general, born in Var in 1785. He left France after the restoration of 1815, and went to Hindostan. He entered the service of Runjeet Singh at Lahore, organized his army after the French system, and became general-in-chief. Died in India in 1839.

Allarde, d′, dä′lȧRd′, (PIERRE GILBERT Leroi—leh-RwÄ′,) BARON, a French political economist, born at Montluçon in 1749; died in 1809.

Allart, ä′lȧR′, (MARY GAY,) a novelist, born at Lyons, in France, in 1750. She lived a long time in Paris, and wrote a successful novel called "Albertine de Saint-Albe," (1818.) She also made an elegant French translation of the "Family Secrets" of Miss Pratt. Died in Paris in 1821.

Allatius, âl-lā′she-us, (LEO,) [It. LEONE ALLACCI, lä-o′nä âl-lät′chee,] an eminent scholar and physician, born at Chios (Scio) in 1586, embraced the Catholic religion, taught Greek in a college of Rome, and was appointed librarian of the Vatican by Pope Alexander VII. He edited and translated into Latin several old Greek works, and wrote some original productions. Died in 1663.

Alle, âl'lȧ, (GIROLAMO,) an Italian writer and ecclesiastic, born at Bologna probably about 1580. He was an admired orator, and author of many works in prose and verse on religious and moral subjects, (1613–54.)

Al-lec'tus, an officer of Carausius, King of Britain. Having murdered Carausius, in 293, he usurped the throne. He was defeated and killed by the Roman army of Constantius Chlorus about 296 A.D.

Allegrain, âl'gRȧN', (CHRISTOPHE GABRIEL,) a distinguished French sculptor, born in Paris about 1710. He excelled in nude figures. Died in 1795.

Allegrain, (ÉTIENNE,) the father of the preceding, was a skilful landscape-painter, who died in 1736, aged eighty.

Allegretti, âl-là-gRet'tee, (ANTONIO,) a Florentine poet, who lived (mostly at Rome) about the middle of the sixteenth century.

Allegretti, (CARLO,) an Italian painter, born at Monte Prandone, lived between 1600 and 1650.

Allegretti, (JACOPO,) an Italian physician and astrologer, born at Forlì in the early part of the fourteenth century, had an extensive reputation as a Latin poet.

Allegri. See CORREGGIO.

Allegri, âl-lā'gRee, (ALESSANDRO,) a satirical poet of the sixteenth century. He was a native of Florence, and excelled in burlesque poetry. The purity of his language was recognized by the Academy Della Crusca. Died about 1596.

Allegri, (GREGORIO,) an eminent musician and composer, born at Rome about 1580, was a singer in the pontifical chapel. He is said to have been a relative of the painter Correggio. His most remarkable work is the "Miserere," which is still performed annually in the pope's chapel during the holy week. Died in 1652.

See BURNEY's "Musical Tour in Italy."

Allegrini, âl-là-gRee'nee, (FRANCESCO,) a distinguished Italian painter, born at Gubbio in 1587. He worked at Rome and Genoa in oil and fresco. Died in 1663.

Allegrini, (FRANCESCO,) a designer and engraver, born at Florence in 1729. Died about 1785.

Allein or **Alleine,** âl'len, (JOSEPH,) an English nonconformist divine, born at Devizes in 1633, was educated at Oxford. He became curate to Mr. Newton at Taunton in 1655, and was ejected for nonconformity in 1662. Continuing to preach frequently, he was committed to Ilchester jail in 1663, fined one hundred marks, and imprisoned one year. He again suffered similar persecution in 1665, in consequence of which he died prematurely in 1668, leaving several religious works, one of which, "An Alarm to the Unconverted," (1672,) is highly esteemed and has been often reprinted.

See A. DUFF's "Life and Death of the Rev. J. Alleine;" AUGUST RISCHE, "Leben J. Alleins weiland Predigers zu Taunton," Bielefeld, (?) 1850; "Life and Death of J. Alleine," London, 1672.

Allein or **Alleine,** (RICHARD,) an English nonconformist minister, born about 1610, was rector of Batcombe, in Somersetshire. He published, besides other works, a "Vindication of Godliness," ("Vindiciæ Pietatis," 1663,) which was highly esteemed. Died in 1681.

Allemand. See LALLEMAND.

Allemand, âl'môN', (GEORGES,) a French historical painter, born at Nancy, lived in Paris about 1650.

Allemand, (JEAN BAPTISTE,) a French painter, was a pupil of J. Vernet. He lived at Rome, and painted some fine landscapes in the Corsini palace in 1750.

Allemand, âl'môN', (ZACHARIE JACQUES THÉODORE,) a French admiral, born at Port Louis, in Lorient, in 1762. He commenced his career as a cabin-boy. In 1792 he was made captain, and captured many British merchant-vessels between 1793 and 1800. He rose gradually by his activity and skill to the station of vice-admiral in 1809. He commanded the fleet which Cochrane attempted to destroy with fire-ships at the Isle of Aix in 1809. Died in 1826.

Allemanni, âl-là-mân'nee, (PIETRO,) of Ascoli, an Italian painter, who flourished between 1470 and 1490.

Allemant. See LALLEMANT and LALAMANT.

Allen, âl'len, (ALEXANDER,) an English philologist, a son of John Allen (1771–1839) noticed below, born at Hackney, near London, in 1814. He was a good classical scholar, and an excellent teacher. He wrote articles for the "Penny Cyclopædia" and for Smith's "Dictionary of Greek and Roman Biography," and published several works for the use of students of the Greek and Latin languages. Died in 1842.

Allen, (DAVID OLIVER,) an American missionary, born at Barre, Massachusetts, in 1800. He laboured many years in India, whither he went about 1827, and published "India, Ancient and Modern," (2d edition, 1858.) Died in 1863.

Allen or **Alen,** (EDMOND,) an English theologian, born in Norfolk. He wrote a number of works. Died in 1559.

Allen, (EPHRAIM W.,) born about 1780, was for more than thirty years editor of the "Newburyport Herald." In his office William Lloyd Garrison learned the art of printing. (See GARRISON.) Died in 1846.

Allen, (ETHAN,) an officer of the Revolutionary war, born at Litchfield, in Connecticut, about 1742. He settled, when young, in Vermont, and became the leader of the famous "Green Mountain Boys." On the 10th of May, 1775, at the head of only eighty-three men, he took the forts Ticonderoga and Crown Point. In September of the same year, while on an expedition to take Montreal, he fell in with a much larger force of British troops, and was made prisoner. He remained in captivity above two years and a half, when he was exchanged for Colonel Campbell, an English officer. After his release he was appointed general of the state militia. He died suddenly, February 13, 1789. Besides a narrative of his captivity, and some writings of a political character, he wrote a work entitled "Reason the only Oracle of Man," in which he advocated pure Deism.

See "Ethan Allen and the Green Mountain Heroes of '76," by H. W. DE PUY; Life of Ethan Allen, in SPARKS's "American Biography;" HUGH MOORE, "Memoir of Colonel E. Allen," Plattsburg, 1834.

Allen, (HENRY,) a religious enthusiast, born at Newport, Rhode Island, in 1748. He was the founder of a sect in Nova Scotia who taught that Adam and Eve, in their state of innocence, had a spiritual existence without bodies, and that all human beings are emanations from the same great Spirit, and were present with our first parents in the Garden of Eden before the fall, and participated in the original transgression. He published a collection of hymns, and several religious treatises and sermons. Died in 1784.

Allen, (JOHN,) an Irish prelate, born at Dublin in 1476, became Archbishop of Dublin in 1528. He was killed in 1534 by Thomas Fitzgerald, a son of the Earl of Kildare, during a rebellion.

Allen, (JOHN,) a Puritan divine, born in England in 1596, emigrated to America, and settled as first minister in Dedham, Massachusetts. Died in 1671.

Allen, (JOHN,) M.D., an English physician, who lived in the early part of the eighteenth century and wrote a valuable work in Latin entitled a "Synopsis of Universal Practical Medicine," ("Synopsis Universæ Medicinæ Practicæ,") which aims to give in a succinct form the opinions of the most eminent physicians in all ages respecting the cause and cure of diseases. He was elected a Fellow of the Royal Society in 1730. Died in 1741.

See NICHOLS, "Literary Anecdotes."

Allen, (JOHN,) a dissenting layman, born at Truro, England, in 1771. He was the master of an academy at Hackney. Besides other writings of a religious character, he was the author of a valuable and learned work entitled "Modern Judaism, or a Brief Account of the Opinions, Rites, and Ceremonics of the Jews," (1816,) said to be the best work on the subject in the language. Died in 1839.

Allen, (JOHN,) M.D., a British writer on constitutional history, metaphysics, etc., was born at Redford, near Edinburgh, in 1770. He studied medicine and metaphysics at Edinburgh, and "was eminent in that famous school of metaphysics," says Brougham, "for his extensive learning and unrivalled power of subtle reasoning." In 1795 he published "Illustrations of Hume's Essay concerning Liberty and Necessity." He contributed many political and historical articles to the "Edinburgh Review," and published, besides other works, a learned and luminous "Inquiry into the Rise and Growth of the Royal Prerogative in England," (1830.) His intimacy with Lord Holland was such, says Lord Brougham, that "in the latter part of his life [Mr. Allen] shared all his thoughts, and was never a day apart from him." He was master of Dulwich College for many years. Died in 1843.

See Brougham, "Statesmen of the Times of George III.," Second Series : Sydney Smith, "Memoirs."

Allen, (Joseph W.,) an English landscape-painter, born at Lambeth, Surrey, in 1803. He was reduced in his youth to the necessity of painting scenes for the theatre, and became principal scene-painter at the Olympic Theatre, the success of which was greatly promoted by his skill. He acquired considerable reputation as a painter of pastoral, landscape, and simple, quiet, rural scenery. The style of his later works was vitiated by "brilliant effects" obtained at the expense of fidelity to nature. Died in 1852.

Allen, (Moses,) an American patriot, a brother of the Rev. Thomas Allen, was born at Northampton in 1748. He served as chaplain in the army, was taken prisoner at Savannah, and was drowned in 1779 in an attempt to escape from a prison-ship.

Allen, (Paul,) an American poet and journalist, born at Providence, Rhode Island, in 1775. He was for several years editor of the "Morning Chronicle," published at Baltimore, where he died in 1826. His principal works are a volume of "Original Poems, Serious and Entertaining," and a large poem in five cantos, entitled "Noah."

Allen, (Richard,) an English Baptist minister of London, published "Ecclesiastical Biography," ("Biographia Ecclesiastica," 2 vols., 1690.) Died in London in 1717.

Allen, (Samuel,) a London merchant, who came to New England about 1690, and was subsequently Governor of New Hampshire. Died in 1705.

Allen, (Solomon,) an American divine and patriot, brother of the Rev. Thomas Allen, was born in Northampton, Massachusetts, in 1751. He rose to the rank of major in the war of the Revolution. While in the army, he was ordered by Lieutenant-Colonel Jameson to carry from André to Arnold the letter which informed the latter of André's capture and enabled Arnold to make his escape. Died in 1821.

Allen, (Stephen,) a distinguished citizen of New York, born in that city in July, 1767. He was elected mayor of New York in 1821. While commissioner for visiting prisons, he proposed the erection of a State prison at Sing Sing. He was one of the principal originators of the project for supplying New York with water from Croton River, and was chairman of the Board. He perished in the steamer Henry Clay, which was burned in July, 1852.

See Hunt's "Lives of American Merchants," vol. ii.

Allen, (Stephen M.,) an American merchant and banker, born at Burton, New Hampshire, in 1819. He distinguished himself by his liberal donations to various literary institutions.

See Livingston's "Portraits of Eminent Americans," New York, 1854.

Allen, Alleyn, or **Allan,** pronounced alike âl′len, (Thomas,) an English mathematician of high reputation, born at Uttoxeter in 1542. He refused a bishopric from the Earl of Leicester, with whom he was intimate, and lived much in the family of the Earl of Northumberland. He was a great collector of manuscripts, historical and antiquarian. Among his few publications is a copy (made with his own hand) of Ptolemy's work on Astrology, ("De Astrorum Judiciis,") to which he added some explanatory notes. Died in 1632.

See Wood, "Athenæ Oxonienses."

Allen, (Thomas,) an English divine, born in 1572 or 1573, was a Fellow of Merton College. Died in 1636.

Allen, (Sir Thomas,) an English naval commander, born in Suffolk. He was appointed in 1664 commodore and commander-in-chief of the fleet sent to punish the

Algerine pirates, and in the same year he gained a victory over the Dutch near Gibraltar. He became a rear-admiral in 1665, and was vice-admiral of the fleet which under the Duke of Albemarle defeated the Dutch near the southeast coast of England in 1666. Died about 1680.

See Charnock, "Biographia Navalis."

Allen or **Allein,** (Thomas,) an English clergyman, born at Oxford in 1682, became rector of Kettering in 1715. Among his works is "The Practice of a Holy Life," (1716.) Died in 1755.

Allen, (Rev. Thomas,) an American divine, born at Northampton, Massachusetts, in 1743, was the first minister of Pittsfield. He graduated at Harvard in 1762, and was ordained at Pittsfield in 1764. In the Revolutionary war he warmly supported the popular cause, and served as chaplain at White Plains, Ticonderoga, etc. Four of his brothers were soldiers in the army. He was the author of several published sermons, letters, etc. Died in 1810. He was the father of William Allen, president of Bowdoin College.

Allen, (Thomas,) an English topographical writer and engraver, born about 1803. He published, among other works illustrated by his own hand, "The History and Antiquities of London, Westminster, and Parts adjacent," (4 vols., 1827–8.) Died in 1833.

See "Gentleman's Magazine," July, 1833.

Allen, Alan, or **Alleyn,** (William,) Cardinal, born in Lancashire in 1532, took the degree of D.D. in the University of Douay in 1571, and was made cardinal by Pope Sixtus V. in 1587, in order that he might superintend the Catholic interests in England after Philip II. of Spain should have conquered that country. He left a number of works in defence of the Catholic Church. Died in Rome in 1594.

See Fitzherbert, "Epitome Vitæ Cardinalis Alani," 1608 ; a "Life of Allen" in the folio Brussels edition of Dodd's "Church History ;" Wood, "Athenæ Oxonienses."

Allen, (William,) a chief justice of Pennsylvania, who assisted Dr. Franklin in establishing the College of Philadelphia ; but in the Revolution he took sides with the royalists. Died in 1780. His son, Andrew Allen, also became chief justice of Pennsylvania, and, like his father, sided in the Revolution with the British.

Allen, (William,) an English chemist and philanthropist, born in London in August, 1770, was a member of the Society of Friends. He became a pupil and assistant of Joseph Gurney Bevan, chemist, of . Plough Court, and acquired distinction as a pharmaceutical chemist. In 1802 he was appointed a lecturer on chemistry at Guy's Hospital, and in 1804 gave a course of lectures on natural philosophy at the Royal Institution, at the request of his friend, H. Davy. He was elected a Fellow of the Royal Society in 1807, and was associated with W. H. Pepys in researches on respiration and carbonic acid. (See Pepys.) William Allen was an active promoter of various benevolent and reformatory enterprises, and devoted much time to the cause of the education of the poor. He began to preach in the meetings of his Society in 1818, and accompanied Stephen Grellet, a noted minister of the Society of Friends, in a religious visit to the continent, from which they returned in 1820, after they had traversed Russia from north to south and visited various cities in Turkey and Italy.

In 1822 he went to Vienna to see Alexander, Emperor of Russia, with whom he had a long and satisfactory interview in relation to schools, the slave-trade, and the Greeks. In 1825 he founded two manual-labour schools, one for boys and one for girls, at Lindfield, Sussex. He visited Germany, France, and Spain on religious and philanthropic missions in 1832 and 1833. He contributed several papers on chemistry to the Philosophical Transactions. Died at Lindfield in 1843.

See "Life of William Allen, with Selections from his Correspondence," 2 vols., 1847.

Allen, (William,) D.D., an American biographer, born at Pittsfield, Massachusetts, in 1784. He graduated at Harvard College in 1802, and was president of Bowdoin College from 1820 to 1839. He succeeded Dr. Channing as regent in Harvard College. In 1809 he published "The American Biographical Dictionary," (3d

€ as *k*; ç as *s*; ḡ *hard*; ġ as *j*; g, h, k, *guttural*; n, *nasal*; r, *trilled*; s as *z* ; th as in *this*. (☞ See Explanations, p. 23.)

edition, enlarged, 1857.) Among his works are "Wunnissoo," a poem, (1856;) and "Psalms and Hymns, with many Original Hymns," (1835.) Died in July, 1868.

Allen, (WILLIAM HENRY,) an American naval officer, born at Providence, Rhode Island, in 1784. He distinguished himself as lieutenant under Captain Decatur in the battle which resulted in the capture of the Macedonian, October 25, 1812. Having been raised to the rank of captain, he sailed in the Argus, and took many prizes. In August, 1813, he was killed in a fight between the Argus and the Pelican, and his vessel was captured.

Allen, (WILLIAM HOWARD,) an American naval officer, born at Hudson, New York, in 1792. He took command of the Argus when Captain William Henry Allen was disabled by a mortal wound in August, 1813. He was killed in a fight with pirates near Matanzas in November, 1822.

Allende, âl-yěn′dȧ, (J.,) a Mexican officer, who in 1810 joined Hidalgo in the revolt against Spain and rendered efficient service to the cause. He was captured and shot in July, 1811.

Allent, ȧ′lôn′, (PIERRE ALEXANDRE JOSEPH,) a French general, born at Saint Omer in 1772. After the restoration he became chief of the staff of the national guard, and counsellor of state. He wrote a "History of the Imperial Corps of Engineers, and of the Sieges it has directed," (1805,) and a few other works. Died in 1837.

Alléon-du-Lac, ȧ′lȧ′ôn′ dü lȧk, (JEAN LOUIS,) a French naturalist, born at Saint Étienne in 1723, was postmaster at that place. He published "Memoirs on the Natural History of Lyonnois, Forez, and Beaujolois," (2 vols., 1765,) and "Mélanges of Natural History," (2 vols., 1762,) both works of merit. He died, it is supposed, about 1770.

Allerstein, Allerstain, âl′lẹr-stīn′, or **Hallerstein,** a German Jesuit, born about 1700, went as a missionary to China. He stated the population of China in 1760 at 196,837,977. Died at Pekin about 1777.

Allestree or **Allestry,** auls′tre, (RICHARD,) an eminent English divine, born in Shropshire in 1619. He served in the royalist army in the civil war, and at the restoration became one of the chaplains of Charles II. In 1663 he was appointed regius professor of divinity at Oxford. His lectures, which were continued about twenty years, are commended by Bishop Fell. A volume of his sermons was published in 1669 and 1684. Died in 1681.

See WOOD, "Athenæ Oxonienses."

Allestry, auls′tre, (JACOB,) an English poet, born about 1653; died in 1686.

Alletz, ȧ′lȧs′,(PIERRE ÉDOUARD,) a French *littérateur,* born in Paris in 1798. He wrote "Walpole," a dramatic poem, (1825,) an "Essay on Man, or the Accordance of Philosophy with Religion," (2 vols., 1835,) and "Sketches of Moral Suffering," ("Esquisses de la Souffrance morale," 2 vols., 1836,) which is his principal work. He was consul at Barcelona when he died in 1850.

Alletz, (PONS-AUGUSTIN—pôn′zō′güs′tȧn′,) a French *littérateur,* born at Montpellier in 1703. He worked for the booksellers of Paris, and compiled a number of successful works, some of which were popular school-books. Among his works are a "History of the Popes," (1776;) "L'Agronome," a treatise on farming, (1760;) an "Epitome of Grecian History," (1764;) and a Synopsis of the Evidences of Christianity, called "Catechism for Adults," ("Catéchisme de l'âge mûr.") Died at Paris in 1785.

See QUÉRARD, "La France Littéraire."

Alley, âl′le, (Rev. JEROME,) a theologian, born probably in Ireland in 1760, was educated at Trinity College, Dublin. He became rector of Beaulieu and Drumcarr. Among his works is "Vindiciæ Christianæ, or a Comparative Estimate of the Genius and Temper of the Greek, the Roman, the Hindu, the Mahometan, and the Christian Religions," (1826.)

Alley or **Alleigh,** âl′le, (WILLIAM,) an English bishop, born at Great Wycombe about 1512. He became a zealous Protestant minister, and in the reign of Mary resigned his cure. On the accession of Elizabeth he was appointed reader of the divinity lecture in Saint Paul's, London. He was consecrated Bishop of Exeter in 1560.

He translated the Pentateuch for the Bishops' Bible, and left several religious works. Died in 1571.

Alleyn or **Allen,** âl′len, (EDWARD,) a celebrated English actor, born in London in 1566, was a friend or companion of Shakspeare. He was one of the two owners and managers of the Fortune Theatre, London, and amassed a large fortune, which he spent in acts of munificence. He founded, for the benefit of the poor, Dulwich College, finished about 1618, and by his last will endowed twenty almshouses. The college was founded for the support of one master, (whose family name must always be the same as that of the founder,) one warden, four fellows, six poor men, six poor women, and for the education and support of twelve boys. Died in 1626.

See J. P. COLLIER, "Memoirs of Edward Alleyn," etc.

Al′lī-bond, (JOHN,) an English divine, born in Buckinghamshire, was rector of Bradwell. He wrote a satirical poem, "Rustic Description of the Oxford Academy lately reformed," ("Rustica Academiæ Oxoniensis nuper reformatæ Descriptio," 1648,) and is called by Anthony Wood an excellent Latin poet. Died in 1658.

Al′lī-bone, (SAMUEL AUSTIN,) an American writer, born in Philadelphia in 1816. He is the author of an excellent work entitled "A Critical Dictionary of English Literature and British and American Authors," of which the first volume (royal 8vo, pp. 1005) was issued in 1858; the second is said to be now (1868) in press. The plan, which is as happy as it is novel, is to give a succinct biography of each author, accompanied by copious extracts from the opinions of the most celebrated critics, or some periodical of acknowledged reputation, by means of which the reader is at once enabled to determine the literary standing of the author concerning whom he may desire information ; and this plan has been so fully and thoroughly carried out as to leave little or nothing to be desired.

Allier, ȧ′le-ȧ′, (ACHILLE,) a French artist and antiquary, born in the Bourbonnais in 1807 or 1808. He described some antiquities of his native province in "Esquisses Bourbonnaises," (1832,) and began, in 1833, to issue, in numbers, "L'Ancien Bourbonnais," a splendid work on the history and antiquities of the Bourbonnais, with plates designed by himself. He died in 1836, leaving it unfinished.

Allier, (ANTOINE,) a French sculptor, born at Embrun in 1793. Among his works are statues of Philopœmen and Eloquence, and busts of Sully and Arago.

Allier, (LOUIS,) called also **Hauteroche,** hōt′rosh′, a French antiquary and numismatist, born at Lyons in 1766. He visited the Troad and Asia Minor, collected many Greek medals, and wrote several antiquarian treatises ; died in 1827.

Allies, âl′lèz, (JABEZ,) an English antiquary, born in Worcestershire in 1787; died in 1856.

Al′ling-ham, (JOHN TILL,) a popular English dramatic writer, flourished about the end of the eighteenth century. He was a native of London, and belonged to the legal profession. He wrote comedies and farces, among which are "The Weathercock," and "Fortune's Frolic," (1799.)

Allingham, (WILLIAM,) a poet, born at Ballyshannon, Ireland, about 1828. He published a volume of poems in 1850, and "Day and Night Songs" in 1854. His poem entitled "Laurence Bloomfield in Ireland" (in 12 chapters, 1864) was very favourably received. He has received an appointment in the Customs in England, and a literary pension was granted him in 1864.

Allio, âl′le-o, (MATTEO,) an Italian sculptor, worked at Milan about 1750. His brother Tommaso was also a sculptor at Milan.

Allioli, âl-le-o′lee, (JOSEPH FRANZ,) a German theologian, born at Sulzbach in 1793. He became professor of theology at Munich in 1826, and provost of the cathedral of Augsburg about 1838. He made a translation of the Bible from the Vulgate into German, (1830, 6th edition, 1839-45,) which was approved by the pope, and wrote several religious works.

Allioni, âl-le-o′nee, (CARLO,) an Italian physician and eminent botanist, born at Turin in 1725. He was professor of botany in the University of Turin, and Fellow of the Royal Societies of London, Madrid, and Göttingen. Like his friend Haller, he was opposed to the artificial system of Linnæus. His principal work is a "Flora of Piedmont," ("Flora Pedemontana, etc.," 3 vols., 1785,) by which he acquired a durable reputation. He wrote an able medical work, entitled "Synopsis of the Present Condition of Diseases," ("Conspectus Præsentaneæ Morborum Conditionis," 1793.) Died in 1804.

See M. F. BUNIVA, "Réflexions sur toutes les ouvrages publiés et inédits du Dr. C. Allioni, avec des notices historiques concernant sa Vie," Turin; ERSCH und GRUBER, "Allgemeine Encyklopaedie;" "Nouvelle Biographie Générale."

Alliot, ăl̄e′o′, (PIERRE,) a French physician of the seventeenth century, born at Bar-le-Duc, had the reputation of great skill in the treatment of cancerous and other malignant ulcers.

Allison. See ALISON.

Al′lĭ-son, (FRANCIS,) a Presbyterian minister, born in Ireland in 1705. He became a professor and vice-provost of the Philadelphia College about 1755. Died in 1777.

Allix, ă′lĕks′, (JACQUES ALEXANDRE FRANÇOIS,) a French general, born at Percy (Manche) in 1776, served as colonel at Marengo, 1800. Died in 1836.

Allix, (PIERRE,) a French Protestant theologian, born at Alençon in 1641, was eminent as a scholar and preacher. He was deeply versed in Hebrew and classical literature. The sermons he preached at Charenton in opposition to Bossuet were much admired. On the revocation of the edict of Nantes in 1685 he took refuge in England, learned the English language, and was appointed treasurer of the cathedral church of Salisbury, (1690.) He was greatly distinguished as a controversial writer. His principal work, "Reflexions on the Books of the Holy Scripture," (1688,) is highly esteemed, and has been often reprinted. Died in 1717.

See WOOD, "Fasti Oxonienses."

Allix. See ALIX.

Alloisi. See GALANINO.

Allori, âl-lo′ree, [It. pron. âl-lò′ree,] (ALESSANDRO,) an eminent Italian painter, born at Florence in 1535, was a pupil of Angelo Bronzino, his uncle, and an imitator of Michael Angelo. He was skilful in drawing, and in the science of anatomy, of which he made an excessive display in his works. He adorned the churches and palaces of Florence with paintings in fresco and oil. His master-pieces are "The Last Judgment," "Christ Disputing with the Doctors," and "The Sacrifice of Abraham." Died in 1607.

See LANZI, "History of Painting in Italy."

Allori, (ANGELO.) See BRONZINO, (ANGELO.)

Allori, (CRISTOFANO,) a celebrated painter, a son of Alessandro, noticed above, was born at Florence in 1577. He studied with Gregorio Pagani, and adopted a style very different from that of his father. He excelled in richness and delicacy of colouring, and was a superior portrait-painter. His works are scarce, and exquisitely finished. Among his master-pieces are a Magdalen, and the "Miracle of San Giuliano," in the Pitti gallery. Died about 1620.

See LANZI, "History of Painting in Italy."

Al′lot, (ROBERT,) is believed to have been the compiler of a valuable collection of early poetry, entitled "England's Parnassus," (London, 1600,) in the compilation of which he showed good taste and judgment.

Allou, ă′loo′, (CHARLES NICOLAS,) a French archæologist, born in Paris in 1787. He wrote an "Essay on the Universality of the French Language," (1828.)

Allouette, de l', deh lă′loo′ĕt′, [Lat. ALAUDA′NUS,] (FRANÇOIS,) a French antiquary, born at Vertus about 1530, was president of the court of Sedan, and master of requests. He wrote many works on genealogy, civil law, the history of the Gauls, etc. Died about 1608.

Allston, aul′stŏn, (JOSEPH,) an American, born in 1778, was Governor of South Carolina in 1812. His wife was Theodosia, the only daughter of Aaron Burr. Died in 1816.

Allston, (ROBERT FRANCIS WITHERS,) an American planter, born in South Carolina in 1801. He was elected Governor of his native State in 1856. He distinguished

himself as an agriculturist, and made improvements in the cultivation of rice.

Allston, (WASHINGTON,) one of the most eminent of American artists, born at Waccamaw, in South Carolina, November 5, 1779. Owing to his delicate health in early childhood, he was sent to Newport, Rhode Island, where he remained at school ten years. He entered Harvard College in 1796, and took the degree of A.B. in 1800. He returned soon after to Charleston, and in 1801 embarked for England, accompanied by Malbone, the painter, whom he had previously known at Newport, and with whom he formed a warm and lasting friendship. The following year he exhibited in London several pictures, one of which, a "French Soldier telling a Story," attracted very favourable notice. He visited Paris in 1804, and subsequently repaired to Italy, where he remained four years. While at Rome he formed an intimacy with Coleridge, of whose extraordinary genius he speaks in enthusiastic terms. In 1809 he returned to America, and soon after married a sister of William E. Channing, the eminent Unitarian divine. He again sailed for England in 1811, and established himself in London, where he had resided but a short time when he met with a severe affliction in the death of his wife. In 1818 he was elected associate of the Royal Academy. The same year, in consequence of failing health, he returned to his home in America. He had previously finished his great historical painting of "The Dead Man revived by Elisha's Bones," for which he obtained the first prize at the British Institution. Among Mr. Allston's most celebrated pictures are "Jacob's Dream;" "Elijah in the Desert;" "The Angel Uriel in the Sun;" and "Spalatro's Vision of the Bloody Hand." He was engaged on a large painting of "Belshazzar's Feast," when he died, July 9, 1843. In addition to his genius as a painter, Allston possessed poetic talent of a high order. He was the author of "The Sylphs of the Seasons, and other Poems," published in 1813.

During his residence at Rome, Allston became acquainted with Washington Irving, who thus describes him: "There was something to me inexpressibly engaging in the appearance and manners of Allston. I do not think I have ever been more completely captivated on a first acquaintance. He was of a light, graceful form, with large blue eyes, and black silken hair waving and curling round a pale, expressive countenance. Everything about him bespoke the man of intellect and refinement. His conversation was copious, animated, and highly graphic, warmed by a genial sensibility and benevolence, and enlivened at times by a chaste and gentle humour. . . . His memory I hold in reverence and affection, as one of the purest, noblest, and most intellectual beings that ever honoured me with his friendship."

See DUNLAP, "Rise and Progress of the Arts of Design in America," vol. i.; TUCKERMAN, "Book of the Artists;" also, article by DR. O. W. HOLMES, in "North American Review," vol. l. p. 358.

Allut, ă′lü′, (ANTOINE,) born at Montpellier, in France, in 1743, was educated at Paris, and became, while very young, a contributor to the "Encyclopédie." He was executed by the Jacobins in 1794.

Ally, (Ăli.) See ALEE.

Almada, de, dâ âl-mä′Dâ, (AL′VARO VAS,) a famous Portuguese warrior, was created Count of Avranches by Charles VI. of France. He was a loyal adherent of Dom Pedro, regent of Portugal, and was killed in battle in 1449.

Almagro, de, dâ âl-mä′gro, (DIEGO,) a bold and enterprising Spanish officer, who was the principal associate of Pizarro in the conquest of Peru. He was a foundling, born about 1464, and went to America to seek his fortune. About 1525, Pizarro, Almagro, and Luque agreed to co-operate in an effort to conquer Peru. This object they effected with a very small force about 1533. (See PIZARRO, FRANCISCO.) In 1534 Almagro was appointed adelantado (governor) of the region which lies southward from Peru. He extended the conquests of the Spanish power into Chili in 1535, after which he captured Cuzco from the army of Pizarro, who had become his perfidious enemy. In a decisive battle, fought near

e as *k*; ç as *s*; ḡ *hard*; ǧ as *j*; G, H, K, *guttural*; N, *nasal*; R, *trilled*; s as *z*; ᵗh as in *this*. (☞See Explanations, p. 23.)

Cuzco in 1538, Almagro was defeated and taken prisoner by Pizarro, who caused him to be put to death.

See ROBERTSON, "History of America;" PRESCOTT, "Conquest of Peru," vol. i.; HERRERA, "Historia."

Almagro, de, (DIEGO,) a son of the preceding, born about 1520, assisted to revenge his father's death by the assassination of Pizarro. After the defeat of his associates by De Castro, he was betrayed and put to death in 1542.

Al-Mahdee or **Al-Mahdî,** (founder of the sect of Almohades.) See ABOO-ABDILLAH-MOHAMMED.

Almahdee or **Almahdî,** âl-mâh′dee′, or, more fully, **Almahdî Billah,** (*i.e.* "the director by the grace of God,") the third caliph of the house of Abbâs, succeeded to the throne in 776 A.D. Died in 785.

Almain, âl′mân′, (JACQUES,) a French theological writer, who was a native of Sens. Died in 1515.

Al-Makhzoomee or **Al-Makhzûmî,** âl-mâk-zoo′-mee, a distinguished historian and poet of Mohammedan Spain, born in 1190. He passed the latter part of his life at the court of the Sultan of Tunis. Died in 1256.

Al-Makkari. See MAKKAREE.

Al-Makin. See ELMACIN.

Al-Makreezee or **-Makrizi.** See MAKREEZEE.

Al-Malek or **Al-Mélik.** See MALIK.

Al-Mamoon. See MAMOON.

Al-Mansoor, Al-Mansûr, Al-Mansour, or **Al-Mançour,** âl-mân′sōōr′, written also **Almanzor** and **Almansor,** ("the Victorious,") the surname by which **Aboo-Amir** (â′bōō â′mir) **-Mohammed,** the minister of Hishâm II., Sultan of Córdova, is generally known. Born near Algeziras in 939 A.D., he began his career as a bookseller and scribe; but he soon found means to recommend himself to the notice of the sultan, and at length, by his talents and address, succeeded in possessing himself of all the real power in the state, Hishâm retaining only the name of sovereign. He exercised the power thus obtained with an ability and success which have scarcely a parallel in the history of Mohammedan Spain. He not only overran the greater part of the Peninsula, but also extended his sway over a considerable portion of Western Africa. His internal administration is said to have been no less distinguished for wisdom and justice, than was his military career for brilliant success. Died in 1002.

See AL-MAKKARI, "History of the Mohammedan Dynasties in Spain," translated by GAYANGOS, 2 vols. 4to, London, 1840–43; CONDE, "Historia de la Dominacion de los Arabes en España;" MARIANA, "Historia general de España."

Al-Mansoor, (ABOO-JAAFAR,) Caliph of Bagdâd. See MANSOOR.

Almanzor. See AL-MANSOOR.

Almeida, âl-ma′e-dâ, (MANOEL,) a Portuguese Jesuit, born at Viseu in 1580. He passed ten years in Abyssinia, (1622–32,) and collected materials for a "History of Ethiopia," which was published by B. Tellez in 1660; it is said to be a work of decided merit. Died at Goa in 1646.

Almeida, de, dâ âl-ma′e-dâ. (ANTONIO,) a Portuguese surgeon, born in Beira about 1760. He published "Surgical Works," ("Obras Cirurgicas," 4 vols., 1814.) Died in 1822.

Almeida, de, (BRITES, bree′tês,) a heroine who has been called "the Portuguese Joan of Arc," was born about the middle of the fourteenth century, and followed the business of a baker. When her native village (Aljubarotta) was attacked by the Spaniards in 1386, she is said to have killed several soldiers with a baker's shovel, which was religiously preserved as a memorial by the inhabitants of Aljubarotta through several generations.

See "Nouvelle Biographie Générale."

Almeida, de, (Dom FRANCISCO,) the first Portuguese Viceroy of India, a son of the Count of Abrantes, was born at Lisbon about the middle of the fifteenth century. Having distinguished himself in the Moorish wars, he was appointed Viceroy of India in 1505, and fixed the seat of his government at Cochin. By his courage and prudence he greatly extended the dominion of Portugal. When Albuquerque arrived in 1508 with a commission to supersede the viceroy, Almeida refused at first to resign the office, and arrested the admiral.

About the end of 1508, Almeida gained a great victory over the Egyptian fleet near the coast of India. Soon after this victory he gave up the command to his rival, and embarked for Portugal in November, 1509; but before the end of the voyage he was killed in an affray with a band of Caffres, near the Cape of Good Hope, in 1510. Thus obscurely perished, by the hands of savages, a man who had humbled the potentates of India and rendered his country's flag triumphant on the Eastern seas.

See BARROS, "Decadas da Asia;" FARIA Y SOUZA, "Asia Portugueza."

Almeida, de, (LORENZO,) a son of the preceding, distinguished for the many noble qualities of his heart, as well as for bravery and military talents, fell in a sea-fight with the Egyptians near Choul, in 1508.

See JOÃO DE BARROS, "Decada quarta;" FARIA Y SOUZA, "Asia Portugueza."

Almeida, de, (NICOLÃO **Tolentino**—to-lĕn-tee′no,) a Portuguese satirical poet, born at Lisbon in 1745. He published a volume of poems in 1802. It is stated that his superiority in satire was such that he had neither rivals nor imitators. Died in 1811.

Almeida, de, (THEODORO.) See ALMEYDA.

Almeida-Garrett, âl-ma′e-dâ gâr-rĕt′,(or gâr′ret,) (J. B. LEITÃO DE,) a Portuguese *littérateur*, and the author of a metrical romance entitled "Adozinda," (London, 1828.) He also wrote a "Historical Sketch of Portuguese Literature."

See LONGFELLOW's "Poets and Poetry of Europe," and an article "On the Poets of Portugal," in the "Foreign Quarterly Review" for 1832, (vol. x.)

Almela, âl-ma′lâ, (DIEGO RODRIGUEZ,) a Spanish historical writer of the fifteenth century, was born in the city of Murcia.

Almeloveen, van, vân âl′mĕh-lo-vân′, (THEODORUS Jansson—yâns′son,) an eminent Dutch physician and scholar, born at Mydrecht in 1657, was professor of Greek and of medicine at Harderwyk. He published good editions of the "Aphorisms" of Hippocrates, and "Celsus de Medicina," (1687,) and wrote several works, among which is "Theological and Philological Amenities," ("Amœnitates Theologico-Philologicæ," 1694.) Died in 1712.

Almeloven, âl′mĕh-lo′ven, (JAN,) a Dutch painter and engraver, born in Holland about 1620. He left a number of spirited etchings of landscapes, some of which are after his own designs.

Almenar, âl-mâ-nar′, (JUAN,) a Spanish physician, lived about 1500, and wrote "De Morbo Gallico," (1502.)

Almendingen, von, fon âl′men-ding′en, (LUDWIG HARSCHER,) a jurist, born of German parents in Paris in 1766. He was a judge or counsellor in the duchy of Nassau. He wrote several legal treatises, and co-operated with Feuerbach in his "Bibliothek," a periodical devoted to criminal law. Died in 1827.

Almer, âl′mer, (JOHANN CHRISTIAN,) a Danish painter, born at Copenhagen in 1742; died in 1792.

Alméras, âl′mâ′râs′,(LOUIS,) an able French general, born at Vienne in 1768. He served on the staff of Kleber in Egypt, and distinguished himself at Heliopolis. Having obtained the rank of general, he joined the grand army in 1809, and was wounded at Wagram. For his conduct at the battle of the Moskwa, in 1812, he was made lieutenant-general. He was taken prisoner in the retreat from Russia. He was appointed commandant of Bordeaux in 1813. Died in 1823.

Almeyda, (FRANCISCO.) See ALMEIDA.

Almeyda, de, dâ âl-ma′e-dâ, (FERNANDO,) a Portuguese sacred poet, born at Alberca in 1459.

See LONGFELLOW's "Poets and Poetry of Europe."

Almeyda, de, (FRANCISCO,) a Portuguese theologian, born at Lisbon in 1701; died after 1750.

Almeyda or **Almeida, de,** dâ âl-ma′e-dâ, (THEODORO,) a Portuguese priest and writer, born at Lisbon in 1722. He promoted the study of philosophy on rational principles in Portugal, and wrote many works, of which the most remarkable is "Philosophical Recreation," ("Recreação Filosofica," 5 vols., 1751.) Died in 1804.

Almici, âl-mee′chee, (CAMILLO,) a learned Italian priest and writer, born at Brescia in 1714; died in 1779.

Almodovar, âl-mo-do'vaR, (Don ILDEFONSO **Dias de Ribera**—de'âs dà re-Bā'rä,) COUNT OF, a Spanish diplomatist and writer of considerable merit. He was successively ambassador to Russia and England, and returned to Spain in 1779. His chief work is a free translation of Raynal's "History of the East and West Indies," (1784-90,) in which he made such changes as enabled it to pass the Spanish censorship. Died in 1794.

See COXE, "Memoirs of the Kings of Spain."

Almohades, âl'mo-hâdz ; singular, **Almohade,** âl'-mo-hâd, [Fr. pron. äl'mo'äd' ; Ger. ALMOHADEN, âl-mo-hä'den ; Lat. ALMO'HADÆ—from the Arabic AL-MOWAHIDOON, (ALMUWAHIDÛN,) signifying "worshippers of ONE God,"] the name of a celebrated Mohammedan dynasty which succeeded in Northern Africa and Spain to the power of the Almoravides. Its founder was ABOO-ABDILLAH-MOHAMMED, (which see,) a religious reformer, who took the surname of AL-MAHDEE, (AL-MAHDÎ,) "the director." His followers called themselves Al-Mowahidoon, that is, "worshippers of the ONE true God" as revealed by Mohammed, and accused the Almoravides of having departed from the original purity of the Moslem faith and of having relapsed into a condition little better than polytheism or paganism. The power of the Almohades lasted from about 1145 until 1269, when it was subverted by the Benee Mereen, (Benî Merîn.) The Almohade dynasty is sometimes called that of Abd-el-Moomen, (or Abd-ul-Mûmen,) because he was the first of the Al-Mowahidoon who took the name of sultan.

See AL-MAKKARI's "Mohammedan Dynasties of Spain," translated by GAYANGOS, London, 1840-43 ; IBN-KHALDOON, "History of the Berbers."

Almon, âl'mon, (JOHN,) an English political writer, born at Liverpool about 1738, was a political friend of John Wilkes. He became a prominent publisher of pamphlets for the opposition party about 1763. Some of these pamphlets were of his own composition. He also published "Anecdotes of Lord Chatham, with his Speeches from 1736 to 1778," (1792,) and "Biographical, Literary, and Political Anecdotes," (3 vols., 1797.) Died in 1805.

See "Gentleman's Magazine," December, 1805.

Almonacid, de, dà âl-mo-nä-thèD', (SEBASTIAN,) a Spanish sculptor, who flourished in the beginning of the sixteenth century.

Almonde, van, vän âl-mòn'deh, (PHILIPPUS,) written also **Allemonda,** a Dutch admiral, born at Briel in 1646. He distinguished himself as captain in the battle against the English in Solebay, 1672. On the death of De Ruyter, 1676, he obtained command of the fleet, and in the following year shared in Tromp's victory over the Swedes. He accompanied William of Orange in his expedition to England in 1688, and commanded the Dutch fleet at La Hogue, (1692,) where the French were signally defeated. Almonde and Sir George Rooke commanded the allies at the destruction of a Spanish fleet in the Bay of Vigo in 1702. Died in 1711.

See VAN DER AA, "Biographisch Woordenboek der Nederlanden."

Almonte, âl-mon'tà, (JUAN N.,) a Mexican general, born about the beginning of the nineteenth century, served under Santa Anna in Texas in 1836, and was sent as ambassador to the United States soon after 1840. He took part in the battles of Buena Vista and Cerro Gordo in 1847. In 1862 he was appointed dictator by a party of Mexicans opposed to Juarez, but he was deprived of power by the French general Forey in September of that year. Died in 1869.

Al-Moohtadee or **Al-Muhtadî Billah,** âl-mooh'-tä-dee' bil'lâh, a caliph of the house of Abbâs. Born in 838 A.D., he ascended the throne in 869, and was killed, after a reign of eleven months, by the rebellious Turkish soldiers.

Al-Mooktadee or **Al-Muktadî,** âl-mook'tä-dee', a caliph of the house of Abbâs, began to reign at Bagdâd in 1075, and died in 1094.

Al-Mooktader, (-Muktader,) âl-mook'tä-der, or **Almook'tader Bil'lah,** a caliph of the house of Abbâs, ascended the throne in 908, and, after a troubled

and inglorious reign, was killed in battle by his rebellious subjects in 931 A.D.

Al-Mooktafee or **Al-Muktafi,** âl-mook'tä-fee', a caliph of the house of Abbâs, who began to reign in 902 A.D., at the age of twenty years, and died in 908.

Al-Mooktafee or **Al-Muktafî** was also the name of another Abbasside caliph, who ascended the throne in 1136. Died in 1160.

Al-Moontaser, Al-Muntaser, or **Al-Muntasir,** âl-moon'tâs-ser, the eleventh caliph of the line of Abbâs, succeeded to the throne by parricide in 862 A.D., and died after a reign of six months.

Al-Mootassem. See MOTASSEM.

Al-Mootenabbee or **Al-Mutenabbî,** âl-moo'teh-nâb'bee, or **El-Motenebbi,** el-mo'teh-neb'bee, one of the most distinguished of the Arabian poets, born at Koofah (Kûfah) in the early part of the tenth century. He was killed, while on a journey, by a party of hostile Arabs, in 965 A.D.

Almoravides, âl-mo'ra-vidz; singular, **Almoravide,** âl-mo'ra-vid, [Fr. pron. äl'mo'rä'vèd' ; Ger. ALMORAVIDEN, âl-mo-rä-vee'den ; Lat. ALMORAV'IDÆ—a European corruption of the Arabic term Almorâbitoon, (or Almorâbitûn,)—in the oblique cases Almorâbiteen, (Almorâbitîn,) an Arabic term signifying "those bound" or "devoted" to the service of God,] the name of a Moslem dynasty which arose in Northern Africa about the middle of the eleventh century. It was founded by ABDALLAH-IBN-YASEEN, (which see,) a religious leader, one of whose generals, Yoosuf-Ibn-Tâshefeen, conquered a large part of Spain and established a dynasty which lasted about one hundred years. The last sultan of this line, Tâshefeen-Ibn-Alee, was deprived of his throne and life by the victorious Almohades in 1145.

See IBN-KHALDOON, "History of the Berbers," (in manuscript,) and AL-MAKKARI, "History of the Mohammedan Dynasties in Spain," translated by GAYANGOS, London, 1840-43.

Almosnino, âl-mos-nee'no, (MOSES,) a learned Jewish rabbi and writer, born at Saloniki in 1523 ; died near the close of the sixteenth century.

Al-Motassem. See MOTASSEM.

Al-Motenebbi. See AL-MOOTENABBEE.

Almquist, âlm'kwist, (KARL JONAS LUDWIG,) a Swedish poet and novelist of the romantic school, was born in 1793. He published several novels, one of which is entitled "Amorina," a number of elementary works on history, mathematics, etc., and a collection of poems entitled "Book of Thorn-Roses," (i.e. "sweet-briers ;" in Swedish, "Törnrosens Bok.") Died in 1844.

See FAHLKRANTZ, "C. J. L. Almquist såsom Författare i Allmänhet och såsom Theolog i synnerhet skärskådad," 2 vols., 1845.

Al-Muhtadî. See AL-MOOHTADEE.
Al-Muktader. See AL-MOOKTADER.
Al-Muktadi. See AL-MOOKTADEE.
Al-Muktafi. See AL-MOOKTAFEE.
Al-Muntaser. See AL-MOONTASER.
Al-Mutassem. See MOTASSEM.
Al-Mutenabbî. See AL-MOOTENABBEE.

Almy, âl'me, (WILLIAM,) an American philanthropist, member of the Society of Friends, born in 1761. He amassed a large fortune, which he employed in promoting objects of benevolence. Among other things, he liberally endowed the Friends' Boarding-School at Providence, Rhode Island. Died in 1836.

Alnander, âl-nän'der, (OLAF JOHAN,) a Swedish antiquary, born at Norrköping, lived about 1510.

Al-Nassir or **Al-Nasir, (An-Nasir.)** See ABD-ER-RAHMAN III.

Aloisi or **Alloisi,** (BALDASSARE.) See GALANINO.

Aloisio, â-lo-ee'se-o, (GIAN-FRANCESCO,) an Italian poet, born near Naples, was accused of heresy, for which he was put to death in 1564.

Aloja, â-lo'yä, (GIUSEPPE,) a Neapolitan engraver, lived about 1750.

Alompra, â-lom'prä, the founder of the present dynasty of Burmah, was born about 1710. He was the chief of the town of Monchaboo, when the King of Pegu conquered Burmah, in 1752. Having raised the standard of revolt, in 1753, he defeated the Peguans in several battles, and made himself master of all Burmah. He took the King of Pegu prisoner in his own capital in

1757. Alompra was faithless and cruel, but possessed superior civil and military talents. Died in 1760.

See DALRYMPLE, "Oriental Repertory;" CRAWFURD, "Journal of an Embassy to Siam," etc.; SYMES, "Account of an Embassy to the Kingdom of Ava in the year 1795."

Alonso or **Alonzo**, (of Spain.) See ALFONSO.

Alonso de los Rios, ä-lon'so dä lòs ree'òs, (PEDRO,) a Spanish sculptor, born at Valladolid in 1650, worked at Madrid. Died in 1700. His father, Francisco, was also an able sculptor.

Alonzo. See ALFONSO.

Alopa, d', dä-lo'pä, (LORENZO,) a learned printer, born at Venice, published at Florence, about 1475–1500, accurate editions of several Greek works, in elegant typography.

Alopæus, ä-lo-pä'ùs, (DAVID,) brother of Maxim, noticed below, born at Viborg in 1769, was sent by the emperor Alexander I. as minister to Sweden in 1809. After the peace of 1815 he was minister from Russia to the court of Berlin, where he died in 1831.

Alopæus, (MAXIM MAXIMOVITCH,) a Russian diplomatist, born at Viborg, in Finland, in 1748. He was appointed by Catherine II., in 1790, minister plenipotentiary to the court of Prussia. Died in 1822.

Alos, ä'lòs, (JUAN,) a Spanish medical writer, became professor of anatomy at Barcelona in 1664.

Aloysius, ä-lo-ish'e-us, an architect who flourished at Rome in the time of Theodoric the Great.

Alpago, äl-pä'go, [Lat. ALPA'GUS,] (ANDREA,) an Italian physician, native of Belluno, lived about the close of the fifteenth century.

Alp-Arslân, älp-ars-län', (the "strong lion,") written also **Alp-Arselan,** a celebrated Seljook sultan, born in Toorkistan in 1030, succeeded to the throne in 1063. In 1071 he defeated and took prisoner Romanus Diogenes, the Byzantian emperor, who is said to have commanded, in this battle, three hundred thousand men. He treated his imperial captive with great generosity and kindness. Alp-Arslân was assassinated in 1072. His person was remarkable for beauty, grace, and strength, and his character appears to have been almost without a stain. His minister, Nizâm-ul-Mulk, (ne-zäm-ool-moolk,) shared the glory of his sovereign. "Under his wise direction," says Sir John Malcolm, "the territories of Alp-Arslân attained the highest prosperity. Justice was well administered; colleges and mosques were erected in every city; learning was encouraged; the poor were protected; and the inhabitants of Persia confessed that the conquest of their country by the savage Tartars, which they had dreaded as the worst of evils, had proved the greatest of blessings."

See MALCOLM, "History of Persia," vol. i. chap. viii.; VON HAMMER, "Geschichte des Osmanischen Reichs;" D'HERBELOT, "Bibliothèque Orientale;" GIBBON, "Decline and Fall of the Roman Empire."

Al-pha'nus or **Alfani,** äl-fä'nee, (FRANCESCO,) an Italian medical writer of Salerno, lived between 1550 and 1600.

Alphée. See ALPHEUS.

Alphege. See ELPHEGE.

Alphen, van, vän äl'fen, (DANIEL,) a Dutch jurist, born in 1713, was professor of law at Leyden. Died in 1797.

Alphen, van, (HIERONYMUS,) a popular Dutch poet, born at Gouda in 1746, became procurator-general at the court of Utrecht, and treasurer-general of the Union. He published "Poems and Meditations," (1777,) "Dutch Songs," ("Gezangen," 1779,) and "Short Poems for Children," (1781,) which are remarkable for simple grace and beauty. His imaginative poem of "The Starry Heavens" ("De Starrenhemel," 1783) is one of his finest productions. Died at the Hague in 1803.

See KAMPEN, "Geschiedenis der Letteren en Wetenschappen in de Nederlanden;" JORISSEN, "Erinnerung an H. van Alphen," 1804.

Alphen, van, (HIERONYMUS SIMON,) a distinguished theologian, an ancestor of the preceding, was born at New Hanau in 1665. He became professor of theology at Utrecht in 1715, and acquired a high reputation as a teacher. He wrote commentaries on the epistles of Paul (1742) and on other books of Scripture. Died in 1742.

HIERONYMUS VAN ALPHEN, (1700–58,) son of the preceding, was professor of theology at Utrecht, and grandfather of the poet Van Alphen.

Alphery, äl'fä-re, (NICEPHORUS,) a Russian, who emigrated to England and became a parson of the Anglican Church. He died at an advanced age in the latter part of the seventeenth century.

Al-phe'us or **Al-phei'us,** [Gr. Ἀλφεός or Ἀλφειός; Fr. ALPHÉE, äl'fä',] a river-god of classic mythology, was a son of Oceanus. The poets fabled that he loved the nymph Arethusa, who fled from him to the island of Ortygia and was metamorphosed into a fountain, and that Alpheus followed her through the sea and was thus united to that fountain.

Alpheus, a Greek poet, native of Mitylene, supposed to have lived in the time of Augustus Cæsar. He was distinguished as a writer of epigrams.

Alpheus, a Greek engraver of gems, lived in the first century of our era.

Alphonse. See ALFONSO.

Alphonso. See ALFONSO.

Alphonso (or Alfonso) Tostado. See ALPHONSUS ABULENSIS.

Al-phon'sus Ab-u-len'sis, (*i.e.* "Alphonso of Avila,") or **Alfonso Tostado,** äl-fon'so tos-tä'do, an eminent Spanish theologian, born in New Castile about 1400, became Bishop of Avila. Died in 1445, leaving many works, among which are "Commentaries on the Scriptures," (13 vols., 1508.)

Alphonsus a Sancta Maria. See ALFONSO OF CARTHAGENA.

Alphonsus Palentinus. See ALFONSO DE PALENCIA.

Alpin. See ALPINUS.

Al-pï'nus, written also **Alpin,** (PROSPER,) [It. PROSPERO ALPINI, pros'på-ro äl-pee'nee,] an eminent Italian botanist and physician, born at Marostica, in the republic of Venice, in 1553. He passed some years in Egypt, and after his return published, in Latin, a work "On the Plants of Egypt," (1591.) He also published a treatise "On the Egyptian Practice of Medicine," ("De Medicina Ægyptiorum," 1591.) In 1593 he became professor of botany at Padua. He was the first European who published an account of the coffee-plant, and he enriched the science of botany with many new facts. He died in 1617, leaving in manuscript a valuable work "On Exotic Plants," ("De Plantis Exoticis," 1628.)

See TOMASINI, "Elogia Virorum Illustrium;" HALLER, "Bibliotheca Botanica."

Alptageen or **Alpteghîn,** älp'ta-geen', a Turkish slave, regarded as the founder of the Gaznevide dynasty in Eastern Persia, (in what is now called Afghanistan.) Died in 976 A.D. His son-in-law Sabuktageen (or Sebektagîn) was the father of the famous Mahmood of Gazna.

Alquié, d', däl'ke-à', (FRANÇOIS SAVINIEN,) a French author of the seventeenth century, wrote, besides other works, "The Delights of France," ("Les Délices de la France," 1670.)

Alquier, äl'ke-à', (CHARLES JEAN MARIE,) a French diplomatist, noted for his tact and amenity, born in La Vendée in 1752. From 1798 to 1813 he was appointed successively ambassador to Bavaria, Madrid, Florence, Naples, Rome, Stockholm, and Copenhagen. In 1816 he was banished from France, on the ground of his having, when in the National Convention, voted for the death of Louis XVI. He was, however, recalled in 1818, and died in 1826.

Als, äls or älss, (PETER, or PEDER,) a Danish painter of history and portraits, born at Copenhagen in 1725; died in 1775.

Alsace, d', däl'sås', (THOMAS LOUIS,) CARDINAL, called also **Alsace de Bossu,** äl'sås' deh bo'sü', (THOMAS PHILIPPE DE Hennin or Hénin—hå'nän',) was born at Brussels in 1680. He was descended from the counts of Flanders and from the counts of Bossu. In 1714 he was appointed by the Emperor of Germany Archbishop of Malines (Mechlin) and Primate of the Austrian Netherlands. In 1719 he was raised to the dignity of cardinal. Died in 1759.

Al-Saffâh or **As-Seffâh.** See ABOO-L-ABBAS-AB-DALLAH.

ā, ē, ī, ō, ū, ȳ, *long;* å, è, ö, same, less prolonged; ă, ĕ, ĭ, ŏ, ŭ, ў, *short;* a, e, i, o, *obscure;* fär, fåll, fåt; mĕt; nŏt; gŏŏd; moo͞ɴ;

Alsario della Croce, äl-sä're-o děl'lä kRo'chà, [Lat. ALSA'RIUS,] a learned physician and writer, born at Genoa about 1576. He gave lectures on medicine in Rome for twenty years or more, and was physician to Pope Gregory XV. Died after 1631.

Al-Sheik, äl-shäk' or äl-shā'ĭk, (MOSES,) a Jewish rabbi, born at Sapheth, in Galilee, was celebrated as an interpreter of the Scriptures, on which he wrote many commentaries. Died about 1595.

Alsloot, van, văn äls-lōt', (DANIEL,) a Flemish landscape-painter, who was born at Brussels about 1550, and died in the early part of the seventeenth century.

Alsop, aul'sop, (ANTONY,) an English divine and eminent classical scholar, who graduated at Cambridge in 1696, and became a prebendary of Winchester. He published a "Selection of the Fables of Æsop," in Latin verse, ("Æsopicarum Fabularum Delectus," 1698.) He also wrote Latin odes with facility. Died in 1727.

Alsop, aul'sop, (RICHARD,) an American poet and journalist, born at Middletown, Connecticut, in 1761. With Theodore Dwight, Hopkins, Trumbull, and others, called the "Hartford Wits," he issued, in 1791, the first number of the "Echo," a satirical journal, directed chiefly against the Democratic party. In 1800 he published a Monody on the Death of Washington. He translated "The Enchanted Lake of the Fairy Morgana," from Berni's "Orlando Innamorato;" and Molina's "Geographical, Natural, and Civil History of Chili." Died in 1815.

See GRISWOLD, "Poets and Poetry of America."

Alsop, (Rev. VINCENT,) an English nonconformist divine, who became minister of a Presbyterian congregation in Westminster. He gained distinction by his strictures on Sherlock's work "On the Knowledge of Christ," and his reply to a sermon by Stillingfleet against nonconformists. Died at an advanced age in 1703.

See NICHOLS, "Literary Anecdotes."

Alsted, äl'stět, [Lat. ALSTE'DIUS,] (JOHANN HEINRICH,) a voluminous German writer on theology and history, born near Herborn, in Nassau, in 1588. His works, which were all written in Latin, were once highly esteemed. Died in 1638.

Alston, auls'ton, (CHARLES,) an eminent Scottish botanist and physician, born at Eddlewood in 1683. He began to read lectures on botany and materia medica at Edinburgh soon after 1720, and was appointed professor of the same in the university of that city about 1740. His principal work is a manual of botany, entitled "Tirocinium Botanicon Edinburgense," (1753,) in which he defended the system of Tournefort and wrote against that of Linnæus. Died in 1760. His lectures on Materia Medica (2 vols., 1770) are highly commended.

See CHAMBERS, "Biographical Dictionary of Eminent Scotsmen."

Alston, (WASHINGTON.) See ALLSTON.

Alston, auls'ton, (WILLIS,) a native of Halifax county, North Carolina, was a representative in Congress from that State from 1799 to 1815, and from 1825 to 1831. During the war of 1812 he was chairman of the Committee of Ways and Means, the most honourable and at the same time the most arduous and responsible position, after the speakership, in the National House of Representatives. Died in 1837.

Alstorph, äls'torf, (JAN,) a Dutch antiquary, born at Groningen about 1680; died in 1719.

Alströmer or **Alstroemer,** äl'strö-mer, (almost äl'-strŭm-er,) (JONAS,) a distinguished Swede, born at Alingsås, in 1685, of poor and obscure parents. He went to seek his fortune, first to Stockholm and afterwards to London, where he set up as ship-broker, in which business he appears to have been very successful. Although he became an English citizen, he still retained the warmest attachment to his native country, to which he returned about 1724. His earnest and untiring efforts were subsequently directed towards the improvement of Swedish commerce and manufactures, by which he merited and obtained the esteem and gratitude of his countrymen, who conferred upon him many honours. He was made, in 1739, a member of the Council of Commerce, and was afterwards ennobled. Died in 1761.

See KRYGER, "Åminnelse-Tal öfver J. Alströmer."

Alströmer or **Alstroemer,** (KLAUDIUS or KLAS,) a Swedish naturalist, born at Alingsås in 1736, was a son of Jonas Alströmer, mentioned above. He studied natural history under Linnæus, and travelled in Spain to obtain information respecting sheep and other subjects. A journal which he wrote during this tour was accidentally destroyed by fire. He published a "Discourse on the Breeding of Fine-Woolled Sheep," (1770,) which is highly praised. Died in 1796.

See DUBB, "Åminnelse-Tal öfver Clas Alströmer," 1796.

Alt, ält, (FRANZ JOSEPH NICOLAUS,) a Swiss historian, born at Freiburg in 1689, bore the title of baron. He wrote in French (of which he was not a perfect master) a "History of Switzerland," (10 vols., 1749–52,) a work of much research, but defective in style and criticism. Died in 1770.

Altani, äl-tä'nee, (ANTONIO,) Bishop of Urbino, an eminent Italian ecclesiastic of the fifteenth century. Died in 1450.

Altani, (ANTONIO,) an Italian poet, born in Friuli about 1510, was of the same family as the preceding. He left in manuscript a great number of sonnets, canzoni, and epigrams, the most of which are lost. Died about 1570.

Altani, (ENRICO,) an Italian dramatic poet, who flourished in the first half of the seventeenth century. Among his productions is "L'Americo," a tragedy. His works are commended by several Italian critics. Died at an advanced age in 1648.

Altaroche, äl'tä'rosh', (MARIE MICHEL,) a successful and witty French writer and journalist, born at Issoire (Puy-de-Dôme) in 1811. He was chief editor of the "Charivari" from 1834 to 1848, and sustained during that period an exuberant flow of ready wit, raillery, and satire. He published a volume of political songs, (1835,) two historical studies entitled the "Reformation," and the "Revolution," (1841,) and other works, which favour democracy. He was elected to the Constituent Assembly in 1848.

Altdorfer, ält'doR'fer, written also **Altorfer,** (ALBRECHT,) a celebrated German painter and engraver, born at Altdorf, in Bavaria, in 1488. There is a doubtful tradition that he was a pupil of Albert Dürer. He worked chiefly in Regensburg, (or Ratisbon,) and is called by the French "Le Petit Albert," either in contradistinction to Albert Dürer or because he seldom painted other than small figures. Among his works is a remarkable picture of the victory of Alexander at Arbela, which contains a great number of figures. The details of costume and accessories are very minutely represented. His engravings on copper and wood are more numerous than his paintings. Died in 1538.

See STRUTT, "Dictionary of Engravers."

Alten, äl'ten, (KARL,) the youngest son of Baron Alten, was born in Hanover in 1764. He entered the English army in 1803, became a major-general in 1812, and commanded with great credit the third division of Wellington's army at the battle of Waterloo, in which he was wounded. He was soon after created a count. Died in 1840.

Altensteig or **Altenstaig,** äl'ten-stīg', (JOHANN or JOHANNES,) a Roman Catholic theologian, a native of Germany, flourished in the first half of the sixteenth century.

Altenstein, äl'ten-stīn, (KARL,) BARON, a Prussian minister of public instruction, born at Anspach in 1770. In 1815 he undertook the recovery of the works of art and literary treasures which the French had removed from Germany to Paris. For the successful accomplishment of this arduous task, all Germany owes him a debt of gratitude. He became minister of public instruction and worship in 1817, and made important changes during the long period of his administration. Died in 1840.

Alter, äl'ter, (FRANZ CARL,) a German Jesuit and eminent classical scholar, born in Silesia in 1749; died in 1804. He published editions of Homer's "Iliad," Lucretius, and other Greek and Latin works.

Althæa, äl-thee'a, [Gr. Ἀλθαία; Fr. ALTHÉE, äl'tà',] in the Greek mythology, was the wife of Œneus, King of Calydon, and the mother of Meleager. (See MELEAGER.)

Althammer, ält'häm'mer, or **Althamer,** (ANDREAS,) a distinguished German divine, born at Brenz, in Suabia, in 1498. He embraced the principles of Luther in 1520, and became, by his learning, energy, and wisdom, one of the chief pillars of the Reformation. Died in 1564. His best-known work is his "Diallage," (*i.e.* "Reconciliation," 1528,) in which he attempts to explain and reconcile those passages of Scripture which at first sight appear to be contradictory.

Althen, äl'tŏn', (EHAN, ě-hän', or JEAN,) a native of Persia, who became a benefactor to France by the introduction of madder, was born in 1711. His father was the governor of a province. He was made captive in his youth by some Arabs, and sold as a slave at Smyrna, whence he escaped to Marseilles. He carried thither some seeds of the madder, the exportation of which was forbidden under penalty of death. Having the advantage of a handsome person, he married a rich heiress of Marseilles, and was thus placed in a situation to pursue at leisure his plans for the culture of madder in France. He had observed that the soil and climate of the Comptat-Venaissin were similar to those of Smyrna and Anatolia, which were most favourable to the cultivation of madder. His experiments in this part of France were crowned with complete success, and the culture of madder has since become extensive and very profitable. Died in 1774.

See A. RASTOUL, "Vie de J. Althen," in "Portraits et Histoire des Hommes utiles."

Althof, ält'hŏf, (LUDWIG CHRISTOPH,) a German physician and medical writer, born at Detmold in 1758; died in 1832.

Althorp, äl'thorp, (Lord JOHN CHARLES SPENCER,) Earl Spencer, a liberal English statesman, the son of George John, Earl Spencer, was born in May, 1782. He was elected to Parliament for Oakhampton in 1804, and was a junior lord of the treasury under the ministry of Fox and Grenville, 1806–7. He represented Northamptonshire in the House of Commons from 1806 until 1834. By his good sense, prudence, probity, and other moral qualities, he acquired great influence, and was commonly called "honest Lord Althorp." In 1830 he became chancellor of the exchequer in the Whig ministry. He inherited the title of Earl Spencer at the death of his father in 1834, and resigned office in the same year. His favourite pursuit was agriculture, to the improvement of which he probably contributed more than any other English nobleman of his time. Died in 1845.

See "Gentleman's Magazine" for November, 1845.

Althusen, ält'hü'sen, [Lat. ALTHU'SIUS,] (JOHANN,) a Dutch jurist, born probably at Emden about 1556, became professor of law at Herborn in 1590, and syndic at Bremen. He was an enlightened friend of liberty, and advocated the doctrine that supreme power is the right of the people. He published a "System of Roman Law," (1586,) and other works. Died about 1638.

See BAYLE, "Historical and Critical Dictionary."

Alticherio, äl-te-kä're-o, or **Aldigieri,** äl-de-jä'ree, (DA ZEVIO—dâd-zä've-o,) a distinguished Veronese painter, who flourished in the latter half of the fourteenth century.

Alticozzi, äl-te-kot'see, (LORENZO,) an Italian Jesuit and theological writer, born at Cortona in 1689. His chief work is "Summa Augustiniana," (6 vols., 1744–61.) Died in 1777.

Altieri. See CLEMENT X.

Altilio, äl-tee'le-o, [Lat. ALTIL'IUS,] (GABRIELLO,) an Italian poet and ecclesiastic, born about 1440. He lived mostly at Naples. He is known as the author of some short Latin poems of great merit, among which is an Epithalamium on the marriage of Galeazzo Sforza, Duke of Milan. Died about 1500.

Alting, äl'ting, [Lat. ALTIN'GIUS,] (HEINRICH,) a Calvinistic theological writer and professor, born at Emden in 1583. He was professor of Frederick, King of Bohemia, professor of theology at Heidelberg, and subsequently at Groningen, 1627–44. Died in 1644.

See "Encyclopædia Britannica," and BAYLE, "Historical and Critical Dictionary."

Alting, (JACOB,) a distinguished biblical scholar, son of the preceding, was born at Heidelberg in 1618. In 1642 he was appointed professor of Hebrew and the Oriental languages at Groningen. He wrote several valuable exegetical and philological works, among which was a Syro-Chaldaic grammar. Died in 1679.

See B. BECKER, "Vita J. Altingii," prefixed to his "Opera Omnia."

Alting, (MENSO,) a zealous Calvinistic preacher and controversialist, born in Drenthe, a district of Holland, in 1541, was the father of Heinrich, above noticed. He was minister at Emden, and leader of his party in a contest against the Lutherans. Died in 1612.

Alting, (MENSO,) a grandson of the preceding, was born in 1636. He became burgomaster of Groningen, and published a valuable work, entitled a "Description of Lower Germany," ("Notitia Germaniæ Inferioris," 1697.) Died in 1712.

See UBBO EMMIUS, "M. Altingii Vita," 1717.

Altissimo, äl-tès'se-mo, (*i.e.* "most sublime,") the surname of a famous Italian poet and improvisatore who lived in the beginning of the sixteenth century. His true name is believed to have been CRISTOFORO FIORENTINO, (kris-tof'o-ro fe-o'rēn-tee'no.) His best work is an Italian metrical version of the first book of the prose romance entitled "Reali di Francia."

Altissimo, dell', dēl-läl-tès'se-mo, (CRISTOFANO,) an eminent Florentine portrait-painter of the sixteenth century.

Altmann, ält'män, (JOHANN GEORG,) a Swiss theologian, born at Zofingen in 1697, was professor of moral philosophy and Greek at Berne. He published, besides other works, "Critical Observations on the New Testament," (3 vols., 1737,) and was one of the two editors of the "Tempe Helvetica," (6 vols., 1735–43.) Died in 1758.

See ERSCH und GRUBER, "Allgemeine Encyklopaedie."

Altmish, ält'mish, surnamed SHEMS (or SHUMS) OOD-DEEN—shĕms or shŭms ōŏd-deen', (the "sun of religion,") a young man of Tartar descent, who, from the condition of a slave, became Sultan of Delhi in 1210 A.D. He died in 1236. He was an able ruler, and was the father of Ruzeea Bêgum and Mahmood Nâsir ōŏd-Deen.

See FERISHTA'S "History of the Mahomedan Power in India," translated by BRIGGS, vol. i.

Altobello, äl-to-bel'lo, (FRANCESCO ANTONIO,) a Neapolitan historical painter of the seventeenth century, was born at Bitonto. He worked at Naples, and excelled in invention and composition.

Altomare, äl-to-mä'rä, (DONATO ANTONIO,) [often called in Latin DONA'TUS AB ALTOMA'RI,] an eminent Neapolitan physician and medical writer. Having been driven from Naples by persecution, he was restored by the mediation of Pope Paul IV. His chief work, "Ars Medica," (1553,) has been often reprinted. Died about 1566.

Altomonte, äl-to-mon'tä, (MARTINO,) an Italian painter, born at Naples in 1657. He worked many years in Vienna with success, and painted portraits of the Austrian emperors. Died in 1745.

Alton, äl'ton, (RICHARD,) COUNT OF, a general in the Austrian service, born in Ireland in 1732, commanded in the Low Countries at the beginning of the insurrection in 1789. He was forced to evacuate Brussels, and died during his retreat towards Vienna in 1790.

His younger brother, EDWARD, Count of Alton, served with distinction against the Turks and French. He fell at the siege of Dunkirk in August, 1793.

Alton, d', dâl'ton, (JOHANN SAMUEL EDUARD,) a physician, born at Saint Goar in 1803. He became professor of anatomy at Halle in 1834, and published a "Manual of Comparative Anatomy of Man," (1850.)

Alton, d', (JOSEPH WILHELM EDUARD,) a German naturalist and antiquary, the father of the preceding, was born at Aquileja in 1772. He studied natural history and the fine arts, and travelled in France, England, Spain, etc. He published a "Natural History of the Horse," (1810,) and a "Comparative Osteology," (1821–28.) About 1821 he was appointed professor of archæology and the history of art in the University of Bonn, where he remained until his death in 1840.

ā, ē, ī, ō, ū, ȳ, *long;* ă, ĕ, ŏ, same, less prolonged; ă, ĕ, ĭ, ŏ, ŭ, ȳ, *short;* ạ, ẹ, ị, ọ, *obscure;* fär, fäll, fät; mēt; nŏt; gŏŏd; mōŏn;

A.ton-Shée, d', dăl'tòǹ' shă', (EDMOND,) COMTE, a French democrat, born in 1810. He was an active promoter of the revolution of February, 1848, advocated a socialist régime, and acted with Ledru-Rollin.

Altorfer. See ALTDORFER.

Altoviti, âl-to-vee'tee, (ANTONIO,) born in 1521, at Florence, was made archbishop of that city in 1548; died in 1573.

Altovitis, âl'to′ve′tèss', or **Altouvitis**, âl′too′ve′tèss', MADEMOISELLE, a poetess, born at Marseilles in 1550. Died in 1606.

Altringer. See ALDRINGER.

Altschul, âlt'shool, (ELIAS,) a German homœopathic physician, born at Prague in 1812. He published a "Dictionary of Ocular Medicine," (2 vols., 1836.)

Altzenbach, âlt'sęn-bȧk', (WILHELM,) the name of two German engravers (father and son) of the seventeenth century. They worked in Paris and Strasburg.

Alunno, ä-loon'no, (FRANCESCO,) an Italian grammarian and calligraphist of the sixteenth century, was born at Ferrara. He is known as the author of two works on the Italian language, which were often reprinted, viz.: "Riches of the Italian Language," (1543,) and a Vocabulary containing the words in Dante, Petrarch, Boccaccio, and others, (1548.) Died in 1556.

Alunno, (NICCOLÒ,) an Italian painter of Foligno, flourished from 1450 to 1500, painted in water-colours, and was an artist of great merit for his time. He was one of those who contributed to the progress of art by the freedom of his style. Among his works is a "Nativity of Christ."

See VASARI, "Lives of the Painters."

Alured. See ALFRED.

Alva, âl'vą, or **Al'ba**, [Sp. pron. âl'vȧ,] (FERNANDO ALVAREZ DE TOLEDO,) [Sp. pron. fêR-nân'do âl'vȧ-rêth dȧ to-lā'Do,] DUKE OF, [Fr. DUC D'ALBE, dük dȧlb,] a celebrated Spanish general under the emperor Charles V. and Philip II., King of Spain, was born in 1508, of a noble and ancient Castilian family. At an early age he entered the army of Charles V., whom he afterwards accompanied in most of his campaigns. In 1556-7 he successfully defended Naples against the allied French and Papal armies, and acquired a high reputation as a prudent and able general. He was sent by Philip II., in 1567, to quell the insurrection which had broken out among the Protestants of the Low Countries. But, although in this war he displayed great abilities as a general, the rigour of his administration, and the extreme cruelty with which he treated the avowed or suspected heretics who fell into his hands, doubtless contributed more than any other cause towards the final separation of those provinces from the Spanish crown. Alva was recalled to Madrid in 1573. He boasted that in the space of four years he had brought no fewer than eighteen thousand persons to the scaffold! In 1580 he invaded Portugal, and, after defeating the Portuguese forces at the mouth of the Tagus, annexed that kingdom to the dominions of Spain. Alva died in 1582.

See WATSON, "Philip II.;" PRESCOTT, "Philip II.," vol. ii.; MOTLEY, "History of the Dutch Republic;" J. ANTONIO DE VERA Y FIGUEROA, "Resultas de la Vida de Fern. Alvarez de Toledo," 1643; "Vie du Duc d'Albe," Paris, 1698; J. V. DE RUSTAUT, "Historia de Fern. Alvarez de Toledo Duque de Alva," 1750; J. MITCHELL, "Biographies of Eminent Soldiers of the Last Four Centuries," 1865.

Alvarado, de, dȧ âl-vä-rä'Do, (ALONZO,) a Spanish officer, who served under Cortez in Mexico, after the conquest of which he went to Peru and obtained a high command in the army of Pizarro. Having been sent with five hundred men to reinforce the brothers of Pizarro at Cuzco, he was defeated and made prisoner by Almagro in 1537. After the death of Pizarro he took arms against Almagro the younger, and joined his troops to those of De Castro, (1542.) He was lieutenant-general of the army which suppressed the rebellion of Gonzalo Pizarro in 1548.

See PRESCOTT, "Conquest of Peru."

Alvarado, de, (PEDRO,) a Spanish officer, born at Badajos at the close of the fifteenth century, was one of the principal companions of Cortez in the conquest of Mexico. He distinguished himself at the battles of Ta-

basco and Otumba, and gained the full confidence of Cortez. He was left in command of the city of Mexico when Cortez marched to encounter Narvaez. In 1523 he led a successful expedition against Zacatula, Tehuantepec, and Guatemala, and received from the King of Spain the title of Governor of Guatemala. He performed an arduous march over the Andes with a design to seize Quito; but, having met the troops of Pizarro, who claimed the command in that place, he retired peaceably after receiving a large indemnity for his expenses. He was killed in a fight with some natives in 1541. Some writers say his death was caused by a horse falling on him down a steep bank.

See PRESCOTT, "Conquest of Mexico," vols. ii. and iii.

Alvares. See ALVAREZ.

Alvarez, âl'vȧ-rêth, (DIEGO,) a Spanish theologian, born in Old Castile about 1550, became Archbishop of Trani, in Italy, in 1606. His chief work is "On the Aids of Divine Grace," ("De Auxiliis Divinæ Gratiæ," 1610.) Died about 1633.

Al'va-rĕz, [Port. pron. âl'vä-rĕz,] (EMANUEL,) a Portuguese Jesuit, born in the island of Madeira in 1526; died in 1582. Among other works, he was the author of an excellent Latin grammar.

Alvarez, (FRANCISCO,) a Portuguese priest, born at Coimbra, became chaplain to King Manoel some time before 1515. Soon after this date he accompanied Duarte Galvam on a mission to the King of Abyssinia, who was then called Prester John. He passed about six years in that strange country, and returned home in 1527. A long and valuable account of this mission was published in 1540, with the title "Prester John of the Indias: a True Account of the Country of Prester John," ("Ho Preste Joam das Indias: verdadera Informaçam das Terras do Preste Joam.") He is regarded as a candid and veracious writer. Died probably about 1540.

See F. DENIS, "Le Monde enchanté," etc.; RAMUSIO, "Viaggi e Navigazioni."

Alvarez, (GOMEZ,) a Spanish poet, born in 1488; died in 1538.

Alvarez, (Don JOSÉ,) one of the most eminent Spanish sculptors, was born at Priego, in the province of Córdova, in 1768. He became a student in the Academy of Madrid in 1794, gained there a prize of the first class, and received from the king a pension of twelve thousand reals (fifteen hundred dollars) in 1799, after which he pursued his studies in Paris. His reputation was increased by a statue of Ganymede, (1804.) He worked chiefly in Rome, and became a member of the Academy of Saint Luke. Among his master-pieces are "Orpheus Sleeping," a "Venus and Cupid," and a group of "Antilochus and Memnon." He received the title of court-sculptor to Ferdinand VII. about 1818. Died at Madrid in November, 1827. His son, a promising sculptor, died in 1830, aged about twenty-five.

See BERMUDEZ, "Diccionario Historico;" NAGLER, "Allgemeines Künstler-Lexikon."

Alvarez, (JUAN,) a Mexican general, born in 1790, was distinguished for his energy and boldness. He took a prominent part in the insurrection which began in 1854 and which deprived Santa Anna of power in 1855. Alvarez became President of Mexico about September, 1855, and abolished the old privilege (*fuero*) of the clergy and the army. He resigned in December, 1855.

Alvarez, (Don MANUEL,) a distinguished Spanish sculptor, born at Salamanca in 1727, was a pupil of Felipe de Castro. He gained the first prize at Madrid in 1754, and became sculptor to the king in 1794. The purity and vigour of his design procured for him the surname of "El Griego," ("the Greek.") Died in 1797.

Alvarez, (Don MARTIN,) Count of Colomera, a Spanish general, born in Andalusia about 1714. He obtained in 1779 the command of the army which besieged Gibraltar without success for several years, and was superseded by the Duc de Crillon in 1782. Having been raised to the rank of captain-general, he commanded in 1794 against the French, whose progress he failed to arrest. He was removed in February, 1795. Died in 1819.

Alvarez, (TOMAS,) a Spanish physician of Seville, published a treatise on the plague in 1569.

Alvarez, de, dà âl′vä-rêth, (BERNARDO,) a Spanish adventurer, born at Seville in 1514, founded several hospitals in Mexico. Died in 1584.

Alvarez de Cabral. See CABRAL.

Alvarez de Castro, âl′vä-rêth dà kâs′tRo, (MARIANO,) a Spanish officer, born at Granada, was distinguished for his resolute defence of Gerona against the French, by whom it was taken in 1809, after a siege of seven months. He died in prison about the end of 1809.

See SOUTHEY, "History of the Peninsular War."

Alvarez de Colmenar. See COLMENAR.

Alvarez de Luna. See LUNA.

Alvarez do Oriente, âl′vä-rêz do o-re-ên′tà, (*i.e.* "Alvarez of the East,") (FERNÃO,) a Portuguese poet of great merit, born at Goa, in India, about 1540. Scarcely anything is known of his life, except that he was bred to the sea and at one time was himself the captain of a vessel. His chief work is entitled "Portugal Transformed," ("A Lusitania transformada," 1607,) a pastoral partly in verse and partly in prose.

Alvarez y Baena, âl′vä-rêth e bä-ä′nä, (JOSÉ ANTONIO,) a Spanish biographer, born at Madrid, wrote the "Illustrious Sons of Madrid," ("Hijos de Madrid illustres," 4 vols., 1789–91.) Died about 1803.

Alvaro, âl′vä-ro, (GIOVANNI,) a Neapolitan painter, who flourished in the first half of the eighteenth century.

Alvarotto, âl-vä-rot′to, (JACOPO,) a distinguished feudal lawyer, born at Padua in 1385; died in 1453.

Alvar Paez, âl′vaR pä′ĕs, or **Alvar Pajo,** âl′vaR pä′zho, [Lat. AL′VARUS PELA′GIUS,] a theologian, born probably in Portugal, became Bishop of Silves in Algarve about 1334. His chief work is "On the Complaint of the Church," ("De Planctu Ecclesiæ,") completed in 1332. He maintains in this the supremacy of the pope. Died about 1350.

Al′va-rus, (PAULUS,) often called **Al′varus Corduben′sis,** (*i.e.* "Alvarus of Córdova,") from the place of his birth, a Christian writer of the ninth century.

Alvarus. See ALVAREZ.

Alvensleben, von, fon âl′vens-lä′bĕn, (ALBRECHT,) COUNT, a Prussian minister of state, born in 1794. He was minister of finances from 1836 to 1842.

Alvensleben, von, (KARL GEBHARD,) a Prussian general, born in 1778. He fought at Jena in 1806, commanded a regiment at Lutzen in 1813, and rendered important service at Bautzen. He became a general in 1817. Died in 1831.

Alvensleben, von, (PHILIP CHARLES,) COUNT, a diplomatist in the service of Prussia, born at Hanover in 1745, was made a count in 1801, and died in 1802.

Alves, âl′vĕs, (ROBERT,) a Scottish poet, born at Elgin in 1745, wrote "The Weeping Bard," and "The Banks of the Esk," (published in 1801.) Died in 1794.

Alviano, âl-ve-â′no, (BARTOLOMMEO,) an Italian general who was famous for his courage, audacity, and skill in the wars that preceded and followed the League of Cambrai, was born about 1455. Having entered the service of Venice, he routed the Imperialists near Cadore in 1508, and was promoted to the position of general-in-chief. He was defeated and taken prisoner by Louis XII. of France at Ghiera d'Adda in 1509. The Venetians and the French having become allies, he was released in 1513. The victory of the French at Marignano, in 1515, is ascribed in great measure to him. He was a lover of literature, and a generous patron of literary men. Died of fever in 1515.

See SISMONDI, "Histoire des Républiques Italiennes."

Alvinczy, Alvinzi, or **Alvinzy, von,** pronounced alike—fon âl-vĭnt′se, (JOSEPH,) BARON, an Austrian general, was born at Vincz, (Vints,) in Transylvania, in 1735, (or, as some authorities say, in 1726.) He became a lieutenant-field-marshal in 1789, and greatly distinguished himself as commander of a division in the campaigns of 1792 and 1793 against the French. After the defeat of Wurmser in Italy in the summer of 1796, Marshal Alvinczy was appointed to the command of a new army of about fifty or sixty thousand men, sent against Bonaparte. He entered Italy from Carinthia, and fought an indecisive action at Bassano on the 6th of November,

1796. In the same month he was defeated by Bonaparte at Arcola, after a battle of three days' duration. "The ruinous fetters of the Aulic Council," says Alison, "paralyzed all the movements of Alvinzi, who in this strife evinced neither the capacity nor spirit of a general worthy to combat Napoleon." Having been again defeated at Rivoli in January, 1797, he resigned his command. Died in 1810.

See BOTTA, "Storia d'Italia;" ALISON, "History of Europe."

Alvintzi or **Alvinczi,** âl-vint′se, (PETER,) a Protestant divine and writer, who lived at Waradin and Kaschau, in Hungary, in the early part of the seventeenth century. Two volumes of his sermons were published in 1632 and 1634.

Al-Waleed or **Al-Walîd** (âl-wä′leed′) I., the sixth caliph of the race of Omeyyah, ascended the throne of Damascus in 705. During his reign, Toorkistan in the East, and Spain in the West, were added to the Arabian Empire, and the Omeyyah dynasty attained the acme of its power. Died in 715 A.D.

See WEIL, "Geschichte der Chalifen."

Alxinger, âlk′sing-ĕr, (JOHANN BAPTIST,) a German scholar and poet, born at Vienna in 1755. He wrote lyric, dramatic, and epic poems. Among his most popular works is "Doolin von Mainz," an epic poem, (1787.) He was well acquainted with the best works in the ancient as well as the modern languages, and is said to have known the whole of the Æneid by heart. As a man he was distinguished by a noble and unostentatious generosity towards all who needed his sympathy or aid. He died in 1797.

Aly. See ALEE.

A-lȳ-at′tēs, [Gr. Ἀλυάττης; Fr. ALYATTE, ä′le-ăt′,] a celebrated king of Lydia, the father of Crœsus, began to reign about 618 B.C. He waged war for five years against Cyaxares, King of Media. A battle between them was interrupted by an eclipse of the sun, in consequence of which they made a treaty of peace. This eclipse, predicted by Thales, is supposed to have occurred in 610 B.C. Alyattes reigned fifty-seven years.

See HERODOTUS, book i.; ROLLIN, "Ancient History;" HAMILTON, "Researches in Asia Minor."

Alyon, ä′le-òN′, (PIERRE PHILIPPE,) a French pharmacist, naturalist, and writer, born at Auvergne in 1758; died about 1820.

A-lȳp′Ĭ-us, [Gr. Ἀλύπιος,] an architect of Antioch, lived in the fourth century. He was charged by Julian the Apostate to rebuild the temple at Jerusalem. But this design was frustrated, if we may credit the statement of an excellent pagan historian, (Ammianus Marcellinus,) by eruptions of fire from the earth.

See GIBBON, "Decline and Fall of the Roman Empire," chap. xxiii.

Alypius, [Ἀλύπιος,] an ancient Greek musician and writer on music. Fragments of his work are extant.

Alypius, a distinguished Greek sophist of the fourth century, born at Alexandria, in Egypt, excelled in dialectics.

Aly Shir. See ALEE-SHEER-AMEER.

Alyy. See ALEE.

Alzate y Ramirez, âl-sä′tà e rä-mee′rĕs, (JOSÉ ANTONIO,) a distinguished astronomer and geographer who lived at Mexico in the early part of the eighteenth century. His numerous works are written in Spanish.

Amac, (a Persian poet.) See AMAK.

Amadei, â-mä-dä′ee, (GIROLAMO,) an Italian priest, born about 1483, preached and wrote against Luther. Died in 1543.

Amadei, (STEFANO,) an Italian painter of history and portraits, born at Perugia in 1589. He excelled in the use of the crayon, and worked in Rome. Died in 1644.

See LANZI, "History of Painting in Italy."

Amadeo, â-mä-dä′o, or **Amadei,** â-mä-dä′ee, (GIOVANNI ANTONIO,) a distinguished Italian sculptor, born at Pavi′a about 1400. Among his principal works are the monuments of the Venetian general Colleoni and his daughter, at Bergamo. Died in 1474.

Amadesi, â-mä-dä′see, (DOMENICO,) a popular Italian poet, born at Bologna in 1657, was a rich merchant. His first poems appeared under the anagram "Simonide de Meaco," (1709.) Died in 1730.

ā, ē, ī, ō, ū, ȳ, *long;* ă, ĕ, ĭ, ŏ, ŭ, ў, *short;* ạ, ẹ, ị, ọ, *obscure;* fär, fâll, fàt; mĕt; nŏt; gōōd; mōōn;

Amadesi, (GIUSEPPE LUIGI,) a distinguished antiquary and scholar, born at Leghorn, of Bolognese parents, in 1701. He contributed to Calogera's "Raccolta di Opuscoli," and published "De Comitatu Argentato," (1763.) Died in 1773.

Am-a-de′us, [It. AMEDEO, â-mà-dā′o, or AMADEO, â-mâ-dā′o ; Fr. AMÉDÉE, ằ′mà′dằ′,] the name of several counts and dukes of Savoy from about 1100 to 1472.

Amadeus I. of Savoy, a son of Humbert, Count of Maurienne, lived in the first half of the eleventh century.

Amadeus II. was a nephew of the preceding, and a son of Oddo by his wife Adelaide of Susa. Died in the eleventh century. He was succeeded by his son, Humbert II.

Amadeus III., Count of Maurienne, succeeded his father, Humbert II., in 1103. He went to Palestine on a crusade with his nephew, Louis VII. of France, in 1147, and died in Cyprus in 1148. His successor was his son, Humbert III.

Amadeus IV. succeeded his father, Thomas I., Count of Savoy, in 1233. He made some additions to his dominions. Died in 1253.

Amadeus V., born in 1249, was a son of Thomas II. of Savoy, Count of Flanders. He succeeded his uncle Philip as Count of Savoy in 1285. He died in 1323, leaving the crown to his son Edward.

Amadeus VI., born in 1334, was a son of Aymon, Count of Savoy, whom he succeeded in 1343. He was one of the most able and powerful princes of the house of Savoy. He defeated the French at Arbrette in 1354, and, having joined a crusade against the Turks, took Gallipoli in 1366 and released the captive emperor John. He acquired large accessions of territory in Piedmont. Died in 1383.

Amadeus VII., born about 1360, succeeded his father, Amadeus VI., at the age of twenty-three. He was styled the "Red Count," from the colour of his armour. He annexed Nice to his dominions. Died in 1391.

Amadeus VIII., son of Amadeus VII., succeeded his father in 1391, being then only eight years old. In 1416 he was created by the emperor Sigismund first Duke of Savoy. He enjoyed a great reputation for wisdom, and was called the Solomon of his age. In 1434 he made his son Louis lieutenant-general of his dominions, and retired to the monastery of Ripaille, which he had founded. Having remained here five years, he was elected pope by the Council of Bâle, in the place of Eugenius IV., whom they had deposed. Amadeus accepted the office, though with great reluctance, taking the name of Felix V. Afterwards, wishing to put an end to the schism in the Church, he publicly renounced his claims to the papacy in favour of Nicholas V., who on the death of Eugenius had been elected at Rome. Died in 1451.

Amadeus IX., a son of Louis, Duke of Savoy, and a grandson of the preceding, was born at Thonon in 1435, and began to reign in 1465. He married Yolande, a daughter of Charles VII. of France. Died in 1472, and was succeeded by his son Philibert.

Am′a-dis de Gaul or **Gau′la,** the hero of a famous romance of chivalry written in the thirteenth century by Vasco de Lobeira, a Portuguese. (See LOBEIRA.) "The Amadis," says Ticknor, "is admitted by general consent to be the best of all the old romances of chivalry."
See TICKNOR, "Spanish Literature," vol. i. chap. xi. p. 221 et seq.

Amador Rebello, â-mâ-doR′ rà-bel′lo, a Portuguese Jesuit and writer, born in 1539 ; died at Lisbon in 1622.

Amaduzzi, â-mâ-doot′see, [in Latin, AMADU′TIUS,] (GIOVANNI CRISTOFORO,) a learned Italian writer, born near Rimini in 1740, was professor of Greek in Rome. He published "Anecdota Literaria," (3 vols., 1774,) and other works. Died in 1792.

Amaia. See AMAYA.

Amak Bokhâree, (or Bokhârî,) âm′âk bo-kâ′ree, (i.e. "Amak the Bokharian,") written also **Amac** and **Amik,** a Persian poet, whose life was nearly coextensive with the eleventh century.

A-mal′ar-ic, [Lat. AMALARI′CUS,] the last king of the Visigoths that reigned in Spain, was a son of Alaric II., who died in 507 A.D. He married Clotilde, a daughter of Clovis, King of the Franks. He was killed during a war against the Franks, in 531 A.D.

Am-a-lā′rĭ-us For-tu-nā′tus, an archbishop of Treves, who was sent by Charlemagne, in 811 A.D., to diffuse Christianity among the Saxons. He established the first church at Hamburg. In 813 he went as ambassador to Constantinople. Died in 814 A.D.

Am′a-lek, [Heb. קֵלָמֲע,] a king of the Amalekites, who opposed the Israelites on their flight from Egypt. He was defeated at the battle of Rephidim. (See Exodus xvii. 8–14 ; Deuteronomy xxv. 17.)

Amalfi. See AVALOS, (COSTANZA.)

Amalie, â-mâ′le-eh, or **Ame′lia,** (ANNA,) Princess of Prussia, and sister of Frederick the Great, was born in 1723. She had a remarkable talent for music, to which she devoted her life. Her musical library was the finest and most complete ever collected. Died in 1787.

Amalie, or **Amelia,** (ANNA,) Duchess of Saxe-Weimar and Eisenach, a daughter of the Duke of Brunswick-Wolfenbüttel, born in 1739, was distinguished as a patron of genius and learning. She assembled at her court the brightest ornaments of German literature, among others Wieland, Herder, Goethe, etc. She was mother of the duke Karl August. Died in 1807.
See BROCKHAUS, "Conversations-Lexikon."

Amalie, (CATHERINE,) a German poetess, born in 1640, married the Count George Lewis (Georg Ludwig) of Erbach. Died in 1696.

Amalie or **Amelia,** (ELISABETH,) a grand-daughter of William I., Prince of Orange, was born in 1602, and in 1619 married William V., Landgrave of Hesse-Cassel. After his death, in 1637, she was made regent, in which capacity she displayed extraordinary energy, wisdom, and virtue. Died in 1651.
See K. W. JUSTI, "Amalie Elisabeth Landgräfin von Hessen."

Amalie or **Amelia,** (MARIE FRIEDERIKE AUGUSTE,) Duchess of Saxony, born in 1794, was a sister of Frederick Augustus II. She cultivated poetry and music, and wrote in German successful dramas, among which are "Falsehood and Truth," "The Marriage-Ring," "Cousin Henry," and "The Young Lady from the Country."
See article by Professor FELTON, in the "North American Review," vol. lii., and "Social Life in Germany, illustrated in the acted Dramas of the Princess Amelia," etc., translated from the German by Mrs. JAMESON.

Amalric OF JERUSALEM. See AMAURY.

Amalric, ằ′mâl′rèk′, (ARNAUD,) a French ecclesiastic of the thirteenth century, distinguished by the energy and sanguinary cruelty which he displayed against the heretics of Languedoc, commonly known as the Albigenses. He was made Archbishop of Narbonne in 1212, and soon after assumed the title of Duke of Narbonne. Died in 1225.

Amalricus. See AMALRIC and AMAURY.

Am-al-a-son′tha, written also **Amalasonte,** [Lat. AMALASUEN′TA,] Queen of the Goths in Italy, distinguished for her wisdom, was a daughter of Theodoric I. She began to reign in 526 A.D., as guardian of her son, who was a minor. The famous Cassiodorus was her prime minister. She was assassinated in 535.
See J. D. RITTER, "Dissertatio de Amalasuenta," 1735.

Amalteo, â-mâl-tā′o, [Lat. AMALTHE′US ; Fr. AMALTHÉE, ằ′mâl′tằ′,] (CORNELIO,) an Italian poet, born at Oderzo about 1530. His profession was medicine. He wrote Latin poems, the best of which is entitled "Proteus," (1572.) Died in 1603.

Amalteo, (FRANCESCO,) the father of the preceding, was born towards the close of the fifteenth century. He taught literature in several cities of Italy, and had some reputation as a writer of Latin verse. He had three sons, who were poets.

Amalteo, (GIOVANNI BATTISTA) an excellent Latin poet, a son of Francesco, noticed above, born at Oderzo in 1525, became secretary to the republic of Ragusa. He wrote Latin eclogues, elegies, and epigrams, and verses in Greek and Italian. His Latin poems are considered equal in elegance to those of any poet of his time. Died in Rome in 1573, soon after he had become secretary to Pope Pius VII. He is regarded as the most eminent poet of all his family.

Amalteo, (GIROLAMO,) a brother of the preceding, born at Oderzo in 1506, was a physician, philosopher, and celebrated Latin poet. He practised medicine with great success at several places. His reputation is founded on two Latin epigrams, entitled "De Gemellis Luscis," ("On the One Eyed Twins,") and "Horologium Pulvereum," ("Hour-Glass,") the former of which has been translated into many languages. Died in 1574.

Amalteo, (GIROLAMO,) a brother and pupil of Pomponio, noticed below, was a historical painter of distinguished ability. His chief works are small pictures, highly finished. He died at an early age.

See ALTAN, "Memorie intorno alla Vita di Pomponio Amalteo;" LANZI, "History of Painting in Italy."

Amalteo, [Lat. AMALTHEUS,] (PAOLO, or PAUL,) an Italian poet, born at Pordenone in 1460, was a brother of Francesco, noticed above. Died in 1517.

Amalteo, (POMPONIO,) an eminent painter of the Venetian school, was born in Friuli in 1505. He was a pupil of Pordenone, whose style he imitated, though with less grandeur of invention. His colouring is brilliant, and his drawing correct. Among his master-pieces are "The Judgment of Solomon," and "The Judgment of Daniel."

Am-al-the'a or **Am-al-thei'a**, [Gr. Ἀμάλθεια; Fr. AMALTHÉE, ä'mäl'tä',] in Greek mythology, the name of the nurse of Jupiter. According to one tradition, she was a goat, whose horn Jupiter broke off and filled with herbs, fruits, flowers, etc., and endowed it with the property of supplying whatever its possessor might desire. This was the origin of the fable of the Cornucopiæ, or "horn of plenty."

Amalthée, the French of AMALTEO, which see.

Amaltheus. See AMALTEO.

Amama, ä-mä'mä, (SIXTI'NUS,) a Dutch Protestant and biblical philologist, born at Franeker in 1593. He was professor of Oriental languages at that city from 1618 until his death, and declined the chair vacated by Erpenius at Leyden. He was the author of a critical work on the historical books of the Old Testament, and a number of Latin treatises. Died in 1629.

Aman, ä'män, (JOHANN,) a German architect, born in Baden in 1765. He designed several public buildings in Austria and other countries. Died about 1834.

Amand, ä'mòn', SAINT, [Lat. SANC'TUS AMAN'DUS,] a bishop of Bordeaux in the fifth century, eminent for his piety and purity of life.

Amand or **Amandus**, SAINT, a French ecclesiastic, born about 590. He was a man of eminent virtues. Died in 679 A.D.

Amand, (JACQUES,) a French engraver, born near Blois in 1730; died in Paris in 1769.

Amand, (PIERRE,) a French surgeon and writer on obstetrics, born at Riez about 1650; died in 1720.

Amanieu des Escas, ä'mä'ne-uh' dä'zès'kä', a troubadour, who flourished in the latter half of the thirteenth century. He passed a part of his life at the court of James II. of Aragon.

Amanton or **Amanthon**, ä'mòn'tòn', (CLAUDE NICOLAS,) a judge at Dijon, in France, and a writer on biography and local history, born in 1760; died in 1835.

Amar, ä'mäR', (ANDRÉ,) (or **Amar**, J. P., according to the "Biographie Universelle,") a French demagogue, born at Grenoble in 1750, was notorious for his cruelty in the reign of terror. He was elected to the Convention in 1792, voted for the death of the king, and became chairman of the committee of *sureté générale* in September, 1793. In October he wrote and presented to the Convention a report which condemned the twenty-two Girondins arrested in June and ordered the arrest of seventy-three other deputies. He acted with the enemies of Robespierre on the 9th of Thermidor, 1794, and defended Barrère, Collot d'Herbois, and Billaud-Varennes in 1795. Died in Paris in 1816.

Amar (or **Amare**) **du Rivier**, ä'mäR' dü re've-å', (JEAN AUGUSTIN,) often called simply **Amar** or **Amare**, an able French critic and miscellaneous writer, born in Paris in 1765. He became conservator of the Mazarin Library in 1809. He made translations of many of the

ancient classics, published several school-books, and wrote many articles for the "Biographie Universelle." Died in 1837.

Amaral, ä-mä-räl', (ANDRES DO,) a Portuguese, who became chancellor of the order of Saint John of Jerusalem while that order had possession of the island of Rhodes. He was defeated as a candidate for the office of grand master in 1521. During the siege of Rhodes by the Turks in 1522 he was put to death on a charge of giving intelligence to the enemy.

See VERTOT, "Histoire des Chevaliers Hospitaliers de St. Jean;' FONTANUS, "De Bello Rhodico," 1524.

Amaral, (ANTONIO Caetano, kä-ä-tä'no) DO,) a Portuguese writer, born at Lisbon in 1747. He wrote a very valuable work on the early history of Portugal, entitled "Memorias sobre a Forma do Governo e Costumes," etc. Died in 1819.

Am'ä-rä Singhä or **Sinha**, äm'ä-ra sing'ha, [modern Hindoo pron. ŭm'ŭr-a sing'ha,] a celebrated Hindoo poet and grammarian, who is supposed to have flourished in the first century B.C. He belonged to the Booddhist sect. His works were all destroyed by the Brahmans, except a vocabulary of the Sanscrit language, entitled "Amara Kosha," which is esteemed a standard work.

Amari, ä-mä'ree, (EMERICO,) an Italian political economist, born at Palermo in 1810. He became professor of law at Palermo in 1841.

Amari, (MICHELE,) an Italian historian, born at Palermo in 1806. His father was condemned to an imprisonment of thirty years for a conspiracy against the government. He published in 1842 his principal work, "The War of the Sicilian Vespers," ("La Guerra del Vespro Siciliano," 2 vols.,) which had great success, but was prohibited by the government. The author was summoned to trial, but escaped to France. He took an active part in the revolution of Sicily in 1848, and was appointed minister of finances in the new government. He resigned office before the end of the year. He has since resided in Paris, and published the first volume of a "History of the Mussulmans in Sicily."

Amariton, ä'mä're'tòn', (JEAN,) a French jurist, born in Auvergne; died in 1590.

Am'a-sa, [אֲמָשָׂא,] a Hebrew warrior, who was appointed by Absalom, when he rebelled, captain of the host instead of Joab. After the suppression of this rebellion he became commander of the army of David, and was treacherously slain by Joab. (See II. Samuel xvii. 25; xx. 4–10.)

Amaseo, ä-mä-sä'o, [Lat. AMASÆ'US,] (POMPILIO,) an Italian scholar, was a son of Romolo, noticed below. Died about 1584.

Amaseo, (ROMOLO,) a celebrated Italian scholar and orator, born at Udine in 1489; died about 1552. He was professor of belles-lettres (literæ humaniores) at Padua, Bologna, and Rome. Among his works may be mentioned a Latin version of Pausanias, (1547,) and a Latin version of Xenophon's "Anabasis," (1533.)

A-mä'sis, [Gr. Ἄμασις,] a celebrated king of Egypt, succeeded Apries about 570 B.C. He is said to have been a man of liberal and independent spirit, and free from the prejudices against foreigners which were common among the Egyptians. His reign was prosperous and peaceful. He built the grand temple of Isis at Memphis, and adorned Egypt with many magnificent monuments. Died about 525 B.C., leaving the throne to his son Psammenitus, (or Psammetichus.)

A-mas'tris, a Persian lady of superior talents, and a niece of Darius Codomannus. She was married successively to Craterus, to Dionysius, tyrant of Heraclea, and to Lysimachus, King of Thrace.

Amat, ä-mät', (FELIX,) an eminent Spanish ecclesiastic and writer, born at Sabadell, near Barcelona, in 1750. He became Archbishop of Palmyra *in partibus infidelium* in 1803, and confessor to Charles IV. in 1806. He was supposed to be favourable to the French during the war which began in 1808. His great work is an ecclesiastical history, entitled "Treatise on the Church of Jesus Christ," ("Tratado de la Iglesia de Jesu Cristo," 12 vols., 1793–1803.) Died in 1824.

See FELIX TORRES AMAT, "Vida de Amat Arzobispo de Palmyra," 1835.

ā, ē, ī, ō, ū, ȳ, *long;* ȧ, ė, ȯ, same, less prolonged; ă, ĕ, ĭ, ŏ, ŭ, ȳ, *short;* ạ, ẹ, ị, ọ, *obscure;* fär, fȧll, fȧt; mēt; nŏt; gŏŏd; mōōn;

Amati, â-mä′tee, (ANDREA,) a celebrated maker of violins, worked at Cremona in partnership with his brother Niccolò about 1550. Their instruments are highly prized at the present time.

Amati. (ANTONIO,) a son of the preceding, born at Cremona about 1565, followed the same business with success. He made for Henry IV. of France, in 1595, a violin, which is said to be now in good order.

Amati, (CARLO,) an eminent Italian architect, born at Milan about 1786. Among his chief works is the Rotunda of San Carlo, at Milan.

Amati, (GIROLAMO,) a distinguished Italian scholar and antiquary, born at Savignano in 1768. He was an assistant librarian in the Vatican, and was regarded as an oracle among antiquaries. He wrote papers on the antiquities of philology and art for the "Giornale Arcadico," and furnished materials for the works of other authors. His sagacity in palæographical science was remarkable. Died in 1834.

Amati, (PASQUALE,) an Italian antiquary, born at Savignano in 1716; died in 1796.

Amatius, a-mä′she-us, (CAIUS,) a famous impostor, who made his appearance at Rome about 45 B.C., claiming to be the grandson of Marius. He was strangled by order of Antony about 43 or 44 B.C.

Amato. See AMATUS.

Amato, d′, dä-mä′to, or **Amati,** â-mä′tee, [Lat. AMA′TUS,] (ELIA,) a literary Italian monk, born at Montalto in 1666. He wrote on various subjects, and displayed a talent for dry humour. Died in 1747.

Amato, d′, (GIOVANNI ANTONIO,) a celebrated historical painter, called "Il Vecchio," ("The Elder,") was born at Naples in 1475. His style resembles that of Perugino in simplicity. He painted religious subjects exclusively, and was also noted as a theologian. Among his master-pieces are a "Dispute on the Sacrament," at Naples, and a "Madonna and Child." He painted in oil and fresco. Died in 1555.

Amato, d′, (GIOVANNI ANTONIO,) a nephew and pupil of the preceding, surnamed IL GIOVANE, (*i.e.* "the younger,") born at Naples in 1535, was a skilful painter. He excelled in colouring, and painted some works which are said to be as finely coloured as those of Titian. His chief work is an altar-piece of the infant Christ, in a church of Naples. Died in 1598.

See DOMINICI, "Vite de' Pittori Napolitani."

Amato, d′, (MICHELE,) an Italian theologian, born at Naples in 1682; died in 1729.

Amato or **A-ma′tus,** (SCIPIO,) an Italian jurist and linguist, flourished between 1600 and 1650.

Amato or **Amati,** [Lat. AMA′TUS,] (VINCENZO,) a Sicilian musician and composer, born in 1629; died in 1670.

Amatrice, dell′, dĕl lä-mä-tREe′chä, (CO′LA,) a Neapolitan architect and painter, who flourished in the early part of the sixteenth century. He worked at Ascoli. His master-piece is a picture of the "Last Supper."

See LANZI, "History of Painting in Italy."

Am-a′tus Lu-sĭ-ta′nus, [Port. JOÃO RODRIGUEZ AMATO, zho-ŏwn′ ro-dREe′ğĕz â-mä′to; Lat. JOAN′NES RODERI′CUS AMA′TUS,] an eminent Portuguese physician and anatomist, born at Castel-Branco in 1511. He lectured in Venice, and practised at Ancona. In 1555 the fear of the Inquisition, which persecuted him as a Jew, induced him to retire to Saloniki, where he joined a synagogue. Died in 1568. He is said to have been the second author who has described the valves in veins. He left, besides other works, one giving an account of seven hundred remarkable cases in medicine and surgery, (1551-66,) which was highly esteemed.

See SPRENGEL, "Biographie Médicale."

Amaury. See AMALRIC.

A-mau′rў, [Fr. pron. ä′mô′re′,] **Aimery,** ä′mĕh-re, [Fr. pron. ĕm′re′,] or **Am-al′ric,** [Ger. AMALRICH, ä′mäl-rik′; Lat. AMALRI′CUS,] **I.,** King of Jerusalem, born in 1135, was a son of Baldwin II. He succeeded his brother Baldwin III. in 1162. He invaded Egypt in 1168, and marched victoriously to Cairo, but was driven out by an army of Turks under Saladin, who invaded the kingdom of Amaury in 1170. The latter defended

his dominions with ability and courage, but with ill success, until his death in 1173, and left the throne to his son, Baldwin IV.

Amaury II. OF JERUSALEM (otherwise called **Amaury de Lusignan**—dęh lü′zĕn′yŏN′) inherited Cyprus from his brother Guy, and received the title of King of Jerusalem in 1194. He was unable to defend the kingdom against the Saracens, and died at Ptolemais in 1205.

Amaury, Amalric, or **Aimeric,** [Lat. AMALRI′CUS,] Patriarch of Jerusalem, succeeded Fulcher in 1159. He contributed much to the election of Amaury I. as King of Jerusalem. Died in 1180.

Amaury, ä′mô′re′, [Lat. AMALRI′CUS,] OF CHARTRES, a French theologian of the twelfth century. He advanced heterodox opinions on the Divine nature (which he identified with the primary matter of Aristotle) in a work called "Physion," now lost. Died about 1205.

Amaury-Duval. See DUVAL.

Amaya, â-mī′ä, a Spanish painter, a pupil of Vincenzo Carducci,. lived about 1682.

Amaya or **Amaia,** (FRANCISCO,) a noted Spanish jurisconsult of the seventeenth century, born at Antequera. He published "Observationes Juris," (1625,) and other works.

Am-a-zī′ah, [Heb. אמציה,] a king of Judah, who ascended the throne 849 B.C. He was killed by a conspiracy, 820 B.C. (See II. Kings xiv.; II. Chronicles xxv.)

Am′a-zons, [Gr. Ἀμαζόνες; Lat. AMAZ′ONES,] the name of a semi-fabulous race of female warriors, supposed to have lived originally on the Thermodon in Pontus, and to have made conquests in Asia Minor and Thrace. During the Trojan war, led by their queen, Penthisile′a, they fought against the Greeks. The battles of the Amazons were favourite subjects of the ancient Greek artists.

See "Encyclopædia Britannica."

Amberger, äm′bĕRğ′er, (CHRISTOPH,) a celebrated German painter, born at Nuremberg about 1490, is supposed to have been a pupil of Hans Holbein. He worked in oil, fresco, and distemper, excelled in perspective, and designed well. The history of Joseph, in twelve pictures, is called his best work. He was patronized by Charles V., of whom he painted a good portrait at Augsburg in 1530. Died at Augsburg about 1570.

Am-bĭ-gā′tus, [Fr. AMBIGAT, ŏN′be′gä′,] an ancient and powerful king of Gaul, supposed to have reigned about 600 or 650 B.C.

Ambillon. See BOUCHET, (RENÉ.)

Am′bĭ-o-rix or **Am-bi′o-rix,** written also **Abriorix** and **Ambriorix,** a king of the Eburones, a Belgic nation, in the time of Julius Cæsar. By stratagem or treachery he succeeded in destroying the army commanded by Cæsar's legates Sabinus and Cotta, 54 B.C.

See CÆSAR, "De Bello Gallico," lib. v.

Ambiveri, äm-be-vä′ree, (FRANCESCO,) an Italian writer, born at Bergamo about 1592; died in 1627.

Am-biv′ĭ-us, (LUCIUS TURPIO,) a famous Roman actor, lived about 175 B.C.

Amblimont, d′, dŏN′ble′mŏN′, (**Fuschemberg,** fü′-shŏN′baiR′,) COUNT, a French naval officer, and writer on naval tactics, was killed in battle in 1796.

Ambly, d′, dŏN′ble′, (CLAUDE JEAN ANTOINE,) a French marquis and field-marshal, born in Champagne in 1711. He emigrated in 1792, and served in the army of the Prince of Condé, after he had been a royalist member of the States-General. Died at Hamburg in 1797.

Ambodik, äm′bo-dik, (NESTOR MAXIMOVITCH,) an eminent Russian physician and accoucheur, born in the province of Pultava in 1740. Died in 1812. He is said to have been the first who wrote on medical subjects in the Russian language. He practised in Saint Petersburg, and published many translations and compilations.

Amboise, (BUSSY D′.) See BUSSY D'AMBOISE.

Amboise, d′, dŏN′bwäz′, (FRANÇOIS,) a French advocate and scholar, born in Paris about 1550; died in 1620. He is chiefly known as the editor of the works of Abelard, (1616.)

Amboise, d′, (GEORGE,) commonly known as CAR-

DINAL D'AMBOISE, a French statesman, born of a noble family at Chaumont-sur-Loire in 1460. He became Archbishop of Rouen in 1493, and prime minister of Louis XII. of France at his accession in 1498, before which he had been his faithful partisan or friend. He displayed great talents for administration, made reforms in legislation and finance, and left the reputation of a wise and virtuous minister. He remained in power until his death in 1510. He was surnamed the "Father of the People."

See LEGENDRE, "Vie du Cardinal D'Amboise," 1726.

Amboise, d', (JACQUES,) [Lat. JACO′BUS AMBOSIA′-NUS,] a French surgeon, brother of François, noticed above, born near the middle of the sixteenth century. His father Jean was surgeon to Henry II., Charles IX., and Henry III. Jacques became in 1594 rector of the university, which he restored to a flourishing condition. Died in 1606.

Ambra, d', dăm′brä, (FRANCESCO,) a distinguished Italian comic poet, born at Florence in the early part of the sixteenth century; died in 1558. His chief works are three comedies, "Il Furto," in prose, (1560,) "La Cofanaria," in verse, (1561,) and "J. Bernardi," in verse, (1563.)

See GINGUENÉ, "Histoire Littéraire d'Italie;" MAZZUCHELLI, "Scrittori d'Italia."

Ambrogi, äm-bRo′jee, (ANTON MARIA,) an Italian Jesuit, born at Florence in 1713. He was professor of rhetoric and poetry at the Collegio Romano, and enjoyed a great reputation as teacher. Died in 1788. His principal work is a translation of Virgil's works into Italian verse, (4 vols., 1758–62.)

Ambrogi, degli, dăl′yee äm-bRo′jee, (DOMENICO,) a skilful Italian painter of the seventeenth century, born at Bologna, was a pupil of Denis Calvart and of Francesco Brizio. He painted landscapes and other works, in oil and fresco, at Bologna. He is said to have had great facility in composition.

Ambrogio, äm-bRo′jo, (GIOVANNI,) a Florentine painter and sculptor, who flourished in the fourteenth century.

Ambrogio or **Ambrosio,** äm-bRo′se-o, (TESEO,) a distinguished Italian Oriental scholar, born at Pavi′a in 1469, became a regular canon of San Giovanni di Laterano at Rome. He was professor of Syriac and Chaldee at Bologna. His principal work is an "Introduction to the Chaldee, Syriac, Armenian, and ten other Languages," (1539.) Died in 1540.

See TIRABOSCHI, "Storia della Letteratura Italiana."

Amboise de Lombez, ŏN′bRwâz′ deh lŏN′bà′, or **de La Peirie,** (deh lä pà′re′,) a French devotional writer, born at Lombez in 1708; died in 1778.

Ambrose, SAINT, sent äm′brŏz, [Lat. SANC′TUS AM-BRO′SIUS ; Fr. SAINT-AMBROISE, săN′tŏN′bRwâz′,] one of the Latin Fathers, was born in Gaul, at Treves, it is supposed, about 340 A.D. His father, a Roman noble, was then prætorian prefect of Gaul. Ambrose was Governor of Liguria (a province of which Milan was the capital) in 374, when Auxentius, the Arian archbishop of Milan, died. In the attempt to elect a successor, the contest between the Catholics and the Arians was very fierce, and the presence of the governor was necessary to appease the tumult. He addressed them with such eloquence and power that the assembled people declared, with one voice, "Ambrose shall be bishop." He accepted the office with great reluctance, but afterwards fulfilled its duties with unequalled ability, zeal, and disinterestedness. He sided with the Catholics, and used all his efforts and influence for the suppression of Arianism. In 390 the emperor Theodosius, incensed at the insolent disobedience of some of the people of Thessalonica, ordered an indiscriminate massacre of all the inhabitants. Ambrose was greatly shocked at this crime ; and when, shortly after, the emperor was about to enter the church at Milan, the archbishop sternly forbade him. Theodosius submitted, and, besides undergoing various other humiliations, was at last obliged to perform public penance. Ambrose died in 397. He left, besides other works, a treatise "De Officiis," on the duties of Christian ministers, which was highly esteemed, and expositions of

Scripture. He was the author of a method of singing known as the "Ambrosian Chant."

"His Letters," says Villemain, "evince a man who, amidst the turbulence and instability of the empire, never had a foible nor stain on his character, whose magnanimity was adequate to all trials, and who in a more auspicious period would have placed himself by his writings in the rank of the first orators and the most noble geniuses."

See PAULINUS, "Vita Ambrosii ;" GODEFROI HERMANT, "Vie de Saint-Ambroise," 1678; J. P. SILBERT, "Leben des heiligen Ambrosius," 1841; BARONIUS, "Annales :" "Saint-Ambroise ; sa Vie et extraits de ses écrits," Lille, 1852; "Nouvelle Biographie Générale ;" "Encyclopædia Britannica ;" VILLEMAIN, "Saint-Ambroise," Paris, 8vo, 1852.

Am′broše, (ISAAC,) an English nonconformist minister and writer, who died in 1664.

Ambrosini, äm-bRo-šee′nee, (BARTOLOMMEO,) a Bolognese physician and writer on botany, born in 1588. He wrote several botanical and medical treatises, and edited four volumes of the works of Aldrovandus on reptiles, quadrupeds, etc. Died in 1657.

Ambrosini, (GIACINTO,) a botanist, born in 1605, was a brother of the preceding, whom he succeeded as professor of botany at Bologna in 1657. He published the first volume of a botanical dictionary, entitled "Phytologia," etc., (1666.) Died in 1672.

Ambrosius, am-bro′she-us, (AURELIA′NUS,) a British chieftain, who lived in the fifth century, was a rival and the successor of Prince Vortigern, whom he defeated about 466. According to tradition, he fought with success against the Saxon invaders under Hengist about 485 A.D.

See PALSGRAVE, "Rise and Progress of the English Commonwealth ;" BEDA, "Chronicon."

Ambrosius OF CAMALDOLI, (kä-mäl-do′lee,) [Fr. AMBROISE LE CAMALDULE, ŏN′bRwäz′ leh kä′mäl′dül′ ; Lat. AMBRO′SIUS CAMALDULEN′SIS,] an Italian monk, born in the Romagna in 1378, became general of his order in 1431. Among his works is an account of an official visitation of nunneries and monasteries, entitled "Hodœporicon." Died in 1439.

Ambrosius or **Ambrose,** Archbishop of Moscow, distinguished for his learning, was born in 1708. Having removed an image of the Virgin, to which the people had resorted for protection from the plague, he was charged with sacrilege, and massacred by a mob, in 1771.

Ambrozy, äm-bRo′ze, (WENZEL BERNHARD,) [Ger. pron. wĕnt′sĕl bĕRn′haRt äm-bRot′se,] a Bohemian historical painter, born in 1723; died in 1806.

Ambühl or **Ambuehl,** äm′bül, (JOHANN LUDWIG,) a German school-teacher and poet, born in Switzerland, in the canton of Saint Gall, in 1750. He wrote novels and historical dramas, which were once popular, and among which was one entitled "Wilhelm Tell." Died in 1800.

Amédée. See AMADEUS.

Ameen- (Amîn- or Amyn-) **Ahmed-er-Râzee,** ä-meen′ äh′med-er-râ′zee, written also **-Ahmed-el-Râzy,** (or **-al-Râzî,**) a Persian geographer, who lived about the close of the seventeenth century.

Ameil, ä′măl′ or ä′mä′ye, (AUGUSTE,) BARON, a French general, born in Paris in 1775. He distinguished himself at the capture of Munich in 1804, and was wounded at Jena in 1806. In 1812 he served in Russia, and obtained the rank of general of brigade. He entered the service of Louis XVIII. in 1814, changed sides twice or oftener during the Hundred Days, and led a corps of Napoleon's cavalry at Waterloo in 1815. Died in exile in 1822.

Ameilhon, ä′mä′lŏN′, (HUBERT PASCAL,) a distinguished French scholar, born in Paris in 1730. He wrote a "History of the Commerce and Navigation of the Ancient Egyptians," (1766,) which caused him to be chosen a member of the Academy of Inscriptions. Having become a partisan of the Revolution, he was elected a member of the Commission of Monuments in 1793. He is said to have preserved from destruction 800,000 volumes which belonged to various libraries and had been confiscated. Ameilhon was librarian of the Arsenal from 1797 until 1811. He contributed many articles to the "Journal des Savants" and the "Journal de

ā, ē, ī, ō, ū, ȳ, *long;* ă, ĕ, ĭ, ŏ, ŭ, ў, *short;* a, e, i, o, *obscure;* fär, fàll, făt; mêt; nŏt; gōōd; mōōn;

Verdun," and some valuable antiquarian treatises to the Memoirs of the Institute. Died in Paris in 1811.

See QUÉRARD, "La France Littéraire;" DACIER, "Notice sur la Vie et les Ouvrages d'Ameilhon."

A-meï'no-clēs, ['Αμεινοκλῆς,] a Corinthian ship-builder, who lived about 700 B.C.

A-meïp'sĭ-as, or **A-mip'sĭ-as**, ['Αμειψίας,] a comic poet of Athens in the time of Aristophanes, over whom he won the first prize in a dramatic contest, with his Κωμασταί, 414 B.C.

Amel, ä'mĕl, (HANS,) an architect who lived in the first half of the fifteenth century. He designed the façade and steeple of Antwerp Cathedral.

Am'ĕl-gard', [Lat. AMELGAR'DUS,] a Flemish historian, who lived in the fifteenth century. He wrote Latin histories of the reigns of Charles VII. and Louis XI.

Amelia or **Amelie** OF GERMANY. See AMALIE.

A-me'lĭ-a, (or a-meel'ya,) an English princess, daughter of George III., was born in 1783. Her character is highly commended. Died in 1810.

Amelin, d', däm'lăN', (JEAN,) the earliest translator of Livy into the French language, was an officer in the army, and lived in the time of Henry II. He published a version of the "Third Decade" in 1559.

Ameline, ăm'lĕN', (CLAUDE,) a French priest, born in Paris in 1624, wrote on the Will, (1684.) Died in 1708.

A-me'lĭ-us or **A-me'rĭ-us**, an Eclectic philosopher, who was born in Italy and flourished in the last half of the third century. He was a disciple of Plotinus. His works have not come down to us.

A-me'lĭ-us, (MARTIN,) a distinguished professor of jurisprudence in the University of Freyburg, in Baden, was born in 1526. He contributed greatly to the introduction of the Protestant religion into Baden about 1556, and was chancellor of Baden for about thirty years. Died about 1590.

Amelot de la Houssaye, ăm'lo' dĕh lä hoo'sä', (ABRAHAM NICOLAS,) a French historical writer and translator, born at Orléans in 1634. He was secretary of embassy at Venice about 1670, and published a "History of the Government of Venice," (3 vols., 1705,) which had a high reputation. Among his other works are "Historical, Political, Critical, and Literary Memoirs," (2 vols., 1722.) He translated the "Prince" of Macchiavelli, (1683,) and the first six books of the "Annals" of Tacitus, (10 vols., 1690,) to which he added notes, historical and political. The last six volumes were translated by Bruys. "His translations with political notes," says Voltaire, "and his histories are very good; his memoirs, very faulty. He is the first writer who has made the government of Venice known." Died in Paris in 1706.

See MORÉRI, "Dictionnaire historique;" QUÉRARD, "La France Littéraire."

Amelotte or **Amelote**, ăm'lot', (DENYS,) a French priest and ecclesiastical writer, born at Saintes in 1606; died in 1678. He made a version of the New Testament which was circulated by Louis XIV. and often reprinted.

Amelunghi, ä-mä-loon'gee, (GIROLAMO,) a burlesque poet of Pisa in the sixteenth century. He wrote a poem called "The War of the Giants," ("La Gigantea," 1566,) one of the first productions of a kind in which the Italians have excelled.

Amendola, ä-mĕn'do-lä, (FERRANTE,) a historical painter of Naples, born in 1664; died in 1724. His chief merit was in colouring. He failed in his effort to imitate Luca Giordano.

Am-e-no'phis or **Am-me-no'phis**, [Gr. Ἀμενῶφις,] the name of several of the early kings of Egypt.

Amenophis I., a powerful king of Egypt of the eighteenth dynasty, ascended the throne about 1778 B.C.

Amenophis II. of Egypt, is reckoned as the seventh Pharaoh of the eighteenth dynasty. He is identified by some authorities with the Memnon of the Greeks, whose statue was one of the seven wonders of the world.

Amenophis III., a famous king of Egypt, a grandson of the preceding, is supposed to have built the palace or temple of Luxor. His conquests are recorded on the obelisk which now stands near the Louvre in Paris.

Amenta, ä-mĕn'tä, (NICCOLÒ,) an Italian poet, lawyer, and philologist, born at Naples in 1659. He composed popular comedies, among which are "Constanza," "Il Forca," "La Fante," and "La Carlotta." His observations on the Italian language, "Della Lingua nobile d'Italia," (1723,) are commended. He wrote the Tuscan language with purity. Died in 1719.

See TIPALDO, "Biografia degli Italiani illustri."

Amerbach, ä'mĕr-bäK', (BASIL,) a jurist, born at Bâle in 1534, was a son of Boniface, noticed below, whom he succeeded as professor. He left some manuscript works on law. Died in 1591.

Amerbach, (BONIFACE,) an eminent scholar, born at Bâle in 1495, was a son of Johann, noticed below. He taught civil law at the University of Bâle for twenty years, and was an intimate friend of Erasmus, who appointed him his residuary legatee. He wrote but little. With the aid of his brothers Basil and Bruno, he corrected an edition of Saint Jerome, (1516-26.) Died in 1562. His Latin style was remarkably good.

See MELCHIOR ADAM, "Vitæ Germanorum Jurisconsultorum."

Amerbach, ä'mĕr-bäK', (JOHANN,) an eminent German printer, born in Suabia. He settled at Bâle about 1480. His principal publications are editions of Saint Ambrose, and of Saint Augustine, (1506,) which was printed in a new kind of type, called Saint Augustin. Died about 1520.

Amerbach, (VITUS.) See AMERPACH.

Amerighi. See CARAVAGGIO.

Amerigo Vespucci or **Americus Vespucius**. See VESPUCCI.

Amerling, ä'mĕr-ling', (FRIEDRICH,) a German painter of high reputation, born in Vienna in 1803. He studied with Horace Vernet in Paris, and visited Italy. He is considered to be eminently successful in portraits. Among his works are "Djdo deserted by Æneas," "Moses in the Desert," and a portrait of the emperor Francis I.

Amerpach, ä'mĕr-päK', (VITUS or VEIT,) [Lat. VI'TUS AMERPA'CHIUS,] a distinguished German scholar, born at Wendingen, in Bavaria, about the close of the fifteenth century, studied at Wittenberg, and was for several years professor of philosophy at Ingolstadt. He wrote, besides other Latin works, one "On the Soul," ("De Anima," 1542,) and "Six Books of Natural Philosophy," (1548.) He also translated some of the speeches of Demosthenes and Isocrates, and wrote commentaries on Cicero and on Horace's "Art of Poetry." Died in 1557.

Amersfoordt, ä'mĕrs-fōRt', or **Amersvoordt**, (JACOB,) an eminent Oriental scholar, born at Amsterdam in 1786; died in 1824. He left "A Discourse on the Popularity of the Christian Religion, or its Adaptation to the Popular Mind," ("Oratio de Religionis Christianæ Popularitate," 1818.)

See J. W. DE CRANE, "Vie d'Amersvoordt," 1824.

Amersfoort, van, văn ä'mĕrs-fōRt', (EVERT,) a Dutch painter, lived in the first part of the seventeenth century.

Ames, āmz, (EDWARD,) a bishop of the Methodist Episcopal Church, born at Athens, in Ohio, in 1806. He was educated at the Ohio University, licensed to preach in 1830, and made a bishop in 1852. Since 1861 he has resided at Baltimore.

Ames, (FISHER,) a celebrated American orator and statesman, born in Dedham, Massachusetts, on the 9th of April, 1758. His father and grandfather were physicians. The former died when Fisher was only six years old. His mother, perceiving the promise of her son, resolved to give him a classical education, and at the age of twelve he was sent to Harvard College. At the preliminary examination he was pronounced a boy of uncommon attainments. He graduated in 1774, but, in consequence of his extreme youth and the straitened circumstances of his family, it was several years before he entered upon his professional studies, the meantime being devoted to teaching and reading the ancient and modern classics. He became a student at law in the office of William Tudor of Boston, and commenced practice in his native town in 1781. Although too young to take an active part in the Revolutionary contest, he watched its progress with deep interest.

ɛ as *k*; ç as *s*; ḡ *hard*; ġ as *j*; G, H, K. *guttural*; N, *nasal*; R, *trilled*; š as *z*; ŧh as in *this*. (☞See Explanations, p. 23.)

He acquired distinction by several political essays which were published in the newspapers under the signature of Brutus and Camillus, and which gave proof of practical wisdom, as well as literary merit, of a high order. They procured his election to the convention which met in Massachusetts in 1788 to ratify the Federal Constitution. In this convention he made, on the subject of biennial elections, a speech characterized by extraordinary eloquence and power. As a member of the legislature of Massachusetts, he was the principal promoter of a law which placed the common-school system of that State upon an improved basis. Having joined the Federal party, he was elected a member of Congress in 1789 by the voters of his native district, which included Boston. He continued to serve in Congress for eight years, during which he constantly supported the administration of Washington and took a prominent part in the debates on all important questions.

"He was," says Griswold, "the leader of the Federal party in the House of Representatives during the administration of Washington, and was applauded for his eloquence and learning, the solidity of his judgment, and the unsullied purity of his public and private conduct."

On the 28th of April, 1796, he supported Jay's treaty with Great Britain in an eloquent and powerful speech, which has been preserved. At the close of this speech, a member of the opposition moved to postpone the subject, on the ground that the House was in a state of too great excitement to come to a just decision. The health of Ames had been for some time very delicate and declining, and on the retirement of Washington, about the end of 1796, he returned to his farm in Dedham. He had married in 1792 Frances Worthington, of Springfield. In 1798 he wrote "Laocoon" and other essays, to arouse the Federalists to a more vigorous opposition to the aggressions of France. On the death of Washington, December, 1799, he pronounced his eulogy before the legislature of Massachusetts. He was elected president of Harvard College in 1804, but he declined the honour, chiefly on account of ill health. He died on the 4th of July, 1808, leaving several sons, of whom one, Nathaniel, acquired some reputation as an author.

In the preparation of his speeches, Fisher Ames did little more, it is said, than draw the outlines, depending for the language, illustrations, and modes of appeal, upon his mental resources at the time of speaking. He was equally distinguished for his delicate wit and brilliant imagination; and his colloquial gifts were considered by his acquaintances not less remarkable than his powers as an orator. His disposition was amiable, and his character without reproach. In person he was of medium height and well proportioned. His letters and other writings were published by his son, Seth Ames, in 2 vols., 1854.

See Dr. J. T. Kirkland's "Memoir of F. Ames," prefixed to his Works, 1854; Griswold's "Prose Writers of America;" also, Parker's "Golden Age of American Oratory," Boston, 1857.

Ames, āmz, (Joseph,) a British naval officer, born in 1619, distinguished himself in a battle against the Dutch in July, 1653. Died in 1695.

Ames, (Joseph,) F.R.S., an English antiquary, born at Yarmouth in 1689. In 1749 he published "Typographical Antiquities : being an Historical Account of Printing in England, with some Memoirs of our Ancient Printers, and a Register of the Books printed by them." An improved edition was published by W. Herbert in 3 vols., 1785–90; and another by Dr. T. F. Dibdin in 1810–19. Died in 1759.

See Gough, "Memoirs of Joseph Ames," prefixed to the "Typographical Antiquities."

Ames, (Nathan P.,) an American machinist and manufacturer of fire-arms, ordnance, and cutlery, born in 1803. He owned extensive works at Chicopee Falls and Cabotville, Massachusetts, and was distinguished as an inventor. Died in 1847.

Ames, (Nathaniel,) a son of Fisher Ames, was the author of several sea-sketches. Died in 1835.

Ames, (William,) D.D., a learned English Puritan divine, born in Norfolk county in 1576. He emigrated to Holland about 1612, and was professor of theology at Franeker for twelve years. He attended the Synod of Dort in 1618. Among his works are "Marrow of Theology," ("Medulla Theologiæ," 1623,) and a book on practical theology, entitled "On the Conscience and its Authority," ("De Conscientia et ejus Jure vel Casibus," 1630,) which had a high reputation even in foreign countries. Died at Rotterdam in 1633.

See Brook's "Lives of the Puritans."

Amestris. See Amastris.

Amfreville, dʹ, dôNʹfr-vĕlʹ, Marquis, a brave French naval officer, commanded the vanguard at the battle of La Hogue in 1692. He obtained the rank of lieutenant-general of the naval armies, and died at an advanced age. Two of his brothers were also distinguished naval captains.

See Quincy, "Histoire militaire de Louis le Grand."

Amherst, amʹẽrst, (Jeffery or Jeffrey,) usually called Lord Amherst, an English general, born at Riverhead, in Kent, in January, 1717. He entered the army in 1731, was aide-de-camp to Lord Ligonier at Fontenoy in 1741, and became a colonel in 1756. Having obtained the rank of major-general in 1758, he commanded at the capture of Cape Breton, and took Ticonderoga from the French in 1759. He performed an important part in the conquest of Canada in 1760, (see Wolfe, General,) after which he was commander-in-chief of the armies in America until 1763, when he was appointed Governor of Virginia. He was made lieutenant-general of the ordnance in 1772, received the title of Baron Amherst in 1776, and became commander-in-chief of the English army in 1778. This command was taken from him in 1782, and restored in 1793. He was superseded as commander-in-chief by the Duke of York in 1795, and was made a field-marshal in 1796. Died in 1797.

See "Gentleman's Magazine," September, 1797.

Amherst, (William Pitt,) Lord, an English diplomatist, born in 1773, was a nephew and heir of the preceding. He was sent as ambassador extraordinary to China in 1816, and arrived at Pekin, but, as he refused to submit to the degrading ceremonies which were the necessary conditions of admission to the Chinese court, his mission was so far a failure. An account of his journey to China was published by Clarke Abel. He was appointed Governor-General of India in 1823, received the title of earl in 1826, and was recalled to England the same year. Died in 1857.

Amhurst, amʹûrst, (Nicholas,) an English political and satirical writer, born at Marden, in Kent, about 1702. Having been expelled from a college of Oxford in 1719, he published, in 1721, a witty satire against that university, in a periodical entitled "Terræ Filius." He afterwards gained distinction as editor of "The Craftsman," a weekly political paper, (commenced about 1730,) which had a very large circulation, (ten or twelve thousand copies,) and in which Lord Bolingbroke and Pulteney were his coadjutors. He was neglected by his political friends when they obtained power in 1742, and died in the same year.

See Cibber, "Lives of the Poets."

Amici, ä-meeʹchee, (Giovanni Battista,) an Italian optician, astronomer, and natural philosopher, born at Módena in 1784. He acquired skill in the construction of optical instruments, especially of mirrors for telescopes and lenses for microscopes. About 1827 he produced a dioptric or achromatic microscope which bears his name and is highly esteemed. At the death of L. Pons, (1835,) Amici was appointed director of the Observatory of Florence, where he gained a high reputation as an observer. He wrote memoirs on double stars, on the diameter of the sun, etc. Died in 1863.

Amici, (Tommaso,) an Italian sculptor of the fifteenth century, was living in 1495.

Amico, ä-meeʹko, (Antonino,) a Sicilian priest, historiographer to Philip IV. of Spain. Died in 1641. He wrote several works on the history and antiquities of Sicily.

Amico, (Bartolommeo,) an Italian Jesuit, born in Lucania in 1562, was professor of philosophy at Naples. He wrote a "Commentary on Aristotle," (7 vols., 1623–48.) Died in 1649.

ā, ē, ī, ō, ū, ȳ, *long;* ă, ĕ, ĭ, ŏ, ŭ, ў, *short;* ạ, ẹ, ị, ọ, *obscure;* fär, fäll, fät; mêt; nŏt; gōōd; mōōn;

Amico, (BERNARDINO,) an Italian monk, born at Gallipoli, near Taranto, passed several years at Jerusalem from 1596 to about 1600. He published at Rome, in 1609, descriptions and designs of sacred buildings in the Holy Land, entitled "Trattato delle Piante ed immagini dei sacri Edifici," etc. The designs were engraved by Callot.

Amico or **A-mi′cus,** (DIOMEDE,) an Italian medical writer, born at Piacenza, lived about 1600.

Amico, (FAUSTINO,) an Italian poet, born at Bassano in 1524. He gave promise of extraordinary talents, but died prematurely in 1558. Among his works is a beautiful Latin epistle to his friend Alessandro Campesano, (1564.) He wrote also Italian verses.

Amico, (FRANCESCO,) an Italian Jesuit and writer on theology, born at Cosenza in 1578; died in 1651.

Amico, (LORENZO,) an Italian monk and writer on philology and other subjects, born at Milazzo in 1633.

Amico, (LUIGI,) an Italian diplomatist, born at Asti in 1757; died in 1832.

Amico, (VITO MARIA,) a learned Sicilian historian and antiquary, born at Catania in 1693. He was for some time professor of philosophy at Catania. He published "Sicilia Sacra," (1733,) and "Catana Illustrata," (4 vols., 1741.) Died in 1762.

Amiconi, â-me-ko′nee, or **Amigoni,** â-me-go′nee, (OTTAVIO,) an Italian painter, born at Brescia in 1605; died in 1661.

Amidano, â-me-dâ′no, (POMPONIO,) an Italian painter, born at Parma in the sixteenth century, was one of the most eminent pupils of Parmegiano. His chief work is an altar-piece in the church of the Madonna del Quartiere at Parma, which is highly praised by Lanzi. Died, it is supposed, about 1600.

See LANZI, "History of Painting in Italy."

Amigoni, â-me-go′nee, or **Amiconi,** â-me-ko′nee, (JACOPO,) an Italian historical painter, whose success appears to have been greater than his merit, was born in Venice in 1675. He worked in London about ten years, (1729–39,) during which he painted many portraits. His style was admired by the purchasers of pictures more than by the critics. Among his works is the History of Judith. He was court painter at Madrid when he died in 1752.

See LANZI, "History of Painting in Italy."

Amik, â′mik or â′meek′, (OF BOKHÂRA,) a Persian poet of the twelfth century.

Amilcar. See HAMILCAR.

Amîn-Ahmed-el-Râzy, (or -al-Râzî.) See AMEEN-AHMED-ER-RÂZEE.

Amiot or **Amyot,** â′me-o′, (JOSEPH,) a French Jesuit and missionary, born at Toulon in 1718. He went to China in 1750, and was invited by the emperor to Pekin, where he remained forty-three years and made great proficiency in the Chinese language. No other writer of the eighteenth century has thrown so much light on the manners and history of the Chinese. He translated several Chinese works, wrote a "Letter on the Genius of the Chinese Language," (1773,) and compiled a Manchoo-Tartar-French Dictionary, (3 vols., Paris, 1789–90,) the first ever published. He was author of a large part of the collection entitled "Memoirs concerning the History, Sciences, Arts, and Customs of the Chinese," (16 vols., 1776–1814.) A life of Confucius by Amiot is included in these Memoirs. Died at Pekin in 1794.

See "Lettres édifiantes et curieuses," xxviii. 158; STAUNTON, "Miscellaneous Notices relating to China;" A. RÉMUSAT, "Recherches sur les Langues Tartares;" ERSCH und GRUBER, "Allgemeine Encyklopaedie."

Amipsias. See AMEIPSIAS.

Am′leth or **Ham′leth,** an ancient and perhaps fabulous prince of Jutland, whose story, as recorded by Saxo Grammaticus, is the foundation of Shakspeare's tragedy of "Hamlet." He is supposed to have lived before the Christian era.

Amling, âm′ling, (KARL GUSTAV,) a celebrated German designer and engraver, born at Nuremberg about 1650. He worked at Munich, was patronized by the elector Maximilian II., and excelled in portraits. He also engraved historical paintings, but with less success.

He was reputed the best German engraver of his time. Died in 1701.

Ammæus, âm-mâ′us, or **Van Amm,** vân âm, (DOMINIC,) a Dutch jurist, born at Leeuwarden in 1579, became professor of law at Jena in 1602. He wrote an important work on public or constitutional law, "Discursus de Jure publico," (1617–23.) Died in 1637.

Amman, written also **Ammann,** âm′mân, (JOHANN,) a German botanist and physician, born at Schaffhausen in 1707, graduated in medicine at Leyden in 1729. In 1733 he became professor of botany at Saint Petersburg, where he died in 1741 or 1742, leaving the first volume of an unfinished work on the plants of Russia, (1739.)

See SPRENGEL, "Geschichte des Botanik."

Amman, (JOHANN CONRAD,) a physician, native of Schaffhausen, who settled in Holland, where he gained a great and deserved reputation for teaching the deaf and dumb to speak. He wrote "Surdus Loquens," (1692.) Died probably about 1725.

Amman, (JOHANN JACOB,) a German surgeon, born at a little village on Lake Zurich in 1586. He published a book of Travels in the Levant, (3 vols., 1618.) Died at Zurich in 1658.

Amman or **Ammon,** âm′mon, (JOST, or JUSTUS,) a famous Swiss engraver and designer, born at Zurich about 1535. He became a citizen of Nuremberg about 1560, and probably passed there the rest of his life, of which little is known. He illustrated many books with his designs, which are exceedingly numerous. He engraved on wood and copper, and excelled in the art of grouping figures. His "Portraits of the Kings of France from Pharamond to Henry III." appeared in 1576. His wood-cuts are better than his copper-plates. Died in 1591.

See HEINECKEN, "Dictionnaire des Artistes;" STRUTT, "Dictionary of Engravers."

Amman or **Ammann,** (PAUL,) an eminent German botanist and physician, born at Breslau in 1634. He obtained a chair of botany at Leipsic in 1674, and a chair of physiology in 1682. He was addicted to paradox, and was a severe critic. Among his works may be mentioned his "Treatment of Deadly Wounds," ("Praxis Vulnerum lethalium," 1690;) and "Natural Character of Plants," ("Character naturalis Plantarum," 1676.) Died in 1691.

See HALLER, "Bibliotheca Botanica."

Ammanati, âm-mâ-nâ′tee, written also **Ammanato** and **Ammanate,** (BARTOLOMMEO,) a distinguished Italian sculptor and architect, born at Florence in 1511, was a pupil of Bandinelli and Sansovino. He imitated Michael Angelo in sculpture. He worked in Rome for Pope Julius III., adorned the Capitol with sculptures, and designed the court and façade of the Roman College. At Florence he constructed the noble bridge called Ponte della Trinità, (which is still standing,) finished the Pitti Palace, and erected several monuments. Among his chief works are three statues which adorn the tomb of Sannazar at Naples, and a colossal statue of Neptune at Florence. Died about 1590. He left a valuable work on public buildings, etc., entitled "The City," ("La Città.") His wife, LAURA BATTIFERRI, was celebrated as a poetess.

See VASARI, "Uomini illustri d'Italia;" CICOGNARA, "Storia di Scultura."

Ammanati, CARDINAL. See PICCOLOMINI.

Ammanati, (GIOVANNI,) an able Italian sculptor, worked at Orvieto from 1331 to 1355.

Ammanati, (LAURA Battiferri—bât-te-fêr′ree,) a distinguished Italian poetess, born at Urbino about 1520. She was married in 1550 to B. Ammanati, above noticed. Died in 1589.

Ammann. See AMMAN.

Ammâr-Ibn-Yâsir, âm-mâr′ Ib'n yâ′sir, a famous Arab and companion of Mohammed. He took part in the battle of the Camel, 658 A.D., and was killed at the battle of Sefayn, where he commanded the cavalry for Alee.

Am′men, (JACOB,) an American general, born in Virginia, graduated at West Point in 1831. He was afterwards professor of mathematics in several colleges in different parts of the United States. He was appointed brigadier-general of volunteers about July, 1862.

ɛ as k; ç as s; ḡ hard; ġ as j; G, H, K, guttural; N, nasal; R, trilled; ṡ as z; th as in this. (☞See Explanations, p. 23.)

8

Am-mĭ-ā′nus, [Ἀμμιανός,] a Greek poet, lived about 100–130 A.D., and wrote epigrams, many of which are found in the Greek Anthology.

Am-mĭ-ā′nus Mar-cel-lī′nus, [Fr. AMMIEN MAR-CELLIN, ă′me′ăN′ măR′să̤′lăN′,] a Roman historian of great merit, born of a Greek family at Antioch in the early part of the fourth century. He entered the army in his youth, took part in a campaign in the East in 350 A.D., and afterwards accompanied Julian in an expedition against Persia. Having retired from the army, he became a resident of Rome, where he wrote his history of the Roman Empire, in thirty-one books, of which the first thirteen are lost. The whole work comprised the period from 96 A.D. to 378 A.D. His fidelity and impartiality are highly commended by Gibbon and other critics. His style, however, is much inferior to the classic models of Roman prose. He died, it is supposed, about 395 A.D. It has been disputed whether he was a Christian or a heathen ; but there would seem to be little ground for doubting that he was a pagan.

See CLAUDE CHIFFLET, "De Ammiani Marcellini Vita ;" GIBBON, "Decline and Fall of the Roman Empire," chap. xxiii.

Ammien Marcellin. See AMMIANUS MARCELLINUS.

Ammirato, âm-me-rä′to, (SCIPIONE,) an Italian historian, born at Lecce, in Naples, in 1531. After various adventures in Venice, Rome, and Naples, he settled at Florence in 1569, and found a patron in the Grand Duke Cosmo, who commissioned him to write the history of Florence. He became a canon in the cathedral of Florence in 1595, and wrote a large number of works, among which is a "Discourse on Cornelius Tacitus," (1594.) His most important work is a "History of Florence," ("Istorie Fiorentine," 1st vol., 1600 ; 2d vol., 1641,) which is the most accurate and complete that has been written on that subject. The Academy Della Crusca styled him "the modern Livy." Died at Florence in 1601.

See DOMENICO DE ANGELIS, "Vita di Scipione Ammirato," 1706 ; TIRABOSCHI, "Storia della Letteratura Italiana."

Am′mon [Gr. Ἀμμων] or **Ham′mon,** an ancient heathen deity, worshipped in Libya, Egypt, Greece, etc., was called Zeus Ammon by the Greeks, and Jupiter Ammon by the Romans. There was a famous temple of Ammon at Thebes in Egypt, and another in the oasis of Siwah, in the Libyan Desert. He was represented in the form of a ram, or as a human being with a ram's head.

Ammon, âm′mon, (CLEMENT,) a German engraver, born at Frankfort, lived about the middle of the seventeenth century.

Ammon, (KARL WILHELM,) a Prussian writer on horses, born at Trakehnen, Prussian Lithuania, in 1777. He published a "Natural History of the Horse," (1815,) and a "Complete Manual of Practical Veterinary Medicine," ("Vollständiges Handbuch der praktischen Pferdearzeneikunst," 2 vols., 1804–7.)

Ammon, von, fon âm′mon, (CHRISTOPH FRIEDRICH,) a German Protestant theologian and popular pulpit orator of wide reputation, was born at Baireuth in 1766. He was professor of theology at Göttingen from 1794 to 1804, in which year he obtained a chair at Erlangen. He removed to Dresden in 1813, and became court preacher to the King of Saxony. He was one of the first apostles of what is called Rationalism in German theology. His principal work is "Development of Christianity into the Universal Religion," ("Fortbildung des Christenthums zur Weltreligion," 4 vols., 1833–40.) Among his numerous works is a "Plan (Entwurf) of a pure Biblical Theology," (3 vols., 1802.) Died in 1820.

See JULIUS PABST, "Lebens- und Charakterumrisse C. F. von Ammons," Dresden, 1850 ; BROCKHAUS, "Conversations-Lexikon ;" and "Ch. F. Ammon nach Leben, Ansichten und Wirken," Leipzig, 1850.

Ammon or **Ammen, von,** (FRIEDRICH AUGUST,) a German physician, son of the preceding, was born at Göttingen in 1799. He became professor in the medical academy of Dresden in 1829, and royal physician, (Leibarzt.) He published, besides other works, "Observations on Diseases of the Eye," (3 vols., 1838–41.) Died in 1861.

Am-mo′nas or **Amoun,** â-moon′, [Gr. Ἀμμώνας or

Ἀμοῦν,] the founder of a celebrated monastic order in Egypt. Died about 320 A.D.

Ammonio, âm-mo′ne-o, written also **Ammon,** (ANDREA,) [Lat. AN′DREAS AMMO′NIUS,] a distinguished Italian scholar, born at Lucca in 1477, was an intimate friend of Erasmus. He became about 1513 Latin secretary to Henry VIII. of England, whose victory at Guinegate he celebrated in a Latin poem called "Panegyricus," which was praised by Erasmus. He afterwards served Pope Leo X. as nuncio to the court of Henry VIII., and died in London in 1517. All his Latin poems are lost, except one eclogue.

See MAZZUCHELLI, "Scrittori d'Italia."

Am-mo′nĭ-us, [Gr. Ἀμμώνιος.] There were among the ancients a number of eminent persons of this name : the following are perhaps most worthy of notice :

Ammonius, a Greek grammarian, who lived at Alexandria about 50 B.C., and wrote commentaries on Homer and Aristophanes.

Ammonius, a Peripatetic philosopher who taught at Athens or Delphi in the latter half of the first century. He was a preceptor of Plutarch, and endeavoured to reconcile the doctrines of Plato and Aristotle. Plutarch wrote a life of him, which is not extant.

Ammonius, a Christian philosopher, who has been confounded with Ammonius Saccas, lived at Alexandria in the third century of our era. He is the reputed author of a Harmony of the Gospels.

Ammonius, a Greek grammarian, was priest of a temple in Alexandria about 380 A.D. He wrote a Dictionary of Greek Synonyms, which has been often printed.

Ammonius surnamed LITHOT′OMUS, a celebrated surgeon of Alexandria, supposed to have lived in the third century B.C. He was the first who contrived a method of breaking the calculus in the bladder when it was too large to be extracted through the opening made by incision ; from which improvement in lithotomy he received his surname.

Ammonius surnamed SAC′CAS, (because in early life he was a porter, and earned a livelihood by carrying sacks,) the founder of that school of Eclectic philosophy commonly known as New Platonism, was a native of Alexandria, in Egypt, where he died 241 A.D. He was the son of Christian parents, but preferred the heathen religion. Among his numerous disciples were Origen, Longinus, and Plotinus. He left no writings, and exacted from his disciples a promise not to divulge the mysteries which he taught.

See RITTER, "History of Philosophy ;" DEHAUT, "Essai historique sur la Vie d'Ammonius Saccas," 1836.

Ammonius, son of Hermias, a Greek philosopher, born at Alexandria, lived at Athens in the last half of the fifth century after Christ. He wrote valuable commentaries on Aristotle and Porphyry, and belonged to the school of New Platonists.

Am′non, a son of David, King of the Jews, was slain by Absalom. (See II. Samuel xiii.)

Amo, â′mo, (ANTONY WILLIAM,) a learned negro, born in Guinea about 1702. He studied at Halle, became a classical scholar, and published a work "On the Law of the Moors," ("De Jure Maurorum," 1729.) He was afterwards a councillor of state at the court of Berlin. On the death of his patron, the Duke of Brunswick, he returned to Africa. He was seen by H. Gallaudet at Axoom, (Axum,) in Abyssinia, in 1753.

See GRÉGOIRE, "De la Littérature des Nègres."

Amolon, â′mo′lôN′, or **Amulon,** â′mü′lôN′, a French ecclesiastic, who became Archbishop of Lyons in 841 A.D. He wrote a treatise against the Jews. Died in 852.

Am-o-me′tus, [Ἀμώμητος,] an ancient Greek author, wrote an account of a voyage on the Nile, of which some fragments are extant.

Amon, â′mon, a son of Manasseh, King of Judah, succeeded to the throne of his father, and was killed by his own servants, who conspired against him. (See II. Kings xxi. 19–23 ; also II. Chronicles xxxiii. 21–24.)

Amontons, â′môN′tôN′, (GUILLAUME,) an ingenious French natural philosopher and mechanician, born in Paris in 1663. He learned architecture, and was empioyed on several public works. He laboured with success to improve the barometer, thermometer, and hygrometer, and wrote a treatise on those instruments, (1695.) "He was the real inventor of the telegraphic art," says Biot, "as it is practised at the present day," (*i.e.* 1811.) He proposed that signals should be transmitted from station to station by operators whose vision was aided by the telescope; but his plan was not executed until fifty years later. Died in 1705.

Amor, the Roman god of love. See CUPID.

Amoretti, ä-mo-ret'tee, (CARLO,) a meritorious Italian naturalist, writer, and translator, born at Oneglia, near Genoa, in 1740 or 1741. He translated Winckelmann's "History of Ancient Art" into Italian, (1779,) wrote an excellent biography of Leonardo da Vinci, (1784,) and became one of the keepers of the Ambrosian Library, at Milan, in 1797. He was a member of the Italian Institute. Amoretti is author of an important work on the geography and natural history of Lakes Como, Maggiore, and Lugano, and the adjacent districts, entitled "Journey from Milan to the Three Lakes," ("Viaggio da Milano ai tre Laghi," 1794.) He translated into French the voyages of Pigafetta and Maldonado. Died in 1816.

See LOMBARDI, "Storia della Letteratura Italiana;" "Nouvelle Biographie Générale."

Amoretti, (MARIA PEREGRINA,) a learned Italian lady, born at Oneglia in 1756. She wrote a work "On the Right of Dowry among the Romans," ("De Jure Dotium apud Romanos.") Died in 1787.

Amoreux, ä'mo'ruh', (PIERRE JOSEPH,) a French physician and miscellaneous writer, born at Beaucaire about 1740. He wrote several works on natural history and rural economy, which were received with favour. Died in 1824.

Amoros, ä-mo'rōs, (FRANCISCO,) a Spanish colonel, born at Valencia in 1769, was the first who introduced gymnastic education into France. During the reign of Joseph Bonaparte he was councillor of state, minister of police, etc. He afterwards became an exile in France, and established a gymnasium with success. In 1831 he was appointed director of a normal gymnasium in Paris. Died in 1843.

Amorosi, ä-mo-ro'see, (ANTONIO,) an Italian painter, born near Ascoli, lived in the first half of the eighteenth century. He painted humorous subjects, which the Italians call *Bambocciate,* and displayed much talent for satire.

See LANZI, "History of Painting in Italy."

Amort, ä'moRt, (EUSEBIUS,) a German theologian and monk, born near Tolz, in Bavaria, in 1692. He wrote a "History of Indulgences," (1735,) and attacked prevailing superstitions in a work "On Revelations, Visions, and Apparitions," (1744.) Died in 1775.

See SAVIOLI-CORBELLI, "Ehrendenkmal E. Amorts," 1777.

Am'o-rȳ, (THOMAS,) an eccentric English writer, a zealous Unitarian, was born about 1690. He published memoirs of several ladies of Great Britain, (1755,) and is supposed to have represented his own character and experience in "The Life of John Buncle, Esq.; containing Various Observations and Reflections made in Various Parts of the World," (2 vols., 1756–66.) Died in 1788.

Amory, (THOMAS,) a distinguished Presbyterian divine, born at Taunton, England, in 1700. He was ordained in 1730, and became principal tutor of a dissenting academy at Taunton in 1738. In 1759 he removed to London, and in 1766 became sole pastor of the chapel at Old Jewry, where he had preached seven years as colleague of Dr. Chandler. He published, besides other works, two volumes of sermons, (1758, 1766,) and "Grove's System of Moral Philosophy, revised, corrected, and improved," (1749.) Died in 1774.

Amos, ä'mos, [Heb. עָמוֹס,] one of the minor Hebrew prophets, lived about 800 B.C. He was a herdsman and gatherer of sycamore-fruit. His book is the third in order of position among the minor prophets, and contains several eloquent and admirable passages.

Amoudrou, ä'moo'dRoo, (ANTOINE,) a French architect, born at Dôle in 1739; died in 1812. He built some palaces in Warsaw.

Amour, (SAINT.) See SAINT-AMOUR.

Ampach auf Grünfelden, (or **Gruenfelden,**) von fon äm'päk öwf grün'fěl'den, (JOHANN GEORG,) a German physician, born in 1784, wrote several veterinary treatises. Died in 1832.

Am-pe'lĭ-us, (LUCIUS,) a Roman, known only as the author of a work called "Book of Memory," ("Liber Memorialis,") which was edited by Salmasius. It is a compendium of history, geography, etc.

Ampère, öN'pair', (ANDRÉ MARIE,) a celebrated French mathematician and natural philosopher, born at Lyons on the 20th of January, 1775, was the son of a merchant. He learned mathematics in early youth at home without a teacher, and eagerly read the poems of Virgil and Horace in the original. He married Julie Carron in 1799. In 1802 he attracted the public attention by a curious work "On the Mathematical Theory of Gaming." In 1805 he obtained by the favour of Delambre the place of *répétiteur* of analysis in the Polytechnic School, Paris. He became inspector-general of the university in 1808, professor of analysis in the Polytechnic School in 1809, and a member of the Institute in 1814.

In 1820 he announced the remarkable discoveries in electro-magnetism which constitute, perhaps, his chief title to celebrity. He demonstrated the influence of a spiral wire conducting a galvanic current, in magnetizing a needle, proved that two voltaic conductors attract each other when the currents have the same direction and repel each other when the currents flow in opposite directions, and inferred from his experiments that the phenomena of natural magnetism depend on electrical currents which constantly pass around the earth from east to west. These results, which he obtained by the application of the most difficult parts of mathematical analysis, were communicated to the Academy of Sciences, in several papers, in the autumn of 1820. "The vast field of physical science," says Arago, "perhaps never presented so brilliant a discovery conceived, verified, and completed with such rapidity."

Ampère gave the name of Electro-Dynamics to his new science. In 1822 he published a "Collection of Observations on Electro-Dynamics." His theory and discoveries in this science were more amply developed in his work entitled "Theory of Electro-Dynamic Phenomena deduced from Experiments only," ("Théorie des Phénomènes électro-dynamiques uniquement déduite de l'Expérience," 1826.)

Among his later works is a treatise on the undulatory theory of light, ("Mémoire sur la Détermination de la Surface courbe des Ondes lumineuses, etc.," 1828;) also, an "Essay on the Philosophy of the Sciences, or Analytic Exposition of a Natural Classification of all Human Knowledge," ("Essai sur la Philosophie des Sciences, ou Exposition analytique d'une Classification naturelle de toutes les Connaissances humaines," 1834.)

He wrote numerous treatises on optics, natural history, etc., which were printed in the "Mémoires" of the Institute, and in other journals. He was a Fellow of the Royal Society of London. Died in Paris in 1836. He is said to have resembled La Fontaine in good nature, (*bonhomie,*) simplicity, and absence of mind.

See ARAGO, "Éloge d'Ampère;" SAINTE-BEUVE et M. LITTRÉ, notice in the "Revue des Deux Mondes," February, 1837; QUETELET, "Notice sur M. Ampère," 1836; LOUIS DE LOMÉNIE, "Galerie des Contemporains illustres."

Ampère, (JEAN JACQUES,) a son of the preceding, was born at Lyons in August, 1800. He devoted himself to literary pursuits, and obtained access to the select society which met at the salon of Madame Récamier. In 1830 he became an assistant or substitute of Villemain as professor at the Sorbonne, and in 1833 succeeded Andrieux as professor of French literature at the College of France. He was admitted into the Academy of Inscriptions in 1842, and into the French Academy in 1847. Among his works are "The Literary History of France before the Twelfth Century," ("Histoire littéraire de la France avant le douzième Siècle," 3 vols., 1839,) and a collection of charming articles called "Littérature et Voyages," (1833.) Died in 1864.

See QUÉRARD, "La France Littéraire."

Am-phĭ-a-rā'us, [Gr. Ἀμφιάραος,] a famous soothsayer

---

and hero of Argos. He took part in the Argonautic expedition, and married Eriphyle, who, bribed by the fatal necklace of Harmonia, persuaded him against his will to join in the expedition of the Seven against Thebes. Tradition adds that the earth opened and swallowed him, and that he was afterwards worshipped as a hero.

Am-phic′ra-tēs, [Gr. Ἀμφικράτης,] an Athenian orator, who flourished about 70 B.C. For some unknown cause he was banished from Athens, and went to Asia, where he died.

Am-phic′ty̆-on, [Gr. Ἀμφικτυών,] a fabulous king of Attica, was a son of Deucalion, (or, as some say, an autochthon.) He was expelled from his kingdom and succeeded by Erichthonius. He is supposed to have lived about 1490 B.C.

Am-phĭ-lo′chĭ-us, [Gr. Ἀμφιλόχιος; Fr. AMPHILOQUE, ȯṅ′fe′lok′,] a bishop of Iconium, and a zealous opponent of Arianism, was born in Cappadocia. About 383 A.D. he went to the court of the emperor Theodosius, and instigated him to issue a decree prohibiting the public assemblies of the Arians. Died about 395 A.D. His works are nearly all lost.

Am-phī′on, [Gr. Ἀμφίων,] a Theban prince, who received a golden lyre from Mercury, and cultivated music with such success that he built the walls of Thebes by the sounds which he drew from that instrument, the stones arranging themselves obsequiously at his will. The meaning of this fable appears to be that by his eloquence and persuasive manners he prevailed upon his rude and hitherto intractable subjects to build the walls of their city. He married the famous Niobe.

Amphi′on [Ἀμφίων] OF CNOS′SUS, a Greek statuary, who lived about 420 B.C.

Am′phis, [Ἄμφις,] an Athenian comic poet, who was a contemporary of Plato. His works are not extant.

Am-phis′tra-tos, [Ἀμφίστρατος,] a Greek sculptor, mentioned by Pliny as the author of a good statue of Callisthenes. He lived about 320 B.C.

Am-phĭ-trī′te, [Ἀμφιτρίτη,] a Nereid of the Greek mythology, represented as the wife of Neptune, and mother of Triton. She was sometimes styled by the poets the goddess of the sea.

Am′pĭ-us, (TITUS FLAVIANUS,) a Roman general, who fought for Vespasian against Vitellius about 70 A.D.

Ampsing, âmp′sing, or **Amp′zing**, (JOHN ASSUE-RUS,) a Dutch medical writer, born in 1559; died in 1642.

Ampsing, (SAMUEL,) a Dutch poet, a son of the preceding, lived in the early part of the seventeenth century.

Ampudia, âm-poo′de-â, (PEDRO DE,) a Mexican general, who obtained that rank in 1840. He commanded an army which besieged Campeachy in 1842–43. In 1846 he was in command at Monterey, which was besieged by General Taylor, and was taken prisoner in September of that year.

Amreeta. See AMRITA.

Am′rĭ-tă, [Hindoo pron. ŭm′rĭ-ta, from ă, privative, and mrĭtă, "dead," also "death,"] sometimes written, but less correctly, **Amreeta**, the name given by the Hindoos to the water of immortality which was produced by the churning of the ocean. (See KŪRMÂ-VATÂRA.) The term Amrita or Amrit is also applied to the food as well as to the drink of the gods, and hence to any delicious drink.

Amroo, Amrû, or **Amrou,** âm′roō,* or, more fully, **Amroo-Ibn-Al-Aâs,** (or -**Ass,**)—Ib′n âl âss, (*i.e.* "Amroo the son of Al-Aâs,") a famous Arabian general, who conquered Egypt in the reign of the caliph Omăr, about 640 A.D. He was afterwards governor of Egypt until Omăr's death. In the civil war which followed the death of Othmân he fought against Alee. Died in 663 A.D.

See IRVING, "Mahomet and his Successors," vol. ii.; ABULFEDA, "Annales Moslemici;" GIBBON, "Decline and Fall of the Roman Empire," chap li.; WEIL, "Geschichte der Chalifen," vol. i.

Amrool-kays, Amrulkais, or **Amroulcays,** âm′rool-kīs′, written also **Amrolkaïs,** a distinguished Arabian poet, who lived about 600 A.D. He was author of one of the Mo'allakât, poems suspended on the Kaaba at Mecca.

Amrou or **Amru.** See AMROO.

Amr-Seebawayh or **Amr-Sibawayh,** âm′r see′-bâ-wīH′, the greatest of the Arabian grammarians, lived at Bagdâd in the reign of Haroun-al-Raschid.

Amsdorf, von, fon âms′dorf, (NIKOLAUS,) a German Reformer, born near Wurzen, in Saxony, in 1483. He became professor of divinity at Wittenberg in 1511, and a zealous adherent of Luther, whom he accompanied to the Diet of Worms in 1521. He was appointed superintendent and minister at Saint Ulrich in Magdeburg in 1524, and Bishop of Naumburg in 1542. Amsdorf took part in Luther's translation of the Bible, and wrote numerous polemical treatises on theology. Died in 1565.

See MELCHIOR ADAM, "Vitæ Theologorum Germanorum."

Amsler, âms′ler, (SAMUEL,) an excellent German engraver, born in Switzerland in 1791. He was professor at the Academy of Fine Arts in Munich, and engraved many pieces after Michael Angelo, Raphael, and Thorwaldsen. Among his works is a "Holy Family" of the second, and "The Triumph of Alexander" of the last-named artist. Died at Munich in 1849.

Amstel, (CORNELIS PLOOS VAN.) See PLOOS.

Amstel, Gijsbrecht or **Gysbrecht van,** gīs′brĕKt or Hīs′brĕKt vån âm′stel, a Dutch nobleman of the thirteenth century, infamous as the betrayer of Floris V., Count of Holland, in 1296. (See FLORIS V.) The odium of this crime contributed much to the ruin of the power of the Dutch aristocracy.

Amthor, âm′tōr, (CHRISTOPH HEINRICH,) a German jurist, born at Stollberg in 1678. He entered the service of Denmark, and was made a counsellor of justice at Copenhagen about 1718. He wrote some successful political tracts and works on law. Died in 1721.

Amulio, â-moo′le-o, or **Da Mula,** dâ moo′lâ, (MARC-ANTONIO,) CARDINAL, an Italian scholar, born at Venice in 1505. He gained the confidence of Pope Pius IV., who employed him in important commissions, and made him a cardinal in 1561. He wrote Latin poems and orations, and other works of some merit, nearly all of which remain in manuscript. Died in 1570.

A-mu′lĭ-us, King of Alba, was a younger brother of Numitor, whom he dethroned about 714 B.C. (See ROMULUS.)

Amurath, â-moo-rât′, or **Moorad,** (**Mourad** or **Murad,**) moo′râd′, (written also **Amurat, Amurad,** and **Mürad,**) **I.,** the first of the Ottoman sultans who made conquests in Europe, succeeded his father Orkhan in 1360. He took Adrianople in 1362, and made it the capital of his European dominions. During a reign of twenty-nine years his arms were everywhere crowned with success. A formidable insurrection having at length broken out in Servia, he hastened to meet this new danger, accompanied by his son, the famous Bayazeed, (Bajazet,) surnamed Ilderim, or "the lightning." His army was inferior in numbers to that of the insurgents; but, yielding to the ardour of Bayazeed, he resolved at once to give battle. After a long and terrible conflict on the plain of Kossovo, the forces of Amurath gained a complete victory. The sultan rejoiced all the more over this success because, as the Moslem historians inform us, he had dreamed the night before that he met his death from the weapon of an assassin. While he lingered on the field of battle, one of the bodies on which he chanced to tread suddenly started up and plunged a dagger into the heart of Amurath, who died a few moments afterwards, (June 15, 1389,) aged sixty-three years. Amurath I. has the distinction of having formed the Janissaries (who had been first levied by his father Orkhan) into a thoroughly organized and disciplined body of troops.

See "Nouvelle Biographie Générale;" VON HAMMER, "Histoire de l'Empire Ottoman."

Amurath or **Moorad (Murad) II.,** born about 1405, succeeded his father Mahomet I. in 1422. His reign was marked by various vicissitudes of fortune. At one time (1422) he threatened Constantinople with a formidable army. In 1429 he took Thessalonica from the Venetians, and in 1433 took possession of Vánina and razed its fortifications to the ground. In 1442 the famous Huniades defeated the troops of Amurath in two successive battles, in the latter of which the Turks lost

---

* See remarks on Oriental names, in the Introduction.

ā, ē, ī, ō, ū, ȳ, *long;* ă, ĕ, ĭ, ŏ, ŭ, y̆, *short;* a, e, i, o, *obscure;* fâr, fâll, fât; mêt; nôt; gŏŏd; moͦon;

two hundred banners and five thousand prisoners, including their general-in-chief. In the following year Huniades gained in rapid succession several victories over the Ottoman forces. In one engagement in which the sultan himself was present, Amurath lost six thousand men, so that he was compelled to sue for peace. A treaty of peace for ten years was signed between the sultan and the King of Hungary, but it was soon after broken by the latter at the instigation of the papal legate Julian. This want of good faith on the part of the Christians was signally avenged the same year by the defeat of the Hungarians near Varna, and the death of Vladislaus, their king, who was unhorsed by Amurath himself and slain by a janissary. Again in 1448 the Hungarians under Huniades suffered a total defeat in the battle of Kossovo, (October, 1448.) This engagement lasted three days ; at last Huniades fled, and his troops were almost annihilated. Twice during his reign Amurath II. abdicated the supreme power and sought in retirement that peace of mind which he could not find on the throne ; but in both instances he was speedily recalled by the wishes of his people to the post which he had so lately left. He died in 1451, leaving behind him the reputation of an able, just, and humane ruler. He was succeeded by his son, Mahomet II., the conqueror of Constantinople.

See " Nouvelle Biographie Générale ;" Von Hammer, " Histoire de l'Empire Ottoman."

Amurath or **Moorad (Murad) III.,** born in 1545, succeeded his father, Selim II., in 1574. On the first day of his reign he caused his five brothers to be strangled. He was weak and sensual as well as cruel ; but his mind was not altogether without taste and cultivation. Died in 1595.

See "Nouvelle Biographie Générale ;" Von Hammer, " Histoire de l'Empire Ottoman."

Amurath or **Moorad (Murad) IV.,** born about 1610, succeeded his uncle Mustafa in 1623. In 1638 he took Bagdâd, which was thenceforward incorporated with the Ottoman Empire : this was the only important event of his reign. He had a vigorous, athletic frame, but a feeble, passionate, and tyrannical disposition ; and these evil traits in his character seemed to increase with his years. He was almost continually intoxicated ; in a fit of drunken rage he would sometimes rush from his palace into the street, sword in hand, killing all whom he met ; at other times he would amuse himself by shooting with his bow from the palace-windows those who happened to be passing beneath. Happily for his people, he died (1640) before he had completed his thirtieth year. He has been styled "the Turkish Nero."

See " Nouvelle Biographie Générale ;" Von Hammer, " Histoire de l'Empire Ottoman."

Amussat, ä′mü′sä′, (Jean Zuléma—zü′lä′mä′,) a French surgeon, born in Deux-Sèvres in 1796. He invented several instruments, among which is a probe used in lithotrity, and published a number of treatises. His memoir on " The Torsion of Arteries" (1829) obtained a prize of the Institute. Died in 1856.

Amy, ä′me′, a French advocate of Aix, wrote some interesting works on rivers and fountains, among which is "Observations expérimentales sur les eaux des rivières de Seine, de Marne, etc.," (1749.) Died in 1760.

Amyn or **Amin.** See Alameen.

A-mȳn′tas, [Gr. Ἀμύντας,] the name of three kings of Macedonia between 510 and 330 B.C. Also, a Macedonian general in the service of Alexander the Great.

Amyntas I., King of Macedonia, began to reign about 510 B.C. He presented earth and water to the Persian ambassadors in token of submission to the supremacy of Darius.

Amyntas II. of Macedonia, ascended the throne in 394 B.C. He was defeated in battle by the Illyrians, and recovered his kingdom by the aid of the Thessalians. He afterwards strengthened himself by an alliance with Sparta. Died in 370 B.C., leaving three sons, Alexander, Perdiccas, and Philip called the Great.

Amyntas III. was a grandson of the preceding, and a son of Perdiccas. He was an infant at the death of his father in 359 B.C., and was the lawful heir to the throne which was usurped by his uncle Philip. He was

put to death on the charge of a conspiracy against Alexander a short time before the latter invaded Asia.

Amyntas, one of the generals of Alexander the Great. During the campaign in Asia he conducted reinforcements from Macedonia to the army at Babylon. About 330 B.C. he was tried on a charge of complicity in a plot alleged to have been formed by his friend Philotas, and acquitted.

Amyntas, son of Antiochus, a Macedonian officer who was in the service of Persia when Alexander invaded that country. He commanded some Greek auxiliaries that fought for Darius at Issus, 333 B.C., after which he led an expedition against Egypt, then in the possession of the Persians. After he had gained a victory near Memphis, he was surprised by the Persians and killed, about 330 B.C.

Amyntas, a king of Galatia, fought for Antony at Philippi, and against him at the battle of Actium, 31 B.C. Died about 30 B.C.

Amyntianus, a-min-she-ā′nus, [Ἀμυντιανός,] a Greek author, lived about 170 A.D., and wrote a " Life of Alexander the Great," which is lost.

Amyot, ä′me-o′, (Jacques,) a French writer and translator of great merit, born at Melun in 1513. He became professor of Greek and Latin at Bourges about 1540, and was appointed tutor to the sons of Henry II. in 1558. He was made grand almoner of France on the accession of Charles IX. in 1560, and Bishop of Auxerre in 1570. In 1559 he published an excellent translation of Plutarch's " Lives," which is especially celebrated as a model of French style. He also translated from the Greek seven books of Diodorus Siculus, (1554,) Longus's romance of " Daphnis and Chloe," (1559,) and the " Moral Treatises of Plutarch." Died at Auxerre in 1593. Amyot is ranked among the prose writers who have contributed most to the perfection of the French language.

See De Thou, " Histoire," book viii. ; Nicéron, " Mémoires ;" "Éloge d'Amyot," in the "Mémoires de l'Académie Française ;" " Nouvelle Biographie Générale ;" Bayle, " Historical and Critical Dictionary."

Amyot, (Joseph.) See Amiot.

Am′yot, (Thomas,) an English antiquary, born at Norwich about 1775. He embraced the legal profession, and became private secretary to Mr. Windham while the latter was secretary at war in 1806. In 1812 he published the speeches of Windham, with a short notice of his life. He contributed several treatises to the " Archæologia," and was for many years secretary to the Society of Antiquaries. Died in 1850.

Amyraut, ä′me′ro′, [Lat. Amyral′dus,] (Moses,) a distinguished French Protestant divine and writer, born at Bourgueil, in Anjou, in 1596. He became professor of divinity at Saumur in 1633. In order to promote union among the Protestant churches, he wrote a Latin " Treatise on Secession from the Roman Church, and on Peace among the Evangelical Churches," and was, in consequence, involved in a controversy with certain Calvinistic divines by his attempt to explain Calvin's views on predestination, which he wished to reconcile with the doctrine of universal grace. He was author of many works in French and Latin, among which is "Christian Morality," (6 vols.,) a work of much merit. He was esteemed for his talents and worth by both Catholics and Protestants. Died in 1664.

See Charles E. Saigey, " M. Amyraut, sa Vie et ses Écrits," 1849 ; Bayle, " Historical and Critical Dictionary."

Amyrtæus, am-ir-tee′us, [Gr. Ἀμυρταῖος ; Fr. Amyr-tée, ä′mĕr′tä′,] King of Egypt, obtained the throne about 450 B.C. by a revolt against the King of Persia.

Anacaona, ä-nä-kä-o′nä, surnamed Golden Flower, was the wife of Caonabo, a cacique of Hayti when Columbus discovered that island in 1492. She was put to death by Ovando, the Spanish governor.

See Irving's " Life of Columbus."

An-a-char′sis, [Gr. Ἀνάχαρσις,] a Scythian philosopher, contemporary and friend of Solon. He was, it is said, the only barbarian admitted to the citizenship of Athens. He was reckoned by some writers among the Seven Wise Men of Greece. On his return to his native country he was shot dead with an arrow by the Scythian king for performing the Greek rites to the goddess Cybele. Some of his witty sayings have been preserved by Diogenes Laertius, Plutarch, and Lucian.

An-a-cle′tus, [Fr. ANACLET, ả′nả′clả′,] sometimes called **Cletus,** the second or third bishop of Rome, was a native of Athens. He is variously represented as the successor or predecessor of Clement. Died, it is supposed, about 100 A.D.

Anacletus THE ANTIPOPE, was elected by a part of the cardinals in 1130, and disputed the claim of Innocent II. to the popedom. Supported by the populace of Rome, he maintained possession of that city until his death in 1138, though his rival was recognized by nearly all the European powers.

See ARTAUD DE MONTOR, "Histoire des souverains Pontifes."

A-nac′re-on, [Gr. Ἀνακρέων,] a celebrated Greek amatory lyric poet, born at Teos, in Ionia, about 560 B.C. He passed many years in the prime of his life at the court of Polycrates, tyrant of Samos, to which it is supposed he was invited about 540. After the death of Polycrates, whose bounty he had largely enjoyed, he removed to Athens, which he left probably about 514 B.C. According to some accounts, he attained the age of eighty-five. His death is said to have been caused by a grape-stone or dried grape, by which he was choked. He left odes and songs on love and wine, which are regarded as models of that species of poetry named from him Anacreontic; also elegies, epigrams, etc. Numerous fragments of his poems are extant.

See MÜLLER, "Histoire de la Littérature de l'ancienne Grèce;" BODE, "Geschichte der lyrischen Dichtkunst der Hellenen;" VOSSIUS, "De Poetis Græcis."

An-a-dў-om′e-ne, [Gr. Ἀναδυομένη,] (*i.e.* the goddess "rising up out" of the sea,) a surname given to Venus, in allusion to the story of her origin.

Au-a-fes′tus or **Anafesto,** â-nä-fěs′to, (PAOLUCCIO, pŏw-loot′cho,) the first Doge of Venice. Died in 717 A.D.

A-na-ï′tis or **Anahid,** [Gr. Ἀναῖτις,] a goddess worshipped in Armenia and Asia Minor, was supposed to be identical with the Greek Aphrodite or the Persian goddess of nature.

A′nan, (Ben David,) a Jewish rabbi of the eighth century, is represented as the restorer of the Karaite doctrines and defender of the pure law.

Anania, ä-nä′ne-ä, (GIOVANNI LORENZO,) a learned Italian of the sixteenth century, born at Taverna, in Calabria. Among other works, he wrote a treatise on the nature of demons, (1581; 5th edition, 1669.)

Anania, d′, dä-nä′ne-ä, or **Anagny, d′,** dä-nân′yee, written also **Agnany,** (JOANNES,) an Italian jurist and canonist. Died in 1458.

An-a-nī′as or **Hananiah,** called **Sha′drach,** one of three Hebrew captives whom the King of Babylon ordered to be thrown into a fiery furnace. (See Daniel i. and iii.)

Ananias, a Jewish general, was a son of Onias who erected a Hebrew temple at Heliopolis, in Egypt. He and his brother Chelcias commanded an army which Cleopatra, Queen of Egypt, sent into Judea against her son, Ptolemy Lathyrus, in 103 B.C.

Ananias, a Jew, who was appointed high-priest at Jerusalem about 45 or 50 A.D. He was a party to the persecution of the Apostle Paul, and appeared as his accuser before Felix. (See Acts xxiii. 2; xxiv. 1; xxv. 2.) He was killed by robbers, or, according to some accounts, by the seditious Jews, about 66 A.D.

See JOSEPHUS, "Jewish Antiquities."

Ananias, one of the primitive Christians, was a resident of Damascus, and eminently devout. He was sent by the Lord, who appeared to him in a vision, to restore sight to Saul of Tarsus, who had just been converted. (See Acts ix. 10-18.)

A-năn′tă, [Hindoo pron. ŭn-ŭn′ta—from ăn, privative, and ăntă, "end,"] a name signifying "without end," sometimes applied to the great serpent Sêsha, the symbol of eternity. (See SESHA.)

A-nā′pī-us and **Am-phin′o-mus,** two brothers, who lived at Catania before the Christian era and acquired celebrity by saving their parents from an eruption of Mount Etna.

Anar. See NÖRVI.

Añasco, de, dä än-yȧs′ko, (JUAN,) a Sevillian officer, who served under Hernando de Soto in his expedition into Florida in 1539-43.

Anassagora. See ANAXAGORAS.

Anastase. See ANASTASIUS.

Anastasia, an-as-tä′she-a, [Fr. ANASTASIE, ả′nȧs′-tả′ze′,] SAINT, the wife of Publius, a pagan. After his death, having made a public profession of Christianity, she suffered martyrdom in 303 A.D., during the reign of Diocletian.

Anastasius, an-as-tä′she-us, [Gr. Ἀναστάσιος; Fr. ANASTASE, ả′nȧs′tȧz′,] **I.,** a Byzantine emperor, born at Dyrrachium (now Durazzo) about 430 A.D. On the death of the emperor Zeno, in 491, his widow, the empress Ariadne, gave her hand in marriage to Anastasius, and raised him to the throne. He persecuted or differed with the orthodox, who rose in arms, and, under the command of Vitalianus, defeated his army in 514. Died in 518 A.D., and was succeeded by Justin I.

See GIBBON, "Decline and Fall of the Roman Empire."

Anastasius II., Emperor of the East, succeeded Philippicus by election in 713 A.D. The army which he sent against the Arabs revolted, proclaimed Theodosius emperor, and captured Constantinople. Anastasius was deposed in 716, and put to death by order of Leo III. about 720 A.D.

See GIBBON, "Decline and Fall of the Roman Empire."

Anastasius, Patriarch of Constantinople, was raised to that dignity by Leo about 730 A.D. He favoured the Iconoclasts. The Catholic writers represent him as a disgrace to his profession. Died in 753 A.D.

Anastasius, an-as-tä′she-us, [Fr. ANASTASE, ả′nȧs′-tȧz′,] **I.,** POPE, a Roman by birth, succeeded Siricius about 398 A.D. He was strongly opposed to the doctrines of Origen. Died in 402, and was succeeded by Innocent I.

Anastasius II., a native of Rome, was elected pope in 496, in place of Gelasius I. He wrote a letter to Clovis, King of the Franks, on his conversion to Christianity. Died in 498 A.D.

Anastasius III. became pope after the death of Sergius III. in 911. Died in 913, and was succeeded by Lando.

Anastasius IV., a native of Rome, was elected pope in 1153, as successor to Eugenius III. He is represented as wise and virtuous. He died at an advanced age in 1154, and was succeeded by Adrian IV.

Anastasius surnamed BIBLIOTHECA′RIUS, (*i.e.* "Librarian,") a Roman priest of the ninth century, translated from Greek into Latin several works, among which is "Historia Ecclesiastica," composed chiefly of extracts from Nicephorus and Syncellus. Died probably about 890 A.D.

Anastasius, surnamed SINAITA (sī-nȧ-ī′ta) from having been a monk on Mount Sinai, became Bishop or Patriarch of Antioch in 561 A.D. He was a zealous defender of the orthodox Catholic faith, for which he was expelled from his see by Justin II. in 570; but he was restored by the emperor Maurice in 593. Died in 599 A.D.

Anastasius, SAINT, called "the Apostle of Hungary," was born in 954 A.D., and died in 1044.

An-a-to′lī-us, [Fr. ANATOLE, ả′nả′tol′,] an eminent philosopher of Alexandria, lived in the latter part of the third century. He opened a school in Alexandria, and was the first Christian who taught the philosophy of Aristotle. He became Bishop of Laodicea about 270 A.D.

Anatolius, a Platonic philosopher, contemporary with the preceding, was a master of Iamblichus and friend of Porphyry. A fragment of work, entitled "Sympathies and Antipathies," is ascribed to him.

See FABRICIUS, "Bibliotheca Græca."

Anatolius, a Greek jurist, born at Berytus, was employed by Justinian in the compilation of the Digest, about 530 A.D.

An-ax-ag′o-ras, [Gr. Ἀναξαγόρας; Fr. ANAXAGORE, ả′nȧk′sả′goR′; It. ANASSAGORA, ä-nȧs-sȧg′o-rä,] a celebrated Greek philosopher, born at Clazomenæ, near Smyrna, 500 B.C. He came to Athens about 460 B.C., or, according to some writers, twenty years earlier, and remained there about thirty years. Socrates and Eu-

---

ā, ē, ī, ō, ū, ȳ, *long;* ȧ, ė, ȯ, same, less prolonged; ă, ĕ, ĭ, ŏ, ŭ, ў, *short;* ạ, ẹ, ị, ọ, *obscure;* fär, fȧll, fȧt; mėt; nŏt; gōōd; mōōn;

ripides are said to have been among his disciples. In 432 B.C. he was prosecuted on a charge of impiety. Pericles, who had been his pupil, assisted in his defence. To escape from death he fled from Athens, and died at Lampsacus, in Asia Minor, 428 B.C. Anaxagoras wrote a treatise on Nature, of which some fragments have been preserved. He maintained the eternity of matter, the elements of which were, he held, in a state of confusion, till another distinct principle, self-existent, infinitely subtile and powerful, which he termed Nous, (or Mind,) reduced them to order : generation and destruction were only the union and separation of elemental particles which could neither be created nor annihilated ; there was no such thing as chance or accident, these being nothing more than names for unknown causes.

Anaxagoras may be regarded as the father of modern science. Of all the ancient philosophers he appears to have been the first to combine, in the investigation of Nature and her laws, close reasoning with careful observation and experiment. He demonstrated that air was a substance, and not mere vacuity according to the popular notion, by showing that when it was confined, as in bladders, it offered a positive resistance and displaced other bodies. His observation that there is no such thing as chance, but that "chance" is merely the name for a "cause unperceived by the human intellect," (τὴν τύχην, ἄδηλον αἰτίαν ἀνθρωπίνῳ λογισμῷ,) evinced rare sagacity, as well as subtlety of thought ; and in teaching that the destruction and production of material bodies are nothing more than the separation and reunion of the elemental particles, he anticipated one of the most important discoveries of modern chemistry.

See RITTER, "History of Philosophy," 3 vols. 8vo, Oxford, 1838 ; G. H. LEWES, "Biographical History of Philosophy ;" DE RAMSAY, "Anaxagoras," the Hague, 1778 ; J. T. HEMSEN, "Anaxagoras Clazomenius sive de Vita ejus atque Philosophia," 8vo, 1821 ; SCHAUBACH, "De Anaxagora ;" DIOGENES LAERTIUS.

Anaxagoras, a Greek statuary, born at Ægina, lived about 480 B.C. He executed a statue of Jupiter placed at Elis after the battle of Platæa.

Anaxagore. See ANAXAGORAS.

An-ax-an'dri-dēs, [Gr. Ἀναξανδρίδης,] a king of Sparta, reigned from about 560 to 520 B.C. He was the father of Cleomenes and Leonidas.

Anaxandrides, a Greek comic poet, lived in the fourth century B.C. He wrote many successful dramas.

An-ax-ar'ehus, [Gr. Ἀναξάρχος ; Fr. ANAXARQUE, ă'năk'sărk',] a Greek philosopher, a native of Abdera, was intimate with Alexander the Great, whom he accompanied on his expedition into Asia in 334 B.C. He appears to have been a man of respectable character. After the death of Alexander, Anaxarchus is said to have been put to death by the tyrant Nicocreon, by being pounded in a large mortar ; he bore the torment with stoical fortitude.

See ARRIAN, "Anabasis."

A-nax'ĭ-las, [Ἀναξίλας,] an Athenian comic poet, contemporary with Plato, lived about 340 B.C.

A-nax-ĭ-lā'us [Gr. Ἀναξίλαος] or **An-ax'ĭ-las,** a tyrant or prince of Rhegium, (now Reggio,) in the south of Italy, in the fifth century B.C.

Anaxilaus, [Gr. Ἀναξίλαος,] a Pythagorean philosopher, born in Larissa, lived at Rome in the reign of Augustus, and was banished from Italy on a charge of magic.

A-nax-ĭ-man'der, [Gr. Ἀναξίμανδρος; Fr. ANAXIMANDRE, ă'năk'se'môNDR',] an eminent Greek philosopher, born at Miletus, in Asia Minor, about 610 B.C., is said to have been a disciple or friend of Thales. The invention of the sun-dial is attributed to him, and Pliny states that he discovered the obliquity of the ecliptic. He taught that the earth is a sphere, that the sun is a globe of fire as large as the earth, and that there is an infinite number of worlds. The statement of his opinions given by Plutarch differs from the above. A book which he wrote is the oldest prose work on philosophy mentioned among the Greeks. Died about 546 B.C.

See RITTER, "History of Philosophy ;" G. H. LEWES, "Biographical History of Philosophy ;" DIOGENES LAERTIUS.

An-ax-im'e-nēs, [Gr. Ἀναξιμένης ; Fr. ANAXIMÈNE, ă'năk'se'mån',] a Grecian philosopher, born at Miletus, flourished probably about 500 B.C. Little is known of his life. His opinions were recorded by Theophrastus. He maintained that *Aer* (air) is the original principle of which all things are formed and into which all things are resolved, and that this aer is in eternal motion.

See RITTER, "History of Philosophy ;" G. H. LEWES, "Biographical History of Philosophy ;" J. H. SCHMIDT, "De Anaximenis Vita et Physiologia," 1689 ; DIOGENES LAERTIUS.

Anaxim'enes OF LAMP'SACUS, a historian who lived about 350 B.C. He wrote a history of Philip of Macedon and of his son Alexander, which is lost. According to Suidas, he was one of the instructors of Alexander the Great. Pausanias relates that he once saved his native city by his ready wit. When he came as an intercessor to Alexander, (who was greatly exasperated against the citizens of Lampsacus for siding with' the Persians,) the conqueror, anticipating his intention, exclaimed, " I swear I will not grant your request !" "I implore you, then," said Anaximenes, "to destroy Lampsacus and reduce its citizens to slavery." Alexander had the magnanimity to keep his word.

Anaya y Maldonado, ä-nī'ä e mäl-do-nä'DO,(DIEGO,) born at Salamanca about 1350, was made Archbishop of Seville in 1417 ; died in 1437.

Ancæus, an-see'us, [Gr. Ἀγκαῖος ; Fr. ANCÉE, ôN'så',] a fabulous son of Neptune, and King of Samos, was the pilot of the ship Argo in the Argonautic expedition. He planted a vineyard, but was warned by a seer that he would never drink any wine of his own production. He made some wine, and was raising a cup of it to his mouth, when he was told that a wild boar was in his vineyard. He left the wine untasted, and attacked the boar, by which he was killed. This event is said to have given rise to the proverb, "There is many a slip between the cup and the lip."

An-can'ther-us, (CLAUDIUS,) a physician and historical writer, lived at Vienna between 1550 and 1600.

Ancarano, än-kä-rä'no, (GASPARO,) an Italian priest and poet of Bassano, lived between 1550 and 1600.

Ancarano, d', dän-kä-rä'no, (PIETRO GIOVANNI,) an Italian jurist and poet, born at Reggio, in Lombardy, lived about 1550.

Ancée. See ANCÆUS.

Ancelot, ôNss'lo', (JACQUES ARSÈNE FRANÇOIS POLYCARPE,) a French dramatic author, born at Havre in 1794. He was in his youth a clerk in the bureau of the navy department. In 1819 he produced "Louis IX.," a tragedy in verse, which had a great success, and obtained from the king a pension of two thousand francs. His tragedy of "Fiesco" (1824) was also favourably received. He afterwards composed many dramas, comedies, and vaudevilles, and succeeded De Bonald in the French Academy in 1841. Died in 1850.

His wife, originally MARGUERITE VIRGINIE CHARDON, a painter and authoress, was born at Dijon in 1792. She wrote several plays, and a volume of tales called "Empruns aux Salons de Paris," of considerable merit.

See "Nouvelle Biographie Générale ;" QUÉRARD, "La France Littéraire."

Ancharano, d', dän-kä-rä'no, (PIETRO,) an Italian jurist, born about 1350 ; died probably about 1420.

Anchères, ôN'shair', (DANIEL,) a French poet, born near Verdun in 1586, was patronized by James I. of England.

Anchersen, ăng'ker-sen, (JOHAN PEDER,) a Danish antiquary, born at or near Ribe about 1700, was professor of elocution at Copenhagen. He wrote "Origines Danicæ," (1747,) and other works on Danish antiquities. Died in 1765.

See ERSCH und GRUBER, "Allgemeine Encyklopaedie."

Anchersen, [Lat. ANSGA'RIUS or ANSGA'RII,] (MATTHÆUS,) a Danish Oriental scholar, born at Colding in 1682, was made Bishop of Ribe in 1731, and died in 1741.

Ancheta, än-chä'tä, (MIGUEL,) a Spanish sculptor of the sixteenth century, was born at Pamplona. He was reputed one of the best sculptors of his time.

See BERMUDEZ, "Diccionario Historico."

Anchieta, de, dä än-she-ä'tä, (JOSÉ,) a distinguished Portuguese Jesuit and missionary, commonly called "the Apostle of Brazil," was born at Laguna, in Teneriffe, in 1533. He went to Brazil in 1553, and the same year founded a college for the creoles and natives. After a

---

є as k; ç as s; ğ hard; ġ as j; G, H, K, guttural; N, nasal; R, trilled; ṣ as z; ᵵh as in this.   (☞See Explanations, p. 23.)

life of peril and unceasing toil, he died, near Espiritu Santo, in 1597.

See VASCONCELLOS, "Vida do Padre Joseph de Anchieta," 1672; "Vida dei Padre J. de Anchieta," by RODRIGUEZ, 1618.

Anchilus, âng'Ke-lus, [Fr. pron. ŏN'she'lüs',] (N.,) a Flemish painter, an imitator of Teniers, born at Antwerp in 1688, and worked in London. Died in 1733.

An-chi'sēs, [Gr. 'Αγχίσης; Fr. ANCHISE, ŏN'shēz',] a Trojan prince, who was said to have been the father of Æneas by Venus. On the destruction of Troy he escaped w.tn his son, and afterwards died in Sicily.

Ancillon, ŏN'se'yŏN', (CHARLES,) a French writer, son of David, noticed below, was born at Metz in 1659. He accompanied his father to Berlin, where, under the Elector of Brandenburg, (afterwards King of Prussia,) he enjoyed various honourable offices. He left several mediocre works. Died in 1715.

Ancillon, (DAVID,) a learned French Protestant divine, born at Metz in 1617. He was pastor of a church at Metz from 1653 to 1685. After the revocation of the edict of Nantes in the latter year, he went to Berlin, where he died in 1692. He wrote an "Apology for Luther," and a few other works.

See "Discours sur la Vie de M. Ancillon," by CHARLES ANCILLON, 1698.

Ancillon, (JOHANN PETER FRIEDRICH,) an eminent German writer and statesman, of French extraction, born at Berlin in 1766. He was a Protestant minister in early life. In 1806 he was appointed instructor to the crown prince, and received the title of councillor of state, and afterwards held other important offices. He was minister of foreign affairs from 1831 until his death. He belonged to the French family of Ancillons, and wrote in the language of his ancestors with as much facility as in the German. Among his works are "Mélanges of Literature and Philosophy," in French, (1801,) and "On the Spirit of Constitutions, and its Influence upon Legislation," in German, (1825.) His "View of the Revolutions of the Political System of Europe since the Fifteenth Century" (in French, 4 vols., 1803) was very popular. Died in 1837.

See F. A. A. MIGNET, "Notice sur la Vie et les Travaux de M. Ancillon," 1847.

Ancillon, (JOSEPH,) an eminent lawyer, born at Metz in 1626, was a brother of David, noticed above. He emigrated to Berlin about 1685, and became a counsellor of the Elector of Brandenburg. He published a "Treatise on the Difference between Personal Property and Real Estate," (1698.) Died at Berlin in 1719.

Ancillon, (LUDWIG FRIEDRICH,) the father of Johann Peter Friedrich, noticed above, was born in 1744. He was a man of superior talents, and wrote some works on religious philosopny and sacred literature, among which is one on the Cartesian argument for the existence of God, (Berlin, 1792.) Died in 1814.

Ancina, ân-chee'nâ, (GIOVANNI GIOVENALE,) an Italian ecclesiastic, born at Fossano in 1545, became Bishop of Saluzzo in 1602: died in 1604. He wrote several short Latin poems.

Anckarström. See ANKARSTRÖM.

Ancona, d', dân-ko'nâ, (CIRIACO,) an Italian traveller, writer, and antiquary, born at Ancona about 1390. He travelled much in the Levant, where he copied inscriptions and collected manuscripts. He left, besides other works, an "Itinerarium." Died about 1450.

Ancora, d', dân'ko-râ, (GAETANO,) an Italian miscellaneous writer and antiquary, born at Naples in 1757, was professor of Greek in the university of that city. Died in 1816. Among his works are a "Memoir on the Observance of Silence by the Ancients," (1782,) and "Researches on some Metallic Fossils of Calabria," (1791.)

Ancourt. See DANCOURT.

Ancre, d', dôNKR, [It. D'ANCORA, dân'ko-râ,] (Con-cino Concini, kon-chee'no kon-chee'nee,) LE MARÉ-CHAL, an Italian courtier, born at Florence, went to France in 1600 in the retinue of Maria de Medici, queen of Henry IV. He married Eleonora Galigai, who was the favourite attendant of the queen and had great influence at court. After the death of Henry, in 1610, he became first gentleman of the chamber, Marquis d'Ancre,

and marshal of France. He even assumed the power of prime minister, and made many enemies by his insolence and rapacity. He was assassinated in 1617 by De Luines, De Vitry, and others, who appear to have performed the will of the king in this action. His wife was tried, convicted of sorcery and *lèse-majesté*, and executed, in the same year. It is said that when asked by what magic art she gained an ascendency over the queen, she replied, "By that power which strong minds exercise over the weak."

See BAZIN, "Histoire de France sous le Règne de Louis XIII;" G. SALEI, "Cenni storico-critichi su la Vita di C. Concini," 1839; SISMONDI, "Histoire des Français;" D. SANDELLIUS, "De D. Concini Vita," 1767.

An'cus Martius or **Marcius,** (mar'she-us,) fourth king of Rome, a grandson of Numa Pompilius, succeeded Tullus Hostilius about 634 B.C. He is considered the lawgiver or founder of the plebeian order, which seems to have received in his reign a distinct political existence. He waged war with success against the Latins, founded Ostia, and built the Pons Sublicius, (Bridge of Piles.) He died about 610, and was succeeded by Tarquinius Priscus.

See NIEBUHR, "Roman History."

Ancwitz. See ANKWITZ.

Andala, ân'dâ-lâ, (RUARD,) a learned professor of the Cartesian philosophy, and afterwards of theology, in the University of Franeker, was born in Friesland in 1665. He wrote "Descartes in reality the Overturner of Spinosism and the Architect of Experimental Philosophy," (1719.) Died in 1727.

Andelot. See DANDELOT.

Anderloni, ân-děR-lo'nee, (PIETRO,) an Italian engraver, born near Brescia in 1784. He became director of the School of Engraving at Milan in 1831, and engraved several works of Raphael and Titian. Died in 1849.

An'der-sen, (HANS CHRISTIAN,) one of the most gifted writers of the present age, was born at Odense, in the island of Fünen, April 2, 1805. His father was a shoemaker in very indigent circumstances, although he belonged to a family that had once been rich. He used to seek relief from the bitterness of his lot by relating to his children and friends stories of the wealth and splendour of his ancestors. Hans was only nine years old when his father died. His mother wished to apprentice him to a tailor, but was prevailed on by a fortune-teller to send him to Copenhagen. Here he tried to obtain a situation at the theatre; but he was refused because he was so meagre and thin. Having a fine voice, he found employment for a time as a singer. But after six months he lost his voice, and was again thrown upon the world. He was, however, so fortunate as to meet with generous and enlightened patrons. Councillor Collin, who had the sagacity to perceive Andersen's uncommon powers, obtained permission of the king to send the boy to a free academy, to be educated at the expense of the state.

At an early age Andersen had written several short poems, among which "The Dying Child" was particularly admired. Having obtained pecuniary aid from the King of Denmark, he travelled through Germany, France, and Italy. After his return he produced a classical romance, entitled "The Improvisatore," (1834.) The delineations in this work of the scenery and manners of Southern Europe have never been surpassed by any writer. Another, called "O. Z.," appeared in 1835, containing descriptions of life in the North. "Only a Fiddler" presents some striking pictures from the story of his own early life.

The "Poet's Bazaar" (1842) was the result of a visit to the Levant. His original genius is most conspicuous in his fairy-tales, of which he has published several volumes. They are characterized by quaint humour, rich imagination, and sometimes by deep pathos. His numerous works have been translated into most of the European languages.

"For vividness and reality of detail, for breadth and boldness, too, in the description of scenery, and for skill in conveying the impression made on a fine mind and earnest heart by all that is beautiful in nature and true in art, he stands without a rival among recent writers of romance." ("Quarterly Review," March, 1845.)

See HOWITT's "Literature and Romance of Northern Europe," London, 1852; also, "Blackwood's Magazine," vol. lxii. p. 387.

An'der-son, (ADAM,) a Scottish political economist, born about 1690, was a clerk in the South Sea House for forty years. He was author of a well-known History of Commerce, entitled an "Historical and Chronological Deduction of the Origin of Commerce, etc.," (2 vols., 1762,) a work of great research. Died in 1765.

See CHAMBERS, "Biographical Dictionary of Eminent Scotsmen."

Anderson, (ALEXANDER,) an eminent Scottish mathematician, born at Aberdeen about 1580, became professor of mathematics at Paris, and died in the early part of the seventeenth century. He published, besides other works, "Supplementum Apollonii Redivivi," (1612.)

See CHAMBERS, "Biographical Dictionary of Eminent Scotsmen."

Anderson, (ALEXANDER,) M.D., a British botanist, who passed many years in the West Indies, and was superintendent of the botanic garden of Saint Vincent. He wrote an "Account of a Bituminous Lake or Plain in the Island of Trinidad," (1789;) a "Description of the Bread-Fruit Tree," (1798;) and an "Essay on the Cultivation of the Clove," (1802.) Died about 1813.

Anderson, (ARTHUR,) M.P., a Scottish gentleman noted for his public spirit and enterprise, was born in Shetland in 1792. He was the principal founder, and for many years the director, of the Peninsular and Oriental Steam Navigation Company.

Anderson, (CHRISTOPHER,) a British Baptist minister, born in Edinburgh in 1782. He founded the Edinburgh Bible Society. His chief works are the "Domestic Constitution," (1826,) and "Annals of the English Bible," (2 vols., 1845.) Died in 1852.

See "Life and Letters of Christopher Anderson," by his nephew, 1854; CHAMBERS, "Biographical Dictionary of Eminent Scotsmen."

An'der-son, (Sir EDMOND,) an English judge, noted for his learning, born at Broughton about 1530. He was chief justice of the court of common pleas from 1582 until his death, and was one of the commissioners who tried Mary, Queen of Scots, and Sir Walter Raleigh. He treated the Puritans with rigour, but his judicial conduct is said to have been generally moderate and correct. His "Reports of Cases argued and adjudged in the Common Bench" are esteemed good authority. Died in 1605.

See FOSS, "Judges of England;" LLOYD, "State Worthies."

An'der-son, (GEORGE,) a traveller, born in Sleswick. He traversed Persia, India, China, and other countries, between 1644 and 1650, and published a narrative of his travels, in German, (1669.)

Anderson, (GEORGE,) an English writer and mathematician, born at Weston in 1760; died in 1796.

Anderson, (GEORGE B.,) an American general, born at Wilmington, North Carolina, about 1834, graduated at West Point in 1852. He commanded a brigade of Lee's army at the battle of Antietam, and received there a wound at which he died in October, 1862.

Anderson, (HENRY J.,) professor of mathematics, etc. in Columbia College, New York, from 1825 to 1843. He was associated with Lieutenant Lynch in the exploration of the Dead Sea, and published "Geology of Lieutenant Lynch's Expedition," (1848.)

Anderson, (ISAAC,) an American Presbyterian minister, born in Rockbridge county, Virginia, in 1780. He was distinguished as a pioneer preacher or missionary in the Western States, and as the founder of a theological seminary at Maryville, Tennessee. Died in 1857.

Anderson, (JAMES,) a Scottish antiquary and historical writer, born at Edinburgh in 1662. He became a resident of London soon after the union of England and Scotland. He wrote an "Essay showing that the Crown of Scotland is Independent," (1705,) and spent many years in making a collection of ancient Scottish charters, etc., which was published under the title of "Choice Treasury (or Collection) of the Charters and Coins of Scotland," ("Selectus Diplomatum et Numismatum Scotiæ Thesaurus," 1739.) He also published "Collections relating to the History of Mary, Queen of Scotland," (4 vols., 1724–28.) Died in 1728.

See CHAMBERS, "Biographical Dictionary of Eminent Scotsmen."

Anderson, (JAMES,) an ingenious writer on agriculture and political economy, born near Edinburgh in 1739 was a practical farmer. He published valuable "Essays relating to Agriculture and Rural Affairs," (3 vols., 1777,) and edited a weekly periodical called "The Bee," (1790–94,) which is highly commended. In 1797 he removed to the vicinity of London, where he issued a monthly periodical called "Recreations in Agriculture, Natural History, Arts, and Literature," (1799–1802,) in which he developed a new theory on rent, that was afterwards adopted by Malthus and others. His scientific information was extensive and accurate. Besides his other writings, he has contributed several articles to the "Encyclopædia Britannica." Died in 1808.

See CHAMBERS, "Biographical Dictionary of Eminent Scotsmen."

Anderson, (JAMES,) was physician-general of the East India Company's army at Madras, in the last quarter of the eighteenth century. He was noted for long and diligent efforts to introduce the cochineal, mulberry-tree, silkworm, and other productions, into Hindostan. He published letters to Sir Joseph Banks and others on these subjects. Died about 1810.

Anderson, (JAMES,) M.D., an American physician, born in 1752; died in Maryland in 1820.

See THACHER, "Medical Biography."

Anderson, (JAMES STUART MURRAY,) an English writer, born about 1798, graduated as B.A. at Oxford in 1820. He became rector of Tormarton about 1850, and published "The History of the Church of England in the Colonies and Foreign Dependencies of the British Empire," (3 vols., 1851.)

Anderson, ân'der-son, (JOHANN,) an accomplished publicist, was born at Hamburg in 1674, and took the degree of doctor of laws at Leyden in 1697. He was afterwards employed by the citizens of Hamburg in various negotiations at different European courts. He became successively syndic, burgomaster, and senior burgomaster of his native city. Died in 1743. He left an "Account of Greenland, Iceland, and Davis' Straits," (1746.)

Anderson, (JOHN,) born in Dumbartonshire, Scotland, in 1726, was appointed professor of natural philosophy in the University of Glasgow in 1760. Died in 1796. He deserves honourable and grateful remembrance for having founded in Glasgow an institution, called the Andersonian Institution, for the purpose of imparting by popular lectures a knowledge of the useful sciences to mechanics and others not able to go through a full collegiate course. He published a popular work, entitled "Institutes of Physics," (1786.)

See CHAMBERS, "Biographical Dictionary of Eminent Scotsmen."

Anderson, (JOHN,) a Scottish surgeon, born in Mid-Lothian in 1789, wrote "Memoirs of the House of Hamilton," (1825.) Died in 1832.

Anderson, (Rev. JOHN,) a Scottish Presbyterian divine, born about 1671. He became minister of Dumbarton in 1704, and removed to Glasgow in 1720. His chief work is a "Defence of the Church Government, Faith, Worship, and Spirit of the Presbyterians," (1714.) Died about 1722.

See CHAMBERS, "Biographical Dictionary of Eminent Scotsmen."

Anderson, (JOSEPH,) United States Senator, born near Philadelphia in 1757. He was appointed by Washington, in 1791, judge of the territory south of the Ohio. Upon its organization into the State of Tennessee, in 1797, he was elected to the United States Senate, of which he continued an influential member for nineteen years, being twice chosen president *pro tempore*. From 1815 to 1836 he was First Comptroller of the United States Treasury. Died in 1837.

Anderson, (LARS.) See ANDREÆ, (LAURENTIUS.)

Anderson, (RICHARD C.,) an American diplomatist, born in Kentucky about 1750. He was a representative in Congress from Kentucky from 1817 to 1821, United States Minister to the Republic of Colombia in 1823, and in 1826 Envoy Extraordinary to the Assembly of American Nations at Panama. Died at Panama in 1826.

Anderson, (RICHARD HENRY,) an American general, born in South Carolina about 1822, graduated at West Point in 1842. He became a captain in 1855, resigned his commission in 1861, and was made a brigadier-general in the confederate army. He commanded a division at Gettysburg, July, 1863.

Anderson, (ROBERT,) M.D., a Scottish critic and biographer, born in Lanarkshire in 1750. He resided in Edinburgh from 1790 until his death, and had an extensive correspondence with literary men. He is best known as editor of a good edition of "The Works of the British Poets; with Prefaces Biographical and Critical," (14 vols., 1792–1807.) He also published "The Life of Dr. Johnson," (1795,) and "The Life of Dr. Smollett," (1803.) Died in 1830.

See CHAMBERS, " Biographical Dictionary of Eminent Scotsmen."

Anderson, (ROBERT,) a British poet, born at Carlisle in 1770; died in 1833. Many of his ballads and other poems are in the Cumberland dialect. His works are chiefly of a humorous cast.

See "Autobiography of Robert Anderson."

Anderson, (ROBERT,) an American general, born near Louisville, Kentucky, in 1805, graduated at West Point in 1825. He served as captain in the Mexican war, 1846–47, and became a major of artillery in 1857. In the autumn of 1860 he took command of the forts of Charleston harbour. He removed his garrison, December 26, from Fort Moultrie to Fort Sumter, which he refused to surrender on the demand of Governor Pickens. The insurgents besieged Fort Sumter, and began to bombard it on the 12th of April, 1861. The bombardment was kept up with red-hot shot and with unremitting fury for many hours. Major Anderson's position having at length been rendered untenable by want of provisions and by the combustion of part of the fort, he surrendered on the 13th of April. He was promoted to be a brigadier-general in the regular army in May, 1861. In consequence of ill health, or some other reason, he took no further part in the civil war.

See GREELEY's "American Conflict."

Anderson, (WALTER,) a historical and critical writer, who was minister of Chirnside, Scotland, for about fifty years. Among his works are "The History of Croesus, King of Lydia," (1755,) and "The Philosophy of Ancient Greece investigated in its Origin and Progress, etc.," (1791,) which has some merit, but was superseded by Enfield's "Abridgment of Brucker." Died in 1800.

See CHAMBERS, " Biographical Dictionary of Eminent Scotsmen."

Anderson, (WILLIAM,) a British naturalist who was surgeon on the Resolution in Cook's second voyage round the world, 1772–75. He wrote several short treatises.

Anderson, (WILLIAM,) a British horticulturist, born about 1766, was for many years curator of the botanic garden at Chelsea. Died in 1846.

Andersson, ân'der-son, (CHARLES JOHN,) a traveller, born in Sweden in the nineteenth century. Between 1850 and 1855 he passed several years in the exploration of Southern Africa, and made contributions to the natural history and geography of that region. He published a narrative of his adventures. While on a hunting expedition in Southern Africa, he was attacked and killed by a wounded elephant in 1856.

An'der-ton, (HENRY,) an English painter of history and portraits; died about 1665.

Anderton, (JAMES,) an English Roman Catholic controversial writer, who died in 1643.

Andhrimnir or **Andrimner,** ân-drim'ner, in the Norse mythology, the name of the cook who boils every day, in the kettle Eldhrimnir, the flesh of the boar Sæhrimnir, for the table of the gods and heroes.

See THORPE, "Northern Mythology," vol. i.; MALLET, "Northern Antiquities," vol. ii., Fable xx.

Andlo (ând'lo) or **Andlau,** ând'löw, written also **Andelo,** ân'deh-lo, (PETER HERMAN OF,) [Lat. PE'TRUS DE AND'LO or AND'ELO,] a German jurist, of Italian descent, lived in the fifteenth century, and wrote in Latin on the Germanic Empire a work which is remarkable as the first attempt in Germany to compile a system of public law.

An-doç'I-dēs, ['Ανδοκίδης,] an Athenian orator, born about 467 B.C., was called one of the "Ten Orators." He was appointed with Glaucon to command a fleet in

432, and acted a prominent part in political affairs. When the thirty tyrants obtained power in 404 B.C., he went into exile, from which he soon returned. He died about 390 B.C. A few of his orations are extant.

Andoque, ôN'dok', a French writer of the seventeenth century, author of a History of Languedoc, (1648.)

Andrada, ân-drâ'dâ, (FRANCISCO,) a Portuguese poet, flourished about 1600.

Andrada, de, dâ ân-drâ'Dâ, or **Andrade, de,** dâ ân-drâ'Dâ, (ALFONSO,) a Spanish Jesuit, born at Toledo in 1590, wrote many works on theology. Died in 1658.

Andrada, de, dâ ân-drâ'dâ, or **Andrade, de,** dâ ân-drâ'dâ, (ANTONIO,) a Portuguese Jesuit, born in Alentejo about 1580. He went as a missionary to India and Thibet, and published a "New Discovery of the Grand Cathay, or Kingdom of Thibet," (1627.) Died at Goa in 1633.

Andrada, de, or **Andrade, de,** (DIOGO LOPEZ,) a Portuguese preacher, born in Santarem in 1569; died in 1635.

Andrada, de, or **Andrade, de,** (FERNAN PEREZ,) a Spaniard, surnamed (in the Galician dialect) O Bo, ("the Good,") was a friend of Henri de Trastamara. He built, about 1388, a noble bridge across the Eume.

Andrada, de, (FERNÃO PEREZ,) a Portuguese naval officer, commanded a ship in the fleet of Albuquerque, who in 1511 appointed him admiral of a fleet of ten ships at Malacca. He defeated the Sultan of Java in a sea-fight in 1513, and commanded the first European fleet that appeared on the coast of China, (1518.) He was successful in opening commercial intercourse with the Chinese.

Andrada, de, or **Andrade, de,** (FRANCISCO RADES,) a Spanish writer of great merit, born at Toledo, was author of a "History of the Three Spanish Orders of Chivalry," (1572.) He lived in the latter half of the sixteenth century, and was chaplain to Philip II.

Andrada, de, or **Andrade, de,** (JACINTO,) an excellent Portuguese writer, born at Beja in 1597. He was abbot of the monastery of Santa Maria das Chãs. Died in 1657. His principal work is the Life of Dom João de Castro, Viceroy of India, (1651,) which is a model of fine writing.

Andrada, de, (PAOLO GONZALEZ,) a Portuguese lyric poet of the early part of the seventeenth century. He wrote a volume of Spanish poems, (published at Lisbon in 1629.)

Andrada e Sylva, (or **Silva,**) ân-drâ'dâ à sèl'vâ, (JOSÉ BONIFACIO,) a distinguished Brazilian, born at Santos in 1765. He studied at the University of Coimbra in Portugal, and returned to Brazil in 1819. He was a man of great courage, ability, and eloquence, and took the lead in those measures which in 1822 severed Brazil from Portugal and created it an independent empire. He was prime minister of Brazil for a short time in 1822–23, and was appointed guardian of the emperor's minor children in 1831. He died in 1838, leaving several scientific treatises.

His brothers, ANTONIO CARLOS and MARTIN FRANCISCO DE ANDRADA, born towards the close of the eighteenth century, were both distinguished for their talents and eloquence, and both held high positions under the Brazilian government. Antonio Carlos died in 1845.

See J. M. PEREIRA DA SYLVA, "Plutarco Brasileiro," 1847; E. JOAQUIM DA SYLVA MAIA, "José Bonifacio de Andrada e Sylva, Elogio historico," 1838; FLETCHER and KIDDER, "Brazil and the Brazilians," 1868.

Andrade or **Andrada,** (DIOGO de Payva—dâ pī'vâ,) a learned Jesuit, born at Coimbra, in Portugal, in 1528. He distinguished himself by his talents and eloquence at the famous Council of Trent, and afterwards wrote an elaborate defence of its doctrines against Chemnitz, a Protestant controversialist. Died about 1575.

Andral, ôN'drâl', (GABRIEL,) an eminent French physician, born in Paris in 1797, was a son of Guillaume, noticed below. He published "Clinique Médicale," (4 vols., 1824–27,) and a "Summary of Pathological Anatomy," (3 vols., 1829,) which had a great success. He wrote also various other medical works. In 1830 he became professor of pathology, and in 1839 succeeded Broussais in the chair of pathology and therapeutics, in

ã, ē, ĩ, ō, ū, ȳ, *long;* à, è, ò, same, less prolonged; ă, ĕ, ĭ, ŏ, ŭ, ў, *short;* a, e, i, o, *obscure;* fär, fàll, fàt; mêt; nŏt; gōŏd; mōōn·

Paris. He was admitted into the Institute in 1842. The wife of Dr. Andral was a daughter of Royer-Collard. Died in 1853.

See QuÉRARD, "La France Littéraire."

Andral, (GUILLAUME,) a distinguished physician, the father of the preceding, was born in Lot in 1769. He became a physician to the army of Italy, and obtained a high position under Murat at Naples about 1808.

Andray. See ANDRÉ.

André. See ANDREÆ.

André. See ANDREAS.

André, ŏn′drä′, called SYL′VIUS, [in French, DU BOIS, dü bwä′,] a French chronicler of the twelfth century.

Andre, än′drä, (CHRISTIAN KARL,) a German teacher and writer, born at Hildburghausen in 1763. He taught near Gotha and at Brünn, and was editor of a popular magazine called "Hesperus," (1809-31.) Among his numerous works are "Useful Walks for Every Day in the Year," (1790,) and a valuable "Geographico-Statistical Description of the Austrian Empire," (1813.) Died at Stuttgart in 1831.

Andre, (EMIL,) a German writer on the culture and management of forests, was born at Schnepfenthal in 1790.

André, ŏn′drä′, or **Saint-André,** săN′tŏn′drä′, (FRANÇOIS,) a French medical writer, lived about the close of the seventeenth century.

André, sometimes written **Andray,** ŏn′drä′, (JEAN,) a French historical painter, born at Paris in 1662; died in 1753.

Andre, (JOHANN,) a celebrated German composer, kapellmeister to the Prince of Prussia, was born at Offenbach in 1741. He composed many operas and songs. Died in 1799.

Andre, (JOHANN ANTON,) a musical composer, son of the preceding, was born at Offenbach in 1775. He composed masses, concertos, symphonies, etc., and published some works which Mozart left in manuscript. Died about 1845.

André, an′drä or an′dre, (JOHN,) an adjutant-general in the British army of the American Revolution, celebrated for his complicity in the treason of Arnold, was born in London in 1751. His parents were from Geneva, in Switzerland, where he was educated with a view to becoming a merchant. But, being crossed in love, he abandoned the counting-house for the camp, and received his first commission in the British army in 1771. In 1774 he came to America as a lieutenant in the Royal Fusiliers, and was among the officers captured at Saint John's early in the war by Montgomery. His varied and graceful talents and his engaging manners appear to have obtained for him the appointment of adjutant-general with the rank of major, without his performing any distinguished military services. He held, moreover, a facile and at times satirical pen, and occasionally amused himself with caricaturing in rhyme the appearance and exploits of the "rebel" officers. After the evacuation of Philadelphia by the British he was employed to carry on a correspondence with a body of loyalists near the Chesapeake, who were conspiring to restore the royal government. He first introduced himself to the notice of Arnold by means of a letter, written August 16, 1779, to Mrs. Arnold, whose acquaintance he had formed in Philadelphia.

Major André was employed by Sir Henry Clinton to conduct the secret negotiations with Benedict Arnold for the surrender of West Point; and for this purpose he assumed the name of John Anderson. On the 21st of September, 1780, Major André and Arnold had an interview at the house of Joshua H. Smith. Arnold furnished André a number of papers relating to West Point, including maps and plans and memoranda of the weakest points where an attack might be made with the best advantage. He also gave him a passport through the American lines. After he parted from Arnold, Smith accompanied him beyond the American outposts, and André proceeded towards New York City by land. André now pursued his journey in confident security until he had crossed a small stream near Tarrytown, when three men, armed with muskets, emerged from a thicket and brought him to a stand. Losing all caution,

he exclaimed, "Gentlemen, I hope you belong to our party?" "What party?" asked the leader. "The lower party," said André. "We do," was the reply. André then declared himself a British officer on important business, who must not be detained a moment. To his consternation, the party now declared themselves Americans, and told André he was their prisoner. Recovering himself, he attempted to pass off his former declaration as a subterfuge, saying he was a Continental officer procuring information from below, and showed a pass from General Arnold. The suspicions of his captors, however, were fully aroused, and, on searching his person, the papers furnished him by Arnold were found between his stockings and the soles of his feet. As a last resort, André offered them his horse and watch, or any reward they might name, if they would let him go. But the sturdy republicans were not to be bribed. They conducted him ten or twelve miles to North Castle, and delivered him to Lieutenant-Colonel Jameson. Recognizing the handwriting of Arnold in the papers found, and perceiving that they were of a dangerous nature, Colonel Jameson forwarded them by express to Washington at Hartford, and then, with an obtuseness almost incredible, was about to send André to Arnold with a letter stating the circumstances of his arrest and the character of the papers found on him. Major Talmadge, arriving soon after, immediately suspected Arnold, and, by earnest entreaty, prevailed on Jameson to detain André; but the letter was suffered to go on and furnish Arnold timely warning to make his escape. André was tried by a court-martial and condemned to be hung as a spy. He admitted freely who he was, and for what purpose he came within the American lines, but declined disclosing anything implicating any other person. Sir Henry Clinton made great efforts to secure his release. It was intimated to him that André would be given up on the surrender of Arnold; but this was not to be thought of. André requested that his sentence might be commuted to being shot; but the magnitude of the plot in which he was implicated forbade any indulgence being shown him. He was executed at Tarrytown on the morning of October 2, 1780, conducting himself with great fortitude to the last. The day before his execution he sketched, with pen and ink, a miniature likeness of himself, which is now in the Trumbull Gallery of Yale College. In 1821 his remains were transferred to England and interred in Westminster Abbey. The names of his captors were John Paulding, David Williams, and Isaac Van Wart. They were liberally rewarded by Congress, and in 1853 a monument was erected to their memory on the site of André's arrest. Joshua H. Smith was tried for treason, but acquitted on the plea of his ignorance of Arnold's traitorous designs.

See Life of Benedict Arnold, in SPARKS's "American Biography;" WINTHROP SARGENT, "Life and Career of Major John André," 1861; "Atlantic Monthly" for December, 1860.

André, ŏn′drä′, L'ABBÉ, a French writer, born at Marseilles, lived between 1750 and 1800. He published an edition of the works of D'Aguesseau, (13 vols., 1759-90.)

Andre, (RUDOLPH,) a German writer on rural economy, born at Gotha in 1792, was a brother of Emil, above noticed, and was a practical cultivator. It is stated that he first described the art of improving races of animals. Died in 1825.

André, (Marshal SAINT.) See SAINT-ANDRÉ.

André, (VALÈRE.) See ANDREAS, (VALERIUS.)

André, (YVES MARIE,) a French Jesuit writer, and professor of mathematics at Caen, born in 1675 in Brittany; died in 1764. He is known as the author of an "Essay on the Beautiful," (1741,) a work of considerable merit.

Andrea, än-drä′ä, (ALESSANDRO,) an Italian historical writer, born at Barletta in 1519.

Andrea, (GIOVANNI,) an Italian scholar, born at Vigévano in 1417, became Bishop of Aleria in Corsica. He is chiefly remembered as the editor of several classical works published at Rome, among which are "Cæsar's Works," (1469;) "The Decades of Livy," (1470;) "The Works of Virgil," (about 1470;) "Pliny's Natural History," (1470,) and "Cicero's Orations," (1471.) Died in 1475.

ɛ as k; ç as s; ğ hard; ġ as j; G, H, K, guttural; N, nasal; R, trilled; s̄ as z; th as in this. (☞See Explanations, p. 23.)

Andrea, written also **Andreas,** (ONUFRIO,) a Neapolitan poet, wrote, besides other works, a heroic poem, called "Italia Liberata," (1646.) He was ranked among the best Italian poets of his time by Crescimbeni. Died about 1650.

Andrea PISANO, (pe-sä'no,) a celebrated Italian sculptor and architect, born at Pisa about 1270, was a pupil of Nicola and Giovanni Pisani. He was one of the first who abandoned the Gothic style for the antique models of Greece. He was invited to Florence to execute the sculptures of the façade of Santa Maria del Fiore. At the death of Arnolfo di Lapo, Andrea was appointed superintendent of the public works of Florence. He designed the Castello di Scarperia and the church of San Giovanni at Pistoja. His master-piece of sculpture is the bronze rilievi of the gates of the baptistery of San Giovanni at Florence, (1339.) Died at Florence in 1345.

His son NINO was an able sculptor, and finished some of his father's works.

See CICOGNARA, "Storia della Scultura."

Andrea, (ZOAN or GIOVANNI,) a skilful Italian engraver, who lived in the early part of the sixteenth century. He copied and imitated the prints of Mantegna. His works are rare, and command high prices.

See OTTLEY, "Early History of Engraving."

Andrea, d', dân-drä'ä, (FRANCESCO,) an eminent jurist of Naples, born near Amalfi in 1625 ; died in 1698.

Andrea del Castagno. See CASTAGNO.

Andrea del Sarto or **Vannucchi.** See SARTO.

Andrea di Luigi. See LUIGI.

Andreæ, ân-drä'ä, (ABRAHAM,) a Swedish prelate, born in Ångermannland. He was elected Archbishop of Upsal in 1593, before which date he had opposed the attempt of King John to restore the Roman Catholic religion in Sweden. He died in prison in 1607.

Andreæ or **Andreä,** ân-drä'ä, (or **Andreas,** ân-drä'äs,) (JACOB or JAMES,) an eminent German Protestant theologian, born at Waiblingen, in Würtemberg, in 1528. He was ordained deacon at Stuttgart in 1546, after which he became professor at Tübingen. He performed many long journeys in Germany to organize the Lutheran worship, and acquired great influence by his learning, energy, and eloquence. He was president of a board of five who, in 1580, produced the "Formula Concordiæ," a summary and symbol of faith then adopted, and still recognized, by the Lutheran Church. He wrote many polemical works against the Calvinists and Papists. Died in 1590.

See MELCHIOR ADAM, "Vitæ Germanorum Theologorum ;" J. V. ANDREÆ, "Fama Andreana reflorescens," etc., 1630; LEBRET, "Programmata III. de J. Andreæ Vita," 1799.

Andreæ, ân'dre-ē or ân-drä'ä, [Fr. ANDRÉ, ôn'drâ',] (JOHANNES or GIOVANNI,) an eminent professor of canon law, was born near Florence about 1275. He was professor at Bologna for many years. Died in 1348. He was reputed the most celebrated canonist of the fourteenth century. His "Commentaries on the Decretals" were highly esteemed.

See FANTUZZI, "Scrittori Bolognesi ;" MAZZUCHELLI, "Scrittori d'Italia."

Andreæ, (JOHANN GEORG REINHARDT,) a German apothecary, born at Hanover in 1724. He wrote treatises on chemistry, botany, etc., which appeared in the "Hanover Magazine," and "Letters from Switzerland," (2d edition, 1776.) Died in 1793.

Andreæ or **Andreä,** [Fr. ANDRÉ, ôn'drâ',] (JOHANN VALENTIN,) a German satirical writer of great merit, born at Herrenberg, in Würtemberg, in August, 1586, was a grandson of Jacob Andreæ, (1528–90.) He became deacon at Vaihingen in 1614, town-pastor at Calw in 1620, court preacher at Stuttgart in 1639, and ecclesiastic counsellor to the Duke of Brunswick-Wolfenbüttel in 1642. The institution of the order of Rosicrucians is ascribed to him by some writers ; but the disputes on this question have not dispelled its obscurity. His principal work is a "Hundred Satirical Dialogues," ("Menippus, sive Dialogorum Satiricorum Centuria," 1617.) He showed a liberal philosophical spirit in his Latin work entitled "The Images of the Virtues and

Vices of Human Life," (1619.) He also published poems in German, which are praised by Herder. Died in 1654. "Andreæ," says Hallam, "was a man above his age, and a singular contrast to the narrow and pedantic herd of German scholars and theologians."

See SEYBOLD, "Selbstbiographien berühmter Männer," 1799; W. HOSSBACH, "J. V. Andreæ und seiner Zeitalter dargestellt," 1819; FLÖGEL, "Geschichte der Komischen Literatur."

Andreæ, (LAURENTIUS,) [Sw. LARS AN'DERSON,] one of the principal agents in the introduction of the Reformation into Sweden. He was converted to the Protestant faith in 1520, and appears to have become soon after the principal adviser of Gustavus Vasa, who appointed him chancellor. In 1526 he published a translation of the New Testament into Swedish. He afterwards incurred the suspicion and displeasure of his sovereign, and died in obscurity in 1552.

See GEZELIUS, "Biographiskt-Lexicon."

Andreæ, (TOBIAS,) a German Cartesian philosopher, born at Braunfels in 1604, was professor of Greek at Groningen. Died in 1676.

Andreæ, (TOBIAS,) a German physician and professor of philosophy, was born at Bremen in 1633 ; died at Franeker in 1685.

Andreani, ân-drä-ä'nee, (ANDREA,) a noted Italian engraver, surnamed MANTUANO, (i.e. the "Mantuan,") born at Mantua about 1540 ; died in 1623. He carried to great perfection the art of engraving on wood in chiaroscuro. His master-piece is "The Triumph of Cæsar."

An'dre-as, [Gr. Ἀνδρέας,] the name of several ancient physicians, none of whom is of sufficient note to deserve a place here.

An'dreas, an archbishop of Cæsarea in Cappadocia, supposed to have lived about the close of the fifth century. He wrote a commentary on the Apocalypse.

An'dreas surnamed CRETEN'SIS, ("of Crete,") a native of Damascus, who became Archbishop of Crete near the end of the seventh century.

Andreas, (Italian.) See ANDREA.

Andreas, ân-drä'äs, Archbishop of Lund, in Sweden, wrote "Hexaemeron," a Latin poem on the Creation, and was author or compiler of the "Laws of Zealand." Died in 1228.

An-dre'as or **An'drew,** (OF NAPLES,) called also **Andreasso,** ân-drä-äs'so, born about 1324, was the second son of Carobert, King of Hungary. His marriage with Joanna, heiress of the throne of Naples, was celebrated in 1331, and she became queen regnant in 1334. A conspiracy having been formed against him by several princes and barons of Naples, he was assassinated in 1345.

Andreas, ân-drä'äs, a liberal German prelate, Archbishop of Crain, (Carniola,) attempted to reform the Romish Church, the corruptions of which he boldly exposed. He was committed to prison and strangled in 1484.

See ERSCH und GRUBER, "Allgemeine Encyklopaedie."

Andreas or **Andrew,** (JOHN,) surnamed RATISBONEN'SIS, (i.e. "of Ratisbon,") sometimes called ANDREAS MAGISTER, (i.e. "Andrew the Master,") a learned German chronicler who lived about the year 1400.

Andreas, (ONUPHRIUS.) See ANDREA, (ONUFRIO.)

Andreas, ân-drä'äs, or **André,** ôn'drâ', (VALERIUS,) a Flemish bibliographer, born in Brabant in 1588. He became professor of Hebrew and of law at Louvain. His reputation is founded chiefly on his "Bibliotheca Belgica," (1623,) a work of some value on the life and writings of eminent Belgians. Died in 1656.

See FÉLIX NÈVE, "V. André professeur d'Hébreu, etc.," 1846; E. VANDERLINDEN, "V. Andreæ Præconium," 1850.

Andreasi or **Andreassi,** ân-drä-äs'see, (IPPOLITO,) an Italian painter, born at Mantua, was a pupil of Giulio Romano, and lived about 1600.

André-Bardon. See DANDRÉ.

Andre du Bois. See ANDRÉ SYLVIUS.

Andreevsky, ân-drä-êv'ske, (STEPAN,) a Russian physician, who became minister of finances in 1807 ; died in 1818.

Andrei, ân-drä'e or ân-drä', or **An'drew,** (YAROSLAVITCH, yâ-ro-slä'vitch,) a younger brother of Alexander-Nevsky, waged war against Batoo- (or Batou-) Khan the Mogul. Died in 1264.

Andrei or **Andrew,** surnamed YOOREVITCH or YOU-REVITCH, yoo′rĕ-vitch, Grand Duke of Russia, born in 1110, was a warlike prince, and extended his dominions by conquest. He was assassinated in 1174.

Andreini, ân-dRà-ee′nee, (FRANCESCO,) an Italian actor and writer of comedies, born at Pistoja, lived about the close of the sixteenth century. He is supposed to have died about 1620.

Andreini, (GIOVANNI BATTISTA,) son of the preceding, also an actor and writer, was born at Florence about 1578; died about 1650. Besides other successful works, he wrote a sacred drama entitled "L'Adamo," (lå-då′mo,) (or "Adam," 1613,) from which Milton is by some supposed to have derived the idea of "Paradise Lost."

Andreini, (ISABELLA,) a native of Padua, the wife of Francesco, noticed above, was both an accomplished actress and a poetess. Though greatly admired for her personal attractions, she maintained an irreproachable character. Died in 1604, aged forty-two. Among her poems is "Mirtilla, a Pastoral Fable," (1588.)

Andreini, (PIETRO ANDREA,) a learned Italian antiquary, born at Florence about 1650; died in 1720.

Andrelini, ân-dRà-lee′nee, (PUBLIO FAUSTO,) [in Latin, PUB′LIUS FAUS′TUS ANDRELI′NUS,] an Italian writer of Latin poetry, was born at Forlì about 1450. In 1489 he was appointed by Charles VIII. professor of classical literature in the University of Paris, where he died in 1518. His pretensions as a poet were ridiculed by Erasmus, who said his verses lacked only one syllable, *i.e. sense.*

Andreoli, ân-dRà-o′lee, (GIORGIO da Gubbio—då goob′be-o,) an Italian sculptor and worker in terra-cotta, lived about 1500.

Andréossi or **Andréossy,** ŏN′drà′o′se′, (ANTOINE FRANÇOIS,) COUNT OF, a distinguished French military officer and engineer, born at Castelnaudary, in Languedoc, in 1761. He served with distinction in Italy, (1796,) became general of brigade about 1797, and went to Egypt in 1798. He contributed, as a member of the Institute of Cairo, to the labours of the "Commission of Egypt," and wrote excellent memoirs on Lake Menzaleh and the natron lakes. He officiated as chief of the staff of Bonaparte on the 18th Brumaire, 1799, and was made general of division, and appointed successively ambassador to London, Vienna, and Constantinople. On the restoration of the Bourbons (1814) he was recalled from the Ottoman Porte, and remained in private life till the revolution of March, 1815, when he again accepted office under Napoleon as the head of the war department. After the defeat of Napoleon at Waterloo, he was one of the five commissioners sent to negotiate an armistice with the allied powers, on which occasion he gave his ready consent to the recall of the Bourbons. He became a member of the Academy of Sciences in 1826, was elected to the Chamber of Deputies in 1827, and died in 1828. He left, besides other works, a "Journey to the Mouth of the Black Sea, or Essay on the Bosphorus and Delta of Thrace," (1818.)

See MARION, "Notice nécrologique sur le Comte Andréossi," 1843; "Nouvelle Biographie Générale."

Andréossy or **Andréossi,** (FRANÇOIS,) an ancestor of the preceding, born in Paris in 1633. He was an eminent mathematician and engineer, and deserves especial notice as the projector of the Canal of Languedoc. Died in 1688.

Andreozzi, ân-dRà-ot′see, (GAETANO,) an Italian dramatic composer, born at Naples in 1763; died in 1826.

Andres, ân′dRĕs, (BONAVENTURA JOHANN,) a learned Jesuit, born at Nuremberg in 1744; died in 1822.

Andrés, ân-dRĕs′, (CARLOS,) a Spanish lawyer, born near Valencia in 1753. He translated into Spanish several works of his brother Juan Andrés. Died in 1820.

Andrés, (JUAN,) a most learned Spanish author, born at Planes, in the province of Valencia, in 1740, joined the Society of Jesuits in 1754. When the Jesuits were expelled from Spain in 1767, he went first to Corsica and afterwards to Italy. The most important and best-known of his numerous works is that entitled "On the

Origin, Progress, and Present State of all Literature," ("Dell' Origine, de' Progressi, e dello Stato attuale d'ogni Letteratura," 7 vols., 1782–99.) He was appointed by Joseph Bonaparte prefect or keeper of the royal library at Naples in 1806. His best works are in Italian, although he sometimes wrote in Latin, and occasionally in Spanish. His "Essay on the Philosophy of Galileo" (1776) is particularly commended. Died in 1817.

See TIPALDO, "Biografia degli Italiani illustri."

Andrés de Gusseme, ân-dRĕs′ då goos′så-mä, (TOMAS,) a Spanish numismatist of the eighteenth century.

Andrés de Uztarroz, ân-dRĕs′ då ooth-târ-rŏth′, (JUAN FRANCISCO,) an eminent Spanish historian and antiquary, born at Saragossa about 1606. He obtained the title of chronicler of the kingdom. Among his numerous works is one called "Annals of the Crown and Kingdom of Aragon," (1663.) Died in 1653.

An′drew, [Gr. Ἀνδρέας; Fr. ANDRÉ, ŏN′dRà′; Lat. AN′DREAS,] SAINT, one of the twelve apostles, was a brother of Saint Peter, and a fisherman of Galilee. He appears to have found the Messiah and become his disciple before any other of the twelve, with perhaps one exception. (See John i. 40.) He is supposed to have preached the gospel in Greece, Thrace, and the countries north of the Danube. Tradition adds that he suffered martyrdom at Patræ, (now Patras,) in Achaia. See Matthew iv. 18, x. 2; Mark i. 16, xiii. 3; Luke vi. 14; John vi. 8, xii. 22.)

An′drew or **András,** ŏn′drås, the name of three Hungarian kings of the line of Arpád, between 1046 and 1301. Andrew I. ascended the throne about 1046; died about 1060.

Andrew II. of Hungary, born about 1176, began to reign in 1205. In 1222, seven years after King John of England had granted the Magna Charta to his barons, Andrew II., scarcely less weak than his English contemporary, promulgated the Golden Bull, or Magna Charta of Hungary, in which the following remarkable clause occurs: "If we, or any of our successors, ever at any time wish to act contrary to this our ordinance, then let our bishops and the other barons and nobles of our kingdom, all and sundry, present and to come, have the free power of resisting and contradicting us and our successors, as a perpetual privilege, without the reproach of any want of fidelity." This provision was confirmed and sworn to by every successive king of Hungary for more than four hundred years. In 1687 it was modified with the consent of the states. Andrew died in 1235, and was succeeded by his son Bela.

Andrew III., King of Hungary, a grandson of Andrew II., was born at Venice. He began to reign in 1290. The pope claimed Hungary as a fief of the popedom, and made a donation of it to Charles Martel, son of the King of Naples, whose army was defeated by Andrew (1291) at Agram. He died in 1301, and was the last king of the line of Arpád.

Andrew OF CRETE. See ANDREAS.

Andrew, PRINCE OF RUSSIA. See ANDREI.

Andrew OF PISA. See ANDREA PISANO.

An′drew, (JAMES,) a Scottish mathematician and grammarian, born in 1774; died in Edinburgh in 1833.

An′drew, (JOHN ALBION,) an American statesman, born at Windham, Maine, in May, 1818. He graduated at Bowdoin College about 1837, studied law, and was admitted to the bar in Boston in 1840. He gained distinction by his opposition to slavery, and was elected a member of the legislature by the Republicans of Boston in 1858. In 1860 he was elected Governor of Massachusetts for one year. Within a week after President Lincoln's call for seventy-five thousand men, April 15, 1861, he dispatched five regiments in answer to that summons. He was elected Governor the second time, in 1861, and afterwards re-elected at three successive elections. In his message of January, 1862, he said, "The great rebellion must be put down, and its promoters crushed beneath the ruins of their own ambition. The greatest crime of history must receive a doom so swift and sure that the enemies of popular government shall stand in awe while they contemplate the elastic energy and concentrative power of democratic institu-

---

€ as *k;* ç as *s;* ḡ *hard;* ḡ as *j;* G, H, K, *guttural;* N, *nasal;* R, *trilled;* s as *z;* s as in *this.* (☞See Explanations, p. 23.)

tions and a free people." Governor Andrew acquired great and well-deserved popularity by his assiduous attention to the wants of the soldiers in the field, by the fervid eloquence with which he animated the people during the civil war, and by his persistent efforts for the arming and liberation of the negroes. He died, deeply lamented, in October, 1867. A meeting of members of the legislature of Massachusetts passed a resolution— "That in his decease the commonwealth and the nation alike have suffered an irreparable loss ; that his reputation had become national, and we might well have hoped for him the highest national offices and honours." "Among the many heroic men," says Mrs. Stowe, "who have sacrificed their lives in the great battle of liberty in our country, there is no one who deserves a more honoured memory than John A. Andrew of Massachusetts."

See HARRIET BEECHER STOWE, "Men of Our Times," 1868 ; P. C. HEADLEY, "Massachusetts in the Rebellion," p. 18 ; "Notice of the Official Life of Governor Andrew," (anonymous,) 1868.

An'drews, (ANNIE M.,) an American lady, born about 1835. She devoted herself to the relief of the sick as a nurse during the prevalence of the yellow fever at Norfolk, Virginia, in 1855.

Andrews, (EBENEZER S.,) an American publisher, born in Boston in 1766. As a partner of Isaiah Thomas, he established a publishing house at Baltimore in 1794, and another at Albany in 1796. Died in 1851.

Andrews, (ETHAN ALLEN,) LL.D., an American scholar and writer, born at New Britain, in Connecticut, in 1787, graduated at Yale College in 1810. He was for several years professor of the ancient languages in the University of North Carolina. He was the author of a number of school-books, chiefly designed for those commencing the study of the Latin language. Andrews and Stoddard's "Latin Grammar" in particular has had an extensive circulation. His most important work is an excellent Latin-English Lexicon, (1850,) on the basis of Freund's "Wörterbuch der Lateinischen Sprache." Died in 1858.

An'drews, (HENRY,) an English artist and botanist, who resided in London. He published a series of coloured engravings with descriptions of rare plants, entitled "The Botanist's Repository," (10 vols., 1797–1814.) Among his other works is a "Monograph of the Genus Rosa," with coloured figures.

Andrews, (JAMES PETIT,) an English historical writer, born near Newbury, in Berks, in 1737. He published a "History of Great Britain connected with the Chronology of Europe," (vol. i., part i., 1794, part ii., 1795,) a work of some merit, which was never finished. It is composed on a new plan, and comprises the period from Cæsar's invasion to the accession of Edward IV. Among his other works is a curious and amusing collection of "Anecdotes, etc., Ancient and Modern," (1789,) and a "Continuation of Henry's History of Great Britain" (1 vol., 1796) to the accession of James I. Died in 1797.

See "Gentleman's Magazine," September, 1797.

Andrews, (JOHN,) LL.D., an English historian, for whose biography we find scanty materials. His principal works are a "History of the Revolutions of Denmark," (2 vols., 1774,) and a "History of the War with America, France, Spain, and Holland," (4 vols., 1785–86). He died in his seventy-third year, in 1809. "By his death," says the "Gentleman's Magazine," "the nation is deprived of an able historian and a profound scholar."

See "Gentleman's Magazine," February, 1809.

Andrews, (JOHN,) D.D., an Episcopal clergyman, born in Cecil county, Maryland, in 1746. In 1789 he was appointed professor of moral philosophy in the University of Pennsylvania, and in 1810 became provost of that institution. He published "Elements of Logic." Died in 1813.

Andrews or **Andrewes,** an'drŭz, (LANCELOT,) an English divine of great learning, was born in London in 1555, and educated at Cambridge. Having attained distinction as a preacher, he became one of the chaplains of Queen Elizabeth, who appointed him Dean of Westminster in 1601. He was one of the ten divines selected to translate the Pentateuch in the reign of James I., and

was chosen Bishop of Chichester in 1605. At the request of the king, he wrote a work called "Torture of Tortus," ("Tortura Torti," 1609,) in which he defended the authority of kings in ecclesiastical affairs, in answer to Matthew Tortus. He was translated to the see of Ely in 1609 and made a privy councillor. In 1618 he was promoted to the see of Winchester, and became dean of the royal chapel. He died in 1626, leaving a high reputation for piety, moderation, and charity. Among his most popular works we may name his "Manual of Private Devotions and Meditations for every Day in the Week," and a "Manual of Directions for the Visitation of the Sick." He was probably more learned in canon law and ecclesiastical antiquities than any of his English contemporaries. His style was once greatly admired, but is too affected and pedantic to please the critics of the present age. His death was deplored by Milton in a Latin elegy.

See CASSAN, "Lives of the Bishops of Winchester ;" FULLER, "Worthies of England," and his "Church History ;" ISAACSON, "Life of Bishop Andrews," 1650.

Andrews, (MILES PETER,) M.P., an English dramatist, but more noted as a man of fashion than as an author, was a son of a merchant of London, and inherited a fortune. He wrote several comedies, one of which is called "Better Late than Never," (1790.) He represented Bewdley in Parliament from about 1790 till his death. His dinners and entertainments were celebrated. Died in 1814.

See "Biographia Dramatica."

An'drews, (THOMAS,) M.D., F.R.S., a chemist, born in Belfast, graduated at Edinburgh in 1835. He received from the Royal Society, in 1845, a medal for his researches into the heat produced by chemical combination. He became professor of chemistry at Belfast in 1849.

Andri. See ANDRY.

Andria, ân'dRe-â, (NICOLA or NICCOLÒ,) an able Italian scientific writer, born in Otranto in 1748. He became successively professor of natural history, (1775,) physiology, (1801,) and the theory of medicine, (1808,) at the University of Naples. Among his works are "Elements of Chemical Philosophy," in Latin, (1786,) "Institutes of the Practice of Medicine," ("Institutiones Medicinæ Practicæ," 1790,) and "General Observations on the Theory of Life," (1804.) Died in 1814. His Latin works have been translated into Italian, and the last of the above-named into French.

See CALLISEN, "Medicinisches Schriftsteller-Lexikon."

Andrian-Warburg, von, fon ân'dRe-ân ŵaR'boôRG, (VICTOR,) BARON, an Austrian writer on politics and government, born near Göritz in 1813.

Andriessens, ân'dRès'sĕns, (ANTON,) a skilful Dutch landscape-painter, born at Amsterdam in 1746. He was a member of the Academy of that city. Died in 1813.

Andriessens, (J.,) a brother of the preceding, born at Amsterdam in 1742, was a painter of history and landscape, and a distinguished teacher of art. Several eminent artists were pupils of his school at Amsterdam. Died in 1819.

See DESCAMPS, "Vies des Peintres Hollandais," etc.

Andrieu or **Andrieux,** ôN'dRe'uh', (BERTRAND,) a celebrated French medallist and mint engraver, born at Bordeaux about 1760. He worked in Paris, and excelled in minuteness and correctness of execution. He engraved medals for the most important events of the reign of Napoleon. Among his master-pieces are "Napoleon crossing the Alps," "The Battle of Marengo," and "The Peace of Vienna." Died in 1822.

Andrieu, ôN'dRe'uh', (MARIE MARTIN ANTOINE,) a French military officer, born in 1768, became adjutant-general in 1797. Died in Saint Domingo in 1802.

Andrieux, ôN'dRe'uh', (FRANÇOIS GUILLAUME JEAN STANISLAS,) a popular French dramatist and poet, born at Strasburg in 1759. He studied law, which he practised for some years. In 1787 he produced a successful comedy, "The Giddy-Heads," ("Les Étourdis.") He hailed the Revolution with joy ; he was chosen a member of the Council of Five Hundred in 1798, and of the Tribunat in 1800. Having been removed from this office, on account of his independence, in 1802, he re-

ă, ĕ, ĭ, ŏ, ŭ, ȳ, *long;* ä, ė, ĭ, ŏ, ŭ, ȳ, *short;* ạ, ẹ, ị, ọ, *obscure;* fär, fåll, fåt; mĕt; nŏt; gŏŏd; mŏŏn;

nounced politics. In 1804 he became professor of grammar and belles-lettres in the École Polytechnique, and librarian of the Senate. He was chosen, at the unanimous desire of the members of the French Academy, professor of literature in the College of France in 1814, which position he held nearly twenty years. As a lecturer he was very popular. In 1829 he was elected perpetual secretary of the French Academy. Among his numerous works are several comedies in verse, one of which is called "La Comédienne," (1816,) occasional poems, and "Lectures on the Philosophy of the Belles-Lettres." Died in Paris in 1833.

See A. H. TAILLANDIER, "Notice sur la Vie et les Ouvrages d'Andrieux," 1850; M. THIERS, "Discours sur Andrieux," in the "Recueil de l'Académie Française," 1830–39; also article by A. H. TAILLANDIER, in the "Nouvelle Biographie Générale."

Andrioli, ân-dRE-o′lee,(GIROLAMO,) an Italian painter of Verona, lived about 1610.

Andriolli, ân-dRE-ol′lee, (MICHEL ANGELO,) a physician and medical writer of Verona, lived about the end of the seventeenth century. He wrote a "Manual of Practical Medicine," (1700,) and other medical works of some merit.

An-dris′cus, [Gr. Ἀνδρίσκος,] a native of Adramyttium, in Asia Minor, declared himself, about 150 B.C., the son of Perseus, King of Macedon, assumed the name of Philip, (whence he was called Pseudo-Philippus, *i.e.* the "false Philip,") and made himself master of all Macedonia. He defeated one Roman army, but was at length defeated himself and taken prisoner by Cæcilius Metellus, 148 B.C.

Androcle. See ANDROCLES.

An′dro-clēs, [Ἀνδροκλῆς,] an Athenian demagogue, enemy of Alcibiades, after whose exile, 415 B.C., he became the chief of the democratic party at Athens. He was assassinated in 411 B.C.

Androcles or **An′dro-clus,** [Fr. ANDROCLE, ôN′-dRok′l′,] a slave who lived at Rome about the beginning of the Christian era, was the subject of a well-known story, which is briefly as follows. He ran away from his master, and hid himself in a wild region of Africa, where he extracted a thorn from the foot of a lion that he met in a cave. The grateful animal, in return, shared with Androcles the products of the chase for several years. Having been caught by his master, Androcles was condemned to fight in the circus with a lion, which proved to be his former friend, and received him with caresses. Androcles was then pardoned and set free. This remarkable narrative is related by Aulus Gellius on the authority of one who affirmed that he had witnessed the scene at the amphitheatre.

See "The Guardian," No. 139, by ADDISON; DION CASSIUS; AULUS GELLIUS.

An′dro-clus, a son of Codrus, King of Athens, led a colony to Asia Minor, and became King of Ephesus, probably about 1050 B.C.

An-dro-çȳ′dēs, [Ἀνδροκύδης,] a Greek painter, a native of Cyzicus, was a rival of Zeuxis, and lived about 400 or 375 B.C.

Androcydes, a Greek physician who lived about 330 B.C.

An-dro′ge-us, [Gr. Ἀνδρόγεως; Fr. ANDROGÉE, ôN′-dRo′zhȧ′,] a son of Minos, King of Crete, vanquished all the Greek athletes at the games of the Panathenæa. It was fabled that Ægeus, moved by envy, caused him to be assassinated, and that Minos waged war against Athens to avenge his death.

An-drom′a-ehē, [Gr. Ἀνδρομάχη; Fr. ANDROMAQUE, ôN′dRo′mȧk′,] a Trojan lady, the wife of Hector, celebrated for her beauty and virtue. On the fall of Troy she became the captive of Pyrrhus. She was afterwards the wife of Helenus, a son of Priam.

An-drom′a-ehus, [Gr. Ἀνδρόμαχος,] an ancient physician, native of Crete, who became "Archiatros" (*i.e.* "chief physician") to the Roman emperor Nero. He invented or improved a famous medical compound called "'Theri′aca Androm′achi."

Andromaque. See ANDROMACHE.

An-drom′e-dạ, [Gr. Ἀνδρομέδη; Fr. ANDROMÈDE, ôN′dRo′mȧd′,] a daughter of Cepheus, King of Ethiopia, and of Cassiopeia. According to the Greek poets, she

was rescued from a sea-monster by Perseus, and was transformed into a constellation of the celestial sphere.

Andronic, the French of ANDRONICUS, which see.

An-dro-nī′cus [Gr. Ἀνδρόνικος] OF OLYN′THUS, a general of Alexander the Great. In 314 B.C. he fought for Demetrius against Ptolemy.

Andronicus, an Egyptian Jew, who lived in the reign of Ptolemy Philometor, in the second century B.C. In a judicial contest between the Jews and Samaritans, respecting the authority of the temples at Jerusalem and Gerizim in Samaria, Andronicus pleaded the cause of the Jews with success before the king.

Andronicus, a Greek poet of high reputation, born in Egypt, lived about 360 A.D. His works are not extant.

Androni′cus, (JOAN′NES CALLIS′TUS,) a Greek teacher, born at Thessalonica, (Saloniki,) was learned in grammar and philosophy. After the capture of Constantinople in 1453, he fled to Italy, and taught the Greek language at Rome and Florence. He was afterwards a professor in the University of Paris. Died about 1478.

Andronicus, (MARCUS LIVIUS.) See LIVIUS ANDRONICUS.

Andronicus, (MARCUS POMPILIUS,) an Epicurean philosopher of Syria, taught at Rome about 60 B.C.

Androni′cus RHO′DIUS, (*i.e.* "of Rhodes,") a Peripatetic philosopher, who collected, revised, and arranged the works of Aristotle about 80 B.C. He is said to have invented the term Metaphysics. His works are lost.

Andronicus An′ge-lus, a nephew of Alexis Comnenus, was a general in the reign of Manuel, 1143–80. His sons Isaac and Alexis became emperors.

Androni′cus I., Com-nē′nus, [Gr. Ἀνδρόνικος Κομνηνός; Fr. ANDRONIC, ôN′dRo′nèk′,] a Byzantine emperor, remarkable for his talents, personal beauty, strength, profligacy, and cruelty. He was born about 1115, and was a grandson of Alexis I. Comnenus. He succeeded in getting himself appointed regent during the minority of Alexis II.; but, abusing the powers thus conferred, he put that prince and his mother the empress Maria to death, and usurped the throne, in 1183. Some of the nobles having formed a conspiracy against him, he determined to exterminate the whole body of the aristocracy. When multitudes had already perished, and his cruel purpose seemed on the point of being completely fulfilled, the people of Constantinople rose in insurrection, seized Andronicus, and, after inflicting on him every species of indignity, put him to death, in 1185.

See NICETAS, "Andronicus Comnenus;" GIBBON, "Decline and Fall of the Roman Empire."

Androni′cus Cyrrhes′tes, (sIr-rês′tèz,) [Κυρρήστης,] a Greek architect, who is supposed to have designed the Tower of the Winds at Athens, which was intended to show the direction of the wind.

Andronicus II., Palæologus, (pa-le-ol′o-gus,) [Gr. Παλαιόλογος,] a son of the emperor Michael, was born about 1260, and began to reign in 1283. He manifested a decided hostility to the Roman Pontiff, by whom he was excommunicated in 1307. He waged war with various success against the Turks. In 1328 he was deposed by his grandson Andronicus, and died about 1332.

See GIBBON, "Decline and Fall of the Roman Empire."

Andronicus III., Palæologus, grandson of the preceding, was born about 1296. The emperor his grandfather resolved, on account of his dissolute habits, to deprive him of his right to the succession. After a civil war of several years between the young prince and his grandfather, the latter abdicated in 1328. Andronicus III. was defeated by the Turks in 1330, and was, from the time of his accession, involved in almost continual wars. Died in 1341, aged forty-five, and was succeeded by his son John.

See GIBBON, "Decline and Fall of the Roman Empire."

An′dros, (EDMUND,) an English gentleman, born in London in 1637, was in 1672 major in Prince Rupert's regiment of dragoons. In 1674 he was appointed Governor of New York. He was recalled in 1681, and received the honour of knighthood. In 1686, James II., having resolved to unite the whole of New England under one government, appointed Sir Edmund Andros

---

e as k; ç as s; g̃ hard; g̃ as j; G, H, K, guttural; N, nasal; R, trilled; s̃ as z; th as in this. (☞See Explanations, p. 23.)

Governor of the same, and subsequently, in 1688, of New York. In consequence of his arbitrary proceedings, his administration became very unpopular. On the news of the landing of the Prince of Orange in England, the inhabitants of Boston rose in insurrection, (April, 1689,) imprisoned Andros, and restored Bradstreet, the former Governor. In the following July, orders came from King William to send Andros to England; but, the charges against him having been withdrawn, he escaped unpunished, and afterwards, in 1692, was appointed Governor of Virginia. He was removed in 1698, and died in England in 1713 or 1714.

See BELKNAP, "History of New Hampshire;" NEAL, "History of New England;" BANCROFT, "History of the United States," vols. ii. and iii.; HILDRETH, "History of the United States."

An'dros, (THOMAS,) an American divine and patriot, born at Norwich, Connecticut, in 1759. He fought at the battles of Long Island and White Plains, was afterwards taken prisoner, and confined in a prison-ship, from which he escaped. He preached more than forty years at Berkeley, Massachusetts. Died in 1845.

An-dros'the-nēś, [Gr. Ἀνδρόσθενης,] a Greek sculptor of Athens, lived about 420 B.C., and adorned the temple of Apollo at Delphos.

Androsthenes of Thasos, a general of Alexander the Great, accompanied Nearchus in the expedition to explore the Persian Gulf.

An-dro'tĭ-on, [Ἀνδροτίων,] an Athenian orator and demagogue, a pupil of Isocrates, lived about 350 B.C. We have an oration of Demosthenes against a political measure which Androtion advocated.

Androuet du Cerceau, ŏn'drŏo'ả' dü sĕR'sō', (JACQUES,) a skilful French architect, born at Paris, (or, as some writers state, at Orléans,) was a Protestant. He was appointed royal architect about 1578, and designed the Pont Neuf, at Paris. He was employed by Henry IV. in the extension of the Tuileries, and is supposed to have commenced the gallery of the Louvre. He published several architectural works, one of which is called "The Most Excellent Buildings (*Bâtiments*) of France," (1576.) Died about 1592, in exile for his religion.

See DEZALLIER D'ARGENVILLE, "Vies des fameux Architectes."

Andry, ŏn'dre', (CHARLES LOUIS FRANÇOIS,) a French physician, born in Paris in 1741. He wrote an able "Treatise on the Induration of Cellular Tissue in New-born Infants," (1788.) He was one of the consulting physicians of Napoleon I. Died in 1829.

Andry, (NICOLAS,) surnamed BOISREGARD, (bwăR'-găR',) a French physician and medical writer, born at Lyons in 1658, became dean of the faculty of medicine in the University of Paris in 1724. He lost this position after the lapse of two years. His "Treatise on the Generation of Worms in the Human Body" (1700) was reprinted and translated into English, German, Italian, and Dutch. Died in 1742.

Aneau or **Anneau,** ả'nŏ', (BARTHÉLÉMY,) a French poet and historian, born at Bourges, was favourable to the Protestant faith. He was killed by a mob in 1561.

Anel, ả'nĕl', (DOMINIQUE,) a distinguished French surgeon, born at Toulouse in 1678. He introduced important improvements in the operations for aneurism and fistula lachrymalis. His method for the former was further improved by John Hunter. He practised in Paris with high reputation, chiefly as an oculist, and wrote several surgical works. Died probably about 1725.

See "Biographie Médicale."

Aneley. See ANNESLEY.

Anelli, â-nel'lee, (ANGELO,) an Italian poet and professor, born near Brescia in 1761. He became professor of history and eloquence at Brescia in 1802, and of forensic eloquence at Milan in 1809. Among his works are odes, elegies, comedies, and a humorous satirical poem called "The Chronicles of Pindus," ("Le Cronache di Pindo," 1811,) which is commended. Died in 1820.

Anerio, â-nā're-o, (FELICE,) a celebrated Italian composer, was born at Rome about 1560. He composed both sacred and secular music, and succeeded Palestrina as composer to the chapel of the pope. Died about 1630.

See FÉTIS, "Biographie Universelle des Musiciens."

Anerio, (GIOVANNI FRANCESCO,) a composer and musician, a brother of the preceding, was born at Rome about 1567; died after 1603.

Anesi, â-nā'śee, (PAOLO,) a painter, born at Florence, lived in the first half of the eighteenth century.

An'eu-rin, a Welsh poet of the sixth century. Among his works is a poem of nine hundred lines, called the "Gododin," which is still extant.

See E. JONES, "Relicks of the Welsh Bards."

Anfossi, ân-fos'see, (PASQUALE,) a successful Italian dramatic composer, born at Naples about 1733. He lived in Paris, London, and Rome, and composed many operas, oratorios, masses, and motets. Among his best operas are "Antigone" and "L'Avaro." He died at Rome about 1795.

Anfosso, ân-fos'so, (JACOPO,) an able Italian engraver, worked at Pavia in the sixteenth century.

Ange de Saint-Joseph, ŏnzh deh săN'zho'zĕf', or JOSEPH **Labrosse,** (lẳ'bRoss',) a French missionary, born at Toulouse in 1636, laboured in Persia. Died in 1697.

Ange de Sainte-Rosalie, ŏnzh deh săNt'ro'zả'le', or FRANÇOIS **Raffard,** (rẳ'fảR',) a French monk, born at Blois in 1655. He wrote a History of the House of France. Died in 1726.

Angela OF BRESCIA, or **Angela Merici,** ân'jả-lâ mả-ree'chee, who founded the order of Ursuline nuns, was born near Brescia in 1511; died in 1540.

Angeli, (French and German.) See ANGELY.

An'ge-lī, (singular, **An'ge-lus,**) the name of a Byzantine family, several of whose members were emperors of Constantinople; viz., Isaac Angelus, who died in 1204, Alexis III., (see ALEXIS,) and Alexis IV.

Angeli, ân'jả-lee, (BONAVENTURA,) an Italian writer and jurist, born at Ferrara about 1525; died about 1592. His most important work is a "History of Parma," (1591.) He also wrote several legal treatises.

Angeli, ân'jả-lee, (FILIPPO,) an Italian painter of landscapes and battles, born in Rome, was esteemed one of the best landscape-painters of his time. He worked at Florence, to which he removed in 1612, and was patronized by the Grand Duke Cosmo. In his works the aerial perspective is well expressed, and he is said to have been the first painter who applied the strict rules of perspective to landscapes. He was sometimes called FILIPPO NAPOLITANO, because he lived at Naples in his youth. Died about 1645.

See LANZI, "History of Painting in Italy."

Angeli, (STEFANO,) an able Italian mathematician, who lived about 1650, was a pupil of Cavalieri. He taught mathematics at Padua, advocated the Copernican system, and published, besides other works, "Problemata Geometrica," (1658.)

Angelico, (FRA.) See FIESOLE.

Angelico, ân-jĕl'e-ko, (MICHEL ANGELO,) an Italian apothecary, born at Vicenza, lived about 1600.

Angelico, (MICHEL ANGELO,) an Italian poet, born at Vicenza. He entered the service of the emperor Leopold in 1690 as imperial poet, and lived at Vienna. Among his works is a volume of "Lyric Poems," ("Poesie liriche," 1665.) Died at Vienna in 1697.

Angelio, ân-jā'le-o, or **degli Angeli,** dẳl'yee ân'-jả-lee, (PIETRO,) [Lat. PE'TRUS ANGE'LIUS,] a distinguished Italian scholar and writer of Latin poetry, was born at Barga, (whence he was called BARGÆUS, bar-jē'us,) in Lucca, in 1517. He was professor of belles-lettres, etc. at Pisa for about twenty-five years. Among many other poems, he wrote a Latin epic on the conquest of Jerusalem by the crusaders, entitled "The Syriad," ("Syriados Libri XII.," 1591,) a work which was greatly admired by his contemporaries and was even compared to Tasso's immortal poem. In the estimation, however, of more recent critics, it possesses but little merit. His poem on hunting, "Cynegeticon, vel de Venatione," (1562,) is commended as his best work. Died in 1596.

See MAZZUCHELLI, "Scrittori d'Italia;" GINGUENÉ, "Histoire Littéraire d'Italie."

Angelis, ân'jả-lĕs, or **degli Angeli,** dẳl'yee ân'jả-lee, (ALESSANDRO,) an Italian astronomer, born at Spoleto in 1562; died in 1620.

ā, ē, ĭ, ō, ū, ȳ, *long;* ả, ĕ, ŏ, same, less prolonged; ă, ĕ, ĭ, ŏ, ŭ, ў, *short;* ạ, ẹ, ị, ọ, *obscure;* fär, fảll, fåt; mêt; nŏt; gōōd; mōōn;

Angelis, (FILIPPO.) See ANGELI.

Angélis, ȯṉ'zhȧ'lẽss', (PIERRE,) a French painter of landscapes and conversation-pieces, born at Dunkirk in 1685. He worked several years in England with success, visited Rome in 1728, and afterwards settled at Rennes, where he died in 1734. "His manner," says Walpole, "was a mixture of Teniers and Watteau, with more grace than the former, more nature than the latter." See WALPOLE, "Anecdotes of Painting."

Angelis, de, dȧ ân'jȧ-lès, (DOMENICO,) a Neapolitan biographer, born at Lecce in 1675; died in 1719.

Angelis, de, (GIROLAMO,) a devoted Jesuit missionary, born in Sicily in 1567. He visited the Japanese islands in 1602, and, after having made many thousand converts, was burnt alive in 1623.

Angelis, de, (PAOLO,) an Italian antiquary, born in Syracuse; died in 1647.

Angelis, de, dȧ ân'zhȧ-lès, (PEDRO,) a Portuguese publicist, born in Italy, resided at Buenos Ayres. He published in Spanish a work on the history of the provinces of Rio de la Plata (in seven volumes, the first of which appeared in 1836.) It is entitled "Coleccion de Obras y Documentos relativos a la Historia," etc.

Angell, ân'jęl, (JOSEPH K.,) a distinguished American writer on law, born at Providence, Rhode Island, in 1794. He published, besides other works, a "Treatise on the Right of Property in Tide-Waters," (1826.) In conjunction with Samuel Ames, he wrote a "Treatise on the Law of Private Corporations Aggregate," (2d edition, 1843,) which, says Chancellor Kent, is a "very learned, full, and finished treatise, and cannot be too highly praised." Died in 1857.

Angelo, ân'jȧ-lo, (F.,) an Italian poet of Florence, wrote "I Lucidi," a comedy, and other poems. Died at Rome in 1548.

Angelo di Buonarotti, (MICHAEL.) See MICHAEL ANGELO.

Angelo, (POLICIANO.) See POLIZIANO.

Angelo, di, de ân'jȧ-lo, (JACOPO,) a Tuscan, who lived in the fourteenth and fifteenth centuries and was distinguished for his successful efforts to introduce into Italy the study of Greek literature.

Angeloni, ân-jȧ-lo'nee, (FRANCESCO,) an Italian antiquary, born at Terni, in the Roman States, was the uncle and instructor of Bellori. He was secretary to Cardinal Aldobrandini. Among his principal works is "Istoria Augusta," and "The History of Rome from Julius Cæsar to Constantine the Great, illustrated by Ancient Medals," (1641.) Died in Rome in 1652.

Angeloni, (LUIGI,) an Italian politician, born in the Roman Campagna about 1758. He became a tribune in the Roman republic in 1798, and emigrated or fled to Paris in 1799. He entered into a conspiracy against Bonaparte, and was imprisoned for a number of months, about 1810. In 1811 he published a work on the life and writings of Guido d'Arezzo, who has been called the restorer of music. He also wrote several political treatises. Died in London in 1842.

Angelo Rocca. See ROCCA.

Angelucci, ân-jȧ-loot'chee, (TEODORO,) an Italian poet and physician, born near Tolentino, in the march of Ancona. He was an admirer of Aristotle's philosophy, in behalf of which he wrote against Patrizzi. He left, besides several medical works, a translation of Virgil's Æneid into blank verse, (1649,) which is praised by some Italian critics. Died at Montagnana in 1600.

An'ge-lus, (CHRISTOPHER,) a Greek scholar, who came to England in 1608, and, after studying in Trinity College, taught at Oxford, where he died in 1638. He left a few unimportant works written in Greek and also in English, and some others written in Greek and Latin.

An'ge-lus Sile'sius, (se-lee'she-us,) [Ger. pron. âng'-gȧ-lŭs se-lā'ze-ŭs,] otherwise called JOHANN Schef'fler, a German poet, born at Breslau in 1624. He was author of "The Angelic Book of Wonders," ("Cherubinisches Wunderbuch," 1674.) Died in 1677.

Angely or **Angeli,** ȯnzh'le', or **L'Angely,** lȯnzh'le', a witty court fool to Louis XIII. of France. His name is preserved in Boileau's 1st Satire.

Angely, ȯnzh'le', (LOUIS,) a popular German dramatic writer and actor, born at Berlin about 1775, of a family originally from France. He particularly excelled as a ready and rapid translator of French comedies and vaudevilles. His "Feast of the Craftsmen," and "Seven Girls in Uniform," had great success. Died in 1835.

Angennes, d', dȯN'zhěn', (CHARLES,) a brother of Claude, noticed below, was born in 1530, and made cardinal in 1570. Died in 1587.

Angennes, d', (CLAUDE,) Bishop of Mans, an influential ecclesiastic in the time of Henry III. and Henry IV. of France. Born in 1538; died in 1601.

Angerbode or **Angerboda.** See ANGURBODA.

Angermayer, âng'ęr-mī'ęr, (CHRISTOPH,) a Bavarian sculptor, born at Weilheim; died in 1653.

Angerstein, âng'ęr-stīn, (JOHN JULIUS,) a patron of the fine arts, born at Saint Petersburg in 1735. He removed to England, where he became an eminent merchant. His rich collection of paintings forms part of the National Gallery in London. Died in 1822.

Anghiera, de, dȧ ân-ge-ā'rȧ, (PIETRO **Martire**—mar'te-rȧ,) [Lat. PE'TRUS MAR'TYR ANGLE'RIUS,] an Italian scholar, statesman, and historian, born at Arona, on Lake Maggiore, of a noble Milanese family, in 1455, went to Spain in 1488, and spent several years at the court of Ferdinand and Isabella, whence he was sent in 1501 on an embassy to Venice and Cairo. He was afterwards appointed a member of the Council of the Indies. Died at Granada in 1526. He left a valuable historical work on the progress of American discovery, entitled "Concerning the Things of the Ocean and the New World," etc., ("De Rebus Oceanicis et Orbe Novo Decades," 1530.)

See PRESCOTT, "History of Ferdinand and Isabella," vol. ii. part ii.

Angilbert, ang'gil-bęrt, or **En'gil-bert,** [Fr. pron. ȯN'zhěl'baiR'; Lat. ANGILBER'TUS or ENGILBER'TUS,] SAINT, a pupil of Alcuin, and confidential friend of Charlemagne, became abbot of Saint-Riquier in 793, and died in 814 A.D. He was the author of some short Latin poems. Bertha, a daughter of Charlemagne, was his wife, or at least mother of his children. Angilbert was called the Homer of his time.

See MABILLON, "Acta," etc., p. 101 *et seq.*; "Histoire Littéraire de France."

Angiolello, ân-jo-lel'lo, or **Anzolello,** ân-zo-lel'lo, (GIOVANNI MARIA,) an Italian, who was taken captive in 1469, and became the slave of the sultan Mahomet II. He accompanied the Turkish army in 1473 in its invasion of the dominions of Uzun Cassim, King of Persia, of which expedition he wrote a historical account. Died about 1530.

Angiolini, ân-jo-lee'nee, (FRANCESCO,) an Italian Jesuit and scholar, born at Piacenza in 1738. He translated Josephus into Italian, (1780,) also some dramas of Sophocles and Euripides. Died at Polotsk in 1788.

Angiviller, d', dȯN'zhe've'yȧ', (CHARLES CLAUDE Labillarderie—lȧ'be'yȧRd're',) COUNT, a French patron of arts and sciences, a favourite of Louis XVI., became director of the royal buildings, gardens, manufactures, etc. Died in 1810.

Anglada, ȯN'glȧ'dȧ', (JOSEPH,) a French physician, born at Perpignan in 1775. He was professor of medicine or chemistry at Montpellier, and author of a "Treatise on the Mineral Waters of the Pyrenees," (2 vols., 1833,) and a "Treatise on Toxicology," (1835.) Died in 1833.

Angleberme or **Engleberme, d',** dȯN'g'l-bȧRm', (JEAN PYRRHUS,) a French jurist, born at Orléans in 1470, was instructed in Latin and Greek by Erasmus. He became professor of law at Orléans, and published, besides other works, a treatise "On the Salic Law," (1613.) Died in 1521.

Anglesey, (ARTHUR.) See ANNESLEY.

Anglesey, EARL OF. See ANNESLEY.

Anglesey, ang'g'l-see, (HENRY WILLIAM Pag'et,) MARQUIS OF, a British general and statesman, born in 1768, was the eldest son of the Earl of Uxbridge, and was styled Lord Paget in his youth. He served in the campaign of Flanders in 1794, and commanded the cavalry of the army of the Duke of York in Holland in 1799. Having obtained the rank of major-general in 1808, he distinguished himself as a cavalry officer in

€ as *k*; ç as *s*; ḡ *hard*; ġ as *j*; G, H, K, *guttural*; N, *nasal*; R, *trilled*; s̆ as *z*; th as in *this*. (☞See Explanations, p. 23.)

9

Spain under Sir John Moore. On the death of his father in 1812 he succeeded to the earldom, and entered the House of Lords. He was appointed commander of the cavalry of the British army in the spring of 1815, and rendered important services at Waterloo, where he lost a leg. A few days after this action he was rewarded with the title of Marquis of Anglesey. In 1819 he was promoted to the rank of general. He became master-general of the ordnance on the formation of the ministry of Canning in 1827, and lord-lieutenant of Ireland in 1828. Having declared in favour of Catholic emancipation, he was recalled about the end of 1828, but was appointed again to that office by Earl Grey in 1830. He resigned office in 1833, and was master of the ordnance from 1846 to 1852. Died in 1854, leaving several sons.

See LODGE's "Portraits;" "Gentleman's Magazine," June, 1854.

Anglicus. See GILBERTUS.

Angliviel. See BEAUMELLE.

Anglure, d', dǒN'glür', (OGER, o'zhaiR',) a French gentleman, who made a pilgrimage to Palestine in 1395 and wrote a narrative of his journey.

Anglus, (THOMAS.) See WHITE.

Ango or **Angot** (ǒN'go') OF DIEPPE, a rich French ship-owner, who, in 1530, blockaded Lisbon on his private account and obtained compensation for injuries which his vessels had sustained from the Portuguese. Died in 1551.

Ango, (PIERRE,) a writer on optics, lived at Caen between 1650 and 1700.

Angosciola. See ANGUISCIOLA.

Angot, ǒN'go', (ROBERT,) a French poet of moderate talents, born at Caen in 1581. He published in 1603 a collection of odes, sonnets, epigrams, etc., called "Le Prélude poétique."

Angot des Rotours. See DESROTOURS.

Angoulême, d', dǒN'goo'lễm', COMTE, was the title of Francis I. before his accession. Charles IX. was styled the Duke of Angoulême before he was king.

Angoulême, d', (CHARLES de Valois—děh vǎ'lwǎ',) DUC, a natural son of Charles IX. of France, was born in 1573. He distinguished himself at the battles of Arques and Ivry, (1590,) where he fought for Henry IV. He was condemned to imprisonment for life in 1604 for a plot against that king, but was released in 1616. He opened the famous siege of Rochelle in 1628, and was commander-in-chief there until the arrival of the king. He displayed address and talent in civil and military affairs, but was destitute of principle. Died in 1650.

See SISMONDI, "Histoire des Français."

Angoulême, d', (JACQUES,) an eminent French sculptor, who worked at Rome about the middle of the sixteenth century. Among his works (which were compared to those of Michael Angelo) was a statue of Autumn, at Meudon, near Paris.

Angoulême, d', (LOUIS ANTOINE de Bourbon—děh booR'bǒN',) DUC, a son of Comte d'Artois, afterwards Charles X. of France, was born in 1775. He emigrated with his father in 1789, and resided some time at Turin. In 1799 he married his cousin Marie Thérèse Charlotte, a daughter of Louis XVI. Having been refused the privilege of asylum by several powers of the continent, they lived in England from 1806 to 1814. He commanded the French army which invaded Spain in 1823 and restored Ferdinand VII. to absolute power. He assumed the title of dauphin when his father became king in 1824. Died at Göritz in 1844.

Angoulême, d', (MARIE THÉRÈSE CHARLOTTE,) DUCHESS, wife of the preceding, was a daughter of Louis XVI. and Marie Antoinette. She was born at Versailles in 1778, and imprisoned in the Temple in August of 1792, with the king and queen. In 1795, by the mediation of Austria, she was released and exchanged for Camus and other members of the Convention. She returned to France with her husband in 1814, and was at Bordeaux when Bonaparte arrived from Elba. The duke, having received a high command as lieutenant-general of the kingdom, assembled an army to oppose the Bonapartists. The duchess is said to have acted with more en-

ergy and spirit in this crisis than the other Bourbons. She again became an exile in 1830, and died in 1851.

See MRS. ROMER, "Memoirs of the Duchess of Angoulême."

Angran d'Alleray, ǒN'gRǒN' dǎl'rǎ', (DENIS FRANçOIS,) a benevolent French judge, born in Paris in 1715. He was executed in 1794 for sending money to his son-in-law, who had emigrated.

Anguier, ǒN'ge-ǎ', (FRANÇOIS,) an excellent French sculptor, born at Eu, in Normandy, in 1604. He studied at Rome, and after his return was appointed by Louis XIII. keeper of his cabinet of antiques. Among his best productions are a tomb of Cardinal de Bérulle and a mausoleum of the Duke of Montmorency at Moulins. His works are remarkable for truth of expression. Died in 1669.

See "Vies des fameux Sculpteurs."

Anguier, (MICHEL,) a celebrated sculptor, a brother of the preceding, born at Eu in 1612. He was a pupil of Algardi at Rome, where he studied and worked ten years. In 1651 he returned to Paris, where he became rector of the Academy. His master-piece is ι group of the Nativity, in the church of Val de Grace. Died in 1686.

Anguillara, än-gwèl-lä'rä, (LUIGI,) an eminent Italian botanist, born at Anguillara, in the Papal States. He became superintendent of the botanic garden at Padua about 1546, and, according to Sprengel, was professor in that city. In 1561 he resigned his office and retired to Florence. Having travelled in Greece and other foreign lands, and collected many plants, he endeavoured to identify them with those described by the ancient Greek and Roman writers. He was author of a work on "Simples," ("Semplici di Luigi Anguillara," 1561,) which had a high reputation. Died about 1570.

See MAZZUCHELLI, "Scrittori d'Italia;" HALLER, "Bibliotheca Botanica;" ERSCH und GRUBER, "Allgemeine Encyklopaedie."

Anguillara, dell', děl-län-gwèl-lä'rä, (GIOVANNI ANDREA,) a popular Italian poet, born at Sutri, in the Papal States, about 1517, is said to have ruined himself by debauchery, gaming, and other vices. His principal work is a translation, or rather a free imitation, of Ovid's "Metamorphoses," (1554–61,) which has been extravagantly praised by Italian critics, some of whom have preferred it to the original. Died at Rome after 1565; but the exact date of his death is not known.

See MAZZUCHELLI, "Scrittori d'Italia;" TIRABOSCHI, "Storia della Letteratura Italiana."

Anguillesi, än-gwe-lä'see, (GIOVANNI DOMENICO,) an Italian writer and scholar, born at or near Pisa in 1766. Died in 1833. He translated Châteaubriand's "Génie du Christianisme," and other French works, into Italian.

Anguisciola, än-gwe-sho'lä, or **Angussola,** än-goos'so-lä, (SOFONISBA,) a celebrated Italian painter, born at Cremona about 1535, was a pupil of Bernardino Gatti. She excelled in portraits. Having been invited by Philip II. of Spain, she went to Madrid and painted portraits of the king and queen. She afterwards worked in Genoa, and was married to Don Fabrizio de Moncada. About the age of sixty-seven she became blind. It is stated that Van Dyck said he had learned more from her conversation on art than from the study of the best masters. Died about 1620. Her sisters Lucia, Europa, and Anna Maria were skilful painters.

See BERMUDEZ, "Diccionario Historico;" SOPRANI, "Vite de' Pittori Genovesi."

Angurboda or **Angerboda,** äng'ger-bo'dä, (**Angrboda,**) *i.e.* "anguish-boding," written also **An'gerbode,** (Norse Myth.,) a female Jötun, who by Loki became the mother of the wolf FENRIR, the MIDGARDS SERPENT, and HELA, (the goddess of death,) which see.

Angus, EARLS OF. See DOUGLAS.

Angus, ang'gus, (SAMUEL,) a captain in the American navy, born in Philadelphia in 1784. In 1814 he commanded the vessel which took Adams and Clay to Ghent to conclude the treaty of peace with Great Britain. Died in 1840.

Anhalt, än'hält, (ANTON Gunther–gŏon'ter,) PRINCE OF, a general, born in 1653, fought for the allies against Louis XIV. at Steenkerke and Neerwinden. He received in 1703 the command of a Prussian army of 15,000 men in the service of Holland and England. Died in 1714.

Anhalt-Bernberg, ân'hâlt bĕRn'bĕRG, (CHRISTIAN,) PRINCE OF, born in 1568, was an ambitious man, of superior talents. He was the master-spirit of the negotiations which resulted in a union of the Protestant German princes against the emperor about 1608, and was appointed second commander of the army of that "Union." He was successively offered the chief command of the armies of Venice and of France; but he refused both positions. He commanded the army of Frederick, Elector Palatine, which was defeated at Prague in 1620. Died in 1630.

Anhalt-Coethen, (or **-Köthen,**) ân'hâlt kö'tẹn, (LUDWIG,) PRINCE OF, born at Dessau in 1579, was a good classical scholar. He fought for the Protestant party in the Thirty Years' war. Died in 1650.

Anhalt-Dessau, ân'hâlt dĕs'sŏw, (LEOPOLD,) PRINCE OF, a distinguished Prussian general, born in 1676. He displayed able generalship at the battle of Blenheim, (1704,) and commanded the Prussian forces under Prince Eugene in Italy and Flanders from 1706 to 1712. About 1712 he was made a field-marshal. He was commander-in-chief, next to the king, of the army which in 1715 marched against Charles XII. of Sweden. In 1745 he gained a victory for Frederick the Great at Kesselsdorf. Died in 1747.

See VARNHAGEN VON ENSE, "Biographische Denkmale."

Anhalt-Dessau, (LEOPOLD MAXIMILIAN,) a son of the preceding, born in 1700, served the King of Prussia in the war against Austria, and became field-marshal-general. Died in 1751.

Anhalt-Zerbst-Dessau, ân'hâlt tsĕRpst dĕs'sŏw, (GEORGE IV.,) PRINCE OF, born in 1507, was eminent as a scholar and Protestant divine. He was ordained a priest in 1524, and became an eloquent preacher, both in German and Latin. He was intimate with Luther and Melanchthon. Died in 1553. Some of his sermons were published in 1570.

See MELCHIOR ADAM, "Vitæ Germanorum Theologorum."

Anhalt-Zerbst-Dessau, (RUDOLPH,) PRINCE OF, born about 1460, was distinguished as a warrior. He commanded the Imperial army in the war against the Venetians from 1508 till his death in 1513.

Aniano. See ANIANUS.

A-nī-ā'nus, a native of Campania, was a deacon and a friend of Pelagius, whose doctrines he defended at the Council of Diospolis in 415 A.D. He translated the homilies of Chrysostom into Latin. His skill and fidelity as a translator are praised by Huet, Simon, and others.

Anianus, [It. ANIANO, ä-ne-ä'no; Fr. ANIEN, ắ'ne'-ằN',] secretary of Alaric II., King of the Visigoths. His name is connected with a remarkable code of laws promulgated by Alaric about 506 A.D.

Anianus, an astronomer and poet of the fifteenth century, wrote in verse "Computus Manualis," (1488.)

Aníbert, ắ'ne'baiR', (LOUIS MATTHIEU,) a French poet and antiquary, born in 1742; died in 1782.

Anicet-Bourgeois. See BOURGEOIS.

A-nī-ce'tus, [Fr.ANICET, ắ'ne'sắ',] SAINT,was Bishop of Rome about 155 A.D. The date of his death is uncertain.

Anich, ä'niK, (PETER,) a German peasant, born near Innspruck in 1723, studied mathematics and astronomy, and was employed, under the patronage of the empress Maria Theresa, in making maps. Died in 1766.

Anichini, ä-ne-kee'nee, (LUIGI,) a noted Italian cameo- and gem-engraver, born at Ferrara, worked at Venice in the sixteenth century.

Anicii, a-nish'e-ī, a patrician family of Rome, especially distinguished in the later periods of the empire.

Anicius, a-nish'e-us, (LUCIUS GALLUS,) a Roman prætor, who conquered Illyricum in 168 B.C.

Aniello, (TOMMASO.) See MASANIELLO.

Anien. See ANIANUS.

Animuccia, ä-ne-moot'chä, (GIOVANNI,) an Italian musician, born at Florence about 1500. He became chapel-master of St. Peter's, at Rome. Died about 1570.

See FÉTIS, "Biographie des Musiciens."

Animuccia, (PAOLO,) a musician and composer, a brother of the preceding, lived at Rome; died in 1563.

Anisio, ä-nee'se-o, (GIOVANNI,) a Latin poet, born at Naples about 1472. He sometimes wrote his name JANUS ANYSIUS. He published a volume of Latin poems in 1531, and had once a high reputation, which has since declined. Died about 1540.

Anisson, ắ'ne'sŏN', the name of a noted family of printers at Lyons in the seventeenth and eighteenth centuries.

Anisson, (JEAN,) a Frenchman, who edited the Greek Lexicon of Du Cange. In 1690 he was appointed director of the royal printing-office of the Louvre. Died after 1713.

Anisson-Duperron, ắ'ne'sŏN' dü'pắ'rŏN', (ALEXANDRE JACQUES LAURENT,) a French economist, born in 1776, was a son of Étienne Alexandre Jacques, noticed below. He was appointed director of the imperial printing-office at Paris in 1809, and master of requests. From 1833 to 1842 he sat in the Chamber of Deputies, and was made a peer in 1844. Among his works is a treatise in favour of free trade, (1829.)

Anisson-Duperron, (ÉTIENNE ALEXANDRE JACQUES,) born in Paris in 1748, was a grandson of Jean Anisson. He was director of the royal printing-office, 1788–92. He was guillotined in 1794.

Anitchkov, ä-nitch-kov', or **Anitchkof,** (DMITRI S.,) a Russian philosopher and mathematician, born in or before 1740. He published several works, one of which was publicly burnt because a friend to whom he had lent it added some heretical or skeptical opinions. Died in 1788.

Anjoo, Anju, or **Andjou,** ân'joo, a Persian writer, lived about 1600, was one of the chief compilers of the great Persian Dictionary called "Ferhenkee Jehangeeree," ("Ferhenkî Jehangîrî,") in honour of Jehangeer, the Mogul emperor under whose auspices it was completed.

See ERSCH und GRUBER, "Allgemeine Encyklopaedie."

Anjou, ân'joo, [Fr. pron. ŏN'zhoo',] DUKE or COUNT OF, the title of an old and noble house of France which was powerful in the middle ages. Fulke, Count of Anjou, was a leader of one of the crusades, and became King of Jerusalem in 1131. His son, Geoffroy le Plantagenet, married Matilda, the daughter and heiress of Henry I. of England, and founded the royal house of Plantagenet, leaving a son, who became King of England, (Henry II.) The second house of Anjou was a branch of the royal family of France. (See CHARLES I. OF NAPLES.) Louis, a son of John, King of France, became Duke of Anjou about 1360. He assumed the title of King of Sicily, or Naples, in 1382, after which he attempted to conquer Naples, (which Queen Joanna I. had bequeathed to him,) but failed. Died in 1384. The title of Duke of Anjou was also borne by several sons of Henry II., by two sons of Louis XIV., and by a grandson of Louis XIV., who became Philip V. of Spain.

Anjou, (CHARLES OF.) See CHARLES I. OF NAPLES; also CHARLES OF ANJOU, COUNT OF MAINE.

Anjou, (FRANÇOIS,) DUC D'. See ALENÇON.

Anjou, (RENÉ OF.) See RENÉ OF ANJOU.

Ankarkrona, ân'kaR-kroo'nä, (THEODOR,) a Swedish admiral, born at Carlscrona in 1687. He served in the French and British navies in his youth, and returned to the Swedish service in 1711. He conveyed Charles XII. from Stralsund to Stockholm in 1715, after which he obtained the rank of admiral. Died in 1750.

See GEZELIUS, "Biographiskt-Lexicon."

Ankarström or **Anckarstroem,** âng'kạr-ström', (JOHAN JACOB,) a Swedish nobleman, born in 1759, assassinated King Gustavus III. at a masked ball, March 16, 1792. He was condemned to be beaten with rods on three successive days, and on the fourth to be beheaded, his right hand being first cut off.

Anker, âng'kẹr, or **Ancher,** (PE'DER KO'FOD,) a Danish lawyer and writer on law, born in 1710, on the island of Bornholm, was appointed professor of law in the University of Copenhagen in 1741, and died in 1788.

See ERSCH und GRUBER, "Allgemeine Encyklopaedie."

Ankwitz, ânk'ẅits, or **Anewitz,** COUNT, a Pole of

noble family and great talents, born about 1750. He is generally believed to have been a traitor to his country, and to have assisted in the second iniquitous dismemberment of Poland in 1793. In an insurrection of the people of Warsaw in 1794 he was taken and hung.

An'na, a Jewish prophetess, who died about the beginning of the Christian era. (See Luke ii. 36.)

Anna, a sister of Dido, Queen of Carthage. (See Virgil, "Æneid," book iv.) See also ANNA PERENNA.

An'na Com-ne'na, [Fr. ANNE COMNÈNE, än kom'nän',] the daughter of Alexis I., Emperor of Constantinople, a princess of distinguished beauty, talents, and learning, was born in 1083. At her father's death, in 1118, she conspired to place the crown on the head of her husband, Nicephorus Bryennius, but without success. Her "Alexiad," (or "Alexias,") a biography of her father, (in Greek,) is a remarkable work, and one of great historic value, although it is sometimes disfigured by prejudice, as well as by a pedantic and affected style. Died in 1148.

See FABRICIUS, "Bibliotheca Græca."

An'na Ivanovna, Iwanowna, (e-vä-nov'nä,) or **Joanovna,** (yo-ä-nov'nä,) Empress of Russia, born at Moscow in 1694, was a daughter of Iván, (or John,) who was a brother of Peter the Great. She was married in 1710 to Frederick William, Duke of Courland, who died the next year. She ascended the throne as successor to Peter II. in 1730. Her army invaded Poland in 1733, deposed Stanislaus, and placed his rival, Augustus III., on the throne. The reign of Anna was disgraced by the tyranny and cruelty of her favourite, Biren or Biron, who had an entire ascendency over her. She died in October, 1740, and was succeeded by her great-nephew, Iván.

See LÉVESQUE, "Histoire de la Russie."

An'na Pe-ren'na, a goddess of the Roman mythology, was, according to Virgil and Ovid, a daughter of Belus and a sister of Dido. After the death of Dido, she went to Italy and was kindly received by Æneas. The Romans invoked her favour to obtain long life and health.

An'na Pet-rov'na, the eldest daughter of Peter the Great by his empress Catherine, born in 1708, was married in 1725 to Charles Frederick, Duke of Holstein. She was the mother of Peter III. of Russia. Her beauty and talents are spoken of in high terms. Died in 1727.

An-Nadîm, (or **-Nadeem.**) See IBN-ABI-YAKOOB.

Annæus, (LUCIUS.) See FLORUS and SENECA.

Annæus, (MARCUS.) See SENECA.

An'nand, (WILLIAM,) a Scottish minister of the Anglican Church, born in 1633, became Dean of Edinburgh. He wrote "Mysterium Pietatis," etc. Died in 1689.

See CHAMBERS, "Biographical Dictionary of Eminent Scotsmen."

An-Nâsir, (OF CORDOVA.) See ABD-ER-RAHMAN III.

An-Nâsir (or **Al-Nassir**) **Ledeenillah,** (or **Lidini-l-lah,**) än-nä'sir le-deen-il'läh, (*i.e.* "the defender of the religion of God,") one of the later caliphs of the house of Abbâs, began to reign in 1180. He attempted to restore the power and splendour of the caliphate, and was successful in maintaining his dominions against the encroachments of the neighbouring powers. He died in 1225, leaving the character of a just and enlightened prince and a liberal patron of literature and science.

See WEIL, "Geschichte der Chalifen," vol. iii. chap. xi.

Annat, ä'nä', (FRANÇOIS,) a French Jesuit, born at Rodez in 1590, (or, according to the "Biographie Universelle," in 1607.) His proper name was CANARD. He was confessor of Louis XIV. from 1654 until 1670, and was a zealous opponent of the Jansenists. The seventeenth and eighteenth of Pascal's "Lettres Provinciales" were addressed to Annat, who had written several works against Jansenism. The "Biographie Universelle" calls him "the soul of the party opposed to Port-Royal." Died in 1670.

See SAINTE-BEUVE, "Port-Royal."

Annat, (PIERRE,) a French theologian, born in Rouergue in 1638, was a nephew of the preceding. Died in Paris in 1715.

Annaya, de, dä ä-nä'yä, (PEDRO,) a Portuguese admiral, who conquered Sofala in 1508.

Anne, än, [Ger. pron. än'neh,] of Austria, Queen of France, was a daughter of Philip III. of Spain, and mother of Louis XIV. of France. She was born in 1601, and was married in 1615 to Louis XIII., by whom she was treated with neglect. Cardinal Richelieu became her enemy, and artfully used his influence to alienate the king from her. By the will of Louis XIII., who died in 1643, she was appointed, nominally, regent during the minority of her son, but was required to act with the concurrence of a council of five, of which Mazarin was president. The Parliament, however, gave her the regency without limitations, and she chose Mazarin as prime minister. The civil war of the Fronde, which began in 1648, ended in the triumph of the court over the Parliament and a faction of discontented nobles. (See MAZARIN.) Died in 1666.

See SAINT-AULAIRE, "Histoire de la Fronde;" AUBÉRY, "Histoire du Cardinal Mazarin;" SISMONDI, "Histoire des Français."

Anne of Bohemia, called the "Good Queen Anne," a daughter of the emperor Charles IV., was married to Richard II. of England about 1380. She was a friend of Wickliffe, and promoted the reformation of the church. Died in 1394.

Anne of Brittany, (or Bretagne,) Queen-consort of France, born at Nantes in 1476, was the heiress of the Duke of Brittany, and an object of eager competition among various princes. She was married in 1491 to Charles VIII. of France, and after his death (1499) to his successor, Louis XII. Her character is represented as excellent, and she had much influence in the affairs of state. Died in 1514.

See "Memoirs of Anne, Duchess of Brittany," by LOUISA S. COSTELLO.

Anne of Cleves, the fourth queen of Henry VIII., to whom she was married in January, 1540. She was divorced in July of the same year.

See FROUDE, "History of England," vol. iii. chap. xvii.; STRICKLAND, "Lives of the Queens of England"

Anne of Cyprus, a daughter of Janus, King of Cyprus, was married in 1431 to Louis, Duke of Savoy, over whom she acquired great influence. Died in 1462.

Anne of Denmark, a daughter of Frederick II. of Denmark, born in 1574, was married to James I. of England in 1589. She was the mother of Charles I. Died in 1619.

Anne, än, Queen of England, the last sovereign of the house of Stuart, was born at Twickenham on the 6th of February, 1664. She was second daughter of James II. and Anne Hyde, who was a daughter of Lord Clarendon. She was educated in the Protestant religion, and was married in 1683 to Prince George of Denmark, a brother of Christian V. Before this event she had formed an intimacy with Sarah Jennings, who became her favourite adviser and for a time exerted an almost unlimited influence over her. (See MARLBOROUGH, DUCHESS OF.) During the reign of James II. unsuccessful attempts were made to convert Anne to the Roman Catholic religion. A few days after William of Orange entered England in 1688 to dethrone her father, she wrote to the former and assured him of her warm wishes for his success. She lost in 1699 or 1700 her son, the Duke of Gloucester, aged eleven, all her other children having died in infancy.

Anne succeeded William III. on the 8th of March, 1702, and declared her purpose to pursue his foreign policy, which involved England in the war of the Spanish succession, as the enemy of France and the ally of Austria and Holland. (See MARLBOROUGH, DUKE OF.) In her domestic administration she favoured the Tory party. Godolphin, who was considered a moderate Tory, became lord of the treasury, or prime minister. Eventually, Godolphin formed a coalition with the Whigs, and, the Duchess of Marlborough having been supplanted by a new favourite, Mrs. Masham, the Tories, under Lords Oxford and Bolingbroke, (then known as Harley and Saint John,) came into power in 1710. "The great party which had long swayed the destinies of Europe," says Macaulay, "was undermined by bed-chamber women at Saint James." Marlborough was deprived of command in 1711, and the new ministry opened the long war with the French court negotiations which ended the long war by the treaty of Utrecht, April 11, 1713,

---

ā, ē, ī, ō, ū, ȳ, *long;* ă, ĕ, ĭ, ŏ, ŭ, ў, same, less prolonged; ă, ĕ, ĭ, ŏ, ŭ, ў, *short;* ạ, ẹ, ị, ọ, *obscure;* fär, fäll, fät; mêt; nŏt; gōōd; mōōn;

when the allies recognized Philip V., a Bourbon prince, as King of Spain and the Indies.

In the last year of her reign Anne co-operated with her ministers in secret designs and intrigues to secure the succession to her half-brother the Pretender, whose devoted partisan, Lord Bolingbroke, became lord treasurer on the 27th of July, 1714. Three days later the queen was seized with an apoplectic fit, which terminated fatally on the 1st of August, 1714. The plans of the Jacobites were disconcerted by her sudden death, and George I., of the house of Hanover, obtained peaceable possession of the throne. Anne was a woman of moderate or inferior abilities, and not distinguished for generous moral qualities. The period in which she reigned is sometimes called the Augustan age of English literature, which was then illustrated by the genius of Addison, Pope, Bolingbroke, Arbuthnot, and Swift. The victories of Marlborough, which are considered to have reflected more lustre on the English arms than any other since the time of Henry V., were achieved during this reign.

See Coxe, "Memoirs, etc. of John Duke of Marlborough," and Swift, "Works;" Burnet, "History of his Own Times;" "Mémoires du Duc de Saint-Simon;" Voltaire, "Siècle de Louis XIV;" "Pictorial History of England;" "Account of the Conduct of the Duchess of Marlborough," edited by Hooke, 1742; J. Oldmixon, "Life of Queen Anne," 1716; Strickland, "Lives of the Queens of England."

Anne of Hungary, born in 1503, was married to Ferdinand of Austria. She was the heiress of the crowns of Hungary and Bohemia. Died in 1547.

Anne de Beaujeu, ȧn dĕh bō'zhŭh', a daughter of Louis XI. of France, was born about 1462. She was regent during the minority of her brother Charles VIII., and suppressed with vigour a revolt of princes, of whom the Duke of Orléans was chief. Died in 1522.

Annebaut or **Annebaud, d',** dȧn'bō', (Claude,) a French general, born about the end of the fifteenth century. He was taken prisoner with Francis I. at Pavía, (1525,) after which he served with distinction in Italy and Flanders, and was made marshal of France. Died in 1552.

Annese, ȧn-nā'sȧ, (Gennaro,) one of the principal actors in the Neapolitan insurrection of July, 1647. (See Masaniello.) After the restoration of the Spanish authority in 1648, he was beheaded.

Annesley, ȧnz'le, (Alexander,) an English writer on law and political economy, published several works between 1800 and 1808. Died in 1813.

Annesley, ȧnz'le, (Arthur,) Earl of Anglesey, was born at Dublin in 1614. He was a member of the Parliament called by Richard Cromwell in 1659. As president of the new Council of State appointed in February, 1660, he aided Monk in his efforts for the restoration of Charles II. He was created Earl of Anglesey in 1661, and became lord privy seal in 1673. He wrote several political and theological works, among which are "Truth Unveiled in behalf of the Church of England," (1676,) and a "History of the Wars in Ireland," which is lost. Died in 1686.

See Wood, "Athenæ Oxonienses;" Walpole, "Royal and Noble Authors."

Annesley, originally written **Aneley,** (Rev. Samuel,) an eminent English nonconformist minister, a first-cousin of the preceding, was born at Kenilworth in 1620. He obtained the living of Cliffe in Kent about 1646, and was chosen minister by the parishioners of Saint John, London, in 1652. In 1657 Cromwell appointed him preacher at Saint Paul's. After the restoration he was pastor of a Presbyterian congregation in London. He was the grandfather of John Wesley, the founder of the Methodist Church. His sermons have been published. Died in 1696.

See Wood, "Athenæ Oxonienses."

An'nett or **An'net,** (Peter,) an English deistical writer, published "Tracts of a Certain Free Enquirer," (1766.) Died in 1778.

Annibal. See Hannibal.

Annibale, ȧn-ne-bȧ'lȧ, surnamed Padovano, pȧ-do-vȧ'no, an Italian musician, born at Padua, was organist of the church of Saint Mark, Venice. Died about 1655.

An-nĭ-bal-lĭ-ā'nus, (Flavius Claudius,) a nephew of Constantine the Great, was murdered at Constantinople in 337 A.D.

An-nĭç'e-ris, ['Αννικερις,] a Greek philosopher of Cyrene, supposed to have lived about 300 B.C. He was a follower of Aristippus.

An'nĭ-us of Viterbo, [It. Annio da Viterbo, ȧn'ne-o dȧ ve-tĕR'bo,] an Italian Dominican monk, whose proper name was Giovanni Nanni, was born at Viterbo about 1432. He was well versed in Greek and Latin, and in some Oriental languages. He wrote a "Treatise on the Empire of the Turks," ("De Imperio Turcorum," 1471,) and acquired notoriety by the publication of "Seventeen Volumes of Antiquities with Commentaries," ("Antiquitatum Volumina XVII. cum Commentariis," 1498.) In this work he professed to give passages from the lost works of Berosus, Fabius Pictor, and other ancient writers. It is generally admitted that these are forgeries. Died in 1502.

See D. W. Moller, "Disputatio de J. Annio Viterbiensi," 1692.

Anno. See Hanno.

An'no or **Han'no,** Saint, an archbishop of Cologne in the eleventh century. He was an able but overbearing prelate, and for a time exercised great influence over the youthful emperor Henry IV. Died in 1075.

Annone, ȧn-no'nȧ, or **Annoni,** ȧn-no'nee, (Johann Jakob,) a Swiss naturalist and antiquary, born at Bâle in 1728, was professor of eloquence and law in that city. He wrote scientific essays, and made rich collections in natural history and antiquities. Died in 1804.

An-Noowaïree or **An-Nuwayrî,** ȧn-noo-wī'ree' called also simply **Noowaïree,** an eminent Arabian writer, born in Egypt about 1283; died in 1332.

Annot, ȧ'no', (Pierre Nicolas,) a French writer, born in 1762; died in 1823.

Anquetil, ŏNk'tèl', (Louis Pierre,) a French historian, a brother of Abraham Hyacinthe, noticed below, was born in Paris in 1723. He became prior of the abbey of Château-Renard before the Revolution, and a member of the Institute, second class, in 1795. He wrote numerous works, which show marks of haste and carelessness, but which obtained success, especially a "Compendium of Universal History," (9 vols., 1797,) and a "History of the Civil Wars of France in the Sixteenth and Seventeenth Centuries," (3 vols., 1767.) Died about 1808.

See Bon Joseph Dacier, "Notice sur la Vie et les Ouvrages de M. Anquetil," 1810; Quérard, "La France Littéraire."

Anquetil-Duperron, ŏNk'tèl' dü'pȧ'rôN', (Abraham Hyacinthe,) a celebrated Orientalist, born in Paris in 1731. He visited India in 1755 for the purpose of discovering the religious books of the Parsees. After encountering difficulties and toils exceeded only by his zeal, he at last obtained the objects of his search. In 1762 he returned to Europe, rich in Oriental manuscripts, and in 1771 published his "Zend-Avesta," the first translation of the original work of this name that had appeared in any European language. He left other works, among which is "India in Relation with Europe," (2 vols., 1798.) Died in 1805.

See Langlois, "Notice sur Anquetil-Duperron;" Von Bohlen, "Das Alte Indien;" Bon Joseph Dacier, "Notice sur la Vie et les Ouvrages de M. Anquetil-Duperron," 1808; L. P. Anquetil, "Notice sur la Vie de M. Anquetil-Duperron."

Anraat, van, vȧn ȧn'rȧt, (Pieter,) a skilful Dutch painter of conversation-pieces and portraits, flourished at Amsterdam in the latter part of the seventeenth century.

Ansaldi, ȧn-sȧl'dee, (Casto Innocente,) a distinguished Italian antiquary and professor, born at Piacenza in 1710, became a Dominican monk. He was professor of philosophy at Turin from 1760 to 1779, and author of several works of merit, among which are a treatise "On the Recognition of a Future State by the Hebrews," ("De futuro Sæculo ab Hebræis cognito," 1748,) "On the Necessity of Natural and Revealed Religion," (1755,) and "Vindiciæ Maupertuisianæ," (1756.) Died in 1779.

See Mazzuchelli, "Scrittori d'Italia."

Ansaldi, (Innocenzio,) a Tuscan painter, born in 1734; died in 1816. He wrote a poem named "The Accomplished Painter," ("Il Pittore istruito," 1820.)

Ansaldo, ȧn-sȧl'do, (Andrea,) a celebrated Genoese

painter, born at Voltri in 1584, was a pupil of Cambiaso. He worked in fresco and oil at Genoa and other places. Among the best of his numerous works are a "Last Supper," an altar-piece of the martyrdom of Saint Sebastian, (at Cadiz,) and frescos in the Palazzo Spinola, illustrating the exploits of General Spinola in Flanders. Died at Genoa in 1638.

See NAGLER, "Neues Allgemeines Künstler-Lexikon."

Ansaloni, ân-sä-lo'nee, (GIORDANO,) a Sicilian missionary, who in 1632 visited Japan, where he was put to death in 1634.

Ansaloni, (VINCENZIO,) an able Bolognese painter, flourished about the beginning of the seventeenth century. His "Virgin seated on the Clouds" is highly praised by Lanzi.

Ansaree or **Ansarî,** ân'sä-ree', (written also **Unsaree,**) a celebrated Persian poet and scholar, who lived at the court of Mahmood of Ghiznee, (or Gazna.) Died in 1040.

Ansart, ôN'säR', (ANDRÉ JOSEPH,) a French ecclesiastic and historian, born in Artois in 1723; died in 1790.

Ansbert, ans'bert, [Ger. pron. âns'bĕRt,] a German chronicler of the twelfth century, accompanied Frederick Barbarossa to Palestine, and wrote an account of that crusade, which was first published in 1827.

Ans-cä'rǐ-us or **Ans-gä'rǐ-us,** [Fr. ANSCHAIRE, ôN'-shäR',] called "the Apostle of the North," the most successful propagator of Christianity in Denmark and Sweden, was born in Picardy about 800 A.D. About 831 he was created the first archbishop of Hamburg. Died in 864 A.D.

Anseaume, ôN'sōm', (N.,) a French dramatic poet, born at Paris about 1720; died in 1784.

An-se-ĝī'sus or **An-sī-ĝī'sus,** [Fr. ANSÉGISE, ôN'-sä'zhĕz',] a distinguished French ecclesiastic in the time of Charlemagne and his son Louis le Débonnaire.

Ansegisus was also the name of an archbishop of Sens in the ninth, and a bishop of Troyes in the tenth century.

Anselin, ôNs'lâN', (JEAN LOUIS,) a French engraver, born in Paris in 1764; died in 1823.

Anselm, ân'sĕlm, of Havelberg, a Saxon bishop, wrote a work on the dogmatic disputes between the Latin and Greek Churches, entitled 'Αντικείμενα. Died in 1159.

An'selm, SAINT, [Lat. SANC'TUS ANSEL'MUS; Fr. SAINT-ANSELME, sâN'tôN'sĕlm',] Archbishop of Canterbury, was born at Aosta, in Piedmont, about 1034. He became a pupil of Lanfranc at the abbey of Bec in Normandy, where he assumed the monastic habit in 1060, and succeeded Lanfranc as prior in 1063. He was chosen abbot of Bec in 1078, and Archbishop of Canterbury in 1093. He had a long contest with King William Rufus, who confiscated the revenues of the archbishopric in 1097. Died in 1109. The intellect of Anselm was of a high order, and his writings evince a profound and original mind. He is considered as the reviver of metaphysics after the decline of the Roman Empire. Among his greatest works are "Cur Deus Homo;" "Monologium;" "Proslogium;" and "The Agreement (or Compatibility) of Predestination and the Grace of God with Free Will," ("Concordia Praedestinationis necnon Gratiæ Dei cum libero Arbitrio.")

See EADMER, "Life of Saint Anselm," in Latin; MÖHLER, "Life of Saint Anselm," in German, translated by COX; W. F. HOOK, "Lives of the Archbishops of Canterbury," vol. ii. chap. iii., 1860; FRANCK, "Anselme de Canterbéry," 1842; HASSE, "Vie d'Anselme de Cantorbéry," 1843; RAINERI, "Historical Panegyric (Istorico panegirico) on Saint Anselm," 4 vols., 1693-1706; "Foreign Quarterly Review," vol. xxx.

Anselme, (Italian.) See ANSELMO.

Anselme, an'sĕlm or ôN'sĕlm', [Lat. ANSEL'MUS,] Count of Ribemont, (re'bĕh-môN',) was one of the nobles who accompanied Godfrey of Bouillon to the Holy Land, where he was killed in 1099. He wrote a narrative of the events of this crusade.

Anselme, an'sĕlm, [Fr. pron. ôN'sĕlm',] or **Ansel,** ôN'sĕl', OF LAON, [Lat. ANSEL'MUS LAUDINEN'SIS,] a famous teacher of theology, born at Laon, France, about 1050, was one of the founders of the University of Paris. A school which he afterwards directed at Laon became

the most celebrated in Europe. His chief work is a Gloss on the Bible. Died in 1117.

Anselme of Liege, a Flemish historian, lived about 1050, and wrote a "History of the Bishops of Liege."

Anselme, ôN'sĕlm', (ANTOINE,) an eminent French preacher, born in the comté of Armagnac in 1652. He was admired as an orator in the principal churches of Paris, and became preacher-in-ordinary to the king. Several volumes of his sermons were published. Died in 1737.

See MADAME DE SÉVIGNÉ, "Lettres."

Anselme, d', dôN'sĕlm', (JACQUES BERNARD MODESTE,) a French general, born at Apt in 1740, was appointed commander-in-chief of the army of Italy in 1792. He was soon after suspended from his command, was imprisoned in 1793, recovered his liberty after the revolution of July, 1794, and lived in retirement till his death in 1812.

Anselme de Sainte-Marie, ôN'sĕlm' dĕh sâNt'-mä're', (PIERRE,) a French genealogist, born in Paris in 1625, published a "Genealogy of the House of France," (2 vols., 1674.) Died in 1694.

Anselmi, ân-sĕl'mee, (MICHEL ANGELO,) an able Italian painter, born at Lucca about 1490, studied at Sienna, whence he is often surnamed DA SIENNA, ("of Sienna.") He is said to have worked with Correggio at Parma. Died in 1554.

Anselmo, ân-sĕl'mo, or **An'selme,** (GIORGIO,) a writer of Latin poetry, born at Parma, lived in the first part of the sixteenth century. A volume of his poems was printed in 1528.

Anselmo, ân-sĕl'mo, (GIORGIO,) an Italian astronomer, born at Parma, was a grandfather of the Latin poet of the same name. Died in 1440.

Ansel'mo, [Lat. ANSEL'MUS; Fr. ANSELME, ôN'sĕlm'; It. SANT' ANSELMO, sânt ân-sĕl'mo,] SAINT, Bishop of Lucca, an eminent Italian ecclesiastical writer, born about 1036; died in 1086. Among his works is "Collectio Canonum."

See ROTA, "Notizie istoriche di Sant' Anselmo," 1733.

Ansgarius or **Ansgarii.** See ANCHERSEN.

Ansiaux, ôN'se'ō', (EMMANUEL ANTOINE JOSEPH,) a Belgian jurist, born at Liege in 1761; died in 1800.

Ansiaux, (JEAN JOSEPH ÉLÉONORE ANTOINE,) an eminent painter of the modern French school, born at Liege in 1764. He produced many good portraits and historical works, among which are "The Assumption," "The Conversion of St. Paul," and "The Return of the Prodigal Son." Ansiaux was living in 1831.

Ansidei, ân-se-dä'ee, (GIUSEPPE,) an Italian poet, born at Perugia in 1642. He wrote sonnets and other short poems, and a "Tract against the Long Continuance of Private Enmities," (1691.) Died in 1707.

Ansigisus. See ANSEGISUS.

Anslay (anz'le) or **Anneslay,** (BRIAN,) an English writer, known only as the translator of a curious work called "The Citie of Dames," or "Cyte of Ladyes," printed in 1521.

Anslo, ân'slo, (REINIER,) a Dutch poet, born at Amsterdam about 1625. He emigrated to Italy about 1650, and became a Roman Catholic. His principal works are "The Martyr Crown of Stephen," (1646,) "The Plague at Naples," and a drama on the Massacre of Saint Bartholomew, entitled "Parijsche Bruiloft," (i.e. the "Paris Wedding,") written before his became a Catholic. Died at Perugia in 1669.

See LONGFELLOW's "Poets and Poetry of Europe."

An'son, (GEORGE,) LORD, a distinguished naval commander, born in Staffordshire, England, in 1697. He entered the navy early, and in 1724 was made post-captain. He was soon after ordered to the Carolina station, where he purchased land and built a town, called, after his own name, Ansonburg. He was subsequently appointed to the command of the South Sea expedition which sailed from England in 1740; and throughout the whole of that voyage, which extended round the world, amid dangers and difficulties of every kind, he displayed a prudence, skill, fortitude, and courage that have seldom if ever been surpassed. After his return, in 1744, he was successively created rear-admiral of the blue, commissioner of the admiralty, and vice-admiral. In 1747 he commanded the Channel fleet, and captured six French ships of war. As a reward for this brilliant exploit he was created a peer, with the title of Lord Anson, Baron of Soberton. He was first commissioner of the admiralty from 1751 to 1756. In 1757 Anson was made admiral, and in the same year placed at the head of the admiralty, where he remained till his death in 1762. He left no issue. A· Narrative of his Voyage round the World was published.

See "Life of Lord Anson," by Sir JOHN BARROW; KIPPIS, "Life of Lord Anson," in "Biographia Britannica;" J. CAMPBELL, "Lives of the British Admirals."

Anson, (GEORGE,) a British general, born in London in 1797, was a younger son of Thomas, Viscount Anson, and uncle of the Earl of Lichfield. He was a Whig member of Parliament for many years, (1828–53,) and became a major-general about 1851. He was appointed commander-in-chief of the armies of India in 1855, and died there in May, 1857, soon after the breaking out of the mutiny among the Sepoys. ,

Anson, ŏn'sŏn', (PIERRE HUBERT,) a French writer and able financier, born in Paris in 1744. He became a member of the Constituent Assembly, and afterwards administrator-general of the posts of France. He translated into French the Odes of Anacreon, and the Letters of Lady Montagu, (2 vols., 1795.) He also wrote several short poems and prose works. Died in 1810.

Anspach, äns'pak or äns'päK, (CHRISTIAN FRIEDRICH KARL ALEXANDER,) MARGRAVE OF, was born in 1736. His mother was a sister of Frederick the Great. He sold his principality to the King of Prussia in 1791 for an annuity of four hundred thousand thalers, and married Lady Craven, noticed below. Died in 1806.

Anspach, (ELIZABETH BERKELEY,) MARGRAVINE OF, the daughter of Augustus, Earl of Berkeley, was born in 1750. In 1767 she was married to William, afterwards Lord Craven, and on his death, in 1791, to the Margrave of Anspach. Died at Naples in 1828. She possessed great versatility of genius. She wrote a number of dramas, was an accomplished musician and actress, and had considerable skill in sculpture. Unhappily, little can be said in favour of her moral character. Two years before her death she published her "Memoirs," a work full of egotism, but withal very entertaining.

See COLLINS's "Peerage."

Ans'prand, [Lat. ANSPRAN'DUS,] a Longobard whom King Cunibert appointed tutor to his infant son Liutbert. After the death of this prince he became king in 712, and died the same year.

Ansse de Villoison. See VILLOISON.

An'sted, (DAVID THOMAS,) a distinguished English geologist, born in London about 1812, was educated at Cambridge, and was a pupil of Professor Sedgwick. He succeeded John Phillips as professor of geology in King's College, London, and became editor of the journal and proceedings of the Geological Society. He gained a high reputation by his well-written and systematic work entitled "Geology, Introductory, Descriptive, and Practical, with numerous illustrations," (2 vols., 1844.) In 1847 he published a popular treatise called "The Ancient World, or Picturesque Sketches of Great Britain." Among his other works are "The Gold-Seeker's Manual," "The Great Stone Book of Nature," (1863,) "Science of Physical Geography," and "The World we live in," (1869.) He has travelled on the Eastern Continent and in America, and has applied his science to the exploration of mineral resources.

An'ster, (JOHN,) an Irish poet, born at Charleville, in Cork county, about 1796. He published in 1819 a volume of "Poems and Translations from the German," which procured for him the friendship of Coleridge. He was called to the Irish bar in 1824, and was afterwards regius professor of civil law in Trinity College, Dublin, till near the time of his death. His "Faustus; from the German of Goethe," (1835,) is commended by the "Edinburgh Review," and by Coleridge. Anster contributed many articles to "Blackwood's Magazine." His version of Faust has been reprinted in Germany. Died in June, 1867.

Anstett, von, fon än'stĕt, (JOHANN Protasius— pRo-tä'ze-ús,) a diplomatist, born at Strasburg about

1755. He entered the service of Russia about 1790. In conjunction with Nesselrode, he negotiated the treaty of Reichenbach in 1813, after which he represented Russia at the Congress of Prague. He was minister plenipotentiary to the German Diet at Frankfort in the latter years of his life. Died in 1835.

Anstey, än'ste, (CHRISTOPHER,) an English satirical poet, born in Cambridgeshire in 1724, was educated at King's College, Cambridge. He published in 1766 "The New Bath Guide," a scandalous poem, which had great popularity. His satire was directed chiefly against physicians and Methodists. Among his other poems is "The Election Ball." Died in 1805.

Anstey, (THOMAS CHIS'HOLM,) an English lawyer, born in London in 1816. He represented Youghall in Parliament from 1847 to 1852. He published a useful "Guide to the Laws of England affecting Roman Catholics," (1842.)

An'stis, (JOHN,) an English antiquary, distinguished for his knowledge of heraldry, was born at Saint Neots, in Cornwall, in 1669. He became a member of Parliament in 1702, and Garter king-at-arms in 1718. He published many accurate works, among which are "Curia Militaris, or a Treatise of the Court of Chivalry," (1702,) and "The Register of the Most Noble Order of the Garter," (1724.) Died in 1744.

See NICHOLS's "Literary Anecdotes."

Anstruther, än'stru-thẹr or än'stẹr, (Sir JOHN,) a British judge, born in 1753, became chief justice of Bengal in 1798. Died in 1811.

Antæus, an-tee'us, [Gr. 'Ανταῖος; Fr. ANTÉE, ŏn'tä',] a Libyan giant, represented as a son of Neptune and Terra, was a famous wrestler. He resisted Hercules with success for a time, and was invincible so long as he touched his mother Earth; but at last the hero raised Antæus into the air and squeezed him to death.

An-tag'o-ras, ['Ανταγόρας,] a Greek poet and noted gourmand, a native of Rhodes, lived about 250 B.C.

An-tal'çi-das, ['Ανταλκίδας,] a Spartan ambassador, notorious as the author of a disgraceful peace concluded between the Grecian States and Persia, 387 B.C. One condition of the "peace of Antalcidas" was that all the Greek cities in Asia should be surrendered to Persia.

An'tar, (more properly **Antarah-Ibn-Sheddâd,** än'tä-rä ïb'n shed'däd',) a celebrated Arabian warrior, supposed to have lived about the middle of the sixth century. He was himself a poet, and his exploits furnished a copious theme for Arabian song and romance. He composed a poem which is numbered among the Mo'allakât or seven famous poems suspended in the temple of Mecca. He is the hero of an Arabian romance which was translated into English by T. Hamilton and entitled "Antar, a Bedouin Romance," (1819.)

"Nothing can be more delightful," says "Blackwood's Magazine" for January, 1819, "than the feeling which attends us in our first perusal of Antar. We are transported into a scene of which we have before seen nothing, but in which we recognize at once, as if by intuition, the glow, the wildness, the vastness—all the unchanged and unchangeable features—of the eternal desert."

See DE SACY, "Notices des anciens Poëmes Arabes, etc."

Antelami, degli, däl'yee än-tä-lä'mee, (BENEDETTO,) an Italian sculptor and architect of the twelfth century.

Antelmi or **Anthelmi,** ŏn'tĕl'me', the name of several ecclesiastics of the south of France in the seventeenth and eighteenth centuries. The most noted, perhaps, was Joseph Antelmi.

Antelmi or **Anthelmi,** (JOSEPH,) a French ecclesiastic, born at Fréjus in 1648. He became grand-vicar and official of the Bishop of Pamiers in 1684. He left a work "On the Dangers of the Life of Canons," ("De Periculis Canonicorum,") and other writings. Died in 1697.

Antelmi, (PIERRE THOMAS,) a French writer and mathematician, born in Provence in 1730; died in 1783.

An-te'nor, [Gr. 'Αντήνωρ; Fr. ANTÉNOR, ŏn'tä'noR',] a Trojan noted for his wisdom, was the father of Acamas, Agenor, and many other sons. He advised the Trojans to restore Helen to her husband. He has been accused, by writers of little authority, of a design to betray Troy to the Greeks.

€ as k; ç as s; ğ hard; ġ as j; G, H, K, guttural; N, nasal; R, trilled; ṣ as z; th as in this. (☞ See Explanations, p. 23.)

Antenor, a Grecian sculptor, who lived at Athens about 500 B.C. He made bronze statues of Harmo'dius and Aristogi'ton, which were carried away by Xerxes in 480 B.C.

An'te-ros, in the Greek mythology, was originally a being opposed to Eros, (or the god of Love;) but afterwards the name was applied to the deity who avenges unrequited love.

Antésignan, ŏN'tä'sĕn'yŏN', (PIERRE,) a French grammarian, born at Rabastens, in Languedoc, lived about 1550.

Anthelmi. See ANTELMI.

An-thel'mus or **An-tel'mus,** [Fr. ANTHELME, ŏN'-tĕlm',] SAINT, of Savoy, became in 1163 Bishop of Belley, (bĕl'lȧ',) in the south of France, where he died in 1178.

An-the'mĭ-us, an able and upright minister, who was appointed by Arcadius Prefect of the East in 405 A.D., before which date he had been consul under Stilicho. At the death of Arcadius, in 408, he became prime minister, and guardian of the infant heir, Theodosius II. He retired from office in 414 A.D.

Anthemius, (or **Anthe'mius Proco'pius,**) Roman Emperor of the West, a grandson of the preceding. He became a favourite general of Leo, Emperor of the East, who, having been solicited by the Roman senate to give a ruler to Italy, selected Anthemius for that position. He began to reign in 467 A.D. His son-in-law, Ricimer, raised an army and marched against the capital, near which Anthemius was defeated in battle in 472 and put to death.

Anthemius, [Gr. Ἀνθέμιος,] an eminent architect and mathematician, surnamed TRALLIA'NUS, from Tralles, in Lydia, where he was born, was a brother of Alexander Trallianus. He was employed at Constantinople by Justinian, for whom he designed and commenced the celebrated church of Saint Sophia, which, after his death, was finished by Isidorus about 537 A.D., and is now a Turkish mosque. Its dimensions are two hundred and sixty-nine feet long by two hundred and forty-three wide. It is surmounted by a large dome, and is considered the original type of the Byzantine style. Died about 534 A.D.

An'ther-ic or **An'thar-ic,** [Lat. ANTHERI'CUS,] son of Clefo, the successor of Alboin, was elected King of the Longobards about 585, and died in 590 A.D.

Anthing, ân'ting, (FRIEDRICH,) a German painter, born at Gotha about the middle of the eighteenth century. He was for some time an aide-de-camp to the Russian general Suwarrow. He painted portraits in profile, at Vienna, Berlin, etc. Died in 1805.

Anthing, (KARL,) a German general, who became Governor-General of the Dutch possessions in India. Died at Gotha in 1823.

Anthoine, ŏN'twân', (ANTOINE IGNACE,) a French merchant, noted for public spirit, was born at Embrun in 1749. He was the pioneer in opening an extensive commerce with Russia by the Black Sea, and wrote a "Historical Essay on the Commerce and Navigation of the Black Sea," (1805.) He was mayor of Marseilles from 1805 to 1813. His wife, whose maiden name was Clary, was a sister-in-law of Joseph Bonaparte and General Bernadotte. Died in 1826.

Anthoine, (FRANÇOIS PAUL NICOLAS,) a French general and politician, born in 1720. He was elected in 1789 to the States-General, in which body he was an earnest advocate of the establishment of the trial by jury. Died in 1793.

An'thon, (CHARLES,) LL.D., an American classical scholar, born in the city of New York in 1797. He entered Columbia College in 1811, and graduated with distinguished honour in 1815. He studied law, and was admitted to the bar in 1819; but his strong predilection for classical pursuits induced him in 1820 to accept the position of adjunct professor of the ancient languages in Columbia College; and on the resignation of Professor Moore in 1835 he became principal professor of the classics in that institution. He published an edition of Horace, (1830,) a "Dictionary of Greek and Roman Antiquities," and a "Classical Dictionary," (1841.) He also edited many Greek and Latin authors for the use of schools. His works have been reprinted in England,

a distinction rarely if ever before accorded to American classical school-books. Died in 1867.

For an interesting notice of some of the personal traits of Dr. Anthon, see "The Galaxy," New York, September, 1867.

Anthon, (JOHN,) an American jurist, a brother of the preceding, was born at Detroit in 1784. He published, besides other works, "An Essay on the Study of Law," an "Analysis of Blackstone," (2d edition, 1832,) and "Nisi Prius Cases." He practised for many years in the city of New York, where he died in March, 1863.

Anthonie or **Anthony,** an'to-ne, (FRANCIS,) [Lat. FRANCISCUS ANTO'NIUS,] an English physician and alchemist, born in London in 1550. He practised medicine with success, and professed to cure all diseases with a solution of gold called *aurum potabile,* ("potable gold,") on which he published a treatise, entitled "Golden Panacea," ("Panace'a Au'rea," 1619.) Died in 1623.

An'thony or **An'tony,** [Lat. ANTO'NIUS; Fr. ANTOINE, ŏN'twän',] SAINT, surnamed ABBAS, one of the Christian Fathers, the reputed founder of monachism, was born near Heracle'a, in Upper Egypt, in 251 A.D. It is said that in his youth he obeyed in a literal sense the scripture which says, "Sell that thou hast, and give to the poor," and retired from the world to the desert, where he lived as a hermit. Having acquired a wide reputation by his austerities, he founded a monastery near Faioom, (or Phaiûm,) about 305. Many years afterwards he visited Alexandria, to testify against Arianism. His life was written by Athanasius. Some of his letters are extant. He died about 356 A.D.

Anthony. See ANTONIUS, ANTONY, or ANTOINE.

Anthony de Bourbon. See ANTONY OF BOURBON.

Antiboul, ŏN'te'bool', (CHARLES LOUIS,) a French Girondist and lawyer, born at Saint-Tropez about 1752. He was elected in 1792 to the Convention, in which he voted for the detention of the king. On his return from a mission to Corsica he was executed as an accomplice of the Girondists, in October, 1793.

An-tĭ-cli'dēs, [Gr. Ἀντικλείδης; Fr. ANTICLIDE, ŏN'-te'klĕd',] a Greek historian, born at Athens, is supposed to have lived about 300 B.C. His works are lost.

An-tid'o-tus, [Ἀντίδοτος,] a Greek painter, who lived about 350 B.C., was the master of Nicias, the great Athenian painter.

An-tig'e-nēs, [Gr. Ἀντιγένης,] one of the generals of Alexander the Great. He distinguished himself at the siege of Halicarnassus, 331 B.C., and in the battle against Porus, 327. After the death of Alexander he was a faithful officer of Eumenes, and fought against Antigonus, who put him to death in 316 B.C.

Antigenes was also the name of several ancient Greek physicians.

Antigenes, [Ἀντιγένης,] a Greek historian, wrote a Life of Alexander the Great.

An-tĭ-gen'ĭ-das, [Ἀντιγενίδας,] a famous flute-player of Thebes in the fourth century B.C.

Antigna, ŏN'tèn'yä', (JEAN PIERRE ALEXANDRE,) a French painter of genre, born at Orléans in 1818. He gained a first medal in 1851.

Antignac, ŏN'tèn'yåk', (ANTOINE,) a noted French song-writer, born in Paris about 1770; died in 1823. His works have some merit, but do not rank among the best of their class.

Antigone, the French of ANTIGONUS, which see.

An-tig'o-ne, [Gr. Ἀντιγόνη,] the heroine of one of the tragedies of Sophocles, was a daughter of Œdipus, King of Thebes. She was immured alive by Creon for having performed the rites of burial to the body of her brother Polynices.

Antigone, Queen of Egypt, was a daughter of Cassander, and the wife of the Egyptian king Ptolemy Lagus.

An-tig'o-nus, [Gr. Ἀντίγονος,] a king of the Jews, was a son of Aristobu'lus II., after whose death he was driven from Judea by Antipater and his son Herod. He recovered the throne by the aid of the Parthians about 38 B.C., but was declared an enemy by the Roman senate. The army of Antony, who favoured Herod, took Jerusalem, and put Antigonus to death, about 36 B.C.

Antigonus, [Gr. Ἀντίγονος; Fr. ANTIGONE, ŏN'te'-gon',] King of Asia, surnamed CYCLOPS, or "one-eyed," an able general, and successor of Alexander the Great, was born in Macedonia about 382 B.C. He had a high command in the expedition against Persia, and was appointed Satrap of Phrygia in 333 B.C. In the partition of the conquered provinces which was made at the death of Alexander in 323, Antigonus obtained Lycia, Pamphylia, and Greater Phrygia. He was soon involved in a war against Perdiccas, and formed an alliance with Antipater and Ptolemy. After the death of Perdiccas, in 321, he found a formidable adversary in Eumenes, who commanded a Macedonian army in Asia for the cause of the royal family. In 316 Antigonus gained a victory over Eumenes, and put him to death. He had made himself master of a large portion of Asia, when a coalition was formed against him in 315 by Ptolemy, Lysimachus, Cassander, and Seleucus. A long war ensued, in which Antigonus professed to fight for Alexander, the minor son of Alexander the Great by Roxana. Demetrius Poliorcetes, a son of Antigonus, gained a naval victory over Ptolemy, near Cyprus, in 306 B.C., soon after which Antigonus assumed the title of .king. A new coalition having been formed against him in 302 by Cassander, Seleucus, Lysimachus, and Ptolemy, he was defeated and killed at Ipsus, in Phrygia, in 301 B.C.

See Diodorus Siculus; Thirlwall, "History of Greece;" Plutarch, "Eumenes," and "Demetrius."

Antig'onus Ca-rȳs'tĭ-us, ['Αντίγονος Καρύστιος,] a Greek philosopher, who is supposed to have lived in the reign of Ptolemy Philadelphus, 285–247 B.C. He was the reputed author of an extant "Collection of Marvellous Stories," and of some other works, which are lost.

Antig'onus Do'son, [Gr. 'Αντίγονος Δώσων,] a great-grandson of Antigonus the general of Alexander the Great, was a son of Demetrius, and a nephew of Antigonus Gonatas. He became regent or king of Macedonia during the minority of his cousin Philip, 229 B.C. As general-in-chief of the Achæan League, he gained victories over Cleomenes of Sparta and his allies in the Peloponnesus.· Died in 221 B.C., leaving the throne to Philip above mentioned.

Antig'onus Gon'a-tas, [Gr. 'Αντίγονος Γονατᾶς,] a son of Demetrius Poliorcetes, was born in 319 B.C. at Gona, or Gonni, in Thessaly, whence his surname Gonatas. He made himself master of Macedonia in 277, after he had defeated Antipater, a nephew of Cassander, and also an army of Gauls. About 273 his kingdom was invaded by Pyrrhus, the renowned King of Epirus. Antigonus, being unable to resist "the fierce Epirote," fled from the country, but afterwards recovered his throne, on the death of Pyrrhus, in 271 or 272 B.C. He annexed the Peloponnesus to his kingdom, and captured Athens in 262. His death is variously dated 243, 240, or 239 B.C. He was succeeded by his son Demetrius II.

Antiles. See Antyllus.

Antillon, ân-tĕl-yòn', (Isidore,) a Spanish savant, born in Aragon about 1760, became professor of astronomy and geography at Madrid. He wrote, besides other scientific works, " Elements of the Astronomical and Natural Geography of Spain and Portugal," (2d edition, 1815,) which was highly esteemed. Died in 1820.

An-til'o-chus, [Gr. 'Αντίλοχος; Fr. Antiloque, ŏn'-te'lok',] a son of Nestor, distinguished for courage and personal beauty, was one of the suitors of Helen, and a friend of Achilles. He was killed at the siege of Troy by Memnon, or, as others say, by Hector.

Antiloque. See Antilochus.

An-tim'a-chus, [Gr. 'Αντίμαχος; Fr. Antimaque, ŏn'te'mȧk',] an eminent Greek epic poet, who flourished about 400 B.C., was a native of Colophon or Claros. He enjoyed the friendship of Plato. He was the author of an epic poem entitled "Thebais," which the Alexandrian critics thought worthy to be compared to Homer's Iliad. His works, among which was a celebrated elegy called "Lyde," are lost, except small fragments. They are more remarkable for learning than genius.

Antimachus, a Greek epic poet, born at Heliopolis, in Egypt, lived before the Augustan age. He wrote a poem on "The Creation of the World."

Antimaco, ân-tim'ȧ-ko or ân-tee'mȧ-ko, (Marcantonio,) an Italian professor, writer, and critic, born at

Mantua about 1473. He taught Greek at Ferrara, and translated part of the " Ars Rhetorica" of Dionysius of Halicarnassus into Latin. Died about 1550.

Antimaque. See Antimachus.

Antine, d'. See D'Antine.

Antinori, ân-te-no'ree, (Antonio Ludovico,) an Italian antiquary and priest, born in Abruzzo in 1704; died in 1788. He left " Historical Memoirs of the Provinces of the Abruzzi," (4 vols., 1781–84.)

An-tin'o-us, [Gr. 'Αντίνους,] a beautiful youth, a favourite of the Roman emperor Hadrian, was born in Bithynia. He accompanied Hadrian to Egypt, and was drowned in the Nile in 132 A.D. A city, called Antinoöp'olis, was built by the emperor near the spot where he perished, and countless statues were erected in honour of him; some of these, of remarkable beauty, still exist. A new impulse was given to the fine arts by the emulous efforts of sculptors and painters to idealize his form as a type of beauty.

An-ti'o-chus, ['Αντίοχος,] a Greek historian, son of Xenophanes, born at Syracuse, flourished about 440 B.C. He wrote histories of Sicily and of Italy, which were highly prized by the ancients, but are not extant.

Anti'ochus I., surnamed So'ter, (i.e. " Saviour,") the son of Seleucus, King of Syria and Babylonia, was born about 324 B.C., and succeeded his father in 280 B.C. A victory gained by him over the Gauls, by means of his elephants, won for him the name of Soter. He was killed in battle against the Gauls in 261 B.C.

Antiochus II., The'os, a son of the preceding, succeeded his father in 261 B.C. Having delivered the Milesians from their tyrant Timarchus, he received from them the impious title of Theos, (or "God.") Among the important events of his reign was the successful revolt of the Parthians (250 B.C.) under Arsaces, who became the founder of the Parthian Empire. In fulfilment of a treaty with Ptolemy of Egypt, (252 B.C.,) Antiochus repudiated his queen Laodice, and married Berenice, a daughter of Ptolemy. At the death of Ptolemy, he again took Laodice into favour; but she poisoned him in 246, in order to secure the throne for her son Seleucus Callini'cus.

See Appian, "Syriaca."

Antiochus III. surnamed the Great, was a grandson of the preceding, and son of Seleucus Callini'cus. He was only fifteen years old when he succeeded his brother Seleucus Ceraunus, in 223 B.C. His kingdom, of which Antioch was the capital, included, besides Syria proper, Babylonia, Media, and a part of Asia Minor. In a war with Ptolemy, King of Egypt, he at first gained some advantages, but he was afterwards defeated by Ptolemy in a hard-fought battle at Raphia, in Palestine, in 217 B.C. About 214 he suppressed a revolt of Achæus in Asia Minor. While he was engaged in these wars, Arsaces the Parthian had occupied Media. Antiochus recovered Media in 212, and afterwards pursued Arsaces into Parthia. He also made a successful expedition to India, and formed alliances with several Indian princes. His encroachment on the territory of Egypt, and his ambitious designs against Thrace, which he invaded in 196 B.C., involved him in a war with the Romans. His resolution to reject the ultimatum of the Romans was confirmed by the advice of Hannibal, who took refuge at his court in 195. Having invaded Greece in 191 B.C., he was defeated at Thermopylæ by the Roman consul Acilius Glabrio, and withdrew to Asia the same year. In 190 B.C., with an army of above 80,000 men, he encountered the Romans under L. Cornelius Scipio, near Magnesia, and was utterly defeated. It is stated that he left 50,000 dead on the field. Peace was granted to him on condition that he should give up all Asia to the west of Taurus, and pay the expenses of the war, which were estimated at fifteen thousand talents. Having attempted to plunder the temple of Jupiter Belus in order to raise money for the Romans, he provoked an insurrection, in which he was killed, in 187 B.C. A prediction of his death may be found in Daniel xi. 18, 19. He was succeeded by his son Seleucus Philopator.

See Plutarch, and Eusebius, "Chronicon;" Polybius, "History;" Appian, "Roman History;" Justin, "History."

Antiochus IV., inappropriately surnamed Epiph'-

ANES, (or the "Illustrious,") was a younger son of the preceding, by whom in 188 B.C. he was given as a hostage to the Romans. After a captivity of twelve years, he was released, and ascended the throne of Syria in 175 B.C., on the death of his brother Seleucus Philopator, whose son Demetrius was detained as a hostage at Rome. He invaded Egypt in 170, subdued the greater part of the country, and captured the king, Ptolemy Philometor, but he retired from Egypt, in obedience to the peremptory order of the Romans, in 168 B.C. He plundered the temple of Jerusalem, and cruelly persecuted the Jews, who, under Judas Maccabæus and his brother, gained several victories over his armies. (See I. Maccabees ii.) He died in 164 or 165 B.C., of a loathsome disease, which was regarded both by Jews and Greeks as a divine punishment for his impiety.

See ROLLIN, "Ancient History;" JOSEPHUS, "History of the Jews."

Antiochus V., surnamed EU'PATOR, was a son of the preceding, whom he succeeded at the age of nine years, about 164 B.C., under the regency of Lysias. He was put to death in 162 by his cousin-german Demetrius Soter, who succeeded him on the throne.

Antiochus VI., a son of Alexander Balas, was a minor at the death of his father in 146 B.C. Diodotus Tryphon affected to support him as a rival to Demetrius Nicator, who then possessed the throne. The latter was defeated, and Antiochus reigned nominally until he was put to death by Tryphon in 142 B.C.

Antiochus VII., surnamed SIDETES, (sī-dee'tĕz,) born about 164 B.C., was a younger son of Demetrius Soter. Having driven the usurper Tryphon from the throne, he began to reign in 138. He waged war against the Jews, whom he reduced to the state of tributaries, and afterwards against the Parthians, whom he defeated in three battles. He was killed in a battle against the same, in 129 or 128 B.C.

See APPIAN, "De Bello Syriaco;" JOSEPHUS, "History of the Jews."

Antiochus VIII., surnamed GRY'PUS, a son of Demetrius Nicator and Cleopatra, was born about 140 B.C., and was sometimes styled EPIPHANES. Having expelled the usurper Alexander Zabinas, he began to reign about 124 B.C. His reign was disturbed by a civil war caused by his half-brother Antiochus Cyzicenus. He was assassinated in 96 B.C.

Antiochus IX., surnamed CYZICE'NUS, because he was educated at Cyzicus, was a son of Antiochus Sidetes and Cleopatra. He took arms against Antiochus Grypus about 116 B.C., and compelled him, in 112, to divide the kingdom. Antiochus IX. obtained for his share Cœle-Syria and Palestine. In 95 B.C. he was defeated and killed by Seleucus, a son of Grypus.

Antiochus X., surnamed EU'SEBES, (the "Pious,") was a son of Antiochus IX. He took the title of king in 95 B.C., but his claim was contested by Philip and Demetrius, sons of Antiochus Grypus, who prevailed for a time. Tigranes, having been invited by the Syrians, ended the strife, by seizing the kingdom for himself, in 83 B.C.

Antiochus XI., surnamed ASIAT'ICUS, a son of Antiochus Eusebes, was the last king of Syria of the dynasty of the Seleucidæ. While Tigranes was occupied with a war against the Romans, Antiochus made himself master of part of Syria, about 69 B.C. He was deposed by Pompey in 65 B.C., and Syria then became a Roman province.

Antiochus, a physician, who is supposed to have lived at Rome in the second century, and who attained a great age. Galen gives a minute account of his way of living. Another physician of this name was a native of Mauritania, and is said to have suffered martyrdom about 120 A.D. He is venerated as a saint by the Roman Church.

Antiochus OF ÆGÆ, in Cilicia, a Greek sophist, lived about 200 A.D. He served under Alexander Severus in the war against the Parthians, and, to raise the courage of the soldiers, rolled himself in the snow, for which he was well rewarded by the emperor. He afterwards deserted to the Parthians. He had a high reputation as a declaimer or forensic speaker.

Antiochus OF ASCALON, an eminent Platonic philosopher, was a friend of Cicero and of L. Licinius Lucullus. He was a pupil of Philo, whom he succeeded as the head of the New Academy, and taught philosophy at Athens, (where Cicero was his pupil about 80 B.C.,) and afterwards at Alexandria. He laboured to confute the skepticism of Philo and Carneades, and to effect a union or compromise between the principles of the Academy and those of the Stoics. He wrote several works, which are lost; but his doctrines are explained in Cicero's "Academics."

Antiochus OF COMMAGENE was an ally of Tigranes in the war against the Romans under Lucullus, about 69 B.C. He made peace with Pompey, who gave him Seleucia, and he furnished troops to that general in the civil war against Cæsar. He was reigning in 36 B.C.

Anti'ochus surnamed EPIPH'ANES, a younger son of Antiochus Grypus, assumed the title of King of Syria. He was defeated by Antiochus X. in 93 B.C.

Antiochus surnamed HI'ERAX, a son of Antiochus II. of Syria, waged war against his brother Seleucus, and was defeated. Died in 227 B.C., aged about thirty-three.

Antiochus OF SEBA or SABA, lived about the commencement of the seventh century. He wrote a treatise on Christian morals, which is extant.

An-ti'o-pe, [Gr. Ἀντιόπη,] a daughter of Nycteus, King of Thebes, became the mother, by Jupiter, of AMPHION and ZETHUS, (which see.)

Antipas, (HEROD.) See HEROD ANTIPAS.

An-tip'a-ter, [Gr. Ἀντίπατρος,] a pupil of Aristotle, who was made regent of Macedonia. He had been employed as general and minister by Philip of Macedon, by whom he was highly esteemed for his prudence and fidelity. He was appointed regent by Alexander the Great when the latter set out on his expedition against Persia in 334 B.C. In 331 he gained a victory over the Spartans near Megalopolis. He was superseded as regent by Craterus, and ordered to conduct an army of recruits to Babylon in 323. At the division of provinces after the death of Alexander, the generals agreed that Antipater and Craterus should jointly govern Macedonia and Greece. He defeated the Athenians and their allies, who made an effort to recover their independence, in 322 B.C. In the treaty which ended this war, called the Lamian war, it was stipulated that Demosthenes should be delivered to Antipater. The latter joined Antigonus and Ptolemy in a coalition against Perdiccas in 321, and was marching through Syria on his way to Egypt, when Perdiccas was killed by his own troops. Soon after this event he was appointed regent of the empire in place of Perdiccas, and guardian of the young king, Alexander IV., with whom he returned to Macedonia. Died in 319 B.C., leaving a son, Cassander.

See THIRLWALL, "History of Greece;" DIODORUS SICULUS, "History;" PLUTARCH, "Life of Phocion;" JUSTIN, "History;" DROYSEN, "Geschichte der Nachfolger Alexanders."

Antipater, a grandson of the preceding, was the second son of Cassander. He succeeded his brother, Philip IV. of Macedon, in 296 B.C., and, after a contest with his brother Alexander, was deposed by Demetrius Poliorcetes in 294. According to Justin, he was put to death by Lysimachus of Thrace.

Antipater, a Greek epigrammatic poet of Macedonia, lived in the reign of Philip V., 220-179 B.C.

Antipater, a son of •Herod the Great and his first wife Doris, was notorious for cruelty. He conspired against his father, and was put to death in 1 B.C., or in the last year of his father's reign. He is called by Josephus a "mystery of iniquity."

Antipater OF HIERAPOLIS, a Greek rhetorician, who was private secretary of Septimius Severus, who reigned from 193 to 211 A.D.

Antipater (THE IDUME'AN) was a son of Antipas, Governor of Idumea, and the father of Herod the Great. He ruled Judea by permission of the high-priest Hyrcanus, who had been raised to the priesthood by the aid and influence of Antipater. About 46 B.C. he was appointed Procurator or Governor of Judea by Cæsar, to whom he had rendered some service in his war against the Egyptians. Died in 43 B.C.

Antipater OF SIDON, a Greek poet, who probably flourished about 100 B.C. Pliny relates that he had a fever every year on his birthday. A number of his epigrams are extant.

Antipater OF TARSUS, a Stoic philosopher, who lived about 140 B.C., was a disciple and successor of Diogenes the Babylonian. He wrote several works on philosophy, divination, morality, etc., and seems to have been a man of great merit. Cicero praises his subtlety or acuteness. Antipater had a controversy with Carneades, whose skepticism he combated.

Antipater OF TYRE, a Stoic philosopher, died at Athens about 44 B.C. He is favourably mentioned by Cicero.

Antipater, (L. CŒLIUS.) See CŒLIUS.

An-tiph'a-nēs, [Ἀντιφάνης,] an Athenian comic poet of considerable merit, flourished about 360 B.C. He wrote, it is said, not less than two hundred and sixty plays, of which many fragments are extant. He died, says Suidas, in 330 B.C.

Antiphanes, a Greek physician of Delos, of uncertain date, mentioned by Galen.

Antiphanes OF ARGOS, a Greek sculptor, the master of Cleon, lived about 400 B.C.

An-tiph'ĭ-lus, [Gr. Ἀντίφιλος; Fr. ANTIPHILE, ŏN'-te'fēl',] a celebrated Greek painter, born in Egypt, is supposed by many to have flourished about 330 B.C. But Lucian, in his treatise against Calumny, states that he accused his rival Apelles of complicity in a conspiracy which was formed in the reign of Ptolemy Philopator, about 318 B.C. Antiphilus excelled in facility of execution, and is the reputed inventor of the grotesque figures called *grylli*. Pliny notices several of his works, among which are "Cadmus and Europa," and a "Boy blowing a Fire."

Antiphilus, a Greek epigrammatic poet, lived probably between 10 and 70 A.D.

Antipho. See ANTIPHON.

An'tĭ-phon or **An'tĭ-pho,** [Ἀντιφῶν,] one of the Ten Attic Orators, a son of Sophilus, a sophist, was born at Rhamnus, in Attica, about 479 B.C. He made improvements in the art of rhetoric, and was one of the teachers of Thucydides, who expresses a favourable opinion of his oratory. He is said to have been a successful commander in the Peloponnesian war. He seldom spoke in public, but composed speeches or orations for accused persons or politicians. Fifteen of his orations are still extant. He acted a very prominent part in the revolution by which the Council of Four Hundred obtained power in 411 B.C. Before the end of that year a counter-revolution occurred, and Alcibiades, the enemy of Antiphon, was recalled. Antiphon was tried for treason, and made an eloquent speech in his own defence, but was punished with death. Thucydides represents him as a man of superior virtue and wisdom.

See D. RUHNKEN and P. VAN SPAAN, "Dissertatio de Antiphonte Oratore Attico," 1763; A. DRYANDER, "Commentatio de Antiphontis Rhamnusii Vita," 1838.

Antiphon, a Greek epic poet and sophist, who was contemporary with Socrates. He is supposed to be the Antiphon who wrote a work on Truth, to which several ancient writers refer.

Antiphon, a younger brother of Plato, who has preserved the remembrance of his name in his dialogue Parmenides."

Antiphon, a Greek tragic poet, who flourished about 400 B.C. He lived at the court of Dionysius the Elder, by whom he was put to death. Several of his works are cited by Aristotle. When the tyrant asked him what was the best kind of brass or bronze, he answered, "That of which the statues of Harmodius and Aristogi'ton are made."

Antiquario, ân-te-kwä're-o, (JACOPO,) [Lat. JACO'-BUS ANTIQUA'RIUS,] a learned Italian writer, born at Perugia about 1444. He was secretary to the Duke of Milan. Died at Milan in 1512. A volume of his Latin letters was published in 1519.

Antiquus, ân-tee'kwus, (JOANNES or JAN,) a distinguished Dutch painter, born at Groningen in 1702. He went to Italy in his youth, and worked in Florence, Rome, Naples, and Venice. After his return to Holland he was patronized by the Prince of Orange. Among his works are "The Fall of the Giants," a "Scipio Africanus," and "Parnassus." Descamps calls him a good designer and a good colorist. He painted many portraits. Died in 1750.

See DESCAMPS, "Vies des Peintres Hollandais."

An-tis'ta-tēs, [Ἀντιστάτης,] a Greek architect of the sixth century B.C., laid the foundation of the temple of Jupiter Olympius at Athens.

An-tis'the-nēs, [Gr. Ἀντισθένης; Fr. ANTISTHÈNE, ŏN'tès'tȧn',] an eminent Greek Cynic philosopher, and the reputed founder of the Cynic school, was born at Athens, and flourished about 400 or 375 B.C. He was a disciple and friend of Socrates, after whose death he established a school in the gymnasium of Cynosarges. He is said to have been an enemy of Plato. Among his pupils was the witty and eccentric Diogenes. Antisthenes was very temperate and simple in his way of life, and professed a contempt of riches. As he seemed to make a display of his disregard for the ordinary usages of life, Socrates once said to him, "I can see thy pride (or vanity) through the holes in thy robe." Xenophon, in his "Banquet," gives a favourable impression of his character. Many of his sententious and pithy sayings are recorded. He wrote works on various subjects, which are lost, except perhaps two declamations which are ascribed to him. His doctrines were chiefly moral and practical. He taught that virtue is all-sufficient for happiness, and approved those healthy pleasures that are consequent on labour. In one of his works he says, "There are many popular gods, but only one natural God." He survived the battle of Leuctra, 371 B.C.

See RICHTER, "Dissertatio de Vita, Moribus et Placitis Antisthenis Cynici;" RITTER, "History of Philosophy;" G. H. LEWES, "Biographical History of Philosophy;" DIOGENES LAERTIUS.

Antoine, (of Germany.) See ANTON.

Antoine, (of Italy.) See ANTONIO.

Antoine, ŏN'twän', (JACQUES DENIS,) an eminent French artist, born in Paris in 1733. He built the staircase of the Palais de Justice, and the Mint, (Hôtel des Monnaies,) the unity and simplicity of which presented a strong contrast with the then prevailing style in French architecture. It was finished in 1789. Died in 1801.

See QUATREMÈRE DE QUINCY, "Histoire des Architectes."

Antoine, (PAUL GABRIEL,) a French Jesuit, born at Lunéville in 1679, was professor of philosophy in several colleges. He published, besides other works, "Theologia Moralis Universa," (3 vols., 1726 and 1731,) often reprinted. Died at Pont-à-Mousson in 1743.

Antoine, (SÉBASTIEN,) a French engraver, born at Nancy, flourished between 1720 and 1750.

Antoine de Bourbon. See ANTONY OF BOURBON.

Antoine de Messine. See ANTONELLO.

Antoinette, (MARIE.) See MARIE ANTOINETTE.

Antolinez, ân-to-lee'nêth, (Don JOSÉ,) a Spanish landscape-painter, who excelled in colouring, was born at Seville in 1639. He painted some historical pictures. Died at Madrid in 1676.

Antolinez y Sarabia, ân-to-lee'nêth e sȧ-rä-Bee'ä, (FRANCISCO,) a nephew of the preceding, born at Seville in 1644, was a skilful painter. He studied with Murillo, whose colouring he imitated with success, and worked at Madrid. Died in 1700.

Antolini, ân-to-lee'nee, (GIOVANNI,) an architect of Milan, born in 1755; died in 1841. He published, among other works, a treatise on civil architecture.

Antommarchi, ân-tom-maR'kee, (FRANCESCO,) an Italian anatomist, born in Corsica. He became, in 1812, anatomical dissector to a hospital of Florence, attached to the University of Pisa, and was afterwards physician or surgeon to Napoleon at Saint Helena, 1818–21. He published "The Last Moments of Napoleon," (2 vols., 1823,) and "Anatomical Plates of the Human Body," (1823–26.) Died in Cuba in 1838, or, according to some authorities, about 1844.

See "Mémoires du Docteur F. Antommarchi."

Anton, ân'ton, or **An'tony,** [Fr. ANTOINE, ŏN'twän',] I., (CLEMENS THEODOR,) King of Saxony, born in 1755, was the second son of Frederick Christian, Elector of Saxony. He married Maria Theresa of Austria, whose father became emperor Leopold I. In 1827 he succeeded his brother Frederick Augustus, but, on account of his age and lack of abilities, took little part in the government. Died in 1836.

See MEYNERT, "Anton König von Sachsen."

Anton, (CONRAD GOTTLOB,) a German philologist, born at Lauban in 1745 ; died at Wittenberg in 1814.

Anton, (GOTTFRIED,) [Lat. GOTHOFRE′DUS ANTO′-NIUS,] an eminent professor of feudal and Roman law, born in Westphalia about 1570 ; died in 1618.

Anton or **An-to′nǐ-us,** (PAUL,) a German Protestant theologian, born at Hirschfeld, in Lusatia, in 1661, became professor of theology at Halle about 1695. His work, called "The Doctrine of the Council of Trent," (1697,) has been often reprinted. Died at Halle in 1730.

Anton, von, fon ân′ton, (KARL GOTTLOB,) a German historian and lawyer, born at Lauban in 1751, was noted for his critical sagacity. He wrote, besides other works, a "History of Agriculture in Germany," (3 vols., 1799-1802,) and a "History of the German Nation," (unfinished, 1793.) Died in 1818.

Antonelle, ǒN′to′nĕl′, (PIERRE ANTOINE,) a French marquis, born at Arles in 1747, became a zealous revolutionist, was elected to the Legislative Assembly in 1792, and took an active part against the Girondists. Died in 1817.

Antonelli, ân-to-nel′lee, (GIACOMO,) an Italian cardinal and able politician, born near Terracina on the 2d of April, 1806. He became second treasurer under the papal government in 1844, and grand treasurer of the two apostolic chambers in 1845. By the suppleness of his character and the energy disguised under an affable exterior, he acquired great influence with Pius IX., who appointed him minister of finances. He opposed the liberal movement which resulted in the formation of a republic at Rome in 1848, and became the pope's secretary of state for foreign affairs (or first minister) in April, 1850. He has shown himself an ultra-conservative, and determinedly hostile to the cause of Italian unity.

Antonelli, (GIOVANNI CARLO,) an Italian bishop and distinguished writer on canon law, who became Bishop of Ferentino in 1677, was born at Velletri. Among his chief works is one "On the Government of the Episcopal Church," (or "of the church by bishops,") ("De Regimine Ecclesiæ Episcopalis," 1650.) Died in 1694.

Antonelli, (LEONARDO,) an Italian cardinal, born at Sinigaglia in 1730, distinguished himself as a friend of the Jesuits, and as an advocate of the most extravagant claims of the Roman Church. Died in 1811.

Antonelli, (NICCOLÒ MARIA,) COUNT, an eminent Italian historian and theologian, born at Pergola in 1698, was made cardinal in 1759. He wrote on "The Rights of the Apostolic See to Parma and Piacenza," (4 vols., 1742,) and other works. Died in 1767.

Antonello, ân-to-nel′lo, or **Antonelli,** ân-to-nel′lee, (ANTONIO,) surnamed DA MESSINA, dâ mês-see′nä, from the place of his birth, [Fr. ANTOINE DE MESSINE, ǒN′-twän′ dĕh mä′sĕn′,] a celebrated painter, born at Messina about 1414, is generally supposed to be the first Italian who painted in oil. His admiration of an oil-painting by J. Van Eyck induced him to visit Bruges, where he gained the friendship of Van Eyck, who imparted to him his secret method of mixing his paints. He returned to Italy about 1445, worked at Milan, and acquired a high reputation by the brilliancy of his colouring. About 1470 he settled in Venice, where he lived twenty years, and painted subjects from the Scriptures, among which is a picture of the Virgin reading. Died about 1495.

See LANZI, "History of Painting in Italy," and "Lives of the Early Flemish Painters."

Antoni, d′, dân-to′nee, (ALESSANDRO VITTORIO **Papacino**—pä-pä-chee′no,) a distinguished Piedmontese artillery officer and writer on the military art, born at Villa Franca in 1714. He entered the army at an early age, and passed successively through the various grades until he attained the rank of lieutenant-general in 1784. Among his works are a treatise on "Military Architecture," (6 vols., 1778,) and one on "Gunpowder," (1765.) Died in 1786.

Antoni, degli, dâl′yee ân-to′nee, (VINCENZO BERNI,) an Italian jurist, born at Bologna in 1747; died about 1810.

See CARLO PEPOLI, "Vie d'Antoni."

An-to′nǐ-a, (MA′JOR, or "the Elder,") a daughter of Mark Antony the Triumvir, and Octavia, a sister of Augustus Cæsar, was born in 39 B.C. She became the wife of L. Domitius Ahenobarbus, and mother of Cneius Domitius, who was the father of the emperor Nero.

Anto′nia, (MI′NOR, or "the Younger,") a younger daughter of Mark Antony and Octavia, was born about 36 B.C. She was married to Claudius Drusus Nero, (who died in 9 B.C.,) and became mother of the celebrated Germanicus, and of Claudius, who was afterwards emperor. She was admired for her beauty and esteemed for her virtues. The emperor Caligula was her grandson. Died in 37 or 38 A.D.

Antoniano, ân-to-ne-ä′no, (SILVIO,) a celebrated Italian improvisatore and cardinal, born at Rome in 1540. He improvised verses on various subjects, and in all the measures of Italian poetry. As professor of classical literature in the College of Sapienza at Rome, he lectured with great reputation. He was made a cardinal in 1598. He wrote a "Treatise on Education," (1584,) and a volume of Latin Orations, (1610.) Died in 1603.

See GINGUENÉ, "Histoire Littéraire d'Italie."

Antoniasso, ân-to-ne-âs′so, an Italian painter, who lived in the first part of the sixteenth century.

Antonides, ân-to′ne-dĕs, (THEODORUS,) a Dutch theologian, lived in the first half of the eighteenth century.

Antonides Nerdenus, ân-to′ne-dĕs nĕR-dä′nŭs, (HENDRIK,) also called **Hendrik Antonius van der Linden,** (vân dẹr lin′dẹn,) a Dutch theologian, born at Naerden in 1546. He wrote, in Latin, a "System of Theology," (1613.) Died in 1604.

Antonides van der Goes, ân-to′ne-dĕs vän dẹr HOOS, (JOHANNES,) a popular Dutch poet, born at Goes in 1647. He practised medicine in his youth, and afterwards obtained an office in the admiralty. His chief work is a national poem descriptive of the Dutch river Y or Ij, entitled "The Y Stream," ("Ijstroom," 1671,) which was very popular. Died in 1684.

Antonides van der Linden, (JOHANNES.) See LINDEN.

Antoniles, (JOSÉ.) See ANTOLINEZ.

Antonilez. See ANTOLINEZ.

Antonin, the French for ANTONINUS, which see.

An-to-ni′nạ, the wife of Belisarius, born in 499 A.D., was eminent for her beauty, energy, and powers of fascination. She had great influence in public affairs. She was once imprisoned by Belisarius for her infidelity, but he was afterwards reconciled to her. Died after 565.

See GIBBON, "Decline and Fall of the Roman Empire."

Antonini, ân-to-nee′nee, (ANNIBALE,) born near Salerno, in Naples, settled in Paris, where he was known as the Abbé Antonini. He wrote an Italian-French Dictionary, and other works. Died in 1755.

Antonini, (FILIPPO,) an Italian antiquary, born at Sarsina in the sixteenth century. Died about 1630.

Antonini, (GIUSEPPE,) an Italian antiquary and jurist, lived between 1700 and 1750.

An-to-ni′nus, [It. ANTONIO, ân-to′ne-o, or ANTONINO, ân-to-nee′no ; Fr. ANTONIN, ǒN′to′nĂN′,] SAINT, a learned and pious archbishop of Florence, born in 1389 ; died in 1459. His numerous works are principally theological. His "Summa Theologica" (4 vols., 1478) has been often reprinted.

Antoninus, (MARCUS AURELIUS.) See AURELIUS ANTONINUS.

An-to-ni′nus Lib-er-ā′lis, a Greek writer, who is supposed to have lived about 150 A.D., but is not mentioned by any ancient author. There is extant a work entitled a "Collection of Metamorphoses," which is ascribed to him.

An-to-ni′nus Pi′us, or, more fully, **Ti′tus Au-re′lǐ-us Ful′vus Boi-o′nǐ-us Ar′rǐ-us An-to-ni′nus,** [Fr. ANTONIN, ǒN′to′nĂN′,] an excellent Roman emperor, a son of Aurelius Fulvus, was born at Lanuvium in 86 A.D. He became consul in 120 A.D., after which he governed the province of Asia, as proconsul, with wisdom and equity. He married Annia Galeria Faustina, and was adopted by Hadrian in 138, on condition that he should adopt Marcus Annius Verus. (See AURELIUS, (MARCUS,) and LUCIUS VERUS.) Antoninus succeeded Hadrian in July, 138, and began under happy auspices his peaceful and prosperous reign. He appears to have treated the Christians with moderation, if not clemency. It has been stated that he issued an edict for the protection of Christians; but some writers ascribe this edict to his successor. According to Capitolinus, from whom we derive nearly all our knowledge of Antoninus, he was temperate, humane, amiable, learned, and eloquent. The name of Pater Patriæ ("Father of his Country") was conferred on him by the senate. He died in 161 A.D., and was succeeded by Marcus Aurelius. His memory was so greatly venerated that five of his successors assumed the name of Antoninus.

See J. CAPITOLINUS, "Vita Antonini;" GAUTIER DE SIBERT, "Vie d'Antonin."

Antonio, ân-to'ne-o, DOM an illegitimate son of Dom Luis, son of King Emmanuel of Portugal, claimed the throne in opposition to his uncle Henry, and on the death of the latter, in 1580, was proclaimed king. He was totally defeated by the Duke of Alva the same year. After various attempts to recover his kingdom, he died in Paris in 1595.

Antonio OF FLORENCE. See ANTONINUS, (SAINT.)

Antonio, (MARC.) See RAIMONDI.

Antonio, ân-to'ne-o, (NICOLAS,) [Lat. NICOLAUS ANTONIUS,] a distinguished Spanish bibliographer and critic, born at Seville in 1617. He was appointed in 1659 by Philip IV. his general agent at the court of Rome, where he remained eighteen years. During this time he was employed on his great work, which is a complete list of the Spanish authors and a catalogue of their writings. In 1672 he published a part of this work, entitled "New Spanish Library," ("Bibliotheca Hispana Nova," in 2 vols.) The "Old Library" ("Bibliotheca Vetus," in 2 vols.) appeared in 1696. He became fiscal of the royal council at Madrid about 1677. Died in 1684. His "Bibliotheca Hispana" is considered by many critics the best work on Spanish literature. He also wrote a "Critique on Fabulous Histories," ("Censura de Historias fabulosas," 1742.)

See ARANA DE VARFLORA, "Hijos de Sevilla;" MAYANS, "Vida de N. Antonio," prefixed to his "Censura de Historias fabulosas;" TICKNOR, "History of Spanish Literature."

Antonio (ân-to'ne-o) OF PADUA, a Franciscan monk and celebrated preacher, born at Lisbon in 1195; died at Padua in 1231. He is regarded by the Roman Catholics of Italy and Portugal as one of the greatest of their saints.

Antonio, (PEDRO,) a Spanish historical painter, born at Córdova in 1614; died in 1675.

Anto'nio surnamed VENEZIANO, (vå-nêd-ze-â'no,) or the "Venetian," an eminent painter in fresco, born in Venice, or, according to some authorities, in Florence, about 1310. He worked chiefly in Florence and Pisa. His design was correct and graceful. The truth and harmony of his chiaroscuro are praised by Vasari. His works are nearly all destroyed. Died in 1384.

See NAGLER, "Allgemeines Künstler-Lexikon."

Antonio da Messina. See ANTONELLO.

Antonio da Vegu, ân-to'ne-o då vå-goo', or **da Veggia,** då vêd'jå, an able Italian sculptor, lived about 1500 or 1550. He adorned the cathedral of Milan.

Antonio de Lebrixa. See NEBRISSENSIS.

Antonio di Locate, ân-to'ne-o de lo-kå'tå, an Italian sculptor, who was employed on the façade of the Certosa di Pavía about 1473.

Antonio Margarita, ân-to'ne-o maR-gå-ree'tå, or **Margalitha,** maR-gå-lee'tå, was converted from Judaism to Christianity in 1522. He wrote an exposition of the Jewish religion, (1530,) which was praised by Luther.

Antonio Morosini, ân-to'ne-o mo-ro-see'nee, an Italian poet, lived at Florence about 1650–1700.

Antonisze, ân-to-nis'seh, (KORNELIS,) a skilful Dutch painter of cities, born at Amsterdam about 1500. He was elected a member of the council of Amsterdam in 1547. His name is sometimes written TEUNISSEN.

An-to'nï-us, [Fr. ANTOINE, ôN'twän',] (CAIUS,) a younger brother of Mark Antony the Triumvir, was sent in 49 B.C., as Cæsar's lieutenant, to Illyricum, and became prætor of the city, as a colleague of Brutus, in 44 B.C. In the same year he led a small army into Macedonia, which he found occupied by a hostile force under Brutus, to whom he surrendered in the spring of 43 B.C. He was put to death in retaliation for the death of Cicero and D. Brutus.

Antonius, (CAI'US HYB'RIDA,) an uncle of the preceding, and a son of M. Antonius the Orator, became prætor in 66, and the colleague of Cicero in the consulship in 63 B.C. In the canvas for this office, Catiline and Antonius worked together to defeat Cicero. Antonius was a man of profligate habits, and did not cordially co-operate with Cicero in the contest with Catiline. He was banished for extortion or malversation in 59 B.C. Died about 44 B.C.

Antonius, (FELIX.) See FELIX ANTONIUS.

Antonius, (FRANCISCUS.) See ANTHONIE.

Antonius, (IULUS,) a son of Mark Antony and Fulvia, married Marcella, a niece of Augustus. By the favour of Augustus, he was chosen prætor in 13 B.C., and consul in the year 10. He was condemned to death in 2 B.C. for an intrigue with Julia, daughter of the emperor. Horace addressed the second ode of his fourth book to I. Antonius, who was himself the author of a poem called "Diomedeis."

Antonius, (LUCIUS,) a younger brother of Antony the Triumvir, was elected tribune of the people for 44 B.C., and, after the death of Cæsar, promoted the designs of his brother Marcus. In 41 he was consul with P. Servilius Isauricus, and joined Fulvia in her efforts to alienate Mark Antony from Octavius. He raised an army against the latter, but was forced to surrender at Perugia, (41 B.C.,) and was sent to Spain to take command in that country.

Antonius, (MARCUS,) commonly called THE ORATOR, one of the most eloquent of Roman orators and lawyers, was born in 142 B.C. He was grandfather of Mark Antony the Triumvir. He obtained the government of Cilicia, with the title of proconsul, in 103, and became consul in 99. He favoured the aristocratic party, and was an adherent of Sulla in the civil war against Marius, by whose order he was assassinated in 87 B.C. His great power as an orator is commemorated by Cicero in his treatise "De Oratore," and in his "Brutus." He left no written orations. In the judgment of Cicero, Marcus Antonius and L. Crassus were the first Roman orators who equalled the great orators of Greece.

See PLUTARCH, "Marius;" DRUMANN, "Geschichte Roms," vol. i.

Antonius, (MARCUS,) surnamed the TRIUMVIR, called in English MARK ANTONY, [Fr. MARC-ANTOINE, mårk'-ôN'twän',] a famous Roman general and politician, a son of M. Antonius Creticus, was born about 83 B.C. His mother was Julia, a daughter of L. Julius Cæsar, who was consul in 90 B.C. He distinguished himself in his youth by his talents, extravagance, and audacious defiance of the laws. He commanded the cavalry under Gabinius in Syria and Egypt in 57–56 B.C., and was elected quæstor in 53 or 52. In the latter year he served in Gaul as lieutenant of Cæsar, by whose influence he obtained the offices of augur and tribune in 50 B.C. Antony used his power as tribune to promote the interest of Cæsar in his contest with the senate. In January, 49, he fled from the city to the camp of Cæsar, and in the civil war which ensued he became the lieutenant of that chief, who, when he passed from Italy to Spain, intrusted to Antony the chief command in the former country. He proved himself a brave and able general, and commanded the left wing at the battle of Pharsalia, 48 B.C. When Cæsar became dictator, 47 B.C., Antony was appointed his master of the horse. He married Fulvia, the widow of P. Clodius, in the year 46, and was the colleague of Cæsar in the consulship in 44. Many of the conspirators who killed the dictator wished to involve Antony in the same fate; but this design was overruled by Brutus.

Having obtained possession of the papers of Cæsar, he aspired to supreme power, but opened insidious negotiations with Brutus and Cassius, consented to an amnesty, and procured from the senate a decree to ratify the acts of the late dictator. By his artful and eloquent funeral oration over the body of Cæsar, he aroused the fury of the populace against the conspirators, who were, in consequence, driven out of Rome. He found a powerful rival in young Octavius, (the adopted son and heir of Cæsar,) whom he at first treated with contempt. Antony's popularity was also damaged by the Philippics of Cicero. The consuls Hirtius and Pansa raised an army against Antony, who was defeated at Mu'tina (now Módena) in 43 B.C. Before the end of this year, Octavius deserted the cause of the senate, and united with Antony and Lepidus to form a triumvirate. It was on the demand of Antony that Cicero was included in the fatal proscription-list of the triumvirs. The conduct of the war against Brutus and Cassius devolved chiefly on Antony, to whose skill the victory at Philippi, 42 B.C., must be ascribed.

In the division of the provinces, Asia and the East in general were allotted to Antony, who there indulged without restraint his love of luxury and dissolute vices. He was captivated by the charms of Cleopatra, Queen of Egypt, and became so infatuated as almost wholly to neglect his affairs. The intrigues of Fulvia caused a rupture between Antony and Octavius in 41, but after her death in 40 B.C. they were reconciled, and the former married Octavia, the sister of Octavius. Antony's army, under Ventidius, defeated the Parthians in the year 38. About the end of that year the triumvirate was renewed for a second period of five years. Antony soon renewed his connection with Cleopatra, and divorced Octavia. The rival triumvirs began to prepare for war in 32 B.C., or earlier, and fought in 31 a decisive naval battle at Actium, where Antony was defeated. (See AUGUSTUS.) He retreated to Alexandria, and was deserted by his fleet. Finding his case desperate, he killed himself, in 30 B.C. He had by Fulvia two sons, Iulus and Antyllus, who survived him. Antony is a conspicuous character in two of Shakspeare's dramas,—"Julius Cæsar" and "Antony and Cleopatra."

See "Antony," in PLUTARCH's "Lives;" DION CASSIUS, "History of Rome;" DRUMANN, "Geschichte Roms;" APPIAN, "Bellum Civile."

Anto'nius surnamed CRET'ICUS, (MARCUS,) a son of M. Antonius the Orator. He became prætor in 75 B.C., and in the next year received command of the whole Roman fleet, with instructions to clear the Mediterranean Sea of pirates. He disgraced himself by plundering Sicily. Having afterwards attacked Crete, he was totally defeated. He died or was killed in Crete about 70 B.C.

Anto'nius, (MARCUS Gnipho—nī'fo,) a learned rhetorician and grammarian, born in Gaul about 114 B.C. He opened a school in Rome, and numbered among his pupils Cicero and Cæsar. His writings have not come down to us. Died about 64 B.C.

Antonius, (NICOLAUS.) See ANTONIO, (NICOLAS.)

Antonius, SAINT. See ANTHONY.

Antonius Castor. See CASTOR.

Antonius (MARCUS) **de Dominis.** See DOMINIS.

Antonius Musa. See MUSA.

Anto'nius Pol'e-mo, a sophist and orator of high reputation, was born at Laodice'a, in the reign of Hadrian. He lived mostly at Smyrna, where he taught rhetoric with success. "I heard Polemo declaim thrice," says Herodes Atticus; "the first time as a critic; the next as a lover; the last time with unmingled wonder at his powers." He died in the reign of Antoninus Pius, 138-161 A.D.

Anto'nius Pri'mus, (MARCUS,) an able Roman general, born at Tolosa (Toulouse) about 20 A.D. He contributed to the elevation of Vespasian to the throne by victories over the partisans of Vitellius, at Bedriacum, and near Rome, in 69 A.D.

Antonius Saturninus. See SATURNINUS.

Antony, (MARK.) See ANTONIUS, (MARCUS.)

An'to-nÿ OF BOURBON, (boor'bọn,) [Fr. ANTOINE DE BOURBON, ŏN'twăn' dẹh boor'bǒN',] Duke of Vendôme, and King of Navarre, born in Picardy in 1518, was the first prince of the blood, (next to the king's sons.) He was a brother of the Prince of Condé. He married in 1548 Jeanne d'Albret, heiress of the King of Navarre. At the accession of Charles IX. in 1560 he was appointed lieutenant-general of the kingdom, and entered into a coalition or triumvirate with his enemy the Duke de Guise, and Constable de Montmorency. About this time he abandoned the Reformed communion and turned Roman Catholic. In the civil war which began in 1562 he commanded the royal army until he was mortally wounded at the siege of Rouen. He died in 1562, and left a son, who became Henry IV. of France.

See DAVILA, "The Civil Wars in France;" DE THOU, "Historia sui Temporis;" BRANTÔME, "Vies des Hommes illustres," etc.; SISMONDI, "Histoire des Français."

Antraigues. See ENTRAIGUES.

An-tÿl'lus, the Greek name of Marcus, a son of Mark Antony the Triumvir and Fulvia. He was born about 45 B.C., was invested with the toga virilis at Alexandria in 30 B.C., and about the end of that year was taken prisoner by Octavius and put to death.

Antyllus [Gr. Ἀντυλλος] or **An-til'lus,** sometimes incorrectly written **Antiles,** an eminent physician and surgeon of antiquity, is supposed to have lived in the third or fourth century after Christ. He wrote in Greek several works, which are quoted by Oribasius, but are not extant.

A-nu'bis, [Gr. Ἀνουβις,] an Egyptian deity or idol, represented as the offspring of Osiris, and worshipped in the form of a dog.

Anund, ä'nŭnd, (JAKOB,) King of Sweden, reigned from 1024 to 1035.

Anvari. See ANWAREE.

Anville, d', (JEAN BAPTISTE Bourguignon —booR'gĕn'yôN',) one of the greatest geographers that ever lived, was born in Paris in 1697. He early devoted himself to studies connected with his favourite science, which he may be said to have almost created. In 1773 he was elected to the chair of geography in the Academy of Sciences, and appointed first geographer to the king. Our limits will not permit us to name more than a small portion of the works of D'Anville. Suffice it to say that his maps embrace almost every country in the world in ancient as well as modern times. He is admitted to be the first who raised geography to the dignity of an exact science. "He was endowed," says Rossel, "with a surprising fineness of tact, which enabled him nearly always to distinguish truth from error." The accuracy of his maps of Egypt was confirmed by the survey made by the French about 1799. Among his works are "Orbis Véteribus notus;" "Orbis Romanus;" and a "Compendium of Ancient Geography," ("Géographie Ancienne abrégée," 3 vols., 1768.) He died in 1782.

See CONDORCET, "Éloge de M. D'Anville," 1782; "Encyclopædia Britannica;" "Nouvelle Biographie Générale."

Anwaree or **Anwarî,** än'wä-ree', written also **Anvari,** one of the most celebrated of the Persian lyric poets, was born in Khorassân in the early part of the twelfth century. He began his career in great poverty, but was soon invited to the court of the sultan Sanjar, and at length raised to the highest honours in the state. About 1148 his sovereign was defeated and taken prisoner by a tribe of Toorkomans, and Anwaree's native country presented a scene of universal outrage and desolation. On this occasion he implored the aid of the Prince of Samarcand, in one of the most beautiful and touching poems in the Persian language, entitled the "Tears of Khorassân." Anwaree lived to see his country delivered from its oppressors, and died about 1200.

See D'HERBELOT, "Bibliothèque Orientale;" FERISHTA, "History."

An'ÿ-te OF TEGEA, [Ἀνύτη Τεγεάτης,] a Greek poetess of high reputation, is supposed to have lived about 300 B.C. Some fragments of her works are extant.

An'ÿ-tus, [Ἀνυτος,] an Athenian demagogue, notorious as an accuser of Socrates, after whose death he was banished from Athens, and is said to have been stoned to death at Heracle'a in Pontus.

Aoust, d', doo, (EUSTACHE,) a French general, born at Douai in 1763, was executed in Paris in July, 1794.

Apáczai or **Apátzai,** ŏp'ät-sī, (JOANNES,) a distinguished Hungarian scholar, native of Apatza, in Transylvania. He was the author of the first Hungarian Encyclopædia, ("Magyar Entziklopedia.") Died in 1659.

Apafi, ŏp'pŏf-ee, (MIHÁLY—me'hȧl',] the name of two Transylvanian princes, father and son, the first of whom died in 1690, the second in 1713, leaving no issue.

Ap'ạ-mạ [Gr. Ἀπάμα] or **Ap'a-me,** [Ἀπάμη,] a Persian or Bactrian lady, who was married about 325 B.C. to Seleucus Nicator. She was the mother of Antiochus Soter.

Aparicio, ä-pä-ree'the-o, (JOSÉ,) a Spanish painter, born in 1780, was a pupil of the celebrated French painter David. Among his works is a picture of "The Plague in Spain." He was living in 1822.

Apchon, d', däp'shòn', (CLAUDE MARC ANTOINE,) a French prelate, noted for his beneficence, was born at Montbrison about 1723. Died in 1783.

Apel, ä'pel, (JOHANN,) [Lat. JOHAN'NES APEL'LUS,] a German professor of law, and a devoted follower of Luther, born at Nuremberg in 1486 ; died about 1536.

Apel, (JOHANN AUGUST,) a German writer, who was once popular, was born at Leipsic in 1771. He composed verses with facility, and wrote for several journals and periodicals. Among his works are songs, elegies, tragedies, and a mediocre treatise on classical prosody called "Metrik," (1816.) Died in 1816.

Apelchasem, (a Turkish general.) See ABOO-L-KASIM.

A-pel'las, ['Ἀπελλᾶς,] a Greek statuary, lived about the fourth century B.C. According to Pliny, he made statues of bronze.

Apellas or **A-pol'las,** ['Ἀπολλᾶς,] a Greek geographer, born at Cyrene, is supposed to have lived about 235 A.D.

A-pel'lēs, [Gr. 'Ἀπελλῆς; Fr. APELLE, ä'pêl',] the most celebrated painter of antiquity, was born in the island of Cos, according to Pliny and Ovid ; but others state that he was a native of Colophon or Ephesus. He attained the height of his celebrity about 330 B.C. He studied first under Ephorus, and afterwards under Pamphilus at Sicyon. His success was partly due to close and long-continued application. *Nulla dies sine linea* is a saying which originated in one of his maxims. He obtained the special favour of Alexander the Great, of whom he painted many portraits. It is said that he had the exclusive privilege of painting this king. Apelles surpassed other painters in elegance and grace, the *charis* (χάρις) of the Greeks, in respect to which Correggio is perhaps pre-eminent among the moderns. Pliny maintained that Apelles contributed more towards perfecting the art than all other painters, and painting was called the "Apellean art" ("ars Apellea") by the Roman poets Statius and Martial. Among his masterpieces was a portrait in profile of King Antigonus on horseback. His most celebrated work was the "Venus Anadyomene, or Venus rising from the sea and wringing her hair with her fingers," which was painted for the people of Cos, and which, after the lapse of three hundred years, was taken by Augustus Cæsar as the equivalent of one hundred talents (about 100,000 dollars) in payment of tribute. It is said that Apelles was enamoured of Campaspe, (the model from which this picture was painted,) a favourite of Alexander, who gave her to the artist. Apelles appears to have survived Alexander, who died in 323 B.C. He is praised for his generous conduct to the painter Protogenes of Rhodes, whose works were not appreciated until Apelles purchased some of them at a high price and circulated a report that he would sell them as his own. Ovid alludes to the picture of Venus, above noticed, in these elegant lines :

    " Sic madidos siccat digitis Venus uda capillos
    Et modo maternis tecta videtur aquis."[*]

Many interesting anecdotes are recorded of this artist. He is supposed by some writers to have followed Alexander the Great in his expedition to Asia.

See PLINY, "Natural History ;" SUIDAS, "Apelles ;" PLUTARCH, "Aratus," and "Alexander ;" CARLO DATI, " Vite de' Pittori antichi," 1667.

Apelles, [Gr. 'Ἀπελλῆς,] a heretic, who lived about 150 A.D., was at first a disciple of Marcion, from whom he afterwards differed. He is said to have rejected the authority of the Old Testament, and to have taught strange doctrines respecting the Divine nature. He

founded a sect called Apellists, and wrote a work entitled the "Gospel of Apelles."

See EUSEBIUS, " Historia Ecclesiastica ;" LARDNER, " History of Heretics."

Apelles OF EPHESUS, a Greek painter, mentioned by Lucian in his treatise on Calumny. He worked in Egypt, and was patronized by Ptolemy Philopator, about 220 B.C. He was falsely accused by a rival painter, Antiphilus, of a conspiracy against the king ; but his innocence was proved, and the accuser was condemned to be the slave of Apelles.

A-pel'lĭ-con OF TEOS, [Gr. 'Ἀπελλικῶν,] a rich Peripatetic philosopher, who was distinguished by his fondness for collecting old and rare manuscripts. He became a citizen of Athens, and commander of a force in the island of Delos, where he was defeated by the Romans. It is said that the world is indebted to him for the preservation of the works of Aristotle, and that he purchased the library collected by that philosopher, including his autograph manuscripts. Died about 86 B.C

A'per, (MARCUS,) a distinguished Roman orator of the time of Vespasian. He was a Gaul by birth. None of his works are extant.

Apezteguia, ä-pěth-tä-ḡee'ä, (Don JUAN FELIPE,) a Spanish sculptor, worked at Madrid. Died in 1785.

A-phā'reūs, (or af'a-rūs,) ['Ἀφαρεύς,] an Athenian poet and orator, who flourished about 350 B.C., was an adopted son of Isocrates the orator. He composed many tragedies, some of which were successful. None of his works are extant.

Aph-ro-dis'ĭ-us OF TRALLES, a sculptor, mentioned by Pliny among the artists who adorned the palace of the Cæsars. He lived in the first century of our era.

Aph-ro-dī'te, ['Ἀφροδίτη,] the Grecian name of the goddess VENUS, which see.

Aph-tho'nĭ-us ['Ἀφθόνιος] of Antioch, a noted Greek rhetorician, supposed to have lived in the fourth century of our era. He wrote a popular book of rhetorical exercises, called "Progymnasmata," which was often printed and used in schools in the sixteenth and seventeenth centuries.

Apian, ä'pe-än, [Lat. APIA'NUS,] or **Appian,** äp'-pe-än, (PETER,) a noted German astronomer and mathematician, born in Misnia in 1495. His real name was BIENEWITZ, (bee'neh-ẅits.) He taught mathematics at Ingolstadt, and first suggested the method of ascertaining the longitude by the distance of the moon from a fixed star. His work on Cosmography (1524) had a wide reputation. He also published a treatise on astronomy, entitled "Astronomicon Cæsareum," (1540.) He was patronized and ennobled by Charles V. Died in 1552.

Apian or **Appian,** (PHILIP,) a son of Peter Apian, noticed above, born in 1531, succeeded him in the chair of mathematics. He wrote "On the Utility of the Cylinder," (" De Cylindri Utilitate,") and several other small works. Died at Tübingen in 1589.

See LIPENIUS, " Bibliotheca realis Philosophica ;" CELLIUS, " Oratio de Vita et Morte P. Apiani," 1591.

Apicius, a-pish'e-us, (MARCUS GABIUS,) a celebrated epicure, lived at Rome in the time of Augustus and Tiberius. It is related by Seneca that after spending on rare culinary dainties one hundred million sesterces, (about $3,600,000,) Apicius was obliged to look into his accounts. He discovered that he had only ten million sesterces ($360,000) remaining ; upon which, unwilling to starve on such a pittance, he poisoned himself ! His name has become proverbial for gluttony, both in ancient and modern times.

Apin, ä-peen', (JOHANN LUDWIG,) a German physician, born at Hohenlohe in 1668 ; died in 1703. He was author of several medical works.

Apin or **Apinus,** ä-pee'nŭs, (SIGISMUND JAKOB,) a philologist, a son of the preceding, was born near Nuremberg in 1693. He became rector of a school at Brunswick. Among his works is a dissertation "On Pure Intellect," (" De Intellectu puro.") Died in 1732.

A'pĭ-on [Gr. 'Ἀπίων] surnamed PLISTONI'ÇES, a learned Greek grammarian and historian, was born in Oasis, Egypt, and lived in the reigns of Tiberius, Caligula, and Claudius, (A.D. 15–54.) He became master of

---

[*] The following is a nearly literal translation : " So Venus wrings her dripping hair with her fingers, and appears covered (or clothed) with the maternal waters," (*i.e.* the waters from which she sprang.)

a school in Rome about the year 45. He wrote a "History of Egypt," a lexicon to Homer, and other works, among which were annotations on the poems of Homer, and a book against the Jews, in reply to which Josephus wrote his "Antiquities of the Jews." He was called "Cymbalum Mundi" (" Cymbal of the World") by Tiberius, probably on account of his vanity and egotism. His works are lost, except small fragments.

See SCHOELL, "Histoire de la Littérature Grecque."

A'pis, [Gr. Ἆπις,] a mythical king of Argos, and a son of Phoroneus. He is said to have called Peloponnesus APIA, and to have reigned also in Egypt.

Apis, the Bull of Memphis, the chief idol or object of worship among the ancient Egyptians. According to some accounts, he was sacred to Osiris, in whom the sun was worshipped. The death of this animal caused great mourning among the Egyptians.

See GUIGNIAUT, "Religions de l'Antiquité," vol. i.

Ap'john, (JAMES,) F.R.S., an Irish chemist, born at Sunville, county of Limerick, in 1796. He became professor of chemistry in the University of Dublin in 1850. He wrote a number of treatises on chemistry.

A-po-cau'cus, [Gr. Ἀπόκαυκος; Fr. APOCAUQUE, ä'po'kōk',] a powerful and corrupt favourite of the emperor Androni'cus, was assassinated in 1345.

Apolinarius. See APOLLINARIUS.

Apollinaire. See APOLLINARIUS.

A-pol-lĭ-nā'ris, A-pol-ĭ-nā'rĭ-us, or **A-pol-lĭ-nā'-rĭ-us,** THE ELDER, a grammarian, born at Alexandria, lived about 330 A.D. He taught at Berytus and Laodice'a, and became a presbyter in the Christian Church. He wrote a "Grammar for Christians," and other works.

Apollinaris or **Apollinarius** THE YOUNGER, a son of the preceding, was Bishop of Laodicea, and author of the Apollinarian heresy. He was distinguished as an orator and philosopher, and was a man of great abilities and learning. He obtained the bishopric as early as 362 A.D., and died in the reign of Theodosius the Great, between 380 and 392 A.D. He was author of many volumes of commentaries on the Bible, of "Thirty Books against Porphyry," and of numerous other works, which are nearly all lost. About 375 A.D. he was charged with heresy in relation to the Incarnation. It appears that he taught that Christ had not a rational or human soul, but that it was replaced by the *logos,* or Divine Spirit.

See SOZOMEN, "Historia Ecclesiastica;" WERNSDORFF, "Dissertatio de Apollinare Laodiceno," 1694; TILLEMONT, "Mémoires;" "Vitæ Apollinaris Historia," Paris, 1571.

Apollinaris, (SULPITIUS CAIUS,) a distinguished grammarian, said to have been a native of Carthage, taught at Rome in the second century.

Apollina'ris Sĭ-do'nĭ-us, [Fr. APOLLINAIRE SIDOINE, ä'po'le'nȧR' se'dwȧn',] (CAIUS SOL'LIUS,) SAINT, a bishop and Latin poet, born at Lugdunum (Lyons) in 430 A.D. He married a daughter of Avitus who became Emperor of Rome in 455 and was deposed the next year. He was appointed by Anthemius chief of the senate, prefect of the city, and afterwards patrician. In 471 A.D. he was elected Bishop of Clermont, (Augustonemetum.) He died about 488, leaving various works, some of which are lost. His "Carmina" ("Poems," or "Songs") and "Epistolæ" are extant, and are prized for the historical information they afford.

See GERMAIN, "Essai sur Apollinaris Sidonius," 1840; FAURIEL, "Histoire de la Gaule méridionale."

Apollinarius. See APOLLINARIS.

A-pol-lĭ-nā'rĭ-us or **A-pol-ĭ-nā'rĭ-us,** [Gr. Ἀπολλινάριος; Fr. APOLLINAIRE, ä'po'le'nȧR',] (CLAUDIUS,) SAINT, a bishop of Hierapolis, in Phrygia, lived in the reign of Marcus Antoninus. He wrote, besides other works, a defence of Christianity, which Saint Jerome calls an excellent book. His works are not extant.

A-pol'lo, [Gr. Ἀπόλλων; Fr. APOLLON, ä'po'lôN'; It. APOLLONE, ä-pol-lo'nȧ,] the god of archery, music and poetry, medicine, and prophecy, was the son of Jupiter and Latona. He was born on the island of Delos, whence he is often called Delius, while Diana, his sister, is named Delia. He is also styled Pythius, or the "Pythian," because his first great exploit was to slay with his arrows the serpent Python. Apollo was likewise regarded by the later poets of antiquity as the god of

the sun. Homer represents Apollo and the sun-god as entirely distinct personages. Under the name of Pæan, Apollo was invoked in the character both of a healer or protector and a destroyer—for his arrows were supposed to produce the pestilence. Some of the poets represented Pæan as the healing god, but distinct from Apollo; but this was not the general opinion. Although Apollo was regarded as the author of the healing art, the title of the "god of medicine" is usually given to his son Æsculapius. The "god of the unerring bow" ("Childe Harold," canto iv.) was often called Phœbus, or Phœbus Apollo, from the Greek Φοῖβος, "bright," or "shining." Apollo is usually represented as a beautiful young man, crowned with laurel, and having in his hand a harp or bow and arrows.

See BUTTMANN, "Mythologus;" G. HERMANN, "Dissertatio de Apolline et Diana;" HARTUNG, "Die Religion der Römer;" GUIGNIAUT, "Religions de l'Antiquité," translated from the German of CREUZER, vol. ii.; KEIGHTLEY, "Mythology."

Apollodore. See APOLLODORUS.

Apollodoro, ä-pol-lo-do'ro, (FRANCESCO,) sometimes called IL PORCIA, èl poR'chä, an Italian portrait-painter, born in Friuli, lived in the first half of the seventeenth century.

A-pol-lo-do'rus, [Gr. Ἀπολλόδωρος; Fr. APOLLODORE, ä'po'lo'doR',] a celebrated Greek artist, the founder of a new school of painting, was born at Athens about 440 B.C., and was surnamed the "Shadower." He was a rival of Zeuxis, and is said to have been the first who represented the effects of light and shade with success. His works are highly praised by Pliny, who says he was the first who painted men and things as they really appeared, (*hic primus species exprimere instituit.*) Among his works was a picture of "Ajax Wrecked."

See PLINY, "Natural History."

Apollodorus, a Greek sculptor, born probably about 350 B.C. He bestowed great labour on his works, and often destroyed them because they did not satisfy him.

Apollodorus, a Greek comic poet of high repute, a native of Carystus in Eubœa, lived probably in the last half of the fourth century B.C.

Apollodorus, an Epicurean philosopher, who became head of the school of Epicurus. He was succeeded by his pupil, Zeno of Sidon, about 84 B.C. According to Diogenes Laertius, he wrote four hundred books, (βιβλία,) one of which was a Life of Epicurus.

Apollodorus, the name of several ancient physicians, one of whom wrote a treatise "On Venomous Animals."

Apollodorus, a jurist, employed by Theodosius the Younger in the compilation of a system of laws known as the Theodosian Code. He lived about 425 A.D.

Apollodorus of Athens, a celebrated grammarian and historian, flourished about 150 B.C., and was a pupil of Aristarchus. He wrote many valuable works, which are all lost except a "Bibliotheca," a manual of Greek mythology, which is incomplete and is regarded by some critics as an abridgment of his original work. It is, however, highly prized as the best work extant on that subject. Some fragments remain of his versified chronicle of the History of Greece.

See FABRICIUS, "Bibliotheca Græca;" SCHOELL, "Histoire de la Littérature Grecque."

Apollodorus of Damascus, an eminent architect, born at Damascus in the first century. He was employed at Rome by Trajan, for whom he erected many grand edifices, among which were the Forum and Column of Trajan, (which still exists,) a theatre, an odeum, and the Basilica Ulpia. The Forum of Trajan was considered the most splendid in Rome. His greatest work was a magnificent bridge over the Danube, near the confluence of that river with the Aluta, (Alt,) built in 105 A.D. He was put to death by Hadrian, whose motive is supposed to have been envy or anger because Apollodorus had ridiculed a temple built after the design of Hadrian.

See DION CASSIUS, "History;" ÆLIUS SPARTIANUS, "Hadrian."

Apollodorus of Gela, a Greek comic poet, who lived probably about 320 B.C. His works are not extant.

Apollodorus of Pergamus, a Greek rhetorician, born about 100 B.C. He taught rhetoric at Rome, and was one of the teachers of Octavius, (afterwards the emperor Augustus.) He was the founder of a new school of rhetoric; but he wrote very little. Died about 22 B.C.

ā, ē, ī, ō, ū, ȳ, *long;* ă, ĕ, ĭ, ŏ, ŭ, ў, *short;* a, e, i, o, *obscure;* fär, fȧll, fȧt; mêt; nŏt; gŏŏd; mōōn;

Apollodorus of Phalerum, (or Phaleron,) in Attica, a disciple and friend of Socrates. He was a man of eccentric character, and appears to have been deficient in firmness and in intellectual power.

Apollodorus surnamed EPH'ILUS, a Stoic, who wrote on Ethics and Physics, before the Christian era.

Apollon. See APOLLO.

A-pol-lon'ĭ-dēs or **A-pol-lon'Ĭ-das,** [Ἀπολλωνίδης,] a Greek poet of unknown date, supposed to have been born at Smyrna. He left a number of admired epigrams, which are extant in the Greek Anthology.

Apollonides, a Greek officer, appointed governor of Argos by Cassander about 315 B.C.

Apollonides of Cos, a Greek physician, who practised at the court of Artaxerxes Longimanus of Persia, and is said to have seduced Amytis, a sister of that king, for which offence he was put to death.

Apollonides of Nicæa, a Greek grammarian, of whom little is known. He is supposed to have lived in the reign of Tiberius. His works are lost.

Apollonio, ä-pol-lo'ne-o, (JACOPO,) an Italian painter, born at Bassano about 1585, was a grandson of Jacopo da Ponte. Among his master-pieces are a Saint Sebastian, a Saint Francis, and a Magdalen, in the churches of Bassano. Died in 1654.

See LANZI, "History of Painting in Italy."

A-pol-lo'nis or **A-pol-lo'nĭ-a,** the wife of Attalus I., King of Pergamus. She was the mother of four sons, who were noted for filial piety, and who erected a temple to her memory.

A-pol-lo'nĭ-us, [Gr. Ἀπολλώνιος,] an eminent sculptor of Rhodes, lived probably about 200 B.C. He and his brother Tauriscus were the sculptors of a marble group of Zethus and Amphi'on tying Dirce to the horns of a bull, which Pliny says was brought to Rome by Asinius Pollio. Many critics have identified this work with the group called "Toro Farnese" which is at Naples.

Apollonius, a Greek physician, a pupil of Herophilus, often quoted by Galen, lived about 180 B.C.

Apollonius, an excellent Athenian sculptor, a son of Nestor, is supposed to have lived before the Christian era. He is known only as the sculptor of a marble statue of Hercules, of which a fragment, called the Torso of the Belvedere, is preserved at Rome. It is one of the most admirable extant specimens of ancient art. The head, arms, and legs have been broken off.

Apollonius, a sophist and grammarian of Alexandria, lived in the time of Augustus. He left a Homeric Lexicon to the Iliad and Odyssey, which is still extant and is highly prized. It was published by Villoison in 1773.

Apollonius OF ALABANDA. See APOLLONIUS MOLON.

Apollonius of Athens, a rhetorician, who taught at Athens about 200 A.D., and held several high offices. He gained the victory in a rhetorical contest over Heracli'des in the presence of the Roman emperor.

Apollonius of Chalcis, a Stoic philosopher, who had so high a reputation that he was invited to Rome by Antoninus Pius to direct the education of Marcus Aurelius, by whom his merit as a teacher is commended.

Apollonius of Myndus, an astronomer, who lived in the time of Alexander the Great. His works are all lost.

Apollonius of Pergamus, a Greek physician, who lived in the first century B.C.

Apollo'nius CITIEN'SIS, a physician, born at Citium, in Cyprus, lived in the first century B.C. He wrote a curious Greek treatise on Articulations, (Περὶ ἄρθρων,) which is called the most ancient commentary on Hippocrates that has come down to us.

Apollo'nius surnamed DYS'COLUS, (the "morose,") a celebrated Greek grammarian of Alexandria, lived in the reigns of Hadrian and Antoninus, (117–161 A.D.) He was the father of Ælius Herodian. He wrote, besides many works which are lost, an able treatise :"On the Syntax of the Parts of Speech," (Περὶ συντάξεως τοῦ λόγου ἱερῶν,) which is extant. Priscian calls him the greatest of grammarians.

See SUIDAS, "Apollonius;" FABRICIUS, "Bibliotheca Græca."

Apollonius THE EMPIRIC, a Greek physician, who lived probably about 200 B.C.

Apollonius, (LÆVI'NUS,) a geographer and historian of the sixteenth century, was born near Bruges. He

died in one of the Canary Islands, while on a voyage to Peru. He was author of two works of some merit,—an "Account of the Discovery of Peru," (1567,) and "On the Expedition of the French to Florida," ("De Navigatione Gallorum in Terram Floridam," 1568.)

Apollo'nius MO'LON, an eminent Greek rhetorician, born at Alabanda, in Caria. He was sent by the people of Rhodes as an envoy to Rome in 81 B.C. He taught at Rhodes both before and after this date. Cicero and Julius Cæsar were among his pupils about 78 B.C. His works are not extant.

Apollo'nius surnamed PERGÆ'US, [Fr. APOLLONIUS LE PERGÉEN, ă'po'lo'ne'üs' lĕh pĕr'zhä'ŏN',] one of the most profound and original of all the ancient geometers, was born at Perga, in Pamphylia, about the middle of the third century B.C. He lived at Alexandria in the reign of Ptolemy Philopator, (B.C. 222–205.) Little or nothing is known of his life in addition to the facts above stated. It is supposed that he survived Archimedes. His principal work is a "Treatise on Conic Sections," (in Greek,) seven books of which have been preserved. The eighth book is lost. He also wrote another mathematical treatise, of which an Arabic version is extant, and other works, which are lost. Apollonius was also an astronomer, and is said to have been the first who discovered the method of representing by epicycles the phenomena of the stations and retrogradations of the planets.

See MONTUCLA, "Histoire des Mathématiques;" SCHOELL, "Histoire de la Littérature Grecque;" FABRICIUS, "Bibliotheca Græca;" "Encyclopædia Britannica."

Apollo'nius RHO'DIUS, [Gr. Ἀπολλώνιος ὁ Ῥόδιος,] a celebrated Greek epic poet and rhetorician, born at Alexandria (or, as some say, at Naucratis) about 235 B.C. He was a son of Silleus or Illeus, and a pupil of the poet Callimachus, with whom he quarrelled. He removed in his youth to Rhodes, where he taught rhetoric for many years with great success and obtained the honour of citizenship. Having returned to Alexandria, he was appointed keeper of the celebrated library of that place, as successor to Eratosthenes, about 194 B.C. Only one of his works is extant, namely, the "Argonautica," an epic poem in four books on the expedition of the Argonauts, which in general displays more erudition than poetic inspiration. "It is," says Quintilian, "a respectable work, but generally mediocre." Some modern critics, however, think they find in this poem beauties of detail of the first order.

See WEICHERT, "Ueber das Leben und Gedicht des Apollonius," 1821; SCHOELL, "Histoire de la Littérature Grecque," 1813; E. GERHARD, "Lectiones Apollonianæ."

Apollo'nius TYANÆ'US, (tī-a-nee'us,) (or "Apollonius of Tyana,") [Gr. Ἀπολλώνιος Τυαναῖος; Fr. APOLLONIUS DE TYANE, ă'po'lo'ne'üs' dĕh te'ăn',] a Pythagorean philosopher who lived about the middle of the first century, was born at Tyana, in Cappadocia. He is the subject of marvellous stories, and is considered by some writers to have been an impostor, by others a magician of wondrous skill. It appears that he was venerated for his wisdom by his contemporaries, who believed that he had the gift of prophecy and the power of working miracles. His life has been written by Flavius Philostratus, who says he went to India, conversed with the Brahmins, and after his return assumed the character of a moral reformer in Greece and Rome. The only work of Apollonius that has come down to us is his "Apology" in reply to Euphrates. His miracles have been compared to those of Christ by some ancient and modern infidels.

See BRUCKER, "History of Philosophy;" RITTER, "History of Philosophy;" PHILOSTRATUS, "Life of Apollonius," in English, 1809, translated by E. BERWICK; JOHN HENRY NEWMAN, "Life of Apollonius Tyanæus," 8vo, 1853; F. C. BAUR, "Apollonius von Tyana und Christus," 1832; KLOSE, "Dissertationes III. de Apollonio Thyanensi," 1724.

A-pol-lo'nĭ-us, (WILLEM,) a Dutch Reformed theologian, born at Veere ; died in 1657.

Apollonius Collatius. See COLLATIUS.

Apollonius de Tyane. See APOLLONIUS TYANÆUS.

A-pol-loph'a-nēs, [Gr. Ἀπολλοφάνης,] an ancient physician, born at Seleucia, lived 200 or 250 B.C. He was physician to Antiochus the Great, (or, according to

є as *k;* ç as *s;* g̃ *hard;* g̃ as *j;* G, H, K, *guttural;* N, *nasal;* R, *trilled;* s̃ as *z;* th as in *this.* (☞See Explanations, p. 23.)

10

some accounts, Antiochus Soter.) with whom he is said to have had much influence.

A-pol'los, a Jew who became an able and eloquent preacher of Christianity. (See Acts xviii. 24; I. Corinthians i. 12; iii. 4; iv. 6.)

Aponus, (PETRUS.) See ABANO, (PIETRO DI.)

Apostoli, ä-pos'to-lee, (FRANCESCO,) an Italian writer, born at Venice about 1750. He was once minister from San Marino to Napoleon I. He published, at Milan, a "View or Picture of the Eighteenth Century," ("Rappresentazione del Secolo XVIII.," 3 vols.,) "History of the Gauls, Franks, and French," ("Storia dei Galli, Franchi e Francesi," 1 vol.,) and other works. Died poor at Venice in 1816.

Apostoli, (GIOVANNI FRANCESCO,) a Latin poet, born in Montferrat, lived in the latter half of the sixteenth century. He published in 1580 a volume of satirical Latin poems, entitled "Leisure Hours," ("Succisivæ Horæ.")

Apostoli, degli, dàl'yee ä-pos'to-lee, (PIETRO FRANCESCO,) an Italian ecclesiastic, born at Novara; died about 1650.

A-pos-to'lĭ-us, (MICHAEL,) a learned Greek who was born at Constantinople, and fled to Italy soon after the capture of that city in 1453. He published or edited a collection of Greek and Latin Proverbs, printed in 1538. Died about 1480, leaving a son, Arsenius, Bishop of Malvasia.

Apostool, ä-pos-tōl', (SAMUEL,) a Dutch Mennonite theologian, born in 1638. He became in 1662 one of the ministers of the Baptist congregations at Amsterdam. A doctrinal dispute between him and one of his colleagues resulted in a division of the sect into two parties, called Apostolians and Galenists.

Appel, äp'pel, (JACOB,) a Dutch painter, born at Amsterdam in 1680, excelled in landscapes, portraits, and history. He worked at the Hague and at Amsterdam. Died in 1751. His son, of the same name, was a successful painter.

Appelius, äp-pā'le-ŭs, (JOHAN HENDRIK,) a Dutch financier, born at Middelburg about 1767, was minister of finance for many years. Died in 1828.

Appelman, äp'pel-män', (BAREND, or BERNARD,) a Dutch landscape-painter, born at the Hague in 1640. He studied in Italy, and painted many admired landscapes of Roman scenery. Died in 1686.

Appendini, äp-pen-dee'nee, (FRANCESCO MARIA,) an Italian priest and scholar, born near Turin in 1768; died in 1837. He is the author of the best political and literary history of the little state of Ragusa, (2 vols., 1802,) and of a "Life and Examination of the Works of Petrarch," ("La Vita e l'Esame delle Opere del Petrarca.")

See COSNACICH, "Memoria storica sulla Vita del P. F. M. Appendini," 1838.

Ap'per-ley, (CHARLES JAMES,) an English gentleman, noted as a fox-hunter and a writer on sporting subjects under the pseudonym of "Nimrod," was born in Denbighshire in 1777. Besides many articles for sporting journals, he wrote "Remarks on the Condition of Hunters, the Choice of Horses, and their Management," (1831,) "Nimrod's Hunting Tours," (1835,) and "The Chase, the Turf, and the Road," (1837.) The last appeared in the "Quarterly Review" in 1827. Died in 1843.

Appert, ä'pair', (BENJAMIN NICOLAS MARIE,) a French philanthropist, born in Paris in 1797. He began about 1816 to establish schools among the poor and others, for mutual instruction, which were eminently successful. Since 1822 he has devoted his time chiefly to the improvement of the condition of prisons and convicts. He has written a "Treatise on the Education of Prisoners," (1822,) "Travels in Belgium," (1846,) and other works.

Appert, (FRANÇOIS,) a brother of the preceding, has given his name to a well-known process for preserving alimentary substances in vessels of tin hermetically sealed.

Ap'pĭ-an, [Gr. Ἀππιανός; Lat. APPIA'NUS; Fr. APPIEN, ä'pe-äN',] an ancient historian, who was born at Alexandria, and removed to Rome probably in the reign of Trajan. He became eminent as an advocate, and obtained the high office of procurator. He is supposed to have died in the reign of Antoninus Pius, (138–161 A.D.,)

or soon after the end of that reign. He is the author of a valuable "Roman History" written in Greek, (Ῥωμαϊκὴ Ἱστορία,) in which he treats of the different nations of the Roman Empire separately. His style is clear and easy, and his work appears to have been carefully compiled; but he is not ranked among historians of the first order.

See FABRICIUS, "Bibliotheca Græca;" DOMENICUS, "Programma de indole Appiani Alexandrini," 1844.

Appian, (PETER.) See APIAN.

Appiani, äp-pe-ä'nee, (ANDREA,) a celebrated Italian painter, born at or near Milan in 1754. He imitated the style of Correggio, and painted both in oil and in fresco. In fresco he was probably unrivalled by any painter of his time. About 1805 he was appointed principal painter of Napoleon, (in Italy,) and was made a knight of the Iron Crown. Among his greatest works are the frescos of the church Santa Maria Vergine, Milan, and the frescos of the royal palace of Milan. He made good portraits of Napoleon and others of the Bonaparte family. His works are admired for grace, purity of design, and brilliancy and harmony of colour. Died in 1817 or 1818.

See NAGLER,"Neues Allgemeines Künstler-Lexikon;" G. LONGHI, "Elogio storico di A. Appiani," 1826.

Appiani, (ANDREA,) an able painter, worked at Milan in the first half of the nineteenth century. He was a grandson of the preceding.

Appiani, (FRANCESCO,) an Italian painter, born at Ancona in 1702. He worked at Rome and Perugia, and acquired a fair reputation as a fresco-painter. Among his best works is the "Death of San Domenico," at Rome. He continued to paint until his ninetieth year. Died in 1792.

See LANZI, "History of Painting in Italy."

Appiano, äp-pe-ä'no, (NICCOLÒ,) an Italian painter of the fifteenth century, was a pupil of Leonardo da Vinci.

Appiano, (PAOLO ANTONIO,) an Italian preacher and biographer, born at Ascoli in 1639; died at Rome in 1709.

Appiano, d', däp-pe-ä'no, (GHERARDO,) a son of Jacopo, noticed below, succeeded his father as lord or master of Pisa in 1398. In 1399 he sold Pisa to the Duke of Milan, reserving for himself the sovereignty of Piombino and the island of Elba. His descendants ruled these dominions, with the title of Prince of Piombino, for two centuries. Died in 1405.

Appiano, d', (JACOPO,) an Italian politician, who by the assassination of Pietro Gambacorti (which Appiano appears to have procured, or at least connived at) obtained the chief power in Pisa in 1392, and assumed the title of Lord, (Signore.) Died in 1398.

Appianus, (the historian.) See APPIAN.

Appien. See APPIAN.

Appion. See APION.

Appius Claudius. See CLAUDIUS.

Applegath, ap'p'l-gath, (AUGUSTUS,) born near London in 1790, invented improved machines for printing. About 1846 he constructed a rotary vertical machine for printing the London "Times."

Appleton, ap'p'l-ton, COMMODORE, an English naval commander, fought in the harbour of Leghorn in 1652 against the Dutch, who, having a larger number of guns, obtained a dearly-bought victory.

Appleton, ap'p'l-ton, (DANIEL,) the founder of the publishing-house of Appleton & Company, New York, one of the largest establishments of the kind in the United States, was born in Haverhill, Massachusetts, in 1785. He first opened a bookstore in Boston, but subsequently removed to New York, where he died in 1849.

Appleton, (JESSE,) D.D., an American divine, born at New Ipswich, New Hampshire, in 1772. He graduated at Dartmouth in 1792, and in 1797 was ordained pastor at Hampton, New Hampshire. He was chosen president of Bowdoin College in 1807, and continued in the office until his death, in 1819.

Appleton, (JOHN,) an American politician and editor, born in Beverley, Massachusetts, in 1815. He was for some years editor of the "Eastern Argus," at Portland, Maine. He was appointed Minister to Russia by President Buchanan in 1860.

Appleton, (NATHAN,) a Boston merchant, brother of Samuel, noticed below, born in New Ipswich, New Hampshire, October 6, 1779, was one of the three original founders of Lowell. He was elected to Congress in 1831, and re-elected in 1842. He was author of various pamphlets on banking, the tariff, etc., and of a memoir of the Honourable Abbott Lawrence in Hunt's "Lives of American Merchants." Died in 1861.

Appleton, (SAMUEL,) an eminent American merchant and philanthropist, was born at New Ipswich, New Hampshire, in June, 1766. He established himself in business in Boston about 1794 in partnership with his brother Nathan. He was early distinguished for his benevolence, making large donations—for many years $25,000 annually—to worthy charitable objects. He liberally endowed the academy of his native town, and gave $10,000 to Dartmouth College. The needy and suffering ever found in him a kind friend and benefactor. He died without children in 1853, worth nearly $1,000,000, bequeathed to his widow $200,000, and placed in the hands of his executors an equal amount to be applied to "scientific, literary, religious, and charitable purposes."

Appony, von, fon âp′poñ′, (ANTON RODOLPH,) COUNT, an Austrian diplomatist, born in 1782, was ambassador at Paris from 1828 to 1849.

Appuleius. See APULEIUS.

Appuleius, ap-pu-lee′yus, (MARCUS,) a Roman, who became quæstor in 44 B.C., and supplied Brutus with money and men in the civil war.

Appuleius Saturninus. See SATURNINUS.

Apraxin, â-prȧk′sin, (FEODOR MATVEIEVITCH, mȧt-vā′ĕ-vitch,) a Russian admiral, the grandfather of the following, was born in 1671. He obtained the favour of Peter the Great, and was one of his principal coadjutors in his projects of reform. Having been appointed Governor of Azov in 1700, he built several vessels of war and a haven at Taganrog. He became an admiral and president of the admiralty in 1707, and captured Viborg from the Swedes in 1710. In 1713 he commanded with success against the Swedes on the coast of Finland. He afterwards received the titles of admiral-general and senator, and rendered important services in the war which was ended by the treaty of Nystad in 1721. Died in 1728.

See HALEM, "Leben Peters des Grossen."

Apraxin, (STEPAN FEODOROVITCH,) a Russian general, born in 1702. He served in the war against the Turks, and obtained in 1756 the rank of field-marshal. In 1757 he was appointed commander-in-chief of a large Russian army sent against Frederick the Great, and in August of that year he defeated the Prussians at Gross-Jägerndorf. In obedience to secret orders from Bestuzhef, the chancellor, he omitted to improve the victory, and was recalled in disgrace. Died in 1758 or 1760.

See HALEM, "Leben Peters des Grossen."

Après de Mannevillette, d', dȧ′prȧ′ dĕh mȧn′vĕ′-lĕt′, (JEAN BAPTISTE NICOLAS DENIS,) often called simply **D'Après,** a distinguished French hydrographer, born at Havre in 1707. He produced a collection of charts of the Eastern Seas, entitled "Le Neptune oriental," (1743.) Died in 1780.

A′prĭ-ēs, [Gr. Ἀπρίης, Ἀπρίας,] a king of Egypt, was a son of Psammuthis, (or Psammis,) whom he succeeded about 595 B.C. He is probably the Pharaoh-hophra of Scriptures, (Jeremiah xliv.) He sent against the Greeks of Cyrene an army which was defeated and afterwards revolted. Apries was dethroned and put to death about 568 B.C., and was succeeded by Amasis.

Ap-ro′nĭ-us, (LUCIUS,) a Roman general, flourished between 8 and 28 A.D.

Aprosio, â-pRO′se-o, (ANGELICO,) a learned Italian writer and Augustine monk, born at Ventimiglia in 1607, was a noted bibliographer. He acquired a high reputation by his numerous works on literary criticism and other subjects, among which are a moral essay against luxury, entitled "The Shield of Rinaldo," ("Lo Scudo di Rinaldo," 1642,) and "La Biblioteca Aprosiana," (1673.) He founded in his native city a library called "Aprosiana." Died in 1681.

See MAZZUCHELLI, "Scrittori d'Italia."

Ap′sȧ-rȧ [Hindoo pron. ŭp′sạ-rȧ′] or **Ap′sạ-ras,** English plural **Ap′sarȧs** or **Ap′sarases,** in the Hindoo mythology, a race of celestial nymphs, produced by the churning of the ocean. (See KŬRMȦVATȦRA.) The

Apsaras (or Apsarases) are described as possessing incomparable beauty, sweetness, and grace. It is common among the Hindoo writers to say of a woman of extra ordinary beauty and elegance, that she rivals the Apsa-rạs. These charming beings are unfortunately wanting in one important attribute—virtue ; they are the dancing girls of Swerga, (the heaven of Indra,) and seem to correspond nearly to the Peris of the Persians.

See MOOR, "Hindu Pantheon," pp. 96 and 97, also 259, etc.

Apshoven, van, vȧn âps′ho′vẹn, (THEODORUS,) a Dutch painter of still life, of the seventeenth century. He was a pupil or imitator of Teniers.

Ap′sĭ-nēs, [Ἀψίνης,] a Greek teacher of rhetoric, born at Gadara, in Phœnicia, taught at Athens in the third century. A work attributed to him, entitled "Art of Rhetoric," is extant, but in a defective state.

Aps′ley, (Sir ALLEN,) an English officer, born about 1618, was a son of Sir Allen Apsley, Lieutenant of the Tower of London, and a brother of Lucy Hutchinson the authoress. He fought for the king in the civil war and was governor of the fort at Exeter when that place was taken in 1646. After the restoration, he was treasurer of the household and receiver-general to the Duke of York. He was the author of a poem entitled "Order and Disorder, or the World Made and Undone," (1679.) Died in 1683.

See Mrs. HUTCHINSON, "Memoirs of Colonel Hutchinson."

Apsley, LORD. See BATHURST, (HENRY.)

Ap-syr′tus, [Ἀψυρτος,] written also **Absyrtus,** a Greek veterinary surgeon, born at Prusa or Nicomedia, in Bithynia, is supposed to have lived in the first half of the fourth century.

Ap′thorp, (EAST,) an eminent divine, born in Boston, Massachusetts, in 1733. He studied at the University of Cambridge, in England. In 1778 he published four letters in reply to Gibbon's attack on Christianity. This work was very favourably received, and was even commended by Gibbon himself. Shortly after, Apthorp received the title of D.D. In 1793 he was appointed to the prebend of Finsbury. Died in 1816.

Apulée, the French for APULEIUS, which see.

Apuleius, â-pu-lee′yus, sometimes called **Apule′ius Platon′icus,** and **Lu′cius Apule′ius Bar′barus,** a naturalist, of whom little is known except that he was author of an extant Latin work on plants, entitled "Herbarium." It describes one hundred and twenty-eight plants, and indicates their medicinal properties. He is supposed to have lived in the fourth or fifth century.

Apuleius or **Appuleius,** âp-pu-lee′yus, [Fr. APULÉE, ả′pü′lả′,] a Latin writer and pagan philosopher of the Platonic school, born at Madaura, in Africa, lived about 150 A.D. He was highly distinguished for talents and eloquence, and possessed a fertile imagination. Having married a rich widow at Œa, (Tripoli,) he was prosecuted by her relatives on a charge that he had in his courtship made use of magical arts. He defended himself on that occasion by an "Apology," which is still extant, and has some literary merit. His most remarkable work is a fable or romance called "Metamorphosis, or the Golden Ass," which is supposed by some to be designed as a satire on magicians, priests, and debauchees. It has been translated into several languages, and often reprinted. He wrote a treatise "On the Doctrines of Plato," which is extant, and several other works, that are lost.

See BÉTOLAND, "Notice sur la Vie, etc. d'Apulée;" FR. HILDEBRAND, "Commentarius de Vita et Scriptis Apuleii," 1835 ; D. W. MOLLER, "Dissertatio de Lucio Apulejo," 1691 ; BAYLE, "Historical and Critical Dictionary."

Apuleius Celsus. See CELSUS.

Aquapendente. See FABRIZIO.

A-qua′rĭ-us, [It. AQUARIO, â-kwä′re-o,] (MATTHIAS,) an Italian monk, who wrote on the philosophy of Aristotle. Died in 1591.

Aquaviva, (ANDREA MATTEO.) See ACQUAVIVA.

Aquaviva, â′kwä-vee′vä, (CLAUDIO,) a general of the Jesuits, born at Naples in 1543, was a son of the Duke of Atri. He wrote a "Plan or Method of Studies," ("Ratio Studiorum," 1586.) Died in 1615.

Aquaviva, (OCTAVIUS,) an Italian cardinal, abridged the "Summa" of Thomas Aquinas. Died in 1612.

€ as *k*; ç as *s*; ğ *hard*; ğ as *j*; G, H, K, *guttural*; N, *nasal*; R, *trilled*; ŝ as *z*; ŧh as in *this*. (☞See Explanations, p. 23.)

Aquiba. See AKIBA-BEN-JOSEPH.

Aq'uï-la, a Jew, who was born in Pontus, and, after his conversion to Christianity, became a companion of the Apostle Paul in a voyage from Corinth to Syria. (See Acts xviii. 2, 18, 26.)

Aquila, å'kwe-lå, (CASPAR,) an eminent German Protestant theologian, born at Augsburg in 1488. His name was originally ADLER, (signifying "Eagle,") which, according to the usage of those times, he changed to its Latin equivalent AQUILA. He became professor of Hebrew at Wittenberg about 1524. He was an intimate friend of Luther, and assisted him in his translation of the Old Testament. For his opposition to the "Interim," in 1548, Charles V. declared him an outlaw and set a price on his head. Aquila saved himself by flight. After the treaty of Passau (1552) he returned to his pastorship at Saalfeld, which Luther had procured him in 1527. He published a number of works, mostly controversial. Died at Saalfeld in 1560.

See CHR. SCHLEGEL, "Bericht vom Leben und Tode C. Aquilæ," 1737 ; J. AVENARIUS, " Kurze Lebensbeschreibung Casparis Aquilæ," 1718 ; F. W. STRIEDER, "Hessische Gelehrten-Geschichte ;" HILLINGER, "Memoria Aquilina oder Leben Casp. Aquilæ," 1731 ; GENSLER, "Vita Mag. C. Aquilæ," 1816.

Aq'uila, (JULIUS,) a Roman jurist of unknown date, is called Gallus Aquila in the "Index Florentinus." The Digest contains two excerpts from his "Book of Answers."

Aquila, å'kwe-lå, (PIETRO,) a distinguished Italian engraver, born at Palermo, was a priest in his youth, and lived at Rome in the latter part of the seventeenth century. His best work is the Farnese Gallery, etc., after Annibale Carracci. He engraved also some works of Raphael.

His brother, FRANCESCO FARAONE, (få-rå-o'nå,) was also an engraver, but inferior to Pietro. He worked at Rome, and engraved after Raphael, Correggio, and other masters.

Aquila, (POMPEO.) See AQUILANO.

Aq'uila surnamed PON'TICUS, the author of a celebrated Greek version of the Old Testament, lived about 100 or 120 A.D. According to Epiphanius, he was a native of Sinope, in Asia Minor, and was employed by Hadrian to superintend the building of the city Ælia Capitolina on the site of Jerusalem. He was converted by the Christians, but was afterwards excommunicated for practising astrology, and became, it is said, a proselyte to the Jewish faith. His version (of which some fragments now remain) was adopted by the Jews in preference to that of the Septuagint, and was admitted by Origen into his great work the "Hexapla."

Aquila, dell', dêl lå'kwe-lå, or **Aquilano, dell',** dêl lå-kwe-lå'no, (SERAFINO,) a celebrated Italian poet and improvisatore, born at Aquila, in Abruzzo, in 1466. He composed many sonnets, epistles, and capitoli, which were more admired by his contemporaries than by modern critics. He was patronized by Ferdinand II. of Naples, and Cæsar Borgia. Died prematurely at Rome in 1500.

See TIRABOSCHI, "Storia della Letteratura Italiana."

Aquilano, å-kwe-lå'no, or **Dell' Aquila,** dêl lå'kwe-lå, (POMPEO,) a good Italian fresco-painter, born in the Abruzzo, lived about 1580. Among his works is a "Deposition from the Cross," at Rome.

Aquilano, [Lat. AQUILA'NUS,] (SEBASTIANO,) an Italian physician, who flourished towards the close of the fifteenth century. He was professor of medicine at Ferrara in 1495, and wrote several medical works. Died about 1513.

A-quil'I-us, (HENRI,) a Belgian historical writer, lived about 1550.

A-quil'I-us, (SABINUS,) a Roman jurist, surnamed "the Cato of his age," was consul in 214 A.D.

Aquilius (or Aquillius) Gallus. See GALLUS.

A-quil'lI-us, (MANIUS,) a Roman general, became consul in 101 B.C. He subdued the revolted slaves of Sicily, in which war he received several wounds. The display of these scars in court, and the eloquence of M. Antonius, saved him from condemnation in a trial for malversation in 98 B.C. In 88 B.C. he was sent as proconsular legate to Asia, where he was defeated and taken

prisoner by Mithridates, who put him to death by pouring molten gold down his throat.

Aquin, d', då'kåN', (LOUIS CLAUDE,) a French organist, born in Paris in 1698; died in 1772.

Aquin, d', (PIERRE LOUIS,) a son of the preceding, and a mediocre writer ; died in 1797.

Aquin, d', då'kåN', or **Aquino, d',** då-kwe'no, (PHILIPPE,) a learned Jew, born at Carpentras, and converted to Christianity in the early part of the seventeenth century. He was baptized at Aquino, in Naples, whence he received his surname. Died about 1650. He published a Hebrew, Chaldee, Talmudic, and Rabbinical Dictionary, (1620,) and other works.

A-qui'nas, (THOMAS,) [It. TOMMASO D'AQUINO, tom-mä'so då-kwee'no ; Fr. THOMAS D'AQUIN, to-mä' då'kåN',] SAINT, surnamed THE ANGELIC DOCTOR, was perhaps the most eminent scholastical teacher that ever lived. He was born of a noble family, probably at Aquino, in the kingdom of Naples, about 1225. His father was a nephew of Frederick I., Barbarossa. He joined the order of Saint Dominic about the age of sixteen, and became a pupil of Albertus Magnus. His extraordinary talents and attainments soon spread his fame over Europe ; but he steadily refused all ecclesiastical preferment. He taught and preached for some years at Paris and Rome. Died in 1274. He left numerous works, chiefly theological, moral, and metaphysical, among which the most important is his "Sum of Theology," ("Summa Theologiæ.") "The greatest of the schoolmen," says Hallam, "were the Dominican Thomas Aquinas, and the Franciscan Duns Scotus. They were founders of rival sects, which wrangled with each other for two or three centuries." Aquinas was remarkable for modesty and exemplary obedience to his superiors, as well as for purity of life ; but he was not deficient in independence. When he once entered the presence of Innocent IV., before whom a large sum of money was spread out, the pope observed, "You see that the Church is no longer in that age in which she said, 'Silver and gold have I none.'" "True, holy father," replied Aquinas ; "neither can she any longer say to the lame, 'Rise up and walk.'" (See Acts iii. 2-8.)

See RENN DICKSON HAMPDEN, "Life of Thomas Aquinas," in the "Encyclopædia Metropolitana," and 18mo, 1848 ; ANTOINE TOURON, "Vie de S. Thomas d'Aquin," 1737 ; ARRIAGA, "Vida de S. Tomas de Aquino," 1648 ; MAFFEI, "Vita di Tommaso d'Aquino," 1842 ; THOLUCK, "Dissertatio de Thoma Aquinate," etc., 1842 ; P. J. CARLE, "Histoire de la Vie et des Écrits de Thomas d'Aquin," 1846 ; C. MORELLES, "Vita S. Thomæ Aquinatis," Antwerp, 1612 ; BUTLER, "Lives of the Saints."

Aquino, d', då-kwee'no, (CARLO,) an Italian writer and Jesuit, born at Naples in 1654. He became professor of rhetoric at the College of Rome, and obtained a high reputation by his works in Latin and Italian, among which are Latin poems, "Carmina," (3 vols., 1701-03.) "Lexicon Militare," (1724,) and a translation into Latin verse of Dante's "Divina Commedia, "(1728,) which is regarded as his greatest poetical production. Died at Rome in 1737.

Aquino, d', (TOMMASO.) See AQUINAS.

Arabella Stuart. See STUART.

A-ra'bi-us Scho-las'tI-cus, a Greek epigrammatic poet, who lived probably about 550 A.D. Several of his epigrams are found in the Greek Anthology.

Arabshah or Arabschah. See AHMED-IBN-ARAB-SHAH.

A-rach'ne, [Gr. Ἀράχνη ; Fr. ARACHNÉ, å'råk'nå',] (Myth.,) a Lydian maiden, very skilful in the art of weaving, in which she challenged Minerva to a trial of skill. The offended goddess changed her into a spider.

Aradon, å'rä'dòn', (JÉRÔME,) a French general, fought for the League against Henry IV. about 1590.

Arago, år'a-go or å'rä'go', (DOMINIQUE FRANÇOIS,) a celebrated French astronomer and natural philosopher, was born at Estagel, near Perpignan, (Eastern Pyrenees,) on the 26th of February, 1786. He entered the Polytechnic School in 1803, after a profound study of the works of Euler and Laplace, and in 1805 was attached to the Observatory of Paris as secretary to the Bureau of Longitudes. In 1806 Arago and Biot were ordered by the emperor to continue the grand geodesical operations of Delambre and Méchain, and extend the measurement of the arc of the meridian from Barcelona to the Balearic Isles. In the performance of this task he was exposed to severe hardships among the mountains of Spain, and in 1808 he escaped from the violence of the Spaniards (who suspected that he was a spy) by flight to Algiers. On his voyage from Algiers to France he was taken by a Spanish privateer, and detained in the hulks at Palamos until he was liberated on the demand of the Dey of Algiers. After other dangers and disasters, which he describes in his "History of my Youth," he returned to France in the summer of 1809. To reward him for these labours, he was admitted into the Academy of Sciences in that year, although he had not attained the age required by their rules. He succeeded Monge as professor of analysis in the Polytechnic School in 1809, and lectured there more than twenty years.

He was associated with Malus and Fresnel in their optical discoveries, advocated the undulatory theory of light, and made some discoveries in the science of electromagnetism. He showed that there is no substance which is not capable, under certain conditions, of exhibiting signs of the magnetic virtue, and he proved that the best magnet is a bar of steel enclosed by a helix of copper wire. For his discovery of magnetism developed by rotation, he received the Copley medal of the Royal Society of London about 1829. In 1830 he was appointed Director of the Observatory, and became perpetual secretary of the Academy of Sciences.

The eulogies which he composed on Fourier, Condorcet, Ampère, James Watt, Carnot, and others, are regarded as models in this species of composition. He was elected to the Chamber of Deputies in 1830 or 1831, and became a leader of the *extrême gauche*, the advanced republicans.

Arago was a prominent member of the provisional government formed in February, 1848, in which crisis he united with Lamartine in efforts to enforce order and moderate measures. He acted for a few months as minister of war and the marine, and was one of the executive commission of five chosen by the Assembly in May, 1848. He opposed the election of Louis Napoleon, and refused to take the oath of allegiance after the *coup d'état* of December, 1851. In consideration of his eminent merits, his compliance with the law in respect to this oath was dispensed with. He died on the 2d of October, 1853, leaving a son Emmanuel, noticed below, and a son Alfred, who is a historical painter.

Arago was a man of ardent temperament, and was distinguished for his courage, generosity, and eloquence. He rendered great services to science, less perhaps by his discoveries than by the admirable talent with which he popularized science, in his lectures on astronomy at the Observatory, in his academical memoirs or reports, and in his notices published in the "Annuaire du Bureau des Longitudes." His articles on lightning, steam, and astronomy gave to that journal an immense vogue. "The popularity of M. Arago," says Loménie, "the European reputation which he enjoys, his marked position in politics, have all combined to attach to his name the idea of a species of intellectual royalty." The same writer asks "Whether a marvellous faculty of illumining with bright and unexpected radiance the most abstract theories; an obstinate ardour in the cultivation of what the learned in *x* and *y* call the *subaltern science*, . . . whether all this does not give genuine claims upon public gratitude, and constitute one of the finest attributes of genius."

Arago and Gay-Lussac founded, about 1816, a scientific periodical entitled "Annales de Chimie et de Physique." He was a member of all the principal scientific academies of Europe, and a friend of Humboldt, Brougham, Brewster, and Faraday. It is said that he was a favourite of Napoleon I., and that the latter, after the battle of Waterloo, intended to select Arago as his companion and retire with him to the United States, to devote himself to the study of science. Referring to his powers of application, De Loménie says, "Ask the young astronomers attached to the Observatory; they will tell you that never did a human brain encounter a more enormous mass of labour; that he deems every one an idler who does not work fourteen hours a day. They will tell you that this formidable man busies himself with politics, chemistry, physics, mechanics, astronomy philosophy . . . ; and that amid all his various and absorbing occupations he finds time to play the part of one of the most brilliant and delightful talkers of the saloons of Paris."

See "History of my Youth," by D. F. ARAGO; M. DE LOMÉNIE, "Galerie des Contemporains," tome ii.; English version of the same, by ROBERT WALSH, entitled "Sketches of Conspicuous Living Characters," Philadelphia, 1841; CHARLES ROBIN, "Biographie de D. F. Arago," 1848; QUÉRARD, "La France Littéraire," Supplément; J. A. BARRAL, "F. Arago," 8vo, 1853; D. F. ARAGO, "Histoire de ma Jeunesse," précédée d'une préface par ALEXANDRE DE HUMBOLDT, etc., 1854.

Arago, (EMMANUEL,) a son of the preceding, born in Paris in 1812. He studied law, and practised at the bar with success, especially as counsel for the defence in political causes. In 1839 he was one of the defenders of Martin-Bernard and Barbès. He was an active promoter of the revolution of February, 1848, and was selected on the 24th of that month, by a reunion of republicans at the office of the "National," to oppose the proclamation of the regency in the Chamber of Deputies. A few days later he was sent by the new government, as commissary-general, to Lyons, and his efforts are said to have saved that city from a disastrous agitation. He was elected in April to the Constituent Assembly, and in May was sent as minister to Berlin. On the election of Louis Napoleon, in December, 1848, he resigned his position and returned to France. He renounced political life after the *coup d'état* of December, 1851.

Arago, (ÉTIENNE,) a dramatic writer and politician, a brother of the celebrated D. F. Arago, was born at Estagel, near Perpignan, in 1803. He began about 1824 to produce a long series of comedies and vaudevilles, in which he was assisted by various persons. Many of these were performed with success. His works evince a genius for satire, a talent for observation, and great skill in producing dramatic effect. He is the sole author of the "Aristocrats," (1847,) a successful comedy in verse. In the revolution of 1830 he fought in Paris against the soldiery of Charles X. He became a contributor of political articles to the "Siècle" and "National," and in 1834 was one of the founders of the "Réforme," a daily democratic journal. M. Arago was director-general of the post-office department from the revolution of February, 1848, until the end of the administration of Cavaignac, in December of the same year. In the Constituent Assembly he voted with the *gauche*, and supported the motion to impeach the President for sending an army to Rome. He was exiled for his part in the insurrection of June, 1849.

See "Nouvelle Biographie Générale."

Arago, (JACQUES ÉTIENNE VICTOR,) a *littérateur* and traveller, brother of the preceding, was born at Estagel in 1790. In 1817 he accompanied as draughtsman the exploring expedition of Freycinet. After having been wrecked on the Falkland Islands, he returned to France in 1821, and published a "Tour round the World in the Uranie," etc., ("Promenade autour du Monde sur les Corvettes l'Uranie et la Physicienne," 2 vols., 1822.) He produced several dramas, among which is the "Cadet de Gascogne," (1836,) and a "Voyage round the World," (with engravings, 5 vols., 1838–40,) which has been often reprinted. Died in 1855.

See QUÉRARD, "La France Littéraire."

Ar'a-gon, de, [Sp. pron. dà à-rä-gòn',] (FERNANDO,) a Spanish historian, became Archbishop of Saragossa in 1539. His father was a natural son of King Ferdinand V. Died in 1575.

Aragon, de, (MARTIN,) Duke of Hermola, a Spanish numismatist of the sixteenth century.

Aragona, d', dä-rä-go'nä, or **Aragon, d',** dä-rä-gòn', (TULLIA,) a celebrated Italian poetess and musician, born in the beginning of the sixteenth century. She was the illegitimate daughter of Tagliavia, (afterwards cardinal,) a descendant of the royal house of Aragon. She lived at Rome, Venice, and Florence. She was distinguished for her beauty, as well as for her genius and learning. Her chief works are a "Dialogue on the

---

ċ as *k*; ç as *s*; g̃ *hard*; ġ as *j*; G, H, K, *guttural*; N, *nasal*; R, *trilled*; s̃ as *z*; ŧh as in *this*. (☞ See Explanations, p. 23.)

Infinity of Love," ("Dialogo dell' Infinità d'Amore," 1547,) and a romance in verse called "Il Meschino o il Guerino," (1560.) Died about 1560.

Aragonese, â-rä-go-nä′sà, (SEBASTIANO,) an Italian painter and designer of Brescia, lived in the latter part of the sixteenth century. He worked chiefly with the pen, and made drawings of sixteen hundred ancient medals.

Araja, â-rä′yä or â-rī′à, (FRANCESCO,) a dramatic composer, born at Naples in 1700. In 1735 he visited Saint Petersburg, where he produced "Cephalus and Procris," (1755,) the first opera written in the Russian language. He returned to Italy in 1759.

Araktcheief, â-räk-shä′yêf, written also **Arakcheev** and **Arakcejeff,** (ALEXIS ANDREEVITCH,) a Russian count and general, born in Novogorod in 1769. He became inspector-general of artillery in 1803, and minister of war about 1808. He made reforms in several departments of the army, especially in the artillery, and rendered important services in the war of 1812, after which he established the system of military colonies. Died in 1834.

Araldi, â-räl′dee, (ALESSANDRO,) an Italian painter, a pupil of Giovanni Bellini, was born at Parma, and painted in what is called the Gothic style. He is praised by Lanzi. Died about 1528.

Araldi, (MICHELE,) an eminent Italian physician and physiologist, born at Módena in 1740. He became professor of physiology and anatomy at Módena about 1770, and was distinguished for his attainments in a variety of studies. He was perpetual secretary of the National Institute of Italy from 1804 until his death. His chief work is "On the Use of Anastomoses in the Vessels of Animal Machines," (1816.) Died at Milan in 1813.

See ROVIDA, "Elogio d'Araldi," 1817.

Aram, ā′ram, (EUGENE,) remarkable for his talents and acquirements, as well as his untimely end, was born in 1704 in Yorkshire, England. While acting as an assistant to his father, who was a gardener, he studied mathematics, and gave some attention to the languages. On marrying, he became a school-master, and prosecuted his studies with such diligence and success as to obtain a good knowledge of the Latin, Greek, Hebrew, Chaldee, Arabic, Welsh, and Irish languages. In 1759 he was tried for the murder of Daniel Clark, a shoemaker of Knaresborough, and found guilty. At the trial he made an elaborate and able defence, but after his condemnation he confessed his guilt. On the night before his execution he made an attempt to commit suicide, by opening the veins of his arms; but he was discovered before he had bled to death, and the sentence of the law was carried into effect. The story of Eugene Aram forms the subject of one of Bulwer's novels.

See "Biographia Britannica;" "Account of the Trial of Eugene Aram," London, 1759; SCATCHERD, "Memoirs of Eugene Aram," 1832.

Aramont or **Aramon,** d′, dä′rä′môn′, (GABRIEL de Luetz—dęh lü′à′,) BARON, a French diplomatist, born, it is supposed, about 1500. He was sent as ambassador to the Ottoman Porte in 1546, and induced the sultan Solyman the Magnificent to send a fleet to operate against Charles V. He accompanied the sultan to Persia. An account of his journeys, written by his secretary, Chesnau, was afterwards published. Died in 1553.

Aranda, dä â-rän′dä, (EMANUEL,) of Spanish extraction, was born at Bruges about 1608. He was captured at sea by Algerine pirates in 1640, and remained in slavery at Algiers until March, 1642. After his release he published an entertaining narrative of his adventures, with a description of Algiers, (1657.)

Aranda, (FRANCISCO,) a Spanish sculptor, worked at Toledo about 1500. His brother Juan was also a sculptor.

Aranda, (JUAN,) a Spanish writer, born at Jaen, lived about 1550 or 1600.

Aranda, (Don PEDRO Abarca y Bolea—â-baR′kä e bo-lä′à,) COUNT OF, an able Spanish diplomatist and statesman, born of a noble family at Saragossa in December, 1718. He served some years in the army, and in 1759 obtained the chief command of the artillery. In 1763 he commanded an army which invaded Portugal and took Almeida. He became prime minister, with the title of President of the Council of Castile, in 1766, and initiated various measures of reform. Among the important acts of his administration were the suppression of the order of Jesuits in 1767, and the reduction of the power of the Inquisition. The intrigues of the court of Rome and the hostility of the clergy to Aranda induced the king to dismiss him from power in 1773, but at the same time he was appointed ambassador to France. It is stated that, about the close of the American war, the British ministry having offered to Spain the choice of Gibraltar or Florida, Aranda chose the latter, and signed the treaty of 1783. He was recalled about 1785, and was prime minister for a few months in 1792, before the end of which year he was supplanted by the royal favourite Godoy. Died in 1799, or, according to some authorities, in 1794.

See MASDEU, "Historia de España;" R. SAINT-HILAIRE, "Histoire d'Espagne;" ERSCH und GRUBER, "Allgemeine Encyklopaedie;" COXE, "Memoirs of the Kings of Spain."

Aranda de Duero, â-rän′dä dà doo-ā′ro, (ANTONIO,) a Spanish monk, published a Description of Palestine, (1545,) which he visited in 1530. Died in 1555.

Arantius, a-ran′she-us, or **Aranzio,** â-rän′ze-o, (JULIUS CÆSAR,) an eminent and accurate Italian anatomist, born at Bologna about 1530, was professor in the university of his native city for many years. Died in 1589. He left several works, among which is one "De humano Fœtu," (1564.)

Arany, ŏr′ŏñ, (JÁNOS,) a popular Hungarian poet, born at Nagy Szalonta in 1819. He produced in 1843 a prize poem called "The Lost Constitution." His second poem, "Toldi," (1847,) was also successful. He afterwards wrote the "Conquest of Murany," (1848,) and "Catharine," ("Katalin," 1850.)

Aranzio, (GIULIO CESARE.) See ARANTIUS.

A-rā′tor, [It. ARATORE, â-rä-to′rà,] a poet, born at Milan or Brescia about 490 A.D., was appointed "comes privatorum" (count of the domestics) by Athalaric. Having resigned this office, he entered the Church of Rome, and became a subdeacon. He wrote, in Latin verse, the "History of the Apostles," ("Historiæ Apostolicæ,") which is said to be superior to the poetry of his contemporaries. Died about 560 A.D.

A-rā′tus, [Ἄρατος,] a celebrated Greek poet and astronomer, was born at Soli, in Cilicia, and lived between 300 and 250 B.C. He was invited by Antigonus Gonatas to his court, where he passed the latter part of his life. He was the author of an astronomical Greek poem, entitled "Phenomena," which was greatly admired by the ancients and is remarkable as being the oldest treatise of the kind. It has often been printed. Cicero made of this poem a Latin version, some fragments of which have come down to us, and Hipparchus wrote a commentary on it, which is extant. Aratus is supposed to be the poet quoted by Saint Paul in his address to the Athenians in the twenty-eighth verse of the seventeenth chapter of the Acts. He wrote a poem on the weather, etc., called "Prognostica," which, however, is considered as a division or portion of the "Phenomena." This poem was so much admired by Ovid that he said,

"Cum Sole et Lunâ semper Aratus erit."*—*Amor,* i. 15.

A good edition of Aratus was published by Buhle in 1793–1801.

See FABRICIUS, "Bibliotheca Græca;" DELAMBRE, "Histoire de l'Astronomie ancienne;" and a "Life of Aratus," published by P. VETTORI, Florence, 1567.

Aratus, a celebrated Greek statesman and general, born at Sicyon in 271 B.C. On the murder of his father Clinias, Aratus, then seven years old, escaped to Argos. He liberated his native city from the tyrant Nicocles in 251 B.C., and became the founder of the famous Achæan League, of which he was chosen general (*strate′gos*) in 245, and many times afterwards. He captured Corinth from the Macedonian garrison in 243, obtained the accession of Argos to the league, and proved himself a consummate politician by his successful efforts to counteract Macedonian influence in Southern Greece. The Achæans were involved in war against Sparta in 226 B.C., after which Aratus was defeated in several cam-

* "Aratus will always be [associated] with the sun and moon;" in other words, his fame will last as long as the sun and moon endure.

paigns by Cleomenes of Sparta. The latter, however, was totally defeated in 222 B.C. by Antigonus of Macedon, with whom the Achæans had formed an alliance. Aratus died in 213 B.C., leaving "Commentaries," or memoirs of his life, which were praised by.Polybius, but which, unhappily, have not come down to us.

See article "Aratus," in PLUTARCH's "Lives;" POLYBIUS, "History."

Aratus, an Achæan general, son of the preceding, obtained command of the army in 219 B.C. He was poisoned by Philip II.

Araujo, â-rŏw′zho, (ANTONIO,) a Portuguese missionary, born in the Azores in 1566, laboured in Brazil. Died in 1632.

Araujo or **Arauxo,** â-rŏw′HO, (FRANCISCO,) a Spanish musician, who wrote on the Organ. Died in 1663.

Araujo, de, dà â-rŏw′zho, (JOSÉ,) a Portuguese philosopher, born in Lisbon in 1667; died in 1743.

Araujo, de, dà â-rŏw′HO, (PEDRO,) a Spanish sculptor, received the title of sculptor to the king about 1700.

Araujo d'Azevedo, â-rŏw′zho dâ-zà-vā′do, (ANTONIO,) COUNT DA BARCA, a Portuguese minister of state, born at Ponte de Lima in 1754. He became a proficient in the Greek, Latin, French, and English languages, and was distinguished for his literary and scientific attainments. After he had resided some years as minister at the Hague, he was sent to Paris in 1797 to negotiate a peace, and in the same year signed a treaty. The cabinet of Lisbon delayed the ratification of this treaty so long that the French Directory annulled it. A report having gained currency that Araujo expected to procure the assent of the Directors by bribery, they resolved to prove their innocence by an act of rigour, and confined him in prison several months. He became secretary of state, or minister of foreign affairs, in 1804, and was the principal minister after 1806, but showed his incapacity to guide the state in critical times. A French army entered Lisbon in November, 1807, the house of Braganza ceased to reign, and Araujo retired to Brazil, where he was made minister of marine in 1814. He had been chief minister for a few months, when he died at Rio Janeiro in 1817. He translated the "Elegy" and other poems of Gray into Portuguese verse.

See MENDO TRIGOSO, "Vida do Araujo," and the article on ARAUJO, by FERDINAND DENIS, in the "Nouvelle Biographie Générale."

Arauxo, â-rŏw′sho, (SALGADO—sâl-gä′do,) a Portuguese ecclesiastic and historian, lived about 1600.

Ar-bā′çēs, [Gr. Ἀρβάκης,] a Median general under Sardanapa′lus, against whom he revolted, overthrew the Assyrian monarchy, and established the kingdom of Media, about 876 B.C.

Arbasia, âR-bä-see′â, (CESARE,) an excellent Italian painter, born at Saluzzo. He was one of the founders of the Academy of Saint Luke at Rome. He worked at Córdova and Málaga, in Spain, about 1580. Among his works are a picture of the Incarnation, at Málaga, and some frescos in the town-hall of Saluzzo. He is supposed to have died in 1614.

See BERMUDEZ, "Diccionario Historico."

Arbaud de Porchères, d', dåR′bō′ deh poR′shaiR′, (FRANÇOIS,) a French poet, born in Provence in the sixteenth century, was a friend and imitator of Malherbe. He wrote several odes, and a version or paraphrase of the Psalms, (1633.) He was one of the first members of the French Academy, and received a pension from Richelieu. Died in 1640.

Ar-be′tĭ-o (ar-bee′she-o) or **Ar-be′tĭ-on,** a Roman general, noted for his ambitious intrigues, was consul in 355 A.D. In 361 he commanded the army of Constantius against the Parthians. Having sided with Valens, so that the rebellion of the latter came to naught, in 365 A.D.

Arbiter. See PETRONIUS ARBITER.

Arblay. See D'ARBLAY.

Ar′bo-gast, [Gr. Ἀρβογάστης; Lat. ARBOGAS′TES; Fr. ARBOGASTE, âR′bo′gåst′,] a Frank who became an able and distinguished general in the Roman service. He commanded with success against the Germans in the reign of Gratian. Under Valentinian II. he was commander in Gaul, and, having won the favour of his army, defied the authority of the emperor, who was found dead

in his chamber in 392 A.D. It is supposed that he was killed by order of Arbogast. The latter was defeated by Theodosius near the river Frigidus (Wippach) in 394, soon after which he killed himself.

Arbogast, SAINT, a French ecclesiastic, who obtained the favour of King Dagobert, and was made Bishop of Strasburg about 669 A.D. Died in 678.

Arbogaste, âR′bo′gåst′, written also **Arbogast,** (LOUIS FRANÇOIS ANTOINE,) a distinguished French mathematician, born in Alsace in 1759. He became rector of the university at Strasburg, and afterwards professor of mathematics in the Central School of that place. He was a member of the National Convention about 1793, but took no part in politics. His principal work is entitled "Du Calcul des Dérivations," (1800,) in which is found the first use of symbols of operation independently of symbols of quantity. Died in 1803.

Arborio di Gattinara, âR-bo′re-o de gât-te-nä′rä, (ANGELO ANTONIO,) Archbishop of Turin, born at Pavía in 1658; died in 1743.

Arborio di Gattinara, (GIOVANNI MERCURINO,) a brother of Mercurino, noticed below, was born at Lucca in 1685. He became Bishop of Alexandria. Died in 1743.

Arborio di Gattinara, (LUIGI,) Abbé de Brème, (or Brema,) an accomplished Italian scholar and writer, born at Turin in 1781, was a son of the Marquis de Brème. He became governor of the pages at the court of Eugene, Viceroy of Italy, and a friend of Silvio Pellico. He contributed literary articles to "Il Conciliatore," a celebrated journal of Milan, and wrote a number of occasional poems. Died in 1820.

Arborio di Gattinara, (LUIGI GIUSEPPE,) the father of the preceding, was born in Paris in 1754. He served the King of Sardinia as ambassador to Vienna about 1785, and was minister of the interior under Eugene, Viceroy of Italy. Died in 1828.

Arborio di Gattinara, (MERCURINO,mêR-koo-ree′no,) COUNT, often called simply COUNT OF GATTINARA, an eminent diplomatist and jurist, born at Vercelli, in Piedmont, in 1465. He became president of the Parliament of Burgundy in 1507; after which he was employed as negotiator by the emperor. In 1520 he was appointed chancellor by Charles V., whose favour and confidence he enjoyed until the end of his life. He was the principal negotiator of the treaty of Cambrai in 1529, and was made a cardinal the same year. He was a friend of Erasmus, and a constant advocate of moderate and liberal measures for the reformation of the Church. Died at Innspruck in 1530.

See AUBERY, "Histoire des Cardinaux;" GUICCIARDINI, "History of Italy;" CARLO DENINA, "Elogio storico di M. di Gattinara," 1782; P. EKERMAN, "Dissertatio de M. Gattinara," 1761.

Ar-bo′rĭ-us, (ÆMILIUS MAGNUS,) a Roman advocate, noted for eloquence, born in Gaul about 270 A.D., was a son of the following, and an uncle of the poet Ausonius. The emperor Constantine appointed him preceptor of one of his children at Constantinople. Died about 335 A.D.

Arborius, (CÆCIL′IUS ARGIÇ′IUS—ar-jish′e-us,) a learned citizen of Gaul, settled on the site of Bayonne in 264 A.D. His daughter was the mother of the poet Ausonius.

Arbrissel or **Arbrisselles, d',** dåR′bRe′sĕl′, (ROBERT,) the founder of the abbey of Fontevrault, was born at Arbrissel, in Brittany, about 1047; died in 1117.

Arbuckle, ar′buk-k'l, (JAMES,) the author of a mock-heroic poem entitled "Snuff," (1719,) born at Glasgow in 1700; died in 1734.

See CAMPBELL, "Introduction to the History of Poetry in Scotland."

Ar′buckle, (MATTHEW,) an American general, born in Greenbrier county, Virginia, in 1776. He served in the Mexican war, 1846–47. Died in 1851.

Ar-buth′not or **Ar-buth′net,** (ALEXANDER,) a Scottish Protestant divine and poet, born about 1538. He was appointed principal of the University of Aberdeen in 1568, and was twice chosen moderator of the Assembly, 1573 and 1577. He is the reputed author of several vernacular poems of some merit, one of which is entitled "The Praises of Women." Died in 1583.

See CHAMBERS, "Biographical Dictionary of Eminent Scotsmen."

Arbuthnot, (ALEXANDER,) a Scottish printer, who printed the first Scotch Bible, in 1579. Died in 1585.

Ar'buth-not, [Scottish pron. ar-bŭth'nọt,] (JOHN,) a British author, satirist, and physician, celebrated for his wit, genius, and learning, was born at Arbuthnot, near Montrose, in Scotland, in 1675. He was educated at Aberdeen, where he took the degree of M.D., and became a resident of London in his youth. His "Examination of Dr. Woodward's Account of the Deluge" (1697) first brought him into notice. His "Tables of the Grecian, Roman, and Jewish Measures, Weights, and Coins" (1705) have a high reputation, and are regarded as a standard. In 1709 he was appointed physician-in-ordinary to Queen Anne. He became intimate with Pope, Swift, and Bolingbroke, and was employed as a political writer by the Tory ministry. He produced in 1712 the humorous "History of John Bull," an excellent political allegory, in which the belligerent powers of Europe were personated by John Bull the Clothier, Nick Frog the Linen-draper, Louis Baboon, (Bourbon,) etc. Macaulay calls this work "the most ingenious and humorous political satire extant in our language." ("History of England," vol. v. chap. xxiv.)

About 1714 he united with Pope and Swift in the formation of the famous "Scriblerus Club," the design of which was to ridicule all false tastes in literature or abuses of learning. His "First Book of the Memoirs of Martinus Scriblerus" is regarded as a master-piece of wit and irony. Among his other works is an "Essay on the Effects of Air on Human Bodies," (1733.)

He died in 1735, leaving a son George and two daughters. In 1751 appeared "The Miscellaneous Works of Dr. Arbuthnot," (2 vols.;) but the genuineness of some of these works was denied by his son. Referring to the writers of Queen Anne's reign, Dr. Johnson said, "I think Dr. Arbuthnot the first man among them. He was the most universal genius, being an excellent physician, a man of deep learning, and a man of much humour." (Boswell's "Life of Johnson.") His benevolence and integrity are highly commended. "He has more wit than we all have," said Swift, "and his humanity is equal to his wit."

See CHAMBERS, "Biographical Dictionary of Eminent Scotsmen;" SWIFT'S "Letters."

Arbuthnot, (MARIOT,) a British admiral, born in 1711. He became a post-captain in 1747. Having been raised to the rank of vice-admiral in 1779, he obtained the chief command on the American station, and was blockaded by Count D'Estaing in the harbour of New York. He co-operated with Sir Henry Clinton in the capture of Charleston, South Carolina, in 1780, and became an admiral of the blue in 1793. Died in 1794.

Arc, Joan d'. See JOAN OF ARC.

Arc, d', or **Arcq, d',** dȧrk, (PHILIPPE AUGUSTE de Sainte-Foix—dẹh sȧNt'fwȧ',) a French historical writer, published a "History of Commerce and Navigation," (1758,) and other works. Died at Tulle, in 1779.

Arcade. See ARCADIUS.

Arcadelt, ȧR'kä-dĕlt', or **Arcadet,** ȧR'kä'dȧ', (JACQUES,) an eminent Dutch or Flemish musician and composer. He went to Rome in 1536, and was employed in the pontifical chapel in 1540. He composed masses, madrigals, etc.

Arcadio, ȧR-kä'de-o, (ALESSANDRO,) an Italian medical writer, lived in Piedmont in the seventeenth century.

Arcadio, (GIAN-FRANCESCO,) an Italian medical writer, born at Bistagno; died about 1620.

Ar-cā'dĭ-us, ['Αρκάδιος,] a Greek grammarian, born at Antioch, lived about 200 A.D. He wrote an "Onomasticon," which is praised by Suidas, and a "Treatise on Accents," which is extant.

Arcadius, [Gr. 'Αρκάδιος; Fr. ARCADE, ȧr'kȧd',] Emperor of the East, born in Spain in 383 A.D., was the eldest son of Theodosius the Great, who at his death, in 395, divided the empire, leaving the eastern part to Arcadius, and the western part to his other son, Honorius. Byzantium was the capital of the Eastern Empire, which included Thrace, Asia Minor, Syria, etc. Rufinus became guardian or regent, in accordance with the will of Theodosius, but was assassinated by Gainas before the end of the year. (See GAINAS.) Arcadius was a very

weak prince, and was controlled by his empress Eudoxia. He was partial to the orthodox creed, and issued edicts against the Arians. Died in 408 A.D., leaving the throne to his son, Theodosius II.

See SOCRATES, "Historia Ecclesiastica;" SOZOMEN, "Historia Ecclesiastica;" GIBBON, "History of the Decline and Fall of the Roman Empire."

Arcæus, ar-see'us, (FRANCISCUS) [Sp. FRANCISCO DE ARCE, frȧn-thĕs'ko dȧ aR'sȧ,] a distinguished Spanish physician and surgeon, born at Fresno about 1494; died probably about 1575. He left an able treatise "On the Treatment of Wounds," (1574,) which was translated into English, German, and Dutch.

Arcagna. See ORCAGNA.

Arcano, d', daR-kä'no, (MAURO, mŏw'ro,) commonly called "Il Mauro," a celebrated burlesque poet of Italy, was born of a noble family of Friuli about 1490. He was intimate with the poet Berni, and an enemy to Aretin. His works are similar, and, in the opinion of some critics, almost equal, to those of Berni. They are generally satirical, and are censured for indecency and levity. Died in 1536.

Arcasio, aR-kä'se-o, (GIOVANNI FRANCESCO,) an Italian jurist, born at Bisagno, in Piedmont, in 1712, was professor of law at Turin. Died in 1791.

Arce, de, dȧ aR'thȧ, (Don CALEDONIO, kä-lä-do'ne-o,) a Spanish sculptor, patronized by Charles IV., born at Burgos in 1739; died in 1795.

Arce, de, (FRANCISCO.) See ARCÆUS.

Arce, de, (JOSÉ,) a Spanish sculptor, who executed in 1657 some statues for the cathedral of Seville.

Arcère, ȧR'saiR', (LOUIS ÉTIENNE,) a French ecclesiastic, poet, and historian, born at Marseilles in 1698. Among his works is a "History of Rochelle and of Aunis," ("Histoire de la Rochelle et de l'Aunis," 2 vols., 1756–57.) Died in 1782.

Arcésilas, the French of ARCESILAUS, which see.

Ar-çes-ĭ-lā'us, ['Αρκεσίλαος,] a Greek painter of Paros, whom Pliny calls one of the first painters in encaustic. He is supposed to have lived in the fifth century B.C.

Arcesilaus, a Greek sculptor, of whom little is known. Among his works was a statue of Diana, on which Simonides wrote some verses.

Arcesilaus IV., the last king of Cyrene, was extolled by the poet Pindar. Died about 431 B.C.

Arcesilaus, [Gr. 'Αρκεσίλαος; Fr. ARCÉSILAS, ȧr'sȧ'ze'-lȧs',] a Greek skeptical philosopher, born at Pitane, or Pitana, in Æolia, in 316 B.C., was the founder of the New, or, as it is sometimes called, the Middle Academy. He studied philosophy under Theophrastus and Polemo, and admired Plato, but modified his doctrines so much that he was considered as the head of a new school. He opposed the dogmatism of the Stoics, and maintained that man knows nothing with certainty,—that the evidence of the senses is deceitful. His oratorical talents and ingenuity in argument are highly commended. It is not known that he left any written record of his principles. He used the Socratic method of teaching, was in the habit of maintaining alternately both sides of an argument, and was noted for the keenness of his replies. Died in 241 B.C.

See RITTER, "History of Philosophy;" G. H. LEWES, "Biographical History of Philosophy;" DIOGENES LAERTIUS; SEXTUS EMPIRICUS, "Adversus Mathematicos."

Arcesilaus, an eminent sculptor, who flourished at Rome in the first century B.C. "His models," says Varro, "were more highly prized than the finished works of other artists." Among his productions was a "Venus Genitrix."

Arcet. See DARCET.

Ar-chag'a-thus, a Greek surgeon, who is said to have introduced the practice of surgery into Rome. He lived about 220 B.C.

Archange de Clermont, ȧR'kŏNzh' dẹh klĕR'mŏN', a French historian, lived in the first half of the seventeenth century.

Archange de Rouen, ȧR'kŏNzh' dẹh rwŏN, a French theologian, lived about 1690–1700.

Ar-chan'ge-lus or **De Archangelo,** dȧ aR-kän'-jȧ-lo, (OTTAVIO,) an Italian poet, born at Catania, lived in the first half of the seventeenth century.

Arch'bold, (J. F.,) an eminent English writer on law, of the present century, has published many legal works, which have been often reprinted, and among which are a "Digest of the Pleas of the Crown," (1813;) "The Practice of the Court of King's Bench in Personal Actions," (9th edition, 1855;) a "Summary of the Law relative to Pleading and Evidence in Criminal Cases," etc., (18th edition, 1856.)

Arch'dale, (JOHN,) an Englishman, born in Buckinghamshire, was originally a member of the Society of Friends. In 1694 he became Governor of Carolina, or South Carolina, which enjoyed new prosperity under his administration. He introduced the cultivation of rice, and wrote a "Description of the Province of Carolina," (1707.)

See BANCROFT's "History of the United States," vol. iii. chap. xix.

Arch'dall, (Rev. MER'VYN,) an antiquary, born in Dublin in 1723. He published in 1786 "Monasticon Hibernicum," or a "History of the Abbeys, Priories, and other Religious Houses in Ireland." He was afterwards rector of Slane, in the county of Meath, where he died in 1791.

Arch-de'kin or **Ars-de'kin,** (RICHARD,) an Irish Jesuit, born in the county of Kilkenny about 1619. He published a system of theology, entitled "Controversies concerning Faith reduced to an Easy Method," ("Controversiæ Fidei ad facilem Methodum redactæ," 1617,) which was often reprinted. Died at Antwerp in 1693.

Ar-che-bu'lus, [Gr. Ἀρχέβουλος; Fr. ARCHÉBULE, ȧR'shȧ'bül',] a Greek poet, born at Thebes, flourished in the second half of the third century before Christ.

Archedamus. See ARCHIDEMUS.

Ar-ched'ĭ-cus, an Athenian comic poet, flourished about 302 B.C.

Ar-che-la'us, [Ἀρχέλαος] a king of Sparta, of the race of Agidæ, began to reign about 884 B.C.

Archelaus, a son of Herod the Great and Malthace, was appointed heir to the kingdom by the last will of his father. His claim was disputed by his brother Herod Antipas, who had many partisans. About 1 A.D. Archelaus went to Rome to procure the recognition of Augustus Cæsar, who divided the kingdom and decided that Archelaus should rule Judea Proper, Samaria, and Idumea, with the title of Ethnarch, ("ruler of nations.") He was banished by Augustus for cruelty in 7 A.D. (See Matthew ii. 22.)

Archelaus, an Egyptian writer, of unknown date, four of whose epigrams are found in the Greek Anthology. He is supposed to be the author of a work called a "Description of Strange or Curious Animals," which is not extant.

Archelaus, a Greek poet, who wrote a work on alchemy, lived probably in the fifth century after Christ.

Archelaus, a native of Cappadocia, was general-in-chief of the army of Mithridates VI. in his first war against the Romans. In 87 B.C. he led a large army into Greece, and occupied Athens, where he was attacked by Sulla. He defended himself in the Piræus in a long and famous siege. In 86 he retired to Thessaly, and was defeated by Sulla at Chæronea and Orchomenus. By order of his sovereign, he signed a treaty of peace with Sulla in 85 B.C. He deserted to the Romans in 81.

Archelaus, a son of the preceding, obtained the office of high-priest of Comana about 63 B.C. He won the hand of Berenice, Queen of Egypt, by pretending to be a son of King Mithridates. He was defeated by the Romans and killed in 55 B.C., after a reign of several months. His son Archelaus succeeded him as high-priest, and was deposed by Cæsar in 47 B.C.

Archelaus, the last king of Cappadocia, was a grandson of the preceding and Glaphyra. He obtained the throne in 34 B.C. by the favour of Mark Antony, who is said to have been captivated by the beauty of Glaphyra. Having given offence to Tiberius, he was summoned to Rome and detained until his death in 17 A.D.

Archelaus, Bishop of Carrha, in Mesopotamia, lived about 276 A.D. He challenged Manes the heretic to a public dispute, in which the latter was worsted. His account of this disputation was highly esteemed.

Archelaus, King of Macedonia, was a son and suc-

cessor of Perdiccas II. He reigned from 413 to 399 B.C., and encouraged Greek literature and arts by attracting to his court several eminent poets and artists, among whom were Euripides and Zeuxis. Socrates also was invited by him, but declined the favour. Archelaus was succeeded by his son Orestes.

Archelaus of Miletus, (or, according to some writers, of Athens,) a Greek philosopher, who flourished about 450 B.C., was surnamed PHYSICUS, because he directed his attention to physical rather than moral science. He was a pupil of Anaxagoras, and an instructor of Socrates at Athens. His works, if he wrote any, are entirely lost, and the merits of his system are not well understood. He admitted two principles of generation—heat, which moves, and cold, which remains at rest.

Archenholz. See ARCKENHOLTZ.

Archenholz, aR'ḳen-holts', (JOHANN WILHELM,) a popular German writer of history, etc., was born at Dantzic in 1741. He served in the Seven Years' war, attained the rank of captain, and after the peace of 1763 spent many years in travelling in England, France, and Italy. He gave evidence that he was a shrewd observer and agreeable writer, in his descriptive work called "England and Italy," (2 vols., 1785,) often reprinted. He edited for about twenty years the "Minerva," a successful historical and literary journal of Hamburg, which was first issued in 1792. His "History of the Seven Years' War" (2 vols., 1793) was very popular, and was translated into many languages. He was author of other histories. Died in 1812.

See ERSCH und GRUBER, "Allgemeine Encyklopaedie."

Ar'cher, (JOHN,) physician to Charles II. of England, wrote a book called "Every Man his Own Doctor," (1673.)

Archer, (JOHN WYKEHAM,) an English painter, engraver, and antiquary, born at Newcastle-on-Tyne about 1806. He produced several hundred drawings or sketches of the antiquities of London and its environs, and a book entitled "Vestiges of Old London." Died in 1864.

Archer, (Sir SIMON,) an English antiquary of Warwickshire, born in 1581; died after 1654.

Archer, (THOMAS,) an English architect, a disciple or imitator of Vanbrugh, lived in the first half of the eighteenth century. He designed, besides other works, St. Philip's Church at Birmingham, (1719,) and St. John's at Westminster, (finished about 1728,) a remarkable structure of stone, which has been compared to "an elephant lying on its back, with its legs sprawling in the air." Died in 1743.

See WALPOLE, "Anecdotes of Painting."

Ar'cher, (WILLIAM S.,) an American Senator, born in Amelia county, Virginia, in 1789. He was a member of Congress from 1820 to 1835, and took a leading part in all matters of national importance. In 1841 he was elected a Senator of the United States by the Whigs of Virginia for six years, during which he was chairman of the Committee on Foreign Relations. Died in 1855.

Ar-ches'tra-tus, [Ἀρχέστρατος,] an Athenian general, who succeeded Alcibiades as commander of the fleet in 407 B.C.

Archestratus, [Fr. ARCHESTRATE, ȧR'shĕs'tRȧt',] a Greek poet, born in Sicily, is supposed to have lived about 350 B.C. He wrote a poem on Gastronomy, which is lost. His descriptions of animals were accurate, and were used by Aristotle in his "History of Animals."

Archevesque, ȧRsh'vĕk', (HUE, hü,) a French troubadour of the thirteenth century, born in Normandy.

Archiac, d', dȧR'she-ȧk', (ÉTIENNE JULES ADOLPHE **Desmier de Saint-Simon**—dez'me-ȧ' deh sȧN'se'-mŏN',) VICOMTE, a French geologist, born at Rheims in 1802. He published "Zizim, or the Chivalry of Rhodes," a romance, (3 vols., 1828.) His most important work is a "History of the Progress of Geology from 1834 to 1851," in French, in six or more vols., (1847–56,) published under the auspices of the minister of public instruction.

Ar-chi'a-das [Ἀρχιάδας] or **Ar-chi'a-dēs,** [Ἀρχιάδης,] a Greek philosopher of the fifth century after Christ, was a friend of Proclus.

Ar'chi-as [Gr. Ἀρχίας] of Corinth, founded the city of Syracuse about 733 B.C.

€ as *k*; ç as *s*; g̃ *hard*; g̃ as *j*; G, H, K, *guttural*; N, *nasal*; R, *trilled*; ṣ as *z*; ṯh as in *this*. (☞ See Explanations, p. 23.)

Archias surnamed the HUNTER OF FUGITIVES gained an infamous notoriety by pursuing the Athenian orators who were proscribed by Antipater about 322 B.C.

Archias, (AU'LUS LICIN'IUS,) an accomplished Greek poet of Antioch, in Syria, became a resident of Rome in 102 B.C. He enjoyed the friendship of Lucullus and Cicero, and was admitted to the rights of citizenship. Among his works were a poem on the Cimbric war of Marius, and one on the Mithridatic war, both of which are lost. His right of citizenship having been contested, Cicero advocated his cause, about 60 B.C., in an admirable oration, (" Pro Archia,") and expressed himself deeply indebted to his client for the direction of his youthful studies and the development of his mental powers. About thirty epigrams, of little merit, bearing the name of Archias, are preserved in the Greek Anthology; but it is doubtful whether they were actually written by him. The oration of Cicero is the only source of information respecting him.

See WALLENIUS, "Dissertatio de Aulo Licinio Archia," 1806; SCHOELL, "Histoire de la Littérature Grecque;" JACOBS, "Anthologia Græca."

Ar-chĭ-dā'mus ['Αρχίδαμος] **I.,** King of Sparta, reigned probably about 600 B.C. He was one of the Proclid (or Euŕypontid) line.

Archidamus II., King of Sparta, was a grandson of Leotychides, and began to reign about 470 B.C. In the Peloponnesian war he commanded an army which invaded Attica in 431 B.C. ; but he could not provoke the Athenians to risk a battle. He again invaded Attica in 428, and died in 427 B.C.

Archidamus III., King of Sparta, was a son of the great Agesilaus. In 367 B.C. he defeated the Argives and Arcadians in a battle which was called "the tearless," because it was won without the loss of a man on the Spartan side. He resisted with success the attack of Epaminondas at Sparta in 362, and ascended the throne in 361 B.C. Having passed over to Italy to aid the Tarentines, he was killed in battle in 338 B.C. He was succeeded by his son, Agis III.

Archidamus IV., King of Sparta, was a son of Eudamidas. He was defeated near Mantinea by Demetrius Poliorcetes in 296 B.C.

Archidamus V., the last king of Sparta of the Proclid line, was a brother and successor of Agis IV., who died 240 B.C. According to Polybius, he was put to death by Cleomenes not long after that date.

Archidamus, a Greek physician mentioned by Galen, lived probably about 400 B.C.

Ar-chĭ-de'mus, a Stoic philosopher of Tarsus, in Cilicia, lived about 160 B.C. He was author of a Greek work "On the Elementary Principles of Matter."

Ar-chĭǵ'e-nēs, [Gr. 'Αρχιγένης; Fr. ARCHIGÈNE, äR'-she'zhǎn',] a celebrated Greek physician, born at Apamea, Syria. He practised in Rome with great success in the reigns of Domitian, Nerva, and Trajan, (81–117 A.D.,) and wrote numerous works, of which some fragments have been preserved by Galen, Oribasius, and others.

Ar-chĭl'o-ehus, [Gr. 'Αρχίλοχος ; Fr. ARCHILOQUE, äR'she'lok',] a celebrated Greek lyric poet and satirist, born in the island of Paros, flourished about 680 or 700 B.C. He emigrated to Thasos in the prime of life, and joined the Thasian army, but fled from the first battle, and threw away his shield. He wrote odes, elegies, and satires, and is regarded as the inventor of the Iambic verse, or the first Greek who composed Iambic verses according to fixed rules.

"Archilochum proprio rabies armavit Iambo."*
HORACE, "Art of Poetry."

The invention of the Epodic, Trochaic Tetrameter, and other forms of metre is also ascribed to him. Some fragments of his works are extant. According to Quintilian, he was a very vigorous, nervous, versatile, and elegant

* "Rage armed Archilochus with his own Iambics," (*i.e.* Iambics of his own invention.) This line has allusion to a generally received but doubtful story, that Lycam'bes, having promised his daughter Neobu'le to Archilochus, afterwards broke his word and gave her in marriage to a more wealthy suitor. This exasperated the poet, who wrote against the father and daughter an invective so scathing that they hung themselves in despair.

writer. *Summa in eo vis ; elegantes, vibrantesque sententiæ ; plurimum sanguinis et nervorum.* He was especially distinguished by the severity of his sarcasm. Some ancient critics placed him above all other poets except Homer. There is a tradition that he was killed in a battle between the Parians and the Naxians.

See MÜLLER, "Literature of Ancient Greece;" BENTLEY, "Phalaris;" FABRICIUS, "Bibliotheca Græca;" BODE, "Geschichte der lyrischen Dichtkunst;" HUSCHKE, "Dissertatio de Fabulis Archilochi," 1803.

Archiloque. See ARCHILOCHUS.
Archimede. See ARCHIMEDES.

Ar-chĭ-me'dēs, [Gr. 'Αρχιμήδης; It. ARCHIMEDE, ar-ke-mā'dà ; Fr. ARCHIMÈDE, äR'she'mảd',] the greatest geometer of antiquity, was born in the state of Syracuse, Sicily, about 287 B.C., and was of Greek extraction. He is supposed to have been a pupil of Conon of Egypt, and a relative of Hieron II., King of Syracuse. He enjoyed the favour and patronage of Hieron and of his son Gelon. Among the few recorded incidents of his life is the following. He was consulted by the king in regard to a gold crown which the latter suspected to be alloyed with silver by a fraudulent artificer. While he was pondering the mode of detecting this fraud, he immersed himself in a full bathing-tub, and, with the thought that the water which overflowed must be equal in bulk to his body, he discovered the mode of ascertaining the bulk of the crown compared with an equally heavy mass of pure gold. He was so transported with joy that he ran home undressed, exclaiming, *Eurēka,* (or, rather, *Heurēka,*) " I have found it !"

Archimedes was profoundly versed in mechanics and hydrostatics, in which he made many discoveries, and was the inventor of several powerful machines. Nearly eighteen hundred years elapsed after his discoveries before any progress was made in theoretical mechanics. It was he who uttered that famous saying, Δὸς ποῦ στῶ καὶ τὸν κόσμον κινήσω, "Give me where I may stand, and I will move the world," (or "universe.") The long resistance of Syracuse to the Romans under Marcellus is ascribed to the warlike engines invented by Archimedes. The story that he burned the Roman ships by means of mirrors is discredited, as it is not confirmed by Polybius, Livy, or Plutarch. He was killed at the capture of Syracuse, 212 B.C. Of this event Plutarch gives several versions, one of which is as follows : A Roman soldier entered his room and ordered him to follow him to Marcellus, but the geometer refused to do so until he had finished his problem, and the soldier, in a passion, drew his sword and killed him. (See article "Marcellus," in Plutarch's "Lives.") He left a number of works, eight of which are extant, viz. : "On the Sphere and Cylinder," (the proportions of which he discovered ;) "The Measurement of the Circle," (in which he proves that the circumference is to the diameter nearly as 3.1428 to 1 ;) "On the Equilibrium and Centre of Gravity of Planes ;" "On Conoids and Spheroids ;" "On Spirals ;" "The Quadrature of the Parabola ;" "The Arenarius," (Ψαμμίτης;) and "On Floating Bodies."

"That his [Archimedes'] intellect was of the very highest order," says Professor Donkin, of Oxford, "is unquestionable. He possessed in a degree never exceeded, unless by Newton, the inventive genius which discovers new provinces of inquiry and finds new points of view for old and familiar objects ; the clearness of conception which is essential to the resolution of complex phenomena into their constituent elements ; and the power and habit of intense and persevering thought, without which other intellectual gifts are comparatively fruitless." (See article "Archimedes," in Smith's "Greek and Roman Biography and Mythology.")

When Cicero was quæstor in Sicily, he found overgrown with briers, the tomb of Archimedes, marked by the figure of a sphere inscribed in a cylinder, in commemoration of his discovery.

See G. LIBRI, "Histoire des Mathématiques en Italie;" MAZZUCHELLI, "Notizie istoriche e critichi intorno alla Vita ed Invenzioni di Archimede," 1737; HENNERT, "Dissertation sur la Vie d'Archimède," 1766; J. A. SCHMIDT, "Dissertatio de Archimede," 1683; DOMENICO SCINÀ, "Discorso intorno ad Archimede," 1823; "Quarterly Review," vol. iii.

Ar-chĭ-me'lus, ['Αρχίμηλος,] a Greek poet, flourished

ā, ē, ī, ō, ū, ȳ, *long;* à, ĕ, ŏ, same, less prolonged; ă, ĕ, ĭ, ŏ, ŭ, ў, *short;* a, ȩ, į, ǫ, *obscure;* fär, fàll, fàt; mêt; nŏt; gōōd; mōōn;

about 225 B.C. One of his epigrams is preserved by Athenæus.

Archinto, aR-kĕn'to, (ALESSANDRO,) a theologian, who received from Charles V. the title of count. Died at Milan in 1567.

Archinto, (ALESSANDRO,) a Jesuit and writer, born at Milan in 1577; died in 1645.

Archinto, (CARLO,) COUNT, a learned Italian nobleman, born at Milan in 1669. He founded an academy of cavalieri, (knights,) (1702,) and an association called Società Palatina, by which Muratori's great work was printed. He wrote, besides other works, "Tables of Sciences and Arts." Died in 1732.

Archinto, (CARLO ANTONIO,) an Italian ecclesiastic and writer, lived in the first half of the seventeenth century.

Archinto, (FILIPPO,) Archbishop of Milan, an Italian theologian, born in 1500; died in 1558.

Archinto, (FILIPPO,) COUNT, an Italian jurist, born at Milan in 1649. He held several high offices. Died about 1720.

Archinto, (GIROLAMO,) born at Milan about 1671, became Archbishop of Tarsus. Died in 1721.

Archinto, (GIUSEPPE,) an Italian prelate, born in 1651. He became Archbishop of Milan and a cardinal in 1699. Died in 1712.

Archinto, (OTTAVIO,) COUNT, an Italian antiquary, born at Milan. He wrote several treatises on the antiquities of the Milanese. Died in 1656.

Ar-chi'nus, ['Αρχῖνος,] an Athenian, who with Thrasybu'lus expelled the thirty tyrants in 403 B.C. and restored the democracy. According to Demosthenes, he acted the principal part in this revolution, and distinguished himself as a statesman on other occasions.

Ar-chip'pus, an Athenian comic poet, of whom little is known. He gained a victory with one of his comedies in 416 B.C. His most celebrated play was entitled "The Fishes." Only small fragments of his works remain.

See Vossius, " De Poetis Græcis."

Archon, ăr'shŏn', (LOUIS,) a French ecclesiastical writer, born at Riom in 1645; died in 1717.

Ar-chy'tas, [Gr. Ἀρχύτας,] an eminent Greek philosopher, mathematician, and general, born at Tarentum, lived about 350 B.C. He belonged to the Pythagorean sect, and is said to have saved the life of Plato from the anger of Dionysius the Tyrant. He commanded the army of Tarentum for seven years, and perished in a shipwreck on the coast of Apulia, leaving a high reputation for public and private virtue. Archytas passes for one of the first who applied geometry to mechanics and framed powerful machines on mathematical principles. He left a number of works, which have not come down to us. Fragments of a treatise " On Wisdom," ascribed to him, are extant. Horace calls him

"——maris et terræ, numeroque carentis arenæ,
Mensorem,"*

in an ode "Ad Archytam," Carm. i. 28.

See G. LIBRI, " Histoire des Mathématiques en Italie ;" G. NAVARRA, " Tentamen de Archytæ Tarentini Vita," 1820; O. F. GRUPPE, " Ueber die Fragmente des Archytas, etc.," 1840.

Archytas, a Greek epigrammatic poet, mentioned by Diogenes Laertius.

Archytas of Mitylene, a writer on music, mentioned by Diogenes Laertius.

Arcimboldi, aR-chĕm-bol'dee, (ANTONELLO,) an Italian Hellenist and priest, was a son of Giovanni Angelo, noticed below. He translated some works of the Greek Fathers into Latin. Died in 1578.

Arcimboldi, (GIOVANNI,) an Italian cardinal and writer, became Archbishop of Milan in 1484. Died in 1491.

Arcimboldi, (GIOVANNI ANGELO,) Archbishop of Milan, born in 1485, published a " Catalogue of Heretics," (1554.) Died in 1555.

Arcimboldi, (GIUSEPPE,) an Italian painter, born at Milan in 1533, excelled in portraits. He worked for the emperor Ferdinand I., and his successor, at Prague. Died in 1593.

* "The measurer of the sea and land, and of the innumerable sands."

Arcimboldi, (GUIDO ANTONIO,) brother of Giovanni the cardinal, became Archbishop of Milan in 1488. Died in 1497.

Arcimboldi, (OTTAVIO,) a learned prelate, born at Milan in 1471, was versed in Hebrew, Greek, and Latin. Died about 1503.

Arcis, ăr'se', (MARC,) a French sculptor, born at Toulouse, became a member of the Royal Academy in 1684. Died about 1740.

Arciszewski, aRt-se-shĕv'ske, (CHRISTOPHER,) a Polish noble and general, born towards the close of the sixteenth century. He entered the Dutch service about 1630, and fought with distinction in Brazil against the Spaniards and Portuguese. He became second in command under Maurice of Nassau, in Brazil, in 1637. Some authorities state that he was Governor of Brazil. Died at Lissa in 1656, (or, as some writers state, in 1668.)

Arckenholtz or **Arkenholz**, aR'ken-holts', (JOHANN,) a Swedish historical writer, born in Finland in 1695. He published, in French, " Memoirs of Christina, Queen of Sweden," (4 vols., 1750–60,) valuable as a collection of materials, but not well written, and assisted Mauvillon in a " History of Gustavus Adolphus," (1764.) Died in 1777.

See PORTHAN, "Åminnelse-Tal öfver J. Arckenholtz," 1781.

Arco, aR'ko, (FILIPPO,) an Italian general in the Imperial army, was beheaded for treason in 1704.

Arco, d', daR'ko, (GIAMBATTISTA GHERARDO,) an Italian political economist, born at Arco in 1739. He became a resident of Mantua, and wrote a number of works, among which are " The Influence of Commerce on Talents and Customs," (" Costumi,") and " On the Political and Economical Relations between the City and the Country belonging to it," (" Dell' Armonia politico-economica trà la Città e il suo Territorio," (1771.) He was appointed governor of the duchy of Mantua by the emperor Joseph II. Died in 1791.

Arco, d', (NICCOLÒ,) COUNT, a good Latin poet, born at Arco, in the Tyrol, in 1479. He was learned in ancient and modern languages, and was intimate with Annibal Caro, Fracastor, and Paolo Giovio. A volume of his poems was published in 1546. His " Dirge for the Death of his Mother," (" Nænia de Morte Matris,") which resembles Cowper's " Lines on his Mother's Picture," is greatly admired. Died in 1546.

Arco, del, dĕl aR'ko, (ALONSO,) a Spanish painter, who was a deaf-mute, called EL SORDILLO DEL PEREDA, ĕl soR-dĕl'yo dĕl pȧ-rā'Dȧ, (" The Little Deaf Man of Pereda,") was born at Madrid in 1625. He studied under Pereda, was a good colorist, and excelled in portraits. His master-piece, in the opinion of some, is the " Baptism of John the Baptist." Died in 1700.

Arcoleo, aR-ko-lā'o, (ANTONIO,) an Italian dramatic poet, born in the island of Candia, lived in the seventeenth century.

Arçon, d', dȧr'sòn', (JEAN CLAUDE ÉLÉONORE le Michaud—lĕh me'shŏ',) a French military engineer, born at Pontarlier in 1733, distinguished himself in the Seven Years' war. He was the inventor of floating batteries, which attracted much attention in 1782, although they proved unsuccessful in the siege of Gibraltar. These vessels, the decks of which were covered with a shell-proof blindage forming two inclined planes, presented to the guns of the fort a thick layer *(cuirasse)* of green wood, partly defended by an armour of cables. He wrote, besides other works, " Political and Military Considerations on Fortifications," (1795.) He was a member of the Institute and of the Senate. Died in 1800.

See DRINKWATER, " Account of the Siege of Gibraltar ;" GIROD-CHANTRANS, " Notice sur la Vie du Général d'Arçon," (1801.)

Ar-co-na'tus, (JEROME,) a German poet, born in Silesia in 1553; died in 1599.

Arconi, d', dȧr'ko'ne', (CÉSAR,) a French writer on physical science and theology, was born at Viviers ; died in 1681.

Arconville, d', dȧr'kòn'vèl', (MARIE,) a learned French authoress, born in 1720. She published many works, among which were romances, poems, biographies, and a " History of Francis II. of France," (2 vols., 1783.) Died in 1805.

€ as k; ç as s; ğ hard; ġ as j; G, H, K, guttural; N, nasal; R, trilled; ŝ as z; ŧh as in this. (☞See Explanations, p. 23.)

Arcos, aR'kòs, (Don RODRIGO **Ponz de Leon**—pônth dà là-òn',) DUKE OF, a Spaniard who was appointed Viceroy of Naples in 1646. His exactions provoked a formidable insurrection in 1647, (see MASANI-ELLO,) and he was obliged to make concessions to the people. Don Juan of Austria in the mean time was sent with a fleet to enforce the royal authority, and the fight was renewed between his troops and the Neapolitans, who proclaimed a republic. The Duke of Arcos was removed from office about the end of 1647, and returned to Spain in disgrace.

See LEO and BOTTA, "Histoire d'Italie."

Arc-tī'nus ['Αρκτῖνος] of Miletus, an ancient Greek epic poet, is supposed to have lived before 700 B.C. Little or nothing is known of his life. His works, among which was a poem called "Æthiopis," are all lost.

Arcudi, aR-koo'dee, (ALESSANDRO TOMMASO,) an Italian satirical writer, born at Galatina, in Naples, in 1655, wrote "The Anatomy of Hypocrites," (1699.) Died in 1718.

Ar-cu'dĭ-us or **Arcudio,** aR-koo'de-o, (PETER,) a Roman Catholic priest, born at Corfu about 1570. He was sent by the pope to Poland and Muscovy, where he laboured as a missionary about twenty years. He wrote in Greek "On the Harmony of the Western and Eastern Churches in the Use of the Seven Sacraments," (2d edition, 1619.) Died about 1635.

Ar-cul'phus, written also **Arculf** and **Arculfe,** a French or Gallic priest who visited and explored the Holy Land about 650 A.D. An account of his travels was written by Adomnan.

Arcussia, d', dàR'kü'se-à', (CHARLES,) a French gentleman, born in Provence about 1548, was known as the author of a work on Falconry, (1598,) which had great success. Died in 1617.

Arcy, d'. See D'ARCY, (PATRICK.)

Ar-da-bu'rĭ-us, [Gr. 'Αρδαβούριος,] a general of the Eastern Empire, the father of Aspar, commanded an Imperial army which invaded Persia in 422 A.D. and besieged Nisibis without success.

Ardasheer. See ARDSHEER.

Ardell, (JAMES MAC.) See MACARDELL.

Ardemans, aR-dà-màns', (TEODORO,) a Spanish architect and painter, born at Madrid in 1664. He was appointed cabinet-painter to the king about 1704. He designed the principal part of the palace and collegiate church of San Ildefonso. Died in 1726.

Ar'den, (EDWARD,) an English gentleman and Roman Catholic, a third-cousin to Mary Arden the mother of Shakspeare, was born in 1531. In 1583 Arden was executed on a charge of treason, with his son-in-law Somerville. Many persons believed that Arden was innocent, and that he was the victim of the enmity of the Earl of Leicester, with whom he had quarrelled. He left a son Robert, who was a lawyer.

Arden, (JOHN.) See ARDERN.

Arden, (RICHARD PEPPER,) LORD ALVANLEY, an English lawyer and judge, born at Bredbury, near Stockport, in 1745. He became a personal and political friend of William Pitt, and was appointed solicitor-general in 1782. Having resigned when Fox and Lord North came into power in 1783, he was reappointed to that office about the end of the same year by Pitt. He was attorney-general from 1784 to 1788, and was made master of the rolls in the latter year. In 1801 he succeeded Lord Eldon as lord chief-justice of the court of common pleas, and was created a peer, by the title of Baron Alvanley. Died in 1804.

See Foss, "The Judges of England," vol. viii.

Ardène, àR'dàn', (ESPRIT JEAN DE ROME, ês'pRe' zhôn deh rom,) a French poet, born at Marseilles in 1684. He published a collection of Fables in verse, (1747,) and wrote odes, epigrams, and other verses, (4 vols., 1767.) Died in 1748.

Ardène, (JEAN PAUL DE ROME,) a brother of the preceding, born at Marseilles in 1689, was a priest and horticulturist. He published treatises on "Tulips," (1760,) "Carnations," (1767,) and other plants; also a work on gardening and rural economy, called the "Rural Year,"

("Année champêtre," 3 vols., 1769,) which was considered one of the best on those subjects. Died in 1769.

Ardenne, d', dàR'dèn', [Lat. ARDUEN'NA,] (REMACLE, rĕh-màkl',) a Latin poet, born near Maubeuge about 1480. He was secretary of Margaret of Burgundy. He wrote, besides other mediocre poems, "Palamedes," a drama, (1512.)

Ardente, aR-dèn'tà, (ALESSANDRO,) an Italian painter, born at Faenza, worked mostly at Turin. He painted portraits and history with success. Among his works are a "Conversion of Saint Paul" and a "Baptism of Christ." Died in 1595.

See LANZI, "History of Painting in Italy."

Ar'dern, (JOHN,) or **Johannes de Arderne,** an eminent English surgeon, who practised at Newark from 1349 to 1370, when he removed to London. He made some important improvements in surgery, and wrote several works, one of which is a "Treatise on Fistula," (1588.)

Ar'derne, (JAMES,) an English clergyman, founded a library at Chester. Died in 1691.

Ardeschir. See ARDSHEER.

Ardha-Nari. See SIVA.

Ar'dĭ-çēs of Corinth, an ancient Greek painter, who, according to Pliny, painted monochromatic pictures.

Ardingelli, aR-dèn-jel'lee, (NICCOLÒ,) an Italian cardinal, whom Pope Paul III. sent to France to negotiate a peace between Francis I. and Charles V. Died in 1547, aged about forty-five.

Ardizzon, aR-dèt-sòn', or **Ardizzoni,** aR-dèt-so'nee, (ANTONIO,) an Italian writer, died at Naples in 1699.

Ardoin. See ARDUIN.

Ardoina, aR-do-ee'nà, (ANNA MARIA,) an Italian poetess, born in 1672, was a daughter of the Prince of Palizzo. Died in 1700.

Ardsheer (Ardshir or **Ardeschir) Bâbegan,** ard-sheer' bà'bĕh-gàn', a famous king of Persia, the founder of the dynasty of Sassanides, was a man of humble origin. He rebelled against King Artabanus or Arda-van, who was defeated and killed in battle. After he had extended the limits of Persia by conquests, he reigned many years in peace, and had a wide reputation for virtue and wisdom. His maxims are still preserved by the Persians. He died probably about 260 A.D., and left the throne to his son, Shapûr or Sapor. He was called Artaxerxes by the Greeks.

See MALCOLM, "History of Persia;" GIBBON, "Decline and Fall of the Roman Empire."

Ardshir (or Ardsheer) Darazdast. See ARTAX-ERXES LONGIMANUS.

Arduenna. See ARDENNE.

Arduin, ard'win, **Ardoin,** or **Ardoino,** aR-do-ee'no, sometimes written **Ardouin** and **Ardwig,** King of Italy, was chosen by several Italian nobles as successor to Otho III. in 1002. War ensued between him and Henry, Emperor of Germany, who became master of Milan and other cities of Lombardy. Died in 1015.

See PROVANA, "Studj critichi sovra la Storia d'Italia a' tempi del Rè Ardoino," 1849; MURATORI, "Annali d'Italia."

Arduini, aR-doo-ee'nee, or **Arduino,** aR-doo-ee'no, (LUIGI,) an Italian agriculturist, born at Padua about 1750. He became professor, at Padua, of rural economy, and wrote several works on that science. Died in 1833.

Arduini, (PIETRO,) an Italian botanist, the father of the preceding, was born at Verona. He published in 1766 a work on the culture and use of plants employed in domestic and rural economy.

Arduino, aR-doo-ee'no, (MAESTRO,) a Venetian sculptor and architect of the fifteenth century.

Ar'dÿs, [Gr. 'Αρδυς,] King of Lydia, succeeded his father Gyges about 680 B.C., and reigned about forty-nine years.

Aregio, à-rā'He-o, (PABLO,) a skilful Spanish painter, born in the fifteenth century. He painted subjects from the life of the Virgin, in the cathedral of Valencia, about 1506.

Areius, (the heresiarch.) See ARIUS.

A-reï'us, [Gr. 'Αρειος,] a Stoic philosopher of Alexandria, was a friend and preceptor of Augustus Cæsar.

Arellano, de, dà à-rĕl-yà'no, (GIL RAMIREZ,) a Spanish antiquary of the first part of the seventeenth century. He wrote "Vindication of the Ancient Grandeur of the Counts of Aguilar," (" Memorial en justificacion de la Grandeza antigua de los Condes de Aguilar,") which is a model in its kind.

Arellano, de, (JUAN,) the best Spanish flower-painter of his time, was born in 1614. Died at Madrid in 1676.

A-rel′li-us, a Roman painter, who lived in the first century B.C. The senate ordered his pictures to be removed from the temples because he took courtesans as his models.

Aremberg, ȧ′rĕm-bĕRG,(AUGUSTE MARIE RAYMOND,) PRINCE OF, a son of Karl Leopold, noticed below, was born at Brussels in 1753. He was elected to the French States-General in 1789, and favoured the doctrines of the Revolution. About 1792 he emigrated to Austria, in the army of which he attained the rank of major-general. He was a friend of Mirabeau. Died in 1833.

Aremberg, (JOHN OF LIGNE,) COUNT, a general of Philip II. of Spain, was probably born in Flanders. He was appointed governor of Friesland and Overyssel by Philip II., and took sides against the Prince of Orange about 1563. In 1567 he commanded a small army sent by Alva against the French Huguenots. He was defeated and killed in a battle at Groningen in May, 1568.

See MOTLEY, "Rise of the Dutch Republic," vol. ii. chap. ii.

Aremberg, (LEOPOLD PHILIPP KARL JOSEPH VON LIGNE,) DUKE OF, a general born at Mons in 1690, was the father of Karl Leopold, noticed below. He fought for Austria at Malplaquet in 1709, and as major-general contributed to Prince Eugene's victory at Belgrade in 1717. In 1737 he obtained the rank of field-marshal, and the chief command of the army in Flanders. He commanded an army of Maria Theresa in the war which began in 1741. Died in 1754.

Aremberg, von, fon ȧ′rĕm-bĕRG, (KARL LEOPOLD,) a field-marshal in the Austrian service, son and successor of the preceding, distinguished himself in the Seven Years' war. He led the right wing of the Austrians at Hochkirchen in 1758, and was defeated by Wünsch in 1759.

Arena, ȧ-rā′nȧ, (BARTOLOMMEO,) a politician, born in Corsica about 1760. He was elected to the French Legislative Assembly in 1792, and was a partisan of the Revolution and an enemy of Paoli. As a member of the Council of Five Hundred, he opposed Bonaparte in the contest of the 18th Brumaire, 1799, after which he lived in exile. Died at Leghorn about 1830.

Arena, (GIUSEPPE,) a conspirator, born in Corsica, was a brother of the preceding. He served as adjutant-general at the siege of Toulon in 1793, and was elected to the Council of Five Hundred in 1796. In October or November, 1801, he was arrested at the Opera as an accomplice of Ceracchi and others in a conspiracy to kill Napoleon, and was executed in 1802.

Arena, (GIUSEPPE,) an Italian musician and composer, flourished between 1725 and 1750.

Arena, ȧ-rā′nȧ, or **Harena,** (JACOBUS,) a Belgian or Italian jurist, born in the thirteenth century, is said to have taught civil law at Padua in 1300. He wrote several legal works, which were printed in the sixteenth century.

Arena, d', dȧ′rȧ′nȧ′, (ANTOINE,) the Latinized name of LA SABLE, (lȧ sȧbl,) a French jurist and macaronic poet, born at Souliers, near Toulon. Died in 1544.

Arenales, ȧ-rȧ-nȧ′lĕs, (JOSÉ,) a South American geographer, was a lieutenant-colonel in the army of Buenos Ayres in 1833.

Arend, ȧ′rĕnt, or **Arents,** ȧ′rĕnts, (BALTHASAR,) a son of Caius, noticed below, born in Holstein about 1640, was a minister, and published several works, chiefly sermons. Died in 1687.

Arend or **Arents,** (CAIUS or KAY,) a German orthodox divine, born in Holstein in 1614. He was minister at Glückstadt from 1661 to 1678, and afterwards at Meldorf. He published several sermons. Died in 1691.

Arends, ȧ′rĕnts, (JAN,) a Dutch painter, born at Dort in 1738. He painted marine pieces and other subjects, at his native place and Middelburg, with success. Died in 1805.

Arends, written also **Arents,** (THOMAS,) a Dutch merchant and poet, born at Amsterdam in 1652. He composed fugitive poems and dramas. Died in 1700.

Arendt, ȧ′rĕnt, (MARTIN FREDERIK,) a Danish antiquary, born at Altona in 1769. He traversed many countries of Europe on foot in order to investigate antiquities, copy runic inscriptions, etc., having no resources but the bounty of strangers. He wrote several short antiquarian treatises. Died near Venice in 1824.

Arensbeck, ȧ′rĕns-bĕk′, (PETER DIETRICH,) a Swedish linguist, was minister of a church at Stockholm, and teacher of Oriental languages. Died in 1673.

Arents. See AREND.

Ar′e-sas, [᾽Αρέσας,] a Greek Pythagorean philosopher, lived in Italy, and succeeded Tydas as head of the school.

Aresi, ȧ-rā′see, (PAOLO,) an Italian ecclesiastic, eminent as a preacher and writer, was born at Cremona in 1574. He became Bishop of Tortona in 1620. His principal work is "Sacred Emblems," etc., (" Imprese sacre con triplicati Discorsi illustrate," 1613.) He afterwards enlarged it to seven volumes, (1621–35.) Died in 1644.

Areson, ȧ′rĕh-son, (JON,) a bishop and poet of Iceland, born in 1484. He became Bishop of Iceland in 1522, and resisted the efforts of the King of Denmark to establish the Protestant religion in that island. Having taken up arms against the king, he was defeated and put to death in 1550.

Aresti, ȧ-rĕs′tee, (FLORIANO,) an Italian composer of operas, born at Bologna, lived about 1700.

Aretæus, ȧr-e-tee′us, [Gr. ᾽Αρεταῖος; Fr. ARÉTÉE, ȧ′rȧ′tȧ′,] an eminent Greek medical writer, born probably in Cappadocia, is supposed to have lived in the first or second century of the Christian era. Nothing is known of his life. He wrote a work in eight books on the Causes, Symptoms, and Cure of Acute and Chronic Affections, which is still extant, and is highly prized for its matter and the elegance of its style. His work has often been printed in Greek and Latin since 1552.

See SPRENGEL, "Histoire de la Médecine;" SURINGAR, "Dissertatio de Aretæo medico," 1837.

Ar′e-tas, [Gr. ᾽Αρέτας,] the name of several kings of Arabia, who reigned between 170 and 40 B.C. One of these defeated Antiochus XII. about 90 B.C., and afterwards gained a victory over Alexander Jannæus.

One king of this name was the father-in-law of Herod Antipas. He appears to have been the Aretas who reigned in Damascus when the Apostle Paul escaped from that city. (See II. Corinthians xi. 32.) He waged war against Herod Antipas, who, having been defeated, applied for aid to the emperor Tiberius. The latter ordered Vitellius to march against Aretas ; but the death of Tiberius, in 37 A.D., prevented the execution of this design.

A-re′te, [Gr. ᾽Αρήτη,] a daughter of the celebrated Aristippus, was versed in philosophy, which she learned of her father. She had a son, Aristippus, who was surnamed Μητροδίδακτος, (*i.e.* "Mother-taught.")

Arétée. See ARETÆUS.

Ar-e-thu′sa, [Gr. ᾽Αρέθουσα; Fr. ARÉTHUSE, ȧ′rȧ′tüz′,] a Nereid and an attendant of Diana, was, according to a poetical legend, beloved and pursued by Alpheus, and was changed into a fountain in Ortygia, near Syracuse. (See ALPHEUS.) She was invoked by Virgil as a source of poetical inspiration, (Eclogue x. 1.)

Aretin or **Aretino,** (BERNARDO.) See ACCOLTI.

Aretin, von, fon ȧ′rĕh-teen′, (JOHANN ADAM CHRISTOPH JOSEPH,) BARON, a Bavarian diplomatist, born at Ingolstadt in 1769. He represented Bavaria in the Germanic Diet at Frankfort from 1817 until his death, and published, besides a few other works, a " Manual of the Philosophy of Life," (1793.) Died in 1822.

Aretin, von, (JOHANN CHRISTOPH ANTON MARIA,) BARON, a brother of the preceding, was born at Ingolstadt in 1772 or 1773. He became aulic counsellor at Munich in 1793, and vice-president of the Munich Academy of Sciences in 1804. He published many and various works, among which are a "History of the Jews in Bavaria," (1803,) and an "Introduction to Mnemonics," (1810.) Died in 1824.

Aretin, von, (JOHANN GEORG,) BARON, a German writer on rural economy, born in 1771, was a brother of the preceding.

Aretin, von, (KARL MARIA,) BARON, a German historian, born at Munich in 1796, was a son of Johann Christoph Anton Maria, noticed above. He was appointed keeper of the archives of Bavaria, and privy counsellor. Among his works is a "History of the Elector Maximilian I.," (1842.)

Aretino, â-râ-tee'no, [Lat. ARETI'NUS; Fr. ARÉTIN, ä'râ'tăn',] (ANGELO,) an Italian jurisconsult of the fifteenth century, born at Arezzo. His family name was GAMBIGLIONI. He was professor of law at Ferrara and Bologna, and wrote a "Treatise on Misdemeanours and Crimes," ("Tractatus de Maleficiis," 1472,) and other works, which were highly esteemed. He died after 1450.

Aretino, (CARLO.) See MARSUPPINI, (CARLO.)

Aretino, (FRANCESCO.) See ACCOLTI.

Aretino, (LEONARDO.) See BRUNI.

Aretino, [Lat. ARETI'NUS; Fr. ARÉTIN,] (PIETRO,) a satirical Italian writer, surnamed THE SCOURGE OF PRINCES, was born at Arezzo in 1492. He had superior talents, but little learning. In 1527 he became a resident of Venice, and wrote a libel on Pope Clement VII., then imprisoned or besieged by the Imperialists. He associated with eminent authors and artists, and corresponded with several monarchs of Europe, among whom were Francis I. of France, and the emperor Charles V., from whom he received a pension. His conduct was extremely licentious and venal. He wrote numerous works, among which were Dialogues, Comedies, Letters, (6 vols., 1538–57,) Sonnets, and other poems. He died at Venice (where the greater part of his mature life was passed) in 1557.

See BERNI, "Vita di P. Aretino," 1537; DUJARDIN, "Vie de Pierre Arétin," 1750; MAZZUCHELLI, "Vita di Pietro Aretino," 1763; DUBOIS-FONTANELLE, "Vie de Pierre Arétin," 1768.

Aretino, (SPINELLO,) an eminent Italian painter, born at Arezzo about 1315. He adorned the chapel of Santa Maria Maggiore, and other churches of Florence, with frescos. Those of San Miniato, in the same city, are still preserved. The "History of Pope Alexander III.," in the town-hall of Sienna, is called his principal work. In the opinion of Vasari, he was a better painter than Giotto. Died about 1400.

See VASARI, "Lives of the Painters."

Aretius, a-ree'she-us, [Ger. pron. â-rět'se-ùs,] (BENEDICT,) a Swiss Calvinist theologian and botanist, born at Berne. He became professor of languages and theology at that city about 1563. He published, besides other works, "Theological Problems," ("Problemata Theologica," 1574, often reprinted,) and a "Description of the Mountains Stockhorn and Niesen, and the Plants growing on the Same," (1561.) He was a friend of Conrad Gesner. Died in 1574.

Aretius, (CLAUDIUS MARIUS.) See AREZZO.

Aretusi, â-râ-too'see, (CESARE,) also called CESARE Modenese, (mo-dâ-nā'sà,) a skilful portrait-painter, born at Módena (or, as some say, at Bologna) about the middle of the sixteenth century. He imitated with success the style of various masters. His copy of Correggio's "Notte ' is highly commended. Died at Parma about 1610.

Areus, ā'rūs or ā're-us, [Gr. Ἀρεύς,] **I.,** King of Sparta, succeeded his grandfather Cleomenes II. in 309 B.C. He repulsed Pyrrhus, King of Epirus, who attacked Sparta in 272 B.C. He was slain at Corinth in 265, in a battle against the Macedonians, and was succeeded by his son Acrotatus.

Areus II. of Sparta, a son of Acrotatus, died while still a child, about 256 B.C.

Arevalo. See CANO DE AREVALO.

Arezzo, â-rět'so, (CLAUDIO MARIO,) [Lat. ARE'TIUS, CLAU'DIUS MA'RIUS,] a learned Italian, who was a native of Syracuse and lived about 1550. He was imperial historian to Charles V., whose armies he followed in Italy and Germany. He wrote, besides other works, "Chorographia sive de Situ Siciliæ Libellus," (1537,) a description of Sicily.

Arezzo, (TOMMASO,) an Italian cardinal, born in Tuscany in 1756, was a grandson of the preceding. He was sent to Saint Petersburg by the pope in 1801 to negotiate for the reunion of the Greek and Roman Churches. In 1808 he was appointed Vice-Governor of Rome, and arrested by the French. He was imprisoned in Corsica, whence he escaped in 1813, and was created a cardinal in 1816. Died in 1833.

Arezzo, (F. M.) See CASINI.

Arezzo, d', dâ-rět'so, (BETRICO, bâ-tree'ko,) an Italian poet of the fourteenth century.

Arezzo, d', (FRANCESCO,) an Italian pulpit orator and writer on theology, born in 1553; died in 1616.

Arezzo, d', (GUITTONE, gwět-to'nà,) a poet who is called one of the founders of Italian poetry, and of whose life little is known. He wrote thirty-eight sonnets, several canzoni, and a number of letters in prose. His sonnets are remarkable for regularity in rhythm and rhyme. Petrarch ranked him with Dante and Cino da Pistoja. Died in 1294.

See GINGUENÉ, "Histoire Littéraire d'Italie."

Arezzo, d', (GUY.) See GUY.

Arezzo, d', (SCIPIONE Burali-boo-râ'lee,) an Italian cardinal, born near Gaeta in 1511. He employed his great influence with success against the introduction of the Inquisition into Italy. Died about 1577.

Arfe, de, dâ AR'fâ, written also **Arphe** or **Darphe,** (HENRIQUE,) a silversmith, born in Germany in the latter part of the fifteenth century, removed to Spain. He made silver tabernacles, designed with great taste, for the cathedrals of Leon, Córdova, and Toledo. His son Antonio was also a skilful artist and worker in silver.

Arfe, de, (JOSÉ,) a Spanish sculptor, born at Seville in 1603, made statues of silver for the cathedral of that city. Died in 1666.

Arfe y Villafane, de, dâ AR'fâ e věl-yâ-fâ'nà, (JUAN,) a son of Antonio, was born at Leon in 1535. He designed the tabernacles of Avila, (1571,) Seville, (1587,) and Osmas, which are among the most beautiful in Spain, and was employed by Philip II. to adorn the Escurial. He wrote "Assayer of Gold, Silver, and Stones," ("Quilatador de Oro, Plata y Piedras," 1572.)

See BERMUDEZ, "Diccionario Historico."

Arfian, de, dâ AR-fe-ân', (ANTONIO,) an excellent Spanish fresco-painter, a pupil of Luis de Vargas, flourished at Seville about 1550. His son Alonzo was also an able painter.

Argaiz, de, dâ AR-gïth', (GREGORIO,) a Spanish monk of the seventeenth century, wrote a History of the Spanish Church, (1667,) derived from spurious documents fabricated by himself.

Ar'gall, (Rev. JOHN,) an English scholar, born in London, graduated at Oxford about 1565. He wrote "Introduction to the Art of Logic," ("Introductio ad Artem Dialecticam," 1605.) Died in 1606.

Argall, (RICHARD,) an English poet who wrote in the reign of James I. Among his works is a poem called "The Bride's Ornaments," (1621.)

Argall, (SAMUEL,) an English adventurer, born at Bristol in 1572. He was deputy-governor of Virginia for two years, (1617–19) and was accused of many acts of tyranny and rapacity. Died in 1639.

Argand, ăr'gôn', (AIMÉ, à'mà',) a Swiss chemist, born at Geneva about the middle of the eighteenth century, is known as the inventor of the Argand lamp. The wick of this lamp is in the form of a hollow cylinder, through which a current of air passes. He made the first model of the lamp, in England, in 1782, and added a glass chimney to it. A person named Quinquet deprived him of the profit of the invention. Died in 1803.

Argelander, AR'gĕh-lân'der, (FRIEDRICH WILHELM AUGUST,) an eminent Prussian astronomer, born at Memel in 1799. He was a pupil of Bessel, and afterwards his assistant in the Observatory of Königsberg. In 1823 he became director of the Observatory of Åbo, Finland, which was removed to Helsingfors about 1832. He was appointed professor of astronomy at Bonn in 1837, and published a good celestial atlas, entitled "Uranometria Nova," (1843.) Continuing the great work of Bessel, he determined the position of 22,000 stars, which he made known in his "Observations at the Observatory of Bonn," (1846.)

For many years he has been employed in observing the variations in the luminosity and apparent magnitude of certain fixed stars. He also demonstrated the theory that the solar system has a progressive motion in absolute space.

Argellati, AR-jĕl-lâ'tee, (FILIPPO,) a learned and meritorious Italian writer, born at Bologna in 1685. He

ā, ē, ī, ō, ū, ȳ, *long;* à, ė, ò, same, less prolonged; ă, ĕ, ĭ, ŏ, ŭ, ў̌, *short;* ạ, ẹ, ị, ọ, *obscure;* fär, fâll, fàt; mêt; nŏt; gōŏd; mōōn·

assisted Muratori in the publication of his "Rerum Italicarum Scriptores," and edited or republished the works of several Italian authors. He was the author of "Library of Milanese Writers," (" Bibliotheca Scriptorum Mediolanensium," 2 vols., 1745,) and of a few other works. Died in 1755.

Argellati, (FRANCESCO,) a son of the preceding, born at Bologna in 1712. He studied law, and took his doctor's degree in 1736. In 1740 he became a royal engineer. He wrote, besides other works, "Practice at the Venetian Bar," ("Pratica del Foro Veneto," 1737,) and a "History of the Origin of Science and Literature," (1st vol., 1743; the other volumes were never finished.) Died in 1754.

Argens, d', dăr'zhŏn', (JEAN BAPTISTE de Boyer— dẹh bwā'yà',) MARQUIS, a French littérateur, born at Aix, in Provence, in 1704. He served in the army until a fall from his horse, after the siege of Philipsburg, disabled him. Having written his famous "Jewish Letters" (" Lettres Juives," 6 vols., 1738-42) and "Chinese Letters," (6 vols., 1739-42,) he obtained the patronage of Frederick the Great, who appointed him chamberlain and director of belles-lettres in the Academy. D'Argens was one of the intimate associates of that king. He was also the author of "The Philosophy of Good Sense," and "Cabalistic Letters." Died at Toulon in 1771.

Argens evinced great ardour in the pursuit of every kind of knowledge. He took Bayle for his model ; but he was very far inferior to the author of the "Critical Dictionary" in wit and intellect as well as in style.

See THIEBAULT, "Mes Souvenirs de vingt Ans de Séjour à Berlin ;" QUÉRARD, " La France Littéraire."

Argensola, de, dà ar-hên-so'lä, (BARTOLOMÉ LEONARDO,) an excellent Spanish poet, born at Barbastro, in Aragon, about 1565. He was appointed a canon of Saragossa, and *coronista* or historiographer of Aragon, about 1616. He published a "History of the Conquest of the Moluccas," (1609,) and wrote a number of poems ("Rimas,") which were printed with those of his brother Lupercio. These brothers, whose genius and works were similar, were called " the Horaces of Spain." Died in 1631.

See N. ANTONIO, " Bibliotheca Hispana Nova ;" LONGFELLOW, " Poets and Poetry of Europe."

Argensola, de, (LUPERCIO (loo-pĕR'the-o) LEONARDO,) a brother of the preceding, was born at Barbastro about 1563. At an early age he became secretary to the ex-empress Maria of Austria, at Madrid, and produced three successful tragedies,—"Filis," "Isabela," and "Alejandra." In 1610 he was appointed secretary of state by the Viceroy of Naples. He died at Naples in 1613. His fame rests on his lyric poems. " An understanding at once solid and ingenious," says Bouterwek, "subject to no extravagant illusion, yet full of true poetic feeling, and an imagination more plastic than creative, impart a more perfect Horatian colouring to the odes and sonnets of Lupercio."

See TICKNOR, "History of Spanish Literature ;" LONGFELLOW, " Poets and Poetry of Europe ;" BOUTERWEK, "History of Poetry and Eloquence from the Close of the Thirteenth Century ;" SEDANO, "Parnaso Español ;" N. ANTONIO, " Bibliotheca Hispana Nova."

Argenson, d', dăr'zhŏn'sŏn', (MARC ANTOINE René de Paulmy—rẹh'nà' dẹh pŏ'me',) a son of René Louis Voyer, noticed below, was a member of the French Academy. He collected one of the richest libraries ever owned by a private person, and sold it to the Count d'Artois in 1785. It is now the "Bibliothèque de l'Arsenal." He published "Miscellanies from a Large Library," (" Mélanges tirés d'une grande Bibliothèque," 65 vols.) Died in 1787.

Argenson, d', (MARC PIERRE,) COUNT, a son of Marc René de Voyer, (1652-1721,) noticed below, was born in 1696. He was secretary of war from 1742 to 1757, and was an able administrator. The Encyclopédie of D'Alembert and Diderot was dedicated to him as a liberal patron of letters. He was a friend of Voltaire, to whom he furnished materials for his "Siècle de Louis XIV." Died in 1764.

See VOLTAIRE, "Correspondance Générale ;" C. LEBEAU, "Éloge dẹ M. le Comte d'Argenson," 1765.

Argenson, d', (MARC RENÉ,) Marquis de Voyer, a French general, born in 1722 ; died in 1782.

Argenson, d', (MARC RENÉ de Voyer—dẹh vwā'yà',) a French magistrate, born of a noble family in 1652. He became president of the council of finance and keeper of the seals in 1718. He was a member of the French Academy. Died in 1721.

See FONTENELLE, " Éloge de M. R. de Voyer d'Argenson," 1721.

Argenson, d', (MARC RENÉ DE VOYER,) a grandson of Count Marc Pierre, born in 1771. He married the widow of Prince Victor de Broglie. He was prefect of Deux-Nèthes from 1809 to 1813, and, as a member of the Chamber of Deputies during the Hundred Days, was joined with La Fayette in a deputation to the allies to obtain the exclusion of the Bourbons. After the restoration he was often elected as a deputy, and voted with the opposition. Died in 1842.

See " Notice sur la Vie de Voyer d'Argenson," Paris, 1845.

Argenson, d', (RENÉ DE VOYER,) COUNT, a diplomatist employed by Cardinal Richelieu and Mazarin ; died about 1650.

Argenson, d', (RENÉ LOUIS VOYER,) MARQUIS, a son of Marc René, (1652-1721,) noticed above, was born in 1696. He was appointed minister of foreign affairs in November, 1744, and resigned office in January, 1747. He was a friend of Voltaire, and author of "Considerations on the Government of France," (1764,) which Rousseau commended. Died in 1757.

See VOLTAIRE, "Correspondance Générale."

Argenta, aR-jĕn'tä, (JACOPO,) an Italian painter, born at Ferrara, flourished about 1560.

Argental, d', dăr'zhŏn'täl', (CHARLES AUGUSTIN Fériol—fä're'ol',) COUNT, a literary Frenchman, born in Paris in 1700, was a nephew of Madame de Tencin, the mother of D'Alembert. He corresponded with Voltaire, who treated him as a confidential friend. He wrote some short verses, and was suspected of being the author of "Anecdotes of the Court of Edward," which appeared among the works of Madame de Tencin. Died in 1788.

See VOLTAIRE, "Correspondance Générale."

Argentelle, d', dăr'zhŏn'tèl', (LOUIS MARC ANTOINE Robillard—ro'be'yäR',) a French naturalist, born at Pont-l'Évêque in 1777, was skilled in making wax models of plants, fruits, etc. Died in 1828.

Argenterio, aR-jĕn-tä're-o, [Lat. ARGENTE'RIUS ; Fr. ARGENTIER, ăR'zhŏn'te-à',] (GIOVANNI,) an Italian physician, born at or near Chieri, in Piedmont, in 1513. He was professor of medicine successively at Naples, Pisa, Rome, and Turin. He wrote many medical works, in some of which he attacked the system of Galen and displayed more learning than judgment. Died in 1572.

Argenti, aR-jĕn'tee, sometimes written **Arienti,** (AGOSTINO,) an Italian poet of Ferrara, wrote a pastoral drama, called "The Unfortunate," (" Lo Sfortunato," 1568.) Died in 1576.

Argenti, (GIOVANNI,) an Italian Jesuit and writer, born at Módena about 1564 ; died in 1629.

Argentier. See ARGENTERIO.

Argento, aR-jĕn'to, (GAETANO,) an able Italian jurist, born at Cosenza in 1662. He was appointed to a high judicial office in 1709. In 1714 the emperor Charles VI. raised him to the dignity of president of the royal council, and gave him the title of duke. He died in 1730, leaving several legal works.

Argentré, d', dăr'zhŏn'trà', (BERTRAND,) a learned French jurist, born at Vitré in 1519. He was one of the commissioners appointed for the reformation of the law of Brittany, but opposed the efforts of Dumoulin to introduce general or equal laws and diminish the power of feudal lords over their vassals. He wrote a "History of Bretagne," (1582,) a work of little merit, and several legal treatises. Died in 1590.

See M. DE KERDANET, " Vie d'Argentré," 1820.

Argentré, d', (CHARLES du Plessis — dü plǎ'se',) a French theologian, born near Vitré in 1673. He was appointed Bishop of Tulle in 1725. Among his works are " Elementa Theologica," (1702,) and "Lexicon Philosophicum," (1706.) Died in 1740.

Argenville. See DEZALLIER.

Arger, ăR'zhair' or ăR'zhà', (PIERRE,) a Flemish conspirator, who attempted to assassinate Henry IV. of France. He was detected and executed in 1589.

Arghoun or Arghun. See ARGOON.

Arghûn Khân. See ARGOON.

Argillata, de, då aR-jèl-lä'tå, or Argellata, de, då aR-jĕl-lä'tå, (PIETRO,) called also Pietro della Cerlata pe-ä'tRo dĕl-lå chĕR-lä'tå, an eminent Italian physician and anatomist, was professor of logic and medicine at Bologna. He made improvements in surgery, on which he wrote a work, "Chirurgiæ Libri Sex," (1480.) Died in 1423.

Argis, d', (BOUCHER.) See BOUCHER.

Argoli, aR-go'lee or aR'go-lee, (ANDREA,) an Italian mathematician, born in the kingdom of Naples about 1570. He was professor of mathematics at Padua, and published, besides other works, "Ephemerides," extending to 1700. Died in or after 1650.

Argoli, (GIOVANNI,) a son of the preceding, was born at Tagliacozzo about 1610. He published, in 1626, a poem called "Endymion," which was successful. He was author of several treatises on classical antiquities, among which was a series of notes on Onuphrius Panvinius "On the Games of the Circus" ("De Ludis Circensibus") and "On Triumphs," ("De Triumphis,") (1642.) Died about 1660.

Argonautæ, ar-go-nau'tee, [Gr. 'Αργοναῦται; Eng. AR'GONAUTS, (i.e. the "sailors of the Argo,")] the heroes celebrated in the old Greek traditions as the companions of Jason in a maritime expedition to Colchis, on the Euxine, for the purpose of obtaining the golden fleece. (See JASON.) They derived their name from the ship Argo, in which they made the voyage. The expedition of the Argonauts forms the subject of an epic poem by Apollonius Rhodius.

Argonne, d', dåR'gon', (NOËL, no'ĕl',) a French Carthusian monk, born in Paris about 1635. He entered a monastery at Rouen about 1668, and changed his name from Noël to Bonaventure. He published a "Treatise on the Right Method of Reading the Fathers," ("Traité de la Lecture des Pères de l'Église," 1668,) which is highly praised by Mabillon and others, and "Mélanges of History and Literature," (3 vols., 1699-1701,) under the name of Vigneul-Marville. Died in 1704.

Argoon, Argoun, or Argûn, ar'gōon', written also Arghoun or Arghûn, a son of Abâka Khan, succeeded his father as sovereign of Persia (or rather of Central and Western Asia) in 1281. Through the influence of his minister, Saad-ud-Dowlah, the Christians residing in the dominions of Argoon were protected and treated with great favour. And while the pope (Nicholas IV.) was sending deputations to express his gratitude to Argoon, the "true believers," if we may trust the statement of some of the Moslem historians, "trembled lest the sacred temple of Mecca should be converted into a cathedral." Argoon Khan died in 1291.

See MALCOLM, "History of Persia," vol. i. chap. x.; PRICE, "Mahomedan History."

Argote, de, då aR-go'tå, (JERONIMO Contador-kon-tå-dôR',) a Portuguese writer and monk, born at Collares in 1676. Among his principal works are a "History of the Archbishopric of Braga," ("Memorias para a Historia ecclesiastica de Braga," 3 vols., 1732-44,) and "Rules of the Portuguese Language, the Mirror of the Latin Language," (" Regras da Lingua Portugueza, Espelho da Lingua Latina," etc., 1721.) Died in 1749.

Argote de Molina, aR-go'tå då mo-lee'nå, (GONZALVO or GONÇALO,) a Spanish writer on history and genealogy, born at Seville in 1549. He wrote, besides other works, "Nobility of Andalusia," ("Nòbleza del Andaluzia," 1588.) Died about 1590.

Argou, åR'goo', (GABRIEL,) a French lawyer, born in the Vivarais. He gained distinction by his work called "Institutes of French Law," ("Institution au Droit français," 1692,) often reprinted. Died about 1705.

Argoun. See ARGOON.

Argout, d', dåR'goo', (ANTOINE MAURICE APOLLINAIRE,) COUNT, a French financier, born in Isère in 1782. He became auditor to the Council of State in 1810, and a peer of France in 1819. In July, 1830, he acted as mediator between Charles X. and the popular leaders, and obtained concessions from the former when it was too late. He was appointed minister of the marine in November, 1830, minister of commerce in 1831,

minister of the interior in 1833, governor of the Bank of France in 1834, and minister of finances in 1836. Before the end of that year he exchanged that office for the post of governor of the Bank, which he continued to hold under the republic of 1848. About 1852 he was appointed president of the section of finances, by Louis Napoleon. Died in 1858.

Argüelles, aR-gwêl'yês, (AUGUSTIN,) a Spanish minister of state, born in the Asturias in 1775. He was a member of the committee which formed the liberal constitution of 1812, and rendered himself popular by his talents and liberal principles. He was proscribed in 1814 and sentenced to an exile of ten years. He was minister of the interior for about one year, in 1820. In 1841 he was appointed tutor to the young queen Isabel. Died in 1844.

See LABRADOR Y ORTIZ, "Biografia de A. Argüelles," Madrid, 1844; EVARISTO SAN MIGUEL, "Vida de D. A. Arguelles," 1850.

Arguelles, (JOSÉ DE CANGA.) See CANGA.

Argues. See DESARGUES.

Arguijo, de, då aR-ḡee'ho, Arguiso, de, då aR-ḡeč'-so, or Arguizo, de, då aR-ḡee'tho, (JUAN,) a Spanish poet of high reputation, born at Seville in the latter part of the sixteenth century, was a man of fortune. He was eulogized by Lope de Vega and other poets who had enjoyed his bounty. He wrote sonnets and other short poems, the style of which is elegant and natural. Died about 1625.

See VARFLORA, "Hijos de Sevilla."

Argun. See ARGOON.

Ar'gus, [Gr. 'Αργος,] a fabulous personage, whom the Greek poets imagined to have had one hundred eyes, some of which were always awake. Having been employed by Juno as guardian of a cow into which Io was transformed, he was killed by Hermes. Tradition adds that Juno transferred his eyes to the tail of a peacock.

Argus, a mythical king of Argos, supposed to bᴇ a son of Jupiter and Niobe, and the successor of Apis.

Argyle or Argyll, DUKES, MARQUISES, and EARLS OF. See CAMPBELL.

Argyll, ar-ḡil', or Argyle, (GEORGE DOUGLAS CAMPBELL,) DUKE OF, a British statesman and author, born in 1823. He was styled Marquis of Lorn before the death of his father, which occurred in 1847. He published, in 1848, "Presbytery Examined." In the House of Lords he has acted with the Liberal party. He was appointed lord privy seal in 1852, and postmaster-general in 1855; he again became lord privy seal in the cabinet of Palmerston in 1859. In 1855 he was elected president of the British Association assembled at Glasgow. He is distinguished as a parliamentary debater and popular lecturer. He resigned office about July, 1866, and was appointed secretary for India in December, 1868, in the new cabinet formed by Mr. Gladstone. He published, towards the close of 1866, a philosophical work, entitled "The Reign of Law," which has attracted much attention.

Argyrammos, år-ḡe-räm'mos, (ALEXANDER,) a public-spirited Greek patriot, who about 1810 established a printing-office in order to publish a large Greek lexicon, called Κιβωτός.

Ar-gy̆-rop'y̆-lus, Ar-gy̆-rop'u-lus, or Ar-gy̆-rop'-u-lo, (JOANNES,) a learned Greek professor, born at Constantinople, emigrated to Italy between 1434 and 1442. He taught Greek at Florence about fifteen years, ending in 1471, after which he was professor of Greek at Rome. He was a man of superior talents. His chief works are Latin translations from Aristotle. He is supposed to have died about 1490.

Ar'gy̆-rus, [Gr. 'Αργυρος; Fr. ARGYRE, åR'z̄hèR',] (ISAAC,) a Greek monk and astronomer, born at Constantinople about 1322. He wrote, besides other astronomical works, "Paschal Canon," ("Kanōn Paschᴇ lios.")

Ari, å're, or Ara, å'rå, Hin Frodi (—fro'de,) a historian of Iceland, was born in that island about 1068. He wrote the first part of "Landnamabok," a "History of the Settlement of Iceland," which was continued by other writers, and is extant. Died in 1148.

A-rĭ-ad'ne, [Gr. 'Αριάδνη; Fr. ARIANE, å're'ån',] a daughter of Minos, King of Crete, was beloved by Theseus. It is said that she gave Theseus a clew of thread which enabled him to find his way through the mazes of the Cretan labyrinth. (See THESEUS.)

Ariadne, a daughter of Leo I., Emperor of the East, was married to Zeno, who ascended the throne in 474 A.D. According to some authors, she caused him to be buried alive while he was in a fit of epilepsy or apoplexy; but this statement is extremely improbable. After the death of Zeno, (491,) she became the wife of his successor, Anastasius I. Died in 515 A.D.

Ariæus, a-rī-ee'us, or **Aridæus,** âr-e-dee'us, [Gr. 'Αριαῖος or 'Αριδαῖος,] a general who fought for Cyrus the Younger, of Persia, at Cunaxa, 401 B.C.

A-rī-al'dus, an archdeacon of the Church of Milan, whose zeal against simony and the marriage of the clergy produced violent tumults and a schism in the church about 1056. He was resisted by the majority of the Milanese clergy, (who were opposed to celibacy,) and was supported by the pope, and by the mob, who, under his direction, plundered and pulled down the houses of the priests. In 1066 the Archbishop of Milan, who had been excommunicated by the pope, laid an interdict on the diocese of Milan, to continue so long as Arialdus remained in it. Arialdus was killed in the same year by some partisans of the clergy.

See BARONIUS, "Annales;" MURATORI, "Annali d'Italia."

Ariane. See ARIADNE.

A-rī-a-rā'thēs [Gr. 'Αριαράθης] **I.,** King of Cappadocia, born about 400 B.C., succeeded his father Ariamnes. In the partition that followed the death of Alexander the Great, Cappadocia was allotted to Eumenes, and Perdiccas sent an army to occupy it. Ariarathes was defeated in battle and put to death in 322 B.C.

Ariarathes II., a nephew of Ariarathes I. After the death of Eumenes, 315 B.C., he received aid from the King of Armenia, expelled the Macedonians, and recovered the throne of Cappadocia, which he left to his son Ariamnes II.

Ariarathes III., a son of Ariamnes II., reigned more than twenty years, and died about 220 B.C.

Ariarathes IV., a son of the preceding, was a child when his father died. He married a daughter of Antiochus the Great, and was an ally of that king in his war against the Romans about 190 B.C. Died about 164 B.C.

Ariarathes V., also called **Mithridates,** succeeded his father Ariarathes IV. He formed an alliance with the Romans. In 158 B.C. he was driven from the throne by Holofernes, a pretender, but was restored by the Romans. While fighting for the Romans against Aristoni'cus of Pergamus, he was killed in battle in 130 B.C. He left a minor son, Ariarathes VI., who was assassinated by order of Mithridates, King of Pontus, in 96 B.C.

Ariarathes VII., a son of Ariarathes VI., was placed on the throne by Mithridates, by whom he was assassinated after a short reign. A son of Mithridates obtained the throne; but the people revolted, and crowned Ariarathes VIII., who was a brother of Ariarathes VII. He reigned but a short time.

Ariarathes IX. of Cappadocia began to reign about 42 B.C. He was deposed by Mark Antony in 36 B.C.

Arias, ä're-âs, (FERNANDEZ ANTONIO,) a Spanish painter of the seventeenth century, born at Madrid. He excelled in colour and chiaroscuro, and was patronized by the Duke of Olivarez. Died about 1684.

See BERMUDEZ, "Diccionario Historico."

Arias, (FRANCISCO,) a Spanish writer of devotional works, born at Seville in 1533; died in 1605.

Arias, ä're-âs, (FRANCISCO **Gabino**—gâ-bee'no,) a South American officer and traveller, who explored the wild or desert region called the "Gran Chaco," and the valley of the Vermejo, about 1780. Died about 1808.

A'rī-as Mon-tā'nus, (BENEDICTUS,) [Sp. BENITO **Arias Montano** — ä're-âs mon-tâ'no,] an eminent Spanish linguist and biblical scholar, was born at Frexenal, in Estremadura, in 1527. He distinguished himself at the Council of Trent in 1562, and about 1568 was selected by Philip II. to edit a polyglot Bible, which was published at Antwerp in 1572 and is a beautiful and celebrated edition. Arias Montanus was accused of heresy, and of corrupting the text of Scripture, by Leon de Castro, a professor of Salamanca, but was not convicted. He was an adversary of the Jesuits. His mod-

esty and sincere piety are attested by various writers. He wrote a number of works, among which is one entitled "Jewish Antiquities," (1593.) Died at Seville in 1598.

See ROSENMÜLLER, "Handbuch für die Litteratur der Biblischen Kritik;" N. ANTONIO, "Bibliotheca Hispana Nova;" LOUMYER, "Vie de B. A. Montano," 1842.

Ar'ī-bert [Fr. pron. ä're'baiR'] **I.,** King of the Longobards or Lombards, was a native of Bavaria. He was elected king in 653 A.D. He favoured the Catholic party, and proscribed Arianism. Died in 661 A.D.

Aribert II., King of the Lombards, a descendant of Aribert I., began to reign in 701 A.D. He was defeated in battle by Ansprand in 712, and died, or was killed, soon after that event.

Arici, ä-ree'chee, (CESARE,) an Italian poet, born at Brescia in 1782. He studied law, and was a judge under the régime of Napoleon. In 1824 he became professor of Latin at Brescia. His principal work is "La Pastorizia," (1814,) a didactic poem on the breeding of sheep which is praised by competent judges. Died in 1830.

See TIPALDO, "Biografia degli Italiani illustri."

Aridæus. See ARRHIDÆUS.

Arienti. See ARGENTI.

Arienti, degli, dàl'yee â-re-ên'tee, (CECCO, chek'ko,) an Italian physician, born about 1418; died in 1508.

Arier. See ARYA.

Arif-al-Harwee- (or **Al-Harwî-) Moulana, (Maulâna,)** ä'rif âl-har'wee' mŏw-lä'nä, a Persian poet, who lived in the first half of the fifteenth century.

Ar-I-gī'sus [Fr. ARIGISE, ä're'zhêz'] **I.,** Duke of Beneventum, reigned from 591 to 641 A.D.

Arigisus II., Duke or Prince of Beneventum, began to reign in 758 A.D. He contended for thirteen years against Charlemagne, to whom he at last became tributary. Died in 787.

Ar-ig-no'te [Gr. 'Αριγνώτη] of Samos, a daughter or pupil of Pythagoras. According to Suidas, she wrote on the Mysteries of Ceres and Bacchus.

Arigoni, â-re-go'nee, (GIOVANNI GIACOMO,) an Italian musical composer, lived in the seventeenth century.

Arigoni or **Arrigoni,** ar-re-go'nee, (ONORIO,) an Italian numismatist, born at Venice in 1668. He had a rich collection of medals, of which he published a description, (1741.)

Arimanes or **Arimanius.** See ORMUZD.

Arimino, de, dà â-ree'me-no, (GREGORIUS or GREGORIO **da Rimini**—dä ree'me-nee,) an Italian scholastic philosopher and Augustin monk, born at Rimini. He was remarkable for the subtlety of his intellect as well as for his learning. Died in 1358.

Aringhi, â-rên'gee, (PAOLO,) an Italian priest and antiquary, born in Rome. He published a treatise on the Catacombs of Rome, ("Roma Subterranea Novissima," 1651.) Died in 1676.

Arioald, ä're-o-âld', was elected King of Lombardy in 625 A.D. He was an Arian, and married Gundaberga. Died about 636 A.D.

A-rī-o-bar-zā'nēs [Gr. 'Αριοβαρζάνης; Fr. ARIOBARZANE, ä're'o'bäR'zän'] **I.,** King of Cappadocia, began to reign about 93 B.C. He was several times driven out by Mithridates and restored by the Romans.

Ariobarzanes II. was a son of the preceding, whom he succeeded about 63 B.C.

Ariobarzanes III., a son of the preceding, began to reign about 50 B.C. He aided Pompey against Cæsar in the civil war, but was pardoned by the latter. He was put to death by Cassius in 42 B.C.

Ariobarzanes, the name of three kings of Pontus, descended from one of the seven Persian chiefs who killed Smerdis the Magian in 521 B.C.

Ariobarzanes I. reigned in the fifth century B.C., and was the father of Mithridates I.

Ariobarzanes II. was a son of Mithridates I., whom he succeeded in 363 B.C.; died in 337 B.C.

Ariobarzanes III., a son of Mithridates III., began to reign about 266 B.C.; died about 240.

A-rī'on, ['Αρίων,] an ancient Greek poet and musician, who is supposed to have lived about 700 B.C. Herodotus has preserved the following curious fable respecting him. During a voyage at sea, the crew of the ship in which he sailed resolved to kill him for his money, and ordered

---

e as k; ç as s; g̃ hard; ġ as j; G, H, K, guttural; N, nasal; R, trilled; s̃ as z; th as in this. (☞See Explanations, p. 23.)

him to jump overboard. Arion, having obtained permission to sing one song to his cithara, threw himself into the sea, and was received on the back of a dolphin, which carried him safely to land. (See Herodotus, book i.)

See also MÜLLER, "Histoire de la Littérature de l'ancienne Grèce."

Arioste. See ARIOSTO, (LODOVICO.)

Ariosti, â-re-os′tee, (ATTILIO,) an Italian dramatic composer, born at Bologna about 1660. At the invitation of the Royal Academy of Music, he went to London in 1720, and became a rival of Handel. He produced in London several operas, which were performed with success, and among which "Coriolano" was the most popular. Having ceased to enjoy the public favour, he left England about 1730.

See BURNEY, "History of Music."

Ariosto, â-re-os′to, (ALESSANDRO,) an Italian monk, born at Bologna, was sent about 1476 on a mission to the Maronites of Lebanon. He wrote a "Description of Palestine."

Ariosto, (FRANCESCO,) a great-uncle of the famous poet, was professor of philosophy and civil law at Ferrara. He wrote a treatise on a spring of petroleum at Mont Gibbio, (1690.) Died in 1492.

Ariosto, (GABRIELLO,) a brother of the great poet Ariosto, had also some talent for poetry. He was a cripple from infancy. His poetry is praised by Lilio Giraldi. After his death a volume of his Latin poems was published in 1582.

Ariosto, [Lat. ARIOS′TUS; Fr. ARIOSTE, å′re′ost′,] (LODOVICO or LUDOVICO,) an eminent Italian poet, born at Reggio, near Módena, September 8, 1474. In his boyhood he dramatized the story of Pyramus and Thisbe. After he left the College of Ferrara he studied law for several years, in compliance with the will of his father; but his strong love of poetry impelled him to renounce that profession. By his early lyric poems, remarkable for elegance and facility, he attracted the notice of Cardinal Ippolito d'Este, whose service he entered in 1503. He was employed by the cardinal and his brother Alfonso, Duke of Ferrara, in missions to several Italian courts. About 1505 he began to compose his celebrated romantic and fantastic poem, "Orlando Furioso," the subject of which are the fabulous and chivalrous adventures of the paladins of the age of Charlemagne. It was published in 1516. It is stated that Cardinal Ippolito, when a copy of this poem was presented to him by Ariosto, exclaimed, "Master Ludovico, where the devil did you pick up so many absurdities?"

The "Orlando Furioso" has been translated into nearly all the languages of Europe. The best English translations are those of Harrington and Rose. "No poet has equalled him," says Ginguené, "in this kind of épopée, where the imagination has another race to run than in the purely heroic poem. No one has blended with such skill the serious with the amusing, the graceful with the terrible, the sublime with the familiar."

Ariosto offended Cardinal Ippolito in 1517 by his refusal to accompany him to Hungary, although he pleaded ill health as his excuse; and about the end of that year he entered the service of Duke Alfonso. In 1522 he was appointed commissary or governor of the district of Garfagnana, which was infested by brigands and inhabited by rude and lawless people. He acquitted himself well in this office, which he resigned in 1524. He married, late in life, a widow named Alessandra Benucci, but the marriage was kept a secret until his death, probably because he held some small ecclesiastical benefices. About 1526 he built for himself in Ferrara a commodious but not very costly house, which is now, or was recently, standing. He published in 1532 a new and improved edition of his great poem. He died at Ferrara on the 6th of June, 1533, leaving two natural sons, Giovanni Battista and Virginio.

Among his works are seven satires, which are composed in the Horatian manner and are remarkable for urbanity, and five comedies in verse, entitled "La Cassaria," "I Suppositi," "Il Negromante," ("The Magician,") "La Lena," and "La Scolastica," which were performed at Ferrara a few years before his death. He also wrote Italian elegies, sonnets, canzoni, etc., and a number of Latin poems, which were printed in 1553.

"Ariosto," says Hallam, "has been, after Homer, the favourite poet of Europe. His grace and facility, his clear and rapid stream of language, his variety and beauty of invention, his very transitions of subject, so frequently censured by critics, but artfully devised to spare the tediousness that hangs on a protracted story, left him no rival in general popularity. Above sixty editions of the 'Orlando Furioso' were published in the sixteenth century. . . . Corniani observes of the style of Ariosto, . . . that he is sparing in the use of metaphors, contenting himself generally with the plainest expressions; by which, if he loses something in dignity, he gains in perspicuity. . . . Doubtless this transparency of phrase, so eminent in Ariosto, is the cause that he is read and delighted in by the multitude as well as by the few. . . . His similes are conspicuous for their elaborate beauty: imitated, as they usually are, from the ancients, they maintain an equal strife with their models, and occasionally surpass them. . . . The 'Orlando Furioso,' as a great single poem, has been very rarely surpassed in the living records of poetry. He must yield to three, and only three, of his predecessors. He has not the force, simplicity, and truth to nature of Homer, the exquisite style and sustained majesty of Virgil, nor the originality and boldness of Dante." ("Introduction to the Literature of Europe.")

See GAROFALO, "Vita di Ariosto;" MAZZUCHELLI, "Scrittori d'Italia;" BARUFFALDI GIUNIORE, "La Vita di Lodovico Ariosto," 1807; FABRONI, "Elogj di Dante, di Poliziano, di Ariosto e di Tasso," 1800; HARRINGTON, "Life of Ariosto," 1634; PIGNA, "I Romanzi," 1554; LONGFELLOW, "Poets and Poetry of Europe;" CORNIANI, "I Secoli della Letteratura Italiana;" BAROTTI, "Vita di L. Ariosto," 4 vols., 1766; CARL L. FERNOW, "Lebenslauf L. Ariosto's des Göttlichen," 1809.

Ariosto, (ORAZIO,) a son of Gabriello, noticed above, was born at Ferrara in 1555, and became a canon of the cathedral of that city. He was a friend of Tasso, for whom he wrote in verse the "Arguments" ("Argomenti") one of which is prefixed to each canto of the "Jerusalem Delivered." He also wrote some comedies, and left unfinished a poem entitled "L'Alfeo." Died in 1593.

Ariostus. See ARIOSTO, (LODOVICO.)

Arioviste. See ARIOVISTUS.

A-rī-o-vis′tus, [Ger. EHRENVEST, ä′ren-vĕst, and ARIOVIST; Fr. ARIOVISTE, å′re′o′vĕst′,] a German chief of the Suevi, who, after aiding the Sequani in war against the Ædui, settled in Gaul and subjected both of those tribes to his dominion. During the consulship of Julius Cæsar he obtained the alliance of the Romans, who recognized him as a king. In 58 B.C. he was defeated in a great battle by Cæsar, whom the Gauls had solicited to liberate them. Ariovistus escaped across the Rhine in a boat.

See P. L. HAUS, "J. Cæsars Krieg mit dem Germanier-König Ariovist," 1790; CÆSAR, "De Bello Gallico."

Ar′ī-phron, [Ἀρίφρων,] a Greek poet of Sicyon, who is supposed to have lived about 550 B.C. He composed a beautiful ode or pæan to Health, (Ὑγίεια,) which has been preserved by Athenæus.

Arisi, â-ree′see, (FRANCESCO,) an Italian *littérateur* and eminent lawyer, born at Cremona in 1657. He published many works in prose and verse, among which were "Lyrical Poems," ("Poesie liriche," 1680,) and "Cremona Litterata," (3 vols., 1702-41.) Died in 1743.

Arista, â-rès′tä, (MARIANO,) a Mexican general, born about 1800. He served as an officer in various civil wars, became general of brigade about 1833, and general of division in 1841. He was defeated by the United States army, under General Taylor, at Palo Alto, May 8, 1846. In 1848 he was appointed minister of war, and in 1850 was elected President of Mexico. Santa Anna having headed a successful insurrection, Arista was banished in the early part of 1853. He died in Spain in 1855.

Aristænetus, âr-is-ten′e-tus, [Gr. Ἀρισταίνετος; Fr. ARISTÉNÈTE, å′rès′tå′nåt′,] a Greek rhetorician of Nicæa, in Bithynia, was a friend of Libanius. He was appointed governor of a district of Bithynia by the emperor Constantius, and was killed by an earthquake at Nicomedia in 358 A.D. There are extant about fifty fictitious erotic letters, of little merit, under the name of Aristænetus;

ā, ē, ī, ō, ū, ȳ, *long;* ă, ĕ, ĭ, ŏ, ŭ, ў, *same, less prolonged;* ă, ĕ, ĭ, ŏ, ŭ, ў, *short;* ạ, ẹ, į, ọ, *obscure;* fär, fâll, fät; mĕt; nŏt; gŏŏd; mŏŏn

but many critics think that the author of these is a different person from the friend of Libanius.

See SCHOELL, "Histoire de la Littérature Grecque."

Aristænus, är-is-tee′nus, [Gr. Ἀρίσταινος; Fr. ARIS-TÈNE, ä′rèss′tàn′,] of Megalopolis, was chosen general (strate′gos) of the Achæans in 198 B.C., and persuaded them to form an alliance with the Romans, rather than with Philip of Macedon. He was a political opponent of Philopœmen. He was re-elected strategos in 195 and 186 B.C.

Aristæon, är-is-tee′on, a Greek philosopher, of whom little is known. He wrote a work on Harmony, a fragment of which is preserved by Stobæus.

Aristæus, är-is-tee′us, [Gr. Ἀρισταῖος; Fr. ARISTÉE, ä′rèss′tà′,] a personage in the Greek mythology, supposed to have been the son of Apollo and Cyrene. He was worshipped as the god who presided over flocks and herds and who taught men the art of managing bees.

See VIRGIL's "Georgics," book iv.

Aristæus, an ancient Greek geometer, the reputed author of two works, one of which was entitled Κωνικά, ("Conics.") Euclid appears to have made use of these works, which are not extant. This geometer is by some writers identified with Aristæus or Aristæon of Croton, a philosopher whom Iamblichus calls the successor of Pythagoras.

Aristæus or **A-ris′te-as,** a Greek sculptor, who probably lived about 130 A.D. Among his works are two statues of centaurs, found at Tivoli in 1746.

Ar-is-tag′o-ras, [Gr. Ἀρισταγόρας,] tyrant of Miletus, revolted against the King of Persia about 500 B.C., and made an alliance with the Athenians, who furnished him twenty ships. The allies took Sardis and burned it, but were defeated by the Persians. Aristagoras fled to Thrace, where he was killed about 498 B.C.

Aristagoras, a Greek geographer, lived about 350 B.C., and wrote on the cities and antiquities of Egypt.

Ar-is-tan′der of Paros, a Greek sculptor, lived about 400 B.C.

Aristander, [Gr. Ἀρίστανδρος; Fr. ARISTANDRE, ä′rèss′tòNdR′,] a Greek soothsayer, was a skilful interpreter of dreams, and was often consulted by Alexander the Great, whom he accompanied in his expedition to Persia.

Ar-is-tar′chus [Gr. Ἀρίσταρχος; Fr. ARISTARQUE, ä′rèss′tàRK′,] a Greek astronomer of Samos, flourished probably about 260 B.C. Nothing is known of his life. He is mentioned in the "Arenarius" of Archimedes, who says, "Aristarchus of Samos supposes that the stars and sun are immovable, and that the earth revolves around the sun in the circumference of a circle." The only extant work of Aristarchus is a treatise "On the Magnitudes and Distances of the Sun and Moon," in which he gave an ingenious method of measuring the distances from the earth, although the results which he obtained were far from exact. He invented a dial which is noticed by Vitruvius. There is a passage in Plutarch from which it is inferred that Aristarchus conceived or maintained both the annual motion and the diurnal rotation of the earth.

See DELAMBRE, "Histoire de l'Astronomie ancienne;" FORTIA D'URBAN, "Histoire d'Aristarque de Samos," 1810; ERSCH und GRUBER, "Allgemeine Encyklopaedie."

Aristarchus, [Fr. ARISTARQUE,] a celebrated Greek grammarian and critic, born in Samothrace, was a pupil of Aristophanes of Byzantium. He passed the greater part of his life at Alexandria, in Egypt, where he founded a school which flourished for a long time. Suidas states that he lived about 156 B.C., and other writers date his birth at 160 B.C. He is said to have died in Cyprus at the age of seventy-two. He is regarded by some as the greatest critic of antiquity. It is generally admitted that his merits as an editor and commentator of Homer are greater than those of any other; and the division of the Iliad and Odyssey into twenty-four books is attributed to him. He wrote commentaries on other Greek poets, and several works on grammar, none of which are preserved entire. A fragment of his treatise "On Analogy" is extant.

See SCHOELL, "Histoire de la Littérature Grecque;" C. L. MAT-THESIUS, "Disputatio de Aristarcho Grammatico," 1725; K. LEHRS, "De Aristarchi Studiis Homericis," 1833.

Aristarchus of Athens, a violent opponent of the democracy, was one of the chiefs of the government in 411 B.C. He was executed for treason about 406.

Aristarchus of Tegea, a Greek tragic poet, who lived about 450 B.C. He composed sixty tragedies, which are all lost. One of them, entitled "Achilles," is said to have been translated into Latin by Ennius.

Aristarchus, a disciple and companion of the Apostle Paul, was a native of Thessalonica. (See Acts xx. 4; Colossians iv. 10.)

Aristarque. See ARISTARCHUS.

Aristeas. See ARISTÆUS and ARISTEUS.

A-ris′te-as, [Ἀρίστεας,] a Greek poet, who is supposed to have lived six centuries or more B.C. According to some writers, he was a contemporary of Homer. He wrote an epic poem entitled "The Arimaspea," (Τὰ Ἀριμάσπεια,) six verses of which are preserved by Longinus.

Aristeas, the supposed author of a Greek letter entitled "The History of the Seventy Interpreters," which is extant and gives an account of the translation of the Pentateuch, or Old Testament, under the auspices of Ptolemy Philadelphus, King of Egypt. Josephus calls him a friend of that king, and quotes his letter. It is now the prevalent opinion that this letter is a forgery. The name is written Aristæus by Josephus.

Aristée. See ARISTÆUS and ARISTEUS.

Aristeides. See ARISTIDES.

Aristène. See ARISTÆNUS.

Aristénète. See ARISTÆNETUS.

A-ris′teūs (or a-ris′te-us) or **A-ris′te-as,** [Gr. Ἀριστεύς or Ἀριστέας; Fr. ARISTÉE, ä′rèss′tà′,] a Corinthian general, commanded the troops which were sent by Corinth to aid Potidæa against the Athenians in 432 B.C. In 430 he was associated with some Spartans in an embassy to the King of Persia, but on his way to that country fell into the power of the Athenians, who put him to death.

See THIRLWALL's "History of Greece."

Aristide. See ARISTIDES.

Ar-is-ti′dēs or **Aristei′des,** [Gr. Ἀριστείδης; Fr. ARISTIDE, ä′rèss′tèd′,] surnamed THE JUST, an Athenian statesman and general of great eminence and merit, the son of Lysimachus, was born in Alopeke, a demos of Attica. He belonged to the aristocratic party, and became a political rival of Themistocles. When Greece was invaded by the Persians, in 490 B.C., he was one of the ten generals who commanded alternately each for one day. According to Plutarch, Aristides resigned his turn of command to Miltiades, and thus procured for the army the advantage of a skilful general at the battle of Marathon. Having been selected to guard the spoils found in the Persian camp at Marathon, he maintained his high character for integrity, and was elected archon eponymus, or chief archon, in 489. The intrigues of Themistocles and the envy excited by the eminent virtue of Aristides conspired with such success against him that he was ostracized, in 483 B.C., on the pretext that his influence was becoming dangerous to public liberty. It is related that during the process by which he was ostracized, he was requested by a voter, who could not write, to write Aristides on a shell or tile used as a voting-tablet. He complied, but first inquired, "Has Aristides done you an injury?" "No," replied the voter, "nor do I even know him; but I am tired of hearing him always called 'Aristides the Just.'"

On the invasion of Greece by Xerxes, in 480 B.C., Aristides was recalled, and recovered his influence. In reply to Mardonius, who offered to bribe the Athenians to desert the cause of the Greeks, he declared, "So long as this sun shall shine, the Athenians will wage war against the Persians for their ravaged country and for their violated temples." He commanded the Athenian force of eight thousand at the battle of Platæa, 479 B.C., and contributed greatly to the victory.

Aristides and Cimon obtained command of the troops which Athens contributed in 477 B.C. to an expedition of the allies against the Persians. Pausanias of Sparta was commander-in-chief of the allies at first, but rendered himself unpopular by his haughtiness and severity. Aristides by prudence and mildness gained the favour of the allies, and transferred to his own state the supremacy or precedence in the Greek confederation. He was appointed to determine the amount which each state should pay towards the expenses of the war, and gave general satisfaction in the performance of this duty. He died about 468 B.C.

Aristides is considered as one of the most illustrious statesmen and patriots of antiquity, and one of the most virtuous public men of any age or nation.

See the article "Aristides," in PLUTARCH'S "Lives," where he is compared with Cato the Censor; "Life of Aristides," by CORNELIUS NEPOS; GROTE, "History of Greece," chap. xxxvi.; THIRLWALL, "History of Greece;" EPKEMA, "Dissertatio de Aristide," 1829.

Aristides, a Greek statuary, who lived in the latter part of the fifth century B.C., and was a pupil of Polycletus of Sicyon.

Aristides, (Æ'LIUS,) a distinguished sophist and rhetorician, born at Hadriani, in Bithynia, about 117, or, as some say, in 129 A.D., was a pupil of Polemon and Herodes Atticus. He became a resident of Smyrna, and after that city had been ruined by an earthquake, in 178 A.D., he persuaded the emperor Marcus Aurelius to rebuild it. He was very vain of his eloquence, and compared himself to Demosthenes. His orations, many of which are extant, have little merit except the choice and arrangement of the words.

See FABRICIUS, "Bibliotheca Græca;" PHILOSTRATUS, "Vitæ Sophistarum."

Aristides of Athens was the author of an apology for the Christians, which was presented or addressed to the emperor Hadrian about 125 A.D., and is not extant.

Aristides of Miletus, a Greek writer of fiction, lived in the second century B.C. He wrote tales called "Milesiaca," (Μιλησιακά.)

Aristides of Thebes, an eminent Greek painter, a contemporary of Apelles, flourished between 360 and 330 B.C. He excelled in expression, and, according to Pliny, was the first painter that expressed the passions and movements of the soul. When Alexander the Great stormed Thebes, he saw and appropriated a picture by Aristides of the sack of a city. He was a brother of the eminent painter Nicomachus.

A-ris-tī'dēs Quin-til-ĭ-a'nus, a Greek writer on music, of an uncertain period. He quotes Cicero, and is supposed to have lived in the second century of the Christian era. His treatise "On Music" is extant, and is highly prized.

A-ris'tǐ-on, ['Αριστίων,] otherwise called Athe'nion, a Greek philosopher, who persuaded the Athenians to become the allies of Mithridates against the Romans. About the same time he made himself tyrant of Athens, the people of which he cruelly oppressed. He was put to death by Sulla at the capture of Athens in 86 B.C.

Aristipp or **Aristippe.** See ARISTIPPUS.

Ar-is-tip'pus, [Gr. 'Αρίστιππος; Fr. ARISTIPPE, ä'rès'-tèp'; Ger. ARISTIPP, ä-ris-tip',] a celebrated Greek philosopher, the founder of the Cyrenaic school, was born at Cyrene, in Africa, about 425 B.C. He was a pupil of Socrates, but differed from him widely in his principles and life. He passed some years at the court of Dionysius of Syracuse, and travelled extensively. His system of philosophy favoured the free indulgence in sensual pleasure, and he is said to have regarded pleasure as the chief object of life, although he observed moderation in the enjoyment of it. He was intimate with the courtesan Laïs. His works, if he wrote any, are not extant ; but concurrent traditions enable us to form a probable estimate of his character and opinions. He neglected mathematics and the physical sciences, and avoided public affairs. His versatility, equanimity, and faculty of adapting himself to the varieties of fortune and circumstance are noticed by Horace, who says, felicitously,

"Omnis Aristippum decuit color et status et res."*

A number of his sharp sayings and repartees are recorded by Diogenes Laertius. When King Dionysius remarked that the philosophers seek the favour of the rich, but the rich do not pay court to philosophers, Aris-

* "All fortune fitted Aristippus well."—CREECH.

tippus said, "That is because the philosophers know what they need, while the rich do not know." He was living in 366 B.C. After his death his doctrines were propagated by his daughter Arete, and by her son Aristippus. Wieland wrote a romance of "Aristippus and his Contemporaries," ("Aristipp und seine Zeitgenossen," 4 vols., 1800–02.)

See RITTER, "History of Philosophy;" G. H. LEWES, "Biographical History of Philosophy;" F. MENTZ, "Aristippus Philosophus Socraticus, sive de ejus Vita," etc., 1719; H. KUNHARDT, "Dissertatio philosophico-historica de Aristippi Philosophia morali," 1795; SEXTUS EMPIRICUS, "Adversus Mathematicos;" DIOGENES LAERTIUS.

Aristippus THE YOUNGER, a Greek philosopher, grandson of the preceding, whose doctrines he professed. He flourished about 360 B.C.

Aristippus, tyrant of Argos, was defeated by Aratus and killed about 242 B.C.

A-ris'to or **A-ris'ton,** ['Αρίστων,] an ancient Greek physician, is supposed to have lived in the fifth century B.C. Some ancient critics ascribed to him the work "On Wholesome Diet," which has often been included among the works of Hippocrates.

Aristo or **Ariston** of Alexandria, a Peripatetic philosopher, lived about 30 B.C.

Aristo or **Ariston,** the son of Aristocles, was an Athenian and the father of Plato.

Aristo or **Ariston** of Ceos, a Peripatetic philosopher, succeeded Lycon as head of the Peripatetic school about 230 B.C. His works are lost. According to Cicero, they gave evidence of a refined and elegant mind.

Aristo or **Ariston** of Chios, (surnamed THE SI'REN, for his persuasive eloquence,) a Stoic philosopher, was a disciple of Zeno, and lived about 275 B.C. He opened a school at Athens, and lectured on ethics, which he considered the only part of philosophy worthy of study. He did not follow strictly the doctrines of Zeno, but taught that the highest good consisted in indifference to everything except virtue and vice. His works, if he wrote any, are not extant.

See N. SAAL, "Commentatio de Aristone Chio," 1852.

Aristo or **Ariston** of Cyrene, was the chief of the democratic party in a civil war which occurred at Cyrene about 403 B.C.

Aristo or **Ariston** of Pella, the reputed author of a Greek work called a "Dialogue between Papiscus and Jason," which was probably written in the second century, and is not extant. It was designed to prove that the prophecies concerning Christ apply to Jesus, and was commended by Origen.

Aristo or **Ariston,** a king of Sparta, of the Eupontid or Proclid line, a son of Agesicles, ascended the throne about 560 B.C., and after a long reign was succeeded by his son, Demaratus.

Aristo or **Ariston,** a Spartan sculptor, who made a colossal statue of Jupiter, at Olympia, noticed by Pausanias.

Aristo or **Ariston,** a Greek painter, who lived about 330 B.C., was a son of Aristides of Thebes, and was the master of Euphranor.

Aristo, (TITUS,) a Roman jurist of the time of Trajan, was a friend of the younger Pliny, who speaks highly of his virtue and learning.

Aristobule. See ARISTOBULUS.

A-ris-to-bu'lus, [Gr. 'Αριστόβουλος; Fr. ARISTOBULE, ä'rès'to'bül',] a Greek historian who lived about 330 B.C., and wrote a history of the Asiatic expedition of Alexander the Great, which he had accompanied. This history, which is not extant, had a high reputation, and was used as a guide by Arrian. Plutarch and Lucian mention an Aristobulus of Cassandria, who was probably the same person.

See VOSSIUS, "De Historicis Græcis."

Aristobulus, a Jew and Peripatetic philosopher, who lived in Egypt in the reign of Ptolemy Philometor and his successor, (181–117 B.C.) He wrote a commentary on the law of Moses.

Aristobulus, a son of Herod the Great and Mariamne, was sent to Rome to be educated. Having been accused of a plot against Herod, he was put to death about 1 B.C.

ă, ē, ī, ō, ū, ȳ, *long;* ă, ĕ, ŏ, same, less prolonged; ă, ĕ, ῐ, ŏ, ŭ, ў, *short;* ạ, ẹ, ị, ọ, *obscure;* fär, fåll, fåt; mět; nŏt; gōōd; mōōn;

Aristobulus THE YOUNGER, a grandson of Herod the Great, passed his life in a private station. He died after 44 A.D.

Aristobulus, a son of Herod, King of Chalcis, was placed on the throne of Armenia by Nero about 55 A.D.

Aristobulus I., high-priest of the Jews, was a son of Joannes Hyrcanus, at whose death, in 107 B.C., according to Josephus, he assumed the title of king. He died in 105 B.C., and was succeeded by his brother Alexander Jannæus.

Aristobulus II., a younger son of Alexander Jannæus, obtained the throne about 70 B.C., after he had defeated his brother Hyrcanus. In 63 B.C. Pompey took Jerusalem, placed Hyrcanus on the throne, and carried Aristobulus as a captive to Rome. He escaped in the year 57, renewed the war in Judea, and was retaken. Having been released by Cæsar in 49 B.C. and sent home to fight against Pompey, he was poisoned by the partisans of the latter.

Aristobulus, a grandson of the preceding. was a brother of Mariamne, the wife of Herod. He was made high-priest at the age of seventeen, and was put to death by Herod in 35 B.C.

Aristocle. See ARISTOCLES.

A-ris'to-clēē, [Gr. Ἀριστοκλῆς ; Fr. ARISTOCLE, ä′rès′-tok′l′,] a sculptor of Cydonia, is supposed to have lived about 500 or 600 B.C. Pausanias says he was among the most ancient sculptors of Greece.

Aristocles, a Greek physician, lived probably in the first century after Christ. Some of his formulas have been preserved by Galen.

Aristocles of Messana or Messina, a Greek Peripatetic philosopher, lived in the second century after Christ. He wrote on Ethics, etc.

Aristocles of Pergamus, a rhetorician and Peripatetic philosopher, was a disciple of Herodes Atticus. He flourished between 100 and 135 A.D.

Aristocles of Rhodes, a Greek grammarian, contemporary with Strabo.

Aristocles of Sicyon, a Greek sculptor, and a brother of Canachus, lived about 400 B.C.

Aristocrate. See ARISTOCRATES.

Ar-is-toc'rạ-tēē I., King of Arcadia, lived about 770 B.C.

Aristocrates II., a grandson of the preceding, reigned about 660 B.C. He was put to death by his subjects as a traitor.

Aristocrates, [Gr. Ἀριστοκράτης; Fr. ARISTOCRATE, ä′rès′to′krǎt′,] an Athenian politician, was a member of the government of Four Hundred formed in 411 B.C., which he aided Theramenes to subvert. He was one of the ten generals chosen in 407, and one of those who commanded at Arginusæ in 406 B.C. He was put to death for his conduct at this battle.

Aristocrates, a Greek physician mentioned by Galen, lived probably between 100 B.C. and 100 A.D.

Aristocrates, a Greek historian, was a native of Sparta, and appears to have lived later than 188 B.C. He wrote a work on the history of Laconia, which is not extant.

Aristodème, the French of ARISTODEMUS, which see.

Ar-is-to-de'mus, [Gr. Ἀριστόδημος; Fr. ARISTODÈME, ä′rès′to′dặm′,] a Greek painter of the fourth century B.C., was the father of two more eminent painters, Aristides of Thebes and Nicomachus.

Aristodemus, a tragic actor of Athens, took an active part in politics, as a supporter of the Macedonian party, and was an opponent of Demosthenes.

Aristodemus, a Greek statuary, lived about 300 B.C., and made a statue of Seleucus, King of Babylon.

Aristodemus of Caria, a Greek painter, lived about 50 A.D.

Aristodemus, tyrant of Cuma, in Italy, was a contemporary of Tarquin the Proud, of Rome. He was killed by conspirators about 490 B.C.

Aristodemus, a general of the first Messenian war, gained several victories, and became King of Messenia about 730 B.C.

Aristodemus of Miletus, a general of Antigonus, King of Asia, who sent him in 315 B.C. to the Pelopon-

nesus to oppose Cassander. He took several fortified places.

Aristodemus of Nysa, a Greek grammarian, a pupil of Aristarchus, lived about 100 B.C. His works are all lost.

Aristodemus of Nysa, a grammarian, a relation of the preceding, taught at Rome about 80 B.C. The great Pompey was one of his pupils.

Aristodemus, a Spartan soldier who escaped from the battle of Thermopylæ in 480 B.C. and was stigmatized as a coward. To retrieve his honour he fought with signal bravery at Platæa, where ·he was killed, 479 B.C.

Ar-is-to-ḡī'ton or **Aristogeī'ton,** [Gr. Ἀριστογείτων,] an Athenian who. conspired with Harmodius against Hippias and Hipparchus. See HARMODIUS.

Aristogiton, an Athenian orator and demagogue, who was surnamed the "Dog," and was a political opponent of Demosthenes. His orations are not extant.

Aristogiton, a Greek statuary, lived about 400 B.C.

Ar-is-to-lā'us, an eminent Greek painter, a son and pupil of Pausias of Sicyon, lived about 300 B.C. His style was remarkable for severity.

Ar-is-tom'a-ẹhus, [Gr. Ἀριστόμαχος ; Fr. ARISTOMAQUE, ä′rès′to′mǎk′,] a Greek Peripatetic philosopher, born at Soli, in Cilicia, spent much time in the study of bees. He was a pupil of Lycon.

Aristomaque. See ARISTOMACHUS.

Ar-is-to-me'dēē, [Gr. Ἀριστομήδης ; Fr. ARISTOMÈDE, ä′rès′to′mặd′,] a sculptor of Thebes, lived in the time of Pindar, who dedicated a statue of Cybele made by this artist.

Aristomène. See ARISTOMENES.

Ar-is-tom'e-nēē, [Gr. Ἀριστομένης; Fr. ARISTOMÈNE, ä′rès′to′mặn′,] a Messenian general, famous for his daring exploits, commanded the Messenians in the war against the Lacedæmonians which began in 685 B.C. and ended in 668 B.C., when the Messenians emigrated to Sicily. The memory of Aristomenes was perpetuated by songs and annual sacrifices for many centuries.

See JOURDAN, "Histoire d'Aristomène," 1749; NORRMANN, "Aristomenes Messenius vir heroicus," 1690.

Aristomenes, an Athenian comic poet, lived about 420 B.C. His works are not extant.

Ar-is-to-nī'cus of Alexandria, a grammarian and contemporary of Strabo. His works are not extant.

Aristonicus [Ἀριστόνικος] of Marathon, an Athenian orator, who co-operated with Demosthenes against the Macedonian party. He was one of the prominent public men whom the Athenians delivered to the victorious Antipater, by whom he was put to death in 322 B.C.

Ar-is-ton'ĭ-das, a Greek statuary, who, according to Pliny, by a combination of different metals, imitated the complexion of the human face.

Ar-is-ton'o-us [Ἀριστόνοος] or **A-ris'to-nus** [Ἀριστόνους] of Ægina, a Greek statuary of uncertain epoch.

Ar-is-ton'ȳ-mus, [Ἀριστώνυμος,] an Athenian comic poet, contemporary with Aristophanes. His works are not extant.

Aristophane. See ARISTOPHANES.

Ar-is-toph'a-nēē, [Gr. Ἀριστοφάνης ; Fr. ARISTOPHANE, ä′rès′to′fän′,] the most celebrated comic poet of Greece, was born about 444 B.C., and is generally supposed to have been an Athenian by birth. He produced in 427 his first comedy, "The Feasters," which is not extant. His next work was "The Babylonians," (426,) in which he attacked Cleon, a powerful demagogue, who was his personal and political enemy. He also lashed and ridiculed Cleon with great success in "The Knights" or "Demagogues," which gained the prize in 424 B.C. and is esteemed one of his most admirable works. It is said that Aristophanes acted the part of Cleon in this drama, as no other actor was bold enough to personate him.

Among his master-pieces is "The Clouds," (423,) a powerful· satire against the Sophists, which, however, was not successful in gaining the first prize. In this play he ridiculed and misrepresented Socrates, whom he unjustly confounded with the Sophists. Plato, in his "Apology," identifies Aristophanes with the accusers of Socrates, and with those who excited the popular prejudice against · him as a skeptic and a corrupter of the youth.

Aristophanes was the author of about fifty comedies, of which eleven are extant, viz.: "The Acharnians," (425 B.C.;) "The Knights," (424;) "The Clouds," (423;) "The Wasps," which gained the first prize; "The Peace," (419;) "The Birds," (414;) "Lysistrata;" "Thesmophoriazusæ," (411;) "Plutus," (408;) "The Frogs," (395;) and "The Female Orators," (392 B.C.) He is praised for his wit, comic humour, originality, good sense, and fidelity in the delineation of Athenian manners. His style is considered a model of Attic purity. He is one of the interlocutors in the "Banquet" of Plato, who is said to have been a great admirer of his comedies. "The Acharnians," "The Knights," "The Birds," and "The Frogs" have been translated into English by J. Hookham Frere. He died probably about 380 B.C.

See THIRLWALL, "History of Greece," iv. 250; H. T. RÖTJCHER, "Aristophanes und sein Zeitalter," 1827; H. POL, "Dissertatio de Aristophane," 1834; C. F. RANKE, "Commentatio de Aristophanis Vita," 1845.

Aristoph'anes OF BYZANTIUM, a celebrated grammarian and critic, called the founder of the Alexandrine school of criticism, flourished between 250 and 200 B.C. He was a pupil of Callimachus and Zenodotus, the master of the famous Aristarchus, and keeper of the royal library at Alexandria. The invention of the Greek system of punctuation and accents is attributed to him. Among his works, which are all lost, except small fragments, were commentaries on Homer and on other poets. He shares with Aristarchus the honour of establishing the Alexandrine canon of classic writers.

See SCHOELL, "Histoire de la Littérature Grecque."

A-ris'to-phon ['Αριστοφῶν] of Azenia, an Athenian statesman and orator. In 403 B.C. he procured the passage of a law to confine the right of citizenship to persons whose parents were both free citizens. He exerted great influence in the state throughout a career of unusual length. In 355 B.C. he defended the law of Leptines against Demosthenes.

Aristophon of Colyttus, an influential Athenian statesman, younger than the preceding, was a contemporary of Demosthenes.

Aristophon, a Greek comic poet, whose works are lost, except small fragments.

Aristophon, an eminent painter of Thasos, of the fifth century B.C., was a brother of the great painter Polygnotus.

Aristote. See ARISTOTLE.

Aristoteles. See ARISTOTLE.

Aristotile, â-rès-tot'e-là, [Fr. ARISTOTE, ả'rès'tot',] called FIORAVANTI, fe-o-rã-vân'tee, an Italian architect, born at Bologna or Venice. By the invitation of the Czar Iván, he went to Moscow about 1474. He repaired or rebuilt the Kremlin, and erected the magnificent church of the Assumption, (1479,) and the palace of the Belvedere, (1497,) at Moscow. He wished to return to Italy, but was forcibly detained by the Czar. His family name was ALBERTI.

See BAYLE, "Dictionnaire Historique."

Aristotile or **Bastiano da San Gallo**, bâs-te-â'no dã săn gãl'lo, an Italian painter and architect, born at Florence in 1481, was a nephew of Giuliano and Antonio San Gallo, and a pupil of Pietro Perugino. He excelled in perspective and architectural painting, and was much employed in decorations for festivals and princely entertainments. Among his works was a copy of Michael Angelo's cartoon of Pisa, and the Expulsion of Adam and Eve from Paradise. Died in 1551.

See VASARI, "Lives of the Painters."

A-ris-to-ti'mus, [Gr. 'Αριστότιμος; Fr. ARISTOTIME, ả'rès'to'tèm',] a tyrant who usurped the supreme power of Elis, lived about 250 B.C.

Aristotle, ằr'is-tot'l, [Gr. 'Αριστοτέλης; Lat. and Ger. ARISTOT'ELES; Fr. ARISTOTE, ả'rès'tot'; It. ARISTOTILE, â-rès-tot'e-là; Sp. ARISTOTELES, â-rès-to-tã'lès; Persian and Arabic, ARISTÂTÂLÎS, ả'ris'tã'lèss',] one of the most illustrious philosophers of antiquity, and, if considered with respect to the intellect alone, perhaps the most remarkable man that ever lived, was born at Stagira, (or Stageira,) in Thrace, on the western side of

the Gulf of Strymon, 384 B.C. From the place of his birth, he was surnamed THE STAGIRITE, (Σταγειρίτης.)*

His father, Nicomachus, who was physician to Amyntas, King of Macedon, is said to have been the author of several works on medicine and natural history. Being left an orphan at an early age, Aristotle was placed under the guardianship of Proxenus, who had him carefully educated. When he was seventeen years old, he visited Athens, then the great centre of Grecian art, literature, and philosophy. He arrived in that city while Plato was absent in Sicily. Aristotle, however, applied himself meanwhile to such sources of philosophic instruction as were open to him; and as soon as Plato returned, he became his pupil. The extraordinary powers and zeal in the pursuit of knowledge evinced by the young Stagirite made him a great favourite with his master, who used to call him the "Intellect" of his school. He remained at Athens about twenty years. He seems to have regarded his illustrious teacher with the highest respect, and even affection; but he did not accept all his doctrines; and, as his own views became more definite and more matured, the difference between the philosophic systems of the master and the pupil became more strongly marked. This divergence of opinion appears to have furnished the sole foundation for the stories of a personal disagreement between the two philosophers, and of Aristotle's disrespect and ingratitude towards his great teacher. During the latter part of the period of twenty years above referred to, Aristotle commenced a school of his own, in which he gave lessons on rhetoric and other subjects. About 347 B.C. he received an invitation from Hermias, the prince or ruler of Atarneus, in Asia Minor, who had been one of his pupils, to visit his court. While here, he married Pythias, the adopted daughter of Hermias. But this prince having been assassinated about 344 B.C., Aristotle fled with his wife to Mitylene. Here he remained two years, when he received an invitation from Philip of Macedon to become the instructor of his son, Alexander. In the letter† which the king is said to have addressed to the philosopher on that occasion, he says (in substance) that he thanks the gods not so much that they have given him a son, as that he was born in the time of Aristotle, under whose instructions he hopes the young prince may become worthy of his high destiny. Aristotle appears to have been always treated with the greatest respect both by Philip and Alexander. The latter, indeed, regarded his master with an affection and reverence that he seems to have felt for no other mortal. He caused to be rebuilt, at Aristotle's desire, the city of Stagira,‡ which had been destroyed during the wars of Philip. He is said not only to have given him eight hundred talents (more than eight hundred thousand dollars) to enable him to prosecute his researches in natural history, but to have procured for him, during his campaigns, many rare animals and other curiosities. Alexander having ascended the throne in 336 B.C., Aristotle soon after repaired to Athens, where he opened a school called the Lyce'um, from its proximity to the temple of Apollo Lyceius, (Λύκειος.) He is said to have been of so active and restless a temperament that he gave his lectures while walking up and down, and that hence his school was called the "Peripatetic School," (from περιπατέω, to "walk about.") Others say that the term was derived from ὁ περίπατος, (i.e. "the walk,") a name which had already been given to the place where Aristotle taught. The new school was largely attended, and numbered among its scholars many distinguished men, including, among others, Callisthenes, Demetrius Phalereus, and Theophrastus.

After the death of Alexander, Aristotle, being regarded by many of the Athenians with distrust as the friend of Macedon, was, as a mere pretext, it would seem, accused

---

* Thus, Pope, in his "Temple of Fame," says,

"There, in a shrine, that cast a dazzling light,
    Sat, fixed in thought, the mighty Stagirite."

† See AULUS GELLIUS, "Noctes Atticæ," lib. x.
‡ In regard to this subject there is considerable diversity in the statements of different writers: thus much, however, may be regarded as certain, that the city was rebuilt, and that this was due to Aristotle's influence at the Macedonian court.

ā, ē, ī, ō, ū, ȳ, *long;* ă, ĕ, ĭ, ŏ, ŭ, ў, *short;* ạ, ẹ, į, ọ, *obscure;* fâr, fãll, fãt; mêt; nŏt; gōōd; mōōn;

of impiety. Without awaiting his trial, that the Athenians might not, as he said, be guilty of "twice sinning against philosophy,"* he withdrew to Chalcis, in Euboea. Here he died, at the age of sixty-two.

In the history of Western civilization there is no example of any other philosopher having exerted so great and so permanent an influence on the minds of men as Aristotle. For nearly two thousand years his authority was not only predominant, but almost despotic, in all countries where the light of learning had penetrated, whether in Europe, Northern Africa, or Western Asia. During the period known as the "dark ages," when little attention was paid to learning, even in the most favoured portions of Christian Europe, the philosophy of Aristotle was encouraged, and his works diligently studied, in the Moslem capitals of Bagdâd and Córdova. On the revival of letters in Italy and other parts of Europe, Aristotle reigned for a time in the schools without a rival. Dante (1265–1321) speaks of him as "the master of those that know:"

"Vidi il Maestro di color che sanno
Seder tra filosofica famiglia.
Tutti lo miran, tutti onor gli fanno."†
Inferno, canto iv., l. 131.

Unfortunately, his influence, like that of the Roman pontiff, had come to be established on the basis of authority rather than of reason; and that great reaction against authority, in Christendom, which accompanied or caused the Reformation, did not, in its aggressive march, spare the prescriptive throne of the Stagirite. For nearly two hundred years after the time of Bacon, the works of Aristotle were almost universally neglected among the learned in Europe. Towards the close, however, of the last century, attention was again directed to them by several distinguished Germans, including Lessing, Wolf, Schneider, and afterwards more particularly by Hegel, who deemed the philosophical writings of Aristotle worthy of the profoundest study. Thus, after having been for ages the object of a blind, irrational homage, and then of an almost equally blind and irrational contempt, the time is near, we may hope, when at last he will be estimated at his real worth and assume his true position in the realm of intellect. This position, after a thorough and impartial examination of his various claims, must be admitted to be fully equal, if not superior, to that of any other of the great masters of thought that the world has ever seen. Not only was his intellect in the highest degree penetrating, comprehensive, and profound, but the different powers of his mind were so justly balanced, that he seemed equally fitted to excel in each of the various departments of thought. There was scarcely any branch of learning or science known to the ancients to which he did not make important contributions; while some branches he may be truly said to have created. He was the founder of the science of logic, and brought it to such a degree of perfection that subsequent philosophers have added little or nothing of any value; and, in the language of one pre-eminently qualified to judge of such questions, he is "high above comparison with any subsequent logician." (See Sir William Hamilton's "Logic," lecture ii., p. 19).

It is scarcely too much to say that he was also the father of the "science" of natural history; for he appears to have been the very first who introduced anything like a true scientific arrangement into this department of study. Cuvier has called attention to his extraordinary sagacity as a naturalist, in which character he was certainly in advance of his age twenty-two hundred years. "He is," says Cuvier, "not only the most ancient author of comparative anatomy whose works have come down to us but he is one of those who have treated this branch of natural history with the most genius, and best deserves to be taken for a model."

It is common to speak of the scientific process known as "Induction" as if it were wholly a modern invention. But a conception, more or less complete, of induction was common to several of the ancient philosophers.

* In allusion to Socrates' having been put to death on a similar accusation.
† "I saw the master of those that know, sitting amid a family of philosophers; all gaze upon him, all do him honour."

Aristotle evidently refers to this process when, in his work on "Metaphysics," he says, "Science begins when from a great number of experiences one general conception is formed which will embrace all similar cases." "Aristotle," says one who has evidently studied his works with great care, "may be truly styled the father of the Inductive Philosophy, since he first announced its leading principles, and announced them with a completeness and precision not surpassed by Bacon himself." (See G. H. Lewes's "Aristotle," p. 108.)

The moral character of Aristotle seems to have been in every way estimable. In his friendships he was warm and constant. He appears to have cherished the memory of his friend and patron Hermias with a deep and devoted affection. Of his poetical productions there remains a beautiful pæan, full of noble simplicity and pathos, written on the occasion of the death of his beloved prince. Besides other charges brought against him by the Athenians, he was accused of paying divine honours to Hermias. Although a measure of Alexander's aversion and hatred to Callisthenes extended to Aristotle, there is ground for believing that the latter never lost his regard and affection for his royal pupil. And so far was he from furnishing just occasion for the charge against him of disrespect and ingratitude to Plato, that he shows towards his great master an affectionate regard in those very passages wherein he expresses his dissent from him. While clearly intimating that Plato is dear to him, he maintains that truth ought to be dearer to us than any personal considerations. This, in all probability, is the true origin of the proverb, "Amicus Plato, sed magis amica veritas," ("Plato is dear, but truth is more dear.") He did not accept Plato's theory of Ideas, nor the doctrine of Reminiscence which was so intimately connected with that theory. (See PLATO.) Although he fully recognizes the existence of a supreme spiritual (or immaterial) Intelligence as the creative power of the universe, there is nothing in his writings to show that he believed in the immortality of the soul, as this expression is commonly understood,—that is, the continuation of a man's personal identity in a future state of existence.

Only a comparatively small portion of Aristotle's writings have come down to us; but these treat of a great variety of subjects, and prove the universality of his genius. They may be divided under the following heads: 1. Dialectics and Logic; 2. Physics; 3. Mathematics; 4. Metaphysics; 5. Ethics; 6. Politics; 7. Œconomics; 8. Historical Writings; 9. Miscellaneous Writings. The best edition of Aristotle's entire works is that of Bekker, Berlin, 1831. Of the earlier editions, the first Aldine, (Aldina editio princeps,) published at Venice in 5 vols., (1495–98,) is the most valuable.

See RITTER, "History of Philosophy;" G. H. LEWES, "Aristotle," 1 vol. 8vo, London, 1864; ADOLPH STAHR, "Aristotelia," 1830; AMMONIUS, "Vita Aristotelis;" FABRICIUS, "Bibliotheca Græca;" DIOGENES LAERTIUS; ANDREAS SCHOTT, "Vitæ comparatæ Aristotelis et Demosthenis," 1603; FÉLIX RAVAISSON, "Essai sur la Métaphysique d'Aristote," 2 vols., 1837–46; article "Aristote," in the "Nouvelle Biographie Générale," by DR. HOEFER; "Encyclopædia Britannica;" "Biographie Universelle."

Aristoxène. See ARISTOXENUS.

Ar-is-tox'e-nus [Gr. Ἀριστόξενος; Fr. ARISTOXÈNE, à′rès′tok′sån′] of Tarentum, a Greek philosopher and writer, a pupil of Aristotle, lived about 330 B.C. He wrote many works, which are lost, and three extant books on music, which are esteemed valuable and are the oldest on that subject that have come down to us. He rejected the arithmetical system of Pythagoras in music.

Aristoxenus, a Greek physician, who lived about the beginning of the Christian era, and whose opinions are quoted by Galen.

A-ris'tus [Ἄριστος] of Salamis, in Cyprus, a Greek historian of uncertain date. He wrote a History of Alexander the Great, which is lost. Some statements derived from his work have been preserved by Arrian and Strabo.

Aristus, an Academic philosopher, who was a friend of Cicero, and a brother of the philosopher Antiochus. He taught philosophy at Athens, where Marcus Brutus was among his pupils, and where Cicero visited him in 51 B.C.

Ar-is-tȳl′lus, [Gr. Ἀρίστυλλος; Fr. ARISTYLLE, ȧ′rès′-tĕl′,] a Greek astronomer, lived in the third century B.C.

Ariu, ȧ′re-oo, (EMILIO,) a Venetian sculptor of the fifteenth century.

A-rī′us or **Á-reī′us,** popularly called **A′rĭ-us,** [Gr. Ἄρειος,] the founder of Arianism, and author of the greatest schism that ever divided the Christian Church before the Reformation, was born at Cyrene, in Africa, shortly after the middle of the third century. He was ordained a deacon at Alexandria by the patriarch Peter, and promoted to the highest rank among the clergy by the patriarch Alexander.

The controversy which arose between Alexander and Arius about 318 A.D. caused Constantine to summon the first general council, which met at Nicæa (or Nice) in 325 A.D., and condemned with great unanimity the doctrines of Arius, who denied that the Son is coeternal and coessential with the Father. Arius, who had attended this council, was exiled to Illyricum by Constantine, but this sentence was revoked two or three years later. Arianism spread rapidly in Syria and Asia Minor, and was approved by the Synods of Tyre and Jerusalem in 335 A.D.

Soon after this date he returned to Alexandria; but his presence excited there so great a disturbance that Constantine recalled him to Constantinople, where the Arians were numerous and powerful. According to some writers, he avowed his submission to the creed adopted by the Council of Nice, and was about to be restored to communion, when he died suddenly near 336 A.D. Authorities differ respecting the place of his death and many events of his life. Arianism was patronized as the religion of the state by the emperor Constantius, and by Valens. The contest between the Arians and Athanasians (see ATHANASIUS) raged for more than two centuries, and carnal weapons were resorted to by each party to enforce its arguments. The Goths, Vandals, and Suevi of the fifth and sixth centuries were nearly all Arians.

The sect became divided into two portions, called "Hetero-ousians" (who were strict or ultra-Arians) and Semi-Arians or "Homoiousians," who admitted the "similar essence" of the Son with the Father.

The followers of Arius were often called Eusebians, from Eusebius, Bishop of Nicomedia.

See NEANDER, "History of the Christian Church;" MAIMBOURG, "Histoire de l'Arianisme;" STARK, "Essay on Arianism," (in German,) 1783; G. M. TRAVASA, "Storia critica della Vita di Ario," 1748; EUSEBIUS, "Vita Constantini;" SOZOMEN, "Historia Ecclesiastica;" EPIPHANIUS, "Panarium;" THEODORET, "Historia Ecclesiastica;" REUTERDAHL, "Memorabilia Arii ejusque Hæreseos," 1813.

Arivey, de l′, dĕh lȧ′re′vȧ′, (PIERRE,) a French comic writer, born at Troyes, flourished about 1550–80.

Arja, a German spelling of ARYA, which see.

Arjâsp or **Argiasp,** aR′jȧsp′, a king of Turân or Tartary, reigned about five or six centuries before Christ. He waged war against Gushtâsp, King of Persia, because the Persians had adopted the religion of Zoroaster. He was defeated and killed by the Persian prince Isfendiyâr.

See MALCOLM's "History of Persia."

Arje, aR′Hȧ, (R. JACOB JUDAH,) a learned Spanish rabbi and antiquary, born about 1602, resided at Amsterdam, and wrote a number of works. His great work called "Tabnith Hecal" ("The Model of the Temple," 1642) was highly esteemed.

Arje or **Arié,** (R. JUDAH.) See LEO OF MODENA.

Arjona, de, dȧ aR-Ho′nȧ, (MANUEL,) a Spanish poet, born at Osuna in 1761, passed the greater part of his life at Seville. He became *doctoral* of the royal chapel of San Fernando at Seville, and obtained other offices in the church. He wrote an "Ode to the Spanish Nobility," ("Oda a la Nobleza Española,") and other poems of some merit, none of which were published during his life. Died in 1820.

See QUINTANA, "Tesoro del Parnaso Español."

Ar′ju-nă, Ar′joon, or **Ar′jun,** [Hindoo pron. ŭr′-jōō-nạ or ŭr′jōōn,] a mythic hero among the Hindoos, supposed to represent courage, (or, according to some writers, prudence.) He was a companion of Krishna.

Arkenholtz. See ARCKENHOLTZ.

Arkevolti, aR-kȧ-vol′tee, a celebrated Italian rabbi, grammarian, and poet, died in his native town of Padua in 1611.

Arkwright, ark′rīt, (Sir RICHARD,) an Englishman, whose ingenuity has contributed greatly to the prosperity of Great Britain, was born at Preston, Lancashire, in 1732, and was a barber in his youth. He is the reputed inventor of a machine for spinning cotton, which produced an immense extension of the cotton-manufacture in the British Empire. He set up the machine at Preston in 1768, and obtained a patent for it in 1769, about which date he formed a partnership with Need and Strutt of Nottingham. In 1771 they built a spinning-mill on the Derwent at Cromford, which was moved by water-power. This enterprise was very successful. He became the proprietor of other cotton-mills, and controlled the market of cotton yarn for some years. His right to the patent was contested, and a verdict was given against him in 1781; but his business continued to prosper. He was knighted by George III. in 1786. Died in 1792. It is stated that he left property valued at nearly half a million sterling.

Arkwright is celebrated not only as an ingenious inventor, but also as the founder or pioneer of the factory system. He was a man of wonderful energy and perseverance. "It required," says Dr. Ure, "a man of Napoleon nerve and ambition to subdue the refractory tempers of workpeople accustomed to irregular paroxysms of diligence, and to urge on his multifarious and intricate constructions in the face of prejudice, passion, and envy. Such was Arkwright, who, suffering nothing to turn aside his progress, arrived gloriously at the goal, and has forever affixed his name to a great era in the annals of mankind."

See DR. URE, "Cotton Manufacture of Great Britain," vol. i., and "Philosophy of Manufactures," p. 14; "Pursuit of Knowledge under Difficulties," vol. ii.; "Edinburgh Review" for June, 1827, (vol. xlvi.;) BAINES, "History of the Cotton Manufacture in Great Britain;" "Encyclopædia Britannica."

Arkwright, (RICHARD,) the only son of the preceding, was born in 1755, and inherited excellent talents for business. He was also a manufacturer of cotton, and accumulated an immense fortune, which, after his death, was sworn by the executors to exceed one million pounds; but this was a mere statement of form: his actual wealth was far beyond that sum. It has been stated that he was the richest commoner of England. He was well versed in political economy. Died in 1843.

Arlanibœus, aR-lȧ-ne-bö′ŭs, (FILIP,) a Swedish historian of the seventeenth century, wrote a work entitled "Swedish Arms," ("Arma Suecica," 1631.)

Arlaud, aR′lō′, (BENOÎT,) a Swiss portrait-painter, born at Geneva, worked in London. Died in 1719.

Arlaud, (JACQUES ANTOINE,) an eminent miniature-painter, born at Geneva in 1668, had great success in his art, both in Paris and London. He formed a friendship with Newton, and, after his return to Geneva, corresponded with him. Died at Geneva in 1746.

See WALPOLE, "Anecdotes of Painting."

Ar-len′sis de Scu-dạ-lu′pis, (PETER,) an alchemist, lived in the last part of the sixteenth century.

Ar′ler or **Arleri, von,** fon aR-lȧ′ree, (PETER,) an architect, born in Bologna about 1333, exercised his art in Germany, and particularly at Prague, where he was for thirty years engaged on the cathedral of Saint Vitus, a fine specimen of the Gothic style. He was living in 1386.

Arlincourt, d′, dȧR′lăN′koor′, (VICTOR,) VICOMTE, a French poet and novelist, born near Versailles in 1789. He was appointed auditor to the Council of State by Napoleon I. He published in 1818 an epic poem called "Charlemagne, ou la Caroléide." His most popular romance is "Le Solitaire," (1825.) His style is eccentric, and not approved by the critics. Died in 1856.

Arlington, EARL OF. See BENNET.

Arlotti, aR-lot′tee, (DECIO,) an Italian dramatist of the eighteenth century, was born at Reggio; died in 1759.

Arlotti, (LUDOVICO,) an Italian poet and priest, lived in the first half of the sixteenth century.

Arlotti, (MARCANTONIO,) an Italian poet, lived in the second half of the sixteenth century.

Arlotti, (POMPEO,) an Italian physician, born at Reggio in the latter part of the sixteenth century, wrote a work on Bleeding in Fevers.

Arlotti, (RIDOLFO,) an Italian poet, born at Reggio, in Lombardy, about the middle of the sixteenth century. He was a friend of Tasso, and had a fair reputation as a poet. Among his works was a poem on the Conquest of Granada by Ferdinand V. of Castile and Aragon. Died in 1613.

Arlotto, AR-lot'to, called IL PIOVANO, èl pe-o-vä'no, ("The Curate,") or **Arlotto Mainardi,** AR-lot'to mī-naR'dee, a celebrated Italian wit, born at Florence in 1396, was originally a wool-comber, but afterwards took holy orders, and travelled extensively. He was a favourite with sovereigns for his bonmots, which have been published at various times and in different languages. He died about 1483.

Ar-lo'tus or **Ar'lot de Pra'to,** an ecclesiastic, born probably in Tuscany, is said to have compiled the first Concordance of the Bible. Died at Paris in 1287.

Arluno, AR-loo'no, (BERNARDINO,) an Italian jurist and historian, who lived at Milan about 1500, wrote, besides other works, a history of his native city, (" Historia Patriæ,") which was never printed.

Arluno, (GIOVANNI PIETRO,) brother of the above, was a physician of eminence. He practised at Milan, and wrote several medical works.

Arma, AR'mä, (GIOVANNI FRANCESCO,) an Italian physician, born in Piedmont. He was appointed first physician to the Duke of Savoy in 1553, and had a respectable reputation as a medical writer.

Armagnac, d', däR'män'yäk', (BERNARD,) COUNT, Constaole of France, succeeded to his title and estate in 1391. He was ambitious, unscrupulous, and skilful in war. He became the head of the league formed in 1410 by the princes of the blood against the Duke of Burgundy, and was the chief instigator of the civil war which raged between the "Armagnacs" and the "Burgundians." (See CHARLES VI.) Called by Queen Isabeau to defend the kingdom against the English in 1415, he insisted on being appointed constable and chief minister. Having obtained these offices, he treated the royal family with contempt, and rendered himself odious to the people of Paris by his tyranny. In 1418 Paris was taken by the Burgundians, who massacred the Count of Armagnac, with many of his partisans.

See RYMER, "Fœdera;" SISMONDI, "Histoire des Français."

Armagnac, (JEAN,) I., COUNT OF, succeeded to his county in 1319, and distinguished himself in the French service under the kings Philip of Valois, John, and Charles V., taking a prominent part in most of the military movements of those sovereigns. Died in 1373.

Armagnac, (JEAN,) III., COUNT OF, was a brother of Bernard, and grandson of Jean I. He was appointed captain-general in 1385, and commanded an expedition for the conquest of Milan from Galeazzo Visconti in 1391. He was killed in battle before he reached Milan, in the same year.

Armagnac, (JEAN,) IV., COUNT OF, succeeded his father Bernard VII. in 1418, taking sides with the English against Charles VII. He assumed independent powers, but was subdued by Louis XI. (then dauphin) in 1444, and imprisoned for a year. Died in 1450.

Armagnac, (JEAN,) V., COUNT OF, a son of Jean IV., was born about 1420. He was excommunicated by the pope for incest, and was notorious for various crimes. He joined the League of the Public Good in rebellion against Louis XI. about 1465. After this rebellion was terminated by the treaty of Conflans, he again revolted. He was taken prisoner and killed by the royal troops in 1473.

Armand, äR'môN', (ALFRED,) a French architect, born in Paris in 1805. He built railway-stations at Versailles, Amiens, Paris, Calais, etc.

Armand, (CHARLES,) MARQUIS DE LA ROUARIE, dẹh lä roo'ä're', a French officer who served in the American war of the Revolution and rose to the rank of brigadier-general. He died in France in 1793.

Armand, (FRANÇOIS HUGUET,) a celebrated French comedian, born at Richelieu in 1699, and died at Paris in 1765.

Armand de Bourbon. See CONTI.

Armandi, AR-män'dee, (PIERRE DAMIEN,) a general born at Fusignano, in Italy, in 1778. He served in the French army during the empire, and obtained on the field of Bautzen (1813) the rank of colonel. After the restoration of 1815 he was governor of the eldest son of Louis Bonaparte. He fought for the Italian insurgents in 1848–49, and commanded the artillery at Venice. He wrote a valuable work entitled "Military History of Elephants," ("Histoire Militaire des Éléphants," 1843.) Died in 1855.

Armani, AR-mä'nee, or **Armanni,** AR-män'nee, (GIOVANNI BATTISTA,) an excellent Italian improvisatore, born in Venice in 1768, performed in many cities of Italy, and held several civil offices under Napoleon in his native country. He translated into Italian Châteaubriand's "Genius of Christianity" and "Martyrs," and wrote two dramas which added nothing to his reputation. Died in 1815.

See TIPALDO, "Biografia degli Italiani illustri."

Armani, (PIERMARTIRE, pe-äR-maR'te-rà,) an Italian painter, born near Módena in 1613; died in 1669.

Armann, AR'män, (VINCENZ,) called by the Italians VINCENZO ARMANNO, a Flemish landscape-painter of great ability, worked a number of years at Rome, and painted in oil, fresco, and distemper. Died at Venice in 1649.

Armansperg, von, fon aR'män-spĕRG', (JOSEPH LUDWIG,) COUNT, a liberal German statesman, born at Kötzing, in Bavaria, in 1787. He attended the Congress of Vienna in 1815, and was elected to the chamber of deputies in 1825. He became minister of finances in 1826, and minister of foreign affairs in 1828. In 1832 he was appointed president of the council of the regency formed for Otho, King of Greece, who was a minor. He directed the affairs of Greece until February, 1837. Died in 1853.

Armati, AR-mä'tee, (SALVINO, säl-vee'no,) a Florentine, who is the reputed inventor of spectacles. Little is known of his life. His epitaph, preserved by L. del Migliore in "Firenze Illustrata," designates him as the inventor of spectacles, and dates his death in 1317. Vanni del Busca, who wrote in 1299, mentions spectacles as a recent invention.

Armelle, äR'mĕl', (NICOLE,) a French mystic, born in 1606, was celebrated for her piety. Her life was published under the title of "School of the Pure Love of God," (Paris, 1704.) Died in 1671.

See ZIMMERMANN'S "Solitude."

Armellini, AR-mĕl-lee'nee, (CARLO,) an Italian patriot and eminent lawyer, was born at Rome about 1780. He was an adherent of the Roman republic formed under French influence in his youth, and continued to be a republican to the last. He was a member of the provisional government formed at Rome in 1848, and one of the committee of three to whom the executive power was confided in 1849. On the restoration of the pope by the French army he went into exile. Died in 1863.

Armellini, (MARIANO,) an Italian monk, antiquary, and writer, born at Ancona about 1662; died in 1737.

Armenini, AR-mà-nee'nee, (GIOVANNI BATTISTA,) an Italian painter, born at Faenza, published in 1587 "True Precepts of Painting," ("Veri Precetti della Pittura.")

Armero y Peneranda, AR-mä'ro e pà-nà-rän'dä, (FRANCISCO,) a Spanish admiral of the present age. He was minister of the marine several times between 1840 and 1850, and attained the rank of chief admiral in 1855. He succeeded Narvaez as prime minister in 1857.

Armessin, de l', dẹh lär'mä'säN', (NICOLAS,) a French engraver, born in Paris in 1684. He engraved portraits and history with success, and received the title of engraver to the king. Died in 1755.

His father, of the same name, born in 1640, was an engraver of inferior skill.

Armfelt or **Armfeldt,** aRm'fĕlt, (CARL,) BARON OF, an eminent Swedish general, born in Finland in 1666. He was employed by Charles XII. to defend Finland against the Russians, and displayed great skill and valour in a battle near Storkyro, in 1718, but was overpowered by superior numbers. Died in 1736.

Armfelt or **Armfeldt,** (GUSTAF MAURITZ,) a Swedish general and courtier, born in the province of Åbo in 1757, was a great-grandson of the preceding. He was a favourite of Gustavus III., and, just before the death of that king in 1792, was appointed governor of Stockholm. In 1794 he was charged with treason by the regent, who, during the absence of Armfelt on a mission to Naples, procured a sentence of death against him. He was restored to his former dignities by Gustavus IV. in 1799, and appointed governor-general of Finland in 1805. In 1808 he commanded an army which was sent to conquer Norway, but failed. He entered the Russian service in 1810, and obtained several high offices. Died in 1814.

See "Autobiography of G. M. Armfelt," 1830.

Ar'min or **Ar'mўn**, (ROBERT,) an English actor in Shakspeare's company, licensed in 1603. He was author of a small work called "A Nest of Ninnies," (1608,) which is of little value. "The Valiant Welshman," a play, (1615,) is attributed to him.

Arminius. See HERMANN.

Ar-min'i-us, (FULGENTIUS, fŭl-jĕn'she-us,) the Latin name of an Italian writer who became Bishop of Nusco in 1669.

Ar-min'i-us, [Dutch pron. aR-mee'ne-ŭs,] (JACOBUS,) a celebrated Dutch theologian, from whom the system of theology called Arminianism takes its name, was born at Oudewater in 1560. His Dutch name was JACOB HARMENSEN, in place of which he used the Latinized form Arminius. The surname VETERAQUINAS (sometimes given to him) was derived from "Veteres Aquæ," the Latin for Oudewater. He was educated at Marburg, Leyden, and Geneva, 1575–85, visited Rome in 1586, and was ordained a minister at Amsterdam in 1588. He succeeded Francis Junius as professor of divinity at Leyden in 1603. Before this date he had entertained doubts of the Calvinistic doctrine of predestination, and had incurred the suspicion of heterodoxy. In 1604 he propounded tenets on grace and predestination which were opposed by Francis Gomar and others and excited a violent controversy. His adversaries accused him of Pelagianism, but he denied the charge. Among his adherents were Grotius and Olden-Barneveldt. The Supreme Court of the Hague, after hearing a discussion between Arminius and Gomar in 1608, declared that the difference in their doctrines was of little importance. A national synod was convoked to settle this dispute; but, before the appointed time, Arminius died in 1609, leaving several able theological treatises, which were published in one volume, (1629.) He was a man of blameless life and moderate temper. His device was, "A good conscience is Paradise." The national synod which met at Dort in 1618 condemned the five articles of the Arminian creed, the adherents of which were severely persecuted in Holland by Maurice, Prince of Orange. The principles of Arminius have been adopted by the Wesleyan Methodists, and by many members of the Anglican Church.

See CASPAR BRANDT, "Life of Arminius," (in Latin,) 1724; MOSHEIM, "Ecclesiastical History;" PETRUS BERTIUS, "Oratio in Obitum J. Arminii," 1629; Professor MOSES STUART, "The Creed of Arminius, with a Brief Sketch of his Life and Time," in "The Biblical Repertory," 1831.

Ar'mis-tead, (LEWIS A.,) an American general, born in Virginia. He served in the Mexican war, 1846–47, and became a brigadier-general in the Confederate army in 1861. He was killed at Gettysburg, July, 1863.

Armistead, (WALKER KEITH,) an American general, born in Virginia about 1780. He was educated at West Point, and in the second war with Great Britain was chief engineer to the army on the Niagara, and afterwards at Norfolk. In 1828 he was breveted a brigadier-general, and in 1836–37 commanded in the war against the Florida Indians. Died in 1845.

Ar'mI-tage, (EDWARD,) an eminent English painter of the present age, has executed, besides other works, some excellent frescos for the new Houses of Parliament.

Armonville, ăR'môN'vèl', (JEAN BAPTISTE,) a French Jacobin member of the Convention, born at Rheims in 1756; died in 1808.

Arm'strong, (ARCHIBALD,) commonly called **Archy** or **Archee**, jester to James I. of England, lost his place by his sarcasms on Archbishop Laud, and died in 1672.

Armstrong, (FRANCIS,) an English physician, lived at Uppingham; died in 1789.

Armstrong, (GEORGE,) M.D., a brother of John the poet, gave peculiar attention to the diseases of children, and founded a dispensary for the relief of the infant poor in London in 1769. Died about 1780.

Arm'strong, (JAMES,) an American general, born in Pennsylvania in the early part of the eighteenth century. He took part in the defence of Fort Moultrie and in the battle of Germantown. He was a representative in Congress from 1793 to 1795. Died in 1795.

Armstrong, (JOHN or JOHNNIE,) the hero of a ballad in Scott's "Border Minstrelsy," famous for his freebooting expeditions and levies of black mail in the neighbourhood of Langholm. He was hung, by order of James V., about 1529, with thirty-six followers who had come with offers of service.

Armstrong, (JOHN,) an eminent British poet and physician, born at Castleton, Roxburghshire, Scotland, about 1709. He took his degree in medicine at Edinburgh in 1732, soon after which he settled in London and practised with little success. He published anonymously in 1735 a satirical "Essay for Abridging the Study of Physic;" and in 1737, "The Economy of Love," a poem, which is censured for indecency. His principal work is "The Art of Preserving Health," (1744,) a didactic poem, which was received with favour by eminent critics of that age, and often reprinted. "There is a classical correctness and closeness of style in this poem," says Dr. Warton, "that are truly admirable, and the subject is raised and adorned by numberless poetical images." ("Reflections on Didactic Poetry.")

He afterwards produced "Benevolence, a Poetical Epistle," (1751,) "Taste, an Epistle to a Young Critic," (1753,) and several other works. He was physician to the army in Germany from 1760 until the peace of 1763, after which he lived on half-pay. In 1773 he published a volume of "Medical Essays." He was a friend of the poet Thomson. Died in 1779.

See CHAMBERS, "Biographical Dictionary of Eminent Scotsmen;" CHALMERS, "Lives of the English Poets."

Armstrong, (JOHN,) an English military engineer, wrote a "History of Minorca," (1752.) Died in 1758.

Armstrong, (JOHN,) an American general, born at Carlisle, in Pennsylvania, about 1758. He served as an officer in the Revolutionary war, at the end of which he wrote the celebrated "Newburg Addresses," in order to obtain redress or relief for the officers of the army. He was sent as minister to France in 1804, and became secretary of war in January, 1813. For his ill success in defending Washington against the British, he was removed in September, 1814. He died in 1843. (Allen says 1855.)

Armstrong, (JOHN,) an eminent English medical writer, born near Sunderland, in the county of Durham, in 1784. He studied in Edinburgh, and practised with success in Sunderland. In 1814 he published a treatise on "Puerperal Fever." His reputation was widely extended by "Practical Illustrations of Typhus Fever," (1816,) which was a very popular work. He removed to London in 1818, and, though rejected at his examination by the College of Physicians, obtained great professional success in the metropolis. He was also a popular lecturer in the Webb Street School of Medicine, of which he was one of the founders. It appears that he expressed a great contempt for medical learning, and regarded himself as a reformer of the science. He was author of other works besides the above-named. Died in 1829.

See "Memoir of the Life of J. Armstrong," by F. BOOTT, M.D., 1834.

Armstrong, (JOHN,) an English writer and prelate, born near Sunderland in 1813. He became Bishop of Grahamstown, South Africa, about 1853. Died in 1856.

Armstrong, (Rev. JOHN,) a Scottish poet and political writer of much promise, born at Leith in 1771, removed to London, and, while expecting church preferment, supported himself by writing for periodicals. He died of consumption, induced by excessive occupation, at the early age of twenty-seven. Many of his poems appeared in the daily papers of that time.

See "Gentleman's Magazine," September, 1797.

Armstrong, (JOHN MOSTYN,) an English geographer of the eighteenth century, published an "Essay on the Contour of the Coast of Norfolk," (1791.)

Armstrong, (ROBERT,) a general in the Florida war, was born in Tennessee about 1790. Died at Washington in 1854. General Jackson bequeathed to him his sword.

Armstrong, (SAMUEL T.,) a noted bookseller of Boston, mayor of the city, and Governor of Massachusetts for the unexpired term occasioned in 1836 by the election of Governor Davis to the United States Senate. Died in 1850, aged sixty-six.

Armstrong, (Sir THOMAS,) a British subject, born at Nymwegen, was twice imprisoned by Cromwell for his adherence to the royal cause ; released and rewarded at the restoration, he fell under suspicion of the court as an intimate friend of the Duke of Monmouth and an accomplice in the Rye-House Plot, and suffered death in 1684, under circumstances of great injustice. A committee of the House in 1689 reported that "his execution was illegal, and was murder under pretence of justice."

Armstrong, (Sir WILLIAM GEORGE,) .F.R.S., an English engineer, inventor of the Armstrong gun, was born at Newcastle-upon-Tyne in 1810. He became proprietor of an establishment for the manufacture of hydraulic engines for the use of mines, etc. About 1856 he invented the wrought-iron rifled cannon which bears his name and is extensively used. Since that date he was appointed engineer-in-chief for rifled ordnance, and superintendent of a foundry at Woolwich.

Armstrong, (WILLIAM JOSEPH,) an American Presbyterian divine, born at Mendham, New Jersey, in 1796. He was pastor of the First Presbyterian Church in Richmond, Virginia, from 1824 to 1834. He was lost at sea in the steamer Atlantic in November, 1846. A volume of his sermons, with a memoir of his life, has been published.

Armyn, (ROBERT.) See ARMIN.

Arnal, AR-nȧl', (JUAN PEDRO,) a learned Spanish architect, born at Madrid in 1735. He was appointed vice-director of the Academy of San Fernando in 1774, and director of architecture in the same Academy in 1786. The latter appointment was made by the king. Died in 1805.

Ar'nald, (RICHARD,) an English divine, born in London near the close of the seventeenth century, became a fellow of Emmanuel College, Cambridge, and rector of Thurcaston, Leicestershire, in 1733. His principal work is a "Critical Commentary on the Apocryphal Books," which is esteemed judicious and valuable. It is usually printed as a continuation of the commentaries of Lowth and Patrick. Died in 1756.

See J. NICHOLS, " History and Antiquities of Leicester."

Arnald, (WILLIAM,) son of the above, and preceptor to the Prince of Wales, was for twenty years insane, and died in 1802.

Arnaldi, AR-nȧl'dee, (ENEA, ȧ-nā'ȧ,) an Italian count who was born at Vicenza in 1716, and devoted much attention to architecture. He wrote a work on the construction of theatres, and another " On Ancient Basilicas, and particularly those of Vicenza," (" Delle Basiliche antiche, e specialmente di quella di Vicenza," 1767.)

Arnaldo (AR-nȧl'do) or **Arnold** of BRESCIA, brĕsh'ȧ, [in Latin, ARNAL'DUS, ARNUL'PHUS, or ARNOL'DUS BRIXIEN'SIS ; Fr. ARNAUD (ȧr'nō') DE BRESCIA,] an eloquent Italian agitator and reformer, was born at Brescia about the end of the eleventh century. He studied under the celebrated Abelard in France, and on his return to Italy became a monk and preacher. At this time the corruption of the clergy was general and notorious. He began to preach openly that the clergy ought not to possess temporal property or power, and ought to be contented with their tithes and the free offerings of the people. His doctrines were received with favour by many nobles and others, and produced much excitement. For this cause he was banished from Italy by Pope Innocent II. in 1139. He retired to France and Switzerland, where he obtained many adherents. In 1143 the populace of Rome, who favoured the opinions of Arnaldo, revolted against the pope. On learning this event, Arnaldo went to Rome and raised

there the standard of civil liberty and religious reform. Excited by his harangues, the Romans established a senate, defied the temporal power of the pope, and some of the more violent committed great excesses against the persons and property of the cardinals. The pope, Eugenius III., was driven out of Rome in 1146. His successor, Adrian IV.. reduced the people to submission by placing Rome under an interdict in 1154. Arnaldo was driven out of the city, and afterwards seized by Frederick Barbarossa. who delivered him to his enemies. He was put to death at Rome in 1155. His violent enemy Saint Bernard admits that his morals were pure.

See J. D. KÖLER, "Dissertatio de Arnoldo Brixiensi," 1742; D. H. FRANKE, "Arnold von Brescia," Zurich, 1825; HODGSON, "Reformers and Martyrs," Philadelphia, 1867; GUADAGNINI, "Difesa di Arnoldo da Brescia," 2 vols., 1790; D'ACHÉRY, "Spicilegium;" SAINT BERNARD, "Epistolæ;" BECK, "Arnold von Brescia;" QUIRIN, "Essai historique sur Arnaud de Brescia," 1848.

Ar-nal'dus Vil-la-no-va'nus, [Fr. ARNAUD DE VILLENEUVE, ȧr'nō' dėh vėl'nUv'; It. ARNALDO DI VILLANOVA, AR-nȧl'do de vėl-lȧ-no'vȧ,] written also **Arnal'dus Novicomen'sis,** a celebrated physician, born about 1235. He studied at Paris, at Montpellier, and in Italy, seems to have possessed all the medical and chemical knowledge of his day, and paid particular attention to alchemy. His medical essays are numerous, as well as others on alchemy and religion. He incurred the charge of heresy at one time for his religious speculations. He was also employed in diplomatic affairs by the Kings of Sicily and Naples, and died in 1313 on his way to Avignon to visit, as a physician, Clement V., who had sent for him.

See CAMPEGIUS, "Arnaldi Vita;" PIERRE JOSEPH HAITZE, "Vie d'Arnauld," 1719; N. ANTONIO, "Bibliotheca Hispana Vetus."

Ar'nall, (WILLIAM,) a political pamphleteer, editor of the "British Journal," "Free Briton," and an instrument of Sir Robert Walpole's, has been condemned to notoriety in Pope's "Dunciad." He died about 1740.

Arnas Magnæus. See ARNI-MAGNUSSON.

Arnason, AR'nȧ-son, (JON,) a Danish jurist, born in Iceland about 1727 ; died in 1777.

Arnason, (JON,) an Icelandic writer, born at Hof in 1819. He published, besides several biographies and other works, "Icelandic Popular Tales and Adventures," (Leipsic, 1862–64,) an English version of which appeared in 1864.

Arnason, (MAGNUS JON,) Bishop of Skalholt, and a man of great learning, was born in Iceland in 1665, but studied in Copenhagen. He appears to have been a faithful but rigid ecclesiastical ruler. He died in 1743.

Arnau, ȧR-now', (JUAN,) a Spanish painter, born at Barcelona in 1595, excelled as a colorist. Died in 1693.

Arnaud, ȧr'nō', (DANIEL,) a celebrated French Provençal poet, born in Périgord, is supposed to have lived in the latter part of the twelfth century.

See LONGFELLOW's " Poets and Poetry of Europe."

Arnaud, (FRANÇOIS,) a French abbé, writer, and critic, born near Carpentras in 1721. He published in 1754 a "Letter on Music to the Count de Caylus," which was received with favour. He was associated with M. Suard as joint editor of the "Journal Étranger," (1760–62,) and of the "Gazette littéraire de l'Europe," (8 vols., 1764–66.) In 1771 he was admitted into the French Academy, and became reader and librarian to MONSIEUR, afterwards Louis XVIII. Died in 1784.

Arnaud, (GEORGE,) a jurist and classical scholar, of French extraction, born at Franeker, in Holland, in 1711. Before he attained the age of twenty, he excelled as a classical antiquary and critic. He became professor of law at Franeker in 1739, and died in 1740, leaving several critical and legal works, which have a high reputation.

Arnaud, (HENRI,) a warlike pastor of the Waldenses, born at La Tour or La Torre, in Piedmont, in 1641, was noted for his sagacity and ability as a military leader. He led a successful expedition of the Waldenses, (Vaudois,) who in 1689 recovered by arms their homes, from which they had been expelled by the Duke of Savoy on account of their religion. In their march among or over the Alps towards their native valleys, they defeated the French armies in several battles. An account of this expedition, written by Arnaud, was published in English in 1827. He served as colonel in the armies of the allies 'n the war against the French which began about 1702. Died at Schönberg in 1721.

Arnaud, d', dăr'nō', (FRANÇOIS THOMAS MARIE **Baculard**—bä'kü'lăr',) a voluminous French writer of plays, novels, etc., born in Paris in 1718, was patronized in his youth by Voltaire. He afterwards corresponded with Frederick the Great, who addressed to him some complimentary verses. His biographers record with admiration his [answer to Frederick, who, after several atheists had just professed their creed, asked the opinion of Arnaud on the subject. He replied, "I rejoice to believe in the existence of a being greater and wiser than kings." He wrote many novels, which had a temporary popularity. Among his principal works is a collection of anecdotes and essays called "Recreations of the Man of Sensibility," ("Les Délassements de l'Homme sensible," 12 vols., 1784.) Died in 1805.

See QUÉRARD, "La France Littéraire."

Arnaud de Marsan, ăR'nō' dĕh măR'sôN', a Provençal troubadour, and the author of a poem illustrating the society of the age of the troubadours.

Arnaud de Nobleville. See ARNAULT DE NOBLEVILLE.

Arnaud de Ronsil, ăR'nō' dĕh rôN'sèl' or rôN'se'ye, (GEORGE,) a skilful French surgeon, born about 1700, devoted himself especially to the treatment of hernia. He practised in Paris, and subsequently in London, with a high reputation. His writings are praised for clearness and profoundness. His chief work is a "Dissertation on Hernias," (2 vols., 1749.) Died in 1774.

Arnaud de Villa Nova. See ARNALDUS.

Arnauld, ăR'nō', (ANGÉLIQUE,) called also **Angélique de Saint-Jean,** ôN'zhä'lèk' dĕh säN'zhôN', an eminent nun, born in 1624, was a niece of Marie Angélique and a daughter of Robert Arnauld d'Andilly. She was elected prioress of Port-Royal in 1669, and abbess in 1678, after which she was persecuted by the Jesuits. She was considered a prodigy of piety and learning, and it is stated that her father said, "All my children and myself are fools in comparison of Angélique." She was the principal author of a biographical work called "Mémoires pour servir à l'Histoire de Port-Royal," (3 vols., 1742.) Died in 1684.

See SAINTE-BEUVE, "Port-Royal," and MARY ANNE SCHIMMELPENNINCK, "Memoirs of Port-Royal," 2 vols., 1853.

Arnauld, (ANTOINE,) procureur-général to Catherine de Médicis, was a man of eminent abilities, and, though a Huguenot, was saved from the Massacre of Saint Bartholomew by Catherine. He died in 1585.

Arnauld, formerly written **Arnaud,** (ANTOINE,) surnamed L'AVOCAT, (lä'vo'kä',) or "the Advocate," a celebrated orator, born in Paris in 1560, was the most eloquent French pleader of his day, and the father of the eminent Arnaulds of Port-Royal. He succeeded his father as procureur-général in 1585. His most celebrated speech was a "plaidoyer" for the University of Paris against the Jesuits in 1594, which is supposed to have been the cause of the persecution which the recluses of Port-Royal suffered after his death. He died in 1619, leaving six daughters and four sons, all of whom were distinguished.

Arnauld, (ANTOINE,) Doctor of the Sorbonne, a celebrated theologian and philosopher, born in Paris on the 6th of February, 1612, was a son of the preceding and Catherine Marion. He was the most celebrated member of the family of Arnauld, and was sometimes called "le grand Arnauld." He was ordained a priest in 1641, and became a doctor of the Sorbonne about the same time. In 1643 he published an able work "On Frequent Communion," ("De la fréquente Communion,") which made a powerful impression, and gave great offence to the Jesuits, of whom he was always a determined antagonist. This work produced a reform in the style of French theologians, and set an example of a purer taste, which was soon followed by Pascal and Bossuet.

In the controversy respecting grace which arose between Jansenius and his opponents, Arnauld became a zealous Jansenist. He passed some years in the retirement and seclusion of Port-Royal, (a convent near Paris,) and wrote many works on theology and philosophy. In 1656 he was expelled from the Society of the Sorbonne for a work which he wrote on the Jansenist question. This affair gave rise to the "Provincial Letters" of Pascal, for which Arnauld furnished some materials. During the persecution to which his party was exposed from 1656 to 1668, he lived in concealment. He published in 1669 "The Perpetuity of the Faith of the Catholic Church touching the Eucharist defended against Sieur Claude de Charenton," which added to his reputation. A large part of it was written by Nicole. He sought refuge from the enmity of the Jesuits in exile in 1679, after which he lived in various cities of Flanders and Holland until his death, which occurred at Brussels in 1694.

Arnauld was remarkable for his simplicity of character and habits, his impetuosity, and his industry. Boileau wrote his epitaph, and designated him "the most learned mortal that ever wrote," ("le plus savant mortel qui jamais ait écrit.") His fellow-worker Nicole having expressed a desire for repose and respite from their long literary and dogmatical strife, Arnauld exclaimed, "Will you not have all eternity to rest in?" ("N'aurez-vous pas pour vous reposer l'éternité toute entière?")

Among his works, which were collected in a good edition of forty-five closely-printed quarto volumes, (1775-83,) are "La Logique, ou l'Art de Penser," (1662,) an excellent treatise, generally called "The Port-Royal Logic;" "Elements of Geometry," (1667;) a "Treatise on True and False Ideas," (1683—in opposition to the theory of Malebranche;) and "The Practical Morality of the Jesuits," ("Morale pratique des Jésuites," 8 vols., 1683-94.) He aided Lancelot in the composition of the "Grammaire générale et raisonnée."

See "Histoire de la Vie et des Ouvrages de M. Arnauld," by P. QUESNEL, 1697; "Vie d'Antoine Arnauld," by LARRIÈRE, 1783; "Histoire de la Vie et des Ouvrages de M. Arnauld;" SAINTE-BEUVE, "Port-Royal," vol. ii.; VARIN, "La Vérité sur les Arnauld," 2 vols., 1847; C. JOURDAIN, "Notice sur les Travaux philosophiques d'A. Arnauld," 1843; "Biographie Universelle."

Arnauld, (ANTOINE,) commonly called THE ABBÉ, born in 1616, was the son of Robert Arnauld d'Andilly. He first joined the army, but, failing of promotion, resorted to the Church. He was a moderate Jansenist. In 1674 Louis XIV. conferred on him the abbey of Chaumes-en-Brie. He died in 1698, leaving some valuable historic Memoirs, published in 1756.

Arnauld or **Arnaud,** ăR'nō', (ANTOINE,) a French general, born at Grenoble in 1749, was of humble birth, but, joining the army in 1791, he distinguished himself under Dumouriez, in the campaign on the Rhine, at Hohenlinden and other places. He died in Holland in 1804.

Arnauld, (HENRI,) Bishop of Angers, the sixth child of "L'Avocat" before mentioned, was born in 1597. In his early career he pursued the law, and spent several years at Rome as attaché to Cardinal Bentivoglio. On his appointment to the bishopric of Angers, from a complete worldling he became a self-denying, charitable, and laborious pastor. He died at Angers in 1692.

See BESOIGNE, "Vie de Henri Arnauld," 2 vols., 1750.

Arnauld, (MARIE ANGÉLIQUE,) DE SAINTE-MADELEINE, a sister of Antoine Arnauld, (1612-94,) was born in 1591. Her original name was Jacqueline Marie. She became in early youth abbess of Port-Royal, in which she made a reform by enforcing a rigid ascetic regimen, and acquired a high reputation for virtue and intelligence. Died in 1661. Her sister Agnes was also abbess of Port-Royal, and author of two religious books. These sisters were Jansenists. Agnes died in 1671.

Arnauld, (SIMON,) MARQUIS DE POMPONNE. See POMPONNE.

Arnauld d'Andilly, ăR'nō' dôN'de'ye', (ROBERT,) the eldest brother of the great Antoine Arnauld, and father of Angélique, (de Saint-Jean,) noticed above, born in Paris in 1589, was distinguished for probity, piety, and literary ability. In early life he had much favour and influence at the court of Louis XIII., who, it is said, offered him the office of secretary of state, which he declined. He accepted the place of intendant of the army in 1634. About 1645 he retired from the world and entered the monastery of Port-Royal. His principal works are interesting autobiographical Memoirs, published in 1734, and an elegant translation of Josephus's History, (1667–69.) He died in 1674, leaving a son, Simon, Marquis de Pomponne.

Arnauld (Arnold) de Chartres, ȧR'nō' dĕh shȧRtR, [Lat. ARNJL'DUS CARNOTEN'SIS,] a French writer on theology, became abbot of Bonneval in 1138. He wrote, besides other works, "On the Principal Works of Christ," ("De Cardinalibus Christi Operibus.") His style is elegant.

Arnauld de Marveil, ȧR'nō' dĕh mȧR'vȧl' or mȧR'vȧ'ye, written also **Arnaud de Merueil** or **de Maruelh,** a Provençal troubadour, whom Sismondi places highest as an amatory poet of his day. He died in the latter part of the twelfth century.

Arnault, ȧR'nō', (LUCIEN ÉMILE,) a French dramatic writer, son of Vincent Antoine, noticed below, was born at Versailles in 1787. He was appointed auditor to the council of state in 1808. He produced a number of tragedies, one of which, entitled "Regulus," was successful. After the revolution of 1830 he was prefect of several departments.

Arnault, (VINCENT ANTOINE,) a French poet and dramatist, born in Paris in 1766. He began his career by the tragedy of "Marius at Minturnæ," (1791,) which had great success. He was author of two other popular tragedies, entitled "Lucrèce," (1792,) and "Germanicus," (1816,) and of a number of poems, fables, etc. In 1797 he was charged by Napoleon to organize the government of the Ionian Isles. In 1808 he was appointed chief or director of public instruction. He succeeded Andrieux in 1833 as perpetual secretary of the French Academy, and published "Souvenirs of a Sexagenarian," (4 vols., 1833.) Died in 1834.

See JOURDAIN, "Poëtes Français."

Arnault (ȧR'nō') or **Arnaud de Nobleville,** dĕh nobl'vĕl', (LOUIS DANIEL,) a French physician, noted for his benevolence, born at Orléans in 1701. He devoted himself to the gratuitous service of the poor in his native city. He wrote a "Manual for Charitable Ladies," ("Manuel des Dames de Charité," 1747,) often reprinted, and a "Natural History of Animals," to serve as a supplement to the Materia Medica of Geoffroy, (6 vols., 1756.) Died in 1778.

Arnavon, ȧR'nȧ'vǒN', (FRANÇOIS,) a French theologian, born near Vaucluse about 1740; died in 1824.

Arnay, d', dȧR'nȧ', (JOHANNES RUDOLPHUS,) a Swiss writer, born in the canton of Berne in 1710. He became professor of eloquence and history at Lausanne, and wrote, besides other works, a "Treatise on the Private Life of the Romans," (1732.) Died in 1766.

Arnd, ȧRnt, (CHRISTIAN,) a German writer on philosophy and logic, born in 1623; died in 1653.

Arnd, Arnt, or **Arndt,** ȧRnt, (JOHANN,) a German Lutheran divine of great merit, born at Ballenstädt, duchy of Anhalt, in December, 1555. He was minister at Quedlinburg from 1590 to 1599, and then removed to Brunswick. He was an earnest teacher of practical religion. About 1595 he published the first part of his great work "On True Christianity," ("Vom wahren Christenthum,") which produced a powerful impression, was admired as a master-piece of composition, and translated into nearly all the languages of Europe. There are English versions of it by Boehm (1712) and W. Jacques, (1815.) Probably no other book except the Bible has been so often printed in Germany. In 1611 he became general superintendent at Zelle, where he died in 1621, leaving several other works.

See "Johann Arnd, ein biographischer Versuch," von FR. ARNDT, 1838; F. W. KRUMMACHER, "J. Arnds Leben," 1842; WILDENHAHN, "J. Arnt: Zeitbild aus Braunschweigs Kirchen- und Stadtgeschichte," etc., 2 vols., 1847; WEHRHAN, "Lebensgeschichte J. Arndts," 1848; H. L. PERTZ, "Commentatio de J. Arndtio," 1852.

Arnd, [Lat. ARN'DIUS,] (JOSUA or JOSIAH,) a German Lutheran minister and prolific writer, born at Güstrow in 1626. He became professor of logic at Rostock in 1653, and resigned that chair in 1656, after which he preached at Güstrow. He wrote in Latin on theology, philosophy, history, etc. Among his works is a "Lexicon of Ecclesiastical Antiquities," (1667,) and several Latin poems. Died in 1684.

Arnd, (KARL,) one of the earliest bibliographical

writers, a son of the preceding, was born at Güstrow in 1673. He became professor of Hebrew at Rostock in 1708, and published several learned works. Died in 1721.

Arndt, ȧRnt, (ERNST MORITZ,) a popular German poet and political writer, born in the Prussian island of Rügen on the 26th of December, 1769. His first work was a book of "Travels in Germany, Hungary, and Italy," (1797–98.) He became a professor at Greifswalde in 1806, and successfully invoked the spirit of German nationality against the aggressions of Napoleon, in his "Spirit of the Time," ("Geist der Zeit," 1806.) He zealously promoted the war of independence (1812–13) by a number of spirited songs, poems, and pamphlets, which were considered master-pieces. His famous song, "Was ist des Deutschen Vaterland?" ("What is the German's Fatherland?") is called the most popular song of Germany. He was appointed professor of history at the University of Bonn in 1818; but he was suspended from his functions in 1819, because he insisted on the constitutional reforms which the king had promised. Arndt was restored to his chair at Bonn in 1840, and was deputed to the National Assembly of Frankfort in 1848. Among his works are a tract entitled "Ueber Landwehr und Landsturm," ("On the Militia and the Levy en Masse," 1812,) and "Souvenirs of my Life," (1840.) He died in 1860.

See W. NEUMANN, "E. M. Arndt: eine Biographie;" E. M. ARNDT, "Erinnerungen aus dem äussern Leben," 1840; LONGFELLOW, "Poets and Poetry of Europe."

Arndt, (GOTTFRIED AUGUST,) a German writer on history and law, born at Breslau in 1748. He became professor of moral philosophy and political economy at Leipsic in 1791. He published, besides other works, "Archives of the History of Saxony," (3 vols., 1784–86.) Died in 1819.

Arndt, (JOHANN GOTTFRIED,) a German historian, born at Halle in 1713. He was rector of a gymnasium at Riga, and published a valuable work entitled "Chronicles of Livonia," (1740–50.) Died in 1767.

Arndt, von, fon ȧRnt, (C. GOTTLIEB,) a German writer, and imperial councillor of Catherine II. of Russia, published a work "On the Origin of European Dialects." Died in 1829.

Arndts, ȧRnts, or **Arendts,** ä'rēnts, (LUDWIG,) a German jurist, born at Arnsberg, in Prussia, in 1805. He was successively professor of law at Bonn, Munich, and Vienna, and wrote a "Manual on the Pandects," and other works.

Arne, arn, (CECILIA,) (originally **Young,**) one of the most distinguished singers of her time, was the wife of Thomas Arne. Died in 1776.

Arne, (MICHAEL,) an English composer, son of Thomas, noticed below, was born in London about 1740. He inherited a moderate portion of his father's talent. His principal work was the opera of "Cymon," (1767.) He composed several popular songs, among which is "The Topsails shiver in the Wind." Died in 1785.

Arne, (SUSANNA.) See CIBBER.

Arne, (THOMAS AUGUSTINE,) an eminent English musician and composer, born in London in 1710, was the son of an upholsterer who is identified by some with a person of that trade mentioned by Addison in "The Spectator," No. 50. He composed the music for Addison's opera of "Rosamond," which was performed with success in 1733, and also that for Milton's "Comus," (1738,) which increased his reputation. "The melody of Arne at this time," says Dr. Burney, "and of his Vauxhall songs afterwards, forms an era in English music: it was so easy, natural, and agreeable to the whole kingdom that it had an effect on the national taste." In 1740 he married Cecilia Young, a popular vocalist, and in 1745 was engaged as composer by the manager of Vauxhall Gardens. Among his most celebrated works is the opera "Artaxerxes," (1762.) The two principal national songs of England, "God save the King" and "Rule Britannia," owe their popularity chiefly to his music. Died in 1778.

See BURNEY, "History of Music;" FÉTIS, "Biographie Universelle des Musiciens."

Arnemann, ȧR'nĕh-mȧn', (JUSTUS,) a German medical writer, born at Lüneburg in 1763, practised some years at Altona. He published numerous works of

ϵ as *k*; ç as *s*; g̃ *hard*; g̃ as *j*; G, H, K, *guttural*; N, *nasal*; R, *trilled*; s̃ as *z*; th as in *this*. (☞ See Explanations, p. 23.)

moderate merit, among which is a treatise on Materia Medica, ("Entwurf einer praktischen Arzeneimittellehre," (2 vols., 1792.) He committed suicide in 1807.

Ar'nest or **Er'nest** [Lat. ARNES'TUS] of Pardubicz, first Archbishop of Bohemia, minister to Charles IV. of that kingdom, and first chancellor of the University of Prague, died in 1364.

Arn'grims-son,(Eystein—ī'stīn,) an Icelandic monk of the fourteenth century, celebrated for his "Lily," reputed the best poem in the Icelandic language. It enjoyed great popularity during the reign of Catholicism in the North. He died in 1361.

See KRAFT og NYERUP, "Almindeligt Litteraturlexicon.

Arnheim, von, fon ARN'hīm, or **Arnim**, äR'nim, (JOHANN GEORG,) a distinguished German diplomatist and general, born in the Mark of Brandenburg about 1581. He entered the army of the emperor Ferdinand II. in 1626, and won the favour of Wallenstein, who employed him in a negotiation with Gustavus Adolphus. In 1628 he obtained the rank of field-marshal. He passed in 1630 into the service of the Elector of Saxony, who gave him the chief command of his army, and he commanded the left wing under Gustavus Adolphus at Leipsic in 1631. Arnheim and Wallenstein commanded opposing armies in 1632 and 1633; but the former was suspected of collusion with the enemy. He defeated the Imperialists at Liegnitz in May, 1634, and detached Saxony from the Swedish alliance in 1635. He resigned his commission the same year. Died in 1641.

See PUFENDORF, "De Rebus Suecicis;" WALDSTEIN, (WALLENSTEIN,) "Briefe," 3 vols., 1829.

Arnigio, AR-nee'jo, (BARTOLOMMEO,) an Italian poet, born at Brescia in 1523 ; died of the plague in 1577.

Arnim. See ARNHEIM.

Arnim, aR'nim, (ELISABETH or BETTINA—bĕt-tee'nä,) a celebrated German authoress, born at Frankfort-on-the-Main in 1785. She was a sister of the poet Clemens Brentano, and became the wife of L. A. von Arnim, also a poet. She was in her youth a passionate admirer of Goethe, with whom she corresponded. Her imagination was ardent and eccentric. Her principal works are "The Correspondence of Goethe with a Child," (3 vols., 1835,) which she translated into English, and "Die Günderode," (2 vols., 1840,) a collection of letters and charming idyllic poems. Died in Berlin in January, 1859.

See "Blackwood's Magazine," vol. lviii., and "Foreign Quarterly," vol. xxxiv.

Arnim, von, fon aR'nim, (LUDWIG **Achim**—ä'kim,) a popular, original, and romantic German poet, born at Berlin in 1781. He studied the natural sciences, and published in 1799 a "Theory of Electricity." In partnership with his friend Clemens Brentano, whose sister Bettina he afterwards married, he published a collection of popular songs, called "The Boy's Wonder-horn," ("Des Knaben Wunderhorn," 3 vols., 1806.) His novel entitled "Poverty and Riches, Guilt and Repentance of the Countess of Dolores," (2 vols., 1810,) is highly commended, and is perhaps his best work. His productions display great imagination, depth of feeling, and a tendency to the romantic simplicity of the middle ages. Among his admired prose works are the tale called "Angelica the Genoese and Cosmus the Rope-dancer," ("Angelica die Genueserin und Cosmus der Seilspringer,") and "Isabella of Egypt," (1811.) Died in 1831.

See GERVINUS, "Neuere Geschichte der poëtischen national Literatur der Deutschen."

Arni-Magnusson, aR'ne mäg'nŭs-son, [Lat. AR'NAS MAGNÆ'US,] an eminent archæologist of Iceland, born in 1663, studied at Copenhagen, where he subsequently became professor of history and antiquities. He was sent to Iceland, in 1702, by Frederick IV., and, during a residence of ten years in that country, made a large and valuable collection of manuscripts. The Arna-Magnæan Commission, having for its object the publication of these works, was named in his honour. Died in 1730.

See the Introduction to KEYSER's "Religion of the Northmen," translated by PENNOCK, pp. 22, 23.

Arnisæus or **Arnisäus**, aR-ne-zä'ŭs, (HENNIN'GUS,) a miscellaneous writer, born near Halberstadt, in Prus-

sian Saxony, in the sixteenth century. In 1620 he removed to Copenhagen and became physician to Christian IV. Died in 1636.

Arnkiel, aRn'keel, (FRIEDRICH,) a historian, a son of Trogillus, noticed below, lived at Apenrade in the first part of the eighteenth century.

Arnkiel, (TROGILLUS, tRo-ḡil'lŭs,) a divine and antiquary, born near Apenrade, in Sleswick. He became superintendent of the Lutheran Church in Holstein in 1686. His work "On the Philosophy and School of Epicurus" (in Latin, 1671) was received with favour. He also wrote an able treatise on the ancient religion and the moral and political state of the Saxons, Goths, etc., entitled "Cimbrische Heiden-Religion," (1691.) Died at Apenrade in 1713.

Ar'no, first Archbishop of Salzburg, in Germany, was a man of great influence in his day, being councillor to the Duke of Bavaria, and held in high esteem by Charlemagne and Pope Leo III. Died about 820.

Arnobe. See ARNOBIUS.

Ar-no'bī-us, [Fr. ARNOBE, äR'nob',] (A'FER,) sometimes called THE ELDER, a rhetorician and eloquent apologist for Christianity, was a native or resident of Sicca, in Numidia, and flourished about the end of the third century. Little is known of his life. He was converted from paganism to Christianity, and wrote an able work called "Disputations against the Gentiles," ("Disputationes contra Gentes,") in which he attacks the absurdities of the pagan religion with powerful sarcasm. This is supposed to have been written soon after the persecution under Diocletian, which began in 302 A.D. His doctrines are not considered strictly orthodox. M. Villemain, in the "Nouvelle Biographie Générale," remarks that certain circumstances give this work a character of originality and a real importance in relation to philosophy and history. "Writing at the end of persecution and before the ruin of paganism, he is full of ardent recriminations and of curious details." Lactantius was a pupil of Arnobius.

See CAVE, "Historia Literaria;" NEANDER, "History of the Christian Church;" BAYLE, "Historical Dictionary;" MORÉRI, "Dictionnaire Historique."

Arnobius THE YOUNGER, [Fr. ARNOBE LE JEUNE, äR'nob' leh zhŭn,] a semi-Pelagian ecclesiastic, who flourished about 460 A.D. His chief work was a Commentary on the Psalms. He opposed the doctrines of Saint Augustine.

Ar'nold, Duke of Gueldres, (or Geldern,) of the house of Egmond, (or Egmont,) was born in 1410. He was defeated in battle by the Duke of Berg in 1444, and lost the duchy of Jülich. His son Adolphus rebelled against him with success, and confined Arnold in prison for about five years. He was released by the intervention of Charles the Bold of Burgundy, to whom he sold his duchy in 1472. Died in 1473.

See PONTANUS, "Historia Gelrica."

Arnold, aR'nolt, Abbot of Lubeck, a German chronicler of the twelfth century.

Arnold, (ANDREAS,) a German theologian, and professor of Greek at Nuremberg, where he was born in 1656 ; died in 1694.

Ar'nold, (BENEDICT,) succeeded Roger Williams as Governor of Rhode Island in 1657, and held the office for many years. Died in 1678.

Arnold, (BENEDICT,) an American general, infamous for his attempt to betray his country, was born at Norwich, Connecticut, January 3, 1740. During his boyhood he was noted for his turbulence, audacity, and love of mischief. Having been apprenticed to an apothecary, he ran away and enlisted as a soldier, but soon deserted, and afterwards became a merchant of New Haven and engaged in an extensive trade with the West Indies. His speculations ended in bankruptcy, under circumstances which left a stain upon his reputation for honesty. Soon after the battle of Lexington, April, 1775, he received a commission as colonel in the service of Massachusetts. He aided Ethan Allen in the capture of Ticonderoga in May, 1775, and in the autumn of that year commanded a body of about twelve hundred men sent to take Quebec. In the long and difficult march through the pathless forests he displayed the qualities

ā, ē, ī, ō, ū, ȳ, *long;* ȧ, ė, ȯ, *same, less prolonged;* ă, ĕ, ĭ, ŏ, ŭ, y̆, *short;* ạ, ẹ, ị, ọ, *obscure;* fär, fȧll, fȧt; mĕt; nŏt; gōōd; mōōn;

of an able commander. He joined the army of General Montgomery, who had the chief command, and who attacked Quebec about the end of December, but was defeated and killed. Arnold was wounded in the leg at Quebec, and his services in this campaign were rewarded with the rank of brigadier-general.

Having obtained command of a flotilla of small vessels on Lake Champlain, he encountered a superior force on the 11th of October, 1776, and, although he was not victorious, he fought with such skill and determined courage that this action tended to animate and revive the hopes of the patriots. Early in 1777 he was deeply offended because Congress promoted five of his juniors to the rank of major-general. He was soon after raised to the same rank, but the affront still rankled in his heart, for the five previously appointed continued to be above him. He was frequently involved in difficulties by his violent and imperious temper and his dishonesty in pecuniary transactions.

He commanded the left wing at the battle of Bemus Heights, September 19, 1777, and there quarrelled with General Gates, who appears to have been jealous of Arnold. In consequence of this dispute, Arnold resigned his command soon after the date just named; but during the battle of Stillwater, October 7, he entered the field without the permission of General Gates, and displayed desperate courage or temerity. According to Sparks, "Arnold received no orders during the day, but rode about the field in every direction, seeking the hottest parts of the action, and issuing his commands wherever he went. Being the highest officer in rank that appeared in the field, his orders were obeyed when practicable; but all accounts agree that his conduct was rash in the extreme, indicating rather the frenzy of a madman than the considerate wisdom of an experienced general." In this battle he received a severe wound, which disabled him for several months, during which Congress accorded to him his full rank.

In June, 1778, he was appointed to the command of Philadelphia, which had just been evacuated by the British. He ran deeply into debt, and lived in an extravagant style, which he endeavoured to support by peculation and acts of rapacity. He married about 1779 Margaret, a daughter of Edward Shippen, an eminent citizen of Philadelphia. A court-martial called to investigate his official conduct in Philadelphia sentenced him to receive a reprimand from the general-in-chief, (January, 1780.) Although the reprimand was administered by General Washington in very mild and conciliatory terms, the vindictive spirit of Arnold was not appeased. About six months before the date last named, he had made treasonable overtures to the enemy. To enhance the value of his treachery, he solicited and obtained command of West Point, (perhaps the strongest and most important position in the United States,) which he proposed to betray into the hands of Sir Henry Clinton. The latter employed Major André as his agent in this negotiation. The plot was detected and defeated by the capture of André, September 23, 1780, (see ANDRÉ, JOHN,) and Arnold narrowly escaped (September 25) in the British sloop Vulture, which was stationed below West Point. It is stated that he received from Sir Henry Clinton £6315 as the reward of his treason or as an indemnity for what he had lost by desertion.

Arnold entered the British army as a colonel, and issued two proclamations or addresses to the Americans, designed to vindicate his own course and to persuade others to desert. He was appointed to command an expedition against Virginia, and sailed from New York to Hampton Roads in December, 1780. He ascended the James River, and inflicted much damage on the people of that region, by burning and pillage. In September, 1781, he commanded a body of troops which took Fort Griswold, Connecticut, massacred the garrison after they had surrendered, and burned New London. This was his last exploit in the war of the Revolution. He passed the rest of his life mostly in England, where, according to Sparks, "he was shunned and despised by everybody" except the king and a few persons in authority. He died in London in June, 1801, leaving a son, James Robertson Arnold, who became a

major-general in the English army. (See Sparks's "Life of Benedict Arnold," in his "Library of American Biography," vol. iii.)

Arnold, aR'nolt, (CHRISTOPH,) a German peasant, distinguished for his knowledge of astronomy, born near Leipsic in 1646. He is said to have discovered the comet of 1683 eight days before Hevelius; and he was the first to call attention to that of 1686. He also observed the transit of Mercury across the sun's disc in 1690. Died in 1695.

Arnold, (CHRISTOPH,) a German philologist, born at Nuremberg (or, according to some authorities, at Hersbruck) in 1627, became a professor of history and eloquence. He wrote a number of works, among which was the "Ornament (or Beauty) of the Latin Language," ("Ornatus Linguæ Latinæ," 1657.) Died in 1685.

Arnold, (DANIEL HEINRICH,) professor of philosophy and divinity at Königsberg, born in that city in 1706, was the author of a history of the Königsberg University. Died in 1775.

Arnold, (FRANZ,) a priest of Cologne, and a violent opposer of Luther, against whom he wrote several works.

Arnold, (FRIEDRICH,) a German engraver, born in Berlin in 1780; died in 1809.

Arnold, (GEORG,) a German jurist, born at Chemnitz in 1531, wrote in Latin a "Life of Maurice, Elector of Saxony." Died in 1588.

Arnold, (GEORG,) an organist, born in the Tyrol, lived towards the close of the seventeenth century.

Arnold, (GEORGE DANIEL,) a jurist, born at Strasburg in 1780. He was appointed professor of Roman law at his native city in 1811, published a text-book of Roman law, (1812,) and gave in the Alsatian dialect a remarkable picture of manners in his popular comedy of "Whit-Monday," ("Le Lundi de Pentecôte,") which was eulogized by Goethe. He also wrote fugitive poems of some merit. Died in 1829.

Arnold, (GOTTFRIED,) a German Protestant theologian of high reputation, born at Annaberg, Saxony, in 1666. He preached at Werben and at Perleberg, and received the title of historiographer to Frederick I. of Prussia. He wrote, besides many other theological works, a mystical book called "Sophia, or the Mysteries of Divine Wisdom," (1700,) and a "History of the Church from the Christian Era to 1688," (3 vols., 1699–1700,) which offended the orthodox Lutherans, and was noticed in foreign countries. He died in 1714, leaving an autobiography, (1716.)

See also COLERUS, "Historia G. Arnoldi," 1718; PETERSEN, "Geretteter Bruder Arnold," 1718; ADOLPHE RIFF, "G. Arnold, Historien de l'Église," 1847.

Arnold, (HALDRENIUS VESALIENSIS.) See ARNOLDUS.

Arnold, (JOHANN CHRISTIAN,) professor of philosophy, and afterwards of physics, in the University of Erlangen, was born at Weissenfels in 1724; died in 1765.

See REINHARD, "Memoria J. C. Arnoldi," 1765.

Arnold, (JOHANN GERHARD,) a German publicist and historian, born in 1637; died in 1717.

Arnold, (JOHANN GOTTFRIED,) an eminent musical composer for the violoncello, was born in Hohenlohe in 1773; died in 1806.

See FÉTIS, "Biographie Universelle des Musiciens."

Arnold, (JOHANN von Bergel—fon bĕR'gĕl,) a German poet of the sixteenth century. He wrote a poem "On the Invention of the Art of Engraving on Copper or Brass," ("De Chalcographiæ Inventione," 1541.)

Arnold, (JOHN,) one of the greatest improvers of the chronometer, was born at Bodmin, in Cornwall, in 1744. He removed to London, and was patronized by George III. Among his improvements are the detached escapement, the expansion balance, the cylindrical balance spring, etc. Died in 1799.

Arnold, (JOSEPH,) M.D., an English naturalist, born in Suffolk in 1783, entered the navy as assistant surgeon, visited New South Wales, and made a large collection of natural objects, which was destroyed by fire at Batavia. He afterwards accompanied Sir Stamford Raffles to Sumatra, where he died in 1831.

Arnold, (LEMUEL H.,) born at Saint Johnsbury, Vermont, in 1792, was elected Governor of Rhode Island in

1831, re-elected in 1832, and was a member of Congress from 1843 to 1845. Died in 1852.

Arnold, (LEWIS G.,) an American general, born in New Jersey, graduated at West Point in 1837, and distinguished himself in the Mexican war, and also in the Florida war of 1856. He was appointed a brigadier-general in the Union army in January, 1862.

Arnold, (MATTHEW,) an English poet, a son of Dr. Thomas Arnold of Rugby, was born at Laleham, near Staines, in Middlesex, December 24, 1822. He was educated at Rugby and Oxford, and elected a Fellow of Oriel College in 1845. He became in 1847 private secretary to Lord Lansdowne, and lay inspector of schools, under the Committee of the Council of Education, in 1851. In 1848 he published "The Strayed Reveller, and other poems," and in 1856 appeared a "new and complete edition" of his poems. He was elected professor of poetry at Oxford in 1857. "For combined culture and fine natural feeling in the matter of versification," says the "Edinburgh Review" for October, 1856, "Mr. Arnold has no living superior." In 1865 appeared a volume of "Essays in Criticism," in which Mr. Arnold shows himself to be a critic of no common order: his observations "On Translating Homer" are among the very best that have ever been written on that subject. A volume of "New Poems" by Matthew Arnold" was published in 1867.

Arnold or **Arnoldus,** (NICOLAUS,) a Protestant divine and eminent preacher, born at Lesna, in Poland, in 1618. He became professor of theology at Franeker in 1651, and wrote in Latin several works on theology. Died in 1680.

Arnold, AR'nolt, (OLORI'NUS or CYGNÆ'US,) a Dutch writer on theology ; died in 1622.

Arnold, (RICHARD,) an English chronicler and merchant of London, born about 1450, was the author of a work commonly called "Arnold's Chronicle," but sometimes named "The Statutes of London," (about 1500.)

Arnold, (SAMUEL,) a successful English musical composer, born in London in 1740. His opera of the "Maid of the Mill" (1765) was greatly applauded. Among his most popular works are the oratorio of "The Prodigal Son ;" and operas entitled "Rosamond," (1767,) "Inkle and Yarico," (1787,) and "The Castle of Andalusia," (1782.) He was appointed organist and composer to the king in 1783, and organist of Westminster Abbey in 1793. At the request of the king, he published a magnificent edition of Handel's Works, (36 vols.) Died in 1802.

See FÉTIS, "Biographie Universelle des Musiciens."

Arnold, (SAMUEL BENEDICT,) a German painter of history and portraits, born at Dresden in 1744 ; died in 1817.

Arnold, (SAMUEL J.,) a son of Samuel Arnold the composer, published a number of dramatic pieces, among which are "Auld Robin Gray," (1794,) "Irish Legacy," (1797,) and "Britain's Jubilee," (1809.)

Arnold, (THOMAS,) D.D., of Rugby, an English historian and teacher of great merit, was born at Cowes, in the Isle of Wight, on the 13th of June, 1795. He entered Corpus Christi College, Oxford, in 1811, took a first-class degree in 1814, and gained the chancellor's prize for a Latin Essay in 1817. He was distinguished at college for the liberality of his opinions and the independence of his character. In 1820 he married Mary, a daughter of the Rev. John Penrose.

He passed several years at Laleham, near Staines, where he was employed as a private tutor. In 1827 or 1828 he was ordained a priest, and became headmaster of Rugby School, where he found a proper sphere for the exercise of his rare qualifications as a teacher. He raised the character of that school by the influence of Christian principles, enforced by his own example, and diligently cultivated a sense of duty and responsibility in the students.

He published a pamphlet on Church Reform in 1833, and a valuable edition of Thucydides, (in 1830–35.) His principal work is a "History of Rome," (3 vols., 1838–40–42,) which comprises the period from the origin of Rome to the end of the second Punic war, and was interrupted by his death. This is a work of high reputation, composed on the basis of Niebuhr's discoveries.

He contributed articles to the "Quarterly Review" and "Edinburgh Review." In August, 1841, he was appointed regius professor of modern history at Oxford. Soon after he had finished the introductory course of lectures, he died at Rugby, in June, 1842. Among his works are five volumes of sermons, (1828–42,) and "Introductory Lectures on Modern History," (1842.)

"He will strike those who study him more closely," says the "London Quarterly Review" for October, 1844, "as a complete character,—complete in its union of moral and intellectual gifts ; . . . for his greatness did not consist in the pre-eminence of any single quality, but in several remarkable powers, thoroughly leavened and pervaded by an ever-increasing moral nobleness."

"His sermons," says Arthur Penrhyn Stanley, "are remarkable as being, by their simple and natural language, one of the first practical protests raised in the nineteenth century against the technical and unreal phraseology generally used in English preaching, and as uniting a high religious standard, a strong imagination, and a living spirit of devotion with unaffected good sense, and moral energy and sincerity."

"As an historian, his moral qualifications consisted chiefly in his love of truth, his conscientiousness, and his high Christian judgment of all political transactions. Intellectually, his chief excellence lay not so much in the philosophical and biographical department of history as in analyzing laws, parties, and institutions."

See "Life and Correspondence of Dr. Arnold," (2 vols., 1844,) by A. P. STANLEY, "Encyclopædia Britannica ;" "Edinburgh Review" for January, 1843 ; "Tom Brown's School-Days at Rugby."

Arnold, (THOMAS,) an English physician, born in 1742. He took his degree at Edinburgh, and settled at Leicester, where he became senior physician to the infirmary, and physician to the lunatic asylum. His principal work is "Observations on the Nature, Kinds, Causes, and Prevention of Insanity, Lunacy, or Madness," (2 vols., 1782–86,) which displays much learning. Died in 1816.

Arnold, (THOMAS KER'CHEVER,) an English clergyman, rector of Lyndon, noted as editor of numerous popular text-books, was born about 1800. Among his publications are school-manuals for the Greek, Latin, French, and German languages. Died in 1853.

Arnold, (WILLIAM DEL'AFIELD,) a son of Dr. Thomas Arnold of Rugby, born in 1828, became an officer in the British army, and afterwards director of public instruction in the Punjab. He was author of a novel called "Oakfield ; or, Fellowship in the East," an exposition of the trials of a young officer who resolves to set an example of fidelity to Christian principles in the army. He died at Gibraltar, on his passage homeward from India, in April, 1859. His brother Matthew has written some beautiful and touching lines on his death.

Arnold of Brescia. See ARNALDO.

Arnold or **Arnolt von Bruck,** AR'nolt fon BRŌŌk, (or **de Prug,** dĕh pRŌŌG,) a German musician of the sixteenth century.

Arnold von Büderich, AR'nolt fon bü'dĕh-rik', a German theologian, lived in the second half of the fifteenth century.

Arnold Melchthal. See MELCHTHAL.

Arnold of Meldorp, a German theologian of the twelfth century.

Ar'nold or **Ar'nould of Rotterdam,** a Dutch theologian, whose family name was Geilhoven. Died in 1442.

Ar'nold von Wink'el-ried, [Ger. pron. AR'nolt fon ŵink'ĕl-reet',] a brave Swiss patriot, who broke the Austrian phalanx at the battle of Sempach in 1386, by rushing against the points of their spears and gathering within his arms as many as he could. He fell pierced with mortal wounds, but decided the victory in favour of the Swiss.

See "Histoire de la Confédération Suisse," translated from the German of J. von Müller by MONNARD and VUILLEMIN, Paris, 1840–46.

Arnoldi, AR-nol'dee, or **di Arnoldo,** de AR-nol'do, (ALBERTO,) an eminent Florentine sculptor and architect of the fourteenth century, executed a colossal marble group of the Madonna and Child, in the church of Santa Maria del Bigallo, Florence, (1364,) which was formerly attributed to Andrea Pisano.

ā, ē, ī, ō, ū, ȳ, *long;* à, è, ò, same, less prolonged; ă, ĕ, ĭ, ŏ, ŭ, ў, *short;* ạ, ẹ, ị, ọ, *obscure;* fär, fäll, fåt; mêt; nŏt; gōōd; mōōn;

Arnoldi, aʀ-nol′dee, (BARTHOLOMEW,) a German friar and philosopher, born at Usingen, was an adversary of Luther. Died in 1532.

Arnoldi, (DANIEL,) a German philologer, born at Bergedorf in 1595; died in 1651.

Arnoldi, (WILHELM,) Bishop of Treves, was born at Budan, in the district of Treves, in 1798. He was elected bishop in 1839. In 1844 he induced a great multitude of people to make a pilgrimage to Treves to see or worship a relic called "the holy coat of Treves." This proceeding caused great excitement, and resulted in a schism of the Church. (See RONGE.)

Arnoldi, von, fon aʀ-nol′dee, (JOHANN,) a German diplomatist and historian, born at Herborn, in Nassau, in 1751. He was employed as a negotiator by the Stadtholder William V. About 1803 he entered the service of William I., King of the Netherlands, who appointed him a privy councillor in 1815. He wrote a "History of the Countries ruled by the House of Orange-Nassau," ("Geschichte der Oranien-Nassauischen Länder," 3 vols., 1799-1816.) Died in 1827.

Ar-nol′dus or **Arnold,** aʀ′nolt, (HALDRE′NIUS VESALIEN′SIS,) a learned theological writer, born at Wesel, on the Lower Rhine. He taught Greek at Cologne, and was chosen canon of the metropolitan chapter of that city. Died in 1534.

Arnoldus de Villa Nova. See ARNALDUS.

Arnolfini, aʀ-nol-fee′nee, (GIOVANNI ATTILIO,) an able Italian hydraulic engineer, born at Lucca in 1733. He was charged with the hydraulic department of public works at Lucca in 1761, after which he improved the river Serchio by confining it between new rocky banks. He died in 1791, leaving in manuscript many volumes on physics, hydrostatics, etc.

Ar-nol′fo, [Lat. ARNUL′FUS,] written also **Arnoul,** of Milan, a historian, who lived near the end of the eleventh century. He wrote a "History of Milan," (from 925 to 1076,) prized for its fidelity and accuracy. It is commended by Muratori.

Arnolfo, written also **Arnoul,** became Archbishop of Milan in 1093, and preached a crusade in company with Urban II.

Arnolfo di Lapo. See LAPO.

Arnolt von Bruck. See ARNOLD VON BRUCK.

Arnone, aʀ-no′nà, (ALBERTO,) a skilful Neapolitan portrait-painter, born in the seventeenth century, was a pupil of Carlo Maratta. Died at Naples in 1721.

Ar′not, (HUGO,) a Scottish writer and advocate, born at Leith in 1749. His original name was Pollock, which he changed when he became heir to the maternal estate of Balcormo. He published an entertaining and valuable "History of Edinburgh," (1779,) a "Collection of Celebrated Criminal Trials in Scotland," (1785,) which displays great research, and an "Essay on Nothing," (1777.) Died in 1786.

See CHAMBERS, "Biographical Dictionary of Eminent Scotsmen."

Ar′nott, (ARCHIBALD,) a Scottish physician, born in 1771, served as surgeon in the army in Egypt, Spain, and other countries. His regiment was stationed at Saint Helena while Bonaparte was confined there. In April, 1821, he was called to attend the imperial captive, at whose death he was present. He received from his dying patient a silver snuff-box as a token of his esteem, and published "An Account of the Last Illness, Decease, and Post-Mortem Appearance of Napoleon Bonaparte," (1822.) Died in 1855.

Arnott, (JAMES MONCRIEFF,) a British surgeon, born in 1794. He settled in London about 1817, and became professor of surgery in King's College of that city.

Arnott, (Dr. NEIL,) a Scottish physician and eminent experimental philosopher, born near Montrose in 1788, was a pupil of Sir Everard Home. He began to practise in London about 1812, and delivered a course of lectures on natural philosophy in its application to medicine, (1823-24,) which he published in 1827 under the title of "Elements of Physics or Natural Philosophy, General and Medical, explained in non-technical Language." This work was received with great favour and translated into nearly all the European languages. He became one of the physicians-extraordinary to the queen in 1837, and was chosen a Fellow of the Royal Society in

1838. The Rumford medal of this society was awarded to him in 1854 for his inventions, among which are the water-bed or floating mattress for the sick, and the "Arnott Stove." He received also a gold medal from the jurors of the Universal Exposition of Paris in 1855. He is author of an "Essay on Warming and Ventilating," (1838.)

Arnoul. See ARNULFO.

Arnoul, äʀ′noo′, written also **Arnulf,** one of the most learned and eloquent French prelates of his time, was appointed Bishop of Orléans in 986.

Arnoul, written also **Arnulf** or **Ernulf,** born at Beauvais about 1040, became Bishop of Rochester in 1114. Died in 1124. He was author of some documents relating to the church and see of Rochester, which were published by Hearne in 1720.

Arnoul, written also **Arnulf,** a Norman priest, who served Robert II. of Normandy as chaplain in the first crusade. He obtained by intrigues in 1111 the office of Patriarch of Jerusalem. Died in 1118.

Arnoul, written also **Arnulf,** a French prelate, who became Bishop of Lisieux about 1140, was a friend of Thomas A Becket. He died in 1182, leaving many letters, which have some historical value.

Arnoul of Milan. See ARNOLFO.

Arnoul, (RENÉ,) a French poet, born at Poitiers in 1569; died in 1639.

Arnould. See ARNULF.

Arnould, äʀ′noo′, (AMBROISE MARIE,) a French political economist, born at Dijon about 1750. He published a successful work "On the Balance of Trade," (1791,) and was one of the leaders of the party which revolted against the Convention on the 13th Vendémiaire, 1794. Having supported Bonaparte in the Council of Five Hundred in the crisis of the 18th Brumaire, 1799, he was appointed a member of the Tribunat, after the suppression of which he was a counsellor of state. Among his important works is "The Political Maritime System of the Europeans during the Eighteenth Century," ("Système maritime politique," etc., 1797.) Died in 1812.

Arnould, (SOPHIE,) a popular French actress and opera-singer, born in Paris about 1744, was noted for her conversational powers and bonmots. Died in 1803.

See A. DEVILLE, "Arnoldiana," 1813.

Arnould of Rotterdam. See ARNOLD OF ROTTERDAM.

Arnoult, äʀ′noo′, (CHARLES,) a French jurist, born at Bèze in 1750; died in 1793.

Arnoult, (JEAN BAPTISTE,) a French writer, born in 1689, published, besides a few other works, "The Preceptor," (1747,) which contains treatises on grammar, the Christian religion, and other subjects. Died at Besançon in 1753.

Arnoux, äʀ′noo′, (JEAN,) a French Jesuit, born at Riom about 1560, or, as one account states, in 1575. He became distinguished as a preacher and skilful controversialist, and was appointed confessor to Louis XIII. in 1617, but was removed from this position in 1621. He wrote several theological works, some of which were against Calvinism. Died in 1636.

Arntzen, aʀnt′sęn, or **Arnt-ze′nĭ-us,** [Ger. pron. aʀnt-sā′ne-ůs,] (JOHANN,) a German philologist, born at Wesel in 1702. He succeeded Burmann as professor of history and eloquence at Franeker in 1742. His reputation is founded on excellent editions of Aurelius Victor, (1733,) of Pliny's Panegyricus, (1738,) and of the Panegyricus of Drepanius Pacatus, (1753.) Died in 1759.

See ERSCH und GRUBER, "Allgemeine Encyklopaedie."

Arntzen or **Arntzenius,** (JOHANN HEINRICH,) a learned philologist, a son of the preceding, born at Nymwegen in 1734. He became in 1774 professor of law at Utrecht, where he died in 1797, leaving valuable editions of Arator's poems, (1769,) and of the "Panegyrici Veteres," (1790.)

Arntzen or **Arntzenius,** (OTTO,) a brother of Johann, born at Wesel in 1703, was a good Latin scholar. He was professor or rector at Utrecht and Amsterdam. His edition of Dionysius Cato's "Disticha" (1735) is said to be the best. Died in 1763.

See ERSCH und GRUBER, "Allgemeine Encyklopaedie."

Arntzenius. See ARNTZEN.

€ as k; ç as s; ḡ hard; ġ as j; G, H, K, guttural; N, nasal; R, trilled; s̄ as z; ŧh as in this. (☞See Explanations, p. 23.)

12

Arnu, ăr′nü′, (NICOLAS,) a French theologian of considerable reputation, born near Verdun (Meuse) in 1629. Died at Padua in 1692.

Arnulf. See ARNOUL.

Ar′nulf, [Lat. ARNUL′PHUS,] written also **Arnoul** or **Arnould,** Emperor of Germany, was a son of Carloman of Bavaria, and a great-grandson of Charlemagne. He was elected King of Germany in 887 or 888 A.D., and defeated the Normans near Louvain in 892, after which he invaded Italy and captured Rome in 896. He was then crowned as emperor by the pope. He died at Ratisbon in 899, and was succeeded by his son, Louis IV.

See SCHWARZ, "Historia Arnulphi Imperatoris," 1744; GAGERN, "Arnulfi Imperatoris Vita," 1837.

Arnulf, a natural son of Lothaire, King of France, became Archbishop of Rheims in 988. Died in 1023.

Arnulf, SAINT, or **Arnoul,** an ancestor of Charlemagne, was born about 580 A.D., and became Bishop of Metz in 611. He was a confidential adviser of King Clotaire, and had a high reputation as a statesman. Died about 640 A.D.

Arnulfus or **Arnulphus.** See ARNULF.

Arnulfus OF MILAN. See ARNOLF.

Arn′way, (JOHN,) D.D., an English divine, born in 1601, suffered much for his attachment to the cause of Charles I., and during his exile in Holland wrote "An Alarum to the Subjects of England," (1650,) containing, among other things, a defence of the character of the late king. He died in Virginia in 1653.

Aromatari, degli, däl′yee â-ro-mä-tä′ree, (GIUSEPPE,) a learned physician and naturalist, born at Assisi, in the Papal States, about 1586. He practised medicine at Venice for about fifty years with such success that he was invited to England by James I.; but he preferred to remain where he was. He published in 1611 a "Reply to the Criticisms of Alessandro Tassoni on the Poems of Petrarch." His most important production is a short treatise on the reproduction of plants, "De Generatione Plantarum ex Seminibus," which was prefixed to his work on Hydrophobia, (1625.) He showed the analogy which exists between the seeds of plants and the eggs of animals, and first suggested those principles of germination which have been recognized by modern physiologists. Died in 1660.

See MAZZUCHELLI, "Scrittori d'Italia;" HALLER, "Bibliotheca Botanica."

Aronce. See ARUNS.

Arooj, Aroudj, or **Aruj,** â-rooj′, written also **Aruch** or **Arouds,** corrupted into **Horush, Horuc,** etc., a Turkish pirate, the elder of two brothers who about 1510–40 were the terror of Christendom. See BARBAROSSA.

Aroon. See ARUNA.

Arouet. See VOLTAIRE.

Arpád, aR′pâd, founder of the kingdom of Hungary, was a chief of the Magyars, who about 890 A.D. migrated from Galicia and conquered the Slavonic princes who then possessed Hungary. A part of his army invaded Italy and defeated Berengarius, on the Brenta, in 900. Died in 907. Andrew III., who died in 1301, was the last king of the Arpád dynasty.

See ERSCH und GRUBER, "Allgemeine Encyklopaedie;" MAILATH, "Geschichte der Magyaren."

Arpajon, d', dăR′pä′zhôN′, (LOUIS,) DUKE, and Marquis of Séverac, a French general, distinguished himself at the siege of Montauban in 1621. He had a high command in the Thirty Years' war. In 1645 he was appointed generalissimo by the grand master of Malta, for the defence of which against the Turks he raised two thousand men. Died in 1679.

Arpajon, d', (LOUIS,) MARQUIS, a French general, was a grandson of the preceding. Died in 1736.

Arpe, aR′peh, (PETER FRIEDRICH,) a learned jurisconsult and writer, born at Kiel in Holstein, in 1682. He was professor of law at Kiel from 1717 until 1722. In his "Laicus Veritatis Vindex" (1717) he maintained that the division of Christians into clergy and laity is contrary to the law of Moses and to the Gospel. Among his works is "Themis Cimbrica," (1737,) which treats of the institutions and manners of the Cimbri and other Teutonic tribes. Died about 1745.

See MOLLER, "Cimbria Literata;" ADELUNG, Supplement to JÖCHER'S "Allgemeines Gelehrten-Lexikon."

Arpino. See CESARI, (GIUSEPPE.)

Arpino, aR-pee′no, (JACOPO FRANCESCO,) an Italian physician, philosopher, and naturalist, was born in Piedmont in the early part of the seventeenth century.

Arquato, aR-kwä′to, (GIOVANNI FRANCESCO,) an Italian physician who wrote a work called "Medicus Reformatus," (1608,) was born in the Venetian States, and lived about the commencement of the seventeenth century.

Arquier. See DARQUIER.

Ar-Râdhee- (or **Ar-Râdhî-**) **Billah,** ar-rä′dee bil′-läh, one of the Abbasside caliphs, was raised to the caliphate in 934 A.D. Died about 940.

Arraes, ar-rä′ĕs, or **Arraiz,** ar-rä′iz, almost ar-rīz′, (AMADOR, â-mä-doR′,) a Portuguese classic writer, born at Beja in 1530. He became Bishop of Portalegre in 1581, and wrote "Moral Dialogues," (1589,) a work of high reputation, in which he took Plato for his model. Died in 1600.

Arraes or **Arrais,** (DUARTE MADEIRA,) a Portuguese physician, born near Lamego. He became physician to John IV., and wrote several medical works which were often reprinted. Died in 1652.

Arragos, ä′rä′go′, (GUILLAUME,) [Lat. GULIEL′MUS ARRAGO′SIUS,] a French physician, born near Toulouse in 1513; died at Bâle in 1610.

Arraiz. See ARRAES.

Arran, EARL OF. See HAMILTON, (JAMES.)

Arras, d', dă′râs′, (MATHIEU,) a French architect, born at Arras about 1300. He was employed by John, King of Bohemia, to build the cathedral of Prague, commenced in 1344. Before the completion of this work, he died, in 1352.

Ar-Rasheed or **Ar-Rashîd,** ar-rä-sheed′, (**Aboo-** (**Abû-**) **Mohammed-Abdul-Wahed,** ä′boo′ mo-häm′med äb′dool wä′hed,) a sultan of Western Africa, commenced his reign in 1232, after a hard struggle with his rival, Yahya An-Nâsir, in which he took Morocco by siege. He died in 1242.

Ar-Rashid. See HAROUN-AL-RASCHID.

Arrault, ä′ro′, (CHARLES,) a French jurist, born in the Gatinais in 1643; died in 1718.

Arreboe, ar′reh-bo′eh, (ANDERS,) a popular Danish poet, born in the island of Arröe in 1587. He was chosen Bishop of Drontheim in 1618, but was deposed for disorderly conduct in 1621. Having partially retrieved his reputation, he became pastor at Vordingborg in 1626. He was considered the greatest poet that Denmark had produced before Tullin. His principal work is "Hexaemeron," (1641,) a poetical paraphrase of the French poem of Du Bartas. Died in 1637.

See MOLBECH, "Danske Anthologie;" KRAFT og NYERUP, "Almindeligt Litteraturlexicon for Danemark," etc.

Arredondo, ar-rà-DON′do, (ISIDORO,) a Spanish historical painter, born at Colmenar de Oreja in 1653. He was patronized by Charles II., who gave him the title of painter to the king. Died in 1702.

Ar-rhe′nî-us, [Swed. pron. ar-rī′ne-ús,] (CLAS or CLAUDIUS,) a Swedish historian, eminent for learning and sagacity, was born at Linköping in 1627. He became professor of history at Upsal in 1668. His chief work is an "Ecclesiastical History of Sweden," ("Historiæ Svecorum Gothorumque Ecclesiasticæ Libri IV.," 1689.) He was appointed royal historiographer in 1678, and ennobled in 1684, when he assumed the name of Oernhielm, (Eagle-Helmet.) Died in 1695.

See GEZELIUS, "Biographiskt-Lexicon öfver namnkunnige Svenska Män;" P. LAGERLOEF, "Memoria C. Arrhenii," 1696; THYSELIUS, "Dissertatio de Meritis literariis C. Arrhenii," 1791.

Arrhenius, (JACOB,) a Swedish scholar, a brother of the preceding, born in 1642, was professor of history at Upsal from 1687 until 1716. He wrote many able treatises on points of ancient history, among which are a "Short Sketch of Ancient Egypt," ("Brevis Adumbratio Veteris Ægypti," 1694,) and an essay on the office of Roman Consul, ("De Consule Romano," 1705.) Died in 1725.

See GEZELIUS, "Biographiskt-Lexicon."

Arrhidæus, är-re-dee′us, or **Aridæus,** [Gr. Ἀῤῥιδαῖος or Ἀριδαῖος; Fr. ARRHIDÉE, ä′re′dà′,] a son of Philip of Macedon and of a courtesan named Philinna, was a half-brother of Alexander the Great. He had a weak mind, which, according to Plutarch, was the result of poison administered by Olympias. On the death of Alexander he was proclaimed king at Babylon, under the name of Philip. He was controlled by his wife Eurydice, and, after a nominal reign of six years, was put to death by order of Olympias, the mother of Alexander, about 315 B.C.

See JUSTIN, books ix., xiii., and xiv.

Arrhidæus, a Macedonian general, who was one of the two regents appointed at the death of Perdiccas in 321 B.C. He and the other regent, Python, resigned in the same year because they were unable to enforce their authority against Eurydice. In the division of provinces made about 320 he received a part of Phrygia.

Arrhidée. See ARRHIDÆUS.

Ar'rĭ-a, a Roman matron, eminent for fortitude, was the wife of Cæcina Pætus, who was condemned to death in 42 A.D. She killed herself in order to set an example of courage and fortitude to her husband.

Arriaga, de, dȧ ar-re-ȧ'gȧ, (JUAN CRISOSTOME,) a Spanish composer of great genius, born at Bilboa in 1808, studied in Paris under Fétis. He displayed great inventive power in his fugue for eight voices, called "Et Vitam Venturi," which Cherubini pronounced a masterpiece. In 1824 he published a set of quartets, which are highly praised. Died prematurely in 1825 or 1826.

See FÉTIS, "Biographie Universelle des Musiciens."

Arriaga, de, (PABLO JOSÉ,) a Spanish Jesuit and missionary, born at Vergara in 1562, laboured in Peru. Died about 1622.

Arriaga, de, (RODRIGO,) a Spanish philosopher and Jesuit, born at Logroño in 1592. He taught philosophy with great success for thirteen years at Prague, where he resided from 1624 until his death. He attempted to revive the philosophy of the schoolmen in his "Philosophical Course," ("Cursus Philosophicus," 1632,) which evinces an acute and subtle mind. He also wrote a work on theology, (8 vols., 1643–55.) Died in 1667.

See ADELUNG, "Geschichte der Philosophie."

Ar'rĭ-an, [Gr. Ἀῤῥιανός; Lat. ARRIA'NUS FLA'VIUS; Fr. ARRIEN, ȧ're-ȧN',] an eminent Greek historian, born at Nicomedia, in Bithynia, was a pupil and friend of Epictetus. He committed to writing, edited, or digested the philosophic doctrines of Epictetus, (who published nothing himself.) There are now extant a "Manual ("Enchiridion") of Epictetus," compiled by him, and four books of a work called the "Epictetus of Arrian." He obtained the favour of the emperor Hadrian, who in 136 A.D. appointed him governor of Cappadocia. We have no evidence that he held this office, or any other, after the death of Hadrian, 138 A.D. He was at one time priest of Ceres and Proserpine in his native city. His principal work is a "History of the Expedition of Alexander the Great," Ἀνάβασις Ἀλεξάνδρου, (The Ascent of Alexander,) which is highly prized on account of its intrinsic merit, and because we have no other history of Alexander worthy of equal confidence. Among his qualifications for a historian were a good judgment, accuracy in geographical and strategical details, and a correct and simple style. In style, and in other respects, he proposed Xenophon as his model. He was author of many other works, some of which are lost. Among those extant are a "Treatise on Tactics," a "Discourse on Hunting," a "Circumnavigation of the Euxine Sea," and a small but interesting work called "Indica," describing India, its people, customs, products, etc. The date of his death is not known. His abstract of the philosophy of Epictetus, or "Enchiridion," was highly esteemed, both by the pagans and early Christians.

See FABRICIUS, "Bibliotheca Græca;" ELLENDT, "De Arrianeorum Librorum Reliquiis," 1836; MAUERMANN, "Arrianus Nicomediensis et Quintus Curtius Rufus," 1835.

Arrianus, (the historian.) See ARRIAN.

Ar-rĭ-a'nus, [Gr. Ἀῤῥιανός; Fr. ARRIEN, ȧ're-ȧN',] a Greek author of uncertain date, wrote a treatise on meteors and comets.

Arrianus, a Roman jurist, who is supposed to have lived in the time of Trajan, wrote a work on law, entitled "De Interdictis," ("Concerning Interdicts.")

Arrianus, a Greek poet, who wrote a poem on Alex-

ander, called "The Alexandriad," and translated Virgil᾽ Georgics into hexameter verse.

Arriaza, ȧr-re-ȧ'thȧ, (JUAN BAUTISTA,) an eminent Spanish poet, born at Madrid in 1770, was sometime called ARRIAZA Y SUPERVIELA, (e soo-pêR-ve-ȧ'lȧ.) He published a volume of poems entitled "First-Fruits," or first productions of his genius, ("Las Primicias," 1797,) and soon after that date went to England as secretary of legation. In 1803 appeared his poem "Emilia," on the influence of the fine arts. He returned to Spain in 1807, and took a prominent part in politics as a friend of absolute monarchy. After the restoration of 1814 ne was minister of foreign affairs. Among his works are "Poesias patrioticas," (1810.) Died in 1837.

See BROCKHAUS, "Conversations-Lexikon;" LONGFELLOW, "Poets and Poetry of Europe."

Arribas, ȧr-ree'bȧs, (PABLO ANTONIO,) a Spanish minister of state, born in 1771, held office under Joseph Bonaparte. Died in 1828.

Arrien. See ARRIAN and ARRIANUS.

Arrighetti, ȧr-re-ḡet'tee, (FILIPPO,) an Italian ecclesiastic, born at Florence in 1582, was distinguished for his knowledge of philosophy and theology. Died in 1662.

Arrighetti, (NICCOLÒ,) a disciple and friend of Galileo, also a poet, born at Florence in the sixteenth century. Died in 1639.

Arrighetti, (NICCOLÒ,) a learned Jesuit, born at Florence in 1709, wrote a "Theory of Fire," ("Ignis Theoria," etc., 1750.) Died in 1767.

Arrighetto, or **Arrigo da Settimello,** ȧr-ree'go dȧ sêt-te-mel'lo, a Latin poet and ecclesiastic, born near Florence in the latter part of the twelfth century. He wrote an elegiac poem on "The Mutability of Fortune and the Consolation of Philosophy," ("De Diversitate Fortunæ et Philosophiæ Consolatione,") which is said to have been used in schools and esteemed as a model by mediæval teachers.

Arrighi, ȧr-ree'ḡee, (ANTONIO MARIA,) an Italian jurist, and professor of civil law at Padua, born in Corsica in 1689, was naturalized as a citizen of Venice in 1741. He wrote, besides other works, one "On Universal Pontifical Law," ("De Jure Pontificum Universo," 1727,) and a "Life of F. Morosini," (1749.) Died about 1760.

Arrighi, (GIUSEPPE,) an Italian historical painter, born at Volterra, lived in the second half of the seventeenth century.

Arrighi, (JEAN Toussaint—too'sȧN',) Duke of Padua, an able general, born in Corsica in 1778. He entered the French service, and was wounded at Saint-Jean-d'Acre in 1798 or '99, a few years after which Napoleon gave him the title of Duke of Padua. As colonel he distinguished himself near Ulm in 1805, and he was made a general of division on the field of battle at Essling, 1809. He rendered important services at Leipsic in 1813, and was appointed governor of Corsica on the return of Napoleon from Elba. He lived in exile from 1815 to 1820. In 1852 he became a senator. Died in 1853.

See "Nouvelle Biographie Générale."

Arrighi Landini, ȧr-ree'ḡee lȧn-dee'nee, (ORAZIO,) a native of Florence, born in 1718, is reckoned among the good Italian poets of the eighteenth century. Arrighi was the family name of his father, and Landini that of his mother. He served for some time in the Neapolitan army, and afterwards settled at Venice. His principal works are "The Tomb of Isaac Newton," a poem in blank verse, (1751,) and "La Bibliade," a poetical description of the great libraries, ancient and modern.

See MAZZUCHELLI, "Scrittori d'Italia."

Arrigho. See ARRIGHETTO.

Arrigoni, (HONORIO.) See ARIGONI.

Arrigoni, ȧr-re-go'nee, (CARLO,) an Italian musician and composer, born at Florence. He went to London in 1732, and entered into competition with Handel, with but poor success.

Arrigoni, (FRANCESCO,) an Italian writer, born at Bergamo in 1610; died in 1645.

Arrigoni, (GIOVANNI BATTISTA,) an Italian poet, born at Mantua in the sixteenth century. He published "Madrigali," (1602,) and "Rime," (1604.)

Arriquibar, ȧr-re-kee'bȧR, (Don NICOLAS,) a Span-

ε as k; ç as s; ḡ hard; ġ as j; G, H, K, guttural; N, nasal; R, trilled; ŝ as z; th as in this.   (☞See Explanations, p. 23.)

ish merchant of Bilboa, who about 1770 composed a work of some merit on political economy, called "Recreacion politica." Died about 1778.

Ar'rĭ-us, (QUINTUS,) Roman prætor in 72 B.C., distinguished himself in the servile war and also as an orator.

Arrius, (QUINTUS,) son of the above, was a friend of Cicero.

Arrivabene, âr-re-vä-bā'nà, (ANDREA,) a Venetian printer and translator of the sixteenth century.

Arrivabene, (FERDINANDO,) an Italian jurist and philologist, born at Mantua in 1770, was president of a court at Brescia. He wrote, besides two legal treatises, a historical Commentary on Dante, and an Essay on Forensic Language. Died in 1834.

Arrivabene, (GIOVANNI FRANCESCO,) an Italian poet, born at Mantua, flourished about the middle of the sixteenth century. His chief works are two maritime eclogues, called "Cloanto" and "Idromanzia," (1547.)

Arrivabene, (GIOVANNI PIETRO,) a poet, born at Mantua in the fifteenth century. He wrote a Latin poem, called "Gonzagidos Libri quatuor," in honour of Ludovico Gonzaga, Marquis of Mantua, which was first printed in 1738. Died about 1504.

Arrivabene, (IPPOLITO,) an Italian physician, practised at Rome. Died in 1739.

Arrivabene, (JOHN,) COUNT, an Italian patriot and economist, born about 1785, was a friend of Silvio Pellico. He was arrested in 1821 by the Austrian government, and only escaped imprisonment by exile from his native country.

See "Memoirs of Count John Arrivabene," written by himself, (London, 1862.)

Arrivabene, (LUDOVICO,) an Italian poet, flourished about 1600.

Ar'rōw-smith, (AARON,) an eminent English geographer, born at Winston, Durham, in 1750. He became a resident of London about 1770, and made himself master of the theory and practice of map-engraving. In 1790 he published a large map of the world on Mercator's projection. He collected a large fund of new information from navigators and other sources, and published more than one hundred maps, which had a high reputation on the continent, and among which is a "Map of the World on a Globular Projection, with a Companion of Explanatory Letter-press," (1794.) Died in 1823. His son Aaron published several school atlases and manuals of geography.

Arrowsmith, (JOHN,) D.D., an eminent English divine, born near Newcastle-upon-Tyne in 1602. He was educated at Cambridge, and was regarded as one of the ablest as well as most worthy Puritan divines of that age. He preached at Lynn about twelve years, (1631-42,) and became regius professor of divinity at Cambridge in 1651. He was master of Trinity College from 1653 until his death. His chief works are "Tactica Sacra," (1657,) and a "Chain of Principles," ("Armilla Catechetica," 1659.) Died in 1659.

See NEAL, "History of the Puritans."

Arroyo, de, dà âr-ro'yo, (DIEGO,) an excellent Spanish miniature-painter, born in 1498, worked at Toledo and Madrid. He was appointed cabinet-painter to Charles V. Died in 1551.

Arruntius, ar-rŭn'she-us, a Roman physician mentioned by Pliny, lived probably about 50 A.D.

Arruntius, (LUCIUS,) a Roman consul, 22 B.C., is supposed to have been the author of a "History of the First Punic War," referred to by Seneca.

Arruntius, (LUCIUS,) a son of the above, was consul in 6 A.D., and eminent for his wealth and integrity. Augustus is said to have considered him worthy of the empire. His merits excited the jealousy of Tiberius, and brought upon him annoyance and persecution, which induced him to commit suicide in 37 A.D.

Arsace. See ARSACES.

Ar-sā'çēs or **Ar'sạ-çēs,** [Gr. Ἀρσάκης; Fr. ARSACE, âr'sȧss'; Persian, AR'SHAK,] the founder of the kingdom of Parthia and of the dynasty of the Arsacidæ. He probably flourished in the third century B.C.; but his history is involved in much obscurity. He is supposed to have been the chief of a nomade tribe of Scythians, Bac-

trians, or Parthians. His memory was so highly honoured that his successors assumed the name of Arsaces.

Arsaces I., King of Parthia, is identified by some historians with the preceding; others have regarded him as his son or grandson. In the reign of Antiochus Theos of Syria, the Parthians, who had been subject to the Syrian monarchy, revolted with success about 250 B.C., and Arsaces became their king. After a reign of two years, he was succeeded by his brother Tiridates.

Arsaces II., (Tĭr-ĭ-dā'tēs,) brother of Arsaces I., began to reign about 248 B.C. He gained a decisive victory, about 238, over Seleucus Callinicus, who attempted to regain possession of Parthia. This event was celebrated by the Parthians as a new era, from which their national independence was dated. He is supposed to have died about 220 B.C.

Arsaces III. (Aĭ-ta-bā'nus) was the son and successor of Arsaces II. He was defeated about 212 B.C. by Antiochus the Great, who invaded Parthia. Peace was restored soon after that event. The length of his reign is unknown.

Arsaces IV. (Priapetius, prī-a-pe'she-us) was a son of the preceding. According to Justin, he reigned fifteen years.

Arsaces V., (Phra-ā'tēs I.,) King of Parthia, son of the above, succeeded his father about 170 B.C. He conquered the Mardi.

Arsaces VI., (Mith-rĭ-dā'tēs I.,) brother of the preceding. This king extended his conquests to the Indus. He reigned twenty-five years or more, and died about 135 B.C.

Arsaces VII., (Phraates II.,) son of Arsaces VI., after being himself defeated three times by Antiochus VII., King of Syria, conquered and killed the latter in 128 B.C., but was in turn overcome and slain by the Scythians.

Arsaces VIII., (Artabanus II.,) uncle of the preceding, was slain, after a short reign, by the Scythians.

Arsaces IX. (Mithridates II.) surnamed THE GREAT, was a son of Arsaces VIII. He waged war against the Scythians with success. An embassy sent by him, in 92 B.C., to Sulla, (who was then in Asia,) was the first intercourse between the Parthians and Romans of which we have an authentic account.

Arsaces X. Of this king scarcely anything is known.

Arsaces XI. (San-ạ-tro'çēs) seems to have been in exile among the Scythians, who restored him to his throne about 70 B.C. He reigned only seven years.

Arsaces XII. (Phraates III.) succeeded his father Arsaces XI. in 70 B.C., during the Mithridatic war. His alliance was courted by the Romans and by Mithridates, but he resolved to remain neutral. He made or renewed a treaty with Pompey in 66 B.C., after which he was offended because Pompey cast into chains his son-in-law Tigranes the Armenian, and because he refused to address him (Arsaces) as "King of Kings." He was murdered by his sons Mithridates and Orodes about 60 B.C.

Arsaces XIII., (Mithridates III.,) a son of Arsaces XII., was expelled from his throne by the Parthian senate on account of his cruelty, and put to death by his brother Orodes about 55 B.C.

Arsaces XIV., (O-ro'dēs,) a son of Arsaces XII., was King of Parthia when the war began between the Romans and Parthians. His army, under Surena, gained a great victory over Crassus, who was slain, in 53 B.C. The Parthians under Pacorus, a son of Orodes, invaded Syria in 50 B.C., and were defeated by Cassius. He maintained neutrality in the civil war between Cæsar and Pompey; but after the battle of Philippi, 42 B.C., the war was renewed between him and the Romans. The Parthians were defeated by Ventidius, an officer of Antony, in 39 and 38 B.C., and Arsaces was murdered by his son Phraates about 37 B.C.

Arsaces XV. (Phraates IV.) was a son of the preceding. In 36 B.C. the war was renewed by Antony. who led a large army through Armenia, but was repulsed by the Parthians and pursued as far as the Araxes. About 23 B.C. Arsaces made a treaty of peace with Augustus, to whom he restored the prisoners and standards taken at the defeat of Crassus. Died in 4 A.D.

ā, e, ī, ō, ū, ȳ, *long;* à, è, ò, same, less prolonged; ă, ĕ, ĭ, ŏ, ŭ, ў, *short;* ạ, ẹ, ị, ọ, *obscure;* fâr, fàll, fàt; mêt; nŏt; gōōd; mōōn;

Arsaces XVI., (**Phra-ạ-tā′çēs,**) said to have been accessory to the death of his father Arsaces XV. He was put to death, after a reign of a few months, in consequence of a rebellion caused by his vices.

Arsaces XVII. (**Orodes II.**) was also put to death by his subjects, on account of his cruelty, in the same year as his predecessor.

Arsaces XVIII., (**Vo-no′nēs I.,**) son of Phraates IV., lived a long time at Rome as a hostage, where he acquired habits which made him unpopular among the Parthians and led to his expulsion from the throne. He was assassinated, it is supposed, by the order of Piso, a Roman officer, about 19 A.D.

Arsaces XIX., (**Artabanus III.,**) a Median king, who expelled Arsaces XVIII., had a stormy reign of twenty-eight years, during which he was twice driven from his throne by the aid of Rome, but died at last in possession of Parthia about 44 A.D.

Arsaces XX. (**Go-tar′zēs**) and **Arsaces XXI,** (**Bar-dā′nēs,**) after a struggle for the empire, settled it by the former retiring to Hyrcania and the latter retaining Parthia; but, Bardanes having been assassinated, Gotarzes resumed the royal authority. Gotarzes died about 50 A.D. He was succeeded by Arsaces XXII., whose reign was very short.

Arsaces XXIII., (**Vol-o-ġe′sēs I.,**) one of the most distinguished of the Parthian kings, was involved in a long contest with Rome in relation to the sovereignty of Armenia, over which he had placed his brother Tiridates. The difficulty was finally compromised by Tiridates going to Rome to receive the crown from Nero. Vologeses died in 90 A.D.

Arsaces XXIV., (**Pac′o-rus,**) son of the above, after a reign of nearly eighteen years, died about 107 A.D.

Arsaces XXV., (**€hos′ro-ēs,**) [Gr. Χοσρόης; Persian, KHOS′ROO′ or KOSREW,] brother of the preceding, was defeated by Trajan in 114, and finally driven from his throne, on which Parthamaspates was placed by the Roman emperor; but on the death of Trajan, in 117, Chosroës expelled his rival, and died probably in 122, greatly esteemed by his subjects.

Arsaces XXVI, (**Vologeses II.,**) a son of Arsaces XXV., is said to have gained great advantages over the Romans for a period, but afterwards, having been driven back into his own dominions, he is supposed to have died in 149 A.D.

Arsaces XXVII., (**Vologeses ·III.,**) son of the preceding, seems, like all his predecessors, to have been involved in wars with Rome. Died in 216 A.D. Some writers suppose two or more kings to have reigned between Arsaces XXVI. and XXVIII., (as we have numbered them :) on thi⁀̃point see article "Parther," in Ersch and Gruber's "Allgemeine Encyklopaedie," by KRAUSE.

Arsaces XXVIII., (**Artabanus IV.,**) also called **Ardavan,** was a son of Arsaces XXVII., and was the last king of Parthia of the dynasty of the Arsacidæ. He began to reign about 216 A.D. In 217 he fought an indecisive battle against the Romans, under Macrinus, near Nisibis. He then turned his arms against the Persians, who had revolted and were led by Ardsheer or Artaxerxes. Having been defeated and taken prisoner, he was put to death by Ardsheer about 226 A.D.

Ar-sā′çēs (or ar′sạ-sēz) **I.,** King of Armenia, was a son of Arsaces XIX. (Artabanus III.) of Parthia. He obtained the throne by the aid of his father in 35 A.D. About a year later he was murdered by his own officers, who were bribed by Mithridates the Iberiàn.

Arsaces II. was placed on the throne of Armenia in 222 or 223 A.D. by his brother Artabanus IV., King of Parthia. He joined Alexander Severus in his expedition against Persia, by which alliance he saved his own kingdom. He died before 260 A.D.

Arsaces III. of Armenia succeeded his father Tiridates III. about 340 A.D. He waged war against Sapor, King of Persia, about 360, and entered into an alliance with Julian the Apostate. In the campaign of 363 A.D. he deserted Julian, whose defeat and death near Ctesiphon are attributed to the treachery of Arsaces. His nobles having rebelled against him, he applied for aid to Sapor, who detained him in captivity until his death.

See AMMIANUS MARCELLINUS, books xx., xxi., xxiii., xxv., and xxvii.

Arsaces IV. was probably a grandson of Arsaces III. He began his reign conjointly with his brother Valarsaces in 382, but, the latter dying the next year, he reigned alone, till his deposition by Sapor and Theodosius, who divided his kingdom between them about 387 A.D.

Arsachel. See ARZACHEL.

Arsacid or **Arsacide,** ar-sas′sid, the English singular of ARSACIDÆ; employed also as an adjective. The plural form **Arsacids** or **Arsacides** is rarely used.

Arsacidæ, ar-sas′e-dē, [Fr. ARSACIDES, ȧr′sȧ′sèd′; Ger. ARSACIDEN, aR-sȧt-see′dẹn, and ARSAKIDEN, aR-sȧ-kee′dẹn; a patronymic from **Arsaces,** which appears to have been a very common name among the ancient Persians, Parthians, etc.,] an appellation given to several Asiatic dynasties, but especially to the dynasty of Parthian kings who reigned from Arsaces I., about 250 B.C., to the death of Artabanus IV., (Arsaces XXVIII.,—or XXXI., according to some authorities,) in 226 A.D., and to a dynasty of Armenian kings who reigned between 150 B.C. and 430 A.D.

Arsakes. See ARSACES.

Arsakiden. See ARSACIDÆ.

Ar-sa′mēs, [Gr. Ἀρσάμης,] the father of Hystaspes, and grandfather of Darius I., King of Persia. Another of the same name, son of Darius I., accompanied Xerxes in his expedition against Greece. A third was a favourite (illegitimate) son of Artaxerxes Mnemon. A fourth is supposed to have been a king of Armenia in the time of Seleucus II., and the founder of Arsamosata.

Arsdekin. See ARCHDEKIN.

Arsène. See ARSENIUS.

Ar-se′nĭ-us, [Gr. Ἀρσένιος; Fr. ARSÈNE, ȧr′sȧn′,] SAINT, written also **Arsennus,** born at Rome in 354 or 355 A.D., was appointed tutor to Arcadius, son of the emperor Theodosius, in 383, and remained at the court of Constantinople eleven years, having gained the favour of the emperor. In 394 he retired to a desert in Egypt, where he became noted for his ascetic piety. Died in 449 A.D.

Arsenius surnamed AUTORIA′NUS, Patriarch of Constantinople, was born in that city about the end of the twelfth century. He was appointed in 1259, by the Greek emperor Theodore Lascaris II., guardian of the prince his son, an office for which he seems to have been wholly unfitted. He was circumvented by Michael Palæologus, who usurped the throne and banished the patriarch for his refusal to grant him absolution. Died in 1273.

Arsenius, a distinguished Greek scholar and philologist, son of Michael Apostolius, born in the latter part of the fifteenth century, was, it is supposed, a native of Candia (Crete) or of Italy. He became Roman Catholic Archbishop of Malvasia, or Monembasia, in the Morea. He edited his father's "Apophthegmata," and a collection of scholia on several dramas of Euripides, (1534.) Died in 1535.

See HODIUS, "De Græcis illustribus."

Arsenius, a Greek bishop, who accompanied Jeremiah II., Patriarch of Constantinople, to Russia, about 1588, when he established the Russian Patriarchate, of which Arsenius wrote an account.

Arsenius, a Greek monk, founder of a Greek and Latin school at Moscow in the early part of the seventeenth century, and inventor of a type still called the Arsenian.

Arsenne, ȧr′sèn′, (LOUIS CHARLES,) a French painter, born in Paris in 1790, was a pupil of David. He produced some remarkable paintings of religious subjects, among which was "Christ in the Garden of Olives." He also derived from the works of Châteaubriand and Lamartine subjects of some designs.

Arsennus. See ARSENIUS.

Ar′sēs, [Gr. Ἀρσης,] **Nar′sēs,** [Gr. Νάρσης,] or **Oar′-sēs,** [Gr. Ὀάρσης,] a son of Artaxerxes III., King of Persia, was placed on the throne in 339 B.C. by Bagoas, who had killed Artaxerxes. After a reign of three years, he was put to death by Bagoas. He was succeeded by Darius Codomannus.

Arshenevsky, aR-shĕ-nĕv′ske, (BASIL,) a Russian mathematician, born at Kiev in 1758; died in 1808.

Arshi, aR′shee, also called **Chaki,** a Turkish poet, born in Roumelia; died in 1570.

Arsilli, aR-sèl′lee, (FRANCESCO,) an Italian poet and

physician, born at Sinigaglia about 1470. He practised in Rome many years, and was a friend of Paulus Jovius. He wrote in verse a descriptive catalogue of contemporary Roman poets, "De Poetis Urbanis," (1524,) which is interesting to students of literary history. Died in 1540.

See TIRABOSCHI, "Storia della Letteratura Italiana."

Ar-sin'o-ë, [Gr. Ἀρσινόη,] a concubine of Philip of Macedon, became the wife of Lagus and the mother of Ptolemy I., King of Egypt.

Arsinoë, a daughter of Ptolemy I., King of Egypt, and Berenice, was born about 316 B.C., and was married to Lysimachus of Thrace in 300 B.C. In order to secure the succession for her son, she excited the suspicion of Lysimachus against Agathocles, his son by a former marriage, who was put to death in prison. After the death of Lysimachus, in 281 B.C., she went to Thrace with her sons, who were put to death by Ptolemy Ceraunus. She then fled to Egypt, and became the queen of her own brother, Ptolemy Philadelphus. A gold medal of Arsinoë is extant.

Arsinoë, a daughter of Lysimachus, King of Thrace, and Nicæa, became the wife of Ptolemy Philadelphus of Egypt, by whom she had three children, Ptolemy, Lysimachus, and Berenice. She was banished by the king before her marriage with Arsinoë above noticed.

Arsinoë, wife of Magas, King of Cyrene, brother of Ptolemy II. of Egypt.

Arsinoë, daughter of Ptolemy III., became the wife of her brother, Ptolemy IV., Philopator, by whom she was put to death to make way for Agathoclea, his second wife. She appears to have been the queen whom Livy calls Cleopatra.

Arsinoë, daughter of Ptolemy XI., Auletes, and sister of Cleopatra, assumed the sovereignty during the siege of Alexandria by Cæsar in 48 B.C., who, on the capture of the city, carried her to Rome to grace his triumph. She was put to death by Antony, at Cleopatra's instigation, 41 B.C.

Arslan. See ALP-ARSLAN.

Artabanus OF PARTHIA. See ARSACES III. and XXVIII.

Artabasdes. See ARTAVASDES.

Artabaze. See ARTABAZUS.

Artabazes. See ARTAVASDES.

Ar-ta-ba'zus, [Gr. Ἀρτάβαζος; Fr. ARTABAZE, ȧr'tȧ-bȧz',] a Persian general, who lived about 450 B.C. He and Megabysus suppressed the revolt of Inarus in Egypt.

Artabazus, a Median, who formed a devoted attachment to Cyrus, King of Persia.

See XENOPHON'S "Cyropædia."

Artabazus, a distinguished Persian general and favourite of Xerxes, whom he accompanied on his invasion of Greece in 480 B.C. He was present at the battle of Platæa, 479 B.C.

Artabazus, a general of Artaxerxes I., quelled a revolt of the Egyptians about 460 B.C.

Artabazus, a Persian general, was a satrap of Asia Minor in the reign of Artaxerxes III., against whom he revolted in 356 B.C. With the aid of the Athenian Chares and other Greeks, he gained several victories. He was afterwards defeated, and fled with his brother-in-law, Memnon of Rhodes, to the court of Philip of Macedon. Having obtained pardon, he returned to Persia, and proved his loyalty to King Darius at the battle of Arbela. He was appointed Satrap of Bactria by Alexander the Great about 330 B.C. He died, at a very advanced age, about 320 B.C.

See THIRLWALL, "History of Greece;" DIODORUS SICULUS, books xv. and xvi.

Artachæes, ar-tạ-kee'ĕz, [Gr. Ἀρταχαίης,] a Persian, who cut the canal for Xerxes near Mount Athos, by which his fleet avoided the dangerous voyage round the promontory.

Artaldus. See ARTAUD.

Artale, ar-tä'lȧ, or **Artali,** ar-tä'lee, (GIUSEPPE,) an Italian poet, born at Mazzareno, in Sicily, in 1628. He served with distinction in the defence of Candia against the Turks, and was noted as a swordsman and duellist. He published several poetical works of no great merit. Died at Naples in 1679.

Artapherne. See ARTAPHERNES.

Ar-tạ-pher'nēs, [Gr. Ἀρταφέρνης; Fr. ARTAPHERNE, ȧr'tä'fȧRn',] a half-brother of King Darius Hystaspes, by whom he was appointed satrap of the Asiatic coast of the Ægean Sea and of other parts of Asia Minor in 506 B.C. He intervened in favour of Hippias, who had been expelled from Athens, and ordered the Athenians to receive him again; but they refused. He suppressed, about 498, a revolt of the Ionians, who were aided by the Athenians.

Artaphernes, a son of the preceding, was appointed in conjunction with Datis to the command of the Persian army which invaded Greece in 490 B.C., and which was defeated at Marathon. He appears to have been the second in command under Datis in this campaign; and he commanded the Lydians in the expedition of Xerxes against Greece in 480 B.C.

Artaphernes, a Persian ambassador, sent in 425 B.C. by Artaxerxes I. on a mission to Sparta.

Artario, ar-tä're-o, (JOSEPH,) a Swiss sculptor and modeller, born near Lugano in 1697. He worked in Germany and England, and his productions are called good imitations of the antique. He died at Cologne in 1760.

Ar-tạ-sī'rēs, [Gr. Ἀρτασίρης,] a corruption of the Armenian **Ar'dạ-shîr'** or **Ar'dạ-sheer',** i.e. ARTAXERXES, written also **Ardashes,** a son of King Bahram Sapor, was the last king of Armenia of the dynasty of the Arsacidæ. He was deposed in 428 A.D. by Bahram V. of Persia, who annexed Armenia to his own empire. This result was promoted by the Armenian nobles, who were opposed or indifferent to Christianity. Artasires was nominally a Christian.

Artaud, ȧr'tō', [Lat. ARTAL'DUS,] an archbishop of Rheims in the first half of the tenth century.

Artaud, (ANTOINE FRANÇOIS MARIE,) a French antiquary, born at Avignon in 1767. His chief work is "The Mosaics of Lyons," ("Les Mosaïques de Lyon," 1818.) Died in 1838.

See DUMAS, "Éloge de A. F. M. Artaud," 1840.

Artaud, (JEAN BAPTISTE,) a French dramatist, born at Montpellier in 1732. Among his works is "Le Centenaire de Molière," (1773,) which was performed with success. Died in 1796.

Artaud, (JOSEPH PIERRE,) a French prelate, born in Venaissin in 1706, became eminent as a preacher, and was appointed Bishop of Cavaillon in 1756. He wrote a "Panegyric on Saint Louis," (1754,) and "Pastoral Instructions," which are commended. Died in 1760.

Artaud, (NICOLAS LOUIS,) a French writer and translator, eminent as a Greek scholar, was born in Paris in 1794. After the revolution of 1830, he became inspector of the Academy of Paris, and inspector-general of letters. In 1840 he was commissioned to organize instruction in Algeria. He was a member of the council of public instruction a few years before his death. He translated the tragedies of Sophocles, (3 vols., 1827,) the comedies of Aristophanes, (6 vols., 1830,) and the tragedies of Euripides, (1832.) Among his works is a "Literary Essay on the Poetical Genius of the Nineteenth Century," (1825.) Died in 1861.

Artaud de Montor, ȧr'tō' dẹh môN'toR', (ALEXIS FRANÇOIS,) CHEVALIER, a French author, born in Paris in 1772. In his early life he was secretary to several embassies to Rome and other cities of Italy. He afterwards devoted himself to literature and arts, and was admitted into the Academy of Inscriptions. Among his works are "Lives of Artists," "Machiavel, his Genius and Errors," (1833,) a "History of the Sovereign Pontiffs," 8 vols., and a "Life of Pope Pius VII.," which passed through eleven editions and obtained a prize of the French Academy in 1838. Died in 1849.

See "Nouvelle Biographie Générale."

Ar-tạ-vas'dēs, [Gr. Ἀρταουάσδης; Fr. ARTAVASDE, ȧr'tä'väsd',] **Ar-ta-bas'dēs,** [Gr. Ἀρταβάσδης,] or **Ar-ta-ba'zēs,** [Gr. Ἀρταβάζης; in Armenian, AR'DA-WAZT' or AR'TA-WAZT',] King of Armenia, was a son of Tigranes. He formed an alliance with the Roman Crassus against the Parthians in 54 B.C. After Crassus persisted in meeting the enemy in an open level country against the advice of Artavasdes, the latter retired into Armenia and made peace with Orodes the Parthian. He offered his assistance to Antony in his expedition against Parthia in 36 B.C., but deserted him in the same year. In 34 he was enticed by Antony to the Roman camp, and detained as a captive until 31 B.C., when he was put to death by Cleopatra.

See DION CASSIUS, "History;" TACITUS, "Annals."

Artavasdes II., placed by Augustus on the throne of Armenia in 6 B.C., was driven out by his subjects the following year.

Artavasdes III. was King of Armenia and ally of Sapor I., King of Persia, in 260 A.D., when the latter conquered and took prisoner the emperor Valerian.

Artavasdes or **Ar-ta-bas′dus** [Gr. Ἀρτάβασδος; Fr. ARTAVASDE, ȧr′tȧ′väsd′] surnamed CUROPALA′TES, was the political chief of the orthodox party at Constantinople in the reign of Constantine V., who was an iconoclast. He rebelled in 742 A.D., and was proclaimed emperor by his party. In the civil war that ensued, he was defeated, taken prisoner, and executed about the end of 743 A.D.

Artaxerce. See ARTAXERXES.

Ar-tax-erx′ēs I., Lon-ǵim′a-nus, [Gr. Ἀρταξέρξης Μακρόχειρ; Fr. ARTAXERCE LONGUE-MAIN, ȧr′tȧk′sȧrss′ lôñḡ′mâÑ′; Persian, ARD′SHEER′ DARÂZDȦST,] a celebrated king of Persia, the son of Xerxes I., whom he succeeded in 465 B.C. He was surnamed Longimanus (*i.e.* Longhanded) because his right hand was longer than his left. He killed with his own hand Artabanus, who had murdered his father. Among the events of his reign was a revolt of the Egyptians, (460,) who were aided by the Athenians. About 455 B.C., Egypt, with the exception of the marshes of the Delta, was subjected to the power of Persia. The Persians, however, were defeated by the Athenians, under Cimon, near Salamis, in Cyprus, in 449 B.C. The reign of Artaxerxes is described by Plutarch as wise and moderate. He died in 425 B.C., and was succeeded by his son Xerxes II.

See DIODORUS SICULUS; THIRLWALL, "History of Greece."

Artaxerxes II., surnamed MNEMON (nee′mon) from the excellence of his memory, was the eldest son of Darius II. and Parysatis, and began to reign in 405 B.C. His younger brother Cyrus, who was satrap of the western part of Asia Minor and aspired to the throne of Persia, collected a large army, in which were ten thousand Greeks. Artaxerxes having taken the field in person, the armies met at Cunaxa in 401 B.C., and Cyrus was killed. (See CYRUS and XENOPHON.) His provinces in Asia Minor were invaded by the Spartan Agesilaus, who gained several victories; but this danger was averted by the peace of Antalcidas, in 387 B.C. His reign was disturbed by many revolts, and his efforts to recover Egypt failed. His eldest son Darius was detected in a conspiracy against the king, by whose order he was put to death. Artaxerxes died in 362 B.C., aged about ninety-four.

See article "Artaxerxes," in PLUTARCH'S "Lives;" DIODORUS SICULUS; XENOPHON, "Anabasis;" THIRLWALL, "History of Greece."

Artaxerxes III. (or **O′chus**) was a son and successor of the preceding. He massacred his father's surviving children, and became notorious for cruelty. By the aid of Mentor the Rhodian, and other Greeks, he reduced Egypt to his domination about 350 or 345 B.C. He abandoned himself to sensuality, and left the direction of the government to Bagoas, a eunuch, by whose order he was poisoned in 339 B.C. His son Arses succeeded him.

Ar-tax′ĭ-as [Gr. Ἀρταξίας] or **Ar-tax′ēs,** [Ἀρτάξης,] according to the Greek and Roman historians, founded the kingdom of Armenia in 190 B.C. After the defeat of Antiochus the Great (whose general he was) by the Romans, he made himself independent in Armenia.

Artaxias II., King of Armenia, whose father was dethroned and carried to Alexandria by Mark Antony in 34 B.C., was chosen king by the Armenians, but expelled by the Romans, and reinstated by Phraates IV. of Parthia. He was murdered by his nobles for his cruelty.

Artaxias III. This sovereign, whose Greek name was ZE′NO, a son of the King of Pontus, was placed on the throne of Armenia by the Romans in 18 A.D., after an interregnum of two years in consequence of the flight of Vonones.

Arteaga, ȧr-tȧ-ä′gä, (ESTEBAN,) a Jesuit, born in Madrid near the middle of the eighteenth century, re-

moved to Italy after the suppression of his order. He published at Bologna a history of the Italian lyrical drama, ("Le Rivoluzioni del Teatro musicale italiano," etc., 2 vols., 1783,) which is called the best work on that subject. Died in Paris in 1799.

Arteaga, (HORTENSIO.) See ARTIAGA.

Arteaga y Alfaro, ȧr-tȧ-ä′gä e äl-fä′ro, (MATIAS,) a Spanish painter and engraver, one of the founders of the Academy of Seville, was born in that city in the first half of the seventeenth century. Died in 1704.

See BERMUDEZ, "Diccionario Historico."

Artedi, ȧr-tä′dee, (PETER,) [Lat. PE′TRUS ARCTE′-DIUS,] an eminent Swedish naturalist, born at Anund in 1705. He entered the University of Upsal in 1724, and studied natural sciences and medicine. About 1728 he formed, at Upsal, an intimate friendship with Linnæus. They entered into a scientific partnership, and agreed to divide the field of labour in natural history. Artedi, having chosen the departments of fishes and reptiles, departed, in 1734, to England, where he had access to the museum of Sir Hans Sloane. He met Linnæus again at Leyden in 1735, and was employed by Seba, a rich apothecary of Amsterdam, to describe his collection of fishes. Before he had finished this task, he fell into a canal in the night and was drowned, in December, 1735. He left an excellent work on fishes, which was published by Linnæus in 1738, with the following title, "Petri Artedi Ichthyologia sive Opera omnia de Piscibus," etc. This was the most complete work that had appeared on that subject. In the opinion of Du Petit-Thouars, "it was worthy to be proposed as a model to natural historians, and was a master-piece which has not yet been surpassed."

See "Life of Artedi," by LINNÆUS, prefixed to his "Opera Omnia," 1738; GEZELIUS, "Biographiskt-Lexicon;" "Biographie Universelle."

Artefius. See ARTEPHIUS.

Artémidore. See ARTEMIDORUS.

Ar-tem-ĭ-do′rus, [Gr. Ἀρτεμίδωρος; Fr. ARTÉMIDORE, ȧr′tȧ′me′doR′,] a Greek grammarian, who lived about 240 B.C., was a pupil of Aristophanes of Byzantium. His works are not extant.

Artemidorus, a Greek physician, born in Pamphylia in or after the third century B.C. He taught that the œsophagus or stomach was the seat of hydrophobia.

Artemidorus, a native of Cnidos, grammarian, and friend of Julius Cæsar, lived in Rome. According to Plutarch, he was informed of the plot to kill Cæsar, and warned him of his danger in a letter which Cæsar held in his hand (but had not read) when he entered the senate-house on the Ides of March.

Artemidorus, a painter at Rome in the time of the poet Martial, by whom he is ridiculed.

Artemido′rus CAP′ITO, a Greek physician and grammarian, who lived at Rome in the time of the emperor Hadrian, and published a valuable edition of Hippocrates, which was highly esteemed by Hadrian.

Artemido′rus CORNE′LIUS, an ancient physician, an accomplice of Verres in his iniquities in Cilicia and Sicily. He is mentioned by Cicero in this connection.

Artemido′rus DALDIA′NUS, a native of Ephesus, who lived about 160 A.D., wrote a curious work on dreams and their interpretations, (Ὀνειροκριτικά,) which is valuable for the light it throws on ancient customs and opinions.

See FABRICIUS, "Bibliotheca Græca."

Artemido′rus OF EPH′ESUS, a geographer, who lived about 103 B.C., and who is frequently quoted by Strabo.

Artemis, [Ἄρτεμις,] the Greek name of the goddess DIANA, which see.

Artémise. See ARTEMISIA.

Artemisia, ar-te-mish′e-ạ, [Gr. Ἀρτεμισία; Fr. ARTÉMISE, ȧr′tȧ′mèz′,] a warlike queen of Halicarnassus, who reigned after her husband's death. She joined the fleet of Xerxes, with her ships, in the expedition against the Greeks, and distinguished herself by bravery and skill at the naval battle of Salamis, fought against her advice in 480 B.C. Being pursued by an Athenian ship, she artfully eluded the danger by attacking a Persian vessel, and thus led her pursuers to think she was not their enemy. A doubtful tradition adds that, in consequen'e of disappointed love, she jumped from the Leucadian rock into the sea.

See HERODOTUS, "History," vii. and viii. ; PAUSANIAS, iii.

Artemisia, an Oriental princess, celebrated for her grief at the death of her husband and for her devotion to his memory, was the wife of Mausolus, Prince of Caria, who died in 352 B.C. She erected for him at Halicarnassus a magnificent tomb, which was reckoned one of the seven wonders of the world, and from which such monuments, in succeeding times, have derived the generic name of *mausoleum*. It is stated that she invited the eminent poets and orators of that time to compete with each other in composing a eulogy on Mausolus, that she mingled his ashes with her drink, and died of grief about two years after his death.

See DIODORUS SICULUS; STRABO, xiv. ; CICERO, "Tusculanæ;" J. C. AVENARIUS, "Dissertatio de Artemisia et Mausoleo," 1714.

Artemius. See ANASTASIUS II.

Ar-te'mĭ-us [Gr. Ἀρτέμιος] or **Ar-the'mĭ-us,** [Ἀρθέμιος,] a Christian commander-in-chief of the Roman army in Egypt in the reign of Constantius. He was put to death on the accession of Julian, (362 A.D.,) on account of his severity towards the pagans.

Ar'te-mon, [Ἀρτέμων,] a Greek painter of uncertain period, who is classed by Pliny among artists of the second rank. Among his master-pieces mentioned by Pliny was the "Apotheosis of Hercules."

Artemon, a sculptor, who lived in Rome about the time of Pliny. His works adorned the palace of the Cæsars.

Artemon, a rhetorician, often quoted by Seneca, is supposed to have lived under Augustus or Tiberius.

Artemon or **Ar'te-mas,** the founder of the sect of Artemonites, who denied the divinity of Christ, lived in the third century.

Artemon of Cassandria, a learned grammarian, who flourished about 300 B.C.

Artemon of Clazomenæ, a famous engineer, the reputed inventor of the testudo and battering-ram, was employed by Pericles in the siege of Samos.

Ar-te'phĭ-us or **Ar-te'fĭ-us,** an alchemist, who appears to have lived in the twelfth century.

Arteveld, van, văn aR'teh-vĕlt', or **Artevelde, van,** văn aR'teh-vĕl'deh, (JACOB,) a famous demagogue, born at Ghent near the beginning of the fourteenth century. He was a wealthy brewer, and by his eloquence and other talents acquired great influence over the people of Ghent, who, having revolted against the Count of Flanders, chose Arteveld as the commander of their forces. He confirmed his power by proscribing the nobles, and ruled the city in a violent and arbitrary manner. In 1335 he formed an alliance with Edward III. of England, whom he aided in his war against France. In 1340 he induced the Flemings to do homage to Edward as King of France. He afterwards formed a project to make the English Black Prince Count of Flanders. The citizens of Ghent, led by Gherard Denys, revolted against him for this cause and killed him in 1345. He is called James d'Arteville by Hume, and Jacques d'Artvelle by French writers.

See FROISSART, "Chronicles;" MEYER, "Annales Rerum Flandricarum;" ÉCREVISSE, "Redevoering op J. van Artevelde," 8vo, 1846; J. DE WINTER, "J. van Artevelde," 8vo, 1846.

Arteveld, van, (PHILIP,) a son of the preceding, was born at Ghent about 1540, and inherited his father's riches. He passed the prime of life in a private station, which he suddenly left to become, like his father, a powerful popular leader. In 1379 the people of Ghent revolted against Louis, Count of Flanders, who besieged that city so effectually that famine was imminent. Finding that their leaders were inadequate for the crisis, they nominated Arteveld captain by acclamation in 1381. In May, 1382, he gained a decisive victory over Count Louis at Bruges, which was captured by the victors, and he assumed the title of regent. Charles VI. of France soon after sent an army under Clisson to aid the Count of Flanders against the insurgents, who were defeated with great loss at Roosebeke or Rosebec in November, 1382. Arteveld was killed in this battle, and Count Louis became master of Ghent.

See FROISSART, "Chronicles;" M. DE BARANTE, "Histoire de Bourgogne."

Artevelde. See ARTEVELD.

Arteveldt, van, (ANDREW.) See ARTVELT.

Arteville or **Artvelle.** See ARTEVELD.

Ar'thur or **Ar'tus,** written also **Artur,** a semi-fabulous prince of Britain, and hero of the famous romances of the Round Table, is supposed to have flourished in the fifth or sixth century, during the dark period which occurred between the evacuation of Britain by the Romans and the conquest of that island by the Saxons. The authentic accounts of his deeds are so scanty that his existence has been doubted by some antiquaries. According to popular tradition, he gained several victories over the Saxons, and over Cerdic, the founder of the West Saxon kingdom, after which he was killed in battle against his rebellious nephew Modred or Medrod at Camlan. His exploits were the favourite subjects of mediæval poets and romancers. Hume calls him Prince of the Silures. ("History of England.")

See TURNER, "History of the Anglo-Saxons;" OWEN, "Cambrian Biography;" LELAND, "Assertio Arthuri;" JOSEPH RITSON, "Life of King Arthur," 1825.

Ar'thur I., Duke of Brittany, born in 1187, was a grandson of Henry II. of England. He was put to death by his uncle John Lackland in 1202.

Arthur II. of Brittany, born in 1262, was a son of John II. Died in 1312.

Arthur III., Duc de Bretagne, (or Brittany,) born in 1393, was a son of John (Jean) V. He fought for the Orléans faction, was wounded at Agincourt, and became Constable of France about 1424. He succeeded to the dukedom at the death of his nephew Pierre in 1456. Died in 1457.

Ar'thur, Prince of Wales, the eldest son of Henry VII. and Elizabeth of York, was born in 1486. He married Catherine of Aragon in 1501, and died without issue in 1502, after which his widow became the wife of his brother, Henry VIII.

Ar'thur, (ARCHIBALD,) a Scottish divine of liberal principles, was born in Renfrewshire in 1744, and licensed as a preacher in 1767. Soon after that date he was appointed chaplain to the University of Glasgow. He became the assistant of Dr. Reid as professor of moral philosophy at Glasgow in 1780, and succeeded to the chair vacated by Dr. Reid at his death in 1796. He died in June, 1797, leaving "Discourses on Theological and Literary Subjects," (1803.)

Ar'thur, (TIMOTHY S.,) an American writer of fiction, born near Newburg, Orange county, New York, in 1809. He was educated in Baltimore, and became a clerk or agent of a banking company. Since 1841 he has resided in Philadelphia. He has written many popular tales illustrative of domestic life and designed to promote morality. Among his works are "Lights and Shadows of Real Life," "Tales for Rich and Poor," (6 vols.,) "Library for the Household," (12 vols.,) "The Good Time Coming," (1855.)

Arthus, aR'toos, **Ar'tus,** or **Ar-thu'sĭ-us,** (GOTTHARD,) a translator and compiler, born at Dantzic about 1570. Among his publications is a "History of the East Indies," ("Historia Indiæ Orientalis," 1608.) He supplied many Latin translations for De Bry's "Collection of Voyages."

Artiaga, or **Paravicino y Artiaga,** pä-rä-ve-thee'-no e aR-te-ä'gä, (HORTENSIO FELIX,) a Spanish poet and priest, born at Madrid in 1580, was appointed preacher to Philip III. in 1616. As a poet he was a disciple of Gongora, and was much admired by his contemporaries. Died in 1633.

Artieda, de, dä aR-te-ä'Dä, (ANDRES **Rey**—rā or rā'e,) a Spanish writer, born at Valencia about the middle of the sixteenth century. He served in the army for many years, and distinguished himself at Lepanto. He wrote "The Lovers," ("Los Amantes," 1581,) and other dramas. His reputation rests chiefly on his "Discourses, Epistles, and Epigrams," (1605.) Died in 1613.

Artiga, de, dä aR-tee'gä, (Don FRANCISCO,) a Spanish landscape-painter and engraver, born at Huesca about the middle of the seventeenth century. He founded and endowed a chair of mathematics at Huesca, and taught in it himself. He wrote treatises on mathematics and other subjects. Died in 1711.

ā, ē, ī, ō, ū, ȳ, *long;* ă, ĕ, ĭ, ŏ, same, less prolonged; ă ĕ, ĭ, ŏ, ŭ, ў, *short;* ạ, ẹ, ị, ọ, *obscure;* fär, fåll, fåt; mĕt; nŏt; gōŏd; mōōn;

Artigas, aR-tee′gȧs, (Don JUAN or FERNANDO JOSÉ,) a South American general, born at Montevideo about 1760. He entered the service of the Junta or republic of Buenos Ayres about 1811, before which he had been a leader of the lawless Gauchos. He gained victories over the royalists, made himself master of the Banda Oriental, and became a general. Having quarrelled with Posadas, the director of the new state, he raised an army of Gauchos, defeated the troops of Buenos Ayres, and compelled the Junta to recognize him as independent chief of the Banda Oriental in 1814. He waged war with various success against the Portuguese, who invaded the Banda Oriental in 1816. In 1820 he captured the city of Buenos Ayres, but before the end of the year he was driven into exile. Died in Paraguay in 1825 or 1826.

See ARMITAGE, "History of Brazil."

Artigny, d′, däR′tèn′ye′,(ANTOINE **Gachat**—gä′shä′,) a French *littérateur*, born at Vienne in 1706, became a canon of the church in that city. He published a valuable work entitled "New Historical, Critical, and Literary Memoirs," ("Nouveaux Mémoires d'Histoire, de Critique et de Littérature," 7 vols., 1749–56.) Died in 1778.

Artis, d′, däR′te′, (GABRIEL,) a French Protestant and controversial writer, noted for his zeal against Socinianism, was born in Aveyron in 1660. He became minister of a church in Berlin, but was deprived of that office about 1692 on account of his contentious spirit. Died about 1730.

Artis, d′, [Lat. ARTIS′IUS,] (JEAN,) a French writer on canon law and kindred subjects, born at Cahors in 1572, was appointed professor of canon law in the University of Paris in 1623. Died in 1651.

Artisjosky. See ARCISZEWSKI.

Artmann, aRt′mȧn, (JEROME,) a celebrated organ-maker of Bohemia, born at Prague in the latter part of the seventeenth century.

Artner, von, fon aRt′ner, (MARIA THERESE,) a German poetess, daughter of an Austrian officer, born at Schnitau, in Hungary, in 1772. She produced several successful dramas, among which was "Quiet Greatness," ("Stille Grösse," 1824.) Her most popular works are lyric poems, published under the name of Theone, "Field-Flowers from Hungary's Plains, gathered by Minna and Theone," ("Feldblumen auf Ungarns Fluren gesammelt von Minna und Theone," 1800.) Died at Agram in 1829.

See DÖRING, "Vie d'Artner," 1829.

Artois, van, vȧn äR′twä′, (JACQUES,) an excellent Flemish landscape-painter, born at Brussels in 1613. His works are commended for good taste, and for the richness and variety of the details. Many of the figures in his landscapes were painted by the younger Teniers. He obtained high prices for his pictures, but his habits were so extravagant that he remained poor. He is supposed to have died about 1665.

See HOUBRAKEN, "Groote Schouburg;" HEINECKEN, "Dictionnaire des Artistes."

Ar-to′mĭ-us, (PETER,) a Polish poet and Lutheran minister at Thorn, was born in 1552; died in 1609.

Artopœus, aR-to-pee′us, or **Artopöus,** aR-to-pö′us, (JOHANN,) a German writer and professor of law, born at Worms in 1520; died about 1580.

Artopœus, aR-to-pee′us or aR-to-pö′us, sometimes written **Artopæus,** (PETER,) a learned Protestant divine, born in Pomerania in 1491, was the author of many polemical and religious works. Died at Stettin in 1563.

Artopœus or **Artopöus,** (JOHANN CHRISTOPH,) a philologist and historian, originally named BECKER, born at Strasburg, on the Rhine, in 1626. He was professor of Latin in the gymnasium of his native city for many years. He wrote many historical and antiquarian treatises, and was the reputed author of a curious Latin "Essay on the State and Place of Souls after Death," ("De Statu, Loco et Vita Animarum," etc.) Died in 1702.

See JÖCHER, "Allgemeines Gelehrten-Lexikon."

Ar-to′rĭ-us, [Gr. Ἀρτώριος,] (MARCUS,) a medical writer of Rome, was physician to the emperor Augustus, whom he attended in the campaign against Brutus and Cassius, 42 B.C. By his advice, Augustus removed from his camp at Philippi just before it was taken by the

enemy. Artorius was drowned at sea in 31 B.C. He was the author of a work on Hydrophobia, which is lost.

Artot, äR′to′, (JOSEPH,) a Belgian violinist, born at Brussels in 1815; died in Paris in 1845.

Artur or **Artus.** See ARTHUR.

Artus, (GOTTHARD.) See ARTHUS.

Artus, äR′tüss′, (THOMAS,) Sieur d'Embry, a French *littérateur*, born at Paris about 1550, was a coadjutor of Blaise de Vigenère.

Artusi, aR-too′see, (GIOVANNI MARIA,) a writer on music, born at Bologna about the middle of the sixteenth century, was a canon in the church of that city. He published "The Art of Counterpoint," (1586,) and a work "On the Imperfections of Modern Music," (1600.) He is supposed to have died about 1610.

See BURNEY, "History of Music."

Artusini, aR-too-see′nee, (ANTONIO,) an Italian poet and jurist, born at Forli in 1554; died about 1630.

Artvelt, van, vȧn aRt′vèlt, (ANDRIES,) a good marine painter of Antwerp, flourished about 1620, and was a contemporary of Van Dyck, who painted his portrait. He excelled in depicting storms.

Aruajo de Azevedo Pinto Pereyra, ä-roo-ä′zho dä ä-zä-vä′do pèn′to pȧ-rā′e-rä, (ANTONIO,) Count of Barca, a Portuguese poet and diplomatist of the latter part of the eighteenth century. Died in 1816.

See LONGFELLOW'S "Poets and Poetry of Europe."

Arum, ä′rŭm, (DOMINIC,) a Dutch jurist, born at Leeuwarden in 1579, became professor of law at Jena about 1605. "He rendered," says Guizot, "importan services to the public law of Germany." Among his works are "Academic Discourses on Public Law," ("Discursus academici de Jure publico," 5 vols., 1617–23,) and a "Treatise on the Diets of the German Empire," ("De Comitiis Imperii Romano-Germanici," 1630.) Died at Jena in 1637.

See FOPPENS, "Bibliotheca Belgica."

Ar′u-na or **Ar′un,** [Hindoo pron. ŭr′ŏŏ-na, and ŭr′ŏŏn,] in the Hindoo mythology, the charioteer of the Sun, (Sŏŏrya or Sûrya.) He is a son of Kasyapa, and brother-german of Garuda, the eagle of Vishnu. As a personification of the dawn, he may be said to correspond to the Aurora or Eos of classic mythology.

See MOOR'S "Hindu Pantheon."

Ar′un-del, (Lady BLANCHE,) the wife of Thomas, Lord Arundel, and daughter of Edward Somerset, Earl of Worcester, was born in 1583. She gained distinction by her defence of Wardour Castle against the Parliament about 1642. Died in 1649.

Arundel, EARL OF. See HOWARD.

Arundel, (HENRY,) third Baron of Wardour, succeeded to his title in 1648. He was one of the five Roman Catholic lords who were imprisoned upon the perjured testimony of Titus Oates. On the accession of James II. he became lord keeper of the privy seal. Died in 1694.

Arundel, (MARY,) COUNTESS OF, a learned English lady and writer of the sixteenth century, was the wife of Henry Howard, Earl of Arundel.

Arundel, (THOMAS,) Archbishop of Canterbury, born at Arundel Castle, Sussex, in 1353, was a younger son of Richard Fitz-Alan, Earl of Arundel. He became Bishop of Ely in 1375, lord high-chancellor in 1386, and Archbishop of York in 1388. In 1396 he was translated to the see of Canterbury. This was the first instance that occurred of a translation from the see of York to that of Canterbury. In 1397 he was impeached for high treason, and banished by·Richard II. He took a prominent part in the revolution by which Richard was dethroned, and was restored to the see of Canterbury by Henry IV. in 1399. He prohibited the translation of the Scriptures into English, and persecuted the Lollards,—*i.e.* the disciples of Wickliffe. Died in 1413.

See FULLER, "Church History:" HOLINSHED, "Chronicle;" RAPIN, "History of England;" W. F. HOOK, "Lives of the Archbishops of Canterbury," vol. iv. chap. xvii., (1860.)

Arundel, (THOMAS,) first Lord Arundel of Wardour, was a son of Sir Matthew Arundel of Wardour Castle, Wilts, and was born about 1540. In his youth he entered the service of the German emperor, who rewarded his remarkable exploits in the war against the Turks with the title of Count of the Roman Empire, (1595.) He was created Baron Arundel by James I. in 1605. Died in 1639.

Arundel, (THOMAS,) the second baron, a son of the preceding, fought for Charles I. in the civil war, and was mortally wounded at Lansdowne in 1643.

Arundel, (Sir THOMAS,) was a grandfather of the first Lord Arundel of Wardour. He was a friend of the Duke of Somerset, and was charged with being his accomplice in treason and in a conspiracy to kill the Duke of Northumberland. Though he was probably innocent, he was executed in February, 1551–52. His wife was a sister of Catherine Howard, a queen of Henry VIII.

A'runs or **Aruntius,** a-run'she-us, [Fr. ARONCE, ǎ'rôNss',] a son of Demaratus of Corinth, who is said to have emigrated to Etruria, was a brother of Tarquin the Elder, of Rome.

Aruns, a Roman prince, was a brother of Tarquin the Proud, (Superbus,) the last king of Rome. According to the legend, he was killed by his wife Tullia, (a daughter of Servius Tullius,) who was notorious for cruelty.

Aruns, a son of Tarquin the Proud. After the expulsion of that king, an army of Etruscans marched against Rome to reinstate him, and encountered the Roman army, led by the consul Brutus. Aruns, who fought for his father in this battle, engaged Brutus in a single combat, in which both were killed.

Aruns, a son of Porsena, who accompanied his father in his invasion of Rome.

Aruns, an Etrurian, who is said to have invited the Gauls into Italy to revenge himself for an insult offered to his wife by a noble of that country.

Aruns, a Roman historian, lived about 60 B.C., and wrote a History of the Punic War.

Arusianus, a-ru-she-a'nus, (MESSUS or MESSIUS,) a Roman grammarian, of whom nothing is known except that his name is connected with a work called "Quadriga vel Exempla Elocutionum," a vocabulary of remarkable phrases found in Virgil, Sallust, Terence, and Cicero. The value of this is enhanced by many fragments of the lost works of Sallust and Cicero which are preserved in it.

Ar-van'dus, a prefect of Gaul from 467 to 472, was condemned to death by the Roman senate for malpractices in his office; but his punishment was commuted to perpetual exile and confiscation of property.

Arvidsson, aR'vids-son, written also **Arwidsson,** (TRULS or TROILS,) a Swedish engraver, born at Westervik, studied at Upsal about 1680, and became learned in Oriental languages, especially Hebrew. He was copper-plate engraver to the Antiquarian Archives, and published a singular work on the original music of the first seven Psalms of David, (1705.) Died in 1705.

Arvieux, d', dǎR've'uh', (LAURENT,) CHEVALIER, a French traveller and Oriental scholar, born at Marseilles in 1635. He showed much tact in negotiating a treaty with the Dey of Tunis in 1668, and rendered important services to the French ambassador at Constantinople in 1672. He was consul at Aleppo from 1679 to 1686, and refused the office or title of Bishop of Babylon, which was offered him by the pope. His "Treatise on the Manners and Customs of the Arabs" (1717) is commended. His accuracy and veracity have been attested by Niebuhr. He left papers from which Labat compiled "Memoirs of Chevalier D'Arvieux, containing his Travels in Asia, Syria, etc.," (6 vols., 1735.) Died in 1702.

See ERSCH und GRUBER, "Allgemeine Encyklopaedie."

Arwidsson. See ARVIDSSON.

Arwidsson, aR'wids'son, (ADOLF,) a Swedish scholar, born in Finland in 1791. He was exiled in 1822 from Finland for a political article in a journal. Having removed to Stockholm, he was appointed keeper of the royal library. He published, besides other works, a collection of old popular Swedish songs, (3 vols., 1834–42.) Died in 1858.

Arya, âr'ya, [Ger. ARJA,] English plural **Ar'yas,** the name of an ancient race of men who are supposed to have dwelt originally near the sources of the Oxus, (Amoo,) and who first crossed the Indus from the north probably about two thousand years before the Christian era. The Aryas were the ancestors of the modern Hindoos, and were nearly related (as is shown by a com-

parison of their respective languages) to the ancient Persians. The Aryan language was the Sanscrit, generally regarded as the most ancient of all the Indo-European tongues. Using the term in a more comprehensive sense, the Aryas may be said to have been the ancestors of the entire Indo-European (otherwise called Aryan) family of nations. The word would seem to have signified originally "agriculturists," used in contradistinction to the Turanian or Tartar nations, who were nomadic shepherds, though its later Sanscrit signification is "of good family," "noble," "honourable," and hence it was applied only to the higher castes among the Hindoos. (See BRAHMANISM.)

See MAX MÜLLER'S "Science of Language," pp. 237, 238, 239; WHITNEY'S "Language and the Study of Language," particularly lectures v. and vi.

☞ **ARYAN,*** the adjective derived from ARYA, is also used as a noun, with the same signification as Arya. [The Germans use ARIER, â're-er, singular and plural.]

Aryabhatta, âr-ya-bat'ta, called by the Arabs **Aryabahr,** aR'ya-bâHR', a celebrated Hindoo mathematician and astronomer, who lived probably about the beginning of the Christian era. He was the earliest known writer on algebra. He announced the diurnal rotation of the earth, and made a near approximation to the truth in his statement of the earth's diameter.

See COLEBROOKE'S "Essays."

A-rym'bas [Gr. Ἀρύμβας] **I.,** sometimes written **Arrybas,** King of the Molossi, is supposed to have reigned about 390 B.C., and to have been the first to give a well-organized government to the Molossi.

Arymbas II., also a king of the same people. Died in 346 B.C.

Ar-ys-dā'ghĕs, SAINT, a Christian bishop, born in Cappadocia about 280 A.D., was Patriarch of Armenia. Died in 339.

Arysdaghes, an Armenian grammarian, born in 1178; died in 1239.

Arzachel, aR-thâ-chĕl', a noted astronomer, who lived in Spain in the latter half of the eleventh century.

Arzan, aR'zăn, an Armenian high-priest and pagan, opposed Christianity by arms. He was killed in 302 A.D.

Arzão, aR-zŏwN', (ANTONIO RODRIGUEZ,) a Brazilian traveller, who, about 1694, explored the province of Minas and the river Doce.

Arzere, dell', del-laRd-zā'rà, (STEFANO,) an Italian fresco-painter of note, lived in the sixteenth century, at Padua. He imitated Titian.

See LANZI, "History of Painting in Italy."

As or **Asa.** See ÆSIR.

A'sa, [Heb. אָסָא; Gr. Ἀσά,] King of Judah, and a son of Abijam or Abijah, began to reign in 970 B.C. according to Hales, or 955 according to Usher. He was distinguished by his zeal against idolatry. He died about 929 B.C. (See I. Kings xv.; II. Chronicles xiv., xv., xvi.)

Asadi (â'sâ'dee) OF TOOS, a Persian poet, who flourished about 950 A.D., was a preceptor of Firdousee, and chief poet at the court of Mahmood of Gazna. Among his works is Gushtâsp Nâmeh, an epic poem. It is said that he wrote the last part of the Shâhnâmeh, which Firdousee left unfinished at his death in 1020.

See "Annals of Oriental Literature," 1820.

Asam, â'sâm, a Bavarian painter, born in the seventeenth century. He acquired a great reputation by his frescos, and, with his brother Egid, adorned many churches in Bavaria. Among their works are the pictures in the Johannes-Kirche at Munich. Died in 1739.

See HEINECKEN, "Dictionnaire des Artistes."

· **A'san,** [Gr. Ἀσάνης; Lat. ASA'NES,] King of Bulgaria, reigning about the close of the twelfth century, restored his country to independence by throwing off the yoke of the Greek Empire.

Asan II., (JOANNES,) son of the preceding, having been compelled to flee to Russia by the usurpation of a relative, returned about 1217 with a Russian army and drove out the usurper. Died in 1241.

Asan III., (JOANNES,) the last Bulgarian king of the Asanian dynasty, (whose father King Mitzes was an exile

---

* Pronounced âr'yan or âr'e-an, to distinguish it from *Arian,* (*i.e.* "belonging to Arius," the great heresiarch.)

ă, ē, ī, ō, ū, y̆, *long;* à, è, ò, same, less prolonged; ă, ĕ, ĭ, ŏ, ŭ, y̆, *short;* a, e, i, o, *obscure;* fâr, fàll, fàt; mêt; nŏt; gōŏd; mōōn

at the time of his death,) recovered his kingdom in 1279, but was expelled in 1281 by the usurper Terter or Terteres, and died at Constantinople.

A-san'der, [Gr. 'Ασάνδρος; Fr. ASANDRE, ä'zôNdR',] a Macedonian officer, was a brother of Parmenio, and son of Philotas. He was appointed in 334 B.C. governor of Lydia by Alexander the Great, after whose death he obtained the satrapy of Caria. He formed an alliance with Ptolemy the son of Lagus, and extended his power by the conquest of Lycia. From 315 to 313 B.C. he waged war against Antigonus. The time of his death is unknown.

Asander, appointed governor of the Bosphorus in the Tauric Chersonesus by Pharnaces II. in 47 B.C., revolted from his master and formed a kingdom in which he was confirmed by Augustus. He is reputed to have built the wall across the Tauric Chersonesus.

Asandre. See ASANDER.

A'saph [Heb. אָסָף] or **As'saph,** a Hebrew musician or psalmist, who was contemporary with King David. He was the chief of certain Levites whom David appointed to minister before the ark and to thank and praise the Lord. (See I. Chronicles xvi. 5 and xxv. 1.) The name occurs at the beginning of many of the Psalms. (See Psalms l., lxxiii. et seq.)

As'aph, SAINT, a prelate of the seventh century, supposed to have been the first Bishop of Saint Asaph in Wales. Several theological works are attributed to him.

See H. WHARTON, "Historia de Episcopis et Decanis Londinensibus, etc."

As'both, [Hun. pron. ŏsh'bot,] (ALEXANDER,) a Hungarian patriot, born in 1811, distinguished himself as an engineer in the war of 1848–49. Having come to the United States, he was made, in 1861, a brigadier-general of volunteers under General Fremont, in Missouri. Died in 1868.

Asar. See ÆSIR.

Asbury, as'ber-e, (FRANCIS,) was born in Staffordshire, England, in 1745. He was sent by John Wesley to America as a missionary about 1770, and was appointed in 1784 the first bishop of the Methodist Church then organized upon a new basis in the United States. Died in Virginia in 1816.

See "Asbury and his Coadjutors," by W. C. LARRABEE.

Ascagne. See ASCANIUS.

Ascalus, ăs'kä-lŭs, (CONRAD,) a German philosopher, lived about 1600–20. He published "Physica et Ethica Mosaica," (1613,) and other works.

As-ca'nI-us [Gr. 'Ασκάνιος; Fr. ASCAGNE, ăs'kän'] was, according to Virgil and Livy, a son of Æneas and Creusa, and the founder of Alba Longa. He was also called Iulus (Julus) or Ilus, and was claimed by the Julia gens of Rome as one of their ancestors. There are various traditions about him, according to one of which he succeeded his father as King of the Latins.

Ascanius, ăs-kä'ne-ùs, (PETER,) a Swedish naturalist, who lived about 1750, was for many years inspector of the mines in the north of Norway. He corresponded with Linnæus, and published a work on natural history, entitled "Figures enluminées d'Histoire naturelle," 1767.

Ascarelli, ăs-kä-rel'lee, written also **Ascariel,** (DEBORA,) a Jewish poetess, born at Rome, lived about 1600.

As'ca-rus, ['Ασκαρος,] a Theban sculptor, lived about 300 B.C. He made a statue of Jupiter, at Olympia.

As'çe-lin, or **Ascelino,** ä-shä-lee'no, (NICOLA,) a Dominican who was sent by Innocent IV. on a mission to Tartary about 1245.

Ascensius. See BADIUS.

Asch, van, vän ăsk, (PIETER **Janzen**—yän'zen,) a skilful Dutch landscape-painter, born at Delft in 1603. He lived to an advanced age, but left few works.

Asch, von, fon ăsh, (GEORG THOMAS,) a physician and anatomist, born at Saint Petersburg in 1729, studied at Göttingen, of which university he was subsequently a liberal benefactor. He was the companion and friend of Haller. He served for some years as a surgeon in the Russian army. Died in 1807.

Asch, von, (PETER ERNST,) brother of the above, one of the most esteemed physicians of his time in Moscow, wrote a work "De Natura Spermatis."

Ascha. See MAIMOON-BEN-KAIS.

Ascham, ăs'kam, (ANTHONY,) an English astrologer and writer on herbs, lived about 1550.

Ascham, (ANTHONY,) an Englishman, born at Boston, in Lincolnshire, entered Cambridge University in 1633. He supported the Parliament in the civil war, and was appointed tutor to the captive Duke of York in 1646. He wrote a work "On the Confusions and Revolutions of Government," (1648.) He was sent soon after as ambassador to Madrid, where he was murdered in 1650 by some English royalists, who were tried and condemned, but released by the influence of the pope. One of them, however, was retaken and executed.

See CLARENDON's "History of the Rebellion."

Ascham, (ROGER,) an eminent English classical scholar and writer, was born near Northallerton, in Yorkshire, in 1515. He was educated at Saint John's College, Cambridge, and was elected a Fellow of the same in 1534. In 1544 he was chosen orator of the university, and in 1545 published "Toxophilus, or the School of Shooting." "He designed not only to teach the art of shooting," says Dr. Johnson, "but to give an example of diction more natural and more truly English than was used by the common writers of that age. He has not failed in either of his purposes." He was appointed in 1548 tutor of the Princess Elizabeth, whom he instructed in Greek and Latin until 1550, when he resigned that situation. His motive appears to have been the offensive conduct of some attendants of his pupil.

On a visit to Lady Jane Grey at her father's country-seat, he found her reading Plato's "Phædon," in the original. "While the horns were sounding and the dogs in full cry," says Macaulay, "she sat in the lonely oriel with eyes riveted to that immortal page which tells how meekly and bravely the first great martyr of intellectual liberty took the cup from his weeping jailer." ("Essay on Lord Bacon.") He was appointed (notwithstanding his Protestantism) Latin secretary to Queen Mary in 1553, and was continued in this office by Queen Elizabeth, (1558,) who also after her accession took lessons in Greek and Latin from him. He resided constantly at court from this time until his death, which occurred in 1568. He left a son Giles, and other children. Ascham appears to have had the rare felicity of passing through the worst of times without persecution or dishonour. His greatest work is "The Schole-Master, or Plain and Perfite Way of teaching Children to understand, read, and write the Latin Tonge," (1571,) which is a production of great merit. Dr. Johnson speaks of it as "perhaps the best advice that was ever given for the study of languages."

See a "Life of Ascham" (probably by DR. JOHNSON) appended to an edition of his English works, 1761; GRANT, "De Vita Rogeri Ascham;" WOOD, "Fasti Oxonienses;" "Retrospective Review," vol. iv., (1821.)

Aschaneus, ăs-kä-nä'ùs, (MARTIN,) a Swedish writer of the seventeenth century, obtained the office of "royal antiquarian" about 1630, before which he was a chaplain in the army. He published a translation of the Psalms, (1619,) and left in manuscript several works, among which was a drama "On the Creation and Fall of Man."

Aschbach, ăsh'bäk, (JOSEPH,) a German historian, born at Höchst, near Frankfort-on-the-Main, in 1801. He became professor of history at Bonn about 1842. Among his works are a "History of the Visigoths," (1827,) and a "History of the Omeyyades in Spain," ("Geschichte der Omaijaden in Spanien," 2 vols., 1829–30,) which are commended.

Ascheberg, von, fon ăs'keh-bĕRg', or **Aschenberg, von,** fon ăs'ken-bĕRg', (RUTGER, rüt'gĕr,) COUNT, an able Swedish general, born at Afgülden in 1621. He was made a colonel in 1655 for his victory over a greatly superior force of Poles, and defeated the Danes in several actions in 1658–59. In 1670 he attained the rank of lieutenant-general. During the war between Sweden and Denmark, which was renewed in 1675, he was charged with the defence of Sweden. The victories of the Swedes at Halmstadt, Lund, and Carlscrona, in 1676, are ascribed to his skill, although the king had the nominal command. He was made a field-marshal in 1680. Died in 1693.

See SVEN LAGERBRING, "Rütger von Aschebergs Lefverne," 1751.

Aschenbrenner, ăsh'en-bren'ner, (CHRISTIAN HEIN-

RICH,) a German violinist, born at Alt Stettin in 1654. Died in 1732.

Asciano, d', dä-shä'no, (GIOVANNI,) a Siennese painter, lived towards the close of the fourteenth century.

Ascione, â-sho'nà, (ANGELO,) a Neapolitan fruit-painter, who lived towards the close of the seventeenth century.

Asclepi, âs-klä'pee, (GIUSEPPE,) an Italian natural philosopher, born at Macerata in 1706; died in 1776.

Asclepiad or **Asclepiade,** as-klee'pe-ad, the English singular of ASCLEPIADÆ; used also as an adjective. ☞ The plural form **Asclepiads** or **Asclepiades** rarely occurs in English.

Asclepiadæ, as-kle-pī'ạ-dē, [Gr. Ἀσκληπιάδαι; Fr. ASCLÉPIADES, ås'klä'pe'ắd',] the name of the descendants of Æsculapius, who, during several centuries, were the most celebrated physicians of Greece.

As-cle-pī'ạ-dēṣ, [Gr. Ἀσκληπιάδης; Fr. ASCLÉPIADE, ås'klä'pe'ắd',] a Greek lyric poet, inventor of a kind of verse called *Asclepiad,* is supposed to have lived about 600 B.C.

Asclepiades, one of the bishops of Antioch, was distinguished as a writer of commentaries.

Asclepiades of Myrleia, a native of Bithynia, said to have taught at Rome in the time of Pompey the Great. To him, or a person bearing the same name, are ascribed various literary works, including a " History of Bithynia," a work on Spain, and a commentary on the Odyssey.

Asclepiades of Phlius, a Greek philosopher, who was a pupil or friend of Menedemus, and lived about 350 B.C. Nothing is known of his opinions or works.

Asclepiades, an eminent physician, born in Prusa, in Bithynia, in A.D. 88, was presented by Trajan with the freedom of seven cities.

Asclepiades of Samos, a Greek poet, who lived about 280 B.C., is said to have been a teacher of Theocritus. A number of epigrams preserved in the Greek Anthology are ascribed to him.

Asclepiades of Tragilos, (a town of Thrace,) supposed to have been a pupil of Isocrates, was the author of some critical works.

Asclepi'ades BITHY'NUS, a celebrated Greek physician, born at Prusa, in Bithynia, in the second century B.C. He practised with great success at Rome, where he founded a school which was very popular. Among his pupils were Artorius (noticed in this work) and Themison. His system exercised an important influence on medical science for a long time. He indulged the inclinations of his patients in the use of wine and other things, and professed that a physician's duty consists in healing his patients safely, speedily, and pleasantly. He adopted the corpuscular theory of Epicurus as the basis of his pathology. His works were numerous; but only small fragments of them remain. He died at a great age, probably between 90 and 60 B.C.

See GUMPERT, "Asclepiadis Bithyni Fragmenta," 1798; A. COCCHI, "Discorso primo sopra Asclepiade," 1758; BIANCHINI, "La Medicina d'Asclepiade," 1769.

Asclepi'ades PHARMA'CION, a Greek physician, lived about 100 A.D. He wrote a work on Pharmacy, in ten books, which is not extant, but is often quoted by Galen.

See C. F. HARLESS, "De Medicis veteribus 'Asclepiades' dictis," 1828.

As-cle-pĭ-o-do'rus, [Gr. Ἀσκληπιόδωρος; Fr. ASCLÉPIODORE, ås'klä'pe'o'doR',] an excellent Greek painter, born at Athens, was a contemporary of Apelles, and lived about 330 B.C. According to Pliny, he surpassed Apelles in symmetry.

Asclepiodorus, a general of Alexander the Great, and a satrap of Syria, lived about 330 B.C.

As-cle-pĭ-od'o-tus, [Gr. Ἀσκληπιόδοτος; Fr. ASCLÉPIODOTE, ås'klä'pe'o'dot',] a Stoic philosopher, who was a pupil of Posidonius.

Asclepiodotus, a Greek physician and mathematician, flourished about 470–500 A.D.

Asclepiodotus, a New-Platonic philosopher of Alexandria, was a disciple of Proclus.

Asclepios or **Asklepios.** See ÆSCULAPIUS.

As-cle'pĭ-us, [Gr. Ἀσκληπιός,] the supposed author of a dialogue in Greek on God, Man, and the World, between Hermes and himself.

Asclepius, an ancient Greek commentator on Hippocrates, whose period is unknown. He wrote a commentary on the "Aphorisms," which is not extant.

Asclepius of Tralles, a Christian writer, who lived in the sixth century. He composed a commentary on part of the "Metaphysics" of Aristotle.

As-cle'pĭ-us, (NICHOLAS,) a German theologian, surnamed BARBA'TUS, was a native of Cassel. He published numerous works in Latin. Died in 1571.

Ascoli, d', (CECCO.) See CECCO.

Ascoli, d', dâs'ko-lee, (DAVID,) a Jew who lived about 1550, and wrote "Defence of the Hebrews," ("Apologia Hebræorum," 1559,) for which he was imprisoned.

Ascoli, d', (TROJANO MARULLI, tRo-yắ'no mâ-rool'-lee,) DUKE, a Neapolitan officer and personal friend of Ferdinand IV., was remarkable for his loyalty. In 1800 or 1801 he was appointed director-general of the police of the kingdom. He is praised for the prudence and humanity with which he restored order after the disturbances of 1798–1800. Died in 1823.

Ascondo, âs-kon'do, (FRANCISCO,) a Spanish architect, born in the province of Biscay in 1705; died in 1781 at Valladolid. He built several churches and convents in Castile.

As-co'nĭ-us Pe-dĭ-ā'nus, (QUINTUS,) an eminent Roman critic and commentator, who flourished about 50 A.D., is supposed to have been a native of Padua. He wrote a Life of Sallust, which is lost, and valuable commentaries on Cicero's orations, some of which are extant. In 1416, Poggio Bracciolini found at Saint Gall, in Switzerland, a manuscript containing commentaries on the following orations: "In Verrem;" "In Divinationem;" "Pro Cornelio;" "In Toga Candida;" "In Pisonem;" "Pro Scauro;" and "Pro Milone." His explanations and comments are historical, legal, and constitutional, rather than grammatical. He became blind at the age of seventy-three, and survived the loss of his sight about twelve years.

See MADVIG, "De Q. Asconii Pediani Commentariis Disputatio Critica," 1828.

Ascough, (ANNE.) See ASKEW.

Ascough, (Sir GEORGE.) See AYSCUE.

Asdrubal. See HASDRUBAL.

Asdrubali, âs-dRoo-bâ'lee, (FRANCESCO,) an eminent obstetrical practitioner and teacher at Rome, died in 1832. He published a useful work, entitled "Elements of Obstetrics," ("Elementi di Ostetricia," 3 vols., 1793.)

Aseer-ed-Deen Oománee or **Assîr-ud-Dîn Umânî,** â-seer' ed- (or ōōd-) deen' oo-mâ'nee, a Persian poet of wit and learning, lived in the thirteenth century.

Aselli, â-šel'lee, or **Asellio,** â-šel'le-o, [Lat. ASEL'-LIUS,] (GASPARO,) an Italian anatomist, born at Cremona about 1580, became professor of anatomy at Pavía, after he had served as surgeon-in-chief in the army. He was at Milan when, in 1622, he made the important discovery of the lacteal vessels, which has rendered his name memorable. This discovery was announced in a work entitled "On the Lacteal Veins," ("De Lactibus sive Lacteis Venis," etc., 1627.) Died in 1626.

See HALLER, "Bibliotheca Anatomica;" "Nouvelle Biographie Générale."

A-sel'lĭ-o, (PUBLIUS SEMPRONIUS,) a Roman historian, lived about 130 B.C., and was military tribune under Scipio Africanus. He wrote a "History of the Punic Wars," which is not extant.

Asellius. See ASELLI.

A-sel'lus, (TIBERIUS CLAUDIUS,) a Roman knight, whom Scipio Africanus in his censorship reduced to a lower rank in 141 B.C. He became tribune of the people in 139 B.C.

Asen. See ÆSIR.

As'e-nath, a daughter of Poti-pherah, an Egyptian priest, became the wife of the patriarch Joseph. (See Genesis xli. 45, 50.)

Asensio y Mezorada, â-sĕn'se-o e mâ-tho-râ'Dà, (FRANCISCO,) a Spanish engraver, born in Old Castile. Died at Madrid in 1794.

Asfandiyâr. See ISFENDIYÂR.

Asfeld, d', dâs'fĕld', (ALEXIS Bidal—be'dằl',) BARON, a French officer of German extraction, born about 1650. He served with distinction in several campaigns against the Germans, and became maréchal-de-camp in 1688. He defended Bonn with great obstinacy for about four months against a large army, and was mortally wounded in that siege in 1689.

Asfeld, d', (BENOÎT BIDAL,) BARON, a brother of the preceding, born in 1658. He fought at Fleurus, (1690,) Steenkerke, (1692,) and Charleroi, (1693,) and obtained the rank of maréchal-de-camp in 1696. He was an able and active officer of cavalry. Died in 1715.

Asfeld, d', (CLAUDE FRANÇOIS BIDAL,) MARQUIS, an able general, brother of the preceding, born in 1667. He served in Flanders in 1690–97, and in 1703 obtained a high command in Spain, where he besieged and took many fortified places. In 1704 he became a lieutenant-general. He contributed to the victory of Almanza, where he commanded the French cavalry, in 1707. He was rewarded with the title of marquis by Louis XIV. about 1714. In 1733 he was second in command under Villars in Italy, and gained several victories. He succeeded Berwick as commander-in-chief in Germany in 1734, was made a marshal of France, and maintained the field against Prince Eugene until the peace. Died in 1743.

See PINARD, "Chronologie historique militaire."

Asfeld, d', (JACQUES VINCENT BIDAL,) a French Jansenist theologian, brother of the preceding, born in 1664. Died in 1745.

Asgard. See ÆSIR.

As'gill, (Sir CHARLES,) the first baronet of that name, rose from the station of a clerk to great wealth. He was elected lord-mayor in 1757, and created a baronet in 1761.

Asgill, (Sir CHARLES,) son of the preceding, born about 1763, served under Cornwallis in America, and was selected, by lot, to be hung in retaliation for an American officer who had been put to death by a party of English; but he was pardoned through the intercession of Marie Antoinette. He served under the Duke of York in 1793, and took a conspicuous part in putting down the rebellion in Ireland. He rose to the rank of general, and died in 1823.

Asgill, (JOHN,) an English lawyer and pamphleteer, born in the seventeenth century. He published in 1700 "An Argument proving that Men may be translated to Heaven without Dying, etc.," which caused a great sensation. The House of Commons, of which he was elected a member in 1707, condemned his book as blasphemous, and expelled the author. He attributed death to the power of custom and to the fear of death, rather than to necessity. Asgill advocated the cause of the House of Hanover, in several pamphlets. He died in prison for debt in 1738, aged eighty or more.

See KIPPIS, "Biographia Britannica."

Ash, (EDWARD,) an eminent English physician of London, took the degree of M.D. at Oxford in 1796. He was a good scholar, and had excellent conversational powers. He wrote critical articles for a literary paper called "The Speculator," (1790.) About 1797 he discovered that when plates of zinc and silver moistened are placed in contact, the zinc is rapidly oxydated. This was a step towards the discovery of the chemical changes and laws on which the action of the galvanic battery depends. The discovery of Dr. Ash was published in 1797 by Humboldt, to whom he had written a letter. Died in 1829.

Ash, (Dr. JOHN,) F.R.S., an uncle of the preceding, born in 1723, was educated at Oxford. He had a high reputation as a physician, and practised for many years in Birmingham and London. Among his works is a treatise on the mineral waters of Spa and Aix-la-Chapelle, (1788.) He was president of the Eumelian Club, of which Sir Joshua Reynolds and others were members. Died in 1798.

Ash, (Rev. JOHN,) an English philologer and dissenting minister, born in Dorsetshire about 1724. He was minister of a Baptist congregation at Pershore from 1751 until his death. His principal work is a "New and Complete English Dictionary," (2 vols., 1775,) which is not considered a high authority. Died in 1779.

Ash or **Ashe,** ash, (SAINT GEORGE,) an Irish prelate, who was born about 1658. During the troubles of James II.'s reign he left for England, and became an attaché to Lord Paget, who was ambassador for King William at

the court of Austria. On his return to Ireland he was made successively Bishop of Cloyne, of Clogher, and of Derry. He was also a member of the Irish privy council. Died in 1718.

Ash'burne, de, (THOMAS,) an English friar, lived about 1350, and wrote a treatise against the "Trialogus" of Wickliffe.

Ash-burn'ham, (JOHN,) an English gentleman, a native of Sussex, was a confidential agent of Charles I. in the civil war. He was one of the commissioners for the treaty of Uxbridge in 1644, and was employed in other important missions. Ashburnham and Berkeley were the principal agents and attendants of the king in his escape from Hampton Court in November, 1647, and in his surrender to Colonel Hammond. He was suspected of treachery in this transaction; but his character has been vindicated from this suspicion. He became groom of the bedchamber to Charles II. about 1660. Died in 1671. His grandson was created Earl of Ashburnham.

See CLARENDON, "History of the Rebellion;" WHITELOCKE, "Memorials."

Ashburton, LORD. See DUNNING.

Ash'bur-ton, (ALEXANDER BARING,) LORD, an English financier and diplomatist, born in 1774, was a son of Sir Francis Baring, a merchant of London. He passed some of his early years in the United States as a commercial agent of his father, and married a daughter of William Bingham of Pennsylvania, a United States Senator. In 1810 he succeeded his father as head of the great firm of Baring Brothers & Company. He was elected to Parliament in 1812 and in several subsequent years. In politics he was a Whig until his opposition to the Reform Bill of 1831 converted him into a supporter of Sir Robert Peel. For a few months in 1834–35 Mr. Baring was president of the Board of Trade in the cabinet of Peel, through whose influence he was created Baron Ashburton in 1835. Soon after the return of Peel to power in September, 1841, Lord Ashburton was sent on a special mission to the United States to negotiate on the subject of a long-disputed boundary between Maine and the British Colonies. For this important service he was selected because his sentiments and antecedents were favourable to peace and conciliation. The negotiation on the part of the United States was conducted in a similar spirit by Mr. Webster, and the treaty was signed in 1842. This is usually called the Ashburton Treaty. He was a liberal patron of the fine arts. He died in May, 1848, and left his title to his son, William Bingham Baring, born in 1799.

See "Gentleman's Magazine" for July, 1848.

Ashbury, ash'ber-e, (JOSEPH,) a distinguished tragic actor, born in London in 1638. Accompanying the Duke of Ormond to Ireland, he became connected with the Dublin stage, and died in that city in 1720.

Ash'by, (Rev. GEORGE,) an English antiquary, born in 1724, obtained the living of Barrow, Suffolk, in 1774. He contributed to the works of Bishop Percy, Richard Gough, and Nichols. Died in 1808.

Ashby, (HENRY,) an English penman and engraver of writing, born in 1744; died in 1818.

Ashby, (Sir JOHN,) an English admiral, who became a captain before the revolution of 1688. He led the van at the battle of Bantry Bay in 1689, soon after which he was made a vice-admiral of the red. After the defeat of the Earl of Torrington in 1690, the command of the fleet was given to Ashby and two other admirals jointly. As admiral of the blue, he commanded a squadron of the fleet which gained a victory over the French at La Hogue in 1692. Died in 1693.

See CAMPBELL, "Naval History."

Ash'by, (TURNER,) a Virginian general, born in Fauquier county, Virginia, about 1824. He took arms against the Union in 1861, and distinguished himself as an officer of cavalry. In May, 1862, he became a brigadier-general in the army of Stonewall Jackson. He was killed near Harrisonburg, Virginia, in June of the same year.

Ashdowne, ash'down, (WILLIAM,) a writer in defence of Unitarianism, lived at Canterbury, England, from about 1760 to 1800. Among his works is one entitled the "Unitarian, Arian, and Trinitarian Opinion respecting Christ, examined and tried by Scripture alone," (1789.)

Ashe, ash, (ANDREW,) an excellent flute-player, born at Lisburn, in Ireland, about 1758. He performed at the Italian Opera-House, London. Died in 1838.

Ashe, (JOHN,) a patriot of the American Revolution, born in England in 1721, emigrated to North Carolina. He led an expedition against Fort Johnson in 1775, and served as brigadier-general in Georgia in 1778 and 1779. Died in 1781.

Ashe, (SAMUEL,) a brother of the preceding, born in 1725. He became chief-justice of North Carolina in 1777, and Governor of that State in 1796. Died in 1813.

His son, John Baptist, born in 1748, was an officer in the Revolutionary war, and afterwards a member of Congress. Died in 1795.

Ashe, (SIMEON,) an English Puritan minister, who preached many years in London. He became chaplain to the Earl of Manchester about 1642, and favoured the Parliament in the civil war, but after the death of Charles I. was an opponent of the dominant party. He actively promoted the restoration of 1660. A number of his sermons were published. According to Baxter, he was a nonconformist of the old stamp, and was eminent for a holy life. Died in 1662.

See NEAL, "History of the Puritans."

Ashe, (THOMAS,) an English writer, called CAPTAIN ASHE, published, besides other works, "Travels in America," (1808.) Died in 1835.

See "Life and Correspondence of T. Ashe," 3 vols., 1814.

Ash'e or **Ash'i,** sometimes written **Asser,** (RAB or RAV,) a celebrated Babylonian rabbi, born in 353 A.D. He is said to have been the original author or compiler of the "Babylonian Talmud," which is a vast body of traditions, commentaries, and illustrations of the Hebrew laws, especially of the oral law recorded in the "Mishna," which forms the text of the Talmud. This work was not finished until many years after his death. He was considered a man of great learning, genius, and piety. Died in 427 A.D. For many centuries the Jews regarded the Babylonian Talmud as the chief object of their study and the highest authority for the decision of legal questions. In 1554 the Talmud was burnt, by order of the pope, throughout Italy.

See WOLF, "Bibliotheca Hebraica;" "Talmud Babylonicum," Amsterdam, 1644.

Ash'er, [Heb. אָשֵׁר,] a son of the Hebrew patriarch Jacob and Zilpah, was the head of one of the twelve tribes of Israel. (See Genesis xxx. 13 ; Deuteronomy xxxiii. 24.) The name signifies *happy.*

Ash'er, (R. BEN JECHIEL,) was head of the Jewish college of Toledo, in Spain, where he was very highly esteemed. His works, all relating to the Jewish laws and religion, are very numerous. Died in 1321.

Ash'field, (EDMUND,) an English portrait-painter, who lived in the age of Charles II. He is said to have been the first artist who drew in coloured crayons (now termed *pastels*) in imitation of oil-painting.

Ashi. See ASHE, (RAB.)

Ashik, ash'ik, a Turkish poet and biographer, born in Roomelia about 1518. He officiated as judge in several towns. He wrote biographies of about four hundred Turkish poets, and a number of lyrical poems, mostly erotic. His ode on the Danube is called one of the finest specimens of Oriental poetry. Died about 1570.

See VON HAMMER, "Geschichte der Osmanischen Dichtkunst."

Ash'ley, (CHESTER,) born in Westfield, Massachusetts, in 1790, was elected in 1844 from Arkansas to the United States Senate, in which he served as chairman of the Committee on the Judiciary until his death in 1848.

Ash'ley, (JOHN,) an English musician and dealer in music. He had a son, General Ashley, an excellent violinist, who died in 1818. Another son, John James, was noted as an organist.

Ashley, LORD. See SHAFTESBURY.

Ashley, (ROBERT,) an English translator, born in Wiltshire in 1565. He published translations of "Uranie" from the French of Du Bartas, (1589,) of the "Life of Almansor, King of Spain," from the Spanish, (1627,) and of a few other works. Died in 1641.

Ash'mole, (ELIAS,) an English antiquary, alchemist, and herald, born at Lichfield in 1617, was the founder of the Ashmolean Museum of Oxford. He studied law and astrology, in which he had strong faith. In the civil war he favoured the royal cause. He published in 1652 "Theatrum Chemicum Britannicum," a work which consists of treatises on alchemy by various authors. In 1660 he was appointed Windsor herald by Charles II. His principal work, "The Institution, Laws, and Ceremonies of the Order of the Garter," (1672,) was received with great favour, and is still esteemed. About 1682 he presented to the University of Oxford a collection of curiosities, medals, coins, and botanical specimens, the most of which he had received as a gift from the botanist Tradescant and his son. The museum thus commenced still bears his name. Died in 1692. He left Memoirs of his own life, (1717.)

See also ALLEN's "History of Lambeth."

Ash'more, (JOHN,) an English poet and translator, who lived in the first half of the seventeenth century.

Ash'mun, (JEHUDI,) a zealous and efficient promoter of colonization in Liberia, whither he sailed in 1822, from which period he devoted all his time to the cause. He died in Boston in 1828, while on a visit for the recovery of his health.

See the "Life of Jehudi Ashmun," by R. R. GURLEY; "North American Review," vol. xli., (1835:) and "Foreign Quarterly Review," vol. xxvi., (1841.)

Ash'mun, (JOHN HOOKER,) a distinguished American jurist, born at Blandford, Massachusetts, in 1800. He graduated at Harvard in 1818, and, on the organization of the department of law in that university in 1829, was appointed its first professor. Died in 1833. "He had gathered about him," says Judge Story, "all the honours which are usually the harvest of the ripest life."

Ashoka. See ASOKA.

Ashraf, äsh'raf, a tyrannical and cruel Afghan chief, who occupied the throne of Persia from 1725 to 1729. He was defeated by Nâdir Shâh, who espoused the cause of the deposed prince Tahmâsp, and soon after killed, by a follower of the latter, in 1729.

See MALCOLM, "History of Persia;" SIR WILLIAM JONES, "Histoire de Nadir Chah," London, 1770.

Ash'ton, (CHARLES,) an English classical critic, born at Bradway, Derbyshire, in 1665. He obtained a prebendal stall in Ely, and became master of Jesus College, Cambridge, in 1701. His chief work is an edition of Justin Martyr's "Apologies," (1768.) Died in 1752.

Ashton, (JOHN,) a gentleman in the service of James II. of England, was executed in 1691, on the charge of conspiring to restore that sovereign.

Ashton, (THOMAS,) a popular English clergyman, born in 1716, was a friend of Horace Walpole. He was elected preacher of Lincoln's Inn in 1762, and published a volume of sermons in 1770. Died in 1775.

Ashton, (Sir THOMAS,) an alchemist in the reign of Henry VI., who had a patent for transmuting the baser metals into gold.

See FULLER, "Worthies of England."

Ash'to-reth [Heb. עַשְׁתֹּרֶת; Gr. Ἀστάρτη] or **Ash'ta-roth,** the name of a Syrian goddess, who was worshipped also by the people of Israel. (See Judges ii. 13 and x. 6; I. Samuel vii. 3; and I. Kings xi. 33; also, Milton's "Paradise Lost," book i.)

Ash'urst, (HENRY,) an English gentleman, who acquired considerable wealth in London and was noted for his benevolence. He contributed liberally to the support of Puritan preachers, but he professed to belong to no sect. Died in 1680.

Ash'well, (GEORGE,) an English theologian, born in London in 1612, was rector of Hanwell, near Banbury, from 1658 until his death. He published "Fides Apostolica," (1653,) an argument for the Apostles' Creed, and a treatise on Socinianism, (1680.) Died in 1693.

Ash'worth, (CALEB,) D.D., an English dissenting minister, born in Lancashire in 1722. He succeeded Dr. Doddridge in 1752, in accordance with the will of that divine, as principal of the academy in which young men were educated for the ministry, and which was removed from Northampton to Daventry, where Ashworth was then pastor. He fulfilled the duties of this position in

ā, ē, ī, ō, ū, ȳ, *long;* ă, ĕ, ĭ, ŏ, ŭ, ў, *short;* ą, ę, į, ǫ, *obscure;* fär, fäll, fät; mĕt; nŏt; gōōd; mōōn;

such a manner as fully to justify the recommendation of Dr. Doddridge. Died in 1775.

See CHALMERS's "Biographical Dictionary."

Asinari, ä-se-nä′ree, (FEDERIGO,) Count of Camerano, an Italian poet, born at Asti, in Piedmont, in 1527. He was sent as ambassador to Florence in 1570. He wrote, besides sonnets, madrigals, and other lyrical poems, a tragedy in verse, called "Tancred," (" Tancredi," 1587,) which was highly praised by Italian critics. Died in 1576.

Asinari, (OTTAVIANO,) an Italian poet, was a son or brother of the preceding. According to some authorities, he was author of " Tancredi," above referred to.

Asinelli, ä-se-nel′lee, (GERHARDO,) an Italian architect, lived about 1110. He and his brother erected the famous tower of Bologna which bears their name.

A-sin′i-us, (GIOVANNI BATTISTA,) an Italian jurist, lived in the second half of the sixteenth century.

Asinius Gallus. See GALLUS.

Asinius Pollio. See POLLIO.

Asioli, ä-se-o′lee, (BONIFAZIO,) an Italian composer, born at Correggio in 1769. He was appointed chapelmaster to the viceroy Eugene at Milan, and director of the Conservatorio, about 1800. He composed operas, cantatas, and notturnos, which were admired especially for their ease and grace. Died in 1832.

Asir. See ÆSIR.

Asîr-ud-Dîn Umâni. See ASEER-ED-DEEN.

A′sî-us, (or ä′she-us,) [ʹΑσιος,] of Samos, one of the earliest of the Greek poets, composed both epic and elegiac poetry, some extracts from which have come down to us. He is supposed to have lived about 700 B.C.

See VOSS, "De Poetis Græcis;" ULRICI, "Geschichte der Hellenischen Dichtkunst."

ʹ **Askelof,** äs′keh-lof′, (JOHAN CHRISTOPH,) a Swedish journalist and editor, born in 1787.

As′kew, written also **Ays′cough** and **As′cough,** (ANNE,) an English martyr, born in Lincolnshire in 1521. Having been convinced of the Reformed doctrines by reading the Bible, she was turned out of doors by her husband, whose name was Kyme. She was arrested in 1545, questioned on the subject of the sacrament, and burned at the stake in 1546, after giving proof of invincible fortitude.

See HODGSON, "Reformers and Martyrs," Philadelphia, 1867; FULLER, "Church History;" FOX, "Book of Martyrs."

Askew, (ANTHONY,) F.R.S., an English physician, noted as a Greek scholar and a collector of classical books and manuscripts, was born at Kendal in 1722. He travelled in the Levant, and after his return practised in London. He was a friend of Dr. Mead, Dr. Parr, and Sir William Jones. Died in 1774. His books were sold at auction for about four thousand pounds sterling.

See DIBDIN, "Bibliomania;" NICHOLS, "Literary Anecdotes."

Askew, (GEORGE.) See AYSCUE.

Asklepiadæ. See ASCLEPIADÆ.

Asklepiades. See ASCLEPIADES.

Asklepiodorus. See ASCLEPIODORUS.

Asklepiodotus. See ASCLEPIODOTUS.

Asklepios. See ÆSCULAPIUS.

Aslacus, äs′lä-kŭs, (CUNRADUS,) a Norwegian, a pupil of Tycho Brahe, born at Bergen in 1564. He became professor of philosophy and theology at Copenhagen about 1600. He wrote, besides other works, a treatise on the "Moral and Physical Doctrines of Moses," (" Physica et Ethica Mosaica," 1613.) Died in 1624.

Asmai, Al. See ABD-EL-MALEK.

As′mar, (MARIA THERESA,) born near Nineveh in 1804, was a daughter of the Emir Abdallah-Asmar, and was educated in the Christian faith. She travelled over the principal part of Asia Minor, and subsequently visited Italy, France, and England, where she published in 1844 an account of her adventures.

See "Memoirs of a Babylonian Princess," London, 1844; "London Quarterly Review."

Asmonæans, as-mo-nee′ans, or **As-mo-ne′ans,** [Fr. ASMONÉENS, ăs′mo′nä′ŏn′,] a family or dynasty of Jewish princes, some of whom were called Maccabees. The name is derived from Asmonæus or Asamonæus, an obscure person who lived about 300 B.C. His great-grandson Mattathias was eminent as a zealous patriot,

and left several sons, who ruled Judea and repulsed the armies of their Syrian persecutors. (See MACCABÆUS.) The sovereignty of Judea remained in this family until the death of Antigonus, about 37 B.C.

See JOSEPHUS, "Jewish Antiquities;" and the Apocryphal Books of Maccabees.

Asmoneans. See ASMONÆANS.

Asne, l′, lân, (MICHEL,) an able French designer and engraver, born at Caen in 1596. He engraved after Rubens, Titian, and other masters. Died in Paris in 1667.

Asôkă or **Açôka,** a-so′kă, sometimes written **Asho′ka,** called also **Dhar-mă-so′kă,** King of Maghada, one of the greatest sovereigns that ever ruled in India, (the Sandracottus of the Greek historians.) He was born at Pâtaliputtra about three centuries before Christ. Having attempted the life of his father, he was banished to a distant province. On hearing that his father was at the point of death, he hastened to Pâtaliputtra, and killed all his brothers except one, who was a son of the same mother with himself, and placed himself upon the throne. But, having at length been converted to Boodhism, his character became entirely changed; and whereas he had formerly been called CHANDÂSOKA, (*i.e.* the "raging Asoka,") he now received the name of DHARMÂSOKA, (the "Asoka of the law,") on account of his zeal for the law of Booddha. He is said (with Oriental hyperbole, no doubt) to have erected eighty-four thousand monasteries (vihârs) in honour of the eighty-four thousand discourses of Booddha. (See GAUTAMA.) He has left monuments with inscriptions in different parts of India, proving that his dominion extended over a large part of what is now known as Hindostan.

See KÖPPEN, "Religion des Buddha," p. 168 *et seq.*

Asola. See ASULA.

Asolano. See ASOLANUS.

Asoora or **Asoor.** See ASURA.

A-sop-o-do′rus, a Greek statuary, mentioned by Pliny, was a disciple of Polycletus.

Asp, âsp, (MATTHIAS,) a Swedish scholar, noted for his knowledge of Greek, born at Norrköping in 1696. He became professor of poetry and eloquence at Upsal about 1730, and professor of theology there in 1737. He wrote many academical dissertations on ancient literature. Died in 1763.

Asp, (PEHR OLOF,) a nephew of the preceding, born at Stockholm in 1745, was minister to Constantinople from 1790 to 1795, and to London from 1796 to 1799. He wrote a treatise on "Political Economy," (1800,) and "Travels in the Levant," (1805.) Died in 1808.

As′par, [Gr. ʹΑσπαρ,] a general of the Eastern Empire, was a son of Ardaburius. In 425 A.D. he and his father defeated the usurper John, at Ravenna. He acquired so much power that at the death of Marcian in 457 A.D. he procured the accession of Leo I., whom he caused to be consecrated by a bishop. This is said to have been the first instance of the consecration of an emperor by a bishop. His Arianism, it seems, prevented Aspar from making himself emperor. In 471 A.D. he was killed in the palace by order of Leo.

Aspasia, as-pä′she-a, [Gr. ʹΑσπασία; Fr. ASPASIE, ås′på′ze′,] a Grecian woman, celebrated for her beauty, talents, and political influence, was a native of Miletus. She removed to Athens in her youth, and gained the affection of Pericles, with whom she lived as his wife. The laws of Athens. however, did not permit him to marry a foreigner. The comic poets and other scandal-mongers reported that she instigated Pericles to wage war against the Samians. Her house was frequented by the *élite* of Athens, and even by Socrates, who called himself her disciple. According to Plutarch, who refers to Plato's "Menexenus" as his authority, many Athenians resorted to her on account of her skill in the art of speaking. It was commonly reported that she composed part of the famous funeral oration which Pericles pronounced over the Athenians who fell in battle. She was once prosecuted by the poet Hermippus on a charge of impiety, but was acquitted through the efforts of Pericles. She survived Pericles, who died in 429 B.C., and is said to have formed a similar connection with Lysicles.

є as *k*; ç as *s*; ḡ *hard*; ḡ as *j*; G, H, K, *guttural*; N, *nasal*; R, *trilled*; š as *z*; ŧh as in *this*. (☞See Explanations, p. 23.)

There is an antique bust which bears the name of Aspasia and is supposed to be a portrait of the subject of this article. "Aspasia," says Madame de Staël, "was considered a model of female loveliness, as Alexander of heroism," ("Aspasie signifiait la plus aimable des femmes, comme Alexandre le plus grand des héros.")

See PLUTARCH, "Pericles;" SUIDAS, 'Ασπασία; BURIGNY, "Vie d'Aspasie."

Aspasia THE YOUNGER, a beautiful Ionian lady, became the wife of Cyrus the Younger, who changed her original name, Milto, to Aspasia. She was distinguished for virtue and intelligence. After Cyrus had been killed at Cunaxa, 401 B.C., she was taken as a captive by the king Artaxerxes, whose favour she gained. When this king appointed his son Darius as his successor, the latter requested his father to give him Aspasia; but the old king preferred to consecrate her as a priestess of Anaitis.

See PLUTARCH, "Life of Artaxerxes."

Aspasius (as-pā′she-us) [Gr. 'Ασπάσιος] THE PERIPATETIC, a Greek writer, lived probably in the first century of the Christian era. His commentaries on Aristotle's "Nicomachean Ethics" are extant.

Aspasius of Byblos, a teacher of rhetoric, lived about 150 A.D., or later, and wrote several works.

Aspasius of Ravenna, a sophist of the third century, was secretary of the emperor Alexander Severus, who appointed him principal teacher of eloquence in the school of Rome.

Aspegren, ås′peh-grēn′, (GUSTAF CARSTEN,) a Swedish naturalist, a baker by trade, born at Carlscrona in 1791. He contributed to Nilsson's Fauna, Agardh's works on Algæ, and other Swedish works on natural history. He published "An Essay at a Flora of Bleking," his native province, (1823.) Died in 1828.

Aspelin, ås′peh-lin′, (DAVID,) a Swedish poet, born at Långasjö in 1780. He became minister of a church at Tolg, and composed several successful poems on public events. His poem on the union of Norway and Sweden gained the first prize of the Swedish Academy in 1813. Died in 1821.

Aspelmayer or **Aspelmeyer,** ås′pel-mī′er, (FRANZ,) a German composer, died at Vienna in 1786.

As′per, a Latin critic and grammarian, of whom little is known, wrote a commentary on Virgil, and a treatise on grammar. He is quoted by Saint Augustine, Saint Jerome, and other writers.

Asper, (CAIUS JULIUS,) an eminent Roman, whom Caracalla raised to high honour, but in a fickle moment afterwards degraded and banished.

Asper, ås′per, (HANS,) an eminent Swiss painter, born at Zurich in 1499. He painted landscapes, portraits, and animals of various kinds. His style was similar to that of Holbein, his contemporary, whom he nearly rivalled in portraits. He made the original drawings for Gesner's Natural History. His works are very scarce, unless some of those sold as the works of Holbein were painted by Asper. Died in 1571. His sons Hans and Rudolph were painters.

Asper, d′, ås′per, or **Aspre,** d′, dåspR, (CONSTANT GHILAIN CHARLES van Hoobrouck—vån hō′bRŏwk,) BARON, a general, born at Ghent in 1754. He served with distinction in the Austrian army in the war against the French republic, and became a general-major in 1798. In 1805, while covering the march of General Mack, he was taken prisoner near the Danube. He obtained command of sixteen thousand men in 1809, and was rewarded for his conduct at Essling with the rank of general of the ordnance. He was mortally wounded at Wagram in 1809.

Asper, d′, or **Aspre,** (CONSTANTIN,) BARON, a son of the preceding, was born at Brussels in 1789. He entered the Austrian army in 1806, after which he served several campaigns against the French. In 1825 he became a colonel. He fought against the insurgents in Italy in 1830, and obtained the rank of general of division about 1840. He contributed greatly to the defeat of the revolted Italians in 1848–49, and became a general of the ordnance. Died at Padua in 1850.

See BROCKHAUS, "Conversations-Lexikon."

Aspertini, ås-pêR-tee′nee, or **Aspertino,** ås-pêR-tee′no, (AMICO, ä-mee′ko,) a skilful and eccentric painter,

born at Bologna in 1474, was called MAESTRO AMICO. He painted with both hands at the same time, had great facility of execution, and excelled as a painter of animals. His style was a mixture of all styles, from that of Giotto to that of Giorgione. Died in 1552.

See VASARI, "Lives of the Painters."

Aspertini, (GUIDO,) a brother of the preceding, was a painter, and probably a native of Bologna. Among his works is an "Adoration of the Magi." He died about the beginning of the sixteenth century, at the age of thirty-five.

As-per′tus or **Ans-ber′tus,** Bishop of Ratisbon in 891, but previously private secretary to King Arnulf of Germany. He is thought to have been the author of a part of the "Annales Fuldenses."

Aspetti, ås-pet′tee, (TIZIANO,) an Italian sculptor, born at Padua in 1565, was said to be a nephew of the painter Titian. He worked at Venice, Padua, Florence, and Pisa. His works are highly commended. Vasari calls him "Tiziano Padovano," ("Titian of Padua.") He died at Pisa in 1607. Among his master-pieces are a statue of Saint Anthony at Padua, and the statues of Saint Peter and Saint Paul which adorn the façade of Saint Mark at Venice. M. Weiss argues that he could not be a nephew of Titian, who was born eighty-eight years earlier.

See VASARI, "Lives of the Painters, Sculptors, etc."

Aspilcueta, ås-pêl-kwā′tä, (JUAN,) a Spanish missionary, born in Navarre. He went in 1549 to Brazil, where he laboured with success. Died at Bahia in 1555.

Aspilcueta, (MARTIN.) See AZPILCUETA.

As′pin-wåll, (WILLIAM,) an American physician, born at Brookline, Massachusetts, in 1743, was noted for his skill in treating small-pox, and erected hospitals for inoculation. He served as a volunteer at the battle of Lexington, April, 1775. Died in 1823.

See THACHER, "Medical Biography."

As′pland, (ROBERT,) an eminent English dissenting minister, born at Wicken, in Cambridgeshire, in 1782. He was ordained as a Baptist minister about 1802, after which he became a Unitarian. He preached at the Gravel-pit Chapel, Hackney, from 1805 until his death, in 1845. He began about 1815 to issue the "Christian Reformer," a monthly magazine, and was author of numerous works.

See "A Memoir of the Life of R. Aspland," by his son, ROBERT B. ASPLAND, 1850.

Asplund, ås′plŏŏnd, (ARNOLD,) an eminent Swedish ecclesiastic, born at Stockholm in 1736, had a high reputation as a preacher, and published several sermons. He was a member of the National Diet about 1790. His life appears to have been passed in Stockholm. Died in 1815.

Aspre. See ASPER.

Aspremont, d′, dåspR′mòN′, VICOMTE, was governor of Bayonne in the reign of Charles IX. He distinguished himself by his refusal to massacre the Huguenots in 1572.

Aspremont, d′, (FRANÇOIS de la Mothe Villebert—deh lä mot vèl′bair′,) VICOMTE, a French general and engineer, who commanded with success at several sieges in Flanders, 1655–72. He was wounded at Condé, Valenciennes, and Gravelines. Died in 1678.

Aspruck, ås′prŏŏk, (FRANZ,) a German painter and engraver, lived at Augsburg about the beginning of the seventeenth century.

As′pull, (GEORGE,) an excellent English musician, born at Manchester in 1813. He performed on the piano with applause before the king in 1824, and about the same time gave public concerts. Before he was eleven, he executed with ease the most difficult pieces which were composed as tests of manual skill by Kalkbrenner and Czerny. It is stated that Rossini pronounced him "the most extraordinary creature in Europe." Died in 1832.

See FÉTIS, "Biographie Universelle des Musiciens."

Asquini, ås-kwee′nee, (BASILIO,) an Italian priest and artist, born at Udine in 1682, designed a fine church for his native town, and published a volume of biographies of eminent men born in Friuli, (1735.) Died in 1745.

ā, ē, ī, ō, ū, ȳ, *long;* à, ê, ô, same, less prolonged; ă, ĕ, ĭ, ŏ, ŭ, ў, *short;* a, ę, į, o, *obscure;* fär, fåll, fåt; mêt; nŏt; gōōd; mōōn;

Asquini, (FABIANO,) COUNT, a meritorious rural economist of Italy, was born at Udine in 1726. He is entitled to the greater part of the honour of introducing the cultivation of silk into Friuli. He is said to have been the first to promote in Italy the use of potatoes as food and of turf as fuel. He also enriched himself and the country by extensive plantations of trees. Died in 1818. His treatise "On the Means of Obviating the Scarcity of Timber" was published after his death.

See TIPALDO, "Italiani illustri del Secolo XVIII."

Assaeed- (âs-sâ-eed′) **Abool-Hassan-Alee,** (or **As-sa′îd-Abûl-Hassan-Alî,**) â′bool′ hâs′san â′lee′, twelfth Sultan of Western Africa, was raised to the throne in 1242 A.D., under the title of Al-Moo�225adhed Billah, and was killed in 1246 in battle at Tlemcen.

See CONDÉ, "Histoire de la Domination des Arabes," etc.

Assafadee or **Assafadî,** âs-sâf′a-dee′, an Arabian biographer, born at Safada in 1296; died in 1362.

Assalini, âs-sâ-lee′nee, (PIETRO,) an Italian physician, born at Módena about 1765. He served in the French army in the campaign of Egypt, 1798, and was afterwards appointed by Napoleon first surgeon to the court and surgeon-in-ordinary to the viceroy Eugene. He published "Observations on the Plague," (1803,) and a work on diseases of the eye, (1811.) Died about 1840.

As-Sâmaânee or **As-Sâmaânî,** âs-sâ-mâ-â′nee, surnamed KAWÂM-ED-DEEN or KAWWÂM-UD-DÎN, kâ-wâm′ ed-deen′, (the "support or pillar of religion,") a famous Mohammedan writer, born at Merv, in Khorassân, in 1113, was the author of a History of Bagdâd, in 15 vols., a History of Merv, and a work on Genealogy. Died about 1166.

As-Sameel-Ibn-Hâtim-al-Kelâbee or **As-Sa-mîl-Ibn-Hâtim-Al-Kelâbî,** âs-sâ-meel′ Ib′n hâ′tim âl-kẹ-lâ′bee, a distinguished Mohammedan general and governor of Spain under the caliphs, flourished about 750 A.D. He was afterwards poisoned in prison by the order of Abd-er-Rahman.

As-samh-Ibn-Mâlik-Al-Khoulanee, (or **Al-Khaulânî,**) âs-sâmh′ Ib′n mâ′lik âl-kŏw-lâ′nee, governor of Mohammedan Spain under the caliphs. He was appointed to that office in 719. In 721 he took Carcassonne and Narbonne, in France, but was defeated and killed by the Duke of Aquitaine in the same year.

Assandro, âs-sân′dRo, (GIOVANNI BATTISTA,) an Italian jurist, lived at Cremona in the early part of the seventeenth century.

Assaph. See ASAPH.

Assarino, âs-sâ-ree′no, (LUCA or LUCAS,) an Italian historian and popular novelist, son of a Genoese merchant, born at Seville in 1607. He resided mostly in Italy. He wrote "La Stratonica," (1635,) "L'Armelinda," (1640,) and other novels, which had a great success for a time; also a history of the wars in Italy between 1613 and 1630, ("Delle Guerre e Successi d'Italia," etc., 1665.) Died at Turin in 1672.

See SOPRANI, "Scrittori della Liguria."

Assarotti, âs-sâ-rot′tee, (OTTAVIO GIOVANNI BATTISTA,) a benevolent priest, born at Genoa in 1753, is known as the founder of the Italian institutions for the education of the deaf and dumb. He was for many years a teacher in the schools of his order, called *Scuole Pie,* (benevolent schools.) About 1802 he began to teach in his own chamber a few deaf-mutes, being almost entirely ignorant of what had been done for that class in other countries. He received aid from the government in 1812. Died in 1829.

See TIPALDO, "Biografia degli Italiani illustri."

Assas, ä′sä′, (NICOLAS,) a French officer, was captain of the regiment of Auvergne. In 1760, while he was inspecting the outposts near Klostercamp, he found himself in the hands of a party of the enemy who were about to surprise the French. He was threatened with instant death if he gave the alarm; but he cried out, "A moi, Auvergne! voilà les ennemis!" and fell pierced with wounds.

See VOLTAIRE, "Siècle de Louis XV."

Asscherades, âsh′er-â′dẹs, (CARL GUSTAV **Schultz** shŏŏlts,) a Swedish diplomatist and historian. Died in 1799.

Asseline, äss′lẽn′, (GILLES THOMAS,) a mediocre French poet, born at Vire in 1682, was a friend of Thomas Corneille, on whose death he wrote an ode. He became president of the college of Harcourt, Paris, and composed, among other poems, one entitled "Religion," (1725.) Died in 1767.

See QUÉRARD, "La France Littéraire."

Asseline, (JEAN RENÉ,) a French ecclesiastic, born in Paris in 1742, was professor of Hebrew at the Sorbonne. In 1790 he was appointed Bishop of Boulogne, but he refused to conform to the civil constitution of the clergy, and went into exile. On the death of Abbé Edgeworth he became confessor to Louis XVIII. He published several religious works. Died in 1813.

See QUÉRARD, "La France Littéraire."

Asselyn, âs′sẹh-lîn′, (JAN,) an excellent painter of landscapes, horses, and battles, born in Holland, or at Antwerp, in 1610, was a pupil of J. Vandevelde. He studied in Rome, and painted a number of landscapes taken from the vicinity of that capital. He imitated the manner of his friend Peter Laer. About 1645 he settled in Amsterdam, where he gained a high reputation. His colouring is brilliant and warm, his touch fine, and his composition displays good taste. Died at Amsterdam in 1660.

See HOUBRAKEN, "Groote Schouburg;" D'ARGENVILLE, "Abrégé de la Vie des plus fameux Peintres."

Assemani, âs-sâ-mâ′nee, (GIUSEPPE LUIGI or ALOYSIO,) a theological writer, a nephew of Giuseppe Simone, noticed below, was born in Syria about 1710, but educated at Rome, where he was appointed professor of Syriac, and afterwards professor of Oriental languages at the Propaganda. He died in Rome in 1782.

Assemani, (GIUSEPPE SIMONE,) a learned Maronite, born at Tripoli, in Syria, about 1686, was educated at Rome. He was sent to the Levant by the pope, in search of manuscripts, in 1715, and was appointed keeper of the Vatican Library about 1730. His principal work is "Bibliotheca Orientalis Clementino-Vaticana," (4 vols., fol., 1719-28,) which is probably the most ample fund of information on Syriac literature that has ever been amassed. He wrote a valuable work on Oriental Church History, in which he was well versed. Died at Rome in 1768.

See ERSCH und GRUBER, "Allgemeine Encyklopaedie;" SAX, "Onomasticon;" "Nouvelle Biographie Générale."

Assemani, (SIMONE,) an Orientalist of high reputation, born at Tripoli, or, as some writers state, at Rome, in 1752, was a relative of Giuseppe Luigi. He became professor of Oriental languages in a seminary of Padua about 1785, and professor of the same in the university of that city in 1807. Among his works are an "Essay on the Origin, Religion, Literature, and Customs of the Arabs before the Time of Mohammed," (1787,) and "Globus Cœlestis Cufico-Arabicus," (1790,) the description of a celestial globe which belonged to one of the Sultans of Egypt. Died in 1821.

Assemani, (STEFANO **Evodio**—à-vo′de-o,) a nephew of Giuseppe Simone, was born at Tripoli about 1707. He was the principal compiler of a valuable catalogue of the manuscripts of the Vatican Library, (3 vols., 1756-59,) and succeeded his uncle as keeper of that library in 1768. He published catalogues of the Oriental manuscripts in the Florentine libraries, viz., Medicea, Laurentiana, and Palatina, (1742.) Died in 1782.

See TIPALDO, "Biografia degli Italiani illustri."

Assen, van, vän âs′sẹn, (JAN,) a Dutch historical and landscape painter of considerable merit, born at Amsterdam about 1635. His style of painting is very bold, and he is said to have used the prints of Antonio Tempesta for his own pictures. Died in 1695.

See NAGLER, "Neues Allgemeines Künstler-Lexikon."

Assen, van, (JAN WALTHER,) a Dutch engraver on wood, born at Amsterdam about 1480. His heads have much expression, but his design is not very correct. His prints are in great request among amateurs.

Assenede, van, vän âs-sẹh-nâ′dẹh, (DIDERIK,) a Flemish poet of the middle of the fourteenth century, translated into Flemish verse the romance of "Flores et Blanche."

See PAQUOT, "Mémoires pour servir à l'Histoire littéraire des Pays-Bas."

ɛ as *k;* ç as *s;* ḡ *hard;* ġ as *j;* G, H, K, *guttural;* N, *nasal;* R, *trilled;* s as z; th as in *this.* (☞ See Explanations, p. 23.)

Asseolo. See OSCEOLA.

Asser. See ASHÉ, (RAB.)

As′ser, or **As-se′rĭ-us Men-e-ven′sis,** a learned English monk of the ninth century, passed much time at the court of Alfred the Great, who treated him as a friend and employed him as his reader. His name is connected with a Latin "Life of Alfred the Great," (which comprises only the period from 849 to 889,) but some critics maintain that it is the work of some other author. Died about 910.

Assereto, âs-sà-rā′to, (GIOVACCHINO,) an Italian painter in oil and fresco, born at Genoa about 1600, was a pupil of Andrea Ansaldo, whose design he imitated with success. He worked at Genoa, Sarzana, and Rome, and gained a high reputation. Died in 1649.

See LANZI, "History of Painting in Italy."

Assezan, d′, dås′zŏN′, a French dramatic author, born at Toulousé in 1654. His principal works were the tragedies of "Agamemnon" and "Antigone." Died in 1696.

See PARFAIT, "Histoire du Théâtre Français."

Assheton, ash′tŭn, (WILLIAM,) an English clergyman, born in Lancashire in 1641. He became rector of Beckenham, Kent, in 1676, and wrote many religious works, among which is "Toleration Disapproved and Condemned," (1670.) He was the projector of an unsuccessful scheme for the maintenance of the widows of clergymen and others. Died in 1711.

See WATT, "Life of William Assheton," and WOOD, "Athenæ Oxonienses."

Ass′hod, written also **Aschod,** the name of several princes and kings of Armenia, of the dynasty of the Pagratidæ, who were of Jewish origin, but who appear to have adopted the Christian religion about 600 A.D.

Asshod I. restored the kingdom of Armenia about 856 A.D., and ruled with wisdom and moderation, extending the bounds of his dominions. Died in 889.

Asshod II. ascended his throne in 914, after a long warfare with the Arabs, who had usurped for a period the government of Armenia. Died about 930.

Asshod III. succeeded his father in 952, and was distinguished for his patronage of industry, trade, and architecture, and for his wars with the Mohammedans. Died in 977.

Asshod IV. shared the kingdom of Armenia with his brother John, and both afterwards became tributary to the Greek Empire. In this reign Armenia was much harassed by the Turks. Died in 1039.

Assignies, d′, då′sèn′ye′, (JEAN,) a Flemish monk, and writer of devotional works, born in 1562; died in 1642.

Assigny, d′, då′sèn′ye′ or dås-seen′ye, (MARIUS,) a clergyman of the Anglican Church, of French extraction, born in England in 1643, wrote "The Art of Memory," (1699,) and other works. Died in 1717.

Assing, âs′sing, (ROSA MARIA,) a German poetess, a sister of Varnhagen von Ense, was born at Dusseldorf in 1783. She was married in 1816 to Dr. Assing, a physician, who soon after settled at Hamburg. She wrote numerous poems and tales of some merit. Died in 1840. A volume of her works, entitled "Poetical Remains," ("Rosa Maria's poetischer Nachlass,") appeared in 1841.

See BROCKHAUS, "Conversations-Lexikon."

Assisi, d′, (ANDREA.) See LUIGI, (ANDREA.)

Asso. See ADSO.

Assollant, å′so′lôN′, (JEAN BAPTISTE ALFRED,) a French novelist, born at Aubusson, Creuse, about 1827. He published, besides other works, "Acacia," "Brancas," (1859,) "Les Aventures de Karl Brunner," (1861,) "Rose d'Amour," (1862,) and "Scenes from Life in the United States," ("Scènes de la Vie des États-Unis," 1858.)

Assomption, de l′, deh lå′sŏmp′se-ôN′, (CHARLES,) a Flemish Carmelite, and writer on theology, born in 1625; died in 1686.

Assoucy, d′, då′soo′se′, (CHARLES Coypeau—kwå′-pŏ′,) a French satirical poet of considerable notoriety for his imprudence and misfortunes, was born at Paris about 1604. Died in 1678 or 1679.

See FLÖGEL, "Geschichte des Burlesken."

Asso y del Rio, de, då âs′so e dĕl ree′o, (IGNAZIO

Jordan—HOR-dân′,) a Spanish jurist and naturalist of the eighteenth century. He published in 1775 "Institutes of the Civil Law in Spain," ("Instituciones del Derecho civil de Castilla,") which is considered the best work on the subject. He also wrote a treatise on the plants of Aragon, ("Synopsis Stirpium indigenarum Aragoniæ," 1799.)

See WATT, "Bibliotheca Britannica."

Assumpção, de, då âs-soomp-sŏwN′, (JOSÉ,) a Portuguese theologian, noted as a writer of Latin verse. Died in 1751.

Assumpção-Velho, da, då âs-soomp-sŏwN′ vĕl′yo, (JOACHIM,) a Portuguese natural philosopher, born in 1753, was a canon regular of the congregation of Saint Croix. He studied physical science with great success, and published "Meteorological Observations made in 1783–84," and "Observações fysicas por Occasião de seis Raios," etc. Died in 1793. "He left unfinished works which," says Correa da Serra, "would have procured for him a great reputation in Europe."

Assunto, dell′, dĕl lås-soon′to, (ONORIO,) an Italian monk, and writer on theology, born in 1639; died in 1716.

Ast, âst, (GEORG ANTON FRIEDRICH,) a German scholar and teacher of great eminence, was born at Gotha in 1778. He was educated at Gotha and Jena, and became in 1805 professor of classical literature in the University of Landshut. In 1826, when this university was transferred to Munich, Ast removed thither and retained his professorship. His lectures were eminently suggestive. Among his works (which are mostly philological or philosophical) are a metrical German version of the tragedies of Sophocles, (1804,) a "Manual of Æsthetics," (1805,) an "Introduction to Philology," (1808,) "Elements (Grundlinien) of Philosophy," (1809,) and "The Life and Writings of Plato," ("Platons Leben und Schriften," 1816.) He published an edition of all the works of Plato, with a Latin version and commentary, (11 vols., 1819–32.) Few modern critics have done more to illustrate the works of Plato. Died at Munich in December, 1841.

See BROCKHAUS, "Conversations-Lexikon."

Asta, dell′, dĕl lâs′tâ, (ANDREA,) a Neapolitan historical painter, born at Bagnuoli about 1673, was a pupil of Solimena. Among his chief works is a Nativity. Died in 1721.

As-ta′rĭ-us or **As-tĭ-a′rĭ-us,** (BLASIUS,) [It. BIASIO ASTARIO, be-â′se-o âs-tâ′re-o,) an Italian medical writer, born at Pavia, lived in the first half of the sixteenth century.

Astarloa y Aguirre, de, då âs-tâR-lo′å e å-gwèr′rå, (Don PABLO PEDRO,) a Spanish linguist, born at Durango in 1752. He devoted his life chiefly to the study of languages. His principal work is an argument for the antiquity of the Basque language, ("Apologia de la Lengua Bascongada," 1803,) in which he proves its identity with the language of the ancient Iberi. "Astarloa was the first," says W. von Humboldt, "who studied the Basque language in a really searching spirit." Died in 1806.

Astarrita, âs-târ-ree′tâ, (GENNARO,) an Italian dramatic composer, born at Naples about 1750. He composed many operas, which were for the most part successful, but he was deficient in originality. His most popular production was "Circe and Ulysses," ("Circe e Ulisse.")

As-tar′te, [Gr. Ἀστάρτη; see ASHTORETH,] a goddess worshipped by the Phœnicians and Syrians, who erected to her a famous temple at Hierapolis. (See I. Kings xi. 33.) She has by some mythologists been identified with Aphrodite or Venus.

Astbury, ast′ber-e, (J.,) an Englishman who made great improvements in the manufacture of pottery, was born about 1678. It is stated that by feigning to be an idiot he obtained admission into the workshop of a foreign potter and learned a secret process used by him. He began business at Shelton, and produced a white stoneware of a very superior quality by mixing pipeclay with Shelton marl. He was the first British potter who used calcined flint as an ingredient of his fabrics. Died in 1743.

See SHAW, "History of the Staffordshire Potteries."

ā, ē, ī, ō, ū, ȳ, *long*; à, è, ò, same, less prolonged; ă, ĕ, ĭ, ŏ, ŭ, ў, *short*; a, e, i, o, *obscure*; fâr, fàll, fàt; mêt; nŏt; gŏŏd; mŏŏn;

As'tẹll, (MARY,) an English authoress, born at Newcastle-upon-Tyne in 1668. In 1697 she published a "Serious Proposal to the Ladies for the Advancement of their True and Greatest Interest," which provoked the ridicule of certain writers of the "Tatler," who gave her the name of Madonella. One of her religious treatises having been attacked by Lady Masham, she defended her opinions in "The Christian Religion as professed by a Daughter of the Church of England," (1705,) which was praised for logical ability. She was esteemed by several eminent divines and authors. Died in 1731.

See BALLARD, "Memoirs of Several Learned Ladies of Great Britain," Oxford, 1752.

Astemio. See ABSTEMIUS.

Aster. See ASTERIUS.

Aster, ȧs'tẹr, (ERNST LUDWIG,) a Prussian general and engineer, born at Dresden about 1778, planned the fortifications of Coblentz and Ehrenbreitstein.

Astère. See ASTERIUS.

As-te'rï-a, [Gr. Ἀστερία; Fr. ASTÉRIE, ȧs'tȧ're',] in classic mythology, was a daughter of the Titan Coeus, a sister of Latona, and the wife of Perses. The poets feigned that to escape from Jupiter she assumed the form of a quail.

As-te'rï-us, [Gr. Ἀστέριος,] a Sophist and advocate of Arianism, lived in Cappadocia about 320 A.D. During Maximian's persecution of the Christians, in the early part of the fourth century, he is said to have relapsed into paganism; but he afterwards renounced this error. He wrote several works, which are not extant.

Asterius, [Gr. Ἀστέριος; Fr. ASTÈRE, ȧs'taiR',] written also **Aster,** SAINT, a Father of the Church, supposed to have been born at Antioch about 340 A.D. He became Bishop of Amasea, in Pontus; but the date of this promotion and nearly all the events of his life are unknown. His extant homilies contain some eloquent passages, and teach doctrines considered sound by the Roman Catholics.

Astesano, ȧs-tȧ-sȧ'no, (ANTONIO,) an Italian poet, born near Asti in 1412.

Astesati, ȧs-tȧ-sȧ'tee, (GIOVANNI ANDREA,) an Italian historian, born at Brescia in 1673; died in 1747.

Astiarius. See ASTARIUS.

Astle, as's'l or as't'l, (THOMAS,) F.R.S., an eminent English antiquary, born in Staffordshire in 1734. He was appointed about 1775 chief clerk in the record office in the Tower, and became keeper of the records several years later. His principal work is "The Origin and Progress of Writing, as well Hieroglyphic as Elementary, illustrated by engravings, etc.; also, some Account of the Origin and Progress of Printing," (1784,) which is said to be the best work in the language on that subject. Died in 1803.

See NICHOLS, "Literary Anecdotes;" SHAW, "History and Antiquities of Staffordshire;" "Gentleman's Magazine," vol. lxiv., (1804.)

Ast'ley, (Sir JACOB,) afterwards LORD ASTLEY, an English royalist general, who had served under Gustavus Adolphus. Having been made a major-general by Charles I. in 1642, he fought at Edgehill, where he was wounded, and commanded the garrison of Reading in 1643. In 1644 he repulsed Waller at the Cherwell, and was created Lord Astley of Reading. He led a division at Naseby in 1645, and commanded the last remnant of the royal army which was defeated at Stow in 1646. Died in 1651. "Sir Jacob," says Clarendon, "was an honest, brave, plain man, and as fit for the office he exercised, as major-general of foot, as Christendom yielded."

See CLARENDON, "History of the Great Rebellion."

Astley, (JOHN,) an English portrait-painter, born in Shropshire in the early part of the eighteenth century, was a pupil of Hudson. He visited Rome, and subsequently worked with success in London and Dublin. He married the widow of Sir William Daniel, whose large fortune he inherited a few years after his marriage. Died in 1787.

See EDWARDS, "Anecdotes of Painters."

Astley, (PHILIP,) an excellent equestrian, and founder of Astley's Amphitheatre, London, was born at Newcastle-under-Line in 1742. He served with distinction in the Seven Years' war, and, having left the army about 1765, began to exhibit equestrian feats to the public. He published "The Modern Riding-Master," (1775,) a "System of Equestrian Education," (1801,) and other works. Died in 1814.

See "Gentleman's Magazine," 1814.

As-tol'phus or **As-tul'phus,** [Fr. ASTOLPHE, ȧs'tolf',] written also **Aistulf,** King of the Lombards or Longobards, succeeded his brother Ratchis in 749 or 750 A.D. He seized Ravenna and the Pentapolis about 752, after which he marched against the duchy of Rome. The pope called to his aid Pepin, King of the Franks, who defeated Astolphus in 754, and compelled him to cede the provinces called the Exarchate and Pentapolis to the see of Rome. This was the origin of the temporal power of the popes. Died in 756 A.D.

As'tọn, (ANTONY,) an English writer of comedies, appeared as actor at Drury Lane about 1700. He is supposed to have died about 1750.

See "Biographia Dramatica."

Aston, (Sir ARTHUR,) an English royalist, whom Hume calls "an officer of reputation," commanded the dragoons at Edgehill, (1642,) and distinguished himself in the defence of Reading. He afterwards went to Ireland and became commander of a garrison of three thousand men at Drogheda, which was taken by Cromwell in 1649. Aston and nearly all his men were massacred by the victors.

See HUME, "History of England."

Aston, (Sir THOMAS,) an Englishman, who wrote a "Remonstrance against Presbytery," (1640.) In the civil war he fought for Charles I., was taken prisoner, and in an attempt to escape was mortally wounded. Died in 1645.

See WOOD, "Athenæ Oxonienses."

Aston, (Sir WALTER,) of Tixall, in Staffordshire, born about 1580, was a patron of Drayton the poet. He was sent as ambassador to Spain in 1619. Died in 1639.

Astor, de, dȧ ȧs-toR', (DIEGO,) a Spanish copper-plate and die engraver, lived at Toledo. In 1609 he was appointed engraver to the mint of Segovia.

See BERMUDEZ, "Diccionario Historico."

As'tọr, (JOHN JACOB,) a celebrated New York merchant, was born near Heidelberg, in Germany, in 1763. At the age of sixteen he joined his brother in London in the business of making musical instruments, and four years later (1783) embarked for Baltimore, taking a stock of instruments with him. In New York he exchanged his stock for furs, which he took to London and disposed of to great advantage. Thus encouraged, he resolved to devote himself to the fur trade, and with this view made himself acquainted with the various European markets and carefully studied the different kinds of furs. On returning to America he established himself in New York, which was henceforth his usual place of residence. His enterprise and thrift soon enabled him to ship his furs in his own vessels, which brought back cargoes of foreign produce, thereby reaping a double profit. In sixteen years he had acquired a fortune of two hundred and fifty thousand dollars. Such was his diligence, and so great were his talents for business, that when his commerce covered the seas, he was enabled to control the action of his shipmasters and supercargoes in the minutest details, and rarely if ever was he known to have erred either in judgment or in a knowledge of the facts. He conceived the vast scheme of connecting the fur trade with the Pacific by means of a line of trading-posts extending from the great lakes along the Missouri and Columbia to the mouth of the latter river, where he founded Astoria in April, 1811, to be used as a central depot, and then, by getting possession of one of the Sandwich Islands as a station, to supply China and the Indies with furs directly from the Pacific coast. The disasters which befell two of the expeditions sent out to the Pacific for this purpose, and the desertion of one of the principal agents or partners in the enterprise, and his betrayal of Astor's plans to the Northwest (British Fur) Company, prevented the success of this scheme. Astor invested largely in real estate, erected numerous buildings, both public and private, and thus, from the almost unexampled rise in the value of this kind of property in New York during the first half of the present century, added immensely to his rapidly increasing wealth. At his death in 1848 his property was estimated at not less than twenty millions of dollars. For many years Fitz-Greene Halleck, the poet, was his private secretary.

Astor no doubt owed much to fortuitous circumstances, but his great success was chiefly due to sagacity and close application to business through a long course of years. Among his bequests were four hundred thousand dollars for the establishment of a library in New York, and fifty thousand dollars to his native village in Germany; but almost the whole of his property was left to his son, William B. Astor. William B. Astor subsequently added to his father's bequest nearly as much more, so that the Astor Library is now one of the most liberally endowed institutions of the kind on the American continent.

See WASHINGTON IRVING, "Astoria," 1836, and "Adventures of Captain Bonneville," 1837; HUNT's "Merchant's Magazine" for August, 1844; HUNT's "Lives of American Merchants," vol. ii.

Astorga, ås-toʀ′gå, (ANTONIO PEDRO Alvarez Osorio—ȧl′vȧ-rêth o-so′re-o,) MARQUIS OF, a Spanish statesman and diplomatist, born near the beginning of the seventeenth century, filled the office of ambassador to Rome with great credit. He was also Viceroy of Naples from 1672 to 1675.

See GIANNONE, "Storia civile del Regno di Napoli."

Astorga, d', dås-toʀ′gå, (EMANUELE,) BARON, an excellent musical composer, born in Sicily about 1680. Astorga was a name which he assumed after his father had been executed for a political offence. He was patronized by Leopold I., at whose death (1705) he left Vienna. He afterwards visited many capitals of Europe, but did not perform in public. Among his works are an admirable "Stabat Mater," and cantatas entitled "Quando Penso," and "Torna Aprile."

See FÉTIS, "Biographie Universelle des Musiciens."

Astorga, de, då ås-toʀ′gå, (JUAN LORENZO,) a Spanish poet, lived in the middle of the thirteenth century.

See LONGFELLOW's "Poets and Poetry of Europe."

Astori, ås-to′ree, (GIOVANNI ANTONIO,) an Italian antiquary, classical scholar, and priest, born at Venice in 1672, became canon of the ducal church of Saint Mark. Among his works is a treatise "On the Cabiri Gods," ("De Diis Cabiris," 1703.) Among his friends were A. Zeno, Scipio Maffei, and Poleni. Died in 1743.

See MAZZUCHELLI, "Scrittori d'Italia."

Astorini, ås-to-ree′nee, (ÉLIA,) a learned Italian priest, born in Calabria in 1651. He was a Cartesian in philosophy, and appears in his youth—during a residence in Germany—to have adopted or favoured Protestant doctrines. About 1688 he returned to Italy and to the Roman Church. He became professor of mathematics at Sienna in 1690. Among his works are "Elementa Euclidis," (1691,) and a treatise entitled "On the True Church against the Lutherans," (1700.) Died in 1702.

See MAZZUCHELLI, "Scrittori d'Italia," and JÖCHER, "Allgemeines Gelehrten-Lexikon."

As-tor-pil′co, a son of Francisco Pizarro and Angelina, who was a daughter of Atahualpa, Inca of Peru.

See HUMBOLDT, "Tableaux de la Nature."

Astræa, as-tree′a, [Gr. Ἀστραῖα; Fr. ASTRÉE, ȧs′trȧ′,] a mythical personage, regarded as a daughter of Jupiter and Themis, was sometimes called the goddess of justice. According to tradition, she lived on the earth during the golden age, at the end of which she ascended to a more congenial sphere among the stars, being the last of the immortals to leave the earth.

As-tram-psy′chus, [Gr. Ἀστράμψυχος,] the name of several Persian Magi. One of this name, mentioned by Suidas, wrote a work on the Interpretation of Dreams.

Astrée. See ASTRÆA.

As-tron′o-mer, THE, [in Latin, ASTRON′OMUS; Fr. L'ASTRONOME, lȧs′tro′nom′,] is the appellation given to the unknown writer of a valuable "Life of Louis le Débonnaire." It appears that he was attached to the court of that monarch, and wrote from personal knowledge, about the middle of the ninth century.

See GUIZOT, "Collection des Historiens de la France."

Astros, d', dås′tros′, (PAUL THÉRÈSE DAVID,) a French prelate, born in Var in 1772. He was imprisoned by Napoleon for several years, ending in 1814, because

he was an agent of the pope in his contest with the emperor. In 1830 he became Archbishop of Toulouse. He published several theological works. Died in 1851.

See PICOT, "Mémoires pour servir à l'Histoire ecclésiastique du dix-huitième Siècle."

Astruc, ås′trük′, (JEAN,) a French medical writer and teacher of high reputation, born at Sauve, in Languedoc, in 1684. By the aid of an excellent memory and methodical habits, he acquired great erudition. He became professor of anatomy at Toulouse in 1710, and of medicine at Montpellier in 1716 or 1717. About 1728 he removed to Paris, and was appointed consulting physician to the king, and professor of medicine in the Royal College, in 1730. In 1736 he published his capital work "On Venereal Diseases," ("De Morbis Venereis,") which, according to the "Biographie Universelle," is the most complete work on the subject, in respect to erudition and historical research. Among his works is a "History of the Faculty of Medicine of Montpellier," ("Mémoires pour servir à l'histoire," etc.) Died in 1766.

See LORRY, "Vie d'Astruc;" and ASTRUC, "Autobiographie," in "Mémoires de la Faculté de Montpellier."

Astulphus. See ASTOLPHUS.

As-ty′a-ĝēs, [Gr. Ἀστυάγης; Fr. ASTYAGE, ȧs′te′-ȧzh′,] King of the Medes, was the son and successor of Cyaxares, and grandfather of Cyrus the Great. He was dethroned by Cyrus about 560 B.C., and is called the last king of Media. (See CYRUS I.) Herodotus is the authority for this statement. According to Xenophon, Astyages had a son Cyaxares, who succeeded him.

As-ty′a-nax, [Gr. Ἀστυάναξ,] also called **Scamandrius,** son of Hector and Andromache, was killed in infancy by the Greeks at the capture of Troy.

As-ty′d̄-a-mas, [Gr. Ἀστυδάμας,] an Athenian tragic poet, was a son of Morsimus, also a tragic poet. He lived about 380 B.C., and gained prizes for many of his dramas, none of which are extant. The people erected to him a statue, on which he wrote an egotistical inscription. He had a son Astydamas, who was a tragic poet. Only the titles of his works remain.

See BRUNCKS and JACOBS, "Anthologia Græca."

As-ty̆-me′dēs, [Gr. Ἀστυμήδης; Fr. ASTYMÈDE, ȧs′-te′mȧd′,] a prominent citizen of Rhodes, who sided with the Romans against Perseus of Macedon, about 170 B.C.

As-ty′o-chus, [Gr. Ἀστύοχος,] a Spartan admiral, who obtained chief command of the fleet in 412 B.C. He sailed to Chios and Lesbos to expel the Athenians, but failed; and is said to have sold himself to Tissaphernes. He was deprived of his command in 411 B.C.

Asula, ȧ′soo-lå, or **Asola,** ȧ′so-lå, (GIOVANNI MATTEO or G. MARIA,) an Italian composer, a native of Verona, lived about 1580-1620.

A-su-la′nus, Asolano, ȧ-so-lȧ′no, or **D'Asola,** dȧ′-so-lå, (ANDREA,) one of the earliest Italian printers, born at Asola, flourished about 1490-1520. He was the father-in-law of the celebrated Aldus Manutius.

See RENOUARD, "Annales de l'Imprimerie des Aldes," 1825.

As′u-ra or **As′oo-ra,** [Hindoo pron. ŭs′oo-ra,] in common language **Asur** or **Asoor,** usually pronounced ŭs′oor. In the Hindoo mythology, the Asuras, children of Kas′yapa and Diti, are a race of powerful demons, who are represented as constantly opposing the Suras, (Sooras,) or gods. (See SURA.) The Asuras may be said to correspond, in some of their leading attributes, to the giants, (Jötuns,) and the Suras to the Æsir, of the Northern mythology.

See MOOR's "Hindu Pantheon."

As′y̆-chis, [Gr. Ἄσυχις,] an Egyptian king, whose period is uncertain, but who built the eastern propylæa of the great temple of Phtha (Vulcan) at Memphis, regarded as the finest work of the kind in Egypt. He also built a brick pyramid, and established the law of giving the dead body of the debtor's father as security for debt.

Atabalipa. See ATAHUALPA.

Atahualpa or **Atahuallpa,** ȧ-tä-hwȧl′pä, sometimes written **Atabalipa,** the last Inca of Peru, was a son of Huayna Capac and a princess of Quito. About 1525 he became King of Quito by the will of his father, who left Peru to Atahualpa's brother Huascar, the lawful heir of the whole empire. Atahualpa, who was warlike and ambitious, invaded, with a large army, the dominions of Huascar, whom he defeated and took prisoner, (1532.) According to Garcilasso de la Vega, he massacred of the royal family all who had the blood of the Incas in their veins, except Huascar and his brother Manco Capac. In the same year that he thus usurped the throne of the Inca, Pizarro entered upon the conquest of Peru. After mutual professions of amity, Atahualpa and Pizarro met in an interview, (November, 1532,) during which the former was seized by the Spaniards and loaded with chains.

To obtain his release, the Inca offered to fill with gold, as high as he could reach, the room in which he was confined, twenty-two feet long and seventeen feet wide. Pizarro accepted this offer. Before the full amount had been collected, the Spaniards became impatient, and divided the spoil. Rumours of a rising among the natives afforded Pizarro a pretext to arraign the captive Inca before a military court. He was condemned to be burned alive, but by abjuring his religion he obtained the privilege of being strangled by the *garrote*, in August, 1533. "He is allowed to have been bold, highminded, and liberal," says Prescott. "All agree that he showed singular penetration and quickness of perception. His exploits as a warrior had placed his valour beyond dispute."

See PRESCOTT, "Conquest of Peru," vol. i.; GARCILASSO DE LA VEGA, "Historia general del Peru;" A. VON HUMBOLDT, "Tableaux de la Nature."

Ataide, â-tâ-ee′dâ, written also **Atayde,** (Dom LUIS,) Count of Tougia, a Portuguese nobleman, who was twice Viceroy of India. He first landed in that country in 1568, at a period when there was a conspiracy between the Nizâm and other native princes to drive out the Portuguese, which he frustrated. He embarked for Portugal in 1572, but returned to India in 1580, where he died shortly after.

See A. PINTO PEREIRA, "Historia da India, etc.," 1616.

Atâjee, Atâjî, â-tâ′jee, or **Athadschi,** a distinguished Turkish poet, born at Constantinople about 1583; died in 1635.

See VON HAMMER, "Geschichte der Osmanischen Dichtkunst."

At-a-lan′ta or **At-a-lan′te,** [Gr. Ἀταλάντη; Fr. ATALANTE, ă′tă′lŏNt′,] in ancient mythology, the most swiftfooted of mortals, was distinguished also for courage and martial exploits. She promised her hand to the man who should outstrip her in the race, with the condition that if he failed he must forfeit his life. Milanion won the race by dropping three golden apples which he received from Venus, and which tempted her to stop and pick them up.

Ata-Malek, ăt′ä mâl′ek, written also **Atha-Melik,** (Ala-ed-Deen or Ala-ed-Dîn, â-lâ-ed-deen′,) a Persian historian, born in Khorassân about 1227, was appointed prefect of Bagdâd after its capture by the Moguls in 1258. He was author of a history of the Moguls, entitled "The Conquest of the World." Died in 1282.

Atanagi, â-tâ-nâ′jee, (DIONIGI,) a distinguished Italian *littérateur* and editor, born at Cagli, in the duchy of Urbino. About 1532 he went to Rome, where he remained twenty-five years in indigence. He removed to Venice in 1560, and died there between 1567 and 1574. He is regarded as a judicious and accurate editor. Among his publications are "Familiar Letters of Thirteen Illustrious Men," (1554,) and "Poems of Several Eminent Tuscan Poets," ("Delle Rime di diversi nobili Poeti Toscani," 2 vols., 1565.)

See MAZZUCHELLI, "Scrittori d'Italia."

Atanasio. See ATHANASIUS and ATHANASIO.

Atar, ă′tar, (BEN DAVID,) a Jewish rabbi and .poet, lived at Amsterdam in the second half of the seventeenth century, translated the Psalms into Spanish verse.

Atar, (BEN SAMUEL,) a Jew of the sixteenth century, published a work on Hebrew traditions.

At′a-ulf, Ad′a-ulf, or **Ad′olf,** [Gr. Ἀτάουλφος; Lat. ATAUL′PHUS,] was brother-in-law of Alaric I., King of the Visigoths, whom he succeeded in 411 A.D. He married Placidia, (a sister of the emperor Honorius,) whom he had taken captive at the capture of Rome in 410. In 412 he evacuated Italy and marched into Gaul, where he took Narbo, Burdigala, (Bordeaux,) etc. After

he had conquered Aquitaine, he crossed the Pyrenees to expel the Vandals and Suevi from Spain. He was assassinated by one of his officers at Barcelona in 415 A.D.

See MURATORI, "Annali d'Italia."

Atayde. See ATAIDE.

Atch′i-son, (DAVID R.,) an American politician, born in Fayette county, Kentucky, in 1807, removed in 1830 to Missouri. He was appointed in 1841 to fill an unexpired term in the United States Senate, of which he continued a member till 1855. He at first acted with the Benton wing of the Democratic party, but soon after embraced the extreme views of Calhoun. In the troubles attending the organization of the territory of Kansas in 1854, '55, and '56, he not only lent his countenance to the outrages committed by armed men from Missouri, by which the free-soil voters of Kansas were driven from the polls, but also took an active part in those civil disturbances and conflicts in that territory, which may be said to have foreshadowed the war of the great rebellion.

A′te, [Gr. Ἀτη,] a personage of classic mythology, was said to have been a daughter of Eris, (Discord,) or, according to Homer, of Jupiter. She was called the goddess of evil, or the goddess that avenges crimes.

A-te-nul′fus or **At′e-nulph,** written also **Atenolphe,** became Prince of Beneventum by conquest about 900 A.D., before which he was Count or Prince of Capua. He died in 910, leaving two sons, Landulphus and Atenulphus, who reigned jointly. They defeated the Saracens on the Liris in 916, and subjected nearly all Apulia. Atenulphus II. died about 940 A.D.

See GIANNONE, "Storia civile del Regno di Napoli."

Atenulphus II. of Beneventum, reigned jointly with his brother Landulphus. He waged war against the Saracens, who were driven out of Italy in 933. Died in 933.

Atha-Ben-Hakim. See AL-HAKEM-IBN-ATTÂ.

Athaji or **Athadschi.** See ATÂJEE.

A-thal′a-ric or **A-thal′ric,** [Lat. ATHALARI′CUS,] a Gothic prince, a son of Euthelric or Eutharic, and a grandson of Theodoric I., reigned nominally over the Gothic kingdom of Italy (his mother being regent) from 526 until 534 A.D., when he died, aged eighteen.

Ath-a-lī′ah, [Heb. עתליה; Fr. ATHALIE, ă′tă′le′,] Queen of Judah, a daughter of Ahab, King of Israel, and the notorious Jezebel. She was married to Jehoram, King of Judah, and became a zealous patron of idolatry. At the death of her son Ahaziah, she usurped the throne, and murdered all the males of the royal family except Joash, by whose adherents she was killed about 878 B.C. The history of Athaliah forms the subject of one of Racine's most admired tragedies. (See II. Kings viii. 18, 26, and xi.; II. Chronicles xxii. and xxiii.)

Ath′a-mas, [Gr. Ἀθάμας,] a mythical person, was a son of Æolus, and a brother of Sisyphus and Salmoneus. He married Nephele, and afterwards Ino, a daughter of Cadmus. It is said that he became insane and killed his son. (See INO.)

Atha-Melik. See ATA-MALEK.

A-than-a-ġil′dus [Fr. ATHANAGILDE, ă′tă′nă′zhĕld′] became king of the Spanish Visigoths in 554 A.D. by the aid of the emperor Justinian. He fixed his court at Toledo, where he died in 567 A.D. His daughter Brunehaut was married to Siegbert, King of Austrasia, and her sister Galswinda to King Chilperic.

See MARIANA, "Historia general de España."

A-than′a-ric, an able chief of a tribe of Visigoths who inhabited Dacia, made a treaty of peace about 370 A.D. with the emperor Valens, against whom he had waged war several years. He failed in an effort to resist a horde of wild Huns who rushed like a torrent from the north in 376 A.D. Died in 381.

Athanase. See ATHANASIUS.

Athanasio, â-tâ-nâ′se-o, or **Atanasio,** (Don PEDRO,) a Spanish painter and excellent colorist, born at Granada in 1638, was a pupil of Alonzo Cano. Died in 1688.

Athanasius, ath-a-nā′she-us, [Gr. Ἀθανάσιος; Fr. ATHANASE, ă′tă′năz′; It. ATANASIO, â-tâ-nâ′se-o,] SAINT, an illustrious Greek Father and pillar of the Church, was born at Alexandria about 296 A.D. He was a pupil and secretary of the archbishop Alexander. He attended in 325 A.D. the famous Council of Nice, in which he distinguished himself by his eloquence and zeal against the doctrine of Arius. In the next year he was elected Archbishop of Alexandria by the clergy and the people. It is said that he refused to obey an order which Constantine the Great issued in 331, to restore Arius to communion. Having been accused of sacrilege and other crimes by his enemies, he was summoned, in 334 or 335 A.D., before a council at Tyre, which condemned him without proof. He was exiled to Treves by Constantine, at whose death (337) he was restored to his see by the favour of Constantine II. The Arians prevailed in the Council of Antioch, 341 A.D., and were patronized by the emperor Constantius. Athanasius was again deposed, and retired to Rome, where he was cordially received by the bishop Julius, and found many friends. In 347 his cause and doctrines were approved by the Council of Sardica, and in 349 he returned in triumph to Alexandria. He was considered the leader of the orthodox party, who were sometimes called Athanasians.

Athanasius is commended for the fortitude with which he endured long persecution, and the firmness with which he defended the faith against imperial power and presented himself as a barrier against despotism. His influence and reputation were so great that Constantius did not venture to use open violence against him, but by artful and indirect means he procured his condemnation at the Council of Milan, 355 A.D. Athanasius then found a safe refuge among the anchorites of Upper Egypt, where he remained six years and composed several works. On the death of Constantius, 361 A.D., he was restored to his office. He was exiled by Julian (362) and by Valens, (367 ;) but he passed his last five years in the possession of his see, and died in 373 A.D.

Among his most important works are, a "Discourse on the Incarnation," "Five Books against Arius," a "Discourse against the Greeks or Gentiles," a "Disputation (Διάλεκτος) with Arius in the Council of Nice," "Epistles to Serapio," "An Apology to the Emperor Constantius," and an "Apology for his own Flight." His style is clear, simple, and forcible. His character appears to have been a rare combination of genius, wisdom, practical ability, courage, and discretion.

It is now generally admitted that the Athanasian Creed, which was a standard of orthodoxy in the Middle Ages, was not composed by this Athanasius, to whom it was formerly ascribed.

See HERMANT, "Vie d'Athanase," 1671; MÖHLER, "Athanasius der Grosse," 1827; SOCRATES, "Historia Ecclesiastica;" SOZOMEN, "Historia Ecclesiastica;" E. RENAUDOT, "Histoire des Patriarches d'Alexandrie," 1713; PHOTIUS, "Bibliotheca."

Athanasius, Bishop of Ancyra in 360 A.D., was a strenuous advocate of the Nicene Creed against the Eunomians and others. Died about 372 A.D.

Athanasius, presbyter of Alexandria, of which city he was a native, lived about 450 A.D.

Athanasius, a jurist of Emesa, in Syria, lived in the sixth century.

Athanasius, BISHOP, was elevated to the see of Naples in 877 by his brother Sergius, duke of that city, whom he afterwards conspired against, put out his eyes and delivered him a captive to Pope John VIII., and took possession himself of the dukedom.

See GIANNONE, "Storia civile del Regno di Napoli."

Athanasius, Patriarch of Constantinople, attained that dignity in 1289, and abdicated in 1310.

Athanasius called THE RHETORICIAN, was born at Constantinople (or, according to some authorities, in Cyprus) about 1552. He removed to Paris, where he died in 1663, leaving several Greek works, among which is "The Delight of the Soul, etc.," (1639,) and a "Compendium of Moral Philosophy," (1641.)

A'the-as, a warlike and prudent king of Scythia, lived about 350 B.C. and waged war against Philip of Macedon.

Athelard. See ADELARD.

Atheling. See EDGAR ATHELING.

Ath'el-stän', more correctly **Æthelstan** or **Ethelstan—êth-el-stän',** written also **Adelstan** and **Edelstan,** one of the wisest and ablest of the Anglo-Saxon kings, born about 895 A.D., was the eldest son of Edward the Elder, and a grandson of Alfred the Great. He succeeded his father in 925, and soon after annexed to

his kingdom Northumbria, which had been ruled by Sigtric or Sithric, a Danish chief. In 934 he invaded Scotland. Among the important events of his reign was a great victory which he gained in 937 A.D. at Brunenburg, Brunsbury, or Brunford, over an army of Danes, Scots, Picts, etc., led by Anlaf, (a son of Sigtric,) and by Constantine of Scotland. His power exceeded that of any previous Anglo-Saxon king. He reigned over all the island except Cumbria, Wales, Cornwall, and Scotland, which were tributary to him. His liberality, and respect for laws, learning, and religion, are commended by William of Malmesbury. He died without issue in 941, and was succeeded by his brother Edmund.

See HUME, "History of England," chap. ii.; FREEMAN, "Norman Conquest," vol. i. chap. ii.

A-the'na, [Gr. Ἀθήνη or Ἀθηνᾶ,] the goddess of wisdom, one of the great divinities of the Greek mythology, was fabled to have sprung in full armour from the head of Jupiter. She presided over agriculture, inventions, sciences, laws, and industry, and was the reputed creator of the olive-tree. She was the great national divinity of the Athenians, whose capital derived its name from her. Athena, sometimes called Pallas Athena, corresponds to the Minerva of the Romans. (See MINERVA.)

Athenæus, ath-a-nee'us, [Gr. Ἀθήναιος; Fr. ATHÉNÉE, ä'tä'nà',] a Peripatetic philosopher, born at Seleucia, in Cilicia, lived about 50 B.C. He was a party leader in his native city, and was intimate with Lucius Murena, who conspired against Augustus in 22 B.C. He was arrested on this account, but was released because there was no proof against him.

Athenæus, the author of an extant Greek work on Military Engines, addressed to Marcellus, (probably the conqueror of Syracuse.) He is said to have been a contemporary of Archimedes.

Athenæus, an eminent physician, the founder of the medical sect of "Pneumatici," was born in Cilicia, at Tarsus or Attalia, probably in the first century after Christ. He practised at Rome with success, and wrote many works, of which only small fragments remain. The name of his sect is derived from πνεῦμα, *spirit,* an active principle which they considered a fifth element.

Athenæus, a distinguished Greek *littérateur* and antiquary, born at Naucratis, in Egypt, flourished about 200 A.D. Little is known of his life, except that he became a resident of Rome, and wrote or compiled an interesting work entitled Δειπνοσοφισταί, "The Banquet of the Learned," or, perhaps, "The Contrivers of Feasts,"which is extant. It is in the form of a dialogue, and purports to be a description of a banquet given by Laurentius or Larensius, a noble Roman, to a number of eminent men, among whom was Galen. It is an immense mass of anecdotes, criticisms, facts in natural history, and extracts from the works of about seven hundred poets, dramatists, historians, etc., and derives its value chiefly from these extracts from authors whose works are lost. As a work of art it has little merit ; but it affords much information about the private life of the ancient Greeks, and gives proof of great antiquarian research.

A good edition of Athenæus was published by W. Dindorf, Leipsic, 3 vols., 1827.

See FABRICIUS, "Bibliotheca Græca;" SCHOELL, "Histoire de la Littérature Grecque;" "Edinburgh Review," vol. iii., (1803;) "Blackwood's Magazine," vol. iv., (1818.)

Athenæus, a Greek epigrammatic poet mentioned by Diogenes Laertius. Two of his epigrams are found in the Greek Anthology.

Ath-e-nag'o-ras, [Gr. Ἀθηναγόρας; Fr. ATHÉNAGORE, ä'tä'nä'goR',] an ancient physician to whom is ascribed an extant unedited Latin treatise on the Pulse and Urine. He is supposed to have lived before the Christian era.

Athenagoras, a Greek philosopher, born at Athens, was converted to Christianity in the second century, and wrote "An Apology for the Christians," which is still extant. It was addressed to Marcus Aurelius, or, as some say, to Hadrian and Antoninus. He also left an extant treatise in defence of the doctrine of the Resurrection. His works have considerable literary merit, and are highly esteemed in other respects. They have been translated into English by David Humphreys. Athenag-

ä, ē, ī, ō, ū, ȳ, *long;* à, è, ò, same, less prolonged; ă, ĕ, ĭ, ŏ, ŭ, ў, *short;* ą, ę, į, ǫ, *obscure;* fär, fàll, fàt; mêt; nôt; gōŏd; mōŏn;

oras has been accused of alloying Christianity with Platonic philosophy.

See NEANDER, "History of the Christian Church."

Athénagore. See ATHENAGORAS.

Athenais. See EUDOCIA.

Athénas, ă'tă'nȧs', (PIERRE LOUIS,) a Frenchman distinguished for his efforts to improve agriculture, commerce, and the useful arts, was born in Paris in 1752. He opened a manufactory of sulphuric acid at Nantes, invented a plough which was much used, discovered the tin-mines of Piriac, and wrote treatises on agriculture, rural economy, etc. He introduced and naturalized the Guinea grass, (*Panicum altissimum,*) which is valuable for pasture or fodder. Died in 1829.

See QUÉRARD, "La France Littéraire."

Athénée. See ATHENÆUS.

Athenion. See ARISTION.

A-the'nǐ-on, ['Αθηνίων,] a famous Greek encaustic painter, born at Maronea, in Thrace, lived about 320 B.C., and was a pupil of Glaucion of Corinth. He is said to have excelled Nicias, compared with whom he was more austere in colouring. Among his works were "Ulysses detecting Achilles in a female dress," and a "Groom breaking in a horse." Pliny expresses the opinion that he would have surpassed all men in painting if he had not died young.

See PLINY, "Natural History."

Athenion, a Greek comic poet of the middle comedy, from whose play "The Samothracians" we have a long extract in Athenæus.

Athenion or **Athe'nio,** a leader of the insurgents in a servile war in Sicily, is said to have been a Cilician by birth. He was defeated by the consul Manius Aquillius, who killed Athenion with his own hand, in 102 B.C.

See DIODORUS SICULUS, "Fragments."

Athenion, a Greek physician, mentioned by Soranus as being a follower of Erasistratus, lived probably between 200 B.C. and 100 A.D,

A-then'o-clēs [Gr. 'Αθηνοκλῆς] of Cyzicus, a commentator upon Homer, is spoken of by Athenæus as a better critic of Homer's poems than Aristarchus. Another Athenocles is mentioned by Athenæus as an excellent engraver, and embosser of drinking-cups.

Athénodore. See ATHENODORUS.

A-then-o-do'rus, [Gr. 'Αθηνόδωρος; Fr. ATHÉNODORE, ă'tă'no'doR',] a Greek statuary, was a native of Arcadia and a pupil of Polycletus the elder. He was particularly successful in representing women of rank. He flourished about 350 B.C.

Athenodorus, one of the three sculptors of the celebrated group of "Laocoon and his Sons," was a son of Agesander of Rhodes. (See AGESANDER.)

Athenodorus, a Greek physician, who was probably a contemporary of Plutarch. He wrote a work "On Epidemic Diseases," (not extant.)

Athenodorus, [Fr. ATHÉNODORE,] a Stoic philosopher, called CANANI'TES, (from Cana, in Cilicia, the birthplace of his father,) was born at Tarsus. He was probably the person whom Cicero calls Athenodorus Calvus, ("Ad Atticum," xvi.) He taught at Apollonia, where Octavius appears to have taken lessons from him, and afterwards removed to Rome. His influence over Octavius, before and after he became emperor, tended to restrain him from excessive severity. Among the lost works attributed to Athenodorus is a treatise against the "Categories" of Aristotle. He died aged eighty-two.

See DIOGENES LAERTIUS; FABRICIUS, "Bibliotheca Græca."

Athenodorus surnamed CORDYL'IO, of Tarsus, a Stoic philosopher, was keeper of the great library of Pergamus. He removed to Rome, where he lived in the same house with Cato Uticensis until his death.

Athenodorus of Ænos, a Greek rhetorician, taught at Athens between 150 and 200 A.D.

Athenodorus of Teos, a Greek, who performed on the harp at the marriage of Alexander the Great and Statira in 324 B.C.

Ath'er-stone, (EDWIN,) an English poet, born at Nottingham about 1788, was the author of "Abradates and Panthea," (1821,) "The Last Days of Herculaneum," and "The Fall of Nineveh," (1828,) which are highly commended. He contributed to the "Edinburgh Review."

See "Blackwood's Magazine," vol. xxvii., and "Edinburgh Review," vol. xlviii.

Ath'er-ton, (CHARLES G.), an American Democratic politician, son of Charles H. Atherton, was born at Amherst, New Hampshire, in 1804. He graduated at Harvard in 1822. In 1837 he was elected to Congress, and the next year introduced a series of resolutions, which passed the House of Representatives, requiring that all petitions or papers relating in any way to the subject of slavery should be laid on the table without being debated, printed, or referred. These resolutions formed the basis of the famous "gag-law," in the repeal of which John Quincy Adams won immortal renown. In 1843 Mr. Atherton was elected to the United States Senate, and re-elected in 1852. Died in 1853.

Atherton, (HUMPHREY,) a major-general in New England, much employed in negotiations with the Indians, came from England to Dorchester, Massachusetts, in 1650. Died in 1653.

Athias, â-tee'ȧs, (ISAAC,) a Spanish Jew and writer, lived at Amsterdam about 1600–20.

Athias, (Rabbi JOSEPH,) an eminent Jewish printer of Amsterdam, published editions of the Hebrew Bible (1661 and 1667) which were highly esteemed. He was presented with a gold chain by the States-General for these services. The majority of modern editors of the Bible have followed the text of Athias. Died in 1700.

Athlone, EARL OF. See GINKEL.

Atia, ā'she-ą, the mother of the Roman emperor Augustus, was a daughter of M. Atius Balbus and Julia, the sister of Julius Cæsar. She is praised for the care and wisdom with which she educated her son. Died in 43 B.C.

Atienza Calatrava, â-te-ĕn'thâ kâ-lâ-trâ'vâ, (MARTIN,) a Spanish painter, one of the founders of the Academy of Seville, lived about 1660.

A-til-ǐ-çī'nus, a Roman jurist, who lived in the first century of our era. His works are cited in the Digest.

A-til'ǐ-us, a freedman in the reign of Tiberius, chiefly famous for an amphitheatre for gladiators which he erected near Fidenæ, but so slightly that it fell when filled with spectators, in 27 A.D., and from twenty to fifty thousand persons are said to have been killed and wounded. He was banished.

Atilius, (CAIUS and MARCUS,) Roman decemviri in 216 B.C.

Atilius, (LUCIUS,) was tribune of the people, 311 B.C.

Atilius, (LUCIUS,) a quæstor, 216 B.C., fell at Cannæ.

Atilius, (LUCIUS,) commanded the Roman garrison at Locri, 215 B.C.

Atilius, (LUCIUS,) prætor in 197 B.C.

Atilius, (LUCIUS,) a Roman jurist in the second century B.C.

Atilius, (LUCIUS,) surnamed SAPIENS, a Roman jurist, lived between 200 and 150 B.C.

Atilius, (MARCUS,) an early Latin comic poet, whose period is unknown. His works are not extant. Cicero calls him a very rugged poet,—*poeta durissimus.*

At'kins, (HENRY,) a Boston navigator, who in numerous trading voyages to Davis Straits, between 1729 and 1758, explored much of the coast of Labrador. A brief account of his observations is published in the "Massachusetts Historical Collections."

At'kins, (JOHN,) born at Plaistow, Essex, in England, entered the navy as surgeon about 1703. He served in various parts of the world, and published an interesting work entitled "Voyage to Guiana, Brazil, and the West Indies," (1737,) and "The Navy Surgeon, or a Practical System of Surgery," (1737.)

Atkins, (RICHARD.) See ATKYNS.

Atkins, (ROBERT,) an English nonconformist divine, born in Somersetshire about 1625. He preached at Exeter, and was ejected for nonconformity in 1662. Died in 1685.

At'kin-son, (BENJAMIN ANDREW,) an English Presbyterian minister, preached in London about 1715–35, and wrote against Popery.

Atkinson, (HENRY,) an English mathematician, born near Newcastle-upon-Tyne about 1786. He contributed to the Ladies' and Gentlemen's Diaries, and was one of the editors of the "Newcastle Magazine." Died in 1831.

At′kin-son, (HENRY,) an American general, born in North Carolina about 1780. Having in 1820 been made a brigadier-general, he commanded the Western Army at the battle of Bad Axe, in which he defeated the Indians under Black Hawk, August 2, 1832. Died in 1842.

Atkinson, (THEODORE,) a chief-justice of New Hampshire, born at New Castle in 1697; died in 1779.

Atkinson, (THOMAS,) an English clergyman and Latin poet, was rector of Islip, where he died in 1639. He left in manuscript a Latin tragedy, entitled "Man," ("Homo.")

At′kin-son, (THOMAS,) a Scottish writer, born about 1800, lived in Glasgow. Died in 1833.

Atkinson, (THOMAS WITLAM,) an English artist and traveller, born in Yorkshire in 1799. He painted landscapes, passed about seven years in the exploration of Siberia, and published "Oriental and Western Siberia, a Narrative of Seven Years' Explorations and Adventures," etc., (1858,) and "Travels in the Regions of the Upper and Lower Amoor," (1860.) Died in 1861.

At′kyns, (JOHN TRACY,) an English lawyer, who was called to the bar in 1732. He was appointed cursitor baron of the exchequer in 1755. His "Reports of Cases argued and determined in Chancery from 1736 to 1754" are considered good authority.

See FOSS, "Judges of England," vol. viii.

Atkyns or **At′kins,** (RICHARD,) an English gentleman, born in Gloucestershire about 1615, raised a troop of horse for the king in the civil war. In a work "On the Origin and Growth of Printing," (1664,) he attempted to deprive Caxton of the credit of introducing printing into England. (See CAXTON.) Died in 1677.

Atkyns, (Sir ROBERT,) an eminent English lawyer and judge, a son of Edward Atkyns, who was a baron of the exchequer, was born in Gloucestershire in 1621. He was knighted at the coronation of Charles II., and appointed a judge of the court of common pleas in 1672. Refusing to be subservient to the designs of the corrupt court, he resigned or was removed in 1680. After the revolution which dethroned James II. he was appointed chief baron of the exchequer in 1689. Among his works are an "Inquiry into the Power of dispensing with Penal Laws," (1689,) and a "Defence of Lord Russell's Innocency," (1689.) Died in 1709.

See FOSS, "Judges of England," vol. vii.

Atkyns, (Sir ROBERT,) a son of the preceding, born near London in 1646 or 1647. He devoted much time to researches in the history and antiquities of the county in which he resided, and is chiefly known as author of "The Ancient and Present State of Glo'stershire," (1712.) Died in 1711.

See "Biographia Britannica."

At-lan′tĭ-dēş, [Gr. Ἀτλαντίδες,] the daughters of Atlas, were also called Hesperides, Pleiades, and Hyades.

At′las, [Gr. Ἄτλας,] a mythical personage represented by the ancient poets sometimes as bearing the heavens on his shoulders, and sometimes as the keeper of the pillars which support the heavens. Hesiod calls him a son of Japetus and Clymene. In later traditions the conception of his superhuman personal existence is blended or lost in the idea of the celebrated mountain in Northern Africa. By some he was represented as the leader of the Titans in their war against Jupiter.

At′lee, (SAMUEL JOHN,) an American colonel in the Revolutionary war, born in Pennsylvania in 1738, was elected to Congress from Lancaster in 1780. Died in 1786.

Âtmăn, ât′man, or **Âtmâ,** ât′mâ, (*i.e.* "soul,") called also **Părămâtmâ,** ("first or great soul,") the Sanscrit name of the great soul of the world, [in German, WELT-SEELE,] alluded to in the Vedas as the original or primary principle of nature. This idea is regarded as the germ or commencement of the Brahminical philosophy.

See KÖPPEN, "Religion des Buddha," p. 29.

Atondo y Antillon, â-ton′do e ân-têl-yôn′, (Don ISIDORO,) a Spanish admiral who explored Lower California and planted a colony there about 1682.

See VENEGAS, "Noticias de la California."

A-tos′sa, [Gr. Ἄτοσσα,] a daughter of Cyrus, King of Persia, became successively the wife of Cambyses, of Smerdis the Magian, and of Darius Hystaspes, over whom she had great influence. She was the mother of Xerxes. According to Hellanicus, she was the first person who wrote epistles.

Atrée. See ATREUS.

A′treūs, [Gr. Ἀτρεύς; Fr. ATRÉE, ȧ′trȧ′,] an ancient king of Mycenæ, supposed to have been a son of Pelops and Hippodami′a, and father or grandfather of Agamemnon and Menelaus. The crimes and calamities of Atreus and his family afforded a prolific subject for the Greek poets and fabulists.

A-trī′dēş, [Gr. Ἀτρείδης,] plural **A-trī′dæ,** [Ἀτρείδαι,] a patronymic from Atreus. In the singular it commonly designates Agamemnon, but in the plural the two brothers Agamemnon and Menelaus. (See Homer's "Iliad," *passim.*)

A-tro-çĭ-ā′nus, [Ger. pron. â-trot-se-â′nûs,] (JOANNES,) a German poet and botanist, lived at Bâle and Colmar in the first half of the sixteenth century. He was a teacher of languages, and published, besides other works, a Latin poem on "The Peasants' War of 1525," ("De Bello Rustico Anni 1525,") (published in 1528,) and an edition of Æmilius Macer "On the Virtues of Plants."

A-trop′a-tēş, [Gr. Ἀτροπάτης,] a Persian general, commanded a division at the battle of Arbela, 331 B.C., and was made Satrap of Media by Alexander, 330 B.C.

Atropos. See PARCÆ.

At′sȳll, (RICHARD,) an English engraver, worked for Henry VIII. about 1510-40.

See WALPOLE, "Anecdotes of Painting in England."

At′ta, (TITUS QUINTIUS,) a Roman dramatic poet, wrote comedies about 80 B.C. Some fragments of his writings have been preserved.

At-ta-ġĭ′nus, [Gr. Ἀτταγῖνος,] a Theban, who favoured the cause of Xerxes on his invasion of Greece, 480 B.C.

Attaignant, ȧ′tăn′yôN , (PIERRE,) a French printer of Paris, said to have been the first who printed music with movable types. Died in 1556.

See PANZER, "Annales Typographicæ."

Attaignant, de l′, dĕh lȧ′tăn′yôN′, (GABRIEL CHARLES,) a French versifier, born in Paris in 1697, became a canon of Rheims. His works, comprising songs, madrigals, etc., were published in four volumes in 1757. Died in 1779.

See QUÉRARD, "La France Littéraire."

Attâjî. See ATAJEE.

Attale. See ATTALUS.

At′ta-lī′a-tēş or **Attali′ata,** [Gr. Ἀτταλειάτης,] (MICHAEL,) compiled a compendium of law at Constantinople in the eleventh century.

At′ta-lus, [Gr. Ἄτταλος; Fr. ATTALE, ȧ′tăl′,] a general of Philip of Macedon, was uncle of Cleopatra whom Philip married in 337 B.C. At a feast which followed this event, he offended the prince Alexander by a wish or prayer for a *legitimate* successor to the throne. Attalus insulted or injured Pausanias, who complained to King Philip ; but the latter, from favouritism to Attalus, refused to give him redress. This offence is supposed to have caused the assassination of Philip by Pausanias. Attalus was put to death, by order of Alexander, in 336 or 335 B.C.

See DIODORUS SICULUS, book xvi.; JUSTIN, books ix. and xii.

Attalus, [Fr. ATTALE,] an officer of Alexander the Great, and brother-in-law of Perdiccas, was one of the officers left with part of the army in Bactria in 328 B.C., and accompanied Alexander in the invasion of India in 326. In 321 he commanded the fleet of Perdiccas in his expedition against Ptolemy of Egypt. He was defeated in Pisidia and taken prisoner by Antigonus in 320 B.C. His ultimate fate is unknown.

See ARRIAN's "Anabasis."

Attalus I., King of Pergamus, succeeded his cousin Eumenes I. in 241 B.C. He gained a decisive victory over the Gauls, who had occupied Galatia. Before the year 226 he had made himself master of all Asia Minor west of Mount Taurus. As ally of the Romans and Ætolians, he waged war against Philip of Macedon be-

ā, ē, ī, ō, ū, ȳ, *long;* ă, ĕ, ŏ, same, less prolonged; ă, ĕ, ĭ, ŏ, ŭ, ȳ, *short;* ą, ę, į, ǫ, *obscure;* fär, fȧll, fȧt; mĕt; nŏt; gōōd; mōōn;

tween 210 and 204. In 200 B.C. he met at Athens a Roman embassy and formed another league against Philip. He died in 197 B.C., and left the throne to his son Eumenes II. Attalus had the reputation of a just and wise ruler, and a very able general.

See POLYBIUS, "History," books iv., v., x., xvi., xvii., xviii., xxii., etc.; LIVY, books xxvi., xxvii., xxviii., xxix., xxxi., etc.

Attalus II., surnamed PHILADEL'PHUS, was the second son of Attalus I., and was born about 220 B.C. He began to reign in 159, before which he had served Eumenes II. as general and ambassador to Rome. He adhered constantly to the Roman alliance, and waged war against Prusias of Bithynia. He founded Philadelphia in Lydia, and patronized the arts and sciences. Horace is supposed to refer to the flourishing finances of Attalus in the phrase "Attalicis conditionibus," (Ode I. "Ad Mæcenatem.") Died in 138 B.C.

See POLYBIUS, "History," books iii., xxii., xxv., xxx., xxxi.; LIVY, books xxxv., xxxvii., xxxviii., xlii., xlv.

Attalus III., (PHILOME'TOR,) a nephew of the preceding, and son of Eumenes II., ascended the throne in 138 B.C., soon after which he murdered many of his friends and relatives. Having been seized with remorse, he abandoned public affairs, and applied himself to sculpture, and to gardening, on which he wrote a book. He died in 133 B.C., having made a will, in which the Roman people were appointed his heirs.

See DIODORUS SICULUS, book xxiv.; JUSTIN, book xxxvi.

Attalus, a mathematician, who wrote a commentary on the "Phenomena" of Aratus, is supposed to have flourished between 162 and 128 B.C.

Attalus, a Greek physician of the second century, A.D., was a pupil of Soranus, and belonged to the medical school called *Methodici*, (or "Methodists.")

Attalus, an Athenian sculptor of unknown date, who executed the statue of the Lycian Apollo at Argos.

Attalus, an able and eloquent Stoic philosopher, who lived at Rome in the reign of Tiberius. He was a teacher of the philosopher Seneca, who speaks of him in very favourable terms and quotes a number of his sayings. He was banished through the influence of Sejanus.

See FABRICIUS, "Bibliotheca Græca."

Attalus, a rhetorician or sophist, who appears to have been a native of Laodicea. He settled at Smyrna, and flourished in the reign of Marcus Aurelius.

Attalus, a presbyter of the Christian Church in the fourth century, was condemned for Arianism, 381 A.D.

Attalus, (FLAVIUS PRISCUS,) probably an Ionian by descent, was a pagan by birth, and was converted to Arianism. He was prefect of Rome when that capital was taken by Alaric in 409 A.D., and was then proclaimed emperor by Alaric in place of Honorius. He refused the offer of Honorius to be his associate in the empire. In 410 he was deposed by Alaric, and in 416 A.D. was banished by Honorius to Lipari. His subsequent fate is not known.

See SOZOMEN, "Historia Ecclesiastica;" GIBBON, "Decline and Fall of the Roman Empire."

Attalus, (MARTYN,) one of the Christians put to death at Lugdunum (Lyons) in the reign of Marcus Aurelius, 177 A.D.

Attameemee, (or **Atamîmî**,) an Arabian physician, a native of Jerusalem, gave much attention to pharmacy and materia medica, and wrote numerous medical works. He was living in Egypt in 980 A.D.

Attâr, ât-tâR', or, as he was usually called, **Co'gi** (or **Kho'jah**) **Attar**, was nominally the vizier, but really the ruler, of Ormuz when Albuquerque first arrived before that city. He successfully resisted until his death all the attempts of the Portuguese to take Ormuz. He is believed to have died in 1513.

Attardi, ât-taR'dee, (BONAVENTURA,) an Italian theologian and Augustine monk of the early part of the eighteenth century, became in 1738 provincial of his order in Sicily and Malta.

See MAZZUCHELLI, "Scrittori d'Italia."

Attâr-Fereed-ed-Deen, (or **Ferîd-ed-Dîn**,) ât-târ' fêh-reed' ed-deen', a celebrated Persian poet, who was distinguished for his profound knowledge of the Soofee doctrines, was born in a suburb of Nishapoor, in Khorassân, about 1120 A.D. He wrote forty poetical works, one of which was published at Paris in 1819, with a

memoir. He is said to have been killed by a soldier of Jengis Khan, 1221 A.D., aged one hundred and one years.

Attavante, ât-tâ-vân'tà, (FIORENTINO,) an Italian illuminator and miniature-painter of the latter part of the fifteenth century, worked principally at Venice.

See LANZI, "History of Painting in Italy."

Attavanti, ât-tâ-vân'tee, (PAOLO,) an Italian friar and eloquent preacher, born at Florence in 1419, entered the order of Servites, of which he wrote an account, (1727.) Among his works are "Compendium of Canonical Law," ("Breviarium totius Juris canonici," 1479,) and an "Exposition of the Penitential Psalms," (1479.) Died in 1499.

See TIRABOSCHI, "Storia della Letteratura Italiana."

At-te'ius surnamed PRÆTEXTA'TUS, a grammarian, and afterwards called PHILOLOGUS. He lived in the latter half of the first century B.C., and taught many noble Roman youths, and prepared a Compendium of Roman History for the use of Sallust.

Atteius Capito. See CAPITO.

Attendolo, ât-tên'do-lo, or **Attendoli**, ât-tên'do-lee, (DARIO, dâ-ree'o,) an Italian jurist of the middle of the sixteenth century, was born in the duchy of Ferrara. Among his works is a treatise on the Duel, ("Duello diviso in tre Libri," 1560.)

See MAZZUCHELLI, "Scrittori d'Italia."

Attendolo, (GIOVANNI BATTISTA,) an Italian priest, distinguished as a poet and a linguist, was born at Capua. In the dispute respecting Tasso's "Jerusalem Delivered," he defended that poet against the Academy della Crusca. He left, besides other works, "Rime," ("Poems," 1584.) Died in 1592.

See MAZZUCHELLI, "Scrittori d'Italia."

Atterbom, ât'ter-bom', (PETER DANIEL AMADEUS,) a Swedish poet, born in East Gothland, or in the county of Christianstadt, in 1790. He became German teacher of Prince Oscar about 1820, and professor of philosophy at Upsal in 1828. For many years he edited the "Poetical Almanac," ("Poetisk Kalender.") His poems are admired for grace and harmony. He first introduced sonnets and octaves into Swedish poetry. Among his chief works is "The Seers and Poets of Sweden," a contribution to literary history, in five or six volumes, the first of which appeared in 1841. Died in 1855.

See LONGFELLOW, "Poets and Poetry of Europe;" BROCKHAUS, "Conversations-Lexikon;" "Nouvelle Biographie Générale."

Atterbury, ât'ter-ber-e, (FRANCIS,) Bishop of Rochester, an eminent English writer, pulpit orator, and politician, born at Milton, near Newport-Pagnell, in Buckinghamshire, in March, 1662, was a son of Lewis Atterbury, noticed below. He entered Christ Church, Oxford, in 1680, published a Latin version of Dryden's "Absalom and Achitophel" in 1682, and married Miss Osborn, a relative of the Duke of Leeds, in 1690. In 1691 he became lecturer at Saint Bride's Church, London. Having distinguished himself as an eloquent preacher, he was appointed one of the chaplains to William and Mary about 1694. He was the chief author of a witty answer to Bentley's "Dissertation on the Epistles of Phalaris." (See BENTLEY and BOYLE.) He wrote, in answer to Dr. Wake, "The Rights, Powers, and Privileges of an English Convocation stated and vindicated," (1700.) He was appointed chaplain to Queen Anne in 1702, Dean of Carlisle in 1704, and Bishop of Rochester in 1713.

Atterbury was a zealous Tory and Jacobite, and was intimate with Pope and Swift. He was an able and adroit politician, and would probably have been primate if Queen Anne had survived a few years longer. It is reported that on her death (1714) he urged Bolingbroke to proclaim the Pretender James. He was committed to the Tower in 1722 on a charge of being engaged in plots to restore the Stuart family, and was convicted by the House of Lords in May, 1723. The sentence was deprivation of all his offices and benefices and banishment for life. He retired to France, and continued to be a favourite agent and adviser of the Pretender. He died in Paris in February, 1732. Four volumes of his sermons were published in 1740.

According to Boswell, Dr. Johnson reckoned Atterbury's sermons among the best in the language for style. "He is the glory of our English orators," says Doddridge. "In his writings we see language in its strictest purity and beauty." Among his works is an eloquent vindication of Luther, in "An Answer to some Considerations on the Spirit of Martin Luther and the Original of the Reformation," (1687.)

See his "Epistolary Correspondence," 4 vols., 1783, edited by J. NICHOLS; THOMAS STACKHOUSE, "Memoirs of the Life of Francis Atterbury," 1727; HALLAM, "Constitutional History;" SWIFT, "Four Last Years of the Reign of Queen Anne;" KIPPIS, "Biographia Britannica."

Atterbury, (LEWIS,) the father of the preceding, was born in 1631. He became rector of Milton or Middleton Keynes, in Bucks, about 1657, and retained that living under the reign of Charles II. Three of his sermons were published. He was drowned near his residence in 1693.

Atterbury, (LEWIS,) a son of the preceding, was born in the parish of Newport-Pagnell in 1656. He was admitted to priest's orders in 1681, and elected preacher at Highgate Chapel, London, in 1695. He was one of the chaplains of Queen Anne, who presented him to the rectory of Shepperton. He also obtained the rectory of Hornsey in 1719, but continued to preach at Highgate until his death. Two volumes of his sermons were published in 1699 and in 1703. Died in 1731.

Atterbury, (LUFFMAN,) an English composer of glees and songs, born about 1740; died in 1800.

At'tĭ-cus, [Gr. Ἀττικός,] a philosopher of the Platonic school, lived in the reign of Marcus Aurelius, about 175 A.D. His works are not extant.

Atticus, an Athenian, who was raised from indigence to affluence by the discovery of a vast treasure in his house or land near Athens. He was the father of Herodes Atticus the rhetorician. (See HERODES.) He announced his discovery of the treasure to the emperor Nerva, who answered that he might use it or *abuse* it as he pleased. He left by will an annuity of one mina* to each citizen of Athens.

Atticus, a native of Sebaste, in Armenia, was irregularly chosen Patriarch of Constantinople in 406 A.D., in place of John Chrysostom, who had been deposed. Pope Innocent refused to recognize the appointment; but they were finally reconciled. He wrote a treatise "On Faith and Virginity," ("De Fide et Virginitate,") not extant. Died in 425 A.D.

Atticus, (DIONYSIUS,) a Greek rhetorician, a native of Pergamus, lived at Athens about 50 B.C.

Atticus, (TITUS POMPONIUS,) a Roman philosopher and scholar, celebrated for his benevolence, moderation, and mediatorial services, was born in 109 B.C. He belonged to the equestrian order, and inherited an ample fortune. On becoming heir to his uncle Quintus Cæcilius, he assumed that name, or prefixed it to his original name. During the civil war between Sulla and Marius, he retired to Athens, where he remained many years, and gained the favour of the Athenians by his munificence. He returned to Rome about 65 B.C., and devoted his time chiefly to literature, adhering constantly to a resolution, which he had formed in early life, to accept no public office and to maintain neutrality between hostile parties. He was an intimate friend of Cicero, with whom he corresponded regularly for many years, and was on friendly terms with Cæsar, Pompey, Brutus, Mark Antony, and Augustus. When Brutus was forced to fly from Italy, Atticus sent him a million sesterces.† He also afforded relief to the wife of Antony in her adversity. In philosophy he favoured the sect of Epicurus. He wrote an epitome of Roman history, entitled "Annales," comprising a period of seven centuries, and several other works, which are all lost. He was distinguished for fine literary taste, and excelled in the composition of epigrammatic inscriptions. His daughter Pomponia (or Attica) was married to M. Vipsanius Agrippa, the chief minister of Augustus, and his granddaughter Vipsania Agrippina was the wife of the emperor Tiberius. Many letters of Cicero to Atticus are extant. Died in 32 B.C.

See "Life of Atticus," by CORNELIUS NEPOS; CICERO, "Letters to Atticus," in Middleton's "Life of Cicero;" HÜLLEMANN, "Diatribe in T. Pomponium Atticum," 1838; DRUMANN, "Geschichte Roms;" BAYLE, "Historical and Critical Dictionary."

---

* About twenty dollars of our money; but, owing to the comparative scarcity of the precious metals in that age, its relative value was probably very much greater.
† About forty thousand dollars. See preceding note.

At'tĭ-la, [Gr. Ἀττίλας; in German, ETZEL, êt'sĕl, or ATZEL, ât'sĕl,] a famous heathen conqueror, chief of the Huns, surnamed THE SCOURGE OF GOD, was a son of Mundzuk or Mundzuccus. About 432 A.D. he succeeded his uncle Roas as king of the nomadic Huns who lived in Pannonia and north of the Danube. In a few years he extended his domination over Scythia and Germany. He invaded the Roman Empire in 447 or 446, defeated the armies of Theodosius, Emperor of the East, in several battles, and obliged him to treat for peace, which he obtained by the payment of an annual tribute. Marcian, who began to reign in 450 A.D., refused to pay tribute, and said, in reply to the messengers of Attila, "I have gold for my friends, and iron for my enemies." The haughty barbarian sent to the Emperors of the East and West a message in these terms: "Attila, my master and thy master, commands thee to prepare without delay a palace for his reception." He demanded in marriage Honoria, a sister of the emperor Valentinian, but the latter refused his consent. Having led a large army (estimated at seven hundred thousand men) into Gaul, he was defeated in a great battle by the Roman general Aëtius and Theodoric the Visigoth near Châlons-sur-Marne in 451 A.D. Soon after this date he invaded Italy, the northern part of which he ravaged without meeting any resistance. The emperor sued for peace by the mediation of Pope Leo I., who, in a personal interview with Attila, induced him to grant a truce and to retire from Italy. He died in Hungary in 453 or 454 A.D., and was buried by night. It is reported that he said "the grass could not grow where his horse had passed." He left sons named Ellac and Dengezic; but they did not inherit his abilities nor his power. Attila is the hero of many old German legends and songs, especially of the Niebelungen-Lied.

See JORNANDES, "De Rebus Geticis;" "Attila," an epic poem, (with notes,) by Rev. WILLIAM HERBERT, 1828; GIBBON, "Decline and Fall of the Roman Empire," chaps. xxxiv. and xxxv.; CALLIMACHUS EXPERIENS, "De Gestis Attilæ," 1541; JUVENCUS CÆLIUS CALLANUS, "Vita Attilæ," 1502; J. M. BARBIERI, "La Guerra d'Attila," 1568; FESSLER, "Attila König der Hunnen," 1794; AMÉDÉE THIERRY, "Attila dans les Gaules," 1852; LINK, "Ueber Attila König der Hunnen," 1780; DR. HOEFER, in the "Nouvelle Biographie Générale."

Attinghausen, ât'ting-hŏw'zĕn, a Swiss patriot, who was landamman of the canton of Uri in 1306, and one of the founders of the federation between the cantons of Uri, Schwitz, and Unterwalden.

Attiret, ▲'te'r▲', (CLAUDE FRANÇOIS,) a French sculptor, born at Dole in 1728, worked at Dijon. By order of the magistrates of Dole, he executed a statue of Louis XVI., the first erected to that prince. Died in 1804.

Attiret, (JEAN DENIS,) a French painter and Jesuit, an uncle of the preceding, born at Dole in 1702. He worked at Lyons and Avignon. In 1737 he went to Pekin, in consequence of a request from the French missionaries that an artist should be sent to them. He gained the favour of the emperor Kien-Lung, by whom he was employed in his palace for many years. Kien-Lung also required the artist to accompany him in a military expedition and to paint the battles or pomps which he witnessed. Attiret, from motives of policy, conformed to the Chinese taste, and used water-colours, or distemper, because the emperor disliked the gloss of oil-colours. Died at Pekin in 1768.

See "Nouvelle Biographie Générale."

Attius, (L.,) a Roman poet. See ACCIUS.

At'to or **Ac'to** [Fr. ATTON, â'tôN'] **Ver-çel-lĭ-en'-sis,** a French monk, who was chosen Bishop of Vercelli about 924 A.D. His works were published in 1768.

At'tucks, (CRISPUS,) a half-breed Indian or mulatto, was the leader of the mob in the fray known as the "Boston Massacre," which occurred on the 5th of March, 1770. He was killed by the soldiers on that occasion, and was buried with much pomp.

Attumonelli, ât-too-mo-nel'lee, (MICHELE,) a distinguished physician and medical writer, born at Andria, in Naples, 1753, in 1799 removed to Paris, where he had an extensive practice. Died in 1826.

Att'wâ-tẽr, (RUSSELL,) a soldier of the American Revolution, born in Cheshire, Connecticut, in 1762. In the attack of the British on New Haven he was wounded

---

ā, ē, ī, ō, ū, ȳ, *long;* ă, ĕ, ĭ, ŏ, ŭ, ў, *same, less prolonged;* ă, ĕ, ĭ, ŏ, ŭ, ў, *short;* a, ẹ, ị, ọ, *obscure;* fär, fåll, fåt; mĕt; nŏt; gŏŏd; mŏŏn;

and left for dead on the field, but recovered. After the defeat of Napoleon at the battle of Waterloo he was employed by the friends of the emperor to purchase a tract of land in Northern New York, which they intended as a retreat for the emperor should he succeed in making his escape. But on hearing that Napoleon had given himself up to the English, the project was abandoned. Died in 1851.

Att′wood or **At′wood**, (THOMAS,) an English judge, who officiated in the island of Dominica. He wrote "Observations on the true Method of Treatment of the Negro Slaves in the British West-India Islands," (1790,) and "History of Dominica," (1791.) Died in prison for debt in 1793.

Attwood or **Atwood**, (THOMAS,) a distinguished English composer for the church, theatre, etc., born in 1767, was a favourite pupil of Mozart, at Vienna. He was patronized by the Prince of Wales, (George IV.,) and was elected organist of Saint Paul's Cathedral in 1795, and composer to the chapel royal in 1796. His anthem "The King shall rejoice," composed for the coronation of George IV., was much admired. He became organist to the chapel royal in 1837. He composed a number of popular songs and glees, among which are "The Harp's Wild Notes," and "In this Fair Vale," several operas, and a grand anthem for the coronation of William IV., (1830.) Died in 1838.

See FÉTIS, "Biographie Universelle des Musiciens."

At′well, (GEORGE,) of Cambridge, England, published a "Defence of Astrology," (1660,) and "The Faithful Surveyor," (1662.) Sir Isaac Newton is said to have expressed a favourable opinion of him.

At′wood or **Att′wood**, (GEORGE,) an English mathematician, eminent as a lecturer on natural philosophy, was born in 1745. He became a Fellow and tutor of Trinity College, Cambridge. In 1784 he published a "Treatise on the Rectilinear Motion and Rotation of Bodies," which was highly esteemed, and contained the first account of the machine since called by the name of "Atwood," by which the laws of simply accelerated motion are verified. His "Dissertation on the Construction of Arches" (1801) is a work of much merit. According to some writers, he was financial private secretary to William Pitt. Died in 1807.

Atwood, (WILLIAM,) an English constitutional and political writer, was chief-justice of New York, and lived about 1700. He wrote, besides several historical or legal treatises, a tract entitled "The Superiority and Direct Dominion of the Crown of England over the Crown and Kingdom of Scotland," (1704,) which was answered by James Anderson.

Atzel. See ATTILA.

Aubais, d′, dō′bȧ′, (CHARLES de Barchi—deh bȧR′-she′,) a French marquis, noted as a patron of literature, was born near Nîmes in 1686. He published, with Léon Ménard, "Documents for the History of France, with Notes," ("Pièces fugitives pour servir à l'Histoire," etc., 3 vols., 1759.) Died in 1777.

Auban. See SAINT-AUBAN.

Aubenton. See DAUBENTON.

Auber, ō′baiR′, a French economist, born at Rouen about the middle of the eighteenth century. He wrote several able reports on Agriculture, Internal Improvements, etc., as secretary of the "Société d'Émulation" of Rouen. Died in 1804.

Auber, (DANIEL FRANÇOIS ESPRIT,) an eminent French composer, born at Caen in January, 1784, was a pupil of Cherubini. His first production, "Le Séjour militaire," (1813,) was coldly received, but his comic opera "La Bergère Châtelaine" (1820) was a complete success. In partnership with Eugène Scribe, he composed the music of many popular operas which are remarkable for originality and grace. His opera "La Muette de Portici," (1828,) commonly known as "Masaniello," had great success, and is called his master-piece. "In this are found," says M. Denne-Baron, "situations strong and impassioned, rendered with admirable energy, *nuances* which the composer has seized with exquisite delicacy, displaying all the riches of a style diversified to infinity." Among his most popular comic operas are "Fra Diavolo," (1830,) "Lestocq," (1834,) "Le Domino noir,"

(1837,) and "Haydée," (1847.) He was chosen a member of the Institute in 1829. He was recently director of music in the chapel of Napoleon III.

See FÉTIS, "Biographie Universelle des Musiciens;" "Nouvelle Biographie Générale;" LOMÉNIE, "Galerie des Contemporains."

Auberi. See AUBERY.

Auberlen, ŏw′bĕr-len, (SAMUEL GOTTLOB,) a German composer and organist, born near Stuttgart in 1758. He composed symphonies, cantatas, duets, and music for various instruments. About 1816 he founded a school for choral singing. He was afterwards organist of the cathedral of Ulm. Died about 1830.

See S. G. AUBERLEN, "Leben, Meinungen," etc.; FÉTIS, "Biographie Universelle des Musiciens."

Aubernon, ō′bĕR′nôN′, (PHILIPPE,) a French administrator, born in 1757, became commissary of the army of the Alps in 1792. Died in 1832.

Aubert, ō′baiR′, (ANAÏS, ȧ′nȧ′,) MADEMOISELLE, a French dramatic artist, born about 1800.

Aubert, (AUGUSTIN,) a French painter, born in 1781, lived at Marseilles. He painted history, landscapes, and portraits with success. Died in 1832.

Aubert, (ESPRIT,) born near Avignon, was the author of a dictionary in Latin, with synonyms in Greek and French, published at Lyons in 1613.

Aubert, FATHER, a Jesuit, who lived in the first half of the eighteenth century, and wrote several works, principally on natural history.

Aubert, (FRANÇOIS,) a French physician and medical writer, born at Dormans, in Champagne, in 1695; died about 1760.

Aubert, (FRANÇOIS,) a canon and religious writer, born at Paris in 1709. He wrote a "Refutation of Rousseau and his Oracles"—*i.e.* Rousseau, Voltaire, etc., (1768.)

Aubert, (FRANÇOIS HUBERT,) a French advocate, born at Nancy in 1720. He wrote a "Life of Stanislas Lecszinski, King of Poland and Duke of Lorraine,"(1769,) which was praised by Fréron. He passed about twenty-five years in the service and at the court of this prince.

Aubert, (GUILLAUME,) an eloquent French advocate, born at Poitiers about 1534. He published a fragment called a "History of the Wars waged by the Christians, under Godfrey of Bouillon, against the Turks," (1559.) Died about 1600.

Aubert, (JACQUES,) a French physician, born at Vendôme. He wrote a "Treatise on the Plague," ("Libellus de Peste," 1571,) and other works. Died in 1586.

Aubert, (JEAN LOUIS,) ABBÉ, a French poet, fabulist, and critic, born in Paris in 1731, was for many years editor of the "Petites Affiches," a journal, which he made popular. In 1756 he published a collection of fables, which had a European reputation. Voltaire found in them philosophy adorned with the charms of wit, and wrote to Aubert, "You have the merit of style and of invention in a department where every thing seemed to have been said. You have placed yourself beside La Fontaine." His drama, in verse, on "The Death of Abel," was less successful. He was appointed professor of French literature in the Collège Royal, Paris, in 1773. Died in 1814.

See QUÉRARD, "La France Littéraire."

Aubert, (MICHEL,) a French engraver, born in Paris in 1700. He engraved some works of Rubens and of several Italian masters, also portraits of painters for D'Argenville's work, "The Lives of the Most Famous Painters." Died in Paris in 1757.

Aubert, (PIERRE,) a literary French lawyer, born at Lyons in 1642. He published a new and enlarged edition of Richelet's "Dictionary of the French Language," (3 vols., 1728,) and presented to the city of Lyons a large library for the public use. Died in 1733.

Aubert, (PIERRE FRANÇOIS OLIVIER,) a violoncellist, musical composer, and author of a History of Music, born at Amiens in 1765.

See FÉTIS, "Biographie Universelle des Musiciens."

Aubert, SAINT, became Bishop of Avranches, in France, in the early part of the eighth century. He founded the monastery of Mont Saint-Michel, on a high rock in the sea, on the coast of France.

Aubert de la Chesnaye des Bois, ō′baiR′ deh lä shȧ′nȧ′ dä bwä, (FRANÇOIS ALEXANDRE,) a French compiler, born at Ernée, in Mayenne or Maine, in 1699. He published "Historical, Philosophical, and Critical Correspondence in answer to the *Lettres Juives*," (3 vols., 1739,) a "Military Dictionary," and other dictionaries; also, "Critical Letters on the Romans, English, and French," (1743.) Died in Paris in 1784.

Aubert (or **Gaubert**) **de Puicibot**, ō'baiʀ' dĕh pwe'se'bo', a French troubadour, born in Limousin, after a life of dissipation entered a monastery. Died in 1263.

Aubert de Vertot. See VERTOT.

Aubert de Vitry, ō'baiʀ' dĕh ve'tʀe', (FRANÇOIS JEAN PHILIBERT,) a French writer and translator, born in Paris in 1765. He published in 1792 "Studies on Education," and wrote against the Jacobins in 1793. During the republic and the empire of Napoleon he filled several civil offices. He translated "Memoirs of Goethe" from the German, (1823,) and several works from- the English. Died in 1849.

See QUÉRARD, "La France Littéraire."

Aubert du Bayet, ō'baiʀ'dü bā'yȁ', (JEAN BAPTISTE ANNIBAL,) a French general, born in Louisiana in 1759. He fought under La Fayette for the United States, and was elected in 1791 to the French legislative assembly, in which he acted with the popular party. Having re-entered the army, he rose to the rank of general of division, and in 1793 commanded at the famous siege of Mentz, which he surrendered to the Prussians, He was minister of war about three months in 1795, and was ambassador at Constantinople, where he died in December, 1797.

Aubert du Petit-Thouars. See DU PETIT-THOU-ARS.

Aubertin, ō'bĕʀ'tȁn', (DOMINIQUE,) an adjutant-general in the French army, and author of "Memoirs on the War of La Vendée," born at Lunéville in 1751; died in 1825.

Aubertin, (EDME, êdm,) a learned French Protestant, born at Châlons-sur-Marne in 1595, became minister at Charenton, near Paris. He published in 1629 "The Conformity of the Creed of the Church with Saint Augustine in Relation to the Eucharist," which was received with favour by the Protestants, and was answered by the great Arnauld. Died in 1652.

See BAYLE, "Historical and Critical Dictionary."

Aubert-Roche, ō'baiʀ' rosh, (LOUIS,) a French physician, graduated in Paris in 1833, and passed some years in the service of Mehemet Ali, Viceroy of Egypt. In 1839 he published a treatise "On the Plague and Typhus of the East," in which he argues that the plague is not contagious.

Aubery, ō'bʀe', (ANTOINE,) a French historical writer, born in Paris in 1616. He published a "General History of Cardinals," (5 vols., 1642-49,) a "History of Cardinal Richelieu," (1660,) "Mémoires pour l'Histoire du Cardinal de Richelieu," (2 vols., 1660,) and a "History of Cardinal Mazarin," (2 vols., 1695,) which Beuchot calls glossed over (*fardée*) and inexact. Died in 1695.

See NICÉRON, "Mémoires."

Aubery, (CLAUDE,) a French physician, who lived in the sixteenth century. Having adopted the Reformed religion, he removed to Lausanne, where he became professor of philosophy. His works, on religious and medical subjects, display great erudition. Died in 1596.

Aubery, (JACQUES,) a French jurist and advocate, lived at Paris between 1550 and 1600.

Aubery, (JEAN,) physician to the Duke of Montpensier, was born in the Bourbonnais in the latter part of the sixteenth century. He wrote several medical works, and a "History of the City of Autun."

Aubery, (LOUIS,) Sieur du Maurier, (mō're-à',) a French historical writer of the seventeenth century, studied at Leyden, and travelled in the north of Europe. His chief work is "Memoirs to illustrate the History of Holland and the other United Provinces," ("Mémoires pour servir à l'Histoire de Hollande," etc., 1680,) which passed through many editions and is praised for its veracity and impartiality. Died in 1687.

Aubespine, de l', dĕh lō'bĕs'pĕn', (CHARLES,) Marquis de Châteauneuf, and Abbé de Préaux, a French diplomatist, notorious for intrigues, born in Paris in 1580, was a son of Guillaume de l'Aubespine. After he had served in several foreign missions, he appointed

keeper of the seals in 1630. He is censured for his severity or injustice to Marshals de Marillac and de Montmorency, at whose trial he presided. He was deprived of office and imprisoned by Richelieu in 1633. Died in 1653.

Aubespine, de l', (CLAUDE,) born about 1508, was secretary of state and finance for a long period, and was employed by several kings in important diplomatic missions. He was one of the ablest negotiators of his time. He left a son Guillaume. Died in 1567.

Aubespine, de l', (GABRIEL,) a brother of Charles, and grandson of Claude, noticed above, was born in 1579. He became Bishop of Orléans in 1604, and displayed much learning in several works, one of which is entitled "On the Ancient Rites of the Church," ("De veteribus Ecclesiæ Ritibus," 1623.) Died in 1630.

Aubespine, de l', (MADELEINE,) a daughter of Claude, and aunt of Gabriel, was celebrated for her beauty, talents, and accomplishments. She wrote some poetical and prose compositions, and translated Ovid's Epistles.

Aubeterre, d', dōb'taiʀ', (DAVID **Bouchard**—boo'-shãʀ',) VICOMTE, a French officer, born at Geneva, of a Protestant family. He became a Roman Catholic, and was appointed governor of Périgord by Henry IV. He was killed at the siege of L'Isle in 1598.

Aubeterre, d', (FRANÇOIS **d'Esparbès de Lussan** —dĕs-pãʀ'bǎ' dĕh lü'sǒn',) VICOMTE, a French officer who fought for Henry IV. in the civil war, became a marshal of France in 1620. Died in 1628.

Aubeterre, d', (JOSEPH HENRI **Bouchard d'Esparbez**—boo'shãʀ'dĕs'pãʀ'bǎ',)MARQUIS, a French general, born in 1714, served with distinction in several campaigns, became maréchal-de-camp in 1748 and lieutenant-general in 1758. He was afterwards ambassador to Vienna, Madrid, and Rome, and proved himself an able negotiator. In 1783 he was made marshal of France. Died in 1788.

Aubignac, d', dō'bĕn'yǎk', (FRANÇOIS **Hédelin**—hǎd'lǎn',) ABBÉ, a mediocre French critic and dramatist, a grandson of Ambroise Paré, born in Paris in 1604. He wrote "Pratique du Théâtre," (1669,) which, says La Harpe, "is a dull and tedious commentary on Aristotle;" "Zénobie," a tragedy in prose, (1647;) and epigrams and *brochures* against Corneille and Ménage. Died in 1676.

Aubigné, d', (MERLE.) See D'AUBIGNÉ.

Aubigné, d', dō'bĕn'yà', (THÉODORE **Agrippa**—ȁ'gʀe'pȁ',) a French Huguenot historian, warrior, and poet, remarkable for his learning, wit, and audacity, was born at Saint-Maury, in Saintonge, in 1550. He was grandfather of Madame de Maintenon. It is reported that he translated the "Crito" of Plato in his eighth year. At the age of thirteen he was sent to a college in Geneva, from which he ran away two years later. He fought for the Huguenots in 1567 and 1568, a few years after which he entered the service of Henry of Navarre, who prized him highly as a partisan and companion in perilous adventures, and also employed him in negotiations. He sometimes, however, offended Henry by his bold sarcasms and epigrams. In 1586 he raised a regiment at his own expense to fight against the League. He rendered important services at the battle of Coutras, (1587,) and was intrusted by Henry IV. with the custody of Cardinal Bourbon, a competitor for the crown. In 1616 he published the first volume of his valuable History of his own Time, entitled "Histoire universelle depuis l'An 1550 jusqu'à l'An 1601," (3 vols., 1616-20,) which is his greatest work. A sentence of death was passed against him by the French court in 1621, but he had previously escaped to Geneva. The pretext for this sentence was that he had used the materials of a ruined church to repair a fortress. He died at Geneva in 1630. Among his works are a satire called "Catholic Confession of Sieur de Sancy," "Adventures of Baron de Fœneste," a satirical romance, (1617-20,) and interesting autobiographic memoirs, ("Histoire secrète de T. A. d'Aubigné, écrite par lui-même," (1729-31.)

See M. A. SAVOUS, "Vie d'Aubigné;" BAYLE, "Historical and Critical Dictionary;" DAVILA, "History of the Civil Wars in France;" "Nouvelle Biographie Générale."

Aubigné de la Fosse, d', dō'bĕn'yà' dĕh lǎ fos, (NATHAN,) [called in Latin ALBIN'EUS or ALBINÆ'US,] a French physician, born near Pluviers in 1601, was a son of Théodore Agrippa d'Aubigné, (according to Beuchot of the "Biographie Universelle.") He practised at Geneva, the citizenship of which he obtained in 1627, and published "Bibliotheca Chemica Contracta," (1654.) He died at an advanced age.

Aubigny, d', dŏ'bĕn'ye', (ROBERT STEWART,) marshal of France, served under Charles VIII. in Italy, and was made a marshal in 1514. He died in 1544.

Aubin. See SAINT-AUBIN.

Aubin, ō'bằN', (N.,) a French Protestant minister, born at Loudun in the seventeenth century. He took refuge in Holland on the repeal of the edict of Nantes, 1685. His principal work is "Histoire des Diables de Loudun," (1693,) an account of some nuns said to have been possessed by devils.

Aublet, ō'blằ', (JEAN BAPTISTE CHRISTOPHE **Fusée**—fü'zà',) a French botanist, born at Salon, in Provence, in 1720. He passed about nine years (1752–61) in the Isle of France, and published a list of plants growing there. In 1762 he was sent by the government as apothecary-botanist to French Guiana, in which he collected many specimens. His greatest work is a description of these, with figures, "Histoire des Plantes de la Guiane Françoise," (4 vols., 1775,) which was highly esteemed. It describes nearly four hundred new species. His herbarium was purchased by Sir Joseph Banks. Died in 1778.

See "Biographie Médicale;" "Nouvelle Biographie Générale."

Aubrée, ō'brà', (RENÉ,) a French general, born at Rennes in 1763, was killed at Saragossa in 1808.

Aubrey, aw'bre, (JOHN,) F.R.S., an eminent English antiquary, born at Easton-Piers, Wiltshire, in March, 1626, inherited several valuable estates. He was educated at Oxford, and became a diligent collector of literary and antiquarian materials. In 1656 he was a member of the club of Commonwealth's Men, founded on the principles of Harrington's "Oceana." Soon after 1666 he was reduced to poverty by law-suits and other causes. As a writer he shows much credulity, particularly in his "Miscellanies," (1696,) in which he treats of omens, apparitions, oracles, knockings, etc. Anthony Wood's account of Milton was transcribed from a manuscript of Aubrey, who was acquainted with that poet. Died in 1697. He left in manuscript "The Natural History and Antiquities of Surrey," which was published in 1719, and valuable memoirs of English poets, etc., published in 1813, under the title of "Letters written by Eminent Persons in the Seventeenth and Eighteenth Centuries."

See "Memoir of John Aubrey," by JOHN BRITTON.

Aubrey or **Aw'brey,** (WILLIAM,) an eminent civilian, born in the county of Brecon, Wales, in 1529 or 1530, belonged to the same family as the preceding. He was appointed regius professor of civil law at Oxford in 1553, and afterwards a member of the council of the marches of Wales and a master in chancery. He was distinguished for wisdom and learning. Died in 1595.

See TANNER, "Bibliotheca Britannico-Hibernica."

Aubriet, ō'bre'ằ', (CLAUDE,) a French painter of flowers, and an able botanist, born at Châlons-sur-Marne in 1651. He accompanied Tournefort to the Levant, and on his return was appointed painter to the king at the Jardin des Plantes. He added to the collection of designs of plants on vellum commenced by Nicolas Robert, designed the plates of Sebastien Vaillant's "Botanicon Parisiense," (1727,) and illustrated Tournefort's "Éléments de Botanique." Died in 1743.

See NAGLER, "Allgemeines Künstler-Lexikon."

Aubrion, ō'bre'ŏN', (JEAN,) a French historian of the fifteenth century, was a burgess of Metz, and wrote a "Chronicle of Metz from 1464 to 1500." Died about 1500.

Aubriot, ō'bre'o', (HUGUES,) a prévôt (provost) of Paris, who fortified and drained that city by subterranean channels, (*égouts*,) and, by his strict police, made some powerful enemies, who prosecuted him for heresy and other crimes. He was condemned and imprisoned in 1381, and liberated by a party of insurgents in 1382. He is said to have died the same year.

Aubrussel, l', lō'brü'sĕl', (IGNACE,) a French Jesuit and writer, born at Verdun in 1663; died in Spain in 1730.

Aubry, ō'bre', (CHARLES,) a French Latin poet, flourished about 1700.

Aubry, (CHARLES LOUIS,) a French economist and writer, born at La Ferté-Milon in 1746; died in 1817.

Aubry, (CLAUDE CHARLES,) a French general, born at Bourg-en-Bresse in 1773. For his services on the Danube in 1809 he was made a general of brigade. He distinguished himself by the construction of a bridge across the Berezina, which saved the remains of Napoleon's army retreating from Moscow. He was rewarded with the title of count and the rank of general of division. He was killed at Leipsic in 1813.

Aubry, (ÉTIENNE,) a successful French painter of portrait and *genre*, born at Versailles in 1745; died in 1781.

Aubry, (FRANÇOIS,) a French revolutionist, born in Paris about 1750, became in 1792 a member of the Convention, in which he acted with the *Plaine*. He protested against the proscription of the Girondists, May 31, 1793, and was arrested by the Jacobins. In April, 1795, he was appointed a member of the Committee of Public Safety, and succeeded Carnot in the direction of military operations. Among the acts of his administration was his refusal to employ Bonaparte, who solicited a command in 1795. Aubry belonged to the party which was defeated September 4, 1797, and he was deported to Guiana. Died in exile about 1800.

Aubry, (JACQUES CHARLES,) a French jurist, born in 1688; died in 1739.

Aubry, (JEAN,) a French alchemist and quack doctor, practised in Paris about 1650–60. According to Gui-Patin, he was *merus et ignarus nebulo,* (an "arrant and ignorant knave.")

Aubry, (JEAN BAPTISTE,) a learned French Benedictine, born near Épinal in 1736. He wrote "The Philosophic Friend," ("L'Ami philosophique," 1776,) and other works. Died in 1809.

Aubry, (JEAN FRANÇOIS,) physician-in-ordinary to Louis XVI. of France, was a native of Luxeuil, where he died in 1795. He published a well-known work called "The Oracles of Cos," (1778.) He was a great admirer of Hippocrates.

Aubry, (MARIE.) See GOUGES.

Aubry, (PHILIPPE CHARLES,) a French translator and poet, born at Versailles in 1744, was a teacher of languages. He published the "Wit of Addison," ("Esprit d'Addison,") a French version of Goethe's "Sorrows of Werther," (1777,) and a volume of lyric poems, called "Le Pétrarque Français," (1799.) Died in 1812.

Aubry, d', dŏ'bre', or **Aubery, d',** dŏb're', (JEAN,) commonly known as ABBÉ AUBRY, an ecclesiastic, afterwards a physician and medical writer of considerable celebrity, born at Montpellier about 1700.

Aubry de Montdidier, ō'bre' dĕh mŏN'de'de-à', a French knight, murdered by Richard de Macaire in 1371. His dog pursued Macaire until the king ordered that the affair should be decided by a combat between the dog and the suspected assassin, who, having been conquered in the contest, confessed his crime.

Aubry du Bouchet, ō'bre' dü boo'shằ', a deputy of the States-General, and originator of the general registry of estates, was born in 1740 at La Ferté-Milon, in Aisne.

Aubry-Lecompte, ō'bre' lçh kŏNt', (HYACINTHE LOUIS VICTOR JEAN BAPTISTE,) a French designer and lithographer, born at Nice in 1797, produced lithographs of "The Holy Family," after Poussin, and of some works of Raphael, among which is the Sistine Madonna. Died in 1858.

Aubusson, d', (FRANÇOIS,) DUC DE FEUILLADE. See FEUILLADE.

Aubusson, d', dŏ'bü'sŏN', (JEAN,) a troubadour of the thirteenth century, was patronized by Frederick II., Emperor of Germany.

See MILLOT, "Histoire littéraire des Troubadours."

Aubusson, d', (JEAN,) a French writer, who lived about 1550.

Aubusson, d', (PIERRE,) grand master of the order of Saint John of Jerusalem, was born of French family in 1423. He entered that order (at Rhodes) about 1450, and was employed in important missions to Paris and Rome. In 1476 he was elected grand master. He fortified Rhodes and prepared for a vigorous defence against Mahomet II., who besieged the city of Rhodes in 1480 with an army of about one hundred thousand men. The Turks were repulsed with great loss, after a severe fight, in which Aubusson was wounded in several places. In 1501 he was chosen captain-general of a league of Christian princes against the Moslems, the formation of which had been the great object of his life. This enterprise failed, partly from the jealousies of the allies. Died in 1503.

See BOUHOURS, "Histoire de Pierre d'Aubusson," 1676; "Nouvelle Biographie Générale."

Auchmuty, ä′mu-te, (?) [Scotch pron. äн′moo-te,] (ROBERT,) an eminent lawyer of Massachusetts, born in the north of Scotland, settled in Boston early in the eighteenth century. He published a pamphlet entitled "The Importance of Cape Breton to the British Nation." Died in Boston in 1750.

Auchmuty, (ROBERT,) a son of the preceding. He devoted himself to the law, and in 1768 became judge of the court of admiralty. In 1770 he was associated with John Adams in the trial of Captain Preston, but upon the breaking out of the war sided with the royalists. Died in England.

Auchmuty, (SAMUEL,) D.D., a distinguished Episcopal clergyman, brother of the preceding, was born in Boston in 1725. He graduated at Harvard in 1742, studied divinity at Oxford, and, on returning to America, became assistant rector of Trinity Church, New York, and afterwards had charge of all the Episcopal churches in the city. Died in 1777.

Auchmuty, ä′mu-te, (?) (Sir SAMUEL,) a British general, a son of the preceding, born in New York in 1756. He served in several campaigns against the United States, 1776–78, after which he was employed about twelve years in India. He acted as adjutant-general to the army in Egypt in 1801 and 1802. Having obtained in 1806 command of the British troops in South America, with the rank of brigadier-general, he took the strongly fortified city of Montevideo from the Spaniards in 1807. He was appointed to the chief command at Madras in 1810, and captured Java in 1811. In 1813 he returned to England, and became a lieutenant-general. Died at Dublin in 1822.

See "Narrative of the Operations of a Small British Force employed in the Reduction of Montevideo," London, 1807.

Auck′land, (GEORGE EDEN,) EARL OF, a son of William Eden, noticed below, was born in 1784. On his father's death in 1814, he entered the House of Lords, as an adherent of the Whig party. In 1834 he was appointed first lord of the admiralty, and in 1835 sent to India as Governor-General. Among the important events of his administration was the disastrous war against the Afghans, (1838–39.) He was recalled in 1842. Died in 1849.

Auckland, (WILLIAM EDEN,) LORD, an English diplomatist, born about 1750, was one of three commissioners appointed in 1778 to negotiate with the revolted American colonies and restore the British dominion over them. In 1785 he was sent as ambassador to France, with which he negotiated a commercial treaty. He published "The Principles of the Penal Laws," (1771,) a treatise "On the Population of England," (1786,) and other works. Died in 1814.

Auclère, ō′klaiʀ′, (GABRIEL ANDRÉ,) a revolutionist, born in Argenton, France, about 1750, sought to substitute paganism for Christianity. Died in 1815.

Aucour. See BARBIER D'AUCOUR.

Auda, ŏw′dä, (DOMENICO,) a Franciscan monk and medical writer, born near Nice towards the end of the sixteenth century.

Audæus, au-dee′us, [Gr. Αὐδαῖος,] or **Au′dï-us,** [Gr. Αὔδιος; Fr. AUDÉE, ō′dà′,] the founder of a sect in the fourth century A.D., was born in Mesopotamia. Epiphanius ascribes his secession from the church to persecution which his zeal against the luxury and vices of the clergy had provoked, rather than to heterodox opinions.

Aude, ōd, (JEAN,) a French dramatist, born at or near Apt in 1755. He was secretary to the celebrated Buffon, and author of several dramas. He is said to have written a Life of Buffon. Died in 1841.

Audebert, ō′daiʀ′, (GERMAIN,) a French lawyer and Latin poet, born at Orléans in 1518, was the author

of three Latin poems in praise of Venice, Rome, and Naples, entitled "Venetia," (1583,) "Roma," (1585,) and "Parthenope," (1585.) He was decorated with the collar of Saint Mark by the senate of Venice. Died in 1598.

Audebert, (JEAN BAPTISTE,) an eminent French painter, engraver, and naturalist, was born at Rochefort in 1759. He first attained success as a miniature-painter, and afterwards became an enthusiastic student of natural history. He published, in 1800, a "Natural History of Apes, Lemurs, and Galeopitheci," with sixty-two plates, designed and engraved by himself, and printed in oil-colours by a new method which he invented. The description and engravings of this work are highly commended. His costly and splendid "History of Humming-Birds, Fly-Catchers, Jacamars, and Promerops" (1 vol., 1802) "is regarded," says Du Petit-Thouars, "as the most perfect work of the kind which has ever appeared." He died in 1800, leaving unfinished works on birds, which were edited by Vieillot and Desray.

See "Biographie Universelle;" LE BAS, "Dictionnaire encyclopédique de la France."

Audebert, SAINT. See AUBERT, SAINT.

Audée. See AUDÆUS.

Audefroi (ōd′fʀwä′) THE BASTARD, one of the most celebrated troubadours of the Langue d'Oil in the twelfth and thirteenth centuries. He is thought by some to have been the inventor of the "Romance."

Audenaerde, Audenarde, or **Oudenaerde, van,** pronounced alike vân ŏw-deh-nähʀ′deh, (ROBERT,) a Flemish portrait-painter and celebrated engraver, born at Ghent in 1663. He was a pupil of Carlo Maratta, many of whose works he engraved. He painted but few pictures. Died in 1743.

See DESCAMPS, "Vies des Peintres Flamands."

Audentius, aw-den′she-us, a Spanish theological writer of uncertain age, supposed to have lived in the third or fourth century. He wrote a treatise against heretics.

Audhumla, (Auðumla,) ŏw-tнŭm′la or ö-tнŭm′la, written also **Audhumbla** and **Œdumla,** [from auðr, "desert," and hum, "darkness,"] a mythic cow, which, according to the Norse mythology, came into existence simultaneously with the giant Ymir, who was nourished by her milk. She licked the salt frost-covered rocks, and there came forth a mighty being called Buri, whose son Bör was the father of Odin. Her name doubtless has reference to the primeval chaotic darkness in which she arose.

See THORPE'S "Northern Mythology," vol. i., pp. 4 and 140.

Audibert, ō′de′baiʀ′, an antiquary, born at Toulouse about 1720, wrote a treatise on the origin of that city. Died in 1770.

Audibert, (LOUIS FRANÇOIS Hilarion—e′lä′re′ŏn′,) a French *littérateur*, born at Marseilles about 1798, was master of requests several years, and resigned in 1830. Among his works is a "Mélange of Literature and History," (1839.)

Audibert, (URBAIN,) a French botanist, born at Tarascon (Bouches-du-Rhône) in 1789, was a pupil of De Candolle. He cultivated a nursery near Tarascon, and co-operated with Dunal and Requien in the completion of "Flore du Midi." He took an important part in the redaction of the "Nouveau Duhamel" and "Annals of French Agriculture." Died in 1846.

Audierne, ō′de′ärn′, (JACQUES,) a French geometer, born at Beauchamps about 1710. He taught mathematics in Paris, and published a "Treatise on Trigonometry," (1756,) and "Elements of Geometry," (1765.) Died about 1785.

Audiffred, ō′de′fʀĕd′, (J. P.,) a French mathematician of the eighteenth century, was joint author (with F. N. Babeuf) of a "Cadastre perpetuel," (1789.)

Audiffredi, ŏw-dĕf-fʀä′dee, (GIOVANNI BATTISTA,) an astronomer and bibliographer, born at Saorgio, near Nice, in 1714, resided at Rome. He published, besides other works, "Celestial Phenomena observed," ("Phænomena Cœlestia observata," 1753–56.) Died in 1794.

See DELAMBRE, "Histoire de l'Astronomie moderne."

Audiffret, ō′de′fʀä′, (HERCULE, ĕʀ′kül′,) a French theologian, born at Carpentras in 1603, was considered one of the most eloquent writers of his day. His "Ouvrages de Piété" (3 vols.) were published in 1675. He was an uncle of the pulpit orator Fléchier, whose education he directed. Died in 1659.

Audiffret, (JEAN BAPTISTE,) a French geographer, born at Marseilles about 1658, published "Geography, Ancient, Modern, and Historical," (2 vols., 1689–91.) Died in 1733.

See WATT's "Bibliotheca Britannica."

Audiffret, (POLYEUCTE, po'le'ükt',) a French monk and numismatist, born in Provence about 1750, had a rich cabinet of medals. Died in 1807.

Audiffret, d', dŏ'de'frȧ', (CHARLES LOUIS **Gaston**—gȧs'tôn',) MARQUIS, a French financier and senator, born of an Italian family at Paris in 1787. He served many years as chief clerk in the administration of the finances, and became president of the court of accounts (*cour des comptes*) in 1829. His "Financial System of France" (1839) was regarded as the best work to consult on the actual state of French finances. He was appointed a senator in 1852.

Audigier, ō'de'zhe-ȧ', a French historical writer of the seventeenth century, wrote a work on the Origin of the French, (1676.)

Audigier, a French historian of the eighteenth century, born at Clermont, was the author of a History of Auvergne, which remains in manuscript.

Audiguier, d', dŏ'de'ge-ȧ', (VITAL, ve'tȧl',) Sieur de la Ménor, (mȧ-noR',) a French writer, born near Villefranche, Guienne, about 1570. He fought for Henry IV. in several campaigns against the League. He gained an extensive but transient reputation by his novels, verses, and other works, among which are "La Philosophie soldade," (1604,) and "The Portrait of the World," ("Pourtrait du Monde," 1604.) His versions of Cervantes's Tales ("Novelas," 1618) were included by the French Academy among the best specimens of French writing. He was assassinated about 1625, or, according to some authorities, in 1630.

See BAYLE, "Historical and Critical Dictionary;" GOUJET, "Bibliothèque Française."

Audin, ō'dȧN', (J. M. V.,) a French historian and biographer, born at Lyons in 1793, became a resident of Paris. Among his chief works are a "History of the Life and Works of Luther," (2 vols., 1839,) and a "History of Leo X. and his Age." Died in 1851.

See QUÉRARD, "La France Littéraire."

Audinot, ō'de'nŏ', (NICOLAS **Médard**—mȧ'dȧR',) a French actor and writer of plays, born at Nancy about 1740; died at Paris in 1801.

Audin-Rouvière, ō'dȧN'roo've-air',(JOSEPH MARIE,) a French physician, born at Carpentras in 1764, lived chiefly in Paris. He published "La Médecine sans Médecin," ("Physic without a Doctor," 1794,) which was very popular and was translated into many languages. He vended a medicine called "Grains of Life," ("Grains de Vie.") Died in 1832.

See QUÉRARD, "La France Littéraire."

Audius. See AUDÆUS.

Audley, awd'le, originally **de Aldithley,** (HENRY, the first of the line of Lords Audley.) He supported John in his contest with the barons, and otherwise took a conspicuous part in the events of his time.

Audley, (JAMES,) LORD, son and successor of the preceding, took a prominent part in the support of Henry III. against the barons and the Welsh rebels. Died about 1272.

Audley, (JAMES,) Lord Audley of Helegh, an English nobleman, born about 1314, has been confounded with Sir James Audley, noticed below. He served with distinction in the army of Edward III. Died about 1386.

Audley or Audeley, (Sir JAMES,) a chivalrous attendant of the Black Prince, and one of the original knights of the order of the Garter. He displayed signal courage at the battle of Poictiers, (1356,) in which he was severely wounded. The Black Prince immediately retained him as his own knight, and several years later appointed him governor of Aquitaine. Died in 1369. The order of the Garter was instituted in 1344.

Audley or Awdeley, (JOHN,) a noted English printer, who lived about 1570, was the reputed author of several ballads and short poems.

Audley, (THOMAS,) Lord Audley of Walden, lord chancellor of England, was born in Essex about 1488. He became Speaker of the House of Commons about 1529, lord keeper of the great seal in 1532, and lord chancellor in 1533. He presided at the trial of Sir Thomas More, and is censured for his servile compliance with the arbitrary will of Henry VIII. in that affair and in other proceedings. He was created Baron Audley of Walden in 1538. Died without male issue in 1544.

See FULLER, "History of the Worthies of England;" LORD CAMPBELL, "Lives of the Lord Chancellors;" FOSS, "The Judges of England."

Audoin. See ALDUIN.

Audoin de Chaignebrun, ōd'wȧN' deh shȧñ'brŭn', (HENRI,) a French physician and medical writer, born in 1714; died in 1781.

Au-do'le-on, [Gr. Αὐδολέων,] a king of the Pæonians, reigned about 300 B.C.

Audouard, ō'doo-ȧR', (MATHIEU FRANÇOIS **Maxence**—mȧk'sôNss',) a French physician, born at Castres, in Tarn, in 1776. He served for many years as physician in the army. About 1822, the legislature voted him an annual pension of two thousand francs. He wrote treatises on intermittent fevers and on the yellow fever, (1807 –24.) Died in 1856.

Audouin, ō'doo-ȧN', (FRANÇOIS XAVIER,) a French revolutionist and economist, born at Limoges in 1766. He was commissioner in La Vendée about 1792, and during the republic was a judge of the court of cassation. He wrote a treatise "On Maritime Commerce and its Influence on the Power and Riches of States," (1800,) and a "History of the Administration of the War," (4 vols., 1811,) which are commended. Died in 1837.

Audouin, (JEAN VICTOR,) an eminent French entomologist and comparative anatomist, born in Paris in April, 1797, was educated as a physician. He began in 1818 to contribute, to various journals and the Transactions of Societies, numerous and valuable treatises on insects, which procured for him the friendship of Cuvier. He was associated with Milne-Edwards in researches upon the Crustacea and Annelida. In 1827 he married a daughter of Alexandre Brongniart. He succeeded Latreille as professor at the Muséum in 1833, and was admitted into the Academy of Sciences in 1838. Among his chief works is a "History of Insects which infest the Vine, especially the Pyrale, etc.," (1840–43.) He was one of the editors of the "Annales des Sciences naturelles," and left in manuscript several volumes on the economy of insects when he died, in November, 1841.

See "Éloges de J. V. Audouin," par MM. SERRES, CHEVREUL, and MILNE-EDWARDS, in the "Annales des Sciences naturelles;" "Nouvelle Biographie Générale."

Audouin, (PIERRE,) a skilful French engraver, born in Paris in 1768. He engraved, for Laurent's "Collection du Musée," "La belle Jardinière" of Raphael, the "Jupiter and Antiope" of Correggio, and other works. Died in 1822.

Audouin de Géronval, ō'doo-ȧN' deh zhȧ'rôn'vȧl', (MAURICE ERNEST,) a French writer and economist, born in Paris in 1802, was secretary of the Académie de l'Industrie. He wrote, besides several historical treatises and tales, a "Project of a Model Farm," adopted by the Institute in 1830. He is said to have originated the idea of a model farm. Died in 1839.

See QUÉRARD, "La France Littéraire."

Audoul, ō'dool', (GASPARD,) an advocate, and member of the Council of the Duke of Orléans, was born in Provence in the last half of the seventeenth century. He wrote a work upon the origin and powers of the régale.

Audra, ō'drȧ', (JOSEPH,) a French abbé and historian, born at Lyons about 1712, was a friend of Voltaire. He became professor of history at Toulouse about 1768, and published a "General History from the Time of Charlemagne to the Present Day," (1 vol., 1770,) which was eulogized by Voltaire, but censured as irreligious by the Archbishop of Brienne, who deprived him of his office. His chagrin on this account induced a brain-fever, of which he died in 1770.

See VOLTAIRE, "Correspondance," and GRIMM, "Correspondance."

ᵉ as *k*; ç as *s*; ḡ *hard*; ġ as *j*; G, H, K, *guttural*; N, *nasal*; R, *trilled*; ṡ as *z*; ŧh as in *this*. (☞See Explanations, p. 23.)

Audrade, ŏ'drȧd', [Lat. AUDRA'DUS,] called **Mod'-icus,** a French visionary, who professed to be inspired. He wrote a poem called the "Fountain of Life," ("Fons Vitæ.") Died about 854 A.D.

Audran, ŏ'drŏN', (BENOÎT,) an eminent French designer and engraver, a son of Germain, was born at Lyons in 1661, and became a pupil of his uncle Girard Audran. Among his best works are "The Seven Sacraments," after Poussin, and "The Brazen Serpent," after Le Brun. He also engraved some works of Raphael, Paul Veronese, and other Italians. He was patronized by Louis XIV. Died in 1721.

Audran, (CHARLES,) a French engraver, born in Paris in 1594, studied in Rome. He engraved prints after Titian, the Caracci, Domenichino, and other Italian masters. Died in 1674.

Audran, (CLAUDE,) a mediocre engraver, born in Paris in 1592, was a brother of the preceding. He settled at Lyons, where he died in 1677, leaving three sons, Germain, Girard, and Claude, all distinguished engravers or painters.

Audran, (CLAUDE,) a son of the preceding, born at Lyons in 1639 or 1640, was a painter of history. He assisted Le Brun in his "Battles of Alexander," and was an imitator of his style. He was admitted into the Academy of Paris in 1675, and became a professor in the same in 1681. Among his chief works is "The Miracle of the Five Loaves." Died in 1684.

Audran, (CLAUDE,) eldest son of Germain, a painter of grotesque subjects, was born at Lyons in 1658. Died in 1734.

Audran, (GERMAIN,) an engraver, born at Lyons in 1631, was a son of Claude I. He worked at his native city, and died in 1710, leaving four sons, Claude, Benoît, Jean, and Louis, who were artists.

Audran, (GIRARD or GÉRARD,) regarded by some as the greatest historical engraver that ever lived, was a son of Claude I., and was born at Lyons in 1640. After he had received instruction from his father, he studied several years in Rome, where he designed antique statues, copied with the crayon some works of Raphael, and became an excellent draughtsman. He returned to Paris about 1670, and was appointed engraver to the king, for whom he engraved Le Brun's "Battles of Alexander." These are Audran's masterpieces. Among his other works are two cartoons of Raphael, (the "Death of Ananias" and "Paul and Barnabas at Lystra,") "Coriolanus," after N. Poussin, and the "Martyrdom of Saint Agnes," after Domenichino. The point and graver in his hand assumed the powers of the pencil. By a bold mixture of free hatchings and dots, he gave to his works the harmony and effect of a picture in which the colours of objects are finely distinguished. He published a work called "The Proportions of the Human Figure," (1683.) Died in 1703.

See FONTENAI, "Dictionnaire des Artistes;" STRUTT, "Dictionary of Engravers;" HUBER, "Manuel des Amateurs;" NAGLER, "Neues Allgemeines Künstler-Lexikon."

Audran, (JEAN,) son of Germain, born at Lyons in 1667, was, next to Girard, the most eminent artist of this family, and was a pupil of his uncle Girard. He engraved after more than fifty eminent painters, among whom are Poussin, Rubens, Le Brun, and Van Dyck. "The Rape of the Sabines," after Poussin, is called his master-piece. Among his best works are "Galatea," after C. Maratta, and "The Victories of Alexander," after Le Brun. He was appointed engraver to the king in 1707. Died in 1756.

See FONTENAI, "Dictionnaire des Artistes;" HUBER, "Manuel des Amateurs."

Audran, (LOUIS,) a brother of the preceding, born at Lyons in 1670, was a skilful engraver. He studied with his uncle Girard in Paris. Among his works, which are not numerous, is "The Massacre of the Innocents," after Le Brun. He died prematurely in 1712.

See HUBER, "Manuel des Amateurs."

Audran, (PROSPER GABRIEL,) a French lawyer, born at Paris in 1744. He became professor of Hebrew in the University, and wrote a Hebrew and Arab grammar. Died in 1819.

Audrein, ŏ'drăN', (YVES MARIE,) a French politician and writer, was one of the teachers of Robespierre. He became a warm but humane partisan of the principles of the Revolution, and a member of the Convention, in which he voted for the death of Louis XVI. with a respite. He was elected Bishop of Quimper-Corentin in 1798, and was assassinated by the Chouans (royalists) in 1800. He left a treatise on national education, and an "Apology for Religion against Pretended Philosophers," (1797.)

Audren de Kerdrel, ŏ'drŏN' dĕh kĕR'drĕl', (JEAN MAURE—mōr,) a French monk, author of a History of Bretagne, (1707.) Died in 1725.

Audri. See AUDRY.

Audrichi, ŏw-dRee'kee, (EVERARDO,) an Italian ecclesiastic of the eighteenth century, who taught philosophy and mathematics, published a collection of Latin plays, and a work on Antiquities.

See MAZZUCHELLI, "Scrittori d'Italia."

Audry, Audri, ŏ'dre', or **Aldric,** ăl'drĕk', [Lat. ALDRI'CUS,] SAINT, a French ecclesiastic, born about 775, became Archbishop of Sens. Died in 840.

See "Vita Sancti Aldrici;" MORÉRI, "Dictionnaire Historique."

Audry de Puyraveau, ŏ'dRe' dĕh pü-e'rȧ'vo', (PIERRE FRANÇOIS,) a French revolutionist, born at Puyraveau in 1783. He was elected to the Chamber of Deputies in 1827, boldly avowed himself a republican and was a leader of the popular party in the revolution of 1830. His manufactory in Paris was the rendezvous of the insurgents, whose efforts he directed with great efficiency. It is stated that he was the first to nominate La Fayette as commander of the national guard.

Au'du-bon, (JOHN JAMES,) an American ornithologist of great eminence, born in Louisiana on the 4th of May, 1780. He was the son of a French naval officer who settled as a planter in Louisiana. He manifested in childhood a passion for observing the habits of birds. Educated partly in Paris, to which he went at the age of fifteen, he studied design in the school of the celebrated painter David. Having returned to America about 1798, he inherited from his father a good farm in eastern Pennsylvania, and married. About 1810 he commenced a series of excursions through the vast primeval forests, which he explored alone, and in which he passed the greater portion of his time for many years. He produced coloured designs of all the birds he could find, being impelled to this pursuit by his love of nature rather than an ambition to make himself famous. He removed to Henderson, on the Ohio River, where he resided for several years with his wife and children.

In 1826 he went to England, and began in London the publication of a great work on ornithology. He visited France in 1828, and was received with great honour by Cuvier, Humboldt, and other savants. He obtained numerous subscribers, at one thousand dollars a copy, for his magnificent work entitled "The Birds of America," in folio, illustrated with about four hundred and forty-eight plates of one thousand and sixty-five species of birds of the natural size, beautifully coloured, (1830-39.) It consists of five volumes of engravings designed by himself, and five volumes of letter-press.

Cuvier expressed the opinion that this work "is the most magnificent monument that art has ever erected to ornithology," ("*C'est le plus magnifique monument que l'art ait encore élevé à l'ornithologie.*") Audubon returned to America in 1830, after which he explored the coasts, the lakes, the rivers, and the mountains from Labrador and Canada to Florida. He visited England again, to superintend the publication of his "Birds of America." He also published his "Ornithological Biography," or an Account of the Habits of the Birds of the United States of America, accompanied by a Description of the Objects represented in the Work entitled The Birds of America," (Edinburgh, 5 vols., 1831-39.) Having crossed the Atlantic homeward for the last time about 1840, he settled on the Hudson River, in New York. He published a popular and cheaper edition of his "Birds of America," (7 vols. 8vo, 1844,) and "The Quadrupeds of North America," (3 vols. of letter-press and 3 vols. of plates, 1846-50.) In the latter work he was assisted by his sons Victor Gifford and John Woodhouse.

To excellent skill in designing natural objects he added

an admirable talent for describing them in graphic language. His character is eulogized by Professor Wilson, of Edinburgh, in the following terms: "The hearts of all warmed towards Audubon, who were capable of conceiving the difficulties, dangers, and sacrifices that must have been encountered, endured, and overcome before genius could have embodied these, the glory of its innumerable triumphs. . . . The man himself is just what you would expect from his production, full of fine enthusiasm and intelligence, most interesting in his looks and manners, a perfect gentleman, and esteemed by all who know him for the simplicity and frankness of his nature. He is the greatest artist, in his own walk, that ever lived." He died in New York City, in January, 1851.

See article on "American Ornithology" in the "London Quarterly Review" for July, 1832; GRISWOLD, "Prose Writers of America;" DUNLAP, "History of the Rise and Progress of the Arts of Design," etc., (vol. ii. chap. xxviii. ;) "Brief Biographies," by SAMUEL SMILES; Rev. C. C. ADAMS, "Journal of the Life and Labours of J. J. Audubon ;" "Audubon the Naturalist in the New World," by Mrs. HORACE SAINT JOHN, London, 1856; "Democratic Review" for May, 1842.

Audwin. See ALDWIN.

Auenbrugger von Auenbrug, ŏw'ĕn-brŏŏg' gĕr fon ŏw'ĕn'brŏŏg, (called **Avenbrugger** by French and English writers,) (LEOPOLD,) a German physician, who invented percussion as a means of detecting diseases of the thorax or lungs, was born at Grätz, in Styria, in 1722. He became physician to the Spanish hospital of Vienna. He announced his great discovery in his "Inventum novum ex Percussione Thoracis humani," etc., ("New Discovery by Percussion of the Human Chest," etc., Vienna, 1761.) This was translated into English by Dr. Forbes in 1824. The practice of percussion was neglected until it was revived by Corvisart about 1808. Auenbrugger wrote two treatises on insanity. Died in 1809.

See "Biographie Médicale."

Aue. See HARTMANN VON AUE.

Auer, ŏw'ĕr, (ANTON,) considered the founder of the present school of Bavarian porcelain-painters, was born at Munich in 1778. He was patronized by Prince Ludwig, (afterwards king.) Died in 1814.

Auer, (JOHANN PAUL,) a distinguished historical and portrait painter, was born at Nuremberg in 1636, and died in 1687.

Auerbach, ŏw'ĕr-bâk', (BERTHOLD,) a popular German author, born of Jewish parents at Nordstetten, in Würtemberg, in 1812. He published "Spinoza," a historical romance, in 1837, "The Poet and Merchant," a novel, (1839,) and "The Cultivated Citizen," ("Der gebildete Bürger," 1842.) His reputation rests chiefly on his "Village Tales of the Black Forest," ("Schwarzwälder Dorfgeschichten," 2 vols., 1843,) which were translated into English and other languages. His novel entitled "Auf den Höhen" ("On the Heights") has also been translated into English.

See BROCKHAUS, "Conversations-Lexikon."

Auerbach, (JOHANN GOTTFRIED,) a German portrait-painter, born in Saxony in 1697; died at Vienna (where he was court-painter) in 1753.

Auerell, (WILLIAM.) See AVERELL.

Auernhammer. See AURENHAMMER.

Auersperg, von, ŏw'ĕr-spĕRG', (ANTON ALEXANDER,) COUNT, a German poet, whose assumed name is ANASTA'SIUS GRÜN, was born at Laybach in 1806. He has published successful poems, among which are "The Last Knight," ("Der letzte Ritter," 1830,) and "Promenades" (or "Excursions") of a Poet of Vienna," ("Spaziergänge eines Wiener Poeten," 1831,) which is remarkable for wit and humour.

See LONGFELLOW'S "Poets and Poetry of Europe."

Auersperg or **Auersberg, von,** (HERBARD,) BARON, hereditary marshal of Carniola, (Krain,) was famous as the defender of Germany against the Turks. Born in 1525; killed in battle in 1575.

Auerstädt or **Auerstedt.** See DAVOUST.

Auffenberg, von, fon ŏwf'fĕn-bĕRG', (JOSEPH,) FREIHERR, a German dramatic poet, born at Freiburg, in Brisgau, in 1798. After serving in the army of Baden, he settled in Baden about 1836, and received the title of marshal of the court (hoffmarschall) of the grand duke in 1839. His principal works are "The Alhambra," a

dramatic poem, (3 vols., 1829–30,) and "Louis XI. in Péronne." Died in 1857.

Auffmann, ŏwf'mân, (JOSEPH ANTON XAVER,) a German organist and composer, born about 1720; died in 1778.

Auffray, ō'frâ', (JEAN,) a French political economist, who considered the art of printing an injury to literature, but was an advocate of free trade. Born at Paris in 1733; died in 1788.

Auffschnaiter, ŏwf'shnī'tĕr, (BENEDICT ANTON,) a German musician, lived at Passau about 1700.

Au-fid'ï-us, (CNEIUS,) a Roman quæstor in 119 B.C., and tribune in 114. He was the author of a Greek history of Rome.

Aufidius, (TITUS,) a jurist, who was quæstor in 84 B.C., and afterwards prætor of Asia.

Aufidius, (TITUS,) a Sicilian physician, lived in the first century B.C.

Aufrere, ō'frair', (ANTHONY,) an English writer, who translated a number of works from the German of Goethe and others, and the editor of the "Lockhart Letters," was born at Norfolk in 1756, and died at Pisa in 1833.

Aufréri, ō'frâ're', (ÉTIENNE,) a distinguished French jurist, who wrote on civil and canon law. He became the official of the Archbishop of Toulouse in 1483. Died about 1510.

Aufresne, ō'frĕn', (JEAN **Rival**—re'vâl',) an eminent French actor, was born in Geneva in 1709, and died in Russia (where Catherine II. gave him a distinguished reception) in 1806.

Augaron, ō'gâ'rŏn', (JACQUES,) a French surgeon, employed by the King of Navarre about 1570.

Auge, d', dŏzh, [Lat. AUGE'TIUS,] (DANIEL,) a French philologist and writer, born at Villeneuve-l'Archevêque died about 1595.

Augeard, ō'zhâr', (JACQUES MATHIEU,) a farmer-general, (the last who held the office,) and secretary of commands to Marie Antoinette, was born at Bordeaux, 1731. He left memoirs on the intrigues of the French court in his time, which remain in manuscript. Died in Paris in 1805.

Augeard, (MATHIEU,) a French jurist and advocate of the parliament of Paris. Died in 1751.

Au'ge-as, (or au-ge'as,) [Gr. Αὐγέας or Αὐγείας; Fr. AUGÉAS, ō'zhâ' âs',or AUGÉE, ō'zhâ',] a mythical king of Elis, said to be a son of Neptune, (or of the Sun.) One of the tasks imposed on Hercules was to cleanse the stables of Augeas, who kept a great number of oxen. He was killed by Hercules because he refused to pay the reward which he had promised for this work.

Augée. See AUGEAS.

Augenio, ŏw-ja'ne-o, (ORAZIO,) an Italian physician and medical writer, born in the Romagna about 1527, became professor of medicine at Turin in 1577, and at Padua in 1593. Died in 1603.

Auger, ō'zhâ', (ATHANASE, â'tâ'nâz',) ABBÉ, a French classical scholar and translator of great learning, was born in Paris in 1734. He was appointed vicar-general by the Bishop of Lescars. He published a translation of the "Complete Works of Demosthenes and Æschines," (4 vols., 1777,) which is generally correct, but is deficient in spirit. He also translated the works of Isocrates, (3 vols., 1783,) and the Orations of Cicero, (3 vols., 1787.) In 1792 he published an able work "On the Constitution of the Romans under the Kings and during the Republic," (3 vols.) Died in 1792.

See HÉRAULT DE SÉCHELLES, "Éloge d'Athanase Auger;" QUÉRARD, "La France Littéraire."

Auger, (EDMOND,) a French Jesuit, born near Troyes in 1515. He was one of the missionaries sent by his superiors to convert the Protestants in the south of France, and became confessor of Henry III. about 1575. His eloquence is praised by Catholic writers. Died in 1591.

See MORÉRI, "Dictionnaire Historique."

Auger, (HIPPOLYTE NICOLAS JUST,) a French novelist and dramatist, born at Auxerre in 1797. He wrote "Marpha," (1818,) "Rienzi," (1825,) and other novels. Among his successful dramas are "Peter the Great," (1836,) and "Poor Mother!" ("Pauvre Mère!" 1837, with F. Cornu.)

Auger, (LOUIS SIMON,) a successful French critic and littérateur, born in Paris in 1772. He edited with ability

ę as k; ç as s; ḡ hard; ġ as j; G, H, K, guttural; N, nasal; R, trilled; s as z; ᵵh as in this. (☞See Explanations, p. 23.)

14

the works of numerous French authors, and began to write for the "Journal of the Empire" in 1808. In 1816 he was elected to the French Academy, of which he became perpetual secretary in 1827. He wrote many articles for the "Biographie Universelle," among which are those on Molière and Voltaire, and the "Preliminary Discourse" of the same work. He also published "Mélanges philosophiques et littéraires." He was found drowned in the Seine in 1829, having probably committed suicide.

See QUÉRARD, "La France Littéraire."

Augereau, ŏzh'rō', [in Latin, AUGUREL′LUS,] (ANTOINE,) a French printer of Paris. Died in 1544.

Augereau, (PIERRE FRANÇOIS CHARLES,) Duc de Castiglione, (kȧs'tēg′le′on′,) a celebrated French general, born in Paris in 1757, was a son of a mechanic or domestic, and had few opportunities of acquiring an education. He was a fencing-master at Naples before the Revolution. Having enlisted in 1792 as a private, he rose rapidly, and became a general of division about the end of 1793. He contributed mainly to the victory at Loano, in November, 1795, and was one of the most active and successful of Bonaparte's generals in the campaign of 1796. He took Lodi, in April, and decided the victory of Lodi, by his charge along the bridge, in May, 1796. Among his brilliant exploits were the defence of Castiglione and his charge at Arcola in the same year. In August, 1797, he was appointed commander of the seventeenth military division, (which included Paris,) having been selected because he was a devoted partisan of the new régime. He obeyed the commands of a majority of the Directors with audacity in the *coup d'état* of the 18th Fructidor, (4th of September,) 1797, and was elected to the Council of Five Hundred in 1799. Before this date Augereau and Bonaparte regarded each other with distrust or jealousy.

He commanded the Gallo-Batavian army in 1800 and 1801, was made a marshal of France in 1804, and Duke of Castiglione in 1805. He took part in the battle of Jena, 1806, and was severely wounded at Eylau. In 1809 he was employed in Spain. When Napoleon invaded Russia in 1812, he left Augereau in command of an army in Germany to cover his rear. He maintained his reputation at Leipsic in 1813. Having declared his adhesion to Louis XVIII. in 1814, he was confirmed in his rank and dignities ; but he deserted to Napoleon in March, 1815. Died in June, 1816.

See LAS CASES, "Mémorial de Sainte-Hélène ;" BOURRIENNE, "Mémoires sur Napoléon ;" "Nouvelle Biographie Générale."

Augetius. See AUGE.

Augier, ō′zhe-À′, (ÉMILE,) a French dramatist and poet, a grandson of Pigault Lebrun, was born at Valence, in Drôme, in 1820. He produced in 1844 a drama entitled "La Ciguë," (" Hemlock,") which had a great success. His "Aventurière," a comedy, (1848,) was received with favour, and his comedy of "Gabrielle" (1849) obtained the Monthyon prize of the French Academy. These comedies are in verse. He published a volume of poems in 1856, and was elected to the French Academy in 1857 in place of M. Salvandy.

Augier, (JEAN BAPTISTE,) a French lawyer and general, born at Bourges in 1769. He served under Napoleon, and was governor of Königsberg. During the Russian campaign, as a member of the Chamber of Deputies, he took an active part in the restoration. Died in 1819.

See "Dictionnaire historique des Généraux Français."

Augier-Dufot, ō′zhe-À′ dü′fo′, (ANNE AMABLE—ȧ′-mȧbl′,) a French physician, born at Aubusson in 1733, was author of works on various subjects. Died at Soissons in 1775.

See QUÉRARD, "La France Littéraire."

Auguis, ō′gèss′, (PIERRE JEAN BAPTISTE,) a French revolutionist, born at Melle, in Deux-Sèvres, about 1745. He was elected to the Convention in 1792, voted for the detention or banishment of the king, and courageously opposed the power of Robespierre in 1794. In 1799 he was a member of the Council of Five Hundred. Having supported Bonaparte on the 18th Brumaire, he obtained a seat in the legislative body. Died in 1810.

Auguis, (PIERRE RENÉ,) a French *littérateur*, son of the preceding, was born at Melle, near Niort, in 1786.

He published "The New Odyssey," a poem, (1812,) a "History of Catherine II. of Russia, and of Paul I.," (1813,) "The Genius of the French Language," (1820,) and various other works. In 1830 he was elected to the Chamber of •Deputies, in which he acted with the opposition. Died in 1846.

Au'gur, (CHRISTOPHER COLON,) an American general, born in New York, graduated at West Point in 1843. He served as lieutenant in the Mexican war, (1846–47,) and gained the rank of captain in 1852. He commanded a division at Cedar Mountain, Virginia, in August, 1862, and became a major-general in November of that year. He served under Banks, in Louisiana, in 1863, and commanded the department of Washington from October, 1863, to August, 1866. He holds the rank of colonel in the United States regular army.

Augur, (HEZEKIAH,) an American sculptor and inventor, born in New Haven, Connecticut, in 1791. Among his works may be mentioned "Jephthah and his Daughter," in the Trumbull Gallery of Yale College. He invented a machine for carving, now in general use. Died in 1858.

See TUCKERMAN, "Book of the Artists ;" DUNLAP, "History of the Rise and Progress of the Arts of Design," etc.

Augurelli, ŏw-goo-rel′lee, or **Augurello,** ŏw-goo-rel′lo, (GIOVANNI AURELIO—ŏw-rā′le-o,) a Latin poet and critic of superior merit, born at Rimini about 1454, (or, according to Ginguené, about 1441.) He taught Greek and Latin at Venice, and wrote odes, elegies, epistles, and Iambics, which were printed collectively in 1491 or 1492, and a longer poem entitled "Chrysopoiia," (or "Chrysopoia,") 1515. Died at Treviso in 1524 or 1537.

Au-gu-rī′nus, (LUCIUS MINUCIUS,) a Roman, who was *præfectus annonæ* during a famine in 439 B.C. He exposed the designs of Spurius Melius.

Augurinus, (MARCUS GENUCIUS,) a Roman consul in 444 B.C. Under his consulate the law (Lex Canuleia) permitting marriage between patricians and plebeians was passed.

Augurinus (PUBLIUS MINUCIUS) was a Roman consul (492 B.C.) in a year of dreadful famine, which he and his colleague mitigated by importing corn from Sicily, and by founding a colony at Norba, to which many of the poor were sent.

Augurinus, (QUINTUS MINUCIUS,) Roman consul in 457 B.C., led an army against the Æqui and Sabines, and compelled them to abandon the Roman territory and shut themselves up in their own towns.

Augurinus, (SENTIUS,) a Roman poet, who was the friend of the younger Pliny, by whom his verses are highly commended.

Augurinus, (TIBERIUS MINUCIUS,) a Roman consul, who defeated the Samnites in 305 B.C.

Augurinus, (TITUS GENUCIUS,) brother of Marcus, noticed above, became consul in 451 B.C., and was afterwards one of the first Decemvirate.

August, the German of AUGUSTUS, which see.

AU-GUS′TA, a Latin word signifying "majestic," or "venerable," given as a title to the wives of the Roman emperors. The first who received it was Livia, the wife of Augustus Cæsar.

Augusta, ŏw-goos′tȧ, (CRISTOFORO,) a painter of the sixteenth century, born near Cremona, gave great promise of future eminence, but died young.

See LANZI, "History of Painting in Italy."

Augusta, ŏw-gōōs′tȧ, (JOHANN,) a friend of Luther, born at Prague in 1500, became a minister of the sect of Bohemian Brethren, which is regarded as the origin of the Moravian Church. He was chosen bishop of all their churches in Bohemia about 1538. He differed from Luther in religious opinions. He was imprisoned sixteen years by Ferdinand I. (from 1548 to 1564.) He published several works. Died in 1575.

See PELZER, "Portraits de Savants Bohêmes."

Augustenburg, PRINCE OF. See CHARLES AUGUSTUS, PRINCE ROYAL OF SWEDEN.

Augusti, ŏw′gōōs′tee, (CHRISTIAN JOHANN WILHELM,) an eminent German theologian, born at Eschenberg, near Gotha, in 1771. He became professor extraordinary at Jena in 1800, and succeeded Ilgen as professor of Oriental literature in that city in 1803. In 1807 he obtained the chair of theology at Jena. As an orthodox Lutheran he opposed the philosophical or speculative school. From 1811 to 1819 he was professor at Breslau, and removed to the University of Bonn in 1819. His chief work is "Memorable Things from Christian Archæology," ("Denkwürdigkeiten aus der Christlichen Archaeologie," 12 vols., 1817–35,) which he condensed into a "Manual of Christian Archæology," (3 vols., 1836.) Died in 1841.

See BROCKHAUS, "Conversations-Lexikon."

Augusti, (FRIEDRICH ALBRECHT,) a grandfather of the preceding, born at Frankfort-on-the-Oder in 1696, was the son of a Jew. He was converted to Christianity in 1721, and became a Lutheran minister at Eschenberg. He published several learned works on theology. Died in 1782.

Augustin, (ANTONIO.) See AUGUSTINUS.

Augustin, ō′güs′tăN′, (JEAN BAPTISTE JACQUES,) a distinguished French miniature-painter in oil and enamel, was born at Saint-Diez, in Vosges, in 1759. He worked in Paris, was patronized by Louis XVIII., and painted portraits of many eminent persons. He was appointed painter to the king in 1819. Died in 1832.

Au′gus-tine, [Lat. AURE′LIUS AUGUSTI′NUS; Fr. AUGUSTIN, ō′güs′tăN′; It. AUGUSTINO, ŏw-goos-tee′no,] SAINT, the most illustrious Latin Father of the Church, was born at Tagasta, in Numidia, on the 13th of November, 354 A.D. He was instructed in religion by his mother Monnica (or Monica,) who was a devout Christian. He also studied Greek, rhetoric, and philosophy at Madaura and Carthage. About the age of nineteen he was captivated with the heresy of the Manichæans, to which he adhered for nine years. Having taught grammar and rhetoric at Tagasta, Carthage, and Rome, he was appointed professor of rhetoric and philosophy at Milan in 384. Amidst a career of immorality into which strong youthful passions had impelled him, he was seriously impressed by the sermons of Saint Ambrose. He experienced a decided conversion in 386, after deep conflicts, which he has described in his "Confessions," an autobiography. Soon after this event he returned to Africa.

He was ordained a priest about 391 by Valerius, Bishop of Hippo, whom he succeeded in 396. He distinguished himself as the adversary of the Donatists at the Council of Carthage in 401 A.D., and had a high reputation as an eloquent preacher. About 418 he produced two works against the Pelagians, "On the Grace of Christ," ("De Gratia Christi,") and "On Original Sin," ("De Peccato Originali.") His capital work, entitled "On the City of God," ("De Civitate Dei,") was intended to subvert the foundations of paganism and establish those of Christianity, and to refute the opinion that the capture of Rome by Alaric, and other calamities of the empire, were caused by the prevalence of the new religion. It was finished about 426. He wrote many other works, among which are those "On Faith and Works," ("De Fide et Operibus,") and "On the Soul and its Origin," ("De Anima et ejus Origine.") He died at Hippo, during the siege of that city by the Vandals, on the 28th of August, 430 A.D. His habits were simple and temperate, rather than ascetic. The best edition of his works is that published by the Benedictines at Paris, (11 vols., 1679–1700.) "Of all the Fathers of the Latin Church," says Villemain, "Saint Augustine manifested the most imagination in theology, the most eloquence, and even sensibility, in scholasticism. . . . He writes as well on music as on free will; he explains the intellectual phenomena of memory as well as he reasons on the decline of the Roman Empire. His subtile and vigorous mind has often consumed on mystical problems an amount of sagacity which would have sufficed for the most sublime conceptions."

See "Confessions of Saint Augustine;" POSSIDIUS, "Vie de Saint-Augustin;" GEORGE MORINGO, "Vie de Saint-Augustin," 1533; GODEAU, "Vie de Saint-Augustin," 1657; TILLEMONT, "Mémoires ecclésiastiques," (vol. xiii.,) 1702; RIVIUS, "Vita Sancti Augustini," 1646; POUJOULAT, "Vie de Saint-Augustin," 2d edition, 1852; BINDEMANN, "Augustines Leben," 1844; BUTLER, "Lives of the Saints;" BÄHR, "Christliche Römische Theologie;" VILLEMAIN, "Tableau de l'Éloquence chrétienne au quatrième Siècle," 1849; "Nouvelle Biographie Générale."

Augustine or **Austin,** SAINT, "the Apostle of England," was prior of a Benedictine monastery at Rome, before he was sent by Gregory I. to convert the Anglo-Saxons. He arrived in the island in 596 or 597 A.D., and was well received by Ethelbert, whose wife Bertha was a Christian. The king and many of his subjects were soon after baptized. Augustine was appointed Archbishop of Canterbury. The year of his death is variously dated 604, 607, and 614.

See W. F. HOOK, "Lives of the Archbishops of Canterbury," vol. i. chap. ii.

Augustini (ŏw-gōōs-tee′nee) **ab Hor′tis,** (CHRISTIAN,) a Hungarian physician, born at Zips in 1598. He became a physician to the emperor Ferdinand, and formed a botanic garden at Vienna. Died in 1650.

Augustino. See AGOSTINO.

Augustino, (VENEZIANO.) See AGOSTINO.

Au-gus-ti′nus, (ANTONIUS,) [Sp. ANTONIO AUGUSTIN, an-to′ne-o ŏw-goos-teen′,] Archbishop of Tarragona, one of the most learned jurists of Spain, was born at Saragossa about 1516. He gained a high reputation by his "Emendations and Opinions of Civil Law," ("Emendationes et Opiniones Juris Civilis," 1538–43.) In 1555 he was sent as papal nuncio to England, to promote the interests of the Roman Church in that country. He became Bishop of Lerida in 1560, and Archbishop of Tarragona in 1574. He wrote several works on Roman and canon law, which are called classical, and among which is "De Emendatione Gratiani Dialogi," (1581.) "His works," says Correa da Serra, in the "Biographie Universelle," "will preserve his celebrity in all ages." Died in 1586.

See "A. Augustini Vitæ Historia," by GREGORIUS MAYANSUS SISCARIUS; N. ANTONIO, "Bibliotheca Hispana Nova."

Augustinus, (AURELIUS.) See AUGUSTINE, SAINT.

Augusto, ŏw-goos′to, [Lat. AUGUS′TUS,] of Udine, an Italian poet, lived in the first half of the sixteenth century.

Au-gus′tu-lus, (ROMULUS,) the last Roman Emperor of the West, was a son of the patrician Orestes. He became emperor in 475 A.D., and was deposed by Odoacer in the following year.

AU-GUS′TUS, a name conferred by the Roman senate on Caius Julius Cæsar Octavianus, 27 B.C. The word signifies "noble," "majestic," or "venerable." This name was adopted as a title by Tiberius and his successors. The Greek equivalent of Augustus is *Sebastos.*

Augustus. See AUGUSTUS CÆSAR.

Au-gus′tus [Ger. AUGUST, ŏw′gŏŏst] **I.,** (or **II.,**) (FREDERICK,) King of Poland, was born at Dresden in 1670. He was the second son of John George III., Elector of Saxony, and Anna Sophia of Denmark. He was endowed with superior talents, which were well cultivated, and possessed extraordinary physical strength. In 1690 and 1691 he served with distinction in the Imperial army against the French. He succeeded his brother John George IV. as Elector of Saxony in 1694, formed an alliance with the emperor, and obtained from him the chief command in the war against the Turks, by whom he was defeated in Hungary in 1697.

Augustus was elected King of Poland in May or June, 1697, having abjured the Protestant religion for the sake of this prize. His rival, the Prince of Conti, was the choice of a strong party in the Diet; but Augustus obtained possession of the throne without difficulty. He joined Peter the Great of Russia in a league against Charles XII. of Sweden, and invaded Livonia in 1700. His army was defeated by the Swedes on the Duna in 1701 and at Klissow in 1702. He was expelled from Poland, on the throne of which Charles XII. placed Stanislas Leszczynski, in July, 1704. To save his Saxon dominions from the victorious Swede, he signed a treaty in 1706, by which he renounced the crown of Poland.

The defeat of Charles XII. at Pultowa enabled Augustus to recover the throne of Poland in 1709, when Stanislas retired without a contest. The Diet in 1712 demanded the removal of the Saxon troops from Poland, but the king refused to remove them, and thus provoked an insurrection, which was at last appeased by the king's complying with the demand of the Diet. The latter part of his reign was comparatively quiet. He died in February, 1733, leaving a son, Augustus, who succeeded him, and a natural son, Maurice of Saxony, the famous general. Augustus was ambitious, licentious, prodigal, and extremely fond of luxury and splendour. His court at Dresden was more splendid than any other in Europe, except that of Louis XIV.

See FASSMANN und HORN, "Friedrich August des Grossen Leben," 1734; DESROCHES DE PARTHENAY, "Histoire de Pologne sous le Roi Auguste II," 4 vols., 1734.

Augustus (or **August**) **II.**, (or **III.**,) (FREDERICK,) a son of the preceding, born at Dresden in 1696, did not inherit his father's talents. He was educated as a Protestant, but was converted to the Roman Catholic Church about 1712. He married Maria Josephine, a daughter of Joseph I., Emperor of Austria, in 1719. In 1733 he succeeded as Elector of Saxony, and was elected King of Poland by a party in the Diet, another party choosing Stanislas. In the contest which ensued, Augustus, supported by Russia and Austria, prevailed about 1736. He joined the league formed by France and Prussia against Maria Theresa of Austria in 1740 or 1741, but in 1743 he became an ally of that empress against Frederick the Great, who defeated the Saxon army and took Dresden in 1745. In the Seven Years' war, 1756–63, the Saxons were defeated, and Saxony was ravaged by the victorious Prussians. He died in October, 1763, and was succeeded in Saxony by his son, Frederick Christian August.

See BÖTTIGER, "Geschichte des Kurstaates und Königreiches Sachsen."

Au-gus'tus (or **August**) **I.**, Elector of Saxony, a son of Henry the Pious, born in 1526, succeeded his brother Maurice in 1553. He was distinguished as a legislator, and had the reputation of a wise ruler ; but he was intolerant to the Calvinists. Under his auspices, a creed of Lutheran orthodoxy, called "Formula Concordiæ," was adopted about 1580. He died in 1586, and was succeeded by his son Christian I.

See HOMMEL, "Elector Augustus Saxoniæ Legislator," 1765; EICHHORN, "Deutsche Staats- und Rechts-Geschichte."

Augustus II. OF SAXONY. See AUGUSTUS I. (or II.) OF POLAND.

Augustus I., KING OF SAXONY. See FREDERICK AUGUSTUS.

Augustus II., KING OF SAXONY. See FREDERICK AUGUSTUS.

Augustus, Duke of Saxony, and last Archbishop of Magdeburg, born at Dresden in 1614. He was dispossessed and repossessed of his archbishopric several times during the wars between Gustavus Adolphus and the Emperor of Germany. Died in 1680.

Augus'tus, [Ger. AUGUST, ŏw'gŏost,] (EMIL LEOPOLD,) Duke of Saxe-Gotha and Altenburg, born at Gotha in 1772, was the eldest son of Duke Ernest II., whom he succeeded in 1804. He was an admirer of Napoleon, and joined the Rhenish Confederation about 1807. He was a liberal patron of the fine arts, and author of several æsthetical novels, among which is "Kyllenion, oder Auch ich war in Arcadien," ("I also was in Arcadia," 1805.) He died in 1822, and was succeeded by his brother Friedrich. The daughter of Duke August was the mother of Prince Albert, consort of Queen Victoria.

Au-gus'tus, (FRIEDRICH WILHELM HEINRICH,) Prince of Prussia, born in 1779, was a nephew of Frederick the Great, and a son of Prince Augustus Ferdinand. He fought at Jena in 1806, where he was taken prisoner. Having obtained in 1813 the rank of lieutenant-general, he displayed skill and courage at Dresden, Kulm, and Leipsic. In 1815 he was appointed commander of a corps-d'armée, and besieged and took many fortified French towns. He was reputed the first artillery officer in the Prussian army. Died in 1843.

See "Preussische National-Encyklopädie."

Augustus, [Ger. AUGUST, ŏw'gŏost,] (PAUL FRIEDRICH,) Grand Duke of Oldenburg, was born in 1783. He served against the French in Russia in 1812, and began to reign in 1829. He is represented as an enlightened and liberal prince. About 1848 he granted a constitution which increased the civil and religious freedom of his subjects. Died in 1853.

Augus'tus, (WILLIAM,) Prince of Prussia, an able

general, born at Berlin in 1722, was a younger brother of Frederick the Great. He studied the military sciences with zeal, and distinguished himself at Hohen-Friedberg in 1745. As general of infantry, he gave proof of skill at Lowositz in 1756. After the defeat of the Prussians at Kollin, in 1757, Augustus was appointed commander of thirty thousand men who covered the rear of the retreating army. He failed in his effort to check the superior force of the enemy, and for this failure was deprived of his command. He died in 1758, leaving a son, Frederick William, who became King of Prussia.

See ARCHENHOLZ, "History of the Seven Years' War," (in German.)

Augus'tus Cæ'sar, called by Suetonius **Octavius Cæsar Augustus**, [Fr. OCTAVE CÉSAR AUGUSTE, ok'-täv' sà'zȧr' ō'güst'; It. OTTAVIO CESARE AUGUSTO, ot-tä've-o chà'sà-rà ŏw-goos'to,] and subsequently named, as the heir of Julius Cæsar the dictator, **Ca'ius Ju'lius Cæ'sar Octavia'nus**, the first Roman emperor, was born at Velitræ, not far from Rome, in 63 B.C. He was the son of Caius Octavius and Atia, the daughter of Julia, who was the sister of Julius Cæsar. His father died about the year 60, and his mother married L. Marcius Philippus, who was consul in 56 B.C., and who superintended the education of young Octavius. At the age of twelve he pronounced a funeral oration in praise of his grandmother Julia, and four years later he assumed the *toga virilis*. He was adopted as a son by Julius Cæsar the dictator, whom he followed to Spain in 45 B.C. According to some writers, he was present at the battle of Munda. He was pursuing his studies at Apollonia when he learned that Cæsar was killed, in 44 B.C., and that he had been appointed the heir of his uncle. In company with his friend Vipsanius Agrippa, he went to Rome to claim his inheritance. He found a dangerous rival in Mark Antony, who had possession of the money and papers of the dictator and refused to give them up. Octavius pursued an artful and temporizing course, by which he gained the support of Cicero and other senators, and showed himself an equal match for old and experienced players in the game of political intrigue. In January, 43, the senate gave him command of an army, and sent him with the consuls Hirtius and Pansa to fight against Antony, who was in Cisalpine Gaul. The army of the senate defeated Antony near Mutina, (Módena,) but Hirtius and Pansa were killed in the battle. Soon after this event the command of the army was transferred to D. Brutus by the senate, which had resolved to check the growing power and ambitious efforts of Octavius. In defiance of the authority of the senate, he marched with an army to Rome, was elected consul in August, 43 B.C., (before he had reached the legal age,) and formed a coalition or triumvirate with Antony and Lepidus against M. Brutus and the other republicans. Antony and Octavius, commanding in person, gained a decisive victory over Brutus and Cassius at Philippi, 42 B.C. According to Suetonius, he treated the vanquished with merciless cruelty. Thousands of persons perished as victims of the proscription which the triumvirs ordered. Octavius and Antony soon quarrelled, but postponed hostilities by a feigned reconciliation, and combined their forces against Sextus Pompey, who was master of Sicily and Sardinia. Octavius gained a decisive victory over Pompey in 36 B.C., and, while Antony was engaged in Eastern campaigns or in dalliance with Cleopatra, established his power in Italy. He became consul for the second time in 33 and for the third time in 31 B.C. At length, owing in part to Antony's infatuation for Cleopatra, and his neglect of Octavia, (the sister of Augustus,) whom he had recently married, the breach became irreconcilable. Octavius gained a decisive victory at the naval battle of Actium, (31 B.C.,) which rendered him sole master of the Roman empire. He entertained or professed a design to restore the republic ; but he allowed himself to be persuaded to usurp imperial power, partly disguised under the form of a republican government. He was elected consul several times after the year 30, and received the title of Augustus from the senate in 27 B.C. His chief ministers or advisers were Agrippa, Mæcenas, and Asinius Pollio. He accepted in the year 23 the *tribunitia potestas* (tribunitian power) for life.

Augustus was a liberal patron of the poets Virgil and Horace, whose genius rendered the Augustan age the most illustrious in the history of Roman literature. He greatly increased the architectural splendour of Rome, and boasted that he left that a city of marble which he had found a city of brick. Under his rule the people enjoyed such a share of peace and prosperity as reconciled them to the loss of their liberty. He married several wives, namely, Clodia, Scribonia, and Livia Drusilla. Scribonia bore him a daughter Julia, his only child. In his domestic relations he was not happy. He was temperate or abstemious in his diet, and lived in a comparatively simple style.

He applied himself with great diligence to the study of eloquence from his early youth. Although he could speak very well extemporaneously, he never addressed the senate, the soldiers, or the people, unless he had carefully prepared himself beforehand. He was partial to the study of Greek literature and philosophy, but he never wrote in that language, and did not speak it fluently. According to Suetonius, Augustus composed many works in prose on various subjects, including a history of his own life, which extended only to the Cantabrian war. He also wrote some epigrams and other verses. Having adopted Tiberius (his step-son) as his successor, he died in August, 14 A.D.

See Suetonius, "Life of Augustus," ("Vita Augusti;") Nicolas Damascenus, "De Vita Augusti;" Tacitus, "Annales;" Drumann, "Geschichte Roms;" Plutarch's "Life of Marcus Antonius;" Nougarède, "Histoire du Siècle d'Auguste," 1840; Larrey, "Vie d'Auguste," 1840.

Augus′tus Fred′erick, Prince of Great Britain, and Duke of Sussex, the sixth son of George III., was born in 1773. He married, at Rome, in 1793, Lady Augusta Murray, a daughter of the Earl of Dunmore. The prerogative court having declared this marriage to be null and void, the parties were separated, after the birth of a son, Sir Augustus Frederick d'Este. The Duke of Sussex was liberal in politics, voted for the abolition of the slave-trade and slavery, and favoured religious toleration. He was chosen president of the Royal Society in 1830, and retired from that position in 1839. He contributed liberally to benevolent institutions. Died in 1843.

Au′laf, written also **Anlaf**, a Danish chief, who ravaged Ireland and the north of England, and finally, having conquered Edmund at Leicester, obtained the northern part of the kingdom, which he ruled until his death about 943.

Aulaf, King of Norway. See Olaf.

Aulagnier, ō′lȧn′ye-ā′, (Alexis François,) a French medical writer, born in Grasse in 1767; died in 1839.

Aulaire. See Saint-Aulaire.

Au-la′nï-us E-van′der, an Athenian sculptor, who lived in Rome in the time of Augustus.

Aulard, ō′lȧr′, (Pierre,) a French general, born in Languedoc in 1763, was killed at Waterloo in 1815.

Aulber, (Erasmus.) See Alber.

Aulber, ȯwl′bẹr, (Johann Christoph,) a German historian, born at Waiblingen in 1671; died in 1743.

Aulber, (Matthaeus,) a German reformer, born at Blaubeuren in 1495, became a disciple of Luther about 1518. He preached at Reutlingen, and induced that city to adopt the Augsburg Confession in 1530. In 1548 he was appointed cathedral preacher at Stuttgart by Duke Ulrich.

Aulbéry, ō′bä′re′, (George,) secretary to Charles III., Duke of Lorraine, was author of several poems, a life of Saint Sigisbert, King of Austrasia, and a description of Lorraine and Nancy.

Auletta, ȯw-let′tä, (Pietro,) an Italian composer of operas, lived in the first half of the eighteenth century.

Aulich, ȯw′lĭk, (Louis,) a Hungarian general, born at Presburg in 1792. He was made a general in the spring of 1849, and contributed to the success of the Hungarians over Windischgrätz. He succeeded Görgey as minister of war in July or August, 1849. After the surrender of Görgey, he was hung as a rebel by the Austrians at Arad in October, 1849.

See Brockhaus, "Conversations-Lexikon."

Auliczeck. See Aulizeck.

Aulisio, d′, dȯw-lee′se-o, [Lat. Aulis′ius,] (Dome-

nico,] an Italian jurist, linguist, and writer, eminent for his learning, was born at Naples about 1645. He was well versed in the ancient and modern languages, numismatics, and various sciences, and was professor of civil law at Naples for many years. Among his numerous works are, "On the Architecture of the Mausoleum," ("De Mausolei Architectura,") "On the Timaic Harmony," ("De Harmonia Timaica,") and "Commentaries on Civil Law," ("Commentaria Juris Civilis," 3 vols., 1719-20.) Died in 1717.

See "Vita di Aulisio," prefixed to his "Scuole Sacra" by Troisio, 1723.

Aulizeck, ȯw′lit-sĕk′, or **Aulizeck**, ȯw′lit-chĕk, (Dominic,) a Bohemian sculptor, born at Policzka in 1734; died at Munich in 1803.

Aulnaye, de l′, dẹh lō′nā′, (François Henri Stanislas,) a French writer, born at Madrid in 1739. He translated "Don Quixote" into French, (1824,) and wrote many articles for the "Biographie Universelle." Among his numerous works are a "History of the Religions and Worships of all Nations," (1791,) "Pax Vobis, or the Anti-Mason," (Philadelphia, 1791,) and an essay "On the Pantomime of the Ancients," ("De la Saltation théâtrale," 1790.) "His version of Don Quixote," says Weiss, "is the best in the language." He lived mostly in Paris. Died in 1830.

See Quérard, "La France Littéraire."

Aulon, d′, dō′lôn′, (Jean,) a French gentleman, known as a companion-in-arms of Joan of Arc. He was appointed by the king to attend her as *intendant* or *maître-d'hôtel*. He fought at the siege of Orléans. In the campaign of 1449 he was made a chevalier.

Aultanne, d′, ōl′tän′, (Joseph Augustin de Fournier—dẹh foor′ne-ā′,) Marquis, a French general, born at Valréas in 1759, served at the battles of Zurich and Hohenlinden, but, having connected himself with Moreau, became suspected by Napoleon for a time. He afterwards distinguished himself at Austerlitz and Jena, and was made governor of Warsaw and Toledo. Died in 1828.

Aulu-Gelle. See Gellius, (Aulus.)

Au′lus, the name of one or more gem-engravers, who lived under early Roman emperors.

Aulus Gellius. See Gellius.

Aulus Postumius. See Postumius.

Aumale, d′, dō′mäl′, (Charles de Lorraine—dẹh lo′rȧn′,) Duc, a French prince, born about 1555, was a son of Claude II., and a first-cousin of Henry, Duke of Guise. After the death of the latter, (1588,) Aumale and the Duke of Mayenne became the chiefs of the League formed against the Huguenots and Henry IV. Aumale commanded a wing of the army of the League at the battle of Ivry, (1590,) and afterwards joined in a treasonable design to transfer France to the King of Spain. He was sentenced to death by Parliament in 1595, but had escaped from their power. Died at Brussels in 1631.

See De Thou, "Historia sui Temporis;" Sismondi, "Histoire des Français."

Aumale, d′, (Claude de Lorraine,) Duc, a French duke, born about the end of the fifteenth century, was a son of René II. of Lorraine. He conquered the duchy of Luxembourg in 1542, and was created Duke of Guise by Francis I. Died in 1550.

Aumale, d′, (Claude II.,) Duc, the son of the preceding, born about 1525, was a brother of François, Duke of Guise. He had a high command in the war against Charles V., and fought against the Huguenots at Dreux, (1562,) Saint-Denis, (1567,) and Moncontour, (1569.) He was one of the principal instigators of the Massacre of Saint Bartholomew, (1572.) He was killed at the siege of La Rochelle in 1573, and left a son Charles, noticed above.

See De Thou, "Historia sui Temporis."

Aumale, d′, (Claude,) a Knight of Malta, son of Claude II., was born in 1563. He was an active, fierce, and cruel member of the League, and declared he would make a Saint Bartholomew of the royalists all over France. He was killed at Saint-Denis in 1591.

Aumale or Albemarle, d′, dȧl′bẹh-mȧrl′, (Étienne, or Stephen,) Count of, was son of Eudes, first Count

---

ē as *k*; ç as *s*; ḡ *hard*; ǧ as *j*; G, H, K, *guttural*; N, *nasal*; R, *trilled*; s̄ as *z*; th as in *this*. (☞See Explanations, p. 23.)

of Aumale, (and Earl of Holderness,) and nephew of William the Conqueror. In 1095 a conspiracy was formed to place him on the English throne, but being defeated he was condemned to the loss of his eyes ; William Rufus, however, pardoned him. He twice rebelled against Henry I., who burnt his castle in Aumale. He made two pilgrimages to the Holy Land, in the last of which he died, in 1127.

Aumale, d', or Albemarle, (EUDES or ODO,) COUNT, son of Étienne II., Count of Champagne, being deprived of his inheritance by his uncle Thibaut III., took refuge with the Duke of Normandy, whose half-sister he married, and to whom he rendered good service in the conquest of England, for which he was created Earl of Holderness. Having joined Mowbray's rebellion, in 1094, he was imprisoned by William Rufus the rest of his life.

Aumale, d', or Albemarle, (GUILLAUME, or WILLIAM,) COUNT, son of Étienne, succeeded his father in Aumale and Holderness in 1127. He supported Stephen in his contest for the crown of England against the empress Matilda. In 1173 he joined the rebellion of Prince Henry against his father Henry II., but afterwards submitted. Died in 1180.

Aumale, d', (HENRI EUGÈNE PHILIPPE LOUIS d'Orléans—doR'lä'ôN',) DUC, the fourth son of King Louis Philippe, was born in Paris in 1822. He entered the army in 1839, served in Africa in 1840, and became maréchal-de-camp in 1842. In 1843 he gained a victory over Abd-el-Kâdér, whose camp and treasures fell into the hands of the French. He was rewarded with the rank of lieutenant-general, and in September, 1847, was appointed Governor-General of Algeria. Soon after that date Abd-el-Kâdér surrendered to him. When the news of the revolution of 1848 arrived in Algeria, the Duc d'Aumale submitted to the new régime in a manner that was generally applauded. He retired as an exile to England.

Aumale, d', (JEAN d'Arcourt—dǎR'kooR',) COMTE, a French soldier, born in 1396, defeated the English in 1423 between Laval and Vitré. He was killed at the battle of Verneuil in 1424.

Aumont, d', (dô'môN', (JACQUES,) DUC, an officer in the national guards in the Revolution, (who was maltreated by the mob for supposed aid to Louis XVI. in his escape,) served till 1793. He died in 1799.

Aumont, d', (dô'môN', (JEAN,) an able French general, born in 1522 of a noble family. He fought against the Protestants in the war which began in 1562, and was made a marshal of France in 1579. In 1589 he became an adherent of Henry IV., for whom he fought with distinction at Ivry, in 1590. He was killed in battle in 1595. He was renowned for courage and magnanimity. His grandson Antoine, Duc d'Aumont, (1601–69,) was a marshal of France.

See DE THOU, "Historia sui Temporis ;" and L'ESTOILE, "Mémoires."

Aumont, d', (LOUIS MARIE ALEXANDRE,) DUC, a brother of Jacques, born in 1736, was a member of the States-General in 1789, and an adherent of the Bourbons. Died in 1814.

Aumont, d', (LOUIS MARIE CÉLESTE de Pienne—deh pe'ên',) DUC, a royalist general, born in 1770, was a son of Jacques, above noticed. He commanded a band of royalists who entered Normandy from the sea during the Hundred Days. Died in 1831.

Aumont, d', (LOUIS MARIE VICTOR,) DUC, a French general, a son of Antoine, born in 1632. He distinguished himself as an officer in the wars of Louis XIV. in Flanders. Died in 1704.

Au-na'rĭ-us or **Au-na-chä'rĭ-us,**[Fr. AUNAIRE, ô'nǎR',] SAINT, Bishop of Auxerre, is known by various names. He was born of a noble family at Orléans about 540 A.D., and enjoyed a high reputation for learning and sanctity.

Aungerville. See RICHARD DE BURY.

Aunillon, ô'ne'yôN', (PIERRE CHARLES Fabiot—fá'be'o',) ABBÉ, born in 1684, was the author of "The Disguised Lovers," a comedy, "Azor, a Fairy Tale," and "The Force of Education," a novel. Died in 1760.

Aunoy, ô'nwä', (MARIE CATHERINE,) COUNTESS OF,

a distinguished ornament of the court of Louis XIV., born about 1650. She is known in our times chiefly by her fairy-tales, which have run through numberless editions and been translated into various languages. She also wrote several novels; and, among them, "The History of the Count of Warwick," "Memoirs of the Court of England," and other historical memoirs and romances. Died at Paris in 1705.

See QUÉRARD, "La France Littéraire ;" DUNLOP, "History of Fiction ;" "Histoire Littéraire des Femmes Françaises."

Aupick, ô'pĕk', (JACQUES,) a French general, born at Gravelines in 1789. He served in several campaigns of Napoleon, became a colonel in 1834, and a general of division in 1847. In 1851 he was ambassador to London. He was appointed a senator in 1853. Died in 1857.

Auramazda. See ORMUZD.

Aurang-Zebe. See AURUNG-ZEB.

Aurat, d'. See DORAT.

Aurbach, von, fon ôwR'bâk, or **Aurpach,** ôwR'pâk, (JOHANN,) a German jurist of Bamberg, lived in the second half of the fifteenth century.

Aurbacher, ôwR'bâk-ęr, (LUDWIG,) a German schoolmaster, born in Bavaria in 1784, wrote, besides other works, "The Adventures of Seven Suabians," (1846.) Died in 1847.

Au-re'lĭ-a, the mother of Caius Julius Cæsar the dictator, was a woman of superior character. Died in 54 B.C.

Aurelia Gens, a plebeian family in Rome, of Sabine origin, containing many illustrious names. C. Aurelius Cotta was the first who obtained the consulship, 252 B.C.

Au-re'lĭ-an or **Au-re-lĭ-ā'nus,** [Fr. AURÉLIEN, ô'rā'le'âN',] (CLAUDIUS DOMITIUS,) a Roman emperor, who was born of obscure parents about 212 A.D., at Sirmium, in Pannonia, or, according to some, in Lower Dacia, or in Mœsia. He rose by his talents and courage from the rank of private to the highest position in the army of Valerian, and was appointed consul in 258 A.D. On the death of Claudius in 270, Aurelian was proclaimed emperor by the army. About the same time the north of Italy was invaded by the Alemanni, who were defeated at Fanum, in Umbria. The principal event of his reign was an expedition against Zenobia, Queen of Palmyra, who reigned over Syria, Egypt, etc., and whose army he defeated near Emesa. Palmyra and the queen were captured by him in 273 A.D. (See ZENOBIA.) He punished a revolt of the Palmyrenes, which occurred soon after, with a general massacre, and acted with extreme severity on other occasions. He was very successful in his military enterprises, and was called the restorer of the empire, but was more competent to command an army than to govern a nation. He was assassinated by his own officers in 275 A.D., and was succeeded by Tacitus.

See VOPISCUS, "Vita Aureliani ;" TREBELLIUS POLLIO, "Odenatus," and "Zenobia ;" TILLEMONT, "Histoire des Empereurs ;" GIBBON, "Decline and Fall of the Roman Empire," chap. xi.

Aurelian or **Aurelianus,** SAINT, was born about 500 A.D. He became Bishop of Arles, and the pope's vicar for Gaul, about 546. He died at Lugdunum, (Lyons,) 551 A.D.

Aurelianus, SAINT. See AURELIAN, SAINT.

Aurelianus Cælius. See CÆLIUS AURELIANUS.

Aurélien, the French of AURELIAN, which see.

Aurelio, ôw-rā'le-o, King of Asturias, reigned from 768 to 774 A.D. He bound himself by treaty to deliver annually a number of maidens to the Moorish king as tribute.

See PAQUIS and DOCHEZ, "Histoire d'Espagne."

Aurelio, ôw-rā'le-o, (AURELIO,) a Venetian poet flourished between 1660 and 1720.

Aurelio, Aurelli, ôw-rel'lee, or **Arelli,** â-rel'lee, (GIOVANNI Muzio—moot'se-o,) [in Latin, JOAN'NES MU'TIUS AURE'LIUS,] a Latin poet, born at Mantua, lived in the early part of the sixteenth century. He was appointed governor of Mondolfo by Leo X., became unpopular, and was assassinated a few months after his appointment. He left a hymn to John the Baptist and an epistle to Leo X., which are highly praised by J. C. Scaliger.

See BAILLET, "Jugements des Savants," and SCALIGER, "Poetica."

ā, ē, ī, ō, ū, ȳ, long; ă, ĕ, ŏ, same, less prolonged; ă, ĕ, ĭ, ŏ, ŭ, ў, short; ạ, ẹ, ị, ọ, obscure; fär, fåll, fåt; mêt; nŏt; gōōd; mōōn;

Aurelio, (LUDOVICO,) an Italian historian and Jesuit, born at Perúgia, was distinguished for his proficiency in Greek, Latin, and German. He became a canon of the Lateran at Rome. Among his works are a "History of the Rebellion of the Bohemians against the Emperors Matthias and Ferdinand," (1625,) and an "Epitome of the Annals of Cardinal Baronius," (2 vols., 1634.) Died in 1637.

See MAZZUCHELLI, "Scrittori d'Italia."

Au-re′lĭ-us, a famous Roman painter, lived in the reign of Augustus.

Aurelius, ŏw-rā′le-ûs, (ÆGIDIUS,) a learned Swedish writer and translator, born at Upsal, lived about 1650.

Aurelius, (JOANNES MUTIUS.) See AURELIO, (GIOVANNI MUZIO.)

Au-re′lĭ-us An-to-nī′nus, (MARCUS,) commonly called **Mar′cus Aure′lius,** [Fr. MARC-AURÈLE, mǎr′kō′rāl′,] sometimes surnamed THE PHILOSOPHER, a Roman emperor, celebrated for his wisdom, learning, and virtue, was born at Rome in April, 121 A.D. He was a son of Annius Verus, who once held the office of prætor. His own original name was Marcus Annius Verus. He was educated by able teachers, among whom were Fronto, Apollonius of Chalcis, and Herodes Atticus. In philosophy he was a disciple of the Stoics, of which sect he became an illustrious ornament by his practice as well as by his writings. Having been adopted by Antoninus Pius in 138 A.D., he assumed the name of M. Ælius Aurelius Verus Cæsar. In 139 Antoninus, who had just become emperor, associated him in the administration. Aurelius married Faustina, a daughter of Antoninus, about 146 A.D., and succeeded his adopted father in 161, after he had been urged by the senate to accept the throne. He associated with himself in the empire Lucius Commodus, *alias* Lucius Verus. They reigned harmoniously together until the death of Verus in 169 A.D.

His reign was disturbed by many insurrections, and by inroads of northern barbarians, especially the German tribes of the Marcomanni and Quadi. Though he preferred peace, he was almost continually involved in war, in which he acted on the defensive and was generally victorious. He is said to have shown himself a skilful general. He commanded in person the army that drove the Marcomanni out of Pannonia. His victory over the Quadi in 174 A.D. is attributed to a miracle by some writers, who affirm that the thirsty Romans were refreshed by a shower during the battle, while the enemy were assailed by a violent storm of hail and lightning. An ancient tradition ascribes this miracle to the prayers of a Christian legion which formed part of the army of Aurelius.

In 175 A.D., Avidius Cassius, an able general, who commanded the Roman army in Syria, revolted, declared himself emperor, and made himself master of Egypt and of the part of Asia which lies east of Mount Taurus. He was killed by his own officers in the same year. Aurelius visited Syria, Egypt, Athens, etc., in 176. He was initiated into the Eleusinian mysteries at Athens, and on other occasions conformed to the established religious rites. In 177 he associated his son Commodus with himself in the empire. He was engaged in a campaign against the Marcomanni and Quadi, when he died at Sirmium, or at Vindebona, (Vienna,) in March, 180 A.D. Commodus erected to his memory the Antonine column, which stands at Rome in the Piazza Colonna. His thoughts and doctrines were recorded by himself in a Greek work, called "Meditations," which is considered an excellent manual of moral discipline. His biographers find it difficult to explain the persecution which the Christians suffered in his reign, and which is perhaps the only stain on his memory. We learn from one short passage of his writings that he was prejudiced against the Christians. No monarch was ever more beloved by his subjects. He acquired the boasted equanimity of the Stoic philosophy, without the asperity which was a characteristic of the Stoics in general. A good English version of "The Thoughts of Marcus Aurelius Antoninus," by George Long, appeared in 1862.

See CAPITOLINUS, "Marcus Antoninus Philosophus;" TILLEMONT, "Histoire des Empereurs;" RIPAULT, "Histoire de l'Empereur Marc-Antonin," 5 vols., 1820; DION CASSIUS, lib. lxxi.; FA-

BRICIUS, "Biblioth′ca Græca;" DE SUCKAU, "Étude sur Marc Aurèle," 1857; AURELIUS VICTOR, "De Cæsaribus Historia." See also the notice of Marcus Aurelius in MATTHEW ARNOLD's "Essays in Criticism."

Aurelius Arcadius Charisius. See CHARISIUS.

Aurelius Augustinus. See AUGUSTINE, SAINT.

Au-re′lĭ-us Cor-ne′lĭ-us, the Latin name of a Dutchman whose family name was SOPSEN, better known as the friend of Erasmus (whose preceptor he is said to have been) than by his works,. which were principally Latin elegies. He was a native of Gouda.

See ERASMUS, "Epistolæ."

Aurelius Cornelius Celsus. See CELSUS.

Aurelius Cotta. See COTTA.

Au-re′lĭ-us Vic′tor, (SEXTUS,) a Roman historian, who flourished between 350 and 400 A.D., is supposed to have been a pagan. He was appointed prefect of Pannonia Secunda by the emperor Julian about 360, and was prefect of the city of Rome under Theodosius. The materials for his biography are very scanty. He wrote "De Cæsaribus Historia," which contains the lives of the emperors from Augustus to Constantius, and is extant. He is also the reputed author of two extant works, entitled "Lives of Illustrious Romans," ("De Viris illustribus Urbis Romæ,") and "On the Life and Character of the Emperors," ("De Vita et Moribus Imperatorum," or "Aurelii Victoris Epitome.")

Aurelli, (GIOVANNI MUZIO.) See AURELIO, (GIOVANNI MUZIO.)

Aureng-Zebe. (or **Zeyb.**) See AURUNG-ZEB.

Aurenhammer, ŏw′ren-hâm′mer, or **Auernhammer,** ŏw′ern-hâm′mer, (JOSEPHA,) a celebrated pianoforte player at Vienna, and a composer of some reputation. She lived at the close of the eighteenth century.

Au-re′o-lus, (CAIUS,) one of the various usurpers called the "Thirty Tyrants" that arose in different parts of the Roman Empire during the reign of Gallienus, was born in Dacia, of an obscure family, and rose by his military merit. After having put down two pretenders to the imperial throne, he assumed the purple about 267 A.D. Having by treachery procured the assassination of his rival Gallienus, he soon after submitted to Claudius II., (the successor of Gallienus,) but subsequently, re volting, was slain, 268 A.D.

Aurgelmir. See YMIR.

Auria, ŏw-ree′ä, (VINCENZO,) an Italian antiquary and historian, born at Palermo in 1625, is said to have been chancellor of Sicily. He published numerous useful works, among which are a "History of the Viceroys of Sicily," ("Istoria de' Signori Vicerè di Sicilia," 1697,) and a "Treatise on Tournaments," (1690.) He also wrote verses in Latin and Italian. Died in 1710.

See MONGITORE, "Vita di Auria," in CRESCIMBENI's "Vite degli Arcadi illustri."

Auria, d′, (GIOVANNI DOMENICO,) an eminent Neapolitan sculptor and architect of the sixteenth century. His master-piece is the Fontana Medina in the Piazza del Castelnuovo at Naples. Died in 1585.

See CICOGNARA, "Storia della Scultura."

Auria, d′, (GIUSEPPE,) an Italian mathematician, who lived in Naples in the sixteenth century. He wrote a work on the best method of study. He also translated various works of the Greek mathematicians.

Aurifaber, ŏw′re-fä′ber, (ANDREAS,) a Latin form of the name of ANDREAS GOLDSCHMIDT, a German physician, born at Breslau in 1512, became professor in the University of Königsberg. He published a treatise "On the Management of Dogs, ("De Cura Canum," 1545,) and wrote a "History of Amber," ("Succini Historia," 1561.) Died in 1559.

Aurifaber, (JOHANN,) a brother of the preceding, born at Breslau in 1517, was a Lutheran divine. He gained distinction by settling some religious differences at Lubeck, and became professor of divinity at Königsberg about 1555. Died in 1568.

Aurifaber, (JOHANN,) a German divine, born in the county of Mansfeld about 1519. He is said to have been private secretary of Luther, at whose death he was present. He was appointed court preacher at Weimar in 1551, and minister of the principal Lutheran church at Erfurt in 1566. He edited the "Letters of Luther" and his "Table-Talk," and was one of the editors of Luther's óther works. Died in 1575.

See JÖCHER, "Allgemeines Gelehrten-Lexikon."

Auriferi, ŏw-ree′fâ-ree, (BERNARDIUS,) a botanist of distinction, was born in Sicily, of very poor parents, in 1739. He published a work entitled "Hortus Panormitanus," (1789.) Died in 1796.

Aurigny, d′, dō′rĕn′ye′, (GILLES,) a French poet, born at Beauvais, became an advocate in the Parliament of Paris. He produced a number of imaginative works, which were once popular. Among the most admired of these is "The Guardian of Love," ("Tuteur d'Amour," 1546,) a poem. Died in 1553.

Auriol, d′, dō′re′ol′, (BLAISE,) a French poet and jurist, born at Castelnaudary, became professor of canon law at Toulouse. His chief poem is "Le Départ d'Amour," ("The Departure of Love," 1508,) intended as a continuation of "La Chasse d'Amour" of Octavien de Saint-Gelais. Died about 1540.

Auriol, d′, (PIERRE,) [in Latin AURE′OLUS or AURI′OLUS,] a French theologian, born at Toulouse, became Archbishop of Aix about 1320.

See CARDINAL SERNANO, "Vie de Pierre d'Auriol."

Aurisicchio, ŏw-re-sĕk′ke-o, an Italian composer, who died about the middle of the eighteenth century.

Aurispa, ŏw-rès′pȃ, (GIOVANNI,) an eminent Italian scholar, who contributed much to the restoration of classical learning among his countrymen. He was born at Noto, in Sicily, about 1370. Having visited Constantinople in 1418, he returned with a rich store of Greek manuscripts, many of which were almost, if not wholly, unknown in Europe. He also contributed not a little to the popularity of Greek literature by his zeal and success as a teacher. Died at Ferrara in 1459. He translated into Latin "Hieroclis Liber in Pythagoræ Aurea Carmina."

See TIRABOSCHI, "Storia della Letteratura Italiana."

Au-rĭ-vil′lĭ-us, (or ŏw-re-vil′le-ûs,) (CARL,) an eminent Swedish Orientalist, born at Stockholm in 1717, studied at Jena, Halle, and Paris. He became professor of Oriental languages at Upsal in 1772, and was appointed a member of a commission to translate the Bible into Swedish. He translated the Pentateuch, Job, the Psalms, and the Prophets. His academical dissertations are highly commended. Died in 1786.

See "Biographiskt-Lexicon öfver namnkunnige Svenska Män."

Aurivillius, (ERIC,) a Swedish jurist, born at Knutby in 1643; died in 1702.

Aurivillius, (MAGNUS,) a Swedish minister, who served Charles XII. as chaplain at Pultowa and Bender, was born in 1673.

See "Biographiskt-Lexicon öfver namnkunnige Svenska Män."

Aurivillius, (PEHR FABIAN,) a son of Carl, born in 1756, was for forty years keeper of the principal library of Sweden, at Upsal, of which he compiled a catalogue, (1814.) He was professor of humanities at Upsal, and wrote a biography of Bergman the chemist. Died in 1829.

See "Biographiskt-Lexicon öfver namnkunnige Svenska Män."

Aurivillius, (SAMUEL,) a Swedish physician, and professor of anatomy at Upsal. Died in 1767.

Au-ro-gal′lus, (MATTHAEUS,) a distinguished scholar, cotemporary and friend of Luther, was born in Bohemia about 1480. He was for some time professor of Hebrew, Greek, and Latin in the University of Wittenberg, and afterwards rector in that institution. He published several works, and aided Luther largely in his translation of the Bible. Died in 1543.

See BAYLE, "Historical and Critical Dictionary."

Auroux des Pommiers, ō′roo′ dȃ po′me-ȃ′, (MATHIEU,) a French ecclesiastic and legal commentator, who lived in the first half of the eighteenth century.

Aurpach. See AURBACH.

Au-run′cus, (POSTHUMIUS COMINIUS,) a Roman general, who was consul in 493 B.C., when the plebeians asserted their rights on Mons Sacer.

Aurung-Zeb, (Aureng (or Aurang)-Zebe,) ō′rŭng-zȃb′, the "ornament of the throne," afterwards surnamed ALUM-GEER or ALAM-GÎR, ȃ′lŭm-ğeer, ("conqueror of the world,") a celebrated emperor of Hindostan,

was born in 1618. Though the third son of Shah Jehân, he managed, by creating dissension among his brothers, and finally by the assassination of the two elder, Dârâ and Shujâ, and the imprisonment of the younger, Môorâd, to possess himself of the whole empire, even in the lifetime of his father, whom he detained in captivity for seven years. Notwithstanding the unscrupulous means by which he possessed himself of power, he seems to have used it not unwisely nor very unjustly, so far as his Mohammedan subjects were concerned; though his bigoted intolerance towards the Hindoos created discontent and was the cause of the first formidable insurrection among the warlike Marhattas. Though cool and crafty, he seems not to have been cruel, except from motives of policy. During a severe famine which afflicted his empire in the third year of his reign, he showed both wisdom and humanity in the relief of his famishing subjects. He added Beejapore and Golconda to his dominions, and increased the imperial revenue to £40,000,000. He died in 1707, in the fiftieth year of his reign. The Mussulmans of India regard him as one of the greatest of their monarchs; but the decadence of the empire may be traced to his policy. As in the case of Louis XIV. of France, whom he resembled, his religious intolerance and habits of duplicity ruined the resources and prosperity of the country.

See ELPHINSTONE, "History of India;" BERNIER, "Voyages et Description de l'Empire Mogol;" J. MILL, "History of British India;" DOW, "History of Hindustan."

Au′sĭ-us, (or ŏw′se-ûs,) (HENRY,) a Swedish Hellenist, born in Smalånd in 1603, was professor of Greek at Upsal. Died in 1659.

Ausone. See AUSONIUS.

Au-so′nĭ-us, [Fr. AUSONE, ō′son′,] (DECIMUS MAGNUS,) a celebrated Latin poet, born at Burdigala (Bordeaux) about 310 A.D. He taught grammar and rhetoric at that city with such success that his fame induced Valentinian to appoint him tutor of his son Gratian in 367. After the accession of Gratian to the throne, 375 A.D., Ausonius enjoyed the favour of his former pupil, and obtained, besides other high offices, that of consul in 379. He appears to have been a Christian in profession; but Muratori and others have affirmed or supposed he was a pagan. He wrote epigrams; "Idyllia;" a descriptive poem on the Moselle; and "Series of Noble Cities," ("Ordo nobilium Urbium.") His poems were greatly admired by his contemporaries, but are less agreeable to the taste of modern critics, who consider his style faulty in many respects. His poem on the Moselle has considerable merit, and is called the oldest specimen of descriptive poetry. Died about 394 A.D.

See M. DE PUYMAIGRE, "Vie d'Ausone;" SOUCHAY, "Dissertatio de Vita et Scriptis Ausonii;" FABRICIUS, "Bibliotheca Latina;" J. DEMOGEOT, "Études historiques et littéraires sur Ausone," 1837.

Ausonius, [Fr. AUSONE,] SAINT, born in the French province of Saintonge, is supposed to have been consecrated first bishop of Angoulême (Engolisma) in 260 A.D., and to have been slain by the Vandals about 270; but his history is doubtful.

Auspicius, aw-spish′e-us, SAINT, Bishop of Toul, was a learned and distinguished ornament of the Church in France in the fifth century. Died about 480 A.D.

Aussigny, d′, dō′sĕn′ye′, (THIBAULD,) was Bishop of Orléans, France, in the fifteenth century. He wrote a "History of the Acts of Joan of Arc."

See SAINTE-BEUVE, "Tableau de la Poésie Française au seizième Siècle."

Aus′ten, (Miss JANE,) an English authoress, born at Steventon, Hampshire, in December, 1775, was a daughter of a clergyman who was rector of that parish for many years. After the death of her father, she resided at Southampton and at Chawton, to which she removed in 1809. In 1811 she published anonymously her first novel, "Sense and Sensibility," which was very favourably received. Her other works are "Pride and Prejudice," "Mansfield Park," "Emma," (1816,) "Northanger Abbey," (1818,) and "Persuasion," (1818.) Her characters belong to the middle rank of English society, and are not extraordinary either morally or intellectually. She is considered almost unrivalled in fidelity to nature. Her writings are free from sentimental extravagance, but

---

ā, ē, ĭ, ō, ū, ȳ, *long;* ȧ, ė, ȯ, same, less prolonged; ă, ĕ, ĭ, ŏ, ŭ, y̆, *short;* ạ, ẹ, ị, ọ, *obscure;* fâr, fȧll, fȧt; mĕt; nŏt; gōŏd; mōŏn;

not deficient in tenderness. They have been translated into French, and are admired in France. "Edgeworth, Ferrier, Austen," says Sir Walter Scott, "have all given portraits of real society far superior to anything vain man has produced of like nature." Died in May, 1817.

See LOCKHART, "Life of Sir Walter Scott;" "Quarterly Review" for January, 1821; "Atlantic Monthly" for February, 1863; MRS. ELWOOD, "Memoirs of the Literary Ladies of England from the Commencement of the Last Century," vol. ii., 1843.

Austen, (RALPH,) a writer on horticulture, fruit-trees, etc., was born in Staffordshire about 1610.

Austen or **Aus'tin,** (WILLIAM,) an English metal-founder in the reign of Henry VI., was one of the artists employed to execute the splendid tomb of Richard, Earl of Warwick, in Saint Mary's Church at Warwick.

See DUGDALE, "Antiquities of Warwickshire."

Aus'tin, (BENJAMIN,) an American political writer of the democratic school, born about 1752. He was a sup-porter of Jefferson. A collection of his writings in the "Boston Chronicle," under the signature of "Old South," was published in 1803 in a volume entitled "Constitutional Republicanism." He died in Boston in 1820.

Austin, (CHARLES,) a son of Benjamin, noticed above, was shot in the streets of Boston (1806) in an attempt to inflict castigation upon one who had attacked his father in the public papers.

Austin, (JAMES TRECOTHIC,) an American lawyer and writer, son of Jonathan L. Austin, born in Boston in 1784. He graduated at Harvard in 1802, was advocate of Suffolk county for twenty-nine years, and attorney-general of Massachusetts from 1832 to 1843. He published a "Life of Elbridge Gerry," and other works.

Aus'tin, (JOHN,) an English writer, born in Norfolk county in 1613, became a Roman Catholic about 1640, and afterwards resided mostly in London. He wrote, besides other works, "The Christian Moderator; or, Persecution for Religion condemned," (1651,) the style of which is commended. Died in 1669.

See BUTLER, "Historical Memoirs respecting the English, Irish, and Scotch Catholics."

Austin, (JOHN,) an English jurist, born in 1797, was author of "The Province of Jurisprudence determined," (1832,) which is said to be one of the most valuable con-tributions to the philosophy of law and legislation that has been produced in modern times. Died in 1860.

Austin, (JONATHAN LORING,) an American patriot, born in Boston in 1748. In 1777 he was sent to Paris with the news of the surrender of Burgoyne. Here he remained two years as Franklin's secretary, and after-wards spent two years as his agent in England. On his return to the United States he was liberally rewarded by Congress. Died in 1826.

Austin, (MOSES,) an American pioneer, born in Dur-ham, Connecticut, about the commencement of the Amer-ican Revolution. He sold his property in 1820, and pen-etrated to the interior of Texas. At Bexar he forwarded to the Mexican government an application for permission to establish in that country an American colony of three hundred families, and, without waiting for a reply, he set out on his return to Missouri for settlers. He died soon after (June, 1821) from the effect of the hardships to which he had been exposed. His application, however, was successful, and the colony was established by his son, Stephen F. Austin.

Austin, (ROBERT,) an English clergyman, who de-fended the Parliament in a pamphlet entitled "Alle-giance not impeached," etc., (1644.)

Austin, SAINT. See AUGUSTINE, SAINT.

Austin, (SAMUEL,) an English poet, son of Rev. Sam-uel, noticed below, was born in 1636; died in 1661.

Austin, (SAMUEL,) D.D., president of the University of Vermont, was born in New Haven, Connecticut, in 1760. He graduated at Yale with distinguished honours in 1783, and, after studying divinity, preached for several years in Fair Haven, and about twenty-five years in Wor-cester, Massachusetts. Died in 1830.

Austin, (Rev. SAMUEL,) an English poet, born in Cornwall in 1606. His principal work is "Austin's Urania, or the Heavenly Muse," (1629.)

See WOOD, "Athenæ Oxonienses."

Austin, (Mrs. SARAH,) an English writer, distin-guished as a translator from the German, was a member of the Taylor family of Norwich. She became the wife of John Austin, barrister, of London. She published "Characteristics of Goethe," (3 vols., 1833,) which had a great success, "Considerations on National Education," "Sketches of Germany from 1760 to 1814," and other original works. She also made excellent translations of Prince Pückler-Muskau's "Travels in England," and of Ranke's "History of the Popes," (3 vols., 1840,) of which Macaulay remarks, "It is such as might be expected from the skill, the taste, and the scrupulous integrity of the accomplished lady who, as an interpreter between the mind of Germany and the mind of Britain, has already deserved so well of both countries." (Review of Ranke's "History of the Popes.") Died in 1867.

See "Gentleman's Magazine" for September, 1867.

Austin, (STEPHEN F.,) the founder of the State of Texas, was a son of Moses Austin, noticed above. He explored the region watered by the Colorado and Brazos Rivers in 1821, and conducted from New Orleans a party of emigrants, who settled where the city of Austin now stands. About the end of 1822 the grant made to his father was confirmed to him by the Mexican government. In the spring of 1833 the Texan colonists formed a con-stitution and applied for admission to the Mexican con-federacy; but Austin, who visited the city of Mexico on this mission, found that country in a state of anarchy, and failed to obtain the ratification of the Texan constitu-tion. He was detained at Mexico as a prisoner or hos-tage until September, 1835. About that time the Texans took arms to drive the Mexicans out of Texas, and ap-pointed Austin commander-in-chief. In November, 1835, he went as commissioner to the United States to pro-mote the liberation of Texas from the Mexican domi-nation, and to obtain the recognition of Texas as an independent State. Died in December, 1836.

Austin, (WILLIAM,) of Lincoln's Inn, London, was the author of a poem on the passion of Christ, some prose works of a religious character, and a translation of Cicero on "Old Age." Died in 1633.

Austin or **Aus'ten,** (WILLIAM,) a designer and en-graver, who lived in London about 1750. Views of buildings in Palmyra and Rome are his most noted works.

Austin, (WILLIAM,) an English physician and chemist of high reputation, was born in 1753. He practised at Oxford and in London, and was chosen physician to Saint Bartholomew's Hospital in 1786. He published a "Treatise on the Origin and Component Parts of the Stone in the Bladder," (1791,) and wrote several papers on gases. Died in 1793.

Austin, (WILLIAM,) an American lawyer and writer, born in 1778, rose to eminence at the Boston bar. His principal works are his "Letters from London," in 1802 and 1803, and "Essay on the Human Character of Jesus Christ," in 1807. Died in 1841.

Aus-tre-ber'ta, SAINT, born in Artois in 633 A.D., was related to the royal family. She died in 704.

Austregilde, ōs't'r-zhĕld', the wife of Gontran, King of Burgundy, notorious for her crimes. Died in 560 A.D.

Austremoine, SAINT, săn'tōs't'r-mwän', [Lat. STRE-MO'NIUS,] the first Bishop of Auvergne, converted many pagans in Gaul about 250 A.D.

Autelli, ŏw-tel'lee, (JACOPO,) an Italian worker in mosaic, flourished in the first half of the seventeenth century. There is said to be a curious mosaic in the mu-seum at Florence upon which he worked sixteen years.

See LANZI, "History of Painting in Italy."

Autelz, des, dȧ zō'tĕl', (GUILLAUME,) a French poet of considerable reputation in his day, but of no great merit, born in Burgundy in 1529. He is supposed to have died about 1600.

See NICÉRON, "Mémoires."

Autenrieth, von, fon ŏw'ten-reet',(HERMANN FRIED-RICH,) a physician, born at Tübingen in 1799, succeeded his father as professor of anatomy in 1835. He has published, besides other works, one "On the Diseases of the Common People of Great Britain," ("Ueber die Volkskrankheiten in Gross-Britannien," 1824.)

See CALLISEN, "Medicinisches Schriftsteller-Lexikon."

e as k; ç as s; g hard; g as j; G, H, K, guttural; N, nasal; R, trilled; s as z; th as in this. (☞See Explanations, p. 23.)

Autenrieth, von, (JOHANN HERMANN FERDINAND,) an able German medical writer and physiologist, born at Stuttgart in 1772, was the father of the preceding. He practised about one year (1794) at Lancaster, Pennsylvania, and became professor of anatomy, etc. at Tübingen in 1797. He was distinguished for his varied knowledge and powers of observation, and wrote numerous works, the principal among which is a "Manual of Human Physiology," ("Handbuch der empirischen menschlichen Physiologie," 3 parts, 1801-02.) Died at Tübingen in 1835.

Auteroche,(CHAPPE D'.) See CHAPPE D'AUTEROCHE.

Autharis. See ANTHERIC.

Authon. See AUTON.

Authville des Amourettes, d', dōt'vĕl' dă ză'-moo'rĕt', (CHARLES LOUIS,) a French tactician, who published several works on military subjects. He was born at Paris in 1716, and died there in 1762.

Autichamp, d', dō'te'shŏN', (ANTOINE JOSEPH Eulalie de Beaumont—uh'lȁ'le' dĕh bō'mŏN',) COUNT, born in 1744, was a brother of the marquis Jean T. Louis, noticed below. He fought for the American cause at Yorktown. Died in 1822.

Autichamp, d', (CHARLES,) a son of the preceding, born in 1770, was a royalist chief in the Vendean war of 1793. Died in 1852.

Autichamp, d', (CHARLES,) Seigneur de Miribel, a French officer, entered the army about 1640. He distinguished himself at Lerida and Lens. Died in 1692.

Autichamp, d', (JEAN THÉRÈSE LOUIS de Beaumont—dĕh bō'mŏN',) MARQUIS, was born at Angers, of a distinguished French family, in 1738. He took an active part in the royalist cause during the Revolution until 1797, when he entered the service of Paul I. of Russia, where he obtained considerable distinction. Returning to France with the Bourbons in 1815, he was made lieutenant-general, and governor of the Louvre. Died in 1831.

See DE COURCELLES, "Dictionnaire historique des Généraux Français."

Au'to-clēs, [Αὐτοκλῆς,] an Athenian general and orator, commanded in Thrace in 362 B.C.

Au-toc'ra̢-tēs [Αὐτοκράτης] of Athens, one of the earliest Greek dramatic poets.

Autoin. See ALDUIN.

Au-tol'ў-cus, [Αὐτόλυκος,] a Greek mathematician, born at Pitane, in Æolis, lived about 320 B.C. He taught mathematics to the philosopher Arcesilaus, and wrote two extant works, "On the Moving Sphere," and "On the Risings and Settings of the Stars."

See SCHOELL, "Histoire de la Littérature Grecque."

Autolycus, a famous thief of antiquity, the son of Hermes. (See SISYPHUS.)

Au-tom'e-don, [Αὐτομέδων,] the name of a poet to whom are attributed a number of epigrams in the Greek Anthology. He is supposed to have been a native of Cyzicus, and to have lived in the reign of Nerva.

Automne, ō'ton', [Lat. AUTUM'NUS,] (BERNARD,) a French jurist, born near Auch about 1570. He wrote, besides other legal works, a "Commentary on the Common Law (Coutume) of Bordeaux." Died in 1666.

Auton, Authon, d', dō'tŏN', or **Autun,** ō'tŭN', written also **Anton** and **D'Anton,** (JEHAN or JEAN,) a French poet and chronicler, who is supposed to have been born about 1470. His reputation as a poet brought him to the notice of Anne of Brittany, queen of Louis XII., through whom he received the appointment of chronicler to the king. His "Annals of the Reign of Louis XII." are distinguished for their truth and fidelity. Died in 1527.

See GOUJET, "Bibliothèque Française."

Au-ton'o-ē, [Gr. Αὐτονόη,] a daughter of Cadmus, and a sister of Ino, was the wife of Aristæus, and mother of Actæon.

Au-toph-ra̢-dā'tēs, [Gr. Αὐτοφραδάτης,] a Persian general in the time of Artaxerxes III. and Darius II. He suppressed the revolt of Artabazus, Satrap of Lydia, and commanded the fleet of Darius in the war with Alexander the Great, in conjunction with Pharnabazus.

Autran, ō'trŏN', (JOSEPH,) a French poet, born at Marseilles in 1812. He produced in 1838 "Sports for the Winds," ("Ludibria Ventis,") which was received

with favour, and in 1848 "The Daughter of Æschylus," a drama in five acts, which shared the prize of the Academy with the "Gabrielle" of Augier. His "Poems of the Sea" (1852) are admired.

Autreau, ō'trō', (JACQUES,) a French artist of the seventeenth century, was respectable both as a painter and dramatic writer. His comedy of "Port à l'Anglais" (1718) was eminently successful. Died in poverty, at Paris, in 1745, aged eighty-nine.

See HEINECKEN, "Dictionnaire des Artistes."

Autrey, ō'trȁ', (HENRI JEAN BAPTISTE Fabry de Moncault—fȁ'bre' dĕh mŏN'kō',) COUNT, born in Paris in 1723. He was commander of a brigade of cavalry of Brittany ; but was chiefly noted for the works he wrote in opposition to the Encyclopædists, (as the infidel philosophers of the French Revolution were called.) Died in 1777.

See GRIMM, "Correspondance littéraire."

Autrive, d', do'trĕv', (JACQUES FRANÇOIS,) an eminent French violinist and composer, was born at Saint-Quentin in 1758, and died in 1824.

Autroche, d', dō'trosh', (CLAUDE de Loynes—dĕh lwǎn,) a French translator, born at Orléans in 1744. He published in 1804 a metrical version of Virgil's "Æneid," which he considered an improvement on the original. He proposed to give an edition of the Æneid such as he supposed Virgil would have written if he had lived long enough to make it perfect. In 1808 he produced a mediocre version of "Paradise Lost, separated (dégagée) from the superfluous parts which disfigure it." Died in 1823.

See QUÉRARD, "La France Littéraire."

Au-tro'nĭ-us Poe'tus was consul of Rome in 66 B.C., after which he was banished as an accomplice of Catiline.

Autumnus. See AUTOMNE.

Autun. See AUTON.

Auvergne, ō-vȩrn', [Fr. pron. ō'vărñ',] (BERNARD,) the first Count of, obtained his title in 864. He joined the league of Charles the Bald in 877, but made his peace with the king in the following year, and afterwards rendered distinguished services to Louis II., who appointed him guardian to his son Louis III. He was killed in war in 884.

Auvergne, d', ȁō'vărñ', (ANTOINE,) a French operatic composer, born at Clermont-Ferrand in 1713, went to Paris, where he became director of the Opera. Died in 1797.

Auvergne, d', (EDWARD,) an English historical writer, born in the island of Jersey about 1660. He was chaplain to William III., whom he accompanied in his wars in the Spanish Netherlands, of which he afterwards wrote the history. Died in 1737.

See WOOD, "Athenæ Oxonienses;" SALMON, "History and Antiquities of Essex."

Auvergne, d', (GUILLAUME,) [Lat. GULIEL'MUS ARVER'NUS or ALVER'NUS,] Bishop of Paris, was born at Aurillac in the latter part of the twelfth century. A doctor of the Sorbonne, he was distinguished by his philosophical, mathematical, and theological studies, having written voluminously on the last subject. His chief work is a treatise on "The Universe," ("De Universo.") Died in 1249.

Auvergne, d', (LATOUR.) See LATOUR D'AUVERGNE.

Auvergne, d', (MARTIAL,) called also **Martial of Paris,** an eminent French lawyer, poet, and wit, was born in Paris about 1440. Among his works may be mentioned the "Decrees of Love," ("Les Arrests d'Amour,") partly in prose and partly in poetry, in imitation of the subjects treated in the courts of Love as established in that age, and a poem entitled "Vigils of the Death of Charles the Seventh." Died in 1508.

See LONGFELLOW's "Poets and Poetry of Europe."

Auvergne, d', (PEYROLS, pā'rol',) a distinguished Provençal poet, many of whose songs are preserved in the Vatican and the Royal Library of Paris, flourished in the twelfth century.

See MILLOT, "Histoire littéraire des Troubadours;" SISMONDI, "De la Littérature du Midi de l'Europe."

Auvergne, d', (PIERRE,) also called **Petrus de Alvernia (or Arvernia)** and **Petrus de Cros,** a pupil of Thomas Aquinas, was born in Auvergne about 1250,

---

ā, ē, ī, ō, ū, ȳ, long; ă, ĕ, ĭ, ŏ, ŭ, ў, short; ą, ȩ, į, ǫ, obscure; fär, fâll, fât; mĕt; nŏt; gōōd; mōōn;

and became one of the most distinguished philosophers and theologians of his day. He wrote several commentaries on Aristotle's works, was a socius of the Sorbonne, and canon of the Cathedral of Paris.

See BULÉE, "Historia Universitatis Parisiensis."

Auvergne, d', (PIERRE,) written also **Peyre d'Auvergne,** a famous troubadour of Clermont, flourished about the middle of the twelfth century. He afterwards renounced the world and became a monk. He died, it is supposed, about 1215.

See LONGFELLOW, "Poets and Poetry of Europe ;" MILLOT, "Histoire littéraire des Troubadours."

Auvergne, d', (PIERRE,) a celebrated French scholar, who became rector of the University of Paris in 1272. Died probably about 1300.

Auvergne, d', (THÉOPHILE MALO CORRET DE LA TOUR.) See LATOUR D'AUVERGNE.

Auvigny, d', dō'vĕn'ye', (JEAN **du Castre** — dü kȧst'r,) a French *littérateur*, born in Hainaut about 1710, is said to have been addicted to pleasure no less than to literature. Among his works are "Lives of Illustrious Men of France," (10 vols., 1739–57,) and a romance called "Memoirs of Madame de Barneveldt," (1732 or 1735.) He was killed at the battle of Dettingen in 1743.

See MORÉRI, "Dictionnaire Historique."

Auvity, ō've'te', (JEAN ABRAHAM,) for several years a surgeon of the Foundling Hospital at Paris, was noted for his skill in treating the diseases of children. He wrote several medical essays. Died in 1821.

Auvray, ō'vrȧ', (FÉLIX,) a French historical painter, born in 1800, was one of the most distinguished pupils of Baron Gros. Died in 1833.

Auvray, (JEAN,) a French poet of considerable merit, but whose works are too often disfigured by indelicate allusions and coarseness of expression, born about 1590; died in 1633. His "Sacred Treasure" seems to have been the best of his productions.

Auvray, (LOUIS MARIE,) a French colonel, born in 1762, was prefect of La Sarthe from 1800 until 1814. He published "Statistics of the Department of La Sarthe," (1802.) Died in 1833.

Auvray, (PHILIPP PETER JOSEPH,) a portrait-painter, born at Dresden in 1778 ; died in 1815.

Auwera, ōw-ŵā'rä, (JOHANN GEORG,) an artist who was educated at Rome, but afterwards became court-sculptor in Bavaria, resided at Würzburg, where he died in 1756.

See JÄCK, "Leben und Werke der Künstler Bambergs."

Auxbœuff, ō'buf', (PIERRE,) a French priest, eminent as a pulpit orator, lived at Paris about 1400.

Auxentius, awk-sen'she-us, [Fr. AUXENCE, ōk'-sŏNss',] Bishop of Milan, (Mediolanum,) born in Cappadocia about 310 A.D. He was at first an Arian, but afterwards recanted, and enjoyed the favour of the emperor Valentinian until his death in 374.

Aux-Epaules, ō'zȧ'pōl', [Lat. DE HU'MERIS, AD HU'MEROS, or DE SCAP'ULIS,] a French soldier of fortune of the fifteenth century, took an active part in the civil wars under Charles VII., and served for a time in the English army. Died in 1643.

See JEAN CHARTIER, "Chronique," and "La Mer des Histoires," Lyons, 1512.

Aux-il'ĭ-us, a French theologian, lived about 900, and wrote some treatises against Pope Sergius III.

Auxiron, ōk'se'rŏN', (JEAN BAPTISTE,) a French mathematician, born at Baume-les-Dames about 1680; died in 1760.

Auxiron, d', dōk'se'rŏN',(CLAUDE FRANÇOIS JOSEPH,) a French officer, born in Besançon in 1728, wrote some works on the best method of supplying Paris with water, and one (2 vols. 12mo) on "Government." Died in 1778.

Auxiron, d', (JEAN BAPTISTE,) a French jurist, born at Besançon in 1736; died in 1800.

Auzanet, ō'zȧ'nȧ', (BARTHÉLEMI,) a French lawyer of high repute, born in Paris in 1591. He was engaged with De Lamoignon in an effort to produce a uniform system of laws throughout France, which, though it failed of its object, produced some valuable legal works. Died in 1673.

See MORÉRI, "Dictionnaire Historique."

Auziron, ō'ze'rŏN', (JEAN BAPTISTE,) a French engineer, and writer on political economy, born at Besançon in 1728 ; died in 1778.

Auzoles, d', dō'zol', (JACQUES,) Lord of La Peyre, and author of several works on Chronology and the Bible, was born in Auvergne in 1571, and died at Paris in 1642.

See NICÉRON, "Mémoires."

Auzou, ō'zoo', (LOUIS NAPOLÉON,) a nonconformist French priest, born at Versailles in 1806, was a disciple of Abbe Châtel, founder of the "French Catholic Church." He wrote "On Sacerdotal Usurpations," (1832,) and other works, and protested against the celibacy of the clergy. In 1839 he retracted his heterodox opinions.

See QUÉRARD, "La France Littéraire."

Auzout, ō'zoo', (ADRIEN,) an able French astronomer, mathematician, and instrument-maker, born at Rouen, became one of the first members of the Academy of Sciences, founded in 1666. He was the inventor of the movable wire micrometer, and published a "Treatise on the Micrometer," (1667.) "He shares with Picard," says Biot, "the honour of having applied the telescope to graduated instruments or quadrants." Died at Rome about 1692.

See DELAMBRE, "Histoire de l'Astronomie moderne;" CONDORCET, "Éloges."

Auzoux or **Auzou,** ō'zoo', (LOUIS,) a French physician, born in the department of L'Eure in 1797. He is distinguished by the invention of a new art of imitating anatomical preparations with paste or pulp, (*pâte de carton,*) which becomes hard when it dries. He gave the name of *anatomie clastique* to his method, which is considered a very valuable invention.

Av-a-lo'nĭ-us, (ELVAN,) an English missionary, who is said to have preached the gospel to the Bretons in the second century.

See GODWIN, "De Episcopiis Anglicis;" MORÉRI, "Dictionnaire Historique."

Avalos, d', dä-vä'lōs, sometimes written **Davalo** (dä-vä'lo) by the Italians, the name of a noble family of Spanish origin, who migrated to the kingdom of Naples in the fifteenth century.

Avalos, d', (ALFONSO,) Marquis of Pescara, an officer and friend of Ferdinand II. of Naples, to whom he rendered good service in his war against the French. He died from the effects of a wound in 1495, leaving a son Ferdinand, who was a famous general.

Avalos, d', (ALFONSO,) Marquis del Vasto, (written also Del Guasto,) an able general, born at Naples in 1502, was a son of Iñigo, noticed below, and a first-cousin of the Marquis of Pescara. He entered the army of Charles V. at an early age, and greatly contributed to the victory of Pavia in 1525. He succeeded the Marquis of Pescara in command of the army in November of the same year. In the expedition against Tunis in 1535 he had the chief command of the land-forces. He succeeded De Leyva as captain-general of the Imperial forces in Italy, and became governor of Milan in 1536 or 1537. He was defeated with great loss by the French under Condé, at Cérisoles, in 1544. Died in 1546. His sonnets and *Rime* are commended.

See BOTTA, "Storia d'Italia ;" VERRI, "Storia di Milano ;" BRANTÔME, "Vies des grands Capitaines."

Avalos, d', (COSTANZA,) a distinguished poetess, sister of the preceding, lived about 1520. She became the wife of Alfonso Piccolomini, Duke of Amalfi. Her poetical talents, beauty, and virtue are highly praised by contemporary writers.

Avalos, d', (FERDINANDO,) Marquis of Pescara, [in French, Le Marquis de Pescaire,] a famous general, born at Naples about 1490, was a son of Alfonso the elder, noticed above. About 1508 he married Vittoria Colonna, a poetess. (See COLONNA, VITTORIA.) He was taken prisoner by the French at Ravenna in 1512, and appointed general of the infantry in Italy by Charles V. about 1518. In 1521 he captured Milan from Lautrec, and in 1522 pillaged Genoa after he had taken it by storm. Pescara and the Duke of Bourbon invaded Provence in 1524, but were forced to retreat. The former formed the plan of the battle of Pavia, (1525,) and appears to be entitled to the honour of the victory, although he was not nominally the first in command. (See LANNOY, and BOURBON, DUC DE.) Sismondi says Pescara had the greatest share in gaining this battle, in which he was wounded. Lannoy having gone to Spain with the royal captive, the chief command devolved on Pescara. At this juncture, several Italian princes formed a secret league to drive the Spaniards out of Italy, and attempted to seduce Pescara into the project; but he divulged the secret to Charles V. Died at Milan, in November, 1525.

See PAOLO GIOVIO, "La Vita di Don Ferrando Davalo;" BRAN-TÔME, "Vies des Hommes illustres;" GIANNONE, "Storia civile del Regno di Napoli;" GUICCIARDINI, "Istoria d'Italia;" BOTTA, "Storia d'Italia;" VERRI, "Storia di Milano."

Avalos, d', (IÑIGO,) Marquis del Vasto, a younger brother of Alfonso, Marquis of Pescara, noticed above, served under the great captain Gonzalo de Córdova, and died in his service in 1503.

Avalos, de, dä ä-vä'lôs, (IÑIGO,) a Spanish general, who was a constant adherent of Alfonso V. of Aragon. Died in 1481.

Avalos, de, (RUY LOPEZ,) father of the preceding, was Grand Constable of Castile, and a noted warrior. Died about 1427.

A-van-ci'nus, [Ger. pron. ä-vänt-see'nůs,] (NICO-LAUS,) a learned Jesuit, rector of the colleges of Grätz, Passau, and Vienna, and author of several works on biography, criticism, and theology, was born in the Tyrol in 1612, and died in 1685.

See JÖCHER, "Allgemeines Gelehrten-Lexikon."

Avançon, d', dä'vôN'sôN', (GUILLAUME,) Archbishop of Embrun, born about 1530, was a violent adversary of the Protestants. Died in 1600.

Avantio. See AVANZI.

Avantius, (HIERONYMUS.) See AVANZI, (GIROLAMO.)

Avanzi, ä-vän'zee, or **Avantio,** ä-vän'te-o, [Lat. AVAN'TIUS,] (GIOVANNI MARIA,) a distinguished Italian jurist and poet, born at Rovigo in 1549, was a friend of Torquato Tasso. He resided at Padua from 1606 until his death. He wrote "Il Satiro, Favola pastorale," a drama, (1587,) "The Glow-Worm," ("La Lucciola," a poem, 1627,) and other works in prose and verse, which remain in manuscript. Died in 1622.

See MAZZUCHELLI, "Scrittori d'Italia."

Avanzi, (GIROLAMO,) an Italian philologist and editor, born at Verona probably about 1460. He assisted Aldus Manutius in preparing the works of Latin authors for the press, and was rather bold and unscrupulous in his conjectural emendation of texts. Among the classics which he edited were Catullus, (1493,) Lucretius, (1500,) and the Younger Pliny, (1504.) He was living in 1534.

Avanzi, (GIUSEPPE,) an Italian painter, born at Ferrara in 1655, was more noted for the number than the quality of his productions. Lanzi says that he seems to have painted against time. He executed figures, land-scapes, etc. His master-piece is the "Beheading of John the Baptist." Died in 1718.

See LANZI, "History of Painting in Italy."

Avanzi, (NICCOLÒ,) a distinguished engraver of gems, of the sixteenth century. He was born at Verona, but worked mostly at Rome.

See VASARI, "Lives of the Painters."

Avanzi, d', dä-vän'zee, (JACOPO DI PAOLO,) an emi-nent Italian painter of the fourteenth century, supposed to have been a native of Bologna or Padua. He worked at Bologna between 1370 and 1400. In his youth he painted Madonnas almost exclusively. He afterwards formed a partnership with Simone de' Crocefissi. His style resembled that of Giotto, whom he surpassed in attitude and expression. The frescos which he exe-cuted in San Felice, Padua, in 1376 were partly restored in 1773 by F. Zanoni.

See LANZI, "History of Painting in Italy."

Avanzini, ä-vän-zee'nee, (GIUSEPPE,) an Italian ma-thematician and natural philosopher, born at Gaino, in Venetia, in 1753. He became professor of mathematics at Padua about 1797. Having been deprived of this place by the political events of 1801, he was restored in 1806. He was chosen in 1805 a member of the National Institute. He wrote essays on the resistance of fluids, and a "Treatise on the Theory of the Hydraulic Ram," (1815.) Died in 1827.

See TIPALDO, "Biografia degli Italiani illustri."

Avanzini, (GIUSTINIANO,) an Italian painter, who flourished in the first half of the nineteenth century.

Avanzini, (PIETRO ANTONIO,) an Italian painter, born at Piacenza; died in 1733.

Avanzino, ä-vän-zee'no, a painter of many frescos in the churches of Rome, born at Città di Castello in 1552; died in 1629.

Avanzino, (GIUSEPPE MARIA,) an Italian physician of Roveredo, became professor at Florence. He was a pupil of Vallisnieri, and defended the opinion of his master respecting the origin of springs, in a treatise, (1725.) Died in 1739.

Avanzo. See AVANZI.

Avaray, d', dä'vä'rä', (ANTOINE LOUIS,) DUC, a French officer, born in 1759, chiefly distinguished for aiding the escape of Monsieur (afterwards Louis XVIII.) from Paris in June, 1791, of which Louis in gratitude published a full account after his accession to the throne. Died in Madeira (whither he had gone for his health) in 1811.

Avaray, d', (CLAUDE ANTOINE de Bésiade—deh bä'ze'ǎd',) DUC, father of the preceding, was born in 1740. He served in the Seven Years' war, was a deputy in the States-General, a member of the Constituent As-sembly, (1790,) and a zealous royalist. He only escaped the guillotine by the death of Robespierre. In 1814 he carried the address of the Senate to Louis XVIII. Died in 1829.

Avaray, d', (CLAUDE THÉOPHILE DE BÉSIADE,) MARQUIS, a French general, born in 1655. He served in several campaigns before the peace of Ryswick, (1697,) and became maréchal-de-camp in 1702. He commanded a wing with great success at the battle of Almansa in 1707, and served under Villars in Flanders in 1710-12. Died in 1745.

Avas, ä-väs', (R. MOSES JUDAH,) a Jewish theological writer and poet, lived in the seventeenth century.

Avâtâr, av'ạ-târ', or **Avâtârâ,** av'ạ-tä'ra, [from ăvă, "off," "away," "down," and târă, a "crossing over" or passing from one thing to another,] a term signifying "descent" or "transformation," applied in the Hindoo mythology to an incarnation of one of the principal dei-ties, particularly of Brahma, Siva, and Vishnu. The avatars of Vishnu are especially celebrated; they are named as follows: 1. Matsya, the "Fish;" 2. Kûrma, (kōōrmạ,) the "Tortoise;" 3. Varâha, the "Boar;" 4. Narasingha, the "Man-Lion;" 5. Vâ'mana, (or Wâ'ma-na,) the "Dwarf;" 6. Parasurâ'ma, (called in the com-mon dialect Pŭr'asoorâm';) 7. Râma Chandra; 8. Krish-na; 9. Bōōddha, (Buddha;) the tenth, which is yet to come, is called Kalki. The particular Avatars of Vishnu will be treated of more fully under their respective heads. (See MATSYA, KÛRMA, etc.)

Avaux. See FÉLIBIEN.

Avaux, d', dä'vō', a violin-player and composer, who lived in Paris in the latter part of the eighteenth century.

Avaux, d', (CLAUDE de Mesmes—deh měm,) COUNT, one of the most distinguished French diploma-tists of the seventeenth century, was born about 1595. He was sent on a mission to Venice in 1627. About 1643 he was appointed a plenipotentiary to conduct the intri-cate negotiations required to terminate the Thirty Years' war. He passed several ensuing years at the Hague, at Münster, and at various German courts, and is said to have gained the confidence of foreign powers by his integrity. Before he had completed the negotiations which resulted in the peace of Westphalia, (1648,) he was recalled by Mazarin, in consequence of the in-trigues and jealousy of Servien, who had been sent as his colleague. He died in 1650. He left diplomatic memoirs, which were published in 1674.

See RETZ, "Mémoires;" FLASSAN, "Histoire de la Diplomatie Française."

Avaux, d', (JEAN ANTOINE de MESMES,) COUNT, a French diplomatist, born in 1640, was a nephew of the preceding, whose talents he is said to have inherited. He was one of the plenipotentiaries who negotiated the treaty of Nymwegen, (1678,) after which he was ambas-sador to Holland until 1688. In 1689 he was envoy ex-traordinary to James II. in Ireland. He also had some agency in the treaty of Ryswick, (1697.) Died in 1709.

The "Negotiations of Count d'Avaux" were published in 6 vols., 1753.

See MACAULAY, "History of England," especially chap. xii. of vol. iii.; SAINT-SIMON, "Mémoires."

Avaux, d', (JEAN ANTOINE DE MESMES,) COUNT, a judge and academician, born in Paris in 1661, was a grand-nephew of Claude, noticed above. He became first président of the Parliament of Paris in 1712, and courageously headed that Parliament in opposition to several measures of the regency, especially to the financial schemes of Law in 1718. He was elected in 1710 to the French Academy. He was noted for his bon-mots. Died in 1723.

See D'ALEMBERT, "Histoire des Membres de l'Académie."

Avaux, d', (JEAN JACQUES DE MESMES,) a French judge, born in 1640, was a member of the French Academy. Died in 1688.

Aved, ä'vĕd', (JACQUES ANDRÉ JOSEPH,) a successful French portrait-painter, born at Douay in 1702, was a pupil of La Belle. He was elected a member of the Academy of Paris in 1734, soon after which he was appointed portrait-painter to the king. Among his works are portraits of Mehemet-Effendi, J. B. Rousseau, and Mirabeau. He is said to have been particularly successful in representing character. Died in 1766.

See HEINECKEN, "Dictionnaire des Artistes."

Av'e-dik, Patriarch of Armenia. Having persecuted or offended the Catholics, he was abducted by the Jesuits about 1704, and imprisoned at Messina.

Aveelen. See AVELEN.

Aveen, ä-vān', (ADRIAN,) a Dutch engraver, born at Amsterdam, lived about 1700.

Aveiro, ä-vā'e-ro, (Don JOSÉ de Mascarenhas—dä mäs-kä-rĕn'yȧs,) DUKE OF, a Portuguese nobleman of infamous character, born in Lisbon about 1710, is chiefly noted for his having been one of the prime actors in an attempt to assassinate the king (José I.) in 1758, for which he was broken on the wheel, and his property confiscated. This conspiracy was originated by the Jesuits and discontented nobles in revenge for the protection which the king gave to the Marquis of Pombal.

See SMITH, "Memoirs of the Marquis of Pombal," and "Gentleman's Magazine" for February, 1759.

Aveis or Aveys, a-vās' or ä-vīs', written also Avis, SULTAN, second sovereign of the Persian dynasty of Ilkhânian princes. He became sultan in 1356. He is represented as the benefactor of his people and a munificent patron of learning. Died in 1374.

Avelen, van den, vȧn dĕn ä'vĕh-lĕn, or Aveelen, ä'vä'lĕn, also written Aveele, (JOHAN,) a Dutch engraver of moderate ability, worked at Stockholm from 1702 to 1712.

Aveline, ȧv'lĕn', (ANTOINE,) a French engraver and designer, born in Paris about 1660. He engraved many landscapes and views of cities. Died in 1712.

Aveline, (FRANÇOIS ANTOINE,) an engraver of mediocre abilities, was born in Paris in 1718. He worked chiefly for the booksellers. Died in London in 1762.

Aveline, (JEAN,) an engraver, born in Paris, was a brother of the preceding.

Aveline, (PIERRE,) a designer and engraver, born in Paris in 1710, was a cousin of the preceding. He was the most able artist of the family. He engraved after Jordaens, Watteau, Teniers, Rubens, Albani, and his own designs. Died about 1760.

See BASAN, "Dictionnaire des Graveurs."

Avellaneda, de, dä ä-vĕl-yä-nä'Dä, (ALONSO FERNANDEZ,) the assumed name of a Spanish author who in 1614 published a sequel to the first part of "Don Quixote," before Cervantes had published his second part. This spurious continuation, entitled "Segundo Tomo del ingenioso Hidalgo Don Quixote," was translated into French by Le Sage, (1704,) and into English in 1805. Avellaneda's work is much inferior to that of Cervantes, but has some literary merit. His real name is not known. His prologue contains a scurrilous attack on Cervantes.

See N. ANTONIO, "Bibliotheca Hispana Nova."

Avellaneda, de, (Don GARCIA—gaR-thee'ä,) Count of Castrillo, a distinguished Spanish statesman, born

about 1600. He was sent by Philip IV. as viceroy to Naples in 1653. During his administration two hundred thousand people are said to have died of plague in the city alone in six months. Avellaneda has been justly censured for the inefficiency of his measures of prevention.

See GIANNONE, "Storia civile del Regno di Napoli."

Avellaneda, de, (GERTRUDIS GOMES,) a popular Spanish poetess, born in the island of Cuba in 1816, was a daughter of a naval officer. She settled at Madrid about 1840, and published a volume of "Lyric Poems" in 1841. Her tragedies, "Alfonso Munio," "Principe de Viana," and "Egilona," had great success. She was married in 1846 to Don Pedro Sabator, who died the same year. She afterwards produced two poems, "The Cross," ("La Cruz,") and the "Last Accent of my Harp," and several dramas, among which are "The Glories of Spain," (1850,) "The Flower-Girl," ("La Hija de las Flores,") and "La Sonambula."

Avellani. See AVELLONI, (GIUSEPPE.)

Avellar, de, dä ä-vĕl-laR', (FRANCISCO GOMES,) a Portuguese prelate, born in 1739, became Bishop of Algarve in 1789. He merited the title of public benefactor by his improvements in agriculture. Died in 1816.

Avellino, ä-vĕl-lee'no, (FRANCESCO MARIA,) an Italian antiquary and numismatist, born at Naples in 1788. He became professor of Greek in the University of Naples in 1815. In 1839 he was appointed director of the Museo Borbonico. He wrote many treatises on medals and antiquities. Died in 1850.

Avellino, (GIULIO,) a Sicilian landscape-painter, called IL MESSINESE, ("the Messinese,") was a pupil of Salvator Rosa. His style resembles that of his master, but is not so wild. He worked at Ferrara, where he died about 1700.

See LANZI, "History of Painting in Italy."

Avellino, (ONOFRIO,) a skilful Italian painter of history and portraits, born at Naples in 1674, was a pupil of Solimena. He was especially successful in portraits. He worked at Naples and at Rome, where he died in 1741. Among his best works is a fresco in the church of San Francesco di Paolo in Rome.

See LANZI, "History of Painting in Italy."

Avellone. See AVELLONI.

Avelloni, ä-vĕl-lo'nee, (FRANCESCO,) a prolific Italian dramatist, born at Venice in 1756. His first play, "Giulio Assassino," was performed with success at Naples. He wrote many plays which were brought on the stage of Naples under the name of the Prince of Sangro, who paid him eight ducats apiece. He was most successful in the sentimental drama, sometimes called the "lachrymose." Among his works are the "Lantern of Epictetus," and "Il Sogno d'Aristo," ("Aristo's Dream.") Died at Rome in 1837.

See TIPALDO, "Biografia degli Italiani illustri."

Avelloni or Avellani, ä-vĕl-lä'nee, (GIUSEPPE,) an Italian poet of great imagination, born at Venice in 1761. Among his works is "Padova Riacquistata," ("Padua Recovered," 1790.) Died at Venice in 1817.

A'ven, Da'ven, Davent, dä'vôn', or D'Avesnes, an engraver, the time and place of whose birth are unknown. He engraved on copper several works of Primaticcio and Giulio Romano.

Avenant. See DAVENANT.

Av-e-nä'rĭ-us, (JOHANN,) a German theologian, born at Eger in 1520. His German name was Habermann, (or Hafermann, *i.e.* "Oatman,") which, according to the custom of the time, he changed to the Latin equivalent *Avenarius.* He was professor of theology at Jena. He published a Hebrew Lexicon, (1568,) and other works. Died in 1590.

Avenarius, (JOHANN,) a Protestant minister, born at Steinbach in 1670. He preached at Berka and Gera, and wrote several theological and musical works, among which is "Evangelic Doctrine, or Song-Sermons," ("Evangelische Lehr, oder Lieder-Predigten," 1729.) Died at Gera in 1736.

Avenarius, (JOHANN,) a grandson of Johann, (1520 –90,) noticed above, was professor of eloquence. He wrote "Synopsis Œconomica," and other works, dated 1608–28.

Avenarius, (THOMAS,) a German composer, born near Leipsic, published some songs in 1614.

Avenbrugger. See AUENBRUGGER.

Avendanno, â-vĕn-dân′no, (PEDRO Nuñez—noon′-yĕth,) a Spanish jurist, lived about 1540.

Avenelles, des, dặ zằv′nĕl′, (ALBIN or AUBIN,) a French satirical poet, born in 1480, was canon of Soissons. He translated into verse the "Remède d'Amour" of Æneas Sylvius, (Pius II.)

See GOUJET, "Bibliothèque Française."

Avenelles, des, (PHILIPPE,) a French translator of Plutarch's "Lives," (Paris, 1558.)

Avenelles, des, (PIERRE,) an advocate of the Parliament of Paris, chiefly known by his disclosure of the Amboise conspiracy (formed in 1560 by the Prince de Condé) to remove the Guise family from about the person of Francis II.

Avenpace, ä′vĕn-pä′thà, **Avempace,** ä′vĕm-pä′thà, **Abenpace,** or more properly **Ibn-Bâjah,** ĭb′n-bâ′jah, (**Aboo-Bekr-Moham′med-Ibn-Yahya**—yâh′hyȧ,) a celebrated Arabian philosopher, born probably at Saragossa. He practised medicine at Seville, which he quitted about 1120 A.D. He afterwards became vizier at the court of Fez, where he is supposed to have died about 1130. He was one of the teachers of Averroës, and was a devoted admirer of Aristotle. Avenpace wrote treatises on philosophy, metaphysics, etc.

See N. ANTONIO, "Bibliotheca Hispana Vetus;" CASIRI, "Bibliotheca Arabico-Hispana;" WÜSTENFELD, "Geschichte der Arabischen Aerzte."

Avenport, d', dâv′en-port, (FRANCIS CHRISTOPHER,) an English monk, born at Coventry about 1598, was chaplain to Charles II. Died in 1665.

Av-en-ti′nus, (or â-vĕn-tee′nŭs,) (JOHANNES,) a historian of much merit, whose family name was THÜRMAIER or THÜRNMAIER, was born at Abensberg, in Bavaria, in 1466. Having taught eloquence, etc. at Vienna and Ingolstadt, he was invited to Munich in 1512, and became the tutor of the duke's sons. His chief work is a "History of Bavaria," ("Annales Boiorum," 1554,) which was generally esteemed, and highly praised by Leibnitz. The editor of this work suppressed some passages unfavourable to the Romish Church, which were restored in an edition published by Cisner in 1580. Died in 1534.

See J. ZIEGLER, "Vita Aventini;" D. W. MÖLLER, "Dissertatio de J. Aventino," 1698.

Av′en-zo′ạr, written also **Avenzohar** or **Abenzohar,** a corruption of the Arabic name **Ibn-Zohr,** (ĭb′n zṓhR,) a celebrated Arabian physician, born probably near Seville, Spain, about 1075. According to some modern authorities, he was a Jew. He was a son of an eminent physician of similar name who wrote several works and died in 1130. The son became vizier of the Sultan Abdel-Moomĕn. Died at Seville in 1162. His principal work, commonly called "Teiseer," ("Teisîr," "Taisir," or "Theizir,") is one of the most valuable works of the Arabian physicians.

See LEO AFRICANUS, "De Viris illustribus;" FABRICIUS, "Bibliotheca Græca;" CASIRI, "Bibliotheca Arabico-Hispana."

Avenzoar THE YOUNGER, a son of the preceding, born at Seville about 1114, was a distinguished physician and poet. He succeeded his father as chief physician to the Sultan Abdel-Moomĕn, and was raised to the rank of vizier. He wrote several medical works, which are not extant. Died at Morocco about 1200. By Arabian writers he was accounted the most eminent of the family.

See FABRICIUS, "Bibliotheca Græca;" N. ANTONIO, "Bibliotheca Hispana Vetus."

Aver. See AUER.

Aver, ä′vẹr, (JOHANN PAUL,) a German painter, born at Nuremberg in 1636; died in 1687.

Averani, ä-vä-rä′nee, (BENEDETTO,) an eminent Italian professor and classical scholar, born at Florence in 1645, became in 1676 professor of Greek, and afterwards of humanities, in the University of Pisa. He was very successful as a teacher of the Greek and Roman languages and antiquities. His lectures on Thucydides, Euripides, Cicero, Livy, and Virgil were published in three volumes, (1716.) He wrote other works, in prose and verse. Died at Pisa in 1707.

See G. AVERANI, "Benedicti Averani Vita;" FABRONI, "Vitæ Italorum doctrina excellentium."

Averani, (GIUSEPPE,) a celebrated jurist, brother of the preceding, born at Florence in 1662, was also distinguished for his attainments in the physical sciences. He became in 1684 professor of law at Pisa, where he lectured with high reputation for many years. He wrote, besides other works, a "Discourse on the Law of War and Peace," ("Disputatio de Jure Belli et Pacis," 1703,) and "Interpretations of Law," ("Interpretationes Juris," 1716–36.) His Latinity is admired by Italian critics. Died in 1738.

See FABRONI, "Vitæ Italorum doctrina excellentium;" TIPALDO, "Biografia degli Italiani illustri;" MAZZUCHELLI, "Scrittori d'Italia."

Averani, (NICCOLÒ,) brother of the preceding, an eminent Italian advocate and mathematician, who edited the works of Gassendi, was born at Florence about 1650; died in 1727.

See MAZZUCHELLI, "Scrittori d'Italia."

Averara, ä-vä-rä′rä, (GIOVANNI BATTISTA,) an Italian fresco-painter, born at Bergamo, was an imitator of Titian. He was a good colorist, and excelled in painting infants and landscape-backgrounds. He was in the prime of life when he died in 1548.

See LANZI, "History of Painting in Italy."

Averari, ä-vä-rä′ree, (ANTONIO,) an Italian writer and famous preacher, born in Lombardy, lived about 1500.

See MAZZUCHELLI, "Scrittori d'Italia."

Averdy, de l', dẹh lằ′vĕR′de′, called also **Laverdi,** (CLÉMENT CHARLES FRANÇOIS,) a French statesman, born in Paris about 1720, was made comptroller-general of the finances in 1763. He recommended the abolition of the transit-duties on grain, which was afterwards carried into effect, and proposed other salutary measures, but was soon after removed from office. He perished by the guillotine in 1793.

See LACRETELLE, "Histoire de France," and "Vies des Surintendants des Finances et des Contrôleurs-généraux."

A′vẹr-ell, also written **Auerell,** (WILLIAM,) an English pamphleteer of the sixteenth century, wrote a "Dial for Daintie Darlings," (London, 1590,) and other works.

A′vẹr-ill or **A′vẹr-ell,** (WILLIAM W.,) an American general, born in the State of New York, graduated at West Point in 1855. In the autumn of 1862 he was appointed a captain in the regular army, and brigadier-general of volunteers. He commanded a troop of cavalry in several actions fought in Virginia in 1863. In December of that year he conducted a raid into Southwestern Virginia and destroyed a large amount of stores at Salem. He served under Sigel and Hunter in West Virginia in 1864.

Averkam, van, vän ä′vẹr-kăm′, written also **Averkampen,** (HENDRIK,) a Dutch landscape and marine painter, born at Kampen about the end of the sixteenth century, was called "the Mute of Kampen." His history is unknown. His drawings are more prized than his pictures, the colours of which have been injured by time.

Averois or **Averoys.** See AVERROES.

Averoldi, ä-vä-rol′dee, (GIULIO ANTONIO,) an Italian antiquary, born at Venice in 1651, became a resident of Brescia. He formed a rich collection of medals, marbles, etc., and wrote a treatise on the paintings and antiquities of Brescia, (1700.) Died in 1717.

See BRULLIOT, "Dictionnaire des Monogrammes."

Averoni, ä-vä-ro′nee, (VALENTINO,) an Italian theologian, born at Florence, lived between 1550 and 1600.

Averrhoës. See AVERROËS.

Averroës,* ä-vĕr′ro-ĕz, or **A-ver′ro-is,** written also **Averois, Averoys,** or **Averrhoes,** the common form of the name of **Ibn-Roshd,** (ĭb′n rŏsh′d,) one of the most famous of all the Arabian philosophers and physicians, was born at Córdova, in Spain, probably in the first quarter of the twelfth century. He was a pupil of Avenpace and Avenzoar. He became cadi (judge) at Seville and Córdova, and enjoyed a high degree of favour at the court of Aboo-Yoosuf-Yakoob-Al-Mansoor-Billah, at Morocco. His celebrity as a writer rests chiefly on his Commentary on Aristotle, which in the middle ages

* Chaucer, after Dante, writes the name AVERROIS. (See Prologue to the "Canterbury Tales.")

ā, ē, ī, ō, ū, ȳ, *long;* ă, ĕ, ŏ, same, less prolonged; ă, ĕ, ĭ, ŏ, ŭ, ў, *short;* ạ, ẹ, ị, ọ, *obscure;* fär, fâll, fât; mĕt; nŏt; gṓd; mṓn;

obtained for him the title of "The Commentator." He is mentioned by Dante, in the "Inferno," canto iv., as "Averroïs che il gran comento feo."[*]
His works are extremely numerous. He wrote on medicine, theology, law, logic, etc. Some of his works have been translated into Latin and Hebrew. He died at Morocco in 1198. He seems to have been a more devout believer in the philosophy of Aristotle than in the religion of Mohammed. In the fifteenth and sixteenth centuries the disciples of Aristotle in Italy were divided into two sects, the Averroists and the Alexandrists.

See LEO AFRICANUS, "De Viris illustribus;". N. ANTONIO, "Bibliotheca Hispana Vetus;" BRUCKER, "History of Philosophy;" TENNEMANN, "Geschichte der Philosophie;" E. RENAN, "Averroës et Averroïsme," 1852; DR. F. HOEFER's article on AVERROES, in the "Nouvelle Biographie Générale."

Aversa, â-vĕr′så, (TOMMASO,) an Italian poet and dramatist, born at Amistrato, in Sicily. He was patronized by several cardinals and dukes, and gained considerable reputation by his poems, among which are "Piramo e Tisbe," an idyl, (1617,) and "The Pilgrim," ("Il Pellegrino," a drama, 1641.) He translated Virgil's "Æneid" into Sicilian verse, (1654-60.) Died in 1663.
See MAZZUCHELLI, "Scrittori d'Italia."

A′ver-ÿ, (WAITSTILL,) an American lawyer and patriot, born in Norwich, Connecticut, near the middle of the last century. He removed to North Carolina, of which State he became attorney-general in 1777. Died in 1821.

Avesani, â-và-så′nee, (GIOACHINO,) an Italian poet, born at Verona in 1741, became professor of rhetoric at Verona in 1775. In 1807 he published a volume of elegant Latin and Italian poems, ("Poesie Italiane e Latine.") Among his works is "The Metamorphoses," ("Le Metamorfosi," a poem, 1812.) His edition of "Orlando Furioso," in which the licentious passages are suppressed, appeared in 1820. Died in 1818.
See MOSCHINI, "Della Letteratura Veneziana del Secolo XVIII."

Avesbury, (ROBERT OF.) See ROBERT OF AVESBURY.

Avesne, d′, (BAUDOUIN.) See BAUDOUIN D'AVESNE.

Avesne, d′, då′vĕn′, (FRANÇOIS,) a French fanatic of the seventeenth century, who claimed a divine mission for himself, and made virulent attacks upon the king and his ministers. He is supposed to have died about 1660.
See NICÉRON, "Mémoires."

Aveyro. See AVEIRO.

Avezac, d′, dåv′zåk′, (AUGUSTE GENEVIÈVE VALENTIN,) nephew of Jean Pierre Valentin, noticed below, was a native of Saint Domingo. Having settled in the United States, he became a successful lawyer, and in 1831 was appointed chargé-d'affaires to the Netherlands. Died in 1850.

Avezac, d′, (JEAN PIERRE VALENTIN,) son of Pierre Valentin, noticed below, was born in 1756, and was one of the deputies sent to France in 1790 to oppose the revolutionary ideas then prevalent. Died in Saint Domingo in 1803.

Avezac, d′, (PIERRE VALENTIN,) a French lawyer, born at Tarbes in 1719, emigrated in 1748 to Saint Domingo, where he became a planter and was distinguished for his zeal in promoting public improvements. Died in 1781.

Avezac, d′, (PIERRE VALENTIN DOMINIQUE JULIEN,) son of the preceding, born in Saint Domingo in 1769, removed to New Orleans, where he died in 1831. He translated Scott's "Marmion" into French.

Avezzana, â-vĕt-zä′nå, (GIUSEPPE,) an Italian patriot, born in Piedmont in 1797, fought in the republican campaigns of 1821-23, afterwards served in Mexico under Santa Anna, and took part in the Italian revolution of 1848.

Aviani, â-ve-â′nee, an excellent Italian painter of architecture, landscapes, and marine views, born at Vicenza, adorned the ceilings of several churches in that city. Some of his works contain figures painted by Carpioni. He flourished in the first half of the seventeenth century.
See LANZI, "History of Painting in Italy."

Aviano, â-ve-â′no, (GIROLAMO,) an Italian poet, born at Vicenza, was, according to Ginguené, one of the most

successful burlesque poets of his time. He published three satirical chapters, ("Capitoli," 1603,) which are praised by several Italian critics. Died about 1608.
See MAZZUCHELLI, "Scrittori d'Italia."

A-vĭ-ā′nus, (FLAVIUS,) a Roman poet, who is often confounded with Rufus Festus Avienus, was the author of numerous fables in verse, which are sometimes printed with those of Æsop. His date is uncertain. He probably lived between 200 and 350 A.D.

Aviau du Bois de Sanzay, â′ve-ō′ dü bwä dęh sŏN′zȧ′, (CHARLES FRANÇOIS,) Archbishop of Bordeaux, noted for his piety and benevolence, was born in 1736, in the diocese of Poitiers. He emigrated in the Revolution, but, returning in disguise, visited all parts of his diocese, at great personal hazard. Though appointed archbishop by Napoleon, he sided with the pope in his contests with the French emperor. He was named a peer in 1815, and died in 1826.
See J. TOURNON, "Précis de la Vie de Monseigneur C. F. d'Aviau," 1829.

Av′ĭ-bus, (GASPARO OSELLO, gâs-pâ′ro o-sel′lo, or GAS′PAR AB OSEL′LO,) an Italian engraver of Padua, lived about 1560-80. He imitated the style and copied some of the prints of Giorgio Ghisi surnamed Mantovano.
See STRUTT, "Dictionary of Engravers."

Avicebron, â-ve-thà-brŏn′, (SOLOMON IBN GABIROL,) a Spanish Jew and philosopher, was author of a work called "Source of Life," ("Fons Vitæ,") which was often noticed by Albertus Magnus and Aquinas. He applied the philosophy of Aristotle to the Mosaic doctrines. M. Munck has recently proved the identity of Avicebron with Solomon Ibn Gabirol, who was distinguished as a religious poet, and died at Malaga in 1070.
See "Nouvelle Biographie Générale."

Av-ĭ-çen′nȧ, [It. pron. â-ve-chĕn′nå; Fr. AVICENNE,[*] â′ve′sĕnn′,] the Latin form of **Ibn-Sînâ,** ĭb'n-see′nâ, the most illustrious of Arabian physicians, born at Afshena, a village in Bokhara, 980 A.D. He was a remarkable instance of precocity as well as activity of intellect. He is said to have been a thorough master of Moslem theology, and of the chief branches of mathematical and physical science then cultivated, including arithmetic, algebra, Euclid's elements, and the Almagest of Ptolemy, before he was sixteen. At this age he began the study of medicine, of natural science, and of the metaphysical writings of Aristotle. Before he was twenty he had the reputation of being the most learned and gifted man of his time. He was patronized in turn by several Mohammedan princes, among whom he had acquired great fame by his extraordinary skill in the cure of diseases. Although he applied himself intensely to study and to the composition of his numerous works, he appears to have given himself with scarcely less ardour to the pursuit of pleasure, to the ruin of his constitution, so that it was said of him that his philosophy could not procure him wisdom nor all his medical skill procure him health. He died in 1037, in the fifty-seventh year of his age. Among his numerous writings we may particularly mention his "Rule" or "System of Medicine," ("Canon Medicinæ,") a great work, the different parts of which treat of anatomy and physiology, materia medica, and the various diseases to which man is subject, with their appropriate remedies. It was originally written in Arabic, and has been translated into Hebrew as well as into Latin. He wrote various other works, including a book on animals, said to be little more than a paraphrase of Aristotle's "History of Animals," and a work on the "Soul," ("De Anima;") also several small treatises on alchemy and other subjects. No man, except Aristotle and Galen, exercised so absolute an authority in science, during the middle ages, as Avicenna. For five centuries his "Canon" was regarded as the highest authority in the schools of Europe.

See IBN-KHALLIKÂN's "Biographical Dictionary," published by De Slane, Paris, 1842; FREIND, "History of Physic;" BRUCKER, "History of Philosophy;" WÜSTENFELD, "Geschichte der Arabischen Aerzte;" S. KLEIN, "Dissertatio de Avicenna medico," 1846; CHOULANT, "Handbuch der Bücherkunde für die ältere Medicin;" ABULFARAJ, "Oriental History;" ABULFEDA. "Universal History."

---

[*] Chaucer writes the name AVYCEN. (See the "Pardoneres Tale.")

€ as *k*; ç as *s*; g *hard*; ġ as *j*; G, H, K, *guttural*; N, *nasal*; R, *trilled*; š as *z*; th as in *this*. (☞See Explanations, p. 23.)

A-vid'ĭ-us Cas'sĭ-us, a brave and able Roman general, born in Syria, was noted for his extreme severity as a disciplinarian. He commanded under Marcus Aurelius the army which defeated the Parthians in 165 A.D., and a few years later was appointed governor of Syria. Having several legions under his command, he revolted in 175 A.D. and declared himself emperor. He made himself master of Egypt and of Asia east of Mount Taurus. Marcus Aurelius was about to march against him, when Avidius was killed by his own officers in 175 A.D.

A-vĭ-e'nus, (RUFUS FESTUS,) a Roman poet, who probably lived about 400 A.D. He is supposed to have been a native of Italy, and to have been a pagan. The works which have come down to us under his name are a Latin paraphrase, in hexameters, of the "Periegesis" of Dionysius, a translation of the "Phenomena" and "Prognostica" of Aratus, and a fragment (seven hundred and three lines) of a poem called "The Maritime Region," ("Ora Maritima.") His style is superior to that of contemporary writers.

See WERNSDORF, "Poetæ Latini minores."

Avigador, ă-ve-gä-dȯR', (SOLOMON BEN ABRAHAM,) a Jewish philosopher and writer, lived about 1400.

Avila, de, (ALFONSO.) See ALPHONSUS ABULENSIS.

Avila, de, dă ä've-lä, (FRANCISCO,) a Spanish portrait-painter of Seville, lived in the first part of the seventeenth century. His portraits were celebrated for their fidelity.

Avila, de, (GIL GONZALEZ,) a Spanish biographer and antiquary, born at Avila about 1577. He published in 1606 "The Antiquities of Salamanca, with the Lives of its Bishops," and in 1623 a description of Madrid, with the lives of the principal natives, in his "Theatre of the Greatness (or "Glories") of Madrid," ("Teatro de las Grandezas de Madrid.") His chief work, "Ecclesiastical Theatre," ("Teatro eclesiastico," 4 vols., 1645-53,) giving the biographies of the bishops and archbishops of the two Castiles, was left unfinished at his death. Died in 1658.

See N. ANTONIO, "Bibliotheca Hispana Nova."

Avila, de, (HERNANDO,) was painter and sculptor to Philip II. of Spain. He appears to have worked chiefly in Toledo, where about 1568 he painted two altar-pieces, —a "John the Baptist" and an "Adoration of the Kings." Died about 1600.

See BERMUDEZ, "Diccionario Historico."

Avila, de, (JUAN,) an eloquent and zealous Spanish preacher, born in La Mancha about 1500, was called "the Apostle of Andalusia," in which province he laboured with success as home-missionary for twenty years. Among his converts were Saint Francisco Borja and Saint Teresa de Jesus. He died in 1569, leaving, besides other religious works, "Spiritual Letters," which were translated into French and (partly) into English.

See LUIS DE MUÑOZ, "Vida de Juan de Avila," 1635.

Avila, de, (Don SANCHO,) a Spanish general, born at Avila in 1523. He was an officer in the expedition against the corsair Dragut, in Africa, in 1550. He went to the Netherlands in 1567 with the Duke of Alva, of whose guard he was then commander. It was Avila who arrested the Counts Egmont and Hoorn at Brussels. He failed in an attempt to relieve Middelburg in 1574, but in the same year defeated Count Louis of Nassau at Mook or Mookerheide. In 1577 he withdrew with his army from the Low Countries in compliance with the treaty of Ghent. Died at Lisbon in 1583. According to the Dutch historians, he was as cruel as Alva.

See BRANTÔME, "Capitaines étrangers;" DE THOU, "Histoire Universelle;" MOTLEY, "Rise of the Dutch Republic," vol. ii.

Avila y Zuñiga, de, dă ä've-lä e thoon-yee'gä, (LUIS,) a Spanish historian who lived in the reign of Charles V., whose favour he enjoyed. He was ambassador to Rome in the time of Paul IV. and Pius IV., served in the war against the Protestant German princes, and commanded the Spanish cavalry at the siege of Metz in 1552. He wrote "Commentaries of the War of Charles V. in Germany in the Years 1546 and 1547," (1548,) which was translated into English and other languages. This work has been praised for the elegance and conciseness of its style, but is considered partial by some judges. He appears to have died about 1560.

See N. ANTONIO, "Bibliotheca Hispana Nova;" DE THOU, "Histoire Universelle."

Aviler, ă've-lā', (AUGUSTIN CHARLES,) a French architect, born in Paris in 1653, studied in Rome, with the aid of a pension from the king. He worked some time with Mansard, in Paris, and afterwards erected several fine buildings at Carcassonne, Nîmes, and Toulouse, among which is the palace of the Archbishop of Toulouse. He published a "Course of Architecture," (1691,) often reprinted, and a good "Dictionary of all the Terms of Architecture, Civil and Hydraulic." Died at Montpellier in 1700.

See FONTENAI, "Dictionnaire des Artistes."

Avis. See AVEIS.

Avisenna. See AVICENNA.

Av'ĭ-son, (CHARLES,) an eminent English musician and musical critic, born about 1710, passed nearly all his life at Newcastle-upon-Tyne, where he was church organist. He was a pupil of Geminiani, and published an ingenious and able "Essay on Musical Expression," (1752,) which displays good taste, scholarship, and sound judgment. It was, however, severely and bitterly criticised by Dr. Hayes, professor of music at Oxford. Avison's reputation as a composer rests chiefly upon his concertos. Died in 1770.

See FÉTIS, "Biographie Universelle des Musiciens."

Avisse, ă'vèss', a blind French versifier, born in 1772, became professor in the Institution for the Blind at Paris. Died in 1801. A volume of his poems was published in 1802.

Avisse, (ÉTIENNE FRANÇOIS,) a French comic poet, born in Paris about 1694. He wrote "The Divorce," and other comedies, which had a temporary success. Died in 1747.

Avitabile, ă-ve-tä'be-lä, (PIETRO,) an Italian missionary, died at Goa in 1650.

See F. MAGGI, "Vita d'Avitabile Pietro."

Avitabile, d', dă-ve-tä'be-lä, or **Avitable,** ă-ve-tä'blä, (BIASIO **Magoli**—mä-go'lee,) an Italian writer of poetry and biography, lived at Naples in the seventeenth century.

Avitus. See ELAGABALUS.

A-vī'tus, (AL'CIMUS ECDIÇ'IUS,) SAINT, Bishop of Vienne, was born in Auvergne about the middle of the fifth century. He obtained great reputation for learning, and succeeded his father as bishop about 490 A.D. He was a zealous adversary of Arianism, from which he converted Sigismund, Prince of Burgundy. He wrote letters, homilies, and other works, some of which are lost. Among his extant works is a poem, or series of poems, "On the Creation of the World," "On Original Sin," "On the Deluge," ("Diluvio Mundi,") etc. "The analogy of these two poems," says Guizot, referring to Milton's epic, "is a curious literary fact, and that of Saint Avitus deserves the honour of being compared to that of Milton." Died in 525.

See CEILLIER, "Auteurs sacrés;" BOLLANDUS, "Acta Sanctorum."

Avitus, (GALLONIUS,) a governor of Thrace in the time of Aurelian.

Avitus, (JULIUS,) successively governor of Mesopotamia, Asia, and Cyprus, which appointments he held under Seve'rus and Caracalla. He was the husband of Mœsa, and grandfather of the emperors Elagabalus and Alexander Severus.

Avitus, (MARCUS MÆCILIUS,) one of the emperors of the Western Roman Empire, is supposed to have been born in Auvergne about 400 A.D. Before his accession to the empire he had been Prefect of Gaul, and had distinguished himself in the wars against the Huns and Vandals. On the sack of Rome by the latter, and the death of Maximus in 455, he assumed the purple, and after a reign of fourteen months was deposed by Ricimer, and appointed Bishop of Placentia. Died in 457. He was the father-in-law of Sidonius Apollinaris.

See GIBBON, "Decline and Fall of the Roman Empire."

Avity, d', dă've-te', (PIERRE,) a French writer and soldier, was born at Tournon in 1573. His productions are very miscellaneous, embracing poetry, history, fiction, morals, etc.; but his greatest work appears to have been "A General Description of the Four Quarters of the Globe, its Empires, Kingdoms, States, and Republics," (1st vol., 1626.) Died in 1635.

Avogadro, â-vo-gä′dRo, (ALBERTO,) an Italian poet, born at Vercelli, lived at Florence in the fifteenth century.

Avogadro, (CAMILLO,) an Italian poet, born at Milan; died in 1617.

Avogadro, not **Avogrado,** as sometimes spelled, (GIROLAMO,) an Italian philologer, jurist, and patron of learning, born at Brescia, lived between 1450 and 1500.

Avogadro, (GIUSEPPE,) Count of Casanova, an Italian nobleman, born at Vercelli in 1731. He wrote several treatises on rural economy, (1783–1810.) Died in 1813.

Avogadro, (LUCIA,) an Italian poetess of the sixteenth century, born at Bergamo. She had the distinction of being praised by Tasso. Died about 1570.

Avogadro, (LUDOVICO,) was the chief of a band which conspired to expel the French from Brescia in 1512, and was killed in the attempt.

Avogadro, (NESTORE DIONIGI,) an Italian philologist and friar of Novara, lived in the latter half of the fifteenth century. He composed a Latin Lexicon, which passed through many editions. The oldest known edition is dated 1488.

See MAZZUCHELLI, "Scrittori d'Italia."

Avogadro, (PIETRO,) an Italian painter of considerable merit, lived in Brescia in the first half of the eighteenth century. "The Martyrdom of San Crispino" is called his master-piece.

See LANZI, " History of Painting in Italy."

Avogadro or **Avvocati,** âv-vo-kä′tee, (VINCENZO MARIA,) an Italian writer on theology, born at Palermo in 1702.

Avogaro or **Avogari,** (AZZONI RAMBALDO.) See AZZONI AVOGARI.

Avolo, â′vo-lo, (CESARE,) an Italian philosopher of the sixteenth century, wrote "On the Causes of Sympathy and Antipathy," (" De Causis Sympathiæ et Antipathiæ," 1580.)

Avondano, â-von-dä′no, (PIETRO ANTONIO,) an Italian composer, lived at Naples in the first half of the eighteenth century.

Avont, van, vän â′vont′ or â′vòN′, (PIETER,) a Flemish painter and etcher of Antwerp, flourished about 1650. He painted landscapes with figures from sacred history or from mythology. His pictures and etchings are scarce and highly prized.

See HUBER, "Manuel des Amateurs;" HEINECKEN, " Dictionnaire des Artistes."

Avosani, â-vo-sä′nee, (ORFEO, OR-fä′o,) an Italian organist and composer of sacred music of the seventeenth century.

Avost, d', dä′vo′, (JÉRÔME,) a French poet, born in Brittany in 1558 or '59, had an office in the household of Margaret, queen of Henry IV. He translated into French the "Jerusalem Delivered" of Tasso, and other works, and wrote some original verses.

Avrigny, d', dä′vRèn′ye′, (CHARLES JOSEPH Lœillard—luh′yäR′,) a French poet and dramatist, born in the island of Martinique about 1760, lived mostly in Paris. He wrote several operas and vaudevilles, which were moderately successful, and in 1801 an elegant and vigorous "Essay on the Origin and Progress of the British Power in India." His poem on "The Departure of La Pérouse," (1807,) and his tragedy of "Joan of Arc," (1819,) are highly commended. He was a censor of the press under the empire. Died in 1823.

See QUÉRARD, "La France Littéraire."

Avrigny, d', (HYACINTHE Robillard—ro′be′yäR′,) a French Jesuit, and a historian of high and merited reputation, was born at Caen in 1675. By his impartial and candid statements of the actions of the Jesuits, he incurred the censure of his superiors, who mutilated his writings. His grief on this account is said to have hastened his death, which occurred at Alençon in 1719. His chief work is "Memoirs contributory to a General His-

tory of Europe from 1600 to 1716," (4 vols., 1725,) which we have only in a mutilated state.

See MORÉRI, "Dictionnaire Historique;" LE LONG, "Bibliothèque Historique."

Avril, ä′vRèl′ or ä′vRe′ye, (JEAN JACQUES,) BARON, a French general, born at Loudun in 1752 ; died in 1839.

Avril, (JEAN JACQUES,) an eminent French engraver, born in Paris in 1744, was a pupil of J. G. Wille. His numerous works are executed with much taste and technical skill. Among his best plates are "Virginia and Icilius," after Lebarbier, "The Family of Darius," after Lebrun, and several after Rubens and N. Poussin. Died in 1832.

See HUBER, "Manuel des Amateurs."

Avril, (JEAN JACQUES,) a son and pupil of the preceding, born in Paris in 1771, was an able engraver. He obtained in 1810 a gold medal for a plate of "The Woman of Cana," after Drouais. Died in 1831.

Avril, (PHILIPPE,) a French Jesuit, who in 1685 made an effort to go by land to China as a missionary. Having reached Astrachan, he encountered some obstacle, and resolved to try another route through Russia. He performed his journey as far as Moscow ; but the government would not permit him to proceed farther. Having returned to France, he published "Travels in various States of Europe and Asia," (1692,) a work of some value.

Avrillon, ä′vRe′yòN′, (JEAN BAPTISTE ÉLIE,) an eloquent French monk. and voluminous author of religious works, was born in Paris in 1652, and died in 1729.

Avrillot, ä′vRe′yo′, (BARBE,) or MADAME Acarie—ä′kä′re′, a French devotee, called the founder of the order of Carmelites in France, was born in Paris in 1565. Died in 1618.

See TRONSON DE CHENEVIÈRE, "Vie de Barbe Avrillot."

Avvocati. See AVOGADRO, (VINCENZO MARIA.)

Avy, ä′ve′, (ANTOINE SYLVAIN,) BARON, a French general, born in 1776, was killed at Antwerp in 1814.

Avycen. See AVICENNA.

Awbrey, (WILLIAM.) See AUBREY.

Awdeley, (JOHN.) See AUDLEY.

Awdeley, (THOMAS.) See AUDLEY, (THOMAS.)

Awhadi (ä′wä-dee′) of Marâgha, a Persian poet, of the Soofee (Sûfi) sect, was the author of "Jâm-i-Jam," a mystical work treating of the doctrines of the Soofees, which is still extant. Died at Ispahân in 1297.

Axajacatl, â-hä-hä-kä′tl, sometimes written **Axajatl,** emperor of the Mexicans or Aztecs, was the father of the celebrated Montezuma. He reigned about fourteen years, and added a number of provinces to the empire. Died about 1477.

Axehielm, äx′ê-hyêlm, (JOANNES,) a Swedish antiquary, born at Norrkjöping in 1608, became assessor at the superior court of law at Åbo in 1637. He left in manuscript several treatises on the antiquities of Sweden. Died in 1692.

Axel. See ABSALON.

Axel, äk′sel, (ISAAC,) a Swede, who was secretary to Gustavus Adolphus, and wrote a treatise on morality, (1662.)

Axelson, äk′sel-son′, (IVER, ee′ver,) a Dane, who renounced allegiance to Denmark in 1453, and reigned over the island of Gothland. He delivered that island to the King of Denmark about 1467.

Axelt, äk′sêlt or **Atzelt,** ät′sêlt, (JOHANN,) a German engraver of portraits, born at Nuremberg in 1654.

Axen, äk′sen, (PETRUS,) a German philologist and lawyer, born at Husum, in Sleswick, in 1635. He translated into Latin Galeazzi Gualdi's "History of the Peace between Louis XIV. and Philip IV.," (1667,) and published "Phædri Fabulæ Æsopicæ," (1671.) Died in 1707.

Ax-ĭ-o-ni′cus, [Ἀξιόνικος,] an Athenian dramatic author, who lived about 380 B.C.

Ax-ĭ-o′the-a, [Ἀξιοθέα,] a Greek woman who lived about 300 B.C. and came to Athens disguised in male apparel to attend the lectures of Plato.

Axmann, äks′män, (JOSEPH,) an Austrian engraver, born at Brunn in 1793. He illustrated various works, chiefly those of Schiller and Stolberg.

See NAGLER, "Neues Allgemeines Künstler-Lexikon."

Ax′tel, (DANIEL,) COLONEL, was an adherent of Par-

ϵ as k; ç as s; ḡ hard; ġ as j; G, H, K, guttural; N, nasal; R, trilled; s̄ as z; ᵵh as in this. (☞See Explanations, p. 23.)

15

fiament in the civil war, and served under Cromwell in Ireland. He was executed by the royalists in 1660.

Axtelmayer, åks′tel-mī′er, (STANISLAUS REINHARD,) a German natural philosopher, who lived about 1700–25, and wrote on various subjects.

Ax′tĭ-us, or **Axt,** åkst, (JOHANN CONRAD,) a German physician, who graduated in 1670. He published a "Treatise on Coniferous Trees and their Products," (1679,) and other works.

Axtman, åkst′mån, (LEOPOLD,) a clever Austrian painter of animals, born at Fulneck, in Moravia, in 1700. He settled in Prague, where he died in 1748. He excelled in painting dogs and horses.

See JÄCK, "Leben und Werke der Künstler Bambergs."

Axular, åk′sü′lår′, (PIERRE,) a French writer in the Basque language, was born in Gascony. He became parish priest of Sare, and published in 1642 a popular treatise "On Repentance," which is called the most remarkable work ever written in the Basque language.

See AUGUSTIN CHAHO, "Voyage en Navarre," Paris, 1836; LARRAMENDI, "Diccionario trilingue del Castellano, Bascuence y Latin," 1745.

Ayala, â-yå′lå, (SEBASTIANO,) a learned Jesuit, born in Sicily in 1744, was a friend of Metastasio, of whom he wrote a biography. He was once minister from the republic of Ragusa to the court of Vienna. He edited the posthumous works of Metastasio, (3 vols., 1785,) wrote a pamphlet against the doctrines of the French Revolution, (1792,) and an "Essay on the Faults of the Dictionary della Crusca." Died in 1817.

See TIPALDO, "Biografia degli Italiani illustri."

Ayala, de, då â-yå′lå, (BALTHASAR,) a learned writer of Spanish extraction, was born at Antwerp about 1548. He was judge-advocate of the army of Philip in the Low Countries. He wrote a treatise "Upon the Rights and Duties of War and Military Discipline," ("De Jure et Officiis Bellicis et Disciplinâ Militari," 1582,) which is said to be the first that systematically reduced the practice of nations in the conduct of war to legitimate rules. Died in 1584.

See FOPPENS, "Bibliotheca Belgica."

Ayala, de, (BARNABÉ,) a Spanish painter of Seville. Died about 1670.

Ayala, de, (DIEGO LOPEZ,) a canon of Toledo, lived in the sixteenth century. He made elegant Spanish versions of the "Philocopo" of Boccaccio, and of the "Arcadia" of Sannazar, (1547.)

Ayala, de, (JUAN Interian—èn-tå-re-ân′,) [Lat. JOAN′NES INTERAMNEN′SIS AJALÆ′US,] a Spanish poet and prose writer, born about 1656, was professor of Hebrew and theology at Salamanca. His best works are Latin poems, "Opuscula Poetica," (1723,) which are praised for their grace and elegance, and the "Learned Christian Painter," ("Pictor Christianus Eruditus," 1730,) a treatise on the errors which painters often commit in the representation of religious subjects. He wrote many letters to Emanuel Marti, which are published with those of his correspondent. Died in 1730.

See MAYANS, "Specimen Bibliothecæ Hispano-Majansianæ."

Ayala, de, (PEDRO LOPEZ,) the most popular of the early Spanish historians, was born in Murcia in 1332. He fought for Henry de Trastamarre at the battle of Nagera, (1367,) where he was taken prisoner by the English. He was afterwards a member of the council of King Henry (Enrique) of Castile, and filled the office of high chancellor in the reign of John I. His chief work is a "History of Castile," ("Cronicas de los Reyes de Castilla, Don Pedro, Don Enrique II., Don Juan I. y Don Enrique III.," 1495,) which is highly esteemed for fidelity. He was probably the most learned Spaniard of his time. He translated Livy's History, and other works, into Spanish. Died in 1407.

See N. ANTONIO, "Bibliotheca Hispana Vetus;" LOPEZ DE AYALA, "Cronicas;" SANCHEZ, "Coleccion de Poesias Castellanas."

Aybar, ī-bar′, (XIMENES PEDRO,) a Spanish painter who lived at Calatayud in the latter half of the seventeenth century, was a pupil and imitator of Francisco Ximenes.

Aybek. See AIBEK.

Aycard, å′kår′, (MARIE,) a French novelist, was

born at Marseilles in 1794. He published, besides other works, novels entitled "Flora," "Marie de Mancini," (1830,) and "The Count of Horn," (1834.) Died in 1859.

Ayer, ā′er, (PETER,) a soldier of the American Revolution, and subsequently one of the founders of the society of Shakers, was born in 1760, in Canterbury, New Hampshire; died in 1857.

Ayeshah or **Aieshah,** ā′e-shạh or ī′e-shạh, [Ger. spelling, AISCHAH or AYESCHAH,] the daughter of Aboo-Bekr, and favourite wife of Mohammed, to whom she was married when only nine years of age. In the events that took place after his death she bore a conspicuous part,—particularly against the caliph Othmân, and afterwards Alee, whom she resisted in arms, but by whom she was finally subdued. She was held in great veneration by all Moslems. Died at Medina in 677.

See IRVING, "Mahomet and his Successors;" OCKLEY, "History of the Saracens."

Aylesbury or **Ailesbury,** ālz′ber-e, (FRANCES,) a daughter of Sir Thomas, noticed below, was the wife of the Earl of Clarendon, and grandmother of Queens Mary and Anne.

Aylesbury or **Ailesbury,** (Sir THOMAS,) an English mathematician and patron of learning, was born in London in 1576. He was appointed master of requests and master of the mint, and created a baronet in 1627. He patronized Thomas Hariot, and welcomed to his table all men of science, some of whom received pensions from his private income. Having adhered to the royal cause in the civil war, he went into exile in 1649. Died at Breda in 1657.

See WOOD, "Fasti Oxonienses;" "Biographia Britannica."

Aylesbury, (WILLIAM,) a son of the preceding, born in Westminster about 1612, became tutor to the young Duke of Buckingham. By the order of Charles I., he translated (with the aid of Sir C. Cotterell) Davila's "History of the Civil Wars of France," (1647.) He was for some time secretary to the Governor of Jamaica, where he died in 1657.

See WOOD, "Athenæ Oxonienses."

Aylett, ā′let, (ROBERT,) an English poet, born about 1580, obtained the office of master in chancery. He published in 1622 a volume of four poems, entitled "Peace with her four Garders," "Susanna," "Thrift's Equipage," and "Joseph or Pharaoh's Favourite." Among his other works are "Divine and Moral Speculations," (1654.)

Ayliffe, ā′lif, (JOHN,) a learned English jurist, who lived in the eighteenth century, and styled himself a Fellow of New College, Oxford. We have little information of the events of his life. He published in 1714 "The Ancient and Present State of the University of Oxford," (2 vols.) He manifested his hostility to the Romish Church in his "Supplement to the Canons and Constitutions of the Church of England," (1726.) In 1734 he published a "Pandect of the Roman Civil Law." The time of his death is unknown.

Aylini, ī-lee′nee, or **Ailino,** ī-lee′no, (GIOVANNI,) an Italian historian, lived between 1350 and 1400.

Ayllon, de, då ïl-yòn′, (LUCAS VASQUEZ,) a Spaniard, of the early part of the sixteenth century, who was instrumental in inducing the men of Narvaez to desert to Cortez, and was among the first to land on the territories of the (now) United States, for the purpose of carrying off Indians for slaves. He formed a settlement in South Carolina, (which was afterwards abandoned,) where he died in 1526.

Aylmer, ål′mer, called also **El′mer,** (JOHN,) an English bishop, born at Tilney, in Norfolk, in 1521. Soon after he left college, he became tutor to Lady Jane Grey, who expressed her opinion of him in these terms : "He teaches me so gently, so pleasantly, with such fair allurements to learning, that I think all the time nothing whiles I am with him." He was a zealous Protestant, and lived in exile on the continent during the reign of Mary. In 1559 he published an "Harborowe (harborough) for faithful and true Subjects against the late-blown Blast," in answer to John Knox's "Blast of the Trumpet against the Monstrous Regiment of Women." He became Bishop of London in 1576, after which he distinguished himself by his intolerance and persecution of the Puritans and the Catholics. Died in 1594.

See WOOD, "Athenæ Oxonienses;" FULLER, "Worthies of England;" STRYPE, "Annals and Ecclesiastical Memorials."

Ayl'mer, (MATTHEW,) LORD, born probably in Ireland about 1643, became a rear-admiral in 1692, after he had distinguished himself at the battle of La Hogue. In 1709 he was appointed lord commissioner of the admiralty, admiral, and commander-in-chief of the fleet. He was deprived of his command in 1710, but reinstated in 1714. In 1718 he was raised to the Irish peerage as Lord Aylmer, Baron of Balrath. Died in 1720.

Ayloffe, ā'lof, (Sir JOSEPH,) a distinguished antiquary, born in Sussex, England, about 1708. He was chosen a Fellow of the Royal Society in 1731, and became auditor-general of the hospitals of Bridewell and Bethlem in 1750. His chief work is "Calendars of the Ancient Charters, and of the Welsh and Scotch Rolls, now remaining in the Tower of London," (1772.) He contributed some papers to the Society of Antiquaries, and edited several works, among which was Leland's "Collectanea," (6 vols., 1770.) Died in 1781.

See THOMSON'S "History of the Royal Society."

Ayl'ward, (THEODORE,) an English composer of music, was organist of Saint George's chapel, Windsor. Died in 1801.

Aymar. See ADEMAR.

Aymar, ă'mǎr', (JACQUES,) a successful French impostor, who was born a peasant in 1662. He professed, by his skill in divination, to discover hidden treasures, mines, and even the guilt of suspected persons. He obtained a wonderful degree of credence,—even scientific men maintaining controversies as to the source of his marvellous powers. After several years of successful imposture, he finally confessed the fraud.

Aymard, ă'mǎr', (ANTOINE,) a French general, born at Lezignan, in Aude, in 1773, became a colonel in 1807, and served with distinction in Spain from 1808 to 1812. Having been made a general of brigade in 1813, he adhered to Napoleon during the Hundred Days. He commanded the troops which, after a severe fight, suppressed an insurrection at Lyons in 1834. Died in 1861.

Aymar Rivault. See RIVAULT.

Aymé, ă'mā', (JEAN JACQUES,) better known by the name of **Job Aymé,** a French advocate, born at Montélimart in 1752, took an active part in the French Revolution, and escaped the guillotine only by the fall of Robespierre. He was elected a member of the Council of Five Hundred in 1795, but was banished to Guiana in 1798, on suspicion of being a royalist. On his return he received an appointment from Napoleon, and published a work on Guiana. Died in 1818.

Aymé, (JOB.) See AYMÉ, (JEAN JACQUES.)

Aymé de Chatillon. See AYMÉ DE VARENNE.

Aymé de Varenne, (or **Varranne,**) ă'mā' deh vǎ'rěn', (or vǎr'rǎn',) sometimes called **Aymé de Chatillon,** (deh shǎ'te'yôN',) a French poet of the twelfth century, is chiefly known as the author of the "Romance of Florimont."

Aymon, Aimon, ā'mon, [Fr. pron. ă'môN',] written also **Haimon,** Count of Ardennes, and his four sons Alard, Regnaud, (Rinaldo or Renaud,) Richard, (or Richardet,) and Guichard, (or Guiscard,) ("les quatre fils Aymon,") were celebrated characters in the romances and poems of the Middle Ages. It is doubtful if they had a real existence. Rinaldo is one of the principal characters of Ariosto's great poem.

See FERRARIO, "Storia ed Analisi degli antichi Romanzi."

Ay'mon, [in Italian AIMONE, ī-mo'nȧ,] Count of Savoy, was born in 1291. He sent troops to the assistance of France in the war against Edward III. of England, created the office of chancellor, and introduced other reforms calculated to maintain a pure administration of justice. Died in 1343.

Aymon, ă'môN', (JEAN,) a French ecclesiastic, born in Dauphiné. He turned Protestant about 1700, after which, it is said, he stole some manuscripts from the royal library of Paris and fled to Holland. He published, besides other works, a satirical "Tableau of the Court of Rome," (1707,) and "Acts of all the National Synods of the Reformed Churches of France," (1710.)

Aynès, ă'nês', (FRANÇOIS DAVID,) a French *littérateur*, born at Lyons in 1766, published a "Universal Dictionary of Geography," (3 vols., 1814.) Died in 1827.

Aynsworth, (HENRY.) See AINSWORTH.

Ayo or **Aïo,** ā'yo, Duke of Beneventum, succeeded to the dukedom in 641 A.D.

Ayolas, de, dǎ ā-yo'lȧs, or **d'Ayolas,** dȧ-yo'lȧs, (JUAN,) a Spanish adventurer, who sailed with Pedro de Mendoza, in 1534, on a voyage of conquest and discovery to the La Plata. Mendoza, having been disabled by disease in 1536, deputed his command to Ayolas, who ascended the Paraguay to Asuncion, where he defeated a body of natives and remained six months. Leaving a garrison at Asuncion, he ascended the river about eighty leagues, and then marched westward by land with two hundred Spaniards. He never returned. According to the report of an Indian, Ayolas and his men were decoyed into a morass and killed by the Payagos.

See SOUTHEY, "History of Brazil," and HERRERA, "Historia general."

Ayrault or **Airault,** ă'rō', [Lat. ÆRO'DIUS,] (PIERRE,) a French jurist, born at Angers in 1536. He practised in the Parliament of Paris with a high reputation, and wrote, besides other legal works, a treatise "On the Paternal Authority," ("De Patrio Jure," 1593,) composed on the occasion of his son René having joined the Jesuits against his father's will; also "On the Judicial Order and Instruction employed by the Ancient Greeks and Romans in Public Accusations," ("De l'Ordre et Instruction judiciaire dont les anciens Grecs et Romains ont usé en Accusations publiques," 1575.) Died in 1601.

See TAISAND, "Vies des plus célèbres Jurisconsultes;" "Vita Petri Ærodii," by his grandson, GILLES MÉNAGE, 1675.

Ayrault, (RENÉ,) a Jesuit and writer, born in Paris in 1567, was a son of the preceding. Died in 1644.

Ayrenhoff, von, fon ī'ręn-hof', (CORNELIUS HERMANN,) a German dramatic poet of decided talent, was born in Vienna in 1733, and died there in 1819. He took the French dramas as his models. His most successful works were comedies; but they are now little known. He attained the rank of lieutenant-field-marshal in the army in 1794.

See his "Autobiography," published in 1810, and WOLFF, "Encyklopädie der Deutschen Nationalliteratur."

Ayrer, ī'ręr, (CHRISTOPH HEINRICH,) a German medical writer, lived about 1600.

Ayrer, (EMANUEL WILHELM,) a German medical writer, born at Nuremberg in 1647; died in 1690.

Ayrer, (GEORG HEINRICH,) a German jurist, born in Meiningen in 1702. He was professor of law at Göttingen, and author of many legal treatises. Died in 1774.

Ayrer or **Eyer,** ī'ręr, (JACOB,) a German dramatic poet, who flourished in the latter part of the sixteenth century, and practised as a notary and advocate at Nuremberg. Little else is known of his life, except that he wrote sixty-six dramas for his own amusement, the earliest of which are dated about 1585. They display great dramatic power, but are little more than stories in the form of dialogue, without unity of action or of time. Died about 1605.

See TIECK, "Deutsches Theater;" WOLFF, "Encyklopädie der Deutschen Nationalliteratur."

Ayrer, (JOHANN WILHELM,) a son of Emanuel Wilhelm, noticed above, born in 1671, was a physician at Altorf.

Ayrer, (MELCHIOR,) a German physician and chemist, born at Nuremberg in 1520, was a pupil of Melanchthon. He left some works in manuscript.

Ayres, ārz, (JOHN,) an eminent English penman, published a Treatise on Penmanship, (1697.) Died about 1705.

Ayres, (PHILIP,) an English writer, who flourished between 1650 and 1700. He published "Emblems of Love," (1683,) "Lyric Poems," (1687,) and other works.

Ayrmann, īr'mȧn, (CHRISTOPH FRIEDRICH,) a German scholar, born at Leipsic about 1695, became professor of history at Giessen in 1721, and began several historical works, but finished nothing. He edited Vei leius Paterculus, Florus, Eutropius, Cæsar, Suetonius, Justin, and Terence. Died in 1747.

See JÖCHER, "Allgemeines Gelehrten-Lexikon."

ê as k; ç as s; ğ hard; ğ as j; G, H, K, guttural; N, nasal; R, trilled; ş as z; th as in this. (☞ See Explanations, p. 23.)

Ayrton, är'ton, (EDMUND,) an English composer of cathedral music, was born at Ripon, Yorkshire, in 1734. He was appointed vicar-choral of Saint Paul's Cathedral about 1765, and master of the children of the royal chapels in 1780. His compositions are highly commended. Died in 1808.

See FÉTIS, "Biographie Universelle des Musiciens."

Ayrton, (WILLIAM,) a critical writer on music, born in London between 1777 and 1781, was a son of the preceding. He was a successful teacher of music, and editor of "The Harmonicon," a monthly musical review, 1823–33. Died in 1858.

Ayscough, (ANNE.) See ASKEW.

Ayscough, ās'kū, (?) (FRANCIS,) an English clergyman, entered Oxford in 1717. He was preceptor to George III. before his accession, and became Dean of Bristol. He married a sister of George, Lord Lyttleton. Died about 1766.

Ayscough, (Sir GEORGE.) See AYSCUE.

Ayscough, (GEORGE EDWARD,) a son of Francis, noticed above, edited the works of his uncle, Lord Lyttleton, in 1774, and published "Semiramis," a tragedy, in 1776. Died in 1779.

See NICHOLS, "Literary Anecdotes;" "Biographia Dramatica."

Ayscough, (JAMES,) an English optician, lived in London about 1720–40, and wrote a treatise on Spectacles, (1750.)

Ayscough, (SAMUEL,) an Englishman, noted as a maker of indexes, was born about 1745. He was appointed assistant librarian in the British Museum in 1785, of the manuscripts of which he had published a good catalogue in 1782. He made indexes for the "Gentleman's Magazine," (56 vols., 1731–86,) for the "Remarkable Passages and Words of Shakspeare," (1790,) and for other works. Died in 1804.

See "Gentleman's Magazine," 1805.

Ayscue, ās'kū, written also **Ayscough, Ascough,** or **Askew,** (Sir GEORGE,) a distinguished English admiral, who had acquired the reputation of an able officer before the end of the reign of Charles I. He adhered to the Parliament when, in July, 1648, the greater part of the navy revolted and went over to the Prince of Wales, and for his fidelity was raised to the rank of vice-admiral in 1649. He conveyed Cromwell's army to Ireland in that year, and took Barbadoes from the royalists about the end of 1651. He commanded in an indecisive battle against the Dutch admiral De Ruyter, near Plymouth, in 1652, a few months after which he resigned, or was dismissed. In 1665 he led a squadron in the battle which the Earl of Sandwich gained over the Dutch, and greatly contributed to the victory. As admiral of the blue, he took part in a great battle in June, 1666, and was taken prisoner by the Dutch after his ship had struck on a sand-bank. This was the last action in which he was engaged. The date of his death is unknown.

See CAMPBELL, "Lives of British Admirals;" CHARNOCK, "Biographia Navalis," 1794; CLARENDON, "History of the Rebellion."

Ayta, ī'tä, or **Aytta,** īt'tä, (ULRICH **Viger van Zuichm**—ve-hair' vän zoiKm,) usually called **Vig'lI-us Zui'chemus,** an eminent Dutch jurist and statesman, of Spanish extraction, was born at Leeuwarden in 1507. He lectured on the Institutes at the University of Padua, and became very popular as a teacher. He was appointed an imperial senator in 1543, and president of the imperial council of the Netherlands in 1549. In the contest which resulted in the independence of the United Provinces, he adhered to the King of Spain, but opposed some of the violent measures of the Duke of Alva. His "Commentaries on Ten Titles of the Institutes," relating to wills, (1534,) were regarded at that time as the very highest authority. According to Motley, he was crafty, plausible, adroit, and pusillanimous. He died at Brussels in 1577.

See TAISAND, "Vies des plus célèbres Jurisconsultes;" MOTLEY, "Rise of the Dutch Republic," vols. i. and ii. ; FOPPENS, "Bibliotheca Belgica"

Ay'ton or **Aytoun,** ä'ton, (Sir ROBERT,) a Scottish poet, born at Kinaldie, Fifeshire, in 1570. On the accession of James I., (1603,) he complimented that king in a Latin poem, for which he was rewarded with the offices of private secretary to the queen and master of requests.

He wrote other Latin poems, and some in the vernacular, which were admired by Burns. Died in 1638.

See CHAMBERS, "Biographical Dictionary of Eminent Scotsmen."

Ay'toun, (WILLIAM EDMONDSTOUNE,) an eminent British critic and poet, born in Fifeshire in 1813, was a son-in-law of Professor John Wilson. In 1831 he gained a prize at the University of Edinburgh for his poem of "Judith." Having studied law, he was called to the bar in 1840. He was appointed professor of rhetoric in the University of Edinburgh in 1845. "His literary connection," says "Blackwood" for April, 1868, "with Maga,* became so intimate and so well known that common repute attributed the editorship to him, as it had to his father-in-law, Professor Wilson,—in either case without foundation." His *nom de plume* was Augustus Dunshunner. In 1849 he published "Lays of the Scottish Cavaliers, and other Poems," which reached the tenth edition in 1857. "A volume of verse," says the "London Quarterly Review," "which shows that Scotland has yet a poet. Full of the true fire, it now stirs and swells like a trumpet tone, now sinks in cadences sad and wild as the wail of a Highland dirge." Among his most successful works are "Bothwell, a Poem," (1856,) and a parody on certain poets of the spasmodic school, entitled "Firmilian, a Spasmodic Tragedy, by T. Percy Jones," (first published in 1854.) In a later volume, with the last-named work are included Aytoun's "Bon Gaultier Ballads." Died in 1865.

See "Memoir of William Edmondstoune Aytoun," by THEODORE MARTIN; "Blackwood's Magazine" for April, 1868.

Ayyub or **Ayyoub.** See AIYOOB.

Ayyubiah. See AIYOOBITES.

Ayyubites or **Ayyoubites.** See AIYOOBITES.

Azâd Khân, â-zâd' Kân, an Afghan chief, who served under Nâdir Shâh. Six years after the death of that conqueror, (in 1753,) he became a powerful competitor for the throne of Persia with Kareem (Karîm) Khân, whom he at one time nearly drove from his kingdom ; but, being afterwards surprised in a mountain-pass, his army was utterly destroyed by the forces of Kareem. He at first fled to Georgia, but afterwards returned, and, throwing himself on the mercy of Kareem, was not only pardoned, but admitted to his intimate friendship.

Azad-ud-Daulah, â'zad (or ŭz'ąd) ōōd dǒw'lah, second prince of the Deelamee (Dilami) dynasty, who ruled over the western part of Persia in the tenth century. He was a mild and beneficent sovereign, who fostered letters and promoted public improvements. Died in 983.

Azâiri (â-zī're) of Rai, a Persian poet, who lived about 1000 A.D., at the court of Mahmood of Gazna, (or Ghiznee.)

Azaïs, ä'zä'ěss', (PIERRE HYACINTHE,) a French philosopher, born at Sorèze in 1766, was a son of Pierre Hyacinthe, noticed below. Having written against the excesses of the Revolution, he was condemned to deportation, but escaped by concealing himself. Under the empire he was inspector of books at Nancy. His favourite study was the doctrine of compensations, on which he published a work, "The Compensations in Human Destinies," (1809.) In 1812 he published a larger work, called "Système universel," 8 vols. Died in 1845.

See J. GUADET, "Notice sur Azaïs," prefixed to the fifth edition of his "Compensations," and "Nouvelle Biographie Générale."

Azaïs, (PIERRE HYACINTHE,) a French musician and composer, born in Languedoc in 1743; died in 1793.

See FÉTIS, "Biographie Universelle des Musiciens."

Azambuja, de, dä â-zăm-boo'zhä, (JOÃO ESTEVES,) a Portuguese prelate, became Archbishop of Lisbon in 1402, and afterwards cardinal. Died in 1415.

Azambuza, de, dä â-zăm-boo'zä, (DIOGO,) an able and humane Portuguese commander, was sent out in 1481 by João II. at the head of an expedition, and established a settlement on the coast of Guinea.

See MARMOL, "Description générale de l'Afrique."

Azanza, de, dä â-thän'thä, (MIGUEL JOSÉ,) an able Spanish statesman, born in Navarre (Navarra) in 1746, was appointed minister of war in 1793. He was Viceroy of Mexico from 1796 to 1799, and governed that colony

---

* Another name for "Blackwood's Magazine."

with unusual equity. In March, 1808, he was appointed minister of finance by Ferdinand VII. As a member of the Supreme Junta, to which the king committed the government on his departure to Bayonne, Azanza appears to have favoured the French party. He was minister of the Indies and minister of justice under Joseph Bonaparte, (1809–13,) and followed him into exile. Died at Bordeaux in 1826.

See ALISON, "History of Europe;" SOUTHEY, "History of the Peninsular War."

Azara, de, dâ â-thä'râ, (Don FELIX,) a Spanish naturalist, born near Balbastro, in Aragon, in 1746. He had obtained the rank of lieutenant-colonel of engineers, when in 1780 he was sent to South America to survey the disputed boundary between the Spanish and Portuguese possessions. He remained there about twenty years, during which he prepared a map of Buenos Ayres and Paraguay and studied the natural history of those regions. Amidst his arduous labours he was greatly hindered and harassed by jealous and ignorant officials. An account of his observations on the mammalia and birds of Paraguay was published in French in 1801. He published, in Spanish, "Observations on the Quadrupeds, Reptiles, and Birds of Paraguay and La Plata," (5 vols., Madrid, 1802.) These works entitle him to a high rank as an original observer. His "Travels in South America," with notes by Cuvier, were published in French (4 vols., 1809) by Walckenaer, at the request of the author. Percival Hunter translated into English the volume of his Spanish work which treats of the quadrupeds of Paraguay, etc., (1836.) Died in Aragon in 1811.

See WALCKENAER, "Notice sur F. Azara," prefixed to the "Voyage dans l'Amérique Méridionale;" P. HUNTER, "Natural History," etc."

Azara, de, (Don JOSÉ NICOLAS,) a brother of the preceding, distinguished as a writer, diplomatist, and patron of literature and art, was born at Barbunales, near Balbastro, in 1731. He succeeded Grimaldi as ambassador at Rome in 1785, before which date he had for some years performed the functions of that office without the title. He acquired great influence with the court of Rome, where he remained until 1798. He patronized many artists, especially Raphael Mengs, of whom he wrote an entertaining biography, (1780.) In 1790 he produced an elegant Spanish version of Middleton's "Life of Cicero." He was sent to Paris as ambassador about 1800, and died there in January, 1804.

See BOURGOING, "Notice historique sur le Chevalier d'Azara," 1804; SEMPERE Y GUARINOS, "Biblioteca Española."

Azaree or **Azari,** ä'zä-ree, a celebrated Persian poet of the Soofee sect, was the author of many religious works. Died in 1460.

Azariah. See ABEDNEGO.

Az-ạ-rī'ah, [Heb. הירזע,] a king of Judah, succeeded his father Amaziah. (See II. Kings xiv. 21, 22.)

Azariah di Rossi, â-zä-ree'â de ros'see, (or **De Ru'beis,**) a very learned Jewish rabbi and writer of the sixteenth century, was a native of Mantua. He displayed a spirit of liberal criticism in his work called "The Light of the Eyes," (1574,) which treats on history, chronology, etc., and is highly esteemed by Christian scholars.

See LELONG, "Bibliotheca Sacra."

Azario, âd-zä're-o, (PIETRO,) an Italian chronicler, born at Novara in the early part of the fourteenth century. He compiled a chronicle of Lombardy from 1250 to 1362, called "Book of Achievements in Lombardy," ("Liber Gestorum in Lombardia.")

Azeezee or **Azîzî,** â-zee'zee, a Turkish statesman, historian, and poet, born at Constantinople about 1590; died in 1657.

Azeglio, d', dâd-zàl'yo, (CESARE,) MARQUIS, born at Turin in 1763, served in the army against the French, by whom he was taken prisoner in 1792. About 1815 he was ambassador from the King of Sardinia to Rome. He founded in 1822 a journal called the "Friend of Italy," ("Amico d'Italia,") which he edited until 1829. Died in 1830.

Azeglio, d', (MASSIMO Taparelli—tâ-pâ-rel'lee,) MARQUIS, an illustrious Italian statesman, author, and artist, son of the preceding, was born at Turin about 1800. He passed about eight years (1821–29) at Rome,

and gained distinction as a painter of landscapes, etc. He married a daughter of the celebrated author Manzoni, and began his literary career by a popular romance, "Ettore Fieramosco," (1833,) which was received with enthusiasm by the Italians. His historical romance "Niccolò di Lapi" (1841) had also a great success, and gave a powerful impulse to Italian patriotism. He manifested his liberal principles in a political treatise called "The Late Events in the Romagna," (1846.) In 1848 he took arms against the Austrians, and was severely wounded at Vicenza. In May, 1849, he was appointed president of the council (prime minister) by Victor Emmanuel. He was succeeded by Cavour in 1852. His policy was too moderate or conservative to satisfy the zealous republicans. Died in 1866.

See "M. Azeglio prima et dopo la Guerra della Indipendenza," Turin, 1850; BROCKHAUS, "Conversations-Lexikon;" "Gentleman's Magazine" for March, 1866.

Azelt. See AXELT.

Az'e-mar' (or **Az'ī-mar'**) **le Noir**—lẹh nwâR, a Provençal troubadour, lived in the first half of the thirteenth century.

Azémar, ä'zà'mär', (FRANÇOIS BAZILE,) a French general, born at Cabannes in 1776, was killed at the battle of Gross Drebnitz in 1813.

Azevedo. See ACEVEDO and ACEBEDO.

Azevedo, (FELIX ALVARES.) See ACEVEDO.

Azevedo, â-zà-vä'do, (JOÃO,) a Portuguese theologian, born at Santarem in 1665; died in 1746.

Azevedo, (LUIZ,) a Portuguese Jesuit and linguist, born at Chaves in 1573, educated at Goa, was afterwards sent to Abyssinia, where he was greatly beloved, and where he died in 1634. He spoke fluently the Geëz and Amharic dialects, into which he translated the New Testament and other works.

Azevedo, â-thä-vä'DO, (PEDRO,) a Spanish physician, born in the Canaries, wrote a treatise on the plague, (1589.)

Azevedo, (PEDRO,) a Spanish medical writer, who lived about 1720.

Azevedo, de, dâ â-thä-vä'DO, (ALONSO,) a Spanish lawyer and legal writer, died in his native city of Plasencia in 1598.

Azevedo, de, (ALONSO,) a Spanish poet, who published at Rome, in 1615, a poem entitled the "Creation of the World."

Azevedo, de, dâ â-zà-v⁼'do, (ANGELA,) a Portuguese dramatic authoress, lived about 1650. She wrote in Spanish, and was attached to the court of Philip IV. of Spain.

Azevedo, de, (FRANCISCO,) a Portuguese poet, born at Lisbon; died in 1680.

Azevedo, de, (IGNAZIO,) a Portuguese Jesuit missionary, born at Oporto in 1527, was noted for his self-denial and ascetic piety. He laboured several years in Brazil, and returned to Europe. On a second voyage to Brazil, of which he was appointed provincial, the ship in which he sailed was attacked near the Canary Islands in 1570 by a fanatical sea-captain in the service of the Queen of Navarre, who massacred Azevedo and many other Jesuit missionaries.

See BEAUVAIS et CAROURA, "La Vie et le Martyre d'Azevedo," 1745.

Azevedo, de, (JERONYMO,) a brother of the preceding, was Governor-General of Ceylon from 1595 to 1612, and Viceroy of the Portuguese dominions in India from 1612 to 1617. He returned to Portugal in 1617, and died in prison, to which he is said to have been committed for alleged disloyal intrigues.

Azevedo, de, (LUIS ANTONIO,) a Portuguese grammarian, lived at Lisbon about 1800.

Azevedo, de, (LUIZA,) a Portuguese poetess, born at Villa de Paredes in 1655; died in 1679.

Azevedo-Coutinho, â-zà-vä'do kō-tèn'yo, (Jozĕ JOAQUIM,) a Portuguese bishop and writer on commerce, was born in Brazil in 1742. Died in 1821.

Azevedo-Morato, de, dâ â-zà-vä'do mo-râ'to, (MANOEL,) a Portuguese poet, born at Coimbra, lived about 1710.

Azevedo-Tojal, de, dâ â-zà-vä'do to-zhâl', (P.,) a Portuguese poet, published, in 1716, "Carlos reduzido,

---

€ as *k;* ç as *s;* ğ *hard;* ğ as *j;* G, H, K, *guttural;* N, *nasal;* R, *trilled;* ş as *z;* ŧh as in *this.* (☞See Explanations, p. **23.**)

Inglaterra illustrada," ("Charles restored or reclaimed, and England enlightened,") a heroic poem, of which the conversion of Charles II. of England to Catholicism forms the chief subject.

Azevedo y Zuñiga, de, då å-thå-vä′Do e thoon-yee′gä, (CASPAR,) Count of Monterey, was made Viceroy of Peru in 1603, having previously filled the office of viceroy in Mexico. Died at Lima in 1606.

Azim-ed-Dowlah-Bahâdur,(or -**Behauder,**) å′zim ed dŏw′läh ba-hå′der, (or ba-hå′dōōr,) the last nabob of the Carnatic in India. He ceded the Carnatic to the East India Company in 1801. Died in 1819.

Azinhero, å-zěn-yä′ro, (CHRISTOVÃO RODRIGUEZ,) a Portuguese jurist and historian, born at Evora in 1474.

Azizî. See AZEEZEE.

Aznar, åz-naR′, or **As-ï-na′rï-us,** Count of Gascony or Vasconie, died in 836 A.D., and left a son Sancho, who became Count of Navarre.

Azo, Azzo, åt′so, or **A-zo-li′nus,** (PORTIUS,) one of the most celebrated jurists of the middle ages, was born at Bologna near the middle of the twelfth century. He lectured at the University of Bologna. His chief works, "Summa Codicis" and "Summa Institutionum," were the highest authority in his time. Died about 1220.

See TAISAND, "Vies des plus célèbres Jurisconsultes."

Azolinus. See AZO.

Azopardi, åd-zo-paR′dee, (FRANCESCO,) an Italian musician, lived at Malta about 1750, and published "Practical Music," ("Il Musico prattico.")

Azor, å-thôR′, [Lat. AZO′RIUS,] (JUAN,) a Spanish Jesuit and casuist, born at Zamora in 1533. He published at Rome "Institutes of Morals," ("Institutiones Morales,") the principles of which were censured by Pascal in his "Provincial Letters." Died in 1603.

Azpilcueta, åth-pêl-kwä′tå, (MARTIN,) a celebrated Spanish doctor of canon law, often called the "Navarrese" or "Navarro," was born near Pampeluna about 1490. He wrote a number of works, which were published in 3 vols., 1590. At the age of eighty he appeared as counsel for Carranza, an archbishop who was tried for heresy at Rome. He was remarkable for his charitable disposition. Died at Rome in 1586.

See N. ANTONIO, "Bibliotheca Hispana Nova."

Azraki, åz′rå-kee, a Persian poet and sage, born at Herât in the eleventh century, flourished at the court of Tugân Shâh, at Nishapoor. He was the author or reviser of a work of philosophical and moral maxims called the "Book of Sinbad."

Azulai, å-zoo′lī, (ABRAHAM,) a Jewish cabalistic writer, lived at Fez. Died in 1644.

Azuni, åd-zoo′nee, (DOMENICO ALBERTO,) a distinguished jurist and antiquary, born at Sassari, in the island of Sardinia, in 1749. He published in 1786–88 a valuable "Universal Dictionary of Mercantile Jurisprudence," and in 1795 "The General System of the Principles of the Maritime Law of Europe," ("Sistema universale dei Principii del Dritto maritimo dell' Europa," 4 vols.,) a work of high reputation. An improved French version was published by him in 1805. He was appointed by Napoleon president of the court of appeal at Genoa in 1807, and was one of the compilers of the French Code of Commerce. Among his works is a "Civil and Natural History of Sardinia," (1802.) Died at Cagliari in 1827.

See G. MANNO, "Vita d'Azuni;" TIPALDO, "Biografia degli Italiani illustri."

Azurara, de, då å-zoo-rå′rå, or **Zurara,** zoo-rå′rå, (GOMEZ,) a Portuguese historian, born in the first half of the fifteenth century, was appointed keeper of the Torre do Tombo in 1454. Among his works is a "Chronicle of the Discovery and Conquest of Guinea." He was living in 1472.

Azzanello, åt-så-nel′lo, (GREGORIO,) an Italian writer, born at Cremona, lived about 1400.

Azzari, åt-så′ree, (FULVIO,) a historian, born at Reggio, in Lombardy, about the middle of the sixteenth

century. He wrote a "History of Reggio," in Latin, (1623.)

Az-zarkâl, åz-zar-kål′, **Abool-** (or **Abûl-**) **Kâsim-Ibn-Abderrahman.** å′bōōl kå′sim ïb'n åb-der-råн′-mån, a distinguished astronomer and mathematician, born at Córdova about 1000 A.D., was the inventor and improver of some astronomical instruments, and the propounder of some ingenious theories in astronomy.

Azzemino, åt-sà-mee′no, (PAOLO,) a Venetian artist, who flourished about 1500–20. He excelled in the art of inlaying on gold, silver, and iron, called in French *damasquinage.*

Azzi, åt′see, (ORAZIO,) an Italian writer on theology, born at Parma, lived about 1700–25.

Azzi, degli, dål′yee åt′see, (FRANCESCO MARIA,) an Italian poet, born at Arezzo in 1655. His sonnets have been commended by Italian critics. Died in 1707.

Azzi ne' Forti, degli, dål′ye åt′see nä foR′tee, (FAUSTINA,) a sister of Francesco Maria, noticed above, wrote verses which were received with favour. Died in 1724, aged about seventy-four.

Azzio, åt′se-o, [Lat. ACTIUS,] (TOMMASO,) an Italian jurist, born in the latter part of the sixteenth century, was the author of a treatise on the game of chess.

Azzo, åt′so, **I.,** (ALBERT,) Marquis of Este, was involved in war against the Emperor of Germany about 1014. Died in 1029.

Azzo II., son of Azzo I., the wealthiest of the Italian nobles, played a conspicuous part in the affairs of Italy, as also did his successors Azzo III., V., and VI. Azzo VII. was a distinguished leader of the Guelph faction, in which he experienced great variety of fortune, but finally triumphed, and died in Ferrara in 1264.

Azzo, (ALBERTO,) called also **Atto** or **da Alberto,** a nobleman of Lucca, who took a distinguished part in the defence of the towns of Lombardy in the latter half of the tenth century, and was created by Otho the Great Marquis of Reggio and Módena.

See SISMONDI, "Histoire des Républiques Italiennes."

Azzoguidi, åt-so-gwee′dee, (GERMANI,) an Italian physician, born at Bologna in 1740, was the author of an excellent work on the structure of the uterus, and was the founder of the museum of comparative anatomy and physiology in his native city. Died in 1814.

Azzoguidi, (VALERIO FELICE,) an Italian antiquary, born at Bologna in 1651. He published a work "On the Origin and Antiquity of Bologna," ("De Origine et Vetustate Bononiæ," 1716.) Died in 1728.

See MAZZUCHELLI, "Scrittori d'Italia."

Azzolini, åt-so-lee′nee, (DECIUS,) an Italian cardinal and poet, born at Fermo in 1623 ; died in 1689.

Azzolini or **Mazzolini,** måt-so-lee′nee, (GIOVANNI BERNARDINO,) a Neapolitan painter, who worked at Genoa about 1610, or, according to some authorities, in 1510. He excelled in expression.

See SOPRANI, "Vite de' Pittori Genovesi."

Azzolini, (LORENZO,) an Italian poet, born at Fermo, was a nephew of Cardinal Azzolini. He became secretary to Pope Urban VIII., who appointed him Bishop of Ripatransone in 1630. He wrote, besides other poems, a "Satire against Luxury," (1686,) which was much admired by Italian critics. Died in 1632.

See MAZZUCHELLI, "Scrittori d'Italia."

Azzoni Avogari, degli, dål′yee åt-so′nee å-vo-gå′-ree, (RAMBALDO,) an Italian antiquary, born at Treviso in 1719, became a canon of the cathedral in that town. He founded a public library at Treviso. His knowledge of the ancient documents and inscriptions of Italy was remarkable. He wrote, besides other works, a treatise "On the Origin and Antiquities of Treviso," (1840.) Died in 1790.

See a "Life of Azzoni," prefixed to his "Considerazioni sopra le prime Notizie di Trivigi," 1840.

Azzoobeydee or **Az-zubeydî,** åz-zōō-bä′dee, a Moslem lexicographer and grammarian, born at Seville about 927 ; died about 990.

ā, ē, ī, ō, ū, ȳ, *long;* å, ê, ô, same, less prolonged; ă, ĕ, ĭ, ŏ, ŭ, ў, *short;* a, e, i, o, *obscure;* fär, fåll, fåt; mêt; nŏt; gōōd; mōōn,

B.

Baader, bä′dẹr, (CLEMENS ALOIS,) brother of Franz Xaver, noticed below, born in 1762, published a work entitled "Learned Bavarians," ("Gelehrten Baiern.") Died in 1838.

Baader, (FRANZ JOSEPH,) born at Ratisbon in 1733, was physician to the Elector of Bavaria. Died in 1794.

Baader, (TOBIAS,) a German sculptor, born in Bavaria, lived in the second half of the seventeenth century.

Baader, von, fon bä′dẹr, (FRANZ XAVER,) a German philosopher, born at Munich in 1765, became professor of speculative theology in that city. He was an adherent of Jacob Böhme, and published several works in opposition to the philosophy of Hegel and Schelling; also many well-written pamphlets or short treatises. Died in 1841.

See F. HOFFMANN, "F. v. Baader in seinem Verhältniss zu Hegel, etc.," 1850.

Baader, von, (JOSEPH,) brother of Franz Xaver, born at Munich in 1763, was the author of a number of treatises on mechanics. Died in 1835.

Baah-Deen or **Baahdîn,** bä′äh-deen′, a learned Persian, supposed to have lived in the seventeenth century, wrote, by command of Abbâs the Great, a "Summary of Civil and Canon Law," (left unfinished.)

Baak-Hattigh, bäk-hät′tiG, (JEAN,) a Flemish landscape-painter, flourished about 1640.

Bä′ạl, (or bäl,) | Heb. בַּעַל,] written also **Bel,** the principal god of the Phœnicians and several other Oriental nations, represented the sun, while Baaltis, Astarte, or Ashtoreth, the correlative female deity, corresponded to the moon, (queen of heaven.) Baal was also the Bel or Belus of the Babylonians, and his worship became almost universal under several of the Jewish kings. (See I. Kings xviii. 22.)

Baale, van, vän bä′lẹh, (HENDRIK,) a Dutch dramatic poet, born at Delft, wrote "De Saracenen." Died in 1822.

Baan, van, vän bän, (JACOB,) an able Dutch portrait-painter, son of Jan, noticed below, was born at the Hague in 1673. He accompanied William III. to England in 1688, and worked for some years in London. Died in Vienna in 1700.

Baan, van, (JAN,) a Dutch portrait-painter of high reputation, born at Haarlem about 1633, imitated Van Dyck. He was invited to England by Charles II., whose portrait he painted. Among his master-pieces was a portrait of John de Witt, which was torn in pieces by the mob that murdered that statesman. Van Baan refused to paint Louis XIV. in 1672, because he waged an aggressive war against Holland. Died at the Hague in 1702.

See DESCAMPS, "Vie des Peintres Flamands, Hollandais, etc.;" NAGLER, "Neues Allgemeines Künstler-Lexikon."

Baardt or **Baart,** bärt, (PETER,) a Flemish physician of the seventeenth century, was the author of agricultural poems, which have been compared by his countrymen to Virgil's "Georgics."

Baarland or **Barland, van,** vän bär′länt, (ADRIAN,) a Flemish writer and professor of rhetoric at Louvain, born in 1488; died in 1542.

See NICÉRON, "Mémoires."

Baarland, van, (HUBERT,) a medical writer, born at Baarland, in Holland, flourished between 1510 and 1550.

See DE LA RUE, "Geletterd Zeeland."

Baarsdorp. See BAERSDORP.

Baart. See BAARDT.

Baart or **Baert,** bärt, (ARNAUD,) a Flemish jurist, born at Brussels in 1554; died in 1629.

Baasha, bä′a-sha, [Heb. בַּעְשָׁא,] a captain of Israel and son of Ahijah, slew King Nadab and usurped the throne about 950 B.C. Died 926 B.C. (See I. Kings xv. and xvi.)

Baaz, bäts, or **Baazius,** bät′se-ůs, (BENEDICT,) a Swedish writer on morals, etc., was governor of the royal castle at Stockholm. Died in 1650.

Baazius, bät′se-ůs, (JOHAN,) a bishop of Wexiö, and author of the "Ecclesiastical History of Sweden," born

in 1581, was a brother of the preceding. He had three sons, who distinguished themselves—John, (Archbishop of Upsal,) Eric, and Benedict. Died in 1649.

Bab, bäb, (JOHN,) an Armenian theologian, died about the end of the ninth century.

Baba, bä′bä, a Turkish prophet or impostor, flourished about 1240.

Baba-Alee or **Baba-Ali,** bä′bä′ ä′lee′, the first independent Dey of Algiers, was elected successor to Ibra-heem, who was slain in an insurrection of the people in 1710. He was a man of great abilities and worth. He succeeded in inducing the Turkish sultan to recognize in Algiers an ally instead of a subject. He died in 1718, lamented by Europeans as well as Moslems.

Babarczy, bä-bäRt′se, (ANTON,) born at Pesth, in Hungary, was a partisan of Austria in the revolution of 1848, and rose to be chief commissioner of civil affairs for Hungary.

Bab′bage, (CHARLES,) F.R.S., an eminent English mathematician, born about 1790, was educated at Trinity College, Cambridge, where he was Lucasian professor from 1828 to 1839. In 1832 he published an important work on the "Economy of Manufactures and Machinery," which was often reprinted, and translated into several languages. He contributed many papers to the "Philosophical Transactions" and other scientific publications. Among his works is "The Ninth Bridgewater Treatise," (1837.) He invented about 1822 a calculating machine, and expended a large sum of money (about £17,000) in its construction; but the government, which had supplied him with funds, having abandoned the enterprise, the machine was never completed.

See "London Quarterly" for January and March, 1827, (vol. xxxv. ;) "Passages from the Life of a Philosopher;" "Edinburgh Review" for January, 1833, (vol. lvi. ;) "Fraser's Magazine," vol. viii.

Bab′bard, (RALPH,) an English mechanical inventor, lived in the reign of Queen Elizabeth.

Babbini. See BABINI.

Babek (bä′bek) **Khor′remee** or **Kho′remi,** i.e. "the Sensualist," a famous Persian impostor, who is said to have inculcated an unbounded libertinism. He propagated his doctrines with the sword, and for a time defied the utmost power of the caliph Motassem, but was at last taken and put to death in 837 A.D.

Babel, bä′bȇl, (HUGH,) a writer on logic and grammar, was professor of Hebrew, Greek, etc. at Louvain. Died in 1556.

Bä′bell, (WILLIAM,) an English composer and organist, born about 1690, lived in London. Died in 1722.

See FÉTIS, "Biographie Universelle des Musiciens."

Babeno Sanct Huber, bä-bä′no sänkt hoo′bẹr, (LUD-WIG,) a German philosopher and Benedictine, born at Leiningen in 1660. He was professor of theology at Salzburg, and published several works. Died in 1726.

Bâber, bä′bẹr, written also **Babour,** a Persian prince, was a grandson of Tamerlane. He dethroned in 1451 his brother Mohammed, who reigned over Irâk and Fars. Died about 1460.

Bâber (or **Babur**) **Mohammed,** bä′bẹr mo-hȁm′-med, written also **Babour** and **Baubur,** surnamed ZA-HEER ED-DEEN, (ZAHÎR EDDÎN,) zạ-heer′ ẹd-deen′,("protector of religion,") the illustrious founder of the Tartar or Mogul Empire in India, was born of the race of Tamerlane in 1482 or 1483. In 1494, when not more than twelve years of age, he succeeded to the throne of his father, King of Ferghâna. The career of Bâber was marked by a series of extraordinary vicissitudes and wonderful exploits unparalleled even in Oriental history. On one occasion, having been expelled from his paternal kingdom, he resolved to attack with less than three hundred followers Samarcand, then one of the strongest cities of Asia, and defended by a large army. He scaled the walls in the night, and was joined by many of the inhabitants. A panic having seized upon the troops of the city, the king fled, leaving his capital in the hands of Bâber. The latter was compelled soon after, by the vicissitudes of

ẽ as k; ç as s; g̃ hard; g̃ as j; G, H, K, guttural; N, nasal; R, trilled; s̃ as z; th as in this.   (☞ See Explanations, p. 23.)

wai, to retire to Cabool. Here he was at first received with great favour; but, a formidable insurrection having been raised against him, he successively challenged and slew in single combat five of the principal leaders of the opposing faction. The others, filled with admiration or fear, accepted him as their king. Our limits will not permit us to pursue the various changes of his fortune. Suffice to say that, after having made two incursions into India, one in 1505 and the other in 1519, he crossed the Indus the third time in 1524, and defeated and slew Ibraheem, King of Delhi, thus putting an end to the second Gaurian dynasty, in 1526. Bâber died in 1530, leaving his throne to his son Humâyoon. Bâber possessed not only great bodily strength and dexterity, but abilities of a very high order, and was not less distinguished for his courage and generosity. He was, moreover, a master of the arts of music and poetry. He left an interesting as well as highly instructive history of the events of his own life, of which there is an able review in Lord Jeffrey's "Essays."

See "Life of Bâber, Emperor of Hindostan," by R. M. CALDE-COTT; "Retrospective Review," vol. ii., second series, 1828; "History of British India," in Harper's Family Library, vol. i.; FERISHTA, "Mahomedan Power in Ind.a," translated by J. BRIGGS, 4 vols. 8vo, London, 1829.

Babeuf, bǎ'buf', (ÉMILE,) a son of François, noticed below, born in 1785, was a zealous partisan of Bonaparte, whom he followed to Elba in 1814.

Babeuf, (FRANÇOIS NOËL,) a French conspirator and political theorist, born at Saint-Quentin in 1764, assumed the name of CAIUS GRACCHUS. He founded in 1794 a journal called the "Tribune of the People," in which he advocated absolute equality and community of property. He became the chief of a numerous band of conspirators who designed to revolt against the Directory and establish the régime of *babouvisme*. Having been betrayed by one of his accomplices, he was executed in 1797.

See BUONAROTTI, "Conspiration pour l'Égalité dite de Babeuf," 2 vols., 1828; SUDRE, "Histoire du Communisme," Paris, 1849.

Babey, bǎ'bǎ', (ATHANASE MARIE PIERRE,) a member of the French Constituent Assembly, born in 1744, was chosen one of the Council of Five Hundred in 1795. Died in 1815.

Babi, bǎ'be', (JEAN FRANÇOIS,) a French anarchist, born at Tarascon in 1759, was one of a party which attacked the camp at Grenelle, for which he was executed in October, 1796.

Babié de Bercenay, bǎ'be-à' deh bĕRss'nà', (FRANçois,) a prolific French author on history, etc., born at Lavaur in 1761. Died about 1830.

See QUÉRARD, "La France Littéraire."

Babin, bǎ'bǎN', (FRANÇOIS,) a French ecclesiastical writer, and professor of theology at Angers, born in 1651. Died in 1734.

Babinet, bǎ'be'nǎ', (JACQUES,) a French natural philosopher, born at Lusignan in 1794, became professor of physics in the College of Saint Louis, Paris. He published a number of valuable treatises on meteorological optics and terrestrial magnetism, and made important improvements in the air-pump, hygrometer, etc. He became a member of the Academy of Sciences in 1840. Among his works is "Studies and Lectures on the Sciences of Observation," etc., ("Études et Lectures sur les Sciences d'Observation," etc.)

Bab'ing-ton, (ANTHONY,) an English gentleman, and a zealous Catholic, devoted to the cause of Mary Stuart, was executed in 1586 for having conspired against the life of Queen Elizabeth.

See HUME, "History of England," chap. xlii.; FROUDE, "Reign of Elizabeth."

Babington, (CHARLES CARDALE,) F.R.S., an English botanist, born about 1808. He became professor of botany at Cambridge, and published, besides other works, a "Manual of British Botany."

Babington, (GERVASE,) an English prelate, born in Nottinghamshire about 1550, became Bishop of Worcester in 1597. Died in 1610.

Babington, (WILLIAM,) F.R.S., a chemist and mineralogist, was born near Coleraine, Ireland, in 1756. He began to practise medicine in London about 1797, and lectured on chemistry at Guy's Hospital. In 1799

he published a "New System of Mineralogy." He was one of the founders of the Geological Society, of which he was chosen president in 1822. Died in 1833.

See RICHARD BRIGHT, "Memoir of the Life and Writings of William Babington."

Babini, bâ-bee'nee, or **Babbini**, bâb-bee'nee, (MATTEO,) a celebrated Italian vocalist, born at Bologna in 1754. Died in 1816.

See FÉTIS, "Biographie Universelle des Musiciens."

Babo, bä'bo, (JOSEPH MARIA,) a German dramatist, born at Ehrenbreitstein in 1756, was the author of the historical tragedy of "Otto von Wittelsbach," which is ranked among the best dramas of its kind in the language. He lived at Munich. Died in 1822.

Babo, von, fon bä'bo, (LAMBERT,) a German cultivator, born at Manheim in 1790, published several valuable treatises on the culture of the vine.

Babois, bä'bwä', (MARGUERITE VICTOIRE,) a French poetess, born at Versailles in 1760, was a niece of Ducis. Her "Elegy on the Death of her Daughter" (1805) was greatly admired. Died in 1839.

Babou, bä'boo', (JEAN,) Baron de Sagonne, a French general, commanded the artillery at the battle of Saint-Denis in 1567. Died in 1569.

See DE COURCELLES, "Dictionnaire historique des Généraux Français."

Babr. See BABER.

Bā'bri-us [Βάβριος] or **Bā'bri-as**, [Βαβρίας,] a Greek fabulist, supposed to have lived a short time previous to Augustus, made a collection of Æsop's Fables, which he turned into choriambic verse.

See TYRWHITT, "Dissertatio de Babrio," 1776.

Babuer or **Babure**, bä'bür, (THEODORE,) a Dutch painter of interiors, worked about 1600–40.

See NAGLER, "Neues Allgemeines Künstler-Lexikon."

Bab'ȳ-las, Bishop of Antioch, suffered martyrdom under Decius in 251 A.D. He was esteemed one of the most faithful and virtuous prelates of his time.

Bac, bâk, (THÉODORE,) a French jurist, born at Limoges in 1808, was associate editor of the journal "L'Europe monarchique," in 1837. He was a deputy to the Constitutional Assembly in 1848.

Baccaini, bâk-kä-ee'nee or bâk-ki'nee, (BENEDETTO,) an Italian writer, born in 1657, was professor of ecclesiastical history at Módena. Died in 1721.

Baccalar y Sanna, bâk-kä-lar' e sän'nä, (VINCENTE,) Marquis of Saint Philip, a Spanish historian and statesman, who occupied important posts under Charles II. and Philip V. He wrote, in Spanish, a "History of the Jewish Monarchy" and a "History of Philip V." Died in 1726.

Baccanelli, Bacchanelli, bâk-kä-nel'lee, or **Baccanel'cius**, (GIOVANNI,) an Italian physician and medical writer of the sixteenth century, born at Reggio.

Baccarini, bâk-kä-ree'nee, (GIACOMO,) an Italian painter, was born at Reggio; died in 1682.

See LANZI, "History of Painting in Italy."

Baccelli, bât-chel'lee, (GIROLAMO,) an Italian writer and physician, born at Florence in 1515, translated Homer's "Odyssey" into Italian verse. Died in 1581.

Bacchanelli. See BACCANELLI.

Bac-chei'us [Βακχεῖος] or **Bac-che'us**, written also **Vacceus**, a Greek musician, surnamed THE ELDER, flourished in the early part of the fourth century. He was the author of an "Introduction to the Art of Music."

Bac-chi'dēs, a general of Demetrius Soter, invaded Judea 160 B.C., and fought a battle against Judas Maccabæus, who was killed in this action.

Bacchini, bâk-kee'nee, (BENEDETTO,) a learned Benedictine monk, born in the duchy of Parma, or at Florence, in 1651. He published several religious and miscellaneous works. Died in 1721.

See IRENEO AFFO, "Vita del P. Bacchini," 1797.

Bac'chus, [Gr. Βάκχος,] called also in Greek **Diony'-sus**, [Διώνυσος,] the god of wine, is commonly said to have been the son of Jupiter and Semele. He taught men the culture of the vine and the mode of extracting the juice of the grape. According to one account, Bacchus was the son of Ammon, King of Libya, and a beautiful woman named Amalthe'a. Ammon, fearing the jealousy of his wife Rhea, had young Bacchus and his mother conveyed to a town called Nysa, on a delicious island formed by the river Triton. He became, according to this legend, a mighty conqueror and benefactor of mankind, by whom he was at last deified. Among the most important events of his history is his expedition to India. From this and other circumstances, many writers suppose the worship of Bacchus to have been derived from India. His chariot drawn by panthers or tigers, and the Indian origin of the vine, are cited as incidental evidences of that fact. Bacchus is usually represented as an effeminate young man crowned with vine- and ivy-leaves, with a thyrsus in his hand.

See KEIGHTLEY, "Mythology;" GUIGNIAUT, "Religions de l'Antiquité," vol. ii. ; G. F. CREUZER, "Dionysus seu Commentationes de Rerum Bacchicarum Orphicarumque Origine et Causis," 2 vols. 4to, 1808-09.

Bac-chȳl'ī-dēs, [Gr. Βακχυλίδης; Fr. BACCHYLIDE, bȧ'ke'lĕd',] an eminent Greek lyric poet, born about 512 B.C., in the island of Ceos, was a nephew of Simonides and a rival of Pindar. His extant works have been published in Bergk's "Poetæ Lyrici Græci."

Bacci, bȧt'chee, (ANDREA,) an Italian physician, naturalist, and writer, who lived about 1580.

Bacciarelli, bȧt-chä-rel'lee, (MARCELLINO,) an Italian artist, born at Rome in 1731, was employed by Augustus III. of Poland as designer of the gallery of engravings at Dresden. He also painted portraits and historical pieces. He settled at Warsaw about 1765, and was patronized by the king Stanislas Poniatowski. Died at Warsaw in 1818.

Bacciccio. See BACICCIO.

Baccio, bȧt'cho, or **Bacci,** bȧt'chee, [Lat. BAC'CIUS,] (ANDREA,) an Italian physician and naturalist of the sixteenth century, was a native of Milan.

Baccio d'Agnolo. See AGNOLO.

Baccio da Monte-Lupo, bȧt'cho dä mon'tȧ-loo'po, a Florentine sculptor and architect, born about 1445. His bronze statue of Saint John the Evangelist is regarded as his master-piece. He was the father of the sculptor Raphael da Monte-Lupo. Died about 1533.

See VASARI, "Lives of the Painters and Sculptors."

Baccio della Porta, bȧt'cho dĕl-lä-poR'tä, an eminent Italian painter, known also as FRA BARTOLOMMEO DI SAN MARCO, (fRȧ baR-to-lo-mä'o de sän maR'ko,) was born at Savignano, near Florence, in 1469. He was a pupil of Cosimo Rosselli, and subsequently studied the works of Leonardo da Vinci. He was an adherent and friend of the celebrated reformer Savonarola, and was so deeply affected by his martyrdom that in 1500 he took the habit of Saint Dominic. After four years, passed chiefly in the convent of San Marco, at Florence, which he adorned with some of his finest pictures, he visited Rome, where his intercourse with Raphael was productive of benefit to both. Among his master-pieces are the magnificent fresco of the "Last Judgment" in the chapel of Santa Maria Nuova at Florence, the figure of "Saint Mark" in the Pitti palace, the "Marriage of Saint Catherine," a "Virgin on a Throne," and a "Saint Paul" at Rome, which was finished by Raphael. Baccio's productions display great knowledge of chiaroscuro, richness of colouring, and grace in the disposition of the draperies, united to a dignity and sweetness of expression little inferior to those of Raphael. Died in 1517.

See VASARI, "Lives of the Painters;" LANZI, "History of Painting;" MRS. JAMESON, "Memoirs of Early Italian Painters;" WINCKELMANN, "Neues Maler-Lexikon;" "Nouvelle Biographie Générale."

Bacciochi, bȧt-cho'kee, (ADORNO,) a Corsican officer, who entered the French army in 1761, was an emigrant in 1792, after which he served under Condé until 1801.

Bacciochi, (FELICE PASQUALE,) Prince of Lucca and Piombino, born in Corsica in 1752. He married in 1797 Maria Elisa, sister of Napoleon. He was made a senator, and obtained the rank of general, and other distinctions. Died in 1841.

Baccusi, bȧk-koo'see, (IPPOLITO,) an Italian composer, lived at Verona about 1590-1600.

Bacellar. See BARBOSA BACELLAR.

Bach, bȧK, the name of a German family which for more than two centuries was celebrated for musical talent, and produced upwards of fifty distinguished artists. VEIT BACH, the founder of the family, a native of Presburg, in Hungary, settled in Thuringia about 1600.

Bach, (ALEXANDER,) an Austrian statesman, born at Loosdorf in 1813. He became in 1848 minister of justice, and was elected to the Constituent Assembly, where he advocated the centralization of the Austrian monarchy and strongly opposed the democratic party. He favoured the policy which provoked the revolt of Hungary in 1848. In 1849 he succeeded Count Stadion as minister of the interior.

See C. WURZBACH, "A. Bach, politisches Charakterbild," 1850; BROCKHAUS, "Conversations-Lexikon."

Bach, (JOHANN AUGUST,) a German jurist, and professor of law at Leipsic, born in 1721. He wrote, in Latin, a "History of Roman Jurisprudence." Died in 1759.

Bach, (JOHANN CHRISTIAN,) youngest son of Johann Sebastian, noticed below, born in 1735, was surnamed the Milanese or English Bach. He resided five years as organist at Milan, and in 1759 became chapel-master at London. He produced a number of popular operas and instrumental pieces. Died in 1782.

Bach, (JOHANN CHRISTOPH,) born at Arnstadt, in Thuringia, in 1643, enjoyed the highest reputation as an organist, composer, and contrapuntist. His works are numerous, including ecclesiastical and secular music. He died in 1703, leaving two sons, Johann Nicholas and Johann Christoph, who were distinguished musicians.

Bach, (JOHANN CHRISTOPH FRIEDRICH,) a musical composer, a son of Johann Sebastian, born in 1732. He lived at Bückeburg, where he died in 1795.

Bach, (JOHANN SEBASTIAN,) the most illustrious member of the family, born at Eisenach on the 21st of March, 1685, was the son of Johann Ambrosius Bach. Having received his first instruction from his brother Johann Christoph, he became for a time a chorister at Lüneburg. In 1704 he was appointed organist at Arnstadt, and in 1708 court organist at Weimar. During the seven years that he occupied this post, he produced many of his finest compositions for the organ. In 1723 he became musical director at the Saint Thomas School of Leipsic, which situation he filled till his death. Having been invited to the Prussian court by Frederick II., in 1747, he surprised and delighted that monarch by his wonderful extemporaneous performances. The works of Bach are very numerous, embracing almost every variety of sacred and secular music, and so admirable for their grandeur, science, and inventive power as to entitle him to rank among the greatest composers that have ever lived. As an organist, he was esteemed equal to Handel, who was his contemporary ; and his skill as a performer on the piano and other keyed instruments was unsurpassed. Among his best compositions are his oratorio of "The Nativity," (" Passions-Musik,") and a collection of preludes and fugues, entitled "The Well-tempered Clavier." Bach was twice married, and had eleven sons and nine daughters. Died at Leipsic in 1750.

See the "Life of John Sebastian Bach," translated from the German ; FÉTIS, "Biographie Universelle des Musiciens;" J. N. FORKEL, "Ueber J. S. Bach's Leben, Kunst und Kunstwerke," 1802, and the English translation of the same; C. L. HILGENFELDT, "J. S. Bach's Leben, Wirken und Werke," 1850.

Bach, (KARL PHILIPP EMANUEL,) son of Sebastian, noticed below, born at Weimar in 1714. He was appointed chamber-musician to Frederick the Great of Prussia in 1740, and in 1767 became director of music at Hamburg. Among his principal compositions are the oratorio of "The Israelites in the Wilderness," and numerous sonatas, symphonies, and songs of great originality and beauty. He also wrote an "Essay on the True Art of playing the Harpsichord," (1797.) Died in 1788.

See BROCKHAUS, "Conversations-Lexikon."

Bach, bȧk, (VICTOR,) a French physician and Jacobin, born at Villefranche about 1770, practised in Paris. He killed himself about the end of 1799.

Bach, (WILHELM Friedemann—fRee'deh-mȧn',) eldest son of Johann Sebastian, born at Weimar in 1710, was surnamed BACH OF HALLE, from his residence in that city. He studied music under his father, and became organist at the church of Saint Sophia, Dresden, (1733,) and afterwards at Halle, (1747.) He attained great excellence both in the theory and practice of music, and as a performer was second only to his father. Owing to his dissipated habits, he died in great poverty in 1784.

See FÉTIS, "Biographie Universelle des Musiciens."

Bachartier-Beaupuy, bȧ'shȧR'te-ȧ' bō'pü-e', (MICHEL ARMAND,) a French general, born in 1755, was killed at the battle of Reutlingen in 1796.

Bachaumont, bȧ'shō'mòN', (LOUIS,) a French literary gossip and scandal-monger, published a collection of anecdotes, songs, facetiæ, etc., entitled "Mémoires secrets," (6 vols., 1777.) Died in Paris in 1771.

See LE BAS, "Dictionnaire encyclopédique de la France."

Bachaumont, de, dẹh bȧ'shō'mòN', (FRANÇOIS le Coigneux—lẹh kwȧn'yuh',) a French lawyer and littérateur, born in Paris in 1624, was the author of a number of witty and satirical poems against Cardinal Mazarin, during the war of the Fronde. Died in 1702.

Bache, bätch, (ALEXANDER DALLAS,) an American philosopher and savant, born in Philadelphia in July, 1806, was a great-grandson of Dr. Franklin. He graduated at the military academy at West Point in 1825, and was appointed professor of mathematics in the University of Pennsylvania in 1827. In 1836 he was chosen president of Girard College, and visited Europe to study various systems of instruction. He published in 1839 a "Report on the European System of Education." He became in 1841 the first principal of the Philadelphia High School, which he had organized. In 1843 he was appointed Superintendent of the United States Coast Survey. His services in this position were most important, and gave general satisfaction. Besides his voluminous official reports, he contributed many valuable scientific papers to the Proceedings of the American Association for the Advancement of Science. Died in 1867.

Bache, (BENJAMIN FRANKLIN,) an American printer and journalist, son of Richard Bache, was born in Philadelphia about 1768. He accompanied Dr. Franklin to Paris, and there learned the business of printing and type-founding in the celebrated establishment of the brothers Didot. After his return to the United States, he began, in 1790, the publication of the "General Advertiser," afterwards called the "Aurora," a paper which, under his editorial management and that of his successor, Mr. Duane, exerted a powerful influence in opposition to the administrations of Washington and Adams. Died in 1799.

Bache, (FRANKLIN,) a physician and chemist, son of the preceding, and cousin of Alexander Dallas, noticed above, was born in Philadelphia in 1792. He graduated as M.D. in the University of Pennsylvania in 1814, published a "System of Chemistry for the Use of Students of Medicine" in 1819, and became professor of chemistry in the Franklin Institute in 1826. In 1831 he was appointed professor of chemistry in the Philadelphia College of Pharmacy, and in 1841 obtained the same chair in the Jefferson Medical College. He was one of the authors of Wood and Bache's "Dispensatory of the United States," (1 vol. 8vo, 1833, 13th edition, 1869,) a work of the highest character, and an acknowledged standard in the department of which it treats. He was elected president of the American Philosophical Society in 1853. Died in 1864. (See WOOD, GEORGE B.)

See "Biographical Memoir of Franklin Bache, M.D.," by GEORGE B. WOOD, Philadelphia, 1865.

·Bache, (RICHARD,) born in England in 1737, emigrated to the United States, where he married, in 1767, Sarah, only daughter of Benjamin Franklin. He was appointed postmaster-general of the United States in 1776. Died in 1811.

Bache, (SARAH,) only daughter of Dr. Benjamin Franklin, and wife of Richard Bache, was born in Philadelphia in 1744. She was a lady of superior accomplishments, and was remarkable for her humane and patriotic efforts to relieve the sufferings of the sick and destitute soldiers of the Revolution. Died in 1808.

Bachelet-Damville, bȧsh'lȧ' dòN'vèl', (LOUIS ALEXANDRE,) a French general of brigade, born at Saint-Aubin in 1771, was killed in Saxony in 1813.

Bachelier, bȧsh'le-ȧ', (JEAN JACQUES,) a French painter of landscapes, fruit, and flowers, born in Paris in 1724. He devoted his fortune of sixty thousand francs to the establishment of a free school of design. He was for many years director of the porcelain manufactory at Sèvres. Died in 1805.

See NAGLER, " Neues Allgemeines Künstler-Lexikon."

Bachelier, (NICOLAS,) a French sculptor and architect, born at Toulouse, was a pupil of Michael Angelo.

Bachelin. See BASSELIN.

Bachelot, bȧsh'lo', (JEAN ALEXIS AUGUSTIN,) . French theologian, born in 1790. He went as a missionary to the Sandwich Islands about 1826, but he was expelled by the English. Died in 1838.

Bachelot de la Pylaie, bȧsh'lo' dẹh lȧ pe'lȧ', (A. J. M.,) a French naturalist and antiquary, born at Fougères in 1786. He published a "Manual of Conchology," (1828,) and a "Flora of Newfoundland," (1829.)

See QUÉRARD, "La France Littéraire," (Supp.)

Bachelu, bȧsh'lü', (GILBERT DÉSIRÉ JOSEPH,) BARON, a French general, born in Dole in 1777, served with distinction in the Egyptian, Austrian, and Russian campaigns, and in 1814 was created lieutenant-general by Louis XVIII., having previously been made an officer of the Legion of Honour. In 1838 he represented Châlons-sur-Saône in the Chamber of Deputies, where he acted with the opposition. Died in 1849.

Bacher, bȧ'shȧ', (ALEXANDRE ANDRÉ PHILIPPE FRÉDÉRIC,) son of George Frédéric, noticed below, was born about 1730. He was for many years editor of the "Journal de Médecine." Died in 1807.

Bacher, [Lat. BACHE'RIUS,] (GEORGE FRÉDÉRIC,) a French physician, born in Upper Alsace in 1709, published several works on the Treatment of Dropsy.

Bacher, (THÉOBALD,) a French diplomatist, born in Alsace in 1748, was chargé-d'affaires at Ratisbon and Frankfort. He died in 1813, leaving "Memoirs on Germany and Switzerland."

Bachet. See MEZIRIAC.

Bacheville, bȧsh'vèl', (ANTOINE,) a French adventurer, born at Trévoux, served in the army from 1804 to 1814. Having been accused of a political conspiracy in 1816, he escaped and went into exile. He died at Muscat in 1820.

Bacheville, (BARTHÉLEMI,) a brother of the preceding, was his companion in his campaigns and in exile, but returned to France, and died in 1835.

See "Voyages des Frères Bacheville en Turquie et en Asie," 1822.

Bachiacca, bȧ-ke-ȧk'kȧ, a surname of Francesco Ubertini, frȧn-chês'ko oo-bĕR-tee'nee, an Italian painter, born at Florence, was a pupil of Perugino. Died in 1557.

See VASARI, "Lives of the Painters."

Bachman, bak'mạn, (JOHN,) D.D., an American naturalist, born in Dutchess county, New York, in 1790. He became pastor of the German Lutheran church of Charleston, South Carolina, about 1815. He assisted Audubon in the composition of his great work on Ornithology, and was the principal author of a work on the Quadrupeds of North America, illustrated by Audubon and his sons. He wrote various other works.

Bachmann, bȧk'mȧn, (GOTTLOB,) a German composer, born in 1763; died about 1810.

Bachmann, (GOTTLOB LUDWIG ERNST,) a German philologist, and professor of classical literature at Rostock, born at Leipsic in 1792. He published an excellent edition of Lycophron's "Alexandra," a collection of "Anecdota Græca," from the Royal Library of Paris, and other learned works.

See BROCKHAUS, "Conversations-Lexikon."

Bachmann, (KARL FRIEDRICH,) a German philosopher, born at Altenburg in 1785, was professor of moral and political economy at Jena, and wrote several works on philosophy. Died in 1855.

Bachmann, de, dẹh bȧk'mȧn, (JACQUES JOSEPH ANTOINE LEGER,) BARON, a Swiss general, born in 1733, commanded the Swiss guard which defended Louis XVI. in August, 1792. He was executed the same year.

Bachmann-Anderletz, bȧk'mȧn ȧn'der-lĕts, (NICOLAUS FRANZ,) BARON, a Swiss general, born in the canton of Glarus in 1740, served during the Seven Years' war in the French army, and rose to be major-general under the King of Sardinia. Under the Bourbons he was created commander of Saint Louis. Died in 1831.

See GIRARD, "Histoire des Officiers Suisses qui se sont distingués aux Services étrangers," 1781.

Bachovius, bạ-ko've-ùs, (REINHART,) called also Bachov (bȧk'of) OF ECHT, (ekt,) a German theologian, born in 1544, was the author of several treatises in defence of Calvinism. Died in 1614. His son, of the same name, born in 1575, was professor of law at Heidelberg in 1613.

See ERSCH und GRUBER, "Allgemeine Encyklopaedie."

Baciccio, bȧ-chĕt'cho, **Bacciccio**, bȧt-chĕt'cho, or **Bacici**, bȧ-chee'chee, (GIAMBATTISTA **Gauli**—gŏw'lee,) a Genoese painter of portraits and scriptural subjects, born in 1639. His pictures, both in fresco and oil, are numerous. Died in 1709.

See LANZI, "History of Painting in Italy."

Bacici. See BACICCIO.

Baciochi. See BACCIOCHI.

Bäck or **Baeck**, bĕk, (ABRAHAM,) a Swedish physician, naturalist, and scientific writer, born at Söderhamn in 1713. He became physician-in-ordinary to the king, and president of the Royal College of Medicine, in 1749. He was intimate with Linnæus, who named the genus Bæckia in his honour. Died in 1795.

See GEZELIUS, "Biographiskt-Lexicon."

Back, (Sir GEORGE,) an English navigator, born at Stockport in 1796. After serving against the French in 1809, he accompanied Sir John Franklin on his Arctic expedition in 1819 and 1823. In 1833 he undertook another voyage in search of Captain Ross. Being informed of Ross's safety, he continued his journey, and made several discoveries, of which he gave an account after his return, entitled "A Narrative of the Expedition along the Shores of the Arctic Ocean in 1833-34."

See "Quarterly Review" for April, 1836; "Edinburgh Review" for July, 1836.

Back, de, dĕh bȧk, (JAMES,) a Dutch physician, born at Rotterdam, lived about 1650. He was one of the first to accept the doctrine of the circulation of the blood.

Back'er, (GEORGE,) an English physician of the eighteenth century, was the author of "Researches on the Advantages of Inoculation," (1776,) and other medical works.

Backer, bȧk'ḳer, (PETER,) a Prussian sculptor, a pupil of Schlutter, worked at Berlin in the second half of the seventeenth century.

Backer, van, vȧn bȧk'ẹr, (ADRIAN,) a Dutch painter of history and portraits, born in 1643, worked at Amsterdam. Died in 1686.

Backer, van, (FRANCIS,) an able Dutch painter, lived about 1720, and was court painter to the elector-palatine Johann Wilhelm.

Backer, van, (JACOB,) a Dutch painter, brother of Adrian, born at Haarlem in 1608. He worked at Amsterdam, and had great facility of execution. Died in 1651.

See HOUBRAKEN, "Vies des Peintres."

Backer, van, (JAMES or JACOB,) sometimes called **James of Palermo**, a distinguished historical painter and excellent colorist, born at Antwerp in 1530; died in 1560.

Backereel, bȧk'ẹh-rāl', (GILES,) a Flemish or Dutch painter, born about 1572, worked at Antwerp. His design is said to be as correct as that of Rubens.

See NAGLER, "Neues Allgemeines Künstler-Lexikon."

Backhouse, bak'kŭs, (WILLIAM,) an English writer on astronomy and alchemy, born in 1593, was the author of "The Golden Fleece," and "The Complaint of Nature." He also translated, from the French, "The Pleasant Fountain of Knowledge." Died in 1662.

Backhuysen or **Bakhuysen**, bȧk-hoi'zẹn, (LUDOLF,) an eminent Dutch marine painter and engraver, born at Emden in 1631. He was the pupil of Van Everdingen, but owed his great excellence chiefly to the study of nature. It was his custom to put out to sea during a storm, to observe the motion of the waves and the agitated vessels, and, on his return, finish the sketches he had made. Among his master-pieces is a marine view, for which the burgomasters of Amsterdam gave him thirteen hundred florins, and subsequently presented to Louis XIV. of France. Died in 1709.

See NAGLER, "Neues Allgemeines Künstler-Lexikon."

Backhuysen, (LUDOLF,) a painter of martial scenes, grandson of the preceding, born in 1717. He died at Rotterdam about 1782.

Backmeister, bȧk'mī-stẹr, (HARTMANN LUDWIG CHRISTIAN,) director of the German College at Saint Petersburg, born at Dillenburg, in Nassau, in 1736. He wrote, in German, a "History of the Swedish Nation," (1767,) "Bibliotheca Russica," (11 vols., 1778,) and other useful works. Died in 1806.

Backmeister, (LUCAS,) a German theologian, born at Lüneburg in 1530, was the author of a number of commentaries on the Bible. Died in 1608.

Backmeister, (LUCAS,) a son of the preceding, born in 1570, published several theological and controversial works. Died in 1638.

See J. CUSTERUS, "Memoria L. Bacmeisteri Oratione parentali, etc."

Backmeister, (MATTHEW or MATTHAEUS,) a German physician, born at Rostock in 1580, was the author of a "General Treatise on Practical Medicine," and other medical works. Died in 1626.

Back'us, (AZEL,) D.D., the first president of Hamilton College, New York, born in Norwich, Connecticut, 1765. He graduated at Yale in 1787, and succeeded the celebrated Dr. Bellamy as pastor of the church in Bethlehem Connecticut. Died about 1817.

Backus, (CHARLES,) D.D., an American Baptist divine, uncle of President Azel Backus, was born in Norwich, Connecticut, in 1749. Dr. Backus was an eloquent preacher and an able theologian. Died in 1803.

Backus, (ISAAC,) an American Baptist minister, born in Norwich, Connecticut, in 1724. He published numerous works, among which is a "History of the Baptists in New England." Died in 1806.

Bacler d'Albe, bȧk'laiR'dȧlb, (LOUIS ALBERT **Ghislain**—gèz'lȧN',) a skilful French painter and engineer, born at Saint-Pol in 1762. He served in the Italian campaign of 1796, and took a distinguished part in the battle of Arcola, which forms the subject of one of his best pictures. In 1802 he prepared an excellent chart of the theatre of war in Italy, with 54 plates. He was appointed by Bonaparte director of his topographical bureau, and became general of brigade in 1813. He published "Annales pittoresques et historiques des Paysagistes," (1803.) Died in 1824.

See "Nouvelle Biographie Générale."

Bā'con, (ANNE COOKE,) a daughter of Sir Anthony Cooke, born about 1528, was married to Sir Nicholas Bacon, and was the mother of Lord Bacon. She was versed in the Greek, Latin, and Italian languages, and translated Bishop Jewel's "Apology for the Church of England" from Latin into English. Died in 1600.

Bacon, (ANTHONY,) an English politician, born about 1558, was a son of Sir Nicholas, and a half-brother of Lord Bacon. He was a friend of the Earl of Essex and of Henry of Navarre, whom he visited about 1585.

Bacon, (FRANCIS,) [Lat. FRANCIS'CUS BACO'NUS,[*]] BARON VERULAM, (vêr'u-lạm,) VISCOUNT SAINT ALBAN'S, (commonly called LORD BACON,) one of the most illustrious philosophers of modern times, was born in London, the 22d of January, 1561. His father was Sir Nicholas Bacon, lord keeper of the great seal under Elizabeth. His mother was Lady Anne, the daughter of Sir Anthony Cooke, and the sister of Mildred, Lord Burleigh's second wife. She is represented as a person of bright talents, no inconsiderable learning, and very decided religious opinions. While still a child, Bacon was remarkable for his ready wit, as well as for his general intelligence. When the queen once asked him how old he was, he replied, "Just two years younger than your majesty's happy reign." Queen Elizabeth used to call him, it is said, her "little lord keeper."

It is related that on one occasion, while his young companions were playing and amusing themselves in Saint James's Park, near his father's house, he stole away to the brick conduit, to find out the cause of a singular echo which was heard there. "Every tale told of him in his childhood," says Dixon, "wins on the imagination, whether he hunts for the echo in Saint James's Park, or eyes the jugglers and detects their trick, or lisps wise words to the queen and becomes her young lord keeper." When a little more than twelve years of age, he and his brother

---

* BACO'NUS (genitive BACO'NI) is the usual Latin form of Bacon's name. Sometimes, though rarely, it is made a noun of the third declension—in the nominative BACON, (genitive BACO'NIS.)

Anthony were sent to Cambridge, and entered Trinity College, of which Dr. Whitgift, afterwards Archbishop of Canterbury, was then master. Francis was a diligent and successful student, and before he was sixteen years old he is said to have conceived a decided dislike to the Aristotelian philosophy, as then taught in the schools. On leaving the University, he entered Gray's Inn as a student of law, and soon after visited France, for the purpose of becoming acquainted with the French language, as well as the institutions and customs of the continent. But the death of his father, in 1579, made it necessary for him to return to England. The other brothers had been well provided for, but Sir Nicholas had delayed making any provision for Francis, his youngest son, though intending to do so, when all his plans were cut short by his sudden death. In 1582 young Bacon was admitted to the bar ; he was made a bencher in 1586, and in 1589 became counsel-extraordinary to the queen, at the early age of twenty-eight ; "a grace," says his biographer Rawley, "scarce known before." He had been elected to Parliament for Melcombe Regis in 1585, at the early age of twenty-four, and appears to have sat in every House of Commons from that time until 1614. Ben Jonson, in his "Discoveries," gives the following description of Bacon's oratory while he was in Parliament : "There happened in my time one noble speaker who was full of gravity in his speaking. His language, when he could spare or pass a jest, was nobly censorious.* No man ever spake more neatly, more pressly, more weightily, or suffered less emptiness, less idleness, in what he uttered. No member of speech but consisted of his own graces. His hearers could not cough or look aside from him without loss. He commanded when he spoke, and had his judges angry or pleased at his devotion. No man had their affections more in his power. The fear of every man that heard him was lest he should make an end."

Although a near connection of Burleigh, whose influence during the greater part of Elizabeth's reign was unrivalled, Bacon appears to have owed little or nothing to the favour of that powerful minister. Nevertheless, the Cecils procured him the reversion of the place of Register of the Star Chamber, an office worth £1600 per annum ; but it did not fall to him until nearly twenty years later, in the reign of King James. Without adopting the suggestion of Rawley, that Burleigh† sought in every way, especially by secret means, to keep Bacon down, "lest if he had risen he might have obscured his glory," it is sufficiently evident that the Cecils were little inclined to favour his promotion, possibly because they regarded him as a man of speculation rather than of practical ability. The intellectual powers of Bacon were of a character too original and profound to be understood and appreciated by those whose chief talent consisted in the facility with which they could adapt themselves to the servile routine of courts. And, although Burleigh may have been somewhat raised above the class referred to, still his mind appears to have been of a very ordinary stamp. Prudence and fidelity to his sovereign were almost the only virtues he possessed ; and even his prudence was of a low and vulgar type, the offspring of a cold and plodding experience, rather than the inspiration of an original and far-seeing intellect ; and hence, in an extraordinary emergency, he was really less prudent than many men who had far less experience.‡

Bacon, being thus left to his own unaided exertions, applied himself diligently to the law, and in time acquired a lucrative if not an extensive practice. In 1592 appeared his first publication, a pamphlet, in reply to a little book, (or "Libel,") entitled "A Declaration of the True Causes of the Great Troubles." In 1594 he became a candidate for the office of solicitor-general, but was not successful. The Earl of Essex, a kinsman and favourite of the queen, had greatly interested himself in Bacon's behalf, but he was overborne by the superior influence of the Cecils. Essex felt deeply the disappointment of his friend, and generously gave him an estate, near Twickenham, worth £1800, a sum very greatly superior in value to what would be represented by the same figures at the present time. Mr. Dixon endeavours to prove that Bacon was under no real obligation to Essex for this magnificent present,—that it was indeed nothing more than a just, though scarcely adequate, payment for Bacon's professional services. But Bacon himself evidently did not regard it in that light ; for he says, referring to the gift of his friend, that it was made "with so kind and noble circumstances as the manner was worth more than the matter."

For many years Bacon appears to have entertained the project of making his fortune by a wealthy marriage. About the year 1596 he was paying court to a rich widow named Hatton. Essex again warmly interested himself in the cause of his friend, but with no better fortune than before. "This suit, happily for Bacon," says Macaulay, "was unsuccessful." Lady Hatton afterwards married "that narrow-minded, bad-hearted pedant," Sir Edward Coke, "and did her best," adds the same writer, "to make him as miserable as he deserved to be."

Bacon was not insensible to the kindness of his noble friend ; but the difference of character, and still more the difference of policy, of the two men, led necessarily to a coldness between them and to their final estrangement. Bacon could not approve the rash and criminal schemes of Essex, and his remonstrances were lost upon the headstrong and infatuated earl. Nevertheless, when fortune and everything else seemed to desert his former friend, he did not desert him, but appears to have used all his influence and eloquence with the queen, even to the risk of her favour, in order to soften her resentment towards her misguided kinsman. And when at length he was called to act as one of her majesty's counsel, he seems to have availed himself of his official position to mitigate, as far as possible, the severity of the charges against Essex. It is, indeed, difficult wholly to excuse Bacon for the part which he took in this trial ; but it is altogether probable that he sincerely believed—at least in the earlier stages of the business—that what he did was the best for Essex that could be done under the circumstances. But if, when he found that all his efforts to save his former friend and benefactor were unavailing, he had absolutely declined to take any further part in the prosecution, his character would have been cleared from one of the darkest shadows now resting upon it. According to Mr. Dixon, having done all in his power to satisfy the claims of friendship, Bacon was perfectly right in turning against one who had "proved himself a rebel and a traitor," and that in this "he did no more than discharge his necessary duty to his country and his queen." This might be a valid defence, if there was any good reason to believe that without Bacon's efforts to secure the conviction of Essex the safety of his country would have been seriously imperilled. But, as the case now stands, the common sense and common feeling of mankind are naturally arrayed against one who, whatever may have been his secret motives, did actually promote his worldly interests and his advancement at court—the object of his life-long ambition—by seeking to convict and bring to the block one to whom he was once closely bound by gratitude and friendship.

After the accession of James I., (in 1603,) Bacon's advancement was all that a man of reasonable ambition could desire. He was raised to the knighthood the day before the king's coronation. Having soon after been chosen by the House of Commons to make a representation of the oppressive acts of the royal purveyors, he performed the duty with such ability and address as to give satisfaction both to the king and to the Parliament. The House gave him a vote of thanks, and the king appointed him one of his counsel.

---

* Censor-like—in other words, severe and dignified in his style.

† Alluding to Bacon's failure to obtain any present provision, Rawley's words are, it "might be imputed not so much to her Majesty's averseness or disaffection towards him, as to the arts and policy of a great statesman then who laboured, by all industrious and secret means, to suppress and keep him down, lest if he had risen he might have obscured his glory." Some suppose that the person here alluded to was Burleigh's son Robert, a view which, perhaps, better corresponds to the known facts of history, although at that date young Cecil could scarcely be termed a "great statesman." "The Cecils," says Lord Campbell, "not only refused to interest themselves for their kinsman, but, that he might receive no official assistance from others, they spread reports that he was a vain speculator, and totally unfit for real business."

‡ See Motley's account of Burleigh's conduct during the preparations for the Spanish invasion. ("History of the United Netherlands.")

ā, ē, ī, ō, ū, ȳ, *long;* à, è, ò, same, less prolonged; ă, ĕ, ĭ, ŏ, ŭ, ў, *short;* ạ, ẹ, ị, ọ, *obscure;* fär, fäll, fät; mêt; nôt; gŏŏd; mōōn;

In May, 1606, Bacon married Alice Barnham, the daughter of a wealthy London merchant and alderman. In 1607 he was made solicitor-general. In 1611 he became one of the judges of the knights-marshal's court, and in 1613 he was appointed attorney-general, and was made a member of the privy council. His law practice was now very lucrative, and the emoluments arising from his various offices afforded him what for those times may be called an immense income. He was selected by the king as his agent in the prosecution of Peacham, a clergyman who was accused of treason on account of some passages in a sermon found in his house. The sermon had never been preached, and there was no proof that he had any intention of preaching it. Bacon is charged with having sought, contrary to law and justice, to obtain the opinions of the judges before the case came up for trial.

In March, 1617, Bacon was appointed keeper of the great seal, and in January, 1618, he became lord high chancellor of England, the highest civil office to which an English subject could then attain. In July of the same year he was created Baron Verulam, and took his seat in the House of Peers. In 1620 he was made Viscount Saint Alban's. His sixtieth birthday (January 22, 1620) was celebrated with great state, Ben Jonson furnishing a poem to be recited on that occasion, in which he speaks of the lord chancellor as one

"Whose even thread the Fates spin round and full
Out of their choicest and their whitest wool."

The same year he published his "Novum Organum," embodying the ripest and richest results of his life-long studies.

In contemplating the life of Bacon, we cannot help calling to mind those words of our great poet, descriptive of the career of one who, though far inferior to him in genius, was in worldly power and splendour fully his equal:

"This is the state of man; to-day he puts forth
The tender leaves of hope, to-morrow blossoms,
And bears his blushing honours thick upon him.
The third day comes a frost, a killing frost.
*   *   *   *   *   *
Farewell, a long farewell, to all [his] greatness!"

A man named Wraynham, against whom Bacon had decided a suit in chancery, accused the chancellor of accepting bribes; and, though he did not make good his accusation in regard to his own case, his complaints led to the appointment of a committee in the House of Commons, to inquire into the abuses of the courts of justice. In consequence of this inquiry, a number of cases of alleged corruption on the part of the lord chancellor were presented. The Commons referred the case to the House of Lords, as the only proper tribunal for trying it. In the course of the trial it was shown that in a majority of the cases the presents were received after the suits were terminated, and in some others that the chancellor had decided against the donors. But, unfortunately, the accusations could not all be thus disposed of. It was alleged that in one instance, when the decision was drawn up but not yet delivered, a timely and liberal present prevailed on the chancellor to reverse his decree. In another, when one of the parties had administered a liberal bribe and was encouraged to hope that the decision would be in his favour, a subsequent and larger gift from the opposite party turned the scale in favour of the latter. At the commencement of the trial Bacon strongly asserted his innocence, but he afterwards abandoned his defence and acknowledged his guilt. His words were, "I do plainly and ingenuously confess that I am guilty of corruption, and do renounce all defence."* So that either some of the accusations were well founded, or else, from some motive difficult to conceive of, he was induced to cast away his good name by telling a falsehood. His apologists suggest that he did this to please

* No greater stigma can be cast upon the memory of Lord Bacon than to charge him with insincerity in making the above confession. After the paper containing it had been read in the House of Peers, twelve lords were appointed to wait on him, to ascertain if the signature appended to the confession was genuine. He passionately exclaimed, "My lords, it is my act, my hand, my heart! I beseech your lordships to be merciful to a broken reed!" (For a full account of the case the reader is referred to the State Trials.)

the king. But such a defence from his friends dishonours him, if possible, even more than the accusations of his enemies. An honourable man, to please his sovereign, might indeed sacrifice his life, but not his honour, not his good name for all coming time. On the 3d of May, 1621, he was sentenced to pay a fine of forty thousand pounds and to be imprisoned during the king's pleasure. "The sentence of Bacon," says Macaulay, "was scarcely pronounced when it was mitigated. He was indeed sent to the Tower; but this was a mere form. In two days he was set at liberty." Not long after, his fine was remitted. He was even permitted to present himself at court. He was allowed a pension of twelve hundred pounds, no inconsiderable income for that age. The rest of his life was passed in retirement, and was chiefly occupied in scientific pursuits. He died on the 19th of April, 1626, leaving no children.

In person Bacon was of a middling stature, well formed, but not robust. His forehead was high and broad, and the expression of his face was benevolent as well as intellectual. "In advanced life," says Lord Campbell, "his whole appearance was venerably pleasing, so that a stranger was insensibly drawn to love before knowing how much reason there was to admire him." In society he is represented to have been "a most delightful companion, adapting himself to company of every degree, calling, and humour," and "bringing out with great effect his unexhausted stores of jests new and old." Prominent among his good qualities was his entire freedom from all mean jealousy of others, and his disposition to patronize merit wherever found. Towards his servants and dependants he appears to have been uniformly kind and generous; if he had a fault in this respect it was in being too indulgent, and their extravagance contributed to his ruin.

In contemplating the fall of so great a man, we should not lose sight of the principal cause. With his many and rare accomplishments, and with all the strength of his transcendent intellect, Bacon had one "weakest weakness," an inordinate love of splendour and display. The consequence was that he was often embarrassed and in debt, and he was tempted to eke out the deficiency of his large income by accepting presents and bribes.

Bacon's greatest work was his "Instauratio Magna,"* of which the "Novum Organum,"† already referred to, is but a part, although the most important part, and his treatise "De Augmentis Scientiarum" ("On the Advancement of the Sciences"‡) the opening chapter. Believing, as Bacon did, that the then prevailing mode of studying science (particularly the science of nature) had become greatly perverted, his aim was to bring men back, so to speak, to the right employment of their powers, and to direct them into such a path of inquiry and examination as would best promote the cause of true science. This he proposed to effect by teaching them a new method of exploring or investigating nature, the principles of which are laid down with great explicitness and fulness in his "Novum Organum."

Among Bacon's other works we may mention his "Essays," (first published in 1598,) perhaps the most popular of all his writings; "On the Wisdom of the Ancients," ("De Sapientia Veterum,") which appeared in 1610, and of which a good translation, by Sir Arthur Gorges, was published in 1619. His collection of Apothegms constitutes one of the most attractive portions of his various works.

In regard to Bacon's attainments as a lawyer, and his qualifications as a judge, Lord Campbell observes that "his mind was thoroughly familiar with the principles of jurisprudence," and "that he had made himself complete master of the common law of England." The same able critic pronounces Bacon's "History of the Alienation Office" "a treatise worthy of Hale, showing a most copious and accurate acquaintance with existing law and with our legal antiquities." "No one ever sat in Westminster Hall with a finer judicial understanding; no one

* Literally, the "Great Instauration," (or "Restoration.")
† "New Instrument," or new method of pursuing science.
‡ Or, as Bacon himself translates it, [On] "the Advancement of *Learning*," using the word in a wider sense than is common at the present day.

ever more thoroughly understood the duties of a judge." ("Lives of the Lord Chancellors," vol. ii. chap. lvi.)

Respecting Bacon's rank as a philosopher a great diversity of opinion prevails. While some claim that to his improved method of studying nature are chiefly to be attributed the prodigious strides which have been made by modern science, others deny to him not merely pre-eminent but even eminent mc.it in this respect, asserting that the present method of scientific investigation is quite different from the method laid down by Bacon. The truth will probably be found between the two extremes. If Bacon's method was not in all respects the same as that pursued by the most enlightened interrogators of nature at the present day, there can scarcely be a reasonable doubt that by his writings and influence he has contributed far more than any other philosopher to pave the way for that wonderful "advancement of the sciences" which forms the peculiar distinction and glory of modern philosophy. Our narrow limits preclude us from entering, in this place, more fully into the consideration of the subject. All that remains for us is to direct the reader's attention to such sources of information as may enable him to form a correct judgment for himself. Respecting this question, see particularly Professor Napier's Essay on this subject, published in the "Transactions of the Royal Society of Edinburgh," (1818,) and G. H. Lewes's article on Bacon, in his "Biographical History of Philosophy;" Hallam's "Introduction to the Literature of Europe;" also Macaulay's very interesting "Essay on Lord Bacon," one of the ablest and most brilliant of his many able and brilliant review-articles.

See, also, "Personal History of Lord Bacon," by WILLIAM HEPWORTH DIXON, (1859,) who has brought to light some interesting facts which had escaped the researches of previous biographers; MONTAGU, "Life of Bacon," added to Bacon's collected works; CAMPBELL, "Lives of the Lord Chancellors," containing one of the most impartial and, on the whole, one of the best of all the Lives of Lord Bacon; WILLIAM RAWLEY, "Life of Lord Bacon," 1658; DAVID MALLET, "Life of Francis Bacon, Lord Chancellor," 1740; ROBERT STEPHENS, "Life of Lord Bacon," 1734; G. L. CRAIK, "Bacon, his Writings and his Philosophy," 3 vols., 1846-47; JOSEPH SORTAIN, "Life of Lord Bacon," 1851; RÉMUSAT, "Bacon, sa Vie et son Influence," 1857; DE VAUZELLES, "Histoire de la Vie de F. Bacon de Verulam," 2 vols., 1833; POUILLOT, "Vie du Chancelier F. Bacon," 1755; KUNO FISCHER, "Franz Bacon von Verulam," 1856, (a work of great merit;) OZANAM, "Deux Chanceliers d'Angleterre: Bacon de Verulam et S. Thomas (Becket archevêque de Cantorbéry," 1835; W. DUGDAL, "Life of Lord Bacon," in the "Baconiana" of THOMAS TENISON, 1679; WILHELMY, "Dissertatio de Vita et Philosophia F. Baconis," 1843; J. SPEDDING, "Life of Bacon," in his very complete edition of Bacon's works, of which 11 vols. 8vo have already (1869) appeared.

Bacon, (JOHN,) an eminent English sculptor, born in Surrey in 1740. Having gained a number of prizes from the Society for the Encouragement of Arts, he became in 1770 an associate of the Royal Academy. His principal works are a statue of Mars, a bust of George III., the monument to Lord Chatham in Guildhall, the statue of Blackstone at Oxford, and the statues of Howard and Dr. Johnson at Saint Paul's, London. Died in 1799.

See RICHARD CECIL, "Memoirs of John Bacon," 1801; CUNNINGHAM, "Lives of Painters, Sculptors," etc.

Bacon, (JOHN.) See BACONTHORP.

Bā'con, (LEONARD,) an American divine, born at Detroit, Michigan, in 1802, graduated at Yale College in 1820, and became pastor of the Centre Church, New Haven, Connecticut, in 1825. He has published many theological works, and distinguished himself as a champion of orthodoxy and of the Congregational Church polity. About 1850 he became one of the editors of the "Independent." Among his works is "Slavery discussed in Occasional Essays from 1833 to 1846," (1846.)

Bacon, (NATHANIEL,) an English lawyer, a grandson of Sir Nicholas, was a member of the Long Parliament, and a republican in the civil war. Died in 1660.

Bacon, (NATHANIEL,) a Virginian leader of insurgents, was born probably in England about 1630. He was an eloquent lawyer, and a popular favourite among the Virginians. He took command of a body of malcontents who, in 1676, rose in arms partly to defend the province against the Indians and partly to maintain their rights against Governor Berkeley. Bacon obtained successes over both the Indians and the governor, but before the end of the contest he died, in 1677.

See SPARKS, "American Biography," vol. iii. of new series.

Bacon, (Sir NATHANIEL,) an English landscape-painter, a-half-brother of Lord Bacon, studied in Italy. Died about 1615.

Bacon, (Sir NICHOLAS,) an eminent English statesman, born at Chiselhurst, in Kent, in 1510, was the father of the great philosopher Lord Bacon. He was educated at Cambridge, and studied law. In 1537 he was appointed solicitor to the court of augmentations. He was attorney to the court of wards from 1546 until the death of Edward VI., when, having become a Protestant, he was removed by Queen Mary. He was appointed lord keeper of the great seal by Elizabeth in 1558, and became a friend of Sir William Cecil, who was his brother-in-law. He held the office of lord keeper for twenty years, during which, by a moderate and prudent policy, he contributed much to the prevalence of the reformed religion in England. His mind was sound, well balanced, and vigorous. Referring to Bacon and other ministers of Elizabeth, Macaulay says, "It is needless to relate how dexterously, how resolutely, how gloriously they directed the politics of England during the eventful years which followed; how they succeeded in uniting their friends and separating their enemies; how they humbled the pride of Philip; how they backed the unconquerable spirit of Coligni. . . . Among these statesmen Sir Nicholas Bacon was generally considered as ranking next to Burleigh. He was called by Camden *sacris conciliis alterum columen*." ("Essay on Lord Bacon.") Died in 1579.

See "A Remembrance of the Woorthie and Well Employed Life of the Right Honourable Sir Nicholas Bacon, etc.," by GEORGE WHETSTONES; LORD CAMPBELL'S "Lives of the Lord Chancellors."

Bacon, (PHANUEL,) an English divine and humorous writer, born in 1700, became rector of Balden, in Oxfordshire. He was the author of dramatic pieces, entitled "The Moral Quack," "The Insignificants," and "The Trial of the Time-Killers," (1757.) Died in 1783.

Bacon, (ROBERT,) an English divine, writer, and popular preacher, born about 1168; died in 1248.

Bacon, sometimes written **Bakon** or **Bacun,** (ROGER,) a celebrated English philosopher and monk, called THE ADMIRABLE DOCTOR, was born near Ilchester, in Somersetshire, about 1214. He was educated at Oxford and Paris, took the vows of the Franciscan order at Oxford, and found a liberal patron in Robert Greathead, Bishop of Lincoln. He was profoundly versed in Latin, Greek, Hebrew, metaphysics, theology, philosophy, and several sciences. His learning and skill in mechanics were so great that he was suspected of dealing in magic. He wrote in Latin many works on astronomy, chemistry, optics, physics, theology, etc. "The mind of Roger Bacon," says Hallam, "was strangely compounded of almost prophetic gleams of the future course of science and the best principles of the inductive philosophy, with a more than usual credulity in the superstitions of his own time." "It seems hard to determine whether or not he be entitled to the honours of a discoverer in science; that he has not described any instrument analogous to the telescope is now generally admitted, but he has some new and important notions in optics. That he was acquainted with the explosive powers of gunpowder, it seems unreasonable to deny." His principal work is entitled "Opus Majus," which was composed about 1265, and first printed in 1733. It treats of nearly all the sciences. In 1278 a council of Franciscans condemned his writings and committed Bacon to prison, in which he was confined ten years. He died probably at Oxford, in 1292. He is regarded as the greatest philosopher of the thirteenth century. "The resemblance between Roger Bacon and his greater namesake," says Hallam, "is very remarkable. Whether Lord Bacon ever read the 'Opus Majus,' I know not; but it is singular that his favourite quaint expression *prærogativa scientiarum* should be found in that work. And whoever reads the sixth part of the 'Opus Majus' upon experimental science must be struck by it as the prototype in spirit of the 'Novum Organum.'" ("Introduction to the Literature of Europe.")

See ANTHONY À WOOD'S "History and Antiquities of Oxford;" LELAND'S "Commentarii de Scriptoribus Britannicis;" "Biographia Britannica;" F. HOEFER, "Histoire de Chimie," vol. i., and his article in the "Nouvelle Biographie Générale."

Bacon, (SAMUEL,) an Episcopal clergyman, employed with two other persons by the United States government as an agent for establishing a colony of blacks in Southern Senegambia, where they arrived in charge of eighty-two free blacks in 1820. All three of the agents died soon after.

Bacon-Tacon, bắ'kôN' tắ'kôN', (PIERRE JEAN JACQUES,) a French antiquary, born at Oyonnax in 1738. He was the author of a "Numismatical History of Different Nations, Ancient and Modern." Died in 1817.

See QUÉRARD, "La France Littéraire."

Bā'cǫn-thorp, Bā'con-dorp, or **Bā'con,** (JOHN,) an English monk of the fourteenth century, born in Norfolk, was surnamed THE RESOLUTE DOCTOR. He had a high reputation for learning, and professed the philosophy of Averroës. He wrote, among other works, a commentary on the "Master of Sentences." Died about 1346.

Bacoue, bắ'koo', (LÉON,) a French Catholic theologian of the seventeenth century, became Bishop of Pamiers in 1685. He was the author of a Latin poem "On the Education of a Prince," (1671.) Died in 1694.

See MORÉRI, "Dictionnaire Historique."

Bacquère, de, deh bắ'kaiʀ', (BENOÎT,) a French writer of the seventeenth century, was the author of a medical work entitled "Physician for Old Men," (" Senum Medicus.")

Bacquet, bắ'kắ', (JEAN,) a French jurist and legal writer of the sixteenth century; died in 1597.

Bacsányi, bŏh-chắn'yee, (JÁNOS,) a Hungarian writer, born at Tapolcza in 1763. He was one of the founders of the "Magyar Museum," and the author of a poem entitled "The Bravery of Hungary." Died in 1845.

Bactishua. See BAKHTISHWA.

Bacun, (ROGER.) See BACON.

Baczko, bâtch'ko, called also **Glodzlaus,** a Polish chronicler of the thirteenth century, was keeper of the library of Posen. He wrote a continuation down to 1271 of the chronicle of Poland, begun by Bagalulphus, Bishop of Posen.

See JÖCHER, "Allgemeines Gelehrten-Lexikon."

Baczko, von, fon bâts'ko, (LUDWIG,) a German writer, born at Lyck, in East Prussia, in 1756, became blind at the age of twenty-one. He was the author of several romances and dramas, and a "History of Prussia." Died in 1823.

See his "Geschichte meines Lebens," 3 vols., 1824.

Bada, bä'Dä, (JOSÉ,) a Spanish architect, born at Malaga about 1690, finished the cathedral of that city. Died in 1756.

Badajos, bä-Dä-hòs', (JUAN DE,) a Spanish architect, a native of the city of that name, lived in the sixteenth century. One of his greatest works is the cloister of the monastery of Saint Zoil at Carrion, in Old Castile.

Badakhshi, bä-dǎk'shee, a Persian poet of the tenth century, was the author of a *divan* or collection of poems which enjoyed great popularity with his countrymen.

Badalocchio, bä-dä-lok'ke-o, sometimes called **Sisto Rosa,** an Italian painter and engraver, born at Parma in 1581, was a pupil of Annibal Caracci, who highly commended his skill in design. Among his master-pieces we may name a "Saint Francis," and "Galatea." His engravings after Correggio's cupola at Parma are greatly admired. Died in Rome in 1647.

See LANZI, "History of Painting in Italy."

Badaracco, bä-dä-räk'ko, (GIOVANNI RAFFAELLO,) a skilful painter, son of Giuseppe, noticed below, born at Genoa in 1648. Died in 1726.

See LANZI, "History of Painting in Italy."

Badaracco, (GIUSEPPE,) an Italian painter, called IL SORDO, born at Genoa about 1588. He imitated Andrea del Sarto with success. Died in 1657.

Badaro, bä-dä'ro, (GIOVANNI,) an Italian botanist and writer, born near Genoa in 1793; died in 1831.

Bad'by, (JOHN,) an English Lollard of the fourteenth century, perished at the stake during the persecutions of his sect under Henry IV., (1409.)

Bad'cock, (RICHARD,) an English botanist, lived about 1745, and wrote on the structure of anthers.

Badcock, (SAMUEL,) an English divine, born in Devonshire in 1747. He opposed the doctrines of Priestley,

and was the author of a number of able criticisms in the "Monthly Review." Died in 1788.

Badehorn, bä'deh-horn', (SIGISMUND,) a German theologian, born in 1585, was professor of Hebrew at Leipsic. Died in 1626.

Baden, bä'den, (JAKOB,) a Danish philologist, born at Vordenborg in 1735. He studied at Göttingen and Leipsic, and became in 1779 professor of eloquence and the Latin language at Copenhagen. He published school editions of Virgil, Horace, and Phædrus, and translated several classics into Danish. He was editor of the "University Journal" from 1793 to 1801. His Danish Grammar is highly esteemed. Died in 1804.

See KRAFT og NYERUP, "Almindeligt Litteraturlexicon;" G. L. BADEN, "Bidrag til Professoren J. Baden," 1800.

Baden, (JAKOB GUSTAV LUDWIG,) son of the preceding, born in 1764, was the author of several legal and historical works. Died in 1840.

See KRAFT og NYERUP, "Almindeligt Litteraturlexicon."

Bä'den, (RICHARD DE,) founder of University Hall, Cambridge, in 1326. After that building was destroyed by fire, another was erected, which is called Clare Hall.

Baden, (TORKEL,) a Danish philologist, born at Fredericksburg in 1765, became professor of eloquence at Kiel in 1794. Died in 1804.

Baden, (TORKEL,) a Danish philologer, born in 1668, wrote "A Demonstration of the Affinity of the Danish and Latin Languages," ("Roma Danica, Affinitatem Linguæ Danicæ cum Romana exhibens," 1699.) Died in 1732.

Baden-Baden, bä'den bä'den, (LUDWIG WILHELM I.,) MARGRAVE OF, a distinguished general, born in Paris in 1655. He served under Montecuccoli against the French, and in 1683 assisted Sobieski in defending Vienna against the Turks. He subsequently defeated the Turks in two engagements. He constructed the celebrated fortifications called the lines of Stollhofen. Died in 1707.

See A. SCHREIBER, "Badische Geschichte," 1827.

Baden-Baden, (WILHELM I.,) MARGRAVE OF, a German general, born in 1593, was appointed by Ferdinand II. to command the army of the Upper Rhine, which was defeated by Gustavus Adolphus, (1631.) He made several unsuccessful attempts to unite the Catholics and Protestants, at the Diet of Ratisbon. Died in 1677.

Badenius, bä-dä'ne-ùs, (ANDREAS,) a German theologian, died in 1667.

Badenius, (CHRISTOPH,) a son of the preceding, published, in 1710, "John's Testimony to the Truth."

Badens, bä'dens, [Fr. pron. bä'dôn',] (FRANCIS,) a Flemish painter of history and portraits, born at Antwerp in 1571, was surnamed THE ITALIAN, from his merits as a colorist. Died in 1604.

Badens, (JOHN,) a brother of the preceding, born in 1576, was a skilful portrait-painter. Died in 1603.

See NAGLER, "Neues Allgemeines Künstler-Lexikon."

Bader, bä'der, (KARL ADAM,) a celebrated German vocalist, born at Bamberg in 1789.

Badesi, bä-dä'see, (GIROLAMO,) an Italian poet, lived in the second half of the sixteenth century.

Badessa, bä-dês'sä, (PAOLO,) an Italian poet, born at Messina, flourished about 1560. He translated the first five books of Homer's "Iliad" into Italian verse.

Badg'er, (GEORGE E.,) an American statesman and jurist, born at Newbern, North Carolina, in 1795, graduated at Yale College in 1813. President Harrison appointed him in 1841 secretary of the navy, in which office he was continued by Tyler, but resigned on the President's vetoing the bill to recharter the United States Bank. In 1846 he was elected to the United States Senate, and was re-elected for a full term in 1848.

Badger, (JOSEPH,) an American missionary, born at Wilbraham, Massachusetts, in 1757. Having served four years in the army, he went to Ohio,where he laboured more than thirty years as a missionary. Died in 1846.

Bad'ham, (DAVID C.,) a British physician and naturalist, born about 1805. He became a curate of Wymondham, in Norfolk, about 1846. He wrote on natural history, particularly on insects. Died in 1857.

Badia, bä-dee'ä, (CARLO AGOSTINO,) an Italian composer of the eighteenth century, was chapel-master to Leopold I. at Vienna.

Badia, (CARLO FRANCESCO,) an eloquent Italian preacher, born at Ancona in 1675, became president of the University of Turin about 1730 ; died in 1751.

Badia, (TOMMASO,) an Italian cardinal, born at Módena about 1483, attended the Diet of Worms in 1540. Died in 1547.

Badia y Leblich. See ALEE BEY.

Badiale, bä-de-ä'lä, (ALESSANDRO,) an Italian painter and skilful engraver, born at Bologna. He is supposed to have died about 1650.

Badie, de la, deh lä bä'de', (LOUIS AUGUSTIN,) a French general, born in 1696 ; died in 1765.

Badier, bä'de-à', (JEAN ÉTIENNE,) a French monk and writer, born at Dole in 1650 ; died in 1719.

Badile, bä-dee'lä, (GIOVANNI ANTONIO,) an Italian painter and admirable colorist, born at Verona in 1480. He was the uncle and preceptor of Paul Veronese, and numbered Zelotti among his pupils. Died in 1560.

See LANZI, "History of Painting in Italy."

Ba-di'nus or **Badino,** bä-dee'no, (LUIGI DONATO,) an Italian priest and Latin poet, born at Mondovì in 1675. Died in 1742.

Badius, bä'de'üs', (CONRAD,) a learned printer, born in Paris in 1510, was a son of Jodocus, noticed below, and a brother-in-law of Robert Estienne. Having been converted to Calvinism, he removed in 1549 to Geneva, where he published fine editions of many works. Died about 1560.

See A. F. DIDOT, "Essai sur l'Histoire de l'Imprimerie."

Badius, bä'de-us, (JODOCUS, yo-do'kus, or JOSSE, zhoss,) a celebrated Flemish printer and Latin poet, born in 1462, was surnamed ASCENSIUS, from Asche, near Brussels, his birthplace. About 1500 he established a large printing-house in Paris, called "Prælum Ascensianum," which issued many fine editions of the classics. Died in 1535.

See LA CAILLE, "Histoire de l'Imprimerie ;" D. M. MANNI, "Vita di G. Badio," 1757; BAYLE, "Historical and Critical Dictionary."

Badius, bä'de-oos, (RAOLFO,) an Italian theologian, born at Florence, lived in the second half of the seventeenth century.

Badoaro, bä-do-ä'ro, (FEDERIGO,) an Italian diplomatist, born in Venice in 1518, was employed by the republic in embassies to the court of Charles V. and Philip II. In 1556 he founded at Venice the Academy della Fama. Died in 1593.

Badoaro, (GIACOMO,) an Italian dramatic poet of the seventeenth century, was a friend of Paolo Sarpi.

Badoaro, (GIOVANNI,) an Italian cardinal and writer on theology. Died in 1714.

See "Vita del Cardinale G. Badoaro," 1766.

Badoaro, (LAURO,) an Italian bishop and poet, born at Venice about 1546, wrote "Rime Spirituali," and other works. Died in 1593.

Badoero. See BADUERO.

Badoero, bä-do-ä'ro, (PIETRO,) was Doge of Venice from 939 to 942 A.D., during which period the independence of Venice was recognized by Berenger II. of Italy.

Badolet, bä'do'lä', (JEAN,) a Protestant minister, was professor of the humanities at Geneva about 1650. Among his works is "Anatomy of the Human Conscience," ("Conscientiæ humanæ Anatomia," 1659.)

Badon, bä'dòn', (EDMOND,) a French dramatist and novelist, wrote a "Duel under Richelieu," (1832,) and other works. He died prematurely in 1849.

Badoureau, bä'doo'rō', (J. F.,) a French engraver, lived in the first half of the nineteenth century. He engraved some works of Raphael and Titian.

Badstüber, bäd'stü'ber, (ANDREW,) a Danish jurist, born at Copenhagen in 1728 ; died in 1808.

Baduel, bä'dü'êl', (CLAUDE,) a French Protestant minister. born at Nimes in the fifteenth century. He preached at Geneva, and wrote a work to prove the utility of marriage to literary men, (1544.) Died at Geneva in 1561.

Baduero, bä-doo-ä'ro, or **Badoero,** (URSUS I.,) Doge of Venice from 864 to 881 A.D., defeated the Saracens.

Baduero, (URSUS II.,) was elected Doge of Venice in 912, and retired to a convent in 932.

Baeck. See BÄCK, (ABRAHAM.)

Baeck, bäk, or **Baecx,** bäks, (JOACHIM,) a Dutch theologian, born at Utrecht in 1548 ; died in 1619.

Baehr. See BÄHR.

Baehrens. See BÄHRENS.

Baeli, bä-ä'lee, (FRANCESCO,) an Italian poet and antiquary, born at Milazzo, in Sicily, in 1639 ; died in 1710.

Baena, bä-ä'nä, (ANTONIO LADISLAU Monteiro—mon-tä'e-ro,) a Portuguese historian and geographer, served in Brazil as officer in the army. He wrote some valuable works, one entitled "Chorographic Essay on the Province of Pará," ("Ensaio corografico sobre a Provincia do Pará," 1839.) Died about 1851.

Baer. See BÄR.

Baer, bä'air', [Ger. pron. bär,] (FRÉDÉRIC CHARLES,) a French Protestant professor of theology, and miscellaneous writer, born at Strasburg in 1719 ; died in 1797.

Bærebistes, bèr-e-bis'tèz, or **Berebistes,** [Fr. BÉRÉBISTE, bä'rä'bèst',] a king of the Dacians about 40–20 B.C., drove the Sarmatians beyond the Dnieper, and rendered Thrace and Macedonia tributary to his kingdom.

Baerle, van, vän bär'leh, [Lat. BARLÆ'US ; Fr. BARLÉE, bär'lä',] (GASPARD,) a Dutch theologian and distinguished Latin poet, born at Antwerp in 1584. He was professor of logic at Leyden in 1617, and obtained the chair of philosophy and eloquence at Amsterdam about 1633. Besides numerous Latin poems and orations, he was the author of a valuable "History of Brazil under Maurice of Nassau." He was also engaged in the defence of Arminius against the Gomarists. Died in 1648.

See CORVINUS, "Oraison funèbre de G. Baerle."

Baerle, van, [Lat. BARLÆ'US,] (MELCHIOR,) an uncle of the preceding, born at Antwerp, lived between 1550 and 1600. He wrote several Latin poems.

Baermann. See BÄRMANN.

Baersdorp, van, (CORNELIS,) a Dutch physician and medical writer of the sixteenth century, was first physician to Charles V., who also made him his chamberlain and a councillor of state. Died in 1565.

See MERSSEMAN, "Notice sur C. van Baersdorp," 1844

Baersius, bär'se-us, or **Bek'en-stil,** a Dutch mathematician of the sixteenth century, was a resident of Louvain. He wrote "Tables of the Latitudes and Longitudes of the Planets."

Baerstrat, bär'strät, a Dutch marine painter of the seventeenth century. Died in 1687.

Baert, bä'air' or bärt, (ALEXANDRE BALTHASAR FRANÇOIS de Paule- -deh pōl,) BARON OF, a French geographer and statesman, born at Dunkirk about 1750. He became a member of the Legislative Assembly, (1791,) and of the Chamber of Deputies, (1815.) Among his principal works is his "Picture of Great Britain, Ireland, and the English Possessions," (1800,) which was highly esteemed by Napoleon. Died in 1825.

See QUÉRARD, "La France Littéraire."

Baert, [Lat. BAER'TIUS,] (FRANCIS,) a Flemish Jesuit, born at Ypres in 1651, wrote a "Commentary on the Life of Saint Basil," and was a contributor to the "Acta Sanctorum." Died in 1719.

Baeumer. See BÄUMER.

Baeza, dä bä-ä'thä, (DIEGO,) a Spanish theologian, born in Galicia in 1582 ; died in 1647.

Baf, SAINT. See BAVO, SAINT.

Baffa, bäf'fä, or **Baffi,** bäf'fee, (FRANCESCA,) an Italian poetess of the sixteenth century, resided at Venice.

Baffi, bäf'fee, (BARTOLOMMEO,) an Italian ecclesiastic, published a number of Latin orations. Died at Milan about 1578.

Baffi, (GIOVANNI BATTISTA,) an Italian poet and physician, born at Perugia ; died in 1596.

Baffi or **Baffo,** bäf'fo, [Lat. BAF'FUS,] (LUCULLO,) an Italian poet and physician, born at Perugia ; died about 1622.

Baf'fin, (WILLIAM,) a celebrated English navigator, born about 1580. He made three successive voyages to the Arctic regions in 1612, 1615, and 1616, and, during the last, discovered the large bay between Greenland and British America, since called by his name. In his account of his voyage in 1612 is first given a method for determining the longitude at sea by an observation of the heavenly bodies. Baffin was killed at the siege of Ormuz while fighting against the Portuguese, in 1622.

Baffo. See BAFFI.

Baffo, bâf'fo, surnamed THE PURE, a beautiful Venetian lady, who, being captured by pirates in 1580, was sold as a slave to Amurath III. She subsequently became his sultana, and exercised great influence over him and his successor, Mahomet III.

Baffo, (GIORGIO,) a Venetian of the eighteenth century, of the same family as the preceding, was called the most licentious poet of his time. Died in 1768.

See TIPALDO, "Biografia degli Italiani illustri."

Bafor, von, fon bâ'for, (BALTHASAR,) a German diplomatist of the sixteenth century, was counsellor of state under the emperors Rudolf, Matthias, and Ferdinand. Died in 1620.

Bagæus, bâ-jee'us, a Persian general of cavalry, defeated Agesilaus the Spartan, near Dascylium, in 396 B.C.

Bagard, bâ'gâR', (CÉSAR,) a French sculptor, born at Nancy in 1639. Among his principal works is a bust of Louis XIV. Died in 1709.

Bagarotto, bâ-gâ-rot'to, or **Bagarato,** bâ-gâ-râ'to, an Italian jurist and legal writer of the thirteenth century, was a native of Bologna. Died about 1242.

Bagarris, bâ'gâ'rèss', (PIERRE ANTOINE Rascas—râs'kâ',) SIEUR, a French antiquary and collector of medals, lived about 1600. He received in 1608 from Henry IV. the title of "Maître des cabinets, médailles," etc.

Bagatti, bâ-gât'tee, (FRANCESCO,) an Italian composer, who was court organist at Milan about 1610.

Bag'by, (ARTHUR P.,) an American Senator, born in Virginia in 1794. He settled in Alabama about 1818, and represented that State in the Senate of the United States from 1842 to 1849. Died in 1858.

Bagd-ed-Deen or **Bagdeddîn,** bâgd'ed-deen', **(Mohammed,)** an Arabian mathematician of the tenth century, wrote, among other works, a "Treatise on the Division of the Superficies," which was translated into Latin by John Dee.

Bâge, (ROBERT,) an English novelist, born at Derby in 1728. Among his works we may mention "Barham Downs," "The Fair Syrian," and "James Wallace." His life has been written by Sir Walter Scott. Died in 1801.

See SCOTT, "Miscellaneous Prose Works;" WILLIAM HUTTON, "Memoirs of Robert Bage," 1802.

Bagelaar, bâ'Geh-lâR', (ERNEST WILLEM,) a Dutch designer and engraver, born in 1775; died at Ghent in 1836.

Baget, bâ'zhâ', (HENRI JEAN,) a French anatomist of the eighteenth century, was the author of a valuable "Treatise on Osteology," (1731.)

Baget, de, deh bâ'zhâ', (JEAN CHEVALIER,) a French general, born in 1743; died in 1821.

Bagetti, bâ-jet'tee, or **Baggetti,** bâd-jet'tee, (GIUSEPPE PIETRO,) an Italian landscape-painter, born at Turin in 1764; died in 1831.

Bag'ford, (JOHN,) an English antiquary, born in London in 1651, made a valuable collection of ancient books and manuscripts for the libraries of Bishop Moore and the Earl of Oxford. Died in 1716.

Baggaert, bâg'gârt, (JAN,) a Dutch physician, born at Flushing about 1657, was the author of treatises on smallpox, measles, and scurvy. Died in 1710.

See VAN DER LINDEN, "De Scriptoribus Medicis."

Bagge, bâg'geh, (JAKOB,) a Swedish admiral, born in the province of Aland in 1499. He served against the Russians in 1555, and afterwards defeated the Danes at Bornholm, but in 1564 was captured by them, and subsequently died in prison.

See GEYER, "Histoire de la Suède."

Bagge, von, fon bâg'geh, (KARL ERNST,) BARON, a German amateur musician of the eighteenth century, was chamberlain to the King of Prussia. He is the subject of one of Hoffmann's tales. Died in 1791.

See FÉTIS, "Biographie Universelle des Musiciens."

Bagger, bâg'ger, (JOHN,) a learned Lutheran, Bishop of Copenhagen, born in Holstein in 1646. He was a violent opponent of the Calvinists and Huguenots, and used his influence to prevent the Danish government from giving an asylum to the latter. Died in 1693.

Bagger, (KARL CHRISTIAN,) a Danish poet, born in 1807. Among his principal works is a tale entitled "My Brother's Life." Died in 1846.

Bag'ge-sen, (or bâG'Geh-sen,) (JENS IMMANUEL,) a celebrated Danish poet, born at Körsor, in Zealand, in 1764. In 1789 he visited Germany, France, and Switzerland, and while at Bern married the granddaughter of the illustrious Haller. Having become thoroughly versed in German literature and acquired the friendship of several eminent German writers, he wrote a number of his principal works in that language, and made Klopstock, Voss, and Wieland his models. His "Comic Tales," ("Comiske Fortällinger,") in Danish, published in 1785, were very well received, and in 1808 he brought out a collection of German poems, entitled "Heath-Flowers," ("Haideblumen.") His "Parthenais, or the Alpine Journey," in German, (1812,) is an epic idyll in hexameter verse, and is esteemed one of his finest productions. In 1811 Baggesen was appointed professor of the Danish language and literature at Kiel. Among his other works may be mentioned his "Labyrinthen, or Wanderings of a Poet in Europe," (4 vols., 1792,) a memoir of his own early life, written in Danish prose, and "Adam and Eve," a humorous epic, (1826.) Died in Hamburg in 1826.

See D. FRICKE, "In Memoriam J. J. Baggesen," (1827;) LONGFELLOW, "Poets and Poetry of Europe;" HOWITT, "Literature and Romance of Northern Europe," 1852; AUGUST BAGGESEN, "J. Baggesen's Biographie udarbeitet vornemmeligen efter hans egne Haandskrifter," 2 vols. 8vo, 1842–43; MICHEL BERR, "Notice sur Baggesen, poëte Danois," Paris, 1805.

Baggetti. See BAGETTI.

Bagieu, bâ'zheh-uh', (JACQUES,) a French writer on surgery, lived about 1750.

Baglione, bâl-yo'nà, or **Baglioni,** bâl-yo'nee, (CESARE,) an Italian painter of landscapes, fruits, and flowers, born at Bologna about 1525. Died in 1590.

See LANZI, "History of Painting in Italy."

Baglione, (GIOVANNI,) an Italian painter, born at Rome about 1573, was patronized by Pope Paul V. His works in fresco and oil enjoyed a high reputation in his time. He was the author of a valuable work entitled "Lives of Painters, Sculptors, and Architects from 1572 to 1642." He worked mostly in Rome. Died about 1650.

See LANZI, "History of Painting in Italy."

Baglioni. See BAGLIONE.

Baglioni, bâl-yo'nee, (ASTORRE,) a relative of Gian Paolo, noticed below, served under Charles V. in the war of Tunis, and was afterwards made governor of Famagosta, in Cyprus, by the Venetians. After a brave defence of that city against the Turks in 1570, he was forced to capitulate, and was executed by order of Mustafa Pasha in 1571.

See DARU, "Histoire de Venise."

Baglioni, (GIAN PAOLO,) an Italian soldier, of a noble family, born in the fifteenth century, rose to be sovereign of Perugia. In 1520 he was summoned to Rome and executed by order of Leo X., who then took his possessions.

Baglioni, bâl-yo'nee, (LELIO,) a Florentine professor of theology. Died in 1620.

Baglioni, (MALATESTA,) son of Gian Paolo, noticed above, became governor of Perugia, but was deprived of his power by the allied army of the pope and emperor in 1529. Died in 1531.

Baglivi, bâl-yee'vee, (GIORGIO,) an Italian physician, born at Ragusa in 1669. In 1692 he studied under the celebrated anatomist Malpighi, and was afterwards appointed professor of anatomy and medicine at the College of Sapienza, at Rome. He was chosen a Fellow of the Royal Society of London in 1698. His complete works were published in 1704, under the title of "Opera omnia Medico-practica," and often reprinted. Baglivi is regarded as the founder of the system of *solidism,* as opposed to the previous theories, which maintained that in diseases the fluids of the body are the first to be affected. He had a wide reputation as a medical writer. Died in Rome in 1707.

See FABRONI, "Vitæ Italorum doctrina excellentium," etc.; FILIPPO FERRARIO, "Della Vita e delle Opere di G. Baglivi," 1839.

e as k; ç as s; g̃ hard; g̃ as j; G, H, K, guttural; N, nasal; R, trilled; s as z; th as in this. (See Explanations, p. 23.)

16

Bagnacavallo, bȧn-yȧ-kȧ-vȧl'lo, (BARTOLOMMEO,) originally **Bartolommeo Ramenghi,** (rȧ-mĕn'ḡee,) the greatest painter of the Bolognese school, born near Bologna in 1484. He was a pupil of Raphael, whom he assisted in the decoration of the Vatican. Among his master-pieces are a "Virgin and Child with Saint John," and "The Coronation of Charles V. at Bologna." His works were admired and studied by Guido and the Caracci. Died in 1542.

See VASARI, "Lives of the Painters," etc.; LANZI, "History of Painting in Italy."

Bagnacavallo, (BARTOLOMMEO,) THE YOUNGER, a nephew of the preceding, was a skilful painter of architecture and ornaments.

Bagnacavallo, (GIOVANNI BATTISTA,) a painter, was a son of Bartolommeo the Elder. He worked with Primaticcio in France. Died in 1601.

See LANZI, "History of Painting in Italy."

Bagnara, da, bȧn-yȧ'rȧ, (PIETRO,) a painter of the Roman school, and a pupil of Raphael, worked about 1550.

Bagnasco, bȧn-yȧs'ko, or **Bagna Sacco,** bȧn'yȧ sȧk'ko, (ANTONIO,) an Italian jurist of the sixteenth century, was the author of a treatise "On the Succession of the Kingdom of Gaul," ("De Successione Regni Galliæ.")

Bagnoli, bȧn'yo-lee, or **Bagnioli,** bȧn-ye-o'lee or bȧn-yo'lee, (GIULIO CESARE,) an eminent Italian poet, born at or near Ferrara, wrote "The Judgment of Paris," and other works. Died about 1630.

Bagnolino, bȧn-yo-lee'no, (GIROLAMO,) an Italian poet, lived about 1520–40.

Bagnolo, bȧn'yo-lo, (GIAN FRANCESCO GIUSEPPE,) COUNT, an Italian jurist and mathematician, born at Turin in 1709. His principal work is an "Explanation of the Tables of Gubbio," (1748.) Died in 1760.

Bagnuolo, bȧn-yoo-o'lo, COUNT, an Italian general, born in the kingdom of Naples. He commanded an army for Philip II. in Brazil, and opposed Maurice of Nassau with success in 1638.

Ba-go'as, [Gr. Βαγώας,] a Persian eunuch and soldier under Artaxerxes Ochus, said to have been a native of Egypt. In 338 B.C. he poisoned the king and his sons, with the exception of Arses, whom he raised to the throne. Having subsequently put him to death, and made Darius Codomannus king in his stead, Bagoas was seized by the latter, and executed about 336 B.C.

Ba-go'as Cā'rus, a favourite of Herod the Great, conspired against that king, and was put to death.

Bagolino, bȧ-go-lee'no, (GIOVANNI BATTISTA,) a learned Italian physician of Verona, lived about 1580.

Bagolino, (GIROLAMO,) a learned Italian physician of the sixteenth century, was a native of Verona. He wrote a number of medical and philosophical treatises.

Bagolino, (SEBASTIANO,) an Italian poet and painter, born at Alcamo, in Sicily, in 1560; died in 1604.

Ba-goph'a-nēs, a Persian general, commanded the citadel of Babylon, which he surrendered to Alexander the Great, with the royal treasure, in 331 B.C.

Bag'ot, (Sir CHARLES,) an English diplomatist, son of William, Lord Bagot, born in 1781. He was successively minister to France, (1814,) ambassador to Saint Petersburg, (1820,) and to Holland, (1824.) He afterwards succeeded Lord Sydenham as Governor-General of Canada, where he died in 1843.

Bagot, bȧ'go', (JEAN,) a French Jesuit and writer, born at Rennes in 1580, was engaged in the controversy with the Port-Royalists. Died in 1664.

Bagot, (LEWIS,) an English prelate, born in 1740, was successively Bishop of Bristol, of Norwich, and of Saint Asaph. He wrote "Sermons on the Prophecies." Died in 1802.

Bagot, (RICHARD,) brother of the preceding, born in 1782, became Bishop of Oxford in 1829, and of Bath and Wells in 1845. He was an adherent of Dr. Pusey. Died in 1854.

Bagration, bȧ-grä'shon, [Russ. pron. bȧ-GRÄ-te-òn',] (PETER,) PRINCE, a celebrated Russian general, of the Georgian family of the Bagradites, born about 1765. He served under Suwarrow in the campaigns of Italy and Switzerland, and was everywhere conspicuous for his impetuous and unyielding courage. He commanded the van-guard under Kootoosov in the Austrian campaign of 1805, and on the 16th of November successfully opposed the greatly superior force of Murat and Lannes, thus allowing Kootoosov, with the main army, to reach Znaim in safety. Being appointed lieutenant-general soon after, he commanded the van-guard under Liechtenstein at Austerlitz, and displayed the greatest bravery and skill in the subsequent engagements of Eylau and Friedland. After having several times defeated the Swedes and the Turks, he was mortally wounded at the battle of Borodino, in 1812.

See SÉGUR, "Histoire de Napoléon et de la Grande Armée."

Bag'shaw, (CHRISTOPHER,) an English scholar and theologian, born in Derbyshire; died about 1626.

See WOOD, "Athenæ Oxonienses."

Bagshaw, (EDWARD,) an English lawyer of the seventeenth century, was elected to the Long Parliament in 1640, and distinguished himself by his opposition to the cause of the king and of episcopacy. He wrote, among other works, "The Right of the Crown of England as established by Law." Died in 1662.

See WOOD, "Athenæ Oxonienses."

Bagshaw, (HENRY,) an English divine, son of the preceding, born in 1632, was chaplain to the Earl of Danby. He was the author of "Discourses against Papists and Socinians." Died in 1709.

Bagshaw, (WILLIAM,) an English nonconformist divine and theological writer; died in 1703.

Bagutti, bȧ-goot'tee, (PIETRO MARTIRE,) an Italian sculptor, lived at Bologna about 1780–90.

Bag'well, (WILLIAM,) an English astronomer, who wrote "The Mystery of Astronomy made plain," (1673.)

Bahadar- or **Bahadur-Shah.** See BEHADAR-SHAH.

Baharam-Kooree, (or **Curi,**) bȧh'ȧ-rȧm koo'ree, Sultan of Persia, reigned in the first half of the fifth century.

Bahier, bȧ'e-à' or bȧ'yȧ', (JEAN,) a French ecclesiastic and Latin poet; died in 1707.

Bahil, bö'hĕl', (MATTHIAS,) a Hungarian theologian, lived in the second half of the eighteenth century.

Bahn, bȧn, (JEROME,) a German theologian, born at Hamburg; died in 1744.

Bahn, (NICOLAS,) a German writer on theology, born in 1664; died in 1704.

Bahnsen, bȧn'sen, (BENEDICT,) a German mystic, born in Holstein, lived about 1660–90.

Bähr or **Baehr,** bȧR, (JOHANN CHRISTIAN FELIX,) a distinguished German scholar, born at Darmstadt in June, 1798, studied at Heidelberg, where in 1826 he became professor of classical literature. His "History of Roman Literature" (2 vols., 1828) is esteemed a standard work. He published editions of the "Alcibiades" of Plutarch, and other classics, and made numerous contributions to Ersch and Gruber's "Encyklopaedie," and to other publications. Among his other productions is a valuable edition of the works relating to Herodotus, (4 vols., 1832.) Bähr became chief librarian at Heidelberg in 1833, and has since been created aulic councillor.

See BROCKHAUS, "Conversations-Lexikon."

Bahr, bȧR, (JOSEPH FRIEDRICH,) a German Protestant bishop, and writer on theology, was born in 1713. He preached at Schönfeld and other places. Died in 1775.

Bahrdt, bȧRt, (KARL FRIEDRICH,) a German Protestant theologian, born at Bischofswerda in 1741. He was successively professor of Biblical philology at Leipsic, and of philosophy at Erfurt, but was obliged to give up these offices on account of his profligacy and his bold criticisms on the Bible. He published, among other deistical works, "Letters on the Bible in a Popular Style." Died in 1792.

See his Autobiography, "Geschichte meines Lebens und meiner Schicksale," 4 vols., 1790; ERSCH und GRUBER, "Allgemeine Encyklopaedie;" D. POTT, "Leben und Schicksale C. F. Bahrdts," 1790.

Bährens or **Baehrens,** bȧ'rens, (J. E. F.,) a German writer on agriculture, born in 1760; died in 1830.

Bai, bī, or **Bais,** bȧ'ĕss, (TOMMASO,) an Italian composer, born at or near Bologna, was master of the chapel of the Vatican. He composed a *Miserere*, which is much admired. Died in 1714.

See FÉTIS, "Biographie Universelle des Musiciens."

Baian, bī-ân', written also **Baion,** [Lat. BAIA'NUS,] (ANDREW,) an Indian convert to Christianity, born at

Goa, was ordained a priest at Rome about 1635. He translated the "Æneid" into Greek verse, and the "Lusiad" of Camoens into Latin verse.

See CHAUDON et DELANDINE, "Dictionnaire Historique."

Baiardi. See BAJARDI.

Baiardi, bâ-yaR'dee, or **Baiardo,** bâ-yaR'do, (OTTAVIO ANTONIO,) an Italian antiquary, born about 1690, was the author of a work entitled "Prodromus of the Antiquities of Herculaneum," (1742.) Died about 1765.

Baidu-Khan, bī'doo-kân, called also **Baidu-Ogul,** a Tartar or Mongol king of the race of Jengis Khan, died in 1294, after a reign of eight months.

Baier, bī'ẽr, (JOHANN DAVID,) a German theologian, born at Jena in 1681, was a son of Johann Wilhelm the elder, noticed below. Died at Altdorf in 1752.

Baier, (JOHANN JACOB,) a German physician and naturalist, brother of the preceding, born at Jena in 1677. He wrote a number of scientific and medical treatises, (in Latin.) Died in 1735.

See "Allgemeines Gelehrten-Lexikon," Supplement.

Baier, (JOHANN WILHELM,) a German Lutheran theologian, born in 1647, became professor at Halle, (1694.) He was the author of a "Compendium of Theology," (1686,) and other works. Died in 1695.

Baier, (JOHANN WILHELM,) a theologian and naturalist, born at Jena about 1676, was a son of the preceding. He wrote a "Dissertation on the Fossil Monuments of the Universal Deluge," ("Disputatio de Fossilibus Diluvii universi Monumentis," 1712.) Died in 1729.

Baïf, de, dẽh bâ'ẽf', (JEAN ANTOINE,) a French littérateur, son of Lazare, noticed below, born at Venice in 1532, was an intimate friend of the poet Ronsard. He was the author of sonnets and various other poems. He was one of seven poets called the "Pléiade," and was the reputed founder of the first literary society in France. Died in 1589.

See LONGFELLOW, "Poets and Poetry of Europe;" SAINTE-BEUVE, "Tableau de la Poésie Française au seizième Siècle."

Baïf, de, (LAZARE,) a French diplomatist and learned writer of the sixteenth century, born near La Flèche, in Anjou, was a counsellor of Francis I. He translated the "Electra" of Sophocles and the "Hecuba" of Euripides into French verse, and wrote, among other works, in Latin, a treatise "On Naval Affairs." Died in 1547.

See LA CROIX DU MAINE et DUVERDIER, "Bibliothèque Française."

Bail, bâl or bâ'ye, (CHARLES JOSEPH,) a French writer and officer, born at Béthune in 1777, served in the Belgian war of 1793. He was the author of "Statistics of the Kingdom of Westphalia," esteemed one of the best works of the kind, a work "On the Jews in the Nineteenth Century," and several other treatises. He also edited "Bernadotte's Correspondence with Napoleon," (1819.) Died in 1827.

See QUÉRARD, "La France Litteraire."

Bail, (LOUIS,) a French theologian of the sixteenth century, born at Abbeville, was a doctor of the Sorbonne, and superior of the monastery of Port-Royal. He wrote a treatise "On the Benefit of the Cross," and other religious works, which had considerable reputation in his time. Died in 1669.

See MORÉRI, "Dictionnaire Historique;" LELONG, "Bibliothèque Française."

Baila, bī'lâ or bâ-ee'la, (GIUSEPPE,) an Italian jurist, born at Monreale in 1585; died in 1645.

Bailay. See BAILEY.

Bail'don, (JOSEPH,) an English musician and composer, lived about 1750–70.

Bailey. See BAYLEY.

Bailey, bâ'le, (ANSELM,) an English theologian and writer on music; died in 1724.

Bailey, bâ'le, (GAMALIEL,) an American journalist, distinguished as an opponent of slavery, born at Mount Holly, New Jersey, in 1807. He was a physician in early life, removed to Cincinnati in 1831, and joined James G. Birney in 1836 as the publisher of an anti-slavery paper called "The Philanthropist." The first year their office was twice attacked by a mob, who threw their press into the river. In 1837 he became the sole or chief editor of the "Philanthropist." He removed to Washington, District of Columbia, in 1847, and began to edit "The National Era," which under his judicious management exerted a considerable influence on political affairs. Mrs. Stowe's celebrated novel "Uncle Tom's Cabin" first appeared in the columns of the "National Era." Died in 1859.

Bailey, (JACOB WHITMAN,) an American microscopist, born at Ward, Massachusetts, about 1808, became professor of chemistry at West Point. He wrote many treatises on infusoria, algæ, etc., inserted in Silliman's "Journal of Science," and in other periodicals. He acquired distinction by his microscopic researches in botany and zoology, and made improvements in the construction of microscopes. Died in 1857.

Bai'ley, (JOHN,) a dissenting divine, born in Lancashire, England, in 1644, emigrated in 1684 to America and settled as a pastor at Boston. Died in 1697.

Bai'ley, (JOHN,) a Scotch mechanician and agriculturist, born in the latter part of the eighteenth century. He was the inventor of a plough which he described in a treatise, afterwards translated into German, (1805.)

Bailey or **Bai'ly,** sometimes written **Bailay,** (NATHAN or NATHANIEL,) an English lexicographer and school-master at Stepney, published an Etymological English Dictionary, which is said to have formed the basis of Dr. Johnson's work, also a "Domestic Dictionary," and other educational books. Died in 1742.

Bailey, (PETER,) an English writer, born in Cheshire, was editor of a journal called "The Museum." He published "Sketches from Saint George's Fields," a humorous poem, and "A Queen's Appeal," written in the Spenserian measure. Died in 1823.

Bailey, (PHILIP JAMES,) an English poet, born at Nottingham in 1816. He completed his studies at Glasgow, and subsequently practised law for a short time. His principal poem, "Festus," published in 1839, produced a great sensation. In the words of a judicious critic, "its defects and merits alike gained for it immediate and wide success. Its subject was the highest questions of philosophy and religion, and it abounded in bold and glowing passages. Yet, unlike the 'Faust' of Goethe, which doubtless suggested 'Festus,' its art was chaotic; it was wildly extravagant, and often as unintelligible as it was fervent, and its few finely imaginative utterances have not been able to retain for the work its first popularity." He was author of two other poems, entitled "The Angel World" and "The Mystic."

See "Blackwood's Magazine" for April, 1850; R. H. HORNE, "New Spirit of the Age."

Bailey, (SAMUEL,) an English writer, born at Sheffield in 1787. His "Essays on the Formation and Publication of Opinions" (1820) was very favourably received, and was commended by Sir James Mackintosh. He afterwards published "Essays on the Pursuit of Truth and Progress of Knowledge," "Theory of Reasoning," and other works on mental philosophy, political economy, etc.

Bailey, (THEODORUS,) an American rear-admiral, born in the State of New York about 1804, entered the navy in 1818. He became a lieutenant in 1827, a commander in 1849, and captain in 1855. He was second in command under Farragut in the great naval battle against the defences of New Orleans in April, 1862. He rendered important services in this action, and was the foremost in entering New Orleans, having been sent by Farragut to demand the surrender of that city on the 25th. In November, 1862, he was appointed commander of the Eastern Gulf Blockading Squadron. It is stated that in about one year and a half he captured more than one hundred and fifty blockade-runners.

Bailey, (THOMAS,) father of Philip James, noticed above, born in 1785, was the author of the "Advent of Charity," and a "History of Nottinghamshire." Died in 1856.

Bailey or **Baley,** (WALTER,) born in Dorsetshire in 1529, was appointed royal professor of medicine at Oxford in 1561, and was subsequently physician to Queen Elizabeth. He wrote "Directions for Health," and other works. Died in 1592.

Bai'lies, (WILLIAM,) a celebrated physician, of English extraction, was employed by Frederick the Great of Prussia. He wrote an "Essay on the Bath Waters," and other medical works. Died in 1787.

See "Biographic Médicale."

Baillarger, bả'yăr'zhả' or bằl'yăR'zhả', (JULES GA-BRIEL FRANÇOIS,) a French physician, born at Mont-bazon in 1806, was distinguished for his skill in mental maladies, on which he published several works.

Baille. See BAYLE.

Baillès, bằ'yĕs', (JACQUES MARIE JOSEPH,) Bishop of Luçon, and Vicar-General of Toulouse, born in that city in 1798.

Baillet. See SAINT-JULIEN.

Baillet, bả'yả', (ADRIEN,) a French writer and scholar, born near Beauvais in 1649. His most important pro-duction is entitled "Judgments of the Learned upon the Principal Works of Authors," (Jugements des Savants," etc., 1685, 9 vols. 12mo, unfinished.) He also wrote a "Life of Descartes," a "History of Holland from the Truce of 1609 to the Present Time," (1690,) and other works. Died in 1706.

See NICÉRON, "Mémoires."

Bailleul. See BALIOL.

Bailleul, bả'yul' or bả'e-yul', (JACQUES CHARLES,) a French advocate, born near Havre in 1762, was a mode-rate member of the Convention in 1792, and was pro-scribed in 1793. Died in 1843.

See TISSOT, "Éloge de Bailleul," 1843.

Bailleux, bả'yuh' or bằl'yuh', (ANTOINE,) a French composer and professor of music at Paris, produced a number of symphonies. Died in 1791.

See FÉTIS, "Biographie Universelle des Musiciens."

Baillie, bả'le, (JOANNA,) one of the most eminent British female poets, was born near Glasgow in 1762. She published in 1798 the first volume of a series of "Plays on the Passions," which was very well received. Her tragedy of "The Family Legend" was brought out at Edinburgh in 1810 with brilliant success, Sir Walter Scott having written the epilogue, and one of the prin-cipal parts having been performed by Mrs. Siddons. Among her other dramas, "De Montfort" and "Basil" enjoy perhaps the highest reputation. Besides the above-named works, she was the author of "Metrical Legends of Exalted Characters," and a number of ballads and songs of great beauty. Miss Baillie resided during the greater part of her life at Hampstead, near London, where her brother, the celebrated Matthew Baillie, was court physician. During her life, which was prolonged almost to ninety years, her house was the resort of the most distinguished persons of her own and other coun-tries. She was a very intimate friend of Sir Walter Scott, who admired her genius and highly esteemed her for her moral and social qualities. She died at Hamp-stead in 1851. "This great work," says the "Edinburgh Review" for April, 1836, referring to her "Plays on the Passions," "is then completed, and in a manner worthy of its commencement : a noble monument of the power-ful mind and the pure and elevated imagination of its author."

See also "Quarterly Review," vols. xxxvii., lv. ; "Edinburgh Re-view," vols. ii., v., xix. ; "Blackwood's Magazine" for August, 1824; CHAMBERS, "Biographical Dictionary of Eminent Scotsmen."

Baillie, (JOHN,) a Scottish Orientalist, born at Inver-ness about 1770, became professor of the Arabic lan-guage and Mussulman law in the College of Fort Wil-liam, Bengal. He published several works upon Arabic grammar, which are ranked among the most valuable that have appeared on the subject. Died in 1833.

Baillie, (Lady GRIZEL.) See HUME, (GRIZEL.)

Baillie, (MATTHEW,) a celebrated physician and ana-tomist, born in Lanarkshire, Scotland, in 1761, was a brother of Joanna Baillie. He studied at the University of Glasgow, where his father, the Rev. James Baillie, was professor of divinity. Through the influence of his maternal uncle, the eminent anatomist William Hunter, he applied himself to the study of medicine at Oxford, where he graduated in 1789, and soon after was made a member of the College of Physicians. In 1783 he suc-ceeded Hunter as lecturer on anatomy. He became phy-sician to George III. and the royal family about 1810, and acquired a very extensive practice in London. He was distinguished for his skill in diagnosis. His "Mor-bid Anatomy of some of the most Important Parts of the Human Body" (1795) is esteemed a standard work, and has been translated into German, French, and Ital-

ian. He also wrote "Lectures and Observations on Medicine," (1825.) He died in 1823, bequeathing to the College of Physicians his medical library and anatomical collection.

See CHAMBERS, "Biographical Dictionary of Eminent Scotsmen," and "An Account of Baillie's Life," prefixed to his works, by JAMES WARDROP.

Baillie, [Lat. BAY'LIUS,] (ROBERT,) a Scottish theo-logian, born at Glasgow about 1602. In 1640 he was sent to London by the Scottish lords to protest against the innovations of Archbishop Laud, and was subse-quently principal of the university at Glasgow. In 1649 he was one of the commissioners charged to compliment Charles II. at the Hague in the name of the general as-sembly of the clergy. He was a man of profound learn-ing, and wrote several theological and historical works in English and in Latin. Died in 1662.

See CHAMBERS, "Biographical Dictionary of Eminent Scotsmen;" "Westminster Review" for January, 1842.

Baillie OF JERVISWOOD, (ROBERT,) a Scottish patriot, eminent for ability and virtue, was identified with the party or cause of which Lord Russell and Algernon Sidney were the chiefs. He was arrested in 1684, and charged with complicity in the Rye-House plot. He was condemned without evidence, and executed in De-cember, 1684.

See CHAMBERS, "Biographical Dictionary of Eminent Scotsmen."

Bail'lie, (WILLIAM,) a distinguished engraver, born in Ireland about 1736, served for a time in the army, and obtained the rank of captain. His engravings after Rembrandt are greatly esteemed.

See STRUTT, "Dictionary of Engravers."

Baillif, (LE ROCHE.) See RIVIÈRE, (ROCHE LE BAILLIF.)

Baillon, bả'yòN', (EMMANUEL,) a French naturalist, who was a proficient in ornithology and vegetable physi-ology. He furnished valuable information to Buffon, and wrote several works, one of which was "On the Means of counteracting the Encroachments of Moving Sands on the Sea-Coast." Died at Abbeville in 1802.

See LE BAS, "Dictionnaire encyclopédique de la France."

Baillot, bả'yo', (PIERRE MARIE FRANÇOIS de Sales —dĕh sằl,) one of the most celebrated French violinists, born at Passy in 1771, was a pupil of Viotti. He visited Russia, Holland, and England, where his performances obtained great applause. Died in 1842.

Baillou, de, dĕh bả'yoo', [Lat. BALLO'NIUS,] (GUIL-LAUME,) a French physician, born in Paris in 1538. He was appointed by Henry IV. first physician to the Dau-phin in 1601. He was the author of several medical works of great merit, among which we may cite "Medical Counsels, in Three Books," (1649,) and "Adversaria Medicinalia." He is said to have been the first who made known the nature of the croup. Died in 1616.

See RENÉ MOREAU, "Vita G. de Baillou Doctoris Medici," 1641 ; "Biographie Médicale ;" SPRENGEL, "Geschichte der Medicin."

Baillu, bả'yü' or bằl'yü', written also **Balliu** and **Bail-lieu,** (PETER,) a Flemish engraver of the seventeenth century, executed numerous prints after Rubens, Van Dyck, Rembrandt, and other masters.

See DESCAMPS, "Vies des Peintres Flamands."

Bailly, bả'ye' or bả'e-ye', (ANTOINE,) a French in-spector-general of finances. He wrote a "Financial His-tory of France," ("Histoire financière de la France,") a work of merit. Died in 1851.

Bailly, bả'le, (DAVID,) a Dutch painter, born at Ley-den in 1588, acquired a high reputation for his portraits drawn with a pen.

See NAGLER, "Allgemeines Künstler-Lexikon."

Bailly, (GEORGE,) a French general, born in 1685 ; died in 1759.

Bailly, (JACQUES,) a French painter, born at Graçay in 1629 ; died in 1679.

Bailly, (JACQUES,) a French dramatist, painter, and keeper of the royal pictures, born at Versailles in 1701. The celebrated Jean Sylvain Bailly was his son. Died in 1768.

Bailly, bả'le, [Fr. pron. bả'ye',] (JEAN SYLVAIN,) an eminent French astronomer, philosopher, and elo-quent writer, was born in Paris on the 15th of Septem-ber, 1736. He was a pupil and friend of La Caille. In

ā, ē, ī, ō, ū, ȳ, *long;* ă, ĕ, ĭ, ŏ, ŭ, ў, *same, less prolonged;* ă, ĕ, ĭ, ŏ, ŭ, ў, *short;* ạ, ẹ, ị, ọ, *obscure;* fär, fàll, fàt; mĕt; nŏt; gŏŏd; mōōn;

1763 he was elected to the Academy of Sciences, to which he had presented some lunar observations. He produced in 1766 an able "Essay on the Theory of the Satellites of Jupiter," and in 1771 a remarkable "Memoir on the Light of the Satellites of Jupiter," which light he had measured by an ingenious method. His eulogy on Leibnitz gained the prize offered by the Academy of Berlin, and his eulogy on Molière obtained an *accessit* at the French Academy. He published in 1775 the first volume of his great work, "The History of Astronomy, Ancient and Modern," (4 vols., 1775-83,) which is written in a brilliant, attractive style and abounds in ingenious ideas. It obtained great popularity. He was elected to the Académie Française in 1784, and to the Academy of Inscriptions in 1785. Except Fontenelle, he was the only Frenchman who had the honour to be a member of the three great Academies of Paris.

Having won the favour of the public by his probity and other virtues, he was chosen a deputy to the States-General in 1789. He was the first president of this assembly, over which he presided during the famous session of the Tennis-court, and was elected mayor of Paris on the 16th of July, 1789. His efforts, in concert with La Fayette, to maintain order and moderate the violence of the Revolution, were not successful. By his order, the national guard fired on a riotous crowd which had assembled in the Champ-de-Mars in July, 1791, for the purpose of making a demonstration against the king. This act gave great offence to the popular party. Bailly offered his resignation in September, but was persuaded to retain his office until November, 1791.

He was arrested by the Jacobins at Melun in 1793, taken to Paris, and condemned to death in November, one of the charges against him being his part in the affair of the Champ-de-Mars. He was executed, after he had suffered many insults and refinements of cruelty, on the 12th of November, 1793. To one of the bystanders who said, "Bailly, you tremble," "Yes," he replied, "but it is with cold." "The name of Bailly," says Lamartine, "was an inscription on the frontispiece of the Revolution. He was on a level with this destiny by his character, if not by his genius. His administration had been a series of triumphs of the people over the court. When bloody tumults began to stain the victories of the people, he spoke like a sage, and acted like a magistrate." ("History of the Girondists.") He left Memoirs of the Revolution, ("Mémoires d'un Témoin oculaire," etc., 3 vols., 1804.)

See "Biographie de Bailly," par F. ARAGO, 1852; "Éloge de Bailly," par LALANDE, 1794; "Éloge de Bailly," par LACRETELLE; English version of Arago's "Biographie," Boston, 1859; "Vie privée et politique de Bailly," Paris, 1790; "Edinburgh Review" for April, 1805.

Bailly, (JOSEPH,) a French physician, born in 1779, wrote an "Essay on Artesian Wells." Died in 1832.

Bailly, (JOSEPH A.,) a skilful sculptor, born at Paris in 1825, came to Philadelphia in 1850. He executed, besides other works, the groups of "Adam and Eve," "Eve and her two Children," and the monument of Washington placed (1869) in front of the State-House in Philadelphia.

Bailly de Juilly, bȧ'ye' (or bȧ'e-ye') deh zhü'e-ye', (EDME LOUIS BARTHÉLEMI,) a French politician, born at Troyes in 1760. He was a moderate member of the National Convention in 1792-95, and opposed the execution of Louis XVI. Died in 1819.

Bailly de Monthion, bȧ'ye' deh môN'te'ôN', (FRANÇOIS GÉDÉON,) COMTE, a French general, born in the Isle of Bourbon in 1776. He fought at Marengo, and gained the rank of colonel at Austerlitz, 1805. He was wounded at Waterloo, where he acted as general of division. Died in 1846.

Baily, bā'le, (EDWARD HODGES,) an eminent English sculptor, born at Bristol about 1788. He was a pupil of Flaxman, and also studied at the Royal Academy, where he successively won the silver and the gold medals. He became an academician in 1820. Among his masterpieces in the department of classic and poetic sculpture we may mention "Eve at the Fountain," "Hercules casting Hylas into the Sea," "Psyche," "The Graces Seated," and "Eve Listening to the Voice." He has also produced statues of Earl Grey, Lord Mansfield, Nelson, and other celebrated men.

Baily, (FRANCIS,) an English astronomer, and writer on assurances, annuities, etc., born in 1774, was a member of the Stock Exchange, London. He was one of the founders of the Astronomical Society of London. Among his most useful labours was the reorganization of the "Nautical Almanac," the revision of the society's catalogue of stars, and the republication in England of the catalogues of Lalande and La Caille. He also made valuable contributions to the "Memoirs of the Astronomical Society," and published, among other esteemed works, "The Doctrine of Life Assurances and Annuities," (1810.) He was the author of a "Life of Flamsteed." Died in 1844.

See the "Philosophical Magazine."

Baily, (NATHAN.) See BAILEY, (NATHAN.)

Bain, (ALEXANDER,) a distinguished Scottish writer, born at Aberdeen about 1818. He graduated at Marischal College, in his native town, in 1840. In 1860 he became professor of logic in the University of Aberdeen. He has written on a great variety of subjects, including logic, psychology, etc.

Bain'bridge or **Bam'bridge,** (CHRISTOPHER,) an English prelate, born in Westmoreland about 1450, rose to be Archbishop of York in 1508. Being afterwards sent by Henry VIII. on an embassy to Pope Julius II., he was made Cardinal of Saint Praxede by the latter. He died at Rome in 1514, and is supposed to have been poisoned.

Bainbridge, (JOHN,) an English astronomer and physician, born at Ashby-de-la-Zouch in 1582, was first Savillian professor of astronomy at Oxford. Among his writings is a "Description of the Comet of 1618." Died in 1643.

See "Biographie Médicale."

Bain'bridge, (WILLIAM,) an American commodore, born at Princeton, New Jersey, in 1774. He became a captain in 1800, and took command of the frigate Philadelphia, which, having run aground near Tripoli, was captured, with all the crew, in October, 1803, by the gunboats of Tripoli. He was detained in captivity about nineteen months. Having obtained the rank of commodore, he was appointed, in September, 1812, commander of a squadron consisting of the Constitution, of forty-four guns, the Essex, and the Hornet. He captured the British frigate Java, of forty-nine guns, in December, 1812, after an action in which the British loss was about one hundred and seventy-four killed and wounded, and the American loss thirty-three. After the end of the war, he commanded a fleet in the Mediterranean. Died in 1833.

See THOMAS HARRIS, "Life of Commodore William Bainbridge," Philadelphia, 1837.

Baines, bānz, (EDWARD,) an English journalist, born in Lancashire in 1774. He was for many years editor and proprietor of the "Leeds Mercury," in which he showed himself an able advocate of Catholic emancipation and of other important reforms. He represented Leeds in Parliament from 1834 till 1841. He wrote a "History of the Reign of George III.," a "History of the County Palatine of Lancaster," (4 vols.,) and several other works. Died in 1848.

See the "Life of Edward Baines," by his son, 1851.

Baines, (EDWARD,) a son of the preceding, born at Leeds about 1800, succeeded his father as editor of the "Leeds Mercury." He wrote a "History of the Cotton Manufacture," (1835,) and a "Life of Edward Baines," (his father, 1851.) In 1859 he was elected member of Parliament for Leeds, and was again elected in 1868. He is a decided Liberal in politics.

Baines, (JOHN,) an English mathematician, born in Yorkshire about 1786, published valuable contributions to the "Mathematical Repository," "Ladies' Diary," and other periodicals. Died in 1835.

Baines, (MATTHEW TALBOT,) an English lawyer, a son of Edward Baines, born at Leeds in 1799. He was returned to Parliament by the Liberal voters of Hull in 1847, and was president of the poor-law board from 1849 to 1855. As chancellor of the duchy of Lancaster, he had a seat in the cabinet from 1855 to 1858. He represented Leeds in the House of Commons. Died in 1860.

Baini, bä-ee'nee or bē'nee, (GIUSEPPE,) an Italian musician, born about 1775, was director of the pontifical chapel at Rome. He composed a number of sacred pieces, and wrote "Historical and Critical Memoirs of the Life and Works of Palestrina," (1828.) Died in 1844.

See J. ADRIEN DE LAFAGE, "Notice sur J. Baini," 1845.

Bains, bänz, [Fr. pron. bȧN,] (MICHAEL,) a Calvinistic divine, born in 1513, was a deputy from Louvain to the Council of Trent. Died in 1589.

Bainville, bȧN'vèl', (CHARLES,) a French painter and versifier, was a relative of Boileau, who advised him to cultivate painting. Died in 1754.

Bairaktar, bī'râk-tȧR', or **Beirakdar,** bī'râk-dȧR', (MUSTAFA PASHA,) a Turkish officer, born in 1755. In the contest between Selim III. and Mustafa he was the adherent of the former. After the murder of Selim by Mustafa, Bairaktar, having deposed the usurper and raised Mahmood to the throne, was made by him grand vizier. On a revolt of the janissaries, in 1808, he put an end to his life.

See JUCHEREAU DE SAINT-DENYS, "Révolutions de Constantinople en 1807-1808," Paris, 1819.

Baird, bârd, (ABSALOM,) an American general, born at Washington, Pennsylvania, in 1824, graduated at West Point in 1849. He became a captain in the regular army in 1861, and a brigadier-general of volunteers in May, 1862. He served at Chattanooga, November, 1863, and commanded a division of Sherman's army in the campaign against Atlanta in 1864.

Baird, bârd, (Sir DAVID,) a distinguished general, born in Aberdeenshire, Scotland, in 1757. Having entered the service in India, he was made prisoner by Hyder Ali in the engagement at Peramboucum, and detained captive four years. After his release, he was created general of brigade about 1797, and in 1799 headed the assault on Seringapatam, which resulted in the capture of that place. For this splendid achievement he received the thanks of Parliament, while Colonel Wellesley, afterwards Duke of Wellington, was made governor of the town, though he had taken no prominent part in the assault. He accompanied Lord Cathcart to Denmark in 1807, and afterwards served in the Spanish campaign, where he was severely wounded at the battle of Corunna, (1808.) He was soon after created a baronet, and obtained the order of the Bath. Died in 1829.

See THEODORE HOOK, "Life of Sir David Baird," 1832; CHAMBERS, "Biographical Dictionary of Eminent Scotsmen."

Baird, (ROBERT,) D D., an American theologian, born in Fayette county, Pennsylvania, in 1798, studied theology at Princeton, New Jersey. He took a prominent part in the organization of the system of public schools in New Jersey. In 1835 he went to Europe, where he devoted several years to the promotion of Protestant Christianity and the cause of temperance. He became the agent and secretary of the American and Foreign Christian Union. He published, besides other works, a "Visit to Northern Europe," "A View of Religion in America," (1842,) and a "History of the Waldenses, Albigenses, and Vaudois." Died in 1863.

See "Life of Robert Baird," by his son, 1866.

Baird, (SPENCER F.,) LL.D., an eminent American naturalist, born at Reading, Pennsylvania, in 1823, became professor of natural science in Dickinson College, and afterwards assistant secretary of the Smithsonian Institution. Besides his other labours, he has translated and edited the "Iconographic Encyclopædia," (4 vols. 8vo, 2 vols. steel plates,) and published reports on the collections in natural history made by Stansbury, Gilliss, Marcy, and others. He has also published, in conjunction with J. Cassin, "The Birds of North America," (2 vols. 4to, 1860,) and the "Mammals of North America," (1 vol. 4to, 1861.) He has studied, with great success, the various divisions of the vertebrata and their distribution, and has made valuable contributions to the Journal of the Academy of Sciences of Philadelphia, to the publications of the Smithsonian Institution, etc.

Baireuth, (FREDERICA, MARGRAVINE OF.) See FREDERICA SOPHIA WILHELMINA.

Bairo, bī'ro, (PIETRO,) an Italian physician and medical writer, born at Turin in 1468; died in 1558.

Baiter, bī'ter, (JOHN GEORGE,) a Swiss philologist, born at Zurich in 1801, was professor in the university of that city. He published "Oratores Attici," (1838-43,)

and, in conjunction with Orelli, "The Works of Plato, (21 vols., 1839-42.)

Baithe, bī'tĕ, written also **Beithe,** (STEPHEN,) a Hungarian botanist and Protestant theologian of the sixteenth century, published several works on Botany.

See JÖCHER, "Allgemeines Gelehrten-Lexikon," (Supplement.)

Baitz, bīts, (JOHANN ANDREAS HARTMANN,) a celebrated organ-maker, born at Utrecht about 1708. Among the best may be named those of the churches of Zierikzee, of Groningen, and of the Mennonites at Utrecht. Died in 1770.

See FÉTIS, "Biographie Universelle des Musiciens."

Baius, bī'us, (JACQUES,) a Flemish theologian, was a nephew of Michael, noticed below. Died in 1614.

Baius, bȧ'yus, the Latinized name of **De Bay,** dĕh bā, (MICHAEL,) a learned Flemish theologian, born at Melin, in Hainault, in 1513. He was appointed by Charles V. professor of divinity at Louvain in 1551, and subsequently became chancellor of that university, and inquisitor-general of the Netherlands. Having published, about 1565, his works on free will and grace, in which he advocates the doctrines of Saint Augustine, his dogmas were denounced by Pope Pius V., and Baius was obliged to retract. His views were afterwards adopted by the Jansenists. Died in 1589.

See SWEERT, "Athenæ Belgicæ;" BAYLE, "Historical and Critical Dictionary."

Bajardi or **Baiardi,** bȧ-yaR'dee or bī-aR'dee, or **Bajardo** or **Baiardo,** bȧ-yaR'do, (ANDREA,) a mediocre Italian poet, born at Parma; died after 1520.

Bajardo, bȧ-yaR'do, (GIOVANNI BATTISTA,) a skilful Italian painter, born at Genoa; died prematurely in 1657.

Bajazet, or **Bajazîd.** See BAYAZEED.

Bajon, bȧ'zhòN', a French naturalist, went to Cayenne in 1763, and practised there as surgeon for many years. He published "Memoirs towards the History of Cayenne and Guiana, etc.," (2 vols., 1778.)

Bajus. See BAIUS.

Bajza, bī'zŏh, (ANTON,) a Hungarian writer, born in 1804. In 1830 he succeeded Kisfaludy as editor of a literary journal entitled "The Aurora." He was the author of "Lyric Poems," and several historical works.

Bakacs, bŏh'kŏtch', (THOMAS,) a Hungarian statesman of the fifteenth century, who rose from the condition of a peasant to be secretary of the emperor Matthias Corvinus. On the accession of Vladislaus II. to the throne, he was made cardinal primate of Hungary, and papal legate. He afterwards preached a crusade against the Turks, which, however, resulted in a civil war among the Hungarian nobles. Died in 1521.

Bake, bȧ'kĕh, (JAN,) a Dutch philologist, born in 1787 at Leyden, where he became professor of Greek and Roman literature in 1817. His editions of Posidonius and Cleomedes (1820) are highly esteemed. He was a contributor to the "Bibliotheca Critica Nova," and wrote, in Latin, a number of philological essays of remarkable elegance.

Bake, (LAURENT,) a Dutch poet, born at Amsterdam about 1650, was lord of Wulverhorst. He was the author of "Biblical Poems." Died in 1714.

Bâkî or **Bâkî,** bȧ'kee, or **Abd-el-Bâkee,** (-Bâkî,) âbd-el-bȧ'kee, the greatest of Turkish lyric poets, born near the beginning of the sixteenth century. In genius he ranks with the Persian poet Hafiz. Died in 1600, or, according to Ersch and Gruber, in 1599.

See HAMMER-PURGSTALL, "Geschichte der Osmanischen Dichtkunst, bis auf unsere Zeit;" ERSCH und GRUBER, "Allgemeine Encyklopaedie."

Bâ'kĕr, (CHARLES,) an English philanthropist, became in 1829 superintendent of the Yorkshire institution for the deaf and dumb at Doncaster. He contributed valuable articles on the deaf, dumb, and blind, to the "Penny Cyclopædia" and other publications.

Baker, (DAVID or AUGUSTINE,) a learned English Benedictine monk, born near Monmouth in 1575, made a valuable collection of documents, which were afterwards used by Cressy in his "Church History," and by Reyner in his "Apostolatus Benedictinorum." Died in 1641.

See WOOD, "Athenæ Oxonienses."

Baker, (DAVID ERSKINE,) an English biographical writer of the eighteenth century, was a son of Henry

Baker, mentioned below. His "Companion to the Playhouse" forms a part of the work afterwards published with the title of "Biographia Dramatica." Died in 1774.

Bā′ḳẹr, (EDWARD DICKINSON,) COLONEL, a Senator of the United States, born in England in 1811, was brought to Pennsylvania in his childhood. He studied law in Illinois, served as colonel in the Mexican war, (1846–47,) was elected to Congress in 1848, and removed to California in 1852. Having gained distinction as an orator of the Republican party, he was elected a Senator of the United States for Oregon in 1860. He made an eloquent speech against disunion in the Senate, in answer to John C. Breckinridge. He raised a regiment in New York and Philadelphia, called the California regiment, (afterwards the Seventy-first Pennsylvania,) of which he became colonel, and commanded a brigade at Ball's Bluff, where he was killed in October, 1861.

Baker, (GEOFFROY,) an English monk and historian of the fourteenth century. He translated into Latin the history of the reigns of Edward I. and Edward II., written originally in French by Thomas de la More.

Baker, (GEORGE,) an English surgeon of the sixteenth century, wrote "On the Nature and Properties of Quicksilver," "The Book of Distillations," and other medical works. He was surgeon-in-ordinary to Queen Elizabeth.

Baker, (Sir GEORGE,) an English physician and medical writer, born in Devonshire in 1722. He was a Fellow of the Royal Society, of the Society of Antiquaries, and of the Royal College of Physicians, of which he was made president in 1797. He was appointed physician-in-ordinary to George III. Died in 1809.

Baker, (HENRY,) an English naturalist, born in London in 1698. About 1720 he opened a school for the instruction of the deaf and dumb, which was very successful; but his method was kept secret. He published a treatise entitled "The Microscope made Easy," (1743,) and "Employment for the Microscope," (1764.) He obtained in 1744 the Copley medal for his microscopic experiments on saline particles. He had married in 1729 the daughter of the eminent novelist Defoe. He was a Fellow of the Royal Society and of the Society of Antiquaries, and founded the Bakerian Lecture of the Royal Society. Died in 1774.

See "Biographia Britannica."

Baker, (HUMPHREY,) an English mathematician, published an arithmetical work entitled "The Well-Spring of Sciences," (1562,) which was esteemed at the time.

Baker, (JOHN,) an English admiral under the reign of Queen Anne and George I., distinguished himself in the expedition against the French which resulted in the capture of Gibraltar, (1704.) He was afterwards employed in several important missions. Died in 1716.

Baker, (Sir JOHN,) an English statesman under Henry VIII., Edward VI., and Mary, rose to be chancellor of the exchequer in 1545. As one of the privy council, he signalized himself by his refusal to sign the bill of Edward VI. excluding his sisters Mary and Elizabeth from the throne. Died in 1558.

Baker, (OSMAN C.,) an American bishop, born at Marlow, New Hampshire, in 1812. He became a professor in the Methodist Biblical Institute in 1847, and a bishop of the Methodist Episcopal Church in 1852.

Baker, (RICHARD,) an English mathematician, wrote a work entitled "An Idea of Arithmetic," (1655.)

Baker, (Sir RICHARD,) an English historian, born about 1568, was the author of a "Chronicle of the Kings of England," which had great popularity in its time. It was composed during the author's residence of more than twenty years in Fleet prison, where he had been confined for debt. Died in 1644.

See WOOD, "Athenæ Oxonienses."

Baker, (ROBERT,) an English physician of the latter part of the seventeenth century, was the author of a treatise on the bones, entitled "Cursus Osteologicus."

Baker, (Sir SAMUEL WHITE,) an English traveller, born in 1821. He explored in 1861–64 the region lying around the sources of the White Nile. He published accounts of his explorations, entitled "The Albert N'yanza, Great Basin of the Nile," (1866,) and "The Nile Tributaries of Abyssinia," (1867,) besides various other works. He was knighted in November, 1866.

Baker, (THOMAS,) an English mathematician, born in 1625, was the author of "The Geometrical Key; or the Gate of Equations unlocked," (1684.) Died in 1690

Baker, (THOMAS,) an English antiquary, born near Durham in 1656. He is principally known from his valuable manuscript collections on the history and antiquities of the University of Cambridge, which comprise in all thirty-nine volumes folio. He also rendered important assistance to Bishop Burnet, Dr. Conyers Middleton, and other contemporary writers, in their works. Died in 1740.

See MASTERS, "Memoirs of the Life of Thomas Baker," 1784.

Baker, (WILLIAM,) an English printer, born in 1742, wrote "Peregrinations of the Mind, by the Rationalist," (1770,) and "Remarks on the English Language."

Bake′well, (ROBERT,) an English agriculturist, born in Leicestershire about 1726. He is celebrated for the improvements he introduced into stock, the principal of which are the long-horned breed of cattle and the sheep called by his name. Died in 1795.

Bakhtishwa, bâk′tish′wâ, a Nestorian of the eighth century, was physician to Haroun-al-Raschid. Being unable to cure the caliph in his last illness, he was ordered by the latter to be put to death; but the death of the sovereign prevented the execution of the order.

Bakhuysen. See BACKHUYSEN.

Bâkî or Abd-el-Bâkî. See BÂKEE.

Bakker, bâk′ḳẹr, (GERBRAND, hĕR′brânt,) a Dutch physician, and professor of anatomy and physiology at Groningen, born at Enkhuisen in 1771. He wrote a treatise, in Dutch, "On Animal Magnetism," and other works in Latin. Died in 1828.

See LA FAILLE, "Hulde aan de Nagedachtenis van G. Bakker," 1828.

Bakker, (PETER Huizinga—hoi-zing′Hâ,) a Dutch poet, born about 1718. He wrote "Satires against the English," a poem on the inundation of 1740, etc. Died in 1801.

See WAGENAAR, "Notice sur Bakker."

Bakon. See BACON, (ROGER.)

Baksai, bŏk′shī′, (ABRAHAM,) a Hungarian jurist and historian of the sixteenth century, wrote, in Latin, a "Chronology of the Dukes and Kings of Hungary."

Balaam, bā-la-am or bā′lam, [Heb. בִּלְעָם,] a famous Oriental seer, lived about 1490 B.C. (See Numbers xxii., xxiii., and xxiv.)

Balâdori. See BELÂDORI.

Balæus. See BALE.

Balamio, bâ-lâ-mee′o, or Bal'amy, (FERDINAND,) physician to Pope Leo X., was a native of Sicily. He translated into Latin several works of Galen.

See VAN DER LINDEN, "De Scriptoribus Medicis."

Balanzac, de, dẹh bǎ′lôN′zǎk′, (FRANÇOIS de Bremond—dẹh brẹh-mòN′,) BARON, a French Calvinist and Protestant leader, who fought with distinction under Henry of Navarre, in the battles of Jarnac, Coutras, etc.

See SULLY, "Mémoires;" ANSELME, "Histoire des grands Officiers de la Couronne."

Balarama, (Bǎlǎrâmǎ,) commonly pronounced bŭl′-ạ-rä′mạ, [from bǎlǎ, "strength," and râmǎ, "beautiful," "pleasing," denoting perhaps a union of beauty and strength,] the name of a famous Hindoo warrior, the elder brother of Krishna, whom he assisted in his wars. He is regarded as an incarnation of Vishnu.

See MOOR's "Hindu Pantheon."

Balard, bǎ′lǎR′, (ANTOINE JÉRÔME,) a French chemist, born at Montpellier in 1802, discovered in 1826 the substance called bromium. He became a member of the Academy of Sciences in 1844, and in 1851 professor of chemistry in the College of France. He was a contributor to the "Annales de Chimie et de Physique."

Balard, (MARIE FRANÇOISE JACQUÈTE ALBY,) a French poetess, born at Castres in 1776; died in 1822.

See QUÉRARD, "La France Littéraire."

Ba-las′sạ, (or bŏl′ösh-shŏh,) (VALENTINE,) COUNT, a Hungarian nobleman of the sixteenth century, wrote Latin poems, and a number of popular lyrics in Hungarian. He was killed in 1594, at the storming of Gran.

See HORANYI, "Memoria Hungarorum."

Balassi, bâ-lâs′see, (MARIO,) a Florentine painter, born in 1604; died in 1667.

See LANZI, "History of Painting in Italy."

Balban-Geias-ed-Deen, or **Balban-Gheias-ed-dîn,** bâl'bån gi'ås ed-deen', King of Delhi, rose from an obscure position to be vizier of Nâsir-ed-Deen-Mahmood, whom he succeeded in 1265. Balban was a man of ability, and was celebrated for the splendour of his court, and for his generosity. His name is sometimes written BULBUN, according to the common Hindoo pronunciation. He died in 1286, and was succeeded by Kai-Kobâd.

See FERISHTA, "History of the Mahomedan Power in India," translated by General BRIGGS.

Balbastre, bâl'båstr', (CLAUDE LOUIS,) a celebrated French organist, born at Dijon in 1729, was a pupil and friend of Rameau. He was chiefly distinguished for his great skill as a performer. By substituting the piano for the harpsichord, he effected a revolution in this department of music. Died in 1799.

See FÉTIS, "Biographie Universelle des Musiciens."

Balbe, the French of BALBO, which see.

Balbi, bâl'bee, (ADRIANO,) an eminent geographer, born at Venice in 1782. Having visited Portugal in 1820, he obtained materials for his "Statistical Essay on the Kingdom of Portugal and Algarve compared with other States of Europe," (in French, 2 vols., 1822.) He brought out in Paris in 1826 the first volume of his "Ethnographical Atlas of the Globe, or Classification of Ancient and Modern Nations according to their Language," (in folio.) This work, in which he has drawn information from the writings of Humboldt, Champollion, Adelung, and other savants, is ranked among the most valuable productions of its kind. He also published a "Compendium of Geography," ("Abrégé de Géographie," 1 vol. 8vo,) which has been translated into the principal European languages and is esteemed one of the very best works on geographical science. His works are written in French. He resided many years in Paris, which he quitted in 1832. Died in 1848.

See "Nouvelle Biographie Générale;" BROCKHAUS, "Conversations-Lexikon."

Balbi, (DOMENICO,) an Italian dramatist of the seventeenth century, was a resident of Venice.

Balbi, (GASPARO,) a celebrated Venetian traveller and merchant, lived in the latter half of the sixteenth century. He visited India, where he spent nearly ten years, and published, in 1590, "Travels in the East Indies," an interesting and valuable work.

See GINGUENÉ, "Histoire Littéraire d'Italie."

Balbi, (GIOVANNI,) a Dominican monk of the thirteenth century, sometimes called JANUENSIS, was born at Genoa, in Italy. He was the author of a kind of encyclopædia, entitled "Catholicon," treating of theology, natural history, and other branches of knowledge. It was one of the first works printed by Faust and Schaeffer; the original edition is dated at Mentz, 1460.

See ALTAMURA, "Bibliotheca Ordinis Prædicatorum."

Balbi or **Balbo,** bâl'bo, (GIROLAMO,) a Venetian ecclesiastic and scholar, born in the fifteenth century, was a pupil of Pomponio Leto. He was successively professor of belles-lettres at the University of Paris, and of German law at Vienna. Having been made Bishop of Göritz, in Carinthia, he assisted at the coronation of Charles V., on which occasion he wrote a treatise "On the Coronation of Princes." Died in 1535.

See "Nouvelle Biographie Générale."

Balbi, [Lat. BAL'BUS,] (PIETRO,) an Italian prelate and writer of the fifteenth century, was a relative of Æneas Sylvius, afterwards Pope Pius II., under whom he became Bishop of Tropea. Died in 1479.

Balbi, de, deh bâl'be', LA COMTESSE, born in 1753, was a favourite or confidante of the Count of Provence before he became King Louis XVIII. She was discarded about 1792. Died in 1836.

Balbian, van, vån bâl'be-ân, (JUST,) a Dutch physician, born at Alost, was the author of a work which was translated into Italian under the title of "Il Specchio della Chimia," ("The Mirror of Chemistry.") Died in 1616.

See HOEFER, "Histoire de la Chimie."

Balbin. See BALBINUS.

Balbin, bâl-bèn', or **Balbino,** bâl-bee'no, (PAOLO,) an Italian philosopher and poet, became professor of medicine at Bologna about 1724.

Bal-bi'nus, (ALOYSIUS BOLESLAUS,) a Bohemian Jesuit and historian, born at Königgrätz about 1611. He wrote, in Latin, an "Epitome of Bohemian History," and "Historical Miscellanies of the Kingdom of Bohemia." Died in 1688 or 1689.

See STANISLAUS WYDRA, "Leben A. B. Balbinus," 1788.

Bal-bi'nus, [Fr. BALBIN, bâl'båN',] (DECIMUS CÆLIUS,) a Roman senator who, in conjunction with Maximus, was proclaimed emperor in opposition to Maximinus. The prætorian guards, dissatisfied with the new emperors elected by the senate, seized them in their palace, and, having put them to death, proclaimed Gordianus emperor, 238 A.D.

See JULIUS CAPITOLINUS, "Vita Balbini;" GIBBON, "Decline and Fall of the Roman Empire."

Balbis, bâl'bis or bâl'bèss, (GIAMBATTISTA,) an Italian botanist, born in Piedmont in 1765, succeeded Allioni as professor of botany at Turin in 1800, and in 1819 filled the same chair at Lyons. In conjunction with his friend Nocca, he published the "Flora Ticinensis." Died in 1831.

Balbis, (SILVIO,) an Italian *littérateur*, born at Caraglia, in Piedmont, in 1737, wrote, among other works, a poetical paraphrase on the prophet Nahum. Died in 1796.

Balbo, (CESARE,) an Italian writer and statesman, born at Turin in 1789, was appointed by Napoleon, in 1812, commissioner of the Illyrian provinces. In 1843 he published a work entitled "Hopes of Italy," ("Speranze d'Italia,") which created a great sensation and obtained extensive popularity. In 1848 he was an earnest advocate of the moderate party and the administration of D'Azeglio, and contributed a number of able articles to the Turin journal "Il Risorgimento." His "History of Italy from the Beginning till 1814," published in 1849, is a work of superior merit. Balbo also translated from the German, into Italian, Leo's "Exposition of the Constitutions of the Lombard States." Died in 1853.

See BROCKHAUS, "Conversations-Lexikon."

Balbo, (GIROLAMO.) See BALBI.

Balbo, [Fr. BALBE, bâlb,] (PROSPERO,) COUNT OF, a Sardinian diplomatist and writer, born in 1762, was ambassador to the French republic in 1796. He became successively rector of the University of Turin, minister of the interior, and president of the Academy of Sciences. Died in 1837.

See L. CIBRARIO, "Notizie biografiche del Conte P. Balbo," 1837.

Balboa, bâl-bo'â, (MIGUEL Cavello—kâ-vêl'yo,) a Spanish missionary who visited South America about 1566 and collected materials for a "History of Peru," which was published in French, (Paris, 1840.)

Balboa, de, (Don FRANCISCO,) a native of Italy, who became counsellor of the Spanish Inquisition, lived in the seventeenth century. He wrote, in Latin, a treatise "On the Law of Monarchy," (1630.)

Balboa, de, (VASCO NUÑEZ,) a celebrated Spanish navigator and discoverer, born at Xeres de los Caballeros, in Estremadura, about 1475. Having accompanied Bastidas in his expedition to the West Indies in 1501, he joined, while at Hayti, in 1510 the party of Enciso, a lieutenant of the navigators Ojeda and Nicuesa, both then absent. They founded on the Isthmus of Panama the town of Santa Maria de la Antigua; but dissensions soon after breaking out between them, the partisans of Balboa prevailed, and he was chosen leader of the expedition. Having obtained reinforcements from Columbus at Hispaniola, he proceeded to explore the Isthmus of Darien, and on the 29th of September, 1513, discovered from the summit of a mountain the vast expanse of the Pacific Ocean. Kneeling, he returned thanks to God for permitting him to make this great discovery, and, having erected a cross upon the spot, he descended to the shore, and, standing in the water, took possession of the sea and the adjacent countries in the name of the sovereigns of Castile. Meanwhile, his rival Enciso had traduced him to the Spanish government, and Pedrarias Davila was sent to supersede and try him for having usurped Enciso's command. Balboa was at length appointed deputy under Pedrarias, but eventually fell a victim to the jealousy and ill will of the latter, who caused him to be executed on a charge of treasonable designs, (1517.) In his intercourse with the Indians. Balboa displayed

ā, ē, ī, ō, ū, ȳ, *long;* å, ė, ȯ, same, less prolonged; ă, ĕ, ĭ, ŏ, ŭ, ў, *short;* a, ẹ, ị, ọ, *obscure;* får, fåll, fåt; mêt; nŏt; gōod; mōōn.

great humanity and prudence, and, in the words of a contemporary writer, "was the best lance and the best head that ever protected a camp in a land of idolatrous savages."

See W. IRVING, "Voyages and Discoveries of the Companions of Columbus;" M. J. QUINTANA, "Vidas de Españoles celebres;" "Nouvelle Biographie Générale."

Balbuena, de, då bâl-bwā′nå, (BERNARDO,) a Spanish poet and ecclesiastic, born at Val-de-Peñas in 1568, was appointed Bishop of Porto Rico, in the West Indies, in 1620. He was the author of a pastoral romance entitled "The Age of Gold," ("El Siglo de Oro,") which was republished by the Spanish Academy, (1821,) "El Bernardo," an epic poem, and a number of lyrics. Died at Porto Rico in 1627.

See TICKNOR, "History of Spanish Literature."

Bal′bus, (L. CORNELIUS,) surnamed MA′JOR, a native of Gades, lived in the first century B.C., served under Metellus, Memmius, and Pompey, and in 61 B.C. accompanied Cæsar to Spain. In the contest between Pompey and Cæsar he was an adherent and intimate friend of the latter, and was intrusted by him with the management of his affairs at Rome. After Cæsar's death, Balbus attached himself to Octavius, through whose influence he was made consul in 40 B.C., being the first one not born a Roman citizen who had received that honour. He wrote a diary (not extant) of the prominent events of his own and Cæsar's life.

Balbus, (L. CORNELIUS,) called MI′NOR, nephew of the preceding, born at Gades, was quæstor to Asinius Pollio in Spain in 43 B.C. After acquiring a large fortune by oppression and fraud, he went to Africa, where he subsequently became proconsul. For his victory over the Garamantes, a triumph was decreed him at Rome. He built a theatre at Rome supported by pillars of onyx.

Ballus, (L. LUCILIUS,) a Roman jurist, supposed to have been a brother of the Stoic philosopher Q. Lucilius Balbus. He was a pupil of Mucius Scævola.

Balbus, (L. OCTAVIUS,) an eminent Roman lawyer, who, being informed of his proscription by the triumvirs Augustus, Antony, and Lepidus, effected his escape, but, on hearing that his son's life was in danger, returned to his house, where he was slain by the soldiers.

Balbus, (M. ATIUS,) a Roman, who became prætor in 62 B.C., and governor of Sardinia. He married the sister of Julius Cæsar, and their daughter Atia was the mother of Octavius.

Balbus, (Q. LUCILIUS,) a Stoic philosopher, and pupil of Panætius, highly commended by Cicero, who makes him one of the interlocutors in his Dialogue "On the Nature of the Gods."

Balbus, (SP. THORIUS,) a Roman orator, became tribune about 111 B.C. He introduced an agrarian law, some fragments of which still remain on bronze tablets.

Balbus, (T. AMPIUS,) a tribune in 63 B.C., and again in 59, was a partisan of Pompey during the civil war. He was subsequently banished by Cæsar, but was afterwards pardoned through the intercession of Cicero.

Balbus surnamed MEN′SOR, (the "Measurer,") a Roman engineer, lived in the reign of Augustus, and compiled and superintended a register or census of the Roman Empire.

Băl′can-quăl, (WALTER,) a Scottish prelate in the time of James I. of England, became Bishop of Durham. He wrote "Letters on the Synod of Dort," and "Declaration of Charles I. concerning the Late Tumults in Scotland." Died in 1642.

Băl-căr′res or **Bal-căr′ras,** (COLIN,) EARL OF, a Scottish writer, born in 1649, published a "Brief Account of the Affairs of Scotland relating to the Revolution of 1688," (1714.) Died in 1722.

See MACAULAY'S "History of England," vol. iii.

Bâl′chen, (Sir JOHN,) an English admiral, born in 1669, served with distinction in the Spanish wars of 1707 and 1739, and was sent in 1744 to the assistance of Sir Charles Hardy, then blockaded in the Tagus by the French. On his return, he perished by shipwreck off the coast of Jersey, together with nearly twelve hundred men.

See "Biographia Britannica."

Baldacchini, bâl-dåk-kee′nee, (FILIPPO,) an Italian poet, born at Cortona, lived in the early part of the sixteenth century. He was patronized by Leo X., and held the offices of prothonotary and apostolic referendary at Rome.

See MAZZUCHELLI, "Scrittori d'Italia."

Baldassari, bâl-dås-så′ree, (GIUSEPPE,) an Italian naturalist and physician, born about 1705, was a resident of Sienna. He made several useful discoveries in chemistry, and wrote treatises on the mineral waters of Tuscany.

See MAZZUCHELLI, "Scrittori d'Italia."

Baldasseroni, bâl-dås-så-ro′nee, (GIOVANNI,) an Italian statesman, born at Leghorn in 1790, became in 1847 minister of finance of Tuscany. As president of the new conservative cabinet, (1849,) he advocated the laws restraining the liberty of the press.

Baldasseroni, (POMPEO,) an Italian jurist, born at Leghorn about 1750. He wrote, among other works, "Laws and Customs of Exchange," (3 vols., 4th edition, 1805,) which has a high reputation. Died in 1807.

Baldassini, bâl-dås-see′nee, (GIROLAMO,) an Italian writer, born at Jesi about 1720, was the author of "Historical Memoirs of the City of Jesi." Died in 1780.

Baldaya, bâl-då′yå or bâl-dī′å, (ALFONSO GONÇALES,) a Portuguese explorer in the service of the Infant Don Henry, visited the western coast of Africa in 1434. He penetrated thirty leagues beyond Cape Bojador, and the following year arrived at the port since named Puerto da Cavallero.

See JOÃO DE BARROS, "Asia Portugueza, Decada Primeira."

Balde, bâl′deh, (JAKOB,) a learned Jesuit, and one of the best Latin poets of modern times, born at Ensisheim, in Alsace, in 1603. He became court chaplain to the Prince-Elector of Bavaria. His satires, odes, elegies, idyls, and lyrics are highly commended by Schlegel and Herder, and a number of his songs have been translated by the latter. Died in 1668.

See F. C. F. CLESCA, "Balde's Leben und Schriften," 1842.

Balde, bâl′deh, [Lat. BALDÆ′US,] (PHILIP,) a Dutch missionary of the seventeenth century, resided ten years in Ceylon. He wrote, in Dutch, a "Description of the Island of Ceylon, Malabar, and Coromandel," (1672.)

See MORÉRI, "Dictionnaire Historique."

Baldelli, bâl-dêl′lee, (FRANCESCO,) an Italian scholar and Latin poet, lived in the latter half of the sixteenth century, was a native of Tortona. He made translations from Philostratus, Eusebius, Dio Cassius, and other classics.

Baldelli, (GIAMBATTISTA,) an Italian *littérateur*, born at Cortona in 1766, published editions of Macchiavelli, Boccaccio, and Marco Polo, and wrote an "Essay on Petrarch and his Works." Died in 1831.

See TIPALDO, "Biografia degli Italiani illustri."

Balder, bâl′der, or **Baldur,** bâl′dûr, [from *balldr,* "strong," "brave," "good,"*] in the Norse mythology, the second son of Odin, often designated as "Balder the Good," is supposed to represent the brightness of the summer sun. He is very beautiful, and makes all things bright and cheerful: hence he has been called the Apollo of the North. He is the comforter of the unfortunate, and is beloved by all. His dwelling-place is Breidablik, (*i.e.* "widely shining,") where nothing impure can enter. It is related that Balder dreamed one night that his life was in imminent peril. When he told his dream, the gods were exceedingly distressed, and his mother Frigga exacted an oath from all things—from fire, water, iron, stones, from beasts and birds and venomous reptiles—that they would not in any way injure her beloved Balder. But from the mistletoe she exacted no oath, because it seemed so feeble and insignificant that it could not possibly be a source of danger. After she had thus bound all nature, as she supposed, to spare her favourite son, the gods were accustomed, by way of sport, to have Balder stand forth while they shot at him with their bows and threw stones at him, to all which assaults he was completely invulnerable. But when Loki, the god of evil, discovered that the mistletoe had

* Grimm supposes that, like the Lithuanian *baltas,* the name originally signified both "white" and "good."

€ as *k;* ç as *s;* g̃ *hard;* ġ as *j;* G, H, K, *guttural;* N, *nasal;* R, *trilled;* s̃ as *z;* ⱨh as in *this.* (☞See Explanations, p. 23.)

taken no oath not to injure Balder, he procured the plant, and came to the assembly of the gods. There he found the blind god Hoder standing apart by himself. Loki asked him why he did not throw something at Balder as well as the rest. "Because I am blind," said he, "and have nothing to throw." "Come," said the tempter, "do like the rest; show honour to Balder by casting this trifle at him, and I will direct your hand." Hoder did as he was told, and Balder, pierced through by the fatal mistletoe, fell dead. When they saw what had been done, all the gods were struck speechless, and became paralyzed with astonishment and grief. But after a time Hermod, at Frigga's desire, visited the realm of death, riding Odin's horse Sleipnir. Having reached the world of shades, he besought Hela to release Balder, so greatly beloved by all, that he might return to Asgard, (the habitation of the gods.) Hela answered that if Balder was indeed so universally beloved he would be universally lamented; and if it came to pass that everything wept for him, then he should return to the gods, but if anything whatever failed to weep, he must remain in the realm of death. Thereupon the Æsir sent messengers over all the world, entreating all things to weep for Balder. And all did so—everything animate and inanimate —until the messengers came to a cavern where dwelt a giant hag named Thok, (or Thökt.) She answered their request with jeers:

"Is Balder dead? and do ye come for tears?
Thok with dry eyes will weep o'er Balder's pyre.
Weep him all other things, if weep they will—
I weep him not: let Hela keep her prey."*

It afterwards appeared that it was no other than Loki himself (see LOKI) who had thus assumed the form of the hag Thok, in order to prevent Balder's restoration to life. The explanations usually given of the myth of Balder are not very satisfactory.

See THORPE'S "Northern Mythology," vol. i., particularly pp. 185-6; KEYSER'S "Religion of the Northmen," pp. 144-5; MALLET'S "Northern Antiquities," vol. ii., Fables xii., xxviii., and xxix.; PETERSEN'S "Nordisk Mythologi."

Balderic, baul'der-ik, or **Baudry,** bō'dre, [Fr. pron. bō'dRE'; Lat. BALDERI'CUS,] a French ecclesiastic, born at Meun-sur-Loire about 1050, was created Bishop of Dol in 1107. Among his works are a "Life of Robert d'Arbrissel," an enlargement of "Theudebode's History of the First Crusade," and a Latin poem on the Conquest of England by the Normans. Died in 1130.

See "Histoire Littéraire de la France," tome viii.

Balderic or **Balderi'cus,** surnamed RU'BEUS, or THE RED, a French chronicler of the eleventh century, was Bishop of Noyon and Tournay. His principal work is a "Chronicle of Cambray and Arras, from the Reign of Clovis to 1090." Died in 1097.

Baldeschi. See BALDUS, (ANGELO.)

Baldi, bâl'dee, [Lat. BAL'DUS,] a Florentine physician, and professor of medicine in the College di Sapienza at Rome, was employed by Popes Urban VIII. and Innocent X. Died in 1645.

Baldi, (BERNARDINO,) called also **Baldi d'Urbino** —dooR-bee'no, [in French, BALDI D'URBIN—dük'bȧn',] abbot of Guastalla, an Italian scholar, celebrated for profound and varied learning, born at Urbino in 1553. He studied mathematics and classical literature at Padua, where Commandino was one of his teachers. Among his works, which amount to nearly one hundred, we may mention a "History of Calvinism," "Life of Federigo Commandino," a number of eclogues, sonnets, and other poems, and a "Chronicle of Mathematicians." He translated the "Automata" of Hero, and wrote valuable commentaries on Vitruvius and the "Mechanics" of Aristotle, (1621.) He also prepared vocabularies of the Turkish and Hungarian languages, and translated into Italian the Geography of Edrisi. Died at Urbino in 1617.

See BAFFO, "Vita di Bernardino Baldi;" ISIDORO GRASSI, "Baldus redivivus seu B. Baldi Vita," Parma, 1717; IRENEO AFFÒ, "Vita di Monsignor B. Baldi d'Urbino," 1783.

Baldi, (CAMILLO,) an Italian philosophical writer, born at Bologna about 1547, was professor of logic in his native city. Died in 1634.

Baldi, (GIUSEPPE,) a Florentine physician of the seventeenth century, was the author of a valuable work on mushrooms.

Baldi, (LAZARRO,) an Italian painter, born at Pistoia about 1623, was a pupil of Pietro da Cortona. Among his master-pieces are the "Repose in Egypt," and an "Annunciation." Died in 1703.

See LANZI, "History of Painting in Italy."

Baldi, (VALENTINO,) a painter of the Florentine school, born at Pistoia in 1744; died in 1816.

Baldi de Ubaldis, bâl'dee dȧ ஂo-bâl'dèss, (PIETRO,) an Italian jurist and legal writer of the fourteenth century, was a native of Perugia, where he became professor of law. Died in 1400.

See MORÉRI, "Dictionnaire Historique."

Baldi d'Urbin. See BALDI, (BERNARDINO.)

Baldinger, bâl'ding-er, (ERNST GOTTFRIED,) an eminent German physician, born near Erfurt in 1738. He became professor of medicine at Göttingen in 1773. Among his pupils were Blumenbach and Akermann. He published, besides many other medical and botanical works, a treatise "On the Diseases of Soldiers," (1763.) Died at Marburg in 1804.

See G. F. CREUZER, "Memoria E. G. Baldingeri," 1804.

Baldini, bâl-dee'nee, (BACCIO, bât'cho,) a Florentine engraver of the fifteenth century, was originally a goldsmith. He executed, among other prints, a number of illustrations for Dante. He was the contemporary, and is said to have been the pupil, of Finiguerra.

See LE BLANC, "Manuel de l'Amateur d'Estampes."

Baldini, (BACCIO,) professor of medicine at Pisa, and first physician to Cosimo I., Grand Duke of Tuscany, was director of the Laurentian Library. He wrote a "Life of Cosimo I.," (1578,) and other works. Died in 1585.

Baldini, (BERNARDINO,) an Italian mathematician and physician, born near Lake Maggiore about 1515; died in 1600.

Baldini, (FRA TIBURZIO,) an Italian painter of Bologna, is supposed to have lived about 1610.

Baldini, (GIOVANNI,) a Florentine painter, lived about 1500, and was the master of Garofalo.

Baldini, (GIOVANNI FRANCESCO,) an Italian naturalist and priest, born at Brescia in 1677; died in 1765.

Baldinucci, bâl-de-noot'chee, (FILIPPO,) an Italian writer on art, born at Florence about 1624, was patronized by the Grand Duke Cosimo III. He published an important work entitled "Notices of the Professors of Design (Painters) from Cimabue, 1260–1670," ("Notizie de' Professori del Disegno," etc., 6 vols. 4to, 1681–88, 4th edition, 14 vols., 1808,) which is highly esteemed. Died in 1696.

See MAZZUCHELLI, "Scrittori d'Italia."

Baldit, bâl'de', (MICHEL,) a French physician of the seventeenth century, wrote "Wonders of the Waters of Bagnols," (1651,) and other works.

Bâl'dǫck or **Bau'dǎke, de,** (RALPH,) an English prelate and statesman of the thirteenth century, was created Bishop of London in 1304. He was lord chancellor of England for a short time under Edward I. He is said to have written a "History of England," which has been lost. Died in 1314.

See "Biographia Britannica."

Baldovinetti, bâl-do-ve-net'tee, or **Balduinetti,** bâl-doo-e-nêt'tee, (ALESSIO,) a Florentine painter and worker in mosaics, born in 1424, was a pupil of Uccello, and the teacher of Domenico Ghirlandaio. Died in 1499.

See VASARI, "Lives of the Painters."

Baldovini, bâl-do-vee'nee, (FRANCESCO,) a Florentine poet, born in 1635, was the author of a comic idyl entitled "The Lament of Cecco da Varlungo," (1694,) which is very popular in Italy. Died in 1716.

See MAZZUCHELLI, "Scrittori d'Italia;" DOMENICO MARIA MANNI, "Vita del priore dottore F. Baldovini," 1769.

Baldovino. See BALDWIN.

Baldrighi, bâl-dRee'ġee, (GIUSEPPE,) a painter of the school of Parma, born at Pavia about 1722; died in 1802.

Balducci, bâl-doot'chee, (FRANCESCO,) a Sicilian poet of the seventeenth century, was a native of Palermo. His lyrics in the Sicilian dialect are highly esteemed, and

* See the fine poem by Matthew Arnold, entitled "Balder Dead," which is itself almost an epitome of Northern mythology.

he is regarded by some critics as one of the best Anacreontic poets of Italy. Died at Rome in 1642.

See MAZZUCHELLI, "Scrittori d'Italia."

Balducci, (GIOVANNI,) an Italian sculptor and architect, born at Pisa in the latter part of the thirteenth century. Among his master-pieces is the sculptured shrine of Saint Peter in the church of Saint Eustorgio at Milan. He was living in 1347.

See LANZI, "History of Painting in Italy."

Balducci, (GIOVANNI,) surnamed COSCI, an Italian painter of the sixteenth century, was a native of Florence. Among his best works is "The Finding of the Cross," in the church of La Crocetta. He painted frescos in Florence, Rome, and Pistoia. Died at Naples in 1600.

See LANZI, "History of Painting in Italy."

Balduin. See BALDWIN, (THOMAS.)

Balduin, bâl′doo-een, (CHRISTIAN ADOLF,) a German savant, born near Meissen in 1632, was the author of a work entitled "Hermes Curiosus," and other chemical treatises. Died in 1682.

Balduin, (FRIEDRICH,) a German Lutheran writer, born at Dresden in 1575, was professor of theology at Prague. Died in 1627.

See J. G. NEUMANN, "Programma de Vita F. Balduini," 1709.

Balduinus. See BALDWIN and BAUDOUIN.

Baldung, bâl′doong, (HANS,) sometimes called **Grün,** an eminent German painter and engraver, born at Gmünd, in Suabia, about 1470. His works include historical pictures and portraits; among the latter may be named those of Maximilian I. and Charles V. His "Crucifixion," in the cathedral of Freiburg, is ranked among his master-pieces. He was a friend of Albert Dürer, to whom he is considered nearly equal. He executed a number of wood-cuts and copper-plates. Died about 1550.

Baldus, the Latin of BALDI, which see.

Bal′dus or **Baldeschi,** bâl-dĕs′kee, (ANGELO,) sometimes called **Angelus Baldus de Ubaldis,** an eminent Italian jurist, born at Perugia about 1325, was professor of law successively at Pisa, Bologna, Florence, and Padua. He wrote "Commentaries on the Old and the New Digests," "Lectures on the Three Books of Decretals," and other legal works of great merit. Died in 1400.

See SAVIGNY, "Geschichte des Römischen Rechts im Mittelalter."

Baldwin, bauld′win, [Fr. BAUDOUIN, bōd′wâN′, or BALDUIN, bâl′dwâN′; Lat. BALDUI′NUS; It. BALDOVINO, bâl-do-vee′no,] first Count of Flanders, surnamed BRAS DE FER, ("Iron Arm,") acquired his title about 860 A.D. Having married Judith, daughter of Charles the Bald, King of France, against the will of the latter, he was excommunicated by the pope, Nicholas I., at the instigation of Charles. He afterwards obtained absolution from the pope, and was reconciled to the king, who made Flanders a county. Died in 877.

See LE BROUSSART, "Mémoires sur les Baudouin, Comtes de Flandre," Brussels, 1820.

Baldwin II., Count of Flanders, a son of the preceding, was engaged in wars against Charles the Simple, King of France, and Eudes, Count of Paris. He married Alfrith, daughter of Alfred the Great of England. Died in 918.

Baldwin III., Count of Flanders, grandson of the preceding, began to reign in 958. He died about 1034.

Baldwin IV., Count of Flanders, surnamed THE BEARDED, succeeded his father, Baldwin III. He increased his dominions by the conquest of Valenciennes, and established commercial fairs in the Flemish cities. Died in 1036.

Baldwin V., Count of Flanders, surnamed OF LILLE, and sometimes LE DÉBONNAIRE, (lĕh dâ′bo′nêR′,) was the son of Baldwin IV. He obtained by conquest several considerable districts in Germany, which he retained as a fief of the empire. On the death of Henry I. of France, Count Baldwin became guardian to his son Philip, and regent of the kingdom. He gave his daughter Matilda in marriage to William of Normandy, whom he accompanied in the invasion of England. Died in 1067.

Baldwin VI., Count of Flanders, was the son of Baldwin V., and was surnamed THE GOOD, and also OF MONS. He assigned the county of Flanders to Arnoul, his eldest son, and Hainault to Baldwin, the second son. Died in 1070.

Baldwin VII., Count of Flanders, surnamed HAPKIN, from a kind of axe used in the execution of outlaws in his reign. He was an ally of Louis le Gros of France against Henry I. of England. Died in 1119.

Baldwin VIII., Count of Flanders and Hainault, was the enemy of Philip Augustus of France until 1192, when he was reconciled and did homage to him. The counties of Flanders and Hainault were united in his reign. Died in 1195.

See LE BROUSSART, "Mémoires sur les Baudouin, Comtes de Flandre."

Baldwin IX., [Gr. Βαλδονῖνος; Lat. BALDUI′NUS,] son of the preceding, Count of Flanders, was born in 1171. He joined the fourth crusade in 1200, and on arriving at Zara with a fleet commanded by Dandolo was solicited by Alexius, son of the deposed emperor Isaac, to aid in restoring his father to the throne. He promised them in return to acknowledge the supremacy of the pope and to grant them pecuniary assistance. The crusaders succeeded in defeating the usurper; but, the people being unwilling to perform the promises of Alexius, hostilities broke out between them, and after a siege of three months Constantinople was taken in 1204, and Baldwin elected emperor. He was subsequently defeated and made prisoner by the Bulgarians in 1205. He died in 1206, and was succeeded by his brother Henry.

See LE BEAU, "Histoire du Bas-Empire;" A. CAHOUR, "Baudouin de Constantinople," 1850; J. J. DE SMET, "Mémoire historique sur Baudouin IX," 1846.

Baldwin II., Emperor of Constantinople, born in 1217, ascended the throne in 1228. In 1261 his capital was taken by Michael Palæologus, and Baldwin effected his escape to Italy, where he died. He was a nephew of Baldwin I.

Baldwin I., [Fr. BAUDOUIN, bōd′wâN′; It. BALDOVINO, bâl-do-vee′no,] King of Jerusalem, and a brother of the celebrated Godfrey of Bouillon, whom he accompanied in 1096 on the first crusade. He fought with distinguished bravery against the infidels, and, being afterwards invited by the Christian inhabitants of Edessa to become their ruler, he assumed the title of Count of Edessa. On the death of his brother Godfrey in 1100 he succeeded him as King of Jerusalem. He gained important victories over the Saracens, and captured Sidon, Ascalon, Acre, and other cities. He died in 1118. Tasso, in his "Jerusalem Delivered," has finely contrasted the character of Baldwin with that of Godfrey, and represents the former as actuated wholly by ambitious motives.

See GIBBON, "Decline and Fall of the Roman Empire;" LE BEAU, "Histoire du Bas-Empire."

Baldwin II., surnamed DU BOURG, (dü booR,) a cousin of the preceding, whom he succeeded in 1118. He was engaged in numerous wars against the Arabs and Saracens. During his reign the military orders of Saint John and the Templars were established for the defence of the Holy Land. He died in 1131, leaving the crown to his son-in-law, Foulques of Anjou.

See ORDERICUS VITALIS, "Historia."

Baldwin III., born in 1130, was the son of Foulques of Anjou, whom he succeeded in 1142. His country was invaded in 1145 by Zenghi, Sultan of Aleppo, who took possession of Edessa. Baldwin fought with varying success against the celebrated Noor-ed-Deen, (Noureddin,) son of Zenghi. He died in 1163, and was succeeded by his brother, Amalric or Amaury.

Baldwin IV., King of Jerusalem, surnamed THE LEPER, born in 1160, was the son of Amaury, whom he succeeded in 1174. In 1182 he gained a signal victory over the famous Saladin near Tiberias, but was afterwards several times defeated by him. He died in 1186, and was succeeded by his nephew, Baldwin V., who died in childhood about 1187.

See LE BEAU, "Histoire du Bas-Empire."

Bâld′win, (THOMAS,) surnamed DEVO′NIUS, (i.e. "of Devonshire,") an English prelate, born at Exeter, Devonshire, about 1150, became Bishop of Worcester and afterwards Archbishop of Canterbury, (1184.) Having crowned Richard I. in 1189, he accompanied him the following year to the Holy Land, but died at Acre soon after his arrival.

See W. F. HOOK, "Lives of the Archbishops of Canterbury," vol. ii. chap. ix.

Bàld′win, (ABRAHAM,) an American statesman, born in Connecticut in 1754. Having removed to Savannah, Georgia, he was elected a delegate to Congress in 1786, and was a member of the convention which formed the Constitution of the United States. He was elected a Senator of the United States by the legislature of Georgia in 1799. He was a brother-in-law of Joel Barlow. Died in 1807.

Baldwin, (HENRY,) an American jurist, born at New Haven, Connecticut, in 1779. He removed to Pennsylvania, where he was several times elected to Congress. He was appointed judge of the supreme court of the United States in 1830. Died in 1844.

Baldwin, (ROGER SHERMAN,) a United States Senator, born in New Haven, Connecticut, in 1793. He graduated at Yale in 1811. In 1844 he was elected by the Whig party Governor of the State, and was re-elected in 1845. From 1847 to 1851 he was a United States Senator. In 1841 Governor Baldwin distinguished himself as associate counsel with John Quincy Adams in the famous African Amistad trial before the supreme court of the United States. Died in 1863.

Baldwin, (THOMAS,) D.D., an eminent Baptist divine, born in Norwich, Connecticut, in 1753. He became pastor of the Second Baptist Church in Boston in 1790. He took an important part in establishing Waterville College, Maine, also Columbia College, in the District of Columbia. Dr. Baldwin was author of a work in defence of the religious views of the Baptists, and of numerous published sermons. Died in 1825.

Baldwin, (WILLIAM,) an English divine and moralist, published a "Treatise of Moral Philosophy," (1549,) and was one of the authors or editors of a "Mirror for Magistrates." Died about 1564.

Bàle, [Lat. BALÆ′US,] (JOHN,) a learned prelate and biographical writer, born in Suffolk in 1495. Being persecuted on account of his conversion to Protestantism, he repaired to Holland, where he remained till the accession of Edward VI. After his return he was created in 1552 Bishop of Ossory in Ireland. He was again obliged to leave England during the reign of Mary, and resided in Switzerland until the accession of Elizabeth. His most important work is entitled "Catalogue of the Illustrious Writers of Great Britain," (in Latin.) He also wrote a number of dramatic pieces on religious subjects, and several theological treatises. His severe attacks on the Catholics have caused his writings to be prohibited by that church. Died in 1563.

See TANNER, "Bibliotheca Britannico-Hibernica;" PITSEUS, "De Scriptoribus Angliæ."

Bale, (ROBERT,) a Catholic theologian of the fifteenth century, was prior of the Carmelites at Norwich. Died in 1503.

Baléchou, bȧ′là′shoo′, (JEAN JOSEPH NICOLAS,) a celebrated French engraver, born at Arles in 1715. His full-length portrait of Augustus, King of Poland, is esteemed a master-piece of its kind. Among his other works are "The Calm" and "The Tempest," after Vernet, and "Saint Genevieve," after Vanloo. Died in 1765.

See HEINECKEN, "Dictionnaire des Artistes."

Balen, van, vȧn bä′lẹn, or Ballen, bȧl′lẹn, (HENDRIK,) an eminent Flemish painter, born at Antwerp in 1560, was a pupil of Adam van Oort, and excelled both in design and colouring. His "Judgment of Paris," "Saint John in the Wilderness," and "Festival of the Gods," are among his master-pieces. He numbered among his scholars Van Dyck and Snyders. Died in 1632.

His son JOHN, born in 1611, was a painter. Died after 1650.

See DESCAMPS, "Vies des Peintres Flamands."

Bales, bȧlz, (PETER,) a celebrated English calligrapher, born in London in 1547. It is related by Evelyn that he wrote within the circle of a penny the Lord's Prayer, the Decalogue, the Creed, two Latin prayers, his own name, motto, and date. Died in 1610.

See "Biographia Britannica."

Balestra, bȧ-lĕs′trȧ, (ANTONIO,) an eminent Italian painter, born at Verona in 1666, was a pupil of Carlo Maratta. His "Defeat of the Giants" gained a prize from the Academy of Saint Luke. His "Saint Theresa"

and "Descent from the Cross" are also esteemed master-pieces. Died in 1740.

See LANZI, "History of Painting in Italy."

Baley. See BAILEY, (WALTER.)

Balfe, bȧlf, (MICHAEL WILLIAM,) an eminent musician and composer, born in Dublin, Ireland, in 1808. He performed on the violin in his youth, and went to Italy about 1825, after which he produced many operas, and became distinguished as a singer. Among his operas are "Joan of Arc," "The Daughter of Saint Mark," "The Bohemian Girl," which had a great success, "The Maid of Honour," and "The Rose of Castile."

See "Nouvelle Biographie Générale."

Balfour, bȧl′foor or bȧl′fur, (ALEXANDER,) a Scottish *littérateur*, born in Forfarshire in 1767, was the author of novels entitled "Campbell, or the Scottish Probationer," and "The Foundling of Glenthorn," (1823.) He also published a volume of poems, and contributed to the "Edinburgh Review." Died in 1829.

See CHAMBERS, "Biographical Dictionary of Eminent Scotsmen."

Balfour, (ANDREW,) a Scottish naturalist of the seventeenth century, founded at Edinburgh a botanical garden and museum. The "Balfouria," a genus of Australian plants, was named in his honour.

Balfour, (FRANCIS,) a Scottish physician of the eighteenth century, was a native of Edinburgh. He resided many years in Calcutta, and published a treatise "On the Influence of the Moon in Fevers," (1784,) and several works on the diseases of hot climates.

Balfour, (Sir JAMES,) a Scottish courtier and intriguer of the sixteenth century. He became a lord of session about 1563, and was implicated in the conspiracy against Darnley. In 1567 he was appointed by Queen Mary captain of Edinburgh Castle, which he afterwards delivered to her enemies. He became in 1568 a partisan of Regent Murray, who promoted him to the office of lord president of the court of session ; but he soon deserted to the party of Queen Mary, and was attainted by Parliament in 1571. He betrayed all parties in turn, and was accessory to the destruction of the regent Morton, who was executed for the murder of Darnley in 1581. Died in 1583.

See KNOX, "History of the Reformation;" CHAMBERS, "Biographical Dictionary of Eminent Scotsmen;" BURTON, "History of Scotland."

Balfour, (Sir JAMES,) a Scottish antiquary and annalist. He wrote some treatises on heraldry, and a brief history of the kings of Scotland, which remained in manuscript until 1824. Died in 1657.

See CHAMBERS, "Biographical Dictionary of Eminent Scotsmen."

Balfour, (JOHN HUTTON,) F.R.S., an eminent British botanist and physician, was born in Edinburgh in 1808, and succeeded Dr. Hooker as professor of botany at Glasgow about 1840. He published a "Manual of Botany," (1849,) and a valuable "Class-Book of Botany," (1852.) He also wrote the articles on Botany for the "Encyclopædia Britannica," (8th edition.) In 1845 he succeeded Professor Graham in the chair of botany and medicine at Edinburgh.

Balfour OF PILRIG, (JAMES,) a Scottish jurist and philosophical writer, born near Edinburgh about 1705, was appointed in 1754 professor of moral philosophy in that city. He was the author of "Philosophical Essays," (1768,) and two treatises against the doctrine of Hume, written, however, with such kindness and candour as to gain for him the friendship of that writer. Died in 1795.

Balfour, (ROBERT,) a learned Scottish philosopher of the seventeenth century, was profoundly versed in mathematics and ancient languages. He wrote commentaries on Aristotle, and edited the works of Cleomedes.

See CHAMBERS, "Biographical Dictionary of Eminent Scotsmen."

Balfour, (WALTER,) a prominent Universalist minister, born in Stirlingshire, Scotland, in 1776, emigrated to Massachusetts, where he died in 1852.

Balguy, baul′ge, (?) (JOHN,) an English divine, born at Sheffield in 1686, became in 1729 vicar of Northallerton, in Yorkshire. He was the author of a "Brief Inquiry concerning the Moral Perfections of the Deity," (1730,) "Letter to a Deist concerning the Beauty and Excellence of Moral Virtue," and other similar works. Died in 1748.

See "Biographia Britannica."

ā, ē, ī, ō, ū, ȳ, *long;* ȧ, ė, ȯ, same, less prolonged; ă, ĕ, ĭ, ŏ, ŭ, y̆, *short;* ạ, ẹ, ị, ọ, *obscure;* fär, fȧll, fȧt; mĕt; nŏt; gōōd; mōōn;

Balguy, (THOMAS,) an English divine, son of the preceding, born in 1716, became vicar of Alton, in Hampshire, in 1771. He published "Discourses on Various Subjects," and "Divine Benevolence asserted and vindicated from the Reflections of Ancient and Modern Skeptics," (1782.) Died in 1795.

Băl'ĭ or **Beli,** written also **Baly,** [Hindoo pron. bŭl'ĭ,] called also **Mahâbali,** mạ-hâ'bạ-lĭ, (*i.e.* the "great Bali,") (Indian Myth.,) the name of a mighty prince, who, though generally virtuous, was so elated with his great power that he omitted the appropriate ceremonies and offerings to the gods. To humble and punish him, Vishnu took the form of a pitiful dwarf, (see VAMANA,) and, presenting himself before Bali, asked as a boon as much land or territory as he could pass over in three steps. The incautious monarch unhesitatingly granted and ratified the request. Thereupon Vishnu revealed himself in his true character, and with two steps deprived Bali of earth and heaven, but, in consideration of his virtues, left him Pâtâla, or the Lower World. As king of the lower regions, Bali is by some supposed to be the same as Yama, the god of justice and judge of departed spirits.

See MOOR's "Hindu Pantheon."

Balicour, bȧ'le'kooR', (MARGUERITE THÉRÈSE,) a popular French actress, born about 1700; died in 1743.

Balin, bȧ'lȧN', (JEAN,) a French ecclesiastic and historian, born at Vesoul about 1570, wrote, in Latin, a "History of the War in Flanders under Ambrosio Spinola," (1609.)

Bă'lĭ-ol or **Băl'lĭ-ol,** (EDWARD,) son of John Baliol the rival of Bruce, entered Scotland in 1332, and, having with the aid of Edward III., King of England, gained several victories over the Scots, was crowned king of that country, but was compelled to resign the dignity in less than three months. With the assistance of Edward, he was victorious in 1333 at Halidon Hill; but, the English king having crossed over into France, the cause of Baliol declined, and David Bruce became king. Died in 1363.

See CHAMBERS, "Biographical Dictionary of Eminent Scotsmen."

Bă'lĭ-ol or **Băl'lĭ-ol,** [Fr. BAILLEUL, old French pron. bȧl'yul',] (JOHN,) an English baron of the thirteenth century, was patronized by Henry III., whose cause he espoused against the revolted barons. Having married the Scottish princess Dervorgill, he became the father of the Baliol who disputed the crown of Scotland with Bruce. He made arrangements for founding the college at Oxford called by his name, but, dying before they were completed, it was founded by his widow. Died in 1269.

Bă'lĭ-ol or **Băl'lĭ-ol,** de, [Fr. BAILLEUL,] (JOHN,) Lord of Galloway, the son of the preceding, born about 1259, is celebrated as the rival of Bruce for the crown of Scotland. On the death of Margaret, granddaughter of Alexander III., the succession was disputed between Robert Bruce, John Hastings, and John Baliol, the nearest relatives of the deceased king. The case was referred to Edward I. of England as arbiter, who decided in favour of Baliol, on condition that he should do homage to the King of England for his crown. His coronation took place at Scone in 1292. During his short reign he was called King John. He soon repented of his oath to Edward, and, renouncing his allegiance, marched against the king, who had invaded Scotland. Baliol's army was signally defeated, and he himself, being made prisoner, resigned to the English king his title to the crown. After several years of confinement, he retired to France, where he died in 1314.

See BURTON, "History of Scotland," vol. ii. chaps. xix., xx.; LINGARD, "History of England;" CHAMBERS, "Biographical Dictionary of Eminent Scotsmen."

Ba-lis'tạ, a Roman commander, was prefect of the prætorians under Valerian. When the emperor was defeated by the Persians in 260, Balista was placed at the head of the army, and obtained several victories over the enemy. He is supposed to have been put to death in 264 A.D., by order of Odenatus, King of Palmyra.

Balk, bȧlk, (DANIEL GEORG,) a German physician, born at Königsberg in 1764, was professor of medicine in the University of Dorpat. He wrote a poem entitled "Human Grandeur," and other works. Died in 1826.

Ball, (Sir ALEXANDER JOHN,) a distinguished naval officer, was a native of Gloucestershire. He entered the navy at an early age, and in 1798 commanded the Alexander in the battle of the Nile, where he was conspicuous for his bravery. He was afterwards appointed Governor of Malta. Coleridge, in his publication entitled "The Friend," speaks in high terms of Sir Alexander Ball, with whom he was intimate. Died in 1809.

Ball, (JOHN,) an English preacher, who took a prominent part in the insurrection of Wat Tyler in 1381, and was executed in the same year at Coventry, with a number of his fanatical companions.

Ball, (JOHN,) an English Calvinistic divine, born near Woodstock in 1585. He was the author of a "Treatise on Faith," and a "Treatise containing all the principal Grounds of the Christian Religion." The latter passed through many editions, and was translated into several languages. The piety and learning of Ball are highly commended by Fuller and Baxter. Died in 1640.

See S. CLARKE, "Lives of XXXII Divines."

Ball, (ROBERT,) an Irish naturalist, born in the county of Cork in 1802, was secretary of the Royal Zoological Society, and director of the museum of Trinity College, Dublin. Died in 1857.

Ballabene, bȧl-lȧ-bā'nȧ, (GREGORIO,) an Italian composer, born at Rome about 1730. His principal work is a mass of forty-eight notes. Died in 1800.

See FÉTIS, "Biographie Universelle des Musiciens."

Ballanche, bȧ'lôNsh', (PIERRE SIMON,) a French philosopher and writer on social reform, born at Lyons in August, 1776. Among his principal works are an "Essay on Social Palingenesis," "The Vision of Hebal," and two historic prose poems, entitled "Antigone" and "Orpheus." He was a member of the French Academy, and an intimate friend of Châteaubriand, Madame Récamier, Nodier, and other celebrated writers. Died in June, 1847. He is considered by some French critics as a great writer and profound thinker, but by others his writings are regarded as mystical and obscure.

See VICTOR LAPRADE, "Ballanche, sa Vie et ses Écrits;' LoMÉNIE, "M. Ballanche, par un homme de rien," 1841, (first published in Loménie's "Galerie des Contemporains;") J. J. AMPÈRE, "Ballanche," 1849; ALBERT AUBERT, "P. S. Ballanche," 1847.

Ballantyne. See BELLENDEN.

Băl'lạn-tӯne, (JAMES,) a Scottish printer and journalist, born at Kelso in 1772. At the grammar-school of Kelso he first became acquainted with Walter Scott, and laid the foundation of a friendship which continued through their lives. Having removed in 1799 to Edinburgh, he established a printing-house, from which he issued in 1802–3 Scott's "Minstrelsy of the Scottish Border." He continued for more than twenty years to print the various works of that celebrated writer, and shared in his failure in 1826. He was also editor and proprietor of the "Edinburgh Weekly Journal." Ballantyne's abilities as a critic were highly prized by Scott, and his fine social qualities and admirable recitations are commended in the warmest terms by Lockhart and Professor Wilson. Died in 1833. (See SCOTT, SIR WALTER.)

Ballantyne, (JOHN,) brother of the preceding, born at Kelso in 1774, was for a time clerk in the publishing-house of Ballantyne & Company, of which he became nominal head in 1808. He was distinguished for his wit and humour, and is said by Lockhart to have surpassed the comedian Mathews as a mimic. Died in 1821.

Ballard. See BALARD, (ANTOINE.)

Băl'lạrd, (GEORGE,) an English writer, born in Gloucestershire, published in 1752 a popular work entitled "Memoirs of British Ladies celebrated for their Writings or Skill in the Learned Languages, Arts, or Sciences." Died in 1755.

Ballard, (VOLANT VASHON,) an English naval commander, born about 1774, accompanied the expedition of Vancouver to the northwest coast of America. He afterwards had a share in the capture of Guadeloupe, and was made rear-admiral in 1825. Died in 1833.

Ballarini, bȧl-lȧ-ree'nee, (IPPOLITO,) an Italian ecclesiastic and writer, born at Novara; died in 1558.

Ballarini, (PAOLO,) an Italian painter, born at Bologna in 1712; died after 1782.

ᴄ as *k*; **ç** as *s*; **ḡ** *hard;* **ġ** as *j;* G, H, K, *guttural;* N, *nasal;* R, *trilled;* š as z; th as in *this.* (☞See Explanations, p. 23.)

Balle, bâl′lẹh, (NIKOLAI **Edinger**—ā′ding-ẹr,) a Danish theologian, born on the island of Laaland in 1744. He became successively professor of theology at Copenhagen, (1772,) court preacher, (1774,) and Bishop of Seeland, (1783.) He published a "Manual of Religion," "Theological Theses," (1776,) and other esteemed works. Died in 1816.

Ballenden or **Ballanden.** See BELLENDEN.

Ballenstedt, bâl′lẹn-stĕt′, (JOHANN GEORG JUSTUS,) a German theologian, born at Schöningen in 1756, was the author of a valuable geological work entitled "The Primitive World," ("Die Urwelt.") He was pastor at Pabstorf in Prussia.

See ERSCH und GRUBER, "Allgemeine Encyklopaedie."

Ballerini, bâl-là-ree′nee, (PIETRO,) an Italian theologian, born at Verona in 1698; died about 1760.

Ballester, bâl-yĕs-taiR′, (?) or **Balester,** bâ-lĕs-taiR′, (JOAQUIN,) a Spanish engraver, born about 1750. He executed a number of the plates for Yriarte's work on Music; also the engravings for the splendid edition of "Don Quixote" published at Madrid in 1780. Died in 1795.

See NAGLER, "Neues Allgemeines Künstler-Lexikon."

Ballesteros, bâl-yĕs-tā′ròs, (Don FRANCISCO,) a Spanish general, born at Saragossa in 1770, served against the French in the campaigns of 1793 and 1795. He was for a short time minister of war under Ferdinand VII. Died in Paris in 1832.

Ballesteros, (LUIS LOPEZ,) brother of the preceding, born in Galicia in 1778, succeeded Garay as minister of finance in 1825.

Ballet, bâ′là′, (FRANÇOIS,) a French theologian, who wrote a "History of Pagan, Jewish, and Christian Temples," (1760.)

Ballexserd, bâ′lĕk′saiR′, (JACQUES,) a Swiss physician, born at Geneva in 1726. He was the author of a "Dissertation on the Physical Education of Children," (1762,) which obtained a prize from the Academy of Haarlem. Died in 1774.

Balleydier, bâ′là′de-à′, (ALPHONSE,) a French historical writer, born at Lyons in 1820, published, besides other works, a "History of the Revolutions of the Austrian Empire," (2 vols., 1853.)

Balleydier, (C. J. C.,) a French officer, born at Annecy in 1762, served with distinction in Holland and Prussia. Died in 1807.

Balli, bâl′lee, (ANTONIO,) THE ELDER, an Italian jurist and legal writer, born at Trapani; died in 1591.

Balli, (ANTONIO,) THE YOUNGER, a nephew of the preceding, was judge of the royal court of Palermo.

Balli, (FABIO,) an Italian, who was the author of "Sicilian Songs," and a poem in the Neapolitan dialect, entitled "Palermo Liberato," 1612. Died in 1632.

See MAZZUCHELLI, "Scrittori d'Italia."

Balli, (GIUSEPPE.) See BALLO.

Balliani, bâl-le-à′nee, (GIAMBATTISTA,) a learned Genoese senator, born in 1586, was the author of a valuable treatise "On the Natural Motions of Heavenly Bodies." Died in 1666.

See MAZZUCHELLI, "Scrittori d'Italia."

Ballière de Laisement, bâ′le-aiR′ dẹh làz′mòN′, (CHARLES LOUIS DENIS,) a French littérateur and writer on music, born in Paris in 1729; died in 1800.

Ballin, bâ′lâN′, (CLAUDE,) a celebrated French goldsmith, born in Paris in 1615, executed a number of exquisite works in gold and silver for Cardinal Richelieu and Louis XIV. Died in 1678.

See LE BAS, "Dictionnaire encyclopédique de la France."

Ballin, (CLAUDE,) a nephew of the preceding, was also highly distinguished in the same department of art.

Ballineri, bâl-le-nā′ree, (GIOVANNI,) an Italian painter, born at Florence about 1580, was a pupil of Cigoli.

Balling, bâl′ling, (EMANUEL,) a Danish novelist, born in 1743; died in 1795.

Bâl′lin-gâll′, (GEORGE,) professor of military surgery in the University of Edinburgh, born at that city in 1786. He was the author of "Outlines of Military Surgery," "Observations on the Diseases of European Troops in India," and other medical works. Died in 1855.

Balliol. See BALIOL.

Ballo, bâl′lo, or **Balli,** bâl′lee, (GIUSEPPE,) an Italian priest and savant, born at Palermo in 1567; died at Padua in 1640.

Ballois, bâ′lwâ′, (LOUIS JOSEPH PHILIPPE,) a French writer, born at Périgueux in 1778, founded, in 1802, the "Annales de Statistique." Died in 1803.

Ballon, de, dẹh bâ′lòN′, (LOUISE BLANCHE THÉRÈSE Perrucard—pạ̈′rü′kăR′,) a French nun, born in Savoy in 1591, founded, in the convent of Annecy, the sisterhood of the reformed Bernardines. Died in 1668. Her "Religious Works" were published in 1700.

Ballonius. See BAILLOU.

Ballou, bal-loo′, (HOSEA,) an eminent American preacher and controversialist, the author or founder of "Universalism" in the modern acceptation of this term, was born in Richmond, New Hampshire, April 30, 1771. After he had laboured many years in different parts of New England, he settled at Boston in 1817. He published several theological works, among which the most worthy of notice is, perhaps, his "Examination of the Doctrine of Future Retribution." In 1819 he established the "Universalist Magazine," the first weekly newspaper devoted to the doctrines of Universalism ever published, and in 1831, in connection with his nephew of the same name, he issued the first number of the "Universalist Expositor," now known as the "Universalist Quarterly Review." The doctrine preached by Mr. Ballou in the early part of his career was that known as "Restorationism," which teaches that all souls will ultimately be saved, after undergoing, for a longer or shorter period, punishment designed simply for their purification and preparation for a higher state of happiness; but in the latter portion of his life he taught the doctrine that there is no punishment whatever in a future state of existence, but that the wicked receive their full punishment in this world, and that all men will be saved without exception, whatever may have been the sins or crimes of their earthly life. His biography has been published by his son, M. M. Ballou, and in three volumes 12mo by the Rev. Thomas Whittemore. Died in 1852. (See MURRAY, JOHN.)

Bally, bâ′le′, (VICTOR,) a French physician, born at Beaurepaire, published a treatise "On the Typhus Fever of America," (1814,) and "History of the Yellow Fever in Spain in 1821."

See QUÉRARD, "La France Littéraire."

Bal′mer, (ROBERT,) a Scottish theologian, born in Roxburghshire in 1787. He preached at Berwick for many years, and became professor of theology in the United Secession (or Presbyterian) Church in 1834. He was highly esteemed for talent and moral worth. Died in 1844. His "Academical Lectures and Pulpit Discourses" were published in two volumes, 1845.

See CHAMBERS, "Biographical Dictionary of Eminent Scotsmen," (Supplement.)

Balmés, bâl-mês′, written also **Balmis,** (FRANCISCO XAVIER,) surgeon to the Spanish court, introduced vaccination into the Spanish Colonies in 1803, and subsequently into the Canary and Philippine Islands and China.

Balmés, (JAIME LUCIO,) an eminent Spanish theologian and philosopher, born at Vich, in Catalonia, in 1810. He was the author of "Political Considerations on the Situation of Spain," (1840,) and "Protestantism compared with Catholicism in its Relations to European Civilization," (3 vols., 1848.) The latter, esteemed his ablest work, was written in reply to Guizot. His "Filosofia fundamental" was translated into English. Died in 1848.

See ANTONIO SOLER, "Biografia del D. J. Balmes," 1850; GARCIA DE LOS SANTOS, "Vida de Balmés," 1848; BLANCHE-RAFFIN, "J. Balmés, sa Vie et ses Ouvrages," Paris, 1849, and a German version of the same, by KARKER, 1852.

Balnaves, bâl-nav′ẹss, or **Balnav′is,** (HENRY,) surnamed of HALHILL, a Scottish statesman and Protestant writer, born in Fifeshire. He became in 1538 one of the lords of session, and secretary of state under the regent Arran in 1543. In this post he promoted the passing of Lord Maxwell's act for allowing the Scriptures to be read in the vulgar tongue. Being accused of sharing in the conspiracy against Cardinal Beatoun, he was imprisoned, together with Knox and other reformers, at Rouen, in France, where he wrote his "Confession of Faith." Having returned to Scotland, he was appointed in 1563 one of the commissioners to revise the "Book of Discipline." Died in 1571.

See MACKENZIE, "Lives of Scottish Writers;" CHAMBERS, "Biographical Dictionary of Eminent Scotsmen."

Balog, bä-log, or **Balogh,** (JÁNOS,) a Hungarian statesman, born in 1800, defended the rights of the people against the nobility, in the Diet of 1825. After the defeat of the patriots in 1849, he escaped with Kossuth into Turkey.

See BROCKHAUS, "Conversations-Lexikon."

Baloufeau, bä'loo'fō', or **Balouffeteau,** bä'loof'tō', (JACQUES,) a French adventurer and impostor, born at Saint-Jean-d'Angély. After having,under assumed names, married many women in different parts of Europe, he obtained two hundred crowns from the King of France as a reward for revealing a pretended conspiracy, and two thousand pounds sterling from the English government for a similar service. He was at last arrested in France and executed in 1627.

Balsamina, bäl-sä-mee'nä, (CAMILLA,) an Italian vocalist, born at Milan, was prima donna at the court of Prince Eugene, Viceroy of Italy, in 1807. Died in 1810.

See FÉTIS, "Biographie Universelle des Musiciens."

Balsamo, (GIUSEPPE.) See CAGLIOSTRO.

Balsamo, bäl'sä-mo, (PAOLO,) a distinguished agriculturist and writer, born at Termini, in Sicily, in 1763. He was professor of agriculture at Palermo, and translated into Italian Arthur Young's "Pleasures of Agriculture." Died in 1818.

See TIPALDO, "Biografia degli Italiani illustri."

Bäl'sạ-mo or **Bäl'sạ-mon,** (THEODORE,) a Greek prelate, who became Patriarch of Antioch in 1186. He wrote a "Commentary on the Canons of the Apostles, and the Seven Œcumenical Councils." Died in 1204.

Bäl'sham, written also **Belesale, de,** (HUGH,) an English prelate, and founder of Saint Peter's College, Cambridge, born in Cambridgeshire, became, in 1257, Bishop of Ely. Died in 1286.

Baltacchini, bäl-täk-kee'nee, (MICHELE,) an Italian philosopher, born in Naples in 1803. He published, besides other works, a "History of Masaniello," (1834,) and "The Life and Works of Campanella," (1840–43.)

Baltadschi or **Baltadji.** See BALTAJEE.

Baltajee (Baltaji, Baltadji, or **Baltadschi) Mohammed,** bäl-tä'jee mo-hâm'med, a Turkish statesman and commander, rose to be grand vizier under Ahmed III. He was appointed in 1710 to command the Turkish forces acting with Charles XII. of Sweden against the Russians. After gaining a decided victory over the enemy, he was induced by the empress Catherine to sign a treaty, by which he lost all the advantages he had won, and gave great offence to Charles. Died in 1712.

See VON HAMMER, "Histoire de l'Empire Ottoman ;" VOLTAIRE, "Histoire de Charles XII."

Baltard, bäl'tåR', (LOUIS PIERRE,) a celebrated French architect and engraver, born in Paris in 1765. He furnished the design for the Palace of Justice at Lyons, and constructed the chapels for the houses of detention of Saint-Lazare and Sainte-Pélagie. Among his engravings we may name "Paris and its Monuments," (1803,) and "Saint John baptizing on the Banks of the Jordan," after Poussin. Died in 1846.

See J. M. DALGABIO, "Éloge historique de M. Baltard," 1846.

Baltard, (VICTOR,) a French architect, born in Paris in 1805, published in 1847 a "Monography of the Villa Medicis."

Baltazarini, bäl-tåd-zä-ree'nee, called also **Beaujoyeulx,** bō'zhwä'yuh', an Italian musician, who was a favourite at the court of Catherine de Médicis.

See FÉTIS, "Biographie Universelle des Musiciens."

Balten, or **Baltens.** See BALTON.

Balthasar, the French for BELSHAZZAR, which see.

Balthasar, bäl'tä'zäR', (CHRISTOPHE,) a French jurist, born at Villeneuve-le-Roi in 1588, was royal advocate at Auxerre. He wrote a "Treatise on the Usurpations of the Kings of Spain upon the Crown of France." Died in 1670.

Balthasar, (JOSEPH ANTOINE FÉLIX,) a Swiss jurist,

born at Lucerne in 1737, contributed several articles on Swiss history to Haller's "Bibliotheca Helvetica," and wrote a "Defence of William Tell." Died in 1810.

Balthasar, bäl'tä-zaR, or **Balthazari,** bäl-tä-tsä'ree, (THEODOR,) a German savant, and professor of mathematics at Erlangen, is supposed to have invented the solar microscope, of which he published a description, (1710.) This invention is attributed by some to Lieberkühn.

See FISCHER, "Geschichte der Physik."

Balthasar, von, fon bäl'tä-zaR, (AUGUSTIN,) a German jurist and writer, born at Greifswalde in 1701 ; died in 1779.

Baltimore, (LORD.) See CALVERT, (GEORGE.)

Balton, bäl'ton, **Baltens,** or **Balten,** bäl'tŏN', (PETER,) a Flemish painter, born at Antwerp in 1540. He painted in the style of Breughel, and his miniature landscapes and historical pieces are highly esteemed. Died in 1579.

See FIORILLO, "Geschichte der Malerei."

Baltus, bäl'tüs', (JEAN FRANÇOIS,) a French Jesuit, born at Metz in 1667, wrote a reply to Fontenelle's "History of Oracles," and other works. Died in 1743.

Baltzar, bäl'sår, (THOMAS,) a celebrated German violinist, who in 1658 visited London, where he was appointed director of concerts by Charles II. Died in 1663.

See BURNEY, "General History of Music."

Balue, de la, deh lä bä'lü', (JEAN,) a French cardinal, born at Poitiers in 1422, was a favourite of Louis XI., by whom he was made Bishop of Evreux and prime minister. For his efforts to abolish the "Pragmatic Sanction" he was made a cardinal by Pope Paul II. in 1467. After having been for many years the instigator and partner of his sovereign's tyranny and vices, he endeavoured to excite a quarrel between Louis and his brother. For this crime he was imprisoned by the king in an iron cage for eleven years. He was released in 1480, on the intercession of Pope Sixtus IV. He was afterwards appointed protector of the order of Malta, and obtained other high preferments from Pope Innocent VIII. Died in 1491.

See AUBERY, "Histoire des Cardinaux."

Baluffi, bä-loof'fee, (CAJETANO,) an Italian ecclesiastic, resided many years in New Granada, and published in 1848 a "Religious History of America."

Baluze, bä'lüz', (ÉTIENNE,) a French historian, born at Tulle in 1630, was charged by Colbert with the care of his library, and afterwards appointed inspector of the Royal College by Louis XIV. He published in 1709 his "History of the House of Auvergne," in which he proves that the family of Bouillon are descended from the ancient dukes of Guienne, and, consequently, owed no allegiance to the French crown. This work gave great offence to the king, who caused it to be suppressed, the author exiled, and his estates confiscated. Baluze also wrote the "Lives of the Popes of Avignon," (1693.) Died in Paris in 1718.

See "Vie de Baluze, par lui-même, continuée par MARTIN ;" J. B. VITRAC, "Éloge de Baluze," 1777.

Balzac, bäl'zäk', (CHARLES LOUIS,) a French architect, born in 1798, accompanied the expedition to Egypt in 1798, and contributed valuable architectural designs to the Description of Egypt afterwards published by the government. Died in 1820.

See QUÉRARD, "La France Littéraire."

Balzac, de, deh bäl'zäk', (HONORÉ,) a celebrated French novelist, born at Tours in May, 1799. He published in 1822 a series of tales, under the names of Horace de Saint-Aubin, and other pseudonyms, and in 1829 brought out, in his own name, a historical romance entitled "The Last Chouan," ("Le dernier Chouan.") His next works, the "Physiologie du Mariage," and "La Peau de Chagrin," were very successful, and were soon followed by a series of novels and tales entitled "Comédie humaine," intended to delineate every phase of French society. Among the most popular of these may be named "Le Père Goriot," "Eugénie Grandet," and "Balthasar Claes." In 1848 Balzac married the Countess Hanska, a Polish lady to whom he had dedicated his novel of "Séraphita." He died in Paris in

August, 1850, and a glowing eulogy was pronounced over his grave by Victor Hugo. Balzac's works enjoy great popularity in France, and have been translated into the principal European languages. He had great acuteness of observation and brilliant fancy; but his delineations are often unnatural and extravagant, and his writings are deficient in moral elevation.

See GUSTAVE DESNOIRESTERRES, "Vie de Honoré de Balzac;" LOUIS DE LOMÉNIE, "Notice sur H. de Balzac," 1842; GEORGE SAND, "Notice biographique sur H. de Balzac," 8vo, 1853; A BASCHET, "H. de Balzac," 1852; also, a critique on the novels of Balzac, in the "North American Review" for July, 1847, (by J. L. MOTLEY.)

Balzac, de, (JEAN LOUIS Guez—gȧ,) SEIGNEUR, a French *littérateur,* born at Angoulême in 1594. He contributed greatly to the improvement of his native language, and was esteemed the best French prosaist of his time. He was patronized by Cardinal Richelieu, and in 1634 was elected unanimously to the French Academy. His brilliant success as an author and his innovations in literature caused him to be severely assailed by Goulu and other contemporary writers. He was the author of a work entitled "The Christian Socrates," (1652,) "Aristippus," (a treatise on the duties of sovereigns, dedicated to Christina of Sweden,) and a number of Latin poems; but his fame rests chiefly on his "Familiar Letters," (1624,) which have passed through several editions. Died in Paris in 1654.

See A. MALITOURNE, "Notice sur la Vie de Balzac," prefixed to his "Œuvres Choisies," 2 vols., 1823; P. H. MARRON, "J. L. Guez de Balzac;" BAYLE, "Historical and Critical Dictionary;" MOREAU DE MERSAN, "Notice sur la Vie de Balzac," prefixed to the "Pensées de Balzac," 1807.

Balzani, bȧl-zä'nee, (GIOVANNI,) an Italian portrait-painter, born at Bologna in 1658; died in 1735.

Balze, bȧlz, (NICOLAS,) an able French advocate, born in Languedoc in 1735, wrote odes, tales, etc. Died in 1792.

Bambam, bȧm'bȧm, (HARTWIG,) a German Lutheran theologian, lived at Hamburg; died in 1742.

Bamberger, bȧm'bĕRG-ẹr, (JOHANN PETER,) a German theologian and *littérateur,* born at Magdeburg in 1722. He was editor of the "British Theological Magazine" at Halle, and translated "Knox's Essays," Anderson's "History of Commerce," and other English works, into German. Died in 1804.

Bambini, bȧm-bee'nee, (GIACOMO,) an Italian painter, born at Ferrara about 1590. He died prematurely in 1629.

Bambini, (NICCOLÒ,) an Italian painter, born at Venice in 1651, possessed great skill in design, but was deficient as a colorist. Died in 1736.

See LANZI, "History of Painting in Italy."

Bamboccio, bȧm-bot'cho, (ANTONIO,) an Italian sculptor, born at Piperno about 1368. Among his best works are the mausoleum of Cardinal Filippo Minutolo, celebrated by Boccaccio, and the monument of Ludovico Aldemareschi. Died about 1430.

Bamboccio. See LAER, (PETER VAN.)

Bamboche. See LAER, (PETER VAN.)

Bambridge, (CHRISTOPHER.) See BAINBRIDGE.

Bamesbier, bȧ'mess-beer', (HANS or JAN,) a Dutch painter, born at Amsterdam in 1500, was a pupil of Lambert Lombard. He lived to the age of a hundred, notwithstanding his intemperate habits. Died in 1600.

See NAGLER, "Neues Allgemeines Künstler-Lexikon."

Bamfield. See BAMFYLDE.

Bam'ford, (SAMUEL,) an English writer and radical politician, born near Manchester in 1788, was a weaver by trade. He was several times imprisoned on account of his political opinions. He was the author of a collection of poems of great merit, a prose work entitled "Walks in South Lancashire," and "Passages in the Life of a Radical."

See "Brief Biographies," by SAMUEL SMILES.

Bam'fylde or **Bam'field,** (FRANCIS,) an English theologian, was the author of "An Argument in Favour of the Observance of the Jewish Sabbath," (1672,) and other religious works. Died in 1684.

Bamp'ton, (Rev. JOHN,) Canon of Salisbury, born in 1689, was the founder of the series of lectures called by his name. He gave his estates to the University of Oxford for the endowment of eight divinity lecture sermons, to be delivered annually. Died in 1751.

Ban'as-tẹr, (GILBERT,) an English poet and musi-

cian, whose only extant poem is entitled "The Miracle of Saint Thomas," (1467.)

See COLLIER, "History of Dramatic Poetry," etc.

Bancal des Issarts, bȯN'kȧl' dạ'ze'sȧR', (JEAN HENRI,) a French magistrate, born in the diocese of Montpellier in 1750. He was a deputy to the National Convention in 1792, where he voted against the union of Savoy with France, and opposed the execution of the king. Being sent with other commissioners to Dumouriez, he was given up by him to the Austrians and imprisoned in 1793. With his colleagues he was exchanged in 1795 for the Duchess of Angoulême. In 1796 he became a member of the Council of Five Hundred. He wrote, among other works, a treatise "On New Social Order, founded on Religion." Died in 1826.

See "Nouvelle Biographie Générale."

Bancel, bȯN'sĕl', (LOUIS,) a learned French theologian, born at Valence, lived at Avignon. Died in 1685.

Banchero, bȧn-kä'ro, (ANGELO,) an Italian painter, born at Sestri, near Genoa, about 1774; died in 1793.

Banchi, bȧn'kee, (SERAPHINO,) a Dominican monk, born at Florence. Having informed Henry IV. of France of Barrière's project to assassinate him, he was offered by that monarch the bishopric of Angoulême, which he refused. Died in 1622.

Banchieri, bȧn-ke-ä'ree, (ADRIANO,) an Italian poet and writer on music, born at Bologna; died in 1634.

Banck, bȧnk, (LAWRENCE,) a Swedish jurist, was a native of Norrköping. He became professor of law at Franeker, and wrote in Latin several treatises against the usurpations of the pope. Died in 1662.

See BAYLE, "Historical and Critical Dictionary."

Banck or **Bank, van der,** vȧn dẹr bȧnk, (PETER,) a skilful Flemish engraver, born in Paris in 1649, worked in London, where he died in 1697.

Banco, bȧn'ko, (NANNI D'ANTONIO, nȧn'nee dȧn-to'-ne-o,) an Italian architect and sculptor, born at Sienna in 1374, had a share in the construction of the cathedral of Florence. Died in 1421.

See VASARI, "Lives of the Painters," etc.

Ban'croft, (AARON,) D.D., an American Congregational divine, born at Reading, Massachusetts, in 1755, graduated at Harvard in 1778. He settled as pastor at Worcester in 1785, and remained there for fifty years or more. Besides a great number of sermons, he published a "Life of Washington," which obtained great popularity. He was the father of George Bancroft the historian. Died in 1839.

Ban'croft, (EDWARD,) an English physician and naturalist, published an "Essay on the Natural History of Guiana," (1769,) and "Experimental Researches on the Philosophy of Permanent Colours," (1794.) He was a Fellow of the Royal Society and of the Royal College of Physicians, and was intimate with Dr. Franklin and Dr. Priestley. Died in 1821.

Bancroft, (GEORGE,) a distinguished American historian, son of the Rev. Aaron Bancroft, was born at Worcester, Massachusetts, on the 3d of October, 1800. He entered Harvard College in 1813, and graduated with distinguished honours in 1817. In 1818 he went to Germany, entered the University of Göttingen, and studied history, philology, etc., under Heeren, Bunsen, and other distinguished professors. He took the degree of doctor of philosophy at Göttingen in 1820, after which he passed some time in Berlin and Heidelberg in the society of Wilhelm von Humboldt, Varnhagen von Ense, and Schlosser. Having returned home in 1822, he served as Greek tutor in Harvard College for one year, published a volume of Poems in 1823, and opened the Round Hill School at Northampton. In 1824 he produced a translation of Heeren's "Reflections on the Politics of Ancient Greece." His reputation was increased by the first volume of his "History of the Colonization of the United States," which appeared in 1834.

He had been an active supporter of the Democratic party for many years when he was appointed in 1838 collector of customs for the port of Boston. The third volume of his History appeared in 1840, and was commended by the "Edinburgh Review" in the following

---

ā, ē, ī, ō, ū, ȳ, *long;* ȧ, ė, ȯ, same, less prolonged; ă, ĕ, ĭ, ŏ, ŭ, ў, *short;* ạ, ẹ, ị, ọ, *obscure;* fär, fȧll, fȧt; mĕt; nŏt; gŏŏd; mōŏn;

terms: "The real liberality, the general fairness, the labour and conscientious research, it evinces, deserve, and we are assured will receive, his [the reader's] warmest approbation." (Vol. lxxxv., January, 1847.) He was the Democratic candidate for the office of Governor of Massachusetts in 1844, but was not elected. In March, 1845, he became secretary of the navy in the cabinet of Mr. Polk. He established a naval school at Annapolis, and improved the Astronomical Observatory at Washington. In 1846 he resigned his place in the cabinet and was appointed minister plenipotentiary to England. During his residence in Europe he examined the archives and libraries of Paris and London, in which he collected materials for his great work on American history. He returned to the United States in 1849, became a resident of the city of New York, and devoted himself to literary pursuits. He contributed to the "North American Review." In 1852 he published the fourth volume of his History, which is the first volume of the "History of the Revolution." This work has extended to nine volumes octavo, but is not yet (1869) completed.

"We know few modern historic works," says Professor Heeren, "in which the author has reached so high an elevation at once as an historical inquirer and an historical writer. The great conscientiousness with which he refers to his authorities, and his careful criticism, give the most decisive proofs of his comprehensive studies."

In a notice of the third volume, William H. Prescott remarks, "The reader will find the pages of the present volume filled with matter not less interesting and important than the preceding. He will meet with the same brilliant and daring style, the same picturesque sketches of character and incident, the same acute reasoning and compass of erudition." ("North American Review" for January, 1841.)

In February, 1866, he delivered at Washington, in presence of Congress and the foreign diplomatic corps, an oration in honour of Abraham Lincoln, which attracted much attention.

He was appointed minister to the court of Berlin in 1867, and negotiated with the North German Confederation a treaty by which Germans who emigrate and become naturalized as citizens of the United States are released from their allegiance to the government of their native country and are assured the enjoyment of all the rights of native citizens of the United States.

See, also, "North American Review" for January, 1835, vol. xl., and "Foreign Quarterly" for July, 1841.

Bancroft, (JOHN,) a nephew of Richard Bancroft, noticed below, was a native of Oxfordshire. He became Bishop of Oxford in 1632. Died in 1640.

Bancroft, (RICHARD,) an English prelate, born in Lancashire in 1544, became Bishop of London, (1597,) and Archbishop of Canterbury, (1604.) He was a zealous opponent of the Puritans, and wrote, among other works, "Dangerous Positions and Proceedings published under the Pretence of Reformation, etc." Died in 1610.

See GARDINER, "History of England from 1603 to 1616," chaps. iv. and x.; "Biographia Britannica."

Bancroft, (THOMAS,) an English writer, who made a collection of "Epigrams and Epitaphs," (1649.)

Bandarra, bån-dår'rå, (GONSALO ANNES,) a Portuguese poet, and pretended prophet, born at Villa de Trancoso, was surnamed THE PORTUGUESE NOSTRADAMUS. His verses entitled "Trovas Redondilhas," prophesying the subjugation of Portugal by Spain, and its subsequent restoration, acquired great popularity in Portugal, and were translated into French. Died in 1556.

See General FOY, "Mémoires sur les Guerres de la Péninsule."

Bandel, bån'del, (ERNST,) a distinguished German sculptor, born at Anspach in 1800. He studied at Munich, where in 1820 he exhibited his statue of Mars; he afterwards became a resident of Berlin. Among his master-pieces are a colossal bronze or copper statue of Hermann, (Arminius,) and busts of King Maximilian of Bavaria, and the poet Grabbe.

Bandello, bån-del'lo, (MATTEO,) an Italian novelist and Dominican monk, born at Castelnuovo, in Piedmont, in 1480. Having visited France, he was created Bishop of Agen by Henry II. in 1550. He published

in 1554 the first three volumes of his novels; the fourth came out after his death. Though less elegant in style than those of Boccaccio, they bear a strong resemblance to them in originality of conception and descriptive powers, and are equally immoral. Shakspeare, Massinger, and other English dramatists derived some of their plots from Bandello. Died at Agen in 1561.

See NAPIONE, "Piemontesi illustri," and MORÉRI, "Dictionnaire Historique."

Bandello, de, då bån-del'lo, (VINCENZO,) an Italian Dominican monk and writer, born at Castelnuovo in 1435; died in 1506.

Bandelloni, bån-dêl-lo'nee, (LUIGI,) an Italian poet and musical composer of this century, born at Rome.

Bandettini, bån-dêt-tee'nee, (TERESA,) a celebrated Italian improvisatrice and poetess, sometimes called **Amarilla Etrusca,** born at Lucca in 1763, was the author of a tragedy entitled "Il Polidoro," and "The Death of Adonis," a poem. She was crowned with laurel at Rome in 1794, and her genius and virtues are commended by Alfieri, Monti, and other eminent writers. Died in 1837.

See TIPALDO, "Biografia degli Italiani illustri."

Bandiera, bån-de-ā'rå, (ATTILIO and EMILIO,) Italian patriots, brothers, born at Naples or Venice, the elder in 1817, the second in 1819, were the sons of an Austrian vice-admiral. In 1842 they embraced with ardour the cause of Young Italy, and entered into a correspondence with Mazzini. In the hope of exciting the people to insurrection, they advanced in 1844 with a small force into Calabria, but, being soon after betrayed and arrested, were executed by order of the Austrian government.

See RICCIARDI, "Histoire de la Révolution d'Italie en 1848;" GIUSEPPE MAZZINI, "Ricordi dei Fratelli Bandiera e dei loro Compagni," 1845.

Bandiera, (BENEDETTO,) a painter of the Roman school, born at Perugia in 1557; died in 1634.

Bandinelli, bån-de-nel'lee, (BACCIO, båt'cho,) an eminent Italian sculptor, born at Florence in 1487, was a pupil of Gian Francesco Rustici. Among his master-pieces are the figure of "Christ at the Tomb," in the church of the Annunziata, the group of "Adam and Eve," and the bas-reliefs in the Duomo at Florence. He also attempted painting, in which, however, he did not excel. As a sculptor he is regarded as second only to Michael Angelo, to whom he manifested an envious hostility. Bandinelli enjoyed the favour of the emperor Charles V., Cosimo de Medici, and Pope Clement VII. Died in 1559.

See VASARI, "Lives of the Painters and Sculptors;" CICOGNARA, "Storia della Scultura."

Bandinelli, (CLEMENTE,) a son of the preceding, born at Florence, was a promising sculptor, but died young.

Bandinelli, (MARCO,) a painter of the seventeenth century, born at Bologna, was at first the valet and cook of Guido Reni. He was surnamed MARCHINO DI GUIDO.

Bandinelli, (MICHEL ANGELO,) a Florentine painter, a nephew of Baccio, lived about 1550.

Bandini, bån-dee'nee, (ANGELO MARIA,) a learned Italian writer, born at Florence in 1726, was appointed in 1756 first keeper of the Laurentian Library. Among his principal works are a "Description of the Obelisk of Augustus discovered on the Field of Mars," and a "Life of Amerigo Vespucci," (1745.) Died in 1800.

See GINGUENÉ, "Histoire Littéraire d'Italie."

Bandini, (GIOVANNI,) a sculptor, born at Castello, in Tuscany, worked in the second half of the sixteenth century. He made the statue of Architecture placed on the tomb of Michael Angelo at Florence.

Bandini, (SALLUSTIO,) an Italian economist, born at Sienna in 1677; died in 1760.

Bandino, bån-dee'no, (DOMENICO,) an Italian scholar and writer, born at Arezzo in 1340, was professor of eloquence at Bologna, and afterwards at Padua. He wrote a large work entitled "Fons Memorabilium Universi," treating of theology, astronomy, natural philosophy, etc., (unpublished.) Died about 1415.

See TIRABOSCHI, "Storia della Letteratura Italiana."

Bandtke, bånt'kå, or **Bandtkie,** bånt'kyå, (GEORGE

$\mathfrak{e}$ as k; $\mathfrak{c}$ as s; $\mathfrak{g}$ *hard;* $\dot{g}$ as j; G, H, K, *guttural;* N, *nasal;* R, *trilled;* $\mathfrak{s}$ as z; $\mathfrak{th}$ as in *this.* (☞See Explanations, p. 23.)

17

SAMUEL,) a Polish historian, born at Lublin in 1768, became in 1811 librarian and professor of bibliography at Cracow. He was the author of a "History of the Polish Nation," (in Polish,) which is esteemed a standard work, a "History of Printing in Poland," and "Historico-critical Miscellanies towards the History of Oriental Europe," (in German, 1802.) Died in 1835.

Bandtke, (JOHANN VINCENZ,) brother of the preceding, born at Lublin in 1783, was professor of law at the University of Warsaw. He published in 1831 a collection of Polish legal documents, entitled "Jus Polonicum." Died in 1851.

Banduri, bân-doo'ree, (ANSELMO,) an Italian antiquary and Benedictine monk, born in Dalmatia in 1671. He published "Coins of the Roman Emperors from Trajan to the Last Palæologus," (1718, 2 vols. fol.) Died in Paris in 1743.

Bane, written also **Benn**, (JAMES,) became Archbishop of Saint Andrew's in 1328. Died in 1332.

Banel, bâ'něl', (PIERRE,) a French general, born at Lectoure in 1766, was killed at Cossaria, in Piedmont, in 1796.

Banér, bâ-naiR' or bâ-nīR', written also **Bannier**, **Banier**, or **Banner**, (JOHAN,) a celebrated Swedish general, born near Stockholm in 1595. Having served in the Russian and Polish campaigns of 1626-29, he accompanied Gustavus Adolphus to Germany in 1630, and commanded under him the right wing at the memorable battle of Leipsic. His brilliant achievements upon this occasion won for him the highest commendations from his sovereign. Being appointed to the chief command of the Swedish army on the death of Gustavus, he gained a signal victory over the allied army under the Elector of Saxony, near Wittstock, in 1636. He defeated the Imperial troops near Chemnitz in 1639, and subsequently overran and laid waste a great part of Germany. He died in 1641, long before the conclusion of the Thirty Years' war, in which he had borne so distinguished a part. In the words of Schiller, "He was calm in danger, greater in adversity than in prosperity, and never more formidable than when he was supposed to be on the verge of ruin."

See CARL MANDERFELDT, "Éloge de J. Banér," 1787; SCHILLER, "History of the Thirty Years' War."

Banes, bâ'něs, (DOMINGO,) a Spanish theologian, born at Valladolid in 1527; died in 1604.

Banfi, bân'fee, (GIULIO,) an Italian lute-player, who was taken as a prisoner to Tunis, where his musical talents procured for him the favour of the Bey, who gave him his liberty. He wrote a work entitled "The Guitar-Master," (1653.) Died about 1670.

Banfi, bân'fee, (LADISLAUS,) BARON, a Hungarian patriot, born in 1795, was a coadjutor and intimate friend of Wesselényi. In the Diet of 1839 he advocated the union of Transylvania with Hungary. Died in 1839.

Bang, bằng, (FREDERIK LUDWIG,) a Danish physician and medical writer, born in the island of Seeland in 1747, became in 1782 professor at the University of Copenhagen. Died in 1820.

See KRAFT og NYERUP, "Almindeligt Litteraturlexicon."

Bang, (JOHAN,) a Danish medical writer, born in 1737, lived at Copenhagen; died in 1808.

Bang, bằng, [Lat. BAN'GIUS,] (PETER,) a Swedish theologian, and professor of theology at Abo, born at Helsingborg in 1633. He became Bishop of Viborg in 1696. He wrote, in Latin, a "Treatise on Sacred Chronology," and "Ecclesiastical History of Sweden." Died in 1696.

Bang, [Lat. BAN'GIUS,] (THOMAS,) a Danish philologist and writer, born in the island of Funen in 1600, was professor of Hebrew and afterwards of theology at Copenhagen. Died in 1661.

See MOLLER, "Cimbria Literata;" MORHOF, "Polyhistor."

Bängs, (NATHAN,) an American Methodist minister, born in Fairfield county, Connecticut, in 1778. He preached in the city of New York, and was appointed agent for Methodist books in 1820, after which he edited the "Christian Advocate and Journal," and was president of the Wesleyan University at Middletown, Connecticut. He published, besides other works, a "History of the Methodist Episcopal Church," (4 vols. 12mo.)

Banier. See BANÉR.

Banier, bâ'ne-â', (ANTOINE,) a French *littérateur*, born in Auvergne in 1673, wrote a work entitled "Historical Explanation of Fables," and translated into French Ovid's "Metamorphoses." Died in 1741.

Banières, bâ'ne-aiR', a versatile French genius, born at Toulouse in the early part of the eighteenth century, was successively an ecclesiastic, lawyer, soldier, poet, and comedian. His adventures have furnished Dumas with material for his novel of "Olympe de Clèves."

See LEMAZURIER, "Galerie historique du Théâtre Français."

Bä'nim, (JOHN,) a celebrated Irish novelist, born at Kilkenny about 1800. His delineations of peasant life in Ireland are eminently vivid and truthful, and are regarded as scarcely inferior to those of Miss Edgeworth. Among his most popular works are "Tales of the O'Hara Family," (1825,) "The Battle of the Boyne," (1828,) "The Denounced," (1830,) "The Smuggler," (1831,) and "The Mayor of Wind-Gap." Died in 1842.

See "Life of John Banim," by PATRICK J. MURRAY, 1857; R. H. HORNE, "New Spirit of the Age," 1844.

Banim, (MICHAEL,) a brother of the preceding, born at Kilkenny about 1796, was also a writer of fiction. He aided his brother in the composition of "Tales of the O'Hara Family," and was chief author of "The Croppy." Among his works is "Clough Fionn, or the Stone of Destiny."

Banister. See BANNISTER, (JOHN.)

Ban'is-ter, (JOHN,) an English surgeon, born about 1550, wrote, among other treatises, "The History of Man, sucked from the Sappe of the most approved Anathomistes," (1578,) and "Antidotarie Chyrurgicale," (1589.) Died about 1630.

Banister, (JOHN,) a distinguished English botanist, who travelled in the United States and West Indies. In 1680 he contributed a catalogue of Virginian plants to Ray's "History of Plants." The genus Banisteria was named in his honour. Died about 1689.

Banister, (JOHN,) an English violinist, born about 1630. He composed the music for the opera of "Circe." Died about 1679.

See FÉTIS, "Biographie Universelle des Musiciens."

Banister, (RICHARD,) an English surgeon, distinguished for his skill in the treatment of diseases of the eye, in relation to which he wrote several treatises. Died about 1630.

Bank-Ban, bânk'bân', [Lat. BANCBA'NUS,] a Hungarian nobleman, who, in 1217, assassinated Gertrude, queen of Andrew II., for having aided her brother Eckart to outrage his wife. Bank-Ban was subsequently put to death. Katona's tragedy of "Bank-Ban," esteemed the best drama in the Hungarian language, is founded on this event.

Bankert, van, vằn bânk'ert, (ADRIAN,) a Dutch naval commander, born at Flushing, fought against the English in 1666, and in 1672 against the united French and English fleets. Died in 1684.

Bankert, (JOSEPH van Trappen—vằn trâp'pen,) a Dutch admiral, father of the preceding, born at Flushing about 1590, fought in the battle of Dunkirk, and defeated the Portuguese fleet near Brazil in 1647. Died on his voyage home the same year.

Bankes, bânks, (HENRY,) an English writer, born about 1757, published the "Civil and Constitutional History of Rome," (1818.) He was a member of Parliament from 1780 to 1826. Died in 1835.

Bankes, (Sir JOHN,) an English jurist, born at -Keswick in 1589, succeeded Sir Edward Littleton as lord chief justice of common pleas under Charles I. in 1640. He supported the king against the Parliament, by which he was declared a traitor. Died in 1644.

See Foss, "The Judges of England."

Banks, bânks, (EDUARD,) a German diplomatist, born at Hamburg in 1796, became secretary of the senate, (1826,) syndic of Hamburg, (1837,) and was subsequently ambassador to London.

Banks, (JOHN,) an English dramatist, was the author of tragedies entitled "The Destruction of Troy," "The Rival Kings," "The Unhappy Favourite, or the Earl of Essex," (1685,) "Cyrus the Great," (1696,) and others.

See "Biographia Dramatica."

ā, ē, ī, ō, ū, ȳ, *long;* ă, ĕ, ŏ, same, less prolonged; ă, ĕ, ĭ, ŏ, ŭ, ў, *short;* ą, ę, į, ǫ, *obscure;* fär, fâll, fât; mêt; nŏt; gŏŏd; mōon,

Banks, (JOHN,) born in Berkshire, England, in 1709, was the author of a "Critical Review of the Life of Oliver Cromwell." Died in 1751.

Banks, (Sir JOSEPH,) an eminent English naturalist, born in London on the 4th of January, 1743, was a son of William Banks, Esq., from whom he inherited an easy fortune. He entered Christ Church, Oxford, in 1760, and left it in 1763, with an extensive knowledge of natural history, especially of botany. In 1766 he was chosen a Fellow of the Royal Society, and in 1768 accompanied Captain Cook in his voyage of discovery round the world. His friend Dr. Solander was associated with him as naturalist in this expedition. They returned with rich collections of natural objects in June, 1771, and intended to publish a botanical work; but the death of Solander prevented its completion. Sir Joseph Banks explored Iceland in 1772. He was president of the Royal Society from 1777 until 1820, and distinguished himself as a liberal patron of travellers and scientific men. Several voyages of discovery were performed under his direction or favoured by his influence. He laboured to diffuse over each region of the earth the productions of other climates. He was knighted in 1781, and became a member of the privy council in 1797. In 1802 he was chosen an associate of the Institute of France. He published a "Short Account of the Cause of the Disease in Corn called the Blight, the Mildew, and the Rust," (1803,) and "Circumstances relative to Merino Sheep," (1809.) He died in London in 1820, and left no family. Cuvier composed a eulogy on him, which he read at the Institute in 1821.

See, also, DUNCAN's "Short Account of the Life of Sir Joseph Banks," 1821; "Sir J. Banks and the Royal Society," London, 1844.

Banks, (NATHANIEL PRENTISS,) an American statesman and general, born at Waltham, Massachusetts, in January, 1816, was a son of poor parents, and enjoyed few advantages of education. He learned the trade of a machinist, cultivated his mind at home, lectured before lyceums, and studied law. He became a member of the State legislature for 1849 as a Democrat, and was chosen Speaker of the House of Representatives of Massachusetts in 1851. In 1852 he was elected a member of Congress, in which he voted against the Kansas-Nebraska bill and separated from his party on the question of slavery. He was returned to Congress in November, 1854, by the Republicans and Know-Nothings, and was selected as the Republican candidate for Speaker of the House. After an exciting contest, which lasted more than two months, he was elected Speaker on the one hundred and thirty-third ballot, in February, 1856. He won a high reputation as a presiding officer.

In November, 1857, he was elected Governor of Massachusetts, and was re-elected for 1859 and 1860. On the breaking out of the rebellion in 1861, he was appointed in May a major-general of volunteers, soon after which he commanded a separate army on the Potomac. His army gained a victory at Winchester in March, 1862, and followed the retiring enemy to Harrisonburg. In May he was ordered to fall back to Strasburg, and a large part of his army was withdrawn. On the 24th of May he was attacked by General Stonewall Jackson, and made a rapid retreat to the Potomac, marching thirty-five miles in a day. He commanded a corps which under the orders of General Pope fought a severe battle at Cedar Mountain, Virginia, August 9, 1862. Both sides claimed the victory. In December, 1862, he superseded General Butler at New Orleans as commander of the Department of the Gulf. He took Opelousas in April, 1863, and Alexandria in the ensuing month, after defeating the enemy and capturing two thousand prisoners. About the 25th of May he invested Port Hudson, which was surrendered, with about six thousand prisoners, July 9.

In March, 1864, he began to move his army on an expedition against Shreveport, on the Red River, in which a fleet of gunboats and monitors under Rear-Admiral Porter co-operated. Porter took Alexandria on the 16th of March, and about ten days later Banks assembled his whole army at that place, from which he marched to Grand Ecore. On the 7th of April his advance engaged the enemy at Pleasant Hill and drove him from the field. The insurgents attacked and defeated a part of

his army at Sabine Cross-Roads and Peach Hill on the 8th. During the next night General Banks fell back to Pleasant Hill, where the enemy attacked him on the 9th and was repulsed with loss. The preservation of the gunboats under Porter was mainly due to the efficient aid of Lieutenant-Colonel Bailey, who, by damming the river, enabled the boats to descend in safety, although the water was at this time very low. The Union army, pressed by superior numbers, retreated to Alexandria, which it reached on the 27th of April and evacuated on the 14th of May, 1864. About that date General Banks was relieved from the command. He was elected a member of Congress in the autumn of 1864, and re-elected in 1866 and 1868. He served as chairman of the Committee of Foreign Relations in the Fortieth Congress.

Banks, (THOMAS,) one of the most eminent English sculptors, born at Lambeth in 1735. He studied architecture for a time under Kent, but he soon renounced it for sculpture. He exhibited in 1771 his group of "Mercury, Argos, and Io," which was so much admired that he was sent by the Academy in 1772 to pursue his studies at Rome. While there he produced his exquisite statue of "Psyche and the Butterfly," a model of classic grace, which was afterwards purchased by Catherine II. of Russia, and his group of "Caractacus before Claudius," also esteemed a master-piece. On the invitation of the empress Catherine, he visited Saint Petersburg in 1784; but, becoming dissatisfied, he returned to England, where he was soon after made a Royal Academician. Among his other productions may be named his noble figure of the "Mourning Achilles," and the monument to the daughter of Sir Brooke Boothby, a work of touching beauty, representing a sleeping child. Banks numbered among his friends Flaxman, Fuseli, and Horne Tooke. "He was," says Cunningham, "the first of our native sculptors whose aims were uniformly lofty and heroic and who desired to bring poetry to the aid of all his compositions, and, like Flaxman, added another to the number of those devout sculptors whose purity of life and reach of intellect are an honour to their country." Died in 1805.

See CUNNINGHAM, "Lives of Painters and Sculptors."

Banks, (THOMAS CHRISTOPHER,) an English genealogist, born about 1762, published, besides other works, "Stemmata Anglicana," (1825.) Died in 1854.

Ban'na-tyne, (GEORGE,) born in Scotland in 1545, was the compiler of the manuscripts entitled "Corpus Poeticum Scotorum." The Bannatyne Club, designed to promote the study of Scottish history and antiquities, was founded by Sir Walter Scott in 1823, and the "Memorials of George Bannatyne," edited by Sir Walter conjointly with D. Laing, appeared in 1826.

See CHAMBERS, "Biographical Dictionary of Eminent Scotsmen."

Bannatyne, (Sir WILLIAM,) a Scottish lawyer, born in 1743, was one of the founders of the Highland Society of Scotland, and contributed to the "Mirror" and the "Lounger." Died in 1834.

Ban'ne-ker, (BENJAMIN,) a negro mathematician of Maryland, born in 1731. Thomas Jefferson sent a manuscript copy of Banneker's almanac to the secretary of the Academy of Sciences at Paris. Banneker assisted in running the boundary-lines of the District of Columbia and laying out Washington City. In 1792 he published a letter addressed to Mr. Jefferson, then secretary of state. Died at Baltimore in 1806. Two sketches of his life have been published by the Maryland Historical Society.

See "Atlantic Monthly" for January, 1863.

Banner. See BANÉR.

Ban'ner-man, (ALEXANDER,) an English portrait-engraver, born at Cambridge in 1730; died about 1800.

Bannerman, (Sir ALEXANDER,) born at Aberdeen in 1783, was appointed Governor of Newfoundland in 1857.

Bannier. See BANÉR.

Ban'nis-ter or **Ban'is-ter,** (JOHN,) a distinguished comic actor, born in London in 1760; died in 1836.

See JOHN ADOLPHUS, "Memoirs of John Banister," 2 vols., 1829.

Ban'nis-ter, (WILLIAM B.,) an American lawyer and merchant, was born in Brookfield, Massachusetts, in 1774, or, according to some authorities, in 1783. He died in 1853, and left forty thousand dollars to charitable institutions.

Bannitza, bản-nit′sả, (JOSEPH LEO,) a German jurist, born at Würzburg in 1733; died in 1800.

Ban′quo, a Scottish chieftain of the eleventh century, was Thane of Lochaber, and the accomplice of Macbeth in the murder of King Duncan. He was assassinated by Macbeth in 1066, but his son Fleance escaped, and from him the house of Stuart derives its origin. Shakspeare, in his tragedy of "Macbeth," has somewhat altered the facts of history with regard to Banquo.

See GUTHRIE, "History of Scotland;" BURTON, "History of Scotland."

Banti, bản′tee, or **Bandi,** bản′dee, (GEORGINA BRIGIDA,) a celebrated Italian vocalist, born at Crema in 1757; died in 1806.

Banzer, bảnt′ser, (MARK,) a German medical writer, born at Augsburg in 1592; died in 1644.

Ba′o-dan′, King of Ireland, began to reign about 565 A.D. He was killed soon after by Colman.

Baour-Lormian, bả′oor′ lor′me′ôN′, (PIERRE MARIE FRANÇOIS LOUIS,) a French littérateur, born at Toulouse in 1770. He wrote an imitation of Ossian's poems, which attracted the favourable notice of Napoleon, also a number of poems and dramas, and translated Tasso's "Jerusalem Delivered" into French verse. He was admitted into the French Academy in 1815. Died in 1857.

Ba′phi-us, a Greek, who wrote "Commentaries on the Basilica," is supposed to have lived about 1050 A.D.

Ba-phom′e-tus, the name of a personage mentioned in the documents of the Gnostics, Templars, and Freemasons of the middle ages, conjectured by some to have been Mohammed.

Bapst, bảpst, or **Pabst,** pảpst, (MICHAEL,) a German physician and writer, born at Rochlitz in 1540; died in 1603.

Baptista, bảp-tès′tả, or **Battista,** bảt-tès′tả, a learned Italian lady and nun of the order of Santa Clara, was of the family of Malatesta. Died in 1447.

Baptista or **Battista,** (GIUSEPPE,) an Italian poet and theologian, born at Naples; died in 1675.

Baptiste, (JEAN.) See MONOYER.

Baptiste, bảp′tèst′, (JOHN GASPARD,) a Flemish painter, a pupil of Boschaert, born at Antwerp; died in 1691.

Baptiste, bảp′tèst′, (NICOLAS ANSELME,) THE ELDER, a French actor, born at Bordeaux in 1761, enjoyed a high reputation, particularly in comedy. Died in 1835.

Baptiste, (PAUL EUSTACHE ANSELME,) called THE YOUNGER, a son of the preceding, was likewise distinguished as a comic actor. Died in 1839.

Baptistin. See BATTISTIN.

Baquoy, bả′kwả′, (JEAN CHARLES,) a French engraver, born in Paris in 1721. He executed the vignettes for an edition of Ovid's "Metamorphoses." Died in 1777.

Baquoy, (MAURICE,) a French engraver, father of the preceding, born about 1680; died in Paris in 1747.

Baquoy, (PIERRE CHARLES,) son of Jean Charles, noticed above, was born in Paris in 1759. His engraving after Le Sueur's "Martyrdom of Saint Gervais and Saint Protais" is esteemed his master-piece. Died in 1829.

Bar, bar, (GEORG LUDWIG,) BARON OF, a German writer, born in Westphalia about 1701; died in 1767.

Bar, bảr, (JEAN ÉTIENNE,) a French advocate, born at Anneville in 1748. Being elected to the National Convention, he voted for the death of the king, and, after the fall of Robespierre, became secretary of the Convention. He was subsequently a member of the Council of Five Hundred, and president of the civil tribunal of Thionville. Died in 1801.

See LE BAS, "Dictionnaire encyclopédique de la France."

Bar, de, deh bảr, (ADRIEN AIMÉ Fleury—fluh′re′,) a French general, born at Thiais in 1783, served in the principal campaigns of the first empire, and subsequently distinguished himself in Algeria. He became lieutenant-general in 1844, and a senator in 1852. Died in 1861.

Bar, de, (FRANÇOIS,) a French Benedictine monk and ecclesiastical writer, born near Saint-Quentin in 1538; died in 1606.

Bar, de, (NICOLAS,) a French painter of the seventeenth century.

Bär or **Baer,** bair, [Lat. BÆ′RIUS,] (NICHOLAUS,) a German poet, born at Bremen in 1639, wrote Latin

poems on natural history, one of which is entitled "Ornithophonia." Died in 1714.

Bär or **Baer, von,** fon bair, (KARL ERNST,) an eminent Russian naturalist, of German extraction, born in Esthonia in February, 1792. He studied at Dorpat, and in 1819 became professor of zoology at Königsberg, where he founded a zoological museum. In 1837 he made a voyage to Nova Zembla, of which he afterwards gave an account in the "Memoirs of the Academy of Saint Petersburg." Among his principal works (in German) are a "History of the Development of Animals," (2 vols., 1828-37,) and "Researches on the Development of Fishes," (1835.) Since 1834 he has been a resident of Saint Petersburg, and librarian at the Academy of Sciences there. He made important discoveries in zoology and physiology.

See a sketch of his life, by himself, Saint Petersburg, 1865; also a notice in the "London Quarterly" for April, 1867.

Barabas, bŏr′ŏ-bŏsh, (NICOLAUS,) a Hungarian painter, born in Transylvania in 1810. Among his best works are portraits of Baron Wesselényi, Klapka, and Görgey. He was elected a member of the Academy of Arts at Vienna, and of the Hungarian Academy, (1837.)

Ba′rach or **Ba′rak,** [Heb. ברק,] a judge of the Hebrews, and son of Abinoam, flourished about 1240 B.C. Having, with the assistance of Deborah, defeated Sisera and delivered his people from the yoke of the Canaanites, he ruled over Israel. (See Judges iv.)

Baradæus, bả-rả-dee′us, (JACOBUS,) sometimes called **Zan′zalus,** a monk who distinguished himself by his zeal in reviving the heresy of the Monophysites or Eutychians. He was by his followers (called Jacobites) made Bishop of Edessa. Died in 588 A.D.

Baraguey d'Hilliers, bả′rả′gả′ de′ye-à′ or dèl′ye-à′, (ACHILLE,) a French marshal, son of Louis, noticed below, born in 1795, was aide-de-camp to Marshal Marmont in 1813. Having served successively in Austria, Spain, and Algeria, he was made lieutenant-general in 1843. He was appointed under Louis Napoleon one of the vice-presidents of the senate, and obtained the grand cross of the legion of honour. He was created in 1854 marshal of France.

Baraguey d'Hilliers, (LOUIS,) a French general, born in Paris in 1764, served in the Italian campaigns of 1796-97. Having been created inspector-general of infantry (1801) and grand officer of the legion of honour, (1804,) he commanded the dragoons in the invasion of Austria in 1805. Appointed governor of Venice in 1808, he shared with the viceroy Eugene in the victory of Raab. As commander of a division of the Russian army in 1812, he had the misfortune to fall into the hands of the enemy, with the greater part of his forces. For this he was suspended from his functions by Napoleon, and died soon after, of mortification.

See "Victoires et Conquêtes des Français."

Barahona, bả-rả-o′nả, (PEDRO,) surnamed VALDEVIESO, vẳl-dẳ-ve-ā′so, a Spanish theologian and religious writer of the sixteenth century.

Barahona y Soto, or **Baraona y Soto, de,** dả bả-rả-o′nả e so′to, (LUIS,) a Spanish poet and physician of the sixteenth century, born at Lucena, in Andalusia. He wrote a continuation of the "Orlando Furioso," entitled "The Tears of Angelica," which is eulogized by Cervantes in "Don Quixote," also a number of satires and eclogues, and translated some of Ovid's works into Spanish. Died about 1586.

See TICKNOR, "History of Spanish Literature."

Baraillon, bả′rả′yôN′, (JEAN FRANÇOIS,) a French physician, statesman, and writer, born at Vierzat, in Auvergne, in 1743. He was elected in 1792 to the Convention, where he voted for the imprisonment of the king. He was afterwards secretary of the Council of Five Hundred, and in 1801 president of the legislative body. Died in 1816.

Baraldi, bả-rảl′dee, (GIUSEPPE,) an Italian littérateur, born in 1778; died in 1832.

Baralt, bả-rảlt′, (RAFAEL MARIA,) a Spanish-American writer, born at Maracaibo about 1810. His principal work is entitled "History of Venezuela from its Discovery to 1797," (1 vol., 1841.) Two additional volumes, bringing it down to 1837, were subsequently written by Baralt, conjointly with Ramon Diaz.

Baranof, bä-rä′nof, (ALEXANDER ANDREVITCH,) governor of the Russian possessions in the northwestern part of America, founded in 1796 a colony at Behring Strait. He was ennobled by the emperor Alexander. Died in 1819.

Baranovitch, bä-rä′no-vitch, (LAZAR,) a Russian theologian, became Archbishop of Tchernigov. He was the author of a poem "On the Vicissitudes of Human Life," and other works. Died in 1693.

Baranovski, bä-rä-nov′skee, [Lat. BARANO′VIUS,] (ALBERT,) a Polish archbishop of Gnesen under the reign of Sigismund III. Died in 1615.

Baranovski, (STANISLAS,) of Rzeplin, a Polish biographical writer of the seventeenth century.

Barante, de, deh bä′rôNt′, (AMABLE GUILLAUME PROSPER **Brugière**—brü′zhe-aiR′,) a French statesman, an excellent historian and miscellaneous writer, son of Claude Ignace, (the second of that name,) noticed below, was born at Riom in 1782. He was appointed under Louis XVIII. general secretary in the ministry of the interior, and in 1819 made a peer of France. He was the author of a "Picture of French Literature in the Eighteenth Century," (1808,) "Literary Miscellanies," (1836,) and "History of the Dukes of Burgundy," (13 vols., 1826.) The last-named work has a high reputation. He also published a "History of the National Convention," (1853,) and translated Schiller's dramas. In 1828 he succeeded Desèze in the French Academy. Died in December, 1866.

See a "Memoir of Prosper de Barante," by GUIZOT, 1867.

Barante, de, (CLAUDE IGNACE BRUGIÈRE,) a French critic and dramatist, born at Riom, in Auvergne, in 1670; died in 1745.

Barante, de, (CLAUDE IGNACE BRUGIÈRE,) BARON, grandson of the preceding, born at Riom in 1745. He published, among other works, an "Examination of the Fundamental Principle of Rochefoucauld's Maxims," (1798.) Died in 1814.

See QUÉRARD, "La France Littéraire."

Baranzano, bä-rän-zä′no, (GIOVANNI ANTONIO,) surnamed REDEMP′TUS, a Piedmontese monk and philosopher, born in the diocese of Vercelli in 1590, became professor of philosophy at Annecy. He opposed the doctrines of Aristotle, and was the author of "Uranoscopia," and other works, in Latin. He was a friend and correspondent of Lord Bacon. Died in 1622.

See BAYLE, "Historical and Critical Dictionary;" NICÉRON, "Mémoires."

Baraona y Soto. See BARAHONA Y SOTO.

Barat, bä′rä′, (NICOLAS,) a French Orientalist, born at Bourges, aided Thomassin in his "Glossarium Hebraicum." Died in 1706.

Baratier, bä′rä′te-ä′, written also **Barretier,**(JOHANN PHILIPP,) a German youth, of French extraction, celebrated for precocity of intellect, was born near Nuremberg in 1721. At the age of thirteen he had mastered Latin and Greek and the principal Oriental tongues, and translated from the Hebrew into French the travels of Benjamin of Tudela. In 1735 he was created master of arts by the University of Halle, where he publicly defended fourteen theses. He died in 1740, at the age of nineteen.

See J. H. S. FORMEY, "Vie de J. P. Baratier," 1741; F. BARATIER, "Nachricht von seinem frühzeitig gelehrten Sohne," 1728; DR. JOHNSON'S Works, vol. xiii., 1812.

Baratta, bä-rät′tä, (FRANCESCO,) an Italian sculptor, born at Massa di Carrara. Among his works are a "Hercules," and a colossal statue intended to represent the river La Plata. Died in 1666.

Baratta, (FRANCESCO,) an Italian painter, born at Genoa, removed to Rome in 1824.

Baratta, (PIETRO,) a Venetian sculptor, lived in the second half of the seventeenth century.

Barattieri, bä-rät-te-ä′ree,(BARTOLOMMEO,) an Italian jurist of the sixteenth century, was a native of Placentia. He composed a work "On Feudal Law."

Baratynski, bä-rä-tin′skee, (ABRAM,) an eminent Russian poet, the friend and contemporary of Pushkin, resided during his youth in Saint Petersburg. He afterwards spent eight years in the military service in Finland. His poem entitled "The Gypsy" is a charming picture

of Russian life, and enjoys great popularity. He published in 1833 his complete works, in two volumes. Died in 1844.

See BROCKHAUS, "Conversations-Lexikon."

Barba, baR′bä, (ALVAREZ ALONSO,) a Spanish ecclesiastic, who lived in the early part of the seventeenth century, was the author of a "Treatise on Metallurgy," (1640,) which was translated into French and German.

Barba, baR′bä, (GIOVANNI,) an Italian advocate and prelate, born at Naples, was one of the twelve consistorial advocates at Rome. He published a treatise "On the Art and Method of Languages," (1734.) Died about 1745.

Barba, (JUAN SANCHEZ,) a Spanish sculptor, whose principal work is a statue of the "Dying Saviour," at the convent della Merced at Madrid. Died in 1670.

Barba, (PEDRO,) professor of medicine at Valladolid, became in 1621 first physician to Philip IV. of Spain.

Barba, della, děl′lä baR′bä, (POMPEO,) an Italian naturalist and writer of the sixteenth century, born at Pescia, was physician to Pope Pius IV. Died in 1582.

Barbacena, baR-bä-sä′nä, (F. **Caldeira Brant**—käl-dä′e-rä brânt,) MARQUIS OF, a Brazilian diplomatist and soldier, born at Sabora in 1772. He was appointed by the Emperor of Brazil to conduct the negotiations in relation to the independence of that country, with Portugal, and was afterwards minister of finance. Barbacena was the first to introduce steamboats and steam-engines into Brazil. Died in 1842.

Barbadillo, baR-bä-děl′yo, (ALFONSO GERONIMO de **Salas**—dä sä′läs,) a Spanish novelist and dramatic writer, born at Madrid about 1580, was an intimate friend of Cervantes, whose style he imitated. Died in 1630.

See TICKNOR, "History of Spanish Literature;" BAENA, "Hijos de Madrid."

Barbadino, baR-bä-dee′no, a Portuguese writer of the eighteenth century, was the author of a work on the "True Method of being Useful to the Church and State."

Barbadoro, baR-bä-do′ro, (BARTOLOMMEO,) an Italian scholar of the sixteenth century, was a native of Florence. In conjunction with Jerome Mei, he discovered the "Electra" of Euripides and the "Agamemnon" of Æschylus, subsequently published by P. Victorius.

See ERSCH und GRUBER, "Allgemeine Encyklopaedie."

Barbalho Bezerra, baR-bäl′yo bä-zěr′rä, (AGOSTINHO,) a Brazilian traveller, born at Saint Paul. He was appointed general superintendent of the mines of Brazil in 1664, and explored that region in search of precious stones. Died about 1667.

Barbalunga. See RICCI.

Barbançois, de, deh bäR′bôN′swä′, (CHARLES Hélion—ä′le-ôN′,) MARQUIS, a French nobleman and agricultural writer, born near Châteauroux in 1760. He was the first who introduced Spanish sheep into France, (1776.) Died in 1822.

Barbançon, de, deh bäR′bôN′sôN′, (MARIE,) a French lady of the latter part of the sixteenth century, celebrated for her brave defence of her castle against Montare, governor of Bourbonnais.

Barbanègre, bäR′bä′nägR′, (JOSEPH,) BARON OF, a French general, born at Pontacq, in Basses-Pyrénées, in 1772. He served in Napoleon's Austrian and Russian campaigns, and in 1815 bravely defended Huningen against the allies for nearly two months. Died in 1830.

Bar′ba-ra, SAINT, [Fr. SAINTE-BARBE, säNt′bäRb,] a celebrated martyr, supposed to have been contemporary with Origen and to have been instructed by him. According to some writers, she suffered death under Galerius; while others state that she was martyred at Nicomedia in the reign of Maximin I.

See MRS. JAMESON'S "Sacred and Legendary Art;" MORÉRI, "Dictionnaire Historique."

Barbarelli. See GIORGIONE.

Barbarigo, baR-bä-ree′go,[Lat. BARBARI′CUS,](AGOSTINO,) became Doge of Venice in 1486. During his rule Italy was invaded by Charles VIII. of France, the Turks deprived Venice of her Greek provinces, and Cyprus was reunited to the Venetian republic, on condition of the payment of an annual tribute of eight thousand ducats to the queen of that island. Died in 1501.

See DARU, "Histoire de Venise."

Barbarigo, [Lat. BARBARI′CUS,] (GREGORIO,) born in Venice in 1625, was made a cardinal in 1660. He was distinguished for his learning and piety, and for his liberal patronage of literature. Died in 1697.

See RICCHINI, "De Vita ac Rebus gestis B. G. Barbarici," 1761.

Barbarigo, (NICCOLÒ,) a relative of Agostino, was ambassador from Venice to Constantinople. He wrote, in Latin, the lives of the doge Andrea Gritti and of Cardinal Contarini. Died in 1579.

Barbarini, (FRANCESCO.) See BARBERINI.

Barbaro, baR′bȧ-ro, (DANIELLO,) an Italian ecclesiastic of the sixteenth century, born at Venice, was the author of a treatise "On Eloquence," and of one "On the Architecture of Vitruvius," (1556.) Died in 1570.

Barbaro, (ERMOLAO,) an Italian prelate, born at Venice about 1410, became Bishop of Treviso in 1443. He made a Latin translation of Æsop's "Fables," (unpublished.) Died in 1471.

Barbaro or **Bar′barus,** (ERMOLAO or HERMOLAUS,) an Italian diplomatist and scholar, born at Venice in 1454, was a grandson of Francesco, mentioned below. He studied under Pomponius Lætus, and in 1477 became professor of philosophy at Padua. He was afterwards employed on several important embassies. Among his principal works is a critical commentary on Pliny's "Natural History," entitled "Castigationes Plinianæ." He also made translations from Dioscorides and Aristotle into Latin. Died in 1493.

See TEISSIER, "Éloges des Savants;" NICÉRON, "Mémoires."

Barbaro, (FRANCESCO,) an Italian scholar, orator, and statesman, born at Venice in 1398, rose through several offices to be procurator of Saint Mark. He was the author of a "Treatise on Marriage," and of other works, in Latin. Died in 1454.

See GHILINI, "Teatro de' Uomini letterati."

Barbaro, (JOSAPHAT,) a Venetian traveller of the fifteenth century. His "Journey to the Tanais, Persia, India, and Constantinople" (1543) is to be found in Ramusio's "Collection of Travels." Died in 1494.

See MAZZUCHELLI, "Scrittori d'Italia."

Barbarossa. See FREDERICK I. OF GERMANY.

Bar-ba-ros′sa,* the name of two brothers, who, as corsairs, were the terror of Christendom during almost the whole of the first half of the sixteenth century. The elder, AROOJ, HORUSH, or HORUC, was a native of Mitylene. Having embraced the Mohammedan religion and commenced his career as a corsair, he at length became (about 1517) ruler of a large portion of what is now known as Algeria. In 1518 Charles V. sent an army of Spaniards against Arooj, who, after displaying the most desperate courage, was defeated and slain.

His brother HADHER, (hȧd′ẽr,) usually known by his surname KHAIR-ED-DEEN, (or -EDDÏN′, KÏR′ed-deen′, (*i.e.* the "good of the faith,") was immediately after the death of Arooj proclaimed ruler of Algiers. In order to resist the Spaniards, he offered the sovereignty of Algiers to the Turkish sultan, Selim I., on condition of being made viceroy and obtaining reinforcements of troops. A body of two thousand janissaries was sent to him in 1519, and the dominion of Turkey from that time was established in Algiers. In 1532 Barbarossa, on the solicitation of the people of Tunis, drove away their king, Muley Hassan, and assumed the chief power. Being appointed "capudan pasha," or great admiral, by Solyman, he ravaged the coast of Italy in 1534, but was soon after defeated by the emperor Charles V. and his celebrated admiral, Doria, who captured Tunis. The French king, Francis I., having formed an alliance with the Sultan against Charles V., their united forces laid siege in 1543 to Nice, which they obliged to capitulate. Barbarossa died at Constantinople in 1546.

See MORGAN, "History of Algiers;" ROBERTSON, "Charles V.," chaps. v. and vi.

Barbarossa, baR-bȧ-ros′sȧ, (PAOLO EMILIO,) an Italian poet and mystic, born at Trapani; died in 1614.

Barbaroux, bȧR′bȧ′roo′, (CHARLES JEAN MARIE,) a prominent member of the Girondist party during the French Revolution, born at Marseilles in 1767. He had already distinguished himself by his eloquence as an advocate, when he became in 1791 deputy-extraordinary from Marseilles to the Legislative Assembly in Paris, and there formed an intimacy with Vergniaud, Roland, and other distinguished revolutionists. Elected afterwards to the National Convention, he denounced Robespierre and his colleagues, and, during the trial of the king, voted for his death, but with the appeal to the people. After the proscription of the Girondists by the Jacobins, in May, 1793, Barbaroux left Paris, but, having concealed himself for some days in the neighbourhood of Bordeaux, was at length discovered, and guillotined in that city in 1794.

See his "Mémoires," 1822; LAMARTINE, "History of the Girondists."

Barbaroux, (CHARLES OGER,) a French advocate and writer, son of the preceding, born at Marseilles in 1792. He published a part of his father's "Mémoires," (1822,) a "History of the United States," (1824,) and other works. He was elected a member of the Council of State in 1849, and became Senator in 1858.

Barbat. See BARBUT.

Barbatelli. See POCCETTI.

Barbato, baR-bȧ′to, (BARTOLOMMEO,) an Italian poet, born at Padua. He edited Tasso's great poem, and wrote a "Life of Tasso," (1628.)

Barbato, (GIROLAMO,) an Italian medical writer, first discovered the serum of the blood, on which he wrote a treatise, (1667.)

Barbatus. See ASCLEPIUS, (NICHOLAS.)

Bar-bā′tus, (M. HORATIUS,) a Roman of the Horatian gens, who, having distinguished himself by his opposition to the second decemvirate, became, with Valerius Poplicola, the leader of the plebeian party. They were conjointly elected consuls in 449 B.C., and during their consulship were passed the laws entitled "Valeriæ Horatiæ Leges," confirming the liberties of the people.

Bar′bauld, [Fr. pron. bȧR′bō′,] (ANNA LÆTITIA,) an English writer, born in Leicestershire in 1743. She was the daughter of the Rev. John Aikin, by whom she was early instructed in the classics. In 1773 she brought out a collection of poems, which immediately gave her a high reputation, and which passed through four editions in one year. This was soon followed by "Miscellaneous Pieces in Prose," written conjointly with her brother, Dr. John Aikin. Miss Aikin was married in 1774 to the Rev. Rochemont Barbauld, a dissenting divine of French extraction, who a short time after opened a school for boys at Palgrave, in Suffolk. About this time Mrs. Barbauld wrote, for the use of a few pupils under her charge, "Hymns in Prose for Children," which are full of poetic feeling and moral beauty. In 1775 she published "Devotional Pieces," and "Early Lessons;" the latter, intended for young children, was received with great favour, and still retains its popularity. In 1791 she wrote a poetical epistle to Wilberforce on the rejection of the bill for the abolition of the slave-trade, and in 1792 "Remarks on Mr. Gilbert Wakefield's Inquiry into the Expediency, etc. of Public or Social Worship." She brought out in 1793 a sermon entitled "The Sins of the Government the Sins of the Nation," which, as well as the preceding treatises, displays great ability and the strongest love of justice. Among Mrs. Barbauld's other productions may be named her poem entitled "Eighteen Hundred and Eleven," and her contributions to the popular work "Evenings at Home." She also published a selection from the "Spectator," "Tatler," and "Guardian," with a preliminary essay which shows great critical acuteness, accompanied by the most interesting parts of his correspondence. She died in 1825. Mrs. Barbauld's books for children are among the most useful and attractive of their kind, and her writings are all characterized by the elevated morality and deep devotional feeling which were so conspicuous in her life.

See "Life of Mrs. Barbauld," prefixed to her works, by LUCY AIKIN; MRS. ELWOOD, "Memoirs of the Literary Ladies of England," etc., vol. i., 1843.

Barbault, bȧR′bō′, (ANTOINE FRANÇOIS,) a French

---

* Derived, according to some writers, from *barba,* "beard," and *rossa,* (Italian,) "red," from the colour of their beard; but, according to others, Barbarossa is a corruption of *Baba* ("father")-*Horush,* the name by which Arooj was commonly called by his followers.

---

surgeon, born in Paris in 1705. He was the author of "Principles of Surgery," and other works of the kind. Died in 1784.

Barbault-Royer, bȧr′bō′ rwȧ′yȧ′, (P. F.), a West Indian diplomatist and journalist, (of the coloured race,) was engaged in the insurrection of Saint Domingo in 1792. Being sent to France with complaints against the colonial government, he was unable even to obtain a hearing from the Council of Five Hundred. He was afterwards associate editor of the official journal of the Directory in France, and was employed in the ministry of foreign affairs.

See QUÉRARD, "La France Littéraire."

Barbazan, bȧr′bȧ′zŏn′, (ÉTIENNE,) a French writer, born in the diocese of Auxerre in 1696, published, among other works, "Fables and Stories of the French Poets from the Eleventh to the Sixteenth Centuries," (1756.) Died in 1770.

Barbazan,de, dĕh bȧr′bȧ′zŏn′,(ARNAULD GUILHEM,) SIRE, a celebrated French soldier, was one of the most active defenders of the cause of Charles VII. against the Burgundian faction. In 1430 he defeated the united English and Burgundian army at La Croisette, for which service he was made governor of Champagne and Brie and received the title of restorer of the kingdom and crown of France. Died in 1432.

See DU CHÊNE, "Histoire de la Maison du Plessis de Richelieu."

Barbe, bȧrb, (PHILIPPE,) a learned French priest, born in London in 1723, translated some of the Greek Fathers. Died in France in 1792.

See MATHIEU, "Notice sur le Père Barbe."

Barbe, SAINTE. See BARBARA, SAINT.

Barbé-Marbois. See MARBOIS.

Barbe-Radziwil. See RADZIWIL.

Barbeau de la Bruyère, bȧr′bō′ dĕh lȧ brü′yaiʀ′, (JEAN LOUIS,) born in Paris in 1710, published a valuable "Historical Chart," (1750,) and translated from the German of Strahlemberg the "Description of the Russian Empire." Died in 1781.

Barbedette-Chermelais, bȧrb′dĕt′ shĕrm′lȧ′, (JOSEPH JEAN,) a distinguished French jurist, born in the department of Ille-et-Vilaine in 1784 ; died in 1826.

Bar′ber, (FRANCIS,) an American officer, born at Princeton, New Jersey, in 1751. He became in 1769 rector of an academy at Elizabethtown, and gained a high reputation as a teacher. General Alexander Hamilton was one of his pupils. He entered the army in 1776, obtained the rank of lieutenant-colonel in the same year, and served in the battles of Trenton, Princeton, Brandywine, and Monmouth. In 1781 he was selected by General Washington to suppress a mutiny of the Pennsylvania and New Jersey troops, and performed that mission with success. Colonel Barber was killed accidentally at Newburg, New York, in 1783.

Bar′ber, (JOHN,) an English lawyer of the sixteenth century, was an intimate friend of Archbishop Cranmer. He was a contributor to the compilation entitled "Necessary Doctrine and Erudition of a Christian Man."

Barber, (JOHN W.,) an American writer, born in Windsor, Connecticut, in 1798. His principal works are "Connecticut Historical Collections," (1836,) "Massachusetts Historical Collections," (1839,) and "European Historical Collections," (1855.) In conjunction with Henry Howe, of New Haven, he has also published "Historical Collections" of New York, (1841,) New Jersey, (1844,) Virginia, (1844,) and Ohio, (1847.)

Bar′ber, (MARY,) born at Dublin about 1712, was a friend and protégée of Dean Swift. She published a volume of poems under the patronage of Swift and Lord Orrery. Died in 1757.

Barbereau, bȧrb′rō′ or bȧr′bĕh′rō′, (MATHURIN AUGUSTE BALTHASAR,) a French musician, born in Paris in 1799, composed the music for the opera entitled "The Sybarites of Florence."

Barberet, bȧrb′rȧ′, (DENIS,) a learned French physician, born at Arnay-le-Duc, in Burgundy, in 1714. He was the author of a treatise "On the Epidemic Diseases of Beasts," and other works. Died in 1770.

Barberi, bȧr-bȧ′ree, (FILIPPO,) an Italian theologian, born at Syracuse ; lived about 1480.

Barberi, (FRANCESCO,) an Italian jurist, was fiscal

procurator under Pius VI. He had charge of the prosecution of the celebrated impostor Cagliostro, whom he condemned to perpetual imprisonment. Died about 1800.

Barberi, (GIOVANNI,) an Italian architect and painter of perspective, worked at Rome about 1785.

Barberini, bar-bȧ-ree′nee, (ANTONIO,) surnamed THE ELDER, born at Florence, of a noble family, in 1569, was a brother of Pope Urban VIII. He was created Cardinal of Sinigaglia in 1624. Died in 1646.

Barberini, (ANTONIO,) called THE YOUNGER, born at Rome in 1608, was a nephew of Pope Urban VIII., and was made a cardinal in 1628. Died in 1671.

Barberini, (BONAVENTURA,) an Italian ecclesiastic and Archbishop of Ferrara, where he was born in 1674. He was the author of "Orations," in Italian, which were admired in his time. Died in 1743.

Barberini, (FRANCESCO,) an Italian cardinal, born at Florence in 1597, was a nephew of Urban VIII., by whom he was made librarian of the Vatican and appointed to various high offices. He made a translation of the twelve books of Marcus Aurelius from the Greek into Italian, and was the founder of the celebrated Barberini Library. Died in 1679.

Barberini or **Barbarini,** bar-bȧ-ree′nee, (FRANCESCO,) an Italian poet, born at Barberino, near Florence, in 1264, was a pupil of Brunetto Latini, who has been immortalized by Dante. His principal work is entitled "Documenti d'Amore," being a kind of moral and philosophic treatise in verse. Died in 1348.

Barberini, (FRANCESCO,) a descendant of the noble Roman family of that name, is the present owner of the splendid Barberini palace, which was built in the time of Urban VIII., and, next to the Vatican, is the largest in Rome. It contains several master-pieces of Raphael, Pietro da Cortona, and other eminent painters.

Barberini or **Barberino,** (MAFFEO.) See URBAN VIII.

Barberini, (TADDEO,) a nephew of Pope Urban VIII., who gave him the principality of Palestrina. He attempted to conquer the duchy of Parma, but was defeated. Died in 1647.

Barberousse, the French for BARBAROSSA, which see.

Barbès, bȧr′bês′, (ARMAND,) a French conspirator, born in the island of Guadeloupe in 1810, removed to Paris, and took part in the attack on the Conciergerie in 1839, for which he was condemned to imprisonment for life. On the revolution in 1848 he was released, but soon becoming involved in another conspiracy he was taken and confined in the prison of Belle-Ile-en-Mer.

Barbésieux, de, dĕh bȧr′bȧ′ze′uh′, (LOUIS FRANÇOIS le Tellier,) dĕh tȧ′le-ȧ′,) MARQUIS, born in Paris in 1668, was a son of Louvois. He became minister of state under Louis XIV. Died in 1701.

Barbette, bȧr′bĕt′, (PAUL,) a distinguished physician of the seventeenth century, born at Strasburg, resided at Amsterdam, where he had an extensive practice.

Barbetti, bar-bĕt′tee, (ANGELO,) an Italian artist, born at Sienna in 1803, was celebrated for his skill as a sculptor of wood.

Barbeu-Dubourg, bȧr′buh′ dü′booʀ′, (JACQUES,) a French physician and naturalist, born at Mayenne in 1709. He was a friend and correspondent of Franklin, to whom he dedicated his "Code of Human Reason." He also published "The French Botanist," and "Elements of Medicine," and translated into French Bolingbroke's "Letters on History," (1752.) He edited the works of Franklin, translated into French by Lécuy. The name of Barbeuia has been given to a genus of Madagascar plants. Died in 1779.

Barbeyrac, bȧr′bȧ′rȧk′, (CHARLES,) a French physician of high reputation, born at Céreste, in Provence, in 1629. He is said by John Locke, who was intimate with them both, to have greatly resembled Sydenham both in his views of medicine and his manners. He died in 1699, leaving a number of medical works in Latin and French.

Barbeyrac, (JEAN,) an eminent French jurist, born at Béziers in 1674, was the son of a Calvinistic divine who removed to Switzerland on the revocation of the edict of Nantes. He became professor of history and civil law at Lausanne in 1711, and of public law at Groningen in 1717. Among his principal works are his

" Histury of Ancient Treaties," from the earliest times to the death of Charlemagne, a translation into French of Puffendorf's " Abridgment of the Law of Nature and of Nations," (1706,) and the treatise "De Jure Belli et Pacis" of Grotius. Barbeyrac was a member of the Royal Society of Sciences at Berlin. Died in 1744.

See G. Laissac, " Notice biographique sur Barbeyrac," 1838.

Barbiani, baR-be-â'nee, (GIOVANNI BATTISTA SI-MONE,) a painter of the Bolognese school, born at Ravenna. Died in 1650.

Barbiano, baR-be-â'no, (ALBERICO,) COUNT, an Italian commander of the fourteenth century, was noted as having substituted native troops instead of the foreign mercenaries hitherto employed. Barbiano's forces, called the Company of Saint George, acquired a high reputation, and some of the first generals of the time were trained in his school. In 1384 he was appointed, by Charles III. of Naples, grand constable of the kingdom. Died in 1409.

See Sismondi, " Histoire des Républiques Italiennes."

Barbié du Bocage, bȧR'be-â' dü bo'kȧzh', (ALEXANDRE FRANÇOIS,) a French geographer, born in Paris in 1798, published a " Dictionary of Biblical Geography." Died in 1835.

Barbié du Bocage, (JEAN DENIS,) a distinguished French geographer, born in Paris in 1760, was a pupil of the celebrated D'Anville. He executed the maps for Choiseul-Gouffier's " Voyage pittoresque de la Grèce," (1824,) the atlas for the " Travels of Anacharsis," and a valuable map of the Morea. He also wrote an " Account of the Life and Works of D'Anville," (1802.) Died in 1825.

See Quérard, " La France Littéraire."

Barbier, bȧR-be-â', (ANTOINE ALEXANDRE,) a French bibliographer, born at Coulommiers in 1765. He became successively keeper of the library of the council of state, private librarian to Napoleon, (1807,) and, after the restoration, superintendent of the private libraries of the king. He obtained the decoration of the legion of honour in 1822. He was the author of a " Dictionary of Anonymous and Pseudonymous Works," (4 vols. 8vo, 1806–08,) which is highly esteemed, and a "Catalogue of the Library of the Council of State." Died in Paris in 1825.

See a " Life of Barbier" prefixed to the fourth volume of his Dictionary; Louis Barbier, " Notice biographique sur A. A. Barbier," 1827.

Barbier, (CHARLES,) a French philanthropist, born in the eighteenth century. He spent much time in devising a method to teach the blind to write in characters legible to themselves. Died about 1830.

Barbier, (EDMOND JEAN FRANÇOIS,) a French jurist and littérateur, born in Paris in 1689. He was the author of a " Historical and Anecdotical Journal of the Reign of Louis XV.," (7 vols. 4to,) which contains interesting information not met with elsewhere. Died in 1771.

Barbier, (HENRI AUGUSTE,) a French satiric poet, born in Paris in 1805. His poem entitled " La Curée" came out in 1830, and was soon followed by the " Émeute," " La Popularité," and " The Idol," political satires which caused a great sensation and at once established his fame as a patriot and poet. In 1831 he published a collection of pieces under the title of " Iambics."

See Longfellow's " Poets and Poetry of Europe."

Barbier, (HIPPOLYTE,) a French biographer and ecclesiastic, born at Orléans about 1805. He published a valuable " Biography of Contemporary Clergymen," (10 vols., 1841 et seq.)

Barbier, (JEAN BAPTISTE GRÉGOIRE,) a French physician and botanist, lived at Amiens about 1800–20.

Barbier, (LOUIS,) surnamed the ABBÉ DE LA RIVIÈRE, (lȧ re've'air',) a French prelate, was almoner of Gaston, Duke of Orléans. As a reward for betraying the secrets of his master to Cardinal Mazarin, he was created, by the latter, Bishop of Langres. Died in 1670.

Barbier, (MARIE ANNE,) a French writer, born at Orléans, was the author of the tragedies entitled " Cornelia," " The Death of Cæsar," and " Arria and Pætus," also several poems and operas. Died in 1742.

Barbier d'Aucour, bȧR'be-â' dŏ'kooR', (JEAN,) a French critic and littérateur, born at Langres about 1640. His principal work is entitled " Opinions of Cleanthe on

the Conversations of Ariste and Eugène," by the Jesuit Père Bouhours, (1672,) esteemed a model of able and ingenious criticism. Barbier was a member of the French Academy, and an opponent of the Jesuits. Died in 1694.

See Nicéron, " Mémoires."

Barbier-Vémars, bȧR'be-â' vȧ'mȧR', (JOSEPH NICOLAS,) a French philologist, born at Louvres in 1775. He aided in the compilation of the "Annals of the Arts and Manufactures," (55 vols., 1807–14.)

Barbieri, baR-be-â'ree, (FRANCESCO,) surnamed IL LEGNANO, (èl lȧn-yâ'no,) an able historical and landscape painter of the Venetian school, born at Legnano in 1623 ; died in 1698.

Barbieri, (GIOVANNI FRANCESCO.) See GUERCINO.

Barbieri, (GIOVANNI MARIA,) an Italian philologist, born at Módena in 1519, wrote a history of Attila, (" La Guerra d'Attila," 1569.) Died in 1574.

Barbieri, (LODOVICO,) an Italian painter and engraver, born at Bologna, worked about 1660–1700.

Barbieri, (PAOLO ANTONIO,) an Italian painter of the Bolognese school, was a brother of Guercino. He devoted himself chiefly to painting animals and fruits, in which department he attained great excellence. Died in 1649.

See Lanzi, " History of Painting in Italy."

Barbieri, (PIETRO ANTONIO,) a painter of the Milanese school, born at Pavía in 1663 ; died after 1700.

Barbieri, del, dèl baR-be-â'ree, or **Barbiere**, baR-be-â'rà, [Fr. BARBIER, bȧR'be-â',](DOMENICO,) surnamed THE FLORENTINE, an Italian painter and engraver, born at Florence in 1501. He was a pupil of Rosso, whom he assisted in executing the frescos at Fontainebleau and Meudon, in France. His engravings after Michael Angelo and Titian are highly esteemed.

See Vasari, " Lives of the Painters."

Barbiers, baR-beers', (BARTHOLOMEUS,) a Dutch landscape-painter, born at Amsterdam in 1740, was a son of Pieter, noticed below. Died in 1808.

Barbiers, (PIETER,) a Dutch painter, born in 1717. One of his principal works represents the burning of the Opera-House at Amsterdam. Died in 1780.

Barbiers, (PIETER Bartsz—bȧRts,) son of Bartholomeus, noticed above, born at Amsterdam in 1772, produced historical pictures and landscapes of superior merit. Died in 1837.

Bar-bil'lus, a Roman astrologer of the first century, was patronized by the emperor Vespasian, while others of the profession were excluded from the city.

Barbo, (PETER.) See PAUL II.

Barbolani, baR-bo-lȧ'nee, (TORQUATO,) an Italian poet and soldier, born at Arezzo, rose to be lieutenant-colonel in the service of the emperor Francis I. He was the author of Latin and Italian poems, and translated the " Orlando Furioso" into Latin verse. Died in 1756.

See Tipaldo, " Biografia degli Italiani illustri."

Barbosa, baR-bo'sȧ, (AGOSTINHA DA SYLVA,) a Portuguese lady, who lived about 1680, and published, under the pseudonym of Pedro do Albornoz, a "Treatise on Architecture and Arithmetic."

Barbosa, (AGOSTINHO,) a Portuguese prelate and jurist, born in 1590, was created Bishop of Ugento by Philip IV. of Spain. He was the author of theological and legal works. Died in 1649.

Barbosa, (AYRES (ī'rês) or ARIUS,) a Portuguese poet and scholar of the fifteenth century, studied Greek at Florence, and subsequently contributed greatly to revive classical literature in Spain and Portugal. After teaching at Salamanca, he was appointed tutor to the Portuguese princes Alfonso and Henry. He died in 1530, leaving several Latin poems and grammatical works.

See Barbosa Machado, " Bibliotheca Lusitana."

Barbosa, (CAETANO,) surnamed CONSTANTINO, (konstȧn-tee'no,) born at Evora, in Portugal, in 1660, was one of the most celebrated preachers of his time.

Barbosa, (DUARTE,) a Portuguese navigator, born at Lisbon about 1480, visited India and the Moluccas, and wrote an account of those countries, which is contained in Ramusio's collection. Having accompanied Magellan in his voyage around the world, Barbosa was assassinated in the island of Zebu in 1521.

Barbosa, (JOZÉ,) a Portuguese historian, born aᵗ Lisbon in 1674, was a brother of Barbosa Machado. He

ā, ē, ī, ō, ū, ȳ, long; ă, ĕ, ŏ, same, less prolonged; ă, ĕ, ĭ, ŏ, ŭ, ў, short; ą, ę, į, ǫ, obscure; fär, fȧll, fȧt; mêt; nŏt; gōōd; mōōn;

was appointed historiographer of the house of Braganza, and wrote a work entitled "Chronological Catalogue of the Queens of Portugal and their Sons," (1727.) Died in 1750.

Barbosa, (MANOEL,) a Portuguese jurist, the father of Agostinho, flourished about 1570–1630.

Barbosa, (PEDRO,) a celebrated Portuguese jurist of the sixteenth century, was professor of law at Coimbra. Though he opposed Philip II. of Spain as the usurper of the crown of Portugal, he was created by him a councillor of state and chancellor of the kingdom. He wrote a number of valuable legal works, in Latin. Died in 1606.

See JÖCHER, "Allgemeines Gelehrten-Lexikon."

Barbosa, (VINCENT,) a Portuguese monk, born in 1663, left a work on Borneo and the missions of that island, (1692.) Died in 1711.

Barbosa Bacellar, baʀ-bo'să bă-sĕl-laʀ', (ANTONIO,) a celebrated Portuguese jurist, poet, and historian, born at Lisbon in 1610. He wrote, among other works, a defence of the house of Braganza. Died in 1663.

See BARBOSA MACHADO, "Bibliotheca Lusitana."

Barbosa Machado, baʀ-bo'să mă-shă'do, (DIEGO,) a Portuguese biographical and historical writer, born at Lisbon in 1682. His principal work, entitled "Bibliotheca Lusitana," (4 vols. folio, 1741–59,) is a historical and critical notice of Portuguese writers, and, though containing some errors, is esteemed the most valuable production of the kind in that language. Died in 1770.

See "Nouvelle Biographie Générale."

Barbot, băʀ'bo', (JEAN,) a French traveller of the seventeenth century, was inspector of the establishments of the French West India Company. He wrote a "Description of the Western Shores of Africa and the Adjacent Countries." Died in 1720.

Barbot, (MARIE ÉTIENNE,) a French general, born at Toulouse in 1770; died in 1839.

Barbotan, băʀ'bo'tôn', (CLAIRE JOSEPH,) a French general, born about 1719, was elected to the States-General in 1789, and executed in 1794.

Barbou, băʀ'boo', (HUGUES,) a son of Jean, noticed below, published at Limoges, in 1580, an excellent edition of Cicero's "Letters to Atticus."

Barbou, (JEAN,) a celebrated French printer and resident of Lyons, published, in 1539, an edition of the works of Clément Marot, printed with remarkable elegance and accuracy.

Barbou, (JEAN JOSEPH,) a French printer of Paris, noted for the correctness and beauty of his editions. Died in 1752.

Barbou, (JOSEPH,) a brother of the preceding, became a printer in Paris about 1722. Died in 1737.

Barbou, (JOSEPH GÉRARD,) established himself as a bookseller in Paris in 1746, and issued about 1750 the series of Latin classics called by his name. He also printed in superior style the "New Testament" in Latin, and various other works.

Barbou - Descourières, băʀ'boo' dǎ'koo're-aiʀ', (GABRIEL,) a French general, born in 1761, served with distinction under Napoleon in Austria, Spain, and Italy, and became governor of Ancona in 1810. Having made his submission to the Bourbons, he was appointed grand officer of the legion of honour, and chevalier of Saint Louis. Died in 1817.

Bar'bour, (JAMES,) an American statesman, born in Orange county, Virginia, in 1775. He was elected Governor of Virginia in 1812, and a Senator of the United States in 1815. In accordance with the wish of President Madison, he presented a bill to establish a United States Bank, which was approved by the Senate. He was appointed secretary of war by President Adams in 1825, and minister to England in 1828. Having been recalled by President Jackson in 1829, he retired from the public service. He was president of the Whig National Convention in 1839. Died in 1842.

See "Encyclopædia Americana," Supplement.

Bar'bour, Bar'ber, or **Barbere,** (JOHN,) the most eminent of the early Scottish poets, born at Aberdeen about 1320, was contemporary with Chaucer. After being appointed Archdeacon of Aberdeen, he visited Oxford in order to complete his studies. His principal

work, entitled "The Bruce," is a history, in verse, of the life and deeds of Robert Bruce, which, besides its merit as a poem, has great value as a historical record.

See CHAMBERS, "Biographical Dictionary of Eminent Scotsmen."

Barbour, (JOHN S.,) a relative of James Barbour, noticed above, born in Culpepper county, Virginia, in 1790, was a representative in Congress from 1823 to 1833. Died in 1855.

Barbour, (PHILIP N.,) a nephew of James Barbour, noticed above, was born near Bardstown, Kentucky, in 1817. He served as an officer in the Mexican war, and was killed at Monterey in September, 1846.

Barbour, (PHILIP PENDLETON,) a lawyer and judge, born in Orange county, Virginia, in 1783, was a brother of Governor James Barbour. He was elected a member of Congress in 1814, and was subsequently chosen Speaker of the House of Representatives. He advocated the admission of Missouri as a slave State in 1821, and continued to serve in Congress until 1825. In 1829 he presided over the convention which formed a new constitution for Virginia. He was appointed an associate justice of the supreme court of the United States in 1836. Died in 1841.

See "Encyclopædia Americana," Supplement.

Barbour, (THOMAS,) COLONEL, a Virginian officer, born in 1735, was the father of James and Philip Pendleton Barbour. He served as a colonel in the Revolutionary war, before which he had been a prominent member of the House of Burgesses. Died in 1825.

Bar-bu-cal'lus, (JOANNES,) lived in the sixth century, and is supposed to have been a native of Barbucale, in Spain. Eleven of his epigrams are extant in the Greek Anthology.

Bar'bu-la, (L. ÆMILIUS,) son of Q. Æmilius, became consul in 281 B.C. He gained important victories over the Tarentines, Samnites, and Etruscans.

Barbula, (Q. ÆMILIUS,) a Roman consul in 317 B.C., in which year Apulia was subdued, became a second time consul in 311.

Barbuo, baʀ'boo-o, or **Barbo-Soncino,** baʀ'bo son-chee'no, (SCIPIONE,) an Italian jurist of the sixteenth century, resided at Padua. He wrote "Lives of the Dukes of Milan."

Barbut or **Barbat,** baʀ'bŭt, written also **Barbud,** a famous but semi-fabulous Persian musician, who is supposed to have lived in the earliest times. He was the reputed inventor of a sort of lyre called by his name, whence possibly the Greek *barbitos* derives its origin.

Barca. See HAMILCAR.

Barca. See CALDERON DE LA BARCA.

Barca, baʀ'kă, (ALESSANDRO,) an Italian chemist, born at Bergamo in 1741; died in 1814.

Barca, (FRANCISCO,) a Portuguese musician, born at Evora, lived about 1600–30.

Barca, (GIOVANNI BATTISTA,) an Italian painter, born at Mantua, worked at Verona in 1650.

Barca, baʀ'kă, (JOSÉ,) a captain-general in the Spanish service, was born at Milan, and lived between 1600 and 1650.

Barca, (PIETRO ANTONIO,) an Italian artist and engineer, born at Milan, lived about 1670.

Barca, de la, dǎ lă baʀ'kă, (FRANCISCO JOAQUIN CALDERON,) a learned ecclesiastic, of Creole extraction, lived in the eighteenth century, and became preacher-general of the order of the Franciscans. He was the author of a "Treatise on Practical Astronomy."

Barcali, baʀ-kă'lee, surnamed MOHAMMED-BEN-PIR-ALI, (mo-hăm'med bĕn peer ă'lee,) a Mohammedan theologian and writer of the sixteenth century.

Barcellos, de, dă baʀ-sel'lôs, (FRANCISCO,) a Portuguese poet and ecclesiastic, was the author of Latin poems which were highly esteemed in his time. Died in 1570.

Barceloneta, di, de baʀ-chă-lo-nā'tă, (UGONE,) an Italian theologian and celebrated preacher, born in Piedmont about 1230, was Cardinal of Saint Sabina. He wrote several religious works in Latin.

Barcena, baʀ-thā'nă, (ALFONSO,) a Spanish Jesuit, born at Córdova, resided as a missionary in South America. He wrote, for the use of the natives, several religious and educational works in the Indian dialects. Died in 1598.

Barc'ham or **Bark'ham**, (JOHN,) an English divine and antiquary, born at Exeter about 1570. He contributed to Speed's "History of England" the lives of Henry II. and King John, and had a considerable share in Guillim's "Display of Heraldry." Died in 1642.

See WOOD, "Athenæ Oxonienses."

Barchetta, baR-kĕt'tả, (ANDREA,) an Italian sculptor, born in Naples, lived about 1630.

Barchou de Penhoen, bȧR'shoo' dẹh pẹh-no'ŏN', (AUGUSTE THÉODORE HILAIRE,) BARON, a French writer, born at Morlaix in 1801. He published, besides other works, a "History of German Philosophy from Leibnitz to Hegel," (2 vols., 1836,) "The Philosophy of Schelling," (1834,) and a French version of Fichte's "Destiny of Man," (1833.) He was one of the first redacteurs of the "Revue des Deux Mondes." Died in 1855.

Barcia, de, dả baR-thee'ả, (ANDREA GONZALEZ,) a Spanish historian, who lived about 1700, was the author of a "General History of Florida," and a work entitled "First Historians of the West Indies."

Barckhausen, baRk'hŏw'zẹn, (JOHANN CONRAD,) a German chemist and physician, born at Horn in 1666, became professor of chemistry at Utrecht, in Holland. He wrote, among other scientific works, a "Synopsis Pharmaceutica," (1690,) and "Historia Medicinæ," and made several important discoveries in chemistry. A genus of plants has been named Barkhausia in his honour. Died in 1723.

Bar'clay (bark'le) or **Bar'klay,** (ALEXANDER,) an eminent British writer of the sixteenth century. He studied at Oxford, and subsequently visited Germany and France. He translated an allegorical French poem entitled "The Castle of Labour," also Sallust's "Jugurthine War," into English, and wrote the lives of several saints. His most popular work is a free translation of the "Ship of Fools," from the German of Sebastian Brandt. Died in 1552.

See WARTON, "History of English Poetry."

Bar'clay, (GEORGE,) a Scottish Jacobite conspirator, formed in 1696 a plot to seize or kill William III. Some of the conspirators were executed, but Barclay escaped by flight.

Barclay, (HENRY,) D.D., an Episcopal clergyman, born in Albany, New York, in the early part of the eighteenth century, was for several years a missionary among the Mohawk Indians, and was afterwards appointed rector of Trinity Church, New York. In connection with W. Andrews and J. Ogilvie, he translated the Liturgy into the Mohawk language. Died in 1765.

Barclay, bȧR'klả', (JEAN,) an eminent French writer, of Scottish extraction, born at Pont-à-Mousson in 1582. His most admired work is an allegorical romance in prose and verse, written in ·Latin, entitled "Argênis," (1621.) It has been translated into the principal languages of Europe, and has been eulogized by Leibnitz, Coleridge, and other eminent men. He also wrote, in Latin, several controversial treatises, and the "Satyricon of Euphormio," a satire. Died at Rome in 1621. He was a son of William Barclay, noticed below.

See D. DALRYMPLE, (LORD HAILES,) "Sketch of the Life of J. Barclay, author of the Argenis," 1786; CHAMBERS, "Biographical Dictionary of Eminent Scotsmen;" "Encyclopædia Britannica."

Barclay, (JOHN,) a Scottish theologian, born in 1645. He wrote a "Description of the Roman Catholic Church," (1689.) Died in 1710.

Barclay, (JOHN,) a Scottish physician, who lived about 1620, was the author of a eulogy on tobacco, entitled "Nepenthes, seu de Nicotianæ Herbæ Viribus."

Barclay, (JOHN,) born in Perthshire, Scotland, in 1734, was the founder of a religious sect called Barclayans, or Bereans, a name derived from a passage in the Acts of the Apostles xvii. 11. His theological works were published in three volumes. Died in 1798.

Barclay, (JOHN,) a Scottish physician and writer on anatomy, born in Perthshire in 1760. He died in 1826, leaving to the Royal College of Surgeons his anatomical collection, since called the Barclayan Museum.

Barclay, (ROBERT,) an eminent writer and an apologist for the Society of Friends, was born at Gordonstown, in Morayshire, Scotland, on the 23d of December, 1648. He was the eldest son of Colonel David Barclay of Ury

and Catherine Gordon, who was descended from the noble family of Huntley. He was educated in Paris at the Scots College, of which his uncle was principal. He learned to write and speak Latin with facility and correctness, and after he left Paris studied Greek and Hebrew. About 1664 he returned to Scotland, in obedience to the will of his father, who had recently adopted the principles professed by George Fox. Robert Barclay entered into fellowship with the Society of Friends in 1667, and became a minister of the gospel. He was endowed by nature with talents of a high order, and possessed the moral courage and energy requisite for a reformer.

In 1670 he began to defend the principles of the Friends against the erroneous charges and misrepresentations of their opponents, by a treatise entitled "Truth cleared of Calumnies." He married Christian Mollison about 1670. In 1672 he felt himself impelled by a sense of duty to walk through the streets of Aberdeen clothed in sackcloth and ashes. To explain and defend the doctrines of the Friends, he published a "Catechism and Confession of Faith," (1675,) "The Anarchy of the Ranters," (1676,)* and "Theological Propositions," ("Theses Theologicæ," about 1676.)

In company with George Fox and William Penn, he visited Germany on a religious mission in 1677. About this date he and his father were imprisoned in Aberdeen on account of their religious profession. His principal work is "An Apology for the True Christian Divinity, as the same is held forth and preached by the People called in scorn Quakers," (1678,) which was originally written and published in Latin, and afterwards translated into English by the author. This work is characterized by great logical acumen, and has been highly commended by eminent critics of different denominations.

In 1679 he obtained from Charles II. a charter for erecting his estate of Ury into a free barony with civil and criminal jurisdiction. He published in the same year a vindication of his "Apology," which had been attacked by several writers. In 1682 he was appointed governor of the province of East Jersey; but he sent a deputy, and never went to America himself. During the last years of his life he enjoyed the favour of James II. He died at Ury in October, 1690, aged about forty-two, leaving three sons and four daughters. One of the sons, named David, was a merchant of London, and is said to have entertained three successive monarchs, George I., George II., and George III., when they visited the city.

See JOSEPH GURNEY BEVAN, "Life of Robert Barclay," 1802; SEWEL, "History of the Quakers;" JOHN BARCLAY, "History of Friends in Scotland."

Barclay, (WILLIAM,) a Scottish jurist, born in Aberdeenshire about 1540. He studied in France under the celebrated Cujas and Leconte, and in 1578 became professor of law at Pont-à-Mousson. In 1603 he visited England; but, failing to meet with patronage from James I., on account of his being a Catholic, he soon returned to France, and in 1605 was appointed professor of law at Angers. Among his principal works are a treatise on regal power, ("De Regno et Regali Potestate," 1600,) and "On the Power of the Pope." The latter was published after his death by his son John Barclay, the author of "Argénis." Barclay is ranked among the first jurists of his time. Died in 1606.

See BAYLE, "Historical and Critical Dictionary;" NICÉRON, "Mémoires;" CHAMBERS, "Biographical Dictionary of Eminent Scotsmen."

Barclay de Tolly, bȧR'klả' dẹh to'le', (MICHAEL,) PRINCE, a celebrated Russian field-marshal, of Scottish extraction, born in Livonia about 1755, early distinguished himself in the wars against Turkey, Sweden, and Poland, between 1788 and 1794, and in 1806 took part in the Polish campaign against the French. He was made lieutenant-general after the battle of Eylau, where he was severely wounded, and in 1810 was appointed minister of war. In 1812 he obtained the command of the army of the West, but after the battle of Smolensk he was superseded by Kootoosov. At Borodino, Barclay commanded the right wing, and by his skilful retreat contributed to save the remnant of the Russian army.

* This title was afterwards exchanged for a "Treatise on Christian Discipline."

He subsequently held the chief command at Bautzen, Culm, and Leipsic, and in 1814 was created a field-marshal. He died in 1818, having been previously made a prince of the empire.

See "Nouvelle Biographie Générale."

Bar′co, del, (ALONSO,) an eminent Spanish landscape-painter, born at Madrid in 1645; died in 1685.

Barco, del, (JUAN RODRIGUEZ GARCIA,) a Spanish painter who was employed by the Duke of Alva to adorn with frescos his castle of Barco d'Avila, which received its name from the artist.

See QUILLIET, "Dictionnaire des Peintres Espagnols."

Barcokheba, bar-kok′e-bâ, also written **Bar-Cochba** or **Barchochebas,** (originally **Simeon,**) a celebrated Jewish impostor under the reign of Hadrian. Claiming to be the Messiah, he excited an insurrection among the Jews, A.D. 131, and took possession of Jerusalem and many fortified places. After a sanguinary contest and immense loss on both sides, the city was retaken by the Roman general Julius Seve′rus, and Barcokheba, after an obstinate defence in the fortress of Bethar, killed, in 136 A.D.

Barcos, de, deh bâr′kos′, (MARTIN,) a French theologian, born at Bayonne in 1600, studied at Louvain under the celebrated Jansenius. In 1644 he succeeded his uncle, Duvergier de Hauranne, as abbot of Saint-Cyran. He was a friend of Arnauld, and published, among other works, in defence of Jansenism, an "Exposition of the Faith of the Church touching Grace and Predestination," (1697.) Died in 1678.

Bard, (JOHN,) an American physician, born near Philadelphia in 1716. He practised many years in the city of New York, to which he removed in 1743, and attained eminence in his profession. He was elected president of the Medical Society of New York about 1788. Died in 1799.

Bard, (SAMUEL,) an eminent physician, born in Philadelphia in April, 1742, a son of Dr. John Bard, and a grandson of Peter Bard, a French Protestant refugee. He was educated at the University of Edinburgh, where he passed about three years and was received as an inmate in the family of Dr. Robertson the historian. Having graduated as M.D. in 1765, he began to practise in the city of New York in 1767. About the end of the Revolutionary war he was selected by General Washington as his family physician. He published a treatise on "Angina Suffocativa," and a treatise on "Obstetrics," (1807.) In 1813 he was chosen president of the College of Physicians and Surgeons of New York. Dr. Bard was an active and efficient promoter of benevolent enterprises. Died in May, 1821.

See Rev. JOHN McVICKER, "Life of Samuel Bard," 1822; S. D. GROSS, "American Medical Biography," 1861.

Bard, (WILLIAM,) an American merchant, born in the city of New York in 1777. He was the first president of the New York Life Insurance Company, which he and others organized about 1830. Died in 1853.

Bardaji y Azara, de, dâ bar-dâ-hee′ e â-thâ′râ, (Don EUSEBIO,) a Spanish statesman, born in the province of Cuenca in 1765, was employed in various important missions, and rose to be minister of foreign affairs and *procer* of the kingdom in 1834. He favoured the French policy, and opposed the ministry of Calatrava. Died in 1844.

Bar′das, brother of the empress Theodora, was, on the death of the emperor Theophilus of Constantinople, appointed one of the tutors to his son Michael III. Having caused his colleague Theoctistes to be put to death, and confined his sister in a cloister, he assumed the title of Cæsar, but was afterwards supplanted in the favour of Michael by Basil the Macedonian, and assassinated by order of the emperor, 866 A.D.

See LE BEAU, "Histoire du Bas-Empire."

Bar′das Scle′rus, a distinguished general under the Byzantine emperor John Zimisces, who had married his sister. After the death of Zimisces, he revolted against the emperor Basil II., and was for a time nearly always victorious. But at length, having been worsted by Bardas Phocas, and weary of his stormy life, he became reconciled to the emperor. Died about 990 A.D.

See LE BEAU, "Histoire du Bas-Empire."

Barde, de la, deh lâ bârd, [Lat. LABARDÆ′US,] (JEAN,) a French diplomatist, born at Marolles-sur-Seine about 1600, was patronized by Cardinal Mazarin. He was for many years French ambassador in Switzerland. He wrote, in Latin, a valuable history of his own times. Died in 1692.

Bardeleben, von, fon bar′deh-lâ′ben, (KURT,) a Prussian statesman, born in 1796, was a deputy from Königsberg to the National Assembly at Frankfort, and in 1848 to the National Assembly of Prussia.

Bar-de-sā′nēš, an eminent Syrian writer, and founder of a sect called Bardesanians, was born at Edessa, and lived about 170–200 A.D. He is called a heretic by some writers. It is said, however, that he wrote several works against heretics. He composed in the Syriac language many psalms or hymns of remarkable beauty, and a dialogue on Fate.

See F. STRUNZ, "Historia Bardesanis," 1710; HAHN, "Bardesanes Gnosticus;" MOSHEIM, "De Rebus Christianorum."

Bardet, bâr′dā′, (PIERRE,) a French advocate, born in Bourbonnais in 1591, published "Recueil d'Arrêts du Parlement de Paris," 1690. Died in 1685.

Bardi, (DONATO.) See DONATELLO.

Bardi, bar′dee, (GIOVANNI,) Count of Vernio, an Italian miscellaneous writer, born at Florence, was patronized by Pope Urban VIII.

Bardi, (GIROLAMO,) an Italian monk and historian, born at Florence about 1544. Among his works we may name his "Universal Chronology from the Creation of Adam to 1581." Died in 1593.

Bardi, (GIROLAMO,) an Italian physician and philosopher, born at Rapallo in 1603, became professor of philosophy at Pisa. He wrote, in Latin, several treatises on theology and medicine. He lived at Rome from 1651 to 1667. Died in 1670.

Bardi, (PIETRO,) Count of Vernio, son of Giovanni, noticed above, an Italian *littérateur*, born at Florence, lived about 1640. He translated into Italian the essays of Maximus Tyrius.

Bardi, de′, dâ bar′dee, (DEA,) an Italian nun of the fifteenth century, was the author of a burlesque poem entitled "Ode on the Death of a Jackdaw."

Bardili, bar-dee′lee, (CHRISTOPH GOTTFRIED,) a German metaphysical philosopher, born at Blaubeuren in 1761, became professor of philosophy at Stuttgart in 1794. His principal work is entitled "Sketch of First Logic," in which he opposes the system of Kant and favours the philosophy of absolute identity, ("Identitäts-Philosophie.") Died in 1808.

Bardili, (JOHANN **Wendel**—wĕn′del,) a German writer of travels, born at Reutlingen; died in 1740.

Bardin, bâr′dĕN′, (ÉTIENNE ALEXANDRE,) a French general, born in Paris in 1774, was a son of Jean Bardin the painter. Died in 1840. His most important work is a very extensive and complete military dictionary, entitled "Dictionnaire de l'Armée de Terre," the last part of which has been published since his death.

See QUÉRARD, "La France Littéraire."

Bardin, (GUILLAUME,) a French jurist, wrote a "Chronicle of Languedoc," (from 1031 to 1454.)

Bardin, (JEAN,) a French painter, born at Montbar in 1732, was director of the School of Fine Arts at Orléans, and a member of the Institute. He numbered among his pupils Regnault and David. Died in 1809.

See CHAUDRUC DE CRAZANNES, "Notice sur la Vie de M. Bardin," 1809.

Bardin, (PIERRE,) an eminent French jurist, born at Toulouse about 1420.

Bardin, (PIERRE,) a French *littérateur*, born at Rouen in 1590, was a member of the French Academy. Died in 1637.

Bardon, a French painter. See DANDRÉ-BARDON.

Bardon de Brun, bâr′dôN′ deh brŭN, (BERNARD,) a French ecclesiastic, born at Limoges, wrote a tragedy in verse entitled "Saint James." Died in 1625.

See ÉTIENNE PETIOT, "Vie de B. Bardon," 1636.

Bardou, bâr′doo′, (JEAN,) a French *littérateur* and ecclesiastic, born in 1729, wrote, among other works, "The History of Laurent Marcel, or the Unprejudiced Observer," (1770.) Died in 1803.

Bardou, (OSCAR FRANÇOIS,) a French actor, born at Montpellier about 1804.

Bardozzi, baR-dot'see, (JÁNOS,) a Hungarian writer, born about 1740, wrote a continuation of Wagner's "Analecta Scepusii." Died in 1819.

Bar-dȳl'lis [Gr. Βάρδυλλις] or **Bardylis,** a robber chief, who lived about 400 B.C., rose to be King of Illyria. He made war upon Perdiccas III. of Macedonia, whom he defeated and killed in 360 B.C.

Bardzinski, baRd-zin'skee, (JAN ALAN,) a Polish theologian and scholar of the seventeenth century. He translated Lucan's "Pharsalia" into Polish verse, and also made a translation of Seneca's tragedies and Boethius's "Consolations of Philosophy."

Baré, bā'rā', or **Baret,** a Frenchwoman, born in Burgundy in 1741, accompanied the botanist Commerson, disguised as a man, in his voyage with Bougainville in 1766. Commerson named several plants in her honour.

Bare'bone or **Bar'bone,** (PRAISE-GOD,) a noted English fanatic, originally a leather-dealer, was a member of Cromwell's Parliament in 1653, which is known in history by his name. On the arrival of General Monk, Barebone headed a large procession of the people with a petition to Parliament against the restoration of Charles II.

See "Biographia Britannica."

Barella, bä-rĕl'lä, (GIOVANNI BATTISTA,) an Italian Jesuit and writer, born at Milan; died in 1687.

Barellas, bä-rĕl'yäs, (ESTEBAN,) a Spanish writer, published a historical romance entitled "History of the Counts of Barcelona, Bernardo Barcino and his son Zinofre," (1600.)

Barendsen. See BARENTS.

Barentin, bä'rŏN'tăN', (CHARLES LOUIS FRANÇOIS de **Paule**—dĕh pōl,) a French statesman, born in 1738, succeeded Lamoignon in 1788 as keeper of the seals under Louis XVI. He was the originator of several unpopular measures, for which he was denounced by Mirabeau as one of the most dangerous advisers of the king. Upon this, he resigned his post; but after the restoration he was appointed honorary chancellor by Louis XVIII. Died in 1819.

Barentin-Montchal, de, dĕh bä'rŏN'tăN' mŏN'shăl', (LOUIS,) VISCOUNT, a French general and *littérateur,* brother of the preceding, born in Paris in 1737. He served in the Seven Years' war, and subsequently commanded the guard of Louis XVIII. at Mittau. He wrote a treatise "On Ancient and Historical Geography," (1807.) Died in 1824.

See QUÉRARD, "La France Littéraire."

Barentin-Montchal, de, MADAME, wife of the preceding, wrote an "Abridged History of the Old and New Testament for Children and Youth," (1804.)

Barents, bä'rĕnts, or **Barendsen,** bä'rĕnt-sĕn, (DIETRICH,) also called **Bernard Dirk,** a Dutch painter, born at Amsterdam in 1534. He studied in Italy under Titian, with whom he formed an intimate friendship, and whose portrait he painted. His picture of "Judith" is ranked among his master-pieces. Died in 1592..

See DESCAMPS, "Vies des Peintres Flamands," etc.

Barentz or **Barendz,** bä'rĕnts, written also **Barentzen,** (WILLEM,) a Dutch navigator of the sixteenth century, who attempted, in 1594, a voyage to China by way of the Arctic Sea, and reached 78° of latitude. His account of the expedition, translated into French, is contained in the "Histoire générale des Voyages."

Barère de Vieuzac, bä'rair' dĕh veŭh'zăk', (BERTRAND,) a French Jacobin demagogue, born at Tarbes, in Gascony, in 1755. He entered public life as deputy to the States-General in 1789, and was elected to the Convention in 1792. He voted for the death of the king, and for some time acted with the Girondists. In April, 1793, he was chosen a member of the committee of public safety. He deserted the Girondists at the critical time of their contest with the Jacobins; and after the supreme executive power was usurped by a committee of nine, (July, 1793,) he was the reporter or organ of that atrocious committee. The flowery style with which he adorned the measures of a merciless proscription procured him the designation of the "Anacreon of the guillotine." He first proposed that "terror should be the

order of the day." In 1794 a schism occurred in the committee. On one side were Robespierre, Saint-Just, and Couthon; on the other, Billaud and Collot. Barère waited to see which side should prove the stronger. On the 9th Thermidor he spoke against Robespierre in the Convention, and moved that his head be cut off without trial. Barère, Collot, and Billaud were condemned to deportation in 1795, but the first escaped from prison and found means to avoid that penalty. He was banished as a regicide in 1816, and returned to France in 1830. Died in 1841. The "Mémoires de Barère" were edited by H. Carnot and David d'Angers, (4 vols., 1843.)

"Compared with him," says Macaulay, "Fouché seems honest; Billaud seems humane; Hébert seems to rise into dignity. . . . He had become a murderer merely for his safety, and continued to be a murderer merely for his pleasure."

See MACAULAY'S "Essays;" M. CARNOT, "Notice historique sur Barère," 1842.

Baret, bä'rā', (JACQUES de la Galanderie—dĕh lä gä'lôNd'RĔ',) a French lawyer and writer, born at Tours in 1579; died about 1650.

Baret, (JEAN,) a French jurist and legal writer, born at Tours in 1511.

Baret, (JEAN,) a French historian, published a "History of the Last Troubles in Moldavia," (Paris, 1620.)

Baret, (RENÉ,) grandson of the jurist Jean Baret, lived about 1650–70. He wrote a work on the "Knowledge of Horses and their Diseases," (1661.)

Baretti, bä-ret'tee, (GIUSEPPE,) an Italian writer, born at Turin in 1716. In 1751 he visited London, where he taught Italian, and, having been befriended by Dr. Johnson and other distinguished men, was appointed secretary for the foreign correspondence of the Royal Academy. He published an "Italian and English Dictionary," (1760,) an "Italian Grammar," an "Account of the Manners and Customs of Italy," (1768,) and (in English) "Travels through Spain, Portugal, and France," (1770,) which is praised in the highest terms by Dr. Johnson. The first-named work is still in use. He also wrote, in French, an essay "On Shakspeare and Voltaire," in which he exposes the ignorance of the latter with regard to the English language and literature. Died in 1789. Dr. Johnson observes of Baretti, "There are strong powers in his mind. He has not, indeed, many hooks, but with what hooks he has he grapples very forcibly."

See BOSWELL, "Life of Johnson;" GIUSEPPE FRANCHI, "Notizie intorno alla Vita de G. Baretti," 1790.

Barezzi, bä-rĕt'see, (STEFANO,) a Milanese painter of the nineteenth century, noted as having discovered a process for transferring frescos to wooden tables.

Barfod, baR'fod, (PAUL FREDERIK,) a Danish historian, born at Grenaae, in Jutland, in 1811. He wrote a "History of Denmark and Norway under Frederick III.," "The Jews in Denmark," and "Biography of the Ranzau Family." He edited for a time a journal advocating the union of Sweden, Norway, and Denmark.

See BROCKHAUS, "Conversations-Lexikon."

Barfuss, baR'fōōss, (JOHANN ALBRECHT,) COUNT OF, a Prussian general, born in 1631, served with distinction against the Turks in Hungary in 1691. Died in 1704.

Bargagli, baR-gäl'yee, (GIROLAMO,) an Italian jurist and dramatic writer, brother of Scipione, noticed below, was the author of "La Pellegrina," a comedy, and a work entitled "Dialogo dei Giuochi," an explanation of the social games of Italy. Died in 1586.

See MAZZUCHELLI, "Scrittori d'Italia."

Bargagli, (SCIPIONE,) a distinguished Italian writer, born at Sienna, published a series of historical sketches and tales entitled "Trattenimenti," ("Entertainments,") and a treatise "On Devices," ("Dell' Imprese,") explaining the origin and signification of devices in the age of chivalry. He was created a count palatine by the emperor Rudolph II. Died in 1612.

See MAZZUCHELLI, "Scrittori d'Italia."

Bargedé, bäRzh'dä', (NICOLAS or NICOLLE,) a French *littérateur* and poet, born at Vezelay about 1550.

Bargeo or **Bargæus.** See ANGELIO.

Bargès, bäR'zhĕs', (ANTOINE,) a musician, apparently

of French extraction, was chapel-master at the Casa Grande at Venice about 1530.

Bargès, (JEAN JOSEPH LÉANDRE,) a French ecclesiastic and Orientalist, born at Auriol in 1810, was appointed in 1842 professor of Hebrew in the faculty of theology in Paris. He published treatises on the church history and antiquities of Africa and the city of Tlemcen, and "On the Temple of Baal at Marseilles."

See "Nouvelle Biographie Générale."

Bargeton, bȧrzh'tòn', (DANIEL,) a French jurist, born at Uzès about 1678, was the author of a collection of letters advocating taxation of the clergy. Died in 1757.

Barginet, bȧr'zhe'nȧ', (ALEXANDRE PIERRE,) a French political writer and novelist, born at Grenoble in 1798. Died in 1843.

Bar'grave, (ISAAC,) an English divine, born in 1586, became Dean of Canterbury. Died in 1642.

Bar'ham, (HENRY,) an English naturalist of the eighteenth century, resided many years in the West Indies. He wrote an account of the vegetable productions of South America and the West Indies, entitled "Hortus Americanus."

Barham, (RICHARD HARRIS,) an English divine and humorous writer, born at Canterbury in 1788. He studied at Oxford, and was subsequently appointed rector of Saint Augustine and Saint Faith in London. His "Ingoldsby Legends," a series of tales in verse, appeared in "Bentley's Miscellany" in 1837, and were received with great favour. He was also one of the principal contributors to Gorton's "Biographical Dictionary," and wrote for "Blackwood's Magazine" a story of college life, entitled "My Cousin Nicholas." Barham was a friend of Sydney Smith, Theodore Hook, and other celebrated wits of the time. For a severe but not unjust criticism on the "Ingoldsby Legends," see the "New Spirit of the Age," (London, 1844.) Died in 1845.

See a "Life of R. H. Barham," in an edition of his "Ingoldsby Legends," 1847; "Men I have known," by WILLIAM JERDAN, 1866.

Barhebræus. See ABOOLFARAJ, (GREGORIUS.)

Baricelli, bâ-re-chel'lee, or **Baricello,** bâ-re-chel'lo, (GIULIO CESARE,) an Italian physician, born at San Marco about 1598.

Barile, bâ-ree'lâ, (GIOVANNI,) an Italian painter and skilful sculptor in wood, born about 1520. He was the master of Andrea del Sarto.

Barile, (GIOVANNI DOMENICO,) an Italian theologian, flourished between 1700 and 1725.

Barili, bâ-ree'lee, (ANTONIO DI NERI,) an Italian sculptor and architect, worked at Sienna from 1485 till 1511.

Barilli, bâ-rèl'lee, (LUDOVICO,) a celebrated Italian vocalist, born at Módena about 1767, was for many years director of the Italian Opera in Paris.

Barillon, bâ're'yòn', a French diplomatist, was ambassador at the court of London in the reign of James II. He was ordered to leave England by William of Orange about the end of 1688. "His political career," according to Macaulay, "had brought great calamities both on the house of Stuart and on the house of Bourbon." ("History of England," vol. iii. chap. xii.)

Barillon, (JEAN,) called also **Jehan Bourdel,** a French historian, born at Issoire, wrote a "History of the First Six Years of the Reign of Francis I.," (unpublished.) Died in 1553.

Barillon, de, dęh bâ're'yòn', (HENRI,) Bishop of Luçon, born in Auvergne in 1639; died in 1699.

See C. F. DUBOS, "Abrégé de la Vie de M. H. de Barillon," 1700.

Baring, (ALEXANDER.) See ASHBURTON, LORD.

Baring, bâ'ring, (DANIEL EBERHARD,) a German scholar, born near Hildesheim in 1690, was the author of a work on diplomacy, entitled "Clavis Diplomatica." Died in 1753.

Baring, (EVERARD,) a German scholar and teacher, born at Lubeck in 1608, taught at Hanover. Died in 1659.

Bâ'ring, (Sir FRANCIS,) an English financier and capitalist, born at or near Exeter in 1740, was the father of Lord Ashburton, and founder of the great banking-house of Baring & Company, London. Died in 1810.

Baring, (Sir FRANCIS THORNHILL,) a liberal English statesman, born in 1796, was a grandson of the preceding, and a son of Sir Thomas Baring. He was a lord of the treasury from 1830 to 1834, joint secretary to the treasury from 1835 to 1839, and chancellor of the exchequer from 1839 to 1841. In the cabinet of Lord John Russell he was first lord of the admiralty, 1846–52.

Baring, (THOMAS,) an eminent financier, brother of Sir Francis T. Baring, was born in 1800. In 1835 he was elected to Parliament for Great Yarmouth, and in 1844 for Huntingdon. He was for a time the principal manager of the banking-house of Baring & Company.

Baring, (Sir THOMAS,) eldest son of Sir Francis, born in 1772, was a member of Parliament from 1830 to 1832. He was a patron of art, and the owner of a choice collection of pictures.

Barisani, bâ-re-zâ'nee, (JOSEPH,) a German physician and medical writer, born in 1756; died in 1787.

Barisano, bâ-re-sâ'no, (FRANCESCO DOMENICO,) an Italian physician and scientific writer, born at Alba about 1650.

Barison, bâ're-sòn', or **Bar'riso,** the heir of the kingdom of Sardinia, was made king of that country in 1154 by the assistance of Frederick Barbarossa, to whom he offered a tribute of four thousand silver marks. He was subsequently detained a prisoner by the Genoese, as a hostage for the money they had advanced for the tribute.

See CARL ANDREAS BEL, "Dissertatio de Barrisone," 1766.

Barisoni, bâ-re-so'nee, (ALBERTINO,) an Italian jurist and ecclesiastic, born in 1587, became professor of the Pandects at Padua in 1631, and Bishop of Ceneda in 1653. Died in 1667.

See MAZZUCHELLI, "Scrittori d'Italia."

Baritu, bâ're-too, (GEORGE,) a distinguished Wallachian scholar and journalist, born in Transylvania in 1812, published in 1853 a "German-Roumanian Dictionary."

Barjaud, bȧr'zhò', (JEAN BAPTISTE,) a French littérateur and soldier, born at Montluçon in 1785. He served under Napoleon in the campaigns of 1812 and '13, and was mortally wounded at the battle of Leipsic, (1813.) He was the author of "National Odes" and other works.

Bar-Jesus. See ELYMAS.

Bar'kah Khân I., called also **Barbacan,** a famous Kharizmian chief, who, having formed an alliance with Nejm-ed-Deen, Aiyoobite Sultan of Egypt, took Jerusalem from the Christians in 1244 and slaughtered all the inhabitants who had not escaped. A quarrel breaking out soon after between the Sultan and Barkah Khan, the latter was slain in battle in 1246.

See MALCOLM's "History of Persia."

Barkah Khan, sometimes called **Bor'ga,** second Mogul ruler of Kapchak, succeeded his brother Bâtoo (Bâtu) in 1255, and waged war against the Russians and Persians. He founded the city of Serai, on the Volga, and was a liberal patron of learning. Died about 1265.

Bar'ker, (ANDREW,) an English merchant of Bristol, in 1576 fitted out two vessels to the West Indies at his own expense, in order to avenge the injuries he had received from the Spaniards at Teneriffe.

See HAKLUYT, "Collection of Voyages."

Barker, (BENJAMIN,) an English landscape-painter of superior merit, was a brother of Thomas Barker, the inventor of the panorama. Died in 1838.

Barker, (EDMUND HENRY,) an English classical scholar, born in Yorkshire in 1788. He published a "Greek and English Lexicon," (1831,) "Classical Recreations," and "Parriana," a collection of criticisms and anecdotes relating to his friend Dr. Parr. He was also a contributor to the "Classical Journal," and edited several Latin classics, and the "Thesaurus Græcæ Linguæ" of Henri Estienne, (Stephanus.) Died in 1839.

See "Gentleman's Magazine," May, 1839.

Barker, (GEORGE,) F.R.S., of Birmingham, an Englishman noted for his public spirit and liberal support of benevolent enterprises. Died in 1845, aged about seventy.

Barker, (HENRY ASTON,) a skilful panorama-painter, son of Robert Barker, noticed below, born at Glasgow in 1774. Died in 1856.

Barker, (JACOB,) an American merchant and financier, born in Kennebec county, Maine, in 1779. He has for many years resided at New Orleans.

See "Incidents in the Life of Jacob Barker," by himself, New York, 1855.

Barker, (JOHN,) an English physician, who wrote an "Essay on the Conformity of Ancient and Modern Medicine in the Treatment of Acute Diseases." Died in 1748.

Barker, (JOHN,) an English diplomatist, born in Derbyshire, became in 1826 British consul to Alexandria, and subsequently consul-general in Egypt. Died in 1850.

Barker, (MATTHEW HENRY,) an English novelist, born about 1790. His novels are mostly sketches of sea-life, and first appeared in the "Literary Gazette," "Bentley's Miscellany," and other journals, under the name of "The Old Sailor," and other pseudonyms. Among the most popular of these are "The Greenwich Pensioners," "Tough Yarns," and "Hamilton King." In 1828 Barker became editor of the "Nottingham Mercury." Died in 1846.

Bar'ker, (ROBERT,) a distinguished artist, and inventor of the panorama, born in the county of Meath, Ireland, in 1739. He exhibited in Edinburgh in 1788 a panoramic view of that city, and subsequently a panorama of London in Leicester Square. Among his most admired pieces are the battles of Trafalgar and Copenhagen. Died in 1806.

See NAGLER, "Neues Allgemeines Künstler-Lexikon."

Barker, (THOMAS,) an English painter of landscapes and rural subjects, born in Monmouthshire in 1769. Among his master-pieces is the "Woodman and the Gypsy." Died in 1847.

Barkey, baR'kī, (NICOLAUS,) a German scholar and theologian, born at Bremen in 1709. He published the "Museum of the Hague," ("Museum Haganum,") "Bibliotheca Bremensis Nova," (1760,) and other miscellaneous works. Died in 1788.

Barkham. See BARCHAM, (JOHN.)

Barkhausen, bark'höw'zen, (HEINRICH LUDWIG WILLIBALD,) a German writer on political economy, born in 1742, was the author of "Letters on the Policy of the Corn Trade," and other works. Died in 1813.

See ERSCH und GRUBER, "Allgemeine Encyklopaedie."

Barkiarokh or **Barkyaroc,** bark'yâ-rok', fourth Persian prince of the Seljookian dynasty, succeeded his father Malik-Shah in 1092. He died in 1104.

Bark'ly, (Sir HENRY,) born in London in 1815, was appointed Governor of Victoria, in Australia, in 1856.

Bar'kok', first Sultan of the Circassian Mamelukes, or Borgites, possessed himself of the throne of Egypt in 1390, after overthrowing the Baharite or Tartar dynasty. He was a promoter of learning, and founded a college at Cairo. Died in 1398.

Barkow, bar'ko, (HANS KARL LEOPOLD,) a German anatomist and physiologist, born in the isle of Rugen about 1798, published "Monstra animalium duplicia per anatomen indagatâ," (1830-36.)

Barks'dale, (CLEMENT,) an English divine and writer born in Gloucestershire in 1609, was the author of a "Life of Grotius," and a collection of poems. Died in 1687.

Barks'dale, (WILLIAM,) an American general, born in Tennessee in 1821. He removed to Mississippi, studied law, and was elected to Congress about 1853. He was a violent partisan of slavery and disunion. He was killed at Gettysburg, July 2, 1863.

Bar'la-am, a monk of the order of Saint Basil, whose original name was **Bernard,** born at Seminara, in Calabria, about 1290. He resided several years at Constantinople, where he became thoroughly versed in the Greek language, and, after his return, was appointed in 1342 Bishop of Geraci, in the kingdom of Naples. Died in 1348.

Barland. See BAARLAND.

Barlæus. See BAERLE, (CASPAR VAN.)

Barles, bǎrl, (LOUIS,) a French physician of the seventeenth century, translated several medical works from the Dutch of De Graaf.

Barlesio, baR-lā'ze-o, written also **Barlezio,** [Lat. BARLE'TIUS,] (MARINO,) a historian, born at Scutari, in Albania, wrote, among other works in Latin, "The Life and Actions of Scanderbeg," (1506,) which has been translated into several languages.

See SAX, "Onomasticon."

Barletta, baR-let'tâ, (GABRIELLO,) a popular Italian preacher, born in the kingdom of Naples, lived about 1450-80. His sermons have been often reprinted.

See BAYLE, "Historical Dictionary;" NICÉRON, "Mémoires."

Barlotta, baR-lot'tâ, (GIUSEPPE,) a Sicilian poet and *littérateur,* born at Trapani in 1654.

Bar'low, (FRANCIS,) a distinguished English painter and engraver, born in Lincolnshire about 1625. His representations of landscapes, birds, and fishes are particularly admired. Among his best works are the illustrations for an edition of Æsop's "Fables," which he also etched, and a "Book of Birds," engraved by Faithorne.

See STRUTT, "Dictionary of Engravers."

Bar'low, (FRANCIS CHANNING,) an American general, born at Brooklyn, New York, in 1834. Before the breaking out of the rebellion he followed the legal profession. He enlisted as a private in April, 1861, became a colonel about May, 1862, and served with distinction at the battles of Fair Oaks, June 1, and Antietam, September 17. He was appointed a brigadier-general about September, 1862. He commanded a division at the battles of the Wilderness and Spottsylvania Court-House, May, 1864; also in an assault on the defences of Petersburg in June. In November, 1865, he was elected secretary of state by the Republicans of New York.

Barlow, (JOEL,) an American poet and patriot, born at Reading, Connecticut, in 1755, graduated at Yale College in 1778. He studied theology, was licensed as a Congregational minister, and joined the army as a chaplain. When the army was disbanded, in 1783, he settled at Hartford, began to study law, and was admitted to the bar in 1785. Before this date he had married a sister of Abraham Baldwin. In 1787 he published "The Vision of Columbus," a poem, which obtained great popularity. He visited Europe in 1788, became a resident of Paris about 1792, and wrote several works to promote the principles of the French Revolution. During his residence in France he wrote a humorous poem on "Hasty Pudding," which was much admired.

Having enriched himself by commercial speculations in France, he returned to the United States in 1805, and settled on the Potomac near Washington. In 1808 he published his most elaborate work, "The Columbiad," an epic poem, which proved, however, in the opinion of most critics, a complete failure. He was appointed ambassador to France in 1811, and was invited by the French minister in the autumn of 1812 to a conference with Napoleon at Wilna, but before he arrived at that place he died, near Cracow, in December, 1812. "As an author," says R. W. Griswold, "he belonged to the first class of his time in America; and for his ardent patriotism, his public services, and the purity of his life, he deserves a distinguished rank among the men of our golden age." ("Poets and Poetry of America.")

See, also, C. E. OELSNER, "Notice sur la Vie de J. Barlow," Paris, 1813; "Edinburgh Review" for October, 1809; "Encyclopædia Americana;" DUYCKINCK, "Cyclopædia of American Literature."

Barlow, (NICHOLAS,) an English watchmaker, who invented a repeater clock about 1676.

Barlow, (PETER,) F.R.S., a distinguished English mathematician, born at Norwich in 1776. He became in 1806 one of the mathematical masters in the Royal Academy at Woolwich. He was afterwards a professor in that academy many years, and resigned the chair in 1847. He published an "Elementary Investigation of the Theory of Numbers," (1811,) and a "Mathematical and Philosophical Dictionary," (1814.) His "Essay on Magnetic Attractions" (1820) was highly prized. For his researches on magnetism he received the Copley medal in 1825. Among his valuable discoveries is a method of compensating or rectifying errors in the compass caused by the attraction of iron in ships. Died in 1862.

See "Nouvelle Biographie Générale."

Barlow, (THOMAS,) an English divine and theologian, born in Westmoreland in 1607, became Bishop of Lincoln in 1675. He was the author of "The Case of Toleration in Matters of Religion," and several works on civil and canon law. Died in 1691.

See WOOD, "Athenæ Oxonienses."

Barlow or **Bar'lowe,** (WILLIAM,) born in Essex county, England, became Bishop of Chichester in 1559. He wrote a work entitled "Cosmography," and several controversial treatises. Died in 1568.

Barlow or **Barlowe,** (WILLIAM,) an English divine and mathematician, son of the preceding, born in

ă, ē, ī, ō, ū, ȳ, *long;* ă, ĕ, ŏ, same, less prolonged; ă, ĕ, ĭ, ŏ, ŭ, ўy, *short;* ạ, ẹ, ị, ọ, *obscure;* fär, fâll, fât; mêt; nŏt; gŏŏd; mōŏn;

Pembrokeshire, was appointed Archdeacon of Salisbury in 1614. He was the first of his countrymen who wrote on the properties of the magnet, and he made important improvements in the mariner's compass. His principal work is entitled "The Navigator's Supply," (1597.) Died in 1625.

Bärmann or **Baermann,** baiR'män, (GEORGE FRIEDRICH,) a German mathematician of the eighteenth century, became professor of mathematics at Wittemberg. He published an edition of Euclid, and translated Lucian's "Master of Eloquence" into German. Died in 1769.

Bärmann or **Baermann,** (GEORG NIKOLAUS,) a German *littérateur,* born at Hamburg in 1785, was the author of a number of romances, tales, and dramas. He also made translations from the English, French, Spanish, and Italian, among which are several dramas of Calderon and Gozzi, and Sir Walter Scott's works. Died in 1850.

Barmecides, bar'mȩ-sīdz, (singular **Bar'mȩ-çide,**) or **Bar'ma-çīdes,** [Fr. BARMÉCIDES, bȧr'mȧ'sèd'; Ger. BARMECIDEN, baR-mĕt-see'dȩn ; Lat. BARMAÇ'IDÆ,] written also **Barmekides,** a celebrated Persian family, which derived its name from Barmak or Barmek. His son Khaled-ben-Barmek was first minister of Al-Mahdee, by whom he was appointed tutor to his son the famous Haroun-al-Raschid. Yahya, son of Khaled, became vizier to Haroun, and by his eminent services contributed in a great degree to the glory of his sovereign's reign. Yahya's three sons, namely, Yahya, Jaafar, and Fadhl, after enjoying for a long time the favours and friendship of Haroun-al-Raschid, at length incurred his displeasure, and were put to death by his orders, together with nearly all their family, about 802 A.D. The virtues and the tragic fate of the Barmecides have been a favourite subject with Arabian poets and historians.

See ERSCH und GRUBER, "Allgemeine Encyklopaedie."

Bar'na-bạs, [Gr. Βαρνάβας; Fr. BARNABÉ, bȧr'nȧ'bȧ',] SAINT, one of the early Christian apostles, was a native of the island of Cyprus, and was originally named Joseph. He accompanied Saint Paul on a religious mission to Antioch, and afterwards visited Cyprus with Mark. According to tradition, Barnabas founded the church in Milan, of which he was the first bishop. The writings attributed to him are generally regarded as apocryphal. The time and manner of his death are unknown.

See Acts xiii.-xv.; P. PUCCINELLI, "Vita di S. Barnaba," 1649.

Bar'nạrd, (Sir ANDREW FRANCIS,) a British general, born in 1773 ; died in 1855.

Barnabé. See BARNABAS, SAINT.

Bar'nạrd, (DANIEL D., LL.D.,) United States minister to Prussia, born in Berkshire county, Massachusetts, in the early part of the nineteenth century. In 1827 he was elected a representative to Congress, and was re-elected in 1839, 1841, and 1843. He was appointed minister to Prussia in 1850. For several years he has edited a journal of education in New York.

Bar'nạrd, (Lady ANNE,) a Scottish poetess, whose maiden name was **Lindsay,** born in Fifeshire in 1750, was a daughter of the Earl of Balcarres. She wrote the ballad of "Auld Robin Gray." Died in 1825.

Barnard, (FREDERICK A. P., LL.D.,) an American teacher and educational writer, born in Sheffield, Massachusetts, in 1809. He graduated at Yale College, and became professor of mathematics, natural philosophy, etc. in the University of Alabama, (1838 to 1854,) and professor of mathematics and astronomy in the University of Mississippi, of which he was chosen president in 1856. His principal work is "Letters on College Government and the Evils inseparable from the American College System in its Present Form," (1855.)

Bar'nạrd, (HENRY,) a British general, born in Oxfordshire about 1800. He served in the Crimea in 1854, and obtained command of an army in India in June, 1857. Died at Delhi in July of that year.

Barnard, (HENRY,) an eminent American writer on education, born at Hartford, Connecticut, in January, 1811. He graduated at Yale College in 1830, and studied law. As a member of the legislature of Connecticut, to which he was elected about 1837, he rendered important services by the reorganization of the system of public schools. He became secretary of the board of educa-

tion of Connecticut, and in this capacity wrote a number of able reports on public schools. He published, besides other works, "School Architecture," "Normal Schools in the United States," "Hints and Methods for the Use of Teachers," and "National Education in Europe." He has recently been appointed United States Commissioner of Education. "Mr. Barnard," says the "Westminster Review" for January, 1854, "in his work on 'National Education in Europe,' has collected and arranged more valuable information and statistics than can be found in any one volume in the English language."

Barnard or **Bernard,** (JOHN,) an English divine and controversialist, born in Lincolnshire ; died in 1683.

Barnard, (JOHN,) an American divine, born in Boston in 1681. He was minister of Marblehead for more than fifty years, and published numerous sermons. He was distinguished for his sagacity in temporal affairs. Died in 1770.

Barnard, (Sir JOHN,) an English merchant and statesman, born in Berkshire in 1685. He was elected in 1722 a member of Parliament for London, which he continued to represent for nearly forty years, voting generally against the administration of Sir Robert Walpole. He was made a knight in 1732, and in 1737 lord-mayor of London. Died in 1764.

See "Biographia Britannica."

Barnard, (JOHN G.,) an able American general and engineer, born in Essex county, Massachusetts, in 1815. He graduated at West Point in 1833, obtained a commission in the corps of engineers, and was employed many years on the defences of the coast. He became a captain in 1838, and served as engineer in the Mexican war, 1846–47. In the spring of 1861 he planned and superintended the fortifications of Washington. He was appointed chief of engineers of the army of the Potomac about July 2, 1861, and served at the battles of Gaines' Mill, June 27, and Malvern Hill, July 1, 1862. He was chief engineer of the armies in the field, on the staff of General Grant, from June 5, 1864, to April 9, 1865. In December, 1865, he obtained the rank of colonel of engineers. During the war he was a member of many boards and commissions. He has published a number of scientific and military works.

Barnaud, bȧr'nō', (NICOLAS,) a French writer on alchemy and philosophy, born at Crest, in Dauphiny. He published, among other works, "The Mirror of the French," (1582,) a political treatise.

Barnave, bȧr'nȧv',(ANTOINE PIERRE JOSEPH MARIE,) a French revolutionist and orator, born at Grenoble in 1761. He acquired distinction as an advocate in his youth, and was elected to the States-General in 1789. He was one of the founders of the club called "Friends of the Constitution," one of the leaders of the popular party, and for a short time had much influence in the Assembly. He was the adversary of Mirabeau in a celebrated debate on the subject of the king's power to make war and peace. In 1791 he and two others were appointed as a committee to attend the king in his compulsory return from Varennes to Paris. His sympathy was excited for the royal captives, and he then became a defender of the throne with the constitution. His political career ended with the dissolution of the Assembly in September, 1791, and he was executed in November, 1793. He left several political treatises, one of which is entitled "Réflexions politiques." Lamartine represents him as an honest man, of moderate capacity, and calls him "the first orator of the Assembly which held the fate of the monarchy suspended," (in June, 1791.) "Barnave, though the best debater in the National Assembly," says Macaulay, "flinched before the energy of Mirabeau."

See M. DE SALVANDY, "Vie de Barnave," 1833 ; LAMARTINE, "History of the Girondists."

Barner, baR'nȩr, (JAMES,) a German chemist and physician, born at Elbing in 1641 ; died in 1686.

Barnes, barnz, (ALBERT,) an eminent American divine, born at Rome, in the State of New York, in 1798. He graduated at Hamilton College in July, 1820, and in the autumn of the same year entered the Theological Seminary at Princeton. Having been licensed to preach in 1823, he was soon after ordained pastor of the Presbyterian Church of Morristown, New Jersey. In 1830 he was called to the pastoral charge of the First Presbyterian Church of Philadelphia, a position which he held for more than thirty years. In the controversy which led to a division of the church into the Old and New Schools he took an important part, and he is perhaps the most prominent and influential representative of the New-School doctrines. As a commentator on the Scriptures, Mr. Barnes has deservedly a high reputation. It is admitted, even by those who do not agree with him in many of his religious views, that in his scriptural notes he combines extensive learning with great simplicity and clearness of exposition. His writings are highly prized by the religious community on both sides of the Atlantic. It is estimated that the circulation of his "Notes on the New Testament" (of which there are eleven volumes) has up to this time (1869) reached above a million volumes. Among his numerous other works may be mentioned his "Inquiry into the Scriptural Views of Slavery," "The Church and Slavery," (1857,) and "The Atonement in its Relations to Law and Moral Government," (1859.)

Many years since, Mr. Barnes took a decided stand, both in his sermons and in his writings, against the iniquities of slavery; he has the honourable distinction of having firmly and fearlessly declared his views on this subject at a time when such a course was as unpopular as it was unusual among the clergy of the United States.

It may be proper to state that Mr. Barnes declines on conscientious grounds the title of doctor of divinity, a title to which perhaps few divines, either in this country or in Europe, could present a better claim, whether we consider his great learning or the purity and consistency of his Christian character.

Barnes, barnz, (BARNABY,) an English poet, born about 1569. He was the author of a "Divine Century of Spiritual Sonnets," and a tragedy entitled "The Devil's Charter." He also translated Cicero's "De Officiis."

Barnes, (DANIEL H.,) a Baptist minister and distinguished American conchologist, was one of the founders and teachers of the New York High School. He contributed to "Silliman's Journal" a number of articles on conchology, etc. Died in 1828.

Barnes, (JOHN,) an English Catholic theologian, who condemned in his writings some of the dogmas of the Romish Church, and was imprisoned nearly thirty years in the Inquisition, where he died. His principal works are "Catholico-Romanus Pacificus," (1680,) and an "Essay against Equivocations."

Barnes, (JOSHUA,) an English scholar, born in London in 1654, published editions of Euripides, Homer, and Anacreon. He also wrote a "History of Edward the Third," and a number of poems. Died in 1712.

Barnes, written also **Berners,** (JULIANA,) born in Essex, was prioress of the convent of Sopewell, near Saint Alban's. She wrote a treatise on hunting, hawking, etc., known as the "Book of Saint Alban's," (1486.)
See LINGARD, "History of England."

Barnes, (ROBERT,) an English Protestant theologian under the reign of Henry VIII., who appointed him one of his chaplains. He afterwards incurred the displeasure of the king, and was burnt at the stake by his order, (1540.) He wrote "Lives of the Popes from Saint Peter to Alexander II.," (1536,) with a preface by Luther.
See BURNET, "History of the Reformation."

Barnes, (SUSAN REBECCA,) an American poetess, born in New Hampshire. Her works are included in Griswold's "Female Poets of America."

Barnes, (THOMAS,) an able English editor, born about 1786. He was chief editor of the London "Times" for about twenty years, and one of the proprietors of the same. Died in 1841.

Barnes, (WILLIAM,) an English philologist, clergyman, and poet, born in Dorsetshire about 1810. He published various works.

Bar'nett, (JOHN,) an English musician and composer, born at Bedford in 1802. He has composed popular songs, masses, and a successful English opera, entitled "The Mountain Sylph."

Barnett, (MORRIS,) an English actor who successfully adapted the French drama "Monsieur Jacques," and others, to the English and American stage. Died in 1856.

Barneveldt, baR'neh-vĕlt, (JOHAN van Olden—vãn old'en,) an eminent and liberal Dutch statesman, born at Amersfoort in 1549. He began to practise law at the Hague about 1570, soon after which he served in the army against the Spaniards, and was chosen pensionary of Rotterdam in 1576. He was at the head of a deputation which, in 1585, after the death of William of Orange, offered the sovereignty of the Dutch provinces to Queen Elizabeth. On his return he was appointed advocate-general or grand pensionary of Holland, and successfully opposed the designs of the Earl of Leicester, who had command of the army. He acquired great influence in the state, and became the chief of the republican party, the opponents of which followed Maurice of Nassau. In his negotiations with the Spanish court, which, despairing of the conquest of the revolted provinces, had made pacific overtures, he was impeded by Maurice and his partisans, who denounced him as a traitor; but he extorted the recognition of the independence of the United Provinces, and in April, 1609, concluded a truce for twelve years. Before and after this event he was grand pensionary, the highest civil officer of the state.

The fierceness of faction was increased by fanaticism. A bitter contention had lately risen in Holland between the Arminians and Gomarists, (rigid Calvinists.) Barneveldt having identified himself with the former, Prince Maurice took sides with the Gomarists. (See ARMINIUS and GROTIUS.) The army, the ignorant multitude, and the majority of the clergy adhered to Maurice, who procured the convocation of a national synod to agree upon a standard of compulsory conformity. This measure Barneveldt opposed, because he favoured universal toleration. The Synod met at Dort in 1618, and condemned the Arminians. Barneveldt was arrested the same year, convicted on imaginary charges, and beheaded in May, 1619.
See MOTLEY, "History of the United Netherlands;" DE THOU, "Historia sui Temporis;" MORÉRI, "Dictionnaire Historique."

Bar'ney, (JOSHUA,) an American commodore, born in Baltimore in 1759. He became a lieutenant in 1775 or 1776, was captured by the British in 1777 and again in 1781. Having obtained command of the Hyder Ali, he captured the General Monk in 1782. In the autumn of that year he was sent to France with despatches. He received a commission as captain in the French service in 1795, but resigned it in 1800. He commanded a flotilla in Chesapeake Bay in 1813, and was wounded at the battle of Bladensburg in August, 1814. Died in 1818.
See MARY BARNEY, "Memoir of Commodore J. Barney," 1832.

Barn'field, (RICHARD,) an English poet, born about 1574, was the author of "Cynthia," (1595,) and several other poems. Died after 1605.

Barni, bǎR'ne', (JULES,) a French philosopher, born at Lille in 1818. He has published French versions of the works of Kant, with critical remarks.

Barnstorf, baRn'stoRf, (BERNARD,) a German physician and scientific writer, born at Rostock in 1625; died in 1704.

Barnstorf, (EBERHARD,) son of the preceding, born at Rostock in 1672, became professor of mathematics and medicine at Halle. He was the author of several medical works in Latin. Died in 1712.
See "Biographie Médicale."

Bar'num, (PHINEAS T.,) a famous American speculator, born at Bethel, Connecticut, in 1810. In 1841 he established in New York City a museum, which, through its real and pretended wonders, soon acquired great celebrity. For further particulars of his history, see his "Life," written by himself, (New York, 1855.)

Baro, bǎ'ro', (BALTHASAR,) a French poet and jurist, born at Valence in 1600, was the author of an "Ode on the Death of Marshal Schomberg," and several dramatic poems. Died in 1650.

Barocci, bä-rot'chee, [Fr. BAROCHE, bä'rosh',] or **Baroccio,** bä-rot'cho, (FIORI FEDERIGO d'Urbino—dooR-bee'no,) a celebrated Italian painter, born at Urbino in 1528. He studied the works of Raphael and

ä, ē, ī, ō, ū, ȳ, *long;* ă, ĕ, ĭ, ŏ, ŭ, ў, *short;* ą, ę, į, ǫ, *obscure;* fär, fâll, fåt; mêt; nŏt; gōōd; mōōn·

Titian, but formed his style chiefly upon the model of Correggio. Among his master-pieces are a "Descent from the Cross," at Perugia, a "Holy Family," in the Museum at Naples, and "Saint Francis in Ecstasy at the Appearance of the Saviour and the Virgin," which he was seven years in completing. Barocci possessed great merit as a colorist, and skill in the management of chiaroscuro. He also engraved several of his pictures in superior style. Died in 1612.

See BELLORI, "Vite dei Pittori," etc.

Baroccio, bȧ-rot'cho, or **Barocci,** (AMBROGIO,) a Milanese painter and sculptor of the fifteenth century, was an ancestor of F. Federigo d'Urbino, noticed above.

Baroccio or **Barozzio.** See VIGNOLA.

Baroche, the French of BAROCCI, which see.

Baroche, bȧ'rosh', (PIERRE JULES,) a French advocate and minister of state, born in Paris in 1802. He was a member of the Constituent Assembly in 1848–49, and minister of the interior in 1850. From April to October, 1851, he was minister of foreign affairs. Having become a partisan of Louis Napoleon, he was appointed president of the council of state just after the *coup d'état* of December, 1851. In June, 1863, he became minister of justice and keeper of the seals.

Baroero, bȧ-ro-a'ro, (?) (GIACOMO,) an Italian professor of surgery at Turin, born at Soglio in 1790, wrote a "Treatise on Practical Surgery." Died in 1831.

Bär'on, (ALEXANDER,) a physician, born in Scotland in 1745, emigrated to Charleston, South Carolina, about 1770. He practised there with distinction, and was one of the founders of the medical society of South Carolina. Died in 1819.

Bär'on, written also **Baro,** (BONAVENTURA,) an Irish monk, originally named Fitzgerald, born at Clonmel about 1600. Died in 1696.

Baron, bȧ'rôn', (ÉGUINAIRE, à'ğe'nâr',) a distinguished jurist, born at Saint-Pol-de-Léon in 1495, was styled by Cujas the French Varro. He published several Latin treatises on the Pandects. Died in 1550.

See TAISAND, "Vies des plus célèbres Jurisconsultes."

Baron, bȧ-rōn', (ERNST GOTTLIEB,) a celebrated German lute-player and writer on music, born at Breslau in 1696. He published, among other works, "Historical, Theoretical, and Practical Researches on the Lute." Died in 1760.

Baron, (HYACINTHE THÉODORE,) a French physician and medical writer, born in Paris in 1686, was elected in 1730 dean of the medical faculty. Died in 1758.

Baron, (HYACINTHE THÉODORE,) a physician, son of the preceding, born in Paris in 1707; died in 1787.

Bar'on, (JOHN,) an English physician, wrote a "Life of Dr. Jenner," (2 vols., 1827–38.) Died in 1851.

Baron, (MICHEL,) originally **Boyron,** a dramatic writer, and one of the most celebrated French actors, born in Paris in 1653. At an early age he attracted the notice of Molière, who became his intimate friend and gave him valuable instructions in his art. He was called the Roscius of his time. Died in 1729.

Baron, written also **Baro,** (PIERRE,) a French Protestant, became professor of divinity at Cambridge, England, about 1574. Died in London in 1599.

Baron, (RICHARD,) an English dissenting divine and political writer, was a native of Leeds. He published a compilation entitled "The Pillars of Priestcraft and Orthodoxy shaken," and edited Milton's prose works. Died in 1768.

Baron, (VINCENT,) a French theologian, born at Martres in 1604, published several works. Died in 1674.

Baron d'Hénouville, bȧ'rôn' dà'noo'vèl', (THÉODORE,) brother of Hyacinthe Théodore Baron the younger, noticed above, born in Paris in 1715, wrote several valuable works on chemistry and pharmacy. Died in 1768.

Baroni, bȧ-ro'nee, (ADRIANA BASILIO,) an Italian lady, celebrated for her beauty, talents, and accomplishments. A volume of poems in praise of her graces was published in 1633.

Baroni, (LYONORA,) daughter of Adriana Baroni, was likewise distinguished for her beauty and wit, and enjoyed a high reputation as a vocalist.

Baroni-Cavalcabo, bȧ-ro'nee kȧ-vȧl-kȧ'bo, (CLE-

MENTE,) an Italian *littérateur*, born near Roveredo in 1726, wrote "Memoirs towards Literary History," and other works. Died in 1796.

Baroni-Cavalcabo, (GASPAR ANTONIO,) a painter, born in 1682 near Roveredo, in the Tyrol. Died in 1759.

Baronio. See BARONIUS.

Ba-ro'nĭ-us or **Baronio,** bȧ-ro'ne-o, (CESARE,) an eminent Italian cardinal and writer on church history, born at Sora, in the kingdom of Naples, in 1538. He studied theology at Rome under the celebrated Filippo di Neri, whom in 1593 he succeeded as superior of the congregation of the Oratory. He became successively confessor to Pope Clement VIII., cardinal, and librarian of the Vatican. His principal work is entitled "Ecclesiastical Annals," 12 vols. folio, (in Latin, 1588–1607,) which, though not free from errors, is characterized by great learning and research, and cost its author thirty years of labour. Among his other productions is a treatise "On the Sicilian Monarchy," in which he opposes the claims of the King of Spain to Sicily. At an election for pope he once received thirty-one votes. Died in Rome in 1607.

See NICÉRON, "Mémoires;" J. BARNABÆUS, "Vita purpurati principis C. Baronii Cardinalis," 1651; LA CROZE, "Vie de Baronius;" T. LE FEBVRE, "Vie de C. Cardinal de Baronius," 1668.

Baronius, (JUSTUS,) a Calvinistic theologian of the seventeenth century, born at Xanten, in the duchy of Cleves, was converted to Catholicism, in defence of which he wrote several treatises.

Barotti, bȧ-rot'tee, (GIOVANNI ANDREA,) an Italian *littérateur*, born at Ferrara in 1701 ; died about 1775.

Barou du Soleil, bȧ'roo' dü so'là'ye, (or so'lȧl',) (PIERRE ANTOINE,) a French writer, born at Lyons in 1742, was executed during the reign of terror in 1793.

Barozzi or **Barozzio.** See VIGNOLA.

Barozzi, bȧ-rot'see, or **Barocci,** bȧ-rot'chee, (FRANCESCO,) an Italian jurist, was professor of canon law at Padua. He was related to the popes Eugene IV and Paul II., and was appointed by the latter Bishop of Treviso. Died in 1471.

Barozzi or **Barocci,** (FRANCESCO,) an Italian mathematician and scholar, lived about 1570.

Barozzi, (GIACOMO,) nephew of the preceding, wrote a "Treatise on Mathematics" and "Commentary on the Sphere."

Barra, bȧ'rȧ', (PIERRE,) a French physician and medical writer, lived at Lyons about 1650.

Barraband or **Barraban,** bȧ'rȧ'bôn',(PIERRE PAUL,) a French artist and excellent bird-painter, born at Aubusson in 1767. Among his best productions are the illustrations for Le Vaillant's "Natural History of African Birds," for Sonnini's edition of Buffon, and for Latreille's "History of Insects." Died in 1809.

Barrabino, bȧr-rȧ-bee'no, (SIMONE,) an Italian painter, born near Genoa ; died in 1640.

Barrados, bȧr-rȧ'dȯs, or **Barradas,** bȧr-rȧ'dȧs, [Lat. BARRA'DIUS,] (SEBASTIÃO,) a Portuguese Jesuit, born in 1542, was venerated as a saint. Died in 1615.

Barragan, bȧr-rȧ-gȧn', (MIGUEL,) a Mexican general who became president of Mexico in 1835 and died a few months afterwards.

Barral, bȧ'rȧl', (JEAN AUGUSTIN,) a French chemist, born at Metz in 1819, first extracted nicotine from the tobacco-leaf and made known its highly poisonous qualities. He also wrote several treatises on the application of chemistry to agriculture and the arts.

Barral, (PIERRE,) a French writer and zealous Jansenist, born at Grenoble, was one of the principal contributors to the "Historical, Literary, and Critical Dictionary of Celebrated Men." Died in 1772.

Barral, de, deh bȧ'rȧl', (ANDRÉ HORACE FRANÇOIS,) VISCOUNT, a French general, born at Grenoble in 1743, served in the last campaigns of the Seven Years' war, and in 1792 under Kellermann in the army of the Alps. Died in 1829.

Barral, de, (JOSEPH MARIE,) Marquis of Montferrat, brother of André Horace, a French magistrate, born at Grenoble in 1742, became first president of the imperial court at Grenoble. Died in 1828.

Barral, de, (LOUIS MATHIAS,) COUNT, brother of André Horace, noticed above, born in 1746. He be-

---

€ as k; ç as s; ğ hard; ğ as j; G, H, K, guttural; N, nasal; R, trilled; š as z; ŧh as in this. (☞See Explanations, p. 23.)

came successively Bishop of Meaux, almoner to the empress Josephine, and Archbishop of Tours.

Barranco, bâr-rän′ko,(FRANCISCO,) a Spanish painter, lived in Andalusia about 1650.

Barras, de, dẹh bȧ′rä′, (LOUIS,) COUNT, a French naval officer, born in Provence, served under De Grasse in the American war in 1782, and afterwards took possession of the English colonies of Nevis and Montferrat.

Barras, de, (PAUL FRANÇOIS JEAN NICOLAS,) COUNT, one of the first five Directors of the French Republic, was born of a noble family at, Foy-Emphoux, in Provence, in 1755. He favoured the popular cause in 1789, and in 1792 was elected to the Convention, in which he was a prominent partisan of the Mountain. In October, 1793, Barras and Fréron were sent on a mission to the south of France. They are charged with instigating the cruel execution of many royalists of Toulon after that city had been taken by the army. Barras was one of the conspirators who triumphed over Robespierre on the 9th Thermidor, 1794. Having been appointed by the Convention commander of the national guard on that day, he distinguished himself by his successful audacity. In October, 1795, with the aid of Bonaparte, whom he selected as general of the artillery, he defeated the insurgents of the sections in Paris, and was chosen a member of the Directory. After the *coup d'état* of the 18th Fructidor, Barras was the most powerful of the directors. He was the only man who kept his place in the Directory from its first appointment until its subversion by Bonaparte in 1799, which was the end of his political career. He died near Paris in 1829. He was indolent and dissolute, and possessed only moderate abilities.

See "Mémoires de Barras;" THIERS, "History of the French Revolution;" C. DORIS, "Amours et Aventures du Vicomte de Barras," 4 vols., 1816.

Barrau, bä′rō′, (THÉODORE HENRI,) a French teacher and educational writer, born at Toulouse in 1794.

Barraud, bä′rō′, (JACQUES,) an eminent French jurist and legal writer, born at Poitiers in 1555; died in 1626.

Barraud, (JACQUES,) a son of the preceding, was also noted as a jurist and Latin poet.

Barré, bä′rä′, (GUILLAUME,) a German publicist of French extraction, born about 1760. Having visited Paris in the early part of the Revolution, he became interpreter to Napoleon. He published in 1804 a "History of the French Consulate under Bonaparte." Died in 1829.

Barré, (ISAAC,) COLONEL, an officer of the British army, born in Dublin in 1726, was a son of a Frenchman. He served in Canada under General Wolfe, was patronized by Lord Shelburne, and was elected a member of Parliament in 1761. He gained the favour of the Americans by a spirited speech against the Stamp Act in 1765, and by his subsequent course during Lord North's administration. In 1766 he was appointed a privy councillor. The "Letters of Junius" have been ascribed to Colonel Barré. Died in 1802.

Barre, bȧR, (JEAN AUGUSTE,) a French sculptor, a son of Jean Jacques, noticed below, born in Paris in 1811. He gained a first medal in 1840.

Barre, (JEAN JACQUES,) a French engraver of medals, born in Paris in 1793. He became *graveur-général* of the mint in 1842. Died in 1855.

Barre, (JOSEPH,) a French ecclesiastic and chancellor of the University of Paris, was the author of a "General History of Germany," (11 vols., 1748,) and other works. Died in 1764.

Barré, (LOUIS,) a French *littérateur*, born at Lille in 1799, translated Walter Scott's poems into French, and published in 1844 a "New Classical Biography."

Barré, (PIERRE YVES,) born in Paris in 1749, was the author of several popular dramas, one of which is entitled "The Marriage of Scarron." Died in 1832.

Barre, de la, dẹh lä bȧR, (ANTOINE le Fèvre—leh′-fĕvr′ or fȧvr′,) a French general, appointed Governor of Guiana in 1663, re-took Cayenne from the Dutch, and was made Governor of Canada in 1682. He was recalled in 1685, and died in 1688.

See CHARLEVOIX, "Histoire de la Nouvelle France."

Barre, de la, (CÉSAR ALEXIS Chichereau—shĕsh′-

rō′,) CHEVALIER, a French *littérateur*, born at Langeais about 1630, was the author of "Fables" in verse.

Barre, de la, (FRANÇOIS Poulain—poo′lȧN′,) a French miscellaneous writer, born in Paris in 1647. He published, among other works, a treatise "On the Equality of the Sexes." Died in 1723.

Barre, de la, (JEAN,) a French lawyer and *littérateur*, born in Paris about 1650, wrote a continuation of Bossuet's "Discourse on Universal History." Died about 1711.

Barre, de la, (JEAN,) a French antiquary of the seventeenth century, was a resident of Corbeil.

Barre, de la, (JEAN FRANÇOIS le Fèvre—leh′fĕvr′ or fȧvr′,) CHEVALIER, grandson of Antoine le Fèvre, noticed above, born at Abbeville in 1747. He was condemned to death by the tribunal of that city for having mutilated a crucifix, and was executed in 1766, at the age of nineteen. This act of barbarity and intolerance is severely commented upon by Voltaire in his "Account of the Death of the Chevalier de la Barre."

See VOLTAIRE, "Correspondance," and his "Relation de la Mort du Chevalier de la Barre," 1766.

Barre, de la, (JEAN JACQUES,) a Protestant theologian, born at Geneva in 1696, was a son of François Poulain, noticed above. He published "Philosophic Thoughts" and "Dialogues on Different Subjects." Died in 1751.

Barre, de la, (LOUIS FRANÇOIS JOSEPH,) a French scholar and critic, born at Tournay in 1688, was a brother of Antoine Barre de Beaumarchais. He published editions of the "Vetera Analecta" of Mabillon, of Moréri's "Dictionary," and other valuable works. Died in 1738.

Barre, La, lä bȧR, (MICHEL,) a celebrated French musician and composer of operas, born in Paris about 1680. Died in 1744.

Barre de Beaumarchais, de la, dẹh lä bȧR dẹh bō′mȧr′shȧ′, (ANTOINE,) a French *littérateur*, born at Cambrai, was the author of "Letters, Serious and Playful, on the Works of Savants," (1729.) Died about 1757.

Barré de Saint-Venant, bä′rä′ dẹh sȧN′vẹh-nôN′, (JEAN,) a French agricultural writer, born at Niort in 1737, became a resident of Saint Domingo. He wrote a work "On the Modern Colonies under the Torrid Zone," (1802.) Died in 1810.

Barreau, bä′rō′, (ALEXANDRINE ROSE,) a French heroine, born at Sartens about 1770, served as soldier in nearly all the campaigns of the republic and empire. Died in 1843.

Barreau, (FRANÇOIS,) an ingenious French mechanician, born at Toulouse in 1731. One of his masterpieces was an ivory sphere of exquisite and complicated workmanship, called a *kiosk*, which he presented to Napoleon. Died in 1814.

Barreaux, des, dȧ bä′rō′, (JACQUES Vallée—vä′lä′,) SEIGNEUR, an indifferent French poet, born in Paris in 1602. Died in 1673.

Barreiros, bär-rä′e-ròs, (GASPAR,) a Portuguese geographer, was a nephew of the celebrated historian João de Barros. His principal work is entitled "Chorographia;" besides which he was the author of "Cosmographic Observations." Died in 1574.

Barrelier, bȧR′le-ȧ′, (JACQUES,) a French botanist, born in Paris in 1606. In 1635 he entered the order of Saint Dominic, and, while visiting the convents of France, Spain, and Italy, made a valuable collection of plants and shells. He was engaged upon a large botanical work when he died in 1673. His manuscripts were subsequently destroyed by fire; but the copper-plates were preserved, and were collected by Antoine de Jussieu, and published with accompanying descriptions, under the title of "Plants of France, Spain, and Italy." The work contains thirteen hundred and ninety-two figures of plants, and three plates of shells. Plumier has named the genus Barrelia in honour of this botanist.

Barrême, bä′rĕm′, (FRANÇOIS,) a French arithmetician of the seventeenth century, was a native of Lyons, and the author of valuable arithmetical works. Died in 1703.

Barrère. See BARÈRE.

Barrère, bä′rair′, (PIERRE,) a French naturalist and physician, born at Perpignan about 1690. He was the author of an "Essay on the Natural History of Equi-noctial France," being a mere list or enumeration of the natural productions of Guiana and Cayenne, where he resided nearly three years. Died in 1755.

See "Biographie Médicale."

Barres, (JOSEPH FREDERICK.) See DESBARRES.

Barretier. See BARATIER.

Barreto, bâr-rā'to, (FRANCISCO,) a Portuguese mis-sionary and Jesuit, born at Montemor-o-Novo in 1588. He wrote, in Italian, an "Account of Missions, etc. in the Province of Malabar," (1645.) Died at Goa in 1663.

Barreto, de, dà bâr-rā'to, (FRANCISCO,) a Portuguese who was appointed in 1555 governor of the Indies. In an attempt to conquer that portion of Africa called Mo-nomotapa, after suffering great hardships, he died in 1574. It was by his orders that the poet Camoëns was exiled to Macao.

Barreto, de, (MUÑOZ, moon-yŏz',) a Portuguese under the reign of Sebastian, was Viceroy of the Indies in 1573, and in 1589 governor of the eastern shores of Africa.

Barreto de Resende, bâr-rā'to dà rà-sèn'dà, (PE-DRO,) a Portuguese historian, who left in manuscript a work on the history of India. Died in 1651.

Bär'rett, (EATON STANNARD,) an Irish writer of satire and fiction, born about 1785. He published poems en-titled "Woman," and "All the Talents," (1807;) also "The Heroine," a satirical romance. Died in 1820.

Barrett, (ELIZABETH.) See BROWNING.

Barrett, (GEORGE,) a distinguished landscape-painter, born at Dublin about 1730, was one of the first members of the Royal Academy of Painting. He was a friend of Edmund Burke. Died in 1784.

Bär'rett, (GEORGE HORTON,) an English actor, born in 1794, removed to the United States, where he gained considerable popularity, and became manager of the Bowery Theatre in New York.

Bar-rett', (or bä'rà',) (JEAN JACQUES,) a French *littéra-teur,* of English extraction, born at Condom in 1717. He made translations from Cicero, Ovid, Virgil, and Tacitus, and also translated Macchiavelli's "History of Florence," and "The Praise of Folly" by Erasmus. Died in 1792.

Barrett, (JOHN,) a distinguished classical scholar, born in Ireland about 1750. He studied at Trinity College, where he became vice-provost in 1806. He wrote an "Inquiry into the Origin of the Constellations that com-pose the Zodiac," and an "Essay on the Life of Swift." Dr. Barrett discovered, among the manuscripts of the college library, a palimpsest, containing fragments of the Gospel of Saint Matthew, supposed by some to have been written in the second century. He was noted for his eccentricities; and many anecdotes are related of his simplicity and ignorance of common life. Died in 1821.

Barrett, (WILLIAM,) an English antiquary and sur-geon, resided at Bristol. His principal work is entitled "History and Antiquities of Bristol," (1788.) He was a fellow of the Antiquarian Society. Died in 1789.

Barrey, bä'rà', (CLAUDE ANTOINE,) a French physi-cian, born at Besançon in 1771, was a zealous promoter of vaccination. Died in 1837.

Barri. See GIRALDUS CAMBRENSIS.

Barri, bâr'ree, (GABRIELLO,) an Italian scholar and antiquary, born at Francica, in Calabria, wrote, in Latin, a treatise "On the Antiquity and Situation of Calabria," (1571,) and other works.

Barri, (GIACOMO,) a Venetian painter and engraver, born about 1630, imitated Titian and Tintoretto. He published "Viaggio pittoresco," (1671,) which was trans-lated into English by Lodge. Died after 1684.

Barrientos, bâr-re-ên'tôs, (BARTOLOMÉ,) a Spanish scholar and commentator of the sixteenth century, was a native of Granada.

Barrientos, (GENES, Hà'nês,) a Spanish theologian, preached in the Philippine Islands. Died in 1694.

Barrière, bä're-aiR', (JEAN FRANÇOIS,) a French *lit-térateur,* born in Paris in 1786, published, among other works, "Memoirs of Madame Campan."

Barrière, or Labarre, là'bäR', (PIERRE,) a French soldier, notorious from his attempt on the life of Henry IV. He was executed in 1593, declaring that he had been incited to the deed by the Catholic priests.

Barrière, (THÉODORE,) a French dramatist, born in Paris in 1823. Among his works is "Les Filles de Marbre," (1853.)

Barrière, de la, dèh là bä're-aiR', (Dom JEAN,) the founder of the order of the Feuillants, born at Saint-Céré in 1544. In 1586 his institution was recognized by a brief from Pope Sixtus V. Died in 1600.

Bär'rin-ġer, (DANIEL MOREAU,) an American poli-tician, born in Cabarras county, North Carolina, in 1807. He represented a district of his native State in Congress from 1843 to 1849, and was minister to Spain from 1849 to 1853.

Bär'ring-ton, (Hon. DAINES,) a distinguished English jurist and naturalist, born in 1727, was a son of John Shute, Viscount Barrington, noticed below. He pub-lished in 1766 "Observations upon the Statutes, chiefly the more Ancient, from Magna Charta to the 21 Jac. I. c. 27," which is esteemed a standard work. He wrote also a "Dissertation on the Linnæan System," and a tract "On the Probability of reaching the North Pole," (1775,) which is said to have suggested to Captain Phipps his voyage to the Arctic regions. Barrington contributed to the "Archæologia" and to the "Philosophical Transac-tions." He was vice-president of the Royal Society. Died in 1800.

Barrington, (JOHN,) son of the first Viscount Bar-rington, a major-general who commanded the British forces at the capture of Guadeloupe. Died in 1764.

Barrington, (JOHN Shute,) first VISCOUNT, an able English writer and politician, born in Hertfordshire in 1678. He became a member of Parliament about 1714, after which he was raised to the Irish peerage. "He is reckoned the shrewdest head in England," says Dean Swift. His principal work, "Miscellanea Sacra; or a New Method of considering so much of the History of the Apostles as is contained in Scripture," (2 vols., 1725,) was highly esteemed. Died in 1734.

Barrington, (Sir JONAH,) an Irish lawyer and writer, born in Queen's county in 1767. He became in 1790 a member of the Irish Parliament, where he acted with the popular party and voted against the Union. He was subsequently made a knight and a judge of the admiralty court. He was the author of "Historic Memoirs of Ire-land" and "Personal Sketches of his Own Times." The latter was very popular: it abounds in amusing though extravagant anecdote, and presents a tolerably correct picture of Irish society at that time. Died in 1834.

Barrington, (Hon. SAMUEL,) fifth son of the first Lord Barrington, entered the navy at an early age. He was promoted to the rank of vice-admiral, and in 1778 took Saint Lucia from the French. Died in 1800.

See CAMPBELL, "Lives of the British Admirals."

Barrington, (SHUTE,) the youngest son of the first Lord Barrington, born in Berkshire in 1734, rose to be Bishop of Durham in 1791. He wrote a "Life of Wil-liam, Viscount Barrington." Died in 1826.

Barrington, (WILLIAM WILDMAN,) second Viscount Barrington, eldest son of John Shute, Lord Barrington, born in 1710. He was elected to Parliament for Ply-mouth in 1754, which he continued to represent for more than twenty years. He was successively appointed sec-retary at war, (1755,) chancellor of the exchequer, (1761,) and treasurer of the navy, (1762.) Died in 1793.

See SHUTE BARRINGTON, "Political Life of W. Wildman Bar-rington," 1815; "London Quarterly Review" for January, 1816.

Barrios, bâr're-ôs, or **De Barros,** dà bâr'rôs, (MI-GUEL,) sometimes called **Daniel Levi,** a Spanish Jew of the seventeenth century, wrote, among other works, an "Account of the Spanish Poets and Writers of Jew-ish Origin."

Barris, bä'rèss', (PIERRE JOSEPH PAUL,) a French statesman, born at Montesquieu in 1759, was a deputy to the Legislative Assembly in 1791, and subsequently president of the court of cassation. Died in 1824.

Barroilhet, bä'rwä'là', (PAUL,) a French vocalist, born at Bayonne in 1810. He performed in the Opera of Paris.

Barrois, bä'rwä', (JACQUES MARIE,) a learned French bookseller, born in Paris in 1704, published a great num-ber of valuable catalogues. Died in 1769.

Bär'ron, (JAMES,) an American commodore, born in Virginia in 1768. He commanded the Chesapeake, which the British ship Leopard attacked and captured in 1807, in time of peace, because Barron refused to allow his vessel to be searched for deserters. For his conduct in this affair he was suspended for several years. In 1820 he killed Commodore Decatur in a duel, and was at the same time severely wounded himself. Died in 1851.

Barron, (SAMUEL,) a naval officer, brother of the preceding, born in Virginia about 1764. He commanded a squadron sent against Tripoli in 1805. Died in 1810.

Barron, (SAMUEL,) an American officer, born in Virginia, entered the navy about 1812. He became a commander in 1847, and captain in 1855. As commodore of the rebel navy, he commanded at Fort Hatteras, which he surrendered in August, 1861.

Barros, bår'ròs, (ANDREA,) a Portuguese Jesuit, native of Lisbon, lived about 1700–30. He wrote a "Life of Antonio Vieyra."

Barros, de, då bår'ròs, (JoÃo,) the most eminent of the Portuguese historians, born at Viseu in 1496. He was patronized by the Infant of Portugal, afterwards John III., on whose accession he was appointed governor of the Portuguese establishments on the coast of Guinea. He subsequently filled the post of agent-general for those colonies for more than thirty years. The first two decades of his great work, entitled "Asia, or the History of the Discoveries and Conquests of the Portuguese in the East Indies," came out in 1552–53, and the third decade ten years later. The fourth, which brings the history down to 1539, was published in 1615, with notes by Lavanha. A continuation of this history has been written by Diego de Couto. Barros was the author of a historical romance called "Chronicle of the Emperor Clarimundo," and a number of moral and scientific treatises. His writings are remarkable for elegance of style, and his merits as a historian have procured for him the name of "the Portuguese Livy." Died in 1570.

See MANOEL SEVERIM DE FARIA, "Vida de João de Barros," 1624; BARBOSA MACHADO, "Bibliotheca Lusitana," and an able essay on "Portuguese Literature" in the "London Quarterly Review" for May, 1809.

Barroso, bår-ro'so, (MIGUEL,) a Spanish painter, born at Consuegra, in New Castile, in 1538, was employed by Philip II. to adorn a part of the Escurial. Died in 1590.

Barrot, bå'ro', (CAMILLE HYACINTHE **Odillon—** o'de'yòn',) an eloquent French advocate and statesman, born at Villefort, in Lozère, in 1791. Having gained distinction as an advocate, and adopted liberal opinions, he began his political career as president of the society which took for its name *Aide-toi et le ciel t'aidera*. He was an active promoter of the revolution of 1830, and, it is said, advised or persuaded Lafayette to refuse the presidency of the republic. In August, 1830, he was appointed prefect of the department of Seine at Paris, and a few months later was elected to the Chamber of Deputies, in which he became a leader of the opposition, or *gauche modérée*. He favoured electoral reform, and won popularity by his speeches against the administration of Guizot, between 1840 and '48. He was a member of the brief ministry which the king appointed in February, 1848, as a concession to the victorious revolutionists. On the abdication of Louis Philippe, he advocated the appointment of the Duchess of Orléans as regent. He was minister of justice and president of the council in the first cabinet of Louis Napoleon from December, 1848, to September, 1849. He protested against the *coup d'état* of December, 1851, after which he retired from political life.

See LOUIS BLANC, "Histoire de dix Ans."

Barrot, (FERDINAND,) brother of Odillon Barrot, born in 1806, became minister of the interior in 1849, a member of the council of state in 1851, and a senator in 1853.

Barrot, (JEAN ANDRÉ,) a French politician, the father of Odillon, was born about 1752. As a member of the Convention in 1793, he voted against the execution of the king. Died in 1845.

See ODILLON BARROT, "Notice sur la Vie de J. A. Barrot," 1814.

Bär'rōw, (ISAAC,) an eminent English divine, mathematician, and pulpit orator, born in London in October, 1630, was educated at Cambridge, where he took the degree of M.A. in 1652. After an extensive tour on the Continent, he was ordained in 1660, and chosen professor of Greek at Cambridge. In 1662 he obtained the chair of geometry in Gresham College, and in 1663 the Lucasian professorship of mathematics. He resigned this in favour of his friend and pupil, the illustrious Newton, in 1669, and was appointed master of Trinity College by the king in 1672. As a mathematician he is estimated more highly by the English than by the French. By the invention of the method of tangents he prepared the way for the application of the differential calculus to geometry. He published, besides other works, "Euclidis Elementa," (1655,) "Lectiones Opticæ," (1669,) and "Lectiones Geometricæ," (1670.) Among his posthumous works are "Lectiones Mathematicæ," (1683,) and an admirable "Treatise on the Pope's Supremacy." His Sermons and other theological works, edited by Dr. Tillotson, appeared in three volumes, 1685. He was never married. His moral character was irreproachable. Died in London in May, 1677.

"We admire," says Robert Hall, "as much as it is possible for our readers to admire, the rich invention, the masculine sense, the exuberantly copious yet precise and energetic diction, which distinguish Barrow, who, by a rare felicity of genius, united in himself the most distinguishing qualities of the mathematician and the orator." "The sermons of Barrow," says Hallam, "display a strength of mind, a comprehensiveness and fertility, which have rarely been equalled." ("Introduction to the Literature of Europe.")

See ARTHUR HILL, "Life of Barrow," prefixed to his collected works, 1685; WARD, "Lives of the Professors of Gresham College."

Barrow, (JOHN,) an English writer of the last century, chiefly known as the compiler of a "Geographical Dictionary," and a "History of Discoveries made by Europeans in Different Parts of the World," (1756.)

Barrow, (JOHN,) an English physician, who published a "New Medicinal Dictionary," (1749,) and a "New Essay of the Practice of Physic."

Barrow, (Sir JOHN,) an English traveller, and one of the founders of the Geographical Society, born in Lancashire in 1764. He accompanied Lord Macartney, as his secretary, to the Cape of Good Hope in 1797, and in 1804 was appointed by Lord Melville second secretary to the admiralty, a position which he held for forty years. During this period he rendered important services to geographical science, and was active in promoting voyages to the Arctic regions. Among his principal works are "Travels in South Africa," (1803,) "Memoirs of Naval Worthies of Queen Elizabeth's Reign," (1845,) and "Voyages of Discovery and Research in the Arctic Regions." He was also a contributor to the "Encyclopædia Britannica" and "Quarterly Review." He became a Fellow of the Royal Society in 1805, and was subsequently president of the Geographical Society. Died in 1848.

See "An Autobiographical Memoir of Sir John Barrow."

Bär'rōw-bӯ, (WILLIAM,) an English physician, born in London about 1700, translated from the Latin some of the works of Astruc.

Bär'rōwe or **Bär'rōweš,** (HENRY,) an English nonconformist, of the sect called Brownists, was executed in 1592 on a charge of publishing seditious books against the queen and government. He was the author of "A Brief Discoverie of the False Church," (1590.)

Barruel, de, deh bȧ'rü-êl', (AUGUSTIN,) a learned French Jesuit, born near Viviers in 1741. He published, among other works, a treatise "On the Pope and his Religious Rights," (1803.) Died in 1820.

Barruel-Beauvert, de, deh bȧ'rü-êl' bo'vaiR', (ANTOINE JOSEPH,) COUNT, a French *littérateur*, born near Bagnols, in Languedoc, in 1756, was the author of a "Life of Rousseau," and several political works in favour of the royalists. Died in 1817.

Bär'rӯ, (Sir·CHARLES,) an eminent English architect, born at Westminster in 1795. Among his master-pieces are the church of Saint Peter's at Brighton, King Edward's Grammar-School at Birmingham, and the Athenæum at Manchester. In 1840 he began the new Parliament-House, which, though he did not live to see it completed, is a splendid monument of his genius and taste. Sir Charles was a Fellow of the Royal Society, and a member of the Institute of Architects, and of various learned societies in Europe. Died in 1860.

See a "Memoir of Sir Charles Barry," by his son, the Rev. ALFRED BARRY, 1867.

Bär′rў, (Sir DAVID,) a learned physician, born in the county of Roscommon, Ireland, in 1780, was the author of "Researches on the Influence exercised by Atmospheric Pressure upon the Progression of the Blood in the Veins," etc. Died in 1835.

Barry, (EDWARD,) an English divine, born at Bristol about 1759; died in 1822.

Barry, (Sir EDWARD,) an English physician and medical writer, studied under Boerhaave at Leyden. He became professor of medicine at Dublin, and was a Fellow of the Royal Society. Died in 1776.

Barry, (GARRET,) an officer, born in Ireland, published in 1634 a "Discourse of Military Discipline."

Bär′rў, (GEORGE,) a Scottish divine, born in Berwickshire in 1747, was the author of a "History of the Orkney Islands," (1805.) Died in 1804.

Barry, (GERALD.) See GIRALDUS CAMBRENSIS.

Barry, (JAMES,) Lord of Santry, writer on law, born in Dublin in 1598, became lord chief-justice of the king's bench in Ireland. Died in 1673.

Barry, (JAMES,) an eminent historical painter, born at Cork in 1741. He was the son of the master of a coasting-vessel, who destined him for his own profession. He manifested a passion for art at a very early age, passing whole nights in drawing, and "spending all his pocket-money on pencils and candles." One of his first productions represented the conversion of a king of Cashel by Saint Patrick: it attracted general admiration, and procured for the artist the friendship and patronage of Edmund Burke, by whose pecuniary assistance he was soon after enabled to visit Rome. Having studied five years in that city, he returned to England in 1770, and was subsequently elected an associate of the Royal Academy. In 1775 he published an "Inquiry into the Real and Imaginary Obstructions to the Progress of Art in England," an able refutation of Winckelmann's theory that the climate of England was unfavourable to the high development of art. In 1777 he began a series of six pictures designed to illustrate human improvement. Of these works, which are esteemed his master-pieces, the "Victors at Olympia" deserves particular mention. Barry was elected professor of painting at the Academy in 1782; but his unfortunate irritability of temper kept him constantly embroiled with his colleagues, and having, as was alleged, made some false accusations against members of the Academy, he was deprived of his office in 1797. He died in 1806, in destitute circumstances. "Barry," says Cunningham, "was the greatest enthusiast in art which this country ever produced: his passion for it almost amounted to madness;" and the same writer adds, "his imagination was second only to that of Fuseli."

See CUNNINGHAM'S "Lives of Painters and Sculptors;" "Encyclopædia Britannica;" "Edinburgh Review" for August, 1810; "Blackwood's Magazine" for December, 1820.

Barry, (JOHN,) COMMODORE, a naval officer, born in Wexford county, Ireland, in 1745, emigrated to America about 1760. Having obtained command of a United States frigate in 1776, he captured the British vessel Atalanta in May, 1781, and commanded the Alliance, which conveyed La Fayette to France about the end of that year. Died in 1803.

Barry, bä′re′, (MARIE JEANNE Gomart de Vaubernier—go′mȧR′ deh vō′bĕR′ne-ȧ′,) COUNTESS OF, a mistress of Louis XV., of France, was born at Vaucouleurs in 1746. She exercised a powerful influence at court, and received the homage of Chancellor Maupeou and other distinguished men, who obtained through her the most important offices and privileges. During the reign of terror she was arrested as a royalist, and executed in November, 1793.

See "Nouvelle Biographie Générale."

Barry, (MARTIN,) a distinguished English physiologist, born in Hampshire in 1802, graduated in medicine at Edinburgh, and finished his studies at Heidelberg in 1834. His principal work, entitled "Researches in Embryology," first appeared in the "Philosophical Transactions" from 1838 to 1842, and obtained for him the gold medal of the Royal Society. He also published a treatise "On Fibre," and other works relating to animal development. He was elected a Fellow of the Royal Society in 1840. Died in Suffolk in 1855.

Barry, (RENÉ,) a French *littérateur* and royal historiographer, lived about 1630. Among his works is a "Life of Louis XIII.," (in Latin.)

Barry, (SPRANGER,) a celebrated actor, born at Dublin in 1719, performed with great success in his native city and in London. He is said to have been in some characters scarcely inferior to Garrick. Died in 1777.

See "Biographia Dramatica."

Bär′rў, (WILLIAM F.,) an American general, born in New York City in 1818, graduated at West Point. He was made captain in 1852, and major of artillery in May, 1861. In August of that year he became a brigadier-general of volunteers, and served as chief of artillery, under General McClellan, in the battles near Richmond, June, 1862.

Barry, (WILLIAM TAYLOR,) an American politician, born in Lunenburg county, Virginia; in 1785. He became a citizen of Kentucky, was elected to Congress in 1810, and was subsequently chief justice of that State. He was appointed postmaster-general under President Jackson in 1829, and was the first incumbent of that office who was a member of the cabinet. In 1835 he was sent as minister to Spain. He died at Liverpool, while on his way to Madrid, the same year.

Barry or **Barri, de,** deh bä′re′, (PAUL,) a French Jesuit, born near Narbonne in 1587, wrote a number of mystical religious treatises, which were satirized by Pascal in his "Provincial Letters." Died in 1661.

Barry Cornwall. See PROCTER.

Barsony, (baR-shoñ′) OF LOVAS BERENY, (lo-vŏsh′ bä-reñ′,) (GEORGE,) a Hungarian Catholic bishop, distinguished for his zeal against the Protestants. Died in 1678.

Bar-su′mas or **Bar-sau′mas,** a prominent leader of the Nestorians, became Bishop of Nisibis in 435 A.D.

Bart or **Barth,** bȧR, (JEAN,) a celebrated French seaman, born at Dunkirk in 1651, signalized himself as a privateersman against the Dutch in 1672. After performing many brilliant exploits as a cruiser in the Mediterranean, he was appointed by Louis XIV. chief of a squadron in 1697. He obtained letters of nobility from the French king for having captured a Dutch fleet laden with corn, in 1694. Died in 1702.

See MACAULAY, "History of England," vol. iv.; A. RICHER, "Vie de Jean Bart," 1780; VANDEREST, "Histoire de Jean Bart," 1841.

Barta, baR′tä, (BALTHASAR,) a Hungarian chronicler, born at Szoboszlo, lived about 1770.

Bartalini, baR-tä-lee′nee, (FRANCESCO,) an Italian painter, born at Sienna about 1560; died in 1609.

Bartas, du, dü bȧR′tä′, (GUILLAUME de Salluste—deh sȧ′lüst′,) an eminent French poet and negotiator, born at Montfort, in Armagnac, in 1544, was a Protestant. He was sent by Henry IV. on missions to several foreign courts. His chief work is a poem entitled "The Week of Creation," ("La première Semaine, ou la Création,") which was once greatly admired, and was translated into Latin, Italian, English, and German. He received several wounds at the battle of Ivry, survived a few months, and died in 1590. "His imagination, though extravagant, is vigorous and original." (Hallam's "Introduction to the Literature of Europe.")

See, also, SAINTE-BEUVE, "Tableau de la Poésie Française."

Bartels, baR′tĕls, (ERNST DANIEL AUGUST,) a German physician, born at Brunswick in 1778, became professor of medicine at Berlin in 1827, and published many works on physiology, etc. Died in 1838.

See CALLISEN, "Medicinisches Schriftsteller-Lexikon."

Bartenstein, baR′ten-stīn′, (JOHANN CHRISTOPH,) born in 1690, rose to be vice-chancellor of Austria and Bohemia. He wrote "The Law of Nature and of Nations." Died in 1766.

Bartenstein, (LORENZ ADAM,) a German mathematician and scholar, born at Heldburg in 1711, was the author of several critical and mathematical treatises. Died in 1796.

See J. C. BRIEGLEB, "Vita L. A. Bartensteinii," 1793.

Barth, bȧRt, (FRIEDRICH GOTTLIEB,) a German phi-

---

lologist, born at Wittenberg in 1738, published an edition of Propertius with notes, and a "German and Spanish Grammar," (1778.) Died in 1794.

Barth, (GOTTFRIED,) a German jurist and professor of law at Leipsic, born in that city in 1650; died in 1728.

Barth, (HEINRICH,) a celebrated German explorer, born at Hamburg in 1821. He visited Northern Africa in 1845, whence he proceeded to Arabia and Asia Minor, and in 1849 published his "Wanderings along the Shores of the Mediterranean." About this time he received proposals from the British government to join the expedition which was then being fitted out for Central Africa. In company with Mr. Richardson and Dr. Overweg, he set out in December, 1849. Having spent nearly six years in his explorations, during which time his two companions died, Dr. Barth returned to Europe in 1855. He published in 1857 his "Travels and Discoveries in North and Central Africa." Died in 1865.

See "Edinburgh Review" for January and April, 1859, vol. cix.

Barth, (JEAN.) See BART, (JEAN.)

Barth, bår, (JEAN RAPHAEL PHILIPPE,) a French medical writer, born at Sarreguemines, in Moselle, about 1812. His chief work is a "Practical Treatise on Auscultation," (1840.) He was assisted by Henri Roger in the composition of this work.

Barth, bårt, (KARL,) a German engraver, born at Hildburghausen in 1792. He engraved some works of Cornelius and Overbeck.

Barth, [Lat. BAR'THIUS,] (MICHAEL,) a German physician, born at Annaberg, in Saxony, about 1650, was the author of "Letters on Medicine," and a number of Latin poems. Died in 1684.

Barth, (PAUL,) a German Orientalist, born at Nuremberg in 1635; died in 1688.

Barth, von, fon bårt, [Lat. BAR'THIUS,] (CASPAR,) a German scholar, born at Cüstrin in 1587, wrote a Latin work entitled "Adversaria," and commentaries on Claudian, Statius, and other classics. Died in 1658.

See KROMAYER, "Programma in C. Barthii obitum," 1658; NICÉRON, "Mémoires."

Barth-Barthenheim, bårt-bårt'en-hīm', (JOHANN BAPTIST LUDWIG EHRENREICH,) COUNT OF, a distinguished statesman and jurist, born at Hagenau, in Alsace, in 1784. He rose, through various offices under the Austrian government, to be aulic councillor. He wrote several legal and political works. Died in 1846.

Barthe, bårt, (FÉLIX,) a French jurist and statesman, born at Narbonne in 1795. He became minister of public instruction in 1830, and in 1831 minister of justice under Casimir Périer. In 1834 he was made first president of the court of accounts, and a peer of France.

See "Notice sur la Vie de M. Barthe," 1846.

Barthe, (NICOLAS THOMAS,) a French writer, born at Marseilles in 1734, wrote an epistle "On Genius considered in its Relation to the Fine Arts." Died in 1785.

Barthel, baR'tel, (JOHANN CASPAR,) a German jurist, born at Kissingen in 1697, became vice-chancellor of the University of Würzburg. He wrote several Latin treatises on canon law. Died in 1771.

See "Vita J. C. Bartheli," 1752.

Barthel, written also **Bartel,** (JOHANN CHRISTIAN FRIEDRICH,) a German engraver, born at Leipsic in 1775. Among his best works are the "Castle of Heidelberg," after Primavesi, and a view of Vaucluse. He also produced several paintings.

Barthel, (MELCHIOR,) a German sculptor, born in Saxony, worked at Venice; died in 1674.

Barthélemy or **Barthélemi,** SAINT. See BARTHOLOMEW, SAINT.

Barthélemy, bår'tål'me', (AUGUSTE Marseille-mår'sȧ'ye,) a French satiric poet, whose works had great popularity, born at Marseilles in 1796. Among the principal we may name the "Villéliade," an attack on the ministry of Villèle, (1826,) "Satire against the Capuchins," and "Napoleon in Egypt," (1828.) In conjunction with his friend Méry, he wrote the "Dupinade," (1831,) a mock-heroic poem, and a number of political satires. He resided mostly in Paris.

Barthélemy, (FRANÇOIS,) MARQUIS OF, a French statesman, born at Aubagne in 1747, was a nephew of the author of "Anacharsis." He held various offices

under Napoleon, and at the fall of the empire in 1814 presided over the commission of the senate which dethroned the emperor. Under Louis XVIII. he was made a peer and grand officer of the legion of honour, and was subsequently appointed minister of state. Died in 1830.

Barthélemy, (JEAN JACQUES,) a celebrated French writer and scholar, born near Aubagne, in Provence, in 1716. Having studied theology and ancient languages under the Jesuits at Marseilles, he visited Paris, where he acquired the friendship of Gros de Boze, keeper of the royal cabinet of medals. In 1753 he succeeded De Boze in this post, having previously been elected to the Academy of Inscriptions. He subsequently travelled in Italy, where he spent several years in antiquarian researches and made a large and choice collection of medals for the royal cabinet. Having obtained several lucrative offices through the favour of the Duke of Choiseul, Barthélemy devoted himself to literary pursuits, and published a number of valuable treatises, chiefly on numismatics and ancient inscriptions. In 1788 he brought out his principal work, entitled "Travels of Anacharsis the Younger in Greece," ("Voyage du Jeune Anacharsis en Grèce,") on the composition of which he had spent thirty years. It soon obtained great popularity both in France and other countries, and was translated into several languages. In 1789 Barthélemy became a member of the French Academy. Died in Paris in 1795.

See MANCINI-NIVERNAIS, "Essai sur la Vie de J. J. Barthélemy," 1795; M. G. C. VILLENAVE, "Notice sur les Ouvrages de J. J. Barthélemy," 1821; "Encyclopædia Britannica."

Barthélemy, (JEAN SIMON,) a French historical painter, born at Laon in 1742; died in Paris in 1811.

Barthélemy, (LOUIS,) a French writer on grammar, history, etc., born at Grenoble in 1759; died in 1815.

Barthélemy, (NICOLAS,) a French Benedictine, born in Touraine in 1478, was the author of Latin epigrams and idylls, and a treatise "On Active and Contemplative Life," (1523.) Died about 1535.

Barthélemy Saint-Hilaire, bår'tål'me' sånt'e'lår', (JULES,) a French journalist and scholar, born in Paris in 1805, was assistant editor of the "Globe," the "National," and other journals. He became in 1838 professor of Latin and Greek philosophy in the College of France. He wrote, among other works, a "Commentary on Aristotle," which obtained a prize from the Academy.

Barthelmont. See BARTLEMANN.

Barthès. See BARTHEZ.

Barthez, bår'tå', or **Barthès,** bår'tå', (PAUL JOSEPH,) a celebrated French physician and physiologist, born at Montpellier in 1734. In 1757 he was appointed royal censor, and became associate editor of the "Journal des Savants" and the "Encyclopédie Méthodique." He obtained the chair of medicine at Montpellier in 1759. Having settled in Paris in 1780, he was made consulting physician to the king, and a councillor of state. He was the author of "New Doctrine of the Functions of the Human Body," (in Latin, 1774,) "New Elements of the Science of Man," (1778,) a "Discourse on the Genius of Hippocrates," (1801,) and other valuable works. Died in 1806.

See LORDAT, "Mémoires sur la Vie de P. J. Barthez," 1818.

Barthez, de, deh bår'tå', (ANTOINE CHARLES ERNEST,) a French medical writer, born at Narbonne, in Aude, about 1800. Among his works is a "Treatise on the Diseases of Children," (3 vols., 1843.)

Barthez (or **Barthès**) **de Marmorières,** deh mår'mo're-air', (ANTOINE,) BARON, son of Guillaume, noticed below, was born at Saint Gall, in Switzerland, in 1736. He wrote a tragedy entitled "The Death of Louis XVI.," and other works. Died in 1811.

Barthez (or **Barthès**) **de Marmorières,** (GUILLAUME,) a French engineer of bridges, etc., and writer on mechanics, lived about 1750.

Barthius. See BARTH, (CASPAR VON.)

Barthold, baR'tolt, (FRIEDRICH WILHELM,) a German historian, born in Berlin in 1799, became a professor at Greifswalde in 1834. He published a number of well-written works on German history, among which is a "History of the German Cities and Corporations," ("Bürgerthums,") 1851.

Bartholdy. See MENDELSSOHN, (FELIX.)

Bartholdy, bȧR-tol'dee, (JAKOB SALOMO,) a German soldier, diplomatist, and writer, of Jewish extraction, born at Berlin in 1779. He served in the campaigns against the French from 1809 to 1814, and subsequently became consul-general at Rome. He wrote a "History of the Tyrolese War of 1809," and a "Life of Cardinal Consalvi," (1825.) Died in 1825.

Barthole. See BARTOLI.

Bartholin, bȧR'to-lin', [Lat. BARTHOLI'NUS,] (ERASMUS,) a Danish physician and savant, born at Roskild in 1625, was a son of Kaspar, noticed below. He became professor of geometry and medicine at Copenhagen.

See NICÉRON, " Mémoires."

Bartholin, written also **Bartholine,** (KASPAR,) a learned physician and medical writer, born at Malmö, in Scania, in 1585, was professor of medicine at Copenhagen, and in 1618 rector of the university in that city. Died in 1629.

See HALLER, " Bibliotheca Anatomica."

Bartholin, (KASPAR,) a Danish physician, born in 1655, was a son of Thomas Bartholin, (the first of that name.) He became physician to the King of Denmark, and published a number of medical and scientific works, in Latin. Died in 1738.

Bartholin, bȧR-to-leen', or **Bartolini,** bȧR-to-lee'nee, (RICARDO,) an Italian *littérateur* of the sixteenth century, was a native of Perugia.

Bartholin, (THOMAS,) son of Kaspar the elder, noticed above, born at Copenhagen in 1616, was one of the most eminent physicians of his time. Having studied at Leyden and afterwards visited the principal countries of Europe, he was appointed in 1648 professor of anatomy at Copenhagen. Among his works, which are written in Latin, are a treatise on the lymphatic vessels, (the discovery of which he claimed,) a dissertation on the functions of the liver, and his "Anatomia," (1641,) which had a high reputation as a text-book and passed through numerous editions. Died in 1680.

See HALLER, " Bibliotheca Anatomica;" G. HANNÆUS, " Oratio in obitum T. Bartholini," 1680.

Bartholin, (THOMAS,) a Danish jurist, son of the preceding, born in 1659, was appointed keeper of the royal archives, and held other important offices. He was the author of several works on northern antiquities and history. Died in 1690.

Bartholine. See BARTHOLIN.

Bartholinus. See BARTHOLIN.

Bartholomæus, bar-thol-o-mee'us, an English bishop of Exeter, wrote a compilation entitled a "Penitential," and "Dialogues against the Jews." Died about 1187.

Bartholomæus, bȧR-to-lo-mä'oos, Bishop of Urbino, in Italy, lived about 1350.

Bartholomæus, bȧR-to-lo-mä'ŭs, [Fr. BARTHÉLEMI, bȧR'tȧl'me' ; Sp. BARTOLOMÉ, bȧR-to-lo-mä',] (A MARTYR'IBUS ; so named from the church of the Martyrs,) a Portuguese prelate, born in 1514. In 1559 he became Archbishop of Braga. At the Council of Trent he distinguished himself by his advocacy of reform in the Catholic Church. Died in 1590.

See LEMAISTRE DE SACY, "Vie de Barthélemi," 1663; L. MUÑOZ, "Vida de Fr. Bartolomé de los Martyres," 1645 ; F. A. VITORIA, "Vida do arcebispo Fr. Bartholomeo dos Martyros," 2 vols., 1748–49.

Bar-thol-o-mæ'us Co-lo-nĭ-en'sis, or **Bartholomew of Cologne,** a distinguished scholar and writer, born at Cologne about 1460, studied at Deventer, where he became acquainted with Erasmus. Died about 1514.

Bartholomæus (or **Bar-thol'o-mew) de Glan'ville,** a Franciscan monk, called ANGLICUS, (the "Englishman,") born in Suffolk, lived about 1370. His principal work is a kind of encyclopædia, entitled "On the Properties of Things," ("De Proprietatibus Rerum,") which had a high reputation in his time.

Bar-thol'o-mew, [Gr. Βαρθολομαῖος; Lat. BARTHOLO-MÆ'US,] SAINT, (believed by many to be the same as the **Nathanael** spoken of in John i. 45–49,) one of the twelve apostles, is supposed to have been a native of Galilee. It is stated by Eusebius that he preached the gospel in India. The time and place of his death are unknown, and none of his writings are extant. His relics are said to have been brought to Rome, where a church was erected in his honour. (See Matthew x., Mark iii., and Luke vi.)

Bartisch, baR'tish, (GEORG,) a German surgeon, who lived about 1570, and wrote "On Diseases of the Eye."

Bar'tle-mann, [Fr. BARTHELMONT, bȧR'tĕl'môN',] written also **Barthelemon,** (HIPPOLYTE,) a French musician and composer of operas, born at Bordeaux in 1731 ; died in London in 1808. He was an excellent violinist.

See "Fraser's Magazine," vol. xlviii.

Bar'tle-mann, (JAMES,) an English vocalist, especially distinguished as a bass singer, born at Westminster in 1769 ; died in 1821.

Bart'lett, (ELISHA,) an American physician, born at Smithfield, Rhode Island, in 1804 or 1805, graduated in 1826. He practised several years at Lowell, Massachusetts, obtained the chair of medicine in the University of Maryland in 1844, and afterwards lectured on medicine at Lexington and Louisville, Kentucky. In 1850 he was appointed professor of medicine in the University of New York. He was a popular teacher, and acquired distinction by his medical works, among which is an "Essay on the Philosophy of Medical Science." Died in 1855.

See GROSS, "American Medical Biography."

Bartlett, (ICHABOD,) a distinguished American lawyer, born at Salisbury, New Hampshire, in 1786. He graduated at Dartmouth College in 1808, and afterwards practised law at Portsmouth. He was a representative in Congress from 1833 to 1839. Died in 1853.

Bartlett, (JOHN RUSSELL,) an American writer, born at Providence, Rhode Island, in 1805. He was a merchant in New York in early life, and was appointed in 1850 commissioner to determine the boundary-line between the United States and Mexico. He published a "Dictionary of Americanisms," (1848,) and a "Personal Narrative of Explorations and Incidents in Texas, New Mexico, California, etc.," (2 vols., 1854.)

Bartlett, (JOHN SHERREN,) M.D., a physician and journalist, born in England in 1790. He emigrated to the United States, and in 1822 established in New York "The Albion," a journal of the English conservative school of politics, which he conducted with signal ability. On the introduction of ocean steam-navigation he founded "The European" in Liverpool, intended to furnish the American public a weekly summary of foreign news. His latest enterprise in journalism was "The Anglo-Saxon," commenced in Boston in 1855.

Bartlett, (JOSEPH,) an American satiric poet, born in Plymouth, Massachusetts, about 1763. He graduated at Harvard in 1782. In 1799 he delivered a poem on Physiognomy before the Phi Beta Kappa Society of Harvard. An edition of this poem was published in 1823, together with a number of aphorisms on various subjects. On the 4th of July, 1823, he delivered an oration in Boston, and recited a poem called "The New Vicar of Bray." Died in 1827.

Bartlett, (JOSIAH,) M.D., an American patriot, born in Amesbury, Massachusetts, in 1729. He was a delegate to the Continental Congress in 1776–78, and signed the Declaration of Independence. He was appointed chief justice of the common pleas in 1779, and soon after chief justice of the superior court of New Hampshire. In 1790 he became President of New Hampshire, and in 1793 was chosen the first Governor under the new constitution.

See CHARLES A. GOODRICH, "Lives of the Signers to the Declaration of Independence."

Bartlett, (JOSIAH,) an American physician, born in Charlestown, Massachusetts, in 1759. He delivered orations on various subjects. Died in 1820.

Bartlett, (WILLIAM,) a wealthy American merchant, one of the principal founders and benefactors of the Theological Seminary at Andover, was born at Newbury, Massachusetts, in 1748; died in 1841.

Bartlett, (WILLIAM HENRY,) an English artist, born in London in 1809, travelled extensively in the East, and published several works illustrated with drawings by himself. Among them are "Walks in and about Jerusalem," (1844,) "Forty Days in the Desert," (1848,) and "The Nile Boat, or Glimpses of the Land of Egypt," (1849.) Died at sea in 1854 or 1855.

See WILLIAM BEATTIE, "Memoir of William Henry Bartlett," 1855.

Bartlett, (WILLIAM H. C.,) an American scientific writer, born in Lancaster county, Pennsylvania, in 1804, published treatises on "Optics," "Mechanics," and "Spherical Astronomy," and contributed to "Silliman's Journal," etc.

Bar'tol, (CYRUS AUGUSTUS,) an American Congregational minister, born at Freeport, Maine, in 1813. He became pastor of a church in Boston about 1837. He published, besides other works, "Pictures of Europe," and "Discourses on the Christian Spirit and Life."

See a notice, by E. P. WHIPPLE, in the "North American Review" for January, 1850.

Bartoldy, baR-tol'dee, (GEORG WILHELM,) a learned German writer, born at Colberg in 1765. He translated Bacon's "Novum Organum." Died in 1815.

Bartoli, baR'to-lee, or **Bartolo,** baR'to-lo, [Lat. BAR'-TOLUS; Fr. BARTHOLE, bǎR'tol',] an Italian jurist and legal writer, born at Sasso-Ferrato in 1313, was professor of law at Perugia. He enjoyed a very high reputation in his time. Died in 1356.

Bartoli, (COSIMO,) an Italian *littérateur,* lived at Florence, and wrote several scientific, historical, and moral treatises. He was one of the founders of the Academy degli Umidi, formed in 1540. Among his works is a "Life of Frederick Barbarossa," (1559.)

See GINGUENÉ, "Histoire Littéraire d'Italie."

Bartoli, (DANIELE,) an Italian Jesuit and distinguished writer, born at Ferrara in 1608. His greatest work is a "History of the Company of Jesus," (1653-63,) which gives an interesting account of the missions of the Jesuits in the various parts of Asia, including Japan. He also wrote a "Life of Ignatius Loyola," (1689,) and several moral and scientific treatises, which are highly esteemed. Died in Rome in 1685.

See TIRABOSCHI, "Storia della Letteratura Italiana."

Bartoli, (DOMENICO,) an Italian poet, born near Lucca in 1629, assisted Beverini in translating the "Æneid" into Italian. Died in 1698.

Bartoli, (FRANCESCO,) an Italian painter of the school of Módena, was a pupil of Bibbiena. Died in 1779.

Bartoli, (GIUSEPPE,) an Italian antiquary, born at Padua in 1717, became professor of belles-lettres at Turin in 1745. He was a corresponding member of the French Academy of Inscriptions. Died in 1788.

Bartoli, (MINERVA,) an Italian poetess, born at Urbino, lived about 1580.

Bartoli, (PIETRO SANTI,) a celebrated Italian engraver and painter, born at Perugia about 1635. He studied painting under Nicolas Poussin, whose style he imitated with great success. He is chiefly known from his engravings, which are for the most part illustrations of ancient art from the Catacombs and the ruins of Rome. Died at Rome in 1700. He engraved some works of Raphael.

See LANZI, "History of Painting in Italy."

Bartolini, baR-to-lee'nee, (GIUSEPPE MARIA,) an Italian painter of the Bolognese school, born at Imola in 1657; died in 1725.

Bartolini, (LORENZO,) a celebrated Florentine sculptor, born about 1778. Having studied in Paris under Lemot, he soon after established his reputation by a bas-relief of great beauty, representing "Cleobis and Biton." He was charged by Napoleon with the execution of a number of works, and founded by his order the school of sculpture at Carrara. His colossal bust of Napoleon is ranked among his master-pieces; also the group of "Hercules and Lycas," and the monument of Lady Stratford Canning at Lausanne, in Switzerland. Bartolini is esteemed by his countrymen as second only to Canova. "No artist," says M. Breton, "not even Canova, approached as near as Bartolini to the ideal purity and the noble simplicity of the works of the age of Pericles." ("Nouvelle Biographie Générale.") He died at or near Florence in January, 1850.

Bartolo. See BARTOLI.

Bartolo, baR'to-lo, or **Bartoli,** baR'to-lee, (DOMENICO,) sometimes called **Domenico d'Asciano,** an Italian fresco-painter, born about 1450, was a nephew and pupil of Taddeo, noticed below.

Bartolo or **Bartoli,** (TADDEO,) an Italian painter of

Sienna, born about 1350. Among his master-pieces are the frescos in the public palace at Sienna.

See LANZI, "History of Painting in Italy."

Bartolocci, baR-to-lot'chee, [Lat. BARTOLOC'CIUS,] (GIULIO,) an Italian scholar and ecclesiastic, born in 1613, is sometimes called **di Celano,** (de châ-lā'no,) from the place of his birth. He was professor of Hebrew in the college di Sapienza at Rome. His principal work is entitled "Bibliotheca Magna Rabbinica," (4 vols., 1675-93,) a valuable synopsis of rabbinical literature. Died in 1687.

See WOLF, "Bibliotheca Hebraica."

Bartolommei, baR-to-lom-mā'ee, (GERONIMO,) an Italian *littérateur,* born at Florence about 1584, was the author of several tragedies and poems, among which is "Didascalia, sive Doctrina Comica." Died in 1662.

Bartolommei, (MATTEO MARIO,) an Italian dramatist, born at Florence in 1640, was a son of the preceding. Died in 1695.

Bartolommei, (SIMONE PIETRO,) an antiquarian writer, born in the Tyrol in 1709; died in 1764.

Bartolommeo, baR-to-lom-mā'o, a Florentine painter who worked about 1250.

Bartolommeo, (MAESTRO,) a Venetian sculptor and architect, lived about 1390. He designed the "Porta della Carta," the chief entrance to the doge's palace at Venice.

Bartolommeo della Porta. See BACCIO DELLA PORTA.

Bartolommeo, di, de baR-to-lom-mā'o, (DIONISIO,) an Italian architect, worked at Naples about 1580.

Bartolommeo, di, (LEONARDO,) a Sicilian politician, born at Palermo; died in 1450.

Bartoloni, baR-to-lo'nee, (PIETRO DOMENICO,) an Italian physician and miscellaneous writer, born at Empoli, near Florence, about 1640.

Bartolozzi, baR-to-lot'see, (FRANCESCO,) an eminent Italian engraver, born at Florence about 1725. He studied under Wagner at Venice, and, after residing for a time at Rome, removed to England, where he executed a series of plates from Guercino. On the invitation of the Prince-regent of Portugal, about 1805, he settled in that country, where he died about 1816. Bartolozzi excelled in every department of engraving, and is justly esteemed one of the greatest masters of the art. Among his most admired works are the "Virgin and Child," after Carlo Dolce; Guido's "Massacre of the Innocents;" and the "Death of Lord Chatham," after Copley. The number of his prints is estimated at more than two thousand.

See LE BLANC, "Manuel de l'Amateur d'Estampes."

Bartolus. See BARTOLI.

Bar'ton, (BENJAMIN SMITH,) an American naturalist and physician, born at Lancaster, Pennsylvania, in 1766, was a nephew of David Rittenhouse. He studied medicine in London and Edinburgh, and graduated at Göttingen about 1788. He obtained in 1789 the chair of natural history in the College of Philadelphia, which was incorporated with the University of Pennsylvania in 1791. He was appointed professor of materia medica in 1795, and succeeded Dr. Rush as professor of the theory and practice of medicine in 1813. He promoted the diffusion of natural science by his writings, among which are "Elements of Botany," (1803,) and "Collections for an Essay towards a Materia Medica of the United States," (1798.) Died in 1815.

See a "Biography of Benjamin S. Barton," by his nephew, W. P. C. BARTON; THACHER, "Medical Biography."

Bar'ton, (BERNARD,) a member of the Society of Friends, popularly known as "the Quaker poet," was born in London in 1784. He was the author of "Napoleon, and other Poems," (1822,) "Devotional Verses," (1826,) "Poetic Vigils," "A Widow's Tale, and other Poems," (1827,) and "The Reliquary," (1836.) "His works are full of passages of natural tenderness, and his religious poems, though animated with a warmth of devotion, are still expressed with that subdued propriety of language which evinces at once a correctness of taste and feeling." ("Gentleman's Magazine.") Died in 1849.

See "Memoirs, Letters, etc. of Bernard Barton," edited by his daughter; "Edinburgh Review" for November, 1820; "Blackwood's Magazine" for December, 1822.

ā, ē, ī, ō, ū, ȳ, *long;* ă, ĕ, ĭ, ŏ, ŭ, ў, *short;* ạ, ẹ, ị, ọ, *obscure;* fär, fåll, fåt; mêt; nŏt; gōŏd; mōon;

Barton, (ELIZABETH,) an English fanatic or impostor under the reign of Henry VIII., commonly called "the Holy Maid of Kent." Having acquired a reputation for being inspired, she was instigated by the partisans of Queen Catherine to prophesy against the marriage of the king with Anne Boleyn. The excitement produced by these revelations among the people was so great that the government, becoming alarmed, caused her to be arrested in 1533, together with a number of priests, her accomplices, and she was executed with them at Tyburn in 1534.

Barton, (THOMAS,) a learned Episcopal minister, born in Ireland in 1730. He married a sister of David Rittenhouse in 1753, and officiated for many years as rector at Lancaster, Pennsylvania. He was the father of Benjamin Smith Barton, M.D. Died in New York in 1780.

Barton, (WILLIAM,) LIEUTENANT-COLONEL, an American officer, born about 1747. He commanded a small party which surprised and captured General Prescott near Newport, Rhode Island, in July, 1777. Died in 1831.

Barton, (WILLIAM P. C.,) an American botanist and physician, born in 1786. He was a nephew of Benjamin Smith Barton, whom he succeeded as professor of botany in the University of Pennsylvania. He published "Vegetable Materia Medica of the United States, or Medical Botany," (2 vols., 1817–25,) "Compendium Floræ Philadelphicæ," (2 vols., 1818,) and "Flora of North America, illustrated by coloured figures," (3 vols., 1821–23.) Died in 1856.

Bar'tram, (JOHN,) an eminent American botanist, born in Marple, Delaware county, Pennsylvania, in 1701. His attainments in natural history attracted the attention of Linnæus, who pronounced him "the greatest natural botanist in the world." He was the first American to establish a botanical garden, which he enriched with exotics and rare native plants. Sir Hans Sloane, Linnæus, and other eminent European botanists furnished him with books and apparatus, and he in return sent them new and curious specimens of the natural productions of America. He was chosen a member of several learned societies in Europe, and appointed American botanist to George III. of England, a position which he held till his death in 1777. The results of his observations on the inhabitants, animals, climate, soil, productions, etc., in a journey to Lake Ontario, were published in London in 1751, and a journal of a tour to East Florida in 1766. He also contributed various papers to the "Philosophical Transactions." Mr. Bartram was distinguished in other departments of natural history, possessed some knowledge of medicine, and was an ingenious mechanic. He had a fine botanic garden in the environs of Philadelphia.

See WILLIAM DARLINGTON, "Memorials of John Bartram and Humphrey Marshall," 1849; "Encyclopædia Americana."

Bartram, (WILLIAM,) a botanist and traveller, born near Philadelphia in 1739, was a son of the preceding. He passed about five years in the exploration of the natural productions of the Carolinas, Georgia, and Florida, and published "Travels through North and South Carolina, Georgia, and East and West Florida," (1791.) He produced a list of American birds, which was the most complete that appeared before the work of Wilson. Died in 1823.

See "Encyclopædia Americana."

Bartsch, baRtsh, (JAN,) a Dutch physician and savant, born about 1720, was a friend of Boerhaave and Linnæus. The latter named the genus Bartsia in his honour.

Bartsch, von, baRtsh, (JOHANN ADAM BERNHARD,) a German engraver and writer upon art, born at Vienna in 1747, was keeper of the imperial library and of the prints in the royal collection. His principal work is entitled "The Painter-Engraver," ("Le Peintre-Graveur," 21 vols., 1821,) besides which he prepared a "Catalogue of all the Prints of Rembrandt," with several other similar works. Among his engravings and etchings, which amount in all to more than five hundred, we may mention his prints after Rembrandt and Potter. Died in 1820.

See LE BLANC, "Manuel de l'Amateur d'Estampes."

Barucco, bä-rook'ko, (GIACOMO,) a painter of the Venetian school, born about 1620.

Baruch, bä'rŭk, [Heb. ברוך,] the son of Neriah, was the friend and companion of the prophet Jeremiah, whom he served as a scribe. He accompanied Jeremiah in 588 B.C. into Egypt, where, as stated by some writers, he died; while others assert that he died in Babylon. The book of Baruch is recognized as canonical by the Catholics, but it is regarded by the Protestants as apocryphal. (See Jeremiah xxxii. 12–16; xxxvi. 4, 17, 27.)

Baruffaldi, bä-roof-fäl'dee, (GERONIMO,) an Italian littérateur, born at Ferrara in 1675; died in 1753.

Baruffaldi, (GERONIMO,) an Italian Jesuit and writer, born at Ferrara in 1740, was a nephew of the preceding. Died in 1817.

Bar'wick, (JOHN,) an English divine, born in Westmoreland in 1612, distinguished himself by his zeal in promoting the restoration of Charles II. Died in 1664.

See PETER BARWICK's "Life of John Barwick," 1721.

Barwick, (PETER,) brother of John Barwick, was appointed in 1660 physician-in-ordinary to Charles II. He wrote, among other works, a "Defence of Harvey's Discovery of the Circulation of the Blood." Died in 1705.

Bary, bä're', (HENRY,) a Flemish engraver, born about 1625. Among his master-pieces are portraits of Grotius and Admiral Van Tromp, and "Summer and Autumn," after Van Dyck.

See DESCAMPS, "Vie des Peintres Flamands," etc.

Barye, bä're', (ANTOINE LOUIS,) a French sculptor and engraver, born in Paris in 1795. Among his master-pieces are a "Lion strangling a Boa," a "Group of Young Bears," "Charles VI. in the Forest of Mans," and "The Three Graces."

Barzena. See BARCENA.

Barzini, baRd-zee'nee, (FRANCESCO,) a Florentine writer on astrology and philosophy, born about 1667.

Barzizzio or **Barziza.** See GASPARINO.

Barzoni, baRd-zo'nee, (VITTORIO,) an Italian political and historical writer, born at Lonato in 1768; died in 1829.

See WILLIAM THOMPSON, "Life of Vittorio Barzoni," London, 1831; "Quarterly Review" for March, 1813.

Bas or **Basse,** bâs, (MARTIN,) a Dutch engraver, who lived about 1600, left several portraits of superior merit.

Bas or **Basse,** (WILLIAM,) an engraver, whose principal work is a "Virgin with the Infant Jesus and Saint John." Nothing is known of his life.

See STRUTT, "Dictionary of Engravers."

Bas, Le. See LE BAS.

Basadonna, bä-så-don'nä, (GIOVANNI,) an Italian poet, born at Venice, wrote "Latin Dialogues," (1518.)

Basaiti, bä-sï'tee, (MARCO,) sometimes called del Friuli, an eminent Italian painter of the fifteenth century, was a native of Friuli. His "Calling of Saint Peter," in the Academy at Venice, is esteemed his master-piece. He painted other pictures of great merit, among which we may name an "Assumption," and "The Prayer in the Garden."

See VASARI, "Lives of the Painters."

Basan or **Bazan,** bä'zŏn', (PIERRE FRANÇOIS,) a French engraver, born in Paris in 1723. Among his best works are a "Bacchus and Ariadne," after Giordano, and "Antiope," after Correggio. He was the author of a "Dictionary of Ancient and Modern Engravers," which is highly esteemed, (3 vols., 1767.) Died in 1797.

See LE BLANC, "Manuel de l'Amateur d'Estampes."

Basanier, bä'zä'ne-â', (MARTIN,) a French musician and mathematician, born about 1540, wrote a work on the theory and practice of music.

Bascape, bås-kä'pä, (GERONIMO,) an Italian jurist and legal writer; died in 1641.

Baschenis, bås-kä'nèss, (EVARISTO,) an Italian painter, born at Bergamo in 1617, was celebrated for his skilful representations of musical instruments, books, and similar objects of still life. Died in 1677.

See LANZI, "History of Painting in Italy."

Baschi, bâs'kee, (MATTEO,) an Italian monk, born in the duchy of Urbino, was the founder of the order of Capuchins, so called from a hood of peculiar form (cappuccio) worn by them. Died in 1552.

See BAVERIUS, "Annales Capucinorum."

Baschiera, bâs-ke-â'rä, (NICCOLÒ,) an Italian artist,

who designed the magnificent marble front of Saint Peter's at Mantua. Died about 1760.

Baschilow. See BASHILOF.

Bas'com, (HENRY B.,) an American Methodist bishop and pulpit orator, born in Western New York in 1796. He was ordained bishop at Saint Louis, Missouri, in 1849 or 1850, and died in the latter year.

See M. M. HENKLE, "Life of Bishop Bascom," 1857.

Basedow, bä'zeh-do', (JOHANN BERNHARD,) originally JOHANN BEREND Bassedau, (bäs'seh-dŏw,) a celebrated German teacher and educational reformer, was born at Hamburg in 1723. He published in 1774 an elementary school-book entitled "Orbis Pictus," in three volumes and illustrated with one hundred engravings, which soon became widely popular. About the same time he founded at Dessau a school called a "Philanthropin," in which he sought to render knowledge attractive and adapt it to the comprehension of the young. Died at Magdeburg in 1790.

See J. C. MEYER, "Basedows Leben und Schriften," 2 vols., 1791; H. RATHMANN, "Beiträge zur Lebensgeschichte J. B. Basedow's," 1791.

Baseilhac. See COSME, (Frère JEAN.)

Ba-se'lǐ-us or **van Basel,** vän bä'zel, written also **Basle,** (JACOBUS,) a Dutch historian and theologian, born in 1530, wrote an "Account of the Siege of Bergen-op-Zoom in 1588." Died in 1598.

Baselius, (JACOBUS,) a grandson of the preceding, born at Leyden, was the author of an "Ecclesiastical History of Belgium," (1657.)

Baselius, (NICHOLAS,) a Flemish surgeon and writer, wrote, in Latin, a "Description of the Comet of 1577."

Baselli, bä-šel'lee, (BENEDETTO,) an Italian physician and surgeon, born at San Pellegrino. Having been refused admission to the College of Physicians because he practised surgery, he wrote, in Latin, a vindication of the nobility of surgery. Died in 1621.

See "Biographie Médicale."

Basevi, bas'e-ve, (GEORGE,) a distinguished English architect, born at Brighton in 1794. Among his principal works are the Fitzwilliam Museum at Cambridge, and Saint Mary's Hall at Brighton. He also furnished the designs for Belgrave Square. Died in 1845.

Bash'aw, (EDWARD,) an English nonconformist minister of Exeter. For refusing to take the oath of allegiance he was imprisoned in Newgate, where he died in 1671.

Bashilof, bäsh'I-lof, or **Baschilow,** (SEMEN,) a Russian savant, born at Moscow in 1740. He was secretary of the senate at Saint Petersburg, and translated several French works, among which was the "Candide" of Voltaire. Died in 1770.

Bashkin, bäsh'kin, (MATTHEI SEMENOF,) a Russian heresiarch of the sixteenth century, who professed doctrines resembling those of the Arians.

Bashuysen, von, fon bäs'hoi'zẹn, (HEINRICH JAKOB,) a German Oriental scholar, born at Hanau in 1679, was appointed to the chair of Oriental languages and history at Zerbst. He published a number of Latin commentaries on the Hebrew writers. Died in 1758.

See E. L. D. HUCH, "Programma continens Vitam H. J. de Bashuysen," 1759.

Bä'sǐl, Bishop of Thessalonica, called **Ascolius** or **Acholius,** was a friend of Saint Ambrose. He baptized the emperor Theodosius. Died about 384 A.D.

Bä'sǐl or **Ba-sil'I-us,** [Gr. Βασίλειος or Βασίλιος; It. BASILIO, bä-šee'le-o; Fr. BASILE, bä'zèl',] SAINT, surnamed THE GREAT, one of the most eminent of the Christian Fathers, born at Cæsarea, in Cappadocia, about 329 A.D. He studied law and rhetoric at Constantinople, and subsequently at Athens, where Julian (afterwards emperor) and Gregory Nazianzen were his fellow-students. With the latter he formed an intimate friendship, which lasted through life. About 358 A.D. he abandoned his profession, and retired to a cloister in a mountainous region of Pontus, where he was soon joined by Gregory. He here established a system of monastic discipline, which still prevails in Greek and Oriental monasteries. On the death of Eusebius in 370, Basil was elected Bishop of Cæsarea. In this station he was distinguished for his extensive charities, his zeal for the reformation of church discipline, and his opposition to the Arian

heresy, at that time maintained by the emperor Valens. Among his chief productions (in Greek) are "Nine Homilies on the Six Days' Work," "Two Books on Baptism," "Homilies on the Psalms," and a collection of "Letters." His writings are characterized by great purity of style, and an elevated moral tone combined with fervent piety. Died in 379 A.D.

See SOCRATES, "Historia Ecclesiastica;" GODFREY HERMANT, "Vie de Saint-Basile," 1674; SOZOMEN, "Historia;" A. AGRESTA, "Vita del protopatriarca S. Basilio Magno," 1658; J. E. FEISSER, "Dissertatio de Vita Basilii Magni," 8vo, 1828; KLOSE, "Basilius der Grosse nach seinem Leben," etc., 1835.

Basil or **Basilius** of Cilicia, Bishop of Irenopolis, an ecclesiastical writer of the fifth century. He was the author of a "History of the Church," and several controversial works.

Basil I., [Lat. BASIL'IUS; Fr. BASILE, bä'zèl',] surnamed THE MACEDO'NIAN, Emperor of the East, was born about 820, in humble circumstances. He succeeded in winning the favour of the emperor Michael III., who raised him to be his colleague in the empire, (866;) but Basil did not long retain his favour, and, believing his own life to be in danger, he caused Michael to be assassinated in 867. He commenced the compilation of the code of laws entitled "Basilica," which was completed by his son Leo. Having conquered a considerable part of Asia Minor, he drove the Saracens out of Italy in 885. He died in 886, and was succeeded by his son, Leo VI.

See LE BEAU, "Histoire du Bas-Empire;" G. IMPACCIANTI, "Basilio il Macedone," 2 vols., 1809.

Basil II., [Lat. BASILIUS,] Emperor of the East, born in 958, was a son of Romanus II. On the death of the usurper John Zimisces, (975,) Basil succeeded to the throne, his brother Constantine having a nominal share in the government. Basil was one of the greatest commanders of his time, and was engaged in almost continual wars with the Saracens, Bulgarians, and Germans.

See GIBBON, "Decline and Fall of the Roman Empire."

Basil or **Basilius,** made Bishop of Ancyra in 336 A.D. in opposition to Marcellus, who was deposed by the party of Eusebius. He was a zealous opponent of the Arians.

Basil, Bishop of Seleucia. See BASILIUS.

Basil, the founder of the heretical sect of Bogomiles in Bulgaria. He was burnt at the stake, by order of the emperor Alexius Comnenus, in 1118.

See "Nouvelle Biographie Générale."

Basil, Prince of Moldavia in the seventeenth century, was deposed for his tyranny.

Bä'sǐl-Väl'en-tīne, [Lat. and Ger. BASIL'IUS VALENTI'NUS,] a celebrated German writer on chemistry and alchemy, born about 1410. He was the author of a treatise entitled "The Triumphal Car of Antimony," ("Currus Triumphalis Antimonii,") and other scientific works, which had a high reputation among his contemporaries.

See F. HOEFER, "Histoire de la Chimie."

Basile, the French of BASIL, which see.

Basile, bä-šee'lä, (ADRIANA,) a sister of Giambattista, noticed below, was distinguished for her beauty, and her talent for music and poetry.

Basile, (GENNARO,) a Neapolitan painter, who about 1756 resided at Brünn, in Moravia, where are most of his works.

Basile, (GIAMBATTISTA,) an Italian poet, born about 1580; died in 1637.

Basiletti, bä-še-let'tee, (LUIGI,) an Italian painter of history and landscapes, born at Brescia; died about 1845.

Basili, bä-šee'lee, (PIER-ANGELO,) an Italian painter, born at Gubbio about 1540; died in 1604.

Basilico, bä-šee'le-ko or bä-šil'e-ko, (CIRIACO,) an Italian littérateur, lived about 1670, and translated into Italian verse the "Satyricon" of Petronius Arbiter.

Basilico, (GERONIMO,) an Italian jurist, born at Messina, was the author of some legal and other works. Died in 1670.

Bas-ĭ-lī'dēs, [Gr. Βασιλείδης; Fr. BASILIDE, bä'ze'lèd',] the founder of a sect, lived in Egypt under the reign of Trajan and Hadrian. His doctrine is said to have been a reflection of that of Zoroaster. He taught that the world was produced by two principles, Good or Light, and Evil or Darkness. Died about 130 A.D.

See RITTER, "History of Philosophy."

Bas-I-li'na, the second wife of Julius Constantius, and the mother of Julian the Apostate. She is said to have favoured the doctrines of the Arians. Died in 331 A.D.

Basilio. See BASIL, SAINT.

Basilio da Gama, bä-see'le-o dä gä'mä, (JOZÉ,) born at San Jozé, in Brazil, in 1740, was one of the founders of the Brazilian Academy. He was the author of a popular poem entitled "Uruguay," and a number of lyrics. Died about 1795.

Bas-I-lis'cus, [Gr. Βασιλίσκος; Fr. BASILISQUE, bǎ'-ze'lêsk',] Emperor of the East, was a brother of the empress Verina, wife of Leo I. In 468 A.D. he was appointed, under Leo I., commander-in-chief of the great expedition against Genseric, King of the Vandals, who had taken possession of Carthage. His army suffered a total defeat, and Basiliscus was banished to Thrace. On the death of Leo, 474, he usurped the throne, of which Zeno was the rightful heir. In 476 Zeno defeated and took captive the usurper, who died in prison in 477 or 478. During his reign the great library of Constantinople was destroyed by fire.

See GIBBON, "Decline and Fall of the Roman Empire."

Basilisque or **Basilique.** See BASILISCUS.

Basilius. See BASIL, SAINT.

Ba-sil'I-us, Bishop of Seleucia from 448 till 458, was the author of a collection of homilies.

Basil'ius OF GLEMO'NA, a missionary to China, published a "Chinese Dictionary," (1726,) which has been translated into several languages. Scarcely anything is known of his life.

Basilovitch. See IVAN, Czar of Russia.

Bas'I-lus, (L. MINUCIUS,) sometimes called M. **Satrius**, a Roman soldier, served under Cæsar in Gaul in 54 and 52 B.C. Though a professed friend of Cæsar, he took part in his assassination, and was afterwards murdered by his own slaves, whom he had treated cruelly.

Basin, bǎ'zǎN', (SIMON,) a French ecclesiastic and writer, born in Paris in 1608, was chaplain to Anne of Austria, wife of Louis XIII. Died in 1671.

Basin or **Bazin**, bǎ'zǎN', (THOMAS,) a French historian, born at Caudebec in 1402. He became professor of canon law at Caen, and in 1447 Bishop of Lisieux. He wrote, in Latin, a "History of Charles VII. and Louis XI.," which is highly interesting, a "Justification of the Maid of Orléans," and other works. Died in 1491.

See "Nouvelle Biographie Générale."

Basine or **Bazine**, bǎ'zèn', was originally married to the King of Thuringia, whom she abandoned, and became the wife of Childeric I. of France, and the mother of the celebrated Clovis.

Bā'šing or **de Bā'šing-stoke**, (JOHN,) an English scholar, born in Hampshire, studied at Oxford, and subsequently at Athens, where he collected a number of Greek manuscripts. He introduced the Greek numeral letters into England. He wrote several learned works, and translated into Latin a Greek treatise on grammar, entitled "Donatus of the Greeks," ("Donatus Græcorum.") Basing was appointed Archdeacon of Leicester. Died in 1252.

See SCHOELL, "Histoire de la Littérature Grecque."

Basinio di Basanii, bä-see'ne-o de bä-sä'ne-ee, an Italian poet, born at Parma about 1425, became professor of Latin eloquence at Ferrara. He wrote a Latin poem entitled "Hesperides." Died in 1457.

Basire, (CLAUDE.) See BAZIRE.

Basire, bä-zeer', (ISAAC,) an English divine, born in the island of Jersey in 1607. He was appointed chaplain to Charles I. about 1640, and held the same office under Charles II. He wrote a "History of the English and Scotch Presbytery." Died in 1676.

Basire, (JAMES,) an English engraver, born in 1730. Among his works are "Pylades and Orestes," after West, and "The Field of the Cloth of Gold; or the Interview between Francis I. and Henry VIII." The last-named plate was one of the largest ever engraved. Died in 1802.

Basire, (JAMES,) son of the preceding, born in 1769, succeeded his father as engraver to the Royal and Anti-

quarian Societies. His prints of the English cathedrals after John Carter are among his best works. Died in 1822.

Bas'ker-ville, (JOHN,) an English printer, celebrated for the great improvements he effected in typography, was born in Worcestershire in 1706. His English Bible, Book of Common Prayer, and editions of the classics are still admired and sought for. Died in 1775.

Baskerville, (Sir SIMON,) an eminent English physician, died in 1641.

Basmaison Pougnet, de, dęh bä'mǎ'zòN' poon'yǎ', (JEAN,) a French jurist and legal writer, born about 1540, was a native of Riom.

Basmaji, bäs-mǎ'jee, or **Basmadji**, (IBRAHEEM,) a Hungarian renegade, who, in conjunction with Seid-Effendi, established the first printing-press in Turkey. He was permitted by the Sultan Ahmed III. to print anything except the Koran and the canonical writings. Died in 1746.

Basmanov, bäs-mä'nov, (PETER,) a Russian general, who, having in 1605 aided the false Demetrius to usurp the throne, was killed in attempting to enter the Kremlin.

Basnage, bä'nǎzh', (ANTOINE,) a French Protestant divine, son of Benjamin, noticed below, born in 1610. He took refuge in Holland after the revocation of the edict of Nantes, and died as pastor at Zutphen in 1691.

Basnage, (BENJAMIN,) a Protestant theologian, born at Carentan in 1580. He was pastor in his native town, and in 1637 became president of the synod at Alençon. He wrote a "Treatise on the Church," (1612.) Died in 1652.

Basnage de Beauval, bä'nǎzh' dęh bō'vǎl', (HENRI,) son of Basnage du Fraquenay, born at Rouen in 1656, was advocate of the parliament in his native city. He was the author of a "Treatise on Religious Toleration," (1684,) and edited a journal entitled "History of the Works of Savants." He became an exile for religion about 1686. Died at the Hague in 1710.

See BAYLE, "Historical and Critical Dictionary."

Basnage de Beauval, (JACQUES,) an eminent scholar and theologian, brother of the preceding, born at Rouen in 1653. He studied at Saumur under the celebrated Tannegui Le Fèvre, and acquired a profound knowledge of the ancient and modern languages. He subsequently devoted himself to theology at Geneva and Sedan, and in 1676 became Protestant pastor at Rouen. He emigrated to Holland about 1685. Through the influence of his friend the grand pensionary Heinsius, he was appointed pastor at the Hague in 1709. About this time he was employed in several political negotiations, in which he displayed such diplomatic ability that Voltaire said of him, "he was fitter to be minister of state than of a parish." Among his numerous and valuable works may be named "The Holy Communion, or Treatise on the Necessity and Means of Communing Worthily," (1688,) "History of the Church from Jesus Christ to the Present Time," (2 vols., 1699,) and "History of the Jews from Jesus Christ to the Present Time," (5 vols., 1706.) Died in 1723.

See NICÉRON, "Mémoires."

Basnage de Flottemanville, bä'nǎzh' dęh flot'-mòN'vèl', (SAMUEL,) grandson of Benjamin, noticed above, born at Bayeux in 1638. He became pastor at Zutphen, where he died in 1721. He wrote several ecclesiastical works in French and Latin.

Basnage du Fraquenay, bä'nǎzh' dü frǎk'nǎ', (HENRI,) a French jurist, son of Benjamin Basnage, born at Sainte-Mère-Église in 1615, was one of the most learned and eloquent advocates in the parliament of Normandy. He wrote a "Treatise on Mortgages," (1687,) and other legal works. Died in 1695.

See TAISAND, "Vies des plus célèbres Jurisconsultes."

Basque, le, lęh bäsk, (MICHEL,) a French buccaneer, who, in concert with L'Olonnais, captured the towns of Maracaibo and Gibraltar, in the Gulf of Venezuela, about 1660, and obtained immense booty.

See CHARLEVOIX, "Histoire de la Nouvelle France."

Bass, (GEORGE,) an English navigator, discovered in 1798 the strait which separates Australia from Tasmania, since called Bass's Strait.

See FLINDERS, "Journey of Discovery, etc."

€ as *k*; ç as *s*; ḡ *hard*; ġ as *j*; G, H, K, *guttural*; N, *nasal*; R, *trilled*; s̄ as *z*; țh as in *this*. (☞See Explanations, p. 23.)

Bass, bâss, [Lat. BAS'SIUS,] (HEINRICH,) a German physician and medical writer, born at Bremen in 1690, was for many years professor of anatomy and surgery at Halle. Died in 1754.

Bassa, bâs'så, (Don PEDRO HOLASCO,) a Spanish general, born at Reus, in Catalonia, in 1790. He served with distinction against the French, and was appointed in 1834 governor of Barcelona, where he was killed in a riot, (1835.)

Bassæus, bâs-sā'us, (NICHOLAS,) a German printer, born at Frankfort-on-the-Main about 1550, published several valuable botanical works with plates.

Bassal, bâ'sål', (JEAN,) a French priest and revolutionist, born at Béziers in 1752. As a member of the National Convention, he voted for the death of the king, and was subsequently elected by the Jacobins president of their society. Died in 1802.

Bassan, the French of BASSANO, which see.

Bassand, bâ'sôn', (JEAN BAPTISTE,) a French physician, born in Franche-Comté in 1680. He studied at Leyden under Boerhaave, with whom he afterwards maintained a correspondence, which was published at Vienna in 1778. Died in Vienna in 1742.

Bassani, bâs-sä'nee, or **Bassanio,** bâs-sä'ne-o, (ALESSANDRO,) an Italian lawyer, born at Padua; died in 1495.

Bassani, (CESARE.) See BASSANO.

Bassani, (GIACOMO ANTONIO,) an Italian Jesuit and pulpit orator, born at Vicenza in 1686. He wrote a number of sermons and poems in Latin and Italian. Died in 1747.

Bassani, (GIAMBATTISTA,) an Italian violinist and composer of church music and operas, born at Padua about 1657. He numbered Corelli among his pupils.

See FÉTIS, "Biographie Universelle des Musiciens."

Bassani, (GIOVANNI,) an Italian musician and composer, born about 1600, resided at Venice. He invented a musical instrument called the *bassanello.*

Bassanino, bâs-sâ-nee'no, (FRANCESCO,) a Venetian writer, was the author of a work entitled "Life and Death of Saint Rosalie," (1733.)

Bassanio. See BASSANI.

Bassano, bâs-sä'no, (ANNIBALE,) an Italian architect, born at Padua about 1440.

Bassano or **Bassani,** bâs-sä'nee, (CESARE,) an Italian engraver, born at Milan about 1580.

Bassano, DUKE OF. See MARET.

Bassano, [Fr. BASSAN, bâ'sôN',] (FRANCESCO da Ponte—dâ pon'tâ,) called THE ELDER, an Italian painter, born at Vicenza, belonged to the first Venetian school. He worked mostly at Bassano, from which he derived his surname. Died in 1530.

See LANZI, "History of Painting in Italy."

Bassano, (FRANCESCO,) called THE YOUNGER, eldest son of Giacomo, noticed below, born in 1548. Among his master-pieces are the fresco representing "The Capture of Pavia," in the ducal palace at Venice, and "The Rape of the Sabines." Died in 1591.

Bassano, (GERONIMO DA PONTE,) youngest son of Giacomo, born in 1560. His principal work is an altarpiece in the church of San Giovanni at Bassano, representing "Saint Barbara and the Virgin." Died in 1622.

Bassano, (GIOVANNI BATTISTA DA PONTE,) born in 1553, was the second son of Giacomo. He copied his father's works with such exactness that the copies are frequently mistaken for the originals. Died in 1613.

See VASARI, "Lives of the Painters."

Bassano, [Fr. LE BASSAN, lęh bâ'sôN',] (JACOPO or GIACOMO DA PONTE,) son of the elder Francesco, born at Bassano in 1510. He studied at Venice the works of Titian and other great masters of the Venetian school. Among his best historical pictures are "The Birth of Jesus Christ," "The Flight into Egypt," and a "Mater Dolorosa." He also painted landscapes, animals, and domestic and tavern scenes, with admirable skill and fidelity. Bassano had a profound knowledge of chiaroscuro, and as a colorist was scarcely inferior to Titian. He likewise produced several excellent portraits, among which we may name those of Tasso and Ariosto. He died in 1592, leaving four sons, who were distinguished painters.

See VASARI, "Lives of the Painters ;" LANZI, "History of Painting in Italy ;" MRS. JAMESON, "Memoirs of Early Italian Painters."

Bassano, (LEANDRO DA PONTE,) called THE CHEVALIER, third son of Giacomo, born in 1558, produced historical pictures and portraits of superior merit. He painted the portrait of the doge Grimani, who created him Chevalier of Saint Mark. Died in 1623.

Bas'san-tin, Bas'sin-toun, or **Bas'sen-tin,** (JAMES,) a Scottish mathematician, born about 1500, was the author of several astronomical and mathematical works which were esteemed in his time. Died in 1568.

See CHAMBERS, "Biographical Dictionary of Eminent Scotsmen."

Bassaraba. See BESSARABA.

Basse. See BAS.

Basse, bass, (WILLIAM,) an English poet of the seventeenth century, was the author of "The Sword and Buckler," "Great Brittaines Sunnes-set, bewailed with a Shower of Teares," composed on the death of Prince Henry, and an epitaph on Shakspeare.

Bassée, de la, dęh lâ bâ'sâ', (BONAVENTURE,) a French Capuchin, sometimes called LOUIS le Pippre, (lęh pêpR,) born in Artois about 1580. He wrote, in Latin, a work entitled "The Obedient Parishioner."

Basselin, bâs'lâN', or **Vasselin,** vâs'lâN', written also **Bachelin** and **Bisselin,** (OLIVIER,) a French poet, born in the Val-de-Vire, Normandy, about 1350, was a fuller by trade. His works, which are chiefly convivial and bacchanalian songs, were called "vaux-de-Vire" from the residence of the writer. The modern term vaudeville is supposed to be derived from vau-de-Vire. Died about 1419.

See NICOT, "Trésor de la Langue Française."

Bassen, van, vân bâs'sęn, (B.,) a Dutch painter and sculptor, born about 1590, resided for some time in London, where he painted the portraits of Charles I. and his queen. He excelled in perspective and in architectural pictures.

Bassenge, bâ'sôNzh', (JEAN NICOLAS,) a Flemish poet, born at Liege in 1758. He published, in conjunction with his friends Reynier and Henkart, a work entitled "Leisures of Three Friends." Died in 1811.

Bassentin. See BASSANTIN.

Basseporte, bâs'poRt', (MADELEINE FRANÇOISE,) a French lady, celebrated as a painter of flowers and birds, born in Paris in 1700, held the position of designer of the Jardin des Plantes. Her principal work is the continuation of the collection of plants painted on vellum for Gaston, Duke of Orléans. Died in 1780.

Bassermann, bâs'ser-mân', (FRIEDRICH DANIEL,) a German politician, born at Manheim in 1811, became in 1848 under-secretary of state in the ministry of the interior, which post he held till the resignation of Gagern. He died by suicide in 1850.

Basset, bâ'sâ', (CÉSAR AUGUSTE,) a French Benedictine monk and educational writer, born in Paris about 1760; died in 1828.

Bas'set, (PETER,) an English historian, born in Staffordshire about 1390, was chamberlain to Henry V., whom he accompanied to France. His work entitled "Acts of King Henry" ("Acta Regis Henrici") remains in manuscript.

Basset de la Marelle, bâ'sâ' dęh lâ mâ'rêl', (LOUIS,) a French jurist, born at Lyons about 1730, rose to be president of the grand council in Paris. He was condemned to death by the Jacobins, and executed in 1794.

Bassetti, bâs-set'tee, (MARCANTONIO,) an Italian painter of the Venetian school, born at Verona in 1588. He was a good colorist. Died in 1630.

See RIDOLFI, "Vite dei Pittori Veneti."

Bassetti, (SIMONE,) an Italian writer, born about 1590, wrote, in Latin, a work entitled "Monomachia of Virtues and Vices."

Bassewitz, bâs'wits, (HEINRICH FRIEDRICH,) a German diplomatist and historian, born in 1680, was ambassador to the court of Peter the Great. He was the author of "Historical Memoirs of Russia from 1713 to 1725." Died in 1749.

Bassi, bâs'see, a celebrated Italian buffo singer, died at Vicenza in 1825.

Bassi, (BARTOLOMMEO,) a Genoese painter, born about 1615, was noted for his skill in perspective.

Bassi, (FERDINANDO,) an Italian naturalist, born at Bologna. A genus of trees indigenous to the coast of

Malabar was named by Linnæus Bassia in his honour. Died in 1774.

Bassi, (FRANCESCO,) a painter of Bologna, was a pupil of Barbieri. Died in 1732.

Bassi, (FRANCESCO,) born at Cremona in 1642, was surnamed IL CREMONESE DEI PAESI, ("the Cremonese of landscapes,") from his excellence in that department of painting. Died in 1700.

See LANZI, "History of Painting in Italy."

Bassi, (GIOVANNI MARIA,) an Italian sculptor of Bologna, lived about 1710.

Bassi, (GIUSEPPE,) Count of Velletri, an Italian philosophical and satirical writer, lived at Rome about 1630.

Bassi, (LAURA MARIA CATARINA,) an Italian lady, born at Bologna in 1711, was celebrated for her profound knowledge of philosophy, mathematics, and languages. She was appointed in 1732 professor of philosophy in her native city, having previously received the title of doctor. In 1738 she was married to Dr. Joseph Verati. Died in 1778.

See J. FANTUZZI, "Elogio de Laura Bassi," Bologna, 1778.

Bassi, (MARTINO,) an Italian architect of the sixteenth century, was a native of Milan, and assisted in the construction of the great cathedral in that city.

Bassi, (UGO,) an Italian patriot and eloquent preacher, born in the Roman States about 1804. He fought against the Austrians in 1848, and served as chaplain to Garibaldi. Having been taken prisoner, he was put to death in August, 1849.

Bassi, de', dà bâs'see, (UGO VISCONTI,) the natural son of a wealthy gentleman of Sardinia. The Pisan government having refused him, on account of his illegitimacy, the large possessions of his father, Bassi resolved to betray Sardinia into the hands of James II. of Aragon. For this purpose he treacherously invited a number of Pisans to assist in defending the island against the King of Aragon, and, having separated them into small bodies, caused them to be massacred, (1323.)

See SISMONDI, "Histoire des Républiques Italiennes."

Bassiano, bâs-se-ä'no, (LANDI,) [Lat. BASSIA'NUS LAN'DUS,] an Italian physician, born at Piacenza, wrote a number of medical works in Latin. Died in 1562.

Bassiano, (ULISSE,) an Italian poet, born at Bologna, lived at Rome about 1550.

Bassianus. See CARACALLA.

Bassignana, da, dà bâs-sèn-yä'nä, (GIOVANNI STEFANO,) an Italian Carmelite monk and religious writer, flourished about 1480.

Bassinet, de, dęh bä'se'nà', (ALEXANDRE JOSEPH,) a French ecclesiastic and writer, born at Avignon in 1733. He was editor for a time of the "Magasin Encyclopédique," and wrote, among other works, "The Sacred History of the Old and New Testaments," (8 vols., 1804.) The last volume was written by the Abbé Lecuy. Died in 1813.

Bassintoun. See BASSANTIN.

Bassius. See BASS, (HEINRICH.)

Basso, bâs'so, (ANTONIO,) an Italian poet and jurist, who was put to death by order of the Duke of Guise for having been engaged in the insurrection of 1647.

Basso, del, dèl bâs'so, (ANDREA,) an Italian poet and prose-writer, lived about 1470.

See LONGFELLOW's "Poets and Poetry of Europe."

Bas'sol, (JOHN,) a Scottish philosopher, was the author of "Philosophic and Medical Miscellanies," (in Latin.) Died in 1347.

See CAVE, "Historia Literaria."

Bassompierre, bä'sòn'pe-aiR', (FRANÇOIS,) BARON OF, Marquis d'Harouel, and marshal of France, was born in Lorraine in 1579. At an early age he became distinguished at the French court, where his personal advantages and brilliant accomplishments procured for him the friendship and patronage of Henry IV. Having served in Savoy, and subsequently against the Turks in 1603, he was appointed colonel-general of the Swiss guards. After the death of Henry, Bassompierre enjoyed in an equal degree the favour of Louis XIII., who created him marshal of France in 1622. He was soon after employed in important embassies to Spain, Switzerland, and England. He married privately Louise de Lorraine, Princess of Conti. In 1631 he was imprisoned in the Bastille by order of Cardinal Richelieu, whom he had offended, and was not released until the death of the cardinal in 1642. He died in 1646, leaving two volumes of "Memoirs," written while in prison, and published in 1665; they are considered to present a faithful picture of the profligacy of the French court at that time. His style is said to be animated and *spirituel.*

See "Mémoires du Maréchal de Bassompierre," 1665; PUYMAIGRE, "Vie de Bassompierre," 1848; "Nouvelle Biographie Génerale."

Bassot, bä'so', (JACQUES,) a French writer, to whom has been attributed a "History of the Giant Teutobochus, King of the Teutons, etc.," (1613.)

Bassotti, bâs-sot'tee, (GIOVANNI FRANCESCO,) an Italian painter, born at Perugia, flourished about 1660.

Bassuel, bä'sü-el', (PIERRE,) a French surgeon and medical writer, born in Paris in 1706; died in 1757.

Bas'sus, (CÆSIUS,) a Roman lyric poet of the first century, to whom the sixth satire of Persius is addressed. Fragments of his works are in the "Corpus Poetarum."

Bassus, (CESELLIUS,) a Roman of Carthaginian extraction, promised the emperor Nero to discover the treasures concealed by Dido. Having failed, he committed suicide.

Bassus, (CNEIUS AUFIDIUS ORESTES,) a Roman historian and orator in the time of Augustus. He wrote a history of the Roman wars in Germany, also a general history of Rome, which was continued by Pliny the Elder. His works are not extant.

Bassus, (LOLLIUS,) a Greek poet, a native of Smyrna, flourished about 20 A.D. He was the author of ten Epigrams which are contained in the "Greek Anthology."

Bassus, (SALEIUS,) a Roman poet, lived about 60 A.D. He was highly esteemed and patronized by Vespasian, and his genius was commended by Quintilian. None of his works are extant.

Bassville, de, dęh bäs'vèl', (NICOLAS JEAN **Hugou** (hü'goo') or **Husson**—hü'sòn',) a French journalist and diplomatist, was editor for a time of the "Mercure National." Being sent as secretary of legation to Naples in 1792, he was soon after summoned to Rome, and, while attempting to exhibit the republican cockade, was killed in a riot.

See "Nouvelle Biographie Générale."

Bast, bâst, (FRIEDRICH JAKOB,) a German scholar and diplomatist, born in the duchy of Hesse-Darmstadt in 1772, was secretary of legation at Paris. He published a "Critical Letter on Antoninus Liberalis, Parthenius, and Aristænetus," (1805,) written in French and addressed to M. Boissonade; also "Notes and Palæographical Dissertations" in Schaefer's edition of "Gregory of Corinth." Both of these works are ranked among the best of their kind. Died in 1811.

See QUÉRARD, "La France Littéraire."

Bast, bâst, (PETER,) a Dutch painter and engraver; died in 1605.

Bast, de, dęh bâst, (LIEVIN AMAND MARIE,) nephew of Martin Jan, noticed below, born at Ghent in 1787. He was keeper of the cabinet of medals at Ghent, and the author of several works on art. Died in 1832.

See A. VOISIN, "Notice sur L. A. M. de Bast," 1833.

Bast, de, dęh bâst, (LOUIS AMÉDÉE,) a French novelist, born in Paris in 1795.

Bast, de, (MARTIN JAN,) a Flemish ecclesiastic and writer on antiquities, born at Ghent in 1753, was a member of the Academy of Brussels and the Society of Antiquaries in France. Died in 1825.

Basta, bâs'tä, (GIORGIO,) an Italian soldier, born at Naples, served with distinction under the Duke of Parma in 1579. He was the author of two works on military science, which have a high reputation. Died in 1613.

Basta, (GIUSEPPE,) an Italian jurist and legal writer, born in 1743; died in 1819.

Bastard, bâs'täR', (T.,) a French botanist, was director of the botanic garden at Angers in 1814. He wrote a "Flora of Maine-et-Loire," (1807.)

Bas'tard, (THOMAS,) an English epigrammatist in the time of Queen Elizabeth, born at Blandford, in Dorsetshire. He wrote, besides his epigrams, a Latin poem entitled "Magna Britannia." Died in 1618.

See "Biographia Britannica."

Bastard, de, dẹh bȧs'tȧr', (DOMINIQUE,) a French jurist, born at Toulouse in 1683; died in 1777.

His son FRANÇOIS, born in 1722, became first president of the Parliament of Toulouse. Died in 1780.

Bastard or **Bastart, de,** dẹh bȧs'tȧr', (GUILLAUME,) Vicomte de Fussy, (fü'se',) born at Bourges, held several important offices under Charles VI. and Charles VII. Died in 1447.

Bastard d'Estang, de, dẹh bȧs'tȧr' dês'tôN', (DOMINIQUE FRANÇOIS MARIE,) COMTE, an able French judge, born at Nogaro in 1783. He became a member of the Chamber of Peers in 1819. Died in 1844.

See A. DE BASTARD D'ESTANG, "Notice historique sur F. de Bastard Comte d'Estang," 1844.

Bastardi, bȧs-taR'dee, (ZACCHERIA,) an Italian ecclesiastical writer, born at Módena; died about 1650.

Bastaro, del, dĕl bȧs-tȧ'ro, (GIUSEPPE,) an Italian painter of the Roman school, born about 1590.

Baste, bȧst, (PIERRE,) a French naval commander, born at Bordeaux in 1768, served against the English at the siege of Malta, the battle of Aboukir, (1798,) and in the Spanish campaign of 1808. In 1809 he was created by Napoleon count of the empire, and rear-admiral in 1811. Died in 1814.

Baster, bȧs'tẹr, (JOB,) a Dutch botanist, born at Zierikzee, in Zealand, in 1711. He published "Observations on some Marine Plants and Insects," (1753,) and other scientific works. The name Bastera has been given in his honour to several genera of plants. Died in 1775.

See HALLER, "Bibliotheca Botanica."

Basterio, bȧs-tȧ're-o, (NICCOLÒ **di Carmagnola—**de kaR-mȧn-yo'lȧ,) an Italian professor of theology and philosophy at Pavía, lived about 1620.

Bastholm, bȧst'holm, (CHRISTIAN,) an eminent Danish theologian, born at Copenhagen in 1740. He became court preacher in the Danish capital, and published numerous works, among which are "Spiritual Eloquence," (1775,) "Philosophy for the Unlearned," (in German, 1787,) and "Principal Doctrines of the Christian Religion," (1783.) Died in 1819.

See ERSCH und GRUBER, "Allgemeine Encyklopaedie."

Bastiani, bȧs-te-ȧ'nee, (GIUSEPPE,) an Italian painter, born at Macerata, was a pupil of Gasparini, and lived about 1580.

Bastianino. See GRATELLA.

Bastiano di San Gallo, bȧs-te-ȧ'no de sȧn gȧl'lo, an Italian painter of perspective and theatrical decorations, was a pupil of Perugino and a friend of Raphael.

See VASARI, "Lives of the Painters."

Bastiat, bȧs'te'ȧ', (FRÉDÉRIC,) an able French writer on political economy, born at Bayonne in 1801. He published in 1844, in the "Journal des Économistes," a treatise "On the Influence of French and English Tariffs on the Future of the Two Nations," in which he opposed the protective system. Having visited England and made the acquaintance of Cobden, he brought out after his return a translation of various addresses of the free-traders, to which was prefixed an introduction, entitled "Cobden and the League." He subsequently edited in Paris the "Libre Échange," a journal devoted to the cause of free trade. His "Harmonies Économiques" (1849) is regarded as his greatest work. Died at Rome in 1850.

See "Nouvelle Biographie Générale."

Bastide, bȧs-tee'Dȧ, (FERNANDO,) a Spanish Jesuit of the sixteenth century, was professor of theology and chancellor of the University at Valladolid.

Bastide, bȧs'tĕd', (JULES,) a French republican journalist and statesman, born in Paris in 1800. He became about 1836 chief editor of the "National," a daily journal, and in 1846 was one of the founders of the "Revue Nationale." He was minister of foreign affairs under Cavaignac from June to December, 1848.

Bastide, (LOUIS,) a French jurist and theologian, born about 1680, was the author of several esteemed religious works.

Bastide, (MARC,) a French Benedictine monk and ecclesiastical writer; died in 1668.

Bastide, (MARC ANTOINE,) a French Protestant theological writer and diplomatist, born at Milhau-en-

Rouergue about 1624. He wrote in 1672 a reply to Bossuet's "Explanation of the Doctrine of the Catholic Church," a "Treatise on the Eucharist," and other similar works. Died in 1704.

Bastide, (PHILIPPE,) a French Benedictine, born in the diocese of Bourges in 1620; died in 1690.

Bastide, de, dẹh bȧs'tĕd', (JEAN FRANÇOIS,) a French *littérateur,* born at Marseilles in 1724, was editor of the "Spectateur Français," and other journals. His works are of a frivolous character: they were severely criticised by Voltaire and other writers of the time. Died in 1798.

Bastien, bȧs'te-ȧN', (JEAN FRANÇOIS,) a French bookseller, born in Paris in 1747, compiled a number of valuable works on agriculture and gardening. Died in 1824.

Bastiou, bȧs'te-oo', (YVES,) a French teacher and educational writer, born at Pontrieux, in Brittany, in 1751; died in 1814.

Baston, bȧs'tôN', (GUILLAUME ANDRÉ RENÉ,) born at Rouen in 1741, became in 1813 Bishop of Seez. Died in 1825.

Bas'ton, (ROBERT,) an English writer, born near Nottingham, was the author of Latin poems on various subjects. Died about 1312.

Bastoul, bȧs'tool', (LOUIS,) a French general, born at Montolieu in 1753, was killed at Hohenlinden in December, 1800.

Bast'wick, (JOHN,) an English physician and controversial writer, born in Essex in 1593. For his violent attacks on episcopacy he was condemned to imprisonment for life; but the sentence was afterwards reversed.

Baszko, bȧsh'ko, (GODISLAS,) a Polish historian, author of a "Chronicle of Great Poland," lived about 1820.

Batacchi, bȧ-tȧk'kee, (DOMENICO,) a licentious Italian writer, born at Leghorn in 1749; died in 1802.

Bataillard, bȧ'tȧ'yȧr', (CHARLES,) a French writer, was the author, among other works, of a "Political and Moral Picture of France," (1801.)

Bat'a-lus [Βάταλος] or **Bat'ta-lus,** a Greek fluteplayer, noted for his effeminacy, lived about 420–400 B.C.

Bate, (GEORGE,) a distinguished English physician and historian, born in Buckinghamshire in 1608. He was first physician successively to Charles I., Cromwell, and Charles II. He wrote, in Latin, several medical works, and a "History of the Civil War between Charles I. and Cromwell," in which he favours the Puritans. Dr. Bate was a member of the Royal Society and of the College of Physicians. Died in 1668.

See "Biographie Médicale."

Bate, [Lat. BA'TUS,] (JOHN,) an English scholar and theologian, born about 1350; died in 1429.

Bate, (JULIUS,) an English divine, published a "Hebrew and English Lexicon." Died in 1771.

Bate'cumbe or **Bade'combe,** (WILLIAM,) an English mathematician, born about 1390, wrote, in Latin, a treatise "On the Solid Sphere," and other works.

Batélier or **Bathélier, le,** lẹh bȧ'tȧ'le-ȧ', (JACQUES,) a French jurist, was the author of "Commentaries on the Common Law of Normandy," (1626.)

Bateman, bȧt'man, (CHARLES PHILIP BOTELER,) an English admiral, born in 1775, assisted in the defence of Cadiz against the French in 1812.

Bateman, (THOMAS,) an eminent English physician, born in Yorkshire in 1778, was for a time associate editor of the "Edinburgh Medical and Surgical Journal." He wrote a number of medical treatises, chiefly on diseases of the skin, and contributed the principal articles on medicine to Rees's "Cyclopædia." Died in 1821.

See J. RUMSEY, "Account of the Life, etc. of Thomas Bateman," 1826.

Bateman, (WILLIAM,) an English prelate, born at Norwich, was the founder of Trinity Hall, Cambridge. He became Bishop of Norwich in 1343. Died in 1355.

Baten, bȧ'tẹn, (HENRY,) a Flemish astronomer of the thirteenth century, wrote a work entitled "Mirror of Divine and Natural Things," ("Speculum Divinorum et Naturaliam,") unpublished.

Bates, (BARNABAS,) a distinguished advocate of cheap postage in the United States, was born in England in 1785. About 1825 he established "The Christian Enquirer" at New York. He devoted himself for years to the work of effecting a reduction in the rates of postage,

ā, ē, ī, ō, ū, ȳ, *long;* ȧ, ė, ȯ, same, less prolonged; ă, ĕ, ĭ, ŏ, ŭ, ў, *short;* a, ẹ, į, ǫ, *obscure;* fär, fȧll, fȧt; mēt; nŏt; gŏŏd; mōōn;

and to his labours we are greatly indebted for our present system of cheap letter-carriage. Died in 1853.

Bates, (EDWARD,) an American statesman, born in Goochland county, Virginia, about 1792. He emigrated to Missouri at an early age, studied law, and became an eminent lawyer. He was a political friend of Henry Clay in 1824, was elected a member of Congress in 1827, and voted for John Quincy Adams in 1828. After the expiration of his first term in Congress, he devoted himself exclusively to his profession for many years. He was president of the national convention of the friends of internal improvement which met in Chicago in 1847, and he maintained in an able speech that it is the duty of the Federal government to develop the resources of the country by great public works. He opposed the repeal of the Missouri Compromise in 1854, after which he acted with the friends of free labour in the Kansas question. He was appointed attorney-general of the United States by President Lincoln in March, 1861, and resigned about September, 1864.

Bates, (JOAH,) a distinguished English musician and composer, born in Yorkshire in 1740. He was appointed in 1784 to conduct the commemoration of Handel at Westminster Abbey. Died in 1799. His wife, originally Miss Harrop, was an excellent vocalist.

Bates, (JOSHUA,) born in Weymouth, Massachusetts, in 1788, established in 1826, in connection with John Baring, son of Sir Thomas Baring, a mercantile house in London under the name of Bates & Baring. Subsequently the firm was merged into the celebrated house of Baring Brothers & Company. In 1854 he filled the position of umpire to the British and American commissioners for settling the claims of citizens of the United States and Great Britain growing out of the war of 1812, and appears to have discharged its delicate and responsible duties with entire satisfaction to all parties. But that which confers the greatest lustre on Mr. Bates's memory is his munificent endowment of the Boston Library, with the express condition that it should be "PERFECTLY FREE TO ALL, with no other restrictions than may be necessary for the preservation of the books." He may thus be said to have been the founder not only of the most useful, but—if we consider the variety and character as well as the number of its books—of perhaps the most magnificent library of which this continent can boast. When the project of establishing a public library in Boston was made known to Mr. Bates, he wrote to the mayor, offering the sum of fifty thousand dollars towards the library, that it might be commenced "at once;" he afterwards added to this munificent donation books to the value of not less than fifty thousand dollars more. On his death, in 1864, the trustees passed a resolution that the large hall of the library, in which the rarest and most valuable books are contained, should thenceforward be designated as Bates Hall.

See "Memorial of Joshua Bates, from the City of Boston," 1865.

Bates, (JOSHUA,) an American clergyman, born at Cohasset, Massachusetts, in 1776. He was president of Middlebury College, Vermont, from 1818 to 1839, and afterwards minister at Dudley, Massachusetts. Died in 1854.

Bates, (THOMAS,) an English farmer, who lived at Kirkleavington, was distinguished for his success in improving the breed of cattle. Died in 1849.

Bates, (WILLIAM,) an eminent English dissenting minister, born in 1625, was a Presbyterian and a royalist. He preached in London until he was ejected by the Act of Uniformity in 1662. He was a person of great learning and superior talents, and had a high reputation both as a preacher and a writer. Among his intimate friends were Archbishop Tillotson and John Howe. He published, besides other works, "The Lives of Pious and Learned Men," (in Latin, 1681.) Died in 1699.

See MACAULAY'S "History of England," vol. ii. chap. viii.

Bāte'sǫn, (THOMAS,) a celebrated English composer of madrigals, was organist of the cathedral at Chester about 1600.

Bath, EARL OF. See PULTENEY, (WILLIAM.)

Bathe, bâth, (WILLIAM,) an Irish Jesuit and writer, born at Dublin about 1532, became director of the Irish seminary at Salamanca. Died in 1614.

Bathélier. See BATÉLIER.

Bathem, van, văn bȧ'tem, written also **Battem** or **Battum,** (GERARD,) a Dutch landscape-painter of superior merit, lived in the seventeenth century.

Ba-thil'da or **Ba-til'da,** [Fr. BATHILDE or BATILDE, bȧ'tèld',] SAINT, originally an Anglo-Saxon slave, became the wife of Clovis II., King of France, who, dying young, left her regent of the kingdom. She was celebrated for her talents and piety, and was canonized by Pope Nicholas I. Died in 680.

See BAILLET, "Vita Sanctæ Bathildis."

Báthori, bȧ'to-ree, (ELIZABETH,) PRINCESS OF, a niece of Stephen Bathori, King of Poland, and wife of the Hungarian count Nadasdi, was one of the most striking examples of fiendish cruelty recorded in history. With the assistance of three servants, she enticed to her castle a great number of young girls, whom she caused to be massacred, in order that she might restore her beauty by bathing in their blood. Her crimes being discovered, she was sentenced to perpetual imprisonment. Died in 1614.

Báthori, (GABOR or GABRIEL,) became Prince of Transylvania in 1608. Matthias, King of Hungary, having invaded his country, was repulsed with the assistance of Bethlen Gabor ; but the life of the latter being threatened by his cousin Bathori, Bethlen Gabor was made Prince of Transylvania by the Turks, and Bathori was killed soon after, (1613.)

Báthori, (LADISLAS,) a Hungarian monk, born about 1490, translated the Bible and the "Lives of the Saints" into Hungarian.

Báthori, (SIGISMUND,) a prince of Transylvania, born about 1550. Having married a princess of the house of Hapsburg, he promised to the emperor Rudolph that, in case of his dying without children, the crown of Transylvania should be united to that of Austria. Through the influence of the Jesuits, he soon after abdicated in favour of Rudolph. His subjects, dissatisfied with this arrangement, reinstated him in 1601 ; but, having been defeated by the Austrians, Bathori again abdicated, in consideration of a large pension and other advantages. Died in 1613.

See HORANYI, "Memoria Hungarorum."

Báthori, (STEPHEN,) was elected in 1571 Prince of Transylvania, and in 1576 succeeded to the throne of Poland. He reconquered Lithuania from the Russians, and obtained other important advantages over them. Died in 1586.

See WARSEWITZ, "Vita et Res gestæ Stephani Regis Polonorum," 1587.

Bath'urst, (ALLEN,) Earl Bathurst, born at Westminster in 1684, was a son of Sir Benjamin Bathurst, treasurer of the household to the princess Anne, afterwards queen. In 1705 he was elected to Parliament for Cirencester, and signalized himself by his opposition to Marlborough and other Whig leaders. He obtained the title of Lord Bathurst in 1711. Throughout his public career he firmly opposed the administration of Sir Robert Walpole. Lord Bathurst (who was created an earl in 1772) was distinguished for his literary tastes and attainments, and was intimate with Pope, Swift, Addison, and other eminent men. Pope dedicated to him the third epistle of his "Moral Essays." Died in 1775.

See the "Annual Register" for 1775.

Bathurst, (BENJAMIN,) an English diplomatist, born in London in 1784. Having been sent on a mission to Vienna in 1807, he disappeared mysteriously near Hamburg, and is supposed to have been assassinated.

Bathurst, (HENRY,) second Earl Bathurst, and Lord Apsley, an English judge, son of Allen Bathurst, born in 1714. He was appointed a judge in the court of common pleas in 1754, and lord chancellor of England in 1770 or 1771. He resigned the great seal in 1778, and became president of the council in 1780. Died in 1794.

See LORD CAMPBELL, "Lives of the Lord Chancellors ;" Foss, "The Judges of England," vol. viii.

Bathurst, (HENRY,) a nephew of Allen, Lord Bathurst, born in Northamptonshire in 1744. He was created in 1805 Bishop of Norwich. Died in 1837.

See "Memoirs of Dr. Henry Bathurst, Bishop of Norwich," by Rev. H. BATHURST, 1837.

Bathurst, (HENRY,) son of Baron Apsley, mentioned

above, born in 1762. Having filled several important offices, he became secretary of the colonies, (1812,) and president of the council, (1828.) He was a decided Tory in politics. Died in 1834.

Bathurst, (RALPH,) an English physician, divine, and scholar, born in Northamptonshire in 1620, was one of the founders of the Royal Society, of which he was elected president in 1668. He was appointed chaplain to Charles II., (1663,) and vice-chancellor of the University of Oxford, (1673.) He was the author of Latin poems and other works. Died in 1704.

See WARTON, "Life of R. Bathurst," 1761.

Bathurst, (THEODORE,) a relative of Dr. Ralph Bathurst, translated Spenser's "Shepherd's Calendar" into Latin verse, (1653.)

Bathyani. See BATTHYÁNYI.

Bath-y̆-clēs, [Βαθυκλῆς,] a Greek sculptor, native of Magnesia, supposed to have been contemporary with Solon. His principal work was the colossal throne of the Amyclæan Apollo, which he covered with bas-reliefs.

Bathylle, the French of BATHYLLUS, which see.

Ba-thy̆l'lus, [Gr. Βάθυλλος; Fr. BATHYLLE, bȧ'tèl',] a celebrated comedian, who lived about 30 B.C., was a native of Alexandria and a freedman of Mæcenas. He excelled in comic pantomime, and his performances were exceedingly popular with the Romans. His partisans were styled Bathyllians, while those of his rival Pylades the tragedian were called Pyladians.

Batilda, SAINT. See BATHILDE.

Batinskof, bȧ-tins'kof, (CONSTANTINE NICOLAEVITCH,) a Russian poet and critic, born at Vologda in 1787. He was the author of lyric poems and elegies, which are highly esteemed, and essays on Russian and Italian literature. He also translated into Russian Schiller's "Bride of Messina." Died in 1855.

Batista. See BATTISTA.

Batizi, bȧ-tee'zee, (ANDREW and MICHAEL,) Hungarian Protestants of the sixteenth century. The former was the author of national hymns, the latter of religious works.

Batka, bȧt'kȧ, (LORENZ,) a German musician, born at Lischau, in Bohemia, in 1705, was director of music at Prague. He died in 1759, leaving five sons, who were noted as vocalists and musicians.

Batlowski, bat-lov'skee, a Polish painter, lived in the latter part of the seventeenth century.

Bat'man, (STEPHEN,) an English divine and writer, born in 1537. He published, among other works, a poem entitled "The Travayled Pilgrime, bringing Newes from all Parts of the Worlde." Died in 1587.

Bat'man-son, (JOHN,) an English Carthusian monk, who lived in the sixteenth century, wrote several works, in Latin, against Erasmus and other reformers.

Bā'ton, [Βάτων,] a Greek comic poet, lived about 300 B.C. A few fragments of his comedies are extant.

Baton of Sinope, a Greek historian, supposed to have lived about 277 B.C. He wrote "Commentaries on Persian Affairs," a "History of Attica," and other works, which are mentioned by several ancient writers.

Batoni, bȧ-to'nee, (POMPEO GIROLAMO,) a celebrated Italian painter, born at Lucca in 1708. He studied in Rome, where he soon acquired the reputation of one of the first artists of his time. Among his master-pieces in historical painting are "Saint Catherine of Sienna," "The Fall of Simon Magus," and "Saint Celso." His portraits of Joseph II. and Leopold II. of Austria are also highly esteemed: the former procured for him letters of nobility from the empress Maria Theresa. His style is graceful, and free from the prevalent mannerism of his time. He had great facility of execution. Died at Rome in 1786 or 1787.

See LANZI, "History of Painting in Italy;" ONOFRIO BONI, "Elogio del Cavaliere P. Batoni," 1787.

Batoo- (**Batou-** or **Batu-**) **Khan,** bȧ'too' kȧn, supposed to have been the grandson of Jengis Khan, assumed the government of Kapchak in 1223. By the command of the great khan Oktai, whom he acknowledged as his superior, he made war on Poland and Hungary, and conquered Russia, which he held in subjection for ten years. Died in 1255.

See D'HERBELOT, "Bibliothèque Orientale."

Batootah, Batoutah, or **Batûtah,** bȧ-too'tȧ, written also **Battuta, (Moham'med-Ibn-Abdil'lah,)** commonly called **Ibn-Batootah,** (or -**Batûtah,**) a famous Moorish traveller of the fourteenth century, visited Egypt, and the principal part of Asia, including China and the Indian archipelago. Only fragments of his travels have been discovered and published.

See "Blackwood's Magazine" for May, 1841.

Batou-Khan. See BATOO-KHAN.

Batoutah. See BATOOTAH.

Bat'ra-chus, [Gr. Βάτραχος, a "frog,"] a Greek architect of the time of Augustus. With his countryman **Saurus,** [Σαῦρος, a "lizard,"] he built two temples at Rome. As they were not allowed to inscribe their names on their work, they carved, it is said, a lizard and a frog on the columns.

Batsch, bȧtsh, (AUGUST JOHANN GEORG KARL,) a German naturalist, born at Jena in 1761. He wrote, among other works, a monograph of the mushrooms in the vicinity of Jena, entitled "Elenchus Fungorum," (1783,) and "Elements of Systematic Chemistry," (1789.) Gmelin has given the name Batschia to a genus of the order Boraginæ. Batsch was professor of natural history, etc. at Jena, where he died in 1802.

See "Nouvelle Biographie Générale."

Batt, bȧt, (BARTHOLOMEW,) a Flemish Protestant, born at Alost in 1515, wrote, in Latin, a treatise "On Christian Economy."

Batt, (CHARLES,) a Flemish physician, translated several medical works from the French. He lived at Dort from 1593 to 1598.

Batt, bȧt, (CONRAD,) a Dutch or German physician, born at Rostock in 1573; died in 1605.

Batt, (CORNELIUS,) son of James, noticed below, born in Zealand in 1470, was the author of a "Description of the World." Died in 1517.

Batt, (JAMES,) born in Zealand, was secretary of the town of Bergen-op-Zoom. He was an intimate friend of Erasmus.

Batt, (LIEVIN,) a Flemish physician, son of Bartholomew, noticed above, born at Ghent about 1540, was professor of mathematics at Rostock. Died in 1591.

Batt, (WILLIAM,) an English physician, born at Collingham in 1744, became in 1778 professor of chemistry at Genoa, where he introduced vaccination. Died in 1812.

Battaglia. See CERQUOZZI.

Battaglia, bȧt-tȧl'yȧ, an Italian architect of the eighteenth century, celebrated for having completed the magnificent convent of Catania, in Sicily.

Battaglia, (CESARE,) an Italian ecclesiastic, born at Milan in 1605.

Battaglia, (DIONISIO,) an Italian painter of the Venetian school, born at Verona, lived about 1520-40.

Battaglia, (FRANCESCO,) a Venetian senator, who distinguished himself by his zeal in the cause of the French Revolution, and proposed an alliance between the republics of France and Venice. Died in 1799.

Battaglini, bȧt-tȧl-yee'nee, (MARCO,) an Italian prelate, born near Rimini in 1645, was Bishop of Cesena. He wrote a "Universal History of Councils," (1686,) and other works. Died in 1717.

Battalus. See BATALUS.

Battara, bȧt-tȧ'rȧ, (GIOVANNI ANTONIO,) an Italian naturalist and physician, born at Rimini, published several botanical works. Died in 1789.

Bat'tel, (ANDREW,) an English traveller, born in Essex about 1565, was made prisoner by the Portuguese and detained many years in their settlements in Africa. His adventures are related in Purchas's "Collection of Voyages."

Battelli, bȧt-tel'lee, (GIOVANNI CRISTOFORO,) an Italian antiquary, born near Urbino in 1658, became Archbishop of Amasia. Died in 1725.

Battely, bȧt'le, (JOHN,) a learned English divine, born at Bury Saint Edmund's in 1647, became Archdeacon of Canterbury. His principal work is an account of the antiquities of Richborough and Reculver, entitled "Antiquitates Rutupinæ." Died in 1708.

Battem. See BATHEM.

Bat'ten, (ADRIAN,) an English composer of sacred music, became organist of Saint Paul's Cathedral in 1624.

ā, ē, ī, ō, ū, ȳ, *long;* ȧ, ė, ȯ, *same, less prolonged;* ă, ĕ, ĭ, ŏ, ŭ, y̆, *short;* ạ, ẹ, ị, ọ, *obscure;* fär, fȧll, fȧt; mȇt; nŏt; gŏŏd; mŏŏn;

Batteux, bȧ'tuh', (CHARLES,) a French *littérateur*, born near Vouziers in 1713, was appointed professor of Greek and Latin philosophy in the College of France. He wrote, among other works, a "Treatise on the Fine Arts," and also made a translation of Horace, (1750,) which is valued for its accuracy. He was a member of the French Academy, and of the Academy of Inscriptions. Died in 1780.

See MADAME DACIER, "Éloge de Batteux," and a "History of First Causes," or "Exposé sommaire des Pensées des Philosophes sur le Principe des Etres," 1769.

Batthyányi, bŏt'yȧn-yee, or **Bathyanyi**, (CASIMIR,) COUNT, a Hungarian nobleman and patriot, born about 1817. He took an active part in the revolution of 1848, and in 1849 was appointed minister of foreign affairs. After the defeat of the Hungarians he was imprisoned for a time, and on his release went to Paris, where he died in 1854.

Batthyányi or **Bathyani**, written also **Battyany**, (IGNATIUS,) COUNT, a canonist, born in Transylvania in 1741, became Bishop of Weissenburg. He founded an observatory at Carlsburg, and published several works. Died in 1798.

Batthyányi, (CHARLES,) PRINCE, a Hungarian general, born about 1697. He performed a prominent part in the war of the Austrian succession, which ended in 1745. He also had a high command in the Austrian service during the Seven Years' war. Died in 1772.

Batthyányi or **Bathyányi**, (LOUIS,) COUNT, a Hungarian patriot and liberal statesman, born at Presburg in 1809. He contended for religious liberty, and became chief minister of the government formed in March, 1848. In consequence of the hostile movements of Jellachich, Ban of Croatia, who was instigated by the imperial court, he resigned in September, 1848. Civil war ensued, in which the friends of Batthyányi were vanquished. He was tried by a court-martial, and shot in October, 1849.

See HORVATH, "Louis Bathyányi, ein politischer Märtyrer," 1850; and "Graf L. Batthyányi, sein Leben, Wirken und Ende," Leipsic, 1850.

Battie, bȧt'te, (WILLIAM,) an English physician, born in Devonshire in 1704, was celebrated for his skilful treatment of insanity. His principal work is a "Treatise on Madness," (1758.) He was a Fellow of the Royal Society. Died in 1776.

See "Biographie Médicale."

Battier, bȧ'te-à', (SAMUEL,) a Swiss physician, born at Bâle in 1667, was a friend of Malebranche and Tournefort. He published several philosophical and scientific works in Latin. Died in 1744.

Battiferri, (LAURA.) See AMMANATI.

Bat'tis-hill, (JONATHAN,) an English musical composer, born in 1738. His anthems, glees, and songs are highly esteemed. Died in 1801.

See FÉTIS, "Biographie Universelle des Musiciens."

Battista, bȧt-tès'tȧ, (FULGOSO,) a Doge of Venice, who, being exiled about 1480, wrote, in Latin, a work entitled "Memorable Examples."

Battista or **Baptista**, (GIUSEPPE,) an Italian writer, born in the kingdom of Naples. He was the author of Latin epigrams, Italian lyrics, and several prose works. Died in 1675.

Battista, (IGNAZIO,) an Italian writer, who lived about 1540, wrote a "History of the Roman Emperors," and a work "On the Origin of the Turks," both in Latin.

Battista, (SPAGNUOLI,) an Italian ecclesiastic and Latin poet, surnamed THE MANTUAN, born at Mantua about 1436. His works were greatly admired by his contemporaries, but are now forgotten. Died in 1516.

Battista d'Agnolo, bȧt-tès'tȧ dȧn'yo-lo, or **Battista del Moro**, bȧt-tès'tȧ del mo'ro, an Italian painter of the sixteenth century, born at Verona. He worked at Verona and Venice.

Battista del Moro. See BATTISTA D'AGNOLO.

Battista di Ferrara, bȧt-tès'tȧ de fêr-rȧ'rȧ, an Italian writer, born about 1380, was the author of "Chronicles of Ferrara," and other works.

Battisti, bȧt-tès'tee, (BARTOLOMMEO,) born at Roveredo, in the Tyrol, in 1755, was appointed about 1784 physician to the Emperor of Austria. Died in 1831.

Battistin, bȧt-tès-teen', written also **Baptistin**, (JOHN BAPTIST STUCK,) an Italian musician and composer, of German extraction, born at Florence about 1677. He was an excellent performer on the violoncello, which he is said to have first introduced into France. Died in 1755.

Battistini, bȧt-tès-tee'nee, (FRANCESCO,) a noted Italian improvisatore, born in 1747, became professor of Latin and Italian eloquence in the college De Propaganda at Rome. Died in 1825.

Batton, bȧ'tòn', (DÉSIRÉ ALEXANDRE,) a French composer of operas, born in Paris in 1797, was a pupil of Cherubini.

Battoni, (POMPEO.) See BATONI.

Battori. See BÁTHORI.

Battum. See BATHEM.

Bat'tus I., a Lacedæmonian, born at Thera, was the founder of the colony of Cyrene, about 630 B.C. He received divine honours after his death.

Battus II., surnamed FELIX, was grandson of the preceding, and succeeded Arcesilaus as King of Cyrene. Under his reign the colony was greatly increased by the arrival of colonists from various parts of Greece. Died about 575 B.C.

Battus III., son of Arcesilaus II., reigned about 544 B.C.

Battuta. See BATOOTAH.

Battyany. See BATTHYÁNI.

Batu-Khan. See BATOO-KHAN.

Batus. See BATE.

Batûtah. See BATOOTAH.

Batz, de, (deh bȧts, (JEAN,) BARON, a French general, born near Tartas in 1760, made several unsuccessful attempts during the Revolution to save Louis XVI. and the royal family. Died in 1822.

Baubur or **Bauber**. See BÂBER.

Bau'çis, (Myth.,) a Phrygian peasant, who, with her husband Philemon, kindly received Jupiter and Mercury when travelling in disguise. For this favour Jupiter changed their cottage into a temple, and made them his priests. At their death they were changed to trees.

Baudake. See BALDOCK.

Baudart, bō'dȧr', (WILLIAM,) a Protestant theologian, born at Deinse, in Flanders, in 1565. In conjunction with Bucer and Bogerman, he translated the Old Testament into Dutch. Died in 1640.

Bauddha or **Baudha**, bōw'd'hạ, worshipper of BOODDHA, which see.

Baude, bōd, (HENRI,) a French poet and satirist, born at Moulins about 1430; died about 1495.

See V. DE VIRIVILLE, "Nouvelles Recherches sur H. Baude," 1853

Baudeau, bō'dō', (NICOLAS,) a French writer on political economy, born at Amboise in 1730. He was a contributor, conjointly with Mirabeau, to the journal entitled "Ephemerides of the Citizen;" and published, among other works, an "Exposition of the Natural Law." Died about 1792.

See QUÉRARD, "La France Littéraire."

Baudelaire, bōd'lȧr', (CHARLES,) a French poet, born in India in the early part of the present century. He wrote, among other things, "Les Fleurs du Mal," ("The Flowers of Evil,") and made translations of the works of Edgar A. Poe. His productions exhibit a mind of uncommon force, but intensely morbid. Died in 1867.

See "Atlantic Monthly" for February, 1869.

Baudelocque, bōd'lok', (JEAN LOUIS,) a celebrated French surgeon, born at Heilly, in Picardy, in 1746. He studied under Solayrès, and became chief surgeon and accoucheur of the hospital de la Maternité. He was also appointed by Napoleon first accoucheur to the empress Marie Louise. Among his writings, which are esteemed standard works, we may name his "Art des Accouchements," (2 vols., 1781.) Died in 1810.

See LE BAS, "Dictionnaire encyclopédique de la France."

Baudelot de Dairval, bōd'lo' deh dȧr'vȧl', (CHARLES CÉSAR,) a French antiquary, born in Paris in 1648, was the author of a popular work "On the Utility of Travels," etc. He became a member of the Academy of Inscriptions in 1705. Died in 1772.

See NICÉRON, "Mémoires."

Baudens, bō'dôn', (JEAN BAPTISTE LOUIS,) a French surgeon, born at Aire in 1804, was the author of a "New Method of Amputations," and other surgical works.

є as *k*; ç as *s*; ğ *hard*; ğ as *j*; G, H, K, *guttural*; N, *nasal*; R, *trilled*; ŝ as *z*; ŧh as in *this*. (☞See Explanations, p. 23.)

19

Bauder, bŏw'dẹr, (JOHANN FRIEDRICH,) born at Hersbruck in 1713, wrote on Fossils, etc. Died in 1791.

Bauderon, bōd'rŏN', (BRICE,) a French physician, born about 1540, was the author of a "Pharmacopœia," which passed through many editions. Died in 1623.

Baudesson, bō'dạ̊'sôN', (NICOLAS,) a French flower-painter, born at Troyes in 1609; died in 1680.

Baudet, bō'dạ̊', (ÉTIENNE,) a French engraver, born at Blois in 1643, executed a number of prints after Poussin and Le Brun. His "Adam and Eve," after Domenichino, is regarded as his master-piece. Died in 1716.

Baudier, (DOMINICUS.) See BAUDIUS.

Baudier, bō'de-ạ̊', (MICHEL,) historiographer of France, born in Languedoc about 1590. He published a "History of the War in Flanders from 1559 to 1609," "Life of Cardinal Ximenes," "General History of the Religion of the Turks," (1626,) and other works. Died in 1645.

Baudin, bō'dåN', a French priest, afterwards a moderate Jacobin, born about 1766; died in 1830.

Baudin, (NICOLAS,) a French naturalist, born in the Isle of Ré in 1750, was captain of a vessel sent in 1800 on a scientific expedition to New Holland. He died in the Isle of France in 1803.

Baudin des Ardennes, bō'dåN' dạ̊'zäR'dĕn', (CHARLES,) son of Pierre Charles Louis, noticed below, born at Sedan in 1784. He served with distinction against the English in 1808–12, and took the fortress of San Juan de Ulloa from the Mexicans in 1838. He was made vice-admiral and obtained the grand cordon of the legion of honour in 1848. Died in 1854.

Baudin des Ardennes, (PIERRE CHARLES LOUIS,) a French revolutionist and political writer, born at Sedan in 1748. As a member of the National Convention, he voted for the imprisonment of the king, and the appeal to the people. He was a member of the Institute. Died in 1799.

Baudis. See BAUDISSIN.

Baudissin, bŏw'dis-sin' or bō'de'sån', (OTTO FRIEDRICH MAGNUS,) a German general, born in 1792.

Baudissin, written also **Bauditz** or **Baudis,** (WOLF HEINRICH,) COUNT OF, a distinguished general, of Danish extraction, served under Gustavus Adolphus in the Thirty Years' war, from 1625 to 1633. Died about 1650.

Baudissin, (WOLF HEINRICH FRIEDRICH KARL,) COUNT OF, a German *littérateur*, brother of Otto Friedrich, noticed above, born at Rantzau in 1789. He translated into German "Henry VIII.," "Othello," "Lear," "Much Ado about Nothing," and other dramas of Shakspeare, which are accompanied with notes by Tieck.

Bauditz. See BAUDISSIN.

Bau'dĭ-us or **Baudier,** bō'de-ạ̊', (DOMINICUS,) a Flemish historian and scholar, born at Lille in 1561. He became professor of history and eloquence at Leyden in 1602. His "History of the Twelve Years' Truce" is written in elegant Latin, and his Latin poems were likewise greatly admired. Died in 1613.

See SWEERT, "Athenæ Belgicæ."

Baudoin or **Baudoin de Condé,** bō'dwåN' dẹh kôn'dạ̊', a French poet, lived about 1220.

Baudoin, (JEAN.) See BAUDOUIN.

Baudory, du, dü bō'do're', (JOSEPH,) a French Jesuit and miscellaneous writer, born at Vannes in 1710. Died in 1749.

Baudot, bō'do', (AUGUSTE NICOLAS,) a French general, born at Rennes in 1765, served under Moreau and Kleber, and was mortally wounded at Alexandria in 1801.

Baudot, (MARC ANTOINE,) a French Jacobin, member of the National Convention, voted for the death of the king within twenty-four hours. Died in 1830.

Baudot, (PIERRE LOUIS,) a French antiquary, and writer on numismatics, born at Dijon in 1760; died in 1816.

Baudot de Juilly, bō'do' dẹh zhü'e'ye' or zhwe'ye', (NICOLAS,) a French historian, born in Paris in 1678. He wrote a "History of the Conquest of England by William of Normandy," and other works. Died in 1759.

Baudouin, the French of BALDWIN, which see.

Baudouin, bō'dwåN', (BENOÎT,) a French antiquary, born at Amiens; died in 1632.

Baudouin, [Lat. BALDUI'NUS,] (FRANÇOIS,) an emi-nent French jurist and writer, born at Arras in 1520. He was professor of law successively at Angers, Paris, Strasburg, and Heidelberg, and was created a councillor of state by Henry III. Died in 1573.

See NICÉRON, "Mémoires."

Baudouin, (GABRIEL,) a French priest, born at Avesnes in 1689, founded a hospital at Warsaw. Died in 1768.

Baudouin or **Baudoin,** bō'dwåN', (JEAN,) born at Pradelles about 1590, wrote translations of the Latin classics. Died in 1650.

Baudouin, (PIERRE ANTOINE,) a French miniature-painter, born in Paris in 1723; died in 1769.

Baudouin d'Avesne, bō'dwåN' dȧ'vĕn', a French chronicler of the thirteenth century, wrote "The Genealogical History of the Counts of Hainault."

Baudouin de Ninove, (ne'nov',) a Flemish monk, author of a chronicle from the birth of Christ till 1294.

Baudouin (bō'dwåN') OF PADERBORN, a priest, lived about 1420, and wrote a "Universal History."

Baudoux or **Beaudoux,** bō'doo', (ROBERT,) a Flemish engraver, born at Brussels, lived about 1620.

Baudrais, bō'drạ̊', (JEAN,) a French *littérateur*, born at Tours in 1749, held several offices under the government, and was one of the witnesses of the last testament of Louis XVI. He passed thirteen years as an exile in the United States, (1804–17.) His works are chiefly romances, tales, and dramas. Died in 1832.

Baudran or **Baudrand,** bō'drôN', (MICHEL ANTOINE,) a French geographer, born in Paris in 1633. He wrote, in Latin, a "Geographical and Historical Dictionary," (2 vols.,) which was translated into French. Died in 1700.

Baudrand, bō'drôN', (MARIE ÉTIENNE FRANÇOIS HENRI,) COUNT, a French general, born at Besançon in 1774, served under Napoleon, and in 1830 became lieutenant-general. He was created a peer in 1832, and appointed tutor to the Count of Paris in 1838. Died in 1848.

Baudrexel, bŏw-drĕk'sẹl, (PHILIPP JAKOB,) a German musical composer, born in Suabia about 1635; died about 1700.

Baudricourt, de, dẹh bō'dre'kooR', (JEAN,) a French marshal, born at Blois, served successively under Charles the Bold, Louis XI., and Charles VIII. Died in 1499.

Baudrigeen. See BAUDRINGHEEN.

Baudrillart, bō'dRe'yȧR', (HENRI,) a French economist, born in Paris in 1821. He gained the prize of the French Academy for his "Éloge de Turgot," (1846,) and his "Éloge de Madame de Stael," (1850.) He also wrote several works on political economy.

Baudrillart, (JACQUES JOSEPH,) a French agriculturist, born at Givron, in Ardennes, in 1774, published a "Dictionary of Arboriculture and the Management of Forests," (1821,) and other works. Died in 1832.

See "Notice biographique sur M. Jacques Joseph Baudrillart," by BARON DE SILVESTRE.

Baudrimont, bō'dRe'môN', (ALEXANDRE ÉDOUARD,) born at Compiègne in 1806, was a professor of chemistry at Bordeaux, and wrote "On General and Experimental Chemistry," and other works.

Baudringheen, bŏw'dking-hān', or **Baudrigeen,** bŏw'dRe-hān', a Dutch painter, lived at Amsterdam about 1640.

Baudron, bō'drôN', (ANTOINE LAURENT,) a French musician, born at Amiens in 1743; died in 1834.

Baudry d'Asson, bō'dRe' dȧ'sôN', (ANTOINE,) a French Jansenist, born in Poitou, was a friend of the celebrated Arnauld. He published various religious and controversial works. Died in 1668.

Baudry d'Asson, (GABRIEL,) a royalist officer, born in Poitou, in France, in 1755, took an active part in the defence of La Vendée, and was killed at Mans in 1793.

Baudry des Lozières, bō'dRe' dạ̊ lo'ze-aiR', (LOUIS NARCISSE,) a French traveller, born in Paris in 1761, published, besides other works, a "Voyage to Louisiana and South America," (1802.) Died in 1841.

Bauduer, bō'dü'ạ̊', (GILLES ARNAUD,) a French scholar and theologian, born near Auch in 1744; died in 1787.

Bauduin, bō'dwåN', (DOMINIQUE,) a Flemish theologian, born at Liege in 1742, was professor of history at

Maestricht. He wrote, among other works, a defence of the Christian religion. Died in 1809.

Bauduins, bō'dwăN', (ADRIAN FRANCIS,) a Flemish painter and engraver, born at Dixmude in 1640, executed several prints after Van der Meulen, who was his brother-in-law. Died in 1700.

Baudus, bō'düss', (JEAN LOUIS AMABLE,) a French journalist, born at Cahors in 1761, removed to Hamburg in 1791, and became editor of the "Spectateur du Nord." Died in 1822.

Bauer. See BAUR.

Bauer, bŏw'er, a German jurist and legal writer, born at Leipsic in 1695; died in 1763.

Bauer, (ANTON,) a German jurist, and professor of law at Göttingen, born at Marburg in 1772. He was the author of a "Manual of Natural Law," (1808,) "Introduction to the Practice of Criminal Law," (1837,) and other works. Died at Göttingen in 1843.

Bauer, (AUREL REINHARD EDUIN,) a German theologian, and preacher of the German Catholic congregation at Dresden, born near Grossenhain in 1816. He wrote, among other works, a "History of the Foundation and Development of the German Catholic Church," (1846,) and a treatise "On Primitive Christianity." In 1849 he embraced Protestantism.

Bauer, (BRUNO,) a German rationalistic theologian, distinguished for the boldness or recklessness of his biblical criticisms, was born at Eisenberg in 1809. In 1838 he published a "Critical Exposition of the Religion of the Old Testament." Among his numerous other works is a "Critique of the Gospels, and History of their Origin," (2 vols., 1850.)

See BROCKHAUS, "Conversations-Lexikon."

Bauer, (CHRISTIAN FRIEDRICH,) a German Protestant writer, and professor of theology at Wittenberg, was born at Hofgarten in 1696; died in 1782.

Bauer, (CHRYSOSTOM,) a distinguished German organ-builder, born in Würtemberg, lived about 1700.

Bauer, (EDGAR,) a German political writer, a brother of Bruno, noticed above, born at Charlottenburg in 1821. He was imprisoned four years at Magdeburg for a work entitled "The Contest of Criticism with the Church and State," ("Der Streit der Kritik mit der Kirche und Staat," 1843.)

Bauer, (FERDINAND,) a German painter of objects of natural history, born at Feldsperg in 1744. He accompanied Dr. Sibthorp to Greece in 1784, and furnished the exquisite designs for the "Flora Graeca," published after the death of Sibthorp. He subsequently joined Captain Flinders's expedition to Australia, and published, after his return, "Illustrations of the Flora of New Holland," (1813,) one of the most superb works of the kind. Died in 1826.

Bauer, (GEORG LORENZ,) a German rationalistic theologian, born at Hiltboltstein in 1755. He studied at Altdorf, where in 1789 he became professor of eloquence, Oriental languages, and moral philosophy, and in 1805 obtained the chair of Oriental literature and exegesis at Heidelberg. Among his principal works are his "Hermeneutica Sacra Veteris Testamenti," (1797,) "Biblical Theology of the New Testament," (4 vols., 1800-2,) and "Hebrew Mythology of the Old and New Testament," (1802-3.) He also translated from the Arabic into German the History of Abool-Faraj. Died in 1806.

See MEUSEL, "Gelehrtes Deutschland."

Bauer, (JOHANN GOTTFRIED,) a German jurist and legal writer, born at Leipsic in 1695; died in 1763.

Bauer, (JOHANN JAKOB,) a German bookseller, born at Strasburg in 1706, began the publication of the "Universal Library of Rare Books," ("Bibliotheca Librorum rariorum universalis.") Died in 1772.

Bauer, (KARL LUDWIG,) a German philologist, born at Leipsic in 1730. He published a "German-Latin Dictionary," and other educational works. Died in 1799.

See J. D. DANIEL, "C. L. Bauer, biographisches Denkmal," 1806.

Bauerle, bŏw'êr-leh, (ADOLF,) a German dramatist, born at Vienna in 1784, wrote "The False Prima Donna," "The Friend in Need," and other popular comedies.

Bauernfeld, bŏw'êrn-fêlt', (EDUARD,) a German dramatic writer, born at Vienna in 1804, was the author of "The Confession," and several other successful comedies.

Bauffremont, de, deh bōfR'môN', (ALEXANDRE EMANUEL,) PRINCE, born in Paris in 1773. He fought against the French Republic in 1793-94. Died in 1833.

Bauffremont, de, (ALFONSE,) DUC, a son of the preceding, created a count by Napoleon, served with distinction at the battles of Moskwa and Dresden, 1813.

Bauffremont or **Beauffremont, de,** deh bōfR'môN', (CLAUDE,) Baron of Senescey, son of Nicolas, noticed below, was a zealous partisan of the Duke of Guise in the war of the League. He wrote several political works. Died in 1596.

His son CLAUDE CHARLES ROGER was created Bishop of Troyes in 1562.

Bauffremont, de, (HENRI,) son of Claude, noticed above, held several offices under the government. Died in 1622.

Bauffremont, de, (NICOLAS,) Baron of Senescey, and governor of Auxonne, was a zealous Catholic, and fought in the battles of Jarnac and Moncontour. He was appointed grand provost of France under Charles IX. Died in 1582.

Baugier, bō'zhe-à', (EDME,) a French writer, born about 1680, was the author of "Historical Memoirs of the Province of Champagne," (1721.)

Baugin, bō'zhăN', (LUBIN,) a French painter, called LE PETIT GUIDE, lived in Paris about 1650.

Bauhin, bō'ăN', (GASPARD,) a celebrated anatomist and naturalist, of French extraction, born at Bâle in January, 1560, was a younger son of Jean the elder, noticed below. He studied at Padua under Fabricius ab Aquapendente and other eminent teachers, and was appointed professor of anatomy and botany at Bâle in 1588. He was also made rector of the university, and obtained other distinctions. He was the author of a number of valuable medical and botanical works, among which we may name his "Pinax Theatri Botanici," (1596,) and "Prodromus Theatri Botanici," (1620.) Plumier named the genus Bauhinia in his honour. Died at Bâle in 1624. "Gaspard Bauhin," says Dr. Hoefer, "was not a mere compiler. He had the merit and glory of a legislator; his name for a long time was received as an authority, and even at the present day it is sometimes associated with those of Tournefort and Linnæus."

See "Nouvelle Biographie Générale;" NICÉRON, "Mémoires;" HALLER, "Bibliotheca Botanica."

Bauhin, (JEAN,) born at Amiens in 1511, was first physician to Margaret, sister of Francis I. Having become a Protestant, he removed to Bâle, in Switzerland, where he was made dean of the College of Physicians. Died in 1582.

Bauhin, (JEAN,) an eminent botanist and physician, born at Bâle in 1541, was a son of the preceding. He studied botany at Tübingen under Fuchs in 1560, after which he accompanied Gesner on a scientific excursion in Switzerland. He also travelled and studied in France, but was compelled to leave the country on account of his being a Protestant. In 1566 he was appointed professor of rhetoric at Bâle, and in 1570 he became physician to the Duke of Würtemberg at Montbéliard, where he resided until his death. His reputation is founded on two posthumous works, viz.: "Historiæ Plantarum generalis novæ et absolutæ Prodromus," (1619,) and "Historia universalis Plantarum nova," ("A New Universal History of Plants," 3 vols., 1650-51.) Died in 1613.

See PETER BREBACH, "Christlicher Arzt, Leichenpredigt auf J. Bauhin," 1614; SPRENGEL, "Historia Rei Herbariæ;" HALLER, "Bibliotheca Botanica."

Bauhin, (JEAN GASPARD,) son of Gaspard, noticed above, born at Bâle in 1606, was professor of botany in his native city. In 1659 he was appointed physician-in-ordinary to Louis XIV. Died in 1685.

See SPRENGEL, "Historia Rei Herbariæ;" ZWINGER, "Oratio in obitum J. G. Bauhin," 1687.

Bauhin, (JÉRÔME,) son of the preceding, born in 1637, was also a distinguished physician. Died in 1667.

Bauhuis, bŏw'hois, [Lat. BAUHU'SIUS,] (BERNARDUS,) a Jesuit, born at Antwerp in 1575, was the author of Latin epigrams. Died in 1629.

Bauhusius. See BAUHUIS.

Baulacre, bō'lăkR', (LEONARD,) a Swiss *littérateur*, born at Geneva in 1670; died in 1761.

Bauldri or **Bauldry,** bō'dRe', (PAUL,) a French

scholar, born at Rouen in 1629, became professor of sacred history at Utrecht, where he married the daughter of the celebrated Henry Basnage. He published an edition of the "De Mortibus Persecutorum" of Lactantius. Died in 1706.

Baulieu. See BAULOT.

Baulme Saint-Amour, de la, dẹh lä bōm sȧNt'ä'-moor', (JEAN,) a French scholar and Latin poet, born in Franche-Comté in 1539 ; died about 1578.

Baulot, bō'lo', or **Baulieu,** bō'lẹ-uh', (JACQUES,) a French surgeon, celebrated for his skill in lithotomy, born near Lons-le-Saulnier in 1651 ; died in 1720.

Baumann, (CHRISTIAN JAKOB,) a German Protestant and theological writer, born at Berlin in 1725.

Baumann, (NICHOLAS,) professor of history at Rostock, to whom some writers attribute the authorship of "Reineke Fuchs," was born about 1450; died in 1526.

Baumbach, bŏwm'bȧk, (FRIEDRICH AUGUST,) a German composer and writer on music, born at Leipsic in 1753. He was a contributor to the "Dictionary of the Fine Arts" published in 1794. Died in 1813.

Baumbach, (JOHANN BALTHASAR,) a German Orientalist, was professor of Greek and Hebrew at Heidelberg. Died in 1622.

Bäumchen, boim'kẹn, a German sculptor, born at Dusseldorf, worked in Russia. Died in 1789.

Baumé, bō'mä', (ANTOINE,) a celebrated French chemist, born at Senlis in 1728. His early instruction was very defective, but he acquired by his own exertions so thorough a knowledge of chemistry that he was appointed about 1752 professor in the College of Pharmacy in Paris. He founded a manufactory of sal-ammoniac, hitherto imported from Egypt, perfected the scarlet dye of the Gobelin tapestry, improved the manufacture of porcelain, and invented a method of dyeing cloth of two colours. He was also the inventor of the areometer called by his name, and made several other important inventions and discoveries. He was elected to the Academy of Sciences in 1773. Among his most valuable works are his "Elements of Pharmacy, Theoretical and Practical," (1762, 8vo,) "Plan of a Course of Experimental and Rational Chemistry," (1757,) and "Manual of Chemistry," (1763.) Died in 1804.

See CADET DE GASSICOURT, "Éloge de Baumé," 1806; "Biographie Médicale;" QUÉRARD, "La France Littéraire."

Baume, de la, dẹh lä bōm, (NICOLAS AUGUSTE,) Marquis de Montrevel, born in 1645, distinguished himself by his bravery at the siege of Lille and at the battles of Namur, Luxemburg, and Cassel, and was made a marshal in 1703. While dining with the Duke of Biron, he accidentally overturned a salt-cellar, when he exclaimed, "I am a dead man !" and died a few days after, the victim of his superstitious fears, (1716.)

See SAINT-SIMON, "Mémoires."

Baume des Dossat, de la, dẹh lä bōm dạ do'sä', (JACQUES FRANÇOIS,) a French *littérateur,* born at Carpentras in 1705 ; died in 1756.

Baume Montrevel, de la, dẹh lä bōm môNtR'vĕl', (CLAUDE,) Archbishop of Besançon, in France, born in 1531 ; died in 1584.

Baume Saint-Amour, de la, dẹh lä bōm sȧnt'-ä'moor', (PHILIPPE,) a governor of Franche-Comté, which was conquered from Spain by Louis XIV. of France in 1668. Died about 1670.

Baumeister, bŏw'mī'stẹr, (FRIEDRICH CHRISTIAN,) a German philosophical writer, born in Saxe-Gotha in 1709, studied at Jena under the celebrated Wolf, of whose system he was an advocate. Died in 1785.

See BRIEGLEB, "Epistola de Vita, Moribus, etc. Fr. C. Baumeisteri," 1766.

Baumeister, (JOHANN WILHELM,) a German, born at Gmünd in 1804, was appointed in 1839 professor in the veterinary school at Stuttgart. He wrote several treatises on the diseases and management of animals. Died in 1846.

Baumer, bŏw'mẹr, written also **Bäumer,** (GEORG,) a German sculptor, born in Bavaria about 1763. Among his works are a bas-relief representing a descent from the cross, and a bust of Napoleon. Died about 1830.

Baumer, (JOHANN PAUL,) a German physician, born about 1725, lived at Erfurt ; died in 1771.

Baumer, (JOHANN WILHELM,) a German naturalist, and professor of medicine at Giessen, born at Rehweiler, in Franconia, in 1719. He published "The Natural History of the Mineral Kingdom," (1780,) and other scientific treatises. Died in 1788.

See ERSCH und GRUBER, "Allgemeine Encyklopaedie."

Baumes, bōm, (JEAN BAPTISTE TIMOTHÉE,) a French physician and medical writer, professor in the medical school of Montpellier, was born at Lunel in 1777; died in 1828.

Baumgaertner. See BAUMGÄRTNER.

Baumgarten, bŏwm'gaR'tẹn, (ALEXANDER GOTTLIEB,) a celebrated German philosopher and disciple of Wolf, born at Berlin in 1714, became in 1740 professor of philosophy at Frankfort-on-the-Oder. He is regarded as the founder of the science or philosophy of the Beautiful, to which he gave the name of "Æsthetics." Among his principal works are his "Elements of Belles-Lettres," (3 vols., 1748,) "Metaphysica," "Ethica Philosophia," and "Æsthetica," (2 vols., 1750, unfinished.) Died at Frankfort-on-the-Oder in 1762.

See MEYER, "Leben Alexander G. Baumgartens," 1763; SEMLER, "Ehrengedächtniss," 1758; "Biographie Universelle."

Baumgarten, (JOHANN CHRISTIAN GOTTLOB,) a German botanist, born at Lucknau, in Lusatia, in 1765, published the "Flora of Transylvania," and other botanical works. Died about 1830.

Baumgarten, (MARTIN A.,) a German traveller, born in 1473, visited Egypt, Arabia, and Palestine. An account of his travels was published in Churchill's Collection. Died in 1535.

See NIEBUHR, "Voyage en Arabie."

Baumgarten, (SIGISMUND JAKOB,) a German theologian, and professor of theology at Halle, born at Wolmirstädt in 1706, was a brother of Alexander Gottlieb, noticed above. He was the author of "Moral Theology," (1738,) "Abridgment of Ecclesiastical History," (3 vols., 1742,) and other works. He also translated from the English the "Universal History of the World," (16 vols., 1744,) which was continued after his death by his friend Semler. Died in 1757.

See SEMLER, "Programma in Memoriam S. J. Baumgarten," 1757.

Baumgarten-Crusius, bŏwm'gaR'tẹn kroo'ze-ús, (DETLEV KARL WILHELM,) a German scholar, born at Dresden in 1786. He published editions of Plutarch's "Agesilaus," of Xenophon, Suetonius, and other classics, and was the author of moral and educational treatises. He lived at Meissen, where he died in 1845.

See A. BAUMGARTEN-CRUSIUS, "Leben des Rectors D. C. W. Baumgarten-Crusius," 1853.

Baumgarten-Crusius, (LUDWIG FRIEDRICH OTTO,) a learned German theologian, brother of the preceding, born at Merseburg in 1788. He published, among other works, a "Manual of the History of Dogmas," (1831,) "Compendium of the History of Dogmas," (1840,) and "Observations on some Writings of Lamennais." He was professor of theology at Jena from 1817 until his death in 1843.

Baumgartner, bŏwm'gaRt'nẹr, (G. J.,) a Swiss jurist and politician, born at Saint Gall in 1797.

Baumgärtner or **Baumgaertner,** bŏwm'gȧRt'nẹr, (JOHANN,) a German sculptor, born in Bavaria in 1744 ; died in 1792.

Baumgärtner or **Baumgaertner,** (JOHANN BAPTIST,) a German musician and writer on music, born at Augsburg about 1725 ; died in 1782.

Baumgärtner, (JOHANN WOLFGANG,) a Tyrolese artist and skilful glass-painter, born about 1710.

Baumgärtner, von, fon bŏwm'gaRt'nẹr, (ANDREAS,) a German savant and minister of trade and public works, born at Friedberg, in Bohemia, in 1793. He became professor of physics at Vienna in 1823. He wrote, among other works, "Mechanics in their Application to the Arts and Industry." In 1851 he was elected president of the Academy of Sciences at Vienna.

Baumhauer, bŏwm'hŏw'ẹr, a German sculptor, lived about 1620.

Baumstark, bŏwm'staRk, (ANTON,) a German philologist, born in 1800. He published editions of Cæsar, Quintus Curtius, and other classics, made a German

---

translation of Cæsar, and wrote a "Commentary on the Poetry of Horace."

Baumstark, (EDUARD,) a German writer, brother of the preceding, born near Baden in 1807. He became in 1839 professor of financial science and political economy at Greifswalde, and translated into German Ricardo's "Principles of Political Economy."

Baune, de la, deh lǎ bōn, (JACQUES,) a French Jesuit and Latin writer, born in Paris in 1649; died in 1726.

Bauny, bō'ne', (ÉTIENNE,) a French Jesuit, noted for his works on casuistry, born at Mouzon in 1564; died in 1649.

Baur, bŏwr, (FERDINAND CHRISTIAN,) a German critic and Protestant theologian of much influence, born at Schneiden in June, 1792, is called the founder of the Tübingen school of theology. About 1826 he became professor of theology at Tübingen. He published, besides other works, a "History of the Doctrine of the Atonement," (1838,) and "The Christian Dogma of the Trinity and Incarnation," (1843.) Died in 1861.

Baur, (FRIEDRICH WILHELM,) a German general, born at Bieber, in Hanau, in 1735. He entered the service of Frederick the Great in the Seven Years' war, and was subsequently invited to Russia by Catherine II., who made him engineer-general and conferred on him other distinctions. He wrote, in French, "Geographical and Historical Memoirs of Wallachia." Died in 1783.

See STRIEDER, "Hessische Gelehrten-Geschichte."

Baur, Bawer, or **Bauer,** bŏw'er, (JOHANN WILHELM,) a German painter and engraver, born at Strasburg about 1600, was a pupil of Brendel. Among his best works are prints from his own designs of the "Metamorphoses" of Ovid. Died in 1640.

See LE BLANC, "Manuel de l'Amateur d'Estampes."

Baur, bŏwR, (NICOLAAS,) a Dutch painter of marine views and landscapes, born at Harlingen in 1767. His "Bombardment of Algiers" is regarded as his masterpiece. Died in 1820.

See NAGLER, "Neues Allgemeines Künstler-Lexikon."

Baur, (SAMUEL,) a German scholar and miscellaneous writer, born at Ulm in 1768, was a contributor to Ersch and Gruber's "Encyklopaedie." Died in 1832.

Baurenfeind, bŏw'ren-fīnt', written also **Bauernfeind,** (GEORG WILHELM,) a German artist, born at Nuremberg, executed several of the designs for Niebuhr's "Travels in Arabia." Died in 1763.

Bauria, bŏw're-â, (ANDREA,) an Italian theologian of Ferrara, wrote, in Latin, a "Defence of the Apostolic Power against Martin Luther," (1521.)

Bausa, bŏw'sâ, (GREGORIO,) a Spanish painter, born in 1596, lived at Valencia; died in 1656.

Bausan, bō'zŏn', (JEAN,) a naval officer, born at Gaeta in 1757. He fought for the French, under Massena, at Gaeta, in 1806, and gained a victory over the English and Sicilians in 1808. Died in 1821.

Bausch, bŏwsh, (JOHANN LORENZ,) a German physician, born at Schweinfurt in 1605, was the founder and the first president of the Academy of the Curious in Nature, (1652.) Died in 1665.

Bause, bŏw'zeh, (JOHANN FRIEDRICH,) an eminent German engraver, born at Halle in 1738, was an intimate friend and pupil of Wille, whom he took for his model. Bause was appointed professor of engraving in the Academy of Arts at Leipsic. He executed numerous portraits of the celebrated writers of his time. Died in 1814. His daughter Juliana Wilhelmine was also a skilful engraver.

See LE BLANC, "Manuel de l'Amateur d'Estampes;" NAGLER, "Neues Allgemeines Künstler-Lexikon."

Bause, (THEODOR,) a German jurist and antiquary, born in Saxony in 1752, became professor at the University of Moscow, and corresponding member of the Academy of Sciences at Saint Petersburg. Died in 1812.

Bausner, bŏws'ner, (BARTHOLOMEW,) a physician and writer, born in Transylvania about 1629; died in 1682.

Bausset, de, deh bō'sȧ', (LOUIS FRANÇOIS,) a distinguished cardinal and writer, born at Pondicherry in 1748, came at an early age to France, where he rose through various promotions to be Bishop of Alais in 1784. In 1791 he signed the protest of the French bishops against the civil constitution of the clergy. He entered the Chamber of Peers after the second restoration, and in 1817 was made a cardinal, having previously been elected to the French Academy. His "History of Fénelon" (3 vols.) came out in 1808, and met with the most favourable reception; it was followed in 1814 by the "History of Bossuet," which was less successful. He was also the author of several miscellaneous treatises. Died in 1824.

See M. DE VILLENEUVE, "Notice historique sur le Cardinal de Bausset," 1824; DE QUÉLEN, "Discours sur Bausset," 1829.

Bausset-Roquefort, bō'sȧ' rok'foR', (PIERRE FRANÇOIS GABRIEL RAYMOND IGNACE FERDINAND,) COUNT OF, cousin of Louis François, noticed above, born at Béziers in 1757, became Archbishop of Aix. Died in 1829.

Bautain, bō'tăN', (LOUIS,) a French theologian and philosophical writer, born in Paris in 1796. He was appointed in 1838 dean of the literary faculty at Strasburg, and in 1849 director of the college of Juilly. He was the author of "The Philosophy of Christianity," (1835,) and other similar works.

See QUÉRARD, "La France Littéraire," (Supplément.)

Bauter, bō'tȧ', (CHARLES,) a French dramatic poet, born in Paris about 1580; died about 1630.

Bautru, bō'trü', (GUILLAUME,) Count of Serrant, a French nobleman, diplomatist, and celebrated wit, born at Angers in 1588, was one of the first members of the French Academy. Died in 1665.

Bauvin, bō'văN', (JEAN GRÉGOIRE,) a French littérateur and lawyer, born at Arras in 1714, was professor at the military school in his native city. Died in 1776.

Baux, bō, (PIERRE,) a French physician, born at Nimes in 1679, wrote, among other works, a "Treatise on the Plague." Died in 1732.

Bauza, bŏw'thâ, (Don FELIPE,) a Spanish geographer, born about 1750, became director of the hydrographic depot at Madrid. He published some excellent maps of South America. Died in 1833.

Bava, bâ'vâ, (GAETANO EMANUELE,) Count of San Paolo, a Piedmontese savant, born at Fossano in 1737, published a "Historical Survey of the Changes and Progress of Sciences, Arts, etc. from the Eleventh to the Eighteenth Century." Died in 1829.

See TIPALDO, "Biografia degli Italiani illustri."

Bava, (GIOVANNI BATTISTA,) a general, born at Vercelli, in Piedmont, in 1790, served with distinction in the French armies and in the war of Italian independence.

Bavay, de, deh bâ'vȧ', (PAUL IGNATIUS,) a Flemish physician and chemist, born at Brussels in 1704, was professor of anatomy and surgery and head-physician of the military hospitals in that city. Died in 1768.

Baverel, bȧv'rěl', (JEAN PIERRE,) a French ecclesiastic and littérateur, born in Paris in 1744; died in 1822.

Baverini, bâ-vâ-ree'nee, (FRANCESCO,) an Italian musician, born about 1420, is said to have composed the music for "The Conversion of Saint Paul," ("San Paolo,") the first opera ever represented.

See FÉTIS, "Biographie Universelle des Musiciens."

Bavia, de, dȧ bâ-vee'â, (LUIS,) a Spanish historian, born at Madrid, wrote a continuation of Illesca's "History of the Popes." Died in 1628.

Baviera, bâ-ve-â'râ, (MARCANTONIO,) an Italian jurist, lived about 1490, was professor of civil law at Pisa and Padua.

Baville, bâ'věl', (ARNAUD,) a French general, born at Fronton in 1757, died of a wound received at Liegnitz in 1813.

Bavisano, bâ-ve-sâ'no, (FRANCESCO DOMENICO,) born at Alba, in Montferrat, was appointed in 1570 physician to the Duke of Savoy.

Bā'vĭ-us, a Latin poet in the time of Augustus, who, with his friend Mævius, is known only from his envious and malicious attacks on Horace and Virgil. He is satirized by the latter in his "Bucolics."

Bavo, bâ'vo, or **Baf,** bâf, [Fr. BAVON, bâ'vôN',] SAINT, sometimes called **Allowin,** born in Brabant about 589, was the patron of the city of Ghent. Died about 653.

See JEAN DE THIELRODE, "Chronique de Saint-Bavon à Gand," 1798.

·Bavo, di, de bâ'vo, (GOTTOFREDO,) president of the council of Charles Emmanuel, Duke of Savoy, wrote a valuable work "On Criminal Law," (1607.)

Bavon, the French of BAVO, which see.

Bavoux, bȧ'voo', (ÉVARISTE,) son of François Nicolas, noticed below, was a deputy in 1852 to the legislative body. He was the author of "Political Philosophy," (1840,) and other works.

Bavoux, (FRANÇOIS NICOLAS,) a French jurist and legal writer, born at Saint-Claude in 1774, was elected to the Chamber of Deputies, and about 1830 became counsellor in the court of accounts. Died in 1848.

Bawd'wen, (WILLIAM,) an English divine, who published in 1809–12 two volumes of a translation of the "Domesday-Book." He died soon after, leaving the work unfinished.

Bawr. See BAUR.

Bawr, bŏwr, (ALEXANDRINE SOPHIE **Goury de Champgrand**—goo're' deh shŏN'grŏN',) BARONESS, a novelist and dramatic writer, of French extraction, born at Stuttgart in 1776. She was first married to the celebrated Count de Saint-Simon, who, not long after, requested a divorce on the grounds that it was not fit that he, being the first man in the world, should have any other than the first woman for his wife. She was subsequently married to the Baron de Bawr, who died soon afterwards. Madame de Bawr published a number of popular works, among which we may name the comedy of "Money and Address," and "Raoul ou l'Énéide," a novel.

See QUÉRARD, "La France Littéraire," (Supplément.)

Bax'I-us, (NICAISIUS,) a Flemish scholar and Latin poet, born at Antwerp about 1595.

Bax'ter, (ANDREW,) an eminent Scottish philosopher and metaphysician, born at Aberdeen about 1686. His principal work is entitled "Inquiry into the Nature of the Human Soul," (1737;) it is commended by Dugald Stewart and Bishop Warburton, who observes of the book that it is "one of the most finished of the kind that the present times, greatly advanced in true philosophy, have produced." Died in 1750.

See "Biographia Britannica."

Bax'ter, (RICHARD,) an eminent English nonconformist divine, born at Rowdon, in Shropshire, on the 12th of November, 1615. He was a man of great learning, though not educated at any college. He was ordained in 1638, was chosen vicar of Kidderminster in 1640, and soon became distinguished as an eloquent preacher. In the civil war he was disposed to be neutral, and to mediate between the hostile parties. About 1645 he accepted the place of chaplain to a regiment of Cromwell's army; but he afterwards showed himself hostile to the government of the Protector. He published in 1650 "The Saint's Everlasting Rest," a work which is generally and justly admired. At the restoration (1660) he was appointed one of the chaplains of Charles II.; but he was separated from the Anglican Church by the Act of Uniformity in 1662, after he had refused a bishopric. He subsequently preached at Acton, and after the Act of Indulgence in 1672 he removed to London, where he lectured in Pinners' Hall. Among his principal works are "Methodus Theologiæ," (1674,) "Catholic Theology," and a "Call to the Unconverted," (1669,) of which about twenty thousand copies were sold in one year. In 1685 Baxter was tried before the notorious Jeffries on a charge of sedition, founded on a passage in one of his works. He was fined five hundred marks, for the non-payment of which he was imprisoned about eighteen months. Died in December, 1691. In his character, zeal and moderation were happily united. He was the founder of a new school of theology, which bears his name. "He discovers a manly eloquence," says Doddridge, "and the most evident proofs of an amazing genius, with respect to which he may not improperly be called the *English Demosthenes.*" "Pray read with great attention," says Coleridge, "Baxter's Life of himself; it is an inestimable work. There is no substitute for it in a course of study for a clergyman or public man."

See his own "Narrative of the most memorable Passages of his Life and Times," 1696; E. CALAMY, "Life of Baxter," 1713; Rev. WILLIAM ORME, "Life and Times of R. Baxter," prefixed to an edition of Baxter's works in 23 vols., 1830; AUGUST NEANDER, "R. Baxter ein Mann der Wahrhaft rechten Mitte," etc., Berlin, 1833; MACAULAY, "History of England," vol. i. chap. iv., vol. iii. chap. xi.; "Edinburgh Review" for October, 1839.

Baxter, (THOMAS,) an English mathematician, published "Principles of Astronomy and Natural Philosophy," (1740.)

Baxter, (THOMAS,) an English artist, especially distinguished as a painter of china, born in 1782. Among his master-pieces are copies of the works of Reynolds and West. Died in 1821.

Baxter, (WILLIAM,) an English scholar, born in Shropshire in 1650, was a nephew of the celebrated Richard Baxter. He prepared editions of Horace and Anacreon, and a Latin Grammar, and wrote, in Latin, a "Glossary of British Antiquities." Baxter's edition of Horace formed the basis of the one subsequently published by Gesner. Died in 1723.

See "Biographia Britannica."

Baxter, (WILLIAM EDWARD,) a British Liberal politician, born at Dundee in 1825. He was returned to Parliament for Montrose in 1855. He published "America and the Americans," (1850,) and other works.

See "Quarterly Review" for April, 1850.

Bay, de, deh bȧ, (ALEXANDRE,) MARQUIS, a French general, born at Salins about 1650, served with distinction in the war of the Spanish succession. He was appointed viceroy of the province of Estremadura in 1705, and created a knight of the Golden Fleece in 1708. Died in 1715.

Bayam, bȧ-yŏwn', (JOZÉ PEREIRA,) a Portuguese historian and ecclesiastic, born near Coimbra in 1690, wrote a history of Portugal and the achievements of Don Sebastian, (1737,) also a "Treatise on Purgatory," (1742.) Died in 1743.

Bayanne, bȧ'yȧn', (ALPHONSE HUBERT **de Lattier**—deh lȧ'te-à',) a French cardinal, born at Valence in 1739, held several offices under the empire, and was made a peer by Louis XVIII. He wrote, in Italian, a valuable work on the malaria in Italy. Died in 1818.

Bayard, bȧ'yȧr', (FERDINAND MARIE,) a French writer, born at Moulins-la-Marche in 1763, published "Travels in the Interior of the United States in 1791," and other works. Died about 1818.

Bayard, bi'ard, (GEORGE D.,) an American general, born in New York about 1836, graduated at West Point in 1856. He became a captain of cavalry in the regular army in August, 1861, and a brigadier-general of volunteers in 1862. He distinguished himself as a leader of cavalry in several actions in Virginia under General Pope. He was killed at Fredericksburg in December, 1862.

Bayard, (JAMES A.,) a distinguished American statesman and lawyer, born in Philadelphia in 1767. He graduated at Princeton College in 1784, and commenced the practice of law in Delaware. In 1796 he was elected a member of Congress, in which he acted with the Federal party and acquired a high reputation as an orator and constitutional lawyer. He supported Jefferson for President in preference to Burr when the duty devolved on the House of Representatives to elect one of those two candidates in 1801; and the result of this contest is ascribed chiefly to his influence. He represented Delaware in the Senate of the United States from 1804 to 1813, and opposed the war of 1812. He was one of the commissioners who negotiated the Treaty of Ghent with Great Britain in 1814, soon after which he was appointed minister to the court of Saint Petersburg; but he declined that mission, saying that he had no wish to serve the administration except when his services were necessary. He died in August, 1815, soon after his return from Europe.

His son JAMES A. was elected a Senator of the United States for Delaware in 1850.

Bayard, (JEAN BAPTISTE FRANÇOIS,) a French jurist and legal writer, born in Paris in 1750, was appointed by the Directory a judge of the court of cassation about 1799. Died in 1800.

Bayard, (JEAN FRANÇOIS ALFRED,) a French *littérateur*, born at Charolles in 1796, was the author of numerous very popular comedies and vaudevilles; among others, of "Christine, or the Queen of Sixteen Years," (1828,) and "The Promenade to Vaucluse." Died in Paris in 1853.

Bayard, (JOHN,) a patriot of the American Revolution, born in Cecil county, Maryland, in 1738. At the battle

ā, ē, ī, ō, ū, ȳ, *long;* ȧ, ė, ȯ, same, less prolonged; ă, ĕ, ĭ, ŏ, ŭ, y̆, *short;* ạ, ẹ, ị, ọ, *obscure:* fär, fåll, fåt; mēt; nŏt; gōŏd; mōŏn;

of Trenton he commanded a battalion of Philadelphia militia. In 1785 he was chosen a member of the Congress of the Confederation. Mr. Bayard was an intimate friend of Whitefield. Died in 1807.

Bayard, bā′erd, [Fr. pron. bȧ′yȧʀ′,] (PIERRE **du Terrail**—dü tȧ′rȧl′,) called "le chevalier sans peur et sans reproche," ("the knight without fear and without reproach,") was born at Castle Bayard, near Grenoble, in 1475. Having attracted the notice of Charles VIII. by his skill in horsemanship and knightly accomplishments, he accompanied that monarch on his expedition to Naples in 1494, and performed remarkable feats of valour at the battle of Fornovo. After the death of Charles he took part in the Italian campaigns of Louis XII., and at the "battle of the Spurs," in 1513, he was chiefly instrumental in saving the French army from total rout when pursued by the English cavalry. On the invasion of Italy by Francis I., Bayard took Prosper Colonna prisoner, and had a prominent part in the sanguinary battle of Marignano, (1515,) after which, at the request of Francis I., he conferred upon that sovereign the honour of knighthood. In 1522 he defended the frontier town of Mézières against the forces of Charles V., an exploit which, in the words of Dampmartin, "would have sufficed for the glory of any other than Bayard." Being sent in 1524 against the imperial army under the Duke of Bourbon, Bayard assumed the chief command after Bonnivet was disabled by a wound. While exerting himself to enable the French to effect a retreat, he was mortally wounded, and died soon after on the field of battle. "Perhaps no other person," says Southey, "who acted so unimportant a part in the world ever attained so wide and just a renown." ("Quarterly Review," vol. xxxii.) The same writer adds that he was indebted for his renown to his genuine worth,—his generosity and virtue.

See SYMPHORIEN CHAMPIER, "La Vie et les Gestes de Bayard," 1525; L. A. BAQUILLOT, "Histoire du Chevalier Bayard," 1702; GUYARD DE BERVILLE, "Histoire du Chevalier Bayard," 1760; Rev. JOSEPH STERLING, "Life of Chevalier Bayard," 1781; BUCHOLZ, "Bayard," Berlin, 1801; PILLOT, "Essai sur le Chevalier Bayard," 1816; P. COHEN, "Histoire de Pierre du Terrail," 1821; DELANDINE DE SAINT-ESPRIT, "Histoire de Bayard," 1842; W. G. SIMMS, "Life of Chevalier Bayard," New York, 1847; Major-General JOHN MITCHELL, "Biographies of Eminent Soldiers of the Last Four Centuries," 1865.

Bayard, (SAMUEL,) an American jurist, born about 1765. He published a "Digest of American Cases on the Law of Evidence," 1810, and an "Abstract of the Laws of the United States." Died in 1840.

Bayazeed, Bayazîd, or **Bajasîd,** bȧ′yȧ-zeed′, I., less correctly, **Baj′a-zêt,** Sultan of the Ottomans, surnamed ILDEREEM, (ILDERÎM,) or "Lightning," on account of his rapid movements, born in 1347, was the son of Amurath I. He ascended the throne in 1390, and within a few years subjugated Bulgaria, the greater part of Asia Minor, and a considerable portion of Greece. In 1396 he gained a signal victory over the allied army of the Hungarians, Poles, and French, at Nicopolis, from which Sigismund, King of Hungary, with difficulty escaped. Tamerlane having invaded Asia Minor, a battle was fought between him and Bayazeed near Angora in 1491, in which the army of the latter was totally defeated and he himself taken prisoner. It is related that Bayazeed was confined by his conqueror in an iron cage. He died in 1403, and was succeeded by Mahomet I.

See VON HAMMER, "Geschichte des Osmanischen Reichs."

Bayazeed, Bayazîd, or **Bajazet II.,** born in 1447, succeeded his father, Mahomet II., in 1481. He was engaged in almost constant warfare with the Hungarians, Poles, Venetians, and Persians, and was at length deposed by his son Selim. Died in 1512.

See VON HAMMER, "Geschichte des Osmanischen Reichs."

Baye, bā, (FRANÇOIS **Berthelot** — bĕʀt′lo′,) MARQUIS OF, a French general, wrote an "Account of the Campaigns of Marshal de Créqui in 1677." Died in 1776.

Bayen, bȧ′yŏn′, (PIERRE,) a French chemist and pharmacist, born at Châlons-sur-Marne in 1725, was the author of treatises on the mineral waters of France, and on the metallic oxides. Died in 1798.

See HOEFER, "Histoire de la Chimie."

Bayen y Sabias. See BAYEU Y SUBIAS.

Bayer, bȧ-yair′, (FRANCISCO PEREZ,) a Spanish antiquary, born at Valencia in 1711. He was successively

professor of Hebrew at Salamanca, preceptor of the Infant Don Gabriel, and keeper of the library at Madrid. He wrote, among other works, a treatise "On the Alphabet and Language of the Phœnicians and their Colonies," (1772.) Died in 1794.

Bayer, bī′er, (GOTTLIEB SIEGFRIED,) an eminent German Orientalist, particularly distinguished as a Chinese scholar, born at Königsberg in 1694, was a grandson of the astronomer Johann Bayer. In 1726 he was invited to become professor of Greek and Roman antiquities at Saint Petersburg. His principal work is entitled "Museum Sinicum," (2 vols., 1730.) It contains a Chinese grammar and lexicon, a treatise on Chinese chronology, and extracts from Chinese works. He also wrote, in Latin, a valuable "History of Osrhœna and Edessa, illustrated by Coins," and was a contributor to the "Acta Eruditorum," and the "Memoirs" of the Academy of Saint Petersburg. Died in 1738.

Bayer,(HIERONYMUS JOHANN PAUL,) a German jurist, and professor of law at Munich, born at Rauris in 1792.

Bayer, (JOHANN,) a German astronomer and Protestant preacher, born at Augsburg about 1572. He published in 1603 an excellent work called "Uranometria," a description of the constellations, with charts, in which the stars were for the first time designated by the letters of the Greek alphabet. This very convenient innovation was universally approved. He died in 1660.

See MONTUCLA, "Histoire des Mathématiques;" ERSCH und GRUBER, "Allgemeine Encyklopaedie."

Bayer, (JOHANN WOLFGANG,) a German Jesuit, born at Schlesslitz, in Bavaria, was sent in 1749 as a missionary to Peru.

Bayer de Boppart, bī′er deh bop′paʀt, (CONRAD,) became Bishop of Metz in 1415; died in 1459.

Bayer de Boppart, (THIERRY,) Bishop of Metz, was ambassador of the emperor Charles IV. at Rome. Died in 1384.

Bayes, bāz, (JOSHUA,) a Presbyterian nonconformist minister, born at Sheffield in 1671, preached in London. Died in 1746.

Bayes, (THOMAS,) a son of the preceding, was a Presbyterian minister at Tunbridge Wells, and noted as a writer on mathematics. Died in 1761.

Bayeu y Subias, bī′ê-oo e soo-bee′ȧs, sometimes incorrectly written **Bayen y Sabias,** (FRANCISCO,) an able Spanish painter, born at Saragossa in 1734. He worked at Madrid, and obtained the title of painter to the king. Died about 1795.

See BERMUDEZ, "Diccionario Historico."

Bayeux, bȧ′yuh′, (GEORGE,) a French jurist and littérateur, born at Caen about 1752. He made a prose translation of the "Fasti" of Ovid, accompanied with valuable notes, and wrote, among other works, "Reflections on the Reign of Trajan," (1787.) Having been appointed royal commissioner, he was killed in a mob at Caen in 1792.

Bayf. See BAIF, (LAZARE.)

Bayhoffer. See BAYRHOFFER.

Bayle, bȧl, (ANTOINE LAURENT JESSÉ,) a French physician, nephew of Gaspard Laurent, noticed below, was born at Vernet in 1799. He wrote, among other works, an "Elementary Treatise on Anatomy," and was principal editor of the "Encyclopédie des Sciences."

Bayle, (FRANÇOIS,) a French physician and writer, born at Saint-Bertrand-de-Commines in 1622, was professor of medicine at Toulouse. Died in 1709.

Bayle, (GASPARD LAURENT,) an eminent French physician, born at Vernet, in Provence, in 1774. He graduated in Paris, where he was subsequently appointed physician to the emperor Napoleon. He wrote, among other treatises, "Researches on Pulmonary Consumption," (1810,) a work of high reputation, and was a contributor to the "Dictionnaire des Sciences médicales." Died in Paris in 1816.

Bayle, (MOÏSE,) a French revolutionist and member of the National Convention, born in Languedoc about 1760, voted for the death of the king and the Girondists. He was appointed in 1793 president of the Convention. He was the author of "Letters to Fréron," (1795.) Died about 1815.

Bayle, (PIERRE,) a celebrated philosopher and critic,

born at Carlat, in Ariége, in the south of France, on the 18th of November, 1647, was a son of a Protestant minister. He studied at the college of Toulouse, where he joined the Roman Catholic Church; but he returned to his former religion about a year later, and retired for safety to Geneva, (1670.) For several years he served as private tutor at Geneva, Rouen, and Paris. In 1675 he was appointed professor of philosophy at the Protestant academy of Sedan, which was suppressed by Louis XIV. in 1681. To reassure the public, alarmed by the comet of 1680, he produced his admirable letter on the Comet, ("Pensées diverses sur la Comète," 1682.) He became professor of philosophy and history at Rotterdam in 1681. He defended the Calvinists against the misrepresentations of Maimbourg, in his "Critique générale de l'Histoire de Calvinisme de Maimbourg," (1682,) which was very successful and contributed much to increase his reputation. In 1684 he began to issue monthly a critical journal or review, entitled "Nouvelles de la République des Lettres," which obtained some reputation, but was discontinued in 1687.

His repose was disturbed by the jealous enmity of Jurieu, his former friend, who accused him of being the author of an anonymous work, "Avis aux Réfugiés," which was injurious to the Protestant cause. The magistrates of Rotterdam deprived him of his professorship in 1693, actuated, it appears, by a suspicion that he was not sound in faith. His principal work is a "Historical and Critical Dictionary," ("Dictionnaire historique et critique," 2 vols. folio, 1696,) which obtained extensive popularity but was censured for its skeptical tendency. It appears to have exerted a great influence over the literature and philosophy of Europe. A third and enlarged edition was published by Prosper Marchand, (4 vols., 1720.) This dictionary was translated into English and other languages. As a writer, Bayle was remarkable for wit, vivacity, dialectical skill, and love of paradox. "An admirable dialectician rather than a profound philosopher," says Voltaire, "he knew scarcely anything of physical science." "Bayle is admirable," says Hallam, "in exposing the fallacies of dogmatism, the perplexities of philosophy, the weaknesses of those who affect to guide the opinions of mankind. But, wanting the necessary conditions of good reasoning, an earnest desire to reason well, a moral rectitude, . . . he often avails himself of petty cavils and becomes dogmatical in his very doubts. . . . The sophistry of Bayle, however, bears no proportion to his just and acute observations." ("Introduction to the Literature of Europe.") He died at Rotterdam in December, 1706. He is said to have been strictly moral, disinterested, and indifferent to temporal riches. Warburton speaks of him as one "who with a soul superior to the sharpest attacks of fortune and a heart practised to the best philosophy," yet "struck into the province of paradox as an exercise for the unwearied vigour of his mind." ("Divine Legation," book i.)

See Du Revert, "Histoire de Bayle et de ses Ouvrages," 1716; Pierre des Maizeaux, "Vie de Pierre Bayle," 1712; Feuerbach, "Pierre Bayle, seine Verdienste für die Geschichte der Philosophie," 1838; "Encyclopædia Britannica;" Sainte-Beuve, in the "Revue des Deux Mondes" for December, 1835.

Bayle, sometimes written **Baille,** (Pierre,) a French Jacobin, born at Marseilles, was a member of the National Convention, where he voted for the death of the king. He was arrested at Toulon when that city was given up to the English, and was put to death in prison, (1793.)

Bayley, bā′le, (Edward,) an English physician, wrote an "Account of the Earthquake at Havana in 1734." Died in 1760.

Bayley, (Frederick W. N. B.,) an English *littérateur,* and first editor of the "Illustrated London News," born in 1807. He wrote the "New Tale of a Tub," in verse, "Little Red-Riding-Hood," and other poems. Died in 1852.

Bayley, (Sir John,) an English jurist, born in 1763. He published a "Summary of the Laws of Bills of Exchange," (1789,) and became a justice of the king's bench in 1808. Died in 1841.

Bayley, (Richard,) an American physician, born in Fairfield, Connecticut, in 1745. He began to practise medicine in the city of New York in 1772, and advocated a new mode of treating croup, which was extensively

adopted. He published a "Letter on the Croup," (1781,) and an "Essay on the Yellow Fever," (1797.) In 1793 he became professor of surgery in Columbia College. Died in 1801.

See Thacher, "Medical Biography."

Baylies. See Bailies, (William.)

Baylies, bā′lēz, (Francis,) an American politician, born in 1784, was a member of Congress from Massachusetts. He wrote a "History of the Old Colony of Plymouth," (1828.) Died in 1852.

Bay′ly or **Bai′ley,** (Anselm,) an English scholar, published some theological and critical works.

Bayly, (John,) son of Lewis, Bishop of Bangor, born in 1595, was the author of a work entitled "The Angel Guardian." Died in 1633.

Bayly, (Lewis,) Bishop of Bangor, born in Caermarthen about 1565, was the author of a very popular work, entitled "Practice of Piety." It was translated into Welsh and several other languages. Died in 1632.

Bayly, (Thomas,) an English divine and controversialist, was a son of Lewis, Bishop of Bangor. He was converted to Catholicism about 1650.

Bayly, (Thomas Haynes,) an English lyric poet and miscellaneous writer, born near Bath in 1797. His works include novels and tales and numerous dramatic pieces. His songs enjoy great popularity. Died in 1839.

Bay′lў, (Thomas Henry,) an American politician, born in Accomac county, Virginia, in 1810, was a lawyer. He was a member of Congress from 1844 to 1856, and was chairman of the committee of ways and means during several sessions. Died in 1856.

Bayly, (William,) an English astronomer, sent by the Royal Society in 1769 to the North Cape, to observe the transit of Venus. Died in 1810.

Bāy′nam or **Bāyn′ham,** (William,) an American surgeon and anatomist, born in Caroline county, Virginia, in 1749. He studied in London, where he passed many years, and became an excellent anatomist. He returned to America about 1785, and settled in Essex county, Virginia. He performed many difficult surgical operations with success, and wrote several articles for medical journals. Died in 1814.

See Thacher, "Medical Biography."

Bayne, (Alexander,) a Scottish jurist, born in Fifeshire, was appointed in 1722 to the chair of Scottish law at Edinburgh, then recently established. He wrote a treatise "On the Rise and Progress of the Law of Scotland, and the Method of studying it," and edited Hope's "Minor Practicks," which had remained in manuscript nearly a century. Died in 1737.

Bayne or **Baine,** bān, (James,) a Scottish dissenting divine and eloquent preacher, born in 1710. He preached in Edinburgh. Died in 1790.

See Chambers, "Biographical Dictionary of Eminent Scotsmen."

Bayne, (William,) an English naval officer, was killed in an engagement between the French and English near the West Indies in 1782.

Bayn′ham, (James,) an English lawyer, who was burned at the stake in 1530 for having denied the real presence in the eucharist.

Bayn′tun, (Sir William Henry,) a British admiral, born about 1765; died in 1840.

Bayon, de, deh bā′yòn′, (Jean,) a French monk and ecclesiastical writer, lived at Bayon about 1290.

Bayrhoffer, bīʀ′hof′fer, incorrectly written **Bayhoffer,** (Karl Theodor,) a German philosopher of the school of Hegel, born at Marburg in 1812. He became professor of philosophy in his native city in 1845. He wrote, among other works, a treatise "On Catholicism in Germany," "Idea and History of Philosophy," (1838,) and "Researches on the Essence, History, and Criticism of Religion," (1849.) He was an active radical politician in 1848.

Bayro. See Bairo, (Pietro.)

Bazaine, bā′zȧn′, a French mathematician, born near Metz about the middle of the eighteenth century, wrote a work entitled "French Metrology." Died in 1833.

Bazaine, (François Achille,) a French general, born in 1811. He commanded a brigade at Sevastopol in 1854, and became a general of division in 1855. He obtained, in 1863 or 1864, the chief command of the

French army in Mexico. That army was withdrawn in the latter part of 1866.

Bazaliero, băd-zȧ-le-ā′ro, (CALIGULA,) an Italian poet and bookseller of Bologna, lived about 1480.

Bazan. See BASAN.

Bazancourt, de, dęh bă′zŏṉ′koor′, (JEAN BAPTISTE MARIN ANTOINE **Lecat**—lęh′kă′,) a French general, born at Val-de-Molle in 1767. He served in Egypt and in the Austrian campaign of 1805, and was subsequently created a baron of the empire and commander of the legion of honour. Died in 1830.

See "Victoires et Conquêtes des Français."

Baz′a-rad′, the first Prince of Wallachia of whom history gives a particular account, ruled over that country about 1330.

Bazard, bă′zăR′, (AMAND,) a French journalist, and founder of Carbonarism in France, born in Paris in 1791. He was a principal contributor to the journal entitled "L'Aristarque," and was subsequently associate editor of "Le Producteur," the organ of the Saint-Simonians, whose system he had adopted. Becoming dissatisfied with the extreme doctrines of that sect, he proclaimed himself the head of the new Saint-Simonian hierarchy. Died in 1832.

See MICHAUD et VILLENAVE, "Histoire du Saint-Simonisme," 1847.

Baze, băz, (N.,) a French lawyer, born at Agen in 1800, was elected in 1848 to the Legislative Assembly.

Bazhenof, băzh′ę-nof, (VASILI IVANOVITCH,) an eminent Russian architect, born at Moscow in 1737. He studied at Saint Petersburg, and subsequently in Paris under Duval, and on his return was made adjunct of the Academy of Fine Arts. His principal work is the Saint Michael Palace at Saint Petersburg; he also assisted in the construction of the Kazan church in that city. Bazhenov made a Russian translation of Vitruvius, (4 vols., 1790.) He was vice-president of the Academy of Fine Arts at Saint Petersburg, and member of several foreign Academies. Died in 1799.

Bazicalva, băd-ze-kăl′vȧ, written also **Bazzicaluve,** (ERCOLE,) an Italian designer and engraver of the seventeenth century, was a native of Pisa.

Bazin. See BASIN.

Bazin, bă′zăṉ′, (ANAÏS DE RAUCOU, ă′nă′ĕss′ dęh rō′koo′,) a French historian and lawyer, born in Paris in 1797. He wrote a "History of France under Louis XIII.," (2 vols., 1837,) and other works. Died in 1850.

Bazin, (CLAUDE,) a French physician and professor of pharmacy, born in Paris; died in 1612.

Bazin, (DENIS,) a French physician and professor of surgery at the Royal College; died in 1632.

Bazin, (GILLES AUGUSTIN,) a French naturalist, born in Paris, practised medicine at Strasburg. He wrote several treatises on plants and insects. Died in 1754.

Bazin, (GUILLAUME,) a French physician, born near Chartres, became in 1472 dean of the faculty of medicine in Paris. Died in 1500.

Bazin, (JACQUES RIGOMER,) a French jurist and politician, born at Mans in 1771, was editor for a time of "Le Démocrate," in which he opposed the Directory. He was mortally wounded in a duel in 1820.

Bazin, (JEAN,) a French diplomatist, born at Blois in 1538. He was sent on a mission to Poland in 1572, and procured the election of the Duke of Anjou as King of Poland. Died in 1592.

Bazin, (NICOLAS,) a French engraver, born at Troyes about 1636, was a pupil of Claude Mellan. He executed a number of prints after Correggio, Guido, and Lebrun. Died about 1706.

Bazin, (SIMON,) son of Claude Bazin, noticed above, was dean of the faculty of Paris in 1638. Died in 1660.

Bazine. See BASINE.

Bazinghen, de, dęh bă′zăṉ′gŏṉ′, (FRANÇOIS ANDRÉ Abot—ă′bo′,) a French antiquary and numismatist, born at Boulogne-sur-Mer in 1710. Died in 1791.

Bazire or **Basire,** bă′zèR′, (CLAUDE,) born at Dijon in 1764, was a member of the National Convention, and voted for the death of Louis XVI. He was a partisan of Danton, and was executed in 1794.

Bazius or **Baazius.** See BAAZ.

Baz′ley, (THOMAS,) born in Lancashire in 1797, became president of the Manchester chamber of commerce in 1845.

Bazot, bă′zo′, (ÉTIENNE FRANÇOIS,) a French *littérateur,* born in the department of Nièvre in 1782.

Bazzacco. See PONCHINO.

Bazzani, băt-să′nee, (GASPARO,) an Italian painter, born at Reggio in 1701; died in 1780.

Bazzani, (GIUSEPPE,) an Italian painter, and director of the Academy of Painting at Mantua, executed a number of frescos in that city. Died in 1769.

Bazzani, (MATTEO,) an Italian physician and naturalist, born at Bologna in 1674; died in 1749.

Bazzano, di, de băt-să′no, (FRANCESCO ANGELUCCIO,) an Italian chronicler of the sixteenth century, wrote a "History of Aquila from 1436 to 1585."

Bazzicaluve. See BAZICALVA.

Bazzino, băt-see′no, or **Bazzini,** băt-see′nee, (FRANCESCO,) an Italian composer and organist, born at Lovero, in the Venetian States, about 1600. Died in 1660.

Bazzino, (NATALE,) an Italian musician, was a brother of the preceding. Died in 1639.

Bēach, (ABRAHAM,) D.D., an Episcopal clergyman, born at Cheshire, Connecticut, in 1740, graduated at Yale College in 1757. He became assistant rector of Trinity Church, New York. Died in 1828.

‚Beach, (MOSES YALE,) an American mechanic and projector, born in Wallingford, Connecticut, in 1800. About 1835 he went to the city of New York, and became proprietor of "The Sun," said to be the first penny paper published in this country. Died in 1868.

Beacon. See BECON, (THOMAS.)

Beak. See BEK, (ANTHONY.)

Beale, beel, (BARTHOLOMEW,) an English physician, born in the latter part of the seventeenth century, was a son of Mary Beale, mentioned below.

Beale, (LIONEL,) an English physician and writer, born about 1820. He became professor of physiology, etc. in London.

Beale, (MARY,) an English portrait-painter, born in 1632, was a pupil of Sir Peter Lely. Among her best works are portraits of Dr. Tillotson and the Bishop of Chester. She was also the author of poems, which were admired by her contemporaries. Died in 1697.

See WALPOLE, "Anecdotes of Painting in England."

Beale, [Lat. BE′LUS,] (ROBERT,) an English jurist and diplomatist under the reign of Queen Elizabeth, was a brother-in-law of Sir Francis Walsingham. He was ambassador at the court of the Prince of Orange in 1576, and was employed in other important missions. He possessed one of the most valuable historical libraries in Europe. Died in 1601.

Bēan, (RICHARD,) an English painter and engraver, born in 1792; died in 1817.

Beard, (JOHN,) a distinguished English tenor-singer, born about 1717; died about 1791.

Beard, (JOHN R.,) an English clergyman, born about 1800, published, besides other works, the "People's Dictionary of the Bible," (2 vols.,) and a "Life of Toussaint L'Ouverture." He preached some years in Manchester.

Beard, (THOMAS,) an Irish engraver, lived about 1720.

Beardé de l'Abbaye, băR′dǎ′ dęh lȧ′bǎ′, a French agricultural writer, died in 1771.

Bēaŝ′ley, (FREDERICK,) an Episcopal clergyman, born in 1777, was professor of moral philosophy in the University of Pennsylvania from 1813 to 1828. Among his works are "An Examination of the Oxford Divinity," "A Search of Truth in the Science of the Human Mind," and a "Reply to the Views of Dr. Channing." His writings attracted attention in Europe. Died at Elizabethtown, New Jersey, in 1845.

Beatiano. See BEAZIANO.

Beatillo, bà-â-têl′lo, (ANTONIO,) an Italian Jesuit and popular preacher, born near Naples in 1570; died in 1642.

Bēa′tǫn, [Scottish pron. bā′tǫn,] written also **Beatoun, Beton,** or **Bethune,** (DAVID,) Cardinal, and Archbishop of Saint Andrew's, a formidable opponent of the reformed religion in Scotland, was born in 1494. He finished his studies in Paris, and in 1519 was appointed Scottish resident at the French court. After his return, he took his seat in Parliament, in 1525, as Abbot of Arbroath, and became lord privy seal in 1528. In 1533 he was ambassador, in company with Sir Thomas Erskine, to France, where he negotiated the marriage of

James V. with Madeleine, daughter of Francis I., and, after her decease, prepared the way for a second marriage with the daughter of the Duke of Guise. He succeeded his uncle as Archbishop of Saint Andrew's in 1539, having shortly before been created a cardinal by Pope Paul III. On the death of King James, in 1542, Beaton claimed the regency by right of a forged will which he produced; but the Earl of Arran was appointed regent, and, after a struggle for the supremacy, the cardinal prevailed upon him to abjure Protestantism. From this time he applied himself to the work of persecution, and incurred general odium by his cruelties, especially in the execution of the celebrated George Wishart. In May, 1546, he was assassinated in the chamber of his castle by a band of reformers headed by Norman Leslie.

See Cook, "History of the Reformation in Scotland;" Knox, "History of the Reformation in Scotland;" Froude, "History of England," vol. iv. chaps. xviii.-xxii.; Robertson, "History of Scotland;" Chambers, "Biographical Dictionary of Eminent Scotsmen."

Beaton, (James,) uncle of the preceding, was born about 1470. He rose through several promotions to be chancellor of the kingdom, and Archbishop of Saint Andrew's, in 1522. He was a member of the council of regency appointed in 1524. Died in 1539.

See Chambers, "Biographical Dictionary of Eminent Scotsmen."

Beaton, (James,) an eminent Scottish prelate, born about 1520, was a nephew of Cardinal Beaton. He became Archbishop of Glasgow in 1552. He was a confidential adviser of the queen regent, after whose death, in 1560, he retired for safety to France. Died at Paris in 1603.

Beatoun. See Beaton.

Beatricé. See Beatrizet, (Nicolas.)

Beatrice Portinari, bà-à-tree′chà poR-te-nà′ree, an Italian lady of rare beauty and loveliness of character, immortalized by Dante in his "Divine Comedy," was a native of Florence. She was married to Simone dei Bardi. Died about 1290.

See Balbo, "Vita di Dante."

Be′a-trix, (or be-à′triks,) a daughter of Renaud, Count of Burgundy, was married in 1156 to the emperor Frederick I. of Germany. Died in 1185.

Beatrix, a daughter of Ferdinand of Aragon, King of Naples, was married to Matthias Corvinus, King of Hungary, in 1475. Died in 1508.

Beatrix of Lorraine was the wife of Boniface III., Marquis or Duke of Tuscany, and the mother of the celebrated Countess Matilda. After the death of Boniface she was married to Godefroi le Barbu, Duke of Lorraine. Died in 1076.

See Sismondi, "Histoire des Républiques Italiennes."

Beatrix, Saint, sister of Saint Faustinus and Saint Simplicius, was put to death in 303 for having drawn from the Tiber and buried the bodies of her brothers above named, who had been decapitated by order of Diocletian.

Beatrizet, bà′tRè′zà′, or **Beautrizet,** bo′tRè′zà′, (Nicolas,) a French designer and engraver, sometimes called Beatrici or Beatricé, born about 1507. Among his master-pieces are "Joseph sold by his Brethren," after Raphael, and an "Ascension," after Michael Angelo. Died about 1570.

See Le Blanc, "Manuel de l'Amateur d'Estampes."

Beatson, bèt′son, or beet′son, (Robert,) a Scottish writer and compiler, born in Fifeshire in 1742. Among his principal works we may name the "Naval and Military Memoirs of Great Britain from 1727 to the Present Time," (3 vols., 1790.) Died in 1818.

See Chambers, "Biographical Dictionary of Eminent Scotsmen."

Beattie, bee′te, [Scottish pron. bà′te,] (James,) a Scottish poet and philosophical writer, born in the county of Kincardine in 1735. He was appointed in 1760 professor of moral philosophy and logic at Marischal College, Aberdeen. In 1767 he brought out his "Essay on Truth," written in refutation of the doctrines of Hume. It went through five editions in four years, and was translated into several languages. The first book of "The Minstrel" appeared in 1771, and met with great favour. Beattie soon after this visited London, where he acquired the friendship of Dr. Johnson, Goldsmith, and other eminent literary men; and during a second visit,

in 1773, he obtained from the University of Oxford the degree of D.C.L. About this time he published the second book of "The Minstrel," which was followed in a few years by a number of moral and critical essays, and a treatise "On the Evidences of Christianity," (1786.) In 1790 Dr. Beattie lost his eldest son, James Hay Beattie, a youth of rare promise and endowments; and to this bereavement was added in 1796 that of his only remaining child, a son of eighteen years. His health, which had long been feeble, gave way under these afflictions, and he died in 1803. His most popular work, "The Minstrel," without displaying great originality, is characterized by such melody of versification, tenderness of feeling, and fine perception of the beauty and grandeur of external nature, as have rendered it a favourite with all classes. It is eulogized by Gray, Dr. Johnson, and Byron. Burns sent a copy as a present to a friend with these lines:

"I send you more than India's boast,
In Edwin's simple tale."

Cowper pronounces Beattie the most agreeable and amiable writer he ever met with, "whose critical and philosophical researches are diversified and embellished by a poetical imagination that makes even the driest subject a feast for an epicure in books."

See Sir William Forbes, "Life of James Beattie," 2 vols., 1806; Alexander Bower, "Life of James Beattie," 1804; Chambers, "Biographical Dictionary of Eminent Scotsmen;" "Encyclopædia Britannica;" "Edinburgh Review" for April, 1807.

Beattie, (James Hay,) a son of the preceding, was born at Aberdeen in 1768. He was appointed professor of moral philosophy at Aberdeen before he was nineteen years old. He died in 1790, leaving "Essays and Fragments," (1794.)

See "Life of James H. Beattie," by his father, 1791.

Beattie, (William,) born in 1770, was physician to the fleet, and was present at the death of Nelson, at the battle of Trafalgar. He published an "Authentic Narrative of the Death of Nelson," (1807.) Died in 1843.

Beattie, (William,) M.D., a popular English author and physician, born in Scotland. He graduated about 1820, and removed to London. Among his numerous works are the "Heliotrope, or Pilgrim in Pursuit of Health," a poem, (1833,) and "The Danube: its History, Scenery, etc.," (1844.) He published a well-written "Biography of Thomas Campbell," who was his friend, (3 vols., 1849.)

Be-a′tus Rhe-na′nus, a German scholar, whose original name was **Bild,** (bĭlt,) born in Alsace in 1485. He published the first edition of the Roman history of Velleius Paterculus, and, according to Dupin, first caused the works of Tertullian to be printed. He also wrote, in Latin, a "History of Germany." Died in 1547.

See Vossius, "De Historicis Latinis;" Baillet, "Jugements des Savants."

Beaubreuil, de, dĕh bo′bRul′, (or bo′bRuh′yĕ,) (Jean,) a French lawyer and littérateur of the sixteenth century, was the author of a tragedy entitled "Atilius Regulus." (1582.)

Beaubrun, bo′bRŭn′, (Charles and Henri,) sometimes written **Bobrun,** French portrait-painters, born at Amboise in the early part of the seventeenth century.

Beaubrun, (Louis,) a portrait-painter, born at Amboise, resided in Paris about 1640.

Beaucaire de Péguillon, bo′kăR′ dĕh pă′ge′yòN′, (François,) a French prelate and historian, born in 1514, was an intimate friend of the Cardinal Charles de Lorraine, by whom he was created Bishop of Metz. He wrote, in Latin, a "History of France from 1541 to 1562."

See Baillet, "Jugements des Savants."

Beauchamp or **Beauchamps,** bo′shòN′, (Joseph,) a French astronomer, and member of the Institute of France, born at Vesoul in 1742, was a friend and pupil of Lalande. He was appointed in 1795 consul at Muscat, in Arabia. He contributed a number of treatises to the "Journal des Savants" and the "Memoirs of the Institute of Cairo." He was one of the savants employed in Egypt in 1798. Died in 1801.

Beauchamp, bee′chạm, (Richard,) Earl of Warwick, an English general, born about 1380, served in France under Henry V. He succeeded the Duke of Bedford as regent in France, and died at Rouen in 1439.

ă, ē, ī, ō, ū, ȳ, long; ă, ĕ, ŏ, same, less prolonged; ä, ĕ, ĭ, ŏ, ŭ, ȳ, short; ạ, ẹ, ị, ọ, obscure; fär, fäll, fät; mĕt; nŏt; gōōd; mōōn;

Beauchamp, (RICHARD,) an English prelate, noted for his knowledge of architecture, became Bishop of Salisbury in 1450. He rebuilt the chapel at Windsor under Edward IV., and the great hall in the episcopal palace of Salisbury. Died about 1481.

Beauchamp, de, děh bō′shôN′, (ALFONSE,) a *littérateur* and politician, born at Monaco, in Sardinia, in 1767. He wrote, among other works, a "History of La Vendée," and a "Life of General Moreau," (1814.) He was a contributor to the "Biographie Universelle" and the "Gazette de France." Died in 1832.

See LE BAS, "Dictionnaire encyclopédique de la France."

Beauchamp, de, (CHARLES GRÉGOIRE,) MARQUIS, born in Poitou in 1731, was a deputy in 1789 to the States-General, where he was an advocate of the cause of royalty. Died in 1817.

Beauchamps, de, děh bō′shôN′, (PIERRE FRANÇOIS Godart—go′däR′,) a French *littérateur*, born in Paris in 1689, wrote a number of comedies and romances. Died in 1761.

Beauchâteau, de, děh bō′shä′to′, (FRANÇOIS MATHIEU Chastelet—shät′lă′,) a precocious French poet, born in Paris in 1645. He wrote, at the age of twelve, a collection of poems entitled "The Lyre of the Young Apollo." Died about 1700.

Beauchâteau, de, (HIPPOLYTE CHASTELET,) brother of the preceding, visited England, where he was converted to Protestantism in 1675, and became noted as a pulpit orator.

Beauchêne, de, děh bō′shěn′, (EDME PIERRE Chanvot—shôN′vo′,) a French physician and writer, born at Ville-Franche, near Joigny, in 1748, was consulting physician to Louis XVIII. Died in 1824.

Beauchesne-Gouin, de, děh bo′shěn′ goo-âN′, a French navigator, who discovered in 1699 an island in the Strait of Magellan, to which he gave the name of Louis-le-Grand, and in 1701 an island south of East Falkland, which he called Isle Beauchêne.

See WOOD, "Cruizing Voyage," London, 1718.

Beauclair, de, děh bō′klăR′, (P. L.,) a miscellaneous writer, born in the Isle of France in 1735; died in 1804.

Beauclerc, bō′klęrk′, (DIANA,) an English artist, who lived about 1780, furnished designs for the beautiful edition of "Lenore" translated by W. H. Spencer.

See NAGLER, "Neues Allgemeines Künstler-Lexikon."

Beauclerk, bō′klęrk′, (TOPHAM,) an English gentleman of distinguished talents and wit, born in 1739, was an intimate friend of Dr. Johnson. Died in 1780.

Beaucousin, bō′koo′zăN′, (CHRISTOPHE JEAN FRANÇOIS,) a French jurist and biographical writer, born at Noyon in 1723; died in 1798.

Beaudoux. See BAUDOUX.

Beauffremont. See BAUFFREMONT.

Beaufils, bō′fěss′, (GUILLAUME,) a French Jesuit, born in Auvergne in 1674; died in 1757.

Beaufort, bu′fort, (Sir FRANCIS,) F.R.S., a British rear-admiral, born about 1775, was distinguished as a hydrographer, and produced several charts of sea-coasts. He was hydrographer to the admiralty from 1832 to 1855. Died in 1857.

Beaufort, (HENRY,) CARDINAL, an ambitious English prelate, a half-brother of King Henry IV., was born about 1370. He was a son of John of Gaunt, Duke of Lancaster, and Catherine Swynford. He became Bishop of Winchester in 1404, after which he appears to have acted as lord chancellor. At the death of Henry V., in 1422, the care of the person and education of the infant Henry VI. was intrusted to Beaufort, who, says Hume, "was a prelate of great capacity, but of an intriguing and dangerous character." He had a long contest for the ascendency with his nephew the Duke of Gloucester, over whom he eventually prevailed. (See GLOUCESTER, HUMPHREY, DUKE OF.) Died in 1447. Shakspeare has no doubt followed the commonly-received estimate of Beaufort's character in his "Henry VI."

See LORD CAMPBELL, "Lives of the Lord Chancellors;" AUBERY, "Histoire des Cardinaux."

Beaufort, (MARGARET,) Countess of Richmond and Derby, born in 1441, was descended from John of Gaunt, Duke of Lancaster. She was successively married to Sir Henry

Stafford, and to Lord Stanley, afterwards Earl of Derby Her son by her first marriage became king, under the name of Henry VII. She was distinguished for her charities and her patronage of learning, and was the founder of Christ's College (1505) and Saint John's College, Cambridge. She also established the professorship of divinity called from her name the Lady Margaret professorship. She translated some religious works from the French. Died in 1509.

See "Life of Margaret Beaufort, Countess of Richmond," by C. A. HALSTED; WALPOLE, "Royal and Noble Authors."

Beaufort, de, děh bō′for′, (EUSTACHE,) a French ecclesiastic, born in 1635, was appointed abbot of Sept-Fonts. Died in 1709.

Beaufort, de, (FRANÇOIS DE VENDÔME,) DUC, born in Paris in 1616, was the son of César de Vendôme, and the grandson of Henry IV. In the war of the Fronde he became, with the Prince of Conti and other nobles, one of the leaders of the disaffected party. Being sent in 1669 to assist the Venetians against the Turks, he was killed in the defence of Candia.

See MASCARON, "Oraison funèbre du Duc de Beaufort."

Beaufort, de, (HENRI ERNEST Grout—groo,) CHEVALIER, a French traveller, born at Aubevoye in 1798. He visited Africa in 1824, and explored the Gambia, Bondou, and the country of the Mandingoes. Died in Africa of a fever in 1825.

See E. F. JOMARD, "Notice sur De Beaufort," 1824.

Beaufort, de, (LOUIS,) a distinguished historian, of French extraction, was tutor to the Prince of Hesse-Homburg. He wrote, in French, a "Dissertation on the Uncertainty of the First Five Centuries of Roman History," (1738,) which is commended by Niebuhr, a "History of Germanicus," (1741,) and a "History of the Roman Republic," (1766.) He was a member of the Royal Society of London. Died in 1795.

Beaufort de Thorigny, bō′for′ děh to′rěn′ye′, (JEAN BAPTISTE,) a republican general, born in Paris in 1761, distinguished himself in the war in Flanders, (1793.) Died in 1825.

Beaufort d'Hautpoul, bō′for′ dō′poo′, (ÉDOUARD,) MARQUIS OF, a French officer, born in Paris in 1782; died in 1831.

Beaugeard, bō′zhäR′, (JEAN,) a French Jacobin, and member of the National Convention, born at Vitré in 1764. Died in 1832.

Beaugeard, (JEAN SIMON FERRÉOL,) a French *littérateur*, born at Marseilles in 1754; died in 1828.

Beaugendre, bō′zhôNdR′, (ANTOINE,) a French Benedictine monk, born in Paris in 1628; died in 1708.

Beauharnais, de, děh bō′äR′nâ′, (ALEXANDRE,) VICOMTE, a distinguished general, born in 1760 in the island of Martinique, where in 1779 he married Josephine Tascher de la Pagerie, afterwards Empress of France. He served under Rochambeau in the American war, was a deputy to the States-General in 1789, and was twice president of the National Assembly. In 1794 he served under Custine on the Rhine, but, being accused of treason by the revolutionary tribunal for having failed to deliver Mentz from the allies, he was guillotined in that year.

See LE BAS, "Dictionnaire encyclopédique de la France."

Beauharnais, de, (CLAUDE,) COUNT, born in 1756, was a son of Marie Anne Françoise Beauharnais, noticed below. Died in 1819.

Beauharnais, de, (EUGÈNE,) Viceroy of Italy, born in Paris, September 3, 1781, was the son of Alexandre de Beauharnais and Josephine, afterwards Empress of France. After the marriage of his mother with Napoleon, he accompanied the latter to Egypt in 1798, and was severely wounded at Saint-Jean-d'Acre. For his conduct at Marengo (1800) he obtained the rank of chef d'escadron. In 1805 he was appointed arch-chancellor of state, grand officer of the legion of honour, and Viceroy of Italy. In this high office he distinguished himself by the ability and justice of his administration. In the Austrian campaign of 1809 he defeated the Archduke John at Raab, in Hungary. He had married in 1806 Augusta Amelia, daughter of the King of Bavaria, and was soon after declared by Napoleon his adopted son, and heir-apparent to the crown of Italy. He took a prominent part in the Russian campaign of 1812, and after the defeat of the French succeeded Murat in the command of the army. His conduct on this occasion was commended in the warmest terms by Napoleon, and his masterly retreat from Moscow contributed in a great degree to save the remnant of the French forces. In 1814 Eugene was compelled to relinquish Italy to the Austrians, upon which he retired into Bavaria, where he was made Prince of Eichstadt and Duke of Leuchtenberg. He died in February, 1824, leaving two sons and four daughters.

See LÉONARD GALLOIS, "Histoire du Prince Eugène de Beauharnais," 1821; ANTOINE AUBRIET, "Vie de Eugène Beauharnais," 1824; SCHÖNBERG, "Prinz Eugen und sein Hof," 1825; ARMANDI, "Vie militaire du Prince Eugène," 2 vols., 1843; VAUDONCOURT, "Histoire politique et militaire du Prince Eugène," 3 vols., 1825.

Beauharnais, de, (FRANÇOIS,) MARQUIS, born at La Rochelle in 1756, was a brother of Alexandre. He was a devoted royalist, and rose to be major-general under Condé. He was made a peer under the Bourbons. Died in 1823.

Beauharnais, de, (HORTENSE.) See HORTENSE.

Beauharnais, de, (JOSEPHINE.) See JOSEPHINE.

Beauharnais, de, (MARIE ANNE FRANÇOISE MOUCHARD,) COUNTESS, generally called FANNY BEAUHARNAIS, born in Paris in 1738, was married to Count de Beauharnais, uncle of Alexandre. She was the author of several dramas and poems. Died in 1813.

See MADAME BRIQUET, "Dictionnaire des Françaises."

Beaujeu. See ANNE DE BEAUJEU.

Beaujeu, de, deh bō'zhuh', (CHRISTOPHE,) a French soldier and poet, served under Henry III. and Henry IV.

Beaujeu, de, (ÉDOUARD,) son of Guichard, noticed below, born in 1316. He fought against the English under Edward III., and was present at the battle of Crécy, soon after which he was made marshal of France. He was killed at the battle of Ardres in 1351.

Beaujeu, de, (GUICHARD,) served under Philip the Fair and several succeeding sovereigns, and in 1328 fought under Philip VI. in Flanders. Died in 1331.

Beaujeu, de, (HUMBERT,) fought against the Albigenses under Louis VIII., and became Constable of France in 1240. He accompanied Saint Louis to Palestine, and, according to some authorities, died in Egypt in 1250.

Beaujeu, de, (PIERRE DE BOURBON,) SIRE, was Constable of France. He subsequently married Anne, daughter of Louis XI., and became regent during the minority of Charles VIII. Died in 1502.

See ANSELME, "Histoire généalogique, etc. de la Maison royale de France."

Beaujolais, de, deh bō'zho'lȧ', (LOUIS CHARLES D'ORLÉANS,) COMTE, born in Paris in 1779, was a son of the Duke of Orléans, surnamed ÉGALITÉ, and brother of Louis Philippe, afterwards king. Died in 1808.

Beaujon, bō'zhôN', (NICOLAS,) a wealthy and philanthropic French banker, born at Bordeaux in 1718, was the founder of a hospital in Paris which bears his name. Died in 1786.

Beaujour, bō'zhoor', (LOUIS FÉLIX,) a French diplomatist and writer, born in Provence in 1765; died in 1836.

Beaujoyeulx. See BALTAZARINI.

Beaulac, bō'lǎk', (GUILLAUME,) a French jurist and legal writer, born in the department of Hérault about 1745; died in 1804.

Beaulaton, bō'lȧ'tôN', a French poet, born at Montargis, made an indifferent translation of Milton's "Paradise Lost" into French. Died in 1782.

Beau, Le. See LE BEAU.

Beaulieu. See BAULOT.

Beaulieu, bō'le-uh', almost bōl'yuh', (AUGUSTIN,) a French navigator, born at Rouen in 1589, visited the East Indies in 1616. He wrote an account of his travels, which was published in Thévenot's "Collection of Voyages." Died in 1637.

Beaulieu, (CLAUDE FRANÇOIS,) a French publicist and littérateur, born at Riom in 1754, was editor of the "Assemblée Nationale" and other journals, in which he advocated a constitutional monarchy. He contributed a number of articles to the "Biographie Universelle," and wrote "Historical Essays on the Causes and Effects of the French Revolution," (1801.) Died in 1827.

See LE BAS, "Dictionnaire encyclopédique de la France."

Beaulieu, (EUSTORG,) sometimes called HECTOR, a French poet and musician, born about 1530.

Beaulieu, de, deh bō'le-uh', (CAMUS DE VERNET, kȧ'müs' deh vêR'nȧ',) favourite of Charles VII. of France, who appointed him grand master of the horse and director of the finances. He was assassinated, by order of the constable Artus de Richemont, in 1427.

Beaulieu, de, (CHARLES Gilloton—zhe'yo'tôN',) a French writer on political economy, lived about 1750.

Beaulieu, de, (JEAN BAPTISTE Allais—ȧ'lȧ',) a French calligrapher, was the author of a work entitled "The Art of Writing," (1681.)

Beaulieu, de, (JEAN PIERRE,) BARON, an Austrian general, born in 1725, fought in the Seven Years' war. Being sent in 1796 to Italy, he was signally defeated at Montenotte by Bonaparte. He resigned his command in June, 1796. Died in 1820.

Beaulieu, de, (LOUIS LE BLANC,) a Protestant divine, and professor of theology at the Calvinist Academy of Sedan, born at Plessis-Marly, in Limousin, in 1614. He was the author of "Sedan Theses," ("Theses Sedanenses,") and other religious works. Died in 1675.

See BAYLE, "Historical and Critical Dictionary."

Beaulieu, de, (SÉBASTIEN de Pontault—deh pôN'tō',) first engineer of Louis XIV., wrote a work entitled "The Glorious Conquests of Louis le Grand, or Collection of Plans and Views of Places Besieged and the Sites of Battles." Died in 1674.

See DE COURCELLES, "Dictionnaire des Généraux Français."

Beaumanoir. See LAVARDIN, (JEAN DE.)

Beaumanoir, bō'mǎ'nwȧR', MARQUIS OF, a French littérateur and dramatist, born in Brittany about 1720; died about 1795.

Beaumanoir, de, deh bō'mǎ'nwȧR', (JEAN,) SIRE, a French soldier, and companion-in-arms of the famous Bertrand du Guesclin. He fought on the side of the Count of Blois against John of Montfort, and was the leader of the thirty Breton knights who in 1351 had a combat with and defeated the thirty English champions.

See LE BAS, "Dictionnaire encyclopédique de la France."

Beaumanoir, de, (PHILIPPE,) born in Picardy, was one of the most eminent jurists of his time. His principal work, entitled "The Common Law (Coutume) of Beauvoisis," still enjoys a high reputation, and was republished in 1842 by M. Beugnot. Died in 1296.

See MONTESQUIEU, "Esprit des Lois;" "Nouvelle Biographie Générale."

Beaumarchais, de, deh bō'mǎR'shȧ', (PIERRE AUGUSTE Caron—kȧ'rôN',) a French dramatist and versatile genius, born in Paris in 1732. He was the son of a watchmaker named Caron, and for a time pursued his father's occupation; but his skill in music soon procured him admission to court. About this time he entered into business relations with the famous financier Duverny, by which he was enabled to make a large fortune, and at the commencement of the American Revolution made an advantageous contract to supply the colonies with arms and ammunition. In this affair he was the secret agent of the French government. In 1775 he brought out "The Barber of Seville," an opera which was very successful, and in 1784 "The Marriage of Figaro." The latter, in which the aristocracy was assailed, was prohibited from being acted by Louis XVI.; but in spite of the interdiction it was brought on the stage, and was received with the greatest enthusiasm. Among his other works we may name the drama of "Eugénie," which formed the groundwork of Goethe's "Clavigo;" also a number of memoirs or pleadings written on occasion of lawsuits in which he was engaged, and displaying such powers of wit and satire as to excite the jealousy of Voltaire. He favoured the popular cause in the French Revolution, to which his writings had largely contributed. Died in 1799.

See COUSIN D'AVALON, "Vie de P. A. Caron de Beaumarchais," 1802; M. DE LOMÉNIE, "Beaumarchais, sa Vie et son Temps," in the "Revue des Deux Mondes," October and November, 1852; SAINT-MARC GIRARDIN, "Notice sur la Vie de Beaumarchais," 1835; E. BERGER, "Essai sur la Vie et les Ouvrages de Beaumarchais," 1847; "Edinburgh Review," vol. civ., 1856; "Fraser's Magazine," vol. xlix., 1854; "Westminster Review" for September, 1844.

Beaume, bōm, (JOSEPH,) a French historical painter, born at Marseilles in 1790, worked in Paris.

ā, ē, ī, ō, ū, ȳ, *long;* ȧ, ė, ȯ, *same, less prolonged;* ă, ĕ, ĭ, ŏ, ŭ, y̆, *short;* ą, ę, į, ǫ, *obscure;* fär, fäll, fǎt; mêt; nŏt; gŏŏd; mŏŏn;

Beaumelle, de la, dẹh lä bō'mĕl', (LAURENT **Angliviel**—ŏN'gle've-êl',) a French writer, born at Valleraugue in 1726. Having published a work entitled "My Thoughts," ("Mes Pensées,") which contained remarks offensive to Voltaire, he was imprisoned in the Bastille, chiefly at the instigation of the latter. On his release he wrote a reply to Voltaire's "Supplement to the Age of Louis XIV.," which is esteemed a masterpiece of· wit and polemics. In 1756 he brought out "Memoirs towards the History of Madame de Maintenon," for which he was imprisoned about a year. Died in 1773.

See M. NICOLAS, "Notice sur la Vie, etc. de L. A. de la Beaumelle," 1852; CHARLES NISARD, "Les Ennemis de Voltaire, Desfontaines, Fréron et La Beaumelle," 1853.

Beaumelle, de la, (VICTOR LAURENT ANGLIVIEL,) son of the preceding, born near Mazères in 1772. He served in the Spanish campaign of 1808, and subsequently under Dom Pedro, Emperor of Brazil. He wrote a treatise "On the Brazilian Empire," (1823,) and various other works. Died in 1831.

Beaumes. See BELMEIS.

Beaumesnil, bō'mạ̈'nêl', (HENRIETTE ADELAIDE **Villard**—vê'yằR',) a French comic actress and operasinger, born in 1748; died in 1803.

Beaumetz, de, dẹh bō'mạ̈s', (BON ALBERT **Brioisbre'**wä',) CHEVALIER, a French jurist, member of the Constituent Assembly, born at Arras in 1759. He made important improvements in the laws, and wrote a valuable work, entitled "Penal Code of the Jurymen of the Chief National Court," (1792.) To escape the reign of terror, he emigrated in 1792. Died at Calcutta about 1809.

See QUÉRARD, "La France Littéraire."

Beaumont, bō'mŏnt, formerly bu'mŏnt, (BASIL,) an English naval officer, born in 1669, became rear-admiral under Queen Anne. While on his way to Rotterdam in 1703, he was overtaken in the Downs by a terrible storm; thirteen vessels were sunk, and the admiral, with fifteen hundred seamen, perished.

See BURCHET, "Naval History."

Beaumont, bō'mŏN', (CLAUDE ÉTIENNE,) a French architect, born at Besançon in 1757, studied in Paris under Dumont. His principal work is the "Salle du Tribunat" in Paris. Died in 1811.

Beaumont, bō'mŏnt', (CLAUDIO FRANCESCO,) an Italian painter, born at Turin in 1694. Among his best works are the frescos of the royal palace at Turin. Died in 1766.

See LANZI, "History of Painting in Italy."

Beaumont, bō'mŏN', (ÉTIENNE,) a Swiss lawyer and philosophical writer, born at Geneva in 1718, was the author of an anonymous work entitled "Principles of Philosophy," attributed by some to Diderot. Died in 1758.

See SENEBIER, "Histoire littéraire de Genève."

Beaumont, (FÉLIX BELLATOR,) COUNT, a French soldier and statesman, born in Paris in 1793, served in the campaigns of 1812-15, and became a senator in 1852.

Beaumont, (FRANCIS,) the father of the celebrated dramatist, was one of the judges of the court of common pleas. Died in 1598.

Beaumont, (FRANCIS,) an English dramatic poet, son of the preceding, was born in Leicestershire in 1586. He was educated at Oxford, and studied law in the Temple. In London he associated with Ben Jonson and other wits who met at the Mermaid Tavern. He married Ursula Isley, by whom he had two daughters. He became the intimate friend of John Fletcher, in conjunction with whom he wrote a number of popular dramas. Among these are "Philaster," (1611,) "The Maid's Tragedy," "The Coxcomb," (1613,) and "Cupid's Revenge," (1613.) Beaumont was sole author of "The Masque of the Inner Temple," (1612,) and of minor poems, among which is a "Letter to Ben Jonson." Died in 1615. (See FLETCHER, JOHN.) "It cannot be denied," says Hazlitt, "that they are lyrical and descriptive poets of the highest order; every page of their writings is a *florilegium:* they are dramatic poets of the second class in point of knowledge, variety, vivacity, and effect; they are masters of style and versification in almost every variety of melting modulation or sounding pomp of which they are capable : in comic

wit and spirit they are scarcely surpassed by any writers of our age." ("Lectures on the Dramatic Literature of the Age of Elizabeth.") The elder Coleman's prologue to "Philaster," spoken in 1763, has the following apt and admirable lines :

"Beaumont and Fletcher, those twin stars that run
Their glorious course 'round Shakspeare's golden sun."
(BEAUMONT and FLETCHER'S Works, vol. i. p. 203.)

See "Biographia Dramatica ;" CAMPBELL'S "Lives of the British Dramatists."

Beaumont, (Sir GEORGE HOWLAND,) an English amateur, landscape-painter, and liberal patron of art, was born in Essex in 1753. He had the principal share in the establishment of the National Gallery, to which he presented sixteen paintings, many of them works of eminent artists. He was a friend of Wordsworth and Coleridge. Died in 1827.

Beaumont, (JEAN FRANÇOIS **Albanis**—ȧl'bȧ'nèss',) a French agriculturist, born at Chambéry about 1755, was the author of several books of travels and antiquarian treatises. Died in 1812.

Beaumont, (JEANNE LE PRINCE.) See PRINCE DE BEAUMONT.

Beaumont, (Sir JOHN,) elder brother of the dramatist, born in 1582, was the author of an unpublished religious poem, entitled "The Crown of Thorns," and a collection of poems called "Bosworth Field." Died in 1628.

Beaumont, (JOSEPH,) an English divine, born in Suffolk in 1615, became professor of divinity at Cambridge in 1670. His poem entitled "Psyche, or Lovers' Mysteries," had a transient popularity. Died in 1699.

See "Retrospective Review," vols. xi. and xii., 1825.

Beaumont, (PIERRE FRANÇOIS,) a French engraver, born in Paris in 1720, executed several prints after Wouwerman and Breughel. Died about 1780.

Beaumont, bō'mŏnt', (WILLIAM,) M.D., a surgeon in the United States navy, born in 1796. While stationed at Michilimackinac, in 1822, a young man was brought to him with a wound in his stomach produced by the discharge of a musket at the distance of only three or four feet. By skilful treatment the wound was healed, leaving an aperture of about two and a half inches in diameter, through which could be witnessed the process of digestion. Dr. Beaumont availed himself of this extraordinary phenomenon to prosecute a series of observations and experiments on digestion, the results of which have been received as valuable acquisitions to medical science throughout the world. They were first published in 1833, and have been republished in England and on the continent. Died in 1853.

Beaumont, de, dẹh bō'mŏN', (AMBLARD,) a French jurist, born near Grenoble ; died in 1375.

Beaumont, de, (ANTOINE FRANÇOIS,) VICOMTE, a French naval officer, born in Périgord in 1733, distinguished himself as commander of a squadron against the English in 1781. In 1789 he was a deputy from Agen to the States-General. Died in 1805.

Beaumont, de, (CHRISTOPHE,) Archbishop of Paris, born in Périgord in 1703. He was a zealous opponent of the Jansenists, and excited so much hostility by his violence that he was at length exiled to La Trappe. Died in 1781.

See P. PICHOT, "Éloge de C. de Beaumont," 1822 ; ABBÉ FERLET, "Oraison funèbre de Monseigneur de Beaumont," Paris, 1784 ; "Nouvelle Biographie Générale."

Beaumont, de, (ÉLIE.) See ÉLIE DE BEAUMONT.

Beaumont, de, (GEOFFROY,) born at Bayeux, was Bishop of Laon and papal legate in Lombardy. Died in 1273.

Beaumont, de, (J. T. G. **Leprévot**—lẹh'prȧ'vo',) born in Normandy about 1740. He suffered, during the reigns of Louis XV. and Louis XVI., an imprisonment of more than twenty years, for having discovered a secret coalition for a monopoly of grain, known as the *pacte de famine,* ("contract of starvation,") which was sanctioned by the government.

See LE BAS, "Dictionnaire encyclopédique de la France ;" "Nouvelle Biographie Générale."

Beaumont, de, (JEAN de **Hainaut**—hạ̈'nō',) SIRE, a French soldier, celebrated by Froissart, was a brother of William the Good, Count of Hainaut. He at first favoured the cause of Edward III. of England, who afterwards married his niece Philippa. In 1345 he went over to the party of Philip of Valois, and distinguished himself at the battle of Crécy. Died in 1356.

See FROISSART, "Chronicles."

Beaumont, de, (JEAN LOUIS MOREAU,) a French magistrate, born in Paris in 1715, wrote "Memoirs concerning Taxes in Europe," (1768.) Died in 1785.

Beaumont, van, vän bō'mŏn', (SIMON HERBERT,) a Dutch botanist and Latin poet, born at Dort in 1574; died in 1654.

Beaumont de Brivasac, de, dĕh bō'mŏn' dĕh bRe'-vȧ'zȧk', COMTE, a French geographer, born near Toulouse in 1746, was the reputed author of a work entitled "Europe and its Colonies." Died in 1821.

See QUÉRARD, "La France Littéraire."

Beaumont de Carrière, de, dĕh bō'mŏn' dĕh kȧ'-re-aiR', BARON, a French general of division, was aide-de-camp of Murat. Died in 1813.

Beaumont de la Bonnière, de, dĕh bō'mŏn' dĕh lȧ bo'ne-aiR', (GUSTAVE AUGUSTE,) a distinguished French publicist and writer, born at Beaumont-la-Châtre, in Sarthe, in February, 1802. In 1831 he accompanied M. de Tocqueville to the United States, in order to study the penitentiary systems of that country. Having returned to France, he married in 1836 the granddaughter of La Fayette. In 1840 he was elected to the Chamber of Deputies, and in 1848 became a member of the Constituent Assembly, where he voted with the moderate republicans. In August, 1848, he was sent by General Cavaignac as ambassador to England. He wrote a valuable treatise "On the Penitentiary System of the United States, and its Application in France," (2 vols., 1832,) "Slavery in the United States," ("L'Esclavage aux États-Unis," 1835,) and "Ireland, Political, Social, and Religious," (1839.) The two last-named works obtained the Montyon prize from the Institute. He resigned his office of ambassador on the election of Louis Napoleon, December, 1848. About the end of 1851 he was imprisoned for opposition to the *coup d'état* of December 2. Died in 1866.

See QUÉRARD, "La France Littéraire," (Supplément.)

Beaumont de la Bonnière, de, (MARC ANTOINE,) COMTE, a French general, born in Touraine in 1760. He served in the principal campaigns from 1795 to 1809, and was made general of division, grand officer of the legion of honour, and count of the empire. In 1814 he was created a peer by Louis XVIII. Died in 1830.

See "Victoires et Conquêtes des Français."

Beaumont de Péréfixe. See PÉRÉFIXE.

Beaumont des Adrets. See ADRETS.

Beaune, de, dĕh bōn, (FLORIMOND,) a French geometer, and an intimate friend of Descartes, born at Blois in 1601. He wrote a treatise, in Latin, "On the Limits of Equations," and invented several astronomical instruments. Died in 1652.

Beaune, de, (JACQUES,) a French minister of finance under Francis I. He lent to the queen-mother money provided for the army, for which offence he was executed in 1527.

Beaune, de, (RENAUD,) born at Tours, in France, in 1527, became Archbishop of Sens in 1596. He was instrumental in the conversion of Henry IV. to Catholicism. Died in 1606.

Beaunoir, bō'nwȧR', (ALEXANDRE LOUIS BERTRAND Robineau—ro'be'nō',) a French dramatist, born in Paris in 1746. Beaunoir is an anagram of Robineau, which was his proper name. Died in 1823.

See QUÉRARD, "La France Littéraire."

Beaupère, bō'paiR', (JEAN,) a French priest, notorious as one of the judges who condemned Joan of Arc in 1430. Died about 1450.

Beauplan, de, dĕh bō'plŏn', (GUILLAUME le Vasseur—lĕh vȧ'suR',) a French geographical writer, born in Normandy, published a "Description of the Ukraine," (1650,) which was translated into German and English; also a valuable map of the Ukraine. Died about 1670.

Beaupré, de, dĕh bō'prȧ', (PLAT,) a French priest, a member of the Convention of 1792, voted for the death of Louis XVI.

Beaupuis, de, dĕh bō'pü-e', almost bō'pwe',(CHARLES WALON,) a French ecclesiastic, born at Beauvais in 1621, became director of the Port-Royal schools in Paris, and wrote several "Moral Essays." Died in 1709.

See MORÉRI, "Dictionnaire Historique."

Beaupuy, de, dĕh bō'pü-e', (ARMAND MICHEL BACHELIER,) a French general, born at Mussidan in 1757, served under Moreau on the Rhine, and was killed in the retreat from Bavaria in 1796.

Beaupuy, de, (NICOLAS MICHEL BACHELIER,) a brother of the preceding, born at Mussidan in 1750, was elected to the Council of Ancients in 1799. Died in 1802.

Beaurain, de, dĕh bō'rȧn', (JEAN,) born at Aix-en-Essart in 1696, was appointed in 1721 royal geographer. His principal work is a "Topographical and Military Description of the Campaigns of [Marshal] Luxembourg from 1690 to 1694," (1756.) Died in 1771.

Beauregard. See BÉRIGARD.

Beauregard, bōr'gȧR', (CHARLES VICTOR,) sometimes called **Woirgard,** a French general, born at Metz in 1764, was killed near Badajos in 1810.

Beauregard, (JEAN NICOLAS,) a French Jesuit and popular preacher, born at Metz in 1731; died in 1804.

Beauregard, bō're-gard', [Fr. pron. bō'rĕh-gȧR' or bōR'gȧR',] (PETER GUSTAVUS TOUTANT,) an American general, born near New Orleans about 1816. He graduated at West Point, the second in his class, in 1838, and was appointed second lieutenant of artillery, but was soon after transferred to the corps of engineers. He was breveted as major for his meritorious conduct in the Mexican war, (1846-47.) He obtained in 1853 the rank of captain, which he resigned in February, 1861, to enter the Confederate army. He directed the bombardment of Fort Sumter, which initiated the civil war, April 12, 1861. In June he took command of the army at Manassas Junction. He commanded at the battle of Bull Run, (July 21,) where he gained a decided victory over the Union forces. In this engagement, according to his own statement, he had 27,000 men, of whom 269 were killed and 1483 were wounded. For this service he was promoted to be a general in the regular army of the Southern Confederacy. Early in 1862 he passed from the Army of the Potomac to that of the Mississippi. On the first day of the battle of Shiloh (April 6) he was next in command under General Albert S. Johnston, on whose death he succeeded to the chief command. He was, however, the next day defeated by General Grant. He then retired to Corinth, which was strongly fortified, and which he defended against the Union army in a long siege. He evacuated Corinth about May 30, 1862, and retreated with but little loss. Having been raised to the full rank of general, the highest in the service, he took, in August, 1862, command of the department of South Carolina and Georgia. He defended Charleston with success in 1863 against the Federal navy and army commanded respectively by Dahlgren and Gillmore.

About the 1st of May, 1864, Beauregard moved his forces to Petersburg and reinforced the army of Lee. He was appointed commander of the military division of the West in October, and was sent to Georgia to defend it against Sherman, but proved utterly unable to withstand the advance of the Union army. He had united his forces with those of General J. E. Johnston in North Carolina when that officer surrendered to Sherman in April, 1865.

See "Southern Generals," an anonymous work, 1865; GREELEY, "The American Conflict," vol. ii.

Beaurepaire, bōr'pȧR', (NICOLAS JOSEPH,) born at Coulommiers in 1740, was appointed in 1792 commandant of Verdun, which was immediately afterwards besieged by the Prussians. Finding his efforts to maintain the place unavailing, Beaurepaire destroyed himself.

See "Victoires et Conquêtes des Français."

Beaurepaire, de, dĕh bōr'pȧR', (NICOLAS GIRARD,) a French soldier, born in Poitou, was one of the leaders of the Vendeans in the campaign of 1793, and was mortally wounded the same year.

Beaurepaire-Rohan, de, dĕh bōr'pȧR' ro'ŏn', (HENRI,) a Brazilian traveller, of French extraction, born about 1818. Among his principal works is a "Complete Geography of Matto Grosso."

ā, ē, ī, ō, ū, ȳ, *long*; à, ê, ô, same, less prolonged; ă, ĕ, ĭ, ŏ, ŭ, ў, *short*; a, e, i, o, *obscure*; fär, fȧll, fȧt; mêt; nŏt; gŏŏd; mōŏn;

Beaurieu, de, dẹh bō′Rẹ-uh′, (GASPARD **Guillard—** ẹ′yȧR′,) a French *littérateur,* born at Saint-Paul, in Artois, in 1728, wrote "The Disciple of Nature," and other works. Died in 1795.

See QUÉRARD, "La France Littéraire."

Beausobre, de, dẹh bō′sobR′, (CHARLES LOUIS,) a Protestant divine, born at Dessau, in Germany, in 1690, was a son of Isaac de Beausobre, noticed below. He became a privy councillor of the King of Prussia, and pastor at Berlin. Died in 1753.

Beausobre, de, (ISAAC,) an eminent French Protestant theologian, born at Niort in 1659. On the revocation of the edict of Nantes he took refuge in Rotterdam, (1685,) and in 1694 repaired to Berlin, where he became pastor of one of the French churches, and subsequently court chaplain. He was the author of a "Critical History of Manichæus and the Manicheans," (2 vols., 1739,) which is esteemed a standard work, and of "Critical and Philological Remarks on the New Testament," (1742.) He also contributed a number of valuable articles to the "Bibliothèque Allemande," and wrote a "History of the Reformation," which he left unfinished. Died at Berlin in 1738. Beausobre and Lenfant translated the New Testament into French, (1718.)

See LACHAPELLE, "Vie de Beausobre."

Beausobre, de, (JEAN JACQUES **de Beault**—dẹh bō,) COMTE, a French general and military writer, born in 1704. He assisted at the sieges of Menin and Ypres in 1744, and in 1757 commanded at the blockade of Gueldres, which he forced to surrender. Died in 1784.

See DE COURCELLES, "Dictionnaire des Généraux Français."

Beausobre, de, (LOUIS,) son of Isaac, noticed above, born at Berlin in 1730, was the author of "Letters on German Literature," and other works. Died in 1783.

Beausoleil, bō′so′lȧl′ or bō′so′lạ′yẹ, (JEAN **du Châtelet**—dü shȧt′lạ′,) born in Brabant about 1576, wrote a work on alchemy entitled "Diorismus." Died in 1643.

See HOEFER, "Histoire de la Chimie."

Beaussier, bō′sẹ-ȧ′, (LOUIS ANDRÉ,) an able naval officer, was a nephew of Louis Joseph, noticed below. Died in 1789.

Beaussier de Lille, bō′sẹ-ȧ′ dẹh lèl, (LOUIS JOSEPH,) a French naval officer, born at Toulon in 1700; died in 1765.

Beautemps-Beaupré, bō′tŏN′ bō′pRȧ′, (CHARLES FRANÇOIS,) a celebrated French hydrographer, born near Sainte-Menehould in 1766. Among his principal works are the Atlas accompanying the account of D'Entrecasteaux's voyage in 1791, an "Atlas of the Baltic Sea," and "General Hydrographic Chart." He was appointed, in 1814, chief hydrographer and keeper of the marine depôt, and was a member of the French Institute and of the Royal Society of Göttingen. Died in 1854.

See "Nouvelle Biographie Générale."

Beauteville, de, dẹh bōt′vèl′, (JEAN LOUIS **Dubuisson**—dü′bü-e′sŏN′, Bishop of Alais, born at Beauteville, in France, in 1708; died in 1775.

Beauvais, bō′vȧ′, (CHARLES NICOLAS DAUPHIN,) a French engraver, son of Nicolas, noticed below, born in Paris about 1720.

Beauvais, (CHARLES THÉODORE,) a French general, born at Orléans in 1772, was a son of Charles Nicolas Beauvais de Préaux. He served under Napoleon in Italy, Egypt, and Spain. He published, among other works, "The Official and Confidential Correspondence of Napoleon with Foreign Courts," (7 vols., 1819,) and was principal editor of the compilation entitled "Victories and Conquests of the French," ("Victoires et Conquêtes des Français," 28 vols., 1817.) Died in 1830.

Beauvais, (GILLES FRANÇOIS,) a French Jesuit and moralist, born in Brittany in 1695; died in 1773.

Beauvais, (GUILLAUME,) a French antiquary, born at Dunkirk in 1698, wrote an "Abridged History of the Roman Emperors from Medals," (1767,) and other works on numismatics. Died in 1773.

Beauvais, (JACQUES,) a French engraver, born about 1750.

Beauvais, (NICOLAS DAUPHIN,) a French engraver, born in Paris in 1687, was a pupil of Gérard Adrian. Died in 1763.

Beauvais, (PHILIPPE,) a French sculptor, son of the

preceding, died in 1781. His principal work is a statue of "Immortality," executed for the Empress of Russia.

Beauvais, de, dẹh bō′vȧ′, (BERTRAND PAIRIER,) a French royalist, born at Chinon about 1755, took an active part in the Vendean war, of which he wrote an account, entitled "View of the War of La Vendée." Died in 1827.

See BILLARD DE VEAUX, "Biographie des Personnes marquantes de la Chouannerie."

Beauvais, de, (JEAN BAPTISTE CHARLES MARIE,) an eloquent French prelate, born at Cherbourg in 1731, became Bishop of Senez. He wrote a number of Funeral Orations and Sermons. Died in 1790.

See N. MAILLET, "Éloge de Messire de Beauvais," 1807; N. N. DE SAMBUCY, "Vie de Monseigneur de Beauvais," 1842.

Beauvais, de, (RÉMY,) a French Capuchin, born about 1580, wrote a burlesque poem entitled "La Madeleine."

Beauvais de Préaux, bō′vȧ′ dẹh pRȧ′ō′, (CHARLES NICOLAS,) a French physician and writer, born at Orléans in 1745. As a member of the National Convention in 1792, he voted for the death of the king. Died in 1794.

Beauval, bō′vȧl′, (JEANNE OLIVIER **Bourguignon** —booR′gĕn′yòN′,) a comic actress, born in Holland about 1643, was patronized by Molière. Died in 1720.

Beauvallet, bō′vȧ′lạ′, (PIERRE FRANÇOIS,) a French actor and dramatist, born at Pithiviers in 1801.

Beauvallet, (PIERRE NICOLAS,) a French sculptor, born at Havre in 1749, studied under Pajou. Among his best works are busts of William Tell and Marat. Died in 1828.

Beauvarlet, bō′vȧR′lạ′, (JACQUES FIRMIN,) a French engraver, born at Abbeville in 1731, executed several prints after Giordano. Died in 1793.

Beauvau, de, dẹh bō′vō′, (BERTRAND,) a French statesman, born about 1400, was employed by Charles VII. in several important negotiations, and was appointed royal chamberlain in 1435. Died in 1474.

See S. DE SAINTE-MARTHE, "Histoire généalogique de la Maison de Beauvau."

Beauvau, de, (CHARLES JUSTE,) marshal of France, born at Lunéville in 1720. He commanded the principal attack at the storming of Mahon in 1756, and had a prominent share in the victory of Corbach in 1760. In 1789 he became a member of the cabinet of Louis XVI. Marshal Beauvau was elected to the French Academy and the Academy della Crusca. Died in 1793.

See S. J. DE BOUFFLERS, "Éloge de M. de Beauvau," 1805.

Beauvau, de, (CHARLES JUSTE FRANÇOIS **Victurnien**—vèk′tüR′ne-ȧN′,) PRINCE, son of Marc Étienne, noticed below, was born in 1793. He served in the Russian campaign of 1812, and was created a senator by Louis Napoleon in 1852.

Beauvau, de, (HENRI,) BARON, a French general, served with distinction under Rudolph II. of Germany. He wrote an account of his campaigns and travels, (1619.)

Beauvau, de, (HENRI,) MARQUIS, son of the preceding, wrote "Memoirs of Charles IV., Duke of Lorraine and of Bar." Died in 1684.

Beauvau, de, (LOUIS,) a French statesman, born about 1410, became grand seneschal of Provence, and chamberlain of René, King of Sicily. Died in 1462.

Beauvau, de, (LOUIS CHARLES ANTOINE,) MARQUIS, a French general, born in 1710, was killed at the siege of Ypres in 1744.

Beauvau, de, (MARC,) Prince of Craon, was governor of Francis of Lorraine, afterwards Emperor of Germany, and subsequently became Viceroy of Tuscany. He had a high reputation for learning and accomplishments. Died in 1754.

See MORÉRI, "Dictionnaire Historique."

Beauvau, de, (MARC ÉTIENNE GABRIEL,) born in 1773, bore the title of a prince of the Holy Empire, and was a grandee of Spain. Died in 1849.

Beauvau, de, (RENÉ,) a distinguished French soldier, fought under Charles of Anjou in Italy in 1265, and was mortally wounded at the battle of Benevento in 1266.

Beauvau, de, (RENÉ FRANÇOIS,) an excellent French prelate, born in 1664. Appointed Bishop of Tournay in 1707, he did his utmost to relieve the sufferings of the soldiers and citizens during the siege of that place by

Prince Eugene, and, after it was captured, refused to perform a Te Deum for the conquerors. He was created Archbishop of Narbonne in 1719. Died in 1739.

See MORÉRI, "Dictionnaire Historique."

Beauvilliers, bō've'ye-à', (ANTOINE,) a noted French gastronome, born in Paris in 1754, wrote "The Art of Cookery," (2 vols., 1814.) Died in 1817.

Beauvilliers, de, dẹh bō've'ye-à', (FRANÇOIS HONORAT,) Duke of Saint-Aignan, born in 1607, was a member of the French Academy. Died in 1687.

Beauvilliers, de, (MARIE,) daughter of Count Saint-Aignan, born in 1574, was mistress of Henry IV. until superseded by Gabrielle d'Estrées, after which she became abbess of Montmartre. Died in 1656.

Beauvilliers, de, (PAUL HIPPOLYTE,) Duke of Saint-Aignan, born in 1684, wrote a work entitled "Literary Amusements." He was a member of the French Academy. Died in 1776.

Beauvoir, de, dẹh bō'vwȂr', (AIMÉE LÉOCADIE DOZE,) a French dramatic authoress, the wife of Édouard, noticed below, born in 1823. She wrote several successful dramas, and "Les Confidences et Causeries de Mademoiselle Mars," (3 vols., 1855.)

Beauvoir, de, (ÉDOUARD ROGER,) a French novelist and dramatic writer, born in Paris in 1809.

Beauvois. See BELENVEI.

Beauvois, de, (PALISOT.) See PALISOT.

Beauvollier, de, dẹh bō'vo'le-à', (JEAN Valot—và'lo',) a French officer, born near Loudun, served in the Vendean army in 1793, was afterwards taken prisoner by the republicans at Mans, and executed in 1794.

Beauvollier, de, (PIERRE LOUIS VALOT,) a Vendean leader, brother of Jean Valot, born near Loudun in 1770. He became maréchal-de-camp after the second restoration. Died about 1825.

See DE COURCELLES, "Dictionnaire des Généraux Français."

Beauxalmis, bō'zȂl'me', written also **Beaulxamis,** (THOMAS,) a French ecclesiastic of the order of the Carmelites, born at Melun in 1524. Died in 1589.

Beauzée, bō'zà', (NICOLAS,) a French grammarian and *littérateur,* born at Verdun in 1717. Among his principal works are his "Grammaire Générale," (2 vols., 1767,) for which Maria Theresa bestowed upon him a gold medal, "Dictionary of Grammar and Literature," written conjointly with Marmontel, and "Exposition of the Historical Proofs of Religion," (1747.) Beauzée was a member of the French Academy. Died in 1789.

See LE BAS, "Dictionnaire encyclopédique de la France."

Beā'vẹr, written also **Biever** or **Bever,** (JOHN,) known also by the Latin names of CAS'TOR, CASTO'RIUS, FI'BER, and FIBE'RIUS, was an English Benedictine monk of Westminster, and lived about 1330. He wrote a "Chronicle of England from Brutus down to his own Time."

Beaver, (PHILIP,) an English naval officer of great merit, born in 1760, attempted in 1792 to found a colony on the island of Bulama, off the west coast of Africa, for the purpose of introducing civilization among the natives. Having lost the greater part of his colonists by sickness, he returned to England in 1794, and published soon after an account of his expedition, entitled "African Memoranda," (1805.) Died in 1813.

See "Life and Services of Captain Philip Beaver," by W. H. SMYTH, London, 1829; "London Quarterly Review" for July and November, 1829.

Beaziano, bà-äd-ze-à'no, **Beatiano,** bà-ā-te-à'no, or **Beazzano,** bà-ät-sà'no, (AGOSTINO,) an Italian poet, born at Treviso, lived about 1550.

Bēaz'ley, (SAMUEL,) an English architect and *littérateur,* born in Westminster in 1786. He constructed a number of theatres in England and Dublin, and wrote upwards of a hundred dramas, also novels entitled "The Oxonians" and "The Roué." Died in 1851.

Beazzano. See BEAZIANO.

Bebel, bà'bẹl, (BALTHASAR,) born at Strasburg in 1632, was professor of theology at Wittenberg. He wrote "Antiquitates Ecclesiæ," (3 vols., 1669.) Died in 1686.

Bebel, [Lat. BEBE'LIUS,] (HEINRICH,) a German scholar and *littérateur,* born in Suabia, became in 1497 professor of belles-lettres at Tübingen, and wrote "Face-

tiæ," and other Latin works in prose and verse. Died about 1516.

See G. W. ZAPF, "H. Bebel nach seinem Leben und seinen Schriften," 1802.

Bebenburg, von, fon bà'bẹn-bōŏRG', (LUDOLF,) a German professor of canon law, became Bishop of Bamberg about 1340.

Bebootoff or **Bebutoff,** bà-boo-toff', (VASILI OSIPOVITCH,) PRINCE, a Russian commander, born in 1792, served with distinction in the Caucasian campaigns of 1828–29, and became lieutenant-general in 1843.

Becan, bà'kȁn, [Lat. GORO'PHIUS BECCA'NUS,](JOHN,) a Flemish physician, whose original name was VAN GORP, born in Brabant in 1518; died in 1572.

See MORHOF, "Polyhistor."

Becan, (MARTIN,) a Flemish Jesuit and writer, born in Brabant about 1550, was successively professor of theology at Mentz, Würzburg, and Vienna, and confessor to the emperor Ferdinand II. Died in 1624.

See "Scriptores Societatis Jesu."

Becan, (WILLIAM,) a Flemish poet and Jesuit, born at Ypres in 1608; died in 1683.

Beccadelli, (ANTONIO.) See PANORMITA.

Beccadelli, bek-kà-del'lee, or **Beccatelli,** bȇk-kà-tel'lee, (LUIGI,) an able Italian *littérateur,* born at Bologna in 1502. He wrote, besides other works, a "Life of Cardinal Pole," which was translated into Latin, (1563,) and a "Life of Petrarch." He became Archbishop of Ragusa about 1555. Died at Prato in 1572.

See MAZZUCHELLI, "Scrittori d'Italia."

Beccafumi, bȇk-kà-foo'mee, (DOMENICO,) an eminent Italian painter and sculptor, born at Sienna about 1480, was originally named MECHERINO. Among his masterpieces are his "Saint Sebastian," in the Borghese palace, and the designs of the mosaic pavement of the cathedral of Sienna. He was also a wood-engraver, and was skilled in the art of casting bronze. Died at Genoa in 1549.

See VASARI, "Lives of the Painters, Sculptors," etc.

Beccara, bȇk-kà'rà, or **Bechara,** bà-kà'rà, (CAMILLO,) an Italian poet, born at Placentia, lived about 1550.

Beccari, bek'kà-ree, (AGOSTINO,) an Italian poet, born at Ferrara about 1540, was the author of a pastoral comedy entitled "The Sacrifice," ("Il Sacrifizio,") said to have been the first work of the kind ever written, and to have been the model of Tasso's "Aminta." Died in 1590.

See GINGUENÉ, "Histoire Littéraire d'Italie."

Beccari, (GIACOMO BARTOLOMMEO,) an Italian physician and savant, born at Bologna in 1682. He was an intimate friend of Morgagni and other eminent men, whom he assisted in founding the Academy of the "In quieti," (the "Restless,") which was changed or developed by Count Marsigli into the Institute of Sciences and Arts in 1711. Beccari was soon after appointed professor of physics at that institution, and in 1750 succeeded Bazzano as president, having previously been elected to the Royal Society of London. He wrote several scientific treatises. Died in 1766.

See MAZZUCHELLI, "Scrittori d'Italia."

Beccaria, bȇk-kà-ree'ȁ, (ANTONIO,) an Italian scholar and poet, born at Verona, lived about 1470.

Beccaria, (GIOVANNI BATTISTA,) an Italian savant and natural philosopher, born at Mondovì in 1716, was appointed in 1748 professor of experimental physics at Turin. He published a treatise on "Natural and Artificial Electricity," (1753,) and "Letters on Electricity," (1758.) He contributed several articles to the "Transactions" of the Royal Society of London. Died in 1781.

See A. TANA, "Éloge de J. B. Beccaria," Turin, 1781; G. A. F. G. LANDI, "Memorie storiche intorno a gli Studj G. B. Beccaria," 1783.

Beccaria, di, de bȇk-kà-ree'ȁ, (CESARE BONESANA,) MARQUIS, an eminent philosophical and political writer, born at Milan, in Italy, on the 15th of March, 1738. He early became familiar with the works of Helvétius and Montesquieu, and the latter exercised a powerful influence on the direction of his studies. He published in 1762 a work "On the Abuses of the Coinage in the State of Milan, and their Remedies." In 1764 he brought out his "Treatise on Crimes and Punishments," ("Trattato dei Delitti e delle Pene,") which was most favourably

ā, ē, ī, ō, ū, ȳ, *long;* à, ė, ŏ, same, less prolonged; ă, ĕ, ĭ, ŏ, ŭ, ў, *short;* ạ, ẹ, ị, ọ, *obscure;* fār, fȁll, fȁt; mȇt; nŏt; gōŏd; mōŏn;

received, and at once established the author's reputation. "Never," says a French writer, "did so small a book produce such great effects." It was translated into the principal languages of Europe, including modern Greek, and went through six editions in less than two years. Voltaire, regarding it as the code of humanity, wrote a commentary upon it; and Catherine II. of Russia caused it to be transcribed into her new code. Under the patronage of Count Firmian, he had, in 1764, assisted in founding a periodical called " Il Caffé," on the plan of Addison's " Spectator." In 1768 Beccaria accepted the chair of public economy created for him at Milan by Count Firmian. Died at Milan in November, 1793.

See TIPALDO, "Biografia degli Italiani illustri," vol. iii.; UGONI, "Della Letteratura Italiana," 1820–22; C. P. VILLA, "Vita del Marchese C. Beccaria," 1821; PIETRO CUSTODI, "Vita di C. Beccaria;" "Encyclopædia Britannica."

Beccaruzzi, běk-kā-root'see, (FRANCESCO da Conegliano—dā ko-nāl-yā'no,) an Italian painter, born about 1490 at Conegliano, was a pupil of Pordenone.

See LANZI, " History of Painting in Italy."

Beccatelli, běk-kā-tel'lee, (GIOVANNI FRANCESCO,) an Italian musician and writer on music; died in 1734.

Beccatelli, (LUIGI.) See BECCADELLI.

Becchio, bek'ke-o, [Lat. BEC'CHIUS,] (GUGLIELMO,) Bishop of Fiesole, was a native of Florence. Died in 1480.

Beccold. See JOHN OF LEYDEN.

Bec-Crespin, du, dü běk'krĕs'păN', (JEAN,) a French theologian, born about 1540, became Bishop of Saint-Malo. He wrote a " History of the Great Tamerlane, taken from the Monuments of the Arabs," (1602.)

See " Gallia Christiana."

Beccuci, běk-koo'chee, (DOMENICO MARIA,) an Italian writer, born at Florence in 1730; died in 1800.

Beccuti, běk-koo'tee, or **Beccuci,** běk-koo'chee, (FRANCESCO,) an Italian burlesque poet, surnamed IL COPPETTA, born at Perugia in 1509; died in 1553.

Bec-de-Lièvre, běk'dĕh'le-ȧvR', (ANNE CHRISTOPHE,) a French royalist, served under Condé against the republicans, and was killed at Oudan in 1795.

Becelli, bà-chel'lee, (GIULIO CESARE,) an Italian poet and littérateur, born at Verona in 1683, wrote a number of dramas, and an essay " On Modern Poetry," (1732.) Died in 1750.

See MAZZUCHELLI, " Scrittori d'Italia."

Becerra, bà-thêr'rȧ, (DOMINGO,) a Spanish priest, born at Seville, published a " Treatise on Customs," (" Tratado dos Costumbres," 1589.)

Becerra, (FERNANDO,) a Spanish friar, born about 1580, wrote several religious works.

Becerra, (FRANCISCO,) a Spanish architect, born about 1545, built in Spanish America the cathedral of Lima, the church at Cuzco, and other public edifices.

Becerra, (GASPARO,) an eminent Spanish painter, sculptor, and architect, born at Baeza about 1520, studied at Rome under Michael Angelo, and afterwards worked for Philip II. His master-piece is a statue of the Virgin, at Madrid. Died in 1570.

See BERMUDEZ, " Diccionario Historico."

Becerril, bà-thêr-rèl', (ALONZO,) a Spanish artist, noted for his skilful sculpture in silver, born about 1550.

Becerril, (FRANCISCO,) a brother of the preceding, was also an artist and silversmith. Died in 1573.

See BERMUDEZ, " Diccionario Historico."

Bechada, bà'shā'dā', (GRÉGOIRE,) a French poet, born about 1090, wrote " The Conquest of Jerusalem," (not extant.)

Béchard, bà'shȧR', (FERDINAND,) a French political writer, born at Nîmes in 1799. He published, besides other works, an " Essay on Administrative Centralization," (2 vols., 1837.)

Béchaud, bà'shō', (JEAN PIERRE,) a French general, born at Béfort in 1770, was killed at Orthez in 1814.

Beche, de la. See DE LA BECHE.

Becher, běk'ẹr, (ALFRED JULIUS,) of German extraction, was born at Manchester, in England, in 1804. He studied law at Heidelberg and Berlin, and was subsequently professor of music at the Hague. On the breaking out of the revolution of 1848, he edited " The Radical," a democratic journal, which was suppressed after

the storming of Vienna, and Becher was arrested and put to death, (1848.)

See BROCKHAUS, " Conversations-Lexikon."

Becher, běk'ẹr, (JOHANN JOACHIM,) a German chemist, born at Speyer about 1630. He was successively professor of medicine at Mentz, aulic councillor at Vienna, and chief physician of the Elector of Bavaria, but did not remain long in any place. He was fond of speculation, and was the first who attempted to connect by a theory the scattered facts of chemistry. His theory was the basis of that perfected by Stahl. The most important of his numerous works is his " Physica Subterranea," (1669.) Died in London about 1684; some say in 1682.

See F. HOEFER, " Histoire de la Chimie;" URBAN G. BUCHER, "Muster eines nützlichen Gelehrten in der Person J. J. Bechers," 1722.

Becher, (SIEGFRIED,) a German statistician, born at Plan, in Bohemia, in 1806. He published a treatise " On the Austrian Monetary System from 1524 to 1838," and " Population of the Austrian Monarchy from 1819 to 1843."

See BROCKHAUS, " Conversations-Lexikon."

Becherer, běk'ẹr-ẹr, (FRIEDRICH,) a German architect, born at Spandau in 1746; died in 1823.

Béchet, bà'shā', (ANTOINE,) a French ecclesiastic and littérateur, born at Clermont in 1649; died in 1722.

Béchet, (JEAN BAPTISTE,) a French antiquary and littérateur, born near Salins in 1759, wrote " Historical Researches concerning the City of Salins." Died in 1830.

Bechstein, běk'stīn, (JOHANN MATTHIAS,) a German naturalist, born in the duchy of Saxe-Gotha in 1757. He was appointed in 1800 director of the Academy of Forest Science at Dreissigacker. He published the " Natural History of Germany," " Insectology of the Forest," " Forest and Hunting Science in all its Departments," (5 vols., 1818,) " Natural History of Cage-Birds," (1840,) and other works. He is regarded as the founder of forest science. Died in 1822.

See BROCKHAUS, " Conversations-Lexikon."

Bechstein, (LUDWIG,) a German littérateur, nephew of the preceding, born near Meiningen in 1801. He wrote a number of poems and tales, among which is " Deutsches Mährchenbuch," (1848.)

Bechtold, běk'tolt, (JOHANN,) a German artist, lived in Nuremberg about 1584. He coloured many of the engravings of Albert Dürer.

See NAGLER, " Neues Allgemeines Künstler-Lexikon."

Becichemi, bà-che-kā'mee, (MARINO,) born at Scutari, in Turkey, about 1468, became professor of Latin eloquence successively at Venice, Brescia, and Padua. Died in 1526.

Becius, bā'se-ùs, (JAN,) a Dutch Socinian theologian, born in 1622; died about 1700.

Beck, (CAVE,) an English clergyman, published " The Universal Character by which all Nations may understand one another's Conceptions," (1657.)

Beck, běk, (CHRISTIAN DANIEL,) a German historian and philologist, born at Leipsic in 1757. He became in 1785 professor of Greek and Latin in his native city, and filled other important offices. He published valuable editions of Euripides, Pindar, Apollonius, and other classics, and wrote a " Universal History of the World," (1787–1806.) Died in 1832.

See CARL F. A. NOBBE, " Vita C. D. Beckii," 1837.

Beck, (DAVID.) See BEEK.

Beck, (DAVID,) a German organ-builder, resided at Halberstadt about 1790. His greatest work is the organ in the cathedral of Groningen.

Beck, (DOMINICUS,) a German mathematician and writer, born near Ulm in 1732; died in 1791.

Beck, (FRANZ,) a German musician, born in 1731, composed a number of symphonies and a " Stabat Mater." Died in 1809.

Beck, (GEORGE,) born in England about 1749, was appointed professor of mathematics in the Royal Academy at Woolwich in 1776, and emigrated in 1795 to America. He translated Anacreon, and a large part of Homer, Horace, and Virgil. Died in 1812.

Beck, (HEINRICH,) a German comedian and comic writer, born at Gotha in 1760; died in 1803.

ɛ as k; ç as s; ḡ hard; ġ as j; G, H, K, guttural; N, nasal; R, trilled; s̅ as z; ŧh as in this. (☞See Explanations, p. 23.)

Beck, bĕk, (JAKOB CHRISTOPH,) a Swiss historian, born at Bâle in 1712 ; died about 1770.

Beck, (JOHANN J.,) a German jurist, born at Nuremberg in 1684, became professor of law at Altdorf. Died in 1744.

Beck, (JOHANN LUDWIG WILHELM,) son of Christian Daniel, noticed above, born at Leipsic in 1786, became professor of law at Königsberg in 1812. He wrote "Corpus Juris Civilis," and other legal works.

Beck, bĕk, (JOHN,) BARON OF, a distinguished soldier, fought in the Spanish army in the campaigns of the Netherlands from 1640 to 1648, and became lieutenant-general, and governor of the duchy of Luxemburg.

Beck, (JOHN BRODHEAD,) an eminent physician, born at Schenectady, New York, in 1794, graduated at Columbia College in 1813, and in 1826 succeeded to the chair of materia medica and botany in the College of Physicians and Surgeons in New York City. At the time of his death, in 1851, he was professor of medical jurisprudence in the same institution. He was author of "Infant Therapeutics," (1849,) and was associated with his brother, T. R. Beck, in the authorship of their great work on Medical Jurisprudence.

See S. D. GROSS, "American Medical Biography," 1861.

Beck, bĕk, (KARL,) a Hungarian poet, born at Baja in 1817, wrote "The Poet Traveller," (1838,) "Silent Songs," ("Stille Lieder,") and other lyrics.

Beck, (KARL JOSEPH,) a German surgeon, born in the duchy of Baden in 1794, published a "Manual of Ocular Medicine," (1824,) and other medical treatises. Died in 1838.

See C. H. BAUMGAERTNER, "Gedächtnissrede auf Dr. C. J. Beck," 1839.

Beck, (LEWIS C.,) M.D., an American naturalist, born at Schenectady about 1798, was a brother of John B. Beck, noticed above. He graduated in 1817, was appointed professor of chemistry at Rutgers College, New Brunswick, New Jersey, in 1830, and mineralogist of the survey of the State of New York in 1836. In 1840 he became professor of chemistry in the Medical College of Albany. He wrote numerous treatises on chemistry, botany, etc. His valuable Report on the Mineralogy of New York was published by the State in 1842. Died in 1853.

See S. D. GROSS, "American Medical Biography," 1861.

Beck, (MATTHIAS FRIEDRICH,) a German theologian and Orientalist, born in Suabia in 1649 ; died in 1701.

Beck, (MICHAEL,) a German theologian and scholar, born at Ulm in 1653, became professor of the Hebrew language in his native city. Died in 1712.

Beck, (THEODRIC **Romeyn**—ro′mĭn′,) M.D., an American medical writer, born at Schenectady, New York, in 1791. He graduated at Union College in 1807, practised at Albany until 1817, and then became principal of the Albany Academy, which he directed for more than twenty-five years. In 1826 he was appointed professor of medical jurisprudence in Fairfield Medical College. He obtained the chair of materia medica in the Albany Medical College about 1840. His principal work is "Elements of Medical Jurisprudence," (1823, 10th edition, 2 vols., 1850,) which is highly esteemed. Died in November, 1855.

See S. D. GROSS, "American Medical Biography," 1861.

Becke, von der, fon der bek′kĕh, (JOHANN KARL,) a German jurist and poet, born at Iserlohn in 1750. Died in 1830.

Becker, (BALTHASAR.) See BEKKER.

Becker, bek′ker, (CHRISTIANE AMALIE LUISE,) a celebrated German actress, born in 1777, is the subject of Goethe's poem of "Euphrosyne." Her personations of Schiller's and Lessing's dramatic characters were eulogized in the highest terms by Wieland and other eminent critics. She was married at the age of fifteen, and died about 1796, leaving a daughter, the present Madame Werner.

See BROCKHAUS, "Conversations-Lexikon."

Becker, (DANIEL,) a German physician, and professor of medicine at Königsberg, born at Dantzic in 1594 ; died in 1655.

Becker, (DANIEL,) son of the preceding, born at Königsberg in 1627, was dean of the faculty in his native

city. He died in 1670, leaving a son named Daniel Christopher, also a physician.

Becker, (FERDINAND,) canon of Paderborn, was born at Grevenstein in 1740. He was imprisoned for a time in the convent of Paderborn for having written works containing heresies. Died in 1810.

Becker, (FERDINAND WILHELM,) son of Karl Ferdinand, noticed below, born at Höxter in 1805. He studied at Frankfort-on-the-Main, and subsequently at Edinburgh. In 1829 he settled as a physician at Berlin. He published a valuable treatise "On Cholera," and a Latin essay "On the Historical Explanation of Medicine." Died in 1834.

Becker, (GOTTFRIED WILHELM,) a German physician and littérateur, born at Leipsic in 1778. He published sketches of travel, and other works, and t,anslated some of Cooper's novels, and "My Prisons" ("Le mie Prigioni") of Silvio Pellico, into German.

See BROCKHAUS, "Conversations-Lexikon."

Becker, (JAMES,) a skilful German painter of genre and landscapes, born near Worms in 1810.

Becker, (JOHANN,) a German physician and medical writer, born at Schwerin in 1770 ; died about 1840.

Becker, (JOHANN PHILIPP,) a German patriot, born at Frankenthal in 1809. Being compelled to leave his country on account of his liberal opinions, he went to Switzerland, where he took an active part against the Jesuits and the Sonderbund. In conjunction with Esselen, he published a "History of the Revolution of May, 1849, in Southern Germany."

See "Nouvelle Biographie Générale."

Becker, (JULIUS,) a German composer and writer on music, born at Freiberg in 1811. He published a treatise "On the Science of Harmony," and composed an opera entitled "The Siege of Belgrade."

Becker, (KARL FERDINAND,) a German scholar, born in the electorate of Treves in 1775. He published a "Complete German Grammar," "Organism of the German Language," (1841,) and other works. Died in 1849.

Becker, (KARL FERDINAND,) a German organist, born at Leipsic in 1804, was a son of Gottfried Wilhelm, noticed above. He wrote a "Systematic and Chronological Exposition of Musical Literature," (1836,) and other works.

Becker, (KARL FRIEDRICH,) a German historian, born at Berlin in 1777, wrote a very popular "History of the World for Children and Teachers," (9 vols., 1801.) Five volumes were subsequently added to it by Woltmann, Menzel, and Loebell. Died in 1806.

Bec′ker or **Bajert-Becker,** [Fr. pron. bả′zhair′ bả′kair′,] (LÉONARD NICOLAS,) Comte de Mons, a French general, born at Obernheim in 1770. He was raised to the rank of general of division on the field of Austerlitz. Died in 1840.

Becker, (NIKOLAUS,) a German poet, born at Geilenkirchen in 1816, is chiefly known as the author of a very popular national song beginning, "They shall not have it, the free German Rhine !" (" Sie sollen ihn nicht haben, den freien deutschen Rhein !") It was written in 1840, in response to a proposed annexation of the valley of the Rhine to France. Died in 1845.

See BROCKHAUS, "Conversations-Lexikon."

Becker, (PHILIPP CHRISTOPH,) a German engraver of seals and medals, born at Coblentz in 1674. He was patronized by Joseph I. and Charles VI. of Austria, and Peter the Great of Russia. Died in 1742.

Becker, (PHILIPP JAKOB,) a German painter, born at Pforzheim in 1763, studied at Rome under Raphael Mengs. Died in 1829.

Becker, (RUDOLF ZACHARIAS,) a popular German writer, born at Erfurt in 1752, published a number of moral and educational works for the lower classes. One of these, entitled "Instructive Tales of Joy and Sorrow in the Village of Mildheim," (1787,) was so popular that more than half a million copies of it were soon printed in German and other languages. Died in 1822.

See BROCKHAUS, "Conversations-Lexikon."

Becker, (WILHELM ADOLF,) a son of Wilhelm Gottlieb, noticed below, born at Dresden in 1796, published a "Manual of Roman Antiquities," (1843,) and other works. Died in 1846.

ā, ē, ī, ō, ū, ȳ, *long;* ă, ĕ, ĭ, ŏ, ŭ, ў, *short;* ą, ę, į, ǫ, *obscure;* fär, fåll, fåt; mêt; nŏt; gŏŏd; mōōn;

Becker, (WILHELM GOTTLIEB,) a German writer on antiquities and horticulture, born at Kalenberg in 1753, published "Augusteum, or Description of the Antique Monuments of Dresden," (3 vols., 1805,) and "Manual for Amateurs of Gardens," (1795–99.) Died at Dresden in 1813.

Beckerath, de, dęh bêk'kęh-rȁt', (HERMANN,) a Prussian statesman and financier, born at Crefeld in 1801. He was a deputy in 1848 to the National Assembly at Frankfort, where he sided with the liberal conservative party, and the same year became minister of finance in the ministry of the empire. He resigned both offices in 1849.

Beck'et, (THOMAS À,) Archbishop of Canterbury, was born in London in 1117. He became Archdeacon of Canterbury about 1154, and chancellor of England in 1158. According to Hume, the chancellor in that age kept the great seal, acted as secretary of state, and was a kind of prime minister. Becket lived in splendid style, performed the part of a courtier, and on one or more occasions exposed his person in battle in Normandy, whither he had followed the king. He was appointed Archbishop of Canterbury by the influence of Henry II. in 1162, after which he totally altered his demeanour and affected in his person the greatest austerity. He determined to resist the projects which Henry had formed to limit or diminish the ecclesiastical power. After a contest with the king in relation to the "Constitutions of Clarendon," Becket appealed to the pope, and escaped to France, (1164.) Supported by the pope, he excommunicated Henry's ministers, suspended the spiritual thunder over Henry himself, and persisted in his course with the utmost obstinacy. In 1170 he was permitted to return, and was reinstated in his office without resigning any of those pretensions which had been the origin of the contest. The haughty prelate continued to defy the authority of the king, and excommunicated two bishops for their compliance with Henry's will. Not long after (December 29, 1170) he was assassinated by four barons, servants of Henry. Becket was the first Saxon Archbishop of Canterbury after the Norman conquest. He was regarded as a martyr not only by the devoted adherents of the church, but by thousands of patriotic Saxons, who beheld in him the champion of their race against Norman tyranny. He was canonized by the pope in 1172, and his shrine at Canterbury became the resort of myriads of pilgrims.

See HUME, "History of England," vol. i. chap. viii.; MACAULAY, "History of England," vol. i.; CANDA, "Vie de Saint Thomas Becket," 1615; BATAILLE, "Vie de Saint Thomas Becket," 1843; ROBERT, "Histoire de Saint Thomas Becket," 1844; GILES, "Life and Letters of Thomas à Becket," London, 2 vols., 1846; JAMES C. ROBERTSON, "Biography of Thomas Becket," 1859; IMMANUEL BEKKER, "Leben des heiligen Thomas von Canterbury," 1838; W. F. HOOK, "Lives of the Archbishops of Canterbury," vol. ii. chap. xii.

Becket, (WILLIAM,) an English surgeon and writer on surgery, was born at Abingdon in 1684; died in 1738.

Beck'ett, (ISAAC,) one of the earliest English mezzotint engravers, born in Kent in 1653. Among his masterpieces are portraits of Charles II. and of Lady Williams.

See WALPOLE's "Anecdotes of Painting."

Beck'ford, (WILLIAM,) born in the West Indies in 1690, rose through several offices to be lord mayor of London. Died in 1770.

Beckford, (WILLIAM,) a celebrated English writer, son of the preceding, born in 1760. He inherited from his father the estate of Fonthill, in Wiltshire, and large estates in Jamaica, producing an annual revenue of more than one hundred thousand pounds. At the age of twenty he published "Biographical Memoirs of Extraordinary Painters," which is characterized by a critic in the "London Quarterly" as "a series of sharp and brilliant satires on the Dutch and Flemish schools." His romance of "Vathek" came out in 1784. This work, written in elegant French, was commended in the highest terms by Lord Byron, who says, "As an Eastern tale, even Rasselas must bow before it; his Happy Valley will not bear a comparison with the Hall of Eblis." An able writer in the "London Quarterly" observes, however, that "its inspiration is too often such as might have been inhaled in the Hall of Eblis." Having visited Portugal in 1794, he built a splendid mansion near Cintra, alluded

to by Byron in "Childe Harold," canto i. In 1796 he began the erection of Fonthill Abbey, upon which he expended enormous sums, and filled it with the rarest and most costly works of art. This magnificent establishment was sold in 1822, and Beckford built another palace in the neighbourhood of Bath. In 1834 he brought out a series of letters entitled "Italy, with Sketches of Spain and Portugal," which are ranked by an English critic "among the most elegant productions of modern literature." Died in 1844.

See "London Quarterly Review" for March and June, 1834.

Beck'ing-ham, (CHARLES,) an English dramatist, born in London, wrote, before the age of twenty, his tragedies of "Scipio Africanus," and "Henry IV. of France." Died in 1730.

See "Biographia Dramatica."

Beck'ing-ton, (THOMAS,) an English prelate and diplomatist, born about 1385, was tutor to Henry VI., under whom he became successively secretary of state, lord privy seal, and Bishop of Bath and Wells. In 1432 he was one of the ambassadors charged to negotiate a peace with France. Died in 1465.

See "Biographia Britannica."

Beckmann, bĕk'mȁn, (FRIEDRICH,) a popular German comedian, born at Breslau in 1803, acted at Berlin, and afterwards at Vienna.

Beckmann, (JOHANN,) a German naturalist and agricultural writer, born at Hoya in 1739. He became professor of physics and natural history at the Protestant Gymnasium of Saint Petersburg in 1763, and in 1770 professor of economy at Göttingen, where he lectured forty years or more. He wrote, among other works, "Principles of Rural Economy in Germany," (1769,) and "Contribution to the History of Inventions," ("Beiträge zur Geschichte der Erfindungen," 5 vols., 1786–1805.) Died in 1811.

See G. HEYNE, "Memoria Joan. Beckmanni," 1811; "London Quarterly Review" for January, 1816.

Beckmann, (JOHANN FRIEDRICH GOTTLIEB,) born in 1737, was organist at Celle, in Hanover, and one of the most skilful pianists of his time. Died in 1792.

Beck'with, (Sir GEORGE,) an English general, born in 1753, became successively Governor of Bermuda, (1797,) Governor of Saint Vincent, (1804,) and commander of the South American forces in 1808. He subsequently took Martinique and Guadeloupe from the French. Died in 1823.

Beckwith, (JOHN CHARLES,) an English general and philanthropist, born in 1790. He served on the staff of the Duke of Wellington, and lost a leg at Waterloo, 1815. He devoted much of his time and money to the welfare of the Waldenses, and opened many schools in Piedmont, where he died in 1862.

Béclard, bȁ'klȁr', (PIERRE AUGUSTIN,) a French surgeon and anatomist, born at Angers in 1785, became surgeon-in-chief of the hospital de la Charité in Paris, and in 1818 professor of anatomy at the School of Medicine. He was an excellent teacher of anatomy, and published "Elements of General Anatomy," (1823.) Died in Paris in 1825.

See C. P. OLLIVIER, "Notice sur la Vie, etc. de P. A. Béclard," 1827.

Becmann, bĕk'mȁn, (GUSTAV BERNARD and OTTO DAVID HEINRICH,) brothers, and German jurists, born in the duchy of Mecklenburg in 1720 and 1722, were professors of law at Göttingen. The first-named died in 1783, the latter in 1784.

Becmann, (JOHANN CHRISTOPH,) a German geographer and historian, born at Zerbst in 1641, became professor of Greek and of history at Frankfort-on-the-Oder. Died in 1717.

See "Monumentum Becmannianum, hoc est Vita et Scripta J. C. Becmanni," 1719.

Becœur, bęh-kUR', (CHARLES,) a French painter of history and portraits, born in Paris in 1807.

Be'çon or **Bēa'çon,** (THOMAS,) an eminent English divine, and one of the early Protestant reformers, born in Kent about 1512. He was an excellent writer, and was the author of several works against popery. Froude calls him "the large-minded Becon." Died in 1570.

See FROUDE, "History of England," vol. v. chap. xxviii.

Becquerel, bĕk'rĕl', (ALEXANDRE EDMOND,) a natural philosopher, son of Antoine César, born in Paris in March, 1820. He has distinguished himself by researches on electricity, magnetism, and optics, and has been associated in the labours of his father. He ascertained that oxygen gas has a magnetic power, and discovered a chloride of silver capable of receiving and preserving the coloured impressions of light. In conjunction with his father, he wrote a "Treatise on Terrestrial Physics and Meteorology," (1847.) In 1853 he became professor of physics at the Conservatoire des Arts et Métiers.

Becquerel, (ANTOINE CÉSAR,) a French savant, distinguished for his discoveries in electro-chemistry, was born at Châtillon-sur-Loing, in Loiret, in March, 1788. He studied in the Polytechnic School, served in the army as an officer of engineers from 1810 to 1815, and then retired, with the rank of major, to devote himself to the study of electricity. Among the results of his early researches were the refutation of Volta's theory of contact, and the construction of the first pile with a constant current. He obtained by slow electric action the metals aluminum, silicium, glucium, etc., and invented a method of electrotyping, (*coloration électrique sur or et argent.*) He was admitted into the Academy of Sciences in 1829, and received the Copley medal of the Royal Society of London in 1837 for various memoirs on electricity. Among his works are a "Treatise on Electricity and Magnetism," (7 vols., 1834-40,) and a "Treatise on Electro-Chemistry." He afterwards became professeur-administrateur in the Museum of Natural History. He has presented more than a hundred memoirs to the Institute.

See "Nouvelle Biographie Générale;" QUÉRARD, "La France Littéraire."

Becquerel, (LOUIS ALFRED,) a physician, son of the preceding, was born in Paris in 1814. He wrote several able professional treatises, and was appointed physician to the hospital of Sainte-Perrine in 1851.

Becquet, bặ'kặ', (ANTOINE,) a learned French monk of the order of the Celestines, born in Paris in 1654, wrote several bibliographical works in Latin. Died in 1730.

Becri- (or **Bekri-**) **Mustafa,** bĕk'ree mŭs'tạ-fạ, a favourite of the sultan Amurath IV., lived about 1630.

Bectoz, de, dẹh bĕk'to',(CLAUDINE,) a learned French lady, born near Grenoble about 1480, was surnamed THE SCHOLASTIC SISTER. She was abbess of the convent of Saint-Honorat, in Provence. Died in 1547.

See HILARION DE COSTE, "Éloges des Femmes illustres."

Beczkowski, bĕtch-kov'skee, (JOHANN FRANZ,) a Bohemian historian, born at Deutschbrod in 1658.

Beda, bẹh-dȧ', (NOËL,) a French theologian, born in the diocese of Avranches, was noted for the bitterness and violence of his controversial writings. He published a work against Erasmus, which the latter pronounced a "repertory containing one hundred and eighty-one lies, two hundred and ten calumnies, and forty-seven blasphemies." Died in 1536.

See MORÉRI, "Dictionnaire Historique."

Bedaffa, van, vȧn bà-dȧf'fȧ, or **Bedaff,** be-dȧf', (ANTONY,) a skilful Flemish painter, born at Antwerp in 1787; died in 1829.

Beddevole, bĕd'vol', (DOMINIQUE,) a native of Geneva, in Switzerland, became physician to William III. of England. Died about 1692.

Beddevole, (JEAN,) a Swiss jurist, born at Geneva in 1697, made a French translation of Giannone's "Civil History of the Kingdom of Naples," (1742.) Died about 1760.

See SENEBIER, "Histoire littéraire de Genève."

Bed'doeß, (THOMAS,) an eminent English physician and chemist, born at Shiffnal, in Shropshire, in 1760. He studied in Pembroke College, Oxford, and attained great proficiency in Latin and other languages. He also received instruction in medicine from Dr. Cullen of Edinburgh. About 1787 he was appointed reader in chemistry to the University of Oxford. He resigned this office about 1792 because his liberal political opinions did not accord with those that prevailed at Oxford. He married a younger sister of Maria Edgeworth. In 1798 he established at Bristol a Pneumatic Institution in order to experiment on the cure of disease by the respiration of gases, and employed Humphry Davy—then a young aspirant for fame—as his assistant. He was the author of numerous works, among which are a "Popular Essay on Consumption," (1799,) and "Hygeia, or Essays Moral and Medical," (3 vols., 1802.) "He was a remarkable man," says Sir Humphry Davy, "admirably fitted to promote inquiry, better than to conduct it." Died in December, 1808.

See E. STOCK, "Life of Beddoes," 1811.

Beddoes, (THOMAS LOVELL,) a son of the preceding, born in 1803, was a poet, and an eccentric character. In 1822 he produced "The Bride's Tragedy," a remarkable poem. "With all its extravagancies," says "Blackwood's Magazine," "it shows far more than glimpses of a true poetical genius," (vol. xiv.) His favourite sciences were anatomy and physiology, which he studied in Germany. He died at Bâle in 1849, in consequence of a scratch he received while dissecting at Frankfort. A volume of his poems was published after his death.

Bede, beed, [Lat. BE'DA,] surnamed THE VENERABLE, an English monk and ecclesiastical writer, illustrious for his learning and virtues, was born in the county of Durham about 673, and at the age of thirty was ordained priest. His writings include treatises on astronomy, mathematics, grammar, and music, but his reputation rests chiefly on his "Ecclesiastical History of the English Nation," ("Historia Ecclesiastica Gentis Anglorum.") This work, upon which he was employed many years, was completed about 734, and first printed about 1474. It was translated into Saxon by King Alfred. His severe application to study brought on a consumption, of which he died, about 735. It is related that on the night of his death he continued dictating to his amanuensis a translation of some work, probably of the Gospel of Saint John, into Anglo-Saxon. He asked the scribe how many chapters remained. "Only one," he replied; "but you are too weak to dictate." "No," said Bede; "take your pen and write quickly." After some time the scribe said, "Master, it is finished;" to which Bede replied, "Thou hast said truly, consummatum est," (it is finished;) and, having repeated a short prayer, he expired.

See GEHLE, "De Bedæ Venerabilis Vita et Scriptis;" CAVE, "Historia Literaria;" J. A. GILES, "Life of Bede," prefixed to his complete works, 12 vols. 8vo, 1844.

Bede, (CUTHBERT.) See BRADLEY, (EDWARD.)

Bedeau, bẹh-dō', (MARIE ALPHONSE,) a French general, born at Nantes in 1804. He served in Algeria ten years, (1836-46,) and became a general of division in 1844. Holding a high command in Paris during the revolution of 1848, he favoured the republicans, and was vice-president of the Legislative Assembly in 1849.

Bédé de la Gormandière, bȧ'dȧ' dẹh lȧ goR'môn'-de-aiR', (JEAN,) a French jurist, born at Angers, lived about 1620. He wrote, among other works, a treatise "On the Liberty of the Gallican Church."

Be-dell', (GREGORY TOWNSEND,) D.D., a distinguished Episcopal clergyman, born on Staten Island, New York, in 1793. He graduated at Columbia College in 1811. For the last twelve years of his life he was rector of Saint Andrew's Church, Philadelphia, where he died in 1834. Dr. Bedell was greatly admired as a pulpit orator. He was author of "Ezekiel's Vision," "Onward, or Christian Progression," "Renunciation," two volumes of published sermons, and other religious works.

Be-dell', (WILLIAM,) an eminent English prelate, born in Essex in 1570. He accompanied Sir Henry Wotton, ambassador to Venice, as his chaplain about 1604, and, during his residence in that city, acquired the friendship of the celebrated Paul Sarpi, known as Father Paul. Having become thoroughly versed in Italian, he translated into that language the Book of Common Prayer. After his return to England, he was elected provost of Trinity College, Dublin, and created Bishop of Kilmore and Ardagh, (1629.) He effected a great reformation among the Protestants of Ireland, and made numerous converts from the Catholics. He caused the Old Testament, and the homilies of Chrysostom and Leo in praise of the Scriptures, to be translated into Irish. Died in 1642.

See BURNET, "Life of Bedell," 1685; H. J. MONCK MASON, "Life of W. Bedell," 1842.

ā, ē, ī, ō, ū, ȳ, *long;* ȧ, ė, ȯ, same, less prolonged; ă, ĕ, ĭ, ŏ, ŭ, ў, *short;* ạ, ẹ, ị, ọ, *obscure;* fär, fåll, fåt; mêt; nŏt; gō̎d; mō̎n;

Bédène, bȧ'dȧn', or **Bidène,** be'dȧn', (VITAL,) a French poet, born at Pézénas, lived about 1610.

Bed'er-ic, (HENRI,) surnamed DE BURY, an English monk, born at Bury Saint Edmund's, lived about 1380. He wrote sermons and other religious works in Latin.

See BAYLE, "Historical and Critical Dictionary."

Bed'ford, (ARTHUR,) an English divine, born in Gloucestershire in 1668, wrote a number of treatises against the stage and the corrupt dramatic literature of the time, also a work entitled "The Great Abuses of Music," (1711.) Died in 1745.

Bedford, DUKE OF. See RUSSELL.

Bedford, (—— Russell,) first EARL OF. He attended Henry VIII. in his expedition against France, was knighted in 1522 for his services, and created Lord Russell in 1539. He was afterwards made Earl of Bedford, and died in 1555, leaving the title to his son Francis.

Bed'ford, (GUNNING S.,) M.D., an American physician, professor of midwifery, etc. in the University of New York, was born in Baltimore in 1811. He wrote a treatise on midwifery, a volume of clinical lectures on the Diseases of Women and Children, (which passed through five editions in two years,) and other works.

Bedford, (HILKIAH,) an English divine, born in London in 1663, was fined and imprisoned on a charge of having written the work entitled "Hereditary Right to the Crown of England asserted," of which it is believed George Harbin was the author. Died in 1724.

Bedford, (JOHN Plantagenet,) DUKE OF, the third son of Henry IV. of England, and Mary Bohun, was born about 1390. He was created Duke of Bedford in 1414 or 1415, and commanded the army in England during the absence of his brother Henry V. in France. By the will of Henry V., who died in 1422, he was appointed regent of France, part of which had recently been conquered by the English. In the same year the Parliament appointed him "protector" of England during the minority of Henry VI. He is described by Hume as "the most accomplished prince of his age; whose experience, prudence, and valour qualified him for his high office." Having taken command of the army in person, he gained victories over the French at Verneuil (1424) and other places; but his victorious progress was effectually arrested by Joan of Arc at Orléans in 1429. It appears that he was not supported and reinforced by the English Parliament or the chief ministers. He was one of the chief authors of the judicial murder of Joan of Arc. Died at Rouen in 1435.

See HUME'S "History of England."

Bedford, (JOHN Russell,) sixth DUKE OF, an English peer, distinguished as a patron of fine arts, was born in 1766. He devoted much time and money to the improvement of agriculture, and was noted for his liberality and public spirit. He was the father of Lord John (Earl) Russell. Died in 1839.

Bedford, (THOMAS,) son of Hilkiah, was the author of a "Historical Catechism," and other works. Died in 1773.

See "Biographia Britannica."

Bedford, (WILLIAM Russell,) fourth EARL and first DUKE OF. He was a member of the Long Parliament which met in 1640, and was a general in the army of the Parliament at the battle of Edgehill, (1642.) He was created Duke of Bedford about 1694. Died in 1700. He was the father of Admiral Lord Russell.

Bedinelli, di, de bȧ-de-nel'lee, (FRANCESCO DI PAOLO,) an Italian surgeon and medical writer, who resided at Fano about 1760.

Bed'in-ǧer, (GEORGE M.,) an officer in the American army of the Revolution, settled in Kentucky, and was a representative from that State in Congress from 1803 to 1807.

Bed'lōe, (WILLIAM,) a notorious English adventurer, who was rewarded with £500 for his pretended revelation of the popish plot, and of the circumstances attending the murder of Sir Edmundbury Godfrey. Died in 1680.

See HUME'S "History of England," vol. vi.

Bedmar, de, dȧ bĕd-maR', (ALFONSO de la Cueva—dȧ lȧ kwā'vȧ,) a Spanish marquis, born in 1572. Having been sent by Philip III. as ambassador to Venice in 1607, he entered into a conspiracy to betray that republic into the hands of Spain. The plot was discovered, and Bedmar was compelled to leave the city. He was made a cardinal in 1622. Bedmar's conspiracy is said to have suggested the plot of Otway's "Venice Preserved." Died in 1655.

See DARU, "Histoire de Venise;" SAINT-REAL, "Conspiration contre Venise."

Bédoch, bȧ'dok', (PIERRE JOSEPH,) a French magistrate, born in the department of Corrèze in 1761, was a representative to the Chamber of Deputies in 1818. Died in 1837.

Bedos de Celles, beh'dos' deh sĕl, (Dom FRANÇOIS,) a learned French ecclesiastic, born at Caux in 1706, wrote "Practical Gnomonics, or the Art of Drawing Solar Dials," an excellent work. Died in 1779.

Bedouin, beh-dwȧn', (SAMSON,) a French monk of the abbey de la Couture, near Mans, was the author of a number of dramas, satires, and songs. Died about 1563.

Bédoyère. See LA BÉDOYÈRE.

Bedriaga, bĕd-re-ȧ'gȧ, (MARIA E.,) a Russian lady, born at Tver in 1794, was the author of several tales, etc. Died in 1830.

Beduschi, bȧ-doos'kee, (ANTONIO,) an Italian painter, born at Cremona in 1576, was a pupil of Antonio Campi.

Bed'well, (WILLIAM,) an English divine and Oriental scholar, born about 1562, had a share in the translation of the Scriptures published under James I. Died in 1632.

Bee, (BERNARD E.,) a South Carolinian general, born at Charleston, graduated at West Point in 1845. He became a captain in 1855, and fought against the Union at Bull Run, where he was killed, July 21, 1861.

Bee'cher, (CATHERINE E.,) an American authoress, a daughter of Dr. Lyman Beecher, was born at East Hampton, Long Island, in 1800. She was principal of a female seminary at Hartford, Connecticut, from 1822 to 1832. She published, besides other works, "Domestic Service," a "Treatise on Domestic Economy," "Physiology and Calisthenics," (1856,) and "Common Sense applied to Religion," (1857.)

Beecher, (Rev. CHARLES,) an American writer, son of Dr. Lyman Beecher, born at Litchfield, Connecticut, in 1815. He published "Pen-Pictures of the Bible," (1855,) and several other works.

Beecher, (EDWARD,) an American clergyman, a son of Dr. Lyman Beecher, was born in 1804. He graduated at Yale College in 1822, became a tutor in that institution in 1825, and pastor of Park Street Church, Boston, in 1826. He was president of Illinois College from 1831 to 1844, and pastor of Salem Street Church, Boston, from 1846 to 1856. Among his works is "The Conflict of Ages," (1854.)

Beecher, (HARRIET.) See STOWE, (HARRIET BEECHER.)

Beecher, (HENRY WARD,) a distinguished American minister and writer, a son of Dr. Lyman Beecher, noticed below, was born in Litchfield, Connecticut, on the 24th of January, 1813. He appears to have given in childhood but little promise of future distinction. "He had," says Mrs. Stowe, "precisely the organization which often passes for dulness in boyhood. He had great deficiency in verbal memory; . . . he was excessively sensitive to praise and blame, extremely diffident, and with a power of yearning, undeveloped emotion which he neither understood nor could express. . . . In forecasting his horoscope, had any one taken the trouble to do it, the last success that ever would have been predicted for him would have been that of an orator." But even while a boy he proved that, if he did not inherit the eloquence, he inherited at least something of the controversial ability, of his father. "A forward school-boy among the elder scholars had got hold of Paine's 'Age of Reason,' and was flourishing largely among the boys with objections to the Bible. Henry privately looked up Watson's 'Apology,' studied up the subject, and challenged a debate with the big boy, in which he came off victorious by the acclamation of his school-fellows." This occurred when he was about eleven years old. He manifested at this period little inclination for severe study, but had conceived a passionate desire to go to sea. His father adroitly used this desire to induce him to commence a course of mathematics with a view to qualify himself to become a naval officer. He applied himself energetically to his new studies, "with his face to the navy, and Nelson as his beau ideal." But not long afterwards there occurred in that section of the country a religious "revival," and young Beecher, with many others, was powerfully impressed. The result was that the naval scheme was abandoned, and his thoughts were directed to the pulpit as his natural and proper sphere. After going through the preparatory studies, he entered Amherst College, where he graduated in 1834; and soon after he commenced the study of theology at Lane Seminary, under the direction of his father. (See BEECHER, LYMAN.) He began his ministerial course at Lawrenceburg, Indiana, but removed soon after to Indianapolis. In 1847 he became pastor of the Plymouth Church (of orthodox Congregationalists) in Brooklyn, near New York. Here he has gathered around him the largest congregation, it is said, in the United States. He is also one of the most popular writers and most successful lecturers in America. His success as a public speaker is due not so much to what is popularly termed eloquence, as to an unfailing flow of racy and original thought, which, though often enlivened with flashes of quaint humour, is not without an under-current of deep moral and spiritual earnestness. In 1850 Mr. Beecher published a volume of "Lectures to Young Men." He was one of the originators of "The Independent," a weekly religious paper published in New York, which acquired through his contributions a wide popularity. The articles which he furnished to the paper were signed with an asterisk. A volume of these contributions was published in 1855, with the title of "Star Papers;" and a second series of the same appeared in 1858. His "Life Thoughts" (1858) has had a very extensive circulation. One of his latest productions is a novel, entitled "Norwood," (1868,) which first appeared in the columns of the "New York Ledger." As a reformer, particularly in the causes of temperance and anti-slavery, Mr. Beecher has long stood in the foremost rank in America.

See "Men of Our Times," by HARRIET BEECHER STOWE, 1868.

Beecher, (LYMAN,) D.D., an eminent American preacher and theologian, born at New Haven, Connecticut, on the 12th of October, 1775. He graduated at Yale College in 1797, and studied theology under President Dwight. After he had preached several years at East Hampton, Long Island, he became in 1810 minister of the Congregational church of Litchfield, Connecticut. He was a popular pulpit orator, and acquired great influence in the religious world. About 1826 he removed from Litchfield to Boston, in order to uphold the ancient (orthodox) faith against the influence of the Unitarians. He was installed as minister of the Hanover Street Church, Boston. His zealous efforts to prevent defection from the orthodox church are said to have been very successful. In 1832 he became president of Lane Theological Seminary at Cincinnati, and minister of the Second Presbyterian Church in that city. He was an active and earnest promoter of temperance and other moral enterprises, and was distinguished by the boldness and energy of his character. He quitted Cincinnati about 1842, after which he resided for many years in Boston. He wrote, besides other works, "Views in Theology," and "Skepticism." His sermons on Temperance have had an immense circulation, and have been translated into several foreign languages. His collected works were published under his direction, in Boston, in three volumes. About 1856 he removed to Brooklyn, where he died in January, 1863. Dr. Beecher was thrice married, and had thirteen children, several of whom became distinguished as writers or ministers.

See his "Autobiography and Correspondence," edited by his son, CHARLES BEECHER, 2 vols., 1864.

Beecher, (THOMAS K.,) a son of Dr. Lyman Beecher, noticed above, born at Litchfield, Connecticut, February 10, 1824. He graduated at Illinois College (Jacksonville, Illinois) in 1843. For about fifteen years he has had the pastoral charge of a Congregational church at Elmira, in the State of New York. He is an eloquent preacher, and a zealous philanthropist. He considers it to be especially his duty to discourage the spirit of sectarianism,

and to promote a liberal and fraternal feeling among the various Christian churches.

Bee'chey, (FREDERICK WILLIAM,) an English navigator and naturalist, son of Sir William Beechey, mentioned below, was born in London in 1796. In 1818 he sailed with Franklin on his first Arctic voyage, and in 1819 accompanied Sir Edward Parry to the Polar regions. He was charged in 1821, in conjunction with his brother, H. W. Beechey, to make a survey of the northern coast of Africa. In 1825 he sailed, as commander of the Blossom, on another Arctic expedition, reached 71° 23′ north latitude, and returned in 1828. He had discovered in 1827 two harbours southeast of Cape Prince of Wales, which he named Port Clarence and Port Grantley. He was made rear-admiral of the blue in 1854. He published in 1828 "Proceedings of the Expedition to explore the Northern Coast of Africa from Tripoli eastward," and in 1831 a "Narrative of a Voyage to the Pacific and Behring's Strait," which was followed by two volumes treating of the botany and zoology of the voyage. Died in November, 1856.

See "London Quarterly Review" for 1831; "Edinburgh Review" for March, 1831.

Beechey, (Sir WILLIAM,) a distinguished English portrait-painter, born in Oxfordshire in 1753. He was chosen an associate of the Royal Academy in 1793, and was appointed portrait-painter to Queen Charlotte. Among his principal paintings was one of George III. on horseback; he also painted the Prince of Wales and other members of the royal family, Lord Cornwallis, Lord Nelson, and John Kemble. He became a Royal Academician in 1797. Died in 1839.

Beeck, bāk, (JOHANN MARTIN,) a German Protestant theologian, born at Lubeck in 1665; died in 1727.

Beek, bāk, (DAVID,) a celebrated Dutch portrait-painter, born at Delft in 1621, was one of the most distinguished pupils of Van Dyck. He was appointed by Charles I. of England teacher of drawing to the Prince of Wales and his brothers, and was subsequently patronized by Christina of Sweden, who charged him to paint the portraits of the sovereigns and eminent persons of Europe. Died in 1656.

See DESCAMPS, "Vie des Peintres Flamands, Hollandais," etc.

Beekkerk, bāk'kĕrk, (HERMANN WALTER,) a Dutch painter, born at Leeuwarden in 1756; died in 1796.

Beeldemaker, bāl'deh-mä'ker, or **Beeldemaken**, bāl'deh-mä'ken, (FRANCISCUS,) a Dutch historical painter, son of Jan, noticed below, born at the Hague in 1669.

Beeldemaker, (JAN,) a Dutch painter, born at the Hague in 1636, was distinguished for his hunting-scenes and animals. Died in 1736.

See DESCAMPS, "Vie des Peintres Flamands, Hollandais," etc.

Beer, bār, (CORNELIS,) a Flemish painter, worked in Spain about 1630–50.

Beer, bār, (GEORG JOSEPH,) a German physician and oculist, born at Vienna in 1763. He invented several surgical instruments, and wrote "Practical Observations on the Cataract," (1791,) "Bibliotheca Ophthalmica," (3 vols., 1799,) and other valuable works. Died in 1821.

Beer, (JAKOB MEYER.) See MEYERBEER.

Beer, Bähr, or **Baehr**, bār, (JOSEPH,) a German musician, born at Grünwald, in Bohemia, in 1744; died in 1811.

See SPRENGEL, "Geschichte der Medicin."

Beer, (MARTIN,) a German philosopher and geographer, born at Nuremberg in 1617. He wrote various works. Died in 1692.

See JOHANN FABRICIUS, "Memoria M. Beerii," 1693.

Beer, (MICHAEL,) a German dramatic writer, brother of the celebrated composer Meyerbeer, born at Berlin in 1800. Among his best works are the tragedies of "Struensee" and "The Pariah," (1826,) which are highly commended. Died at Munich in 1833.

See MARMIER, "Revue Germanique," 1834.

Beer, (WILHELM,) a German astronomer, brother of the preceding, born in Berlin in 1797. He was an intimate friend of Mädler, in whose astronomical labours he was associated. They published in 1836 a map of the moon, which obtained the Lalande prize from the French Academy. It was followed in 1837 by a commentary, entitled "The Moon in its Cosmic and Individual Relations." Died in 1850.

Beer-Bing, băr bing, (ISAIAH,) a Jewish scholar, lived about 1810. He translated from German into Hebrew the " Phædon" of Mendelssohn.

Beering. See BEHRING.

Beers, (NATHAN,) an American subaltern officer, born at Stratford, Connecticut, in 1753. He entered the army in 1777, and served until 1783. Died in 1849.

Beethoven, van, văn bā'to-vęn, (LUDWIG,) a celebrated composer, of Dutch extraction, was born at Bonn, in Prussia, on the 17th of December, 1770. He was a pupil of Neefe, whom he succeeded as organist at the court of the Elector of Cologne, who sent him to Vienna to finish his studies under Haydn; but Haydn, who was about to depart to England, placed Beethoven under the tuition of Albrechtsberger. He settled in Vienna at an early age, and gained a high reputation by his extempore fantasias. Desiring to offer homage to the genius of Napoleon, he commenced in 1802 a symphony for that purpose. This master-piece of art and science, in which the genius of the artist is revealed in its greatest majesty, was not finished until 1804. It is said that when he was about to send it to Napoleon he learned that he had usurped imperial power, for which reason he changed the title of the piece to "Sinfonia eroica." In 1805 he produced the celebrated opera of "Leonore" or "Fidelio." He composed many symphonies, overtures, cantatas, sonatas, quintets, quartets, etc., which attest the originality and sublimity of his genius. In 1809 he resolved to accept the office of chapel-master at the court of Jerome Bonaparte, but was induced to remain at Vienna by the promise of a pension. He was extremely reserved in conversation, and, having become deaf in the prime of life, avoided society, and fell into a habit of gloom and distrust. He was never married. Died at Vienna in March, 1827.

"His imagination," says Denne-Baron, "required the vast field of the orchestra to display itself in all its splendour. It is in instrumental music, especially in the symphony, the compass of which he extended beyond the scale laid down by Haydn and Mozart, that Beethoven acquired his chief title to celebrity." In 1831 appeared a volume of "Beethoven's Studies in Thorough Bass, Counterpoint, and the Theory of Composition."

See SCHINDLER, "Biographie von L. van Beethoven," 1840, and an English version of the same, by MOSCHELES, 2 vols., 1841; F. WEGELER und F. RIES, "Biographische Notizien über L. van Beethoven," 1838; "Foreign Quarterly Review" for 1831.

Beets, bāts, (NIKOLAAS,) a popular Dutch humorist and poet, born at Utrecht in the early part of the present century. His "Camera Obscura," a collection of sketches and tales, and a volume of poems entitled "Corn-Flowers," ("Korenbloemen,") have been very favourably received.

See "Fraser's Magazine" for December, 1854.

Beffa-negrini, bĕf-fȧ-nȧ-gree'nee, (ANTONIO,) an Italian historical writer, born at Asola in 1532; died in 1602.

Beffara, bȧ'fȧ'rȧ', (LOUIS FRANÇOIS,) a French *littérateur,* born at Nonancourt in 1751, wrote contributions to the history of the French drama. Died in 1838.

Beffroy de Beauvoir, bȧ'fRwȧ'dẹh bō'vwȧR', (LOUIS ÉTIENNE,) born at Laon in 1754, was a deputy to the National Convention, and voted for the death of the king. He afterwards became a member of the Council of Five Hundred. Died in 1825.

See LE BAS, "Dictionnaire encyclopédique de la France."

Beffroy de Reigny, bȧ'fRwȧ' dẹh rạn'ye', (LOUIS ABEL,) brother of the preceding, known by his pseudonym of "Cousin Jacques," born at Laon in 1757. He was the author of a popular comedy entitled "La petite Nanette," and various other works. Died in 1811.

See QUÉRARD, "La France Littéraire."

Bega, bā'gȧ, (CORNELIS,) a Dutch painter and engraver, born at Haarlem about 1620, was a pupil of Adrian van Ostade, and excelled in the same department of painting. Among his master-pieces are a "Chemist in his Laboratory," and a "Company of Drinkers." Died in 1664.

See NAGLER, "Neues Allgemeines Künstler-Lexikon;" STRUTT, "Dictionary of Engravers."

Begarelli, bȧ-gȧ-rel'lee, sometimes written **Begarilli,** (ANTONIO,) an Italian artist, born at Módena about 1498,

was celebrated for his skill in modelling stucco and clay. He was intimate with Correggio, whom he is said to have instructed in his art. Died in 1565.

See LANZI, "History of Painting in Italy."

Begas, bā'gâs, (KARL,) court painter to the King of Prussia, and professor in the Academy of Arts at Berlin, born at Heinsberg in 1794. He studied under Philippart at Bonn, and subsequently in Paris under Gros. Among his best historical pictures are "The Finding of Moses," "The Sermon on the Mount," and "Henry IV. at the Château of Canossa." He also painted a number of excellent portraits, including those of Alexander von Humboldt, Cornelius, and Meyerbeer. Died in 1854.

See NAGLER, "Neues Allgemeines Künstler-Lexikon."

Begat, bẹh'gȧ', (JEAN,) a French jurist and legal writer, born at Dijon in 1523, became president of the parliament in his native city. Died in 1572.

Bégault, bȧ'gō', (GILLES,) a French ecclesiastic, celebrated as a pulpit orator, born in 1660; died about 1715.

Begein. See BEGEYN.

Beger, bā'gẹr, (LORENZ,) a German antiquary, born at Heidelberg in 1653, wrote, in Latin, a number of treatises on numismatics. Died in 1705.

Begeyn, bȧ-gīn', (ABRAHAM,) a Dutch landscape-painter, born in 1650; died about 1710.

Begh, bĕg, (LAMBERT,) sometimes called **Le Bègue,** a French ecclesiastic, supposed to have founded at Liege, in the latter part of the twelfth century, the religious order of Béguines, consisting of widows and unmarried women. The foundation of this order is ascribed by some writers to Saint Francis of Assisi. Died in 1177.

See "L'Art de vérifier les Dates."

Bégin, bȧ'zhȧN', (AUGUSTE ÉMILE,) a French *littérateur,* born at Metz in 1803. He published a "History of Napoleon, his Family, and his Epoch," (6 vols., 1853 *et seq.*)

Bégin, (LOUIS JACQUES,) a French surgeon and writer, born at Liege in 1793; died in 1859.

Bégon, bȧ'gòN', (ÉTIENNE,) a French lawyer, born about 1658; died in 1726.

Bégon, (MICHEL,) a French magistrate and eminent patron of science, born at Blois in 1638, possessed a choice collection of medals and objects in natural history. Plumier named in his honour the Begonia, a genus of South American plants remarkable for the beauty of their foliage and flowers. Died in 1710.

See MORÉRI, "Dictionnaire Historique."

Bégon, (SCIPION JÉRÔME,) son of the preceding, born at Brest in 1681, became Bishop of Toul. Died in 1753.

Bègue de Presle, le, lẹh bȧg dẹh pRĕl, (ACHILLE GUILLAUME,) a French physician, born near Orléans about 1735. He translated from the English some of the works of Monro and Lewis, and was a contributor to the "Bibliothèque physico-économique." He was a friend of J. J. Rousseau, and wrote an account of his last days. Died in 1807.

See "Biographie Médicale."

Bègue, Le, lẹh bȧg or lẹh bĕg, a celebrated French musician and composer, was organist of the church of Saint-Merry, in Paris. Died about 1720.

Béguelin, de, dẹh bȧg'lȧN', (NICOLAS,) a Swiss physician, born at Courlary in 1714, was tutor to Frederick William, afterwards King of Prussia. He subsequently became director of the Academy of Sciences at Berlin. Died in 1789.

Béguignot, de, dẹh bȧ'gĕn'yo', (FRANÇOIS BARTHÉLEMI,) COMTE, a French general, born in 1747, served in the campaigns of 1795 and 1799. Died in 1808.

Béguillet, bȧ'gẹ'yȧ', (EDME,) a French agricultural writer; died in 1786.

Béguin, bȧ'gȧN', (JEAN,) a French chemist, born about 1600, wrote "Tyrocinium Chymicum."

Behadar- (**Bahadar-** or **Bahadur-**) **Khan,** bẹ-hȧ'dạr or bȧ-hȧ'dŭr kȧn, (**Ala-ed-Deen-Aboo-Saeed,** or **Ala-ed-Dîn-Abû-Saîd,** ȧl'ȧ-ed-deen' ȧ'boo sȧ-eed',) last Sultan of the Mongol dynasty in Persia, born in Azerbaijân in 1302. Died in 1335.

See PRICE, "History of Persia."

Behadar- (**Bahadar-** or **Bahadur-**) **Shah,** second son of Aurung-Zeb, born about 1642, was also called the SULTAN MOAZZEM, (mo-âz'zẹm.) His brother Mohammed having died, Behadar became Emperor of the Moguls on the death of his father in 1707. He died in 1712.

See ELPHINSTONE, "History of India;" FRASER, "History of Nadir Shah," etc.

Behague, de, dẹh bà'ăg', (JEAN PIERRE ANTOINE,) COMTE, a French general, was appointed Governor of Martinique in 1792.

Behaim, bā'hīm, written also **Behem** or **Boehm,** (MARTIN,) an eminent navigator and geographer, born at Nuremberg in 1436, is said to have been a pupil of Regiomontanus. About 1480 he visited Portugal, where he was received with great distinction, and in 1484 was appointed geographer to the African expedition of Diogo Cam, in which they explored the western coast of Africa from the river Gambia to the Congo. After his return to Lisbon he was made a knight by King John II. He subsequently settled in the island of Fayal. In 1492 he made a terrestrial globe, (still in the possession of his family,) which is an interesting monument of the geographical science of that time. He died about 1506, leaving a number of valuable maps and charts.

See "Geschichte des Seefahrers Ritter Martin Behaim," by F. W. GHILLANY, 1853; C. G. VON MURR, "Diplomatische Geschichte des berühmten Ritters M. Behaim," 1778.

Beham, bā'hăm, sometimes written **Bochem,** (BARTHOLOMÄUS,) a distinguished German painter and engraver, born about 1496, was a pupil of Albert Dürer. Among his master-pieces in engraving are "Triton and the Nereids," and "Cleopatra." Died in 1540.

See HEINECKEN, "Dictionnaire des Artistes."

Beham, (HANS SEBALD,) nephew of the preceding, born at Nuremberg in 1500, was one of the best pupils of Albert Dürer. His prints are of very small size, and include engravings on copper, etchings, and woodcuts. Died about 1550.

See NAGLER, "Neues Allgemeines Künstler-Lexikon."

Behem. See BEHAIM.

Behlen, bā'lẹn, (STEPHAN,) a German writer, born at Fritzlar in 1784, published treatises on forest science and hunting. Died in 1847.

Behm, bām, (ERNST LEOPOLD,) a German Protestant theological writer, born in 1700; died in 1742.

Behm, (JOHANN,) a German Protestant divine, born at Königsberg in 1578, published, in Latin, a "Chronology of the World from the Creation to the Destruction of Jerusalem." Died in 1648.

Behm, (JOHANN,) a German Protestant writer on theology, born in 1687; died at Königsberg in 1753.

Behm, (MICHAEL,) a Protestant theologian and writer, born at Königsberg in 1612; died in 1650.

Behmen. See BÖHME, (JAKOB.)

Behmer, bā'mẹr, (FRIEDRICH EHRENREICH,) a German jurist, born at Berlin in 1721; died in 1776.

Behn, bĕn, (Mrs. APHRA,) an English authoress, whose maiden name was JOHNSON, born about 1640. She wrote, besides plays, a number of poems, tales, etc., remarkable for their licentiousness. She is alluded to by Pope under the name of Astrea, which was her pseudonym. Her novel entitled "Oroonoko the American Prince" was very popular. About 1666 she was employed by Charles II. as a secret agent at Antwerp, and captivated several lovers, from one of whom she extorted information of an intended expedition to burn the shipping in the Thames. Died in 1689.

See CIBBER, "Lives of the English Poets."

Behourt, bẹh-ooR', (JEAN,) a French grammarian and dramatist, born in Normandy, lived about 1600.

Behr, bāR, (CHRISTIAN FRIEDRICH,) a German general, born in Pomerania in 1739, served in the French army in the Seven Years' war. Died in 1831.

Behr, (CHRISTOPH,) a German scholar, wrote several works in Latin. Died in 1704.

Behr, (GEORGE HENRI,) a physician, born in Strasburg in 1708, was a pupil of Boerhaave. Died in 1761.

Behr, (JOHANN HEINRICH AUGUST,) a German statesman, born at Freiberg in 1793, became in 1849 minister of finance for the kingdom of Saxony.

Behr, (WILHELM JOSEPH,) a German publicist, born at Sultzheim in 1775. He became professor of law at Würzburg in 1799, and was subsequently twice elected

to the Bavarian Diet, in which he supported liberal principles, and was punished by a long imprisonment. He became a member of the Frankfort Parliament in 1848. He published, besides other works, a "System of Public Law," (3 vols., 1810.) Died in 1851.

Behrens, bā'rẹns, (CONRAD BARTHOLD,) a German physician, born at Hildesheim in 1660. He wrote medical, scientific, and historical treatises. Died in 1736.

Behrens, (GEORG HENNING,) a German physician, born at Goslar in 1662. He wrote "Hercynia Curiosa," a work on the Hartz Forest, (1703.) Died in 1712.

Behrens, (KARL FRIEDRICH,) a German traveller, published in 1739 "Visits to Southern Countries."

Behrens, (MICHAEL,) a German theologian, born at Buxtehude, in Hanover, in 1657; died in 1728.

Behrens, (RODOLF AUGUSTIN,) a German physician and medical writer, born at Brunswick; died in 1747.

Behring, bā'ring, (VITUS,) a Danish historian and Latin poet, born in Jutland in 1617, became historiographer to the King of Denmark. Died in 1675.

See BAILLET, "Jugemens des Savants."

Behr'ing, Beer'ing, or **Be'ring,** [Dan. pron. bā'ring,] (VITUS,) a celebrated Danish navigator, and discoverer of the strait which bears his name, born in Jutland in 1680. Having entered the Russian navy at an early age and served with distinction against the Swedes, he was appointed in 1725 commander of a scientific expedition to the Sea of Kamtchatka. After an absence of more than three years, during which he explored the coast of Kamtchatka as faɪ as 67° 18′ N. lat. and ascertained that Asia was not joined to America, he returned to Russia. Appointed captain-commander in 1732, he set out on a second voyage in 1741, and discovered a part of the North American coast, supposed to have been New Norfolk. Both he and his crew being disabled by sickness, they attempted to return to Kamtchatka, but were wrecked on the island of Avatcha, since called Behring's Island, where Behring died soon after.

See "Nouvelles Découvertes faites des Russes entre l'Asie et l'Amérique," Paris, 1781.

Beidâwee or **Beidâwi, (Al,)** âl bā'dă'wee', written also **Beidhawi** and **Beidhavi, (Abdal'lah-Ben-O'măr,)** a learned Mussulman of the thirteenth century, born at Beda or Beida, in Farsistân, was the author of a "Universal Chronology," (in Persian,) and a "Commentary on the Koran," (in Arabic.) The latter is highly esteemed by Mohammedans.

Beier, bī'ẹr, (ADRIAN,) a German jurist and legal writer, born at Jena in 1634, was professor of law in his native city. Died in 1712.

Beier, (AUGUST.) See BEYER.

Beier, (HARTMANN,) a Protestant theologian, born at Frankfort-on-the-Main in 1516, studied at Wittenberg, where he acquired the friendship of Luther. Died in 1577.

Beil, bīl, (JOHANN DAVID,) a German actor and dramatist, born at Chemnitz in 1734; died in 1794.

Beimiram, bī'me-râm', (ISAAC,) a Jewish physician of the eleventh century, was a contemporary of Avicenna. He wrote several works.

Bein, bīn, (JOHANN,) a designer and engraver, born at Coxweiller (Bas-Rhin) in 1789; died in 1857.

Beinaschi. See BENASCHI.

Beinga-della, bān'gă del'lä, the last king of Pegu, who, after having conquered Ava in 1752, was made prisoner in 1757 by the Burmans, and put to death in 1775.

Beinl von Bienenburg, bīn'l fon bee'nẹn-booRG, (ANTON,) a German physician, and professor of pathology at Vienna, born in 1749. He was physician-in-chief of the Imperial armies. Died in 1820.

Beinville, bâN'vèl', (CHARLES BARTHÉLEMI,) a French publicist and partisan of Richelieu, wrote a work entitled "French Truths opposed to Spanish Calumnies." Died in 1641.

See LELONG, "Bibliothèque historique de la France."

Beireis, bī'rīs, (GOTTFRIED CHRISTOPH,) a German physician and chemist, born at Mühlhausen in 1730. He wrote on medicine and natural history. Died in 1809.

See J. P. GABLER, "Narratio de Vita G. C. Beireisii," 1812.

Beisch, bīsh, written also **Beich,** (JOACHIM FRANZ,) a German landscape-painter and engraver, born in Suabia in 1665. Died in 1748.

ā, ē, ī, ō, ū, ȳ, *long;* à, ė, ò, same, less prolonged; ă, ĕ, ĭ, ŏ, ŭ, ў, *short;* a, ẹ, ị, ọ, *obscure;* fär, fàll, fät; mēt; nŏt; gōōd; mōōn;

Beisler, bīs′lẹr, (HERMANN,) a Bavarian statesman, born at Bensheim in 1790, filled several important offices under the government, and was appointed in 1848 minister of the interior, but held the office only three months.

Beissier, bȧ′se-ȧ′, (JACQUES,) a French surgeon, born in 1623, in Dauphiny, attended Louis XIV. in his campaigns. Died in 1712.

Beisson, bȧ′sȯN′, (FRANÇOIS JOSEPH ÉTIENNE,) a French engraver, born at Aix in 1759; died in 1820.

Beitar. See ABEN-BEITAR.

Beja, bā′zhȧ, (LUIS,) a Portuguese theologian and writer, born at Perestrello, lived about 1600–50.

Beja, de, dȧ bā′zhȧ, (FREY ANTONIO,) a Portuguese priest, born in 1493, wrote a treatise against astrology.

Béjart, bȧ′zhȧR′, (JACQUES,) a French comedian, born in Paris in 1622, was a friend of Molière, and acted some of the characters in his plays. Died in 1659.

Bejot, bẹh-zho′, (FRANÇOIS,) a French *littérateur,* born at Montdidier in 1718, was professor of Greek at Paris, and a member of the Academy of Inscriptions. Died in 1787.

Bek. See BEEK, (DAVID.)

Bēke, (CHARLES TILSTONE,) an English traveller and writer of high reputation, born in 1800, accompanied the expedition of Major Harris to Abyssinia about 1845. He wrote "Origines Biblicæ, or Researches in Primeval History," (1834,) which was severely criticised in Germany by Paulus and others; "Essay on the Nile and its Tributaries," (1847;) "On the Sources of the Nile in the Mountains of the Moon," (1848;) and "On the Geographical Distribution of the Languages of Abyssinia," (1849.)

See "London Quarterly Review" for November, 1834.

Beketof, bĕk′ĕ-tof′, or **Bek′e-toff,** (NIKITA,) a Russian administrator, born in 1729, was governor of Astrachan, and a benefactor to the public. Died in 1794.

Bekiesz, bā′ke-ĕss, (GASPAR,) a Hungarian general in the service of Poland, born about 1530; died in 1579.

Bekk, bĕk, (JOHANN BAPTIST,) a German statesman and jurist, born at Tryberg, in Baden, in 1800, became minister of the interior in 1846, which position he resigned after the revolution of 1848.

Bekker or **Becker,** bĕk′kẹr, (BALTHASAR,) a Dutch theologian, born in Friesland in 1634, was the author of "Researches on Comets," and "The World Bewitched," ("Betoverde Weereld," 1691.) For the latter, in which he condemned the prevailing superstitions of the time respecting sorcery, he was deprived, by the synod, of his office as preacher. Died in 1698.

See J. M. SCHWAGER, "Geschichte der Intoleranz, oder Leben und Schicksale des Dr. B. Bekker," 1780; "B. Bekker in Franeker," Groningen, 1848.

Bekker, (ELIZABETH,) a celebrated Dutch novelist and poetess, born at Flushing in 1738. She was married to Adrian Wolff, a Protestant preacher, and after his death, in 1777, resided with her friend Agatha Deken, in conjunction with whom she wrote her most admired romances, among which are the "History of William Leevend," and "History of Sara Burgerhart." Died in 1804.

Bekker, bĕk′kẹr, (IMMANUEL,) an eminent German philologist and critic, born at Berlin in 1785. He studied at Halle under Wolf, and was appointed professor of philology and Greek at Berlin about 1807. As a member of the Academy of Sciences, he was sent by that body, in 1817, to Italy, in order to assist in deciphering the "Institutes of Gaius," discovered by Niebuhr. In 1814 he had published his "Anecdota Græca," (3 vols.) He produced good editions of the following authors : Plato, (10 vols., 1814–21,) "The Attic Orators," (7 vols. 1823,) Aristotle, (7 vols.,1831,) Thucydides, (3 vols., 1821,) Aristophanes, (3 vols., 1825,) "Scholia for the Iliad," (3 vols., 1827,) and Photius, (2 vols., 1824.)

See BROCKHAUS, "Conversations-Lexikon."

Bektash, Bektasch, or **Bektach.** See BEYGTASH.

Bel. See BELUS and BAAL.

Bel, bĕl, (JEAN JACQUES,) a French *littérateur,* born at Bordeaux in 1693, wrote "Critical Letters on the Marianne of Voltaire," (1726,) and other works. Died in 1738.

See QUÉRARD, "La France Littéraire."

Bel, bĕl, (KARL ANDREAS,) born at Presburg in 1717, was a son of Matthias, noticed below. He became professor of poetry at Leipsic. Died in 1782.

Bel, [Lat. BE′LIUS,] (MATTHIAS,) a Hungarian theolo-

gian, historiographer to the emperor Charles VI., born at Orsova in 1684. He wrote several valuable works, in Latin, on Hungarian history. Died in 1749.

Bel, le, lẹh bĕl, (JEAN,) a Belgian, born about 1305, wrote a chronicle of his own times, which was recently discovered, and published in 1850. Died about 1390.

Be′la I., King of Hungary, succeeded to the throne in 1059. Died in 1063.

Bela II., THE BLIND, succeeded Stephen in 1131.

Bela III. became King of Hungary in 1174. Hungary was first divided into counties in his reign. Died in 1196.

Bela IV., son of Andrew II., ascended the throne in 1235. During his reign the Moguls under Batoo- (Batu-) Khan ravaged Hungary with fire and sword. Died in 1270.

Bela, de, dȧ bā′lȧ, CABALLERO, a Basque historian, born about 1715, wrote a valuable "History of the Basques," of which only an extract has been published.

See QUÉRARD, "La France Littéraire."

Belâdori or **Belâdori,** (Ahmed,) or, more fully, **Aboo-l-Hassan-Ahmed-Ibn-Yahya-al-Belâdori,** (or **-Balâdori,)** ȧ′bŏŏl hȧs′sạn ȧh′med Ib′n yȧh′hyȧ ȧl bạ-lȧ′do-ree, an Arabian historian and poet, lived at Bagdâd in the ninth century. He wrote a history of the early conquests of the Arabs, and translated works from the Pehlevi into Arabic. He died in a hospital for the insane, in 892 A.D.

See IBN-KHALLIKÂN, "Biographical Dictionary;" "Nouvelle Biographie Générale."

Belair, bẹh-lȧR′, (ALEXANDRE PIERRE JULIENNE,) a French general, born in Paris in 1747, served in the army of the North in 1793, and rose to be commander of the National Guards. He wrote several works on fortifications. Died in 1819.

See DE COURCELLES, "Dictionnaire des Généraux Français."

Belair, (CHARLES,) born in Saint Domingo, was a nephew of the celebrated Toussaint L'Ouverture. He took an active part as general of brigade against the French in 1802 ; but, having been taken prisoner, he was condemned by a military commission and shot.

See P. LACROIX, "Mémoires sur les Révolutions de Saint-Domingue."

Belanger, bẹh-lȯN′zhȧ′, (FRANÇOIS JOSEPH,) a French architect, born in Paris in 1744; died in 1818.

Belbeuf, de, dẹh bĕl′buf′, (ANTOINE LOUIS PIERRE JOSEPH Godard—go′dȧR′,) MARQUIS, a French jurist, born at Rouen in 1791, became a senator in 1852.

Bel′camp, van, (JOHN,) a Dutch painter, who worked in London. Died in 1653.

Belcari, de, dȧ bĕl-kȧ′ree, (MAFFEO,) an Italian poet, born in Florence ; died in 1454.

Bel′chẹr, written also **Belchier,** (DABRIDGECOURT,) an English antiquary and dramatic writer. Died in 1621.

Belcher, (Sir EDWARD,) an English naval officer and explorer, born in 1799. He sailed with Captain Beechey to the Arctic regions in 1825, and subsequently, in the ship Sulphur, made a voyage round the world. He joined the expedition to China in 1841, and was knighted in 1843. In 1852 he commanded the expedition in search of Sir John Franklin. He published a "Narrative of the Voyage round the World on the Sulphur," (1836,) and several other works.

Belcher, (JONATHAN,) one of the royal governors in America, born in Cambridge, Massachusetts, in 1681, became one of the principal merchants in New England. He was Governor of Massachusetts and New Hampshire from 1730 to 1741, when his enemies procured his removal. Repairing at once to England, he vindicated his conduct before the king, was restored to the royal favour, and appointed Governor of New Jersey about 1747. Died in 1757.

Belcher, (JONATHAN,) son of the preceding, born in 1711. He graduated at Harvard in 1728, was appointed Lieutenant-Governor of Nova Scotia in 1760, and chief justice in 1761. Died in 1776.

Belchier, bel′chẹr or bel′chĪ-ẹr, (JOHN,) an English surgeon, and Fellow of the Royal Society, born in Surrey in 1706, became governor of Guy's Hospital. Died in 1785.

See WATT, "Bibliotheca Britannica."

Belderbusch, bĕl′dẹr-bŏŏsh′, (KARL LEOPOLD,)

€ as *k;* ç as *s;* g̅ *hard;* g̅ as *j;* G, H, K, *guttural;* N, *nasal;* R, *trilled;* s̄ as *z;* ŧh as in *this.* (☞See Explanations, p. 23.)

COUNT, born in 1749, became a member of the senate of the Netherlands in 1810. Died in 1826.

Beldori, bĕl-do'ree, (GIOVANNI PIETRO,) an Italian antiquary, born at Rome about 1615 ; died in 1696.

Belelli, bȧ-lel'lee, (FULGENCIO,) an Italian ecclesiastic, born at Buccino, in Naples, about 1682 ; died in 1742.

Belenvei, de, deh bel'ŏn-và', or **Beauvois**, bō'và', (AIMERY,) a French troubadour. Died in 1264.

Bel'e-sis or **Bel'e-sȳs**, a priest of Babylon, joined Arbaces in overthrowing the old Assyrian Empire. He was afterwards governor of Babylon, about 826 B.C.

Belestat, de, deh beh-lĕs'tȧ', (GARDOUCH, găr'-doosh',) MARQUIS, a French writer, born at Toulouse in 1725 ; died in 1807.

Belestat, de, (PIERRE LANGLOIS,) a French physician, who lived about 1570, wrote on Egyptian antiquities.

Belèze, beh-làz', (GUILLAUME LOUIS GUSTAVE,) a French *littérateur*, born at Montpellier in 1803. Among his works is a "Universal Dictionary of Practical Life."

Bel'four, (HUGO JAMES,) an English dramatist and poet, born about 1802, published, under the pseudonym of Saint John Dorset, two dramas, entitled "Montezuma," and "The Vampyre." Died in 1827.

Bel'frage, (HENRY,) minister at Falkirk, in Scotland, was born in 1774. He published "Discourses for the Young," (1817,) and other works. Died in 1835.

See MCKERROW, "Life of Henry Belfrage," 1837.

Belfredotti, de, dȧ bĕl-frȧ-dot'tee, (BOCCHINO,) sovereign of Volterra, in Italy, was put to death as a traitor (1361) for attempting to sell his country to the Pisans.

See SISMONDI, "Histoire des Républiques Italiennes."

Belgiojoso, bĕl-jo-yo'so, (CRISTINA TRIVULZIO,) PRINCESS OF, an Italian lady, distinguished for her talents and her patriotism, born at Milan in 1808. About 1830 she removed to Paris, where she acquired the friendship of Augustin Thierry, Mignet, and other eminent men of the liberal party. In 1848 she warmly advocated the Italian revolution, and raised a battalion of volunteers at her own expense. After the defeat of the patriots and the confiscation of her property, she went again to Paris, and became a contributor to the "National."

Bel'gĭ-us or **Bol'gĭ-us**, a leader of the Gauls, who in 279 B.C. gained a signal victory over the Macedonians, in which their king, Ptolemy Ceraunus, was killed.

Belgrado, bĕl-grȧ'do, (GIACOMO,) an Italian Jesuit, born at Udine in 1704, wrote (in Latin) on mechanics and natural philosophy. Died in 1789.

See MAZZUCHELLI, "Scrittori d'Italia."

Belgrand, bĕl'grŏn', (CLAUDE HENRI,) a French general, born in 1748, commanded at the long siege of Malta in 1800. Died in 1839.

Bel-gra'vĭ-us or **Bel-lo-gra'vus**, (RICHARD,) an English Carmelite monk under the reign of Edward II.

Belhomme, bĕl'om' or bȧ'lom', (Dom HUMBERT,) a French Benedictine friar and eloquent preacher, born at Bar-le-Duc in 1653 ; died in 1727.

Belhomme, (JACQUES ÉTIENNE,) a French physician, born in Paris in 1800, wrote several treatises on insanity.

Beli. See BALI.

Belidor, de, dȧ bȧ-le-dŏr', (BERNARD FOREST,) a distinguished engineer and military writer, born in Catalonia in 1693, became professor in the School of Artillery at La Fère, in France. He served in the German campaign of 1742, and afterwards became a member of the Academy of Sciences. Among his principal works are his "Hydraulic Architecture," (1737,) "New Course of Mathematics for the Use of Artillery," (1757,) and a work on engineering. Died in 1761.

See QUÉRARD, "La France Littéraire."

Belière, de la, deh lȧ beh-le-air', (CLAUDE,) a French writer, was born at Charolles, and published, in 1664, "Physionomie raisonnée."

Beligatti, bȧ-le-gât'tee, (CASSIO,) an Italian Capuchin and Orientalist, born at Macerata in 1708, resided as a missionary in Thibet. He published an alphabet of the language of Thibet, and a Hindostanee grammar. Died in 1791.

See ERSCH und GRUBER, "Allgemeine Encyklopaedie."

Belin, beh-lăn' or blăn, (FRANÇOIS,) a French dramatist, born at Marseilles in 1672 ; died in 1732.

Belin, (JEAN ALBERT,) a learned French writer, born at Besançon about 1610, became Bishop of Bellay in 1666. Died in 1677.

Belin de Ballu, beh-lăn' deh bâ'lü', (JACQUES NICOLAS,) a French scholar, born in Paris in 1753, became professor of Greek in the University of Kharkov, in the Ukraine. He translated into French the "Hecuba" of Euripides and the complete works of Lucian, with critical and historical remarks. He also wrote a "Critical History of Eloquence among the Greeks and Romans," (1803.) Died in Saint Petersburg in 1815.

See QUÉRARD, "La France Littéraire."

Beling, bā'ling, (OSWALD,) a German poet, born at Sleswick in 1625 ; died at Cassel in 1646.

Bel'ing, (RICHARD,) an Irish Catholic, born in the county of Dublin in 1613. He first fought for the insurgents in the rebellion of 1641, but afterwards joined the royalist army. He wrote, in Latin, a defence of the Irish Catholics, and other works. He added a sixth book to Sir Philip Sidney's "Arcadia." Died in 1677.

Bélisaire or **Belisar**. See BELISARIUS.

Bel-ĭ-sā'rĭ-us, [Fr. BÉLISAIRE, bâ'le'zăR'; Ger. BELISAR, bā'le-zăR',] a Byzantine general, whose talents were of the highest order, was born at Germania, in Illyria, about 505 A.D. He served in the guard of Justinian before his accession to the throne, (527,) and soon after that event was appointed general-in-chief of the army of the East. He defeated the Persians at Dara, in 530, and quelled a dangerous sedition at Constantinople in 532 A.D. In 533 and 534 he gained decisive victories over the Vandals in Africa, captured their king, Gelimer, and destroyed his kingdom. For this service he was honoured with a triumph, and chosen sole consul, in 535. Between 535 and 540 he was employed against the Ostrogoths, who had obtained possession of Italy. He made himself master of Rome, and had nearly reduced Italy, when he was recalled in 540 A.D. He opposed with success on the eastern frontier a Persian army under Cosroës (or Khosroo) in 542, and at the end of this campaign was degraded by the influence of the empress Theodora. He was fined and threatened with death, but was pardoned on condition that he would be reconciled to his unfaithful and abandoned wife Antonina, who was a favourite of Theodora. In 544 he renewed the war against the Gothic king Totila in Italy, with a small army, which proved to be inadequate to the expulsion of the more numerous enemy. He returned to the capital in 548, and passed about ten years in inaction. His last service was the repulse of the Bulgarians, who invaded the empire in 559 A.D., after which the jealousy of Justinian or the intrigues of courtiers deprived him of command.

In 563 he was falsely accused of a conspiracy against the life of Justinian, for which his fortune was sequestered. According to Gibbon, his innocence was recognized before his death, which occurred in 565 A.D. There appears to be no foundation for the once current tradition or fiction that he was deprived of sight and reduced to support himself by begging. He seems to have been a Christian in outward conformity at least. As a general, he was distinguished for presence of mind and rapidity of movement. He was loyal to the emperor, humane to the vanquished, and patient towards rivals who falsely accused him.

See "Life of Belisarius," by LORD MAHON, 1829; GIBBON, "Decline and Fall of the Roman Empire;" CHRISTIAN FRIEDRICH ZELLER, "Belisarius," Tübingen, 1809; C. L. ROTH, "Ueber Belisars Ungnade," 1846; "Blackwood's Magazine" for May, 1847.

Belknap, bĕl'nap, (JEREMY,) an American historian and clergyman, born in Boston in 1744. He was ordained pastor of a Congregational church at Dover, New Hampshire, in 1767, and in 1787 removed to Boston, where he preached about ten years. He published a "History of New Hampshire," (3 vols., 1784–92,) "American Biography," (2 vols., 1794–98,) and "The Foresters," an apologue. Died in 1798.

See a "Life of J. Belknap," 1847.

Belknap, (WILLIAM G.,) an American officer, born at Newburg, New York, in 1794, served at the battle of Fort Erie in August, 1814, became a captain in 1822, and a major in 1842. He distinguished himself at Buena Vista in 1847. Died in 1852.

ā, ē, ī, ō, ū, ȳ, *long;* ă, ĕ, ĭ, ŏ, ŭ, ў, *short;* ą, ę, į, ǫ, *obscure;* fär, fåll, fât; mĕt; nŏt; gōōd; mōͻn;

Bell, (ANDREW,) the founder of the monitorial system of instruction, also called the Madras system, was born at Saint Andrew's, in Fifeshire, in 1752. He was appointed in 1789 chaplain of Fort Saint George, at Madras, where he devoted himself to the gratuitous instruction of the orphans of the military asylum. On his return to England he published an account of the new method, and soon after a school was established upon this plan by Joseph Lancaster. The success of these experiments caused the system to be generally adopted in England and other countries. Dr. Bell died in 1832, leaving large sums for the endowment of schools on the Madras system. (See LANCASTER, JOSEPH.)

See "Life of the Rev. Andrew Bell," by R. and C. C. SOUTHEY; "London Quarterly Review" for October, 1811; CHAMBERS, "Biographical Dictionary of Eminent Scotsmen."

Bell, (BEAUPRÉ,) an English antiquary, who bequeathed a valuable collection of medals and manuscripts to Trinity College, Cambridge. Died in 1745.

Bell, (BENJAMIN,) F.R.S., a distinguished Scottish surgeon, born at Edinburgh, studied under Professor Monro. He published a "System of Surgery," (6 vols., 1782,) and other works of high reputation, which were translated into French and German. Died in 1806.

See CHAMBERS, "Biographical Dictionary of Eminent Scotsmen."

Bell, (Sir CHARLES,) an eminent physiologist and anatomist, born at Edinburgh in 1774, was a son of the Rev. William Bell. He was a pupil of his brother John, noticed below. About 1804 he became a resident of London, where he practised and lectured on surgery. He published in 1806 an "Essay on the Anatomy of Expression in Painting," which is highly esteemed, and in 1807 his valuable "System of Operative Surgery." In 1814 he was appointed surgeon to the Middlesex Hospital, which he left in a flourishing condition in 1836. He was highly distinguished for his skill as an operator. In 1821 he announced an important discovery in a paper on the "Nervous System," read before the Royal Society. He discovered that the nerves of sensation are distinct from the nerves of motion; that the former, arising from the posterior column of the spinal marrow, convey sensation from the body to the brain; and that the nerves connected with the anterior column convey the mandates of the will to the members, and are essential to voluntary motion. This has been pronounced the most important discovery in physiology since that of the circulation of the blood by Harvey. In 1824 he published "An Exposition of the Natural System of the Nerves of the Human Body," and was appointed to the senior chair of anatomy and surgery in the London College of Surgeons. He was knighted on the accession of William IV., (1830,) and accepted a chair of surgery in the Edinburgh University in 1836. He died in Worcestershire, on a journey to London, in April, 1842.

Among his works are "Illustrations of the Great Operations of Surgery: Trepan, Hernia, Amputation, Aneurism, and Lithotomy," (1821,) "The Hand, its Mechanism and Vital Endowments as evincing Design," (one of the Bridgewater Treatises, 1833,) and an improved edition of his "Anatomy of Expression," with illustrations drawn by himself, (1844.)

See A. SHAW, "Narrative of the Discoveries of Sir Charles Bell in the Nervous System," 1837; "Quarterly Review" for May, 1843, vol. lxxii.; AMÉDÉE PICHOT, "Sur C. Bell," Paris, 1846; CHAMBERS, "Biographical Dictionary of Eminent Scotsmen," (Supplement.)

Bell, (CURRER.) See BRONTÉ.

Bell, (GEORGE JOSEPH,) an eminent Scottish jurist, born near Edinburgh in 1770. He published "Commentaries on the Laws of Scotland," (1810,) which soon passed through six editions. Its rare merit procured for him a vote of thanks from the Faculty of Advocates. He also wrote "Principles of the Law of Scotland," and other standard treatises on law. In 1821 he was appointed professor of Scottish law at Edinburgh. Died in 1843.

Bell, (HENRY,) a Scottish engineer and mechanician, born in Linlithgowshire in 1767. He constructed in 1811 a steamboat, which he launched on the Clyde in 1812, four years after Fulton's first experiment on the Hudson, of which he appears to have been ignorant. He died in 1830, and a monument was erected to his memory near Bowling.

See CHAMBERS, "Biographical Dictionary of Eminent Scotsmen."

Bell, (HENRY GLASFORD,) editor of the "Edinburgh Literary Journal" in 1830, wrote a "Life of Mary Queen of Scots," and a collection of poems.

Bell, (HENRY H.,) an American rear-admiral, born in North Carolina, entered the navy in 1823. He was appointed fleet-captain to Farragut in April, 1862. He commanded a division of the fleet in the great battle with the forts below New Orleans, April 18–25 of that year. On the capture of New Orleans, he took down, in the midst of an angry mob, the flag of the disunionists from the custom-house. During the absence of Farragut in 1863, he commanded the Western Gulf Blockading Squadron, and was promoted to the rank of rear-admiral. He was drowned on the coast of Japan in January, 1868.

Bell, (JAMES,) born at Jedburgh, in Scotland, in 1769, published a "System of Popular and Scientific Geography," (6 vols.) Died in 1833.

See CHAMBERS, "Biographical Dictionary of Eminent Scotsmen."

Bell, (JOHN,) sometimes called BELL OF ANTERMONY, from his residence, a Scottish traveller, born in 1691. In 1714 he visited Saint Petersburg, and in 1715 was appointed by Peter the Great surgeon and physician to the expedition then preparing for Persia. He subsequently travelled in Siberia, China, and the Caucasus, and in 1737 was sent by the Russian government on a mission to Constantinople. He died in Scotland in 1780. His works had been published in 1763, under the title of "Travels from Saint Petersburg to various Parts of Asia:" they are highly interesting, particularly the portion relating to China.

See CHAMBERS, "Biographical Dictionary of Eminent Scotsmen."

Bell, (JOHN,) an English printer, born in 1746, published fine editions of Shakspeare and other English poets. Died in 1831.

Bell, (JOHN,) an English artillery officer, born in 1747, was the inventor of the "gun proof" and several other military machines, for which he obtained a silver medal from the Society of Arts. Died in 1798.

Bell, (JOHN,) a distinguished British surgeon, born in Edinburgh in May, 1763, was a brother of Sir Charles Bell. He began to lecture on anatomy and surgery in Edinburgh about 1790, in a theatre built for himself, and practised surgery with great success. In 1793 he published the first volume of a "System of the Anatomy of the Human Body," (4 vols., 1793–1804.) He was an eloquent lecturer, a powerful writer in controversy, and one of the most skilful operators of his time. His other principal works are "Discourses on the Nature and Cure of Wounds," (2 vols., 1793–95,) "Principles of Surgery," (3 vols., 1801,) and "Observations on Italy," (1825.) Having visited Italy for the benefit of his health, he died at Rome in April, 1820. "His picturesque descriptions of the country are fresh and delightful landscapes, while his remarks on the pictorial and sculptured treasures of Italy are replete with feeling and judgment." ("London Literary Gazette.")

See CHAMBERS, "Biographical Dictionary of Eminent Scotsmen."

Bell, (JOHN,) M.D., a physician and medical writer, born in Ireland in 1796, emigrated in 1810 to America. He was for several years lecturer on the institutes of medicine in the Philadelphia Medical Institute, and afterwards became professor of the theory and practice of medicine in the Medical College of Ohio.

Bell, (JOHN,) an American. statesman, born near Nashville in 1797, studied law, and was admitted to the bar in 1816. He was elected a member of Congress in 1827, and was re-elected six times between that year and 1841. He opposed Calhoun's project of nullification, and supported General Jackson as candidate for the Presidency in 1832, but protested against the removal of the deposits from the Bank of the United States. He acquired distinction as a debater, and was a constant advocate of a protective tariff, and of the improvement of rivers and harbours. About 1833 he separated from the Democratic party and joined the Whigs, who elected him Speaker of the House of Representatives in 1834, when James K. Polk was his competitor. In 1836 he advocated the election of Hugh L. White to the Presidency, and was returned to Congress by the voters of the district which contains Nashville and the Hermitage,

(General Jackson's residence.) He was appointed secretary of war by President Harrison in 1841, but he resigned in September of that year, in consequence of Tyler's defection from the Whig party. Having passed about six years in retirement, he was elected a Senator of the United States from Tennessee in 1847. He favoured the compromise measures of Mr. Clay in 1850, and opposed the repeal of the Missouri Compromise in 1854. In 1853 he was re-elected a Senator for six years. In 1860 a National Convention of a party styling itself the Constitutional Union Party nominated Mr. Bell for President and Edward Everett for Vice-President, with a brief "platform," which insisted only on "The Constitution, the Union, and the Enforcement of the Laws." He received thirty-nine electoral votes, cast by the States of Tennessee, Kentucky, and Virginia. Died in 1869.

Bell, (JOHN,) an English sculptor, born in Norfolk in 1800. Among his master-pieces are "The Eagle-Slayer," (1837,) "Una and the Lion," "Dorothea," (1841,) and "The Babes in the Wood." He has also produced statues of the "Madonna and Child," "Andromeda," and other scriptural and classical subjects.

Bell, (LUTHER V.,) an American physician, born at Chester, New Hampshire, in 1806. He became, in 1837, superintendent of the McLean Insane Asylum at Charlestown, Massachusetts.

Bell, (ROBERT,) a distinguished journalist and miscellaneous writer, born at Cork, in Ireland, in 1800. Having removed to London, he became a contributor to the "New Monthly Magazine," "The Atlas," and Lardner's "Cabinet Cyclopædia." In conjunction with Bulwer and Lardner, he founded, in 1840, "The Monthly Chronicle." He also published a "History of Russia," (3 vols., 1836–38,) "Lives of the English Poets," (2 vols., 1839,) "Outlines of China," (1845,) a "Life of George Canning," (1846,) and other works. Died in London in April, 1867.

Bell, (SAMUEL,) an American Senator and lawyer, born at Londonderry, New Hampshire, in 1770. He was Governor of his native State for five years, (1819–23,) and was a Senator of the United States from 1823 to 1835. Died in 1850.

Bell, (THOMAS,) a distinguished English naturalist, born in Dorsetshire in 1792. He became, in 1825, one of the founders of the "Zoological Journal," and was subsequently elected a Fellow of the Royal Society, and president of the Linnæan Society, (1853.) He published a "Monograph of the Testudinata," (1833,) a "History of British Quadrupeds," (1836,) and a "History of the British Stalk-Eyed Crustacea," (1853.)

Bell, (WILLIAM,) an English divine and religious writer, born about 1731, was chaplain to the princess Amelia, and was appointed, in 1765, prebendary of Westminster. Died in 1816.

Bell, (WILLIAM,) an English painter, born at Newcastle-upon-Tyne. He obtained the gold medal of the Royal Academy, in 1771, for his picture of "Venus requesting Vulcan to forge the Arms for Æneas." Died about 1800.

Bella, bel'lä, (GERONIMO,) an Italian pastoral poet, born in Piedmont, lived about 1630–60.

Bella, della, del'lä bel'lä, (GIANO,) an Italian democrat, who was exiled from Florence in 1294. Died about 1295.

Bella, della, (STEFANO,) an eminent Italian engraver, born at Florence in 1610, was commissioned by Cardinal Richelieu to engrave the "Capture of Arras," and other military exploits of Louis XIII. His works are of small dimensions, and number over fourteen hundred pieces. "No one," says Basan, "has surpassed this excellent artist in delicacy and lightness of point." In drawing human figures, it is said, he always began at the feet and worked upwards. On his return to Florence, he was appointed teacher of design to Prince Cosimo II., afterwards grand duke. Among his master-pieces is a "View of Pont-Neuf, Paris," and "Parnassus." Died in 1664.

See NAGLER, "Neues Allgemeines Künstler-Lexikon."

Bellacato, bĕl-lä-kä'to, (LUIGI,) an Italian physician, born at Padua in 1501, practised in his native city. Died in 1575.

Bellagatta, bĕl-lä-gät'tä, (ANGELO ANTONIO,) an Italian physician, born at Milan in 1704, wrote "Philosophic Letters," and other works. Died in 1742.

Bellaguet, bȧ'lȧ'gȧ', (LOUIS FRANÇOIS,) a French littérateur, born at Sens in 1807, translated several works from the Latin and Italian.

Bel'la-mọnt, (RICHARD,) EARL OF, an English nobleman, who was appointed Governor of New York and Massachusetts in 1695. He was a popular governor, and captured the pirate Captain Kidd. Died at New York in 1701.

Bel'la-mỹ, (ANNE GEORGE,) a noted English actress, born in London in 1733. She died in poverty in 1788, leaving a work entitled "Apology for the Life of G. Anne Bellamy," (London, 1785,) which some writers have attributed to Alexander Bicknell.

Bellamy, bel'lä-me, [Dutch pron. bel'lä-mī,] (JACOBUS,) one of the most eminent of Dutch poets, born at Flushing in 1757. On the occasion of the war of 1785, he published his "Patriotic Poems," ("Vaderlandsche Gezangen.") His other principal works are "Songs of my Youth," ("Gezangen mijner Jeugd,") and a simple and touching story in the ballad form, entitled "Roosje." He contributed greatly to improve the Dutch language and literature and bring them nearer to his favourite German models. He died at the early age of twenty-eight.

See Q. KNIPERS, "Notice sur Bellamy;" A. VEREUL, "Redevoeringen over J. Douza en over J. Bellamy," 1791; OCKERSE en KLEYN, "Gedenkzuil op het Graf van J. Bellamy," 1822; LONGFELLOW, "Poets and Poetry of Europe."

Bellamy, (JOHN,) an English writer, published in 1818 "The Holy Bible, newly translated from the Original Hebrew."

See "London Quarterly Review," vols. xix. and xxiii.; "Eclectic Review," vol. x.

Bel'la-mỹ, (JOSEPH,) a celebrated American theologian, born in Connecticut in 1719, graduated at Yale College in 1735. He was ordained pastor of the church at Bethlehem, Connecticut, in 1740, and also laboured as an itinerant preacher. He was regarded as a powerful preacher and a learned divine. His system of theology is similar to that of Jonathan Edwards. Several volumes of his sermons and other works have been published. Died in 1790.

Bellamy, (THOMAS,) an English writer, born at Kingston-upon-Thames in 1745, wrote a novel entitled "Sadaski," and other works. Died in 1800.

Bellange, bȧ'lôNzh', (JACQUES,) a French engraver, born at Châlons about 1610. Among his best prints are "Saint John . . the Wilderness," and "The Death of Virginia."

See HEINECKEN, "Dictionnaire des Artistes."

Bellangé, bȧ'lôN'zhȧ', (JOSEPH LOUIS HIPPOLYTE,) a French painter of battles and historical pieces, born in Paris in 1800.

Bellange, (THIERRY,) a French painter, pupil of Vouet, born at Nancy about 1596; died about 1650.

Bellanger, bȧ'lôN'zhȧ', (FRANÇOIS JOSEPH,) a French architect, born in Paris in 1744. Among his works is the iron cupola of the grain-market, (Halle au Blé,) Paris, (1812.) Died in 1818.

Bellanger, (JEAN ANTOINE,) a French engraver, who lived about 1745, executed, among other prints, the "Miracle of the Loaves and Fishes," and "The School of Athens," after Raphael.

See HEINECKEN, "Dictionnaire des Artistes."

Bellardi, bĕl-lar'dee,(CARLO LUIGI,) a physician and naturalist, born near Vercelli, in Piedmont, in 1741. He wrote several botanical treatises, and contributed to Allioni's "Flora Pedemontana." He lived many years in Turin. Died in 1828.

See TIPALDO, "Biografia degli Italiani illustri."

Bellarini, bĕl-lä-ree'nee, (GIOVANNI,) an Italian theologian, born at Castelnuovo, entered the society of Barnabites in 1575. He wrote "Mirror of Divine and Human Wisdom," ("Speculum humanæ atque divinæ Sapientiæ," 1630.) Died in 1630.

Bellarmin or **Bellarmine.** See BELLARMINO.

Bellarmino, bĕl-lar-mee'no, [Fr. BELLARMIN, bȧ'lȧR'mäN',] often called in English **Bellarmin** or **Bellar-**

mine, bĕl-lar′min, (ROBERTO,) an eminent Italian cardinal and champion of Catholicism, born at Montepulciano on the 4th of October, 1542. He entered the order of Jesuits at the age of eighteen, and became professor of theology at Louvain in 1570. On his return to Rome in 1576, he was appointed by Gregory XIII. to teach controversial theology in the college he had just founded. He was made a cardinal by Clement VIII. in 1598, and in 1601 Archbishop of Capua, but upon being appointed librarian of the Vatican, in 1605, he resigned his see. He died at Rome in 1621. Among his principal works are his "Controversies," ("Disputationes de Controversiis Fidei adversos hujus temporis Hæreticos," 1581–88, 4 vols., 1688,) "Treatise on the Duty of Bishops," and "On the Power of the Pope in Temporal Affairs," (all in Latin.) Cardinal Bellarmine was distinguished for his elevation of character and mildness of disposition, and, though esteemed one of the ablest controversialists of his time, was accustomed to say that "an ounce of peace was worth more than a pound of victory."

"As the century drew near its close," says Hallam, "the Church of Rome brought forward her most renowned and formidable champion, Bellarmin.... His abilities are best tested by Protestant theologians, not only in their terms of eulogy, but indirectly in the peculiar zeal with which they chose him as their worthiest adversary. More than half a dozen books in the next fifty years bear the title of Anti-Bellarminus." ("Introduction to the Literature of Europe.")

See BELLARMINO's "Autobiography;" G. FULIGATTI, "Vita del Cardinal Roberto Bellarmino," 1622; DANIELLO BARTOLI, "Della Vita di R. Bellarmino," 1678; FRANCESCO MARAZZA, "Ristretto della Vita di R. Bellarmino," 1682; P. FRIZON, "Vie du Cardinal Bellarmin," 1708; and "Leben des Cardinals R. Bellarmin, von einem Priester in Franken," 1846.

Bellart, bȧ′lȧr′, (NICOLAS FRANÇOIS,) a distinguished French advocate, born in Paris in 1761. He was made attorney-general of the royal court, grand officer of the legion of honour, and obtained other distinctions under Louis XVIII. Died in 1826.

See BILLECOQ, "Notice sur Bellart," 1826.

Bellati, bĕl-lä′tee, (ANTONIO FRANCESCO,) an Italian theologian, Jesuit, and pulpit orator, born at Ferrara in 1665, wrote "Sacred and Moral Treatises," and other works. Died in 1742.

See MAZZUCHELLI, "Scrittori d'Italia."

Bellati, (GIOVANNI,) an Italian painter, born in 1745; died in 1808. Some of his works are at Rome.

Bellavène, bȧ′lä′vȧn′, (JACQUES NICOLAS,) BARON, born at Verdun in 1770, was appointed by Napoleon in 1812 inspector-general of military schools. He wrote a "Course of Mathematics for the Use of Military Schools." Died in 1826.

Bellavia, bĕl-lä-vee′ä, (MARCANTONIO,) a Sicilian engraver and painter, lived about 1600.

See LANZI, "History of Painting in Italy."

Bellay, bȧ′lȧ′ or bĕl′lȧ′, (FRANÇOIS PHILIPPE,) a French medical writer, born at Lent in 1762, practised at Lyons. He published, with Dr. Brion, a good medical journal, (1799–1804.) Died in 1824.

Bellay, du, dü bȧ′lȧ′, (GUILLAUME,) Seigneur de Langey, a French diplomatist and soldier, born near Montmirail in 1491. He was appointed by Francis I. Viceroy of Piedmont, and was employed in important embassies to England, Italy, and Germany. He died in 1543, leaving "Memoirs of his Times."

See BRANTÔME, "Mémoires des Capitaines Français."

Bellay, du, (JEAN,) a French cardinal, brother of the preceding, born in 1492, was patronized by Francis I., and became successively Bishop of Paris and of Limoges, and Archbishop of Bordeaux. Died in 1560.

See AUBERY, "Histoire des Cardinaux."

Bellay, du, (JOACHIM,) a distinguished poet, nephew of the preceding, surnamed THE FRENCH OVID, was born near Angers about 1524. He enjoyed the favour of Francis I. and his sister, Margaret of Navarre. He wrote Latin poems and sonnets, which were greatly admired in his time. Died in 1560.

See SAINTE-BEUVE, "Tableau de la Poésie Française au seizième Siècle;" and LONGFELLOW, "Poets and Poetry of Europe."

Bellay, du, (MARTIN,) brother of the cardinal, became

lieutenant of Normandy. He wrote "Historic Memoirs from 1513 to 1547." Died in 1559.

Bellay, du, (RENÉ,) the youngest brother of Cardinal du Bellay, became in 1535 Bishop of Mans. Died in 1546. His nephew, EUSTACHE DU BELLAY, became Bishop of Paris.

Belle, bĕl, (CLÉMENT LOUIS MARIE ANNE,) a historical painter, born in Paris in 1722; died in 1806.

Belle, de, dẹh bĕl, (JEAN FRANÇOIS JOSEPH,) a French officer, born at Voreppe in 1767, served in the Italian campaign of 1799, and subsequently under Le Clerc in Saint Domingo, where he fell in battle in 1802.

Belle, la, bĕl, (ALEXIS SIMON,) a French portrait-painter, born about 1674; died in 1734.

Belleau, bȧ′lō′, (RÉMY,) born at Nogent-le-Rotrou in 1528, was a friend of Ronsard, and was one of the seven poets called "the French Pleiades." He wrote pastorals entitled "Bergeries," and "Amours et nouveaux Eschanges des Pierres précieuses," (1576.) Died in Paris in 1577.

See LONGFELLOW's "Poets and Poetry of Europe."

Bellebuoni, bĕl-là-boo-o′nee, (MATTEO,) an Italian writer, born about 1290, translated from the Latin into Italian "The History of the War of Troy."

See GINGUENÉ, "Histoire Littéraire d'Italie."

Bellecombe, de, dẹh bĕl′kȯmb′, (ANDRÉ URSULE CASSE,) a French littérateur, born at Montpézat, in Lot-et-Garonne, in 1822, wrote a "Universal History," (8th volume, 1858; unfinished.)

Bellecourt, bĕl′koor′, (JEAN CLAUDE GILLES,) sometimes called COLSON, a French comedian, born in Paris in 1725; died in 1778. His wife, ROSE PÉTRONILLE LE ROY DE LA CORBINAYE, was also a popular actress.

Bellée, bȧ′lȧ′, (TEODORO,) an Italian physician, born near Ragusa. He taught medicine at Padua for many years. Died in 1600.

Bellefonds or **Bellefont, de,** dẹh bĕl′fȯn′, (BERNARDIN **Gigault**—zhe′gō′,) MARQUIS, born in 1630, served in Flanders in 1637, and subsequently in Holland, and was made marshal of France in 1668. Died in 1694.

Belleforest, de, dẹh bĕl′fo′rȧ′, (FRANÇOIS,) a French littérateur, born at Sarzan in 1530, was a favourite at the court of Margaret, Queen of Navarre. He published many mediocre works, among which is "Histoires tragiques," translated from Bandello. Died in Paris in 1583.

Bellegarde, de, dẹh bĕl′gȧrd′, (ANTOINE DUBOIS,) a member of the French National Convention, born in Angoumois about 1740. He became subsequently a member of the Council of Five Hundred and of the Council of Ancients, (1798.) Died in 1825.

Bellegarde, de, (GABRIEL DU PAC,) a French Jansenist theologian, born near Carcassonne in 1717. He wrote "Historical Memoirs on the Affair of the Bull Unigenitus," and other works. Died in 1789.

Bellegarde, de, (HENRI,) COMTE, born at Chambéry, in Savoy, in 1755, entered the Austrian service, and fought in the principal campaigns against the French from 1793 to 1800. He was made field-marshal in 1806. Died in 1831.

Bellegarde, de, (JEAN BAPTISTE MORVAN,) generally known as the ABBÉ DE BELLEGARDE, born near Nantes in 1648. He made translations from Saint Chrysostom, Saint Basil, Gregory Nazianzen, and other Fathers, also several of the Latin classics. Died in 1734.

See MORÉRI, "Dictionnaire Historique."

Bellegarde, de, (ROGER de Saint-Lary—dẹh sȧn′-lȧ′re′,) a French marshal, who enjoyed the favour of Catherine de Médicis and Henry III., but, having fallen into disgrace, was poisoned by order of the former, (1579.)

See F. SECOUSSE, "Mémoire historique sur la Vie de Roger de Saint-Lary de Bellegarde," 1764.

Bellegarde, de, (ROGER de Saint-Lary et de Termes—dẹh sȧn′lȧ′re′ ȧ dẹh tȧrm′,) DUC, born al. ut 1563, was a favourite of Henry III., Henry IV., and Louis XIII. Died in 1646.

Bellegingue, bĕl′gȧng′, (PIERRE,) a French physician, born at Besançon in 1759; died in 1826.

Belle-Isle, de, DUC. See FOUQUET, (CHARLES LOUIS AUGUSTE.)

Belle-Isle, de, (LOUIS CHARLES ARMAND FOUQUET,) CHEVALIER. See FOUQUET.

Bel'len-den, Ballantyne, or Ballentyne, (JOHN,) a Scottish poet, who served James V. as "clerk of his comptis," and became Archdeacon of Moray about 1536. He translated Hector Boece's "History of Scotland" from the Latin into the vernacular language, and wrote several poems. Died at Rome about 1550.

See BALLENTYNE, in CHAMBERS's "Biographical Dictionary of Eminent Scotsmen."

Bellenden, Ballantyne, or Ballenden, (Sir JOHN,) a Scottish statesman and jurist, was appointed a lord of session in 1547, and on the arrival of Queen Mary became one of her privy council. Died in 1577.

See CHAMBERS, "Biographical Dictionary of Eminent Scotsmen."

Bellenden, (WILLIAM,) a Scottish writer, celebrated for the elegance of his Latinity. He resided many years in Paris, where he is said to have been professor of humanities. His principal works are a sort of compilation from Cicero, entitled "Ciceronis Princeps," (1608,) dedicated to Prince Henry, "De Statu Reipublicæ," and the "De Statu prisci Orbis," (1615.) Dr. Middleton has been charged with borrowing from these writings in his "Life of Cicero." Died before 1633.

See CHAMBERS, "Biographical Dictionary of Eminent Scotsmen."

Bellenger, bȧ'lôN'zhȧ', (FRANÇOIS,) a French philologist and littérateur, born in the diocese of Lisieux in 1688. He translated Dionysius of Halicarnassus, and wrote several critical essays. Died in 1749.

Bellenghi, bĕl-lĕn'gee, (FILIPPO MARIA ALBERTINO,) an Italian writer on theology and physical sciences, born at Forlimpopoli in 1758. He became Archbishop of Nicosia. Died in 1839.

Belle-Perche, de, dĕh bĕl'pȧrsh', (PIERRE,) a chancellor of France and learned bishop, born in Nivernais; died in 1307.

Beller or Bellere, bȧ'laiR', [Lat. BELLE'RUS,] a Flemish typographer and writer, published at Antwerp a number of elegant editions of the classics. Died in 1595.

Bellermann, bel'ler-mân', (CHRISTIAN FRIEDRICH,) son of Johann Joachim, noticed below, a German Protestant theologian and writer, born at Erfurt in 1793.

Bellermann, (JOHANN FRIEDRICH,) a German littérateur, a brother of the preceding, born at Erfurt in 1795. He published in 1840 an edition of the "Hymns of Dionysius and Mesomedes."

Bellermann, (JOHANN JOACHIM,) a German theologian and antiquary, born in 1754 at Erfurt, where he became professor of theology, (1790.) He wrote a "Manual of Biblical Literature," (1787,) "Remarks on Phœnician and Punic Coins," (1812,) and other works. Died in 1842.

See "J. J. Bellermanni, Vita breviter ab ipso descripta," 1804.

Bel-ler'o-phon, [Gr. Βελλεροφών,] i.e. "Slayer of Bellerus," originally called Hippon'ous, in Grecian mythology, was the son of Glaucus, King of Corinth. Having slain Bellerus, he fled to Prœtus, King of Argos, who, at the instigation of his wife, sent him to Iobates, King of Lycia, requesting the latter to put him to death. Bellerophon being sent by Iobates against the monster Chimæra, slew him, and afterwards defeated the Amazons. Attempting to soar to Olympus on the winged horse Pegasus, Jupiter caused him to be thrown to the earth, and he was made blind by the fall.

Bellerose, bĕl'roz', (PIERRE le Messier—lĕh mȧ'-se-ȧ',) a French comedian, died in 1670.

Bellet, bȧ'lȧ', ABBÉ, a French antiquary and naturalist, lived about 1720. He was canon of Cadillac.

Bellet, (CHARLES,) a French ecclesiastic and religious writer, born in 1702; died in 1771.

Bellet, (ISAAC,) a French physician, who was inspector of the mineral waters of France. Died in 1778.

Bellet-Verrier, bȧ'lȧ' vȧ're-ȧ', (HUBERT,) a French writer, lived about 1680-1725. His principal work is entitled "Alphabetical Memorial concerning the Law, Police, and Finances of France."

Belleteste, bĕl'tĕt', (B.,) a French Orientalist, born at Orléans in 1778, translated from the Arabic a "Treatise on Precious Stones." Died in 1808.

Belleval, de, dĕh bĕl'vȧl', (CHARLES FRANÇOIS Dumeisniel—dü'mȧ'ne-el',) a French botanist, born in 1733; died at Abbeville in 1790.

Belleval, de, (PIERRE RICHER,) a French physician and botanist, born at Châlons-sur-Marne in 1558. He became, in 1596, professor of botany at Montpellier, being the first who taught that science in France except in connection with medicine. The genus Richeria was named in his honour. Died at Montpellier in 1623.

See "Recherches sur la Vie de P. R. de Belleval," Paris, 1822.

Belleville, bĕl'vĕl', or Turlupin, tür'lü'păn', (HENRI Legrand—lĕh'gRôN',) a French comedian. Died in 1634.

Bellevois, bĕl'vwȧ', a skilful painter of marine views. Died at Hamburg in 1684.

Bellevue, de, dĕh bĕl'vü', (ARMAND,) a French Dominican monk, born in Provence about 1290.

Bellevue, de, (JACQUES,) a French jurist, born at Aix, became, in 1314, professor of law at Perugia.

Belley, bȧ'lȧ', (AUGUSTIN,) a French antiquary, born at Sainte-Foi-de-Montgomery in 1697, was a member of the Academy of Inscriptions. Died in 1771.

Belli, bĕl'lee, (CARLO,) an Italian Jesuit and writer, born at Venice in 1742; died in 1816.

Belli, (CHERUBINO,) a Sicilian monk and poet, lived about 1590-1650.

Belli, (FRANCESCO,) an Italian theologian and writer, born at Arzignano in 1577; died in 1644.

Belli, (GIULIO,) an Italian writer, born at Capo d'Istria, wrote a work entitled "Hermes Politicus," (1608.)

Belli, [Lat. BEL'LIUS,] (HONORIUS,) an Italian physician and botanist, born at Vicenza, lived about 1550-90. He practised in the island of Crete, was well versed in the Greek language, and was one of the first that attempted to identify the plants mentioned by the ancients.

See JÖCHER, "Allgemeines Gelehrten-Lexikon."

Belli, (PAOLO,) an Italian Jesuit and Latin writer, born at Messina in 1588; died in 1658.

Belli, (PIETRO,) an Italian jurist, born at Alba in 1502; died in 1575.

See VERNAZZA, "Vie de P. Belli," 1783.

Belliard, bȧ'le-ȧr', (AUGUSTIN DANIEL,) COMTE, a French general, born at Fontenay-le-Comte in 1769. He became a general in 1796, fought successfully in the campaigns of Italy, Egypt, Austria, and Russia, and in 1814 was made colonel-general of the cavalry of the guard. He was created a peer by Louis XVIII., and in 1831 was sent as ambassador to Belgium. Died at Brussels in 1832.

See "Mémoires du Comte Belliard, écrits par lui-même," 3 vols., 1834; "Nouvelle Biographie Générale."

Bellicard, bȧ'le'kȧr', (JÉRÔME CHARLES,) a French architect and engraver, born in Paris in 1726, was professor in the Royal Academy of Architecture. He published "Observations on the Antiquities of Herculaneum," (1754.) He was a member of the Academies of Florence and Bologna. Died in 1786.

See LE BLANC, "Manuel de l'Amateur d'Estampes."

Bellier, bȧ'le-ȧ', (PIERRE,) a French scholar, who translated a part of the works of Philo-Judæus, (1575.)

Bellièvre, de, dĕh bȧ'le-ȧvr', (ALBERT,) a French prelate, son of Pomponne, noticed below, was appointed Archbishop of Lyons by Henry IV. in 1599. In 1604 he resigned his office to his brother Claude. Died in 1621.

Bellièvre, de, (NICOLAS,) brother of the preceding, born in 1583, rose to be president of the parliament of Paris in 1614.

Bellièvre, de, (POMPONNE,) a French jurist and diplomatist, born at Lyons in 1529. He was sent on important missions to Sweden and England, and in 1599 was made chancellor of France by Henry IV. Died in 1607.

See JEAN PAPIRE MASSON, "Elogium P. de Bellièvre," 1607.

Bellin, the French of BELLINI, which see.

Bellin, bȧ'lăn', (JACQUES NICOLAS,) a French hydrographer and engineer of the marine, born in Paris in 1703. He executed the maps for the Abbé Prévost's "Histoire Générale des Voyages," and published a collection of charts entitled "French Hydrography," (1756.) Died in 1772.

Bellincioni, bĕl-lĕn-cho'nee, (BERNARDO,) sometimes called Bellinzona, a Florentine poet. Died in 1491.

Belling, von, fon bel'ling, (WILHELM SEBASTIAN,) a Prussian general and favourite of Frederick the Great, born about 1719, served with distinction in the Seven Years' war. Died in 1799.

See ARCHENHOLZ, "Histoire de la Guerre de Sept Ans."

Bellingen, de, dẹh bặ'lȧN'zhȯN', (FLEURI,) a French grammarian, was the author of "Etymology or Explanation of French Proverbs," (1656.)

Bellingham, bel'ling-ạm, (Sir EDWARD,) an able soldier, and for two years governor or deputy of Ireland under Edward VI. Died in 1549.

See FROUDE, "History of England," vol. v. chap. xxviii.

Bel'ling-ham, (RICHARD,) Governor of Massachusetts, born in England in 1592. He came to America as a lawyer in 1634, and subsequently filled the office of lieutenant-governor for thirteen years and that of governor for ten years. He was first elected in opposition to Governor Winthrop in 1641. Died in 1672.

Bellini, bĕl-lee'nee, or **Bellino,** bĕl-lee'no, an Italian painter of the Venetian school, lived about 1500.

Bellini, (FILIPPO,) an Italian painter, born at Urbino about 1560. His pictures in fresco and oil are praised.

See LANZI, "History of Painting in Italy."

Bellini, [Fr. BELLIN, bặ'lȧN',] (GENTILE,) a celebrated Venetian painter, born in 1421, was a son of Jacopo, noticed below. Among his master-pieces are "The Preaching of Saint Mark," and "Presentation of the Infant Jesus at the Temple." He was invited to Constantinople by the Sultan Mahomet II., who treated him with distinguished favour and employed him to paint several historical pieces. Died about 1507.

See VASARI, "Lives of the Painters;" MRS. JAMESON, "Memoirs of Early Italian Painters."

Bellini, (GIOVANNI,) brother of the preceding, born at Venice about 1426, was the most distinguished member of his family, and is regarded as the founder of the Venetian school. He assisted his brother in the embellishment of the senate-house at Venice, and painted a great number of historical pieces. Of these we may name a "Coronation of the Virgin," a "Madonna and Child attended by the Angels," "Christ at Emmaus," and "The Saviour giving a Benediction." His works display great richness of colouring and superior arrangement of the draperies. Among his numerous pupils were Titian and Giorgione. His death is variously dated 1510, 1512, or 1516.

See VASARI, "Lives of the Painters;" MRS. JAMESON, "Memoirs of Early Italian Painters;" LANZI, "History of Painting in Italy;" "G. Bellini e Pittori contemporanei," Venice, 1840.

Bellini, (JACOPO,) a Venetian painter, chiefly distinguished for his portraits. He was one of the first who painted in oil. Died about 1470.

Bellini, (LAURENTIO,) a celebrated Italian anatomist and physician, born at Florence in 1643. He studied at Pisa under Borelli, whose peculiar system he adopted. (See BORELLI, GIOVANNI ALFONSO.) After having filled the chair of anatomy at Pisa for thirty years, he became first physician to the grand duke Cosimo III. at Florence. He wrote several medical treatises in Latin, which had a high reputation in his time. Died in 1704.

See FABRONI, "Vitæ Italorum doctrina excellentium;" G. ATTI, "Notizie biografiche della Vita di M. Malpighi e di L. Bellini," 1847.

Bellini, [Fr. BELLIN,] (VINCENZO,) a celebrated musical composer, born at Catania, in Sicily, about 1802. He studied at Naples under Zingarelli. Having produced several symphonies and other musical pieces, he brought out at Milan in 1827 his opera of "Il Pirata," which was very successful. It was soon followed by "La Straniera," and "I Capuletti ed i Montecchi." "La Sonnambula" came out in March, 1831, and in December of the same year "La Norma." The two last-named operas were received with enthusiasm throughout Europe, and still retain their popularity. In 1834 he produced "I Puritani," which ranks among his best works. He died near Paris in September, 1835, at the early age of thirty-two.

See FÉTIS, "Biographie Universelle des Musiciens;" F. GERARDI, "Biografia di V. Bellini," 1835.

Bellman, bĕl'mȧn, (KARL MICKEL,) a Swedish poet, born at Stockholm about 1740. His lyrics are principally bacchanalian songs and delineations of low life, and enjoy great popularity in Sweden. Among these

may be named "The Temple of Bacchus" and "Fredman's Sänger og Epistlar." Died in 1795.

See CARL PLOUG, "C. M. Bellman's Liv, og Bellman som comisk Dithyrambiker af J. L. Heiberg," 1844.

Bello, bel'lo, (FILIPPO,) an Italian littérateur, born at Naples in 1666; died in 1719.

Bello, (MARCO,) an Italian painter of the Venetian school, lived about 1450.

Belloc, bặ'lok', (JEAN HILAIRE,) a French painter of history and portraits, born at Nantes in 1787.

Belloc, (JEAN LOUIS,) a French surgeon, born near Agen in 1730, published a number of works on surgery and legal medicine, and invented several surgical instruments. He acquired celebrity as a professor in Paris, where he died in 1807.

Belloc, bặ'lok', (LOUISE SWANTON,) MADAME, a French writer, of Irish extraction, born at La Rochelle in 1799, translated into French a number of the works of Byron, Moore, and Miss Edgeworth, also Goldsmith's "Vicar of Wakefield," and "Uncle Tom's Cabin."

See QUÉRARD, "La France Littéraire."

Bellocq, bặ'lok', (PIERRE,) a French littérateur and satirist, born in Paris in 1645; died in 1704.

Bel-lo'na, [Fr. BELLONE, bặ'lon'; derived from the Latin *bellum*, "war,"] the goddess of war of the ancient Romans. She delights in war and carnage; she is usually represented as the companion, and sometimes as the sister or wife, of Mars. She is described by the poets as armed with a scourge, and bearing a torch in her hand. Her priests were called *Bellonarii*.

See TIESLER, "Dissertatio de Bellonæ Cultu," 1842.

Belloni, bĕl-lo'nee, (GERONIMO,) a Roman banker, patronized by Benedict IV., wrote an "Essay on Commerce," which was translated into several languages. Died in 1761.

See MAZZUCHELLI, "Scrittori d'Italia."

Belloni, (GIOVANNI,) an Italian theologian and jurist, was canon of Padua. Died in 1623.

Belloni, (GIUSEPPE,) an Italian sculptor and architect, resided at Venice about 1600–20.

Belloni, (PAOLO,) an Italian jurist and legal writer, was professor of civil law at Pavia. Died in 1625.

Bellori, bĕl-lo'ree, (GIOVANNI PIETRO,) an Italian antiquary, born at Rome in 1615, wrote a number of treatises on Roman history and antiquities. Christina of Sweden appointed him her librarian and keeper of her cabinet. Died in 1696.

See MAZZUCHELLI, "Scrittori d'Italia."

Bellot, bặ'lo', (JOSEPH RENÉ,) a French naval officer, born in Paris in 1826, accompanied Captain Belcher in search of Sir John Franklin in 1852. Having afterwards joined Inglefield's expedition, he perished in a storm near Cape Bowden in 1853. He discovered a strait connecting Prince Regent's Inlet and Peel Sound, which has been named Bellot's Strait.

Bellot, (PIERRE FRANÇOIS,) a French jurist, born at Geneva in 1776, was professor of civil law. Died at Geneva in 1836.

See CHERBULIEZ, "Notice sur la Vie de P. F. Bellot," 1838.

Bellotti, bĕl-lot'tee, (BERNARDO,) an Italian painter and engraver, surnamed CANALETTO, born at Venice in 1724. Died in 1780.

See LANZI, "History of Painting in Italy."

Bellotti, (PIETRO,) an Italian painter of the Venetian school, born at Volgano; died in 1700.

Bel-lo-ve'sus, the first Gallic chief who passed the Alps, established himself with his band in Etruria, according to Livy, about 590 B.C.

See DUPLEIX, "Mémoires des Gaules."

Bel'lows, (HENRY WHITNEY,) D.D., an eminent Unitarian divine, born in Boston in 1814. He took the degree of A.B. at Harvard in 1832, and afterwards studied in the theological school of that university. In 1838 he became pastor of a church in the city of New York. He was the principal founder of the "Christian Inquirer," (1846,) and was for several years the chief contributor to its columns. Mr. Bellows is an able and eloquent public speaker, and has lectured successfully on a great variety of subjects, especially those connected with social or educational interests, or with patriotic or

---

є as *k*; ç as *s*; g̃ *hard*; ġ as *j*; G, H, K, *guttural*; N, *nasal*; R, *trilled*; s̄ as *z*; ŧh as in *this*. (☞See Explanations, p. 23.)

philanthropic enterprises. Among his publications, his lectures "On the Treatment of Social Diseases," delivered at the Lowell Institute, Boston, in 1857, deserve to be particularly mentioned. He was the principal originator of the United States Sanitary Commission, of which he became the first president in 1862. He held this position as long as that organization continued.

Belloy, de, dẹh bả'lwả', (AUGUSTE,) MARQUIS, a French poet, born in Paris about 1815. He produced, besides other works, "Orfa," (1853,) and "Flowery Legends," ("Légendes fleuries," 1855.)

Belloy, de, (JEAN BAPTISTE,) a French cardinal, and Archbishop of Paris, born near Senlis in 1709 ; died in 1808.

Belloy, de, (PIERRE,) a French jurist, born at Montauban about 1540. His principal work is entitled "The Catholic Apology," being a defence of the rights of Henry of Navarre to the throne independent of his Catholicity. In consequence of this he was imprisoned two years in the Bastille by the Guises.

See MORÉRI, "Dictionnaire Historique."

Belloy, de, (PIERRE LAURENT **Buyrette**—bü-e'rĕt' or bwe'rĕt',) a French dramatist, born at Saint-Flour-en-Auvergne in 1727, wrote a tragedy entitled "The Siege of Calais." He was a member of the French Academy. Died in 1775.

See QUÉRARD, "La France Littéraire."

Bellucci, bĕl-loot'chee, or **Belluzzi,** bĕl-loot'see, (ANTONIO,) an Italian painter, born in 1654, was patronized by Joseph I. of Austria. He excelled in painting small figures. Died in 1726.

See LANZI, "History of Painting in Italy."

Bellucci, (TOMMASO,) an Italian botanist, born at Pistoia. He became professor of botany at Pisa, and published in 1662 an "Index of Plants in the Garden of Pisa," (in Latin.)

Bellune, DUC DE. See VICTOR.

Bellunello, bĕl-loo-nel'lo, (ANDREA,) an Italian painter, born in the Friuli, lived about 1470.

Bellunese, bĕl-loo-nā'sả, (GIORGIO,) an Italian portrait-painter, born in the Friuli, lived about 1550.

Belluno, DUKE OF. See VICTOR.

Belluti, bĕl-loo'tee, (BONAVENTURA,) a Sicilian philosopher and ecclesiastic, born at Catania in 1599. He wrote a "Course of Philosophy," and other works, in Latin. Died in 1676.

Belluzzi. See BELLUCCI.

Belly, bả'le', or **Billy,** be'ye', (JACQUES,) a French painter and engraver, born at Chartres in 1603.

Belmas, bĕl'mả', (LOUIS,) born at Montréal, in the department of Aude, in 1757, became Bishop of Cambrai in 1802. By his advocacy of the liberty of the Gallican Church and his submission to the civil constitution of the clergy, he incurred the displeasure of the pope. He was the last constitutional bishop. Died in 1841.

See LASALVE, "Éloge de M. Belmas," 1848.

Bel'meis or **Bel'meys,** (JOHN,) called also **John of York,** a divine of the twelfth century, was Bishop of Poitou. He wrote against Thomas à Becket.

Belmeis or **Beaumes, de,** (RICHARD,) was consecrated as Bishop of London about 1150.

Belmeis or **Beaumes, de,** (RICHARD,) became Bishop of London in 1108. He expended a large sum of money in the erection of Saint Paul's Cathedral. Died in 1127.

Belmissero or **Belmessere,** bĕl-mĕs-sā'rẻ, (PAOLO,) an Italian physician and Latin poet, born at Lanni, lived about 1530. He was professor of medicine and philosophy at Bologna.

See MAZZUCHELLI, "Scrittori d'Italia."

Belmondi, bĕl'mȯN'de', (PIERRE,) a French littérateur, born at Virieux in 1774 ; died in 1822.

Belmont, de, dẹh bĕl'mȯN', (AIMERI,) a troubadour of Provence, lived about 1270.

Belmontet, bĕl'mȯN'tả', (LOUIS,) a French littérateur and politician, born at Montauban in 1799. He became in 1830 editor of "La Tribune," in which he opposed the Orléans dynasty. He published several republican odes, and a collection of poems entitled "Golden Numbers," ("Les Nombres d'Or," 1846.) In 1835 he married a granddaughter of the famous Vergniaud. Among his works is "Une Fête de Néron," a tragedy, (1829.) He is now a Bonapartist in politics.

See "Nouvelle Biographie Générale."

Belmonti, bĕl-mon'tee, (PIETRO,) an Italian poet, born at Rimini in 1537 ; died in 1592.

Be'lŏe, (WILLIAM,) an English divine and scholar, born at Norwich in 1756. He made several translations from the Greek, of which his "History of Herodotus, with Notes," (4 vols., 1791,) deserves especial mention. He also wrote a number of original works, and was associated with Archdeacon Nares as editor of "The British Critic." Died in 1817.

Belon, bẹh-lȯN' or blȯN, (PIERRE,) one of the most eminent naturalists of his time, born in the department of Sarthe, in France, about 1517. He visited successively Greece, Egypt, and Palestine, and, after an absence of three years, returned to France in 1550. In 1553 he published an account of his expedition, which was translated into Latin by L'Écluse. On his way to Paris, through the Bois de Boulogne, in 1564, he was assassinated by an unknown hand. Belon wrote a number of valuable treatises on natural history, geography, and antiquities. His "History of Birds" (1555) is said to be the most important treatise on that subject produced in the sixteenth century.

See CUVIER, "Histoire des Sciences naturelles."

Beloselsky, bả-lo-sel'skee, (ALEXANDER,) PRINCE, a Russian littérateur, born at Saint Petersburg in 1757, wrote a collection of poems in French. Died in 1809.

Béloste, bả'lost', (AUGUSTIN,) a French surgeon, born in Paris in 1654, published a treatise on surgery, (1695,) and a "Treatise on the Use of Mercury," (1725.) He adopted some good old methods which had fallen into disuse. He practised at Turin, where he died in 1730.

Belot, bẹh-lo' or blo, (JEAN,) a French lawyer, born at Blois about 1590, published an "Apology for the Latin Language." Ménage, in his "Requête des Dictionnaires," remarks "that his generous interest in that language is the more praiseworthy, as he had not the honour to be acquainted with it."

See PELISSON, "Histoire de l'Académie Française."

Belot, (JEAN,) a French ecclesiastic, who lived about 1570, wrote treatises on chiromancy and occult science.

Belot, (OCTAVIE GUICHARD,) MADAME, a French authoress, born in Paris in 1719. She published "Reflections on Rousseau's Discourse concerning the Inequality of Conditions," and translated from the English Dr. Johnson's "Rasselas," and portions of Hume's History. Died in 1805.

See LE BAS, "Dictionnaire encyclopédique de la France."

Below, bā'lo, (JACOB FREDERICK,) a Swedish physician and naturalist, born at Stockholm in 1669. He was appointed by Charles XII., in 1705, physician to the army. He was taken prisoner at the battle of Pultowa, after which he practised in Moscow. Died in 1716.

Bel'pẹr, (EDWARD STRUTT,) LORD, an English politician, born at Derby in 1801. He represented Derby in Parliament from 1830 to 1848, voting with the Liberals.

Belprato, bĕl-prȧ'to, (GIOVANNI VINCENZO,) an Italian littérateur, lived about 1550.

Bel'sham, (THOMAS,) an English Unitarian divine and theological writer, born at Bedford in April, 1750. He became, in 1805, pastor of the Essex Street chapel, London, where he remained until his death. Among his principal works are his "Evidences of the Christian Revelation," and "Elements of the Philosophy of the Human Mind and Moral Philosophy," (1801.) He also published a "Translation of the Epistles of Saint Paul, with an Exposition and Notes," (4 vols., 1822.) Died in 1829.

See JOHN WILLIAMS, "Memoirs of Thomas Belsham," 1833: "London Quarterly Review" for 1823–24, and "Edinburgh Review" for January, 1803.

Belsham, (WILLIAM,) an English historian and political writer of the Whig party, born in 1752, was a brother of the preceding. He published a "History of Great Britain to the Conclusion of the Peace of Amiens in 1802," (12 vols. 8vo, 1806,) "Essays, Historical, Political, and Literary," (2 vols., 1789–91,) and other works. His history was commended by Professor Smyth and other critics. Died in 1827.

Bel-shaz'zar, [Heb. בלשאצר; Fr. Balthasar, bȧl'-tȧ'zȧr',] King of Babylon, began to reign about 554 B.C. He was a descendant of Nebuchadnezzar. In 538 or 539 Babylon was taken by Cyrus the Great, and Belshazzar was killed.

See Book of Daniel, chap. v.; D. S. Goebel, "Dissertatio de Belsasaro," 1757.

Belsunce, de, deh bĕl'sŭnss', Comte, a French royalist officer, was killed in a mob, at Caen, in 1790.

Belsunce, de, (Armand,) a French general, born in 1722. He fought at Fontenoy in 1745, and at Hastenbeck in 1757. Died in Saint Domingo in 1764.

Belsunce de Castel-Moron, de, deh bĕl'sŭnss' deh kȧs'tĕl' mo'rôn', (Henri François Xavier,) a French Jesuit, born in 1671, was made Bishop of Marseilles in 1709, and during the prevalence of the plague in that city (1720) devoted himself to the relief of the sufferers. Died in 1755.

See P. Barbet, "Éloge de Belsunce," 1821.

Beltraffio, bĕl-trȧf'fe-o, (Giovanni Antonio,) an Italian painter, born at Milan in 1467, was a pupil of Leonardo da Vinci. Died in 1516.

See Lanzi, "History of Painting in Italy."

Beltramelli, bĕl-trȧ-mel'lee, (Giuseppe,) an Italian littérateur, born at Bergamo in 1734; died in 1815.

Beltrami, bĕl-trȧ'mee, (Fabrizio,) an Italian writer, born at Cetona, in Tuscany, lived about 1630.

Beltrando, bĕl-trȧn'do, (Hermano Domingo,) a Spanish architect and sculptor, born at Vittoria; died in 1590.

Beltrano, bĕl-trȧ'no, (Agostino,) an Italian painter, born at Naples in 1616; died in 1665.

Beltrano, (Ottavio,) an Italian writer and publisher, who lived about 1650.

Belurger, beh-lür'zhȧ', (Claude,) a French professor of belles-lettres at the College of Navarre. Died about 1622.

Be'lus, [Gr. Βῆλος,] a mythical king of Phœnicia, regarded as a son of Neptune and Libya, a brother of Agenor, and father of Ægyptus. He is by some writers identified with the Hebrew Baal, and in a mythic sense signifies the Sun.

See Guigniaut, "Religions de l'Antiquité," Paris, 1825-29, vol. ii. book iv. chap. iii.

Be'lus or **Bel,** one of the first kings of Babylon, was the father of Ninus. He is sometimes confounded with the preceding.

Belvedere, bĕl-vȧ-dā'rȧ, (Andrea,) an excellent Italian painter of animals, fruits, and flowers, born at Naples about 1646; died in 1732.

See Lanzi, "History of Painting in Italy."

Belvezen. See Belenvei.

Bélyard, bȧ'le-ȧr', (Simon,) a French poet, who lived about 1580, was a partisan of the League, and wrote against Henry III.

Belzoni, bĕl-zo'nee, (Giovanni Battista,) a celebrated traveller and explorer, born at Padua about 1778. In 1803 he visited England, where he married, and for several years gained a livelihood by exhibiting as an athlete. He possessed great muscular strength, and is said to have supported himself by performing the parts of Hercules and Samson. Having studied hydraulics in his youth, he sought in several foreign countries an opportunity to apply his knowledge of that science. Having travelled in Portugal, Spain, and Malta, accompanied by his wife, they arrived in Egypt in 1815. One of his first antiquarian labours was the removal of the colossal head incorrectly styled the young Memnon, in which enterprise he was assisted by Mr. Salt, the British consul. With great difficulty it was shipped to England; and it now forms one of the grandest ornaments of the department of Egyptian antiquities in the British Museum. He soon after visited the temple of Ipsamboul, which he was the first to open, and in 1818 discovered in the valley of Beban-el-Molook a magnificent Egyptian tomb. He made drawings of the chambers and took impressions of the figures and hieroglyphics, which fac-simile he subsequently exhibited in London. This tomb also contained an alabaster sarcophagus, which Belzoni brought to England. He penetrated into the second pyramid of Gizeh, and discovered the ruins of the town

of Berenice. On his arrival in England in 1819 he published a very interesting and well-written narrative of his discoveries. He set out in 1823 for Timbuctoo, in Africa, but died in Benin, after a short illness, in December, 1823.

See Belzoni, "Narrative of the Operations and Recent Discoveries within the Pyramids, Temples, Tombs, and Excavations in Egypt and Nubia," London, 1820; "Household Words," vol. ii., 1851, (republished in the "Living Age," vol. xxix.;) C. L. Brightwell, "Annals of Industry and Genius," 1863.

Bem, bĕm, (Joseph,) a distinguished Polish general, born at Tarnow, in Galicia, in 1795. He served in the campaign of 1812 under Davoust, and about 1819 was made professor in a school of artillery at Warsaw. On the breaking out of the revolution of 1830, he became a major in the Polish service. Having joined the Hungarian patriots in 1848, he obtained command of an army, and defeated the Austrians in several battles. After the defeat at Temesvar he took refuge in Turkey, where he became a Mohammedan, and was made a pasha by the Sultan. Died in 1850.

See Pataky, "Bem in Siebenbürgen," 1850; N. N. Lajos, "Le Général Bem," Paris, 1851.

Be-mar'chI-us, [Βημάρχιος,] a Greek sophist, born at Cæsarea, in Cappadocia, about 320 A.D. He wrote a "Life of the Emperor Constantine," and other works, not extant.

Bembo, bĕm'bo, (Bernardo,) a Venetian senator and liberal patron of learning, born in 1433, was the father of the celebrated Cardinal Bembo. Died about 1520.

Bembo, (Giovanni,) succeeded Marcantonio Memmo as Doge of Venice in 1615. Died in 1618.

Bembo, (Pietro,) an Italian cardinal, celebrated for his learning, born at Venice in May, 1470. He studied Greek under Lascaris, and subsequently became a member of the academy of Aldus Manutius. In 1512 he repaired to Rome, where Leo X. appointed him his private secretary and bestowed upon him numerous ecclesiastical preferments. After the death of Leo he retired to Padua, where he formed a valuable library and a collection of rare medals. He was made a cardinal by Paul III. in 1539. He died in 1547. Among his principal works are a "History of Venice," (in Latin,) which he afterwards translated into Italian, (1552,) dialogues on the nature of love, entitled "Gli Asolani," and a number of Italian sonnets. His writings are all characterized by great elegance of style. Among his friends were the painter Raphael and Cardinal Bibbiena. His chief literary merit consisted in his being one of the restorers of pure Latinity. His collected works were published in Venice, in four volumes, 1729. "If some praise is due," says Hallam, "as it surely is, to the art of reviving that consummate grace and richness which enchants every successive generation in the periods of Cicero, we must place Bembo among the ornaments of literature in the sixteenth century." ("Introduction to the Literature of Europe.")

See Beccadelli, "Vita di P. Bembo;" J. de la Casa, "Vita Bembi;" M. Battaggia, "Elogio del Cardinale Bembo," 1827; Longfellow, "Poets and Poetry of Europe;" Aubery, "Histoire des Cardinaux;" Mazzuchelli, "Scrittori d'Italia;" "Nouvelle Biographie Générale."

Bême or **Besme,** bĕm, (Karl Dianowitz—de-ȧ'no-ẅits,) a Bohemian, notorious as the assassin of Coligny. He was killed by some Protestants at Saintonge in 1575.

Bemetzrieder, bȧ'mĕts-ree'der, writer on music, born in 1747, resided in Paris, and subsequently in London.

Bemmel, van, vȧn bem'mel, (Willem,) a Dutch landscape-painter of great merit, born at Utrecht in 1630. Having visited Italy and England, he established himself at Nuremberg. Died in 1708.

See Descamps, "Vies des Peintres Flamands, Hollandais," etc.

Bemmel, von, fon bem'mel, (Christoph,) a German landscape-painter, son of Peter, noticed below, born in 1707.

Bemmel, von, (Joel Paul,) elder son of Johann Georg, born at Nuremberg in 1713, was a painter of landscapes and historical pieces.

Bemmel, von, (Johann Georg,) a skilful German painter of landscapes and animals, born at Nuremberg in 1669, was a son of Wilhelm, noticed below. Died in 1725.

See Nagler, "Neues Allgemeines Künstler-Lexikon."

ᵿ as k; ç as s; ğ hard; ġ as j; g, h, k, guttural; n, nasal; r, trilled; š as z; ᵺ as in this. (☞ See Explanations, p. 23.)

21

Bemmel, von, (JOHANN NOAH,) brother of Joel Paul, born at Nuremberg in 1716. His works include hunting-scenes, battles, animals, and portraits.

Bemmel, von, (KARL SEBASTIAN,) nephew of Christoph, mentioned above, born at Bamberg in 1743, painted landscapes, sea-pieces, and night and morning scenes, which are greatly admired and sought for. Died in 1796.

See JÄCK, "Pantheon der Literaten und Künstler Bambergs."

Bemmel, von, (PETER,) brother of Johann Georg, born at Nuremberg in 1685, painted landscapes, storms, and winter scenes with great effect. Died in 1754.

Bemmelen, van, văn bem'měh-lĕn, (ABRAHAM,) a Dutch writer on physical science, born in 1755, published "Elements of Experimental Physics," and other works. Died in 1822.

Ben, běn, (SEV,) a Polish Jew, born in 1763, was a good Hebrew scholar, and published a Hebrew Lexicon. Died in Vienna in 1811.

Benaben, běh'nä'bŏn', (LOUIS GUILLAUME JACQUES MARIE,) a French journalist and *littérateur,* born at Toulouse in 1774, was associate editor of "La Minerve," and subsequently edited the "Gazette de France," a journal of Paris. Died in Paris in 1831.

Benaglio, bä-näl'yo, (GIROLAMO,) an Italian painter, worked at Verona in the fifteenth century.

Benalcazar, bä-näl-kä'thăR, or **Belarcazar,** bä-lar-kä'thăR, (SEBASTIAN,) a Spanish soldier, born in Estremadura. In 1514 he accompanied Pedrarias, governor of Darien, to South America, where he assisted Pizarro in the conquest of Peru. He was subsequently appointed governor of Popayan. Died in 1550.

See PRESCOTT, "History of the Conquest of Peru;" TOURON, "Histoire générale de l'Amérique."

Benamati, bä-nä-mä'tee, (GUIDO UBALDO,) an Italian poet, born at Gubbio. Among his works is an epic poem, "The Naval Victory," ("La Vittoria navale," 1640.) Died in 1653.

Benard, běh-năR', (LAURENT,) a French Benedictine monk and writer, born at Nevers in 1573; died in 1620.

Benary, bā'nä-ree, (FRANZ FERDINAND,) a German Orientalist, born at Cassel in 1805. He published in 1830 the Sanscrit poem of "Nalodaya," with a Latin translation and explanation.

Benaschi, bä-näs'kee, (ANGELA,) daughter of Giovanni Battista, by whom she was instructed in painting, was born in 1666. She excelled in portraits. (See next article.)

Benaschi, written also **Beinaschi, Benoschi,** or **Berneschi,** (GIOVANNI BATTISTA,) an Italian painter, born at Turin about 1634, imitated the style of Lanfranco. Among his master-pieces are the frescos of the church of Santa Maria at Naples. Died about 1690.

See LANZI, "History of Painting in Italy."

Benavente, (LUIS,) a Spanish poet, born at Toledo about 1630.

Benavides, bä-nä-vee'Dĕs, (ALFONSO,) a Spanish Franciscan monk, lived about 1600–40.

Benavides, bä-nä-vee'dĕs, [Lat. BENAVID'IUS,] (MARCO,) surnamed MANTUANO, (män-too-ä'no,) an eminent Italian jurist and writer, born at Padua in 1489. He was created count palatine by Charles V., and was professor of law at Padua. He wrote a work entitled "Polymathia," and legal treatises. Died in 1582.

See A. RICCOBONI, "Oratio in obitum M. Benavidii," 1582.

Benavides, (VINCENT,) a painter, born at Oran, in Africa, settled in Spain, where he obtained the title of painter to Charles II. Died in 1703.

Ben'a-zeeh or **Ben'e-zeeh,** (CHARLES,) an English painter and engraver, born about 1740, worked several years in Paris and Rome. Died in England in 1803.

See LE BLANC, "Manuel de l'Amateur d'Estampes."

Benazech, (PETER PAUL,) an English engraver, born in London about 1744.

Ben'bōw, (JOHN,) an English admiral of distinguished bravery, born in 1650, entered the service under James II., and was subsequently employed by William III. In August, 1702, he had a severe engagement near Jamaica with a French squadron under Ducasse; but, after maintaining a running fight for more than four days, he was mortally wounded. He survived until November, 1702.

See SMOLLETT, "History of England;" CAMPBELL, "Lives of the British Admirals."

Benbow, (JOHN,) a son of Admiral Benbow, was shipwrecked on the coast of Madagascar in 1701 or 1702. He was compelled to remain on that island several years.

Benchaim, běn-kä'ĕm, (ABRAHAM,) an Italian rabbi, who published in 1488 an edition of the Bible which is said to have been the first printed in Hebrew.

Benci, běn'chee, (FRANCESCO,) an Italian Jesuit, born at Acquapendente in 1542, wrote a number of treatises in elegant Latin. Died in 1594.

Bencius, běn'she-us, [It. BENCI, běn'chee,] (HUGO,) called also HUGO OF SIENNA, an Italian physician, who translated several works from the Greek and Arabic medical writers. Died in 1448.

See MORÉRI, "Dictionnaire Historique."

Bencivenni, běn-che-ven'nee, (GIUSEPPE,) an Italian *littérateur,* born in 1731, wrote a "Life of Dante," and other works. Died in 1808.

Benckert. See BENKERT.

Bencovich, běn'ko-vik', (FRIEDRICH,) an Austrian painter, sometimes called FEDERIGHETTO DI DALMATIA, lived in the early part of the eighteenth century.

See HEINECKEN, "Dictionnaire des Artistes."

Benda, běn'dä, (FRANZ,) a German musician and excellent violinist, born in Bohemia in 1709, became in 1771 concert-master to Frederick the Great. Died in 1788.

Benda, (GEORG,) brother of the preceding, born in 1721, was patronized by Frederick the Great. He produced several popular operas. Died in 1795. His son FRIEDRICH LUDWIG, a composer, was born in 1746. Died in 1792.

Benda, (JOHANN WILHELM OTTO,) a relative of the preceding, born at Berlin in 1775, translated into German the works of Shakspeare and the poems of Sir Walter Scott. Died in 1832.

Bendavid, běn-dä'vit, (LAZARUS,) a philosopher and mathematician, of Jewish extraction, born at Berlin in 1762, was a disciple of Kant. He wrote, among other works, a treatise "On the Jewish Calendar," and several essays in defence of Kant's philosophy. Died in 1832.

See his "Autobiography," ("Selbstbiographie,") 1804.

Bendeler, běn'děh-ler, or **Bendler,** běnd'ler, (JOHANN CHRISTIAN,) a German landscape-painter, born in 1688; died in 1728.

Bendeler, (JOHANN PHILIPP,) a German musician and writer on music, born near Erfurt about 1660; died about 1712.

Bendeler, (SALOMON,) a German singer, born at Quedlinburg in 1683, is said to have possessed a voice of prodigious strength and compass. Died in 1724.

See FÉTIS, "Biographie Universelle des Musiciens."

Bendemann, běn'děh-mân', (EDUARD,) a German painter, of Jewish extraction, born at Berlin in 1811, was a pupil of Schadow. Among his master-pieces may be named "The Jews by the Rivers of Babylon," "Jeremiah on the Ruins of Jerusalem," (a work of very large dimensions,) and the "Two Maidens at a Fountain." In 1838 he became professor at the Academy of Arts at Dresden. He afterwards decorated the royal palace at Dresden with many grand frescos, which are greatly admired. Some of these represent allegories, religious subjects, and portraits of the heroes and legislators of universal history. According to a French critic, he "is distinguished for a peculiar grace and a profound knowledge of nature. He is one of the few painters of Dusseldorf who have succeeded equally in historical pictures and in genre."

See NAGLER, "Neues Allgemeines Künstler-Lexikon."

Bender, von, fon běn'der, (BLASIUS,) BARON, a mediocre Austrian general, born in Breisgau in 1713. He obtained the chief command in Belgium in 1790. Died in 1798.

Bendinelli, běn-de-nel'lee, (AGOSTINO,) an Italian musical composer, born at Lucca about 1550; died about 1620.

Ben'dish, (BRIDGET,) daughter of General Ireton, and granddaughter of Oliver Cromwell, born about 1650, was noted for her energy of character and her eccentricities. She is said to have strongly resembled Cromwell, both physically and morally. Died in 1727.

Bendler. See BENDELER.

Bendlowes, bĕnd'lŏz, or **Benlowes,** (EDWARD,) an English poet, born in Essex in 1602, published a number of poems in Latin and English. Died in 1676.

See WOOD, "Athenæ Oxonienses."

Bendonsky, bĕn-don'skee, (SYMON SYMONOWICZ,) a Polish poet, born in Galicia in 1557, assumed the name of SIMONIDES. He wrote elegant poems in Latin and Polish. Died in 1629.

Bendtsen, bĕnt'sĕn, (BENDT,) a Danish scholar, born at Copenhagen in 1763. He was director of the college of Frederiksburg, and published several works. Died in 1830.

See J. N. MADVIG, "Mindeord over B. Bendtsen," 1831.

Benecke, bā'nĕh-kĕh, (GEORG FRIEDRICH,) a German philologist, born in the principality of Oettingen in 1762. He wrote "Contributions to the Knowledge of the Old German Language and Literature." He was professor and librarian in the University of Göttingen. Died in 1844.

See BROCKHAUS, "Conversations-Lexikon."

Benedek, von, fon bā'nĕh-dĕk', (LUDWIG,) an Austrian general, born at Oedenburg, in Hungary, in 1804. He served as colonel in the war against the Italians in 1848-49. Having been raised to the rank of general, he fought against the Hungarian patriots in 1849. He obtained in June, 1866, the command of the grand Austrian army of about 200,000 men, with which he was expected to conquer Prussia. Remaining on the defensive in Bohemia, he permitted the two Prussian armies to cross a range of mountains and to effect a junction with each other at Sadowa, where, on the 3d of July, 1866, Benedek was defeated in a battle which decided the issue of the war. The victors took more than one hundred pieces of cannon, and 21,471 prisoners.

Benedette, Le. See CASTIGLIONE, (GIOVANNI.)

Benedetti, bà-nà-det'tee, or **Benedicti,** bà-nà-dĕk'-tee, (ALESSANDRO,) an Italian physician, whose medical and anatomical works had a high reputation in his time. He settled at Venice in 1495. Died after 1510.

Benedetti, (ANTONIO,) an Italian Jesuit and antiquary, born at Fermo in 1715, was professor of rhetoric in the Jesuits' College at Rome. Died in 1788.

Benedetti, (DOMENICO,) an Italian physician, and professor of anatomy at Venice, lived about 1740. He wrote, besides medical works, several poems and dramas.

Benedetti, (FRANCESCO,) an Italian dramatic poet, born at Cortona in 1785, wrote several tragedies, and a "Life of Cola di Rienzo," (1831.) Died in 1821.

See TIPALDO, "Biografia degli Italiani illustri."

Benedetti, (GIOVANNI BATTISTA,) an able Italian mathematician, born at Venice, was a pupil of Tartaglia. He published in 1585 a remarkable work, entitled "Divers Speculations of J. B. Benedetti," ("J. B. Benedicti diversæ Speculationes.") He made many discoveries in mathematics, and advanced many sound ideas in physical philosophy. Died in 1590.

See "Nouvelle Biographie Générale."

Benedetti, (GIULIO CESARE,) an Italian medical writer, born at Aquila, was professor of medicine at Rome. Died in 1656.

Benedetti, (MATTEO,) an Italian painter, born at Reggio about 1650. He painted frescos at Brescia.

Benedetti, (MICHELE,) an Italian painter and engraver, born at Viterbo in 1745, was a member of the Academy of Vienna. Died in 1810.

Benedetti, bà-nà-det'tee, (VINCENT,) born in Corsica about 1815, was appointed by the French government minister to the kingdom of Italy in 1861.

Benedetti, de', dà bà-nà-det'tee, (DOMENICO,) an Italian historical painter, born in Piedmont in 1610; died in 1678.

Benedetti, de', (PIETRO,) an Italian poet of the early part of the seventeenth century, born at Genoa, translated eight of the Odes of Horace into Italian verse.

Benedetto. See BENEDICT.

Benedetto. See JACOPONE.

Benedetto. See MARCELLO.

Benedetto da Majano, bà-nà-det'to dà mà-yä'no, a Florentine sculptor and architect, born in 1444; died 1498.

See VASARI, "Lives of the Painters and Sculptors."

Benedetto da Rovezzano, bà-nà-det'to dà ro-vĕt-sä'no, an Italian sculptor, born near Florence abou. 1480; died about 1550.

Ben'e-dict I., [Lat. BENEDIC'TUS; It. BENEDETTO, bà-nà-det'to; Fr. BENOÎT, beh-nwä',] surnamed BONO'-SUS, became pope in 575 A.D. Under his rule the Longobards extended their conquests in Italy, and threatened Rome. Died in 578.

Benedict II., a native of Rome, succeeded Leo II. as pope in 684. He prevailed upon Constantine IV. to renounce the usurped right of confirming papal elections. He died in 685, and was succeeded by John V.

Benedict III., successor of Leo IV., was elected pope in 855. He was distinguished for his piety and mildness of character. He died in 858, and was succeeded by Nicholas I.

Benedict IV. succeeded John IX. in 900 A.D. The following year he crowned as sovereign of Italy Louis, son of the King of Provence. He died in 903, and was succeeded by Leo V.

Benedict V. was made pope in 964, in opposition to Leo VIII.; but the Emperor Otho I. of Germany, who favoured the cause of Leo, reduced Rome by famine, and exiled Benedict to Hamburg, where he died in 965.

Benedict VI. was elected in 972 successor of John XIII. After the death of Otho I., the Romans rebelled against Benedict and put him to death, (974.)

Benedict VII. succeeded Benedict VI. in 975. He assembled a council and excommunicated the anti-pope Boniface. Died about 984.

Benedict VIII. became pope in 1012. His claims were supported against the anti-pope Gregory by Henry II., whom he crowned at Rome in 1013. He signally defeated the Saracens, who had invaded Tuscany. He died in 1024, and was succeeded by John XIX.

Benedict IX. (THEOPHYLAC'TUS of Tusculum) was the successor of John XIX. in 1034. His vices and oppressive rule caused him to be expelled by the Romans in 1044, and Silvester III. was made pope in his stead. The date of his death is not known.

Benedict X., a native of Capua, succeeded Stephen IX. in 1058, though not regularly elected. He was compelled to give up the tiara to Nicholas II. in 1059.

Benedict XI., (NICCOLÒ **Boccasini**—bok-kä-see'-nee,) Cardinal of Ostia, was a native of Treviso, and succeeded Boniface VIII. in 1303. He died in 1304, and was succeeded by Clement V.

Benedict XII. (originally JACQUES **Fournier**—fooR'-ne-à',) was a native of France, and succeeded John XXII. in 1334. He was the third pope who reigned at Avignon. He laboured zealously to reform the clergy and the monastic orders, and was the author of several ecclesiastical works. He died in 1342, and was succeeded by Clement VI.

See A. DE MONTOR, "Histoire des souverains Pontifes Romains."

Benedict XIII., Cardinal ORSINI, succeeded Innocent XIII. in 1724. He was distinguished for his private virtues and his pacific disposition, and did much to preserve peace among the sovereigns of Europe. He died in 1730, and was succeeded by Clement XII.

See ALESSANDRO BORGIA, "Vita Benedicti XIII.," 1741; MICHAEL RANFT, "Lebensbeschreibung des Papstes Benedict XIII.," 1743; CLEMENTE DA CRUZ, "Vida do Benedicto XIII.," 1739.

Benedict XIV., Cardinal PROSPERO LAMBERTINI, born at Bologna in 1675, succeeded Clement XII. in August, 1740. His talents were of a high order, and he was profoundly versed in theology, history, and classical literature. He founded academies at Rome, built a number of public edifices, and was a munificent patron of learning and the arts. He died in 1758, leaving the reputation of one of the most learned, prudent, and respectable pontiffs who have ever lived. He was the author of several esteemed religious works in Latin. He was succeeded by Clement XIII.

See FABRONI, "Vita di Benedetto XIV.," 1787; "Vie du Pape Benoît XIV.," Paris, 1775; F. GALIANI, "Delle Lodi di Papa Benedetto," 1758.

Benedict XIII., (ANTI-POPE,) PEDRO DE LUNA, (pä'dRo dà loo'nä,) was born in Aragon about 1334. He was elected pope at Avignon in 1394, but his title was disputed by Boniface IX., who reigned in Rome. This schism caused great perplexity in the church for many years. At length, in 1415, the Council of Constance deposed both of the popes. Died in 1424.

Ben'e-dict or **Benoît** OF ANIANE, (ä'ne'än',) SAINT, born in Languedoc about 750, became abbot of the monastery of Aniane. Died in 821.

See BAILLET, "Vies des Saintes."

Benedict OF APPENZELL, (äp'pĕnt-sĕl',) an eminent Swiss musician and contrapuntist, born at Appenzell about 1480. His works are eulogized by Dr. Burney and Fétis.

See BURNEY, "General History of Music."

Benedict, surnamed BIS'COP, an Anglo-Saxon monk, and a noted promoter of learning, of the seventh century, built the monasteries of Wearmouth and Jarrow.

Benedict [Fr. BENOIST, bĕh-nwä'] OF PETERBOROUGH, an English chronicler, became abbot of Peterborough in 1117. He wrote a History of Henry II. and Richard I., and a "Life of Becket."

See "Biographia Britannica."

Benedict, bä'nĕh-dikt, (JULIUS,) a German composer and pianist, born at Stuttgart in 1804. Among his principal works are the operas of "The Brides of Venice," "The Assassins," and "The Gypsy's Warning."

Ben'e-dict, [Lat. BENEDIC'TUS; Fr. BENOÎT, bĕh-nwä'; It. BENEDETTO, bä-nä-det'to; Sp. BENITO, bä-nee'to,] SAINT, a celebrated Italian ecclesiastic, regarded as the founder of the monastic system in the West, was born at Nursia, near Spoleto, in 480 A.D. He founded an establishment at Monte-Casino, near Naples, about 529, and instituted as the rule of his order, in addition to religious duties, various kinds of manual labour, the instruction of the young, and the transcription of valuable manuscripts. He was the author of a work entitled "Regula Monachorum," containing the rules of the order of Saint Benedict. Died in 543.

See JUAN DE CASTANIZA, "Vida de S. Benito," 1583; J. B. PLANCHETTE, "Vie du grand S. Benoît," 1652; ANTON SULGER, "Vita divi Benedicti," 1691; J. G. WAITZMANN, "Leben und Wirken des heiligen Benedict," 1825.

Benedict, (TRAUGOTT WILHELM GUSTAV,) a German medical writer, lived at Breslau about 1820.

Benedicti. See BENEDETTI.

Ben-e-dic'tis, de, (dà,) (BEN. TETIUS,) an Italian canonist, surnamed CAPRA, (kä'prä,) lived about 1440.

Benedictis, de, (GIAMBATTISTA,) an Italian Jesuit, born about 1620. He wrote a number of polemical treatises against the philosophy of Descartes and against the Jansenists. Died in 1706.

See MAZZUCHELLI, "Scrittori d'Italia."

Benedictis, (JACOB.) See JACOPONE DA TODI.

Benedictus. See BENEDICT.

Ben-e-dic'tus, or **Benoît,** a learned Maronite, whose original name was AMBARACH, born in Phœnicia in 1663. He studied at Rome, and subsequently became professor of Hebrew at Pisa. Died in 1742.

Ben-e-dic'tus, (JOHN,) a Polish physician, who published in 1530 a work in Latin on the sweating-sickness.

Benediktov, ben-e-dik'tof, (VLADIMIR,) a Russian poet, published in 1835 a collection of lyrics, which obtained great popularity.

See BROCKHAUS, "Conversations-Lexikon."

Benedix, bä'nĕh-diks, (JULIUS RODERICH,) a German dramatist and littérateur, born at Leipsic in 1811.

Benefiale, bà-nà-fe-ä'là, or **Beneficiale,** bà-nà-fe-chä'là, (MARCO,) CHEVALIER, an Italian painter, born at Rome in 1684; died in 1764.

See LANZI, "History of Painting in Italy."

Ben'e-field, (SEBASTIAN,) an English Calvinistic divine, born in Gloucestershire in 1559, became professor of divinity at Oxford in 1613. He published numerous sermons and commentaries on Scripture. Died in 1630.

Beneke, bä'nĕh-kĕh, (FRIEDRICH EDUARD,) a German philosopher, born in 1798 at Berlin, where he became professor extraordinary of philosophy in 1832. He published "Psychological Sketches," (1825–27,) "Pragmatic Psychology," (1850,) and other works. He was found in 1856, drowned in a canal; and it is supposed he died by suicide.

Benekendorf, bĕn'ĕh-kĕn-dorf, (KARL FRIEDRICH,) a German writer, born in Brandenburg in 1720, published

several popular works on political and rural economy. Died in 1788.

Benese, de, de ben-eez', (RICHARD,) an English ecclesiastic, who wrote a treatise on mensuration, (1535.)

Beneton de Morange de Peyrins, bĕh-nĕh-tòN' dĕh mo'rŏNzh' dĕh pà'rän', (ÉTIENNE CLAUDE,) a French littérateur, published a "History of War," (1741.) Died in 1752.

Benetti, bà-net'tee, (GIOVANNI DOMENICO,) an Italian physician, born in 1658 at Ferrara, where he became a professor in the university. He was physician to the Duke of Mantua, and wrote a work entitled "Corpus Medico-Morale," (1718.)

Benevento or **Benevent,** PRINCE OF. See TALLEYRAND.

Benevoli, bà-nĕv'o-lee, (ANTONIO,) an Italian surgeon and skilful oculist, born in the duchy of Spoleto in 1685, published treatises on the cataract and on hernia. He practised at Florence, where he died in 1756.

Benevoli, (ORAZIO,) an Italian musician and composer, born at Rome in 1602; died in 1672.

Bénézech, bà'nà'zĕk', (PIERRE,) born at Montpellier in 1745, became minister of the interior under the Directory in 1795, and afterwards a counsellor of state. Died in 1802.

See CHALLAN, "Éloge historique de P. Bénézech," 1803.

Ben'e-zet', (ANTHONY,) an eminent philanthropist, born at Saint-Quentin, in France, in 1713, was the son of Protestant parents. He joined the Society of Friends, emigrated to Philadelphia in 1731, and became a schoolteacher. He was a zealous opponent of the slave-trade, and a benefactor of the negroes, for whom he opened an evening school. He wrote on the slave-trade and slavery several tracts, which, it is said, first drew the attention of Clarkson and Wilberforce to that subject. Among his writings is "Some Historical Account of Guinea, with an Inquiry into the Slave-Trade," (1771.) He was distinguished for his generosity and active kindness to the poor and suffering wherever found. Died in 1784.

See VAUX, "Memoir of Anthony Benezet."

Benfatto, bĕn-fät'to, (LUIGI,) an Italian painter, surnamed IL FRISO, (èl free'ṣo,) born at Verona in 1551, was a nephew and pupil of Paul Veronese. Died about 1641.

See LANZI, "History of Painting in Italy."

Benfey, bĕn'fī, (THEODOR,) a German philologist, born near Göttingen in 1809. He published a "Dictionary of Greek Roots," (1839,) which obtained the Volney prize from the French Academy of Sciences; also an edition of the hymns of Sama-Veda, with a translation and glossary, and translated the comedies of Terence. His "Sanscrit-English Dictionary" (London, 1866) is highly esteemed.

See BROCKHAUS, "Conversations-Lexikon."

Beng, bòN, or **Bengy,** bòN'zhe', (ANTOINE,) a French jurist, succeeded Cujas as professor of law at Bourges in 1595. Died in 1616.

Bengel, bĕng'ĕl, [Lat. BENGE'LIUS,] (JOHANN ALBRECHT,) an eminent Lutheran theologian, born at Winnenden, in Würtemberg, in 1687. Having finished his studies in the theological college at Tübingen, he was employed for many years as pastor at Denkendorf, and about 1749 became prelate at Alpirsbach. His edition of the Greek Testament, published in 1734, is esteemed a standard work. He also wrote a treatise on the holiness of God, entitled "Syntagma de Sanctitate Dei," "Gnomon Novi Testamenti," "Explanation of the Revelation of Saint John," (in German, 1740,) and other works of a high character. Died in 1752.

See "Memoir of the Life and Writings of J. A. Bengel," translated from the German; J. P. FRESENIUS, "Zuverlässige Nachricht von dem Leben und den Schriften J. A. Bengels," 1756; J. C. F. BURK, "Dr. J. A. Bengel's Leben und Wirken," 1831.

Bengel, von, fon bĕng'ĕl, (ERNST GOTTLIEB,) grandson of Johann Albrecht, noticed above, born in 1769, became professor of theology at Tübingen. Died in 1826.

Benger, bĕng'gĕr, (Miss ELIZABETH OGILVY,) an English authoress, born at Wells, in Somersetshire, in 1778. She published poems, novels, and dramas; but she owes her reputation chiefly to her historical and biographical works, among which are "Memoirs of Elizabeth Stuart, Queen of Bohemia;" "Memoirs of

ă, ē, ī, ō, ū, ȳ, long; ă, ĕ, ŏ, same, less prolonged; ä, ĕ, ī, ŏ, ŭ, y̆, short; a, e, i, o, obscure; fär, fäll, fät; mĕt; nŏt; gōŏd; mōŏn;

Mary Queen of Scots;" and "Memoirs of Klopstock and his Friends." Miss Benger was an intimate friend of Mrs. Barbauld, Joanna Baillie, and Mrs. E. Hamilton. Died in 1827.

Bengtson, bĕngt'son, (JOHAN,) Archbishop of Upsal, in Sweden, born in 1417; died in 1467.

Ben-hā'dad [Heb. בֶּן־הֲדַד] **I.,** King of Syria, was contemporary with Asa, King of Judah, whom he assisted in repelling the invasion of Baasha, King of Israel.

See I. Kings xv. 20.

Benhadad II., son of the preceding, made war on Ahab, King of Israel, and besieged Samaria. He was afterwards murdered by Hazael, who succeeded him on the throne of Syria.

See II. Kings vi. 24; viii. 7–15.

Benhadad III., King of Syria, was the son of Hazael. He carried on a war against Jehoahaz, King of Israel.

See II. Kings xiii. 3.

Beni, bā'nee, (PAOLO,) a scholar and critical writer, born in the island of Candia about 1552, was successively professor of theology at Perugia, of philosophy at Rome, and of belles-lettres at Padua. Died at Padua in 1625.

See BAYLE, "Historical and Critical Dictionary;" GINGUENÉ, "Histoire Littéraire d'Italie."

Be-nig'nus, [Fr. BÉNIGNE, bā'nĕñ',] SAINT, supposed to have been a disciple of Polycarp, was sent on a mission to Gaul, and suffered martyrdom at Dijon about 179 A.D.

See MORÉRI, "Dictionnaire Historique."

Benincasa, bà-nĕn-kä'sä, (BARTOLOMMEO,) COUNT, a literary Italian nobleman, born near Módena about 1745; died about 1825. He published, in French, "Les Morlaques," (1788,) and founded a journal in Dalmatia.

Benincori, bà-nĕn-ko'ree, (ANGELO MARIA,) an Italian musician and composer, born at Brescia in 1770; died in 1821.

Beninga, bà-ning'hä, (EGGERIK,) a Dutch historian, wrote a "Chronicle of East Friesland." Died in 1562.

Benini, bà-nee'nee, (VINCENZO,) an Italian physician and littérateur, born at Bologna in 1713; died in 1764.

Beniowsky or **Benyowsky,** bà-ne-ov'skee, (MAURITIUS AUGUSTUS,) COUNT, a Hungarian nobleman and adventurer, born in the county of Neutra in 1741. He served in the Seven Years' war, and in 1768 joined the Polish confederation against the Russians. Being taken prisoner, he was exiled in 1770 to Kamtchatka, whence he effected his escape to France in 1772. He was soon after sent by the French government to establish a colony in Madagascar; but, having claimed the sovereignty of that island, he was killed in an encounter with the French in 1786.

See M. A. BENIOWSKY, "Voyages et Mémoires," 2 vols., 1791, and English version of the same, by W. NICHOLSON.

Benit, beh-ne', (ANNE FRANÇOIS,) a French physician, born at Mirecourt in 1796; died in Spain in 1823.

Benito. See BENEDICT, (SAINT.)

Benivieni, bà-ne-ve-ā'nee, (ANTONIO,) a learned Italian physician, was a friend of Marsilio Ficino and Politiano. Died in 1502.

Benivieni, (DOMENICO,) brother of the preceding, an Italian ecclesiastic, born at Florence, was surnamed SCOTTINO (skot-tee'no) from the subtlety of his theology. He became, in 1479, professor of dialectics at Pisa. He was a warm friend of Savonarola, and wrote in defence of his doctrines. Died in 1507.

See MAZZUCHELLI, "Scrittori d'Italia."

Benivieni, (GERONIMO,) brother of the two preceding, born at Florence about 1453. He was a friend of Savonarola, and translated from Latin into Italian his "Treatise on the Simplicity of Christian Life," (1496.) He was one of the first Italians who discarded the low and trivial taste which prevailed in the fifteenth century and returned to the standards of Dante and Petrarch. He published in 1500 "Il Commento di Ieronimo Benivieni." Died in 1542.

See GINGUENÉ, "Histoire Littéraire d'Italie."

Ben'ja-min, [Heb. בְּנִימִין,] youngest son of the patriarch Jacob and Rachel. He was the favourite of his father, who reluctantly permitted him to accompany his brothers to Egypt. (See Genesis xlii., xliii., xliv.)

Benjamin OF TUDELA, a Jewish rabbi and traveller, born in the kingdom of Navarre. He visited, between 1160 and 1173, Egypt, Persia, and the frontiers of China, which countries he describes in his "Itinerary." This work has been translated into several languages, and is interesting as being the first description of those regions given by a European.

See CARMOLY, "Notice sur B. de Tudèle et ses Voyages," 1837.

Ben'ja-min, (JUDAH P.,) an American politician, of Jewish parentage, born in Saint Domingo about 1812. He studied law, which he practised with success in New Orleans. In 1852 he was elected a United States Senator for Louisiana, and re-elected in 1858 or 1859. In politics he was a Democrat and disunionist. He was secretary of war at Richmond from about September, 1861, to February, 1862, when he became secretary of state to the Southern Confederacy. He retired to Europe soon after the capture of Jefferson Davis, May, 1865.

Benjamin, (PARK,) an American poet and journalist, born in 1809 at Demerara, in Guiana, where his father was engaged in trade. He studied at Harvard, and graduated at a college of Hartford, Connecticut. He edited the "American Monthly Magazine" of New York in 1837 and 1838. In 1840 Mr. Benjamin and R. W. Griswold began to publish a literary journal, called "The New York World." He wrote numerous lyrical poems and sonnets. His longest work is entitled a "Poem on the Meditation of Nature." "Many of his pieces," says Griswold, "are distinguished for poetical simplicity of thought and elegance of diction." ("Poets and Poetry of America.") Died in 1864.

Benkendorf, bĕn'ken-dorf, (KARL FRIEDRICH,) a German writer on agriculture and rural economy. Died in 1788.

Benkendorf, (LUDWIG ERNST,) a German general, born at Anspach in 1711. He served in the Seven Years' war, and became in 1775 inspector-general of cavalry. Died in 1801.

Benk'en-dorff, (ALEXANDER,) COUNT, a Russian general and diplomatist, born in Esthonia about 1782. He served in the Russian campaigns against the French, and became aide-de-camp to the grand duke Nicholas, afterwards emperor. After the accession of Nicholas he was made a count, and a member of the imperial council. Died in 1844.

See BROCKHAUS, "Conversations-Lexikon."

Benkendorff, (CONSTANTINE,) brother of the preceding, born in 1784, served against the French in 1813–14, and subsequently in the Persian campaign of 1826, when he was made lieutenant-general. He died soon after.

Benkert or **Benckert,** bĕnk'kert, (JOHANN PETER,) a German sculptor, born at Neustadt in 1709. He adorned with his works the royal palace of Sans-Souci, in Prussia. Died in 1769.

Benkowitz, bĕn-ko'vits, (KARL FRIEDRICH,) a German writer of novels, poems, etc., born in 1764, committed suicide at Glogau in 1807.

Benlowes. See BENDLOWES.

Benn, (WILLIAM,) an English dissenting divine, born in Cumberland in 1600; died in 1680.

Bennati, bĕn-nä'tee, (FRANCESCO,) an Italian physician, born at Mantua in 1788, wrote medical treatises, one of which gained the Montyon prize of the French Institute. Died in Paris in 1834.

Ben'net, (BENJAMIN,) an English nonconformist divine, born in Leicestershire in 1674, published a "Memorial of the Reformation," (1721,) and other works. Died in 1726.

Bennet, (CHRISTOPHER,) an English physician, born in 1617; died in 1655. He practised in London.

Bennet, (HENRY,) Earl of Arlington, an English statesman under Charles II., born in 1618. He was appointed secretary of state in 1662, and was one of the ministry styled "the Cabal," from the initials of their titles forming that word. On the accession of James II. he was continued in the office of lord chamberlain, which he had previously held. Died in 1685.

See MACAULAY's "History of England, vol. i.

Bennet, (JOHN,) a celebrated English composer of madrigals, lived under the reign of Queen Elizabeth.

Bennet, (ROBERT,) an English dissenting divine, wrote a "Theological Concordance of the Synonymous Words in Scripture," (1657.) Died in 1687.

Bennet, bĕn'net, (ROELOF GABRIEL,) a Dutch naval officer and writer, born about 1774, published, in conjunction with Van Wyk, a "History of the Navigation of the Netherlands from the Sixteenth to the Eighteenth Centuries." Died in 1829.

Bennet, (THOMAS,) an English divine and controversialist, born at Salisbury in 1673, published a "Refutation of Popery," "Treatise on Schism," a Hebrew Grammar, and other works. Died in 1728.

See "Biographia Britannica."

Bennet, (WILLIAM,) an English musician and composer, born about 1767, became organist of the church of Saint Andrew's at Plymouth. His sacred compositions are highly esteemed.

Ben'nett, (AGNES MARIA,) an English novelist, was the author of "Anna, or Memoirs of a Welsh Heiress," and other works. Died about 1805.

Bennett, (EDWARD TURNER,) an English zoologist and writer, born near London in 1797; died in 1836.

Bennett, (JAMES,) an English dissenter, born in 1774. He wrote (with David Bogue) a "History of the Dissenters," (3 vols., 1809.) Died in 1862.

Ben'nett, (JAMES GORDON,) an American journalist, born in Banffshire, Scotland, about 1800, emigrated to the United States in 1819. He was employed as reporter or assistant editor of several journals of New York City, and took an active part in politics as a supporter of General Jackson. About 1830 he became associate editor of the "Courier and Enquirer," and in 1833 was chief editor of "The Pennsylvanian," in Philadelphia. He founded in 1835 the "New York Herald," which he has conducted with great ability and success for thirty-four years.

Bennett, (JOHN HUGHES,) an English medical writer, born in London in 1812. He obtained about 1848 the chair of the institutes of medicine in Edinburgh. He published a "Treatise on Clinical Medicine," (1856,) and other works.

Bennett, (WILLIAM COX,) an English poet, born at Greenwich about 1820. He published several volumes of poems, and gained distinction as a writer of songs.

Bennett, (WILLIAM JAMES EARLY,) an English theologian, and a leader of the tractarian party, was born about 1805. He became vicar of Frome about 1852. He published, besides other works, a "Treatise on the Eucharist."

Bennett, (WILLIAM STERNDALE,) an English pianist and composer, born in 1816. Having studied at the Royal Academy of Music, he visited Germany, where he acquired the friendship and patronage of Mendelssohn. In 1838 he was elected a member of the Royal Society of Music.

Benning, bĕn'ning, (JOHN Bodecher—bo'dĕĸ-ẹr,) a Dutch philosopher and poet, born in 1606, was professor of philosophy at Leyden. Died in 1642.

Benningsen, bĕn'ning-sẹn, written also **Bennigsen,** (ALEXANDER LEVIN,) COUNT, a German politician, a son of General Benningsen, noticed below, was born near Wilna in 1809. He was minister of foreign affairs of Hanover from March, 1848, until October, 1850.

Benningsen, written also **Bennigsen,** (LEVIN AUGUST THEOPHIL,) COUNT, a celebrated military commander in the Russian service, born at Brunswick in 1745. He fought in the Turkish campaign of 1788, and against the Poles in 1793. In 1796 he took Derbend from the Persians, and was made lieutenant-general in 1798. Though he headed the conspiracy against the emperor Paul, he was appointed by Alexander, on his accession, Governor-General of Lithuania. He commanded in 1807 at the battle of Eylau, where the victory was claimed by both parties. On the death of Kootoosof, in 1813, he took the command of the army of reserve, and was soon after created a count. Died in Hanover in 1826.

See "Nouvelle Biographie Générale."

Ben'no, [Fr. BENNON, bȧ'nôn',] SAINT, Bishop of Meissen, in Germany, born in 1011, was at first a partisan of Henry IV. against Gregory VII., but afterwards espoused the cause of the pope. Luther wrote on the subject of his canonization (in 1523) a work entitled "The New Idol of Meissen." Died in 1107.

See "Leben und Wunderthaten des heiligen Benno," 1844.

Ben'nor or **Ben'no,** a German cardinal, who lived in the last part of the eleventh century, supported the cause of the anti-pope Clement III. against Gregory VII. He wrote a "Life of Gregory VII.," (in Latin,) which is very unpopular with the Catholics.

See AUBERY, "Histoire des Cardinaux."

Benoist, bẹh-nwȧ', or **Benoît,** [Lat. BENEDIC'TUS,] Bishop of Marseilles, lived about 1230.

Benoist (or **Benedict**) OF SAINT-MAURE, (mōr,) a troubadour in the reign of Henry II. of England, wrote a poem called "The Romance of Troy." "The Chronicle of the Dukes of Normandy" (in French verse) is ascribed to him by some critics.

See ABBÉ DE LA RUE, "Essais sur les Bardes."

Benoist, (MARIE GUILHELMINE Leroux Delavalle —lẹh-roo' dẹh-lȧ'vèl',) MADAME, wife of Pierre Vincent, noticed below, born in Paris in 1767, studied painting under Lebrun and David. Among her best works are portraits of Napoleon and Marie Louise. Died in 1826.

Benoist or **Benoît,** bẹh-nwȧ', (PIERRE VINCENT,) a French statesman and *littérateur,* born at Angers in 1758, rose to be minister of state and member of the privy council in 1828. Died in 1834.

Benoist, [It. BENEDETTO, bȧ-nȧ-det'to,] (ZACHARIE,) a naval officer, of Genoese extraction, gained two victories over the fleet of Pisa in 1284 and 1286. He afterwards became an admiral of France.

Benoît. See BENEDICT.

Benoît, bẹh'nwȧ', (ANTOINE Vernier—vĕʀ'ne-ȧ',) a French *littérateur,* born at Dôle in 1769, wrote a "Treatise on Religious Liberty," and was a contributor to the "Bibliothèque Historique." Died in 1832.

Benoît, (ÉLIE,) a French Protestant theologian, born in Paris in 1640, wrote a "History of the Edict of Nantes," (1693,) and other works. Died in 1728.

Benoît, (JEAN,) called also **Benedicti,** a French theologian and Dominican, was born at Evreux. He wrote "Introductions to Dialectics," ("Introductiones Dialecticæ," 1538.) Died in 1563.

Benoît, (JEAN,) a French ecclesiastic, born at Carcassonne in 1632, wrote a "History of the Albigenses and the Waldenses." Died in 1705.

Benoît, (MICHEL,) a learned French Jesuit, born at Autun in 1715. In 1745 he was a missionary to China, where he introduced the reflecting telescope, the art of engraving, and other useful inventions. Died in 1774.

See "Lettres édifiantes et curieuses."

Benoît, (PIERRE VINCENT.) See BENOIST.

Benoît, (RENÉ,) a French theologian, born near Angers in 1521. He published in 1566 a French translation of the Bible, which was condemned by Pope Gregory XIII. as favouring Protestantism. He was subsequently confessor to Henry IV., who appointed him Bishop of Troyes. Died in 1608.

See MORÉRI, "Dictionnaire Historique."

Benoli, bȧ'no-lee, (IGNAZIO,) called IL BORNO, an Italian painter, born at Verona. He imitated Rubens, whose works he copied, but with reduced dimensions. Died in 1724.

Benomont, bẹh-no'môn', (PIERRE,) a rich French physician and philanthropist, born at Machault in 1679. He practised in Paris, where he died in 1772.

Benoni. See RUFFINI.

Benoschi. See BENASCHI.

Benouville, bẹh-noo'vèl', (FRANÇOIS LÉON,) a French historical painter, born in Paris in 1821. He gained the grand prize in 1845, and a medal of the first class in 1853. Among his most admired works are "Judith," "Esther," and "Raphael seeing La Fornarina for the First Time."

Benouville, (JEAN ACHILLE,) a landscape-painter, brother of the preceding, born in Paris in 1815. He obtained the grand prize of Rome in 1845.

Benozzo. See GOZZOLI.

Bensen, bĕn'sẹn, (KARL DANIEL HEINRICH,) a German writer, born in 1761, was professor of financial science at Würzburg, where he died in 1805.

Benserade, de, dĕh bŏNss′RÄd′ or bŏN′sĕh-RÄd′, (ISAAC,) a French poet, born in Upper Normandy in 1612, was a favourite of Cardinal Richelieu, and acquired great popularity at the court of Louis XIV. by his sprightly and brilliant verses. During twenty years he was employed to compose verses for the *ballets,* which at that time constituted the favourite diversion of the court. In such performances he displayed great ingenuity and finesse, and was unrivalled among his contemporaries. He also wrote several tragedies, elegies, sonnets, etc. He was a member of the French Academy. Died in 1691.

See SENECÉ, "Histoire du Théâtre Français;" C. PERRAULT, "Parallèles des Anciens et des Modernes."

Bensi, bĕn′see, (BERNARDO,) an Italian Jesuit, born at Venice in 1688, was professor of moral theology at Venice. Died in 1760.

Bensi or **Benso,** bĕn′so, (GIULIO,) an Italian painter, born near Genoa in 1601, excelled in painting architectural perspectives. Died in 1668.

Bĕns′ley, (THOMAS,) a celebrated English printer, was associated with König in the construction of the steam press first used in the printing of the "London Times" in 1814. (See KÖNIG.) Bensley published a splendid edition of Shakspeare's Works, and of Hume's "History of England." Died in 1833.

See NICHOLS, "Literary Anecdotes," etc.

Bĕn′son, (GEORGE,) an English dissenting divine, born in Cumberland in 1699, originally a Calvinist, afterwards became an Arian. He wrote, among other works, a "History of the Life of Christ," and a "Treatise on Prayer." Died in 1763.

Benson, (JOSEPH,) an English Methodist minister, born in Cumberland in 1748. He preached in several large towns of England, and acquired extensive influence. He published a "Defence of the Methodists," (1793,) an "Apology for the Methodists," (1801,) a "Life of the Rev. John Fletcher," a number of Sermons, and a "Commentary on the Holy Scriptures," (5 vols., 1811–18,) which is highly esteemed. "He was," says Adam Clarke, "a powerful and able preacher, and a profound theologian." Died in London in 1821.

Benson, (MARTIN,) born in Herefordshire in 1689, became Bishop of Gloucester about 1734. Died in 1752.

Benson, (WILLIAM,) sometimes called AUDITOR BENSON, an English Whig politician, born in 1682, was a member of Parliament in the reign of George I. He published an edition of Virgil's "Husbandry," with notes, and was the first to propose the erection of a monument to Milton in Westminster Abbey. Benson is satirized in Pope's "Dunciad." Died in 1754.

Bent, van der, vän der bĕnt, (JAN,) a Dutch painter born at Amsterdam in 1550, was a pupil of Wouwerman and Van der Velde. Died in 1690.

Bentabolle, bŏn′tȧ′bol′, (PIERRE,) a French Jacobin, became a member of the National Convention and of the Council of Five Hundred. Died in 1798.

Bent-Aichah, bĕnt-ī′kah, daughter of Ahmed, an Arab poet of Córdova, was celebrated for her poetic talent. Died in 1009.

Bentham, bĕn′tȧm, (EDWARD,) an English divine, born at Ely in 1707, became professor of divinity at Oxford. Died in 1776.

Bentham, (JAMES,) an English divine and antiquary, born at Ely in 1708. He published a "History and Antiquities of the Conventual and Cathedral Church of Ely from 675 to 1771." Died in 1794.

Bentham, bĕn′tȧm or bĕn′thȧm, (JEREMY,) a celebrated English jurist and utilitarian philosopher, was born in London on the 15th of February, 1748. He entered Queen's College, Oxford, about the age of fourteen, and studied law, but soon declined the practice of that profession. His motive is said to have been disgust at the unjust charges to suitors. His first publication was an anonymous "Fragment on Government," (1776.) He visited Paris, Constantinople, Smyrna, and White Russia in 1785–86. In 1787 he published a "Defence of Usury," which, says Sir J. Mackintosh, "is perhaps the best specimen of the exhaustive discussion of a moral or political question, leaving no objection, however feeble, unanswered." His "Introduction to the

Principles of Morals and Legislation," though printed in 1780, was not published until 1789.

He devoted his life to the reform of legislation, and maintained the theory that "utility is the test and measure of virtue,"—that the happiness of the greatest number should be the object of legislation. In his long warfare against the iniquities of legislation as he found it, he was ridiculed and denounced as a lunatic by many of the leaders of public opinion in England. His works were first appreciated by foreigners. About 1791 he formed a friendship with M. Dumont, who became to him a valuable coadjutor and translated into French several of his works, viz., "Treatise on Civil and Penal Legislation," ("Traité de Législation civile et pénale," 3 vols., 1802,) and "Theory of Penalties and Rewards," ("Théorie des Peines et des Récompenses," 2 vols., 1818.) These were first published in French. (See DUMONT, ÉTIENNE.)

Among his numerous English works are "Panopticon," a valuable work on prison-discipline, (1791,) "The Rationale of Judicial Evidence," (5 vols., 1827,) and a "Constitutional Code." His "Traité de Législation," etc. (1802) was translated into English by R. Hildreth, Boston, (1840.) "Those who read it," says Lord Jeffrey, "will dissent, we should imagine, from many of the author's fundamental principles; but they will infallibly be delighted with the sagacity and independence which distinguish all his speculations." He died at Westminster on the 6th of June, 1832, having retained to a great age the freshness and serenity of his prime. An edition of his works, in eleven volumes, was published by Dr. Bowring in 1843. "Of Mr. Bentham," says Macaulay, "we would at all times speak with the reverence which is due to a great original thinker and to a sincere and ardent friend of the human race. . . . Posterity will pronounce its calm and impartial decision, and that decision will, we firmly believe, place in the same rank with Galileo and with Locke the man who found jurisprudence a gibberish and left it a science." "In some of the highest departments in which the human intellect can exert itself, he has not left his equal or his second behind him." "Never was there a literary partnership so fortunate as that of Mr. Bentham and M. Dumont. The raw material which Mr. Bentham furnished was most precious, but it was unmarketable. He was assuredly at once a great logician and a great rhetorician. But the effect of his logic was injured by a vicious arrangement, and the effect of his rhetoric by a vicious style. . . . His oracles were of high import, but they were traced on leaves and flung loose to the wind. . . . M. Dumont was admirably qualified to supply what was wanting in Mr. Bentham." (See "Dumont's Recollections of Mirabeau," in Macaulay's Essays.) "It cannot be denied," says Mackintosh, "that Mr. Bentham has done more than any other writer to rouse the spirit of juridical reformation which is now gradually examining every part of law. . . . The true and eminent merit of Mr. Bentham is that of a reformer of jurisprudence. He is only a moralist with a view to being a jurist."

See "Memoirs of Jeremy Bentham," prefixed to his works by DR. BOWRING; "Edinburgh Review" for October, 1843; SIR JAMES MACKINTOSH, "View of the Progress of Ethical Philosophy."

Bentham, (Sir SAMUEL,) a brother of Jeremy, was born in 1757. He was a ship-builder and naval engineer, and was employed by the government as inspector of naval works. Died in 1831.

Bentham, (THOMAS,) born in Yorkshire about 1513, was appointed by Queen Elizabeth in 1559 Bishop of Lichfield and Coventry. Died in 1578.

Ben′tinck, (Lord GEORGE,) a political leader, whose full name was WILLIAM GEORGE FREDERICK CAVENDISH BENTINCK, was the third son of William Henry, fourth Duke of Portland. His mother, Henrietta Scott, was a sister of the wife of George Canning. He was born in February, 1802. In 1826 he became private secretary to his uncle Canning, then a member of the cabinet. He was elected in 1827 a member of Parliament for King's Lynn, which he represented to the end of his life. He was more remarkable for his passion for the turf than for his political knowledge or talents. About 1836 he deserted the Whigs, and became a political friend of

Sir Robert Peel, whom he served efficiently as "whipper-in," urging and coercing absent members of his party to attend and vote on important questions. Like the majority of the Tories, he was opposed to free trade, and on the repeal of the corn-laws, in 1846, was converted into a violent adversary of Peel. He then became the leader of the Protectionist or Tory party, who chose him in consideration of the energy and skill he had shown in his favourite pursuits. He began to study statistics, spoke often in the House, and maintained a spirited contest against the ministry. He died suddenly, of a disease of the heart, in September, 1848.

See B. DISRAELI, "Lord George Bentinck, a Political Biography," 1851; "Edinburgh Review," vol. xcv., 1852.

Bentinck, (HENRY,) son of William, noticed below, was created Duke of Portland in 1716, and became Governor of Jamaica in 1721. Died in 1726.

Bentinck, (WILLIAM,) a Dutch statesman, born in 1648, was a personal attendant and friend of William, Prince of Orange, before his accession to the throne. He came to England with that prince in 1688, was created Earl of Portland in 1689, and served as general in Ireland in 1690. In 1697 he was the principal agent of his government in the negotiation of the treaty of Ryswick. He is said to have possessed the confidence of William III. in a greater degree than any other person. Died in 1709.

See MACAULAY's "History of England," vols. ii., iii., and iv.

Bentinck, (WILLIAM CHARLES CAVENDISH,) LORD, a British general, born in 1774, was the second surviving son of William Henry, third Duke of Portland. Having served in many campaigns, he became Governor of Madras in 1803, and was recalled about 1805. He was commander of the troops sent to aid Ferdinand, King of Sicily, in 1810, and held at the same time the office of plenipotentiary. He gave in 1812 a liberal constitution to Sicily. In 1814 he led a successful expedition against the French in Italy, and took possession of Genoa. He was appointed Governor-General of India by Canning in 1827. In this position he showed himself a humane and enlightened governor. The most important act of his administration was the abolition of the *Suttee*—the custom which required widows to be burned on the funeral piles of their husbands—in 1829. Lord Bentinck resigned, on account of ill health, in 1835. Died at Paris in 1839.

See MACFARLANE, "Our Indian Empire."

Bentinck,(WILLIAM HENRY CAVENDISH,)third Duke of Portland, an eminent statesman, son of the second duke, born in 1738. He began his public life as a Whig, became Lord-Lieutenant of Ireland in 1782, and was prime minister of the new cabinet formed in 1783 by a coalition of Lord North with Mr. Fox. About 1791 he changed his politics and became a supporter of the Tory ministry. He was appointed first lord of the treasury in 1807. Died in 1809.

Bentivoglio, bĕn-te-vòl'yo, (CORNELIO,) an Italian ecclesiastic and writer, born at Ferrara in 1668, was a son of Ippolito, noticed below. He became Archbishop of Carthage, and papal nuncio in France, and was made a cardinal in 1719. Died in 1732.

See SISMONDI, "Histoire des Républiques Italiennes;" LONGFELLOW, "Poets and Poetry of Europe."

Bentivoglio, (ERCOLE,) an Italian poet and diplomatist, born about 1510, wrote sonnets, eclogues, and dramatic works which were greatly admired in his time. Died in 1573.

See GINGUENÉ, "Histoire Littéraire d'Italie."

Bentivoglio, (GIOVANNI,) an Italian nobleman, and leader of the anti-papal party, was proclaimed sovereign of Bologna in 1401, but after a short rule was defeated and put to death. His son Antonio and his grandson Annibal were also rulers of Bologna.

See SISMONDI, "Histoire des Républiques Italiennes."

Bentivoglio, (GIOVANNI II.,) rose to be sovereign of Bologna about 1462. After a rule of more than forty years, he was driven from the city by Pope Julius II. Died in 1508.

Bentivoglio, (GUIDO,) an able writer and diplomatist, born at Ferrara in 1579, became successively Archbishop of Rhodes, papal nuncio in France and Flanders, and

cardinal. He wrote an "Account of the War in Flanders," (1633, in Italian,) a volume of "Memoirs," (1648,) and a collection of "Letters." Died in 1644.

See TIRABOSCHI, "Storia della Letteratura Italiana;" GINGUENÉ, "Histoire Littéraire d'Italie."

Bentivoglio, (IPPOLITO,) a lyric poet and dramatist, born at Ferrara; died in 1685.

See SISMONDI, "Histoire des Républiques Italiennes."

Bentkowski, bĕnt-kov'skee, (FELIX,) a Polish author, born in 1781, was professor of history at Warsaw. He published an important work, entitled a "History of Polish Literature," (2 vols., 1814.) Died in 1852.

Bent'ley, (GIDEON,) an American soldier of the Revolution, born in 1751; died in Oswego county, New York, in 1858, aged one hundred and seven years.

Bent'ley, (Sir JOHN,) a British admiral, was knighted for his conduct in an action off Cape Saint Vincent about 1760. Died in 1772.

Bentley, (RICHARD,) a celebrated critic, regarded as the greatest classical scholar that England ever produced, was born at Oulton, in Yorkshire, on the 27th of January, 1662. He entered Saint John's College, Cambridge, in 1676, and in 1683 became tutor to Dr. Stillingfleet's son, whom he accompanied to Oxford. His first publication was a "Latin Epistle to John Mill, containing Critical Observations on the Chronicle of Joannes Malala," (1691,) which procured him a high European reputation. In 1692 he was honoured with the first appointment to the Boyle lectureship, and chose for his subject the absurdities of atheism. These lectures were much admired, and reached the sixth edition in 1735. He became keeper of the Royal Library in 1693, and chaplain-in-ordinary to the king in 1695. In 1697 he produced his celebrated "Dissertation on the Epistles of Phalaris," in which he affirmed those epistles to be spurious. On this subject he was involved in a controversy with Charles Boyle, Atterbury, Pope, Swift, and other wits, who attacked his personal character with asperity. He replied in another "Dissertation on the Epistles of Phalaris," in 1699. "It was," says Hallam, "the first great literary war that had been waged in England. Both combatants were skilful in wielding the sword: the arms of Boyle, in Swift's language, were given him by all the gods; but his antagonist stood forward in no such figurative strength, master of a learning to which nothing parallel had been known in England ; . . . with a style rapid, concise, amusing, and superior to Boyle in that which he had chiefly to boast, a sarcastic wit." Posterity has decided that Bentley was victorious in this affair. He was appointed master of Trinity College, Cambridge, in 1700, and Archdeacon of Ely in 1701. He became involved in a long contest and lawsuit with the Fellows of Trinity College, in relation to which he is censured for his arrogant and arbitrary conduct. Having been elected regius professor of divinity in 1717, he gave great dissatisfaction by the demand of illegal or unusually large fees from candidates for the degree of D.D. For this offence the senate of the university deprived him in 1718 of all his degrees ; but he was restored by a mandamus of the court of king's bench about 1724. He published an excellent edition of Horace, (1711,) and an edition of Terence, (1725,) which is called one of his best performances. His ill-judged attempt to improve the text of Milton's great poem gave much offence to the admirers of that poet. His last work was an edition of Homer, which, however, he did not live to finish. Died in July, 1742. Bentley's daughter was the mother of Richard Cumberland the dramatist.

See MONK's "Life of Bentley," 1830; HARTLEY COLERIDGE, "Lives of Distinguished Northerns;" "Encyclopædia Britannica ;" "Edinburgh Review" for July, 1830; "London Quarterly Review" for November, 1831.

Bentley, (RICHARD,) son of the preceding, wrote a comedy entitled "The Wishes," and several other works. Died in 1782.

Bentley, (ROBERT,) an English botanist, born about 1820, became professor of botany in London, and wrote a "Manual of Botany."

Bentley, (THOMAS,) a nephew of the famous Richard Bentley, was a Fellow of Trinity College. He published an edition of Cicero "De Finibus" in 1718.

Bentley, (WILLIAM,) an American Unitarian minister

and antiquary, born in Boston in 1758, was ordained pastor of a church at Salem in 1783. He wrote a "History of Salem." Died in 1819.

Ben'ton, (THOMAS HART,) an American Senator, born at or near Hillsborough, North Carolina, on the 14th of March, 1782. Having removed to Tennessee in early youth, he studied law, and began to practise at Nashville about 1811. In 1812 he commanded a regiment under General Jackson, with whom he quarrelled. Jackson attempted to strike Benton with a horsewhip at Nashville in 1813, and was severely wounded with a pistol by Benton's brother. Colonel Benton settled at Saint Louis, Missouri, in 1815, and began to publish a political paper. He was elected a Senator of the United States by the legislature of Missouri in 1820. He acted with the Democrats, became a supporter of General Jackson, and the most prominent politician of Missouri. Having been re-elected to the Federal Senate in 1826, he distinguished himself as an advocate of a gold and silver currency, and received the sobriquet of *Old Bullion.* He supported President Jackson in his hostility against the United States Bank. About 1832 he was again chosen to represent Missouri in the Senate of the United States, of which he continued to be a member for a period of thirty years. He was a political friend of President Van Buren, voted for the annexation of Texas to the United States in 1845, and opposed Calhoun on the subjects of nullification and State rights. In 1850 he made a speech against Clay's compromise bill. In consequence of a division in the Democratic party in relation to slavery, Mr. Benton was defeated as a candidate for the office of Senator about the end of 1850, and retired from the Senate in March, 1851. He was elected a member of the national House of Representatives in 1852, and opposed the repeal of the Missouri Compromise. In 1856 he was supported by one section of the Democracy as candidate for Governor of Missouri, but was not elected. He advocated the election of Buchanan to the Presidency in 1856, in preference to Fremont, who was his son-in-law. He published a voluminous work entitled "A Thirty Years' View, or a History of the Working of the American Government for Thirty Years, from 1820 to 1850," (2 vols., 1854–56,) and "An Abridgment of the Debates of Congress from 1789 to 1856," (15 vols., 1857.) He died at Washington in April, 1858.

Benton, (WILLIAM P.,) an American lawyer and general, born in Maryland, emigrated to Indiana. He became a brigadier-general of the Union army in 1862.

Bentzel-Sternau, von, fon bĕnt'sĕl stĕr'nŏw, (ANSELM FRANZ,) a German statesman, born in 1738, was counsellor to the Elector of Mentz. Died in 1784.

Bentzel-Sternau, von, (CHRISTIAN ERNST,) COUNT, a German statesman and writer, born at Mentz in 1767, became minister of state and finance in the grand duchy of Frankfort, (1812.) He published "The Stone Guest," ("Der Steinerne Gast,") "The Golden Calf," and other popular satirical romances. Died in 1850.

See BROCKHAUS, "Conversations-Lexikon."

Bentzen, bĕnt'sęn, or **Bentzon,** (ADRIAN BENONI,) a Norwegian *littérateur,* born at Tönsberg in 1777.

Benvenuti, bĕn-vȧ-noo'tee, (CARLO,) an Italian mathematician and Jesuit, born at Leghorn in 1716. He wrote, in Latin, a "Synopsis of General Physics," and translated into Italian Clairault's "Elements of Geometry." Died in 1789.

Benvenuti, (GIUSEPPE,) an Italian physician and medical writer, born in the duchy of Lucca about 1728.

Benvenuti, (PIETRO,) an eminent Italian painter, born at Arezzo in 1769. He was regarded by some as the best painter of Tuscany in his time. His design is correct and his style elevated. His chief work is a series of frescos of prophets and evangelists on the dome of the chapel of Medici at Florence. Among his other works is "The Woman of Samaria." Died at Florence in 1844.

See "Nouvelle Biographie Générale."

Benvenuto, bĕn-vȧ-noo'to, (GIOVANNI BATTISTA,) called ORTOLANO, an Italian painter of the school of Ferrara, born about 1480; died in 1525.

Benvenuto Cellini. See CELLINI.

Benvoglienti, bĕn-vŏl-yĕn'tee, (UBERTO,) an Italian *littérateur* and patron of learning, born in 1668; died in 1733.

Benyowsky. See BENIOWSKY.

Benzel, bĕnt'sęl, [Lat. BENZE'LIUS,] (ERIC,) born about 1632, was made, in 1700, Archbishop of Upsal by Charles XII. He superintended the Swedish translation of the Bible published by order of Charles XII., and wrote several religious works. Died in 1709.

See JOHAN ESBERG, "Libri in E. H. Benzelii Tumulum," 1712.

Benzel, [Lat. BENZELIUS,] (ERIC,) son of the preceding, born at Upsal in 1675, became successively Bishop of Gothenburg and of Linköping, and Archbishop of Upsal. He was one of the founders of the Academy of Sciences at Upsal, and wrote several valuable historical and antiquarian works. Died in 1743.

See OLOF DALIN, "Åminnelse-Tal öfver E. Benzelius," 1744.

Benzel, (HENRY,) brother of Eric, mentioned above, born at Strengnäs in 1689, was one of the savants sent by Charles XII., in 1714, on a scientific expedition to the East. He was made Archbishop of Upsal after his return. His journal of his travels is still in manuscript. Died in 1758.

See M. ASP, "Likpredikan öfver H. Benzelius med Personalier," 1758.

Benzel-Sternau. See BENTZEL-STERNAU.

Benzenberg, bĕnt'sęn-bĕRG', (JOHANN FRIEDRICH,) a German mathematician and astronomer, born near Elberfeld in 1777. He wrote, among other works, a "Manual of Geometry," (1810,) and a treatise "On Falling Stars," (1839.) Died in 1846.

Benzi, bĕn'zee, (MASSIMILIANO SOLDANO,) a painter and engraver of medals, born at Florence in 1658.

Benzio, bĕn'ze-o, (TRIFONE,) an Italian diplomatist and poet, born at Assisi, lived in the latter part of the sixteenth century. He was secretary to Pope Julius III., and was employed on several missions.

Benzon, bĕn'zon, (FRIEDRICH WILHELM KARL,) a Danish historian, born at Kiöge in 1791.

Benzoni, bĕn-zo'nee, (GERONIMO,) an Italian traveller, born about 1520, spent many years in America, of which he gave an account in a work entitled "History of the New World," (1565.)

Beolco, bȧ-ol'ko, or **Biolco,** be-ol'ko, (ANGELO,) an Italian dramatic poet, born at Padua in 1502, was surnamed RUZZANTE, from the number of rustic farces he composed. Died in 1542.

Beorn. See BIÖRN.

Beowulf, be-o'wŏŏlf, a semi-fabulous naval hero of Denmark, who forms the subject of a celebrated epic poem in Anglo-Saxon, supposed to have been written in the ninth century. It has been translated into English and German.

See TURNER, "History of the Anglo-Saxons."

Béquet, bȧ'kạ', (ÉTIENNE,) an able French journalist and critic, born in Paris about 1800. He wrote for the "Journal des Débats" for fifteen years. In 1830 he was prosecuted and acquitted for a political article ending with these words : "Unfortunate France ! unfortunate king !" which were afterwards often repeated. Died in 1838.

Berain, beh-rǎn', (JEAN,) a French designer, born at Saint-Michel in 1630; died in 1697.

Berain, (PIERRE MARTIN,) a French historian, lived about 1710.

Béranger, bȧ'rŏN'zhȧ', (CHARLES,) a French painter of landscapes and genre, born at Sèvres in 1816.

Béranger, de, dęh bȧ'rŏN'zhȧ', (PIERRE JEAN,) a celebrated French lyric poet, born in Paris on the 19th of August, 1780. He lived with his grandfather, who was a tailor, until he was nine years old, after which he went to reside with an aunt, who appears to have acted towards him the part of a true mother, and, while giving him the rudiments of an education, instilled into his mind the principles calculated to make him a good man and a true patriot. For a short time he served as apprentice to a printer. When he was about sixteen, he began to write poetry. Several of his lyrics attracted the attention and procured for him the patronage of Lucien Bonaparte, and in 1815 he brought out his first collection of songs. They were received with great favour by the people ; but their bold, patriotic, and often satirical tone gave offence to the government ; and, as Béranger in his succeeding productions abated nothing of the freedom of his satire, he was condemned in 1828 to an imprisonment of nine months and a heavy fine. He was an ardent republican. After the revolution of 1830, which his poems had contributed to bring about, he refused to accept any office under the government. He brought out in 1833 a fifth collection of his songs, leaving memoirs of his life and a number of poems, which were published after his death. In 1848 he was elected to the Constituent Assembly by the voters of the department of Seine, but he declined to serve. He died in July, 1857. He is represented as a man of a generous, noble, and independent character.

"His style," says J. F. Destigny, "has a limpidity, precision, and purity which defy criticism. All ordinary eulogy (*louange banale*) would cast a shade upon his glory." ("Nouvelle Biographie Générale.")

"The great peculiarity of Béranger," says the "Quarterly Review" for January, 1832, "is the mixture of gayety and pathos which he combines with the happiest effect. He indeed mingles 'the grave and gay, the lively and severe,' with a very original and singular felicity."

See a posthumous work of Béranger, entitled "Ma Biographie," 1857; BOITEAU, "Philosophie et Politique de Béranger," 1858; SAVINIEN-LAPOINTE, "Mémoires sur Béranger," 1857; LONGFELLOW, "Poets and Poetry of Europe;" "Edinburgh Review" for July, 1833; LOUIS DE LOMÉNIE, "Notice sur Béranger," 1844.

Bérard, bȧ'rȧr', (AUGUSTE,) an eminent French surgeon, born at Varrains, near Saumur, in 1802. He was the founder of the Société de Chirurgie of Paris. In 1842 he obtained the chair of surgical *clinique* in Paris. He published a number of able treatises on surgery. Died in 1846.

Bérard, (AUGUSTE SIMON LOUIS,) born in Paris in 1783, became master of requests to the Council of State in 1814, and founded (with Chaptal) the first company for the production of illuminating gas. He was a liberal member of the Chamber of Deputies in 1827-30, and took a prominent part in the revolution of 1830 as a partisan of Louis Philippe. Died in 1859.

See "Nouvelle Biographie Générale."

Bérard, (FRÉDÉRIC,) a French physician and medical writer, born at Montpellier in 1789, was a contributor to the "Dictionnaire des Sciences médicales" of Paris. Died in 1828.

See J. A. DUPAU, "Notice historique sur F. Bérard," 1828.

Bérard, (PIERRE,) a French pharmacist and botanist, born at Grenoble about 1630. He wrote a work entitled "Theatrum Botanicum," (unpublished.) The genus Berardia was named in his honour.

Bérard, (PIERRE HONORÉ,) a distinguished French surgeon, brother of Auguste, born at Lichtenberg in 1797. He became in 1831 professor of physiology to the faculty of medicine in Paris, and was subsequently elected to the Academy of Medicine. He began the publication of a "Course of Physiology," (1st vol., 1848.) Died in 1858.

See "Nouvelle Biographie Générale."

Berardi, bȧ-rȧr'dee, (ANGELO,) an Italian musician and composer, born near Bologna about 1650, wrote several treatises on music.

Berardi, (FABIO,) an Italian engraver, born at Sienna in 1728, was one of the most distinguished pupils of Wagner.

Bérardier de Bataud, bȧ'rȧr'de-ȧ' deh bȧ'to', (FRANÇOIS JOSEPH,) a French *littérateur*, born in Paris in 1720; died in 1794.

Berardo, bȧ-rȧr'do, (GERONIMO,) an Italian writer, born about 1500, translated two of the comedies of Plautus.

Béraud, bȧ'ro', (ANTOINE,) a French *littérateur*, born at Aurillac in 1794. He wrote dramas, political songs, etc.

Béraud, (JEAN JACQUES,) a French savant, born near Castellane in 1753, was professor of mathematics and experimental physics at Marseilles. Died in 1794.

Béraud, (LAURENT,) a French Jesuit and astronomer, born in 1703 at Lyons, where he was director of the observatory. He published several valuable scientific works. Died in 1777.

See LE FÈBVRE, "Éloge historique du P. L. Béraud," 1780.

Béraudière, de la, deh lȧ bȧ'ro'de-air', (FRANÇOIS,) Bishop of Périgueux, born at Poitiers, wrote a "Funeral Oration on Henry IV." Died in 1646.

Bérauld, bȧ'ro', (FRANÇOIS,) a French scholar, son of Nicolas, noticed below, born at Orléans about 1510. He wrote Greek and Latin poems, and translated the two books of Appian containing the wars of Hannibal and those of Spain.

See MORÉRI, "Dictionnaire Historique."

Bérauld, [Lat. BERAL'DUS AURE'LIUS,] (NICOLAS,) an eminent French scholar and writer, born at Orléans in 1473. He was a friend of Erasmus, and numbered among his pupils D'Andelot and Admiral de Coligny. He published a Greek-Latin Dictionary (1521) and an edition of Pliny's "Natural History," (1516,) and wrote several Latin treatises. Died in 1550.

See BAYLE, "Historical and Critical Dictionary."

Bérault, bȧ'ro', (CLAUDE,) a French philologist, succeeded D'Herbelot as professor of the Syriac language in the Royal College in Paris. He published an edition of "Statius ad Usum Delphini," (1685.) Died in 1705.

See BAYLE, "Historical and Critical Dictionary."

Bérault, (JEAN,) a French *littérateur*, translated Barclay's "Euphormio" from the Latin, (1640.)

Bérault, (JOSIAS,) a French jurist, and advocate of the parliament of Rouen, born in 1563, wrote a "Commentary on the Common Law of Normandy." Died about 1640.

Bérault, (MICHEL,) a French Protestant theologian, published in 1598 a "Brief and Clear Defence of the Vocation of the Ministers of the Gospel," in reply to Cardinal Perron. He preached at Montauban.

Bérault-Bercastel, bȧ'ro' bĕr'kȧs'tĕl', (ANTOINE HENRI,) a French writer, born near Metz in 1772, wrote a "History of the Church," (24 vols., 1778-90,) and other works. Died in 1794.

Berbiguier, bĕr'be'ge-ȧ', (BENOÎT Tranquille—trȯn'kèl',) a French flutist and composer, born at Carderousse in 1781; died about 1838.

Berbiguier, (CHARLES ALEXIS VINCENT,) a French visionary, born at Carpentras about 1776, wrote a work on demonology. Died in 1851.

Berch, bĕrk, (ANDERS,) a Swedish writer on rural economy, born in 1711; died in 1774.

Berch, (KARL REINHOLD,) a Swedish antiquary, born in 1706, wrote a "History of the Kings and Celebrated Characters of Sweden, taken from Medals." Died in 1777.

See OLOF CELSIUS, "Åminnelse-Tal öfver C. R. Berch," 1781.

Berchelmann, bĕr'kĕl-mȧn', (JOHANN PHILIPP,) a German physician, born at Darmstadt in 1718; died 1783.

Berchem. See BERGHEM.

Berchem, bĕr'kĕm, [Lat. BERCHE'MIUS,] (WILHELM,) a German chronicler, lived about 1480.

Berchény, [Fr. pron. bĕr'shȧ'ne'; Hun. BERCSÉNY, bĕr-chȧñ',] written also **Berkeny,** (LADISLAS IGNAZ,) COUNT OF, son of Nicholas, noticed below, born at Eperies, in Hungary, in 1689. He entered the French service in 1712, and became a marshal in 1758. Died in 1778.

Bercheny or **Bercsény,** bĕr-chȧñ', (NICHOLAS,) a Hungarian nobleman, born in 1664, made an unsuccessful attempt, in conjunction with Prince Ragotsky, to separate Hungary from Austria about 1705. Died in 1725.

Berchet, bĕr'shȧ', (GIOVANNI,) an Italian patriot and poet, born at Milan about 1790, was a friend of Silvio Pellico. After the suppression of the "Conciliatore," a liberal journal to which he had contributed, he removed to Geneva. He published in 1841 a volume of patriotic songs, which were received with enthusiasm, and still enjoy great popularity, though prohibited by the government. Died in Italy in 1851.

Berchet, bĕr'shȧ', (TOUSSAINT,) a French philologist and Protestant writer, born at Langres in 1540. He made a version of Henry Estienne's Greek Catechism, which was often reprinted. Died about 1605.

Berchett, bĕr'shĕt', (PIERRE,) a French painter and engraver, born in 1659, was employed by William III. of England to decorate his palace at Loo. Died in 1720.

See WALPOLE, "Anecdotes of Painting in England."

Bercheure, bĕr'shur', written also **Berchoire,** [Lat. BERCHO'RIUS,] (PIERRE,) a French Benedictine monk, born in Poitou. He translated into French Livy's "Roman History." Died in 1362.

Berchheim, bĕʀ′kăn′, or **Berckheim, de,** dĕh bĕʀk′-hīm, (FRIEDRICH SIGISMUND,) BARON, a French general, of German extraction, born at Ribeauvillé in 1775. He served with distinction in the armies of Napoleon, and attained the rank of general of division. Died in 1819.

Berchoire. See BERCHEURE.

Berchoux, bĕʀ′shoo′, (JOSEPH,) a French poet, born at Saint-Symphorien, near Lyons, in 1765. His first poem was a well-known satire on the ridiculous ambition then prevalent of imitating the Greek and Roman costumes and habits of life, entitled "Qui me délivrera des Grecs et des Romains?" (" Who will deliver me from the Greeks and the Romans?") He published in 1800 "La Gastronomie," which had great success and was translated into English. His later works were less successful. Died in 1839.

See LE BAS, "Dictionnaire encyclopédique de la France."

Berchtold, bĕʀK′tolt, (LEOPOLD,) COUNT OF, a German philanthropist, born in 1738, travelled in Europe, Asia, and Africa, and introduced vaccination where it was previously unknown. He also founded several charitable institutions in his native country. Died in 1809.

See "Nouvelle Biographie Générale."

Berckel, van, văn bĕr′kĕl, (THEODORUS VICTOR,) a Dutch engraver, born at Bois-le-Duc in 1739; died 1808.

Berckheim. See BERCHHEIM.

Berckmann, bĕrk′mân, **Bergmann,** bĕʀG′mân, or **Barkmann,** bârk′mân, (JOHN,) a chronicler, supposed to have been a native of Stralsund. His principal work is entitled "Chronicles of Stralsund," (in manuscript, and written in Low German.) Died in 1560.

Berckmans, bĕrk′mâns, (HENDRIK,) a distinguished Dutch portrait-painter, born near Willemstadt in 1629. He was a pupil of Jordaens and Wouwermans.

See NAGLER, "Neues Allgemeines Künstler-Lexikon."

Berckringer, bĕrk′ring′er, (DANIEL,) a German scholar, born in the Palatinate, was tutor to the children of the King of Bohemia. Died in 1667.

Bercsény. See BERCHENY.

Bére or **Ber,** baiʀ, [Lat. BE′RUS,] (LOUIS,) a Catholic theologian, born at Bâle; died in 1554.

Bere, bä′rĕh, (OSWALD,) a German physician, born at Frankfort in 1472; died at Bâle in 1567.

Berebistes. See BÆREBISTES.

Berecynthia. See CYBELE.

Berednikof, be-rĕd′ne-kof, (YAKOV IVANOVITCH,) a Russian archæologist, born in 1802, contributed to the large Sclavonian Dictionary (1847) of the Academy of Sciences of Saint Petersburg, of which he was a member.

Beregani, bȧ-rȧ-gä′nee, (NICCOLÒ,) an Italian historian and dramatic poet, born at Vicenza in 1627; died in 1713.

Berends, bä′rĕnts, (JOHANN BERNARD JAKOB,) a German physician, born at Frankfort-on-the-Main about 1760. Died about 1830.

Berends, (JULIUS,) a German democratic politician, born at Kyritz in 1817, was elected in 1848 to the Prussian National Assembly.

Berends, (KARL AUGUST WILHELM,) a German physician and medical writer, born in 1753, was professor of medicine successively at Frankfort-on-the-Oder, Breslau, and Berlin. Died in 1826.

See CALLISEN, "Medicinisches Schriftsteller-Lexikon."

Berengaria, bȧ-rĕn-gä′re-ä, [Fr. BÉRENGÈRE, bȧ′rŏN′-zhair′,] a Spanish lady distinguished for beauty and resolution, was the queen of Alfonso VIII. of Castile. Died in 1159.

Berengaria, a sister of the famous Blanche of Castile, was married to Alfonso IX. of Castile, who divorced her in 1209. Died in 1244.

Berengario, bȧ-rĕn-gä′re-o, [Lat. BERENGA′RIUS; Fr. BÉRENGER, bȧ′rŏN′zhȧ′,] (GIACOMO,) an eminent Italian surgeon and anatomist of the sixteenth century, surnamed CARPEN′SIS, was born at Carpi. He was professor of surgery at Pavia and Bologna, and wrote several anatomical works in Latin. He is said to have made important discoveries. Fallopius called him the restorer of anatomy. He lectured at Bologna from 1502 to 1527.

See TIRABOSCHI, "Storia della Letteratura Italiana."

Berengarius or **Berengario.** See BÉRENGER, (kings of Italy.)

Bérenger, the French of BERENGARIO, which see.

Bérenger, bȧ′rŏN′zhȧ′, [It. BERENGARIO, bȧ-rĕn-gȧ′-re-o; Lat. BERENGA′RIUS,] **I.,** grandson of Louis le Débonnaire, was crowned King of Italy about 888, in opposition to Guido, Duke of Spoleto. He was assassinated in 924.

Bérenger (or **Berenga′rius) II.,** called THE YOUNGER, grandson of the preceding, was crowned King of Italy in 950. His country being afterwards invaded by Otho the Great of Germany, Bérenger became tributary to that sovereign, and was at length deposed and imprisoned. Died in 966.

See SISMONDI, "Histoire des Républiques Italiennes."

Bérenger, bȧ′rŏN′zhȧ′, (ALPHONSE MARIE MARCELLIN THOMAS,) a French jurist and magistrate, born at Valence in 1785. He became counsellor at the court of cassation in 1831, and a member of the Chamber of Peers in 1839. Among his principal works is a treatise "On Criminal Justice in France," (1818.) He became in 1831 a member of the Academy of Moral and Political Sciences.

Bérenger, (JEAN,) COUNT, a French legislator, born near Grenoble in 1767. He was elected to the States-General in 1790, and was a member of the Tribunat in 1800. Died about 1845.

Bérenger, (JEAN PIERRE,) a Swiss littérateur, born at Geneva in 1740. He wrote, among other works, a "History of Geneva from its Origin to the Present Time," (6 vols., 1772.) Died in 1807.

Bérenger, (LAURENT PIERRE,) a French littérateur, born at Riez in 1749, became inspector of the Academy at Lyons. Among his works we may name "Morality in Action," ("La Morale en Action,") which has gone through numerous editions. Died in 1822.

See J. B. DUMAS, "Notice historique sur L. P. Bérenger," 1836.

Bérenger, (PIERRE,) a French theologian of the twelfth century, was a native of Poitiers.

Bérenger, (RAYMOND,) grand master of the order of Saint John of Jerusalem, was a native of Dauphiny, in France. He defeated the Egyptian corsairs who infested Cyprus and Rhodes, and took Alexandria after a short siege. Died in 1373.

Bĕr′en-ġer, (RICHARD,) gentleman of the horse to George III. of England, was the author of "The History and Art of Horsemanship," (1771.) Died in 1782.

Bérenger de Palasol, bȧ′rŏN′zhȧ′ dĕh pȧ′lȧ′sol′, a French troubadour of the twelfth century. Died in 1194.

Bérenger de la Tour, bȧ′rŏN′zhȧ′ dĕh lȧ tooʀ, a French poet of the sixteenth century, was the author of "The Golden Age," and other works. Died about 1560.

Bérenger [Lat. BERENGA′RIUS] **de Tours,** bȧ′rŏN′-zhȧ′ dĕh tooʀ, a celebrated French ecclesiastic, born about 998, was a native of Tours. He studied under Fulbert of Chartres, and became in 1039 Archdeacon of Angers. Having opposed the dogmas of transubstantiation and the real presence, his doctrine was condemned by Pope Leo IX. in 1050. He formally retracted his opinions; but, as he still continued to deny the orthodox dogmas, he was compelled, in a council at Rome, to make another recantation. Died in 1088.

See FLEURY, "Histoire ecclésiastique;" HEINRICH MÜLLER, "Berengarii veteris novique Historia," 1674; H. SUDENDORF, "Berengarius Turonensis, oder eine Sammlung ihn betreffender Briefe," 1850.

Berenguer, bȧ-rĕn-gairʹ, (PEDRO JUAN Morales—mo-rȧ′lĕs,) a Spanish theologian of the early part of the seventeenth century. He published a work entitled "Explanation of the Mysteries of our Holy Faith," (1608.)

Berenhorst, bä′rĕn-horst′, (GEORG HEINRICH,) a German officer and military writer, born in 1733, served in the Seven Years' war. His principal work is entitled "Reflections on the Military Art," (1797.)

Ber-e-ni′çe, [Gr. Βερενίκη,] an Egyptian princess, the daughter of Lagus, and niece of Antipater, was married to Ptolemy Soter. Through her influence he appointed as his successor her son Ptolemy Philadelphus, to the exclusion of the children of Eurydice, his other wife.

Berenice II., daughter of Ptolemy Philadelphus, was married to Antiochus Theos, King of Syria, who had divorced Laodice, his former wife. After the death of Ptolemy, Laodice murdered her husband and her rival Berenice (247 B.C.) and placed her own son on the throne.

Berenice III., daughter of Ptolemy Philadelphus and

Arsinoë, was married to Ptolemy Evergetes. During his absence on an expedition to Syria, she made an offering of her hair to Venus for his safe return ; and the astronomer Conon publicly reported that Jupiter had made of it the constellation called "Coma Berenices." Berenice was put to death by her father in 216 B.C.

See CARL W. RAMLER, "Ptolemäus und Berenice," 1765.

Berenice, daughter of Ptolemy Lathyrus, was married to Alexander II., whom Sulla had made king. She was soon after murdered by her husband.

Berenice, daughter of Ptolemy Auletes, and sister of the celebrated Cleopatra, was raised to the throne by the Alexandrians, who had revolted against her father, (58 B.C.) Having poisoned her first husband, Seleucus, she was married to Archelaus, high-priest and King of Comana. In 55 B.C. she was put to death by order of her father, who had regained his crown.

Berenice, (called Berni'çe [Gr. Βερονίκη] in the New Testament,) daughter of Agrippa I., King of Judea, was born about 28 A.D. She was married to Herod, King of Chalcis, and afterwards to Polemon, King of Cilicia. About 75 A.D. she visited Rome, where Titus wished to marry her, but renounced her when he found the match would displease his people. This event has formed the subject of one of Racine's tragedies. Berenice was the sister of Herod Agrippa, before whom Paul preached. (See Acts xxv.)

Bères, baiR, (ÉMILE,) a French political economist, born at Castelnau d'Anzac in 1801, wrote several works on political economy, trade, etc.

Běr'es-ford, (Rev. JAMES,) an English writer, born in 1764, published "The Miseries of Human Life, or The Last Groans of Timothy Testy and Samuel Sensitive," (2 vols., 1806–07.) Died in 1840.

Beresford, (Lord JOHN GEORGE,) Primate of Ireland, a son of the Marquis of Waterford, born at Dublin in 1773. He became Bishop of Cork in 1806, of Clogher in 1819, Archbishop of Dublin in 1820, and was translated to the see of Armagh in 1822. Died in 1862.

Beresford, (WILLIAM CARR,) VISCOUNT, a distinguished general, born in Ireland in 1768, was the natural son of the first Marquis of Waterford. Having served in Egypt and Buenos Ayres, and captured Madeira in 1807, he fought in the Peninsular war under Wellington, and was made a field-marshal of Portugal and Duke of Elvas. After his return to England he was created a viscount in 1823, and in 1828 master-general of the ordnance. Died in 1854.

Berettoni, bà-rĕt-to'nee, written also Berrettoni, (NICCOLÒ,) an Italian painter, born at Montefeltro in 1627, was one of the best pupils of Carlo Maratta. Died at Rome in 1682.

Berg. See BERGIUS, (BENGT.)

Berg, bĕRG, (JENS CHRISTIAN,) a Norwegian jurist and antiquary, born at Drontheim in 1775.

Berg, bĕRG, (JOHANN PETER,) a German theologian and Orientalist, born at Bremen in 1737, became professor of ecclesiastical history and Oriental languages at Duisburg. He wrote valuable commentaries on the Scriptures. Died in 1800.

See MÖLLER, "Denkschrift zur Ehre J. P. Bergs," 1801.

Berg, (MAGNUS,) a Norwegian painter and excellent sculptor in ivory, born in 1666, was patronized by King Christian V. Died in 1739.

Berg, van den, vän děn bĕRG, (MATTHIAS,) a Flemish painter, born at Ypres in 1615, was a distinguished pupil of Rubens, whose works he copied with great accuracy. Died in 1647.

See BRYAN, "Dictionary of Painters."

Berg, von, fon bĕRG, (JOACHIM,) a German diplomatist and philanthropist, born at Herrndorf in 1526, bequeathed all his property to create a fund for the education of the poor in his own country. Died in 1602.

See G. VON BERG, "Memoria Bergeriana;" KELLER, "Joachim von Berge und sein Stiftungen," 1834.

Bergalli, bĕR-gâl'lee, (CARLO,) an Italian ecclesiastic and littérateur, born at Palermo ; died in 1679.

Bergalli, (LUIGIA,) an Italian dramatic authoress, born at Venice in 1703, became the wife of Count Gasparo Gozzi. (See GOZZI.) Died about 1760.

Bergamasco. See CASTELLO.

Bergamini, bĕR-gâ-mee'nee, (ANTONIO,) an Italian poet, born at Vicenza in 1666 ; died in 1744.

Bergamo, bĕR'gâ-mo,(JACOPO FILIPPO FORESTI,) Italian chronicler, born near Bergamo in 1434 ; died in 1520.

Bergamo, da, dâ bĕR'gâ-mo, (FRA DAMIANO,) an Italian Dominican monk, who was celebrated as a sculptor in wood. Died in 1549.

Bergantini, bĕR-gân-tee'nee, (GIOVANNI PIETRO,) an Italian poet and miscellaneous writer, born at Venice in 1685; died about 1760.

Bergasse, bĕR'gâss', (ALEXANDRE,) a French royalist and political writer, brother of Nicolas, noticed below, was born at Lyons in 1747 ; died in 1821.

Bergasse, (NICOLAS,) a French jurist and political writer, born at Lyons in 1750, published in 1787 a memorial in favour of his client Kornmann, which won for him a high reputation, and was answered by Beaumarchais. He also wrote in favour of animal magnetism. Died in 1832.

See LE BAS, "Dictionnaire encyclopédique de la France."

Berge, bĕR'geh, (ERNST GOTTLIEB,) a German writer, born in 1649, visited England in 1678, and published, after his return, an excellent translation of Milton's "Paradise Lost," (1682.)

Berge, bâRzh, (FRANÇOIS Beaudire—bo'dĕR',) born at Collioure, in France, in 1779, served successively in Egypt, Germany, and Spain, and was made lieutenant-general in 1823. Died in 1832.

Ber-gel-la'nus, (JOHANN ARNOLD,) a German typographer, wrote a Latin poem in praise of printing, entitled "Encomium Chalcographiae," (1541.)

Bergelmir, bĕr-gĕl'mir, [originally Berggelmir, a "mountain mass," (?)] the name of one of the Frost-giants in the Norse mythology. It is related that when Odin and his brothers slew the giant Ymir, all the Frost-Jötuns were drowned in his blood except Bergelmir, who, with his wife, escaped, and continued the race of Frost-giants. (See YMIR.)

See THORPE'S "Northern Mythology," vol. i.

Bergen, bĕRG'en, a Dutch painter of rare promise, born at Breda about 1670, died at the age of nineteen. Some of his works are in the Louvre, others at Dresden.

Bergen, (DANIEL.) See BERGER.

Bergen, van, vän bĕR'hen, (DIRK,) a Dutch painter of landscapes and animals, born at Haarlem about 1645, was a pupil of Van der Velde. Died in 1689.

Bergen, von, fon bĕR'gen, (JOHANN GEORG,) a German medical writer, the father of Karl August, born at Dessau ; died at Frankfort-on-the-Oder in 1738.

Bergen, von, (KARL AUGUST,) a German botanist, anatomist, and scientific writer, born at Frankfort-on-the-Oder in 1704. In 1744 he became professor of pathology and therapeutics in his native city. The genus Bergena was named in his honour by Adanson. Died in 1760.

See "Biographie Médicale."

Bergen, von, (RUDIGER,) a German poet, born at Riga in 1603 ; died in 1661.

Bergenhielm, bĕR'gen-he-ĕlm or bĕR'gen-hyĕlm, (JOHAN,) BARON OF, a Swedish statesman and Latin poet, born in Ostrogothia in 1629, rose to be secretary of state and chancellor of the court. Died in 1704.

Berger, bĕR'ger, (ALBRECHT LUDWIG,) a German jurist, born at Oldenburg in 1768 ; died in 1813.

Berger, bĕR'ger, (CHRISTIAN JOHAN,) a Danish physician, born in 1724, became professor of medicine and surgery at Kiel. Died in 1789.

Berger or Bergen, bĕR'gen, (DANIEL,) a German engraver, born in Berlin in 1744. He engraved history and portraits. Died in 1824.

Berger, bĕR'zhâ', (JACQUES,) a painter of history, born at Chambéry, was a good colorist. Died at Turin in 1823.

Berger, (JEAN JACQUES,) a French senator, born at Thiers, in Puy de Dôme, in 1790. He was a member of the Chamber of Deputies from 1837 to 1848, and took an active part in the republican movement of 1848. He became prefect of La Seine about December, 1848, and senator in 1853.

Berger, (JOHAN ERIC,) a Danish savant, born about 1772, was professor of astronomy at Kiel. He wrote "A General Sketch of Science," and other works. Died in 1833.

See H. RATJEN, "J. E. von Berger's Leben," 1835.

Berger, (JOHANN GOTTFRIED EMANUEL,) a German theologian, born at Ruhland in 1773, published, among other works, a "History of the Philosophy of Religions." Died in 1803.

Berger, (JULIEN FRANÇOIS ADOLPHE,) a French classical scholar, born in 1810. He was for several years professor of rhetoric at the College of Charlemagne, Paris.

Berger, (LUDWIG,) a German composer and pianist of great merit, born at Berlin in 1777. His works are chiefly cantatas, operas, and symphonies. He numbered among his scholars the celebrated Mendelssohn. Died in Berlin about 1839.

Berger, (PAUL,) a German theologian and Hebraist, born at Rosenburg, lived about 1730.

Berger, (THEODOR,) a German jurist and historian, born near Coburg in 1683, published legal and historical works in Latin and German. Died in 1773.

Berger, von, fon bĕR'ğĕr, (CHRISTOPH HEINRICH,) a German jurist and aulic councillor, born at Wittenberg about 1680. Died in 1757.

Bergerac, de, dĕh bĕRzh'Răk', (SAVINIEN CYRANO,) a French dramatist and notorious duellist, born in Périgord about 1620. He served in the army in his youth. His principal works are the tragedy of "Agrippina," (1653,) and the "Pédant Joué," a comedy. Died in Paris in 1655. Some writers conjecture that Swift derived the idea of his "Gulliver's Travels" from Bergerac's "Comic History of the States and Empires of the Moon," ("Histoire comique des États et Empires de la Lune," 1656.)

See CHARLES NODIER, "B. Desperriers et Cyrano de Bergerac," 1841.

Bergeret, bĕRzh'Rả', (JEAN,) a French botanist, born at Morlas, in Basses-Pyrénées, published a Flora of the Basses-Pyrénées, (2 vols., 1803.) Died about 1814.

Bergeret, (JEAN PIERRE,) a French physician and botanist, born near Auch in 1751, became surgeon to Monsieur (afterwards Louis XVIII.) in 1785. Died in 1813.

Bergeron, bĕRzh'rŏN', (LOUIS,) a French journalist and littérateur, born at Chauny in 1811, published, among other works, "Campaigns of Spain and Portugal under the Empire," (1833.)

Bergeron, (NICOLAS,) a French jurist and historian, a native of Béthisy, lived about 1560. He is said to have produced the first synchronic tables of history.

Bergeron, (PIERRE,) son of the preceding, born in Paris, wrote a "Treatise on Navigation and Modern Voyages of Discovery and Conquests," (1629,) and other geographical and historical works.

Bergeron, (PIERRE,) a French poet and littérateur, born in Paris in 1787, was professor in a college at Brussels.

Bergery, bĕRzh'Re', (CLAUDE LUCIEN,) a French mathematician, and professor of mathematics in the School of Artillery at Metz, born at Orléans in 1787. He published "Geometry applied to Industry," (1835,) and "Elementary Astronomy," (1832.)

Berghaus, bĕRG'hŏws, (HEINRICH,) an eminent German geographer, born at Cleves in 1797. He was appointed in 1816 geographical engineer in the war department at Berlin, and in 1824 professor of mathematics in the Academy of Architecture. Among his numerous and excellent works are his "Physical Atlas," (with ninety maps, 1838,) an oro-hydrographic map of France, charts of Asia and Africa, "Elements of Geography," (1842,) "Ethnography," (1846,) and "The Nations of the Globe," ("Die Völker des Erdballs," 1845.) He also published a German edition of Catlin's "Indians of North America."

See BROCKHAUS, "Conversations-Lexikon."

Berghe, van den, văn den bĕR'Hĕh, (THOMAS,) a Flemish physician, born at Dixmude about 1615, wrote a treatise on the plague of 1669.

Berghem, bĕRG'hĕm, (NIKOLAAS,) an excellent Dutch landscape-painter, whose original name was VAN HAERLEM, was born at Haarlem in 1624. He was a pupil of Van Goyen, Jan Wils, and Weeninx. He had great executive facility, painted with equal success landscapes, animals, and figures, and gave a fine finish to his works without impairing the general effect. His works are extremely numerous, and present a great variety of subjects. Their peculiar charm results partly from a graceful and

easy touch, a harmonious colouring, and a natural composition. He also left designs and etchings of remarkable beauty. Died at Haarlem in 1683. "The delicate degradation of his aerial perspective," says Bryan, "the light floating of his skies, and the transparence of his water, have never been surpassed by any Dutch painter."

See BRYAN, "Dictionary of Painters;" NAGLER, "Neues Allgemeines Künstler-Lexikon."

Bergier, bĕR'zhe-ả', (CLAUDE FRANÇOIS,) a French jurist and littérateur, born at Darnay, in Lorraine, in 1721. He translated Ferguson's "Essay on Civil Society," and other English works, into French. Died in 1784.

Bergier, (NICOLAS,) a French writer, born at Rheims in 1567, published, among other antiquarian works, a valuable "History of the Great Roads (grands chemins) of the Roman Empire," (1622.) Died in 1623.

See BAYLE, "Historical and Critical Dictionary."

Bergier, (NICOLAS SYLVESTRE,) a French scholar and theologian, born at Darnay in 1718, was a brother of Claude François, noticed above. He wrote several able treatises in defence of the Christian religion against the attacks of Voltaire, Rousseau, and Baron Holbach, and made a translation of Hesiod, (1767,) which is highly esteemed. Died in Paris in 1790.

See QUÉRARD, "La France Littéraire."

Ber'gĭ-us or **Berg,** bĕRg, (BENGT,) a Swedish botanist, born at Stockholm in 1723, wrote a "Treatise on Luxuries," and other works. Died in 1784.

See SCHOENBERG, "Åminnelse-Tal öfver B. Bergius," 1785.

Bergius, (PETER JONAS,) brother of the preceding, was a pupil of the celebrated Linnæus, and became professor of natural history at Stockholm. Linnæus named in his honour the genus Bergia. Born about 1730; died in 1790.

See OLOF SWARTZ, "Åminnelse-Tal öfver P. J. Bergius," 1822.

Bergk, bĕRk, (THEODOR,) a German linguist and classical scholar, born at Leipsic in 1812, became professor of philosophy at Marburg in 1842, and at Freiburg in 1852. He published an edition of Anacreon, (1834,) and "Poetæ Lyrici Græci," (1843.)

Bergklint, bĕRk'lint, (OLAUS,) a Swedish poet of the latter part of the eighteenth century, wrote an "Ode on Adversity," which is very popular in Sweden.

Bergler, bĕRG'lĕr, (JOSEPH,) a statuary and painter, born in the Tyrol in 1718, worked at Vienna, Passau, and Prague. Died in 1788.

Bergler, (JOSEPH,) a German painter, son of the preceding, born at Salzburg in 1753. He executed a series of pictures illustrating the history of Bohemia. Died in 1829.

See NAGLER, "Neues Allgemeines Künstler-Lexikon."

Bergler, (STEPHEN,) a distinguished philologist, born at Cronstadt, in Transylvania, about 1680. He contributed a number of articles to the "Acta Eruditorum" and "Bibliotheca Græca," and edited several Greek and Latin classics. Died at Constantinople in 1746.

See SAX, "Onomasticon."

Bergman or **Bergmann,** bĕRG'mån, (TORBERN OLOF,) a celebrated Swedish chemist and naturalist, born at Catherinberg, in West Gothland, in March, 1735. He studied at Upsal, and devoted himself chiefly to natural history, physics, and mathematics. In 1761 he was appointed adjunct professor of mathematics and natural philosophy at Upsal, where he succeeded Wallerius as professor of chemistry in 1766 or 1767, after which he gave almost exclusive attention to chemistry. He first discovered that fixed air was an acid, and wrote a memoir entitled "On the Aerial Acid," (1774.) He ascertained the distinctive characters of nickel, analyzed many mineral substances with great accuracy, and published a classification of minerals, in which the grand divisions are founded on the chemical nature of the substances. By the application of geometry to the forms of crystals, he laid the basis of crystallography, which was developed by Haüy. "His researches," says Biot, "have placed Bergman in the first rank of chemists." His theory of Elective Attractions, on which he published an essay, (1775,) was admired, and considered as an important contribution to science. He was a member of the Royal Societies of London, Berlin, Turin, etc. He wrote a

€ as k; ç as s; ğ hard; ğ as j; G, H, K, guttural; N, nasal; R, trilled; š as z; ᵗh as in this. (☞See Explanations, p. 23.)

"Physical Description of the Earth," (2 vols., 1770–74,) an "Essay on the Forms of Crystals," a thesis on "Astronomical Interpolation," (1758,) and many other works, published under the title of "Opuscula Physica et Chimica," (6 vols., 1779–90.) He was an early patron of Scheele the chemist. Died at Medevi in 1784.

See P. F. AURIVILLIUS, "Åminnelse-Tal öfver T. O. Bergmann," 1785; ERSCH und GRUBER, "Allgemeine Encyklopaedie;" BIOT, article in the "Biographie Universelle;" PETER J. HJELM, "Åminnelse-Tal öfver T. O. Bergman," 1786; HOEFER, "Histoire de la Chimie."

Bergmann, bĕRG'măn, (GUSTAV,) a German writer on Livonian history, etc., born in 1744; died in 1814.

Bergmann, (JOSEPH,) a German Jesuit and naturalist, born at Aschaffenburg in 1736, became professor of physics and natural history at Mentz. He published several scientific works. Died in 1803.

See ERSCH und GRUBER, "Allgemeine Encyklopaedie."

Bergmann, (MICHAEL ADAM,) born at Munich in 1733, wrote contributions towards the "History of Munich," (1780.) Died in 1783.

Bergmüller, bĕRG'mül'ler, (JOHANN GEORG,) a German engraver, born in Bavaria in 1687, became director of the Academy at Augsburg. Died in 1762.

Bergoeing, bĕR'gwăN', (FRANÇOIS,) born at Saint-Macaire in 1755, was a member of the French National Convention, and voted for the imprisonment of Louis XVI. Died in 1820.

Bergon, bĕR'gôN', (JOSEPH ALEXANDRE,) COUNT, a French statesman, born at Mirabel in 1741, rose to be councillor of state under Napoleon. Died in 1824.

Bergonzoni, bĕR-gon-zo'nee, (LORENZO,) an Italian painter, born at Bologna in 1646, was a pupil of Guercino. Died in 1722.

Bergstrasser, bĕRG'strȁs-ser, (JOHANN ANDREAS BENIGNUS,) an eminent German naturalist, born at Idstein in 1732, was professor of philosophy at Hanau. Among his works is a "Description, with Figures, of all the Diurnal Butterflies of Europe," (1759.) Died in 1812.

See ERSCH und GRUBER, "Allgemeine Encyklopaedie."

Berigard, beh-re'găR', (PIERRE,) a relative of the following, born at Florence, lived about 1620. He translated the "Aphorisms" of Hippocrates into verse.

Berigard, de, deh beh-re'găR', or **Beauregard,** bōR'-găR', (CLAUDE GUILLERMET,) SEIGNEUR, a French mathematician, born at Moulins about 1591, became professor of philosophy at Pisa. Died in 1664.

See NICÉRON, "Mémoires."

Bering. See BEHRING.

Beringer, bā'ring-er, (DIEPHOLD,) a fanatical German peasant, also called **Peringer** and **Shuster,** born about 1490, gained notoriety by preaching against the pope.

Beringer, (JOACHIM,) a German Protestant theologian, lived between 1600 and 1650. He assumed the name of JOACHIM URSINUS.

Beringer, (JOHANN BARTHOLOMÄUS ADAM,) a German physician and naturalist, born about 1680, published several works.

See ERSCH und GRUBER, "Allgemeine Encyklopaedie."

Beringer, (MICHAEL,) a German philologist, born at Uhlbach in 1566, was professor of Hebrew at Tübingen. Died in 1625.

See W. SCHICKARD, "Vita M. Beringeri," 1627.

Beringhen, de, deh beh-rȁN'gôN', (JACQUES LOUIS,) MARQUIS, born in Paris in 1651, was first groom of Louis XIV. He served with distinction as an officer of cavalry. Died in 1723.

Běr'ing-ton, (JOSEPH,) an English Catholic historian, born in Shropshire about 1750, published a "Literary History of the Middle Ages," (1814,) one of the best works on that subject; and a "History of the Reign of Henry II. of England and his Sons," (1790.) Died in 1827.

See BUTLER, "Historical Memoirs of the English, Irish, and Scottish Catholics," etc.; "London Quarterly Review" for April, 1814.

Bériot, de, deh bà're'o', (CHARLES AUGUSTE,) a celebrated Belgian violinist, born at Louvain in 1802, succeeded Baillot as professor at the Conservatory of Music in Paris, (1842.) He had married in 1836 the famous vocalist Madame Malibran.

See FÉTIS, "Biographie Universelle des Musiciens;" FAYOLLE, "Paganini et Bériot," 1831.

Berkel, van, văn bĕr'kel, [Lat. BERKE'LIUS,] (ABRAHAM,) a Dutch philologist, born at Leyden about 1630, published editions of the "Enchiridion" of Epictetus, and other classics. Died in 1688.

See MORÉRI, "Dictionnaire Historique."

Berkeley, berk'le, (FRANCIS HENRY FITZ-HARDINGE,) a liberal English legislator, a younger son of the fifth Earl of Berkeley, born in 1794. He has represented Bristol in Parliament since 1837, and has gained distinction as an advocate of the mode of voting by ballot.

Berkeley, (GEORGE,) an English bishop and metaphysical philosopher of great merit, was born at Kilcrin, near Thomastown, Ireland, on the 12th of March, 1684. He became a Fellow of Trinity College, Dublin, in 1707, and established his reputation as a philosopher by "An Essay towards a New Theory of Vision," (1709.) In 1710 he published a remarkable work, "The Principles of Human Knowledge," in which he maintained his celebrated theory of idealism, affirming that there is no proof of the existence of matter anywhere but in our own perceptions. In 1713 he visited London, where he became intimate with Addison, Pope, Swift, Arbuthnot, and Steele, and wrote several essays for the "Guardian." In 1718 Mrs. Vanhomrigh (Swift's "Vanessa") left Berkeley a legacy of £4000. He was appointed Dean of Derry in 1724, before which he had been chaplain to the Duke of Grafton. He published in 1725 a "Proposal for Converting the Savage Americans to Christianity," and wished to found a college in America for that object, for which he raised a large sum of money by subscription. He also received a grant or promise of £20,000 from government, and, having married a Miss Anne Forster, sailed to Rhode Island in 1728. On this subject he wrote a short poem, ending with these lines:

> "Westward the course of empire takes its way;
> The four first acts already past,
> A fifth shall close the drama with the day:
> Time's noblest offspring is the last."

He preached about two years in Newport, but was compelled to abandon the project of the college because the ministry failed to send the funds, and he returned to England. He defended religion against infidels and skeptics in his "Alciphron, or the Minute Philosopher," (1732,) a dialogue on the model of Plato. He was chosen Bishop of Cloyne in 1734, and about 1745, in order to set a shining example to churchmen, refused the See of Clogher, the revenue of which was twice as great as that of Cloyne. Among his later works are "The Analyst," addressed to an infidel mathematician, (1735,) and "A Word to the Wise," (1749.) He removed to Oxford in 1752, and died there in January, 1753.

"Berkeley," says Dr. Johnson, "was a profound scholar as well as a man of fine imagination." "Ancient learning, exact science, polished society, modern literature, and the fine arts," says Sir J. Mackintosh, "contributed to adorn and enrich the mind of this accomplished man. All his contemporaries agreed with the satirist [Pope] in ascribing

> 'To Berkeley every virtue under heaven.'

Adverse factions and hostile wits concurred only in loving, admiring, and contributing to advance him. . . . His works are beyond dispute the finest models of philosophical style since Cicero. Perhaps they surpass those of the orator in the wonderful art by which the fullest light is thrown on the most minute and evanescent parts of the most subtle of human conceptions." ("View of the Progress of Ethical Philosophy.")

See "Life of Berkeley," by DR. STOCK, prefixed to his works, 1784; also G. N. WRIGHT, "Life of George Berkeley," prefixed to his works, 1843; COUSIN'S French version of TENNEMANN'S "Geschichte der Philosophie;" "Encyclopædia Britannica."

Berkeley, (GEORGE,) an English divine, son of the preceding, born in London in 1733, became prebendary of Canterbury. Died in 1795.

Berkeley, (GEORGE,) EARL OF, published "Historical Applications and Occasional Meditations on Several Subjects." Died in 1698.

Berkeley, (GEORGE CHARLES GRANTLEY FITZHARDINGE,) an English writer, son of the Earl of Berkeley, born in 1802. He published, in 1836, a novel called "Berkeley Castle."

Berkeley, (MAURICE FREDERICK FITZ-HARDINGE,)

M. P., a naval officer, second son of the fifth Earl of Berkeley, born in 1788. He became a vice-admiral in 1857.

Berkeley, (Rev. MILES JOSEPH,) an English naturalist, born at Biggin about 1803, published botanical treatises, among which is "Gleanings of British Algæ." He is distinguished as a mycologist.

Berkeley, (Sir WILLIAM,) born near London, was appointed Governor of Virginia in 1641, took sides with Charles I. in the civil war, and maintained the royal authority in Virginia until the death of the king. He submitted to Cromwell in 1651, and then retired from office. In 1659 he again became Governor of Virginia. He is censured for his cruelty towards the insurgents whom his tyrannical conduct provoked to revolt. (See BACON, NATHANIEL.) He once said, "I thank God there are no free schools nor printing-presses in Virginia." Died in England in 1677.

See "Encyclopædia Americana."

Berkeley, (Sir WILLIAM,) a British vice-admiral, born about 1640, served against the Dutch under the Duke of York, and was killed in a naval engagement in 1666.

Berkeley, de, (THOMAS,) an English baron, owner of Berkeley Castle, in which Edward II. was confined and murdered in 1327. He was not, however, accessary to that crime.

Berkely, berk′le, (GEORGE HENRY FREDERICK,) an English general, born in 1785, served in the Peninsular war, and subsequently represented Devonport in Parliament. Died in 1857.

Berken, written also **Berquen, de,** deh bĕR′kĕn, (LOUIS,) a lapidary of Bruges, discovered in 1476 the art of cutting and polishing diamonds.

Berkenhead. See BIRKENHEAD.

Ber′ken-hout, (JOHN,) an English physician, of Dutch extraction, born at Leeds about 1730, graduated at Leyden in 1765. He published "Outlines of the Natural History of Great Britain and Ireland," (1769,) "Biographia Literaria," (1777,) and a "Botanical Lexicon." Died in 1791.

Berkeny. See BERCHENY.

Berkheiden or **Berkheyden,** bĕRk′hī′dĕn, (GERARD,) a Dutch painter, born at Haarlem about 1645, excelled in architectural pictures. Died in 1693.

See NAGLER, "Neues Allgemeines Künstler-Lexikon."

Berkheiden, sometimes written **Breckberg,** (JOB,) brother of the preceding, born at Haarlem about 1632, painted landscapes and portraits with skill. Died about 1695.

Berkhey, bĕRk′hī, or **Berkey,** (JAN LEFRANCQ,) a Dutch poet and savant, born in 1729 at Leyden, where he became professor of natural history. He published a "Natural History of Holland," (1769,) and other scientific works, and a collection of Idylls. Died in 1812.

Berk′ley, (JOHN,) an English royalist officer in the time of Charles I., wrote "Memoirs of the Negotiations of Charles I. with Cromwell," etc.

Berlepsch, von, fon bĕR′lĕpsh, (EMILIE,) a German authoress, born at Gotha in 1757, published "Miscellanies in Prose and Verse," which are highly esteemed.

Berlichingen, von, fon bĕR′liK-ing′ĕn, (GÖTZ or GOTTFRIED,) a celebrated German knight, surnamed OF THE IRON HAND, from an artificial hand which replaced one lost in battle. Having taken part in the war of the peasants against the nobles, he was put under ban of the empire by Maximilian I., and sentenced to pay a heavy fine. According to some writers, he was afterwards mortally wounded while defending his castle against the Imperial troops, (1562.) His achievements form the subject of one of Goethe's most popular dramas, which has been translated by Sir Walter Scott. He left "Memoirs of his Life."

See CARL LANG, "Ritter G. von Berlichingen," 1825; F. W. PISTORIUS, "Lebensbeschreibung des Ritters G. von Berlichingen," 1738; BÜSCHING, "Leben Götz von Berlichingens," 1814.

Berlichingen, von, (JOSEPH FRIEDRICH ANTON,) COUNT, an officer and *littérateur,* born at Tyrnau in 1759, served in the Austrian army against the Turks in 1788. He translated into Latin verse Goethe's "Hermann and Dorothea." Died in 1832.

See BROCKHAUS, "Conversations-Lexikon."

Berlier, bĕR′le-â′, (THÉOPHILE,) a French jurist, born at Dijon in 1761, was a member of the Convention, 1792–95. Died about 1840.

Berlin, bĕR-leen′, (JOHANN DANIEL,) a German composer and musician, born at Memel in 1710, was organist at Drontheim, in Norway. Died in 1775.

Berlinghieri, bĕR-lĕn-ḡe-ā′ree, (ANDREA VACCA,) an eminent Italian surgeon, born at Pisa in 1772, studied anatomy under Desault in Paris and John Hunter in London. He lectured on surgery at Pisa, and published a number of valuable treatises on lithotomy and other branches of surgery. He also improved several surgical processes, and invented a number of surgical instruments. Died in 1826.

See TIPALDO, "Biografia degli Italiani illustri."

Berlioz, bĕR′le-o′, (HECTOR,) a celebrated French composer, born in the department of Isère in 1803. He visited Rome in 1830 as pensionary of the Academy of Fine Arts, and after his return brought out, in 1833, his symphony of "Harold." His Requiem for General Danrémont, performed in 1837, was received with general applause, and was followed in 1839 by his dramatic symphony of "Romeo and Juliet," one of his most successful productions. He also published a number of valuable treatises on music. He was considered by some as the chief of the romantic musical school. Died in 1869.

See FÉTIS, "Biographie Universelle des Musiciens."

Bermann, de, deh bĕR′mŏN′, a French jurist, born at Nancy in 1741, wrote a "Historic Dissertation on the Ancient Chivalry and Nobility of Lorraine," (1763.)

Bermudes, bĕR-moo′Dĕs, (GERONIMO,) a Spanish ecclesiastic, and professor of theology at Salamanca, born about 1530, published several tragedies and poems. Died about 1589.

See TICKNOR, "History of Spanish Literature."

Bermudes, (JUAN,) a Spanish ecclesiastic, born in Galicia. In 1520 he accompanied the Portuguese embassy to Abyssinia, where he was appointed patriarch. He died in 1575, leaving an interesting account of Abyssinia.

See VEYSSIÈRE LA CROZE, "Histoire du Christianisme d'Éthiopie et d'Arménie."

Bermudez, (JUAN AUGUSTIN CEAN.) See CEAN-BERMUDEZ.

Bermudez de Castro, bĕR-moo′Dĕth dâ kâs′tRo, (SALVADOR,) born at Cadiz in 1817, contributed a number of poems to the "Revista de Madrid," of which he was editor.

Bermudo, bĕR-moo′Do, or **Vermudo,** vĕR-moo′Do, [Fr. BERMUDE, bĕR′müd′,] I., surnamed THE DEACON, was proclaimed King of the Asturias in 788, in opposition to his relative Alfonso II. He subsequently made the latter his colleague on the throne.

Bermudo II., son of Ordoño, became King of Leon and Asturias in 982. In conjunction with the King of Navarre and the Count of Castile, he gained a signal victory over the Moors at Osma about Almanzor, (998.) Died in 999.

Bermudo III. succeeded Alfonso V. as King of Leon and Asturias in 1027. He was killed in 1037, while fighting against Sancho, King of Navrre.

See MORÉRI, "Dictionnaire Historique."

Berna or **Bernia.** See BERNI, (FRANCESCO.)

Bernabei, bĕR-nâ-bā′ee, (GIUSEPPE,) a musician, son of the following, born at Rome about 1643, became chapel-master to the Elector of Bavaria. Died at Munich in 1732.

Bernabei, (GIUSEPPE ERCOLE,) an Italian composer, born at Caprarola, was patronized by the Elector of Bavaria. Died at Munich in 1690.

See FÉTIS, "Biographie Universelle des Musiciens."

Bernabei, (PIER ANTONIO,) an excellent Italian fresco-painter of Parma, flourished about 1550.

Bernacchi, bĕR-nâk′kee, (ANTONIO,) an Italian vocalist, born at Bologna about 1700; died about 1750.

Bernadotte, bĕr′na-dot′, [Fr. pron. bĕR′nä′dot′,] CARL XIV. JOHAN, King of Sweden and Norway, Prince of Ponte-Corvo, and marshal of France, was born at Pau, in January, 1764, and was the son of a lawyer. His original name was JEAN BAPTISTE JULES BERNADOTTE, (zhŏN bâp-tēst′ zhül bĕR′nä′dot′.) In 1780 he enlisted as a private in the royal marines. While a sergeant, in the beginning of the Revolution, he saved the life of his colonel from a mob at Marseilles, in 1790. In politics he was an ardent republican. Promoted rapidly in the wars which followed the Revolution, he gained distinction in Flanders and on the Rhine, under Custine, in 1792. In 1794 he became a general of division under Kleber and Jourdan, and distinguished himself at the battle of Fleurus in that year. He served under Bonaparte in Italy in 1797, and was applauded for his conduct at the passage of the Piave and in other actions. In consequence of a disagreement with Bonaparte, he applied to the Directory for another command, and was appointed minister to Vienna. The mob of that capital having made a ferocious attack on him in his hotel in April, 1798, he suddenly left Vienna, and in the same year married Mademoiselle Clary, a sister-in-law of Joseph Bonaparte. In June, 1799, he was appointed minister of war at Paris, and displayed much ability in directing this department, until he was removed in the autumn of the same year.

Though he refused to join in the movements which made Bonaparte consul and emperor, the latter in 1804 created him marshal of France and gave him command of an army in Hanover. In 1805 he joined the grand army which invaded Austria; and he maintained his reputation at Austerlitz, where he and Lannes commanded the French left wing. He was created Prince of Ponte-Corvo in June, 1806, and in October gained a decisive victory over the Prussians at Halle. In 1807 he received the military command of the Hanse Towns and Northern Germany. His conduct at Wagram, in 1809, was severely censured by the emperor.

On the death of the crown-prince of Sweden, an important question arose, who should be the successor to the Swedish throne. Bernadotte had gained credit for moderation and humanity during the war between France and Sweden in 1807–8. For this and other reasons, the Swedish Diet elected him as heir to the throne in August, 1810. With some difficulty he obtained the assent of Bonaparte, who, it is said, wished Bernadotte had refused the crown, but exclaimed, finally, "Go, then: let our destinies be accomplished!" Bernadotte immediately went to Sweden, and became the colleague of Charles XIII. in the government. They refused to support Napoleon's continental system by the exclusion of English goods. The French army having invaded Pomerania in January, 1812, the Swedish court prepared for hostilities by a treaty of alliance with Russia, in which the annexation of Norway to Sweden was stipulated.

In the campaign of 1813 he joined the allies in Germany with an army of about 28,000 Swedes. Having assumed command of a larger army designed for the protection of Berlin, he gained an important victory over Oudinot at Gross-Beeren in August, and another over Ney at Dennewitz in September. He also contributed to the victory of Leipsic, but was considered rather backward and lukewarm in the cause. The English agent, Sir C. Stewart, having resorted to menaces to drive him into the action, he exclaimed, "Do you forget that I am Prince of Sweden, and one of the greatest generals of the age?" He did not follow the allies in the invasion of France in 1814, and, returning home, he soon effected the conquest of Norway, which was averse to be transferred to the Swedish crown. On the death of the king, February 5, 1818, Bernadotte succeeded as Carl XIV. Johan. His reign was peaceful and prosperous. He introduced many important reforms, and was a zealous promoter of education and internal improvement in his kingdom. He died on the 8th of March, 1844, and was succeeded by his son, Oscar I.

See Touchard-Lafosse, "Histoire de Charles XIV;" Héricourt, "Étude biographique sur Charles XIV," 1844; Sarrans, "Histoire de Bernadotte," 1845; Erik G. Geijer, "Konung Karls XIV. Johan Historia," 1844; M. Runkel, "Carl XIV. Johan," 1841; Wm. G. Meredith, "Memorials of Charles (XIV.) John, King of Sweden," 1829; Carl Grosse, "Carl XIV. Johan von Schweden," 1844.

Bernaert, bĕr'nȧrt, or **Bernaerst,** bĕr'nȧrst, (Nicasius,) a Dutch painter, born about 1600; died about 1665.

Bernaerts, bĕr'nȧrts, [Lat. Bernar'tius,] (Jean,) a Flemish jurist and littérateur, born at Mechlin in 1568.

He wrote a "History of the Life and Martyrdom of Mary Queen of Scots," (in Flemish.) Died in 1601.

See Sweert, "Athenæ Belgicæ."

Bernaldez, bĕr-nȧl'dĕth, (Andres,) often called El Cura de los Palacios, (dȧ lŏs pȧ-lȧ'the-ŏs,) a Spanish historian, born in Leon about 1490, wrote a "History of the Catholic Sovereigns," (still in manuscript.)

See Prescott, "History of Ferdinand and Isabella," vol. ii. part i.; Irving, "Life of Columbus."

Bernal Diaz de Castillo. See Castillo.

Bernaldus. See Bertholdus.

Bernard. See Barnard, (Jean.)

Ber'nard, [Fr. pron. bĕr'nȧr'; It. Bernardo, bĕr-nȧr'do; Lat. Bernar'dus,] King of Italy, and grandson of Charlemagne, succeeded his father Pepin about 812. He was deposed by his uncle Louis, and put to death, about 818.

Bernard, Duke of Septimania and Toulouse, espoused the cause of Louis le Débonnaire against his revolted sons. Being afterwards accused of treason by Charles the Bald, he was put to death in 844.

Bernard of Brussels, a Flemish painter of portraits, hunting-pieces, etc. Died in 1540.

Bernard of Thuringia, a German visionary, who caused great alarm in Europe by predicting the end of the world, lived about 960.

Bernard, bĕr'nȧr', (Adrien Antoine,) called Bernard de Saintes, was born at Saintes in 1750. As a member of the National Convention, he voted for the death of Louis XVI. Died in 1819.

Bernard, (Andrew,) a French monk, born at Toulouse, was historiographer to Henry VII. of England. He wrote, in Latin, a "History of Henry VII. to the Capture of Perkin Warbeck."

Bernard, (Aristide Martin,) a French radical politician, born at Montbrison in 1808. He was imprisoned for political offences from 1840 to 1848.

Bernard, (Auguste Joseph,) a French antiquary and historical writer, born at Montbrison in 1811.

Bernard, (Catherine,) a French poetess, born at Rouen in 1662, was a relative of Corneille and Fontenelle. Her principal works are the tragedies of "Laodamia," (1690,) and "Brutus," (1691.) She wrote several novels, which exhibit much knowledge of the human heart. Fontenelle was her friend and admirer. Died in 1712.

Bernard, (Charles,) historiographer of France under Louis XIII., wrote a "History of the Wars of Louis XIII. against the Rebellious Religionists," (1646.)

Bernard, (Claude,) called the Poor Priest, born at Dijon in 1588, was noted for his benevolence, and spent a large fortune in acts of charity. Died in 1640.

See François de Giry, "Vie de C. Bernard," 1683; F. Gerson, "Vie du Père Bernard."

Bernard, (Claude,) an eminent French physiologist, born at Saint-Julien, in Rhône, in July, 1813. His treatise entitled "Researches on the Uses of the Pancreas" obtained the grand prize of the Institute in 1849. He was admitted into the Institute in 1854, and succeeded Magendie as professor of experimental physiology in the Collége de France in 1855. Among his works are "Researches on the Functions of the Spinal Nerve," and a "Memoir on Animal Heat," (1856.)

See "Nouvelle Biographie Générale."

Ber'nard, (Edward,) an English astronomer and philologist, born near Towcester in 1638, published a "Treatise on Ancient Weights and Measures." He was for many years Savilian professor of astronomy at Oxford. Died in 1697.

See Thomas Smith's "Life of E. Bernard," in Latin.

Bernard, (Sir Francis,) an English lawyer, who was Governor of New Jersey from 1758 to 1760, when he became Governor of Massachusetts. He offended the people by bringing troops into Boston, and showed himself hostile to the popular cause. He was one of the principal instruments employed to enforce the obnoxious measures which produced the Revolution. He was recalled in 1769. Died in 1779.

See Bancroft's "History of the United States."

Bernard, (Herman Hedwig,) of Cambridge, England, a Hebraist, born in 1785, published "The Main Principles of the Creed and Ethics of the Jews," (1832.) Died in 1857.

Bernard, (JACQUES,) a French Protestant divine and scholar, born at Nyons, in Dauphiny, in 1658. He wrote several religious and historical treatises, and succeeded Bayle as editor of the journal entitled "Nouvelles de la République de Lettres." He passed his latter years in Holland. Died in 1718.

See Quérard, "La France Littéraire."

Bernard, bĕR'nȧRt, (JAN FREDERIK,) a writer and bookseller of Amsterdam, published "Memoirs of the Count of Brienne, Minister of Louis XIV.," (1719,) and various other works. Died in 1752.

See Quérard, "La France Littéraire."

Bernard, (JEAN,) a French writer and Latin poet, born at Dijon in 1576.

Bernard, (JEAN,) a French physician and medical writer, born at Nantes in 1702. He became professor of anatomy at Douay in 1744. Died in 1781.

Bernard, (JEAN BAPTISTE,) a French *littérateur*, born in Paris in 1710, became professor of eloquence in the College of Navarre. Died in 1772.

Bernard, (JEAN ÉTIENNE,) a physician and medical writer, of French extraction, born at Berlin in 1718; died in 1793.

Bernard, (JOHN,) an English clergyman, born at Castor, in Lincolnshire, became a Fellow of Lincoln College, Oxford, in 1648. He wrote a "Life of Peter Heylin," (1683,) who was his father-in-law. Died in 1683.

Bernard, (JOHN,) an English actor, born at Portsmouth in 1756, performed with applause in England and the United States, and became one of the managers of the Boston Theatre. Died in London in 1830. (See BERNARD, WILLIAM.)

Bernard, (LOUIS ROSE DÉSIRÉ,) called also BERNARD DE RENNES, a French magistrate and writer, born at Brest in 1788.

Bernard, (NICHOLAS,) an English divine, was a friend of Archbishop Usher, whom he served as chaplain. He took the degree of M.A. at Oxford in 1628. About 1642 he was presented to the rectory of Whitchurch. He wrote a "Life of James Usher," (1656.) Died in 1661.

Bernard, (PIERRE,) a French lawyer and writer, born at Calais in 1640, published "Annals of Calais," (1715.) Died in 1720.

Bernard, (PIERRE,) a French *littérateur*, sometimes called BERNARD D'HÉRY, born near Auxerre in 1756, published ' Poetical Preludes," and other works. He also translated Tasso's "Jerusalem Delivered" into French verse. Died in 1833.

See Quérard, "La France Littéraire."

Bernard, (PIERRE JOSEPH,) a French poet, born at Grenoble in 1710, was styled by Voltaire the "Gentil Bernard." His works are of a frivolous and immoral character. Died in 1775.

Bernard, (PONS JOSEPH,) a French mathematician, born near Draguignan in 1748, published "New Principles of Hydraulics," (1787.) Died in 1816.

Bernard, (RICHARD,) an English Puritan divine, rector of Batcombe, Somersetshire, born about 1566, wrote "The Key of Knowledge for the Opening of the Mysteries of Saint John," "The Faithful Shepherd," and other theological works. He translated Terence into English. Died in 1641.

Bernard, [Fr. pron. bĕr'nȧR'; Ger. BERNHARD, bern'hȧrt; It. BERNARDO, bĕR-nȧR'do,] SAINT, an eminent ecclesiastic, born near Dijon, in Burgundy, in 1091. He entered the Cistercian monastery of Citeaux at an early age, accompanied by his five brothers and a number of associates, whom his eloquence had induced to embrace the monastic life. In 1115 he became Abbot of Clairvaux, near Langres, where, refusing all higher preferment, he exercised a powerful influence on the ecclesiastical affairs of Europe. He prevailed upon the French and English sovereigns to recognize Innocent II. as pope, in opposition to the cardinal Peter of Leon, and in 1140 was chiefly instrumental in procuring the condemnation of Abelard's heretical writings. He was also active in promoting the crusade of 1146. He died in 1153, and was canonized in 1174 by Pope Alexander III. The

best edition of his works, including sermons, epistles, and religious treatises, was published by Mabillon in 1709.

See Lemaître, "Vie de Saint-Bernard," 1649; Bourgoing de Villefore, "Vie de S. Bernard," 1704; A. Neander, "Der heilige Bernard und sein Zeitalter," 1813, (translated into English by Wrench, 1843;) J. L. T. Ratisbonne, "Histoire de S. Bernard," 2 vols., 1841; C. Montalembert, "Histoire de S. Bernard;" Levin Olbers, "Vita Bernardi Claraevallensis," 1810; J O. Ellendorf, "Der heilige Bernhard," 1837; Eugenio de Corral, "Vida de S. Bernardo," 1782; "Nouvelle Biographie Générale."

Bernard, (SALOMON,) a French painter and wood-engraver, called PETIT BERNARD, born at Lyons about 1500.

Bernard, (SAMUEL,) a French painter and engraver, born in Paris in 1615; died in 1687.

Bernard, (SAMUEL,) a French banker, son of the preceding, born about 1651. He acquired an immense fortune, and lent large sums to Louis XIV. and Louis XV. Died in 1739.

See Saint-Simon, "Mémoires."

Bernard, (SIMON,) a French general and engineer, born at Dôle in 1779, served under Napoleon in several campaigns. In 1824 he accompanied La Fayette to America, where he rendered important services as chief engineer of the army. After his return to France he became aide-de-camp to Louis Philippe, lieutenant-general of engineers, and in 1836 minister of war. Died in 1839.

Bernard, (THOMAS,) a wealthy English philanthropist, born at Lincoln in 1750. He procured the erection of a free chapel in Saint Giles's, London, and in conjunction with Count Rumford founded, about 1800, a scientific establishment, which afterwards became the Royal Institution. He wrote several works on the improvement and education of the poor. Died in 1818.

See James Baker, "Life of Thomas Bernard," 1819.

Bernard, (WILLIAM BAYLE,) son of John Bernard the actor, noticed above, born in 1808, wrote "The Nervous Man," "The Middy Ashore," and other popular dramas, and completed and published his father's "Recollections of the Stage."

Bernard, de, dĕh bĕr'nȧR', (LOUIS SIMON JOSEPH,) a French writer, sometimes called BERNARD DE MONTBRISON, was born at Saint-Esprit in 1768. He was rector of the Academy of Strasburg. Died in 1832.

Bernard de Chartres, bĕr'nȧR' dĕh shȧR'tIR, a celebrated Platonic philosopher and theologian of the twelfth century. He directed a school at Chartres, in France, and wrote two works, called "Megacosmus" and "Microcosmus," which are extant.

See Hauréau, "De la Philosophie scolastique."

Bernard del Carpio. See BERNARDO.

Bernard de Menthon, bĕr'nȧR' dĕh mŏN'tôN', SAINT, founder of the celebrated establishments of the "Great and Little Saint Bernard," was born near Annecy, in France, in 923. After having converted the pagan inhabitants of the Alpine country to Christianity, he built, on the ruins of heathen structures, two monasteries for the relief and entertainment of pilgrims. These houses are still inhabited by monks, who render great services to travellers in the Alps. Died in 1008.

See Richard, "Vie de Saint-Bernard de Menthon;" J. C. Legrand, "Vie de S. Bernard de Menthon," 1743; "Four Ecclesiastical Biographies," by J. H. Gurney.

Bernard de Morlaix, bĕr'nȧR' dĕh mor'lä', a Benedictine monk and Latin poet of the twelfth century, wrote a treatise "On Contempt of the World," ("De Contemptu Mundi,") printed in 1597.

Bernard de Palissy. See PALISSY.

Bernard de Saxe-Weimar. See BERNHARD.

Bernard de Varennes, bĕr'nȧR' dĕh vä'rĕn', DOM, a French ecclesiastic, born about 1650, published a "History of Constantine the Great," (1728,) and several religious works. Died in 1730.

See Moréri, "Dictionnaire Historique."

Bernard de Ventadour, bĕr'nȧR' dĕh vôN'tä'dooR', a French troubadour of the twelfth century, was patronized by Éléonore of Guienne. He is noticed and praised by Petrarch in his "Trionfi," iv.

See "Blackwood's Magazine" for April, 1836; Longfellow's "Poets and Poetry of Europe."

Bernard du Grail, de, dĕh bĕr'nȧR' dü grȧl or grȧ'ye, (CHARLES,) a popular French novelist, born at Besançon in 1805. Among his chief works are "The

e as k; ç as s; g̃ hard; g̃ as j; G, H, K, *guttural*; N, *nasal*; R, *trilled*; s̃ as z; th as in *this*. (☞See Explanations, p. 23.)

22

Gordian Knot," (1838,) "Gerfaut," (1838,) and "The Serious Man," (1847.) Died in 1850.

See QUÉRARD, "La France Littéraire;" "Blackwood's Magazine," vol. lxi., 1847.

Bernard Saint-Affrique, bĕR'nȧR' sȧN'tȧ'ïRĕk', (LOUIS,) a French statesman, born in the department of Gard in 1745, became a member of the National Convention and of the Council of Ancients.

Bernardes, bĕR-nȧR'dĕs, (DIOGO,) one of the most eminent Portuguese poets, born at Ponte de Barca about 1540. His pastoral poems are greatly admired by his countrymen, who have styled him the "Portuguese Theocritus." Died in 1596.

See ADAMSON, "Lusitania illustrata;" R. SOUTHEY, "On Portuguese Poetry;" LONGFELLOW, "Poets and Poetry of Europe;" BARBOSA MACHADO, "Bibliotheca Lusitana."

Bernardi, bĕR'nȧR'de', (ARNALD,) a French theologian, born at Cahors, wrote "Postilla super Apocalypsin." Died in 1334.

Bernardi, (AUGUST FERDINAND.) See BERNHARDI.

Bernardi, ber-nar'dee, (JOHN,) an English officer, noted for his zeal in the cause of James II., whom he followed into France and Ireland. Died in 1736.

Bernardi, (JOSEPH ELZÉAR DOMINIQUE,) a French jurist and legal writer, born at Monieux, in Provence, in 1751, became a member of the Council of Five Hundred, and of the Academy of Inscriptions, (1816.) Died in 1824.

Bernardi or **Bernardy,** bĕR'nȧR'de', (PHILIPPE,) a French writer, brother of the preceding, born at Monieux in 1759, was professor of rhetoric at Poitiers. Died after 1815.

Bernardi, bĕR-nȧR'dee, (STEPHEN,) a German composer and writer on music, lived about 1600-40. He was chapel-master at Verona.

Bernardi del Castel-Bolognese, bĕR-nȧR'dee del kȧs'tĕl bo-lôn-yā'sȧ, (GIOVANNI,) an Italian lapidary, born at Castel-Bolognese about 1495, was patronized by Charles V. and Pope Clement VII. Died in 1555.

See NAGLER, "Neues Allgemeines Künstler-Lexikon."

Bernardin. See BERNARDINO.

Bernardin de Péquigny, bĕR'nȧR'dȧN' dĕh pȧ'kĕn'ye', a French theologian and writer, born in Picardy about 1663; died in 1709.

Bernardin de Saint-Pierre. See SAINT-PIERRE.

Bernardini, bĕR-nȧR-dee'nee, (MARCELLO,) an Italian opera-composer, born at Capua about 1752.

Bernardino, bĕR-nȧR-dee'no, [Fr. BERNARDIN, bĕR'nȧR'dȧN',] SAINT, of Sienna, an eloquent Italian ecclesiastic, born at Massa di Carrara in 1380. He became Vicar-General of the order of Saint Francis, and is said to have founded more than three hundred monasteries. Died in 1444.

See DUPIN, "Bibliothèque ecclésiastique."

Bernardo, bĕR-nȧR'do, [Fr. BERNARD, bĕR'nȧR',] an Italian, surnamed IL TREVISANO, (LE TRÉVISAN,) born at Padua in 1406, wrote a number of works, in Latin and French, on alchemy. Died in 1490.

See F. HOEFER, "Histoire de la Chimie."

Bernardo OF PAVIA, an Italian ecclesiastic, became successively professor of canon law at Rome and at Bologna, and Bishop of Pavia. He published a collection of decretals, and several other works. Died in 1213.

Bernardo, (ZENALE,) called **Bernardino,** a painter and architect, born at Treviglio, in the Milanese, was a friend of Leonardo da Vinci, who praises him in his "Treatise on Painting." Died in 1526.

See VASARI, "Lives of the Painters."

Bernardo da Bologna, bĕR-nȧR'do dȧ bo-lôn'yȧ, an Italian theologian and biographer, lived about 1740-50.

Bernardo da Cruz, bĕR-nȧR'do dȧ kROOS, (FREY,) a Portuguese historian, wrote a "History of the Reign of Don Sebastian," (1837.)

Bernardo del Carpio, bĕR-nȧR'do del kȧR'pe-o, a celebrated Spanish hero of the ninth century, was a nephew of Alfonso the Chaste. He displayed the most brilliant courage in the wars against the Moors, and, according to tradition, defeated the famous Roland at Roncesvalles. His exploits form the subject of several dramas by Lope de Vega, and of many popular Spanish ballads.

See MARIANA, "Historia de España."

Bernardoni, bĕR-nȧR-do'nee, (PIETRO ANTONIO,) an Italian poet, born at Vignola in 1672; died in 1714.

Bernasconi, bĕR-nȧs-ko'nee, (ANDREA,) a musician, born at Marseilles in 1712. He produced a number of successful operas. Died at Munich in 1784.

See FÉTIS, "Biographie Universelle des Musiciens."

Bernasconi, (LAURA,) an Italian flower-painter, born at Rome about 1620; died after 1670.

See LANZI, "History of Painting in Italy."

Bernauer, bĕR'nŏw-er, (AGNES,) the beautiful daughter of a citizen of Augsburg, was privately married to Albert, Duke of Bavaria. His father, having discovered the marriage, caused Agnes to be drowned in the Danube, (1435,) on a charge of sorcery.

See "Nouvelle Biographie Générale."

Bernazzano, bĕR-nȧt-sȧ'no, a Milanese painter of landscapes, animals, and still-life, lived about 1540.

Bernd, bĕRnt, (CHRISTIAN SAMUEL THEODOR,) a German writer on heraldry, born at Meseritz in 1775, published "The Principal Points of Heraldic Science."

Bernegger, bĕR'nĕk'ker, (MATTHÄUS,) a German scholar and Latin writer, born at Hallstadt in 1582; died in 1640.

Berner, bĕR'ner, (FRIEDRICH WILHELM,) a German musician and composer, born at Breslau in 1780, was a skilful organist and pianist. Died in 1827.

Berner, (JOHANN BENJAMIN,) a German Protestant theologian, born at Greitz in 1727; died in 1772.

Berneron, de, dĕh bĕRn'rôN', (FRANÇOIS,) a French general, born in 1750, served under Luckner and Dumouriez.

Berners, (JOHN BOURCHIER,) LORD, an English statesman and writer, born about 1474, rose to be chancellor of the exchequer under Henry VIII. He is chiefly celebrated for his translation of Froissart's "Chronicles." Died in 1532.

Berners, (JULIANA.) See BARNES.

Berneschi. See BENASCHI.

Bernet, bĕR'nȧ', (JACQUES,) a French cardinal, born at Saint-Flour in 1770. He became Archbishop of Aix in 1835. Died in 1846.

Bernetti, bĕR-net'tee, (TOMMASO,) born at Fermo in 1779, was one of the thirteen cardinals who refused to attend the marriage of Napoleon and Maria Louisa, who were called black cardinals, from their not being allowed to wear the purple. He assisted in the conclusion of the concordat with the Netherlands, (1827,) and was employed in other important negotiations. Died in 1852.

See "Biographie du Cardinal Bernetti," 1852.

Berneville, de, dĕh bĕRn'vĕl', (GILEBERT,) a famous French poet or *trouvère,* born in Artois, lived about the middle of the thirteenth century.

See A. DINAUX, "Trouvères de la Flandre."

Bernhard, bĕRn'hart, Duke of Saxe-Weimar, one of the most celebrated commanders in the Thirty Years' war, born in 1604, was a son of John III., Duke of Saxe-Weimar. Having previously served in the armies of Holland and Denmark, he joined Gustavus Adolphus on his arrival in Germany, and distinguished himself in various engagements in 1631 and 1632. After the death of Gustavus at Lützen, (1632,) he commanded the left wing of the Swedish army, and by his skill and energy contributed greatly to the victory. In 1633 he obtained the command of half the army, and received the dukedom of Franconia. Dissatisfied with the terms of the peace of Prague, he entered into a personal treaty of alliance with France in 1635. He subsequently gained a signal victory over the Imperial troops at Rheinfelden, (1638,) and soon after captured Breisach. He died in 1639, of pestilential fever, or, according to some writers, of poison administered by order of Cardinal Richelieu.

See SCHILLER, "History of the Thirty Years' War;" "History of the two illustrious Brothers Ernestus the Pious, and Bernard, Great Duke of Saxe-Weimar," London, 1740; J. A. C. VON HELLFELD, "Geschichte Bernhards des Grossen, Herzogs zu Sachsen-Weimar," 1797; BERNHARD ROESE, "Herzog Bernhard der Grosse von Sachsen-Weimar," 2 vols., 1828-29.

Bernhard, (KARL,) Duke of Saxe-Weimar, born at Weimar in 1792. He served in the principal campaigns against the French from 1806 to 1815, and was made lieutenant-general in 1831. He published "Travels in North

America," (1828,) and "Summary of the Campaign in Java in 1811."

See "London Quarterly Review" for July and November, 1829.

Bernhard, bĕRn'haRt, (KARL,) the pseudonym of **Saint-Aubain,** a celebrated Danish novelist, of French extraction. Among his most popular works are "Pictures of Life in Denmark," (1841,) "The Children's Ball," and "Christian II. and his Times," (1837,) a historical romance.

See "Nouvelle Biographie Générale," and BELLMAN, "Poëtes Suédois."

Bernhard or **Bernhardi** (bĕRn-haR'dee) OF BERNITZ, (MARTIN,) a Polish botanist, physician to the King of Poland, lived about 1650.

Bernhard, SAINT. See BERNARD, SAINT.

Bernhardi, bĕRn-haR'dee, written also **Bernardi,** (AUGUST FERDINAND,) a German philologist, born at Berlin about 1769. He was a brother-in-law of Tieck, and published conjointly with him "Bambocciaden," a collection of comic tales. He also wrote "Elements of the Science of Language," ("Anfangsgründe der Sprachwissenschaft," 1805,) and other works. Died in 1820.

See BROCKHAUS, "Conversations-Lexikon."

Bernhardi, (JOHANN JAKOB,) a German botanist and medical writer, born at Erfurt in 1774; died about 1840.

Bernhardi, (KARL CHRISTIAN SIGISMUND,) a German statesman, scholar, and writer, born at Ottrau in 1799. He succeeded Grimm as first keeper of the library of the museum at Cassel in 1829, and was in 1848 a member of the National Assembly at Frankfort.

Bernhardy, bĕRn-haR'dee, (GOTTFRIED,) born at Landsberg, in Prussia, in 1800, became professor of classical philology at Halle in 1829.

Bernhold, bĕRn'holt, (JOHANN BALTHASAR,) a German poet and theologian, born in 1687; died in 1769.

Bernhold, (JOHANN GOTTFRIED,) a son of the preceding, born in 1721, wrote several tragedies. Died about 1755.

Bernhold, (JOHANN MICHAEL,) a learned German physician and medical writer, born in 1736; died in 1797.

Berni, bĕR'nee, or **Bernia,** bĕR'ne-ä, (FRANCESCO,) an eminent Italian burlesque poet, was born at Lamporecchio, in Tuscany, about 1490. He became a priest, and entered the service of Cardinal Bibbiena at Rome. After the death of Bibbiena he passed seven years in the service of Ghiberti, Bishop of Verona, as secretary. He was appointed a canon of the cathedral of Florence about 1530. He wrote a number of burlesque poems and satires, which are remarkable for the elegance of their style, and are considered the best model of a kind of poetry which derives from him its name, "Poësia Bernesca." Berni also produced a modification (*rifacimento*) of Bojardo's "Orlando Innamorato," which some critics regard as superior to the original poem. It was published in 1541. "Berni undertook," says Hallam, "the singular office of writing over the 'Orlando Innamorato,' preserving the sense of almost every stanza, and inserting nothing but a few introductory passages, in the manner of Ariosto, to each canto. The genius of Berni, playful, satirical, flexible, was admirably fitted to perform this labour; . . . and the 'Orlando Innamorato' has descended to posterity as the work of two minds." ("Introduction to the Literature of Europe.") Died in 1536.

See GINGUENÉ, "Histoire Littéraire d'Italie;" MAZZUCHELLI, "Scrittori d'Italia;" REV. H. STEBBING, "Lives of the Italian Poets," 1831; "North American Review" for October, 1824, article "Italian Narrative Poetry," (by PRESCOTT.)

Berni, (FRANCESCO,) an Italian jurist and dramatic poet, born in 1610 at Ferrara, where he became professor of belles-lettres. Died in 1673.

Bernice. See BERENICE.

Bernier, bĕR'ne-à', (ADHELM,) born at Senlis, in France, published several works on French history, dated 1834-37.

Bernier, (ÉTIENNE ALEXANDRE,) a zealous royalist, born at Daon, in La Mayenne, in 1762, was called "the Apostle of La Vendée." He was appointed Bishop of Orléans by Napoleon. Died in 1806.

See THIERS, "Histoire du Consulat et de l'Empire."

Bernier, (FRANÇOIS,) a celebrated French traveller and physician, born at Angers. In 1654 he visited Syria

and Egypt, and subsequently resided many years in India as physician to the Mogul emperor Aurung-Zeb. He published, after his return, a "History of the Last Revolution of the States of the Great Mogul," (1670,) and a "Continuation of Memoirs of the Empire of the Great Mogul," (1671.) These are esteemed standard works, and are written in a spirited and attractive style. Bernier also wrote several scientific treatises, which were popular in his time. Died in 1688.

See WALCKENAER, "Vies de plusieurs Personnages célèbres;" "Retrospective Review," vol. i., second series, 1827.

Bernier, (JEAN,) a French physician, born at Blois in 1622, wrote "Medical Essays," and a "History of Blois." Died in 1698.

Bernier, (NICOLAS,) a French musician and composer, born at Mantes in 1664, became royal chapelmaster. Died in 1734.

See FÉTIS, "Biographie Universelle des Musiciens."

Bernieri, bĕR-ne-ä'ree, (ANTONIO,) a skilful Italian miniature-painter, born in 1516, was a pupil of Correggio. Died in 1565.

See LANZI, "History of Painting in Italy."

Berningroth, bĕR'ning-rōt', (MARTIN,) a German engraver and designer, born in 1670; died in 1733.

Bernini, bĕR-nee'nee, (DOMENICO,) an Italian ecclesiastic, son of Giovanni Lorenzo, noticed below, wrote a "History of all Heresies from the Beginning of Christianity to Innocent XI.," (1705.)

Bernini, [Fr. LE BERNIN, leh bĕR'năN',] (GIOVANNI LORENZO,) often called "the Cavalier Bernini," an eminent Italian sculptor and architect, born at Naples in December, 1598. At a very early age he was taken to Rome, where his first specimens of sculpture procured for him the favour of Paul V. and Cardinal Barberini, afterwards Urban VIII. Among his best works are the Barberini palace, the colonnade before the entrance of Saint Peter's, and the monument of the Countess Matilda. He also executed busts of Charles I. of England, Louis XIV. of France, and other distinguished persons. He was patronized and munificently rewarded by the principal sovereigns of Europe, and left at his death, in November, 1680, a fortune of nearly £100,000 sterling. He died in Rome.

See QUATREMÈRE DE QUINCY, "Dictionnaire d'Architecture;" DOMENICO BERNINI, "Vita del Cavaliere G. L. Bernini suo Padre," 1713; P. B. SILORATA, "Biografia del Cavaliere G. L. Bernini," 1838.

Bernini, (GIUSEPPE MARIA,) a Capuchin missionary to the East Indies, born in Piedmont, translated several works from the Sanscrit. Died in 1753.

Bernini, (PIETRO,) an Italian painter and sculptor, father of Giovanni Lorenzo, above noticed, born in Tuscany in 1562. Died in 1629.

Bernis, de, dĕh bĕR'nĕss', (FRANÇOIS JOACHIM DE PIERRE,) a French cardinal and diplomatist, born at Saint-Marcel de l'Ardèche in 1715. He was ambassador to Venice, was employed in various negotiations by Louis XV., and subsequently became minister of foreign affairs. He held this office during the Seven Years' war, (1755-62.) He was made Archbishop of Albi in 1764, having been previously elected a member of the French Academy. He wrote a number of poems and prose works. In 1769 he was sent as ambassador to Rome, where he remained until his death in 1794.

See VOLTAIRE, "Siècle de Louis XV," and "Correspondance;" "Nouvelle Biographie Générale."

Bernitz, (MARTIN OF.) See BERNHARD, (MARTIN.)

Ber'no, [Fr. BERNON, bĕR'nôN',] a learned Benedictine monk, became Abbot of Reichenau, near Lake Constance. He wrote, in Latin, several treatises on music and theology. Died in 1045.

Bernouilli. See BERNOULLI.

Bernoul. See BERTHOLDUS.

Bernoulli, bĕR'noo'ye', written also **Bernouilli,** (CHRISTOPHE,) nephew of Jacques, (second of the name,) noticed below, was born at Bâle in 1782. He studied at Göttingen, where he became professor of natural history in 1817. He published a treatise "On the Phosphorescence of the Sea," (1802,) and "Physical Anthropology," 1811, (in German.)

Bernoulli, (DANIEL,) a celebrated mathematician and philosopher, son of Jean, (the first of that name,) noticed below, was born at Groningen on the 9th of February, 1700. He studied mathematics and medicine in Italy under Michelotti and Morgagni, and was appointed professor of mathematics at Saint Petersburg about 1725. After his return in 1733 he became professor of anatomy and botany at Bâle, and subsequently of physics and speculative philosophy. In 1748 he succeeded his father as member of the French Academy of Sciences. He obtained the prize of that institution ten times, having shared it once with Euler, and was a member of the principal learned societies of Europe. Among his numerous works, which are written in Latin and French, we may mention his "Treatise on Hydrodynamics," (1738,) and "Physical and Mechanical Researches on Sound," (1762.) Died at Bâle in 1782.

See CONDORCET, "Éloge de Daniel Bernoulli," 1782; D. BERNOULLI, "Vita D. Bernoulli," 1783.

Bernoulli, (JACQUES or JAMES,) an eminent mathematician, born at Bâle, in Switzerland, in December, 1654. He studied the philosophy of Descartes, and in 1687 became professor of mathematics in his native city. He improved the differential calculus invented by Leibnitz, and solved many important problems, among which is the "Isoperimetrical problem." He discovered the properties of the logarithmic spiral, and wrote several treatises on mathematics. In 1699 he was elected a foreign associate of the Academy of Sciences of Paris. Died at Bâle in 1705.

See BATTIER, "Vita Jacobi Bernoulli," 1705.

Bernoulli, (JACQUES,) son of John, (the second of the name,) born at Bâle in 1759. He was instructed in geometry and physics by his uncle Daniel, and became professor of mathematics at Saint Petersburg, where he married the granddaughter of Euler. He was drowned in the Neva in 1789.

Bernoulli, (JEAN or JOHN,) born at Bâle in 1667, was a brother of Jacques, (the first of the name.) He discovered the exponential calculus, and had a share in the principal discoveries of his brother. He became professor of mathematics at Groningen, (1695,) and in the University of Bâle, (1705.) He was a member of the Academies of Paris, Berlin, and Saint Petersburg, and of the Royal Society of London. His contributions to the "Acta Eruditorum," and other journals, were published in four volumes, (1742,) and his "Correspondence with Leibnitz" in 1745. Died in 1748.

He left three sons, NICHOLAS, DANIEL, and JOHN, who are all noticed in this work.

See D'ALEMBERT, "Éloge de J. Bernoulli."

Bernoulli, (JEAN or JOHN,) brother of Daniel, born in 1710 at Bâle, where he became professor of mathematics. He was a member of the Academy of Sciences of Paris and of Berlin, and wrote several scientific works, which obtained the prize from the first-named institution. Died in 1790.

Bernoulli, (JEAN,) son of the preceding, born at Bâle in 1744, became astronomer royal at Berlin. He was a member of the Academy of Saint Petersburg and the Royal Society of London, and published a number of works on astronomy, mathematics, and geography, also "Travels in Germany, Russia," etc., (6 vols., 1779.) Died in 1807.

Bernoulli, (JÉRÔME,) a Swiss naturalist, a relative of the preceding, born at Bâle in 1745; died in 1829.

Bernoulli, (NICOLAS,) eldest brother of Daniel, born at Bâle in 1695. He became professor of law at Berne, and subsequently of mathematics at Saint Petersburg, in conjunction with his brother Daniel. Died at Saint Petersburg in 1726.

Bernoulli, (NICOLAS,) cousin of the preceding, born at Bâle in 1687. He was, on the recommendation of Leibnitz, appointed in 1716 professor of mathematics at Padua. He made several important mathematical discoveries. Died in 1759.

Bernstein, (GEORG HEINRICH,) born near Jena in 1787, became in 1821 professor of Oriental languages at Berlin. He published an edition of the "Arabic Grammar and Chrestomathy" of Michaelis, and of "Hitopadesa," a popular Sanscrit book of stories or fables. He removed to Breslau in 1843.

Bernstein, (JOHANN GOTTLIEB,) a German writer on

surgery, born in 1747 in Berlin, where he was professor from 1810 until 1821. Died in 1835.

Bernstorff, von, fon bĕRN′storf, (ANDREAS PETER,) COUNT, an eminent statesman, born in the duchy of Brunswick-Lüneburg in 1735. He studied at Göttingen and Leipsic, and became minister of state (1769) under the King of Denmark. He died in 1797, leaving a high reputation for ability and integrity. He was a nephew of Johann Hartwig Ernst, noticed below.

See EGGERS, "Denkwürdigkeiten aus dem Leben des Staatsministers Von Bernstorff," 1800; RASMUS NYERUP, "A. P. Bernstorffs Levnetsbeskrivelse," 1812.

Bernstorff, von, (CHRISTIAN GUNTHER,) COUNT, son of the preceding, born at Copenhagen in 1769. He became successively ambassador to Berlin and Stockholm, and minister of state, (1797.) He represented Denmark at the Congress of Vienna in 1814, and in 1815 signed the cession of Norway to Sweden. In 1818 he entered the service of Prussia, and was appointed minister of foreign affairs. Died in 1835.

See "Nouvelle Biographie Générale."

Bernstorff, von, (JOHANN HARTWIG ERNST,) COUNT, a celebrated statesman in the Danish service, born at Hanover in 1712. He was employed in various important negotiations, and became minister of foreign affairs in 1751. In 1773 he concluded a treaty by which Russia exchanged Holstein for Oldenburg. He was a generous patron of learning and the arts, and greatly promoted the commerce and manufactures of his country. Died in 1772. A monument was erected to his memory by the serfs whom he had emancipated.

See MARTIN HÜBNER, "Sörgetale over Greve J. H. E. Bernstorff," 1772; G. L. AHLEMANN, "Ueber das Leben und den Charakter des Grafen von Bernstorff," 1777; G. NAVARRO, "Vie du Comte J. H. E. Bernstorff," 1822.

Bernt, bĕRnt, (JOSEPH,) a German writer on legal medicine, born about 1770. He lectured on medical jurisprudence at Prague and at Vienna. Died in 1842.

Bernward, bĕRn′wȧRt, SAINT, Bishop of Hildesheim, in Lower Saxony, born about 950, was celebrated for his profound and various learning, and his patronage of the arts. He was appointed tutor and court chaplain to the emperor Otho III. Died in 1022.

Béroalde, bā′ro′ȧld′, or **Bérould,** bā′roo′,(MATHIEU,) a French Calvinistic theologian, born near Paris about 1510, was professor of Hebrew at Orléans. Died in 1576.

Béroalde de Verville, bā′ro′ȧld′ deh vĕR-vèl′, (FRANÇOIS,) a French mathematician and littérateur, son of the preceding, born in Paris in 1558; died in 1612.

See "Nouvelle Biographie Générale."

Beroaldo, bā-ro-ȧl′do, (FILIPPO,) called THE ELDER, an Italian scholar and writer of high reputation, born in 1453 at Bologna, where he was for many years professor of belles-lettres. He published numerous commentaries on the Greek and Latin classics, also Orations, and other short works. Died at Bologna in 1505.

See GINGUENÉ, "Histoire Littéraire d'Italie;" GIOVANNI PINI, "Vita P. Beroaldi Senioris," 1505.

Beroaldo, (FILIPPO,) nephew of the preceding, born at Bologna in 1472, became librarian of the Vatican in 1516. Died at Rome in 1518.

Beroaldo, (VINCENZO,) an Italian poet, son of Beroaldo the Elder, was born at Bologna; died in 1557.

Beroldingen, de, deh bā′rol-ding′en, (FRANZ,) BARON, a Swiss mineralogist, born at Saint-Gall in 1740. He wrote a "Treatise on Ancient and Modern Volcanoes," (1791,) and other works, in German. Died in 1798.

See ERSCH und GRUBER, "Allgemeine Encyklopaedie."

Be-ro′sus, [Gr. Βηρωσός; Fr. BÉROSE, bā′roz′,] a Chaldee historian, sometimes called **Bar-Oseas,** ("son of Oseas,") lived in the time of Alexander the Great, and was a priest of Belus at Babylon. His principal work was a "History of Babylonia and Chaldæa," written in Greek; fragments of it are preserved in Eusebius and other Greek writers.

See VOSSIUS, "De Historicis Græcis;" FABRICIUS, "Bibliotheca Græca."

Bérould. See BEROALDE, (MATHIEU.)

Berquen. See BERKEN.

Berquin, bĕR′kăN′, (ARNAUD,) a French writer, born at Bordeaux in 1749, is chiefly celebrated for his "Children's Friend," (6 vols., 1784,) and other popular works for the young. He also made a number of translations from the English. Died in Paris in 1791.

See LE BAS, "Dictionnaire encyclopédique de la France."

Berquin, de, dẹh bĕr′kăN′, (LOUIS,) a French gentleman, born in Artois in 1489, was a counsellor of Francis I. He was a friend of Erasmus, whose works he was active in circulating. Being accused of Lutheranism at the theological faculty of Paris, he was burned at the stake in 1529.

See SISMONDI, "Histoire des Français," chap. xvi.; BAYLE, "Historical and Critical Dictionary;" "Quarterly Review" for July, 1859.

Berr, bĕR, (FRIEDRICH,) a German musician and composer of instrumental music, born at Manheim in 1794; died about 1838.

Berré, bặ′rä′, (JEAN BAPTISTE,) a Flemish painter of animals, born at Antwerp in 1777; died in 1838.

Berredo, de, dȧ bĕr-rä′do, (BERNARDO PEREIRA,) a Portuguese writer and soldier, born at Villa de Serpa. He became Governor of Maranham, Brazil, and wrote annals of that province, (1749.) Died at Lisbon in 1748.

Berrettoni. See BERETTONI.

Berres, bĕr′rĕs, (JOSEPH,) a skilful German surgeon, born at Göding, in Moravia, in 1796. About 1830 he became professor of anatomy in the University of Vienna, and published, besides other works, "Anthropologie," (1821,) which was highly esteemed. Died in 1844.

Berretoni, (NICCOLÒ.) See BERRETTI.

Berretti, bĕr-ret′tee, or **Berretini,** bĕr-rȧ-tee′nee, written also **Berretoni,** (NICCOLÒ,) an Italian painter, one of the best pupils of Carlo Maratta, born about 1637; died in 1682.

See LANZI, "History of Painting in Italy."

Berrettini. See CORTONA, (PIETRO DA.)

Berri. See BERRY.

Berriat. See BERRYAT.

Berriat Saint-Prix, bặ′re-ă′ săN′prĕ′, (CHARLES,) a French jurist and *littérateur,* born at Grenoble in 1802, became a counsellor at the imperial court of Paris in 1857.

Berriat Saint-Prix, (JACQUES,) a French jurist, born at Grenoble in 1769. He published numerous works, and edited the writings of Boileau, (1830–34.) Died at Paris in 1845.

See DUCHESNE, "Notice sur la Vie, etc. de Berriat Saint-Prix," 1847; A. H. TAILLANDIER, "Notice sur la Vie de Berriat Saint-Prix," 1846.

Bĕr′ridge, (JOHN,) born about 1716, became vicar of Everton in 1755, and published "The Christian World Unmasked," (1773.) Died in 1793.

Bĕr′ri-ẹn, (JOHN MCPHERSON,) an American lawyer and Senator, born in New Jersey in 1781, removed to Georgia, where he was elected to the United States Senate in 1824. He was appointed attorney-general of the United States in 1829, and resigned in 1831. He was again made Senator in 1840 and in 1846. Died in 1856.

Berrier, bặ′re-ă′, (JEAN FRANÇOIS CONSTANT,) a French *littérateur,* born at Aire, in Artois, in 1766, wrote birthday odes, vaudevilles, etc. Died in Paris in 1824.

Bĕr′rĭ-man, (WILLIAM,) a learned English divine, born in London in 1688, became chaplain to the Bishop of London in 1720. He wrote, among other works, a "Historical Account of the Trinitarian Controversy," (1725.) He was well versed in Greek, Hebrew, Chaldee, Arabic, etc. Died in 1750.

See "Biographia Britannica."

Berroyer, bặ′rwȧ′yȧ′, (CLAUDE,) a French jurist, born at Moulins in 1655, was an advocate in the Parliament of Paris. Died in 1735.

Berruguete, bĕr-roo-gā′tȧ, (ALONZO,) a Spanish architect and sculptor, born near Valladolid, was a pupil of Michael Angelo. He restored the Alhambra, and executed several important works at Madrid. Among his master-pieces was the choir of the cathedral of Toledo. He was made a chevalier by the emperor Charles V. Died in 1561.

See BERMUDEZ, "Diccionario Historico."

Berruyer, bặ′rü-e′ȧ′, (JEAN FRANÇOIS,) born at Lyons in 1737, served in the Seven Years' war and in the campaigns of the French Revolution, and was made inspector-general of cavalry. Died in 1804.

Berruyer, (JOSEPH ISAAC,) a French Jesuit, born at Rouen in 1681; died in 1758.

Bĕr′rỹ, (HIRAM G.,) an American general, born at Thomaston, (now Rockland,) Maine, in 1824. He served as colonel at Bull Run, July 21, 1861, and became a brigadier-general of volunteers in April, 1862. He distinguished himself by his skill and courage at Fair Oaks, June 1, and in the Seven Days' battles near Richmond, June 26–July 1, 1862. About February, 1863, he was appointed a major-general. He commanded a division at Chancellorsville, where he was killed, May 3, 1863.

Bĕr′rỹ, (Sir JOHN,) an English naval commander, born in Devonshire in 1635; died in 1691.

Berry, (MARY,) an English lady of distinguished talents and beauty, born in 1762, was an intimate friend and correspondent of Horace Walpole. She wrote a work entitled "England and France," and a "Life of Lady Rachel Russell." Her correspondence and that of her sister Agnes with Horace Walpole came out in 1840. Died in 1852.

See "Journals and Correspondence of Miss Mary Berry," edited by LADY THERESA LEWIS, 1866; "London Quarterly Review" for March, 1845; "Edinburgh Review," vol. cxxii., 1865.

Berry, (WILLIAM,) a Scottish seal-engraver, born about 1730; died in 1783.

Berry or Berri, de, dẹh bĕr′re, [Fr. pron. bặ′re′,] (CAROLINE FERDINANDE LOUISE,) DUCHESSE, daughter of Ferdinand I., King of the Two Sicilies, was born at Naples in 1798. She was married in 1816 to the Duke of Berry, second son of Charles X. After the assassination of her husband, in 1820, the legitimists supported the claims of her infant son, the Duke of Bordeaux, to the throne. In 1832 a rising in her favour took place in Brittany, but, being betrayed by a pretended friend, she was taken by the enemy, and, after a short imprisonment, retired to Sicily.

See DERMONCOURT, "La Vendée et Madame," Paris, 1834; ALFRED NETTEMENT, "Mémoires de Madame la Duchesse de Berry," 3 vols., 1836; "London Quarterly Review" for October, 1833; "Foreign Quarterly Review" for July, 1837.

Berry or Berri, de, (CHARLES,) DUC, born in 1446, was a son of King Charles VII., and a younger brother of Louis XI. Impelled by ambition to be king, he conspired with Charles the Bold against Louis XI. This was the origin of the League of the Public Good, (*Bien public.*) (See LOUIS XI.) Died in 1472.

Berry, de, (CHARLES,) DUC, a grandson of Louis XIV., born in 1686. He married in 1710 the daughter of Philip, Duke of Orléans, afterwards regent of France. Died in 1714.

See SAINT-SIMON, "Mémoires."

Berry or Berri, de, (CHARLES FERDINAND d'Artois—dăR′twä′,) DUC, a French prince, born at Versailles in 1778, was the second son of Charles X. He emigrated about 1790, and served in the army under the Prince of Condé. In 1816 he married the Princess Caroline of Naples. He was assassinated by Louvet in Paris in February, 1820.

See CHÂTEAUBRIAND, "Mémoires touchant la Vie et la Mort du Duc de Berry," 1820; F. T. DELBARE, "Vie de S. A. R. le Duc de Berry," 1820.

Berry or Berri, de, (JEAN,) DUC, born in 1340, was the third son of John II., King of France. He was present at the battle of Poitiers, and in 1360 was one of the hostages delivered up to England by the treaty of Brétigny. In 1381 he was, by Charles VI., appointed royal lieutenant for Languedoc, but on account of his tyranny was deprived of his office. After the murder of the Duke of Orléans, he joined the faction of the Armagnacs against the Burgundians. He died in 1416, leaving a valuable collection of manuscripts and works of art.

See RAYNAL, "Histoire du Berry:" FROISSART, "Chronicles."

Berry or Berri, de, (MARIE LOUISE ÉLISABETH d'Orléans—doR′lä′ôN′,) DUCHESSE, eldest daughter of Philip, Duke of Orléans, born in 1695, was married to the Duke of Berry, grandson of Louis XIV. She was noted for her ambition and profligacy. Died in 1719.

See SAINT-SIMON, "Mémoires."

Berryat or Berriat, bặ′re-ă′, (JEAN,) a French physician and medical writer; died in 1754.

Berryer, bặ′re-ă′ or bĕr′yȧ′, (ANTOINE PIERRE,) a celebrated political orator and chief of the legitimist party, a son of Pierre Nicolas, noticed below, born in Paris on the 4th of January, 1790. He studied in the college

Juilly, and made his *début* at the bar of Paris in 1811. Although he favoured the restoration, he thought it expedient to show lenity to the losing party. He was associated with his father in pleading the cause of Marshal Ney in 1815, and defended with success General Cambronne, who had followed Napoleon to Waterloo. As a prelude to his parliamentary career, he gave a course of political lectures, which were very successful, and in 1830 was elected a deputy for Puy, (in Haute-Loire.) In his first speech, March, 1830, he sustained with magnificent eloquence the bold position that the crown has a right to choose the ministry outside of the majority.

After the revolution of July, 1830, he remained as champion of the legitimist cause, although the members of his party retired from the Chamber *en masse.* He maintained a position independent of the ministerial and the opposition parties. His speech against the abolition of the hereditary peerage, in 1831, was very celebrated. In June, 1832, he was arrested as a suspected partisan of the Duchesse de Berry, who attempted to effect a revolution b arms, although he had advised her against that course. He was tried and acquitted. About the period of 1835 he was considered the foremost orator in the Chamber. He opposed, as defective and premature, the motion for the abolition of slavery in 1838, supported the transient coalition of Guizot and Thiers in 1839, and defended the captive Louis Napoleon in 1840. In the Assemblies of 1848 and 1849 he was one of the chiefs of the majority formed by a coalition of several monarchical parties. He opposed the *coup d'état* of Napoleon in December, 1851, after which he remained aloof from politics for some years. He was elected to the French Academy in 1852. Died in November, 1868.

See LOUIS MARIE DE LA HAYE CORMENIN, "Biographie parlementaire de M. Berryer," 1837; "Biographie de M. Berryer," Paris, 8vo, 1839; "Nouvelle Biographie Générale;" "Blackwood's Magazine" for July, 1837; "Edinburgh Review" for October, 1842.

Berryer, (NICOLAS RENÉ,) a French statesman, born in Paris in 1703, became keeper of the seals in 1761. Died in 1762.

See DUCLOS, "Mémoires sur le Règne de Louis XV."

Berryer, (PIERRE NICOLAS,) a French jurist and eloquent pleader, born at Sainte-Menehould in 1757, was the father of Antoine Pierre, noticed above. He had a large practice in commercial causes, and was counsel in several political trials, among which was that of Marshal Ney in 1815. He published an "Allocution of an Old Friend of Liberty to France," (1830,) and "Souvenirs," (1838.) Died in 1841.

See "Souvenirs de M. Berryer de 1774 à 1838," 2 vols., 1838.

Ber'ser-ker, [from *ber,* "bare," and *serk,* "coat of mail,"] a legendary Scandinavian hero of the eighth century, celebrated for his strength and valour. He fought without coat of mail or helmet, whence his name. The name Berserkers was also applied to a class of warriors who, under the influence of a sort of demoniac possession, fought naked, performing marvellous feats of valour, unmindful or insusceptible of wounds.

See BROCKHAUS, "Conversations-Lexikon."

Bersmann, bĕRs′mân,[Lat. BERSMAN′NUS,](GREGOR,) a German scholar, born at Annaberg, in Saxony, about 1536. He translated the Psalms into Latin verse, and published editions of several classics. Died in 1611.

See W. SCHUBERT, "De G. Bersmanno Philologo et Poeta," 1853.

Berta, bĕR′tâ, (FRANCESCO,) born about 1719, at Turin, where he became one of the keepers of the royal library. Died in 1787.

Bertaire or **Berthaire,** SAINT, sân′bĕR′tàR′, born about 810, was descended from the kings of France. He became, in 856, abbot of the monastery of Monte-Casino. He was killed by the Saracens in 884.

See MABILLON, "Acta Sanctorum Ordinis Sancti Benedicti."

Bertana bĕR-tâ′nâ, (LUCIA,) an Italian poetess, born about 1530; died in 1567.

Bertani, bĕR-tâ′nee, or **Bertano,** (GIOVANNI BATTISTA,) an Italian painter and architect, was a pupil of Giulio Romano. He worked at Mantua about 1566.

See VASARI, "Lives of the Painters."

Bertani, (LELIO,) an Italian musician and composer, born at Brescia about 1520; died in 1600.

Bertaut, Bertault, or **Berthaut,** pronounced alike bĕR′tō′, born at Valenciennes about 1705, was an excellent performer on the violoncello, which he first rendered popular in France. Died in 1756.

See FÉTIS, "Biographie Universelle des Musiciens."

Bertaut, (ÉLOI,) a French writer, born at Vesoul in 1782, became professor of mathematics at Besançon about 1800. Died in 1834.

Bertaut, (FRANÇOIS,) a French *littérateur,* born in Paris in 1621, was a favourite with Louis XIII., who appointed him his reader. He was a brother of Madame de Motteville. (See MOTTEVILLE.)

Bertaut, (JEAN,) a French ecclesiastic and popular poet, born at Caen about 1560, rose to be Bishop of Seez in 1606, and almoner to Mary de Médicis, queen of Henry IV. It is said that he contributed much to the conversion of Henry IV. to Catholicism. He composed pastorals, songs, elegies, and other poems, which were much admired. Many of them were translated into Greek and Latin. He was an uncle of Madame de Motteville the authoress. Died in 1611.

See LONGFELLOW, "Poets and Poetry of Europe;" SAINTE-BEUVE, "De la Poésie Française au seizième Siecle."

Bertaut, (LÉONARD,) a French ecclesiastic, born at Autun; died in 1662.

Bertaux, bĕR′tō′, (DUPLESSI,) a French artist, engraved the "Campaigns of Napoleon in Italy," after Vernet. Died in 1815.

Bertel, bĕR′tĕl, or **Bertels,** (JAN,) a Flemish ecclesiastic and historical writer, born at Louvain in 1559; died in 1607.

Ber′tha or **Ber′trade,** called also **E′dith-ber′gą,** a daughter of Caribert, King of Paris, lived about 560 A.D. She was married to Ethelbert, King of Kent, whom she persuaded to embrace Christianity.

See LE BAS, "Dictionnaire encyclopédique de la France."

Ber′thą, [Fr. BERTHE, bàRt,] a daughter of Conrad, King of Burgundy, was married to Robert, King of Paris, her cousin in the fourth degree, about 995, and afterwards divorced on account of relationship.

Berthaire. See BERTAIRE, SAINT.

Berthault, bĕR′tō′, (LOUIS MARTIN,) a French architect, born in Paris about 1771, was commissioned by Napoleon to execute a number of public works. He furnished the designs for the principal parks and gardens of France.

See LE BAS, "Dictionnaire encyclopédique de la France."

Berthault, (PIERRE,) a French ecclesiastic, born at Sens, lived about 1600–50.

Berthault, (RENÉ,) a French *littérateur,* translated the "Golden Book" of Marcus Aurelius. Died in 1534.

Berthaut. See BERTAUT.

Berthe. See BERTHA.

Berthegène. See BERTHEZÈNE.

Berthélemy, bĕR′tàl′me′, (JEAN SIMON,) a French historical painter, born at Laon in 1743; died in 1811.

Berthelet, (GRÉGOIRE.) See BERTHELOT.

Berthelin, bĕR′lân′, (PIERRE CHARLES,) a French writer on lexicography, born in Paris about 1720; died in 1780.

Berthelot, bĕR′tlo′, (CLAUDE FRANÇOIS,) a French mechanician, engineer, and professor of mathematics, born at Château-Châlons in 1718. He published "Mechanics applied to the Arts, Manufactures, Agriculture, and War," (1782.) Died in 1800.

See LE BAS, "Dictionnaire encyclopédique de la France."

Berthelot or **Berthelet,** (GRÉGOIRE,) a French Benedictine writer, born at Berain in 1680; died in 1745.

Berthelot, (JEAN FRANÇOIS,) a French jurist, and professor of law in Paris, where he was born in 1749; died in 1814.

Berthelot, (N.,) a French satiric poet, born about 1580.

Berthereau, bĕRt′rō′, (GEORGES FRANÇOIS,) a French ecclesiastic and philologist, born at Belesme in 1732; died in 1794.

Berthet, bĕR′tà′, (ÉLIE BERTRAND,) a French novelist, born at Limoges in 1815. He became a resident of Paris in 1834, and produced many successful novels, among which are "The Poacher," ("Le Braconnier,"

·1846,) "The Storks' Nest," ("Le Nid de Cigognes," 1848,) and "The Catacombs of Paris," (8 vols., 1854.)

Berthet, (JEAN,) a French Jesuit and writer, born at Tarascon in 1622 ; died in 1692.

Berthezène, bĕrt'zȧN', written also **Berthegène,** (PIERRE,) a French baron, born in Hérault in 1775, gained the rank of general of division by his conduct at Bautzen and Lutzen in 1813. He had a prominent part in the conquest of Algeria.

Berthier, bĕr'te-à',(GUILLAUME FRANÇOIS,) a French Jesuit and critic, born at Issoudun in 1704, wrote a continuation (in 6 vols.) of the "History of the Gallican Church." He edited the "Journal de Trévoux" for many years. Died in 1782.

Berthier, (JOSEPH ÉTIENNE,) a French Cartesian philosopher, born at Aix in 1702, was an Oratorian. He published, besides other works, "The Nature of Comets," ("La Physique des Comètes," 1760,) and "The Principles of Physics," (1763.) Died in Paris in 1783.

Berthier, (LOUIS ALEXANDRE,) Prince of Wagram, was born at Versailles in November, 1753. He served as captain under La Fayette in the United States, (1778–82,) and in 1796 became chief of staff of the army of Bonaparte, with the rank of general of division. He gained in this campaign the favour and confidence of Bonaparte, whom he followed in 1798 to Egypt, and aided in his victory over the Directory in 1799, soon after which he became minister of war. He was made a marshal of France in 1804, distinguished himself in the campaign against Austria in 1805, and received the title of Prince of Neufchâtel in 1806. During the absence of Napoleon, in 1809, Berthier had for a short time the title of general-in-chief of the grande armée. For his services at the battle of Wagram, in 1809, he was created Prince of Wagram. In this and subsequent campaigns he was chief of the staff, and usually rode in the carriage of Napoleon, whose plans and orders he digested and despatched with admirable precision and promptitude. He was not, however, equal to the chief command of an army. He shared the disasters of the Russian campaign. In 1814 he was among the first of the generals to give his adhesion to Louis XVIII., by whom he was raised to the peerage. On the return of Napoleon from Elba, Berthier wished to be neutral, and retired to Bamberg, where he met a violent death in March, 1815. Six men in masks (says the "Nouvelle Biographie Générale") threw him from a window into the street, whence he was taken up in a dying condition ; but this story is discredited by some writers.

See "Mémoires d'A. Berthier," Paris, 1826.

Berthier, (NAPOLÉON LOUIS JOSEPH ALEXANDRE,) Duke of Wagram, the only son of the preceding, was born in Paris in 1810. He entered the Chamber of Peers in 1836, and about 1848 became a partisan of Louis Napoleon. In 1852 he was made a senator. He is distinguished as a practical agriculturist.

Berthier, (PIERRE,) a French mineralogist, born at Nemours in 1772, became a member of the Academy of Sciences in 1827. His chief work is a "Treatise on Assays by the Dry Method," ("Traité des Essais par la Voie sèche," 11 vols., 1833.) Died in August, 1861.

Berthold. See BERTHOLDUS.

Berthold, bĕr'tolt, a Saxon ecclesiastic, who was distinguished for his zeal in converting the Livonians to Christianity. He was killed in 1198, while endeavouring to propagate his doctrines by force of arms.

See ERSCH und GRUBER, "Allgemeine Encyklopaedie."

Berthold, a German ecclesiastic and eminent pulpit orator ; died in 1272.

Berthold, (ARNOLD ADOLF,) a German savant, born at Soest, in Westphalia, in 1803. He published a "Manual of the Physiology of Men and Animals," (2 vols., 1829,) a "Manual of Zoology," (1845,) and several works on comparative anatomy and physiology. He became a professor at Göttingen in 1836. Died in 1861.

See BROCKHAUS, "Conversations-Lexikon."

Ber-thol'dus or **Berthold,** bĕr'tolt, called also **Bernaldus, Bernoul,** and **Bertoul,** a German ecclesiastic, who lived about 1060, wrote, in Latin, a history of his times, and other works.

Bertholet, bĕr'to'lä', (JEAN,) a Flemish Jesuit, born at Salm, wrote the "Ecclesiastical and Civil History of the Duchy of Luxembourg," (1741.) Died in 1755.

Bertholet-Flemalle. See FLEMALLE.

Berthollet, bĕr'to'lä', (CLAUDE LOUIS,) a French chemical philosopher of great eminence, was born at Taillore or Talloire, near Annecy, Savoy, on the 9th of November, 1748. He was educated at Turin, where he took his degree in medicine in 1768. In 1772 he removed to Paris, and by the mediation of Tronchin became physician to the Duke of Orléans, with whom he enjoyed facilities in his chemical investigations. He produced "Researches on the Nature of Animal Substances" in 1780, and about this time was admitted into the Academy of Sciences. In 1785 he announced his conversion to the anti-phlogistic theory of Lavoisier, which no other eminent French chemist had yet adopted, and presented a memoir on oxy-muriatic acid, (chlorine.) He discovered the composition of ammonia in 1785, proved that nitrogen is an essential principle in the composition of animal substances, and in an essay on prussic acid (1787) maintained that oxygen is not necessary to the formation of acids. About this time he rendered an important service by inventing the process of bleaching by chlorine. In 1790 he published a good work on the art of dyeing, "Élémens de l'Art de la Teinture." He was chosen professor of chemistry in the Polytechnic School in 1794, and was sent to Italy with Monge in 1796 to select works of art and science which should be taken to Paris as spoils. He was associated with Lavoisier and others in reforming the nomenclature of chemistry. Berthollet is said to have been the only one to whom Bonaparte confided in advance the secret of his expedition to Egypt, (1798,) which he accompanied. Under the auspices of Monge and Berthollet, the Institute of Egypt was founded ; and a number of their pupils made a grand application of the lessons of the Polytechnic School. He explained the formation of the carbonate of soda at Lake Natron, and discovered a valuable mode of obtaining muriatic acid from common salt, then called muriate of soda.

Berthollet was one of the few select friends who returned to France with Bonaparte in 1799, about the end of which year he was made a senator. His "Researches on the Laws of Affinity" (1801) was translated into English by Farrel, (1804.) In 1803 he published an able "Essay on Chemical Statics," ("Essai de Statique chimique," 2 vols.,) which was translated into English and other languages. In the last-named work he controverted the opinions of Bergman on elective affinity. During the empire he received the title of Count ; but he always preserved his simplicity and love of study. He discovered how to keep water pure in voyages by carbonizing the inside of the cask or other vessel. On the restoration of the Bourbons he was admitted to the Chamber of Peers. He died at Arcueil, near Paris, on the 6th of November, 1822, or, according to some writers, on the 6th of December of that year.

See CUVIER, "Éloge de Berthollet," 1824; E. F. JOMARD, "Notice sur la Vie et les Ouvrages de Berthollet," 1823; JULIA DE FONTENELLE, "Notice historique sur Berthollet," 1826; "Nouvelle Biographie Générale."

Bertholon, bĕr'to'lôN', (PIERRE,) a French physician and savant, born at Lyons in 1742, was a friend of Dr. Franklin. He wrote a treatise on the "Electricity of Meteors," (1787,) and other similar works. Died in 1800.

See "Biographie Médicale."

Berthon, bĕr'tôN', (RENÉ THÉODORE,) a French artist, born at Tours in 1778, painted history at Vienna and Paris.

Berthot, bĕr'to', (CLÉMENT LOUIS CHARLES,) a French writer, born in Haute-Marne in 1758, wrote a "History of the French Revolution," (18 vols., 1792–1803.) Died in 1832.

Berthoud, bĕr'too', (FERDINAND,) a Swiss mechanician and writer, born in the county of Neufchâtel about 1725, was the inventor of marine clocks. He was a member of the Institute of France and of the Royal Society of London. Died in 1807.

Berthoud, (SAMUEL HENRI,) a French journalist and littérateur, born at Cambrai in 1804, was successively associate editor of the "Revue des Deux Mondes," the

" Revue de Paris," and " La Presse." He has published romances, poems, and moral and historical treatises. He settled in Paris about 1832.

See QUÉRARD, "La France Littéraire."

Berti, bĕR′tee, (ALESSANDRO POMPEO,) an Italian ecclesiastic and historical writer, born at Lucca in 1686. Died in Rome in 1752.

Berti, (GIOVANNI LORENZO,) an Italian theologian, and professor of ecclesiastical history at Pisa, born at Saravezza in 1696; died in 1766.

Berti, (PIETRO,) an Italian Jesuit and writer, born at Venice in 1741, was professor of rhetoric at Parma. Died in 1813.

Ber′tie, (RICHARD,) an English Protestant gentleman, who married the Duchess-dowager of Suffolk. In the reign of Mary he retired with his wife to the continent, for refuge from persecution.

His son PEREGRINE, born in 1555, was an eminent officer, and succeeded Leicester as commander of the English troops in the Low Countries. Died in 1601.

Bertie, (ROBERT,) a son of Peregrine, noticed above, born in 1582, was a military officer, and fought for Charles I. in the civil war. He was created Earl of Lindsey about 1626, and was mortally wounded at Edgehill in 1642.

Bertie, (Sir THOMAS HOAR,) an English naval commander, born in London in 1758. He served against the French in 1778–82, and was made vice-admiral in 1813. Died in 1825.

Bertie, (WILLOUGHBY,) fourth Earl of Abingdon, an English statesman and political writer. He published "Thoughts on the Letter of Edmund Burke to the Sheriffs of Bristol." Died in 1799.

Bertier de Sauvigny, bĕR′te-â′ dẹh sõ′vĕn′ye′, (LOUIS BÉNIGNE FRANÇOIS,) a French statesman, born about 1742, was intendant of the district of Paris in 1768. He was killed in a mob in 1789, together with his father-in-law Foulon.

Bertin, bĕR′tăN′, (ANTOINE,) a French erotic poet, born in the Isle of Bourbon in 1752. His reputation was founded on his poem "Des Amours," (1780.) Died in Saint Domingo in 1790.

Bertin, (ANTOINE,) a French ecclesiastic, born at Droup-Saint-Basle in 1761, became professor of theology at Rheims. Died in 1823.

Bertin, (ÉDOUARD FRANÇOIS,) a French landscape-painter, son of Louis François, noticed below, was born in Paris in 1797. Among his master-pieces are "The Forest of Fontainebleau," and a "View of the Apennines." He became editor or director of the "Journal des Débats" in 1854.

Bertin, (EXUPÈRE (ĕk′sü′pair′) JOSEPH,) a French anatomist of high reputation, born at Tremblay in 1712, published a "Treatise on Osteology," (4 vols., 1754,) and other anatomical and medical works. Died in 1781.

See CONDORCET, "Éloge de Bertin."

Bertin, (HENRI LÉONARD JEAN BAPTISTE,) a French statesman, born in Périgord in 1719, became controller-general of finance in 1759. Died in 1792.

See LACRETELLE, "Histoire du dix-huitième Siècle."

Bertin, (JEAN VICTOR,) a French landscape-painter, born in Paris in 1775; died in 1841.

Bertin, (LOUIS FRANÇOIS,) a French journalist and littérateur, born in Paris in 1766. He founded in 1800 the "Journal des Débats," a literary daily paper, to which Châteaubriand and other eminent writers of the time were contributors. Accused by Napoleon of favouring the royalists, he was first imprisoned and afterwards exiled, and in 1811 his journal was confiscated. He had then twenty thousand subscribers or more. In 1814 he resumed its publication. Died in 1841.

See "Nouvelle Biographie Générale."

Bertin, (LOUIS MARIE ARMAND,) son of the preceding, born in Paris in 1801. He succeeded his father as editor of the "Journal des Débats" in 1841. Died in 1854.

Bertin, (LOUISE ANGÉLIQUE,) daughter of Louis François, born at Roches in 1805, studied music under Fétis, and composed the operas of "Esmeralda" and "Faust."

See FÉTIS, "Biographie Universelle des Musiciens."

Bertin, (NICOLAS,) a French painter, born in Paris in 1667. He became a professor in the Academy of Paris in 1716. Among his works is "Saint Philip baptizing the Eunuch." Died in 1736.

Bertin, (RENÉ JOSEPH HYACINTHE,) a French physician and medical writer, son of Exupère Joseph, noticed above, born near Rennes in 1767; died in 1827.

Bertin, (THÉODORE PIERRE,) a French littérateur, born near Provins in 1751. He translated into French the "Curiosities of Literature" and other English works. Died in 1819.

Bertin, SAINT, born at Constance, in Switzerland, became Abbot of Sithieu, at Saint-Omer, about 695. Died in 709.

Bertin d'Antilly, bĕR′tăN′ dŏN′te′ye′, (LOUIS AUGUSTE,) a French dramatic writer, a natural son of Auguste Louis, noticed below, born in Paris about 1760. He died at Saint Petersburg in 1804.

Bertin de Blagny, beR′tăN′ dẹh blăN′ye′, (AUGUSTE LOUIS,) a French littérateur, and member of the Academy of Inscriptions, lived about 1750.

Bertin de Veaux, bĕR′tăN′ dẹh võ, (LOUIS FRANÇOIS,) a French politician and journalist, brother of Louis François Bertin, noticed above, born in Paris in 1771. He was one of the founders and managers of the "Journal des Débats." He was twice elected to the Chamber of Deputies, became a councillor of state in 1827, and a member of the Chamber of Peers in 1832. Died in 1842.

Bertini, bĕR-tee′nee, (ANTONIO FRANCESCO,) an Italian physician, born at Castel-Fiorentino in 1658; died in 1726.

Bertini, (GIUSEPPE MARIA SAVERIO,) a physician and medical writer, son of the preceding, born at Florence in 1694; died in 1756.

Bertini, ber-tee′nee, (HENRI,) a composer and pianist, born in London in 1798, lived many years in Paris. He composed for the piano some works which are highly commended by Fétis.

Bertini, (SALVATORE,) an Italian musician and composer, born at Palermo in 1721, became chapel-master to the king. Died in 1794.

Bertius, bĕR′te-us, (PETER,) born at Baveren, in Flanders, in 1565, was historiographer and cosmographer of Louis XIII., and published a work entitled "Theatre of Ancient Geography," (in Latin, 1619.) Died in 1629.

See NICÉRON, "Mémoires;" WALCKENAER, "Vies de plusieurs Personnages célèbres," 1830.

Bertlef, bĕR′lĕf, (MARTIN,) a German writer, born in Transylvania, was professor at Thorn in 1699. He published "Solemn and Civil Orations," (or "Assemblies,") ("Solennes et Civiles Conciones," 1695.)

Bertling, bĕR′ling, (ERNST AUGUST,) a German theologian, born at Osnabrück in 1721; died in 1769.

Bertola. See BERTOLI.

Bertolacci, bĕR-to-lăt′chee, (ANTONIO,) a magistrate of Corsican extraction, born in England, was appointed by the government administrator and controller-general of the island of Ceylon, which post he filled for seventeen years. He wrote a "View of the Agricultural, Commercial, and Financial Interests of Ceylon," (1817.) Died in 1833.

Bertoli, bĕR′to-lee, or **Bertola,** bĕR′to-lâ, (AURELIO GIORGIO,) an Italian author and monk, born at Rimini in 1753. He lectured on history at Naples, and was afterwards professor of belles-lettres at Pavia. He translated the works of Horace, and Gesner's Idylls, into Italian, and wrote, besides several able critical essays, a poem on the death of Clement XIV., entitled "Le Notti Clementine," which was received with favour. Died at Rome in 1798.

See TIRABO, "Biografia degli Italiani illustri."

Bertoli, (GIOVANNI DOMENICO,) an Italian antiquary, born at Mereto, in the Friuli, in 1676; died after 1750.

Bertolio, bĕR′to′le-o′, (ANTOINE RENÉ CONSTANCE,) a French jurist, born at Avignon, was appointed by Napoleon chief judge of Guadeloupe. Died in 1812.

Bertolotti, bĕR-to-lot′tee, (GIOVANNI LORENZO,) an Italian historical painter, born at Genoa in 1640; died in 1721.

Berton, bĕR′tŏN′, (ÉMILE ADOLPHE JOSEPH,) a French physician and writer, born at Dinant in 1801, was a son of General Berton, executed in 1822. Died in 1855.

Berton, (FRANÇOIS,) son of Henri Montan, noticed

below, born in Paris in 1784, produced a number of ballads and comic operas. Died in 1832.

Berton, (HENRI Montan—mŏn'tŏn',) a popular French composer, son of Pierre Montan, noticed below, born in Paris in 1766. His works include oratorios, songs, and operas, one of which is entitled "Aline, Queen of Golconda." Died in 1844.

See FÉTIS, "Biographie Universelle des Musiciens."

Berton, (JEAN BAPTISTE,) a French general of brigade, born near Sedan in 1769. He was a member of the Carbonari, and in 1822 was executed, by order of Louis XVIII., for having headed an insurrection against the government.

See "Mémoire pour le Général Berton," 1822.

Berton, (LOUIS SÉBASTIEN,) principal of the military school of Brienne, where he was born in 1745. Among his pupils was Napoleon Bonaparte, who, on becoming First Consul, made him director of the Lyceum of Arts at Compiègne. Died in 1811.

See LE BAS, "Dictionnaire encyclopédique de la France."

Berton, (PIERRE MONTAN,) a French composer, born in Paris in 1727. He became director of the Opera in 1767. Died in 1780. A great reform in dramatic music was effected under his administration.

Ber'ton, (WILLIAM,) chancellor of Oxford University, lived about 1380. He wrote several Latin treatises against Wickliffe.

Bertoni, bĕr-to'nee, (FERDINANDO,) an Italian musician, born at or near Venice in 1727, composed successful operas entitled "Orfeo," "Armida," and "Tancredi." Died in Venice about 1800.

Bertotti-Scamozzi, bĕr-tot'tee skä-mot'see, (OTTAVIO,) an Italian architect, born at Vicenza in 1726. He built several fine palaces near Vicenza, and published an edition of Palladio's works. Died about 1800.

Bertoul. See BERTHOLDUS.

Bertoux, bĕr'too', (GUILLAUME,) a French Jesuit and writer, born in 1723.

Bertrade. See BERTHA.

Bertram, bĕr'trăm, (AUGUST WILHELM,) a German physician, born in 1752, became in 1787 professor of medicine at Halle. Died in 1788.

Bertram, bĕr'trŏn', (BONAVENTURE CORNEILLE,) a French Orientalist, born at Thouars, in Poitou, in 1531, became a Protestant minister and professor of Hebrew at Geneva. He wrote, in Latin, a work on the civil and ecclesiastical policy of the Jews, (1580.) Died in 1594.

Ber'tram, (CHARLES,) an English antiquary and philologist, born about 1700, was professor of the English language in the Royal Marine Academy at Copenhagen.

Bertram, (CHRISTIAN AUGUST,) a German littérateur and journalist, born at Berlin in 1751 ; died in 1830.

Bertram, (JOHANN FRIEDRICH,) a German Lutheran theologian, born in 1699 ; died in 1741.

Bertram, (JOHANN GEORG,) a German theologian, born at Lüneburg in 1670 ; died in 1728.

Bertram, (PHILIPP ERNST,) a German jurist and writer, born at Zerbst in 1726, was professor of law at Halle in 1761. Died in 1777.

Bertrand, bĕr'trŏn', (ANTOINE MARIE,) a French revolutionist, was appointed mayor of Lyons in 1792. He was condemned to death by the Directory, and executed in 1796.

Bertrand, bĕr'trŏn', (ÉLIE,) a Swiss naturalist and geologist, born at Orbe in 1712. He became pastor of a church at Berne about 1744, published "Memoirs on the Interior Structure of the Earth," (1752,) a "General Dictionary of Fossils," (2 vols., 1763,) and other scientific works. He also wrote some moral and religious treatises. Died about 1790.

Bertrand, (FRANÇOIS Séraphique—sä'rä'fĕk',) a French jurist and poet, born at Nantes in 1702 ; died in 1752.

Bertrand or **Bertrandi,** bĕr-trăn'dee, (JEAN,) a French statesman and cardinal, born in 1470, was keeper of the seals under Henry II., and afterwards became Archbishop of Sens. Died in 1560.

Bertrand, (JEAN,) a Swiss divine and miscellaneous writer, brother of Élie, noticed above, born at Orbe in 1708. He wrote several agricultural treatises, and made translations from the English. Died in 1777.

Bertrand, (JEAN BAPTISTE,) a French physician, born at Martigue, in Provence, in 1670, practised at Marseilles. He wrote, among other works, a "Historical Account of the Plague of Marseilles in 1720." Died in 1752.

Bertrand, (JEAN BAPTISTE,) a French ecclesiastic and littérateur, born at Cernay-lès-Reims in 1764, published several works on Etymology. Died in 1830.

Bertrand, (JEAN ÉLIE,) a Swiss moralist and religious writer, born at Neufchâtel in 1737. He was pastor of a French church at Berne. Died in 1779.

Bertrand, (JOSEPH LOUIS FRANÇOIS,) a French mathematician, born in Paris in 1822, was admitted into the Institute in 1856. He published several able works on Algebra, etc.

Bertrand, L'ABBÉ, a French astronomer, born at Autun in 1755, became professor of physics in the college of Dijon, (1782.) Died in 1792.

Bertrand, (LOUIS,) a Swiss mathematician and geologist, born at Geneva in 1731, was a pupil of Euler. He wrote "Elements of Geometry," (1812,) and other mathematical treatises. He obtained a professorship at Geneva in 1761. Died in 1812.

See CUVIER, "Discours sur les Révolutions de la Surface du Globe."

Bertrand, (LOUIS JACQUES NAPOLÉON ALOYSIUS,) a French poet, born in Piedmont in 1807 ; died in 1841.

Bertrand, (PHILIPPE,) a French sculptor, born in Paris in 1664 ; died in 1724.

Bertrand, (PHILIPPE,) a French engineer and geologist, born near Sens in 1730. He published several works on Navigation and Geology, and was engineer of a canal connecting the Rhine with the Rhone. Died in Paris in 1811.

See QUÉRARD, "La France Littéraire."

Bertrand, (THOMAS BERNARD,) a French physician and medical writer, born in Paris in 1682, became dean of the faculty in 1740. Died in 1751.

See "Biographie Médicale."

Bertrand d'Alamanon, bĕr'trŏn' dä'lä'mä'nŏn', or **d'Allamon,** dä'lä'mŏn', a French troubadour, born in Provence about 1100.

Bertrand de Born. See BORN.

Bertrand de la Hosdinière, bĕr'trŏn' dĕh lä ho'-de'ne-air', (CHARLES AMBROISE,) a French magistrate, and member of the National Convention, sided with the Girondists, and voted for the death of the king. He became in 1798 a member of the Council of Five Hundred. Died in 1819.

See LE BAS, "Dictionnaire encyclopédique de la France."

Bertrand de Molleville, de, dĕh bĕr'trŏn' dĕh mol'-vĕl', (ANTOINE FRANÇOIS,) MARQUIS, a French statesman, born at Toulouse in 1744. He was appointed minister of the marine in October, 1791, but held that office only a few months. He wrote a "History of the French Revolution," (14 vols., 1800–1803,) and other works. He was proscribed as a royalist in August, 1792, but escaped by flight. Died in Paris in 1818.

Bertrand, de, dĕh bĕr'trŏn', (HENRI GRATIEN,) COMTE, a French general, born at Châteauroux in 1773. He served in Egypt, Austria, and Russia, and in 1815 accompanied Napoleon to Saint Helena. After his return to France, he was elected to the Chamber of Deputies. He died in 1844, leaving in manuscript "Memoirs of the Campaigns of Egypt and Syria, dictated by Napoleon at Saint Helena." They were published in two volumes (1847) by the son of Count Bertrand.

See "Victoires et Conquêtes des Français ;" L. DE LOMÉNIE, "Galerie des Contemporains ;" PAULIN, "Notice biographique sur le Général Comte Bertrand," 1847.

Bertrandi, bĕr-trăn'dee, (GIOVANNI ANTONIO MARIA,) an Italian surgeon, born at Turin in 1723, wrote several medical and anatomical works, which are highly esteemed. He was professor of surgery in Turin, and chief surgeon to the king. Died in 1765.

See "Biographie Médicale."

Bertrandi, (JEAN.) See BERTRAND.

Bertrandi, bĕr'trŏn'de', (NICOLAS,) a French jurist, and professor of law at Toulouse, wrote a historical account of Toulouse, ("De Tholosanorum Gestis," 1515.) Died in 1527.

Bertrans, bĕr'trŏn', surnamed CLERC, (klĕRk,) a French poet and romance-writer of the thirteenth century.

€ as k; ç as s; g̃ hard; g̃ as j; G, H, K, guttural; N, nasal; R, trilled; s as z; th as in this. (☞ See Explanations, p. 23.)

Bertuch, bĕR'tŏŏK, (FRIEDRICH JUSTIN,) a German *littérateur* and journalist, born at Weimar in 1747. He published, in conjunction with Seckendorf and Zanthier, the "Magazine of Spanish and Portuguese Literature," and translated "Don Quixote" into German. His tragedy of "Elfrida," (1775,) and his "Picture-Book for Children," ("Bilderbuch für Kinder,") enjoy great popularity. Died in 1822.

See BROCKHAUS, "Conversations-Lexikon;" "Nouvelle Biographie Générale."

Bertusio, bĕR-too'se-o, (GIOVANNI BATTISTA,) an Italian painter and pupil of the Caracci. Died about 1650.

Bertuzzi, bĕR-toot'see, (NICCOLÒ,) an Italian painter, born at Ancona, worked at Bologna. Died in 1777.

Bérulle, bå'rül', [Lat. BERUL'LUS,] (PIERRE,) an eminent French cardinal and statesman, born near Troyes in 1575, was the founder of the congregation of the Oratory (Oratoire) in France, and first superior of the order of the Carmelites, which he also instituted. He was sent on embassies to Spain and to Rome, and was afterwards appointed minister of state, in which post his abilities and virtues excited the jealousy of Cardinal Richelieu. He died in 1629, leaving sermons and controversial writings which are highly esteemed. The piety and learning of Cardinal Bérulle are warmly eulogized by Bossuet.

See HABERT DE CÉRISY, "Vie de Bérulle," 1646; M. M. TABARAUD, "Histoire de P. de Bérulle, Cardinal," etc., 2 vols., 1817; LOUIS DONI D'ATTICHY, "De Vita et Rebus gestis P. Berulli Cardinalis," 1649.

Berullus. See BÉRULLE.

Bervic, bĕR'vĕk', (CHARLES CLÉMENT,) an eminent French engraver, born in Paris in 1756, was a pupil of J. George Wille. Among his master-pieces are a full-length portrait of Louis XVI., a print of Laocoon, the "Rape of Dejanira," after Guido, and the "Education of Achilles," after Regnault. Died in 1822.

See LE BLANC, "Manuel de l'Amateur d'Estampes."

Berville, bĕR'vèl', (SAINT-ALBIN, sån'tȧl'bȧn',) an advocate-general in the royal court of Paris, born at Amiens in 1788, was a contributor to the "Revue Encyclopédique" and other journals.

Berwick, bĕr'rik or bĕr'wik, (JAMES FITZ-JAMES,) DUKE OF, born in 1660, was a natural son of James II. of England and Arabella Churchill, sister of the Duke of Marlborough. He served in Austria under Charles of Lorraine, and in 1688, after an unsuccessful attempt to oppose the Prince of Orange, retired with James II. to France. Having been naturalized in 1703, he was appointed commander of the French army in Spain in 1704. He gained a signal victory over the Spaniards at Almanza in 1707, which established Philip V. on the throne. He was created by that sovereign Duke of Liria and Xerica, having previously been made a marshal. He was killed at the siege of Philipsburg in 1734.

See MACAULAY, "History of England," vol. v.; MONTESQUIEU, "Éloge historique du Duc de Berwick;" DUC DE BERWICK, "Mémoires depuis 1685 jusqu'en 1734," 2 vols. 8vo, 1778; "Life of J. Fitz-James, Duke of Berwick," Dublin, 1738.

Be-rȳl'lus, [Gr. Βερυλλός,] Bishop of Bostra or Bozra, in Arabia, maintained that Christ had no existence before his incarnation. He was converted from this belief by Origen in 244 A.D.

Berze, bĕRz, or **Bersil,** bĕR'sèl', (HUGUES,) a French satiric poet, lived about 1230.

Berzel. See BERZELIUS.

Ber-ze'lĭ-us, [Sw. pron. bĕR-zn̄'le-us,] (or **Berzel,** bĕRt'sęl,) (JOHAN JAKOB,) BARON, a celebrated Swedish chemist, was born near Linköping, in East Gothland, on the 20th of August, 1779. He is said to have been the son of a parish schoolmaster. He studied medicine and chemistry at the University of Upsal, where he graduated in 1804. In 1806 he became professor of chemistry at Stockholm, and began to edit, in conjunction with Hisinger, "Memoirs of Physical Philosophy, Chemistry, and Mineralogy," (6 vols., 1806–18,) for which he wrote forty-seven important articles. Among his first publications was an able "Treatise on Animal Chemistry, (2 vols., 1806.) He was chosen president of the Academy of Sciences in 1810, and perpetual secretary of the same in 1818. He was greatly distinguished by his skill and precision as an annalist, and enriched many departments of chemistry by his researches. His great work is a "System of Chemistry," ("Lärebok i Kemien," 3 vols., 1808–18,) which was translated into English and other languages.

He contributed much to perfect the atomic theory after Dalton, and proposed a chemical nomenclature which was received with great favour in the north of Europe. He discovered selenium, thorium, and perhaps other elementary substances. It was his researches that gave the first impulse to modern organic chemistry. We owe to him a greater number of accurate analyses than to any other chemist of his time. At the request of the academy, he produced "Annual Reports on the Progress of Physics, Chemistry, and Mineralogy," (27 vols., 1821–48,) which are highly prized and contain many judicious criticisms. He resigned his professorship about 1832, and received from the king the title of "Freiherr," or baron, soon after that date. He married about the age of fifty-two. Died in August, 1848.

See B. VON BESKOW, "Tal öfver Professoren J. Berzelius," 1848; G. FORCHHAMMER, "J. J. Berzelius," Stockholm, 1849; LOUVET, "Notice sur la Vie et les Travaux de J. J. Berzelius," 1849; L. DE LOMÉNIE, "Galerie des Contemporains."

Berzsényi, bĕR'zhän-yee, (DANIEL,) a Hungarian lyric poet, born at Heteny in 1776; died in 1836.

Besançon, bęh-sŏN'sŏN', (ÉTIENNE MODESTE,) a French *littérateur* and ecclesiastic, born near Beaune in 1730. He wrote "The Old Market Town," ("Le Vieux Bourg,") a mock-heroic and satirical poem, (1779,) which passed through several editions. Died in 1816.

See QUÉRARD, "La France Littéraire."

Besard, bęh-zȧR', (JEAN BAPTISTE,) a French physician and writer, born at Besançon about 1576.

Besborodko, bês-bo-rod'ko, (ALEXANDER,) PRINCE, a Russian statesman, born in Little Russia in 1742, was patronized by Catherine II., who appointed him secretary of state in 1780. Died in 1799.

Bescherelle, bȧsh'rêl', (LOUIS NICOLAS,) an eminent French grammarian and lexicographer, born in Paris in 1802. He was appointed librarian of the Louvre in 1828. He has published, besides several works on grammar, a French dictionary, ("Dictionnaire National," 2 vols., 1843–46,) which is regarded as the best in the language.

A younger brother of the preceding, known as BESCHE-RELLE JEUNE, born at Paris in 1804, has published a "Complete Course of the French Language," (6 vols., 1852.)

See "Notice biographique sur M. Bescherelle aîné," 1847.

Beschi, bês'kee, (CONSTANTINO GIUSEPPE,) an Italian Jesuit and missionary, resided many years in India. He wrote, in Latin, a "Grammar of the High Dialect of the Tamil Language," and other similar works. Died in 1742.

See MAZZUCHELLI, "Scrittori d'Italia."

Beschitzi, bȧ-shĕt'see, (ELIAS,) a Jewish theologian, born at Adrianople about 1420, was surnamed THE BYZANTINE, from his residing at Constantinople. He published "The Mantle of Elias," esteemed a standard work by the Jews. Died in 1490.

See BARTOLOCCI, "Bibliotheca Latino-Hebraica."

Beseler, bä'zęh-lęr, (KARL GEORG CHRISTIAN,) a German jurist, born near Husum in 1809, became professor of law at Rostock in 1837.

Beseler, (WILHELM HARTWIG,) a German politician, a brother of the preceding, born in Oldenburg in 1806. He was an active promoter of the revolt of Sleswick and Holstein against Denmark in 1848.

Besenval, de, dęh bęh-zŏN'vȧl', (PIERRE VICTOR,) BARON, a Swiss officer, born at Soleure in 1722, entered the French service and attained the rank of lieutenant-general. His "Memoirs" (4 vols.) were published in 1805. Died in 1791.

See "Mémoires de M. le Baron de Besenval, écrits par lui-même," Paris, 1805.

Besenzi, bȧ-sen'zee, (PAOLO EMILIO,) an Italian painter, born at Reggio about 1624; died in 1666.

Besiers, bęh-ze-à', (MICHEL,) a French ecclesiastic, born at Bayeux in 1719, wrote a "History of the City of Bayeux," (1773.) Died in 1782.

Beskow, bês'kov, (BERNARD,) a Swedish poet and dramatist, born at Stockholm in 1796. His tragedy of "Torkel Knutsson," esteemed one of the best of Swedish plays, was translated into German and Danish by Oeh-

ā, ē, ī, ō, ū, ȳ, *long;* ȧ, ė, ȯ, same, less prolonged; ă, ĕ, ĭ, ŏ, ŭ, ў, *short;* ạ, ẹ, į, ọ, *obscure;* fär, fȧll, fȧt; mĕt; nŏt; gŏŏd; mŏŏn;

lenschläger, as well as the tragedies of "Hildegarde," "Gustaf Adolf i Tyskland," and others. He also wrote a collection of poems, and "Recollections of Travel," ("Vandrings-minnen.") In 1833 he was appointed marshal of the royal household, and subsequently became perpetual secretary of the Swedish Academy. He obtained the rare distinction of being made a doctor of philosophy by the University of Upsal in 1842.

See BROCKHAUS, "Conversations-Lexikon."

Besler, bĕs'lẹr, (BASIL,) a German botanist and pharmacist, born at Nuremberg in 1561, published several botanical works in Latin. The genus Beslera was named in his honour by Plumier. Died in 1629.

Besler, (MICHAEL ROBERT,) a German physician, nephew of the preceding, born at Nuremberg in 1607; died in 1661.

Besly, bả'le', (JEAN,) a French jurist and writer, born at Coulonges-les-Royaux, in Poitou, in 1572 ; died in 1644.

Besnard, bĕs'nȧr',(FRANÇOIS JOSEPH,) born at Buschweiler, in Alsace, in 1748, became first physician to Maximilian, Count Palatine. He introduced vaccination into Bavaria, and wrote on the abuse of mercury. Died in 1814.

Besnier, bả'ne-ả', (PIERRE,) a French Jesuit, born at Tours in 1648, wrote a "Discourse on the Science of Etymologies." Died in 1705.

Bes'ọ-dun [Lat. BESODU'NUS] or **Bes'tọn,** (JOHN,) a prior of the Carmelites at Lynn, in England, wrote a "Compendium of Moral Theology," (in Latin.) Died in 1428.

Besoigne, bẹh-swȧñ', (JÉRÔME,) a French Jansenist, born in Paris in 1686, wrote a "History of the Abbey of Port-Royal," (8 vols., 1756,) and other works. Died in 1763.

Besold, bä'zolt, or **Besolde,** bȧ-zol'dẹh, (CHRISTOPH,) a German jurist, and professor of law at Tübingen, where he was born in 1577. Died in 1638.

Besombes de Saint-Geniès, bẹh-zòmb' dẹh sȧN'-zhẹh-ne-ả', (PIERRE LOUIS,) a French *littérateur*, born at Cahors in 1719. Died in 1783.

Besozzi, bȧ-sot'see, (ALESSANDRO,) an Italian musician, born in 1700, was patronized by the King of Sardinia. His brothers, GIROLAMO, ANTONIO, and GAETANO, were distinguished musicians.

Besplas, de, dẹh bes'plȧ', (JOSEPH MARIE ANNE Gros—grȯ,) a French theologian, born at Castelnaudary in 1734, wrote an "Essay on Pulpit Eloquence," and other works. Died in 1783.

See QUÉRARD, "La France Littéraire."

Bessa, bả'sȧ', (PANCRACE,) a French painter of flowers and fruits, born in Paris in 1772 ; died after 1830.

Bessaraba, bĕs-sȧ'rȧ'bȧ, a powerful family, which gave a name to Bessarabia, a region comprised between the Pruth and the Dniester.

Bessaraba, (CONSTANTINE BRANCOVAN,) was elected vaivode in 1688, and became the secret agent of Leopold of Austria. In order to relieve himself from the Turkish yoke, he formed an alliance with Peter the Great about 1709. But he proved to be a treacherous ally in the war which Peter waged against the Turks in 1711. He was put to death, by order of the Sultan, in 1714.

See CANTEMIR, "History of the Ottoman Empire."

Bessaraba, (MATTHEW BRANCOVAN,) reigned over Wallachia from 1633 to 1654.

Bessaraba, (MICHAEL,) THE BRAVE, born about 1558, was elected vaivode in 1592. He was a warlike prince, and made himself master of Transylvania by conquest. He was assassinated in 1601.

Bessaraba, (MIRCE,) Vaivode of Wallachia, was a son of Rudolph II., and was elected in 1382. He waged war against the Turks, to whom he was forced to become tributary in 1393. Died in 1418.

Bessaraba, (RUDOLPH,) was the founder of the principality of Wallachia. Died in 1265.

Bes-sa'rĭ-on, (JOHN,) sometimes called **Basil,** a learned Greek cardinal, born at Trebizond about 1390. He was sent in 1438 by the emperor John Palæologus to the Council of Ferrara, to assist in effecting a union between the Greek and Latin Churches. He was created Archbishop of Siponto by Nicholas V., and in 1463 obtained the title of Patriarch of Constantinople from Pius II. He was a zealous promoter of Greek literature, and

translated into Latin the "Metaphysics" of Aristotle and the "Memorabilia" of Xenophon. Died in 1472.

See AUBERY, "Histoire des Cardinaux ;" A. BANDINI, "De Vita et Rebus gestis Bessarionis Cardinalis," 1777 ; O. RAGGI, "Commentario sulla Vita del Cardinale Bessarione," 1844.

Bessé, bả'sȧ', (GUILLAUME,) a French jurist and writer, born at Carcassonne, wrote a "History of the Dukes, Marquises, and Counts of Carcassonne," (1660.) Died in 1680.

Bessé, (PIERRE,) a doctor of the Sorbonne, born at Rosiers, in Limousin, was preacher to Louis XIII. and the Prince of Condé. He had a high reputation for eloquence, and published "The Christian Democritus," and other religious works. Died in 1639.

Bessé, de, dẹh bả'sȧ', (HENRI,) a French writer, was a member and secretary of the Academy of Inscriptions. He is the supposed author of an "Account of the Campaigns of Rocroi and Friburg in 1643 and 1644," (1673.) Died in 1693.

Bessé, de, (JOSEPH,) a French medical writer, born at Peyrusse, in Aveyron, about 1670. He practised in Paris, and published "Analytical Researches on the Structure of the Parts of the Human Body," (2 vols., 1701,) and other works. He died at an advanced age.

Bessel, bĕs'sẹl, (CHRISTIAN GEORG,) a German moralist, born at Minden, wrote in German a curious work, (1673,) which was translated into Latin with the title of the "Artificer of Political Fortune," ("Faber Fortunæ politicæ.")

Bessel, (FRIEDRICH WILHELM,) one of the greatest of modern astronomers, was born at Minden, Prussia, on the 22d of July, 1784. He served an apprenticeship in the counting-house of a merchant of Bremen for about seven years. Among his first scientific labours was the reduction of Harriott's observations on the comet of 1607, which he performed with success at the age of twenty. He was appointed assistant to Schröter at Lilienthal in 1806, and became director of a new observatory, built under his superintendence, at Königsberg, in 1811–12. He was also professor of astronomy in the university of that place. In 1818 he published an excellent work, entitled "Fundamenta Astronomiæ," deduced from the observations of J. Bradley. He undertook about 1837 the arduous task of ascertaining the annual parallax of a fixed star, 61 Cygni. The result which he obtained, and which is almost immeasurably small, $0''.374$, is generally received as the truth. Among his chief works are "Tabulæ Regiomontanæ," (1830,) "Determination of the Length of the Simple Seconds' Pendulum," (1837,) "Measure of the Distance of the Star 61 in the Constellation of Cygnus," (1839,) and "Astronomical Observations," (1841–42.) No observatory has contributed more during the present century to the improvement of every branch of astronomy than that of Königsberg under his direction. Bessel was appointed a privy councillor by the King of Prussia, and received several titles of honour. He was author of a great number of treatises published in the "Astronomische Nachrichten." In early life he married a daughter of Professor Hagen. Died in March, 1846.

See J. F. W. HERSCHEL, "Brief Notice of the Life and Discoveries of F. W. Bessel," 1847; C. T. ANGER, "Erinnerung an F. W. Bessels Leben und Wirken," 1846.

Bessel, von, fon bĕs'sẹl, (GOTTFRIED,) a German chronicler, born at Buchheim in 1672, became abbot of the monastery of Gottwich in 1714. He wrote a "History of Gottwich," in Latin. Died in 1749.

See ERSCH und GRUBER, "Allgemeine Encyklopaedie."

Bessényi, bĕsh'shän-yee, OF GALANTAI, (GEORGE,) a Hungarian *littérateur*, wrote several tragedies, and translated Pope's "Essay on Man." Died about 1810.

Besser, von, fon bĕs'sẹr, (JOHANN,) a German poet, born at Frauenburg in 1654, became counsellor to the Elector of Brandenburg at Berlin. He entered the service of Augustus, Elector of Saxony, after 1713. Died in 1729.

Bessières, bả'se-aiR', (JEAN BAPTISTE,) a distinguished French marshal, born near Cahors in 1768. He served in the campaigns of Italy, Egypt, and Austria, and was made a marshal of France, and grand officer of the legion of honour, in 1804. In 1805 he defeated the Russian army under Kootoosov, and greatly distinguished himsrlf at the battle of Austerlitz. Appointed, in 1808, to a command in Spain, he was chiefly instrumental by his victories in placing Joseph Bonaparte on the throne. He was soon after made Duke of Istria by Napoleon. In 1813 he obtained the chief command of all the cavalry, and, while reconnoitring on the morning before the battle of Lutzen, was killed by a shot from the enemy, the 1st of May, 1813.

See "Victoires et Conquêtes des Français;" C. MIRAMONT, "Vie de J. B. Bessières."

Bessin, bạ′sȧN′, (Dom GUILLAUME,) a French Benedictine monk, born near Evreux in 1654; died in 1736.

Besson, bạ′sŏN′, (ALEXANDRE,) a French Jacobin, born near Ornans about 1757, became a member of the National Convention, and of the Council of Five Hundred. Died in 1826.

Besson, (JACQUES,) a French mathematician and writer, born at Grenoble, became professor at Orléans in 1569. He invented several instruments.

See MORÉRI, "Dictionnaire Historique."

Besson, (JACQUES FRANÇOIS,) born in Ain in 1756. He became Bishop of Metz in 1824. Died in 1842.

See "Notice sur J. F. Besson," 1842.

Besson, (JOSEPH,) a French Jesuit, born at Carpentras in 1607, spent many years as a missionary in Syria. He published in 1660 a work entitled "Missions of the Jesuits in Syria." Died in 1691.

Besson, L'ABBÉ, born at Flumet, in Upper Faucigny, wrote "Memoirs towards the Ecclesiastical History of the Dioceses of Geneva, Tarentaise, Maurienne, etc." Died about 1780.

Bes′sus, [Gr. Βῆσσος,] a satrap of Bactriana, fought for Darius at Gaugamela, accompanied him in his retreat, and murdered him in 330 B.C. He was taken prisoner by the Macedonians and delivered to a brother of Darius, who put him to death.

Best, bĕst, (JEAN,) a French printer and engraver on wood, born at Toul in 1808. He executed illustrations for works published in Prussia, Austria, and other foreign countries, and obtained a medal of the first class at the Exposition of Paris in 1855.

Best, bĕst, (WILLEM,) a Dutch jurist and legal writer, born at Amersfort in 1683, became professor of civil law at Harderwick. Died in 1719.

Bestelmeier, bĕs′tĕl-mī′ẹr, (GEORG,) a German politician and magistrate, born at Schwabach in 1785.

Beston. See BESODUN, (JOHN.)

Bestoozhef or **Bestoujev**, bĕs-too′shĕf, written also **Bestoujef, Bestuschew**, and **Bestouchef**, (ALEXANDER,) a Russian novelist and soldier, born about 1795, was implicated in a conspiracy against the emperor in 1825, and exiled to Siberia. In 1830 he was permitted to join the Russian army, and fell in 1837 in an engagement with the Circassian mountaineers. He had published in 1823, conjointly with Ryleief, a literary journal entitled "The Polar Star." His romances of "Mullah Nur" and "Ammalath Beg" are highly esteemed by his countrymen, and have been translated into German.

See BROCKHAUS, "Conversations-Lexikon."

Bestoozhef, Bestoujev, or **Bestuschew**, (MICHAEL ALEXIS PETROVITCH,) a Russian statesman, born at Moscow in 1693. He enjoyed successively the favour of Peter the Great and the empresses Anna and Elizabeth, by the last of whom he was appointed grand chancellor of the empire. He negotiated important treaties with England, Denmark, and Sweden, and influenced the Russian government to espouse the cause of Austria in the Seven Years' war. In 1758 he was convicted of treason for having endeavoured to exclude the grand duke Peter from the throne, and was stripped of his titles and exiled. He was recalled in 1762 by Catherine II., who created him a field-marshal. He died in 1766. The invention of a chemical preparation called "Tinctura tonica nervina Bestuzewi" is attributed to Count Bestoozhef.

See MANSTEIN, "Histoire de Russie;" RULHIÈRE, "Histoire le l'Anarchie de Pologne."

Bestoozhef, Bestoujev, or **Bestuschew Riumin**, ḃès-too′shẹv re̩-u′min, (or re̩-u′meen′,) (MICHAEL,) a Russian officer, a relative of the preceding, was engaged in the conspiracy of 1825, having for its object the exter-

mination of the imperial family. He was executed in 1826, with three of his accomplices.

See BROCKHAUS, "Conversations-Lexikon."

Besuchet, bẹh-zü′shạ′, (JEAN CLAUDE,) a French physician, was born near Paris in 1790, published a "Treatise on Gastritis," (1837,) and a "History of Free-Masonry from its Introduction into France till 1829."

See QUÉRARD, "La France Littéraire."

Betanços, de, dȧ bȧ-tȧn′thŏs, or **Betanzos**, (DOMINGO,) a Spanish missionary, born at Leon. He visited Hayti about 1514, and afterwards resided in Mexico, where he laboured earnestly to convert the natives and save them from the tyranny of their rulers. He died in Spain in 1549.

See TERNAUX-COMPANS, "Pièces sur la Mexique."

Betanços, de, (JUAN,) a Spanish historian of the sixteenth century, visited the West Indies, of which he wrote an account, (still in manuscript.)

See ANTONIO, "Bibliotheca Hispana Nova."

Bétencourt, de, dẹh bȧ′tŏN′koor′, (PIERRE LOUIS JOSEPH,) a French Benedictine monk and antiquarian writer, born at Arras in 1743. Died in 1829.

Beth′am, (EDWARD,) an English clergyman, who gave two thousand pounds for a botanical garden at Cambridge, and founded a charity-school. Died in 1783.

Betham, (Sir WILLIAM,) an English antiquary and writer on genealogy, born in Suffolk in 1779. In 1812 he was appointed genealogist of the order of Saint Patrick, and soon after deputy-keeper of the records at Dublin. He wrote "On the Origin and History of the Constitution of England and the Early Parliaments of Ireland," (1834,) "On Parliamentary and Feudal Dignities," and "Etruscan Literature and Antiquities Investigated." He was foreign secretary of the Irish Academy, and Fellow of the Society of Antiquaries, London. Died in 1853.

See "London Quarterly Review" for June, 1845; "Blackwood's Magazine" for April, 1845.

Beth′ell, (Sir RICHARD,) an eminent English lawyer and reformer of law, born at Bradford, in Wiltshire, in 1800. He was appointed queen's counsel in 1840, and returned to Parliament for Aylesbury in 1851. About the end of 1852 he became solicitor-general. He was appointed attorney-general in 1856, resigned in 1858, and was reappointed in 1859. He became lord chancellor, with the title of Baron Westbury, in June, 1861, and resigned in July, 1865. He belonged to the Liberal party in politics.

See Foss, "The Judges of England," vol. ix.

Bethencourt or **Bettencourt**, bạ′tŏN′koor′, (JACQUES,) a French physician, who practised at Rouen, lived about 1520.

Bethencourt, (JEAN,) the conqueror of the Canary Islands, was chamberlain of Charles VI. of France. He died in 1425, and his "History of the First Discovery and Conquest of the Canaries in 1402" was published in 1630.

See "Histoire de la première Découverte et Conqueste des Canaries," Paris, 1630.

Bethencourt y Molina, de, dẹh bạ′tŏN′koor′ e mo′le′nȧ′, (AUGUSTIN,) a descendant of the preceding, was born in the island of Teneriffe in 1760. He studied engineering at Madrid, entered the Russian service in 1808, and executed many important public works. Died in 1826.

Béthisy, de, dẹh bȧ′te′ze′, (CHARLES,) COMTE, a French general, son of the following, born in 1770. He served in the royalist army, and in 1820 was created a peer of France, and lieutenant-general. Died in 1827.

Béthisy, de, (EUGÈNE EUSTACHE,) COMTE, a French general, nephew of Jean Laurent, noticed below, was born at Moutiers in 1739. He served under Condé in the campaigns of 1792–93, and, after the restoration, was made lieutenant-general. Died in 1823.

Béthisy, de, (JEAN LAURENT,) a French musician, born at Dijon in 1702, wrote an "Exposition of the Theory and Practice of Music," (1754.) Died about 1770.

Béthisy de Mézières, de, dẹh bȧ′te′ze′ dẹh mȧ′ze-air′, (HENRI BENOÎT JULES,) brother of Eugène Eustache, born in 1744, became Bishop of Uzès in 1780. Died in 1817.

ā, ē, ī, ō, ū, ȳ, *long;* ȧ, ė, ȯ, same, less prolonged; ă, ĕ, ĭ, ŏ, ŭ, ў, *short;* a̩, e̩, i̩, o̩, *obscure;* fär, fȧll, fȧt; mĕt; nŏt; gŏŏd; mōōn

Bethlen, bĕt′lẹn, (GABRIEL,) or **Bethlen-Gabor,** (gä′bor,) an able Magyar general and ruler, born in 1580, became Prince of Transylvania in 1613. He was a Protestant, a friend of religious liberty, and a patron of learning. Having, as commander of the oppressed Hungarians, defeated the emperor Ferdinand of Austria, he was elected King of Hungary in 1620 ; but he soon renounced or lost that kingdom. Died in 1629.

See HORANYI, " Memoria Hungarorum."

Bethlen-Bethlen, bĕt′lẹn-bĕt′lẹn, (JOHN,) COUNT, born in 1613, became Chancellor of Transylvania. He wrote a " History of Transylvania from 1629 to 1663," (in Latin.) Died in 1687.

Bethlen-Bethlen, von, fon bĕt′lẹn bĕt′lẹn, (NICOLAS,) COUNT, a German chronicler, son of the preceding, was born in 1642 ; died in 1716.

Bethlen-Bethlen, von, (WOLFGANG,) COUNT, Chancellor of Transylvania, born in 1648, wrote, in Latin, a " History of Transylvania from 1526 to 1609." Died in 1679.

Bethmann, bāt′män, (FREDERIKE AUGUSTE CONRADINE,) a celebrated German actress, originally named FLITTNER, born at Gotha in 1766 ; died in 1814.

Bethmann, (SIMON MORITZ,) a celebrated German banker and philanthropist, born in 1768, was one of the firm of Bethmann Brothers, at Frankfort-on-the-Main. He was ennobled by the emperor Francis of Austria. Died in 1826.

Bethmann-Hollweg, von, fon bāt′män hol′wĕg, (MORITZ AUGUST,) a German jurist and writer, born at Frankfort-on-the-Main in 1795. He studied under Savigny at Berlin, where he became professor of civil law, and, in 1827, rector of the university.

See BROCKHAUS, " Conversations-Lexikon."

Bethmont, bĕt′môN′, (EUGÈNE,) a French lawyer, born in Paris in 1804, was elected to the Chamber of Deputies in 1846, and was afterwards appointed minister of justice.

Bethune. See BEATON.

Béthune. See SULLY.

Bethune, bĕt′ūn or bā′ton, (ALEXANDER,) a Scottish writer, born in Fifeshire in 1804, was a poor peasant. In conjunction with his brother John, he wrote " Tales and Sketches of the Scottish Peasantry." Died in 1843. His brother JOHN was born in 1810 ; died in 1839.

Béthune, (ARMAND JOSEPH.) See CHAROST.

Bethune, [see next article,] (DIVIE,) a philanthropist, born at Dingwall, Scotland, in 1771, came to America in 1792, and settled in New York as a merchant. One-tenth of his income was devoted to the cause of religion. He supported Sunday-schools, and imported Bibles for distribution ; he printed at his own expense ten thousand tracts, many of which he distributed with his own hand. Died in 1824.

See A. R. VAN NEST, " Memoir of the Rev. Dr. Geo. W. Bethune," New York, 1867.

Bethune, bẹ-thoon′,* (GEORGE W.,) D.D., an American divine, scholar, and poet, a son of the preceding, was born in the city of New York in 1805. He commenced his education at Columbia College, in his native city, and afterwards graduated at Dickinson College, in Pennsylvania. He studied theology at Princeton, and in 1828 became the pastor of a Dutch Reformed church at Rhinebeck, New York. Two or three years afterwards, he removed to Utica. In 1834 he was invited to Philadelphia, where he became pastor of the First Dutch Reformed Church of that city. He was not only an eloquent preacher, but an accomplished scholar and an able and successful public lecturer. In 1849 he removed to Brooklyn, where he continued to reside, for the most part, during the remainder of his life. The anxieties which he felt for his country at the commencement of the civil war in 1861, preyed upon his health, on account of which he visited Europe in the autumn of that year. After passing some time in France, he arrived at Florence in the spring of 1862. Having, while there, imprudently accepted an invitation to preach in public, he was soon after attacked

* The name BETHUNE is the same in its origin as BEATON, BEATOUN, and BETTON ; and it appears, from the Rev. A. Van Nest's "Memoir," that the name of Dr. Bethune's father was pronounced in Scotland precisely like BEATON,—*i.e.* bā′ton or bet′ton.

with cerebral symptoms, and died of apoplexy the following night, April 27, 1862. Dr. Bethune was distinguished for his fine culture, his genial spirit, and his vivid appreciation of the varied beauties of nature. Among his religious publications are three volumes, entitled respectively " The Fruit of the Spirit," " The History of a Penitent," and " Early Lost, Early Saved." He also edited a volume of " British Female Poets," and Walton's "Complete Angler," (1847,) to which he prefixed a valuable bibliographical preface. A collection of his poems, entitled " Lays of Love and Faith, with other Fugitive Poems," appeared in 1848. A volume of his lectures before various literary associations and popular assemblies was published in New York in 1850.

See A. R. VAN NEST's " Memoir of the Rev. Dr. Geo. W. Bethune," New York, 1867, and " Obituary Notice of Dr. Geo. W. Bethune," read before the American Philosophical Society, by DR. ROBLEY DUNGLISON, October, 1862.

Bethune, (JOHN DRINKWATER,) COLONEL, an English officer, born about 1762. He wrote a " History of the Late Siege of Gibraltar," (1785.) Died in 1844.

Bethune, (JOHN ELLIOT DRINKWATER,) an English gentleman, born in 1801, was appointed in 1848 president of the " Council of Education" in India, where he first established schools for the education of native females. Died in 1851.

Béthune, bā′tün′, (QUESNES or COESNES, kwĕn,) a French poet, accompanied Baldwin, Count of Flanders, to Palestine, about 1190.

Béthune, de, dẹh bā′tün′, (HIPPOLYTE,) a benevolent French prelate, grandson of Philippe, noticed below, born in 1647. He became Bishop of Verdun about 1680, and founded a hospital. Died in 1720.

Béthune, de, (PHILIPPE,) Count of Selles and Charost, a French diplomatist and soldier, served under Henry IV. in his principal campaigns. He was employed in several important embassies, and concluded the treaty of Pavía in 1619. Died in 1649.

See MORÉRI, " Dictionnaire Historique."

Be′tis or **Ba′tis,** called also **Bab-e-mes′sēs,** an officer of King Darius, defended Gaza bravely against Alexander the Great ; but that place was at length taken by an assault, in which Betis was killed.

Beton, (CARDINAL.) See BEATON.

Betourné, bẹh-toor′nā′, (AMBROISE,) a French poet, born at Caen in 1795. He wrote fables, ballads, and elegies, some of which were translated into various languages. Died in 1835.

Betta dal Toldo, bet′tä däl tol′do, (FRANCESCO,) an Italian jurist, born at Roveredo in 1526 ; died in 1599.

Bette d'Etienville, bạt dā′te-âN′vĕl′, (JEAN CHARLES VINCENT,) a French *littérateur,* born at Saint-Omer in 1759. He was implicated in some of the intrigues of the notorious Madame La Motte-Valois, for which he was imprisoned for a short time. He published " The Effects of Prejudice," (1788,) and other works. Died in Paris in 1830.

Bettelini, bĕt-tà-lee′nee, (PIETRO,) an Italian engraver, born at Lugano in 1763, was a pupil of Bartolozzi. Among his master-pieces are an " Assumption" after Guido Reni, and an " Ecce Homo" after Correggio. He also engraved several of the works of Thorwaldsen.

See NAGLER, " Neues Allgemeines Künstler-Lexikon."

Bettencourt. See BETHENCOURT.

Bet′tẹr-tọn, (THOMAS,) an English dramatist, and one of the most popular actors of his time, born in Westminster, London, in 1635. He excelled in the rôles of Macbeth, Othello, and Hamlet, and was commended by Addison, Dryden, and Pope. Died in 1710.

See CHARLES GILDON, " Life of T. Betterton," 1710.

Betti, bet′tee, (BIAGIO,) an Italian painter, born near Pistoia in 1545, became a monk in 1572 ; died in 1615.

Betti, (SIGISMONDO,) a Florentine painter and skilful designer, flourished about 1750.

Betti, (ZACCARIA,) an Italian poet, born at Verona in 1732, wrote a poem entitled " The Silk-Worm," (" Del Baco da Seta.") Died in 1788.

See B. DEL BENE, " Elogio del Conte Z. Betti," 1790.

Bettine or **Bettina.** See ARNIM.

Bettinelli, bĕt-te-nel′lee, (SAVERIO,) an Italian Jesuit and author, born at Mantua in 1718. He wrote tragedies, poems, and other works ; but his reputation is chiefly founded on an essay on the "Renaissance of Literature and Art in Italy," ("Risorgimento negli Studj nelle Arti," etc., 2 vols., 1775.) He published his collected works, in twenty-four volumes, 1801. Died in 1808.

See TIPALDO, "Biografia degli Italiani illustri;" G. F. NAPIONE, "Vita de.l' Abate S. Bettinelli," 1809.

Betting de Lancastel, bȧ'tȧN' dęh lôN'kȧs'tĕl', a French publicist, born in the department of Lower Rhine in 1798, wrote "Considerations on the State of 'he Jews in Christian Society," (1824.)

Bettini, bĕt-tee'nee, (ANTONIO,) Bishop of Foligno, born at Sienna in 1396, wrote a religious work entitled ' Il Monte-Santo di Dio," (1477,) chiefly remarkable for containing the first copper-plate engravings. Died in 1487.

See PANZER, "Annales Typographici."

Bettini, (DOMENICO,) a skilful Italian painter of flowers and fruits, born at Florence in 1644, was a pupil of Mario Nuzzi. Died at Bologna in 1705.

See LANZI, "History of Painting in Italy."

Bettini, (MARIO,) an Italian Jesuit and writer, born at Bologna in 1582 ; died in 1657.

Bettkober, bĕt'ko-bęr,(CHRISTIAN HEINRICH FRIEDRICH,) a German sculptor, born in Berlin in 1746 ; died about 1822.

Bettoni, bĕt-to'nee, (CARLO,) COUNT, an Italian agricultural writer, born at Bugliaco, near Lake Garda, in 1735 ; died in 1786.

See F. SOAVE, "Memorie intorno alla Vita del Conte Bettoni."

Bettoni, (NICCOLÒ,) a learned Italian printer and writer, lived about 1800-20. He published a complete edition of " Euripides," and Alfieri's tragedy of "Alceste," (1807.)

Betts, bĕts, (JOHN,) born at Winchester about 1620, studied at Oxford, and became physician to Charles II.

Bet'ty̆, (WILLIAM HENRY WEST,) a precocious English actor, generally called "the young Roscius," born at Shrewsbury in 1791. Before the age of thirteen he performed with unprecedented success in London, Edinburgh, and Cork. Having made a large fortune, he retired from the stage in 1807. He appeared again in public in 1812 ; but, as the popular mania had subsided, he was received without enthusiasm.

Betuleius, bȧ-too-li'ŭs, (SIXTUS,) a German philologist, born at Memmingen, in 1500, was professor of philosophy and belles-lettres at Augsburg. Died in 1554.

Betussi, bȧ-toos'see, (GIUSEPPE,) an Italian *littérateur,* born at Bassano about 1500.

Beuchot,buh'sho',(ADRIEN JEAN QUENTIN,)a French bibliographer, born in Paris in 1773. He wrote many articles for the "Biographie Universelle," and published a new edition of Bayle's Dictionary, (16 vols., 1821,) and an edition of Voltaire's works, (72 vols., 1827-33,) which is said to be the most complete and valuable that has been issued. Died in 1851.

Beudant, buh'dôN', (FRANÇOIS SULPICE,) an eminent French mineralogist and natural philosopher, born in Paris in September, 1787. He explored the minerals of Hungary at the public expense in 1818, and became professor of mineralogy in the Faculty of Sciences of Paris about 1820. He published "Researches on the Causes which determine the Variations of Crystalline Forms of the same Mineral Substance," (1818,) an important work on the geology and mineralogy of Hungary, (3 vols., 1822,) an excellent "Elementary Treatise on Mineralogy," (2d edition, 1831,) and other works. He became a member of the Academy of Sciences in 1824, and was inspector-general of the University. Died in Paris in 1852.

See QUÉRARD, "La Littérature Contemporaine."

Beuf, Le. See LE BEUF.

Beughem, van, vȧn buh'hĕm, (CHARLES ANTOINE FRANÇOIS DE PAULE,) a Flemish writer and Latin poet, born at Brussels in 1744 ; died in 1820.

Beugnot, de, dęh bun'yo', (ARTHUR AUGUSTE,) COMTE, an able French writer and liberal politician, born at Bar-sur-Aube in 1797, was a son of Jacques Claude. His most important work is a "History of the Destruction of Paganism in the West," (2 vols., 1835.) He was elected a member of the Academy of Inscriptions about 1832, became a peer of France in 1841, and a mem-

ber of the Legislative Assembly in 1849. He was an eminent advocate of the freedom of education in that body.

See "London Quarterly Review" for September, 1836.

Beugnot, de, (JACQUES CLAUDE,) COMTE, a French statesman, born at Bar-sur-Aube in 1761. As a member of the Legislative Assembly, (1791,) he was conspicuous for his opposition to the Jacobins. In 1807 he took part in the organization of the kingdom of Westphalia, and became minister of finance under Jerome Bonaparte. He was appointed minister of the interior under the provisional government, (1814,) and director-general of police under Louis XVIII. He acted as minister of the marine for a short time in 1815. Died in 1835. The memoirs of Comte Beugnot have been published by his grandson, Albert Beugnot, in two volumes, Paris, 1866.

See "Edinburgh Review" for April, 1867.

Beuil, de, dęh buI, (JEAN,) a French warrior, born in Touraine in 1346, had a high command in the army, and gained some victories. He was killed at Agincourt in 1415.

Beuil, de, (JEAN,) a son of the preceding, commanded with success in many actions between 1420 and 1450, and was called "the Scourge of the English." Died in 1470.

Beukels, buh'kęls, (WILLEM,) a Dutch fisherman, to whom Charles V. erected a statue for having discovered the method of preserving herrings. Born in 1397 ; died in 1449.

Beulan, bu'lan, [Lat. BEULA'NUS,] an English writer, was contemporary with Saint Gregory the Great. He wrote a Latin work "On the Genealogies of Nations."

See MORÉRI, "Dictionnaire Historique."

Beumler, boim'lęr, (MARKUS,) a Swiss scholar and Protestant theologian, born in the canton of Zurich in 1555. He made translations from Plutarch and Demosthenes. Died in 1611.

Beurée, buh'rȧ', (DENIS,) a French diplomatist in the service of Sweden, was preceptor to Prince Eric, son of Gustavus Vasa. After the accession of Eric to the throne, he was ennobled and made a senator ; but he was subsequently put to death by order of the king, who was insane at the time, (1567.)

Beurer, boi'ręr, (JOHANN AMBROSIUS,) a German naturalist and physician, born at Nuremberg in 1716, was a contributor to the "Opera Botanica" of Conrad Gesner. Died in 1754.

Beurmann, de, dęh bur'môn', (PAIS pȧ) ERNEST,) a French general, born at Strasburg in 1775 ; died in 1835.

Beurnonville, de, dęh bur'nòn'vĕl', (PIERRE DE RUEL,) MARQUIS, a French marshal, born at Champignolle in 1752. He served under Dumouriez in 1792, became successively minister of war, (1793,) commander-in-chief of the army of the North, (1796,) a peer and minister of state under Louis XVIII., (1814,) marshal of France, and commander of the order of Saint Louis, (1816.) Died in 1821.

See "Victoires et Conquêtes des Français."

Beurrier, buh're-ȧ', (LOUIS,) a French monk of the order of the Celestines, born at Chartres, wrote a "History of the Monastery of the Celestines in Paris," (1634.) Died in 1645.

Beurrier, (PAUL,) a French theologian, born in 1610, was Abbot of Sainte-Geneviève. Died in 1696.

Beurrier, (VINCENT TOUSSAINT,) a French preacher and ecclesiastical writer, born at Vannes in 1715 ; died in 1782.

Beurs, burs, (WILLEM,) a Dutch painter of landscapes and portraits, was born at Dort in 1656 ; died near the close of the seventeenth century.

Beust, von, fon boist, (FRIEDRICH CONSTANTIN,) a German geologist, born at Dresden in 1806, wrote, besides other works, a "Critique on Werner's Theory of Veins," (1840.) He became engineer-in-chief of mines in 1851.

Beust, von, (FRIEDRICH FERDINAND,) BARON, an eminent German statesman, brother of the preceding, born at Dresden in 1809. He became minister of foreign affairs in Saxony in February, 1849. In October, 1866, he was appointed minister of foreign affairs (*i.e.* prime minister) of the Austrian Empire. He acquired a high reputation in this position,and effected important changes, which promoted civil and religious liberty, and which

ā, ē, ī, ō, ū, y̆, *long;* ȧ, ė, ò, same, less prolonged; ă, ĕ, ĭ, ŏ, ŭ, y̆, *short;* ạ, ę, į, ǫ, *obscure;* fär, fȧll, fȧt; mêt; nŏt; gŏŏd; mōŏn,

were denounced by the pope in an allocution in the summer of 1868.

Beuth, boit, (PETER CHRISTIAN WILHELM,)•born at Cleves in 1781, became a member of the Prussian council of state.

Beuther, boi'tẹr, sometimes written **Beuthere,** (MICHAEL,) a German theologian and scholar, born at Carlstadt in 1522, studied under Luther and Melanchthon. He wrote "Commentaries on Livy" and other classics, and "Historical and Chronographical Observations," (in Latin.) Died in 1587.

Beutler, boit'lẹr, (CLÉMENT,) a Swiss landscape-painter of great merit, lived in the eighteenth century. Among his master-pieces are "The Garden of Eden," and "Saint Anthony preaching on the Sea-Shore."

Beutler, boit'lẹr, (JOHANN HEINRICH CHRISTIAN,) a German writer, born at Suhl, in Franconia, in 1750; died about 1835.

Beuve, (SAINTE.) See SAINTE-BEUVE.

Beuvelet, buv'lá', (MATHIEU,) a French ecclesiastic and devotional writer, born near Soissons about 1500.

Bev'an, (JOSEPH GURNEY,) a member of the Society of Friends, born in London in 1753, was a chemist and druggist. He published a "Life of Robert Barclay," (1802,) and a "Life of the Apostle Paul," (1807,) which is commended by Horne and Orme. Died in 1814.

Bever. See BEAVER.

Be'vẹr, (THOMAS,) an English jurist and scholar, born in Berkshire in 1725. He published a "History of the Legal Polity of the Roman State," (1781.) Died in 1781.

Beverense, bâ-vâ-rên'sâ, (ANTONIO,) an Italian painter, worked in Venice about 1670.

Bev'ẹr-idge, (WILLIAM,) an eminent English prelate and Orientalist, born at Barrow, in Leicestershire, about 1637. He published in 1658 a Latin treatise on the Hebrew, Chaldee, Syriac, Arabic, and Samaritan languages. On the revolution of 1688 he became chaplain to William and Mary, and in 1704 Bishop of Saint Asaph. Among his principal writings are a "Treatise on Chronology," (1669,) and a valuable work on the "Canons of the Greek Church," (1672,) both in Latin; also "Private Thoughts upon Religion," (1709,) and other esteemed devotional treatises. Died in 1708.

See a "Memoir of Bishop Beveridge," by THOMAS H. HORNE, prefixed to Beveridge's Works, in 9 vols., 1824.

Beverini, bâ-vâ-ree'nee, (BARTOLOMMEO,) an Italian ecclesiastic and *littérateur,* born at Lucca in 1629; died in 1686.

Beverland, bêv'ẹr-lânt, (ADRIANUS,) a Dutch writer and classical scholar, born at Middelburg in 1654. He was fined by the University of Leyden, and afterwards banished from Utrecht, on account of the obscenity and impiety of his works. Died in 1712.

See NICÉRON, "Mémoires."

Bev'ẹr-ley, [Lat. BEVERLA'CIUS,] (JOHN OF,) one of the most learned men of his time, was the tutor of the Venerable Bede. He became Archbishop of York in 687, and in 704 founded at Beverley a college for secular priests. He wrote several theological works, in Latin. Died in 721.

See PITS, "De Scriptoribus Angliæ;" "Biographia Britannica."

Beverley, (JOHN OF,) an English Carmelite monk, was professor of divinity at Oxford about 1390.

Bev'ẹr-lỹ, (ROBERT,) an American writer, born in Virginia. He was clerk of the Council about 1697, and wrote a "History of the Present State of Virginia," (1705.) Died in 1716.

Bevern, bâ'vêrn, (AUGUST WILHELM,) a German general, born at Brunswick in 1715, served in the Seven Years' war. Died in 1782.

Beverningk, van, vản bâ'vẹr-nink', or **Beverning,** (HIERON,) a Dutch statesman, born at Gouda in 1614, was called THE PACIFICATOR, from his successful negotiations. He became curator of the University of Leyden, and contributed greatly to promote the study of botany and other sciences. He first introduced into Europe the Tropæolum majus, or Nasturtium. Died in 1690.

See G. D. J. SCHOTEL, "Jets over H. van Beverning," 1847; BAYLE, "Historical and Critical Dictionary."

Beverwyck, van, vản bâ'vẹr-wĭk', [Lat. BEVEROVI'-

CIUS,] (JAN,) a Dutch physician and writer, born in 1594 at Dort, where he practised and taught medicine. Died in 1647.

Bevilacqua, bâ-vĕ-lâ'kwâ, (AMBROGIO,) a Milanese painter, flourished about 1480.

See LANZI, "History of Painting in Italy."

Bevilaqua or **Bevilagua.** See SALIMBENI.

Bev'in, (ELWAY,) an English musician and composer under the reigns of Queen Elizabeth and King James, became royal chapel-master, and organist of the Bristol Cathedral. He wrote "A Briefe and Short Instruction of the Art of Musicke," (1631.)

See FÉTIS, "Biographie Universelle des Musiciens."

Bev'is, an English astronomer, and secretary of the Royal Society, born in 1696. He assisted in publishing the tables of Halley, and was the inventor of a circular microscope. Died in 1771.

Bévy, bâ've', (Dom CHARLES JOSEPH,) a French Benedictine monk, born near Orléans in 1738, was royal historiographer for Flanders and Hainault. He wrote, among other works, a "History of the Nobility of the Gauls, French, and other European Nations," (1791.) He was a Fellow of the Royal Society of London. Died in 1830.

See QUÉRARD, "La France Littéraire."

Bewick, bū'ik, (JOHN,) an English artist, born in 1760, was a brother and pupil of Thomas, noticed below. He produced some of the designs of the "History of Quadrupeds," and aided his brother in the illustration of other works. Died in 1795.

Bewick, (THOMAS,) an English artist, distinguished for his skill in wood-engraving, was born near Newcastle-upon-Tyne in 1753. He studied under Beilby, by whom he was employed to engrave the diagrams of Hutton's "Treatise on Mensuration," (1770.) Encouraged by the success of this work, he furnished illustrations to Gay's "Fables," for one of which, "The Old Hound," he obtained the premium offered by the Society of Arts for the best wood-engraving. In 1790 he published, conjointly with Mr. Beilby, a "General History of Quadrupeds," for which his brother John furnished a part of the designs. His "History of British Birds," esteemed his greatest work, came out in 1804, in two volumes. He also illustrated Goldsmith's "Traveller" and "Deserted Village," the "Fables of Æsop," and other works. Died in 1828.

See STRUTT, "Dictionary of Engravers;" "Pursuit of Knowledge under Difficulties," vol. ii., 1839; "Blackwood's Magazine" for July, 1825.

Bexley, LORD. See VANSITTART.

Béxon, bạ'sòn', (GABRIEL LÉOPOLD CHARLES AMÉ,) a French ecclesiastic and naturalist, born at Remiremont in 1748, was a friend of Count de Buffon, whom he aided in his work on natural history. He published several treatises on agriculture and natural history, and a "History of Lorraine," (1 vol., 1777, unfinished.) Died in 1784.

Béxon, (SCIPION JÉRÔME,) a French jurist and legal writer, brother of the preceding, born at Remiremont in 1753, was charged in 1806 by the King of Bavaria to draw up a criminal code for his states. Died in 1822.

See "Edinburgh Review" for October, 1809.

Beyer or **Beier,** bī'ẹr, (ADOLPH,) a German mineralogist, lived in Saxony; died in 1768.

Beyer or **Beier,** (AUGUST,) a philologist and minister, born in Saxony in 1707, published several bibliographical works. Died in 1741.

Beyer, (GEORG,) a German jurist, born at Leipsic in 1665; died in 1714.

Beyerlinck or **Beierlynck,** bī'ẹr-lĭnk', (LAURENS,) born at Antwerp in 1578, was canon of the cathedral in his native city. He wrote "The Great Theatre of Human Life," (7 vols.,) and other works, (in Latin.) Died in 1627.

Beygtash or **Beygtach,** bâg'tâsh' or bĕg'tâsh', written also **Bektasch** or **Bektach,** HAJI, (HADJI,) or VELY, (*i.e.* the "Saint,") a Turkish Mussulman, was the founder of an order of dervishes called by his name. Being employed by Amurath I. to bless the standard of his militia, he gave them the name of Yeni-Shery, or "new soldiers," which is the origin of the word Janissary. Died about 1368.

See VON HAMMER, "Geschichte des Osmanischen Reichs."

ɛ as *k;* ç as *s;* ḡ *hard;* ġ as *j;* G, H, K, *guttural;* N, *nasal;* R, *trilled;* s̄ as *z;* th as in *this.* (☞See Explanations, p. 23.)

Beyle, bȧl, (MARIE HENRI,) a popular and versatile French *littérateur*, known also by the pseudonym of STENDHAL, born at Grenoble in 1783. Among his principal works are a "History of Painting in Italy," (2 vols., 1817;) "Lives of Haydn, Mozart, and Metastasio," (1817;) "Rome, Naples, and Florence in 1817;" "Life of Rossini," (1824;) "Memoirs of a Tourist," (1838;) and the romances of "The Carthusian Nun of Parma," (" La Chartreuse de Parme," 1839,) and " Le Rouge et le Noir." His life was adventurous, and diversified by various pursuits. He became intendant of the domains of the emperor Napoleon at Brunswick in 1806, and entered the Council of State as auditor in 1810. He passed seven years at Milan, (1814–21,) and was appointed consul at Civita Vecchia about 1830. Died in Paris in 1842.

See COULOMB, "Notice sur la Vie de M. H. Beyle," 1845; HONORÉ DE BALZAC, "Études sur M. Beyle;" "Edinburgh Review" for January, 1856.

Beyma, van, vȧn bī'mä, (JULIUS,) a Dutch jurist, born about 1539, became successively professor of law at Wittenberg, Leyden, and Franeker. Died in 1598.

Beyme, bī'meh, (KARL FRIEDRICH,) COUNT, a Prussian statesman, born at Königsberg in 1765 ; died in 1838.

Beyrich, bī'riK, (HEINRICH ERNST,) a German geologist, born in Berlin in 1815.

Beys, bȧ, (GILLES,) a French printer ; died in 1593.

Beys, de, deh bȧ, (CHARLES,) a French poet and dramatist, born in Paris in 1610 ; died in 1659.

Beysser, bȧ'sȧ', (JEAN MICHEL,) a French republican general, born at Ribeauvillé, in Alsace, in 1734, distinguished himself in the war of La Vendée. He was executed in 1794, on a charge of favouring the royalists.

Beytz, bīts, (JOSEPH FRANCIS,) BARON OF, a Belgian magistrate, born at Bruges, became, after the union of Belgium with France, a member of the Council of Five Hundred. Died in 1832.

Be'za, [Fr. DE BÈZE, deh bȧz, sometimes written Besze,] (THEODORE,) a celebrated Calvinistic theologian and scholar, was born at Vezelay, in Burgundy, on the 24th of June, 1519. He studied the classics under Melchior Wolmar, professor in the University of Bourges, and subsequently devoted himself to literary pursuits in Paris. Having abjured Catholicism in 1548, he was soon after appointed professor of Greek at Lausanne. He published in 1554 a treatise in defence of the execution of Servetus, entitled "De Hæreticis a Civili Magistratu puniendis." In 1556 he completed his translation of the New Testament into Latin, and in 1559 removed to Geneva, where, through the influence of Calvin, he was appointed rector of the university. On the death of Calvin, in 1564, Beza succeeded him as professor of theology. He died in 1605. He was the author of a "Life of Calvin," "Ecclesiastical History of the Reformed Churches in France from 1521 to 1563," (3 vols., 1580,) and several controversial works. He was profoundly versed in ancient literature, and was one of those in France who contributed most to the great movement of the *renaissance*.

See BOLZEC, "Histoire de la Vie de Théodore de Bèze," 1577; TAILLEPIED, "Vie de T. de Bèze," 1577 ; LA FAY, "De Vita et Obitu T. Bezæ," 1606; VEGA, "De Vita et Miraculis Lutheri, Calvini et Bezæ," 1646; ZIRGENBEIN, "Leben Calvins und Bezas," 1789; SCHLOSSER, "Leben des The. Beza," 1809.

Bézard, bȧ'zȧR', (LÉON LOUIS,) a French painter, born at Toulon in 1800. He painted historical and religious subjects, and gained a first medal in 1836.

Bezborodko. See BESBORODKO.

Bèze. See BEZA.

Beziers, (MICHAEL.) See BESIERS.

Bezons, de, deh beh-zòN', (CLAUDE Bazin—bä'zȧN',) SEIGNEUR, a French magistrate and writer, born in Paris in 1617, succeeded Chancellor Séguier in the French Academy in 1643. Died in 1684.

Bezons, de, (JACQUES BAZIN,) a French marshal, son of Claude, born in 1646, served under Turenne, in Holland, in 1672, and subsequently in the war of the Spanish succession. He became a member of the Council of Regency on the death of Louis XIV. Died in Paris in 1733.

Bezout, beh-zoo', (ÉTIENNE,) a French mathematician, born at Nemours in 1730. He wrote a "Complete Course of Mathematics, for the Use of the Marine, the Artillery, and the Pupils of the Polytechnic School," (6 vols., 1780.) Died in Paris in 1783.

Bezzi, bět'see, (GIOVANNI FRANCESCO,) an Italian painter, born at Bologna about 1500; died in 1571.

Bezzuoli, bět-soo-o'lee,(GIUSEPPE,) an Italian painter, born at Florence in 1784. Among his best works are "The Baptism of Clovis," and "The Entrance of Charles VIII. into Florence."

Bhairȧvȧ, b'hī'rạ-vạ, [a Sanscrit word signifying "terror ;" also "terrible,"] one of the many appellations applied to Siva. It is also the name of one of Siva's sons, who is said to be chiefly worshipped among the Mahrattas.

See MOOR'S "Hindu Pantheon."

Bhȧrȧtȧ-Muni (or -Mouni,) b'hȧr'ạ-tạ mōō'nǐ, [Hindoo pron. b'hŭr'ạ-tạ mōō'nǐ,] sometimes written Bharatu-Wouni, an ancient Hindoo writer and sage, commonly regarded as the inventor of the drama.

Bhȧrȧvi, b'hȧ'rạ-vǐ, a Hindoo poet, author of a poem called "Kîrâtârjuniya."

Bhȧr'trǐ-Hȧr'ǐ, [Hindoo pron. b'hŭr'trǐ hŭr'ǐ,] a Hindoo poet, supposed to have been a brother of King Vikramâditya, wrote, it is said, a grammatical poem entitled "Kârikâ," (or "Câricâ.") Another poet of the same name wrote a poem on Rama, called "Bhatticâvya."

Bhȧt'tȧ Nȧrȧ'yȧnȧ, [Hindoo pron. b'hŭt'tạ nȧ-rȧ'-yạ-nạ,] a Hindoo dramatist, supposed to have lived between 800 and 1000 A.D.

Bhȧv'ȧ-bhȧ'tǐ, [Hindoo pron. b'hŭv-ạ-b'hoo'tǐ,] written also Bhavabhouti, a Hindoo poet of the eighth century, wrote a popular drama, entitled the "Loves of Mâlatî and Mâdhava."

Bhȧvȧnî, one of the names of PȦRVATî, which see.

Bhrǐgu, b'hRǐg'ōō, a famous sage or demigod of the Hindoo mythology, was, according to one account, the son of Brahma, according to another, of Varuna ; but it is stated in the "Institutes of Manu" that Manu produced "ten lords of created beings," among which lords Bhrigu is numbered. (Chap. i., v. 32–35.) According to the Sivapurâna, Bhrigu was the father of Marîchi, who was the father of Kâsyapa.

See MOOR'S "Hindu Pantheon."

Biacca, be-ȧk'kä, (FRANCESCO MARIA,) an Italian *littérateur* and ecclesiastic, born at Parma in 1673, translated the poems of Catullus and Statius. Died in 1735.

Biagi, be-ä'jee, (CLEMENZO,) an Italian antiquary, born at Cremona in 1740, published several works. Died at Milan in 1804.

Biagi, (GIOVANNI MARIA,) an Italian poet and priest, born at Roveredo in 1724 ; died in 1777.

Biagioli, be-â-jo'lee, or Biascioli, be-â-sho'lee, (NICCOLÒ GIOSAFATTE,) an Italian *littérateur*, born at Vezzano, near Genoa, in 1768, published an "Elementary Italian Grammar." In 1799 he was exiled on account of his liberal opinions, and became a resident of Paris, where he taught Italian. He edited Dante's works, (3 vols., 1818,) and Petrarch's works, (3 vols., 1821.) Died in 1830.

Bialobocki, be-â-lo-bot'skee, (JOHN,) a Polish poet of the seventeenth century.

Biamonti, be-â-mon'tee, (GIUSEPPE LUIGI,) an Italian *littérateur*, born at Vintimiglia in 1730, translated into Italian prose the works of Sophocles, Homer's "Iliad," and the "Odes" of Pindar, and wrote several tragedies. He was professor of eloquence at Bologna and at Turin. Died at Milan in 1824.

Bianca Capello. See CAPELLO.

Biancani, be-ân-kä'nee, (GIUSEPPE,) an Italian mathematician and Jesuit, born at Bologna in 1566; died in 1624.

Biancardo, be-ân-kaR'do, (UGOLETTO,) an Italian general, lived about 1370.

Bianchi, be-ân'kee, (ANTONIO,) an Italian poet and gondolier of Venice, lived about 1760. He wrote an epic poem entitled "Il Davide," (1751,) which is highly praised.

Bianchi, (BRIGIDA,) an Italian dramatist, lived about 1650. She wrote several comedies under the name of AURELIA.

Bianchi, (FEDERIGO,) an Italian painter, born at Milan about 1590. According to the "Nouvelle Biographie Générale," he was one of the best Milanese masters of the seventeenth century.

See LANZI, "History of Painting in Italy."

Bianchi, (FRANCESCO,) an Italian composer of operas, born at Cremona in 1752; died in 1811.

Bianchi, (FRANCESCO FERRARI,) sometimes called IL FRARI, an Italian painter, born at Módena in 1447, is said to have been the teacher of Correggio. He was a good colorist. Died in 1510.

Bianchi, [Lat. BLAN'CUS or PLAN'CUS,] (GIOVANNI,) an Italian savant, born at Rimini in 1693, became professor of anatomy at Sienna in 1741. About 1744 he returned to his native place and restored the Academy of the Lyncei. Died in 1775.

Bianchi, (GIOVANNI ANTONIO,) an Italian sculptor and painter, born in Lombardy; died at Genoa in 1657.

Bianchi, (GIOVANNI ANTONIO,) an Italian *littérateur* and dramatist, born at Lucca in 1686; died in 1758.

Bianchi, (GIOVANNI BATTISTA,) an eminent Italian anatomist, born at Turin in 1681, was professor of anatomy in the University of Turin for many years. Among his principal works is a "History of the Liver," (" Historia Hepatica," 2 vols., 1725.) Died in Turin in 1761.

See TIRABOSCHI, "Storia della Letteratura Italiana."

Bianchi, (ISIDORO,) a Milanese painter, born about 1626, was a pupil of Morazzone. Died about 1670.

Bianchi, (ISIDORO,) an Italian monk and philosophical writer, born at Cremona in 1733; died in 1807.

See LOUIS BELLO, "Vie du Père Bianchi."

Bianchi, (MARCANTONIO,) an Italian jurist, born in 1498 at Padua, where he became professor of criminal law in 1544. Died in 1548.

Bianchi, (ORAZIO,) an Italian philologist and translator, born at Rome; died at Milan in 1756.

Bianchi, (PIETRO,) an Italian painter, born at Rome in 1694; died in 1740.

Bianchi, be-ôn'ke', (THOMAS XAVIER,) a French philologist, born in Paris in 1783, became royal secretary and interpreter (secrétaire-interprète) for Oriental languages. He published, among other works, a "Turkish-French Dictionary," in which he was assisted by J. D. Kieffer.

Bianchi, (VENDRAMINO,) an Italian diplomatist, lived about 1730.

Bianchi, von, fon be-ân'kee, (FRIEDRICH,) BARON, an Austrian commander, of Italian extraction, born at Vienna in 1768. He served in the principal campaigns against the French, and in 1809 obtained the rank of lieutenant-field-marshal. In 1815 he gained a signal victory over Murat near Tolentino, and was afterwards created Duke of Casalanza. Died in 1855.

See BROCKHAUS, "Conversations-Lexikon."

Bianchi Giovini. See GIOVINI.

Bianchini, be-ân-kee'nee, (FRANCESCO,) an eminent Italian astronomer and antiquary, born at Verona in December, 1662. He published a number of valuable treatises on the antiquities of Rome, and a "Universal History, proved by Monuments and illustrated with Symbols of the Antique," (1697.) He passed the most of his life at Rome, was patronized by the popes Alexander VIII. and Clement XI., and was appointed by the latter secretary of the commission charged with reforming the calendar. He also drew a meridian-line and erected a gnomon in the church of Santa Maria degli Angeli. Died at Rome in 1729.

See FONTENELLE, "Éloge de Bianchini," 1757; A. MAZZOLENI, "Vita di F. Bianchini," 1735; NICÉRON, "Mémoires."

Bianchini, (GIOVANNI FORTUNATO,) an Italian physician, born in the kingdom of Naples in 1720; died in 1779.

Bianchini, (GIUSEPPE,) an Italian antiquary, born at Verona in 1704, was a nephew of Francesco, noticed above, several of whose works he completed.

Bianco, be-ân'ko, written also Biancho, (ANDREA,) a Venetian geographer, lived about 1420. He executed a number of hydrographic charts.

Bianco, (BARTOLOMMEO,) an Italian architect, born in the province of Como. Among his best works is the palace of the University at Genoa. Died in 1656.

Bianco, del, dêl be-ân'ko, (BACCIO, bât'cho,) an Italian painter, born at Florence in 1604. Having been invited by Philip IV., he went to Madrid, where he died in 1656.

See LANZI, "History of Painting in Italy."

Biancolelli, be-ân-ko-lel'lee, (GIUSEPPE,) an Italian actor, often called DOMENICO, (dom-à-nee'ko,) born at Bologna in 1640, performed the part of Harlequin in Paris. Died in 1688.

Biancolelli, (PIERRE FRANÇOIS,) called likewise DOMINIQUE, (do'me'nèk',) a French actor and dramatic writer, son of the preceding, born in Paris in 1681; died in 1734.

Biancolini, be-ân-ko-lee'nee, (GIOVANNI BATTISTA GIUSEPPE,) an Italian chronicler, born at Verona in 1697; died in 1780.

Bianconi, be-ân-ko'nee, (CHARLES,) an Italian, noted as the inventor or originator of the Irish car system which bears his name, was born in the duchy of Milan about 1787. He emigrated to Ireland in early youth, and began in 1815 to carry passengers in cars. He succeeded, and extended his lines of cars or stages through all parts of Ireland.

Bianconi, (GIAMBATTISTA,) an Italian ecclesiastic and philologist, born in 1698 at Bologna, where he became professor of Greek and Hebrew. Died in 1781.

Bianconi, (GIOVANNI LUIGI,) an Italian physician and philosopher, nephew of the preceding, born at Bologna in 1717. He published "Two Letters on Physics," (1746,) a "Treatise on Electricity," (1748,) and other works. He became physician to the King of Poland about 1750. Died at Perugia in 1781.

Biancucci, be-ân-koot'chee, (PAOLO,) an Italian painter, born at Lucca in 1583, was a pupil of Guido. Died about 1653.

Biandrate, be-ân-drä'tà, (BENVENUTO,) an Italian diplomatist and historian, was commander of the order of Saint John of Jerusalem. Died in 1527.

Biard, be'ôr', (AUGUSTE FRANÇOIS,) a celebrated French painter, born at Lyons in 1800. In 1828 he visited various parts of Europe, Asia, and Africa, and made valuable collections of materials for the exercise of his art. His "Family of Mendicants," exhibited at the Paris Exposition in 1832, obtained the gold medal, and was succeeded in a few years by "The Strolling Players," "The Mad-House," "Attack of Spanish Robbers in the Sierra Morena," "The Wind of the Desert," and "The Slave-Trade."

See L. BOIVIN, "Notice sur M. Biard," etc.; "Examen critique des Tableaux de Biard," Paris, 1842.

Biard, (PAUL,) a French Jesuit, born at Grenoble in 1565, was professor of theology at Lyons. In 1611 he visited Canada, being one of the first Jesuit missionaries to that country. He died in France in 1622.

See CHARLEVOIX, "Histoire de la Nouvelle France."

Biard, (PIERRE,) a French sculptor and architect, born in Paris in 1559; died in 1609.

Biarnoy de Merville, be'âr'nwâ' deh mêR'vèl', (PIERRE,) a French jurist, born in Normandy, published a work entitled "Règles pour former un Avocat," (" Rules for making a Lawyer," 1711,) which obtained great success. Died in 1740.

Bi'as, [Βίας,] one of the seven sages of Greece, was a native of Priene, and is supposed to have lived about 566 B.C. He enjoyed a high reputation for skill and ability as an advocate, as well as for practical wisdom and love of justice. A number of his maxims are preserved in the writings of Diogenes Laertius, Plutarch, and others.

Biascioli. See BIAGIOLI.

Biauzat, de, deh be'ō'zâ', (GAUTHIER,) a French magistrate, became a member of the Council of Ancients, (1798,) and of the court of cassation, (1799.) Died in 1815.

Bi-bac'u-lus, (M. FURIUS,) a Latin satirical poet, born at Cremona about 103 B.C. He wrote, in iambic verse, a poem on the wars of Gaul, entitled "Pragmatia Belli Gallici," and a number of epigrams and satires. He is compared by Diomedes with Horace and Catullus. A few fragments of his works are preserved.

See WEICHERT, "Dissertatio de Turgido Alpino S. M. F. Bibaculo," 1822.

Bibars or Bîbarz, bee'barz, sometimes written Baibars, called also Bundokdâr, bŏŏn'dok-dâr', Sultan of Egypt, was the fourth of the Baharite dynasty of Mamelukes. He ascended the throne in 1260, having murdered his predecessor, Kootooz, (Kûtûz.) He defeated the Tartars and ravaged Armenia, but at length died from accidentally drinking poison, in 1277.

є as k; ç as s; ḡ hard; ġ as j; G, H, K, guttural; N, nasal; R, trilled; š as z: th as in this. (☞ See Explanations, p. 23.)

23

Bibars or **Bibarz,** twelfth Sultan of the Baharite Mamelukes, ascended the throne in 1309, and was deposed and put to death in 1310.

Bibaut, be'bō', [Lat. Bibau'cius,] (Willem,) a Flemish preacher, born at Thielt, became general of the order of Carthusians in 1521. Died in 1535.

Bibbiena. See Galli, (Ferdinando.)

Bibbiena, bĕb-be-ā'nå, (Angelo Dovizio,) nephew of Cardinal Bibbiena, lived about 1570. He held the office of apostolic prothonotary.

Bibbiena, (Bernardo,) called also **Bernardo Dovizio** (do-vĕt'se-o) or **Devizio,** (dȧ-vĕt'se-o,) and **Bernardo di Tarlatti,** (de taR-lȧt'tee,) a celebrated Italian cardinal, born at Bibbiena in 1470. He was intimate with Giovanni de Medici, who afterwards became Pope Leo X. and made Bibbiena a cardinal in 1513. He patronized literary men and artists, and wrote, besides other works in verse and prose, "Calandria," a comedy, which was much admired and passed through many editions. In 1518 Bibbiena was sent on a mission to the French court to promote a crusade against the Turks. He died suddenly in 1520, not without a suspicion of his having been poisoned.

See Paolo Giovio, "Elogio de Bibbiena;" Ginguené, "Histoire Littéraire d'Italie;" A. M. Bandini, "Il Bibbiena, ossia il Ministro di Stato," etc., 1758.

Bibbiena, da, då bĕb-be-ā'nå, (Giovanni Maria Galli,) an Italian painter, born in 1625, was the father of Ferdinando Galli, and a pupil of Albano. Died in 1665.

See Lanzi, "History of Painting in Italy."

Bibbiena, da, or simply **Bibbiena,** bĕb-be-ā'nå, (Giuseppe Galli,) a painter, born at Bologna in 1696. He worked at Vienna and Dresden. Died in 1756.

Biber, bee'bẹr, (George E.,) a theologian, born probably in Germany about 1800, became curate of Roehampton, England, about 1842. He published "Bishop Blomfield and his Times," and many theological works.

Biberstein, bee'bẹr-stīn', (Marschall,) Baron, a German botanist, born at Würtemberg in 1768, travelled in the Crimea and the Caucasus, and published a description of the flora of those countries. Died in 1828.

Biberstein, von, fon bee'bẹr-stīn', (Ernst Franz Ludwig Marschall,) a German statesman, born at Wallerstein in 1770, became in 1806 minister of the Duke of Nassau. Died in 1834.

Bib-ĭ-ā'na, Saint, a Roman virgin, who suffered martyrdom about 360 A.D.

Bib'lĭ-an-dẹr, (Theodore,) an eminent Swiss divine and philologist, whose original name was Buchmann, (bōōk'mȧn,) born at Bischofszell in 1504, was professor of theology at Zurich from 1532 to 1560. He wrote theological treatises in Latin, and translated several books of the Zurich Bible commenced by Leo Juda. Died in 1564.

Bibron, be'bRòN', (Gabriel,) a French zoologist, born in Paris in 1806. He wrote, in conjunction with Duméril, a "Natural History of Reptiles," (about 1833.) Died in 1848.

Bib'u-lus, (L. Calpurnius,) a Roman, who became consul in 59 B.C. He was a partisan of Pompey during the civil war, and was afterwards proconsul in Syria, and commander of the fleet in the Ionian Sea, (49 B.C.)

Bibulus, (L. Calpurnius,) son of the preceding and of Portia, the daughter of Cato, was made governor of Syria by Antony. He died about 40 B.C., leaving a life of his stepfather Brutus.

Bicaise, be'kȧz', (Honoré,) a French physician, born at Aix-en-Provence in 1590, wrote a work "On the Causes and Cure of the Plague."

Bicci, di, de bĕt'chee, (Lorenzo,) a painter of the Florentine school, born before 1400. He painted frescos in the cathedral of Florence. Died about 1460.

Bicci, di, (Neri,) an Italian painter, son of Lorenzo, noticed above. Died after 1466.

See Vasari, "Lives of the Painters."

Bichat, be'shȧ', (Marie François Xavier,) a French physiologist and anatomist of great eminence, was born at Thoirette, in Jura, on the 11th of November, 1771. He went to Paris in 1793, and became a favourite pupil of Desault, who adopted him as his son. In 1797 he collected and edited the "Surgical Works of Desault," and began to lecture on anatomy, surgery, and physiology in a school established by himself. He developed new and important ideas on the anatomy of the tissues, and on the distinction between organic and animal functions, in his "Treatise on the Membranes," (1798,) in "Researches on Life and Death," (1800,) and in his great work, "General Anatomy applied to Physiology and Medicine," ("Anatomie générale appliquée," etc., 4 vols., 1801,) which established his reputation as a profound philosopher. Bichat was the first who reduced the organs of the body to their elementary tissues and explained the chemical, physical, and vital properties of each primitive tissue. He has also the honour of being the first who recognized the importance of the distinction between organic and animal functions and made it the basis of a classification. He was appointed physician to the Hôtel-Dieu in 1799 or 1800. He impaired his health by excessive application to study and experiments, and died prematurely in July, 1802, leaving an unfinished work on "Descriptive Anatomy," of which he published two volumes. His pupils Buisson and Roux added three more volumes. "No one," says Corvisart, "has done so much and so well in so short a time."

See P. Sue, "Éloge de Bichat," 1803; Bilon, "Éloge historique de Bichat," 1802; Miquel, "Éloge de Bichat," 1823; Roux, "Éloge de Bichat," 1851; "Nouvelle Biographie Générale."

Bick'ẹr-staff, (Isaac,) an Irish dramatist, born about 1735, was for some time an officer of marines. He produced, besides other plays, three comic operas, entitled "Love in a Village," (1763,) "The Maid of the Mill," (1765,) and "Lionel and Clarissa," (1768,) all of which were successful. He died after 1787.

Bick'ẹr-steth, (Edward,) D.D., an English writer, born at Acton, in Suffolk, in 1814, became Archdeacon of Buckinghamshire in 1853. He has published several theological works.

Bickersteth, (Rev. Edward,) a distinguished English divine and theological writer, born in Westmoreland in 1786. He published in 1814 a "Help to the Study of the Scriptures," which obtained great popularity. Having taken orders, he visited Africa in 1816, for the purpose of inspecting the stations of the Missionary Society in that country. He officiated as secretary of that society for about fifteen years. In 1830 he became rector of Watton, in Hertfordshire, where he was active in promoting the cause of religious and benevolent associations. He was one of the founders of the Evangelical Alliance. Among his numerous and valuable works may be named "A Practical Guide to the Prophecies," "A Treatise on Baptism," "The Promised Glory of the Church of Christ," and "The Restoration of the Jews." Died in 1850.

See "Memoir of the Rev. Edward Bickersteth," by T. R. Birks, 2 vols., 1851; "Burning and Shining Lights," by the Rev. Robert Steel.

Bickersteth, (Henry,) Lord Langdale, an English judge, brother of the preceding, born at Kirkby-Lonsdale in 1783. He practised in the courts of equity, and attained to eminence as a lawyer. He was appointed master of the rolls, and raised to the peerage, in 1836. Died in 1851.

See Foss, "The Judges of England," vol. ix.

Bick'ẹr-ton, (Sir Richard Hussey,) an English admiral, born in 1759, served under Lord Keith in 1801, and assisted in the blockade of Alexandria. He was created admiral of the blue in 1810, knight-commander of the Bath in 1815, and subsequently general of the royal marines. Died in 1832.

Biclara, be-klā'rå, (João,) a Portuguese historian, born at Santarem, flourished between 550 and 600 A.D.

Bid'dle, (Clement,) an American officer, born in Philadelphia in 1740, was originally a member of the Society of Friends. Before the Revolution he was a merchant, and a decided asserter of the rights of the colonies. He served as colonel at the battles of Trenton, Princeton, Brandywine, and Monmouth. He was appointed marshal of Pennsylvania about 1789 by General Washington, who was his friend and correspondent. Died in 1814.

Biddle, (Clement Cornell,) a son of the preceding, born in Philadelphia in 1784, was a lawyer and political economist. He served as colonel in the war against Great Britain, (1812-15.) He published, with notes and

ā, ē, ī, ō, ū, ȳ, *long;* ȧ, ė, ȯ, same, less prolonged; ă, ĕ, ĭ, ŏ, ŭ, ў, *short;* ą, ẹ, į, ǫ, *obscure;* fär, fȧll, fȧt; mĕt; nŏt; gōōd; mōᵇn;

additions, a translation of J. B. Say's "Treatise on Political Economy," (1821.) Died in 1855.

Biddle, (JAMES,) an American naval officer, born in 1783, was educated in Philadelphia. He entered the navy about 1800, and in 1832 signed a commercial treaty with Turkey. Having obtained the rank of commodore, he commanded a squadron on the coast of China in 1847. Died in Philadelphia in 1848.

Bid'dle, (JOHN,) the founder of Unitarianism in England, born in Gloucestershire in 1615, was a graduate of Oxford. In 1647 he wrote for private circulation a pamphlet in which he attempted to refute the commonly-received opinion respecting the Deity of the Holy Spirit. For this he was summoned before the Parliament, and, after a protracted trial, condemned to five years' imprisonment. While in prison, he wrote (in 1648) a "Confession of Faith concerning the Holy Trinity," and several other tracts in defence of his peculiar doctrines. After the death of Charles I., Biddle was released; but he was soon remanded by Bradshaw, president of the council. The act of indemnity and oblivion having been passed in 1651, he was set at liberty, and soon after formed with his adherents a society to which was given the name of Unitarians. He was subsequently twice imprisoned under Cromwell, and his works publicly burned. After the restoration of Charles II. he was again sent to prison, where he died in 1662.

See J. TOULMIN, "Life of John Biddle," 1815; JOHN FARRINGTON, "Vita J. Bidelli," 1682.

Biddle, (NICHOLAS,) an American naval commander, born in Philadelphia in 1750. He entered the British navy in 1770, and served as midshipman in the same vessel with Lord Nelson. Having returned to America in 1776, he was appointed captain of the Andrew Doria, and captured several prizes from the British. In February, 1777, he took command of the Randolph, a frigate of thirty-two guns. During an action with the British ship Yarmouth, in March, 1778, the magazine of the Randolph exploded, and killed Captain Biddle with nearly all his crew.

Biddle, (NICHOLAS,) an American financier, born in Philadelphia in January, 1786, was a nephew of Commodore Biddle, and a son of Charles Biddle, who was for some time vice-president of the commonwealth of Pennsylvania. He graduated at Princeton in 1801, after which he passed several years in Europe. Having returned in 1807, he edited for a time "The Port-Folio," (a literary journal,) and was elected a member of the legislature of Pennsylvania in 1810. He served in the Senate of that State from 1814 to 1817, and in 1819 was appointed a director of the United States Bank by President Monroe. In 1823 he became president of that bank, which, by virtue of his new financial measures, supplied the country with a uniform currency, until, after an exciting political contest, the bill for the recharter of the bank was vetoed by President Jackson in 1832. In accordance with the limitation of its charter, the bank was closed in 1836. A second "United States Bank," designed as a successor to the old one, having been chartered by the State of Pennsylvania, in whose legislature the Whig or Anti-Jackson party had at that time a majority, Mr. Biddle was made president of the new institution: it failed, however, in 1841. Mr. Biddle was also president of the trustees of the fund (amounting to 2,000,000 dollars) left by Stephen Girard for the establishment of a college for orphans. "To his exertions alone," says Judge Robert T. Conrad, "the country owes one of the most beautiful structures of modern times,—the Girard College. . . . He proposed the present plan, and, in the midst of wild political excitement and opposition, persisted firmly, and secured a building which every citizen now not only approves, but applauds." His eloquence and literary merits are highly extolled by his biographer just quoted. Died in February, 1844.

See a "Memoir of Nicholas Biddle," by ROBERT T. CONRAD, in the "National Portrait-Gallery," vol. iv., 1839.

Biddle, (RICHARD,) an American lawyer and writer, a brother of the preceding, was born in Philadelphia in 1796. He practised law at Pittsburg, and published a "Memoir of Sebastian Cabot; with a Review of the History of Maritime Discovery," (1831.) He was a member of Congress from 1837 to 1840. Died in 1847.

Bid'dŭlph, (THOMAS TREGENNA,) an English divine, born in Worcestershire in 1763, wrote "Essays on the Liturgy," (1798,) and other religious works, which have a high reputation.

See "London Quarterly Review" for December, 1824.

Bidermann. See BIEDERMANN.

Bidermann or **Biedermann,** bee'der-mân', (JAKOB,) a German Jesuit and writer, born at Tübingen; died at Rome in 1639.

Bidermann, (JOHANN GOTTFRIED,) a German writer on genealogy, lived about 1760.

Bidermann, (JOHANN GOTTLIEB,) a German philologist, born at Naumburg in 1705; died in 1772.

See HÜBLER, "Memoria J. G. Biedermann," 1772.

Bidet, be'dà', (NICOLAS,) a French agriculturist, born in 1709, wrote on the culture of grapes. Died at Rheims in 1782.

Biding, be'dâN', (MOSES ISRAEL,) a French Jew, born in 1775, was professor of Hebrew at Metz.

Bid'lake, (JOHN,) an English divine, born at Plymouth in 1755; died in 1814.

Bidloo, bid'lo, (GODFRIED,) a Dutch anatomist, born at Amsterdam in 1649. He became physician to William III. of England, and in 1694 professor of anatomy and surgery at Leyden. He wrote, in Latin, "Anatomy of the Human Body," with one hundred and five plates by G. de Lairesse, (1685,) and other works. Died in 1713.

Bidloo, (LAMBERT,) a Dutch botanist, brother of the preceding, was a resident of Amsterdam.

Bidou, be'doo', (FRANÇOIS SIMON,) a French medical writer, born at Écos (Eure) in 1769; died in Paris in 1824.

Bidpai. See PILPAY.

Bie, van, vän bee, (ADRIAN,) a Flemish painter, born near Antwerp in 1594; died about 1640.

See DESCAMPS, "Vies des Peintres Flamands," etc.

Bie, van, (JAKOB,) a Flemish engraver, born about 1600, resided at Antwerp.

Biedermann. See BIEDERMANN.

Biedermann, bee'der-mân', (FRIEDRICH KARL,) a German publicist, and professor of law at Leipsic, where he was born in 1812. He founded in 1842 the "German Monthly Journal for Literature and Public Life," and published a treatise "On German Philosophy from Kant to the Present Time," (2 vols., 1842,) and "Fundamental Philosophy," (1837.) About 1850 he began to direct the publication of an extensive encyclopædic work, called "Germania."

See BROCKHAUS, "Conversations-Lexikon."

Biedermann, bee'der-mân', written also **Bidermann,** (JOHANN JAKOB,) a Swiss landscape-painter, born at Winterthur, lived about 1780–1820.

Biehl, beel, (CHARLOTTE DOROTHEA,) a Danish authoress and dramatist, born at Copenhagen in 1731, made a translation of "Don Quixote," which is highly esteemed. Died in 1788.

See KRAFT og NYERUP, "Litteraturlexicon for Danemark," etc.

Biel, beel, (GABRIEL,) a German philosophical writer, born at Speyer; died in 1495.

Biel, (JOHANN CHRISTIAN,) a German Lutheran theologian, born at Brunswick in 1687; died in 1745.

Biel, (LUDWIG,) professor of philosophy at Vienna, wrote a treatise entitled "The Utility of Money," ("Utilitates Rei Nummariæ," 1733.)

Biela, von, fon bee'lä, (WILHELM,) BARON, a German astronomer, born near Stolberg in 1782, discovered in 1826 the comet since called by his name. Died in 1856.

Bielefeld, von, fon bee'leh-fĕlt, (JAKOB FRIEDRICH,) BARON, a German publicist and littérateur, born at Hamburg about 1712, became in 1747 inspector of the Prussian universities. Died in 1770.

Bieler, bee'ler, (BENJAMIN,) a German antiquary and theologian, born in Saxony in 1693; died in 1772.

Bieler, (KARL AMBROSIUS,) a German physician, born at Ratisbon in 1693; died in 1747.

Bielinski, be-à-lĕn'skee, (FRANCIS,) a Polish naturalist, was appointed by Augustus III. grand marshal of the crown. Died about 1766.

Bielinski, (PETER,) a Polish magistrate, born in 1754, became senator palatine, and filled other offices under government. Died in 1829.

Bielke, be-êl'keh, written also **Bjelke,** (NICHOLAS,) COUNT, a Swedish mineralogist, was director of the department of mines from 1782 to 1789.

Bielke, (STEN (or STENO) KARL,) a Swedish naturalist and scientific writer, born at Stockholm in 1709; died in 1754.

See GEZELIUS, "Biographiskt-Lexicon;" ROSENADLER, "Åminnelse-Tal ofver Sten Karl Bjelke," 1755.

Bielowski, be-à-lov'skee, (AUGUSTUS,) a Polish *littérateur,* born in Galicia about 1806, published a translation of Goethe's "Faust."

Bielski, be-êl'skee, (MARTIN,) a Polish chronicler, born in 1495. His "Kronika Polska" is admired for the elegance of its style, and is the first important history of Poland written in the Polish language. Died in 1576. His son Joachim wrote a continuation of the "Chronicle of Poland," and published the entire work in 1597.

Bienaimé, be-ân'â'mà',(PIERRE THÉODORE,) a French architect, born at Amiens in 1765 ; died in 1826.

Bienaise, be-ân'âz', (JEAN,) a French surgeon, born at Mazères, wrote "Operations of Surgery by a Short and Easy Method," (1688.) Died in 1681.

Bienaymé, be-ân'â'mà', (PIERRE FRANÇOIS,) a French naturalist, became Bishop of Metz in 1802. He was a friend of Buffon and Daubenton. Died in 1806.

Bienné, be-ân'nà', [Lat. BENENA'TUS,] (JEAN,) a French typographer, published several fine editions of the Greek and Latin classics. Died in 1588.

Bienvenu, be-ân'veh-nü', (JACQUES,) a Genevese *littérateur* and satirist, lived about 1570.

Bienville, de, deh be-ân'vèl', (JEAN BAPTISTE Lemoine—leh-mwân',) a French captain, born in Canada about 1680. He was a brother of Lemoyne d'Iberville, whom he accompanied on his expedition to the mouth of the Mississippi in 1699, and after his death (1706) became governor of the French colony which was planted in Louisiana. He founded the city of New Orleans in 1718. Died in France about 1768.

Bierbrauer, beeR'bRôw'er, (JOHANN JAKOB,) a German magistrate, born at Hesse in 1705 ; died in 1760.

Bierkander or **Bjerkander,** be-êR'kân-der, (KLAUDIUS,) a Swedish savant, born in 1735 ; died in 1795.

See OEDMANN,"Åminnelse-Tal öfver probsten C. Bjerkander,"1798.

Bierling, beer'ling, (CONRAD FRIEDRICH ERNST,) son of Friedrich Wilhelm, born in 1709, was professor of metaphysics and theology at Rinteln. Died in 1755.

Bierling, (FRIEDRICH WILHELM,) a German preacher and theologian, born at Magdeburg in 1676, was a friend and correspondent of Leibnitz. Died in 1728.

Biermann, beeR'mân, (KARL EDUARD,) a German landscape-painter, and professor in the Academy of Arts at Berlin, where he was born in 1803.

Biermann, (MARTIN,) a German physician, and professor of medicine at Helmstedt, lived about 1570–1600.

Biernacki, be-êR-nât'skee or byêR-nât'skee, (ALOIS PROSPER,) a Polish nobleman, distinguished for the agricultural improvements he introduced into Poland, born in the palatinate of Kalisch in 1778 ; died in 1856.

Biernatzki, beeR-nâts'kee, (JOHANN CHRISTOPH,) a German Lutheran divine, born at Elmshorn, in Holstein, in 1795, published "The Hallig, or Shipwrecks in an Island of the North Sea," (1836,) and other tales. Died in 1840.

See C. L. BIERNATZKI, "Biographie von J. C. Biernatzki," 1852.

Bierstadt, beer'stat, (ALBERT,) an eminent landscape-painter, born at Dusseldorf, in Germany, in 1828. His parents emigrated to New England when he was about two years old. In 1853 he visited Germany, studied for a time at the Dusseldorf Academy, and executed several views of German scenery, which attracted very favourable notice. Having spent a winter in Rome, and made the tour of Switzerland and the Apennines, he returned to the United States in 1857. The following year he accompanied General Lander's expedition to the Rocky Mountains, where he spent several months in making sketches. In 1863 he produced his magnificent "View of the Rocky Mountains—Lander's Peak," (six feet by ten.) Among his other works may be mentioned his "Sunlight and Shadow," "The Storm in the Rocky Mountains," and "The Domes of the Yo Semite."

See TUCKERMAN's "Book of the Artists."

Bieselinghen. See BIEZELINGEN.

Biesenthal, bee'zen-tâl', (JOHANNES HEINRICH,) a Hebrew philologist, a friend of the celebrated Neander, born in Posen about 1800. Though born of Jewish parents, he early embraced Christianity. He published in 1840 a Hebrew-Latin Lexicon, and in 1851 a valuable "History of the Christian Church during the First Three Centuries."

Biesmann, bees'mân, (KASPAR,) a German Jesuit and professor of philosophy, born at Dusseldorf in 1639. He wrote on rhetoric and ethics.

Biester, bees'ter, (JOHANN ERIC,) a German *littérateur* and journalist, born at Lubeck in 1749. In 1785 he founded, conjointly with Gedike, the "Berlin Monthly Review," ("Monatsschrift,") and became in 1784 librarian of the royal library. He translated from the French Barthélemy's "Travels of Anacharsis." Died in 1816.

Biet, be-à', (ANTOINE,) a French missionary to Cayenne, born near Senlis about 1620.

Biet, (CLAUDE,) born near Verdun-sur-Saône, became first apothecary to the king. Died in 1728.

Biet, (RENÉ,) a French antiquary, wrote a "Dissertation on the True Epoch of the Establishment of the Franks in Gaul," (1736.) Died in 1767.

Biett, be-êt', (LAURENT,) born in the canton of Grisons, became physician to the hospital Saint-Louis, (Paris,) into which he introduced important improvements. Died in 1840.

Biever. See BEAVER.

Bièvre, de, deh be-êvR', (MARÉCHAL,) MARQUIS, a French *littérateur* and wit, born in 1747, published several dramas, and the "Almanac of Puns," ("Calembours.") Died in 1789.

Biez, de, dü be-à', (OUDARD,) a French marshal, who served against the English in 1523, and in the Italian campaign of 1528. Died in 1553.

Biezelingen or **Bieselinghen, van,** vân bee'zeh-ling'en, (CHRISTIAN JAN) a Dutch portrait-painter, born at Delft in 1558. Among his master-pieces is a portrait of William I., Prince of Orange. Died in 1600.

Biffi, bêf'fee, (ANDREA,) a Milanese sculptor, lived about 1600, and executed works for the Milan cathedral.

Biffi, (GIOVANNI,) an Italian *littérateur* and Latin poet, born near Milan in 1464.

Biffi, (GIUSEPPE,) an Italian musician and composer, born at Milan, flourished about 1580.

Bifield, (NICHOLAS.) See BYFIELD.

Bifröst, bif'röst, the name given in the Norse mythology to the rainbow. See HEIMDALL.

Bigari, be-gâ'ree, (VITTORIO,) an Italian painter and sculptor, born at Bologna about 1692 ; died in 1776.

Bigarré, be'gâ'rà', (AUGUSTE JULIEN,) a French general, born at Palais in 1775 ; died in 1838.

Bigelot, bèzh'lo', (FRANÇOIS EMMANUEL SIMÉON,) a French *littérateur,* born at Nancy in 1789 ; died in 1820.

Big'e-lōw, (ERASTUS,) born at West Boylston, in Massachusetts, in 1814, invented a machine for weaving counterpanes, which was a great improvement on those previously in use.

Bigelow, (JACOB,) M.D., LL.D., an eminent American physician, born in Sudbury, Massachusetts, in 1787, graduated at Harvard in 1806. He was for many years physician to the Massachusetts General Hospital, and professor of materia medica and of clinical medicine in Harvard University. He became president of the Massachusetts Medical Society, and also president of the American Academy of Arts and Sciences. He served on the committee of five appointed in 1820 to form the "American Pharmacopœia," and for ten years delivered lectures at Cambridge on the application of science to the useful arts. As the founder of Mount Auburn Cemetery, he displayed great taste in laying out the grounds, designing the gateway, etc. His first work, entitled "Florula Bostoniensis," appeared in 1814, (3d edition, greatly enlarged, 1840 ;) and his "American Medical Botany" (3 vols. 8vo) in 1817–21. He has also published a work entitled "The Useful Arts considered in Connection with the Applications of Science," an excellent "Discourse on Self-Limited Diseases," and a kindred work, entitled "Nature in Disease."

ā, ē, ī, ō, ū, ȳ, *long;* à, è, ò, same, less prolonged; ă, ě, ĭ, ŏ, ŭ, ў, *short;* a, e, i, o, *obscure;* fär, fàll, fàt; mêt; nôt; gōōd; mōōn;

Bigelow, (JOHN,) an American author and journalist, born in Ulster county, New York, in 1817, graduated at Union College in 1835. He has contributed a number of able articles to the "Democratic Review." From 1845 to 1848 he was prison-inspector at Sing-Sing, and originated some important reforms in the discipline of that institution. In 1850 he became associated with Mr. Bryant as editor of the New York "Evening Post." In the same year he visited Jamaica, and published after his return an excellent work, entitled "Jamaica in 1850; or the Effects of Sixteen Years of Freedom on a Slave Colony." In 1861 Mr. Bigelow was appointed American consul at Paris; on the death of Mr. Dayton, in December, 1864, he became chargé-d'affaires, and in April, 1865, minister plenipotentiary at the court of France. He resigned this position in December, 1866.

Bigelow, (TIMOTHY,) an American lawyer, born at Worcester, Massachusetts, in 1767, graduated at Harvard in 1786. He rose to the first rank in his profession. In 1807 he removed to Medford, and opened an office in Boston. He was an active Federalist, and was Speaker of the House of Representatives of Massachusetts for eleven years. Died in 1821.

Bigeon, be'zhôn', (LOUIS FRANÇOIS,) a French medical writer, born at La Villée in 1773, practised at Dinan about forty years. Died in 1848.

Bigeot, be'zho', (CLAUDE ÉTIENNE,) a French diplomatist in the service of Spain. Died in 1675.

Biget. See MARTHE.

Bigg, (WILLIAM REDMORE,) an English painter of interiors and domestic scenes. Died in 1828.

Bigi, bee'jee, (FELICE,) an Italian flower-painter, worked at Verona about 1680.

Bigio, bee'jo, (MARCANTONIO FRANCIA,) an Italian painter, born at or near Florence in 1445; died in 1525.

Big'land, (JOHN,) an English writer, born in Yorkshire, published "Letters on the Study and Use of Ancient and Modern History," and a "History of Spain," which has been translated into French. Died in 1832.

Bigland, (RALPH,) an English antiquary, born in Westmoreland in 1711, was appointed Garter king-at-arms in 1780. Died in 1784.

Biglia, bêl'yà, (ANDREA,) an Italian scholar, wrote historical works in Latin. Died in 1435.

Big'lōw, (WILLIAM,) a New England teacher and writer, born in 1773. He graduated at Harvard in 1794, and subsequently became principal of the Boston Latin School, which he conducted with distinguished success for several years. Edward Everett was among his pupils. He prepared several text-books for his school, and was an active contributor to the periodical press. Died in 1844.

Bignan, bên'yŏn', (ANNE,) a French poet and translator of the classical school, born at Lyons in 1795, produced good poetical versions of Homer's "Iliad" (1830) and "Odyssey," (1840.) He obtained four prizes of the French Academy for original poems, among which are an "Epistle to Cuvier," and "Napoleon in Russia," (1844.) Died in November, 1861.

Bigne, de la, deh lä bên, (GACES, gäs,) a French poet and ecclesiastic, born in Normandy about 1328, was chaplain successively to Philip of Valois, John II., and Charles V., of France.

Bigne, de la, (MARGUERIN, mårg'răn',) a French doctor of the Sorbonne, born at Bernières-le-Patry about 1546; died about 1590.

Big'nell, (HENRY,) an English divine, born at Oxford in 1611; died about 1660.

Bignicourt, de, deh bên'ye'kooR', (SIMON,) a French *littérateur*, born at Rheims in 1709; died in 1775.

Bignon, bên'yŏn', (ARMAND JÉRÔME,) a French jurist, nephew of Jean Paul, noticed below, whom he succeeded as royal librarian, was born in 1711. He was a member of the French Academy, and of the Academy of Inscriptions. His son Jean Frédéric also became royal librarian. Died in 1772.

Bignon, (JEAN PAUL,) grandson of Jérôme, noticed below, born in Paris in 1662, was appointed preacher to Louis XIV., and in 1718 became royal librarian. He was a member of the French Academy. He was a friend and patron of Tournefort, who named in his honour the genus Bignonia. Died in 1743.

Bignon, (JÉRÔME,) a French magistrate and scholar, born in Paris in 1589, became a page and companion of the dauphin, afterwards Louis XIII. He was subsequently councillor of state, and on the death of De Thou succeeded him as first keeper of the royal library. He was distinguished for his profound learning, and pleaded many important causes with great *éclat.* He wrote, among other works, a treatise "On the Grandeur of our Kings, and their Sovereign Power," (1615,) Died in 1656. According to Voltaire, "he left a great name, rather than great works."

See PÉRAU, "Vie de Jérôme Bignon," 1757.

Bignon, (LOUIS PIERRE ÉDOUARD,) an able French statesman and historian, born at La Meilleraye in 1771. He was minister plenipotentiary to Baden in 1809, and soon after administrator-general of Austria. After the battle of Waterloo he was made minister of foreign affairs by Napoleon, was elected to the Chamber of Deputies in 1817, and created a peer of France in 1837. He was the author of a "History of France from the 18th Brumaire to the Peace of Tilsit," (6 vols., 1829–30,) and a "History of France under Napoleon from the Peace of Tilsit to 1812," (4 vols., 1838,) also of several political treatises. Napoleon bequeathed to M. Bignon 100,000 francs, and charged him to write the history of French diplomacy from 1792 to 1815. Died in Paris in 1841.

See MIGNET, "Notice sur L. P. É. Bignon," 1841.

Bignoni, de, dà bên-yo'nee, (MARIO,) an Italian monk and eminent preacher, born in Venice; died in 1660.

Bignotti, bên-yot'tee, (VINCENZO,) an Italian ecclesiastic and *littérateur,* born at Vercelli in 1764; died in 1831.

Bigoni, be-go'nee, (LUDOVICO,) an Italian poet, born at Brescia in 1712; died in 1785.

Bigonnet, be'go'nà', (JEAN ADRIEN,) a French revolutionist and republican, born in 1755, became a member of the Council of Five Hundred. Died in 1832.

Bigot, be'go', (ÉMERY,) a French scholar, born at Rouen in 1626. He discovered in the library of Florence the Greek text of the "Life of Saint Chrysostom" by Palladius, which he published in 1680. Died in 1689.

Bigot, (GUILLAUME,) a French poet, born at Laval, in Maine, in 1502, became professor of philosophy at Tübingen. He published a "Prelude of Christian Philosophy," ("Christianæ Philosophiæ Præludium," 1549.)

Bigot, (MARIE,) a celebrated pianist, whose original name was KIÉNÉ, born at Colmar in 1786. She was instructed in music by Haydn and Beethoven, by whom her performances were highly commended. Died in 1820.

See LE BAS, "Dictionnaire encyclopédique de la France."

Bigot de Palaprat. See PALAPRAT.

Bigot de Préameneu, be'go' deh prà'ăm'nuh', (FÉLIX JULIEN JEAN,) a French jurist, born at Rennes in 1747, was made a count of the empire and grand officer of the legion of honour under Napoleon, and in 1815 a peer of France. He was a member of the French Academy, and a coadjutor of Portalis and others in the reformation of the civil code. Died in 1825.

See NOUGARÈDE DE FAYET, "Notice sur la Vie de Bigot de Préameneu."

Bigotier, be'go'te-à', [Lat. BIGOTHE'RIUS,] (CLAUDE,) a Latin poet, born at Treffort, in La Bresse, about 1500, was professor of rhetoric at Lyons.

Bigotière, de la, deh lä be'go'te-air', (PERCHAMBAULT, pêr'shŏn'bō',) a French officer, born at Rennes, served in the royalist army in La Vendée. Having been made prisoner at Mans, he was shot in 1794.

Bigotière, de la, (RENÉ DE PERCHAMBAULT,) a French jurist, born at Angers about 1640, wrote a treatise "On the Common Law of Brittany," and other legal works. Died in 1727.

Bigs'by, (ROBERT,) an English antiquary, born at Nottingham about 1806. He published "Poems and Essays," "The Antiquarian Enthusiast," (3 vols., about 1850,) and other works.

Bihârî Lôl, bī-hâ'ree lôl, a Hindoo poet, contemporary with Kabir.

Biheron, be'rŏn' or be'ẹ'rŏn', (MARIE CATHERINE,) a French anatomist, was born in Paris in 1719. She was patronized by the celebrated physicians Jussieu and Villoison in Paris, and by Hunter and Hewson in London.

є as *k*; ç as *s*; g̃ *hard*; g̃ as *j*; G, H, K, *guttural*; N, *nasal*; R, *trilled*; s̃ as *z*; th as in *this*. (☞See Explanations, p. 23.)

Her anatomical cabinet was bought at her death for Catherine II. of Russia. Died in 1786.

See CHAUDON et DELANDINE, "Nouveau Dictionnaire Biographique."

Bilain, be'låN', (ANTOINE,) a French jurist and legal writer, born near Rheims; died in 1672.

Bilderbeck, de, dẹh bĕl'dĕR'bĕk' or bil'dẹr-bĕk', (L. F.,) BARON, a French novelist and dramatist, born at Wissembourg, in Alsace, lived about 1800.

Bilderbeck, von, fon bil'dẹr-bĕk', (CHRISTOPH LORENZ,) a German jurist, born at Schwerin in 1682.

Bilderdijk or **Bilderdyk,** pronounced alike bil'dẹr-dīk', (WILLEM,) an eminent Dutch poet, born at Amsterdam in 1756. He published in 1777 "The True Love of Fatherland," ("De ware Liefde van het Vaderland,") and in 1779 a successful translation of the "Œdipus Tyrannus" of Sophocles. In 1806 he was chosen by King Louis Bonaparte to instruct him in the Dutch language, and afterwards elected one of the first members of the Institute then recently founded at Amsterdam. Among the most important of his numerous works may be named "Elius," (1778,) "Miscellaneous Poems," (1799,) "The Destruction of the First World," ("De Ondergang der eerste Wereld," 1817, unfinished,) "Maladies of Literary Men," "Rural Life," ("Buitenleven,") a free translation of some of Ossian's poems, and a number of tragedies. He was distinguished for his attainments in almost every department of learning. "Willem Bilderdijk," says Bosworth, "is the Samuel Johnson of the Dutch. . . . He was a giant in literature and intellectual strength, the most fertile of the Dutch writers." Died at Haarlem in 1831.

His second wife, KATHARINA WILHELMINA, was the author of the tragedies of "Elfrida" and "Iphigenia," and translated Southey's "Roderick." Died in 1830.

See JAN VAN WALRÉ, "Ter Gedachtenis van W. Bilderdijk," 1832; J. DA COSTA, "Overzicht van het Leven en de Werken van W. Bilderdijk," 1844; VAN KEMPEN, "Histoire Littéraire;" LONGFELLOW, "Poets and Poetry of Europe;" "Fraser's Magazine," vol. l., 1854; BOSWORTH'S "Anglo-Saxon Dictionary," preface, pp. cviii., cix.

Bilderdyk. See BILDERDIJK.

Bilfinger, bil'fing-ẹr, (GEORG BERNHARD,) a German philosopher of the school of Leibnitz, born at Canstadt, in Würtemberg, in 1693. He was curator of the University of Tübingen, and a member of the Royal Academy of Berlin. He wrote a number of philosophical and scientific treatises in Latin. He obtained the prize offered by the French Academy of Sciences for an explanation of the cause of the weight of bodies. Died in 1750.

See ADELUNG, Supplement to JÖCHER, "Allgemeines Gelehrten-Lexikon;" W. G. TAFINGER, "Leichenrede über den hoch zu betrauernden Todesfall des zum seltenen Exempel," etc., 1750.

Bilguer, bĕl'gaiR', (JEAN ULRIC,) a distinguished Swiss surgeon and medical writer, born at Coire in 1720, became surgeon-general of the Prussian army about 1759, and received a title of nobility from the Emperor of Germany. His Latin treatise on the management of gunshot wounds (1761) has been translated into French, German, and English. Died in 1796.

See "Biographie Médicale."

Bilguer, von, fon bĕl'gaiR', (PAUL RUDOLF,) a famous German chess-player, born in 1809. He died in 1840, leaving a "Manual of Chess-Playing," which was completed and published in 1843 by Heydebrand.

Bilhon, be'lôN', (JEAN JOSEPH FRÉDÉRIC,) a French writer on political economy, born at Avignon in 1759; died in 1834.

Bilhuber, bil'hoo'bẹr, (JOSEPH FRIEDRICH,) a German physician, born at Aurich in 1758; died in 1793.

Bilintani, be-lèn-tä'nee, (POMPEO,) an Italian poet, born at Venice, lived about 1530.

Biliotti, be-le-ot'tee, (IVO,) an Italian soldier, who lived about 1530, distinguished himself by his brave defence of Florence against the forces of Charles V.

Bilistein, de, dẹh be'le'ståN', (CHARLES LÉOPOLD ANDREU,) BARON, a French writer, born in Lorraine in 1724, published an "Essay on the Navigation of Lorraine," and other works.

Biliverti, be-le-vĕR'tee, (GIOVANNI,) a skilful painter, born at Florence in 1576, was a pupil of Cigoli. Among

his master-pieces are a "Holy Family," and the "Chastity of Joseph." Died in 1644.

See LANZI, "History of Painting in Italy."

Bill, (ROBERT,) an English mechanician, distinguished for his zealous efforts to introduce the use of gas into England, was born in 1754; died in 1827.

Billard, be'yåR', (CHARLES MICHEL,) a French physician, born near Angers in 1800, translated from the English Thomson's "Elements of Chemistry." Among his works is a "Treatise on the Diseases of Infants," (1828.) Died in 1832.

Billard, (CLAUDE,) a French poet and dramatist, was counsellor to Queen Margaret of Valois. Died in 1618.

Billard, (ÉTIENNE,) a French comic writer, born at Nancy; died in 1785.

Billard, (JEAN PIERRE,) a French physician and medical writer, born at Vesoul in 1726; died in 1790.

Billard, (PIERRE,) a French theologian, born in the department of Maine in 1653, wrote against the Jesuits a work entitled "The Beast with Seven Heads," (1693.) Died in 1726.

Billaud-Varenne, (or **-Varennes,**) be'yō' vȧ'rễn', (JACQUES NICOLAS,) a French Jacobin, born at La Rochelle in 1756. As a member of the National Convention in 1792, he voted for the death of the royal family and the ministers, and in various ways distinguished himself by the violence of his measures. He was subsequently made president of the Convention, and a member of the Committee of Public Safety. He was exiled to Cayenne, in company with Collot d'Herbois, in 1795, and afterwards went to Hayti, where he died in 1819.

See "Mémoires de Billaud-Varennes," 2 vols., 1821; THIERS, "Histoire de la Révolution Française."

Billault, be'yō', (AUGUSTE ADOLPHE MARIE,) a French jurist and politician, born at Vannes in 1805. He was elected to the Chamber of Deputies in 1837, and distinguished himself as a legislator. In 1848 he was a republican member of the Constituent Assembly. Having given his adhesion to the policy of Napoleon, he became president of the legislative body in 1851. He was minister of the interior from July, 1854, to 1858, and succeeded Walewski as minister of state in June, 1863. Died in October of the same year.

Billaut, (ADAM.) See ADAM-BILLAUT.

Bille, bil'lẹh, (STEEN ANDERSEN,) a Danish admiral, born in Funen in 1751, took part in the blockade of Tunis, (1796,) and the battle of Copenhagen, (1801.) Died in 1833.

Bille, (STEEN ANDERSEN,) son of the preceding, born at Copenhagen in 1797, served in the French army in the campaign of 1823. He was made by the King of Denmark minister of the marine, and rear-admiral, in 1852. He commanded a scientific expedition around the world in 1845-47, and published a narrative of the same, (3 vols., 1849-51.)

Billeberg, bil'lẹh-bĕRG', (JOHAN,) a Swedish savant, professor of mathematics at Upsal. Died in 1717.

Billecocq, be'yẹ-kok, (JEAN BAPTISTE LOUIS JOSEPH,) an eminent French advocate and *littérateur,* born in Paris in 1765; died in 1829.

See DUPIN, "Notice sur Billecocq."

Billemaz, bĕl'mȧ' or be'yẹ-mȧ', (FRANÇOIS B.,) a French Jacobin, born at Belley about 1750, was executed in 1793 on a charge of being an agent of the Girondists.

Billerbek, von, fon bil'lẹr-bĕk', (CONSTANTINE,) born at Janikow in 1713, served in the Prussian army in the principal campaigns of the Seven Years' war, and was made lieutenant-general and chevalier of the Black Eagle in 1784. Died in 1785.

Billerey, bĕl'rằ' or be'yẹ-rằ', (CLAUDE NICOLAS,) a French physician, born about 1667 at Besançon, where he was professor of medicine. Died in 1759.

Billet, be'yằ', (PIERRE,) a French scholar and Latin poet, born in 1656, was professor of rhetoric in the college du Plessis. Died in 1719.

Billi, (JACQUES.) See BILLY.

Billican, bil'le-kȧn', (THEOBALD,) also called **Gerlach,** a German reformer, born at Billigheim, was converted by Luther about 1518. He preached at Nordlingen, and lectured on law at Heidelberg. Died in 1554.

Billich, bil'lik, [Lat. BILLICH'IUS,] (ANTON GUN-

THER,) a German physician and chemist, wrote a treatise "On the Three Chemical Principles," in Latin.

Billing, be′yȧN′, (SIGISMOND,) a French officer, born at Colmar in 1773. He was commandant of the national guard of Paris during the Hundred Days, and was appointed chief of the staff by La Fayette in 1830. Died in 1832.

Bil′lingṡ, (JOSEPH,) an English navigator, commanded an expedition sent out in 1787 by Catherine II. of Russia, and discovered some islands in the Northern Ocean.
See " Découvertes des Russes dans le Nord."

Billings, (WILLIAM,) said to have been the first American musical composer, was born in Boston in 1746. He introduced a new style of church music, which obtained great popularity in New England. He was an intimate friend of Samuel Adams. Died in 1800.

Bil′lingṡ-ley, (Sir HENRY,) an English mathematician, translated Euclid's "Elements of Geometry" into English, with notes by Whitehead. Died in 1606.

Bil′ling-ton, (Mrs. ELIZABETH **Weichsel**—wīk′sęl,) a celebrated English vocalist, of German extraction, born in London in 1770. She was married when very young to Mr. Billington, a musician of Drury Lane Theatre, with whom she visited the principal cities of Europe. She was everywhere received with enthusiasm, and is said to have realized ten thousand pounds in one year by her engagements. Died in 1818.
See her "Autobiographic Memoirs," 1792; OXBERRY, "Dramatic Biography."

Billot, be′yo′, (JEAN,) a French preacher, born at Dôle in 1709; died in 1767.

Billouet, bẹl′yoo′ȧ′ or be′yoo′ȧ′, (PHILIPPE,) a French Hebraist, born at Rouen in 1684; died at Orléans in 1720.

Billuart, bẹl′yü-ȧR′ or be′yü-ȧR′, (CHARLES RENÉ,) a French theologian, and professor of philosophy in the college of Douay, born in 1685; died in 1757.

Billy. See BELLY.

Billy, de, dęh be′ye′, (JACQUES,) a French scholar, born at Guise in 1535, translated into Latin the works of Saint Gregory Nazianzen, Saint John Chrysostom, and John of Damascus. Died in 1581.

Billy, de, (JACQUES,) a French mathematician and scientific writer, born at Compiègne in 1602; died in 1679.

Billy, de, (NICOLAS ANTOINE,) a French ecclesiastic and writer, born at Vesoul in 1753; died in 1825.

Bi′lon or **Pi′lon,** an Armenian historian, born in 643 A.D. He wrote a "History of the Patriarchs of Armenia," and translated into Armenian the " Ecclesiastical History" of Socrates. Died in 711.

Bilon, be′lŏN′, (FRANÇOIS MARIE HIPPOLYTE,) a French physician, born at Grenoble in 1780, was a pupil of Bichat. He was a contributor to the "Dictionnaire des Sciences médicales." Died in 1824.

Bilotta, be-lot′tȧ, (GIAMBATTISTA,) an Italian jurist, wrote some legal works. Died in 1636.

Bilotta, (GIOVANNI CAMILLO,) an Italian jurist and legal writer, born in 1557; died in 1588.

Bilotta, (OTTAVIO,) son of Giambattista, noticed above, was a jurist at Naples. Died about 165c.

Bilotta, (SCIPIONE,) an Italian jurist and legal writer. Died in 1581.

Bils, van, vȧn bils, [Lat. BIL′SIUS,] (LODEWIJK,) a Dutch anatomist, who lived about 1670–90, pretended to have a secret process by which he could preserve bodies from decomposition.

Bil′son, (THOMAS,) a learned English prelate, born at Winchester in 1536, became Bishop of Worcester in 1596, and of Winchester in 1597. He published "The Perpetual Government of Christ's Church," "The True Difference between Christian Subjection and Unchristian Rebellion," (1595,) and "The Survey of Christ's Sufferings for Man's Redemption, etc.," (1604.) Died in 1616.

Bimard. See LA BASTIE.

Bimbi, bèm′bee,(BARTOLOMMEO,) a Florentine painter of flowers and fruit, born in 1648; died in 1725.

Bimet, be′mȧ′, (PIERRE,) a French littérateur, born at Avignon in 1687; died in 1760.

Binasco, be-nȧs′ko, or **Binaschi,** be-nȧs′kee, (FILIPPO,) an Italian poet, born at Binasco, in the duchy of Milan; died in 1576.

Binchois, bȧN′shwȧ′, (GILLES,) a musician, who lived about 1400–20, made improvements in harmony and the notation of music.
See FÉTIS, "Biographie Universelle des Musiciens."

Binck. See BINK.

Binder, bin′der, (WILHELM CHRISTIAN,) a German writer, born at Weinsberg in 1810. In 1846 he became editor of the "Encyclopædia for Catholic Germany." He published, besides other works, "The German Horace," (3d edition, 1841,) and "Prince Metternich and his Times," (3d edition, 1845.)

Bineau, be′nō′, (AMAND,) a French chemist, born about 1810, became professor of chemistry at Lyons. He collected and published in 1837 a series of lectures on chemical philosophy, by Thénard.

Bineau, (JEAN MARTIAL,) a French engineer and financier, born at Gennes, in Maine et-Loire, in 1805. He was elected to the Legislative Assembly in April, 1849, and was minister of public works from October of that year to January, 1851. He became minister of finance in January, 1852. Died in September, 1855.

Binet, be′nȧ′, (CLAUDE,) a French poet, born at Beauvais, was a friend of Ronsard, who intrusted to him the publication of his works.

Binet, (ÉTIENNE,) a French Jesuit, born at Dijon in 1569, is satirized in Pascal's "Provincial Letters." Died in 1639.

Binet, (ÉTIENNE,) a French surgeon, practised in the army, and was killed at the siege of Rochelle in 1627 or 1628.

Binet, (FRANÇOIS ISIDORE,) a French preacher and Capuchin monk, born at Niort in 1720.

Binet, (JACQUES PHILIPPE MARIE,) an eminent French mathematician and astronomer, born at Rennes in 1786. He succeeded Delambre in 1823 as professor of astronomy in the College of France, and in 1843 replaced Lacroix in the department (section) of geometry at the Academy of Sciences. He wrote a number of valuable treatises on geometry and natural philosophy, among which is a "Memoir on the Composition of Forces and the Composition of Momenta," (1815.) Died in 1856.
See QUÉRARD, "La France Littéraire," (Supplément.)

Binet, (RENÉ,) a French littérateur, born near Beauvais in 1729. He published a "History of the Decline of Morals among the Romans," (1795,) and a good translation of the works of Virgil and Horace. Died in 1812.
See BOULARD, "Notice sur la Vie de R. Binet," 1817.

Bing. See BEER-BING.

Bingham, bing′am, (GEORGE,) an English divine, born in Dorsetshire in 1713, wrote a "Vindication of the Doctrine and Liturgy of the Church of England," (1774,) "Essay on the Millennium," and other works. Died in 1800.

Bingham, (Sir GEORGE RIDOUT,) an English major-general, born in 1777, served in the Peninsular war. He was subsequently charged to convey Napoleon to Saint Helena. Died in 1833.

Bing′ham, (JOHN A.,) an American lawyer and legislator, born in Pennsylvania in 1815. He was admitted to the bar in 1840, and was elected a member of Congress, in 1854, by the Republicans of the twenty-first district of Ohio. He was re-elected at five subsequent elections, and acquired distinction as a debater. On the 24th of February, 1868, Thaddeus Stevens and Mr. Bingham were appointed a committee to impeach Andrew Johnson, President of the United States, at the bar of the Senate. He was also chairman of the managers who conducted the impeachment in April, 1868, and was re-elected to Congress in October of that year.

Bingham, (JOSEPH,) an eminent English scholar and divine, born in Yorkshire in 1668. He published, m 1722, "Antiquities of the Christian Church," ("Origines Ecclesiasticæ," 10 vols.,) esteemed one of the most valuable works of the kind. Died in 1723. His son Joseph prepared an edition of the "Story of the Theban War," published after his death.
See RICHARD BINGHAM, "Life of Joseph Bingham," 1829.

Bingham, (PEREGRINE,) an English writer on law, born about 1788. He published several legal treatises, (1820–40,) and "Reports in the Common Pleas," (1822–34.) Died in 1864.

Bingham, (Sir RICHARD,) an English general, who had a high command in the reign of Elizabeth. He served with distinction against the Irish insurgents about 1586–92. He was the ancestor of the Earls of Lucan.

Bingham, (WILLIAM,) an American Senator, born in 1752. He married Miss Willing, of Philadelphia, in 1780. He represented Pennsylvania in the Senate of the United States from 1795 to 1801. Died at Bath, England, in 1804. His daughter was married to Sir Francis Baring's son.

Bingham. See LUCAN, EARL OF.

Bing'ley, a celebrated actor, of English extraction, born at Rotterdam in 1755; died in 1818.

Bingley, (WILLIAM,) an English divine and miscellaneous writer, born in Yorkshire. He published, among other works, "Memoirs of British Quadrupeds," (1819,) "The Economy of a Christian Life," "Animal Biography," and "Useful Knowledge," (3 vols. 8vo, 1816.) Died in 1823.

Bini, bee'nee, (CARLO,) an Italian writer and republican, born at Leghorn in 1806, was a friend of Mazzini and devoted to his political principles. Died in 1842.

Bini, bee'nee, [Lat. BIN'IUS,] (SEVERIN,) a German ecclesiastic, and professor of theology at Cologne, was born in Rhenish Prussia. Died in 1641.

Bink or **Binck,** bĭnk, (JAKOB,) a celebrated painter and engraver, born at Cologne about 1500, is supposed to have studied under Albert Dürer. He became portrait-painter to Christian VIII. of Denmark. Died about 1560.

Binkes, binks, (JAKOB,) a Dutch mariner, who in 1676 defended the island of Tobago for a time against Admiral D'Estrées. He perished by an explosion the same year.

Bin'ney, (AMOS,) M.D., an American naturalist, born in Boston in 1803, was noted as a patron of art and science. He possessed an ample fortune, which he expended liberally in the promotion of science and the patronage of art. He was president of the Boston Society of Natural History at the time of his death. Among his works is "Terrestrial and Air-Breathing Mollusks of the United States," illustrated by beautiful engravings, (3 vols., 1851.) Died at Rome in 1847.

See a notice of A. BINNEY, prefixed to the above work, by A. A. GOULD, who edited the same.

Binney, (HORACE,) a distinguished lawyer of Philadelphia, was born in that city in 1780. At an early age he entered Harvard College, where he graduated in 1797, dividing the first honours with his classmate, the late Judge White, of Salem, Massachusetts. He is now (1869) the only surviving member of his class. He studied law in Philadelphia, in the office of Jared Ingersoll, and was admitted to the bar in 1800. He devoted himself with great assiduity to his profession, and in a few years stood at its head with John Sergeant, Charles Chauncey, and other eminent lawyers. He took a leading part in the most important cases in the higher courts of Pennsylvania, and was frequently called to the supreme court of the United States. More than once he had tendered to him high judicial positions, which he declined. Towards the close of President Jackson's first administration Mr. Binney was elected to Congress, where his ability and eloquence soon gave him a commanding position. He appeared in court for the last time in 1843, when he made his celebrated argument in the supreme court of the United States in the case of Vidal versus the Mayor of Philadelphia. This argument, which was exhaustive and is regarded as unanswerable, is often cited as authority, by the bench and bar throughout the United States, on questions involving the law of charitable uses, and it has been referred to in England by eminent jurists in terms of the highest commendation. Mr. Binney's last appearance before his legal brethren was on the occasion of the death of his friend, the Honourable John Sergeant; and in delineating the character of that distinguished man he spoke with eloquence and touching pathos.* His great and varied learning, his large experience and profound judgment in all matters pertaining to his profession, joined to his consistent and upright character, have given Mr. Binney a position of authority and influence to which few men have attained. Among his most important writings we may mention "An Inquiry into the Formation of Washington's Farewell Address," (1859,) and his Eulogiums on Chief-Justice

* His remarks on that occasion are to be found in "Wallace's Circuit Court Reports," vol. ii.

Tilghman (1827) and on Chief-Justice Marshall, (1836.) His argument in the Vidal case, before referred to, was published in Philadelphia in 1844, (1 vol. 8vo.) Binney's "Reports of Cases in the Supreme Court of Pennsylvania," in six volumes, are esteemed models of their kind.

See "Quarterly Review" for April, 1860.

Bin'ney, (THOMAS,) an eloquent English nonconformist minister, born at Newcastle-upon-Tyne about 1800. He settled in London about 1830, and preached many years in the Weigh-House Chapel. He is the author of numerous popular works, among which are "The Closet and the Church," "The Practical Power of Faith," and "Is it possible to make the Best of both Worlds?"

Bin'ning, (HUGH,) a Scottish Presbyterian minister, born in Ayrshire in 1627, became professor of moral philosophy at Glasgow. Died in 1654.

See CHAMBERS, "Biographical Dictionary of Eminent Scotsmen."

Binninger, bin'ning-ẹr, (JEAN NICOLAS,) born at Montbelliard in 1628, was physician to the Duke of Würtemberg.

Binos, de, dẹh be'nos', L'ABBÉ, a French traveller, born in 1730, published in 1786 an account of his travels in Egypt and Palestine. Died in 1803.

Binterim, bin'tẹr-im, (ANTON JOSEPH,) a German Catholic theologian, born at Dusseldorf in 1779, published "Memorable Things (*Denkwürdigkeiten*) respecting the Catholic Church," (7 vols., 1825–32,) and other works. Died in 1855.

Bintinaye, de la, dẹh lä băn'te'nạ', (AGATHON MARIE RENÉ,) a French naval officer, born at Rennes in 1758; died in 1792.

Bioern. See BIÖRN.

Biolco. See BEOLCO.

Bi'on, [Βίων,] a Greek tragic poet, mentioned by Diogenes Laertius, lived probably in the first century B.C.

Bion of Abde'ra, a Greek mathematician, who lived in the third or fourth century B.C.

Bion of Borysthenes, a philosopher, who lived about 280 B.C. After professing nearly all the systems of philosophy in turn, he embraced that of the Peripatetics.

Bion [Gr. Βίων] of Smyrna, a celebrated bucolic poet, lived under the reign of Ptolemy Philadelphus II. of Egypt. He was a contemporary and friend of Moschus, who composed an elegy in his honour. His style is elegant, and his versification harmonious. His principal extant poem is a lament for Adonis. He is supposed to have died by poison.

Bion, be'ôn', (JEAN,) a French priest, born at Dijon in 1668, was converted to Protestantism, and subsequently took charge of an English congregation in Holland. He wrote a "Narrative of the Sufferings of the Protestants in the Galleys of France," (1708.)

Bion, (JEAN MARIE,) a French jurist, and member of the National Convention, (1792,) voted for the imprisonment of the king. He became secretary in the Council of Five Hundred about 1795.

Bion, (NICOLAS,) a French engineer and mechanician, born in 1652. He wrote a "Treatise on the Construction, etc. of Mathematical Instruments," etc. Died in 1733.

Biondi, be-on'dee, (ANGELICA LUCIA,) an Italian poetess, daughter of the architect Zucchi, was born in Piedmont in 1771; died in 1805.

Biondi, (GIOVANNI FRANCESCO,) an Italian *littérateur* and diplomatist, born in Dalmatia in 1572. Having been introduced by Sir Henry Wotton to James I. of England, he was employed by that sovereign in several embassies. He wrote, in Italian, a "History of the Civil War between the Houses of Lancaster and York," (1637.) Died in 1644.

See NICÉRON, "Mémoires."

Biondo, be-on'do, [Lat. BLON'DUS,] (MICHAEL ANGELO,) an Italian physician and medical writer, born at Venice in 1497; died about 1560.

Biondo Flavio. See FLAVIO.

Biörn, Bioern, or **Björn,** be-ÖRN', I., King of Sweden in the eighth century, was surnamed IRONSIDES.

Biörn III. reigned in the ninth century. He favoured the introduction of Christianity into Sweden.

Biörn or **Björn,** be-ÖRN' or björn, sometimes written **Beorn,** a historian of the seventeenth century, born in Iceland, was the author of a work on the discoveries in Greenland, "De Novitiis Grœnlandorum Indiciis."

Biot, be'o', (Édouard Constant,) a French Orientalist, son of Jean Baptiste, noticed below, was born in Paris in 1803. He was a member of the Academy of Inscriptions. He translated several works from the Chinese, and was a contributor to the "Journal Asiatique." Died in 1850.

Biot, be'o' or be'ot', (Jean Baptiste,) a celebrated French astronomer, optician, and natural philosopher, born in Paris on the 21st of April, 1774. He was educated in the college Louis-le-Grand and in the Polytechnic School, and became professor of physics in the College of France in 1800. Having written some mathematical essays, he was elected to the Academy of Sciences in 1803, and accompanied Gay-Lussac in his ascension by a balloon in 1804. His "Analytic Treatise on Curves and Surfaces of the Second Degree" (1802) was highly esteemed and often reprinted. In 1805 he published an "Elementary Treatise on Physical Astronomy," (3d edition, 6 vols., 1850.) He was appointed a member of the bureau of longitudes, and in 1806 was employed by the government, in conjunction with Arago, in the measurement of the arc of the meridian in Spain. He obtained the chair of physical astronomy in the Faculty of Sciences in 1809. Biot was chosen a member of the Royal Sociey of London about 1815. He was sent to the Shetland Islands, in 1817, to perform a geodesic operation. His "Treatise on Experimental Physics and Mathematics" (4 vols., 1816) is called one of the best on that subject. In 1821 he published "Geodesical, Astronomical, and Physical Observations made in Spain, France, England, and Scotland, to determine the Variation of Gravity, etc." He contributed many articles to the "Journal des Savants" and the "Annales de Chimie et de Physique." For the "Biographie Universelle" he wrote many able notices of scientific men, among whom were Descartes, Dr. Franklin, and Galileo. In his "Memoir on Circular Polarization and its Application to Organic Chemistry" (read in 1833) he announced a new discovery, which has been applied with success in testing the quality of sugar. He received in 1840 the Rumford medal of the Royal Society of London for his researches in the circular polarization of light. He was admitted to the French Academy in 1856, in consideration of the beauty and eloquence of his writings, among which we should notice his "Researches on Ancient Astronomy." He married in early life a daughter of Professor Brisson. Died in 1862, in his eighty-eighth year.

See Le Bas, "Dictionnaire encyclopédique de la France;" "Nouvelle Biographie Générale;" "Blackwood's Magazine" for July, 1818.

Birago, be-rä'go, (Carlo,) Baron of, a distinguished military engineer, born near Milan in 1792, was the inventor of the system of bridges called by his name. Died in 1845.

Birago, (Francesco,) an accomplished Italian gentleman and writer, born at Milan in 1562. He was well versed in the *scienza cavalleresca, i.e.* the laws of honour and chivalry, on which he wrote several works of much merit. He was appealed to as an oracle or arbiter on questions of chivalry. Died about 1640.

See "Nouvelle Biographie Générale."

Birago, (Jacopo,) sometimes called **Lapo** or **Lampo,** an Italian scholar and Hellenist, born in Tuscany about 1420. He became professor of literature and philosophy at Bologna, and translated Plutarch's "Lives" into Latin.

Birago Avogadro, be-rä'go ä-vo-gä'dro, (Giambattista,) an Italian historian and jurist, wrote an "African History," (1650,) which has been translated into French.

Birague, be-rä'gä, (Clemente,) a Spanish artist, born about 1560, is said to have been the inventor of engraving on diamonds. Among his works of this kind is a portrait of Don Carlos, son of Philip II.

Birague, de, deh be'räg', (Flaminio,) a French poet, nephew of René, noticed below, lived about 1570.

Birague, de, (René,) a statesman and cardinal under Henry II. and Charles IX., was born at Milan in 1510. He became keeper of the seals in 1570, and on the death of L'Hôpital obtained the title of chancellor. He is said to have been one of the principal instigators of the Massacre of Saint Bartholomew. Died in 1583.

See De Thou, "Historia sui Temporis;" Moréri, "Dictionnaire Historique."

Biran. See Maine de Biran.

Birch, beĕrK, (Johann Georg,) a Danish author, born in 1750, lived at Seeland; died in 1795.

Birch, (Peter,) an English divine, born in 1652, became prebendary of Westminster.

Birch, (Samuel,) an English antiquary, born in London about 1813. He has written on Greek and Roman antiquities and Egyptian hieroglyphics.

Birch, (Thomas,) D.D., an English historian and biographer, born in London in 1705. He was originally a member of the Society of Friends, but he subsequently entered into orders in the Church of England. He became a Fellow of the Royal Society in 1734, and one of its secretaries in 1752. He published, in 1741, his "General Dictionary, Historical and Critical," (10 vols.,) being a translation of Bayle's work, with great additions. He also wrote a "Life of Archbishop Tillotson," "Life of Henry, Prince of Wales, Son of James I.," and other works. Died in 1766.

Birch'ing-ton, written also **Brychington,**(Stephen,) an English monk and chronicler, wrote a "History of the Archbishops of Canterbury down to 1368," published in Wharton's "Anglia Sacra."

Birch-Pfeiffer, beĕrK'pfi'fer, (Charlotte,) a popular German actress and dramatic writer, born at Stuttgart in 1800, was the author of "The Favourites," ("Die Günstlinge,") "Hinko," and other plays. Died in December, 1868.

Birck'beck, (Simon,) an English divine, born in Westmoreland in 1584, published a work entitled "The Protestant's Evidence."

Birckner, beĕrK'ner, (Michael Gottlieb,) a Danish author, born at Copenhagen in 1756, was vicar at Korsoer. He gained a high reputation by his writings, among which is a "Plea for the Liberty of the Press," (1797.) Died in 1798.

See his "Autobiography," 1797, and a German translation of the same, 1812; also Kraft og Nyerup, "Litteraturlexicon."

Bird, (Charles Smith,) an English theologian and controversialist, born about 1795; died in 1862.

Bird, (Edward,) an eminent English painter of rural and domestic scenes, born at Wolverhampton in 1772. His pictures of the "Choristers Rehearsing," "Good News," and "The Will," established his reputation, and caused him to be elected an academician. He was appointed painter to the Princess Charlotte about 1813. Among his other works we may name "The Surrender of Calais," "The Field of Chevy Chase the Day after the Battle," "The Gipsy Boy," "The Country Auction," and "The Death of Eli." For the last-named picture he obtained from the Marquis of Stafford the sum of five hundred guineas. Died in 1819.

See Cunningham, "Lives of Painters, Sculptors, and Architects."

Bird, (Francis,) an English sculptor, born in London in 1667. Among his works are Dr. Busby's monument, in Westminster Abbey, and a statue of Queen Anne. Died in 1731.

Bird, (Golding,) an English medical writer, born in 1815, practised in London with success. He contributed many treatises to medical periodicals, and published "Elements of Natural Philosophy," (2d edition, 1843.) Died in 1854.

Bird, (John,) an English mechanician and instrument-maker, published a work entitled "Method of Dividing Astronomical Instruments." Died in 1776.

Bird, (Robert Montgomery,) M.D., an American author, born at New Castle, Delaware, in 1803. He began to practise medicine in Philadelphia, and produced successful tragedies, entitled "The Gladiator" and "Oraloosa." In 1834 he published "Calavar, a Romance of Mexico." Among his other works are "The Infidel," a novel, (1835,) and "The Adventures of Robin Day," (1839.) He became in 1847 joint editor and proprietor of the "North American and United States Gazette," published in Philadelphia. He was distinguished for his learning, versatility, and practical ability. Died in 1854.

See Griswold's "Prose Writers of America."

Birde or **Byrd,** bird, (William,) an eminent English composer of church music, born about 1540. He was a pupil of Thomas Tallis, and became, conjointly with him, organist to Queen Elizabeth in 1575. Among

---

ɛ as *k;* ç as *s;* g̃ *hard;* g̃ as *j;* G, H, K, *guttural;* N, *nasal;* R, *trilled;* s̃ as *z;* th as in *this.*   (☞See Explanations, p. 23.)

his best productions are his "Sacred Songs," and his magnificent canon entitled "Non Nobis, Domine," which is still popular. Died in 1623.

See BURNEY, "General History of Music."

Biré, be′rā′, (PIERRE,) a French jurist, lived about 1580.

Biren, bee′ren, **Biron,** bee′ron, or **Buren,** boo′ren, (ERNEST JOHN,) Duke of Courland, born in 1690. He was patronized by Anne, Duchess of Courland, who, on becoming Empress of Russia, made him governor and duke of Courland. He was made regent by the empress at her death, but, having formed a scheme to marry his son the Princess Elizabeth, he was exiled to Siberia. He was afterwards recalled by Peter III. Died in 1772.

See RUEHL, "Geschichte E. J. von Biron," 2 vols., 1764; HEM-PEL, "Leben des Herzogs E. J. von Curland," 1772; KARAMSIN, "Histoire de la Russie."

Birger, beer′ger, King of Sweden, born in 1281, was deposed by his subjects, and died in Denmark in 1321.

Birger de Bielbo, (Bjelbo,) beer′ger dä be ĕl′bo, Duke of Gothia, born about 1210, was a brother-in-law of Eric, King of Sweden, on whose death he became regent of the kingdom. He founded the city of Stockholm, and introduced numerous reforms into the government. Died in 1266.

See SILFVERSTOLPE, "Åreminne öfver Birger Jarl till Bjällbo," 1787.

Biringuccio, be-rèn-goot′cho, (VANUCCI,) an Italian mathematician, lived about 1520. He wrote a work on pyrotechny.

Birk′beck, (GEORGE,) an English physician and educational reformer, born in Yorkshire in 1776. He graduated at Edinburgh, where he made the acquaintance of Jeffrey, Lord Brougham, and Sidney Smith. He became soon after professor in the Andersonian Institution at Glasgow. From 1801 to 1804 he gave a gratuitous course of lectures to the mechanics of that city, which were numerously attended. In 1823 the London Mechanics' Institution was founded, and Dr. Birkbeck was elected its president. Died in 1841.

See KNIGHT, "Dictionary of Arts, Commerce," etc.

Birk′en-head or **Berk′en-head,** (Sir JOHN,) an English journalist, born in Cheshire about 1615. In 1642 he became editor of "The Court Mercury," or "Mercurius Aulicus," a royalist journal. After the restoration he became a member of Parliament for Wilton, and a Fellow of the Royal Society. Died in 1679.

Birk′head, [Lat. BIRCHEA′DUS,] (HENRY,) an English writer and Latin poet, born in London in 1617.

See WOOD, "Athenæ Oxonienses."

Birnbaum, beern′bowm, (JOHANN MICHAEL FRANZ,) a German *littérateur*, born at Bamberg in 1790, became professor of law and chancellor of the University at Giessen, (1848.)

Bir′ney, (DAVID BELL,) an American general, son of James G. Birney, noticed below, born at Huntsville, Alabama, in 1825. He was a lawyer before the rebellion, and resided in Philadelphia. About the end of 1861 he was appointed a brigadier-general. He served with distinction at Fredericksburg, December, 1862, and at Chancellorsville, May, 1863. Having been raised to the rank of major-general, he commanded a division at the battle of Gettysburg, July, 1863, and in several battles between Grant and Lee in 1864. In July of that year he obtained command of the tenth army corps. He died in Philadelphia, October, 1864.

See TENNEY, "Military and Naval History of the Rebellion."

Birney, (JAMES G.,) a distinguished opponent of slavery, born at Danville, Kentucky, in 1792 or 1793. He studied law, which he practised at Huntsville, Alabama. About 1834 he began to advocate publicly the immediate emancipation of slaves, and liberated twenty or more which he owned, thus sacrificing property valued at several thousand dollars. He founded an anti-slavery paper, called "The Philanthropist," at Cincinnati, in 1834 or 1835. His office was attacked by a mob, which threw his press into the Ohio River. About 1836 he was appointed secretary of the American Anti-Slavery Society, and afterwards resided several years in New York City. He acted an important part in the organization of a new political party, called the "Liberty Party," by which he was nominated for the Presidency in 1840. About 1842 he removed to Saginaw, Michigan. He received 62,263

votes as the candidate of the Liberty party in the Presidential election of 1844. He was author of a tract entitled "The American Churches the Bulwarks of American Slavery." Died near Perth Amboy, New Jersey, in 1857, leaving several sons.

Bir′nie, (Sir RICHARD,) a Scottish magistrate, born at Banff about 1760. As a police magistrate in London, he rendered service in the suppression of a riot in 1820. Died in 1832.

See CHAMBERS, "Biographical Dictionary of Eminent Scotsmen."

Biroli, be-ro′lee, (GIOVANNI,) an Italian physician and botanist, born at Novara in 1772, became professor of botany and materia medica at Turin, and published several works on agriculture, etc. Died in 1825.

Biron. See BIREN.

Biron, de, deh be′rôn′, (ARMAND de Gontaut—deh gôn′tō′,) DUC, a French marshal, born about 1524. He fought against the Huguenots at Saint-Denis and Moncontour, and subsequently under Henry IV. at Ivry. He was killed at the siege of Épernay in 1592.

Biron, de, (ARMAND LOUIS DE GONTAUT,) Duc de Lauzun, a nephew of Louis Antoine, noticed below, was born in Paris in 1747. He fought in America for the United States about 1780, and was appointed general-in-chief of the army of the Rhine in July, 1792. He defeated the Vendeans at Parthenay in 1793. Having offended the Committee of Public Safety by insisting on resigning his command, he was executed in December, 1793.

Biron, de, (CHARLES ARMAND,) DUC, a French general, born in 1663. He obtained the baton of marshal in the reign of Louis XV. Died in 1756.

Biron, de, (CHARLES DE GONTAUT,) DUC, son of Armand de Gontaut, noticed above, born in 1562, was a favourite of Henry IV., who gave him the title of marshal of France and appointed him in 1595 Governor of Burgundy. Being afterwards convicted of conspiring with the Duke of Savoy against the French king, he was put to death in 1602.

See DE THOU, "Historia sui Temporis;" MARTIR-RIZO, "Historia de la Vida del Duque de Biron," 1629.

Biron, de, (LOUIS ANTOINE,) a son of Charles Armand, noticed above, born in 1700, served in Italy, Flanders, etc., and became marshal of France. Died in 1788.

Biroteau, be′ro′tō′, (JEAN BAPTISTE,) a French Girondist, born at Perpignan, was a member of the National Convention, and voted at the trial of the king for the appeal to the people. He was executed on a charge of treason in 1793.

See THIERS, "Histoire de la Révolution Française."

Birr, beer, (ANTOINE,) a Swiss physician and critic, born in 1693, became professor of Greek at Bâle.

Bisaccioni, be-sät-cho′nee, (MAJOLINO, mä-yo-lee′no,) COUNT, an Italian soldier, diplomatist, and writer, born at Ferrara in 1582. He was employed in various embassies by the Duke of Savoy and other princes. Died in 1663.

See MAZZUCHELLI, "Scrittori d'Italia."

Bis′bie, (NATHANIEL,) D.D., an English divine, wrote "The Modern Pharisee," and a number of sermons. Died in 1695.

Biscaino, bès-kä-ee′no, (DOMENICO,) an Italian painter and engraver, born at Genoa in 1632; died in 1657.

Bischof, bish′off, (KARL GUSTAV,) a German chemist and geologist, born at Wörd, near Nuremberg, in 1792, became professor of chemistry at Bonn in 1822. He published a "Manual of Chemical and Physical Geology," (2 vols., 1847-55, unfinished,) which is highly esteemed.

Bischof, (NICOLAS.) See FROBEN.

Bischoff, bish′off, (CHRISTOPH HEINRICH ERNST,) a German physician, and professor of pharmacy and therapeutics at Bonn, was born at Hanover about 1780.

Bischoff, (GEORG FRIEDRICH,) born at Ellrich in 1780 was the originator of the musical festivals of Germany. Died in 1841.

Bischoff, (GOTTLIEB WILHELM,) professor of botany at Heidelberg, born at Dürkheim in 1797, published "Elements of Medicinal Botany," (1831,) and "Manual of Universal Botany," (1834.)

Bischoff, (IGNAZ RUDOLF,) of Altenstern, a German physician and surgeon of high reputation, born at Krems-münster in 1784, became professor of clinics at Vienna about 1825. He published a treatise "On Chronic Diseases in general," (1817,) and other medical works. Died in 1850.

Bischoff, (THEODOR LUDWIG WILHELM,) a German physiologist and anatomist, son of Christoph Heinrich Ernst, born at Hanover in 1807. In 1844 he became professor of anatomy and physiology at Giessen, where he founded an anatomical museum and a physiological institute. He wrote several valuable treatises on the development of the mammalia.

See BROCKHAUS, "Conversations-Lexikon."

Bischofsberger, bish'offs-bĕR'gẹr, (BARTHOLOMEW,) a Swiss writer and Protestant divine, born in the canton of Appenzell in 1622, wrote a "History of the Canton of Appenzell." Died in 1678.

Bischofswerder, von, fon bish'ofs-wĕR'dẹr, (JOHANN RUDOLF,) a Prussian officer and statesman under Frederick William II., was employed by him in several important negotiations. Died in 1803.

See ERSCH und GRUBER, "Allgemeine Encyklopaedie."

Bischop (or **Biskop**) **van,** vän bis'KOP, (JAN,) a skilful Dutch designer and painter of landscapes and history, was born at the Hague in 1646. He copied the Italian masters with the crayon. Died in 1686.

See DESCAMPS, "Vies des Peintres Flamands," etc.

Bischop, van, written also **Biskop,** (KORNELIS,) a Flemish or Dutch painter, born in 1630, was a pupil of Bol, whose style he imitated. Died in 1674.

Biscioni, be-sho'nee, (ANTONIO MARIA,) a learned Italian ecclesiastic and eloquent preacher, born at Florence in 1674, was appointed apostolic prothonotary, and chief librarian of the Laurentian Library of Florence. He wrote a "History of the Noble Family of the Panciatichi," and other works. Died in 1756.

See GINGUENÉ, "Histoire Littéraire d'Italie."

Bis'cōe, (RICHARD,) an English divine, born about 1670. He published "The History of the Acts of the Apostles, confirmed from other Authors," etc., "which," says Dr. Doddridge, "shows how incontestably the Acts of the Apostles demonstrate the truth of Christianity."

Biset, be'zạ', (CHARLES EMMANUEL,) a Flemish painter, born at Mechlin in 1633, became director of the Academy of Antwerp in 1674.

See DESCAMPS, "Vies des Peintres Flamands."

Bish'ọp, (GEORGE,) an English astronomer, born in 1784; died in 1861.

Bishop, (Sir HENRY ROWLEY,) an eminent English composer, born in London in 1780. He was elected professor of music at Oxford in 1848, and was one of the first directors of the Philharmonic concerts. Among the most popular of his numerous operas are "The Englishman in India," "Guy Mannering," "The Knight of Snowdon," and "The Slave." His ballads, songs, glees, etc. are esteemed master-pieces of the kind. He was knighted in 1842. Died in 1855.

Bishop, (SAMUEL,) an English divine and poet, born in London in 1731. He is believed to have written the popular farce of "High Life Below-stairs," sometimes attributed to Garrick. Died in 1795.

See T. CLARKE, "Life of S. Bishop," prefixed to his works, 1796.

Bishop, (WILLIAM,) an English Catholic theologian, born in Warwickshire in 1555. In 1623 he was appointed by the pope apostolic vicar, and obtained the title of Bishop of Chalcedon. Died in 1624.

Bisi, bee'see, (BONAVENTURA,) an Italian painter of miniatures, born at Bologna in 1612, was also an etcher. Died at Módena in 1662.

Biskop. See BISCHOP.

Bismark, biz'mȧrk, (FRIEDRICH WILHELM,) a German general and military writer, born at Windheim, in Westphalia, in 1783. He entered the French army, and distinguished himself under Ney in the Russian campaign of 1812.

Bismark- (or **Bismarck-**) **Schönhausen, von,** fon biz'mȧrk shön'höw'zẹn, (KARL OTTO,) a celebrated Prussian statesman, born at Brandenburg in 1813. He studied law at the Universities of Göttingen and Berlin. In 1847 he was elected a member of the United Diet, and became one of the chief orators of the Junkers, or Conservative party. In 1851 he was sent to Frankfort

as first secretary of legation, with the title of Privy Counsellor to the Prussian Embassy. He adopted the political axiom that Prussia could not fulfil its mission in Germany until Austria should be driven out of the Bund. He was sent as ambassador to Saint Petersburg in 1859, about the end of which year he visited Paris, ostensibly for amusement. He represented Prussia at Paris for a short time in 1862, and was appointed prime minister in September of that year. His reactionary policy gave great offence to the Liberals. In October, 1862, he dissolved the chamber, (the majority of which opposed his measures,) and declared that the ministry would govern on their own responsibility. Prussia, with the aid of Austria, conquered Sleswick and Holstein from Denmark in 1864, and signed the Convention of Gastein in relation to those duchies in August, 1865. Bismark designed to annex Sleswick and Holstein to Prussia, but could not obtain the consent of Austria. The long rivalry between these two powers was now brought to a crisis. A majority of the German Bund having voted in favour of Austria, Prussia seceded from the Bund and formed an alliance with the King of Italy. War was declared in June, 1866. The Prussian armies speedily occupied Hanover and Saxony. Advancing into Bohemia, they encountered the Austrian army near Sadowa (Königgrätz) on the 3d of July, and gained a victory so decisive that the Emperor of Austria made overtures of peace; and a treaty was signed in August, 1866, by which Austria was excluded from the German Bund. Hanover, Electoral Hesse, Holstein, and other small states were annexed to Prussia. Bismark negotiated in August, 1866, secret treaties of offensive and defensive alliance with Bavaria, Baden, and Würtemberg. According to these treaties, (which were made public in April, 1867,) the King of Prussia is commander of the armies of the said states. This brief and momentous war rendered Prussia perhaps the foremost power in Europe, united nearly all Germany, (except Austria, Bohemia, and Moravia,) and greatly impaired the influence and prestige of Napoleon III. It is generally admitted that Bismark outwitted the French emperor in the diplomatic intrigues and contests of 1866. "In considering recent events," says M. Thiers, March, 1867, "I am tempted to exclaim, with Bossuet, 'A man was found.' Not that I wish to institute any comparison between Cromwell, to whom the quotation applies, and the bold minister who has so rapidly raised Prussia to greatness. . . . But, considering how wonderfully adapted he has shown himself to the task he has undertaken, I cannot help saying, Yes, a man has been found endowed with rare political sagacity, still greater boldness, and whom his countrymen must consider a great patriot." He was appointed chancellor of the North German Confederation in July, 1867.

See a Memoir of Bismark in the "North American Review" for January, 1868.

Bisot or **Bizot,** be'zo', (JEAN LOUIS,) a French mechanician and pyrotechnist, born at Besançon in 1702; died in 1781.

Bis'sạt, Bis'sẹt, or **Bis'sạrt,** (PETER,) a Scottish philosopher and poet, born in 1500, became professor of canon law at Bologna. Died in 1568.

Bisschop. See EPISCOPIUS.

Bisschop, van, (JAN.) See BISCHOP.

Bisselin. See BASSELIN.

Bis'sẹll, (WILLIAM H.,) an American Governor, born in Otsego county, New York, in 1811. He studied medicine, and removed to Monroe county, Illinois, in 1837. About 1842 he began to practise law. He served as colonel in the Mexican war, (1846-47,) and represented a district of Illinois in Congress from 1849 to 1855. Having separated from the Democratic party in 1854, he was elected Governor of Illinois by the Republicans in 1856. Died at Springfield in 1860.

Bissen, bis'sẹn, (WILHELM,) a Danish sculptor, born near Sleswick in 1798, studied at Rome under Thorwaldsen. He became president of the Academy of Fine Arts at Copenhagen in 1850. Among his master-pieces are "Cupid sharpening his Arrow," an "Apollo," and a "Venus."

Bis'set, (CHARLES,) a Scottish physician and savant, born in Perthshire in 1717. He wrote an "Essay on the

Theory and Construction of Fortifications," and several medical works. Died in 1791.

See CHAMBERS, "Biographical Dictionary of Eminent Scotsmen."

Bisset, (JAMES,) a Scottish *littérateur* and amateur artist, born at Perth in 1752 ; died in 1832.

Bisset, (ROBERT,) a Scottish writer, published a "History of the Reign of George III.," (6 vols.,) a "Life of Edmund Burke," (1798,) and an edition of the "Spectator," with notes and lives of the authors. Died in 1805.

Bis′set, (WILLIAM,) an English divine and political writer under the reign of Queen Anne, wrote several controversial treatises against Dr. Sacheverell.

See NICHOLS, "Literary Anecdotes."

Bisso, bès′so, (FRANCESCO,) a resident of Palermo, was appointed by Philip II. of Spain, in 1581, first physician of the kingdom of Sicily. Died in 1598.

Bisson, be′sŏn′, (LOUIS CHARLES,) Bishop of Bayeux, born in the department of Manche in 1742 ; died in 1820.

Bisson, (Count P. F. J. G.,) a French general, born at Montpellier in 1767, served in the Prussian campaign of 1807, and was created a count in 1808. Died in 1811.

See "Victoires et Conquêtes des Français."

Bissoni, bès-so′nee, (GIOVANNI BATTISTA,) an Italian painter of Padua. Died in 1636.

Bistac, bès′tăk′, (FRANÇOIS,) a French grammarian, and rector of the college at Langres, where he was born in 1677. Died in 1752.

Bitaubé, be′tŏ′bă′,(PAUL JÉRÉMIE,) a German scholar, of French extraction, born at Königsberg in 1732. He published a French translation of the "Iliad" and "Odyssey," and of Goethe's "Hermann and Dorothea." His most esteemed work is a prose poem entitled "Joseph." He was a foreign associate of the French Academy of Inscriptions. Died in 1808.

See DACIER, "Notice sur Bitaubé;" MICHEL BERR, "Essai sur la Vie et les Ouvrages de P. J. Bitaubé," 1809.

Biton. See CLEOBIS.

Bi′ton, [Βίτων,] a Greek writer, known as the author of a work on machines of war, dedicated to a king Attalus, but which one is uncertain.

Bitzius, bit′se-ús, (ALBERT,) a popular Swiss author, who wrote under the assumed name of JEREMIAS GOTTHELF, was born at Morat, in the canton of Freiburg, in 1797. He was pastor of Lützelfluh. He published many tales and other works, among which are "Kathi die Grossmutter," (2 vols., 1848,) and "Uli der Pächter," (1849.) Died in 1854.

Biumi, be-oo′mee, (PAOLO GIROLAMO,) an Italian physician and medical writer, who graduated at Pavia in 1685, was professor of anatomy at Milan. Died in 1731.

Bivar, be-var′, (FRANCISCO,) a Spanish theologian and religious writer, born at Madrid ; died in 1636.

Bivar, de, (RODRIGO DIAZ.) See CID, THE.

Biver, be-vaiR′, or **Bivero,** be-vā′ro, (PEDRO,) a Spanish Jesuit and religious writer, born at Madrid in 1572 ; died in 1656.

Bixio, bèk′se-o, (JACQUES ALEXANDRE,) an able journalist, born at Chiavari, in Sardinia, in 1808. He founded at Paris, with M. Buloz, the "Revue des Deux Mondes," and published a good work, entitled "La Maison rustique." In 1848 he was elected to the Constituent Assembly, and was wounded in a contest with the seditious mob. He was minister of agriculture and commerce for a short time in December, 1848. His public life was abruptly terminated by the *coup d'état* in 1851.

Bizardière, de la, deh lă be′zăR′de-àiR′, (MICHEL DAVID,) SIEUR, a French historian, who published a "History of Louis le Grand," (1712,) and several works on Polish history.

Bizet, be′ză′, (MARTIN JEAN BAPTISTE,) a French ecclesiastic, born near Bolbec in 1746.

Bizot, be′zo′, (PIERRE,) a French antiquary, born in 1630 ; died in 1696.

Bizzarri, bèt-săr′ree, or **Bizari,** bèd-zä′ree, (PIETRO,) an Italian historian and poet, born about 1530. His principal works are a "History of the War in Hungary," (1569,) and a "History of the Cyprian War between the Venetians and Solyman," (1573,) both in Latin.

Bizzelli, bèt-sel′lee, (GIOVANNI,) a Florentine painter of history and portraits, born about 1556 ; died in 1612.

Bjelke. See BIELKE.

Bjering or **Biering,** be-êr′ing, (CHRISTIAN HENRIK,) a Danish author, born in Funen, was pastor of Aastrup. Died in 1804.

Bjerken, be-êr′ken, (PETER,) an able Swedish surgeon, born in Stockholm in 1765, became in 1802 physician-in-ordinary to the king. He obtained the order of the Polar Star, and other distinctions. Died in 1818.

See S. A. HEDIN, "Åminnelse-Tal ŏfver P. af Bjerken," 1819.

Björn or **Bjœrn.** See BIÖRN.

Björner, Bjœrner, or **Biœrner,** be-ŏR′ner, (ERIC JULIUS,) a Swedish antiquary, born in 1696 ; died in 1750.

See ERSCH und GRUBER, "Allgemeine Encyklopaedie."

Björnklow or **Biœrnklow,** be-ŏRn′klŏw, (MATTHEW,) a Swedish statesman and senator, born in 1607, was employed in various embassies. Died in 1671.

Björnson, be-ŏrn′sŏn, (BJÖRNSTJERNE, be-ŏrn′-ste-êR′nĕh,) a popular Norwegian author, born in 1832, has written a few short poems, some dramas, and several charming tales, among which are "Arne," (recently translated into English,) "A Happy Lad," and "The Fisher-Maiden," ("Fiskerjenten," 1868.) The last, which is his latest production, has been translated into German and English. His works have been received with extraordinary favour wherever they have become known. "With M. Björnson," says the London "Athenæum" of April 26, 1862, "a new era begins in Scandinavian literature."

See, also, the London "Spectator," September 8, 1868.

Björnstahl or **Biœrnstahl,** be-ŏrn′stål, (JACOB JONAS,) a Swedish traveller, born in Sudermania in 1731, was sent by Gustavus III. on a scientific expedition to Greece, Syria, and Egypt, but died at Salonica in 1779.

See ERSCH und GRUBER, "Allgemeine Encyklopaedie."

Björnstjerna or **Bjœrnstjerna,** be-ŏRn′shêR′nå, (MAGNUS FREDERICK FERDINAND,) a Swedish general and writer, born at Dresden in 1779, entered the Swedish army, and served against the French in the campaigns of 1809-13. He afterwards concluded the treaty by which Sweden and Norway were united. He became lieutenant-general in 1820, and minister plenipotentiary to England in 1826. He published a treatise "On British Rule in India," ("Det Brittiska Riket i Ostindien," 1839,) and "The Theogony, Philosophy, and Cosmogony of the Hindoos," 1843, (in German and Swedish.) Died in 1847.

Blaarer de Wartensee, blä′rer då ŵaR′ten-så, (JEAN,) a Swiss jurist and *littérateur*, born at Zurich in 1685 ; died in 1757.

Blacas, blă′kås′,(PIERRE LOUIS JEAN CASIMIR,)DUKE OF, a French statesman, born at Aulps in 1770, was employed on important embassies to Rome and Naples, and negotiated the Concordat of 1817. He was the founder of the Egyptian Museum in Paris, and a member of the Institute. He was a constant adherent of the Bourbons. Died in 1839.

See VAULABELLE, "Histoire de la Restauration."

Blacas d'Aulps, blă′kă′dŏps, a French troubadour, born at Aulps about 1160 ; died in 1229.

Blache, blåsh, (ANTOINE,) a French ecclesiastic, born at Grenoble in 1635, was imprisoned in the Bastille in 1709 for having accused the Jesuits of conspiring against the king. Died in 1714.

Black, (ADAM,) a Scottish publisher and statesman, born in Edinburgh in 1784, was twice elected to Parliament from his native city. He has published the "Encyclopædia Britannica," and other standard works.

Black, (JEREMIAH S.,) an American lawyer and Democratic politician, born in Somerset county, Pennsylvania, in 1810. He was elected a judge of the supreme court of Pennsylvania in 1851, and again in 1854. He was attorney-general in the cabinet of Buchanan from March, 1857, to December, 1860, and secretary of state from December, 1860, to March, 1861.

Black, (JOHN,) a distinguished journalist and *littérateur*, born at Dunse, in Scotland, in 1783, became principal editor of the London "Morning Chronicle" in 1819. He translated Goldoni's "Autobiography" from the Italian ; also Schlegel's "Lectures on Dramatic Art and Literature," and Humboldt's "New Spain," from the German. Died in 1855.

Black, (JOSEPH,) an eminent chemist and physician, of Scottish extraction, born at Bordeaux in 1728. He graduated at Edinburgh in 1754, and became professor of anatomy at Glasgow in 1756, and in 1766 of chemistry at Edinburgh, where he lectured with eminent success for thirty years. He published in 1755 "Experiments on Magnesia, Quicklime, and other Alkaline Substances," in which he makes known his important discoveries on the nature of lime and fixed air, (carbonic acid gas.) He also originated the theory of latent heat, in relation to which he made many interesting experiments. Dr. Black was a friend of Lavoisier, and numbered among his pupils the celebrated James Watt. Died in Edinburgh in 1799.

See HOEFER, " Histoire de la Chimie ;" ROBISON's preface to BLACK's "Lectures on Chemistry ;" CHAMBERS, " Biographical Dictionary of Eminent Scotsmen;" "Edinburgh Review" for October,1803.

Black′all or **Black′hâll,** (OFFSPRING,) an English divine and controversialist, born in London in 1654. He was created Bishop of Exeter in 1707. Died in 1716.

Blackbourne, blak′būrn, (JOHN,) an English nonjuring bishop, born in 1683. He published an edition of Bayle's "Chronicle concerning Sir John Oldcastle." Died in 1741.

Blackburne, blak′būrn, (FRANCIS,) an English divine, born in Yorkshire in 1705, became Archdeacon of Cleveland. His principal work is entitled "The Confessional, or a Full and Free Inquiry into the Right, Utility, etc. of establishing Confessions of Faith and Doctrine." It caused a great sensation, and gave rise to a protracted controversy. Died in 1787.

See a Life of Blackburne, prefixed to his works by his son Francis, London, 1804.

Black′burne, (FRANCIS,) an eminent Irish lawyer and judge, born in the county of Meath in 1782. He became attorney-general for Ireland in 1830, master of the rolls in 1842, and chief justice of the court of queen's bench in 1846. He was keeper of the great seal during the brief ministry of Lord Derby, (1852,) and became lord-justice of appeal in 1856.

Blackburne, (THOMAS,) an English physician, son of Archdeacon Blackburne, noticed above ; died in 1782.

Black′et, (JOSEPH,) an English poet, born in Yorkshire in 1786, was the son of a day-labourer. He died in 1810, leaving a collection of poems of superior merit.

See "Remains of Joseph Blacket," with a Life by PRATT, 1811.

Black Hawk, a famous American Indian chief, born about 1768. He waged war against the United States in 1832. Died in Iowa in 1838.

See "Life of Black Hawk," by W. J. SNELLING.

Black′ie, (JOHN STUART,) a Scottish classical scholar and writer, born in Glasgow in 1809. He produced a poetical version of Goethe's "Faust," and a good translation of the works of Æschylus, (1850.) In 1852 he became professor of Greek in the University of Edinburgh. He published in 1866 two volumes entitled "Homer and the Iliad." Besides the above, he has contributed to the "Foreign Quarterly," the "Westminster Review," "Blackwood's" Magazine," and other British periodicals. He has also written several articles for the "Imperial Dictionary of Biography."

See "Fraser's Magazine" for 1860.

Black′lock, (THOMAS,) D.D., a Scottish divine and poet, born at Annan in 1721. He became blind in infancy, but nevertheless acquired at an early age a good English education and some knowledge of the classics. Through the kindness of Dr. Stevenson, he was enabled to study at the University of Edinburgh, where he mastered the Latin, Greek, and Italian languages. In 1762 he was ordained minister of the Church of Scotland at Kirkcudbright. He published poems, also philosophical and theological works. Died in 1791.

See Lives of Blacklock, by H. MACKENZIE and by GORDON; CHAMBERS, "Biographical Dictionary of Eminent Scotsmen."

Black′lõe, (THOMAS,) an English Catholic theologian and controversialist, lived about 1620.

Black′more, (Sir RICHARD,) an English writer, born in Wiltshire about 1650, was physician to William III. He was the author of several epic poems, which were satirized by Pope and other contemporary wits. His poem entitled "The Creation" (1712) is warmly commended by Cowper and Dr. Johnson ; and Addison pronounces it "one of the most useful and noble productions in our English verse." Died in 1729.

See JOHNSON, "Lives of the English Poets."

Black′rie, (ALEXANDER,) a Scottish apothecary, who wrote "A Disquisition on Medicines that dissolve the Stone," (1766.)

Black′stone, (JOHN,) an English botanist and apothecary, who lived in London, and died in 1753.

Black′stone, (WILLIAM,) an Episcopal clergyman, who was one of the first settlers of Boston. Died in 1675.

Blackstone, (Sir WILLIAM,) a celebrated English jurist, born in London in 1723. He practised law, was elected to Parliament in 1761, and appointed solicitor-general in 1763. About 1770 he became one of the justices of the court of common pleas. His reputation is founded on his "Commentaries on the Laws of England," the first volume of which appeared in 1765. Three other volumes were afterwards added to this work, which passed through many editions and is extensively used by students of law. Died in 1780. The very high reputation which Blackstone enjoys as a legal writer is due more to the judgment and taste evinced in the selection and arrangement of his materials, and to the clearness, purity, and classic elegance of his style, than to the extent of his legal knowledge or the force of his intellect. J. Horne Tooke justly characterizes his work as "a good gentleman's law-book, clear but not deep." Nearly the same judgment has been pronounced by Fox, Mackintosh, Lord Eldon, and other competent critics.

See CLITHEROE, "Life of Sir W. Blackstone," 1780; FOSS, "The Judges of England," vol. viii. ; ALLIBONE, "Dictionary of Authors."

Black′wall, (ANTHONY,) an English schoolmaster and critical writer, born in Derbyshire in 1674, published "The Sacred Classics defended and illustrated," (1725.) Died in 1730.

Black′well, (ALEXANDER,) a Scottish physician and agricultural writer, went in 1740 to Sweden, where he was executed in 1748 on a charge of conspiracy against the royal family. His wife, Elizabeth Blackwell, published in 1737–39 a herbal, with coloured plates, of the principal plants used in the practice of physic. Commerson named in her honour the genus Blackwellia.

See CHAMBERS, "Biographical Dictionary of Eminent Scotsmen."

Black′well, (ANTOINETTE L. BROWN,) born in Monroe county, New York, in 1825, studied at Oberlin, where afterwards she finished a three-years course in theology. On leaving Oberlin in 1849, though not licensed, she occasionally preached by invitation in several churches in different parts of the United States. In 1853 she was regularly ordained pastor of a Congregational church at South Butler, New York, which position she relinquished the following year on account of ill health. In 1856 she was married to Samuel C. Blackwell, and has since resided near New York City.

Blackwell, (ELIZABETH.) See BLACKWELL, ALEXANDER.

Blackwell, (ELIZABETH,) the first woman that ever received the degree of M.D. in the United States, was born at Bristol, England, in 1821. She was brought to New York by her parents about 1832, taught school several years, studied medicine, and applied for admission to the medical colleges of Philadelphia, New York, Boston, and other places. Her application was rejected by all except that of Geneva, New York, where she was welcomed by a unanimous vote of the students, and where she graduated in 1849. She afterwards studied midwifery in Paris, and practised medicine with success in New York.

Blackwell, (GEORGE,) an English Catholic theologian, born in Middlesex in 1545, wrote several controversial works. Died in 1612.

Blackwell, (THOMAS,) a Scottish critic and scholar, born at Aberdeen in 1701, became professor of Greek in Marischal College of that city. Among his principal works are "Letters on Mythology," and "An Inquiry into the Life and Writings of Homer," (1735.) He was a brother of Alexander, above noticed. Died in 1757.

See CHAMBERS, "Biographical Dictionary of Eminent Scotsmen."

Black′wood, (ADAM,) a Scottish writer, born at Dunfermline in 1539, studied in Paris, where he was patronized by Mary Queen of Scots. He published, in French, "The Martyrdom of Mary Stuart," (1588,) and several Latin works. Died in 1613.

See CHAMBERS, "Biographical Dictionary of Eminent Scotsmen."

Blackwood, (HENRY,) a Scottish physician and writer, born about 1525, became professor of philosophy at Paris. Died about 1614.

Blackwood, (HENRY,) son of the preceding, born in Paris, became professor of medicine and surgery in that city. Died in 1634.

Blackwood, (Sir HENRY,) a distinguished admiral, born in the county of Down, Ireland, in 1770. He served against the French in 1798, and was present at the battle of Trafalgar. In 1819 he was created a K.C.B., and appointed commander-in-chief on the East India station. Died in 1832.

Blackwood, (WILLIAM,) publisher of the celebrated magazine called by his name, was born in Edinburgh in 1776. He brought out in 1817 the first number of his journal, which soon numbered among its contributors Sir Walter Scott, Lockhart, Hogg, and other eminent writers of Tory principles. Under the editorship of Professor Wilson it became the most popular of British periodicals, and its pages were enriched with the writings of Wordsworth, Lamb, Coleridge, De Quincey, and, at a later period, Bulwer, Douglas Jerrold, W. S. Landor, and Professor Aytoun. Died in 1834.

See "Atlantic Monthly," December, 1865.

Blã'dẹn, (MARTIN,) an English officer and writer, served under Marlborough, and attained the rank of lieutenant-colonel. He was nine times elected to Parliament. He published a translation of Cæsar's "Commentaries," which he dedicated to the Duke of Marlborough. Died in 1746.

Blaes. See BLASIUS.

Blæsus, blee'sus, [Gr. Βλαῖσος,] a dramatic poet, supposed to have lived in the third century B.C., was a native of Capræa. His works were written in Greek, and some of them are mentioned by Athenæus.

Blaeu, blã'uh, **Blaeuw,** or **Blauw,** blŏw, (WILLEM,) a celebrated Dutch geographer and typographer, born at Amsterdam in 1571. He was a friend and disciple of Tycho Brahe. Among his principal works are his "Theatre of the World," ("Theatrum Mundi,") "Atlas of the Seas, or Aquatic World," and "Astronomical Instruction on the Use of Globes, etc." Died in 1638.

Blaeuw, blã'uh, (JAN,) son of the preceding, published a number of beautiful editions of the classics, and wrote several geographical works. Died in 1680.

Blag'dẹn, (Sir CHARLES,) an English physician and chemist, born in 1748, was one of the secretaries of the Royal Society, and an intimate friend of Sir Joseph Banks. He contributed a number of scientific treatises to the "Philosophical Transactions." Died in 1820.

Blag'rave, (JOHN,) an English mathematician, published "The Art of Dialling," "The Mathematical Jewel," and other similar works. Died in 1611.

See WOOD, "Athenæ Oxonienses."

Blagrave, (JOSEPH,) an English physician and astrologer, born in 1610, wrote "The Astrological Practice of Physic," (1682,) and other works. Died in 1679.

Blaine, (JAMES GILLESPIE,) an American legislator, born in Washington county, Pennsylvania, in 1830. He removed to Maine, and became editor of the "Kennebec Journal," and afterwards of the "Portland Advertiser." He was elected a member of Congress by the Republicans in 1862, 1864, 1866, and 1868. In March, 1869, he was chosen Speaker of the House of Representatives.

Blainville, de, dẹh blâN'vèl', (HENRI MARIE DUCRO-TAY,) an eminent French zoologist and physician, born near Dieppe in September, 1777. Having studied medicine for a time, he was attracted by the lectures of Cuvier to the study of comparative anatomy and zoology, and was employed by that great naturalist as assistant lecturer. He obtained the chair of anatomy and zoology in the Faculty of Sciences in 1812, on which occasion he took for his thesis the Ornithorhynchus, or duck-bill. He was admitted into the Academy of Sciences in 1825. In 1830 he was appointed professor of the natural history of mollusks and zoophytes at the Jardin des Plantes, and on the death of Cuvier, in 1832, succeeded him in the chair of comparative anatomy in that institution, now called the Museum of Natural History. About this time he was chosen a Fellow of the Royal Society and of the Geological Society of London. His

most important work is entitled "Osteography, or Comparative Iconographic Description of the Skeleton and Dentary System of the Five Classes of Vertebrated Animals, Recent and Fossil." He died in Paris in May, 1850, leaving the above-named production unfinished. Twenty-four parts (*livraisons*) were issued before his death. He also contributed numerous scientific treatises to the "Revue Zoologique" and other similar periodicals, and published "Lectures on General and Comparative Physiology," (3 vols., 1833.)

See NICARD, "Notice sur De Blainville," 1850; FLOURENS, "Mémoire de Ducrotay de Blainville," and English translation of the same in the "Smithsonian Report" for 1865, p. 175.

Blair, (FRANCIS PRESTON,) an American journalist and politician, born at Abingdon, Virginia, in 1791. He began in 1830 to edit the "Globe," a Democratic paper at Washington, and became a friend and confidential adviser of General Jackson. He ceased to edit the "Globe" in 1845. In 1848 he supported Van Buren for the Presidency, in opposition to the regular candidate of the party. He aided in the organization of the Republican party about 1855.

Blair, (FRANK PRESTON, Jr.,) an American general and lawyer, son of the preceding, was born at Lexington, Kentucky, in 1821. He was elected a member of Congress by the voters of Saint Louis, Missouri, in 1856, was re-elected in 1861, and acted with the Republicans for several years. He commanded a corps in the army of Sherman in its march from Chattanooga to Atlanta in 1864, and in the campaign of South Carolina, February, 1865. He joined the Democratic party about 1865, and was nominated as Democratic candidate for the Vice-Presidency in July, 1868, but was not elected.

Blair, (HUGH,) a celebrated divine of the Church of Scotland, born at Edinburgh in 1718. He became a doctor of divinity in 1757, and in 1758 one of the ministers of the High Church of Edinburgh. In 1762 he was appointed to a chair of rhetoric and belles-lettres recently created by George III. in the University of Edinburgh. He published "Lectures on Rhetoric," (1783,) and several volumes of sermons, which had an extraordinary popularity in his time, and were translated into the principal European languages; but they have not found with modern readers and critics the same favour which they once enjoyed. His "Lectures on Rhetoric" has been extensively used as a text-book for schools in the United States as well as in Great Britain. Died in 1800.

See JAMES FINLAYSON, "Life of Hugh Blair," 1801; CHAMBERS, "Biographical Dictionary of Eminent Scotsmen."

Blair, (JAMES,) a Scottish divine in the time of Charles II., was sent in 1685 as a missionary to Virginia, where he founded William and Mary College, and was appointed its first president. Died in 1743.

See CHAMBERS, "Biographical Dictionary of Eminent Scotsmen."

Blair, (JOHN,) a Scottish chronicler and Latin poet, was chaplain to Sir William Wallace. He wrote the "Life of Wallace," in Latin verse, translated in Hume's "History of the Douglases."

Blair, (JOHN,) a relative of Hugh Blair, born at Edinburgh, published a popular work entitled "The Chronology and History of the World, from the Creation to 1753." He was afterwards elected a Fellow of the Royal Society, appointed tutor to the Duke of York, and obtained other distinctions. Died in 1782.

See CHAMBERS, "Biographical Dictionary of Eminent Scotsmen."

Blair, (JOHN,) an American jurist, born in 1732, was appointed by Washington, in 1789, to the bench of the supreme court of the United States, of which John Jay was chief justice. Died at Williamsburg, Virginia, in 1800.

Blair, (MONTGOMERY,) a brother of General F. P. Blair, was born in Kentucky about 1813. He studied law, which he practised in Saint Louis, Missouri, and became a judge of the court of common pleas. About 1852 he removed to Maryland. He was appointed postmaster-general in March, 1861, and was removed near the end of 1864. Since that event he has assumed an attitude of decided opposition to the Republican party.

Blair, (PATRICK,) a Scottish physician and naturalist, born at Dundee, published "Miscellaneous Observations on the Practice of Physic, Surgery, and Botany," (1718,)

ā, ē, ī, ō, ū, ȳ, *long;* ă, ĕ, ĭ, ŏ, ŭ, ў, same, less prolonged; ă, ĕ, ĭ, ŏ, ŭ, ў, *short;* ạ, ẹ, ị, ọ, *obscure;* fär, fåll, fåt; mêt; nŏt; gōōd; mōōn;

'Anatomy and Osteology of the Elephant," and other scientific works. Died about 1728.

See CHAMBERS, "Biographical Dictionary of Eminent Scotsmen."

Blair, (ROBERT,) a Scottish poet and clergyman, born in Edinburgh in 1699, was a cousin of Hugh Blair, noticed above. He was ordained minister of Athelstaneford in 1731, and married a Miss Law in 1738. He died in 1746, leaving a poem entitled "The Grave," which was printed in 1747 and was highly esteemed by many readers. The poet Campbell expresses the opinion that his "language and imagery are free, natural, and picturesque."

See CAMPBELL, "Specimens of British Poets;" CHAMBERS, "Biographical Dictionary of Eminent Scotsmen."

Blaise, blȧz, (BARTHÉLEMY,) a French sculptor, born at Lyons in 1738. Among his principal works are the monument of Count Vergennes, and a bust of Frederick the Great of Prussia. Died in 1819.

Blaise, blȧz, [Lat. BLA'SIUS,] SAINT, Bishop of Sebaste in Armenia, suffered martyrdom in 316 A.D., under Agricola, governor of Cappadocia and Lesser Armenia.

Blake, (FRANCIS,) an American lawyer, born at Rutland, Massachusetts, in 1774. He graduated at Harvard, and practised law in Worcester, where he died in 1817.

Blake, (GEORGE SMITH,) an American naval officer, born in Worcester, Massachusetts, in 1803, served in the Mexican war, and became in 1857 superintendent of the United States Naval Academy at Annapolis. He was made commodore in 1862.

Blake, (HOMER C.,) an American naval officer, born in Dutchess county, New York, in 1822, entered the navy about 1840. He obtained command of the Hatteras in 1861, and was employed in the Gulf of Mexico near Galveston. In January, 1862, he attacked the Alabama, commanded by Captain Semmes, although his vessel was inferior to that of the enemy. The Hatteras was sunk in the action. He rendered an important service by defeating an attempt of the enemy to bring their rams, etc. down James River against City Point, in January, 1864.

Blake, (JOAQUIN,) a Spanish general, of Irish extraction, served from 1808 to 1811 against the French, by whom he was several times defeated. Died in 1827.

Blake, (JOHN BRADLEY,) an English mathematician and naturalist, born in London in 1745 ; died in 1773.

Blake, (JOHN LAURIS,) an American compiler and biographer, born at Northwood, New Hampshire, in 1788. He served as rector of an Episcopal church at Concord, New Hampshire, and at Boston. He published, besides numerous school-books, a "General Biographical Dictionary," (1 vol. 8vo, 1835,) which passed through several editions. Died in 1857.

Blake, (JOSEPH,) nephew of the celebrated Admiral Blake, succeeded Thomas Smith as Governor of South Carolina in 1694. Died in 1700.

Blake, (ROBERT,) a celebrated British admiral, born at Bridgewater, in Somersetshire, about 1599. Having finished his studies at Oxford, he was elected to Parliament for Bridgewater in 1640. He was a staunch Puritan and republican, and distinguished himself in the civil war by his brave and successful defence of Taunton against the royalists, (1645,) thus rendering a service of great importance to the cause. Being appointed in 1649 commander of a squadron of the line, with the title of "General of the Sea," he blockaded Prince Rupert at Kinsale, and on his effecting his escape pursued him to the Tagus and captured a great number of Portuguese galleons. For these achievements he was made Warden of the Cinque Ports. On the breaking out of the war with Holland, in 1652, he gained a signal victory over Van Tromp in the Straits of Dover, (May 19,) and on the 28th of September defeated the Dutch fleet under Admiral De Witt. In February, 1653, he again encountered Van Tromp, whom he defeated after a running fight of three days, in which the English took eleven men-of-war and thirty merchantmen. On account of his failing health, he retired soon after from the service, and became a member of the first two Parliaments summoned by Cromwell. In 1656 he was sent to blockade Cadiz, and the same year destroyed the Spanish plate-fleet at Santa Cruz, in the island of Teneriffe. He received for this service the thanks of Parliament and a diamond ring worth £500. He is considered as the founder of the naval supremacy of England. He died on his voyage to England in 1657.

See CAMPBELL, "Lives of the British Admirals;" "Robert Blake, Admiral and General at Sea," by HEPWORTH DIXON, 1852; MACAULAY, "History of England," vol. i. ; DR. JOHNSON's Works, vol. xii. ; "Quarterly Review" for July, 1858.

Blake, (THOMAS,) an English Puritan divine, born in Staffordshire in 1597, published "The Covenant Sealed," and other religious treatises. Died in 1657.

Blake, (WILLIAM,) a singularly gifted English artist and poet, born in London in 1757, studied engraving for a time under Basire. A collection of his ballads and songs was published in 1787, partly at the expense of his friend and patron the sculptor Flaxman. These were followed in 1789 by his "Songs of Innocence and Experience," accompanied by etched illustrations of great beauty. He next produced his "Gates of Paradise," in sixteen designs, and soon after a series of twenty-seven designs, entitled "Urizen," both works of a mystical character, but displaying remarkable genius. He subsequently illustrated Young's "Night Thoughts," Hayley's "Life of Cowper," and Blair's "Grave." Among his other works are "Twenty-one Illustrations to the Book of Job," and "The Canterbury Pilgrimage," a picture in water-colours. Blake was a believer in the power of conversing with departed spirits, and painted the portraits of several eminent persons who he alleged were revealed to him. He died in 1828, having passed the latter part of his life in extreme poverty, which he bore without repining, finding in his entire devotion to his art a compensation for all privations.

See CUNNINGHAM, "Lives of Painters and Sculptors;" "Life of William Blake," by ALEXANDER GILCHRIST; "Pictor Ignotus," in the "Atlantic Monthly" for April, 1864.

Blake, (WILLIAM RUFUS,) a comic actor, born in Nova Scotia in 1805, acted with great success in New York and other places. Died in 1863.

Blake'ly or **Blake'ley,** (JOHNSTON,) a naval commander, born in Ireland in 1781, entered the navy of the United States in 1800. He took command of the sloop Wasp in August, 1813, and captured, in June, 1814, the British sloop Reindeer. In September of that year he attacked the Avon, which surrendered. The Wasp never returned to port, and it is not known what became of Captain Blakely.

Blake'ney, LORD, an Irish military commander, born in the county of Limerick in 1672. He was lieutenant-governor of the island of Minorca when it was taken by the French in 1756.

Blake'way, (JOHN BRICKDALE,) an English divine and antiquary, born at Shrewsbury in 1765. He wrote a "History of Shrewsbury," and other works. Died in 1826.

Blā'key, (ROBERT,) an English philosopher, born at Morpeth about 1795. He published a "History of Moral Science," (2 vols. 1833,) a "History of the Philosophy of the Mind, embracing the Opinions of all Writers on Mental Science," (4 vols. 1848,) which was received with favour, a "History of Political Literature," (1855,) and other works.

Blamire, blạ-mīr', (SUSANNAH,) an English poetess, born near Carlisle in 1747. She wrote, in the Scottish dialect, a number of admired lyrics, among which are "The Siller Crown," and "The Nabob." Died in 1794.

Blamont, de, dẹh blȧ'môN', (FRANÇOIS COLLIN,) a French musician and composer, born at Versailles in 1690 ; died in 1760.

Blampin, blôN'pȧN', (THOMAS,) a French Benedictine monk, born at Noyon in 1640, edited the works of Saint Augustine, (8 vols., 1679–1700.) Died in 1710.

Blampoix, blôN'pwȧ', (JEAN BAPTISTE,) a French ecclesiastic, born at Mâcon in 1740, became constitutional Bishop of Troyes. Died in 1820.

Blanc, blôN, (CHARLES,) a French *littérateur*, brother of Louis Blanc, noticed below, born at Castres about 1815. He wrote a "History of the French Painters of the Nineteenth Century," (1845,) and a "History of the Painters of all the Schools," (1st vol. about 1850.)

Blanc, (JEAN DENIS FERRÉOL,) a French jurist, born at Besançon in 1744 ; died in 1789.

Blanc, (Louis,) a celebrated journalist and historian, of French extraction, born at Madrid in 1813. He was educated in Paris, and in 1837 became principal editor of the journal entitled "Bon Sens," ("Good Sense.") He founded in 1839 "La Revue du Progrès," and in 1840 brought out his treatise on the "Organization of Labour," an exposition of his radical views of social and political reform. In 1848 he became a member of the provisional government, and was chiefly instrumental in passing the decree abolishing the death-penalty for political offences. He has published a "History of the Ten Years 1830-40," ("Histoire des dix Ans 1830-1840," 6 vols.,) and has begun a "History of the French Revolution," the seventh volume of which came out in 1855. He was very popular with the operatives and socialists of Paris. Having been accused of complicity in the bloody revolt of May and June, 1848, he escaped to England, where he remains an exile.

See CHARLES ROBIN, "Louis Blanc, sa Vie et ses Ouvrages," 1851; "Blackwood's Magazine" for September, 1844; "Edinburgh Review" for July, 1863.

Blanc, blänk, (LUDWIG GOTTFRIED,) a German writer and preacher, born at Berlin in 1781, was a resident of Halle. He published a popular work, entitled "Manual of Things best worth knowing in Nature," ("Handbuch des Wissenswürdigsten aus der Natur, etc.," 3 vols., 5th edition, 1846-49.)

Blanc, Le. See LE BLANC.

Blancard. See BLANKAARD.

Blancard, blŏN'kȧr', (PIERRE,) a French traveller in Asia, born at Marseilles in 1741, wrote a "Manual of the Commerce of the East Indies and China." Died in 1826.

Blancas, blän'kȧs, (GERONIMO,) a Spanish historian, born at Saragossa, succeeded Zurita as royal historiographer. His principal work is a History of Aragon, ("Commentarii Rerum Aragoniensium," 1588.) His Latin style is eulogized by Prescott for its elegance. Died in 1590.

See PRESCOTT, "History of Ferdinand and Isabella," vol. i. part i.

Blancha, blän'chä, (JUAN,) governor of Perpignan when under Spanish rule, defended that place for eight months against the French in 1474.

Blanchard, blŏN'shȧr', (ALAIN,) a citizen of Rouen, in France, who generously sacrificed himself for the safety of his native city when besieged in 1418 by Henry V., who consented to spare the place only on condition of a number of victims being given up.

See LICQUET, "Notice sur Alain Blanchard."

Blanch'ard, (ALBERT G.,) an American general in the Confederate army, born in Massachusetts about 1810, graduated at West Point in 1829, served in the Mexican war, and was made a brigadier-general in 1861.

Blanchard, (ÉLIE,) a French antiquary and scholar, born at Langres in 1672, was a pupil of Dacier. He was elected to the Academy of Inscriptions in 1714. Died in 1756.

Blanchard, (ÉMILE,) a French naturalist, born in Paris in 1819, published a number of treatises on entomology and other departments of zoology.

Blanchard, (FRANÇOIS,) a French jurist and *littérateur;* died in 1660.

Blanchard, (FRANÇOIS,) a celebrated French aeronaut, born at Andelys in 1738. After the brothers Montgolfier had invented the balloon, Blanchard constructed one with wings and a rudder, in which he made an ascension in 1784. In company with Dr. Jeffries, he crossed the Channel in his balloon in 1785, for which achievement he received from the king twelve thousand francs and a pension. Died in 1809.

His wife, MARIE MADELEINE SOPHIE ARMANT, made several ascensions after his death, and was killed by the explosion of her balloon in 1819.

Blanchard, (GUILLAUME,) son of François, (the first of the name,) was an advocate in the Parliament of Paris. He wrote a "Chronological Compilation of the Statutes of the French Kings." Died about 1724.

Blanchard, (JACQUES,) a French painter, born in Paris in 1600, studied at Rome and Venice. His "Descent of the Holy Ghost," in the church of Nôtre-Dame, in Paris, is esteemed his master-piece. Died in 1638.

Blanchard, (JEAN BAPTISTE,) a French Jesuit, teacher, and educational writer, born in the department of Ardennes in 1731; died in 1797.

Blanch'ard, (LAMAN,) an English journalist and *littérateur,* born at Great Yarmouth in 1803. He became associated with Bulwer as editor of "The New Monthly Magazine" in 1831, and subsequently assisted in editing the "Court Journal," the "Constitutional," and "The Courier." He contributed numerous articles in prose and verse to the leading English periodicals. He committed suicide in a fit of insanity in 1845. His "Essays and Sketches" were published by Bulwer Lytton, accompanied by an interesting Memoir, which see.

See "Fraser's Magazine" for March, 1846, (by THACKERAY.)

Blanchard, (THOMAS,) an eminent American inventor, born in Sutton, Worcester county, Massachusetts, in 1788. Mr. Blanchard has taken out in all, including machinery for locomotives, steamboats, etc., twenty-four patents for his different inventions. Died in 1864.

See HENRY HOWE, "Eminent American Mechanics," etc., 1847.

Blanchard de la Musse, blŏN'shȧr' deh lä müs, (FRANÇOIS GABRIEL URSIN,) a French *littérateur,* born at Nantes in 1752; died in 1837.

Blanche, blänch, [Fr. pron. blŏNsh,] OF ARTOIS, (ȧr'twä',) daughter of Robert, Count of Artois, and niece of Saint Louis, was married in 1270 to Henry I., King of Navarre. She afterwards became the wife of Edmund, Earl of Lancaster, brother of Edward I. of England. Died about 1300.

See MÉZERAY, "Histoire de France."

Blanche OF BOURBON, (boor'bǫn,) a daughter of Peter, Duke of Bourbon, born about 1338, was married at the age of fifteen to Peter the Cruel, King of Castile, who soon abandoned her, and caused her to be imprisoned in the castle of Medina-Sidonia, where she died in 1361. Her tragic fate forms the subject of numerous ballads and poems.

See FROISSART, "Chronicles;" TICKNOR, "History of Spanish Literature."

Blanche OF CASTILE, (kas-teel',) daughter of Alphonso IX., King of Castile, born in 1187, was married in 1200 to the son of Philip Augustus, afterwards Louis VIII. On the death of her husband, she became regent of the kingdom, and governed with great ability and wisdom. She was the mother of Louis IX., commonly known as Saint Louis. Died in 1252.

See MACHECO, "Vie de Blanche de Castile," 1820; VAUVILLIERS, "Histoire de Blanche de Castile," 1841; T. NISARD, "Histoire de la Reine Blanche," 1842.

Blanche OF NAVARRE, daughter of Charles III., (surnamed "the Noble,") was first married to Martin, King of Sicily, (1402,) and in 1420 to John of Aragon, son of Ferdinand I. Died in 1441.

See GALLAND, "Mémoires de Navarre."

Blanchelande, de, deh blŏNsh'lŏNd', (PHILIBERT FRANÇOIS ROUSSEL,) a French general, born at Dijon in 1735. He was appointed in 1792 lieutenant-governor of Saint Domingo, but, being accused of causing the troubles in that country, he was condemned by the Revolutionary tribunal, and executed in 1793.

Blanchet, blŏN'shä', (ALEXANDRE PAUL LOUIS,) a French physician, born at Saint-Lo in 1817, published a work on "Deaf-Dumbness," ("La Surdi-Mutité," 4 vols.)

Blanchet, (FRANÇOIS,) a French *littérateur,* born near Chartres in 1707, was appointed royal censor, and keeper of the books in the royal cabinet. He published "Oriental Tales and Apologues," "Moral and Amusing Varieties," and other works. Died in 1784.

See DUSAULX, "Vie de l'Abbé Blanchet," prefixed to his "Variétés Morales," etc.

Blanchet, (PIERRE,) a French dramatic poet, born at Poitiers about 1459, is supposed to have written the "Farce de Pathelin," which was translated into Latin. Died in 1519.

Blanchet, (THOMAS,) a French historical and portrait painter, born in Paris in 1617. His works are praised by D'Argenville. Died in 1689.

Blancheton, blŏNsh'tŏN', (MARC ANTOINE,) a French medical writer, born at Vervaison in 1784. His chief work is an "Essay on Man considered in his Geographical Relations," (1808.) Died in 1830.

Blanchon, blôN'shôN', (JOACHIM,) a French poet, born at Limoges about 1550.

Blanckhof, blånk'hof, or **Blankoff,** blån'kof, (ANTOON,) called also JOHN MAET, (måt,) a Dutch painter, born at Alkmaar in 1628. His best works are marine pieces. Died in 1670.

Bland, (RICHARD,) an American political writer and antiquary, was a citizen of Virginia. He published in 1766 an "Inquiry into the Rights of the British Colonies," and was elected a delegate to Congress in 1774. Died in 1778.

Bland, (Rev. ROBERT,) an English scholar and divine, born in London in 1779. He published, conjointly with J. H. Merivale, "Translations from the Greek Anthology," (1806,) and wrote several poems, and a poetical romance entitled "The Four Slaves of Cythera." Died in 1825.

Bland, (Colonel THEODORIC,) an American patriot, born in Prince George county, Virginia, in 1742, was an uncle of John Randolph of Roanoke. He joined the army in 1777, and gained the rank of colonel and the confidence of Washington. He served as a member of Congress from 1780 to 1783, was a member of the Convention which ratified the Federal Constitution in 1788, and was again elected to Congress in 1789. Died in 1790.

See a "Memoir of T. Bland," in the "Bland Papers," published by CHARLES CAMPBELL, 1840.

Bland, (WILLIAM,) an English writer, born about 1788. He published, besides other works, "Principles of Agriculture," (1827.)

Blandin, blôN'dåN', (PHILIPPE FRÉDÉRIC,) a French surgeon of high reputation, born at Aubigny in 1798, practised in Paris. He published "Traité d'Anatomie topographique," (1826,) and "Elements of Descriptive Anatomy," (2 vols., 1838.) Died in Paris in 1849.

Blandrata, blån-drå'tå, (GIORGIO,) an Italian physician, born in Piedmont, was the founder of Unitarianism in Poland and Transylvania. He became successively a Lutheran, Calvinist, and Socinian, and being appointed physician to John Sigismund, Prince of Transylvania, about 1563, he made many proselytes in that country. He is supposed to have been assassinated by his nephew about 1590.

See VARILLAS, "Histoire des Hérésies."

Blane, (Sir GILBERT,) F.R.S., an eminent British physician, born at Blanefield, Ayrshire, in 1749. He obtained, about 1780, the high office of physician to the fleet commanded by Rodney, in which he served until the end of the war, and published, in 1785, "Observations on the Diseases of Seamen." From 1785 to 1795 he was physician to Saint Thomas's Hospital, London. In 1819 he published "Elements of Medical Logic," which is highly esteemed. He was elected a member of the French Institute about 1826, and became first physician to William IV. in 1830. Died in London in 1834.

See CHAMBERS, "Biographical Dictionary of Eminent Scotsmen."

Blangini, blån-jee'nee, (GIUSEPPE MARCO MARIA FELICE,) an Italian composer, born at Turin in 1781, produced a number of operas, canzonets, and other musical pieces. Died in 1841.

See ARSÈNE HOUSSAYE, "Philosophers and Actresses," vol. ii.

Blankaard, blån'kårt, written also **Blancard,** (NIKOLAAS,) a Dutch scholar, born at Leyden in 1625. He became professor of the Greek language and history at Franeker in 1669, and published editions of Quintus Curtius, the "Enchiridion" of Epictetus, and other classics. Died in 1703.

Blankaard or **Blancard,** (STEVEN,) a Dutch physician, son of Nikolaas, noticed above, born at Middelburg, published a number of medical and anatomical works in Latin, the most important of which is "Anatomia practica Rationalis," (1688.)

Blankenburg, von, fon blån'ken-bōōrG', (CHRISTIAN FRIEDRICH,) a German littérateur and critic, born at Colberg in 1744. He translated into German Johnson's 'Lives of the Poets," and other English works. Died in 1796.

Blankenstein, blån'ken-stïn', (ERNST,) COUNT, a German commander, born in Thuringia in 1733, served

in the Austrian army in the Seven Years' war, and became lieutenant-field-marshal. Died in 1816.

Blankoff. See BLANCKHOF.

Blanpain, blôN'påN', (JEAN,) a French ecclesiastic and historical writer, born in 1704; died in 1765.

Blanquart de Bailleul, blôN'kår' deh bå'yul',(LOUIS EDMOND MARIE,) born at Calais in 1795, became Bishop of Versailles in 1833, and in 1844 Archbishop of Rouen.

Blanquet, blôN'kå', (SAMUEL,) a French physician and naturalist, born in the diocese of Mende ; died about 1750.

Blanquet du Chayla, blôN'kå' dü shå'lå', (ARMAND SIMON MARIE,) a French vice-admiral, born in the department of Lozère in 1759 ; died in 1826.

See "Notice sur Blanquet du Chayla," Paris, 1852.

Blanqui, blôN'ke', (JEAN DOMINIQUE,) born at Nice in 1759, was a deputy to the National Convention, and in 1795 became a member of the Council of Five Hundred. He wrote a work entitled "My Ten Months' Agony," ("Mon Agonie de dix Mois," 1794.) Died in 1832.

Blanqui, (JÉRÔME ADOLPHE,) a celebrated writer on political economy, born at Nice in 1798. He studied economic science under J. B. Say, and in 1833 succeeded him as professor at the Conservatory of Arts and Trades in Paris. He published a "History of Political Economy in Europe from the Ancients to the Present Time," (1837,) which ranks as a standard work, a "Summary of the History of Commerce and Industry," and a "Journey in England," (1824.) Died in 1854.

Blanqui, (LOUIS AUGUSTE,) brother of the preceding, born at Nice in 1805, has distinguished himself as a political conspirator and socialist. He was several times imprisoned for his seditious attempts previous to 1848. He was a ringleader of the insurgents and outlaws of Paris who took arms against the republic in April and May, 1848. For this offence he was condemned to imprisonment for ten years.

Blarru, de, deh blå'rü', (PIERRE,) a French poet, born in 1437, wrote a heroic poem in Latin, entitled "The Nanceid," (1518,) which was once admired, and has been translated into French. Died in 1505.

Blasche, blås'keh, (BERNHARD HEINRICH,) a German educational writer, born at Jena in 1766; died in 1852.

Blasco, blås'ko, (NICCOLÒ,) an Italian poet, born at Chiusa, in Sicily, taught philosophy and belles-lettres at Naples and Rome about 1600-25.

Blasius, blå'ze-ús', (ERNST,) a German surgeon, born at Nice in 1802, became professor of surgery at Halle in 1834.

Bla'sĭ-us or **Blaes,** blås, (GERARD,) a learned Flemish physician, born near Bruges, settled in 1660 in Amsterdam, where he became professor of medicine. He published several Latin treatises on anatomy and medicine. Died in 1682.

Blasius, SAINT. See BLAISE, SAINT.

Blas'ta̞-rēs̱, (MATTHÆUS,) a Greek canonist and monk of the order of Saint Basil, lived about 1350. He was the compiler of a "Collection of the Canons and Councils of the Fathers, and Laws of the Greek Emperors on Ecclesiastical Matters."

Blau, blŏw, (FELIX ANTON,) a German Catholic theologian, born in 1754, wrote against the abuses of the Romish Church. Died in 1798.

Blaurer, blŏw'rer, (AMBROSE,) a Swiss Lutheran divine, born at Constance in 1492; died in 1568.

Blavet, blå'vå', (JEAN LOUIS,) a French littérateur, son of Michel, noticed below, born at Besançon in 1719. He translated from the English Adam Smith's "Wealth of Nations," and Dalrymple's "Memoirs of Great Britain and Ireland." Died in 1809.

Blavet, (MICHEL,) a French musician and composer, born at Besançon in 1700; died in 1768.

Blavier, blå've-å', (ÉDOUARD,) a French geologist and engineer, born in Paris in 1802.

Blay'ney, (BENJAMIN,) D.D., an English philologist, and regius professor of Hebrew at Oxford, had a high reputation as a Biblical critic. He published new translations of Jeremiah and Lamentations, and of Zechariah. Died in 1801.

Blaze, blåz, (ELZÉAR,) a French littérateur, brother of Castil-Blaze, born at Cavaillon about 1786; died in 1848.

ε as k; ç as s; ğ hard; ġ as j; G, H, K, guttural; N, nasal; R, trilled; ŝ as z; th as in this. (☞ See Explanations, p. 23.)

24

Blaze, (FRANÇOIS HENRI JOSEPH,) called also **Castil-Blaze,** käs'tĕl'blȧz, a French musical critic and composer, born at Cavaillon in 1784. He edited the musical department of the "Journal des Débats" from 1820 to 1831, published a "Dictionary of Modern Music," (1821,) and composed several operas. Died in Paris in 1857.

Blaze, (HENRI SÉBASTIEN,) a French musician and composer, father of the preceding, born at Cavaillon in 1763; died in 1833.

Blé, du, dü blȧ, (NICOLAS,) Marquis d'Uxelles, a French general, born in 1652, became a marshal of France in 1703. Died in 1730.

Blecker, blĕk'kẹr, (JAN GASPAR,) a painter and engraver, born at Haarlem about 1600.

Bleda, blä'DÄ, (JAIME,) a Spanish ecclesiastic, born in the province of Valencia about 1550, wrote a "Chronology of the Moors of Spain." Died in 1624.

Bleeck, van, vȧn blāk, (PETER,) a Flemish painter and engraver, born about 1700. Among his best works is a portrait of Paul Rembrandt. Died in London in 1764.

Bleecker, blee'kẹr, (ANN ELIZA,) an American poetess, whose maiden name was SCHUYLER, born in New York in 1752; died in 1783.

See GRISWOLD, "Female Poets of America."

Bleek, blāk, (FRIEDRICH,) born at Arensbök, in Holstein, in 1793, published several valuable critical works on the Scriptures. He became professor of theology at Bonn in 1829. Died in 1859.

Blefken, blĕf'kẹn, (DITHMAR,) a German traveller, visited Iceland in 1563, and afterwards wrote a description of that country, in Latin.

Bleg'bọ-rọugh, (RALPH,) an English physician, born in Yorkshire in 1769, was a member of the Royal College of Physicians. He published "Facts and Observations respecting the Air-Pump Vapour-Bath in Gout, Rheumatism, etc." Died in 1827.

Blegny, de, dẹh blȧn'ye', (NICOLAS,) a French surgeon and writer, born in 1652, became physician to the king in 1687. Died in 1722.

Blein, blȧn, (FRANÇOIS ANGE ALEXANDRE,) BARON, a French general of engineers, born in Drôme in 1767. He served at Austerlitz, Jena, etc., and wrote several scientific works.

Bleiswick, van, vȧn blīs'ŵik, (PIETER,) grand pensionary of Holland, born at Delft in 1724, wrote a Latin treatise "On Dykes." Died in 1790.

Blekers, blä'kẹrs, (N.,) a Dutch painter of history and landscapes, born at Haarlem about 1635, was patronized by the Prince of Orange.

Blende, de, dẹh blĕn'dẹh or blŏnd, (BARTHÉLEMY,) a Jesuit missionary, born at Bruges in 1675, visited Paraguay, where he was killed by the natives in 1715.

Blenker, blĕnk'ẹr, (LOUIS,) a general, born at Worms, Germany, in 1812. He took an active part in the revolutionary movement in his native city in 1849, and after the defeat of the popular party became an exile in New York. He was appointed a brigadier-general in August, 1861, and commanded a division under General Fremont in Virginia in 1862. Died in New Jersey in 1863.

Blen'ner-has'set, (HARMAN,) a wealthy Englishman, noted as an associate or accomplice of Aaron Burr, was born in Hampshire about 1770. He purchased about 1798 an estate on an island in the Ohio River, and ruined his fortune by advancing money to aid Burr in his projects. He was indicted for treason in 1807, but was released on the acquittal of Burr. Died in 1831.

See "Life of Harman Blennerhasset," by W. H. SAFFORD, 1853.

Blès, de, dẹh blês, or **Bless,** (HENRI,) a Flemish landscape-painter of great merit, born near Dinant in 1480. Died in 1550.

See DESCAMPS, "Vies des Peintres Flamands," etc.

Blessebois, blĕss'bwä', (PIERRE CORNEILLE,) an enigmatical personage, of whom nothing positive seems to be known. The name is attached to several French dramas, satires, and poems, published about 1675. Some of these are said to be scurrilous and indecent.

Blessendorf, blĕs'sẹn-dorf', (SAMUEL,) a German painter in enamel, born in Berlin in 1670, was also an engraver.

Blessig, blês'siG, (JOHANN LORENZ,) a Protestant minister, born at Strasburg on the Rhine about 1748.

He became professor of theology in his native city in 1783, and published several works. Died in 1816.

See C. M. FRITZ, "Leben J. L. Blessig's," 2 vols., 1818.

Bles'sing-tọn, (MARGARET,) COUNTESS OF, an Irish lady, celebrated for her beauty, accomplishments, and social qualities, was born in Tipperary county in 1789. She was married when very young to Captain Farmer, and after his death to the Earl of Blessington in 1818. Lord Blessington dying in 1829, his widow took up her residence at Gore House, in London, which was for many years the resort of the literati and other celebrated persons of England and the Continent. Among her most popular works we may name "The Victims of Society," a novel, "Conversations with Lord Byron," (1832,) "The Idler in Italy," and "The Idler in France." She was a frequent contributor to the magazines, etc. Died in 1849.

See "The Literary Life and Correspondence of the Countess of Blessington," by R. R. MADDEN ; "Edinburgh Review," vol. lxvii.

Blesson, blä'sŏn', (LUDWIG JOHANN URBAN,) a German officer, born at Berlin in 1790, published a "Survey of the Art of Fortification," (1827,) and other works.

Bletterie, de la, dẹh lä blȧ'trẹ' or blĕt're', (JEAN PHILIPPE RENÉ,) a French *littérateur*, born at Rennes in 1696. He was professor of eloquence in the Royal College, and a member of the Academy of Inscriptions. He wrote a "History of Julian the Apostate," (1735,) and made translations from the Latin. Died in 1772.

Bleuland, bluh'lȧnt, (JANUS or JAN,) a Dutch medical writer, born at Utrecht, lived about 1780–1800.

Bleville, blẹh-vĕl', (JEAN BAPTISTE THOMAS,) born at Abbeville in 1692, published "The Universal Banker and Merchant," and other works. Died in 1783.

Blicher, blik'ẹr, (STEEN STEENSEN,) a Danish poet and novelist, born in the stift or province of Viborg in 1782. His "National Novels" are very popular, and in some points have a strong resemblance to those of Sir Walter Scott. He translated the poems of Ossian into Danish. He had studied theology in early life, and in 1819 entered on the duties of a pastor. He wrote several treatises on rural economy, and an "Autobiography," which was published in a collection of his works, (9 vols., 1847–48.) Died in 1848.

See P. L. MÖLLER, "Dansk Pantheon."

Bligh, blī, (Sir RICHARD RODNEY,) a British admiral, born in Cornwall in 1737; died in 1821.

Bligh, (WILLIAM,) an English naval officer, born in 1753. By the orders of George III. he was sent in 1787 to the South Sea Islands, for the purpose of introducing the vegetable productions of those countries into the West Indies. While proceeding with his cargo to Jamaica, his men mutinied, (April, 1789,) and he, with eighteen of the crew, was sent adrift in the launch. After enduring great hardships, they arrived at the island of Timor in June, and in the spring of 1790 landed in England. He published soon after a "Narrative of the Mutiny on Board H.M. Ship Bounty," which excited great interest. He was appointed Governor of New South Wales in 1806, but, owing to his tyrannous conduct, was sent back to England in 1808. He died in 1817. The mutiny of the Bounty suggested to Lord Byron his poem entitled "The Island." (For an account of the mutineers, see ADAMS, JOHN.)

Blin, blȧn, (FRANÇOIS PIERRE,) a French physician, born at Rennes in 1756; died in 1834.

Blin de Sainmore, blȧn dẹh sȧn'mor', (ADRIEN MICHEL HYACINTHE,) a French *littérateur*, born in Paris in 1733, was appointed by Louis XVI. keeper of the archives, and historiographer. He wrote poems, dramas, and historical works. Died in 1807.

See VOLTAIRE, "Correspondance."

Blioul, du, dü ble'ool', (JEAN,) a Flemish ecclesiastic, born in Hainault about 1570.

Bliss, (JAMES C.,) M.D., an American philanthropist, born at Bennington, Vermont, in 1791. He practised medicine in the city of New York about forty years, and was eminent for his skill and beneficence. He was one of the founders of the American Tract Society. Died in 1855.

Blitterswick, van, vȧn blit'tẹrs-wik', (JAN,) a Flemish ecclesiastic and religious writer, born at Brussels; died in 1661.

ā, ē, ī, ō, ū, y, *long*: ȧ, ė, ŏ, same, less prolonged: ă, ĕ, ĭ, ŏ, ŭ, y̆, *short*: a, ẹ, į, ọ, *obscure:* fär, fȧll, fȧt: mĕt: nŏt: gŏŏd: mŏŏn:

Blitterswick, van, (WILLEM,) a Flemish jurist and *littérateur,* born at Brussels ; died in 1680.

Bliz′ard, (Sir WILLIAM,) a celebrated English anatomist and surgeon, born in Surrey in 1748. He became, in 1787, professor of anatomy to the old Corporation of Surgeons, being elected a Fellow of the Royal Society the same year. When the Royal College of Surgeons was founded, he was appointed to the chair of anatomy conjointly with Sir Everard Home, and was afterwards twice president of that college. He was the founder of the Hunterian Society, and of several other learned and benevolent institutions. He published a number of works on Surgery and Sanitary Reform. Died in 1835.

See "A Brief Memoir of Sir William Blizard," by WILLIAM COOKE.

Bloch, blok, (GEORG CASTANEUS,) a Danish botanist, born in 1717, became Bishop of Ribe. Died in 1773.

Bloch, (JOHANN ERASMUS,) a Danish gardener, published, in 1647, a work entitled "Horticultura Danica."

Bloch, blok, (MARKUS ELIESER,) a German physician and naturalist, of Jewish family, born at Anspach in 1723, practised medicine in Berlin. His "Universal Natural History of Fishes" (12 vols., with 432 coloured plates, 1782) is esteemed a standard work. Died in 1799.

Bloch, blok, or **Ballagi,** (MORITZ,) a learned Hungarian Jew, born at Ternova in 1815. He published a "Complete Dictionary of the Hungarian and German Languages," (1846.)

Blochmann, blok′mân, (KARL JUSTUS,) a German teacher and educational writer, born at Reichstadt, in Saxony, in 1786. About 1824 he founded at Dresden a large school called Blochman'sche Institut. Died at or near Geneva in 1855.

Block, (ALBRECHT,) a German agricultural writer, born at Sagan in 1774 ; died in 1847.

Block, (BENJAMIN,) a German portrait-painter, born at Lubeck in 1631.

Block, (DANIEL,) a German portrait-painter, father of the preceding, born in Pomerania in 1580. He was court painter to the King of Denmark and the King of Sweden. Died in 1661.

Block, blok, (JAMES REUGERS,) a Dutch painter, born at Gouda about 1580, excelled in perspective and architectural views. Died m 1632.

See DESCAMPS, "Vies des Peintres Flamands," etc.

Block, (JOANNA **Koerten**—kooR′ten,) an ingenious female artist, born at Amsterdam in 1650, was celebrated for her skill in cutting with her scissors landscapes, portraits, and animals. For such works she was paid immense prices by several sovereigns of Europe. Died in 1715.

Block, blok, (MAGNUS GABRIEL,) a Swedish physician, born at Stockholm in 1669 ; died in 1722.

Blockland, blok′lânt, (ANTHONY DE MONTFORT,) a Dutch painter of history and portraits, born at Montfort in 1532. He worked at Utrecht. Died in 1583.

Blod′get, (SAMUEL,) an American projector, born at Woburn, Massachusetts, about 1720. He raised a valuable cargo from a sunken vessel, and began the canal around the Amoskeag Falls, at Haverhill, New Hampshire, but, before it was finished, was sent to prison for debt. Died in 1807.

Bloemaert, blom′märt, (ABRAHAM,) a celebrated Dutch painter, born at Gorkum about 1564 or 1567. He painted landscapes and portraits, but excelled in historical pieces. He was also a skilful engraver. "The Death of Niobe's Sons" is called his master-piece. Died at Utrecht in 1647.

Bloemaert, (KORNELIS,) an excellent engraver, son of the preceding, born at Utrecht in 1603, studied engraving in Paris and in Rome. Among his master-pieces are the "Adoration of the Shepherds," after Cortona, and "Meleager," after Rubens. His three brothers, Adrian, Henry, and Frederick, were also engravers. Died at Rome in 1680.

See NAGLER, "Neues Allgemeines Künstler-Lexikon."

Bloemen, van, vän bloo′men, (JOHN FRANCIS,) a Flemish painter, born at Antwerp in 1656. He studied in Italy, where he passed his mature life, and where he received the surname of ORIZZONTE from some peculi-

arity of his style. His landscapes are greatly admired, and command high prices. Died at Rome in 1740.

See DESCAMPS, "Vies des Peintres Flamands," etc.

Bloemen, van, (NORBERT,) brother of John Francis born at Antwerp in 1672, painted portraits and conversation-pieces.

See DESCAMPS, "Vies des Peintres Flamands," etc.

Bloemen, van,(PETER,) surnamed STANDAERT,(stän′-däRt,) a Flemish painter, brother of the preceding, was a native of Antwerp. His principal works represent military marches, battles, fairs, caravans, etc. He became director of the Academy of Antwerp in 1699.

Bloeteling, bloo′teh-ling, sometimes written **Bloteling,** (ABRAHAM,) a celebrated Dutch designer and engraver, born at Amsterdam in 1634. Among his principal works are "Daniel in the Lions' Den," after Rubens, and a portrait of Erasmus, after Holbein. Died in 1676.

See NAGLER, "Neues Allgemeines Künstler-Lexikon."

Blois. See BLOSIUS.

Blom, blom, (KARL MAGNUS,) a Swedish naturalist and physician, born in Småland in 1737, was a pupil of Linnæus. He was the first to introduce vaccination into Sweden. He wrote several medical and scientific works in Latin. Died in 1815.

Blomberg, blom′bêRG, (BARBARA,) a lady of distinguished family in Nuremberg, was the mistress of Charles V., and the reputed mother of Don John of Austria.

Blome, blo′meh, (JOHANN,) a learned German writer, born at Hamburg about 1620 ; died in 1672.

Blome, (RICHARD,) an English historical writer, lived about 1670.

Blome′field, (FRANCIS,) born in Norfolk, England, in 1705, published "The Topographical History of Norfolk," (3 vols., 1739–69.) Died in 1751.

Blomfield, blüm′fêld, (CHARLES JAMES,) Bishop of London, born in Suffolk in 1786. He graduated at Trinity College, Cambridge, in 1808, and soon after brought out valuable editions of the "Prometheus" and several other dramas of Æschylus. He also edited the "Adversaria Porsoni," and contributed to various reviews a number of critical essays on the Greek classics. In 1824 he published an edition of Callimachus. He became Bishop of London in 1828. Bishop Blomfield distinguished himself by his efforts to improve the condition of the poor, and promoted the erection of a great number of churches in London. His opinions were decidedly "high-church." Died in 1857.

See DR. BIBER, "Bishop Blomfield and his Times," 1857 ; A. BLOMFIELD, "Life of C. J. Blomfield," 1863 ; "London Quarterly Review" for January and April, 1868.

Blomfield, (EDWARD VALENTINE,) a distinguished English scholar, brother of the preceding, was born in 1788. He published a valuable translation of Matthiae's "Greek Grammar," and was a contributor to the "Museum Criticum." Died in 1816.

Blommaert, blom′märt, (PHILIPPUS,) a Belgian philologist and poet, born about 1809, published editions of several old Flemish poems, and translated the "Niebelungen" into Dutch iambics. His best production is a historical work entitled "Aloude Geschiedenis der Belgen of Nederduitschers," (1849.)

Blond, le, leh blôn, (JACQUES CHRISTOPHE,) a miniature-painter, born at Frankfort in 1670. He worked in London, and made unsuccessful attempts to produce coloured engravings or copies of paintings. Died about 1740.

Blond, Le. See LE BLOND.

Blonde, blônd, (ANDRÉ,) a French jurist, born at Auxerre in 1734 ; died in 1794.

Blondeau, blôn′dŏ′, (ANTOINE FRANÇOIS RAYMOND,) a French general, born in Franche-Comté in 1747, served under Pichegru in 1794, and in the Italian campaign of 1799. Died in 1825.

Blondeau, (CHARLES,) a French jurist and miscellaneous writer, born at Mans ; died in 1680.

Blondeau, (CLAUDE,) a French jurist and legal writer, born in Paris, lived about 1650.

Blondeau, (JEAN BAPTISTE ANTOINE HYACINTHE,) professor of Roman law in the faculty of Paris, was born at Namur in 1784. He became a member of the Academy of Moral and Political Science, and published several works on Roman jurisprudence.

ɛ as *k;* ç as *s;* g̃ *hard;* g̃ as *j;* G, H, K, *guttural;* N, *nasal;* R, *trilled;* s̃ as *z;* ŧh as in *this.* (☞See Explanations, p. 23.)

Blondeau ãe Charnage, blôN'dō' dĕh shăR'nắzh', (CLAUDE FRANÇOIS,) a French *littérateur*, born near Pontarlier in 1710. Died in 1776.

Blondel, blôN'dĕl', [Lat. BLONDELÆ'US,] a French troubadour, and favourite of Richard Cœur de Lion, whom he accompanied on his principal expeditions. He is said to have discovered the place of the king's imprisonment in Germany by singing before the fortress part of a song which was answered from within.

Blondel, (DAVID,) a French Protestant divine and writer, born at Châlons-sur-Marne in 1591. In 1650 he succeeded Vossius as professor of history at Amsterdam. He published a number of theological and historical works in Latin and French. Died in 1655.

See BAYLE, "Historical and Critical Dictionary;" BRUCKER, "History of Philosophy."

Blondel, blôN'dĕl', (FRANCIS,) a Flemish physician, born at Liege in 1613 ; died in 1682.

Blondel, (FRANÇOIS,) a French architect and mathematician, born at Ribemont in 1617. He was appointed professor of mathematics in the Royal College, and was chosen by Louis XIV. to teach that science to the dauphin. He published a "Course of Architecture," and various other treatises. The triumphal arch of the Porte Saint-Denis is esteemed his master-piece in architecture. Died in 1686.

See FONTENAY, "Dictionnaire des Artistes."

Blondel, (FRANÇOIS,) a French physician, born in Paris, graduated about 1631, was noted for his opposition to the use of antimony in medicine. Died in 1682.

Blondel, (JACQUES,) a French surgeon, who lived at Lille about 1580, translated, from the Latin, Godin's "Military Surgery."

Blondel, (JACQUES FRANÇOIS,) a French architect, nephew of François the architect, noticed above, was born at Rouen in 1705. He became professor in the Academy of Architecture in Paris. Died in 1774.

Blon'dĕl, (JAMES AUGUSTUS,) an English physician, of French extraction, wrote several esteemed medical works. He was a member of the Royal College of Physicians. Died in London in 1734.

Blondel, (JEAN,) a French jurist and legal writer, born at Rheims in 1733, became president of the imperial court of Paris in 1803. Died in 1810.

Blondel, (LAURENT,) a French scholar and theological writer, born in Paris in 1671 ; died in 1740.

Blondel, (MARIE JOSEPH,) a French historical painter, born in Paris in 1781, was a pupil of Regnault. Among his works are "Zenobia on the Shore of the Araxis," and "Homer in Athens." He was a member of the Institute.

Blondel, (PIERRE JACQUES,) a French *littérateur*, born in Paris in 1674; died in 1730.

Blondel, (ROBERT,) a French poet and moralist, born in Normandy about 1390, was preceptor to the dauphin Charles, a son of Charles VII. Died about 1460.

Blondin, blôN'dăN', (JEAN NOËL,) a French grammarian, born in Paris in 1753, became secretary and interpreter at the Royal Library. He published a "Polyglot Grammar, French, Latin, Italian, Spanish, Portuguese, and English." Died in 1832.

Blondin, (PIERRE,) a French botanist, born at Vaudricourt in 1682, was a pupil of Tournefourt. Died in 1713.

Blondus, (FLAVIUS.) See FLAVIO BIONDO.

Blood, blŭd, (Colonel THOMAS,) a notorious Irish adventurer, born about 1628, served for a time in Cromwell's army. Having failed in his attempt to surprise the castle of Dublin and take the Duke of Ormond, then lord-lieutenant, he seized the person of that nobleman in his coach in London, (1670,) and was only prevented from hanging him by the resistance of his servants. In 1671 he nearly succeeded in possessing himself of the crown jewels ; but, after a short imprisonment for this crime, he was pardoned by Charles II., and received from him a pension. Died in 1680.

See KENNET, "History of England."

Bloom'field, (ROBERT,) an English poet, born at Honington, in Suffolk, in 1766. He was the son of a tailor, and was apprenticed at an early age to a shoemaker in London. While in this situation he composed his rural poem of "The Farmer's Boy," which, after being refused by several booksellers, was published under

the patronage of Mr. Capel Lofft. It was received with extraordinary favour, and was translated into French, Italian, and Latin. Among his other poems we may name "Good Tidings, or News from the Farm," "May-Day with the Muses," and "Ballads and Songs." Of the "Farmer's Boy," Dr. Nathan Drake observes, in his "Literary Hours," that "in true pastoral imagery and simplicity no production can be put in competition with it since the days of Theocritus ;" and a critic in "Blackwood's Magazine" pronounces it "by far the best-written, as to style and composition, of any work of our uneducated poets." Died in Bedfordshire in 1823.

See "Blackwood's Magazine" for June, 1822, vol. xi. ; "Pursuit of Knowledge under Difficulties," vol. ii., 1839.

Bloomfield, (S. T.,) D.D., an English divine and scholar, born about 1790. He has published an edition of Dr. Robinson's "Greek and English Lexicon to the New Testament," with important additions and corrections, which is highly commended by the "Church of England Quarterly ;" also the "Greek Testament, with English Notes, Critical, Philological, and Explanatory," (1832,) and other valuable works of the kind. He brought out in 1829 an excellent translation of Thucydides.

Bloot, blōt, (PIETER,) a Dutch or Flemish painter, whose favourite subjects are drunken frolics, quarrels of peasants, etc. Died in 1667.

Blo'sĭ-us or **De Blois,** dĕh blwâ, (FRANCIS LOUIS,) a Flemish Benedictine monk of noble family, born near Liege in 1506, became abbot of the monastery of Liesses, in Hainault. He was educated with Prince Charles, afterwards the emperor Charles V. Died about 1565.

Blot, blo, Baron de Chauvigny, (dĕh sho'vĕn'ye',) a French wit and *littérateur* in the reign of Louis XIII., wrote a number of satires and epigrams against Cardinal Mazarin. Died in 1655.

Blot, (MAURICE,) a French painter and engraver, born in Paris in 1754, was a pupil of Saint-Aubin. Died in 1818.

Bloteling. See BLOETELING.

Blouet, bloo'ậ', (JEAN FRANÇOIS NICOLAS,) a French journalist and *littérateur*, born at Metz in 1745, wrote on agriculture, commerce, and other subjects. Died in 1809.

Blount, blŭnt, (CHARLES,) Lord Mountjoy and Earl of Devonshire, born in 1563, lived in the reign of Queen Elizabeth, by whom he was treated with great favour. He succeeded to the title of Lord Mountjoy, and became governor of Portsmouth in 1594, and lord deputy of Ireland in 1600. Having put down the Irish rebellion in 1603, he was created Earl of Devonshire by James I., and obtained other distinctions. Died in 1605 or 1606. He was an intimate friend of the Earl of Essex, whose sister he married. She was a great beauty, and previously the wife of Lord Rich. Lord Devonshire and Lady Rich had five children born before their marriage.

Blount, (CHARLES,) an English writer, son of Sir Henry, mentioned below, born at Upper Holloway in 1654, published a deistical work entitled "Anima Mundi," (1678,) and several others of a similar nature. He also translated from the Greek the "Life of Apollonius Tyanæus," by Philostratus. He committed suicide in 1693.

See MACAULAY'S "History of England," vol. iv.

Blount, (Sir HENRY,) born in Hertfordshire in 1602, travelled in Greece, Palestine, and Egypt, of which countries he gave an account in his "Voyage into the Levant," published in 1636. It was translated into French and Dutch. Died in 1682.

Blount, [Lat. BLON'DUS,] (JOHN,) an English writer, who was prebendary and chancellor in the church of York. He wrote theological works which were highly esteemed by his contemporaries, but they are not known to be extant. Died in 1248.

See WOOD, "Athenæ Oxonienses."

Blount, (THOMAS,) an English jurist and writer, born in Worcestershire in 1618. He published "Glossographia," or a dictionary of legal terms, "Lamps of the Law and Lights of the Gospel," (1658,) "The Academy of Eloquence," and other works. Died in 1679.

Blount, (Sir THOMAS POPE,) son of Sir Henry, noticed above, born in 1649, was several times elected to Parliament for Saint Alban's and Hertfordshire. He published a "Critique on Celebrated Writers," ("Censura celebriorum Authorum," 1690,) which is commended by

Hallam, Sir Egerton Brydges, and other eminent critics. Died in 1697.

Blount, blŭnt, (WILLIAM,) an American Senator, born about 1744. He was appointed governor of the territory south of the Ohio River in 1790, and was elected a Senator of the United States by the legislature of Tennessee in 1796. He was expelled from the Senate, in 1797, on a charge that he had abetted an attempt of the British to conquer from Spain part of the lower valley of the Mississippi. Died at Knoxville in 1800.

Blount (blŭnt) **Mount-joy',** Lord Mountjoy, born about 1598, was the eldest son of Charles Blount and Lady Rich. He was created Earl of Newport in 1628, and appointed Constable of the Tower in 1641, but was removed in the same year because the king distrusted his loyalty. He adhered to the royal cause in the civil war, but was regarded as lukewarm. Died in 1665.

Blōw, (JOHN,) an English musician and composer, born in Nottinghamshire in 1648, became organist of Westminster Abbey. Among his principal compositions are a "Gloria Patri," and a collection of secular pieces entitled "Amphion Anglicus." The celebrated Purcell was one of his pupils. Died in 1708.

See BURNEY, "History of Music."

Blücher, von, fon bloo'ker, [Ger. pron. fon blü'ķer,] (GEBHARD LEBRECHT,) a celebrated Prussian field-marshal, born at Rostock in 1742. At an early age he entered the Swedish army, and was taken prisoner by the same Prussian regiment (then under the command of Colonel von Belling) which he afterwards commanded with such distinction. He was prevailed upon by Von Belling to join the army of Frederick the Great, and, after the accession of Frederick William, distinguished himself in the campaigns of 1793-94 against the French. In 1806 he commanded the Prussian vanguard at Auerstadt, and effected a masterly retreat to Lubeck, though pursued by Soult, Bernadotte, and Murat. Appointed in 1813 to the chief command of the allied Russian and Prussian army, he obtained a signal victory over Macdonald on the Katzbach, and soon after took a prominent part in the battle of Leipsic. After various engagements with the French, he advanced to Paris in March, 1814, and, having stormed the heights of Montmartre, entered the city with the allied sovereigns. On this occasion he was created Prince of Wahlstadt by the King of Prussia, and received other high distinctions. In 1815 he again took command of the Prussian army, and though defeated at Ligny, June 16, he appeared on the field of Waterloo in the evening of the 18th and decided the fortunes of that eventful day. With his fresh troops he pursued the flying enemy through the night, and, having arrived in Paris, assisted in re-establishing the Bourbon dynasty. He died in 1819, at the age of seventy-seven. Blücher was chiefly remarkable for his impetuous courage and the rapidity of his movements, which procured for him the name of "Marshal Vorwärts," ("Forwards.") For the plans of his battles he relied principally upon Scharnhorst and Gneisenau, generals of his staff. When praised for one of his victories, he said, "It is owing to my rashness, Gneisenau's prudence, and the mercy of the great God."

See "Life and Campaigns of Blucher," London, 1815; FOERSTER, "Blücher und sein Umgebung," 1821; PISCHON, "Blüchers Leben, Thaten und Ende," 1842; VARNHAGEN VON ENSE, "Blüchers Lebensbeschreibung," 1827; W. BURCKHARDT, "G. L. von Blücher nach Leben, Reden und Thaten geschildert," 1835; "Vie de Blücher," Paris, 1816.

Bludoff or **Bloudoff,** bloo'doff, (DMITRI,) COUNT, a Russian statesman, born at Moscow about 1783. He has been employed in various embassies, appointed secretary of the interior, and president of the legislative department in the council of the empire.

Bluet d'Arbères, de, deh blü-â' (almost blwä) dâR'-baiR', (BERNARD,) a French *littérateur,* and fool by profession, sometimes called the COMTE DE PERMISSION, was born near Savoy about 1560. He wrote eulogies on his patrons, and a number of prophecies for the people. A copy of his works was sold for five hundred francs at the McCarthy sale in 1816.

See FLÖGEL, "Geschichte des Burlesken."

Bluf, bloof, (MATTHÄUS JOSEPH,) a German physician and medical writer, born at Cologne in 1805; died in 1837.

Bluhme, bloo'mĕh, (CHRISTIAN ALBERT,) a Danish statesman, born at Copenhagen in 1794, became minister of foreign affairs in 1851, and in 1852 president of the council.

Bluhme or **Blume,** bloo'mĕh, (FRIEDRICH,) a German jurist, born at Hamburg about 1798. He became profoundly versed in the Roman law, and was appointed professor of law at Bonn. Among his works are "Iter Italicum," (4 vols., 1824-36,) containing the results of his researches in Italy, "Canon Law of the Jews and Christians, especially in Germany," (1826,) and a "Sketch of the Law of the Pandects," (1829.)

Blum, bloŏm, (JEAN,) a Swiss architect, resided ·at Zurich. He published in 1596 a "Book of Architecture."

Blum, bloŏm, (JOACHIM CHRISTIAN,) a German *littérateur,* born at Rathenau in 1739; died in 1790.

Blum, (KARL,) a German composer, and director of the Royal Opera at Berlin, born in that city about 1785. He composed numerous operas and songs. Died in 1844.

Blum, (ROBERT,) a German democratic politician, born at Cologne in·1807. In 1840 he founded the Schiller Association at Leipsic, and soon after became a leading contributor to the "Sächsischen Vaterlandsblättern," a political journal. He was the founder of the German Catholic church at Leipsic in 1845. In the revolution of 1848 he was a prominent leader of the Liberal party, and was one of the deputation sent to Vienna with the address of the parliamentary opposition. On the capture of that city by Windischgrätz, he was arrested and shot, November 9, 1848.

See EDUARD DULLER, "R. Blums Leben und Tod," 1848; EDUARD FRANKE, "Leben, Wirken, etc. des R. Blum," 1848; LUDWIG WITTIG, "Blums letzte Stunden in Wien," 1848.

Blumauer, bloo'mŏw'ĕr, (ALOYS,) a German poet, born at Steyer in 1755, published a burlesque poem entitled "Virgil's Æneid travestied," (1784,) which was very popular in Germany and was translated into Russian. Died in 1798.

Blumberg, bloŏm'bĕRG, (CHRISTIAN GOTTHELF,) a German Lutheran divine and philologist, born near Querfurt in 1664; died in 1735.

Blume. See BLUHME.

Blumenbach, bloo'mĕn-bâk, [Ger. pron. bloo'mĕn-bâk,] (JOHANN FRIEDRICH,) a celebrated German comparative anatomist and physiologist, was born at Gotha on the 11th of May, 1752. He studied at Jena, and afterwards at Göttingen, where he took his degree in medicine in 1775. On this occasion he wrote a thesis on the "Varieties of the Human Race," ("De Generis humani Varietate Nativa,") which was translated into many languages. He became ordinary professor of medicine and anatomy at Göttingen in 1778, and continued to lecture there more than fifty years. He published in 1780 a popular "Manual of Natural History," (10th edition, 1830,) and in 1786 a "Description of the Bones of the Human Body." He explained with success the functions of the human system in his "Institutiones Physiologicæ," (1787,) which was translated into English and other languages and used as a text-book in schools.

Blumenbach was the first who divided the human species into five races,—viz., the Caucasian, Mongolian, Malay, American, and African or Ethiopian. He advocated the unity of the human species. "He was the first," says Dr. Hoefer, "who placed natural history on a scientific basis,—comparative anatomy." Among his important works is a "Manual of Comparative Anatomy," (1805.) In the number of his pupils was Alexander von Humboldt. He was a member of about seventy learned societies, and corresponded with the most eminent philosophers of Europe. He was created a knight of the Guelphic order about 1821. Died at Göttingen in January, 1840.

See "Éloge de Blumenbach," par FLOURENS, 1846; C. F. H. MARX, "Zum Andenken an J. F. Blumenbach," 1840; "Nouvelle Biographie Générale."

Blumröder, von, fon bloŏm'rö'der, (AUGUST FRIEDRICH,) a German *littérateur* and soldier, born at Gehren in 1776, served against the French in the campaigns of 1814-15.

Blun'dell, (JAMES,) a British physician and medical writer, born about 1810, practised in London.

Blun'de-ville, (THOMAS,) an English mathematician,

published in 1594 a popular work, entitled "Exercises, containing Six Treatises."

Blunt, (EDMOND,) an American hydrographer, son of Edmond M. Blunt, noticed below, born in Newburyport, Massachusetts, in 1799. He was for many years engaged in making surveys of the sea-coast of the United States, the West Indies, Guatemala, etc., and since 1833 has been first assistant in the United States Coast Survey at Washington.

Blunt, (EDMOND MARCH,) an American writer on nautical subjects, born in Portsmouth, New Hampshire, in 1770. In 1796 he published his "American Coast Pilot," which has since passed through many editions and been translated into several European languages. It contains descriptions of every seaport in the United States and of most of those in America, with sailing-directions, lists of light-houses, etc. He has also published many other valuable nautical works, charts, etc.

Blunt, (HENRY,) an English religious writer, born about 1794. In 1835 he became rector of Streathan, Surrey. He published, besides sermons, "Lectures on the History of Saint Paul," (1833,) "Lectures on the History of Elisha," and other popular works. It is said that some of his works have passed through forty editions. Died in 1843.

Blunt, (JAMES G.,) an American general, born in Hancock county, Maine, in 1826. He settled in Kansas about 1856, and became a leader of the Free State party. He was appointed a brigadier-general about April, 1862. He defeated the enemy at Kane Hill, Arkansas, in November, and at Prairie Grove in December, 1862. Having been promoted to the rank of major-general, he commanded the department of Kansas in 1863, but was relieved in October of that year.

Blunt, (JOHN JAMES,) an English divine and scholar, born at Newcastle-under-Lime in 1794. He became in 1839 Lady Margaret professor of divinity at Cambridge. He published "Undesigned Coincidences in the Writings both of the Old and New Testaments an Argument of their Veracity," (1847,) "Vestiges of Ancient Manners in Italy and Sicily," and other works. Died in 1855.

See "London Quarterly Review" for July, 1858, (vol. civ.)

Blunthli, blōont′lee, or **Bluntschli,** blōont′shlee, (JEAN HENRI,) born at Zurich in 1656, wrote a chronicle of the city and canton of Zurich, entitled "Memorabilia Tigurina." Died in 1722.

Bluntschli, blōont′shlee, (JOHANN KASPAR,) a Swiss jurist, born in 1808 at Zurich, where he became professor of law in 1836.

Bluteau, blü′to′, (Dom RAPHAEL,) a learned writer, of French extraction, born in London in 1638, became preacher to Henrietta Maria, queen of Charles I. He published a "Portuguese-Latin Dictionary," (1712, 8 vols. fol.) Died in 1734.

Blutel, blü′tĕl′, (CHARLES AUGUSTE ESPRIT ROSE,) a French jurist, and member of the National Convention, born at Caen in 1757. He was a member of the Council of Five Hundred. Died in 1806.

See "Notice sur M. Blutel," Paris, 1847.

Blyenburg, blī′ĕn-bŭRG′, (ADRIAN,) a Latin poet, nephew of Damasus, born at Dort in 1560; died in 1599.

Blyenburg, van, vän blī′ĕn-bŭRG′, (DAMASUS,) a Dutch *littérateur,* born at Dort in 1558, published a compilation of the modern Latin poets.

Bô, bō, (JEAN BAPTISTE JÉRÔME,) a French physician, born near Mur-de-Barrez in 1753, was elected to the National Convention in 1792, and voted for the immediate death of the king. Died in 1811.

Boabdil, bo-äb-dēl′,[corrupted from **Aboo-Abdillah** or **Aboo-Abdallah,**] surnamed EL CHICO, (chee′ko,) (or THE LITTLE,) the last Moorish king of Granada. His claim to the throne was contested by his uncle, Abdallah-el-Zagal. This dispute was settled by Ferdinand of Aragon, who conquered Granada in 1491, when Boabdil ceased to reign. He retired to Africa in 1496, and died about 1536.

Boaden, bō′dĕn, (JAMES,) an English writer, born at Whitehaven in 1762, was an intimate friend of John Kemble. He published several dramas, a "Life of John Philip Kemble," a "Life of Mrs. Jordan," and one of Mrs. Siddons. Died in 1839.

Bo-ad-ĭ-çe′a, [Fr. BOADICÉE, bo′ä′de′så′,] written also **Boadicea, Boodicia,** and **Voadica,** wife of Prasutagus, king of the British tribe of the Iceni, flourished about the middle of the first century. After the death of her husband, Boadicea, incensed by the rapacity and insults of the procurator Catus, took up arms against the Roman colonists and their allies, seventy thousand of whom, according to Tacitus, fell in battle. She was subsequently defeated by Suetonius Paulinus with immense loss, and took poison to avoid falling into the victor's hands.

See TACITUS, "Annales," book xiv.

Boadicée, the French of BOADICEA, which see.

Bŏard′man, (GEORGE D.,) an eminent Baptist missionary, born at Livermore, Maine, in 1801. He graduated at Waterville College in 1821, studied divinity at the Theological Seminary at Andover, and in 1825 sailed for the East under the auspices of the Baptist Board of Foreign Missions. He arrived at Calcutta in December following, and, after devoting some fifteen months to the study of the Burmese language, established a mission at Maulmain, on the Tenasserim coast. This place subsequently became the principal seat of the Baptist missions in that region. The next year he founded another mission at Tavoy. Mr. Boardman continued his work with great zeal and success until his death in 1831.

Boardman, (HENRY AUGUSTUS,) D.D., an eloquent American divine, born at Troy, New York, January 9, 1808. He graduated at Yale in 1829 as valedictorian of his class, and studied theology at Princeton. For more than thirty years he has had the pastoral charge of the Tenth Presbyterian Church in Philadelphia. In 1853 he was elected by the general assembly to fill the chair of pastoral theology at Princeton, but he declined the honour.

See ALLIBONE'S "Dictionary of Authors."

Boaretti, bo-ä-ret′tee, (FRANCESCO,) an able Italian *littérateur,* born near Padua in 1748, became professor of sacred eloquence at Venice about 1785. He translated some of the works of Sophocles and several tragedies of Euripides into Italian, (versi sciolti,) and Homer's "Iliad" into ottava rima, (1788.) Died in 1799.

Boas, bo′äs, (EDUARD,) a German novelist, born at Landsberg in 1815, published a supplement to the works of Goethe, (3 vols., 1841,) and other works. Died in 1853.

Boat. See BOOT.

Boaton, de, dĕh bo′ä′tòn′, (PIERRE FRANÇOIS,) born near Aubonne, in the Pays de Vaud, in 1734, translated into French verse Gessner's "Idyls" and "Death of Abel," and Wieland's "Oberon." Died in 1794.

Bobadilla, de, dȧ bo-bȧ-dèl′yä, (FRANCISCO,) a Spanish magistrate, who was charged, in 1500, to ascertain the condition of the colony at Saint Domingo under Columbus. On his arrival he caused that illustrious man to be arrested and sent in chains to Spain, where he was kindly received by his sovereigns and reinstated in his honours. Bobadilla was soon after obliged to resign his post to Nicholas Ovando.

See IRVING'S "Life of Columbus."

Bobart, bo′baRt, (JACOB,) a German botanist and physician, born at Brunswick about 1598, became superintendent of the botanical garden at Oxford in England. Died in 1679.

Bobart, (JACOB,) son of the preceding, became professor of botany at Oxford in 1683. Died in 1719.

Bobolina, bo-bo-lee′nä, a modern Greek heroine, who in the revolution of 1821 equipped three ships at her own expense, one of which she commanded. She offered her vessels to the government for the blockade of Nauplia, which was maintained fourteen months. She was assassinated in 1825 by the friend of a person supposed to have been wronged by a member of her family.

See POUQUEVILLE, "Histoire de la Régénération de la Grèce."

Bobrof, bo′bRof, (SEMEN SERGEEVITCH,) a Russian poet, whose principal poem is entitled "Khersonida," being a history and description of Taurida, in Southern Russia. Died in 1810.

Bobrun, bo′bRŭn′, (CHARLES,) a French painter, born at Amboise in 1604, executed a number of portraits in conjunction with his cousin Henri, noticed below. Died in 1692.

Bobrun, (HENRI,) a French portrait-painter, born at

Amboise in 1603, was patronized by Louis XIV. Among his master-pieces are portraits of Louis and of Anne of Austria. Died in 1677.

See HEINECKEN, "Dictionnaire des Artistes."

Bocaccino, bo-kât-chee'no, (BOCCACCIO,) an Italian painter, born at Cremona about 1460. He is praised by Lanzi. Died about 1518.

See VASARI, "Lives of the Painters."

Bocaccino, (CAMILLO,) surnamed IL BOCCALINI, (èl bok-kâ-lee'nee,) born at Cremona in 1511, was a son of the preceding. Among his master-pieces are the frescos in the church of Saint Sigismund at Cremona. Died in 1546.

See LANZI, "History of Painting in Italy."

Bocace. See BOCCACCIO.

Bocandé, bo'kôN'dà', (BERTRAND,) a French naturalist and geographer, born at Nantes about 1820, resided many years in Africa. He published "Notes on Portuguese Guinea, or Southern Senegambia."

Bocanegra, bo-kâ-nā'grâ, (PEDRO ATANASIO,) a Spanish painter, born at Granada about 1638, was a pupil of Alonzo Cano. Died in 1688.

Bocarro, bo-kâr'ro, (ANTONIO,) a Portuguese historian, wrote a continuation of the "Asia Portugueza" of João de Barros, (in manuscript.)

Bocarro Francez, bo-kâr'ro fRân'sĕs, (MANOEL,) a Portuguese astronomer and physician, born at Lisbon in 1588, received lessons from Galileo. Died at Florence in 1662.

Boccaccio, bo-kât'cho, [Old English, BOCCACE or BOCACE, bo-kâss'; Fr. BOCCACE, bo'kâss'; Lat. BOCCA'-TIUS and BOCCAC'CIUS,] or, more fully, **Boccaccio di Certaldo,** bok-cât'cho de chĕR-tâl'do, (GIOVANNI,) the most celebrated of Italian novelists, born in Paris in 1313, was the illegitimate son of a Florentine merchant and a Frenchwoman. At his father's desire he engaged in mercantile pursuits, and afterwards studied canon law, which, however, he soon abandoned. Among his first productions were the romance of "Il Filicopo," and a poem in ottava rima, entitled "La Teseide," written at the request of his mistress, the Princess Mary, natural daughter of Robert, King of Naples. After the accession of Joanna to the throne of Naples, Boccaccio wrote, at her desire, his "Decamerone, or Hundred Tales," (1353,) which are esteemed models of Italian prose composition ; but many of them are disgustingly licentious. About this time he was sent on several diplomatic missions, and formed an intimacy with Petrarch, which continued for the remainder of their lives. He was appointed in 1373 to lecture on Florence on Dante, and wrote a commentary on the "Inferno," and a "Life of Dante." Besides his works in Italian, Boccaccio was the author of a number of Latin eclogues and prose essays, and, like his friend Petrarch, rendered important services to classical learning by collecting and transcribing ancient manuscripts. He died in 1375, having for many years previously been in a great measure reformed from the profligacy of his early life and writings. The "Decamerone" has furnished Shakspeare with the subjects of several of his dramas, and Chaucer derived from it his poem of "The Knight's Tale." Hazlitt, after remarking that Shakspeare's play of "All's Well that Ends Well" is from Boccaccio, adds, "The poet has dramatized the original novel with great skill and comic spirit, and has preserved all the beauty of character and sentiment *without improving upon it, which was impossible.* There is indeed in Boccaccio's serious pieces a truth, a pathos, and an exquisite refinement of sentiment which is hardly to be met with in any other prose writer whatever. . . . The invention implied in his different tales is immense ; but we are not to infer that it is all his own. He probably availed himself of all the common traditions which were floating in his time, and which he was the first to appropriate." (See Hazlitt's "Characters of Shakspeare's Plays.")

See also BALDELLI, "Vita di Giovanni Boccaccio," 1806: MAZZU-CHELLI, "Scrittori d'Italia ;" LONGFELLOW, "Poets and Poetry of Europe ;" GIANOTTI MANETTI, "Specimen Historiæ literariæ Florentinæ Seculi XIII. ac XIV., seu Vitæ Dantis, Petrarchæ ac Boccaccii," 1747 ; J. F. ADRY, "Notice sur Boccace," 1802 : "Lives of the Italian Poets," by the Rev. HENRY STEBBING, London, vol. i., 1831.

Bocca di Ferro, bok'kâ de fĕR'ro, (GIROLAMO,) an

Italian jurist, nephew of Luigi, born at Bologna in 1552 ; died in 1623.

Bocca di Ferro, Bucca Ferri, book'kâ fĕR'ree, or **Bucca Ferra,** book'kâ fĕR'râ, (LUIGI,) an Italian physician and philosopher, born at Bologna in 1482. He became professor of logic in his native city, and numbered among his pupils J. C. Scaliger and Benedict Varchi. He wrote several Latin commentaries on the works of Aristotle. Died in 1545.

Boccage, du, dü bo'kâzh',(MANOEL MARIA BARBOSA,) a celebrated Portuguese poet and improvisatore, of French extraction, born at Setuval in 1771. He published numerous sonnets, odes, elegies, and epigrams, and made several translations from the French and Latin. It is stated that he could speak French, Italian, and Latin with facility. He became the chief of a poetic school known under the name of *Elmanismo.* Died in 1806.

See LONGFELLOW's "Poets and Poetry of Europe."

Boccage, du, (MARIE ANNE LE PAGE,) a French poetess, born at Rouen in 1710, was the wife of P. J. Fiquet du Boccage, noticed below. She was the author of a tragedy entitled "The Amazons," imitations of "Paradise Lost" and of Gessner's great "Death of Abel," and other poems, which enjoyed great popularity in her time, but are now nearly forgotten. She was a member of several foreign academies, as well as of those of Lyons and Rouen. Her letters to her sister, Madame Duperron, are still admired. Died in 1802.

See GUILBERT, "Notice sur Madame Boccage," 1807.

Boccage, du, (PIERRE JOSEPH Fiquet—fe'kâ',) a French *littérateur,* born at Rouen in 1700, wrote "Letters on the English Theatre," and translated several works from the English. Died in 1757.

Boccalini, bok-kâ-lee'nee, (TRAJANO,) a witty Italian satirist, born at Loretto in 1556, was the author of "News from Parnassus," ("Ragguagli di Parnaso," 1612,) and other works, which were translated into several languages. Among these is a satire called "Pietra del Paragone politico," (1626.) Died at Venice in 1613.

See MORHOF, "Polyhistor."

Boccanera, bok-kâ-nā'râ, (EGIDIO,) a Genoese admiral, was a brother of Simone, Doge of Genoa. Having entered the Spanish service, he assisted in the capture of Algesiras in 1344, and in 1372 defeated the English fleet under the Earl of Pembroke, whom he made prisoner. Died about 1373.

See SISMONDI, "Histoire des Républiques Italiennes."

Boccanera,(GUGLIELMO,) a Genoese nobleman, raised by the democratic party in 1257 to the sovereign power in Genoa, was deposed in 1262.

Boccanera, (SIMONE,) was elected Doge of Genoa in 1339, removed in 1344, and re-elected in 1356. He gained victories over the Turks and Moors. Died about 1363.

See SISMONDI, "Histoire des Républiques Italiennes."

Boccherini, bok-kâ-ree'nee, (LUIGI,) an Italian composer of instrumental pieces, born at Lucca in 1740, was patronized by Charles IV. of Spain. Died in 1806.

See FÉTIS, "Biographie Universelle des Musiciens."

Bocchi, bok'kee, [Lat. BOC'CHIUS,] (ACHILLE,) an Italian scholar, born at Bologna in 1488, became professor of Greek and Latin literature in his native city. He wrote several Latin works, in prose and verse, on history, philosophy, etc. Died in 1562.

Bocchi,(FAUSTINO,) an Italian painter, born at Brescia in 1659 ; died about 1742.

Bocchi,(FRANCESCO,) born at Florence in 1548, wrote essays on various subjects, and eulogies on eminent Italians. Died in 1618.

Boc'chus [Gr. Βόκχος] I., King of Mauritania, was the father-in-law of Jugurtha, and an ally of that prince in the war against the Romans. Having been defeated by Marius, he betrayed Jugurtha to the Romans in 106 B.C.

Bocchus II., supposed to have been a son of the preceding, fought for Cæsar against Juba, King of Numidia, and was rewarded with a part of the kingdom of Massinissa. In a war between Antony and Octavius, Bocchus was a partisan of the latter.

Bocciardo, bot-chaR'do, (CLEMENTE,) an Italian

pair'ter, born at Genoa in 1620, was surnamed CLEMEN-TONE, from his large stature. Died in 1658.

Boccoue, bok-ko'nà, (PAOLO,) a distinguished Sicilian naturalist, born at Palermo in 1633. He published a large number of Latin and Italian treatises on botany and mineralogy. Died in 1704.

Bocconio, bok-ko'ne-o, (MARINO,) a Venetian conspirator, who, having failed in his attempt to overthrow the aristocracy of Venice, was executed in 1299.

Boccuci, bok-koo'chee, (?) or **Bocous,** (JOSÉ,) a Spanish dramatist, probably of Italian origin, born at Barcelona in 1775, resided for some years in Paris. He wrote successful dramas, and was a contributor to the "Biographie Universelle."

Bocerus. See BOCKER, (JOHANN.)

Boch, bok, or **Bochius,** bo'ke-us, (JOHN,) a Flemish poet, called "the Belgian Virgil," born at Brussels in 1555, wrote Latin poems which were much admired. Died in 1609.

Bochart, bo'shăr', (MATHIEU,) a French Protestant theologian, was the author of a "Treatise against Relics," and a work entitled "Diallacticon," (1662,) advocating the union of Lutherans and Calvinists.

Bochart, (SAMUEL,) an eminent French scholar and Protestant theologian, born at Rouen in May, 1599. He studied divinity and the Oriental tongues under Caméron and Louis Cappel, and was subsequently instructed by Erpenius, at Leyden, in Arabic, Syriac, and Chaldee. He was appointed in 1625 pastor at Caen, where he remained forty-three years and acquired great influence and reputation as a preacher. In 1628 he acquitted himself with credit in a public dispute with the Jesuit Véron, who was employed by Cardinal Richelieu. His greatest works are his "Hierozoicon," (1663,) or an account of animals mentioned in the Bible, and "Geographia Sacra," (1646.) They are commended by Cuvier and Baron Humboldt. Bochart died at Caen in 1667, with the reputation of one of the most learned men of his time. Several volumes of his sermons were published after his death. "No one," says Hallam, "has left a more durable reputation in this literature [Rabbinical or Hebrew] than Bochart. His 'Geographia Sacra' displays great learning and sagacity." ("Introduction to the Literature of Europe.")

See MORIN, "De Vita et Scriptis S. Bocharti," 1692; EDWARD HERBERT SMITH, "S. Bochart: Recherches sur la Vie et les Ouvrages de cet Auteur illustre," 1833.

Bochart de Sarron, bo'shăr' deh să'rôn', (JEAN BAPTISTE GASPARD,) a French mathematician and astronomer, born in Paris in 1730. He was a member of the Academy of Sciences, and first president of the Parliament of Paris. He was guillotined in 1794.

See MONTJOYE, "Éloge historique de B. de Sarron," 1800.

Bochat, bo'shă', (CHARLES GUILLAUME LOYS,) a Swiss historian and miscellaneous writer, born at Lausanne in 1695; died in 1753.

· **Bocholt, von,** fon boK'olt, (FRANZ,) one of the earliest German engravers, lived about 1470. Among his principal works are "The Judgment of Solomon," and "Christ and the Twelve Apostles," (in thirteen plates.)

Bochsa, bok'să', written also **Bocska,** (ROBERT NICOLAS CHARLES,) a French musician and composer, born at Montmédy in 1789. He studied in Paris under Méhul, and attained great excellence as a performer on the harp. In 1822 he became professor of the harp at the Royal Academy of Music, London. His compositions are chiefly pieces for that instrument. Died in Australia in 1856.

Bock, bok, (FRIEDRICH SAMUEL,) a naturalist, born at Königsberg in 1716, was professor of Greek and theology in his native city. He wrote a "History of Socinianism in Prussia," (1753,) and several works on natural history. Died in 1786.

See ERSCH und GRUBER, "Allgemeine Encyklopaedie."

Bock, bok, [Fr. LE BOUCQ, leh book; Lat. TRA'GUS,] (HIERONYMUS,) a German botanist, born at Heidesbach in 1498, was one of the greatest promoters of botanical science in his time. The genus Tragia was named in his honour by Plumier. Died in 1554.

Bock, (KARL AUGUST,) a German anatomist and physician, born at Magdeburg in 1782, published, among other works, a "Manual of Practical Anatomy of the

Human Body," (1819.) He lived many years at Leipsic. Died in 1833.

Bock, (KARL ERNST,) an anatomist, a son of the preceding, born at Leipsic in 1809, published a "Manual of Pathological Anatomy and Diagnostic," (1848.)

Bock, de, deh bok, (JEAN NICOLAS ÉTIENNE,) BARON, a French *littérateur*, born at Thionville in 1747. He wrote an "Essay on the History of Sabeism," and translated from the German the "Life of Baron Trenck," and several works of Wieland and Kotzebue. Died in 1809.

See "Nouvelle Biographie Générale."

Bockelmann, bok'kel-mân', (JOHANN FRIEDRICH,) a German jurist, born at Steinfurt in 1633; died at Leyden in 1681.

Bockenberg, van, vån bok'ken-bĕRG', [Lat. COR-NELISSO'NIUS BUCKENBER'GIUS,] (PIETER,) a Dutch chronicler, born at Gouda in 1548, was historiographer of the States of Holland. Died in 1617.

Bocker, bok'ker, [Lat. BOCE'RUS,] sometimes written **Boedeker,** (JOHANN,) a German writer, Latin poet, and professor of law at Rostock, born near Minden in 1525; died in 1565.

See J. C. OPITZ, "De Vita, Fatis et Scriptis J. Boceri," 1750.

Böckh or **Boeckh,** bök, (AUGUST,) an eminent German philologist and antiquary, born at Carlsruhe on the 24th of November, 1785. He studied at Halle under F. A. Wolf, and became in 1811 professor of eloquence and the Greek language at Berlin. He published an edition of Pindar with a continuous commentary, a Latin translation, and a treatise on Greek versification, (1811,) and in 1817 brought out his "Political Economy of the Athenians," ("Die Staatshaushaltung der Athener,") a work displaying profound learning and research. He likewise published "Metrological Investigations concerning the Weights, Coins, and Measures of Antiquity," (1838,) a "Dissertation on the Silver Mines of Laurium in Attica, and other treatises. He began the "Corpus Inscriptionum Græcarum," continued by his pupil Franz, and still unfinished. (The third volume was published in 1850.) He was a member of the principal learned societies of Germany and other countries. Died in Berlin in August, 1867. The works of Böckh have marked an era in the history of archæology and philology. According to his ideal, the aim of those studies should be to reproduce the entire social and political life of a people during a determinate epoch.

See KLAUSEN, "Biographie von Böckh," forming part of HOFF-MANN's "Lebensbilder berühmter Humanisten," 1837.

Böckh or **Boeckh,** bök, (CHRISTIAN GOTTFRIED,) a German educational writer, born at Memmingen in 1732. He assisted in publishing the "Universal Library of Education," (1774.) Died in 1792.

Böckh or **Boeckh, von,** fon bök, (FRIEDRICH,) a German minister of state, brother of the preceding, born at Carlsruhe in 1777. He became a counsellor of finance in 1810, and was minister of finance (in Baden) from 1828 to 1844. He was president of the cabinet about two years, (1844-46.) Died in 1855.

Bockhorst, van, vån bok'hoRst, (JAN,) a Dutch painter, born at Dentekoom in 1661, studied under Kneller in London. Died in 1724.

See DESCAMPS, "Vies des Peintres Flamands, Hollandais," etc.

Bockhorst, von, fon bok'horst, (JOHANN,) a German painter, born at Münster about 1610, was surnamed LANGHEN JAN, from his tall stature. He was a pupil of Jordaens, in Holland, and ranked high among the artists of the time.

See DESCAMPS, "Vies des Peintres Flamands, Hollandais et Allemands."

Böcking or **Boecking,** bök'king, (EDUARD,) a German jurist and legal writer, born at Trarbach, Prussia, in 1802. He became professor of law at Bonn in 1835.

Böckler or **Boeckler,** bök'kler, (GEORG ANDREAS,) a German architect and mechanician, wrote a treatise "On Hydraulic Architecture," (1663.)

Böckmann or **Boeckmann,** bök'mân, (JONAS,) a Swedish physician, born at Windberg in 1716. He studied anatomy at Berlin under Budæus, and in 1753 was appointed physician to the King of Sweden. Died in 1760.

Böcler or **Boecler,** bök'ler, (JOHANN,) a German

physician, born at Ulm in 1651, settled at Strasburg, where he died in 1701. His son John, born at Strasburg in 1681, became professor of medicine in his native city. Died in 1733.

Böcler or **Boecler**, (JOHANN HEINRICH,) one of the most learned Germans of his time, born at Cronheim, in Franconia, in 1611. He was invited in 1648 to fill the chair of eloquence at Upsal by Christina of Sweden, who appointed him her historiographer. He wrote a number of historical and critical works in Latin, and edited several classic authors. Died in 1692.

See MORHOF, "Polyhistor."

Böcler or **Boecler**, (JOHANN PHILIPP,) son of Johann, (the second of the name,) born at Strasburg in 1710. In 1738 he succeeded Salzmann as professor of chemistry, botany, and materia medica at Strasburg. Died in 1759.

Böcler or **Boecler**, (PHILIPP HEINRICH,) born at Strasburg in 1718, was a brother of Johann Philipp. Died in 1759.

Bocquillot, bo'ke'yo', (LAZARE ANDRÉ,) a French ecclesiastic, born at Avallon in 1649, published a number of theological works, and a "History of the Chevalier Bayard," (1702.) Died in 1728.

See LETORS, "Vie de L. A. Bocquillot," 1745.

Bocska. See BOCHSA.

Bocskai, botch'kī, (STEPHAN,) a nobleman of Transylvania, who in 1604 joined the Hungarians in a revolt against Austria. Having defeated the Imperial troops, he was proclaimed hereditary King of Hungary by Sultan Ahmed I. In 1606 a peace was concluded with the emperor Rudolph, by which religious freedom was secured to the Protestants of Hungary, and Bocskai was acknowledged Prince of Transylvania. Died in 1606.

See BROCKHAUS, "Conversations-Lexicon."

Bocthor, bok'tor', (ELIE or ELLIOUS,) a distinguished Orientalist, born at Sioot, in Upper Egypt, in 1784. He settled in France, where he was appointed professor of Arabic in the Royal Library. He published a "French-Arabic Dictionary," and several translations from the Arabic into French. Died in 1821.

See QUÉRARD, "La France Littéraire," (Supplément.)

Bodæus a Stapel, bo-dā'ŭs â stä'pel, (JAN,) a Dutch botanist and physician of Amsterdam, died young in 1636.

Bodard, bo'dåR', (PIERRE HENRI HIPPOLYTE,) a French botanist and physician, lived about 1800.

Bodard de Tezay, bo'dåR' deh teh-zå', (NICOLAS MARIE FÉLIX,) a French littérateur and diplomatist, born at Bayeux in 1757; died in Paris in 1823.

Boddaert, bod'dåRt, (PIETER,) a Dutch poet, born at Middelburg in 1694, published several original works, and translated into Dutch verse the "Atreus" and "Thyestes" of Crébillon. Died in 1761.

See "Levensgeschiedenis van den vermaarden Dichter P. Boddaert," Amsterdam, 1836.

Boddaert, (PIETER,) a Dutch physician and naturalist, a relative of the preceding, born in Zealand about 1730. He translated into Dutch the "Elenchus Zoophytorum" of Pallas, and John Hunter's "Natural History of the Teeth" (1773) into Dutch and Latin. Died about 1790.

See BROCKHAUS, "Conversations-Lexikon."

Bode, bo'deh, (CHRISTOPH AUGUST,) a German philologist, born at Wernigerode in 1722, became professor of Oriental languages at Helmstedt in 1754. He published an Ethiopic version of the New Testament, and several commentaries on the Scriptures. Died in 1796.

See WIDEBURG, "Memoria C. A. Bodii," 1796: ERSCH und GRUBER, "Allgemeine Encyklopaedie."

Bode, (JOHANN ELERT,) an eminent German astronomer, born at Hamburg in January, 1747. He published in 1768 a popular work entitled "Introduction to the Knowledge of the Starry Heavens," ("Anleitung zur Kenntniss des gestirnten Himmels,") and discovered in the same year a comet, which was the first one having a very short period. He was invited to Berlin by Frederick the Great, and admitted into the Academy of Sciences. Bode has the credit of discovering a law of the planetary system respecting the distances of the planets from each other, called "Bode's Law." Among his chief works is "Uranographia," or "Great Celestial Atlas,"

(1801,) by which, it is said, twelve thousand stars are added to former catalogues. Died in Berlin in 1826.

See "Nouvelle Biographie Générale," and BROCKHAUS, "Conversations-Lexikon."

Bode, (JOHANN JOACHIM CHRISTOPH,) a German littérateur, born at Brunswick in 1730. He is chiefly noted for his excellent translations from the English of Goldsmith's "Vicar of Wakefield" and Sterne's "Sentimental Journey," and of Montaigne's "Essays" and Marmontel's "Incas" from the French. He was a zealous advocate of free-masonry, upon which he wrote several treatises. He was also distinguished as a musician and composer. Died in 1793.

See C. A. BOETTIGER, "J. J. C. Bodes literarisches Leben," 1796.

Bodega y Quadra, bo-dā'gä e kwä'DRä, (JUAN FRANCISCO,) a Spanish navigator, who explored the west coast of North America. Died in 1794.

Bodekker, bo-dek'ker, (JAN FRANCISCUS,) a Dutch portrait-painter, born in the duchy of Cleves in 1660; died in 1727.

Bodel, bo'děl', (JEHAN,) a French troubadour, lived about 1270.

Bodelschwingh-Velmede, von, fon bo'del-shwing' vĕl'meh-deh, (ERNST,) a Prussian, born at Velmede, near Hamm, in 1794, became minister of the interior in 1844.

Bodenschatz, bo'den-shâts', (JOHANN CHRISTOPH GEORG,) a German scholar and antiquary, born at Hof in 1717. He wrote an "Explanation of the New Testament from Jewish Antiquities." Died in 1797.

Bodenstedt, bo'den-stĕt', (FRIEDRICH MARTIN,) a German writer and journalist, born in the kingdom of Hanover in 1819. He resided as a tutor in the family of Prince Galitzin at Moscow, where he perfected himself in the Russian language and translated some of the works of Pushkin and other poets into German. He subsequently travelled in Turkey, Greece, and Asia Minor, and published in 1848 "The Nations of the Caucasus." In 1850 he became editor of the "Weser Zeitung." He has also made a successful German translation of the Persian poems of Meerzâ Shaffee, (Mirza Shaffy.)

See BROCKHAUS, "Conversations-Lexikon."

Bodenstein. See CARLSTADT.

Bodenstein, von, fon bo'den-stīn', (ADAM,) a German physician and alchemist, born in 1528, was a disciple of Paracelsus. Died in 1577.

See SCHMIEDER, "Geschichte der Alchemie," 1832.

Bodewyns, bo'deh-wīns', (NIKOLAAS,) a Flemish or Dutch landscape-painter, was associated with Francis Bout, who painted figures for the landscapes of Bodewyns. The latter died at Brussels in 1700. Pilkington states that Bout was born at Brussels in 1660.

Bödiker or **Boediker**, bö'de-ker, (JOHANN,) a German writer, born in 1641, published Latin and German poems. Died in 1695.

Bodin, bo'dåN', (JEAN,) a celebrated French political writer, born at Angers in 1530. He studied law, and became secretary to the Duc d'Alençon. His principal work is a treatise on government, published in French, "De la République," (1576,) and afterwards translated by him into Latin, "De Republica," (1586.) He maintains that a limited monarchy is the best form of government. This work is analyzed at length by Hallam, who says, "No former writer on political philosophy had been either so comprehensive in his scheme or so copious in his knowledge ; none, perhaps, more original, more independent and fearless in his inquiries. Two names alone, indeed, could be compared with his,—Aristotle and Machiavel." "Bodin and Montesquieu are, in this province of political theory, the most philosophical of those who have read so deeply, the most learned of those who have thought so much." (" Introduction to the Literature of Europe.") Died at Laon in 1596.

See LYSER, "Selecta de Vita et Scriptis J. Bodini," 1715; E. COLOMBEL, "Jean Bodin: Suite d'Études sur le seizième Siècle," 1845; BAUDRILLART, "J. Bodin et son Temps," 1853; BAYLE, "Historical and Critical Dictionary;" GUHRAUER, "Das Heptaplomeron des J. Bodin," 1841.

Bodin, (JEAN FRANÇOIS,) a French magistrate, born at Angers in 1776, wrote "Historical Researches concerning Angers and Lower Anjou." Died in 1829.

Bodin, (LAURENT,) a French physician and medical writer, born in the department of Indre-et-Loire in 1762.

---

e as *k*; **ç** as *s*; **g** *hard*; **g** as *j*; G, H, K, *guttural*; N, *nasal*; R, *trilled*; **s** as *z*; **th** as in *this*. (☞See Explanations, p. 23.)

Bodin, (PIERRE JOSEPH FRANÇOIS,) a deputy to the French National Convention in 1792, voted for the imprisonment of the king. He afterwards became a member of the Council of Five Hundred. Died in 1810.

Bo-dis´co, (ALEXANDER,) a Russian diplomatist, born about 1780. He was appointed Russian minister at Washington about 1837, and retained that position until his death in 1854.

Bod´ley, (JOHN,) an English physician, published a "Critical Essay on the Works of Physicians," (1741.)

Bodley, (Sir THOMAS,) founder of the library at Oxford called by his name, was born at Exeter in 1544. He studied theology and the ancient languages at Geneva, whither his father had repaired during the persecutions of Queen Mary's reign. Having returned to England on the accession of Elizabeth, he graduated at Oxford in 1566. He became gentleman-usher to the queen in 1583, and was afterwards employed by her on important embassies to Denmark, Germany, and France. He was sent in 1588 to the Hague, where he resided many years and was admitted to the Council of State. Soon after his return, in 1597, he founded the Bodleian Library, and, on the accession of James I., was made a knight. Died in 1612.

See THOMAS HEARNE, "Reliquiæ Bodleianæ."

Bodmer, bod´mer, (GEORG,) a Swiss mechanician, born at Zurich in 1786, invented numerous machines, and made an improvement in the method of spinning cotton.

Bodmer, (JOHANN JAKOB,) a Swiss critic and *littérateur*, born near Zurich in 1698. In 1721 he became associated with Breitinger as editor of a literary journal entitled "Discurse der Maler," having for its object the reformation of German poetry. They succeeded, notwithstanding the opposition of Gottsched and other partisans of French taste, in bringing to their views several of the principal writers of Germany, and laid the foundation of the German school soon after made illustrious by Klopstock, Goethe, and Schiller. Bodmer translated the "Paradise Lost" and Pope's "Dunciad" into German, and also published versions of the "Niebelungen" and other ancient poems. He died in 1783, having for fifty years filled the chair of Swiss history at Zurich.

See MEISTER, "Ueber Bodmer;" J. J. HOTTINGER, "Acroama de J. J. Bodmero," 1783; LONGFELLOW, "Poets and Poetry of Europe."

Bodoni, bo-do´nee, (GIAMBATTISTA,) an eminent Italian printer and scholar, born at Saluzzo in 1740. He studied the Oriental languages at Rome, and in 1768 became superintendent of the royal press in Parma. Among his works, which are esteemed models of typographic beauty, may be named editions of "Homer," "Virgil," "Horace," Tacitus's "Annals," and Tasso's "Gerusalemme Liberata." He also wrote a "Typographic Manual," (1818.) Died in 1813.

See GREGORI, "Biographie de Lagrange, Denina et Bodoni," 1814; LAMA, "Vita del Cavaliere G. B. Bodoni," 1816.

Bodwell. See BOTHWELL.

Boece or **Boyce,** boiss, [Lat. BOE´TIUS or BOE´THIUS,] (HECTOR,) one of the early Scottish historians, born at Dundee about 1465. He finished his studies and graduated at the University of Paris, where he subsequently became professor of philosophy. While there, he acquired the friendship of Erasmus, by whom he was highly esteemed. His "History of Scotland" (in Latin, 1526) ranks among the best historical works of that period. It was subsequently translated into the Scottish dialect by Bellenden, at the command of James V. Died about 1536.

See CHAMBERS, "Biographical Dictionary of Eminent Scotsmen."

Boëce, the French of BOETHIUS, which see.

Boecio, the Italian of BOETHIUS, which see.

Boeckel. See BÖCKEL.

Boeckel, book´kel, [Lat. BOCKE´LIUS,] (JAN,) a Flemish physician and medical writer, born at Antwerp in 1535, became professor of medicine at Helmstedt in 1575. Died in 1605.

Boeckh. See BÖCKH.

Boeckhout, van, vän book´hŏwt, (JAN JOSEPH,) a Belgian publicist and political writer, born at Brussels; died in 1827.

Boecking. See BÖCKING.

Boeckler. See BÖCKLER.

Boeckmann. See BÖCKMANN.

Boediker. See BÖDIKER.

Boehm, or **Boehme.** See BÖHME and BÖHM.

Boehmer. See BÖHMER.

Boehmius. See BÖHME.

Boel, bool, (KORNELIS,) a Flemish engraver, born at Antwerp about 1580, worked in England.

Boel, (PIETER,) a skilful Flemish painter of animals, fruits, and flowers, born at Antwerp in 1625. One of his master-pieces is called "The Four Elements." Died 1680.

Boemondo, the Italian of BOHEMOND, which see.

Boerhaave, (ABRAHAM KAAU.) See KAAU.

Boerhaave, bŏr´hav, [Dutch pron. book´hä-vĕh; Lat. BOERHA´VIUS,] (HERMAN,) a Dutch physician and philosopher, whose celebrity has scarcely been equalled by that of any physician in modern times, was born at Voorhout, near Leyden, on the 31st of December, 1668. He was educated for the ministry at Leyden, where he took the degree of doctor of philosophy in 1689, and wrote an inaugural thesis "On the Distinction between the Soul and the Body." At the age of twenty-two he began the study of medicine. He read Hippocrates diligently, and took his degree as doctor of physic at Harderwick in 1693, after which he practised in Leyden, and in 1701 was chosen the successor or substitute of Drelincourt, who lectured on the theory of medicine in the university of that city. His precise definitions, brilliant eloquence, and immense erudition rendered him a very popular lecturer. He obtained in 1709 the chair of medicine and botany vacated by Hotton at Leyden, on which occasion he pronounced a discourse in favour of simplicity in the practice of medicine.

Before this period he had deviated from the Hippocratic method, and adopted mechanical and chemical hypotheses, which he advocated in his treatise "De Usu Ratiocinii Mechanici in Medicina," (1703.) His reputation was widely extended by an excellent systematic work entitled "Medical Institutes," etc., ("Institutiones Mediciæ in usus annuæ Exercitationis domesticos," 1708.) He gave a classification of diseases, and explained their causes, nature, and treatment, in his "Aphorisms on the Diagnosis and Cure of Diseases," ("Aphorismi de cognoscendis et curandis Morbis," 1709,) which is considered a master-piece of learning and of style. His medical system was generally adopted by his contemporaries. Boerhaave was also distinguished as a botanist and a chemist. He published in 1710 a "Description of Plants growing in the Botanic Garden of Leyden." In 1718 he became professor of chemistry, without ceasing to fill the chairs of medicine and botany. He was the first, according to the "Biographie Universelle," who rendered chemistry popular by treating it in a clear and beautiful style. His "Elements of Chemistry" ("Elementa Chemiæ," 1724) is called his chef-d'œuvre by the work just referred to. In consequence of severe attacks of gout, he resigned his chairs of botany and chemistry in 1727 and 1729. He was elected rector of the University of Leyden for the second time in 1730. About this date he was chosen a Fellow of the Royal Society of London. He died on the 23d of September, 1738, leaving one child, a daughter. He was a man of sincere and earnest piety. Among his admired works are two orations, viz., "De Comparando certo in Physicis," (1715,) and "De honore Medici Servitute," (1731.)

The reputation of Boerhaave as a physician and a man of learning is perhaps without a parallel in history. His fame extended not only to every part of Christendom, but to the farthest bounds of Asia. A Chinese mandarin addressed a letter to him with this superscription, "To Boerhaave, Physician in Europe," and the missive was duly received. Although he spent his money freely in the interests of science, yet so extensive and lucrative was his practice that at his death he left, it is said, more than two million florins. His intense application to study, and the exposure incident to his professional duties, had brought upon him in 1732 a severe illness, which confined him to his bed for several months. When he recovered, the inhabitants of Leyden celebrated the joyful event by a public illumination.

See MATY, "Éloge historique de H. Boerhaave," 1747; FONTENELLE, "Éloge de Boerhaave," 1763; DR. S. JOHNSON, "Life of H. Boerhaave;" BURTON, "Life and Writings of H. Boerhaave," 2 vols., 1743; CARL WILHELM EBERT, "Dissertatio historico-medica de H. Boerhavio," 1843; "Biographie Médicale."

Boerhavius. See BOERHAAVE.

Boerio, bo-ā′re-o, (GIUSEPPE,) an Italian jurist and legal writer, born at Lendinara in 1754; died in 1832.

Boerne. See BÖRNE.

Boerner. See BÖRNER.

Bo-e′thī-us, [It. BOECIO, bo-ā′cho, or BOEZIO, bo-àt′-se-o; in French, BOËCE, bo′ass′,] (ANICIUS MANLIUS SEVERINUS,) a celebrated Roman philosopher and statesman, born about 475 A.D. He was liberally educated, and well instructed in Greek philosophy. When about thirty-three, he was elected consul. His administration was beneficent and favourable to the oppressed. He translated the works of Plato and other Greek writers into Latin, wrote commentaries on Aristotle, and acquired a great reputation as an author. He held several high offices under Theodoric the Goth, but, having been accused by some envious courtiers of conspiring against the government, he was unjustly condemned by that king and executed about 525 A.D. His principal work is "On the Consolation of Philosophy," ("De Consolatione Philosophiæ,") which was written in prison, where he was confined just before his death. It is composed of alternate portions of verse and prose. "Few books," says Hallam, "are more striking from the circumstances of their production. Last of the classic writers, in style not impure, . . . in elevation of sentiment equal to any of the philosophers, and mingling a Christian sanctity with their lessons, he speaks from his prison in the swanlike tones of dying eloquence. Quenched in his blood, the lamp he had trimmed with a skilful hand, gave no more light; the language of Tully and Virgil soon ceased to be spoken." ("Introduction to the Literature of Europe.") His great work was very popular in the middle ages, and was translated into various languages. It was translated into Anglo-Saxon by Alfred the Great, and imitated by Chaucer. English versions of it have been produced by W. Causton, Rev. Philip Ridpath, R. Duncan, and others.

See PROCOPIUS, "History;" BARBERINI, "Exposizione della Vita de Boezio," 1783; DOM GERVAISE, "Histoire de Boëce," 1715; HEYNE, "Censura ingenii Boethii," 1806; "Life of Boethius," prefixed to RIDPATH's translation, 1785; GIBBON, "Decline and Fall of the Roman Empire," chap. xxxix.; ERSCH and GRUBER, "Allgemeine Encyklopaedie;" FABRICIUS, "Bibliotheca Latina;" SIRO COMI, "Memoria storico-critica sopra S. Boecio."

Boëthius, (HECTOR.) See BOECE.

Boëthius, bo-ā′te-ŭs, (JACOB,) professor of theology at Upsal, in Sweden, born in 1647. He was condemned to perpetual imprisonment for having opposed the absolute monarchy introduced by Charles XI., but he was released in 1710. Died in 1718.

See ERIK M. FANT, "Vita J. Boëthii," Upsal, 1812.

Boëtie, de la, dĕh lä bo′ā′te′, (ÉTIENNE,) a French *littérateur,* born at Sarlat, in Périgord, in 1530. He was an intimate friend of Montaigne, who refers to him in his chapter "On Friendship." He was the author of Latin and French poems, and a political treatise "On Voluntary Servitude," (written about 1546,) a work of much merit, sometimes called "Le Contr'un." Died in 1563. "La Boëtie, in fact," says Hallam, "is almost a single instance of a thoroughly republican character till near the period of the Revolution. Montaigne, the stanchest supporter of church and state, excuses his friend, *le plus grand homme, à mon avis, de notre siècle,* (the greatest man, in my opinion, of our age,) assuring us that he was always a loyal subject."

See LA FEUGÈRE, "Études sur la Vie de La Boëtie," 1845; J. F. PAYEN, "Notice bio-bibliographique sur É. de la Boëtie," 1853.

Boëtius, (HECTOR.) See BOECE.

Boëtius Epo, bo-ā′te-ŭs ā′po, a Dutch jurist and writer, born in Friesland in 1529; died in 1599.

Boettger or **Boettcher.** See BÖTTGER.

Boettiger. See BÖTTIGER.

Boetzlaer, boots′lär, BARON OF, a Dutch general, born about 1720, distinguished himself by his brave defence of Willemstadt against Dumouriez.

Boezio. See BOETHIUS.

Boffrand, bo′frôN′, (GERMAIN,) a French architect and engineer, born at Nantes in 1667. Among his works are the palace of Nancy, the castle of Lunéville, and the castle de la Favorite, near Mentz. Died in 1754.

Bogaert, bo′gärt, (ADAM,) a Flemish physician, born

at Dort in 1413, was professor of medicine at Louvain for more than thirty years. Died in 1483.

Bogaert, (JACOB,) son of the preceding, born at Louvain in 1440, succeeded his father as professor of medicine in that city. Died in 1520.

Bogaert, van den, (MARTIN.) See DESJARDINS.

Bogaerts, bo′gärts, (FÉLIX,) a Belgian poet and novelist, born at Brussels in 1805. Among his works are "Bibliothèque des Antiquités," (1834,) and "Lord Strafford," (1843.) Died in 1851.

See E. DE BUSSCHER, "F. Bogaerts, Notice biographique," 1851.

Bo′gan, (ZACHARIAH,) an English philologist, born in Devonshire in 1625, wrote a "View of Scriptural Threats and Punishments." Died in 1659.

Bo-gar′dus, (EVERARDUS,) the first minister of the Reformed Dutch Church in New York, came to this country about 1633. He was drowned on his passage to Holland in 1647.

Bo′gart, (ELIZABETH,) an American poetess, born in New York in the early part of this century, has contributed to the "New York Mirror," under the *nom de plume* of "Estelle." A number of her poems are published in Griswold's "Female Poets of America," which see.

Bogatzky, von, fon bo-gäts′kee, (KARL HEINRICH,) a German theological writer, author of "The Golden Treasury," was born in Silesia in 1690; died in 1774.

Bogdane, bog′dan, (JAMES,) a Hungarian painter of flowers, fruits, and birds, worked in England for Queen Anne. Died about 1720.

Bogdanovitch, bog-dä-no′vitch, (HIPPOLYTUS FEDOROVITCH,) an eminent Russian lyric poet, born in Little Russia in 1743. He was appointed in 1761 inspector at the University of Moscow. His principal work, entitled "Dushenka," ("Psyche,") came out in 1775. It ranks among the finest poems of its kind in the language, and was received with the greatest favour by all classes. He also translated from the French Vertot's "History of the Revolutions of the Roman Republic." He was appointed in 1788 president of the archives of the empire. Died in 1803.

See BOWRING, "Russian Anthology;" KARAMZIN, "Biographie de Bogdanovitch."

Bogdanus, bog-dä′nus, (MARTIN,) a Prussian physician, born at Driesen about 1640.

Bogerman, bo′ğer-män, [Lat. BOGERMA′NUS,] (JAN,) a Dutch theologian and controversialist, born in Friesland in 1576. He sided with Gomarus in his dispute with Arminius, and wrote a polemical treatise against Grotius. He was president of the Synod of Dort, and was one of the translators of the Bible into Dutch. Died in 1637.

Boggs, (CHARLES STEWART,) an American commodore, a nephew of Captain James Lawrence of the Chesapeake, was born at New Brunswick, New Jersey, in 1811. He entered the navy in 1826, and gained the rank of commander in 1855. He commanded the gunboat Varuna in the battle by which Farragut captured New Orleans, in April, 1862. In that action he sunk or burned six gunboats, partly iron-clad. The Varuna having fatally damaged by an iron-clad running against her, Captain Boggs ran her ashore, tied her to a tree, and continued to fight as long as his guns remained above the water, or "till the water was over the gun-truck."

Bogin, bo′zhäN′, [It. BOGINO, bo-jee′no,] (JEAN BAPTISTE,) born at Turin in 1701, became grand chancellor of Victor Amadeus, King of Sardinia, in 1730, and in 1750 minister of state under Charles Emmanuel. Died in 1784.

Bog′o-ris, Prince of Bulgaria, succeeded Baldimir, (or Valdimir.) He was converted to Christianity in 853 A.D., and induced or compelled his subjects to adopt the same religion. Died in 896.

Bogros, bo′gRo′, (ANNET JEAN,) a distinguished French anatomist, born in the department of Auvergne in 1786; died in 1823.

See VERNIÈRE, "Notice sur A. J. Bogros," 1824.

Bogsch, bogsh, (JOHANN,) an agricultural writer, born at Deutschendorf, in Hungary, in 1745; died in 1821.

Bogue, bōg, (DAVID,) a Scottish divine, born in Berwickshire in 1750, was one of the founders of the London Missionary Society in 1795. He was one of the first editors of the "Evangelical Magazine," and took an active part in promoting the principal religious associations of the day. Died in 1825.

See JAMES BENNETT, "Memoir of Dr. Bogue;" CHAMBERS, "Biographical Dictionary of Eminent Scotsmen."

Boguet, bo'gā', (HENRI,) a French magistrate and miscellaneous writer, born in Franche-Comté about 1550.

Boguphal, bo'goo-făl, Bishop of Posen, in Poland, wrote a Latin "Chronicle of Poland," (1729,) continued by Baczko. Died in 1253.

Boguslawski, bo-gus-lav'skee, (ADALBERT,) a Polish dramatist and actor, born in 1752, translated dramas from the French, Italian, and Spanish. Died in 1829.

Boguslawski, bo'goo-slăv'skee, (PALM HEINRICH LUDWIG,) a Prussian astronomer, of Polish extraction, born at Magdeburg in 1789. Appointed director of the observatory at Breslau in 1831, he discovered in 1834 the comet called by his name. In 1836 he became professor of astronomy at Breslau. Died in 1851.

See BROCKHAUS, "Conversations-Lexikon."

Bohadsch, bo'hădsh, (JOHANN BAPTIST,) a German physician and naturalist, was professor of natural history at Prague. Died in 1772.

Bohâ-ed-Deen or **Bohâ-eddîn,** bo'hâ-ed-deen', (Ibn-Shedâd, Ïb'n shĕ-dâd',) an Arab historian, born at Mosul in 1145, was distinguished by the favour of the Sultan Saladin, who appointed him cadi of Jerusalem. His principal work is a "Life of Saladin," which has been translated into Spanish by Borbon. Died in 1232.

Bohaire-Dutheil, bo'äR' dü'tĭl', a French dramatist and satirical writer, born about 1750; died in 1825.

Bohan, de, dĕh bo'ôN',(FRANÇOIS PHILIPPE LOURAT,) BARON, a French tactician and military writer, born at Bourg-en-Bresse in 1751; died in 1804.

Bohemond, bo'he-mŏnd,[Fr. BOHÉMOND, bo'â'mŏN'; It. BOEMONDO, bo-à-mon'do; Lat. BOHEMUN'DUS,] I., a famous chief of the crusaders, was the son of Robert Guiscard, Duke of Apulia and Calabria. Accompanied by his cousin Tancred and several Norman princes, he joined the first crusade, at the head of a large army, in 1096. Having assisted at the capture of Nicæa, he gained possession of Antioch by a strategem, and succeeded in obtaining the sovereignty of that city. He subsequently married the daughter of Philip I. of France. He died in 1111, and was succeeded by his son, Bohemond II.

See MICHAUD, "Histoire des Croisades."

Bohemond II. became Prince of Antioch in 1126. He assisted Baldwin, King of Jerusalem, in his wars against the Saracens. Died in 1130.

Bohemond III., grandson of Bohemond II., succeeded to the throne of Antioch in 1163. Died in 1201.

Bohemundus. See BOHEMOND.

Bohic, bo'ĕk', written also **Bouhic** or **Boich,** (HENRI or HERVÉ,) an eminent French jurist, born in Bretagne in 1310; died about 1390.

Bohier, de, bo'e-â', [Lat. BOE'RIUS,] (NICOLAS,) a French jurist, born at Montpellier in 1469; died in 1539.

Bohl, bōl, (JOHANN CHRISTIAN,) a German physician, and professor of medicine at Königsberg, where he was born in 1703; died in 1785.

Bohle, bo'lĕh, (SAMUEL,) a German theologian and Hebraist, born in Pomerania in 1611; died in 1689.

Bohlen, bo'lĕn, (HENRY,) born in Germany, emigrated to the United States in his youth, and became a rich merchant in Philadelphia. In April, 1862, he was appointed a brigadier-general. He served under Fremont and Sigel in Virginia, and was killed near the Rappahannock in August, 1862.

Bohlen, von, fon bo'lĕn, (PETER,) an eminent German Orientalist, born near Jever in 1796. Owing to the poverty of his family, he enjoyed few advantages of education, until enabled to enter the University of Halle through the kindness of several wealthy patrons. He became in 1830 professor of Oriental languages at Königsberg. Among his principal works are a dissertation on the Arabic poet Montenabbi, ("Commentatio de Montenabbio,") an excellent treatise on Indian antiquities, entitled "Das Alte Indien," (2 vols., 1830,) an edition of Bhartrihari's "Sententiæ," and "Genesis Historically and Critically explained," (in German.) He also wrote

a very interesting "Autobiography," published in 1841. Died in 1840.

Böhm or **Boehm,** böm, (ANDREAS,) a German mathematician and philosopher, born at Darmstadt in 1720. He published, among other works, a "Magazine for Engineers." Died in 1790.

Böhm, (JACOB.) See BÖHME.

Böhm or **Boehm,** böm, (JOHN DANIEL,) a Hungarian sculptor, born at Wallendorf in 1794.

Böhm or **Boehm,** (JOSEPH,) a German violinist, born at Pesth in 1798, became professor at Vienna.

Böhm or **Boehm,** (THEOBALD,) a German flutist, born in Bavaria about 1802, made improvements in the construction of the flute. He also composed music for that instrument.

Böhm or **Boehm,** (WENZEL AMADEUS,) a German engraver, born at Prague in 1771. His best works are a Saint Paul, after Sereta, and a portrait of the King of Denmark. Died in 1823.

Böhme, bö'mĕh, **Böhm,** or **Boehm,** böm, written also **Behmen,** [Fr. BŒHM or BŒHME, bặm; Lat. BOEH'MIUS,] (JACOB,) a celebrated German mystic, was born near Görlitz, in Upper Lusatia, in 1575. He served an apprenticeship to a shoemaker, and followed that trade at Görlitz. He was a devout reader of the Scriptures from his youth, and was a member of the Lutheran Church, which he probably never forsook. According to his own statement, he was divinely illuminated, and thus enabled to perceive the mysteries of nature and grace. He wrote, about 1610, a religious book called "Aurora, or the Morning Redness," which Hallam says was not published until 1641. He was generally accounted a visionary by the clergy, but his opinions were adopted by many in Germany, Holland, and England. Among his admirers or disciples were many men of high rank and high cultivation. He wrote numerous works, which were published, in 10 vols., 1682. They were translated into English (1764) by the eminent divine William Law, who was an admirer of Böhme. He died at Görlitz in 1624. "His supernatural illumination," says Hallam, "came without the gift of transferring the light to others, for scarce any have been able to pierce the clouds in which his meaning has been charitably supposed to lie hid."

See LA MOTTE-FOUQUÉ, "Notice sur J. Boehm," 1831; WULLEN, "Jacob Böhms Leben," 1836; JOHANN ADAM CALOV, "Dissertatio de Vita J. Boehmii," 1707; G. L. GMELIN, "Disputatio de J. Boehmio," 1708; J. F. SILLIG, "J. Boehme: biographischer Versuch," 1801.

Böhme or **Boehme,** (JOHANN EUSEBIUS,) a German writer, and professor of history at Leipsic, born at Wurzen in 1717; died in 1780.

Böhmer or **Boehmer,** böh'mẹr, (GEORG LUDWIG,) a younger son of Justus Henning, noticed below, was born at Halle in 1715. He became professor and dean of the faculty of law at Göttingen. Died in 1797.

Böhmer or **Boehmer,** (GEORG RUDOLF,) a German physician and botanist, born at Liegnitz in 1723. He became professor of therapeutics at Kemberg in 1783, and afterwards dean of the university in that city. The genus Boehmeria was named in his honour. Died in 1803.

See CALLISEN, "Medicinisches Schriftsteller-Lexikon."

Böhmer or **Boehmer,** (GEORG WILHELM RUDOLF,) a Protestant theologian and writer, born near Magdeburg in 1800, became professor of divinity at Greifswalde in 1830.

Böhmer or **Boehmer,** (JOHANN BENJAMIN,) a German physician, born at Liegnitz in 1719; died in 1753.

Böhmer or **Boehmer,** (JOHANN FRIEDRICH,) a German historian and compiler, born at Frankfort-on-the-Main in 1795, published "The Archives of the Roman Kings and Emperors from Conrad I. to Henry VII.," (1831,) and "Fontes Rerum Germanicarum," (1843-53.) Died in 1863.

Böhmer or **Boehmer,** (JOHANN SAMUEL FRIEDRICH,) son of the following, became counsellor to the King of Prussia and director of the University of Frankfort-on-the-Oder. Died in 1772.

Böhmer or **Boehmer,** (JUSTUS HENNING,) a German jurist, born at Hanover in 1674. He became chancellor of the University of Halle, and was created by Frederick the Great a member of his state council. His principal work is an "Introduction to Public Universal Law," in Latin, (1709.) Died at Halle in 1749.

See ERSCH und GRUBER, "Allgemeine Encyklopaedie;" A. STRUENSEE, "Das grünende und fruchtbare Alter: Gedächtniss-Predigt zum Andenken des J. H. Boehmer," 1749.

Böhmer or **Boehmer**, (PHILIPP ADOLF,) brother of Georg Ludwig, born at Halle in 1717, was first physician to the Duke of Saxe-Weimar. He became professor of anatomy at Berlin in 1741, and in 1787 royal counsellor and dean of the university. Died in 1789.

Bohn, bōn, (HENRY G.,) a distinguished London publisher, of German extraction, born in London about 1800. Among his numerous and valuable publications may be named his "Standard Library," (130 vols.,) "Library of French Memoirs," "Library of British Classics," and "Guinea Catalogue," which describes three hundred thousand volumes. He has made several translations from the German, and edited the "Bibliotheca Parriana."

Bohn, bōn, [Lat. BOH'NIUS,] (JOHANN,) an eminent German medical writer, born at Leipsic in 1640. He became professor of anatomy at Leipsic in 1668, and was the first who attacked successfully the chemical system of physiology maintained by F. de la Boë. He was distinguished in medical jurisprudence. Among his chief works are "Circulus anatomicus physiologicus," (1680,) and "Medicinæ forensis Specimina Tria," (1690.) Died in 1718.

See "Biographie Médicale."

Bohomolec, bo-ho-mo'lĕts, (FRANCIS,) a Polish writer of dramas, biography, etc. Died in 1790.

Bohren or **Bohra.** See BORA.

Bohse, bo'zĕh, (AUGUST,) also called **Talander,** tä'län-der, a German writer of little merit, born at Halle in 1661. He wrote novels, operettas, etc. Died about 1735.

Böhtlingk, böt'link, (OTTO,) a distinguished Orientalist, of German extraction, born at Saint Petersburg in 1815. He has published, among other works, "Kâlidâsa's Sakuntalâ," (text with a translation, 1842;) a "Sanscrit Chrestomathia," (1845,) and (in conjunction with Roth) a "Sanscrit-German Lexicon," (not yet finished,) a work of unrivalled merit in this department of literature.

See BROCKHAUS, "Conversations-Lexikon."

Bohtori, boh'to-ree, (Al-Waleed or Al-Walîd, âl-wâ-leed',) an Arabian poet, born about 821. His verses were styled, by his countrymen, chains of gold.

Bohtz, bōts, (AUGUST WILHELM,) born at Stettin in 1799, became professor of philosophy at Göttingen in 1842.

Bo'hun, (EDMUND,) an English writer, was the author of a "Historical, Geographical, and Poetical Dictionary," (1694,) and several political works.

See MACAULAY, "History of England," vol. iv.; WOOD, "Athenæ Oxonienses."

Bohusz, bo'hōōsh, (XAVIER,) a Polish historian, born in 1746, published "Researches on the Historical Antiquities and Language of Lithuania." Died in 1825.

Boianus. See BOJANUS.

Boiardo or **Bojardo,** bo-yaR'do, (MATTEO MARIA,) Count of Scandiano, a celebrated Italian poet, born at Scandiano about 1430. His principal work, the "Orlando Innamorato," (left unfinished,) was published about 1495, and was afterwards continued by Ariosto under the title of "Orlando Furioso." It was also written over and so greatly improved by Berni that the original is nearly forgotten. The "Orlando Innamorato of Boiardo," says Hallam, "has hitherto not received that share of renown which seems to be its due. In point of novel invention and just keeping of character, especially the latter, he has not been surpassed by his illustrious follower Ariosto; and whatever of this we find in the Orlando Innamorato is due to Boiardo alone." ("Introduction to the Literature of Europe.") Died in 1494.

See LONGFELLOW, "Poets and Poetry of Europe;" GINGUENÉ, "Histoire Littéraire d'Italie;" W. H. PRESCOTT, critique on Boiardo in the "North American Review" for October, 1824, vol. xix.; G. F. CREMONA, "Elogio del Conte M. M. Bojardo," 1827; "Lives of the Italian Poets," by the Rev. HENRY STEBBING, London, 1831; "Quarterly Review" for April, 1819, article "Narrative and Romantic Poetry of the Italians."

Boiceau, bwä'sō', (JEAN,) a French jurist, born at Poitiers about 1520; died in 1589.

Boichot, bwä'shō', (GUILLAUME,) a French sculptor, born at Châlons-sur-Saône in 1738; died in 1814.

See LE BAS DE GOURMONT, "Vie de Guillaume Boichot," 1823.

Boie or **Boje,** bo'yĕh, (HEINRICH CHRISTIAN,) a German littérateur, born at Meldorp, in Holstein, in 1745. In 1770 he published, conjointly with Gotter, the first "Musenalmanach," and in 1776 became associate editor of the "Deutschen Museum." Died in 1806.

Boieldieu, bwâl'dṛ-uh', (FRANÇOIS ADRIEN,) an eminent French composer, born at Rouen in 1775. Among his best operas are "The Caliph of Bagdad," "The White Lady," ("La Dame blanche,") and "My Aunt Aurora," ("Ma Tante Aurore.") In 1803 he was appointed by the emperor Alexander of Russia his chapel-master. Died in 1835.

See FÉTIS, "Biographie Universelle des Musiciens;" RÉFUVEILLE, (alias ANDRÉ RELOI,) "Boieldieu, sa Vie, ses Œuvres," Rouen, 1751.

Boigne, bwäñ, (BENOÎT le Borgne—lĕh boRñ,) COUNT, a French general, born at Chambéry in 1741, entered the service of the Rajah of the Mahrattas about 1783. He made an immense fortune, a great part of which he bequeathed to charitable purposes in his native city. Died in 1830.

See TURINA, "Éloge historique du Comte de Boigne."

Boileau, bwâ'lō', (CHARLES,) a French ecclesiastic, and member of the French Academy, was a native of Beauvais. Died in 1704.

See D'ALEMBERT, "Éloge de Charles Boileau."

Boileau, (GILLES,) a French magistrate, born in 1584, father of the celebrated Nicolas Boileau. Died in 1657.

Boileau, (GILLES,) a French littérateur, a brother of the celebrated poet of that name, born in Paris in 1631. He wrote a "Life of Epictetus," and a number of poems and satires. He also translated the "Enchiridion" of Epictetus. He was a member of the French Academy. Died in 1669.

Boileau, (GILLES de Buillon—dĕh bü-e'yòN',) a Flemish littérateur of the sixteenth century, translated, from the Latin into French, Albert Dürer's treatise on Fortifications, and made translations from the Spanish.

Boileau, (JACQUES,) brother of Nicolas Boileau, born in Paris in 1635, was a doctor of the Sorbonne. He wrote several ecclesiastical works. Died in 1716.

Boileau, (JEAN JACQUES,) a French biographer and writer on morals, born near Agen in 1649; died in Paris in 1735.

Boileau, boi'lō or bwâ'lō', or, more fully, **Boileau-Despréaux,** bwâ'lō' dä'pRâ'ō', (NICOLAS,) an eminent French poet and satirist, born in Paris (or at Crosne, near Paris) on the 1st of November, 1636, was a son of Gilles Boileau, registrar of the great chamber of the Parliament. He was educated for the law or the church; but his tastes did not incline to either, and he followed no profession but that of author. He was a friend of Racine and La Fontaine. His first production was a satire called "Adieu of a Poet to the City of Paris," (1660,) remarkable for purity of style and elegance of versification. In 1666 he published seven satires, which had great success. He afterwards wrote five other satires, at various dates. In the maturity of his poetical power he composed twelve Epistles, which are even more admired than his satires.

Among his best works are "The Reading-Desk," ("Le Lutrin," 1674,) and "The Art of Poetry," ("L'Art poétique," 1674,) which, in the opinion of Michaud, excels the poem of Horace in the felicity of the transitions and in the sustained elegance of the style. "Boileau is the analogue of Pope," says Hallam, "in French literature. 'The Art of Poetry' has been the model of the 'Essay on Criticism;' few poems more resemble each other. Both are uncommon efforts of critical good sense, and both are distinguished by their short and pointed language, which remains in the memory. The 'Lutrin' is the most popular of the poems of Boileau. Its subject is ill chosen. . . . But the poignant wit and satire, the elegance and correctness of numberless couplets, as well as the ingenious adaptations of classical passages, redeem this poem, and confirm its high place in the mock-heroic line." ("Introduction to the Literature of Europe.")

Boileau was appointed historiographer jointly with Racine, by Louis XIV., and was elected a member of the French Academy in 1684. He has the honour of having effected a revolution in the poetical taste of the French, which was greatly vitiated when he began to write.

He was visited in 1700 by Addison, whose Latin poems Boileau had read and greatly admired. "He certainly opened himself to Addison with a freedom which was a sure indication of esteem. The old man talked on his favourite theme, literature, long and well; indeed, as his young hearer thought, incomparably well. Boileau had undoubtedly some of the qualities of a great critic. He wanted imagination, but he had strong sense. In mere style, abstracted from the ideas of which style is the garb, his taste was excellent. . . . It is easy, we think, to discover in the 'Spectator' and the 'Guardian' traces of the influence, in part salutary and in part pernicious, which the mind of Boileau had on the mind of Addison." (Macaulay, "Review of the Life of Addison.")

He was an intimate friend of Racine, and co-operated with Madame Dacier in the vindication of the merits of the ancient classical authors. His poems, it is said, contain no line that would offend the strictest moralist. Probity and benevolence were prominent traits of his character. "He had the spirit," says Macaulay, "to tell Louis XIV., firmly and even rudely, that his majesty knew nothing about poetry." Died in Paris in March, 1711.

See D'ALEMBERT, "Éloge de Boileau;" DESMAIZEAUX, "Vie de Boileau," 1712; DAUNOU, "Éloge de Boileau," 1787; MICHAUD, article on Boileau in the "Biographie Universelle;" LOUIS SIMON AUGER, "Éloge de Boileau-Despréaux," 1805; LONGFELLOW, "Poets and Poetry of Europe;" "Lives of the Most Eminent French Writers," by MRS. SHELLEY, vol. i.

Boileau, de, dẹh bwả'lō', (MARIE LOUIS JOSEPH,) a French jurist and *littérateur*, born at Dunkirk in 1741; died in 1817.

Boileau de Maulaville, bwả'lō' dẹh mō'lả'vèl', (EDME FRANÇOIS MARIE,) a French archæologist, born at Auxerre in 1759, published several antiquarian treatises, and was a contributor to the "Biographie Universelle." Died in 1826.

Boileux, bwả'luh', (JACQUES MARIE,) a French jurist, born at Caen in 1803. He published a "Commentary on the Civil Code," (3 vols., 1828–44.)

Boillot, bwả'yo', (HENRI,) a French Jesuit and *littérateur*, born in Franche-Comté in 1698; died in 1733.

Boillot, (JOSEPH,) a French architect and writer, born at Langres in 1560.

Boilly, bwả'ye', (LOUIS LÉOPOLD,) a French painter of portraits and genre, born in 1761; died in 1830.

Boindin, bwằN'dăN', (NICOLAS,) a French *littérateur*, born in Paris in 1676; died in 1751.

Boinvilliers-Desjardins, bwằN've'yả' dả'zhăr'dăN', (JEAN ÉTIENNE JUDITH **Forestier**—fo'rả'te-å',) a French *littérateur*, born at Versailles in 1764; died in 1830.

Boirel, bwả'rèl', (ANTOINE,) a French surgeon, born in 1625; died about 1700.

Boiron. See BORRON.

Bois, (JOHN.) See BOYSE.

Boisard, bwả'zăr', (J. J. F. M.,) a French fabulist, born at Caen in 1743; died in 1831.

Bois de la Pierre, bwả dẹh lả pe-aiR', (LOUISE MARIE de Lanfernat—dẹh lŏN'fèR'nả',) a French poetess, born at Verneuil, in Normandy, in 1663; died in 1730.

Bois, du. See DUBOIS.

Bois-Duval, bwả'dü'vål', (JEAN ALPHONSE,) a French naturalist, born at Ticheville (Orne) in 1801, wrote several works on insects, and a "French Flora," (3 vols., 1828.)

Boisgelin, de, dẹh bwảzh'lăN', (JEAN DE **Dieu Raymond de Cucé**—de-uh' rả'mŏN' dẹh kü'sả',) a French theologian, born at Rennes in 1732, became successively Archbishop of Aix and of Tours, and a cardinal about 1803. He was elected to the French Academy in 1776. He was the author of several theological and miscellaneous works. Died in 1804.

See DE BAUSSET, "Notice historique sur M. de Boisgelin," 1804.

Boisgelin, de, (LOUIS BRUNO,) COMTE, a French diplomatist, brother of the preceding, born at Rennes in 1773. He was executed in 1794 by order of the Revolutionary tribunal.

Boisgelin de Kerdu, de, dẹh bwảzh'lăN' dẹh kèR'dü', (PIERRE MARIE LOUIS,) brother of the preceding, born in the diocese of Saint-Brieuc in 1758. He wrote a continuation of Vertot's "History of the Revolutions of Portugal," (1809,) and a work entitled "Ancient and Modern Malta," in English. Died in 1816.

See QUÉRARD, "La France Littéraire," (Supplément.)

Boisgérard, bwả'zhả'răR', (MARIE ANNE FRANÇOIS BARBUAT,) born at Tonnerre in 1767, served in the army of the republic, and was mortally wounded in 1799 at the battle of Capua.

Bois-Guilbert or **Bois-Guillebert,** bwả'gèl'baiR', (PIERRE **le Pesant**—lẹh pẹh-zŏN',) a French *littérateur*, translated the "History" of Herodian, and published several original works. Died in 1714.

Boisjolin, bwả'zho'lăN', (JACQUES FRANÇOIS MARIE **Vieilh**—ve'ål',) a French poet, born at Alençon in 1761. He was a member of the Tribunat in 1800–1801. Died in 1841.

Boisjolin, de, dẹh bwả'zho'lăN', (CLAUDE AUGUSTIN VIEILH,) a French *littérateur*, born in Paris in 1788, succeeded Rabbe as editor of the "Biographie portative des Contemporains." Died in 1832.

Boislandry, de, dẹh bwả'lŏN'dRe', (LOUIS,) a member of the French Constituent Assembly, born at Versailles in 1749; died in 1834.

Boislève, bwả'lȧv', (PIERRE,) a French ecclesiastic, born at Saumur in 1745, became honorary canon of Nôtre-Dame. In 1810, as official of the diocese of Paris, he pronounced the sentence of divorce between the emperor Napoleon and Josephine. Died in 1830.

Boismont. See BRIÈRE DE BOISMONT.

Boismont, de, dẹh bwả'mŏN', (NICOLAS **Thyrel**—te'rèl',) a distinguished French preacher, born in Normandy about 1715. He was a member of the French Academy, and was appointed preacher-in-ordinary to the king. Died in 1786.

See RULHIÈRE, "Éloge de Boismont," prefixed to his "Oraisons funèbres, etc."

Boismorand, bwả'mo'rŏN', (CLAUDE JOSEPH,) a French writer and priest, born at Quimper in 1680. He published "Anecdotes of the Court of Philip Augustus," and other works, and translated "Paradise Lost" into French. Died in 1740.

Boismortier, de, dẹh bwả'moR'te-å', (N. **Bodin**—bo'dăN',) a French composer, born at Perpignan in 1691; died in 1768.

Boisot, bwả'zo', (JEAN BAPTISTE,) a learned French ecclesiastic, born at Besançon in 1638. He was a contributor to the "Journal des Savants." Having obtained the library of Cardinal Granvelle, he arranged and preserved the important documents, treaties, etc. which it contained, and thus rendered a great service to history. Died in 1694.

Boisrobert, de, dẹh bwả'ro'baiR', (FRANÇOIS LE METEL,) a French ecclesiastic and *littérateur*, born at Caen in 1592. His wit and gayety procured for him the favour of Cardinal Richelieu, who made him his companion and gave him many preferments. He wrote a number of dramas, poems, and tales. He was one of the first members of the French Academy, which Richelieu established at his suggestion. Once, when Richelieu was indisposed, his physician advised him that the company of Boisrobert would be more efficacious than any drugs, and wrote this prescription:—*Recipe Boisrobert.* He was sometimes called ABBÉ MONDORI. Died in 1662.

See HIPPEAU, "Notice sur Boisrobert," 1852; OTPEAU, "Notice sur Boisrobert," 1852.

Boissard, bwả'săR', (GEORGE DAVID FRÉDÉRIC,) a French Protestant minister, born at Montbelliard in 1783. He preached for many years in Paris, and wrote numerous religious works. Died in 1836.

See RODOLPHE CUVIER, "Éloge de Boissard," 1837.

Boissard, (JEAN JACQUES,) a French Protestant antiquary and Latin poet, born at Besançon in 1528. He went to Rome, where he formed a collection of antiquities. He published numerous works, among which are "Emblemata Latina et Gallica," (1584,) "Portraits and Lives of Illustrious Men," ("Icones et Vitæ Virorum illustrium," 1592,) and "Romanæ Urbis Topographia et Antiquitates," (1597.) Died at Metz in 1602.

See BAYLE, "Historical and Critical Dictionary;" MORHOF, "Polyhistor."

Boissat, bwả'să', (PIERRE,) a French jurist and Hellenist, born at Vienne about 1550.

Boissat, de, (PIERRE,) son of the preceding, born at Vienne, was the author of a "History of the Knights of Saint John of Jerusalem," (1612.) Died in 1613.

ā, ē, ī, ō, ū, ȳ, *long;* ȧ, ė, ȯ, same, less prolonged; ă, ĕ, ĭ, ŏ, ŭ, y̆, *short;* ạ, ẹ, ị, ọ, *obscure;* fär, fȧll, fȧt; mēt; nŏt; gōōd; mōōn;

Boissat, de, (PIERRE,) poet and soldier, son of the preceding, born at Vienne in 1603. He composed Latin poems, and several prose works. He was admitted into the French Academy. Died in 1662.

See CHORIER, "De P. Boessatii Vita, Amicisque literatis," 1680.

Boisseau, bwä′sō′, (FRANÇOIS GABRIEL,) a French medical writer, born at Brest in 1791 ; died at Metz in 1836. He left many valuable works, among which is "Nosographie organique," (4 vols., 1828-30.)

Boissel de Monville, bwä′sĕl′ dẹh mŏn′vĕl′, (THOMAS CHARLES GASTON,) BARON, councillor to the Parliament of Paris, born in that city in 1763. He was the author of fables and dramatic works. Died in 1832.

Boisserée, bwäss′rä′, (MELCHIOR,) brother of Sulpice, noticed below, born in 1786, was distinguished for his skill in painting on glass, (see next article.) Died in 1851.

Boisserée, (SULPICE,) an eminent Prussian architect and antiquary, of French extraction, born at Cologne in 1783. In conjunction with his brother Melchior and his friend J. B. Bertram, he formed the celebrated collection of paintings called by his name and now in the possession of the King of Bavaria at Munich. In 1824 he began the restoration of the cathedral of Cologne. He published "The Monuments of Architecture on the Lower Rhine, from the Seventh to the Thirteenth Centuries," (1830,) and "Views, Plans, and Details of the Cathedral of Cologne," etc., (in folio, 1823.) Died in 1854.

See BROCKHAUS, "Conversations-Lexikon."

Boisset, bwä′sä′,(JOSEPH ANTOINE,) a French Jacobin, born at Montélimart in 1748, became a member of the National Convention, and subsequently of the Council of Ancients. Died in 1813.

Boissier, bwä′se-ä′, (ÉDOUARD PIERRE,) a Swiss botanist, born at Geneva in 1810, published "Diagnoses Plantarum Orientalium," (3 vols., 1849-59.)

Boissière, de, dẹh bwä′se-air′, (CLAUDE,) a French mathematician, who was born near Grenoble, lived in the latter half of the sixteenth century.

Boissieu, de, dẹh bwä′se-uh′, (BARTHÉLEMY CAMILLE,) a French physician, born at Lyons in 1734 ; died in 1770.

Boissieu, de, (DENYS Salvaing—säl′vän′,) a French jurist and diplomatist, born at Vienne, in Dauphiny, in 1600 ; died in 1683.

See A. DE TERREBASSE, "Vie de Salvaing de Boissieu," 1850.

Boissieu, de, (JEAN JACQUES,) a French engraver and painter, born at Lyons in 1736. His prints are highly esteemed, particularly those after Ruysdael. Died in 1810.

See DUGAS-MONTBEL, "Éloge de J. J. de Boissieu," 1810.

Boissonade, bwä′so′nåd′, (JEAN FRANÇOIS,) an eminent French philologist, born in Paris on the 12th of August, 1774. In 1812 he succeeded Larcher as professor of Greek literature in the Academy of Paris, and also took his place in the Academy of Inscriptions. He became professor of Greek in the College of France in 1828. Among his works, which relate principally to Greek literature, are editions of Philostratus, Holstentius, Nicetas Eugenianus, and other classics. He also published a "Sylloge Poetarum Græcorum," (24 vols., 1825,) and a collection of one hundred and twenty-three fables of Babrius, with a commentary and Latin version. He also edited several French classics, and contributed numerous articles to the "Biographie Universelle," and other works of high reputation. "His lectures," says a French biographer, "have been the honour and pride of the university which could match him against the most renowned Hellenists of foreign universities." Died in September, 1857.

See QUÉRARD, "La France Littéraire ;" "Nouvelle Biographie Générale ;" "Classical Journal," March, 1825.

Boissy, bwä′se′, (JEAN BAPTISTE Thiaudière—te′ō′de-air′,) a French antiquary, and member of the Academy of Inscriptions, born in Paris in 1666 ; died in 1729.

Boissy, (LOUIS MICHEL,) a French historical writer, son of Louis de Boissy, noticed below. Died in 1793.

Boissy-d'Anglas, de, dẹh bwä′se′ dŏn′glä′, (FRANÇOIS ANTOINE,) a French statesman and revolutionist, born at Saint-Jean-Chambre, in Ardèche, in 1756. As a member of the National Convention, he voted for the detention of the king and the appeal to the people. He became successively secretary of the Council of Five Hundred, president of the tribunat, (1802,) commander of the legion of honour, and senator, (1805.) In 1816 he was elected to the Academy of Inscriptions. He published a number of political essays. Died in 1826.

See QUÉRARD, "La France Littéraire."

Boissy, de, dẹh bwä′se′, (CHARLES Desprez—dä′-prä′,) a French jurist and legal writer, born in Paris about 1730 ; died in 1787.

Boissy, de, (LOUIS,) a French littérateur, born at Vic in 1694, was the author of a successful comedy entitled "The Man of the Day," ("L'Homme du Jour.") In 1754 he succeeded Destouches as a member of the French Academy. Died in 1758.

Boiste, bwäst, (PIERRE CLAUDE VICTOIRE,) a celebrated French lexicographer, born in Paris in 1765. His "Universal Dictionary of the French Language" (2 vols. 8vo, 1800) is esteemed a standard work, holding the same rank in France that Johnson's does in England. He also published a "Dictionary of Universal Geography, Ancient and Modern." Died in 1824.

See QUÉRARD, "La France Littéraire."

Boistuau de Launai, bwäs′tü′ō′ dẹh lō′nä′, (PIERRE,) a French historian, lived in the first half of the sixteenth century. His "Théâtre du Monde" was printed twenty times or more. He wrote other works.

Boisville, de, dẹh bwä′vĕl′,(JEAN FRANÇOIS MARTIN,) a French theologian, born at Rouen in 1755, was canon of the cathedral of that city. Died in 1829.

Boisy, de, dẹh bwä′ze′, (ARTUS GOUFFIER, är′tüs′ goo′fe-ä′,) SEIGNEUR, a French statesman and soldier, born about 1475. He served in Italy under Charles VIII. and Louis XII., and was appointed by the latter tutor to the young prince, afterwards Francis I. On the accession of Francis, he became grand master of France and governor of Dauphiny. Died in 1519.

See ANSELME, "Histoire généalogique de la Maison de France."

Boitard, bwä′tăr′, (PIERRE,) a French naturalist and writer on agriculture, born at Mâcon in 1789. He edited several journals, and published numerous works, among which are "The Cabinet of Natural History," (1821,) "Gardener's Manual," "Natural History of European Birds of Prey," (1824,) and "Manual of Entomology," (1828.)

Boiteau, bwä′tō′, (DIEUDONNÉ ALEXANDRE PAUL,) a French littérateur, born in Paris in 1830. He wrote, besides other works, "The Philosophy and Politics of Béranger," (1858.)

Boitel, bwä′tĕl′, (PIERRE,) a French littérateur, lived about 1620.

Boitet de Frauville, bwä′tä′ dẹh frō′vĕl′, (CLAUDE,) born at Orléans in 1570, translated Homer's "Odyssey" into French. Died in 1625.

Boivin, bwä′vän′, (JACQUES DENIS,) a French general of brigade, born in Paris in 1756, served in the republican army from 1793 to 1805. Died in 1831.

Boivin, (LOUIS,) a French scholar and historical writer, born in the diocese of Lisieux in 1649, became a member of the Academy of Inscriptions in 1701. Died in 1724.

Boivin, (MARIE ANNE VICTOIRE Gillain—zhe′yän′,) born near Versailles in 1773, studied anatomy and obstetrics, and obtained the degree of M.D. from the University of Marburg. She was patronized by Madame Elizabeth, sister of the king, and was appointed in 1801 chief superintendent of the hospital de la Maternité, in Paris. She wrote several treatises relating to her profession. Died in 1841.

See QUÉRARD, "La France Littéraire."

Boivin, (RENÉ,) a French engraver, born at Angers in 1530. Among his master-pieces are "Portraits of Ancient Philosophers and Poets," and "Æneas saving his Father." Died in 1598.

Boivin, de, dẹh bwä′vän′, (FRANÇOIS,) a French historical writer, born about 1550 ; died in 1618.

Boivin de Villeneuve, bwä′vän′ dẹh vĕl′nuv′,(JEAN,) brother of Louis Boivin, noticed above, born in 1663. He became in 1705 professor of Greek in the Collége de France. He translated the "Œdipus" of Sophocles and "The Birds" of Aristophanes into French, and wrote in reply to Lamotte an "Apology for Homer, and the Shield of Achilles," (1715.) Died in 1726.

See QUÉRARD, "La France Littéraire."

Boizot, bwä'zo', (LOUIS SIMON,) a French sculptor, born in 1748. He executed statues of Joseph Vernet, Joubert, and Daubenton. Died in 1809.

Bojanus or **Boianus,** bo-yä'nŭs, (LUDWIG HEINRICH,) a German anatomist, born in Alsatia in 1776; died at Darmstadt in 1827.

Bojardo. See BOIARDO.

Bojer, bo'yer, (WENCESLAUS,) a German botanist, born at Prague about 1798. He visited Madagascar and other islands near Africa, and published "Hortus Mauritianus," (1837.) Died in 1856.

Bo-joc'a-lus, a German warrior and ally of Rome, lived in the first century of the Christian era. He is supposed to have been put to death under Nero, for having refused to take up arms against his people, the Ansibarians.

Bo'ker, (GEORGE H.,) an American poet, born in Philadelphia in 1824. After graduating at Princeton in 1842, he made a tour of Europe, and has since resided in Philadelphia. His first volume, "The Lesson of Life, and other Poems," appeared in 1847; followed in 1848 by "Calaynos," a tragedy, which has been played with success both in England and America. Among his other productions are "Anne Boleyn," a tragedy, "Leonore de Guzman," and his "War Lyrics," which have been much admired.

Bokhâree, Bokhâri, or **Bokhâry,** bo-kä'ree, (Aboo Abdallah Mohammed—ä'boo äb-däl'läh mohäm'mĕd,) a celebrated Mussulman theologian, born in 810 A.D., compiled a collection of traditions or sentences borrowed from Mohammed. Died in 870.

Bol, bol, (FERDINAND,) a Dutch painter and engraver, born at Dort about 1610, was a pupil of Rembrandt. Among his best engravings are a "Sacrifice of Abraham," and "Saint Jerome holding a Crucifix." His portraits are highly esteemed. Died about 1685.

See DESCAMPS, "Vies des Peintres Flamands, Hollandais," etc.

Bol or **Boll,** bol, (HANS, or JOHN,) a skilful Flemish painter of landscapes, animals, and flowers, born at Mechlin in 1534. He worked at Amsterdam, and was also an engraver. Died about 1590.

See DESCAMPS, "Vies des Peintres Flamands," etc.

Bol, (KORNELIS,) a Dutch painter, who lived in London in 1666, and painted views of the great conflagration which occurred in that year.

Bolanger, bo'lôn'zhä', (JOHN,) a painter of history, born in 1606, was a pupil of Guido, and worked for the Duke of Módena. Died in 1660.

Bolchowitinow. See BOLKHOVITINOV.

Bold, (SAMUEL,) an English clergyman, who was vicar of Shapwick, Dorsetshire. He published several theological works. Died in 1737.

Boldetti, bol-det'tee, (MARCANTONIO,) an Italian antiquary, born at Rome in 1663; died in 1749.

Boldoni, bol-do'nee, (SIGISMONDO,) an Italian physician, and professor of philosophy at Pavía, born at Milan about 1597; died in 1630.

Bolduc, bol'dük', (JACQUES,) a French ecclesiastic and theological writer, born in Paris about 1580.

Boleslaw, bo'lĕs-läv', or **Boleslaus,** bo'lĕs-lä'ŭs, I., [Fr. BOLESLAS, bo'lĕs'läs',] surnamed THE BRAVE, succeeded his father Mieczislaw (Micislaus) as Prince of Poland in 992. He was engaged in a war with Henry II. of Germany, and conquered a portion of Silesia from the Prussians. He died in 1025, and was succeeded by his son, Mieczislaw II.

Boleslaw or **Boleslaus II.,** surnamed THE BOLD, born in 1042, was a son of Casimir I., whom he succeeded in 1058. Having slain at the altar the Archbishop of Cracow, who had remonstrated against his tyranny, he was anathematized by the pope, and, being deserted by his subjects, fled to Carinthia, where he died about 1090.

Boleslaw or **Boleslaus III.,** surnamed THE WRY-MOUTHED, was the son of Ladislaus, whom he succeeded in 1102. He was engaged in frequent wars with the Hungarians and Russians, and is said to have been victor in more than forty battles. Died in 1138.

Boleslaw or **Boleslaus IV.,** surnamed CRIS'PUS, second son of the preceding, ascended the throne in 1147, having deposed his brother Wladislaw, (Ladislaus.) His country was invaded by the emperor Frederick Barbarossa in 1157; but the following year a peace was concluded between them. Died in 1173.

Boleslaw or **Boleslaus V.,** surnamed THE CHASTE, succeeded his father Leszko in 1237. His country was laid waste by the Tartars in 1240 and 1260. Died in 1279.

Boleyn or **Bullen,** pronounced alike bŏŏl'en, (ANNE,) was a daughter of Sir Thomas Bullen, afterwards Viscount Rochford and Earl of Wiltshire, who was allied to the principal nobility in the kingdom. Her mother was Lady Howard, a daughter of the Duke of Norfolk. She was born in 1507, and passed some years at the court of France. About the age of twenty she became a maid of honour to Queen Catherine, and captivated the fancy of Henry VIII., who, from his desire to marry Anne Boleyn, urged the pope to grant him a divorce from Catherine. Henry married her privately in the early part of 1533. She was crowned publicly in June of that year, and became the mother of Princess Elizabeth in September. She favoured the cause of the Reformers. In 1536 she lost the favour of the king, and was accused of criminal intercourse with several men. She was condemned by a jury of peers and beheaded in May, 1536.

See "Memoirs of Anne Boleyn," by MISS BENGER; STRICKLAND'S "Queens of England;" also the Histories of HUME and LINGARD. For an examination into the character of Anne Boleyn, see FROUDE'S "History of England," vol. ii. chap. xi.

Bolgeni, bol-jä'nee, written also **Boligeni,** (GIOVANNI VINCENZO,) an Italian Jesuit, born at Bergamo in 1733, became professor of theology and philosophy at Macerata. He wrote a number of treatises against the Jansenists. Died in 1811.

Bolingbroke, bol'ing-brŏŏk, (HENRY SAINT JOHN,) VISCOUNT, an eminent English author, orator, and politician, born at Battersea, Surrey, on the 1st of October, 1678, was a son of Sir Henry Saint John, afterwards viscount. He was educated at Christ Church, Oxford, and became extremely dissipated. In 1701 he was elected to Parliament, in which he acted with the Tory party. He was appointed secretary of war in 1704, and retained the office until the change of the ministry in 1708. A violent political change occurred in 1710. The queen, always partial to the Tories, and no longer influenced by the Duchess of Marlborough, dismissed the Whigs from power, and formed a ministry in which Harley was premier and Saint John secretary of state for foreign affairs. The great question which divided the nation in the ensuing four years was, whether England should make peace with France without exacting from Philip V. a resignation of the crown of Spain. After a violent contest, the Tories—the peace party—prevailed. Saint John was the principal (English) negotiator of the treaty of Utrecht, (April, 1713,) which ended the long war of the Spanish succession. He was created Viscount Bolingbroke in 1712, and about that time became a rival of Harley, Earl of Oxford, who had been his friend. Seconded by the influence of Lady Masham over the queen, he became prime minister in place of Harley on the 27th of July, 1714. But his triumph was of short duration. The death of Queen Anne (August 1, 1714) deprived him of power, and frustrated the plans which he is known to have entertained for the restoration of the Stuart dynasty. In the spring of 1715 he escaped to France and entered the service of the Pretender, who appointed him his prime minister. He was impeached of high treason in the same year, and, having failed to appear before his judges, was attainted by Parliament.

In his exile he corresponded with his old friends Pope and Swift. He married in 1720 the widow of the Marquis de Villette, a niece of Madame de Maintenon. He was permitted to return to England in 1723, and recovered his estate, but was not admitted into the House of Lords. He maintained a long opposition to Walpole by articles published in the "Craftsman." Among his works are a "Dissertation on Parties," (1735,) "Remarks on the History of England," in twenty-four letters, first published in the "Craftsman," (1743,) and "The Idea of a Patriot King," (1749.) His works have little merit except the style. His talents were rather brilliant than solid. "In his reasonings," says Dr. Blair, "he is for the most part flimsy and false ; in his political writings, factious ; in what he calls his philosophical ones, sophistical and irreligious in the highest degree." He was brilliant in conversation, and had a high reputation as an orator. He died in December, 1751, having bequeathed some manuscript essays on metaphysics and morals to David Mallet, who published an edition of his works in five volumes, (1754.) "His political writings," says the "Edinburgh Review" for October, 1835, "are the works of a skilful partisan—a master in the arts of insinuation and sarcasm. They abound in animated and splendid passages, and contain many sound constitutional truths which are now trite and common, but which had never been so clearly stated nor so well expressed before."

See GOLDSMITH's "Life of Bolingbroke:" CHESTERFIELD's "Memoirs and Letters;" "Memoirs of Lord Bolingbroke," by G. W. COOKE, 1835: "Edinburgh Review" for October, 1835, and October, 1863: "Life of Lord Bolingbroke," London, 1770; THOMAS HUNTER, "Sketch of the Philosophical Character of Lord Bolingbroke," 1770; FRIEDRICH VON RAUMER, "Lord Bolingbroke und seine Werke," 1841; CHARLES DE RÉMUSAT, "Bolingbroke, sa Vie et son Temps," 1853.

Bolivar, bo-lee'vȧR, (GREGORIO,) a Spanish missionary to Mexico and South America, lived about 1620.

Bol'í-var, [Sp. pron. bo-lee'vȧR,] or, more fully, **Bolivar y Ponte,** bo-lee'vȧR e pon'tà, (SIMON,) the liberator of South America, was born at Caraccas in July, 1783, and inherited a large estate from his father. He was liberally educated at Madrid, and returned to his native land in 1809. In 1811 he joined the insurgents who had taken up arms to liberate their country from the Spanish domination, and became a colonel under Miranda. He obtained the command of an army in 1813, defeated the royalists, and declared himself dictator, but was driven out of Venezuela in 1814. In 1815 he took refuge from the victorious Spaniards by flight to Jamaica. He returned to the scene of contest in 1816, and raised another army, which defeated the Spaniards under Morillo in February, 1817. At a congress of the republic of Venezuela, held in February, 1819, he resigned his dictatorship, or exchanged it for the title of president. His army in the same year defeated the royalists at Bojaca and other places, and liberated New Granada. In December, 1819, Venezuela and New Granada united to form the republic of Colombia, of which Bolivar became the first president. He gained a decisive victory at Carobobo in June, 1821, and in 1822 marched with an army to Peru, which, with his aid, was quickly liberated from the Spaniards. The independence of the South American republics was recognized by England and the United States. About the end of 1823 Bolivar was appointed Dictator of Peru. The war having been ended by a decisive victory over the royalists at Ayacucho in December, 1824, Bolivar resigned the office of Dictator of Peru in January or February, 1825. The same year he visited Upper Peru, which was formed into a separate state, called Bolivia, of which he was declared perpetual protector. He framed for this state a code or constitution by which the executive power was vested in a president for life with irresponsible powers. This caused him to be suspected of designs against popular liberty. During his absence from Colombia, Paez rebelled against the government, which was too feeble to suppress his rebellion. The enemies of Bolivar intimated that he fomented this revolt in order to impress on the minds of the people the necessity of a dictator. He returned in 1826, and restored order by his presence. In December of that year he was declared president for life of Peru, which had adopted the Bolivian code. About this date he was again elected President of Colombia. He was, however, regarded with distrust by the republicans, and formally resigned in February, 1827 ; but, as the Congress refused to accept his resignation, he remained in power. Some writers state that he retired to private life some months before his death. He died at San Pedro in December, 1830. The result of his military services was the independence of three large states, which he also organized with ability.

See the "North American Review" for January, 1829, vol. xxviii., (by C. CUSHING;) DUCOUDRAY-HOLSTEIN, "Mémoires de S. Bolivar," 1829, and English translation of the same, 2 vols., 1830.

Bolkhovitinov or **Bolchowitinow,** bol-ko-vee'te-nov, a Russian archbishop and historical writer, born in

1761. He wrote, besides other works, "Literary Russia," which was translated into German by Strahl in 1828. Died in 1837.

Bolla, bol'lä, (BARTOLOMMEO,) an Italian burlesque poet, born at Bergamo about 1540. He wrote verses called "macaronic."

Bol'lan, (WILLIAM,) a lawyer, born in England, removed to Massachusetts about 1740. He was sent to England in 1745 as agent of the colony, and remained there many years, during which he rendered valuable services to Massachusetts and wrote several political tracts. Died in 1776.

Bollandus, bol-lân'dŭs, (JOHN,) a Flemish Jesuit, born in the province of Limburg in 1596. He was the first of the theological writers called Bollandists, the contributors to the great work entitled "Acta Sanctorum," or Lives of the Saints. In 1643 he published, conjointly with Godfrey Henschen, the first two volumes, in folio. Died in 1665. The "Acta Sanctorum" was continued by several learned men, and in 1794 had reached fifty-four volumes.

See L. P. GACHARD, "Mémoire historique sur les Bollandistes," 1835.

Bollandus, bol-lân'dŭs, or **De Bollandt,** dęh bol'-lânt, (SEBASTIAAN,) a Dutch theologian and philosopher, born at Maestricht. Died in 1645.

Bollemont, de, dęh bol'môn', (FRANÇOIS CHARLES ROBERT CHOUET,) a French general, born at Arrancy in 1749, served under Jourdan in Austria, and rose to be inspector-general of artillery. Died in 1810.

Bollet, bo'là', (PHILIPPE ALBERT,) a French Jacobin, and member of the National Convention, (1792,) voted for the death of the king. He subsequently became a member of the Council of Five Hundred, and of the legislative body. Died in 1811.

Bollioud-Mermet, bo'le-oo' mĕR'mȧ', (LOUIS,) a French littérateur, born at Lyons in 1709 ; died in 1793.

Bollman, bol'mȧn, (ERIC,) a German physician, born in Hanover about 1770. He made an unsuccessful effort to release La Fayette from prison at Olmutz, and afterwards passed some years in exile in the United States. Died in 1821.

Bologna, bo-lòn'yä, (ANTONIO,) an Italian writer, born about 1580.

Bologna, (GIOVANNI BATTISTA,) a Latin poet, born at Milan about 1580, wrote the "Crown of Poets," ("Corona Poetarum," 1616.)

Bologna, da, dä bo-lòn'yä, (GIOVANNI, or JOHN,) [Fr. JEAN DE BOLOGNE, zhŏN dęh bo'loñ',] generally called JOHN (GIOVANNI) OF BOLOGNA, an eminent sculptor and architect, born at Douai, in Flanders, in 1524. He passed the greater part of his life in Italy, principally at Florence, where he became acquainted with Michael Angelo. He was one of the first members of the Academy of Florence. Among his master-pieces in that city are the bronze statue of Mercury in the Imperial Gallery, the "Rape of the Sabines," a statue of Saint Luke, and a "Centaur vanquished by Hercules." The fountain at Bologna, with a colossal bronze figure of Neptune, is ranked among the finest works of the kind; and from this production the artist received his name. He also executed a number of excellent pieces of sculpture at Genoa. As a sculptor he is regarded as inferior only to Michael Angelo. Died in 1608.

See VASARI, "Lives of the Painters and Sculptors;" CICOGNARA, "Storia della Scultura;" FONTENAY, "Dictionnaire des Artistes;" TICOZZI, "Dizionario;" DUTHILLOEUL, "Éloge de Jean de Bologne," 1820.

Bologna, de, (LATTANZIO.) See MAINARDI.

Bologne, de, dęh bo'loñ', (PIERRE,) a lyric poet, of Italian extraction, born in Martinique in 1706 ; died in 1790.

Bolognese. See GRIMALDI.

Bolognetti, bo-lòn2yet'tee, (FRANCESCO,) an Italian poet, born at Bologna about 1540.

Bolognetti, (POMPEO,) an Italian physician, born at Bologna about 1590.

Bologni, bo-lòn'yee, (GIROLAMO,) born at Treviso in 1454, was the author of Latin poems, and edited several Latin classics. He became a priest in 1479, after he had married. He was crowned as poet-laureate by the emperor Frederick III. Died at Treviso in 1517.

---

e as k; ç as s; ğ hard; ğ as j; G, H, K, guttural; N, nasal; R, trilled; s as z; ±h as in this. (☞ See Explanations, p. 23.)

Bolognini, bo-lòn-yee'nee, (ANGELO,) an Italian physician and surgeon, born near Padua about 1490, wrote "On the Cure of External Ulcers," (" De Cura Ulcerum exteriorum," 1514.) He was professor at Bologna.

Bolognini, (CARLO,) an Italian painter of architecture, born at Bologna in 1678; died at Vienna in 1718.

Bolognini, (GIACOMO,) a painter, a nephew of the following, was born at Bologna in 1664; died in 1734.

Bolognini, (GIOVANNI BATTISTA,) called THE ELDER, an Italian painter, born at Bologna in 1611. He was a pupil of Guido, whose works he copied with great success. He also etched some works after that master. Died in 1688.

Bolignini, (GIOVANNI BATTISTA,) THE YOUNGER, an Italian sculptor, son of Giacomo, noticed above, born at Bologna; died in 1760.

Bolognini, (LUIGI,) an Italian jurist, legal writer, and diplomatist, born at Bologna in 1447; died in 1508.

Bolomier, de, dęh bo'lo'me-à', (GUILLAUME,) secretary of Amadeus VIII. of Savoy, rose to be chancellor of the kingdom. He was put to death, on a charge of 'calumny, in 1446.

Bolot, bo'lo', (CLAUDE ANTOINE,) a French jurist, and member of the National Convention, born in Franche-Comté about 1740. He voted for the death of Louis XVI. with a delay of the sentence. Died in 1812.

Bolsec, bol'sek', (JÉRÔME HERMÈS,) a French physician, born in Paris, wrote virulent attacks on Calvin and Beza. Died in 1585.

Bolswert, bol'swĕRt, or **Bolsward,** bol'swåRt, (BOETIUS ADAM,) an eminent Dutch engraver, born in Friesland about 1580, lived at Antwerp. Among his works are a "Last Supper," a "Resurrection of Lazarus," after Rubens, and landscapes after Bloemaert. Died in 1634.

See NAGLER, "Allgemeines Künstler-Lexikon;" HUBER, "Manuel des Amateurs."

Bolswert or **Bolsward,** (SCHELTIUS,) an excellent engraver, brother of the preceding, born at Bolsward in 1586, resided in Antwerp. His prints after Rubens, Van Dyck, and Jordaens are highly esteemed.

See HEINECKEN, "Dictionnaire des Artistes."

Boltin, bol'tin, (IVAN,) a Russian *littérateur* and historian, born at Saint Petersburg in 1735; died in 1792.

Bōl'tǫn or **Bōul'tǫn,** (EDMUND,) an English antiquary and historical writer, published "The Elements of Armories," a "Life of Henry II.," and "Nero Cæsar, or Monarchie Depraved," (1624.)

Bolton, (JAMES,) an English naturalist, who lived about 1770–1800. He published a "History of British Ferns," (1795,) "Natural History of British Song-Birds," (2 vols., 1794–96,) and other works.

Bolton, (MATTHEW.) See BOULTON.

Bolton, (ROBERT,) an English scholar and Puritan divine, born in Lancashire in 1572, published "Helpes to Humiliation," and other works. Died in 1631.

See E. BAGSHAW, "Life of Robert Bolton."

Bolton, (ROBERT,) Dean of Carlisle, born in 1697, published "Letters and Tracts on the Choice of Company," and other treatises. Died in 1763.

Bōl'tǫn, (SARAH T.,) an American poetess of the present century, born in Ohio, was a contributor to the "Home Journal" of New York, and other periodicals.

See GRISWOLD'S "Female Poets of America."

Bolts, bolts, (WILLEM,) born in Holland about 1740, entered the service of the English East India Company, and acquired an immense fortune. He wrote "Considerations on the Affairs of India," and a work on Bengal. Died in 1808.

Bolzani, bol-zå'nee, or **Bolzanio,** bol-zå'ne-o, (URBANO VALERIANO,) an Italian monk and Greek scholar, born in 1440, published a Greek grammar. Died in 1524.

Bolzano, bol-zå'no, (BERNHARD,) a German Catholic theologian and philosophical writer, born at Prague in 1781. He published, among other works, "Athanasia, or Proofs of the Immortality of the Soul." Died in 1848.

Bom, bom, (PETER,) a Flemish landscape-painter, born at Antwerp in 1530, painted in distemper. Died in 1572.

Bomare. See VALMONT DE BOMARE.

Bombaci, bom-bå'chee, (GASPARO,) an Italian, born at Bologna in 1607, wrote a "History of Bologna," (1666.)

Bombardini, bom-bâR-dee'nee, (ANTONIO,) an Italian jurist, and professor of law at Padua, where he was born in 1666; died in 1726.

Bombasio, bom-bå'se-o, written also **Bombace,** (GABRIELLO,) an Italian poet and orator, born at Reggio about 1540. He was patronized by the Duke of Parma. He wrote "Alidoro," a tragedy, and other works.

Bombelles, de, dęh bom'bêl', (HENRI FRANÇOIS,) COMTE, a French general and military writer, born in 1680, distinguished himself at the battles of Oudenarde, Malplaquet, and Belgrade, (1717.) Died in 1760.

Bombelles, de, (MARC MARIE,) MARQUIS, son of the preceding, was born at Bitche in 1744. He served in the Seven Years' war, and was subsequently employed in various embassies to the courts of England, Holland, and Austria. He afterwards entered into orders, and was made Bishop of Amiens, (1819.) Died in 1822.

See DE COURCELLES, "Dictionnaire des Généraux Français."

Bombelli, bom-bel'lee, (RAFAELLO,) a distinguished Italian mathematician, born at Bologna. His principal work is a "Treatise on Algebra," (1572.) He appears to have been one of the first Europeans who were aware that the Arabs derived their knowledge of algebra from the Hindoos.

See G. LIBRI, "Histoire des Sciences mathématiques en Italie."

Bombelli, (SEBASTIANO,) an Italian portrait-painter, born in Friuli in 1635; died about 1685.

See LANZI, "History of Painting in Italy."

Bomberg, bom'bêRG, (DANIEL,) a printer of Antwerp, celebrated for the beauty of his Hebrew characters. Among his works are several editions of the Hebrew Bible, the "Hebraic Concordance" of Isaac Nathan, and the "Babylonish Talmud." Died in 1549.

See BAYLE, "Historical and Critical Dictionary."

Bombino, bom-bee'no, (BERNARDINO,) an Italian jurist, born at Cosenza in 1523; died in 1588.

Bomfim, bòn-fêN', (JOZÉ JOAQUIM,) a distinguished Portuguese general and statesman, born in Estremadura in 1790, was one of the partisans of Dom Pedro in Portugal, and of Donna Maria on her accession to the throne. He was appointed minister of war and of the marine in 1837. After the downfall of the constitution, he was banished to Africa, whence he was recalled in 1847.

See BROCKHAUS, "Conversations-Lexikon."

Bo-mil'car, [Gr. Βομίλκας or Βοαμίλκας,] a Carthaginian admiral, who commanded a fleet which was sent about 209 B.C. to support the army which defended Syracuse against the Romans. He avoided a battle by a hasty retreat, and returned to Carthage.

Bomilcar, a Carthaginian general, who aspired to be king of Carthage about 308 B.C., but failed and was put to death.

Bommel, van, văn bom'męl, [Lat. BOMME'LIUS,] (HENDRIK,) a Dutch historical writer. Died in 1542.

Bommel, van, (KORNELIS RICHARD ANTOÖN,) a Catholic theologian, born at Leyden in 1790, became Bishop of Liege in 1829. Died in 1852.

Bompard, bòn'pâR', (ALEXIS,) a French physician, born at Conflans in 1782, wrote, besides other works, a "Treatise on the Diseases of the Digestive Passages," (" Traité des Maladies des Voies digestives," 1829.)

Bompiano, bom-pe-å'no, (IGNAZIO,) an Italian Jesuit and historical writer, born at Frosinone in 1612, became professor of Hebrew and belles-lettres in the Roman College. Died in 1675.

Bon, bòn, (FLORENT,) a French Jesuit and poet, born about 1580, resided at Rheims.

Bon, bon, (GIOVANNI FILIPPO,) an Italian physician, and professor in the University of Padua, born in 1520.

Bon, (LOUIS ANDRÉ,) a French general, born at Romans, in Dauphiny, in 1758. He served with distinction under Augereau in Italy, and subsequently in the campaigns of Egypt and Syria. He was killed at the siege of Saint-Jean-d'Acre in 1799.

See DE COURCELLES, "Dictionnaire des Généraux Français."

Bon de Saint-Hilaire, bòn dęh sånt'e'lâR', (FRANÇOIS XAVIER,) a French savant, born at Montpellier in 1678, was a member of the Academy of Inscriptions, and of the Royal Society of London. He published a number of scientific treatises, one of which, entitled a "Dissertation on the Spider," (1710,) obtained extensive popularity and was translated into Chinese. Died in 1761.

See LE BAS, "Dictionnaire encyclopédique de la France."

Bona, bo′nȁ, (GIOVANNI,) an Italian cardinal, born at Mondovì in 1609, was the author of several ecclesiastical and religious works in Latin. Died in 1674.

See BERTOLOTTI, "Vita J. Bonæ," 1677; GOUGET, "Vie du Cardinal Bona."

Bona, della, del′lȁ bo′nȁ, (GIOVANNI,) an Italian physician, born near Verona in 1712, was professor at the University of Padua.

Bonac, de, dĕh bo′nȁk′, (JEAN LOUIS d'Usson—dü′sŏN′,) MARQUIS, a French diplomatist, born about 1672, was employed by Louis XIV. in important embassies to Sweden, Poland, and Spain. In 1716 he was ambassador to Constantinople, where he resided nine years. Died in 1738.

Bonacci, (LEONARDO.) See LEONARDO OF PISA.

Bonaccioli, bo-nât-cho′lee, or **Bonacciuoli,** bo-nât-choo-o′lee, (ALFONSO,) an Italian *littérateur*, born about 1540. He translated the first and second parts of Strabo's Geography into Italian; also portions of Pausanias.

Bonaccioli, (LUIGI,) an Italian physician, born at Ferrara about 1480.

Bonacina, bo-nȁ-chee′nȁ, (MARTINO,) an Italian ecclesiastic and theological writer, born at Milan; died in 1631.

Bonacossi, bo-nȁ-kos′see, (BARDELLONE,) son of Pinamonte, noticed below, having imprisoned his father and brother, caused himself to be proclaimed sovereign of Mantua in 1292. He was deposed in 1299 by his nephew Bottesella. Died about 1302.

Bonacossi, (PASSERINO,) a relative of the preceding, expelled the Guelphs from Mantua, and obtained from the emperor Henry VII. the title of imperial vicar. He was killed in a riot about 1328.

Bonacossi, (PINAMONTE,) Prefect of Mantua, became sovereign of that city about 1275, having murdered his colleague, and sided alternately with the Guelph and Ghibeline factions. He is mentioned in Dante's "Inferno." Died in 1293.

See SISMONDI, "Histoire des Républiques Italiennes."

Bo-na-cos′sus or **Buoncossa,** boo-ŏn′kos′sȁ, (ERCOLE,) an Italian physician, and professor in the University of Bologna, was a native of Ferrara. Died in 1578.

Bo′na De′a, [Fr. BONNE DÉESSE, bon dȁ′ĕss′,] (" The Good Goddess,") a Roman divinity, supposed to be the sister or wife of Faunus, and by some authors identified with Ops. She was worshipped by the Roman matrons at an annual festival and with mysterious rites, from which all males were strictly excluded.

Bonafide, bo-nȁ-fee′dȁ, or **Buonafede,** boo-ŏn-ȁ-fȁ′dȁ, (FRANCESCO,) an Italian botanist, born at Padua in 1474. He founded the botanic garden in that city in 1540. Died in 1558.

See R. DE VISIANI, "Notizie della Vita di Bonafede," 1845.

Bonafous, bo′nȁ′foo′, (?) (MATHIEU,) an agriculturist, born at Turin in 1794, wrote on the production of silk and on other branches of rural economy. Died in 1852.

Bonair, bo′nȁr′, (HENRI STUARD,) a French historical writer, lived about 1650.

Bonal, de, dĕh bo′nȁl′, (FRANÇOIS,) born in the diocese of Agen, in France, in 1734, was appointed Bishop of Clermont in 1776, and was afterwards elected to the States-General. Died in 1800.

Bonald, de, dĕh bo′nȁl′,(LOUIS GABRIEL AMBROISE,) VICOMTE, a French statesman and journalist of the royalist party, born near Milhau-en-Rouergue in 1754. He was associated in 1806 with Châteaubriand and Fiévée as editor of the "Mercure," became minister of state in 1822 and a peer of France in 1823. He was the author of "The Theory of Political and Religious Power," (3 vols., 1796,) "La Législation primitive," (3 vols., 2d edition, 1821,) and other works, in which he favours absolutism. He was a member of the French Academy. Died in 1840.

See HENRI DE BONALD, "Notice sur le Vicomte de Bonald," 1841.

Bonald, de, (LOUIS JACQUES MAURICE,) son of the preceding, born at Milhau in 1787, was made Archbishop of Lyons in 1839, became a cardinal in 1841, and a senator in 1851. He is a legitimist in politics.

Bonami, bo′nȁ′me′, (FRANÇOIS,) a French naturalist and scientific writer, born at Nantes in 1710. Du Petit-Thouars has called by his name the genus Bonamia. Died in 1786.

Bonamici. See BUONAMICI.

Bonamy, bo′nȁ′me′, (CHARLES AUGUSTE JEAN BAPTISTE LOUIS JOSEPH,) born at Fontenay-le-Comte in 1764, served with distinction in the army of Napoleon in Italy, Austria, and Russia, and rose to be general of brigade. Died in 1830.

Bonamy, (PIERRE NICOLAS,) a French historical writer, born at Louvres in 1694; died in 1770.

Bonanni, bo-nân′nee, or **Buonanni,** boo-o-nân′nee, (FILIPPO,) an Italian naturalist and antiquary, born in Rome in 1638, published, besides other works, " Gabinetto armonico," (1716.) Died in 1725.

Bonaparte, bo-nȁ-paR′tȁ, (CARLO,) a Corsican lawyer, born in 1756, was the father of Napoleon I. He was a partisan of Pascal Paoli, with whom he fought against the Genoese. He married the beautiful Letitia (Letizia) Ramolino in 1767, and had five sons and three daughters. Died at Montpellier in February, 1785.

Bonaparte, (CAROLINE MARIE ANNONCIADE,) Queen of Naples, a sister of Napoleon I., was born at Ajaccio in 1782. She was married in 1800 to General Murat, who became King of Naples in July, 1808. She is said to have exercised a great influence over her husband, and to have taken an active part in the government. After the death of Murat (1815) she assumed the title of Countess of Lipona, and resided at Trieste for many years. Died at Florence in 1839.

Bonaparte, (CHARLES LUCIEN JULES LAURENT,) Prince of Canino, an eminent naturalist, born in Paris in 1803, was the eldest son of Lucien Bonaparte. He married his cousin Zénaïde, a daughter of King Joseph, in 1822, soon after which he became a resident of Philadelphia and devoted himself to ornithology. He published a valuable work, entitled "American Ornithology, or History of the Birds of the United States," (Philadelphia, 3 vols., 1825–33,) which is complementary to Wilson's Ornithology. In 1828 he settled in Italy. He took a prominent part in organizing the Roman republic, (1848–49.) Among his chief works is " Illustrations of the Italian Fauna," (" Iconografia della Fauna Italica," 3 vols., 1832–41,) which has a high reputation. He had four sons and eight daughters. Died in Paris in 1857.

Bonaparte, (JÉRÔME,) King of Westphalia, the youngest brother of Napoleon I., was born at Ajaccio in November, 1784. He entered the navy in 1800, obtained the rank of lieutenant, and served in the West Indies. During a visit to the United States he became acquainted with Miss Paterson, of Baltimore, whom he married in 1803 without the consent of his family. His marriage was declared null in 1805 by Napoleon, who would not permit the wife to enter France; but he promoted Jerome to the rank of rear-admiral in 1806. In the same year he passed from the navy into the army as a general of brigade. He commanded a corps which gained some successes in Silesia in 1807, and was placed on the throne of the new kingdom of Westphalia in July, 1807. In the ensuing month he married Catherine, a daughter of the King of Würtemberg. Cassel was the capital of his kingdom. He ceased to reign in October, 1813. After the return of Napoleon from Elba, he joined his standard, and commanded a division at Waterloo. He resided as an exile at Trieste, Rome, and Lausanne until 1847, when he returned to France. He became a marshal of France in 1850. He died in June, 1860, leaving two sons, Jerome, (whose mother was Miss Paterson,) and Napoleon Joseph Charles Paul, called Prince Napoleon, issue of his second marriage.

See "Nouvelle Biographie Générale," (under the head of NAPOLÉON.)

Bonaparte, (JOSEPH,) the eldest brother of Napoleon I., was born at Corte, in the island of Corsica, on the 7th of January, 1768. He was sent to the College of Autun about 1777, and returned to Corsica in 1784, after which he studied law at Pisa, and was received as an advocate in Bastia in 1788. Expelled from Corsica by the partisans of Paoli in 1793, he retired to France, and married Julie Clary. In May, 1797, he was sent as ambassador to the court of Rome, and received from Napoleon instructions in which occur the following sentences : " Display a grand character. If the pope dies, permit not another to be chosen." On the murder of the French general Duphot by the Papal troops, December, 1797, he returned to Paris, and became a member of the Council of Five Hundred. He negotiated the treaty of Lunéville with Austria in February, 1801, and the treaty of Amiens with the English in March, 1802. His manners and talents are said to have been well adapted to diplomacy. He seems to have been rather unambiti.ous ; but, urged by the imperious will of Napoleon, he accepted the throne of Naples, February, 1806. On this occasion the imperial egotist addressed to him these words : " All sentiments of affection yield now to reasons of state. I recognize as relatives only those who serve me." In May, 1808, he quitted Naples, and was transferred to the throne of Spain, where he encountered a far more determined resistance. He entered Madrid with the French army in July, 1808, but received little support from the Spaniards, many thousands of whom took arms against the French. He was forced to retire from Madrid, July 31; but Napoleon arrived in November, gained several victories in rapid succession, and occupied the capital in December, 1808. In 1809 a large portion of Spain was occupied by the French armies, severally commanded by Soult, Victor, and Suchet, over whom the authority of the king was only nominal. Disgusted with his anomalous and vexatious position, he offered his resignation or abdication, (March, 1809,) which Napoleon would not accept. His army fought an indecisive battle against the English under General Wellesley, at Talavera, in July, 1809. The war was prosecuted with various success for several years. (See MASSENA ; SOULT ; WELLINGTON.) Joseph was appointed general-in-chief of all the French armies in Spain in March, 1812, and was defeated by Wellington at Vittoria in June, 1813, soon after which event he ceased to reign. When Napoleon departed from Paris for the army, in January, 1814, he left Joseph at that capital, with the title of lieutenant-general. After the battle of Waterloo, he emigrated to the United States, styled himself Count de Survilliers, and resided at Bordentown, New Jersey, with his two daughters. After the accession of Louis Philippe to the throne of France, in 1830, Joseph Bonaparte returned to Europe. He passed several years in England, and afterwards settled at Florence, in Italy, where he died in 1844. (See BONAPARTE, NAPOLEON.)

See A DU CASSE, " Mémoires et Correspondance du Roi Joseph," 10 vols., 1854 ; THIERS, " Histoire du Consulat et de l'Empire ;" " Biographical Sketch of Joseph Bonaparte," London, 1833 ; " Nouvelle Biographie Générale," (under NAPOLÉON.)

Bonaparte, (LETIZIA or LETITIA **Ramolino** (râ-mo-lee'no) or **Ramolini,**) the mother of Napoleon I., was born in Corsica in 1750. She was celebrated for her beauty ; she was also a woman of amiable character and good sense. Napoleon once declared, " It is to my mother and her good principles that I owe my fortune and all the good that I have ever done ;" and again, " Madame Mère had a great character, energy of soul, much elevation and pride." After her son became emperor, she was styled MADAME MÈRE, and resided in Paris. Died in 1839.

Bonaparte, (LOUIS,) King of Holland, a brother of Napoleon I., was born at Ajaccio in 1778. He entered the army about 1794, and served in Italy at the battles of the Brenta, Arcola, (1796,) and Rivoli, (1797.) Having aided Napoleon in the *coup d'état* of the 18th Brumaire, 1799, he was raised to the rank of colonel. In 1802 he was induced to sacrifice his own inclinations and peace by a marriage with Hortense de Beauharnais, who was also averse to the union. They separated finally in 1807. He became a general of division in April, 1804, and was raised to the dignity of prince in May of that year. In compliance with the will of Napoleon, he accepted the title of King of Holland in June, 1806. The Dutch submitted quietly, perhaps contentedly, to the authority of Louis, who was disposed to respect their rights and consult their interests ; but Napoleon insisted that the policy of Holland should be subservient to his own designs. Louis was compelled to sacrifice the mercantile

interests of Holland by co-operation with the "Continental System," *i.e.* the paper blockade of the British ports. On this and other subjects he and the emperor had disputes which ended in a total suspension of friendly relations. In December, 1809, there occurred at Paris a meeting of allied sovereigns, which Louis attended. When he was about to return, he found himself treated as a prisoner, and was not permitted to leave Paris until he submitted to certain conditions which Napoleon imposed. In January, 1810, the French army began to occupy Holland. Louis abdicated in July, 1810, and Holland was then annexed to the French Empire. He retired to private life, and resided successively at Rome and Florence. Died at Leghorn in 1846. He was author of several works, among which may be noticed " Historical Documents and Reflections on the Government of Holland," (3 vols., 1820.) He had three sons,—Napoleon, who died in 1807 ; Napoleon Louis, who died in 1831 ; and Louis Napoleon, now Emperor of France.

See " Mémoires sur la Cour de Louis Napoléon et sur la Hollande," Paris, 1828 ; THIERS, " Histoire du Consulat et de l'Empire ;" F. WOUTERS, " Les Bonaparte depuis 1815 jusqu'en 1846," 1848.

Bonaparte, (LOUIS LUCIEN,) a son of Lucien, and nephew of Napoleon I., was born in England in 1813. He was elected to the Constituent Assembly of France in 1848. In 1852 he became a senator, and received the title of prince.

Bonaparte, (LOUIS NAPOLEON.) See NAPOLEON III.

Bonaparte, (LUCIEN,) Prince de Canino, a brother of Napoleon I., born at Ajaccio in March, 1775, was one of the ablest members of the family. He was educated at the College of Autun and the school of Brienne. In the French Revolution he showed himself a zealous republican, and acted with much energy and moderation on several occasions. In 1795 he married Christine Boyer, a poor girl of Provence, and was appointed commissary of war. He was elected to the Council of Five Hundred in April, 1798, acquired great influence, and became an opponent of the Directory,—or rather of the policy of the Directors ; for he supported the Constitution of the year III. He united with Siéyès, who was elected a Director in May, 1798, and counteracted the Jacobins. After the return of Napoleon from Egypt, October, 1799, Lucien was elected president of the Five Hundred. He co-operated most efficiently with Napoleon in the revolution of the 18th Brumaire, November 9, 1799. According to some authorities, he acted with more resolution and firmness in this affair than Napoleon himself. Lucien was appointed minister of the interior in December, 1799, was sent as ambassador to Spain in November, 1800, and became a member of the Tribunat in 1802. He offended the First Consul by marrying, in 1803, a widow named Madame Jouberthon. His first wife had died about 1800. He went into exile in 1804, settled at Rome, and exchanged politics for literature and art. The emperor offered him a throne on condition that he must dissolve his marriage ; but he declined the offer. He was ordered, it is said, to quit the continent of Europe. He embarked for the United States in 1810, was captured during the voyage by an English cruiser, and detained in England until 1814. He was reconciled to Napoleon in 1815, supported him actively during the Hundred Days, and after his abdication advocated in the House of Peers the claim of Napoleon II. He passed the remainder of his life in exile in Italy, and wrote, besides other works, a poem entitled " Charlemagne," (2 vols., 1814,) and " Autobiographic Memoirs," (1836.) He had six daughters and five sons, Charles Lucien the naturalist, Paul, Louis Lucien, Pierre Napoleon, and Antoine. Died at Rome in 1840.

See P. W. FORCHHAMMER, " Denkrede auf den Fürsten von Canino L. Bonaparte," 1840.

Bonaparte, (LUCIEN,) CARDINAL, a son of Charles Bonaparte, Prince of Canino, was born about 1828. His mother was Zénaïde Charlotte Julie, a daughter of Joseph Bonaparte. He was ordained a priest in 1853, and became a cardinal in 1868. He is said to be remarkable for his personal resemblance to Napoleon I.

Bonaparte, (MARIE ANNE ÉLISA,) usually called **Elisa,** Princess de Piombino, a sister of Napoleon I., was born at Ajaccio in 1777. She was married in 1797 to Félix Bacciochi, a captain of the French army, and went to reside in Paris in 1798. In 1805 Lucca and Piombino were erected into a principality by Napoleon, who gave the sovereignty of the same to his sister Élisa. She became Grand Duchess of Tuscany in March, 1809, and governed that country with ability until 1814. Died near Trieste in 1820.

Bonaparte, bo'nȧ-part, or **Buonaparte,** (NAPO'-LEON,) |Fr. NAPOLÉON BONAPARTE, nä'po'lä'ôn' bo'-nä'pårt'; It. NAPOLEONE BONAPARTE, (or BUONAPARTE,) nä-po-lå-o'nå bo'nå-par'tȧ, (or boo-o'nå-par'tȧ,)] NAPO-LEON I., Emperor of the French, the greatest general of modern times, was born at Ajaccio, in Corsica, August 15, 1769. His father, Carlo Buonaparte, was an officer under General Paoli, and distinguished himself as one of the bravest and most energetic defenders of the liberties of his country against the French. In the hardships and dangers of that contest he was accompanied by his wife Letitia, (whose maiden name was RAMOLINO, rȧ-mo-lee'no,) a young woman of rare beauty as well as courage. It is said that she was suddenly taken in labour at mass, and, having reached her home in haste, her child was born on a piece of old tapestry on which were represented the battle-scenes of the Iliad. The child thus ushered into the world, the offspring of warlike parents and surrounded by the images of war, is said to have been not only singularly beautiful, but very gentle and easily managed until he was two years old. At this age his character suddenly changed: he became imperious, and was invincibly obstinate to those who sought to control him by menaces or by force. In the childish disputes that occurred between him and his elder brother Joseph, Napoleon, it is said, invariably came off conqueror. His mother, however, by combining moderation with firmness, succeeded at length in obtaining a complete ascendency over him. He afterwards said, "It is to my mother, and to the principles which she instilled into me, that I owe my fortune and all the good that I have ever done." "Nevertheless," says his biographer in the "Nouvelle Biographie Générale," "we may well believe that this education, with all its efficiency, was somewhat wanting in tenderness. Napoleon was educated to be one of Plutarch's heroes. He was not, perhaps, sufficiently imbued with those gentle, refined, and benevolent sentiments which form the very essence of the moral sense. The standard of virtue on which his character was moulded was that of antiquity: it was force mastering itself in order that it might become the master of others." Before he was ten years old, (April, 1779,) Napoleon left Corsica for the military school at Brienne, where he remained until he went (October, 1784) to the military school at Paris to complete his education. While at Brienne he was for some time under the instruction of Pichegru. He was distinguished for his proficiency in mathematics ; but he manifested no fondness for classical studies or for belles-lettres in any form. He was studious, of regular habits, well-behaved, and enjoyed excellent health. He took a particular interest in history, in which his favourite authors were Plutarch, Cæsar, Arrian, and others of this class. His father died in February, 1785, at the early age of thirty-six. In September of the same year Napoleon received a commission as sub-lieutenant of artillery ; but he was soon after made first lieutenant in a regiment of artillery stationed at Valence. Having gone to Corsica on a furlough, he expressed himself in 1789 very warmly in favour of the revolutionary movement in France. In February, 1792, he was made captain of artillery. While he was in Ajaccio, in April of that year, a serious dispute having occurred between the troops and the inhabitants of the town, Bonaparte was accused of having given orders to fire on the people ; he was in consequence summoned to Paris to answer for his conduct. He was, however, acquitted. While in the capital he witnessed the insurrection of June 20. He was at a coffee-house, when, seeing the mob pass by armed with pikes, axes, etc., he said to his friend Bourrienne, "Let us follow this canaille." He saw them break into the palace of the Tuileries without meeting any resistance. When the king appeared at the window, wearing the *bonnet rouge*, he exclaimed, "It's all over with that poor man ! How could

they permit those wretches to enter the palace ? A few discharges of grape would have sent them all flying. He afterwards witnessed the rising of the 10th of August. Having returned to Corsica, he found the people of that island divided into two parties. Much the larger number, with Paoli, were in favour of seeking the protection of England. The Bonaparte family, though once strongly attached to General Paoli, adhered to the cause of France and the Convention. In the civil war that ensued in Corsica, Napoleon was closely besieged in a tower with only fifty men, who for three days were reduced to the necessity of living on horse-flesh. He afterwards succeeded in making his escape, and in conveying his mother and the family in safety to Nice, and subsequently to Marseilles.

Napoleon spent a portion of the summer of 1793 in Paris. In the autumn he was ordered to Toulon, then in possession of the Spanish and English. He found the French artillery at that place in a miserable condition, and the troops without any competent commander. A commissioner having arrived from Paris about this time, a council of war was called, and, Bonaparte's plan for the reduction of the place having been decided upon, the execution was intrusted to the young Corsican. It proved a brilliant success, and the name of Bonaparte at once became distinguished throughout France. He was made soon after a brigadier-general. On the fall of Robespierre in July, 1794, Bonaparte was suspended in his command and put under arrest, but was released after a short detention. We find him again actively engaged in military operations towards the close of that year and during the early part of the ensuing year. But in the spring of 1795, the army having been reorganized, Bonaparte, for some unexplained cause, was suspended from his duties and placed upon half-pay. He immediately repaired to Paris, and complained to the proper authorities of this unworthy treatment. But his remonstrances were without avail : he received for answer only that he was too young to command the artillery of an army. He replied, "One grows old very quickly on the field of battle." His protestations were, however, in vain. He remained for some months without any regular employment. But Fortune seemed resolved not to neglect her favourite son. The 13th Vendémiaire, (October 4,) the famous Day of the Sections, was at hand. A formidable insurrection, headed by the National Guards, threatened the total overthrow of the power of the Convention, which, though provided with troops and artillery, had no officer competent to command them. Menou had been selected by the Convention for this duty ; but his indecision had increased the confidence of the insurgents and greatly disheartened his own party. Barras, Tallien, and the other leaders were in the greatest perplexity and alarm. Barras had fortunately become acquainted with Bonaparte at the siege of Toulon. He said to his colleagues, Tallien and Carnot, "I have just the man for our purpose,—a little Corsican officer, who will not stand upon ceremony." The Corsican was accordingly appointed to the command. He had more than five thousand regular troops, about fifteen hundred volunteers, and two hundred pieces of cannon, which his science and skill rendered more effective than ten times the number under the command of an ordinary officer. The insurgents, amounting to more than thirty thousand, fell before the Corsican's terrible artillery like grass before the scythe. Although the National Guards fought with the greatest bravery, the fate of the day was quickly decided. The Convention used the victory thus obtained with great moderation. Only two persons, it is said, suffered death after the conflict was over. Soon after, Barras proposed that the Convention should approve Bonaparte's appointment as second in command of the army of the interior, Barras himself remaining commander-in-chief. The proposal was adopted by acclamation. Although nominally the second in rank, he became by this appointment virtually the commander-in-chief of the army of the interior.

Among the intimate friends of Madame Tallien was Josephine Beauharnais, a young widow of rare beauty and accomplishments. She was the daughter of M. de la Pagerie, a naval officer of Martinique, where she was born in 1763. Having gone to France with her father in 1779, she became acquainted with the young Marquis of Beauharnais, to whom she was soon after married, being then scarcely more than sixteen. Her husband had in 1793 risen to the rank of general in the army of the Republic; but, as he belonged to the *noblesse*, he naturally incurred the suspicion of those in power, and suffered death by the guillotine in the summer of 1794. Soon after the arrest of General Beauharnais his wife also was imprisoned, and would in all probability have shared his fate had she not been delivered by the timely fall of Robespierre. Bonaparte became acquainted with her, and was deeply smitten with her charms. He had been appointed, March 2, 1796, commander-in-chief of the army of Italy. He married Josephine on the 9th of March, and a few days afterwards set out for Nice to take command of the army. The events of the war which followed belong to history rather than to biography: suffice to say that the exploits of young Bonaparte surpassed in splendour everything before recorded of modern warfare. To heighten the romance of the story, the youthful hero, all in the midst of the hardships, excitements, and anxieties of that unequalled campaign, seems to have abandoned himself wholly to the "sweet delirium" of his first love. We find him writing frequent and most impassioned letters to Josephine,—at one time expressing all the tenderness and devotion which he felt for her, at another bitterly reproaching her that she wrote to him so coldly, so briefly, or so seldom. He had sent for his wife to join him in Italy. She arrived at Milan towards the end of June, and spent some days with him at the Serbelloni palace. As she was about to set out under an escort towards Brescia, they found the passage obstructed by the enemy. She saw the Austrian uniforms and heard the musketry at a little distance. Trembling and weeping, she returned. Bonaparte, touched at the sight of her distress, exclaimed, with emotion, "Wurmser shall pay me dearly for the tears which he has caused you to shed." Having defeated and almost annihilated three Austrian armies in succession, and compelled Wurmser, their ablest and bravest general, to take refuge in Mantua, Bonaparte at length brought the war to a triumphant close by the capture of that city. Wurmser surrendered on the 2d of February, 1797, having received from the victor the most honourable terms. With true magnanimity, the French commander declined to be present at the capitulation; and thus the Austrian general was spared the mortification of delivering up his sword to a conqueror so much younger than himself. Having subdued the Austrians in Northern Italy, Napoleon turned his victorious arms against the pope, who, after sustaining several defeats, was compelled to purchase a precarious peace by the payment of thirty millions of livres, besides delivering up to the French a number of statues, paintings, and manuscripts. It was resolved at Vienna that another army, under the Archduke Charles, who had distinguished himself in the recent campaigns on the Rhine, should take the field against Bonaparte. But nothing could resist the genius or the fortune of the French commander. By a masterly movement he surprised the archduke, who occupied a very strong position on the Tagliamento, and succeeded in crossing the river before the Austrians were prepared to offer any effectual resistance. Nothing remained for them but to retreat. Napoleon, following up his advantages with his accustomed promptitude, advanced by rapid strides towards the Austrian capital. On the 7th of April he arrived at Leoben, and pushed his advanced guard to within two cr three days' march of Vienna. But as his own situation, s> far from France, and without sufficient forces to keep open the line of his retreat, was not free from danger, he offered terms of peace, which the Austrian court, trembling for the safety of the capital, eagerly accepted. Having returned to Italy, the young conqueror was for some months occupied in regulating the affairs of that country, of which he claimed to be the liberator. By the treaty of Campo Formio, signed October 17, 1797, Austria acknowledged the independence of the new Cisalpine Republic, which included the larger part of her former possessions in Northern Italy, and guaranteed to France the extension of her boundary to the left bank of the Rhine. In return for these concessions, the French gov-

ernment gave up to Austria Venice and the Venetian territory as far as the Adige, besides Istria and Dalmatia. Genoa, having offered some opposition to the French arms, was required, by way of reparation, to establish a democratic form of government, taking the name of the Ligurian Republic. The terms granted to Austria were thought by many of the friends of France to be much too favourable. This treaty appears, indeed, to have been afterwards a subject of regret and mortification to Bonaparte himself. This may be inferred from the great anxiety he manifested to defend or apologize for it. The Directory had enjoined it upon him not to make peace with the Emperor of Austria, except on condition that the latter should renounce all claim to Venice and all the Venetian territory except Istria and Dalmatia. But Napoleon, having discovered that some persons connected with the government of Venice had made proposals for an alliance with Austria, determined to sacrifice that republic to the interests of France and his own ambition, abandoning, apparently without scruple, those of the democratic party who had been faithful to France, as well as the aristocrats who had sought the protection of the emperor. The Directory, it is said, had thoughts at one time of bringing him to trial for disobeying its orders; but his unbounded popularity rendered such a step not merely unwise, but extremely perilous. In the early part of 1798 the French government contemplated the invasion of Great Britain; and the preparations for this great undertaking were intrusted to Bonaparte. With this object he made a survey of the French coast along the British Channel. It was, however, soon after determined to attack the power of England in her remote possessions: A formidable expedition, destined for Egypt and the eastern coast of the Mediterranean, was fitted out, as it was believed that the British empire in India could be most conveniently reached from that side. This enterprise was regarded by the Directory with the more favour, on account of the growing influence and ascendency of Bonaparte: the members of the government were not unwilling to send far from France, into a sort of honourable banishment, the object of their anxiety and fears. On the other hand, the scheme was perhaps still more agreeable to Napoleon. Visions of boundless conquest and glory floated before his youthful imagination. It seemed not unreasonable that a young commander, who in his first campaigns had rivalled, if he did not surpass, the most brilliant achievements of Alexander, should think he might carry his victorious banners as far as the Macedonian hero had done two thousand years before. The expedition was got ready with the utmost secrecy. The land-force, consisting principally of the army of Italy, is said to have amounted to near 30,000 men. The armament set sail from Toulon on the 19th of May, 1798, and was joined soon after by a large fleet of transports carrying the land-forces under General Desaix. They reached Malta on the 10th of June, and Bonaparte, having come to an understanding with some person within the place, took possession of it without the slightest opposition. As they were passing the impregnable defences, constructed by the famous Knights of Malta, one of his officers said to him, "It is well, general, that there was some one within to open the gates for us; for we should have had more trouble in entering had the place been empty." The expedition arrived at Alexandria on the 29th of June, having by great good fortune escaped the fleet of Nelson, who had rightly guessed the destination of the French armament, and had actually reached Alexandria before the arrival of Bonaparte; but, hearing nothing of the hostile fleet, the English admiral had set sail for Rhodes. As France was at that time at peace with the Sultan, who had then an ambassador in Paris, the invasion of Egypt was wholly unexpected, and Bonaparte met with little resistance until the French troops had arrived near Cairo, in sight of the Pyramids, where they encountered a large body of Mamelukes with their Arab auxiliaries. Bonaparte, galloping to the front of the army, exclaimed, with enthusiasm, "Soldiers, from the summit of yonder monuments forty centuries look down upon your actions!" The battle was fiercely contested, the Mamelukes fighting with all the bravery of desperation; but nothing could withstand the tactics and artillery of the French. The

---

Mamelukes were almost annihilated: the few who escaped fled to Upper Egypt and Syria, no one offering any further resistance to the progress of the invading army. Thus ended the famous "battle of the Pyramids."

In his endeavour to regulate the government of the country, Bonaparte earnestly strove to conciliate the good will of the conquered people. With this view, he not only attended with his army the yearly festival of the Nile, but celebrated with great pomp the Feast of the Prophet, which took place the 20th of August. He has been accused by some of childish folly in supposing that by his expressions of respect or reverence for Mohammed he could impose upon the minds of the Moslems or delude them into the hope that he was about to turn Mussulman. But, in a secular point of view, it was certainly not unwise for a conqueror to show the people whom he had just conquered that he was not an enemy to their religion. It cannot be doubted that they would submit far more patiently to the rule of one who was even indifferent than of one who was hostile to their faith, as they would naturally have supposed him to be—coming from Europe, and especially from the country of Saint Louis—had he not taken the pains to convince them of the contrary. The statements about Bonaparte's having made a distinct profession of the Mohammedan faith appear to be erroneous or much exaggerated. But he certainly made use of some expressions which were designed to give an impression to the Mohammedans that he was very favourable towards their religion. At the same time, assuming an exaggerated or, as we might say, an Oriental style of speech, which indeed seemed to be in perfect harmony with his natural character, he assured them that he, like their prophet, was a man appointed by destiny, whom it would be as vain as it was impious to resist. He even went so far as to declare that he could call them to account for their most secret thoughts. But these declarations did not prevent the Arabs and Turks from perceiving that his claims to a supernatural power were made simply with a view to establish more firmly an earthly domination.

Meanwhile the Porte, assisted by England, was making vigorous preparations for war. Napoleon resolved to be first in the field. Leaving Cairo on the 10th of February, 1799, he crossed the desert through the Isthmus of Suez, taking successively El Arish, Gaza, and Jaffa, the last of which was carried by storm. From 1200 to 1500 Turks and Arabs were taken prisoners, and two days afterwards marched out of the town and put to death in cold blood by volleys of musketry or by the bayonet. The reasons alleged for this inhuman massacre were that the victims had been taken prisoners previously at Gaza and El Arish, and had violated their parole. But the utmost severity of the laws of war could require no more than that they should receive no quarter while they were fighting with arms in their hands: it could never justify the victor in first offering them life, and then taking it again after they had been for two days his prisoners. The apologists for Napoleon allege that it was found impossible to furnish food to the prisoners, or even to guard them, surrounded as Bonaparte was by swarms of active and exasperated enemies, and that they were at last reluctantly sacrificed to the urgent demands of the army.* The French general next marched against Acre. But the plague had broken out in the army, and he had no guns suitable for carrying on a siege. The place was ably and obstinately defended by Djezzar Pasha, assisted by an English force commanded by Sir Sidney Smith. Repeated and desperate assaults were made by the attacking forces, but in vain. One day three hundred chosen men, presenting themselves before the French commander, took an oath that they would enter the town or perish in the attempt. They kept their word: not one of them returned. Napoleon was at last under the necessity of abandoning the place. He afterwards said, "If Acre had fallen, I would have changed the face of the world." "My fortune was arrested by a grain of sand;" alluding to some little contingencies which had

prevented his success. The encampment before Acre was broken up on the 21st of May, 1799, and the army commenced its retreat towards Egypt. Nelson having destroyed the French fleet, August, 1798, all communication with Europe was cut off. Bonaparte could hope neither for reinforcements nor supplies. The retreating army reached Cairo about the middle of June. Having learned (July 15) that the Turkish and English fleets had landed an army of 18,000 men at Aboukir, the French commander instantly made preparations to attack them. After a bloody contest, (July 25,) almost all the Turks were either cut to pieces or perished in the sea, into which they had thrown themselves in the hope of reaching their ships. A few who had sought refuge in the fort of Aboukir were compelled to surrender a few days afterwards. Soon after this victory, Napoleon, having heard of the defeats that had recently been sustained by the French armies in Italy, and of the unpopularity of the Directory, at once resolved to return to France. He made preparations for his departure with the utmost secrecy, taking with him only a few of his best and most attached officers. Kleber was left in command of the army of Egypt, now reduced, by disease and war, to less than 20,000 men. Bonaparte, and the officers who accompanied him, embarked (August 22) in two frigates, and, after a long passage and several narrow escapes from the English cruisers, he landed at Fréjus on the 14th of October. He found the French nation thoroughly dissatisfied with the existing government, and disheartened by the recent disasters. Taking advantage of the uncertainty and confusion among the political parties, he contrived to have himself chosen First Consul, with a power little short of absolute. The First Consul was assisted by two other consuls, of whom he had the appointment, and a senate entirely dependent upon his will. This revolution is known as that of the 18th and 19th Brumaire, (9th and 10th of November.) The news of Bonaparte's elevation to the supreme power was received by the French nation with transports of joy. The people were in truth tired of revolutions, and they longed for a government which should possess the ability and the will to maintain itself unmoved against all enemies from abroad and all factions at home. Commercial confidence was at once restored. Many of the royalists and priests who had fled from their native country during the reign of terror were allowed to return; and Christian worship, which had been forbidden under the different revolutionary governments, was again permitted throughout France. The reason Napoleon afterwards gave for having recourse to the Concordat furnishes the key to this new policy: "The restoration of the public worship will give me the hearts of the people." In this he was not deceived. In return for the contemptuous smiles of a comparatively few skeptics, he won the admiration and gratitude of millions in every quarter of the empire. On his return from Egypt, Napoleon found France at war with Austria, England, and Turkey. His first aim, after he felt himself established in his new power, was to restore to the banners of France the prestige which they had lost during his absence. Early in May, 1800, he set out for Italy. On the 14th of June he fought the great battle of Marengo. In the afternoon a large part of the French army was routed, and seemed to be in irretrievable disorder. At this moment Desaix, at the head of an army of reserve, arrived on the field. He observed to Napoleon, "The battle is lost: I suppose all I can do now is to secure your retreat." "By no means," replied the First Consul: "the battle is, I trust, gained. Push forward your column: I will rally the disordered troops in your rear." This order was gallantly obeyed, and what seemed a disastrous defeat was changed into a complete victory; but General Desaix himself fell dead, being shot through the breast in the first charge. Moreau, at the head of the army of the Rhine, had made a scarcely less successful, though a less brilliant, campaign than Napoleon; and Austria was compelled to sue for peace. The conditions were settled by the treaty of Lunéville. Soon after, negotiations with England were begun, and at length the definitive treaty of Amiens was signed, March 27, 1802. A decree was passed, April 26, 1801, granting a general amnesty to all

* Thiers, who will scarcely be accused of hostility to Bonaparte, throws upon him the whole responsibility of this atrocious act, calling it "the only cruel act of his life." (See "Révolution Française," livre xliv.)

emigrants who wished to return to France, on condition that they would take the oath of fidelity to the government. From this amnesty were excepted the leaders of armed bodies of royalists, those who had held rank in the armies of the allies, or had been encouragers of war against France, those who had been guilty of treason to the republic, and those who had belonged to the household of the Bourbon family. Such of their property as had not been sold was ordered to be restored to the emigrants who should avail themselves of the amnesty. Soon after the battle of Marengo, negotiations were begun with the pope for the establishment of a treaty known as the Concordat, of which the principal provisions were, on the one hand, that the Catholic religion should be acknowledged as the national faith, and its services openly performed, subject to such police regulations as the government should deem necessary; and, on the other, that there should be, under the supervision of the pope and of the French government, a new division of the dioceses, that the bishops should take an oath of fidelity to the government, and observe a ritual containing forms of prayer for the consuls; those bishops who should decline to conform to the terms of the treaty were to be removed, and their places filled by the pope on nominations made by the French government. Lastly, the pope renounced all right to dispute or change the sales of church property which had taken place since the Revolution. This important treaty was ratified on the 18th of September, 1801. The measure was received very coldly by the members of the government, and with murmurs of dissatisfaction by the army; but it doubtless contributed immensely towards attaching the mass of the people, especially in the provinces, to Napoleon's government and person. The First Consul next directed his earnest efforts towards the organization of a thorough system of police. This was the more necessary because not only the restraints of religion and morality, but the habit of obedience to authority so influential with the mass of the people, had, to a great extent, lost their power. The secret police was organized under the supervision of Fouché, who at a later period was himself carefully watched by four counsellors of state, (*conseillers d'état,*) appointed for this purpose. The whole nation, from the highest officer under the First Consul to the lowest peasant, was subjected to a system of the strictest espionage, from which even the privacy of domestic life afforded no shelter. In a society thus organized there was little room for men of character or virtue, except perhaps in the army. In the civil government, men of suppleness and address alone were in request. Fear and self-interest, the lowest motives of human action, were the chief springs by which the machinery of government was set or kept in motion. Under these circumstances, the freedom of the press became an impossibility, if not an absurdity. Yet homage was so far paid to liberty that the very restrictions by which she was fettered were enacted in her name. The decree establishing the censorship of the press began with these words: "Pour assurer la liberté de la presse," etc., ("In order to insure the liberty of the press," etc.)

To this period belong the preparation and completion of Napoleon's celebrated Civil Code, by which, even in the judgment of those least favourable to him, he rendered an inestimable service to France. That he might establish an order of nobility based upon merit, Napoleon instituted what he called the "Legion of Honour," designed to embrace all those, whether in the civil or military ranks, who were sufficiently distinguished by their worth or services to the state. Having established his power at home, he next sought to change the form of government in the Cisalpine Republic. Between four and five hundred deputies from that republic were, at the instance of Napoleon, assembled at Lyons for the purpose of drawing up a new constitution. Anticipating the wishes of the First Consul, they adopted a report, inviting him to take upon himself the office of protector, of which their state, being still in its infancy, stood so much in need,—an office which none but himself was capable of filling. He graciously acceded to their wishes, promising them the protection of the strongest nation in Europe. Taking advantage of the political dissensions

that prevailed among the different Swiss cantons, he offered himself as a mediator in their disputes, at the same time enforcing his authority by the presence of a French army, so that from that time forward, so long as his power lasted, Switzerland was a mere dependant of France. The negroes of Saint Domingo, having been given their freedom during the invasion of the island by the Spaniards and English in 1793, and their liberty having been confirmed by the National Convention at Paris, had for some years been governed as citizens of a free and independent state by their able ruler, Toussaint L'Ouverture. In 1801 the First Consul resolved to reduce them again to complete subjection. For this purpose General Leclerc, who had married Napoleon's sister Pauline, was despatched with a fleet and an army of more than 20,000 men. They arrived at Saint Domingo in January, 1802. After a war of great atrocity on both sides, during which the yellow fever was perhaps even more fatal to the French troops than the arms of their enemies, the invaders were all-but exterminated. General Leclerc himself had died of the fever; and his successor, in order to save the feeble remnant of that once fine army, was obliged to surrender at discretion to the English squadron. Meanwhile, Bonaparte had taken possession of the island of Elba and of Parma, and had formally annexed Piedmont to France. These encroachments excited the jealousy of Europe; England, in particular, complained of them as infractions of the treaty of Amiens, and at length, on the 18th of May, 1803, declared war against France, laying an embargo on all the French vessels found in the British ports. Bonaparte retaliated by seizing on all the English who, as travellers, or from whatever cause, happened to be in the French dominions. In the early part of 1804 a conspiracy was detected at Paris among the partisans of the Bourbons. The Duke d'Enghien, grandson of the Prince of Condé, was reported to be in correspondence with the conspirators. Although he was living at Ettenheim, in Baden, on neutral territory, the First Consul ordered him to be arrested. A body of French soldiers entered the territory of Baden, seized the duke in his own château, and conveyed him to the citadel of Strasburg, whence he was taken to the castle of Vincennes, near Paris. After a nominal trial, in which he was not allowed to have any counsel or to call any witnesses, he was condemned to death. He asked for a confessor in his last moments, but was refused. The trial, or rather inquisition, had commenced at midnight; and the next morning, a little after daybreak, the prisoner was shot on the margin of a grave which had been dug even before the sentence of death was pronounced against him.

Napoleon was chosen "Emperor of the French" in May, 1804. About this time he made great preparations for the invasion of England; but he afterwards abandoned the project, and turned all his energies against Austria, who, aided by Russia, had renewed the war. Sweden and England were also members of the coalition against France. Our limits will permit us to do scarcely more than allude to the chief events of the ensuing struggle. The Austrian general Mack was surrounded and compelled to surrender, with above 20,000 men, at Ulm, October 17, 1805. A few days after the surrender of Mack's army, the great naval battle of Trafalgar was fought, resulting in the almost total destruction of the French fleet. The combined Austro-Russian army, consisting of 80,000 men, commanded by the emperor Alexander in person, was defeated with terrible loss in the great battle of Austerlitz, fought on the 2d of December. An armistice was concluded between Napoleon and Alexander, and soon after a treaty of peace with Austria was signed at Presburg. The French emperor, being thus left free to carry out his ambitious schemes, appointed (March, 1806) his brother Joseph King of Naples and Sicily, and in June of that year made his brother Louis King of Holland. Napoleon had previously (May 26, 1805) been crowned King of Italy at Milan. Soon after he annexed the Ligurian Republic (Genoa) to France. Prussia had for some time been a sort of timid ally of France. Napoleon, since his recent successes against Austria and Russia, had begun to treat her with supercilious contempt. The King of Prussia, offended at the tone of Napoleon, had the imprudence to demand that the French troops should be withdrawn from the German territory. The French emperor replied, with contemptuous defiance, that "to provoke the enmity of France was as senseless as to attempt to withstand the waves of the ocean." The battle of Jena, fought October 16, 1806, seemed to justify the arrogant boast of Napoleon, and laid Prussia completely prostrate at the feet of the conqueror. On February 8, 1807, the great battle of Eylau was fought between the armies of France and Russia, with tremendous loss on both sides, though neither could justly claim the victory. Bonaparte, having been reinforced at the battle of Friedland, (June 13,) defeated the Russians, and compelled them to retreat, but without the loss of their baggage or artillery. The treaty of Tilsit between the French and Russian emperors was signed July 7, 1807. Two days afterwards, at the same place, a treaty was signed between France and Prussia. From the time that Bonaparte became First Consul, Spain had been the submissive ally of France ; but, a misunderstanding and dispute having occurred between Charles IV. and his son and heir, the Prince of Asturias, Napoleon made it a pretext for interfering with the internal affairs of that country. The result was that Joseph Bonaparte was removed from the kingdom of Naples and placed on the Spanish throne. This event was followed by a long, obstinate, and most cruel war, which ended only with the downfall of Napoleon in 1814. The French emperor himself had gone to Spain, in order to establish his brother firmly on the throne at Madrid. A despatch from Paris caused him to return with the utmost expedition. Austria was preparing for another war. Napoleon took the field with his usual celerity. After gaining a victory at Eckmühl, and a still more decisive one at Wagram, where 20,000 Austrians were taken prisoners, he made peace (October 14, 1809) with Austria, who was obliged to give up to the conqueror Trieste, Carniola, and a part of Croatia and Galicia. On his return to Paris the French emperor announced to Josephine his purpose of obtaining a divorce ; and an act to that effect was passed on the 16th of December, 1809. The reason given for this step was that Josephine had never borne him any children, and it was necessary, for the interests of the empire, that he should have an heir. Not quite three months from that date his marriage was celebrated at Vienna (March 11, 1810) with Maria Louisa, daughter of the Emperor of Austria. Napoleon was not present, but he was represented in the ceremony by his favourite Berthier. The young bride, accompanied by the Queen of Naples, set out for Paris a few days afterwards.

Although Napoleon's power at this time appeared to be at its greatest height, those who looked beyond the surface might discern not a few elements which were calculated to impair, if not destroy, the stability of that magnificent edifice which he had just succeeded in erecting. In every campaign where he commanded in person he had been successful against the ablest generals and mightiest armies of Europe. His empire extended from Denmark to Naples. The pope, having launched a bull of excommunication against the conqueror of Italy, was seized at midnight in his own palace on the Quirinal by a body of French soldiers, and held a prisoner ; and out of the territories of the Church were formed two French departments. But, while Napoleon sought to extend his sway more and more widely, he neglected to strengthen his empire by any attempts to soothe the irritation or win the affections of the nations whom he had conquered. On the contrary, elated and rendered arrogant by his unparalleled successes, he appears to have aimed at nothing less than to completely break the spirit, as he had broken the armies, of those who had opposed him. The instructions which he wrote to his brothers Joseph and Louis reveal his temper and policy, and show us clearly why such a power as his could not, in the nature of things, be durable. Joseph, then King of Naples, was desirous of governing his subjects mildly, and, if possible, of gaining their affections. Napoleon wrote to him, "Vos proclamations ne sentent assez le maître. . . . Quel amour voulez-vous qu'ait pour vous un peuple pour qui vous n'avez rien fait ?" ("Your proclamations have not enough of the tone of a master. What love do you expect a people for whom you have done nothing, will have for you ?") and he ends with virtually recommending his brother not to rely upon their love, but upon their fears and his own power. To Louis, at that time King of Holland, he wrote, reproving him for some indulgence he had shown the people, "Never forget that your *first* duty is towards ME, your *second* towards FRANCE : all your other duties, even those towards the people whom I have called you to govern, must be subordinate to these." Of all the European powers, England alone continued to offer any effectual resistance to the encroachments of Napoleon ; but her resources seemed as nothing in comparison with those of the conqueror. To crown the good fortune which appeared ever to attend him, on the 20th of March, 1811, Maria Louisa bore him a son, who received the title of "King of Rome ;" Rome being the second capital of his vast empire. (See REICHSTADT, DUKE OF.) But, while his extended dominions excited their jealousy and fear, the haughty and imperious tone which he assumed deeply wounded the pride of those nations whom he had not yet subdued. A coolness gradually took place between him and Alexander. He had demanded of Sweden and Russia that they should strictly enforce his decrees prohibiting all commerce with the English. Both nations had evaded his demands. Napoleon at first contented himself with simply making complaints to Russia ; but Sweden, being a far less formidable power, was treated with less ceremony. His armed vessels in the Baltic captured a great number of Swedish merchantmen. These were confiscated, on the ground of their being engaged in the contraband trade with Britain. To resist these aggressions, Sweden signed a treaty of alliance with Russia in the early part of 1812. Then followed the memorable campaign of 1812. Napoleon approached the confines of Russia with an army of about 480,000 men. After the great battles of Smolensk, August 16, and Borodino, September 7, Napoleon entered Moscow, and took up his residence in the Kremlin, the ancient palace of the Russian emperors. Soon after a fire broke out, and was spread by the winds to every part of the city, all efforts to extinguish it being in vain. It is still a disputed point whether Moscow was purposely set on fire by the Russians, or whether the destruction of the city was the result of accident. But, whatever may have been the cause, the effect was fatal to the power of Napoleon. He had designed to take up his winter-quarters in Russia, but the conflagration of Moscow made it necessary for him to retreat ; and, the winter having set in much earlier than usual, nearly the whole of his magnificent army were either taken prisoners, or else perished in battle or with hunger and cold. At Smorgoni, on the 5th of December, Napoleon took leave of his generals, to whom he committed the wreck of his grand army, and, accompanied by Caulaincourt, set out in a sledge for Warsaw and Paris. He reached the French capital on the 18th of December. The Russian historian Bootoorlin (Buturlin) states the total loss of the French in the campaign of 1812 at 450,000 men ; of which number, according to his estimate, 125,000 were killed in battle, 132,000 died of fatigue, hunger, and cold, and 193,000, including 3000 officers and forty-eight generals, were taken prisoners. More than nine hundred pieces of cannon belonging to the grand army fell into the hands of the Russians.

On his arrival in Paris, Napoleon began immediately to prepare for another campaign. By fresh conscriptions, and by recalling from distant places all the troops that could be spared, he succeeded in assembling on the German frontier, in the spring of 1813, an army of 350,000 men. He won in May the indecisive victories of Lutzen and Bautzen over the combined Russo-Prussian army. Austria at first stood neutral, and offered her mediation ; but, as it was not accepted, she at length, in August, joined the allies. Napoleon might now perceive the fatal mistake he had made not merely in neglecting to use the means in his power to attach the conquered nations to his person and government, but in recklessly wounding and outraging their feelings of national pride and patriotism. When the French soldiers first entered Germany, not a few of the people seem to have regarded them as liberators, and a large proportion were almost indifferent as to the success of either army; but, after experiencing the insolence and oppression of the French rule, the mass of the population had become so exasperated that the moment there appeared to be some reasonable prospect of throwing off the yoke, they arose as with one mind against their oppressors, in unconquerable numbers. The war which ended in the downfall of Napoleon was commonly called in Germany "der Volkskrieg," ("the people's war,"*) because it was not so much a contest of princes to recover their ancestral dominions, as a struggle of the people to regain the liberty which, imperfect as it was, they had enjoyed under their German rulers. In most of the battles which Napoleon fought during the campaign of 1813, his transcendent military genius gave him the superiority over his foes. But the latter were becoming stronger every moment; and at last, in the fatal battle of Leipsic, about 10,000 of his Saxon allies left him in a body and went over to his enemies. After a disastrous retreat, he crossed the Rhine with only about 70,000 men out of the army of 350,000 with which he had entered Germany in the spring.

The French people had at last become weary of the long and ruinous wars which they were compelled to wage under Napoleon. The legislative body, though hitherto it had seemed to be little more than a pageant designed to add dignity to the imperial court, now ventured to advise the emperor to take the necessary steps for obtaining peace, so far as this could be done consistently with the honour and welfare of the country. A new conscription, however, was ordered; but France had become completely exhausted, and Napoleon was under the necessity of again taking the field, with an army of less than 80,000 men. After the most extraordinary display on his part of courage, promptitude, and military skill, against desperate odds, the allies at last succeeded in taking possession of Paris, on the 31st of March, 1814. Soon after he signed an act of abdication, and retired to the island of Elba, of which he was to have the sovereignty, with the title of emperor, and an annual allowance of six millions of francs, to be paid by France. He remained in Elba only about ten months. During the latter part of his sojourn on the island, he kept up a correspondence with the disaffected parties in France. On the 15th of February, 1815, he left Elba, and landed (March 1) in France, near Fréjus. His journey to Paris was a triumphal procession. The Bourbons were everywhere deserted by the troops. Marshal Ney, who had been sent by Louis XVIII. to check Napoleon's progress, went over to his old commander. Napoleon was received in Paris as the Emperor of France, on condition of his reigning as a constitutional sovereign. Early in June, having assembled an army of about 125,000 men, he hastened to meet the allied Prussian and English armies in Flanders. He repulsed Blücher at Ligny, (June 16,) and forced him to retreat with considerable loss. On the 18th of June the battle of Waterloo was fought between the French army, under Napoleon, and that of the allies, commanded by Wellington. We shall not attempt to give a particular account of this great conflict, as the most contradictory statements are found even among those who are regarded as the best authorities on the subject. Suffice to say that the opposing forces were probably nearly equal, each comprising about 75,000 men. The English troops, however, constituted less than one-half of Wellington's army. The battle began between eleven and twelve o'clock, and continued with the utmost fury till near nightfall, when, the Prussian general Blücher having come up with fresh troops, the French were defeated at every point. The loss of the allies at Waterloo is admitted by Wellington to have been "immense;" but the army of Napoleon was irretrievably ruined. After the rout once began, the French fled in the utmost confusion, leaving cannon, baggage, and everything in the hands of the victors. Napoleon seems still to have entertained hopes of re-

sisting his enemies; but France had become utterly exhausted with her long contest against the combined powers of Europe, and was at last thoroughly weary of war. The Chamber of Representatives at Paris declared itself permanent, and demanded the abdication of the emperor. When Lucien Bonaparte spoke to them of the services which his brother had formerly rendered to the state, La Fayette insisted that the three millions of Frenchmen whom Napoleon had sacrificed upon the altar of his ambition should not be left out of the account. "We have followed your brother," he said, "over the sands of Africa and the frozen deserts of Russia: the bones of Frenchmen scattered over every part of the globe attest our long fidelity." The representatives remained resolute. Some of them declared that there was but one man between France and peace, and demanded that he should be sacrificed to the common good. On the 22d of June Napoleon signed his second abdication. Thus ended the history of the Hundred Days, (the period between the date of his resuming power after leaving Elba, and that of his final abdication.) He then went to Rochefort, for the purpose of embarking for America; but, finding that there was little hope of escaping the British cruisers, he voluntarily gave himself up to Captain Maitland, of the British line-of-battle ship Bellerophon. He was, according to an agreement among the allied powers, who alleged that the peace of the world required that he should not again be allowed to regain his liberty, carried to Saint Helena, having been removed from the Bellerophon to the Northumberland, commanded by Sir George Cockburn. He reached Saint Helena on the 15th of October, 1815. After an imprisonment of nearly six years, he died, of cancer of the stomach, May 5, 1821.

There has probably never been in the history of the world any man who has combined those attributes of intellect and will which confer upon their possessor transcendent military and administrative power, in so high a degree as Napoleon. It has been said, not without reason, that as a general Cæsar gave proof of greater originality of genius, inasmuch as he never repeated the same stratagem or mode of warfare, but always had a fresh invention for every new emergency. But, even if it be admitted that in fertility of invention Napoleon was inferior to Cæsar, it may, on the other hand, be safely affirmed that not only in his power of combination,— of embracing in one harmonious plan a great number of distinct and independent elements,—but also of watching over and directing at one and the same time the complicated movements of mighty armies, the tone of the public press, the operations of foreign and domestic commerce, in addition to the endless intricacies and details of his system of police, and the great measures of his government, not merely in France, but through the whole extent of his vast empire,—he was unequalled by any commander or sovereign that ever lived.

But, whatever may be thought of the genius of Napoleon as compared with that of other great commanders, it cannot be denied that in some respects his career was the most extraordinary, and his destiny the most wonderful, of any recorded in the annals of mankind. Other rulers may have wielded a power as extensive and even more absolute; but they cannot, like Napoleon, boast of having been the sole architects of their own fortunes,—of having risen, like him, from an absolutely private station to the highest pinnacle of greatness. Cyrus and Alexander inherited each, as his birthright, a powerful kingdom; Hannibal and Cæsar were respectively the recognized representatives of high and influential families. Napoleon, on the contrary, besides his energy and his genius, possessed not a single advantage that might not have fallen to the lot of the humblest citizen of France. No other sovereign of whom history makes mention ever maintained himself, even for a single day, against such a combination of gigantic powers; yet Napoleon not only maintained himself, but for twelve years was constantly adding to his dominions in the face of an opposition such as was never before or since arrayed against any single ruler. And he fell at last, so to speak, by his own hand. He seems to have possessed every intellectual endowment except wisdom, and every form of power except

* It was likewise often called "der Freiheitskrieg," ("the war of freedom.")

morai power. His ambition, and the desire to exert his imperious will, often led him to embrace measures which his cooler judgment disapproved.* His invasion of Spain was a remarkable instance of this. No one saw more clearly than he the difficulties and dangers to be encountered in such a war. In a letter addressed to Murat, March 29, 1808, he says, "Do not imagine that you have only to make a display of your troops in order to conquer Spain. . . . They may raise levies against us *en masse* which will render the war eternal. I have at present partisans, but if I show myself in the character of a conqueror I cannot retain one of them." Again, with prophetic forecast, he says, "If war once break out, ALL IS LOST." Yet, in spite of what he so clearly foresaw, he adopted a course which rendered war inevitable. He afterwards said, bitterly, "That wretched war was my ruin : it divided my forces, multiplied the necessity of my efforts, and *injured my character for morality.*" Having lost his reputation for morality, his subjects and allies ceased to have any confidence in his word, and his vast empire, no longer cemented by "that faith which binds the moral elements of the world together," was already beginning to crumble, when his fatal campaign in Russia annihilated his grand army and involved him in irretrievable ruin. With all his sagacity, he committed the stupendous error of supposing that he could, in the nineteenth century, hold Europe in subjection by the mere force of his intellect and will, without the exercise of any strictly moral attributes, and without laying the foundations of his power in the affections of the people.

Among the writings or productions of Napoleon may be mentioned a "History of Corsica," ("Histoire de la Corse,") which having been shown by the Abbé Raynal to Mirabeau, the latter observed that this little history seemed to him "to indicate a genius of the highest order." Napoleon's Correspondence, extending to twelve volumes or more, has recently been published in Paris, by order of the present emperor. But his most important contribution to literature is the work entitled "Memoirs towards the History of France under Napoleon," etc., ("Mémoires pour servir à l'Histoire de la France sous Napoléon," etc.,) dictated by him at Saint Helena, and written by his generals Gourgaud and Montholon, published in nine volumes 8vo, Paris, 1830. To these may be added his "Military Maxims," ("Maximes de Guerre,") prepared by General Husson, Paris, 1830, and the "Religious Conversations" ("Conversations religieuses") of Napoleon, edited by Beauterne, Paris, 1841. We should fail to do justice to the literary labours of Napoleon did we omit to mention his important contributions to the public journals during the consulship and empire. As soon as he became First Consul, he selected the "Moniteur" to be the official organ of his government, and he became, so to speak, its chief editor ; for if he did not dictate he at least inspired the greater number of the articles that appeared in its columns. In it were published, from time to time, such vindications or explanations of his policy, and such statements respecting the measures of his domestic and foreign administration, as he wished the world to receive. It is almost needless to remark that the truth or accuracy of those statements and explanations was never regarded by the imperial editor as a point of vital importance, the great object being to produce the requisite impression upon the mind of France and of Europe.

Those who desire fuller information respecting the life and character of Napoleon may consult, besides the publications above referred to, the following works :

Biographie des premières Années de Napoléon, etc., (Biography of the First Years of Napoleon,) by the BARON DE COSTON, 2 vols. 8vo, Paris, 1840.

Mémoires sur l'Enfance et la Jeunesse de Napoléon jusqu'à l'Age de vingt-trois Ans, (Memoirs relating to the Infancy and Youth of Napoleon until the Age of Twenty-Three Years,) by T. NASICA, 1 vol. 8vo, Paris, 1852.

Souvenirs de la Jeunesse de Napoléon, (Recollections of the Youth of Napoleon,) published in the "Revue des Deux Mondes," March, 1842.

L'Enfance de Napoléon depuis sa Naissance jusqu'à sa Sortie de l'École militaire, (The Childhood of Napoleon from his Birth until his Departure from the Military School,) by the CHEVALIER DE BEAUTERNE, 1 vol. 12mo, Paris, 1846.

Mémoires anecdotiques sur l'Intérieur du Palais et sur quelques Événements de l'Empire, etc., (Anecdotical Memoirs relating to the Interior of the Palace and to some Events of the Empire, etc.,) by L. F. J. DE BAUSSET, prefect of the palace, 4 vols. 8vo, Paris, 1827-29.

Mémoires de Constant, premier Valet-de-chambre de l'Empereur, etc., (Memoirs of Constant, first Valet-de-chambre of the Emperor, etc.,) 6 vols. 8vo, Paris, 1830.

Mémorial de Sainte-Hélène, etc., by the COMTE DE LAS CASES, 8 vols. 8vo, Paris, 1823.

Voice from Saint Helena, by DR. BARRY O'MEARA.

Mémoires du Docteur Antommarchi, ou les derniers Moments de Napoléon, (Memoirs of Dr. Antommarchi, or the Last Moments of Napoleon,) 2 vols. 8vo, Paris, 1825.

Récits de la Captivité de l'Empereur Napoléon, etc., (Account of the Captivity of the Emperor Napoleon, etc.,) by GENERAL MONTHOLON, 2 vols. 8vo, Paris, 1847.

History of the Captivity of Napoleon on the Island of Saint Helena, from the Official Documents and Unpublished Manuscript of Sir Hudson Lowe, by W. FORSYTH.

CHABOULON's Mémoires.

Vie politique et militaire de Napoléon, (Political and Military Life of Napoleon,) by JOMINI, 4 vols. 8vo, Paris, 1827.

Memoirs of Count Segur, 3 vols. 8vo, Paris, 1827.

Mémoires du Duc de Rovigo, (Memoirs of Savary, Duke of Rovigo,) 8 vols. 8vo, Paris, 1828.

Memoirs of Bourrienne, 10 vols. 8vo, Paris, 1829.

Bourrienne et ses Erreurs, etc., (Bourrienne and his Errors, etc.,) 2 vols. 8vo, Paris, 1830.

Mémoires sur les Cent Jours, (Memoirs in relation to the Hundred Days,) by BENJAMIN CONSTANT, 1 vol. 8vo, Paris, 1829.

Memoirs and Souvenirs of the Comte Lavalette, 2 vols. 8vo, Paris, 1831.

LORD HOLLAND's Diplomatic Souvenirs, etc.

Memoirs of the Duke of Ragusa, (Marshal Marmont,) 9 vols. 8vo, Paris, 1857.

Histoire générale de Napoléon Bonaparte, de sa Vie privée et publique, etc., (General History of Napoleon Bonaparte, of his Private and Public Life, etc.,) by A. C. THIBAUDEAU, 5 vols. 8vo, Paris, 1827.

Le Consulat et l'Empire, (The Consulate and the Empire,) by A. C. THIBAUDEAU, 8 vols. 8vo, Paris, 1834-35. (This work is especially complete in regard to the civil history of France under Napoleon.)

Histoire de France sous Napoléon, etc., (History of France under Napoleon, etc.,) by LOUIS PIERRE ÉDOUARD BIGNON, 14 vols. 8vo, Paris, 1829-50. (Very complete in regard to the foreign relations of France during the period referred to.)

Histoire de la République et de l'Empire, (History of the Republic and of the Empire,) by FÉLIX WOUTERS, 1 vol. 4to, Brussels, 1849.

Histoire de la Révolution Française, (History of the French Revolution,) by LOUIS ADOLPHE THIERS, 10 vols. 8vo, Paris, 1823-27.

Histoire du Consulat et de l'Empire, (History of the Consulate and of the Empire,) by LOUIS ADOLPHE THIERS, 20 vols. 8vo, Paris, 1845-62.

ALISON's History of Europe, from the Commencement of the French Revolution to the Battle of Waterloo, 10 vols. 8vo, 1833-42.

Life of Napoleon Bonaparte, by SIR WALTER SCOTT, 9 vols. 8vo, London, 1827.

Histoire de Napoléon, by M. DE NORVINS, 4 vols. 8vo, Paris, 1827.

Histoire de Napoléon, by ELIAS REGNAULT, 4 vols. 12mo, Paris, 1846.

Histoire de Napoléon, de sa Famille, etc., (History of Napoleon, of his Family, etc.,) by M. E. BÉGIN, 5 vols. 8vo, Paris, 1853-54.

Histoire de Napoléon, by ABEL HUGO, 1 vol. 8vo, Paris, 1833.

Histoire des deux Restaurations, etc., (History of the Two Restorations, etc.,) by A. DE VAULABELLE, 6 vols. 8vo, Paris, 1844-47.

Histoire de Napoléon, by BARON MARTIN, (DE GREY,) 3 vols. 8vo, Paris, 1858. (A work of rare merit.)

Histoire de la Restauration, (History of the Restoration,) by LAMARTINE, 6 vols. 8vo, Paris, 1851-53.

Souvenirs contemporains d'Histoire et de Littérature, (Contemporaneous Recollections of History and Literature,) by A. F. VILLEMAIN, 2 vols. 8vo, Paris, 1857.

Victoires et Conquêtes, Désastres, Revers et Guerres civiles des Français de 1792 à 1815, (Victories and Conquests, Disasters, Reverses, and Civil Wars of the French from 1792 to 1815,) by a Society of Military Men and Men of Letters, 27 vols. 8vo, the first of which was issued in 1818.

Histoire de Napoléon et de la grande Armée pendant l'Année 1812, (History of Napoleon and of the Grand Army during the Year 1812,) by the COMTE DE SEGUR, 16th edition, 2 vols. 8vo, Paris, 1852.

Histoire de l'Expédition de Russie, (History of the Campaign in Russia,) by the MARQUIS OF CHAMBRAY, 3 vols. 8vo, Paris, 1838.

Les derniers Jours de la grande Armée, (The Last Days of the Grand Army,) 2 vols. 8vo, Paris, 1847.

Mémoires pour servir à l'Histoire militaire sous le Directoire, le Consulat et l'Empire, (Memoirs towards the Military History [of France] under the Directory, the Consulate, and the Empire,) by MARSHAL SAINT-CYR, 4 vols. 8vo, Paris, 1831.

Mémoires du Maréchal Ney, published by his Family, 2 vols. 8vo, Paris, 1833.

Among the smaller publications relating to Napoleon, the reader is particularly referred to DR. W. E. CHANNING's able and eloquent review of the life and character of that extraordinary man. Although very severe, it has the merit of being (unlike many of the works published in France and England) totally free from any partisan or national animosity.

See also the article "Napoléon Ier" in the "Nouvelle Biographie Générale," which contains a very complete bibliography of Napoleon's works and of those publications which relate to his life and history, from which the foregoing bibliographical list is principally taken.

* The writer of the excellent notice of Napoleon I. in the "Nouvelle Biographie Générale" says, "En son génie il y avait plus de volonté que de raison," ("In his genius there was more of will than of reason.") That notice, it may be remarked, though extremely favourable, not to say partial, to Napoleon, contains perhaps the best résumé of his policy that has yet appeared.

Bonaparte, (NAPOLÉON JOSEPH CHARLES PAUL,) commonly styled PRINCE NAPOLEON, a son of Jérôme, King of Westphalia, by his second wife, was born at Trieste in September, 1822. His features are said to present a very striking likeness to those of his uncle Napoleon I. He passed his youth in various foreign countries until the Revolution of 1848, and was then permitted to enter France. He was elected to the Constituent and Legislative Assemblies, in which he voted with the democrats. In 1852 he was recognized as a French prince, and heir to the throne in case of the failure of issue of Napoleon III. He commanded a division in the Crimean war, (1854,) and was appointed minister of Algeria and the colonies in 1858. In 1859 he married Clotilde, a daughter of Victor Emmanuel of Sardinia, and commanded a corps in the Italian campaign against Austria. He made in 1862 two eloquent speeches, in which he advocated Italian nationality, the principles of the Revolution of 1789, etc., and opposed the temporal power of the pope. About the end of 1862 he visited the United States.

Bonaparte, (PAULINE or MARIE PAULINE,) Princesse Borghese, a sister of Napoleon I., born at Ajaccio in 1780. She was the most beautiful of the family, but was inferior to Élisa in talents. In 1801 she was married to General Leclerc, whom she accompanied to Saint Domingo in 1802. Having lost her first husband by death, she became the wife of Prince Camillo Borghese of Rome, in August, 1803. This prince was a man of feeble character, and soon separated from her. She was prodigal and voluptuous, but is praised for generosity to the poor. Canova made a statue of her, which is said to resemble the Venus of Praxiteles. She died at Florence in 1825.

Bonaparte, (PIERRE NAPOLÉON,) the third son of Lucien, was born at Rome in 1815. After many adventures in America, Italy, and Greece, he became in 1848 a republican member of the French Constituent Assembly. After the *coup d'état* of 1851 he retired to private life.

Bon'ar, (HORATIUS,) D.D., a sacred lyric poet of great merit, born in Edinburgh in 1808, published in 1856 "Hymns of Faith and Hope," and a second series of the same in 1861.

See CLEVELAND, "Literature of the 19th Century," new ed., 1866.

Bonarelli della Rovere, bo-nä-rel'lee del'lä ro-vä'rä, (GUIDUBALDO, gwe-doo-bäl'do,) an Italian poet and *littérateur*, born at Urbino in 1563, was the author of "Filli di Sciro," (1607,) a pastoral, which obtained great success and was translated into French, English, German, and Spanish. Died in 1608.

See F. RONCONI, "Vie de G. Bonarelli della Rovere."

Bonarelli della Rovere, (PIETRO,) an Italian dramatist, son of Prospero, noticed below, lived about 1650.

Bonarelli della Rovere, (PROSPERO,) an Italian poet and dramatist, brother of Guidubaldo, noticed above, born about 1588; died in 1659.

Bonasoni, bo-nä-so'nee, or **Bonasone,** bo-nä-so'nä, (GIULIO,) an Italian painter and engraver, born at Bologna, lived about 1540–72. He is supposed to have been a pupil of Sabbatini. His engravings after Michael Angelo, Raphael, and Titian possess great merit.

See GEORGE CUMBERLAND, "Some Anecdotes of the Life of J. Bonasoni," 1793.

Bonassieux, bo'nä'se-uh', (JEAN MARIE,) a French sculptor, was born at La Panissière in 1810. He obtained medals of the first class in 1844 and 1855.

Bonati, bo-nä'tee, (GIOVANNI,) an Italian historical painter of high reputation, born at Ferrara about 1635. He worked in Rome. Died in 1681.

Bonati, Bonato, bo-nä'to, or **Bonatti,** (GUIDO,) an Italian astrologer, born at Florence; died in 1596.

See BONCOMPAGNI, "Della Vita, etc. di Guido Bonati," 1851.

Bonati, (TEODORO MASSIMO,) an Italian mathematician, physician, and scientific writer, born near Ferrara in 1724. He became professor of mechanics and hydraulics at Ferrara. Died in 1820.

Bonaventura, bo-nä-vĕn-too'rä, (FEDERIGO,) an Italian scientific writer, born at Ancona in 1555; died in 1602.

Bonaventura, SAINT, [Fr. BONAVENTURE, bo'nä'-vôN'tüR',](GIOVANNI di Fidenza—de fe-dĕn'zä,) an eminent scholastic theologian, born at Bagnarea, in Italy, in 1221, was styled "the Seraphic Doctor." He became suc-

cessively professor of theology in Paris, (1253,) general of the order of Franciscans, Bishop of Albano, (1273,) and cardinal, (1274.) Among his principal writings are a "Life of Saint Francis," (in Latin,) and a work entitled "Progress of the Mind towards God," ("Itinerarium Mentis in Deum.") He is regarded by the Franciscans as the greatest scholiast of their order; and Dante has given him a place in his "Paradiso." Died in 1274. He was canonized in 1482 by Sixtus IV.

See VOSSIUS, "De Historicis Latinis;" J. C. BOULE, "Histoire de la Vie de Saint-Bonaventure," 1747; IGNAZ A. FESSLER, "Bonaventura's mystische Nächte oder Leben und Meinungen desselben,' 1807.

Bonaventure de Saint-Amable, bo'nä'vôN'tüR' deh sâNt'ä'mäb'l', a French Carmelite monk, wrote a "Life of Saint Martial," (1685.)

Bonavino. See FRANCHI.

Boncenne, bôN'sĕn', (PIERRE,) a French jurist, born at Poitiers in 1775, published "The Theory of Civil Procedure," (4 vols., 1828.) Died in 1840.

Boncerf, bôN'sĕRf', (CLAUDE JOSEPH,) a French *littérateur*, born in Franche-Comté in 1724; died in 1811.

Boncerf, (PIERRE FRANÇOIS,) a French publicist and economist, born in Franche-Comté about 1745. He wrote, besides other works, an argument against feudal privileges, (1776,) which attracted much attention and was translated into many languages. Died in 1794.

Bonchamp, de, deh bôN'shôN', (CHARLES MELCHIOR ARTUS,) a French royalist general, born in the province of Anjou in 1759. He distinguished himself in the Vendean war, and was mortally wounded at Chollet in 1793. By his dying words he saved the lives of five thousand prisoners whom his soldiers were about to massacre.

See CHAUVEAU et DUSSIEUX, "Vie de Bonchamp," 1817.

Bonciario, bon-chä're-o, (MARCANTONIO,) an Italian writer, born near Perugia in 1555; died in 1616.

Boncompagni, bôn-kom-pän'yee, (BALDASSARE,) one of the most eminent Italian *literati* of the present age, born at Rome in 1821, inherited a large fortune. He is a liberal patron of learning, and has published a number of biographies and other works.

Boncore, bôn-ko'rä, (TOMMASO,) an Italian physician and jurist, lived about 1620.

Boncuore, bôn-koo-o'rä, (GIOVANNI BATTISTA,) an Italian historical painter, born about 1645; died in 1699.

Bond, (GEORGE PHILLIPS,) an American astronomer, son of William Cranch Bond, was born at Dorchester, Massachusetts, in 1825. He graduated at Harvard College about 1845, and aided his father in the observatory at Cambridge. He acquired a high reputation as an observer, and wrote several astronomical works, among which are a "Treatise on the Construction of the Rings of Saturn," and "Elements of the Orbits of Hyperion and the Satellite of Neptune." Died in 1865.

Bond, (JOHN,) an English scholar, born in Somersetshire in 1550, wrote commentaries on Horace and Persius. Died in 1612.

See WOOD, "Athenæ Oxonienses."

Bond, (OLIVER,) an Irish revolutionist, born in 1720, was associated with Wolfe Tone and others in the rebellion of 1797. He was arrested in 1798, and was soon after found dead in his prison.

Bond, (THOMAS,) an American physician, born in Maryland in 1712. He practised in Philadelphia with distinction, and delivered the first clinical lectures in the Pennsylvania Hospital. He was associated with Franklin, Bartram, and others in a literary society. Died in 1784.

See THACHER, "Medical Biography."

Bond, (THOMAS EMERSON,) an American physician and Methodist minister, born in Baltimore in 1782. He practised medicine in his native city, and obtained a chair in the Medical College of Maryland. He was for many years a local preacher among the Methodists, and acquired distinction as a defender of Episcopal Methodism during the controversy which resulted in the organization of the Methodist Protestant Church. He edited "The Christian Advocate and Journal" for many years. Died in 1856.

Bond, (WILLIAM CRANCH,) an American astronomer, born at Portland, Maine, in 1789 or 1790. He was a watchmaker in early life. In 1838 he was appointed by the government to make observations in connection with the exploring expedition sent to the South Sea. He became director of the observatory of Harvard University about 1840. He gained distinction by his observations on Saturn and the fixed stars, and by his operations in celestial photography. Died in 1859. He and his son discovered a satellite of Neptune and the eighth satellite of Saturn.

Bondam, bon'dăm, (PIETER,) a Dutch jurist, and professor of law at Utrecht, born at Campen in 1727; died in 1800.

Bonde, bon'deh, (GUSTAF,) COUNT, a Swedish savant, born at Stockholm in 1682, became chancellor of the University of Upsal. He died in 1764, leaving "Memoirs of Sweden in the Reign of Frederick I.," (in manuscript.)

See D. TILAS, "Åminnelse-Tal öfver G. Bonde," 1766.

Bondi, bon'dee, (CLEMENTE,) an Italian poet and Jesuit, born in the duchy of Parma in 1742, became professor of history and literature at Vienna in 1815. He translated into Italian verse Virgil's "Æneid," "Georgics," and "Bucolics." His version of the "Æneid" is considered one of the best in the Italian language. He also translated Ovid's "Metamorphoses." Among his original works are odes, epigrams, idyls, satires, and didactic poems. His style is commended as noble, simple, and refined. Died in Vienna in 1821.

See TIPALDO, "Biografia degli Italiani illustri;" A. PEZZANA, "Intorno a C. Bondi, Epistola," 1821.

Bondioli, bon-de-o'lee, (PIETRO ANTONIO,) a distinguished physician and medical writer, born in Corfù in 1765, became professor of materia medica at Bologna, (1803.) Died in 1808.

See MARIO PIERI, "Elogio di P. A. Bondioli," 1810.

Bondt, bont, (NIKOLAAS,) a Dutch scholar, born at Voorburg in 1732, wrote a "History of the Confederation of the United Provinces," (1756,) and other works. Died in 1792.

Bondy, de, deh bŏn'de', (PIERRE MARIE **Taillepied**—tāl'pe-å' or tȧ'ye-pe-å',) COMTE, born in Paris in 1766, became chamberlain to the emperor Napoleon in 1805. He was afterwards created count of the empire and member of the state council, and in 1816 was elected to the Chamber of Deputies. Died in 1847.

Bone, (HENRY,) a celebrated English enamel-painter, born at Truro, in Cornwall, in 1755. He became an academician in 1811, and was appointed enamel-painter successively to George III., George IV., and William IV. Among his master-pieces may be named "Bacchus and Ariadne," after Titian; a "Virgin," after Raphael; and a collection of eighty-five portraits of eminent persons in the reign of Elizabeth. Died in 1834.

Bonefons. See BONNEFONS.

Bonelli, bo-nel'lee, (BENEDETTO,) an Italian theologian, born near Trent in 1704.

Bonelli, (FRANCESCO ANDREA,) a naturalist and scientific writer, born in Piedmont in 1784, became professor of natural history at Turin in 1809. Died in Turin in 1830.

See TIPALDO, "Biografia degli Italiani illustri."

Bonelli, (GIORGIO,) an Italian physician and botanist, whose principal work, the "Roman Garden," ("Hortus Romanus," 8 vols. fol., 1772,) has 800 coloured plates.

Boner, bo'ner, [Lat. BONE'RIUS,] (ULRICH,) a German fabulist, who lived in the fourteenth century and wrote a collection of a hundred fables, entitled "The Jewel," ("Der Edelstein," 1461.)

See LONGFELLOW's "Poets and Poetry of Europe."

Bonet, bo-nĕt', (JUAN PABLO,) a Spanish philanthropist, who lived about 1590–1630, published a work on the instruction of deaf-mutes, (Madrid, 1620.)

Bonet, (THÉOPHILE.) See BONNET.

Bonet de Lates, bo'nȧ' deh lȧt, a French physician and astrologer, of Jewish extraction, born about 1480.

Bonfadio, bon-fȧ'de-o, (JACOPO,) born near Salo, became professor of philosophy at Genoa in 1545. He wrote a history of the republic of Genoa, ("Annalium Genuentium," 1528 to 1550,) which was translated into Italian. He was executed in 1550, on a charge of having libelled several distinguished persons in his history. He left poems, which are highly commended.

See MAZZUCHELLI, "Vita di J. Bonfadio," 1746.

Bonfante, bon-fȧn'tȧ, (ANGELO MATTEO,) an Italian poet and naturalist, born at Palermo; died in 1676.

Bonfiglio, bŏn-fēl'yo, or **Buonfigli,** boo-on-fēl'yee, (BENEDETTO,) an able Italian painter, born at Perugia about 1420, is said to have been the master of Perugino. Died about 1500.

Bonfini, bon-fee'nee, (ANTONIO,) an Italian *littérateur*, born at Ascoli in 1427. He was patronized by Matthias Corvinus, King of Hungary, at whose request he wrote a "History of Hungary," in Latin. Died in 1502.

See BAYLE, "Historical and Critical Dictionary;" VOSSIUS, "De Historicis Latinis."

Bonfos, bŏn'fos', (MANAHEM,) a learned Jew of Perpignan, in France, published a book of definitions in Hebrew, (1567,) explaining scientific and technical terms.

Bonfrère, bŏn'frair', [Lat. BONFRE'RIUS,] (JACQUES,) a Flemish Jesuit and Hebrew scholar, born at Dinant in 1573, was professor of theology and Hebrew at Douai. He wrote valuable commentaries, in Latin, on the Pentateuch and other books of the Scriptures. Died in 1643.

See SWEERT, "Athenæ Belgicæ."

Bongars, bŏn'gȧr', (JACQUES,) a learned French Calvinist, born at Orléans in 1546, was employed by Henry IV. in several important negotiations. He wrote "Epistles," and other works, in Latin, which are admired for the elegance of their style. Died in 1612.

See BAYLE, "Historical and Critical Dictionary."

Bongars, de, deh bŏn'gȧr', (JEAN FRANÇOIS MARIE,) BARON, born in the department of Lower Seine in 1758, served in several campaigns of the Revolution, and was appointed general of division in 1812. He translated into French the "Military Institutes" of Vegetius, (1772.) Died about 1820.

Bongarten, bon'gar'ten, (ANICHIUS,) a German soldier of fortune, lived about 1380, and served under several Italian princes.

See SISMONDI, "Histoire des Républiques Italiennes."

Bongiovanni, bon-jo-vȧn'nee, [Lat. BONJOHAN'NES,] (ANTONIO,) an Italian scholar, born near Verona in 1712, published editions of several classics, and in conjunction with Zanetti, librarian of Saint Mark at Venice, completed a catalogue of the manuscripts in that library.

Bongo, bon'go, [Lat. BUN'GUS,] sometimes written **Bonges,** (PIETRO,) an Italian ecclesiastic and scholar, born at Bergamo; died in 1601.

Bon'ham, (MILLEDGE L.,) an American general, born in South Carolina about 1815, was a member of Congress from 1856 to 1860. At the battle of Bull Run, July 21, 1861, he commanded a brigade under Beauregard. He was elected Governor of South Carolina in January, 1863.

Bonheur, bo'nUR', (AUGUSTE,) brother of Rosa Bonheur, born at Bordeaux in 1824. He has painted landscapes, portraits, etc.

Bonheur, (ISIDORE,) a French sculptor, brother of the preceding, born at Bordeaux in 1827. Among his favourite subjects are horses and cattle.

Bonheur, (ROSA,) a celebrated French painter of animals, born at Bordeaux in 1822, was instructed in drawing by her father, an artist of talent. Her principal studies, however, were from living models, which she represented with admirable skill and fidelity. Having previously executed several pieces of great merit, she exhibited in 1850 "The Nivernais Ploughing," ("Labourage Nivernais,") which is esteemed her masterpiece and has obtained a place in the gallery of the Luxembourg. Among her other works may be named "The Horse-Fair," "The Three Musketeers," and "Cows and Sheep in a Hollow Road."

Boni, bo'nee, (GIACOMO ANTONIO,) an Italian fresco-painter, born at Bologna in 1688; died in 1766.

Boni, (MAURO,) an Italian Jesuit, born at Genoa in 1746, published a number of treatises on antiquities and bibliography. Died in 1817.

Boni, (ONOFRIO,) an Italian architect and antiquary, born in 1743. He wrote several antiquarian treatises, and a "Eulogy" on his friend Lanzi. Died in 1818.

Bonichi, bo-nee'kee, (BINDO,) an Italian poet, born at Sienna; died in 1337.

Bonichon, bo'ne'shŏn', (FRANÇOIS,) a French ecclesiastic, wrote "Pompa Episcopalis." Died in 1662.

ɛ as k; ç as s; g̃ hard; g̃ as j; G, H, K, *guttural;* N, *nasal;* R, *trilled;* s̃ as z; th as in *this.* (☞See Explanations, p. **23.**)

Boniface, bon'e-fass, [Fr. pron. bo'ne'fãss'; Lat. Bo-NIFA'CIUS; It. BONIFAZIO, bo-ne-fãt'se-o,] I., POPE, succeeded Zozimus as Bishop of Rome in 419 A.D. His claims were opposed by a party in favour of Eulalius; but the emperor Honorius decided in favour of Boniface. He was a patron of learning, and Saint Augustine dedicated to him some of his works. He died in 422, and was succeeded by Celestinus I.
See BARONIUS, "Annales."

Boniface II., born at Rome, succeeded Felix IV. in 530; died in 532.

Boniface III., born at Rome, was elected pope in 607, and died the same year. He obtained from the emperor Phocas permission for the pope to be entitled universal bishop.

Boniface IV., a native of Valeria, in Italy, succeeded Boniface III. in 608. He dedicated the Pantheon to the Virgin and saints, having first removed the heathen images. Died in 615.

Boniface V., a native of Naples, succeeded Deusdedit in 619. He was noted for his efforts to convert the Britons to Christianity. He died in 624, and was succeeded by Honorius I.

Boniface VI., born at Rome, was the successor of Formosus in 895, and survived his election but fifteen days. He was succeeded by Stephen VII.

Boniface VII., the anti-pope, (Cardinal FRANCONE, frãn-ko'nà,) was elected in 974, during the rule of Benedict VI., who was soon after put to death. Though driven from Rome the following year, he returned in 985, and imprisoned Pope John XIV., who is said to have been starved to death. He died in 985, and was succeeded by John XV.
See PLATINA, "Vitæ Pontificum."

Boniface VIII., (Cardinal BENEDETTO **Gaetani**—gã-à-tã'nee,) born at Anagni about 1228, succeeded Celestine V. in 1294. The Colonna family having disputed his election, he excommunicated them and all their adherents, and destroyed their city of Præneste, with a number of their castles. He was subsequently involved in a contest with Philip the Fair of France, whom he excommunicated. Philip, in return, charged him with heresy and other crimes, and had him arrested and imprisoned at Anagni. He was rescued after a few days by his followers, but died soon after, in 1303. Dante, in his "Inferno," mentions Boniface as one of the simonists, and dwells on his persecution of the Ghibelines. (See "Inferno," canto xxvii.)
See RUBEIS, "De Vita et Rebus gestis Bonifacii VIII.," 1651; WILHELM DRUMANN, "Geschichte des Papstes Bonifacius VIII.," 2 vols., 1852; LUIGI TOSTI, "Storia di Bonifazio VIII.," 1847.

Boniface IX., (Cardinal PIETRO Tomacelli—to-mã-chel'lee) a Neapolitan, succeeded Urban VI. in 1389. He had a competitor in Benedict XIII., the anti-pope, who held his court at Avignon. Boniface died in 1404, and was succeeded by Innocent VII.

Boniface, [Lat. BONIFA'CIUS,] a Roman general, born in Thrace, gained the confidence of the empress Placidia, who began to exercise royal power in 424 A.D. By insidious arts Aetius induced her to recall him from Africa, where he had the chief command. Boniface then revolted, and, contrary to the advice of his friend Saint Augustine, invited Genseric the Vandal to invade Africa. Having returned to the service of Placidia, he came to Italy, and was killed in a battle against Aetius in 432 A.D.
See GIBBON, "Decline and Fall of the Roman Empire."

Boniface, bo'ne'fãss', (HYACINTHE,) a French jurist, born at Forcalquier in 1612; died in 1695.

Boniface, [Lat. BONIFA'CIUS,] (WIN'FRID,) SAINT, born in Devonshire, England, about 680, was styled "the Apostle of Germany," and distinguished himself by his zeal in converting the Germans to Christianity. He resided among them more than thirty years, and founded numerous cathedrals, schools, and monasteries. In 732 he was appointed by Gregory III. Archbishop and Primate of Germany, and subsequently created Archbishop of Mentz by Pepin le Bref, whom he consecrated King of the Franks in 752. He was assassinated in 755, with a number of his companions, by an armed troop of pagans.
See WILLIBALD, "Life of Saint Boniface;" GEORGE W. COX, "Life of Saint Boniface," 1853; J. C. SEITERS, "Bonifacius der Apostel der Deutschen."

Bonifacio, bo-ne-fã'cho, (BALDASSARE,) nephew of Giovanni, noticed below, born at Crema about 1586, became Bishop of Capo d'Istria in 1653. He published poems and treatises on various subjects, in Latin and Italian. Died in 1659.

Bonifacio, (GIOVANNI,) an Italian jurist and writer, born at Rovigo in 1547, wrote a "History of Treviso," ("Storia Trivigiano.") Died in 1635.

Bonifacius. See BONIFACE.

Bonifazio. See BONIFACE.

Bonifazio, bo-ne-fãt'se-o, or **Bonifacio**, bo-ne-fã'cho, (called IL VENEZIANO, èl vã-nèt-se-ã'no; i.e. "the Venetian,") a skilful painter of Verona, born about 1490, is supposed to have been a pupil of Titian. Among his principal works, which are to be seen at Venice and Rome, is "The Traffickers driven from the Temple." Died in 1553.
See VASARI, "Lives of the Painters," etc.

Bonifazio, (FRANCESCO,) an Italian painter, born at Viterbo in 1637, was a pupil of Pietro da Cortona.

Bonilla, de, dã bo-nèl'yã, (ALONSO,) a Spanish poet, born at Baeza, in Andalusia, about 1580.
See LONGFELLOW's "Poets and Poetry of Europe."

Bonin, von, fon bo-neen', (EDUARÐ,) a Prussian general, born at Stolpe in 1793. He commanded the army which fought against the Danes in Sleswick-Holstein in 1848 and 1849.

Bon'ing-ton, (RICHARD PARKES,) an English painter of landscapes and coast-scenery, born near Nottingham in 1801. He studied in Paris under Baron Gros, and subsequently visited Italy. Among his master-pieces are "Views of Venice and Bologna;" "The Tomb of Saint Omer;" and "The Turk in Repose." Died in 1828.

Bonini, bo-nee'nee, (GIROLAMO,) an Italian painter, born at Ancona; died about 1680.

Bonisoli, bo-ne-so'lee, or **Bonizoli**, bo-nèd-zo'lee,(?) (AGOSTINO,) an Italian historical painter, born at Cremona in 1633; died in 1700.

Bonito, bo-nee'to, (GIUSEPPE,) a Neapolitan portrait-painter, born in 1705; died at Naples in 1789.

Bonjean, bòn'zhòn', (LOUIS BERNARD,) a French jurist and legal writer, born at Valence, in Drôme, in 1804. He was appointed a senator in 1855.

Bonjour, bòn'zhoor', two brothers, noted as the founders of a new sect of Flagellants, lived about 1780.

Bonjour, (CASIMIR,) a French littérateur, born at Clermont in 1795, published "The Rival Mother," "The Two Cousins," and other popular comedies.

Bonjour, (FRANÇOIS JOSEPH,) a French chemist, born near Salins in 1754, was a pupil and assistant of Berthollet. He published a translation of Bergman's "Chemical Affinities," (1788.) Died in 1811.

Bonjour, written also **Bonjours**, (GUILLAUME,) a French Augustine monk, born at Toulouse in 1670, went as a missionary to China, where he died in 1714.

Bon, Le. See LE BON.

Bonn, bon, (ANDREAS,) a Dutch surgeon and medical writer, born at Amsterdam in 1738. He was a member of the Academy of Brussels. Died in 1819.

Bonnaire, bo'nãr', (JEAN GÉRARD,) a French general, born in 1771, was condemned to exile on a charge of being concerned in the attack on Colonel Gordon at Condé in 1816. He died the same year.

Bonnaire, de, dĕh bo'nãr', (LOUIS,) a French ecclesiastic and moralist, born about 1680; died in 1752.

Bonnal, (FRANÇOIS.) See BONAL.

Bonnard, bo'nãr', (CHARLES LOUIS,) a French mathematician and engineer, born at Arnay-le-Duc in 1769; died in 1828.

Bonnard, (ENNEMOND,) a French general of division, born in Dauphiny in 1756, served in the Revolutionary campaigns from 1793 to 1798. Died in 1819.

Bonnard, (JACQUES CHARLES,) a French architect, born in Paris in 1765, was a pupil of Renard, whom he aided in restoring the palace of the Tuileries. Died in 1818.

Bonnard, (JEAN LOUIS,) a French missionary to China, born in 1824. He arrived in China in 1850, and was put to death by order of the government in 1852.

Bonnard, de, dĕh bo'nãr', (BERNARD,) a French poet, born at Semur-en-Auxois in 1744; died in 1784.

Bonnard, de, (ROBERT ALEXANDRE,) a French geologist, son of the preceding, born in Paris in 1781. He was a member of the Institute, and wrote on geognosy and metallurgy. Died in 1857.

Bonna-Sforza, bon'nä sfort'sä, daughter of Galeazzo Sforza, Duke of Milan, was married in 1518 to Sigismund I., King of Poland. Died in 1557.

Bonnaterre, bo'nä'taiR', (J. P.,) a French naturalist, born in Rouergue about 1750, was one of the founders of the "Encyclopédie Méthodique." He published in this work his "Picture of the Three Kingdoms of Nature," being a continuation of the natural history of Daubenton, in the same work. Died in 1804.

See QUÉRARD, "La France Littéraire."

Bonnaud, bo'nō', (JACQUES PHILIPPE,) a French general of division, born in 1757. He served under Pichegru and Hoche, and was mortally wounded at Giessen in 1797.

Bonnaud, (JEAN BAPTISTE,) a Jesuit, of French extraction, born in America in 1740, was educated in Paris. He wrote several political works, which offended the Jacobins, by whose orders he was executed in 1792.

Bonnay, de, deh bo'nä', (FRANÇOIS,) MARQUIS, a French statesman and diplomatist, born in 1750, was elected president of the National Assembly in 1789, and sent in 1814 on a mission to Copenhagen. Died in 1825.

Bonne, bon, (RIGOBERT,) a French hydrographer and engineer, born in 1727. He published a "Picture of France," (in 27 maps,) and "Neptune Américo-septentrional," (in 18 maps.) Died in 1794.

See QUÉRARD, "La France Littéraire."

Bonneau, bo'nō', (JEAN IVES ALEXANDRE,) French consul to Poland, born at Montpellier in 1739. He was arrested and imprisoned by Catherine II. for having opposed the dismemberment of Poland. He died in 1805, soon after his release.

Bonne-Carrère, de, deh bon'kä'raiR', (GUILLAUME,) a French revolutionist, born at Muret, in Languedoc, in 1754, was employed by the Directory in several important negotiations. Died in 1825.

Bonnechose, de, deh bon'shoz', (FRANÇOIS PAUL ÉMILE Boisnormand—bwä'noR'môN',) a distinguished dramatist and historian, born at Leyderdorp, in Holland, in 1801. His "History of France" (Paris, 1834) enjoys a high reputation: he has also published a "History of the Four Conquests of England," and a popular tragedy entitled "Rosamond."

Bonnechose, de, (HENRI MARIE GASTON,) born in Paris in 1800, became Bishop of Carcassonne in 1847.

Bonnechose, de, (LOUIS CHARLES BOISNORMAND,) brother of François Paul, noticed above, born at Nymwegen in 1812, was one of the pages of Charles X. He was mortally wounded soon after the battle of La Pénissière, in 1832.

Bonnecorse, de, deh bon'koRss', (BALTHASAR,) a French poet, born at Marseilles, wrote a collection of madrigals entitled "The Watch of Love," ("La Montre d'Amour.") Died in 1706.

Bonnefoi, bon'fwä', (ENNEMOND,) [Lat. ENIMUN'DUS BONEFID'IUS,] a French jurist, born at Chabeuil in 1536, became professor of law at Geneva. He published a valuable work on Oriental jurisprudence. He was a friend of Cujacius, and numbered De Thou among his pupils. Died in 1574.

Bonnefoi, (JEAN BAPTISTE,) a French surgeon, born in 1756, published a treatise "On the Application of Electricity to the Art of Healing." Died in 1790.

Bonnefons, bon'fôn', (AMABLE,) a French writer of devotional works, born at Riom in 1600; died in Paris in 1653.

Bonnefons, (ÉLIE BENOÎT,) a French Benedictine monk, born at Mauriac in 1622; died in 1702.

Bonnefons, written also **Bonefons,** (JEAN,) a French jurist and littérateur, born at Clermont-en-Auvergne in 1554, wrote amatory poems in Latin, which are commended by Ménage. Died in 1614.

Bonnegarde, bon'gäRd', a French compiler, who published a "Historical and Critical Dictionary," (1771.)

Bonnelier, bon'le-à', (HIPPOLYTE,) a contemporary French littérateur, has published a number of tales and other works.

Bon'nell or **Bon'nel,** (JAMES,) son of an English merchant at Genoa, born in 1653, published "Meditations and Prayers." Died in 1699.

Bon'ner, (EDMUND,) an English prelate, infamous for his persecutions, born in Worcestershire about 1490. He was patronized by Henry VIII., who made him his chaplain, employed him in several important negotiations, and in 1540 promoted him to the see of London. Having on the accession of Edward VI. refused to take the oath of supremacy, Bonner was deprived of his bishopric and imprisoned. After the death of Edward he was reinstated in his office by Mary, and took an active part in the persecution which has made her reign infamous. The number of those who suffered martyrdom through his agency is estimated at more than a hundred. On the accession of Elizabeth, Bonner was the only one of the Catholic bishops whom she would not permit to kiss her hand. The queen appears to have fully sympathized with the feeling of the people, among whom he was known as "Bloody Bonner." Bonner's brutality and cruelty contributed greatly to promote the Protestant cause. A published letter, addressed to him by a lady of that time, contains the following passages : "The very papists themselves begin now to abhor your bloodthirstiness and speak shame of your tyranny. . . . You have lost the hearts of twenty thousand that were rank papists within this twelvemonth." He was imprisoned for life in the Marshalsea for refusing to take the oath of supremacy. Died in 1569.

See FROUDE'S "History of England," vol. vi. chap. xxxiii., and vol. vii. chap. i. ; HUME'S "History of England;" FOXE'S "Book of Martyrs ;" "Life and Defence of Bonner, Bishop of London.'

Bonnet, bo'nä', (AUGUSTE BERNARD,) a French medical writer, born at Miramont about 1790, resided at Bordeaux.

Bonnet, bo'nä', (CHARLES,) an eminent naturalist and philosopher, born at Geneva in March, 1720. He published in 1745 his "Treatise on Insectology," in which he gives the result of his important discoveries on the modes of reproduction and animal functions of butterflies, caterpillars, etc. His treatise "On the Use of Leaves in Plants" came out in 1754. It is commended by Cuvier as one of the best works extant on vegetable physiology. Having impaired his sight by the use of the microscope, he turned his attention to philosophy, and published in 1762 "Considerations on Organized Bodies." This was followed by his "Contemplation of Nature," (1764,) "Philosophical Palingenesis," (1769,) and "Philosophical Researches on the Evidences of Christianity," (1770.) The genus Bonnetia was named in his honour by Wahl. Died at Geneva in 1793.

See H. B. DE SAUSSURE, "Éloge historique de C. Bonnet," 1787; J. TREMBLEY, "Mémoire de la Vie et des Ouvrages de C. Bonnet," 1794; ALBERT LEMOINE, "C. Bonnet de Genève, Philosophe et Naturaliste," 1850; article "Bonnet," in "Biographie Universelle," (by CUVIER.)

Bonnet, (JACQUES,) a French writer on music, born in 1644. He published a "History of Music and its Effects," (1715.) Died in 1724.

Bonnet or **Bonet,** bo'nä', (JEAN,) a skilful Swiss physician, brother of Théophile, noticed below, born at Geneva in 1615 ; died in 1688.

Bonnet, (PIERRE,) physician to the Duchess of Burgundy, brother of Jacques, noticed above, born in Paris in 1638 ; died in 1708.

Bonnet, (SIMON,) a French theologian, born at Puyen-Velay about 1653, expended some years on a work called "Biblia maxima Patrum." Died in 1705.

Bonnet, written also **Bonet,** (THÉOPHILE,) a celebrated physician, born at Geneva in 1620. His principal works are entitled "Sepulchretum seu Anatomia Practica," and "Labyrinthus Medicus extricatus," (1679.) Died in 1689.

See NICÉRON, "Mémoires."

Bonnetty, bo'nä'te', (AUGUSTIN,) a French theologian and Orientalist, born in the department of Lower Alps in 1798. He founded in 1830 a religious journal, entitled "Annales de Philosophie chrétienne."

Bonneval, de, deh bon'väl', (CLAUDE ALEXANDRE,) COMTE, a French adventurer, born in Limousin in 1675, served in the Austrian army under Prince Eugene. He subsequently went over to the Turks, and became an officer in their army, under the name of Ahmed (Achmet) Pacha. Died in 1747.

See "Mémoire sur le Comte de Bonneval," by the PRINCE DE LIGNE, 1817; DAVID FASSMANN, "Leben des Grafen von Bonneval," 1740; "Memoirs of the Bagshaw Count Bonneval," London, 1750.

Bonneval, de, (MICHEL,) a native of Mans, was the author of a number of operas and ballets. Died in 1766.

Bonneval, de, (RENÉ,) a French critic and controversialist, born at Mans; died in 1760.

Bonneval, de, (SIXTE LOUIS CONSTANT RUFFO,) a French ecclesiastic, born at Aix in 1742, was a deputy from the clergy of Paris to the States-General in 1789. Died in 1820.

Bonneville, bon'vil, (BENJAMIN L. E.,) an officer and traveller, born in France, graduated at West Point, United States, about 1815. He served in the Mexican war, (1846-47,) and obtained the rank of lieutenant-colonel. He published a "Journal of an Expedition to the Rocky Mountains." In 1837 Irving published a work entitled "Adventures of Captain Bonneville."

Bonneville, de, deh bon'vèl', (C.,) a French engineer and military writer, born at Lyons about 1710; died about 1780.

Bonneville, de, (NICOLAS,) a French journalist and *littérateur*, born at Evreux in 1760, was imprisoned as a Girondist in Paris in 1793-94. He wrote a "History of Modern Europe," (3 vols., 1792,) and other works. Died in 1828.

Bonnier, bo'ne-à', (ÉDOUARD,) a French jurist, born at Lille in 1808, was the author of several legal works.

Bonnier d'Alco, bo'ne-à' dȁl'ko', (ANGE ÉLISABETH LOUIS ANTOINE,) a member of the French National Convention, born at Montpellier in 1750, voted for the death of the king. He was killed by some Austrian hussars while returning from an embassy to Rastadt in 1799.

Bonnières, de, deh bo'ne-air', (ALEXANDRE JULES BENOÎT,) a French jurist, born at Grancy in 1750. He favoured the royalists, and became a member of the Council of Five Hundred in 1795. Died in 1801.

Bonnivard, de, deh bo'ne'vȁr', (FRANÇOIS,) born at Seyssel, in the department of Ain, in 1496. Having adopted republican opinions, he took sides with the Genevese against Duke Charles III. of Savoy; but he had the misfortune in 1530 to fall into the power of the latter, who confined him six years in the castle of Chillon. Bonnivard is the hero of Byron's "Prisoner of Chillon." He wrote a "Chronicle of Geneva," and bequeathed to that city his library and other possessions. He was a man of noble character, and a friend of the Reformation. Died in 1570.

See BYRON, notes to the "Prisoner of Chillon."

Bonnivet, de, deh bo'ne'và', (GUILLAUME **Gouffier**—goo'fe-à',) SEIGNEUR, a French admiral, born about 1488, was a favourite of Francis I., who sent him on embassies to England and Germany. It was by the advice of Bonnivet that Francis I. fought the disastrous battle of Pavia, (1525;) and the admiral, unwilling to survive a defeat of which he was the principal cause, sought and found death in the thickest of the fight.

See BRANTÔME, "Vie de Bonnivet;" "Nouvelle Biographie Générale."

Bonnycastle, bon'e-kas'sęl, (JOHN,) an eminent English mathematician, born in Buckinghamshire, became professor at the Royal Military Academy of Woolwich. His "Introduction to Mensuration," (1782,) "Elements of Geometry," (1789,) "Treatise on Trigonometry," (1806,) and "Elements of Algebra," (1813,) are esteemed standard works. Died in 1821.

Bono, bo'no, (GIAMBATTISTA AGOSTINO,) an Italian jurist, born near Saluzzo in 1738, became in 1768 professor of canon law at Turin. Died in 1799.

Bonomi, bo-no'mee, (GIOVANNI FRANCESCO,) an Italian, born at Cremona in 1536, was patronized by the cardinal Carlo Borromeo, who made him Bishop of Vercelli in 1572. He wrote, in Latin, "The Life and Death of Carlo Borromeo," and other works. Died in 1587.

See MAZZUCHELLI, "Scrittori d'Italia."

Bonomi, (GIOVANNI FRANCESCO,) born at Bologna in 1626, published a number of poems in Latin and Italian.

Bonomi, (GIUSEPPE,) an Italian architect, born at Rome in 1739, resided mostly in England. He became an associate of the Royal Academy. Among his principal works are the Duke of Argyll's mansion at Roseneath, and Eastwell House in Kent. Died in 1808.

Bo-no'mī, (JOSEPH,) an antiquary, born in London about 1796, was a son of the preceding. He published "Nineveh and its Palaces," the "Discoveries of Botta and Layard applied to the Elucidation of Holy Writ," (1852,) and other works.

Bononcini, bo-non-chee'nee, (GIOVANNI BATTISTA,) a famous musical composer, born at Módena about 1670, was a son of Giovanni Maria, noticed below. He had composed several operas, when in 1716 the Royal Academy of Music engaged him to go to London. There he became the rival of Handel, and produced a number of operas, among which were "Erminia" and "Astyanax." The Tories were the partisans of Handel, and the Whigs patronized Bononcini. He quitted England about 1733. Died after 1748.

Bononcini, (GIOVANNI MARIA,) an Italian composer, born at Módena about 1640, was the author of a work entitled "The Practical Musician." His sons Antonio and Giovanni were noted as musicians.

Bonone, bo-no'nà, (CARLO,) an Italian painter, born at Ferrara in 1569. His best works are the frescos in the church of Campo Santo at Ferrara, and of Santa Maria in Vado, which are highly commended. As a pupil and imitator of the Carracci, Bonone is sometimes called "the Carracci of Ferrara." Died in 1632.

See LANZI, "History of Painting in Italy."

Bonours, de, deh bo'noor', (CHRISTOPHE,) a French officer in the Spanish service, born at Vesoul about 1590, published "The Memorable Siege of Ostend."

Bonpland, bòn'plòn', (AIMÉ,) an eminent French naturalist and traveller, born at La Rochelle in 1773. He studied medicine under Corvisart, in Paris, where he formed an intimate friendship with Humboldt, and in 1799 accompanied him on a scientific tour to South America. They published, after their return, "Travels in the Equinoctial Regions of the New Continent," (12 vols., 1815 *et seq.*) Bonpland presented to the Museum of Natural History his large and valuable collection of dried plants, (6000 new species,) and was appointed by the empress Josephine superintendent of her gardens at Malmaison. In 1816 he sailed for Buenos Ayres, where he became professor of natural history. At the end of five years he set out on a journey to the Andes, but in passing through Paraguay was captured by the troops of the dictator Francia. After a residence of nearly ten years under strict surveillance, he was released in 1831. He afterwards resided in Uruguay, and died in 1858. Among his other productions we may name his "Nova Genera et Species Plantarum," (7 vols. fol., with 700 plates, 1815,) a magnificent work, in which he was assisted by Kunth, a "Monograph of the Melastomeæ," (2 vols., 120 plates,) and "Equinoctial Plants collected in Mexico, Cuba, etc.," (2 vols. fol., 140 plates.)

See "Nouvelle Biographie Générale."

Bonsi, bon'see, (FRANCESCO,) COUNT, an Italian writer on veterinary medicine, born at Rimini about 1720.

Bonsi, (LELIO,) an Italian *littérateur*, born at Florence about 1552.

Bonstetten, de, deh bon'stȅt'ten, written also **Bonstettin,** (CHARLES VICTOR,) a Swiss philosopher, born at Berne in 1745. He was a friend of Voltaire, Rousseau, and the historian Müller. Among his principal works are "Researches on the Nature and Laws of Imagination," (1807,) "Studies on Man," (in French, 1821,) an essay on "National Education," and other treatises, in German. Died at Geneva in 1832.

See "Souvenirs de Bonstetten," 1832; and his "Autobiography," contained in a collection of his letters, published by H. FUESSLI in 1827; (two other volumes of his "Letters" were published in 1829;) ERSCH und GRUBER, "Allgemeine Encyklopaedie;" "Edinburgh Review" for April, 1864.

Bontekoe, bon'tęh-koo', (KORNELIS,) a Dutch physician and medical writer, born at Alkmaar in 1648; died in 1685 or 1686.

See OVERKAMP, "Reden over het Leven en de Dood van C. Bontekoe," 1685; "Biographie Médicale."

ā, ē, ī, ō, ū, ȳ, *long;* à, ė, ȯ, same, less prolonged; ă, ĕ, ĭ, ŏ, ŭ, ȳ, *short;* a, ę, į, ǫ, *obscure;* fär, fàll, fât; mêt; nŏt; gōŏd; mōōn;

Bontekoe, (WILLEM ISBRAND,) a Dutch sea-captain, who sailed in 1618 to the East Indies. His ship having taken fire and exploded when near Batavia, Bontekoe was thrown unhurt into the sea, and saved himself by means of a mast. He wrote an account of his adventure, which was translated into French.

See THÉVENOT, "Relation de divers Voyages curieux."

Bontempi, bôn-têm'pee, or **Buontempi,** boo-ôn-têm'pee, (GIOVANNI ANDREA ANGELINI,) an Italian musician and composer, born at Perugia about 1630, wrote "Musical History," (1695,) and other works. Died about 1700.

Bontemps or **Bontems,** bôn'tôN', (MARIE JEANNE de Chatillon—dĕh shä'te'yôN',) a literary French lady, born in Paris in 1718, was the first translator of Thomson's "Seasons" into French. Died in 1768.

Bontius, bon'te-ŭs, (GERARD,) a Dutch physician, born at Ryswick about 1536, became professor of medicine at Leyden. Died in 1599.

Bontius, (JACOB,) son of Gerard, born about 1590, obtained a high reputation as a naturalist. He visited India and Persia, and in 1625 settled as a physician in Batavia. He wrote several valuable works on medicine and botany. Plumier named in his honour a genus of American plants. Died in 1631.

Bonvicino, bôn-ve-chee'no, written also **Buonvicino,** (ALESSANDRO,) an eminent Italian painter, born in 1514, was sometimes called IL MORETTO DA BRESCIA, (ĕl mo-ret'to dä bRĕsh'yä.) He was a pupil of Titian, whom he imitated admirably. He painted portraits with success, and altar-pieces the dignity and grace of which are highly praised. "Inspired with ardent admiration for Raphael," says E. Breton, "he formed for himself a new style, simple, graceful, and elevated." Died in 1564.

See RIDOLFI, "Vite de' Pittori Veneti."

Bonvicino, (AMBROGIO,) a skilful Italian sculptor, born at Milan in 1552; died in 1622.

Bonwicke, bon'wik, (AMBROSE,) an English non-juring divine, born in 1652, became master of Merchant-Taylors' School. He wrote "Pattern for Young Students in the University."

See W. BEVERIDGE, "Life of A. Bonwicke," 1846.

Bonzi, (PAOLO.) See GOBBO.

Booddha or **Buddha,** bōōd'dạ or bōōd'd'hạ, [Fr. BOUDDHA, boo'dä',] the name of an Asiatic divinity, whose worshippers, called Booddhists, (or Buddhists,) are supposed to constitute about one-third of the human race. The name is derived from the Sanscrit verb bŭd, to "understand," to "know," and signifies "wisdom," also the "wise one," or the "sage." The term Booddha has been applied to many different individuals or beings. The Booddhists of India and Ceylon teach that, throughout the countless ages of the past, there have appeared, at long intervals, sages who, by the merit they have acquired during innumerable transmigrations, have at last attained to unlimited intelligence and power. (See BRAHMANISM.) During the long period of their probation, the Bôdhisattvas (or "Aspirants to the Booddhaship") are sometimes born as devas, (inferior deities,) and sometimes in the forms of various animals, even insects, but more frequently as men : in their last and most perfect manifestation as supreme Booddhas, they are always born in the human form. Of these divine sages the most recent and best-known is GAUTAMA, (which see.)

Some of the Nepaulese Booddhists believe in an eternal, self-existent Being, whom they style AdÏ Bōōddha, that is, the "First Booddha," who created all things in heaven and earth, (see Hodgson's "Literature and Religion of the Buddhists," page 63;) but the Ceylonese Booddhists, who appear to have departed the least from the primitive doctrines of Booddhism, are atheists, that is, they do not recognize the existence of any God, properly so called. According to their belief, the highest forms of being are those of glorified men, who, having become supreme Booddhas, are thereby deified ; though they enjoy but a very brief existence in this exalted state, and then pass into Nirwâna, which signifies "annihilation," according to the Ceylonese Booddhists, but, according to the Aishwarikâs of Nepaul, "absorption" into the eternal essence of AdÏ Booddha. For a more par-

ticular account of the doctrines, and for the history, of Booddhism, see GAUTAMA.

See HARDY, "Manual of Budhism;" KÖPPEN, "Religion des Buddha," Berlin, 1857; GUIGNIAUT, "Religions de l'Antiquité," Paris, 1825, vol. i. book i. chap. v.; MOOR, "Hindu Pantheon."

Boodt, bōt, (ANSELM BOETIUS,) a Flemish physician and naturalist, born at Bruges about 1580; died in 1634.

Boogrof, Bougrov, or **Bugrow,** boo'gRof, a Russian astronomer, published a "Dissertation on the Elliptic Motion of the Stars." Died in 1822.

Boo'ker, (Rev. LUKE,) rector of Tedstone, an English writer, born at Nottingham in 1762. He wrote theological and other works. Died in 1835.

Boole, bool, (GEORGE,) an English mathematician, born about 1820. He published a "Mathematical Analysis of Logic," (1847,) and an "Investigation of the Laws of Thought." Died in 1864.

Boolgarin, Boulgarine, or **Bulgarin,** bool-gä'rin or bool-gä'rĕn, (THADDEUS,) a celebrated Russian writer, born in Lithuania in 1789. He studied at the Institution of Military Cadets at Saint Petersburg, and, having made several campaigns in the Russian army, entered the French service. After the fall of Napoleon he became in 1825 associated with Gretsch as editor of "The Northern Bee." He published in 1827 a collection of essays and tales, among which the "Recollections of the War in Spain" deserves especial mention. His novel of "Ivan Vuizhegin" (1829) enjoys great popularity, and has been styled "the Russian Gil Blas." He also wrote a work entitled "Russia in a Historical, Statistical, Geographical, and Literary Point of View."

See FRIEDRICH OTTO, "Lehrbuch der Russischen Literatur."

Boo'mer, (GEORGE BOARDMAN,) an American general, born in Worcester county, Massachusetts, in 1832. He was killed in an attack on Vicksburg in May, 1863.

Boon, bōn, or **Boone,** bō'neh, (DANIEL,) a Dutch painter, who worked in England. He painted drunken revels, etc. Died in 1698.

Boone, (DANIEL,) an American pioneer and explorer, born in Bucks county, Pennsylvania, in 1735, was a famous hunter from his youth. During his minority he emigrated with his father to North Carolina, where he married. In 1769 Boone and five companions penetrated into the unexplored forests of Kentucky, where he passed many months in the pursuits of the chase. He was captured by some Indians, but escaped from them, and returned home in March, 1771. Having resolved to emigrate to Kentucky with his family, he left North Carolina, accompanied by five other families, in September, 1773. After several fights with the Indians, he built a fort at Boonesborough, on the Kentucky River, in 1775. He repulsed several attacks which the savages made on this fort in 1777. In February, 1778, he was surprised and captured by the Indians, who carried him to Chillicothe and Detroit. He, however, gained the favour of the savages, and was adopted as a son by an Indian family. He escaped in June, 1778, and returned to the fort, which was attacked in August by a party of Indians, about four hundred and forty-five in number, fighting under the British flag. Boone, who had about fifty men under him, defended the fort with great resolution and success. Two of his sons were at different times killed by the Indians.

Having lost his lands in Kentucky in consequence of a defective title, he removed to Missouri about 1795, and settled on the Femme Osage River. He continued to follow the occupation of hunter and trapper in Missouri, and obtained a large tract of land in that territory, which then belonged to Spain; but when it was ceded to the United States his title was not admitted to be valid. He died in Missouri in 1820 or 1822.

See SPARKS, "American Biography," vol. xiii., Second Series; W. H. BOGART, "Life of Daniel Boone," 1857.

Boonen, bō'nen, (ARNOUD,)an eminent Dutch painter, born at Dort in 1669. Among his master-pieces are portraits of Peter the Great, the Duke of Marlborough, and the painter Van Huysum. Died in 1729.

See DESCAMPS, "Vies des Peintres Flamands, Hollandais," etc.

Boonen, (KASPAR,) a portrait-painter, brother of the preceding, born at Dort in 1667; died in 1729.

e as k; ç as s; ḡ hard; ğ as j; G, H, K, guttural; N, nasal; R, trilled; ŝ as z; ŧh as in this. (☞See Explanations, p. 23.)

Boorinski or **Burinski,** boo-rin'ske or boo-rĕn'skee, a Russian lyric poet, lived in the early part of the present century.

Boos, bōs, (MARTIN,) a German theologian, born in 1762; died in 1825.

See "M. Boos der Prediger der Gerechtigkeit die vor Gott gilt: seine Selbstbiographie," 1826; C. BRIDGES, "Life of M. Boos," 1836.

Boos, (ROMAN ANTON,) a German sculptor, born in 1735, worked mostly at Munich, where he died in 1810.

Booseeree, (or **Busîrî,**) bŏō-see'ree, written also **Bousyry, (Shereef-ed-Deen Aboo-Abdallah-Mohammed,)** an Arabian poet, born in Upper Egypt in 1210; died in 1294.

Boot, bŏt, written also **Boat,** (GERARD,) a brother of the following, born at Gorkum in 1604, became physician to Charles I. of England. He wrote a work entitled "Ireland's Natural History." Died in 1650.

Boot, van, vän bŏt, (ARNOUD,) a Dutch physician, born at Gorkum in 1606; died in 1650.

Booth, (ABRAHAM,) a Baptist minister, born in Derbyshire in 1734, published "Pædo-Baptism Examined," (1784.) Died in 1806.

Booth, (BARTON,) a celebrated English actor, born in Lancashire in 1681, was a relative of the Earl of Warrington. His performances in "Hamlet," "Othello," and Addison's "Cato" were everywhere received with the highest applause. He wrote "The Death of Dido," a drama. Died in 1733.

See T. CIBBER, "Life of B. Booth."

Booth, (EDWIN,) a popular American tragedian, a son of Junius Brutus Booth, noticed below, was born in Baltimore in 1833. He visited England and the continent of Europe in 1861. He has since acted with great applause in different parts of the United States.

See "Atlantic Monthly" for May, 1866.

Booth, (Sir FELIX,) a wealthy English manufacturer, of the firm of Booth & Co., London, born in 1775. He was knighted as a reward for his generous donation of £20,000 for promoting the expedition of Sir John Ross to the Arctic regions. The most northern tract of land was called, in his honour, Boothia Felix. Died in 1850.

See SIR JOHN ROSS'S Narrative of his Second Voyage in Search of a Northern Passage, etc.

Booth, (GEORGE,) son of Henry, whose title he inherited, published "Considerations upon the Institution of Marriage," (1739.) Died in 1758.

Booth, (HENRY,) Earl of Warrington, born in 1651. As a member of Parliament for Cheshire, under the reign of Charles II., he was conspicuous for his opposition to the Papists. In 1689 he was appointed chancellor of the exchequer by William III. He wrote a number of political tracts, and a vindication of his friend Lord Russell. Died in 1694.

Booth, (JOHN WILKES,) an American actor, notorious as the assassin of President Lincoln, was born in Baltimore. He was a son of the English actor Junius Brutus Booth. He sympathized with the Southern secessionists in the civil war, and, in order to avenge their defeat, formed a conspiracy with J. H. Surratt, Lewis Payne Powell, D. Harold, and others. On the night of the 14th of April, 1865, he entered the private box of the theatre, shot the President in the head, and, rushing to the front of the box, brandished a dagger in his hand, exclaimed, "*Sic semper tyrannis!*" and leaped down to the stage. In his descent his spur caught in the American flag, and he broke his leg. He then mounted a horse, which was standing at the back-door, and escaped to Virginia. He secreted himself in a barn near Bowling Green, to which he was tracked by detectives, and, refusing to surrender, was shot, on the 26th of April, 1865.

Booth, (JUNIUS BRUTUS,) a popular English tragedian, born in London in 1796. He visited America in 1821, where he performed with great applause. He was pre-eminently successful in the character of Richard III. He died in 1852, while returning from California.

See "Life of Junius Brutus Booth," by his daughter, New York, 1866; OXBERRY, "Dramatic Biography."

Booth'bў, (Sir BROOKE,) an English writer, published "Fables and Satires," and "Sorrows sacred to the Memory of Penelope," (1796.)

See "London Quarterly Review" for February, 1810.

Booth'royd, (BENJAMIN,) D.D., an English dissenting divine and bookseller, born in Yorkshire in 1768. He published an edition of the Hebrew Bible without points, which is commended by Horne and other able critics. Died in 1836.

Bootoorlin, (or **Bootoorleen,**) **Boutourline,** or **Buturlin,** boo-tooR-leen' or boo-tooR-lin', (DMITRI PETROVICH,) a Russian general and distinguished military writer, born at Saint Petersburg in 1790. He published, in French, an "Account of the Italian Campaign in 1799;" also a "History of Napoleon's Campaign in Russia," (1820, in Russian.) He was a senator, and director of the Imperial Library. Died in 1850.

See OTTO, "Lehrbuch der Russischen Literatur."

Bopp, bop, (FRANZ,) a distinguished German Orientalist, who may be said to be the founder of the modern science of comparative philology, was born at Mentz, in Hesse-Darmstadt, in 1791. He studied in Paris, where he acquired the friendship of S. de Sacy and A. W. Schlegel; he subsequently visited London and Göttingen, and soon after was appointed professor of Oriental languages at Berlin. He published in 1816 a treatise "On the Conjugation-System of the Sanscrit Language," which was succeeded by a "Glossarium Sanscritum," and "Critical Grammar of the Sanscrit Tongue." His greatest work is entitled "Comparative Grammar of the Sanscrit, Zend, Greek, Latin, Lithuanian, Old Sclavonian, Gothic, and German Languages," (1833,) which has been translated into English under the care of H. H. Wilson, late professor of Sanscrit at Oxford, (1845.) He also published portions of the Indian poem "Mahâbhârata," with a German version and notes.

"Professor Bopp," says Wilson, "may be considered to have established, beyond reasonable question, a near relationship between the languages of nations separated by the intervention of centuries and the distance of half the globe, by differences of physical formation and social institutions,—between the forms of speech current among the dark-complexioned natives of India and the fair-skinned races of ancient and modern Europe; a relationship of which no suspicion existed fifty years ago, and which has been satisfactorily established only within a recent period." Died in Berlin in October, 1867.

See preface to the English translation of Bopp's "Comparative Grammar," London, 1845; also an excellent article by Professor WHITNEY, on Dr. Key and M. Oppert, in the "North American Review" for October, 1867, and "Blackwood's Magazine" for February, 1841.

Boquin, bo'kän', or **Bouquin,** boo'kän', (PIERRE,) a French Protestant theologian, succeeded Calvin as professor of divinity at Strasburg, and was afterwards preacher to the Queen of Navarre. Died in 1582.

Bör or **Bore.** See ODIN.

Bor, (PIETER KRISTIAAN,) a Dutch historian, born at Utrecht in 1559, published a "History of the Netherlands," (1621,) and several other works. Died in 1635.

Bora, von, fon bo'râ, or **Bohren,** bo'ren, (KATHARINA,) the wife of Martin Luther, born at Loeben in 1499, was originally a nun in a convent of Saxony. Having, with a number of her companions, been converted to the doctrines of Luther, they were assisted by him in effecting their escape. (See LUTHER.) Died in 1552.

See WALCH, "Geschichte der Catharina von Bora," 2 vols., 1754, MAYER, "De Catharina Martini Lutheri Conjuge," 1669; HOFFMANN "Catharina von Bora," 1845.

Borâk, bo-râk', or **Burâk,** bŏō-râk', (or, with the article prefixed, **Al-Borâk,** *i.e.* the "lightning,") written also **Burâq,** (Myth.,) the name of a creature on which, according to Mohammedan legends, the prophet rode from Mecca to Jerusalem, and afterwards to heaven, under the guidance of Jabreel, (Gabriel.) It is variously represented, but usually as an animal, in size between an ass and a horse, having a human face, two wings, and, according to some accounts, a tail like a peacock.

See SHEA's translation of MIRKHOND's "Early Kings of Persia," p. 441; SPRENGER's "Life of Mohammad," p. 127.

Borastus, bo-râs'tus, (GREGORIUS LARS,) a Swedish publicist, born at Norrköping about 1584, became secretary to the King of Poland.

Borch, boRK, (MICHAEL JOHN,) COUNT OF, a Polish naturalist, published several treatises on mineralogy, and translated Wieland's "Oberon" into French verse. Died in 1810.

Borch, BORK, or **Borrich,** bor'rĭk, [Lat. BORRICH'-IUS,] (OLAUS or OLUF,) a learned Dane, born in Jutland in 1626, became professor of chemistry and botany at Copenhagen. He founded in that city a college for indigent students. He wrote several valuable scientific works in Latin. Died in 1690.

See BORNEMAN, "Ligpraediken over O. Borch," 1690; NICÉRON, "Mémoires."

Borcholten, bork'ol'tĕn, [Lat. BORCHOL'DUS,] (JOHANN,) a German jurist, born at Lüneburg in 1535, studied under Cujacius, (Cujas,) and became professor of law at Helmstedt. Died in 1593.

Borcht, van der, vȧn dĕr borKt, (HENDRIK,) a Flemish painter and engraver, born at Brussels in 1583, worked for Charles I. of England. Died in 1660.

Borcht, van der, (PIETER,) a Flemish painter and engraver, born at Brussels about 1540; died in 1608.

Borck, bork, (KASPAR WILHELM,) a German diplomatist and writer, born in Pomerania in 1650, rose to be minister of state. He translated into German Shakspeare's "Julius Cæsar." Died in 1747.

Borda, bor'dä', (JEAN CHARLES,) a celebrated French mathematician and engineer, born at Dax in 1733. He studied military engineering, and wrote in 1756 a "Memoir on the Motion of Projectiles," which procured him admission into the Academy of Sciences. In 1757 he fought at the battle of Hastenbeck, soon after which he entered the navy. He published a "Memoir on the Resistance of Fluids," (1763.) In 1767 he explained the principles of the calculus of variations discovered by Lagrange, in a memoir of pure analysis, which is highly commended by Biot. About 1776, Lieutenant Borda improved the method of determining the position of points on a coast, for which he adopted astronomical bearings obtained by reflecting instruments. Having obtained the rank of major-general of the naval army, he served in the American war, (1778–82.) He perfected in 1777 an instrument of great value to mariners, called "circle of reflection," or reflecting circle, (*cercle à réflexion.*) The utility of the repeating circle invented by him was proved in the measurement of an arc of the meridian from Dunkirk to the Balearic Isles, a vast enterprise, of which Borda was the master-spirit. "It is to Borda and Coulomb," says Biot, "that we owe the *renaissance* of sound experimental philosophy in France. Borda should also be regarded as one of the men who have most contributed to the progress of the nautical art." Died in Paris in February, 1799.

See M. BIOT, "Notice sur Borda," in "Mémoires de l'Académie des Sciences;" "Nouvelle Biographie Générale."

Borda, bor'dä, (SIRO,) an Italian physician, born in 1761 at Pavia, where he became professor of materia medica in 1800. Died in 1824.

See G. DEL CHIAPPA, "Memorie intorno alla Vita del Cavaliere S. Borda," 1834.

Bordazar de Artazu, bor-dä-thär' dä är-tä-thoo', (ANTONIO,) a Spanish printer and writer, born at Valencia in 1671, published "Spanish Orthography," and other works. Died in 1744.

Borde or **Boorde,** bōrd, (ANDREW,) [Lat. ANDRE'A PERFORA'TUS,] an English physician, born in Sussex about 1500. He was the author of "The Breviary of Health," "Merrie Tales of the Wise Men of Gotham," and other works. He was patronized by Henry VIII. The designation "Merry-Andrew" was originally applied to him. Died in 1549.

See WOOD, "Athenæ Oxonienses;" "Retrospective Review," vol. i., new series, 1853.

Borde, bord, (CHARLES,) a French poet and skeptical writer, born at Lyons in 1711, was a friend of Voltaire. Among his works is "Le Catéchumène," (1766.) Died in 1781.

See ANTOINE PÉRICAUD, "Notice sur la Vie de C. Borde," 1824.

Borde, de la, dĕh lä bord, (JEAN BENJAMIN,) a French *littérateur*, a favourite of Louis XV., born in Paris in 1734. He was put to death by the Jacobins in 1794.

Bordeaux, de, dĕh bor'dō', DUC, a French prince, son of Charles Ferdinand, Duc de Berry, and grandson of Charles X., was born in Paris in 1820. He is sometimes called COUNT DE CHAMBORD. He is recognized by the Bourbonists as the legitimate heir to the throne, and is styled Henri V.

Bordelon, bord'lôn', (LAURENT,) a French *littérateur*, born at Bourges in 1653; died in 1730.

Bor'den, (SIMEON,) an American civil engineer and mechanician, born in Fall River, Massachusetts, in 1798. Having invented a valuable instrument for determining the base-line in the trigonometrical survey of Massachusetts, he was appointed in 1834 to superintend the work, which he completed in 1841. This is said to have been the first geodetic survey ever accomplished in the United States. He afterwards ran the boundary-line between Massachusetts and Rhode Island, and directed the construction of several railroads. Died at Fall River in 1856.

Bordenave, bord'nȧv', (TOUSSAINT,) a French surgeon, born in Paris in 1728, wrote an "Essay on Physiology," (1756,) and translated Haller's "Elements of Physiology," (1766.) Died in 1782.

Bordereau, bord'rō', (RENÉE,) a French heroine of the Revolution, born near Angers in 1770, served with distinction in the Vendean army. Died in 1828.

See "Mémoires de Renée de Bordereau," etc.

Borderie, bord're', a French poet, born in Normandy in 1507.

Borderies, bord're', (ÉTIENNE JEAN FRANÇOIS,) born at Montauban in 1764, became in 1827 Bishop of Versailles. Died in 1832.

Bordessoulle, de, dĕh bord'sool', (ÉTIENNE TARDIF,) COUNT, a French general, born at Luzeret in 1771. He gained the rank of colonel at Austerlitz, (1805,) and displayed courage and ability in numerous battles during the first empire. Died in 1837.

See MACDONALD, (ÉTIENNE J. J. A. DE TARENTE,) "Éloge du Général de Bordessoulle," 1839.

Bordeu, de, dĕh bor'duh', (ANTOINE,) a French physician, born in Béarn in 1696, wrote a "Dissertation on the Mineral Waters of Béarn," (1749.)

Bordeu, de, (FRANÇOIS,) a French medical writer, son of the preceding, born at Pau in 1734.

Bordeu, de, (THÉOPHILE,) a French medical writer of high reputation, son of Antoine, born at Iseste, in Béarn, in 1722. He settled in Paris about 1750, and became physician of the hospital La Charité. Among his important works are "Researches on the Pulse," (4 vols., 1772,) and a "Treatise on Chronic Diseases," (2 vols., 1776–1801.) Died in 1776.

See ROUSSEL, "Éloge historique de M. de Bordeu," 1778; RICHERAND, "Notice sur la Vie de T. de Bordeu," 1817.

Bording, bor'ding, (ANDERS,) a Danish poet, born at Ribe in 1619, published a literary periodical in Copenhagen. Died in 1677.

See KRAFT OG NYERUP, "Litteraturlexicon."

Bording, bor'ding, (JAKOB,) a Dutch physician, born at Antwerp in 1511, became principal of the college at Carpentras, and subsequently physician to Christian III. of Denmark. Died in 1560.

See M. ADAM, "Vitæ Eruditorum."

Bord'ley, (JOHN BEALE,) an American writer on agriculture, born in 1728; died in Philadelphia in 1804.

Bordone, bor-do'nä, (PARIDE,) a celebrated Italian painter of the Venetian school, born at Treviso about 1510. He studied first under Titian, but he subsequently formed his style on the model of Giorgione. Among his master-pieces are a "Holy Family," "Fisherman presenting the Ring of Saint Mark to the Doge," "The Martyrdom of Saint Andrew," "The Sibyl," and a "Paradise." His portraits are nearly equal to those of Titian. Died in Venice in 1588, or, according to some writers, in 1570.

See LANZI, "History of Painting in Italy;" RIDOLFI, "Vite de' Pittori Veneti;" WINCKELMANN, "Neues Maler-Lexikon."

Bordoni, bor-do'nee, (BENEDETTO,) an Italian geographer, born at Padua, wrote a "Description of Italy." Died about 1530.

Bordoni, (PLACIDO,) an Italian *littérateur*, born at Venice about 1740, made several translations from the French and Latin. Died in 1800.

See FILIASI, "Elogio storico di P. Bordoni," 1820.

ɛ as k; ç as s; ğ *hard;* ġ as j; G, H, K, *guttural;* N, *nasal;* R, *trilled;* ş as z; ŧh as in *this.* (☞See Explanations, p. 23.)

Bordonio, boR-do'ne-o, (GIUSEPPE ANTONIO,) an Italian Jesuit, and professor of rhetoric at Turin, where he was born in 1682. Died in 1742.

Bo're-as, [Gr. Βορέας or Βορὑς; Fr. BORÉE, bo'rȧ',] the North Wind personified by classic poets, who represent him as a son of Astræus and Aurora, and the father of Zetes and Calais.

Boreau, bo'rō', (VICTOR,) a French poet and miscellaneous writer, published a "History of the Middle Ages," (1838,) and other works.

Borée, the French for BOREAS, which see.

Borée, bo'rȧ', (VINCENT,) a French tragic poet, born about 1530.

Borel, bo'rȇl', (PETRUS,) a French *littérateur* and journalist, brother of André François, born at Lyons in 1809.

Borel, (PIERRE,) physician to Louis XIV., born at Castres, in Languedoc, about 1620, published a treatise "On the True Inventor of the Telescope," (in Latin, 1655,) and other scientific works. Died in 1689.

See F. HOEFER, "Histoire de la Chimie."

Borel d'Hauterive, bo'rȇl' dōt'rȇv', (ANDRÉ FRANÇOIS JOSEPH,) a French historian, born at Lyons in 1812.

Borelli, bo-rel'lee, [Lat. BOREL'LUS,] (GIOVANNI ALFONSO,) a celebrated Italian physician and savant, born at Naples in January, 1608, was one of the founders of the so-called iatro-mathematical school, which attempted to apply mathematics to medicine. He studied at Florence and Rome, and became professor of mathematics at Pisa in 1656. His greatest work is entitled "On the Motion of Animals," ("De Motu Animalium," 1680,) and is dedicated to his patroness, Christina of Sweden. He also wrote (in Latin) an "Account of the Eruption of Etna in 1669," and a number of medical and scientific treatises in Latin and Italian. Died at Rome in 1679.

See Eulogy on G. A. Borelli, prefixed to his "De Motu Animalium;" NICÉRON, "Mémoires;" HALLER, "Bibliotheca Anatomica."

Borelli, bo'rȧ'le' or bo-rel'lee, (JEAN ALEXIS,) a French *littérateur*, born in Provence in 1738, resided at Berlin, where he was patronized by Frederick the Great. He published moral and critical essays, and edited some posthumous works of Frederick. Died about 1810.

Borelli, (JEAN MARIE,) a French Jesuit and poet, born in Provence in 1723; died in 1808.

Borellus, (G. A.) See BORELLI.

Borga. See BARKAH KHAN.

Borgarucci, boR-gȧ-root'chee, [Lat. BORGARU'TIUS,] (PROSPERO,) an Italian physician, born near Gubbio, became professor of anatomy at Padua in 1564.

Borger, boRG'er or boR'Her, (ELIAS A.,) born in Friesland in 1785, became, in 1815, professor of theology at Leyden. He published poems, and several critical and theological works. Died in 1820.

See LONGFELLOW, "Poets and Poetry of Europe;" WILLEM BROES, "Leerrede op E. A. Borger," 1820; JAN TICHLER, "Jets over E. A. Borgers Kanselwelsprekenheid," 1835.

Borghese, boR-gā'sȧ, (CAMILLO,) born in 1552, was elected pope in 1605, under the name of Paul V.

Borghese, (CAMILLO,) son of Marcantonio III., born at Rome in 1775. On the entrance of the French into Italy, he attached himself to their cause, and in 1803 received from Napoleon the hand of his sister Pauline, widow of General Leclerc. He was afterwards created Duke of Guastalla, and governor-general of the transalpine provinces, (1810.) He died in 1832, having previously separated from his wife. He left his immense fortune to his brother, Francesco Borghese Aldobrandini.

See TIPALDO, "Biografia degli Italiani illustri."

Borghese, (GIOVANNI VENTURA,) an Italian painter, born at Citta di Castello about 1640, was a pupil of Pietro da Cortona. Died in 1708.

Borghese, (IPPOLITO,) a Neapolitan painter, lived about 1620.

Borghese, (MARCANTONIO I.,) nephew of Paul V., was created by him Prince of Sulmona and a grandee of Spain. One of his relatives, MARCANTONIO II., became Viceroy of Naples in 1721. MARCANTONIO III., of the same family, was celebrated for his patronage of the arts, and his magnificent collection of statues and antiquities in his villa on the Pincian Hill.

Borghesi, boR-gā'see, (BARTOLOMMEO,) an eminent Italian archæologist and numismatist, born at Savignano,

near Rimini, about 1780. His principal work is entitled "Nuovi Frammenti di Fasti Consolari Capitolini," (2 vols., 1820.) He has also made valuable contributions to various scientific journals, and is a member of the principal learned societies of Europe. His collection of coins and medals is esteemed one of the best in Italy. His researches and writings have contributed greatly to elucidate the military, political, sacerdotal, and municipal institutions of the ancient Romans.

See "Nouvelle Biographie Générale."

Borghesi, (DIOMEDE,) an Italian poet and orator, born at Sienna, was an able critic and philologist. He published several volumes of poems and of letters, (1566–1584.) Died in 1598.

See GINGUENÉ, "Histoire Littéraire d'Italie."

Borghi-Mamo, boR'gee-mȧ'mo, (ADELAIDE,) an Italian vocalist, born at Bologna in 1830.

Borghini, boR-gee'nee, (RAFAELLO,) an Italian poet and *littérateur*, wrote a pastoral play called "La Diana pietosa," (1585,) and "Il Riposo in cui si tratta della Pittura e della Scoltura," (1584.)

Borghini, (VINCENZO,) a learned Italian antiquary and ecclesiastic, born at Florence in 1515, wrote a work on the "Antiquities of Tuscany," (1584.) He refused an archbishopric which was offered him by Cosimo de Medici. Died in 1580.

Borgi, boR'jee, (GIOVANNI,) an Italian mechanic and philanthropist, born at Rome about 1735, is called "the founder of ragged schools." He was encouraged and assisted in his benevolent labours by Pope Pius VII. Died about 1802.

Borgia. See ALEXANDER VI.

Borgia, boR'jȧ, (ALESSANDRO,) an Italian theologian, born at Velletri in 1682, became Archbishop of Fermo. Died in 1764.

Borgia, (CESARE,) Duc de Valentinois, (vä'lŏN'te'-nwȧ',) was an illegitimate son of Pope Alexander VI., by whom he was made a cardinal in 1492. He was distinguished for cunning, cruelty, and perfidy. In 1498 he was sent to France with a bull of divorce for Louis XII., who gave him the title of Duc de Valentinois. He married a daughter of Jean d'Albret, King of Navarre, in 1499. Having raised an army, he undertook the conquest of the Romagna, the cities of which were ruled by feudatories of the Roman See. He took Imola, Forlì, Pesaro, Rimini, etc. before the end of 1501, and put to death prisoners in violation of his oath. After the death of Alexander VI., in 1503, his power rapidly declined. (See ALEXANDER VI.) His army having been defeated, he was taken prisoner and sent to Spain in 1504. He escaped in 1506, entered the army of the King of Navarre, and was killed in battle in 1507.

See TOMASI, "Vita del Duca di Valentino," 1655; French version of the same, 1739; and "Leben des C. Borgia," Berlin, 1782.

Borgia, (FRANCISCO.) See FRANCISCO, SAINT.

Borgia, boR'jȧ, sometimes written **Borja,** (FRANCISCO,) a Spanish poet, highly esteemed in his time, was a descendant of Pope Alexander VI., and on his mother's side of Ferdinand the Catholic, King of Spain. He was appointed Viceroy of Peru in 1614. Died in 1658.

See ANTONIO, "Bibliotheca Hispana Nova."

Borgia, (LUCREZIA,) a daughter of Pope Alexander VI., and a sister of Cesare Borgia, was distinguished for beauty and talents. She was married to Giovanni Sforza, Lord of Pesaro, in 1493, to Alfonso, a natural son of Alfonso, King of Naples, in 1498, and to Alfonso of Este, a son of the Duke of Ferrara, in 1501. Her conduct gave rise to scandalous reports, which were generally believed by her contemporaries. She patronized at Ferrara several literary men, especially Bembo, who celebrated her in his works. "The compliments of the literati whom she rewarded," says Sismondi, with covert sarcasm, "seem at present to counterbalance the unanimous testimony of the historians, who accuse her of infamous conduct." Died in 1523.

See BOTTA, "Histoire d'Italie."

Borgia, (STEFANO,) an Italian cardinal, nephew of Alessandro, noticed above, born at Velletri in 1731. He published several antiquarian treatises. and made a valuable collection of medals and manuscripts. Died in 1804.

See AUBIN LOUIS MILLIN, "Notice sur la Vie du Cardinal Borgia."

Borgiani, boR-jä′nee, or Borgianni, boR-jân′nee, (Orazio,) an Italian painter and engraver, born in Rome about 1580, worked in Spain and in Rome. Died about 1630.

Borgo, boR′go, (Carlo,) an Italian Jesuit, born at Vicenza in 1731, was professor of theology at Módena. He wrote a panegyric on Ignatius Loyola, and a work on fortifications, which he dedicated to Frederick the Great. Died in 1794.

Borgo, [Lat. Bor′gus,] (Pietro Battista,) an Italian soldier and historian, served in the Swedish army in the Thirty Years' war, of which he wrote an account in Latin, entitled "Commentaries on the Swedish War," (1633.)

See Mazzuchelli, "Scrittori d'Italia."

Borgo, di, (Luca.) See Pacioli.

Borgognone. See Courtois, (Jacques.)

Borgognone, boR-gôn-yo′nà, (Ambrogio,) a distinguished Italian painter, born at Fossano about 1480. Among his master-pieces are the frescos in the church of San Ambrogio at Milan, and a "Madonna with Two Angels" in the Museum at Berlin.

See Lanzi, "History of Painting in Italy."

Borgondio. See Burgundio.

Borgt, van der, vän der boRkt, (Hendrik,) a Flemish painter, born at Brussels in 1583.

Borhân-ed-Deen or Borhân-Eddîn, bor-hân′ ed-deen′, a learned Arab, born about 1200, published "Advice to Students on the Manner of Studying," which has been translated into Latin and Turkish.

Borhân-ed-Deen or Borhân-Eddîn, (Ibrâheem,) an Arab writer, who wrote a "Treatise on the Customs and Maxims of the Ancient Philosophers," and other works. Died in 1480.

Borie, bo-ree′, (Adolph E.,) an American merchant, of French extraction, born in Philadelphia about 1810. He acquired a large fortune in foreign commerce. During the civil war he was an active and liberal supporter of the Union cause. He was appointed secretary of the navy by President Grant in March, 1869.

Borie, bo′re′, (Pierre Rose Ursule Dumoulin,) a French ecclesiastic, born at Beynat, in the diocese of Tulle, in 1808. He set out on a mission to Tonquin in 1831, where he laboured successfully for seven years; but in 1838 he was put to death by order of the king.

See "Vie de Monseigneur Borie," etc., 1844; "Nouvelle Biographie Générale."

Borie-Cambort, bo′re′ kôN′boR′, (Jean,) a French jurist, and member of the National Convention, voted for the death of Louis XVI. Died in 1805.

Bories, bo′re′, (Jean François Louis Leclerc,) born at Villefranche in 1795, attempted in 1821, with several accomplices, to excite a revolt against the government; but they failed in their enterprise, and were executed in 1822.

Boris. See Godoonof.

Borjon, boR′zhôN′, (Charles Emmanuel,) a French jurist and legal writer, born at Pont-de-Vaux, in Bresse, in 1633; died in 1691.

Borkhausen, boRk′how′zen, (Moritz Balthasar,) a German naturalist, born at Giessen in 1760, published the "Natural History of the Butterflies of Europe," (1788,) "Fauna of Germany," (1797,) and other scientific works. Died at Darmstadt in 1806.

See "Biographie Médicale."

Bor′lace or Bor′lase, (Edmund,) an English physician and historical writer, published the "History of the Execrable Irish Rebellion, etc.," (1680,) and other works on Ireland. Died in 1682.

See "Biographia Britannica."

Bor′land, (Solon,) an American general, born in Virginia, removed to Arkansas. He was elected a Senator of the United States for Arkansas about 1848. He fought against the Union in the civil war. Died in Texas in 1864.

Borlase, (Edmund.) See Borlace.

Borlase, bor′lạs, (William,) an English divine and eminent naturalist and antiquary, born in Cornwall in 1696. He was appointed in 1732 vicar of Saint Just, in Cornwall, and in 1750 became a Fellow of the Royal Society. Among his works are "Observations on the Antiquities, Historical and Monumental, of the County of Cornwall," (1754,) "Natural History of Cornwall," (1758,) and "Observations on the Ancient and Present State of the Islands of Scilly." He also wrote several religious treatises. He was an intimate friend and correspondent of Pope. Died in 1772.

See "Biographia Britannica."

Born, boRn, (Jakob,) a German jurist, born at Leipsic in 1638; died in 1709.

Born, (Jakob Heinrich,) a German jurist, born at Leipsic in 1717; died at Dresden in 1775.

Born, de, deh boRn, (Bertran or Bertrand,) a French troubadour and warrior, born in Périgord, took a prominent part in the wars between Henry II. of England and his sons, and between Philippe Auguste and Richard Cœur de Lion, about 1185–1200. According to Dante, ("Inferno,") Bertran de Born by his verses fomented war, and incited the sons of Henry II. to fight against him and against each other.

See Millot, "Histoire des Troubadours;" Villemain, "Cours de Littérature;" Longfellow, "Poets and Poetry of Europe."

Born, von, fon boRn, (Ignaz,) an eminent German mineralogist, born at Karlsburg, in Transylvania, in 1742. He wrote "Letters on the Minerals of Hungary," (1774,) "Index of Fossils," ("Lithophylacium Bornianum, seu Index Fossilium," 2 vols., 1772–75,) "Index Rerum Naturalium Musei Cæs. Vindobonæ," (1778,) and other works. He made important improvements in mining precious metals, among which was a new method of amalgamation. Died in Vienna in 1791.

See Ersch und Gruber, "Allgemeine Encyklopaedie;" Johann Pezzl, "Lebensbeschreibung Montecuculi's, W. Liechtenstein's und Born's," 1792.

Börne or Boerne, bör′neh, (Ludwig,) a celebrated journalist, critic, and politician, of Jewish extraction, born at Frankfort-on-the-Main in 1786. He studied at Heidelberg and Giessen, and subsequently became editor of the "Staats-Ristretto," a democratic journal, which was soon suppressed. Having been previously converted to Christianity, he edited in 1818–21 the "Wage," a periodical for literature, science, and art. After the revolution of 1830, he founded in Paris "Le Balance," in which he displayed great powers of satire and caustic wit. Among his best works are "Memorial of Jean Paul," ("Denkrede auf Jean Paul,") "Letters from Paris," (1832,) and "Menzel the Frenchman-Eater," ("Menzel der Franzosenfresser,") in reply to that critic's attack on the French. Börne was involved in a controversy with Heine, who wrote a severe attack upon him, entitled "Heine über Börne." Died in Paris in 1837.

See Karl Gutzkow, "L. Börnes Leben," 1840; Eduard Beurmann, "L. Börne als Charakter in der Literatur," 1837; Karl Boelsche, "Zwei Republikaner," 1850; "Foreign Quarterly Review" for August, 1832.

Borneil, de, deh boR′nàl′ or boR′nà′ye, (Giraud,) a French troubadour, born about 1150, is mentioned by Dante in his "Divine Comedy."

Bornemann, boR′neh-mân′, (Wilhelm,) a German jurist, born in Pomerania in 1794, became councillor of state in 1842, and in 1848 minister of justice.

Börner or Boerner, bör′ner, (Caspar,) a German theologian and mathematician, born at Hayn, in Misnia, lived at Dresden. Died in 1547.

See J. A. Ernesti, "Eulogium C. Boerneri," 1740.

Börner or Boerner, (Christian Friedrich,) born at Dresden in 1683, was professor of theology at Leipsic. He published several religious and philosophical works, in Latin. Died in 1753.

See Christian Boerner, "Vitæ suæ Descriptio," 1753.

Börner or Boerner, (Friedrich,) brother of the preceding, born at Leipsic in 1723, was a distinguished physician and writer. Died in 1761.

Börner or Boerner, (Nikolaus,) a German physician, born in Thuringia in 1693; died about 1770.

Bornier, boR′ne-à′, (Philippe,) a French jurist, was born at Montpellier in 1634; died in 1711.

Borowlaski, bor-ro-las′ke, Count, a Polish dwarf, who settled in England, is mentioned in Lockhart's "Life of Scott." He is said to have had uncommon intelligence and culture. Died in 1837.

e as k; ç as s; g̃ hard; g as j; g, h, k, guttural; n, nasal; r, trilled; s as z; th as in this. (☞ See Explanations, p. 23.)

Borowski, bo-rov'skee, (GEORG HEINRICH,) a naturalist, born in 1746 at Königsberg, in Prussia, published
the "Natural History of the Animal Kingdom," and other
works. Died in 1801.

Borowski, von, fon bo-rov'skee, (LUDWIG ERNST,)
a German Protestant divine, born at Königsberg in 1740,
became Archbishop of Prussia about 1829. Died in 1831.

Borri. See BORRUS.

Borri, bor'ree, or Bor'ro, [Lat. BUR'RUS,] sometimes
written Burrhi, (GIUSEPPE FRANCESCO,) an Italian adventurer, born at Milan in 1627. He professed to have
discovered the philosopher's stone, on the strength of
which he obtained considerable sums from Christina of
Sweden and the King of Denmark. He was afterwards
arrested as a heretic, and died in prison in 1695.

See HOEFER, "Histoire de la Chimie."

Borrich. See BORCH, (OLAF.)

Borrichius. See BORCH.

Borromée or Borromæus. See BORROMEO.

Borromeo, bor-ro-mā'o, (ANTONIO MARIA,) COUNT,
an Italian littérateur, born at Padua in 1724, wrote poems
of some merit, and published "Catalogo de' Novellieri
Italiani." Died in 1813.

Borromeo, [Fr. BORROMÉE, bo'ro'mà'; Lat. BOR-
ROMÆ'US,] (CARLO,) SAINT, an Italian cardinal, illustrious for his virtue and piety, born at Arona in 1538.
He was a nephew of Pope Pius IV., by whom he was
made Cardinal and Archbishop of Milan in 1560. He
devoted himself to reforming the morals of the clergy and
providing charitable institutions for the poor. During
the prevalence of the plague at Milan in 1576, he gave
his personal attendance to the sick at the risk of his life,
and spent all he possessed in administering to their
wants. He died in 1584, reverenced as a saint and martyr.
He was canonized by Paul V. in 1610. He was the author
of several theological works, and an exposition of the
doctrines of the Roman Church, entitled "Catechismus
Tridentinus," ("Trent Catechism.")

See BIMIUS, "Vita di S Carlo Borromeo," 1585; MAGNAGO, "Vita
di S. Carlo Borromeo," 1587; POSSEVINO, "Vita di Carlo Borromeo,"
1591; BESOZZI, "Vita Cardinalis C. Borromæi," 1601; GIUSSANO,
"Vita di S. Carlo Borromeo," 1610; GODEAU, "Vie de Saint Charles
Borromée," 1748; TOURON, "Vie de Saint Charles Borromée," 3 vols.,
1761; DIERINGER, "Der heilige C. Borromäus und die Kirchen-
verbesserung seiner Zeit," 1846; LUIS MUÑOZ, "Vida de S. C.
Borromeo," 1624; ALBAN BUTLER, "Vita di S. C. Borromeo," 1835;
ALEXANDER MARTIN, "Histoire de la Vie de S. C. Borromée," 1847.

Borromeo, (FEDERIGO,) Cardinal and Archbishop
of Milan, born in that city in 1564, was the nephew or,
as some writers state, the cousin of Saint Carlo. He
was distinguished for his profound attainments in the
classics and Oriental tongues, and was the founder of the
Ambrosian Library at Milan, for which he caused a great
number of manuscripts to be collected. He was, like
his predecessor, eminent for his exalted character and
active benevolence, which were conspicuous during the
famine and plague at Milan in 1627 and 1630. Of his
conduct on these occasions Manzoni has given a most
interesting picture in his celebrated novel, "I Promessi
Sposi." Died in 1631.

See RIVOLA, "Vita di Federigo Borromeo," 1656.

Borromini, bor-ro-mee'nee, (FRANCESCO,) an Italian
architect, born in the district of Como in 1599. He assisted his relative Maderno, and subsequently the celebrated Bernini, in the completion of Saint Peter's. He
was employed by Urban VIII. in several works at Rome,
which, though displaying much talent, are disfigured by
extravagance and bad taste. He committed suicide in
1667, in a fit of insanity.

See NAGLER, "Allgemeines Künstler-Lexikon."

Borron, bo'rôn', or Bouron, boo'rôn', written also
Boiron, Beron, Bosron, or Burons, (ROBERT and
HELIS,) two Norman-English writers, supposed to have
been brothers or near relatives, were patronized by
Henry II.

See WILKEN, "Histoire des Croisades."

Borroni, bor-ro'nee, (GIOVANNI ANGELO,) an Italian
painter, born at Cremona in 1684, worked many years in
Milan. Died in 1772.

Bor'row, (GEORGE,) an English writer, born at Norwich in 1803. He early distinguished himself by his
attainments in modern languages, including that of the

gipsies, with whom he associated. He published in
1841 "The Zincali; or an Account of the Gipsies of
Spain;" being the result of his observations in that country. He was soon after sent by the London Bible Society on a mission to Spain. In 1843 he brought out his
"Bible in Spain; or Journeys, Adventures, and Impris-
onments of an Englishman in an Attempt to circulate
the Scriptures in the Peninsula." It was received with
extraordinary favour, and is regarded as one of the most
original and attractive works ever written on that country.
Among his works are "Lavengro," (1851,) and "Romany
Rye," (1857,) which are partly autobiographical.

"We conceive," says the "Quarterly Review" for December, 1842, "that Mr. Borrow has come out in these
pages" ("The Bible in Spain") "as an English author of
high mark. Considering the book merely as one of adventure, it seems to us about the most extraordinary one
that has appeared in our own, or indeed in any other,
language, for a very long time."

See, also, "Edinburgh Review" for February, 1843; "Blackwood's
Magazine" for September, 1841, and March, 1851; "Brief Biographies," by SAMUEL SMILES.

Bor'rus or Borri, bor'ree, (CRISTOFORO,) born at
Milan, went on a mission to the East, and was afterwards
professor of mathematics at Lisbon. Died in 1632.

Borsato, boR-sä'to, (GIUSEPPE,) a skilful Italian painter
of the present century, has painted landscapes and architectural pieces. He was for some time professor of painting in the Academy of Venice.

Borsieri de Kanifeld, boR-se-ā'ree dä kä'ne-fĕlt,
[Lat. BURSE'RIUS,] (GIOVANNI BATTISTA,) a Tyrolese
physician and medical writer, born at Trent in 1725.
He studied. at Padua, and in 1770 was appointed by
Maria Theresa professor of materia medica at Pavia.
Died in 1785.

See LEONARDO DEI CLOCK, "Notizie biografiche intorno G. B.
Borsieri de Kanifeld," 1839.

Borsini, boR-see'nee, (LORENZO,) an Italian satirical
poet, born at Sienna in 1800. He was in his youth successively soldier, comedian, and musician, and led an
adventurous life. In 1837 he published a "Sentimental
Journey." His chief works are a poem entitled "The
Ass," ("Asino," 1844,) and "Novissimo Galateo," (1851,)
a satire in verse, which had considerable popularity.

Borsum, van, vän boR'sŭm, (ADAM,) a Dutch painter
of landscapes and animals, lived about 1666.

Borth'wick, (DAVID,) a Scottish jurist in the time
of James I. of England, rose through various offices to
be lord advocate of Scotland. Died in 1581.

Borthwick, (PETER,) a noted Tory politician, born
in Scotland in 1804. About 1833 he had a public discussion with Mr. George Thompson, in which he advocated gradual, instead of immediate, emancipation
of the slaves. He subsequently became manager of the
"Morning Post." Died in 1852.

Boru, (BRIAN.) See BRIAN BOROIMHE.

Bory, de, deh bo're', (GABRIEL,) a French savant,
born in Paris in 1720, contributed several scientific treatises to the "Memoirs of the Academy of Sciences," and
other journals. He was appointed in 1761 Governor-
General of Saint Domingo. Died in 1801.

Bory de Saint-Vincent, bo're' deh săN'văN'sôN',
(JEAN BAPTISTE GEORGE MARIE,) a distinguished French
naturalist and geographer, born at Agen in 1780. He
set out with Baudin's scientific expedition to Australia
in 1800, but proceeded no farther than Mauritius, where
he made a survey of the neighbouring islands. On his
return to France he published his "Essays on the Fortunate Isles and the Ancient Atlantis," (1803,) and "Voyage among the African Islands," (1804, 3 vols.,) with an
atlas.) He was charged in 1829 with the command of
the scientific expedition to the Morea. He was principal
editor of the "Dictionnaire classique d'Histoire naturelle," and contributed numerous articles to other scientific journals. Died in 1846.

See "Justification de la Conduite, etc. de J. B. Bory de Saint-
Vincent," by himself, 1816; HÉRICART DE THURY, "Notice sur le
Baron Bory de Saint-Vincent," 1848; "Edinburgh Review" for April,
1805.

Borzoni, boRt-so'nee, or Borzone, boRt-so'nä,
(FRANCESCO MARIA,) a painter of Genoa, son of Luciano,
noticed below, born in 1625; died in 1696.

ā, ē, ī, ō, ū, ȳ, long; ă, ĕ, ĭ, ŏ, ŭ, ȳ, short; ạ, ẹ, ị, ọ, obscure; fär, fâll, fât; mêt; nŏt; gŏŏd; mōŏn;

Borzoni, (LUCIANO,) a painter of portraits and history, born at Genoa in 1590. His chief merit was truth of expression. Died at Genoa in 1645.

Bos, bos, Bosch, bosk, or **Bosco,** (HIEROM,) a Dutch painter and engraver, born at Bois-le-Duc, in Brabant, about 1450, was surnamed LE JOYEUX. He is supposed to have spent part of his life in Spain, where several of his best works are to be seen. Among these we may name the "Flight into Egypt," "Temptation of Saint Antony," and a "Crucifixion" in the Escurial. He excelled particularly in delineating spectres, demons, and other supernatural subjects. He is said by Descamps to have been one of the first artists who painted in oil. According to some authors, he died about 1500.

See DESCAMPS, "Vies des Peintres Flamands, Hollandais," etc.

Bos, Bus, bŭs, or **Van den Bosch,** vän den bosk, (KORNELIS,) a Dutch engraver, born at Bois-le-Duc about 1510. He engraved after Raphael and Giulio Romano.

Bos, (LAMBERT,) a Dutch philologist, born in Friesland in 1670, became professor of Greek at Franeker in 1704. Among his numerous and learned works we may name "Ellipses Græcæ," "Description of Greek Antiquities," ("Antiquitatum Græcarum Descriptio," 1713,) which is highly esteemed, and an edition of the Septuagint, (1709.) Died in 1717.

See SCHULTENS, "Oratio funebris in Obitum L. Bos," 1718.

Bos, de, deh bos, (JAN LUDWIG,) a Dutch painter of flowers, fruits, and insects, born at Bois-le-Duc. Died in 1507.

See DESCAMPS, "Vies des Peintres Flamands, Hollandais," etc.

Bos, du. See DUBOS.

Bosc, bosk, (LOUIS AUGUSTIN GUILLAUME,) an eminent French naturalist, son of Bosc d'Antic, noticed below, born in Paris in 1759. Having narrowly escaped death during the reign of terror, he visited America in 1796, where he spent two years in scientific investigations. After his return he became a member of the Academy of Sciences, and professor at the Jardin des Plantes, and obtained other distinctions. He published the "Natural History of Shells," (5 vols., 1824,) "History of Worms and Crustacea," (2 vols., 1829,) a "Dictionary of Agriculture," (1809,) and a "Complete Course of Agriculture." He was charged by Madame Roland with the publication of her memoirs, and appointed guardian of her daughter. Died in 1828.

See SILVESTRE, "Notice biographique sur L. A. G. Bosc," 1829; "Nouvelle Biographie Générale."

Bosc d'Antic, bosk dôn'tèk', (PAUL,) born in Languedoc in 1726, published a treatise, "On the Best Means of uniting Perfection and Economy in the Glass-Manufacture in France." Died in 1784.

Bosc, du, dü bosk, (CLAUDE,) a French engraver, who worked in England in 1715, engraved "Marlborough's Battles," and other works.

Bosc, du, (PIERRE THOMINES,) a French Protestant theologian, born at Bayeux in 1623; died in 1692.

See P. LEGENDRE, "Vie de Pierre Thomines du Bosc," 1694.

Boscager, bos'kȧ'zhȧ', (JEAN,) a French jurist, born at Béziers in 1601; died in 1687.

Boscan Almogaver, bos-kän' äl-mo-gä-vaiR',(JUAN,) a celebrated Spanish poet, born at Barcelona about 1500. Through the influence of his friend the Venetian ambassador Navagero, he attempted, conjointly with Garcilasso de la Vega, to reform Spanish poetry by adopting the metre and forms of the Italian. This innovation, though at first strongly opposed, was eventually successful. He was the author of sonnets and canzones in the style of Petrarch, and several epistles of great beauty. He also made an excellent translation of the Greek poem of "Hero and Leander," by Musæus. Died in 1544.

See TICKNOR, "History of Spanish Literature;" LONGFELLOW, "Poets and Poetry of Europe;" NICÉRON, "Mémoires."

Bos'ca-wen, (EDWARD,) an English admiral, born in 1711, was a son of Viscount Falmouth, and related on the mother's side to the Duke of Marlborough. In 1747 he fought under Anson in the engagement off Cape Finisterre, and in 1748 against the French in India. As admiral of the blue, he commanded in 1758 the expedition to America, where he gained several victories. The following year he defeated the French in the Mediterranean, taking several ships and two thousand prisoners.

He was for these services made general of the marines and a member of the privy council, and obtained a pension. Died in 1761.

See CAMPBELL, "Lives of the British Admirals."

Boscawen, (WILLIAM,) a nephew of the preceding, born in 1752, wrote a poetical "Essay on the Progress of Satire," and translated the works of Horace. Died in 1811.

Bosch. See BOS.

Bosch, van, vän bosk, (BERNARDUS,) a Dutch poet, born in 1709, wrote "Poetic Recreations." Died in 1786.

Bosch, van, (HIEROM,) a Dutch scholar and bibliopole, and one of the best Latin poets of his time, born at Amsterdam in 1740; died in 1811.

See J. D. VAN LENNEP, "Memoria H. de Bosch," 1817.

Bosch, van den, vän den bosk, (BALTHASAR,) a Flemish painter, born at Antwerp in 1675. Among his master-pieces is the portrait of the Duke of Marlborough on horseback. Died at Antwerp in 1715.

See DESCAMPS, "Vies des Peintres Flamands," etc.

Bosch, van den, (JAKOB,) a Dutch painter of fruit and still life, born at Amsterdam in 1636; died in 1676.

Bosche, van den, vän den bos'kėh, [Lat. BOS'CHIUS,] (PIETER,) a learned Flemish Jesuit, born at Brussels in 1686, was a contributor to the "Acta Sanctorum," begun by Bollandus. Died in 1736.

Böschenstein or **Boeschenstein,** bösh'ėn-stīn', (JOHANN,) a German philologist, born in 1471, was professor of Hebrew at Augsburg and Wittenberg. Melanchthon was one of his pupils. His "Hebrew Grammar" was printed in 1514, under the direction of Melanchthon.

Boscheron-Desportes. See DESPORTES.

Boschi, bos'kee, (FABRIZIO,) a skilful Italian painter, born at Florence about 1575; died in 1642.

Boschini, bos-kee'nee, (MARCO,) a Venetian painter, engraver, and writer on art, born in 1613; died in 1678.

Boschius. See BOSCHE.

Boscoli, bos'ko-lee, (ANDREA,) an Italian historical painter, born at Florence about 1550; died in 1606.

Boscovich, bos'ko-vik,?[Lat. BOSCOVI'CHUS,] (RUGGIERO GIUSEPPE,) a voluminous writer on mathematics, astronomy, and natural philosophy, was born at Ragusa, in Dalmatia, in May, 1711. He entered the order of Jesuits in 1725, and became distinguished by his talents and attainments in various sciences. He was appointed professor of philosophy and mathematics at the Roman College about 1740. He was among the first savants on the continent who adopted the Newtonian philosophy, which he explained in "Philosophiæ Naturalis Theoria," (1758,) a work of much merit. About 1750 he was employed by the pope to measure an arc of the meridian in the Papal States. An account of this operation was published in 1755. His Latin poem "On Eclipses of the Sun and Moon" (London, 1760) is praised by Walckenaer. Boscovich is ranked among the best modern Latin poets by several French critics. After the suppression of his order, (about 1765,) he became professor at Pavia. About 1775 he removed to Paris, and was appointed "Directeur de l'Optique de la Marine." Among his chief works are "Elementa universa Matheseos," (3 vols., 1754,) and treatises on Optics and Astronomy, ("Opera pertinentia ad Opticam et Astronomiam," (5 vols., 1785.) He died at Milan in February, 1787.

See LALANDE, "Éloge de Boscovich," in the "Journal des Savants," 1792; FABRONI, "Vitæ Italorum doctrina excellentium;" RICCA, "Elogio storico dell' Abate R. G. Boscovich," 1789.

Bose, bo'zeh, (ERNST GOTTLOB,) a German physician and scientific writer, born at Leipsic in 1723, became professor of therapeutics in his native city. Died in 1788.

Boselli, bo-sėl'lee, (ANTONIO,) a painter of the Venetian school, lived about 1500–40.

Bosellini, bo-sėl-lee'nee, (CARLO,) an Italian jurist and writer on political economy, born at Módena in 1765; died in 1823.

Bosio, bo'se-o, (ANGIOLINA,) an Italian vocalist, born at Turin in 1829, performed with brilliant success at Copenhagen, Madrid, Paris, and in the United States. She was married about 1856 to Signor Xindavelonis.

Bosio, (ANTONIO,) an Italian antiquary of Rome, author of "Roma Sotterranea," (1632,) a treatise on the catacombs of Rome. Died in 1629.

Bosio, (FRANÇOIS JOSEPH,) BARON, a distinguished Italian sculptor, born at Monaco in 1769, studied under Pajou, in France. He was employed by the emperor Napoleon in numerous works, among which are the bas-reliefs of the column of the Place Vendôme, busts of Napoleon, the empress Josephine, Queen Hortense, and Pauline Borghese. His "Cupid Darting Arrows" is esteemed one of his best poetic works. He was a member of the French Institute and of the Academy of Arts at Berlin. Died in 1845.

See "Nouvelle Biographie Générale."

Bosio, [Lat. Bo′sius,] (GIACOMO,) an Italian ecclesiastic and historical writer, lived about 1560.

Bosman or **Bosmann,** bos′mân, (WILLEM,) a Dutch traveller, published in 1704 "Travels in Guinea," which has been translated into French and English.

Bosquet, bos′kà′, (PIERRE FRANÇOIS JOSEPH,) a marshal of France, born at Pau in 1810. He served in nearly all the campaigns of Algeria from 1834 to 1852, became general of brigade in 1848, and general of division in 1853. His conduct at Alma was applauded, and his skilful dispositions contributed to the victory at Inkerman, November, 1854. He performed a prominent part at the siege of Sebastopol, and was wounded in the final assault in September, 1855. In 1856 he became marshal of France. Died in 1862.

Bosquet, de, deh bos′kà′, (FRANÇOIS,) born at Narbonne in 1605, became Bishop of Montpellier. He wrote a Latin "History of the Gallican Church." Died in 1676.

Bosquillon, bos′ke′yòn′, (ÉDOUARD FRANÇOIS MARIE,) a French physician and scholar, born at Montdidier in 1744. He settled in Paris, became professor of Greek in the College of France in 1774, and was afterwards royal censor. He was the owner of a library of more than thirty thousand volumes, including the most valuable medical works in ancient and modern languages. He produced translations of English medical works, to which he added valuable notes. Died in 1816.

See QUÉRARD, "La France Littéraire."

Bosron. See BORRON.

Bosscha, bos′kâ, (HERMAN,) an eminent Dutch philologist and Latin poet, born at Leeuwarden in 1755. He studied at Franeker, and in 1804 became professor of ancient literature at Groningen. A collection of his Latin poems, entitled "Musa Daventriaca," was published at Deventer in 1820. He also translated into Dutch Schiller's "Revolt of the Netherlands," Denon's "Travels in Egypt," and Plutarch's "Lives." Died in 1819.

See VAN KAMPEN, "Histoire Littéraire."

Bosschaert, bos′kȁrt, (THOMAS WILLEBRORD,) a Dutch painter of great merit, born at Berg-op-Zoom in 1613, was director of the Academy at Antwerp. His works are in the style of Van Dyck. Died in 1656.

See DESCAMPS, "Vies des Peintres Flamands, Hollandais," etc.

Bosse, bos, (ABRAHAM,) a French engraver and writer on art, born at Tours in 1611; died in 1678.

Bosseck, bos′sĕk, (HEINRICH OTTO,) M.D., a German botanist, born at Leipsic in 1726; died in 1776.

Bosselet, bos′là′, (HIPPOLYTE,) a French political writer, born in Paris in 1824.

Bossi, bos′see, (GIUSEPPE,) an eminent Italian painter and poet, born near Milan in August, 1777, was a friend of Canova. He was elected president of the Academies of Milan, Venice, and Bologna, and published in 1810 "Il Cenacolo di Leonardo da Vinci," which is an admirable monument of learning and taste. He produced a number of sonnets, canzones, etc. Among his paintings are "The Italian Parnassus," and "Aurora and Night." Died in 1815.

See TIPALDO, "Biografia degli Italiani illustri;" G. CALVI, "Versi in Morte di G. Bossi," 1816.

Bossi, bos′see, (GIUSEPPE CARLO AURELIO,) BARON, an able Italian diplomatist and poet, born at Turin in 1758. He was employed by the King of Sardinia on embassies to Prussia, Russia, and Venice. About 1800 he entered the service of Bonaparte, and promoted the annexation of Piedmont to France. Among his poems are "American Independence," (1785,) and "Oromasia," (1805-12.) Died in Paris in 1823.

See TIPALDO, "Biografia degli Italiani illustri."

Bossi, (LUIGI,) an Italian antiquary and *littérateur*, born at Milan in 1785. He published an "Introduction to the Study of the Arts of Design," and other works. Died in 1835.

See G. B. CARTA, "Cenni biografichi intorno al Cavaliere L. Bossi," 1835.

Bos′sĭ-us or **Bo′sĭ-us,** (BENIGNUS,) an engraver, surnamed THE BELGIAN, lived about 1510, and worked at Rome.

Bosso, bos′so, (MATTEO,) a learned Italian ecclesiastic, born at Verona in 1428, was the friend and patron of Politian and other eminent scholars. He wrote, in Latin, several moral essays, among which is one "On the Culture of True Wisdom," ("De vero Sapientiæ Cultu," 1509.) His letters and orations are highly commended. Died at Padua in 1502.

Bossu, bo′sü′, (N.,) a French navigator, was one of the first who explored the State of Louisiana. He published, in 1777, "New Voyages in North America."

See QUÉRARD, "La France Littéraire."

Bossuet, bo′sü-à′, almost bos′swà′, (JACQUES BÉNIGNE,) a celebrated French divine and pre-eminent pulpit orator, born at Dijon, September 27, 1627, was a son of a counsellor of the parliament of Metz. In 1642 he became a student in the College of Navarre, in Paris. His favourite studies were Greek, Latin, philosophy, and the theology of the Bible. In 1648 he pronounced a thesis in the presence of the Prince of Condé, who was thenceforth his friend. He received the degree of doctor and the order of priesthood in 1652, and removed to Metz, of which he had been appointed canon. He is said to have converted many Protestants at Metz by his sermons and by a tract which he wrote against their doctrines in 1655. Having become renowned for eloquence, he was appointed to preach the Advent sermons before the court in 1661, and the Lent sermons of 1662. Between 1661 and 1669 he preached in nearly all the pulpits of Paris, converted from Protestantism Marshal Turenne, and composed his celebrated "Exposition of the Doctrine of the Catholic Church on Subjects of Controversy," ("Exposition de la Doctrine de l'Église catholique sur les Matières de Controverse," 1671,) which was circulated in manuscript three years before it was printed. He became Bishop of Condom in 1669, and pronounced in that year a funeral oration on Henrietta Maria, Queen of England, which is an admirable model of eloquence.

In 1670 he was appointed preceptor to the dauphin, and in 1671 was elected a member of the French Academy. He wrote for the instruction of the dauphin a "Treatise on the Knowledge of God and Oneself," and his "Discourse on Universal History," ("Discours sur l'Histoire universelle," 1681,) "which," says Hallam, "is perhaps the greatest effort of his wonderful genius. Every preceding abridgment of so immense a subject had been superficial and dry. He first irradiated the entire annals of antiquity, down to the age of Charlemagne, with flashes of light that reveal a unity and coherence which had been lost in their magnitude and obscurity. . . . It is written in that close, nervous style which no one certainly in the French language has ever surpassed." Bossuet, who was now the recognized champion of the Roman Church in France, had a "regular conference" on church authority with the Protestant minister Claude in 1678. He was appointed Bishop of Meaux in 1681, and was the organ and master-spirit of the assembly of clergy which met in 1682, on the subject of a quarrel between Pope Innocent XI. and Louis XIV. in relation to the *régale*. Bossuet was the author of the four articles which this assembly adopted as the Gallican creed on the limitations of the papal authority, and which were confirmed by the king. In 1688 appeared his greatest polemical work against the Protestants, a "History of the Variations of the Protestant Churches," ("Histoire des Variations des Églises protestants," 2 vols.) "Never did his genius," says Hallam, "find a subject more fit to display its characteristic impetuosity, its arrogance, or its cutting and merciless spirit of sarcasm." ("Introduction to the Literature of Europe.")

He was engaged in a long correspondence (1691-1700) with Leibnitz in relation to a proposed treaty for the union of the Lutheran and Roman Churches. He offered

ā, ē, ī, ō, ū, ȳ, *long;* à, ė, ȯ, same, less prolonged; ă, ĕ, ĭ, ŏ, ŭ, ў, *short;* ạ, ẹ, ị, ọ, *obscure;* fär, fäll, fȁt; mêt; nŏt; gōŏd; mōŏn;

no important concession in doctrine, and assumed the tone of a dictator rather than a mediator, but was disposed to concede the sacramental cup to the laity. Bossuet and Fenelon clashed with each other in the controversy of Quietism, which originated in the writings of Madame Guyon. He treated Fénelon with remarkable harshness, and procured the condemnation at Rome of his "Maximes des Saintes" in 1699. He died in Paris on the 12th of April, 1704. Even during his life he had received from La Bruyère the title of a Father of the Church.

Among his most admired productions are six funeral orations, viz., "On the Queen of England," "On the Duchess of Orléans," (1670,) "On Maria Theresa, Queen of France," (1683,) "On Anne, Princess Palatine," (1685,) "On M. Letellier," (1686,) and "On the Prince de Condé," (1687.) "Few works of genius, perhaps, in the French language," says Hallam, "are better known or have been more prodigally extolled. In that style of eloquence which the ancients call demonstrative, or rather descriptive, the style of panegyric or commemoration, they are doubtless superior to those justly celebrated productions of Thucydides and Plato that have descended to us from Greece; nor has Bossuet been equalled by any later writer. . . . In moral wisdom Bossuet was pre-eminent; his thoughts are never subtle or far-fetched; they have a sort of breadth, a generality of application, which is peculiarly required in those who address a mixed assembly." ("Introduction to the Literature of Europe.")

Among the best editions of his complete works is that published at Versailles in 43 vols., (1815 et seq.)

See SAINT-MARC-GIRARDIN, "Éloge de Bossuet," 1827; "Life of Bossuet," in English, by CHARLES BUTLER, 1812; "Vie de Bossuet," by BURIGNY, 1761; "Éloge de Bossuet," by D'ALEMBERT; "Histoire de Bossuet," by M. DE BAUSSET, 4 vols., 1814; HENRI PATIN, "Éloge de Bossuet," 1827; J. J. E. ROY, "Histoire de J. B. Bossuet," 1840; "Edinburgh Review" for January, 1858; "London Quarterly Review" for January, 1814; LAMARTINE, "Memoirs of Celebrated Characters," 1856.

Bossuet, (JACQUES BÉNIGNE,) nephew of the preceding, born in 1664, became Bishop of Troyes in 1716. He edited his uncle's works, and wrote several theological treatises. Died in 1743.

Bos'su-lus, (MATHIEU,) a rhetorician, born in France or Italy, was preceptor to Don Carlos, the son of Philip II. of Spain. He lived in Paris in 1583.

Bossut, bo'sü', (CHARLES,) an eminent French geometer, born near Lyons in 1730, studied in the Jesuits' College at Lyons. He was a friend of Fontenelle and D'Alembert, and assisted the latter in preparing the mathematical articles for the "Encyclopédie." In 1752 he became professor of mathematics in the school of engineers at Mézières. He obtained several prizes of the Academy of Sciences, of which he became a member in 1768. Among his works are a "Treatise on Mechanics and Hydrodynamics," (1763,) "Complete Course of Mathematics," and "Essay on the General History of Mathematics," (2 vols., 1802.) He also published an edition of Pascal's works, 5 vols. 8vo. Died in 1814.

See DELAMBRE, "Éloge de Bossut;" "Mémoires," (of the Institute.)

Bostkai, bost'ki, (STEPHEN,) a Hungarian chief, was leader of a revolt against Rudolph II., who by the treaty of Comorn confirmed him in the possession of Transylvania. Died in 1606.

Bos'ton, (JOHN,) a monk of Bury Saint Edmund's, in England, of the fifteenth century, wrote a "History of Monachism."

Bos'ton, (THOMAS,) a Scottish Presbyterian divine and Hebrew scholar, born at Dunse in 1676. He published a "Body of Divinity," "Human Nature in its Fourfold State," and several other works, which are highly esteemed by his sect. He preached many years at Ettrick, Selkirkshire. Died in 1732.

See "Memoir of the Life, Time, etc. of Thomas Boston," 1776; CHAMBERS, "Biographical Dictionary of Eminent Scotsmen."

Bos'well, (ALEXANDER,) son of the biographer of Dr. Johnson, born in Scotland in 1775, was a friend of Sir Walter Scott. He published "Songs chiefly in the Scottish Dialect," and other works. He was killed in 1822, in a duel arising from a political quarrel.

Boswell, (JAMES,) a Scottish lawyer and famous biographer, born at Edinburgh in 1740, was a son of the Laird of Auchinleck, (pronounced af'flek.) He published in 1763 a volume of Letters which had passed between himself and Andrew Erskine, and was introduced to Dr. Johnson in the same year. He afterwards made a tour in France, Germany, and Italy, and returned home in 1766 a warm admirer of Paoli, whom he had visited. He is said to have exhibited himself in public with a placard on his hat bearing the inscription of *Corsica Boswell*, and he published in 1768 a "Journal of a Tour in Corsica." Having become intimate with Dr. Johnson, he made a journey with him to the Western Islands in 1773. His vanity, curiosity, or other questionable motive, prompted him to seek the society of eminent men, and not unfrequently rendered him the laughing-stock of those whose favour he courted. Dr. Johnson said that Boswell had missed his only chance of immortality by not having been alive when the "Dunciad" was written. His "Life of Johnson" (2 vols., 1791) was received with great favour. "The Life of Johnson," says Macaulay, "is assuredly a great, a very great work. Homer is not more decidedly the first of heroic poets, Shakspeare is not more decidedly the first of dramatists, . . . than Boswell is the first of biographers. He has no second. . . . We are not sure that there is in the whole history of the human intellect so strange a phenomenon as this book. Many of the greatest men that ever lived have written biography. Boswell was one of the smallest men that ever lived, and he has beaten them all." Died in 1795.

See MACAULAY's critique on Croker's edition of BOSWELL's "Life of Johnson," published in the "Edinburgh Review," 1831; also "London Quarterly Review" for April, 1857; "Edinburgh Review" for April, 1857; "Fraser's Magazine" for March, 1857.

Boswell, (JAMES,) son of the preceding, born in 1779. He published Malone's edition of Shakspeare, to which he made some additions. Died in 1822.

Bos'worth, (JOSEPH,) an eminent English philologist and divine, born in Derbyshire in 1788. He studied at Aberdeen, where he took the degree of LL.D., and in 1839 received that of D.D. at Trinity College, Cambridge. He had been previously appointed British chaplain at Rotterdam, (1832,) where he resided eight years. His studies were principally directed to the Anglo-Saxon and kindred dialects; and he has published "Elements of Anglo-Saxon Grammar," (1823,) "A Dictionary of the Anglo-Saxon Language," (1838,) and an edition of "King Alfred's Anglo-Saxon Version of the History of the World, from the Latin of Orosius." Dr. Bosworth's distinguished attainments in philology have procured him admission to the Royal Institution of the Netherlands, and other learned societies of Europe; he is also a Fellow of the Royal Society, and of the Society of Antiquaries, London.

See "Edinburgh Review" for October, 1839.

Botal, bo-tâl', or **Botalli,** bo-tâl'lee, (LEONARDO,) a distinguished physician and medical writer, born at Asti, in the Sardinian States, about 1530. He studied under Fallopius, and was subsequently physician to Charles IX. and Henry III.

See BAYLE, "Historical and Critical Dictionary."

Botalli. See BOTAL.

Botelho, bo-têl'yo, or **Botello,** (NUNO ALVAREZ,) a Portuguese navigator, was appointed in 1628 Governor of the Portuguese Indies. Died in 1630.

Botero, bo-tâ'ro, (GIOVANNI,) surnamed BENIS'IUS, an Italian ecclesiastic and writer, born at Bene, in Piedmont, in 1540. He was secretary to Saint Carlo Borromeo, and in 1599 was appointed by Charles Emmanuel tutor to his children. His political treatise entitled "Della Ragione di Stato" had a high reputation in his time. Died in 1617.

Botetourt, bot'e-toort, (NORBORNE BERKELEY,) LORD, born about 1738, was sent to Virginia as governor in 1768. Although he dissolved the house of burgesses (1769) for passing resolves against the obnoxious measures of the British Parliament, he was very much respected in the colony. Died in 1770.

Bot'field, (BERIAH,) F.R.S., an English antiquary, born in Salop in 1807. He wrote a "Tour in Scotland," and other works. Died in 1863.

є as k; ç as s; ğ hard; ġ as j; G, H, K, guttural; N, nasal; R, trilled; š as z; ŧh as in this. (☞See Explanations, p. 23.)

Both, bōt, (JOHN and ANDREW,) brothers and distinguished painters, born at Utrecht about 1610, were pupils of Bloemaert, and worked for some years in Italy. John is said to have painted the landscapes, while his brother supplied the figures and animals. They died about 1650. According to some authors, Andrew died in 1656.

See DESCAMPS, "Vies des Peintres Flamands," etc.

Bothwell, both′well, or **Bodwell,**(JAMES HEPBURN,) EARL OF, a Scottish courtier and conspirator, noted for his audacity and profligacy, was born about 1526. He was the son and heir of Patrick, Earl of Bothwell, who died in 1556. On the accession of Queen Mary (1561) he joined the Protestant party, against which he had before fought, and became a member of the privy council. In 1562 he formed a conspiracy to seize the queen, but was detected and imprisoned. He escaped to France, and in his absence was outlawed. He returned in 1565, and gained the favour of the queen, "whose measures," says Hume, "were all directed by his advice and authority." When Darnley was killed in 1567, public opinion designated Bothwell as the author or accomplice of the crime. He was tried, but no accuser dared to appear; and he was acquitted, with circumstances that confirmed the general opinion of his guilt. "The favour which Mary openly bore to Bothwell," says Hume, "kept every one in awe." A large number of nobles signed a paper in which they recommended Bothwell to Mary as a husband. In 1567 he seized the queen (who was returning from a visit to Stirling) and carried her to Dunbar Castle, with an avowed design to force her to marry him. He effected this object without difficulty. (See MARY STUART.) The principal nobility having taken arms against him, he escaped to the Orkneys, where, according to a doubtful story, he subsisted for some time by piracy. According to Burton, he simply made his escape from the Orkneys in a pirate vessel to Denmark. He afterwards died in the castle of Draxholm, about 1577.

See BURTON, "History of Scotland," vol. iv. chaps. xlv., xlvi., and xlvii.; ROBERTSON, "History of Scotland;" FROUDE, "Reign of Elizabeth."

Bothwidi, bot′we-dee, (JOHAN,) Bishop of Linköping, in Sweden, was preacher to Gustavus Adolphus, whom he accompanied in his campaigns. Died in 1635.

Botin, bo′tin, (ANDERS,) a Swedish historian, born in 1724, wrote a "History of the Swedish Nation to the Reign of Gustavus I.," (1757.) Died in 1790.

Botschild or **Bottschild,** bot′shĭlt, (SAMUEL,) a German painter and engraver, born in Saxony about 1640; died in 1707.

Bott or **Bodt, de,** dĕh bot, (JEAN,) a French architect, born in 1670, was employed by Frederick I. of Prussia to construct the arsenal at Berlin. Died in 1745.

Bott, (THOMAS,) an English dissenting divine, born at Derby in 1688, published, among other works, an answer to Warburton's "Divine Legation of Moses," (1743.)

Bot′ta, (ANNE CHARLOTTE LYNCH,) an American poetess, born at Bennington, Vermont, was married in 1855 to Vincenzo Botta, noticed below. A volume of her poems has been published.

Botta, bot′tä, (CARLO GIUSEPPE GUGLIELMO,) an eminent Italian historian, born at San Giorgio, in Piedmont, about 1768. He graduated in medicine at Turin, and in 1795 was appointed surgeon to the French army in Italy. He became in 1800 a member of the Consulta of Piedmont, and in 1803 was elected to the French legislative body. He published in 1809 a "History of the War of American Independence," translated into English by G. W. Otis of Boston, and in 1824 his "History of Italy from 1789 to 1814," (4 vols.,) which is written with impartiality, in a spirited and attractive style, and is ranked among the best productions of the kind in recent Italian literature. His "Continuation of Guicciardini's History of Italy down to 1789" (10 vols.) came out in 1832. He also wrote a "History of the Nations of Italy from Constantine to Napoleon," (1825,) "Description of the Isle of Corfu," a poem entitled "Il Camillo, o Vejo conquistato," and other works. Died in Paris in 1837.

See TIPALDO, "Biografia degli Italiani illustri;" F. BECCHI, "Elogio storico di C. Botta," 1839.

Botta, (PAOLO EMILIO,) a distinguished archæologist and naturalist, son of the preceding, born about 1800. Being appointed French consul to Alexandria, he visited Arabia in 1837, and in 1844 published an "Account of a Journey in Yemen in 1837 for the Museum of Natural History, Paris." While consul at Mosul in 1843, he excavated at the village of Khorsabad, on the Tigris, in the neighbourhood of Mosul, the remains of an Assyrian palace containing stones with cuneiform inscriptions, and statues similar to those since discovered by Layard. A number of these sculptures are now at the Louvre in Paris. Botta published, conjointly with Letronne, Burnouf, and other savants, a splendid work entitled "Monuments of Nineveh discovered and described by P. E. Botta, with Designs by Flandrin," (5 vols. fol., 1847.)

See "Journal des Débats" for December, 1844.

Botta, (VINCENZO,) an Italian statesman, born in Piedmont, became professor of philosophy at Turin, and in 1849 was elected to the Sardinian Parliament.

Bottalla, bot-täl′lä, (GIOVANNI MARIA,) an Italian painter, born at Savona in 1613, was surnamed IL RAFAELLINO, from the resemblance of his style to that of Raphael. He was a pupil of Pietro da Cortona, and executed several works of great merit at Rome and Genoa. Died in 1644.

See LANZI, "History of Painting in Italy."

Bottani, bot-tä′nee, (GIUSEPPE,) an Italian painter, born at Cremona in 1717, became professor in the Academy of Mantua. Died in 1784.

Bottari, bot-tä′ree, (GIOVANNI GAETANO,) an eminent Italian scholar and ecclesiastic, born at Florence in 1689. He published in 1738, in conjunction with other learned men, a new edition of the "Vocabolario della Crusca," (6 vols. fol.) He was subsequently appointed director of the grand duke's printing-establishment at Florence, professor of ecclesiastical history in the college di Sapienza, librarian of the Vatican, and prelate of the pontifical court. He wrote, among other antiquarian works, an account of the monuments found in the catacombs of Rome; also a number of valuable critical essays. He published in 1741 his excellent edition of the "Vatican Virgil," with the different versions and notes. Died in 1775.

See MAZZUCHELLI, "Scrittori d'Italia;" F. GRAZZINI, "Elogio di G. G. Bottari," 1818.

Bottazzi, bot-tät′see, (FRANCESCO,) an Italian poet and Latin scholar, born about 1770, translated into Latin verse Monti's "Bard of the Black Forest," ("Bardo della Selva nera.")

Böttcher or **Boettcher,** böt′kẹr, **Böttger** or **Boettger,** böt′gẹr, (ADOLPH,) a German poet and translator, born in Leipsic in 1815. He wrote several original poems, among which is "Till Eulenspiegel," (1850,) and produced translations of the poems of Byron, (12 vols., 1840–50,) Milton, (1846,) and other English poets.

Böttcher or **Boettcher,** (CHRISTIAN,) a German painter, born near Aix- -Chapelle in 1818. Among his works are "Evening in the Black Forest," and "Young Villagers of the Rhine."

Böttcher, Boettcher, Böttger, or **Boettger,** böt′-gẹr, written also **Boettiger,** (JOHANN FRIEDRICH,) the inventor of Dresden china, born at Schleitz, in Voigtland, about 1681. Having devoted himself for several years to the study of alchemy and chemistry, he succeeded in manufacturing a porcelain nearly equal in beauty and strength to that of China. Died in 1719.

See ENGELHARDT, "Life of J. F. Boettcher," (in German,) Leipsic, 1837.

Bottée de Toulmon, bo′tä′ dẹh tool′môn′, (AUGUSTE,) a French antiquary and writer on music, born in Paris in 1797; died in 1850.

See VINCENT, "Notice sur la Vie de M. A. Bottée de Toulmon," 1851.

Bottex, bo′tĕks′, (ALEXANDRE,) a French medical writer, born in 1796, lived at Lyons. Died in 1849.

Botticelli, bot-te-chel′lee, (SANDRO or ALESSANDRO,) an eminent Italian painter, surnamed FILIPEPI, (fe-le-pä′pee,) born at Florence about 1440, was a pupil of Filippo Lippi. He was patronized by the popes Sixtus IV. and Pius IV., and painted in the chapel of the Vatican frescos which display great power of imagination. Having

ā, ē, ī, ō, ū, ȳ, *long;* à, ė, ò, same, less prolonged; ă, ĕ, ĭ, ŏ, ŭ, ȳ, *short;* ą, ẹ, į, ǫ, *obscure;* fär, fäll, fät; mĕt; nŏt; gŏŏd; mōŏn;

returned to Florence, he became a disciple of Savonarola, and neglected his art. Died in 1515.

See VASARI, "Lives of the Painters."

Böttiger or **Boettiger**, böt'te-ğɐr, (KARL AUGUST,) an eminent German archæologist and *littérateur*, born at Reichenbach, in Saxony, in 1760, resided at Weimar, and was a friend of Goethe, Wieland, and other eminent German writers. A collection of his essays, etc. ("Kleine Schriften") was published in 3 vols., 1837-38. Died in 1835.

See KARL WILHELM BÖTTIGER, "Karl August Böttiger: biographische Skizze," 1837; NOSTIZ und JAENKENDORF, "K. A. Böttiger: sein Bild, sein Denkmal," 1836; "Foreign Quarterly Review" for January, 1836.

Böttiger or **Boettiger**, böt'te-ğɐr, (KARL WILHELM,) an eminent Swedish poet, of German extraction, born at Westerås in 1807, is a son-in-law of Tegnér. He obtained the degree of doctor in philosophy at Upsal in 1833, and has been twice crowned by the Swedish Academy. He has published poems of great merit, and produced a translation of Tasso's "Gerusalemme Liberata," and of Uhland's ballads.

Böttiger or **Boettiger**, (KARL WILHELM,) a German historian, and professor of literature and history at Erlangen, born at Bautzen in 1790, wrote a "History of Germany," (1838,) and "History of the Electorate and Kingdom of Saxony."

Bottoni, bot-to'nee, (ALBERTO,) an Italian physician, born at Padua, where he became professor of medicine. Died in 1596.

Bottoni, (DOMENICO,) a learned physician, and corresponding member of the Royal Society of London, born at Leontini, in Sicily, in 1641; died in 1731.

Bottrigari, bot-tRe-gå'ree,(ERCOLE,) an Italian mathematician and miscellaneous writer, born at Bologna in 1531; died in 1612.

Botts, (JOHN MINOR,) an American statesman, born at Dumfries, Prince William county, Virginia, in 1802. He studied law, joined the Whig party, and was elected a member of Congress in 1839. He was re-elected in 1841, supported Mr. Clay in 1844, and was returned to Congress in 1847. He was one of the few Southern members who co-operated with John Quincy Adams in his defence of the right of petition. After the dissolution of the Whig party he acted with the American party. He opposed the repeal of the Missouri Compromise in 1854, and was a constant adherent of the Union during the civil war, after which he supported the Republican party. Died in January, 1869.

Bottschild. See BOTSCHILD.

Boturini Benaduci, bo-too-ree'nee bå-nå-doo'chee, (LORENZO,) a native of Milan, who visited Mexico in 1735, and was afterwards appointed historiographer of the Indies. He wrote a "General History of North America," (in manuscript.) Died about 1750.

See PRESCOTT, "History of the Conquest of Mexico," vol. i. book i.

Botzaris. See BOZZARIS.

Boubée, boo'bå', (NÉRÉE,) a French geologist, born at Toulouse in 1806, published several works on geology.

Bouchard or **Bouchart**, boo'shåR', (ALAIN,) a French chronicler and jurist, born about 1470.

Bouchard, (AMAURY,) a French statesman, born at Saint-Jean-d'Angély about 1480.

Bouchard, (DAVID.) See AUBETERRE.

Bouchardat, boo'shåR'då', (ADOLPHE,) a French chemist and pharmacist, born about 1810 in Paris, where he became professor of hygiene in the Faculty of Medicine. He has written various scientific works.

Bouchardon, boo'shåR'dôN', (EDME,) an eminent French sculptor, born at Chaumont-en-Bassigny in 1698. He studied under the younger Coustou in Paris, and subsequently passed ten years at Rome. He became, after his return, professor in the Academy of Fine Arts. The "Fountain of Grenelle" in Paris is esteemed his master-piece; his equestrian statue of Louis XV., upon which he was employed twelve years, was destroyed by a mob in 1792. He executed a number of bas-reliefs and bronze statues of great merit, and was also skilled in etching and design. Died in 1762.

See A. C. P. DE CAYLUS, "Vie d'E. Bouchardon," 1762; FONTENAY, "Dictionnaire des Artistes."

Bouchaud, boo'shō', (MATHIEU ANTOINE,) a French jurist, born in Paris in 1719, became professor of law in the College of France in 1774. He was a member of the Academy of Sciences, and contributed a number of legal articles to the "Encyclopédie." Died in 1804.

Bouche, boosh, (HONORÉ,) born at Aix in 1598, wrote a "Description of Provence." Died in 1671.

Bouche, boosh, (MARTIN,) a Flemish engraver of portraits, supposed to have been born at Antwerp, flourished about 1680.

Bouchel, boo'shĕl', (LAURENT,) a French jurist and legal writer, born at Crespy in 1559; died in 1629.

Boucher, boo'shä', (ALEXANDRE JEAN,) a French musician, surnamed THE ALEXANDER OF VIOLINS, born in Paris in 1770. He was patronized by Charles IV. and Ferdinand VII. of Spain.

Boucher, (FRANÇOIS,) a celebrated French painter, born in Paris in 1703. He studied under Le Moine, and in 1765 succeeded Vanloo as painter to Louis XV. Among his master-pieces we may name "Venus ordering Arms for Æneas," and "The Bath of Diana." His works are censured for mannerism, meretricious attractions, and wanton tendencies. Died in 1770.

See C. BLANC, "Histoire des Peintres;" GRIMM et DIDEROT, "Correspondance Littéraire."

Boucher, (JEAN,) a French theologian, born in Paris about 1548, was a violent partisan of the league against Henry IV., and a "trumpet of sedition." Died in 1644.

See MÉZERAY, "Histoire de Henri IV."

Boucher, (JEAN,) a French ecclesiastic, born at Besançon, published his Travels in Palestine, (1626.)

Boucher, bōw'cher, (JONATHAN,) an English philologist and political writer, born near Wigton, in Cumberland, about 1738. He emigrated to Virginia about 1756, and became rector of Hanover, King George county, in 1761. He adhered to the royal cause in the Revolution, was forced to resign his charge, and returned to England in 1775. About 1784 he obtained the vicarage of Epsom, in Surrey. He published in 1797 a "View of the Causes and Consequences of the American Revolution." He spent many years in compiling a "Glossary of Archaic and Provincial Words," which was unfinished when he died in 1804. Parts 1 and 2 of this work appeared in 1832.

Boucher d'Argis, boo'shä' dăR'zhe', (ANDRÉ JEAN,) son of Antoine Gaspard, born in Paris in 1751. Having publicly denounced Marat, he was condemned to death by the Revolutionary tribunal, and executed in 1794.

Boucher d'Argis, (ANTOINE GASPARD,) a French jurist, born in Paris in 1708, contributed legal treatises to the "Encyclopédie Méthodique." Died in 1791.

Boucher de la Richarderie, boo'shä' deh lä re'-shåRd're', (GILLES,) a French *littérateur*, born at Saint-Germain-en-Laye in 1733, published a "Universal Library of Travels," (6 vols., 1808.) Died in 1810.

Boucher de Perthes, boo'shä' deh pårt, (JACQUES,) a French archæologist, born at Rethel in 1788. He wrote several dramas, and a dictionary of passions and sensations, entitled "Hommes et Choses," ("Men and Things," 4 vols., 1851.) His reputation is founded chiefly on his work called "La Création," (5 vols., 1839-41,) and his "Celtic and Antediluvian Antiquities," (1847.) Died at Abbeville in August, 1868. He has been called the founder of the science of archæo-geology.

Boucherie, boosh're', (AUGUSTE,) a French chemist, born at Bordeaux in 1801. He invented a method of rendering wood incorruptible by impregnating it with sulphate of copper.

Boucheron, boosh'rôN', (CARLO,) an Italian scholar and writer, of French extraction, born in Turin in 1773. Died in 1838.

See T. VALLAURI, "De C. Boucherono," 1838.

Boucheseiche, boosh'såsh', (JEAN BAPTISTE,) a French *littérateur*, born at Chaumont in 1760, translated the "Historical and Geographical Description of Hindostan," from the English of Rennel. Died in 1825.

Bouchet, boo'shä', (CLAUDE ANTOINE,) a French surgeon, born at Lyons in 1785, originated a method of healing by the first intention after amputations. Died in 1839.

See CASTELLAN, "Notice sur le Docteur Bouchet," 1840.

Bouchet, (Frédéric Jules,) a French architect and designer, born in Paris in 1799. He published several professional works, among which is "Compositions antiques," (1850.)

Bouchet, (Guillaume,) a French *littérateur*, born at Poitiers in 1526; died in 1606.

Bouchet, (Jean,) a French writer, born at Poitiers in 1476, published "Annals of Aquitaine," (1524.) Died about 1550.

See Nicéron, "Mémoires."

Bouchet, du, dü boo'shǎ', (Jean,) a French writer on genealogy, born in 1599; died in 1684.

Bouchetel, boosh'těl', or **Bochetel,** bosh'těl', (Guillaume,) born in the province of Berry, became secretary to Francis I., King of France. Died in 1558.

Boucheul, boo'shŭl', (Joseph,) a French jurist and legal writer, born at Dorat; died in 1706.

Bouchitté, boo'she'tǎ', (Louis Firmin Hervé,) a French *littérateur*, and professor of history at Versailles, born in Paris in 1795, published a "History of the Proofs of the Existence of God," (1841,) and other works.

Bouchon-Dubournial, boo'shôn' dü'booR'ne'ǎl', (Henri,) a French *littérateur*, born at Toul in 1749, translated "Don Quixote," and other works of Cervantes. Died in 1828.

Bouchotte, boo'shot', (Jean Baptiste Noël,) born at Metz, in France, in 1754, was minister of war from April, 1793, until April 1, 1794. Died in 1840.

Boucicault, boo'se'kō', sometimes written **Bourcicault,** (Dion,) a dramatist and actor, born in Dublin in 1822. He produced about 1841 a successful comedy called "London Assurance," and afterwards numerous dramas, some of which he translated from the French.

Boucicaut, de, deh boo'se'kō', (Jean le **Meingre**—leh mǎngR',) a French soldier, who became a marshal under Charles V. of France. Died in 1370.

Boucicaut, de, (Jean le Meingre,) son of the preceding, born at Tours in 1365, distinguished himself in the war against the Turks in 1396, and became marshal of France in 1412. Being taken prisoner at the battle of Agincourt, he died in England in 1421.

See De Pilham, "Histoire du Maréchal Boucicaut," 1697; D'Aubigny, "Vies des Hommes illustres," tome vii.

Boucquet, boo'kǎ', (Victor,) a Flemish painter of history, born at Furnes in 1619. "The Judgment of Cambyses" is called his master-piece. Died in 1677.

Bouddha or **Boudha.** See Booddha.

Boudet, boo'dǎ', (Charles Ernest,) a French medical writer, born in 1813; died in 1849.

Boudet, (Jean,) Comte, a French general of division, born at Bordeaux in 1769. He fought against the English in the West Indies in 1794, and in the subsequent campaigns of Holland and Austria. For his services at Aspern and Essling, he was created by Napoleon grand officer of the legion of honour. Died in 1809.

See De Courcelles, "Dictionnaire des Généraux Français."

Boudewyns, bow'deh-wĭns', (Antoon Franciscus,) a Flemish painter, born at Brussels about 1660, was a pupil of Van der Meulen. His landscapes are highly praised.

See Descamps, "Vies des Peintres Flamands," etc.

Boudewyns, (Michael,) a physician of Antwerp, was professor of anatomy and surgery in that city. Died in 1681.

Boudinot, boo'de-not, (Elias,) an American patriot and philanthropist, born in Philadelphia in 1740. He studied law, which he practised in New Jersey, and was a zealous advocate of the patriotic cause in the Revolution. In 1777 he was appointed commissary-general of prisoners, and elected a delegate to Congress, of which he became president in 1782. He was director of the mint at Philadelphia from 1796 to 1805, after which he resided at Burlington, New Jersey. He was chosen the first president of the American Bible Society in 1816. Among his writings is "The Star of the West; or, An Attempt to discover the Lost Tribes of Israel." He bequeathed large amounts of money and land to charitable institutions. Died in 1821.

Boudon, boo'dôn', (Henri Marie,) a French ecclesiastic and religious writer, born in the department of Aisne in 1624; died in 1702.

Boudot, boo'do', (Jean,) a French printer and bookseller, published in 1704 a "Latin-French Dictionary," which was long popular in schools. Died in 1706. His son, of the same name, was distinguished as a printer and bibliographer. Died in 1754.

Boué, boo'ǎ', (Ami,) a French geologist, born at Hamburg in 1794, published several works on geology, and "Turkey in Europe," ("La Turquie en Europe," 1840.)

Bouelles, boo'ěl', sometimes written **Bouilles,** [Lat. Bovil'lus,] (Charles,) a French mathematician and philologist, born at Sancour, in Picardy, about 1470, published "The Book of the Art and Science of Geometry," (1511,) and "Three Books of Common Proverbs," ("Proverbiorum vulgarium Libri tres," 1531.) Died about 1550.

Bouffé, boo'fǎ', a popular French comedian, born in Paris about 1800; died in 1853.

Bouflers, de, deh boo'flaiR', (Louis François,) Duc, a celebrated French marshal, born in 1644, served under Turenne in Holland and Germany. He had a principal share in the victory of Steenkerke in 1692, and in 1693 obtained the rank of marshal. In 1695 he defended Namur a long time against the allies under William III. of England, and in 1708 maintained Lille for nearly three months against Prince Eugene. He received from Louis XIV. the order of Saint Louis and many other distinctions, and was created a knight of the Golden Fleece by the King of Spain. The last battle in which he was engaged was that of Malplaquet, (1709,) where he commanded the right wing; and his retreat on that occasion was esteemed a master-piece of military skill. Died in 1711.

See "Vie du Maréchal de Bouflers," Lille, 1852; Charles de la Rue, "Oraison funèbre de M. le Maréchal de Bouflers," 1711.

Bouflers, de, (Marie Françoise Catherine de Beauvau Craon—deh bō'vō' krǎ'ôn',) Marchioness, a French lady of distinguished talents and accomplishments, was the wife of the Marquis de Bouflers-Remiencourt, captain of the guards to Stanislaus Augustus, King of Poland. She was a friend and correspondent of Voltaire. Died in 1787.

Bouflers, de, (Stanislas,) Marquis, a mediocre French writer, son of the preceding, born at Lunéville in 1737; died in 1815.

Bouflers-Rouvrel, boo'flaiR'roov'rěl',(Marie Charlotte Hippolyte,) Countess, born in Paris in 1724, was a friend of Rousseau and other celebrated French writers, and a correspondent of Hume. Died in 1800.

See J. J. Rousseau, "Correspondance;" Hume, "Private Correspondence."

Bougainville, boo'gǎn'věl', (Jean Pierre,) a French *littérateur*, brother of the navigator, born in Paris in 1722, was a member of the French Academy and secretary of the Academy of Inscriptions. Died in 1763.

Bougainville, de, deh boo'gǎn'věl', (Louis Antoine,) a celebrated French navigator, born in Paris in 1729, accompanied Montcalm to America in 1756, as his aide-de-camp. In 1766 he set sail with the frigate La Boudeuse and the ship L'Étoile for the Falkland Islands, being charged by the government with the transfer of the French colony of Port Louis, on one of those islands, to the Spaniards. Continuing his voyage, he discovered a number of islands in the South Sea, and gave the name of Navigator's Islands to the Samoan Archipelago. He also saw part of the group afterwards called New Hebrides by Captain Cook. He returned to France in 1769, having been the first French navigator who made the circuit of the world. His account of his voyage ("Voyage autour du Monde") appeared in 1771, and was translated into English and German. Bougainville was a Fellow of the Royal Society of London. Died in 1814.

See Marius Pascal, "Essai historique sur la Vie de Bougainville," 1831.

Bougeant, boo'zhôn', (Guillaume Hyacinthe,) a French Jesuit and historical writer, born at Quimper in 1690, wrote a "History of the Treaty of Westphalia," and other works. Died in 1743.

Bougerel, boozh'rěl', (Joseph,) a French ecclesiastic and *littérateur*, born at Aix in 1680, wrote "Memoirs of Illustrious Men." Died in 1753.

Bouget, boo'zhả', (JEAN,) a French Orientalist, born at Saumur in 1692, became professor of Hebrew in the college of the Propaganda at Rome. He published "Rudiments of Hebrew Grammar," and other learned works. Died in 1775.

Boughton, baw'tọn, (GEORGE H.,) a distinguished contemporary painter of landscapes and genre, was born in England, and resided many years in London and on the continent. He afterwards settled at Albany, in New York, where he has produced many works of great merit. Among these may be named his "Coming through the Rye," "The Ambush," and "Passing into the Shade."

See TUCKERMAN, "Book of the Artists."

Bougouinc, boo'gwȧn', (SIMON,) a French *littérateur,* born about 1490, was a valet of Louis XII.

Bougrov. See BOOGROV.

Bouguer, boo'gair', (PIERRE,) a celebrated French mathematician, born at Le Croisic, in Lower Brittany, in 1698. Having obtained several prizes from the Academy of Sciences, he became an associate of that body in 1731. His "Treatise on the Gradation of Light" came out in 1729, and in 1736 he accompanied La Condamine and Godin to Peru, in order to measure a degree of the meridian. He published an account of this operation, entitled "Theory of the Figure of the Earth," (1749.) He also wrote a "Treatise on Mechanics and Dynamics," and a "Treatise on Navigation and Pilotage," (1753,) and invented an instrument which he named the heliometer. He was a Fellow of the Royal Society of London. Died in 1758.

See article "Bouguer" in the "Biographie Universelle," by BIOT; LABERTHONIE, "Relation de la Conversion et de la Mort de Bouguer," 1784.

Bouhier, boo'e-ả', (JEAN,) a learned jurist, and member of the French Academy, born at Dijon in 1673, became president of the parliament of Dijon in 1704. He published a number of legal works, and valuable criticisms on classical subjects. "He was," says Abbé Olivet, "a savant of the first order." Died in 1746.

See OUDIN, "Commentarius de Vita J. Bouhierii," 1746; D'ALEMBERT, "Éloges."

Bouhours, boo'oor', (DOMINIQUE,) a French Jesuit and etymologist, born in 1628 in Paris, where he became professor of rhetoric and belles-lettres. He published in 1671 "Conversations of Aristes and Eugenius," and "Remarks and Doubts on the French Language." These works were received with great favour by some critics, and severely assailed by Ménage and others. He also wrote a "Life of Francis Xavier," which was translated into English by Dryden. Died in 1702.

See NICÉRON, "Mémoires;" "Nouvelle Biographie Générale;" ANDRÉ DACIER, "Éloge de Bouhours," 1702.

Bouillard, boo'yȧr', (JACQUES,) a French engraver, born in 1744; died at Paris in 1806.

Bouillart, boo'yȧr', (JACQUES,) a French ecclesiastic and historian, born at Meulan in 1669; died in 1726.

Bouillaud, boo'yō', or **Bouilliaud,** boo'ye-ō', (ISMAEL,) a French astronomer, born in Loudun in 1605; died in 1694.

Bouillaud, (JEAN BAPTISTE,) professor of clinics in the Medical Faculty of Paris, born at Angoulême in 1796. He contributed numerous articles to the "Revue Médicale" and other journals, and published a "Treatise on Medical Nosography," (5 vols., 1846.)

Bouillé, de, dẹh boo'yȧ', (FRANÇOIS CLAUDE AMOUR,) MARQUIS, a distinguished French general, born in Auvergne in 1739. In the war of American independence, while Governor of Guadeloupe, he defended the French Antilles against the English, and captured several of their islands. He was a devoted royalist, and active in promoting the escape of Louis XVI. from Paris: on the failure of that enterprise, he repaired to Russia, in order to obtain assistance from the empress Catherine. He died in England in 1800, leaving interesting "Memoirs of the French Revolution," which were published in English, (1797,) German; (1798,) and French, (1801.)

See THIERS, "Histoire de la Révolution Française;" RENÉ DE BOUILLÉ, "Essai sur la Vie du Marquis de Bouillé," 1853; CARLYLE, "French Revolution."

Bouilles. See BOUELLES.

Bouillet, boo'yȧ', (JEAN,) a French physician, born near Béziers in 1690; died in 1777.

Bouillet, (JEAN BAPTISTE,) a French geologist, born at Cluny in 1799, has written on minerals and fossils, and on the geology of Auvergne and Puy-de-Dôme.

Bouillet, (MARIE NICOLAS,) a French lexicographer, became inspector of the University of Paris, where he was born in 1798. He published a "Classical Dictionary of Sacred and Profane Antiquity," (1841,) and other works.

Bouillier, boo'ye-ả', (FRANCISQUE,) a French philosopher, born at Lyons in 1813, published a "History of the Cartesian Philosophy," (2 vols., 1854.)

Bouillon. See GODFREY.

Bouillon, de, dẹh boo'yòN', (EMMANUEL THÉODORE de la Tour d'Auvergne—dẹh lả tooR dō'vȧRñ',) a French cardinal, son of Frédéric Maurice, noticed below, was born in 1644. He became chief almoner to Louis XIV. Died in 1715.

Bouillon, de, (FRÉDÉRIC MAURICE DE LA TOUR D'AUVERGNE,) DUC, elder brother of Marshal Turenne, was born at Sedan in 1605. He fought under his uncle the Prince of Orange, and subsequently entered the French service. Appointed lieutenant-general in 1642, he shared with Prince Thomas of Savoy the command of the army of Italy. During the wars of the Fronde he was an adherent of the princes fighting against Mazarin. Died in 1652.

See "Mémoires de la Vie de F. M. de la Tour d'Auvergne," edited by AUBERTIN, 1692; PINARD, "Chronologie Militaire."

Bouillon, de, (HENRI DE LA TOUR D'AUVERGNE,) DUC, a French marshal, originally Viscount Turenne, born in 1555, was a grandson of the Constable of Montmorency. At an early age he became a Calvinist, and was a zealous partisan of Henry of Navarre, who appointed him lieutenant-general of his armies. He married for his second wife Elizabeth of Nassau, daughter of William Prince of Orange. One of the sons of this marriage was the celebrated Turenne. Marshal Bouillon was a patron of learned men, and founded at Sedan a college and library. Died in 1623.

See J. MARSOLLIER, "Histoire de H. de la Tour d'Auvergne, Duc de Bouillon," 1709; ANSELME, "Histoire généalogique des Pairs de France."

Bouillon, de, (ROBERT DE LA MARCK,) DUC, a French marshal, born in 1492, became lieutenant-general of Normandy. Died in 1556.

See BRANTÔME, "Vies des grands Capitaines."

Bouillon-Lagrange, boo'yòN' lả'grŏNzh', (EDME JEAN BAPTISTE,) a French chemist, physician, and writer, born in Paris about 1765, became apothecary to the imperial household. Died about 1840.

Bouilly, boo'ye', (JEAN NICOLAS,) a French dramatist and miscellaneous writer, born in the department of Indre-et-Loire in 1763; died in Paris in 1842.

See E. LEGOUVÉ, "J. N. Bouilly," 1842.

Boulage, boo'lȧzh', (THOMAS PASCAL,) a French jurist, born at Orléans in 1769, became professor of French law in Paris. He was one of those who offered themselves as a hostage for the liberty of Louis XVI. Died in 1820.

Boulainvilliers, de, dẹh boo'lȧN've'ye-ả', (HENRI,) a French historian, born in Normandy in 1658, was a son of François, Count of Saint-Saire. He wrote a "Chronological Abridgment of the History of France," and other works on French history, also a "Life of Mohammed," (1730.) Died in 1722.

See BAYLE, "Historical and Critical Dictionary;" QUÉRARD, "La France Littéraire."

Boulanger, boo'lŏN'zhả', (JEAN,) a French engraver, born at Amiens in 1607; died in 1680.

Boulanger, (LOUIS,) a French painter, born in Piedmont in 1806, was a friend of Victor Hugo, whôse works he illustrated. He gained a first medal in 1836.

Boulanger, (NICOLAS ANTOINE,) a French *littérateur,* born in Paris in 1722, wrote a work entitled "Antiquity Unveiled," published after his death. Died in 1759.

Boulard, boo'lȧr', (ANTOINE MARIE HENRI,) born in Paris in 1754, was appointed by La Harpe his executor, and published the last part of his "Cours de Littérature." He was the owner of a very large and valuable library. Died in 1825.

Boulard, (MICHEL,) a French philanthropist, born in Paris in 1761, became upholsterer (*tapissier*) to the emperor. He gave large sums of money to the poor, and left a million francs to found a hospital. Died in 1825.

Boulay, boo′lå′, (JACQUES,) a French agricultural writer of Orléans. Died about 1730.

Boulay de la Meurthe, boo′lå′ dęh lå murt, (ANTOINE JACQUES CLAUDE JOSEPH,) COMTE, a French statesman, born in 1761. He became successively a member of the Council of Five Hundred and of the council of regency, (1810,) minister of state, and minister of justice conjointly with Cambacérès. He had a principal part in drawing up the Civil Code of Napoleon. Died in 1840.

See "Biographie de M. Boulay de la Meurthe," 1836.

Boulay de la Meurthe, (HENRI GEORGE,) COMTE, son of the preceding, born at Nancy in 1797. In 1837 he represented the department of Meurthe in the Chamber of Deputies. He was vice-president of the republic from December, 1848, to December 2, 1851. Died in Paris in 1858.

Boulay, du, dü boo′lå′, [Lat. BULÆ′US,] (CÉSAR ÉGASSE,) born in the department of Mayenne, was rector and historiographer of the University of Paris. Died in 1678.

Boulay-Paty, boo′lå′ på′te′, (ÉVARISTE FÉLIX CYPRIEN,) son of Pierre Sébastien, noticed below, born at Donges, in Brittany, in 1804. He published a collection of "National Odes," (1830,) and other poems, and received in 1851 the Montyon prize of the French Academy for his "Sonnets on Human Life."

Boulay-Paty, (PIERRE SÉBASTIEN,) a French jurist, born in Brittany in 1763, filled several offices during the Revolution, and became a member of the Council of Five Hundred in 1798. Died in 1830.

Boulduc, bool′dük′, (GILLES FRANÇOIS,) a French chemist, son of Simon, noticed below, born in 1675, became professor of chemistry in the Jardin du Roi in 1729. Died in 1742.

Boulduc, (SIMON,) professor of chemistry at the Jardin du Roi, and member of the Academy of Sciences in Paris. Died in 1729.

Boule, bool, (ANDRÉ CHARLES,) a French cabinetmaker, born in Paris in 1642, adorned his works with mosaics. He worked for nearly all the sovereigns of Europe. Died in 1732.

Boulée, boo′lå′, (ÉTIENNE LOUIS,) a French architect, born in Paris in 1728; died in 1799.

Boulen. See BOLEYN, (ANNE.)

Boulgarine. See BOOLGARIN.

Boullanger, boo′lôN′zhå′, (ANDRÉ,) a popular French preacher, born in Paris about 1578; died in 1657.

Boullemier, bool′me-å′, (CHARLES,) a French ecclesiastic and writer, born at Dijon in 1725; died in 1803.

Boullenger de Rivery, boo′lôN′zhå′ dęh rèv′re′, (CLAUDE FRANÇOIS FÉLIX,) a French jurist and *littérateur*, born at Amiens in 1725; died in 1758.

Boullenois or Boulenois, bool′nwå′, (LOUIS,) a French jurist and legal writer, born in Paris in 1680; died in 1762.

Boulliau, boo′le-ō′, or Bouillaud, boo′yō′, [Lat. BULLIAL′DUS,] a distinguished French astronomer, born at Loudun in 1605. He wrote "Astronomia Philolaica," (1682,) and other learned works. Died in 1694.

Boullier, boo′le-å′, (DAVID RENAUD,) a Protestant theologian, of French extraction, born at Utrecht in 1699; died in London in 1759.

Boullongne, boo′lôNñ′, (BON,) a French painter, son of Louis, noticed below, (the first of the name,) born in Paris in 1649. He became professor in the Academy of Fine Arts; at Paris, in 1678. His design and composition are praised. Died in 1717.

Boullongne, (LOUIS,) a French painter and engraver, born in Picardy about 1609, worked in Paris. He had remarkable skill as a copyist. Died in 1674.

Boullongne, (LOUIS,) son of the preceding, born in Paris in 1654, became first painter to the king, and director of the Academy of Fine Arts. Died in 1733.

See HEINECKEN, "Dictionnaire des Artistes."

Boulogne, de, dęh boo′loñ′, (ÉTIENNE ANTOINE,) born at Avignon in 1747, became Bishop of Troyes in 1807, was deposed by Napoleon in 1811, and appointed Archbishop of Vienne in 1817. His collected works were published in 8 vols., (1827 *et seq.*) Died in 1825.

Boul′ter, (HUGH,) born in or near London in 1671, became in 1723 Archbishop of Armagh, in Ireland. He was distinguished for his charities, and his zeal in the cause of education. Died in 1742.

Boul′ton, (MATTHEW,) an English mechanician, born at Birmingham in 1728. He was the friend and coadjutor of the celebrated Watt, in conjunction with whom he effected great improvements in the steam-engine, which he also applied to new purposes. His coining-apparatus was particularly distinguished for its excellence. His services are mentioned in terms of the highest praise by Watt. Died in 1809.

See a "Life of M. Boulton," published at Birmingham, 1809; HENRY HOWE, "Eminent American and European Mechanics," 1847.

Bouma, bǒw′må, (DOMINICK ACRONIUS,) a Dutch publicist, was professor of eloquence and political history at Franeker. Died in 1656.

Bouquet, boo′kå′, (Dom MARTIN,) a French Benedictine monk, born at Amiens in 1685, published a "Collection of the Historians of Gaul and France," which has been continued by several other writers. Died in 1754.

Bouquier, boo′ke-å′, (GABRIEL,) a French *littérateur*, born in Périgord about 1750, was a Jacobin member of the Convention, (1792–95.) Died in 1811.

Bouquin. See BOQUIN.

Bourbon, boor′bon, [Fr. pron. booR′bòN′,] the name of a famous French dynasty, which reigned over France from 1589 to 1848, excepting the period of the republic and the empire of Napoleon I. Henry IV. was the first king of the house of Bourbon. The house of Orléans is a younger branch of the same family, the founder of which was Robert, Count de Clermont, a younger son of King Louis IX. Robert died in 1317. (See ORLÉANS.)

LOUIS DE BOURBON, first Duke, and Count of Clermont, was a son of Robert, and was born in 1279. He fought with success against the English for Charles le Bel, and was created Duke of Bourbon. He died in 1341.

PIERRE, the second duke, a son of Louis I., was born in 1310. He was a brave warrior, and was killed at the battle of Poitiers in 1356.

His son, LOUIS II., third Duke of Bourbon, born in 1337, distinguished himself in battle against the English. In 1391 he led a successful crusade against the pirates of Tunis. Died in 1410.

JEAN, the fourth duke, born in 1381, was the eldest son of Louis II. He was a leader of the Armagnac party in the civil war. He was taken prisoner by the English at Agincourt, and confined until his death in 1434.

His son CHARLES I., born in 1401, became fifth Duke of Bourbon. He rendered important military services to the dauphin, (Charles VII.,) and defended Orléans against the English in 1428. Died in 1456.

JEAN II., the sixth duke, born about 1426, was the eldest son of Charles I. He joined the Duc de Bretagne and others in the league against Louis XI., (*ligue du bien public.*) In 1483 he became Constable of France. Died in 1488.

The seventh duke was CHARLES, Cardinal de Bourbon, a son of Charles I., born in 1437. He was a diplomatist and a favourite counsellor of Louis XI.

See DESORMEAUX, "Histoire de la Maison de Bourbon," 5 vols., 1772–88.

Bourbon, (NICOLAS,) surnamed THE ELDER, a French scholar and distinguished Latin poet, born near Bar-sur-Aube in 1503; died in 1550.

Bourbon, (NICOLAS,) THE YOUNGER, nephew of the preceding, born near Bar-sur-Aube in 1574. He became professor of Greek at the Royal College in 1611, and was a member of the French Academy. Died in 1644.

Bourbon, de, (ANTOINE.) See ANTONY OF BOURBON.

Bourbon, de, dęh booR′bòN′, (CHARLES,)DUC, usually called CONSTABLE BOURBON, (Connétable de Bourbon,) a famous French general, born in February, 1490, was a son of Gilbert Bourbon, Count of Montpensier. He married the heiress of the Duke of Bourbon, and obtained with her the title of duke. Having served several campaigns in Italy, he received in 1515 the office of constable, the highest military office in the kingdom of France. He contributed to the victory of Marignano, (1515,) and in the next year was chosen viceroy of the Milanese. His loyalty to Francis I. was shaken by various injuries and acts of ingratitude, which historians attribute to the influence of the king's mother, Louisa of Savoy. Her motive is supposed to have been resentment for the coldness or contempt with which he treated her amorous overtures. About 1521 he was deprived by legal process of his estates, which were claimed by Louisa of Savoy. This transaction determined the haughty duke to accept the brilliant offers which he had received from Charles V., for whose service he raised a large body of Germans in 1523. He became lieutenant-general of the emperor in Italy, and had a high command at the battle of Pavía, (1525.) The victory at this place is attributed by some writers to his skill. (See AVALOS, MARQUIS OF PESCARA.) He was regarded with distrust by Charles V., who neglected to pay the German troops commanded by Bourbon Disgusted by the conduct of Charles, he resolved to become an independent prince and to satisfy his mutinous troops with the spoils of conquest. His first enterprise was extremely bold, and conducted with great ability. He led his army three hundred miles or more through a hostile country, and assaulted Rome. He was the first who mounted the wall, and was killed among the first, on the 6th of May, 1527. His victorious army (which contained many Lutherans) pillaged the city, and committed frightful excesses. He was reputed the ablest French general of his time. The Constable Bourbon forms a prominent character in Byron's drama entitled "The Deformed Transformed."

See ROBERTSON, "History of Charles V.;" BRANTÔME, "Vies des grands Capitaines;" GUICCIARDINI, "Historia d'Italia;" GAILLARD, "Histoire de François I;" N. BAUDOT DE JUILLY, "Histoire secrète du Connétable de Bourbon," 1612; VON SCHWARTZENAU, "Der Konnetable Karl von Bourbon, Bilder aus seinem Leben," 1852; Major-General JOHN MITCHELL, "Biographies of Eminent Soldiers of the Last Four Centuries," 1865.

Bourbon, de, (CHARLES,) CARDINAL, born in 1520, was a brother of Antoine de Bourbon, and an uncle of Henry IV. of France. He was one of the chiefs of the Catholic League, and was proclaimed king, with the title of Charles X., in 1589. He was recognized as such by the Parliament of Paris and the majority of the people. Died in 1590.

See J. DUBREUL, "Vie de Charles de Bourbon," 1612; SISMONDI, "Histoire des Français."

Bourbon, de, (CHARLES,) Cardinal Vendôme, a relative of the preceding, born about 1560. He was a son of Louis, first Prince de Condé. Died in 1594.

Bourbon, de, (LOUIS HENRI,) DUC, son of Louis, born at Versailles in 1692. After the death of Louis XIV., he was placed at the head of the council of regency, and was subsequently first minister of Louis XV. Died in 1740.

Bourbon, de, (LUIS ANTONIO,) a younger son of Philip V. of Spain, born in 1727, was made a cardinal about the age of eight, but renounced that office when he arrived at manhood. Died in 1785.

Bourbon, de, (LUIS MARIA,) a Spanish prelate, born in 1777, was a son of the preceding. As president of the regency, he promulgated the Constitution of 1812, and abolished the Inquisition. Died in 1823.

Bourbon, de, (MATHIEU,) surnamed LE GRAND BÂTARD, was a son of Jean II., Duke of Bourbon, and was distinguished as a warrior. Died in 1505.

Bourbon Condé, de, deh boor′bôn′ kôn′dȧ′,(LOUIS,) DUC, a French nobleman and soldier, born in 1668, was a grandson of the great Condé. Died in 1710.

Bourbotte, boor′bot′, (PIERRE,) a French Jacobin, and member of the National Convention, born near Avallon in 1763. Having excited an insurrection, he was defeated, and executed in 1795.

See THIERS, "Histoire de la Révolution Française."

Bourcet, boor′sȧ′, (PIERRE JOSEPH,) a French tactician and military writer, born near Châtellerault in 1700. Died in 1780.

Bourchenu, de, deh boorsh′nü′, (JEAN PIERRE MORET,) Marquis de Valbonnais, a French historical writer, born at Grenoble in 1651; died in 1730.

Bourchier, (JOHN.) See BERNERS, LORD.

Bourchier, boor′chĭ-er, [Fr. pron. booR′she̦-ȧ′,] **Bourgchier,** or **Bouchier,** (THOMAS,) an English ecclesiastic, rose to be Archbishop of Canterbury in 1454, cardinal, and lord chancellor of England. He crowned Edward IV., Richard III., and Henry VII., and performed the marriage-ceremony between the last-named sovereign and Elizabeth of York. Died in 1486.

See W. F. HOOK, "Lives of the Archbishops of Canterbury," vol. v. chap. xxi., 1860.

Bourcicault. See BOUCICAULT.

Bourcier, boor′se-ȧ′, (JEAN LÉONARD,) Baron de Montureux, (deh môN′tü′ruh′,) a French jurist and magistrate, born at Vézelise, in Lorraine, in 1649. He was the principal author of the Leopold Code, adopted in Lorraine. Died in 1726.

See M. SALMON, "Étude sur le Président Bourcier," 1846.

Bourcier, (JEAN LOUIS,) Comte de Montureux, a French magistrate and jurist, son of the preceding, born at Luxembourg in 1687; died in 1737.

Bourdaille, boor′dȧl′ or boor′dȧ′ye̦, (MICHEL,) a French theologian, and doctor of the Sorbonne. Died in 1694.

Bourdaisière, de la, deh lȧ boor′dȧ′ze-aiR′, (JEAN BABOU,) SEIGNEUR, a French statesman, lived about 1570.

Bourdaloue, boor′dȧ′loo′, (LOUIS,) an eminent French pulpit orator and Jesuit, born at Bourges on the 20th of August, 1632. Having been successively professor of rhetoric, philosophy, and moral theology, he was appointed in 1669 court preacher in Paris, where for more than twenty years he preached the sermons during Lent and Advent. His discourses were enthusiastically admired by Louis XIV. and his court; and the king observed that Bourdaloue's "repetitions were better than the novelties of others." His main object was to convince, and his chief weapon was logic, compared with which he considered pathos of secondary importance. His proofs fortify each other by their connection, and respond by their gradation to the auditor's desire to receive impressions more and more vivid. He is said to have been a shining example of modesty, consistency, and other virtues appropriate to his office. His sermons were published in 16 vols., 1707–34. Died in 1704.

See PRIGNY, "Vie de Bourdaloue," 1705; VILLENAVE, "Notice sur Bourdaloue," 1812; JEAN LABOUDERIE, "Notice sur Bourdaloue," 1825; DE SAINT-AMAND, "Notice biographique sur le P. Bourdaloue," 1842.

Bourdeille, de, (CLAUDE.) See MONTRÉSOR.

Bourdeilles, de, (PIERRE.) See BRANTÔME.

Bourdelot, boord′lo′, (JEAN,) a celebrated French scholar, published valuable editions of Lucian, Heliodorus, and Petronius. Died in 1638.

Bourdelot, (PIERRE MICHON,) ABBÉ, a distinguished French physician, born in 1610 at Sens, was patronized by Christina of Sweden. He wrote an "Account of Mount Ætna," and "The History of Music and its Effects," (1715.) Died in 1685.

Bourdic-Viot, de, deh boor′dèk′ ve′o′, (MARIE ANNE HENRIETTE **Payan de l'Etang**—pȧ′yôN′ deh lȧ′tôN′,) an authoress, born at Dresden in 1746, was successively married to the Marquis d'Antremont, the Baron de Bourdic, and M. Viot. She published eulogies on Montaigne and Tasso, and other works. She was eulogized by Voltaire. Died near Bagnols in 1802.

See QUÉRARD, "La France Littéraire."

Bourdigné, de, deh boor′dèn′yȧ′, (CHARLES,) a French poet, born at Angers; died in 1531.

Bourdin, boor′dăN′, (GILLES,) a French scholar, born in Paris in 1515, published esteemed commentaries on several of the classics. Died in 1570.

Bourdin, (JACQUES,) a French statesman under Henry II., Francis II., and Charles IX., became secretary of finance in 1549. He wrote in defence of the rights of the Gallican Church. Died in 1567.

Bourdin, (MAURICE,) a French prelate, born in Limousin, became Archbishop of Braga, and was subsequently elected pope by the German emperor Henry V., in opposition to Gelasius II. He was soon after deposed, and died in prison in 1122.

See ARTAUD DE MONTOR, "Histoire des souverains Pontifes."

Bourdois de la Mothe, boor′dwȧ′ deh lȧ mot, (EDME JOACHIM,) a French physician, born at Joigny in

1754. He was physician to Louis XVIII. and Charles X. Died about 1830.

Bourdoise, boor'dwâz', (ADRIEN,) a French theologian, born near Chartres in 1584 ; died in 1655.

See DESCOURVEAUX, "Vie de M. Bourdoise," 1714; BOUCHARD, "Vie de M. Bourdoise," 1784.

Bourdon, boor'dôN', (AIMÉ,) a French physician, born at Cambray in 1638. He published an "Anatomical Description of the Human Body," and "New Anatomical Tables." Died in 1706.

Bourdon, (ISIDORE,) an eminent French physician and writer, born at Merry, in Orne, in 1796. He practised in Paris, and published numerous and valuable works, among which are "Principles of Medical Physiology," (2 vols., 1828,) "Principles of Comparative Physiology, or History of the Phenomena of Life in all Beings which are endowed with it," (1830,) and "Illustrious Physicians and Naturalists of Modern Times," (1844.) He is said to be one of the most brilliant writers of his time.

See QUÉRARD, "La France Littéraire."

Bourdon, (PIERRE LOUIS MARIE,) a French mathematician, born at Alençon in 1799, published "Elements of Algebra," (1843,) and other works. Died in 1854.

Bourdon, (SÉBASTIEN,) one of the most celebrated French painters, born at Montpellier in 1616. At an early age he visited Rome, where he formed an intimacy with Claude Lorrain, whose pictures he copied with admirable exactness. He became in 1648 one of the founders and first rector of the Royal Academy of Painting and Sculpture in Paris. In 1652 he visited Sweden, where Queen Christina appointed him her first painter. Among his master-pieces are his "Crucifixion of Saint Peter," in the Louvre, and the "Woman taken in Adultery." Bourdon excelled in historical painting, portraits, landscapes, and grotesque subjects, and worked with wonderful rapidity and facility. His engravings and designs are also highly esteemed. Died in Paris in 1671.

See R. DUMESNIL, "Le Peintre-Graveur Français;" J. POITEVIN, "Notice historique sur S. Bourdon," 1812 ; FÉLIBIEN, "Entretien sur les Peintres."

Bourdon de la Crosnière, boor'dôN' deh lå kRo'ne-air', (LÉONARD JEAN JOSEPH,) a French Jacobin, and member of the National Convention, born at Longné-au-Perche in 1758. He voted for the death of the king, and for other violent measures of his party. Having quarrelled with Robespierre, he joined Barras as leader of the National Guards, and seized the person of his former chief and others of the Jacobin faction. He was afterwards a member of the Council of Five Hundred, where he was publicly denounced as an assassin. He wrote a "Memoir on National Education," and other works. Died about 1816.

See LE BAS, "Dictionnaire encyclopédique de la France."

Bourdon de l'Oise, boor'dôN' deh lwâz, (FRANÇOIS LOUIS,) a French revolutionist, born near Compiègne, was a member of the National Convention. He advocated the most violent measures of the Jacobins, but joined with the enemies of Robespierre on the 9th Thermidor. He was elected to the Council of Five Hundred, and subsequently opposed the republican party. He was transported by the Directory to Cayenne, where he died in 1797.

See THIERS, "Histoire de la Révolution Française."

Bourdon de Sigrais, boor'dôN' deh se'grâ',(CLAUDE GUILLAUME,) a French writer, born near Lons-le-Saulnier in 1715, was a member of the Academy of Inscriptions. He published, among other works, a "History of Rats," and translated into French the "Military Institutes" of Vegetius. Died in 1791.

See QUÉRARD, "La France Littéraire."

Bourdon de Vatry, boor'dôN' deh vâ'tre', (MARC ANTOINE,) BARON, a French administrator, born at Saint-Maur in 1761. He was minister of the marine, for a short time, about 1800, after which he was prefect of Havre, Vaucluse, and Maine-et-Loire. Died in 1828.

Bourdonnaie. See LA BOURDONNAIE.

Bourdounais. See LA BOURDONNAIS.

Bourdot de Richebourg, boor'do' deh resh'boor', (CHARLES ANTOINE,) a French jurist, born in Paris in 1685, edited a collection of the common laws of France. Died in 1735.

Bouré, (PAUL JOSEPH,) a Belgian statuary, born in 1823 ; died in 1848.

See SOUST DE BORKENFELDT, "Notice sur la Vie de P. Bouré," 1849.

Bourette, boo'rêt', (CHARLOTTE,) a French authoress, born in 1714, published a collection of works in prose and verse. She kept in Paris a *café* which was a resort of literary men. Died in 1784.

Bourg, du, dü boor, (ANNE,) a French magistrate and Calvinist, born at Riom, in Auvergne, in 1521. Being falsely accused of the assassination of Minard, one of the Catholic judges, he was executed in 1559.

See SISMONDI, "Histoire des Français;" HENRI DONIOL, "Notice historique sur A. du Bourg," 1846; HOFFMANN VON WESTHOFFEN, "Le Martyr évangélique, A. du Bourg," 1841.

Bourgade, boor'gâd', (FRANÇOIS,) a French missionary, born at Ganjou in 1806, laboured in Algeria, and published "Evenings at Carthage," ("Soirées de Carthage.")

Bourgeat, boor'zhâ', (LOUIS ALEXANDRE MARGUERITE,) a French *littérateur*, born at Grenoble in 1787 ; died in 1814.

Bourgelat, boorzh'lâ', (CLAUDE,) the founder of veterinary schools in France, born at Lyons in 1712. He wrote numerous treatises on veterinary medicine, and in 1772 established the Royal Veterinary School at Lyons. Died in 1799.

See GROGNIER, "Notice sur C. Bourgelat," 1805.

Bourgeois, boor'zhwâ', (ANICET,) a French dramatist, born in Paris in 1806, produced a large number of successful melodramas, vaudevilles, and farces.

Bourgeois, (DOMINIQUE FRANÇOIS,) an ingenious French mechanician, born in 1698; died in 1781.

Bourgeois, bŭr-joiss', (Sir FRANCIS,) an English painter, of Swiss extraction, born in London in 1756. He was appointed, in 1791, painter to the King of Poland, and in 1792 became a member of the London Royal Academy. He died in 1811, leaving his choice collection of more than three hundred pictures to Dulwich College, together with a large sum of money for building a gallery.

See NAGLER, "Neues Allgemeines Künstler-Lexikon.

Bourgeois, (N.,) a French historian, born at La Rochelle in 1710; died in 1776.

Bourges, de, deh boorzh, (CLÉMENCE,) a French lady, born at Lyons, enjoyed a high reputation among her contemporaries as a poetess and musician. Died in 1562.

Bourgo or Bourgh. See BURGHO.

Bourgogne, de, Ducs. See BURGUNDY, DUKES OF.

Bourgogne, de, DUKES. See PHILIP THE GOOD; CHARLES THE BOLD.

Bourgoing, boor'gwâN', (FRANÇOIS,) a French theologian and religious writer, born in Paris in 1585, became confessor to Gaston, Duke of Orléans, and superior-general of the order of the Oratory, (Oratoire.) Died in 1662.

See BOSSUET, "Oraison funèbre du P. Bourgoing."

Bourgoing, de, deh boor'gwâN', (CHARLES PAUL AMABLE,) BARON, a diplomatist and statesman, son of Jean François, noticed below, born at Hamburg in 1791. He was minister plenipotentiary from France to Saxony in 1832, and was made a senator in 1853.

Bourgoing, de, (JEAN FRANÇOIS,) BARON, a French diplomatist and writer, born at Nevers in 1748. He was appointed in 1777 secretary of the embassy to Spain, where he resided seven years, and in 1791 was minister plenipotentiary at Madrid. His "Picture of Modern Spain" (1803) has been translated into English and other languages. He also wrote "Historical and Philosophical Memoirs on Pius VI. and his Pontificate," (1798,) and made several translations from the German. Died in 1811.

See "Nouvelle Biographie Générale;" "London Quarterly Review" for October, 1802; "Edinburgh Review" for October, 1804.

Bourgoing de Villefore. See VILLEFORE.

Bourguet, boor'gâ', (LOUIS,) a French naturalist and antiquary, born at Nîmes in 1678, became professor of philosophy and mathematics at Neufchâtel. He wrote a "Treatise on Petrifactions," (1762,) "Philosophical Letters on the Formation of Salts and Crystals," etc., (1729,) and other works. He was a friend and correspondent of Leibnitz. He is said to have discovered the explanation of the Etruscan alphabet. Died in 1742.

See "Nouvelle Biographie Générale."

Bourgueville, de, dẹh booʀg′vẹl′, (CHARLES,) Sieur de Bras, (bʀâ,) a French antiquary, born in 1504, was patronized by Francis I. He published "Antiquities of the Province of Neustria, now Duchy of Normandy," (1588.) Died in 1593.

Bourguignon, (F. M.) See BOURIGNON.

Bourguignon, (the painter.) See COURTOIS.

Bourignon, boo′rẹn′yôn′, (ANTOINETTE,) a French visionary, and founder of a sect called by her name, was born at Lille in 1616. She pretended to have revelations from heaven, in which she was commanded to restore the true church. She travelled over a considerable part of Europe, making many converts, and while at Amsterdam renounced Catholicism. Her works amount to twenty-one large octavo volumes. Died in 1680.

See "Vie d'Antoinette Bourignon," prefixed to her works.

Bourignon or **Bourguignon,** booʀ′gẹn′yôn′, (FRANÇOIS MARIE,) a French antiquary, born at Saintes in 1753, published "Topographic Researches on the Gallic and Roman Antiquities of Saintonge and Angoumois." Died in 1796.

Bourke, bŭrk, (Sir RICHARD,) a general in the British service, born at Dublin in 1777, distinguished himself in the Peninsular war, and afterwards became Governor of New South Wales and Van Diemen's Land. Died in 1855.

Bourlet de Vauxcelles. See VAUXCELLES.

Bourlie, de la, dẹh lả booʀ′le′, (ANTOINE de **Guiscard**—dẹh gẹs′kǎʀ′,) ABBÉ, a French politician, born in 1658. Having failed in an attempt to excite an insurrection of the Protestants against the government, he took refuge in England, where he obtained a pension from Queen Anne. Being convicted of treason before the privy council, he stabbed the chancellor, Lord Oxford, for which he was sent to prison, where, it is said, he committed suicide, (1711.)

See BAYLE, "Historical and Critical Dictionary."

Bourmont, de, dẹh booʀ′môn′, (LOUIS AUGUSTE VICTOR,) Comte de Ghaisne, (gân,) marshal of France, born in the department of Maine-et-Loire in 1773. He was a royalist during the Revolution, and fought against the republic in the Vendean war from 1794 to 1799. Having refused to serve under the First Consul as a general, he was imprisoned about the end of 1800. He made his escape in 1804, and took refuge in Portugal. He entered the service of Napoleon in 1809 or 1810, distinguished himself in the Russian campaign, and was made lieutenant-general in 1814. On the fall of the emperor he gave in his adhesion to Louis XVIII., after whose flight he again went over to Bonaparte. Unwilling to subscribe to the Acte Additionnel, (by which the Bourbons were proscribed,) he offered his resignation to Napoleon, and, after the second restoration, was appointed in 1823 to a command in Spain. He became minister of war in 1829, and in 1830 commander-in-chief of the expedition which resulted in the conquest of Algiers. He was created a marshal the same year. During the revolution of 1830 he was superseded by General Clausel, and, after an exile of several years, died in France in 1846.

See DE LANSAC, "Notice biographique sur le Comte de Bourmont," 1847; MERSON, "Notice biographique sur le Maréchal de Bourmont," 1847; ALISON, "History of Europe."

Bourn, boorn, (SAMUEL,) an English dissenting divine, born in Birmingham in 1713; died in 1796.

See R. FLEXMAN, "Life of S. Bourne," 1799; J. TOULMIN, "Memoirs of the Rev. S. Bourne," 1809.

Bourne, boorn, (HUGH,) founder of the sect of Primitive Methodists, was born in Staffordshire in 1772. This connection, first established in 1810, numbered in 1853 108,926 members. Mr. Bourne successively visited Scotland, Ireland, and the United States, where he was received with great favour. Died in 1852.

Bourne, (VINCENT,) a distinguished English scholar and writer, born about 1698, wrote Latin poems which rank among the most elegant of modern times. Several of them were translated into English by Cowper. He was an usher of Westminster School. Died in 1747.

Bourne, (WILLIAM STURGES,) an English statesman, born at Winchester in 1769. He became a lord of the treasury in 1807, privy councillor in 1814, and secretary of state for home affairs under Canning in 1827. Died in 1845.

Bournon, de, dẹh booʀ′nôn′, (JACQUES LOUIS,) COMTE, a French mineralogist, born at Metz in 1751, was a Fellow of the Royal Society and of the Geological Society of London. He was appointed by Louis XVIII. director of his mineral cabinet. He died in 1825, leaving a "Treatise on Carbonate of Lime," and other works.

Bournonville, booʀ′nôn′vẹl′, (ANTON AUGUST,) a Danish composer of ballets, born at Copenhagen in 1805.

Bournouf. See BURNOUF.

Bouron. See BORRON.

Bourquelot, booʀk′lo′, (LOUIS FÉLIX,) a French antiquary and *littérateur,* born at Provins in 1815. He succeeded Louandre in the editorship of the "Littérature Française contemporaine," a continuation of a work commenced by Quérard.

Bourrienne, de, dẹh boo′re-ên′,(FAUVELET,) a French diplomatist and biographer, born at Sens in July, 1769. He was a fellow-student and friend of Bonaparte at the school of Brienne. On leaving school they made mutual promises of eternal friendship. He and Bonaparte again met at Paris in 1792, and renewed their intimate relations. In 1796 he became confidential secretary to his friend, then general-in-chief of the army of Italy, whom he followed to Egypt. He was dismissed from that office in 1802, and was appointed minister or chargé-d'affaires to Hamburg in 1804 or 1805. Having been accused of peculation, he was recalled in 1810. He deserted the cause of Napoleon in 1814, and was appointed minister of state by Louis XVIII. in 1815, after the battle of Waterloo. He published "Memoirs of Bourrienne," (10 vols., 1829-31,) which produced a great sensation and was translated into many languages. This work is considered particularly interesting as throwing light on the character of Napoleon; although it is not entirely reliable. Died at Caen in 1834.

See "Nouvelle Biographie Générale."

Bourrit, boo′re′, (MARC THÉODORE,) a Swiss naturalist, born at Geneva about 1739, wrote a "Description of the Glaciers of Savoy," (1774,) "Description of the Pennine and Rhetian Alps," (1781,) and other works. He ascended to the top of Mont Blanc with Saussure in 1787. Died near Geneva in 1815.

See "Notice biographique sur M. T. Bourrit," 1836.

Bourru, boo′rü′, (EDME CLAUDE,) a French physician and writer, born in Paris in 1737; died in 1823.

Boursault, booʀ′so′, (EDME,) a French dramatist, born at Mucit-l'Évêque, in Burgundy, in 1638, published the comedies of "Le Mercure galant," "Æsop in Town," and "Æsop at Court." Died in 1701.

See NICÉRON, "Mémoires."

Boursier, booʀ′se-à′, (LAURENT FRANÇOIS,) a French theological writer, born at Écouen in 1679, wrote a work called "Action de Dieu sur les Créatures." Died in 1749.

Bourvalais, de, dẹh booʀ′vả′lả′, (PAUL POISSON,) a wealthy French financier under the reign of Louis XIV. Died in 1719.

Bousbecq. See BUSBECQ.

Bourzeïs, de, dẹh booʀ′zả′ẹss′, (AMABLE,) a French *littérateur* and theologian, born near Riom in 1606; died in 1672.

Bousmard, de, dẹh boo′mǎʀ′, (HENRI JEAN BAPTISTE,) a military engineer in the Prussian service, born at Saint-Mihiel in 1749, was killed at the siege of Dantzic in 1807. He wrote an "Essay on Fortification," (4 vols., 1803.)

Bousseau, boo′so′, (JACQUES,) a French sculptor, born in 1681, was a pupil of Coustou, and became first sculptor to Philip V. of Spain. Died in 1740.

Boussingault, boo′sǎn′go′, (JEAN BAPTISTE JOSEPH DIEUDONNÉ,) a French chemist, born in Paris in 1802, served in his youth on the staff of Bolivar in South America. In conjunction with Dumas, he determined the proportions of the gases which constitute air. He made contributions to meteorology, and published a "Treatise on Rural Economy," (2 vols., 1844,) and other works. He was a member of the Institute.

Bousyry, (Cherif-Eddin.) See BOOSEEREE.

Boutard, boo′tǎʀ′, (FRANÇOIS,) a French *littérateur* and Latin poet, born at Troyes in 1664; died in 1729.

Boutaric, de, dẹh boo′tả′rẹk′, (FRANÇOIS,) a French jurist and writer, born at Figeac in 1672; died in 1733.

ϵ as *k;* ç as *s;* ḡ *hard;* g̃ as *j;* G, H, K, *guttural;* N, *nasal;* R, *trilled;* s̄ as *z;* th as in *this.* (☞ See Explanations, p. 23.)

27

Boutauld, boo'tō', (MICHEL,) a French Jesuit and theological writer, born in Paris in 1607 ; died in 1688.

Boutelle, boo'tĕl', (TIMOTHY,) a distinguished American lawyer, born at Leominster, Massachusetts, in 1777, practised at Waterville, Maine. Died in 1855.

Bouteroue, boot'roo', (CLAUDE,) a French antiquary, born in Paris ; died about 1680.

Bouterwek, boo'ter-wĕk', (FRIEDRICH,) a German philosopher and critic of high reputation, born near Goslar, in Hanover, in 1766. He published in 1791 a popular romance entitled "Count Donamar." In 1802 he became professor of philosophy at Göttingen. His "History of Modern Poetry and Eloquence" (12 vols., 1801-19) is ranked among the best works of the kind, and portions of it have been translated into French, English, and Spanish. He also wrote a treatise "On Æsthetics," (1806,) and a "Manual of Philosophical Science," (1813.) Died at Göttingen in 1828.

See J. F. BLUMENBACH, "Memoria T. Bouterwekii," 4to, 1832; "Nouvelle Biographie Générale."

Bouteville, de, dęh boot'vĕl', (FRANCOIS de Montmorency—dęh mŏn'mo'rŏn'se',) SEIGNEUR, a noted French duellist and soldier, born in 1600, fought with distinction against the Protestants in the wars of the League. He was condemned to death for one of his duels, and executed in 1627. He was the father of the celebrated Marshal Luxembourg.

Bouthilier, le, (ARMAND JEAN.) See RANCÉ.

Boutillier, boo'te'ye-ą', (MAXIMILIEN JEAN,) a French dramatist, was born in Paris in 1745; died in 1811.

Boutrays, boo'trą', or **Boutterais,**boot'rą',(RAOUL,) [Lat. RODOL'PHUS BOTHE'RIUS,] a French writer and Latin poet, born at Châteaudun about 1552 ; died in 1630.

Boutwell, bŏwt'wel, (GEORGE S.,) an American statesman, was born in Norfolk county, Massachusetts, in 1818. He studied law, and was elected Governor of Massachusetts in 1850, and re-elected in 1851. Having joined the Republican party, he represented the seventh district of Massachusetts in Congress in 1863-69. In February, 1868, he advocated, in an able speech, the impeachment of President Johnson, and was placed at the head of the committee appointed to report articles of impeachment. He was one of the seven managers who conducted the impeachment of Johnson in April. In March, 1869, he was appointed by President Grant secretary of the treasury.

Bouvard, (ALEXIS.) See BOUVART, (ALEXIS.)

Bouvard, boo'vȧr', (CHARLES,) a French physician, born near Vendôme in 1572, became professor in the College of France in 1625, and first physician to Louis XIII. in 1628. Died in 1658.

Bouvart or **Bouvard,** boo'vȧr', (ALEXIS,) a French astronomer, born in Faucigny, near Mont Blanc, in 1767. He became an assistant in the Observatory of Paris in 1795, and afterwards a member of the Institute. He worked with Laplace, who confided to him all the researches of detail and calculations of his "Mécanique Céleste." He rendered important services to practical astronomy by his tables of the planet Uranus, (the perturbations of which were first noticed by him,) as suggesting the existence of a planet then undiscovered. Died in 1843.

See ALFRED GAUTIER, "Notice sur A. Bouvard," 1844.

Bouvart, (MICHEL PHILIPPE,) a French physician and writer, born at Chartres in 1717, enjoyed a high reputation in his time, and became professor of medicine in the College of France. Died in 1787.

Bouvenot, boov'no', (LOUIS PIERRE,) a French physician, born at Arbois in 1756 ; died at Sens in 1830.

Bouverie, boo'veh-re', (EDWARD PLEYDELL,) an English politician, son of the Earl of Radnor, was born in 1818. He became paymaster-general, and president of the poor-law board, in 1855. He is a member of the privy council.

Bouvet, boo'vą', (JOACHIM,) a French missionary to China, born at Mans about 1662. He died in 1732, leaving several works on China.

Bouvet de Cressé, boo'vą' dęh krȧ'sȧ', (AUGUSTE JEAN BAPTISTE,) a French writer of history and educational works, born at Provins in 1772 ; died in 1839.

Bouvier, boo've-ą', (ANDRÉ MARIE JOSEPH,) a French physician, was born at Dôle in 1746. He practised in Paris, and was employed by the mother of Napoleon I. Died in 1827.

Bouvier, boo-veer', [Fr. pron. boo've-ą',] (JOHN,) a jurist and legal writer, born at Codognan, in the south of France, in 1787. He emigrated to America about 1802, and studied law, which he practised in Philadelphia. In 1838 he became a judge of the court of criminal sessions. He published a "Law Dictionary," (2 vols., 1839,) which enjoys a high reputation, and a valuable work, entitled "Institutes of American Law," (4 vols., 1851,) which has received the commendation of several eminent jurists. Died in 1851.

Bouys, boo'e', (ANDRÉ,) a French portrait-painter and engraver, born at Hyères, in Var, in 1657 ; died in Paris in 1740.

Bovadilla. See BOBADILLA.

Boverio, bo-vā're-o, [Lat. BOVE'RIUS,] (ZACCARIA,) an Italian theologian, born at Saluzzo in 1568 ; died in 1638.

Boves, bo'vĕs, (JOSÉ TOMAS,) a Spanish royalist soldier, notorious for ferocity, born in Castile. He fought in South America, and defeated Bolivar at San Matéo in February, 1814. He was killed in battle in December of the same year.

Bovet, de, dęh bo'vą', (FRANÇOIS,) a French ecclesiastic, born in 1745, became Archbishop of Toulouse in 1817. He published a work "On Egyptian Dynasties," ("Des Dynasties Égyptiennes.") Died in 1838.

Bovillus. See BOUELLES.

Bŏw'dȩn, (JOHN,) a clergyman of the Anglican Church, born in Ireland in 1751, emigrated to America in 1770. He became professor of moral philosophy in Columbia College, New York, in 1805. Died in 1817.

Bowdich, bŏw'ditch, (THOMAS EDWARD,) an English traveller and savant, born at Bristol in 1790. About 1816 he accompanied a mission to the King of Ashantee, and published, after his return, "A Mission to Ashantee," (1819,) which was received with great favour. In 1822 he again set out for Africa, but on reaching the mouth of the Gambia died of a fever, January, 1824. He wrote, besides other works, an "Essay on the Geography of North-Western Africa," and an "Essay on the Superstitions, Customs, and Arts common to the Ancient Egyptians, etc."

See "London Quarterly Review" for March and November, 1820.

Bŏw'ditch, (NATHANIEL,) an eminent American mathematician, born at Salem, Massachusetts, in March, 1773. He was the son of a cooper, who was not able to give him a liberal education. He served an apprenticeship to a ship-chandler, and passed about nine years at sea, as an inferior officer of a merchant-vessel, after he attained the age of twenty-one. He learned Greek, Latin, and other languages. About 1802 he published a work called "The Practical Navigator," which was highly esteemed. He was president of an insurance company from 1804 to 1823, and removed to Boston in the latter year. He was offered the chair of mathematics in Harvard College, which he declined. His reputation is founded chiefly on a translation of the "Mécanique Céleste" of Laplace, with a copious commentary, published in 4 vols. 4to, (1829-38.) Referring to this subject, the "London Quarterly Review" of July, 1832, remarks, "The idea of undertaking a translation of the whole 'Mécanique Céleste,' accompanied throughout with a copious running commentary, is one which savours at first sight of the gigantesque. . . . The first volume only has as yet reached us ; and when we consider the great difficulty of printing works of this nature, to say nothing of the heavy and probably unremunerated expense, we are not surprised at the delay of the second. Meanwhile, the part actually completed (which contains the first two books of Laplace's work) is, with few and slight exceptions, just what we could have wished to see, —an exact and careful translation into very good English, exceedingly well printed, and accompanied with notes appended to each page, which leave no step in the text of moment unsupplied, and hardly any material difficulty, either of conception or reasoning, unelucidated. To the student of 'Celestial Mechanism,' such a work must be invaluable." Bowditch was actuary of the Mas-

ā, ē, ī, ō, ū, ȳ, *long;* ȧ, ė, ȯ, same, less prolonged; ă, ĕ, ĭ, ŏ, ŭ, ў, *short;* a, ę, į, o, *obscure;* fär, fȧll, fȧt; mȇt; nŏt; gŏŏd; mŏŏn;

sachusetts Life Insurance Company from 1823 until his death. He was a Fellow of the Royal Society of London. He married in early life, and had several children. Died in Boston in March, 1838.

See a "Memoir of N. Bowditch," by his son N. J. BOWDITCH, 1839; notice of Bowditch in the "American Journal of Science," vol. xxxv.

Bŏwd'lẹr, (HANNAH,) sister of Thomas, noticed below, published "Poems and Essays," and "Sermons on the Doctrines and Duties of Christianity." Died in 1830. Her sister Jane was also distinguished as a writer.

Bowdler, (JOHN,) brother of the preceding, born in London in 1783, published "Select Pieces in Verse and Prose," and other works. Died in 1815.

See "Memoir of John Bowdler and Thomas Bowdler;" "London Quarterly Review" for January and April, 1819; "Edinburgh Review" for August, 1817.

Bowdler, (THOMAS,) an English physician, born near Bath in 1754, wrote "Letters from Holland," and edited "The Family Shakspeare." Died in 1825.

Bowdoin, bŏ'd'n, (JAMES,) a patriotic American governor, born in Boston in 1727, was descended from a Huguenot refugee. He graduated at Harvard College in 1745, and inherited an ample fortune. He was elected president of the Council of Massachusetts in 1775, before which he had served many years in the council and general court. In 1778 he was president of the convention which formed the Constitution of Massachusetts. He was chosen Governor of the State in 1785, and again in 1786. Among the events of his administration was Shays's rebellion, which he suppressed with vigour. He was one of the chief founders of the American Academy of Arts and Sciences at Boston. Died in 1790.

Bowdoin, (JAMES,) a son of the preceding, was born at Boston in 1752. In 1805 he was sent on a mission to Spain to negotiate the cession of Florida to the United States, and to settle other affairs. He was a benefactor of Bowdoin College. Died in 1811.

Bŏw'ẹn, (FRANCIS,) an American scholar and author, born at Charlestown, Massachusetts, in 1811, graduated with distinction at Harvard University in 1833. He edited the "North American Review" from 1843 until 1854, and published, in 1849, "Lowell Lectures on the Application of Metaphysical and Ethical Science to the Evidences of Religion." In 1853 he became Alford professor of natural religion, moral philosophy, and civil polity in Harvard University. He contributed several articles to Sparks's "American Biography" and to the "Imperial Dictionary of Biography." Among his works is "Principles of Political Economy applied to the Condition of the American People," (1856,) favourably noticed in the "North American Review" for April, 1856.

Bowen, (JOHN S.,) an American general, born in Georgia about 1831, graduated at West Point in 1853. He became a major-general in the Confederate service, and commanded the army which General Grant defeated at Port Gibson in May, 1863. He died at Raymond, Mississippi, in July or August of that year.

Bowen, (PARDON,) M.D., a physician, born in Providence, Rhode Island, in 1757. He published an "Account of the Yellow Fever at Providence." Died in 1826.

Bowen, (WILLIAM C.,) an American physician, born probably in Rhode Island, in 1785. He was a pupil of Sir Astley Cooper of London, and was appointed professor of chemistry in Brown University in 1812. His experiments on the bleaching-properties of chlorine produced a disease or injury of which he died in 1815.

Bŏw'ẹr, (ARCHIBALD,) a Scottish writer, born at Dundee about 1686, originally a Catholic, professed Protestantism for a time, and afterwards returned to Catholicism. He was a contributor to the "Historia Literaria" and the "Universal History," and wrote a "History of the Popes." Died in 1766.

See CHAMBERS, "Biographical Dictionary of Eminent Scotsmen."

Bŏw'ẹr-bank, (JOHN SCOTT,) an English naturalist, born in London about 1797, published a "History of the Fossil Fruits and Seeds of the London Clay."

Bowle, bōl, (JOHN,) an English divine, was a contributor to the "Archæologia" and the "Biographical History of England," and defended Milton against the attacks of Lauder. Died in 1788.

Bowles, (CAROLINE.) See SOUTHEY.

Bowles, bōlz, (WILLIAM,) a distinguished naturalist, born in Ireland, resided in Spain, where he published, in 1775, an "Introduction to the Natural History and the Physical Geography of Spain," (in Spanish.) It has been translated into French and Italian.

Bowles, (WILLIAM A.,) was born in Maryland. During the American Revolution he instigated the Indians to commit atrocities against the whites. He afterwards incited the savages against the Spaniards, who took him prisoner. He died in prison, at Havana, in 1805.

Bowles, (WILLIAM LISLE,) an eminent English poet, born at King's Sutton, on the border of Northamptonshire, in September, 1762. He was educated at Trinity College, Oxford, and chose the clerical profession. After he had been disappointed in love by the death of a lady to whom he was engaged, he composed, in 1789, "Fourteen Sonnets," which were remarkable for grace of expression and an air of melancholy tenderness. He became rector of Dumbleton in 1797, married a daughter of the Rev. Dr. Wake, and obtained the valuable living of Bremhill, Wiltshire, in 1805. He published in 1804 "The Spirit of Discovery," which is his longest poem. Among his numerous other poems are "The Grave of Howard," (1790,) "The Missionary of the Andes," (1822,) and "Saint John in Patmos," (1832.) In 1828 he became a canon of Salisbury Cathedral. He edited the works of Pope, (1807,) and made some criticisms on that author which provoked a long controversy between himself and the two poets Byron and Campbell. He published in 1825 his "Final Appeal to the Literary Public relative to Pope." Died in 1850.

The poems of Bowles were admired by Coleridge, Wordsworth, and Southey, the last of whom wrote to a friend, "My poetical taste was much meliorated by Bowles." "The Sonnets of Bowles," says Hallam, "may be reckoned among the first-fruits of a new era in poetry. They came in an age when a commonplace facility in rhyming, on the one hand, and an almost nonsensical affectation in a new school, on the other, had lowered the standard so much that critical judges spoke of English poetry as of something nearly extinct." ("Address before the Royal Society of Literature.")

See a "Life of Bowles," by a relative and ALARIC WATTS; "Men I have known," by WILLIAM JERDAN, London, 1866; "London Quarterly Review" for April and December, 1818, and May and July, 1820.

Bŏw'man, (WILLIAM,) F.R.S., an English surgeon, born at Nantwich about 1816. He became professor of physiology and anatomy in King's College, London. He published "Lectures on Operations on the Eye," and other works.

Bŏw'ring, (Sir JOHN,) LL.D., an English statesman and linguist, noted for his attainments in the Sclavonic languages, was born in Exeter in 1792. He published "Specimens of the Russian Poets," (1821,) "Ancient Poetry and Romances of Spain," "Poetry of the Magyars," "Servian Popular Poetry," (1829,) and "Cheskian Anthology," (1832.) He had become in 1825 editor of the "Westminster Review," for which he wrote numerous articles on political economy and in favour of free trade. He was elected to Parliament in 1835, re-elected in 1841, continuing in office till 1849, when he was appointed British consul at Hong-Kong and superintendent of trade in China. He was knighted in 1854, and made governor of Hong-Kong. He had published in 1838–39 "The Works of Jeremy Bentham," who was his intimate friend and had appointed him his executor. He returned from China about 1858.

See "Edinburgh Review" for January, 1831; "Dictionnaire d'Économie politique."

Bŏw'yẹr, (Sir GEORGE,) an English jurist, born in Berkshire in 1811, published a "Treatise on Modern Civil Law," and other works. He became in 1852 a member of Parliament, where he has distinguished himself as a zealous defender of the policy of the Roman Catholic powers.

Bowyer, (WILLIAM,) a celebrated English printer and scholar, born in London in 1699. Among the numerous and excellent works which issued from his press we may name his "Novum Testamentum Græcum," the "Greek Lexicon" of Schrevelius, the "Works of Selden," ("Seldeni Opera Omnia,") Pocock's "Description of the East," Vertot's "Knights of Malta," and "The Coptic Pentateuch." These editions are not only of great typographic beauty and accuracy, but are enriched with valuable notes, prefaces, and indexes. He also wrote "Remarks on Greek and Roman Money," a treatise "On the Origin of Printing," and "Critical Conjectures and Observations on the New Testament," a work of the highest reputation, which was translated into German by Schulz. He was a Fellow of the Society of Antiquaries. He was distinguished for the benevolence and integrity of his character, and numbered among his friends many of the most eminent scholars of his time. Died in 1777.

See "Biographical and Literary Anecdotes of William Bowyer," by JOHN NICHOLS, 1778.

Box'er, (EDWARD,) an English admiral, born at Dover in 1784, served against the French in the campaigns of 1801 and 1809, and subsequently took part in the Crimean war. Died near Balaklava in 1855.

Boxhorn, boks'horn, (MARCUS Zuerius—zü-ā're-ŭs,) an eminent Dutch critic and historian, born at Berg-op-Zoom in 1612. He succeeded Heinsius as professor of history and politics at Leyden. He wrote a large number of Latin works, in prose and verse, among which are "Quæstiones Romanæ," (1637,) "Chronicle of Zealand," (1643,) and a "Universal History," (1675.) Died in 1653.

See NICÉRON, "Mémoires;" L. BARLÆUS, "Oratio funebris in Excessum M. Z. Boxhornii," 1653.

Boyardo. See BOIARDO.

Boyce. See BOECE.

Boyce, (WILLIAM,) an eminent English composer, born in London in 1710. He studied under Dr. Greene, and in 1758 became organist to the Chapel Royal. Among his best works are his grand anthem, "Lord, Thou hast been our Refuge," a "Te Deum," six anthems, and a Jubilate in Dr. Arnold's "Collection of Cathedral Music," and "Solomon," a serenata. He also published a work entitled "The Cathedral Music of the English Masters of the Last Two Centuries," (3 vols. fol., 1760.) Died in 1779.

See FÉTIS, "Biographie Universelle des Musiciens."

Boyd, (ANDREW K. H.,) a popular Scottish writer and divine, born in Ayrshire in 1825. He published in "Fraser's Magazine" a number of essays, which appeared in 1860 under the title of "Recreations of a Country Parson." He has also been a contributor to the "Atlantic Monthly."

Boyd, (HENRY,) an Irish *littérateur*, published "Dramatic and Lyric Poems," and translated Dante's "Divine Comedy" into English verse. Died in 1832.

Boyd, (HUGH MACAULEY,) a jurist and political writer, born in the county of Antrim, Ireland, in 1746. In 1781 he accompanied Lord Macartney to Madras, where he died about 1792. The "Letters of Junius" were for a time attributed to him.

See "Biographia Britannica."

Boyd, (HUGH STUART,) an English writer and Greek scholar. He translated into English some of the works of Chrysostom, Gregory Nazianzen, and Basil, (1806,) and wrote several treatises on theology. Died in 1848.

See "Edinburgh Review" for November, 1814.

Boyd, (JAMES,) an English classical scholar, born about 1795. He edited, besides other works, Adams's "Roman Antiquities." Died in 1856.

Boyd, (JOHN PARKER,) an American general, born at Newburyport, Massachusetts, in 1768, commanded a small corps in the service of Holkar and other East Indian princes. He served as a brigadier-general in the American army in the war of 1812, and took part in the battle of Williamsburg, Canada, in November, 1813. Died in 1830.

Boyd, (LINN,) from 1853 to 1855 Speaker of the National House of Representatives, was born at Nashville, Tennessee, in 1800. In 1835 he was elected to Congress, and, with the exception of 1837-38, was regularly reelected till 1855, a period of twenty years. Died in 1859.

Boyd, (MARK ALEXANDER,) a Scottish writer, born at Galloway in 1562, published "Epistolæ Heroidum," and other esteemed Latin poems. Died in 1601.

See CHAMBERS, "Biographical Dictionary of Eminent Scotsmen."

Boyd, (ROBERT,) a Scottish statesman, and one of the lords of the regency during the minority of James III. He afterwards declared himself sole regent, and promoted a marriage between his son, subsequently Lord Arran, and the sister of the king. Being summoned to Parliament by James to answer for his conduct, Boyd escaped to England, where he died in 1470.

See BURTON's "History of Scotland," chap. xxix.

Boyd, (ROBERT,) a Scottish divine, born at Glasgow in 1578; died in 1627.

Boyd, (WILLIAM,) Earl of Kilmarnock, a Scottish Jacobite, born in 1704. He was taken prisoner at Culloden, tried for treason, and executed in 1746.

Boyd, (ZACHARY,) a Scottish theologian, lived at Glasgow, and wrote "Zion's Flowers," in verse, and other works. Died in 1653.

Boy'dell, (JOHN,) an English engraver and amateur, born in Shropshire, or, as some writers assert, in Staffordshire, in 1719. Having previously published a collection of engravings, among which were upwards of one hundred of his own views in England and Wales, he began business as a print-seller, by which he acquired an immense fortune. By his patronage of the best English painters and engravers he rendered the greatest services to art in his native country. His "Shakspeare Gallery," consisting of illustrations of Shakspeare's dramas, by the most eminent English painters, whom he employed, is a splendid monument of his munificence. The engravings from these pictures were published under his patronage in a superb folio volume, (1803.) Boydell had been elected in 1790 lord mayor of London. Died in 1804.

See STRUTT, "Dictionary of Engravers."

Boye, bo'yĕh, (CASPAR JOHANNES,) a distinguished poet and divine, born at Kongsberg, in Norway, in 1791, wrote several poems and tragedies. He also translated Sir Walter Scott's romances, and several German works.

See ERSLEW, "Forfatter-Lexicon."

Boyen, bo'yen, (HERMANN,) a Prussian statesman and general, born at Kreuzburg in 1771. He served against the French in the campaigns of 1810-12, and became minister of war about 1814. In 1847 he was made a field-marshal, and governor of the House of Invalids at Berlin. Died in 1848.

Boyer, bwä'yà', (ABEL,) a French lexicographer, born at Castres in 1664, published a "French Dictionary" and "Grammar," a "Dissertation on French Prosody," and other works. Died in 1729.

Boyer, (ALEXIS,) a celebrated French surgeon, born in Limousin in 1757. He became about 1804 first surgeon of the emperor Napoleon, who made him a baron of the empire and conferred on him the cross of the legion of honour. He was appointed in 1823 consulting surgeon to Louis XVIII., which post he continued to hold under Charles X. and Louis Philippe. He was afterwards chief surgeon of the Hospital of Charity, in Paris, and a member of the Institute. He published a "Complete Treatise on Anatomy," (4 vols., 1799,) and a "Treatise on Surgical Maladies," (11 vols., 1814-26.) Died in Paris in 1833.

See a "Notice sur la Vie et les Œuvres de Boyer," prefixed to an edition of his "Traité des Maladies chirurgicales," 7 vols., 1844-53; ROUX, "Éloge de Boyer;" "Nouvelle Biographie Générale."

Boyer, (JEAN BAPTISTE,) Marquis d'Aguilles, (dā'gèl' or dā'ge'ye,) a French painter and engraver, born at Aix about 1640; died in 1709.

Boyer, (JEAN BAPTISTE NICOLAS,) a French physician, born at Marseilles in 1693, was conspicuous for his skill and humanity during the prevalence of the plague in that city in 1720. He wrote an "Historic Account of the Plague of Marseilles," and several treatises on infectious diseases. Died in 1768.

See QUÉRARD, "La France Littéraire."

Boyer, (JEAN FRANÇOIS,) a French theologian, born in Paris in 1675, became Bishop of Mirepoix in 1730, and subsequently preceptor to the dauphin, father of Louis XVI. He was a member of the French Academy and of the Academy of Sciences, and in 1741 succeeded Cardinal de Polignac in the Academy of Inscriptions. Died in 1755.

Boyer, boi'ẹr, [Fr. pron. bwȧ'yà',] (JEAN PIERRE,) President of the republic of Hayti, born at Port-au-Prince in 1776, was the son of a white creole and a free negress. After the capture of Toussaint L'Ouverture in the revolution of 1802, he attached himself to the party of the mulatto general Alexander Pétion, then at war with Christophe, and rose to the rank of general of division. On the death of Pétion he succeeded him as President of the republic in 1818. The Haytians becoming dissatisfied with his rule, he was deposed in 1842 and obliged to leave the country. He was succeeded by Hérard, also a mulatto. Died in Paris in 1850.

See MADION, "Histoire d'Haïti," 1847.

Boyer, (PIERRE,) a French theological writer, born at Arlanes in 1677 ; died in 1755.

Boyer, (PIERRE DENIS,) a French ecclesiastic and controversialist, born at Caissac in 1766, became professor of dogmatic theology in the Seminary of Saint-Sulpice, Paris. Died in 1842.

Boyer-Fonfrède. See FONFRÈDE.

Boyle, (CHARLES,) Earl of Or'rery, a son of Roger, Earl of Orrery, and nephew of the great Robert Boyle, was born at Chelsea in 1676. While a student at Christ Church, Oxford, he published, at the age of nineteen, an edition of the "Epistles of Phalaris," with some reflections on the incivility of Bentley, who was keeper of the king's library, and who had lent to Boyle a manuscript of the Epistles, with a remark that they were spurious. (See BENTLEY, RICHARD.) In 1698 appeared a witty and personal attack on Bentley, entitled an "Examination of the Dissertation on the Epistles of Phalaris, by the Hon. Charles Boyle," which was written mostly by Atterbury. Boyle fought as major-general at the battle of Malplaquet in 1709. Soon after the accession of George I., he became a favourite courtier of that king. Died in 1731.

See BUDGELL, "Memoirs of the Lives and Characters of the Family of the Boyles," 1732.

Boyle, (HENRY,) an able politician, a son of Charles, Lord Clifford, and a great-grandson of the first Earl of Cork. He was chancellor of the exchequer from 1701 to 1708, and in the latter year became secretary of state. He was created Lord Carleton in 1714, and appointed president of the council. He was a nephew of the famous Robert Boyle. Died in 1725.

Boyle, (HENRY,) a grandson of Roger, Lord Broghill, became Speaker of the Irish House of Commons in 1732. About 1756 he received the title of Earl of Shannon. Died in 1764.

Boyle, (JEREMIAH T.,) an American general and lawyer, born in Mercer county, Kentucky, in 1818. He entered the Union army in 1861, and commanded a brigade at Shiloh, April, 1862.

Boyle, (JOHN,) son of Charles Boyle, fourth Earl of Orrery, born about 1707. As a member of the House of Lords, he was conspicuous for his opposition to Sir Robert Walpole. He published "Imitations of Two of the Odes of Horace," and "Remarks on the Life and Writings of Swift." Died in 1762.

Boyle, (RICHARD,) the first Earl of Cork, called "the Great Earl of Cork," was born at Canterbury in 1566. He settled in Ireland, acquired a large estate, and held several high offices. In 1620 he was created Earl of Cork. He contributed greatly to the suppression of the Irish Rebellion of 1641. He had seven sons. Died in 1643 or 1644.

Boyle, (RICHARD,) second Earl of Cork, a son of the preceding, born in 1612. He was a partisan of Charles I. in the civil war, and received the title of Earl of Burlington. Died in January, 1698.

Boyle, (RICHARD,) fourth Earl of Cork and third Earl of Burlington, born in 1695, was an amateur architect, and a friend of Pope. Died in 1753.

Boyle, (ROBERT,) a celebrated chemist and experimental philosopher, born at Lismore, in Ireland, on the 25th of January, 1626, was the seventh son of Richard, the "great Earl of Cork." He studied at Eton and at Geneva, which he left in 1641, and afterwards travelled in Italy. In 1644 he returned to England, and devoted himself to study and experiments. He resided at Oxford from 1654 to 1668. He improved the air-pump, and discovered the law of the air's elasticity,—namely, that its

bulk is inversely as the pressure. By his "Skeptica. Chymist" (1661) he contributed to subvert the theories of the iatro-chymists. He taught that the elements of bodies are atoms of different shapes and sizes, the union of which gives origin to what are vulgarly called elements. He was one of the founders of the Royal Society, of which he was chosen president in 1680, but he declined the honour.

"No one Englishman of the seventeenth century after Lord Bacon," says Hallam, "raised to himself so high a reputation in experimental philosophy as Robert Boyle. . . . His 'Disquisition on Final Causes' was a well-timed vindication of that palmary argument against the paradox of the Cartesians, who had denied the validity of an inference from the manifest adaptation of means to ends in the universe to an intelligent Providence. Boyle takes a more philosophical view of the principle of final causes than had been found in many theologians." ("Introduction to the Literature of Europe.")

Boyle learned the Hebrew and Greek languages to qualify himself to write in defence of revealed religion, and printed at his own expense a translation of the Gospels into the Malay language. He refused a peerage, which was offered to him repeatedly. It has been remarked that he was born in the year of Bacon's death, as the person destined by nature to succeed him ; and he may be accounted the most zealous and successful disciple of Bacon in inductive philosophy. His merits were commemorated by Boerhaave in terms like these : "Mr. Boyle, the ornament of his age and country, succeeded to the genius and talents of Lord Verulam. We owe to him the secrets of fire, air, water, animals, plants, and fossils." He was distinguished for his liberality and active benevolence.

Among his works are a "Free Inquiry into the Received Notion of Nature," "Excellency of Theology," a "Discourse of Things above Reason," "On the Great Veneration that Man's Intellect owes to God," "Considerations on the Style of the Holy Scriptures," and "Hydrostatical Paradoxes," (1666.) An edition of his complete works (with a Life of the author prefixed) was published by Dr. Birch in 5 vols. folio, 1744. By his last will he left a fund to endow eight sermons in a year in defence of the Christian religion, which are called the "Boyle Lectures." He was never married, and took no part in political affairs. From 1668 until his death he resided mostly in London, where he died on the 30th of December, 1691. A narrative of his early life, written by himself, may be found prefixed to the edition of his works published by Dr. Birch in 1744.

See BUDGELL, "Memoirs of the Lives and Characters of the Family of the Boyles;" THOMAS BIRCH, "Life and Writings of the Hon. R. Boyle," 1741; HOEFER, "Histoire de la Chimie;" "Encyclopædia Britannica."

Boyle, (ROGER,) Baron Broghill, son of the first Earl of Cork, was born in 1621. Originally a partisan of Charles I., he afterwards fought under Cromwell, and distinguished himself at the siege of Clonmel, in Ireland. He became one of Cromwell's privy council, and, after the restoration of Charles II., filled the same office, was made lord president of the province of Munster, and created Earl of Orrery. He wrote several poems, and a romance called "Parthenissa." Died in 1679.

See HUME, "History of England."

Boyleau, Boyleaux, bwä'lō', sometimes written **Boilesve**, (ESTIENNE,) an eminent French magistrate and jurist, born about 1200. He accompanied Saint Louis in the crusade of 1248, and was appointed after his return provost of Paris.

Boyl'stọn, (NICHOLAS,) the founder of the Boylston professorship of rhetoric and elocution of Harvard University, was born in 1716; died in 1771.

Boylston, (ZABDIEL,) a physician, noted as the first who practised inoculation for the small-pox in America, was born at Brookline, Massachusetts, in 1680. He began to inoculate in Boston in 1721, and excited an opposition so violent that the populace threatened to hang him. He was chosen a Fellow of the Royal Society of London. Died in 1766.

Boym, boim, (MICHAEL,) a Polish Jesuit, was a missionary to India and China, where he died in 1659. He wrote an "Account of China," and other works.

Boyne, Loin, (GUSTAVUS HAMILTON,) LORD, a British general, born about 1640. Having enlisted in the service of William of Orange, he was appointed governor of Enniskillen in 1689. He served with distinction at the battle of the Boyne, (1690,) and in other battles in Ireland. He was created Viscount Boyne in 1717. Died in 1723.

Boyse, Boys, or **Bois,** boiss, (JOHN,) an English scholar, born in Suffolk in 1560, assisted in the translation of the Bible under James I., and was one of the committee of six charged to revise it. He also co-operated with Sir Henry Saville in the publication of the works of Saint Chrysostom. Died in 1643.

See PITS, "De Scriptoribus Angliæ."

Boyse, (JOSEPH,) an English dissenting divine, born in Yorkshire in 1660, belonged to the sect of Brownists, and was a coadjutor of Thomas Emlyn. Died in 1728.

Boyse, (SAMUEL,) an English poet, son of the preceding, born in Dublin in 1708. Although patronized by several persons eminent for rank and talents, he died in extreme poverty, owing to his dissolute habits, (1749.) He contributed numerous poems to the "Gentleman's Magazine," and published separately "Chaucer's Tales in Modern English," "Albion's Triumph," and other works.

Boyseau, de, deh bwȧ'zō', (PIERRE,) Marquis de Châteaufort, (deh shȧ'tō'for',) born near Namur in 1659, fought on the side of Philip V. in the war of the Spanish succession, and became Captain-General of Old Castile. Died in 1741.

See DE STASSART, "Notice sur P. Boyseau," 1846.

Boysen, boi'zen, (FRIEDRICH EBERHARD,) a German historian, born at Halberstadt in 1720. He produced a "Universal History," (10 vols., 1767–72,) and other works. Died in 1800.

See ERSCH und GRUBER, "Allgemeine Encyklopaedie;" "F. E. Boysen's Lebensbeschreibung," 2 vols., 1795.

Boyssières, de, deh bwȧ'se-air', (JEAN,) a French poet, was born at Clermont-Ferrand in 1555.

Boz. See DICKENS.

Boze, de, deh boz, (CLAUDE GROS,) an eminent French archæologist, born at Lyons in 1680. He became in 1706 perpetual secretary of the Academy of Inscriptions, and in 1715 succeeded Fénelon in the French Academy. He published an "Historical Treatise on the Jubilee of the Jews," (1702,) a "Dissertation on the Janus of the Ancients," and several treatises on numismatics. Died in 1753.

See QUÉRARD, "La France Littéraire."

Boz'man, (JOHN LEEDS,) an American lawyer, poet, and historian, born in Oxford, Maryland, in 1757. He was a contributor to "Dennie's Port-Folio" and other periodicals, and was author of a "History of Maryland," (2 vols. 8vo,) and of several legal works. Died in 1823.

Bozzaris or **Botzaris,** bot'sȧ-ris, popularly called boz-zȧr'is, (MARCOS,) a celebrated modern Greek patriot, born at Suli, in Albania, about 1790. He enlisted in the French army about 1808, and retired in 1815 to the Ionian Isles, where he married. In the war of independence which began in 1820 he was an able leader and performed many heroic exploits. He was appointed *Stratarch* of Western Greece late in 1822, and passed the winter in Missolonghi. In the summer of 1823 he attacked by night a greatly superior force of Turks, and fell mortally wounded in the action, which resulted in a decisive victory of the Greeks.

See C. PAGANEL, "Tombeau de M. Botzaris," 1826; POUQUE-VILLE, "Histoire de la Régénération de la Grèce."

Bozzoli, bot'so-lee, (GIUSEPPE,) an Italian *littérateur*, born at Mantua in 1724, translated Homer's "Iliad" and "Odyssey," and Virgil's "Æneid," into Italian verse. Died about 1790.

Brabant, brȧ'bȧnt or brȧ-bȧnt', (HENRY,) DUKE OF, surnamed LE GUERROYEUR, or "the Warrior," went on a crusade to the Holy Land. He was the first who bore the title of Duke of Brabant. Died in 1235.

Brabant, (JOHN IV.,) DUKE OF, married in 1418 his cousin Jacqueline, Countess of Holland and Hainault, who afterwards separated herself from him in order to marry Humphrey, Duke of Gloucester. In 1425 he obtained from the pope a bull for the erection of the Uni-

versity of Louvain. He died in 1427, being the last of the sovereign dukes of Brabant. (See JACQUELINE.)

Braccio da Montone, brȧt'cho dȧ mon-to'nȧ, (ANDREA,) a famous Italian mercenary commander or *condottiere*, born in 1368. He took Rome in 1417, and fought in the service of Naples against Sforza. Died in 1424.

Bracciolini. See POGGIO.

Bracciolini, brȧt-cho-lee'nee, (FRANCESCO,) an Italian poet, surnamed DELL'API, dèl-lȧ'pee, born at Pistoia in 1566. He became secretary to Cardinal Barberini, afterwards Pope Urban VIII. He wrote "The Cross Regained," (" La Croce Riacquistata,") a heroic poem, ranked by some critics next to Tasso's "Jerusalem Delivered." Died at Pistoia in 1646.

See GINGUENÉ, "Histoire Littéraire d'Italie;" VOSSIUS, "De Historicis Latinis;" PAOLO GIOVIO, "Elogia."

Brace, (CHARLES LORING,) an American writer and clergyman, born at Litchfield, Connecticut, in 1826. He travelled in Europe, and published "Hungary in 1851," "Home-Life in Germany," (1853,) and "Norsefolk: Travels in Norway and Sweden," (1857.) He was the principal founder of the Children's Aid Society of New York.

Brace, (JONATHAN,) an American jurist, born at Harrington, Connecticut, in 1754. He graduated at Yale College in 1779, and in 1798 was elected to Congress. Died in 1837.

Brace, (JULIA,) a blind deaf-mute, born near Hartford, Connecticut, in 1806. She lost by a severe illness both sight and hearing when she was four years old. She had previously learned to speak and spell a little. After her misfortune she continued to speak for nearly a year, but gradually forgot the few words she had learned.

For a very interesting notice of her case, see DUNGLISON'S "Physiology," vol. ii. pp. 160, 161.

Bracelli, brȧ-chel'lee, (JACOPO,) an Italian historian, born at Sarzana, became chancellor of the republic of Genoa. He wrote a "History of the Spanish War," and other works, in Latin. Died in 1460.

Brachmann, brȧk'mȧn, (LUISE KAROLINE,) a German poetess and novelist, born at Rochlitz in 1777. At an early age she acquired the friendship of Novalis and of Schiller, who in 1799 published some of her first productions in his "Musenalmanach" and "Horen." She committed suicide in 1822.

See "Life of Luise Brachmann," prefixed to her works, edited by SCHÜTZ.

Bracht, van, vȧn brȧkt, (TIELMAN,) a Dutch Protestant theologian, born at Dort in 1625, was pastor of the Mennonites in his native city. Died in 1664.

Brack'en-ridge, (HENRY M.,) an American judge and writer, born at Pittsburg, Pennsylvania, in 1786. He published a "History of the Second War with Great Britain." In 1817 he accompanied as secretary the commission to the South American republics, and in 1820 produced a "Voyage to South America," which was commended by Humboldt. He also wrote "Recollections of Persons and Places in the West," (2d edition, 2 vols., 1869.) He was appointed a judge of the western district of Louisiana in 1821. In 1840 he was elected a member of Congress.

Brackenridge, (HUGH HENRY,) a writer and politician, the father of the preceding, born near Campbelton, Scotland, in 1748. Having studied law, he settled at Pittsburg, Pennsylvania, about 1782, and was appointed a judge of the supreme court of the State in 1799. He wrote, besides other works, a humorous and satirical work, entitled "Modern Chivalry, or the Adventures of Captain Farrago," (1792.) Died in 1816.

Brac'ton, de, (HENRY,) an eminent jurist, and one of the earliest English writers on law, lived under the reign of Henry III. His principal work is entitled "De Consuetudinibus et Legibus Angliæ," being a complete treatise on legislation and jurisprudence.

See PRINCE, "Worthies of Devon;" "Biographia Britannica."

Brad'bury, (THOMAS,) an English nonconformist divine and writer, born in London; died about 1759.

Brad'dock, (EDWARD,) a British general, born about 1715, commanded the army in America in the war against the French and Indians. He was defeated and killed near Pittsburg in 1755.

Brad'don, (MARY ELIZABETH,) an English novelist, born in London about 1837. She wrote poems entitled "Garibaldi" and "Lady Lisle," and a number of popular novels, among which are "Lady Audley's Secret," "Aurora Floyd," "Eleanor's Victory," and "Henry Dunbar."

Brad'ford, (ALDEN,) LL.D., an American divine and author, born at Duxbury, Massachusetts, in 1765. His principal work is a "History of Massachusetts from 1764 to 1820." Died in 1843.

Bradford, (ANDREW,) son of William Bradford, (printer,) was born about 1686. In 1719 he commenced the publication of the "American Weekly Mercury," the first newspaper issued in Philadelphia. Died in 1742.

Brad'ford, (JOHN,) an English Protestant divine under the reign of Henry VIII., born at Manchester, became chaplain to Edward VI., and was a popular preacher. After the accession of Mary, he suffered martyrdom at the stake, (1555.) His sermons and other writings were published after his death.

See WILLIAM STEVENS, "Life of John Bradford," 1832; W. W. HORNE, "Life of John Bradford," 1800.

Bradford, (ROBERT,) a major in the army of the American Revolution, descendant of Governor Bradford, was born in Plymouth, Massachusetts, in 1750. He served in the principal battles of the Revolution, commencing with that of Bunker Hill and ending with the capture of Cornwallis. For his gallant conduct La Fayette presented him with a sword. Died in 1823.

Bradford, (SAMUEL,) born in 1652, became Bishop of Rochester in 1723. Died in 1731.

Bradford, (WILLIAM,) one of the Pilgrim Fathers, born in Yorkshire, England, about 1590. While still very young, for the sake of religious liberty he emigrated to Holland. He was one of the enterprising band who crossed the Atlantic in the Mayflower in 1620. In 1621 he was elected Governor of Plymouth Colony, and by annual re-elections held that office for about thirty years. One of his first acts was a treaty of peace with the Indian Sachem Massasoit. In 1630 the English government granted to William Bradford, his heirs, associates, and assigns, a patent for the colony. He wrote a history of Plymouth People and Colony from 1602 to 1647, which was published in 1856. He is said to have been distinguished for piety and wisdom. Died in 1657.

See BELKNAP, "American Biography;" "New England Register" of 1850.

Bradford, (WILLIAM,) the first printer in Pennsylvania, born in Leicester, England, in 1658. Having resided for a time in Philadelphia, he removed (1693) to New York, where for upwards of fifty years he was printer to the government. In 1725 he issued the first newspaper ("New York Gazette") published in New York City. Died in 1752.

Bradford, (WILLIAM,) attorney-general of the United States, born in Philadelphia in 1755. Having graduated at Princeton, he served in the war of the Revolution, attained the rank of lieutenant-colonel, and in 1780 became attorney-general of Pennsylvania. In 1794 he was appointed United States attorney-general by Washington. Died in 1795.

Bradford, (WILLIAM,) an American landscape-painter of great merit, born at New Bedford, Massachusetts. His favourite subjects are coast-views, rocky shores, and icebergs. Among his chief pictures are "Hailing the Sloop in Martha's Vineyard," "Light-House in Saint John's Harbour," and "The Coast of Labrador."

See TUCKERMAN, "Book of the Artists."

Brad'ley, (Rev. EDWARD,) an English author, whose assumed name is CUTHBERT BEDE, born in 1827, became rector of Denton in 1859. Among his works are "Verdant Green," a popular novel, and "The Curate of Cranston," (1862.)

Bradley, (JAMES,) an eminent English astronomer, who united the qualities of observer and theorist in a degree perhaps never surpassed, was born in Gloucestershire in 1693. He was educated at Balliol College, Oxford, was chosen a Fellow of the Royal Society in 1718, and Savilian professor of astronomy at Oxford in 1721. In order to observe with the utmost exactitude the variations in the positions of the fixed stars, he erected a zenith-sector at Wansted in 1727, about which date he discovered the cause of the phenomenon called the "aberration of light." This important discovery furnished the first demonstration of the earth's motion around the sun. He was appointed astronomer royal in 1742, and by a series of observations arrived at another great discovery, the "nutation of the earth's axis," which he announced in 1747. "These two discoveries," says M. Biot, "have had the greatest influence on all astronomy ; for as long as the cause of these petty motions was unknown, they were confounded with errors in observations, and rendered it impossible to detect those errors." The same writer calls Bradley's twelve hundred observations of the moon "a monument of inimitable patience, address, and fidelity." He made successful researches on the law of refraction, for which he produced an empirical formula. He died at Chalford in July, 1762, leaving in manuscript thirteen volumes of valuable observations, which were presented to the University of Oxford, and published 1798–1805. Bessel has rendered a great service to astronomy by the reduction of these observations. (See BESSEL, F. W.) Sir Isaac Newton pronounced Bradley "the best astronomer in Europe."

See a good biographical notice of Bradley, by Professor RIGAUD, in the edition of his works published at Oxford in 1832; "Biographia Britannica;" "Edinburgh Review" for July, 1837.

Bradley, (RALPH,) an English lawyer, born in the county of Durham in 1717; died in 1788.

Bradley, (RICHARD,) an English physician and botanist, became in 1724 professor of botany at Cambridge. He wrote a "Treatise on Agriculture and Gardening," (1724,) and other works. Died in 1732.

Brad'shaw, (HENRY,) an English Benedictine monk, wrote poems and chronicles. Died in 1513.

See WOOD, "Athenæ Oxonienses."

Bradshaw, (JOHN,) an English republican judge, born about 1586, of a Cheshire family. He studied law in Gray's Inn, and practised with success before the civil war. He was appointed chief justice of Chester by the Parliament in 1647, and was chosen president of the high court of justice which tried Charles I. in January, 1649. In answer to Charles, who denied the authority of the court, he firmly maintained its superiority above the prisoner. His dignity and moderation on this occasion are commended by some writers; but Hume says "his style will be esteemed to the last degree audacious and insolent." He was afterwards president of the Council of State, and courageously opposed the assumption of supreme power by Cromwell. After the death of Cromwell he was president of the council for a short time. He died in November, 1659, leaving the reputation of a staunch and consistent friend of liberty. He was a kinsman and friend of Milton, who in his "Defensio Secunda" has highly extolled Bradshaw's virtue and talents, saying, among other things, that "he was an eloquent pleader, and discharged all the duties of an uncorrupt judge." John Forster ranks Bradshaw among "the purest and loftiest-minded" statesmen of the Commonwealth. ("Life of Henry Marten.")

See HUME, "History of England."

Bradshaw, (WILLIAM,) an English Puritan, born in Leicestershire in 1571, preached in London, and wrote several works on theology, among which is "English Puritanism," (1605.) Died in 1618.

Brad'street, (ANNE,) an English poetess, born at Northampton in 1613, was married to Governor Simon Bradstreet, noticed below. Died in 1672. For specimens of her poems, see Griswold's "Female Poets of America."

Bradstreet, (JOHN,) a general of the British army in America, commanded a force which took Fort Frontenac in 1758. Died at New York in 1774.

Bradstreet, (SIMON,) born in Lincolnshire, England, in 1603, emigrated to New England in 1630. He was Governor of Massachusetts from 1679 to 1686, and from May, 1689, to May, 1692. Died at Salem in 1697.

Brad'street, (SIMON,) an American divine, born in 1669, was minister at Charlestown, Massachusetts. Died in 1741.

Brad'war-din, (THOMAS,) an eminent English prelate, surnamed THE PROFOUND DOCTOR, born in Sussex in 1290. He was confessor to Edward III., and subsequently Archbishop of Canterbury. He wrote mathematical works, and a theological treatise entitled "The Cause of God against Pelagius," ("De Causa Dei contra Pelagium,") etc. Died in 1348.

See W. F. Hook, "Lives of the Archbishops of Canterbury," vol. iv. chap. xi.

Brā'dȳ, (Hugh,) an American general, born in Pennsylvania in 1768; died at Detroit in 1851.

Brady, (James T.,) an eloquent American lawyer, born in New York City in 1815, was admitted to the bar in 1836. He distinguished himself as counsel for the defence in criminal cases. During the civil war he was an influential leader of the party known as "War Democrats." Died in 1869.

Brā'dȳ, (Nicholas,) D.D., a learned divine, born at Bandon, in Ireland, in 1659. He graduated at Dublin University, and subsequently became chaplain to William III. and Mary. He translated Virgil's "Æneid," and made a popular version of the Psalms in conjunction with Mr. Tate. Died in 1726.

See Cibber, "Lives of the Poets."

Brady, (Robert,) an English physician and historian, born in Norfolk in 1643, was professor of medicine at Cambridge, which town he represented in Parliament. He wrote an "Introduction to the Old English History," and other works. Died in 1700.

Braganza, brȧ-gȧn'zȧ, the name of a royal family of Portugal, descended from Alfonso the first Duke of Braganza, who was an illegitimate son of King John I. Died in 1461. James the fourth Duke of Braganza was a favourite of King Emmanuel, who in 1489 designated him as his successor in case he should leave no issue. (See John IV. of Portugal.)

Bragelongne, de, dĕh brȧzh'loññ', (Christophe Bernard,) a French mathematician and philologist, born in Paris in 1688, was a member of the Academy of Sciences, and a friend of Malebranche. Died in 1744.

Bragg, (Braxton,) an American general, born in Warren county, North Carolina, about 1815, graduated at West Point in 1837. He served with distinction in the Mexican war under General Taylor, with the rank of captain, and resigned his commission in 1856. He became a brigadier-general in the Confederate service in 1861, commanded at Pensacola until February, 1862, and was raised to the rank of major-general about that time. He commanded a corps at the battle of Shiloh, April 6 and 7, 1862. In May ensuing he succeeded Beauregard as commander of the army in Mississippi, with the rank of general. Moving from Chattanooga in August, he invaded Kentucky with a large army and threatened Louisville. He was opposed by an army under General Buell, with part of which he fought a severe and indecisive battle at Perryville, October 8, 1862. General Bragg retired in the night after this action, and returned to Tennessee loaded with spoils captured at Lexington and other places. General Rosecrans, who took command late in October, followed Bragg to Murfreesborough, near which they fought the great battle of Stone River, December 31, 1862–January 2, 1863. The Union army, which remained master of the field, lost here 1533 killed and 7245 wounded. General Bragg reported that he lost 9000 killed and wounded, and had about 35,000 when the battle began. He retired to Tullahoma, followed slowly by Rosecrans, and thence to Chattanooga. A flank movement of Rosecrans compelled him to evacuate that important point on the 9th of September. Having been reinforced, he turned back and attacked the Union army at Chickamauga on the 19th of September, 1863. Bragg drove his opponent from the field, and claimed the victory; but he is said to have lost 15,000 men in this battle, which lasted two days. He was defeated by General Grant in a great battle on Missionary Ridge, near Chattanooga, November 25, 1863. About the 2d of December, 1863, he was relieved from his command. He led a small army from North Carolina to Georgia in the autumn of 1864.

See "Southern Generals," (anonymous,) New York, 1865.

Bragi, brȧ'ge, written also **Brage,** [supposed to be derived from the Icelandic *bragga,* to "adorn," and related to the German *pracht,* "splendour,"] in the Norse mythology, a son of Odin, is the god of eloquence and poetry. From him poetry is called "bragr," and men distinguished for the gift of speech are styled "bragr-men." His wife Iduna keeps the apples of immortality, partaking of which the gods never grow old. This myth doubtless refers to the power of poetry to confer immortality. Bragi is represented as an old man with a flowing beard, the type of an ancient minstrel.

See Thorpe, "Northern Mythology," vol. i.; Keyser, "Religion of the Northmen;" Petersen, "Nordisk Mythologi."

Brā'ham, (John,) a celebrated English vocalist, born in London about 1774. He performed with brilliant success in London, Paris, and the principal cities of Italy. He composed several operas and popular songs. Died in 1831.

See Fétis, "Biographie Universelle des Musiciens;" Oxberry, "Dramatic Biography."

Brahe, brä or brȧ, [Dan. pron. brȧ'ĕh,] (Tycho,) a celebrated astronomer, descended from a noble Swedish family, was born in December, 1545, at Knudsthorp, in Scania, which at that time belonged to Denmark. He entered the University of Copenhagen in 1559, and was destined for the profession of the law; but the great eclipse of the sun, August 21, 1560, gave a new direction to his studies. In 1562 he was sent to Leipsic to study law under the charge of a tutor. While the tutor was asleep, Tycho read astronomical works, watched the motions of stars and planets, and, with no better instrument than a pair of compasses, detected a large error in the Alphonsine Tables. He became in 1569 a resident of Augsburg, where he found two congenial spirits, named John and Paul Hainzel, and employed skilful artists to make a quadrant of fourteen cubits' radius.

Having returned to his native land in 1571, he fitted up an observatory, and cultivated alchemy in order to replenish his purse. In 1573 he published a notice of a new star, brighter than Sirius, which suddenly appeared in the constellation of Cassiopeia in November, 1572, and disappeared finally in March, 1574. He offended his noble relatives by marrying a peasant-girl in 1573. At the request of the king, he delivered a course of lectures on astronomy at Copenhagen in 1574, having gradually overcome his aristocratic prejudice against the occupations of teacher and author. He proposed to settle in Germany, but was retained by the liberal offers of the king, Frederick II., who gave him a grant for life of the island of Huen, Hven, or Hoëne, situated about fourteen miles from Copenhagen, and built for him an observatory on the island. This magnificent structure, called Uraniberg or Oranienberg, ("City of the Heavens,") was ready for use in 1577, and was the most splendid observatory that had ever been erected in Europe.

Tycho spent there twenty years, during which he made vast additions to astronomical science by his observations, and merited the title of "the restorer of astronomy." He formed a catalogue of seven hundred and seventy-seven stars, and discovered, it is said, the true theory of comets. He rejected the Copernican system, for which he substituted a hypothesis that seemed more consistent with the language of Scripture,—namely, that the earth is stationary in the centre of the universe, and that the sun and stars revolve around that centre.

After the death of his royal patron in 1588, a powerful party was formed against Tycho Brahe by courtiers who envied his honours and coveted his revenues. He was deprived of his pensions about 1594, and, being unable to support the expense of his establishment, resolved to transfer his instruments to another place. He emigrated to Germany in 1597, and, having obtained the patronage of the emperor Rudolph, settled at Prague in 1600. In the same year Kepler became the assistant of Tycho, who had invited him to Prague. Among his principal works is "Astronomiæ Instauratæ Progymnasmata," (1587–89.) Died at Prague on the 13th of October, 1601. "As a practical astronomer," says Sir David Brewster, "Tycho has not been surpassed by any observer of ancient or modern times. The splendour and number of his instruments, the ingenuity which he exhibited in inventing new ones, and his skill and assiduity as an observer, have given a character to his labours and a value to his observations which will be appreciated to the latest posterity. . . . His improvements in the lunar theory were still more valuable. He discovered the important inequality called the *variation*, and also the annual inequality which depends on the position of the earth in its orbit."

See BREWSTER, "Martyrs of Science," 1841; P. GASSENDI, "Vie de Tycho Brahé," 1654; P. PEDERSEN, "Den Danske Astronom T. Brahe's Liv og Levnet," 1838; A. G. KAESTNER, "Ueber T. de Brahe's Wahlspruch," 1771; OLAUS SCHILLING, "Dissertatio de Meritis T., Brahe in Astronomiam," Upsal, 1792; P. VON DER WEISTRITZ, "Lebensbeschreibung des Sternsehers T. von Brahe," 2 vols., 1756.

Brăhm, [Hindoo pron. brŭhm or br'hm,] a Sanscrit word, signifying originally "earnest, intense prayer,"* but now used as the name of the eternal self-existent Being, of whose attributes or powers the gods of the Indian triad, Brahma, Vishnu, and Siva, are personifications. His image is the outward universe. In the "Institutes of Manu" (chap. i.) he is spoken of as follows : "He whom the mind alone can perceive, whose essence eludes the external organs, who has no visible parts, who exists from eternity,—even he, the soul of all beings, whom no being can comprehend, shone forth in person," in other words, his creative power was manifested or personified, in Brahma. (See the two following articles.) "Of that infinite, incomprehensible, self-existent Spirit," says Moor, "no representation is made ; to his direct and immediate honour no temples rise ; nor dare a Hindoo address to him the effusions of his soul otherwise than by the mediation of a personified attribute, or through the intervention of a priest." The Hindoos have no images of Brahm, but the pious Brahmans meditate in profound and silent awe upon his unspeakable attributes.

See MOOR, "Hindu Pantheon;" "Religions de l'Antiquité," translated by M. GUIGNIAUT from the German of DR. CREUZER, Paris, 1825, vol. i. p. 150 *et seq.*

Brăhmâ, bră'ma, [Hindoo pron. brŭh'mâ,] a Sanscrit word signifying "worship" or "prayer,"† forming the name of one of the great deities of the Hindoos. Brahma is a personification of the creative power, (see BRAHM,) and is usually styled the "Creator." It may be observed that Brahma has no temples or rites exclusively dedicated to him, and he is far less worshipped or honoured by the Hindoos than Siva or Vishnu. The votaries of the last-named deities are stimulated by the most powerful of human motives,—hope and fear ; but, as the act of creation is past, the worshippers of Brahma are influenced only by the comparatively feeble principle of gratitude. Images of Brahma are sometimes found in temples dedicated to other gods. He is commonly represented with four faces or heads, having reference probably to the four corners of the world. The pictures of him are usually red, or of a reddish hue, which is supposed to have allusion to the colour of the all-producing earth, of which Brahma is regarded as a personification. As fire is the symbol of Siva, and water of Vishnu, so earth is the symbol of Brahma. In another relation, Brahma represents matter, Vishnu spirit, and Siva time. (See articles SIVA and VISHNU.)

See, also, MOOR, "Hindu Pantheon;" COLEMAN, "Mythology of the Hindus," London, 1832; GUIGNIAUT, "Religions de l'Antiquité," Paris, 1825, vol. i. book i. chap. iv.

BRAH'MAN-ISM or **BRAH'MIN-ISM,** [Fr. BRAHMANISME, bră'mâ'nèzm' ; Ger. BRAHMAISMUS, bră-mâ-is'mŭs, or BRAHMANISMUS, bră-mâ-nis'mŭs,] the name of the religious system taught by the Brahmans‡ of India. We first find this system developed in the "Institutes of Manu," (or Menu,) a work whose date (like that of all the early writings of the Hindoos) it is impossible

to fix with any approximation to exactness.* It is remarkable that the Vedas (the oldest of all the books of the Hindoos) contain so few traces—only a few scattered germs, so to speak—of that elaborate religious system which is presented to us in the "Institutes of Manu" and other later works. In the Vedas the gods are mostly such as would be suggested by the objects or phenomena of external nature : for example, Varuna, (Uranus,) or Heaven, (see VARUNA ;) Agni, or the god of fire ; Indra, the god of the atmosphere and clouds ; Mitra, the sun, etc. As, however, the Brahmanical system gradually becomes developed, these divinities retreat into the background and are replaced by the gods of the Hindoo triad, Brahma, Vishnu, and Siva, who appear as manifestations of Brahm, the eternal, self-existent Spirit. (See BRAHM.) Brahma first makes his appearance as the creator of the visible universe, and becomes the source and centre of an endless system of divine sages, inferior gods, celestial nymphs, genii, giants, demons, animals, etc.

In the early ages the head of each family among the Aryas (see ARYAS) appears to have been his own priest, making offerings to the deities in his own name ; but, as the people abandoned the primitive customs of their ancestors, they had recourse to professional priests, who were supposed to know the mind and wishes of the deities and how best to propitiate their favour. The priesthood, having thus become an indispensable necessity, was not long in becoming the dominant power in the state ; and the Brahmans, having once obtained the ascendency, took every precaution to fortify their power and make it perpetual.

With this object, they introduced the distinctions of caste,† not merely as a civil institution, but as resting on and inseparably connected with the very foundations of their religious system. Like the modern advocates of slavery, they taught that these distinctions had been established by the Creator himself. They ingeniously feigned that the priestly class, or Brahmans, were produced from the mouth of Brahma, becoming thus his spokesmen ; while the Kshatriyas,‡ or warrior caste, sprang from his arm ; the Vaisyas,§ (herdsmen, agriculturists, or merchants,) from his thigh ; and the Soodras, (or labourers,) from his foot. The three higher castes are supposed to be of pure Aryan descent ; the Soodras (written also Çûdras) were not improbably the earlier inhabitants of India, whom the Aryas subdued and reduced to slavery. In the Mahâbhârăta the Brahman is called white, the Kshatriya red, the Vaisya yellow, and the Soodra black. It may be proper to observe that Brahmans are not all priests ; but from the Brahmanical caste alone the priests must be chosen.

In order to preserve the sanctity of the priestly caste and defend it against all encroachments, a man of any of the lower castes is strictly forbidden to marry a Brahman woman, (Brahmanî or Brahmanee,) and the children of such marriages are regarded as irredeemably base. The offspring of a Soodra and a Brahmanî is called a Chandâla, and is accounted the lowest of mortals. His very shadow is shunned as pollution ; and a Brahman is forbidden to take shelter under the same tree with one of those wretched outcasts. The Institutes of Manu abound with passages exhibiting the boundless pretensions of the Brahmans, setting forth their godlike dignity and the respect and adoration due them from persons of the other classes. "From his high birth alone, a Brahman is an object of veneration even to the gods." (chap. xi. 85.) "A Brahman, whether learned or ignorant, is a powerful divinity. . . . Though Brahmans employ themselves in all sorts of mean occupation, they must invariably be honoured ; for they are something transcendently divine." (ix. 317, 319.) "Let

---

* "Brăhm" and "Brăhmâ" are from the same root, (brih,) and seem originally to have had essentially the same signification. (See KÖPPEN, "Religion des Buddha," pp. 27, 28.) Brahm is also written Brahmă ; but in the popular pronunciation it has but one syllable.

† Brahmâ appears to have originally signified that "earnest, allprevailing prayer" by which the gods were compelled (according to the Hindoo belief) to grant the request of the suppliant. (See next article.) In like manner, Agni, (or Agnis,) the god of fire, carrying the incense and offerings of mortals to heaven, prevailed upon the gods to grant the prayers of their worshippers. Hence in very early times Agni and Brahma may be said to have been scarcely more than different names for one and the same power. (See KÖPPEN, "Religion des Buddha," p. 27.) Afterwards Brahma came to be regarded not as a mediator between the gods and men, but as the external manifestation of the creative power of Brahm. (See BRAHM.)

‡ The term Brahman (or Brahmin) appears to have been derived not from the god Brahma, but from brahmâ, "prayer," or "worship;" and hence it properly signifies a "praying-man," or "priest." (See BRAHMA.)

---

* Sir William Jones supposes that the work in question received its present form about 880 B.C. ; and it seems to be generally admitted that the greater part, if not the whole of it, was composed some centuries before the rise of Booddhism, (about 500 B.C.)

† We do not, of course, mean to say that the system as it existed in after-ages was definitely and fully planned from the first, but simply that those who laid its foundations did so in the interest of the priesthood ; and the same motives which prompted its commencement presided over its completion.

‡ Kshatriya is pronounced kshŭt're-ya by the modern Hindoos.

§ Pronounced vis'yaz.

є as k; ç as s; g *hard;* g as j; G, H, K, *guttural;* N, *nasal;* R, *trilled;* s̄ as z; th as in *this.* (☞See Explanations, p. 23.)

not a king, although in the greatest distress for money, provoke Brahmans to anger by taking their property; for they, once enraged, could immediately, by sacrifices and imprecations, destroy him, with his troops, elephants, horses, and cars. . . . What prince could gain wealth by oppressing those who, if angry, could frame other worlds and regents of worlds?—could give being to new gods and mortals?" (ix. 313, 315.) "No greater crime is known on earth than slaying a Brahman. . . . Never shall the king slay a Brahman, though convicted of all possible crimes : let him banish the offender from his realm, but with all his property secure and his body unhurt." (viii. 380, 381.) "A Brahman is born above the world, the chief of all creatures. . . . Whatever exists in the universe is in effect, though not in form, the wealth of the Brahmans: . . . through the benevolence of the Brahmans, indeed, other mortals enjoy life." (i. 99, 100, 101.)

The doctrine of "emanation," as it has been termed, may be said to form the basis of the Brahmanical system. According to this doctrine, Brahm is the source and centre of all existence, and the various creatures of the universe are nothing more than emanations from Him ; in other words, they are so many parts or members of the Universal Being, as the bays and creeks on the sea-coast are parts or members of the ocean. And as Brahm is the source whence all things have proceeded or been evolved, so all things will at last return to Him and be absorbed into His essence. This final absorption is regarded by the devout Hindoo as his salvation. In consequence of his dislike to motion and excitement, the notion of absolute repose becomes a necessary part in his ideal of perfect happiness. Hence the aim of all his efforts is to bring his transmigrations to an end, that his individual existence may wholly cease, and that his soul may be completely absorbed and swallowed up in Brahm. The same general doctrine, though with important modifications, may be said to form the foundation of Booddhism. (See BOODDHA.)

The doctrine of the transmigration of souls (called by the Greeks Metempsychosis, and by the Germans Seelenwanderung, or "soul-wandering") became a powerful engine, in the hands of the Brahmans, for curbing and breaking the spirit of the laity. For neglecting the smallest duties or ceremonies enjoined by the priests, one might have to pass ages in unhappy transmigrations ; while, on the other hand, by an implicit and faithful observance of those duties and ceremonies he might at length acquire such an accumulation of merit as to raise him above the power of the gods themselves. There is no other example in the history of mankind of an ascendency of one class over another so despotic and absolute as that which has been obtained by the Brahmans through the institution of caste. And this has been effected not by any punishment applied to the body, or by any external force, but by gradually acquiring, through an artful employment of hope and fear, an unlimited control over the mind. No inconsiderable part of the twelfth chapter of the Institutes of Manu is occupied in stating the kind and number of transmigrations which one must undergo for each of a long list of sins therein enumerated. Thus, for example, he who steals the gold of a priest (unless he makes in this life expiation by some voluntary and cruel penance) will be born a thousand times in the form of a spider or of some disgusting reptile ; if a man steal meat, he will in the next life become a vulture ; if he steal grain, he will become a rat ; and so on. He who kills a Brahman (after "having passed through terrible regions of torture for a great number of years") may, according to the circumstances of his crime, be born as a dog, a boar, or other low animal, or as a Chandâla. A priest who has drunk spirituous liquor will become a worm or insect feeding on filth. Some learned Hindoos hold that there is no expiation by penance for a voluntary sin ; but this is not the general opinion. To a Brahman who knows the Vedas, all expiation is rendered easy. Although the ancient Hindoos appear to have regarded women with far more tenderness and respect than most other Asiatic nations, Manu shows but scant indulgence towards those who err. He says, in substance, that since a woman is not permitted to know the Vedas, by which her guilt might be

expiated, she has no right whatever to commit any sin : her son, however, can perform expiation for her by the repetition of holy texts. (Chap. ix. 18 *et seq.*)

Not the least remarkable feature in the religious system of the Brahmans is the immense importance which it attaches to the performance of prayer and penance. The most efficacious prayer is the committing to memory and repetition of portions of the Vedas. "As fire consumes in an instant with its bright flame the wood that is placed upon it, so with the flame of knowledge a Brahman who understands the Veda consumes all sin." ("Institutes of Manu," chap. xi. 247.) "A priest," says Manu, "who should retain in his memory the whole Rig-Veda would be absolved from guilt even if he had slain the inhabitants of the three worlds," (chap. xi. 262,) a statement which acquires additional force when we consider the tender regard for life which distinguishes the Hindoos from most other nations.*

The Hebrew and Christian Scriptures teach us that prayer and sacrifice, to be availing, must be acceptable to God.† The Brahmans, on the contrary, believe that prayers, even though prompted by the most unworthy motives and uttered for the most unrighteous purposes, if repeated according to the prescribed form and duly persevered in, can *compel* the gods to grant the wishes of the suppliant. By the persevering performance, moreover, of prayer, penance, and sacrifice, a man may in time acquire a power superior to that of the highest gods.‡

See, besides the "Institutes of Manu," already referred to, MOOR, "Hindu Pantheon ;" COLEMAN, "Hindu Mythology ;" KÖPPEN, "Religion des Buddha," (first part ;) PROFESSOR H. H. WILSON'S Introductions to the several volumes of his translation of the "Rig-Veda," 1850 *et seq.*, and "Essays on the Religion of the Hindus," vol. ii. ; COLEBROOKE, "On the Vedas," in "Asiatic Researches," vol. viii. ; SIR W. JONES, "On the Gods of Greece, Italy, and India," in vol. i. of "Asiatic Researches ;" MAX MÜLLER, "Chips," etc. ; DUNCKER, "Geschichte des Alterthums ;" see, also, the "Vedas," the two Hindoo epics "Mahâbhârâta" and "Râmâyâna," and the "Purânas."

Braid'wood, (THOMAS,) one of the first teachers of the deaf and dumb in Great Britain, founded about 1760 an institution at Edinburgh, and subsequently at Hackney, near London. Died in 1806.

Braillé, brå'yà', (LOUIS,) born near Paris in 1809, was blind from his birth, and was distinguished for his intelligence and his rapid acquisition of knowledge, particularly music. He invented a method of writing with points, which has been generally adopted.

Brai'nard, (JOHN G. C.,) an American poet, born at New London, Connecticut, in 1796, graduated at Yale College in 1815. He edited "The Connecticut Mirror" (published at Hartford) for about six years, and produced a volume of poems in 1825. Died in 1828.

See GRISWOLD, "Poets and Poetry of America ;" JOHN G. WHITTIER, "Memoir of Brainard," prefixed to his Poems, 1832.

Brai'nerd, (DAVID,) an American divine and missionary to the Indians, born in 1718 at Haddam, Connecticut. He entered Yale College in 1739, but in February, 1742, was expelled for expressing his belief that one of the tutors was wholly without the grace of God. Says President Edwards, "I never knew his equal of his age and standing for clear, accurate notions of the nature and essence of true religion, and its distinctions from its various false appearances." Among his works may be mentioned a narrative of his labours among the Indians in Massachusetts, Pennsylvania, and New Jersey, published in 1746,

* According to Manu, he who does not willingly inflict pain upon any creature, but "seeks the good of all sentient beings, enjoys bliss without end." (chap. v. 46.)

It is not, however, true, as many suppose, that the Brahmans or other Hindoos are absolutely forbidden to eat flesh : we are expressly told that the Self-existent created beasts for sacrifice. "He who eats according to law commits no sin, even though every day he tastes the flesh of such animals as may lawfully be tasted." Those animals, moreover, "which have been destroyed for the purpose of sacrifice attain in the next world exalted births." But he who eats the flesh of animals which have not been duly consecrated for sacrifice to the gods or manes "will, unable to save himself, be devoured in the next world by those animals whose flesh he has thus illegally swallowed." (See, on this subject, the "Institutes of Manu," chap. v. 26-52, and the "Miscellaneous Notice of the Brahmans and Hindus" in MOOR'S "Hindu Pantheon.")

† See Isaiah i. 15, lix. 2 : Proverbs xv. 8 and 29, xxi. 27, xxviii. 9 ; John ix. 31 ; James iv. 3, v. 16., etc.

‡ This doctrine furnishes the groundwork, so to speak, of Southey's celebrated poem, the "Curse of Kehama ;" and in the notes to that work the reader will find some curious and striking illustrations of the foregoing remarks.

ā, ē, ī, ō, ū, ȳ, *long;* ă, ĕ, ĭ, ŏ, ŭ, ў, same, less prolonged; ă, ĕ, ĭ, ŏ, ŭ, ў, *short;* a, ẹ, į, ǫ, *obscure;* fär, fåll, fåt; mĕt; nŏt; gōōd; mōōn;

"Mirabilia Dei inter Indicos," and "Divine Grace Displayed;" the two latter being portions of his journal, edited and published by Sereno Dwight Edwards in 1822. His life was written by President Edwards. His journal is one of the most interesting and instructive narratives of the kind ever written.

See, also, SPARKS's "American Biography," vol. viii.

Brainerd, (JOHN,) a missionary among the Indians, brother of the Rev. David Brainerd, whom he succeeded in his labours in New Jersey about 1748. Born in 1720; died in 1781.

See "Life of John Brainerd," by the Rev. THOMAS BRAINERD, 1865.

Braith'waite, (JOHN,) an English writer, born about 1690, published an "Account of the Political Events which, on the Death of the Emperor Muley Ismael, took Place in the Empire of Morocco." It was translated into several languages.

Braithwaite, (JOHN,) an English mechanician, who, by means of a diving-bell, recovered a considerable amount of the property sunk in the Royal George and other vessels. Died in 1818.

Braithwaite, (WILLIAM,) an English theologian, born about 1560, assisted in the translation of the Bible in the reign of James I.

Brakel, van, văn brä'ķel,(JAN,) a Dutch naval officer, born in 1618, distinguished himself in several engagements with the English, and attained the rank of rear-admiral. He was killed in a battle against the French in 1690.

See ERSCH und GRUBER, "Allgemeine Encyklopaedie."

Brakenburg, brä'ķen-büRG', (REINIER,) a Dutch painter, born at Haarlem in 1649.

See DESCAMPS, "Vies des Peintres Flamands," etc.

Brā'mạh, (JOSEPH,) a celebrated English mechanician and engineer, born in Yorkshire in 1749. Among his numerous and very valuable inventions are the safety-lock called by his name, the hydrostatic press, the beer-machine for drawing liquor from a cellar, improvements in fire-engines, pumps, steam-engines, and paper-making machinery, and the construction of mains or large water-pipes in London. Died in 1814.

See STUART, "Anecdotes of Steam-Engines;" SAMUEL SMILES, "Industrial Biography," 1864; HENRY HOWE, "Eminent American and European Mechanics," 1847.

Bramante, brä-mȧn'tä, (DONATO LAZZARI,) a celebrated Italian architect and painter, born near Urbino in 1444, was a relative of Raphael. He passed many years of his early manhood at Milan, whence he removed to Rome and built the Cancellaria, or palace of the chancery, (about 1495,) a fine specimen of the architecture of the Renaissance. He was patronized by Pope Julius II., and was the architect of the vast structures which joined the Belvedere to the palace of the Vatican. Among his master-pieces is the small round oratory or temple in the cloister of San Pietro in Montorio, in the genuine antique style. Bramante was the author of the original design of the basilica or church of Saint Peter, which he began to build in 1513, (some say in 1506.) He had finished the four great piers which support the dome, when he died, in 1514. His plan was not adhered to by the succeeding architects, among whom was Michael Angelo. Some critics think the work would have been more noble if Bramante's design had been carried out. His style is admired for its simplicity, grace, and harmony of proportions. He was a benefactor of Raphael, who through the influence of Bramante obtained the patronage of Julius II.

See VASARI, "Lives of the Painters," etc.; PUNGILEONI, "Memoria intorno alla Vita di Donato Bramante," 1837; QUATREMÈRE DE QUINCY, "Vies des Architectes célèbres;" SALVETTI, "Anedotti sulla Patria dell' Architetto Bramante," 1824.

Bramantino, da, dä brä-mȧn-tee'no, (AGOSTINO,) a Milanese painter, flourished about 1525.

Bramantino, (BARTOLOMMEO,) an Italian architect and painter, who lived about the middle of the fifteenth century, and built the church of San Satiro in the Milanese.

Brambilla, brȧm-bèl'lä, (GIOVANNI BATTISTA,) an Italian painter, who worked in Turin about 1770.

Bramer, brä'mẹr, (LEONARD,) a skilful Dutch painter, born at Delft in 1596. He worked in Italy, and imitated the Italian style. He excelled in the treatment of nocturnal conflagrations and illumined caverns. Among his works is a "Raising of Lazarus."

See DESCAMPS, "Vies des Peintres Flamands," etc.

Bram'hall, (JOHN,) born in. Yorkshire about 1593, graduated in divinity in 1630, and in 1634 became Bishop of Londonderry. As one of Strafford's coadjutors, he was impeached by the Irish House of Commons in 1640, and was imprisoned for a time. After the restoration he was created Archbishop of Armagh and Primate of Ireland. Bramhall is chiefly known from his controversy with Hobbes, entitled "The Question concerning Liberty, Necessity, and Chance, clearly stated and debated," (1656.) Died in 1663.

See "Biographia Britannica."

Bramp'stọn or **Bram'stọn,** (Sir JOHN,) an English judge, born in Essex about 1576. He was chief justice of the king's bench from 1635 to 1642. His conduct was vacillating in the civil war. Died in 1654.

See LORD CAMPBELL, "Lives of the Chief Justices;" FOSS, "The Judges of England."

Brampʹtọn, de, (WILLIAM,) an English judge justiciar, who was convicted of peculation in 1288 and fined forty thousand marks.

Bram'stọn, (Rev. JAMES,) an English satirical poet, took his degree at Oxford in 1720. He wrote the "Art of Politics." Died in 1744.

Brancaccio, brän-kȧt'cho, (FRANCESCO MARIA,) an Italian cardinal, patronized by Urban VIII. Died in 1675.

Brancadori-Perini, brän-kȧ-do'ree pȧ-ree'nee, (GIAMBATTISTA,) an Italian writer on chronology, born at Sienna in 1674; died in 1711.

Brancaleone, brän-kȧ-lȧ-o'nȧ, (DANDOLO, dȧn'do-lo,) Count of Casalecchio, (kȧ-sȧ-lek'ke-o,) born at Bologna, was made a senator by the Romans in 1253, and invested with the powers of a dictator, in order to repress the quarrels of the nobles. He compelled Pope Innocent IV. to acknowledge the power of the people, waged war with the barons, and restored peace to Rome. Died in 1258.

See SISMONDI, "Histoire des Républiques Italiennes."

Brancas, brŏN'kä', (ANDRÉ,) a French officer, known as ADMIRAL DE VILLARS, (ve'yȧR',) served for a time in the army of the League, but afterwards went over to Henry IV. Being made prisoner at the siege of Doullens, he was killed by the Spaniards for his desertion.

See MOTLEY, "History of the United Netherlands," chap. xxxi.; ANSELME, "Histoire générale des Pairs de France."

Brancas, de, Duc. See LAURAGUAIS.

Brancas, de, dẹh brŏN'kä', (LOUIS,) Marquis de Céreste, (sȧ'rêst',) served with distinction under Louis XIV. and Louis XV., and was made marshal of France in 1740. Died in 1750.

Brancas-Villeneuve, de, dẹh brŏN'kä' vèl'nuv', (ANDRÉ FRANÇOIS,) a French astronomer. Died in 1748.

Brancato, brän-kä'to, (FRANCESCO,) an Italian missionary to China, published a "Treatise on the Eucharist," and other works, (in Chinese.) Died in 1671.

Branch, (JOHN,) born at Halifax, North Carolina, in 1782, became a Senator of the United States in 1823, was secretary of the navy from March, 1829, till 1831, and was appointed Governor of Florida in 1843. Died in 1863.

Branch, (LAWRENCE O'BRIEN,) an American general, born in Halifax county, North Carolina, in 1820, was a son of the preceding, and represented a district of that State in Congress for several years between 1855 and 1861. He was killed at the battle of Antietam (where he fought against the Union) in September, 1862.

Brand, brȧnt, (BERNARD,) a Swiss jurist and magistrate, born at Bâle in 1523, wrote a "Universal History," (in German.) Died in 1594.

See BRANDMÖLLER, "Vie de Bernard Brand," Bâle, 1650.

Brand, brȧnt, (CHRISTIAN,) a German painter, born at Vienna in 1722, was director of the Academy of Landscapes. Died in 1795.

Brand, (JOHN,) an English antiquary, born at Newcastle-upon-Tyne about 1741, published "Observations on Popular Antiquities," and "History and Antiquities of the Town of Newcastle," (2 vols., 1789.) Died in 1806.

See "London Quarterly Review" for July, 1814.

Brand, (JOHN,) an English divine and writer on political economy; died in 1809.

Brandan, SAINT. See BRENDAN.

Brandão, brăn-dŏwn', (ALEXANDRE,) a Portuguese, who lived about 1650–90, wrote a "History of the War by which Portugal was separated from Spain," (2 vols., 1689.)

Brandão, (ANTONIO,) a Portuguese historian, succeeded De Brito as chief historiographer of the kingdom, (1617.) Died in 1637.

See BARBOSA MACHADO, "Bibliotheca Lusitana."

Brande, brand, (WILLIAM THOMAS,) F.R.S., an eminent English chemist, was born in London in 1788. He became professor of chemistry in the Royal Institution in 1813, and acquired a high reputation as a lecturer. He published a "Manual of Chemistry," (6th edition, 1848,) and an excellent "Dictionary of Science, Literature, and Art," (1842.) He was for many years superintendent of a department in the Mint. Died in 1866.

See "Edinburgh Review" for November, 1811, and October, 1813; "Gentleman's Magazine" for April, 1866.

Brandel, brăn'del, (PETER,) a German painter of history and portraits, born at Prague in 1660; died in 1739.

Brandenburg, ELECTOR OF. See ALBERT ACHILLES, and FREDERICK WILLIAM.

Brandenburg, brăn'den-bŏŏrg', (FRIEDRICH WILHELM,) COUNT OF, son of Frederick William II. of Prussia by his morganatic marriage with the Countess von Doenhoff, was born at Berlin in 1792. He served in several campaigns against the French, and became lieutenant-general. He was appointed prime minister in 1848. Died in 1850.

Brander, brăn'der, (GUSTAVUS,) a Swedish naturalist, resided in London, and was a contributor to the "Philosophical Transactions." Died in 1787.

Brandes, brăn'dĕs, (ERNST,) a German statesman and writer, born at Hanover in 1758, published an "Analysis of Burke's Reflections on the French Revolution," and other works. Died in 1810.

See HEYNE, "Memoria Ernesti Brandes," 1810; ERSCH und GRUBER, "Allgemeine Encyklopaedie."

Brandes, [Lat. BRANDE'SIUS,] (HEINRICH WILHELM,) born at Groben in 1777, studied at Göttingen, and became professor of mathematics at Leipsic in 1826. He wrote a "Manual of Higher Geometry," and several treatises on astronomy and hydraulics. Died in 1834.

See G. HERMANN, "Exequiæ H. Brandesii," 1834.

Brandes, (JOHANN CHRISTIAN,) a German dramatist and actor, born at Stettin in 1735. His wife, Esther Charlotte, was a popular actress, and his daughter, Minna, a distinguished vocalist. Died in 1799.

See ERSCH und GRUBER, "Allgemeine Encyklopaedie," and his "Autobiography," 3 vols., 1802–07.

Brandes, (RUDOLF,) a German pharmacist, born in Lippe-Detmold in 1795. He was the founder of the "Archives of Pharmacy," to which he made numerous contributions. Died in 1842.

See L. F. BLEY, "Leben des Dr. R. Brandes," 1844.

Brandi, brăn'dee, (GIACINTO,) an Italian painter, born in the Roman States in 1623, was a pupil of Lanfranc. Died in 1691.

Brandis, brăn'dis, (CHRISTIAN AUGUST,) professor of philosophy at Bonn, a son of Joachim, noticed below, was born at Hildesheim in 1790. He published, conjointly with Niebuhr, the "Rhenish Museum for Philology, History, and Greek Philosophy," (1827–30,) and wrote several critical works. He was chosen a foreign associate of the French Institute in 1855. Died in 1867.

Brandis, (JOACHIM DIETRICH,) an eminent German physician and medical writer, born at Hildesheim in 1762. He graduated at Göttingen, became professor of medicine at Kiel in 1803, and in 1809 physician to Frederick VI. of Denmark. Died in 1846.

Brandmüller, brănt'mŭl'ler, (GREGORIUS,) a Swiss painter, born at Bâle in 1661, was a pupil of Lebrun, and worked at Prague and Bâle. Among his best works, the design, expression, and colour of which are highly commended, is a "Descent from the Cross." Died in 1691.

Brandmüller, (JOHANN,) a Swiss theologian, born in 1533, was professor of Hebrew at Bâle. Died in 1596.

Brando, brăn'do, **Brand,** brănt, or **Brands,** brănts, (JOHANN,) a Flemish chronicler, born near Hulst, wrote a history of the world from the creation to 1413. Died in 1428.

Brandolese, brăn-do-lā'sä, (PIETRO,) an Italian bibliographer, born in 1754; died in 1809.

Brandolini, brăn-do-lee'nee, (AURELIO,) an Italian poet and *littérateur,* surnamed IL LIPPO, born at Florence about 1440. He was a celebrated pulpit orator, was patronized by Matthias Corvinus, King of Hungary, and became professor of eloquence at Buda. Among his works is one "On the Condition of Human Life," (" De Vitæ humanæ Conditione," 1541.) Died in 1497.

See GINGUENÉ, "Histoire Littéraire d'Italie;" BAYLE, "Historical and Critical Dictionary."

Brandolini, (RAFFAELLO,) a blind Italian *littérateur,* brother of the preceding, lived about 1460–1520, and was professor of eloquence at Rome. He had a rare talent for improvising Latin verse. He was patronized by Leo X., who became pope in 1513.

Bran'don, (CHARLES,) Duke of Suffolk, a favourite of Henry VIII. of England. He married Mary, a sister of King Henry, the widow of Louis XII. of France. Died in 1545.

Brandt or **Brand,** brănt, a German alchemist, who, in attempting to find the philosopher's stone, is said to have first discovered phosphorus. Died about 1695.

See F. HOEFER, "Histoire de la Chimie."

Brandt, brănt, (GEORG,) a Swedish chemist, born in 1694, made various interesting experiments upon metals, of which he gave an account in the "Memoirs of the Academy of Upsal." Died in 1768.

See GEZELIUS, "Biographiskt-Lexicon."

Brandt, brănt, (GERARD,) a Dutch Arminian theologian, born in Amsterdam in 1626. He preached in his native city, and published, besides other works, a "History of the Reformation in the Low Countries," (2 vols., 1671–74.) Died in 1685.

See JAN VAN HAES, "Leven van G. Brandt," 1740.

Brandt, (SEBASTIAN,) a German poet, born at Strasburg in 1458, wrote "The Ship of Fools," (" Das Narrenschiff," 1494,) a satirical poem, which enjoyed extraordinary popularity in its time and was translated into Latin and the principal European languages. Died in 1521.

See FLÖGEL, "Geschichte der Komischen Literatur;" GERVINUS, "Geschichte der Deutschen Literatur."

Brandt, von, fon brănt, (HEINRICH,) a Prussian general, born in Westphalia in 1789, published a "History of the Art of War in the Middle Ages," (1828,) a "Manual of Grand Strategy," (1829,) and other military works.

Branicki, brä-nits'kee, (FRANCIS XAVIER,) a Polish statesman, took an active part in the dismemberment of Poland by Russia, and was one of the leaders of the confederation of Targowicza. Having been declared a traitor to his country, he retired to the Ukraine, where he died in 1819.

See FERRAND, "Histoire des trois Démembrements de la Pologne," 1820.

Branicki, (JOHN CLEMENT,) grand general of the crown of Poland, born in 1688, was distinguished as champion of the nobility against the king, Augustus II. Died in 1771.

See RULHIÈRE, "Histoire de l'Anarchie de Pologne," 1807.

Braniss, brä'niss, (CHRISTLIEB JULIUS,) a German philosophical writer, born at Breslau in 1792. He wrote a "History of Philosophy since Kant," (1842,) and other works.

Brank'er, (THOMAS,) an English mathematician and scientific writer, lived about 1650.

Bran'nan or **Bran'non,** (JOHN M.,) an American general, born in the District of Columbia about 1821, graduated at West Point in 1841. He became a brigadier-general in September, 1861, and commanded a division at the battle of Chickamauga, September 19 and 20, 1863. He served under General Sherman in the campaign against Atlanta, May–September, 1864.

Brant, (JOSEPH,) THAYENDANEGA, (tī-ĕr.-dă-ne'gä,) a famous Indian chief of the Mohawk tribe, was born in 1742. He fought against the American colonists in the Revolution, and had a commission in the British service. After the end of the war he went to England, and published the Gospel of Mark in Mohawk. Died in 1807.

See W. L. STONE, "Life of Brant."

Brantôme, bRŏN'tōm', (PIERRE de Bourdeilles— dĕh booR'dȧl' or booR'dȧ'yĕ,) a popular French historian, born of a noble family about 1540, was a brave soldier, and a witness of many military events of his time. He was for some time chamberlain to the Duke of Alençon, and obtained great favour at the court of Charles IX., who gave him a pension. As a historian he is sprightly, *naïf*, and sometimes eloquent, but never profound. His history is valued as a vivid picture of the epoch in which he lived, and of the characters of the principal actors in it. His chief work, entitled "Lives of Illustrious Men and Great Captains, both French and Foreign," (" Les Vies des Hommes illustres et grands Capitaines Français et étrangers,") was not published until after his death. Died in 1614.

See NICOLAS DE MONMERQUÉ, "Notice historique sur Brantôme," 1824; "Nouvelle Biographie Génerale."

Brants or **Brantz,** brȧnts, written also **Brant,**(JOHN,) a Flemish writer, born at Antwerp in 1559, was father-in-law of the celebrated Rubens. Died in 1639.

Bran'white, (PEREGRINE,) an English poet, born in Suffolk in 1745 ; died in 1794.

Brard, brȧR, (CYPRIEN PROSPER,) a French mineralogist, born at L'Aigle, in Orne, in 1786. He published, besides other works, "Mineralogy applied to the Arts," (3 vols., 1821,) and "New Elements of Mineralogy," (1824.) Died in 1838.

See JOUANNET, "Notice sur C. P. Brard," 1839.

Brarens, brȧ'rẹns, (HENDRIK,) a Danish naval officer, born in 1751, was the author of a "System of Practical Navigation." Died in 1826.

Brascassat, brȧ'kȧ'sȧ', (JEAN,) a French painter of landscapes and animals, born at Bordeaux in 1805. He gained a first medal in 1831, and was elected a member of the Institute in 1846. Among his works, which are praised for a rare solidity of colour, are "Mercury and Argus," and the "Campagna of Rome," (1833.)

Braschi, brȧs'kee, (GIAMBATTISTA,) an Italian antiquary, and Bishop of Sarsina, born at Cesena in 1664 ; died in 1727.

Braschi-Onesti, brȧs'kee o-nês'tee, (LUIGI,) DUKE OF, an Italian statesman, born at Cesena in 1748, was a nephew of Pius VI. He was one of the signers of the treaty of Tolentino in 1797, and was afterwards appointed mayor of Rome. Died in 1818.

Brash'ẹr, (ABRAHAM,) an American patriot and colonel in the war of the Revolution, born in New York in 1734, was the author of numerous popular ballads. Died in 1782.

Bras'ĭ-das, [Gr. Βρασίδας,] a celebrated Spartan commander in the Peloponnesian war, gained several victories over the Athenians, and rendered important services as negotiator. In Plato's "Symposium" he is compared to Achilles. He was killed in battle at Amphipolis in 422 B.C., after which annual sacrifices were offered to him as a hero.

See THUCYDIDES, books iii., iv., and v.

Brassac, de, dĕh brȧ'sȧk', (JEAN GALLARD de Béarn—dĕh bȧ'ȧRn',) COMTE, a French minister of state under Louis XIII., born in the province of Saintonge in 1579 ; died in 1645.

Brassavola, brȧs-sȧ-vo'lȧ, (ANTONIO MUSA,) an Italian physician, born at Ferrara in 1500, was patronized by Francis I., Charles V., the popes Paul III. and Clement VII., and other distinguished persons. Died in 1570.

See GIGUANNÉ, "Histoire Littéraire d'Italie;" CASTELLANI, "De Vita M. Brassavolæ Commentarius," 1767.

Brasseur, brȧ'suR', (PHILIP,) a Flemish writer and Latin poet, born at Mons about 1597 ; died about 1650.

Brassicanus, brȧs-se-kȧ'nŭs, (JOHANN ALEXANDER,) a German philologist and Latin poet, whose original name was KOHLBURGER, born at Wittenberg in 1500; died in 1539.

Brathwayte, brath'wāt,(RICHARD,) an English writer, born in 1588, published "The Prodigal's Tears," "The Golden Fleece," and other poems. Died in 1673.

Brattle, brat't'l, (THOMAS,) an American merchant and scientific writer, born at Boston in 1657 ; died in 1713.

Brault, bRŏ, (CHARLES,) born at Poitiers in 1752, became Archbishop of Albi in 1823, and was afterwards made a peer of France. Died in 1833.

Braun, brŏwn, (ALEXANDER KARL HERMANN,) a German statesman, born at Plauen in 1807, became minister of justice and president of the Council in Saxony. (1848.) He resigned office in 1849.

Braun, (AUGUST EMIL,) a German archæologist, born at Gotha in 1809. He resided many years in Rome, where he became pro-secretary to the Archæological Institute. He wrote a treatise "On the Mythology of Art," (" Kunst-Mythologie," with 100 plates,) and "Antique Marbles," (1843.) Died at Rome in 1856.

Braun, (JOHANN WILHELM JOSEPH,) a German Catholic theologian, born near Düren in 1801. He studied at Bonn, under Hermes, whose peculiar views he adopted. He became professor of ecclesiastical history at Bonn in 1833, and was one of the founders of the "Journal of Philosophy and Catholic Theology."

See BROCKHAUS, "Conversations-Lexikon."

Braur. See BRAUWER.

Brauwer or **Brouwer,** brŏw'wẹr, written also **Brawer** or **Braur,** (ADRIAAN,) a celebrated Dutch painter, born in 1608 at Oudenarde, or, as some writers state, at Haarlem. He was a pupil of Franz Hals, and was patronized by Rubens, but, owing to his dissipated habits, died in poverty at the age of thirty-two. His works are chiefly tavern-scenes, and other delineations of low life, and rank among the best of their kind. Died in 1640.

See DESCAMPS, "Vies des Peintres Flamands, Hollandais," etc.

Bravais, brȧ'vȧ', (AUGUSTE,) a French natural philosopher, born at Annonay in 1811. He has written able treatises on meteorology, crystallography, and astronomy. In 1854 he was admitted into the Institute, (section of geography and navigation.) His brother LOUIS F. is a botanist and writer.

Bravo, brȧ'vo, (BARTOLOMÉ,) a Spanish Jesuit, poet, and grammarian, born about 1560.

Bravo, (JUAN,) a Spanish physician, born in Castile, lived in the second half of the fifteenth century.

Bravo, brȧ'vo, (NICOLAS,) a Mexican general, born about 1780 or 1790, was elected vice-president in 1824. He took arms against President Vittoria in 1827, but was quickly defeated, and was banished. Died about 1854.

Bravo de Sobramonte-Ramires, brȧ'vo dȧ so-brȧ-mon'tȧ rȧ-mee'rēs, (GASPAR,) professor of medicine and surgery at Valladolid, was physician to Philip IV. and Charles II.

Bravo-Murillo. See MURILLO.

Brawe, brȧ'wẹh, (JOACHIM WILHELM,) BARON OF, a German tragic poet, born at Weissenfels in 1738. His tragedies entitled "Der Freigeist" and "Brutus" were edited and published by Lessing after his death, which took place in 1758.

Brawer. See BRAUWER.

Brax'tọn, (CARTER,) one of the signers of the Declaration of American Independence, was born at Newington, King-and-Queen county, Virginia, in 1736. In 1775 he was elected to Congress as successor to Peyton Randolph. Died in 1797.

Bray, (ANNA ELIZA,) an English novelist, whose maiden name was KEMPE, born in Surrey about 1800. She was married to Charles Stothard in 1818, and to Rev. Edward A. Bray about 1825. She published a number of novels, among which are "Gaston de Foix," (1826,) "The White Hoods," (1828,) "Talba," (1834,) and "Trelawney," (1837 ;) also, "Traditions and Legends of Devonshire," (1838.)

See "London Quarterly" for October, 1837.

Bray, (Sir REGINALD,) an English architect, and a favourite of Henry VII., whose chapel at Westminster is supposed to have been designed by him. He also constructed the nave of Saint George's Chapel at Windsor. Died in 1503.

Bray, (THOMAS,) an English divine, born in Shropshire in 1656, made several voyages to America as a missionary, and founded in 1697 a society for the propagation of the gospel in the colonies. Died in 1730.

See "Biographia Britannica."

ɛ as *k*; ç as *s*; ḡ *hard*; ġ as *j*; G, H, K, *guttural*; N, *nasal*; R, *trilled*; ŝ as *z*; ŧh as in *this*. (☞See Explanations, p. 23.)

Bray, (WILLIAM,) an English antiquary, born in 1736, published the "Diary and Memoirs of Evelyn," and was a contributor to the "Archæologia." He was a Fellow of the Society of Antiquaries. Died about 1830.

Bray, de, dĕh brȧ, (FRANÇOIS GABRIEL,) a French diplomatist, born at Rouen in 1765, was minister to Berlin and Saint Petersburg, (1808.) He published a "Critical Essay on the History of Livonia," (1817,) and several scientific works. A genus of plants has been called Braya in his honour. Died in 1832.

See MARTIUS, "Éloge académique du Comte de Bray," 1835.

Bray, de, dĕh brī, (JAKOB,) an excellent Dutch painter of portraits and history, son of Salomon, noticed below, born at Haarlem about 1600 ; died in 1664.

Bray, de, (SALOMON,) a Dutch painter, born at Haarlem in 1579 ; died in 1664.

Bray'brooke, (RICHARD CORNWALLIS NEVILLE,) LORD, an English antiquary, born in London in 1820 ; died in 1861.

Braybrooke, (RICHARD NEVILLE GRIFFIN,) LORD, an English antiquary, born about 1783. He published a "History of Audley End, Essex." Died in 1858.

Brayer de Beauregard, brȧ'yȧ' dĕh bōr'gȧr', (JEAN BAPTISTE LOUIS,) a French *littérateur*, born at Soissons in 1770, wrote several works on political economy. Died in 1834.

Bray'ley, (EDWARD WEDLAKE,) an English antiquary and topographer, born in London in 1773. He published numerous works on the antiquities and topography of England, among which is "Londoniana," (4 vols., 1829.) Died in 1854.

Bray'man, (MASON,) an American officer, born at Buffalo, New York, in 1813, entered the Union army in 1861, and became brigadier-general of volunteers in 1862.

Brea, brā'ȧ, (LODOVICO,) an Italian painter, born at Nice, flourished from about 1480 to 1515. He worked mostly at Genoa. His heads and draperies are commended.

Bréard, brȧ'ȧr', (JEAN JACQUES,) born at Marennes, in France, in 1760, was a member of the National Convention, where he voted for the death of the king. Died in 1840.

Brébeuf, de, (GUILLAUME,) a French poet, born at Thorigny in 1618. He produced a metrical version of Lucan's "Pharsalia," which was once popular, but was severely criticised by Boileau in his "Art Poétique." Died in 1661.

Brébeuf, de, (JEAN,) a French missionary, born in 1593, laboured in Canada, where he was killed by savages in 1649.

Brebiette, brĕh-be-ĕt', (PIERRE,) a French painter and engraver, born about 1596.

Brechten, brĕk'tĕn, or **Verbrechten,** vĕr-brĕk'tĕn, (NIKOLAAS,) a Dutch poet, born at Haarlem about 1240.

Breckburg. See BERKHEIDEN.

Breck'en-ridge, (JAMES,) an American politician, born in Botetourt county, Virginia, in 1763, was a representative in Congress from 1809 to 1817, and was an active leader of the Federal party. Died in 1833.

Breckenridge, (JOHN,) attorney-general of the United States under Jefferson from 1805 to 1806, was born in Virginia near the middle of the eighteenth century. Having removed to Kentucky, he was elected in 1801 to the United States Senate. In this body he proposed the repeal of the judiciary system established at the close of Adams's administration, and took a prominent part in the great debate which followed. Died in 1806.

Breckenridge, (JOHN,) D.D., an eminent Presbyterian divine, son of the preceding, and uncle of John C. Breckinridge, (Vice-President of the United States,) was born at Cabell's Dale, Kentucky, in 1797. He graduated at Princeton in 1818, and subsequently became a professor in that institution.

Breckenridge, usually written **Breckinridge,** (JOHN C.,) an American statesman and general, a nephew of Robert J. Breckenridge, was born near Lexington, Kentucky, in 1821. He studied law, became a Democrat in party politics, and was elected to Congress from Kentucky in 1851, and re-elected in 1853. Having been nominated as Democratic candidate for Vice-President, he was elected in November, 1856, when James Buchanan was

chosen President. He was nominated for the Presidency in 1860 by the disunion Democrats, after they had seceded from the convention which nominated Douglas as a Union Democrat. He had two other competitors,—John Bell and Abraham Lincoln. He received seventy-two electoral votes, Lincoln received one hundred and eighty, Bell thirty-nine, and Douglas twelve. All the Southern States, except Virginia, Kentucky, Tennessee, and Missouri, voted for Breckinridge. He was elected to the Senate of the United States by the legislature of Kentucky, and took his seat in March, 1861. After he had defended the cause of the new confederacy by several speeches in the Senate, he went to the South in September, 1861, and took arms against the Union, with the rank of brigadier-general. He commanded a division at Stone River, December 31, 1862–January 2, 1863, and at Chickamauga, September 19 and 20, 1863. He defeated General Sigel near Newmarket, Virginia, in May, 1864. His corps formed part of the army of Early, which Sheridan defeated near Winchester in September, 1864. He was appointed Confederate secretary of war in January, 1865. Soon after the surrender of General Lee, he sailed for Europe. He returned to the United States in 1868.

Breckinridge, (ROBERT J.,) an American Presbyterian divine, born at Cabell's Dale, Kentucky, in 1800, is a son of John Breckenridge, (the first of the name,) noticed above. He studied at Yale College, graduated at Union College in 1819, practised law eight years in Kentucky, and became pastor of a church in Baltimore in 1832. About 1847 he removed to Lexington, Kentucky. He gained distinction as a preacher and a writer, had much influence in the church, and was appointed professor of theology in a seminary at Danville, Kentucky, in 1853. Among his works are "Travels in Europe," (1839,) and "The Knowledge of God objectively considered," (1857.) He is said to be the principal author of the common-school system of Kentucky. During the civil war he was a decided and earnest supporter of the Union.

Breckinridge, (JOHN C.) See BRECKENRIDGE.

Brecling, brĕk'ling, (FREDERIK,) a Danish Protestant theologian and writer, born near Flensburg in 1629 ; died in 1711.

Brécourt, de, dĕh brȧ'koor', (GUILLAUME MARCOUREAU,) a French actor and dramatic poet. Died in 1685.

Breda, van, vȧn brĕh-dȧ', (JAN,) a Flemish painter of landscapes, fairs, battles, etc., born at Antwerp in 1683. He copied the works of Breughel and Wouwerman with remarkable skill. His touch and skies and distances are praised by Descamps. Died in 1750.

See DESCAMPS, "Vies des Peintres Flamands," etc.

Breda, van, (PIETER,) a Flemish landscape-painter, born at Antwerp in 1630 ; died in 1681.

Bredahl, brȧ-dȧl', (CHRISTIAN DAVID,) a Danish poet, born in 1784, wrote "Dramatic Scenes taken from an Old Manuscript," and other works.

See ERSLEW, "Forfatter-Lexicon."

Bredahl, (NIELS KROG,) a Danish dramatist, born about 1732, wrote several plays, and translated Ovid's "Metamorphoses" into Danish verse. Died in 1778.

Bredenbach, brȧ'dĕn-bȧk', (TILMANN,) a historical writer, born at Emmerich about 1535 ; died in 1587.

Brederode, brȧ'dĕh-ro'dĕh, (GERBRAND,) a Dutch poet, born at Amsterdam in 1585. Among his principal works are "The Meditative Song-Book," "The Great Fountain of Love," and a comedy entitled "Spaanschen Brabander." Died in 1618.

See LONGFELLOW's "Poets and Poetry of Europe."

Brederode, brȧ-dĕh-ro'dĕh, (HENDRIK,) COUNT, a Flemish nobleman, born in Brussels in 1531, was an adherent of Egmont and Horn. In 1566 he presented a petition to the Duchess of Parma for the removal of the Inquisition. He was also one of the principal members of the association called "Les Gueux," ("The Beggars.") Having fought unsuccessfully against the Spaniards, he took refuge in Germany, where he died in 1568.

See P. SCHELTEMA, "H. van Brederode te Amsterdam in 1567," 1847 ; SCHILLER, "History of the Revolt of the Netherlands;" MOTLEY, "Dutch Republic;" M. C. VAN HALL, "H. Graaf van Brederode verdedigd," 1845.

Brederode, (PIETER KORNELIS,) a Dutch jurist, born at the Hague, flourished about 1600.

ā, ē, ī, ō, ū, ȳ, *long;* ȧ, ė, ȯ, same, less prolonged; ă, ĕ, ĭ, ŏ, ŭ, ў, *short;* ą, ę, į, ǫ, *obscure;* fär, fȧll, fȧt; mĕt; nŏt; gōŏd; mōōn;

Bredow, brā'do, (GABRIEL GOTTFRIED,) born at Berlin in 1773, became professor of history at Breslau in 1811. He published a "Manual of Ancient History," etc., (1803,) "Memorable Events of Universal History," (1810,) and a series of tables entitled "Historische Tabellen," which were translated into English by Major Bell. Died at Breslau in 1814.

See KUNISCH, "Bredows Leben," 1816; ERSCH und GRUBER, "Allgemeine Encyklopaedie."

Bredsdorff, brĕds'dorf, (JAKOB HORNEMANN,) a Danish naturalist, born in Seeland in 1790, became in 1828 professor of botany and mineralogy at Soröe. He published "Elements of Geognosy," and other scientific works. Died in 1841.

See ERSLEW, "Forfatter-Lexicon."

Brée, brå, (MATHIEU IGNACE,) a distinguished historical painter, born at Antwerp in 1773, was director of the Academy of Fine Arts in that city. Died in 1839.

See F. BOGAERTS, "M. van Brée," 1842.

Bree, (ROBERT,) an English physician, born in Warwickshire in 1759, practised in London. He published "An Inquiry into Disordered Respiration," (1797.) Died in 1839.

Breenberg, brān'bĕrG, or **Breemberg,** brām'bĕrG, (BARTHOLOMEUS,) a Dutch painter and engraver, born at Utrecht about 1620, excelled in small landscapes and animals. Died in 1660.

See DESCAMPS, "Vies des Peintres Flamands, Hollandais," etc.

Brégis or **Brégy, de,** dĕh brå'zhe', (CHARLOTTE Saumaise de Chazan—sō'måz' dĕh shä'zŏN',) COMTESSE, a witty and accomplished French lady, born in Paris in 1619, was a niece of the celebrated Salmasius. She was maid of honour to Anne of Austria. Died in 1693, leaving a collection of letters and poems.

See "Mémoires de Madame de Motteville."

Bréguet, brå'gå', (ABRAHAM LOUIS,) a celebrated Swiss mechanician and watchmaker, born at Neufchâtel in 1747. He made improvements in watches, and invented numerous astronomical, nautical, and other instruments, distinguished for the perfection of their workmanship. He was a member of the French Bureau of Longitude, and of the Academy of Sciences of Paris. Died in 1823.

See FOURIER, "Éloge de Bréguet."

Bréguet, (LOUIS,) a French watchmaker and natural philosopher, grandson of the preceding, was born in Paris in 1804. He is said to have been the first Frenchman who applied himself seriously to the electric telegraph, on which he produced a treatise in 1845.

Brégy. See BRÉGIS.

Brehm, brām, (CHRISTIAN LUDWIG,) a German ornithologist, born at Schönau in 1787. He published a "Manual of the Natural History of European Birds," (2 vols., 1823-24,) and other works.

Brehmer, brā'mĕr, (HEINRICH,) a German jurist and diplomatist, born at Lubeck in 1800.

Breislak, brīs'låk, (SCIPIO,) an eminent geologist, of German extraction, born at Rome in 1748. Having been appointed professor in the Nazarene College at Rome, he made valuable contributions to the mineralogical cabinet of that institution. He subsequently visited Paris, where he became acquainted with Cuvier and other celebrated savants. He published "Physical Topography of the Campagna," (1798,) "Introduction to Geology," (1811,) and other works, in which he favours the vulcanic theory. He died in 1826, leaving his cabinet of minerals to the Borromeo family.

See CONFIGLIACHI, "Memorie intorno alle Opere, etc. del Geologo S Breislak," 1827; "Edinburgh Review" for April, 1804, and September, 1816.

Breithaupt, brīt'hŏwpt, (JOACHIM JUSTUS,) a German Protestant divine and sacred poet, born in Hanover in 1658, became professor of theology at Halle.

Breithaupt, (JOHANN AUGUST FRIEDRICH,) a distinguished German mineralogist, born near Saalfeld, Saxe-Meiningen, in May, 1791, was a pupil of Werner. He became professor of oryctognosy at Freiberg in 1827. He discovered a number of new species of minerals. His chief work is a "Complete Manual of Mineralogy," (3 vols., 1836-47)

Breitinger, brī'ting'ĕr, (JOHANN JAKOB,) a Swiss scholar and writer, born at Zurich in 1701, became professor of Greek and Hebrew in his native city. He was associated with Bodmer in his efforts to reform German literature, and took a prominent part in the controversy with Gottsched. He was the author of a "Critique on the Art of Poetry," ("Kritische Dichtkunst,") and other works. Died in 1776.

See J. C. LAVATER, "Éloge historique de J. J. Breitinger," 1771.

Breitkopf, brīt'kopf, (JOHANN GOTTLOB EMMANUEL,) a distinguished German typographer, born at Leipsic in 1719, introduced great improvements into the form of types, and wrote a work on the invention of printing. Died in 1794.

See ERSCH und GRUBER, "Allgemeine Encyklopaedie;" HAUSIUS, "Biographie J. G. E. Breitkopfs," 1794.

Brembati, brĕm-bä'tee, (ISOTTA,) an Italian poetess, born at Bergamo; died in 1586.

Bre'mer, [Sw. pron. brī'mĕr,] (FREDERIKA or FREDRIKA,) a celebrated Swedish novelist, born at Åbo, in Finland, in 1802. Her parents having removed to Sweden while she was yet a child, her education was finished at Stockholm, where she was subsequently teacher in a female seminary. She early became familiar with German literature, and was an especial admirer of the works of Schiller. Her novel of "The Neighbours" was first made known to the English and American public in 1842, through the excellent translation of Mrs. Mary Howitt. It was followed by "The Home," (1843,) "The President's Daughters," "The Diary," "The H. Family," "Strife and Peace," "Nina," "Brothers and Sisters," and several others, also translated by Mrs. Howitt. They enjoy great popularity in England and the United States, and have been translated into German, French, Dutch, and other languages. Having visited the United States in 1850, she published, after her return, "The Homes of the New World," (1853,) of which an English and a German translation soon appeared. Among her more recent works are "England in 1851," and a novel entitled "Hertha," (1856.) Died in 1866.

See "Life, Letters, and Posthumous Works of Frederika Bremer," edited by her sister CHARLOTTE, New York, 12mo, 1868; "Fraser's Magazine" for November, 1843; and an article in the "North American Review" for April, 1844, (by LOWELL.)

Brémond, brå-môN', (GABRIELLE,) a French lady, born at Marseilles, travelled in Egypt, Palestine, and Syria, and wrote an account of her journey, which was translated into Italian, (1673.)

See BAYLE, "Historical and Critical Dictionary."

Bremond, de, dĕh brĕh-môN', (CHARLES,) Marquis d'Ars, (dåR,) a French naval officer, born in Saintonge in 1738, was killed in battle against the English in 1761

Brémond, de, dĕh brå'môN', (FRANÇOIS,) a French natural philosopher, born in Paris in 1713. He produced a good translation of the "Philosophical Transactions of the Royal Society of London," (4 vols., 1738.) Died in 1742.

Brémond, de, (GABRIEL,) a French romance-writer, lived about 1670-1703.

Bremond d'Ars, de, dĕh brĕh-môN' dåRs,(CHARLES,) a French captain, born in 1538, rendered important services to the king and Catholic party in the civil wars. Died in 1599.

See DUPLEIX, "Histoire de France."

Bremond d'Arses, (or **d'Ars,**) brĕh-môN' dåRs, (LOUIS,) a French commander, born in Saintonge, distinguished himself in Italy in the reign of Louis XII., and had a high command at Ravenna in 1511.

Brémontier, brå'môN'te-å', (NICOLAS THÉODORE,) a French engineer and inspector-general of bridges and highways, born in 1738; died in 1809.

Bremser, brĕm'sĕr, (JOHANN GOTTFRIED,) a German physician and naturalist, born at Wertheim, on the Main, in 1767. He practised in Vienna, and wrote on intestinal worms. Died in 1827.

Bren'dan, SAINT, written also **Brandan,** was born in Ireland in the fifth century. According to a legend which obtained currency for several centuries, he made a long voyage in the Atlantic and discovered an island called by his name. Died in 577 A.D.

See "Blackwood's Magazine" for June, 1836.

ᴄ as *k*; ç as *s*; ğ *hard*; ġ as *j*; G, H, K, *guttural*; N, *nasal*; R, *trilled*; s as z; ᴛh as in *this*. (☞See Explanations, p. 23.)

Brendel, bRĕn′dĕl, (ADAM,) a German physician, was professor of anatomy and botany at Wittenberg. Died in 1719.

Brendel, (JOHANN GOTTFRIED,) a German physician, born at Wittenberg in 1712, became professor of medicine at Göttingen. Died in 1758.

Brendel, (ZACHARIAS,) a German medical writer, born at Jena in 1592; died in 1638.

Brenius, brā′ne-ŭs, (DANIEL,) a Dutch theologian, born at Haarlem in 1594, was a disciple of Episcopius. Died in 1664.

Brenkenhoff, bRĕnk′ĕn-hof′, (LEOPOLD,) a German writer on the art of war, born at Dessau in 1750; died in 1799.

Brenkenhoff, von, fon bRĕnk′ĕn-hof′, (FRANZ BALTHASAR SCHOENBERG,) a German rural economist, born near Halle in 1723; died in 1780.

See MEISSNER, "Leben des F. B. Schoenberg von Brenkenhoff," 1782.

Brenkmann, bRĕnk′măn, (HENDRIK,) a Dutch jurist, born at Rotterdam about 1680; died in 1736.

See ERSCH und GRUBER, "Allgemeine Encyklopaedie."

Brenner, bRĕn′nẹr, (ELIAS,) a Swedish antiquary and artist, born in 1647, was appointed miniature-painter to Charles XI. Died in 1717.

See ERSCH und GRUBER, "Allgemeine Encyklopaedie."

Brenner, (HENRIK,) a Swedish scholar and historian, born in 1669. He translated into Latin the "History of Armenia" of Moses Chorenensis, and wrote an account of the expedition of Peter the Great against Persia. Died in 1732.

Brenner, (SOFIA ELISABET WEBER,) a Swedish poetess, born about 1660, was the wife of Elias, above noticed. Died about 1730.

Bren′nus, a famous chief of the Sen′ones, a tribe of Gauls, invaded the Roman State about 390 B.C. Having defeated the Roman army, he entered Rome, which he found deserted except by a number of aged senators sitting in ivory chairs, whom the Gauls massacred. The Capitol, however, was defended by a garrison, whom Brennus attempted to surprise by night; but Manlius and his companions, alarmed by the clamour of some geese, repulsed the Gauls. Brennus was induced to depart by the payment of one thousand pounds of gold—plus the weight of his sword, which he threw into the scale, exclaiming, "Væ victis!" According to the popular story, Camillus, who had been previously banished, came to the relief of his countrymen at the very moment when they were weighing out the money which was to purchase peace with the Gauls: the latter were so utterly defeated that, it is said, not one remained to carry home the news of their overthrow. (See CAMILLUS.)

See LIVY, "History of Rome," book v.

Brennus, a Gallic chieftain, invaded Greece about 280 B.C. with an immense army, and committed great devastation. He was defeated at Delphi, and died soon after that event.

Brent, (NATHANIEL,) an English jurist and *littérateur*, born in Warwickshire in 1573. He translated into English and Latin Paul Sarpi's "History of the Council of Trent." Died in 1652.

Brenta, bRĕn′tä, [Lat. BREN′TIUS,] (ANDREA,) an Italian physician and *littérateur*, born at Padua about 1450, was secretary to Cardinal Caraffa. Died in 1483.

Brentana, bRĕn-tä′nä, (SIMONE,) an Italian painter, born in 1656 at Verona, or, as stated by some writers, at Venice. Among his master-pieces is a "Martyrdom of Saint Sebastian," at Verona. Died about 1736.

See LANZI, "History of Painting in Italy."

Brentano, bRĕn-tä′no, (CLEMENS,) a German novelist and dramatist, born at Frankfort-on-the-Main in 1777, was the brother of Bettina von Arnim, the friend of Goethe. Among his most popular works are the dramas of "Ponce de Leon" and "The Foundation of Prague," ("Die Gründung Prags,") a tale entitled "History of the Brave Kaspar and the Fair Annerl," and a collection of national ballads called "Des Knaben Wunderhorn," written conjointly with his brother-in-law, A. von Arnim. Died in 1842.

See BROCKHAUS, "Conversations-Lexikon."

Brentano, (LORENZ,) a German politician, born at Manheim in 1810, took an active part in the Baden revolution of 1848. Being afterwards compelled to leave his country, he took refuge in America.

Brentano, (SOPHIE,) wife of Clemens, noticed above, born at Altenburg in 1761, was originally named SCHUBART. She published several poems and romances. Died in 1806.

Brentel, bRĕn′tĕl, (FREDERICK,) a painter of Strasburg, born about 1580, numbered William Bawer among his pupils.

Brentius. See BRENTZ and BRENTA.

Bren′ton, (Captain EDWARD PELHAM,) an English naval officer, born in 1774, wrote a "Naval History of Great Britain from 1783 to 1822," (5 vols.) Died in 1839.

See "Memoir of Capt. E. Pelham Brenton," by SIR J. BRENTON.

Brenton, (Sir JAHLEEL,) a British rear-admiral, brother of the preceding, born in 1770. He published "The Hope of the Navy," (1839,) and other works. Died in 1844.

See HENRY RAIKES, "Memoir of Sir Jahleel Brenton," 1845; "London Quarterly Review" for March, 1847.

Brentz, bRĕnts, or **Brentzen,** bRĕnt′sẹn, [Lat. BREN′TIUS,] (JOHANN,) a German Protestant theologian, and coadjutor of Luther, born at Weil, in Suabia, in 1499. He assisted at the Diet of Augsburg in 1530, drew up the "Confession of Würtemberg," and was present at the Council of Trent. Pursued by the emissaries of Charles V., he was at length protected by Duke Ulric of Würtemberg. Died in 1570.

See J. W. CAMERER, "J. Brentz der Würtembergische Reformator," 1840; CARL DIETRICH, "Leben des J. Brentz," 1841; VAIHINGER, "Leben und Wirken des Reformators J. Brentz," 1841.

Brentzen. See BRENTZ.

Bréquigny, de, dẹh brā′kĕn′ye′, (LOUIS GEORGE OUDARD **Feudrix**—fuh′dRe′,) a French historian and antiquary, born at Granville in 1716, was a member of the French Academy and of the Academy of Inscriptions. He wrote, in conjunction with Mouchet, a continuation of the "Memoirs of the Chinese," begun by Amiot and others, and assisted in the publication of the "Collection of Laws and Ordinances of the Kings of the Third Race." Died in 1795.

See GRIMM, "Correspondance."

Brera, brā′rä, (VALERIANO LUIGI,) an Italian physician and medical writer of great merit, born at Pavía in 1772, became professor of therapeutics and clinics in his native city. Died in Venice in 1840.

See TASSINARI, "Raccolta della Cure e Scritti del Professore V. L. Brera," 1840.

Brere′ton, (JANE HUGHES,) an English poetess, born in Flintshire in 1685; died in 1740.

Brere′wood, (EDWARD,) an English mathematician and antiquary, born at Chester in 1565. He published "The Patriarchal Government of the Ancient Church," a treatise "On the Weights and Values of Ancient Coins, etc.," ("De Ponderibus et Pretiis Veterum Nummorum,") and other works, in English and Latin. Died in 1613.

See WOOD, "Athenæ Oxonienses."

Brès, bRĕ, (JEAN PIERRE,) a French *littérateur*, born at Limoges in 1782, was one of the editors of the "Revue Encyclopédique." Died in 1832.

Breschet, brĕ′shĕ′, (GILBERT,) a French physician, medical writer, and professor of anatomy in the Faculty of Paris, born at Clermont-Ferrand in 1784. He was a member of the Institute. Died in 1845.

Brescia, da, dä brĕsh′yä or brä′shä, or **Bresciano,** brä-shä′no, (GIOVANNI MARIA,) an Italian painter and engraver, born at Brescia about 1460. His brother GIOVANNI ANTONIO, born about 1461, was an engraver.

See LANZI, "History of Painting in Italy."

Bresmal, brä′măl′, (JEAN FRANÇOIS,) a Flemish medical writer of Liege, lived about 1700.

Bressani, brĕs-sä′nee, (GREGORIO,) an Italian philosopher, born at Treviso in 1703, wrote against the doctrines of Galileo, and in favour of Aristotle. Died in 1771.

See GINGUENÉ, "Histoire Littéraire d'Italie."

Bret, bRĕ, (ANTOINE,) a French *littérateur*, born at Dijon in 1717, wrote a "Commentary on the Works of Molière," and other works. Died in 1792.

ā, ē, ī, ō, ū, ȳ, *long;* ă, ĕ, ŏ, same, less prolonged; ă, ĕ, ĭ, ŏ, ŭ, y̆, *short;* ạ, ẹ, ị, ọ, *obscure;* fär, fȧll, fȧt; mĕt; nŏt; gŏŏd; mōŏn;

Bretagne, de, (ANNE.) See ANNE OF BRITTANY.

Bretagne, de, (ARTHUR.) See ARTHUR.

Breteuil, de, dęh bręh-tul', (LOUIS AUGUSTE le Tonnelier—lęh ton'lę-ạ',) BARON, a French diplomatist of the royalist party, born in Touraine in 1733, was employed in missions to Russia, Sweden, and Naples, and became minister of state about 1783. Died in 1807.

Breton, bręh-tòN', (FRANÇOIS PIERRE HIPPOLYTE ERNEST,) a French artist and antiquary, born in Paris in 1812. He published "Monuments of All Nations," (2 vols., 1843, with 300 engravings designed by himself,) which was translated into several languages, and "Pompéia," (1855.) He wrote many articles on painters for the "Nouvelle Biographie Générale."

Breton, (GUILLAUME,) sometimes called **Gulielmus Brito-Armoricus,** a French ecclesiastic and historian, born in Brittany about 1150. He was chaplain at the court of Philip Augustus, and wrote two histories of his reign,—one, entitled "Philippis," in Latin verse, the other in prose. Died in 1226.

See NICÉRON, "Mémoires."

Breton, brit'on, (NICHOLAS,) an English poet, born in 1555. He wrote pastorals, sonnets, etc. Died in 1624.

Breton, (RAYMOND,) a French missionary to the West Indies, born in 1609, published a "French-Carib and Carib-French Dictionary," and a "Carib Grammar." Died in 1679.

Breton de los Herreros, brȧ-tòn' dȧ lòs ęr-rā'ròs, (MANUEL,) a Spanish dramatist and poet, born in the province of Logroño in 1796.

Bretonnayau, bręh-to'nȧ'yo', (RENÉ,) a French surgeon and writer, lived about 1540–90.

Bretonne, de la. See RÉTIF.

Bretonneau, bręh-to'no', (FRANÇOIS,) a French Jesuit, theological writer, and pulpit orator, born in Touraine in 1660; died in 1741.

Bretonneau, (PIERRE,) a French physician and medical writer, born at Tours in 1771. He obtained celebrity as a practitioner, and is the reputed inventor of the operation called tracheotomy. Died in 1862.

See CALLISEN, "Medicinische Schriftsteller-Lexikon."

Bretschneider, brĕt'shni'dęr, (HEINRICH GOTTFRIED,) a German littérateur, born at Gera in 1739. He was the author of fables, poems, romances, and satires, and "Travels to London and Paris," a translation of which appeared in "Blackwood's Magazine." He is also supposed to have furnished the principal material for Nicolai's "Travels." Died in 1810.

See ERSCH und GRUBER, "Allgemeine Encyklopaedie."

Bretschneider, (KARL GOTTLIEB,) a German rationalist theologian, born at Gersdorf in 1776, was general superintendent in Gotha. He published a "Dogmatic Manual of the Evangelical Lutheran Church," (1814–18,) and "Corpus Reformatorum, or Philippi Melanchthonis Opera quæ supersunt Omnia," (15 vols., 1834–48.) Died in 1848.

See his "Autobiography," ("Selbstbiographie,") 1851.

Brett, (THOMAS,) an English nonjuror, born in Kent in 1667. He became rector of Ruckinge in 1705. He wrote several polemical treatises. Died in 1743.

Bretteville, de, dęh brĕt'vĕl', (ÉTIENNE DUBOIS,) a French theologian, born near Caen in 1650; died in 1688.

Breughel, bruh'gęl or bruh'Hęl, (ABRAHAM,) surnamed THE NEAPOLITAN, an excellent painter of birds and of still life, born at Antwerp, resided many years in Rome and Naples. Died in 1690.

See DESCAMPS, "Vies des Peintres Flamands," etc.

Breughel, (JAN,) an eminent Flemish painter, brother of Peter the younger, born at Brussels about 1570, was called VELVET BREUGHEL, from the usual material of his dress. He painted landscapes, fruit, flowers, and animals with admirable skill. Among his master-pieces is the landscape of "Adam and Eve in Paradise," now in the Museum of the Louvre, for which Rubens furnished the figures. In conjunction with that great artist he executed "The Four Elements," and "Vertumnus and Bellona." His death is variously dated from 1625 to 1642.

See DESCAMPS, "Vies des Peintres Flamands," etc.

Breughel, (PETER or PIETER,) an eminent Flemish painter, surnamed THE DROLL, born near Breda about 1525, excelled in village festivals and comic subjects. Died about 1590.

Breughel, (PETER,) son of the preceding, born at Brussels about 1569, was surnamed THE HELLISH, from the nature of the subjects he painted. Died about 1625.

See DESCAMPS, "Vies des Peintres Flamands," etc.

Breuil, du. See DUBREUIL.

Brev'al, de, (JOHN DURAND,) an English officer and writer, published a "History of the House of Nassau," and several poems. Died in 1739.

Brèves, de, dęh brȧv, (FRANÇOIS SAVARY,) COMTE, a French diplomatist, born in 1560, was ambassador to Constantinople and to Rome. Died in 1628.

Brev'int, (DANIEL,) a Protestant theologian, born in the island of Jersey in 1616. After the restoration of Charles II. he became Dean of Lincoln. Died in 1695.

Brew'er, (ANTHONY,) an English dramatist, lived about 1615–30, and wrote a play entitled "Lingua."

Brewer, (SAMUEL,) an English botanist, was a friend of Dillenius, whom he assisted in publishing his "History of Mosses," ("Historia Muscorum.") Died in 1743.

Brewer, (THOMAS,) an English musician and lyrical composer, lived under the reign of Charles I.

Brews'ter, (Sir DAVID,) an eminent British optician and experimental philosopher, born at Jedburgh, Scotland, December 11, 1781. He was educated at the University of Edinburgh, for the ministry, and was licensed to preach; but his fondness for scientific research led him to abandon the profession of divine and devote himself to his favourite pursuits. He was editor of the "Edinburgh Encyclopædia" from its commencement, in 1808, until its completion, about 1829, and wrote many articles for that valuable work. After he had been engaged some years in optical researches, he published, in 1812, a "Treatise on Burning Instruments, containing the Method of building Large Polyzonal Lenses." In 1815 the Royal Society of London awarded him the Copley medal for his essay "On the Polarization of Light by Reflection," and elected him a Fellow. He invented the kaleidoscope about 1816. In the same year he received from the French Institute half of the prize of three thousand francs awarded for the two most important discoveries made in Europe in physical science during the two years preceding. Dr. Brewster and Professor Jameson founded the "Edinburgh Philosophical Journal" in 1819, and the "Edinburgh Journal of Science," of which sixteen volumes were issued. He invented an improved system of illuminating light-houses by polyzonal (or polygonal) lenses, which was adopted in 1833. He married a daughter of Macpherson, the author or editor of "Ossian's Poems."

Among his chief works are a "Treatise on Optics," (1831,) "More Worlds than One, the Creed of the Philosopher and the Hope of the Christian," (1854,) and "Memoirs of the Life, Writings, and Discoveries of Sir Isaac Newton," (2 vols., 1855.) Among his chief titles to celebrity are his discovery of the law of the polarization of light by reflection, and his researches on colour refraction.

"In the earlier compositions of Sir David, always severe in style and sternly scientific in form," says Hugh Miller, "there is comparatively little indication of that rich flow of fancy and imagination and that fertility of happy illustration which his later writings exhibit." He was a contributor to the "North British Review" and the "Encyclopædia Britannica." In 1841 he was appointed principal of Saint Leonard's College at Saint Andrew's. In 1849 he was elected one of the eight foreign associates of the Institute of France, in place of Berzelius. Died in February, 1868.

Brewster, (WILLIAM,) one of the Pilgrim Fathers, was born at Scrooby, England, in 1560. He was one of a company of Puritans who emigrated to Holland, and he removed to Plymouth in 1620. He was a ruling elder in the church. Died in 1644.

See "Life and Times of William Brewster," by A. STEELE, 1857.

Breydel, brī'dęl, (CARL,) a Flemish painter of landscapes, battles, etc., born at Antwerp in 1677; died in 1744.

See DESCAMPS, "Vies des Peintres Flamands," etc.

€ as k; ç as s; ğ hard; ğ as j; G, H, K, guttural; N, nasal; R, trilled; ŝ as z; ᵗh as in this. (☞See Explanations, p. 23.)

28

Breydel, (FRANTS,) a Flemish painter of portraits, carnivals, and feasts, brother of the preceding, born at Antwerp in 1679; died in 1750.

See DESCAMPS, "Vies des Peintres Flamands," etc.

Breyn, brīn, [Lat. BREY′NIUS,] (JAKOB,) a German botanist, born at Dantzic in 1637; died in 1697.

Breyn, (JOHANN PHILIPP,) a German physician and scientific writer, born at Dantzic in 1690; died in 1764.

Brez, brà, (JACQUES,) a botanist, and Protestant minister, born in Piedmont in 1771, published a "History of the Waldenses," (2 vols., 1797.) Died in 1798.

Brézé. See MAILLÉ-BRÉZÉ.

Brézin, brà′zăN′, (MICHEL,) a French philanthropist, and manufacturer of locks, machinery, etc., born in 1758. He founded a hospital for aged operatives. Died in 1828.

Brial, bre′àl′, (MICHEL JEAN JOSEPH,) DOM, a French ecclesiastic, born at Perpignan in 1743. He was a contributor to the "Literary History of France," and wrote other works. Died in Paris in 1828.

Bri′an Boroihme, (or **Bo-ru′,**) a king of Ireland, succeeded his father Kennedy on the throne of Munster in 978 A.D. He obtained numerous victories over the Danes, but was killed at the battle of Clontarf, after defeating the King of Leinster and his Danish allies, (1014.)

Briarée, the French of BRIAREUS, which see.

Bri-ā′re-us, (or brī′a-rŭs,) [Gr. Βριαρεύς; Fr. BRIARÉE, bRe′à′rà′,] a giant or monster who was said to have a hundred arms. According to Homer, he was called Ægæon by men and Briareus by the gods. He and his two brothers, Gyges and Cottus, conquered the Titans.

Bricheteau, brĕsh′tō′, (ISIDORE,) a French medical writer, born in the department of Aude in 1789, was a favourite pupil and assistant of Pinel. He contributed important articles to the "Dictionary of Medical Sciences," and published several works, which are highly esteemed.

Briçonnet, bre′so′nà′, (GUILLAUME,) a French ecclesiastic and statesman, rose to be superintendent of finance, and minister of Charles VIII. He was also Archbishop of Narbonne and Cardinal of Saint-Malo.

Briçonnet, (GUILLAUME,) a son of the preceding, was Bishop of Meaux, and a patron of learning. Died in 1533.

Bridaine or **Brydaine,** bRe′dăn′, (JACQUES,) a celebrated French preacher, born at Chuslan (Gard) in 1701. His eloquence is highly commended by Massillon, La Harpe, and other eminent writers. He published "Cantiques spirituels," (1748.) Died near Avignon in 1767.

See LA HARPE, "Cours de Littérature;" MAURY, "Essai sur l'Éloquence de la Chaire."

Bridan, bre′dôN′, (CHARLES ANTOINE,) a French sculptor, born at Ruvière, in Champagne, in 1730; died in 1805.

See C. F. VIEL, "Notice sur Bridan," 1807.

Bridault, bRe′dō′, (JEAN PIERRE,) a *littérateur* of Paris, published "The Manners and Customs of the Romans," (1745.) Died in 1761.

Bridel, bRe′dêl′, (JEAN LOUIS,) a Swiss *littérateur*, born in 1759, became professor of the Oriental languages at Lausanne. Died in 1821.

Bridel, (SAMUEL ÉLISÉE,) BARON, a Swiss naturalist and poet, brother of the preceding, born in 1761. He published "Muscologia Recentiorum," (1797,) and other botanical works. He was secretary to the Prince of Saxe-Gotha. Died near Gotha in 1828.

Bridge, (WILLIAM,) an English Puritan and Independent minister, born in 1600, was ejected from Great Yarmouth in 1662. Died in 1670.

Bridge′man, (Sir ORLANDO,) an English judge, presided at the trial of the regicides, (1660,) and succeeded Lord Clarendon as keeper of the great seal in 1667. His reputation is similar to that of the other ministers of Charles II. Died in 1674.

See FOSS, "The Judges of England."

Bridges, brĭj′iz, (JOHN,) an English antiquary, born in Berkshire about 1666; died in 1724.

Bridg′et, SAINT, patroness of Ireland, born in the county of Armagh, lived about 520 A.D.

Brídg′et or **Bri-git′ta,** written also **Birgite,** SAINT. [Fr. SAINTE-BRIGITTE, săNt′bRe′zhĕt′,] born in 1302,

was the daughter of Birger, Prince of Sweden. Her work entitled "Revelations" was translated into several languages. Died in 1373.

See BAILLET, "Vies des Saints;" ÉTIENNE BINET, "Vie de Sainte-Brigitte," 1634.

Bridge′wâ-ter, (FRANCIS EGERTON,) third DUKE OF, an English peer, born in 1736, was a younger son of Scroop, the first Duke of Bridgewater. His mother was Lady Rachel Russell. He succeeded to the dukedom in 1748. In consequence of his delicate health, his education was neglected. His reputation is founded on important improvements of inland navigation. He projected a canal from Worsley to Manchester,—the first navigable canal constructed in England. It was completed at his expense in 1761. He died, without issue, in 1803.

Bridgewater, (FRANCIS HENRY EGERTON,) EARL OF, and Baron Ellesmere, born in 1758, was a son of John, Bishop of Durham. He succeeded to the earldom on the death of his elder brother in 1823. He is noted as the originator of the Bridgewater Treatises. In his will he left eight thousand pounds as a premium for the production of several treatises "On the Power, Wisdom, and Goodness of God." In accordance with his will, the president of the Royal Society selected for this task Rev. Thomas Chalmers, John Kidd, M.D., Peter Mark Roget, Charles Bell, William Whewell, Dr. Buckland, Rev. William Kirby, and William Prout, M.D. Died in 1829.

Bridgewater, [Lat. AQUAPONTA′NUS or AQUIPONTANUS,] (JOHN,) an English Catholic theologian and Jesuit, born in Yorkshire, lived about 1560–1600.

See WOOD, "Athenæ Oxonienses."

Bridg′man, (LAURA,) a blind deaf-mute, who furnishes a remarkable example of the development of intelligence under circumstances apparently the most adverse, was born at Hanover, in New Hampshire, in 1829. She had the enjoyment of all her faculties until she was about two years old, when, in consequence of a severe attack of illness, she lost her sight, hearing, and smell, and the sense of taste was at the same time much impaired. When about eight years old, she was placed under the tuition of Dr. S. G. Howe, principal of the Perkins Institution, in Boston. She learned in a few months to spell and read with a manual alphabet. She afterwards learned to write, and to play skilfully on the piano.

See DUNGLISON's "Physiology," vol. ii. p. 161; also, "Annual Reports of the Perkins Institution" for 1837 *et seq.*

Brid′pôrt, (ALEXANDER HOOD,) LORD, an English admiral, brother of the celebrated Admiral Hood, born about 1724. He served with distinction against the French in 1793 and 1794. Died in 1816.

Brienne, de, dĕh bre′ên′, (JEAN,) a French nobleman, married Isabella, daughter of Conrad of Montferrat, and heiress of the kingdom of Jerusalem. He was subsequently crowned King of Jerusalem, and gained several victories over the Saracens. Died in 1237.

See LAFITAU, "Histoire de Jean de Brienne," 1727.

Brienne Loménie. See LOMÉNIE.

Brière (or **Brierre**) **de Boismont,** bRe′aiR′ dĕh bwâ′môN′, (A.,) a French physician, born at Rouen in 1796, practised in Paris. He wrote "Elements of Botany," (1825,) a treatise on hygiene, and a work entitled "Hallucinations," ("Des Hallucinations," Paris, 1852,) which has attracted considerable attention.

Briet, bre′à′, [Lat. BRIE′TIUS,] (PHILIPPE,) a French Jesuit, born at Abbeville in 1601, wrote "Parallels of Ancient and Modern Geography," and other works. Died in 1668.

Briey, de, dĕh bre′à′, (CAMILLE,) COMTE, a Belgian diplomatist, born in 1799, was minister of foreign affairs from August, 1841, to April, 1843. He was a leader of the Catholic party.

Brifaut, bre′fō′, (CHARLES,) a French *littérateur*, born at Dijon in 1781, became a member of the French Academy in 1826. His drama called "Ninus II." was very successful. Died in Paris in 1857.

Briggs, (CHARLES FREDERICK,) an American writer, born in the island of Nantucket, became in early life a resident of New York City. He edited "Putnam's Magazine" from 1853 to 1856, and afterwards became an editor

ā, ē, ī, ō, ū, ȳ, *long;* à, ė, ò, same, less prolonged; ă, ĕ, ĭ, ŏ, ŭ, y̆, *short;* a, e, i, o, *obscure;* fär, fàll, făt; mĕt; nŏt; gōōd; mōōn;

of the New York "Times." Among his works is "The Adventures of Harry Franco, a Tale of the Great Panic," (1839.)

Briggs, (GEORGE NIXON,) an American statesman and philanthropist, born in Berkshire, Massachusetts, in 1796. He was elected to Congress in 1830, and in 1844 was chosen Governor of Massachusetts. He was an earnest advocate of the temperance cause and other important reforms, and became president of the American Temperance Union in 1860. Died in 1861.

See "Great in Goodness: Memoir of George N. Briggs," by WILLIAM C. RICHARDS.

Briggs, (HENRY,) an eminent English mathematician, born at Warleywood, near Halifax, about 1556. He was educated at Saint John's College, Cambridge. In 1596 he was chosen professor or reader in geometry in Gresham House, (since called Gresham College,) London. He became in 1619 first Savilian professor of geometry at Oxford. He is chiefly distinguished for the improvement and construction of logarithms. "Napier found," says Hallam, "a coadjutor well worthy of him in Henry Briggs, professor of geometry at Gresham College. It is uncertain from which of them the change [*i.e.* from the hyperbolical to the decimal method] in the form of logarithms proceeded." Briggs published in 1624 a great work, "Arithmetica Logarithmica," containing the logarithms of all natural numbers as high as 20,000, and again from 90,000 to 100,000, calculated to fourteen places. Died in 1630.

See WARD's "Lives of the Gresham Professors."

Briggs, (HENRY PERRONET,) an English painter of history and portraits, among whose master-pieces may be named the "First Interview between the Spaniards and the Peruvians," and "Othello relating his Adventures to Desdemona." In 1832 he was elected an Academician. Died in 1844.

Briggs, (HENRY SHAW,) born in Berkshire, Massachusetts, in 1824, served in the campaign of 1861, and was made brigadier-general of volunteers in 1862.

Briggs, (WILLIAM,) an English physician, born in 1641, published a "Theory of Vision," and a work entitled "Ophthalmographia," or description of the eye. Died in 1704.

Brigham, brig'am, (AMARIAH,) an American physician, born in Berkshire county, Massachusetts, in 1798, began to practise medicine in 1821. He became superintendent of the Retreat for the Insane at Hartford, Connecticut, in 1840, and obtained the same office in the New York State Lunatic Asylum at Utica in 1842. He wrote, besides other works, "Mental Cultivation and Excitement," and "The Anatomy, Physiology, and Pathology of the Brain," (1840.) Died in 1849.

Brigham, brig'am, (NICHOLAS,) an English poet, born at Caversham, wrote "Memoirs of Eminent Persons," and other works. Died in 1559.

Brigham Young. See YOUNG, (BRIGHAM.)

Bright, (JESSE D.,) an American politician, born in Chenango county, New York, removed to Indiana, and was elected to the United States Senate in 1845. He was expelled in 1861 for a treasonable correspondence with Jefferson Davis.

Bright, (JOHN,) a celebrated English orator and Radical statesman, was born at Greenbank, near Rochdale, on the 16th of November, 1811. He is a member of the Society of Friends. He was the son of Jacob Bright, a cotton-spinner, and is a partner in the firm of John Bright and Brothers, manufacturers of cotton, at Rochdale. In 1835 he travelled on the continent and visited Palestine. He enlisted in the Anti-Corn-Law League in 1839, and became a zealous champion of the repeal of the corn-laws. About this time he formed an intimate friendship with Richard Cobden. He addressed many public meetings with powerful and impassioned declamation, and was considered second only to Cobden among the advocates of the Anti-Corn-Law League.

He was elected to Parliament for the city of Durham in 1843. The repeal of the corn-laws was followed by a general election in 1847, when Mr. Bright was one of the two members sent from Manchester. He was not identified with either of the great political parties, but, in co-operation with Cobden, formed the Manchester school of politics, advocates of electoral reform and non-intervention in foreign wars. He was re-elected by the voters of Manchester in 1852, but, in consequence of his opposition to the war against Russia, was defeated in 1857. Since that year he has represented Birmingham in Parliament. As a consistent friend of liberty and equal rights, he testified his sympathy with the American Republicans in the civil war, by several eloquent public speeches. In the great debate on the Reform Bill of Russell and Gladstone (1866) he took a prominent part. After the defeat of this bill he made speeches on the subject of Reform at immense meetings held in Manchester, Birmingham, Glasgow, London, and other places. "He is endowed," says the "Saturday Review," "with a voice that can discourse most eloquent music, and with a speech that can equally sound the depths of pathos or scale the heights of indignation." Alluding to Mr. Bright's recent efforts in the cause of Reform, the "European Times" of December 8, 1866, remarks, "In all Mr. Bright's previous career, he has never put forth such extraordinary power, such floods of the very highest order of eloquence on the great question of the day, as during the last four months ; and it is not too much to say that no orator of the century has stirred the heart of the country in so short a time, or so effectually, by his own unaided intellect." On the 15th of August, 1867, the queen signed a Reform bill which granted the right of suffrage to every householder in a borough.

He made, in March, 1868, a speech on Ireland, which is commended by the London "Spectator," March 21, in these terms: "Mr. Bright's grand speech did more to draw the noblest men of all parties nearer to each other than long years of discussion had effected before." At the general election of November, 1868, he was returned for Birmingham. He declined the office of secretary for India, which was offered to him, but he entered the cabinet of Mr. Gladstone as president of the Board of Trade in December, 1868. Two volumes of his "Speeches on Questions of Public Policy" were published in 1868.

See "Edinburgh Review" for January, 1869.

Bright, (RICHARD,) an English physician, born in Bristol in 1789. He settled in London, and published an important work entitled "Original Researches into the Pathology of Diseases of the Kidney." He was the first to describe an affection of the kidney which is generally known as "Bright's Disease." Died in 1858.

Bright, (TIMOTHY,) an English physician and clergyman, born at Cambridge, wrote, besides other works, a "Treatise on Melancholy," (1586.) Died in 1615.

Bright'man, (THOMAS,) an English clergyman, born at Nottingham in 1557 ; died in 1607.

Brigitte. See BRIDGET, SAINT.

Brignolo-Sale, brĕn-yo'lo sä'lä, [Fr. BRIGNOLE-SALE, brĕn'yol' säl,] (ANTONIO GIULIO,) an Italian writer in prose and verse, born in 1605, was a son of a doge of Genoa. Died in 1665.

See J. M. VISCONTI, "Vita di A. G. Brignolo-Sale," 1666.

Bril, brĕl, (MATTHEUS,) a Flemish painter, born at Antwerp in 1550. He was patronized by Pope Gregory XIII., for whom he painted several frescos in the Vatican. Died in 1584.

Bril, (PAULUS,) brother and pupil of the preceding, born at Antwerp in 1556. At an early age he joined his brother at Rome, where he soon acquired a very high reputation as a landscape-painter. Among his master-pieces are "The Martyrdom of Saint Clement," in the Vatican, two landscapes in the Pitti palace at Florence, and "Building of the Tower of Babel," in the Berlin Museum. The figures in several of his pieces were painted by Annibal Caracci. Died at Rome in 1626.

See DESCAMPS, "Vies des Peintres Flamands," etc.

Brillat-Savarin, bRe'yä' sä'vä'răN', (ANTHELME,) a French *littérateur*, born at Bellay in 1755, published a popular work on gastronomy, entitled "The Physiology of Taste," (1825,) the style of which is highly praised. Died in 1826.

See "London Quarterly Review" for July, 1835.

Brillon, bRe'yôN', (PIERRE JACQUES,) a French jurist and legal writer, born in Paris in 1671 ; died in 1736.

€ as *k*; ç as *s*; g *hard;* g as *j;* G, H, K, *guttural;* N, *nasal;* R, *trilled;* s as z; th as in *this.* (☞See Explanations, p. 23.)

Brind'ley, (JAMES,) an English engineer and mechanician, born at Thornset, in Derbyshire, in 1716, was an apprentice to a millwright. He had a remarkable faculty of invention, and made improvements in the machinery of mills. About 1758 he was employed by the Duke of Bridgewater as engineer of a canal from Worsley to Manchester,—the first navigable canal made in Great Britain in modern times. He performed this difficult enterprise with success, and exhibited great fertility of resources. He superintended the construction of the Trent and Mersey Canal, begun in 1766, and other similar works. Died in 1772.

See "Pursuit of Knowledge under Difficulties," vol. i., 1839; HENRY HOWE, "Eminent American and European Mechanics."

Brink'ley, (JOHN,) an English divine and astronomer, born in 1763, became professor of astronomy at Trinity College, Dublin. He published, among other works, "Elements of Astronomy," which is esteemed a standard work. He was created Bishop of Cloyne in 1826. Died in 1835.

Brinkmann, bRink'mân, (KARL GUSTAF,) BARON, a Swedish diplomatist and poet, born near Stockholm in 1764, was sent as ambassador to London in 1807. In 1829 he became a member of the Royal Academy of Stockholm. He was a friend and correspondent of Madame de Staël. He died in 1848, leaving to the University of Upsal his library of ten thousand volumes.

See BERNARD VON BESKOW, "Tal, etc. öfver C. G. von Brinkmann," 1848.

Brins'ley, (JOHN,) an English nonconformist minister, born in 1600, was a nephew of Bishop Hall, (of Norwich.) He preached at Yarmouth, and wrote several works. Died in 1665.

Brinvilliers, bRăn've'ye-a', (MARIE MARGUERITE d'Aubray—dō'bRă',) MARCHIONESS OF, a Frenchwoman, notorious for her crimes, was the daughter of Dreux d'Aubray, civil lieutenant of Paris, and was married in 1651 to the Marquis de Brinvilliers. She successively poisoned her father and two brothers, having previously exercised her art on the patients at the hospitals. She was at length detected, condemned to death, and executed in 1676.

See "Histoire du Procès de la Marquise de Brinvilliers," Paris, 1676; MADAME DE SÉVIGNÉ's "Letters."

Brion, bRE-ôn', (LUIS,) a South American naval officer, born at Curaçoa in 1782. He acquired great influence, took arms against Spain about 1811, and served under Bolivar with distinction. Died in 1821.

Briot, bRE'o', (CHARLES,) a French mathematician, born at Saint-Hippolyte, in Doubs, in 1817. He became teacher of mechanics and astronomy in the Normal School of Paris in 1855. He published, besides other works, "Lessons in Analytical Geometry," (1851,) in which he was assisted by M. Bouquet.

Bris'bane, (Sir CHARLES,) an English admiral, served with distinction under Rodney, Hood, and Nelson, was appointed Governor of Saint Vincent, and created vice-admiral in 1820. Died in 1829.

Brisbane, (Sir THOMAS MACDOUGAL,) a British astronomer and general, born at Bishopton in 1773. He commanded a brigade in many actions in the Peninsula in 1812-13, after which he was Governor of Jamaica and of New South Wales. He built an observatory on the river Tweed. Died in 1860.

Brissac, de, DUC. See COSSÉ-BRISSAC.

Brisseau, bRE'sō', (PIERRE,) a French physician, born in Paris in 1631, published a "Treatise on the Cataract," and other works. Died in 1717.

Brisson, bRE'sòN', [Lat. BRISSO'NIUS,] (BARNABÉ,) an eminent French jurist and philologist, born in Poitou in 1531. He was appointed first president of the Parliament of Paris in 1588 by the League, and was hung in 1591 by the *Seize*, a committee of sixteen factious persons who had possession of the capital. He was author of a treatise "On the Formulas and Solemn Words of the Roman People," ("De Formulis et solennibus Populi Romani Verbis," 1583,) and other works.

See DE THOU, "Histoire;" DANIEL W. MOLLER, "Disputatio circularis de B. Brissonio," 1696.

Brisson, (BARNABÉ,) a French engineer, born at Lyons in 1777, wrote an "Essay on Navigation," and other works. Died in 1828.

Brisson, (MATHURIN JACQUES,) a distinguished French naturalist, born at Fontenay-le-Comte in 1723, became professor of physics in the College of Navarre, published "The Animal Kingdom," ("Le Règne animal," 1756,) "Ornithology," (6 vols., 1760,) and a treatise "On the Specific Weight of Bodies," (1787.) Died near Versailles in 1806.

Brissot, bRE'so', (PIERRE,) a French physician, born at Fontenay-le-Comte in 1478, wrote an able treatise on bleeding for the pleurisy, (1529.) Died in Portugal in 1522.

Brissot de Warville, bRE'so' dĕh văR'vĕl', (JEAN PIERRE,) a French Girondist leader and political writer, born at or near Chartres in January, 1754. He published in 1781 "Théorie des Lois criminelles," (2 vols.) In 1785 he was confined in the Bastille on suspicion of having written an anonymous libel, of which he was innocent. To promote the abolition of the slave-trade, he formed with several friends, in 1788, the Société des Amis des Noirs, (Society of the Friends of the Negroes,) and made a voyage to the United States to inquire into that subject. Having returned to France on the eve of the Revolution, he became editor of the "Patriote Français," a journal which would have sufficed to render him famous if he had no other titles to celebrity. He was elected in 1791 to the National Assembly by the voters of Paris, advocated a republic, and was recognized as the master spirit of the Girondist party, often called *Brissotins*. In the Convention (1792-93) he strenuously opposed the execution of the king and other excesses of the Jacobins. He was imprisoned in June, 1793, and executed in Paris, with twenty-one other Girondists, in October of the same year. He was author of numerous works.

See LAMARTINE, "History of the Girondists;" "Vie privée et politique de Brissot," Paris, 1792; BRISSOT's "Mémoires pour servir à l'Histoire de la Révolution," published by his son, 4 vols., 1830.

Bris'ted, (CHARLES ASTOR,) an American writer, born in New York in 1820, graduated at Yale College in 1839, and pursued his studies at Oxford, England. He published "Five Years in an English University," (1852.)

Bristed, (JOHN,) an Episcopal clergyman, father of the preceding, born in Dorsetshire, England, in 1779. He emigrated to the United States in 1806, and married a daughter of John Jacob Astor in 1820. He preached at Bristol, Rhode Island, and wrote "The Resources of the United States." Died in 1855.

Bris'tŏw, (HENRY WILLIAM,) an English geologist and scientific writer, born about 1817.

Bri-tan'nĭ-cus, (TIBERIUS CLAUDIUS GERMANICUS,) a Roman prince, born in 42 A.D., was a son of the emperor Claudius and Messalina. He was the heir presumptive to the throne before the death of his mother; but, through the influence of Agrippina, Nero was preferred as the successor of Claudius. Britannicus was poisoned by Nero at a banquet in 56 A.D.

See TACITUS, "Annales."

Britard. See BRIZARD.

Brito, de, dà bree'to, (BERNARDO,) a Portuguese historian, born at Villa de Almeida in 1569, wrote a "History of the Portuguese Monarchy," and "Eulogies of the Kings of Portugal." Died in 1617.

See BEAUVAIS, "Vie de B. de Brito," 1744.

Brito, (FRANCISCO JOZÉ MARIA,) a Portuguese diplomatist, born about 1759. He was minister plenipotentiary to France in 1815. Died in 1825.

Brito, (GULIELMUS.) See BRETON, (GUILLAUME.)

Brito-Armoricus. See BRETON, (GUILLAUME.)

Brito Freire, de, dà bree'to frã'e-rà, (FRANCISCO,) a Portuguese admiral, born about 1610, served with distinction against the Dutch in Brazil. Died in 1692.

Brit-o-mar'tis [Gr. Βριτόμαρτις] or **Bri'to,** [Βριτώ,] a nymph, the daughter of Jupiter, and favourite companion of Diana, was beloved by Minos, to escape from whom she threw herself into the sea. She was worshipped especially by sailors and fishermen.

Britton. See BRACTON.

Brit'ton, (JOHN,) a celebrated English antiquary, born in Wiltshire in 1771. Among his numerous works are "The Cathedral Antiquities of England," (14 vols. fol. and 4to, with nearly 300 engravings,) "Architectural

ā, ē, ī, ō, ū, ȳ, *long;* à, ê, ì, ò, same, less prolonged; ă, ĕ, ĭ, ŏ, ŭ, ў, *short;* a, ȩ, į, o, *obscure;* fär, fàll, fàt; mĕt; nŏt; gŏŏd; mŏŏn;

Antiquities of Normandy," (1825,) "A Dictionary of the Architecture and Archæology of the Middle Ages," (1832,) "Illustrations of Fonthill Abbey," and "Historical Notices of Windsor Castle," (1842.) Died in 1857.

See "Men I have known," by WILLIAM JERDAN, London, 1866; "London Quarterly Review" for June and September, 1826.

Britton, (THOMAS,) an English coal-dealer, born in Northamptonshire about 1650, was celebrated for his proficiency in music. Died in 1714.

See "Annals of Industry and Genius," by C. L. BRIGHTWELL, London, 1863.

Brizard, bre′zăr′, or **Britard,** bre′tăr′, (JEAN BAPTISTE,) a French actor and dramatist, born at Orléans in 1721 ; died in 1791.

Brize, bree′zeh, (KORNELIS,) a Dutch painter of still life, bas-reliefs, etc., lived between 1650 and 1700.

Brizeux, bre′zuh′, (JULIEN AUGUSTE PÉLAGE,) a French poet, born at Lorient in 1806. He produced a successful poem entitled "Marie," (1832,) "The Bretons," (1846,) which was crowned by the French Academy, and "Primel et Nola," (1850.) Died in 1858.

Brizio. See BRIZZI.

Brizzi, brĕt′see, or **Brizio,** brĕt′se-o, (FRANCESCO,) an Italian painter, born at Bologna in 1574, was one of the most distinguished pupils of the Caracci. Among his best works is the "Coronation of the Madonna del Borgo." Died in 1623.

See LANZI, "History of Painting in Italy."

Brocario, bro-kä′re-o, a Spanish typographer, published in 1514–16 the Polyglot Bible of Cardinal Ximenes, (6 vols. fol.)

Brocchi, brok′kee, (GIOVANNI BATTISTA,) an Italian naturalist, born at Bassano in 1772. He became professor of botany at Brescia in 1802, and in 1808 inspector of mines of the kingdom of Italy. Among his principal works are his "Sub-Apennine Fossil Conchology, with Geological Observations on the Apennines and the Adjacent Soil," (2 vols., 1814,) and a work "On the Physical Condition of the Soil of Rome," (1820.) Died at Khartoum, in Nubia, in 1826.

See TIPALDO, "Biografia degli Italiani illustri;" G. LARBER, "Elogio storico di G. B. Brocchi," 1828; "Edinburgh Review" for February, 1816.

Brochant de Villiers, bro′shŏn′ deh ve′ye-à′, (ANDRÉ JEAN FRANÇOIS MARIE,) a French naturalist and scientific writer, born in Paris in 1773. He was a member of the Academy of Sciences, and inspector-general of mines. Died in 1840.

Brochet, bro′shà′, (JEAN ÉTIENNE,) a demagogue of the French Revolution. He was exiled by Bonaparte to Cayenne, but was soon after permitted to return, and passed the rest of his life in merited obscurity. Died in 1823.

Brock, (ISAAC,) a British major-general, whose principal achievement was the capture of General Hull and his army at Detroit, in August, 1812. At the battle of Queenstown, October 13 of the same year, he was killed, being pierced by three balls. As a token of the respect which was felt for his high character, the guns of the American forts were fired during his funeral.

Brockedon, brok′don, (WILLIAM,) an English author and artist, born in 1787. He published "Passes of the Alps," illustrated by elegant engravings, (2 vols., 1828,) "Views in Italy," (1842–44,) and "Excursions in the Alps," (1845.) Died in 1854.

Brockes, brok′kĕs, (BARTHOLD HEINRICH,) a German devotional poet, born at Hamburg in 1680. He translated Thomson's "Seasons" into German. Died in 1747.

Brock′ett, (JOHN TROTTER,) an English antiquary, born in 1788; died in 1842.

Brockhaus, brok′hŏwss, (FRIEDRICH ARNOLD,) a celebrated German publisher, born at Dortmund in 1772, was the founder of the firm of Brockhaus at Leipsic. Having purchased the copyright of the "Conversations-Lexikon," he settled at Altenburg in 1811, and began in 1812 the second edition of that work. In 1813 he edited a patriotic journal, entitled "Deutsche Blätter." He removed in 1817 to Leipsic, where, besides six editions of the "Conversations-Lexikon," he brought out Ebert's "Universal Bibliographical Lexicon," Von Raumer's "History of the Hohenstaufen and their Times," Ersch's

"Manual of German Literature," and other important publications. He died in 1823 ; and the firm was continued by his two eldest sons, Frederick and Henry, under whose auspices the "Conversations-Lexikon" reached the tenth edition. To this were subsequently added three accompanying works, entitled "Conversations-Lexicon of the Most Recent Times and Literature," ("Conversations-Lexikon der neuesten Zeit und Literatur," 4 vols., 1832,) "Conversations-Lexicon of the Present," ("Conversations-Lexikon der Gegenwart," 4 vols., 1838,) and "The Present," ("Der Gegenwart," 1848.) They have also published Ersch and Gruber's "Universal Encyclopædia," ("Allgemeine Encyklopaedie,") the "Pfennig-Magasin," and a number of useful periodicals.

Brockhaus, (HERMANN,) third son of Friedrich Arnold, noticed above, was born at Amsterdam in 1806. He became in 1848 professor of the Sanscrit language and literature at Leipsic. He has published, in German and Sanscrit, a portion of the legends of Somadeva.

Brocklesby, brok′′lz-be, (RICHARD,) a distinguished English physician, born in Somersetshire in 1722, was an intimate friend of Edmund Burke. He graduated at Leyden, and in 1758 was appointed physician to the army, which he accompanied to Germany in the Seven Years' war. He was a Fellow of the Royal Society and of the College of Physicians, and published several medical works. Died in 1797.

See "Biographie Médicale."

Brockmann, brok′măn, (JOHANN FRANZ HIERONYMUS,) a celebrated German actor, born at Grätz, in Styria, in 1745 ; died in 1812.

Brodeau, bro′dō′, (JEAN,) a distinguished French scholar, born in 1500, published "Notes on Martial," a "Commentary on the Tragedies of Euripides," and other critical works. Died in 1563.

Bro′der-ick, (DAVID COLBRETH,) an American Senator, born at Washington, District of Columbia, in 1818 or 1819. He worked at the trade of stone-cutter in New York City in his youth, removed to California in 1849, and became a leading Democrat. In 1856 he was elected a member of the Senate of the United States by the legislature of California. He acquired eminence as a debater, spoke against the admission of Kansas as a slave State under the Lecompton Constitution, and separated from his party, on the question of slavery, in 1858. He was challenged, and killed in a duel near San Francisco in September, 1859, by Judge David S. Terry, a partisan of slavery, whose motive appears to have been revenge for the speeches which Broderick had made against Senator Gwin and others of the pro-slavery party.

Broderip, brŏd′rip, (WILLIAM JOHN,) an English naturalist, born at Bristol. He published "Zoological Recreations," (1847,) and "Leaves from the Note-Book of a Naturalist," (1852,) and contributed numerous articles on natural history to Knight's "Penny Cyclopædia." He was a Fellow of the Linnæan Society and of the Royal Society, and vice-president of the Zoological Society. Died in 1859.

See "London Quarterly Review" for December, 1847; "Fraser's Magazine" for April, 1859.

Brod′head, (JACOB,) D.D., an American clergyman, born in Ulster county, New York, in 1782. He became pastor of a Reformed Dutch church in New York in 1809, removed to Philadelphia in 1813, and returned to New York in 1826. Died in 1855.

Brodhead, (JOHN ROMEYN,) an American historian, son of the preceding, born in Philadelphia in 1814, graduated at Rutgers College, New Jersey, in 1831, and studied law. He devoted himself to the study of American history, and, while attached to the United States legation at the Hague, in 1841, was appointed by Governor Seward an agent to procure information relating to the colonial history of New York. He spent three years in examining the records in Holland, London, and Paris, and returned in 1844 with eighty volumes of documents. In 1849 the legislature passed an act authorizing their publication in ten volumes quarto. The first volume of the "History of New York from 1609 to 1664" (the period of its occupation by the Dutch) appeared in 1853.

€ as *k;* ç as *s;* ğ *hard;* ğ as *j;* G, H, K, *guttural;* N, *nasal;* R, *trilled;* s as z; ŧh as in *this.*   (☞See Explanations, p. 23.)

Bro'die, (Sir BENJAMIN COLLINS,) an eminent English surgeon, born in Wiltshire in 1783. He studied under Sir Everard Home, and became, in 1832, surgeon to the queen. He was elected a Fellow of the Royal Society, corresponding member of the Institute of France, and obtained the degree of D.C.L. from the University of Oxford, (1850.) Among his principal works are "Experiments and Observations on the Different Modes in which Death is produced by Certain Vegetable Poisons," (1811,) "Pathological and Surgical Observations on Diseases of the Joints," and "On Local Nervous Affections." Died in 1862.

See his "Autobiography," 1865; H. W. ACLAND, "Biographical Sketch of B. C. Brodie," 1864; "Fraser's Magazine" for January, 1863, and July, 1865.

Brodie, (GEORGE,) an English historian. He published a "History of the British Empire from the Accession of Charles I. to the Restoration," (4 vols., 1822,) which was written for the purpose of pointing out the faults or errors of Hume.

See "Edinburgh Review" for March, 1824; Professor SMYTH, "Lectures on Modern History."

Brodzinski, brod-zins'kee, (CASIMIR,) a Polish poet and critic of distinguished merit, born at Krolowko in 1791, became professor of æsthetics at Warsaw. He made a number of translations from the English, German, and other languages. Died in 1835.

Broeck, van den, văn dĕn brook, (BARBARA,) a Flemish engraver, born about 1560, was a daughter of Crispin, noticed below, some of whose designs she engraved.

Broeck, van den, (CRISPIN,) a Flemish historical painter and engraver, born at Antwerp about 1530; died about 1601.

Broeck, van den, (ELIAS,) a Flemish painter of flowers, fruits, etc., born in 1657; died in 1711.

See DESCAMPS, "Vies des Peintres Flamands," etc.

Broekhuizen, van, văn brook'hoi'zĕn, (JAN,) [Lat. JA'NUS BROUKHU'SIUS,] a Dutch scholar and poet, born at Amsterdam in 1649. He published editions of Tibullus and other classics, and a collection of Latin poems. Died in 1707.

See LONGFELLOW, "Poets and Poetry of Europe;" JÖCHER, "Allgemeines Gelehrten-Lexikon."

Brofferio, brof-fā're-o, (ANGELO,) an eminent Italian dramatist, orator, and political writer, born at Asti, in Piedmont, in 1802. He produced "Vitiges, King of the Goths," "Salvator Rosa," and other dramas, and a volume of popular songs; also a "History of Piedmont," (1849–52.) In 1848 he became a member of the Chamber of Deputies. In politics he is a radical republican.

Broghill, LORD. See BOYLE, (ROGER.)

Broglia, brol'yä, (FRANCESCO MARIA,) born at Chieri, in Piedmont, in 1611, first distinguished himself in the civil war of Savoy in 1638. He afterwards entered the service of France, where he won a high reputation for bravery and military skill. Died in 1656. He was the founder of an illustrious family of French nobles, of whom the following are, perhaps, the most worthy of notice.

Broglie, de, dĕh brog'le', (ACHILLE LÉONCE VICTOR CHARLES,) DUC, a French statesman, born in Paris in 1785 or 1789, was a son of Claude Victor, noticed below. He married the only daughter of Madame de Staël in 1816, and in the same year became a member of the Chamber of Peers, in which he made a speech against the slave-trade in 1822. After the revolution of 1830, the Duc de Broglie and his friend Guizot were the chiefs of the party called *Doctrinaires*. De Broglie was minister of public instruction for a few months in 1830, and minister of foreign affairs from October, 1832, to April, 1834. He was elected in 1849 to the Legislative Assembly, in which he voted with the conservative *droite*. In 1856 he was elected a member of the French Academy.

Broglie, de, (ALBERT,) PRINCE, a son of the preceding, born in 1821, is distinguished in literature and philosophy. He has contributed several articles to the "Revue des Deux Mondes." Among his works is a history of Constantine the Great, entitled "The Church and the Roman Empire in the Fourth Century," (2 vols., 1856.)

See "Edinburgh Review" for April, 1860.

Broglie, de, (ALBERTINE IDA GUSTAVINE DE STAËL,) DUCHESSE, born in Paris about 1797, was the only daughter of the celebrated Madame de Staël-Holstein, and the wife of Achille, Duc de Broglie, noticed above. She was a zealous Protestant, and the author of "Fragments on Various Subjects of Religion and Morals," (1840,) and other works. Died in 1838. "Whatever might be the éclat of her position," says the "Nouvelle Biographie Générale," "she enhanced it by the admirable example that she gave of all the domestic virtues. Her salon was not only the resort of eminent statesmen, but was one of those to which the élite of Paris came to seek intellectual pleasure."

Broglie, de, (CLAUDE VICTOR,) PRINCE, son of Victor François, noticed below, was born in Paris in 1757. He was president of the National Convention in 1791, and in 1794 was executed by order of the Revolutionary tribunal.

Broglie, de, (FRANÇOIS MARIE,) DUC, grandson of Francesco Maria Broglia, noticed above, and son of Victor Maurice, Count of Broglie, was born in 1671, and made marshal of France in 1734. Ten years before, he had resolutely refused this high promotion, because he believed the claims of his father, who was then still living, were juster than his own. In consequence of this generous refusal, his father was made marshal, which office he held till his death in 1727. The Duke of Broglie was a man of great ability, courage, and nobleness of character. Died in 1745.

Broglie, de, (MAURICE JEAN MADELEINE,) a French ecclesiastic, born in 1766, became in 1803 almoner to the emperor, and subsequently Bishop of Ghent. Died in 1821.

Broglie, de, (VICTOR FRANÇOIS,) DUC, son of François Marie, noticed above, born in 1718. He served with distinction in the Seven Years' war, commanded in several battles, and was created marshal of France in 1759. He became minister of war in 1789, and emigrated about 1790. Died at Münster in 1804.

See "Victoires et Conquêtes des Français."

Broglie, de, (VICTOR MAURICE,) COMTE, Marquis de Brezolles, (dĕh brĕh-zol',) son of Francisco Maria Broglia, noticed above, born about 1647, rendered important services in Flanders, (1672–90,) and became a marshal of France in 1724. Died in 1727.

Brogni, brŏn'yee, CARDINAL OF, (originally GIOVANNI Allarmet—äl-lär-mĕt',) an eminent Italian ecclesiastic, born in 1342, was the son of a peasant of Brogni, a village near Annecy. His talents soon raised him to distinction, and in 1385 he was made cardinal. He presided in 1417 at the Council in which John Huss was condemned. He is said, however, to have manifested the kindest sympathy towards Huss, and to have pronounced his sentence reluctantly, and not till he had tried everything to reclaim him which Christian charity could suggest. Died in 1426.

See MORÉRI, "Dictionnaire Historique;" "Nouvelle Biographie Générale."

Broke. See BROOKE.

Broke, brŏk, (?) (FRANCIS J.,) an officer of the American Revolution, and an intimate friend of Washington, was born near Fredericksburg, Virginia, in 1763. He entered the army with his twin-brother John at the age of sixteen, and served his first campaign as a lieutenant under La Fayette. He afterwards joined the army of General Greene, and continued in service to the end of the war. Died in 1851.

Broke, brŏk, (Sir PHILIP BOWES VERE,) a British rear-admiral, born in 1776. He commanded the Shannon in a fight against the American frigate Chesapeake, which he captured in June, 1813. (See LAWRENCE, JAMES.) Died in 1841.

Brome, (ALEXANDER,) an English poet and lawyer, born in 1620. He wrote a number of satires, songs, and epigrams in ridicule of the Parliamentary party; also a comedy entitled "The Cunning Lovers." Died in 1666.

Brome, (JAMES,) an Englishman, who published "Travels in England, Scotland, and Wales," (1700,) and "Travels through Portugal, Spain, and Italy," (1712.)

ā, ē, ī, ō, ū, ȳ, *long;* ă, ĕ, ĭ, ŏ, ŭ, ў, *same, less prolonged;* ă, ĕ, ĭ, ŏ, ŭ, ў, *short;* ạ, ẹ, ị, ọ, *obscure;* fär, fȧll, fȧt; mĕt; nŏt; gōōd; mōōn;

Brome, (RICHARD,) an English dramatist, was originally a servant of Ben Jonson. He published fifteen comedies, among which may be named "The Jovial Crew, or the Merry Beggars," and "The Northern Lass." Died in 1652.

Bromel, bro'mĕl, (OLAF,) a physician and botanist, father of the following, born in the province of Nericia in 1639; died in 1705.

Bromel, von, fon bro'mĕl, (MAGNUS,) born at Stockholm about 1678, became chief physician to the King of Sweden. Died in 1731.

Brom'field, (JOHN,) an American merchant, born at Newburyport, Massachusetts, in 1779, lived in Boston. He gave twenty-five thousand dollars to the Boston Athenæum. Died in 1849.

Brom'field, (WILLIAM,) an English surgeon, born in 1712, published "Chirurgical Observations and Cases," and other medical works; also a comedy called "The City Match." Died in 1792. He was one of the founders of Lock Hospital, London.

Brom'ley, (Sir THOMAS,) an English judge, born in the county of Salop about 1530. He became solicitor-general in 1570, and lord chancellor in 1579. According to Lord Campbell, "he framed the measures intended to bring Mary Queen of Scots to trial." He presided over the court which condemned her in 1586. Died in 1587.

See LORD CAMPBELL, "Lives of the Lord Chancellors," vol. ii.; Foss, "The Judges of England."

Bromley, (WILLIAM,) an English engraver, born at Carisbrooke, in the Isle of Wight, in 1769. Among his principal works are portraits of the Duke of Wellington and Young Napoleon, and the illustrations to "Macklin's Bible." Died in 1842.

His son JOHN, born at Chelsea in 1795, obtained great excellence in mezzotinto engraving. Died in 1839.

Bromp'ton, (JOHN,) an English monk, the reputed author or editor of a "Chronicon" from 588 to 1198.

Bronchorst, (JAN.) See BRONKHORST.

Brondex, bRŏN'dĕx', (ALBERT,) a French wit and poet, born in 1750; died in 1786.

Bröndsted or Brönsted, bRŏn'stĕd, (PETER OLUF,) a Danish antiquary and scholar, born at Horsens, in Jutland, about 1780. Having visited Italy, Greece, and Asia Minor, he was appointed professor of Greek at Copenhagen, (1813,) director of the Royal Museum of Antiquities, and professor of philology and archæology. He published "Travels and Investigations in Greece," (1826, in German and French,) and other valuable treatises on ancient art. Died in 1842.

See ERSLEW, "Forfatter-Lexicon;" J. P. MYNSTER, "P. O. Bröndsted's Biographie," 1844.

Brongniart, bRŏN'ñe-ǎr', (ADOLPHE THÉOPHILE,) a French botanist, son of Alexandre, noticed below, born in Paris in 1801. He succeeded Desfontaines as a member of the Academy of Sciences in 1834, and about 1840 became professor of botany at the Jardin des Plantes. Among his works may be named "Prodromus of a History of Fossil Vegetables," (1828,) "Botanical and Geological Researches on Vegetables enclosed in the Different Strata of the Earth," (2 vols., 1828 et seq.,) and "Observations on the Interior Structure of the Sigillaria Elegans." He was chosen a foreign member of the Royal Society of London in 1852.

See QUÉRARD, "La France Littéraire," (Supplément.)

Brongniart, (ALEXANDRE,) an eminent French chemist and mineralogist, born in Paris in 1770, was a son of Alexandre Théodore, noticed below. He served as physician or apothecary in the army in his youth, and was afterwards a professor of natural history. In 1800 or 1801 he was appointed director of the manufactory of porcelain at Sèvres. He wrote an "Elementary Treatise on Mineralogy," (1807,) which was used as a text-book by many professors. He is said to have been the first who classified reptiles under the heads of Saurians, Batrachians, Chelonians, and Ophidians. In conjunction with Cuvier, he produced a celebrated "Essay on the Mineralogical Geography of the Environs of Paris," (1810.) He was elected a member of the Academy of Sciences in 1815, after which he travelled in Sweden with Berzelius. Among his works is "A Treatise on the Art

of Pottery," ("Traité des Arts céramiques," 1845.) Died in October, 1847.

See BROCKHAUS, "Conversations-Lexikon."

Brongniart, (ALEXANDRE THÉODORE,) a French architect, and member of the Academy of Architecture, born in Paris in 1739. He was the first architect of the Palais de la Bourse, (Exchange,) but did not live to finish it. Died in 1815.

See "Nouvelle Biographie Générale."

Brongniart, (ANTOINE LOUIS,) a French chemist, brother of the preceding, was professor in the College of Pharmacy, and apothecary to Louis XVI. He wrote an "Analytical View of the Combinations and Decompositions of Different Substances." Died in 1804.

Bronikowski, bRO'ne-kov'skee, (ALEXANDER AUGUST FERDINAND von Ope'ln—fon o'pĕln,) a German writer, of Polish extraction, born at Dresden in 1783, published novels entitled "Olgierd and Olga, or Poland in the Eleventh Century," (1832,) and "Hippolytus Boratynski;" also a "History of Poland." Died in 1834.

See "Foreign Quarterly Review" for December, 1834.

Bronkhorst or Bronchorst, van, bRONK'horst, (JAN,) a distinguished Dutch painter of animals, born at Leyden in 1648; died in 1726.

Bronkhorst, van, (PIETER,) an excellent Dutch painter of architectural pieces and perspective, born at Delft in 1588; died in 1661.

See DESCAMPS, "Vies des Peintres Flamands," etc.

Bronn, bRON, (HEINRICH GEORG,) a German naturalist, born in 1800 near Heidelberg, where he became professor of natural science in 1833. He published, besides other works, "Universal Zoology," (1850,) and "Lethæa geognostica," a treatise on petrifactions which serve to characterize rocky formations, (2 vols., 1834.)

See BROCKHAUS, "Conversations-Lexikon."

Bronner, bRON'ner, (FRANZ XAVER,) a German pastoral poet, born at Höchstädt, on the Danube, in 1758; died in 1850.

See his "Autobiography," 3 vols., 1795-97.

Brönsted. See BRÖNDSTED.

Bronté, bron'te, (ANNE,) an English novelist, whose assumed name was ACTON BELL, was born in Yorkshire about 1820. She was a sister of Charlotte Bronté. She wrote, besides several short poems, a prose tale called "Agnes Grey," (1847,) and "The Tenant of Wildfeld Hall," (1848.) Died in May, 1849.

See a biographical notice prefixed by her sister CHARLOTTE to the edition of "Wuthering Heights" and "Agnes Grey," 1850.

Bronté, (CHARLOTTE,) "CURRER BELL," a popular English novelist, born at Thornton, Yorkshire, April 21, 1816, was a daughter of Patrick Bronté, who became curate of Haworth in 1820. She lost her mother when she was a child. While at a boarding-school her health was injured by impure air and food of bad quality. Her friend Mrs. Gaskell says she was (about 1833 or 1834) a "little, set, antiquated girl, very quiet in manners and very quaint in dress." In 1835 she became a teacher of the school at Roe Head, and in 1841 a governess in a private family. Charlotte and her sister Emily went to Brussels in 1842 to learn French, etc. The former was afterwards employed there as a teacher of English, at a salary of sixteen pounds a year; but she returned to Haworth about the end of 1843. In 1846 the Misses Bronté published a volume entitled "Poems by Currer, Ellis, and Acton Bell," Currer Bell being the assumed name of Charlotte. About two years later, under the pressure of painful domestic trials, she produced "Jane Eyre, an Autobiography, edited by Currer Bell," (3 vols., 1848,) which obtained great popularity and was translated into many languages. "Almost all that we require in a novelist," says "Fraser's Magazine," "the writer has,—perception of character and knowledge of delineating it, picturesqueness, passion, and knowledge of life." Of "Jane Eyre" the "Edinburgh Review" for January, 1850, says, "It is certain that for many years there had been no work of such power, piquancy, and originality. Its very faults were faults on the side of vigour, and its beauties were all original. The grand secret of its success, however,—as of all genuine and lasting success,—was its reality." This work was, however, severely criticised by the "Quarterly Review" for December, 1848. "Any one who has studied her writings," says Mrs. Gaskell, "must have noticed her singular felicity in the choice of words." In 1849 she published "Shirley, a Tale." Before this time the death of her sisters had filled her home with desolation. About the end of 1849 she visited London, and became acquainted with Thackeray and Harriet Martineau. Extreme, intense solitude had rendered her shy and somewhat taciturn in the presence of strangers. "Indigestion, nausea, headache, sleeplessness," says Mrs. Gaskell, "all combined to produce miserable depression of spirits." About the end of 1852 she finished "Villette," another novel, which "was received with one burst of acclamation." In December, 1852, a proposal of marriage was made to her by Arthur B. Nicholls, who had been curate of Haworth for many years, and had seen her almost daily during that period. She at first declined the offer because her father sternly disapproved the match; but she finally consented, and they were married in June, 1854. After a brief taste of domestic happiness, she died at Haworth in March, 1855.

"No one in her time," says "Blackwood" for May, 1855, "has grasped with such extraordinary force the scenes and circumstances through which her story moved, or thrown so strong an individual life into place and locality. Her passionate and fearless nature, her wild, warm heart, are transfused into the magic world she has created,—a world which no one can enter without yielding to the irresistible fascination of her personal influence."

See "Fraser's Magazine" for 1857; E. C. GASKELL, "Life of Charlotte Brontë," 2 vols., 1857.

Brontë, (EMILY,) "ELLIS BELL," a younger sister of the preceding, was born in Yorkshire about 1819. She was one of the authors of a volume entitled "Poems by Currer, Ellis, and Acton Bell," (1846.) She also published "Wuthering Heights," a novel, (1847,) the merit of which was variously estimated. Died in December, 1848.

See a biographical notice of Ellis and Acton Bell, prefixed to an edition of "Wuthering Heights," 1850.

Brontë, (PATRICK,) the father of Charlotte Brontë, was born in Ireland about 1774. He became curate of Haworth, in Yorkshire, in 1820. He wrote "Cottage Poems," (1811.) Died in 1861.

Bronzino, (ALESSANDRO.) See ALLORI.

Bronzino, bron-zee'no, (ANGELO,) an Italian painter, born at Florence in 1501. His "Descent of Christ into Hell" is considered his master-piece. Died in 1570.

See VASARI, "Lives of the Painters."

Brook, (BENJAMIN,) an English writer, born in 1775, published "The Lives of the Puritans," (3 vols., 1813.) Died about 1848.

Brooke, (CHARLOTTE,) an Irish authoress, a daughter of Henry Brooke, noticed below. She published, about 1788, "Reliques of Irish Poetry," translated from the Celtic. Died in 1793.

Brooke, (FRANCES,) an English authoress, wrote the "History of Julia Mandeville," and other novels, also "The Siege of Sinope," a tragedy, and several poems. Died in 1789.

Brooke, (GEORGE MERCER,) an officer in the United States army, served with distinction in 1814 and in the Mexican war, and attained the rank of major-general. Died in 1851.

Brooke, (HENRY,) a political and miscellaneous writer of considerable reputation in his time, was born at Rantavan, in Ireland, in 1706. Among his principal works are a poem entitled "Universal Beauty," the tragedies of "The Earl of Essex" and "Gustavus Vasa," and "The Fool of Quality," a novel, (1766.) Died in 1783.

See DR. JOHNSON's "Lives of the Poets."

Brooke, (JAMES,) an English politician, succeeded Wilkes as editor of "The North Briton." Died in 1807.

Brooke, (Sir JAMES,) a distinguished statesman, of English extraction, born in Bengal in 1803. He sailed in 1838 in his yacht, called the "Royalist," for Borneo,

where, as a reward for services rendered to the sultan of that country, he was appointed in 1841 Rajah and Governor of Sarâwak. He formed a code of laws for the natives, and was zealous in his efforts for the extirpation of piracy. On a subsequent visit to England he was made a K.C.B., and obtained the degree of D.C.L., (1847.) Died in England in June, 1868.

See "Private Letters of Sir James Brooke," edited by J. C. TEMPLER, 1853: "Foreign Quarterly Review" for April, 1846.

Brooke, (JOHN CHARLES,) an English topographer and antiquary, born in 1748, published "The Somerset Herald." Died in 1794.

Brooke, LORD. See GREVILLE, (FULKE.)

Brooke or **Broke,** brŏŏk, (Sir ROBERT,) an English magistrate and legal writer; died in 1558.

Brookes, brŏŏks, (JOSHUA,) a celebrated English anatomist and surgeon, born in 1761. The number of his pupils is said to have amounted to seven thousand; and he formed an anatomical museum of great value. Among his works is a "Treatise on Osteology." Died in 1833.

Brooks, brŏŏks, (Rev. CHARLES,) an American Unitarian divine, born at Medford, Massachusetts, in 1795. He was a member of the Peace Society, and a prominent advocate of the temperance reform from its commencement. He also contributed to the improvement of the public schools of New England and to the establishment of normal schools, which work was finally completed by Horace Mann. In 1839 he visited Europe for the second time, having previously been chosen professor of natural history in the University of New York. After spending four years on the continent, he returned to his professorship, which, however, on account of his failing eye-sight, he did not long retain. He wrote a treatise on "Peace, Labour, and Education in Europe," and other works. Mr. Brooks also published one volume of a work on Ornithology, (finely illustrated.)

See LIVINGSTON's "Portraits of Eminent Americans," 1854.

Brooks, (CHARLES SHIRLEY,) an English dramatist, born in 1815 or 1816. He produced dramas, entitled "The Creole" and "Honour and Riches," also several novels, among which is "Aspen Court," (1857.)

Brooks, (CHARLES T.,) an American Unitarian divine and poet, born in Salem, Massachusetts, in 1813. He graduated at Harvard, and in 1837 was settled as pastor in Newport, Rhode Island. He has published translations of Goethe's "Faust," and of the "Wilhelm Tell," and other poems of Schiller.

Brooks, (ERASTUS,) an American journalist, born at Portland, Maine, in 1815. He became editor of the "New York Express" about 1836, supported the Native American party in 1855 and 1856, and afterwards joined the Democratic party.

Brooks, (JAMES,) an American politician, a brother of the preceding, was born at Portland, Maine, in 1810. He became in 1836 associate editor of the "New York Express," and was elected a member of Congress in 1848. Since the rebellion of 1861 he has served for several terms in Congress, and has acted with the Democrats.

Brooks, (JAMES GORDON,) an American poet, born at Claverack, New York, in 1801, graduated at Union College in 1819. He removed in 1823 to New York, where he edited successively "The Minerva," "The Literary Gazette," and "The Athenæum." He married Mary E. Aikin, a poetess, in 1828. Died in 1841.

See GRISWOLD's "Poets and Poetry of America."

Brooks, (MARIA GOWEN,) called MARIA DEL OCCIDENTE by Southey, an American poetess, born at Medford, Massachusetts, about 1795. She was married at an early age to Mr. Brooks, a merchant of Boston, who died in 1823. She published in 1820 a volume entitled "Judith, Esther, and other Poems." About 1823 she removed to the island of Cuba. Her principal work is "Zophiel, or the Bride of Seven," (1825,) which was highly praised by Southey, who spoke of Mrs. Brooks as the "most impassioned and most imaginative of all poetesses." She visited Southey at Keswick in 1831. Died at Matanzas in 1845.

See GRISWOLD, "Female Poets of America;" "London Quarterly Review" for September, 1840.

ā, ē, ī, ō, ū, ȳ, *long;* à, è, ò, same, less prolonged; ă, ĕ, ĭ, ŏ, ŭ, ў, *short;* a, e, i, o, *obscure;* fär, fàll, fåt; mět; nŏt; gŏŏd; mōŏn;

Brooks, (NATHAN COVINGTON,) an American scholar and poet, born in Cecil county, Maryland, in 1809. In 1848 he became president of the Baltimore Female College, in which position he has acquired a high reputation as a teacher. He has published a "History of the Mexican War," which is regarded as one of the best that has appeared on the subject, and a number of poems, among which we may cite "Shelley's Obsequies," and "The Fall of Superstition."

See LIVINGSTON's "Portraits of Eminent Americans," 1854.

Brooks, (PETER CHARDON,) a distinguished merchant of Boston, born at Medford in 1767. He was active in promoting benevolent enterprises. Died in 1849. His three daughters were married to Hon. Edward Everett, Charles Francis Adams, and the Rev. N. L. Frothingham, D.D.

See EDWARD EVERETT, "Life of P. C. Brooks," in HUNT's "American Merchants."

Brooks, (Rev. PHILLIPS,) a popular American clergyman, born in Boston, December 13, 1835. He graduated at Harvard in 1855, and studied for the ministry in the Episcopal Theological Seminary at Alexandria, Virginia. Having been ordained in 1859, he became pastor of the Church of the Advent, in Philadelphia, and in 1862 of the Church of the Holy Trinity, which position he still holds, (1869.)

Brooks, (PRESTON S.,) an American politician, born in Edgefield district, South Carolina, in 1819. He was elected a member of Congress in 1853 and in 1855. In May, 1856, he acquired notoriety by a personal outrage on Charles Sumner in the chamber of the Senate of the United States. He was censured by the House of Representatives, and resigned his seat, but was re-elected. He died in Washington in January, 1857.

Brooks, (WILLIAM T. H.,) an American general, born in Ohio about 1815, graduated at West Point in 1841. He became a captain in 1851, and a brigadier-general of volunteers about September, 1861. He commanded a division at Chancellorsville in May, 1863, and served in the army of the Potomac at Cold Harbour and Petersburg, June–July, 1864.

Broome, (WILLIAM,) an English poet and divine, who assisted Pope in translating the "Odyssey." Having complained that his services were inadequately paid by Pope, the latter gave him a place in the "Dunciad." Broome's merits as a translator are highly commended by Dr. Johnson. Died in 1745.

See DR. JOHNSON's "Lives of the Poets."

Brosamer, bROs'ä-mer, or **Bros'hamer,** (HANS,) a German painter and engraver, born about 1506, resided at Fulda. Died about 1560.

Brosböll, bROs'böl, (KARL,) a Danish novelist and dramatist, born in Jutland in 1820. Among his works is "Madsalune," (1841.)

Broschi. See FARINELLI.

Broshamer, (HANS.) See BROSAMER.

Brossard, de, deh bRo'sÄR', (SÉBASTIEN,) an eminent French musician, died in 1730. His musical library was one of the most valuable ever formed.

Brosse, bROSS, physician to Louis XIII., and founder of the "Jardin Royal," (or "Royal Garden,") otherwise called the "Jardin des Plantes," of Paris. Died in 1641.

Brosses, de, deh bROSS, (CHARLES,) a French antiquary, born at Dijon in 1709. He was a member of the Academy of Inscriptions, and published, among other works, a "History of Voyages to Australia," ("Terres australes," 2 vols., 1756,) and a "History of the Seventh Century of the Roman Republic," (3 vols., 1777.) He was the first who used the terms Polynesia and Australasia. Died in 1777.

See VILLEMAIN, "Tableau de la Littérature au dix-huitième Siècle."

Brosset, bRo'sÄ', (MARIE FÉLICITÉ,) a French Orientalist, born in Paris in 1802. He removed to Saint Petersburg, where he became keeper of the great public library, (1842.) He published several works on the history and language of Georgia.

Brossette, bRo'sĕt',(CLAUDE,) a French advocate and *littérateur,* born at Lyons in 1671; died in 1743.

Brotero, bRo-tā'ro, (FELIX DE AVELLAR,) an eminent Portuguese botanist, born near Lisbon in 1744, published

"Phytographia Lusitanica," (1827.) He was professor of botany at Lisbon for many years. Died in 1828.

See GUSMÃO, "Notice of the Life of F. A. Brotero," London, 1845.

Brothers, brŭth'erz, (RICHARD,) an English fanatic, who professed to be the prophet of a new religion and that he was sent to restore the Hebrews to the land of Canaan. He made numerous predictions relative to European affairs, and published several works of a blasphemous character. Died about 1824.

Brotier, bro'te-à', (GABRIEL,) a French scholar, born at Tannay in 1723, was librarian in the College of Louis le Grand. He published a valuable edition of Tacitus, and wrote a "Treatise on Roman, Greek, and Hebrew Coins compared with the Coins of France," (1760.) Died in 1789.

Brouart, bROo'ö', (JEAN,) [Lat. JOHAN'NES BREVO'TIUS,] a physician and chemist of merit, lived in the Low Countries about 1590.

See HOEFER, "Histoire de la Chimie."

Brouckère, de, deh bROo'kaiR', (CHARLES MARIE JOSEPH Ghislain—gĕs'lÄN',) a Belgian politician and political economist, born at Bruges in 1796, was minister of war from August, 1831, to March, 1832. He published "Principles of Political Economy," (1851.)

Brouckère, de, (HENRI MARIE JOSEPH GHISLAIN,) a brother of the preceding, was born at Bruges in 1801. He became a leader of the Liberal party, and was appointed minister of state in 1847. In October, 1852, he was directed to organize a new ministry, of which he became president. He resigned in March, 1855.

Broue, de la, deh lä bROo, (PIERRE,) a French theologian, born at Toulouse in 1643, became Bishop of Mirepoix. Died in 1720.

Brougham, broo'am or broo'm, (HENRY,) LORD, a popular British orator, statesman, and author, distinguished for his great learning and versatility, was born in Edinburgh on the 19th of September, 1779. His father was Henry Brougham, Esq., of Brougham Hall, Westmoreland, and his mother was Eleanor Syme, a niece of Dr. Robertson the historian. He began his classical studies in the High School of Edinburgh, and about the age of fifteen entered the university of that city, where Dugald Stewart and Dr. Black were among his teachers. His favourite studies were the mathematics and physical sciences. At the age of seventeen, he wrote a paper on the Refraction and Reflection of Light, which was printed in the "Transactions" of the Royal Society.

Having chosen the profession of the law, he became a member of the Edinburgh Society of Advocates about 1800. In 1802 he united with Francis Jeffrey and Sydney Smith to found the "Edinburgh Review," to which he contributed many able articles during a period of twenty-five years, (1803–28.) He published in 1803 an "Enquiry into the Colonial Policy of the European Powers," (2 vols.)

Having removed to London in 1807 or 1808, he was called to the bar at Lincoln's Inn in the latter year, and chose the courts of common law and the Northern circuit. He had attained a high reputation as a forensic orator, when he was elected a member of Parliament for Camelford by the Whigs in 1810. As a parliamentary debater he soon occupied the first rank, and was pre-eminent in passionate vehemence and invective. For many years he found no equal in the House of Commons except Canning, who was his political adversary. Brougham procured the passage of an address to the king for the suppression of the slave-trade in 1810. He lost his election in 1812, and remained out of Parliament four years. He was returned in 1816 for Winchelsea, which he represented until 1830. In 1819 he married a daughter of Thomas Eden of Wimbledon, a brother of Lord Auckland.

He denounced the Holy Alliance, and the foreign policy of the Tory ministry, on several occasions, and distinguished himself as the advocate of popular education and political reform. His popularity was greatly increased by his forensic arguments in 1821, before the House of Lords and Privy Council, in defence of Queen Caroline, who had appointed him her attorney-general. He supported the measures of Canning after the latter became prime minister in 1827, although he had once vehemently assailed the integrity of Canning's public conduct.

In 1825 he published "Practical Observations on the Education of the People," which was often reprinted, and produced a powerful impression on the public mind. He was chosen lord rector of Glasgow University in 1825, when Sir Walter Scott was his competitor. He rendered an important service to the community as one of the founders of the Society for the Diffusion of Useful Knowledge, (1827,) of which he was the first chairman. His treatise "On the Objects, Advantages, and Pleasures of Science" was the first work published by this society. "There is no second man in the kingdom who could with such admirable art have analyzed, as it were, his mental wealth, and sent it forth in a form at once the simplest, the most convenient, and the most ready of access that it was possible to contrive." ("London Monthly Review.")

In 1830 he was returned to Parliament for Yorkshire, after a contest in which, it is said, he addressed eight different electoral meetings in one day. He avowed himself, at the opening of the session, a champion of Parliamentary reform, which was then the principal issue before the country. In November, 1830, he became lord chancellor of England in the new ministry formed by Earl Grey, and received the title of Baron Brougham and Vaux. Among his most celebrated oratorical efforts was a speech for the Reform Bill in the House of Lords, in October, 1831. He manifested prodigious activity in the performance of his duties as chancellor and legislator. He promoted the abolition of slavery in the colonies, and reforms in municipal jurisprudence. On the dissolution of the Whig ministry in November, 1834, he retired from office, and ceased to act with the Whig party. His political course from that time was independent of party: he supported, however, several liberal measures, and devoted himself especially to the cause of law-reform. In 1843 he published "Letters on Law-Reform, addressed to Sir James Graham." He denounced the Anti-Corn-Law League, but voted for the repeal of the corn-laws in 1846.

Lord Brougham was chosen a foreign associate of the Institute of France (class of moral and political sciences) in 1833. He hailed with enthusiasm, or at least cordial favour, the French revolution of 1848, soon after which he signified his desire to become naturalized as a French citizen, but was officially informed that he could not be received as such unless he ceased to be an English peer. Among his principal works are "Sketches of Statesmen of the Time of George III.," (3 vols., 1839–43,) "Political Philosophy," (3 vols., 1840–44,) "Speeches at the Bar and in Parliament," (4 vols., 1843,) "Lives of the Men of Letters and Science who flourished in the Time of George III.," (2 vols., 1845–46,) and "Contributions to the Edinburgh Review: Political, Historical, and Miscellaneous," (3 vols., 1857.) A complete edition of his works was published, under the superintendence of the author, in ten volumes, 1857. It is stated as a fact without precedent in the history of English chancellors that he retired from the court of chancery without leaving a single case, which had been heard, in arrear for judgment. Died at his rural retreat at Cannes, in France, on the 9th of May, 1868.

See "London Quarterly Review" for December, 1818, and April, 1859; "Edinburgh Review" for January, 1837, and April, 1858; "British Quarterly" for July, 1860.

Brougham, broo'ạm, (JOHN,) a popular Irish comedian, born in Dublin in 1810. He came to the United States about 1842, and performed in New York. He produced several comedies and other works.

Broughton, brŏw'tọn, (ARTHUR,) M.D., an English botanist, published several botanical works, (1782–94.)

Broughton, (HUGH,) an English theological writer and Hebrew scholar, born at Oldbury in 1549, was a protégé of the celebrated Bernard Gilpin. Died in 1612.

See "Biographia Britannica."

Broughton, LORD. See HOBHOUSE, (JOHN CAM.)

Broughton, (RICHARD,) an English theologian, published an "Ecclesiastical History of Great Britain from the Nativity to the Conversion of the Saxons." Died in 1634.

Broughton, (THOMAS,) an English divine, born in London in 1704, published "Christianity distinct from the Religion of Nature," and was a contributor to the "Biographia Britannica." Died in 1774.

Broughton, (WILLIAM GRANT,) an English divine, born at Canterbury in 1789, became in 1835 first Bishop of Australia. He died on the voyage home to England in 1853.

Broughton, (WILLIAM ROBERT,) an English navigator, born in Gloucestershire in 1763. He accompanied in 1790 the expedition of Vancouver, who gave the name of Broughton's Archipelago to some islands in the Pacific, in about 50 degrees north latitude. He published a "Voyage of Discovery to the North Pacific Ocean," (1804,) which see. Died in 1822.

Brouncker or **Brounker,** brŭnk'er, (?) (WILLIAM,) VISCOUNT, a distinguished mathematician, born in Ireland in 1620. He became first president of the Royal Society in 1662, and was subsequently appointed lord of the admiralty and chancellor of the queen. He wrote several scientific treatises, and originated some valuable discoveries in mathematics. Died in 1684.

See "Biographia Britannica."

Broussais, broo'să', (FRANÇOIS JOSEPH VICTOR,) a distinguished French physician and medical writer, born at Saint-Malo in 1772, was professor of pathology in the Faculty of Paris. He was a member of the Institute, and the teacher of a system or theory of medicine called the Physiological. Died in 1838.

See "Essai critique sur Broussais," Paris, 1839; MONTÈGRE, "Notice sur la Vie, les Travaux et les Opinions de Broussais," 1839; J. B. PRIOU, "Notice historique sur F. J. V. Broussais," 1841.

Broussier, broo'se-à', (JEAN BAPTISTE,) COUNT, a French general, born near Bar-le-Duc in 1766. As general of brigade, he contributed to the victory at Marengo in 1800. He became a general of division in 1805, and rendered important services in Italy in 1809. Died in 1814.

See "Victoires et Conquêtes des Français."

Brousson, broo'sôn', (CLAUDE,) a French Protestant theologian and religious writer, born at Nimes in 1647. He was executed in 1698, on a charge of treason.

See LA BEAUMELLE, "Lettres à Voltaire;" A. BORREL, "Biographie de C. Brousson," 1852: "Life of C. Brousson," London, 1853.

Broussonnet, broo'so'nà', (PIERRE AUGUSTE,) a French physician and naturalist, born at Montpellier in 1761. He published "Ichthyologia," and "Memoirs towards the History of the Respiration of Fishes." He was professor of botany at Montpellier, and a member of the Academy of Sciences. Died in 1807.

See CUVIER, "Éloge de Broussonnet," 1808; A. P. DECANDOLLE, "Éloge de Broussonnet," 1809.

Brouwer. See BRAUWER.

Browall, bro'wăl, [Lat. BROWAL'LIUS,] (JOHAN,) a Swedish theologian, naturalist, and scientific writer, born at Westrås in 1707. He became professor of natural history at Åbo in 1737, and was subsequently Bishop of that city. Linnæus named in his honour the genus Browallia. Died in 1755.

See GEZELIUS, "Biographiskt-Lexicon."

Brower. See BRAUWER.

Brown. See BROWNE.

Brown, (AARON VAIL,) an American lawyer, born in Brunswick county, Virginia, in 1795, removed to Nashville, Tennessee. He was a member of Congress from 1839 to 1845, was elected Governor of Tennessee in 1845, and appointed postmaster-general of the United States in 1857. Died in 1859.

Brown, (ALBERT G.,) an American Senator, born in Chester district, South Carolina, in 1813. He was elected Governor of Mississippi in 1843 and in 1845, was a member of the national House of Representatives from 1847 to 1853, and was chosen a Senator of the United States in the latter year. He was re-elected about 1858, and retired from the Senate, as a secessionist, in 1861.

Brown, (ALEXANDER,) an English botanist and surgeon, lived about 1670. The genus Brownia was named in his honour.

Brown, (ALEXANDER,) the founder of a family of eminent merchants, was born in Antrim county, Ireland, in 1764. He settled in Baltimore about 1800. Died in 1834. He was the father of William George, John A., and James Brown.

Brown, (ANTOINETTE.) See BLACKWELL.

Brown, (CATHERINE,) a Cherokee convert to Christianity, born in Alabama in 1800; died in 1823.

Brown, (CHADD,) an American Baptist divine, who fled from the persecutions of Massachusetts in 1636 to Providence, Rhode Island. For more than two centuries his descendants have been among the most distinguished citizens of that State. Died in 1665.

Brown, (CHARLES BROCKDEN,) an eminent American novelist, born in Philadelphia in January, 1771. His ancestors were Quakers, who came to Philadelphia with William Penn. He was liberally educated, and from his early years he manifested a decided inclination for literary pursuits. He published "Wieland, or the Transformation," (1798,) "Ormond, or the Secret Witness," (1799,) and "Arthur Mervyn," (1800.) In the last-named work he gives a graphic account of the scenes exhibited during the prevalence of the yellow fever in Philadelphia in 1793. He was editor of the "Monthly Magazine and American Review," (1799–1800.) He also founded, in 1803 or 1805, "The Literary Magazine and American Register," which he edited about five years. Among his other works are "Clara Howard," (1801,) and "Jane Talbot," (1804.) He married a Miss Linn, of New York, in 1804. He died of consumption in February, 1810, leaving one son. Referring to his characteristics as a writer, Mr. Prescott observes, "He has been said to have formed himself on Godwin, and has certainly in some respects adopted his mode of operation, studying character with a philosophic rather than a poetic eye. But there is no servile imitation in all this. He has borrowed the same torch, indeed, to read the page of human nature, but the lesson he derives from it is totally different. His peculiar merits appeal to a higher order of criticism than is to be found in ordinary and superficial readers. Like the productions of Coleridge or Wordsworth, they seem to rely on deeper sensibilities than most men possess, and tax the reasoning powers more severely than is agreeable to readers who resort to works of fiction only as an epicurean indulgence."

See WILLIAM H. PRESCOTT's "Life of C. Brockden Brown," in SPARKS's "American Biography," vol. i., reprinted in PRESCOTT's "Miscellanies," 1855; W. DUNLAP's "Life of Brown," prefixed to an edition of his works, 1827; GRISWOLD's "Prose Writers of America."

Brown, (DAVID,) an English clergyman, went to Calcutta as chaplain to the East India Company, and became provost of the College of Fort William in 1800. Died in India in 1812.

Brown, (DAVID,) a Cherokee, a brother of Catherine, noticed above, was converted by missionaries, who employed him as an interpreter and teacher. Died in 1829.

Brown, (DAVID PAUL,) an American lawyer, born in Philadelphia in 1795, gained distinction as a pleader in criminal cases. He published "The Forum, or Forty Years' Full Practice at the Philadelphia Bar," (2 vols., 1856.)

Brown, (FORD MADOX,) an English painter, born at Calais in 1821. Among his works are "King Lear," "Chaucer at the Court of Edward III.," and "The Last of England."

See "Fraser's Magazine" for May, 1865.

Brown, (FRANCES,) a blind Irish poetess, born at Stranorlar, in Donegal, about 1816. She published "The Star of Atteghei," and other poems, (1844,) which were received with favour.

Brown, (Sir GEORGE,) a Scottish general, born near Elgin in 1790, served in the Peninsular war, and in the American campaign of 1814. He became lieutenant-general in 1851, and distinguished himself in the Crimean war at Alma, Inkerman, and Sebastopol. He was made a K.C.B. in 1855.

Brown, (GEORGE L.,) an American landscape-painter, born in Boston about 1820. He has executed Italian and American landscapes of great merit: among the latter we may name his "Crown of New England," a view in the White Mountains.

See TUCKERMAN, "Book of the Artists."

Brown, (GOOLD,) an American teacher and grammarian, died at Lynn, Massachusetts, in 1857, aged sixty-six years. His principal works are the "Institutes of English Grammar," (1823,) which obtained an immense circulation, and the "Grammar of English Grammars," (1850; 2d edition, 8vo, 1857, pp. 1070,) probably the most extensive treatise of the kind that has hitherto been published.

Brown, (HARVEY,) an American officer, born at Rahway, New Jersey, about 1795, graduated at West Point in 1818. He served in the Mexican war, (1846-47,) became a colonel of the regular army in April or May, 1861, and conducted a successful expedition for the relief of Fort Pickens, of which he had command from April 16, 1861, to February, 1862.

Brown, (HENRY KIRK,) an American sculptor, born in Leyden, Massachusetts, in 1814. He studied in Italy, and, after his return, produced a bronze statue, said to be the first ever executed in America. One of his most noted works is the colossal equestrian statue of Washington in Union Square, New York. He has also executed "The Four Seasons," "Pleiades," and other works in marble.

See TUCKERMAN, "Book of the Artists."

Brown, (JACOB,) an American general, born in Bucks county, Pennsylvania, in 1775. In 1799 he settled in the northern part of New York. He defended Ogdensburg in 1812, and Sackett's Harbour in 1813. Having obtained the rank of major-general, he commanded an army which invaded Canada in the spring of 1814. He gained victories at Chippewa and Niagara Falls in July, 1814. In 1821 he became commander-in-chief of the army of the United States. Died in 1828.

See "Encyclopædia Americana," (Supplement.)

Brown, (JAMES,) an Englishman, born in 1709, originated, it is said, "The Directory, or List of Principal Traders in London," (1782.) Died in 1787.

Brown, (JAMES,) born in Virginia in 1766, was elected a Senator of the United States from Louisiana in 1813, and re-elected in 1819. He was minister to France from 1823 to 1829. Died in 1835.

Brown, (JAMES,) an American publisher, born in Acton, Massachusetts, in 1800, became a partner of the firm of Little, Brown & Co., Boston. Died in 1855.

Brown, (JOHN,) D.D., an eminent English clergyman and miscellaneous writer, born in 1715; died, by suicide, in 1766. Besides other works, he wrote "Barbarossa," a tragedy, and an "Estimate of the Manners and Principles of the Times." The latter work especially enjoyed an extraordinary popularity.

Brown, (JOHN,) a Scottish linguist and minister, born in Perthshire in 1720 or 1722, preached at Haddington. He published a "Dictionary of the Bible," (1769,) and "The Self-Interpreting Bible," (2 vols., 1791.) Died in 1787.

Brown, (JOHN,) M.D., the author of the Brunonian system of medicine, was born at Dunse, in Berwickshire, Scotland, in 1735. He was a pupil of Dr. Cullen, and afterwards became his enemy. According to some authorities, a desire for revenge induced him to form a new system of medicine, which should supplant that of Cullen, and which he propounded in his "Elementa Medicinæ," (1780.) This work was translated into many languages. His system was more popular in Germany than in Great Britain. He divided diseases into two classes, the sthenic and the asthenic, the former of which resulted from excess and the latter from deficiency of exciting power. He used alcohol as a remedy for one set of diseases, and opium for the other. Died poor, in London, in 1788.

See CHAMBERS, "Biographical Dictionary of Eminent Scotsmen."

Brown, (JOHN,) an American merchant, brother of Joseph, Moses, and Nicholas Brown, was born in Providence, Rhode Island, in 1736. He was a zealous promoter of all benevolent and educational objects, and one of the most liberal benefactors of Brown University. From 1799 to 1801 he was a representative in Congress. Died at Providence in 1803.

Brown, (JOHN,) an American officer, born in Berkshire county, Massachusetts, in 1744. He served with distinction in the expedition against Quebec in 1775, and was raised to the rank of lieutenant-colonel in 1776. He was killed in a fight with Indians in October, 1780.

Brown, (JOHN,) a Scottish painter and writer upon art, born at Edinburgh in 1752, wrote "Letters on the Poetry and Music of the Italian Opera." Died in 1787.

Brown, (JOHN,) an eminent Scottish divine, born in 1784, was a grandson of the author of the "Self-Interpreting Bible." He studied at the University of Edinburgh, and in 1822 became pastor of the Rose Street Church in that city. He was appointed in 1834 professor of exegetical theology to the United Secession Church. His principal works are "An Exposition of our Lord's Intercessory Prayer," (1850,) "Discourses and Sayings of our Lord Jesus Christ," and a commentary "On the Epistle to the Galatians." Died in 1858.

See REV. ROBERT STEEL, "Burning and Shining Lights," 1864.

Brown, (JOHN,) M.D., son of the preceding, a Scottish writer, and Fellow of the Royal College of Physicians at Edinburgh, born about 1830. He published in 1858 an interesting and popular work entitled "Horæ Subsecivæ." He has also written "Pet Marjorie : a Story of Child-Life Fifty Years ago."

See "Fraser's Magazine" for April, 1859.

Brown, (JOHN,) of Ossawatomie, a distinguished champion of liberty, born at Torrington, Connecticut, in May, 1800. His father removed to Ohio in 1805. From the age of fifteen to twenty he worked at the trade of tanner and currier. He married in 1820 Dianthe Lusk. According to Redpath, he conceived in 1839 the idea of becoming a liberator of the Southern slaves. He was a devout member of the Congregational Church, and a man of strict moral character. He possessed unflinching courage and intense earnestness. In 1846 he removed to Springfield, Massachusetts, where he was employed as a dealer in wool. He afterwards visited Europe on business. He emigrated in 1855 to Kansas, where he took an active part in the contest with the pro-slavery party. In August, 1856, he gained some advantages at Ossawatomie over a band of Missourians who had invaded Kansas and were ten times more numerous than his own company. In May, 1859, he called a secret convention of the friends of freedom, which met at Chatham in Canada, organized an invasion of Virginia for the purpose of liberating the slaves, and adopted a constitution. In the following July he rented a farm-house about six miles from Harper's Ferry, and collected there a supply of pikes, guns, etc. On the night of October 16, 1859, aided by about twenty men, he surprised Harper's Ferry, seized the arsenal and armory, and took over forty prisoners. About noon on the 17th the party of Brown was attacked by the Virginian militia. After two of his sons and nearly all of his men had been killed, and he himself had been wounded in several places, he was captured. "Enemies and friends," says Redpath, "were equally amazed at the carriage and sayings of the wounded warrior." He was tried in November, and hung at Charlestown, Virginia, on the 2d of December, 1859. He met his death with serene composure. He was twice married, and had twenty children.

See REDPATH, "Life of Captain John Brown," 1860; "Life and Letters of Captain John Brown," edited by R. D. WEBB, London, 1861; GREELEY, "American Conflict," vol. i.

Brown, (JOHN NEWTON,) a Baptist clergyman and writer, born at New London, Connecticut, in 1803. He published in 1835 the "Encyclopædia of Religious Knowledge," which was received with favour. It is stated that he has been engaged for many years on a history of the Church.

Brown, (JOHN W.,) an American author, born at Schenectady in 1814, was an Episcopal minister. He produced "Christmas-Bells, a Tale of Holy Tide, and other poems." Died in 1849.

Brown, (LANCELOT,) an English landscape-gardener, called CAPABILITY BROWN, was born in Northumberland in 1715. He was at the head of his profession in England. Died in 1773.

Brown, (MATTHEW,) an English historical and portrait painter. Died in 1831.

Brown, (MOSES,) an English poet, born in 1703, was vicar of Olney. He wrote "Percy Lodge," (1756,) and other poems. Died in 1787.

Brown, (MOSES,) an American merchant, born at Providence, Rhode Island, in 1738, was an uncle of Nicholas, noticed below. He joined the Society of Friends in 1773. He was a liberal patron of the Friends' Boarding-School at Providence. Died in 1836.

Brown, (MOSES,) an American merchant, born at Newburyport, Massachusetts, in 1742, was a benefactor of Andover Theological Seminary. He also gave largely to several benevolent institutions. Died in 1827.

Brown, (NICHOLAS,) a distinguished American merchant, and munificent patron of Brown University, (formerly Rhode Island College,) born at Providence in 1760. His donations to the institution at different times amounted in the aggregate to not less than $100,000. He also gave freely to missionary and other charitable objects, and in his will made a bequest of $30,000 towards the erection of a Retreat for the Insane. He died October 27, 1841. For fuller particulars, see Hunt's "Lives of American Merchants."

Brown, (OBADIAH,) a manufacturer, born at Providence, Rhode Island, in 1771. He was a member of the firm of Almy, Brown & Slater, cotton-spinners. He gave large sums for various charitable purposes. Died in 1822.

Brown or Browne, (ROBERT,) an English theologian, the founder of the sect called Brownists and afterwards Independents. He taught that all the members of a church are equal, and that the minister should be elected by the members of his congregation. Died in 1630, aged about eighty. He differed from the Church of England about discipline rather than doctrines.

See "Biographia Britannica."

Brown, (ROBERT,) a Scottish agriculturist, born at East Linton about 1770, published an esteemed work "On Rural Affairs," (2 vols., 1811.) Died in 1831.

Brown, (ROBERT,) M.D., an excellent British botanist, born at Montrose in 1773, was educated at Aberdeen and Edinburgh. He was attached as botanist to the expedition sent out in 1801 under Captain Flinders to explore the coast of Australia. He returned in 1805 with a collection of four thousand species of plants from Australia, and became librarian to Sir Joseph Banks. In 1810 he published "Prodromus Floræ Novæ Hollandiæ." As an appendix to Flinders's "Narrative," Dr. Brown also published "General Remarks, Geographical and Systematical, on the Botany of Terra Australis," a work of great merit. He adopted and illustrated in his writings the natural method of Jussieu. He contributed many able treatises to the "Transactions" of the Linnæan Society, and made important discoveries in vegetable physiology, especially in the fecundation of plants. In 1833 he was elected one of the eight foreign associates of the French Academy of Sciences. His reputation was perhaps higher on the continent than in Great Britain; and Humboldt estimated him as the first of botanists, (*botanicorum facile princeps*.) Died in London in 1858.

See article by Dr. HOEFER in the "Nouvelle Biographie Générale."

Brown, (SAMUEL,) M.D., a Scottish poet and chemical theorist, born at Haddington in 1817, was a grandson of Rev. John Brown, (1722–87.) His talents and attainments are said to have been extraordinary. He devoted much time to the subject of isomerism, and laboured to prove that chemical substances which are usually considered simple can be transmuted into each other. In 1850 he produced "The Tragedy of Galileo." Died in 1856. Two volumes of his Essays and Lectures were published in 1858.

Brown, (Sir SAMUEL,) a civil engineer, born in London in 1776, served in the royal navy, and gained the rank of captain. He acquired distinction by improvements in suspension bridges. Died in 1852.

Brown, (TARLTON,) an American officer, born in Barnwell district, South Carolina, in 1754, served as captain in the Revolutionary war. Died in 1846.

Brown, (THOMAS,) a satirical and facetious English poet, commonly called TOM BROWN, born in 1663, was addicted to buffoonery and immoral practices. Died in 1704.

See CIBBER, "Lives of the English Poets," etc.

Brown, (THOMAS,) one of the most distinguished of the Scottish metaphysicians, was born at Kirkmabreck, near Dumfries, in 1778. He manifested his fondness for metaphysical speculation before he was fifteen years of age. Not long after he attended the lectures of Dugald Stewart in Edinburgh, and attracted the attention of that philosopher by the acuteness of his remarks on a certain theory propounded in one of his lectures. This was the beginning of a life-long friendship between these two eminent men. He published, in 1798, "Observations on Darwin's Zoonomia," which evinced remarkable precocity of intellect and was much admired. Mackintosh calls the "Observations" the "perhaps unmatched work of a boy in the eighteenth year of his age."

About 1803 he took his degree as doctor of medicine. He resigned his practice in 1810, and was appointed colleague of Dugald Stewart in the chair of moral philosophy in the University of Edinburgh. He obtained great popularity as a lecturer. His lectures were published under the title of "Lectures on the Philosophy of the Human Mind," (4 vols., 1820.) He wrote a number of poems, one of which is entitled "The Paradise of Coquettes," (1814.) His principal work is "Observations on the Relation of Cause and Effect," (3d edition, enlarged, 1818.) "His first tract on causation," says Sir J. Mackintosh, "appeared to me the finest model of discussion in mental philosophy since Berkeley and Hume." Died in 1820.

Dr. Brown possessed, besides an acute and powerful intellect, a poetic temperament, with a lively imagination and refined sensibilities. "His mind," says Mackintosh, "soared and roamed through every region of philosophy and poetry; but his untravelled heart clung to the hearth of his father and to the children who shared it with him. . . . His heart sought little abroad, but contentedly dwelt in his family and in his study. He was one of those men of genius who repaid the tender care of a mother by rocking the cradle of her reposing age." Respecting the style of Dr. Brown, the same eminent critic observes, "His prose is brilliant to excess; it must not be denied that its beauty is sometimes womanly; that it too often melts down precision into elegance; that it buries the main idea under a load of illustration. . . . It is darkened by excessive brightness; it loses ease and liveliness by over-dress; and, in the midst of its luscious sweetness, we wish for the striking and homely illustrations of Tucker, and for the pithy and sinewy sense of Paley, either of whom, by a single short metaphor from a familiar, perhaps a low, object, could at one blow set the two worlds of reason and fancy in movement."

See DR. WELSH's "Account of the Life and Writings of Thomas Brown," 1825; MACKINTOSH's "View of the Progress of Ethical Philosophy;" ALLIBONE's "Dictionary of Authors."

Brown, (WILLIAM,) an English botanist, born in 1628, published "Catalogus Horti Oxoniensis." Died in 1678.

Brown, (WILLIAM,) an eminent merchant and banker, born at Ballymena, Ireland, in 1784, settled in Liverpool. He was senior partner of the firm of Brown, Shipley & Co., and represented South Lancashire in Parliament in 1845. He gave £30,000 or more for a public library in Liverpool. Died in 1864.

Brown or **Browne,** (WILLIAM LAURENCE,) a theologian, born at Utrecht in 1755, removed to Scotland in 1795, and became professor of divinity at Aberdeen in that year. He wrote an "Essay on the Folly of Skepticism," (1788,) and an "Essay on the Existence of a Supreme Creator," (1816.) The latter gained a prize of £125. Died in 1830.

See CHAMBERS, "Biographical Dictionary of Eminent Scotsmen;" "Edinburgh Review" for April, 1804.

Browne, (ANDREW,) a Scottish physician and medical writer, lived about 1650–95.

Browne, (EDWARD,) an English writer, born in 1642, was physician to Charles II. He translated some of Plutarch's works, and wrote a book of travels. Died in 1708.

Browne, (GEORGE,) became Archbishop of Dublin in 1535. He promoted the Reformation. Died about 1558.

Browne, (GEORGE,) an Irish general, born in 1698, entered the Russian service and fought against the Poles,

French, and Turks. He was created a field-marshal and Governor of Livonia by Peter III. Died in 1792.

See "Histoire de la Vie de Georges Browne," 1794.

Browne, (ISAAC HAWKINS,) an English poet, born at Burton-upon-Trent in 1706, studied law, and became a member of Parliament. He wrote poems "On Design and Beauty," and "On the Immortality of the Soul," ("De Animæ Immortalitate," 1754.) Died in 1760.

Browne, (JOHN,) an English surgeon and medical writer, born in 1642, was surgeon-in-ordinary to Charles II. Died about 1700.

Browne, (JOHN ROSS,) an American traveller and writer. He published in 1846 "Etchings of a Whaling Cruise, with Notes of a Sojourn on the Island of Zanzibar." After a visit to Palestine, he produced a humorous account of his adventures, entitled "Yusef, or the Journey of a Frangi: a Crusade in the East." He was appointed minister to China in 1868.

Browne, (JOSEPH,) an English physician, born about 1650, published a work entitled "Antidotaria," and wrote against the doctrine of the circulation of the blood.

Browne, (JOSEPH,) D.D., an English scholar, born in Cumberland in 1700, was provost of Queen's College, Oxford. Died in 1767.

Browne, (MARY ANN,) an English poetess, born in Berkshire in 1812. She produced "Ada," (1828,) "The Coronal," (1833,) "Ignatia," (1838,) and other poems. In 1842 she was married to James Gray. Died in 1846.

Browne, brōwn, (MAXIMILIAN ULYSSES,) a distinguished general in the Austrian service, born at Bâle in 1705, was a relative of the field-marshal George Browne. He fought in the Silesian war against Frederick the Great, and commanded the right wing at the battle of Mollwitz in 1741. In 1754 he was made a field-marshal. He was mortally wounded at the battle of Prague in 1757. Frederick the Great was accustomed to call Marshal Browne his teacher in the art of war.

See ARCHENHOLZ, "History of the Seven Years' War."

Browne, (PATRICK,) M.D., born in Mayo county, Ireland, about 1720, published a "Civil and Natural History of Jamaica," (1756.) Died in 1790.

Browne, (PETER,) Bishop of Cork, wrote several works on theology. Died in 1735.

Browne, (ROBERT.) See BROWN.

Browne, (SIMON,) an English Dissenting minister, born in Somersetshire about 1680, preached in London. He wrote against Tindal a "Defence of the Religion of Nature and the Christian Revelation," (1732.) Died in 1732.

Browne, (THOMAS,) a learned English theologian, born in Middlesex in 1604, was chaplain to Charles I. Died in 1673.

Browne, (Sir THOMAS,) an eminent English physician, philosopher, and writer, born in London in 1605. He settled in 1636 at Norwich, where he practised medicine for many years, and married Dorothy Mileham about 1640. In 1642 he published anonymously his "Religio Medici," which was very successful and has often been reprinted and translated. "A superior genius," says Hallam, "was exhibited in Sir Thomas Browne. His mind was fertile and ingenious, his analogies original and brilliant, and his learning so much out of the beaten path that it gives a peculiar and uncommon air to all his writings." Among his principal works is "Pseudodoxia Epidemica, or Inquiries into Vulgar and Common Errors," (1646.) He also wrote a "Treatise on Christian Morals," (1716,) which is highly esteemed. In 1671 he was knighted by Charles II. He died at Norwich, on his seventy-seventh birthday, 1682.

See DR. SAMUEL JOHNSON, "Life of Sir Thomas Browne;" HAZLITT, "Age of Elizabeth:" "Retrospective Review," vol. i.; NICÉRON, "Mémoires;" WOOD, "Athenæ Oxonienses."

Browne, (WILLIAM,) an English poet, born at Tavistock in 1590. He wrote pastoral poems, (1613–16,) which had a temporary popularity. Died about 1645.

See "Retrospective Review," vol. ii., 1820.

Browne, (Sir WILLIAM,) an English physician and writer, born in Norfolk in 1692; died in 1774.

Browne, (WILLIAM GEORGE,) an English traveller, born in London in 1768. He travelled in Egypt, and attempted to explore the interior of Africa, but was detained in captivity in Darfoor for three years. He published, in 1799 or 1800, "Travels in Africa, Egypt, and Syria from 1792 to 1798." Having started on another journey towards Samarcand, he was murdered in Persia in 1813.

Browne, (WILLIAM LAURENCE.) See BROWN.

Brŏwn'ell, (THOMAS CHURCH,) D.D., LL.D., was born in Massachusetts in 1779. He graduated at Union College, with the highest honours of his class, in 1804, and continued his connection with the institution, as tutor and professor, for many years. He was ordained in 1816, and appointed Bishop of Connecticut in 1819. He was chosen the first president of Washington (now Trinity) College, an institution chartered in 1823, and built up at Hartford under his auspices. In 1852 he became Presiding Bishop of the Protestant Episcopal Church in the United States. Died in 1865. Bishop Brownell was the author of several valuable religious works and various occasional sermons, addresses, etc. His "Family Prayer" has passed through numerous editions, and been received with great favour by Episcopalians throughout the country. His "Religion of the Heart" (5 vols., partly a compilation and partly original) is also highly esteemed.

Brownikowski. See BRONIKOWSKI.

Brŏwn'ing, (ELIZABETH BARRETT,) one of the most gifted female poets that have ever lived, was born near Ledbury, Herefordshire, about 1807. She was the daughter of Mr. Barrett, an opulent merchant of London. She was highly educated, and well acquainted with the Greek and Latin languages. She began to write verse about the age of ten, and gave early proofs of poetical genius. Among her first published works was "The Battle of Marathon." In 1826 she published a volume entitled "Essay on Mind, and other Poems." She produced in 1833 "Prometheus Bound," translated from the Greek of Æschylus, which was a remarkable performance for a young woman, though not a very good translation. She afterwards made an amended version of the same. Her reputation was extended by "The Seraphim, and other Poems," (1838.) She contributed to the "Athenæum" a series of able critical papers on the Greek Christian poets. Her health was naturally delicate, and was almost ruined by grief for the death of her brother, who was accidentally drowned. After that event she was confined for several years in a darkened chamber. She published in 1839 "The Romaunt of the Page," "The Drama of Exile," (1840,) and two volumes of poems in 1844. In 1846 she was married to the poet Robert Browning, with whom she resided in Italy for many years. She produced in 1851 "Casa Guidi Windows," a poem which treats of the political condition of Italy. "This," says the "North British Review," "is the happiest of Mrs. Browning's performances, because it makes no pretensions to high artistic character, and is really a simple story of personal impressions." Her greatest or most extensive work is "Aurora Leigh," a poem, or novel in verse, (1856,) which is greatly admired. A new edition of her poems was published in three volumes in 1856. She died at Florence in June, 1861.

"The poetical reputation of Mrs. Browning," says the "North British Review" for February, 1857, "has been growing slowly, until it has reached a height which has never before been attained by any modern poetess, though several others have had wider circles of readers." "She possesses genius," says another critic, "a cultivated mind, a truth-loving heart, quick powers of observation, and luxuriancy of fancy and expression; but that luxuriance too often verges—to say the least—on extravagance."

See "British Quarterly Review" for October, 1865; "Edinburgh Review" for October, 1861.

Browning, (ROBERT,) an English poet, born at Camberwell, a suburb of London, in 1812. He was educated at the University of London, and produced in 1835 his first poem, entitled "Paracelsus," which attracted much attention by its originality and subtlety of thought. His tragedy of "Strafford" (1837) was not successful. He married Elizabeth Barrett the poetess in 1846, since which he has resided at Florence and Paris. He published a collection of his shorter poems, in two volumes,

(1849,) and two volumes of poems, under the title of "Men and Women," in 1855. Among his other works are a drama, called "The Blot in the Scutcheon," (1843,) "Pippa passes," and "The Ring and the Book," (1868.) He is considered by some critics as one of the greatest English poets of his time, but is not popular with the masses.

See "London Quarterly Review" for July, 1865; "Edinburgh Review" for October, 1864; "Fraser's Magazine" for February, 1863; "Brief Biographies," by SAMUEL SMILES; R. H. HORNE, "New Spirit of the Age," 1844.

Brŏwn'lŏw, (WILLIAM G.,) an American politician, born in Wythe county, Virginia, in 1805. He was a Methodist minister in the former part of his mature life. He began about 1837 to edit the "Knoxville Whig," which he continued to publish for many years. He opposed the abolition of slavery before the civil war, but in the crisis of 1861 he showed himself a resolute and uncompromising adherent of the Union. He was persecuted and imprisoned by the secessionists in the winter of 1861–62 for several months. He was elected by the Republicans or Radicals Governor of Tennessee in 1865, and again in 1867. In October of the latter year he was chosen a Senator of the United States.

Brŏwn'rig, (RALPH,) an English prelate, born at Ipswich in 1592, became Bishop of Exeter in 1642. Died in 1659.

Brown'rigg, (Sir ROBERT,) born in Ireland in 1775, became Governor of Ceylon in 1813, and conquered the kingdom of Candy, thus reducing the whole island under the British empire, for which service he received the title of baronet in 1816. Died in 1833.

Brownrigg, (WILLIAM,) M.D., F.R.S., an English natural philosopher, born in Cumberland in 1711. He wrote "The Art of making Common Salt," (1748.) Died in 1800.

Brown-Séquard, brŏwn-se-kaR', [Fr. pron. brŏwn-sȧ'kȧR',] (ÉDOUARD,) an eminent French physiologist, born in the island of Mauritius in 1818. His father, Mr. Edward Brown, a native of Philadelphia, in the United States, married, in Mauritius, a lady of French extraction, named Séquard, and his son, in accordance with a common French usage, adopted the names of both his parents. He studied in Paris, where he graduated as doctor of medicine in 1840. He acquired distinction by his researches and experiments on physiology, especially on the blood, on animal heat, and the spinal cord. His experiments on animal heat indicate that the temperature of the human body is 103° Fahr. He has received several prizes from the French Academy of Sciences. In January, 1869, he was appointed professor in the School of Medicine (École de Médecine) at Paris.

Brŏwn'sọn, (ORESTES AUGUSTUS,) a versatile American writer and theologian, born at Stockbridge, Vermont, in 1803. He joined the Presbyterian Church about 1821, became a Universalist minister in 1825, and a Unitarian pastor a few years afterwards. Having become a resident of Boston, he founded in 1838 "The Boston Quarterly Review," which he edited until 1843. He joined the Roman Catholic Church about 1844. Among his works is "Charles Elwood, or the Infidel Converted," (1840,) a novel.

See GRISWOLD's "Prose Writers of America."

Bruant, brü'ŏN', (LIBÉRAL,) an eminent French architect, designed the Hôtel des Invalides, Paris. He died about 1697.

Bruat, brü'ȧ', (ARMAND JOSEPH,) a French admiral, born at Colmar in 1796. He succeeded Admiral Hamelin as commander in the Black Sea in 1854, and took part in the siege of Sebastopol. Died in December, 1855.

Brucæus, broo-sā'ŭs, (HENDRIK,) a Flemish medical writer, born at Alost in 1531; died at Rostock in 1593.

Bruccioli, (A.) See BRUCIOLI.

Bruce, (DAVID.) See DAVID II. OF SCOTLAND.

Bruce, (EDWARD,) a younger brother of King Robert Bruce, was a brave warrior, but deficient in prudence. He invaded Ireland in 1315, was proclaimed king, and waged war against the English for several years. Having rashly engaged in battle against a vastly superior force of English, he was killed near Dundalk in 1318.

Bruce, (EDWARD,) a Scottish judge and diplomatist, born about 1549. He was sent to England in 1598 on a mission the object of which was to obtain a recognition of James as the heir to the throne of England. He died in 1611. The Earls of Elgin are descended from him.

Bruce, (Sir FREDERICK,) an English diplomatist, brother of the Earl of Elgin, was born in 1814. He was appointed ambassador to the United States in the early part of 1865. Died at Boston in September, 1867.

Bruce, (JAMES,) a celebrated Scottish traveller, born at Kinnaird, in the county of Stirling, in December, 1730. He was related to the royal family of Bruce. He was appointed in 1762 consul at Algiers by Lord Halifax, who proposed that he should explore the antiquities of Barbary. Departing from Algiers in 1765, he spent a year or more in examining and drawing the ruins of Barbary, and afterwards visited Baalbec and Palmyra. In 1768 he undertook a journey to Abyssinia to discover the source of the Nile. Passing through Cosseir, Jidda, and Masuah or Masowa, he arrived at Góndar in February, 1770. He was kindly treated by the king, and remained in Abyssinia about two years. He discovered the source of the Blue Nile in November, 1770. Returning through Nubia, he encountered great danger and hardships, which he overcame by uncommon energy and courage, and arrived in England in 1774. He published "Travels to discover the Source of the Nile," (5 vols., 1790,) which attracted much adverse criticism. His veracity was questioned by many persons ; but more recent researches tend to confirm his statements. He died at Kinnaird in 1794.

See A. MURRAY, "Life of Bruce," 1805 ; CHAMBERS, "Biographical Dictionary of Eminent Scotsmen ;" FRANCIS BOND HEAD, "Life of James Bruce, the African Traveller," 1832.

Bruce, (JAMES.) See ELGIN, EARL OF.

Bruce, (JAMES DANIEL,) a Russian engineer, of Scottish extraction, born at Moscow in 1670, became grand master of artillery in 1711. Died in 1735.

Bruce, (Sir JAMES KNIGHT,) an English judge, born in 1791, was appointed lord justice of appeal in 1852. Died in 1866.

Bruce, (JOHN,) a Scottish writer on ethics, politics, etc., born in 1744, was professor of moral philosophy at Edinburgh. Died in 1826.

Bruce, (JOHN,) an English antiquary, born in London about 1802. He contributed to the "Edinburgh Review" and "Gentleman's Magazine," and edited many old works.

Bruce, (JOHN C.,) an English antiquary, born at Newcastle-upon-Tyne in 1805, published a "Hand-Book of English History," (1848,) and "The Roman Wall,"(1851.)

Bruce, (MICHAEL,) a Scottish poet, born in the county of Kinross in 1746. He died at the age of twenty-one, leaving a collection of poems of great beauty and pathos.

See CAMPBELL, "Specimens of the British Poets ;" CHAMBERS, "Biographical Dictionary of Eminent Scotsmen."

Bruce, (PETER HENRY,) an officer of Scottish extraction, born in Westphalia in 1692, served in Germany and Russia. He died in 1751, leaving "Memoirs" of his travels.

Bruce, (ROBERT,) King of Scots, born on the 21st of March, 1274, was descended from Robert de Brus or Bruys, a Norman, who came over with William the Conqueror. He was the son of Robert Bruce, Earl of Carrick, whose father, also named Robert, was the competitor of John Baliol for the throne. He inherited the title of Earl of Carrick. About 1296 he joined Wallace in resistance to the aggressions of Edward I. of England, but soon after retired from the contest and made peace with the English king. He formed in 1305 a secret compact or compromise with Comyn, his rival, who promised to support him in an effort to liberate Scotland from English domination, on condition that Bruce should give him extensive landed estates. Comyn, however, betrayed the secret to Edward, and was killed by Bruce for his treachery. The latter was crowned at Scone in 1306, and raised a small army, which was quickly routed by the English. After he had performed prodigies of valour, Bruce was forced to take refuge in a small island near the coast of Ireland. His brother Nigel was taken prisoner and executed, and other friends of Bruce were treated with barbarity.

Bruce renewed the contest in the spring of 1307, and defeated a greatly superior force of English at Loudon Hill. After the death of Edward I., which took place in July of that year, he recovered a number of fortresses

from the enemy. A series of successful actions rendered him so strong and bold that he invaded England and ravaged the northern counties. At length, in 1314, Edward II. marched into Scotland with an army estimated at 100,000 men, over which Bruce gained a decisive victory at the great battle of Bannockburn, June 24, 1314. The war was continued until 1328, when the English king recognized the independence of Scotland. Bruce died in 1329. He had a son David, who succeeded to the throne, and a daughter Marjory, married to Walter the Steward, ancestor of the house of Stuart.

See BURTON, "History of Scotland," vol. ii. chaps. xxii., xxiii., and xxiv. ; SCOTT, "Tales of a Grandfather ;" CHAMBERS, "Biographical Dictionary of Eminent Scotsmen."

Bruce, (ROBERT,) an able Scottish clergyman, born about 1554. He became minister of a church in Edinburgh in 1587, and acquired great influence. Died in 1631.

Bruce, (THOMAS.) See ELGIN, EARL OF.

Bruce, de, (ROBERT,) Lord of Annandale, was the grandfather of King Robert Bruce. In 1285 John Baliol and Robert de Bruce were rival claimants of the throne, and referred the question to Edward I. of England, who decided in favour of the former. Bruce died in 1295.

Brucioli, bRoo-cho'lee, or **Bruccioli,** bRoot-cho'lee, (ANTONIO,) an Italian translator, born at Florence, lived about 1525-50. He produced a Tuscan version of the Bible, (1532,) and translated some works of Aristotle, (1547-51.)

Bruck, bRook, (KARL LUDWIG,) BARON, a German statesman, born at Elberfeld in 1798, became Austrian minister of commerce and public works in 1848. He resigned in 1851, and was appointed minister of finance in 1855. He killed himself in 1861. He was noted as the originator or chief director of the enterprising company at Trieste known as the Austrian Lloyds.

Brucker, bRook'ker, (JOHANN JAKOB,) an eminent German historian, scholar, and Protestant divine, born at Augsburg in 1696. He published, besides other works, a "Critical History of Philosophy," ("Historia critica Philosophiæ," 5 vols., 1741-44,) a work of immense labour and high reputation. It was the first complete and methodical history of the various schools of philosophy. His biographies of philosophers are especially valuable. The merit of this work consists in the ample collection of materials ; for it is deficient in critical analysis. Died at Augsburg in 1770.

See "Nouvelle Biographie Générale."

Bruckman, bRook'mån, (FRANZ ERNST,) a German physician and naturalist, born near Helmstedt in 1697 ; died in 1753.

Bruckner, bRook'ner, (ISAAC,) an eminent geometer and mechanician, born at Bâle in 1686 ; died in 1762.

See ERSCH und GRUBER, "Allgemeine Encyklopaedie."

Brué, bRü'å',(ÉTIENNE ROBERT,) a French geographer of merit, born in Paris in 1786 ; died in 1832. Besides several separate maps of great value, he published a "Universal Atlas."

See QUÉRARD, "La France Littéraire."

Bruehl. See BRÜHL.

Bruellow. See BRULLOV.

Bruère, de la, deh lå bRü'air', (CHARLES ANTOINE LECLERC,) a French dramatist, born at Crépy-en-Valois, or, according to some authorities, at Paris, about 1715, wrote a play entitled "Dardamus," (1739.) Died in 1754.

Bruerin, bRü'rån', (JEAN BAPTISTE,) a French physician, born at Lyons about 1500, wrote a treatise on diet, entitled "De Re cibaria." He was physician to Henry II. of France.

Brueys d'Aigalliers, bRü'å' då'gå'le-å', (or då'gål'-yå',) (FRANÇOIS PAUL,) a French admiral, born at Uzès in 1753. He commanded the fleet which conveyed the army of Bonaparte to Egypt in 1798. In August of that year he was attacked by Admiral Nelson in Aboukir Bay. He was defeated and killed in this action, and his ship, the Orient, caught fire and exploded just after his death.

See THIERS, "Histoire de la Révolution Française."

Brueys, de, deh bRü'å', (DAVID AUGUSTIN,) a French dramatist and priest, born at Aix in 1640, wrote "Le Grondeur," ("The Grumbler,") and other comedies. Died in 1723.

See DE LAUNAY, "Vie de David A. de Brueys."

Bruges, (JOHN OF.) See EYCK, (JOHN VAN.)

Bru'geš, van, [Dutch, VAN BRUGGE, vän brŭg'ğĕh,] (RUIGER,) a Flemish painter, was a pupil of John van Eyck. There are several excellent pictures in the Pinakothek at Munich attributed to him.

Brüggemann or **Brueggemann,** brŭg'ğĕh-män, (KARL HEINRICH,) a German publicist and writer on political economy, born at Hopsten in 1810.

Bruggen, van der, vän dĕr brŭg'ğĕn, (JAN,) an excellent Flemish engraver, born about 1650.

See NAGLER, "Neues Allgemeines Künstler-Lexikon."

Brugière de Barante. See BARANTE.

Brugman, brŭg'män, sometimes written **Brugmans,** (JAN,) a celebrated Franciscan preacher of the Netherlands. Died in 1473.

Brugmans, brŭg'mäns, (SEBALD JUSTIN,) a physician, and distinguished professor of natural history in the University of Leyden, born at Franeker in 1763 ; died in 1819.

See VAN DER BOON MESCH, "Lofrede op S. J. Brugmans," 1825.

Brugnatelli, brOon-yä-tel'lee, (LUIGI GASPARO,) an Italian chemist and natural philosopher, born at Pavia in 1761. He became a professor in the University of Pavia in 1796. Among his works are "Annals of Chemistry," (22 vols., 1790–1805,) and "The Physico-Medical Journal," (20 vols., 1792–96.) Died in 1818.

See B. BIZIO, "Elogio storico di L. Brugnatelli," 1832.

Brugnot, brün'yo', (JEAN BAPTISTE CHARLES,) a French poet of merit, born in 1798. His life was one long brave struggle with poverty and misfortune. Died in 1831.

See QUÉRARD, "La France Littéraire."

Bruguières, brü'ğe-air',(JEAN GUILLAUME,)a French traveller and naturalist, was born at Montpellier in 1750 ; died in 1799.

Bruhier d'Ablaincourt, brü-e-â' däb'lân'kooR', (JEAN JACQUES,) a French medical writer, born at Beauvais, practised in Paris. Died in 1756.

Brühl or **Bruehl, von,** fon brül, (HEINRICH,) COUNT, a German statesman, born at Weissenfels in 1700. He was patronized by Augustus II. of Poland, and, on his death, was instrumental in raising to the throne the Elector Augustus III. He was loaded with distinctions by the latter, who in 1747 appointed him prime minister. He impoverished the country by his extravagance to such a degree that, on the breaking out of the Seven Years' war, Saxony could furnish but 17,000 men. His library of sixty-two thousand volumes forms a principal part of the Royal Library at Dresden. Died in 1764.

See JUSTI, "Leben und Charakter des Premierministers H. von Brühl," 3 vols., 1760–65; J. H. SEYFART, "Leben des Grafen von Brühl," 1764.

Bruin. See BRUYN.

Bruix, brü-e', (EUSTACHE,) a French admiral, born at Saint Domingo in 1759. He was minister of the marine about 1798. By a daring effort he carried relief to Massena, besieged in Genoa. He was appointed commander of the flotilla which Napoleon prepared for the invasion of England in 1804. Died in 1805.

See MAZÈRES, "Notice historique sur E. Bruix," 1805.

Bruix, de, dĕh brü-e', a French *littérateur,* born at Bayonne in 1728 ; died in 1780.

Brulart de Sillery. See SILLERY.

Brulliot, brü'le'o', (?) (FRANZ,) a German engraver and writer, born at Dusseldorf in 1780, published a "Dictionary of the Monograms, Initial Letters, etc. by which Artists have designated their Names." He was appointed keeper of the prints of the King of Bavaria. Died in 1836.

Brullof or **Brüllow,** brül'lov, (ALEXANDER,) a Russian architect, brother of Karl, noticed below, built the Observatory of the Academy of Sciences, the Mikhailoff Theatre, and other edifices, at Saint Petersburg.

Brullof or **Brüllow,** (KARL,) an eminent Russian painter, born at Saint Petersburg in 1800. He became court painter to the Czar about 1830. Among his masterpieces is "The Last Day of Pompeii." He excelled in colour and composition. Died in 1852.

Brum'mel, (GEORGE BRYAN,) "BEAU BRUMMEL," an English fop, born in London in 1778, inherited an easy fortune. He studied at Oxford, learned to write Latin verse, and became noted for his elegant taste in dress. He was a favourite and companion of the Prince of Wales, lived in splendid style in London, and associated with the nobility on equal terms. For many years he was regarded as a leader of *haut ton,* and an oracle in questions of dress, fashion, and etiquette. Having dissipated his fortune, he exiled himself to France about 1815. He died poor at Caen in 1840.

See CAPTAIN JESSE, "Life of Beau Brummel," 1844; WILLIAM RUSSELL, "Eccentric Personages."

Brumoy, brü'mwa', (PIERRE,) a French classical scholar and Jesuit, born at Rouen in 1688. He wrote Latin poems ; but his reputation is founded chiefly on his "Théâtre des Grecs," (3 vols., 1730,) consisting of translations from Greek dramatists, with analytical remarks which were highly esteemed. Died in 1742.

Brun, brOon, (FRIEDRIKE SOPHIE CHRISTIANE,) a German authoress, born in the duchy of Gotha in 1765, was the daughter of Balthasar Münter. She was married in 1783 to Constantin Brun. Having visited Russia, Switzerland, and Italy, she published "Letters from Rome," (1808,) and "Episodes of Travel," ("Episoden aus Reisen," 4 vols., 1816.) She also wrote a number of poems and prose essays. She was intimate with Klopstock, Madame de Staël, and other eminent persons of the time. Died in 1835.

See BONSTETTEN, "Briefe an Friedrike Brun," 1829.

Brun, brOon, (JOHAN NORDAHL,) a Norwegian pulpit orator of high reputation, born near Drontheim in 1745, became Bishop of Bergen in 1804. He wrote lyric poems, and a drama entitled "Zarine," said to have been the first original tragedy written in the Danish language. Died in 1816.

Brun, Le. See LE BRUN, (CHARLES and PIERRE.)

Brun, (MALTE.) See MALTE-BRUN.

Brunacci, brOo-nät'chee, or **Brunazi,** brOo-nâd'zee, (GIOVANNI,) an Italian historian and antiquary, born near Padua in 1711 ; died in 1772.

Brunacci, (VINCENZO,) an Italian mathematician and writer, born at Pisa in 1768. He became professor of the higher mathematics at Pavia about 1800. Among his numerous works is a "Course of Higher Mathematics," ("Corso di Matematica sublime," 4 vols., 1804–10.) Died at Pavia in 1818.

See TIPALDO, "Biografia degli Italiani illustri ;" ERSCH und GRUBER, "Allgemeine Encyklopaedie."

Brunazi. See BRUNACCI.

Brunck, brOonk, (RICHARD FRANÇOIS PHILIPPE,) a distinguished classical scholar, born at Strasburg in 1729, was educated in Paris among the Jesuits. Entertaining a passionate fondness for the poets of antiquity, and endowed with an exquisite critical taste, his editions of the Greek and Latin authors possess great merit ; but, unfortunately, his emendations of the ancient text, though for the most part ingenious and even felicitous, are too often rash and unjustified by the authority of the best manuscripts. Died in 1803. Among his principal works are editions of Aristophanes, Sophocles, Anacreon, Apollonius Rhodius, Terence, and Plautus, and a "Greek Anthology," (1776.)

See "Memoria R. F. P. Brunckii," 1803 ; ERSCH und GRUBER, "Allgemeine Encyklopaedie."

Brune, brün,(CHRISTIAN,)a French landscape-painter, born in Paris in 1789 ; died in 1849. His wife, Aimée Pagès, born in 1803, is a painter of history and genre.

Brune, (GUILLAUME MARIE ANNE,) a French general, born at Brives-la-Gaillarde in 1763. He gained the rank of general of division by his services at Arcola and Rivoli, (1796,) and in 1799 commanded an army in Holland, where he gained some victories. He was raised to the rank of marshal about 1804, and became governor-general of the Hanseatic Towns in 1807. Soon after this date he offended Napoleon, who removed him from command. He remained out of service until 1815, when he took a command under Napoleon on his return from Elba. He was assassinated at Avignon by a royalist mob in August, 1815.

See "Notice historique sur la Vie de Maréchal Brune," Paris, 1821 ; "Esquisse historique sur le Maréchal Brune," 2 vols., 1840.

Brune, van, vän brü'nĕh, [Lat. BRUNÆ'US,] (JAN,) a Dutch poet and statesman, born in 1585 ; died in 1658.

See LONGFELLOW's "Poets and Poetry of Europe."

ā, ē, ī, ō, ū, ȳ, *long;* ă, ĕ, ŏ, same, less prolonged; ă, ĕ, ĭ, ŏ, ŭ, ȳ, *short;* ạ, ẹ, ị, ọ, *obscure;* fär, fâll, fât; mĕt; nŏt; gōōd; mōōn;

Brunehaut, brün′ho′, the daughter of Athanagildus, King of Spain, was married in 568 to Sigebert, King of Austrasia, (or Ostrasie,) one of the four sons of Clotaire I. She was distinguished in her youth by several noble traits of character, as well as by beauty, talents, and courage; but after the assassination of her husband in 575, at the instigation of Fredegonda, Queen of Neustria, she abandoned herself to a reckless desire of vengeance and an unprincipled ambition. Having, after a life of vicissitudes, fallen at last into the hands of Clotaire II., son of Fredegonda, she was barbarously murdered in 613. She was tied to the tail of a wild horse, which, being let loose, tore her to pieces.

See THIERRY, "Récits des Temps Mérovingiens;" ALEXIS PAULIN PÂRIS, "Brunehaut," 8vo, 1834.

Bru-nel′, (ISAMBARD KINGDOM,) an eminent British engineer and naval architect, born at Portsmouth in 1806, was a son of Sir Mark Isambard, whose mechanical ingenuity he inherited. He was educated in Paris. He exhibited great energy and skill in the construction of the Thames Tunnel, on which he was employed as assistant or resident engineer. About 1833 he was appointed engineer of the Great Western Railway. He was the chief architect or engineer of the Great Western and Great Eastern steamships, the latter of which was finished about 1859. Among his works is the Hungerford Suspension Bridge over the Thames. He was a Fellow of the Royal Society. Died in 1859.

See "London Quarterly Review" for July, 1862.

Brunel, (Sir MARK ISAMBARD,) a celebrated engineer, born at Hacqueville, near Rouen, France, in April, 1769. He displayed great mechanical ingenuity in early youth, joined with an aversion to study and to books, except works on natural philosophy or mathematics. To escape from the reign of terror, (1793,) he emigrated to New York, where he found employment, and built the Bowery Theatre. He removed to England about 1800, and married Miss Kingdom. He invented an excellent machine for the fabrication of block-pulleys, for which the English government gave him more than £15,000. His greatest work is the Thames Tunnel, which is considered one of the most wonderful triumphs of engineering skill in the world. It was commenced about 1825, and completed in 1843. Died in 1849.

See R. BEAMISH, "Life of M. I. Brunel;" E. FRÈRE, "Notice historique sur la Vie de M. I. Brunel," 1850; WILLIAM JERDAN, "Men I have known," London, 1866.

Brunelleschi, broo-nĕl-lĕs′kee, (FILIPPO,) a celebrated Italian architect and sculptor, born at Florence in 1377. He learned the art of goldsmith, and studied in Rome the monuments of ancient architecture, the principles of which he resolved to restore and illustrate. At that time the Gothic style prevailed almost exclusively. He returned to Florence about 1407, and was appointed architect of the cathedral Santa Maria del Fiore, which Arnolfo di Lapo had left unfinished, and over which he raised a majestic dome, one of the largest and most beautiful in the world. It was nearly finished at his death. He also designed the churches of San Lorenzo and Santo Spirito at Florence. Died in 1444.

See VASARI, "Lives of the Painters, etc.;" QUATREMÈRE DE QUINCY, "Vies des Architectes céiebres;" F. BALDINUCCI, "Vita di F. di Ser Brunellesco," published by D. Moreni, 1812.

Brunet or Brunetto. See LATINI.

Brunet, brü′nȧ′, (FRANÇOIS FLORENTIN,) a French theologian, born in Lorraine, wrote "Parallèle des Religions," (5 vols., 1792.) Died in 1806.

Brunet, (JACQUES CHARLES,) a French bibliographer, born in Paris in 1780, published "Manuel du Libraire et de l'Amateur des Livres," (3 vols., 1810; new edition, 6 vols., 1860–65.) This is probably the most extensive work on the subject, and is called the master-piece of modern bibliography. Died in Paris in November, 1867.

See QUÉRARD, "La France Littéraire."

Brunet, (JEAN BAPTISTE,) a French general, born at Rheims in 1765, distinguished himself in Italy in 1800, and afterwards in Saint Domingo, where he inveigled Toussaint into his power. (See TOUSSAINT L'OUVERTURE.) Died in 1824.

Brunet, (JEAN BAPTISTE,) a commander of the army of Italy in 1793, having been suspected of treasonable

correspondence with the enemy, was condemned by the Revolutionary tribunal, and executed in November, 1793.

Brunet, (JEAN LOUIS,) a French canonist, born at Arles in 1688; died in 1747.

Brunet, (PIERRE,) a French physician and writer, born at Nantes in 1770; died in 1832.

Brunet, (PIERRE GUSTAVE,) a French littérateur, born at Bordeaux in 1807.

Brunetti, broo-net′tee, (SEBASTIANO,) an Italian painter, born at Bologna about 1609, was a pupil of Guido. Died in 1649.

Brunetto or Brunetto Latini. See LATINI.

Brunfels, broon′fĕlss, or **Brunsfeld,** broons′fĕlt, (OTHO or OTTO,) a German botanist and physician, born near Mentz about 1464. He published, in 1530, "Living Figures (Pictures) of Plants in Imitation of Nature," ("Herbarum Vivæ Icones ad Naturæ Imitationem," etc.,) which is said to be a capital work. Died at Berne in 1534.

See M. ADAM, "Vitæ Eruditorum."

Bruni, broo′nee, (ANTONIO,) an Italian poet, became secretary of the Duke of Urbino. He wrote the "Grove of Parnassus," ("Selva di Parnaso," 1615,) "Epistole eroiche," (1626,) and other poems. Died at Rome in 1635.

Bruni, (LEONARDO,) a learned writer of Italy, born in 1369 at Arezzo, whence he was often called LEONARDO ARETINO, (â-rà-tee′no.) He settled at Florence, of which city he was appointed chancellor. Besides other works, he wrote a "History of Florence," (in Latin,) and the lives of Dante and Petrarch. Died in 1444.

See GINGUENÉ, "Histoire Littéraire d'Italie."

Brunier. See BRUNYER.

Brunings, broo′nings, (CHRISTIAN,) a German Protestant divine, born at Bremen in 1702, wrote a "Compendium of Hebrew Antiquities," (1763.) Died in 1763.

Brünings, brü′nings, (CHRISTIAN,) a distinguished hydraulic engineer, born at Neckarau, in Baden, in 1736, became director-general of the dikes in Holland. He made several useful inventions, among which was the strommesser, an instrument for measuring the rapidity of streams. Died in 1805.

Brunius, broo′ne-ûs, (KARL GEORG,) a Swedish antiquary and poet, born at Tanum in 1792, became professor of Greek at Lund in 1824, and wrote several Latin poems, and works on Northern antiquities.

Brunn, broon, (JOHANN JAKOB,) an eminent physician, and medical professor in the University of Bâle, where he was born in 1591. He published a "System of Materia Medica," ("Systema Materiæ Medicæ,") of which numerous editions have been published. Died in 1660.

See G. SEGER, "Memoria J. J. Brunnii," 1660.

Brunner, broon′ner, (BALTHASAR,) a German physician, born at Halle, in Saxony, in 1533; died in 1604.

Bruno. See LEO IX.

Bru′no THE GREAT, Archbishop of Cologne, a brother of Otho I., Emperor of Germany, and a man of great influence on the affairs of his age, was a scholar and a patron of learning. Otho committed to him the administration of the duchy of Lorraine. Died in 965.

See RUOTGERUS, "Vita Brunonis," Hanover, 1841.

Bru′no, [Lat. BRU′NUS,] (GIORDANO,) an eminent philosopher, born at Nola, in the kingdom of Naples, about the middle of the sixteenth century. He entered the order of Dominican monks in his youth, but, having found that position irksome to his independent and speculative spirit, he escaped from the convent, and went to Geneva about 1580. He afterwards visited England, France, etc. About 1584 he published "Spaccio della Bestia trionfante," "Della Causa, Principio e Uno," and "Del infinito Universo e Mondi," ("On the Infinite Universe and Worlds.") He returned to Italy in 1592, and settled at Pavia, where he was arrested by the Inquisition and charged with heresy and apostasy, for which he was burned at Rome in 1600. "His system," says Hallam, "may be said to contain a sort of double pantheism. The world is animated by an omnipresent, intelligent soul, the first cause of every form that matter can assume, but not of matter itself. . . . In his work 'Del

ε as k; ç as s; ğ hard; ġ as j; G, H, K, guttural; N, nasal; R, trilled; ŝ as z; th as in this.   (☞See Explanations, p. 23.)

29

infinito Universo,' he asserts the infinity of the universe and the plurality of worlds. That the stars are suns shining by their own light, that each has its revolving planets, were among the enormous and capital offences of Bruno." ("Introduction to the Literature of Europe.")

See BARTHOLMÈS, "Jordano Bruno," 1847; DEBS, "Bruni Nolani Vita et Placita," 1844; C. G. VON MURR, "Leben und Schriften des G. Bruno," 1805; N. MOELLER, "G. Bruno, sa Vie et ses Doctrines," 1840; F. J. CLEMENS, "G. Bruno und Nicolaus von Cusa: philosophische Abhandlung," 1847.

Bru'no, (JACOBUS PANCRATIUS,) a medical writer, born at Altdorf in 1629, became professor of medicine in his native city in 1662. Died in 1709.

Bru'no, SAINT, sometimes called "the Apostle of Prussia." After several years spent in converting the heathen, he was killed near Lithuania, together with a number of his coadjutors, in 1008.

Bruno, SAINT, founder of the order of Carthusians, was born at Cologne about 1040. He retired in 1086, with several associates, to a mountain near Grenoble, where he formed a religious order which adopted the rule of Saint Benedict. The convent of La Grande Chartreuse was afterwards erected on this spot. He subsequently founded another Carthusian convent in Calabria, where he died in 1101.

See TRACY, "Vie de Saint-Bruno," 1785; E. DUCREUX, "Vie de Saint-Brunon," 1812.

Brunof, Brunov, or **Brunow,** broo'nof, (ERNEST PHILIP,) BARON, an eminent Russian diplomatist, born at Dresden about 1796. He negotiated the famous treaty of July 15, 1840, by which England, Russia, Austria, and Prussia agreed to settle the Eastern Question without the consent of France. He was Russian minister at London from 1840 to 1854, and resumed that position in 1858.

Brunov. See BRUNOF.

Brunow. See BRUNOF.

Brunquel or **Brunnquell,** broon'kwěl, (JOHANN SALOMON,) a German jurist, born at Quedlinburg in 1693, was professor of law at Göttingen, where he died in 1735. He wrote a "History of Romano-German Law," in Latin, (1727.)

See JENICHEN, "Vita J. S. Brunnquelli," 1738.

Brunsfeld. See BRUNFELS.

Bruns'wick, HOUSE OF, an ancient princely family of Germany, descended from the princes of Este. ERNEST OF BRUNSWICK, the Confessor, born in 1497, was a zealous Protestant, and founder of the houses of Brunswick-Lüneburg and Brunswick-Wolfenbüttel. Died in 1546. His descendant ERNEST AUGUSTUS, Duke of Brunswick-Lüneburg, became Elector of Hanover. (See ERNEST AUGUSTUS.)

Brunswick, (CAROLINE OF.) See CAROLINE, QUEEN OF ENGLAND.

Bruns'wick-Lü'ne-burg, [Ger. BRAUNSCHWEIG-LÜNEBURG, brŏwn'shwīg lü'nĕh-boŏrg',] (KARL WILHELM FERDINAND,) DUKE OF, a celebrated German commander, born in 1735, was the eldest son of Duke Karl, and a nephew of Frederick the Great, for whom he fought in the Seven Years' war. He married Augusta, Princess of Wales, in 1764, and succeeded to the dukedom in 1780. In 1792 he was appointed commander-in-chief of the allied armies of Austria and Prussia, and invaded France to fight against the Republic. He was baffled by Dumouriez, and retired from France. In 1793 he fought several battles against Moreau and Hoche, and resigned the command. Having obtained the chief command of the Prussian army in 1806, he was defeated at Jena in October of that year, receiving a wound of which he died in the following November.

See BYRON's "Childe Harold," canto iii. stanza xxiii.

Bruns'wick-Oels, ěls or öls, (FRIEDRICH AUGUST,) DUKE OF, brother of the preceding, born at Brunswick in 1740. He wrote "Reflections on Alexander the Great," and other works. Died in 1805.

Brunswick-Oels, (FRIEDRICH WILHELM,) DUKE OF, born in 1771, was a son of Karl Wilhelm Ferdinand. He fought against the French in 1792 and 1793. In 1815 he joined the allies, and was killed at the battle of Quatre-Bras.

KARL, a son of the preceding, was born in 1804. During his minority Brunswick was governed by George IV. of England, who had married an aunt of Duke Karl. In

1830 the people, provoked by his misrule, revolted, and drove Karl out of Brunswick, which was transferred by an act of the Germanic Confederation to his brother William.

Brun'ton, (MARY BALFOUR,) a British novelist, born in one of the Orkney Islands in 1778, married, about the age of twenty, the Rev. Mr. Brunton. She wrote two successful novels, entitled "Self-Control," (1811,) and "Discipline," (1814.) Died in 1818.

See DR. BRUNTON, "Life of Mary Brunton;" "Memoirs of the Literary Ladies of England," etc., by MRS. ELWOOD, vol. ii.; CHAMBERS, "Biographical Dictionary of Eminent Scotsmen."

Bru'nus, [It. BRU'NO,] an Italian surgeon, was a friend of Petrarch, and lived at Padua. He wrote in 1352 a work called "Chirurgia magna," etc.

Brunyer or **Brunier,** brü'ne-ă', (ABEL,) a French physician, born at Uzès in 1573, practised in Paris. He was physician to the children of Henry IV., and was employed by Richelieu in missions to the Protestants. Died in 1665.

Brusantini, broo-sän-tee'nee, or **Brusantino,** broo-sän-tee'no, (VINCENZO,) an Italian poet, born at Ferrara. He wrote "Angelica innamorata," a sequel to "Orlando Furioso," (1550.) Died about 1570.

See GINGUENÉ, "Histoire Littéraire d'Italie."

Brusasorci. See RICCIO.

Brusati, broo-sä'tee, (P. GIULIO CESARE,) a learned Italian professor of theology, philosophy, and logic, born near Novara in 1693; died at Pavía in 1743.

Brusch. See BRUSCHIUS.

Bruschius, broŏsh'e-ùs, or **Brusch,** broŏsh, (KASPAR,) a German poet and writer of ecclesiastical history, born in 1518. He was assassinated in 1559 by two persons whom he was suspected of having satirized. He is said to have favoured the doctrines of Luther.

See BAYLE, "Historical and Critical Dictionary;" FISHBECK, "Vita C. Bruschii," 1710.

Bruslart, de, děh brü'lăr', (LOUIS Guérin—gă'rän',) CHEVALIER, a French officer, born in 1752, became lieutenant-general in 1823. Died in 1829.

Brusoni, broo-so'nee, (GIROLAMO,) an Italian historian and poet, born at Legnano in 1610. He wrote, besides other works, a "History of Italy from 1635 to 1655," (1656.) Died about 1680.

See GINGUENÉ, "Histoire Littéraire d'Italie."

Brusoni or **Brusonio,** broo-so'ne-o, (LUCIO DOMITIO,) an Italian professor of civil law, born near Rome, lived in the first half of the sixteenth century. He published "Facetiarum Exemplorumque Libri VII.," (1518,) a collection of anecdotes, etc. from classic authors.

Brutel de Larivière, brü'těl' děh lă're've-air', (JEAN BAPTISTE,) a learned Protestant theologian, born at Montpellier in 1667, lived in Holland. Died in 1742.

Bruto, broo'to, or **Bruti,** broo'tee, (GIOVANNI MICHELE,) a distinguished Venetian historian and traveller, born about 1515. He wrote, besides other works of less moment, a history of Florence, in Latin. Died about 1590.

Bru'tus, (DECIMUS JUNIUS,) one of the murderers of Cæsar, had served under him in Gaul, and had been appointed commander of his cavalry. He was slain (B.C. 33) by Camillus, a Gaul, to whom he had fled for refuge, and whom he had formerly loaded with benefits, and his head was sent to Mark Antony.

See DION CASSIUS, "History of Rome," books xlv. and xlvi.

Brutus, (LUCIUS JUNIUS,) a distinguished Roman patriot, son of Tarquinia, the sister of Tarquin the Proud. The king having put to death the father and elder brother of Brutus, the latter feigned idiocy, gave up all his possessions to his tyrannical uncle, and patiently accepted the reproachful surname of BRUTUS, (i.e. "stupid, brutish,") which was destined to become a title of so much glory to his family. Aruns and Titus, the sons of Tarquin, having been sent to Delphi to consult the oracle, took Brutus with them to serve for their amusement. When they were making offerings to the god, Brutus offered a simple staff, which, however, was hollow and contained a gold ring,—a significant emblem of the character of the giver. After the outrage done to Lucretia by Sextus the son of Tarquin, (see LUCRETIA,) Brutus threw aside all disguise, put himself at the head of the people, expelled the reigning family from Rome, and effected the abolition of royalty, (509 B.C.) Shortly after, Titus and Tiberius, the two sons of Brutus, accused of conspiring for the restoration of Tarquin, were brought before the consular tribunal for judgment. Their guilt having been proved, Brutus, then consul, with unconquerable patriotism and inflexible justice, condemned his own sons to death, although the people were willing that he should pardon them. In the year 507 B.C., Tarquin, who had never abandoned the purpose of regaining his kingdom, led an army against Rome, and his son Aruns and Brutus met in the field of battle and slew each other. The corpse of Brutus was carried to Rome in triumph, a statue of bronze was erected to his memory, and the Roman matrons wore mourning a whole year for the avenger of the wrongs of Lucretia.

See C. L. CRELL, "Dissertatio de L. J. Bruto Reipublicæ Romanæ Auctore," 1721 ; P. C. CHOMPRÉ, "Vie de Brutus premier Consul de Rome," 1730.

Brutus, (MARCUS JUNIUS,) a Roman jurist and general, a descendant of Lucius Junius Brutus, was the father of the famous conspirator. He fought for Marius against Sulla in the civil war, and commanded a force which defended Mutina (Módena) against Pompey. He surrendered that place in 77 B.C., and was put to death.

Brutus, (MARCUS JUNIUS,) a noted Roman, son of the preceding, was born in 80 B.C. Cato Uticensis was his maternal uncle, and afterwards his father-in-law, Brutus having married his daughter Porcia. In the civil wars he sided with Pompey. After the battle of Pharsalia he was treated with great kindness by Cæsar, and appears to have been sincerely attached to him for a time. He was, at the instigation of Cæsar's enemies, induced to join the conspiracy against the life of the dictator. Subsequently he and Cassius became the leaders of the republican army against Antony and Octavius. At the battle of Philippi, Brutus, who commanded the right wing, was at first completely successful, and drove the troops of Octavius even to their camp ; but Antony, observing the mistake his enemies had committed in pursuing fugitives, instead of assuring the victory to their own friends, turned upon the exposed flank of Cassius and entirely changed the fortune of the day. The republican troops were totally defeated ; and Brutus, after seeing many of his bravest and most attached followers lay down their lives in order to prevent his falling into the hands of his enemies, killed himself with his own sword, 36 B.C.

See PLUTARCH, "Lives;" APPIAN, "Bellum Civile;" QUEVEDO Y VILLEGAS, "Vida de M. Bruto," 1648.

Bruun, brōōn, (THOMAS CHRISTOFFER,) a Danish poet, born in Zealand in 1750 ; died in 1834.

See ERSLEW, "Forfatter-Lexicon."

Bruyère, de la, dẹh lẳ brü-e'yaiR' or brü'yaiR', (JEAN,) a distinguished French writer and moralist, born at Dourdan, in Normandy, in 1646. His principal work is entitled "Les Caractères de Théophraste, traduits du Grec, avec les Caractères ou les Mœurs de ce Siècle," ("The Characters of Theophrastus, translated from the Greek, with the Characters or Manners of this Age," 1688,) a satire, (in prose,) exhibiting keen powers of observation, accompanied by a refined and good-humoured wit and an elegant and spirited style. Died in 1696.

"The Greek writer, [Theophrastus,] with no contemptible degree of merit," says Hallam, "has been incomparably surpassed by his imitator." ("Introduction to the Literature of Europe.") The judgment of posterity has pronounced it to be one of the best books in the French language. La Bruyère, according to some critics, is the greatest painter of manners and character that has written in French. Through the influence of Bossuet, he was appointed teacher of history to a grandson of the great Prince of Condé.

See SUARD, "Notice sur La Bruyère," 1781 ; SICARD, "Vie de La Bruyère," 1827 ; WALCKENAER, "Étude sur La Bruyère," prefixed to his works, 1847 ; M. J. J. VICTORIN-FABRE, "Éloge de La Bruyère," 1810.

Bruyères, brü-e'yaiR' or brü'yaiR', (JEAN PIERRE,) a French officer, born in Languedoc in 1772, distinguished himself at the battle of Jena in 1806, and was in consequence made general, served under Murat in the Russian campaign of 1812, and was killed by a bullet in battle in 1813.

Bruyn, broin, (KORNELIS,) a Dutch traveller and artist, born at the Hague in 1652. He studied painting in Rome and Venice, and subsequently visited Asia Minor, Egypt, and Russia. His "Voyage to the Levant," published in Dutch and French, (1698–1700,) contains more than two hundred engravings. His "Travels through Muscovy, etc." (1711) has three hundred plates, many of them of superior merit.

See NAGLER, "Allgemeines Künstler-Lexikon."

Bruyn, de, broin, (ABRAHAM,) a Flemish painter and engraver, born at Antwerp about 1540.

Bruyn, de, (NICOLAAS,) son of Abraham, born at Antwerp about 1570, was a skilful painter and engraver.

Bruyn, van, vẳn broin, (JAN,) a learned professor of mathematics, physics, and philosophy in the University of Utrecht, born at Gorcum in 1620 ; died in 1675.

See BAYLE, "Historical and Critical Dictionary."

Bruys, brü-e', (FRANÇOIS,) a French *littérateur* and critic, born at Serrières in 1708, published a "History of the Popes," (5 vols., 1734.) Died at Dijon in 1738.

Bruys, de, dẹh brü-e', (PIERRE,) [Lat. PE'TRUS BRU'SIUS,] a French fanatic and iconoclast, suffered death at the stake, in Languedoc, in 1147. Many of his views corresponded with those of the modern Protestants.

See PERRIN, "Histoire des Vaudois."

Bry, bRe, [Flemish pron. bRī,] (THÉODORE,) an eminent engraver, born at Liège in 1528 ; died, in 1598, at Frankfort-on-the-Main. His sons, John Theodore (1561–1620) and John Israel, were able engravers.

Brȳ'an, (GEORGE,) a patriot of the American Revolution, born at Dublin, Ireland, about 1730. Having emigrated to America, he was appointed, in 1778, president of the supreme executive council of the colony of Pennsylvania. Died in 1791.

Brȳ'an, (MICHAEL,) a noted connoisseur in painting, and author of a "Biographical and Critical Dictionary of Painters and Engravers," (1812,) was born at Newcastle, in England, about 1754 ; died in 1821.

Brȳ'ant, (Sir FRANCIS,) an English soldier and statesman, served with credit under Lord Surrey in 1522, became chief justiciary of Ireland in 1548, and died in 1550.

Bryant, (JACOB,) a learned English antiquary, born at Plymouth in 1715. He became secretary to the Duke of Marlborough in 1756. His reputation is founded chiefly on his "New System or Analysis of Ancient Mythology," (3 vols., 1774–76.) Among his numerous works is a "Treatise on the Authenticity of the Holy Scriptures and the Truth of the Christian Religion," (1792.) Died in 1804.

Brȳ'ant, (JOHN HOWARD,) an American poet, brother of William C. Bryant, born at Cummington, Massachusetts, in 1807. He removed to Princeton, Illinois, about 1832, and became a farmer. He is the author of a number of short poems.

Bryant, (SOLOMON,) an American Indian, born in Massachusetts in 1695, resided at Marshpee, where he preached in his own language to the Indians for many years. Died in 1775.

Bryant, (WILLIAM CULLEN,) an eminent American poet, born at Cummington, Hampshire county, Massachusetts, on the 3d of November, 1794. About the age of thirteen he wrote two poems, "The Embargo," a political satire, and "The Spanish Revolution," which were printed in 1808. He entered Williams College in 1810, distinguished himself by his proficiency in the languages, and became a student of law about 1812. Having been admitted to the bar in 1815, he practised law for several years. In 1816 he published "Thanatopsis," which is by many regarded as his finest poem, and in 1821 a volume containing, besides other pieces, a didactic poem called "The Ages." He married about this date, removed to New York City in 1825, and became, in 1826, one of the editors of the "Evening Post," which he has continued to edit with great ability to the present time. A complete collection of his poems was published in 1832. He visited Europe in 1834, and returned in 1836, since which he has crossed the Atlantic several times, and in 1849 travelled in Egypt and Syria. Among his prose works are "Letters of a Traveller." Since 1845 he has resided at Roslyn, on Long Island. As editor of the "Evening Post," he opposed the extension of slavery, and efficiently supported the Union during the civil war.

"No poet," says Griswold, "has described with more fidelity the beauties of the creation, nor sung in nobler song the greatness of the Creator. He is the translator of the silent language of the universe to the world. His poetry is pervaded by a pure and genial philosophy, a solemn and religious tone, that influence the fancy, the understanding, and the heart." ("Poets and Poetry of America.") "All who have read this article," says Professor Wilson, "will agree with what Washington Irving has said of his friend,—that his close observation of the phenomena of nature, and the graphic felicity of his details, prevent his descriptions from becoming general and commonplace." ("Blackwood's Magazine" for April, 1832.)

See, also. "Foreign Quarterly Review" for August, 1832; "Democratic Review" for March, 1842.

Bry-ax'is, [Βρύαξις,] a noted Greek sculptor, flourished about 380 B.C.

Bryczynski, brĭt-chin'skee, (JOSEPH,) a Polish *littérateur,* born near Warsaw in 1798; died in France in 1823.

Brydaine. See BRIDAINE.

Brўdġes, (Sir SAMUEL EGERTON,) an able English writer, born at Wootton Court, Kent, in 1762. He studied law, but did not practise it. He induced his brother to prefer a claim to the barony of Chandos. The adverse decision of the House of Peers was a severe disappointment to him. He was a prolific writer of sonnets, novels, essays, letters, etc. Among his chief works are "Sonnets and Poems," (1785,) "Censura Literaria, containing Titles and Opinions of Old English Books," (10 vols., 1805–09,) "Res Literariæ," (3 vols., 1821,) and "Letters from the Continent," (1821.) Died near Geneva in 1837.

See "The Autobiography, Times, and Opinions of Sir Egerton Brydges," 2 vols., 1834; "London Quarterly Review" for March and June, 1834.

Brў-dōne', (PATRICK,) a Scottish traveller, author of "Travels into Malta and Sicily." Born in 1741; died in 1819.

Brў-en'nĭ-us, (NICEPHORUS,) [Gr. Νικηφόρος Βρυέννιος; Fr. NICÉPHORE BRYENNE, ne'sȧ'foR' bRe'ĕn',] a Byzantine historian and general, was a favourite minister of Alexis Comnenus, and married Anna Comnena. He wrote "Ὕλη ἱστορίας." Died about 1137.

Buache, bü'âsh', (PHILIPPE,) an eminent French geographer, born at Paris in 1700, became, when only twenty-nine years old, first geographer to the king. Died in 1773. He wrote several valuable works on geography, especially that department of it which is termed hydrography.

Buache de la Neuville, bü'âsh' deh lȧ nuh'vèl', (JEAN NICOLAS,) a French geographer, a relation of the preceding, born at Neuville-en-Pont in 1741, was the last Frenchman who bore the title of "first geographer to the king." ("premier géographe du roi.") Died in 1825.

See WALCKENAER, "Vies des Hommes célèbres;" QUÉRARD, "La France Littéraire."

Buat-Nançay, bü'ä' nŎn'sȧ', (LOUIS GABRIEL,) often called simply COMTE DU BUAT, a French diplomatist and writer, author of an "Ancient History of the Nations of Europe," (2d ed., 12 vols., 1772,) and other works. Born in Normandy in 1732; died in 1787.

Bube, boo'beh, (ADOLPH,) a German poet, born at Gotha in 1802. He published "German Tales," ("Deutsche Sagen,") which had great success, and afterwards "Obolen," (1827,) "Poems," ("Gedichte," 1836,) "New Poems," ("Neue Gedichte," 1840,) and "Naturbilder," (1848.)

Bubna Littiz, boob'nä lit'tits, (FERDINAND,) COUNT OF, (often called simply **Bubna,**) a very distinguished Austrian general, born at Zamersk, in Bohemia, about 1768, particularly signalized himself in the campaign against Napoleon in 1813. Died in 1825.

Bu-bul'cus, (CAIUS JUNIUS,) a Roman statesman who was thrice elected consul, and became dictator in 302 B.C.

Buc or **Buck,** (Sir GEORGE,) an English antiquary and historical writer, was gentleman of the privy chamber to James I. He wrote a "Life of Richard III.," and other works. Died about 1622.

Buc, du, dü bük, (JEAN BAPTISTE,) born in Martinique in 1717, of a noble Norman family, was appointed by Choiseul chief of the bureaus for the two Indias, and in 1770 retired with the title of intendant of the colonies. Died in 1795.

Bucer, boot'ser, (MARTIN,) originally KUHHORN, (koo'hoRn,) a celebrated German reformer, and friend of Luther, born in 1491 near Strasburg, where he was professor of theology for twenty years. He assisted at the Diet of Augsburg in 1548, and strongly condemned the so-called Interim of Charles V. At the invitation of Cranmer, he removed to England in 1549, and became professor of theology at Cambridge. He died about 1550, leaving numerous works in Latin and German, among which is a translation of the Psalms with a commentary. He was an advocate of peace and conciliation among the Protestant sects. His "Commentaries on the Gospels" (1527) are highly esteemed.

See MELCHIOR ADAM, "Vitæ Theologorum;" BAYLE, "Historical and Critical Dictionary;" DE THOU, "Histoire."

Buch, von, fon bōōĸ, (LEOPOLD,) an eminent Prussian geologist, born at Stolpe, in Uckermark, on the Oder, in 1774. He studied mineralogy under Werner at Freiberg, where Alexander von Humboldt was his fellow-student. In 1797 he published an "Essay towards a Geognostic Description of Silesia," and performed a scientific excursion in Italy in 1798–99. During a second visit to Italy he witnessed the eruption of Vesuvius in 1805, and was converted from the Neptunian to the Plutonic theory. The results of his observations appeared in his "Geognostische Beobachtungen auf Reisen durch Deutschland und Italien," (2 vols., 1802–09.) He afterwards explored Sweden and other countries, generally travelling on foot. He was the first who noticed the gradual elevation of Sweden, and he originated the doctrine of the slow upheaval of continents. Among his more important works is a geological map of Germany, (1824.) He was pronounced by Humboldt to be "the greatest geologist of our age, the first to recognize the intimate connection of volcanic phenomena." Died in Berlin in 1853.

See English version of FLOURENS'S "Eulogy on L. von Buch," in the "Smithsonian Report" for 1862, p. 358; HOFFMANN, "Geschichte der Geognosie," 1838; HUMBOLDT, "Cosmos;" "Edinburgh Review" for October, 1813; H. VON DECHEN, "Leopold von Buch, sein Einfluss auf die Entwickelung der Geognosie," 8vo, 1853.

Buchan, bŭk'ạn, (DAVID,) a British navigator, born about 1780. He commanded an expedition sent out in 1818 to discover a passage from the Atlantic to the Pacific Ocean through Behring Strait and the Arctic Sea. Died in 1839.

See BARROW, "Chronological History of Voyages into the Arctic Regions."

Buchan, (DAVID STUART ERSKINE,) EARL OF. See ERSKINE.

Buchan, bŭk'ạn, (ELIZABETH or ELSPETH,) the founder of a sect of enthusiasts called Buchanists, was born in Scotland in 1738; died in 1791.

See CHAMBERS, "Biographical Dictionary of Eminent Scotsmen."

Buchan, (JOHN STUART,) EARL OF, born in 1380, was a son of Robert, Duke of Albany, Regent of Scotland. and a grandson of King Robert II. He entered the service of Charles VII. of France in 1420, defeated the English at Baugé, and was appointed Constable of France. Died about 1424.

Buchan, (PETER,) a Scottish antiquary. He published "Gleanings of Scotch, English, and Irish Scarce Old Ballads," (1825,) and other works. Died in 1854.

Buchan, (WILLIAM,) M.D., born at Ancrum, in Scotland, in 1729; died in 1805. He practised in Sheffield, and finally in London. His "Domestic Medicine," published in 1769, had great success.

See CHAMBERS, "Biographical Dictionary of Eminent Scotsmen;" "Gentleman's Magazine" for 1805. .

Buchanan, bŭk-an'ạn, (CLAUDIUS,) a Scottish divine, vice-provost of the College of Fort William, in Bengal, distinguished by his zeal for the propagation of the gospel in India, was born near Glasgow in 1766; died in 1815. He wrote "Christian Researches in Asia," (1811.)

See PEARSON, "Life of Claudius Buchanan," 1819; CHAMBERS, "Biographical Dictionary of Eminent Scotsmen;" "London Quarterly Review" for December, 1811.

ā, ē, ī, ō, ū, ȳ, *long;* ȧ, ė, ȯ, *same, less prolonged;* ă, ĕ, ĭ, ŏ, ŭ, ў, *short;* ạ, ẹ, ị, ọ, *obscure;* fär, fȧll, fȧt; mêt; nŏt; gōōd; mōōn;

Buchanan, (FRANCIS,) M.D., a Scottish physician, born in Stirlingshire in 1762. Having graduated at Edinburgh, he sailed in 1794 for India, as surgeon in the East India Company's service. He published "Travels in the Mysore," (1807,) which has a high reputation, and a "History of Nepaul," (1818.) He was a Fellow of the Royal Society, of the Royal Asiatic Society, and of other learned institutions. Died in 1829.

See CHAMBERS, "Biographical Dictionary of Eminent Scotsmen;" "Edinburgh Review" for October, 1808.

Buchanan, bŭk-an'an, (FRANKLIN,) an American naval officer, born in Baltimore, entered the navy about 1815. He was a captain when the civil war began, resigned in 1861, and commanded the iron-clad Merrimac when she destroyed several Federal vessels in Hampton Roads, March, 1862. Having been raised to the rank of rear-admiral, he commanded the iron-clad Tennessee in Mobile Bay, August, 1864, where he was defeated by Admiral Farragut, and taken prisoner.

Buchanan, (GEORGE,) a celebrated Scottish historian, scholar, and Latin poet, born near Killearn, in the county of Stirling, in 1506, was educated in Paris. He was employed as tutor to the Earl of Cassilis for several years, and returned to Scotland about 1537. Having adopted Protestant opinions, and written a satire against the monks, entitled "Somnium," he was thrown into prison ; but he escaped to England, and passed thence to France about 1540. He remained in France until 1547, during which period he taught at Bordeaux and Paris and wrote several Latin tragedies. After he had passed several months in the prison of the Inquisition in Portugal, he returned to France in 1553, and to Scotland in 1560. In 1562 he became classical tutor to Mary, Queen of Scots, and in 1570 or 1571 was appointed preceptor to the young king, James VI. He was an adherent of the regent Murray in the civil war. Among his principal works are a metrical Latin version of the Psalms, (1570,) "Franciscanus," a poetical satire, and a "History of Scotland," (" Rerum Scoticarum Historia," 1582.) The last is said to be deficient in impartiality. His Latin writings are celebrated for the purity and elegance of the style. He died at Edinburgh in 1582, after saying, "I am going to a place where there are few kings." His translation of the Psalms shows him to have been a poet of a high order ; though he is perhaps more remarkable for harmony of versification and richness of style than for strength of imagination.

See his "Autobiography," 1608; DAVID IRVING, "Memoirs of the Life and Writings of George Buchanan," 1807; CHAMBERS, "Biographical Dictionary of Eminent Scotsmen;" BAYLE, "Historical and Critical Dictionary;" "Blackwood's Magazine" for June, 1818.

Buchanan, (JAMES,) the fifteenth President of the United States, born in Franklin county, Pennsylvania, in April, 1791. He graduated at Dickinson College, Carlisle, in 1809, studied law, and was admitted to the bar in 1812. He was elected a member of Congress in 1820, and began his political career as a Federalist. In 1828 he supported General Jackson as candidate for the Presidency, and was again elected to Congress. He was sent as ambassador to Saint Petersburg in 1831, and elected a Senator of the United States by the legislature of Pennsylvania in 1833. He supported the administration of Van Buren, (1837–41,) and favoured the annexation of Texas to the United States. Having been re-elected, he sat in the Senate until 1845, and was appointed in that year secretary of state in the cabinet of President Polk. He ceased to hold this office in March, 1849, after which he passed four years in private life. He opposed the Wilmot proviso, and, like most other Democratic leaders, raised his voice against the anti-slavery movement. He was minister of the United States at the court of Saint James from 1853 to 1856. In June, 1856, the National Democratic Convention at Cincinnati nominated him for President of the United States. His competitors were John C. Fremont, supported by the Republicans, and Millard Fillmore, "American." Buchanan was elected, receiving 174 electoral votes out of 303, which was the whole number. In the first year of his administration, great excitement was produced by an attempt to establish slavery in Kansas, which became the scene of civil war. On this question Buchanan showed

himself to be a "Northern man with Southern principles." In his message, December, 1857, he argued that Kansas should be admitted with the "Lecompton Constitution," which the pro-slavery party, aided by executive influence, had framed. The majority of Congress, however, refused to admit Kansas as a slave State.

He used his influence to obtain by purchase the island of Cuba, in order to secure a due balance of power between freedom and slavery. In 1854 he had united with John Y. Mason and Pierre Soulé in the "Ostend Manifesto" on the subject of Cuba. His cabinet was composed principally of disunionists and their friends, namely, John B. Floyd, secretary of war ; Howell Cobb, secretary of the treasury ; Jacob Thompson, secretary of the interior ; Isaac Toucey, secretary of the navy ; and Jeremiah S. Black, attorney-general. Before the Presidential election of 1860, a large number of muskets were removed from Northern armories to the South, for the benefit of the disunionists. In his last message, December, 1860, the President cast on the Northern people the blame for the disruption of the Union, which was then imminent, and decided that the Constitution has not delegated to Congress or to the Executive any power to coerce a State or to prevent the secession of a State. "How easy would it be," says he, "for the American people to settle the slavery question forever, and restore peace and harmony to this distracted country ! They, and they alone, can do it. All that is necessary to accomplish the object, and all for which the slave States have ever contended, is to be let alone. . . . For this [i.e. slavery] the people of the North are not more responsible, and have no more right to interfere, than with similar institutions in Russia or in Brazil." About the 12th of December, Louis Cass resigned the office of secretary of state, because the President declined to reinforce Fort Sumter. The movements which the disunionists initiated to found and fortify a Southern Confederacy were facilitated by the supineness of the outgoing Federal administration. Nearly all the forts, arsenals, and custom-houses in the seceded States were seized by the insurgents in the winter of 1860–61. Mr. Buchanan, after his retirement from office, resided at Wheatland, near Lancaster, where he died in June, 1868. He was never married. He had published in 1866 a work entitled "Mr. Buchanan's Administration."

See GREELEY, "American Conflict," 2 vols., 1864–66 ; "Edinburgh Review," vol. civ., 1858, and October, 1860.

Buchanan, (ROBERT,) of Glasgow, a Scottish divine of the present age. He published "The Ten Years' Conflict, being the History of the Disruption of the Church of Scotland," (2 vols., 1849.)

Buchanan, (ROBERT,) a British poet, born in the early part of the present century, has written works entitled "Undertones," "Idyls and Legends of Inverburn," (London, 1865,) and "London Poems," (1866.)

Buchez, bü'shå', (PHILIPPE JOSEPH BENJAMIN,) a French publicist, republican, and able philosophical writer, born at Matagne (Ardennes) in 1796. He advanced some original views in his "Science of the Development of Humanity," (1833.) In conjunction with M. Roux, he published "The Parliamentary History of the French Revolution," (40 vols., 1833–38.) His most important work is his "Complete Treatise on Philosophy, from the Catholic and Progressive Point of View," (" Essai d'un Traité complet de Philosophie, au Point de Vue de Catholicisme et du Progrès," 3 vols., 1840.) He was president of the Constituent Assembly on the 15th of May, 1848, when that body was invaded by ruffians.

See "Nouvelle Biographie Générale."

Buchholz, bōōk'holts, (ANDREW HEINRICH,) a German writer of fiction, born at Schöningen in 1607 ; died in 1671.

Buchholz, (PAUL FERDINAND FRIEDRICH,) a German littérateur, born at Altruppin in 1768 ; died in 1843.

Buchhorn, bōōk'hoRn, (KARL LUDWIG BERNHARD,) a German artist and amateur, born at Halberstadt in 1770, became professor of engraving in the Academy of Arts at Berlin. He died in 1856, leaving considerable bequests to the Academy.

Buchmann. See BIBLIANDER.

Buchner, bōōk'nẹr, (AUGUST,) a German scholar, professor of poetry and eloquence in the University of Wittenberg, born in 1591; died in 1661.

Buchner, (JOHANN ANDREAS ELIA,) born at Erfurt in 1701, was a writer on materia medica, professor of medicine at Erfurt and afterwards at Halle, and consulting physician to the King of Prussia. Died in 1769.

See BROCKHAUS, "Conversations-Lexikon."

Bucholtzer, bōōk'olt'sẹr, (ABRAHAM,) a German divine, an intimate friend of Melanchthon, born in 1529. He wrote the "Index Chronologicus," and other works. Died in 1584.

See MELCHIOR ADAM, "Vitæ Theologorum."

Bucholz, bōōk'olts, written also **Buchholz,** (SAMUEL,) a German historian, born at Pritzwalk in 1717. He published, besides other works, a "History of the March of Brandenburg," (1759-75.) Died in 1774.

See ERSCH und GRUBER, "Allgemeine Encyklopaedie."

Buchon, bü'shŏn', (JEAN ALEXANDRE,) a French writer, born in the department of Cher in 1791. He published a "Life of Tasso," (1817,) and other works, and was a contributor to the "Biographie Universelle." Died in 1846.

Buchoz, bü'sho', (PIERRE JOSEPH,) a physician and botanist, born at Metz in 1731; died in 1807. He published a "Natural History of France," (14 vols., 1776 et seq.,) and other works.

Buchwald, bōōk'wält, (JOHANN HEINRICH,) a poet and littérateur, born at Vienna in 1787. He became in 1828 professor of French literature at Kiel.

See his "Souvenirs," ("Erindringer,") 2 vols., 1827-29, and ERSLEW, "Forfatter-Lexicon."

Buck, (CHARLES,) an English clergyman, born in 1771. He preached in London and Hackney. He published, besides other works, a "Theological Dictionary," (1802.) Died in 1815.

Buck, (Sir GEORGE.) See l'UC, (Sir GEORGE.)

Bucke, bŭk, (CHARLES,) an English writer, born in Suffolk in 1781. He wrote "The Beauties, Harmonies, and Sublimities of Nature," (new edition, 1837,) an eloquent work, which was praised by Sir James Mackintosh, and "The Book of Human Character." Died in 1847.

Buckeridge, buk'rij, or **Buck'ridge,**(JOHN,) an English ecclesiastic, born in Wiltshire. He became Bishop of Rochester in 1611, and Bishop of Ely in 1626. He wrote "On the Power of the Pope in Temporal Affairs," ("De Potestate Papæ in Rebus temporalibus," 1614.) Died in 1631.

Buckhurst, LORD. See SACKVILLE, (THOMAS.)

Buckinck, bōōk'kink, (ARNOLD,) a German of the fifteenth century, the first who engraved maps on and printed them from copper. An edition of Ptolemy's geography with copper-plate maps, the first known work of this kind, was published at Rome by Buckinck in 1478.

See WALCKENAER, "Vie de Buckinck," in his "Mélanges."

Buckingham, bŭk'ing-ạm, (GEORGE **Villiers**—vil'-yẹrz,) first DUKE OF, an English courtier, born in Leicestershire in 1592, became in his youth the favourite of James I. He obtained in rapid succession the titles of baron, viscount, earl, and marquis, and the office of lord-admiral of England. He induced Prince Charles to present himself in person at Madrid as a suitor of the Infanta of Spain, and accompanied him in this romantic adventure, (1623.) During his absence on this journey he was created Duke of Buckingham. His ascendency continued unimpaired after the accession of Charles I., of whom the duke was the chief favourite and prime minister. He involved England in a war with France. His insolence, incapacity, and destitution of principle rendered him very unpopular. He was assassinated in 1628 by John Felton.

See H. WOTTON, "Short View of the Life of George Villiers," 1642; Mrs. THOMPSON, "Life of George Villiers, Duke of Buckingham."

Buckingham, (GEORGE VILLIERS,) second DUKE OF, born in 1627, was the son of the preceding. He possessed the qualities requisite for a successful courtier, and was a man of profligate habits. In the civil war he fought for the king in one action, and subsequently retired to the continent. After the restoration he obtained the favour of Charles II., and promoted the fall of Clarendon, (1667,) of whom he was a bitter enemy.

About 1670 he formed the ministry called the "Cabal," of which he was president. Their policy was to make the king absolute, by the aid of Louis XIV. of France. Died in 1688.

Buck'ingham, (JAMES SILK,) an English traveller, born in Cornwall in 1786. He visited Egypt and India in 1813, and in 1816 edited a journal in Calcutta, which, owing to its censures of the government, was soon suppressed. After his return to England he published several volumes of travels in Palestine, Arabia, etc., and subsequently "Travels in the United States and Canada," (9 vols., 1841-43.) He became a member of Parliament for Sheffield in 1832. He was an earnest advocate of temperance and other social reforms. He died in 1855, leaving an unfinished "Autobiography."

See "London Quarterly Review" for October and January, 1822, and September, 1841.

Buck'ing-hạm, (JOSEPH TINKER,) an American journalist, born at Windham, Connecticut, in 1779. He edited "The New England Galaxy," (1817-28,) "The Boston Courier," (1824-48,) and "The New England Magazine," (1832-36.) He published "Specimens of Newspaper Literature, with Personal Memoirs," (2 vols., 1850,) and "Personal Memoirs and Recollections of Editorial Life," (2 vols., 1852.) Died in 1861.

Buckingham, (WILLIAM ALFRED,) born in Lebanon, Connecticut, in 1804. He became in early life a merchant at Norwich, and was for many years engaged in the manufacture of carpets. He was elected Governor of Connecticut by the Republicans in 1858, and was re-elected seven times. In 1868 he was chosen a Senator of the United States for six years.

See HARRIET B. STOWE, "Men of our Times," 1868.

Buck'ingham and Chan'dos, (RICHARD GRENVILLE BRYDGES CHANDOS,) first DUKE OF, an English peer, born in 1776, was the son of the second Duke of Temple. He was distinguished as a politician, and voted with the Conservatives. Died in 1839.

Buckingham and Chandos, (RICHARD TEMPLE NUGENT BRYDGES CHANDOS GRENVILLE,) second DUKE OF, born in London in 1797, was a son of the preceding. He published "Memoirs of the Court and Cabinets of George III.," (3 vols.) Died in 1861.

See "Private Diary of Richard, Duke of Buckingham and Chandos," London, 1862.

Buckinghamshire, bŭk'ing-ạm-shịr, (JOHN SHEFFIELD,) DUKE OF, son of the Earl of Mulgrave, born in 1649, learned the art of war under Turenne, became keeper of the privy seal under Queen Anne, and died in 1721. Besides his "Essay on Satire" and "Essay on Poetry," and other poems, he wrote "Memoirs" of the Revolution of 1688.

Buck'lạnd, (CYRUS,) an American inventor, master-machinist to the United States armory at Springfield, Massachusetts, was born at Manchester, Connecticut, in 1779. His principal inventions consist of various kinds of machinery for working the gun-stock, comprising fourteen different machines, which have been introduced into Great Britain and Russia, and a machine for cutting the grooves in the barrel of the new rifled musket, by which eight barrels are turned off in the time required to groove one by the old process, the work being done in a much superior manner.

Buck'lạnd, (FRANCIS TREVELYAN,) an English naturalist, son of Dr. William Buckland, noticed below, was born at Oxford in 1826. He has written, among other works, "Curiosities of Natural History," (1857; 3d series, 2 vols., 1866,) and a valuable treatise on pisciculture, entitled "Fish-Hatching," (1863.)

Buckland, (RALPH,) an English Catholic priest, born in Somersetshire in 1564, laboured as a missionary in England, and wrote several works. Died in 1611.

Buckland, (WILLIAM,) D.D., F.R.S., an English geologist, born at Axminster, Devonshire, in 1784, was educated at Corpus Christi College, Oxford. He obtained the chair of mineralogy at Oxford in 1813, and was appointed reader in geology there about 1818. In 1823 he published "Reliquiæ Diluvianæ." His most important work is the Bridgewater treatise entitled "Geology and Mineralogy considered with Reference to Natural Theology," (1836,) which is highly esteemed.

"The extraordinary and inestimable facts," says the "Edinburgh Review" for April, 1837, "which he has brought under the grasp of the general reader have been illustrated by numerous and splendid embellishments; and, while his descriptions of them are clothed in simple and perspicuous language, the general views to which they lead have been presented to us in the highest tone of lofty and impressive eloquence. We have ourselves never perused a work more truly fascinating or more deeply calculated to leave abiding impressions on the heart." He became Dean of Westminster in 1845. Died in 1856.

See, also, "Edinburgh Review" for October, 1823; "London Quarterly Review" for April and July, 1823, and April, 1824; "Men I have known," by WILLIAM JERDAN, London, 1866.

Buckle, bŭk'el, (HENRY THOMAS,) a popular English writer, born at Lee in 1822. His father was a wealthy merchant, and the son received, it is said, a "liberal education." He does not, however, appear to have enjoyed the advantages of that thorough mental training which would have been so valuable a preparation for the prosecution of those philosophic inquiries to which his subsequent life was devoted. On the death of his father, in 1840, he inherited an ample fortune, which enabled him to indulge his fondness for books and to give himself up wholly to literary pursuits. He is said to have formed one of the finest private libraries to be found in Europe. In 1857 Mr. Buckle published the first volume of his celebrated "History of Civilization in England." This work, characterized as it was by great boldness of thought and vigour of style, produced no little sensation in America, as well as in Great Britain. By one class of critics it was received with the warmest admiration, while by another class it was severely criticised, and by some it was condemned in unmeasured terms. This wide diversity of opinion respecting the merits of the work was doubtless chiefly due to the great diversity in the preconceived views of its readers, but perhaps also in no small degree to the peculiar genius of the writer. Although not remarkable for the closeness of his reasoning or for the accuracy of his knowledge,* Mr. Buckle had

* Those who have carefully read his History and taken the trouble to examine the facts and authorities which he cites to prove his positions, will scarcely question the justice of these strictures. It may not, however, be superfluous to call attention to one or two examples in support of what we have said above. In attempting to prove his theory respecting the predominant influence of physical circumstances on the character of nations, he contrasts Greece and India. In the former, we are told, the people are self-reliant and aspiring; in the latter, they are the victims of a grovelling superstition. He speaks of the religion of India as "a system of complete and unmitigated terror." "In Greece," says Mr Buckle, "we for the first time meet with hero-worship,—that is, the deification of mortals," (vol. i. chap. ii.) Now, it so happens that in India, for the last twenty-five hundred years, the deification of mortals has prevailed to an extent wholly unparalleled in the history of the human race. Not only was every Brahman considered to be "something transcendently divine," but he was supposed to possess the highest attribute of godhead, that of creation,—of "framing other worlds" and "giving being to new gods and mortals." (See "Institutes of Manu," chap. ix. 313, 315. 319.) This was the doctrine of Brahminism. If we look at the great offshoots of that system, viz., the religion of the Booddhists (strictly so called) and of the Jains, the case is still stronger against Mr. Buckle's theory; for with the latter the PRINCIPAL DEITIES, and with the former the ONLY DEITIES, WERE DEIFIED MORTALS. (See "Asiatic Researches," vol. ix. p. 288; Hardy's "Manual of Booddhism;" also article GAUTAMA in the present work.) Mr. Buckle's mistake on this point is the more remarkable, as it has the most vital connection with the fundamental doctrine of his system. It is true, he quotes Mr. Colebrooke to the effect that deified heroes formed no part of the religion of the Vedas: it should, however, be remembered that the religion of the Vedas was that of the Aryans soon after their arrival in India, adopted (as we may reasonab y suppose) before the climate and other physical conditions had yet had time to produce their full effect upon the minds of the new inhabitants; and that the "deification of mortals," which Mr. Buckle cites as proof of a self-reliant or anti-superstitious tendency, prevailed to its fullest extent after all the physical conditions belonging to India had had the amplest scope for exercising their utmost influence. From the foregoing facts and considerations the reader can judge of the truth of Mr. Buckle's assertion that "the tendency of Asiatic [*i.e.* Hindoo] civilization was to widen the distance between men and their deities." (!) Mr. Buckle commits an error scarcely less important in regard to Spain. (See "Edinburgh Review" for July, 1861.)

As one out of many instances of defective reasoning to be found in his works, we may cite his argument intended to prove that in all the great movements of society the progress is due to the intellect alone. (See vol. i. chap. iv.) Having shown to his own satisfaction that the progress of society must be the result either of the intellect or the moral sentiments, and that it cannot be owing to moral influences alone, he jumps to the conclusion that the intellectual power only is "the real mover" of society, assuming, "so contrary to all we know of nature, that a pheromenon cannot have more than one cause." (See Mill's "System of Logic," book v. chap. iii. 7.)

the power of presenting his ideas with extraordinary distinctness and force, so that, however he may fail to convince, he seldom or never fails to arouse attention and awaken thought. If we are not mistaken, his influence upon the minds of his readers is owing not so much to the severity of his logic or the weight of his authorities, as to the ardour of his temperament and the energy of his will. Those who read his pages may be compared to men listening to an earnest and gifted orator, who carries his hearers along with him mainly by the intensity and force of his own convictions. Those alone, it would seem, are able to resist the fascination of his genius who, from prejudice or from philosophy, are predetermined not to yield, or to yield only after their reason is fully convinced. We would not intentionally undervalue Mr. Buckle's extraordinary powers. We freely concede to him the possession of vast stores of information, as well as great affluence of thought. But these seeming advantages may to an ardent mind — especially if it have a strong bias towards controversy* — become an impediment, rather than a help, in its efforts to arrive at the truth. In its eager desire to build up an intellectual system, it will often unconsciously seize with avidity on such facts as may happen to favour its preconceived theories, and as unconsciously reject or ignore those of an opposite character.

In 1861 a second volume of Mr. Buckle's History made its appearance; but it did not excite so great an interest as the first had done. It may be that the novelty which gave attraction to the first was wanting; it is also probable that Mr. Buckle's impaired health prevented him from doing as full justice to his subject as he would have done under more favourable circumstances. In the latter part of 1861, with a view to recruit his failing health, he set out on a tour in the Levant. He died at Damascus on the 29th of May, 1862.

See "Westminster Review," vol. lxviii., 1857; "Edinburgh Review" for April, 1858, and July, 1861, pp. 189–90; "Quarterly Review" for July, 1858; "Blackwood's Magazine" for November, 1861; "Fraser's Magazine" for September, 1862, also October, 1857, and August, 1863; FROUDE, "Lecture on the Science of History," in his "Short Studies on Great Subjects," vol. i., 1867; CHARLES HALE, "Personal Reminiscences of the late Henry Thomas Buckle," published in the "Atlantic Monthly" for April, 1863.

Bückler. See SCHINDERHANNES.

Buck′man, (JAMES,) an English naturalist, born at Cheltenham about 1816, was professor at the Agricultural College of Cirencester for many years. He published several works on botany, geology, and agriculture.

Buck′min-ster, (JOSEPH,) an American orthodox clergyman, born at Rutland, Massachusetts, in 1751, graduated at Yale College in 1770. He was ordained pastor of the North Church of Portsmouth, New Hampshire, in 1779. He was an eloquent and popular preacher, and was distinguished for the fervour of his devotional exercises. His sermons produced emotion rather than conviction. Died in 1812.

See "Memoirs of the Life of J. Buckminster," by his daughter, ELIZA B. LEE, 1851.

Buckminster, (JOSEPH STEVENS,) an eloquent Unitarian minister, a son of the preceding, was born in Portsmouth in 1784. He graduated at Harvard with distinction in 1800, and became in 1804 pastor of the Brattle Street Church, Boston, one of the largest and most intelligent congregations in New England. He acquired a high reputation as a preacher and a scholar. In 1806 he made a voyage to Europe for his health. He superintended the publication of Griesbach's "New Testament" in 1808. Died in 1812.

See a "Memoir of J. S. Buckminster," prefixed to his works, 2 vols.; GRISWOLD, "Prose Writers of America;" SPRAGUE, "American Pulpit," vol. viii.

Buck′ner, (SIMON BOLIVAR,) an American general, born in Kentucky about 1824, graduated at West Point in 1844. He was commander of the State Guard of Kentucky in 1861, and took arms against the Union in the autumn of that year. He was one of the generals of the garrison of Fort Donelson when it was attacked by General Grant. The chief command of the fort was

* "His [Mr. Buckle's] controversial ardour is not only a heat, but a blaze, and frequently dazzles the eye of his understanding." See, in the "Atlantic Monthly" for January, 1863, "Mr. Buckle as a Thinker," an article which is well worthy of perusal by all who would form a just estimate of Mr. Buckle's system of philosophy.

---

e as k; ç as s; g̃ hard; g̃ as j; G, H, K, guttural; N, nasal; R, trilled; s as z; th as in this. (☞See Explanations, p. 23.)

transferred by General Floyd to Buckner, who surrendered on the 16th of February, 1862. He commanded a corps at Chickamauga, September 19 and 20, 1863.

Buckridge. See BUCKERIDGE.

Buckstone, (JOHN BALDWIN,) an English comic actor and dramatist, born in the Isle of Wight about 1800. Among his plays are "Jack Sheppard," "The Wreck Ashore," and "Victorine."

Bucquet, bü'kà', (JEAN BAPTISTE,) a French physician and chemist, born in Paris in 1746; died in 1780.

Bucquoi, bü'kwä', (CHARLES BONAVENTURE de Longueval—dĕh lòng'vȧl',) a celebrated general in the Thirty Years' war, born in 1561, entered early into the Spanish army destined to the war then raging in the Netherlands. Having afterwards passed into the service of Austria, he totally defeated the revolted Protestants of Bohemia, near Prague, in 1620. He was killed while besieging Neuhausel, in Hungary, in 1621.

See ERSCH und GRUBER, "Allgemeine Encyklopaedie."

Bucquoy, van, vȧn bü'kwä', (JAKOB,) a Dutch traveller, born at Amsterdam in 1693; died in 1760.

Buddäus or **Buddaeus,** bōōd-dā'ŭs, or **Budde,** bōōd'dĕh, (JOHANNES FRANCISCUS,) a German Lutheran theologian, historian, and voluminous writer, born at Anclam, in Pomerania, in 1667, became professor of moral philosophy at Halle, and afterwards of theology at Jena. Died in 1729.

See NICÉRON, "Mémoires."

Buddäus or **Buddaeus,** written also **Buddeus,** (KARL FRANZ,) a writer on philosophy, etc., son of the preceding, born at Halle in 1695, filled several high offices at Weimar and Gotha. Died in 1753.

See his autobiographic "Denkwürdigkeiten meines Lebens," 1748; J. A. LOEWE, "Gedächtnisspredigt auf den Vice-Kanzler Buddeus," 1753.

Bud'den, (JOHN,) an English scholar, and professor of civil law at Oxford, born in 1566; died in 1620.

Buddha. See BOODDHA.

Budé, bü'dà', (GUILLAUME,) [Lat. GULIEL'MUS BUDÆ'US,] a distinguished scholar, author of a work of great merit on ancient coins, entitled "De Asse," (1514,) was born in Paris in 1467. He was suspected of favouring the Reformation. Budé is said to have been the most learned man in France at the beginning of the sixteenth century. He was a friend of Erasmus, and was patronized by Francis I., who appointed him in 1522 master of requests. He was well versed in Greek, and wrote "Commentaries on the Greek Tongue." Died in 1540.

See BAYLE, "Historical and Critical Dictionary;" LOUIS LE ROY, "Vita G. Budæi, Parisiensis," 1540; D. REBITTÉ, "G. Budé, Restaurateur des Études Grecques en France," 1846; NICÉRON, "Mémoires;" "Nouvelle Biographie Générale."

Budée, bü'dà', (ADRIEN QUENTIN,) a French littérateur and mathematician, born in Paris in 1748; died in 1826.

Buder, boo'der, (CHRISTIAN GOTTLIEB,) a learned German jurist and historian, born in Upper Lusatia in 1693, became professor of jurisprudence at Jena in 1734, and died in 1763.

Budes, de, dĕh büd, (SYLVESTRE,) a French soldier and companion-in-arms of Du Guesclin. Died in 1379.

Budg'ell, (EUSTACE,) an English essayist, born near Exeter in 1685, was a relative of Joseph Addison, who procured for him a clerkship in the civil service. He wrote for the "Spectator" numerous papers with the signature of "X," and was suspected of forging the will of Tindal, by which £2000 were bequeathed to Budgell. He lost £20,000 in the South Sea bubble. He drowned himself in 1736.

Budg'ett, (SAMUEL,) a wealthy English merchant and philanthropist, born near Bristol in 1794. His extraordinary talent for business and energy of character enabled him to amass a large fortune, a great part of which he spent in acts of beneficence and in efforts to improve the condition of the poor in the vicinity. Died in 1851.

See "The Successful Merchant: Sketches of the Life, etc. of Samuel Budgett," by WILLIAM ARTHUR, London, 1853.

Budha. See BOODDHA.

Budrio. See LIPPI, (GIACOMO.)

Bueil. See BUIL.

Bueil, de, dĕh buĬ or buh'yĕ, (JEAN,) Count of Sancerre, (sòN'saiǹ',) a noted French warrior, contemporary

with Joan of Arc. He became admiral of France about 1450, and was surnamed "the Scourge of the English."

Bu'el, (JESSE,) an American journalist, born at Coventry, Connecticut, in 1778, established about 1813 the Albany "Argus," a Democratic journal, which has had a powerful influence in the politics of New York. Having severed his connection with it in 1821, he applied himself to the pursuits of agriculture, and in 1834 published the first number of the Albany "Cultivator," which he conducted for six years. Mr. Buel contributed to promote a taste for agricultural pursuits by his addresses on agriculture in different parts of the country, served repeatedly in the legislature, and was at one time judge of the county court. He was author of "The Farmer's Instructor" and "The Farmer's Companion." Died in 1839.

Bu'ell, (DON CARLOS,) an American general, born in Ohio about 1818, graduated at West Point in 1841. He gained the rank of captain about 1848. In November, 1861, he was appointed commander of the department of Kentucky, with the rank of brigadier-general of volunteers. He became a major-general in March, 1862, and was ordered to move the army of the Ohio (which he commanded) to Tennessee and to join that of General Grant. He arrived at Pittsburg Landing on the evening of April 6, and contributed to the victory on the 7th of that month. In June, 1862, he moved his army from Corinth towards Chattanooga; but before he reached that place he was required to oppose General Bragg, who invaded Kentucky in September and threatened Louisville. General Buell arrived at Louisville about the 24th of September. On the 1st of October he moved in pursuit of the enemy, who had captured Lexington and Frankfort. An indecisive battle was fought at Perryville, October 8, between the army of General Bragg and a part of Buell's army. General Bragg escaped into Tennessee with immense spoils. General Buell, who was considered dilatory and too "conservative," was removed from the command in October, 1862. He resigned his commission in June, 1864.

Buelow. See BÜLOW.

Buesching. See BÜSCHING.

Buettner. See BÜTTNER.

Buffalmacco, boof-fȧl-mȧk'ko, (BUONAMICO DI CRISTOFANO,) a Florentine painter, born about 1262, was a pupil of Andrea Tafi. He is celebrated in the "Decamerone" of Boccaccio. Died about 1340.

See VASARI, "Lives of the Painters."

Buffier, bü'fe-à', (CLAUDE,) an eminent grammarian and philosopher, born of French parents in Poland in 1661. He entered the order of Jesuits, and settled in Paris. He showed an excellent faculty of analysis in his "French Grammar," which formed part of his "Cours général et particulier des Sciences," (1732.) Among his works (which seem to be more highly esteemed by the British than by the French) is a "Treatise on Primary Truths," (1717.) Died in 1737.

Buffon, de, dĕh bü'fòN', [pron. sometimes Anglicized as bŭf'fọn,] (GEORGES LOUIS LECLERC,) COMTE, an illustrious French naturalist and philosopher, born at Montbard, in Burgundy, on the 7th of September, 1707. He was a son of Benjamin Leclerc, a counsellor of the parliament of Dijon, from whom he inherited a competent fortune, and was liberally educated. After he left college he travelled, in company with Lord Kingston, in Italy and England. In 1735 he produced a translation of Newton's "Treatise on Fluxions." He tested by experiments the probability of the statement that Archimedes set fire to the Roman fleet by burning-mirrors, and he succeeded in igniting wood at the distance of two hundred French feet. In 1739 he was admitted into the Academy of Sciences and appointed intendant of the royal garden, ("Jardin du Roi.") Thenceforth he devoted himself as "the high-priest and interpreter of Nature."

In 1749 he published the first three volumes of his great work, "Histoire naturelle, générale et particulière," in which he was assisted by Daubenton, who had charge of the department of anatomy and of those parts of the work which required patient and minute investigation. All the brilliant passages, all the general theories, the description of the habits and manners of animals and of the grand phenomena of nature, are from the pen of Buffon.

ā, ē, ī, ō, ū, ȳ, *long;* ȧ, ė, ȯ, *same, less prolonged;* ă, ĕ, ĭ, ŏ, ŭ, ў, *short;* ạ, ẹ, ị, ọ, *obscure;* fär, fȧll, fȧt; mêt; nŏt; gōōd; mōōn;

Twelve other volumes were issued between 1749 and 1767, after which were added eight volumes containing the History of Birds, in which Daubenton had no share, his place being supplied by Gueneau de Montbelliard and Abbé Bexon. Buffon himself wrote five volumes on Minerals, published between 1783 and 1785. Commenting on this work, Condorcet remarks, "M. de Buffon is poetical in his descriptions ; but, like all great poets, he knows how to render interesting the delineation of natural objects by blending with them moral ideas which affect the soul, at the same time that the imagination is amused or astonished." Buffon was elected a member of the French Academy in 1753, and married Mademoiselle de Saint-Belin in 1762. Among his greatest productions is the "Époques de la Nature," ("Epochs of Nature,") contained in the Supplement to his Natural History. Never perhaps was any literary reputation more rapidly or more widely established than that of Buffon after his great work was given to the world. By demonstrating the unity of the human species, Buffon prepared the way for the labours of Camper, Blumenbach, and Cuvier. Among his important contributions to the philosophy of natural history is the law of the geographical distribution of animals depending on climate and other physical conditions. He also has the credit of discovering that the test of a species consists in fecundity, or power to propagate itself. About 1776 he received the title of Count de Buffon from the King of France. He had one son, who served in the army, obtained the rank of major or colonel, and was executed in the reign of terror for the crime of belonging to the aristocracy. Buffon died in Paris on the 16th of April, 1788. He had received from nature an imposing figure and an eminently noble countenance, bearing the impress of high intelligence and wisdom. Besides the works above mentioned, he left, unfinished, a "Dissertation on Style," in which occurs the celebrated phrase, *Le style est de l'homme.*

See CONDORCET, "Éloge de Buffon ;" CUVIER, "Éloge de Buffon," prefixed to an edition of the "Natural History," 36 vols., 1826; FLOURENS, "Buffon : Histoire de sa Vie et de ses Ouvrages," 1844 ; enlarged edition of the same, 1850 ; A. DE CHESNEL, "Vie de Buffon," 1843 ; ANDRÉ AUDE, "Vie privée de Buffon," 1788.

Bu′ford, (ABRAHAM,) a native of Kentucky, who became a brigadier-general in the Confederate service in 1861.

Buford, (JOHN,) an American major-general, born in Kentucky about 1827. He graduated at West Point in 1848, and gained the rank of captain before the civil war. In the summer of 1862 he was appointed a brigadier-general of volunteers. He obtained command of a brigade of cavalry about August, 1862, served at the battle of Antietam, September 17, and distinguished himself as a cavalry officer in several actions. He rendered important services at Gettysburg, July 1-3, 1863. Died of fever at Washington in December of the same year.

Buford, (NAPOLEON BONAPARTE,) an American general, a half-brother of the preceding, was born in Kentucky in 1807. He graduated at West Point in 1827. He was appointed a brigadier-general in April, 1862, and obtained command of a brigade of Federal cavalry in July of that year.

Bugeaud de la Piconnerie, bü′zhō′deh lä pe′kon′re′, (THOMAS ROBERT,) Duc d'Isly, a celebrated French marshal, born at Limoges in 1784. He served in the Spanish campaigns from 1810 to 1814, and attained the rank of lieutenant-colonel. He went over to Napoleon on his return from Elba, and in the revolution of 1830 gave in his adhesion to Louis Philippe, by whom he was created marshal of France. Being appointed to a command in Algeria, he gained several victories, and in 1837 he concluded with Abd-el-Kâder the treaty of Tafna. In 1840 he became governor-general of the French possessions in Africa. In the course of the three ensuing years he subjected the whole country from Tunis to Morocco. In 1844 hostilities commenced between the French and the Emperor of Morocco, whom Bugeaud defeated at Isly in the same year. Having been recalled in 1847, he was selected to command the army and national guard at Paris on the 24th of February, 1848. Died in 1849.

See BESANCENEZ, "Biographie complète de M. le Maréchal Bugeaud," 1849 ; C. PITOIS, "Souvenirs du Maréchal Bugeaud," 2 vols., 1845.

Bugenhagen, boo′gẹn-hä′gẹn, (JOHANN,) surnamed POMERA′NUS, a German Protestant reformer, born near Stettin, in Pomerania, in 1485. He became professor of theology, and pastor at Wittenberg, in 1522. He wrote an "Explanation of the Psalms," and other religious works, and assisted Luther in translating the Bible. He was a devoted friend of the great Reformer, and preached his funeral sermon. Died in 1558.

See JAENCKE, "Leben J. Bugenhagen's," 1730 ; J. C. LANGE, "J. Bugenhagens Leben," 1731 ; F. C. KRAFT, "De J. Bugenhagii Pomerani Meritis," etc., 1831 ; BIESNER, "Leben des H. Rubenow und des J. Bugenhagen," 1837 ; F. KOCH, "Erinnerungen an J. Bugenhagen," 1817.

Bugge, bŏŏg′gẹh, (THOMAS,) an eminent Danish astronomer, born in 1740 at Copenhagen, where he became professor of mathematics and astronomy in 1777. He published "Elements of Spherical and Theoretical Astronomy," (1796,) "Elements of Abstract Mathematics," and an excellent treatise on Surveying. He was a member of the French Institute, and perpetual secretary of the Society of Sciences of Denmark. Died in 1815.

See JONAS COLLIN, "Mindetale over T. Bugge og C. Colbjoernsen," 1815.

Bugiardini, boo-jaR-dee′nee, (GIULIANO,) a mediocre Italian painter, born at Florence in 1480, was an associate or friend of Michael Angelo. Died in 1552.

See VASARI, "Lives of the Painters."

Buglio, bool′yo, (LUIGI,) a Sicilian Jesuit and missionary, born at Palermo in 1606, went to China in 1637, where he died in 1682.

Bugnyon, bün′yŏN′, [Lat. BUGNO′NIUS,] (PHILIBERT,) a French advocate and *littérateur,* native of Mâcon. Died in 1590.

Bugrow. See BOOGROV.

Buhle, boo′lẹh, (JOHANN GOTTLIEB,) a learned German writer, born at Brunswick in 1763, became professor of philosophy at Göttingen in 1787, and afterwards taught in his native city. Died in 1821. Besides a multitude of other works, he wrote a "History of Modern Philosophy."

See BROCKHAUS, "Conversations-Lexikon."

Buil, boo-eel′, written also **Bueil,** a Benedictine monk of Catalonia, sent by Ferdinand and Isabella to preach the gospel in the West Indies, of which he is regarded as the first patriarch. He is chiefly known from having been one of the most bitter enemies of Columbus.

Buister, bois′tẹr, (PHILIPPUS,) a Flemish sculptor, born at Brussels in 1595, worked in Paris ; died in 1688.

Bujault, bü′zhō′, (JACQUES,) a French rural economist, born near Bressuire in 1771 ; died in 1842.

Bulæus. See BALBAN.

Bu-lar′chus, [Fr. BULARQUE, bü′lärk′,] a Greek painter mentioned by Pliny, lived about 700 B.C.

Bülau, bü′lŏw, (FRIEDRICH,) a German writer on history and political economy, born at Freyberg, in Saxony, in 1805. He became professor of philosophy at Leipsic in 1836. He published, besides other works, "Historische Hausbibliothek," ("Historical Family Library,") of which the 36th volume appeared in 1855.

Bulbun. See BOULAY.

Bulfinger, bŏŏl′fing′ẹr, (GEORG BERNHARD,) a German professor of theology at Tübingen, born in 1693 ; died in 1750.

Bulgarin. See BOOLGARIN.

Bulgaris. See EUGENIUS BULGARIS.

Bŭlk′ley, (CHARLES,) an English dissenting minister, born in London in 1719, was a grandson of Matthew Henry the commentator. He published "Discourses on the Parables and Miracles of Christ," (4 vols., 1771.) Died in 1797.

Bŭlk′ley, (PETER,) the first minister of Concord, Massachusetts, was born in Bedfordshire in 1583. He emigrated to America in 1635. Died in 1659.

Bull, (GEORGE,) a learned English ecclesiastic, born at Wells in 1634, became Bishop of Saint David's in 1705, and died in 1710. He wrote, besides other works, a "Defence of the Nicene Faith," ("Defensio Fidei Nicenæ," 1685-88,) which has been applauded in all parts of Christendom.

See NELSON, "Life of G. Bull," 1717.

Bull, (JOHN,) an eminent English composer and musician, born in Somersetshire about 1563. He became organist to the Royal Chapel in 1591. The authorship of the anthem "God save the King" is ascribed to him by some writers. He died about 1625.

Bull, bōōl, (OLE BORNEMANN,) a celebrated Norwegian violinist, born at Bergen in 1810. Having studied a short time under Spohr, at Cassel, he went to seek his fortune in Paris. Here he was reduced to such distress that he was on the point of committing suicide, when he was relieved by a lady of rank. A concert which he gave soon after furnished him with the means of visiting Italy, where his performances were received with the greatest enthusiasm. Having met with the same brilliant success in Paris, London, and the principal capitals of Europe, he set out about 1845 for America. He purchased about 120,000 acres of land in Pennsylvania, where he founded a Swedish colony, to which he gave the name of Oleona.

See BROCKHAUS, "Conversations-Lexikon;" "Nouvelle Biographie Générale."

Bull, bōōl, (WILLIAM,) an American physician, born in South Carolina in 1710, became lieutenant-governor of his native State in 1764. Died in 1791.

Bullant, bü'lôN', (JEAN,) a celebrated French architect, born about 1520. He erected for Catherine de Médicis a palace called at first Hôtel de la Reine, and afterwards Hôtel de Soissons. He was architect of some parts of the Tuileries, was patronized by several kings of France, and contributed much to the restoration of the classical or Roman style. Died in 1578.

Bullard, bōōl'lard, (ARTEMAS,) an American divine, born at Northbridge, Massachusetts, in 1802, became in 1838 pastor of the First Presbyterian Church of Saint Louis. He was killed by a railroad-accident in 1855.

Bullard, (HENRY ADAMS,) an American lawyer, born at Groton, Massachusetts, in 1788, removed to Louisiana. He was elected a member of Congress in 1831, and again about 1848. Died in 1851.

Bullen, (ANN.) See BOLEYN.

Buller, bōōl'ler, (Right Hon. CHARLES,) a distinguished Liberal statesman, born at Calcutta in 1806. Having graduated at Trinity College, Cambridge, in 1828, he was elected member of Parliament for West Looe, in Cornwall, in 1830. From 1832 till 1848 he represented Liskeard in Parliament, and distinguished himself by his opposition to the corn-laws and his advocacy of various reforms. He was successively appointed queen's counsel, member of the privy council, 1847, and president of the poor-law commission about the end of the same year. He was a contributor to the "Edinburgh" and "Westminster" Reviews and other periodicals. Died in 1848.

Buller, (Sir FRANCIS,) an English judge, born in Cornwall in 1745, was a grandson of Allen, Earl Bathurst. He published an "Introduction to the Law relative to Trials at Nisi Prius," (1767; 7th ed., 1817.) Died in 1800.

See Foss, "The Judges of England," vol. viii.

Bullet, bü'lå', (JEAN BAPTISTE,) a learned French theologian, born at Besançon in 1699; died in 1775.

Bulleyn, bōōl'lin, (WILLIAM,) an English physician in the time of Henry VIII., born about 1500; died in 1576.

Bulliard, bü'le-ǎR', (PIERRE.) a French botanist and artist, born near Langres about 1742; died in 1793. He wrote "Flora Parisiensis," (6 vols., 1774,) a "History of Poisonous Plants," (1784,) and other works.

Bullinger, bōōl'ling-er, (HEINRICH,) a Swiss Protestant reformer of high reputation, born in the canton of Aargau in 1504. While pursuing his studies he is said to have supported himself for several years as a street-musician. He was an intimate friend of Zwingle, whom he succeeded as pastor at Zurich in 1531. Several volumes of his sermons have been published. Died in 1575.

See LAVATER, "Vom Leben Heinrich Bullingers," 1576; BROCK-HAUS, "Conversations-Lexikon;" MELCHIOR ADAM, "Vitæ Theologorum Germanorum;" JOSIAS SIMLER, "Narratio de Ortu et Vita H. Bullingeri," 1575: SALOMON HESS, "Lebensgeschichte Mag. H. Bullingers," 2 vols., 1828.

Bullinger, (JOHANN BALTHASAR,) a Swiss painter and engraver, born at Langenau in 1713, was first professor in the school of design at Zurich. Died about 1790.

Bullion, de, deh bü'le-ôN', (CLAUDE,) a superintendent of the finances under Louis XIII. Under his direction, in 1640, louis-d'ors (the earliest gold coins of France) were first made. Hence, perhaps, the origin of the English term "bullion."

See BLANCHARD, "Histoire des Présidents de Paris."

Bullions, bōōl'yǫnz, (PETER,) a distinguished scholar and educational writer, professor of Greek and Latin in the Albany Academy, was born in Perthshire, Scotland, in 1791. His series of Latin, Greek, and English grammars and readers are among the most popular in use. Died in 1864.

Bullioud, bü'le-oo', (SYMPHORIEN,) Bishop of Soissons, and governor of Milan, born at Lyons in 1480; died in 1533.

Bull'ock, (WILLIAM F.,) an American jurist, born in Fayette county, Kentucky, in 1807. Having served several terms in the State legislature, he was appointed, in 1846, judge of the fifth judicial district, and in 1849 became professor of the law of real property, etc. in the University of Louisville.

See LIVINGSTON's "Portraits of Eminent Americans."

Bulmer, bōōl'mer, (WILLIAM,) an eminent English printer, born at Newcastle-on-Tyne in 1758. He printed, among other works, a magnificent edition of Shakspeare, regarded as equal to anything ever produced in this department of art. Died in 1830.

Bülow or **Buelow,** bü'lo, (AUGUST FRIEDRICH WILHELM,) a German jurist, born at Vorden, in Westphalia, in 1762; died in 1817.

Bülow, (FRIEDRICH WILHELM,) COUNT, a Prussian general, born in Mecklenburg in 1755, particularly distinguished himself in the campaigns of 1813 and 1815. In the latter he commanded under Blücher; and by the promptitude and celerity of his march to reach the field of Waterloo on the evening of the 18th of June, he contributed materially to the victory gained by the allies on that memorable day. Died in 1816.

See "Nouvelle Biographie Générale."

Bülow, (HEINRICH,) BARON, a German diplomatist, born at Schwerin in 1790, was a son-in-law of the celebrated William von Humboldt, whom he accompanied to London as secretary of embassy in 1817. He was ambassador to London in 1827, and in 1842 was appointed minister of foreign affairs. He resigned in 1844. Died in 1846.

Bülow, (HENRY WILLIAM,) a talented though eccentric and visionary person, brother of Friedrich Wilhelm, noticed above, born about 1760, became successively a soldier, an actor, and a preacher of Swedenborgianism. After trying his fortune in the United States, he went to France, where he wrote a work on military tactics, which, from its singularity, procured him the name of "Tactician Bülow." He subsequently visited England, and then returned to his native country, where, having incurred the suspicion of the government, he was arrested, and died in prison in 1807, (or, according to Oettinger, in 1816.)

See JULIUS VON VOSS, "H. von Buelow; nach seinem Talent-Reichthum, etc.," 1807.

Bülow, (LUDWIG FRIEDRICH VICTOR HANS,) COUNT, a Prussian statesman, born near Brunswick in 1774. After the peace of Tilsit he became a member of the state council of the kingdom of Westphalia, and in 1808 minister of finance, commerce, and the treasury. In 1813 he was appointed minister of state and finance by the King of Prussia. Died in 1825.

See F. CRAMER, "Leben des Grafen von Bülow," 1821.

Bülow, von, fon bü'lo, (JOHANN,) a Danish gentleman, distinguished as a patron of literary men, was born in Funen in 1751. He became a marshal in 1784, and director of the royal museums in 1791. Many Danish authors and artists were liberally patronized by him. Died in 1828.

Bülow, von, fon bü'lo, (KARL EDUARD,) a German novelist and littérateur, born in the duchy of Saxony in 1803. He published in 1834 his "Novellenbuch," containing one hundred tales imitated and selected from the French, Spanish, Italian, etc. He also translated into German Manzoni's "Promessi Sposi," (1828.)

Bülow-Cummerow, von, fon bü'lo kōōm'meh-ro, (ERNST,) a German jurist and writer, born in Mecklenburg-Schwerin in 1775.

ā, ē, ī, ō, ū, ȳ, *long;* ă, ĕ, ĭ, ŏ, ŭ, ў̆, *same, less prolonged;* ă, ĕ, ĭ, ŏ, ŭ, ў, *short;* ą, ę, į, ǫ, *obscure;* fär, fȧll, fȧt; mět; nŏt; gŏŏd; mōōn;

Büloz, bü'lo', (FRANÇOIS,) a Swiss *littérateur*, born near Geneva in 1803. He settled in Paris, and founded in 1831 the "Revue des Deux Mondes," a periodical of high reputation, issued twice a month.

Bul'strode, (EDWARD,) an English jurist, born in 1588, published "Reports in King's Bench." Died in 1659.

Bulstrode, (Sir RICHARD,) a son of the preceding, was a royalist in the civil war. He wrote "Essays on Manners and Morals," (1715.) He is said to have attained the age of one hundred and one years.

Bulteau, bül'tō', (LOUIS,) a French writer, born at Rouen in 1625, published an "Essay on the Monastic History of the East," and other works. Died in 1693.

Bulwer, bōōl'wẹr, (EDWARD GEORGE EARLE LYTTON,) Baron Lytton, a distinguished British novelist, was born at Heydon Hall, in Norfolk, in 1805. His father, William Earle Bulwer, who at one time was brigadier-general in the army, belonged to one of the oldest families of Norfolk. His mother, Elizabeth B. Lytton, a wealthy heiress, was descended from an ancient family of Knebworth, in Hertfordshire. Edward was the youngest of three sons, and was carefully educated under the superintendence of his mother, who possessed a decided taste for literature, and is said to have contributed not a little towards giving form and direction to the intellectual powers of her gifted son. He entered Cambridge, and graduated at Trinity Hall in 1826. The chancellor's prize for English verse had been awarded to him for his poem on "Sculpture" in 1825. On his return from a tour through France, he published in 1827 his first novel, "Falkland." In 1828 appeared "Pelham, or the Adventures of a Gentleman," a work, in spite of its extravagances, of considerable merit, and evincing powers of no common order. It was followed by "The Disowned," (1828,) "Devereux," (1829,) "Paul Clifford," (1830,) "The Siamese Twins," a satirical poem, (1831,) and "Eugene Aram," (1832.) The hero of the last-named novel had taught, it is said, in the family of Bulwer's grandfather, from which circumstance the author had felt a peculiar and deep interest in his tragic history. About the year 1831 he became editor of the "New Monthly Magazine." He was returned to Parliament the same year as member for Saint Ives, and, after the passage of the Reform Bill, was elected by the city of Lincoln, which he continued to represent in the House of Commons till 1841. "England and the English," sketches of English society and literature, appeared in 1833. His health having failed, in consequence of the intense application of his mind, he visited Germany and Italy in 1833–34, and soon after he published "The Pilgrims of the Rhine," and "The Last Days of Pompeii ;" then followed "Rienzi, the Last of the Tribunes," (1835.) The same year appeared "The Student," consisting of his contributions to the "New Monthly Magazine." He published in 1837 a work, historical and critical, entitled "Athens : its Rise and Fall." In 1837 also another novel, "Ernest Maltravers," was given to the world ; and soon after a continuation of the same, entitled "Alice, or the Mysteries." He had brought out in 1836 an unsuccessful play called "The Duchess of La Vallière." In 1838 appeared his drama entitled "The Lady of Lyons," and soon after another, called "Richelieu," both of which were eminently successful. He also produced a comedy entitled "Money," which had a great popularity. Another novel, called "Night and Morning," was published in 1841. "Zanoni," a fiction abounding in the marvellous, appeared in 1842 ; then followed "The Last of the Barons," (1843,) "Lucretia, or the Children of the Night," (1846,) designed to show the influence of atheistical (or Lucretian) opinions on the moral character, and "Harold, the Last of the Saxon Kings," (1848.) "The Caxtons," the first of a new series of novels, was published in 1850, "My Novel : by Pisistratus Caxton," in 1851, and "What will He do with It ?" in 1858. The three last-named works made their first appearance in the columns of "Blackwood's Magazine." Although Bulwer is chiefly distinguished as a novelist, he has attempted almost every species of literary composition, and has written, not without success, on a vast variety of subjects. In addition to the works already named, he published in

1827 a poem in the Byronic style, entitled "O'Niel, or the Rebel." "The Crisis," (1835,) a political pamphlet advocating liberal views, had an immense success, and caused his influence to be recognized in politics no less than in literature. Passing over less important works, we may mention his poems "The New Timon," (1846,) and "King Arthur,"(1848,) which added new laurels to his many-sided fame. His translations of Schiller's poems, (first given to the public in 1844,) though not remarkable for their fidelity to the original, may be regarded on the whole as a decided success, and, by furnishing another proof of his versatility, have contributed to extend his literary reputation. His last fiction, "A Strange Story," which by its marvellous incidents reminds one of "Zanoni," was first published in "All the Year Round" in 1861. Bulwer's novels have been translated into several of the European languages, and are extensively read throughout the civilized world. He is perhaps, after Scott, the most universally popular of all the British novelists.

Bulwer was made a baronet in 1838. Having, on his mother's death in 1844, come into the possession of the Knebworth estates, he assumed, in compliance with the conditions of the will, the name of Bulwer-Lytton. In 1856 he was chosen lord rector of the University of Glasgow ; and other literary distinctions have been conferred on him. During the brief term of the Derby ministry in 1858, he held the office of secretary of state for the colonies. He was raised to the peerage, as Baron Lytton, in 1866. He had married in 1827 Miss Rosina Wheeler, of Limerick, Ireland ; but the union was not a happy one, and the parties were subsequently divorced. Robert Edward Bulwer Lytton, the only son by that marriage, has already obtained some distinction as an author, under the pseudonym of "Owen Meredith."

See "Edinburgh Review" for July, 1837 ; "London Quarterly Review" for July, 1865 ; "Blackwood's Magazine" for February, 1855 ; "Fraser's Magazine" for January, 1850.

Bulwer, (Sir HENRY LYTTON EARLE,) an English diplomatist, brother of the preceding, was born in 1804. He has been employed in missions to Vienna, the Hague, and Brussels, and in 1830 became a member of Parliament for Wilton. From 1834 to 1837 he represented Marylebone in Parliament. He was minister plenipotentiary at Madrid from 1843 to 1848, was sent as minister to Washington in 1849, and created Knight Grand Cross of the Bath in 1851. He was sent as ambassador to Constantinople in 1858. He has published "France, Social, Literary, and Political," "Historical Characters : Talleyrand, Cobbett, Mackintosh, and Canning," (2 vols., 1868,) and several other works.

See "London Quarterly Review" for October, 1867.

Bulwer, (JOHN,) an Englishman, who published in 1648 a work to teach deaf people to understand a speaker by observing the motions of his lips.

See "Biographie Médicale."

Bulwer, (ROSINA WHEELER,) afterwards Lady BULWER LYTTON,was born in Ireland in 1807. In 1827 she was married to Bulwer, the celebrated novelist. (See BULWER, EDWARD.) She has published numerous works of fiction, among which may be named "Bianca Capello," "Cheveley, or the Man of Honour," and "The Budget of the Bubble Family."

Bünau, bü'nŏw, (HEINRICH,) COUNT, a German statesman and historian, born at Weissenfels in 1697. He wrote a "History of the German Emperors and Empire," (4 vols., 1728, unfinished,) and a "History of the War between France,England, and Germany," (in French and German, 1763.) His library of 42,000 volumes now forms a principal part of the Royal Library of Dresden. Died in 1762.

See SAX, "Onomasticon."

Bunbury, bŭn'bẹr-e, (HENRY WILLIAM,) an English artist and caricaturist, born in Suffolk ; died in 1811.

Bunbury, (SELINA,) an English authoress of the present century. She has written "Rides in the Pyrenees," (2 vols., 1844,) "Evelyn ; a Novel," (1849,) "Life in Sweden," and "Russia after the War," (2 vols., 1857.)

Bundokdar. See BIBARS.

Bunel, bü'nĕl', (JACQUES,) a French painter of history, born at Tours in 1558 ; died about 1620.

Bunel, (PIERRE,) a French writer, born at Toulouse '1' 1499; died in 1546.

Bunemann, boo'nęh-mân', (JOHANN LUDOLF,) a German bibliographer, born in 1687; died in 1759.

Bunge, von, fon bŏŏng'ęh, (ALEXANDER,) a Russian botanist and traveller, born at Kiev in 1803. In 1830 he accompanied a mission to Pekin, and made a valuable collection of the plants of China and Siberia. He was appointed professor of botany at Dorpat in 1836, and published several botanical works.

Bunge, von, (FREDERICK GEORGE,) a Russian jurist, brother of the preceding, born at Kiev in 1802, became professor of law at Dorpat.

Buniva, boo-nee'vǎ, (MICHELE FRANCESCO,) an Italian medical writer, and professor of medicine at Turin, born at Pinerolo in 1761; died in 1834.

Bunn, (ALFRED,) an English theatrical manager. He published "The Stage, both before and behind the Curtain, from Observations taken on the Spot," (3 vols., 1840.) Died in 1860.

Bunnick. See BUNNIK.

Bunnik, bŭn'nik, or **Bunnick,** (JAKOB,) a Dutch landscape- and battle-painter, was a brother of Jan, noticed below. Died in 1725.

Bunnik, (JAN,) a noted Dutch landscape-painter, born at Utrecht in 1654, was invited to England by William III. Died in 1707.

See DESCAMPS, "Vies des Peintres Flamands," etc.

Bunon, bü'nôn', (ROBERT,) a French dentist, born at Châlons-sur-Marne in 1702, wrote several works on the teeth. Died in Paris in 1748.

Bunsen, bŏŏn'sęn, (ROBERT WILHELM EBERHARD,) a German professor of chemistry at Breslau, born at Göttingen in 1811. He made some discoveries in chemistry, and contributed to Liebig's "Annales de Chimie."

Bunsen, von, fon bŏŏn'sęn, (CHRISTIAN KARL JOSIAS,) CHEVALIER, an eminent German philologist, diplomatist, and theologian, was born, of poor and obscure parents, at Korbach, in Westphalia, on the 25th of August, 1791. He studied under the famous Heyne at Göttingen, learned Greek, Hebrew, and other languages, and there formed a friendship with Mr. Astor, of New York. He afterwards studied Arabic and Persian in Paris under Silvestre de Sacy. "He was endowed by nature," says the "Edinburgh Review," "with the warmest and broadest sympathies. His knowledge was vast and varied; to no field of intellectual research was he a stranger." About 1816 he became acquainted at Rome with Niebuhr, whom he regarded with peculiar affection and veneration, and of whom he declared, "Him alone I can acknowledge as my lord and master."

In 1817 he married a Miss Waddington, a young English lady of good family and fortune, whose influence gave more regularity and stability to the natural piety of his character. He was appointed secretary to the Prussian embassy at Rome in 1818, through the favour of Niebuhr, who then represented the King of Prussia at that court. There passed twenty happy years, during which he devoted much time to historical research, and published, about 1829, a "Description of the City of Rome." He succeeded Niebuhr as Prussian minister at Rome in 1827. Having been recalled in 1838, he was ordered to take leave of absence for a journey to England, where he made many friends among the higher classes and literati. In 1841 he was appointed Prussian ambassador at the court of Saint James. He enjoyed a high degree of the favour of the crown prince who became King of Prussia in 1840. "He acquired," says the "Edinburgh Review" of April, 1868, "a position and an influence in English society which had never before been possessed by a German diplomatist." He gained a wide reputation as an ecclesiastical historian and Egyptologist. Among his principal works are "The Constitution of the Church of the Future," ("Die Verfassung der Kirche der Zukunft," 1845,) "Egypt's Place in Universal History," ("Ægyptens Stelle in der Weltgeschichte," 5 vols., 1845-57,) "Hippolytus and his Epoch," (4 vols., 1851,) a revised edition of which appeared under the title of "Christianity and Mankind," (7 vols., 1854,) and "God in History; or the Progress of Man's Faith in a Moral Order of the World," (2 vols., 1868,) trans-

lated by Susanna Winkworth. The first and second of these works have been translated into English. He continued to represent Prussia at London until 1854. As he advanced in age, his political principles became more and more liberal. In 1857 he was raised to the peerage, with the title of Freiherr (Baron) von Bunsen. After he left London, he resided at Heidelberg and Bonn, where he died in 1860, leaving a number of children.

See a "Memoir of Baron Bunsen," by [his wife] FRANCES, BARONNESS VON BUNSEN, drawn chiefly from "family papers," 2 vols., 1868; Rev. F. D. MAURICE's article on "Baron Bunsen" in "Macmillan's Magazine" for March, 1861, and a notice in the "Révue Chrétienne," 1860, by M. PRESSENSÉ; "Quarterly Review" for June, 1846; "North British Review" for June, 1868; "Blackwood's Magazine" for September, 1868.

Bŭnt'ing, (EDWARD,) an Irish musician and lyrical composer, born at Armagh in 1773; died in 1843.

Bŭnt'ing, (JABEZ,) an eminent English Wesleyan minister, born in Manchester about 1778, was an eloquent preacher. He published a number of sermons. Died in 1858.

See "Life of J. Bunting," by his son, 1859.

Bŭn'yan, (JOHN,) the celebrated author of "Pilgrim's Progress," was born at Elstow, near Bedford, in England, in 1628. He followed the occupation of his father, who was a tinker, and for some time led a wandering, dissipated life. He married about the age of twenty. During the civil war he served in the army of the Parliament in 1645. Having become deeply impressed with the importance of religion, he joined the Anabaptists of Bedford about 1664, and was distinguished for his zeal. He became a Baptist minister about 1655. After the restoration he was sentenced, as a promoter of seditious assemblies, to transportation for life. This sentence, however, was not executed; but he was detained more than twelve years in prison, from which he was released in 1672. During his imprisonment he wrote part of his immortal work, "Pilgrim's Progress." Besides "Pilgrim's Progress," (1678,) he wrote "The Resurrection of the Dead," "Gospel Truths Opened," (1656,) "The Holy City," (1665,) "Grace Abounding," (1666,) "Justification by Jesus Christ," (1671,) "The Holy War," (1682,) "The Pharisee and Publican," (1685,) and other works. After his release he was minister to a congregation at Bedford, and became extremely popular. Died in 1688.

"He had no suspicion," says Macaulay, "that he was producing a master-piece. He could not guess what place his allegory would occupy in English literature; for of English literature he knew nothing. . . . In puritanical circles, from which plays and novels were strictly excluded, the effect was such as no work of genius, though it were superior to the Iliad, to Don Quixote, or Othello, can ever produce on a mind unaccustomed to indulge in literary luxury. In 1678 came forth a second edition, with additions; and then the demand became immense. . . . We are not afraid to say that, though there were many clever men in England during the latter half of the seventeenth century, there were only two great creative minds. One of those minds produced the 'Paradise Lost,' the other the 'Pilgrim's Progress.'" (Essay on Southey's edition of "Pilgrim's Progress," 1831.)

See MACAULAY, "History of England," vol. ii chap. vii.; IVIMEY, "Life of John Bunyan," 1809; SOUTHEY, "Life of Bunyan;" GEORGE OFFOR, "Life of Bunyan," prefixed to an edition of his works, 3 vols., 1853; "Quarterly Review," vol. xliii., May–October, 1830.

Buol-Schauenstein, von, fon boo'ol shŏw'ęn-stīn', (KARL FERDINAND,) COUNT, an Austrian statesman, born in Switzerland in 1797. He was sent as ambassador to Saint Petersburg in 1848, and to London in 1851. In 1852 he became minister of foreign affairs (*i.e.* prime minister) of Austria, and in December, 1854, signed a treaty which engaged Austria to favour the allies against Russia. He resigned in May, 1859.

Buonaccorsi. See PERINO DEL VAGA.

Buonafede, boo-o'nä-fā'dä, (APPIANO,) an Italian writer, and professor of theology at Naples, born at Comacchio in 1716. He published "Poetical, Historical, and Critical Sketches of Various Literary Men," and other works. Died in 1793.

See MAZZUCHELLI, "Scrittori d'Italia."

Buonamici, boo-o-nä-mee'chee, (CASTRUCCIO, käs-tROOt'cho,) one of the most elegant Latin writers, born at Lucca, in Italy, in 1710. His "Commentaries on the Italian War" ("Commentarii de Bello Italico") is a work of great merit. Died in 1761.

See MAZZUCHELLI, "Scrittori d'Italia."

Buonamici or Bonamici, bo-nä-mee'chee, [Lat. BO-NAMI'CUS,] (LAZZARO,) an Italian scholar and *littérateur*, born at Bassano in 1479; died in 1552.

See JOHANN G. ECK, "L. Bonamicus," 1768; G. B. VERCI, "De Rebus gestis et Scriptis L. Bonamici," 1770.

Buonamico. See BUFFALMACCO.

Buonanni. See BONANNI.

Buonaparte. See BONAPARTE.

Buonarotti. See MICHAEL ANGELO.

Buonarotti, boo-o-nä-rot'tee, or Buonarrotti, (FI-LIPPO,) an Italian republican and revolutionist, born at Pisa in 1761. He was an enthusiastic partisan of the principles of the French Revolution, in which he took an active part. Having gone to Paris in 1792, he was sent to Corsica with extensive powers in 1793. As an accomplice in the conspiracy of Babeuf, he was imprisoned several years, (1797-1800.) Died in 1837.

See TRÉLAT, "Notice sur Philippe Buonarotti," 1838.

Buonarroti, boo-o-när-ro'tee, (FILIPPO,) a distinguished Italian antiquary; died in 1733.

Buonarroti, (MICHAEL (or MICHELE) ANGELO,) an Italian poet, nephew of the famous Michael Angelo, born at Florence in 1568; died in 1646.

Buoncompagni. See BONCOMPAGNI.

Buonconsigli, boo-òn-kon-sèl'yee, (GIOVANNI,) an Italian painter, born at Vicenza, lived about 1500.

Buoncuore. See BONCUORE.

Buonfigli. See BONFIGLIO.

Buonfigli, boo-òn-fèl'yee, (GIUSEPPE COSTANTE,) an Italian historian, born at Messina, wrote a "History of Sicily," (1604,) and other works.

Buoni, de', dà boo-o'nee, (BUONO,) a Neapolitan painter; died about 1465.

Buoni, de', (SILVESTRO,) a son of the preceding, was a painter. Died in 1484.

Buoninsegna. See DUCCIO.

Buonmattei, boo-òn-mât-tä'ee, (BENEDETTO,) an able Italian grammarian, born at Florence in 1581. He wrote a treatise "On the Tuscan Language," (1643,) and other works. Died in 1647.

Buono, boo-o'no, a distinguished Italian architect and sculptor, lived about 1150, and erected, besides other edifices, the famous tower of Saint Mark, at Venice.

Buono, (BARTOLOMMEO,) an Italian architect and sculptor, born at Bergamo. He became architect of the republic of Venice in 1505. Among his greatest works is the "Procuratie Vecchie," at Venice. He also restored the tower of Saint Mark. Died in 1529.

Buononcini, (GIOVANNI BATTISTA.) See BONONCINI.

Buontalenti, boo-òn-tä-lèn'tee, (BERNARDO,) an Italian painter, sculptor, and architect, surnamed DELLA GIRANDOLA, (je-rän'do-lä,) born at Florence in 1536. He was appointed by the grand duke Cosimo de' Medici preceptor to his son. Among his master-pieces are the Casino palace at Florence, and the villa of Bratonilo for the grand duke Francis I. de' Medici. Died in 1608.

See QUATREMÈRE DE QUINCY, "Dictionnaire d'Architecture;" CICOGNARA, "Storia della Scoltura."

Buontempi. See BONTEMPI.

Buonvicino. See BONVICINO.

Bu'pa-lus, a Greek sculptor and architect, born in the island of Chios, lived about 550 B.C., and was noted for the enmity between him and the poet Hipponax.

Burâk or Burâq. See BORÂK.

Buranello. See GALUPPI.

Burbage or Burbadge, bǔr'bij, (RICHARD,) an eminent English actor, was a friend of Shakspeare, whose principal characters he personated. Died in 1619.

Bur'beck, (HENRY,) an American officer, born in Boston in 1754. He served as captain in the war of the Revolution, and obtained the rank of brevet brigadier-general in the war of 1812. Died in 1848.

Burchard, boor'kart, [Lat. BURCAR'DUS,] sometimes written Bouchard, a German theologian, born in Hesse, became Bishop of Worms in 1006. He made a collection of canons, entitled "Magnum Volumen Canonum." Died in 1026.

Burchard, SAINT, first Bishop of Würzburg, born in England; died in 752.

Burchiello, booR-ke-el'lo, (DOMENICO,) a witty Italian poet, published a collection of sonnets, which went through twenty editions. Died in 1448.

See "Lives of the Italian Poets," by REV. H. STEBBING, London, 1831.

Burckhard. See SPALATIN.

Burckhard, boork'härt, (FRANS,) a German philosopher, wrote "De Autonomia," (1586.) Died at Bonn in 1584.

Burckhard, (JAMES, or JAKOB,) a German antiquary, born at Sulzbach in 1681. He wrote (in Latin) "On the Fortunes and Merits of Ulrich Hutten," (1717-23,) and other works. Died in 1753.

Burckhardt, boork'härt, (JOHANN KARL,) a German astronomer, born at Leipsic in 1773. He visited Paris in 1797, and acquired the friendship of Lalande, whom he assisted in his scientific labours. He was afterwards appointed adjunct at the Bureau of Longitude, and in 1807 succeeded Lalande as astronomer in the observatory of the Military School. He translated into German a part of Laplace's "Mécanique Céleste," and wrote several astronomical treatises. Died in 1825.

See ERSCH und GRUBER, "Allgemeine Encyklopaedie."

Burckhardt, bürk'hart, [Ger. pron. booRk'härt,] (JO-HANN LUDWIG,) a celebrated Swiss traveller, born at Lausanne in 1784. Having studied at Göttingen, he visited London, where he was introduced to Sir Joseph Banks and other members of the African Association, then about to send out another traveller to Africa. His services being offered and accepted, he set out in 1809, having prepared himself for the journey by a diligent study of the Arabic language, medicine, chemistry, etc. After spending more than two years in Syria, where he assumed the name of Ibrâhîm and the Oriental dress, he proceeded to Cairo, and, passing through the Nubian desert, arrived in 1814 at Mecca. In the character of a Moslem pilgrim or haji, he performed the pilgrimage to Mount Ararat, and subsequently visited Medina. He returned to Cairo in 1816, and in October, 1817, when about to join the caravan for Fezzan, was attacked with a violent fever, of which he died at Cairo. He was buried by the Mohammedans with distinguished honours. His principal works are entitled "Travels in Nubia," (in English, 1819,) "Travels in Syria and Palestine," (1822,) "Notes on the Bedouins and Wahabees," (1830,) and "Arabic Proverbs," (1831.) He bequeathed his valuable collection of Oriental manuscripts to the University of Cambridge. Burckhardt possessed in an eminent degree the intellectual and moral qualities requisite in an explorer; and his works are esteemed among the best of their kind.

See SUEUR-MERLIN, "Notice sur la Vie du Voyageur Burckhardt," 1829; "Nouvelle Biographie Générale;" "London Quarterly Review" for March, 1820; "Edinburgh Review" for August, 1820.

Burdach, boor'däk, (KARL FRIEDRICH,) a German physician, born at Leipsic in 1776, became in 1811 professor of anatomy and physiology at Dorpat. He wrote a treatise "On the Structure and Life of the Brain and Spinal Marrow," (1819,) and other works. Died in 1847.

See his Autobiography, entitled "Rückblicke auf mein Leben: Selbstbiographie," 1847.

Bur'den, (HENRY,) a Scottish mechanician, born at Dunblane in 1791, emigrated in 1819 to America, where he made a number of valuable inventions. Among these are a cultivator, a suspension water-wheel, and a machine for making horse-shoes.

Bur'der, (Rev. GEORGE,) an English dissenting divine, born in London in 1752. He became in 1803 pastor of the Congregational church in Fetter Lane, London, and soon after editor of the "Evangelical Magazine." He published "Evangelical Truth Defended," (1788,) and "Village Sermons," (6 vols., 1799-1812.) Died in 1832.

Bur-dett', (Sir FRANCIS,) an English Liberal politician, born in 1770. He married Sophia, daughter of Thomas Coutts, a rich banker, and was elected to Parliament about 1795. He opposed the war against France, and advocated reform in representation. In 1807 he was returned for Westminster, which he represented for

---

€ as *k*; ç as *s*; g̃ *hard*; g̈ as *j*; G, H, K, *guttural*; N, *nasal*; R, *trilled*; s̃ as *z*; th as in *this*. (☞See Explanations, p. 23.)

nearly thirty years. For a publication reflecting on the conduct of Parliament he was committed to the Tower for a few months in 1810. Died in 1844.

See "Nouvelle Biographie Générale."

Bur'don, (WILLIAM,) an English writer on politics, ethics, etc., born in 1764. Among his works is "Materials for Thinking," (2 vols., 1803-10.) Died in 1818.

Bure, boo'rĕh, [Lat. BURÆ'US,] (ANDERS,) a distinguished Swedish architect and geographer, born in 1571; died in 1646.

Bure, [Lat. BURÆ'US,] (JOHAN,) a Swedish antiquary, and one of the earliest poets of Sweden, born in 1568, became royal librarian. Died in 1652.

Bure, (KATARINA,) a Swedish scholar and writer, born in 1602, was a daughter of the preceding. Died in 1679.

Bure, de, dĕh bür, (GUILLAUME FRANÇOIS,) a noted French bookseller and bibliographer. Died in 1782.

Buren. See BIREN.

Buren. See EGMOND, (MAXIMILIAN.)

Buren, Van. See VAN BUREN.

Burette, bü'rĕt', (PIERRE JEAN,) a learned French physician, born in 1665; died in 1747. He was the author of several valuable dissertations on the gymnastics and the music of the ancients.

See MORÉRI, "Dictionnaire Historique;" QUÉRARD, "La France Littéraire."

Burette, (THÉODORE,) a French historian, born in Paris in 1804. Among his works are a "History of France," (2 vols., 1839,) and "Modern History," (2 vols., 1843.) Died in 1847.

See QUÉRARD, "La France Littéraire."

Bürg or **Buerg,** bürG, (JOHANN TOBIAS,) a German astronomer, born in Vienna in 1766. He was professor of astronomy at Klagenfurth, and afterwards astronomer at the observatory in Vienna. He produced valuable lunar tables, and received part of a prize offered by the French Institute for the solution of a problem in regard to the moon's motions. Died in 1834.

See ERSCH and GRUBER, "Allgemeine Encyklopaedie."

Bürger or **Buerger,** bür'GER, (GOTTFRIED AUGUST,) a popular German poet, born near Halberstadt in 1748; died in 1794. He particularly excelled in ballads and in romantic poetry. He was thrice married. Among his chief works are "Lenore," (1772,) and "The Wild Huntsman," which have acquired a European celebrity. The former has been translated into English.

See H. DÖRING, "G. A. Bürger; biographisches Denkmal," 1847; ERSCH und GRUBER, "Allgemeine Encyklopaedie;" LONGFELLOW, "Poets and Poetry of Europe."

Burgersdicius, bür-ḡers-dish'e-us, or **Burgersdyck,** bür'Gers-dik', (FRANCISCUS,) a Dutch philosopher, born near Delft in 1590, wrote on logic and moral philosophy. Died in 1629.

Burges, bür'jess, (GEORGE,) an English dramatist and Greek scholar, born in 1786; died in 1864.

Burges, bür'jess, (GEORGE,) D.D., an American divine, was born in Providence, Rhode Island, in 1809. After graduating at Brown University, he continued his studies in the Universities of Bonn, Göttingen, and Berlin. In 1847 he was consecrated Bishop of Maine, becoming at the same time rector of Christ Church at Gardiner. His principal works are a versification of the Book of Psalms, "Pages from the Ecclesiastical History of New England," "Last Enemy Conquering and Conquered," and "Sermons on Christian Life," (1854.) Died in 1866.

Bür'gess, (CORNELIUS,) an English nonconformist minister, entered Oxford in 1611. He preached in London. Died in 1665.

Burgess, (DANIEL,) an English dissenting divine, born at Staines in 1645, preached in London many years. He was noted for his facetious sayings. Died in 1713.

Burgess, (Rev. RICHARD,) an English writer, born about 1796. He became rector of Upper Chelsea. Among his works is "Topography and Antiquities of Rome," (2 vols., 1831.)

Burgess, (THOMAS,) an English theologian, born at Odiham, in Hampshire, in 1756, became Bishop of Salisbury about 1825. He wrote numerous religious works. Died in 1837.

See HARFORD, "Life of Bishop Burgess;" WILLIAM JERDAN, "Men I have known," London, 1866; "London Quarterly Review" for October and January, 1822.

Bür'gess, (TRISTAM,) an American orator and statesman, born in Rochester, Massachusetts, in 1770. Having studied law, he was admitted to the bar in 1799, and rose to great eminence. He became a leader of the Federal party, and chief justice of Rhode Island in 1815. In 1825 he was elected a member of Congress, in which his fervid eloquence, powerful logic, and formidable sarcasm procured for him a national reputation. He continued to serve in Congress until 1835. Died in 1853.

See H. L. BOWEN, "Memoir of Tristam Burgess."

Burggrave, booRG'grä'vĕh, or **Burgrave,** booR'grä-vĕh, (JOHANN,) a German physician, born at Darmstadt in 1673; died about 1746.

Burggrave, (JOHANN PHILIPP,) a medical writer, son of the preceding, born at Darmstadt in 1700; died in 1775.

Burgh. See BURGHO.

Burgh, bür'rĕh, (JAMES,) an estimable moral and political writer, born in Perthshire, Scotland, in 1714, was a cousin of Robertson the historian. He wrote, among other works, "The Dignity of Human Nature," (1754,) and "Political Disquisitions," (3 vols., 1774.) Died in 1775.

Burgh, de, (HUBERT.) See BURGHO or BURGO.

Burgh, de, (ULICK.) See CLANRICARDE, MARQUIS OF.

Bur'gho, Bur'go, or **Bourgo,** boor'go, written also **Burgh, Bourgh,** and **Burke,** a distinguished Norman family, related to William the Conqueror. Hubert de Burgo was the minister of King John and Henry III.; but, though faithful to the interests of those sovereigns, he boldly opposed their crimes. From another branch of the same family sprang those invaders, or rather ravagers, of Ireland, to whom the poet Campbell alludes in his "O'Connor's Child."[*]

Burgho, de, de bur'go or boor'go, (RICHARD,) a powerful baron, became master of Connaught, in Ireland. Died in 1243.

Burgho, de, (WALTER,) son and successor of the preceding, obtained by marriage the earldom of Ulster. Died in 1271.

Bürgi, (JOBST.) See BYRGIUS.

Burgkmair, booRk'mIR, (HANS,) an eminent German painter and wood-engraver, born at Augsburg about 1473. Among his best pictures are a "Saint Sebastian" and a "Virgin and Child" at Nuremberg, and "Saint John at Patmos" in the Pinakothek at Munich. He also executed a great number of admirable engravings, including a series of one hundred and thirty-five plates called the "Triumph of the Emperor Maximilian I." He was a friend of Albert Dürer, in conjunction with whom he produced several engravings. Died about 1559.

See NAGLER, "Neues Allgemeines Künstler-Lexikon."

Burgo. See BURGHO.

Bur'gon, (JOHN WILLIAM,) an English poet and biographer, born in London about 1820, published a "Life of Sir Thomas Gresham," (1839,) "Petra," a poem, (1845,) and other works.

Burgos, de, dä booR'gòs, (Don FRANCISCO XAVIER,) a Spanish author and politician, born at Motel, in Andalusia, in 1778. He produced a version of Horace, (4 vols., 1820-23,) which is commended, and wrote several comedies and poems. His "Ode to Reason" is much admired.

Burgos, de, (PABLO,) a learned Spanish ecclesiastic, born at Burgos in 1353. He was Bishop of Burgos, and wrote several works. Died in 1435.

Burgoyne, bür-goin', (JOHN,) an English general and dramatist. He married a daughter of the Earl of Derby, and was elected a member of Parliament in 1761. In the summer of 1777 he obtained command of an army of about 8000 men, with which he marched from Canada towards Albany. Having been repulsed at Stillwater in September, he was forced to surrender at Saratoga in October, 1777. (See GATES, GENERAL.) This event was one of the most important victories gained by the Americans in the war, and produced great exultation among the patriots. He had the reputation of a wit as

---

[*] "For now De Bourgo's sword and flame
Had ravaged Ulster's boundaries,
And lighted up the midnight skies.
    *   *   *   *
And stemmed De Bourgo's chivalry."

ā, ē, ī, ō, ū, ȳ, *long;* ă, ĕ, ĭ, ŏ, ŭ, ў, *short;* a, e, i, o, *obscure;* fär, fâll, fât; mĕt; nŏt; gōōd; mōōn;

well as of a brave and generous man. He composed three dramas, "The Maid of Oaks," "Bon Ton," and "The Heiress," (1786,) which enjoyed considerable popularity in their day. Died in 1792.

See HILDRETH, "History of the United States," vol. iii. chap. xxxvi.

Burgoyne, (Sir JOHN,) an English general, who distinguished himself in the principal battles of the Peninsular war, and was subsequently appointed inspector-general of fortifications in England, lieutenant-general, (1851,) and Knight Grand Cross, (1852.) In the Crimean war he served till 1855 as chief of the engineering department in the British army. He has also obtained the degree of D.C.L. from the University of Oxford.

Burgrave. See BURGGRAVE.

Burgsdorf, von, fon bōŏRGs'dorf, (FRIEDRICH AUGUST LUDWIG,) a German naturalist and writer, born at Leipsic in 1747 ; died in 1802.

Burgundio, booR-goon'de-o, or **Borgondio,** boR-gon'de-o, (ORAZIO,) an Italian Jesuit and scientific writer, born at Brescia in 1679, became rector of the Roman College. Died in 1741.

Burgundy, DUKES OF. With the exception of LOUIS, noticed below, these will be found under their respective names, as CHARLES THE BOLD, JOHN THE FEARLESS, etc.

Bur'gun-dy̆, [Fr. BOURGOGNE, booR'goñ',] (LOUIS,) DUKE OF, Dauphin of France, grandson of Louis XIV., and father of Louis XV., was born at Versailles in 1682. The celebrated Fénelon was appointed his principal preceptor, and was instrumental in effecting a thorough change in his character, of which Saint-Simon gives the following portrait : "This prince was born terrible, and continued terrible through his infancy ; incapable of bearing the least resistance, even from time and the elements ; obstinate to excess, and given up to all violent passions From the height of the skies he looked down upon men as atoms with whom he had no resemblance ; even his brothers scarcely appeared to him intermediate between him and the human race. From this abyss came forth a prince affable, gentle, and humane, humble and austere towards himself." He died in 1712, greatly regretted by the nation.

See SAINT-SIMON, "Mémoires ;" ABBÉ FLEURY, "Portrait du Duc de Bourgogne," 1714 ; J. MARTINEAU, "Recueil des Vertus de Louis de France," 1712 ; PROYART, "Vie du Dauphin, Père de Louis XV," 2 vols., 1778.

Burhill, bŭr'ril, (Dr. ROBERT,) an English divine, chaplain to Sir Walter Raleigh, whom he is said to have assisted in his "History of the World." Died in 1641.

Buri. See AUDHUMLA, and ODIN.

Bŭr'ī-dăn, (JOHN,) [Fr. JEAN BURIDAN, zhŏN bü're'-dŏN',] a schoolman, born at Béthune, in Artois, about 1315, known as the author of the sophism that, if a hungry ass were placed between two measures of oats so that each should make exactly the same impression on his senses, being incapable of making a choice, he must inevitably die of starvation. He was a professor in the University of Paris, and wrote on logic, etc. Died in 1358.

See BAYLE, "Historical and Critical Dictionary ;" FROBES, "Disquisitio de J. Buridano ejusque Asino," 1748.

Burigny, de, dẹh bü'rèn'ye', (JEAN LÉVESQUE,) a French historian, born at Rheims in 1692. He was the author of a "History of Pagan Philosophy," (2 vols., 1724,) "General History of Sicily," (1745,) "History of the Revolutions of the Empire of Constantinople," (1750,) a "Life of Grotius," (1750,) a "Life of Erasmus," (1757,) and a "Life of Bossuet," (1761.) He was for a time associate editor of the journal entitled "L'Europe Savante," at the Hague. He was a member of the Academy of Inscriptions. Died in 1785.

See DACIER, "Éloge de Burigny," 1786 ; QUÉRARD, "La France Littéraire."

Burinski. See BOORINSKI.

Burkard, bōŏR'kärt, (WALDIS,) a German fabulist of the sixteenth century.

Burke. See BURGHO.

Burke, bŭrk, (ÆDANUS,) a lawyer, born in Ireland in 1743, was appointed a judge of the supreme court of South Carolina in 1778, after which he became a Senator of the United States. He wrote a famous pamphlet against the Society of the Cincinnati. Died in 1802.

Burke or **Bourke,** pronounced alike bŭrk, (EDMUND,) an illustrious orator, statesman, and philanthropist, born in Dublin in 1730, or, according to some authorities, in 1728. His family was of Norman descent, Burke having been originally the same name as Burgh, De Burgh, De Burgho, or De Bourgo.* His father, Richard Burke, was an attorney of the first rank in his profession in Dublin. His mother, whose maiden name was Nagle, was a Roman Catholic, of respectable family. Her great-aunt, Ellen Nagle, was married to Sylvanus Spenser, the eldest son of the immortal poet. Edmund Burke was the second son out of a family of fourteen or fifteen children, all of whom died young except three sons, Garret, Edmund, and Richard, and a daughter, named Juliana. Edmund was of a delicate constitution, and, for the sake of country air, was sent at an early age to Castletown-Roche. O'Halloran, the schoolmaster of this place, used to boast to the end of his life that he was the first who put a Latin grammar into the hands of Edmund Burke. Having spent about five years at Castletown-Roche, he returned to Dublin, and not long after he was placed at Ballitore, under the instruction of Abraham Shackleton, a Quaker schoolmaster of superior learning and rare moral worth. At school he formed for Richard Shackleton, the only son of his preceptor, a warm friendship, which continued to the end of his life. It is related that while at school Burke one day saw a poor man pulling down his own hut, which he had been ordered to do because it was too near the highway. The young philanthropist declared that if he were a man in authority the poor should not be thus oppressed. At Ballitore Burke appears to have imbibed that thorough respect for civil and religious liberty for which he was afterwards distinguished. "He had observed," says Prior, "among the Society of Friends, in which he was domesticated, that differences of opinion on those points made neither worse subjects nor worse men. Reflection, and the remembrance that [his] relatives on the side of one parent were Roman Catholics, probably taught him to extend the same liberality of sentiment towards persons of that persuasion." Having spent three years at Ballitore, he entered Trinity College, Dublin, as a pensioner. The range of his studies was remarkable, including the classics, history, philosophy, general literature, and metaphysics, besides less important pursuits. He was accustomed while at college to spend three hours every day in the public library. While he devoted a large part of his time to studies of the severest and most solid character, he did not neglect the lighter kinds of reading, including poetry, novels, and other works of imagination. It is related that when Richard Burke was found one day in a reverie, shortly after his brother had made a great speech in the House of Commons, and was asked the cause, he replied, "I have been wondering how Ned has contrived to monopolize all the talents of the family ; but then, I remember, *when we were at play he was always at work.*" Burke graduated as A.B. in 1748. From the first his destination was the bar ; and in 1747 his name was enrolled at the Middle Temple. In 1750 he went to London, but in 1751 returned to Ireland, and took the degree of A.M. About the year 1753 he became, it appears, a candidate for the chair of logic in the University of Glasgow, but was not successful. In 1755 Burke felt inclined to try his fortune in America. Several persons whom he consulted on the subject highly approved of it ; but his father was strongly averse to the scheme, and it was in consequence abandoned. In 1756 was published, anonymously, his "Vindication of Natural Society." It was an imitation, or rather an ironical criticism, of Lord Bolingbroke's writings against Christianity. "The imitation of Bolingbroke's style and manner was," says Prior, "so perfect as to constitute identity rather than resemblance. It was not merely the language, style, and general eloquence of the original which had been caught, but the whole mind of the noble author." The work purported to be written by a "late noble writer." Many persons, including Lord Chesterfield and Dr. Warburton, believed it to be a genuine production of Bolingbroke.

* As Campbell writes it in his poem of "O'Connor's Child."

In the same year appeared Burke's "Philosophical Inquiry into the Origin of our Ideas of the Sublime and Beautiful." This work attracted much attention, and was greatly admired by some of the most distinguished critics of that age. Dr. Johnson, it is said, regarded it as a model of philosophical criticism. In 1757 Burke was united in marriage with Mary Jane, daughter of Dr. Nugent, a physician of Bath, whither the young student and author had gone for the re-establishment of his health. This union appears to have been a singularly happy one, since he was accustomed to say that "every care vanished the moment he entered under his own roof." "An Account of the European Settlements in America," a work in two volumes, was published in 1757. There is strong reason to believe that it was written principally or wholly by Burke. In 1758–59 he established, in conjunction with the publisher Dodsley, the "Annual Register," a periodical of great merit. His society was now sought by many of the most distinguished men in the kingdom, including, among others, Johnson, Garrick, Reynolds, Lyttleton, Hume, and Warburton. Johnson, as Prior tells us, would submit to contradiction from Burke, though twenty years younger than himself, but would tolerate it from no other person, whatever might be his talents or experience. The admiration which they conceived for each other at their first acquaintance never afterwards suffered any diminution. Johnson used to say that "no man of sense could meet Mr. Burke by accident under a gateway to avoid a shower without being convinced that he was the first man in England." Grattan, the great Irish orator and patriot, considered Burke the greatest man in conversation he had ever met with.

In 1759 Burke was introduced to William Gerard Hamilton, chief secretary to Lord Halifax, then lord-lieutenant of Ireland. The secretary, better known in political history as "Single-Speech Hamilton," appears to have employed Burke as his private secretary. In 1763 the latter received from the government a pension of £300 per annum, partly or chiefly through Hamilton's influence; but, finding afterwards that the pension was considered to be the price not merely of his services but of his political independence, he threw it up with indignation, having enjoyed it twelve months only. When the Marquis of Rockingham became prime minister, in 1765, Burke was appointed his private secretary. Not long after he was returned to Parliament for Wendover, in Buckinghamshire, and entered the House of Commons January 14, 1766. He took an active part in the discussion on American affairs, and at once proved himself an able and eloquent speaker. Alluding to his extensive and varied knowledge, General Lee (who afterwards took part in the American Revolution) says, in a letter to the Prince of Poland, "An Irishman, Mr. Burke, has sprung up in the House of Commons, who has astonished everybody with the power of his eloquence and his comprehensive knowledge in all our exterior and internal politics and commercial interests." The Rockingham ministry was dissolved July, 1766; and soon after Burke wrote a sort of manifesto in its defence, with the title of "A Short Account of a Late Short Administration." In the latter part of the same year an attempt was made to enlist him in the ministerial ranks by the Duke of Grafton, who, in addressing Chatham, spoke of Burke as "the readiest man upon all points perhaps in the whole House." But the scheme was not approved of either by the premier or by Burke himself. On the dissolution of Parliament in 1768, Burke was again returned for Wendover. About the same time he purchased, for above £20,000, an estate near Beaconsfield, in Buckinghamshire. He wrote to Shackleton, "I have made a push, with all I could collect of my own and the aid of my friends, to cast a little root into this country. I have purchased a house, with six hundred acres of land, in Buckinghamshire, twenty-four miles from London."

"About this time," says Prior, "Junius broke forth upon the English world with a vigour and rancour never surpassed." Universal opinion fixed at once upon Burke as the author of the "Letters." Even his own friends at first, Dr. Johnson among the number, believed him to be the true Junius. No one else was supposed to possess either the ability or the knowledge which those letters displayed. His enemies made it a ground for heaping upon him unmeasured abuse. Although he unequivocally and repeatedly denied the accusation, his denial was not generally credited; and it was only after the publication of the "Grenville Papers" that he was completely cleared from suspicion in regard to this charge. In 1770 Burke published a pamphlet entitled "Thoughts on the Cause of the Present Discontents," which is considered one of the most masterly things of the kind in the language. He was rewarded for his thorough acquaintance with American affairs by being appointed, in 1771, agent to the State of New York, a position worth nearly £700 per annum. As the state of the American colonies claimed at this time a large share of the attention of Parliament, Burke became more and more prominent as the ablest member of the opposition. But his extensive information and superior abilities were acknowledged not only in regard to the affairs of the Western colonies, but also those of the remoter East. He had already made himself acquainted with the condition, population, and resources of India. The affairs of the East India Company having fallen into some confusion, in 1772 Sir Charles Colebrooke offered Burke, in the name of the directors, "the first position in a supervisorship of three, empowered to trace out in detail the whole administrative system of India and to remedy all they could find amiss." (Prior's "Life of Burke.") But he declined the offer. The affairs of America were exciting from day to day a deeper interest; his friends appear to have felt that he could not be spared from Parliament; and he himself was probably unwilling to abandon a field for which he felt himself peculiarly fitted, and in which he had already won, and was still to win, so many laurels. In 1772 he accompanied his son Richard (then about fourteen) to France, and placed him at school at Auxerre. He himself spent some time in Paris, where he saw for the first time the young queen Marie Antoinette, of whom he has given so glowing a description in his "Reflexions on the Revolution in France." The state of religion and morals at the French capital filled him even then with apprehension and alarm. Soon after his return, in a speech in Parliament, among other things he uttered these memorable words: "I see propagated principles which will not leave to religion even a toleration, and make virtue herself less than a name." His foresight in regard to affairs in America was scarcely less remarkable. Indeed, he alone, among all the members of Parliament, appears to have fully comprehended the difficulties and dangers which menaced that portion of the empire. He remarked indignantly that a robbery on Hounslow Heath would excite more attention than the incipient insurrection which then threatened to dissever the colonies from the British crown. On the 19th of April, 1774, he made a speech on American taxation. It was considered by many as the greatest effort of oratory that had, till then, ever been put forth in the House of Commons. On this occasion an intelligent American, a friend of Dr. Franklin, (Mr. Sampson,) is said to have exclaimed, "You have got a most wonderful man here: he understands more of America than all the rest of your House put together." On the dissolution of Parliament, which occurred in the autumn of 1774, Burke was returned for Malton. While he was expressing to his constituents his acknowledgments for the honour done him, a deputation of merchants arrived from Bristol, informing him that he had been nominated to represent their city, and urging him to accept the nomination. Having obtained the ready assent of his Malton friends, he proceeded at once to Bristol. After an obstinate and protracted contest, he was returned on the 3d of November. His speech in Parliament, March, 1775, recommending conciliatory measures towards the American colonies, commanded general admiration. Lord Chatham, on being asked his opinion of it, replied that "it was very seasonable, very reasonable, and very eloquent;" and Fox, nearly twenty years afterwards, said, "Let gentlemen read this speech by day and meditate upon it by night: they would there learn that representation was the sovereign remedy for every evil." Lord Erskine observed, at Edinburgh, "It could only proceed from this cause [the corruption of Parliament] that the im-

ā, ē, ī, ō, ū, ȳ, *long;* à, è, ò, same, less prolonged; ă, ĕ, ĭ, ŏ, ŭ, ў, *short;* ạ, ẹ, ị, ọ, *obscure;* fär, fåll, fåt; mĕt; nŏt; gŏŏd; mōōn;

mortal orations of Burke against the American war did not produce as general conviction as they did unmingled admiration." But the fault lay perhaps still more with the blindness and obstinacy of the king and the people.

At length the arbitrary measures of the government began to produce their legitimate effect. The rejection of all the petitions from the colonies, and the utter disregard not only of the rights but of the feelings of Americans, as exhibited in the furious and insane abuse heaped upon their representative, Dr. Franklin, before the privy council by Wedderburn in 1774, had resulted in a feeling of almost total alienation from the mother-country. Owing, perhaps, to that large foresight which enabled him to realize all the evils and dangers attending such a contest, Franklin had been among the most reluctant to commit his countrymen to war, and one of the last to abandon all hope of reconciliation. The day previous to his finally quitting London in the spring of 1775, he called on Burke and freely stated his views and feelings in regard to the impending crisis, expressing his deep regret that the unaccommodating and obstinate temper of England seemed to render a separation inevitable. Before he reached America the war had already begun, and the battles of Lexington and Concord (April 19) had been fought. That of Bunker Hill took place in the following June; and yet so great was the reluctance of the Americans to separate themselves from the mother-country that more than a year elapsed before they could prevail upon themselves to take the step which rendered reconciliation hopeless, and even then the Declaration of Independence was carried with difficulty through Congress. There cannot be a reasonable doubt that, had the conciliatory measures recommended by Burke been adopted, the war of the Revolution would not have taken place, or, at least, it might have been indefinitely postponed. In 1780, Burke delivered one of his most admirable speeches, usually known as that "On the Economical Reform." By his advocacy of the claims of the Roman Catholics, and by his opposition to the policy of repressing the trade of Ireland,—a policy strongly favoured by the merchants of Bristol,—he had lost his popularity with many of his constituents in that city: accordingly, at the next election he offered himself as the candidate for Malton, which he continued to represent for the remainder of his political life. Lord North having been compelled to resign his post as prime minister in 1782, the Marquis of Rockingham and his friends again came into power. Burke was made a privy councillor and appointed paymaster-general of the forces. His disinterestedness while in this office gave another illustration of that high principle by which the conduct of his whole life was guided. No man, by the consent of all impartial persons, had rendered greater services to the country than he; and none could with a better right have availed himself of the perquisites of this lucrative office to repair the deficiencies of his private fortune. By the reforms which he introduced into the paymaster's department, he saved to the public revenue £47,000 per annum: of this sum above £25,000 consisted of the usual and acknowledged perquisites which all his predecessors had received. Lord Shelburne having become prime minister on the death of the Marquis of Rockingham, (July, 1782,) Burke, and the other friends of the late premier, resigned. By the coalition between Fox and Lord North, the latter came again into power in 1783, and Burke was restored to his former office. He took a prominent part in the debates on India, with the affairs of which he was perhaps better acquainted than any other man in England. One of his greatest speeches was delivered on the East India Bill in December, 1783. The bill passed the House of Commons, but was lost in the upper House. This defeat put an end to Lord North's administration, and Pitt succeeded as prime minister. Burke retired from office, and never afterwards held any position under the government. He had been elected, November, 1783, lord rector of the University of Glasgow, and was re-elected the following year.

Perhaps the most brilliant, and certainly not the least useful, portion of Burke's career was that which he devoted to the cause of India. The affairs of that country had recently occupied nearly all his thoughts. The oppression and cruelty of which Warren Hastings, and other officers of the East India Company, had been guilty, filled his soul with irrepressible pity and indignation. In February, 1785, he made an eloquent and masterly speech on the debts of the Nabob of Arcot. "It was," says Prior, "one of those outpourings of a fertile and vigorous intellect, which, on an unpromising theme, seemed to combine all that could instruct, dazzle, and even overpower the hearer." At the opening of the session in January, 1786, he commenced the most arduous and formidable undertaking of his life,—the prosecution of Hastings. The articles embracing the different charges were delivered in April. They were so numerous and extensive as to occupy no inconsiderable part of the attention of the House for two sessions. In January, 1787, Sheridan made his celebrated speech on the Begum case. A committee of impeachment was then formed. On the 10th of May, Burke, as chairman of the committee, accused Hastings at the bar of the House of Lords, in the name of the Commons of England. After the necessary preliminary proceedings, and delays from various causes, on the 13th of February, 1788, Westminster Hall was opened in form, and Burke, in full dress, proceeded thither, followed by the other managers, the House of Commons, the clerks of Parliament, the masters in chancery, the sergeants-at-law, the judges, the House of Peers, and the royal family, the Prince of Wales closing the procession. (For a brilliant description of this imposing scene, the reader is referred to Macaulay's article on Warren Hastings.) Two days having been occupied with preliminary business, on the 15th Burke made his opening speech, of which it is enough to say that it was every way worthy of the occasion and of his great reputation. After various delays, some of which at least were unavoidable, extending through a series of years, at length, on the 23d of April, 1795, a verdict of acquittal was passed: the lord chancellor, however, voted with the minority, who thought Hastings guilty. But, although the impeachment was not carried, it would be a great mistake to suppose that the unconquerable zeal and herculean labours of Burke in behalf of India were without avail.* They had the effect of directing the earnest attention of the British nation to the misgovernment and oppression of which the agents of the Company had been guilty, and thus led the way to important reforms in the administrative system of that country.

But, long before the trial of Hastings was concluded, the mind of Burke had been intensely occupied with a far different subject, which, in his view, was closely connected not only with the welfare of England, but with her very existence as a nation. He had for some time beheld with apprehension the dissemination in France of principles which threatened the total overthrow of all religion and all government. As he had been prominent in the eyes of Europe as one of the most zealous friends of liberty, he received from time to time, from those in France who favoured the revolutionary movement, the most glowing accounts of the success of their experiment. It was in reply to one of these communications that Burke wrote his "Reflexions on the Revolution in France." The success of this work has never been paralleled in the history of political literature. It was published in November, 1790, and within a few months more than thirty thousand copies are said to have been sold. The work was immediately translated into French, and was read with avidity in every part of Europe. So great was the influence of his name, combined with the masterly logic and powerful eloquence of the "Reflexions," that his work completely arrested the spread of the revolutionary spirit in England, and contributed greatly to check its progress in other European countries. The startling and terrible events which followed soon after in France, by proving that the foresight of Burke was even more remarkable than his eloquence,

* "Never," says Lord John Russell, "has the great object of punishment—the prevention of crime—been attained more completely than by this trial. . . . Hastings was acquitted; but tyranny, deceit, and injustice were condemned. India was saved from abominations disgraceful to the English name." ("Memorials of Charles James Fox," vol. ii. p. 257.)

є as k; ç as s; ğ hard; ǧ as j; G, H, K, guttural; N, nasal; R, trilled; š as z; ŧh as in this.　(☞See Explanations, p. 23.)

30

raised his fame to the highest point, and seemed fully to justify the eulogium that his letter on the French Revolution was "the most magnificent political prophecy ever given to the world." The uncompromising hostility of Burke to the principles of the French Revolution led not long after, May 6, 1791, to an open rupture between him and Fox, who hailed the revolutionary movement as the dawn of a political millennium. Fox and his followers charged Burke with having abandoned the principles of his party, and with being guilty of great inconsistency, in that, after having shown himself a strenuous friend of liberty during the whole of his former life, he had in his late writings and speeches discountenanced and denounced the struggles which a great nation was making to establish its freedom. Burke published a vindication of his course, entitled "An Appeal from the New to the Old Whigs," in which he clearly shows that there is nothing in his recent writings or speeches inconsistent with the political doctrines which had been the guide of his former life.* The truth is, he never had been an advocate of extreme democratic principles; he had no confidence in any political system based solely upon theoretical ideas of right and adopted without reference to experience or to the existing condition and usages of the people among whom it was sought to be established. He may perhaps with more justice be charged with having urged his views with too great vehemence, with an excessive and almost acrimonious zeal. But who shall presume to exactly measure the degree of zeal with which a patriot, who sees, as he believes, his country menaced with imminent and deadly peril, should exert himself in seeking to save her from destruction? It is certain that in regard to personal affronts and injuries Burke often, if not always, manifested a magnanimous forbearance; but in the cause of his country, or in the higher cause of justice and humanity, he displayed a spirit as uncompromising as it was disinterested and lofty. It cannot, however, be denied that after his health had been broken and his nerves shattered by the toils and vexations of a life which was one long battle with the various forms of misgovernment, oppression, and tyranny, he sometimes exhibited an impatience and irritability which were mortifying to his friends and which seriously impaired his political and personal influence. One rather amusing example of this kind may be cited. A rough country gentleman in the House of Commons, seeing Burke rise with papers in his hand, exclaimed, "I hope the gentleman does not mean to read that large bundle of papers, and bore us with a long speech into the bargain." Burke is said to have felt so much irritation that, incapable of utterance, he ran out of the house. "Never before," said the witty Selwyn, "did I see the fable realized,—a lion put to flight by the braying of an ass." His enemies availed themselves of this weakness of the great orator, and when they were wholly unable to answer they often contrived either to reduce him to silence, or to prevent his being heard, by coughing or continual vociferations. This practice was familiarly termed "muzzling the lion."

In 1795 Burke received from the king a pension of £1200 per annum on the civil list, and not long after another of £2500 on the West Indian four-and-a-half per cent. fund. These pensions were granted, it is said, at the express desire of the king, no application having been made on the part of Burke or his personal friends. A part of the design in conferring them was to enable Burke to discharge some serious debts incurred in the performance of a long series of unrequited public services. Nevertheless, his acceptance of this very moderate reward for his great services to his country, caused

his conduct to be assailed from every quarter. Even the dignity of the House of Lords did not save him from attacks upon his character by two of the peers. In reply, he wrote in 1796 his "Letter to a Noble Lord," one of the most successful and popular of all the productions of his pen. Burke died July 9, 1797. His only son, Richard, a man of superior talents and great moral worth, had died in 1794. The grief occasioned by this irreparable loss contributed, there is reason to believe, materially to shorten his father's life.

Of Burke, Macaulay says, he was "ignorant, indeed, or negligent of the art of adapting his reasonings and his style to the capacity and taste of his hearers, but in aptitude to comprehension and richness of imagination superior to every orator, ancient or modern." "If we are to praise a man in proportion to his usefulness," says Schlegel, "I am persuaded that no task can be more difficult than to do justice to the statesman and orator Burke. This man has been to his own country, and to all Europe, a new light of political wisdom and moral experience. He corrected his age when it was at the height of its revolutionary frenzy; and, without maintaining any system of philosophy, he seems to have seen farther into the true nature of society, and to have more clearly comprehended the effect of religion in connecting individual security with national welfare, than any philosopher of any preceding age." "Of all the men who are," says the learned Dr. Parr, "or who ever have been eminent for energy or splendour of eloquence or for skill and grace in composition, there is not one who, in genius or erudition, in philanthropy or piety, or in any of the qualities of a wise and good man, surpasses Burke."

Burke's command of language has always been admired. His style is not a mere trick or artifice designed to give dignity to trivial or point to commonplace ideas: it is simply the clothing of great and glowing thoughts in their most natural and appropriate expression. A collected edition of Burke's works and correspondence (8 vols. 8vo) was published in London in 1852. For some excellent observations on Burke as an orator, see the "Quarterly Review" for January and April, 1858, pages 595–98. We select the following passages in regard to Burke and his style of oratory. Referring to his speeches on the Stamp Act, the writer remarks:

"This was the appropriate start of a man who, whether as a statesman, a thinker, or an orator, was without an equal. Pitt and Fox were great, but Burke belongs to another order of beings, and ranks with the Shakspeares, the Bacons, and the Newtons. . . . Though his style is never stilted, it has a rare majesty both in thought and expression. . . . His language was nervous, his sentences polished, his abundant metaphors grand and original. . . . His commonest fault is a monotony of dignity, which wants the relief of passages dressed in a more familiar garb. . . . His innate genius was undoubtedly wonderful, but he improved it to the uttermost. . . . The immense labour which he bestowed on all he did was his constant boast. . . . By the incessant practice of composition, he learned to embody his conclusions in a style more grandly beautiful than has ever been reached by any other Englishman, with either his tongue or the pen." But one result of all this labour was that his speeches were far less interesting and effective when heard in the House of Commons than when read in print. It is related that on one occasion "Erskine crept under the benches to escape a speech which, when published, he thumbed to rags."

See PRIOR, "Life of Burke," 1 vol. 8vo; BISSET, "Life of Burke," 2 vols. 8vo; McCORMICK, "Memoirs of the Right Honourable E. Burke," 1797; DR. GEORGE CROLY, "Political Life of the Right Honourable Edmund Burke," 2 vols. 8vo, 1840; P. BURKE, "The Public and Domestic Life of Edmund Burke," 1853; LORD JEFFREY, "Miscellanies." For a description of Burke's conversational powers, see MISS BURNEY's letter to S. Crisp.

Burke, (JOHN,) a English genealogist, born in Ireland in 1786. His chief work is a "Dictionary of the Peerage and Baronetage of the British Empire," (1826.) The twentieth edition was published by his son, Sir Bernard, in 1858. Died in 1848.

Burke, (JOHN DOLY,) an Irishman, who emigrated to the United States in 1797 and became an editor in Boston. He wrote a "History of Virginia." Died in Virginia in 1808.

---

* Coleridge, referring to the speeches made by Burke at the commencement of the American war, and those made by him at the breaking out of the French Revolution, remarks "that the principles are exactly the same, and the deductions the same; but the practical inferences almost opposite in the one case from those drawn in the other; yet in both equally legitimate, and in both equally confirmed by the results. Whence gained he this superiority of foresight?" Coleridge answers, "Burke possessed, and had sedulously sharpened, that eye which sees all things, actions, and events in relation to the laws that determine their existence and circumscribe their possibility. He referred habitually to principles. He was a scientific statesman, and therefore a seer. For every principle contains in itself the germs of a prophecy." ("Biographia Literaria," chap. x.)

Burke, (PETER,) an English jurist and writer, son of John Burke, noticed above, published several works on the law of copyright and patents; also, "The Public and Domestic Life of Edmund Burke," (1853.)

Burke, (WILLIAM,) an Irish murderer, was a resident of Edinburgh. In 1828 he was convicted of murder, and he confessed that he and his accomplice had murdered fifteen persons, and had sold their bodies to a surgeon.

Burkhart von Hohenfels, boork'hart fon ho'en-fĕlss, a German minnesinger, born about 1200.

See LONGFELLOW's "Poets and Poetry of Europe."

Bur'kitt. (WILLIAM,) an English theologian, born at Hitcham in 1650, wrote "Expository Notes on the New Testament," (1739.) Died in 1703.

Burlamacchi, boor-lä-mäk'kee, (FRANCESCO,) an Italian revolutionist, who, about 1546, conspired against the party of the pope and the emperor Charles V. The plot being revealed by one of the conspirators, Burlamacchi was executed for high treason.

See "Foreign Quarterly Review" for July, 1846.

Burlamaqui, bür'lä'mä'ke', (JEAN JACQUES,) an eminent Swiss jurist, born at Geneva in 1694. He was for many years professor of law in his native city, and a member of the Council of State. His chief works are "The Principles of Natural Law," ("Principes du Droit naturel," 1747,) and "Principles of the Law of Nations," ("Principes du Droit politique," 1751,) both of which were translated into English, German, Italian, and Spanish. Died at Geneva in 1748.

See SENEBIER, "Histoire littéraire de Genève;" ERSCH und GRUBER, "Allgemeine Encyklopaedie."

Burleigh, LORD. See CECIL.

Burleigh or **Burley,** bur'le, (WALTER,) a learned English philosopher and theologian, born in 1275. He was charged with the education of Edward III., who sent him on a mission to Rome in 1327. Died in 1357.

See BRUCKER, "History of Philosophy."

Bur'leigh, (WILLIAM H.,) an American poet and abolitionist, born at Woodstock, Connecticut, in 1812. He became a printer and editor of several papers, among which was the "Christian Witness" of Pittsburg. He contributed to "The New Yorker," and published in 1840 a volume of poems which were much admired. He is a brother of Charles Burleigh, an anti-slavery orator.

See GRISWOLD, "Poets and Poetry of America."

Burlingame, bur'ling-găm, (ANSON,) an American diplomatist, born in Chenango county, New York, in 1822. He studied law, which he practised in Boston. He was elected a member of Congress by the Republicans of the fifth district of Massachusetts in 1854, in 1856, and again in 1858. He advocated the election of John C. Fremont in several eloquent speeches, (1856.) In 1861 he was sent as commissioner or minister to China. About the end of 1867 he was appointed ambassador from China to the United States and the great powers of Europe.

Burlington, EARL OF. See BOYLE, (RICHARD.)

Burl'ton, (PETER HENRY,) an English geographer, born in 1804. While making scientific researches in India, he was killed by the natives in 1829.

Burmann, bür'mân, (FRANCISCUS,) a Dutch Protestant divine and scholar, born at Leyden about 1628, became professor of theology at Utrecht. Died in 1679.

Burmann, (FRANCISCUS,) son of the preceding, born in 1671, was professor of divinity at Utrecht. He published, among other works, a "Harmony of the Evangelists," (1713.) Died in 1719.

Burmann, (JAN,) son of Francis the younger, born at Amsterdam about 1707, became professor of botany in that city, and published "Thesaurus Zeylonicus," (1737,) and other botanical works. Died in 1780.

Burmann, (KASPAR,) a legal writer and historian, nephew of Peter the elder; died in 1755.

Burmann, (NIKOLAAS LAURENS,) son of Jan, born at Amsterdam in 1734. He published a "Flora Indica," with sixty-seven plates, (1768,) and other botanical works. Died in 1793.

Burmann, (PIETER,) an eminent philologist, brother of Francis the younger, born at Utrecht on the 6th of July, 1668. He became professor of history, eloquence,

and the Greek language at Leyden in 1715, and subsequently obtained the chair of history for the United Provinces. He published editions of Horace, Petronius, Phædrus, Suetonius, Lucan, Quintilian, Virgil, and other classics, a treatise on "The Revenues of the Romans," ("De Vectigalibus Populi Romani," 1694,) and various other works, which are esteemed for their learning and accuracy. Died in 1741.

See DR. JOHNSON's Works; SCHACHT, "Oratio funebris in Obitum P. Burmanni," 1741; "Encyclopædia Britannica."

Burmann, (PIETER,) THE YOUNGER, nephew of the preceding, born at Amsterdam in 1713, became professor of history at Franeker. He published a number of Latin poems, an "Anthology" of the Latin poets, (2 vols., 1759-73,) and several excellent editions of the classics. Died in 1778.

Burmeister, boor'mi'ster, (HERMANN,) a German naturalist, born at Stralsund in 1807. He became professor of zoology at Halle in 1842. He published, besides other works, a "Manual of Entomology," (4 vols., 1832-44,) a "History of Creation," (1843,) and "The Animals of Brazil," (2 vols., 1854-56.)

Burn, (RICHARD,) LL.D., an Englishman, author of several popular works on law, born in Westmoreland, was many years vicar of Orton. Died in 1785.

Bur'na-bў, (ANDREW,) an English divine and traveller, born in 1732, published "Travels in North America," "Journal of a Tour to Corsica," etc. Died in 1812.

Burn'ap, (GEORGE WASHINGTON,) an American Unitarian clergyman, born in Merrimack, New Hampshire, in 1802, graduated at Harvard in 1824. He was ordained pastor of the First Unitarian Church of Baltimore in 1827. He has published several theological and other works.

Bur'nel, (ROBERT,) an English lawyer and bishop, became lord chancellor in 1274. He filled that office for eighteen years, and was the chief adviser of Edward I. He died in 1292. "As a statesman and legislator," says Lord Campbell, "he is worthy of the highest commendation."

See LORD CAMPBELL, "Lives of the Lord Chancellors," vol. i.

Burnes, bŭrnz, (Sir ALEXANDER,) a distinguished Orientalist and traveller, born at Montrose, in Scotland, in 1805, was a relative of the poet Burns. At an early age he became a cadet in the Bombay army. He set out in 1832 on an expedition into Central Asia, which he accomplished in about a year. On his return to England he published his "Travels into Bokhara," which had an immense sale and was soon translated into French and German. He was a member of the Royal Asiatic Society, and also of the Royal Geographical Society, which awarded to him the gold medal "for the navigation of the Indus, and a journey across Central Asia." Returning to India in 1835, he was sent in 1836 on a mission to Cabul. On the breaking out of the insurrection in that city in 1841, he was murdered, with several other British residents.

See J. B. EVRIÈS, "Notice sur A. Burnes," Paris, 1842; CHAMBERS, "Biographical Dictionary of Eminent Scotsmen," (Supplement;) J. W. KAYE, "Lives of Indian Officers," vol. ii., London, 1867; "London Quarterly Review" for November, 1834.

Bur'net, (GILBERT,) a British historian and prelate of great eminence, born in Edinburgh on the 18th of September, 1643. He became minister of Saltoun in 1665, and professor of divinity at Glasgow in 1669. About 1670 he married a daughter of the Earl of Cassilis. Having resigned his professorship in 1674, he removed to London. He published in 1679 the first volume of his "History of the Reformation in England," (3 vols., 1679-1715,) for which he received the thanks of Parliament. Charles II. offered him a bishopric on condition that he should support the measures of the court; but he declined the offer. He published a "Life of Sir Matthew Hale" in 1682. Burnet was a person of much influence in public affairs, and contributed greatly to the revolution of 1688 and the succession of William and Mary. He became chaplain to William III. and Bishop of Salisbury in 1689. "The name of Burnet," says Macaulay, "was odious to the great majority of the Anglican priesthood. . . . This distinction he owed to the prominent place which he held in literature and politics, to the readiness of his tongue and of his pen, and above all to the frankness and boldness of his nature,—frankness which could keep no secret, and boldness which flinched from no danger." The same author adds, "The utmost malevolence of faction could not venture to deny that he served his flock with a zeal, diligence, and disinterestedness worthy of the purest ages of the church." ("History of England.") He published in 1699 an "Exposition of the Thirty-Nine Articles of the Church of England," which is considered a standard work. His most remarkable work is his "History of his Own Times," (2 vols., 1724–34,) which was severely criticised by Swift, Pope, and other Tories. He was author of an interesting tract entitled "Some Passages in the Life and Death of Lord Rochester," (1680.) Died in 1715.

See "Life of Bishop Burnet," by his son THOMAS, prefixed to the "History of his Own Times;" CHAMBERS, "Biographical Dictionary of Eminent Scotsmen;" J. LE CLERC, "Life and Character of Bishop Burnet," London, 1715; "London Quarterly Review" for April and July, 1823; GUIZOT, "Monk's Contemporaries."

Burnet, (GILBERT,) a son of the preceding, was chaplain to George I. He wrote some treatises on theology, and died prematurely.

Bur'net, (JACOB,) LL.D., an eminent American jurist, born at Newark, New Jersey, in 1770, was one of the first settlers of Cincinnati. He graduated at Princeton College, and afterwards studied law under Judge Boudinot. In 1796 he removed to Cincinnati, where he resided for the remainder of his life. He was appointed in 1821 a judge of the supreme court of Ohio, and in 1828 elected to the Senate of the United States. He assisted in founding the Cincinnati College, of which he became the first president, and contributed liberally to the cause of education. He was the author of "Notes on the Early Settlement of the Northwestern Territory." Through the influence of La Fayette, Judge Burnet was elected a member of the French Academy of Sciences. Died in 1853.

See LIVINGSTON'S "Portraits of Eminent Americans."

Bur'net, (JOHN,) a Scottish engraver, born near Edinburgh in 1784. Among his best works are prints after Wilkie's "Blind Fiddler," and "Chelsea Pensioners reading the Gazette of the Battle of Waterloo." He has published a "Practical Treatise on Painting," "Rembrandt and his Works," (1849,) and "Life and Works of J. M. W. Turner," (1852.) The last-named work was written conjointly with Mr. P. Cunningham.

Burnet, (THOMAS,) an English divine and eloquent writer, born at Croft, in Yorkshire, about 1635. He became a Fellow of Christ's College, Cambridge, in 1657, and was elected master of the Charter-House in 1685. He had the moral courage to offer the first opposition to the dispensing power which James II. usurped. His reputation is founded on a fanciful but well-written work, in Latin, entitled "Telluris Theoria Sacra," ("The Sacred Theory of the Earth," 1680,) which he translated into English, (1684.) This work has little scientific merit; but it was greatly admired for the beauty of its imagery and its style. He also wrote "On the State of the Dead," ("De Statu Mortuorum," 1727.) Died in 1715.

See BRUCKER, "History of Philosophy."

Burnet, (THOMAS,) an English theologian, became prebendary of Sarum. He published several works. Died in 1750.

Burnet, (Sir THOMAS,) an English judge and political writer, was a son of Bishop Burnet. He edited his father's "History of his Own Times," and wrote a travesty of the first book of the "Iliad." In his youth he was dissipated, and was supposed to be one of the "Mohocks" of Addison's "Spectator." Died in 1753.

Burnet, (WILLIAM,) a son of Bishop Burnet, was born at the Hague in 1688. He was appointed Governor of New York and New Jersey in 1720, and ruled those provinces with ability for eight years. In 1728 he became Governor of Massachusetts. Died in 1729.

Bur'nett, (GEORGE,) an English writer, published "Letters on the State of Poland," and other works. Died in 1811.

Burnett, (GILBERT THOMAS,) an English naturalist, born in London in 1800, became professor of medical botany at King's College, London. He wrote "Outlines

of Botany," (1833,) and was a contributor to the "Journal of Science and Art," and other periodicals. Died in 1835.

Burnett, (JAMES.) See MONBODDO.

Bur'nett, (JOHN,) a Scottish advocate and legal writer, born in 1765, became judge-admiral of Scotland in 1810. He died the same year.

Bur'nett, (WALDO IRVING,) M.D., an American naturalist and microscopist, born at Southborough, Massachusetts, in 1828. He visited Europe about 1850. He contributed to the "American Journal of Science," and other periodicals. Among his works is an "Essay on the Cell : its Physiology, Pathology," etc. Died at Boston in 1854.

Bur'ney, (CHARLES,) a musical composer and doctor of music, born at Shrewsbury in 1726. His talents and worth procured him the respect and friendship of several of the principal wits of that age,—among others, Dr. Johnson and Burke. In 1773 he was elected a Fellow of the Royal Society. His "General History of Music," completed in 1789, is highly esteemed. Died in 1814.

See "Memoirs of Dr. Burney," by his daughter, MADAME D'ARBLAY; FÉTIS, "Biographie Universelle des Musiciens."

Burney, (CHARLES,) a distinguished Greek scholar, second son of the preceding, born at Lynn in 1757; died in 1817.

See "Edinburgh Review" for May, 1811.

Burney, (FRANCES.) See D'ARBLAY, MADAME.

Burney, (JAMES,) the eldest son of Dr. Burney the musical composer, born about 1745, entered the naval service at an early age, and accompanied Cook in his last two voyages. He became rear-admiral, and died in 1821. Besides other works, he wrote a valuable "History of Voyages of Discovery in the Southern Ocean," (5 vols., 1804–16.)

Burney, (WILLIAM,) master of the Royal (Naval) Academy of Gosport, and author of "Lives of the Naval Heroes of Great Britain," born in 1762; died in 1832.

Burnouf, bür'noof', written also **Bournouf,** (EUGÈNE,) a distinguished French Orientalist, son of Jean Louis, noticed below, born in Paris in 1801. He became a member of the Academy of Inscriptions in 1832, and the same year succeeded De Chézy as professor of Sanscrit in the College of France. Among his principal works are "Commentaries on the Yaçna, one of the Liturgic Books of Persia," and "Introduction to the History of Booddhism," (1845.) He died in 1852, having previously been appointed perpetual secretary of the Academy of Inscriptions.

See CHARLES LENORMANT, "Eugène Burnouf," 1852; "Nouvelle Biographie Générale."

Burnouf, (JEAN LOUIS,) a French philologist, born at Urville in 1775. He was appointed, in 1817, professor of Latin eloquence in the College of France. He published a "Method of Studying the Greek Language," (1814,) a translation of the complete works of Tacitus, and of Cicero's "De Officiis." He was a member of the Academy of Inscriptions, and librarian of the university. Died in 1844.

See "Nouvelle Biographie Générale."

Burns, (JOHN,) an eminent Scottish medical writer, born in Glasgow in 1775. He became regius professor of surgery in the University of Glasgow in 1815. His chief work is "Principles of Midwifery," (10th edition, 1843,) which obtained great success. He also published "Principles of Surgery," (2 vols., 1828–38,) and "Principles of Christian Philosophy," (6th edition, 1846.) He perished in the wreck of the Orion in 1850.

Burns, (ROBERT,) a celebrated Scottish poet, born near the town of Ayr, January 25, 1759. His father, William Burness, (or Burnes—for the name was variously written,) was the son of a farmer, and "was thrown," says the poet, in one of his letters, "by early misfortunes, on the world at large, where, after many years' wanderings and sojournings, he picked up a pretty large quantity of observation and experience, to which I am indebted for most of my little pretensions to wisdom." In early life Burns's father had followed the profession of a gardener ; but afterwards he took a lease of a small farm of seven acres, in order to set himself up in the nursery business, and built with his own hands the dwelling in which the poet was born. Although his life appears to have been one long struggle with adversity, William Burness spared no pains that he might give his children a good education. He sent them to school as he had opportunity, and sometimes in the evening, after the day's work was done, assisted their studies himself. "I owed much," says the poet, "to an old woman who resided in the family. . . . She had, I suppose, the largest collection in the country of tales and songs concerning devils, ghosts, fairies, brownies, witches, warlocks, . . . enchanted towers, dragons, and other trumpery. This cultivated the latent seeds of poetry." Robert was the eldest son: he possessed, with a strong intellect and acute sensibilities, a robust and active body, so that when he was only fifteen he is said to have done the work of a man. He was early familiarized with those hardships and sufferings to which the poor are so often subject, and which he has occasionally touched upon in his poems with such pathos and power. In the letter already referred to, he says, "My father's generous master died, the farm proved a ruinous bargain, and, to clench the misfortune, we fell into the hands of a factor, who sat for the picture I have drawn of one in my 'Tale of Twa Dogs.' My father was advanced in life when he married; I was the eldest of seven children; and he, worn out by early hardships, was unfit for labour. . . . We lived very poorly. I was a dexterous ploughman for my age, and the next eldest to me was a brother, (Gilbert,) who could drive the plough very well and help me to thrash the corn. A novel-writer might perhaps have viewed these scenes with some satisfaction; but so did not I : my indignation yet boils at the recollection of the factor's insolent, threatening letters, which used to set us all in tears." In a very interesting and touching account which he wrote of their early troubles, his brother Gilbert says, "I doubt not but the hard labour and sorrow of this period of his life was in a great measure the cause of that depression of spirits with which Robert was so often afflicted through his whole life afterwards." When the poet was about fifteen, his father gave up his farm near Ayr, and removed to the parish of Tarbolton. A little before Burns had reached his sixteenth year, he "first committed," he says, "the sin of rhyme." In his case, as in that of Sappho, "it was Love that taught [him] Song." A "bonnie sweet sonsie lass" had been assigned as his partner in the labours of the harvest-field, (it was the custom to join a male with a female partner on such occasions.) She sang sweetly, and "the tones of her voice made his heart-strings thrill like an Æolian harp." Her singing first put into his head the idea of writing songs. Somewhat later, he went to a noted school at a distance from home, to learn mensuration, surveying, etc., where he appears to have made good progress in his studies, until a charming young girl, who lived near by, "overset his trigonometry, and set him off at a tangent from the sphere of his studies. It was," he says, "in vain to think of doing any more good at school." This irresistible attraction towards what he terms "the adorable half of the human species" seemed destined to exert a constant and controlling influence upon his life. To use his own words, "My heart was completely tinder, and was eternally lighted up by some goddess or other." The fame which he had acquired by his verses, added to his rare conversational powers, caused his company to be eagerly sought in the social gatherings of the vicinity ; and the promiscuous society into which he was thus thrown appears to have laid the foundation of the irregularities and dissipation which unhappily marked the latter part of his life. In his early youth, as he tells us, he regarded illicit love with horror ; but through the influence of some of his new acquaintance his delicacy of feeling on this subject gradually wore away, and before he had reached his twenty-fourth year we find him speaking of his own unlawful amours lightly and almost boastfully. He had recently been initiated into the mysteries of free-masonry. He was introduced to the lodge at Tarbolton by John Rankin, who, according to Lockhart, was "a very dissipated man, with considerable talents," and who appears to have exerted a most unfavourable influence on the moral character of the poet. Burns afterwards addressed to him a poetical epistle. Burns's

father was a worthy and sincerely pious man. In a beautiful tribute to his memory, the poet speaks of him as

> "The tender father and the generous friend ;
> The pitying heart that felt for human woe ;
> The dauntless heart that feared no human pride ;
> The friend of man, to vice alone a foe ;
> ' For even his failings leaned to virtue's side.'"

There is reason to believe that these noble lines are not chargeable with any of the proverbial falsity of epitaphs. But, unhappily, at the time above referred to, Burns's character was but too truly expressed by those words of the Roman poet, "Video meliora proboque, deteriora sequor."[*] In proportion as he rejected the restraints of morality, he appears to have cast off his reverence for religion. "Polemical divinity," says he, "about this time was putting the country half mad ;" and he appears to have been ambitious to show that, while in argument he was not inferior, in wit he was greatly superior, to most of those whom he encountered. He was one day seen "at the door of a public house, holding forth on religious topics to a whole crowd of country-people, who presently became so shocked with his levities that they fairly hissed him from the ground." (See Lockhart's "Life," page 68.) While in this controversial spirit, he wrote two satirical pieces which excited no little commotion in that part of Scotland, being as much applauded by one party or class as they were condemned by the other. These were "The Twa Herds," (or "The Holy Tulzie,") and "Holy Willie's Prayer." Of the latter, Scott speaks as "a piece of satire more exquisitely severe than any which Burns ever afterwards wrote, but, unfortunately, cast in a form too daringly profane to be received into Dr. Currie's collection."

About the year 1785, Burns formed a *liaison* (which was, as some writers tell us, according to the usage then prevailing in Scotland, a virtual marriage) with a young woman named Jean Armour, somewhat above his own rank in life. She bore him twins. He had previously given her a written acknowledgment of marriage ; but this did not appease the anger of her father, as Burns was then wholly unable to support a family. It was his purpose to quit Scotland and seek his fortune in Jamaica. "But, before leaving my native country forever," he says, "I resolved to publish my poems. I weighed my productions as impartially as was in my power. I thought they had merit ; and it was a delicious idea that I should be called a clever fellow, even though it should never reach my ears. . . . I can truly say that, *pauvre inconnu* as I then was, I had pretty nearly as high an idea of myself and of my works as I have at this moment, when the public has decided in their favour." The poems were accordingly published, and were so favourably received that, after all expenses had been paid, he cleared about twenty pounds. The success of his first experiment as an author, and the encouragement which he received from some who were not unknown in the world of letters, produced an entire change in his plans ; and, instead of going to America, he resolved at once to visit Edinburgh and make the acquaintance of the distinguished men of letters of that city. He was soon introduced to the notice of Dugald Stewart, Dr. Hugh Blair, and many others, eminent in rank and fashion as well as in literature. "The attentions he received," says Stewart, "from all ranks and descriptions of persons, were such as would have turned any head but his own." Scott has left us an extremely interesting account of Burns's appearance at this time, which seems to have made a vivid and deep impression on his youthful mind. "His person was strong and robust, his manners rustic, not clownish, with a sort of dignified plainness and simplicity which received part of its effect, perhaps, from one's knowledge of his extraordinary talents. . . . There was a strong expression of sense and shrewdness in all his lineaments. The eye alone, I think, indicated the poeti-

---

[*] "I see the better course and approve it, but I pursue the worse." One can scarcely doubt that he felt at times all the force of those lines in his admirable " Epistle to a Young Friend :"

> " But ne'er with wits profane to range
> Be complaisance extended :
> *An atheist's laugh 's a poor exchange*
> *For Deity offended.*"

---

cal character and temperament. It was large and of a dark cast, which glowed—I say literally *glowed*—when he spoke with feeling or interest. I never saw such another eye in a human head, though I have seen the most distinguished men of my time. His conversation expressed perfect self-confidence, without the slightest presumption."

Among the persons of rank who showed him marked favour, the most prominent was Lord Glencairn, whose kindness the poet ever remembered with the deepest gratitude, and to whose memory he has dedicated one of the most beautiful and touching of all his productions,—the "Lament for James, Earl of Glencairn." Under the patronage of the distinguished men whose acqua·ntance he had made in Edinburgh, he brought out, about the close of 1787, a new edition of his poems, from which he is said to have realized more than five hundred pounds. But, unfortunately, the intoxication of fame, and the continual excitement of his Edinburgh life, furnished a fresh temptation to those irregularities which began some years before. In 1788 he openly declared his marriage with Miss Armour, and soon after was appointed officer of the excise, with a salary of but fifty pounds a year: it was afterwards increased to seventy pounds. In 1791 he removed to Dumfries, where he spent the remainder of his life. His intemperate habits, aggravated by pecuniary distresses, gained more and more the ascendency over him, but not to the extent, as has sometimes been asserted, of rendering him incapable of discharging the duties of his office. One* who knew him well during the latter period of his life, in refuting the charge against him of "habitual drunkenness," says, "He superintended the education of his children with a degree of care that I have never seen surpassed by any parent in any rank of life whatever."

Burns died on the 21st of July, 1796. His funeral was attended by many thousand persons, including those of every rank and condition, some of whom came from a great distance. Nearly twenty years after the poet's death, a costly mausoleum was erected in the churchyard at Dumfries, whither the remains were transferred, June 5, 1815.

The most striking characteristics of Burns's poetry are simplicity and intensity,—an intensity not limited to feeling or passion merely, but belonging equally to his imagination and his thoughts,—in which qualities he is scarcely, if at all, inferior to any of the greatest poets that have ever lived. Some of his expressions are like brilliant flashes of light: in an instant the thought or sentiment is impressed upon the mind, never to be forgotten. His power of concentration is perfectly marvellous. In two short lines—

"The rank is but the guinea stamp,
The man's the gowd for a' that,"—

he says more than many able men could do in an elaborate essay. His "Tam o' Shanter," as has been well observed, is truly an epic, and one of a high order. As an amatory poet, Burns has no equal among British bards ;

"For love's own strain to him was given,
To warble all its ecstasies,
In Pythian words, unsought, unwilled."†

He appears, however, through some peculiarity either of his genius or his temperament, to have been disinclined to undertake any extended poem or other work of imagination. "His poetical temperament," says Campbell, "was that of fitful transports rather than steady inspiration." But this peculiarity may have been at least as much the result of habit, confirmed, if not induced, by the necessities of his outward life, as of the original cast of his mind. Had his education and external circumstances been different, his genius might perhaps have taken another form, and shown itself no less capable of lofty and sustained flights of imagination than it was of brilliant sallies of wit or of the inimitable expression of passion or sorrow. With his rare insight into the human heart, his intensity of feeling and vividness of imagination, combined with wit and humour as varied as they were exquisite, we can scarcely doubt that had his inclination

and habits of thought led him to attempt some longer work, whether a drama or an epic, he might have written something not unworthy of a place among the world-renowned productions of immortal genius, such as Goethe's "Faust" or Cervantes' "Don Quixote." "In the inimitable tale of 'Tam o' Shanter,'" says Scott, "he has left us sufficient evidence of his abilities to combine the ludicrous with the awful and even the horrible. No poet, except Shakspeare, ever possessed the power of exciting the most varied and discordant emotions with such rapid transitions."*

Respecting Burns's moral character little need be added to what is revealed by his life. He had at least the merit of not seeking to defend or excuse his own faults, though he has occasionally suggested palliations, as when he says,

"What's *done* we partly may compute,
But not what is resisted."

His sins were rarely if ever the result of "malice aforethought ;" and the manner in which he sometimes alludes to them is as full of instruction as of pathos. He could not, indeed, as has been justly observed, have so pathetically enforced the truth of some of his moral lessons had he not preached from the text of his own errors.

See LOCKHART, "Life of Burns," 1 vol. 8vo, 1828; CURRIE, "Life," prefixed to BURNS's "Correspondence ;" A. CUNNINGHAM, "Life and Land of Robert Burns," 1840; ALEXANDER PETERKIN, "Review of the Life of Robert Burns ;" JOHN WILSON, "Genius and Character of Robert Burns," 1845; S. TYLER, "Robert Burns as a Poet and a Man," 1848; R. CHAMBERS, "Life and Times of Robert Burns ;" CAMPBELL, "Specimens of the British Poets ;" CARLYLE, "Miscellanies," article "Burns ;" JEFFREY, "Miscellanies." See, also, FITZ-GREENE HALLECK's beautiful lines on Burns.

Burns, (WILLIAM W.,) an American general, born in Ohio about 1826, graduated at West Point in 1847. He became a brigadier-general of volunteers about September, 1861. He served in several battles near Richmond, June, 1862.

Burn'side, (AMBROSE EVERETT,) an American general, born at Liberty, Union county, Indiana, in 1824, graduated at West Point in 1847. He obtained the rank of first lieutenant, which he resigned about 1853. He became a colonel of volunteers early in 1861, commanded a brigade at Bull Run, July 21, and was appointed a brigadier-general in August. He directed the expedition which, moving by sea and aided by a large naval force, captured Roanoke Island in February, 1862. He took Newbern in the next month, and was promoted to the rank of major-general. In July, 1862, he moved his army to the James River to reinforce that of General McClellan. He commanded a corps at the battle of South Mountain, September 14, and at that of Antietam, —where he distinguished himself,—September 16, 1862. On the 7th of November he succeeded General McClellan as commander of the army of the Potomac. On the 13th of December he crossed the Rappahannock and attacked Lee's army, which held a strong and fortified position near Fredericksburg. He was repulsed with a loss of 10,243 killed and wounded, and during the night of the 14th retired to the left bank of the river. At his own request, he was relieved of the command on the 26th of January, 1863. In March or April of that year he took command of the department of the Ohio. Moving through Kentucky, *via* Mount Vernon and London, into East Tennessee, he occupied Knoxville about the 2d of September. He defended Knoxville with success against General Longstreet, who besieged it in November, 1863. In April, 1864, he obtained command of the ninth corps, which fought under General Grant at the battles of the Wilderness, May 5, 6, of Spottsylvania Court-House, May 9-11, and of Cold Harbour, June 3. He was elected Governor of Rhode Island in 1865, and re-elected several times.

Burons. See BORRON.

Buronzo del Signore, boo-ron'zo děl sĕn-yo'rà, (CARLO LUIGI,) a learned Italian prelate, born at Vercelli in 1731, became Bishop of Turin in 1797. He discovered a manuscript of the works of Bishop Acto or Atto, "Attonis Vercellensis Ecclesiæ Episcopi Opera," which he published in 1768. Died in 1806.

---

* The Rev. James Gray. (See Lockhart's "Life," pp. 334-338.)
† Campbell's "Ode to the Memory of Burns."

* "Quarterly Review," No. 1.

ā, ē, ī, ō, ū, ȳ, *long;* à, è, ò, same, less prolonged; ă, ĕ, ĭ, ŏ, ŭ, ў, *short;* a, ę, į, ǫ, *obscure;* fär, fàll, fàt; mět; nŏt; gŏŏd; mŏŏn;

Bŭrr, (Aaron,) an American theologian, born at Fairfield, Connecticut, in 1715, was a son-in-law of the celebrated Jonathan Edwards. He became in 1748 president of the College of New Jersey, which was removed about 1756 from Newark to Princeton. Died in 1757.

Burr, (Aaron,) an American politician, son of the preceding, and a grandson of the great Jonathan Edwards, was born at Newark, New Jersey, in February, 1756. He graduated at Princeton in 1772, entered the army in 1775, and served in the expedition against Quebec. Early in 1776 he was raised to the rank of major, and in July, 1777, he became lieutenant-colonel. He resigned his commission in March, 1779, studied law, was admitted to the bar in 1782, and practised with great success in the city of New York. He was a very adroit, plausible, and insinuating speaker. In 1782 he married a widow named Mrs. Prevost. Having become an active Democrat, he was appointed attorney-general of New York State in 1789, and elected to the Senate of the United States in 1791. In 1800, Jefferson and Burr were the Democratic candidates for the offices of President and Vice-President, and received an equal number of votes. The election consequently devolved on the House of Representatives, which, after a long and exciting contest, decided that Jefferson should be President and Burr Vice-President. By his effort to supplant Jefferson in this election he lost the favour of the Democrats. In 1804 he presented himself as candidate for the office of Governor of New York, but he was defeated, partly by the agency of General Hamilton, whom with slight provocation he challenged and killed in a duel in July, 1804. This act excited such a storm of popular indignation that he found it expedient to absent himself from the State. After he retired from the Vice-Presidency in 1805 he was suspected of a design to conduct a hostile expedition against Mexico, with the view of establishing a government there which should also include the southwestern part of the United States. He was arrested on a charge of treason, tried at Richmond, Virginia, in 1807, and acquitted. In 1808 he went to Europe, where he passed several years in poverty. He resumed the practice of law in New York in 1812, but could not recover his former standing. Died in 1836.

See Parton, "Life and Times of Aaron Burr," 1858; M. L. Davis, "Life of Aaron Burr," 2 vols., 1836-37.

Bur'rhus, (Afranius,) the commander of the prætorian cohorts, on the death of the Roman emperor Claudius, caused Nero to be proclaimed his successor. He at first restrained, but afterwards yielded to, the sanguinary tendencies of the new emperor. Died A.D. 62.

Burriel, boor-re-êl', (Andrés Marcos,) a Spanish Jesuit and historian, born in 1719. He published, among other works, a "History of California, and its Temporal and Spiritual Conquest." Died in 1762.

See Ersch und Gruber, "Allgemeine Encyklopaedie."

Bŭr'rill, (James,) an American Senator and lawyer, born in Providence, Rhode Island, in 1772. He became chief justice of his native State in 1816, and a Senator of the United States in 1817. He opposed the Missouri Compromise and the admission of Missouri as a slave State. Died in 1820.

Bŭr'ritt, (Elihu,) an American reformer and linguist, called "the Learned Blacksmith," was born in New Britain, Connecticut, in 1811. He was apprenticed to a blacksmith about 1827, and worked at that trade many years, during which he learned, in the intervals of labour, numerous ancient and modern languages. As a public lecturer he advocated temperance and other reforms. He published "Sparks from the Anvil," (1848,) and "Thoughts on Things at Home and Abroad," (1854.)

Burrough, bŭr'ro, (Edward,) an English minister of the Society of Friends, was born near Kendal in 1634. He was convinced by George Fox in 1652, began to preach in London in 1654, and published, besides other works, a "Message to the Present Rulers of England," (1659,) and "The Trumpet of the Lord sounded out of Zion." He also wrote many epistles. In the spring of 1662 he was committed to Newgate prison, where he died in the last month of that year.

See "Friends' Library," vol. xiv.

Burrough, (Stephen,) an English navigator, made a voyage to the Arctic regions in 1556, of which he wrote an account.

See Hakluyt, "Voyages and Discoveries."

Burroughes, bŭr'rọz, (Jeremiah,) an English Puritan minister, born in 1599, preached in London. He wrote several works, which were highly esteemed. Died in 1646.

Bur'roughs, written also **Boroughs,** (Sir John,) an Englishman, who wrote "The Sovereignty of the British Seas proved by Records." Died in 1643.

Bŭr'roughs, (George,) an early New England divine, was executed at Salem, Massachusetts, in 1692, for witchcraft.

Bŭr'rōw, (Sir James,) an eminent English lawyer; died in 1782. He published "Reports," (5th ed., 5 vols. 1812.)

Burrow, (Reuben,) an English mathematician, born in Yorkshire, was appointed professor of mathematics at Calcutta in 1782. He died in 1791, leaving a "Treatise on Projectiles," and other works.

Bŭr'rōwṡ, (George Mann,) an English physician, of London. He published about 1828 "Commentaries on the Causes, Forms, Symptoms, and Treatment of Insanity."

See "London Quarterly Review" for October, 1821.

Bŭr'rows, (William,) an American naval officer, with the rank of lieutenant, born near Philadelphia about 1784. As commander of the brig Enterprise, he captured the British brig Boxer in September, 1813. He was killed in this action.

Burser, bŏoR'ser, (Joachim,) a German physician and botanist, born in Lusatia in 1593. He wrote several botanical works, in Latin. The name of Bursera has been given to a genus of terebinths. Died in 1689.

See Ersch und Gruber, "Allgemeine Encyklopaedie."

Bŭr'tọn, (Asa,) D.D., pastor of the church in Thetford, Vermont, born at Preston, (now Griswold,) Connecticut, in 1752; died in 1836.

Bŭr'tọn, (Cassibelan,) an English poet, a son of William the antiquary, born in 1609. He made a translation of Martial into English verse. Died in 1681.

Burton, (Edward,) D.D., an English divine, born in 1794, became in 1829 royal professor of divinity at Oxford. He published a "Greek Testament with English Notes," (1831,) and other works. Died in 1836.

Burton, (Henry,) an English theologian and dissenter, born in Yorkshire in 1579. He published in 1626 two sermons, for which he was punished with the pillory, the loss of his ears, and an imprisonment of fourteen years. Among his works is "The Baiting of the Pope's Bull," (1627.) Died in 1648.

See "Narration of the Life of H. Burton," 1648.

Burton, (John,) an English philologist and divine, born in Devonshire in 1696, became professor of Greek at Oxford. He published "Opuscula Miscellanea theologica," (2 vols., 1771.) Died in 1771.

Burton, (John,) an English physician and antiquary, born in Yorkshire in 1697, published "The Life and Writings of Boerhaave," (1743,) and other works. Died in 1771.

Bŭr'tọn, (John Hill,) a Scottish advocate and miscellaneous writer, born at Aberdeen in 1809, has published "Benthamianæ, or Extracts from the Works of Jeremy Bentham," "Life and Correspondence of David Hume," (1846,) "The History of Scotland from the Revolution to the Extinction of the Jacobite Insurrection," (1853,) and "History of Scotland from Agricola's Invasion to the Revolution of 1688," (1867.)

See "Edinburgh Review" for July, 1867.

Burton, (Richard Francis,) a celebrated English traveller, born about 1821, published "Sindh, or the Unhappy Valley," (2 vols., 1852.) Under the auspices of the Geographical Society of London, he explored Arabia in 1853, and published a "Personal Narrative of a Pilgrimage to El Medinah and Meccah," (3 vols., 1856,) "The Lake Regions of Central Africa," (1860,) "Abeokuta and the Cameroon Mountains," (1863,) and "The Highlands of Brazil," (2 vols., 1869.) He has received for his services to science the gold medals of the English and French Geographical Societies.

See "British Quarterly Review" for October, 1860; "Edinburgh Review" for October, 1860; "Fraser's Magazine" for September, 1855.

Burton, (ROBERT,) an English philosopher and humorist, born at Lindley, Leicestershire, in 1576, was educated at Oxford. He became vicar of Saint Thomas, Oxford, in 1616, and published in 1621 his famous work "The Anatomy of Melancholy : what it is, with all the Kinds, Causes, Symptoms, Prognostics, and several Cures of it : Philosophically, Medicinally, Historically opened and cut up. By Democritus Junior." He composed this book to cure himself of melancholy. Lord Byron pronounced it "the most amusing and instructive medley of quotations and classical anecdotes I ever perused." Dr. Johnson expressed the following opinion : "There is great spirit and great power in what Burton says, when he writes from his own mind." (Boswell's "Life of Johnson.") Burton obtained the living of Segrave about 1630. Died in January, 1639 or 1640.

See WOOD, "Athenæ Oxonienses;" "Blackwood's Magazine" for September, 1861.

Burton, (WILLIAM,) a brother of the preceding, born in 1575, wrote, among other works, a "Description of Leicestershire, with its Antiquities." Died in 1645.

Burton, (WILLIAM,) an English scholar, born about 1609, taught school at Kingston-upon-Thames, and published "Græcæ Linguæ Historia," (1657.) Died in 1657.

Burton, (WILLIAM EVANS,) a popular English comedian and dramatist, born in London in 1804. He resided in the United States after 1834, and was manager of several theatres in New York and Philadelphia. He published a "Cyclopædia of Wit and Humour," (2 vols., 1858.) Died about 1860.

Bury, bĕr're, (ARTHUR,) an English theologian, was principal of Exeter College in the reign of William III. His work, entitled "The Naked Gospel," was publicly burned in 1690, and the author deprived of his office.

Bury, (Lady CHARLOTTE CAMPBELL,) a British novelist, born in 1775, was a sister of the Marquis of Lorn. She patronized Sir Walter Scott when he was young. Among her works are "The Devoted," and "Flirtation." Died in 1861.

See "London Quarterly Review" for January, 1838.

Bury, (ELIZABETH,) an English scholar, noted for her knowledge of Hebrew, was born in Cambridgeshire in 1644. Died in 1720.

See a "Life of E. Bury," by her husband, SAMUEL BURY.

Bury, de, dĕh bü're', (RICHARD,) a French historian, born in Paris in 1730. He wrote, besides other works, "The Heroic and Private Life of Henry IV. of France," (2 vols., 1765.) Died in 1794.

Bury, de, (RICHARD.) See RICHARD DE BURY.

Bus. See BOS.

Bus, de, dĕh büs, (CÉSAR,) a French ecclesiastic, born at Cavaillon in 1544, founded in 1592 the Congregation of Christian Doctrine. Died in 1607.

See J. DE BEAUVAIS, "Vie de César de Bus," 1645 ; PIERRE DUMAS, "Vie du vénérable C. de Bus," 1703.

Busbecq, büs'bĕk or büs'bĕk', **Bousbecq**, or **Boesbec**, boos'bĕk, (AUGIER GHISLEN,) [Lat. AUGE'RIUS GHISLE'NIUS BUSBE'QUIUS,] an eminent Flemish scholar and traveller, born at Commines in 1522, was sent by the emperor Ferdinand as ambassador to Solyman II. He afterwards wrote, in Latin, an interesting narrative of his sojourn at the court of the Sultan, "Legationis Turcicæ Epistolæ quatuor," (1589,) which is replete with valuable information of various kinds. Besides the above work, he wrote "Letters from France to the Emperor Rudolph." Died in 1592.

See SWEERT, "Athenæ Belgicæ;" "Retrospective Review," vol. xiii., 1826; J. G. ECK, "Dissertatio de A. G. Busbequio," 1768; NICÉRON, "Mémoires."

Büs'bў, (Dr. RICHARD,) born in Lincolnshire, England, in 1606, became master of Westminster School in 1640, and in the fifty-five years during which he held that station he is said to have educated a greater number of distinguished men than any other teacher that ever lived. He died in 1695. Though a very severe disciplinarian, he was kind-hearted and eminently charitable to the poor.*

See WOOD, "Athenæ Oxonienses;" "Biographia Britannica."

---

* "Yet he was kind; or, if severe in aught,
The love he bore to learning was in fault."
GOLDSMITH'S "Deserted Village."

Busby, (THOMAS,) an English musician and writer, born at Westminster in 1755, became organist at the church of Saint Mary Wolnoth. He published a "History of Music," a musical dictionary, "The Age of Genius," a poem, and made a translation of Lucretius. Died in 1838.

See "London Quarterly Review" for April, 1814.

Busch, boŏsh, or **Busel**, boo'zĕl, (AUGUST LUDWIG,) a German astronomer, born at Dantzic in 1804. He was the assistant of Bessel, whom he succeeded as director of the observatory at Königsberg in 1846. Died in 1855.

Busche, von dem, fon dām boŏsh'ĕh, [Lat. BUS'-CHIUS,] (HERMANN,) a learned German friend of Luther, born in 1468 ; died in 1534.

Buschetto, boos-ket'to, surnamed DA DULICHIO, (dä doo-lee'ke-o,) from the place of his birth, a Greek architect and sculptor, built the famous cathedral of Pisa, which was commenced about 1063.

See QUATREMÈRE DE QUINCY, "Vies des Architectes célèbres."

Büsching, bü'shing, (ANTON FRIEDRICH,) an eminent German geographer and theologian, born in Schaumburg-Lippe in 1724. He became professor of philosophy at Göttingen in 1759, and in 1761 was invited to Saint Petersburg as preacher to the Protestant congregation. His "Description of the Earth" (1754) was esteemed the most complete work of the kind that had then appeared, and was translated into the principal languages of Europe. He also published a "Magazine for History and Geography," "Biographies of Celebrated Persons," and a "History of the Lutheran Churches in Poland and Russia," (3 vols., 1784–87.) Died in 1793.

See his Autobiography, entitled "A. F. Buschings Lebensgeschichte," 1789.

Büsching, (JOHANN GUSTAV GOTTLIEB,) son of the preceding, born at Berlin in 1783. He was appointed royal archivist at Breslau in 1811, and professor of archæology in 1823. He published many works on German literature, art, and mediæval antiquities. Died in 1829.

Busel. See BUSCH.

Busenbaum. See BUSENBAUM.

Busenbaum, boo'zĕn-bŏwm', or **Busembaum**, boo'-zĕm-bŏwm', (HERMANN,) a famous German Jesuit, born at Nottelen, in Westphalia, in 1600. His work entitled "Marrow of Moral Theology" ("Medulla Theologiæ Moralis," 1645) went through more than fifty editions ; but it was condemned to be burnt, by the parliaments of Paris and Toulouse, for countenancing regicide. Died in 1668.

Bush, (GEORGE,) an American theologian and biblical scholar, born in Norwich, Vermont, in 1796. He graduated at Dartmouth in 1818, and was appointed in 1831 professor of Hebrew and Oriental literature in the University of New York. In 1832 he published his "Life of Mohammed," and about the same time an elaborate "Treatise on the Millennium," in which he maintained the millennium to have been the period in which Christianity triumphed over Roman paganism. In 1835 appeared his "Hebrew Grammar," in 1836 "Illustrations of the Holy Scriptures," and in 1840 he began his series of "Bible Commentaries," in 8 vols. In 1847 he embraced the doctrines of Swedenborg. He edited the "New Church Repository," and officiated as Swedenborgian minister until within a few months of his death in 1860.

See GRISWOLD, "Prose Writers of America."

Bushe, boŏsh, (Sir CHARLES KENDAL,) an eloquent Irish lawyer and judge, born about 1767, was a member of the Irish Parliament. He became chief justice of Ireland in 1822. Died in 1843.

See BROUGHAM, "Statesmen of the Time of George III.," Third Series.

Bush'ĕl, (THOMAS,) an English royalist, born in 1594, was master of the royal mines in Wales, and published several works. Died in 1674.

Bushnell, boŏsh'nel, (DAVID,) an American inventor, born in Saybrook, Connecticut, about 1742, became a captain in the army. He prepared explosive machines which he placed in kegs, that they might be carried by the tide against the British ships in the Delaware. This affair occasioned Hopkinson's ballad of "The Battle of the Kegs." Died in 1826.

See HENRY HOWE, "Lives of Eminent American Mechanics, etc.," 1847.

ā, ē, ī, ō, ū, ӯ, *long;* ă, ĕ, ĭ, ŏ, ŭ, ў, *short;* a, e, i, o, *obscure;* fär, fåll, fåt; mĕt; nŏt; gŏŏd; mŏŏn;

Bushnell, (HORACE,) D.D., an eminent American divine, born in Litchfield county, Connecticut, in 1802. He graduated at Yale College in 1827, and was afterwards for some time literary editor of the New York "Journal of Commerce." In 1833 he was ordained pastor of the North Congregational Church in Hartford. Dr. Bushnell has long been regarded as one of the most eloquent preachers and accomplished writers in Connecticut. He has published several volumes, and a great number of discourses and addresses on various subjects, chiefly philosophical and theological, including the "Moral Tendencies and Results of Human History," "Unconscious Influence," "Politics the Law of God," "The Age of Homespun," etc. In 1849 he was summoned before the Hartford Central Association of Ministers for the heretical opinions alleged to be contained in his volume entitled "God in Christ." The charge was not sustained ; and in reply Dr. Bushnell published (1851) his "Christian Theology," in which he reviews the various shades of belief that have prevailed in the Church, and arrives at the conclusion that exactness in theological science cannot be attained. In 1858 appeared his most important work, "Nature and the Supernatural as together constituting the One System of God."

Busiri. See BOOSEEREE.

Bu-sī'ris, [Gr. Βούσιρις,] in ancient mythology, a king of Egypt, and son of Neptune, who sacrificed to Jupiter all the foreigners who entered his dominions. He was killed by Hercules.

See P. EKERMANN, "Dissertatio de Busiride," Upsal, 1743.

Busleyden, bŭs-li′den, [Lat. BUSLID′IUS,] (JEROME,) a distinguished patron of literature, and friend of Erasmus, born in the province of Luxemburg about 1470; died in 1517.

Buslidius, the Latin of BUSLEYDEN, which see.

Buss, bŏos, (FRANZ JOSEPH,) a German jurist, born at Zell in 1803, was professor of law and political economy at Freiburg in 1836. He published "The Methodology of Canon Law," and other works.

Bussey, bŭz′ze, (BENJAMIN,) a wealthy merchant of Boston, born at Canton, Massachusetts, in 1757. He bequeathed a large sum to Harvard College. Died in 1842.

Bussières, de, deh bü′se′aiR′, a French writer and poet, born near Lyons in 1607 ; died in 1678.

Bussola, boos′so-là, (DIONIGI,) a Milanese sculptor, flourished about 1600–30.

Busson, bü′sòN′, (JULIEN,) a French physician, born in Brittany in 1717 ; died in 1781.

Bussone. See CARMAGNOLA.

Bussy, bü′se′, (ANTOINE ALEXANDRE BRUTUS,) a French physician and scientific writer, born at Marseilles in 1794, made several discoveries in chemistry. In 1850 he was admitted into the Institute.

Bussy d'Amboise, de, deh bü′se′ dòN′bwâz′, (LOUIS DE CLERMONT,) a French nobleman of the time of Henry III., signalized himself by his cruelty during the Massacre of Saint Bartholomew. He was at length murdered by the Count of Montsoreau, whose wife he had seduced. His adventures form the subject of Dumas' romance "La Dame de Montsoreau."

See DE THOU, "Histoire Universelle."

Bussy-Rabutin, de, deh bü′se′ rä′bü′tăN′, (ROGER,) COMTE, a French satirist, born in Nivernais in 1618. He published "Memoirs" and "Letters," and a work entitled "Amorous History of the Gauls." He was imprisoned a year in the Bastille, and subsequently exiled to his country-seat sixteen years, for writing a satire on Louis XIV. Died in 1693.

See LE BRET, "Mémoires secrets de Bussy-Rabutin," 1767.

Bustamante de la Camara, boos-tä-män′tà dà là kä′mä-rä, (JUAN,) a Spanish naturalist, born at Alcalá de Henares. He wrote a work on the animals mentioned in the Scriptures, (2 vols., 1595.)

Bustamente, boos-tä-men′tà, (ANASTASIUS,) a Mexican general, born about 1782. He became President of Mexico in 1830, was soon after banished, was again chosen President in 1837, and was banished a second time in 1841. Died in 1851.

Bustamente or **Bustamante, de,** dà boos-tä-män′-tà, (Don CARLOS MARIA,) a Mexican archæologist, born

about 1800. He edited, besides other works, Bernardino de Sahagun's "History of New Spain," ("Historia universal de las Cosas de Nueva España," 3 vols., 1839.)

Busti, boos′tee, (AGOSTINO,) a skilful Italian sculptor, sometimes called IL BUSTINO, (èl boos-tee′no,) and BAMBAIA, (bâm-bī′yä,) born in the Milanese in 1470. His chief work was a monument to Gaston de Foix at Milan. Died about 1550.

Bute, (JOHN STUART,) EARL OF, a British statesman, born in Scotland in 1713. He became in 1738 one of the lords of the bedchamber to Frederick, Prince of Wales, and in this station succeeded in obtaining a great ascendency over the mind of that prince's son, afterwards George III. The life of Lord Bute belongs rather to history than to biography. We will merely say here that in 1761 he was made one of the principal secretaries of state, and in May, 1762, he became first lord of the treasury to the young king. As minister he was eminently unpopular ; but although he resigned in April, 1763, he still retained the confidence of the king, and continued (as was generally believed) to exert a great influence over the counsels of the cabinet. He passed the last six or seven years of his life in unbroken retirement, and died in 1792. Lord Bute was a liberal patron of literature and the arts. He was fond of the sciences, especially of botany, and published an expensive work, in nine volumes, on the plants of England.

See CHAMBERS, "Biographical Dictionary of Eminent Scotsmen ;" ERSCH and GRUBER, "Allgemeine Encyklopaedie ;" MACAULAY, "Essay on the Earl of Chatham," in the "Edinburgh Review" for October, 1844.

Butéo, bü′tà′o′, or **Borrel,** bo′rêl′, (JEAN,) a French geometer and writer, born at Charpey in 1492 ; died in 1572.

Bŭt′lęr, (ALBAN,) a learned English Catholic divine, president of the College of Saint-Omer, author of "Lives of the Saints," (5 vols., 1745,) and other works. Born at Northampton in 1710 ; died in 1773.

See CHARLES BUTLER, "Life of Alban Butler," London, 1799.

Bŭt′lęr, (ANDREW PICKENS,) an American politician, born in South Carolina about 1796. He was a United States Senator for South Carolina for a number of years between 1846 and 1857. His kinsman Preston Brooks assaulted Charles Sumner in 1856, on account of some remarks offensive to Butler. Died in 1857.

Butler, (BENJAMIN F.,) an American lawyer, practised at Albany, in New York State. He was attorney-general of the United States from December, 1831, to June, 1834, in the cabinet of President Jackson. Died in 1858.

Butler, (BENJAMIN FRANKLIN,) an American politician and general, born at Deerfield, New Hampshire, on the 5th of November, 1818. According to Parton, he was "a youth of keen vision, fiery, inquisitive, fearless." He graduated at Waterville College, Maine, about 1838. He studied law, was admitted to the bar in 1840, and practised with success. It is said that in fertility of expedients and devices to obtain an acquittal of his client he has seldom if ever been equalled. He was originally what is termed a "hard-shell" Democrat, (i.e. one inflexibly devoted to the principles of the party.) He took an active part in politics, and was a delegate to the National Convention which was held in Charleston in April, 1860, and adjourned to Baltimore, where it separated into two bodies. Butler supported Breckinridge for the Presidency in November, 1860, and thus made himself so unpopular in the North that he received only six thousand votes as candidate for Governor of Massachusetts in that year.

On the breaking out of the civil war in 1861 he took command of a brigade, which he moved at once towards Washington ; but, on hearing of the riot in Baltimore, he made a détour to Annapolis. He occupied Baltimore on the 13th or 14th of May, was appointed a major-general on the 16th, and on the 22d took command of Fortress Monroe, the most important fort in the Union. Three slaves having come to the fort for protection, Butler received them, and applied to them the famous phrase "contraband of war." "An epigram," said Theodore Winthrop, alluding to this expression, "abolished slavery in the United States." Butler commanded the land-forces of the expedition which took Fort Hatteras, North Carolina, in August, 1861. In January, 1862, he obtained command of an army of about 15,000 men sent by sea to co-operate with the navy in the capture of New Orleans. The department of the Gulf was then created, and Butler was appointed commander of the same. Admiral Farragut passed the forts on the 24th of April, and transferred New Orleans to General Butler, who entered it on the 1st of May. By stern and vigorous measures he reduced the city to order, and, by his wise and strict sanitary regulations, preserved it from the yellow fever in the summer of 1862. He ordered William Mumford to be executed for tearing down the flag of the Union from the mint. To obtain funds for the support of the poor, he exacted money from rich secessionists. A great outcry was made against him for his order "that any female who should insult an officer or soldier should be regarded and held liable to be treated as a woman of the town, plying her avocation," which, according to Parton, had a salutary effect. General Butler imprisoned the insolent Mayor Monroe in Fort Jackson in May, 1862. He armed free coloured men, and obtained from that class recruits for his army. In November, 1862, he was removed from the command, and was succeeded by General Banks,—a change which it would perhaps be difficult to defend on any principles of sound policy. "At New Orleans," says Parton, "he was magnificently right both in theory and practice." In December, 1862, Jefferson Davis issued a proclamation in relation to General Butler, whom he declared to be a felon, and ordered him to be treated as an outlaw. Butler had gone to New Orleans a pro-slavery Democrat: he came away a decided anti-slavery man and a Radical. He obtained command of the department of Virginia and North Carolina in the latter part of 1863. Having been instructed to operate on the south side of the James River against Richmond, he moved his army, composed of two corps, up the James River on the 4th of May, 1864, and on the 5th occupied City Point and Bermuda Hundred, where he intrenched himself. His army was attacked on the 16th, near Drury's Bluff, and forced back into its intrenchments, where it was safe, but could not operate efficiently against Richmond. He commanded the land-force of an unsuccessful expedition against Fort Fisher in December, 1864, and soon after this date was removed from command by General Grant, who complained that he had violated his instructions.

He was elected a member of Congress in 1866, and was one of the managers selected March 2, 1868, to conduct the impeachment of President Johnson. He was re-elected to Congress in 1868.

See PARTON, "General Butler in New Orleans; History of the Administration of the Department of the Gulf in 1862," 1864; GREELEY, "American Conflict," 2 vols., 1864–66.

Butler, (CHARLES,) an English clergyman, scholar, and writer on music, etc., born at High Wycombe in 1559. Among his works are "The Feminine Monarchy, or the History of Bees," (1609,) and "The Principles of Music," (1636.) Died in 1647.

Butler, (CHARLES,) an able and learned English jurist and Roman Catholic writer, a nephew of Alban Butler, noticed above, was born in London in 1750. He completed the edition of Coke upon Littleton which Hargrave left unfinished. Among his principal works are "Horæ Biblicæ," (1797,) "Horæ juridicæ subsecivæ," (1804,) "Historical Memoirs of the English, Irish, and Scottish Catholics," and a continuation of Alban Butler's "Lives of the Saints." Died in 1832.

See "Reminiscences of Charles Butler," London, 1822.

Butler, (CYRUS,) an American merchant, born in 1767, lived at Providence, Rhode Island. He gave forty thousand dollars to endow a hospital for the insane at Providence. Died in 1849.

Butler, (FRANCES.) See KEMBLE, (FANNY.)

Butler, (JAMES.) See ORMOND, DUKE OF.

Butler, (JAMES,) an American soldier of the Revolution, born in Prince William county, Virginia, settled in South Carolina, where he distinguished himself in partisan warfare against the British. He was killed in the massacre at Cloud's Creek, near the close of the war.

Butler, (JOHN,) Bishop of Hereford, an English political writer, born at Hamburg in 1717. He wrote pamphlets in support of Lord North's measures. Died in 1802.

Butler, (JOHN,) an American tory, born in Connecticut, was notorious as the leader of the party which massacred the settlers of Wyoming Valley in July, 1778.

Butler, (JOSEPH,) an English bishop and writer of high reputation, was born at Wantage, in Berkshire, in 1692. He commenced his scholastic education at the grammar-school at Wantage, from which he went to an academy in Gloucestershire, where he had for his fellow-student Secker, afterwards Archbishop of Canterbury. While at this academy "he wrote," says Mackintosh, "private letters to Dr. Clarke on his celebrated 'Demonstration,' suggesting objections that were really insuperable, and which are marked by an acuteness which neither himself nor any other ever surpassed." Not long after, he entered Oriel College, Oxford. He was admitted into holy orders about 1716 or 1717. In 1721 he became rector of Houghton, and obtained the rich living of Stanhope in 1725. In 1726 he published fifteen sermons preached at the Rolls Chapel, which are highly esteemed. He was appointed chaplain to Lord-Chancellor Talbot in 1733, and clerk of the closet to the queen in 1736. His reputation rests chiefly on his admirable "Analogy of Religion, Natural and Revealed, to the Constitution and Course of Nature," (1736.) "This," says Sir James Mackintosh, "is the most original and profound work extant in any language on the philosophy of religion." Lord Brougham pronounces it "the most argumentative and philosophical defence of Christianity ever submitted to the world." Butler was appointed Bishop of Bristol in 1738, and Bishop of Durham in 1750. Died in 1752. His character is represented as pure, modest, and amiable. He was never married.

See FITZGERALD, "Life of Bishop Butler," prefixed to an edition of his "Analogy," 1848; MACKINTOSH, "View of the Progress of Ethical Philosophy;" ALLIBONE, "Dictionary of Authors;" THOMAS BARTLETT, "Memoirs of the Life, etc. of Joseph Butler, Bishop of Durham;" "London Quarterly Review" for May, 1830, and October, 1839.

Butler, (PIERCE M.,) COLONEL, born in Edgefield District, South Carolina, in 1798, became Governor of his native State, and was killed at the battle of Churubusco in August, 1847.

Butler, (RICHARD,) a major-general in the American army, was killed while fighting, under General Saint Clair, against the Indians, in 1791.

Butler, (SAMUEL,) a celebrated English wit and poet, the author of "Hudibras," was born in the parish of Strensham, Worcestershire, about 1612. He became in early life a clerk to Mr. Jeffereys, a justice of the peace, and afterwards entered the service of Sir Samuel Luke, an officer under Cromwell. Luke is supposed to be the original of Hudibras. After the restoration, (1660,) Butler was secretary to the Earl of Carbury, who appointed him steward of Ludlow Castle. He married a Mrs. Herbert, who brought him a fortune, which, however, was lost by investment in unsound securities. The first part of his famous poem was published in 1663, the second part in 1664; but the third part did not appear until 1678. He died poor, in London, in 1680.

"'Hudibras,'" says Hallam, "was incomparably more popular than 'Paradise Lost:' no poem in our language rose at once to greater reputation. Nor can this be called ephemeral, like that of most political poetry. . . . The sense of Butler is masculine, his wit inexhaustible, and it is supplied from every source of reading and observation. But these sources are often so unknown to the reader that his wit loses its effect through the obscurity of the allusions." ("Introduction to the Literature of Europe.")

See DR. JOHNSON, "Lives of the English Poets;" A. M. H. BOULARD, "Vie de S. Butler Auteur du Poëme d'Hudibras," Paris, 1816; "Biographia Britannica;" A. RAMSAY, "Butler and his Hudibras;" "Retrospective Review," vol. ii., 1820; "Fraser's Magazine" for March, 1856.

Butler, (SAMUEL,) D.D., an English philologist, born in Warwickshire in 1774. He studied at Saint John's College, Cambridge, and became Bishop of Lichfield in 1836. He published a valuable edition of "Æschylus," a "Praxis on the Latin Prepositions," and other works. Died in 1839.

Butler, (THOMAS,) Earl of Ossory, son of James Duke of Ormond, born in 1634. He was raised to the rank of admiral in 1673, and commanded the English 'roops in Flanders in the war against the French in 1677. Died in 1680.

Butler, (WEEDEN,) an English divine, born at Margate in 1742, became chaplain to the Duke of Kent. He wrote "The Cheltenham Guide," "Sermons," etc. Died in 1823.

Butler, (WILLIAM,) an English teacher and writer of school-books, born near Worcester in 1748. Among his works is "Exercises on the Globes," (1798.) Died in 1822.

Butler, (WILLIAM,) an American general, born in Virginia about 1755, was the father of Andrew P. and Pierce M., noticed above. He represented a district of South Carolina in Congress from 1800 to 1813. Died in 1821.

Butler, (WILLIAM ALLEN,) an American lawyer and poet, son of Benjamin F. Butler the attorney-general, was born in Albany in 1825. His "Nothing to Wear: an Episode in City Life," (1857,) has obtained great popularity both in Europe and in this country. Mr. Butler has made contributions in prose and verse to the "Democratic Review," "Literary World," etc.

Butler, (WILLIAM ARCHER,) a philosopher and poet, born at Annerville, near Clonmel, Ireland, about 1814. He contributed several poems to the "Dublin University Magazine." In 1837 he became professor of moral philosophy in Trinity College, Dublin. He wrote "Letters on Romanism, a Reply to Cardinal Wiseman," (1854,) "Lectures on the History of Ancient Philosophy," (2 vols., 1856,) and other works. Died in 1848.

Butler, (WILLIAM O.,) an American general, born in Kentucky about 1793. He served in the war of 1812, and in the Mexican war, (1846–47.) In 1846 he was raised to the rank of major-general. He was the Democratic candidate for Vice-President of the United States in 1848, but was not elected.

Butret, de, dĕh bü'trĂ', BARON, a French horticulturist of Strasburg. He published in 1794 a treatise on the trimming of fruit-trees, "Taille raisonnée des Arbres fruitiers," which was often reprinted. Died in 1805.

Bütt, (GEORGE,) an English clergyman and poet, born in 1741, published numerous sermons. Died about 1795.

Butt, (ISAAC,) an Irish lawyer and politician, born in Donegal county in 1813. He was elected a member of Parliament in 1852. He published, besides other works, a "History of the Kingdom of Italy," (1860.)

Buttafuoco, boot-tâ-foo-o'co, (MATTEO,) a general, born in Corsica in 1730. He opposed Paoli, and promoted the incorporation of Corsica with France. As a member of the States-General in 1789, he favoured the old régime. Died about 1800.

But'ter-field, (DANIEL,) an American general, born in Oneida county, New York, about 1831. He was appointed a brigadier-general of volunteers in September, 1861. He served at several battles near Richmond in May and June, 1862, after which he was raised to the rank of major-general.

Butt'mann, [Ger. pron. bŏŏt'mân,] (PHILIPP KARL,) a learned and profound German philologist, born at Frankfort-on-the-Main in December, 1764, became in 1796 secretary and in 1811 librarian of the Royal Library at Berlin. Died in 1829. Buttmann devoted his attention chiefly to the study of the Greek language and antiquities. His large Greek Grammar ("Ausführliche Griechische Sprachlehre") is, so far as it goes, perhaps the best work of the kind that has ever been written. Unhappily, he did not live to complete it. He was a friend of Niebuhr. He edited various Greek classics. Among his principal works are his "Greek Grammar for Schools," (1792,) which is an abridgment of a more extensive work, sometimes called the "Intermediate Greek Grammar," (1819,) "Lexilogus, or Explanation of Greek Words," (1818,) and "Mythologus, or a Collection of Treatises on the Traditions of Antiquity," (2 vols., 1828.)

See "Nouvelle Biographie Générale;" BROCKHAUS, "Conversations-Lexikon."

Bütt'ner, (CHRISTIAN WILHELM,) an eminent German philologist and naturalist, born at Wolfenbüttel in 1716. He travelled extensively, and formed rich collections of natural history. He passed many years at Göttingen in researches into the primitive history of nations and the filiation of languages. To him we owe the first essay of a glossography, or geography of languages. He published several works. Died at Jena in 1801.

See ERSCH and GRUBER, "Allgemeine Encyklopaedie."

Buttner, bŏŏt'nẹr, (DAVID SIGISMUND AUGUST,) a German botanist, born in 1724, succeeded Haller in the chair of botany at Göttingen. Died in 1768.

Büt'ton, (THOMAS,) an English navigator, made a voyage to the northeastern part of America in 1612, and discovered the mouth of Nelson River, in about 57° north latitude. He gave the name of Button's Bay to a bay near Nelson River. He is said to have been the first who sailed through Hudson Strait to the western shore of Hudson Bay.

Butts, (Sir WILLIAM,) an English physician, born in Norfolk, is mentioned by Shakspeare in his play of "Henry VIII.," act v. He was physician to Henry VIII. Died in 1545.

Buttura, boot-too'râ, (ANTONIO,) an Italian critic and *littérateur*, born near Lake Garda in 1771. He became professor of the Italian language and literature at Saint-Cyr, in France, and in 1817 succeeded Ginguené as professor at the Athenæum. Died in 1832.

Buttura, bü'tü'ră', (EUGÈNE FERDINAND,) a landscape-painter, son of the preceding, born in Paris in 1812; died in 1852.

Buturlin. See BOOTOORLIN.

Buxbaum, bŏŏks'bŏwm, (JOHANN CHRISTIAN,) a German botanist, born at Merseburg in 1694, founded, at the command of the Czar, a botanic garden at Saint Petersburg about 1720, and died in 1730.

Buxhöwden, bŏŏks'hö'dẹn, sometimes written **Buxhoeden,** (FREDERICK WILLIAM,) COUNT, a Russian general, born in Livonia in 1750. He served in the Polish campaign of 1792, and commanded the left wing of the Russians at Austerlitz. Died in 1811.

Buxtehude, (DIETRICH,) a Dutch musician and composer, born about 1635, became organist to Saint Mary's Church at Lubeck. He was esteemed one of the best performers of his time, and composed sacred pieces of great merit. Died in 1707.

Büx'ton, (CHARLES,) an English writer, son of T. Fowell Buxton, noticed below, born in 1822. He wrote "Memoirs of Sir Thomas Fowell Buxton," (3d edition, 1851.) He became a member of Parliament and of the Liberal party.

Buxton, (JEDEDIAH,) an English arithmetician of singular powers of calculation, born near Chesterfield in 1705. His intellect was below mediocrity, with the exception of a wonderful facility in solving the most difficult problems. When on a visit to London, he was taken to the theatre, and employed himself in counting the words used by the actors. Died about 1774.

Buxton, (Sir THOMAS FOWELL,) an eminent English philanthropist, born at Castle Hedingham, in Essex, in 1786. He married in 1807 Hannah Gurney, of Earlham Hall, a sister of Joseph John Gurney and Elizabeth Fry. He represented Weymouth in Parliament from 1818 to 1837, acquired much influence in public affairs, and succeeded Wilberforce as the leader of the anti-slavery movement. About 1838 he produced a "Treatise on the Slave-Trade." Died in 1845.

See a "Life of T. F. Buxton," by his son, CHARLES BUXTON, 3d edition, 1851; A. VON TRESKOW, "Sir T. F. Buxton; ein Bild des Englischen Lebens, etc.," Berlin, 1853; "London Quarterly Review" for June, 1848; "Edinburgh Review" for September, 1818.

Buxtorf, bŏŏks'torf, [Lat. BUXTOR'FIUS,] (JOHANN,) a distinguished Hebrew scholar, born at Camen, in Westphalia, in 1564. He became professor of Hebrew at Bâle in 1591 and published a "Lexicon Hebraicum et Chaldaicum," (1607,) "Biblia Hebraica Rabbinica," or Hebrew Bible with Rabbinical notes, and several treatises on the writings of the Rabbins. Died in 1629.

See DANIEL TOSSANUS, "Oratio de Vita et Obitu J Buxtorfii," 1630; NICÉRON, "Mémoires;" MORÉRI, "Dictionnaire Historique."

Buxtorf, (JOHANN,) son of the preceding, born at Bâle in 1599, was also celebrated as a Hebraist. In 1630 he succeeded his father as professor at Bâle. He published a "Chaldee and Syriac Lexicon," "Concordance of the Hebrew Bible," (1632,) left unfinished by his father, and other works. Died in 1664.

See L. GERNLER, "Oratio parentalis J. Buxtorfii Memoriæ dicata," 1655; NICÉRON, "Mémoires."

Buxtorf, (JOHANN JAKOB,) son of the preceding, born in 1645 at Bâle, was professor of Hebrew in his native city. Died in 1704.

His nephew JOHN was likewise professor of Hebrew at Bâle. Died in 1732.

See S. WERENFELS, "Vita eximii Viri J. J. Buxtorfii," 1705.

Buy de Mornas, bü-e′ deh moR′nä′, (CLAUDE,) a French geographer, born at Lyons. He published "Methodical and Elementary Cosmography," (1770,) and other works. Died in 1783.

Buys, bois, (PAULUS,) an eminent Dutch statesman, lived about 1550–90. He was honoured with the friendship and confidence of William, Prince of Orange, and held for a considerable time the office of advocate of Holland. During the administration of the Earl of Leicester in the Netherlands, Buys was the leader of the opposition party. He is pronounced by Motley one of the ablest statesmen of Holland.

See MOTLEY, "United Netherlands," vol. i. chap. x.

Buzanval, de, deh bü′zŏn′väl′, (NICOLAS CHOART,) a French prelate, remarkable for his devotion to the duties of his office and for the apostolic simplicity of his character, born in Paris in 1611, became Bishop of Beauvais in 1650. Died in 1679.

See J. BESOIGNE, "Vies des quatre Évêques engagés dans la Cause de Port-Royal," 2 vols., 1756.

Buzot, bü′zo′, (FRANÇOIS LÉONARD NICOLAS,) an eminent French Girondist, born at Evreux in 1760, was an advocate before the Revolution. He was sent as a deputy to the States-General in 1789, and to the National Convention in 1792. In the trial of the king he voted for an appeal to the people. On the 31st of May, 1793, he was proscribed as a royalist with the other chiefs of the Gironde, and fled, first to Calvados; afterwards they attempted to conceal themselves in the south of France. Buzot and Pétion were found dead in a field near Bordeaux in June, 1794. Buzot was an especial favourite of Madame Roland.

See LAMARTINE, "History of the Girondists;" "Vie de Buzot," prefixed to his "Mémoires sur la Révolution," edited by GUADET, 1823; article on Madame Roland in this work, and "Mémoires de Madame Roland," edited by M. P. FAUGÈRE, 1864.

Byˊfield, (NICHOLAS,) an English Puritan divine, born in Warwickshire about 1578, was vicar of Isleworth. He wrote commentaries on some books of the New Testament. Died in 1622.

Bylderdyck. See BILDERDIJK.

Byˊles, (MATHER,) an American clergyman and noted humorist, born at Boston in 1706. He preached many years at Boston. In 1776 he adhered to the royal cause. Died in 1788.

Bynæus, bī-nä′ŭs, (ANTOON,) a Dutch philologist, born at Utrecht in 1654, published several Latin works. Died in 1698.

Byng, bĭng, (GEORGE,) an eminent English naval commander, born in 1663, became rear-admiral in 1703, vice-admiral in 1706, and admiral of the blue about 1708. In 1721 he was raised to the peerage, with the title of Viscount Torrington. Died in 1733.

Byng, (JOHN,) an English admiral, son of the preceding, born in 1704. Having in 1756, in consequence of the improvidence and inefficiency of the English ministry, been unsuccessful in an expedition to relieve Minorca, then blockaded by a French fleet of superior strength, he was accused of cowardice by the ministers, who were anxious to avert the public odium from themselves. By a sentence of extreme rigour, he was condemned to be shot. He met his death with the firmness of a hero, March 14, 1757.

See VOLTAIRE, "Siècle de Louis XV;" "Correspondance Générale;" J. F. SEYFART, "Leben des Admirals J. Byng," 1757.

Bynkershoeck, van, vän bĭn′kers-hook′, (KORNELIS,) a celebrated jurist, born at Middelburg, in Holland, in 1673. He published, besides other works, "Observationes Juris Romani," (1700–33,) and "Quæstiones Juris Publici," (1737.) His death is variously dated 1763, 1743, or 1745.

See SAX, "Onomasticon;" ADELUNG, Supplement to JÖCHER's "Allgemeines Gelehrten-Lexikon."

Byns, van, vän bĭns, (ANNE,) a Flemish poetess, born at Antwerp; died about 1548.

Byrd, (WILLIAM.) See BIRDE.

Byrge, the French of BYRGIUS, which see.

Byr′gĭ-us, (JUSTUS,) [Fr. JUSTE BYRGE, zhüst bĕRzh,] or **Jobst Bürgi,** (yopst büR′Gee,) a Swiss mathematician, born at Lichtensteg in 1552. He was patronized by William IV., Landgrave of Hesse-Cassel, for whom he constructed a celestial globe, afterwards bought by the emperor Rudolph II. He was appointed instrument-maker to the emperor, and distinguished himself by several valuable inventions. The invention of logarithms is ascribed to him by some writers, but is more generally attributed to Napier. Died in 1633.

Byrne, (WILLIAM,) an eminent English engraver, born at Cambridge about 1744; died in 1805.

Byˊrom, (JOHN,) an English writer and poet, born near Manchester in 1691, contributed several pieces to "The Spectator," and invented a system of short-hand which still bears his name. His pastoral of "Colin and Phebe," published in the "Spectator," No. 603, was generally admired. Died in 1763.

Byˊron, (ANNA ISABELLA MILLBANKE,) LADY, an English heiress, born in 1792 or 1793, was the only daughter of Sir Ralph Millbanke, afterwards Noel. She was married in January, 1815, to Lord Byron the poet. They separated the following year. After their separation she inherited the title of Baroness of Wentworth. She was a woman of superior talents. Died in 1860.

Byron, (GEORGE ANSON,) CAPTAIN, an English naval officer, born in 1758, was a son of Admiral Byron, noticed below. He rendered important service in the great naval victory gained by Lord Rodney over the French in April, 1782. Died in 1793.

Byron, (GEORGE GORDON NOEL,) an English poet of rare genius, born in London, January 22, 1788. He belonged to an old family (the name appears to have been originally spelled **Burun** or **Bürün,** afterwards **Biron,** and last of all **Byron**) which traced its origin back to the Norman conquest. His grandfather, John Byron, was an English admiral. His father, Captain Byron, married Catherine Gordon, a Scottish heiress, with whom he lived unhappily, and whose wealth he squandered in a life of vice and dissipation. In 1790 the mother of the poet, having been deserted by her husband, retired to Scotland and took up her residence in Aberdeen. Here her son received the first rudiments of his education at a day-school. Not long after he was sent to the grammar-school of Aberdeen. When he was between six and seven years old his mother took him with her on a visit to the Highlands, the scenery of which is said to have made, even at that early age, a deep and indelible impression on his mind. When he was ten years old he succeeded to the estate and title of William, fifth Lord Byron, his grand-uncle, who had resided at Newstead Abbey, in Nottinghamshire, and had died there in May, 1798. Soon after, his mother took him to London and consulted some able surgeons respecting a congenital deformity and lameness of one of his feet; but the defect proved to be incurable, and continued to the end of the poet's life a source of bitter mortification to him. He was next placed at the school of Dr. Glennie, at Dulwich. During his school-days, Byron exhibited many indications both of the virtues and weaknesses which marked his character in after-life. On the one hand, his sympathetic nature, his generosity and courage, won for him the love and respect of his companions; while, on the other, his morbidly sensitive, wilful, and passionate temper involved him in continual disputes and quarrels. It is related that while at Harrow he saw one day a large tyrannical boy punishing little Peel (the brother of the celebrated Sir Robert Peel) because he refused to be his "fag." Byron was not large enough to resist the tyrant with any hope of success, but, in a voice trembling between terror and indignation, he demanded that he might bear half of the punishment. On another occasion, having seen a small and sickly boy bullied by one much older and stronger than himself, he interfered with success. Soon after he said to his protégé, "If any one bullies you, tell me, and I will thrash him if I can." He kept his word; and they were afterwards inseparable friends. Byron had been with Dr. Glennie rather less than two years, when he left for Harrow. While here he formed a romantic and passionate attachment for Miss Chaworth, the heiress of Annesley, an estate adjacent to Newstead Abbey. Miss Chaworth's father had been killed in a duel (or, as some say, in a drunken fight) by Lord Byron, the poet's great-uncle. This very circumstance may not improbably have tended to inflame young Byron's imagination. Alluding to his love for Miss Chaworth, he says, "Our union would have healed feuds in which blood had been shed by our fathers." He appears to have always regarded this as the deepest and truest passion of his life, and to have fully persuaded himself that if he had married Miss Chaworth he would have been a better as well as a happier man. But she did not return his affection, and not long after she was married to a gentleman named Musters. This union appears, however, not to have been a happy one. In 1805 Byron went to Trinity College, Cambridge, which he left two years after without a degree. During his stay at the University he published a volume of poems entitled "Hours of Idleness," (1807,) which was very severely criticised in the "Edinburgh Review." The poet wrote, by way of retaliation, his "English Bards and Scotch Reviewers," a caustic and scathing satire, which at the time caused a great sensation, and convinced the critics that Byron's genius was not to be terror-stricken or reduced to silence by "paper bullets of the brain." Little, however, can be said in praise of the justice or discrimination shown in this satiric poem. The author reminds one of Molière's blind man with a club, who lays about him so valiantly, striking down, it may be, friend and foe alike. The satirist is, in fact, scarcely less severe against Scott, who had never injured him, than against Jeffrey, the object of his burning and bitter resentment. Byron himself afterwards sincerely regretted the publication of this poem, and did all in his power to suppress its circulation.

In 1809, accompanied by his friend John Cam Hobhouse, (with whom he had become acquainted at Cambridge,) Byron set out on his travels through Europe, visiting Portugal, Spain, Turkey, and Greece. He was absent from England nearly two years. On his return he published the first two cantos of "Childe Harold's Pilgrimage," the success of which was so sudden and extraordinary that, as he tells us, "he awoke one morning and found himself famous." Soon after the publication of "Childe Harold" he took his seat in the House of Lords; and he appears to have thought seriously at one time of devoting himself to politics. He addressed the House three times. His most important speech was on the Catholic claims: it is said to have been listened to with much attention. But he seems to have soon lost his interest in politics, and to have abandoned all hopes of making a figure in public life. In 1813 he published "The Giaour," (i.e. "Infidel,") an Oriental tale in verse, which contains some of the most exquisite poetry to be found in the English language. Towards the close of the same year appeared "The Bride of Abydos," another poem of the same general character, which added to his already brilliant reputation. In January, 1814, was published "The Corsair," of which, it is said, at least 14,000 copies were sold in a single day. His other most important poems of this period were "Lara," "The Siege of Corinth," "Parisina," and "The Prisoner of Chillon."

On the 2d of January, 1815, Byron married Miss Anna Isabella Millbanke, only daughter of the baronet Sir Ralph Millbanke, afterwards Noel. She was esteemed a great heiress. Byron says, however, "All I have ever received, or am likely to receive, (and that has been twice paid back, too,) was £10,000." The match was a very unhappy one; the incompatibility of their tempers, and, still more, Lord Byron's irregular, not to say licentious, habits, rendered domestic harmony and peace impossible. Lady Byron bore him, December 10, 1815, a daughter, Ada, who became afterwards the Countess of Lovelace. Soon after she left him and went to her father's, taking with her the child; and he never saw either of them again. In the spring of 1816 he left England, with the determination of never more returning to his native land. Having passed through Belgium and visited the field of Waterloo, he proceeded to Switzerland, and resided for some time near Geneva. While here he wrote the third canto of "Childe Harold." He

afterwards went to Italy and took up his abode in Venice. He next visited Ravenna: during his sojourn in this city he formed a *liaison* with the beautiful Countess Guiccioli, whose sprightly and imaginative character powerfully attracted him. During his stay at Pisa, in 1822, the tragic death of his friend Shelley, who was drowned in a squall near Leghorn, affected him deeply. In the early part of 1822 he was associated with Shelley and Leigh Hunt in conducting a periodical called "The Liberal;" but, soon after Shelley's death, Byron and Hunt quarrelled, and the journal was discontinued. (See HUNT, LEIGH.) In October of the same year he removed to Genoa. Soon afterwards his sympathies for Grecian liberty became strongly excited, and he resolved to devote all his energies to the cause. During his sojourn in Italy, Byron had written several of his most remarkable productions, including the fourth canto of "Childe Harold," "Mazeppa," "Manfred," "Cain, a Mystery," "Marino Faliero," "The Two Foscari," "Sardanapalus," "Werner," and "Don Juan." Having fully embarked in the cause of Grecian freedom, he left Italy in the summer of 1823, and proceeded first to Cephalonia, where he remained some months. He arrived at Missolonghi in January, 1824. He applied himself to business with great energy, manifesting a good sense and practical judgment which many were not prepared to expect from one who had till then been looked upon merely as a poet and a man of pleasure. The exposure which he incurred while making preparations for the siege of Lepanto, then in possession of the Turks, laid the foundation of the illness of which he died. About the middle of February he had a severe convulsive fit. During the extreme prostration that followed this attack, a crowd of Suliotes, whom he had engaged to fight under him, rose in mutiny, and, bursting into his apartment, brandished their arms and furiously demanded their pay. Byron retained his perfect self-possession, and, by his calm and determined courage, awed them into submission. Count Gamba, (brother of the Countess Guiccioli,) who was almost constantly with Lord Byron during the last few months of his life, says of him, "It is impossible to do justice to the coolness and magnanimity which he displayed upon every trying occasion. Upon trifling occasions he was certainly irritable; but the aspect of danger calmed him in an instant. . . . A more undaunted man in the hour of peril never breathed." Having caught a severe cold on the 9th of April, he was attacked with fever and violent rheumatic pains. At last inflammation seized upon his brain and terminated his life on the 19th of April, 1824.

As a man, Byron certainly had great faults; but in palliation of these it should be remembered that he was not only born with violent passions, but that almost every influence of his early life was adverse to the acquisition of habits of self-denial and self-control. By his mother he was treated at one time with the most foolish indulgence; at another, exasperated with causeless reproaches. The fame which he so easily and suddenly acquired, joined to his distinguished rank, may be said to have completed the miseducation which was begun in the nursery. But, in spite of all the disadvantages of education and hereditary temperament, he exhibited many truly noble traits of character, among which were a princely generosity, and a ready and true sympathy for the suffering even in the humblest condition. We are told, in Moore's "Life," that the "inmates" (domestics) "of his family were extremely attached to him, and would have endured anything on his account," and that "he was most unostentatious in his charities."

With all his professions of liberality in politics, Byron always remained an aristocrat at heart; and he is said to have been more proud of his Norman descent than he was of the rare endowments of his mind.

Among the most remarkable characteristics of Byron's poetry, two are deserving of particular notice. The first is his power of expressing intense emotion, especially when it is associated with the darker passions of the soul. "Never had any writer," says Macaulay, "so vast a command of the whole eloquence of scorn, misanthropy, and despair. . . . From maniac laughter to piercing lamentation, there is not a single note of human anguish of which he was not master." The other is his exquisite taste and marvellous felicity in the use of language. Take for example that passage in the "Giaour" beginning with the lines

"He who hath bent him o'er the dead
Ere the first day of death is fled," etc.*

Nothing can exceed the delicacy of perception and taste with which the words are chosen. Of course such exquisite propriety in the choice of words implies an equally exquisite perception of the proprieties of thought and sentiment.

See MOORE, "Life of Byron," 2 vols. 8vo; GALT, "Life of Byron;" "Recollections of the Last Days of Shelley and Byron," by E. J. TRELAWNEY, 1858; the elaborate and excellent article on Byron in ALLIBONE'S "Dictionary of Authors," containing some interesting recollections of the poet not before published, besides a very complete list of bibliographic references; the notice in the "Biographie Universelle," by M. VILLEMAIN, the celebrated critic; JEFFREY, "Miscellanies;" SIR WALTER SCOTT, "Miscellaneous Prose Works;" "London Quarterly Review" for January and July, 1814, October, 1816, April, 1818, July, 1823, and January, 1831; "Edinburgh Review" for December, 1816, August, 1817, and February, 1822; "Atlantic Monthly" for September, 1869; "Quarterly Review" for October, 1869; "The 'True Story of Lady Byron' established," by MRS. HARRIET BEECHER STOWE, 1870.

Byron, (JOHN,) an English naval commander, born in 1723, was a son of William, Lord Byron. He was to have accompanied Lord Anson as midshipman on the Wager in his voyage round the world. The Wager was wrecked on the coast of South America in 1741. He returned to England in 1745. The narrative which Byron published of this shipwreck on his return to England is one of the most interesting works of the kind in the language. He commanded the Dolphin and Tamar in a voyage of discovery in the South Sea in 1764–66. In 1778 he obtained command of a fleet destined to operate against the French in the West Indies. He fought an indecisive battle against D'Estaing off Grenada in July, 1779, and was promoted about that date to the rank of vice-admiral. He was grandfather of the great poet Lord Byron. Died in 1786.

See CHARNOCK's "Biographia Navalis."

Byström, bü'ström, (JOHAN NILS,) a Swedish sculptor, born at Philipsstadt in 1783. He studied in Rome, and, after his return, produced a colossal statue of the crown prince. Among his other works may be named statues of Gustavus Adolphus and of Linnæus.

Bythner, bit'ner, or **Büttner,** büt'ner, (VICTORINUS,) a physician and philologist, born in Poland, became professor of Hebrew at Oxford. He published "Lyra Prophetica Davidis Regis," (1645.) Died about 1670.

Bzovius, the Latin of BZOWSKI, which see.

Bzowski, bzhov'skee, [Lat. BZO'VIUS,] (ABRAHAM,) a Polish theologian, born in 1567. He became professor of philosophy at Milan, and afterwards of theology at Bologna. He wrote "Lives of Paul V. and Gregory XV.," "Continuation of the Annals of Baronius," and other works. Died in 1637.

C.

Caab or **Cab.** See KAAB.

Ca-bā'dēs or **Ca-vā'dēs,** [in Persian, KOBAD or COBAD, ko-bâd',] a Persian king, father of the celebrated Chosroes, ascended the throne about 486 A.D. He gained several victories over the Romans between 502 and 505, and died in 531.

See GIBBON, "Decline and Fall of the Roman Empire."

Cabakjee Ogloo or **Cabakdji Oglou,** kä-bäk'jee og-loo', an officer of janissaries, one of the ringleaders of the revolt which dethroned Selim III., was assassinated in 1808.

Caballero, kä-bâl-yā'ro, (FERNAN,) the pseudonym of a Spanish novelist, whose maiden name was CÆCILIA BÖHL DE FABER, (böl deh fâ'ber.) She was born at Morgue, in Switzerland, in 1797, has been married several times, and has resided in Spain. She has published "La Gaviota," and other novels, which present brilliant pictures of Andalusian life and are highly seasoned with the "Andalusian wit," ("sal Andaluz.") "No living writer," says the "Edinburgh Review" for July, 1861, "has shed so bright a lustre on Spanish literature."

Caballero, (FIRMIN,) a Spanish journalist and statesman, born at Barajas de Melo in 1800. He first attracted public attention by his witty criticisms on Miñano's "Geographical Dictionary." In 1833 he began to edit the "Boletin del Comercio," and in 1834 established another able journal, the "Eco del Comercio." About 1835 he was elected a deputy to the Cortes, and afterwards became a cabinet minister. He published, besides other works, a "Geographical and Administrative Manual of Spain," (1844.)

Caballero, de, dä kä-bâl-yā'ro, written also **Caballero,** (Don JOSÉ ANTONIO,) a Spanish marquis, of Italian descent, born at Saragossa about 1760. He was one of the ministers of Joseph Bonaparte while King of Spain, and on his deposition in 1814 became an exile in France. Died in 1821.

Caballo, kä-bâl'lo, [Lat. CABAL'LUS,] (FRANCESCO,) an Italian medical writer, born in Venetia, lived at Padua. Died in 1540.

Cabanel, kä'bâ'nêl', (ALEXANDRE,) a French historical painter, born at Montpellier in 1823. He obtained a first medal in 1855.

Cabanis, kä'bä'nèss', (JEAN BAPTISTE,) a French advocate, born at Issoudun in 1723. He introduced improvements in cultivation and rural economy, and wrote a valuable "Essay on Grafting," (1764.) Died in 1786.

Cabanis, (PIERRE JEAN GEORGE,) an eminent French philosopher, author, and physician, son of the preceding, was born at Conac, near Saintes, in 1757. He studied medicine under Dubreuil, and settled at Auteuil, near Paris. By a version of some parts of the "Iliad," he gained access to the highest society of Paris, where he was intimate with Diderot, D'Alembert, Condorcet, Franklin, etc. He became the personal and political friend of Mirabeau, whom he assisted with his pen, and whom he attended in his last hours. He wrote an "Account of the Illness and Death of Mirabeau," (1791.) In 1796 he was chosen a member of the Institute, and in the next year professor of clinical medicine in Paris. He married Charlotte, sister of General Grouchy. In 1802 he produced his most important work, "Relation between the Physical System and the Mental Faculties of Man," ("Rapports du Physique et du Moral de l'Homme,") which obtained celebrity, and will doubtless hold its place among the noble essays of abstruse philosophy. In early life, and until about the beginning of the present century, Cabanis held the atheistical views so prevalent at the time of the French Revolution. He maintained, among other doctrines, that the brain "secretes thought," as the liver secretes bile. He afterwards modified his views so far as to recognize in the "primal causes" ("les causes premières") of the universe the existence of both *intelligence* and *will*, and that the same power or powers (*i.e.* "les causes premières") command us to practise virtue. Died in 1808.

See MIGNET, "Éloge de Cabanis;" also the article "Cabanis" in the "Nouvelle Biographie Générale."

Cabanis-Jonval, kä'bä'nèss' zhôn'vâl', (PIERRE,) a French *littérateur*, born at Alais about 1725; died in 1780.

Cabarrus, kä'bä'rüs', (FRANÇOIS,) a French merchant, born at Bayonne in 1752, settled in Spain at an early age. By his talents and services as financier he acquired great influence in the government about 1780, and a few years later he was councillor of finances. In the reign of Charles IV. he was made a count, and was sent as minister plenipotentiary to the Congress of Rastadt in 1797. In 1808 he became minister of finances under Joseph Bonaparte. Died in 1810. His daughter Thérèse, a famous *belle*, became Marquise de Fontenay, then Madame Tallien, and lastly Princesse de Chimay.

Cabarrus, (TERESA.) See CHIMAY, PRINCESS OF.

* See remarks on this passage in a critique in the "Edinburgh Review" for July, 1813.

ā, ē, ī, ō, ū, ȳ, *long;* ă, ĕ, ĭ, ŏ, ŭ, ў, same, less prolonged; ă, ĕ, ĭ, ŏ, ŭ, ў, *short;* a, e, i, o, *obscure;* fär, fâll, fât; mêt; nŏt; gō̆od; mō̆on;

Ça-bas'ĭ-lạs, (Nɪ'ʟᴜs,) [Νεῖλος Καβασίλας,] a Greek archbishop of Thessalonica, wrote an able treatise against the infallibility and supremacy of the pope. Died about 1350.

NICHOLAS CABASILAS, nephew of the preceding, whom he succeeded as archbishop in 1350, was also a zealous adversary of the Latin Church or hierarchy, and author of several works on theology.

See FABRICIUS, "Bibliotheca Graeca."

Cabassole, du, dü kā'bā'sol', (PHILIPPE,) born at Cavaillon, in Provence, became bishop of his native town in 1334, and was made cardinal by Urban V. in 1368. He is best known as the friend of Petrarch, by whom he was greatly esteemed for his talents and learning. Died in 1371.

See MORÉRI, "Dictionnaire Historique."

Cabassut, kā'bā'sü', (JEAN,) a French priest of the Oratory, born at Aix in 1604 or 1605, was eminent for his knowledge of canon law. He wrote "Theory and Practice of Canon Law," and other works. Died in 1685.

Cabat, kā'bā', (LOUIS NICOLAS,) a skilful French landscape-painter, born in Paris in 1812. He produced in 1840 an admired historical landscape, called "The Samaritan," ("Le Samaritain,") and a view of Lake Nemi near Rome. He was before that date termed a *réaliste;* but his later works indicate a change in his manner.

Cabel or Kabel, van der, vȧn der kā'bĕl, (ADRIAN,) an able Dutch painter of landscapes, seaports, figures, etc., born at Ryswick in 1631 ; died in 1695.

Cabestan, kā'bĕs'tŏN', or Cabestaing, de, dĕh kā'-bĕs'tȧN', (GUILLAUME,) a Provençal troubadour, who lived about 1200.

Cabet, kā'bā', (ÉTIENNE,) a French socialist, and the leader of the "Icariens," was born at Dijon in 1788. He became an advocate, and lived in Paris. In 1830 he was appointed procureur-général for Corsica, but he was recalled in 1831. He became a radical democrat, and was elected to the Chamber of Deputies. In 1842 he published his peculiar socialist or communist notions in his romance entitled "Travels in Icaria," ("Voyage en Icarie.") Having made many proselytes to his utopian scheme among the labourers of Paris, he planted a colony in Texas in 1848. After suffering great privations in Texas, Cabet and his Icariens removed in 1850 to the city of Nauvoo, which the Mormons had recently deserted. They held their property in common, and were subject to the sole authority of Cabet. Died at Saint Louis in 1856.

See "London Quarterly Review" for June, 1848.

Cabeza de Vaca, kā-bā'thā dȧ vā'kȧ, (ALVAR NUÑEZ,) a Spaniard who explored the river La Plata in 1540.

Ça-bī'rī, written also Cabeiri, [Gr. Κάβειροι ; Fr. CABIRES, kā'bèR',] ancient divinities worshipped in various parts of the world, especially at Samothrace and Lemnos. The fable of the Cabiri is very obscure. Their mysteries were celebrated with great solemnity. They were believed, among other things, to preside over metals. Some writers trace the worship of the Cabiri to the Phœnicians.

See CREUZER, "Symbolik," vol. ii.

Caboche, kā'bosh', (SIMONET,) a butcher of Paris, who became notorious about 1412 as the chief of a ferocious band called *Cabochiens.* They were partisans of the Burgundians in the civil war between these and the Armagnacs, and committed many outrages in Paris.

See MICHELET, "Histoire."

Caboos, Cabûs, or Cabous, kā-boos', surnamed THE SUN IN ITS SPLENDOUR, a prince, poet, and astronomer, began to reign in Jorjân in 976 A.D. He had a high reputation for virtue, and was a patron of Avicenna. He was deposed in 1012, and died soon after.

Cab'ọt, (GEORGE,) an American Senator, born at Salem, Massachusetts, in 1751, was distinguished for his knowledge of political economy and commercial affairs. He was elected in 1789 to the Senate of the United States, in which he acted with the Federalists and gained the confidence of Washington. He was highly esteemed for his probity and sound judgment. In 1814 he was president of the Hartford Convention. Died in 1823.

Cab'ọt or Gabotto, gā-bot'to, (GIOVANNI,) a Vene-tian pilot and navigator, who lived some time in England and distinguished himself in maritime discovery. In 1496 Henry VII. granted a patent to him and his sons for the discovery of unknown regions. (See CABOT, SEBASTIAN.)

See HAKLUYT, "Principal Navigations and Discoveries of the English Nation."

Cab'ọt, (SEBASTIAN,) [It. SEBASTIANO GABOTTO, sā-bās-te-ā'no gā-bot'to,] a son of the preceding, and a navigator of great eminence, was born at Bristol, England, about 1477. He made several voyages with his father, of which we have no authentic account. In 1497 they discovered a part of North America, which some suppose was Labrador, and others Newfoundland. A few years later he sailed southward as far as Cape Florida. From 1512 until 1517 he was in the service of the King of Spain, who made him a member of the Council of the Indies. In 1526 he commanded a Spanish expedition which explored the river La Plata. About 1548 he returned to England and obtained the favour of Edward VI., who granted him a pension and consulted him in maritime affairs. He became governor of a new company formed to trade with Russia. He was living in 1557, and probably died soon after that date.

See "Memoirs of Sebastian Cabot," by RICHARD BIDDLE, London, 1831 ; ANDERSON, "History of Commerce ;" "Life of S. Cabot," in SPARKS's "American Biography," vol. ix., First Series.

Cabot, kā'bo', (VINCENT,) an eminent French jurist, born at Toulouse about 1550. He professed law fourteen years at Orléans and twenty-two years at Toulouse. He wrote a "Treatise on Benefices," and other works. Died in 1621.

Cabral, kā-brāl', (PEDRO ALVAREZ,) an eminent Portuguese navigator, was chosen by Emmanuel, King of Portugal, to command the fleet which that prince sent to the East Indies in 1500. He sailed or was driven so far westward that, by a fortunate accident, he discovered Brazil in the same year. Pursuing his voyage, he reached Calicut, made conquests, and established the first Portuguese factories in India. He then sailed homeward, and arrived in June, 1501.

See RAMUSIO, "Voyages ;" LAFITEAU, "Conquêtes des Portugais ;" "Nouvelle Biographie Générale."

Cabral de Vasconcellos, kā-brāl' dȧ vȧs-kon-sel'-los, (PAULINO,) a Portuguese poet, who lived about 1780.

See LONGFELLOW's "Poets and Poetry of Europe."

Cabrera, kā-brā'rā, (LUIS,) a Spanish historian, published a "History of Philip II.," (1619.) Died about 1655.

Cabrera, (Don RAMON,) a Spanish general, noted for his cruelty and audacity, was born at Tortosa about 1810. In the civil war between the Christinos and Carlists he joined the latter, and waged a successful guerilla warfare among the mountains of Aragon and Catalonia. He obtained command of a large force, took Valencia in 1837, surprised Morella in 1838, and was created Count of Morella by Don Carlos. The victories of Espartero compelled him to retire to France in 1840. In 1848 he returned to Spain and instigated another rebellion, but was defeated and wounded at Pasteral in 1849, since which he has lived in exile.

See LAVALLÉE, "Histoire de l'Espagne ;" B. DE CORDOVA, "Vida de R. Cabrera," Madrid, 1844 ; "Blackwood's Magazine" for September, 1846.

Cabrera, de, dȧ kā-brā'rā, (JUAN TOMAS HENRIQUEZ,) Duke of Medina del Rio Seco, (mȧ-dee'nā dĕl ree'o sā'ko,) a Spanish statesman, and admiral of Castile, was related to the royal family. He was prime minister under Charles II. in 1693. In consequence of his attachment to the Austrian interests, he was exiled by Porto Carrero. Died in 1705.

See DE LA TORRE, "Mémoires et Négotiations secrètes."

Cabrillo, kā-brĕl'lo, (JUAN RODRIGUEZ,) a Portuguese navigator in the Spanish service. Died in 1543.

Cabrol, kā'brol', (BARTHÉLEMI,) a French anatomist, born at Gaillac about 1535, became professor at Montpellier in 1590.

Caccia, kät'chä,(GUGLIELMO,) a distinguished painter, born in Piedmont about 1568, was usually called IL MONCALVO, because he worked at a place of that name. He was one of the most skilful fresco-painters of his time, and also executed admired pictures in oil, among which is a "Deposition from the Cross." Died in 1625.

See LANZI, "History of Painting in Italy."

Caccianiga, kät-chä-nee′gä, (FRANCESCO,) an able painter and engraver, born at Milan in 1700, worked in Rome, where he died in 1781.

See LANZI, " History of Painting in Italy."

Cacciatore, kät-chä-to′rä, (NICCOLÒ,) a Sicilian astronomer, born in 1780, became director of the Observatory of Palermo in 1817. He published several works on astronomy, (1807–28.)

Caccini, kät-chee′nee, (GIULIO,) an Italian composer and musician, born at Rome about 1560; died in 1635.

Cachet, kä′shä′, (CHRISTOPHE,) a Swiss medical writer, born at Neufchâtel in 1572; died in 1624.

Ca′cus, a fabulous Italian robber and giant, called a son of Vulcan. He lived in a cave. Having stolen some cattle of Hercules, he dragged them by their tails into his cave, so that they could not be discovered by their tracks; but Hercules heard them bellow, and recovered them, killing Cacus. (See "Æneid," book viii.)

Cadahalso. See CADALSO.

Ca-da-lous′, (?) Bishop of Parma, elected pope in 1061, was styled HONORIUS II. He was deposed in 1064.

Cadalso, de, dä kä-Däl′so, written also **Cadahalso,** (JOSÉ,) a successful Spanish poet and satirist, born at Cadiz about 1740. He wrote "Don Julian," a tragedy of some merit, "Fashionable Learning," a prose satire, and anacreontic verses which were admired. He was colonel in the army, and was killed at the siege of Gibraltar in February, 1782. His "Moorish Letters," a witty and satirical work, has been often reprinted.

See TICKNOR, " History of Spanish Literature ;" LONGFELLOW, " Poets and Poetry of Europe."

Cada Mosto, da, dä kä′dä mos′to, (LUIGI,) a navigator, born at Venice about 1432. In the service of Prince Henry of Portugal, he explored the west coast of Africa as far as the mouth of the Gambia, in 1455 and 1456. His account of the voyage is said to be interesting, and very well written. Died about 1480.

See RAMUSIO, " Prima Navigazione di Cada Mosto ;" ZURLA, " Dei Viaggi e delle Scoperte di Cada Mosto," Venice, 1815.

Cadaval, de, dä kä-dä-väl′, (NUNHO CAETANO ALVARES PEREIRA DE MELLO,) DUKE, a Portuguese statesman, born in 1798. He became president of the council of ministers in 1828. Died in 1838 at Paris.

Cäde, (JOHN,) an Irishman and noted rebel in the time of Henry VI., figures in Shakspeare's play as Jack Cade. In 1450, assuming the name of Mortimer, he led a large body of Kentish insurgents towards London, and defeated an army which the king sent against him. The gates of the capital having been opened to him by the citizens or the magistrates, he entered the city and put to death Lord Say, whose political course was obnoxious. After the lapse of a few days, the mob was dispersed by a promise of pardon, and Cade fled to Lewes, where he was killed.

See HUME, " History of England."

Cadenet, kä′d′nä′, (ELIAS,) a troubadour, born in Provence about 1156; died about 1280.

Cader-Billah. See AL-KÂDER-BILLAH.

Cadet de Gassicourt, kä′dä′ deh gä′se′kooR′, (CHARLES LOUIS,) born in Paris in 1769, was a pharmacist, lawyer, and author, remarkable for his versatile talents and activity. He pleaded some causes with success, espoused the popular side in the Revolution, and in 1806 formed the plan of a new board of health, of which for many years he was secretary. In the campaign of 1809 he accompanied Napoleon, who had appointed him his first apothecary. He published many valuable and successful works, among which are "Memoir of Mirabeau," "The Supper of Molière," a comedy, (1798,) "Domestic Chemistry," (1801,) "History of Templars, Free-Masons, and other Secret Societies," "Dictionary of Chemistry," (1803,) "Travels in Austria, etc.," (1818.) He was a member of many scientific academies. Died in 1821.

See QUÉRARD, " La France Littéraire."

Cadet de Gassicourt, (LOUIS CLAUDE,) an eminent French chemist, father of the preceding, born in Paris in 1731. He was for some years apothecary-in-chief of the army. About 1765 he was received into the Academy of Sciences, to which he contributed many treatises on chemistry. His collection of drugs was regarded as the finest in France. He was appointed a commissioner of the chemical department at the royal manufactory of Sèvres. Died in 1799.

See BOULLAY, " Notice sur la Vie de L. C. Cadet," 1805 ; EUSÈBE SALVERTE, " Notice sur la Vie et les Ouvrages de L. C. Cadet," 1822.

Cadet de Metz, kä′dä′ deh mäs, (JEAN MARCEL,) a French mineralogist, born at Metz in 1751; died in 1835.

Cadet de Vaux, kä′dä′ deh võ, (ANTOINE,) a French writer and apothecary, brother of Louis C. Cadet de Gassicourt, born in Paris in 1743. In conjunction with M. Suard, he established, in 1777, the "Journal de Paris." He was noted for practical benevolence, and wrote many useful treatises on domestic and rural economy, among which was an "Essay on the Culture of the Vine," and one "On the Means of Preventing Famine." Died in 1828.

See QUÉRARD, " La France Littéraire."

Cadijah. See KHADIJAH.

Cad′mus, [Gr. Κάδμος,] a hero or demi-god of Greek mythology, was the son of Agenor, King of Sidon. Having been sent by his father in search of his sister Europa, with the charge not to return unless he found her, he settled in Bœotia and founded the city of Thebes. He is the reputed inventor of sixteen simple letters of the Greek alphabet. Tradition adds that he killed a dragon and sowed its teeth, from which armed men sprang up. (See Ovid's "Metamorphoses," books iii. and iv.)

Cadmus, a native of Miletus, said to have been the first Greek prose writer, flourished about 550 or 600 B.C. He wrote a "History of Ionia," which is not extant.

Ca-do′gan, (HENRY,) the son of Charles Sloane, Earl Cadogan, was born in 1780. He entered the army in 1797, became lieutenant-colonel in 1805, and served with distinction in the Peninsular war. He was killed at the battle of Vittoria in 1813. Wellington in his dispatch paid a high tribute to his merit, and the Commons voted a monument to his memory.

Cadogan, (WILLIAM,) Earl and Baron Cadogan, an able English general, was a devoted friend of the Duke of Marlborough, under whom he served at Blenheim (1704) and Ramillies. Having obtained the rank of major-general, he rendered important services at Oudenarde in 1708 and Malplaquet in 1709. He resigned his commission when Marlborough was deprived of the command about 1712. Between 1715 and 1718 he was several times sent as minister to Holland. He was created a baron in 1716, and Earl Cadogan about 1718. In 1722 he succeeded Marlborough as commander-in-chief of the British army. He died without issue in 1726, leaving the title of baron to his brother, General Charles Cadogan, whose son, Charles Sloane, was afterwards made earl.

Cadogan, (WILLIAM,) M.D., born in London in 1711, was a graduate of Oxford. He published "An Essay on Children," often reprinted, and a "Treatise on Gout." Died in 1797.

Cadogan, (WILLIAM BROMLEY,) the second son of Earl Cadogan, (Charles Sloane Cadogan,) was born in 1751. Having taken orders, he became vicar of Saint Giles, Reading, and afterwards rector of Chelsea. His sermons, letters, etc. were published. Died in 1797.

Cadore, de, DUC. See CHAMPAGNY.

Cadoudal, kä′doo′däl′, (GEORGES,) a famous royalist conspirator, born in Brittany in 1769, fought in the Vendean war in 1793. In 1795 and 1796 he was one of the Chouan chiefs, and was defeated by General Hoche. He instigated another unsuccessful revolt in 1799. It appears that he refused the offers of Bonaparte, who wished to enlist him in his service, in 1800. Having formed with Pichegru a conspiracy to assassinate or dethrone Bonaparte, he went to Paris in 1803, and remained concealed there for several months. In 1804 he was arrested, and after trial was executed with his accomplices.

See THÉODORE MURET, " Vie de G. Cadoudal," 1845 ; CRÉTINEAU-JOLY, " Histoire militaire de la Vendée ;" SCOTT, " Life of Napoleon."

Ca-do′vĭ-us or **Mül′ler,** (JAN,) a Dutch theologian and physician, born in 1650, wrote "Memoriale Linguæ Frisicæ Antiquæ." Died in 1725.

See ERSCH und GRUBER, " Allgemeine Encyklopaedie."

ä, ē, ī, ō, ū, y̆, *long;* ä, ĕ, ŏ, same, less prolonged; ă, ĕ, ĭ, ŏ, ŭ, y̆, *short;* ạ, ẹ, į, ọ, *obscure;* fär, fäll, fät; mĕt; nŏt; gōōd; mōōn;

Cadroy, kä′dRwä′, (PIERRE,) a French lawyer, born at Saint-Sever in 1753, was a member of the Convention from 1792 to '95, and a moderate Girondist. He opposed the execution of the king. After the fall of Robespierre he was one of the commissaries of the Convention in the south of France, and took effectual measures against the terrorists in Marseilles and Toulon. Died in 1813.

Cadwalader, kad-wol′a-der, (GEORGE,) an American lawyer and general, born in Philadelphia. He served as a brigadier-general in the Mexican war in 1847. In June, 1861, he was second in command under General Patterson in Virginia. He was appointed a major-general of volunteers in 1862.

Cadwalader, written also **Cadwallader,** (JOHN,) an American general, born in Philadelphia in 1743. He served as brigadier-general at Princeton, Brandywine, Germantown, and Monmouth, 1777–78. Died in 1786.

Cadwaladyr, kad-wol′a-der, the last king of the Britons. Died at Rome in 703 A.D.

Cadwaladyr, a Welsh bard of the sixteenth century.

Cadwallon, kad-wol′lon, Prince of Wales, the father of Cadwaladyr, was defeated in 622 A.D. by Edwin, and retired to Ireland.

Cā′dy,(DANIEL,) an American lawyer, born in Columbia county, New York, in 1773. He gained distinction as an advocate, became a member of Congress, and afterwards a judge. Died at Johnstown, New York, in 1859.

Cæcilius Calactinus, sē-sil′e-us ka-lak-tī′nus, [Καικίλιος Καλακτῖνος,] a Greek rhetorician, born at Calacte, in Sicily, lived in Rome in the reign of Augustus. He wrote many works on grammar and rhetoric, which were approved by the critics of the first and second centuries, but are not extant.

See PLUTARCH, "Lives of the Ten Orators."

Cæcilius Metellus. See METELLUS.

Cæcilius Metellus, sē-sil′e-us me-tel′lus, a Roman high-priest, (pontifex maximus,) was twice elected consul. He gained a victory over the Carthaginians about 250 B.C., and was chosen dictator in 224 B.C.

Cæcilius Statius, sē-sil′e-us stā′she-us, a popular Latin comic poet, the friend of Ennius, was born at Milan, and was a slave in his youth. He wrote forty comedies, of which short fragments only are extant. Died in 168 B.C. Cicero censures his style of Latinity, but admits that he is perhaps chief among comic poets. Horace appears to have thought him in some respects superior to Plautus and Terence. (Epist. lib. ii. 1.)

See "Quintilian," xi.

Cæcina, sē-sil′na, (AULUS,) a Roman orator, was exiled about 48 B.C. for a libellous work against Cæsar. He wrote a book on the "Etrusca Disciplina," which Pliny cites as an authority for his second book.

Cæcina Alienus, sē-sī′na a-le-ee′nus, (AULUS,) a Roman general, called also **A. Licinius Cæcina.** In 68 A.D. he deserted Galba with a body of troops, and entered the service of Vitellius. In the year 69 he marched with a large force from Germany to Italy, and made a junction with the army of Valens. Cæcina and Valens gained a victory over the army of Otho at Bedriacum, which rendered Vitellius master of Italy. Cæcina soon deserted to Vespasian, and a few years later formed a plot against him, for which he was killed by order of Titus in 79 A.D.

See JOSEPHUS, "De Bello Judaico."

Cæci′na Se-ve′rus, (AULUS,) a Roman general, distinguished in the reigns of Augustus and Tiberius. He was governor of Mœsia in 6 A.D. As legate of Germanicus, he commanded an army in Lower Germany, and defeated Arminius (Hermann) in 15 A.D. He lived five years or more after that date.

Cædmon, kĕd′mon or kad′mon, styled "the father of English song," is first mentioned by Bede, who represents him as a "cowherd" attached to the monastery of Whitby. An ode composed by him in praise of the Creator is the earliest specimen of Anglo-Saxon metrical composition extant. Another and longer poem, treating on the creation and fall of man, is attributed to him. He is supposed to have died in 680 A.D.

See THOMAS WRIGHT, "Biographia Britannica Literaria;" LONGFELLOW, "Poets and Poetry of Europe;" KARL W. BOUTERWEK, "Dissertatio de Cædmone Poeta," 1845.

Cælestius. See CELESTIUS.

Cælius. See CŒLIUS.

Cælius (or Cœlius) Aurelianus, see′le-us au-re-le-ā′nus, an eminent physician and medical writer, born at Sicca, in Africa, was one of the sect of Methodici. He probably lived between 100 and 300 A.D. He left two valuable Latin works on chronic and acute diseases, which are extant, entitled "De Morbis Chronicis" and "De Morbis Acutis." His writings are said to be more practical than those of any other medical author of antiquity.

See CARL J. KUEHN, "Programma de Cælio Aureliano," 1816.

Caermarthen, MARQUIS OF. See DANBY, EARL OF.

Cæsalpin or Cæsalpinus. See CESALPINO.

Cæsar, see′zar, [Fr. CÉSAR, sä′zăR′; It. CESARE, chä′sä-rà,] the cognomen of a patrician family of the Julia gens, which was one of the most ancient in the Roman state, and claimed a descent from Iulus, the son of Æneas. The word is derived by some scholars from the Latin *cæsaries,* or the Sanscrit *kĕsa,* which signify "hair." No other name has obtained such celebrity in profane history. The first person bearing the name, who occurs in history, was Sextus Julius Cæsar, prætor in 208 B.C. The name was assumed by the emperor Augustus, and by his successors; and, although the family of Cæsar became extinct with Nero, the succeeding emperors retained it as a title. After the time of Hadrian, the title of Augustus was confined to the reigning prince, and that of Cæsar was given to the heir-presumptive.

Cæsar, tsä′zar, (AQUILINUS JULIUS,) a German historian, born at Grätz in 1720. He wrote a "History of Styria," (7 vols., 1788.) Died in 1792.

Cæsar, (CAIUS.) See CAIUS CÆSAR.

Cæsar, (CAIUS JULIUS CÆSAR STRABO VOPISCUS,) a distinguished Roman orator and poet. He commenced his public career by a speech against T. Albucius in 103 B.C. He surpassed all the orators of his time in wit. He composed tragedies, which were rather polished than powerful. In 88 B.C. he was supported by the aristocratic party for consul; but his election was violently prevented by the tribunes. This contest was one of the proximate causes of the civil war between Sulla and Marius. Cæsar was killed at Rome by the partisans of Marius in 87 B.C.

See APPIAN, "Bellum Civile."

Cæsar, (JULIUS,) [Fr. JULES CÉSAR, zhül sä′zăR′; It. GIULIO CESARE, joo′le-o chä′sä-rà ; Ger. JULIUS CÄSAR, (or CAESAR,) yoo′le-ûs tsä′zăr,] or, more fully, **Cā′ius Ju′lius Cæ′sar,** one of the greatest generals and greatest men that ever lived, was born in July, 100 B.C. He belonged to the Julian tribe or family, (Julia gens,) one of the most ancient in Rome, since it boasted its descent from Julus or Iulus, the son of Æneas. Through the influence of Marius, who had married Cæsar's aunt Julia, he was elected priest of Jupiter *(Flamen Dialis)* while yet a mere boy. In 83 B.C. he married Cornelia, the daughter of Cinna. This act gave great offence to Sulla, who commanded him to divorce his wife; and, on his refusing to do so, he was proscribed. He escaped from Rome, and concealed himself for a time in the country of the Sabines. At length, at the intercession of some of Sulla's friends, he was reluctantly pardoned by the dictator, who remarked, it is said, that the young Cæsar would some day be the ruin of the aristocratic party, adding, "In that boy there are many Mariuses." Soon after Cæsar went to Nicomedes, King of Bithynia, and subsequently served with distinction in the Roman army in Cilicia. Having heard, while here, of the death of Sulla, he returned at once to Rome. About 76 B.C., while on his way to Rhodes for the purpose of studying oratory under Apollonius Molo, (who was also the instructor of Cicero,) he was taken prisoner by the pirates with whom the Mediterranean was at that time greatly infested. He was detained by them more than a month, until his friends could raise the sum demanded for his ransom. According to Plutarch, he treated his captors with great contempt, and, whenever he wished to sleep, used to send and order them to keep silence. He even threatened—in jest, as they supposed—to crucify them when he got his liberty. The ransom having at length been paid, he manned some Milesian vessels, pursued and took the pirates prisoners in their turn, and crucified

€ as *k*; ç as *s*; g̃ *hard*; ġ as *j*; G, H, K, *guttural*; N, *nasal*; R, *trilled*; ŝ as *z*; th as in *this*. (☞See Explanations, p. 23.)

31

them according to his promise. Having remained for some time in Rhodes, he returned to Rome, and became a candidate for popular favour. His patrimonial estate being insufficient to supply the means for that unbounded liberality by which he sought to ingratiate himself with the people, he borrowed for this purpose vast sums from the usurers. It was cast upon him as a reproach, by his enemies, that he was always in debt, and that his poverty ceased only when he had turned his arms against Rome and robbed the public treasury. "Then for the first time," says Lucan, " Rome was poorer than Cæsar."*

Cæsar was elected quæstor in 68 B.C. ; and in the same year his wife Cornelia died. In 67 he married Pompeia, a relative of Pompey the Great, and granddaughter of Sulla the dictator. This was especially intended to conciliate Pompey ; and by various other means he sought to ingratiate himself with that great leader. He became ædile in 65 B.C., and purchased the favour of the populace by the exhibition of public games surpassing in magnificence anything of the kind ever before seen in Rome. In 64 B.C. he was elected pontifex maximus. Catiline's conspiracy occurred in 63, and Cæsar was by many suspected of being accessory to it. When Cicero called for the opinion of the senators as to the punishment which should be inflicted on the conspirators, all the others gave judgment in favour of their death, until it came to Cæsar's turn to speak. He contended that it was contrary to justice and to the usage of the Roman commonwealth to put men of their birth and dignity to death without an open trial, except in a case of extreme necessity. He recommended that they should be kept in prison in any of the cities of Italy which Cicero might fix upon, and that these cities should be bound by the severest penalties to keep them safely. Cæsar's arguments had great influence with the senate ; but Cato, following in an earnest and powerful speech, in which he accused Cæsar of being connected with the conspiracy, carried most of the senators with him : the conspirators were condemned to death ; and Cæsar himself narrowly escaped. As he was leaving the senate-house, his life was threatened by some of the Roman knights ; and, had it not been for the fear of the common people, it is probable that he might have been included in the accusation with Lentulus, Cethegus, and the rest.

He became prætor in 62 B.C., and the next year was sent as proprætor to Spain, where he gained no little distinction both as a general and a civil magistrate, and was saluted by his army *imperator.* He was elected consul, with L. Calpurnius Bibulus as his colleague, in 60, and in 59 B.C. entered upon the duties of his office. One of his first measures was to propose an agrarian law, by which a rich tract of public land was to be distributed among the poorer citizens, especially those who had several children. Although this measure was strongly opposed by his colleague Bibulus, it was carried, chiefly through the influence of Pompey and Crassus. In order that he might strengthen his interest with Pompey still more, he gave him his daughter Julia in marriage, although she had previously been affianced to Servilius Cæpio. Soon after Cæsar himself married Calpurnia, the daughter of L. Piso, for whom he procured the consulship the ensuing year. He formed a secret alliance with Pompey and Crassus, known as the first triumvirate. Supported by such influence, Cæsar had no difficulty in carrying through the senate whatever measures he pleased. The government both of Transalpine and Cisalpine Gaul, with that of Illyricum, was decreed to him for five years. The following spring, (58 B.C.,) when L. Piso and A. Gabinius were consuls, Cæsar left Rome for Transalpine Gaul, and before winter had ended triumphantly two formidable wars, the one with the Helvetii, and the other with Ariovistus, a German prince who had some time before crossed the Rhine and, being supported by a powerful army, had established himself in the eastern part of Gaul. The next year he subdued the various Belgic tribes or nations dwelling between the Rhine and the Seine. In 56 B.C., having divided his

forces, assigning a part of them to his different generals (*legati*) respectively, he overran nearly all the rest of Gaul, besides quelling the insurrections of several nations who had been subdued the year before. In 55 he surprised and cut to pieces two powerful German tribes who had attempted to establish themselves in Gaul. In order more effectually to strike terror into the Germans, he crossed the Rhine by a bridge which he had constructed for that purpose, and, after ravaging the territories of the Sigambri, he recrossed the river and destroyed the bridge. The same year he invaded Britain, and compelled the submission of several of the tribes. The following year he made another expedition into Britain, defeated Cassivellaunus, one of their princes, who had been chosen generalissimo by the different tribes, and, having demanded hostages and fixed the tribute which Britain should pay to the Romans, he returned to Gaul. The ensuing autumn a most formidable revolt occurred among the Eburones, under their king Ambiorix, who succeeded, by stratagem or treachery, in surprising and cutting to pieces a considerable body of Cæsar's troops under the generals Sabinus and Cotta. Fortunately, Cæsar had not yet set out for Italy, as he was accustomed to do on the approach of winter. Ambiorix, whose army had become much increased in consequence of his recent victory, was soon after defeated by Cæsar with great loss ; but the latter deemed it most prudent to remain in Gaul through the entire winter. During the summer of 53 B.C. Cæsar was chiefly occupied in repressing an extensive conspiracy which had been formed among the different Gallic nations, and in reducing to subjection such as had broken out into an open revolt. The following year a general insurrection took place among the Gauls. It was headed by Vercingetorix, a young nobleman of the Arverni, who proved himself to be a general of no mean capacity ; so that Cæsar's situation was for a time extremely critical. There appeared to be the greatest unanimity among the various Gallic nations. Even the Ædui, who, from the time when Cæsar first obtained the government of Gaul, had been faithful allies to the Romans until now, made common cause with the rest, and joined the revolt. They took Noviodunum, a walled town which Cæsar had made the chief depository of his stores ; and he was obliged to retreat to his lieutenant Labienus, beyond the Loire. But, having received reinforcements, he besieged Vercingetorix in Alesia, and at length compelled him to surrender. In the next year (51 B.C.) Cæsar completed the pacification of Gaul. His daughter Julia, the wife of Pompey, had died in 54 B.C. Crassus, the other member of the triumvirate, had lost his life in the war against the Parthians. A coldness had gradually sprung up between him and Pompey, who appears to have become jealous of the recent brilliant successes of his colleague. From his first entrance into public life Cæsar had attached himself to the popular party, and had constantly studied how he might reduce or overthrow the power of the aristocracy. Pompey, on the other hand, a favourite and connection of Sulla, had been one of the staunchest adherents of the senatorial faction, and, after the death of the dictator, was generally regarded as the chief of the aristocratic party. And although, through the arts and influence of Cæsar, he had been induced for a time to take the other side, on the breaking up of their friendship he naturally fell back to his former position. There had been for some time, on the part of the aristocracy, a growing jealousy of Cæsar's power and influence in the state. Some of the more violent were resolved to crush him, if possible, at all hazards. In the year 50 B.C. it was proposed to the senate, by Claudius Marcellus, that Cæsar, having now finished the Gallic war, should be required to lay down his command. But the tribune Curio, whom Cæsar had by large bribes gained over to his interest, interposed his veto. Cæsar was, however, on different pretexts, deprived of two of his legions. Yet, desirous—or seeming to be so—of avoiding a rupture, if possible, he proposed to the senate, through Curio, to resign his command on condition that Pompey would do the same. The senate, however, refused even to consider the proposition. Afterwards, on the motion of Scipio, it was decreed that Cæsar

---

* " Pauperiorque fuit tunc primum Cæsare Roma."
Pharsalia, lib. iii. l. 168.

should disband his army against a certain day, otherwise he should be held to be an enemy of the republic. This was a virtual declaration of war; for few, if any, could suppose that Cæsar would give up his army without a struggle. On being informed of the resolution of the senate, he assembled his soldiers and harangued them on the subject of his wrongs. When he found that they eagerly espoused his cause, he determined to strike at once, while his enemies were yet unprepared. With only 5000 infantry and 300 horse—for his other forces were still beyond the Alps—he marched towards the confines of Italy, which, with its then limits, was separated on the east from Cisalpine Gaul by the small river Rubicon. When he arrived at the banks of this stream, as Plutarch informs us, he hesitated for some time, revolving in his mind the arguments for and against the momentous step which he was about to take. At last, exclaiming, "The die is cast!"- he crossed the river, and, advancing with the utmost expedition, he occupied successively Ariminum, Arretium, Pisaurum, Ancona, Auximum, besides other places. Owing partly to his popularity and partly to the fear which his name inspired, all the towns of Italy seemed ready to open their gates at his approach. His triumphant progress filled Rome with consternation. In the general panic, Pompey, the two consuls, and most of the senators fled from the city in the direction of Capua. Pompey continued his flight to Brundisium, whither he was closely pursued by Cæsar. He escaped, however, to Greece. Cæsar, being unable to follow, for want of ships, returned to Rome, and not long after set out for Spain, where Afranius and Petreius, Pompey's lieutenants, were at the head of a formidable army. In his first engagement with them Cæsar was worsted; but, after encountering for a time great hardships from the want of provisions, he at length triumphed over every obstacle, and compelled Afranius and Petreius to sue for peace, which he granted on condition that they should disband their forces and not again take arms against him during the war. Having overcome all opposition in Spain,—the conquest of which occupied him only about forty days,—and subsequently reduced Massilia, (Marseilles,) he hastened to Rome. During his absence in Spain he had been declared dictator by the prætor M. Lepidus. After eleven days, during which time several important laws had been passed, he abdicated the dictatorship, and immediately set out for Brundisium, where he had ordered his forces to assemble. But he found it impossible to obtain vessels sufficient for their transportation: he was therefore under the necessity of carrying over to Greece only a part of his troops at the first passage. Meanwhile, his situation was critical in the extreme; for Pompey, on account of the multitude of his ships, had command of the sea, and a strict watch was kept upon the movements of Cæsar's vessels, so that the forces of the latter were for a considerable time divided, one part having been landed in Epirus, while the other was compelled to remain in Italy. At length Bibulus, the commander of Pompey's fleet, died; and, his place not being at once supplied, each of the officers acted according to his own judgment and independently of the others. After a time, the vigilance of the blockade having been somewhat relaxed, the remainder of Cæsar's forces were carried over, under the conduct of his faithful friends Mark Antony and Fufius Calenus. In his first encounter with Pompey, near Dyrrachium, Cæsar was repulsed with some loss, and compelled to retreat. He withdrew to Thessaly, whither he was pursued by Pompey. At last the two opposing armies met on the plains of Pharsalia; and although the forces of Pompey (consisting of about 45,000 infantry and 7000 cavalry) were more than double those of his rival, who had about 22,000 foot-soldiers and 1000 horse, they sustained a disastrous defeat. According to Cæsar's own statement, about 15,000 of Pompey's men fell in the conflict, and more than 24,000 were taken prisoners. Pompey escaped to Egypt, where he was treacherously murdered. (See POMPEY.) The result of the civil war may be said to have been decided by the battle of Pharsalia. But there still remained a formidable army of the Pompeians in Africa, under the command of Scipio and Cato. Cæsar did not, however, proceed at once against

these enemies. Having followed Pompey to Egypt, he became involved in a dispute respecting the claims of Ptolemy and his sister Cleopatra to the throne of that country. Captivated by the charms of Cleopatra, he supported her cause against her elder brother, who perished during the war which ensued. Cleopatra was declared Queen of Egypt; but her younger brother, called also Ptolemy, was associated with her on the throne. Before returning to Rome, Cæsar marched against Pharnaces, son of Mithridates the Great, King of Pontus, and totally defeated him near Zela. It was concerning this victory that he wrote to the senate the famous letter comprised in three words, "Veni, vidi, vici," ("I came, I saw, I conquered.") He arrived at Rome in September, 47 B.C., and before the end of that year set out for Africa. The opposing armies met at Thapsus, near the sea-coast, to the southeast of Carthage. The result was the total defeat, and all-but extermination, of the forces under Scipio. The Cæsarean soldiers, exasperated by the obstinacy with which the war had been protracted, cut to pieces all whom they overtook, killing without mercy even those who offered themselves as prisoners, in spite of the remonstrances and entreaties of Cæsar. The cause of the senatorial party having become utterly desperate, Scipio, Juba, Cato, and several others of the leaders, unwilling to fall into the power of the conqueror, put an end to their lives with their own hands.

Cæsar returned to Rome, the undisputed master of the world. But he had scarcely completed the celebration of his recent victories, when intelligence arrived that Pompey's sons, Cneius and Sextus, had assembled a powerful army in Spain. Cæsar hastened with his usual promptitude to meet the new danger. He engaged his enemies near Munda, and, after a very severe action, put them to a total rout. According to Plutarch, when Cæsar saw his men hard pressed and making but a feeble resistance, he rushed into the thickest of the fight, exclaiming, "Are you not ashamed to deliver up your general into the hands of these boys?"—alluding to the youth of Pompey's sons. After the battle he said to his friends that he had often fought for victory; but then, for the first time, he had fought for his life. This was the last of Cæsar's wars.

Although he had thus risen to the summit of power on the ruins of the republic, in the exercise of that power he appears never to have lost sight of the true interests of his country and of the world. One of the first subjects that claimed his attention was the regulation of the Roman calendar. For this purpose, though well versed himself both in mathematics and astronomy, he availed himself of the skill of the most eminent mathematicians of that age. The improved mode of computing time introduced by him has, with some slight modifications, been adopted by all civilized nations, and his name has become inseparably associated with the new calendar, both in the name of the month July, and in the phrases "Julian year," "Julian period," etc. He procured the enactment of several important and salutary laws, and was revolving in his mind vast projects of public improvements, including the preparation of a complete digest of the Roman laws, the clearing out and enlarging of the harbour of Ostia, (at the mouth of the Tiber,) the draining of the Pontine marshes, the cutting of a canal across the Isthmus of Corinth, and the establishment of public libraries, when death put an end to his labours and undertakings.

After the total overthrow of the partisans of Pompey, he had received from the senate the title of *Imperator* (whence comes our word "emperor") for life; he was also declared dictator, and *Præfectus Morum*, ("prefect of manners," or "customs,") both offices being perpetual. As *pontifex maximus*, or high-priest, he had control of the religion of the state. To all these honours he wished to add the title of king, (*rex*,) and thus to hand down his power and dignities to his successor. Having no legitimate children, he adopted his grand-nephew Octavius, whose mother Atia was the daughter of Julia the sister of Cæsar, as his successor and the inheritor of his name. His devoted adherent Mark Antony, on the occasion of the festival called Lupercalia, perhaps with a view to sound the feelings of the people, publicly offered to

Cæsar a regal crown; but he, perceiving that it displeased the multitude, refused it, though, as it was thought, with some reluctance. The name of king, from the time of the Tarquins, had always been, and still was, peculiarly odious to all classes of the Romans; and this consideration encouraged Cæsar's bitter enemies, of whom there were not a few concealed among the aristocracy, to believe that the taking of his life would meet with many approvers even among the people. There was at length formed against him a conspiracy, in which more than sixty persons were implicated. The principal instigator and leader of the enterprise was Cassius, who had distinguished himself as the lieutenant of Crassus in the Parthian war. M. Brutus was also prominent among the conspirators. He appears to have been actuated by a sincere though mistaken patriotism; while Cassius, there is reason to believe, was chiefly influenced by personal animosity. It is said that Cæsar had many warnings of his approaching fate, and that the night before his death his wife Calpurnia dreamed that he was murdered in her arms. In the morning she entreated him with tears not to go to the senate-house, as he had intended. When he had almost decided to stay at home, Decimus Brutus, one of the conspirators, to whom, as well as to M. Brutus, Cæsar had shown many favours, and in whom he had the greatest confidence, came in, and at length prevailed on him to go with him to meet the senate. It had been arranged, as it appears, that while one of the conspirators, L. Tillius Cimber, was presenting a petition to Cæsar, some of the others should crowd around, as if to urge the same request, when an attack upon him should be made by all at once. At first Cæsar resolutely resisted; but, when he perceived the number of his assailants, he wrapped himself in his toga and resigned himself to his fate. According to one account, Cæsar defended himself with spirit until he saw the dagger of M. Brutus among the rest, when he exclaimed, "Et tu, Brute!" ("Thou too, Brutus!") and yielded without any further struggle. Shakspeare, in his tragedy of "Julius Cæsar," appears to have followed scrupulously and minutely the popular traditions respecting the death of Cæsar. After his death it was found that his body had been pierced with twenty-three wounds. He was assassinated on the Ides of March, 44 B.C., in the fifty-sixth year of his age.

Cæsar was tall in stature, and of a noble and commanding presence. He was naturally of a delicate constitution; but by continual exercise and by a frequent exposure to hardships, with the aid of an indomitable will, he became so hardy that few if any could surpass him in enduring the fatigues and privations of a military life. It would seem, however, that his unremitting mental exertions and anxieties began at last to tell upon his health; for Suetonius speaks of his suffering from ill health, assigning it as a reason why he was so reckless of the warnings given him by the soothsayers, as if his life had not been worth the trouble necessary for its preservation. He was subject to occasional attacks of epilepsy; but they were so rare that they do not appear to have seriously interfered with his attention to his multitudinous affairs.

Considered as a general, a statesman, and a ruler, we must admit that few, if any,—even among the most remarkable men that ever lived,—have equalled him, especially if we take into account the versatility as well as the greatness of his talents. "As a soldier," says Suetonius, "it is hard to say whether he was more cautious or more daring. He never marched his army where he was liable to any ambush from the enemy without taking all possible precaution by his scouts. Nor did he pass over into Britain until he had made due inquiry respecting the harbours and what convenience there was for landing his troops. Yet when information was brought him of the siege of a camp of his in Germany, he made his way to his men in a Gallic dress through the enemy's guards. He also went over from Brundisium to Dyrrachium in winter in the midst of the hostile fleets." In the fertility of his resources he appears to have been superior to every other commander of whom history makes mention. He rarely if ever repeated the same stratagem; but he seems to have had a new expedient or invention for every

new occasion, and one which was always adequate to the emergency.

Speaking of those extraordinary men who have compelled "nations unaccustomed to control" to bow obedient to their will, Macaulay remarks that "in this class three men stand pre-eminent,—Cæsar, Cromwell, and Bonaparte. The highest place in this remarkable triumvirate belongs undoubtedly to Cæsar. He united the talents of Bonaparte to those of Cromwell; and he possessed also what neither Cromwell nor Bonaparte possessed,—learning, taste, wit, eloquence, the sentiments and the manners of an accomplished gentleman." (See his article on Hallam's "Constitutional History," in the "Edinburgh Review," 1828.) In Cæsar the intellect, the passions, and the will appear to have maintained a perfect equipoise. For, strong and fierce as were his passions, he never allowed them to rule him; thus justifying the well-known line of Pope's "Temple of Fame,"—

"Cæsar, the world's great master, and his own."

He never permitted personal pique or animosity to interfere in any way with the grand purposes of his life. Although he was, it must be confessed, very far from being a virtuous man, even in the pagan acceptation of the word, he possessed some very noble and rare moral qualities. He appears to have shunned, as by "an immortal instinct," everything that was petty, narrow, or vindictive. Generosity and magnanimity seem to have been inseparable parts of his nature. Suetonius, who certainly did not err on the side of partiality, says Cæsar was always obliging and kind to his friends, mentioning as an example that when he was on a journey through a wild country with C. Oppius, and the latter was suddenly taken ill, Cæsar gave up to him the only sleeping-apartment, and lay himself on the ground in the open air. The same writer also observes that he never carried a quarrel so far but that he was always ready to lay it down when a reasonable occasion offered. His clemency and generosity were conspicuous in every part of his life, but especially so towards the conquered party in the civil war. He was not only a perfect master in the use of arms, and a most skilful horseman, but he was accustomed, when occasion required, to swim across rivers rather than permit the slightest delay. In oratory he was, in that age, second only to Cicero; and it is thought that had he devoted himself more fully to the study he might have surpassed Cicero himself. He is said to have been a perfect master of all the learning and science of his time. Besides being a general, statesman, jurist, orator, and historian, he was also a poet, a mathematician, an astronomer, and an architect. As a historian he justly holds a very high rank. His style is distinguished for clearness, ease, and simplicity, and is not without elegance. His historical writings consist of the first seven books of the commentaries relating to the Gallic war and the three books concerning the civil war. Besides the above, he wrote various other works, of which only fragments remain. A few of his letters have been preserved among the letters of Cicero.

See PLUTARCH, "Lives;" SUETONIUS, "Lives of the Twelve Cæsars;" CÆSAR, "Commentaries;" DION CASSIUS, "History of Rome;" APPIAN, "Bellum Civile;" DRUMANN, "Geschichte Roms;" JULIUS CELSUS, "De Vita et Rebus gestis C. J. Cæsaris," 1697; RICHARD DE BURY, "Histoire de la Vie de J. César," 2 vols., 1758; ALPHONSE DE BEAUCHAMP, "Vie de J. César," 1823; NAPOLÉON BONAPARTE, "Précis des Guerres de J. César, écrit par M. Marchand sous la Dictée de l'Empereur," 1836; ENRICO BINDI, "Sulla Vita e sulle Opere di C. G. Cesare discorso," 1844; P. VAN LIMBURG-BROUWER, "Cesar en zijne Tijdgenooten," 4 vols., 1845-46; JACOB ABBOTT, "Life of Julius Cæsar," 1849; NAPOLÉON III., "Histoire de Jules César," 2 vols., 1867-68; LUCAN, "Pharsalia;" also BYRON, "Childe Harold," canto iv., 90th stanza.

Cæsar, see'zar, (Sir JULIUS,) an eminent English civilian, born in 1557. He was the friend of Lord Bacon, and a favourite of James I., soon after whose accession he was made chancellor of the exchequer. He wrote the "Authority and Proceedings of the Court of Requests." Died in 1636.

See EDMUND LODGE, "Life of Sir Julius Cæsar," etc., 1810.

Cæsar, (L. JULIUS,) a Roman senator, was a nephew of the orator Caius Julius Cæsar, and an uncle of Mark Antony the triumvir, who was the son of his sister Julia. He was consul in 64 B.C., and in the next year voted for the death of Catiline's accomplices, among whom was his sister's husband, P. Lentulus Sura. He took no active part in the civil war which began in 49. After the death of the great Cæsar in 44 B.C., he joined the senatorial party against Antony, and was included in the proscription by the triumvirs in 43, but was pardoned through the intercession of his sister Julia.

Cæsar, (L. JULIUS,) a son of the preceding, fought for Pompey in the civil war, and in 46 B.C. had a command at Utica under Cato, who at his death committed his son to his care. Having surrendered Utica, he was pardoned by the dictator.

See CÆSAR, "Bellum Civile."

Cæsarianus, sē-za-re-ā'nus, (CÆSAR,) [It. CESARE CESARIANO, chā'sā-rà chà-sā-re-ā'no,] an architect, born at Milan, translated into Italian Vitruvius's work on Architecture, with a commentary, (1521.) Died in 1542.

Cæsarion, sē-zā're-on, [Fr. CÉSARION, sà'zā're'óN',] the son of Julius Cæsar and Cleopatra, was born in Egypt in 47 B.C. He probably accompanied his mother to Rome in the year 46. It is said that Antony once declared in the senate that Cæsar recognized Cæsarion as his son. In the year 34 he received from Antony the title of king of kings. He was put to death, by order of Augustus, in 30 B.C.

Cæsarius, sē-zā're-us, [Fr. CÉSAIRE, sà'zāR',] SAINT, an eminent physician, born about 330 A.D., was the son of Gregory Nazianzen, who is styled a Father of the Church. He was first physician to the emperor Constantius at Constantinople until his death in 360. Julian made an exception in his favour when he removed from his court the officers who professed Christianity, and vainly attempted to pervert him from the faith. He was a brother of Saint Gregory Theologus. Died in 369 A.D.

See BAILLET, "Vies des Saints."

Cæsarius, [Fr. CÉSAIRE,] SAINT, an eminent and influential French prelate, born at Châlons about 470 A.D., was chosen Bishop of Arles in 502. He strenuously opposed Arianism and Semi-Pelagianism. In 505 he was exiled for a short time by Alaric the Goth. He composed a "Rule for Monastic Life," and numerous sermons or homilies, which are still extant. Died in 542.

Cæsius Bassus. See BASSUS.

Caëtan. See CAJETAN.

Caffa, kåf'fä, (MELCHIORE,) an able Italian sculptor, born in Malta about 1632, was called "the Maltese." He worked at Rome. Died in 1687.

Caffarelli. See GAFFARELLI.

Caffarelli, kä'få'rà'le', (FRANÇOIS MARIE AUGUSTE,) a general in the French service, born at Falga in 1766. He served as general of division at Austerlitz in 1805, and was minister of war for the kingdom of Italy from 1806 to 1810, after which he made several campaigns in Spain. In 1814 he escorted the empress Maria Louisa to Vienna. Died in 1849.

See TRÉLAT, "Notice sur le Général A. Caffarelli," 1850.

Caffarelli du Falga, kä'få'rà'le' dü fål'gä', (LOUIS MARIE JOSEPH MAXIMILIEN,) a French general, brother of the preceding, born in Languedoc in 1756. He served in the army before the Revolution, escaped from the proscription of 1793, after a confinement of fourteen months, and distinguished himself near Dusseldorf in 1795. Having obtained the rank of general of division, he went to Egypt with Bonaparte in 1798 as chief of the corps of engineers. After rendering important services, he was killed at the siege of Acre in 1799. He was a member of the Institute, and author of several brief and able scientific treatises. Bonaparte had a high opinion of his merit.

See DEGERANDO, "Vie du Général Caffarelli du Falga," 1802; F. D'ALDÉGUIER, "Étude historique sur la Vie de Caffarelli du Falga," 1849.

Caffaro, kåf'fä-ro, called also TASCHIFELLONE, (tås-ke-fĕl-lo'nä,) a Genoese historian, born about 1080. He joined the crusade in 1100, and fought in Palestine. He wrote a "History of Genoa," in Latin. Died in 1164.

Caffi, kåf'fee, (IPPOLITO,) an Italian painter, born at Belluno in 1814, became a resident of Rome, and devoted himself to monumental views with success. His scene of the Carnival was exhibited at the Paris Exposition of 1855. He wrote a "Treatise on Perspective."

Caffiaux, kä'fe-ō', (PHILIPPE JOSEPH,) a French monk and writer, born in 1712; died in 1777.

Caffieri, käf-fe-ā'ree, (FILIPPO,) an Italian sculptor, born in Rome in 1634; died in France in 1716.

Caffieri, käf-fe-ā'ree or kä'fe'å're', (JEAN JACQUES,) a French sculptor, born probably in Paris in 1723, was the son of Jacques Caffieri, who also was a sculptor. The son became sculptor to the king, and professor in the Academy of Painting. Among his finest works are a bust of Corneille and a statue of Molière. Died in 1792.

See FONTENAY, "Dictionnaire des Artistes."

Cagliari, kål'yä-ree, or **Caliari,** kä'le-à-ree, (BENEDETTO,) a painter of the Venetian school, brother of Paul Veronese, born in 1538. "Saint Agatha in Prison" is called his master-piece. Died in 1598.

See LANZI, "History of Painting in Italy."

Cagliari or **Caliari,** (CARLO,) called CARLETTO, son of Paolo, noticed below, was a painter of merit, and imitated the style of his father with success. He died in 1596, aged twenty-six, after completing some works which his father left unfinished.

See RIDOLFI, "Vite de' Pittori Veneti;" LANZI, "History of Painting in Italy."

Cagliari or **Caliari,** (PAOLO,) a celebrated Italian painter, called PAUL VERONESE, (vå-ro-nā'så,) was born at Verona about 1530. He received lessons in art from his uncle Badile, and in the early part of his life went to Venice, where he was very successful, especially in the ornamental style. He afterwards worked in Rome and other cities of Italy. Among his master-pieces are "The Marriage at Cana," (in the Louvre,) "The Pilgrims of Emmaus," and "The Rape of Europa." He was remarkable for richness of imagination, and ranks among the greatest masters as a colorist. Died in Venice in 1588.

"The sixteenth century," says Ruskin, "produced the four greatest *painters*—that is to say, managers of colour—that the world has seen, namely, Tintoret, Paul Veronese, Titian, and Correggio." ("Modern Painters.")

See CARLO RIDOLFI, "Vita di P. Cagliari," 1648; LECARPENTIER, "Notice sur P. Caliari," 1816; ZABEO, "Elogio di P. Cagliari," 1813.

Cagliostro, kål-yos'tro, (ALEXANDER,) COUNT, a celebrated charlatan and arch-impostor, whose proper name was GIUSEPPE BALSAMO, (joo-sep'på bål'sä-mo,) was born at Palermo, in Sicily, about 1745. He assumed the title of count, travelled in many countries under various names, professed alchemy and free-masonry, practised medicine and sorcery, and raised money by various forms of imposture. He was accompanied in his adventures by his handsome wife Seraphina, who was also a mason. "Masonry," says Carlyle, "with its blazonry and mummery, sashes, drawn sabres, brothers Terrible, brothers Venerable, (the whole so imposing by candle-light,) offered the choicest element for him. Accordingly he goes forth prospering and to prosper," (Carlyle's "Miscellanies," vol. iv.) He travelled in his own coach, with a numerous retinue in rich liveries. His fame and fortune culminated at Strasburg in 1783, where he made a dupe of the Prince Cardinal de Rohan. In 1785 this cardinal and Cagliostro were imprisoned in the Bastille, Paris, for complicity in the notorious affair of the Diamond Necklace. Released at the end of nine months, the count went to England, and thence to Rome, where in 1789 he was arrested and sentenced to perpetual imprisonment for being a free-mason. He died in prison in 1795. Schiller's "Geisterseher" was suggested by the history of this personage, who was also the subject of Goethe's drama "Gross-Kcphta."

See "Lettres de Mirabeau sur Cagliostro et Lavater," 1786; "Mémoires pour servir à l'Histoire du Comte de Cagliostro," 1785; "Compendio della Vita, etc. di Giuseppe Balsamo denominato il Conte Cagliostro," 1790; "Life of Count Cagliostro, with his Trial before the Inquisition," 1791; HILDEBRANDT, "Merkwürdige Abenteuer des Grafen Cagliostro und Anderer," 1839; WILLIAM RUSSELL, "Eccentric Personages," 1866.

Cagnati, kån-yå'tee, (GILBERTO,) an Italian botanist, born at Nocera, lived about 1550. He published the "Praises of Gardens," ("De Hortorum Laudibus.")

Cagnati, (MARSILIO,) [Lat. MARSIL'IUS CAGNA'TUS,] a learned Italian physician, born at Padua, published several medical works, (1581–1602.) Died about 1610.

Cagniard de la Tour, kån'ye-åR' deh lä tooR, (CHARLES,) BARON, a Frenchman, distinguished for his mechanical inventions, was born in Paris in 1777. After 1811 he was attached to the council of state and ministry of the interior. He invented a portable mill for camps; the *sirène*, an acoustic instrument; and other machines. In 1851 he was elected to the Academy of Sciences as successor to Gay-Lussac. Among his works is the suspended aqueduct of Crouzol.

Cagnola, kän-yo′lä, (LUIGI,) MARQUIS, an eminent Italian architect, born in Milan in 1762. His principal works are the triumphal arch of the Porta del Ticino at Milan, (once called Porta di Marengo,) the Campanile at Urgnano, (1829,) the churches at Vavallo and Ghisalba, and the marble Porta del Sempione, Milan, commenced in 1807, and finished under the name of "Arco della Pace," ("Arch of Peace,") about 1835. This is the most magnificent of modern triumphal arches, except perhaps the "Arc de l'Étoile" at Paris. He was chamberlain to the Austrian emperor, and president of the Institute of Milan. Died in 1833.

See VALÉRY, "Voyages historiques, etc. en Italie;" N. GIRONI, "Necrologia del Marchese L. Cagnola," 1844.

Cagnoli, kän-yo′lee, (ANTONIO,) an Italian geometer, born at Zante in 1743. He passed some years in Paris, where he was attached to the Venetian embassy, and applied himself to astronomy. About 1786 he removed to Verona, where he had an observatory. In 1798 he was chosen professor of mathematics at Módena, and he was president of the Italian Society from 1800 until his death. He wrote an excellent "Treatise on Trigonometry," (1786,) one on "Conic Sections," (1801,) and several other works. He was a member of the Institute of France. Died at Verona in 1816.

See LABUS, "Vita di A. Cagnoli," 1816; CARLINI, "Notizie sulla Vita di A. Cagnoli," 1819; ERSCH und GRUBER, "Allgemeine Encyklopaedie."

Cahaignes, kä′än′, or **Cahagnes,** kä′än′, (JACQUES,) a French medical writer, born at Caen in 1548; died in 1612.

Cahen, kä′ôn′, (SAMUEL,) a French Jew and eminent Hebraist, born at Metz in 1796, directed the consistorial school of the Jews in Paris from 1823 to 1836. He published a "Manual of Universal History," (1836,) and other works, the most important of which is a French version of the Old Testament, (1851.) Died in 1862.

Câher-Billah. See AL-KÂHIR-BILLAH.

Cahours, kä′oor′, (AUGUSTE,) a French chemist, born in 1813. He has distinguished himself by his researches in organic chemistry, has been a teacher of chemistry in the Polytechnic School, Paris, and has exhibited the actual state of chemical science in a methodical and complete treatise, entitled "Lessons of General Elementary Chemistry," (1856.)

Cahusac, de, deh kä′ü′zäk′, (LOUIS,) a French dramatist, born at Montauban, became a resident of Paris and secretary to the Count of Clermont. He composed tragedies, comedies, and operas, the last of which were successful, aided by the music of Rameau. Died in 1759.

Caianian, a Persian dynasty. See KAIANIAN.

Caiaphas, kä′e-fas, [Gr. Καϊάφας; Fr. CAÏPHE, kä′èf′,] was high-priest of the Jews in 33 A.D. (See Matthew xxvi. 3; Luke iii. 2; John xviii. 13.)

Caiet. See CAYET.

Caietano. See CAJETAN.

Caigniez, kän′ye-ä′, (LOUIS CHARLES,) a French dramatist, born at Arras in 1762, was called the Racine of the Boulevards. His "Judgment of Solomon" and "Pie voleuse" (1815) were translated into several languages. Died in 1842.

Cailhava, kä′lä′vä′, (JEAN FRANÇOIS,) a French comic writer, was born near Toulouse in 1731. He composed several successful comedies and comic operas, among which are "The Guardian Duped," (1765,) "Harlequin Mahomet," and "Egotism," a comedy in verse, (1777.) He was elected a member of the Institute in 1798. Died in 1813.

Caillard, kä′yäR′, (ANTOINE BERNARD,) a French diplomatist, born at Aignan in 1737. He was ambassador at Berlin in 1795, and received the portfolio of foreign affairs during the absence of Talleyrand in 1801. Died in 1807.

Caillau, kä′yō′, (JEAN MARIE,) a French medical writer, born at Gaillac in 1765; died in 1820.

Caille, de la, deh lä käl or kä′ye, (NICOLAS LOUIS,) a celebrated French astronomer, born at Rumigny, near Rheims, in Picardy, in March, 1713. He was educated for the church, and obtained the title of abbé, but speedily renounced theology, and applied himself to astronomy under J. Cassini, who gave him a lodging in the observatory at Paris. In 1739 he was employed in the important work of the verification of the meridian, and before the end of the year he finished the triangulation from Paris to Perpignan. By this operation, and others connected with it, he demonstrated that the length of a degree gradually increases from the equator to the pole. In 1740 he was appointed professor of mathematics in the Mazarin College, for the use of which he wrote treatises on geometry, mechanics, astronomy, and optics. He undertook to rectify the catalogue of the stars, and in 1751, at the expense of government, performed a voyage to the Cape of Good Hope. Having accurately observed about ten thousand stars, he returned to Paris in 1754. He proposed a form of Nautical Almanac since generally adopted, published "Principles of Astronomy," ("Astronomiæ Fundamenta," 1758,) "Tables of the Sun," and Ephemerides. He died in Paris in March, 1762, after which his Southern catalogue ("Cœlum Australe Stelliferum," *i.e.* "Southern Starry Heaven") was published. Delambre says his observations will compare favourably in accuracy with those of his most celebrated contemporaries who had more perfect instruments. Again, he says, "Having reviewed and verified, with new means, a great part of the labours of La Caille, . . . I have felt, at every step with which I traced his progress, increased admiration for the savant who will ever be the honour of French astronomy."

See G. BROTIER, "Clarissimi Viri N. L. de la Caille, Vita." 1763; FOUCHY, "Éloge de La Caille;" BAILLY, "Éloge de La Caille;" ARAGO, "Notices biographiques," tome iii.

Caillé, kä′yä′, or **Caillié,** kä′e-yä′, (RENÉ,) a French traveller, born at Mauzé (Deux-Sèvres) in 1799. A passion for travel led him to Western Africa as early as 1817. He learned the Arab language, and pretended to be a Mussulman. About 1827 he performed a journey from Sierra Leone to Timbuctoo, from which he crossed the desert with a caravan to Morocco in 1828. He had succeeded with his own small resources in an enterprise that had baffled the efforts of many men aided by their government. On his return to France he received a reward of ten thousand francs promised to any one who should visit Timbuctoo, and he published a journal of his travels. Died in 1838.

See E. F. JOMARD, "Notice historique sur la Vie de René Caillé," 1839; "London Quarterly Review" for March, 1830.

Caillemote, käl′mot′ or kä′ye-mot′, a French Protestant officer, was a younger son of the Marquis de Ruvigny. He was colonel of a French regiment in the service of William III. of England, and was killed at the battle of the Boyne in 1690.

See MACAULAY's "History of England," vol. iii.

Caillet, kä′yä′, (GUILLAUME,) a French peasant, born at Mello, near Beauvais, was the leader of the peasantry who in 1358 made an insurrection against the nobles and burned two hundred castles. They called Caillet "Jacques Bonhomme," and themselves "La Jacquerie." The avowed object of the insurgents, whose number was about 100,000, was to exterminate the nobility. Having been defeated by the dauphin, Caillet was taken and executed in 1359.

See SISMONDI, "Histoire des Français;" FROISSART, "Chronicles."

Cailliaud, kä′e-yō′, (FRÉDÉRIC,) a distinguished French traveller, born at Nantes in 1787. He went to Egypt in 1815, and in the service of Mehemet Ali made explorations along the Upper Nile. He re-discovered in Mount Zabarah the famous emerald-mines which were worked in ancient times, and procured in them ten pounds in weight of emeralds. In 1821 a narrative of his travels, entitled "Journey to the Oasis of Thebes," ("Voyage à l'Oasis de Thebes," etc.,) was published by the government. Having returned to Paris in 1822, he published a "Journey to Meroë, the White River, the Oasis of Siwah," etc., (1823-26,) and "Researches into the Arts and Trades and the Civil and Domestic Customs of the Ancient Egyptians, Nubians, and Ethiopians," (1831,) which are highly interesting works.

Caillié. See CAILLÉ.

Caillot, kȧ'e-yo', (JOSEPH,) a popular French comic actor, born in Paris in 1732. He made his *début* at Paris in 1766, and performed many years with success. In 1800 he was chosen a correspondent of the Institute of France. Died in 1816.

Cailloueté, kȧ'yoo'tȧ', (LOUIS DENIS,) a French sculptor, born in 1791. His works adorn the Louvre and other palaces of Paris.

Cailly, de, deh kȧ'e-ye', (JACQUES,) a French poet, called also **D'Aceilly,** was born at Orléans in 1604; died in 1673.

Cain, kān, [Heb. ‖‖p,] the eldest son of Adam, was the first who committed homicide. (See Genesis, chap. iv.) In the second century a sect of heretics assumed the name of Cainites.

Cain, kȧN, (AUGUSTE,) a French sculptor, born in Paris in 1822. Among his best works are "The Eagle defending his Prey," and "The Frogs wishing for a King."

Caïphe. See CAIAPHAS.

Caird, kȧrd, (JAMES,) a Scottish agriculturist, born at Stranraer in 1816, published, besides other works, "English Agriculture." He was a Liberal member of Parliament from 1857 to 1865, and became in 1863 chairman of the royal commission on the sea-fisheries.

Caird, (Rev. JOHN,) a Scottish minister and eloquent pulpit orator, born at Greenock about 1822. He preached at Edinburgh and Errol, and about 1857 became minister of the Park Church, Glasgow. He published "Religion in Common Life," (1856,) and a volume of Sermons, (1858,) which had an extensive circulation.

See "Blackwood's Magazine" for February, 1856; "Fraser's Magazine" for August, 1858.

Cairnes, kȧrnz, (DAVID,) an Irish lawyer and officer, who distinguished himself by his bravery at the defence of Derry against the forces of James II. in 1689. He afterwards represented that city in Parliament, and became attorney-general. Died in 1772.

Cairns, kȧrnz,(HUGH McCALMONT,) commonly called LORD CAIRNS, an eminent lawyer and orator, born near Belfast, in Ireland, in 1819, has represented Belfast in the House of Commons since 1852, and has been conspicuous as one of the ablest debaters in Parliament. He was solicitor-general for a short time in 1858, became attorney-general on the formation of a new ministry by Lord Derby in July, 1866, was appointed lord justice of appeal in October, 1866, and lord chancellor of England in February, 1868. In December of the same year he resigned with his colleagues. He is now (1869) leader of the Conservative party in the House of Lords.

Cairo, kī'ro, (FRANCESCO,) an Italian painter of the Milanese school, born in 1598, was the favourite pupil of Morazzone, whom he is said to have surpassed in design. Died in 1674.

Caiumers or **Caiumaras.** See PESHDADIAN, (dynasty.)

Caius. See GAIUS.

Caius, kā'yus, a Christian writer on theology, lived at Rome about 210 A.D. His works are not extant.

Caius, kā'yoos, (BERNARDINO,) an Italian medical writer, born in Venice, flourished about 1610.

Caius, keȧz, written also **Kaye, Key,** or **Cay,** (JOHN,) an eminent English physician, born at Norwich in 1510, was a graduate of Cambridge University. After practising in Norwich, he settled in London, and was appointed physician successively to Edward VI., Mary, and Elizabeth. He founded at Cambridge the college which bears his name. His talents and learning as a linguist, antiquary, and physician were proved by numerous works in Latin, among which are a "Treatise on the Sweating Sickness," "On British Dogs," one "On the Antiquity of Cambridge University," and translations from Hippocrates and Galen. Died in 1573.

See "Lives of British Physicians," London, 1857; NICÉRON, "Mémoires."

Caius, kā'yus, SAINT, a native of Dalmatia, was elected Bishop of Rome in 283 A.D. as successor to Eutychian. He died in 296.

See TILLEMONT, "Vie de Saint-Paul."

Caius, (THOMAS,) an English scholar and divine, was a Fellow of All Souls' College, Oxford, and afterwards prebendary of Sarum. He wrote, in 1566, a treatise to prove that Oxford University was more ancient than Cambridge, which was answered by Dr. John Caius. Died in 1572.

Cai'us Cæ'sar, a Roman prince, born 20 B.C., was the son of M. Agrippa and Julia, the daughter of the emperor Augustus. The latter adopted Caius and his younger brother Lucius as his heirs. In 1 A.D. he was sent as proconsul into Asia, and subdued the revolted Armenians. He died in Lycia in the year 4. Lucius died in 2 A.D., aged about nineteen.

Cajado, kȧ-zhȧ'do, (ENRIQUE,) a Portuguese poet, who lived a long time in Italy. He composed Latin poems, ("Eclogæ Silva," etc., 1501,) which were praised by Erasmus. Died in 1508.

Cajetan or **Gaetani,** (BENEDETTO.) See BONIFACE VIII.

Caj'e-tan, (or kȧ'ye-tän,) [It. CAJETANO or CAIETANO, kȧ-yȧ-tȧ'no,] (CONSTANTIN,) a learned Italian monk and writer, born at Syracuse in 1560; died in 1650.

Cajetan, sometimes written **Caëtan,** [Fr. pron. kȧ'ȧ'tôN',] (ENRICO,) an Italian prelate, born about 1550. He was made a cardinal in 1585, and sent by Sixtus V. as legate to France, where he united with the League in opposing the accession of Henry IV. When Paris was besieged and suffering famine, about 1590, he urged the inhabitants to hold out, but offered no remedy for their misery except preachings and processions. Died in 1599.

See SISMONDI, "Histoire des Français."

Cajetan, [It. CAJETANO or CAIETANO,] (THOMAS de Vio—dȧ vee'o,) received his surname of CAJETAN from the city Caieta, (Gaeta,) at which he was born in 1469. He entered while young the order of Saint Dominic, of which he became general in 1508. Leo X. made him a cardinal in 1517, and soon after sent him as legate to Germany in order to bring Luther back to fellowship with the Church. He is regarded as the first who maintained the infallibility of the pope without reserve. He was made prisoner at the sack of Rome in 1527. Died in 1534.

See P. EKERMAN, "Dissertatio de Cardinali Cajetano," Upsal,1761.

Cajetano. See CAJETAN.

Cajot, kȧ'zho', (Dom JEAN JOSEPH,) a French Benedictine, born at Verdun-sur-Meuse in 1726. He published "The Antiquities of Metz," and other works. Died in 1779.

Çakjamuni. See GAUTAMA.

Çâkya. See GAUTAMA.

Çal or **Cala.** See KALA.

Calaber, (QUINTUS.) See QUINTUS CALABER.

Calabrese. See PRETI.

Calado, kȧ-lȧ'do, (MANOEL,) a Portuguese historian, born at Villa Viçosa about 1584; died in 1654.

Calamatta, kȧ-lȧ-mȧt'tȧ, (LUIGI,) an eminent engraver, born at Civita Vecchia, Italy, in 1802, worked many years in Paris, where he exhibited his first production in 1827. Among his master-pieces are a masque of Napoleon I., (1834,) and a portrait of George Sand, after his own design.

Calame, kȧ'lȧm', (ALEXANDRE,) an excellent Swiss landscape-painter and engraver, born at Vevay in 1815, studied and worked in Geneva from his early youth. He painted Mont Blanc and other Alpine scenes, also "The Ruins of Pæstum," "An Autumn Evening," and "The Lake of the Four Cantons." Among his admired lithographs and etchings are Views of Lauterbrunnen.

Cal'a-mis, [Κάλαμις,] a celebrated Greek sculptor and embosser, who flourished at Athens about 450 A.D. He excelled in the imitation of horses, and worked both in marble and in bronze. Among his productions was a colossal bronze statue of Apollo, which was brought to Rome by Lucullus. He executed, in marble, another Apollo, which adorned the garden of Servilius in Rome, and which some suppose to be the same as the Apollo Belvedere.

Căl'a-mỹ, (BENJAMIN,) D.D., a son of Edmund, noticed below, belonged to the High-Church party. He was appointed chaplain to the king in 1677, and in 1683 preached a "Discourse against a Scrupulous Conscience," which made a great sensation. In 1685 he became prebendary of Saint Paul's. His printed sermons are esteemed. Died in 1686.

Calamy, (EDMUND,) an able English divine, born in London in 1600. From 1626 to 1636 he was one of the lecturers of Bury Saint Edmund's. Having separated from the Episcopal Church and become a Presbyterian, he was chosen in 1639 minister of Saint Mary's, in or near London, where he laboured twenty years and was admired for his eloquence. He was one of the five who wrote "Smectymnus," (1641,) a treatise against Episcopacy. At the restoration he was appointed chaplain-in-ordinary to Charles II., and a few years later was committed to Newgate for expressing his mind too freely. Died in 1666.

See "Biographia Britannica."

Calamy, (EDMUND,) an eminent nonconformist divine, grandson of the preceding, born in 1671. He became minister at Blackfriars, London, in 1692, and at Westminster in 1703. He published many sermons, "Baxter's Life and Times," "The Inspiration of the Scriptures," and other esteemed works. Died in 1732.

See his "Autobiography," published by J. T. RUTT, 2 vols., 1830.

Calancha, de la, dä lä kä-län'chä, (ANTONIO,) a Peruvian chronicler and monk, born at Chuquisaca; died in the seventeenth century,

Calandar, kȧl-ȧn-dar', (?) a Mohammedan saint and scholar, died about 1324.

Calandra, kä-län'drä, (GIOVANNI BATTISTA,) an Italian painter of mosaics, born at Vercelli in 1568; died about 1646.

Calandrelli, kä-län-drel'lee, (GIUSEPPE,) an Italian astronomer, born at Zagarola in 1749. He became professor of mathematics in Rome in 1774, and was employed by Pius VII. to make astronomical observations. He published several treatises on astronomy and natural philosophy. Died in 1827.

See B. BONCOMPAGNI, "Biografia dell'Abate G. Calandrelli," 1840.

Calandrini, kä-län-dree'nee, (JEAN LOUIS,) a Swiss botanist and philosopher, born at Geneva in 1703, wrote various scientific works. Died in 1758.

Calandrucci, kä-län-droot'chee, (GIACINTO,) an Italian painter, born at Palermo in 1646; died in 1707.

Ca̧-la̅'nus, [Gr. Κάλανος,] a Hindoo philosopher, of the sect which the Greeks named Gymnosophists. Plutarch reports that his proper name was SPHINES. Having been persuaded to follow Alexander the Great, he became sick at Pasargada, where, at his own request, he was burned alive on a funeral pile. It is stated that his last words to Alexander were, "I shall soon see you again in Babylon." A few months later, that prince died in Babylon.

See ARRIAN, "Anabasis."

Calas, kä'läs' or kä'lä', (JEAN,) a French Protestant, born in 1698, was condemned by eight judges of Toulouse to be broken on the wheel for an alleged crime of which he was innocent, and suffered death in 1762. In consequence of the courageous and generous efforts of Voltaire, the sentence against the family was annulled, and they were partially indemnified. Louis XV. granted them 30,000 livres; but their persecutors were not punished.

See VOLTAIRE's "Works;" "Nouvelle Biographie Générale."

Calasanzio, de, dä kä-lä-sän'the-o, (JOSÉ,) a Spanish priest, born in Aragon in 1556, was noted as the founder of the order of chierici regolari, *(clerici regulares.)* Died at Rome in 1648.

See HOFFMANN, "Leben J. Calasantii," 1753; BARTOLOTTI, "Vita del J. Calasanzio," 1749.

Calasio, de, dä kä-lä'se-o, (MARIO,) an Italian linguist, born at Calasio, near Aquila, in 1550, became professor of Hebrew at Rome. He published a Hebrew Dictionary, and spent about forty years in preparing a Hebrew Concordance of the Bible, which is his most important work. Died in 1620.

Cal-a̧-ti̅'nus, (A. ATILIUS,) a Roman dictator and general in the first Punic war. He was consul in 258 B.C., and again in 254. In 249 he was appointed dictator for the purpose of prosecuting the war against the Carthaginians in Sicily. Though the events of his dictatorship were not important, he left an honourable name in history.

Calatrava, kä-lä-trä'vä, (JOSÉ MARIA,) a Spanish statesman, born at Merida in 1781. He became an eminent lawyer, and an eloquent orator of the Liberal party, by which he was elected to the Cortes several times. He was proscribed and exiled from 1814 to 1820, and from 1823 to 1830. After the accession of Isabella, in 1843, he was appointed a senator. Died in 1846.

Calau, kä'löw, (BENJAMIN,) a German painter, born in Holstein in 1724, noted as the discoverer of *éléodorique,* a substance used by ancient painters. Died in 1785.

Calcagni, kȧl-kän'yee, (TIBERIO,) a sculptor, born at Florence, lived about 1570. He was chosen by Michael Angelo to finish some of his last works.

Calcagnini, kȧl-kän-yee'nee, (CELIO,) an Italian philosopher and poet, born at Ferrara in 1479. He was professor of belles-lettres in the University of Ferrara. His chief work is "Three Books of Epistolary Questions," ("Quæstionum epistolicarum Libri tres," 1608,) in which he discussed the great questions of philosophy, and maintained that the earth revolves around the sun. Died in 1541.

See T. C. CALCAGNINI, "Della Vita, etc. di Celio Calcagnini," 1818; GINGUENÉ, "Histoire Littéraire d'Italie;" P. GIOVIO, "Elogia."

Calcar or **Calkar, von,** fon kȧl'kȧr, or **Calker,** kȧl'kȩr, (JOHANN,) an eminent painter, born at Calkar, in the principality of Cleves, in 1500. He was a pupil of John de Bruges, and formed his style in Italy, where he worked some years. It is stated that his works can hardly be distinguished from those of Titian, whom he imitated. Among his master-pieces is a "Mater Dolorosa." He died in Naples in 1546.

See NAGLER, "Neues Allgemeines Künstler-Lexikon;" VASARI, "Lives of the Painters;" LANZI, "History of Painting in Italy."

Calceolari, kȧl-chä-o-lä'ree, or **Cal-ce-o-lä'ri̅-us,** (FRANCESCO,) an Italian naturalist, lived at Verona about 1550. He wrote a "Journey on Mount Baldo," ("Iter Baldi Montis," 1566.) The genus Calceolaria was named in his honour.

See ÉLOY, "Dictionnaire de la Médecine."

Cal'ȩhas, [Κάλχας,] a famous Greek soothsayer, who acted a prominent part at the siege of Troy. He was consulted in the most important affairs by the Grecian chiefs.

Calchi, kȧl'kȩe, (TRISTAN,) a historian, born in Milan in 1462. He was secretary to Duke Francis Sforza and his successors, and wrote a "History of Milan," which is commended.

See GINGUENÉ, "Histoire Littéraire d'Italie."

Calcia, kȧl'chä, (GIUSEPPE,) an Italian painter of the last century, born at Genoa.

Cal'craft, (JOHN,) an English politician, entered Parliament in 1796, and voted for the Reform Bill in 1831.

Caldani, kȧl-dä'nee, (LEOPOLDO MARCO ANTONIO,) an eminent Italian anatomist, born at Bologna in 1725. He professed anatomy with success in his native city, where he published the results of his experiments on Irritability, (1757.) In 1771 he succeeded Morgagni as professor of anatomy at Padua. He wrote a number of treatises on anatomy, physiology, etc., and published a collection of very accurate plates, "Icones anatomicæ," (4 vols., 1801-14.) Died in 1813.

See TIPALDO, "Biografia degli Italiani illustri."

Caldani, (PETRONIO MARIA,) an Italian geometer, brother of the preceding, born probably at Bologna about 1735. In 1763 he became professor of mathematics at Bologna. He wrote several able treatises on geometry, etc. His talents and attainments were highly commended by D'Alembert. Died in 1808.

See TIPALDO, "Biografia degli Italiani illustri."

Caldara, kȧl-dä'rä, (ANTONIO,) an Italian composer, born at Venice about 1675, composed the music of eight operas of Metastasio. Died in 1763.

Caldara, (POLIDORO,) an eminent Italian painter, often called CARAVAGGIO, (kä-rä-väd'jo,) from the name of the place (in the Milanese) where he was born in 1492. He went to Rome while young, received lessons from Maturino, and soon became so skilful an artist that Raphael employed him to paint the friezes in the Vatican. He excelled in landscapes, and painted some admired historical pieces, among which is a "Christ bearing his

ā, ē, ī, ō, ū, ȳ, *long;* ä, ė, ò, same, less prolonged; ă, ĕ, ĭ, ŏ, ŭ, y̆, *short;* a̧, ȩ, i̧, o̧, *obscure;* fär, fȧll, fȧt; mėt; nŏt; gōōd; mōōn;

Cross." The last years of his life were passed at Messina, where he was murdered by his servant in 1543.

See VASARI, "Lives of the Painters;" LANZI, "History of Painting in Italy."

Caldarone, kâl-dả-ro′nà, or **Calderone,** kâl-dả-ro′-nà, (GIOVANNI GIACOMO,) an Italian chemist and physician, born at Palermo in 1651 ; died in 1731.

Caldas, de, dả kâl′dâs, (FRANCISCO JOSÉ,) a self-taught South American philosopher, born at Popayan, in New Granada, about 1770. He devoted himself to botany, astronomy, and physical geography, assisted Mutis in his exploration, and measured the height of Chimborazo. About 1806 he was appointed director of the observatory at Santa Fé de Bogotá. He published some results of his labours in a periodical named the "Semenario de la Nueva Granada," which he began to edit in 1807. Having joined the movement in favour of national liberty, he was executed by Morillo in 1816.

See J. ACOSTA, " Breve Noticia sobre Francisco de Caldas."

Caldas Pereira de Souza, kâl′dâs pả-rã′e-rả dả sō′zả, (ANTONIO,) a Brazilian poet and ecclesiastic, born at Rio Janeiro in 1762, was educated in Portugal. After his death, which occurred in Brazil in 1814, a volume of his odes and other verses was published, with the title of " Sacred and Profane Poems."

See F. DENIS, " Résumé de l'Histoire littéraire du Portugal," etc.

Caldenbach, kâl′dẹn-bâk′, (CHRISTOPH,) a German professor, born in Silesia in 1613. He wrote, besides other works, a "Compendium of Rhetoric," (" Compendium Rhetorices,") which was a popular school-book. Died in 1698.

Câl′dẹr, (ROBERT,) a Scottish Episcopal clergyman, born at Elgin in 1658. Refusing to acknowledge William III., he was deprived of his curacy in 1689, and was imprisoned for nearly a year in Edinburgh jail. He published "The Divine Right of Episcopacy," (1705,) and other works.

Calder, (Sir ROBERT,) a British admiral, born at Elgin, in Scotland, in 1745. Having obtained the rank of captain, he contributed to the victory off Cape Saint Vincent in 1797, and was knighted for that service. He was made vice-admiral in 1804. The next year, in July, he fought an indecisive battle against the combined fleets of France and Spain, returning from the West Indies, and ordered a retreat, for which he was censured by a court-martial. He afterwards served as post-admiral in one of the English naval stations. Died in 1818.

See CHAMBERS, "Biographical Dictionary of Eminent Scotsmen."

Calderari, kâl-dả-râ′ree, (OTTONE,) COUNT, an excellent Italian architect, born at Vicenza in 1730. He imitated the style of Palladio with great success, in several palaces and other edifices which he built in Vicenza and its vicinity. The Palazzo Cordellina (1776) is regarded by some as his capital work. He was an associate of the Institute of France, and author of a treatise on architecture. Died in 1803. His plans (" Opere di Architettura") were published by Diedo, 1808-17.

See J. LE BRETON, " Notice sur la Vie et les Ouvrages d'O. Calderari," 1804.

˙Calderino, kâl-dả-ree′no, [Lat. CALDERI′NUS,] (DOMIZIO,) an eminent Italian classical scholar, born near Calderio about 1447. He became apostolic secretary to Pope Sixtus IV. He published good editions, with commentaries, of Virgil, Juvenal, Ovid, Martial, and Pausanias. Politian, Valla, and Calderino were associated in a literary triumvirate. Died in 1478.

See BAYLE, " Historical and Critical Dictionary;" NICÉRON, " Mémoires;" P. GIOVIO, " Elogia."

Calderinus, the Latin of CALDERINO, which see.

Calderon, kâl′dả′rồN′, (PHILIPPE HERMOGÈNE,) a painter, born at Poitiers, in France, in 1833. Among his works are " The Return from Moscow," and " The Burial of Hampden," (1864.)

Calderon, kâl-dả-rōn′, (SERAFIN,) a Spanish poet, born at Malaga in 1801. He practised law for some time in his native place, and was appointed civil governor of Logroño in 1836. He has published " Poems of a Solitary," (" Las Poesias del Solitario," 1833,) an ingenious romance called "Christians and Moors," (1838,) and other works. Died in Madrid in 1867.

Calderon, de, COUNT. See CALLEJA.

Calderon de la Barca, kâl-dả-rōn′ dả lâ baR′kâ, MADAME, a Scottish authoress, whose maiden name was FRANCES IN′GLIS. Shé was married in 1838 to Calderon de la Barca, minister from Spain, to the United States, whom she afterwards accompanied in his mission to Mexico. In 1843 she published " Life in Mexico," which was received with favour.

Calderon de la Barca, kâl-dả-ròn′ (or kâl′dẹ-ron) dả lâ baR′kâ, (PEDRO,) a celebrated Spanish dramatic author, born of a noble family in Madrid about 1600. He received a liberal education at the University of Salamanca. About the age of thirteen he produced a drama named " El Carro del Cielo," (" The Chariot of Heaven.") His precocity was equalled by the fertility of his genius, as it is stated that he produced at least five hundred dramas. Having acquired fame by his early works, he was invited to court in 1636 by Philip IV., who made him a knight of Santiago. He had previously served as a private soldier in several campaigns in Italy and the Low Countries. About 1652 he entered the church, and obtained a canonicate or chaplaincy at Toledo, after which he wrote only sacred pieces, (autos sacramentales.) By some critics he is regarded as equal to Lope de Vega, who in the preceding age had held the highest rank among Spanish dramatists. His brilliant imagination is not restrained by conventional rules or dramatic unities, and his works present much that is absurd or extravagant, while abounding in interesting, natural, and sublime passages. Among his most admired productions are " The Constant Prince," (" El Principe constante,") a tragedy, " The Devotion of the Cross," " Heraclius," " Love is no Joke," (which furnished to Molière the idea of his " Femmes savantes,") " The Physician of his own Honour," a tragedy, and " Life is a Dream." Several of his best pieces, including " The Constant Prince" and " Life is a Dream," were translated into German by Augustus Schlegel, and are said to be great favourites on the German stage.

See an elaborate and able critique in the twenty-fifth volume of the " Quarterly Review," quoted and approved by Hallam, from which we extract the following : " His boundless and inexhaustible fertility of invention, his quick power of seizing and presenting everything with dramatic effect, the unfailing animal spirits of his dramas, if we may venture on the expression, the general loftiness and purity of his sentiments, the rich facility of his verse, the abundance of his language, and the clearness and precision with which he embodies his thoughts in words and figures, entitle him to a high rank as to the imaginative and creative faculty of a poet ; but we cannot consent to enrol him among the mighty masters of the human breast." " His total want of truth to nature," says Hallam, " even the ideal nature which poetry embodies, justifies at least this sentence." (" Introduction to the Literature of Europe.") Died in 1683.

See RICHARD C. TRENCH, "The Life and Genius of Calderon," 1856; TICKNOR, "History of Spanish Literature;" LONGFELLOW, "Poets and Poetry of Europe;" J. L. HEIBERG, "Commentatio de Poesëos dramaticæ genere Hispanico, præcipue de P. Calderone de la Barca," 1817; "Blackwood's Magazine" for December, 1839; "Fraser's Magazine" for August, 1849, and April, 1857.

Câl′dẹr-wood, (DAVID,) an eminent Scottish divine, born in 1575, became minister of Crelling in 1604. For his opposition to Episcopacy he was imprisoned about 1617, and afterwards banished. He published, in Holland, " The Altar of Damascus," and returned home in 1625. His " History of the Church of Scotland" was received with favour. Died about 1651.

See CHAMBERS, " Biographical Dictionary of Eminent Scotsmen."

Caldora, kâl-do′râ, (JACOPO,) a famous Italian condottiere in the service of the Queen of Naples. He defeated Braccio da Montone at the battle of Aquila in 1424. Died in 1439.

See SISMONDI, " Histoire des Républiques Italiennes."

Câld′well, (CHARLES,) an American physician, born in Caswell county, North Carolina, in 1772, studied medicine in Philadelphia under Dr. Rush. He became professor of natural history in the University of Pennsylvania about 1816. In 1819 he published " The Life and Campaigns of General Greene." He was professor of medicine in Transylvania University, Kentucky, for many years, ending in 1837. He wrote and translated various works, among which was Blumenbach's "Elements of Physiology," (1795.) Died in 1853.

See his "Autobiography," 1855.

Caldwell, (HOWARD H.,) an American poet, born at Newbury, South Carolina, in 1831. He graduated at South Carolina College in 1851, and settled as a lawyer at Columbia. He has made various contributions to the periodical press, and is the author of two volumes of poems.

Caldwell, (Rev. JAMES,) an American patriot, born in Charlotte county, Virginia, in 1734. He became pastor of a Presbyterian church at Elizabethtown, New Jersey, and during the Revolution was a zealous and very influential supporter of the popular cause. He served as chaplain in the army, and at the same time fought as a soldier. His wife was shot dead by the enemy in 1780. He was killed by a sentinel in November, 1781.

Caldwell, (JOHN C.,) an American general, born in Vermont in 1831. He became a brigadier-general in June, 1862, after which he served in Virginia.

Caldwell, (JOSEPH,) D.D., for thirty years president of the University of North Carolina, was born in Lamington, New Jersey, in 1773. He graduated at Princeton with distinguished honours in 1791, and for several years acted as tutor to the college. In 1796 he was elected to the principal professorship in the University of North Carolina, and in 1804 was chosen its first president. Died in 1835.

Ca'leb, [Heb. כָּלֵב,] the son of Jephunneh, a Hebrew warrior, lived about 1500 B.C. He was one of the two Israelite emigrants or fugitives from Egypt that were favoured to enter the promised land. (See Numbers xiv. 24, 30 ; Deuteronomy i. 36 ; Joshua xiv. and xv.)

Caled. See KHALED.

Cā'lef, (ROBERT,) a Boston merchant, distinguished for his opposition to the witchcraft delusion, published in 1700 a work entitled "More Wonders of the Invisible World," in answer to Cotton Mather's "Wonders of the Invisible World." The book excited great indignation, and was ordered to be burned by Increase Mather, the president of Harvard College. Died in 1719.

Calegari, kā-lā-gā'ree, (ANTONIO,) an Italian sculptor, born at Brescia in 1699 ; died in 1777.

Calendario, kā-lĕn-dā're-o, (FILIPPO,) a Venetian sculptor and architect. Died in 1355.

Ca-le'nĭ-us, (WALTER,) a Welsh historian, flourished about 1120.

Ca-le'nus, (QUINTUS FUFIUS,) a Roman consul, who was a partisan of Cæsar in the civil war, after having served him as legate in Gaul in 51 B.C. In the year 47 he was chosen consul through the favour of Cæsar, after whose death, in 44, he joined the party of Antony. He commanded an army for Antony in Northern Italy, where he died about 40 B.C.

See DION CASSIUS, "History of Rome."

Calenzio, kā-lĕn'ze-o, [Lat. CALEN'TIUS,] (ELISEO,) ·born in Apulia, was reckoned among the good Latin poets of his time. He was appointed preceptor to Prince Frederick, son of Ferdinand II. of Naples. His works consist of epigrams, elegies, epistles, etc. Died in 1503.

See TIRABOSCHI, "Storia della Letteratura Italiana."

Calepino, kā-lā-pee'no, (AMBROGIO,) an Italian philologist, born at or near Bergamo in 1435, published a good Latin Dictionary, (1502,) on which he laboured nearly all his life. It passed through many editions. The French word *calepin,* signifying memorandum- or scrapbook, is derived from his name. Died in 1511.

See ADELUNG, Supplement to JÖCHER's "Allgemeines Gelehrten-Lexikon."

Caletti, kā-let'tee, (GIUSEPPE,) called IL CREMONESE, (ĕl krā-mo-nā'sā,) an Italian painter, born at Ferrara in 1600. He painted small historical pieces, demi-figures, etc., with skill. Died about 1660.

See LANZI, "History of Painting in Italy."

Cā'ley, (JOHN,) an English antiquary, born in 1763. He was secretary to the National Record Commission from 1801 to 1831, and was joint editor of many works

on which the commissioners were employed. He contributed several articles to the "Archæologia." Died in 1834.

Calfhill, kāf'il, written also **Calfill** and **Cawfield,** (JAMES,) an English divine, poet, and distinguished preacher, born in Shropshire in 1530. He was appointed prebendary of Saint Paul's in 1562, and Bishop of Worcester in 1570, but died in the same year. One of his poems is called the "Complaint of the Oxford Academy," ("Querela Oxoniensis Academiæ.")

Calhoun, kāl-hoon', (JOHN CALDWELL,) a distinguished American statesman, born in Abbeville district, South Carolina, in March, 1782, was a son of Patrick Calhoun, an Irishman. He entered Yale College in 1802, graduated with distinction in 1804, and studied law. In 1807 or 1808 he was elected to the legislature of his State, in which he served two years. He was chosen a member of Congress in 1810. He entered public life as a Democrat and leader of the war party, and acquired a national reputation before he had completed his first term in Congress. In 1816 he supported a protective tariff and the United States Bank, for which he reported a bill in Congress. He was appointed secretary of war by President Monroe in October, 1817, and was the only member of the cabinet who expressed the opinion that General Jackson transcended or violated his orders by invading Florida in 1818. Mr. Calhoun, in common with most Southern men, approved the Missouri Compromise of 1820.

In 1824 he was elected Vice-President of the United States by a large majority, receiving the votes of the Jacksonians and also the friends of Adams. Having identified himself with the opposition, (the Jackson party,) he was re-elected Vice-President in 1828, when General Jackson was chosen President. Before this period, the people of South Carolina had adopted the opinion that the tariff was injurious to their interests. Mr. Calhoun changed his course on this question, and became the leader of the party of free trade. To counteract the passage of the tariff-bill of 1828, he asserted the doctrine of the sovereignty of the States, and composed on this subject a paper entitled "The South Carolina Exposition," in which he claimed that a State can nullify unconstitutional laws. During the first term of President Jackson, Calhoun and Van Buren were the prominent competitors for the Presidency. "In the public mind," says Parton, "Calhoun towered above his rival ; for he had been longer in the national councils," etc. But General Jackson favoured Van Buren as his successor, and thus incurred the enmity of Calhoun, who was bitterly disappointed by the result.

In 1832 he resigned the office of Vice-President, and was chosen a Senator of the United States. Under his influence and direction, a convention, held in South Carolina about the end of 1832, adopted an ordinance to nullify the tariff, and prepared to resist by force the collection of the revenue. But they were overawed by the firmness of General Jackson, who determined that, on the first overt act of treason, Calhoun should be arrested as a traitor. Mr. Calhoun supported Mr. Clay's compromise tariff of 1833, and acted with the Whigs against General Jackson in relation to the removal of the deposits from the United States Bank. Still aspiring to the Presidency, he thenceforth used the question of slavery as a means of uniting the South in his support. "Calhoun failed," says Parton, "in all the leading objects of his public life except one ; but in that one his success will be memorable forever. He has left it on record (see Benton ii. 698) that his great aim, from 1835 to 1847, was to force the slavery issue on the North." He advocated the test-measures of Mr. Van Buren's administration, and made several speeches on slavery, which he affirmed to be a positive political and social good. In March, 1843, he retired from the Senate, and in March, 1844, was appointed secretary of state by Mr. Tyler. He signed in April of that year a treaty for the annexation of Texas to the Union, and resumed his seat in the national Senate in December, 1845. He spoke against the Mexican war in 1846, and the Wilmot Proviso. He died at Washington in March, 1850. Among his principal writings is a posthumous "Treatise on the Nature of Government," in which he advocates the election of two Presidents, one for the North and one for the South, each having a veto on all acts of Congress.

See JENKINS, "Life of J. C. Calhoun;" "National Portrait-Gallery of Distinguished Americans," vol. ii.; BENTON, "Thirty Years' View;" GRISWOLD, "Prose Writers of America;" PARTON, "Famous Americans of Recent Times," 1867; "Democratic Review" for April, 1838; "London Quarterly Review" for December, 1840.

Cali. See KÂLÎ.

Câlidâsa, (a Hindoo poet.) See KÂLIDÂSA.

Ca̱-lid'ī-us, (MARCUS,) an eminent Roman orator and contemporary of Cicero, whose recall from exile he advocated. He was prætor in 57 B.C., and supported Milo in 52 after the death of Clodius. He joined Cæsar in the civil war which began in 49. Died in 48 B.C. His oratory is highly praised by Cicero. (See "Brutus," 79.)

Calignon, de, de̱h kȧ'lĕn'yȯN', (PIERRE ANTOINE d'Ambesieux—dȯN'bȧ'ze̱-u̱h',) a French priest, born near London in 1729, was educated in Paris. He preached with success at Geneva, Paris, Lyons, etc. Besides other works, he published a "View of the Greatness of God in the Economy of Religion, the Order of Society, and the Wonders of Nature." Died in 1795.

See QUÉRARD, "La France Littéraire."

Calignon, de, (SOFFREY,) a French diplomatist and poet, born at Saint-Jean-de-Voiron in 1550. He aided De Thou in the preparation of the edict of Nantes, and was employed by Henry IV. in difficult negotiations. Died in 1606.

Caligny, de, de̱h kȧ'lĕn'ye', (JEAN ANTENOR HUE,) a French military engineer, born in 1657; died in 1731.

Ca̱-lig'u-la, (CAIUS CÆSAR,) a Roman emperor, born in 12 A.D., was the son of Germanicus and Agrippina, who was a granddaughter of the emperor Augustus. His childhood and youth were passed among the soldiers, with whom he became a favourite. By deep dissimulation he escaped from being a victim to the suspicion of Tiberius, who was the uncle of Germanicus and had adopted the latter as his heir. At the age of twenty-five Caligula succeeded Tiberius, with a general expression of popular favour. The first acts of his reign gave promise of clemency and moderation, by liberating prisoners of state, recalling exiles, etc. Before many months had elapsed, he became a monster of cruelty, and indulged his vicious passions and appetites to the greatest excess. He caused a temple to be erected to himself, and claimed divine honours. It is said that he wished the Roman people had but one head, that he might decapitate them at a single blow. A conspiracy was formed against him by Cassius Chærea, who assassinated him in the year 41, whereupon his uncle Claudius became his successor.

See SUETONIUS, "Lives of the Twelve Cæsars;" TACITUS, "Annales;" DION CASSIUS, "History of Rome."

Calippus. See CALLIPPUS.

Ca̱-lix'tus or **Cal-lis'tus** [Fr. CALLISTE, kȧ'lèst', or CALIXTE, kȧ'lĕkst'] **I.,** a Bishop of Rome, succeeded Zephyrinus in 219 A.D., and died or was killed in 223. There is a doubtful tradition that he suffered martyrdom.

Calixtus II., son of William, Count of Burgundy, was elected as successor to Gelasius II. in 1119, when the church was disturbed by a quarrel with the emperor Henry V., and when the anti-pope Bourdin or Gregory VIII. was supported by a party. After restoring the peace of the church, Calixtus died in 1124.

Calixtus III., (ALONZO **Borgia**—boR'jȧ,) a Spaniard, born at Valencia, was elected pope in 1455, as successor to Nicholas V. He waged war against the Turks with little success, and died in 1458, when he was succeeded by Pius II. His nephew, Cardinal Borgia, became Pope Alexander VI.

See A. DE MONTOR, "Histoire des souverains Pontifes."

Calixtus, kȧ-liks'tŭs, originally **Callisen,** kȧl'le-ze̱n, (GEORGIUS,) a Protestant divine, eminent for his learning and tolerance, was born at Meelby, in Holstein, in 1586. He was professor of theology at Helmstedt, and wrote treatises against several doctrines of the Roman Catholics. His moderation exposed him to the charge of crypto-papism, Calvinism, and heresy. Among his works is an "Epitome of Moral Theology," (1634.) He was among the first who attempted to systematize theology; and he had numerous followers, called Calixtines.

Calixtus was involved in disputes known as the Syncretistic controversy, by which the Lutheran Church was distracted for a long time. Died in 1656. Bossuet called him "the most able Lutheran of our time."

See W. C. DOWDING, "Life of Calixtus," 1864; B. CELLARIUS, "Leichenpredigt auf G. Calixtus," 1656; J. HILDEBRAND, "Abdankung bei Leichbestattung G. Calixti," 1656; HENKE, "G. Calixtus und seine Zeit," 1833.

Calkar. See CALCAR.

Calkoen (sometimes written **Calkon**) **van Beek,** kȧl'koon vȧn bāk, (JAN FREDERIK,) a distinguished Dutch astronomer, born at Groningen in 1772. He was appointed extraordinary professor of mathematics and astronomy at Leyden in 1799, and ordinary professor of the same in 1804. In 1805 he became professor of those sciences at Utrecht. He wrote an "Inquiry into the Origin of the Mosaic and Christian Religion," to refute Dupuis's "Origine de tous les Cultes," and a treatise on the Beautiful, entitled "Euryalus over het Schone," and other works. Died in 1811.

See J. HERINGA, "Ter Nagedachtenisse van wijlen J. F. van Beek Calkoen," 1813.

Call, (Sir JOHN,) an Englishman, born in 1732, became chief engineer of the Coromandel coast in India. After his return to England, he was elected to Parliament in 1784. Died in 1801.

Call, van, vȧn kȧl, (JAN,) a Dutch designer and engraver, born at Nymwegen in 1655. He visited Rome and Germany, and drew picturesque views of the Rhine and other regions. Having settled at the Hague, he engraved with aqua-fortis his own designs. His works were sold for high prices. Died in 1703.

See DESCAMPS, "Vies des Peintres Flamands," etc.

Call, van, (PIETER,) an able Dutch landscape-painter, son of the preceding. Died in 1737.

Cal'la-nan, (JAMES JOSEPH,) an Irish poet, born at Cork in 1795. While a student in Trinity College, Dublin, he produced a prize poem on the accession of George IV. After he left college he was employed as tutor in private families and in the school of Dr. Maginn. He wrote "The Recluse of Inchidony," and several successful lyrics, among which are "The Virgin Mary's Bank" and "Gouzane Barra," a ballad-ode, much admired for its melody of rhythm and its spirit-stirring power. He went in 1827 to Lisbon, where he died in 1829.

Callard de la Duquerie, kȧ'lȧR' de̱h lȧ dük're', (JEAN BAPTISTE,) a French physician, born in 1630, published an "Etymological Medical Dictionary," ("Lexicon Medicum Etymologicum," 1673.) Died in 1718.

Câll'cȯtt, (Sir AUGUSTUS WALL,) a distinguished English landscape-painter, brother of John, noticed below, born at Kensington in 1779. He was elected a member of the Royal Academy in 1810, when he exhibited his admired view of "Morning." He employed his pencil chiefly in scenes of quiet beauty, and has often been called the English Claude. Among his productions are "Evening," "Returning from Market," "The Ferry," and "Harvest in the Highlands," with figures by Landseer, (1833,) which is esteemed one of his master-pieces. He was knighted in 1837, and appointed conservator of the royal pictures in 1844. He died in the same year. (See CALLCOTT, MARIA.) "He painted everything tolerably, and nothing excellently," says Ruskin.

Callcott, (JOHN WALL,) one of the most eminent English composers, brother of the preceding, born at Kensington in 1766. Without a master, he attained great proficiency in music, which he adopted as his profession. He received three of the four gold medals awarded by the Catch Club in 1785, and in 1789 won all the four prizes. He composed many admired anthems, glees, canons, etc., and published a "Musical Grammar," (1805.) About 1806 he became lecturer on music at the Royal Institution, but was soon compelled by ill health to resign that office. He expended much labour on a Musical Dictionary, which was never finished. Died in 1821.

Callcott, (MARIA,) LADY, daughter of Admiral George Dundas, born in 1788, was first married to Captain Thomas Graham, R.N. In 1809 she went with him to India, where she passed two years. She afterwards travelled in Italy and South America, and in 1827 was married to Sir A. W. Callcott, noticed above. She published "Travels in India," (1812,) "Memoirs of Poussin," (1820,) ın "Essay towards the History of Painting," (1836,) which is commended, and other works. Died in 1843.

Calleja, kâl-lā′Hå, or **Callejas,** kâl-lā′Hås, (Don FELIX DEL REY,) Count de Calderon, (dà kâl-dà-rôn′,) a Spanish general, born in 1750. He commanded the royal forces in Mexico in the civil war which began in 1810, and was appointed Viceroy of Mexico in 1813. Died after 1820.

Callenberg, kâl′len-bêRG′, (GERARD,) a Dutch admiral, born at Willemstadt in 1642. He commanded a vessel in a battle against the French near Sicily, in 1676, when De Ruyter was killed. The command of the fleet devolved on Callenberg, who was made vice-admiral soon after. He gained applause at the battle of Vigo, (1697,) where he had the chief command. About 1704 he bombarded, with the English, the fortress of Gibraltar, which was forced to surrender. Died in 1722.

See CHALMOT, "Biographisch Woordenboek."

Callenberg, kâl′len-bêRG′, (JOHANN HEINRICH,) a German author and Lutheran divine, born at Saxe-Gotha in 1694. He became professor of philosophy at Halle in 1727, and professor of theology there in 1739. He was deeply interested in the missionary cause, to promote which he published from his own printing-press many Arabic and Hebrew works. He wrote several works on the subject of missions and on the conversion of the Jews. Died in 1760.

See ERSCH und GRUBER, "Allgemeine Encyklopaedie."

Căl′len-der, (JAMES THOMPSON,) a political writer, born in Scotland, became editor of a paper in Richmond, Virginia. He was a partisan of Jefferson, and attacked Washington's administration with virulence. Died in 1803.

Callet, kâ′lă′, (ANTOINE FRANÇOIS,) a French historical painter and reformer of the French style, born in Paris in 1741; died in 1823.

Callet, (JEAN FRANÇOIS,) a French mathematician, born at Versailles in 1744, was educated in Paris. He was chosen professor of hydrography at Vannes in 1788. In 1792 he returned to Paris, where he acquired a high reputation as a teacher of mathematics. In 1795 he published a stereotype edition of tables of logarithms, which have been extensively used. Died in 1798.

Calliachi, kâl-le-â′kee, (NICCOLÒ,) an Italian scholar, born in Candia in 1645, wrote treatises on the antiquities of Greece and Rome. Died in 1707.

Cal′lĭ-as, [Καλλίας,] a Greek architect, who lived about 300 B.C.

Callias, a Greek historian, who wrote a "History of Sicily" about 310 B.C.

Callias, a Greek dramatic poet, surnamed SCHŒNION.

Cal′lĭ-clēs, [Καλλικλῆς,] a Greek sculptor, born at Megara, lived about 400 or 425 B.C.

Callicles, a Greek painter, who is supposed to have lived about 320 B.C.

Cal-lic′ra-tēs, [Gr. Καλλικράτης; Fr. CALLICRATE, kâ′le′kRăt′,] was distinguished as one of the architects of the Parthenon at Athens, which was finished 438 B.C. This noble and perhaps incomparable specimen of Grecian art, built under the auspices of Pericles and decorated by the genius of Phidias, after serving as a temple to the Athenians, a church to the Christians, and a mosque to the Turks, was ruined by the explosion of a magazine during a siege in 1687. It was built of fine white marble, and surrounded by forty-six columns of the Doric order. (See ICTINUS.)

See VITRUVIUS, "De Architectura;" FÉLIBIEN, "Recueil historique de la Vie des plus célèbres Architectes."

Callicrates, a general of the Achæan League, was noted for his treachery. Died in 149 B.C.

Cal-lĭ-crat′ĭ-das, [Καλλικρατίδας,] a Spartan general, who in 406 B.C. succeeded Lysander in the command of the fleet during the Peloponnesian war. He took Methymne by assault, and gained a naval victory over Conon, the Athenian general, whom he blockaded in Mitylene. The Athenians sent to the relief of Conon a large fleet, which defeated the Spartans near the Arginusæ, where Callicratidas was killed in 406 B.C. He was a plain, blunt Spartan of the primitive stamp.

See MITFORD, "History of Greece;" PLUTARCH, "Life of Lysander."

Callières, de, deh kâ′le-aiR′, almost kâl′yaiR′, (FRANÇOIS,) a noted French writer and negotiator, born at Thorigny in 1645. He became a councillor of the king, and minister plenipotentiary to Ryswick in 1693. In 1689 he was received into the French Academy in place of Quinault. He published many works on various subjects, among which are "On Wit," ("Du bel Esprit,") a "Treatise on the Manner of negotiating with Princes," (1716,) and "The Knowledge of the World," (1717.) Died in 1717.

See D'ALEMBERT, "Histoire des Membres de l'Académie Française;" MACAULAY, "History of England," vol. iv.

Căl-lĭ-er′gus, written also **Calliergi** or **Calloergi,** (ZACHARIA,) a Greek scholar, born in the isle of Crete, was educated in Venice, where in 1499 he published a "Dictionary of the Greek Language," which was highly esteemed. He afterwards lived in Rome, and edited the works of Pindar and Theocritus.

Cal-lim′a-ehus, [Gr. Καλλίμαχος; Fr. CALLIMAQUE, kâ′le′măk′,] an Athenian officer, who commanded the right wing at the battle of Marathon, where he was killed, 490 B.C.

Callimachus, a celebrated Greek sculptor and architect, was probably a native of Corinth or Athens. He is supposed to have flourished about 400 or 450 B.C. The honour of having invented the Corinthian capital is commonly ascribed to him, on the authority of Vitruvius. His statues were remarkable for an exquisite finish; but his style was censured as too artificial.

See VITRUVIUS, "De Architectura."

Callimachus, [Gr. Καλλίμαχος; Fr. CALLIMAQUE, kâ′-le′măk′,] a celebrated Greek poet and grammarian, was born at Cyrene, and flourished at Alexandria between 260 and 240 B.C. He was patronized by Ptolemy Philadelphus, who gave him a place in his museum. He was chief librarian of the famous Alexandrian Library. Among his pupils were Eratosthenes and Apollonius Rhodius. His celebrity surpassed that of nearly all the other Alexandrine scholars and poets. He was a very prolific writer. Besides several important prose works, which are lost, and among which was a history of Greek literature, "Picture or Account of Writings of all Kinds," ("Πίναξ παντοδαπῶν συγγραμμάτων,") in one hundred and twenty books, he composed epic poems called "Hecale" and "Galatea," several tragedies, comedies, elegies, epigrams, and hymns. His hymns and epigrams are the only portion of his works that time has spared. Quintilian ranks him at the head of Greek elegiac poets. Ovid thought he displayed more art than genius : *quamvis ingenio non valet, arte valet.* Few ancient authors have had more numerous and able commentators, among whom were Vossius and Madame Dacier.

See VOSSIUS, "De Poetis Græcis;" J. G. ZIERLEIN, "Dissertatio de ingenio Callimachi," 1770; SCHOELL, "Histoire de la Littérature Grecque;" "Blackwood's Magazine" for December, 1837, and March, 1838; CLEVELAND, "Compendium of Classical Literature."

Cal-lim′a-ehus-Ex-pe′rĭ-ens, (PHILIP,) an Italian historian, born in Tuscany, was a member of the family of Buonaccorsi. Callimachus was an assumed name. About 1473 he emigrated to Poland, where he was appointed preceptor to the sons of Casimir III. Under the reign of John Albert, which began in 1492, he was a powerful favourite at court. He wrote a work on "The Exploits of Attila," a "History of King Vladislaus," and a few other works. Died in 1496.

See BAYLE, "Historical and Critical Dictionary;" NICÉRON, "Mémoires."

Callimaque, the French of CALLIMACHUS, which see.

Cal-lim′e-don, [Καλλιμέδων,] an Athenian orator, who lived about 330 B.C. He supported the Macedonian party.

Cal-lĭ-nī′cus, [Gr. Καλλίνικος,] an architect, born at Heliopolis, in Egypt, was the inventor of the Greek fire, the secret of which has been lost. It is said that by this fire he destroyed a Saracen fleet which attacked Constantinople about 670 A.D.

Cal-lī′nus [Καλλῖνος] of Ephesus, the most ancient of Greek elegiac poets, is supposed to have lived more than 600 years before Christ. Among the fragments of his works which have come down to us is part of a martial elegy of great beauty. It may be found in various collections of the "Poetæ Græci minores."

See BRUNCK, "Analecta."

Cal-li′o-pe, [Gr. Καλλιόπη,] one of the nine Muses, presided over epic poetry, and was represented as holding a closely-rolled parchment or tablets. She was the reputed mother of Orpheus and Linus. (See Musæ.)

Cal-lip′pus [Gr. Κάλλιππος] or **Ca-lip′pus** [Gr. Κάλιππος; Fr. Callippe, kȧ′lêp′] of Athens, was a disciple of Plato, in whose school he became acquainted with Dion of Syracuse. After Dion had become master of Syracuse, Callippus entered his service and obtained his confidence. He assassinated Dion in 353 B.C., and usurped the government. About a year after that event he was expelled from Syracuse, and in 351 was killed by Leptines, one of his officers.

See Diodorus Siculus, book xvi.

Callippus or **Calippus** of Cyzicus, a Greek astronomer, lived about 330 B.C., and was the author of the Calippic period. He was acquainted with Aristotle, who mentions him in his works. Perceiving the inaccuracy of the golden number or period of Meton, (nineteen years,) he invented a new cycle of seventy-six years, which was adopted by astronomers. The Calippic period began in 331 B.C.

See Delambre, " Histoire de l'Astronomie ancienne."

Callisen. See Calixtus, (Georgius.)

Callisen, [Fr. Calliste, kȧ′le-sen, (Adolf Karl Peder,) a Danish physician, born at Glückstadt in 1786. He became professor in the Academy of Surgery of Copenhagen in 1829, and received the title of councillor of state in 1839. He published an important work, in German, called "Dictionary of Living Physicians, Surgeons, Pharmaceutists, and Naturalists of all Civilized Nations," ("Medicinisches Schriftsteller-Lexikon," etc., 33 vols., 1829-35,) which is said to be an indispensable book for every cultivated physician and naturalist. He was a nephew of Hendrik Callisen, noticed below.

Callisen, (Hendrik,) an eminent Danish surgeon, born at Preez, in Holstein, in 1740. He was appointed surgeon-in-chief of the fleet in 1771, and professor of surgery in the University of Copenhagen in 1773. Having acquired a high reputation, he ,became physician to the royal family in 1801. He published a "System of Modern Surgery," ("Systema Chirurgiæ hodiernæ," 1777,) which is esteemed a standard work, and other professional treatises. Died in 1824.

See Erslew, " Almindeligt Forfatter-Lexicon;" Rahlff, " Laudatio in Memoriam H. Callisenii," 1825.

Callisthène. See Callisthenes.

Cal-lis′the-nēs, [Gr. Καλλισθένης; Fr. Callisthène, kȧ′lès′tạn′,] a rhetorician, born at Olynthus, in Thrace, about 365 B.C., was the son of Hero, a cousin or niece of Aristotle. Having accompanied Alexander the Great in his invasion of Persia in 334 B.C., he rose to a high degree of favour with that prince, who charged him to write a history of the expedition. This history, which is not extant, is said to have been written in a sycophantic spirit. According to Plutarch, he offended Alexander by his austerity, boldness of speech, and refusal to prostrate himself before the throne. He was charged with complicity in a conspiracy against the king, and some historians state that he was executed for that crime about 328 B.C.

See Plutarch, "Life of Alexander;" A. Westermann, "De Callisthenis Olynthii Vita et Scriptis," 1838.

Callisthenes, [Fr. Callisthène, kȧ′lès′tạn′,] an Athenian orator, was one of the eight orators whom Alexander the Great required to be delivered to him after the destruction of Thebes in 335 B.C. On this occasion Demosthenes is said to have applied the fable of the wolf which demanded from the sheep the surrender of their dogs. The orators were saved from that danger by the exertions of Demades, who interceded with the victor.

See Arrian, "Anabasis."

Cal-lis′to, [Gr. Καλλιστώ,] a daughter of Lycaon, King of Arcadia, and a companion of Diana. Having lost her chastity, she was transformed into a bear by Diana or Jupiter, and placed among the constellations, under the name of Arctos or Ursa major.

Cal-lis′tra-tus, [Gr. Καλλίστρατος; Fr. Callistrate, kȧ′lès′trȧt′,] the son of Callicrates, an Athenian, was one of the most eloquent orators of his time. It was the

success and applause which attended one of his forensic efforts (366 B.C.) that inspired the emulation of the youthful Demosthenes and determined him to be an orator. After having performed several embassies, he was exiled from Athens, (in 361,) went to Thrace, and founded the city of Datus, (or Datum.) He returned home without leave, and was put to death.

See Thirlwall, " History of Greece."

Callistratus, a Roman jurist, who lived in the reigns of Severus and his son Caracalla, about 200 A.D. Justinian's "Digest" was partly compiled from his writings.

Calloigne, kȧ′lwȧn′, (Jean Robert,) a Flemish sculptor, born at Bruges in 1775; died in 1830.

Cal′lon, [Κάλλων,] a Greek sculptor, born in Ægina, lived about 430 B.C.

Callot, kȧ′lo′, (Jacques,) an excellent designer and engraver, born at Nancy, France, in 1593. Having studied in Rome, he returned to his native place, and acquired such a high reputation that, in 1628, he was invited by Louis XIII. to design and engrave the siege of Rochelle and the attack on the Isle of Rhé. He declined a pension of three thousand livres from the King of France. Though he sometimes used the burin, his etchings are the most admired of his works, among which are "The Miseries of War," "The Temptations of Saint Anthony," "The Fair of Florence," and the sieges above named. Died in 1635. He was a great painter of manners, and was surpassed by few in fertility of invention or in the expression of his figures.

See G. H. Green, " Description of the Works of Callot;" Maume, " Recherches sur la Vie, etc. de J. Callot."

Cally, kȧ′le′, (Pierre,) a French philosopher and ecclesiastic, born near Argentan, is said to have been the first who professed Cartesianism in France. He was chosen principal of the College of Caen in 1675, and edited, "ad usum Delphini," Boethius "De Consolatione Philosophiæ," ("On the Consolation of Philosophy,") in 1680. He wrote a work entitled "Institutes of Universal Philosophy," ("Universæ Philosophiæ Institutio.") Died in 1709.

Calmeil, kȧl′mạl′ or kȧl′mạ′ye, (Juste Louis,) a French physician, born at Poitiers (Vienne) in 1798, was appointed chief physician to the Asylum for the Insane at Charenton. His principal work is "On Insanity considered under the Pathological, Philosophical, Historical, and Judicial Points of View," (1845.)

Calmels, kȧl′mêl′, (Anatole Célestin,) an eminent French sculptor, born in Paris in 1822. He studied in the School of Fine Arts, and gained in 1839 one of the grand prizes. Among his chief productions are the statue of Denis Papin on the façade of the Hôtel de Ville, and those of Calypso and of Massena for the new Louvre.

Calmet, kȧl′mȧ′, (Augustin,) a French Benedictine monk, born near Commercy (Lorraine) in 1672, was eminent for his learning, and for his labours as a commentator of Scripture. He took the monastic vows in 1689, was appointed abbé of Saint-Léopold-de-Nancy in 1718, and ten years later was transferred to the abbey of Senones, where he passed the rest of his life. Calmet published numerous works, among which are "The Bible in Latin and French, with a Literal and Critical Commentary," (1707-16,) a "Historical and Critical Dictionary of the Bible," (2 vols. folio, 1720,) which is regarded as his best production, and has been translated into English, and "Universal History, Sacred and Profane," (17 vols., 1735-71.) Died in Paris in 1757.

See Dom Fangé, " Vie de Dom Calmet," 1763; "Nouvelle Biographie Générale."

Calmo, kȧl′mo, (Andrea,) a facetious Italian poet and actor, born in Venice about 1510. He composed "Rhodiana" and other comedies, which were popular, and published a collection of sonnets, stanzas, canzoni, etc. Died in 1571.

Calogera, kä-lo-jä′rä, or **Calogiera,** kä-lo-je-ä′rä, (Angelo,) an Italian monk, eminent as a philologist, born at Padua in 1699. For many years he was an inmate of the monastery of San Michele, near Venice. With the assistance of P. Zeno, Muratori, and others, he compiled and published a selection from the treatises read at the various scientific and philological academies of Italy.

This valuable work, entitled "Raccolta d'Opuscoli scientifici e filologici," ("Collection of Scientific and Philological Tracts,") was issued periodically from 1729 to 1766. Died in 1768.

See ADELUNG, Supplement to JÖCHER'S "Allgemeines Gelehrten-Lexikon."

Calogiera. See CALOGERA.

Cal'o-Jo-an'nēs or Joannes II. Com-ne'nus, [Gr. Καλο-Ιωάννης ὁ Κομνηνος; Fr. CALO-JEAN, kǎ'lo' zhôN, or JEAN COMNÈNE, zhôN kom'nản',] Emperor of the East, born in 1088, was a son of Alexis I., whom he succeeded in 1118. The surname CALO is supposed to have referred to his intrinsic merit, as his person was the reverse of beautiful. He is said to have been a wise and good prince. He waged successful wars against the Turks and Servians. After many victories over these and other nations or tribes, he conceived the project of conquering the Latin kingdoms of Jerusalem and Antioch, and entered Cilicia with an army. While hunting wild boars in that province, he wounded his hand with a poisoned arrow, which produced his death in 1143. He was succeeded by his son Manuel.

See LE BEAU, "Histoire du Bas-Empire;" NICETAS, "Joannes Comnenus."

Calomarde, kâ-lo-maR'dǎ, (FRANCISCO TADEO,) a Spanish minister of state, born at Villel in 1773. He chose the profession of law, became a resident of Madrid, and an adherent of the absolutist party. After holding several inferior offices, he was appointed minister of grace and justice in 1823. For the ensuing ten years he was the most powerful member of the cabinet, and appears to have been partly responsible for the evil policy and misrule of that period. Failing in an attempt to make Don Carlos king as successor to Ferdinand VII. in 1833, he was disgraced and exiled. Died at Toulouse in 1842.

See LAVALLÉE, "Espagne depuis l'Expulsion des Maures jusqu'en 1847;" "Nouvelle Biographie Générale."

Calomato, kâ-lo-mâ'to, (BARTOLOMMEO,) a Venetian painter of the seventeenth century.

Calonne, de, deh kâ'lon', (ALPHONSE,) a French journalist, born about 1815. He published, in 1852, "Bérangère," a tale, and in the same year assisted to establish the "Revue Contemporaine," of which he has since been director, and which has obtained an important place in periodical literature.

Calonne, de, (CHARLES ALEXANDRE,) a French courtier and minister of state, born at Douai in 1734. Having studied law, he became master of requests in 1763, and intendant of Metz in 1768. In 1783 he was appointed controller-general of finances, through the influence of Vergennes. The expenses of the state were greater than the revenue. Calonne, who was fertile in resources and possessed great powers of application, adopted the policy of disguising the distress by a show of prosperity and by a profuse expenditure of money. He attempted to supply the deficit by loans and temporary expedients, and in 1786 advised an Assembly of Notables, which met next year, thus unintentionally giving the first impulse to the Revolution. The alarming state of the finances then became known, and Calonne was dismissed in 1787. During the Revolution he lived in exile, chiefly in London, and was a zealous royalist. He published several able political and financial tracts, of which perhaps the most notable are a "View of Europe in November, 1795," and "On the Finances of France." Died in 1802.

See THIERS, "Histoire de la Révolution Française;" J. L. CARRA, "M. de Calonne tout entier," 1788; "Nouvelle Biographie Générale."

Calonne, de, (ERNEST,) a French poet and dramatic author, born in Paris in 1822. He wrote "Love and Psyche," a poem, (1842,) which was received with favour, and a play in prose, called "The Doctor in Love," ("Le Docteur amoureux,") which he ascribed to Molière.

Calov, kâ'lof, [Lat. CALO'VIUS,] originally **Kalau,** kâ'lôw, (ABRAHAM,) a German Lutheran divine, born at Mohrungen, Prussia, in 1612. He lectured on theology at Wittenberg, was a violent opponent of Calixtus, and was much addicted to controversy. Among his works is a "System of Theological Subjects," ("Systema Locorum Theologicorum.") Died in 1686.

Calovius, the Latin of CALOV, which see.

Calprenède, de la, deh lǎ kǎl'pRẹh-nản', (GAUTHIER de Costes—deh kost,) SEIGNEUR, a French writer of fiction, born near Sarlat, (Dordogne,) became a resident of Paris about 1632, and gentleman of the chamber to the king in 1650. He wrote "Cassandre," (1642,) "Cleopatra," (10 vols., 1647,) and ʊther romances, which had a temporary popularity, and several tragedies, of which "The Earl of Essex" (1639) is said to be the best. Died in 1663. "Calprenède," says Hallam, "had but a life-estate in the temple of Fame, though he was a poet of no contemptible powers of imaginatio.."

See LA HARPE, "Cours de Littérature;" MALAME DE SÉVIGNÉ, "Letters."

Cal-pur'nĭ-ạ, a Roman lady, a daughter of L. Calpurnius Piso, (who was consul in 58 B.C.,) was the fourth wife of Julius Cæsar, to whom she was married in 59, and whom she survived. Alarmed by bad dreams, she entreated her husband not to leave home on the fatal Ides of March, 44 B.C.

See PLUTARCH, "Life of Cæsar."

Calpurnia, a Roman lady, was the wife of Pliny the Younger, and lived in the first century.

Cal-pur'nĭ-us, (TITUS JULIUS,) a Latin poet, who was surnamed SIC'ULUS, and is supposed to have lived in the third century of our era. Little is known of his history. Several of his Eclogues are extant. They have some merit, and slightly resemble those of Virgil in style. His versification is smooth and sonorous, and his diction is nearly pure.

See "Nouvelle Biographie Générale."

Calpur'nius Flac'cus, a Latin rhetorician, who is supposed to have lived in the reigns of Adrian and Antoninus Pius.

Caluso. See VALPERGA DI CALUSO.

Calvart or Calvaert, kâl'vâRt, [Fr. pron. kâl'väR',] written also **Calvert,** [Fr. pron. kâl'vair',] (DENIS,) an eminent Flemish painter, called by the Italians IL FIAMMINGO, (èl fe-â-mèn'go,) "the Fleming," was born at Antwerp in 1555. He went to Italy while young, studied with Fontana and Sabbatini, and opened a school in Bologna, which became very celebrated. The Bolognese regard him as one of the restorers of their school in respect to colouring. His master-pieces are a "Saint Michael" and a "Purgatory." Among his pupils were Guido, Domenichino, and Albani. Died at Bologna in 1619.

See LANZI, "History of Painting in Italy;" PILKINGTON, "Dictionary of Painters."

Calvel, kâl'vêl', (ÉTIENNE,) a French writer, who published, besides other works, several treatises on agriculture. Died about 1830.

Cal-ve'nạ, (C. MATIUS,) a learned Roman, usually called MATIUS, was an intimate friend of Cæsar the dictator. After the death of the latter, in 44 B.C., he joined the party of Octavius. Tacitus speaks of the power and influence which Matius possessed. He was also intimate with Cicero, who mentions him in his letters. He was perhaps the same as the C. Matius who translated the "Iliad" into Latin verse and wrote an admired work called "Mimiambi."

Căl'vert, (CECIL or CECILIUS,) second Lord Baltimore, was the first proprietor of Maryland, and the son of the first Lord Baltimore. The charter granted to him, June 20, 1632, conferred ample political powers and the ownership of the soil on him and his heirs forever, who, in recognition of their fealty to the British crown, were required to pay annually two Indian arrows and one-fifth of all the gold and silver ore which might ever be found. (See CALVERT, GEORGE.) Lord Baltimore, who never resided in Maryland himself, and probably never saw it, appointed as his lieutenant his brother Leonard, who arrived in the new colony in 1634 with about two hundred persons, mostly Catholics of gentle birth. The colony formed under auspices so favourable, and named in honour of the queen Henrietta Maria, made rapid progress, and for many years enjoyed a remarkable share of peace and prosperity. The proprietor, who was "the heir of his father's intentions not less than of his father's fortunes," discharged his duties to the colonists in a most liberal spirit, and is entitled to a

---

ā, ē, ī, ō, ū, ȳ, *long;* ă, ĕ, ŏ, same, less prolonged; ă, ĕ, ĭ, ŏ, ŭ, ў, *short;* ạ, ẹ, ị, ọ, *obscure;* fâr, fâll, fât; mêt; nôt; gōōd; mōōn;

share of the honour which belongs to the pioneers of civil and religious liberty. He died, at an advanced age, in 1676. Leonard Calvert had died in 1647. The heirs of Lord Baltimore for several generations were proprietors of Maryland.

See BANCROFT, "History of the United States;" HILDRETH, "History of the United States," vol. i. chap. viii.

Calvert, (DENIS.) See CALVART.

Calvert, (FREDERICK,) Lord Baltimore, born in 1731, was the eldest son of Charles, the sixth Lord Baltimore, who died in 1751. The subject of this article then became proprietor of Maryland. He published in 1767 a "Tour in the East," and soon after became a resident of Naples, where he died in 1771. He was the author of a work composed in Latin, English, and French, entitled "Gaudia Poetica," (" Poetic Joys.")

Calvert, (GEORGE,) Lord Baltimore, the founder and enlightened lawgiver of Maryland, born at Kipling, in Yorkshire, England, about 1580, was descended from a noble Flemish family of the same name. He was educated at Oxford University. By his talents and virtues he gained the confidence of James I., who appointed him in 1619 one of the principal secretaries of state. In 1624, avowing his conversion to the Roman Catholic faith, he resigned his office ; but the king retained him in the privy council, and raised him to the Irish peerage as Baron of Baltimore, in Longford county, Ireland. He had previously obtained from James I. an extensive grant of land in Newfoundland, where in 1621 he planted a colony named Avalon, which he supervised in person and sustained for a few years at great expense. His motive in this enterprise was partly to obtain liberty of worship for his fellow-professors, who were subject to restraints and disabilities in the mother-country. His first experiment having failed on account of the ungenial climate and the hostilities of the French, he visited Virginia in 1628 and explored the adjacent regions. He returned to England, and received from Charles I. a grant of all the territory included in the present State of Maryland. As Calvert died in 1632, before the grant was legally executed, the charter was issued in the name of his son Cecil, under date of June 20, 1632. This charter, which was doubtless drafted by the first Lord Baltimore himself, guaranteed the civil and religious liberties of the colonists and their exemption from English taxation forever. "Calvert deserves to be ranked," says Bancroft, "among the most wise and benevolent lawgivers of all ages. He was the first in the history of the Christian world to seek for religious security and peace by the practice of justice and not by the exercise of power ; to plan the establishment of popular institutions with the enjoyment of liberty of conscience ; to advance the career of civilization by recognizing the rightful equality of all Christian sects." He wrote " The Practice of Princes," several letters of state, and a few other works. Several of his speeches in Parliament were published. (See CALVERT, CECIL.)

See BANCROFT, "History of the United States," vol. i. chap. vii.; J. P. KENNEDY, "Discourse on the Life and Character of George Calvert."

Calvert, (GEORGE HENRY,) an American author, and a great-grandson of Lord Baltimore, was born in Maryland in 1803. He published, besides other works, in prose and verse, " Illustrations of Phrenology," (1832,) "Count Julian, a Tragedy," (1840,) and "Scenes and Thoughts in Europe," (1846,) which were received with favour.

Calvert, (Sir HARRY,) a British general, descended from the Calverts of Hertfordshire. In early life he served in the United States under Clinton, Howe, and Cornwallis, and was made prisoner at Yorktown in 1781. He was aide-de-camp to the Duke of York in 1794, in the Low Countries, and became adjutant-general in 1799. After assisting to organize the military colleges at High Wycombe and Marlow, he was made major-general in 1803, a baronet in 1818, and a general about 1821. Died in 1826.

See "Journals and Correspondence of Sir Henry Calvert," by SIR HENRY VERNEY, London, 1853.

Calvert, (JAMES,) an English nonconformist divine, was rector of Topcliffe. Died in 1698.

Calvert, (LEONARD,) the first Governor of Maryland, born about 1582, was a younger son of George, Lord Baltimore. He governed Maryland from 1634 until his death in 1647.

See SPARKS, "American Biography," vol. ix., Second Series.

Calvert, (THOMAS,) an English dissenting minister, born at York in 1606. He became vicar of Trinity, York, and officiated in the cathedral during the rule of the Protector. By the Act of Uniformity (1662) he was ejected from his living. He published " Honey of Heaven," (" Mel Cœli,") an exposition of Isaiah liii., and a few other works. Died in 1679.

Calvi, kâl'vee, (LAZZARO,) a Genoese painter, born in 1502 ; died in 1607, at the age of one hundred and five years. Among his works is "The Continence of Scipio."

See LANZI, "History of Painting in Italy."

Calvi, (PANTALEONE,) a painter, brother of Lazzaro, noticed above, was born at Genoa ; died in 1595.

Calvidus Lætus. See QUILLETT.

Calvin, kâl'vin, written also **Caulvin, Cauvin,** and **Chauvin,** (JOHN,) [Fr. JEAN CALVIN, zhôn kâl'vâN', (or CHAUVIN, shō'vâN' ;) Ger. JOHANN CALVIN, yo'hân kâl-veen'; It. GIOVANNI CALVINO, jo-vân'nee kâl-vee'no; Lat. JOHAN'NES CALVI'NUS,] after Luther, the greatest of the Protestant Reformers, was born at Noyon, in Picardy, (now the department of Oise,) on the 10th of July, 1509. His father, Gérard Cauvin, (kō'vâN',) secretary of the diocese, and fiscal procureur of the lordship of Noyon, destined him for the church, and gave him a liberal education. When only about sixteen years old, Calvin was appointed curé of Marteville, and, by exchange, of Pont-l'Évêque, two years later, while still pursuing his studies in Paris. His relative Robert Olivetan induced him, while at the university, to read the Bible, and pointed out the contradictions between the doctrines of the Holy Scriptures and the theology taught by the Romish Church. At Bourges, where he was studying law,—having abandoned the purpose of dedicating himself to the church,— Calvin became acquainted with Melchior Wolmar, who instructed him in Greek and confirmed him in the doctrines of the Protestant faith. He began soon after openly to profess and preach the new doctrines. In 1532 he published on Seneca's treatise " De Clementiâ" a Latin commentary, in which he calls himself JOHANNES CALVINUS. The design of this work, it would appear, was to lead the French king (Francis I.) to the practice of clemency or toleration towards the Protestants ; but it seems to have had no effect. Having by his zeal for the new faith incurred the displeasure of the Sorbonne, Calvin retired from Paris to Angoulême. For a short period he was protected from persecution by the favour of Margaret of Navarre, sister to Francis I. But being compelled, in 1534, to fly from his native country, he found refuge in Bâle, where he published (1536) his " Institutes of the Christian Religion," (" Christianæ Religionis Institutio,") which, in an eloquently-written preface, he dedicated to Francis I. The object of this —Calvin's most important work—was to explain and vindicate the views of the Reformed Church. It may, indeed, be pronounced the first systematic and thorough defence of Protestantism that had till then appeared.

The doctrines of the Reformation having begun to spread into Italy, Calvin, with the view of aiding in the great work, visited Ferrara, where he was cordially received by the duchess Renée, (Renata,) daughter of Louis XII. of France, and consort of Hercules (Ercole) d'Este. But even her influence was unable to protect him against the power of the Inquisition ; and he was again compelled to seek safety by flight. Returning to Noyon for the last time, he sold his paternal estate, and, accompanied by his brother, sister, and several devoted friends, withdrew to Switzerland. In one of his letters written about this time, he says, "I am driven from the land of my birth. Every step towards its boundaries costs me tears. Perhaps it is not permitted to Truth to dwell in France : let her lot be mine." In his flight he had arrived at Geneva, (August, 1536,) intending to proceed to Germany. But Farel, through whose influence, chiefly, the reformed religion had been established at Geneva, (1535,) earnestly entreated Calvin to remain with him, and boldly threatened him with the wrath of Heaven if he "would not help to carry on the work of God." Calvin yielded, and was elected preacher and teacher of theology. Along with Farel, he prepared a confession of faith and a plan of ecclesiastical discipline, which were approved in a general assembly of the people, July, 1537. But the severe doctrines and strict discipline of the Reformers were very unpalatable to a large number of the Genevese; a powerful party was excited against Farel and Calvin, and early in the year 1538 they were banished from the city. Calvin withdrew to Strasburg, where, under his care, a Reformed congregation was established, which afforded a pattern to the Protestants of France. During this period (1538–41) he produced the first of his valuable contributions to exegetical theology. He did not, however, forget the Genevese. During his exile, strenuous efforts were made by Cardinal Sadolet, the champion of the Catholic cause, to bring them back to the Church of Rome. Calvin was instrumental in thwarting these designs by a masterly and eloquent refutation (1539) of an epistle which had been addressed to them by Sadolet. They already began to regret the absence of the great Reformer; and in 1540 he received from the Genevese senate a pressing invitation to return. He was, moreover, urged to this course by Farel and many others of his friends. Calvin appears to have greatly enjoyed the peaceful life which he led at Strasburg, and was extremely reluctant to return to the scene of his former conflicts; but as he had never ceased to feel the deepest and most affectionate solicitude for the welfare of the church at Geneva, and, above all, as he regarded that city as the post of duty to which Heaven had especially called him, the final decision could not be doubtful with one whose devoted and only aim was, not to please himself, but, by every means in his power, to promote the glory of God. On the 13th of September, 1541, he again entered Geneva, and was received, both by the magistrates and people, "with every demonstration of affection and triumph." During his sojourn at Strasburg he had married (1539) a widow named Idelette de Bures, who is described as a woman of exalted virtues. They had but one child, a son, who died in infancy. Calvin's wife died in 1549.

The remainder of the life of this great man was spent in untiring efforts to establish the Genevese church and government on a firm foundation, and to render the former a model for all other Protestant churches. Calvin died May 27, 1564, aged nearly fifty-five. The effects of his labours in promoting sound morality and learning, to say nothing of religion, are still felt in Geneva, after a lapse of three hundred years. Montesquieu, referring to the great services which Calvin had rendered to that state, says "the Genevese ought to observe the day of his arrival in their city as a festival."

Nothing relating to Calvin is more remarkable than his contempt of riches and the self-denying simplicity of his life. He received from the Genevese only what was sufficient to support him with the greatest parsimony. Although he lived in such poverty, he would never accept a present except for the poor. He repeatedly refused to take anything in addition to his regular stipend. Once, during his sickness, the council advanced him the sum of twenty-five thalers, desiring him to accept it as a gift; but Calvin insisted on repaying it. When some of his friends urged that a person occupying the conspicuous position which he did before all Europe, ought to live in greater style, he replied by simply referring them to the example of Christ and his apostles.

There is in Calvin's history one point which must not be passed without notice, as it has been made by the misinformed and illiberal the ground of much unjust censure. We refer to the part which he took in procuring the condemnation of Servetus. The utmost that can be justly said against Calvin on this head is that in regard to religious toleration he was not in advance of the age in which he lived; nor was he one whit behind it. The doctrine of toleration in its largest sense was not yet recognized, even by men the most liberal and humane.* It must not be forgotten that Calvin was a

statesman as well as a preacher of the gospel. The community which he had so admirably organized at Geneva was to him both state and church, over which he felt it his duty to watch with the most jealous care. He had reason to fear that the errors of Servetus, associated as they were with great abilities and an arrogant, reckless spirit, might endanger the welfare of that community to which he had devoted his life, and which was dearer to him than anything else on earth. He was not merely a watchful pastor, but a zealous patriot, who sought to defend his country against what he deemed a formidable enemy. That his hostility to Servetus was not so much directed against his religious opinions as against his dangerous character, is at least rendered probable by his friendly relations with Socinus, whose theological views were no less objectionable than those of Servetus.

While deeply regretting this blemish on his character, (shared though it was by all the Reformers of that age,) we must not omit to state that, although Calvin approved of the death of Servetus, he did not wish him brought to the stake, dissenting in this from Farel and some of his other friends, who exhorted him to be "firm and severe." Farel at first, in opposition to Calvin, distinctly recommended that the punishment should be death by fire. Afterwards, however, he repented of his severity, and earnestly implored the council to mitigate the sentence of Servetus; but in vain.*

The doctrine of unconditional election and reprobation was the central idea in Calvin's theological system: it is to this doctrine, and others growing immediately out of it, that the term Calvinism is usually applied.

As a theological writer, Calvin is remarkable for clearness, method, and scientific exactness. As a reasoner, he is distinguished for logical acuteness. According to Scaliger, he stood alone among theologians, ("solus inter theologos Calvinus.") Among his numerous works we may name, besides those already mentioned, his "Commentaries on the Harmony of the Gospels," (Geneva, 1561,) his Commentaries on the New Testament, on the Psalms, etc. His other writings consist chiefly of tracts and letters.

See PAUL HENRY, "Life and Times of Calvin," an excellent and exhaustive work; "Letters of Calvin," collected by DR. BONNET; THÉODORE DE BÈZE, "Histoire de la Vie et la Mort de Calvin," 1564; BOLSEC, "Historia de J. Calvini Vita," 1572; MASSON, "Vita J. Calvini," 1598; TISCHER, "Calvin's Leben," 1794; MACKENZIE, "Memoirs of the Life of J. Calvin," 1809; JOHN SCOTT, "Calvin and the Swiss Reformation," 1838; AUDIN, "Histoire de la Vie de J. Calvin," 1840; T. H. DYER, "Life of John Calvin," 1849; MAIMBOURG, "Histoire du Calvinisme;" BAYLE, "Historical and Critical Dictionary;" GUIZOT, "J. Calvin," 1844; KAHNIS, "Lutheranische Dogmatik," vol. ii.; "London Quarterly Review" for March, 1851.

Cal-vi′nus, (CNEIUS DOMITIUS,) a Roman consul, who entered public life about 62 B.C. In the year 54 he offered himself as a candidate for the consulship, which he obtained by bribery and by the influence of Pompey. He became a partisan of Cæsar in the civil war, and commanded the centre at Pharsalia, (48 B.C.) In the year 40 he was again elected consul, and afterwards commanded an army in Spain for several years.

Calvinus, kâl-vee′nûs, (JOHANN,) a German jurist, whose proper name was KAHL, (kâl,) lived about 1630. He published a "Law Dictionary," ("Lexicon Juridicum," 1609,) often reprinted.

Calvinus, (JOHANNES.) See CALVIN, JOHN.

Calvisius, kâl-vee′ze-ûs, (SETH,) a German astronomer and poet, born at Groschleben, in Thuringia, in 1556. His principal work is "Opus Chronologicum," (1605.) Died in 1615.

Calvo, kâl′vo, or **Calvi,** kâl′vee, (JUAN,) a Spanish physician of the sixteenth century, published several useful medical works.

Calvo, (MARCO FABIO,) an Italian physician, born at Ravenna, made one of the first Latin versions of Hippocrates, (1525.) Died at Rome in 1527.

Calvo, de, deh kâl′vo′, (JEAN SAUVEUR,) surnamed THE BRAVE, a French general, born at Barcelona in 1625. He defended Maestricht against the Prince of Orange in 1676. Died in 1690.

* It should be borne in mind that Calvin died several years before William the Silent, from motives of policy rather than from any higher considerations, recommended toleration as a wise measure of government, and more than a century (and that, too, during a period of almost unexampled progress) before William Penn taught the great truth that for their religious opinions men are responsible to God alone.

* It is a striking proof of the universal intolerance of that age that the gentle and humane Melanchthon approved of the execution of the sentence against Servetus. (See Melanchthon's letters to Calvin and Bullinger on this subject.)

ā, ē, ī, ō, ū, ȳ, *long;* à, è, ò, same, less prolonged; ă, ĕ, ĭ, ŏ, ŭ, ў, *short;* ą, ę, į, ǫ, *obscure;* fâr, fâll, fât; mêt; nŏt; gōōd; mōōn;

Calvör or **Calvoer**, kål'vör, (KASPAR,) a German historian, born at Hildesheim in 1650, wrote, in Latin, a work on the early history of Lower Saxony. Died in 1725.

See J. J. FAHSIUS, "Vita G. Calvoerii," 1727.

Calvus. See LICINIUS STOLO.

Calvus, (C. LICINIUS MACER.) See LICINIUS CALVUS.

Ca-lyp'so, [Gr. Καλυψώ,] a nymph or demi-goddess of Greek mythology. She is described by Homer as the daughter of Atlas, and proprietor of the island of Ogygia, on which Ulysses took refuge after a shipwreck. She detained him some years, and promised him immortal youth if he would remain ; but he declined it for the sake of Penelope. Died in 1580.

Calza, kåld'zå, (ANTONIO,) a landscape-painter of the Venetian school, born at Verona in 1653 ; died about 1714.

Calzolai, kål-zo-lå'ee, or **Calzolari,** kål-zo-lå'ree, (PIETRO,) an Italian monk and historian, born in Tuscany about 1500. He wrote a "Historia Monastica," (1561.) Died in 1580.

Cam, kŏwn, (?) (DIOGO,) a Portuguese navigator, who in 1484 explored the west coast of Africa, south of the equator.

Camadeva or **Camadeo.** See KAMADEVA.

Camargo, kå-maR'go, (ALPHONSO,) a Spanish navigator, who explored the Strait of Magellan in 1540.

Camargo, kǎ'mǎR'go', (MARIE ANNE CUPPI,) a famous danseuse, born at Brussels in 1710. She performed in Paris from 1726 to 1751. Voltaire addressed to her verses beginning, "Ah ! Camargo, que vous êtes brillante !" Died in 1770.

See GRIMM, "Correspondance."

Camassei, kå-mås-så'ee, (ANDREA,) an able Italian painter and engraver, born at Bevagna in 1601, worked in Rome. Died in 1648.

Cambacérès, de, deh kŏN'bǎ'så'rèss', (ABBÉ,) an uncle of the distinguished statesman, born at Montpellier in 1721, was eminent as a pulpit orator. He pronounced before the French Academy, in 1768, a panegyric on Saint Louis, which was warmly applauded. Several volumes of his sermons were printed. Died in 1802.

Cambacérès, de, (ÉTIENNE HUBERT,) a French cardinal, brother of the jurist noticed below, was born at Montpellier in 1756. He was appointed Archbishop of Rouen in 1802, and the next year became a cardinal and grand cordon of the legion of honour. Died in 1821.

Cambacérès, de, (JEAN JACQUES **Régis**—rà'zhèss',) an able French statesman and jurist, born at Montpellier in 1757. He gained distinction as a lawyer before the Revolution, and in 1792 was elected to the National Convention, in which he performed a prominent part, but with such caution and wisdom that he was accused of moderation and temporizing. He mostly voted with the republicans, except in the trial of the king. After the fall of Robespierre (July, 1794) he was president of the committee of public safety, and used his great influence to terminate the reign of terror. He passed into the Council of Five Hundred in 1796, and was one of the first members of the Institute. In 1799, Bonaparte, then first consul, appointed Cambacérès second consul. Under the empire he enjoyed the confidence of his master, to whom he gave good counsels and adhered with constant fidelity. He was made arch-chancellor, Duke of Parma, president of the senate, president of the council of state, grand eagle of the legion of honour, etc. He had the principal part in the compilation of the Civil Code. During the Hundred Days he reluctantly served his former chief as minister of justice, and in 1816 was exiled, but was permitted to return in 1818. He then recovered his civil rights, with the title of duke, but did not hold office under the Bourbons. Died in Paris in 1824.

See AUBRIET, "Vie de Cambacérès," 1825 ; THIERS, "Histoire du Consulat et de l'Empire."

Cambacérès, de, (MARIE JEAN PIERRE HUBERT,) DUC, a French senator, nephew of the eminent statesman, was born at Montpellier in 1798. He was raised to the peerage in 1837, and appointed a senator about 1852. Since that date he has become grand master of ceremonies in the imperial household.

Camberlyn d'Amougies, kåm'ber-lĭn' (or kŏN'bêR'-lǎN') dǎ'moo'zhe', (JEAN BAPTISTE GUILLAUME,) a Belgian poet, born at Ghent in 1760 ; died in 1833.

Cambert, kŏN'baiR', (ROBERT,) a French musician, who was organist of the church Saint-Honoré in Paris. About 1659 Perrin and he composed a comic opera which had a great success. It was called the "première comédie Française en musique." They afterwards produced others, entitled "Ariane" and "Pomone." He died in England in 1677, aged about fifty.

See FÉTIS, "Biographie Universelle des Musiciens."

Cambiagi, kåm-be-å'jee, (JOACHIM,) a historical writer, born in Tuscany in 1740, became a partner of Gaetano Cambiagi, a noted printer of Florence. He published a "History of Corsica," (1770.)

Cambiaso, kåm-be-å'so, (LUCA,) also called LUCHETTO DA GENOVA, (loo-ket'to dǎ jà-no'vǎ,) a celebrated Italian painter, born at or near Genoa in 1527. He received lessons in the art from his father Giovanni, and became remarkably skilful in foreshortening. He painted in fresco the "Rape of the Sabines," which was greatly admired. Invited by Philip II., he went to Spain in 1583, and adorned the Escurial with frescos, one of which represents the celestial paradise. He worked with great facility, both in fresco and oil. "The Martyrdom of Saint George," at Genoa, is called his masterpiece. Died in 1585.

See LANZI, "History of Painting in Italy ;" WINCKELMANN, "Neues Maler-Lexikon."

Cambini, kåm-bee'nee, (ANDREA,) an Italian historian, born at Florence, lived about 1470.

Cambini, (GIUSEPPE,) an Italian composer, born at Leghorn in 1746, produced a great number of symphonies, concertos, oratorios, motets, etc. Died about 1832.

See FÉTIS, "Biographie Universelle des Musiciens."

Cambis-Velleron, de, deh kŏN'be' vèl'rŏN', (JOSEPH LOUIS DOMINIQUE,) MARQUIS, a French historian, born at Avignon in 1706 ; died in 1772.

Cambon, kŏN'bŏN', (JOSEPH,) a French republican financier, born at Montpellier in 1756, was a merchant in early life. He was elected to the National Assembly in 1791, and to the Convention of 1792, in which he voted for the death of the king. In 1793 he was one of the committee of public safety, and took a prominent part in the government. He concurred in the overthrow of Robespierre in 1794. As a member of the committee on finances, he rendered important services to the republic, and made many able financial reports. He is said to have merited an enduring reputation by that report, which caused the adoption of the great-book, or register of the public debt. In 1795 the rivalry between Cambon and Tallien resulted in a decree for the arrest of the former, who escaped by concealment. Under the reign of Napoleon he lived in a private station, was exiled in 1815, and died in Belgium in 1820.

See DE BARANTE, "Histoire de la Convention nationale."

Cambon, de, deh kŏN'bŏN', (JEAN LOUIS AUGUSTE EMMANUEL,) MARQUIS, a French lawyer, born at Toulouse in 1737. He was first president of the Assembly of Notables in 1787. Died in 1807.

Cambray, kŏN'brǎ', (BAPTISTE,) a French peasant, noted as the inventor of a cotton or linen stuff called cambric. He lived in Cambrésis, or Cambray, in the thirteenth century.

Cambray-Digny, de, deh kŏN'brǎ' dĕn'ye', (LOUIS GUILLAUME,) a French physicist, born in Picardy in 1723, became a citizen of Florence. He constructed the first steam-engine used south of the Alps. Died about the end of the eighteenth century.

Cam'bre-leng or **Cam'bre-ling,** (CHURCHILL C.,) an American politician, born in North Carolina in 1786. He became a merchant in New York, served in Congress from 1821 to 1839, was chairman of the committee of ways and means, and was appointed minister to Russia in the latter year. Died in 1862.

Căm'bridge, (ADOLPHUS FREDERICK,) DUKE OF, the seventh son of George III. of England, was born in 1774. He entered the army at the age of sixteen, and was taken prisoner by the French at Hondschoote in 1793. He was appointed Governor of Hanover in 1816, and Viceroy of the same in 1831. Died in 1850.

ϵ as *k*; ç as *s*; g̃ *hard*; g̃ as *j*; G, H, K, *guttural*; N, *nasal*; R, *trilled*; s̃ as *z*; th as in *this.* (☞See Explanati)ns, p. 23.)

Cambridge, (GEORGE WILLIAM FREDERICK CHARLES,) DUKE OF, a British general, son of the preceding, and a cousin of Queen Victoria, born at Hanover in 1819. He became a major-general in 1845, and succeeded to the dukedom in 1850. In 1854 he commanded a division in the Crimea. His conduct at Alma and Inkerman in 1854 was applauded. He was appointed commander-in-chief of the British army in 1856.

Cambridge, (RICHARD OWEN,) an ingenious English writer, born in London in 1714. He became a member of Lincoln's Inn in 1737. He wrote the "Scribleriad," a heroic poem, which has been much admired; twenty-one of the best papers in "The World ;" "The Intruder," a poem; and a "History of the War in India between the French and English from 1755 to 1761." Died in 1802.

See CARY, "Lives of English Poets from Johnson to Kirke White."

Cambronne, de, deh kôn′bRon′, (PIERRE JACQUES ÉTIENNE,) BARON, a French general, born at Nantes in 1770. He distinguished himself as colonel in the campaigns of 1812 and 1813, and accompanied Bonaparte to Elba in 1814. In 1815 he was admitted into the Chamber of Peers. He commanded a division at Waterloo, where, after being surrounded, refusing to surrender, he was severely wounded and taken prisoner.* At the revolution of 1830 he was restored to his rank in the army. Died in 1842.

See "Victoires et Conquêtes des Français;" "Histoire du Général Cambronne," Paris, 1845.

Cambry, kôn′bRe′, (JACQUES,) a French *littérateur*, born at L'Orient in 1749, was prefect of the department of Oise. He wrote a variety of learned works, among which are an "Essay on the Life and Works of Poussin," (1783,) and "Travels in Switzerland and Italy." Died in 1807.

Cambyse, the French of CAMBYSES, which see.

Cam-by′sês, [Gr. Καμβύσης ; Fr. CAMBYSE, kôn′bèz′,] King of the Medes and Persians, succeeded his father, Cyrus the Great, about 530 B.C. Five years later he invaded Egypt, defeated Psammenitus, its king, took Memphis, the capital, and in a few months completed the conquest of the country. He then marched against Ethiopia ; but, having lost many men by famine, he returned without success. The cruelties that he afterwards committed, among which was the execution of his brother Smerdis, are ascribed by some to the loss of his reason. He was accidentally wounded by his own sword, and died in consequence in 521 or 522 B.C., leaving no issue.

See HERODOTUS, "History ;" JUSTIN, "Historia ;" VALERIUS MAXIMUS; RAMSPECK, "Specimen de Cambyse Persarum Rege," 1740.

Cam′den, (CHARLES PRATT,) first EARL OF, an English judge and statesman of great merit, born in 1714, was the son of Chief-Justice Sir John Pratt. At Eton he formed a lasting friendship with William Pitt. Having graduated at Cambridge, he was called to the bar in 1738. For many years he obtained but little practice, until his success in defending a bookseller charged with a libel on the House of Commons, in 1752, brought him into notice. He was appointed attorney-general about 1758, was returned to Parliament, and became chief justice of the common pleas in 1762. He there found the proper sphere for his eminent judicial talents, and gained great popularity by his decision against the legality of general warrants in the case of Wilkes.

In 1765 he was created Baron Camden, and in the next year became lord chancellor. He held the great seal nearly four years, and performed the duties of that office with dignity, firmness, and integrity. "Among the names that adorn the legal profession," says Lord Brougham, "there are few which stand so high as that of Camden. He was, however, more eminent in the senate than the forum. He brought into Parliament a high professional reputation, and his talents were peculiarly suited to shine in debate." The constant and powerful champion of constitutional liberty, he opposed the policy of Lord North in relation to America, and has been called the right arm of Lord Chatham, for his

zealous co-operation with that political chief in his long contest with the court. He was president of the council from the accession of the younger Pitt as premier, until his own death. In 1786 he was created Earl Camden. In 1792 he eloquently and successfully maintained the rights of juries in libel-cases, against Thurlow and all the other law lords. Fox's celebrated Libel Act was then carried through the House of Peers by his exertions. Died in 1794.

See LORD CAMPBELL, "Lives of the Lord Chancellors ;" BROUGHAM, "Statesmen of the Time of George III. ;" FOSS, "The Judges of England."

Camden, (JOHN JEFFREYS PRATT,) MARQUIS OF, the eldest son of the preceding, was born in 1759. About 1780 he was returned to Parliament, and appointed a teller of the exchequer. From 1789 to 1794 he was one of the lords of the treasury ; and in the latter year he inherited his father's title and entered the House of Lords. He was lord lieutenant of Ireland for several years previous to 1798. He afterwards served the public with honour as secretary for the colonies and president of the council, and was raised to the rank of marquis about 1812. Died in 1840.

Camden, (WILLIAM,) an eminent English antiquary and author, born in London in 1551. Having graduated at Oxford, he became second master of Westminster School in 1575. In 1586 he produced, in Latin, his most celebrated work, "Britannia sive Regnorum Angliæ, Scotiæ et Hiberniæ ex intima Antiquitate Chorographica Descriptio," (a "Description of Great Britain," etc.,) which was the result of his antiquarian studies and researches pursued for many years, and is a very important production. The subsequent editions have been enlarged by various editors, and the book has been translated into English by Gibson and Gough. Camden was made head-master of Westminster about 1592, and Clarencieux king-at-arms in 1597. He published, besides a few other works, "Annals of the Reign of Elizabeth," written in elegant Latin, and admired for various merits. "It is written," says Hume, "with simplicity of expression very rare in that age, and with a regard to truth. It would not, perhaps, be too much to affirm that it is among the best historical productions which have yet been composed by any Englishman." He died in 1623, and left an estate with which the Camden professorship of history at Oxford was founded.

See THOMAS SMITH, "Life of Camden," 1691; MOLINÆUS, "Oratio de Vita G. Camdeni," 1652; "Retrospective Review," vol. ix., 1824.

Camdenu. See KAMADHENU.

Camdeo. See KAMADEVA.

Camelli, kä-mel′lee, or **Kamel,** kä′mel, (GEORG JOSEPH,) a German botanist, born at Brunn about 1690. He passed some years as a missionary in the Philippine Islands, the plants of which he described accurately in memoirs sent to the Royal Society of London. Linnæus named the genus Camellia in his honour.

See RAY, "Histoire universelle des Plantes."

Camenæ, ka-mee′nee, [Fr. CAMÈNES, kä′mắn′,] the general name of four divinities or prophetic nymphs in early Roman mythology, viz. : Antevorta, Postvorta, Carmenta, and Egeria or Ægeria. The Roman poets sometimes applied this name to the Muses.

Camènes, the French of CAMENÆ, which see.

Ça-me-nǐ-ā′ta, (JOANNES,) [Καμενιάτα Ἰωάννης,] of Thessalonica, a Greek writer, who witnessed and wrote an account of the capture of that city by the Saracens in 904 A.D.

Camenz, kä′mĕnts, (ERDMANN GOTTFRIED,) a German antiquary, born in Saxony in 1692; died in 1743.

Camerarius, kä-mà-rä′re-ûs, or **Cammermeister,** käm′mer-mīs′ter, (ALEXANDER,) a physician, born at Tübingen in 1695, was a son of Rudolf Jakob, whom he succeeded as professor. Died in 1736.

Camerarius, (ELIAS,) a son of Elias Rudolf, noticed below, born at Tübingen in 1673, became first physician to the Duke of Würtemberg. He wrote many medical works remarkable for singular ideas. Died in 1734.

See ÉLOY, "Dictionnaire de la Médecine."

Camerarius, (ELIAS RUDOLF,) a German physician and medical writer, born at Tübingen in 1641, was professor of medicine at that city. Died in 1695.

---

* He is said to have disowned the famous phrase, "The Guard dies, and never surrenders," which was attributed to him.

ā, ē, ī, ō, ū, ȳ, *long;* à, è, ò, same, less prolonged; ă, ĕ, ĭ, ŏ, ŭ, ў, *short;* a, e, i, o, *obscure;* fâr, fàll, fät; mêt; nôt; gŏŏd; mōŏn,

Camerarius, (JOACHIM,) one of the most eminent German scholars of his time, was born at Bamberg in 1500. His proper name was LIEBHARD, (leep'hȧrt.) He was deputed in 1530 to the Diet of Augsburg, where he took a prominent part as the friend and coadjutor of Melanchthon. In 1535 he became director or principal of the University of Tübingen, and in 1541 reorganized that of Leipsic, of which he was rector for many years. He wrote, besides other Latin works, a "Life of Melanchthon," (1566,) Commentaries on Cicero, Aristotle, and other classics, and "Commentaries on the Greek and Latin Tongues," ("Commentarii Linguæ Græcæ et Latinæ," 1551.) "Budæus, Camerarius, Scaliger, Casaubon," says Hallam, "appear to stand out as the great restorers of ancient learning, and especially of the Greek language." ("Introduction to the Literature of Europe.") Died at Leipsic in 1574.

See P. EKERMAN, "Fata et Merita J. Camerarii," Upsal, 1761; AUGUST W. ERNESTI, "Programma de J. Camerario," 1774; J. F. ECKHARD, "J. Camerarii Memoria," 1774; JÖCHER, "Allgemeines Gelehrten-Lexikon."

Camerarius, (JOACHIM,) a distinguished physician and botanist, son of the preceding, born at Nuremberg in 1534. He practised medicine in his native city, and obtained possession of the botanical library of Gesner, with fifteen hundred wood-engravings which he left. He published several botanical works, among which are the "Medical Garden," ("Hortus Medicus,") and "Epitome Mathioli de Plantis," etc., (1586.) Died in 1598.

See DE THOU, "Mémoires historiques;" M. ADAM, "Vitæ Medicorum Germanicorum."

Camerarius, (LUDWIG,) a German diplomatist, son of Joachim II., born at Nuremberg in 1573; died in 1651.

Camerarius, (PHILIPP,) a jurist, son of Joachim I., born at Nuremberg in 1537, was chosen vice-chancellor of the University of Altorf in 1581. He wrote "Leisure Hours," ("Horæ subsecivæ," 3 vols.,) which passed through several editions. Died in 1624.

See J. G. SCHELHORN, "Commentarius de Vita, Fatis ac Meritis P. Camerarii," 1740.

Camerarius, (RUDOLF JAKOB,) a German physician and botanist, son of Elias Rudolf, born at Tübingen in 1665. He was professor of physics at Tübingen from 1689 to 1695, and was then appointed first professor of medicine, including botany, in the same university. In 1694 he published a Latin letter on the sex of plants. "The real establishment of the sexual theory," says Hallam, "is due to Camerarius, professor of botany at Tübingen, whose letter on that subject did much to spread the theory over Europe." ("Introduction to the Literature of Europe.") Died in 1721.

See HALLER, "Bibliotheca Botanica."

Camerata, kȧ-mȧ-rä'tä, (ANDREA,) an Italian architect, born at Venice in 1714; died in 1793.

Camerata, (GIUSEPPE,) a miniature-painter and engraver, born at Venice about 1700. He worked at Dresden for the Elector of Saxony. Died about 1764.

See LANZI, "History of Painting in Italy."

Camerer, kä'meh-rer, (JOHANN FREDERIK,) a Danish historian, born at Ettingen in 1720; died in 1792.

Cam-e-rī'nus, a Latin poet, who was a contemporary of Ovid.

Cam'er-on, (Sir ALAN,) a British general, born probably in Scotland. In 1793 he raised at his own expense a regiment of Cameron Highlanders, with which he fought against the French. He served in the Peninsula as brigadier-general in 1808 and 1810. About 1820 he was made a lieutenant-general. Died in 1828.

Cameron, (ARCHIBALD,) M.D., a Scottish Jacobite, born about 1698, was a brother of Donald Cameron of Lochiel. He took an active part in the rebellion of 1745, was tried for treason, and hung in 1753.

Cameron, (DONALD,) of Lochiel, a Highland chieftain, who fought for the Pretender in the rebellion of 1745, was called "the gentle Lochiel." He captured Edinburgh by surprise, and was wounded at the battle of Culloden, after which he escaped to France in 1746. The disaster of Culloden forms the subject of Campbell's spirited poem entitled "Lochiel's Warning." Lochiel died in 1748. He is commended as a type and model of the Highland chivalry.

See CHAMBERS, "Biographical Dictionary of Eminent Scotsmen," (Supplement;) "Fraser's Magazine" for December, 1842.

Cameron, (Sir EVAN or EWEN,) of Lochiel, a Scottish chief, called "the Ulysses of the Highlands," was born about 1630. He was a zealous Jacobite, took arms against William III. about 1689, and distinguished himself at Killiecrankie. Died in 1719.

Cameron, (JOHN,) a Scottish divine and statesman, who became keeper of the great seal, and afterwards Bishop of Glasgow, (1426.) He was lord chancellor under James I. and James II., and represented the Church of Scotland at the Council of Bâle about 1431.

Cameron, (JOHN,) a liberal Protestant divine and biblical scholar, born at Glasgow about 1580, became eminent for learning and subtlety as a theologian. He went to France in 1600, lectured on Greek and divinity at Bordeaux, Saumur, and Montauban, and published theological works, one of which is called "Myrothecium Evangelicum." He opposed the Calvinistic dogma of predestination. Died at Montauban in 1625.

See BAYLE, "Historical and Critical Dictionary;" HAAG, "La France protestante."

Cameron, (Sir JOHN,) a British general, born in 1773, served in Spain with distinction. Died in 1844.

Cameron, (RICHARD,) a Scottish minister, the founder of the sect of Cameronians, or "Covenanters," was born at Falkland. In the reign of Charles II. he boldly opposed the attempt to enforce the Episcopal form of worship, and became an itinerant field-preacher. In 1680, attended by about twenty armed followers, he proclaimed at Sanquhar that Charles Stuart had forfeited the crown. A few weeks after that event he was killed in a fight with the royalist troops at Airdsmoss. The sect of Cameronians has at present numerous churches in Scotland and elsewhere. They call themselves "Reformed Presbyterians."

See CHAMBERS, "Biographical Dictionary of Eminent Scotsmen;" G. M. BELL, "Life of Richard Cameron," 1843.

Cam'er-on, (SIMON,) an American politician, born in Lancaster county, Pennsylvania, in 1799. He learned the trade of printer, and became editor of a Democratic journal at Harrisburg about 1822, after which he acquired a large fortune by operations in banking, railroads, etc. In 1845 he was elected a Senator of the United States for Pennsylvania. His term in the Senate expired March 4, 1849. Having separated from the Democratic party about 1855, he supported Fremont for the Presidency in 1856, and was elected a Senator of the United States about the end of that year. He was secretary of war in the cabinet of Lincoln from March 4, 1861, to January, 1862, and was then appointed minister plenipotentiary to Russia. He returned home in 1863, and was again elected to the Senate of the United States by the legislature of Pennsylvania in 1866.

Camers, kä'mers, (GIOVANNI,) originally GIOVANNI RICUZZI VELLINI, (jo-vân'nee re-koot'see vĕl-lee'nee,) an Italian monk and Greek scholar, born at Camerino about 1460. He contributed to the revival of learning by publishing editions of Claudian, Florus, Eutropius, and other classic authors. At one time he was professor of philosophy at Padua. Died about 1550.

Cam'Idge, (JOHN,) an English musician and composer, born at York about 1790; died in 1859.

Ca-mil'la, [Fr. CAMILLE, kä'mēl' or kä'me'yĕ,] a mythical personage, celebrated for swiftness of foot and martial valour, was said to be the daughter of the Volscian king Metabus, and an attendant of Diana. According to Virgil, she fought in the army of Turnus, and was killed by Aruns. (See "Æneid," book xi. 366-830.)

Camille, the French of CAMILLUS and CAMILLA, which see.

Camilli, kä-mèl'lee, (CAMILLO,) an Italian poet, born at Sienna about 1550.

Camillo, kä-mèl'yo, (FRANCISCO,) a Spanish historical painter, born at Madrid in 1610; died in 1671.

Camillo, kä-mèl'lo, (JULIUS,) surnamed DELMINIO, (dĕl-mee'ne-o,) an Italian linguist and writer, born at Forlì in 1479. He wrote verses, and treatises on oratory. Died in 1550.

Ca-mil'lus, (LUCIUS FURIUS,) a son of Marcus Furius, noticed below, was chosen dictator of Rome in 350 B.C.

Camillus, [Fr. CAMILLE, kä'mēl' or kä'me'yĕ,] (MARCUS FURIUS,) a celebrated Roman dictator, whose history has been embellished with many fabulous exploits. After serving as military tribune, he was five times chosen dictator, and gained victories over the Falisci, Capenates, Volscians, and Fidenates. In his first dictatorship, which began in 396, he took Veii, after a long siege. About 390 B.C. he was condemned for peculation, and was exiled to Ardea. The Gauls under Brennus having pillaged Rome, Camillus was recalled, and, according to the popular account, gained two decisive victories over the invaders. He was chosen dictator, for the fifth time, in 367. He is said to have dissuaded the citizens from removing *en masse* from Rome to Veii after the former city had been ruined by the Gauls. Died in 364 B.C. Plutarch has written a life of Camillus.

See LIVY, "History of Rome ;" NIEBUHR, "History of Rome," vol. i.; OBRECHT, "Dissertatio, M. F. Camillum repræsentans," 1693.

Caminade, kȧ'me'nȧd', (ALEXANDRE FRANÇOIS,) a French painter, born in Paris in 1783, was a pupil of David. He gained a grand prize, which procured for him a pension and the privilege of studying in Rome. The "Levite of Ephraim" (1838) is called his best work. Died in May, 1862.

Caminatzin, kȧ-me-nȧt-zeen', (?) a nephew of Montezuma, was Prince of Texcuco. He formed an abortive design to liberate his country from the Spaniards, and was killed at the siege of Mexico in 1521.

Caminer, kȧ-me-naiR', (DOMENICO,) an Italian writer, born in Venice in 1731. He issued a periodical entitled "Literary Europe" ("Europa Letteraria") from 1768 to 1774, when he changed the plan, and called it "The Encyclopedic Journal," ("Giornale Enciclopedico.") He wrote a "Life of Frederick II.," and other historical works. Died in 1796.

Caminer, (ELISABETTA,) a daughter of the preceding, born in Venice in 1751, was a scholar and linguist. She made translations of the works of Shakspeare, Marmontel, Gessner, and others, some of which are esteemed. She also edited the journal above named, after her father relinquished it in 1777. Died in 1796.

See TIPALDO, "Biografia degli Italiani illustri."

Caminha, kȧ-mèn'yȧ, (PEDRO DE ANDRADE,) a Portuguese poet, born at Oporto; died in 1594. His poems were published in 1791.

Caminha, de, dȧ kȧ-mèn'yȧ, (PEDRO VAZ,) a Portuguese explorer, went to India with Cabral in 1500. He formed part of the expedition which discovered Brazil, and wrote a description of that country, published in 1817.

Cammerhof, kȧm'mer-hof', (JOHANN,) a German philologist and Lutheran minister, born at Brunswick, lived about 1650.

Cammermeister. See CAMERARIUS.

Camœnæ. See CAMENÆ.

Camoëns, kȧm'o-ĕns, [Port. DE CAMOENS, dȧ kȧ-mo'ĕNs,] (LUIS or LUIZ,) the most celebrated of Portuguese poets, was born of a noble family, probably at Lisbon. The time of his birth is variously stated at 1517 and 1524. He was educated at Coimbra. Soon after he left school, a lady of honour at court inspired him with a passion which became the source of his misfortunes and perhaps also a stimulus to his genius. In consequence of this amour he was exiled to Santarem, where he sought to beguile the pain of separation by writing elegiac verses. When the King of Portugal sent an expedition against Morocco, Camoens joined it, and distinguished himself by his courage in several battles. Finding that his poetic talents and martial merits were equally neglected and depreciated at court, he embarked for India in 1553, exclaiming, with Scipio, "Ungrateful country! thou shalt not possess my bones !" ("Ingrata patria, non possidebis ossa mea.")

After serving in several warlike enterprises, he was exiled from Goa to Macao for a political satire which he entitled "Follies in India." There he composed his greatest work, "The Lusiad," ("Os Lusiadas,") a heroic poem (first printed in 1572) commemorating the martial and nautical exploits of Vasco de Gama and other Portuguese heroes. "The national glory of the Portuguese," says Madame de Staël, "is there illustrated under all the forms that imagination can devise. The versification is so charming and stately that even the common people know many stanzas by heart, and sing them with delight."

In 1569 he returned to Lisbon in great poverty, which continued to be his portion to the end of his life. His misfortunes were aggravated by the degradation and ruin of his country. He died in a hospital in 1579. He has left admired specimens of nearly every species of poetry, among which are numerous sonnets, odes, elegies, and songs. "Camoens," says Robert Southey, "is the 'well undefiled' of that fine language, which he more than any other author enriched and refined." ("Quarterly Review" for April, 1822.)

See F. MORDANI, "Elogio storico di L. Camoens," 1841 ; JOHN ADAMSON, "Memoirs of the Life and Writings of Luis de Camoens," 1820 ; SOUZA BOTELHO, "Vida de Luiz Camoens," 1817 ; BARRETO-FEIO, "Vida de Camoens ;" HENRIQUES VILHEGAS, "Elogio a Memoria de L. de Camoens ;" "Edinburgh Review" for April, 1805.

Camosio, kȧ-mo'se-o, or **Camoti,** kȧ-mo'tee, (GIOVANNI BATTISTA,) an Italian Hellenist, born at Asolo about 1515. He translated into Latin the "Metaphysics" of Aristotle, and other works. Died in 1581 or 1591.

See DE THOU, "Mémoires historiques."

Campagna, kȧm-pȧn'yȧ, (GIROLAMO,) an Italian sculptor, born at Verona in 1552 ; died in or after 1623.

Campagnola, kȧm-pȧn-yo'lȧ, (DOMENICO,) a skilful Italian painter and engraver, born in 1482, is said to have been a pupil of Titian, whom he imitated. He was an excellent colorist. Died in 1550. Among his engravings are a "Holy Family," and an "Adoration of the Magi."

See LANZI, "History of Painting in Italy."

Campagnoli, kȧm-pȧn-yo'lee, (BARTOLOMMEO,) an Italian violinist of high reputation, born near Bologna about 1750. He composed instrumental pieces, and published "Exercises on the Seven Positions." Died in 1827.

Campailla, kȧm-pȧ-èl'lȧ, (TOMMASO,) an Italian philosopher and naturalist, born in Sicily in 1668. His chief work is "Adam, or the Creation," a philosophic poem, (1709 ; 5th edition, 1757.) Died in 1740.

Campan, kŏN'pŏN', (JEANNE LOUISE HENRIETTE Genest—zheh-nȧ',) MADAME, a French lady, eminent as a teacher, was born in Paris in 1752. At the age of fifteen she was appointed reader to the three daughters of Louis XV. About 1770 she became the wife of M. Campan, and lady of the bedchamber to Marie Antoinette. For nearly twenty years she was the first lady of the chamber, and the most intimate confidante of that queen, and continued to serve her until the attack on the Tuileries by the mob, August 10, 1792, when she narrowly escaped death. She afterwards opened a boarding-school at Saint-Germain, which became celebrated, and was patronized by Bonaparte and Josephine. Hortense and two of Napoleon's sisters were her pupils. About 1806 the emperor founded at Ecouen a school for the daughters and sisters of the officers of the legion of honour, and chose Madame Campan as superintendent. She was deprived of this place in 1814 by the Bourbons, and died in 1822, leaving curious and well-written "Memoirs of the Private Life of Marie Antoinette," (3 vols., 1822,) and other works.

See "Nouvelle Biographie Générale."

Campana, kȧm-pȧ'nȧ, (ANTONIO FRANCESCO,) an Italian physician, born at Ferrara in 1751, obtained a chair of physics at Ferrara, and published several medical works. Died in 1832.

Campana, (CESARE,) an Italian historian, born at Aquila about 1540. Among his works is a "Life of Philip II. of Spain," (1608.) Died in 1606.

Campana, kŏN'pȧ'nȧ', (FRANÇOIS FRÉDÉRIC,) a French general, born at Turin in 1771 ; died in 1807.

Campana, (PIETRO,) an Italian engraver, born in 1727 ; died in 1765.

Campanaio, kȧm-pȧ-nȧ'yo or kȧm-pȧ-nī'o, (LORENZO DI LODOVICO,) surnamed LORENZETTO, (lo-rĕn-zet'to,) a Florentine sculptor and architect, born in 1494. As sculptor he was employed at Rome by Raphael, who esteemed him. He was the architect of the Caffarelli palace, and assisted San Gallo in the repair or completion of Saint Peter's at Rome. Died in 1541.

See CICOGNARA, "Storia della Scultura."

Campanella, kȧm-pȧ-nel'lȧ, (TOMMASO,) an Italian philosopher and Dominican monk, born at Stilo, in Calabria, in 1568. His superior mental powers were very early developed. In 1591 he published, at Naples, "Philosophy demonstrated by the Senses," which excited against him the partisans of Aristotle. Charged with heresy and a conspiracy against the government in 1599, he was confined in a dungeon at Naples for twenty-six years, during which he was put to the rack several times, but confessed nothing. He was released in 1626 by the mediation of Pope Urban VIII., and removed to Rome, where he was well treated. Several of his important works were written or published while he was in prison at Naples, viz., "Introduction to Philosophy," ("Prodromus Philosophiæ instaurandæ," 1617,) "Realis Philosophia Epilogistica," (1623,) to which was annexed "Civitas Solis," ("The City of the Sun, or the Idea of a Philosophic Republic.") The "Civitas Solis" has often been reprinted separately, and translated into several languages. For greater security against the cruelty of the Spaniards, he retired in 1634 to France, where he was kindly treated by Richelieu and pensioned by the king. He died in Paris in 1639. Besides those above named, he was the author of many works, among which are a "Treatise on Metaphysics," (1637,) "The Five Parts of Rational Philosophy," (1638,) and an able "Discourse on the Spanish Monarchy," (1640,) which produced much sensation among politicians. "Campanella," says Hallam, "borrowed his primary theorems from Telesio, but enlarged that Parmenidean philosophy by the invention of his own fertile and imaginative genius. He lays down the fundamental principle that the perfectly wise and good Being has created certain signs and types *(statuas atque imagines)* of himself, all of which, severally as well as collectively, represent power, wisdom, and love, and the objects of these, namely, existence, truth, and excellence, with more or less evidence. . . . The strength of Campanella's genius lay in his imagination, which raises him sometimes to flights of impressive eloquence on this favourite theme," *i.e.* the sensibility of all created beings, including plants and minerals. ("Introduction to the Literature of Europe.")

See "Vita e Filosofia di T. Campanella," by BALDACCHINI, Naples, 1840; CYPRIAN, "Vita et Philosophia T. Campanellæ," Amsterdam, 1705; DARESTE, "Thomas Morus et Campanella," Paris, 1843; TENNEMANN, "Histoire de la Philosophie;" "Fraser's Magazine" for March, 1844.

Campani, kȧm-pȧ′nee, (GIOVANNI ANTONIO,) a learned Italian bishop, born at Cavelli in 1427. He wrote epistles, orations, verses, etc., which were printed in 1495. Died in 1477.

Campani, (GIUSEPPE,) a brother of Matteo, noticed below, was an optician and practical astronomer. He published some observations, (1664.)

Campani, (MATTEO,) an Italian optician, born near Spoleto, was curate of a parish in Rome, in the pontificate of Alexander VII. In 1678 he published a work on the construction of clocks. He surpassed all the artists of his time in polishing telescopic object-glasses of great size, and made for Louis XIV. one of one hundred and thirty-six feet focal length, with which Cassini discovered two satellites of Saturn.

Campanile, kȧm-pȧ-nee′là, an Italian priest, born in 1762, laboured as a missionary in Kurdistan, and wrote a "History of Kurdistan and its Sects." Died in 1835.

Campanius, kȧm-pȧ′ne-ŭs, (THOMAS,) a Swedish writer, published in 1702 "A Description of the Province of New Sweden, now called Pennsylvania," which contains historical and other details of some interest.

Campano, kȧm-pȧ′no, [Lat. CAMPA′NUS,] (GIOVANNI,) an Italian geometer, who first translated Euclid from the Arabic, (printed at Venice in 1482,) the Greek text having not yet been found in his time. He was a native of Novara, and is supposed to have lived in the eleventh or twelfth century.

Campanus, kȧm-pȧ′nŭs, (JOHANN,) a German Protestant theologian, separated from the Lutherans in 1530, and formed a sect called Campanites.

Campbell, kȧm′ĕl,[*] the name of an ancient and powerful clan of the Scottish Highlands, which has performed an important part in history since the thirteenth century. Their original name is said to have been O'Dubbin. Among the warlike chiefs of the clan was Diarmid, from whom they derive the appellation of the "sons of

Diarmid." About the middle of the thirteenth century the chief of the clan was COLIN or CALLUM, surnamed MORE, (the "Great.") NIÉL CAMPBELL, a son of Colin, was an adherent of Robert Bruce, whose sister he married. Died in 1316. His son COLIN fought for Edward Bruce in Ireland, and aided King David in the expulsion of the English from Scotland. Died in 1340.

Campbell, kȧm′ĕl, (ALEXANDER,) D.D., founder of the religious sect known as the "Disciples of Christ," was born in the county of Antrim, in Ireland, in 1788. He came to the United States in 1809. His mind was early impressed with the importance of religion, but he did not find among the various Christian sects any whose religious system he could entirely adopt. He subsequently declared against all human creeds, and commenced forming religious associations with the Bible as their only rule of faith. In 1841, Dr. Campbell founded Bethany College, in Virginia, of which he was long the president, and established the "Christian Baptist and Millennial Harbinger," which became the organ of his peculiar religious system. Died in 1855.

See RICHARDSON's "Memoirs of Alexander Campbell," Philadelphia, 1868.

Campbell, (Sir ALEXANDER,) a British general, born in Perthshire in 1759, entered the army about 1776. After serving with distinction for several years in India, he became colonel in 1803, and succeeded Sir Arthur Wellesley in the command of Seringapatam, Mysore, etc. in 1805. He was wounded at Talavera in 1809, obtained the rank of major-general in 1810, and that of lieutenant-general in 1814. In 1820 he was appointed commander-in-chief at Madras. Died in 1824.

See CHAMBERS, "Biographical Dictionary of Eminent Scotsmen."

Campbell, (ARCHIBALD,) second Earl of Argyle, was killed at the battle of Flodden in 1513.

Campbell, (ARCHIBALD,) fourth Earl of Argyle, was the son of Colin, and grandson of the preceding. He was a zealous Protestant, and the first of his family that adopted the Reformed religion. Died about 1558. His son ARCHIBALD, fifth Earl of Argyle, was also a strenuous promoter of the Reformation. He fought for Mary Queen of Scots at Langside in 1568, and afterwards became lord chancellor. Died without issue in 1575.

Campbell, (ARCHIBALD,) Marquis of Argyle, a patriotic Scottish peer, born in 1598, was the son of Archibald, seventh Earl of Argyle, and was styled "Lord Lorn" in his youth. At the death of his father, in 1638, he became Earl of Argyle, and in the same year avowed himself an adherent of the church in its contest with the court of Charles I., signed the Covenant, and took part in the General Assembly which abolished episcopacy. In 1641 the king visited Scotland, and, in order to strengthen himself against the English Parliament, courted the favour of the Covenanters. Argyle was raised to the rank of marquis. In the civil war that ensued he took arms against the royalists, became the leader of the Covenanters, and commanded the army sent against Montrose, by whom he was defeated in 1644 and 1645. He took a prominent part in the coronation of Charles II. at Scone in 1651, and fought for him against Cromwell. At the restoration of 1660 he was convicted of submission to the usurpation of the Protector, and was executed in 1661. He appears to have possessed political talents of a high order.

See CHAMBERS, "Biographical Dictionary of Eminent Scotsmen;" HUME, "History of England."

Campbell, (ARCHIBALD,) Lord Lorn, the eldest son of the preceding, was the ninth Earl of Argyle. He fought for the royal cause at Dunbar in 1650, and on other occasions. In 1663 the title of earl and the estate of his father were restored to him, and he was appointed one of the lords of the council. Being required to take the oath called the Test, in 1681, he added, by way of explanation or reservation, "as far as is consistent with the Protestant faith." For this offence he was condemned to death; but he escaped to Holland. He returned with armed retainers in 1685, was taken prisoner and executed the same year. It is stated that he slept soundly a few hours before his execution.

See CHAMBERS, "Biographical Dictionary of Eminent Scotsmen;" MACAULAY, "History of England," vol. i. chap. v.

[*] Some families who write their name as above pronounce it kȧm′bel.

Campbell, (ARCHIBALD,) a son of the preceding, tenth Earl of Argyle, was made a lord of the treasury in 1690, and lord of sessions in 1694. He was created Duke of Argyle in 1701, and died in 1703, leaving his title to his son John.

Campbell, (ARCHIBALD,) Earl of Islay, (i'lay,) third Duke of Argyle, born about 1682, was a brother of John the second duke. He had great influence in the political affairs of Scotland, and was for many years keeper of the great seal. Died in 1761.

Campbell, (ARCHIBALD,) a Scottish divine, who became Bishop of Aberdeen about 1720. Besides other works, he wrote "The Doctrines of a Middle State between Death and the Resurrection."

Campbell, (ARTHUR,) an officer of the American Revolution, born in Augusta county, Virginia, in 1742. He served, while a boy, in the frontier wars, was made prisoner by the Indians and adopted by the chief, but escaped after a three years' captivity. He served throughout the Revolution, and rose to the rank of colonel.

Campbell, (COLIN,) first Earl of Argyle, was for a long time chancellor of Scotland. He received the title of earl about 1457, and was succeeded by his son Archibald.

Campbell, (COLIN,) third Earl of Argyle, was the son of Archibald. He was justice-general in the reign of James V. Died in 1542.

Campbell, kăm'el, (COLIN,) an English architect, became surveyor of the works at Greenwich Hospital. He published a work on architecture, called "Vitruvius Britannicus," (1715.) Died in 1734.

Campbell, (COLIN,) Lord Clyde, a British general, born in Glasgow in 1792. He entered the army in 1808, served in the Peninsula until 1814, and obtained the rank of major in 1825. In 1842 he became a colonel, and served in the expedition against the Chinese. As general of brigade, he distinguished himself in India between 1848 and 1852. He commanded the Highland brigade in the Crimean war, and contributed to the victories of the Alma and Balaklava in 1854. In this year he was promoted to the rank of major-general, and in 1855 received the grand cross of the Bath. In July, 1857, Sir Colin was appointed commander-in-chief of the army of India, and departed at once to suppress the rebellion of the Sepoys. His relief of Lucknow in November, 1857, is considered a brilliant achievement. He defeated the Sepoys at Cawnpore, and succeeded in crushing the rebellion in 1858. He was the same year raised to the peerage, with the title of Lord Clyde. Died at Chatham in 1863.

See "Blackwood's Magazine" for October, 1858.

Campbell, (GEORGE,) D.D., a Scottish divine, eminent for talents and learning, born at Aberdeen in 1719. He became minister at Aberdeen in 1756, and principal of Marischal College in 1759. He published in 1762 an able "Dissertation on Miracles," in answer to Hume; and in 1766, "Philosophy of Rhetoric," which is highly commended, and said to be his best work. This was followed by a "Translation of the Gospels, with Notes," "Lectures on Ecclesiastical History," etc. Died in 1796.

See KEITH, "Life of George Campbell;" CHAMBERS, "Biographical Dictionary of Eminent Scotsmen."

Campbell, (GEORGE JOHN DOUGLAS.) See ARGYLL, DUKE OF.

Campbell, (GEORGE W.,) born in Tennessee in 1768, embraced the profession of law. From 1803 to 1809 he was a representative in Congress, and for two years chairman of the committee of ways and means. He was elected to the United States Senate in 1811, and was appointed secretary of the treasury in 1815, but the next year resumed his seat in the Senate, in which he served until 1818, when he was sent by Mr. Monroe as minister to Russia. Died in 1848.

Campbell, (JAMES,) an American jurist, born in Philadelphia about 1812. He was appointed in 1841 judge of the court of common pleas of Philadelphia, and in 1852 attorney-general of the State. He became postmaster-general under President Pierce in 1853.

See LIVINGSTON's "Portraits of Eminent Americans."

Campbell, (Sir JAMES,) a British general, entered the army about 1794. Died in 1835.

Campbell, (JOHN,) second Duke of Argyll, (Argyle,) an able commander, born in 1678, was the son of Archibald, first Duke of Argyle. He inherited his father's title in 1703, and in 1705 was created an English peer, as Baron Chatham and Earl of Greenwich. Between 1705 and 1710 he served with distinction at the battles of Ramillies, Oudenarde, and Malplaquet, and was promoted to the rank of lieutenant-general. On the accession of George I., Argyle was appointed commander-in-chief of all the forces in Scotland. He rendered important services in suppressing the rebellion of 1715, and opposed with success at Dunblane a superior force of the Pretender under the Earl of Mar. He changed sides several times in politics, and was accused of trafficking or intriguing with the Jacobites. He died, without male issue, in 1743, when the dukedom of Argyle passed to his brother Archibald.

See ROBERT CAMPBELL, "Life of the Duke of Argyle," 1745; CHAMBERS, "Biographical Dictionary of Eminent Scotsmen."

Campbell, (JOHN,) LL.D., a Scottish writer on history, biography, politics, etc., was born in Edinburgh in 1708, and was taken to England in childhood. He adopted the profession of author, in which he obtained considerable success. Among his numerous works are "History of Prince Eugene and the Duke of Marlborough," "Lives of British Admirals," and "A Political Survey of Britain," which is variously estimated, but said to be his most important work. He made many and valuable contributions to the "Biographia Britannica" and to the "Universal History." Died in 1775. "I think highly of Campbell," says Dr. Johnson. "In the first place, he has very good parts; in the second place, he has very extensive reading."

See "Biographia Britannica;" CHAMBERS, "Biographical Dictionary of Eminent Scotsmen."

Campbell, (JOHN,) LORD, an eminent British lawyer and statesman, born near Cupar, in Fifeshire, Scotland, in 1779, was a son of the Rev. George Campbell, noticed above. He was called to the bar by the Society of Lincoln's Inn in 1806. In 1830 he entered Parliament as a Whig and an ardent Reformer. He was appointed solicitor-general in 1832, attorney-general in 1834, and lord chancellor of Ireland in 1841. He was raised to the peerage, as Baron Campbell, in the latter year. In 1846 he published "The Lives of the Lord Chancellors and Keepers of the Great Seal of England," (7 vols.,) which the "London Quarterly Review" designates as "a work of sterling merit, one of very great labour, of richly diversified interest, and, we are satisfied, of lasting value and estimation." He was appointed chief justice of the queen's bench in 1850. On the accession of the Liberal ministry in 1859 he became lord chancellor of England. He published several volumes of Reports, and "Lives of the Chief Justices of England," (3 vols., 1849–57.) Died in June, 1861.

See the "Quarterly Review" for December, 1845, and December, 1847; Foss, "The Judges of England;" "Edinburgh Review" for October, 1857.

Campbell, (Rev. JOHN,) born in Edinburgh in 1766, was pastor of the Independent Church in Kingsland from 1804 until 1840, and edited "The Youths' Magazine" for many years. In 1812 he visited the missionary stations of South Africa, and after his return published "Travels in South Africa," (1815,) and other works. Died in 1840.

Campbell, (Rev. JOHN,) a Scottish editor and author, was born in Forfarshire about 1794. He was minister of the Tabernacle, Moorfields, London, for many years, until ill health induced him to retire from the pulpit. Since that time he has edited the "British Banner," commenced in 1849, "The Christian Witness," and other successful journals. He has also written "Jethro," a prize essay, "The Martyr of Erromanga," "Maritime Discovery and Christian Missions," and other religious works.

Campbell, (JOHN N.,) an eloquent American Presbyterian minister, born in Philadelphia in 1798. He preached at Albany, New York, from 1831 until near his death in 1864.

Campbell, (Sir NEIL,) a British officer, born about 1770, served with distinction as colonel in the Peninsula from 1810 to 1812. In March, 1814, while charging the

French at Fère-Champenoise, he was wounded by a Cossack who mistook him for a Frenchman. In the same year he was chosen as commissioner to attend Bonaparte to Elba, to reside with him as a sort of accredited diplomatist and to act as a spy on his movements. While Campbell was absent on a visit to Florence, in February, 1815, the ex-emperor escaped. About 1816 he was sent to explore the sources of the Niger, and in 1826 was appointed Governor of Sierra Leone, where he died in 1827.

Campbell, (SAMUEL,) COLONEL, an American officer, born in New Hampshire in 1738, removed to the State of New York. He served in the French war and in that cf the Revolution. Died in 1824.

Campbell, (THOMAS,) an eminent British poet, born at Glasgow in 1777, was the youngest son of a merchant of that city. At the university of his native place he distinguished himself as a superior classical scholar. When in his thirteenth year, he carried off a prize from a competitor twice his age. His translations of the Greek dramatists were regarded as the best any pupil in the university had ever made. In 1799 he produced "The Pleasures of Hope," of which the success has perhaps had no parallel in English literature. It passed through four editions in the first year, and was pronounced by Lord Byron "one of the most beautiful didactic poems in our language." "No poet at such an age," says Moir, "ever produced such an exquisite specimen of poetic mastery,—that is, of fine conception and high art combined. Sentiments tender, energetic, impassioned, eloquent, and majestic are conveyed to the reader in the tones of a music forever varied,—sinking or swelling like the harmonies of an Æolian lyre." Campbell visited the continent in 1800, and witnessed the battle of Hohenlinden, which furnished him with the subject of one of the most exquisite lyrics to be found in any language. On his return to Scotland, after residing for some time in Edinburgh, he removed to London. Soon after his return from the continent he had published "The Exile of Erin," "Ye Mariners of England," "Lochiel's Warning," and other short poems.

In 1803 he married his cousin, Miss Sinclair, and settled near Sydenham. The government (Fox then being prime minister) granted him in 1806 an annual pension of two hundred pounds. In 1809 he published several of his finest poems,—"Gertrude of Wyoming," which surpasses the "Pleasures of Hope" in simplicity, and, if less perfect as a work of art, is perhaps not inferior in imaginative power ; "O'Connor's Child," which, for a certain wild, romantic beauty and exquisite pathos, is unequalled by any of his other productions ; and "The Battle of the Baltic," one of the most spirited odes in the language. In 1819 Campbell published "Specimens of the British Poets ; with an Essay on English Poetry." From 1820 to 1830 he edited the "New Monthly Magazine," which, under the auspices of his distinguished name, was eminently successful. He was elected lord rector of the University of Glasgow in 1827, and made a journey to Algiers in 1832. Among his later works are a not very accurate "Life of Mrs. Siddons," "The Life and Times of Petrarch," and "The Life of Frederick the Great." He died in 1844, and was buried in Westminster Abbey.

In a conversation with Washington Irving, Scott expressed his regret that Campbell wrote so seldom. "He has," says Scott, "wings that would bear him to the skies, and he does now and then spread them grandly, but folds them up again and resumes his perch, as if he were afraid to launch away. The fact is, Campbell is in a manner a bugbear to himself: the brightness of his early success is a detriment to all his further efforts. *He is afraid of the shadow which his own fame casts before him.*" "It is on his lyrics," says Professor Aytoun, "that the future reputation of Campbell must principally rest. They have taken their place, never to be disturbed, in the popular heart ; and, until the language in which they are written perishes, they are certain to endure."

See "The Life and Letters of Thomas Campbell," edited by WM. BEATTIE, 1850, 3 vols. 8vo ; the "Account of Campbell's Life" in "Fraser's Magazine" for November, 1844; GILFILLAN's "Essay on the Genius and Character of Campbell ;" also the excellent critique on Campbell in HAZLITT's "Miscellaneous Works," vol. v.

Campbell, (WILLIAM,) LORD, a brother of the Duke of Argyle, was the last royal governor of South Carolina. He was expelled by the patriots in 1776, and died in 1778.

Campbell, (WILLIAM,) an American soldier, born in Virginia in 1745. He distinguished himself as a colonel at the battle of Guilford, and was killed at Eutaw Springs in September, 1781.

Campbell, (WILLIAM B.,) an American politician, born in Sumner county, Tennessee, about 1807. He was elected Governor of Tennessee in 1851, after he had served as member of Congress. In 1862 he was appointed a brigadier-general in the Union army. Died in 1867.

Campbell, (WILLIAM W.,) born at Cherry Valley, New York, in 1806. He became a judge of the supreme court of New York. He published "The Border Wars of New York," (1831,) and a "Life of De Witt Clinton," (1849.)

Campe, kâm'peh, (JOACHIM HEINRICH,) a German philanthropist and popular writer on education, was born at Deensen, Brunswick, in 1746. He was appointed superintendent of schools in Brunswick in 1787, and became proprietor of an extensive publishing house. He published a good "Dictionary of the German Language," (5 vols., 1807–11,) and wrote many juvenile books, which were received with great favour. His "Robinson the Younger" ("Robinson der Jüngere") has been translated into many languages. Died in 1818.

See MICHEL BERR, "Notice biographique sur Campe," 1819; ERSCH und GRUBER, "Allgemeine Encyklopaedie."

Campeggi, kâm-pěd'jee, (BENEDETTO,) a poet, born at Bologna, narrated the important events of his time in a Latin poem, "Italidis Libri X.," (1553.) Died in 1566.

Campeggi, (GIOVANNI,) an Italian jurist, born in 1438, wrote numerous works on civil and canon law. Died at Mantua in 1511.

Campeggi or Campeggio, kâm-pàd'jo, (LORENZO,) a learned Italian ecclesiastic, born at Bologna in 1474, was made a cardinal by Leo X., who employed him in important missions to Germany and England. Clement VII. sent him as legate to the Diet of Augsburg, famous for its Protestant Confession of Faith, and to England (1528) as one of the judges in the question of the divorce of Catherine of Aragon. He became Archbishop of Bologna. Died in 1539.

See CARLO SIGONIO, "Vita L. Campegii Cardinalis," 1581; AUBERY, "Histoire des Cardinaux."

Campeggi or Campeggio, (TOMMASO,) Bishop of Feltri, nephew of the preceding, was born in 1500. He was nuncio from Paul III. to the Conference of Worms in 1540, and was a member of the Council of Trent in 1545. Besides other works, he wrote a "Treatise on the Authority of Councils." Died in 1564.

Campeggio or Campegio. See CAMPEGGI.

Campellensis. See CHAMPEAUX.

Campello, kâm-pel'lo, (BERNARDINO de' Conti—dà kon'tee,) an Italian *littérateur*, born at Spoleto in 1595. He wrote a "History of Spoleto," (1672,) and other esteemed works, in prose and verse. Died in 1676.

See TIRABOSCHI, "Storia della Letteratura Italiana."

Campello, (PAOLO DE' CONTI,) an Italian scholar, son of the preceding, born at Spoleto in 1643 ; died in 1713.

Campen. See KAMPEN.

Campen, van, vän kâm'pen, (JAKOB,) a Dutch architect, born at Haarlem. Having studied in Rome, he returned and built the Hôtel de Ville at Amsterdam, one of the grandest edifices of Holland, and designed other buildings in that city. Died in 1638.

See NAGLER, "Neues Allgemeines Künstler-Lexikon."

Campen or Kampen, van, [Lat. CAMPEN'SIS,] (JAN,) called also Van den Campen, a Dutch philologist, born at Campen in 1490. He was professor of Hebrew at Louvain from 1519 to 1531, and produced a Hebrew Grammar, and a good Latin version or paraphrase of the Psalms, (1532.) Died in 1538.

See FÉLIX NÈVE, "Notice sur la Vie et les Travaux de J. Campensis," 1845.

Campenon, kôN'peh-nôN', (VINCENT,) a French poet, born at Guadeloupe in 1772. He was educated at Paris, and afterwards resided in France. In 1795 he wrote, in verse and prose, a "Journey from Grenoble to Chambéry." He became an intimate friend of the poet Ducis in 1802, soon after which he produced an admired didactic poem called "The Country-House," ("La Maison des Champs.") His "Prodigal Son," a poem, (1811,) was also very successful. He was chosen a member of the French Academy in place of Delille in 1813. Died near Paris in 1843.

See "Nouvelle Biographie Générale."

Campensis. See CAMPEN, (JAN VAN.)

Camper, kåm′pẹr, (PIETER,) a distinguished Dutch anatomist and naturalist, born at Leyden on the 11th of May, 1722. He studied medicine under Gaubius and Albinus. Having graduated, in 1746 he visited England and France, associating with the most eminent men of science of both countries. He filled successively the chairs of philosophy, anatomy, and medicine at Amsterdam and Groningen, where he lectured with eminent ability. Among his discoveries is that of the presence of air in the bones of birds, (1771.) He wrote many works on anatomy, physiology, etc., among which are "Anatomico-Pathological Demonstrations," (" Demonstrationes anatomico-pathologicæ," 1760–62,) "Dissertation on the Natural Varieties which mark the Physiognomy of Men of Different Climates," and "The Sense of Hearing in Fishes." In 1785 he was chosen foreign associate of the Academy of Paris,—an honour which had been conferred on only one other Dutchman.* He was also a Fellow of the Royal Society of London. Died at the Hague in 1789.

See CONDORCET, "Éloge de Camper;" VIC-D'AZYR, "Éloge de Camper;" A. G. CAMPER, "Levensschets van P. Camper," 1791, and French version of the same; "Notice sur P. Camper," 1803; J. MULDER, "Verdiensten van P. Camper," Amsterdam, 1809; "Encyclopædia Britannica."

Camperdown. See DUNCAN, ADMIRAL.

Campesani, de′, då kåm-på-så′nee, (BENVENUTO,) an Italian poet of high reputation, was born at Vicenza about 1260. Only fragments of his works are extant. Died about 1324.

Campesano, kåm-på-så′no, (ALESSANDRO,) an Italian poet, born at Bassano in 1521; died in 1572.

Camphausen, kåmp′hŏw′zẹn, (LUDOLF,) a Prussian statesman, born at Hünshoven in 1803. He was chosen representative of Cologne in the diet of the Rhenish provinces in 1842, and president of the council of ministers at Berlin in March, 1848. He resigned in June of the same year, and was appointed minister of state, and ambassador to the central power, (Centralgewalt.) In politics he was a moderate Liberal. He was the author of the circular of January 23, 1849, which proposed a German confederation under the direction of Prussia.

See "Nouvelle Biographie Générale."

Camphausen, (OTTO,) a brother of Ludolf, noticed above, was born at Hünshoven in 1812. He has filled several offices in the public service.

Camphausen, (WILHELM,) a German painter of battles, born at Dusseldorf about 1818. He enlisted in a regiment of hussars in order to study his art. Among his works are "Cavaliers and Roundheads," "Charles I. at Naseby," and "Prince Eugene at Belgrade."

Camphuys, kåmp′hois, (JAN,) an able Dutch officer, born at Haarlem in 1634. At the age of twenty he entered the service of the East India Company, and in 1684 was appointed Governor-General of the Dutch possessions in India. He wrote a "History of the Foundation of Batavia." Died in 1695.

See ZEEMAN, "Leven en Daden van J. Camphuys," 1833.

Camphuysen, kåmp′hoi′sẹn, written also **Kamphuizen,** (THEODORUS RAPHAEL,) an eminent Dutch landscape-painter, born at Gorkum about 1580. He is said to have been the first painter of Holland that executed landscapes in the proper manner. His sunset and winter scenes are especially admired. In early life he renounced painting for theology, joined the Socinians, and wrote a few theological works. Died in 1627.

See DESCAMPS, "Vies des Peintres Flamands," etc.

Campi, kåm′pee, or **Campo,** kåm′po, (ANTONIO,) a skilful Italian architect and painter, born at Cremona. He published a "History of Cremona," illustrated with engravings designed by himself. His favourite model in

* Boerhaave.

art was Correggio, whom he imitated with success. He died in or after 1591.

Campi, (BERNARDINO,) a painter, born at Cremona about 1525, acquired a high reputation for portraits and historical pictures. A "Nativity" in one of the churches of Cremona is among his master-pieces. Died about 1590.

See LANZI, "History of Painting in Italy."

Campi, (GALEAZZO,) a painter, born at Cremona in 1475, was the father of three eminent artists, Giulio, Antonio, and Vincenzo. Died in 1536.

See LANZI, "History of Painting in Italy."

Campi, (GIULIO,) an eminent historical painter, born at Cremona about 1500, was the master of Bernardino and brother of Antonio. He studied under Giulio Romano, and opened a successful school at Cremona. He excelled in colour, grace, and elevation of style. His subjects are mostly taken from sacred history. Died in 1572.

See LANZI, "History of Painting in Italy."

Campi, (MICHELE and BALDASSARE,) two brothers, who were botanists, and lived at Lucca about 1650. They published "Spicilegio Botanico," (1652.)

Campi, (VINCENZO,) an Italian painter, born at Cremona before 1532, was a brother and pupil of Giulio Campi. He was a good colorist, and excelled in portraits and pictures of fruit. He also painted religious subjects. Died in 1591.

See LANZI, "History of Painting in Italy."

Campian. See CAMPION.

Campidoglio, kåm-pe-dòl′yo, (MICHELANGELO,) a skilful painter of fruits and flowers, born at Rome in 1610; died in 1670.

Campiglia, kåm-pèl′yå, (ALESSANDRO,) an Italian historian, who lived about 1600. His principal work is a well-written history of Henry IV. of France, (1614.)

Campiglia, (GIOVANNI DOMENICO,) an excellent designer and painter, born at Lucca in 1692, worked at Rome and Florence. The engravings of the "Capitoline Museum" were chiefly designed by him. Died about 1750.

See LANZI, "History of Painting in Italy."

Cam′pǐ-ọn or **Cam′pǐ-ạn,** (EDMUND,) a Catholic priest, eminent for talents and eloquence, born in London in 1540. He took orders in the Anglican Church, and was soon after converted to that of Rome. In 1573 he went to Rome, and joined the Jesuits, who in 1580 sent him to England. Having challenged the Protestants to dispute with him in print, and having, as Hume says, "been detected in treasonable practices," a confession of guilt was extorted from him by the rack, and he was hanged in 1581. He left a "Universal Chronology," a "History of Ireland," and other works.

See HUME, "History of England;" BOMBINO, "Vita et Martyrium E. Campiani," 1618.

Campion or **Champion,** (THOMAS,) an English poet and musician, lived about 1600.

Campistron, de, dẹh kŏn′pès′tRòn′,(JEAN GALBERT,) a French dramatist, born at Toulouse in 1656. He imitated Racine, and produced several successful tragedies, among which are "Andronicus," "Alcibiades," and "Tiridates." His works ran through ten editions. La Harpe says, "His plans are judicious; but he has no well-marked character, no striking situation nor nervous lines." He was for many years secretary to the Duc de Vendôme, and was received into the French Academy in 1701. Died in 1723.

See QUÉRARD, "La France Littéraire."

Campo. See CAMPI, (ANTONIO.)

Campo-Basso, da, då kåm′po bås′so, (NICCOLÒ,) COUNT, a Neapolitan condottiere, who about 1476 entered the service of Charles the Rash of Burgundy, whom he is said to have betrayed.

See BARANTE, "Histoire des Ducs de Bourgogne;" SIR WALTER SCOTT, "Anne of Geierstein."

Campolo, kåm′po-lo, (PLACIDO,) a historical painter, born at Messina, Sicily, in 1693; died in 1743.

Campolongo, kåm-po-lon′go, (EMMANUELE,) an Italian poet and antiquary, born in Naples in 1732. He became eminent as a professor of humanities in Naples, where he began to lecture in 1765. Among his numerous works are "La Polifemeide," and "The Proteus," ("Il Proteo,") a collection of verses in which he assumes the form of various celebrated poets. Died in 1801.

See M. ROBERTI, "Biographie de Campolongo;" TIPALDO, "Biografia degli Italiani illustri."

Campomanes, kȧm-po-mä′nĕs, (PEDRO RODRIGUEZ,) COUNT, a Spanish author and minister of state, eminent for probity and liberality, was born in Asturias about 1720. Having acquired a high reputation as a jurisconsult, he was appointed in 1765 *fiscal* of the royal council of Castile. He was made president of the same council in 1788, and afterwards minister of state. His writings on political economy acquired for him a European reputation, and were commended by Robertson in his "History of America." On the recommendation of Dr. Franklin, he was chosen an honorary member of the Philosophical Society of Philadelphia. He wrote "A Discourse on the Promotion of Popular Industry," (1774,) "Discourse on the Popular Education of Mechanics," an "Appendix to the Education of Mechanics," (in 4 vols.,) and other works. Died in 1802.

See ROBERTSON, "History of America;" ERSCH und GRUBER, "Allgemeine Encyklopaedie;" "Fraser's Magazine" for June, 1831.

Campra, kôN′pRȧ′, (ANDRÉ,) an eminent French composer, born at Aix in 1660, produced sacred music and many popular operas. Died in 1744.

See FÉTIS, "Biographie Universelle des Musiciens."

Camprédon, kôN′pRȧ′dôN′, (JACQUES DAVID MARTIN,) a French general, born at Montpellier in 1761. He was appointed minister of war by Joseph Bonaparte in 1809, and served in the Russian campaign, (1812.) Died in 1837.

See "Vie du Général Camprédon," 8vo, 1838.

Camps. See DESCAMPS.

Camps, de, dĕh kôN, (FRANCOIS,) a French abbé, born at Amiens in 1643, became grand vicar of Serroni, the Archbishop of Albi. He applied himself to the study of medals, of which he made an excellent collection, and wrote treatises on history and numismatics. Died in 1723.

Camuccini, kä-moot-chee′nee, (VINCENZO,) a distinguished painter of history, born in Rome in 1775. In his youth he copied the works of Raphael and other old masters, and afterwards acquired celebrity by a series of pictures from ancient Roman history, among which were "Horatius Cocles" and "The Continence of Scipio." He also painted "The Conversion of Saul," and other scriptural subjects. He was chosen president of the Academy of Saint Luke, and a member of the Institute of France. His style is rather conventional than natural. Died in 1844.

See NAGLER, "Neues Allgemeines Künstler-Lexikon."

Camus, kä′müs′, (ARMAND GASTON,) a republican legislator and writer, born in Paris in 1740. He published in 1783 a translation of Aristotle's "History of Animals," which procured him admission to the Academy of Inscriptions. Elected to the Constituent Assembly in 1789, he had the principal part in framing the civil constitution of the clergy. He was an active member of the Convention, which appointed him in 1792 one of the committee of public safety. With three other commissaries of the Convention, he attempted in April, 1793, to arrest Dumouriez′at the head of his army; but that general sent them prisoners to the Austrian camp. In 1795 he was exchanged for the daughter of Louis XVI., and passed into the Council of Five Hundred. He was a member of the Institute, and author of several able works, among which is a "Journey through the Departments recently united." Died in 1804.

See TOULONGÉON, "Éloge historique de A. G. Camus," 1806; THIERS, "History of the French Revolution."

Camus, (CHARLES ÉTIENNE LOUIS,) a French mathematician, born at Crécy-en-Brie in 1699. In 1727 he wrote a treatise on the Masting of Vessels, which opened to him the Academy of Sciences. He was one of the Academicians who in 1735 went to Lapland with Maupertuis to determine the figure of the earth. He wrote a work on Hydraulics, and a Course of Mathematics, which was valued at the time. The Royal Society of London elected him a Fellow about 1765. Died in Paris in 1768.

See GRANDJEAN DE FOUCHY, "Eloge de C. E. L. Camus."

Camus, (JEAN PIERRE,) Bishop of Belley, was born in Paris in 1582. He preached and wrote zealously against the mendicant monks. For this Richelieu reprimanded him, and added, "If it were not for this fault, I should canonize you." Camus replied, "We should then both have what we wish: you would be pope, and I would be a saint." He wrote "Dorothée," and other religious romances, which had great success at the time. Died in 1652.

See NICÉRON, "Mémoires;" DÉPERY, "Notice sur la Vie de J. K. Camus."

Camus, de, dĕh kä′müs′, or **des Camus,** dȧ kä′müs′, (FRANÇOIS JOSEPH,) a French mathematician, born in Lorraine in 1672, became a resident of Paris. He was admitted into the Academy of Sciences in 1716, and published in 1722 a curious "Treatise on Moving Forces." Died in England in 1732.

Camus de Mézières, le, lĕh kä′müs′ dĕh mȧ′-ze-aiR′, (NICOLAS,) a French architect, born in Paris in 1721. He designed the Corn-Market *(Halle au blé)* of Paris, and wrote "The Genius of Architecture," (1780,) and other works. Died in 1789.

Camus, le, lĕh kä′müs′, (ANTOINE,) a celebrated French physician, born in Paris in 1722. He was appointed professor in the University of Paris in 1762. His reputation was increased by his literary talents and the original character of his medical works, among which are "The Medicine of the Mind," (1753,) and "Maladies of the Region of the Heart." He wrote "Love and Friendship," a comedy, and "The Medical Amphitheatre," a poem, (1745.) Died in 1772.

See BOURRU, "Éloge historique de M. le Camus," 1772.

Camus, le, (ÉTIENNE,) born in Paris in 1632, became Bishop of Grenoble in 1671, and performed the duties of that office with great charity and diligence. On the occasion of a curate's complaining to Camus that he could not prevent the people from dancing on festival-days, the bishop replied, "Oh, permit them at least to give their misery a shake." He received a cardinal's hat in 1686. Died in 1707.

See LALLOUETTE, "Abrégé de la Vie de M. le Camus," 1720.

Camusat, kä′mü′zä′, (JEAN,) a learned French publisher of Paris, was printer to the Académie Française. Died in 1639.

Camusat, (NICOLAS,) a French priest and antiquary, born at Troyes in 1575. He was a canon of the church of Troyes, and author of "Mélanges historiques," (a collection of acts, treaties, and letters, 1619,) and other works. Died in 1655.

Canaan, kä′nan or kä′nȧ-an, [Heb. כְּנַעַן,] a patriarch, was a son of Ham, and ancestor of the Canaanites who inhabited Palestine before it was conquered by the Israelites. (See Genesis ix. 18, and x.)

Can′a-chus, [Κάναχος,] a Greek sculptor, born at Sicyon, lived about 400 B.C. He was a brother of Aristocles the artist, and a pupil of Polycletus.

Canal, kä-näl′, or **Canaletto,** kä-nä-let′to, a Venetian painter, whose proper name was BERNARDO BELOTTO, (bĕR-naR′do bȧ-lot′to,) born in Venice in 1724. He was a pupil of his uncle, Antonio Canal, whom he imitated with success. He worked in Dresden, London, and other places, and painted buildings and scenes in the environs of towns. He excelled in perspective. Died at Warsaw in 1780.

See LANZI, "History of Painting in Italy."

Canal or **Canaletto,** (ANTONIO,) an eminent Italian painter of perspective views, born at Venice in 1697, was a scene-painter in early life. Having studied in Rome, he returned to Venice, and became a successful artist. His subjects are mostly views of the Venetian palaces, canals, etc., which are highly prized. As he painted with great facility, his works are numerous. He is said to have been the first who used the camera obscura in painting. Died in 1768. His pictures of Venetian buildings, etc. are called admirable by some critics, but by others his art is censured as mere mechanism. "The mannerism of Canaletto," says Ruskin, "is the most degraded I know in the whole range of art." ("Modern Painters.")

See LANZI, "History of Painting in Italy."

€ as *k;* ç as *s;* ğ *hard;* ġ as *j;* G, H, K, *guttural;* N, *nasal;* R, *trilled;* s as *z;* th as in *this.* (☞See Explanations, p. 23.)

Canale, kȧ-nȧ′lȧ, (Niccolò,) a Venetian admiral, who commanded against the Turks in 1469. He was removed in 1470 for his dilatory conduct or timidity.

See Sismondi, "Histoire des Républiques Italiennes;" Daru, "Histoire de Venise."

Canaletto. See Canal.

Canani, kȧ-nȧ′nee, (Giovanni Battista,) a skilful Italian anatomist, born at Ferrara in 1515. He is said to have observed the valves which indicate the circulation of the blood, about 1545, and wrote an able "Treatise on the Muscles," (1572.) Pope Julius III. appointed him his first physician. Died in 1579.

Canaples, de, deh kȧ′nȧpl′, Sire, a brave French officer, who served with distinction in the armies of Francis I. and Henry II., (1520–52.)

See De Thou, "Mémoires."

Canard, kȧ′nȧr′, (Nicolas François,) a French mathematician, born at Moulins, was professor in the Lyceum of Moulins, and wrote a treatise on "Political Economy," (1801,) and a work on "Equations," (1808.) Died in 1833.

Canaveri, kȧ-nȧ-vȧ′ree,(Giovanni Battista,) Bishop of Vercelli, an Italian prelate, eminent for learning and eloquence, was born at Borgomaro in 1753. He published "Pastoral Letters," and other works. He was chaplain to the mother of Napoleon I. Died in 1811.

Canaye, de, deh kȧ′nȧ′, (Étienne,) a French abbé, born in Paris in 1694. He entered the congregation of the Oratory in 1716, and became a member of the Academy of Inscriptions in 1728. The records of this institution contain a few able treatises written by him, one of which is on the Areopagus of Athens. Died in 1782.

Canaye, de la, deh lȧ kȧ′nȧ′, (Philippe,) Sieur de Fresne, (deh frɛn,) a French statesman, born in Paris in 1551. He served Henry IV. in diplomatic missions. Died in 1610.

See Moréri, "Dictionnaire Historique."

Can′by, (Edward R. S.,) an American general, born in Kentucky about 1818, graduated at West Point in 1839. He served in the Mexican war in 1846–47, became a captain in 1851, a major in 1855, and a colonel in May, 1861. When the civil war began, he was in New Mexico, where he defended Fort Craig and defeated the Texan insurgents in February, 1862. He was appointed a brigadier-general of volunteers about March, 1862, and afterwards was raised to the rank of major-general. He succeeded General Banks, as commander of the army in Louisiana and of the departments lying west of the Mississippi River, in May or June, 1864. He invested and took Mobile in April, 1865. Having been promoted to the rank of brigadier-general in the regular army, July, 1866, he was assigned in August, 1867, to the command of the second military district, comprising North and South Carolina.

Cancellieri, kȧn-chĕl-le-ā′ree, (Francesco,) an Italian antiquary and priest, born in Rome in 1751. Having gained reputation by some learned treatises, he became librarian to Cardinal Antonelli, and, in 1802, director of the printing-press of the Propaganda. As a writer he was very prolific, and displays more learning than judgment. His work "On the Office of the Secretary to the Basilica of the Vatican" (1788) was received with favour. He also wrote treatises on the origin and design of the ceremonies which are performed at Saint Peter's and the Vatican on festival-days. Died in 1826.

See Tipaldo, "Biografia degli Italiani illustri;" P. V. Baraldi, "Vita di F. G. Cancellieri," 1827; Visconti, "Elogio di F. Cancellieri," 1827.

Cancer, kȧn′thĕr, (Geronimo,) a Spanish writer of comedies and facetious poems, lived about 1620–50. He obtained a place at the court of Philip IV.

Canclaux, de, deh kŏn′klō′, (Jean Baptiste Camille,) Count, a French general, born in Paris in 1740. As lieutenant-general he defended Nantes against the Vendeans in 1793, became commander-in-chief of the army of the west in 1794, and made prudent and successful efforts to pacify the royalists. Under the consulate of Bonaparte he was inspector-general of cavalry, and in 1804 was elected senator. He was created a peer in 1814. Died in 1817.

See De Muy, "Éloge du Comte de Canclaux," 1818.

Cancrin, kȧn-kreen′, [Lat. Cancri′nus,] (Franz Ludwig,) a German mineralogist, born in Hesse-Darmstadt in 1738. He was appointed in 1783, by Catherine II. of Russia, councillor of the Imperial College, and director of the salt-mines of Staraya-Roossa. He published several works, (in German,) among which is "The Elementary Principles of the Science of Mining and of Salt-Works." This is said to be the most complete work on that subject. Died in 1816.

See Meusel, "Lexikon der jetztlebenden Deutschen Schriftsteller."

Cancrin, (Georg,) Count, a distinguished financier, son of the preceding, born at Hanau, in Germany, about 1775. He entered the military administration of Russia in 1796, and was made a councillor of state in 1811. In 1812 he became intendant-general of the army, and in 1815 obtained the rank of lieutenant-general. By his superior talents and probity he gained the confidence of the emperor, who appointed him minister of the finances in 1823. He held this office twenty-one years, and managed the department with decided ability and success. He published, besides other works, "Military Economy in Peace and War," (1822,) which is highly esteemed. Died in Saint Petersburg in 1845.

Can′da-çe, [Gr. Κανδάκη,] the name or title of several ancient queens of Ethiopia, whose court was in the isle of Meröe, and of whom little is known. One of them is mentioned in Acts viii. 27.

Candale, kŏn′dȧl′, (Charles Louis Gaston—gȧs′-tòn′,) Duke of, born at Metz in 1627, rose to a high command in the army, and passed for the most gallant person of his time. His mother Gabrielle was a daughter of Henry IV. of France. Died in 1658.

Candale, (Henri de Nogaret d'Épernon—deh no′gȧ′rȧ′ dȧ′pĕr′nòn′,) Duke of, born in 1591, was the eldest son of the Duc d'Épernon, and an uncle of the preceding. In 1614 he was chosen first gentleman of the chamber of Louis XIII., and in 1621 served with distinction under the Prince of Orange against the Spaniards. Having entered the service of Venice in 1624, he was appointed general-in-chief of the Venetian armies about 1634. Died in 1639.

Candamo, kȧn-dȧ′mo, (Francisco Bances—bȧn′thĕs,) a Spanish dramatic poet, born at Sabugo in 1662. He was an imitator of Calderon, and author of several successful comedies, one of which is entitled "The Slave in Golden Chains." Died in 1709.

See Ticknor, "History of Spanish Literature."

Can-dau′leş, [Gr. Κανδαύλης,] King of Lydia, was also called **Myr′silus.** According to Herodotus, he provoked the resentment of his wife by exposing her without a veil to a favourite officer, named Gyges. By offering him the alternative of the throne or a violent death, she induced Gyges to kill Candaules, and then received the former as her consort.

Candeille, kŏn′dȧl′ or kŏn′dȧ′ye, (Amélie Julie,) a popular French singer and comic actress, born in Paris in 1767. In 1792 she produced "Catherine la belle Fermière," a comedy, which was very successful and was followed by other dramas. Died in 1834.

See Fétis, "Biographie Universelle des Musiciens."

Candeille, (Pierre Joseph,) a musical composer, born in Flanders in 1744. His opera "Castor and Pollux" (1791) had great success. Died in 1827.

Candiac, de, deh kŏn′de′ȧk′, (Jean Louis Philippe Montcalm,) a precocious French child, brother of the Marquis de Montcalm, was born in 1719. It is said that he could read Greek, Latin, and Hebrew. Died in 1726.

Candiano (kȧn-de-ȧ′no) **I.,** (Pietro,) Doge of Venice, was killed in a battle against the Sclavonians in 887 a.d.

Candiano II. (Pietro) was elected Doge of Venice in 932 a.d. He extended the boundaries of the republic by conquest. Died in 939.

Candiano III., (Pietro,) a son of Candiano II., was elected Doge of Venice in 942. Among the events of his administration was the abduction of a party of patrician brides from a church by the pirates of Istria. The pirates were pursued and slain, and the captives recovered.

Candiano IV., (Pietro,) a son of the preceding, became doge in 959. His tyranny provoked a revolt of the people, by whom he was killed in 976.

ā, ē, ī, ō, ū, y̆, *long;* ȧ, ė, ȯ, same, less prolonged; ă, ĕ, ĭ, ŏ, ŭ, y̆, *short;* ą, ę, į, ǫ, *obscure;* fär, fȧll, fȧt; mĕt; nŏt; gŏŏd; mŏŏn;

Candido, kån'de-do, (PIETRO,) a historical painter and sculptor, whose proper name was PIETER DE WITTE, was born at Bruges between 1540 and 1548. He went to Italy in early youth, and worked in Florence and Rome. He was invited by the Elector of Bavaria to Munich, where he produced his principal works (in fresco) and acquired a high reputation. Died at Munich in 1628.

See MILLIN, "Dictionnaire des Beaux-Arts."

Candido Decembrio. See DECEMBRIO.

Can'dĭ-dus I-sau'rus, [Κάνδιδος Ίσαυρος,] a Byzantine historian, who lived in the reign of Anastasius, (490–518 A.D.) He was a person of great influence, and wrote a Byzantine history of the period from 457 to 491. His work is lost; but a summary of its contents is preserved by Photius.

Candish. See CAVENDISH, (THOMAS.)

Candito. See CANDIDO, (PIETRO.)

Cand'lish, (ROBERT SMITH,) a popular Scottish preacher of the present era, and one of the most influential ministers of the Free Church. He was appointed to Saint George's Church, Edinburgh, several years before the secession from the Established Church, which occurred in 1843. In the contest which resulted in that disruption he took a prominent part as coadjutor of Dr. Chalmers. He has published sermons, "Scripture Characters," a "Treatise on the Atonement," and other works.

Candolle, de, dẹh kôN'dol', (AUGUSTIN PYRAMUS,) a distinguished botanist and naturalist, of French extraction, was born at Geneva on the 4th of February, 1778. He was educated at the College of Geneva, where he received lessons in philosophy from the celebrated Saussure. In 1796 he went to Paris, to perfect himself in physical and medical sciences, and became a favourite pupil of the botanist Desfontaines. He also formed intimacies with Cuvier, A. von Humboldt, and Lamarck. His first production was "History of Fleshy (or Succulent) Plants," ("Histoire des Plantes grasses," 1799–1803.) He took his degree as doctor of medicine in Paris in 1804, presenting for his thesis an able "Essay on the Medicinal Properties of Plants." He acquired a European reputation by an improved edition of Lamarck's "Flora of France," which he revised at the request of the author, and the first volume of which appeared about 1805. In 1808 he was appointed professor of botany in the Faculty of Medicine at Montpellier, and director of the Botanic Garden. He published in 1813 his "Elementary Theory of Botany," ("Théorie élémentaire de la Botanique,") which is remarkable for profoundness of views, and is called by some his master-piece. In this work he developed his new classification of plants according to the natural system. In 1816 he resigned his chair and removed to Geneva, the citizens of which founded for him in 1817 a chair of natural history. Having conceived the plan of a great work which should comprise a description of all known plants, he published in 1818 the first volume, with the title of "Natural System of the Vegetable Kingdom," ("Regni vegetabilis Systema naturale.") After the publication of the second volume, (1821,) he discontinued this work, the plan of which was too vast for one man to execute. His "Introduction to the Natural System of the Vegetable Kingdom," ("Prodromus Systematis naturalis Regni vegetabilis,") which he began to publish in 1824, but did not live to finish, is a modification of the original plan, and is a work of great value. It presents a methodical arrangement of all known plants, by orders, genera, and species. He described the organs of plants, with all their anatomical details, and developed the doctrine of metamorphosis, in his "Vegetable Organography," ("Organographie végétale," 1827.) In 1828 he was elected a foreign associate of the Academy of Sciences of Paris, being the first botanist since Linnæus that had received that honour. He published many other treatises on botany and physiology, and obtained a high reputation as a lecturer. He died at Geneva in September, 1841. After his death his "Prodromus" was continued by his son and other botanists.

De Candolle occupies the highest rank among the botanists of the nineteenth century; and among those who have propounded new botanical theories there has been none whose works have been more influential in promoting the philosophical tendency of the science.

See FLOURENS, "Éloge historique de P. de Candolle," 1842, and an English version of the same, in the "Smithsonian Report" for 1859, p. 271; DUNAL, "Éloge d'A. P. Decandolle," 1842; MORREN, "Notice sur la Vie d'A. P. Decandolle," 1843; A. BRONGNIART, "Notice sur A. P. Decandolle," 1846; DELARIVE, "A. P. Decandolle, sa Vie et ses Travaux," 1851; "Foreign Quarterly Review" for April, 1833.

Cane della Scala. See SCALA.

Cañes, kån'yěs, or **Cannes,** (FRANCISCO,) a Spanish monk, born at Valencia, was for many years a missionary at Damascus. On his return to Spain he published an Arabic Grammar, and a valuable "Spanish-Latin-Arabic Dictionary," ("Diccionario Español-Latino-Arabigo," 1787.) Died in 1795.

Canetta, de, då kå-net'tå, (Don ANDREA Hurtado de Mendoza—oor-tå'Do då měn-do'thå,) MARQUIS, was appointed Viceroy of Peru about 1550. He restored order, and reduced several turbulent leaders to submission. Died at Lima in 1560.

Canevari, kå-nå-vå'ree, (DEMETRIO,) an Italian physician, distinguished as a writer, was born at Genoa in 1559; died in 1625.

Canga Argüelles, kång'gå aR-gwěl'yěs, (JOSÉ,) a Spanish statesman, born in Asturias about 1770. Under the constitutional régime which was initiated by the revolution of 1820, he was minister of finance for a short period. In 1823 the absolutists obtained the ascendency, and he fled or was exiled to England, where he remained about seven years, and wrote several works. His "Dictionary of Finance" ("Diccionario de Hacienda," 5 vols., 1828) is one of his most important productions. Died in 1843.

Cange. See DU CANGE.

Cangiage. See CAMBIASO.

Cangiamilla, kån-jå-měl'lå, (FRANCESCO EMMANUELE,) an Italian theologian, born at Palermo in 1702. He wrote "Embryologia Sacra," (1751,) which was translated into several languages. Died in 1763.

See "Nouvelle Biographie Générale."

Canina, kå-nee'nå, (LUIGI,) CAVALIERE, an Italian architect and antiquary, born at Casal in 1793. He published several esteemed works, among which are a "Topographical Plan (Indicazione) of Ancient Rome," (1831,) "Ancient Architecture described and illustrated by Monuments," (9 vols.; 3d edition, 1844,) and "On the Architecture most proper for Christian Temples," ("Sull' Architetture più propria dei Tempj cristiani," 1843.) He was professor of architecture in the Academy of Turin. Died in 1856.

Canini, kå-nee'nee, [Lat. CANIN'IUS,] (ANGELO,) an eminent Italian linguist and grammarian, born in Tuscany in 1521. He taught Greek, Hebrew, Syriac, etc. in Venice, Rome, and Padua, and was afterwards professor in the University of Paris. He published a good Greek Grammar, and a "Grammar of the Syriac, Chaldee, etc.," (1554.) Died in 1557.

See BAYLE, "Historical and Critical Dictionary."

Canini, (GIOVANNI ANGELO,) a painter and engraver, born in Rome about 1620, was a pupil of Domenichino. He went to France with Cardinal Chigi, and, under the anspices of Colbert, engraved a collection of portraits of the great men of antiquity. The word "iconografia," ("iconography,") invented by him, was first used in the title of this work. Died in 1665.

See LANZI, "History of Painting in Italy."

Canino, PRINCE OF. See BONAPARTE, (CHARLES LUCIEN.)

Canisius, kå-nee'se-us, (HENDRIK,) a Dutch theologian, born at Nymwegen, was eminent for his learning in church antiquities. He professed canon law at Ingolstadt about twenty years, and died in 1610. His principal work is entitled "Ancient Lessons," ("Antiquæ Lectiones.") He was a nephew of Petrus Canisius.

Canisius, (PETRUS,) a Dutch Jesuit, whose proper name was PIETER DE HONDT, (dẹh hònt,) was born at Nymwegen about 1520. He distinguished himself at the Council of Trent in 1545, and was appointed court preacher to the emperor Ferdinand I. Among his works is "Summa Doctrinæ Christianæ." Died in 1597.

See M. RADER, "De Vita P. Canisii," 1612, J. DORIGNY, "Vie du R. P. P. Canisius," 1692; FULIGATTI, "Vita del P. P. Canisio," 1649.

Canisius-Cannius, kȧ-nee′se-us kȧn′ne-us, (NICO-LAAS,) a philologist, born at Amsterdam, was a secretary and friend of Erasmus, who employed him in translation from the Greek. Died in 1555.

Canitz, von, fon kȧ′nits, (FRIEDRICH RUDOLF LUD-WIG,) BARON, a German poet, born at Berlin in 1654. He was appointed a councillor of state, and employed in diplomatic missions by the King of Prussia. He died in Berlin in 1699, and his poems, consisting of odes, satires, and elegies, were published in 1700, with the title of "Nebenstunden unterschiedener Gedichte." "The poems of Canitz," says Guizot, "have neither original-ity nor *verve;* but he had the merit of being simple and natural while a fantastic and rude taste prevailed among his contemporaries." (" Biographie Universelle.")

See ERSCH and GRUBER, "Allgemeine Encyklopaedie."

Canitz und Dallwitz, kȧ′nits ŏont dȧl′ẘits, BARON, a Prussian statesman and soldier, born in 1787, was minister of foreign affairs from 1846 to 1848. Died in 1850.

Cā′nĭ-us, (RUFUS,) a Latin poet, born at Cadiz, was a friend of Martial. He was living in 88 A.D.

Cañizares, de, dȧ kȧn-ye-thȧ′rĕs, (JOSÉ,) a popular Spanish dramatist, born in Madrid. He excelled in comedy, and presents, says Velasquez, "a faithful pic-ture of manners in a very spirited style." Died in 1750.

See TICKNOR, "History of Spanish Literature."

Cannabich, kȧn′nȧ-bik, (JOHANN GUNTHER FRIED-RICH,) a German geographer, born at Sondershausen in 1777. He wrote a "Manual of Geography," (1816,) which soon ran through twelve editions, and other works.

See E. KEYSER, "J. G. F. Cannabich, in seinem Leben," etc., 1854.

Cannamares, kȧn-nȧ-mȧ′rĕs, (JUAN,) a Spaniard, who was executed in 1492 for attempting to kill Ferdi-nand V. It is supposed he was insane.

Canne, kan, (JOHN,) an English preacher, who be-came the leader of the English Brownists at Amster-dam soon after the restoration of 1660. He published an esteemed edition of the Bible, with marginal notes and references, (1664,) which was often reprinted.

Cannegieter, kȧn′neh-ğee′ter, (HERMANN,) a Ger-man jurist, born at Arnheim in 1725, wrote a work on Roman law, (" Observationes Juris Romani," 1768,) which is highly esteemed. Died in 1804.

Cannes. See CAÑES.

Can′ning, (CHARLES FOX,) LIEUTENANT-COLONEL, a British officer, who was aide-de-camp of the Duke of Wellington in the campaigns of the Peninsular war and at Waterloo, (1815,) where he was killed.

Canning, (CHARLES JOHN,) VISCOUNT, the son of the eminent statesman George Canning, was born at Brompton in 1812. He succeeded to the title of Vis-count at the death of his mother in 1837, and joined the Conservative party. In 1841 he was appointed under-secretary of foreign affairs. In 1852 or 1853 he became postmaster-general, and a member of Lord Aberdeen's cabinet. He succeeded Lord Dalhousie as Governor-General of India in 1855. His conduct in the critical period of the Sepoy mutiny was severely censured, in 1858, by Lord Ellenborough, then a cabinet minister; but Canning vindicated himself with such success that his opponent resigned his office. (See ELLENBOROUGH.) He was succeeded by Lord Elgin about August, 1861. Died in England in June, 1862.

Canning, (GEORGE,) a distinguished English states-man, orator, and wit, born in London on the 11th of April, 1770, was the son of George Canning, a lawyer without fortune, who died in 1771. He was educated at Eton and Oxford, where he gained honours and began to write verses. In 1793 he entered Parliament as a Tory and supporter of Pitt, to whom he adhered constantly, and in 1796 was appointed under-secretary of state. The next year Canning, Ellis, Frere, and others began to issue weekly the famous series of political satires called "The Anti-Jacobin," which some eminent critics have pronounced one of the wittiest books in the language. He married a rich heiress, a daughter of General John Scott, about 1800. His success as a parliamentary debater was very brilliant, and rendered him an efficient leader of his party. On the dissolution of Pitt's ministry, in 1801, he shared the fortunes of that chief, and afterwards opposed

the administration of Addington for several sessions. In April, 1807, he was appointed secretary for foreign affairs in the ministry of the Duke of Portland, and favoured the vigorous prosecution of the war against France. " If ever a man was made for the service and salvation of a party," says Brougham, " Canning seemed raised up for that of the Tories." This party, however, preferred to follow Lord Castlereagh, who was secretary of war. A dispute between these rivals, in 1809, led to a challenge from Castlereagh, and an exchange of shots, by which Canning was slightly wounded. In consequence of this affair he retired or was dismissed from the cabinet. He made, in 1812, eloquent pleas for Catholic emancipation, to which cause at various times he rendered important services; but he constantly opposed parliamentary re-form. The city of Liverpool elected him as its repre-sentative in 1812, and at several successive elections. He was censured for serving under his successful rival Castlereagh, who in 1814 gave him an unimportant mis-sion to Portugal. He was appointed Governor-General of India in 1822; but, while he was preparing for the voyage, Castlereagh committed suicide, and Canning succeeded his late rival as secretary of foreign affairs in the cabinet of Lord Liverpool, in September, 1822. His policy in the latter years of his life was more liberal than that of other Tory leaders. In April, 1827, he was ap-pointed first lord of the treasury, or premier, in place of Lord Liverpool. The Duke of Wellington, Lord Eldon, and the other ministers having resigned in con-sequence of that change, Canning was compelled to re-sort to the support of the Whigs, some of whom accepted office under him. His health had been feeble for some time when he made his last speech in Parliament in June, 1827, and he died in August of that year, leaving a son, Charles John, Lord Canning.

" His declamation," says Brougham, " though often powerful, always beautifully ornate, never deficient in admirable diction, was certainly not of the highest class. Of his powers of argumentation, his capacity for the pur-suits of abstract science, his genius for adorning the least attractive subjects, there remains an imperishable record in his celebrated speeches on the 'Currency,' of all his efforts the most brilliant and the most happy." He made an important change in the foreign policy of Eng-land, in consequence of which that country ceased to be subservient to the designs of the Holy Alliance.

See ROBERT BELL, "Life of Canning," 1846; A. G. STAPLETON, "The Political Life of George Canning," 1831 and 1859; "Auto-biography of William Jerdan," vol. ii.; BROUGHAM, "Statesmen of the Time of George III.:" W. T. KRUG, "Canning's Denkmal," etc.," 1827; RUEDER, "G. Canning, seine Leben, seine Politik, etc.," 1827; REDE, "Memoirs of G. Canning," 2 vols., 1828; "Encyclo-pædia Britannica;" "Edinburgh Review" for November, 1822; "Foreign Quarterly" for October, 1831.

Canning, (STRATFORD.) See STRATFORD DE RED-CLIFFE.

Cano, kȧ′no, (ALONZO,) one of the greatest artists that Spain has produced, born at Granada about 1600, was a painter, sculptor, and architect. He has been called the Michael Angelo of Spain. He studied paint-ing under Pacheco and Juan de Castillo, and sculpture under Montanes. Having acquired a high reputation, he went to Madrid, and in 1638 received from Philip IV. the title of painter to the king. He painted many pieces for the churches of Seville, Madrid, Granada, etc. A "Conception of the Virgin," at Granada, is called his master-piece. It is reported that on his death-bed he re-fused the crucifix presented to him by a priest, on account of its bad workmanship. Died in 1664.

See QUILLIET, "Dictionnaire des Peintres Espagnols;" BRYAN, "Dictionary of Painters."

Cano, [Lat. CA′NUS,] (MELCHIOR,) a Spanish theo-logian, born at Tarancon in 1523, entered the order of Saint Dominic. In 1546 he became professor of theology in the University of Salamanca. He opposed the Jesuits, and discountenanced absurd scholastic questions. His treatise "On Theological Subjects" ("De Locis theo-logicis") is highly commended for its sentiments and style. He wrote some other works on theology. Died in 1560.

Cano, del, dĕl kȧ′no, (SEBASTIAN,) a Spanish navi-gator, born in Guipuzcoa, is said to have been the first who circumnavigated the globe. He was captain of one of the ships under Magellan when the latter was killed at the Philippine Isles, and, returning in the Victory by the Cape of Good Hope, he arrived in Spain in 1522. Died in 1526.

See F. DE NAVARRETE, "Relaciones de Viages," etc.

Cano de Arevalo, kä'no dà â-râ-vä'lo, (JUAN,) a Spanish painter, born in 1656; died in 1696.

Canonica, kä-non'e-kä, (LUIGI,) an eminent Italian architect, born at Milan about 1742, designed several theatres in Milan, Mantua, and Brescia. His most remarkable works are the Palazzo Orsini, the Casa Canonica, (his own mansion,) and the amphitheatre of the Porta Vercellina at Milan. Died in 1834.

See NAGLER, "Neues Allgemeines Künstler-Lexikon."

Ça-non'ǐ-cus, an Indian chief of the Narragansett tribe, was born about 1565. He was a friend of Roger Williams, to whom he gave a large tract of land. Died in 1647.

Canonieri, kä-no-ne-ä'ree, [Lat. CANONE'RIUS,] (PIETRO ANDREA,) an Italian physician and doctor of law, born at Genoa, flourished about 1600.

Canoppi, kä-nop'pee, (ANTONIO,) a skilful Italian scene-painter, born in 1773, practised his art for several years in Venice and Mantua. When Italy became subject to the power of the French, whom he had opposed, Canoppi fled to Vienna. In 1807 he removed to Moscow, where he decorated the hall of the senate and some private palaces. He painted for the theatre of Saint Petersburg many scenes, which are greatly admired, and wrote several treatises on art. Died in 1832.

Ça-no'pus or **Ça-no'bus,** a water-god of Egyptian mythology, whose figure was represented on water-vessels.

Canova, kä-no'vä, (ANTONIO,) a celebrated Italian sculptor, born at Possagno, in Venetia, on the 1st of November, 1757, was the son of P. Canova, an architect and sculptor. He received lessons in art in the studios of Torretti and Ferrari, of Venice. Having produced about 1778 a group of "Dædalus and Icarus," which was much admired at Venice, he exhibited the same at Rome the next year. Gavin Hamilton, who was a high authority in art, praised his success in copying nature, and encouraged his innate aspirations towards the classic and ideal style. In 1782 he removed his studio to Rome, and increased his celebrity by his group of "Theseus and the Minotaur," which announced the regeneration of modern sculpture. Then followed a monument of Pope Clement XIV., (1787,) and numerous groups of subjects from ancient mythology, among which are "Cupid and Psyche," "The Graces," and "Venus and Adonis." In 1802 he was invited to Paris by Bonaparte, of whom he executed an admirable statue, which came into the possession of the Duke of Wellington. He was chosen an associate of the Institute of France. In 1805 he produced an exquisite figure of "Venus Victorious," with the features of Pauline Bonaparte. In 1810 he went to Paris to make the portrait of the empress Maria Louisa. On his return to Rome he was chosen president of the Academy of Saint Luke. In 1815 the pope sent him to reclaim the works of art of which the French had despoiled the galleries of Italy. Soon after this event he received the title of Marquis of Ischia. He afterwards executed a statue of Washington, which is not unworthy of his fame. Having produced fifty statues, as many busts, besides numerous cenotaphs, groups, etc., he died at Venice in October, 1822, with the reputation of the greatest sculptor of his age.

See MISSIRINI, "Vita di Canova," 1827; CICOGNARA, "Vita di Canova," 1823; QUATREMÈRE DE QUINCY, "Canova et ses Ouvrages," 1836; "Essai sur la Vie et les Ouvrages de Canova," by RÉVEIL and DE LATOUCHE, 1825; J. S. MEMES, "Memoirs of Antonio Canova," Edinburgh, 1825; "Encyclopædia Britannica;" FERNOW, "Ueber den Bildhauer Canova," 1806; G. ROSINI, "Saggio sulla Vita di A. Canova," 1825.

Canovai, kä-no-vä'ee, almost kä-no-vī', (STANISLAO,) a learned Italian priest, born at Florence in 1740. He taught matnematics at Cortona and Parma. In 1788 he produced a prize essay in support of the claim of Americus Vespucius as the first discoverer of America. Canovai and Gaetan del Ricco translated La Caille's "Elements of Mathematics. He published other esteemed works. Died in 1811.

See POZZETTI, "Elogio di S. Canovai," 1812.

Canrobert, kòN'ro'baiR', (FRANÇOIS CERTAIN,) a French marshal, born in Brittany in 1809. He entered the army about 1828, distinguished himself at the siege of Constantine in 1837, and was rapidly promoted. He fought many campaigns in Algeria, and in 1850 returned to France with the rank of general of brigade. Soon after that date he became aide-de-camp to Louis Napoleon, and was made a general of division in 1853. He commanded the first division of the army sent to the Crimea in 1854, and was wounded at the battle of the Alma. On the death of Saint-Arnaud in September, the chief command devolved on Canrobert, who, in conjunction with Lord Raglan, began the siege of Sebastopol. He was wounded at Inkerman, November 5, 1854. The ill success of the allies, and the difficulty arising from a divided command, rendered his position so painful that he resigned to Pelissier the chief command of the French army in May, 1855. He received a marshal's bâton in 1856, and in the spring of 1859 was assigned to the third corps of the army of the Alps. He commanded the reserve at Solferino, June, 1859.

See VAPEREAU, "Dictionnaire des Contemporains."

Canstatt, kän'stät, (KARL FRIEDRICH,) a German physician and medical writer, born at Ratisbon in 1807, became professor at Erlangen. Died in 1850.

Canstein, von, fon kän'stīn, (CARL HILDEBRAND,) BARON, a German philanthropist, born at Lindenberg in 1667, was the founder of the Canstein Bible Society of Halle. Desiring to diffuse Christian principles, he raised a fund to print the Bible about 1712. The enterprise was very successful, and millions of Bibles and New Testaments were printed and sold at low prices. Died in 1719.

See AUGUST H. FRANCKE, "Memoria Cansteiniana," 1722.

Cant. See KANT.

Cant, (ANDREW,) an eminent Scottish minister, who in the reign of Charles I. zealously supported the Covenant. In 1640 he was one of the chaplains of the army of Covenanters, and about the same time became minister of Aberdeen. He is said to have been a royalist in the civil war. He died about 1664. According to the "Spectator," No. 147, the word *cant* originated in his affected tone.

See CHAMBERS, "Biographical Dictionary of Eminent Scotsmen."

Cant, känt, (AREND,) a Dutch anatomist, died young, at Dort, in 1723.

Cantacuzene. See CANTACUZENUS.

Can-ta-cu-ze'nus, Anglicized as **Can'ta-cu-zēne',** [Gr. Καντακουζηνός; Fr. CANTACUZÈNE, kòN'tä'kü'zȧn',] (JOHN,) a Byzantine emperor of superior talents, prime minister in the reign of Andronicus III., who died in 1341, leaving a son, John Palæologus, aged nine years, during whose minority Cantacuzene was regent. Apocaucus and the empress-mother Anne having conspired against him, he appealed to arms, and was proclaimed emperor by his partisans. After a civil war of several years, Anne and her son agreed, in 1347, to receive him as a partner in the empire. The quarrel, however, was renewed a few years later, and the nation fell into such disorder that Cantacuzene abdicated in 1355 and became a monk. He wrote a work on Byzantine History from 1320 to 1357.

See PARISOT, "Cantacuzène Homme d'État et Historien," 1845.

Cantacuzenus, (MATTHEW,) a son of the preceding, born about 1325. He continued the civil war after his father's abdication, was taken prisoner, and compelled by John Palæologus to enter a cloister.

Can-ta-cu-ze'nus or **Can'ta-cu-zēne',** (SERBAN,) Prince of Wallachia, claimed to be descended from the emperor John Cantacuzene. He designed to liberate Wallachia from the Turkish yoke, and formed an alliance with the Czar of Russia. While he was preparing for hostilities, he died about 1685; and it was reported that he was poisoned by his nephew, Constantine Brancovan Bessaraba.

Cantacuzenus or **Cantacuzene,** (STEPHEN,) a son of Constantine Cantacuzene, became Vaivode of Wallachia in 1714. He was deposed by the Turks, and put to death, in 1716.

Canta-Gallina, kän'tä gȧl-lee'nä, (REMI,) an Italian painter and engraver, was, according to some writers, the master of Callot. Died at Florence about 1630.

Cantalicio, kån-tä-lee'cho, [Lat. CANTALYÇ'IUS,] (GIOVANNI BATTISTA,) a Latin poet, surnamed IL VALENTINO, (èl vä-lên-tee'no,) was born at Cantalice. He wrote a poem of which the "Great Captain" Gonsalvo was the hero, and many epigrams. Died about 1514.

Cantarini, kån-tä-ree'nee, (SIMONE,) an eminent Italian painter and engraver, called THE PESARESE, or SIMONE DA PESARO, (se-mo'nä dä pä'sä-ro,) was born at Pesaro in 1612. He studied under Guido Reni at Bologna, and in some respects rivalled that master. He worked in Rome, Mantua, and Verona, his quarrelsome temper, it is said, preventing him from remaining long in one place. Among his master-pieces are a "San Domenico" and a "Magdalene." He painted portraits with success, and was an excellent colorist. Died at Verona in 1648.

See TICOZZI, "Dizionario;" LANZI, "History of Painting in Italy."

Cante del Gabrielli d'Agobbio, kån'tä dêl gä-bRe-el'lee dä-gob'be-o, an Italian leader of the Guelph party, notorious for his cruelty. He became podesta of Florence in 1301, and banished numerous citizens, among whom was the poet Dante.

Cantel, kôN'têl', (PIERRE JOSEPH,) a French Jesuit and scholar, born in 1645, was employed on the editions of Latin authors for the education of the dauphin. He published Justin, (1677,) and Valerius Maximus, (1679,) with notes. Died in 1684.

Cantemir or **Kantemir,** kan'tęh-mįr or kan'tęh-meer, (ANTIOCHUS,) PRINCE, an eminent writer, born at Constantinople about 1709, was a son of Demetrius Cantemir, noticed below. He was educated in Russia. He wrote a number of satires which are remarkable for good sense and which contributed to polish the Russian language. About 1736 he was sent to Paris as Russian ambassador. He translated several Latin and French works into Russian. He died in 1744, leaving a high reputation as a poet, a diplomatist, and a man. Brockhaus's "Conversations-Lexikon" gives his name as KANTEMIR, (CONSTANTINOS DEMETRIOS.)

See a "Notice sur Cantemir," prefixed to GUASCO's French version of his Satires, 1750.

Cantemir, (DEMETRIUS,) an eminent historian and Orientalist, born in 1673, was a son of the Vaivode or Governor of Moldavia. In 1710 he was appointed Vaivode of Moldavia by the Turkish Sultan, and in 1711 he made an alliance with Peter the Great, then at war with the Turks. He was driven out of Moldavia in the same year, and afterwards lived in Russia. He wrote, besides other works, a "History of the Origin and Decay of the Ottoman Empire," (in Latin,) which is highly esteemed and has been translated into several languages. Died in 1723.

See "Nouvelle Biographie Générale."

Canter, kån'tęr, [Lat. CANTE'RUS,] (THEODORUS,) a Dutch scholar, brother of Willem, noticed below, born at Utrecht in 1545. He became a consul in 1588, and governor in 1594. He published "Various Readings," ("Variæ Lectiones," 1574,) which was commended by Scaliger. Died in 1617.

See "Scaligerana;" BURMANN, "Trajectum eruditum."

Canter, [Lat. CANTE'RUS,] (WILLEM,) an able Dutch critic and philologist, born at Utrecht in 1542, is said to have had no passion except for study. He became a resident of Louvain, and published several philological works, one of which, entitled "New Readings," ("Novæ Lectiones,") "deserves especial notice as almost the first effort of an art which," says Hallam, "has done much for ancient literature,—that of restoring a corrupt text, through conjecture guided by skilful sagacity, and upon principles which we may call scientific." ("Introduction to the Literature of Europe.") He also published good editions of Æschylus, Sophocles, and Euripides. Died at Louvain in 1575.

See MELCHIOR ADAM, "Vitæ Philosophorum;" DE THOU, "Éloges;" NICÉRON, "Mémoires."

Canterbury, kån'tęr-bęr-e, (CHARLES MANNERS SUTTON,) VISCOUNT, an English statesman, son of the Archbishop of Canterbury, born in 1780. He entered Parliament in 1807, and was elected Speaker of the House of Commons in 1817. He performed the duties of this office with dignity until 1835, and passed into the House of Lords with the title of Viscount Canterbury. He died in 1845, and left his title to his son, Charles John.

Canterzani, kån-têR-dzä'nee, (SEBASTIANO,) an Italian mathematician, born at Bologna in 1734. He was professor of mathematics in the University of Bologna for nearly forty years, beginning at 1760. He wrote able elementary treatises on geometry, arithmetic, etc., and became president of the Institute of his native city. Died in 1819.

See SCHIASSI, "Elogium S. Canterzani," 1819.

Can'tha-rus, [Κάνθαρος,] a Greek sculptor, born at Sicyon, lived about 260 B.C.

Cantillon, kôN'te'yôN', (PHILIP,) a merchant, who removed from London to Paris, where he established a banking-house and became rich. It is said he was murdered by his valet in London in 1733. He had written an "Essay on Commerce," and "Analysis of Trade, Commerce, Coin, etc.," which were printed after his death.

See GRIMM, "Correspondance."

Cantipratenus or **Cantipratensis.** See THOMAS CANTIPRATENSIS.

Can-tǐ-unc'u-la, the Latin name of CLAUDE CHANSONNETTE, (klôd shôN'so'nêt',) an eloquent lawyer, born at Metz. He studied at Leipsic and Bâle: the latter city, in 1519, founded for him a chair of law. Erasmus praised the purity and dignity of his Latin style. The Emperor of Germany employed him in several important negotiations. He died about 1560, leaving a few legal treatises.

See ERASMUS, "De Cicerone;" MELCHIOR ADAM, "Vitæ Jurisconsultorum Germaniæ," etc.

Canton, kån'ton, (JOHANN GABRIEL,) a German painter, born at Vienna in 1710; died in 1753.

Can'ton, (JOHN,) an English natural philosopher, born at Stroud in 1718, lived mostly in London, where he taught school many years. He was the first person in England who verified Franklin's hypothesis that lightning is identical with the electric fluid, (1752.) He had previously made some discoveries in electricity, which procured him a Fellowship in the Royal Society about 1750. In 1765 that society awarded him a gold medal for his demonstration that water is compressible. He wrote several treatises, which are inserted in the "Philosophic Transactions." Died in 1772.

See "Life of Canton," by his son, in "Biographia Britannica."

Cantoni, kån-to'nee, (SIMONE,) an Italian architect, born at Maggio, became a resident of Milan, where he erected some fine edifices, among which are the Palazzo Serbelloni and Palazzo Mellerio. He also designed the ducal palace at Genoa. Died in 1818.

Cantù, kån-too', (CESARE,) a popular Italian historian, born at Brivio, near Milan, in 1805. About the age of eighteen he became professor of belles-lettres at Sondrio, and afterwards resided in Milan. He published in 1842 an "Essay on the History of Lombardy in the Seventeenth Century." For the liberal ideas expressed in this, he was imprisoned one year. His great work is his "Universal History," ("Storia universale," 20 vols., 1837-42,) which has been very successful and has been translated into English and French. He also wrote a "History of Italian Literature," several popular hymns and poems, and an educational work called "Juvenile Readings," ("Letture giovanili,") which has passed through more than thirty editions. His style is regarded as a model. In the revolution of 1848 he acted with the Liberal party.

See "Nouvelle Biographie Générale."

Cant'well, (ANDREW,) an Irish physician, born in Tipperary, graduated at Montpellier, in France, in 1729. He was received as doctor in the faculty of Paris in 1742, and was chosen professor of surgery in that city in 1750. He wrote several professional treatises. Died about 1764.

See ÉLOY, "Dictionnaire de la Médecine."

Cantwell, (ANDREW SAMUEL MICHAEL,) a son of the preceding, translated into French Gibbon's "History," and other popular English works. He became librarian to the Hôpital des Invalides, Paris, where he died in 1802.

Canuel, kȧ'nü'êl', (SIMON,) a French general, born in Poitou in 1767, was commandant at Lyons under the Directory. Died in 1841.

Canus. See CANO.

Canut, the French of CANUTE, which see.

Canute, ka̤-nūt′, originally **Cnut, Knut,** or **Knud,** [Danish pron. knoot or knooᴅ; Fr. CANUT, kȧ′nü′,] the second king of Denmark of that name, and the conqueror of England, was the son of Sweyn, King of Denmark, who, after subjecting a great part of England, died in 1014. Canute was then proclaimed king by the Danish army, and after the death of Edmund Ironside, in 1016, the whole Anglo-Saxon nation submitted to his sway. He married Emma, the widow of Ethelred II., and gained the favour of his subjects by his prudent policy and monastic piety. He founded several monasteries, and made a pilgrimage to Rome. Denmark and Norway were also under the dominion of Canute, who was the most powerful monarch of his time. The memorable manner in which he rebuked the flattery of his courtiers, who said that all things were possible to him, is thus related by Hume: "He ordered his chair to be set on the sea-shore while the tide was rising, and, as the waters approached, commanded them to retire, and obey him who was the lord of the ocean. When the sea still advanced, and began to wash him, he turned to his courtiers, and remarked that power resided with one Being alone, who could say to the ocean, 'Thus far shalt thou go, and no farther, and here shall thy proud waves be stayed.'" He died in 1036, leaving three sons, Sweyn, Harold, and Hardicanute.

See HUME, "History of England," vol. i. chap. ii.; FREEMAN, "Norman Conquest," vol. i. chaps. v. and vi.

Canute III., a king of Denmark, known as SAINT CANUTE, was the son of Sweyn II., and grandson of the preceding. He succeeded his elder brother, Harold, in 1080. His partiality to the clergy and severity to the people produced great disaffection, which grew at last into a revolt. Canute was assassinated at Odense in 1086, and left the crown to his brother, Eric the Good.

See ANNIBALE ADAMI, "Vita del Re S. Canuto," 1682; BIRCHE-ROD, "K. Knud des heiliges Historie," 1773; MATTHEW OF WEST-MINSTER, "Flores Historiarum."

Canute IV. (or **V.** according to some authorities) was son of Prince Magnus, and grandson of Nicholas, King of Denmark. At the abdication of Eric in 1147, Canute and Sweyn (or Suenon) III. disputed for the crown of Denmark by civil war, in which the former was defeated, but retained a part of the kingdom. He was assassinated by order of Sweyn in 1156.

Canute V., King of Denmark, the eldest son of Valdemar I., was born in 1162, and ascended the throne at his father's death in 1182. He subdued Mecklenburg, and took the title of King of the Slaves and Vandals. He refused to take part in the crusade which the pope promoted about 1186. Afterwards he waged a successful war against Adolph, Duke of Holstein, whom he took prisoner. Under his wise reign Denmark was more prosperous and powerful than it had ever been. He died in 1202, and was succeeded by his brother, Valdemar II.

See HOLBERG, "Danmarks Riges Historie;" SAXO GRAMMATI-CUS, "Danorum Regum Historia."

Canute, ka̤-nūt′, of Sweden, was the son of Eric IX., King of Sweden, who was killed in 1160. Charles Sverkerson then reigned, by the choice of the bishops and nobles, until 1168, when Canute defeated him in battle, killed him, and became king. His reign was mostly peaceful. He died in 1199, and left a son, Eric X.

Canuti, kä-noo′tee, (DOMENICO MARIA,) a skilful Italian fresco-painter, born at Bologna in 1620, was a pupil of Guido. He excelled in composition and foreshortening, and was a skilful engraver. Died in 1684.

See LANZI, "History of Painting in Italy."

Canz, kȧnts, (ISRAEL GOTTLIEB,) a German philosopher, born at Heinsheim in 1690. "He was," says Guizot, "one of the most profound disciples of Wolf, and was successively professor of eloquence, philosophy, and theology in his native city." According to another account, he occupied these chairs in Tübingen instead of Heinsheim. He published many works, one of which, entitled "The Use or Advantage of the Leibnitzian and Wolfian Philosophy in Theology," ("Philosophiæ Leibnitzianæ et Wolfianæ Usus in Theologia,") contributed much to the diffusion of the philosophy of Leibnitz and Wolf in Germany. Died in 1753.

See ERSCH und GRUBER, "Allgemeine Encyklopaedie;" ADELUNG, Supplement to JÖCHER'S "Allgemeines Gelehrten-Lexikon."

Cap, kȧp, (PAUL ANTOINE,) a French pharmacist and naturalist, born at Mâcon in 1788. He published a prize memoir "On the Classification of Medicaments," (1823,) a "History of Pharmacy," (1851,) and a "Museum of Natural History," (1853.)

Capaccio, kä-pät′cho, (GIULIO CESARE,) an Italian writer, born at Campagna about 1560, was for thirty years secretary of the city of Naples. He wrote a "History of Naples," "The Secretary," and other works. Died in 1631.

Capanée. See CAPANEUS.

Cap′a-neūs, [Gr. Καπανεύς; Fr. CAPANÉE, kä′pä′nȧ′,] an Argive hero, was a son of Hipponous, and one of the seven chiefs who led an expedition against Thebes to restore Polynices. The poets relate that he was killed at Thebes by a thunderbolt of Jupiter, whom he had offended by impiety.

Capasso, kä-päs′so, (NICCOLÒ,) a Neapolitan poet, born at Fratta in 1671, was professor of civil and canon law in the University of Naples. His version of Homer's "Iliad" is called his master-piece, and displays original genius, though not much like the Iliad itself. "His style," says Ginguené, "is regarded as among the most sprightly and piquant." Died in 1746.

See TIPALDO, "Biografia degli Italiani illustri."

Capdueil, de, deh kȧp′dul′ or kȧp′du′ye, or **Capduelh,** kȧp′du′êl′, (PONS,) a French troubadour of noble birth, who preached a crusade, in favour of which he also composed poems. He afterwards joined the crusade which was conducted by Philip Augustus about 1190.

Capece, kä-pä′chä, or **Capecio,** kä-pä′cho, [Lat. CA-PYҪ′IUS; Fr. CAPÈCE, kä′pȧss′,] (SCIPIONE,) an eminent Latin poet, was professor of law in the University of Naples. His principal poem, "On the First Principles of Things," ("De Principiis Rerum," 1546,) was much admired, and compared to the great work of Lucretius. The versification and Latinity are better than the philosophy, which teaches that air is the principle of all things. He also wrote elegies and epigrams, a poem on John the Baptist, and a legal treatise. Died about 1562.

See BAYLE, "Historical and Critical Dictionary."

Capece-Latro, kä-pä′chä lä′tro, (GIUSEPPE,) a liberal Italian prelate, born in Naples in 1744, became Archbishop of Tarentum. He wrote a treatise against the celibacy of priests, which attracted much attention, and other works. He was minister of the interior under Joseph Bonaparte and Murat between 1808 and 1815. Died in 1836.

See NICCOLÒ CANDIA, "Elogio storico di G. Capecelatro," 1837; ERSCH und GRUBER, "Allgemeine Encyklopaedie."

Capefigue, kȧp′fêg′, (BAPTISTE HONORÉ RAYMOND,) a French historian and editor of the royalist party, was born at Marseilles in 1801. He became a resident of Paris in 1821, and soon after that date editor of the "Quotidienne." He subsequently wrote for the "Temps," the "Courrier," the "Gazette de France," and other journals, some of which he edited. He has produced a great number of historical works, among which are a "History of Philippe Auguste," (1829,) "Europe during the Consulate and the Empire," (1839-41,) "History of the Restoration," (1842,) and "Europe since the Accession of Louis Philippe," (10 vols., 1849.) Before the revolution of 1848 he had free access to the archives of state. He is charged with favouring absolutism in his writings.

See QUÉRARD, "La France Littéraire;" "Edinburgh Review" for April, 1836; "London Quarterly Review," 1843.

Cap′el, (ARTHUR,) LORD, an English cavalier of Hertfordshire, who was elected a member of Parliament in 1640. After acting with the popular party, he turned royalist, and was created Baron Capel in 1641. In the civil war he held a high command in the royalist army, and was appointed a counsellor of the Prince of Wales. After having made peace, or "compounded," with Parliament, he joined another revolt in 1648, was taken by Fairfax, tried for treason, and executed in 1649.

See HUME, "History of England."

ɛ as k; ç as s; ḡ hard; ġ as j; G, H, K, guttural; N, nasal; R, trilled; s̄ as z; ᵵh as in this. (☞See Explanations, p. 23.)

Capel, (ARTHUR,) Earl of Essex, the eldest son of the preceding, was born in 1635. He was created Earl of Essex by Charles II. in 1661, and sent on an embassy to Denmark in 1670. In 1672 he was made a privy councillor, and lord lieutenant of Ireland. His eloquence and knowledge of law rendered him one of the most influential members of the House of Lords. He afterwards became an opponent of the court, and in 1683 was committed to the Tower on a suspicion of complicity in the Rye-House Plot. A few days after this event he was found dead, having, according to the verdict of the coroner's inquest, committed suicide.

See MACAULAY's "History of England," vols. i. and iii.

Cap′ell, (EDWARD,) an English critic, born at Troston, Suffolk, in 1713, was distinguished as a commentator on Shakspeare. He lived chiefly at Hastings and London, and spent many years in preparing an edition of Shakspeare, which was published in 1767. The text of this edition is said to be one of the purest extant. He wrote or edited several other works, one of which is "The School of Shakspeare." Died in 1781.

See "Biographia Dramatica;" ERSCH und GRUBER, "Allgemeine Encyklopaedie."

Capell, de, (BROOKE A.,) was author of "Travels through Sweden, Norway, and Finmark to the North Cape," (London, 1823,) and other works.

See "London Quarterly Review" for October, 1823.

Capell Lofft. See LOFFT.

Capella, kâ-pel′lâ, (GALEAZZO FLAVIO CAPRA,) an Italian historian, born at Milan in 1487. He became secretary of state to Francis Sforza, Duke of Milan, who employed him in important missions. He was the orator of the emperor Maximilian, and was retained in his office when Charles V. became master of Milan. Capella wrote several valuable works, among which are a "History of the Wars of the Milanese from 1521 to 1530," (in Latin,) and a "History of Francis Sforza," (1535.) He died in 1537.

See GINGUENÉ, "Histoire Littéraire d'Italie."

Ca̧-pel′la̧, (MARTIANUS MINEUS FELIX,) a Latin writer, of whose personal history nothing is known, is supposed to have lived about 500 A.D. His great work, entitled "Satyricon," was a voluminous compilation, somewhat like an encyclopædia of the seven liberal arts, (Grammar, Dialectics, Rhetoric, Geometry, Astronomy, Arithmetic, and Music,) and was highly esteemed and used in the schools of the middle ages. It was a medley of prose and verse, written in an unclassic, pretentious style. Some persons suppose that Copernicus found the germ of his system in a passage of this work which teaches that Mercury and Venus revolve around the sun.

See FABRICIUS, "Bibliotheca mediæ et infimæ Ætatis;" ERSCH und GRUBER, "Allgemeine Encyklopaedie."

Capellen, van, văn kâ-pel′len, (GODARD ALEXANDER GERARD PHILIPPUS,) BARON, an able Dutch statesman, born in 1778. He was appointed minister of the interior in 1809 by Louis Bonaparte, and resigned on the abdication of that king in 1810. In 1814 he became minister of the colonies under William I. He was Governor-General of the Dutch East Indies for five or more years, ending in 1826. In 1838 he attended the coronation of Queen Victoria as ambassador extraordinary, and in 1840 became grand chamberlain to William II. Died in 1848.

See BROCKHAUS, "Conversations-Lexikon."

Capellen, van, (ROBERT GASPARD BURNE,) one of the chiefs of the popular party in Holland, was born at Zutphen in 1743. He entered the States of Guelderland in 1771, and when the Prince of Orange aspired to absolute power he put himself at the head of the opposition. He was sentenced to death as a traitor in 1788; but he had escaped to France, where he died in 1798.

See ERSCH und GRUBER, "Allgemeine Encyklopaedie."

Capellen, van, (THEODORUS FREDERIK,) a Dutch admiral, of the same family as the preceding, born about 1760. As rear-admiral he commanded in 1799 a Dutch fleet, which, when attacked by the English, he surrendered without a battle. He resided in England from that time until 1813, when he returned home with the Prince of Orange and was made vice-admiral. In 1816 he commanded the Dutch fleet which co-operated with the English in the famous attack on Algiers, and was praised by Lord Exmouth for his conduct in that action. Died in 1824.

Capello. See CAPPELLO, (BERNARDO and MARCO.)

Capello, kâ-pel′lo, (BIANCA,) an ambitious and fascinating woman, born of a noble family in Venice. In 1563 she eloped to Florence with Pietro Bonaventuri, who had obtained her consent by false pretences. She soon formed a *liaison* with Francis de' Medici, Grand Duke of Tuscany, to whom she was privately married in 1578. This marriage was afterwards avowed by him, and ambassadors were sent from Venice to Florence to solemnize the adoption of ·Bianca as the daughter of Saint Mark. She is accused of ordering or instigating the assassination of several persons. Died in 1587.

See SISMONDI, "Histoire des Républiques Italiennes;" G. R. DE SAN-SEVERINO, "Storia della Vita e Morte di B. Capello," 1776, and French version of the same, 1779; CICOGNA, "B. Capello; Cenni storici critici," 1828; SIEBENKEES, "Lebensbeschreibung der B. Capello," 1789, and English version of the same, 1797; CARLO BOTTA, "B. Capello," 1838.

Caperan, kâp′rôN′, (ARNAUD THOMAS,) a French Orientalist and priest, born at Dol in 1754, was preceptor of Châteaubriand. He left several works on Oriental languages. Died in 1826.

Cā′per̜ā, (WILLIAM,) an American Methodist bishop, born in South Carolina in 1790, preached several years at Charleston. He was editor of the "Southern Christian Advocate," and was elected a bishop of the Methodist Episcopal Church South in 1846. Died in 1855.

Cā′pet, (HUGH,) [Fr. HUGUES CAPET,* hüg kâ′pȧ′,] King of France, was the head of the third dynasty, and the ancestor of thirty-two French kings. He was the son of Hugh the Great, Count of Paris, and was born about 940 A.D. At the death of Louis V., the last of the Carlovingians, in 987, he assumed royal power, and obtained the suffrages of the assembled barons; but his crown was disputed by Charles of Lorraine, the legitimate heir of the last dynasty. Having defeated Charles in battle, he afterwards possessed the throne in peace, and, by moderation and policy, confirmed his power, which at first was hardly superior to that of the nobles whose choice had made him king. Paris was chosen as the capital of his kingdom. His posterity continued to reign in France until the Revolution of 1789. He died in 996, and was succeeded by his son Robert.

See GUILLAUME DE JUMIÉGES; CAPEFIGUE, "Hugues Capet et le troisième Race," 4 vols., 1836; SISMONDI, "Histoire des Français;" DEVISMES, "Hugues Capet; Fragment historique," 1804.

Capilupi, kâ-pe-loo′pee, (CAMILLO,) a native of Mantua, wrote a famous work called the "Stratagem of Charles IX. against the Huguenots," (1572,) in which he justified the Massacre of Saint Bartholomew and argued that it was premeditated. Cardinal Lorraine, who was then in Rome, endeavoured to suppress this book, from motives of policy.

See DE THOU, "Historia."

Capilupi, (LELIO,) an Italian writer, brother of the preceding, born at Mantua in 1498; died in 1560.

Capistrano, da, dâ kâ-pès-trâ′no, written also **Capistran,** (GIOVANNI,) an Italian monk, eminent for his talents and virtues, was born at Capistrano, in the Abruzzi, in 1385. He preached with honour in the chief cities of Italy and Germany, and was employed as legate and nuncio by several popes. When Belgrade was besieged by the Sultan in 1456, he shut himself up in that city, and by his zeal contributed greatly to its successful defence. He wrote "The Mirror of Conscience," ("Speculum Conscientiæ,") and other works on theology. Died in 1456.

See BAILLET, "Vies des Saints."

Capisucchi, kâ-pe-sook′kee, or **Capizucca,** kâ-pèd-zook′kâ, (BIAGIO or BIASIO,) Marquis of Monterio, an Italian general, born in Rome. He served under the Duke of Parma in the Low Countries in 1584, and was afterwards lieutenant-general of Ferdinand I. de' Medici, Duke of Tuscany. Died in 1613.

See ADAMI, "Elogj istorici de' due Marchesi Capisucchi fratelli Camillo et Biagio," 1685.

---

* The name CAPET is said to have been given to him as a nickname; but there is the greatest diversity in regard to its signification. One authority says it signifies "big-headed;" another, a "jester;" and so on.

Capisucchi, (CAMILLO,) an Italian general, brother of the preceding, born at Rome in 1537; died in 1597.
See MOTLEY, "History of the United Netherlands," vol. i. chap. v.

Capisucchi, (PAOLO,) born in Rome in 1479, became Bishop of Neocastro. Clement VII. having referred to him the question of a divorce between Henry VIII. of England and Queen Catherine, Capisucchi made a report against Henry. Died in 1539.

Cap'I-to, (C. ATEIUS,) an eminent Roman jurist, who flourished in the reign of Augustus, and was chosen consul in 5 A.D. He was the rival of Labeo, and founder of a numerous school of lawyers. He wrote books on pontifical law, and other legal works. Died in 22 A.D.
See TACITUS, "Annales;" HOFFET, "Esquisses biographiques sur Capito," 1850.

Capito, kä'pe-to, [Fr. CAPITON, kä'pe'tòN',] (WOLFGANG FABRICIUS,) an eminent German theologian and Reformer, born at Haguenau about 1480. His original name was WOLFF KOEPSTEIN. He became secretary of Albert, Archbishop of Mentz, who gave him a title of nobility in 1523. About this date he was converted to the Protestant faith, and became intimate with Bucer. He was deputed to the Diet of Augsburg in 1530, and five years later had an interview with Calvin for the purpose of effecting a union between the Calvinists and the Lutherans. He wrote a "Hebrew Institutes," ("Institutiones Hebraicæ,") a "Life of Œcolampadius," "The Six Days' Work of God explained," ("Hexaemeron Dei Opus explicatum," 1539,) and other works. Died at Strasburg in 1541.
See SAX, "Onomasticon;" SECKENDORF, "Historia Lutheranismi."

Capitolinus. See MANLIUS, and MANLIA GENS.

Cap-I-to-li'nus, (JULIUS,) a Latin biographer, who wrote about the end of the third century, was one of the authors of the "Historia Augusta." The biographies of the following emperors are ascribed to him : Antoninus Pius, Marcus Aurelius, Lucius Verus, Pertinax, Clodius Albinus, Opilius Macrinus, two Maximins, three Gordians, Maximus, and Balbinus.
See VOSSIUS, "De Historicis Latinis;" MOLLER, "Dissertatio de J. Capitolino," 1689: G. HEYNE, "Opuscula Academica."

Capiton, the French of CAPITO, which see.

Capivaccio, kä-pe-vät'cho, or **Capo di Vacca,** kä'po de väk'kä, (GERONIMO,) an Italian physician, born at Padua ; died in 1589.

Capizucca. See CAPISUCCHI.

Capmani or **Capmany, de,** dà käp-mä'nee, (ANTONIO,) an eminent Spanish author and philologist, born at Barcelona in 1742. He resided in Madrid many years, and held several political offices. When the French obtained possession of Madrid in 1808, he retired to Seville. He compiled a good French and Spanish Dictionary, and wrote a variety of works, among which are "The Sentinel against the French," "Historico-Critical Theatre of Spanish Eloquence," and "Philosophy of Eloquence ;" also "Historical Memoirs of Barcelona," (1779–92,) which is commended by Prescott. Died at Cadiz in 1813.
See TICKNOR, "History of Spanish Literature ;" MEUSEL, "Bibliotheca Historica;" PRESCOTT, "History of Ferdinand and Isabella," vol. i.

Capnion. See REUCHLIN.

Capo de Feuillide, kä'po' deh fuh'e-yèd', (JEAN GABRIEL,) a French journalist, born in the Antilles in 1800, removed to France about 1818. He has edited several journals of Paris, and has been republican and royalist by turns. In 1844 he published a "History of the People of Paris." He was transported to Algeria for opposition to Napoleon's coup d'état of December, 1851, but returned to France a few years afterwards.

Capo d'Istria, kä'po dis'tRe-â, (AUGUSTIN,) COUNT OF, a brother of John, noticed below, was born in Corfu. He was invited to Greece in 1829 by his brother, who gave him a high position in the army. He was elected President of Greece in December, 1831; but the opposition became so strong that he resigned in April, 1832. Died in 1842.

Capo d'Istria or **Capodistrias,** kä'po-dis'tRe-âs, (JOHN,) COUNT, and President of Greece, was born in Corfu in 1780. He entered the service of Russia in 1806, as clerk in the foreign office, where he was rapidly advanced. After having been employed by the Czar in several diplomatic missions, he represented Russia in the Congress of Vienna in 1814-15, and signed the treaty of peace at Paris in November, 1815. The next year he was appointed foreign secretary of state, and enjoyed the confidence of the emperor, who found in him an unscrupulous and able minister, devoted to the cause of absolutism. About 1817 he received the title of count, and the cross of the order of Alexander. In April, 1827, he was chosen (probably by Russian influence) President (for seven years) of Greece, which had just thrown off the Turkish yoke. His administration was arbitrary and excited much discontent. He violated the constitution, subverted the liberty of the press, and aimed, it would appear, to make Greece subservient to Russia. Some writers, however, justify or excuse his measures in consideration of the violent and factious character of the Greeks. He was assassinated, October 9, 1831, by George and Constantine Mauromichali.
See S. BULGARI, "Notice sur J. Capodistrias," Paris, 1832; A PAPADOPOULOS VRETOS, "Mémoires sur le Président de la Grèce,' 2 vols., 1838.

Cä'pǫn, (WILLIAM,) an English architect and scenepainter, born at Norwich in 1757. His most admired productions were the scenic decorations of Drury Lane and Covent Garden. Died in 1828.

Caponi, kä-po'nee, (AGOSTINO,) a citizen of Florence, who in 1513 engaged in a conspiracy with Machiavel and others to subvert the power of the Medicis. A list of the conspirators dropped by him accidentally betrayed the secret, and Caponi was executed.

Caporali, kä-po-rä'lee, (CESARE,) a satirical Italian poet, born at Perugia in 1531. He lived some years at Rome in the service of several cardinals, and wrote poems remarkable for originality and elegance, viz., "A Journey to Parnassus," "The Life of Mæcenas," and "The Gardens of Mæcenas." Died in 1601.
See GINGUENÉ, "Histoire Littéraire d'Italie."

Cappe, kap, (NEWCOME,) an English Socinian minister, born at Leeds in 1732. He preached many years in his native place, and had a high reputation for eloquence. He published a number of sermons, and left "Critical Remarks on many Important Passages of Scripture." Died in 1800.

Cappel, kä'pěl', (ANGE,) a French Protestant jurist, born in 1537, was related to Louis, noticed below. He became secretary to Henry IV., and wrote a work on the abuses of litigation, ("Abus des Plaideurs," 1604.) He translated several essays of Seneca into French. Died in 1623.

Cappel, (GUILLAUME,) a French theologian, was an uncle of Jacques, who died in 1542. He was rector of the University of Paris in 1491.

Cappel, (GUILLAUME,) born in 1530, was a son of Jacques, and brother of Ange. He translated the works of Machiavel into French. Died about 1586.

Cappel, (JACQUES,) a French jurist, was a councillor of state under Francis I. He was the father of Ange, Jacques, and Louis Cappel. Died in 1542.

Cappel, (JACQUES,) Sieur de Tilloy, (deh te'lwä',) a French jurist, born in 1525, embraced the Reformed religion in his youth. He became a counsellor at Rennes, and, during the persecution of 1572, found refuge at Sedan. Died in 1586.

Cappel, [Lat. CAPPEL'LUS,] (JACQUES,) a French Protestant minister, a son of the preceding, was born at Rennes in 1570. He was professor of Hebrew and theology in his native place, and author of several valuable works, among which are "A Treatise on Weights and Coins," (1606,) "A Treatise on Measures," (1607,) and "Notes on the Old Testament." Died in 1624.

Cappel, (JACQUES LOUIS,) born in 1639, succeeded his father Louis in the chair of Hebrew at Saumur. When the edict of Nantes was revoked, (1685,) he took refuge in England, where he died in 1722.
See LOUIS CAPPEL, "De Cappelorum Gente," 1689; NICÉRON, "Mémoires."

Cappel, (LOUIS,) a French Protestant minister, born in Paris in 1534, was a son of Jacques, (who died in 1542.) He was an intrepid advocate of the Reformation. In the latter part of his life he was professor of theology at Sedan, where he died in 1586.

ε as k; ç as s; ğ hard; ġ as j; G, H, K, guttural; N, nasal; R, trilled; š as z; ᵵh as in this. (☞See Explanations, p. 23.)

Cappel, [Lat. CAPPEL′LUS,] (LOUIS,) called THE YOUNGER, an eminent French Protestant divine, son of Jacques Cappel de Tilloy, born at Sedan in 1585. He passed nearly all his life at Saumur, where he was minister and professor of Hebrew and theology. He rendered himself memorable by his new system of sacred criticism announced in his "Secret of Punctuation revealed," ("Arcanum Punctuationis revelatum," 1624,) maintaining that the vowel points are a modern invention. In 1650 he published his principal work, "Critica Sacra," in pursuance of his project to reform the Hebrew text of the Bible. These works, which excited much opposition, are said to form an epoch in sacred philology, and gained for Cappel the title of father of Hebrew criticism. Died at Saumur in 1658.

See NICÉRON, "Mémoires;" "Nouvelle Biographie Générale."

Cappel, kåp′pel, (LUDWIG CHRISTOPH WILHELM,) a German medical writer, born in 1772; died in 1804.

Cappellari, kåp-pêl-lå′ree, (GENNARO ANTONIO,) an Italian writer, born in Naples in 1655. He wrote and spoke Latin with facility and elegance, and published several Latin works, among which are "The Praises of Philosophy," and a poem on the comets of 1664 and 1665. He was executed at Palermo in 1702, on a charge of treason. His innocence was afterwards recognized.

See TIRABOSCHI, "Storia della Letteratura Italiana."

Cappelle, van, kåp-pel′leh, (JAN PIETER,) a Dutch writer, born at Flushing in 1783, published "Researches for the History of the Netherlands," (1827,) and other works. He became professor of history at Amsterdam in 1819. Died in 1829.

See DAVID JACOB VAN LENNEP, "Gedachtenisrede op J. P. van Cappelle," 1830.

Cappelle, van der, vån der kåp-pel′leh, (JAN,) an eminent Dutch painter of marine and river views, supposed to have flourished about 1680. We have no materials to compose his biography. He was an excellent colorist, and his works, which include some winter landscapes, command high prices.

Cappelli, kåp-pel′lee, (FRANCESCO,) an Italian painter, born at Sassuolo, was one of the best pupils of Correggio. He was living in 1568.

Cappelli, (MARCANTONIO,) an Italian Franciscan monk and theological writer, born at Este, was an opponent of Pope Paul V. in the affair of the interdict of Venice. Died about 1630.

Cappello, kåp-pel′lo, (BERNARDO,) an Italian poet, born at Venice about 1500, received lessons from Bembo. Having entered the public service, he was banished in 1540 to the island of Arbe, from which he escaped about 1542 to the Papal States. He was afterwards governor of Orvieto and Tivoli. He produced in 1560 a volume of lyric poems, "Rime" or "Canzonieri," which, says Tiraboschi, "are among the most graceful, noble, and polished that appeared in the sixteenth century." Died at Rome in 1565.

See SERRASSI, "Vita di Bernardo Cappello," prefixed to his "Rime;" TIRABOSCHI, "Storia della Letteratura Italiana."

Cappello, (MARCO,) an Italian poet and priest, born at Brescia in 1706. He had a talent for improvisation, witticisms, and burlesque composition. Among his satirical or burlesque poems are "The Scarecrow," ("La Befana,") and "The Cats," ("I Gatti.") Died in 1782.

Cappellus. See CAPPEL.

Cap′per, (JAMES,) an English officer in the service of the East India Company. He made the journey from Europe to India by land in 1778, and published "Observations on the Passage to India," (1782.) Died in 1825.

Capperonnier, kåp′ro′ne-å′, (CLAUDE,) an eminent French linguist and critic, born at Montdidier in 1671, was appointed professor of Greek in the College of France in 1722. He kept this place until his death. He published an edition of Quintilian, and other works. Died in 1744.

See ERSCH und GRUBER, "Allgemeine Encyklopaedie."

Capperonnier, (JEAN,) nephew of the preceding, was born at Montdidier in 1716. He succeeded his uncle as professor at the College of France in 1743, and became librarian to the king. The Academy of Inscriptions was opened to him in 1749. He published editions of Cæsar, Plautus, Justin, and other works. Died in 1775.

Capponi, kåp-po′nee, (GINO,) an Italian statesman, father of Neri, noticed below, born about 1350. He was one of the chief magistrates of the republic of Florence, and directed the military administration with success as decemvir of war. "The conquest of Pisa," (1406,) says Sismondi, "was effected chiefly by him." Died in 1420.

See SISMONDI, "Histoire des Républiques Italiennes."

Capponi, (GINO,) MARQUIS OF, an elegant Italian writer, born at Florence in 1792, was a chief of the constitutional party in Tuscany, and was placed at the head of a brief ministry in 1848. He produced a "History of the Popes," and a "Treatise on Education," and wrote many memoirs for the Academy Della Crusca.

Capponi, (GREGORIO ALESSANDRO,) MARQUIS, an Italian scholar, born in Rome about 1685, was noted for his excellent taste in books and antiquities. He formed a rich collection of medals, cameos, etc., and collected a library of rare books, which by his will was added to that of the Vatican. Died in 1746. The Catalogue of the Capponi Library, with notes by Giorgi, is highly prized by bibliographers.

See ADELUNG, Supplement to JÖCHER's "Allgemeines Gelehrten-Lexikon."

Capponi, (NERI,) one of the chief magistrates of the Florentine republic, born in 1388, was eminent for virtue and talents. The victory of Anghieri in 1440 was ascribed to his skill. He wrote a Commentary on his own administration. Died in 1457.

Capponi, (PIETRO,) a grandson of the preceding, filled for many years the highest offices in Florence. In 1494 Charles VIII. of France, having been hospitably admitted with his soldiers into the city, assumed the part of a master. Capponi boldly asserted the freedom of the city, and by a prompt demonstration of a readiness for battle deterred the king from the execution of his audacious purpose. He was killed at a siege in 1496.

See SISMONDI, "Histoire des Républiques Italiennes."

Capponi della Porreta, kåp-po′nee del′lå por-rå′tå, (SERAFINO ANNIBALE,) an Italian theologian and monk, born at Bologna in 1536, wrote several works in elucidation of the theology of Thomas Aquinas. Died in 1614.

See PIO, "Vita di S. Capponi," 1625.

Capra. See BENEDICTIS.

Capra. See CAPELLA, (GALEAZZO FLAVIO.)

Capra, kå′prå, (BALDASSARE,) an Italian astronomer, born at Milan. He disputed with Galileo the title of inventor of the compass of proportion. Died in 1626.

Capranica, kå-prå-nee′kå, (DOMENICO,) an Italian cardinal, born in 1400, was eminent for learning and talents, and performed a prominent part in political affairs. He wrote, besides other works, a "Treatise on the Art of Dying," and one "On Contempt of the World," (" De Contemptu Mundi.") Died in 1458.

See M. CATALANI, "Commentarius de Vita et Scriptis D. Capranicæ," 1793.

Caprara, kå-prå′rå, (ALBERTO,) COUNT OF, an Italian general, nephew of General Piccolomini, born at Bologna in 1631. He entered the service of Austria, and obtained the rank of general. He was a Knight of the Golden Fleece, and was employed in several foreign embassies. He translated portions of Seneca's works into Italian. Died in 1686.

See ERSCH und GRUBER, "Allgemeine Encyklopaedie."

Caprara, (ENEA SYLVIO,) COUNT OF, a distinguished general, born at Bologna in 1631, was a brother of the preceding, and a nephew of the famous Piccolomini. He entered the service of Austria about 1650, and served in forty-four campaigns. He was defeated by Turenne in Germany in 1674, and was victorious over the Turks in Hungary in 1683 and 1685. Died in 1701.

See ERSCH und GRUBER, "Allgemeine Encyklopaedie."

Caprara, (GIOVANNI BATTISTA,) Archbishop of Milan, and count, was born of a noble family at Bologna in 1733. Having served as nuncio to several courts of Europe, he was made a cardinal in 1792. In 1801 he was sent as legate to Paris, with a view to restore public worship, and there performed the ceremony with which the Concordat was celebrated in 1802. He officiated at the coronation of Napoleon as King of Italy in 1805. Died in 1810.

Capriata, kä-pre-ä'tä, (PIETRO GIOVANNI,) an Italian historian and lawyer, born at Genoa. He wrote a "History of Italy from 1613 to 1646," (1648,) which is esteemed for its accuracy. Died about 1660.

Capuro, kä-poo'ro, (FRANCESCO,) a Genoese painter, who lived about 1630.

Capycius. See CAPECE.

Caqué, kä'kà', (AUGUSTIN ARMAND,) a French engraver of medals, born at Saintes in 1793. He worked some time on the "Gallery of the Kings of France," and in 1831 became a member of the commission of the mint. About 1853 he was appointed engraver of medals for the cabinet of the emperor.

Carabantes, de, dà kä-rä-bän'tês, (JOSÉ,) a Spanish missionary, born in 1628, published several works. Died in 1694.

See QUIROGA, "Vida y Virtudes de J. de Carabantes," 1705.

Car-a-cal'la, (MARCUS AURELIUS ANTONINUS BASSIANUS,) a Roman emperor, born at Lyons in 188 A.D. He was the son of the emperor Septimius Severus, who, dying in 212, left the empire to Caracalla and his brother Geta. The latter was assassinated by order of Caracalla, who sought to confirm his 'power by sacrificing many friends of Geta. Papinian, the jurist, was one of the victims, who, it is said, amounted to thousands. His reign was a series of cruelties, extortions, and follies. He chose for his chief ministers persons of the vilest character. He led his army into Parthia about 216 A.D., ravaged a part of the country, and retired before he had encountered the Parthian army. A conspiracy having been formed by Macrinus, Caracalla was killed by one of his soldiers near Edessa, in Asia, in 217 A.D., and Macrinus reigned in his stead.

See GIBBON, "Decline and Fall of the Roman Empire;" MEISTER, "Dissertatio de Caracalla," 1792 ; SPARTIAN, "Vita Caracallæ."

Caracci, kä-rät'chee, or **Carracci,** kâr-rät'chee, [Fr. CARRACHE, kȧ'rȧsh',] (AGOSTINO,) a celebrated painter and engraver, born at Bologna about 1558, was the brother of Annibal and cousin of Ludovico, noticed below. He studied painting under Prospero Fontana, and engraving under Cornelius Cort. He became the partner of the other Caracci in the Academy at Bologna, and assisted Annibal in the Farnese Gallery at Rome. In invention he was equal or superior to either of his kinsmen. "The Communion of Saint Jerome," at the Louvre, is called the master-piece among his paintings. His engravings are numerous and are highly prized. He wrote a "Treatise on Perspective and Architecture." Died in 1602.

See LANZI, "History of Painting in Italy;" MALVASIA, "Felsina pittrice."

Caracci, (ANNIBAL or ANNIBALE,) one of the great masters of the Bolognese school of painting, brother of the preceding, was born about 1560, and was the pupil of Ludovico Caracci. He had more energy and boldness, but less cultivation, than his brother, and is estimated the greatest painter of the Caracci family. The paintings with which he adorned the Farnese Gallery at Rome (on which he worked eight years) are regarded as his master-pieces, and nearly approach the grace of the works of Raphael. He shares with his cousin and brother the honour of founding a new school, which produced many excellent artists. (See CARACCI, LUDOVICO.) Died at Rome in 1609.

See MALVASIA, "Vite de' Pittori Bolognesi;" BRYAN, "Dictionary of Painters and Engravers."

Caracci, (ANTONIO,) an Italian painter, born at Venice in 1583, was a son of Agostino, and a pupil of Annibal, his uncle. He executed some frescos in the Vatican, and an oil-painting of the Deluge, which is much admired. Died in 1618.

Caracci, (FRANCESCO,) a brother of Annibal, born in 1595, was also a painter. After the death of his brothers he opened a school at Bologna in opposition to Ludovico, but was not successful. He died in Rome in 1622.

Caracci, (LUDOVICO,) the founder of the Bolognese school of painting, was born at Bologna in 1555. His instructors were Fontana of Bologna and Tintoretto of Venice. His slowness of execution was such that he obtained the nickname of "the Ox." Having secured the

co-operation of his cousins, above noticed, whose education he had partly directed, he opened an academy in Bologna, which became very celebrated, and effected a reform in the style of art, which had become languid and degenerate. He excelled in design, and was remarkable for fidelity to nature and for his aptitude as a teacher of art. Among his pupils were Guido Reni and Domenichino. Of his oil-paintings, "The Preaching of Saint John the Baptist" (in the Louvre) is accounted the master-piece. Died in 1619.

See MALVASIA, "Vite de' Pittori Bolognesi."

Caraccio, kä-rät'cho, (ANTONIO,) Baron of Corano, (ko-rä'no,) an Italian poet, born at Nardo in 1630. He published lyric poems, and an epic poem entitled "The Empire Vindicated," ("L'Imperio vendicato," 1690,) much admired by his contemporaries. Died in 1702.

See TIRABOSCHI, "Storia della Letteratura Italiana."

Caraccioli, kä-rät'cho-lee or kä-rät-cho'lee, (ANTONIO,) an Italian theologian, born at Melfi, was a son of Gianni, Prince of Melfi, noticed below. He became abbé of Saint-Victor, in France, about 1543, and afterwards Bishop of Troyes. A few years later he was converted to Calvinism. He wrote "The Mirror of True Religion." Died in 1569.

Caraccioli, (DOMENICO,) MARQUIS, an Italian diplomatist and wit, born at Naples in 1715. From 1770 to 1780 he was ambassador from Naples to the French court, and in the latter year became Viceroy of Sicily. He was chosen minister of foreign affairs in 1786. Died in 1789.

See TIPALDO, "Biografia degli Italiani illustri."

Caraccioli, (FRANCESCO,) PRINCE, an admiral, a relative of the preceding, born at Naples about 1748. He commanded the fleet of the Neapolitan republic in 1799, and repulsed the Anglo-Sicilian fleet between Cumæ and Cape Miseno. Soon after this the royalists prevailed at Naples : he was arrested, tried by a court-martial, and hung by order of Lord Nelson.

Caraccioli, (GIANNI,) a favourite courtier and minister of Joanna, Queen of Naples, exercised almost absolute power for about sixteen years. He was assassinated in 1432.

Caraccioli, (GIANNI,) Prince of Melfi, born in 1480, fought alternately for the French and the Spaniards in the campaigns of 1528–36, and was made a marshal of France in 1544. Died in 1550.

Caraccioli, (LUIGI ANTONIO,) born of a noble Italian family in Paris in 1721, became a member of the order of the Oratory, and tutor of the sons of Prince Rewski in Poland. He afterwards resided in Paris. He published many works, one of which attracted much notice. It purported to be a version of Pope Clement the Fourteenth's letters, but was suspected by many to have originated with Caraccioli. Died in 1803.

See GRIMM, "Correspondance littéraire."

Caraccioli, (ROBERTO,) an Italian theologian and pulpit orator, born at Lecce, in Naples, in 1425, became Bishop of Aquino in 1471. He wrote, in Latin, "The Mirror of the Christian Faith," and other works. Died in 1475.

See DOMENICO DE ANGELIS, "Vita di R. Caraccioli," 1703.

Caracciolo, kä-rät-cho'lo or kä-rät'cho-lo, or **Caracciuolo,** kä-rät-choo-o'lo, (GIOVANNI BATTISTA,) an Italian painter, born in Naples, was an admirer of Annibal Caracci, whose works he studied in Rome and imitated with skill. He adorned the churches and palaces of Naples with admired pictures. Died in 1641.

See LANZI, "History of Painting in Italy."

Caracciuolo. See CARACCIOLO.

Ca̤-rac'ta̤-cus, King of the Silures, a tribe of ancient Britons. After resisting the Roman arms about nine years, he was defeated by Ostorius, and carried captive to Rome, in 51 A.D. The Romans admired his manly deportment in presence of the emperor Claudius, who spared his life and sent him home with presents. He is supposed to have died about 54 A.D.

See TACITUS, "Annales."

Caradoc, kä-rä'dok, or **Ca-ra'dog,** [Lat. CARAC'TACUS,] a Welsh chronicler, born at Llancarvan. He wrote a "History of the Welsh Princes," not extant, but of which an English translation has been preserved. He died about 1154.

See WRIGHT, "Biographia Britannica."

Caraduc, kȧ-rȧ'duk, an ancient Briton or Welsh bard of unknown period. He wrote a lay, the scene of which is laid at the court of King Arthur.

Caraffa, kȧ-rȧf'fȧ, a noble family of Naples, which, since the thirteenth century, has produced many dukes, cardinals, etc. Paul IV., elected pope in 1555, was a Caraffa. His efforts to exalt and enrich his kindred involved him in a bloody war with Spain. He made his nephew Charles a cardinal, and gave the titles of Marquis of Montebello and Duke of Palliano to his other nephews Antonio and Giovanni, for whose interest he confiscated the estates of several nobles. In 1559 they were disgraced and exiled by the same pontiff. The cardinal was put to death, after a legal process, in 1561.

Caraffa, kȧ-rȧf'fȧ, (ANTONIO,) a third-cousin of Pope Paul IV., became a cardinal in 1568, and apostolic librarian to Gregory XIII. He edited the Greek Bible of the Septuagint, published in 1587. Died in 1591.

Caraffa, (ETTORE,) Count of Ruvo, born at Naples in 1767, was the heir of the Dukes of Andria. He was arrested in 1796 on account of his liberal opinions, but escaped and left the kingdom. In 1799 he returned with the French army, and as a general fought bravely for the Parthenopean republic. The republicans were soon dispersed, and the whole country fell into the power of the royalists, by whom Caraffa was executed about 1800.

Caraffa or **Carafa,** kȧ-rȧ'fȧ, (MICHELE,) an eminent musician and composer, born in Naples about 1785. He removed to Paris in 1821, and adopted France as his country a few years later. He composed "Le Solitaire," (1822,) "Il Sonnambulo," and other successful operas, among which "Masaniello" (1828) is called his masterpiece. He was a member of the French Institute.

See FÉTIS, "Biographie Universelle des Musiciens."

Caraglio, kȧ-rȧl'yo, or **Caralio,** kȧ-rȧ'le-o, (GIOVANNI GIACOMO,) a celebrated Italian engraver, was born at Verona about 1510. He was a pupil of Marcantonio Raimondi in Rome, and afterwards worked in Verona. He engraved many of the works of Raphael, Titian, Michael Angelo, Giulio Romano, and other masters. Among these are Raphael's "Holy Family" and Titian's "Annunciation." He devoted his latter years to engraving gems, cameos, and medals, with great success, and was patronized in this branch of art by Sigismund I. of Poland. Died about 1570. He sometimes wrote his name Jacobus Veronensis, and Jacobus Caralius.

See VASARI, "Lives of the Painters and Engravers;" TICOZZI, "Dizionario."

Caralio. See CARAGLIO.

Caramuel de Lobkowitz, kȧ-rȧ-moo-ĕl' dȧ lob-ko-vĕts', written also **Caramuele** (kȧ-rȧ-moo-ā'lȧ) **de Lobkowitz,** (JUAN,) a Spanish ecclesiastic, born in Madrid in 1606, was noted for his learning, but was deficient in judgment. The King of Spain sent him as his agent to the court of Vienna, where he made himself so agreeable that the emperor gave him two abbeys, one of which was at Prague. In 1657 he was made Bishop of Campagna. He wrote many works on theology, logic, metaphysics, mathematics, and other sciences. He pretended to resolve questions in theology by the rules of arithmetic. Died in 1682.

See TADISI, "Memorie della Vita di Caramuele de Lobkowitz," 1760; N. ANTONIO, "Bibliotheca Hispana Nova."

Caraman, de, dĕh kȧ'rȧ'mŏN', (PIERRE PAUL **de Riquet**—dĕh re'kȧ',) COUNT, a French general, born in 1646, was a son of M. de Riquet, who constructed the canal of Languedoc. He saved the army at a battle in Flanders between Nodoue and Diest in 1705, and distinguished himself at Ramillies in 1706. Died in 1730.

Caraman, de, (VICTOR LOUIS CHARLES DE RIQUET,) DUC, a French general, born in 1762, was a son of Victor Maurice. Died in 1839.

Caraman, de, (VICTOR MAURICE DE RIQUET,) COUNT, father of the preceding, was born in 1727. He displayed talents and courage in all the campaigns of the Seven Years' war, (1756–63,) during which he rose to the rank of lieutenant-general. In 1786 he became commandant-

general of Provence. He was the principal owner of the canal of Languedoc made by his ancestor, and lost an immense fortune by the Revolution. Died in 1807.

Cara-Mustafa, (or -**Mustapha,**) kȧ'rȧ' mōos'tȧ-fȧ, written also **Kara-Moustapha,** a famous grand vizier of Turkey, was born at Merzisoor, in Asia Minor, in 1634. He became Pasha of Silistria in 1660, and grand vizier in 1676. He commanded the army of two hundred thousand men which in 1683 attacked Vienna and besieged it for sixty days. John Sobieski, King of Poland, came to the relief of the besieged, and gained a decisive victory over the Turks. Cara-Mustafa was executed the same year, by order of the Sultan, Mahomet IV.

See SALVANDY, "Histoire de J. Sobieski."

Ça-rā'nus, [Κάρανος or Καρανός,] a Macedonian general in the service of Alexander the Great.

Carascosa, kȧ-rȧs-ko'sȧ, (MICHELE,) BARON, an Italian general, born in Sicily. He served in the army of Joachim Murat from 1808 to 1814, during which period he became a general. In 1820 he commanded a body of insurgents, who were dispersed by the Austrians. He was sentenced to death, but escaped, and went into exile.

Ça-rau'sĭ-us, (MARCUS AURELIUS VALERIUS,) an adventurer, born at Menapia, in Belgium, about 250 A.D. Having been promoted to the command of a Roman fleet, he made himself master of Great Britain and assumed the title of emperor. After vain efforts to conquer him, Diocletian recognized him by treaty. He was assassinated in 293 A.D.

Caravage. See CARAVAGGIO.

Caravaggio, da, dä kȧ-rȧ-vȧd'jo, [Fr. CARAVAGE, kȧ'rȧ'vȧzh',] (MICHEL ANGELO,) a celebrated Italian painter, born at Caravaggio, in the Milanese, in 1569. His proper name was MICHEL ANGELO AMERIGHI or MORIGI. He studied in Venice and Rome, imitated no model except nature, and adopted a new manner, which gained him much applause and a crowd of imitators. He was a skilful colorist, especially in the treatment of carnations, but lacks taste and elevation of ideas. Among his master-pieces are a "Supper at Emmaus," and "Christ carried to the Grave by Saint John and Nicodemus." He is said to have been involved by his violent temper in several bloody quarrels. Died in 1609.

See LANZI, "History of Painting in Italy."

Caravaggio, (PIETRO PAOLO,) an Italian poet and geometer, born at Milan in 1617. He taught Greek and mathematics at Milan, and was distinguished as a military architect. He wrote "Inno," a poem, besides several odes and sonnets. Died in 168.

Caravaggio Polidoro. See CALDARA.

Cara-Yoosef (or -**Yousef,**) kȧ'rȧ' yoo'sef, written also **Kara-Yûsuf,** the first prince of the Turcoman dynasty of the Black Sheep. He made himself master of Diarbekir, Kurdistân, Azerbaijân, and Irâk about 1410. Died in 1420.

See VON HAMMER, "Histoire de l'Empire Ottoman."

Carbajal. See CARVAJAL.

Car'bo, (CAIUS PAPIRIUS,) an eloquent Roman orator and consul. He was a tribune of the people in the time of Tiberius Gracchus, who was his friend. About 120 B.C. he was elected consul. Being accused of peculation by L. Crassus, he committed suicide.

Carbo, (CNEIUS PAPIRIUS,) a nephew of the preceding, was a general and a partisan of Marius in the civil war. He was chosen consul, with Cinna for his colleague, in 86 B.C., and raised forces as fast as possible to resist Sulla, who was expected to return soon from the East. Carbo was again elected consul for the year 82, after the return of Sulla and after several indecisive battles had been fought. In one of these, Carbo and Sulla commanded the respective armies at Clusium. Soon after that action Carbo was defeated by Metellus at Faventia, and fled to Africa. Having been taken prisoner, he was put to death, by order of Pompey, in 82 B.C.

See PLUTARCH, "Sulla" and "Pompey.'

Carbon de Flins. See FLINS.

Carbonara, kaʀ-bo-nä'rȧ, (LUIGI,) COUNT, an Italian judge, born at Genoa in 1753. In 1803 he was chosen judge of the supreme tribunal of the Ligurian republic,

ā, ē, ī, ō, ū, ȳ, *long;* ȧ, ė, ŏ, *same, less prolonged;* ă, ĕ, ĭ, ŏ, ŭ, ў, *short;* ạ, ẹ, į, ọ, *obscure;* fär, fȧll, fȧt; mĕt; nŏt; gŏŏd; mōon;

and in 1805 president of the court of appeal. He became a senator and count of the French empire in 1809. After the restoration of the Sardinian king, he was president of the supreme court at Genoa. Died in 1826.

Carbondala, kaR-bon-dä'lä, (GIOVANNI,) an Italian surgeon and physician, was born at Santhio, and practised about 1270–1300 at Cremona, Pavia, and Verona. He was professor at Verona in 1298, and wrote a treatise called "De Operatione Manuali."

Carbone, kaR-bo'nå, (GIOVANNI BERNARDO,) an excellent painter of portraits and history, born at Albaro, near Genoa, in 1614. He painted some frescos in Genoa. "His portraits," says Lanzi, "have been mistaken for the works of Van Dyck." Died in 1683.

See LANZI, "History of Painting in Italy."

Carbone, (LUIGI,) a Latin poet and orator, born at Ferrara in 1436 ; died in 1482.

Carburi. See CARBURIS.

Car-bu'ris or **Carburi,** kaR-boo'ree, (JOHN BAPTIST,) a Greek physician of high reputation, born at Cephalonia, was professor of medicine at Turin from 1750 to 1770. About the latter date he accompanied the Countess of Artois to France, where he was appointed physician to the royal family. Died at Padua in 1801.

Carburis or **Carburi,** (MARCO,) COUNT, a chemist, brother of the preceding, born in Cephalonia in 1731 ; died in 1808.

Carburis or **Carburi,** (MARINO,) COUNT, a Greek engineer, born in Cephalonia, was noted for his mechanical skill. He went to Russia, assumed the name of LASCARIS, and became an officer in the army. He distinguished himself by transporting to the capital, in 1769, an enormous mass of granite, which supports the equestrian statue of Peter the Great. Having returned to his native place, he was killed there, in 1782, by his own workmen, who broke into his house in the night to rob him.

See MAZURAKIS, "Vies des Hommes illustres de Cephalonie."

Carcano, kaR-kä'no, (FRANCESCO,) an Italian writer, born at Milan in 1733, published several esteemed works in prose and verse. Died in 1794.

See CORNIANI, "Elogio del Cavaliere F. Carcano," 1795.

Carcano, (GIOVANNI BATTISTA,) an Italian physician and writer, who was for many years professor in the University of Pavia, and is said to have made some important discoveries in anatomy.

Carcano, (IGNAZIO,) an Italian physician, grandson of the preceding, born at Milan in 1682 ; died in 1730.

Carcavi, de, deh kåR'kä've', (PIERRE,) a French lawyer and bibliographer, born in Lyons. He became a resident of Paris, and a friend of Pascal and Descartes. In 1663 Colbert gave him the charge of the Royal Library. He was one of the first members of the Academy of Sciences, into which he was admitted as a mathematician. Died in 1684.

See BAILLET, "Vie de Descartes."

Car'çi-nus, [Καρκίνος,) an Athenian tragic poet, lived about 375 B.C. Only fragments of his works are extant.

Cardan, kar'dan, [Fr. pron. kåR'dôN'; Ger. kaR-dân' ; It. CARDANO, kaR-dä'no ; Lat. CARDA'NUS,] (JEROME,) an Italian physician, mathematician, and author, celebrated for his science, self-conceit, and absurd vagaries, was born at Pavia in 1501. He graduated as doctor of medicine at Padua in 1525, and successively professed mathematics and medicine at Milan and Bologna. His reputation as a physician was very extensive. In 1552 he visited Scotland, to attend the Archbishop of Saint Andrew's, whom he cured. A few of the last years of his life were passed in Rome, where he received a pension from the pope. He dealt much in astrology, and was a professed adept in magical arts. Among his numerous writings are "Ars Magna," a treatise on algebra, "On the Subtilty of Things," ("De Rerum Subtilitate,") "On the Variety of Things," ("De Rerum Varietate,") a "Life of Himself," ("De Vita propria,") and several medical treatises. His durable reputation is founded on his discoveries in algebra. In 1545 he published in his "Ars Magna" a method of solving equations of the third degree, which is known by the name of "Cardan's Formula ;" but he is said to have

obtained this from Tartaglia by unfair means. He was the first that noticed negative roots ; and he made other discoveries. "Cardan," says Hallam, "made a great epoch in the science of algebra." Died at Rome in 1576.

See CROSSLEY, "Life and Times of Cardan," 1836; H. MORLEY, "Life of Cardan," 1854; CARDAN, "De Vita propria," 1643; TENNEMANN, "History of Philosophy;" BAYLE, "Historical and Critical Dictionary;" "Nouvelle Biographie Générale;" "Blackwood's Magazine" for June, 1854.

Cardano or **Cardanus.** See CARDAN.

Car'der, (PETER,) CAPTAIN, an English mariner, served under Drake, who, after passing through the Strait of Magellan, (1586,) sent back Carder to report his progress. He was wrecked in this homeward voyage, and after much suffering reached England.

Cardi. See CIGOLI, (LUDOVICO.)

Car'di-gan, (JAMES THOMAS BRU'DENELL,) EARL OF, a British general, son of the Earl of Cardigan, born in 1797. He bore the title of Lord Brudenell before the death of his father, (1837,) on which event he entered the House of Lords. After passing through the inferior grades with distinction, he was appointed major-general in 1854, and commanded the light cavalry in the Crimean war. His charge at the battle of Balaklava (October, 1854) attracted great applause as a demonstration of reckless courage. Died in April, 1868.

Cardini, kaR-dee'nee, (IGNAZIO,) a Corsican naturalist, born at Mariana in 1562 ; died about 1600. The monks, whom he had satirized, burned nearly all the copies of a scientific work he had written.

Cardon, kåR'dôN', (ANTOINE,) a skilful Flemish engraver, born at Brussels in 1772. In 1792 he settled in London, where he was employed to engrave the works of Rubens and other masters. Died in 1813.

See NAGLER, "Neues Allgemeines Künstler-Lexikon."

Cardona, de, dä kaR-do'nå, or **Cardone, de,** dä kåR-do'nå, (RAIMUND,) a Spanish general, was appointed Viceroy of Naples by Ferdinand the Catholic in 1509. He was defeated by the French at the great battle of Ravenna in 1512. Afterwards he was sent to chastise the Florentines and Venetians, whom he treated with great cruelty. He was Viceroy of Naples for some time during the reign of Charles V.

See SISMONDI, "Histoire des Républiques Italiennes."

Cardonne, kåR'don', (DENIS DOMINIQUE,) a French Orientalist, born in Paris in 1720. He passed twenty years in Constantinople, where he acquired an extensive knowledge of the Oriental languages and customs. After his return, he was professor of Persian and Turkish in the Royal College, interpreter to the king, royal censor, etc. He published a "History of Africa and Spain under the Saracens," and a successful work entitled "Mélanges of Oriental Literature," selected and translated from Arabic and Persian authors. Died in 1783.

See QUÉRARD, "La France Littéraire."

Cardoso, kaR-do'so, (ISAAC,) a learned Portuguese Jew and physician, born about 1620, was one of the so-called "compulsory Christians," and practised medicine with great success at Madrid. He afterwards renounced the Christian faith, and removed to Italy. Died about 1690.

Cardoso, (JORGE,) an eminent Portuguese author and priest, born in 1606. He wrote "Lives of Portuguese Saints," etc., (1651–57,) which is much esteemed. Died in 1669.

Car-do'zo, (ISAAC N.,) an American journalist, born at Savannah, Georgia, in 1786, was editor of the "Southern Patriot," and other journals, in which he advocated free trade. He published "Notes on Political Economy," (1826.)

Cardross, LORD. See ERSKINE, (HENRY,) and ERSKINE, (DAVID.)

Carducci, kaR-doot'chee, or **Carduccio,** kaR-doot'cho, in Spanish **Carducho,** (BARTOLOMMEO,) a skilful Florentine painter in fresco and oil, was born in 1560. He was a pupil of Zucchero, whom he accompanied to Spain. There he was patronized by Philip II., for whom he painted frescos in the Escurial and pictures for the palace in Madrid. His most admired production is a "Descent from the Cross," which is in a church of

Madrid. After the death of Philip II. he passed into the service of his successor. Died in 1610.

See LANZI, "History of Painting in Italy ;" TICOZZI, "Dizionario."

Carduccio, (VINCENZO,) a brother of the preceding, was an eminent artist, and became painter to Philip III. in 1609. He was the head of a flourishing school, and contributed much to promote the arts in Spain. He painted a gallery in the royal palace of Pardo, and wrote a "Treatise on the Nature and Dignity of Painting," which is highly commended. His illustrations of the life of Saint Bruno are esteemed his best works. Died in 1638.

See LANZI, "History of Painting in Italy ;" TICOZZI, "Dizionario."

Carducho, the Spanish spelling of CARDUCCIO. See CARDUCCI.

Card'well, (EDWARD,) D.D., an English divine, born in 1787. He became principal of Saint Alban's Hall, Oxford, in 1831. He published several important works, among which are "Documentary Annals of the Reformed Church of England," (1839,) and "Synodalia," (Oxford, 1842.) He delivered at Oxford a series of lectures on the coinage of the Greeks and Romans, which were published in 1832, and edited Aristotle's "Ethics." Died in 1861.

See "London Quarterly Review" for September, 1843; "Gentleman's Magazine" for August, 1861.

Cardwell, (EDWARD,) an English statesman, nephew of the preceding, was born at Liverpool in 1813. He studied law, and was called to the bar in 1838. He was returned to Parliament in 1842, and was appointed secretary of the treasury in 1845. From 1852 to 1855 he was president of the Board of Trade, and since the former date has represented Oxford in Parliament. He was attached to the Peelite party while it existed. In 1859 he accepted office in the Liberal ministry of Palmerston, as secretary of Ireland. He was appointed chancellor of the duchy of Lancaster in July, 1861, retaining his seat in the cabinet. On the 4th of April, 1864, he became secretary of state for the colonies. He resigned with his colleagues in June, 1866, and was appointed secretary of war by Mr. Gladstone in December, 1868.

Caregna, kā-rěn'yā or kā-rȧn'yā, (GABRIEL,) a learned physician, born probably in Italy, wrote a compendium of the various questions connected with medical science, published at Bordeaux in 1520.

Carel de Saint-Garde, kǎ'rěl' děh sǎN'gȧrd', (JACQUES,) a French poet, born at Rouen, wrote an epic poem, of which Childebrand was the hero. Boileau satirized him in these lines :

"Oh le plaisant projet d'un poëte ignorant,
Qui de tant de héros va choisir Childebrand !"

Died about 1684.

Carelli, kā-rel'lee, (GIOVANNI BATTISTA,) an Italian astronomer, born at Piacenza, lived about the middle of the sixteenth century. He was the author of various astronomical tables published at Venice from 1555 to 1577.

Carême, kā'rěm', (MARIE ANTOINE,) a French adept in the culinary art, was born in Paris in 1784. He became chief cook successively to Talleyrand, the Czar Alexander, and George IV. of England. He published "The French Steward," "The Picturesque Pastry-Cook," ("Le Patissier pittoresque,") and other works. Died in 1833.

Careño. See CARREÑO DE MIRANDA.

Carera, kā-rā'rȧ, (ANTONIO RAFAELLO,) an Italian writer, born near Milan, lived about 1650. He was the author of a satire against physicians.

Carew, kạ-roo', (BAMFYLDE MOORE,) an English adventurer, called the "King of the Beggars," was born about 1692. He ran away from home in boyhood, and joined a party of gipsies, who elected him king. Died after 1758.

See GOADBY, "Life of Bamfylde M. Carew;" WM. RUSSELL, "Eccentric Personages," 1866.

Carew, (Sir BENJAMIN HALLOWELL,) a British admiral, born about 1760. His family name was Hallowell, to which he added Carew in accordance with the will of a relative. He became a post-captain in 1793, distinguished himself at the battle of the Nile in 1798, and was taken prisoner by the French in 1801. He was

made a rear-admiral in 1811, and was employed in the Mediterranean until the peace of 1815. In 1830 he obtained the rank of a full admiral. Died in 1834.

Carew, (GEORGE,) Earl of Totness, and Baron Carew, a British general, born in 1557. In the wars against the Irish rebels he rose to the rank of lieutenant-general and master of ordnance, and about 1600 was appointed one of the lords justices of Ireland. By his courage and prudence he suppressed a formidable revolt, and repulsed a Spanish invasion. He was created Earl of Totness in 1625. A work called "Pacata Hibernia" ("Ireland Pacified") is ascribed to him. Died in 1629.

See WOOD, "Athenæ Oxonienses."

Carew, (Sir GEORGE,) an English diplomatist, was ambassador to the court of France, from which he returned home in 1609, and addressed to the king "A Relation of the State of France, with the Character of Henry IV., etc." This is said to be an excellent performance. Died about 1612.

See WOOD, "Athenæ Oxonienses."

Carew, (Sir NICHOLAS,) an English courtier, was related to Queen Anne Boleyn. He became a favourite of Henry VIII., who appointed him master of the horse. He was executed in 1539, on a charge of having conspired with the Marquis of Exeter and others to raise Cardinal Pole to the throne.

Carew, (RICHARD,) an English lawyer, brother of Sir George, noticed above, was born in 1555. He was chosen high-sheriff of Cornwall in 1586, and a member of the College of Antiquaries in 1589. He published in 1602 an excellent "Survey of Cornwall," and translated part of Tasso's "Gerusalemme Liberata." Died in 1620.

See WOOD, "Athenæ Oxonienses."

Carew, (THOMAS,) an English nobleman and soldier, born in 1368. He took part in the battle of Agincourt, and other engagements with the French.

Carew, (THOMAS,) an English gentleman, who fought with distinction at Flodden in 1513.

Carew, (THOMAS,) an English poet and courtier, born of a Gloucestershire family in 1589. He was a gentleman of the chamber in the court of Charles I., and wrote sonnets and other short poems, which rendered him a favourite of the literary and fashionable world. "Among the poets that have walked in the same limited path," says Thomas Campbell, "he is pre-eminently beautiful." Died in 1639.

See CIBBER, "Lives of the Poets ;" "Retrospective Review," vol. vi., 1822; "London Quarterly Review" for August, 1810.

Carey, (ALICE.) See CARY.

Cā'rey, (GEORGE SAVILLE,) an English song-writer, born about 1743, was the son of Henry Carey, whose musical talents he inherited. He supported himself by entertaining the public in different towns with songs composed and sung by himself. It is said that he never trespassed against decorum or morality. Died in 1807.

Carey, (HENRY,) Earl of Monmouth, born in 1596, was the son of Robert, first Earl of Monmouth, whose title he inherited in 1639. He was learned in modern languages, and published many translations, among which are "Romulus and Tarquin," by Malvezzi, (1637,) "Historical Relations of the United Provinces," by Bentivoglio, (1652,) and "The History of Venice," by Parata, (1658.) Died in 1661.

Carey, (HENRY,) an English poet and musician, was supposed to be the natural son of G. Saville, Marquis of Halifax. He composed the words and music of several popular songs, and wrote farces and other works, among which are "The Contrivances," and "The Musical Century." He killed himself in 1743. George S. Carey, noticed above, was his son.

See FÉTIS, "Biographie Universelle des Musiciens ;" MACAULAY, "History of England," vol. iv. chap. xx.

Cā'rey, (HENRY C.,) an eminent American political economist, son of Mathew Carey, noticed below, was born in Philadelphia in December, 1793. He was trained to business in the publishing-house of his father, whom he succeeded in 1821, as the head of the firm of Carey & Lea. In 1824 he initiated the practice of periodical trade-sales as a medium of exchange between booksellers. He retired from mercantile business about 1836, and published in that year an "Essay on the Rate of Wages," which he expanded into "The Principles of Political Economy," (3 vols., 1837–40.) This work attracted much attention in Europe, and was translated into Italian and Swedish. He advocates a tariff for the protection of domestic manufactures, and maintains that the real interests of classes are not antagonistic. He produced in 1838 "The Credit System in France, Great Britain, and the United States," and in 1848 a valuable work entitled "The Past, the Present, and the Future," in which he presents some new ideas on the progress of agriculture, wages, and society, and controverts the opinions of Malthus and Ricardo. Among his other important works are "The Harmony of Interests, Agricultural, Manufacturing, and Commercial," and "The Principles of Social Science," (3 vols., 1858–59.) He is recognized as the founder of a new school of political economy, which substitutes for the "dismal science" of Malthus and Ricardo a philosophy of physical, social, and political progress.

See "Nouvelle Biographie Générale."

Ca′rey, (JOHN,) LL.D., an Irish scholar, who published many educational works. He edited fifty volumes of the "Regent's Classics," also "Ainsworth's Latin Dictionary," and "Schleusner's Greek Lexicon." He translated some useful works from the French and German. Died in 1829.

Carey, (MATHEW,) a distinguished bookseller and writer, born in Dublin, Ireland, in 1760, learned the trade of printer, and emigrated to Philadelphia in 1784. He founded "The Pennsylvania Herald" in 1785, and published "The American Museum" from 1787 to 1793. He took a prominent part in political affairs, wrote numerous pamphlets, and advocated the United States Bank. To moderate the violence of party spirit, he produced "The Olive-Branch," which passed through ten editions. Among his works are "Essays on Political Economy," and many pamphlets in advocacy of a protective tariff. He was an influential and much-respected citizen. Died in 1839.

See "Encyclopædia Americana," (Supplement;) HUNT's "Lives of American Merchants," vol. i., 1858.

Carey or **Cā′rȳ**, (ROBERT,) first Earl of Monmouth, a British peer, born about 1560, was a relative of Queen Elizabeth, and father of Henry Carey, noticed above. He left manuscript memoirs of his own life, which were published in 1759 by the Earl of Cork and Orrery. Died in 1639.

Carey, (WILLIAM,) D.D., an English Orientalist and Baptist missionary, was born in Northamptonshire in 1761. He went to India in 1794, laboured a few years in Bengal, founded the Serampore mission, and about 1800 became professor of the Sanscrit, Bengalee, and Mahratta languages at the College of Fort William. He published a "Sanscrit Grammar," a "Bengalee-English Dictionary," and several other works. He and his associates translated the Bible into Bengalee and many other Oriental dialects. He was a member of the Asiatic Society. Died in 1834.

See MARSHMAN, "Life of W. Carey," 1859; EUSTACE CAREY, "Memoir of the Rev. W. Carey," 1836.

Carey, (WILLIAM PAULETT,) an Irish writer and critic, brother of Mathew Carey, noticed above, was born in 1768. He became a resident of England, and was an able advocate of political reform. He wrote critical and poetical articles for several periodicals. Died in 1839.

Carez, kȧ′rȧ′, (JOSEPH,) a French printer of Toul, who made improvements in the process of stereotype printing, and is said to be the inventor of *clichage*, by which he printed a book in 1786. Died in 1801.

Car′gill, (DONALD,) a zealous and uncompromising Scottish Covenanter, was born in Perthshire about 1610. He became minister of a parish in Glasgow, and on the restoration in 1660 refused to conform to the new ecclesiastical regulations. He afterwards refused to accept the indulgence, and was a partisan of Richard Cameron when the latter took arms against the king in 1680. Cargill was executed for treason in 1681.

See CHAMBERS, "Biographical Dictionary of Eminent Scotsmen."

Caribert. See CHAROBERT.

Cȧr′ī-bert [Fr. pron. kȧ′re′baiR′; Lat. CARIBER′TUS] **I,** the eldest son of Clotaire I., became King of Paris in 561. Died in 567 A.D.

Caribert II., a son of Clotaire II., and a younger brother of Dagobert, became King of Aquitaine in 629. Died in 631 A.D.

Carignano, kȧ-rèn-yȧ′no, [Fr. CARIGNAN, kȧ′rèn′-yòN′,] (CHARLES EMMANUEL FERDINAND JOSEPH MARIE,) PRINCE OF, the only son of Victor Amadeus, was born at Turin in 1770. He was taken to France as a hostage in 1799, and died there in 1800, leaving a son, Charles Albert, who became King of Sardinia in 1831.

Carignano, [Fr. CARIGNAN,] (THOMAS FRANCIS DE SAVOY,) PRINCE OF, born in 1596, was a younger son of Charles Emmanuel, Duke of Savoy. About 1635 he obtained the command of the Spanish army in the Low Countries, and was defeated by the French at Avesnes. He took arms against the widow of Victor Amadeus (his sister-in-law) in 1639, and expelled her from Turin, but was reconciled with her in 1642. He was then appointed general-in-chief of the French and Savoyard armies in Italy, and defeated the Spaniards at Mora in 1645. In 1654 he was made grand master or high-steward of France. He died in 1656, leaving two sons,—Emmanuel, who became Prince of Carignano, and Eugene Maurice, who was the father of the famous Prince Eugene.

See SCLOPIS, "Documenti intorno alla Vita di T. F. Principe de Carignano," 1832; ERSCH und GRUBER, "Allgemeine Encyklopaedie."

Carillo, kȧ-rèl′yo, (ALFONSO,) a Spanish prelate, born at Cuenca in the second half of the fourteenth century, was made a cardinal by the anti-pope Benedict XIII. in 1409. Died in 1434.

Carillo, (BRAULIO,) an able statesman of Central America, born at Cartago in 1800, became Dictator of Costa Rica in 1838. He was assassinated in 1845.

Carillo d'Acunha, kȧ-rèl′yo (?) dȧ-koon′yȧ, (ALPHONSO,) an ambitious Spanish prelate, of Portuguese descent. He became Archbishop of Toledo in 1446, and was afterwards chief minister of Henry IV. of Castile, who began to reign in 1454. He rebelled against that king in 1465, took an active part in the civil war that ensued, and was the master-spirit of the party of Isabella of Castile. After her accession in 1474 he changed sides, and fought for Joanna until 1478, when he submitted to the successful party. Died in 1482.

See MARIANA, "Historia de España."

Carin. See CARINUS.

Cą-rī′nus, [Fr. CARIN, kȧ′rȧN′,] (MARCUS AURELIUS,) a Roman emperor, eldest son of the emperor Carus, who committed to him the government of Italy, Africa, and the West, when he set out on an expedition against Persia in 283 A.D. Carus died, or was killed, in 284, soon after which Diocletian was chosen emperor by the army in the East. A battle was fought between Carinus and his rival near Margum, in Mœsia, in which the latter was successful, and Carinus, who was detested for his cruelty, was killed by his own soldiers in 285.

See VOPISCUS, "Carinus;" GIBBON, "Decline and Fall of the Roman Empire."

Carissimi, kȧ-rès′se-mee or kȧ-ris′se-mee, (GIACOMO or GIOVANNI GIACOMO,) one of the greatest composers of his time, was born at Venice about 1582. He was the first who employed cantatas for religious subjects; and he made other reforms in sacred music. His motets and cantatas are very celebrated. He was appointed master of the pontifical chapel in Rome about 1649. "The Sacrifice of Jephthah" is called his master-piece. He formed many eminent pupils, among whom was Alessandro Scarlatti. Died in or after 1672.

See FÉTIS, "Biographie Universelle des Musiciens."

Cariteo, kȧ-re-tā′o, an Italian poet, was born at Barcelona, and lived at Naples. He was a friend of Sannazar, and manifested his devotion to the house of Aragon by several odes. He died before 1509.

Carl, kaRl, (JOHANN SAMUEL,) a learned German, born at Oehringen in 1676, was appointed first physician to Christian VI. of Denmark in 1736. He published "Medicina Universalis," (1740,) a treatise "On the Use and Abuse of Bleeding," and many other medical works. Died in 1757.

See BÖRNER, "Jetztlebende Aerzte."

Carl der Grosse. See CHARLEMAGNE.

Carle, kåRl, (PIERRE,) a French engineer, born in the Cevennes in 1666. He entered in 1688 the service of William of Orange, who employed him as engineer in several campaigns. About 1701 he passed into the service of Portugal, and in the war of the Spanish succession became lieutenant-general, and chief engineer of the King of Portugal. In 1720 he retired to London, where he died in 1730.

Carlén, kaʀ-lān′, almost kaʀ-lĭ′ĭn′, (EMILIE FLYGARE,) a popular Swedish novel-writer, whose maiden name was SCHMIDT, (shmit,) born at Stockholm about 1808. She was married to Mr. Carlén, a lawyer of Stockholm, in 1841, after the publication of her first novel, "Waldemar Klein," which had a decided success. She has since written "The Professor," "The Rose of Tistelön," ("Thistle-Island," 1844,) "Home in the Valley," ("Familier i Dalen," 1850,) and other novels delineating Swedish life. They have been translated into English, and have acquired popularity in England and America.

See BROCKHAUS, "Conversations-Lexikon;" W. and M. HOWITT, "Literature and Romance of Northern Europe," 1852, vol. ii. pp. 456-60.

Carleson, kaʀ′leh-son, (EDUARD,) a Swedish diplomatist and economist, born at Stockholm in 1704. He was appointed secretary of foreign affairs in 1757, and president of the council of commerce in 1762. He wrote "Travels in Palestine," (1768,) and other works. Died in 1767.

See GEZELIUS, "Biographiskt-Lexikon;" A. SCHOENBERG, "Åminnelse-Tal öfver E. Carleson," 1767.

Carleson, (KARL,) a Swedish jurist, economist, and writer, brother of the preceding, was born at Stockholm in 1703. He was one of the editors of the "Svenska Argus," a useful literary periodical, and wrote a "Dictionary of Economy," and other works. In 1757 he was appointed secretary of state. Died in 1761.

See GEZELIUS, "Biographiskt-Lexikon;" P. WARGENTIN, "Åminnelse-Tal öfver C. Carleson," 1763.

Carleton, kaʀl′ton, (Sir DUDLEY,) Lord Dorchester, an English statesman, born in Oxfordshire in 1573. He was sent as ambassador to Venice in 1610, to Holland in 1616, and to France in 1625. In 1628 Charles I. created him Viscount Dorchester, and made him secretary of state. He wrote several political tracts. Died in 1631.

Carleton, (GEORGE,) a learned English bishop, born at Norham Castle, of which his father was governor. He was sent by James I. to the Synod of Dort in 1618, and appointed Bishop of Chichester in 1619. He wrote many works on theology and other subjects, among which are a treatise against Astrology, and one "On Jurisdiction, Regal, Episcopal, etc." Died in 1628.

Carleton, (Captain GEORGE,) wrote "Memoirs of an English Officer," (1728,) which have some historical value, and were once attributed to Defoe or Swift.

Carleton, (Sir GUY,) Lord Dorchester, a British general, born at Strabane, Ireland, in 1724. After serving several years in America, he obtained the rank of major-general in 1772, and was made governor of Quebec, which he defended against the Americans in December, 1775. The next year he commanded the army which invaded New York, and fought with Arnold on Lake Champlain. In 1777 he was superseded by General Burgoyne. He was appointed commander-in-chief, *vice* Sir Henry Clinton, in 1781, and, when the peace was concluded, returned to England. In 1787 he received the title of Lord Dorchester. Died in 1808.

See BANCROFT's "History of the United States."

Carleton, (JAMES HENRY,) an American officer, born in Maine, served in the Mexican war, and, soon after the breaking out of the rebellion of 1861, became brigadier-general of volunteers.

Carleton, (WILLIAM,) an eminent Irish novelist, born at Clogher, Tyrone county, in 1798. He published, in 1830, "Traits and Stories of the Irish Peasantry," which had great success. After that time he resided in Dublin, and produced "Fardorougha the Miser," (1839,) "The Fawn of Spring Vale," (1841,) "Willie Reilly," (1855,) and other popular novels. "Mr. Carleton has caught most accurately the lights and shades of Irish life. His tales are full of vigorous, picturesque description and genuine pathos." ("London Quarterly Review" for October, 1841.) Died in 1869.

Carletti, kaʀ-let′tee, (FRANCESCO,) a Florentine traveller, who between 1597 and 1601 visited India, China, and Japan. Having returned to Florence, he was appointed steward by the duke, Ferdinand I., and wrote a narrative of his travels, which was afterwards printed.

Carletto. See CAGLIARI, (CARLO.)

Carli, or **Carli Rubbi**, kaʀ′lee roob′bee, (GIAN RINALDO,) COUNT, an Italian political economist and antiquary, born at Capo d'Istria in 1720. He became learned in the exact sciences and ancient languages. The Venetian senate founded a chair of astronomy and nautical science, of which Carli was professor from 1744 to 1750. After devoting several years to researches respecting coins and currency, he published in 1754 the first volume of his important work on that subject,"Of Italian Moneys, (or Coins,) and of the Institution of Mints in Italy," ("Delle Monete e delle Istituzione delle Zecche d'Italia.") This work made a great sensation in Italy, and its principles were adopted by the courts of Milan and Turin. The court of Vienna having formed at Milan a supreme council of commerce and public economy, Carli was appointed its president. About 1780 he produced two remarkable works, an "Essay on the Natural and Civil Liberty of Man," and "American Letters," which treat of the antiquities of the New World. His "Antichità Italiche" ("Italian Antiquities," 1788) was very successful, and secured for him among antiquaries a rank equal to that which he had attained among political economists. He was author of various other works. Died in 1795.

See BOSSI, "Elogio storico di Gian Rinaldo Carli;" TIPALDO, "Biografia degli Italiani illustri;" "Nouvelle Biographie Générale."

Carlier, kăʀ′le-à′, (CLAUDE,) a French writer, born at Verberie in 1725. He studied natural history in relation to rural economy, especially to the business of wool-growing. He furnished many articles to the "Journal des Savants," and wrote a "History of the Duchy of Valois," and several treatises on the method of raising sheep and on the production of wool. Died in 1787.

Car′lin, (THOMAS,) born in Kentucky in 1790, removed to Illinois in 1813. He was elected Governor of Illinois in 1838, and was re-elected several times. Died in 1852.

Car′ling-foṛd, (THEOBALD **Taafe**—täf,) EARL OF, a general who rendered important services to Charles I. by his efforts to suppress the rebellion in Ireland about 1640-46. Died in 1677.

Carlino, kaʀ-lee′no, [Fr. CARLIN, kăʀ′lăn′,] (CARLO ANTONIO **Bertinazzi**—bêʀ-te-nat′see,) a noted comic actor, born at Turin in 1713; died in Paris in 1783.

Carlisle, kar-lil′, (Sir ANTHONY,) an eminent English surgeon, born near Durham in 1768. He went to London to complete his education, and attended the lectures of John and William Hunter. He became a member of the College of Surgeons, professor of surgery and anatomy in London, and surgeon-extraordinary to the prince-regent, (George IV.) In 1800 he was chosen a Fellow of the Royal Society, to which he contributed several treatises on physiology, etc. From 1808 to 1825 he lectured on anatomy in the Royal Academy, and in 1829 was chosen president of the College of Surgeons. He published numerous and able treatises on anatomy, and on various sciences connected with medicine, also one on "Galvanic Electricity." Died in 1840.

Carlisle, EARL OF. See HOWARD, (CHARLES, FREDERICK, and GEORGE WILLIAM FREDERICK.)

Carlisle, (ISABELLA BYRON,) COUNTESS OF, born in 1721, was the daughter of William, fifth Lord Byron, and first-cousin to the poet Byron's father. In 1743 she was married to Henry Howard, fourth Earl of Carlisle, by whom she had a son Frederick, who was a poet. Died in 1795.

Carlisle, (NICHOLAS,) a British writer and antiquary, born in 1771. He published topographical dictionaries of England, of Ireland, and of Scotland, which are said to be valuable and accurate. Died in 1847.

Carlo Alberto. See CHARLES ALBERT.

Carlo Magno. See CHARLEMAGNE.

Carlo Quinto. See CHARLES V., (of Germany.)

Car′lo-man or **Karloman**, [Fr. pron. kăʀ′lo′mŏN′,] a French prince, was the son of Charles Martel, and elder brother of Pepin le Bref. At his father's death in 741 A.D., he obtained for his share Austrasia, Suabia, and Thuringia. After fighting for these possessions with the Allemanni (or Germans) and others, he renounced his principality in favour of Pepin, went to Rome in 747, and became a monk. Died in 755.

See SISMONDI, "Histoire des Français."

Carloman, the son of Pepin le Bref, and brother of Charlemagne, was born in 751 A.D. At the death of his father, in 768, he became King of Neustria, Burgundy, and part of Aquitaine or South Gaul. He died in 771, leaving two sons; but Charlemagne obtained the dominions of his brother.

See SISMONDI, "Histoire des Français."

Carloman, a Carlovingian prince of the Franks, was the son of Louis le Bègue. In 879 A.D. he was crowned King of Aquitaine and of part of Burgundy, while his brother, Louis III., obtained Neustria, etc. They lived in amity, and their united arms were victorious over the Normans and other foes. He died without issue in 884.

See SISMONDI, "Histoire des Français."

Carloni, kaR-lo'nee, written also **Carlone** and **Carlon,** (GIOVANNI,) an eminent Genoese painter, born in 1591. He adorned the churches of Genoa with frescos, which are greatly admired, and worked also in Florence and Milan. He excelled in brilliancy of colour, facility of composition, and grace of design. Died at Milan in 1630.

Carloni or **Carlone,** (GIOVANNI BATTISTA,) a brother of the preceding, born about 1595, was an excellent painter, especially in fresco. The finest works of the two brothers (who often worked together) are frescos in the church of the Annunziata in Genoa. The compositions are rich and original, and the colours remarkably splendid. The works of these brothers are similar, but those of G. Battista are superior in some respects. He died in 1680, leaving two sons, Giovanni Andrea and Niccolò, who were painters, but not equal to their father. Andrea was born in 1639, and died in 1697.

See TICOZZI, "Dizionario;" LANZI, "History of Painting in Italy."

Car'los, [Spanish pron. kaR'lôs,] DON, Infante of Spain, born at Valladolid in 1545, was the son and heir-apparent of Philip II. and Maria of Portugal. At an early age he manifested a violent and unhappy temper, which his education did not improve. His physical constitution was also diseased, and his reason was perhaps affected by a fit of sickness in his youth. It is said that he was offended at his father because he married Elizabeth of France after having negotiated a proposal of marriage between Carlos and that princess. Carlos attempted to strike the Duke of Alva with a poniard in 1567; but the blow was warded off. The suspicious king, imagining that Carlos had conspired against him, ordered his son to be arrested and judged by the Inquisition. His fate is involved in mystery. Many historians think he was executed, by order of his father, in 1568; others, that he died of disease in prison. His life has furnished Alfieri, Schiller, and others with the subject for a tragedy.

See LUIS DE CABRERA, "Relatio Vitæ Mortisque Caroli Infantis," 1715; SAINT-RÉAL, "Histoire de Don Carlos;" PRESCOTT, "History of Philip II.," vols. i. and ii.

Carlos of Bourbon, (boor'bǫn,) DON, Count de Molina, (dǎ mo-lee'nǎ,) born in 1788, was the second son of Charles IV., King of Spain. During the French empire he was detained in France from 1808 to 1813, when he returned to Spain. He was heir-presumptive to the throne of his brother, Ferdinand VII., until the latter became a father by the birth of Isabella in 1830. The decree of the king settled the succession on his daughter, though the Cortes some years before had restored the Salic law, which excludes females from the throne. At the death of Ferdinand, in 1833, a civil war broke out between the partisans of Isabella and Carlos. The latter was the favourite of the priests and absolutists. In 1839 the Carlist army was compelled to surrender to Espartero, who fought for the queen, and Don Carlos escaped to France. (See ISABELLA.) He abdicated his claim in 1845 in favour of his son, Don Carlos Luis Maria Fernando, Count de Montemolin. Died in 1855.

See DE LOS VALLES, "Career of Don Carlos since the Death of Ferdinand VII.," London, 1835; RUY SANCHEZ, "Historia de Don Carlos," 2 vols., 1844.

Carlos, or, more fully, **Carlos Luis Maria Fernando,** kaR'lôs loo-èss' mä-ree'ǎ fêR-nän'do, Count de

Montemolin, (dǎ mon-tǎ-mo-lèn',) a son of the preceding, was born in 1818. He is a pretender to the Spanish throne, and a first-cousin of the late queen Isabella. His father abdicated in his favour in 1845, since which the Carlists recognize the son as Carlos VI. In 1848 his friends attempted to renew the civil war, but were quickly defeated.

Carlostadt. See CARLSTADT.

Carlota de Bourbon, kaR-lo'tǎ dǎ booR-bôn', (LUISA,) Infanta of Spain, born in 1804, was a daughter of Francis I., King of the Two Sicilies, and Maria Isabella of Spain. She was an aunt of Isabella, the late Queen of Spain. In 1819 she was married to Don Francisco de Paul, a brother of Don Carlos. Her intrigues, it is said, procured the repeal of the Salic law, and the succession of Isabella in preference to Carlos. She died in 1844, after which her son married Queen Isabella.

Carlowitz, kaR'lo-ŵits', (ALOÏSE CHRISTINE,) BARONESS OF, a French authoress, of German extraction, born at Fiume in 1797. She has written "Caroline," (1833,) "The Peer of France, or the Divorce," (1835,) and other tales. Her French version of Schiller's "History of the Thirty Years' War" was crowned by the French Academy.

Carlstadt, karl'stät, written also **Carlostadt** or **Carolostadt,** (ANDREAS Bodenstein—bo'dęn-stīn',) a German Reformer, born in Franconia about 1483. He was professor of divinity at Wittenberg in his early life. After his conversion to the doctrines of Luther he became an iconoclast. About 1524 he opposed Luther in relation to the eucharist. Died in 1541.

See B. BIELER, "Gesammelte Nachrichten von Carlstadts Leben," 1738; J. C. FUESSLI, "Lebensgeschichte A. Bodensteins," 1776.

Car-lÿle', (ALEXANDER,) D.D., a Scottish Presbyterian divine, born in 1721. He was appointed minister of Inveresk, near Edinburgh, in 1747, and became the associate of Blair, Hume, John Home, and other eminent authors. He published a number of sermons between 1779 and 1794, and wrote memoirs of his own time, entitled "Autobiography of A. Carlyle," (published in 1860.) Died in 1805.

See CHAMBERS, "Biographical Dictionary of Eminent Scotsmen."

Carlyle, (JOSEPH DACRE,) an English Orientalist, born at Carlisle in 1759, was a Fellow of Queen's College, Cambridge. In 1794 he was chosen professor of Arabic in that university. About 1800 he went to Constantinople as chaplain to Lord Elgin's embassy, and travelled in Asia. He published "Specimens of Arabic Poetry," (1796,) and undertook a new edition of the Arabic Bible, which he did not live to finish. He died in 1804, leaving a number of admired poems, which were published in 1805.

Carlyle, kar'līl or kar-līl', (THOMAS,) a distinguished British essayist, historian, and speculative philosopher, born at Ecclefechan, in Scotland, in 1795. He entered, in 1809 or 1810, the University of Edinburgh, where he remained about seven years, and distinguished himself in mathematics. He also became well versed in the German language and literature. Having devoted himself to the profession of author, he contributed several biographical articles to the "Edinburgh Encyclopædia" in 1823, published a well-written "Life of Schiller," (1824,) and a translation of Goethe's "Wilhelm Meister," (begun in 1824,) which attracted much attention. About 1825 he married a Miss Welch, and settled on a farm in his native county. Soon after that year he began to contribute critical essays and biographical notices to the "Edinburgh Review," the "Foreign Quarterly Review," and "Fraser's Magazine." In 1834 he published, anonymously, a remarkable work, entitled "Sartor Resartus," which he professed to have translated from a German treatise on the "Philosophy of Clothes," by Diogenes Teufelsdröckh. "This volume," says Alexander H. Everett, "contains, under a quaint and singular form, a great deal of deep thought, sound principle, and fine writing. . . . The style is a sort of Babylonish dialect, not destitute, it is true, of richness, vigour, and at times a sort of felicity of expression, but very strongly tinged throughout with the peculiar idiom of the German language." ("North American Review," vol. xli., October, 1835.) "Sartor Resartus," which first appeared in "Fraser's Magazine," attained a rapid and wide popularity.

ε as k; ç as s; ḡ hard; ġ as j; G, H, K, guttural; N, nasal; R, trilled; ŝ as z; ŧh as in this. (☞ See Explanations, p. 23.)

In 1834 Mr. Carlyle removed to London, where he resided many years. He produced in 1837 a "History of the French Revolution," (3 vols.,) which was generally admired. "On the whole, no work of greater genius, either historical or poetical, has been produced in this country for many years." ("Westminster Review" for July, 1837.) Some other critics, however, express a very different opinion. "Never, indeed," says "Blackwood's Magazine" of July, 1843, "was history written in so mad a vein,—and that not only as regards style, but the prevailing mood of mind in which the facts and characters are scanned. That mood is for the most part ironical. . . . In fine, turn which way you will,—to philosophy, to politics, to religion,—you find Mr. Carlyle objecting, denouncing, scoffing, rending all to pieces in his bold, reckless, ironical manner, but teaching nothing." In 1839 he published "Chartism," in which he treats of the social and political condition of the English. In 1840 he delivered in London a course of lectures on "Heroes and Hero-Worship," which were afterwards published. Among his favourite heroes are Cromwell, Napoleon I., Mohammed, and Frederick the Great. In 1839 or 1840 appeared five volumes of his essays, under the title of "Miscellanies," republished from various periodicals. He again assumed the character of social and political reformer in his "Past and Present," (1843,) and "Latter-Day Pamphlets," (1850.) Among the most important of his later works are "Oliver Cromwell's Letters and Speeches," (1845,) a "Life of John Sterling," (1851,) and "The Life of Frederick the Great," (4 vols., 1858–64.) He has been a constant opponent of the anti-slavery movement, and professes a great contempt for the African race. In 1867 he denounced the new English Reform Bill, and the tendency of the nations towards democracy, in a strange chaotic essay called "Shooting Niagara."

Besides his excellent translations from the German, Carlyle has contributed much in various ways to promote a knowledge of German literature among the English; and the nation is doubtless much indebted to his efforts in this respect than to those of any other single person. Respecting the merit of his original productions the greatest diversity of opinion, as might naturally be expected, prevails among critics. Probably there never was a writer to whom the saying, "Ubi bene nemo melius, ubi male nemo pejus,"* could be more justly applied than to Carlyle. Not a few of his thoughts are inestimable gems, (although the setting may seem rude or quaint,) and nearly all his earlier works abound with passages illuminated by flashes of rare insight, or enriched with important truths, which, if not always new, are at least presented in such a manner as to arouse attention and awaken thought. It is scarcely too much to say that no other author of this century has exerted a greater influence not merely upon the literature, but upon the mind, of the English nation, than Carlyle. But, if his merits are of a high order, his defects are, in our judgment, neither few nor small. Not to mention others of less importance, it will be enough to instance his well-known admiration for successful power, however acquired or exercised, and the want of sympathy evinced by him for the oppressed and down-trodden.† The glaring faults of his style are more conspicuous, or at least offend us more, in his later works, because unrelieved by the freshness of feeling and richness of thought by which his earlier writings are distinguished.

See "Fraser's Magazine" for December, 1858, and December, 1865; "Blackwood's Magazine" for February, 1859; "Foreign Quarterly" for September, 1840; "Edinburgh Review" for October, 1859; "Westminster Review" for January, 1859. For some severe but not unjust strictures on Carlyle's political and moral theories, see "A Letter to Thomas Carlyle," by D. A. WASSON, in the "Atlantic Monthly" for October, 1863.

* "When [he writes] well, none [can write] better; when ill, none worse."

† It is a consolation to believe that these moral blemishes proceed from a mistaken theory rather than from an unfeeling or depraved heart. Carlyle's works—at least his earlier ones—afford abundant evidence that he is capable of a true and heartfelt sympathy with heroic suffering; and we can only attribute it to the influence of a false moral system, or to the prejudice of race, that one who could feel such compassion for the misfortunes of a Marie Antoinette, or such generous admiration for the heroism of a Bouillé, should feel only an unsympathizing contempt for the greater misfortunes and sublimer heroism of a Toussaint.

Car-lȳ'on, (CLEMENT,) an English physician, born at Truro in 1777, was a friend of S. T. Coleridge. He practised at Truro, and published, besides other works, "Early Years and Late Reflections," (4 vols., 1836–58.) Died in 1864.

Carmagnola, kaR-mân-yo'lâ, [Fr. CARMAGNOLE, kȃʀ'mȃn'yol',] an able Italian general, whose proper name was FRANCESCO BUSSONE, (fɾȃn-chȇs'ko boos-so'nȁ,) was born at Carmagnola in 1390. In the service of Visconti, Duke of Milan, he rose to the chief command of the army, and by his military successes restored the declining power of that prince, who made him a count. In 1424, Visconti, prompted by jealousy, deprived him of his command. The general, who had assumed the name of Carmagnola, then passed into the service of Venice, which declared war against the Duke of Milan in 1426. Carmagnola was chosen captain-general, and defeated the Milanese army in 1427. Having suffered some reverses in the ensuing campaigns, he was perfidiously seized and executed by the Council of Ten in 1432. His life is the subject of Manzoni's tragedy "Il Conte di Carmagnola."

See SISMONDI, "Histoire des Républiques Italiennes;" SANUTO, "Vite de' Duchi di Venezia;" LUIGI CIBRARIO, "La Morte del Conte di Carmagnola illustrata," etc., 1834.

Carmagnole, the French of CARMAGNOLA, which see.

Carmarthen. See CAERMARTHEN.

Carmath and Carmatians. See KARMAT.

Carmeli, kaR-mā'lee, (MICHEL ANGELO,) an Italian monk, noted as a Hebrew and Greek scholar, was born at Cittadella about 1700. He was appointed professor of Oriental languages at Padua in 1744. Among his numerous works are an edition of Euripides with notes and an Italian version, (1743–54,) and a "History of the Various Customs, Sacred and Profane, which have been transmitted from the Ancients to the Present Times," (1750.) Died at Padua in 1766.

See TIPALDO, "Biografia degli Italiani illustri;" FANZAGO, "Elogio storico del P. M. Carmeli," 1779.

Car-men'ta, [Fr. CARMENTE, kȃʀ'mȏNt',] a prophetic divinity of ancient Italy, was one of the Camenæ, and supposed to be the mother of Evander. She was worshipped by the Roman matrons at a festival called "Carmentalia."

Carmer, kaR'mer, (JOHANN HEINRICH,) a Prussian lawyer and chancellor, born in 1721; died in 1801.

Carmichael, kar'mī-kel, (GERRHOM,) a Scottish professor of moral philosophy, born at Glasgow in 1682; died in 1738.

Carmichael, (RICHARD,) an Irish surgeon and medical writer, born in Dublin in 1779; died in 1849.

Carmignani, kaR-mên-yȃ'nee, (GIOVANNI ALESSANDRO,) an Italian jurist, born near Pisa in 1768. He practised law in Florence with success, and was reputed one of the greatest forensic orators of that city. He published "Theory of Civil Laws," (1797,) "Elements of Criminal Law," (1803,) and other works. Died in 1847.

Carminati, kaR-me-nä'tee, (BASSIANO,) an Italian physician, born at Lodi in 1750. He was appointed professor of therapeutics, etc. at Pavía, and afterwards became professor emeritus in the same university. His "Hygiene, Therapeutics, and Materia Medica," written in Latin, is a work of great merit. Died in 1830.

See TIPALDO, "Biografia degli Italiani illustri."

Carmoly, kȃʀ'mo'le', (ÉLIACIN,) a French Jew, born in 1805. He has published a "Biography of the Israelites, Ancient and Modern," (1829,) "Literary History of Jewish Authors from the Twelfth to the Sixteenth Century," (1850,) and many other works.

Carmona, kaR-mo'nâ, (SALVADOR,) a distinguished Spanish engraver, born at Madrid about 1730, was a pupil of Dupuis of Paris, and was patronized by the King of Spain. Among his works is a "Virgin and Child," after Van Dyck. Died in 1807.

Carmontelle, kȃʀ'mȏN'tèl', an ingenious French dramatic writer, born in Paris in 1717. In 1768 he published "Dramatic Proverbs," (6 vols.,) on which his literary reputation is founded. These short comedies were favourites with the performers of private theatres. This work is said to be a mine from which several comic authors have borrowed freely. He had a talent for painting, and painted portraits of the most distinguished persons of the eighteenth century. Died in 1806.

See QUÉRARD, "La France Littéraire."

Carmouche, kȧr'moosh', (PIERRE FRÉDÉRIC ADOLPHE,) a French dramatic author, born at Lyons in 1797. He produced many successful plays, among which are the "Honey-Moon," ("Lune de Miel,") "The Vampire," (1820,) and "The Dreams of Matheus," ("Les Rêves de Matheus," 1852.) He has also written fugitive poems and songs. Died in December, 1868.

Car-nar'von, (HENRY HOWARD MOLYNEUX (mol'e-nooks) HERBERT,) fourth EARL OF, the eldest son of the third earl, was born in 1831. He published in 1860 "The Druses of Mount Lebanon." He became secretary of state for the colonies in June, 1866. Disagreeing with Lord Derby and Disraeli on the Reform Bill, he resigned in March, 1867.

Carnarvon, (HENRY JOHN GEORGE HERBERT,) third EARL OF, an English author, born in 1800. He published "Don Pedro," a tragedy ; "Moor," a poem ; and "Notes on Portugal, Galicia, etc." The last work is said to be one of superior ability and interest. Died in 1849.

Carne, karn, (JOHN,) a British traveller and writer, who passed several years in Asia, and wrote "Recollections of Travels in Syria and Palestine," (1830,) and "Letters from the East." Died in 1844, aged about fifty-five.

Carné, de, deh kȧr'nȧ',(LOUIS Marcein—mȧR'sȧN',) COUNT, a French publicist, born at Quimper in 1804. He was elected to the Chamber of Deputies in 1839, and at first acted with the opposition against Guizot. In 1847 he accepted in the Foreign Office the place of Drouyn de l'Huys, removed from his functions of director for supporting a motion of Carné himself against Guizot. He was deprived of this office by the Revolution of 1848. He has published "Views on Contemporary History," (1833,) and other political works. In 1863 he was elected to the Institute in place of Biot.

See QUÉRARD, "La France Littéraire."

Carnéade. See CARNEADES.

Car-ne'a-dēs,[Gr. Καρνεάδης; Fr. CARNÉADE, kȧr'nȧ'-ȧd',] a Greek philosopher and orator, born at Cyrene, in Africa, about 215 B.C., was the founder of a school called the New Academy. He opposed the dogmas of the Stoics, and maintained that the human mind cannot ascertain the truth. He was celebrated for his subtle and powerful eloquence, which his antagonists were unable to gainsay or successfully resist. In 154 B.C., having been sent as ambassador from Athens to Rome, he charmed the young men of the latter city by his eloquent discourses, so that many were quite possessed with an enthusiastic love of philosophy. After he had harangued one day in favour of justice, on the next day he displayed his specious and audacious eloquence in refuting his former arguments and in confounding the distinctions of good and evil. Cato the Censor took prompt measures to protect the youth from this sophistry, and Carneades was dismissed from the city. He died about the age of ninety.

See DIOGENES LAERTIUS; J. ROULEZ, "De Carneade Philosopho ;" VERBURG, "De Carneade Romam legato," 1826; GOURAUD, "Dissertatio de Carneadis Philosophi Vita et Placitis," 1848; CICERO, "Academica" and "De Natura Deorum."

Carneau, kȧr'nō', (ÉTIENNE,) a French poet and monk, born at Chartres ; died in 1671.

Car'ne-gie, (Sir ROBERT,) of Kinnaird, a Scottish negotiator, was minister to France about 1550, and afterwards held several high offices in Scotland. Having joined the Reformers, he was sent by the lords of the Congregation on missions to England and France. Died in 1566.

Carneiro, kaR-nā'e-ro, or **Carnero,** kaR-nā'ro, (ANTONIO,) a Portuguese historian, born near Elvas. He was commissary and treasurer of the Spanish army sent to Flanders in 1585, and wrote a "History of the Civil Wars of the Low Countries from 1559 to 1609," (1612.)

Carnero. See CARNEIRO.

Carnevale, kaR-nà-vȧ'là, (BARTOLOMMEO CORRADINO,) a celebrated painter of the Roman school, born at Urbino. Having become a friar, he was usually called FRA CARNEVALE. Died about 1478.

See LANZI, "History of Painting in Italy."

Carnio, kaR'ne-o, (ANTONIO,) a painter, born in Friuli, was considered superior to any painter whom that country had produced since Pordenone. Died in or after 1680.

See LANZI, "History of Painting in Italy."

Carnochan, kar'noH-an or kar'nok-en, (JOHN MURRAY,) a skilful American surgeon, born at Savannah, Georgia, in 1817, studied under Dr. Valentine Mott. He became in 1851 professor of surgery in the Medical College of New York.

Carnot, kȧr'no', (JOSEPH FRANÇOIS CLAUDE,) a French jurist, brother of the great statesman Carnot, born at Nolay in 1752. He was a warm friend of the reforms made in 1789, and was appointed attorney-general of his department in 1796. He was judge of the tribunal of cassation from 1801 until 1835. He published valuable commentaries on the penal code, and other legal works. Died in 1835.

See "Nouvelle Biographie Générale."

Carnot, (LAZARE HIPPOLYTE,) a French radical politician, a son of the famous war-minister of the republic, was born at Saint-Omer in 1801. He spent several years in exile with his father, and returned to France in 1823. In his youth he was a partisan of Saint-Simon, and advocated socialism in the "Revue Encyclopédique." He was elected to the Chamber of Deputies by the radical opposition in 1839, 1842, and 1846. In February, 1848, he was appointed minister of public instruction by the provisional government, but resigned in July of that year. During this brief term of office he improved the condition of teachers, and procured a decision that the normal school should be gratuitous. Carnot and Cavaignac were elected by the republican voters of Paris to the Legislative Assembly in 1852 ; but, as they refused to take the oath to Louis Napoleon, they were excluded from their seats.

See LAMARTINE, "History of the Revolution of 1848."

Carnot, (LAZARE NICOLAS MARGUERITE,) an eminent French statesman, geometer, and military administrator, was born at Nolay, in Burgundy, on the 13th of May, 1753. He received lessons from Monge at the military school of Mézières, which he entered in 1771 and quitted in 1773 with the rank of lieutenant of engineers. In his youth he wrote several poems, which have some merit. He gained a prize for his "Éloge de Vauban" in 1783, and published in the same year an important "Essay on Machines," containing a new theorem on the loss of force, which is ranked among the finest discoveries of mechanical science.

Having espoused with ardour the popular cause, he was elected a member of the Legislative Assembly by the voters of Pas-de-Calais in 1791, and acquired a great authority in that body. In 1792 he was elected to the National Convention, in which he voted for the execution of Louis XVI. and kept himself aloof from all intrigues and contentions of party. He was neither a Jacobin nor a Girondist, but an inflexible patriot and republican *pur et simple.* In August, 1793, he was chosen a member of the committee of public safety, and found the proper sphere for his genius in the functions of war-minister of the republic. The formation of plans of the campaigns, the selection of generals, the organization of the army, etc. imposed on him an immense and arduous labour, which he performed with such success that it was said that he had "organized victory." He displayed not only the talents of an administrator of the first order, he showed also the science and genius of a great general in the direction of fourteen armies at once so as to insure co-operative action.

Absorbed in the urgent labours of defending France from invading armies, he had no share in the proscriptions and cruelties of the reign of terror. He was chosen a member of the Institute in 1795. After the dissolution of the Convention, he was chosen at one time as representative by fourteen departments. Although he opposed the establishment of the Directory, he was elected one of the Directors in 1795, and again acted as minister of war. Having opposed the measures of Barras and the majority of the Directors, he was proscribed in 1797, and condemned to deportation ; but he escaped to Germany. He returned about the end of 1799, and was minister of war for a short time in 1800. In 1802 he became a member of the Tribunat, in which he opposed Bonaparte's assumption of imperial power, deeming it absurd to reward the restorer of liberty by the ruin or subversion of that very liberty. He declined to hold office under the empire until 1814, when he served as governor of Antwerp. The small fortune with which he retired from office is mentioned as an evidence of his rare probity. Carnot was appointed minister of the interior during the Hundred Days of Napoleon, who felt the necessity of giving some pledges to the friends of liberty. He was also a member of the provisional government formed in June, 1815. On the restoration of Louis XVIII. he was proscribed, and became an exile in Germany. He died at Magdeburg in 1823.

He published several excellent mathematical works, among which are "Reflections on the Metaphysics of the Infinitesimal Calculus," (1797,) and "Geometry of Position," (1803,) in which he gives many entirely new theorems. He was also author of some political treatises.

See D. F. ARAGO, "Biographie de Carnot," 1850; WILHELM KÖRTE, "Das Leben Carnots," 1820; P. F. TISSOT, "Mémoires historiques sur Carnot," 1824; C. DORIS, "Vie privée, politique et morale de Carnot," 1816; THIERS, "History of the French Revolution;" A. SERIEVS, "Carnot, sa Vie politique et privée," 1816; "North British Review" for 1851.

Carnot-Feulins, kǎR'no' fuh'lǎN', (CLAUDE MARIE,) a French officer, born at Nolay in 1755, was a brother of the preceding. He was a captain of engineers when the Revolution began, and was elected to the Legislative Assembly in 1791. In 1792 he was chosen director of the department of fortifications, and performed several important military missions. He was proscribed with his brother in 1797, but was restored on the fall of the Directory in 1799. He obtained the rank of general of brigade, but resigned about 1802, and did not return to the service until the restoration. In 1815 he retired from the army, with the rank and pension of lieutenant-general. Died in 1836.

See "Nouvelle Biographie Générale."

Caro, kä'ro, (ANNIBALE,) one of the most popular Italian authors of his time, was born at Città Nova, in the March of Ancona, in 1507. In 1543 he became secretary to Farnese, Duke of Parma, and from 1548 until his death he was secretary to Cardinal Farnese. He wrote a pure and elegant Italian style in prose and verse, which spread his reputation throughout Italy. His principal production is a poetical version of Virgil's "Æneid," which is called one of the master-pieces of the language, and is a model of elegance and grace. He wrote also original poems and letters, which were greatly admired. An ode, or canzone, which he composed in honour of the King of France, was criticised by Castelvetro, which occasioned an intemperate and rather scandalous war of words between that critic and the author. Died at Rome in 1566.

See CRASSO, "Eloj d'Uomini letterati;" SEGHEZZI, "Vita del Caro," 1742; MORÉRI, "Dictionnaire Historique."

Caro, kä'ro', (ELME MARIE,) a French littérateur, born at Rennes in 1825. He is one of the editors of the "Revue Contemporaine," and has published, besides a few other works, "Moral Studies on the Present Time," (1855,) which was crowned by the French Academy.

Caro, kä'ro, (Don VENTURA or BONAVENTURA,) a Spanish general, born at Valencia about 1742. He received command of the Spanish army in 1793, when war was declared against the French, and obtained some successes on the frontier. In 1802 he was promoted to the high rank of captain-general of the armies. He died in or soon after 1808.

Carolan. See O'CAROLAN.

Carolina Maria, kä-ro-lee'nä mä-ree'ä, Queen of Naples, born in 1752, was the daughter of Francis I. and Maria Theresa of Austria. In 1768 she was married to Ferdinand, King of the Two Sicilies. Being ambitious and high-spirited, she acquired a paramount and evil influence over that imbecile prince. She induced him to join the coalition against Bonaparte about 1805, in consequence of which they were expelled from Naples in 1806, and retired to the island of Sicily. She died in Vienna in 1814. Her daughter had become the wife of the Emperor of Austria, Francis I.

See "Nouvelle Biographie Générale."

Căr'o-līne, Queen of England, was a daughter of John Frederick, Margrave of Brandenburg-Anspach. She was married in 1705 to the Electoral Prince of Hanover, who became George II. of England. She had great influence over the king as long as she lived, and was popular with the nation. "Her character," says Lord Mahon, "was without a blemish, and her conduct always marked by judgment and good sense." She was the mother of four daughters and two sons, Frederick and William. Died in 1737.

See an excellent notice of her character in "Blackwood's Magazine" for February, 1868.

Căr'o-līne A-me'lĭ-ą E-līz'ą-beth, Queen of England, born in 1768, was the daughter of the Duke of Brunswick, and Augusta of England, who was the sister of George III. In 1795 she was married to her cousin the Prince of Wales, afterwards George IV., who was a reluctant party to the union. His aversion became so decided that a complete separation took place in 1796, after the birth of the princess Charlotte. In 1814 she left England, and passed the ensuing years on the continent, until the accession of George IV. in 1820, when she returned to London. The king then instituted against her a trial for adultery, which made a great excitement. The people mostly sympathized with the queen. Caroline was defended by Henry (afterwards Lord) Brougham, who gained great applause by his successful efforts in her behalf, and the government abandoned the prosecution. She died in 1821.

See THOMAS ASHE, "Memoirs of the Life of Princess Caroline," 1812; BROUGHAM'S Works, vols. ix. and x.; "Mémoires et Documents sur la Vie et le Procès de la Reine Caroline," Paris, 4 vols., 1821.

Căr'o-līne Mą-til'dą, [Dan. CAROLINE MATHILDE, kä-ro-lee'neh mä-til'deh,] Queen of Denmark, born in 1751, was a sister of George III. of England. In 1766 she was married to Christian VII. of Denmark, a weak and profligate prince, by whom she was neglected or ill treated. Struensee, an ambitious physician, acquired great influence over her and the king, and became prime minister. A conspiracy or coup d'état in 1772 resulted in the execution of that favourite, and the banishment of Caroline Matilda to Zelle, where she died, asserting her innocence, in 1775. (See STRUENSEE.)

See LENZEN. "Die letzten Stunden der Königin Caroline Mathilde," 1775; HEIMBÜRGER, "Caroline Mathilde Königin von Dänemark," 1851.

Carolostadt. See CARLSTADT.

Carolus Magnus. See CHARLEMAGNE.

Caron. See BEAUMARCHAIS.

Caron, kä'rôN', (AUGUSTIN JOSEPH,) a French officer and Bonapartist, born in 1774. He served in the army during the first republic and the empire, and rose to the rank of lieutenant-colonel in 1814. In 1822 he formed a plot to rescue some prisoners who were accomplices in the Béfort conspiracy. He failed, was tried by a council of war, and shot at Strasbourg, in 1822.

Caron, kä'rôN', (FRANÇOIS,) born in Holland, of French parents, went to Japan in his youth, and lived there some years. He became a member of the Dutch Council of the Indies. Having entered the service of the French, he was appointed by Colbert director-general of French commerce in India in 1666. In 1674 he was recalled to Europe, and was drowned at Lisbon just as he arrived. He had published a "Description of Japan," (1636.)

Caron, (JEAN CHARLES FÉLIX,) a French surgeon, born at Amiens in 1745. He practised in Paris, and became chief surgeon of the Cochin Hospital in 1782. He wrote treatises on Respiration, on the Croup, etc. Died in 1824.

Caron, (JEAN MARIE,) a meritorious French judge, born at Pornic in 1798. He officiated as judge in several places, and afterwards was justice of the peace (juge de paix) at Nantes. He wrote, besides other legal works, one "On the Civil Jurisdiction of Justices of the Peace." Died in 1841.

Căr'on, (RAYMOND,) an Irish Catholic priest, born in 1605, passed some years on the continent. He defended the doctrine of the Gallican Church on the independence of kings and against the infallibility of the pope, in a Latin work entitled "Remonstrance of the Hibernians against the Ultramontane Censures," (1665,) which made much noise at the time. Died in 1666.

ā, ē, ī, ō, ū, ȳ, long; ă, ĕ, ĭ, ŏ, ŭ, ў, short; ą, ę, į, ǫ, obscure; fär, fäll, fät; mĕt; nŏt; gŏŏd; mŏŏn;

Carondelet, kȧ'rŏnd'lȧ' or kȧ'rŏn'dęh-lȧ', (JEAN,) a Burgundian prelate and writer, born at Dôle in 1469. He was appointed by Charles V. president of the Council of Brussels in 1527. He subsequently became Chancellor of Flanders, secretary to the emperor, and Archbishop of Palermo. Erasmus, who was his friend, dedicated to him his "Saint-Hilaire." Died in 1544.

See M. C. MURRAY, "Mémoire historique sur la Vie de J. de Carondelet," 1786; FOPPENS, "Bibliotheca Belgica."

Caroprese, kȧ-ro-prā'sȧ, (GREGORIO,) a learned Italian writer and critic, born near Cosenza in 1620. He resided mostly in Rome and Naples. He wrote a refutation of Machiavel's "Prince," a letter on "Orlando Furioso," and a few other works. Died in 1715.

Caroselli, kȧ-ro-sĕl'lee, (ANGIOLO,) an Italian painter, born in Rome in 1585. He had a remarkable talent for imitating the manners of different masters. Skilful connoisseurs were deceived by his imitations of Titian, Raphael, etc. He also painted portraits with success. Died in 1653.

See LANZI, "History of Painting in Italy."

Carotto, kȧ-rot'to, or **Caroto**, kȧ-ro'to, (GIOVANNI FRANCESCO,) an eminent Italian painter, born at Verona in 1470, was a pupil of A. Mantegna, whom he surpassed in majesty and harmony. He excelled in portraits. Died in 1546.

See VASARI, "Lives of the Painters."

GIOVANNI CAROTTO, a younger brother of the preceding, was distinguished as an architect.

Carouge, kȧ'roozh', (BERTRAND AUGUSTIN,) a French astronomer, born at Dol in 1741. He went to Paris and associated himself with Lalande, for whom he made calculations which were inserted in Lalande's "Astronomy." He prepared tables for calculating the phases of the moon for sixty years, which were published in the "Connaissances des Temps," (1801.) In 1795 he was appointed *administrateur-général des postes*. Died in 1798.

Carové, kȧ'ro'vȧ', (FRIEDRICH WILHELM,) a German critic and philosophical writer, born at Coblentz in 1789; died in 1852.

Carpaccio, kaR-pȧt'cho, [Lat. CARPA'THIUS,] (VITTORE,) an Italian painter, sometimes called SCARPAZZA, born about 1450. He worked in Venice, and was a rival of Bellini. By some writers he is ranked among the first painters of his time.

See LANZI, "History of Painting in Italy."

Carpani, kaR-pȧ'nee, (GIUSEPPE,) an Italian poet and theologian, born at Rome in 1683. He wrote several Latin tragedies, and other works. Died about 1765.

Carpani, (GIUSEPPE,) an eminent Italian dramatic poet, born at Villa Albese, in the Milanese, in 1752. He became editor of the "Gazette" of Milan in 1792, and wrote against the French Revolution. In consequence of the French invasion in 1796, he removed to Vienna, where he settled permanently about 1810. He became a friend of Haydn, whose oratorio of the "Creation" he successfully rendered into Italian. In 1812 he published "Le Haydine," or "Letters on the Life and Works of Haydn," which are commended as elegant and interesting. He produced numerous operas, dramas, and cantatas, among which are "La Camilla," a drama, and "The Judgment of Apollo," a cantata. Died in Vienna in 1825.

See TIPALDO, "Biografia degli Italiani illustri;" FÉTIS, "Biographie Universelle des Musiciens;" "Nouvelle Biographie Générale."

Car'pen-ter, (GEORGE,) LORD, an English general, born in Herefordshire in 1657, entered the army in 1672. In 1707 he commanded the cavalry at the battle of Almanza, Spain, where his conduct was applauded. He was made a lieutenant-general in 1710, and was second in command at the battle of Almenara. In 1715 he commanded the army which defeated the adherents of the Pretender at Preston. A few years later he received the title of Baron. Died in 1731.

See "Life of George Lord Carpenter," London, 1736.

Carpenter, (LANT,) an English divine, born at Kidderminster in 1780, was the father of Dr. W. B. Carpenter the physiologist. From 1805 to 1817 he officiated as Unitarian minister at Exeter, and during that period he published his "Introduction to the Geography of the New Testament," and "Unitarianism the Doctrine of the Gospel." He became minister of the Unitarian church at Bristol in 1817. In 1839 he visited the continent on account of his health. While passing from Naples to Leghorn, he was drowned, in April, 1840. He left numerous works, among which his "Apostolical Harmony of the Gospels" (1838) is perhaps the principal.

See "Memoirs of the Rev. Lant Carpenter," by his son, 1842.

Carpenter, (MARGARET GEDDES,) an English portrait-painter, born at Salisbury in 1793. She was married to W. H. Carpenter, noticed below, in 1817.

Carpenter, (MARY,) an English philanthropist, daughter of Lant Carpenter, was born about 1820. She founded a reformatory institution for females at Bristol, and wrote several works on education, etc. .

Carpenter, (NATHANIEL,) an English scholar and clergyman, born in Devonshire in 1588. He published, besides other works, "Philosophia Libera," (1621,) one of the first attacks on the philosophy of Aristotle. He lived some years in Dublin, where he died about 1630.

See WOOD, "Athenæ Oxonienses."

Carpenter, (RICHARD,) an English priest, who twice or thrice was converted from Protestantism to Catholicism. He published several works, one of which is entitled "Experience, History, and Divinity," (1642.) He also wrote "The Pragmatical Jesuit," a comedy.

See WOOD, "Athenæ Oxonienses."

Carpenter, (WILLIAM,) an English author and biblical critic, born in London about 1798, published several valuable works, among which are "Calendarium Palestinæ," (1825,) "Scripture Natural History," (1828,) and "A Guide to the Practical Reading of the Bible," (1830.)

Carpenter, (WILLIAM BENJAMIN,) an eminent English physiologist, son of Lant Carpenter, noticed above, was born about 1812. He became a student of medicine in University College, London, in 1833, and graduated in Edinburgh in 1839, before which date he had published a treatise "On the Unity of Function in Organized Beings," and a few other short works. In 1839 he published an important and remarkable work, entitled "Principles of General and Comparative Physiology." About 1840 he settled in Bristol. He produced, in 1846, "Principles of Human Physiology," a work of great merit, and scarcely equalled by any other on that subject. "We know of no work on physiology from which the student is likely to derive so much advantage." ("British and Foreign Medical Review.") Dr. Carpenter is, or was, professor of medical jurisprudence in University College, London, and a Fellow of the Royal Society. Among his later publications are "Zoology and Instinct in Animals," (1848,) and "On the Microscope: its Revelations and Uses," (1856.) In 1849 he received a prize of one hundred guineas for an "Essay on Alcoholic Liquors." His brother, RUSSELL LANT CARPENTER, was Unitarian minister at Birkenhead, and published memoirs of his father, the Rev. Lant Carpenter.

See "Westminster Review" for July, 1863.

Carpenter, (WILLIAM H.,) born in London in 1792, became in 1845 keeper of the prints and drawings of the British Museum.

Carpentier, kȧR'pŏN'te-ȧ', (PIERRE,) a French Benedictine friar and antiquary, noted for his learning, was born at Charleville in 1697. He performed the principal part of the improved edition of Du Cange's "Glossarium mediæ et infimæ Latinitatis," (1736.) In 1766 he published a valuable supplement to the work above named, with the title of "Glossarium novum," etc. Died in Paris in 1767.

See TASSIN, "Histoire littéraire de la Congrégation de Saint-Maur."

Carpi, da, dȧ kaR'pee, (GIROLAMO,) a skilful Italian painter and architect, born at Ferrara about 1500. He imitated Correggio with such success that some of his copies passed for the original works of that artist. He adorned the churches of Bologna and Ferrara with frescos and oil-paintings. "The Adoration of the Magi" is called one of his master-pieces. Died in 1556.

See VASARI, "Lives of the Painters, Sculptors, etc.;" BARUFFALDI, "Vita di G. da Carpi Pittore," 1841.

Carpi, da, (UGO,) an eminent Italian wood-engraver and painter, is said to have been born in Rome about

1486. He is the reputed inventor of *clair-obscur* engraving, or printing in light and shade. Among his works are "Diogenes and his Tub," after Parmegiano, and "Æneas bearing off Anchises," after Raphael. He used three blocks, the first for the outline, the second for the middle tints, and the last for the shadows.

Carpin, kaR-peen', or **Carpini,** kaR-pee'nee, (JOHAN'-NES DE PLA'NO,) an Italian monk, noted for his travels and adventures among the Tartars or Mongols who had ravaged the eastern parts of Christendom. In 1246 he was sent by Pope Innocent IV. on a mission to Tartary, with the design to pacify those barbarians or convert them to Christianity. With great courage and patience he penetrated to the court of the Grand Khan, whom he calls Kujak, and who dismissed him with a letter to the pope. On his return home, in 1248, he wrote a narrative of his journey, which is considered tolerably faithful and accurate, (making allowance for the prevalent ignorance, etc.,) and imparted to Europeans their first knowledge of the country of the Mongols. Hakluyt translated it, and inserted it in his "Collection of Voyages," etc. Carpini afterwards was provincial of Germany, and preached the gospel in Bohemia, Norway, and Denmark.

See DE GUIGNES, "Histoire générale des Huns."

Carpioni, kaR-pe-o'nee, (GIULIO,) an Italian painter and engraver, born at Venice in 1611. He painted fabulous and fantastic subjects with success. Died in 1674.

See LANZI, "History of Painting in Italy."

Carpocrate. See CARPOCRATES.

Car-poc'ra-tēs, [Fr. CARPOCRATE, kȧR'po'kRȧt',] a heresiarch of Alexandria, lived in the reign of Adrian, in the second century. He is said to have taught that the world was created by angels, that Christ was only a human being of pre-eminent goodness, and that the souls of men existed before their entrance into this world. He also taught doctrines subversive of morality, a kind of Gnostic Antinomianism, and had numerous followers.

See MATTER, "Du Gnosticisme," 2d edition, 1838.

Carpov, kaR'pof, (JAKOB,) a German theologian, born at Goslar in 1699. He lectured at Jena, where he made many enemies by attempting to treat theology according to philosophic methods. Having removed to Weimar, he was there chosen professor of mathematics in 1742. He wrote an "Inquiry whether the Earth is a Machine or an Animal," and other works. Died in 1768.

See ERSCH und GRUBER, "Allgemeine Encyklopaedie."

Carpzov, kaRp'tsof, [Lat. CARPZO'VIUS,] (AUGUST,) a German diplomatist, son of Benedict, noticed below, born at Colditz in 1612. He became chancellor of the high court of Saxony, and represented that power at the treaty of Westphalia, (1648.) In 1675 he was appointed a privy councillor at Gotha. Died in 1683.

See STURZ, "Commentatio de Vita A. Carpzovii," 1750.

Carpzov, (BENEDICT,) a distinguished German jurisconsult, born in Brandenburg in 1565. He was appointed professor of law at Wittenberg in 1599, and wrote several volumes of "Legal Disputations," ("Disputationes Juridicæ.") He died in 1624, leaving several sons, who gained distinction in the same career.

Carpzov, (BENEDICT,) a son of the preceding, born at Wittenberg in 1595, was a more able jurisconsult than his father. He was a privy councillor to the Elector of Saxony, and author of many works, among which is "Practice in Criminal Causes," ("Practica Rerum criminalium," 1635.) "He deserved to be regarded," says Boissonade, "as the first of German practitioners." Died in 1666.

See LANGE, "Predigt bei der Leichen-Bestattung B. Carpzovii," 1667; KROMAYER, "Programma in B. Carpzovii funere," 1666.

Carpzov, (JOHANN BENEDICT,) a Protestant theologian, brother of the preceding, born at Rochlitz in 1607. He was professor at Leipsic. Died in 1657.

Carpzov, (JOHANN BENEDICT,) an Orientalist, a son of the preceding, born at Leipsic in 1639, was professor of Hebrew, etc. in that city. He wrote treatises on sacred philology. Died in 1699.

His brother, FRIEDRICH BENEDICT, (1649-99,) was noted as a philologist. He contributed to the "Acta Eruditorum."

See JÖCHER, "Allgemeines Gelehrten-Lexikon;" CYPRIAN, "Programma in funere J. B. Carpzovii," 1699; CRELL, "Oratio F. B. Carpzovii Memoriæ sacra," 1700.

Carpzov, (JOHANN BENEDICT,) a historian and jurist, nephew of the preceding, born at Dresden in 1675. He published several works. Died in 1739.

See ERSCH und GRUBER, "Allgemeine Encyklopaedie;" ERNST F. HAUPT, "Ueber J. B. Carpzov als Historiker," 1842.

Carpzov, (JOHANN GOTTLOB,) a Lutheran theologian, born at Dresden in 1679. He was professor of Oriental languages at Leipsic from 1719 to 1730, and in the last year removed to Lubeck, where he preached many years. He wrote, besides other works, "Sacred Criticism on the Old Testament," ("Critica sacra Veteris Testamenti.") Died in 1767.

See ERSCH und GRUBER, "Allgemeine Encyklopaedie;" PETER H. BECKER, "Leben G. Carpzovs," 1767; OVERBECK, "Memoria Vitæ J. G. Carpzovii," 1767.

Carpzovius. See CARPZOV.

Carr, (EUGENE A.,) an American general, born in Erie county, New York, about 1830, graduated at West Point in 1850. He became a captain about 1858, commanded a division at Pea Ridge, March, 1862, and was appointed a brigadier-general of volunteers the same month. He served in Arkansas in 1864.

Carr, (GEORGE,) a minister of the Anglican Church, born at Newcastle, England, in 1704. From 1737 to 1776 he was senior clergyman of the Episcopal Chapel, Edinburgh. Several volumes of his sermons were published. "To his merits as a preacher, great as they were," says Dr. Beattie, "the lustre of his private character was still superior." Died in 1776.

Carr, (JOHN,) an English architect, born near Wakefield, Yorkshire, in 1721. He gained an extensive practice in the north of England, where he erected many fine edifices. Among them are the Town-Hall of Newark, Harewood House, Yorkshire, and the mausoleum of Lord Rockingham at Wentworth. He was chosen lord mayor of York in 1770, and again in 1785. Died in 1807.

Carr, (JOHN,) LL.D., an English schoolmaster, born in the county of Durham in 1732. He taught a grammar-school at Hertford for many years with credit, and made a translation of Lucian's "Dialogues," which is said to be excellent. He also wrote other works. Died in 1807.

Carr, (Sir JOHN,) an English writer of travels, born in Devonshire in 1772, was educated for the law. During the brief peace which followed the treaty of Amiens he visited France, and produced in 1803 "The Stranger in France," which was very successful, partly because for many ensuing years the scenes which he described were inaccessible to English tourists. He afterwards published "Northern Summer, or Travels around the Baltic," a "Tour through Holland," and a few other works. He was knighted about 1806. Died in 1832.

See "Edinburgh Review" for April, 1807.

Carr, (JOSEPH B.,) an American officer, born at Albany about 1825, served in the campaigns of 1861-62, and was made a brigadier-general in 1862.

Carr, written also **Carre** or **Ker,** (ROBERT,) Earl of Somerset, a Scottish courtier, born about 1589. In 1610 his handsome person attracted the notice of the king, James I., of whom he soon became the prime favourite. "James created him Viscount Rochester," says Hume, ". . . and bestowed on him the supreme direction of all his business and political concerns." In 1613 Carr married Lady Frances Howard, lately divorced from the Earl of Essex, and was created Earl of Somerset. He was for some time on very intimate terms with Sir Thomas Overbury; but they afterwards quarrelled, and in 1616 Somerset and his wife were convicted of procuring the death of Overbury by poison, but, through the favour of the king, they escaped the just penalty of their crime. After an imprisonment of several years, he was released, and died in obscurity.

See GARDINER's "History of England from 1603 to 1616," vol. ii. chaps. x., xi., and xiii.; HUME's "History of England," chap. xlvii.

Carr, (Sir ROBERT,) one of the royal commissioners of New England, appointed in 1664 by Charles II. In conjunction with Nicolls, he took New Amsterdam from the Dutch, and changed the name of that city to New York, in honour of the Duke of York, afterwards James II.

Carr, (Rev. WILLIAM HOLWELL,) an English patron of the fine arts, born in 1759. He bequeathed many pictures to the National Gallery. Died in 1830.

ā, ē, ī, ō, ū, ȳ, *long;* ă, ĕ, ŏ, same, less prolonged; ă, ĕ, ĭ, ŏ, ŭ, ȳ, *short;* a, e, i, o, *obscure;* fȧr, fȧll, fȧt; mĕt; nŏt; gŏŏd; mŏŏn;

Carra, kȧ'rä', (JEAN LOUIS,) a French revolutionist, born at Pont-de-Vesle in 1743. He went to Paris in 1789, and became the editor of a journal called "Annales Patriotiques," which was very radical in politics. He was elected to the Convention in 1792, and, having joined the Girondists, was proscribed by Robespierre, and executed in October, 1793. "He took refuge in the Gironde," says Lamartine, "to oppose the excesses of the people." He had published several historical and scientific works.

See LAMARTINE, "History of the Girondists."

Carra Saint-Cyr, kȧ'rä' săN'sèR', (JEAN FRANÇOIS,) COUNT, a French general, born in 1756. As general of brigade, he contributed to the victories of Marengo and Hohenlinden, (1801.) He became a general of division in 1801, and commanded the army of occupation in Naples in 1805. He was Governor of French Guiana in 1817-19. Died in 1834.

See "Victoires et Conquêtes des Français."

Carracci. See CARACCI.

Carrach, kȧr'rȧK, (JOHANN TOBIAS,) a Prussian jurist, born at Magdeburg in 1702. In 1763 he was chosen rector of the University of Halle, in which he had previously been professor of law. He published many legal treatises. Died in 1775.

See ERSCH and GRUBER, "Allgemeine Encyklopaedie;" KÖNIG, "Leben und Schriften des Herrn J. T. Carrach," 1776.

Carrache. See CARACCI.

Carradori, kȧr-rȧ-do'ree, (GIOACHINO,) an Italian physician, born at Prato, in Tuscany, in 1758. About 1802 he wrote a prize essay "On Fertility of Land," which is regarded as a classic work. He contributed able scientific articles to the journals of Milan and Pavia, and published a treatise on Galvanism. Died in 1818.

See SILVESTRI, "Elogio de G. Carradori," 1818; TIPALDO, "Biografia degli Italiani illustri."

Carranza, kȧr-rȧn'thȧ, (BARTOLOMÉ,) a Spanish prelate, born at Miranda in 1503. Charles V. sent him to the Council of Trent in 1546. He accompanied Philip II. to England, where he became confessor to Queen Mary and displayed a fanatical zeal against the Protestants. About 1556 he was appointed Archbishop of Toledo. This promotion appears to have excited the envy of his enemies, who obtained from the Inquisition a censure of a Catechism which he published, and accused him of perverting the mind of Charles V. in his last illness. He was confined in prison ten years or more, and soon after his release he died, in 1576.

See SALAZAR DE MENDOZA, "Vida y Sucesos de B. de Carranza y Miranda," 1788; PRESCOTT, "History of Philip II.," vols. i. and ii.

Carrara, (GIOVANNI MICHELE ALBERTO,) an Italian physician and author, born at Bergamo, was one of the most learned and prolific writers of his time. Among his works are a "History of Italian Affairs in his Own Times," and a Latin poem "On the Venetian War." In 1488 the emperor Frederick III. made him a count palatine. Died in 1490.

See VOSSIUS, "De Historicis Latinis;" A. SUARDI, "Vita di G. M. A. Carrara," 1784.

Carrara, (PIETRO ANTONIO,) a native of Bergamo, published, in 1701, a version of Virgil's "Æneid" in ottava rima.

Carrara, (UBERTINO,) an Italian poet and Jesuit, born at Sora about 1640. He was for many years professor of belles-lettres in the Roman College, and wrote a heroic poem called "Voyage of Columbus," of which the invention is more poetic than the style. Died in 1715.

Carrara, da, dȧ kȧr-rȧ'rȧ, a noble family of Italy, which ruled over Padua in the middle ages and adhered to the Guelph party.

JACOPO DA CARRARA, after commanding the army in the war against Can della Scala, was elected Lord of Padua in 1318. Died in 1324. His nephew, MARSILIO, who succeeded, made an alliance with Can della Scala, of Verona, to whom in 1328 he transferred the title of Lord of Padua; but he continued to be the actual ruler. The heirs of Della Scala were expelled in 1337. Marsilio died in 1338, and was succeeded by his nephew, UBERTINO. During his government hostilities were renewed with the Lord of Verona, and were terminated by a peace in 1343. He died, without issue, in 1345. FRANCESCO I., a grand-nephew of Jacopo, above noticed, obtained the chief power in 1355, and at the same time was chosen to command the army of the league formed by Ferrara, Mantua, Verona, and Padua against the Visconti of Milan. After several indecisive battles, peace was made in 1358. In 1378 he joined the Genoese in a war against Venice, which brought the latter state to the brink of ruin. About 1387 he was deposed by Gian Galeazzo Visconti, and confined in prison until his death in 1393.

See SISMONDI, "Histoire des Républiques Italiennes."

Carrara, da, (FRANCESCO II.,) called NOVELLO, (novel'lo,) the son of Francesco I., noticed above, recovered the lordship of Padua in 1390, by the favour of the Venetians. He waged war against the Visconti, and, by seizing Verona in 1404, involved himself in war with Venice. Having been vanquished by that power, he was taken prisoner and put to death, with his sons, in 1406, after which Padua was annexed to Venice.

See SISMONDI, "Histoire des Républiques Italiennes."

Carre. See CARR.

Carré or Carrée, kȧ'rä', (FRANÇOIS,) a Dutch painter, father of Hendrik, noticed below, was born in Friesland in 1636; died in 1669.

Carré, kȧ'rä', (GUILLAUME LOUIS JULIEN,) a French jurisconsult, born at Rennes in 1777. He became professor of law in the Faculty of Rennes in 1806, and gained a high reputation as a lecturer. He published "Laws of Civil Practice," (1824,) and other works of merit. Died in 1832.

See A. CHAUVEAU, "Notice sur Carré," 1841.

Carré, (HENDRIK,) a Dutch landscape-painter, born about 1656, was a pupil of J. Jordaens. He became a resident of Amsterdam, where he worked many years with success. Descamps praises his colour and touch. Died in 1721.

See DESCAMPS, "Vies des Peintres Flamands," etc.

Carré, (JEAN BAPTISTE LOUIS,) a French writer and tactician, born at Varennes in 1749. Besides other works, he published one entitled "Panoply," (Panoplie, 1795,) a treatise on armour, weapons, and military affairs in general. Died in 1835.

See QUÉRARD, "La France Littéraire."

Carré, (LOUIS,) a French geometer, born at a village in Brie in 1663. After having served Malebranche as amanuensis, he became a teacher of mathematics and philosophy. In 1697 he was admitted into the Academy of Sciences. His principal work is a "Method for the Measurement of Surfaces, Solids," etc., which was once highly prized. Died in 1711.

See FONTENELLE, "Éloge de Carré;" NICÉRON, "Mémoires."

Carré, (MICHAEL,) a brother of Hendrik, born about 1658, was a pupil of N. Berghem, and a skilful painter. He was employed by Frederick I. of Prussia, after whose death he returned to Amsterdam. Died in 1728.

See DESCAMPS, "Vies des Peintres Flamands," etc.

Carré, (NARCISSE EPAMINONDAS,) a French jurist, born in Paris in 1794, was councillor in the Cour Impériale of Paris. He published an edition of the works of Domat, (9 vols., 1822,) and a "Code des Femmes," (1828.)

Carré, (PIERRE LAURENT,) a French littérateur, born in Paris in 1758, obtained the chair of rhetoric at Toulouse, where he lectured with éclat. He wrote an epistle to his friend Delille the poet. He left many odes, epistles, and other poems. Died in 1825.

Carrel, kȧ'rĕl', (NICOLAS ARMAND,) a celebrated French journalist and publicist, was born at Rouen in 1800. He entered the army as sub-lieutenant about 1820, with sentiments of hostility to the dynasty restored by foreign troops. When the government sent an army to Spain to support the cause of absolutism, he resigned in 1823, and joined the army of Spanish liberals. Having been made prisoner, he was sentenced to death by a council of war; but, on account of informalities in the process, he was released. Finding himself destitute of resources except in his literary talents, he became secretary of the historian Augustin Thierry. He soon quitted this service, which imposed too much constraint on his independent spirit, and began to write for the "Constitutionnel," the "Revue Française," and other journals and reviews of Paris. About 1828 he published a "Résumé of the History of Modern Greece," and a "History of the Counter-Revolution in England," which is highly esteemed. "The reigns of the last two Stuarts," says the "Edinburgh Review," "have been written with the mind of a statesman and the hand of a vigorous writer, by Armand Carrel." In 1830 Thiers and Carrel became chief editors of the "National," a daily journal, which the latter first projected, and which was the organ of the liberal opposition. After the revolution of 1830, (in which Carrel took a prominent part,) Thiers entered the new ministry, and left the chief control of the journal to his late colleague, whose eloquence and judgment soon raised the "National" to the highest point of influence and popularity. He gained much applause by the utterance of his indignant abhorrence of the execution of Marshal Ney, while he was pleading a cause before the Chamber of Peers, the majority of which had pronounced the sentence in that case. He was imprisoned by the government of Louis Philippe on account of his writings, although he was the moderator as well as the champion of the popular party. He was killed in a duel by Émile de Girardin, editor of the "Presse," in July, 1836. "His sterling honesty," says Brougham, "was only exceeded by his brilliant talents."

See "Nouvelle Biographie Générale;" CARL BOELSCHE, "Zwei Republikaner," (containing the life of Carrel and L. Börne, 1850:) C. NISARD's article in the "Revue des Deux Mondes" for October 1, 1837.

Carreño de Miranda, kâr-rån′yo dà me-rån′dä, (Don JUAN,) a skilful Spanish painter of history and portraits, was born in Asturias in 1614. In 1669 Philip IV. gave him the title of First Painter to the King, which he retained under Charles II. His works, which illustrate scriptural subjects, are at Madrid, Toledo, etc. Died in 1685. He was an excellent colorist, in which respect he is ranked by Spaniards between Titian and Van Dyck.

See QUILLIET, "Dictionnaire des Peintres Espagnols;" BRYAN, "Dictionary of Painters;" NAGLER, "Neues Allgemeines Künstler-Lexikon."

Carrer, kâr-râR′, (LUIGI,) an Italian lyric poet, born at Venice in 1801, wrote, besides other poems, "The Ring of Seven Gems." Died in 1850.

Carrera, kâr-râ′rä, (PIETRO,) an Italian antiquary, born in Sicily in 1571, wrote "Ancient Syracuse illustrated," and other works. Died in 1647.

Carrera, kâr-râ′rä, (RAFAEL,) a statesman, of Indian extraction, born at Guatemala about 1814. In the civil war (1837–39) he fought with success against the Federal government, and became commander-in-chief of the insurgents. He was elected President of Guatemala in 1847, and re-elected in 1851.

Carreras, kâr-râ′räs, (JOSÉ MIGUEL, JUAN, and LUIS,) three brothers, citizens of Chili, who were noted as patriots, and took part in the war of independence against Spain in the early part of the present century. Juan and Luis were put to death in 1818, and José Miguel in 1822.

Carrère, kȧ′rair′, (JOSEPH BARTHÉLEMI FRANÇOIS,) a French physician, born in 1740 at Perpignan. In 1773 he settled in Paris, and was appointed inspector-general of the mineral waters of Roussillon, and royal censor. He published many professional works, among which are "A Manual for the Service of the Sick," a "Treatise on Inflammatory Diseases," (1774,) and a "Biographical Dictionary of Medical Writers," (2 vols., 1776,) which was continued only to "Coivart." Died in 1802.

See ÉLOY, "Dictionnaire de la Médecine;" "Biographie Médicale;" "Nouvelle Biographie Générale."

Carrère, (THOMAS,) a French physician, father of the preceding, born at Perpignan in 1714; died in 1764.

Carreri, kâr-râ′ree, (GIOVANNI FRANCESCO GEMELLI,) an Italian, born in Naples, visited Asia in 1693, and published "Tour of the World," (1699.)

Carrero, kâr-râ′ro, (PEDRO GARCIAS,) a skilful Spanish physician, born at Calahorra, lived about 1600, acquired a high reputation, and became physician to Philip III. His commentaries on Galen and Avicenna prove him to have been a man of extensive learning.

See N. ANTONIO, "Bibliotheca Hispana Nova."

Carretto, del, dĕl kâr-ret′to, (FRANCESCO SAVERIO,) MARQUIS, a Neapolitan minister of state, born at Salerno. In his youth he served in the army with distinc-

tion, and rose to a high rank. He was chosen minister of police in 1831, and rendered himself odious by the severe and tyrannical measures with which he suppressed popular revolts. In consequence of a transient success of the popular party in 1848, he was banished by Ferdinand II.; but he was soon recalled, and loaded with favours, by that king.

Carrier, kȧ′re-à′, almost kȧR′yà′, (JEAN B.,) a French Jacobin of infamous memory, was born in 1756. He was elected to the Convention in 1792, and in the next year was sent to Nantes, to execute the bloody will of the dominant party. He sacrificed great numbers of prisoners and citizens without trial, and spared neither women nor children. Multitudes were crowded into boats and sunk in the river Loire, and others were shot or guillotined. The first mode of destruction was called *republican baptism.* Soon after the fall of Robespierre the public voice called for justice against Carrier, who, after a trial by the tribunal at Paris, was executed in 1794.

See DE BARANTE, "Mélanges;" "Nouvelle Biographie Générale."

Carriera. See ROSALBA.

Carrière, kȧ′re-aiR′, (DENIS DÉSIRÉ,) a French poet, born at Nancy in 1813; died in 1853.

Carrière, (JOSEPH,) a French theologian, born in 1795. He became professor of theology in the seminary of Saint-Sulpice, Paris. He has published an esteemed work on theology, written in Latin, comprising the following subjects: "On Matrimony," "On Justice and Law," and "On Contracts."

Carrière, kȧ′re-aiR′, (MORITZ,) a German philosophical writer, was born at Griedel, in Hesse, in 1817. He was appointed professor of philosophy at Giessen in 1849. Among his principal works are a treatise "On Aristotle the Friend of Plato," in Latin, (1837,) "The Philosophic Contemplation of the World at the Time of the Reformation," (1847,) and a poem, "The Last Night of the Girondists," ("Die letzte Nacht der Girondisten," 1849.)

See BROCKHAUS, "Conversations-Lexikon."

Carrières, de, deh kȧ′re-aiR′, (LOUIS,) a French biblical commentator, born near Angers in 1662. His commentary was inserted in the French version of the Bible by Sacy. Died in 1717.

Carrillo, kâr-rèl′yo, (MARTIN,) a Spanish historian, born at Saragossa; died about 1630.

Cȧr′ring-tȯn, (NOEL THOMAS,) an English poet, born at Plymouth in 1777. After serving a short time in the royal navy, which he left about 1797, he taught school at Maidstone and Devonport. He wrote several didactic poems of some merit, among which are "The Banks of Tamar," (1820,) "Dartmoor," (1826,) and "My Native Village." "Dartmoor," which is called his best work, was received with great favour. Died in 1830.

See "Autobiography of William Jerdan," vol. iv. chap. ii.

Carrion, kȧ′re-ȯN′, (LOUIS,) a Flemish critic, born at Bruges about 1547. He became professor of civil law and of canon law at Louvain, where he died in 1595. Among his works are an edition of the "Attic Nights" of Aulus Gellius, and "Commentaries on Ancient Readings," ("Antiquarum Lectionum Commentarii.")

Carrion, de, dà kâr-re-ȯn′, (MANUEL RAMIREZ,) a learned Spaniard, born about 1590. He attained great success in the instruction of deaf-mutes, and is said to have been the first who, in Spain, taught letters to that class.

Carrion-Nisas, kȧ′re-ȯN′ ne′zȧ′, (ANTOINE HENRI FRANÇOIS,) a French author, born at Lézignan in 1794. He has published a "Roman History from the Foundation of Rome to the Reign of Constantine," (1815,) "Principles of Political Economy," (1824,) and other works.

Carrion-Nisas, de, deh kȧ′re-ȯN′ ne′zȧ′, (MARIE HENRI FRANÇOIS,) MARQUIS, a French politician and military officer, born at Montpellier in 1787, was the father of the preceding. Died in 1841.

Carro, de, deh kȧ′ro′, (JEAN,) a Swiss physician, born at Geneva in 1770. He practised many years in Vienna, and was noted for his zealous efforts to propagate vaccination, on which he published a work, (1801.) He lived at Carlsbad from 1825 until his death in 1857.

See WEITENWEBER, "Biographie des Dr. J. de Carro," 1844.

ā, ē, ī, ō, ū, ȳ, *long;* ă, ĕ, ĭ, ŏ, ŭ, ў, *short;* a, e, i, o, *obscure;* fär, fåll, fåt; mêt; nŏt; gōōd; mōōn;

Căr'rǫll, (CHARLES,) of Carrollton, an American patriot, born at Annapolis, Maryland, in 1737. He was educated as a Roman Catholic in France, and studied law in Paris and London. Having returned to America about 1764, he inherited a very large estate in land in his native province, and was reputed to be the richest man in Maryland. Before the Revolution began, he defended, by his writings, the rights of the colonies against the oppressive measures of the British ministry. He was elected a delegate to the Provincial Convention in 1775, and a delegate to Congress in July, 1776. He signed the Declaration of Independence, and, in order to identify himself more fully with the danger as well as honour resulting from that manifesto, wrote his name Charles Carroll of Carrollton, after some one had remarked that there were several persons named Charles Carroll. He was elected a Senator of the United States for Maryland in 1788. In 1810 he retired from public life. He was the last surviving signer of the Declaration of Independence. Having attained the age of ninety-five years, he died in 1832.

See GOODRICH, "Lives of the Signers to the Declaration of Independence;" "National Portrait-Gallery," vol. i., 1839.

Carroll, (JOHN,) a Roman Catholic prelate, born in Maryland in 1735, was a cousin of the preceding. He joined the order of Jesuits. In 1776 he went to Canada, at the request of Congress, in company with Benjamin Franklin and two others, who were sent on a political mission. He was appointed Bishop of Baltimore in 1789, and afterwards received the title of Archbishop. Died in 1815.

See "Encyclopædia Americana."

Carron, kä'ròn', (GUI TOUSSAINT JULIEN,) ABBÉ, a French priest and moralist, noted for his works of charity and benevolence, was born at Rennes in 1760. Refusing to take the prescribed oath in 1791, he was exiled to Jersey, and thence removed to London. In each of these places he founded schools, hospitals, etc. In 1814 he returned to Paris, and took part in various benevolent enterprises. He published "Christian Thoughts," "Lives of the Just," "The Confessors of the Faith in France," and many other works. Died in 1821.

See "Notice sur Carron," prefixed to his works.

Carroza, kår-rod'zå, (GIOVANNI,) an Italian physician, born at Messina in 1678; died after 1730.

Carrucci. See PONTORMO.

Cars, kår, (LAURENT,) a skilful French engraver, born at Lyons in 1703, was a pupil of Lemoyne in Paris. He was received into the Royal Academy in 1733. "Hercules and Omphale" is one of his master-pieces. Died in 1771.

Car'sǫn, (CHRISTOPHER,) commonly known as KIT CARSON, a famous trapper and mountain-guide, born in Kentucky in 1809, passed a large portion of his time in the Rocky Mountains and the adjacent territories. He rendered important services as a guide to Fremont in his explorations. In 1847 he was made lieutenant in the rifle-corps of the United States army. Died in 1868.

Car'stairs or Car'stares, (WILLIAM,) a Scottish theologian and negotiator, born at Cathcart in 1649. Having received a good education and studied theology at Utrecht, he became chaplain and private secretary to William, Prince of Orange, who sent him to England on a secret mission in the reign of Charles II. As accessary to the conspiracy of Monmouth's friends, he was arrested and put to the torture, which he bore with fortitude, and confessed nothing important. After the Prince of Orange became King of England, in 1688, Carstairs enjoyed his confidence, and had great influence in the affairs of Scotland. It is stated that by strenuous efforts he dissuaded the king from severe and impolitic measures against the Scottish Presbyterians. In 1704 he was chosen principal of the University of Edinburgh, and became minister of the Grey-Friars' Church in that city. Died in 1715.

"William had," says Macaulay, "one Scottish adviser who deserved and possessed more influence than any of the ostensible ministers. This was Carstairs, one of the most remarkable men of that age. He united great scholastic attainments with great aptitude for civil business, and the firm faith and ardent zeal of a martyr with the shrewdness and suppleness of a consummate politician."

See MACAULAY, "History of England," vol. ii. chap. ix., and vol. iii. chap. xiii.; CHAMBERS, "Biographical Dictionary of Eminent Scotsmen;" McCORMICK, "Life of W. Carstairs," 1774.

Carstares. See CARSTAIRS.

Carstens, kaR'stẹns, (ADOLF GOTHARD,) a Danish writer and critic, born at Copenhagen in 1713; died in 1795.

See ERSCH und GRUBER, "Allgemeine Encyklopaedie."

Carstens, (ASMUS JAKOB,) an excellent Danish historical painter, born near Sleswick in 1754. After he left school he was compelled to serve an apprenticeship of five years to a wine-merchant, and on obtaining his liberty went to Copenhagen, in the Academy of which he studied painting a few years. In 1783 he performed a pedestrian journey to Milan, intending to visit Rome; but want of funds compelled him to return before he reached that point. He worked in Lubeck about five years, during which he supported himself by painting portraits, and thence removed to Berlin, where he produced "The Fall of the Angels." The merit of this procured his appointment as professor in the Academy of that city. In 1792 he went to Rome, where he studied with fond admiration the works of Michael Angelo and Raphael and acquired a wide reputation by his compositions. Among his master-pieces are "The Visit of the Argonauts to the Centaur Chiron," and "Œdipus Tyrannus." Died in Rome in 1798. His subjects were mostly taken from the great poets, ancient and modern.

See FERNOW, "Leben des Künstler Carstens," 1806; NAGLER, "Neues Allgemeines Künstler-Lexikon."

Carsughi, kaR-soo'gee, (RANIERO,) an Italian Jesuit and Latin poet, born in Tuscany in 1647; died at Rome in 1709.

Cartagena, de, då kaR-tå-hā'nå, (ALONSO,) a Spanish poet, who became Archbishop of Burgos. Died in 1456.

See LONGFELLOW, "Poets and Poetry of Europe."

Cartajo, kaR-tå'yo, (ANTONIO MARIA,) an Italian poet, lived about 1530.

Cartari, kaR-tå'ree, (VINCENZO,) an Italian writer, born at Reggio, lived about 1550. Little is known of his life, except that he was in the service of Cardinal Ippolito d'Este. He wrote a popular work, entitled "Images of the Gods of the Ancients," etc., ("Le Immagini degli Dei degli Antichi," 1556.)

See GINGUENÉ, "Histoire Littéraire d'Italie."

Cartaud de la Vilate, kåR'tō' dẹh lå ve'låt', (FRANÇOIS,) a French author and priest, born at Aubusson about 1700. He published in 1736 a "Historical and Philosophical Essay on Taste," an ingenious and eloquent work, which attracted much attention. He displayed a fondness for paradox in his "Thoughts on Mathematics." Died in Paris in 1737.

Cartaux or Carteaux, kåR'tō', (JEAN FRANÇOIS,) a French general, born in Franche-Comté in 1751. In 1793 he defeated the royalists at Orange, for which service he was made on the same day general of brigade and of division. He commenced the siege of Toulon, where Bonaparte served under his orders, but was deprived of the command before the place was taken, in 1793. During the empire he was not in active service. Died in 1813.

See THIERS, "Histoire de la Révolution Française."

Carte, kart, (SAMUEL,) an English divine and antiquary, born at Coventry in 1653, became prebendary of Lichfield. He published a "Chronological Table of Archiepiscopal and Episcopal Sees in England and Wales," also several sermons. Died in 1740.

Carte, (THOMAS,) an English historian, son of the preceding, was born at Clifton in 1686. Having entered into holy orders, he became reader in the Abbey Church, Bath. From his partiality to the house of Stuart, he refused to take the oaths on the accession of George I. In 1715 orders were issued to arrest him as a party to the rebellion; but he escaped to France, where he remained about twelve years. After his return to England, he published a "History of the Life of James, Duke of Ormond," which, says Dr. Johnson, "is considered as a book of authority; but it is ill written. There is no animation, no compression, no vigour." He also wrote

---

€ as k; ç as s; ğ hard; ġ as j; G, H, K, guttural; N, nasal; R, trilled; ŝ as z; th as in this. (☞ See Explanations, p. 23.)

a "History of England," (4 vols., 1747–55,) which was coldly received. Hume refers to Carte as an "author of great industry and learning, but full of prejudices." Died in 1754.

Carteaux. See CARTAUX.

Cartellier, kǎr'tǎ'le-à', (PIERRE,) an eminent French sculptor, born in 1757 in Paris, was a pupil of C. A. Bridan. His reputation was established by the figure of War which adorns the palace of the Luxembourg. His statues of Aristides and Vergniaud were greatly admired, but exist only in plaster models. In 1810 he was elected a member of the Institute, and about that time produced statues of Napoleon and of Louis Bonaparte. He executed many other excellent works. Several distinguished artists were formed in his school. Died in 1831.

See QUATREMÈRE DE QUINCY, "Notice historique sur la Vie de Cartellier."

Car'ter, (ELIZABETH,) an English lady, distinguished as a profound classical scholar and an authoress, was born at Deal, Kent, in 1717. Her father, Nicholas Carter, D.D., curate of Deal, was a good classical scholar, and instructed her in the learned languages. She also made herself mistress of Italian, German, French, and Spanish. In 1738 she published anonymously a small volume of poems, and the next year acquired reputation by translating a work on Newton's philosophy from the Italian of Algarotti. Her "Ode to Wisdom" (1746) is one of her best poems. At an early period of her authorship she became a friend of Dr. Johnson, for whom she wrote Nos. 44 and 100 of the "Rambler." He once remarked of some eminent scholar, "Sir, he is the best Greek scholar in England except Elizabeth Carter." Her translation of Epictetus from the Greek (1758) extended her celebrity beyond the limits of her own country. Warton expressed the opinion that "it excels the original." She was never married. Her character was adorned by modesty, piety, and other Christian graces. Several volumes of her Letters have been published. Died in London in 1806.

See PENNINGTON, "Memoirs of E. Carter;" MRS. ELWOOD, "Memoirs of the Literary Ladies of England," etc., vol. i., 1843.

Carter, (FRANCIS,) an English writer, who resided some years in Spain, and published "A Journey from Gibraltar to Malaga," (1777.) He left a work in manuscript, entitled "Historical and Critical Account of Early-Printed Spanish Books." Died in 1783.

Car'ter, (JAMES GORDON,) an American educationist, born at Leominster, Massachusetts, in 1795, graduated at Harvard in' 1820. He furnished some valuable contributions on the subject of education to the "Boston Patriot" in 1823. As chairman of the committee on education, in the Massachusetts legislature, he did much to promote the interest of free schools. He drafted the bill establishing the Massachusetts Board of Education, of which he was appointed chairman by Governor Everett. Died in 1849.

Carter, (JOHN,) an eminent architect and antiquary, born in London in 1748. From 1780 to 1794 he issued, in numbers, "Specimens of Ancient Sculpture now remaining in England," which was followed by "Views of Ancient Buildings in England." He was employed more than twenty years on an important national work, entitled "The Ancient Architecture of England," (1795 –1816,) which is highly prized by students of that art. Died in 1817 or 1818.

Carter, (JOHN,) a silk-weaver, born at Coggeshall, England, in 1815. By injuries received in falling from a tree, his body below his neck became paralyzed. He lived for eighteen years in this condition, and learned to draw with wonderful skill, holding the brush in his mouth. His chief work is a "Rat-Catcher and his Dogs," the design and execution of which have been full of interest to the leading artists; and all his productions exhibit great æsthetic powers. Died in 1850.

See WILLIAM JAMES DAMPIER, "Memoir of John Carter," London, 1850; FREDERICK J. MILLS, "Life of John Carter," New York, 1868.

Carter, (NATHANIEL H.,) an American writer, born at Concord, New Hampshire, in 1787 or 1788. He became, about 1820, editor of the New York "Statesman," which supported De Witt Clinton. He published, after a visit to Europe, "Letters from Europe," (2 vols., 1827.) Died at Marseilles in 1830.

Carter, (SAMUEL P.,) an American general, born in East Tennessee in 1819, served in the navy in his youth. He was appointed a brigadier-general about May, 1862. He commanded a division under Schofield, in North Carolina, in February, 1865.

Car'ter, (THOMAS,) an Irish musician and composer of vocal music, born about 1768; died about 1802.

Car'ter-et, (Sir GEORGE,) an English naval officer, born about 1600, was an adherent of Charles I. and Charles II. in the civil war. Died in 1679.

Carteret, (JOHN,) Viscount Carteret and Earl Granville, an able English statesman and orator, born in 1690, was the son of George, Lord Carteret, of Bedfordshire. He graduated with high honours at Oxford, and in 1711 entered the House of Lords, where he soon became prominent as a speaker and a supporter of the Whig ministry. He represented England at the Congress of Cambrai in 1720, and was made secretary of state in 1721. Between 1724 and 1730 he was lord lieutenant of Ireland, and after the latter date he acted with the opposition. "Of all the members of the cabinet," says Macaulay, "Carteret was the most eloquent and accomplished. His talents for debate were of the first order; and his knowledge of foreign affairs superior to that of any living statesman. But there was not room in the government for him and Walpole, and Carteret retired." After the defeat of Walpole (1741) he became secretary of state, and for some months was chief minister,—or sole minister. In 1744 he was removed by the influence of the Pelham party. About 1750 he was appointed president of the council. The historian above named says, "His knowledge of modern languages was prodigious. No public man had such profound and extensive learning." His temper was bold, open, and impetuous. Died in 1763.

See MACAULAY, "Essay on Walpole's Letters to Sir Horace Mann," 1833; also his article entitled "Thackeray's History of the Earl of Chatham," 1834.

Carteret, (PHILIP,) CAPTAIN, an English navigator, who, in 1766, commanded one of the two vessels sent out to make discoveries in the South Sea, under the orders of Captain Wallis. Having discovered numerous small islands, one of which bears his name, Captain Carteret returned home in 1769, after which Hawkesworth published an account of the voyage.

Carteromacho. See FORTEGUERRI.

Cartesius, or **Cartes, Des.** See DESCARTES.

Carthaeuser. See CARTHÄUSER.

Car'tha-lo or **Car'tha-lon,** a Carthaginian general of the first Punic war. He commanded a fleet which was sent against the Romans in 249 B.C. Before any general action was fought, the Roman fleet was destroyed by a storm, from which the superior skill of the Carthaginians saved them.

Carthalon, a commander of the cavalry of Hannibal in his invasion of Italy, and at Cannæ in 216 B.C. Soon after that action he was sent to Rome to negotiate for the ransom of prisoners, but was ordered by a lictor to quit the Roman territory before sunset. He was taken prisoner in 208 B.C., and killed by a Roman soldier.

Carthäuser, Carthaeuser, or **Cartheuser,** pronounced alike kǎrt'hoi'zer, (FRIEDRICH AUGUST,) a German physician, son of Johann Friedrich, noticed below, was born at Halle in 1734. He became professor of medicine and surgery at Giessen in 1766. He published "Elements of Mineralogy," "Rudiments of Hydrology," (both in Latin,) and other works. Died in 1796.

Carthäuser, Carthaeuser, or **Cartheuser,** (JOHANN FRIEDRICH,) a learned German physician, born at Hayn in 1704. He experimented on many plants and medicaments, and made a reform in the materia medica. In 1740 he was chosen professor of chemistry, pharmacy, etc. in the University of Frankfort-on-the-Öder. He published (in Latin) "Elements of Experimental Chemistry, etc.," (1736,) "Elements of Materia Medica, General and Special," (1749,) and other works. Died in 1777.

See ÉLOY, "Dictionnaire de la Médecine;" "Biographie Médicale."

Carticeya or **Cartikeya.** See KARTIKEYA.

Cartier, kȁR'te-ȃ', (JACQUES,) a French navigator, the first discoverer of the Saint Lawrence River, was born at Saint-Malo in 1494. Being sent by Francis I. to explore North America in 1534, he entered the Gulf of Saint Lawrence, advanced as far as Gaspé Bay, and returned to France. He renewed the enterprise in 1535, and ascended the river as far as the site of Montreal. Being kindly treated by the natives, he passed the winter in Canada, and arrived at Saint-Malo in July, 1536. A narrative of the voyage was published.

See "Voyage de Découvertes au Canada, etc.," Quebec, 1843.

Cartier, (LOUIS VINCENT,) a French physician and writer on surgery, born in Dauphiné in 1768; died at Lyons in 1839.

Car-tĭ-mand'u-a or **Car-tis-man'du-a**, Queen of the Brigantes in Britain, lived about 50 A.D. She betrayed Caractacus to the Romans.

Cartouche, kȁR'toosh',(LOUIS DOMINIQUE,) a French robber of extraordinary skill and audacity, born in Paris in 1693, was executed in 1721.

Cart'wright, (CHRISTOPHER,) a learned Englishman, born in 1602, is said to have been the first who applied the more ancient uninspired writings of the Jews to the illustration of the Bible. He published several theological works, including one on the Targum, (1648.) Died in 1658.

Cartwright, (EDMUND,) the inventor of the power-loom, was born at Marnham, England, in 1743. Having taken orders, he obtained the living of Brampton, and afterwards that of Goadby-Marwood. He wrote a number of poems, among which were "The Prince of Peace" and "Armina and Elvira." The latter, a poetical legend, passed through nine editions. About 1785 he invented the power-loom, the use of which was opposed by the weavers, who destroyed five hundred of his machines. He obtained patents for many other inventions. In 1809 Parliament voted him £10,000 for the service he had rendered the public by the invention of the power-loom. Died in 1823.

See "Memoirs of the Life, Writings, and Mechanical Inventions of Edmund Cartwright," London, 8vo, 1843; "Pursuit of Knowledge under Difficulties," vol. ii., 1839.

Cartwright, (GEORGE,) an English traveller, born at Marnham in 1739. In the Seven Years' war he served in Germany and obtained the rank of captain. He afterwards made several voyages to Labrador, and in 1792 published a "Journal of a Residence of Sixteen Years on the Coast of Labrador." "The annals of his campaigns among the foxes and beavers," says Coleridge, "interested me more than ever did the exploits of Marlborough or Frederick." Died in 1819.

Cartwright, (JOHN,) MAJOR, a brother of the preceding, was born at Marnham in 1740, and passed some years in the royal navy previous to the American war. Prompted by his love of liberty, he refused to fight against the United States, and wrote "Letters on American Independence," (1774,) besides other political tracts. He was a zealous advocate of parliamentary reform and universal suffrage. Charles J. Fox thought him "one whose enlightened mind and profound constitutional knowledge placed him in the highest rank of public character, and whose purity of principle and consistency of conduct commanded the most respectful attention to his opinions." He was a coadjutor of Tooke, Hardy, etc. in the cause of reform. Died in 1824.

See F. D. CARTWRIGHT, "Life of Major J. Cartwright," 1826.

Cart'wright, (PETER,) an eminent Methodist preacher, born in Amherst county, Virginia, in 1785. While he was still a child, his parents removed with him to Kentucky. When scarcely sixteen years old, he was converted, and joined the Methodist Episcopal Church. At an early age he began to preach, and continued to labour in the cause with great zeal and success for more than fifty years. It is estimated that he preached in all not fewer than fifteen thousand sermons.

See "Autobiography of Peter Cartwright. the Backwoods Preacher," edited by W. P. STRICKLAND, New York, 1856.

Cartwright, (THOMAS,) an English Puritan divine, eminent for learning and talents, was born in Hertfordshire about 1535. He became a Fellow of a college at Cambridge in 1560, and professor of divinity there in 1570. A few years later he was deprived of these offices, and imprisoned several times, for his Puritanism. He published a "Body of Divinity," (1616,) a "Directory for Church Government," commentaries on several books of the Bible, and other works. Died in 1603.

See B. BROOK, "Memoir of the Life of T. Cartwright," 1845.

Cartwright, (THOMAS,) born in 1634, is supposed to have been a grandson of the preceding. He became Bishop of Chester in 1686, and was one of the commissioners who seconded James II. in his despotic attempt to impose a Roman Catholic president on the Fellows of Magdalen College. Died in 1689.

See MACAULAY, "History of England," vols. ii. and iii.

Cartwright, (WILLIAM,) an English poet, born at Northway in 1611. He graduated at Oxford, took orders in 1638, and became an eloquent preacher. Wood calls him "the most florid and seraphical preacher in the university." He was chosen junior proctor of Oxford University, and reader in metaphysics in 1643, and died the same year. He left tragi-comedies and other poems, which were greatly admired by his contemporaries, but are now neglected, except some of his dramas, one of which is entitled "The Ordinary."

See CAMPBELL, "Specimens of the British Poets;" BAKER, "Biographia Dramatica;" "Retrospective Review," vol. ix., 1824.

Carus, kȁ'rŭs, (FRIEDRICH AUGUST,) a Protestant German theologian, born at Bautzen in 1770. He acquired distinction as professor of philosophy in the University of Leipsic, (1796 to 1807.) He published, besides other works, a "History of Psychology," and a "History of the Psychology of the Hebrews," which is said to be a profound and well-written work. Died in 1807.

See SCHWARZE, "Zum Andenken des Professor Carus;" SCHOTT, "Recitatio de F. A. Cari Virtutibus," etc., 1808.

Carus, (KARL GUSTAV,) an eminent German physiologist and physician, born at Leipsic in 1789. He was appointed assistant professor of anatomy in his native city in 1811, and professor of obstetrics at Dresden in 1815. In 1827 he became physician to the King of Saxony, with the title of privy councillor. He also practised painting with success. Among his principal writings are an "Essay on the Nervous System," (1814,) a "Manual of Zootomy," (1818,) "Principles of Comparative Anatomy and Physiology," (3 vols., 1828,) and a "System of Physiology," (3 vols., 1838–40.)

See CALLISEN, "Medicinisches Schriftsteller-Lexikon;" "Nouvelle Biographie Générale."

Cā'rus, (MARCUS AURELIUS,) a Roman emperor, born at Narbo, (now Narbonne.) Under the emperor Probus he held the high office of prefect of the prætorium. At the death of Probus in 282 A.D., Carus was elected his successor by the army. In 283 he marched against the Persians, leaving his son Carinus to govern Italy. Having taken Seleucia and Ctesiphon, he was about to pursue his conquests, when he died suddenly, (283,) or, as some report, was killed by lightning.

See GIBBON, "Decline and Fall of the Roman Empire;" VOPISCUS, "Carus."

Caruso, kȁ-roo'so, or **Carusio**, kȁ-roo'se-o, (GIOVANNI BATTISTA,) an Italian historian, born near Palermo in 1673. He published "Historical Memoirs of Sicily," (3 vols., 1716–45.) Died in 1724.

Caruso, (LUIGI,) a popular Italian composer of operas, born in Naples about 1750. He was living in 1800.

Carvajal, kaR-vȁ-hȁl', or **Carbajal**, kaR-Bȁ-hȁl', (TOMAS JOSÉ GONZALEZ,) a Spanish writer and statesman, born at Seville in 1753. He was chosen president of the junta of finances in 1812. At the restoration in 1814 he was imprisoned for political reasons. In 1819 he produced a Spanish version of the Psalms, which is greatly admired. He afterwards held several high civil offices, among which was that of a member of the Council of the Indies, and became a peer in 1834. He died the same year.

See BROCKHAUS, "Conversations-Lexikon."

Carvajal, de, dȁ kaR-vȁ-hȁl', or **Carbajal**, kaR-Bȁ-hȁl', (BERNARDINO,) born at Palencia, in Spain, about 1456, was made a cardinal in 1493. In 1511 he supported the interest of Louis XII. of France against Pope Julius

II., for which offence he was excommunicated. Having confessed his fault, he obtained pardon in 1513. Died in 1523.

See FABRONI, "Vita Leonis X. ;" PAOLO GIOVIO, "Elogia."

Carvajal, de, or **Carbajal,** (FRANCISCO,) a famous Spanish captain, born about 1464, was conspicuous for courage at the battle of Pavía in 1525, and at the sack of Rome in 1527. He afterwards went to Mexico and Peru, and in 1542 became a major-general. He joined the party of Gonzales Pizarro in his revolt against the King of Spain, and gained several victories over the royalists about 1546. In 1548 he was made prisoner and hung. He was notorious for cruelty.

See ROBERTSON, "History of America."

Carvajal, de, or **Carbajal,** written also **Caravajal, de,** (JUAN,) an eminent Spanish prelate, born at Truxillo, was made a cardinal in 1446. He gained a high reputation by his missions as papal legate in Germany and Hungary. Died at Rome in 1469.

See ERSCH und GRUBER, "Allgemeine Encyklopaedie."

Carvajal or **Carbajal, de,** (LORENZO GALINDEZ,) was born at Placencia in 1472. He was professor of law at Salamanca, was a councillor of Ferdinand and Isabella, and held high offices under Charles V. He left unfinished a "History of Spain," which, with other works, remained in manuscript. Died in 1527.

See PRESCOTT, "History of Ferdinand and Isabella," vol. iii. chap. xxv.

Carvalho. See FREIRE DE CARVALHO.

Carvalho, kaR-vâl'yo, (ANTONIO NUNEZ,) a Portuguese bibliographer, born about 1790, was living in 1855.

Carvalho, (JOZÉ DA SILVA,) a Portuguese minister of state, born in 1782; died in 1845.

Carvalho d'Acosta, kaR-vâl'yo dä-kos'tä, (ANTONIO,) a Portuguese geographer and priest, born in Lisbon in 1650. He published in 1706 a "Topographical Description of Portugal," which treats of the natural and civil history of the principal places, and is esteemed the best work on that subject. He also wrote a "Compend of Geography," and other works. Died in 1715.

See BARBOSA MACHADO, "Bibliotheca Lusitana."

Carvalho e Mello. See POMBAL.

Carvallo, kaR-vâl'yo, (MANUEL,) a South American jurist and diplomatist, born at Santiago, in Chili, in 1808, was chargé-d'affaires at Washington.

Carvaxal. See CARVAJAL.

Car'ver, (JOHN,) the first governor of Plymouth colony, was born in England. He was one of a company of Puritans who emigrated to Holland, and came over in the Mayflower in 1620. He is said to have been a prudent and able governor. Died in 1621.

Carver, (JONATHAN,) an American traveller, born in Connecticut in 1732, served as captain in the war against the French in Canada. He passed about three years (1766-68) in the exploration of North America, which he crossed to the Pacific Ocean, and published in 1778 "Travels through the Interior Parts of North America." Died in London in 1780.

Cā'ry̌, (ALICE,) an American authoress, born near Cincinnati, Ohio, about 1822. She first attracted attention by her contributions to the "National Era," under the title of Patty Lee; and she has since published several volumes of poems and other works, including three novels,—"Hagar, a Story of To-Day," "Married not Mated," and "Hollywood." Her sketches of Western life, entitled "Clovernook," have obtained extensive popularity both in America and Europe.

PHŒBE CARY, a sister of Alice, has also contributed to periodical literature, and in 1854 published a volume entitled "Poems and Parodies."

See GRISWOLD'S "Female Poets of America;" CLEVELAND'S "Compendium of American Literature."

Cary, (Colonel ARCHIBALD,) a Virginian patriot, born about 1730. He favoured the cause of independence, and took a prominent part in the Convention of 1776 which framed the constitution of Virginia. He was afterwards a member of the Senate of Virginia. Died in 1786.

Cary, EARL OF MONMOUTH. See CAREY, (HENRY and ROBERT.)

Cary, kȧ're', (FÉLIX,) a French antiquary and numismatist, born at Marseilles in 1699, formed a fine collection of antique medals. His principal production is a "History of the Kings of Thrace and of the Cimmerian Bosphorus," which is regarded as a classic work. In 1752 the Academy of Inscriptions chose him as a correspondent. Died in 1754.

Cā'ry̌, (Rev. HENRY,) an English scholar and writer, son of Henry F. Cary the translator of Dante. He has published "Testimonies of the Fathers," (Oxford, 1835,) and "Memorials of the Great Civil War in England from 1646 to 1652," (1842.) He has also edited his father's version of Dante, "Early French Poets," etc.

Cary, (Rev. HENRY FRANCIS,) an English poet, eminent as the translator of Dante, was born at Birmingham in 1772. While a student at Oxford, he gave much attention to Greek, Latin, French, and Italian, and before he left college he had published a number of sonnets and odes. In 1797 he was appointed vicar of Bromley Abbot's. He produced in 1806 an excellent translation, in blank verse, of Dante's "Inferno," and in 1814 completed the other portions of the "Divina Commedia." This version is highly applauded by the most eminent judges, including Southey, who said it was "a translation of magnitude and difficulty, executed with perfect fidelity and admirable skill." He afterwards published "The Early French Poets, a Series of Notices and Translations," and other works. Died in 1844.

See "Memoir of H. F. Cary," by his son, HENRY CARY, 2 vols., 1847; "Fraser's Magazine" for May, 1847.

Cary, (JOHN,) of Bristol, an Englishman, published, between 1695 and 1745, "Treatises on Political Economy, etc." His "Discourse on Trade," a work of little merit, was made the basis of a better work, published in French, at Paris, 1755.

Cary, (LOTT,) an African preacher, was born a slave in Virginia, and accompanied the first emigrants sent to Liberia by the American Colonization Society in 1821. He officiated as pastor, physician, and soldier to the colony, was elected vice-agent in 1826, and on the withdrawal of Mr. Ashmun, whose entire confidence he enjoyed, discharged for about six months the duties of governor. ⁃ He was killed in November, 1828, by the accidental explosion of a magazine.

Cary, (LUCIUS.) See FALKLAND, LORD.

Cary, (ROBERT.) See CAREY, (ROBERT.)

Cary, (ROBERT,) a learned English clergyman, born in Devonshire about 1615. He became Archdeacon of Exeter in 1662, and wrote an esteemed work entitled "Palæologia Chronica." Died in 1688.

Căr'y̌l, (JOHN,) of Sussex, an English dramatic writer, was intimate with Pope the poet. He wrote "The English Princess," a tragedy, and a few other works. He was secretary to Mary, queen of James II., whom he followed into exile in 1688, and who gave him the empty title of Earl Caryl.

Caryl, (JOSEPH,) an English divine of the sect of Independents, born in London in 1602, was ejected for nonconformity in 1662. His principal work is an "Exposition of Job," (in 12 vols.,) which is much praised. Died in 1673.

See NEAL'S "History of the Puritans."

Caryophilus. See GAROFALO, (BLAISE.)

Casa, della, del'lä kȧ'sä, (GIOVANNI,) an Italian poet and priest, born near Florence in 1503, was one of the most elegant writers of his time. He became a resident of Rome, and in 1544 Archbishop of Beñevento. Paul IV. on his election to the papal see made Casa his secretary of state. He wrote lyric poems in Italian, which were much admired, and were compared to those of Bembo for purity of style. The first edition appeared in 1558. His most popular prose work is "Galateo, ovvero de' Costumi," which treats of the rules of politeness. He translated Plato into Latin, and wrote Latin "Carmina," and other works. Died at Rome about 1556.

See "Life of Della Casa," prefixed to his works, by G. B. CASOTTI, (edition of 1707;) LONGFELLOW, "Poets and Poetry of Europe;" FILIPPO GERARDI, "Biografia di Giovanni della Casa," 1836; GINGUENÉ, "Histoire Littéraire d'Italie;" ERSCH und GRUBER, "Allgemeine Encyklopaedie;" NICÉRON, "Mémoires."

Casabianca, kȧ'sä-be-an'kä, (LOUIS,) a naval officer, born at Bastia about 1755. He was sent as a deputy to

ā, ē, ī, ō, ū, ȳ, *long;* ȧ, ė, ȯ, same, less prolonged; ă, ĕ, ĭ, ŏ, ŭ, y̌, *short;* ą, ę, į, ǫ, *obscure;* fär, fȧll, fât; mĕt; nŏt; gōōd; mōōn;

the French National Convention in 1792, and voted for the detention of the king. In 1798 he was captain of L'Orient, the flagship of the fleet which conveyed Bonaparte and his army to Egypt. At the battle of the Nile, August 1, 1798, after he was mortally wounded, he made a heroic defence of the burning ship, which finally was destroyed by a terrific explosion.

Casabianca, (RAPHAEL,) a French general, brother of the preceding, was born in Corsica in 1738, and became general of division in 1794. In 1806 he was made a count. Died in 1825.

See DE COURCELLES, "Histoire des Généraux Français."

Casa-Irujo, de, dả kả'sả e-roo'ho, (CARLOS MARIA MARTINEZ,) MARQUIS, a Spanish statesman, born at Cartagena in 1765. From 1795 to 1808 he was minister to the United States, where he married the daughter of Thomas McKean. He was plenipotentiary at the Congress of Aix-la-Chapelle in 1818, and ambassador to Paris in 1821. In 1823 he was appointed minister of foreign affairs, and president of the council. Died in 1824.

Casal, kả-sảl', (GASPAR,) Bishop of Leiria, in Portugal, born at Santarem in 1510. He became counsellor and confessor of John III., whose preceptor he had once been. He wrote a treatise "On the Justification of Man," (in Latin,) and other works. Died about 1580.

See N. ANTONIO, "Bibliotheca Hispana Nova."

Casal, de, dả kả-sảl', or **Cazal,** kả-zảl', (MANUEL AYRES,) a Portuguese geographer, who emigrated to Brazil in his youth, explored parts of that region, and lived for some time in Rio Janeiro. In 1817 he published a valuable "Historical and Geographical Description of Brazil." He died in Lisbon many years after 1817.

Casali, kả-sả'lee, (GIOVANNI BATTISTA,) a Roman antiquary, who published a treatise "On the Sacred and Profane Rites of the Ancients," "The Splendour of Rome and the Roman Empire in Ancient Times," (1650,) and other esteemed works.

Casali, (GIUSEPPE,) an antiquary and priest, born in Rome in 1744. He formed a rich collection of medals and antique remains, was a liberal patron of artists, and wrote a few treatises on numismatics. Died in 1797.

Casanova, kả-sả-no'vả, (FRANCESCO,) a painter, born of Italian parents, in London, about 1728. At the age of twenty-five he went to Paris, where he gained a high reputation for his battle-pieces and landscapes, and was admitted into the Royal Academy. He afterwards worked in Vienna, where the Empress of Russia employed him to illustrate her victories over the Turks. Died in 1805.

See CHARLES BLANC, "Histoire des Peintres."

Casanova, (GIOVANNI BATTISTA,) an Italian painter, brother of the preceding, was born at Venice about 1725. He was a pupil of R. Mengs, and professor in the Academy of Fine Arts of Dresden. He gained distinction by his "Dissertations on Ancient Monuments of Art." Died in 1798.

Casanova, (GIOVANNI GIACOMO de Seingalt—dẹh sĩn'gảlt or dẹh sản'gảlt',) a celebrated Italian adventurer, remarkable for his wit, accomplishments, learning, and intrigues, was born in Venice in 1725, and was a brother of the preceding. His parents were play-actors. For many years he led a wandering and dissipated life in the various capitals of Europe, frequenting the most aristocratic society, and having no regular business. He was confined about two years in the dungeon of Venice, (1755-57,) and escaped by stratagem. In the course of his life he fought several duels. He became librarian to Count Waldstein, a Bohemian grandee, with whom he passed the last fourteen years of his life, and died in 1803, leaving "Memoirs of his Life," which are sprightly and entertaining. He translated the "Iliad" into *ottava rima,* and wrote a few other works.

See CASANOVA, "Memoirs," in German and French, 8 vols., 1830; BARTHOLD, "Die geschichtlichen Persönlichkeiten in J. Casanova's Memoiren," Berlin, 2 vols., 1846; see, also, "Nouvelle Biographie Générale."

Casanova, (MARCANTONIO,) an Italian poet, born at Rome in 1476. He wrote epigrams against Clement VII. Died about 1527.

Cäsar. See CÆSAR.

Casaregi, kả-sả-rä'jee, [Lat. CASARE'GIS,] (GIOVANNI BARTOLOMMEO,) an Italian poet, born at Genoa in 1676, was a brother of the jurist noticed below. He lived at Rome and afterwards at Florence, and was a member of the Academy della Crusca. He wrote elegant lyric poems, "Sonnetti e Canzoni," and translated the Proverbs of Solomon into verse. Died in 1755.

See LONGFELLOW's "Poets and Poetry of Europe.'

Casaregi, [Lat. CASARE'GIS,] (GIUSEPPE LORENZO MARIA,) a distinguished Italian jurist, born at Genoa in 1670. He was reputed a high authority in questions of commercial law, on which he wrote several treatises,— "Discursus legales de Commercio." Died in 1737.

Casaregis. See CASAREGI.

Casas, de las, dả lås kả'sảs, (BARTOLOMÉ,) a benevolent Spanish missionary, noted for his zeal in behalf of the oppressed Indians, was born at Seville in 1474. In 1493 he accompanied Columbus in his second voyage to America. Some years later, having become a Dominican friar, he went to Hispaniola as a missionary, preaching the gospel to the natives, and humanity to the Spanish conquerors who had enslaved them. His efforts to ameliorate the condition of this class having been opposed and frustrated, he visited the court of Spain in 1516, and afterwards repeatedly crossed the ocean to plead their cause. He also addressed to Charles V. several letters or treatises on the subject. He was appointed Bishop of Chiapa, in Mexico, some years before 1550. In 1551 he returned to Spain, where he died in 1566, leaving a "History of the Indies," still in manuscript. The charge that he advised the importation of negro slaves as a substitute for Indians appears to be without foundation: "it has," says the "Nouvelle Biographie Générale," "been completely refuted by M. Grégoire."

See ARTHUR HELPS, "Life of Las Casas," 1868; RAYNAL, "Histoire philosophique des Deux Indes;" GRÉGOIRE, "Apologie de Las Casas," (published in the "Mémoires" of the Institute;) MORÉRI, "Dictionnaire Historique;" MICHAEL PIO, "Vie de Las Casas," 1618.

Casati, kả-sả'tee, (PAOLO,) a learned Italian Jesuit, born at Piacenza in 1617. He taught mathematics and theology at Rome, and is said to have converted Queen Christina of Sweden to the Catholic faith. He wrote treatises on Mechanics, on Optics, and on Fire. The last is commended. Died at Parma in 1707.

See NICÉRON, "Mémoires."

Ca-sau'bon, [Fr. pron. kả'zo'bôn'; Lat. CASAUBO'-NUS,] (ISAAC,) one of the most eminent critics and scholars of his time, was born of French Protestant parents, at Geneva, on the 8th of Febuary, 1559. In 1582 he became a professor of Greek in the College of Geneva, and soon after began to publish the editions of Greek authors which caused his celebrity as a critic. His "Athenæus" (1600) "has always been deemed," says Hallam, "a noble monument of critical sagacity and extensive erudition. In conjectural emendation of the text, no one hitherto had been equal to Casaubon." He married Florence, a daughter of the eminent scholar Henry Étienne, in 1585. He was professor of Greek at Montpellier from 1596 to 1599. In 1600 Henry IV. invited him to Paris to give lessons in Greek, and appointed him royal librarian. He published an excellent edition of Polybius in 1609. In 1610 he removed to England, where he was received with favour by James I., who made him prebendary of Canterbury. Joseph Scaliger once said of Casaubon, "He is the most learned man now living," although he himself was equal to Casaubon in general learning, but not in a critical knowledge of Greek. Casaubon died in London in 1614. He was a moderate Protestant, and wrote a treatise "De Libertate ecclesiastica," ("On Ecclesiastical Liberty.") Among his productions were editions of Aristotle's Works, (1590,) and of the "Characters" of Theophrastus, (1592.)

See ALMELOVEEN, "Vie de Casaubon;" C. NISARD, "Le Triumvirat littéraire, Juste-Lipse, Scaliger et Casaubon," 1851; WOLF, "Casauboniana," Hamburg, 1710; NICÉRON, "Mémoires;" "Nouvelle Biographie Générale;" "London Quarterly Review" for October, 1853.

Casaubon, (MÉRIC,) the son of the preceding, was born at Geneva in 1599. He took orders in the Anglican Church, and obtained the living of Ickham, and in 1628 a prebend in the church of Canterbury. During the civil war he was deprived of these places, and, it is said, declined the proffered gifts and patronage of Cromwell, who desired him to write a history of the war. At the restoration of 1660 he recovered his benefices. He was a writer of moderate ability, and published a variety of works, among which are a "Treatise on Enthusiasm," and one "On Credulity and Incredulity." Died in 1671.

See Wood, "Athenæ Oxonienses;" Nicéron, "Mémoires."

Casaubonus. See Casaubon.

Cas'ca, (P. Servilius,) a Roman conspirator, was a tribune of the people when he assisted at the assassination of Cæsar in 44 B.C. He fought at the battle of Philippi, (42 B.C.,) and died shortly afterwards.

Cas-çel'li-us, (Aulus,) an eminent and eloquent Roman jurist, was a contemporary of Cicero and Trebatius. He was a firm and consistent republican, and showed his independent spirit by refusing, in 41 B.C., to sanction by legal forms the spoliations of the triumvirs. Horace (in "De Arte Poetica," l. 371) speaks of Cascellius as a jurisconsult of rare learning.

See Grotius, "Vitæ Jurisconsultorum;" Lagemans, "Dissertatio de A. Cascellio," 1823.

Cãse, (John,) M.D., born at Woodstock, England, was noted as a disputant and philosopher. He taught philosophy at Oxford, and published the "Mirror of Moral Questions according to the Ethics of Aristotle," ("Speculum Moralium Questionum in Ethicam Aristotelis,") and other works. Died in 1600.

Case, (John,) a famous English astrologer and quack, born at Lyme-Regis. He flourished in the reign of Queen Anne, (1701-14,) and was the successor of Lilly in astrology. He inscribed on his sign,

"Within this place
Lives Doctor Case,"

and is said to have made more money by that distich than Dryden received for all his works. He published "Compendium Anatomicum," and a few other works.

Case, (Thomas,) an English nonconformist minister, born in Kent about 1598, was ejected from Erpingham, Norfolk. He was afterwards rector of Saint Giles-in-the-Fields. Died in 1682.

Casearius, kå-se-å're-us, (Jan,) a Dutch botanist, who lived in India about 1670, and was one of the authors of the "Hortus Malabaricus."

Casel. See Caselius.

Caselius, kå-zã'le-ùs, [Ger. Casel, kå'zẹl ; Fr. Chessel, shǎ'sĕl',] (Johannes,) an eminent German philologist and writer, born at Göttingen in 1533. He was professor of philosophy in the University of Helmstedt from 1590 to 1613. He wrote Latin with elegance, and was author of many works on philosophy and other subjects. The most generally known of his productions were Letters, (in Latin,) which were addressed to his eminent contemporaries, and which are admired for ingenious thoughts and graces of style. Died in 1613.

See M. Adam, "Vitæ Eruditorum;" J. Sigfried, "De Vita et Obitu J. Caselii," 1613.

Caseneuve, de, dẹh kå'z'nuv', [Lat. Caseno'va,] (Pierre,) a French priest and philologist, born at Toulouse in 1591. He wrote a "Treatise on Freehold," and a dictionary, entitled "Origin of the French Language," ("Origines de la Langue Française.") Died in 1652.

See Medon, "Vita Viri illustris Casenovæ," 1656.

Cases, kåz, (Pierre Jacques,) a skilful French painter of history, born in Paris in 1676. Among his masterpieces is a "Holy Family." Died in Paris in 1754.

Cases, Las. See Las Cases.

Cã'sey, (Silas,) an American general, born in Rhode Island in 1807, graduated at West Point in 1826. He served as captain in the Mexican war, (1846-47,) and became a lieutenant-colonel in 1855. He was appointed a brigadier-general of volunteers in August, 1861, and a colonel of the regular army in October, and commanded a division at Fair Oaks, May 31, 1862.

Cas'ĭ-mir [Polish, Kazimierz, kå'ze-me-àRzh'] **I.** of Poland, surnamed the Pacific, was still an infant when his father, Micislaus (Mieczislaw) II., died in 1034. His mother carried him to France, where he took the monastic vows in the abbey of Cluny. Having been invited by the Poles to reign over them, he was crowned in 1041, and married the sister of Yaroslaf, Duke of Russia. His

reign promoted the prosperity and civilization of Poland. Died in 1058, leaving the throne to his son, Boleslaus II.

Casimir II., King of Poland, born about 1137, was a younger son of Boleslaus III. In 1177 his brother Micislaus was deposed, and Casimir was chosen king. He is said to have ruled with wisdom, and to have gained the favour of the people. He waged a successful war against the Prussians, who procured peace by paying tribute. He died in 1194, and was succeeded by his son, Lesko V.

Casimir III., surnamed the Great, became King of Poland at the death of his father, Vladislaus, (or Ladislaus,) in 1333. He married Anne, daughter of the Duke of Lithuania. About 1345 he defeated the King of Bohemia, and in 1366 subdued Red Russia. He founded hospitals, colleges, etc. He died in 1370, and was the last of the royal line of Piast. His nephew, Louis of Hungary, was his successor.

See "Nouvelle Biographie Générale."

Casimir IV. of Poland, born about 1425, was the second son of Vladislaus IV. or V., (who before his accession was Yagello, Duke of Lithuania.) He succeeded his elder brother, Vladislaus, in 1445, and married the daughter of the emperor Albert II. He waged a long war against the Teutonic knights, who were finally defeated in 1466, when Casimir became master of a great part of Prussia. In this reign the constitution of the Diet was changed by the admission of deputies who were not nobles. He died in 1492, leaving five or six sons, three of whom became successively kings of Poland, —John Albert, Alexander, and Sigismund.

Casimir V. of Poland, second son of Sigismund III. and Constance of Austria, was born in 1609. About 1645 he was made a cardinal. In 1648 he was elected king on the death of his brother Vladislaus. He was involved in a war with the allied Cossacks and Russians, whom he defeated. Poland was afterwards invaded by Charles Gustavus of Sweden, who took Warsaw after a victory over the Poles ; but his progress was arrested by a coalition of several powers, and peace was concluded in 1660. Weary of contending against his foreign and domestic enemies, he abdicated in 1668, and died in France in 1672.

See "Lebensbeschreibung Casimiri V., weyland Königs in Polen," Nuremberg, 1680; "Nouvelle Biographie Générale;" "Histoire générale de Pologne, d'après les Historiens Polonais."

Cas'ĭ-mir Sar-bĭ-e'vĭ-us, a Latin lyric poet and Jesuit, born in Poland in 1595, lived some years at Rome. His verses were praised by Rapin the poet. According to Hallam, he obtained a much higher reputation than Sidonius Hoschius. Died about 1640.

Casiri, kå-see'ree, (Michael,) a learned Orientalist and Maronite, born at Tripoli, in Syria, in 1710. He removed to Spain in 1748, and became chief librarian of the Escurial in 1763. His principal work is "Bibliotheca Arabico-Hispana Escurialensis," ("Arabic-Spanish Library of the Escurial,") which is said to be an indispensable treasure to students of Oriental literature. Died in 1791.

See Zenker, "Bibliotheca Orientalis."

Cas'ley, (David,) an English bibliographer, published a "Catalogue of the MSS. in the King's Library," 1734.

Cas'lon, (William,) an English letter-founder and engraver, born at Hales-Owen in 1692 ; died in 1766.

Casmann, kås'mån, (Otho,) a German theologian, who was rector at Stade, in Hanover. Died in 1607.

Casolani, kå-so-lå'nee, (Alessandro,) an eminent Italian painter, born at Sienna in 1552. He excelled in design and composition. Died in 1606.

Casotti, kå-șot'tee, (Giovanni Battista,) an Italian writer, born at Prato, in Tuscany, in 1669. He was professor of philosophy and history in Florence, and author of several learned works, among which was "Historical Notices of the Life and Works of Giovanni della Casa." Died in 1737.

See Tipaldo, "Biografia degli Italiani illustri."

Caspari, kås'på-ree, (Karl Paul,) a learned German biblical critic, born at Dessau in 1814. He became *lector* and member of the faculty in the University of Christiania. He has published, besides other works, "Studies of Biblical Theology and Apologetic Criticism," (1842,) and an "Introduction to the Book of Isaiah and the History of his Time," (1848.)

Casper, kås′per, (JOHANN LUDWIG,) a distinguished German physician, born in 1796. He became assistant professor in the University of Berlin in 1825, and *geheim-medicinalrath* in 1834. In 1833 he began to edit the "Weekly Journal of Medicine." He was appointed professor of medicine in the University of Berlin in 1839. He is regarded as one of the most renowned practitioners of Germany. Among his works is "Essays on Medical Statistics and Officinal Medicine," (1825-37.)

Cass, (JONATHAN,) an American officer in the war of the Revolution, was born in Salisbury, Massachusetts, in 1753. He entered the army in 1775, obtained the rank of captain, and served until the end of the war. Died in 1830.

Cass, (LEWIS,) an American patriot and statesman, a son of the preceding, was born at Exeter, New Hampshire, in October, 1782. He studied law at Marietta, Ohio, and began to practise at Zanesville about 1802. In 1812 he became colonel of a regiment which, under the command of General Hull, invaded Canada. The campaign was ended by the disgraceful surrender of Hull at Detroit in August, 1812. Colonel Cass was promoted to the rank of brigadier-general about March, 1813, and was appointed Governor of Michigan in 1814. While he governed that unsettled territory, he was also for many years Superintendent of Indian Affairs, and negotiated many treaties with the Indians. He resigned the office of Governor in 1831, and was appointed by President Jackson secretary of war the same year. In 1836 he was sent as ambassador to France, and published in 1840 a work entitled "France, its King, Court, and Government." He returned to the United States in 1842, and was elected a Senator of the United States by the legislature of Michigan in the winter of 1844-45. In his letter to Mr. Nicholson, dated December, 1847, he opposed the Wilmot Proviso, and questioned the power of the Congress to exclude slavery from the territories. "This letter," says Mr. Greeley, "is notable as the first clear enunciation of the doctrine termed "Popular (otherwise Squatter) Sovereignty." ("American Conflict.") Cass was nominated as the Democratic candidate for the Presidency by the Baltimore Convention in 1848, but was defeated in the ensuing election by General Taylor, the Whig candidate, who received one hundred and sixty-three electoral votes, General Cass receiving one hundred and thirty-seven. About 1851 he was again elected to the Senate of the United States for six years. He voted for Douglas's Kansas-Nebraska Bill in 1854. He was appointed secretary of state by President Buchanan, March, 1857. He resigned this office in December, 1860, on account of his dissatisfaction with the do-nothing policy of Buchanan, who, even after the secession of South Carolina, declined to reinforce the garrison of Fort Sumter. Died in June, 1866.

See H. R. SCHOOLCRAFT, "Life of General Cass," 1848; W. L. G. SMITH, "The Life and Times of Lewis Cass," 1856.

Cassagnes, kȧ′sȧñ′, or **Cassaigne,** kȧ′sȧñ′,(JACQUES,) a French writer and priest, born at Nîmes in 1636. His early poems opened for him the French Academy in 1662. He was afterwards librarian of the Royal Library, and one of the four first members of the Academy of Inscriptions. He published a translation of Sallust, and a few other works. Died in 1679.

Cassaigne. See CASSAGNES.

Cassana, kås-sä′nä, (GIOVANNI AGOSTINO,) called ABBÉ CASSANA, a successful Italian painter of portraits and animals, born about 1658 ; died at Genoa in 1720.

See LANZI, "History of Painting in Italy."

Cassana, (GIOVANNI FRANCESCO,) a historical painter of the Genoese school, father of the preceding, was born at Cassana in 1611. He worked in Venice and Mirandola, and gained a high reputation. Died in 1691.

See LANZI, "History of Painting in Italy."

Cassana, (NICCOLÒ,) a portrait-painter, born at Venice about 1656, was the son and pupil of the preceding. Having acquired a high reputation, he was invited to England by Queen Anne, whose portrait he painted, and who appointed him her first painter. Died in 1713.

Cas-san′der, [Gr. Κάσσανδρος; Fr. CASSANDRE, kȧ′sôNdR′,] a Macedonian prince, was the son of Antipater, who, at the death of Alexander the Great, ob-

tained the regency or government of Macedonia. In 318 B.C. Antipater died, having appointed Polysperchon his successor, in preference to his own son. A war ensued between these two parties, and Cassander, aided by Antigonus, soon became master of Athens, where he restored the aristocracy under Demetrius Phalereus about 316. Cassander then invaded Macedonia with success, obtained possession of the infant son of Alexander the Great, and married Thessalonice, the sister of the latter prince. In 311, Antigonus and other generals signed a treaty stipulating that Cassander should be regent of Macedonia and Greece until the young prince should attain his majority. In 309 he put to death that prince and his mother Roxana, and usurped the throne. He died in 297 B.C., and was succeeded by his son Philip.

See ARRIAN, "Anabasis;" THIRLWALL, "History of Greece."

Cassander, kås-sån′der, [Fr. CASSANDRE,kȧ′sôNdR′,] (GEORGE,) a learned theologian, born in the isle of Cadsand, Flanders, about 1515. The emperor Ferdinand referred to him as a mediator the chief points in the controversy between the Reformers and the Catholics ; and, with a view to reconcile them, Cassander wrote his famous "Consultation on the Articles of Faith controverted between Papists and Protestants," ("Consultatio de Articulis Fidei inter Papistas et Protestantes controversis.") He was one of the most moderate of the Catholic writers of that time. Died in 1566.

See ARNOLD, "Kirchen- und Ketzer-Historie ;" NICÉRON, "Mémoires ;" MORÉRI, "Dictionnaire Historique."

Cas-san′dra, [Gr. Κασσάνδρα ; Fr. CASSANDRE, kȧ′sôNdR′,] a daughter of Priam and Hecuba, was celebrated for her prophetic powers ; but, according to tradition, Apollo had ordained that her prophecies, though true, should be disbelieved. During the siege of Troy she predicted the impending calamities, but was treated as a lunatic by Priam and others. Agamemnon became enamoured of her, and took her to Mycenæ, where she was killed by Clytemnestra.

Cassandre. See CASSANDER and CASSANDRA.

Cassandre, kȧ′sôNdR′, (FRANÇOIS,) a French writer, principally known by his excellent translation of Aristotle's "Rhetoric," which was highly prized by Boileau. He wrote several other works, in prose and verse. Died in 1695. His whole life was passed in poverty,—which Voltaire ascribes to his morose temper and unsocial habits.

Cassard, kȧ′sȧr′,(JACQUES,) a brave and skilful French naval officer, was born at Nantes in 1672. As captain of a privateer, he took many prizes from the English. Having obtained command of a small squadron, he reduced the Cape Verd Islands and captured Surinam in 1712. After the peace of 1713 he presented claims for money which he had advanced ; but they were disregarded, and he was confined in the castle of Ham for offensive language to the minister. Died at Ham in 1740.

See GRAINCOURT, "Hommes illustres de la Marine Française ;" "Nouvelle Biographie Générale."

Cassas, kȧ′sås′, (LOUIS FRANÇOIS,) an eminent French landscape-painter and architect, born in the department of Indre in 1756. He accompanied to Constantinople the ambassador Choiseul-Gouffier, who employed him to illustrate his "Travels in Greece." He afterwards visited and sketched the monuments of Baalbec, Palmyra, and the Holy Land. In 1799 he began to publish these sketches, in his "Voyage pittoresque de la Syrie, de la Palestine et de la Basse-Egypte." He also published "Picturesque Views of the Principal Sites and Monuments of Greece, of Sicily, and of the Seven Hills of Rome," (1813.) Died in 1827.

See NAGLER, "Neues Allgemeines Künstler-Lexikon."

Cassel, kås′sel, (JOHANN PHILIPP,) a German philologist, born in 1707 at Bremen, where he became professor of eloquence. He published "Historical Notices and Documents of Bremen," (1766,) and other works. Died in 1783.

See CHARLES, "Vie de Cassel ;" MEUSEL, "Gelehrtes Deutschland."

Cassentino. See CASENTINO.

Casserio, kås-sä′re-o, (GIULIO,) an eminent Italian physician, born at Piacenza in 1555. He became a resident of Padua, where he acquired a high reputation, and in 1609 was appointed professor of surgery in the university. He left, besides other works, a treatise on the anatomy and physiology of the senses, and "Anatomical Plates." Died in 1616.

See THOMASINI, "Elogia."

Cassian, kash'e-ạn, [Fr. CASSIEN, kȧ'se'ȧN'; Lat. CAS-SIA'NUS,] (JOHN,) a monk, born probably in Provence about 350 A.D. In 415 A.D. he went to Marseilles, where he founded the monastery of Saint-Victor. He wrote an esteemed work on "Monastic Institutions," and a "Treatise on the Incarnation." His doctrines on grace were opposed by Saint Augustine, as a modified Pelagianism. Died about 433.

See VOSSIUS, "De Historicis Latinis ;" PHOTIUS, "Bibliotheca ;" LOUIS F. MEYER, "J. Cassien ; sa Vie et ses Écrits," 1840.

Cassiani, kås-se-å'nee, (GIULIANO,) an Italian lyric poet, born at Módena in 1712, became professor of eloquence in the university of his native city. He wrote sonnets and other verses, which were much admired, especially "The Rape of Proserpine," ("Il Ratto di Proserpina.") Died in 1778.

Cas-sĭ-ā'nus Bas'sus, a Greek writer of the third or fourth century, was a native of Bithynia. He is supposed to have been the author of an extant work on agriculture and rural economy, entitled "Geoponica," (printed in Greek in 1539.)

Cassibelan. See CASSIVELAUNUS.

Cassibelaunus. See CASSIVELAUNUS.

Cassien. See CASSIAN.

Cas'sin, (JOHN,) an American ornithologist, born in Delaware county, Pennsylvania, in 1813. He resided many years in Philadelphia, and was a member of the Academy of Natural Sciences. He published "Illustrations of the Birds of California, Texas, Oregon, British and Russian America," (1855,) "Mammalogy and Ornithology of the United States Exploring Expedition under Lieutenant Wilkes," and "American Ornithology: A General Synopsis of North American Ornithology ; containing Descriptions and Figures of all North American Birds not given by former American Authors, etc.," (1856.) Died in January, 1869.

Cassini, kås-see'nee, [Fr. pron. kȧ'se'ne',] (CÉSAR FRANÇOIS,) usually called CASSINI DE THURY, (dẹh tü're',) born in Paris in 1714, was the son of Jacques, noticed below. As an astronomer, he was received into the Academy of Sciences at the age of twenty-one, and in 1756 he became director of the Observatory. His most important contribution to science was the triangulation or geometrical description of France, accompanied with an excellent map of France. This is said to be the greatest piece of topography ever executed. He published "The Meridian of Paris verified, etc.," in 1744 ; and the records of the Academy contain many of his writings. Died in 1784.

See CONDORCET, "Éloge de C. F. Cassini ;" MONTUCLA, "Histoire des Mathématiques ;" QUÉRARD, "La France Littéraire."

Cassini, kås-see'nee, (GIOVANNI DOMENICO, or JEAN DOMINIQUE,) a celebrated astronomer, born near Nice on the 8th of June, 1625. After leaving college in Genoa, he pursued the study of astronomy with success, and in 1650 became professor of that science in Bologna. In 1665 he made the important discovery that the rotation of Jupiter is performed in nine hours and fifty-six minutes, and soon after ascertained the diurnal periods of Mars, Venus, and the Sun. He published in 1668 his Ephemerides of the satellites of Jupiter, which Biot calls "an immense and admirable work." Colbert wished to enlist the talents of Cassini in the service of the new Academy of Sciences in Paris, whither the latter removed in 1669. For more than one century subsequent to that date, Cassini and his descendants for three generations presided over the Observatory of Paris. His celebrity was extended in 1684 by the discovery of four satellites of Saturn, of which Huyghens had before discovered one. A royal medal was struck to commemorate this event. He was more remarkable for his activity and success as an observer than for his power as a philosopher, and appears to have been the most popular astronomer of his time, because his discoveries were level to the most common capacity. In the latter part of his life he was employed for several years in the

measurement of an arc of the meridian. He is reputed the discoverer or first observer of the zodiacal light. His writings on astronomy are numerous. Died in 1712.

See "Vie de J. D. Cassini, écrite par lui-même ;" FONTENELLE, "Éloge de J. D. Cassini ;" NICÉRON, "Mémoires ;" and DR. HOEFER's article in the "Nouvelle Biographie Générale."

Cassini, (JACQUES,) an astronomer, and a son of the preceding, was born in Paris about 1670. He was chosen a member of the Academy of Sciences in 1694, and a Fellow of the Royal Society of London in 1696. In 1712 he succeeded his father as director of the Observatory in Paris, where he made some discoveries respecting the orbits of the moons of Saturn, the obliquity of the ecliptic, etc. He is principally known by his efforts to determine the figure of the earth. About 1700 he co-operated with his father in measuring the arc of the meridian southward to Canigou, and in 1718 he alone continued the work northward to Dunkirk. He published in 1720 a treatise "On the Magnitude and Figure of the Earth," containing results which have since been corrected by La Caille and Delambre. He died in 1756, leaving a few other works, among which is "Elements of Astronomy." His son César François, noticed above, was his successor in the Observatory.

See DELAMBRE, "Histoire de l'Astronomie moderne ;" FOUCHY, "Éloge de J. Cassini ;" in "Histoire de l'Académie des Sciences."

Cassini, de, dẹh kȧ'se'ne', (ALEXANDRE HENRI GABRIEL,) COUNT, a French botanist, born in Paris in 1784, was the son of Count J. D. Cassini, astronomer royal. Having studied law, he was made in 1810 a judge of one of the Parisian tribunals. In 1816 he became a judge of the royal court. In 1827 he was chosen a member of the Academy of Sciences, as a botanist. He wrote several botanical treatises. Died in 1832.

See GOSSIN, "Notice sur A. H. G. de Cassini," 1832.

Cassini, de, (JACQUES DOMINIQUE,) COUNT, a French astronomer, son of Cassini of Thury, was born in Paris in 1748. He was elected a member of the Academy in 1770, and succeeded his father as director of the Observatory in 1784. He was the first of the family that fully adopted the physical principles of Newton. In 1793 the Convention decreed that the direction of the Observatory should be committed to four persons, who should officiate in rotation. Cassini was one of the newly-chosen directors ; but, being displeased with this innovation, he resigned in September, 1793. He was imprisoned for several months by the terrorists in the next year, and thenceforth renounced the pursuit of astronomy. Died about 1845.

See DEVIC, "Histoire de la Vie et des Travaux de J. D. Cassini," 1851 ; QUÉRARD, "La France Littéraire."

Cas-sĭ-o-do'rus, [Fr. CASSIODORE, kȧ'se'o'dor',] (MAGNUS AURELIUS,) a Latin historian and minister of state, born at Scylacium, (Squillace,) in Italy, about 470 A.D. He held a high office under Odoacer, who was deposed and killed by Theodoric the Goth in 493, and he afterwards became secretary or chief minister of Theodoric. He resigned his office in 524, but was again in the public service under the successor of Theodoric, and left the reputation of an eminent scholar and wise minister. He wrote a "History of the Goths," of which only an abridgment is now extant, treatises on grammar, logic, arithmetic, music, and other works. He died about the age of one hundred, at the monastery of Viviers, which he had founded.

See SAINTE-MARTHE, "Vie de Cassiodore," 1694 ; A. OLLERIS, "Cassiodore, Conservateur des Livres de l'Antiquité Latine," 1841.

Cas-sĭ-o-pe'Ĭ-ạ, Cas-sĭ-e-pe'Ĭ-ạ, or **Cas-sĭ'o-pe,** [Gr. Κασσιόπεια, Κασσιέπεια, or Κασσιόπη ; Fr. CASSIOPÉE or CASSIOPÉE, kȧ'se'o'på',] the wife of Cepheus, and mother of Andromeda. According to classic mythology, she was placed among the stars, forming the constellation which bears her name.

Cassito, kås-see'to, (GIOVANNI ANTONIO,) an Italian jurist and littérateur, born at Bonito in 1763 ; died in 1822.

Cassius. See CASSIUS LONGINUS.

Cassius, kash'e-ụs, an ancient Roman physician, who practised in Rome under the reign of Tiberius, and was employed professionally by that emperor. Celsus calls him "the most ingenious physician of his age ;" and Galen also highly praises him. Some scholars have ascribed to him the authorship of a medical work called "Medicinales Quæstiones," etc.

ā, ē, ī, ō, ū, ȳ, *long;* ȧ, ė, ȯ, *same, less prolonged;* ă, ĕ, ĭ, ŏ, ŭ, ў, *short;* ạ, ẹ, į, ọ, *obscure;* fär, fȧll, fȧt; mĕt; nŏt; gŏŏd; mŏŏn;

Cassius, kash′e-us, [Ger. pron. kâs′se-ůs,] (ANDREAS,) a German chemist and physician, born at Sleswick. He graduated as doctor of medicine in 1668, and practised at Hamburg with much success. He invented the mode of producing the oxide of gold, which bears his name (purple of Cassius) and affords a fine purple colour to painters on porcelain.

See HOEFER, "Histoire de la Chimie."

Cassius, (AVIDIUS,) a Roman general, noted for audacity and severity of discipline. He gained several victories over the Parthians in the reign of Marcus Aurelius, against whom he rebelled in 175 A.D. He was proclaimed emperor by his army, but a few months later he was killed by some soldiers who conspired against him.

Cassius, (CHRISTIAN,) brother of Andreas, noticed above, was chancellor of the Bishop of Lubeck, and a friend of Grotius. He performed several diplomatic missions with honour. Died in 1676.

Cassius Chærea. See CHÆREA.

Cassius Dion. See DION CASSIUS.

Cas′sius Fe′lix, surnamed IATROSOPHIS′TA, a Greek medical writer, supposed to have lived in the first century.

Cassius Hemina. See HEMINA.

Cas′sius Lon-gi′nus, (CAIUS,) a Roman, elected consul in 171 B.C., and censor in 154. He erected a theatre which was demolished by the senate.

Cassius Longinus, (CAIUS,) a Roman jurist of high reputation, flourished about 50 A.D., and wrote "De Jure Civili." He was banished by Nero in 66 A.D.

Cassius Longinus, (CAIUS,) a famous Roman patriot and general, who conspired with Brutus against Cæsar. His early zeal for liberty was manifested at school, where he struck Faustus, the son of Sulla, for boasting of his father's absolute power. He married a sister of his friend M. Brutus. He acted as quæstor of Crassus in his disastrous expedition against the Parthians in 53 B.C., and, after the defeat of the Romans, saved the remains of the army by a skilful retreat. Having resumed the offensive, he signally defeated the Parthians in Syria. In the civil war he commanded a fleet for Pompey, and, after the battle of Pharsalia, (48 B.C.,) surrendered to Cæsar. After the fatal event of the Ides of March, 44 B.C., (see CÆSAR and BRUTUS,) he commanded in Syria with success against Dolabella, captured Rhodes, then, effecting a junction with the army of Brutus, was finally defeated at Philippi by Antony, and killed himself in 42 B.C. Brutus is said to have called him "the last of the Romans." Cassius forms a conspicuous character in Shakspeare's "Julius Cæsar."

See PLUTARCH, "Life of Brutus;" DION CASSIUS, "History of Rome;" DRUMANN, "Geschichte Roms."

Cassius Longinus, (LUCIUS,) a Roman judge, noted for his strictness or severity. He became consul in 625 A.U.C., or 127 B.C., and censor two years later. Having been chosen prætor, he was sent in 641 to Numidia, to bring Jugurtha to Rome, in which he was successful. Rigid judges were called, after him, *Cassiani judices.*

Cassius Longinus, (QUINTUS,) a rapacious Roman officer, was quæstor in Spain in 54 B.C., and tribune of the people in 49 B.C. He was a partisan of Cæsar in the civil war. Died about 46 B.C.

Cas′sius Par-men′sis, a Latin poet, whose name is sometimes written **Ca′ius Cas′sius Seve′rus,** was probably born at Parma. By some critics he has been confounded with Cassius Etruscus, who was ridiculed by Horace, (Serm. i. 10, 61.) He was one of the conspirators who killed Cæsar the Dictator, and in the war that ensued fought under Brutus. After the defeat and death of Brutus he entered the service of Antony, and fought against Octavius, by whose order he was put to death about 30 B.C. He wrote epigrams and elegies of some merit, of which only small fragments are extant.

See A. NICOLAS, "De Cassio Parmensi Poeta," 1852; A. WEICHERT, "Commentationes II. de Cassio Parmensi Poeta," 1834.

Cas′sius Se-ve′rus Lon-gu-la′nus, a Roman orator, born at Longula about 50 B.C., was noted for his libels against patricians. He introduced a new style of oratory. It is supposed that the sixth epode of Horace is directed against him.

Cas′sius Vis-cel-li′nus, (SPURIUS,) a Roman general, who was thrice chosen consul, and proposed an agrarian

law. On a charge of aspiring to supreme power, he was put to death in 485 B.C.

Cas-sĭ-ve-lau′nus or **Cas-sĭ-be-lau′nus,** sometimes Anglicized as **Cas-sib′e-lan,** a British chief, who ruled the country which lies on the north side of the Thames. He was commander-in-chief of the Britons when Cæsar invaded their island in 54 B.C.; and he made a brave resistance. Having obtained information from the Trinobantes, Cæsar made a successful attack on the capital of Cassivelaunus, which was surrounded with forests, and compelled him to submit and pay tribute.

See CÆSAR, "De Bello Gallico."

Castaglione, kâs-tâl-yo′nà, or **Castiglione,** kâs-têl-yo′nà, (GIUSEPPE,) an Italian antiquary, born at Ancona; died in 1616.

Castagniza, de, dà kâs-tâg-nee′thà, or **Castaniza,** kâs-tâ-nee′thà, (JUAN,) a Spanish monk, who became almoner of Philip II., censor of theology, etc., and wrote "The Perfection of the Christian Life," which is said to be the original of a famous work called "Spiritual Conflict." Died in 1598.

Castagno, del, dêl kâs-tân′yo, (ANDREA,) a celebrated Florentine painter, born at Castagno about 1408. He adorned several churches of Florence with his works, the best of which have been destroyed. He learned from Domenico of Venice the process of oil-painting, which had been lately invented, and then murdered that artist in the dark. This crime was confessed by him on his death-bed. He excelled most of his predecessors in perspective and foreshortening. Died about 1480.

See VASARI, "Lives of the Painters;" MRS. JAMESON, "Memoirs of Early Italian Painters."

Castaldi, kâs-tâl′dee, (CORNELIO,) an Italian poet, born at Feltre in 1480; died in 1536.

Cas-ta′lĭ-o or **Castalion,** kâs′tȧ′le′ȯN′, sometimes written **Castellio,** (SÉBASTIEN,) a liberal Protestant divine, whose family name was CHÂTEILLON, (shâ′tȧ′-yȯN′,) born in Dauphiné about 1515. He became intimate with Calvin, who procured for him a chair in the College of Geneva about 1542. Dissenting from Calvin in relation to reprobation, etc., he resigned or was deprived of this place, and went to Bâle, where he taught Greek. He is said to have written a tract against the persecution of heretics. He published a new Latin version of the Bible, (1551,) which is censured for its deviation from the simplicity of the original. He also wrote "Sacred Dialogues for the Instruction of Youth," and other esteemed works. Died at Bâle in 1563.

See SAINTE-MARTHE, "Elogia Gallorum;" BAYLE, "Historical and Critical Dictionary;" ARNOLD, "Kirchen- und Ketzer-Historie;" J. C. FUESSLI, "Lebensgeschichte S. Castellio's," 1775.

Castalion. See CASTALIO.

Castanheda, kâs-tân-yā′dà, (FERNANDO LOPEZ,) a Portuguese historian, born about 1500. He went to India while young, and spent many years in collecting materials for a history which he published in 1551, viz., "A History of the Conquest of India by the Portuguese." It is esteemed for fidelity.

Castaniza. See CASTAGNIZA.

Castaños, de, dà kâs-tân′yȯs, (FRANCISCO XAVIER,) Duke of Baylen, (bī-lên′,) an able Spanish general, born at Madrid or in Biscay about 1755. He became a lieutenant-general in 1798, soon after which he was exiled from Madrid by Godoy, whom he had opposed. In 1808 he obtained command of a corps, and defeated the French under Dupont at Baylen, where he took about 18,000 prisoners. He was appointed general-in-chief of the fourth corps of the army in 1811, and displayed great skill at the battle of Vittoria, June, 1813. He became captain-general in 1823, and councillor of state in 1825, and favoured a policy of moderation. After the fall of Espartero, in 1843, he was guardian of Queen Isabella. Died in 1852.

Casteels, kâs′tâls, (PIETER,) a Flemish painter and engraver, born at Antwerp in 1684, went to England in 1708. He painted birds, flowers, etc. Died in 1749.

Castel, kâs′têl′, (LOUIS BERTRAND,) a French mathematician and Jesuit, born at Montpellier in 1688. He became a resident of Paris in 1720, and acquired reputation by his writings, among which are a "Treatise on Universal Gravity," (1724,) and "Universal Mathe-

---

matics," (1728.) The latter gained for him admission into the Royal Society of London. He wrote many articles for the "Journal de Trévoux," and invented a machine named "ocular harpsichord." Died in 1757.

See ABBÉ DE LA PORT, "Esprit et Singularités de L. B. Castel," 1763.

Castel, (RENÉ RICHARD LOUIS,) a French poet and botanist, born at Vire in 1758, was educated in a Parisian college. He was a moderate member of the Legislative Assembly, (1791.) About 1797 he published a descriptive poem on plants, ("Des Plantes,) which was much admired and gained the decennial prize. He was professor of rhetoric in the Imperial Lyceum of Paris about ten years, and inspector-general of the university from 1808 to 1814. He wrote a poem entitled "The Forest of Fontainebleau," and a few other works. Died in 1832.

See "Nouvelle Biographie Générale."

Castel-Cicala. See RUFFO, (FABRIZIO.)

Castel-Melhor, de, dà kâs-těl-měl-yōr', (JOÃO RODRIGO DE Vasconcellos—dà vås-kon-sel'lôs,) COUNT, a Portuguese general, who repulsed the Spanish army in 1643, and was commander-in-chief in 1645. Died in 1658. His son, LUIS SOUZA, was the favourite of Alfonso VI., and prime minister from 1663 to 1667.

Casteleyn, de, děh kâs'těh-līn', (MATHIEU,) a Flemish poet, born at Oudenarde, lived about 1550. He wrote an "Art of Poetry," ("De Konst van Rhetoriken," etc., 1555.)

Cas'tell, (EDMUND,) an English Orientalist, was born in Cambridgeshire in 1606. After graduating at Cambridge, he resided there many years, while compiling his great work, a "Lexicon of the Hebrew, Chaldee, Syriac, Arabic, Samaritan, Persian, and Ethiopian Languages," (1669,) on which he spent £12,000, to the ruin of his fortune. "This work," says Dibdin, "has long challenged the admiration and defied the competition of foreigners." In 1666 he was appointed chaplain to the king, and professor of Arabic at Cambridge. Died in 1685.

See WOOD, "Athenæ Oxonienses."

Castellan, kâs'tȧ'lôn', (ANTOINE LOUIS,) a French landscape-painter and architect, born at Montpellier in 1772. Having visited Italy and Greece, he published several interesting works, illustrated by himself, among which are "Letters on the Morea," (1808,) " Manners and Customs of the Ottomans," (1812,) and "Letters on Italy," (1819.) He wrote numerous articles for the "Biographie Universelle," and "Studies on the Château of Fontainebleau, considered as one of the Types of the Renaissance of the Arts in France," (1840,) which is called an excellent work. Died in 1838.

See HEINECKEN, "Dictionnaire des Artistes."

Castellane, de, děh kâs'tȧ'lȧn', (ESPRIT VICTOR ÉLISABETH BONIFACE,) COUNT, a French marshal, born in Paris in 1788. He entered the army as a private in 1804, fought at Eckmühl, Essling, and Wagram, (1809,) and distinguished himself in the Russian campaign, (1812.) After the restoration he served in Spain, became maréchal-de-camp in 1824, and lieutenant-general in 1833. He was raised to the peerage in 1837. Amidst the agitation which followed the revolution of 1848, he maintained order in Rouen by his firmness. He was created a marshal of France in 1852. At the beginning of the war against Austria in Italy, April, 1859, Castellane was appointed commander of the army of Lyons. Died in September, 1862.

See CHARRAS, "Les trois Maréchaux, Saint-Arnaud, Magnan et Castellane," 1853.

Castellani, kâs-těl-lä'nee, (LUIGI FRANCESCO,) an Italian medical writer, born near Mantua, lived about 1770.

Castellanus. See DUCHÂTEL, (PIERRE.)

Castellesi, kâs-těl-lä'see, (ADRIAN or ADRIANO,) an Italian prelate and accomplished Latin writer, born in Tuscany. He published treatises, in Latin, "On True Philosophy," (1507,) and "On the Latin Language," (1513.) He entered into a conspiracy against Leo X., and was detected and fined.

Castelli, the Italian of CHASTEAU, which see.

Castelli, kâs-těl'lee, (BARTOLOMMEO,) an Italian physician, born at Messina, published a "Lexicon Medicum Græco-Latinum," (1607,) often reprinted.

Castelli or **Castellio,** kâs-tel'le-o, (BENEDETTO,) an Italian monk, and an eminent disciple of Galileo in philosophy, was born at Brescia in 1577. He taught mathematics with honour at Pisa, and at the college di Sapienza, in Rome. He is regarded as the author of a new branch of hydraulics, the theory of running waters. Pope Urban VIII. applied to him for an improved plan of confining the rivers which damaged his territories, on which occasion he wrote a valuable treatise "On the Mensuration of Running Waters," ("Della Misura dell' Acque correnti.") He left other scientific works. Died at Rome in 1644.

See "Vita Benedicti Castelli," Dresden, 1746; TANFOGLIO, "Elogio di B. Castelli," 1819.

Castelli or **Castello,** kâs-tel'lo, (BERNARDO,) an eminent painter, born at Genoa in 1557. He became a resident of Rome, where the pope employed him to paint a picture for Saint Peter's. He was a friend of Tasso, for whose great poem he made some designs, which were engraved by Agostino Caracci. Died in 1629.

See MOSCHINI, "Memoria sulla Vita del Pittore B. Castelli," 1810.

Castelli or **Castello,** (GABRIELLO LANCELOTTO,) an Italian antiquary, born at Palermo in 1727; died about 1792.

Castelli, (GIOVANNI BATTISTA.) See CASTELLO.

Castelli, kâs-tel'lee, (IGNAZ FRIEDRICH,) a popular German dramatic author, born in Vienna in 1781. He produced a great number of comedies, some of which are said to be imitations of Eugène Scribe. In 1809 he composed war-songs for the Austrian army, which were distributed by the government and were very popular. Died in 1862.

See "Nouvelle Biographie Générale."

Castelli, (PIETRO,) a learned physician and botanist, born at Messina. He became a professor of medicine in a college of Rome, and afterwards professor of botany in Messina. He wrote several popular works on medicine, chemistry, and botany. Died about 1656.

Castelli, (VALERIO,) born in 1625, was a son of Bernardo, noticed above, and was a successful painter, especially of battle-pieces. He worked in Genoa, the palaces and churches of which he adorned. His works were in request among the French and English. His design and colour are praised. Died in 1659.

See RATTI, "Vite de' Pittori Genovesi."

Castellio, (BENEDETTO.) See CASTELLI.

Castellio, (SÉBASTIEN.) See CASTALIO.

Castello. See CASTELLI.

Castello, kâs-tel'lo, or **Castelli,** kâs-tel'lee, (GIOVANNI BATTISTA,) a skilful Italian painter and architect, born at or near Bergamo about 1506, was surnamed IL BERGAMASCO, (èl běr-gä-mâs'ko.) He is said to have been a pupil of Michael Angelo. He studied in Rome, where he formed a friendship with Luca Cambiaso, and he worked with that artist in Genoa. After he had painted some admirable frescos in Genoa, he went to Madrid, and became painter to the king. He died at Madrid about 1575. His design was correct, and his colouring excellent.

See LANZI, "History of Painting in Italy;" TICOZZI, "Dizionario."

Castelnau, de, děh kâs'těl'nō', (JACQUES,) MARQUIS, a French general, born in 1620, served with distinction in many campaigns against the Spaniards and Imperialists. At Friburg he received six wounds without leaving his post. In 1655 he commanded with success in Hainault, and, in the absence of Turenne, in 1656, commanded the army of Flanders. He obtained a marshal's bâton in 1658, and was killed at Dunkirk the same year.

Castelnau, de, (MICHEL,) an able French diplomatist and general, grandfather of the preceding, was born in Touraine about 1520. In the reign of Henry II. he performed missions to several foreign courts. In the civil wars that began about 1560 he fought against the Protestants at Rouen, Dreux, etc. He was minister to England from 1574 to 1584. After the accession of Henry IV. he obtained a high command in the army. He died in 1592, leaving "Memoirs" of the events from 1559 to 1570, (3 vols., 1731,) which are said to be impartial and trustworthy.

See LE LABOUREUR, "Vie de Michel de Castelnau," 1659; "Nouvelle Biographie Générale."

ā, ē, ī, ō, ū, ȳ, *long;* ȧ, ė, ȯ, same, less prolonged; ă, ĕ, ĭ, ŏ, ŭ, ў, *short;* ą, ę, į, ǫ, *obscure;* fär, fȧll, fȧt; mět; nŏt; gōŏd; mōŏn;

Castelvetro, kâs-têl-vä'tRo, (Ludovico,) a celebrated Italian critic, born at Módena in 1505. His severe criticism on a canzone of Caro about 1555 occasioned a notorious and acrimonious controversy between the poet and the critic. About 1558 he was imprisoned in Rome on suspicion of favouring the doctrines of the Reformers. Having escaped by night, he was condemned as a contumacious heretic in 1561, and took refuge in Lyons and Geneva. His greatest work is a commentary on the "Poetics" of Aristotle, (1570,) which, though marred by sophisms and minute subtleties, "may justly claim respect," says Hallam, "not only as the earliest exposition of the theory of criticism, but for its acuteness, erudition, and independence." ("Introduction to the Literature of Europe.") Died in 1571.

See Muratori, "Vie de Castelvetro," prefixed to his "Opera varie critiche," 1727; J. B. Venturi, "Elogio di L. Castelvetro," 1778; Ginguené, "Histoire Littéraire d'Italie;" Lebret, "Anecdota de L. Castelvetro ejusque Scriptis," 1763; Nicéron, "Mémoires."

Castex, kâs'têks', (Bertrand Pierre,) Baron, a French general, born in Languedoc in 1771; died in 1843.

Casti, kâs'tee, (Giovanni Battista, or Giambattista,) a popular Italian poet and priest, born in the Roman States in 1721. In his early years he was a professor in an academy at Montefiascone. About 1769 he was presented to Joseph II. of Austria, who was pleased with his witty conversation. Casti accompanied embassies from Vienna to several courts of Europe, and, having returned to Austria, was appointed court poet in 1782. In 1793 he published "Novelle galanti," poetical tales, which are admired for vivacity, originality, and elegance. Between 1790 and 1796 he left Vienna, and became a resident of Florence and Paris. His most celebrated work is a poem called "Speaking Animals," ("Animali parlanti," 1802,) a political satire, which Mr. Rose translated or imitated in his "Court and Parliament of Beasts." He also wrote burlesque dramas, and an amusing poem entitled "The Three Groats," ("I tre Giulj,") which was translated into English, (London, 1826.) Died in Paris in 1803.

See Tipaldo, "Biografia degli Italiani illustri;" "Narrative and Romantic Poetry of the Italians," in the "London Quarterly Review" for April, 1819.

Castiglione, kâs-têl-yo'nà, (Baldassare,) one of the most elegant Italian writers of his time, was born at Casatico, near Mantua, in 1478. In early life he became one of the ornaments of the polished court of the Duke of Urbino, by whom in 1505 he was sent as ambassador to England. He was several times employed on missions to Popes Leo X. and Clement VII. In 1525 the latter sent him as ambassador to Charles V. at Madrid. He died at Toledo in 1529. His principal work is "The Courtier," ("Il Cortegiano," 1528,) which is regarded as excellent in thought and style. He wrote several small poems in Latin and Italian, which are esteemed models of elegance.

See Serassi, "Vita del Castiglione," in an edition of his poems, Rome, 1760; Ginguené, "Histoire Littéraire d'Italie;" P. Giovio, "Elogia;" Nicéron, "Mémoires;" Girolamo Ferri, "De Vita et Scriptis B. Castiglionis," 1780.

Castiglione or **Castiglioni,** kâs-têl-yo'nee, (Carlo Ottavio,) Count, an eminent Italian linguist and antiquary, born at Milan about 1790. He directed his attention to languages and numismatics, and published in 1819 a "Description of the Cufic Coins of the Museum of Milan." In the same year Angelo Mai and Castiglione published fragments of a Gothic version of the New Testament, by Bishop Ulphilas, which Mai had recently found in palimpsests. Castiglione produced in 1826 a valuable work entitled "Geographical and Numismatical Memoir on the Part of Barbary called by the Arabs Afrikiah."

See Tipaldo, "Biografia degli Italiani illustri."

Castiglione, (Giovanni Benedetto,) an excellent Italian painter and engraver, surnamed il Grechetto, (êl grà-ket'to,) was born at Genoa in 1616. He was a pupil of G. B. Paggi and of G. Andrea de' Ferrari. He worked at Florence, Genoa, Venice, Rome, and Mantua, and excelled in history, portraits, landscapes, and animals. As a painter of animals he was not surpassed by any artist of Italy. Among his master-pieces is a "Nativity," in a church of Genoa. He produced numerous admirable etchings, among which are "Diogenes with his Lantern," and "The Entrance of the Animals into the Ark." He died at Mantua in 1670.

See Lanzi, "History of Painting in Italy;" Soprani, "Vite de' Pittori Genovesi;" Bryan, "Dictionary of Painters."

Castiglione, (Valerio,) an Italian scholar and writer, born at Milan in 1593. He wrote "Clio," a poem, (1616,) a "History of the Revolution of Piedmont," and other works. Died in 1668.

Castiglione, de, Duc. See Augereau.

Castiglioni. See Castiglione.

Castil-Blaze. See Blaze.

Castilho, de, dà kâs-têl'yo, (Antonio Feliciano,) a popular Portuguese poet, born in Lisbon in 1800, is sometimes called "the Blind Poet of Portugal." About 1820 he published "Letters from Echo to Narcissus," a poem, which had great success. Among his other works are "Day in the Spring," (1822,) "Night at the Castle," ("Noite do Castello," 1830,) and "Poetical Meditations." He is considered the most pure and harmonious of modern Portuguese poets. He has written several prose works, one of which is "Historical Portraits of Portugal," ("Quadros historicos de Portugal.")

Castilhon or **Castillon,** kâs'te'yòn', (Jean Louis,) a French littérateur, born at Toulouse in 1720. He wrote for many periodicals, and published numerous works, among which are a "History of Philosophic Dogmas and Opinions from Ancient Times to the Present," (3 vols., 1769,) and "The Last Revolutions of the Globe." Died about 1793.

Castilla, kâs-têl'yâ, (Don Ramon,) a Peruvian general and statesman, born at Tarapaca about 1795. He fought against the King of Spain in the war of independence which began in 1821. He was made a general of brigade in 1834, and served in the civil war that ensued. In 1845 he was elected President of Peru, has the credit of restoring order and peace to that country. In 1851 he transmitted the government to his successor, José Rufino Echenique. In 1855 he usurped or obtained the chief power. He was re-elected President in 1858. Died in 1867.

Castille, kâs'têl' or kâs'te'ye, (Charles Hippolyte,) a French political writer and novelist, born at Montreuil-sur-Mer in 1820. He published "The Chase after Chimeras," (1854,) and other novels, and wrote political articles for several journals. His most considerable work is a "History of the Second French Republic," (1855,) in which absolutism and the Revolution are represented as natural allies.

Castillejo, de, dà kâs-têl-yā'ho, (Cristoval,) a Spanish poet, born at Ciudad Rodrigo in 1494. He passed much of his life at the court of Don Ferdinand, brother of Charles V. He wrote canzones of a playful and witty character, and satires. Died in 1556.

See Ticknor, "History of Spanish Literature;" Longfellow "Poets and Poetry of Europe."

Castillo, de, dà kâs-têl'yo, (Augustin,) a Spanish painter, born at Seville in 1565; died in 1626.

Castillo, de, (Enriquez,) a Spanish historian, born at Segovia, was chaplain and historiographer to Henry IV., and a member of his privy council. He wrote a "Chronicle of the Reign of Henry IV.," which was recently published by Don J. M. de Flores, secretary of the Spanish Academy of History.

See Prescott, "History of Ferdinand and Isabella," vol. i part i.

Castillo, de, (Fernando,) a Spanish Dominican, born at Granada about 1529, wrote a "History of San Domingo and his Order," (1584.) Died in 1593.

Castillo, del, dêl kâs-têl'yo, (Bernal Diaz,) a Spanish officer, born at Medina del Campo. He assisted Cortez in the conquest of Mexico, whither he went about 1520, and afterwards settled in that country. He wrote a "History of the Conquest of New Spain," which is said to have some merit, though the style is far from elegant.

See "Memoirs of Bernal Diaz del Castillo," by himself, translated by J. Ingraham Lockhart, 1844; Prescott, "History of the Conquest of Mexico," vol. ii. book v.

Castillo, del, (JOSÉ MARIA,) a South American jurist, was appointed by Bolivar president of the council of state, (1828.)

Castillo, del, (JUAN,) a Spanish historical painter, brother of Augustin, noticed above, was born in Seville in 1584, and was the master of Murillo and Alonzo Cano. Died in 1640.

Castillo Solorzano, del, dĕl kȧs-tĕl'yo so-loR-thä'no, (ALONZO,) a famous Spanish romance-writer and poet of the seventeenth century, who was highly praised by Lope de Vega. He produced numerous works in prose and verse, among which are "La Garduña de Sevilla," and the "Hall of Recreation," ("Sala de Recreacion," 1629,) a novel.

See ANTONIO, "Bibliotheca Hispana Nova."

Castillo y Saavedra, del, dĕl kȧs-tĕl'yo e sä-vä'-DRÄ, (ANTONIO,) a Spanish painter of history, portraits, and landscapes, born at Córdova in 1603, excelled in design and composition. In 1666 he visited Seville, where the works of Murillo appeared to him so inimitable that he gave up in despair, and died in less than a year.

See QUILLIET, "Dictionnaire des Peintres Espagnols."

Castillon. See CASTILHON.

Castillon, de, dĕh kȧs'tĕl'yòN' or kȧs'te'yòN', (GIO-VANNI FRANCESCO SALVEMINI,) an able geometer, born at Castiglione, in Tuscany, in 1709, became professor of philosophy at Utrecht in 1751. Frederick the Great invited him to Berlin, and made him a professor of mathematics. In 1787 he succeeded La Grange as director of the mathematical class in the Academy of Berlin. He translated into French Locke's "Elements of Physics," Cicero's "Academics," ("Academicæ Questiones,") and other works. Died in 1791.

See QUÉRARD, "La France Littéraire."

Castillon, de, dĕh kȧs'te'yòN', (JEAN FRANÇOIS ANDRÉ LE BLANC,) a French lawyer, eminent for his learning, eloquence, and philosophic spirit, born at Aix in 1719. He became attorney-general of the parliament of Provence. Died in 1800.

Castlemain, kas's'l-mān', (ROGER PALMER,) EARL OF, was the husband of the Duchess of Cleveland, and ambassador from James II. of England to the pope about 1686. He wrote, besides other works, "An Account of the Present War between the Venetians and Turks," (1666.) Died in 1705.

Castlereagh, kas's'l-rā', (ROBERT STEWART,) LORD VISCOUNT, Marquis of Londonderry, a British statesman, born in the county of Down, Ireland, in 1769, was the eldest son of Robert Stewart, first Marquis of Londonderry, and Sarah F. Seymour, daughter of the Marquis of Hertford. In 1794 he entered the British House of Commons, with a strong tendency to Toryism. By the promotion of his father in 1796, he became Viscount Castlereagh. He was chosen keeper of the privy seal for Ireland in 1797, and secretary to the lord lieutenant in 1798. He performed a prominent part in the suppression of the Irish rebellion of the latter year. "The union of Ireland with Great Britain," (1800,) says Alison, "was carried in the Irish Parliament chiefly through the powerful abilities of Lord Castlereagh." ("History of Europe.") In 1802 he was appointed by Pitt president of the board of control, and in 1805 secretary of state for the department of war and the colonies. The failure of the Walcheren expedition in 1809 exposed him to censure, and occasioned a duel between him and Canning, his colleague in the ministry. Just before the duel the parties resigned office. In February, 1812, Lord Castlereagh became secretary of state for foreign affairs, (in the ministry of Lord Liverpool,) and the leader of the Tory party, in preference to his rival Canning. He represented England at the peace of Paris and the Congress of Vienna in 1814, at the Congress of Paris in 1815, and at that of Aix-la-Chapelle in 1818. He was one of the master-spirits of the coalition against Bonaparte. In 1821, by the death of his father, he became Marquis of Londonderry. After showing symptoms of insanity, he committed suicide in August, 1822. As he left no issue, the title passed to his half-brother Charles. (See LONDONDERRY.) His success as a statesman is ascribed to great talents for business, invincible firmness or moral courage, and adroitness in the management of men. As he had obtained nobility only in the Irish peerage, his parliamentary services were confined to the House of Commons. His "Memoirs and Correspondence" (8 vols., 1848) forms a very valuable contribution to modern history.

See ALISON, "History of Europe:" HARRIET MARTINEAU, "History of the Thirty Years' Peace;" "Nouvelle Biographie Générale;" "London Quarterly Review" for December, 1848, and January, 1862; "Edinburgh Review" for April, 1862; "Foreign Quarterly" for July, 1831; "Blackwood's Magazine" for March, 1862; "Fraser's Magazine" for December, 1848.

Cas'tor and **Pol'lux** or **Pol-y̆-deū'çēs**, [Gr. Κάστωρ, and Πολυδεύκης,] heroes of the Greek mythology, called also DIOSCU'RI, ("sons of Jove,") were, according to one account, twin-brothers, sons of Leda and Tyndareus, and brothers of Helen, whence they were called Tyndar'idæ. According to another legend, they were the sons of Leda and Jupiter. Castor was an expert horseman and charioteer, and Pollux a renowned pugilist. They took part in the Calydonian hunt, in the Argonautic expedition, and other famous enterprises. The ancient poets feigned that Pollux was immortal, and that when Castor was killed in a fight Pollux offered to share his fate. It was, therefore, permitted that the boon of immortality should be divided between them, and that they should exchange places every day, dying and reviving alternately.

See KEIGHTLEY's "Mythology."

Castor [Κάστωρ] of Rhodes, a Greek grammarian, who is supposed to have lived about 150 B.C.

Castor, (ANTONIUS,) a Roman or a Greek physician, who lived at Rome one hundred years, from the reign of Augustus to that of Titus, (80 A.D.) Pliny speaks of his high reputation, and of his botanic garden, which is the first mentioned in history.

Castracani. See CASTRUCCIO.

Castrejon, kȧs-trȧ-hōn', (ANTONIO,) a Spanish painter, born in Madrid in 1625. He was an excellent colorist, and had great facility of invention, which enabled him to succeed equally in heroic subjects and in domestic or familiar scenes. His "Michael contending with the Dragon" is one of his master-pieces. Died in 1690.

See QUILLIET, "Dictionnaire des Peintres Espagnols."

Castrén, kȧs-trän' or kȧs-trīn', (MATTHIAS ALEXANDER,) an eminent philologist, born in the province of Uleåborg, Finland, in 1813. He was a diligent student of the Finnish language and literature, in the illustration of which he spent his life. In 1838 he travelled through Lapland on foot to obtain information about the ancient mythology and language of that region. In 1841 he produced a Swedish translation, in verse, of the popular Finnish poem "Kalevala," which attracted much admiration. Between 1844 and 1849 he pursued his researches among the Samoieds on the Arctic Sea. In 1851 he was appointed professor of the Finnish language at Helsingfors, where he died in 1852 from the effects of his last journey. He left grammars of several dialects of Northern Russia, and other works.

See "London Quarterly Review" for January, 1854.

Castries, kȧs'tRe', (CHARLES EUGÈNE GABRIEL **de la Croix**—dĕh lȧ kRwȧ,) MARQUIS OF, an able French general, born in 1727. Having distinguished himself in many campaigns, he was made lieutenant-general in 1758, and gained an important victory at Wesel in 1760. He was afterwards Governor-General of Flanders, minister of marine in 1780, and marshal of France in 1783. In the Revolution of 1789 he emigrated, found an asylum with the Duke of Brunswick, and died in 1801.

Castriot, (GEORGE.) See SCANDER-BEG.

Castro, kȧs'tRo, (JOSÉ RODRIGO,) a Portuguese Jew and physician, born about 1545, settled in 1596 in Hamburg, where he became professor of philosophy and medicine. He published several valuable works. Died in 1627.

Castro, da, dȧ kȧs'tRo, (PAOLO,) an eminent jurisconsult, born at Castro, in Italy. He professed Roman law at Padua, Florence, Bologna, etc., and wrote treatises on the Digest and Code. Died about 1450.

Castro, de, dȧ kȧs'tRo, (ALFONSO,) a noted Spanish theologian and pulpit orator, born at Zamora about 1495, entered the order of Saint Francis. He accompanied Philip II. to England when he went to marry Queen Mary. In the latter part of his life he resided in the

Low Countries. His principal work is a Latin treatise on "Heresies," (1534,) which was very successful, and passed through ten editions in twenty-two years. Died in 1558.

See N. ANTONIO, "Bibliotheca Hispana Nova."

Castro, de, (Don ALFONSO NUÑES,) a Spanish historian, who lived about 1670. He was historiographer to Philip IV., and wrote a "Chronicle of the Goths, Castilians, and Austrians," ("Coronica Gothica, Castillana y Austriaca," 1708.)

Castro, de, (ALVAREZ GOMEZ,) a Spanish writer, born in the diocese of Toledo in 1521. He became professor of Greek in Toledo, and wrote, in prose and verse, numerous works, among which are "The Life of Francis Ximenes," (1569.) Died in 1586.

Castro, de, dà kås'tro, (ESTEBAN RODRIGO,) a renowned Portuguese physician, born at Lisbon about 1560. He emigrated to Italy, and was professor of medicine in the University of Pisa for twenty-two years. He composed, in Latin, many works, among which are "De Complexu Morborum," (1624,) "Posthuma Varietas," (1639,) and "Medical Consultations," ("Medicæ Consultationes," 1644.) He was styled "the Phœnix of Medicine." Died in 1637.

See N. ANTONIO, "Bibliotheca Hispana Nova;" VAN DER LINDEN, "De Scriptoribus medicis."

Castro, de, (FELIPE,) an eminent Spanish sculptor, born at Noya (Galicia) in 1711. He studied in Rome, and gained the first prize of the Academy of Saint Luke in 1739. He afterwards worked in Madrid, and was ranked among the greatest Spanish sculptors of the age. Died in 1775.

Castro, de, (GABRIEL PEREIRA,) a Portuguese poet and jurist, born at Braga. He became a senator at Lisbon, and wrote, besides other works, a heroic poem called "Ulisea," (1636.) He has been ranked among the fine geniuses of Portugal. Died in 1630.

Castro, de, (GUILLEM,) a Spanish dramatist, born at Valencia about 1569. He was for some time commander of a citadel in the kingdom of Naples, and passed the latter years of his life in Madrid, where he enjoyed the friendship of Lope de Vega. He acquired a European celebrity by his "Spanish Cid," a drama, which was the original of Corneille's tragedy of the same name. Corneille acknowledged that he owed part of the beauty of his piece to Castro. The latter wrote "Dido and Æneas," "Payar en propria Moneda," and other dramas, a volume of which was printed in 1621. Died in 1631. Some account of his life was published by Lord Holland in 1817.

See TICKNOR, "History of Spanish Literature."

Castro, de, (INEZ.) See INEZ DE CASTRO.

Castro, de, (JOÃO,) a celebrated Portuguese general and navigator, born at Lisbon in 1500. He studied mathematics under Pedro Nuñez, and became profoundly versed in that science, as well as in ancient languages. About 1538, as commander of a vessel, he made a voyage to India with the viceroy Garcia de Noronha. He accompanied the expedition which, under Estevão da Gama, explored the Red Sea in 1540. He wrote an exact scientific description of that sea, of which he also made charts. The results of these hydrographical labours were first published in 1833, with the title of "The Log-Book of Don John de Castro on the Voyage which the Portuguese made to the Red Sea," ("Roteiro de Dom Joam de Castro da Viagem que fizeram os Portuguezes ao Mar roxo.") He was appointed Governor of India in 1545, and gained a great victory over the Moors at Diu, after performing prodigies of valour. He received the title of Viceroy of India in 1547, and died in 1548, in the arms of Saint Francis Xavier. He left in manuscript a "Journal of a Voyage from Lisbon to Goa."

See J. FREYRE DE ANDRADA, "Vida de Joam de Castro," 1651, and English version of the same, 1664; FARIA Y SOUZA, "Asia Portugueza;" LINDAU, "Juan de Castro; Gemälde eines Heldenlebens," 1813; JOÃO DE BARROS, "Decada secunda da Asia;" "Nouvelle Biographie Générale."

Castro, de, (JOSÉ RODRIGO,) a Spanish Orientalist and bibliographer, born in Galicia in 1739. He wrote three poems, (1759,) in Hebrew, Greek, and Latin, on the accession of Charles III., to whom he became librarian.

In 1781 he published the first volume of "Bibliotheca Española," ("Spanish Library,") which had great success. The second volume appeared in 1786. Died about 1798.

See ERSCH und GRUBER, "Allgemeine Encyklopaedie."

Castro, de, (PEDRO,) a Spanish painter of still life, excelled in colouring and perspective. Died in 1663.

Castro, de, (VACA,) a Spanish officer, born at Leon, became a judge of the royal court at Valladolid. In 1540 Charles V. sent him as governor to Peru, which was then disturbed by the rebellion of Almagro. In 1542 a battle was fought at Chupas, in which Almagro was defeated and made prisoner. By the order of Castro, he was executed on the spot. Castro was superseded in 1544, and returned to Spain, where he was imprisoned several years. Died in 1558.

See PRESCOTT, "History of the Conquest of Peru," vol. i.

Castro-Sarmento, de, dà kås'tro saR-měn'to,(JAGO,) a Portuguese physician, born about 1692, practised in London, and became a Fellow of the Royal Society. He wrote "Letters on the Diamonds of Brazil," and "Materia Medica," etc., (1758.) Died in 1762.

Castrucci, kås-troot'chee, (PIETRO,) an Italian composer, born at Rome about 1690, served Hogarth as the model of his "Enraged Musician." Died in London in 1769.

Castruccio-Castracani, kås-troot'cho kås-trä-kä'nee, a chief of the Ghibeline party, born in Lucca about 1282. His family name was ANTELMINELLI or INTERMINELLI. In consequence of a revolution in 1316, he became master or seigneur of Lucca, from which he expelled the Guelphs. He waged a successful war against the Florentines, (1320–25,) gained a great victory over their general, Raymond de Cardona, in 1325, and by his courage and political talents became a powerful prince. The emperor Louis recognized him as Duke of Lucca, Pistoia, Volterra, and Lunigiano, and created him a count palatine. He died in 1328, leaving several minor sons, who did not inherit any share of his power. Macchiavelli has written a romance purporting to be a life of Castruccio, but in which historic truth is not respected. "He joined craft and duplicity," says Sismondi, "to the most brilliant valour and to extraordinary talents."

See SISMONDI, "Histoire des Républiques Italiennes;" NEGRINI, "Vita Castruccii Castracani," 1496; MACCHIAVELLI, "Vita di Castruccio-Castracani," 1534, and French translation of the same, by DREUX DU RADIER, 1753; ALDO MANUCCI, "Azioni di Castruccio-Castracani," 1590 and 1820.

Cas'well, (RICHARD,) an American lawyer and general, born in Maryland in 1729, removed to North Carolina in his youth. He was chosen Governor of North Carolina in 1777, and was re-elected several times. He was a member of the convention which formed the Federal Constitution in 1787. Died in 1789.

Caswini. See CAZWEENEE.

Casy, kä'ze', (JOSEPH GRÉGOIRE,) born in 1787, became vice-admiral of France in 1845, and senator in 1852.

Casyapa. See KÂSYAPA.

Cat, Le. See LE CAT.

Catalan, kå'tä'lôN', (EUGÈNE CHARLES,) a French geometer, born in 1814. He acquired distinction as a teacher, and published several approved works, among which are "Elements of Geometry," (1843,) and "Manual for Candidates for the Polytechnic School," (1858.)

Catalani, kå-tä-lä'nee, (ANGELICA,) a famous Italian vocalist, born at Sinigaglia about 1782. She made her début at Rome in 1802 with immense success, which was repeated in the principal cities of Italy. Her concerts were applauded with the greatest enthusiasm in Paris and London. She was married to a Frenchman named Valabrègue, and passed many years in England and Paris. She retired from the stage about 1830, after which she resided at Florence. Her merit consisted principally in a voice of extraordinary volume and power. Died in Paris in 1849.

See FÉTIS, "Biographie Universelle des Musiciens."

Catalani, (MICHELE,) an Italian antiquary, born at Fermo, in the March of Ancona, in 1750; died after 1800.

Catalano, kå-tä-lä'no, (ANTONIO,) a skilful Italian painter, born at Messina in 1560; died in 1630.

Cataldi, kå-täl'dee, **Cataldo,** kå-täl'do, written also **Catuldi,** (PIETRO ANTONIO,) an able Italian mathema-

---

€ as k; ç as s; ğ hard; ġ as j; G, H, K, guttural; N, nasal; R, trilled; š as z; th as in this. (☞ See Explanations, p. 23.)

tician, born at Bologna about 1548. He was for many years professor of mathematics in Bologna, and wrote several works. which display an inventive genius and extensive learning. One of them is entitled "Algebra Applicata," (1622.) Died in 1626.

Cataldo. See CATALDI.

Cataneo. See CATTANEO.

Cat'cott, (ALEXANDER,) an English theologian, published in 1762 a "Treatise on the Deluge," and a volume of sermons. He was one of the most eminent of the Hutchinsonian philosophical school.

Catel, kȧ'těl', (CHARLES SIMON,) a French musical composer, born at L'Aigle (Orne) in 1773, became professor of harmony in the Conservatory of Paris in 1795. He composed the music of "Semiramis," (1802,) "Wallace," (1817,) and other operas ; also a "Traité de Harmonie," (1802.) In 1815 he was chosen a member of the Institute. Died in 1830.

See FÉTIS, "Biographie Universelle des Musiciens."

Catel, kȧ'těl, (FRANZ,) a German painter of landscapes, history, and genre, born at Berlin in 1778 ; died in 1856.

Catel, (GUILLAUME,) a French historian, born at Toulouse in 1560. He was a councillor in the parliament of Toulouse, and author of an esteemed history of Languedoc. Died in 1626.

Catel, (SAMUEL HEINRICH,) a German scholar, born at Halberstadt in 1758. He was professor of Greek in the French gymnasium of Berlin. He published Bion, Moschus, Anacreon, and Sappho, in German verse, and other works. Died about 1835.

Catelan, kȧt'lȯN', sometimes written **Catalan,** (LAURENT,) a French pharmacist, published a "Discours sur la Thériaque," (1614.) Died after 1639.

Catelinot. See CATHELINOT.

Catellan-Caumont,de, děh kȧ'tȧ'lȯN'kō'mȯN',(JEAN ANTOINE,) MARQUIS, a meritorious French judge, born at Toulouse in 1759 ; died in 1834.

Catellan de la Masquère, kȧ'tȧ'lȯN' děh lȧ mȧs'-kaïr', (CLAIRE PRISCILLE MARGUERITE,) a French poetess, born at Narbonne in 1662 ; died in 1745.

Catellano, kȧ-těl-lȧ'no, (FRANCESCO,) an Italian poet, born at Leghorn ; lived about 1750. He produced a version of Anacreon, (1753.)

Catena, kȧ-tā'nȧ, (PIETRO,) an Italian mathematician, born in Venice, wrote several works. Died in 1577.

Catena, (VINCENZO,) a distinguished Italian painter of history, born at Venice in 1470. Several of his works are preserved in Venice. His style resembles that of Giorgione. Died in 1530.

See LANZI, "History of Painting in Italy."

Caterino, kȧ-tȧ-ree'no, (LUIGI,) an Italian scholar, born at Saint Cyprian in 1786 ; died at Naples in 1834.

Catesby, kȧts'be, (MARK,) F.R.S., an eminent English naturalist and artist, born about 1680. He visited Virginia in 1712, and returned home in 1719. Sir Hans Sloane and others persuaded him in 1722 to go to Carolina to delineate its plants and animals. He returned to England in 1726, and in 1731 began to publish his "Natural History of Carolina, Florida, and the Bahama Islands," with coloured figures drawn and etched by himself,—the finest work of the kind that had appeared in England. He wrote "Hortus Britanno-Americanus," and a few other works. Died in London in 1749.

See ERSCH und GRUBER, "Allgemeine Encyklopaedie."

Catesby, (ROBERT,) an English Roman Catholic and conspirator, who originated the Gunpowder Plot of 1605. He is called "a gentleman of good parts" by Hume, who says he "first thought of a most extraordinary method of revenge, and opened his intention to Percy." When Fawkes was arrested, Catesby and his accomplices hurried down to Warwickshire, where they resolved to make a desperate stand. Catesby was killed in the act of resisting the officers who came to arrest him, in November, 1605. (See FAWKES, GUY.)

Cathala-Coture, de, děh kȧ'tȧ'lȧ'ko'tür', (ANTOINE,) a French antiquary and jurist, born at Montauban in 1632. He wrote a "History of Quercy," (3 vols., 1785.) Died in 1724.

Cathalan, kȧ'tȧ'lȯN', (JACQUES,) a French Jesuit, distinguished as a pulpit orator, was born at Rouen in 1671 ; died in 1757.

Catharin. See CATHARINUS.

Ca-tha-rī'nus, [Fr. CATHARIN, kȧ'tȧ'rȧN',] (AMBROSIUS,) an Italian theologian, born at Sienna in 1483. His original name was LANCELOT POLITUS or POLITI, (po-lee'tee,) which he changed when he became a monk. He acquired celebrity by his numerous writings, among which are "Treatises on Original Sin," and "On Grace." He affected to forsake the beaten routes, and disowned the authority of Saint Thomas and the Fathers. In 1552 he was appointed Archbishop of Conza. Died in 1553.

See NICÉRON; "Mémoires;" TOURON, "Hommes illustres de l'Ordre de Saint-Dominique."

Cath'cart, (CHARLES MURRAY,) second EARL OF, a British general, eldest son of William, the first Earl, born in 1783. In the Peninsular war he distinguished himself at Salamanca and Vittoria, (June, 1813.) He led a regiment of cavalry at Waterloo, (1815.) He was Governor of Canada some time between 1840 and 1846.

Cathcart, (Hon. Sir GEORGE,) a brave English general, born in London about 1790, was the third son of the Earl of Cathcart, noticed below. He went to Russia in 1812 as aide-de-camp of his father, who was ambassador to that country. He made the campaigns of 1813 and 1814 with the allied army, and witnessed the battles of Lutzen, Dresden, Leipsic, etc. In 1815 he became aide-de-camp to the Duke of Wellington, whom he attended at Waterloo. He served several years with honour in Jamaica, Canada, etc. In 1852 he was Governor of Cape Colony, and the next year, having obtained the rank of lieutenant-general, he was sent to the Crimea. He was killed at Inkerman, November 5, 1854. His "Commentaries on the War in Russia and Germany in 1812–13" are highly commended.

Cathcart, (WILLIAM SHAW,) first EARL OF, a British general and diplomatist, born at Petersham in 1755. He took part in the American war, and in 1778 became aide-de-camp of Sir Henry Clinton. In 1788, and at several subsequent periods, he was chosen one of the representatives of the Scottish peerage. He was made major-general in 1794, and served against the French in Holland, etc. In 1807 he commanded the expedition which captured the fleet and capital of Denmark, and was created a British peer, with the title of Viscount Cathcart. He was ambassador to Saint Petersburg in 1813, and became an earl in 1814. Died in 1843.

Cathelineau, kȧt'le'nō', (JACQUES,) a French peasant, born near Saint-Florent about 1760, was one of the leaders of the royalist insurrection which broke out in La Vendée in 1793. By his virtue, eloquence, and talent for command he acquired great influence over the insurgents. Just after the Vendéans had gained a great victory at Saumur, (June, 1793,) where they took eighty pieces of cannon, Cathelineau was chosen general-in-chief. A few days later he was killed in an attack on Nantes.

See MURET, "Vie populaire de Cathelineau," 1845 ; "Nouvelle Biographie Générale."

Cathelinot or **Catelinot,** kȧt'le'no', (Dom ILDEFONSE,) a French monk, noted for learning, was born in Paris in 1670. He left many works in manuscript. Died in 1756.

Catherine, kath'er-in, [in Russian, ECATARINA, ȧ-kȧ-tȧ-ree'nȧ,] I., Empress of Russia, was born, of poor parents, at Marienburg, in Livonia, about 1688. Several contradictory versions of her romantic story have been published. She was taken captive at Marienburg by the Russians in 1702, after having been married to a subaltern Swedish officer. Her beauty attracted the notice of Peter the Great, who in 1711 recognized her as his wife. She accompanied him in a campaign against Turkey in 1711, and rendered him an important service by negotiating a treaty when the Russian army was in a critical position. Peter caused her to be crowned in 1724. She was proclaimed empress at his death in 1725, and died in 1727. She had several children by her second marriage, one of whom became the empress Elizabeth.

See VOLTAIRE, "Histoire de Russie," and "Histoire de Charles XII ;" "Nouvelle Biographie Générale."

Catherine [in Russian, ECATARINA] **II,** Empress of Russia, born at Stettin in 1729, was the daughter of the Prince of Anhalt-Zerbst. Her original name was SOPHIA

ā, ē, ī, ō, ū, ȳ, long; ă, ĕ, ĭ, ŏ, ŭ, ȳ, short; ą, ę, į, ǫ, obscure; fär, fȧll, fȧt; mēt; nŏt; gōōd; mōōn;

AUGUSTA. In 1745 she was married to the nephew of Elizabeth, Empress of Russia, and then took the name of Catherine Alexievna. Her husband, who was much inferior to her in abilities, became emperor in 1762, under the title of Peter III. He had long been estranged from her, and now proposed to repudiate her; but, by a conspiracy of her friends, he was deposed in July, 1762, when she became mistress of the empire. (See PETER III.) Though extremely profligate and cruel, she had too strong a mind to be enslaved by her passions or to allow them to interfere with her ambitious policy. She promoted agriculture, commerce, and education, and liberally patronized scientific men, such as Diderot and Euler. In 1772 she became a party to the infamous partition of Poland, by which she obtained Polotsk and Mohzelev, (Mohîlev.) She waged a successful war against the Turks, and extended her dominions on the Black Sea. In 1793, by a new partition of Poland, she acquired Volhynia and Podolia. She died in 1796, and was succeeded by her son, Paul I. "Her capacity," says Brougham, "was of an exalted order. Her judgment was clear and sure; her apprehension extraordinarily quick; her sagacity penetrating; her providence and circumspection comprehensive. There have been few abler monarchs in any part of the world; and the history of princes affords few examples of such talents and such force of character on a throne, perverted to the working of so much mischief." She wrote "Instructions to the Commission for composing a Code of Laws," and various other works.

See CASTERA, "Vie de Catherine II," 1796; STRUVE, "Vita Catherinæ II.," 1798; TOOKE, "History of Catherine II.," 1803; TANNENBERG, "Leben Catherinens II.," 1797; C. J. DE LIGNE, "Portrait de Catherine II," 1797; SÉGUR, "History;" BROUGHAM, "Statesmen of the Time of George III.," vol. ii.; AUGUIS, "Histoire de Catherine II et de Paul I," 1813; N. KARAMZIN, "Lobrede auf Catherine II.," translated into German from the Russian by J. G. RICHTER, 1820; JOHANN R. FORSTER, "Kurze Uebersicht des Lebens der Kaiserin von Russland Catharina II.," 1797.

Catherine (or **Catharine**) OF ARAGON, written also **Katharine,** Queen of England, born in 1486, was the daughter of Ferdinand and Isabella of Spain. She was married in 1501 to Arthur, the eldest son of Henry VII. of England. Arthur died in 1502, and the next year she was affianced to his brother, Prince Henry, who was six years younger than herself. Soon after he ascended the throne (1509) the marriage was solemnized. In 1516 she gave birth to a daughter, Mary, who afterwards became queen. In 1527 Henry raised the question of divorce, which was pending several years. (See HENRY VIII.) She died in 1536, much respected for her many virtues.

See HUME, "History of England;" LINGARD, "History of England;" STRICKLAND, "Queens of England;" FROUDE, "History of England;" SHAKSPEARE, "Henry VIII."

Catherine OF BOURBON, (boor'bon,) [Fr. CATHERINE DE BOURBON, kȧt'rèn' deh boor'bôN',] Princess of Navarre and Duchess of Bar, born in Paris in 1558, was a sister of Henry IV. of France. She was married to the Duc de Bar in 1599. Died in 1604.

Catherine, OF FRANCE, Queen of England, born in 1401, was the daughter of Charles VI. of France and Isabella of Bavaria. In 1420 she was married to Henry V. of England, and became the mother of Henry VI. Soon after the death of Henry V. (1422) she became the wife of a Welsh gentleman, Owen Tudor; and from this union descended Henry VII. and the house of Tudor. Died in 1438.

Catherine, OF PORTUGAL or BRAGANZA, Queen of England, the daughter of John IV. of Portugal, was born in 1638. She was married to Charles II. of England in 1661, but did not succeed in gaining his affection. In 1693, after Charles's death, she returned to Lisbon, and in 1704 was appointed Regent of Portugal by her brother Pedro. (See CHARLES II.) Died in 1705.

See MACAULAY's "History of England," vol. i.

Catherine, SAINT, OF ALEXANDRIA, supposed to have suffered martyrdom under the reign of Maximin, about 307 A.D., was regarded as the patroness of philosophy, learning, and eloquence; and her history has been illustrated by many artists of the middle ages.

See MRS. JAMESON, "Sacred and Legendary Art."

Catherine, [It. CATERINA, kä-tä-ree'nä,] SAINT, OF GENOA, born about 1448, was the daughter of Giacopo Fieschi, who was Viceroy of Naples. She became the wife of Julian Adorno, a dissolute and prodigal patrician, whom, after many years of sorrow, she converted from the error of his ways. She devoted her latter years to the service of the sick in the hospital of Genoa, and died in 1510, leaving two works which were esteemed by the mystics.

See MIRATOLI, "Vita della B. Caterina di Genova," 1580.

Catherine, SAINT, OF SIENNA, born at Sienna in 1347, took the habit of a nun about 1366, and became distinguished for her fervent charity and devotion. She mediated a peace between the Florentines and Pope Urban VI. in 1378. She favoured the same pope when his authority was contested by Clement VII., and made strenuous efforts to terminate the scandalous schism. She died in 1380, and was canonized in 1461. Her letters, and other writings, are admired.

See CHAVAN DE MALAN, "Histoire de S. Catherine de Sienne," 2 vols., 1846; RAYMOND DE CAPOUE, "Vie de S. Catherine de Sienne," 1853.

Catherine (or **Catharine**) **Hŏw'ard,** Queen of Henry VIII., was the daughter of Edmund, Lord Howard, who was a son of the Duke of Norfolk. She was married to Henry in August, 1540, and was executed in February, 1542, on the charge of unchastity before her marriage, and adultery afterwards.

See FROUDE, "History of England," vol. iv. chap. xix.; STRICKLAND, "Queens of England."

Catherine de' Medici, (dȧ mĕd'de-chee,) [Fr. CATHERINE DE MÉDICIS, kȧt'rèn' deh mȧ'de'sèss',] born at Florence in 1519, was the daughter of Lorenzo de' Medici, Duke of Urbino, who was a nephew of Leo X. In 1533 she was married to Henry of France, who in 1547 became King Henry II. She had five sons, three of whom became kings of France,—namely, Francis II., Charles IX., and Henry III. The death of Francis II., in 1560, rendered her mistress of the kingdom, with the title of regent for Charles IX., who was a minor. She was artful, perfidious, and cruel. To increase her political influence, she corrupted the morals of her sons. She fomented civil war among her subjects, and instigated the Massacre of Saint Bartholomew, August, 1572. (See CHARLES IX.) The palace of the Tuileries is a monument of her munificence as a patron of art,—perhaps the only respectable trait of her character. Died in 1589.

See MOTLEY, "History of the United Netherlands," vol. i. p. 44, and vol. ii. pp. 426 and 559; also his "Rise of the Dutch Republic," vol. iii. pp. 577 and 578; EUGENIO ALBERI, "Vita di Caterina de' Medici," 1834; German version of the same, by BECK, 1847; J. F. DESTIGNY, "Histoire mystérieuse de Catherine de Médicis," 1847; "Foreign Quarterly Review" for October, 1840.

Catherine (or **Catharine**) **Parr,** the sixth and last wife of Henry VIII. of England, was the widow of Lord Latimer when, in 1543, she was married to that king. She once offended him, it is said, by dissenting from his opinions in theology, so that her life was in peril; but she dexterously averted the storm by feigning that she did this to afford him the pleasure of refuting her, and to render their conversation more animated. "Is it so, sweet-heart?" said the king: "then we are perfect friends again." She survived Henry, and in 1548 married Thomas, Lord Seymour, Admiral of England. Died in 1548.

See STRICKLAND, "Queens of England."

Catherine Paulowna, [Ger. pron. kä-teh-ree'neh pŏw-lov'nä,] Queen of Würtemberg, daughter of Paul, Emperor of Russia, was born in 1788. In 1809 she was married to the Duke of Oldenburg, who died in 1812. She was a favourite sister of the Czar Alexander, and is said to have been endowed with noble and amiable qualities. She was married in 1816 to the Prince of Würtemberg, who became King William I. Died in 1819.

Catherinot, kȧt're'no', (NICOLAS,) a French antiquary, born near Bourges in 1628; died in 1688.

Cat'ī-līne, [Lat. CATILI'NA,] (LUCIUS SERGIUS,) a famous Roman demagogue and conspirator, born of a patrician family about 108 B.C. He first appears in history as a partisan of Sulla in the civil war, and rendered himself infamous by his complicity in the murders and robberies that followed the success of his party. In 68 B.C. he was chosen prætor at Rome. Four years later he began to canvass for the consulship, and to organize a faction of desperate and profligate men like himself. A remarkable union of audacity and craft, joined with eloquence and other popular qualities, rendered him a fit leader of such a party. Defeated in the election for consul, he formed a conspiracy against the republic in 63 B.C., (690 A.U.C.) Our knowledge of this affair is derived chiefly from the partial statements of Cicero and from the history of Sallust, who, however, agree in representing that Catiline designed nothing less than a general massacre and conflagration. Cicero, who was then consul, having received notice of the plot from Curius, denounced the treason of Catiline to the senate in October, and the consuls were invested *pro tempore* with absolute power for the emergency. On November 8, Cicero uttered in the senate an oration of great power against Cataline, who attempted to reply; but the senate refused to hear him. He then hastily left Rome and joined the army of his partisans, which had been mustered in Etruria, leaving Lentulus and other conspirators in Rome. Certain deputies from Gaul, who had been tampered with, aided Cicero in obtaining more positive evidence, by which Lentulus and others were convicted and executed. The army of the senate overtook the rebels near Pistoria (now Pistoia) in 62 B.C. Catiline animated his men with an eloquent harangue, and fought the battle with skill and determined valour, but was defeated, and fell in the thickest of the fight, with about three thousand of his partisans.

See SALLUST, "Bellum Catilinarium;" CICERO, "Orationes, in Catilinam;" DION CASSIUS, "History of Rome;" H. WOLF, "Catilinæ Conjuratio ex Fontibus narrata," 1803; ROSE, "History of Catiline's Conspiracy," 1813; G. F. SIDNEY, "History of Catiline's Conspiracy," 1795; MURSINNA, "Catilina; historisches Gemälde," 1797.

Catinat de la Fauconnerie, kǎ'te'nǎ' dẹh lǎ fō'kon're', commonly called simply **Catinat,** (NICOLAS,) a marshal of France, eminent for talents, integrity, and generosity, born in Paris in 1637. He distinguished himself in the campaigns against the Spanish and Austrians in Flanders between 1667 and 1678, and was wounded at Seneffe in 1674. Having been made lieutenant-general, he commanded the army which invaded Savoy, and gained the battle of Staffarda in 1690. In 1693 he received a marshal's bâton. Louis XIV., in reading a list of the marshals, exclaimed, at the name of Catinat, "Here is Virtue crowned!" In 1701 he was placed at the head of the army of Italy, as antagonist to Prince Eugene, but was soon superseded by Villeroi. Died in 1712.

See "Mémoires pour servir à la Vie de Catinat," par M. D. C., Paris, 1775; GUIBERT, "Éloge de Catinat;" LA HARPE, "Éloge de N. de Catinat," 1775; LEBOUVER DE SAINT-GERVAIS, "Mémoires et Correspondance de Catinat," 3 vols., 1818; "Nouvelle Biographie Générale."

Catineau-Laroche, kǎ'te'nō' lǎ'rosh', (PIERRE MARIE SÉBASTIEN,) a French civil officer, born at Saint-Brieuc in 1772. After holding several offices, he was appointed chief clerk in the bureau of commerce and the colonies in 1826. He published a "Portable Vocabulary of the French Language," (1797,) and an "Account of French Guiana," (1822.) Died in 1828.

Catius, kā'she-us, an Epicurean philosopher, born in Gaul, (Transpadane.) Died about 45 B.C.

Cat'lin, (GEORGE,) an American traveller and artist, born in Pennsylvania. He acquired distinction by his adventures and studies among the North American Indians, with whom he passed about eight years. He represented the character and life of the red men in a series of paintings, and published "Illustrations of the Manners, Customs, and Condition of the North American Indians," with engravings, (2 vols., 1841,) which, according to the London "Athenæum," "is a book of extraordinary interest and value." Having exhibited his Indian Gallery and collection in Europe, he published "Notes of Eight Years' Travel and Residence in Europe," (2 vols., 1848.)

See TUCKERMAN, "Book of the Artists;" "Edinburgh Review" for January, 1842.

Cā'to, (DIONYSIUS,) a Latin moralist, for whose biography no materials exist, and respecting whom many conflicting opinions have been adopted. His name is connected with a small work entitled "Disticha de Moribus ad Filium," which was extensively employed

as a catechism of morals in the schools of the middle ages, and was commended for its literary merit by Erasmus and Scaliger. It consists mostly of moral precepts, each of which is expressed in two hexameter verses.

See FABRICIUS, "Bibliotheca Latina."

Cato, [Gr. Κάτων; Fr. CATON,* kǎ'tòn'; It. CATONE, kǎ-to'nà,] (MARCUS PORCIUS,) often called CA'TO CENSO'RIUS, (or CENSORI'NUS,) *i.e.* "Cato the Censor," also surnamed THE ELDER, an eminent Roman patriot and statesman, was born of a plebeian family at Tusculum in 234 B.C. At the age of seventeen he served in the army against Hannibal, and in 209 he took part in the siege of Tarentum under Fabius. He contributed to the victory over Hasdrubal on the Metaurus in 207. In the intervals of war he worked on his Sabine farm, and accustomed himself to a hardy, simple mode of life, disciplined in austere virtues and in all branches of practical and useful knowledge. By pleading causes for the poor, he had become an oracle among his rustic neighbors, when Valerius Flaccus, a liberal patrician, recognized his merit, and persuaded him to seek in the Forum of Rome an ampler sphere of usefulness. He soon gained eminence as an orator, and became a candidate for office. He was elected quæstor (paymaster) in 204, and prætor in 198 B.C., when he obtained Sardinia as his province. In 195 he was raised to the consulship, with his early patron, V. Flaccus, for his colleague, and commanded the army in Spain with ability and success, for which he received a triumph on his return. Elected censor in 184, he reformed many abuses, and enforced his principles of economy and sobriety with a severity which procured him many enemies. He was one of the chief advisers of the third Punic war, and author of the phrase (which he often repeated in the senate) *Delenda est Carthago,* ("Carthage must be destroyed.") He wrote a treatise on agriculture, ("De Re rustica,") which is extant. His son, M. Porcius Cato, became an eminent jurist. Died in 149 B.C. In Plutarch's parallels, Cato the Censor is the counterpart of Aristides. Few names occur in the Latin classics oftener than that of Cato, who was venerated as a model of pristine Roman virtue.

See PLUTARCH, "Lives;" LIVY, "History of Rome;" CORNELIUS NEPOS, "Cato;" CICERO, "Cato Major, seu de Senectute;" DRUMANN, "Geschichte Roms;" E. SCHOBER, "De M. P. Catone Censorino," 1825; WEBER, "Programma de M. P. Catonis Vita et Moribus," 1831.

Cato, (MARCUS PORCIUS,) a Roman general, was an uncle of Cato of Utica. He was tribune of the people in 100 B.C., and in that office opposed Apuleius Saturninus. He defeated the Etruscans in the year 90, and was consul in 89 B.C. He was killed in a skirmish with the Marsians.

Cato, (MARCUS PORCIUS,) surnamed THE YOUNGER, and UTICEN'SIS, (*i.e.* "of Utica,") a celebrated Roman Stoic philosopher and patriot, born in 95 B.C., was a great-grandson of Cato the Censor, whom he took for his model in private and public life. He studied the doctrines of the Stoics under Antipater, and inured himself to hardships and privations. His first campaign was in the servile war against Spartacus, (72 B.C.,) in which he gave proof of courage; but martial pursuits did not prove congenial to his taste. After performing the duties of quæstor with honour, he was elected tribune of the people in the same year that Cicero was consul. He appears to have been the only eminent Roman that heartily seconded Cicero in opposing the traitorous designs of Catiline, 690 A.U.C. His sincere devotion to liberty prompted him to strenuously oppose the ambitious coalition of Cæsar, Pompey, and Crassus; but his success was perhaps hindered by his inflexible and uncompromising policy. In 54 B.C. he was elected prætor, and, by his efforts to prevent bribery at elections, gave great offence to the politicians. He failed in his candidacy for the consulship, because he would not resort to corrupt means to procure his election. When the rivalry of Pompey and Cæsar, whom he vainly attempted to reconcile, ripened into civil war in 49 B.C., Cato joined the party of the former as the lesser evil, and, after the death of Pompey, commanded an army in Africa. He resigned the command to Scipio,

---

* The manuscripts of Chaucer have *Caton* and *Catoun.* (See the "Tale of Melibeus," and the "Nonnes Prestes Tale.")

ā, ē, ī, ō, ū, ȳ, *long;* ă, ĕ, ĭ, ŏ, ŭ, ў, *short;* ạ, ẹ, ị, ọ, *obscure;* fär, fȧll, fȧt; mĕt; nŏt; gōōd; mōōn;

who was defeated in the year 46. Cato then wished to defend Utica against the victor; but other counsels prevailed. Unwilling to survive the ruin of the republic, which he had predicted and opposed with all his power, he died at Utica by his own hand, in his forty-ninth year. Cæsar, on hearing of the event, exclaimed, "Cato, I envy thee thy death, since thou hast deprived me of the honour of saving thy life." Cato has generally been regarded as one of the purest and noblest of all the Romans. His lofty and spotless virtue (as virtue was then understood) seemed almost to justify that fine though somewhat extravagant line of Lucan's "Pharsalia:"

"Victrix causa Deis placuit, sed victa Catoni."*

Plutarch makes a comparison between Cato and Phocion, whose virtues, he says, were perfectly similar in form and colour. It may be said, however, that the former excelled in active, the latter in passive, virtues. Cato's son Marcus was killed at Philippi, fighting for Brutus and Cassius.

See TACITUS, "History," iv. 8; VALERIUS MAXIMUS, vi.; DRUMANN, "Geschichte Roms," vol. v.

Cato, (VALERIUS,) a Roman poet and grammarian, who flourished at Rome in the first century B.C. He had a high reputation for his skill as a teacher, and wrote several treatises on grammar. His poems entitled "Lydia" and "Diana" were his most celebrated works; but they have not come down to us. There is extant, under his name, a small poem called "Diræ," which some persons ascribe to Virgil.

See SUETONIUS, "De Grammaticis illustribus;" BURMANN, "Anthologia."

Cato Censorius or **Censorinus.** See CATO (M. PORCIUS) THE CENSOR.

Cā'to Lǐ-çin-ǐ-ā'nus, (CAIUS PORCIUS,) a son of Marcus Porcius, noticed below, became consul in the year 114 B.C., and commanded an army in Thrace, where he was defeated. He was afterwards employed as legate in Africa, and was charged with a dishonourable intrigue with Jugurtha.

Cato Licinianus, (MARCUS PORCIUS,) an eminent Roman jurist, was the son of Cato the Censor by his first wife, and was esteemed a wise and virtuous man. He entered the army in his youth, and distinguished himself at the battle of Pydna in 168 B.C., soon after which he devoted himself to the law. He wrote several legal works. Died in 152 B.C.

Cato Uticensis. See CATO (M. PORCIUS) THE YOUNGER.

Caton, the French of CATO, which see.

Catone, the Italian of CATO, which see.

Catrou, kǎ'troo', (FRANÇOIS,) a French Jesuit and writer, born in Paris in 1659. He edited the "Journal de Trévoux" about twelve years, (1701–12,) with a fair reputation as a critic. He published, besides other works, a "History of Aurung-Zeb," (1702,) and a "Roman History," in twenty-one volumes, which was popular at the time. Died in 1737.

See MORÉRI, "Dictionnaire Historique."

Catrufo, kȧ-troo'fo, (GIUSEPPE,) an Italian composer, born at Naples in 1771. He composed comic operas.

Cats, kȧts, (JAKOB,) sometimes spelled **Catz,** [Lat. CAT'SIUS,] an eminent and popular Dutch poet, born at Brouwershaven, in Zealand, in 1577, holds a conspicuous place among the creators of Dutch poetry and literature. He studied law, which he practised with success; and he performed with credit the highest functions in the public service. He was ambassador to England in 1627 and in 1651. From 1636 to 1651 he served as grand pensionary of Holland. He wrote a poem entitled "Country Life," ("Buitenleven,") and numerous "Moral Emblems," fables, allegories, songs, etc., which are admired for ease, simplicity, and clearness of style, and display a deep knowledge of the human heart. Bilderdijk, one of the greatest of Dutch poets, says,

"Dear Father Cats,
What endless treasures dost thou not contain!"†

"His imagination," says Hallam, "is gay, his morality

* "The victorious cause was favoured by the gods, but the conquered by Cato."

† "Dierbre Vader Cats,
Wat behelst ge niet al schats."

popular and useful. No one was more read than Father Cats, as the people call him; but he is often trifling and monotonous." Died in 1660.

See LONGFELLOW, "Poets and Poetry of Europe;" ALSCHE, "Commentatio de J. Catsio," 1828; SIEGENBEEK, "Over de Verdiensten van J. Cats als Staatsman," 1836: FOPPENS, "Bibliotheca Belgica;" "Fraser's Magazine" for May, 1854.

Cattaneo, kȧt-tȧ'nȧ-o, (CARLO,) an Italian economist and able writer on philosophy, statistics, and politics, born at Milan about 1815. He is a republican, and took a prominent part in the revolution at Milan in 1848. Among his works are "The Insurrection at Milan in 1848," and "Natural and Political Account of Lombardy," ("Notizie naturali e civili della Lombardia.")

Cattaneo, (DANESE,) an Italian sculptor and poet, born at Carrara about 1500. He worked in Venice and Verona, and was eminent as an artist and poet. He was author of a poem called "The Love of Marfisa," ("L'Amor di Marfisa.")

Cattaneo, (FELICE,) an Italian painter, born at Milan, lived about 1730.

Cattaneo or **Cataneo,** kȧ-tȧ-nȧ'o, (GIOVANNI MARIA,) a learned Italian writer, born at Novara, became a resident of Rome. In early youth he composed a commentary on Pliny the Younger, which was admired, and was printed in 1500. He left an unfinished poem on the "Conquest of Jerusalem by the Crusaders." Died about 1528.

Cattani, kȧt-tȧ'nee, (GAETANO,) an Italian missionary, born at Módena in 1696. He went to Paraguay in 1729, and afterwards wrote three long letters on that country, which Muratori inserted in his collection with high and merited praise. Died in 1733.

Cattani da Diacceto, kȧt-tȧ'nee dȧ de-ȧt-chȧ'to, (FRANCESCO,) an Italian philosopher and writer, born at Florence in 1446. He succeeded Marsilio Ficino as professor of philosophy. Died in 1522.

See B. VARCHI, "Vita di F. Cattani da Diacceto," 1561 and 1843.

Cattapane, kȧt-tȧ-pȧ'nȧ, (LUCA,) an Italian painter, born at Cremona, lived about 1500.

Catteau-Calleville, kȧ'to' kȧl'vėl', (JOHANN PETER WILHELM,) a historian and geographer, of French origin, born at Angermunde, in Prussia, in 1759. He became minister of the French Protestant church at Stockholm in 1783, and settled in Paris in 1810. He published a "General Description of Sweden," (1789,) "Travels in Germany and Sweden," (1810,) a "History of Christina, Queen of Sweden," (1815,) and other works. Died in 1819.

See QUÉRARD, "La France Littéraire."

Cattenburg, van, vȧn kȧt'ten-bŭrG, (ADRIAAN,) a Dutch theologian, born at Rotterdam in 1664. He was one of the chief men of the sect of Remonstrants or Arminians, and author of several works, among which were a "Life of Hugo Grotius," (1727,) and "Treatise on the Wisdom of Moses," ("Syntagma Sapientiæ Mosaicæ," 1737.) Died about 1737.

See FELLER, "Dictionnaire Historique."

Cat'ter-mole, (GEORGE,) an eminent English painter, born at Dickleburgh, Norfolk, in 1800. His works are mostly paintings, in water-colours, of subjects derived from history or from the imaginations of Shakspeare and Scott. Among his capital productions is a large picture of "Luther at the Diet of Spire." At the Exposition of Paris in 1855 he received a first-class medal. After that date he painted chiefly in oil. Died in 1868.

Cattermole, (Rev. RICHARD,) an English author, brother of the preceding, became vicar of Little Marlow, in the county of Bucks. He published "The Literature of the Church of England," (2 vols.,) "Illustrated History of the Great Civil War of the Times of Charles I. and Cromwell," (2 vols., 1846–52,) and other valuable works.

Cattho or **Catto,** kȧt-to', (ANGELO,) a learned bishop, born at Taranto, became chaplain to Louis XI. of France. He was reputed to be skilful in astrology and the prediction of future events. Died in 1494.

Cattier, kȧ'te-ȧ', (ISAAC,) a French medical writer, born in Paris, lived about 1640.

Catuldi. See CATALDI.

Catulle. See CATULLUS.

€ as *k*; ç as *s*; ḡ *hard*; ġ as *j*; G, H, K, *guttural*; N, *nasal*; R, *trilled*; ɜ as *z*; th as in *this*. (☞See Explanations, p. 23.)

Ca-tul'lus, [Fr. CATULLE, kȧ'tül',] (CAIUS VALERIUS,) an eminent Latin poet, born at or near Verona about 77 B.C., (some authorities say 87 B.C.) He went to Rome at an early age, and by his literary merit obtained admission into the society of Cicero, Cæsar, Pollio, and others. His indulgence in vicious and expensive pleasures soon reduced him to poverty, which, however, did not subdue his hilarity. His superior genius as a poet is generally admitted by ancient and modern critics. He wrote numerous poems, which are still extant, including odes and epigrams of great beauty and pathos. He also excelled in heroic verse, and was the first Roman that cultivated lyric poetry with success. His longest poem is "The Nuptials of Peleus and Thetis," in hexameter verse. Some critics estimate the "Atys" as the greatest of his works. "His 'Atys,'" says Professor William Ramsay, "is one of the most remarkable poems in the whole range of Latin literature. Rolling impetuously along in a flood of wild passion, bodied forth in the grandest imagery and the noblest diction, it breathes in every line the fiery vehemence of the Greek dithyramb. . . . We admire by turns, in the lighter efforts of his muse, his unaffected ease, playful grace, vigorous simplicity, pungent wit, and slashing invective." He imitated Greek models, and seemed like a Greek poet writing in Latin. He is supposed to have died about 45 B.C.; though Scaliger maintains that he lived about thirty years after that date.

See SELLAR, "Roman Poets of the Republic," chap. xii.; FABRICIUS, "Bibliotheca Latina;" "Nouvelle Biographie Générale;" 'Foreign Quarterly Review" for July, 1842; "Fraser's Magazine" for March, 1849.

Cat'u-lus, †(CAIUS LUTATIUS,) a Roman commander, was chosen consul for the year 242 B.C., when the first Punic war had been waged more than twenty years. The Roman navy had been defeated in several battles, and was nearly annihilated. Catulus took command of a new fleet, and gained a decisive victory over Hanno in 241 B.C. He then terminated the war on terms favourable to Rome.

Catulus, (QUINTUS LUTATIUS,) a Roman general and scholar, noted for the purity and grace with which he spoke and wrote Latin. After several repulses, he was elected consul with C. Marius for the year 102 B.C., when Italy was threatened by the victorious Cimbri. Two Roman armies, commanded by Catulus and Marius, united and defeated the Cimbri in a great battle near Vercelli in 101 B.C. Plutarch says the whole honour of the day was ascribed to Marius, although the chief brunt of the battle fell on the army of Catulus. He became a partisan of Sulla in the civil war, was proscribed by Marius in 87 B.C., and killed himself. He left a historical work on the Cimbrian war, and several poems. Except two epigrams, none of his works are extant.

See APPIAN, "Bellum Civile;" PLUTARCH, "Marius" and "Sulla;" CICERO, "De Oratore."

Catulus, (QUINTUS LUTATIUS,) a son of the preceding, was a prominent leader of the aristocracy, and one of the most moderate and pure of the statesmen of his time. He was consul in 78 B.C., and censor in 65. He was called "illustrious" (" vir clarissimus") by Cicero in his oration "pro Lege Manilia." Catulus was a strong supporter of Cicero in his efforts to defeat the conspiracy of Catiline in 63 B.C. According to Sallust, he urged Cicero to include Cæsar among the conspirators. Died in 60 B.C.

See SALLUST, "Bellum Catilinarium;" TACITUS, "Historia."

Cauche, kōsh, (FRANÇOIS,) a French traveller, born at Rouen, lived about 1650. He passed several years in Madagascar. On his return to France, he published "An Account of the Voyage of F. Cauche to Madagascar," (1651,) which was commended by Du Petit-Thouars.

Cauchois - Lemaire, kō'shwȧ' leh-mâR', (LOUIS FRANÇOIS AUGUSTE,) a French journalist, born in Paris in 1789. He wrote for the "Constitutionnel" from 1820 to 1832, and was noted for his bold and sarcastic political articles. In 1832 he became chief editor of the "Good Sense," (" Bon Sens,") a democratic journal. He was imprisoned several times for his writings between 1820 and 1830. He wrote a "History of the Revolution of 1830," and other works, mostly political. Died in 1862.

See QUÉRARD, "La France Littéraire."

Cauchoix, kō'shwȧ', (ROBERT AGLAÉ,) a French optician, born in Seine-et-Oise in 1776. His telescopes are said to be among the best in use.

Cauchon, kō'shôN', (PIERRE,) Bishop of Beauvais, in the fifteenth century, was a fanatical partisan of the English. He rendered his memory infamous as judge of Joan of Arc (1431) by the perfidious means he used to effect her condemnation and by the atrocious sentence which he pronounced upon her. Died in 1443.

See SISMONDI, "Histoire des Français;" J. DES URSINS, "Histoire de Charles VII."

Cauchy, kō'she', (AUGUSTIN LOUIS,) a French mathematician, son of Louis François, noticed below, was born in Paris in 1789. After gaining the first prize for Latin poetry in the Central School, he entered the Polytechnic School as second scholar in 1805. He passed from that to the School of "Ponts et Chaussées," and was afterwards employed as engineer at the port of Cherbourg. In his youth he was distinguished for his researches into difficult questions, and demonstrated Euclid's celebrated theorem respecting polyhedra. In 1815 the Institute awarded him the grand prize for his "Memoir on the Theory of Waves," which was destined to become the basis of an admirable theory of light. He was chosen a member of the Academy of Sciences and professor of mechanics in the Polytechnic School in 1816. He published for his pupils a "Course of Analysis," (1821,) "Lectures on the Differential Calculus," (1826,) and other works. Refusing to swear allegiance to Louis Philippe in 1830, he lost his professorship. In 1833 he became tutor to the Duke of Bordeaux at Prague. He returned to Paris in 1838, and resumed his place in the Academy of Sciences, for which he wrote many ingenious memoirs. In 1849 he succeeded Biot as professor of physical astronomy in the Faculty of Sciences. Among his later works was a "Memoir on the Dispersion of Light," (1836.) He displayed considerable poetic power in his verses "On Charles V. in Spain," (1834.) Died in 1857.

See "Nouvelle Biographie Générale;" QUÉRARD, "La France Littéraire."

Cauchy, (LOUIS FRANÇOIS,) a French poet, father of the preceding, was born at Rouen in 1755. He composed an "Ode to the First Consul," (1802,) and "The Battle of Austerlitz," (1806,) both in Latin. He was successively archivist of the senate and of the Chamber of Peers. Died in 1847.

Caulaincourt, kō'lâN'kooR', (AUGUSTE JEAN GABRIEL,) a French general, brother of Armand Augustin Louis, noticed below, born in the department of Somme in 1777. He was wounded at Marengo in 1800, and fought in the Peninsula as general of brigade. For his services in the passage of the Tagus in 1809 he was made a general of division. He was killed at the battle of Borodino, September 7, 1812. He was equally distinguished for courage and talents.

See SÉGUR, "Histoire de la Campagne de Russie."

Caulaincourt, de, deh kō'lâN'kooR', (ARMAND AUGUSTIN LOUIS,) Duke of Vicenza, (ve-chên'zȧ,) a French diplomatist, born of an ancient family of Picardy in 1773. He entered the army as a private soldier, became colonel in 1799, and made the campaign of 1800 under Moreau with distinction. Bonaparte sent him on a mission to Russia in 1801, and after his return employed him as aide-de-camp and grand equerry of the palace, (1804.) In the latter function he acquitted himself with dignity. About 1808 he was appointed minister to Russia, where he performed his duties with loyalty and address until 1811, when he asked to be recalled. He appears to have warned his infatuated master against the invasion of Russia, in which he took part. The emperor signified his continued confidence by choosing Caulaincourt as his companion in his hurried return to Paris in December, 1812. In 1813 he was chosen minister of foreign affairs, which were in such a desperate state that no diplomacy could avail; but he shared the fortunes of Napoleon to the last, and, after the battle of Waterloo, retired with honour to private life. He had been made Duke of Vicenza in 1808. Died in 1827.

See THIERS, "Histoire du Consulat et de l'Empire;" "Nouvelle Biographie Générale."

ā, ē, ī, ō, ū, ȳ, long; ă, ĕ, ĭ, ŏ, ŭ, ў, short; a, e, i, o, obscure; fär, fäll, fât; mēt; nŏt; gŏŏd; mōŏn

Caulet, de, dẹh kō'lȧ', (ÉTIENNE FRANÇOIS,) a French bishop, (of Pamiers,) born in 1610 ; died in 1680.

Caulfield. See CHARLEMONT, EARL OF.

Caul'field, (JAMES,) an English writer, born in London about 1764, became a dealer in engravings. He published "Portraits and Memoirs of Remarkable Persons," (1794,) a "Gallery of British Portraits," and other illustrated works.

Cauliac. See CHAULIAC.

Cauls. See CAUS, (SALOMON.)

Caulvin. See CALVIN.

Caumartin, de, dẹh kō'mȧr'tȧ̃n', (JEAN FRANÇOIS PAUL LEFÈVRE,) born at Châlons-sur-Marne in 1668, became Bishop of Vannes and of Blois. He was admitted into the French Academy in 1694. Died in 1733.

See MORÉRI, "Dictionnaire Historique."

Caumartin, de, (LOUIS URBAIN LEFÈVRE,) a French statesman, brother of the preceding, born in 1653, was successively master of requests, intendant of finances, and councillor of state. At his château of Saint-Ange, Voltaire first formed the idea of his "Henriade." Died in 1720.

See SAINT-SIMON, "Mémoires."

Caumont. See FORCE, (MARSHAL,) and LAUZUN.

Caumont, de, dẹh kō'mòN', (ARCISSE,) a French antiquary, born at Bayeux (Calvados) in 1802. He founded about 1833 the Scientific Congress, a reunion of savants, who meet annually in different cities of France, and a "Society for the Conservation of Monuments." He has published several important works, among which are "Lectures on Monumental Antiquities," (10 vols., 1830,) and a "History of Art in the West of France," (1831-40.)

See RICHELET, "Notice sur M. de Caumont."

Caumont, de, (JOSEPH de Seytres—dẹh sȧtR or sĕtR,) MARQUIS, a French antiquary, born at Avignon in 1688. His various and extensive acquirements caused him to be chosen a Fellow of the Royal Society of London, and correspondent of the French Academy of Inscriptions. Died in 1745.

Caurroy, du, dü kō'rwȧ', (FRANÇOIS EUSTACHE,) a French musician and famous composer, born in Picardy in 1549 ; died in 1609.

Caus, kō, (ISAAC,) a French engineer, a relative of Salomon Caus, noticed below, was born at Dieppe. He published an interesting work, in French, entitled a "New Invention to raise Water higher than its Source," (London, 1644.)

Caus, Cauls, or **Caux, de,** dẹh kō, (SALOMON,) a celebrated French engineer and architect, born in Normandy. He was in the service of Charles, Prince of Wales, in London in 1612. From 1614 to 1620 he lived at Heidelberg as engineer of the Elector Palatine Frederick. In 1615 he published a work on motive powers, "Les Raisons des Forces mouvantes avec diverses Machines," etc., which contains a theorem on the expansion and condensation of steam. The French maintain that the Marquis of Worcester derived from Caus the discovery of the utility of steam as a motive power. Arago calls him "a man whom posterity will perhaps regard as the first inventor of the *machine à feu*," (steam-engine.) Caus is supposed to have died in France about 1630.

See "Nouvelle Biographie Générale."

Causeur, kō'zuR', (JEAN,) a French peasant, noted for longevity, was born at Lanfenot in 1638, and died in 1775, at the age of one hundred and thirty-seven. His habits were temperate.

Caussidière, kō'se'dẹ-aiR', (MARC,) a French radical politician, born at Lyons about 1809. He fought on the side of the revolutionists of Paris in February, 1848, was appointed prefect of police by the provisional government which was then formed, and was afterwards elected to the Constituent Assembly. In August, 1848, the Assembly passed a vote of accusation against him in relation to the revolt of May 15, which he was suspected of secretly favouring. He escaped to London. "His heart was honest and generous," says Lamartine : "one could confide in his nature, if not in his opinions." Died in 1861.

Caussin, kō'sȧN', (NICOLAS,) a French writer and priest, born at Troyes about 1582, joined the Jesuits in 1607. His success as a preacher attracted the notice of Richelieu, who made him confessor to Louis XIII. For attempting to supplant Richelieu in the favour of the king, he was dismissed nine months after his appointment. He published, besides other devotional works, "The Holy Court," (5 vols.,) which had an immense circulation. Died in 1651.

See BAYLE, "Historical and Critical Dictionary."

Caussin de Perceval, kō'sȧN' dẹh pĕRs'vȧl', (ARMAND PIERRE,) a French Orientalist, son of Jean Jacques Antoine, noticed below, was born in Paris in 1795. He studied and travelled in Turkey and Syria several years, and about 1822 was appointed professor of Arabic in the College of France. In 1824 he became Arabic interpreter to the ministry. He published an "Arabic Grammar," and "Essays on the History of the Arabs before Islamism, during the Time of Mohammed, and down to the Reduction of all the Tribes under his Dominion," (1847.) He became a member of the Academy of Inscriptions in 1849.

See QUÉRARD, "La France Littéraire."

Caussin de Perceval, (JEAN JACQUES ANTOINE,) a French scholar, father of the preceding, was born at Montdidier in 1759. In 1783 he became professor of Arabic in the College of France, Paris, and in 1809 a member of the Institute. He translated from the Arabic a "Sequel to the Thousand and One Nights," and other works. He published a good edition of the Fables of Lokmân. Died in 1835.

Cauvin. See CALVIN.

Cau'vin, (JOSEPH,) an English scholar, chiefly known as an assistant editor of Brande's "Dictionary of Science, Literature, and Art," (1842.) (See BRANDE, W. T.) He published an improved edition of "Lempriere's Classical Dictionary," (1845.)

Caux. See CAUS, (SALOMON.)

Caux, de, dẹh kō, (GILLES,) a French poet, born about 1682, was a descendant of the great Corneille. His best works are the tragedy of "Marius," (1715,) and "The Hour-Glass," a small poem. Died in 1733.

Caux de Cappeval, kō dẹh kȧp'vȧl', a mediocre French poet, born near Rouen. He published "Parnassus, or an Essay on the Campaigns of the King," (1752,) and other poems, and produced a Latin version of Voltaire's "Henriade." Died in 1774.

See GRIMM, "Correspondance."

Cavacci, kȧ-vȧt'chee, (JACOPO,) a historian and monk, born at Padua in 1567 ; died in 1612.

Cavaceppi, kȧ-vȧ-chep'pee, (BARTOLOMMEO,) a Roman sculptor, who flourished about 1770.

Cavagna, kȧ-vȧn'yȧ, (GIOVANNI PAOLO,) a skilful Italian painter, born at Bergamo about 1560. He took Paul Veronese for his model. Died in 1627.

Cavaignac, kȧ'vȧn'yȧk', (GODEFROY,) a French republican chief, brother of General Louis Eugène Cavaignac, was born in Paris in 1801. He fought on the side of the revolutionists in the three days of July, 1830, was one of the founders of the "Society of the Friends of the People," and became one of the most popular leaders of his party. In 1834 he was imprisoned for political reasons, but escaped in 1835 and went into exile. He returned to France in 1841, and became assistant editor of the journal called "La Réforme." He died in 1845. "Godefroy Cavaignac," says Lamartine, "was a name equal to the name of Carrel in republican estimation. He had died before the triumph (*avènement*) of his idea, and that idea rendered homage to him [in 1848] in the person of his brother." He published a work called "Cardinal Dubois ; or, Every Road leads to Rome."

See QUÉRARD, "La France Littéraire."

Cavaignac, (JEAN BAPTISTE,) a French revolutionist, born at Gordon in 1762, was the father of General Louis Eugène Cavaignac. In 1792 he represented Haute-Garonne in the Convention, and voted for the death of the king. In the insurrection of the sections of Paris against the Convention, October, 1795, he was chosen to co-operate with Barras in directing the army of the Convention. He was one of the Council of Five Hundred in 1796. The fall of his friend Barras, in 1799, injured his political prospects. He was afterwards councillor of state under

Murat, King of Naples. He was exiled from France as a regicide in 1816, and died in Brussels in 1829.

See GONON, "Biographie de J. B. Cavaignac," 1848.

Cavaignac, (LOUIS EUGÈNE,) a distinguished French general and republican statesman, a son of the preceding, was born in Paris in 1802. He entered the Polytechnic School in 1820. In 1828 and 1829 he served in the Morea as captain of engineers. He was sent to Africa in 1832, and soon became eminent for the best qualities of a soldier and an officer. In 1836 he was selected for the perilous post of commander of the garrison of Tlemcen, which he defended with success for more than a year. He became a lieutenant-colonel of zouaves in 1840, and colonel in 1841. For his services at Isly in 1844 he obtained the rank of maréchal-de-camp. He was appointed governor of the province of Orân in 1847, and was in Algeria when the revolution of 1848 occurred. In March of that year the provisional government appointed him Governor-General of Algeria, with the rank of general of division. In April, Lamartine, through the mediation of Madame Cavaignac, (who was called "the mother of the Gracchi,") invited General Cavaignac to come to Paris for the defence of the government against the mob. He arrived in Paris on the 17th of May, two days after a great insurrection had begun, and was appointed minister of war when that office was generally considered an unenviable position. As commander-in-chief of the army and of the national guard, he defeated the insurgents in a great battle in Paris which began on the 23d of June and continued three days. He was appointed dictator by the Assembly on the 24th, and displayed great skill and energy on that occasion. Having resigned the dictatorship, he was recalled to power on the 28th of June, with the title of *chef du pouvoir exécutif,* or President of the republic.

He maintained order in the capital, and pursued a moderate policy, by which many ultra-republicans were alienated from his support. The Assembly on the 25th of November declared that he had deserved well of the country. About this time an election for President by universal suffrage resulted in the choice of Louis Napoleon Bonaparte, who received about 6,000,000 votes, while Cavaignac received 1,448,302. On the 20th of December, 1848, Cavaignac retired from power, and took his seat in the Assembly among the moderate republicans. He was arrested in December, 1851, and detained a few days. In 1852 he was elected a deputy by the voters of Paris; but, as he refused to swear allegiance to the emperor, he did not obtain the seat, and retired from political life. He was again elected a deputy from Paris to the corps législatif, but died a few weeks later, in October, 1857. He had published in 1839 a work entitled "De la Régence d'Alger." Few men who have possessed the chief power in difficult circumstances have preserved so pure a reputation.

See HENRI MONTFORT, "Biographie du Général Cavaignac," 1848; "Lebensbeschreibung des Generals Cavaignac," Strasburg, 1848; "Nouvelle Biographie Générale."

Cavaignac, de, dĕh kȧ'vȧn'yȧk', (JACQUES MARIE,) VICOMTE, a French general, born at Gordon in 1773, was an uncle of the preceding. He served with distinction in the armies of the republic in Italy, and in 1806 was nominated by Napoleon commandant of the legion of honour at the battle of Austerlitz. As general of brigade, he took part in the expedition to Moscow in 1812. He was afterwards raised to the rank of lieutenant-general. The date of his death is unknown.

Cavalca, kȧ-vȧl'kȧ, (DOMENICO,) an Italian ascetic writer, born in Tuscany, was contemporary with Dante. He wrote "The Fruits of the Tongue," and other works, which are cited by the Academy Della Crusca as authority. Died about 1340.

Cavalcabo-Baroni, kȧ-vȧl-kȧ'bo bȧ-ro'nee, (GASPARO ANTONIO,) a painter of the Venetian school, born near Roveredo in 1682; died in 1759.

Cavalcanti, kȧ-vȧl-kȧn'tee, (BARTOLOMMEO,) an Italian writer, born of a noble family at Florence in 1503. Having removed to Ferrara, he was sent by Cardinal Ippolito II. on a mission to the French court. Pope Paul III. also employed him as a negotiator. He wrote a "Treatise on Rhetoric," (1559,) and other works. Died in 1562.

Cavalcanti, (GUIDO,) a Florentine poet, was a friend of Dante, and an ardent Ghibeline. He was one of the poets of that age who made the nearest approach to a good style. His canzone on "Love" was the most popular of his works. Died in 1300.

See GINGUENÉ, "Histoire Littéraire d'Italie."

Cavaleri. See CAVALIERI.

Cavalier, kȧ'vȧ'le-ȧ', (JEAN,) a French peasant, born at Ribaute in 1679, was the most able and popular chief of the Camisards, (persecuted Protestants of Cévennes,) who revolted in 1702. By his courage and skill he foiled the generals of the king and obtained an honourable treaty from Villars, (1704.) He afterwards entered the service of the English, fought at Almanza in 1707, and became a general in the English army. Died in 1740.

See ANTOINE COURT, "Histoire des Camisards."

Cavaliere, kȧ-vȧ-le-ȧ'rȧ, or **Cavalieri,** kȧ-vȧ-le-ȧ'ree, an Italian composer, born about 1550, made some improvements or inventions in music. Died about 1600.

Cavalieri, kȧ-vȧ-le-ȧ'ree, or **Cavaleri,** kȧ-vȧ-lȧ'ree, (BONAVENTURA,) an eminent Italian geometer, born in Milan in 1598, was one of the few whose discoveries form an epoch in the history of geometry. He entered the order of Hieronymites or Jesuates, and became a pupil of Galileo at Pisa. Having devoted himself to researches respecting the proportions of different solids, he discovered, about 1626, his method of indivisibles. He conceived that a line is formed of an infinite number of points, a surface of an infinity of lines, etc., and published in 1635 his "Geometry of Indivisibles." A few years earlier he had been chosen professor of mathematics at Bologna. He wrote a "Treatise on Conic Sections," and several other works. Died at Bologna in 1647.

See MONTUCLA, "Histoire des Mathématiques;" PAOLO FRISI, "Elogio di Galileo Galilei e di B. Cavalieri," 1776; G. PIOLA, "Elogio storico di B. Cavalieri," 1844.

Cavallerii, da, dȧ kȧ-vȧl-lȧ're-ee, (GIOVANNI BATTISTA,) a mediocre Italian engraver, born at Lagherino about 1530, engraved many works after Raphael, Michael Angelo, and Titian. Died in 1597.

Cavallero. See CABALLERO.

Cavallero, kȧ-vȧl-yȧ'ro, or **Caballero,** kȧ-bȧl-yȧ'ro, (Don JUAN,) a Spanish general, born in Naples in 1712, commanded the engineers at the siege of Gibraltar in 1779. Died in 1791.

Cavalli, kȧ-vȧl'lee, (FRANCESCO,) born at Venice, was an organist, and one of the first composers of his time. He became chapel-master of the church of Saint Mark, and was one of the first who composed grand operas. Between 1637 and 1669 he produced thirty-eight successful operas. Died in 1676.

See FÉTIS, "Biographie Universelle des Musiciens."

Cavallini, kȧ-vȧl-lee'nee, (PIETRO,) a celebrated painter and sculptor, born in Rome about 1270, is said to have been a pupil of Giotto. He adorned with frescos the churches of Rome, Florence, and Assisi, where some of them may still be seen. His "Crucifixion" at Assisi is well preserved, and is called his master-piece. Died about 1350.

See LANZI, "History of Painting in Italy;" VASARI, "Lives of the Painters," etc.

Cavallino, kȧ-vȧl-lee'no, (BERNARDO,) a historical painter, born in Naples about 1620. His works are admired for grace, colouring, and charming expression. He excelled most in pictures of small proportions. Died in 1656.

Cavallo, kȧ-vȧl'lo, (TIBERIO,) a philosopher, distinguished for his experiments in electricity, was born at Naples in 1749. In 1771 he went to London, where he passed the most of his mature years. Having made discoveries or inventions in electricity and magnetism, he was chosen a Fellow of the Royal Society in 1779. He invented a micrometer, an electrometer, and a condenser of electricity, and made interesting experiments with a kite in relation to the electric state of clouds. He wrote, besides other works, "A Complete Treatise on Electricity," and a "Treatise on the Nature and Properties of Air." Died in 1809.

Cavallucci, kȧ-vȧl-loot'chee, (ANTONIO,) an Italian historical painter and excellent colorist, born at Sermo-

ā, ē, ī, ō, ū, ȳ, *long;* ȧ, ė, ŏ, same, less prolonged; ă, ĕ, ĭ, ŏ, ŭ, ў, *short;* ą, ę, į, ǫ, *obscure;* fär, fȧll, fȧt; mėt; nŏt; gōōd; mōōn;

neta in 1752. A picture of "Saint Bona taking the Veil," at Pisa, is called his master-piece. Died in Rome in 1795.

See LANZI, "History of Painting in Italy."

Cavâm-(or **Cawâm-)ed-Dowlah,** kâ-vâm' ed-dŏw'-lạh, originally **Ket-bo'gạ,** Prince of Mosul, a Turkish general, defeated by the crusaders at Antioch in 1098.

Cavanilles, kâ-vä-nèl'yĕs, (ANTONIO JOSÉ,) a Spanish priest and eminent botanist, was born at Valencia in 1745. He was professor of philosophy at Murcia, when he was chosen preceptor of the children of the Duke del Infantado, ambassador to Paris. He passed twelve years in Paris, (1777 to 1789,) in which time he produced his dissertations on the class Monadelphia. Having returned to Spain, he published "Icones et Descriptiones Plantarum," etc., an excellent description of Spanish plants, with fine engravings drawn by himself, (6 vols., 1791.) This was followed by "Observations on the Natural History, Geography, etc. of Valencia," (2 vols., 1795–97,) which is said to be the most useful work of that kind ever published in Spain. In 1801 he was chosen director of the royal botanic garden of Madrid. He adhered to the artificial or Linnæan system of botany. Died at Madrid in 1804.

See ERSCH und GRUBER, "Allgemeine Encyklopaedie;" "Nouvelle Biographie Générale."

Cavarazzi, kâ-vä-rât'see, (BARTOLOMMEO,) called CRESCENZI, (krÀ-shĕn'zee,) an Italian painter, born at Viterbo about 1590; died in 1625.

Cavazzi, kâ-vât'see, (GIOVANNI ANTONIO,) an Italian monk, born at Montecuculo. He was sent as a missionary to Congo in 1654. In 1670 he was chosen superior-general of the missions in Congo, Angola, etc., where he laboured many years. He published a "Description of Congo, Angola, and Matamba." Died at Genoa in 1692.

Cave, (EDWARD,) an English printer, born at Newton in 1691, is memorable as the founder of "The Gentleman's Magazine," first issued in January, 1731, under the name of Sylvanus Urban. It was very successful in his hands until his death, and still flourishes, with a high reputation. He patronized Dr. Johnson when the latter was a young and needy author; and Johnson wrote a biography of Cave. Died in 1754.

See DR. JOHNSON'S Works.

Cave, (WILLIAM,) D.D., a learned English divine and scholar, born in Leicestershire in 1637, became vicar of Islington in 1662, canon of Windsor in 1684, and vicar of Isleworth in 1690. He devoted much attention to ecclesiastical antiquities, and wrote many esteemed works, among which are "Primitive Christianity," (1672,) "History of Christ and the Apostles," (1675,) "Lives of the Fathers of the Church in the Fourth Century," (1682,) and "Literary History of Ecclesiastic Writers from the Birth of Christ to the Fourteenth Century," ("Scriptorum ecclesiasticorum Historia litteraria," 2 vols., 1688–89.) The three first named are said to be the best works on those subjects. Died in 1713.

See "Biographia Britannica;" WOOD, "Athenæ Oxonienses."

Cavedone, kâ-vä-do'nȧ, (GIACOMO,) an eminent Italian painter, born at Sassuolo, near Módena, in 1577. He studied under the Caracci and Guido, and worked at Bologna, both in oil and fresco. He excelled in design and colouring, and had great facility of execution. Among his master-pieces are a "Nativity," a "Virgin and Child borne upon the Clouds," a "Holy Family," and "The Adoration of the Magi." Died at Bologna in 1660.

See LANZI, "History of Painting in Italy."

Caveirac, de, dẹh kâ'vȧ'rȧk', (JEAN NOVI,) a French ecclesiastic, born at Nîmes in 1713. He wrote, besides other works, "An Apology for Louis XIV. and his Council in Relation to the Revocation of the Edict of Nantes, with Observations on Saint Bartholomew," (1758.) Voltaire designated this work an "Apology for Saint Bartholomew." Died in 1782.

Cavelier. See LASALLE, (ROBERT.)

Cavelier, kȧv'le-ȧ', (PIERRE JULES,) an eminent French sculptor, born in Paris in 1814, was a pupil of David of Angers and of Delaroche. He obtained in 1842 the grand prize of sculpture, and passed the five ensuing years in Rome. In 1849 he produced "Penelope Asleep," which was greatly admired, and in 1853 a

statue of "Truth," which was placed in the palace of Luxembourg. His works are remarkable for elegance of form and grace of attitude.

Cav'ẹn-dish, (CHARLES,) a younger son of the second Earl of Devonshire, born in London in 1620, was a royalist general in the civil war. He defeated the army of Parliament at Donnington in 1643, and was killed soon after in an engagement with Cromwell near Gainsborough.

Cavendish, (Lord FREDERICK,) a British general, born about 1730, was a younger son of the third Duke of Devonshire. Died in 1803.

Cavendish, (GEORGE,) of Glemsford, an English writer, a brother of Sir William Cavendish, noticed below. He is said to have been the author of a well-written "Life of Cardinal Wolsey," which was once ascribed to Sir William. It was first printed in 1641.

Cavendish, (HENRY,) an eminent English chemist and natural philosopher, born at Nice in 1730 or 1731, was the younger son of Lord Charles Cavendish, and grandson of the Duke of Devonshire. Having been educated at Cambridge, he devoted himself exclusively to scientific pursuits, renounced society, and was remarkable for his eccentric habits. He was a profound mathematician, and ranks among the first of chemical philosophers. He first discovered the distinctive properties of hydrogen gas, laid the foundation of pneumatic chemistry, and demonstrated the proportions of oxygen and nitrogen in common air, (1783.) By burning oxygen and hydrogen in a tight glass vessel, he made the brilliant discovery of the composition of water, in 1784. The results of his experiments (which had never been surpassed in accuracy) were published in the "Philosophical Transactions" from 1766 to 1809. He was chosen an associate of the French Institute in 1803. About 1773 he had inherited an immense fortune from an uncle. He was never married. Died in London in 1810. "Whatever he accomplished," says Sir Humphry Davy, "was perfect at the moment of its production. His processes were all of a finished nature. . . . The accuracy and beauty of his earliest labours have remained unimpaired amidst the progress of discovery, and their merits have been illustrated by discussion and exalted by time." ("Chemical Philosophy.") "He was well versed in high geometry," says Biot, "and made a happy application of this knowledge in a very important question of physics,—the determination of the mean density of our globe."

See G. WILSON, "Life of H. Cavendish;" F. HOEFER, "Histoire de la Chimie," tome ii. ; "Encyclopædia Britannica."

Cavendish, (Lord JOHN,) an English Whig statesman, brother of Frederick, noticed above. He was an opponent of Lord North, whom he succeeded as chancellor of the exchequer in 1782. Died in 1796.

Cavendish, (MARGARET,) an English authoress, was the daughter of Sir Charles Lucas, and wife of William Cavendish, Duke of Newcastle. She wrote various works, among which are poems and plays, remarkable for absurdity and bad grammar. She became a maid of honour to the queen of Charles I. in 1643, and was married in 1645. Horace Walpole calls her "a fertile pedant, with an unbounded passion for scribbling." Died in 1673.

See Rev. ALEXANDER DYCE, "Specimens of British Poetesses;" SIR E. BRYDGES, "Imaginative Biography;" and "Retrospective Review," vol. i., 1853.

Cavendish, (Sir ROBERT SPENCER,) an English naval officer, born in 1791. He served against the French and the Americans, 1812–14. Died in 1830.

Cavendish or **Can'dish,** (THOMAS,) an English navigator, born in Suffolk in 1564, was the second of his nation that circumnavigated the globe. In July, 1586, he sailed with three small ships, chiefly fitted out at his expense, with the design to plunder the Spaniards in Peru, Chili, etc. Having taken rich prizes, among which was the Spanish galleon laden with silver, he crossed the Pacific, and, returning by the Cape of Good Hope, reached England in September, 1588. He rendered some services to the sciences of geography and hydrography. Died in 1593.

See J. BARROW, "Memoirs of the Naval Worthies of Queen Elizabeth's Reign," 1845.

Cavendish, (WILLIAM,) Duke of Newcastle, an English general and author, born in 1592. He was raised to the peerage about 1620, as Baron Ogle, and in 1643 became Marquis of Newcastle. In the civil war he commanded the king's army in the north, and gained several battles in 1643, especially at Atherton Moor. In 1644 Prince Rupert effected a junction with the army at York, and, pretending positive orders from the king, involved the royalists in a decisive defeat at Marston Moor, against the advice of Newcastle. The latter then abandoned the cause and went to France. He returned home in 1660, and was made a duke in 1664. He wrote a treatise on horsemanship, several bad comedies, and other works. Hume represents him as "the ornament of the court and of his order, polite and elegant in his taste." Died in 1676.

See CLARENDON's "History of the Great Rebellion."

Cavendish, (WILLIAM,) first Duke of Devonshire, an eminent English statesman, eldest son of the third Earl of Devonshire, was born in 1640. In the reign of Charles II. he represented Derby in the Commons, with the title of Lord Cavendish, and opposed the measures of the court. In 1679 he was chosen one of the new privy council. On the death of his father, in 1684, he became Earl of Devonshire. He promoted the accession of William III., who appointed him lord steward of the royal household in 1689, and created him a duke in 1694. He wrote an "Ode on the Death of Queen Mary," which Dryden is said to have praised, and other works. His mansion at Chatsworth is an admired monument of art and taste. Died in 1707.

See MACAULAY's "History of England."

Cavendish, (Sir WILLIAM,) the founder of the English house of Devonshire, was born about 1505. After he had served Cardinal Wolsey as gentleman-usher, he became a privy councillor of Henry VIII. about 1546. He is the reputed author of a "Life of Wolsey." (See CAVENDISH, GEORGE.) Died in 1557.

Cavendish, (WILLIAM CHARLES.) See BENTINCK.

Caventou, kǎ'vɔN'too', (JOSEPH BIENAIMÉ,) a French chemist, born at Saint-Omer in 1797, became a resident of Paris. He published a "New Chemical Nomenclature," (1816,) and an "Elementary Treatise on Pharmacy," (1819.) He was associated with Pelletier in the discovery of sulphate of quinine about 1820, for which the Institute awarded them a prize of 10,000 francs in 1827.

See QUÉRARD, "La France Littéraire."

Caviceo, kǎ-ve-chā'o, (JACOPO,) an Italian priest, born at Parma in 1443. He wrote "Il Peregrino," a romance. Died in 1511.

Cavino, kǎ-vee'no, (GIOVANNI,) a skilful Italian engraver, surnamed "the Paduan," and "the prince of forgers." Antique medals being sought for with avidity by students in his time, he employed his talents in counterfeiting them with success. About 1565 he and Bassiano fabricated a great number of spurious medals, which were bought by the antiquaries as genuine.

Cavoie, de, dęh kǎ'vwǎ', (LOUIS D'OGER,) MARQUIS, a French courtier, born in 1640. He was celebrated for his bravery, honour, and politeness, and was admired at court as "the glass of fashion and the mould of form." He accompanied Louis XIV. in his campaigns, and shared his bounty. He was the friend of Turenne and of Racine. Died in 1716.

See SAINT-SIMON, "Mémoires."

Cavolini, kǎ-vo-lee'nee, (FILIPPO,) an Italian naturalist, born at Naples in 1756. He became professor of zoology in the University of Naples, and was distinguished for his researches in marine polypi. He wrote a "Treatise on Marine Polypi," one on the "Generation of Fish," (1787,) and other works. Died in 1810.

See MONTICELLI, "Vita Philippi Cavolini," 1812; TIPALDO, "Biografia degli Italiani illustri."

Cavour, di, de kǎ-voor', (CAMILLO BENSO,) COUNT, an illustrious Italian statesman, born at Turin on the 10th of August, 1810, was a son of the Marquis Michele Giuseppe Benso di Cavour, a merchant of Nice, who acquired a large fortune in trade and was ennobled by King Charles Albert. His mother was a Swiss or French lady of Geneva, named Adelaide Sellon. The French was the

language of his infancy. In his youth he assisted his father in the grain-trade, and passed several years in foreign travel. In 1847 he founded, with Count Balbo, a liberal journal, "Il Risorgimento," ("The Uprising,") which was very successful. During the war against Austria in 1848–49, he defended the cause of Italian independence in his speeches and editorial articles. He was elected to the Chamber of Deputies in 1849, proved himself to be a powerful debater, and succeeded in uniting the moderate democrats and liberal conservatives in a party of which he became the leader. He was appointed minister of commerce in 1850, and minister of finance in 1851. In 1852 he became president of the council, or prime minister of Sardinia. He secured the liberty of the press, and favoured religious toleration and free trade. Among the important measures of his administration were his rebellion against papal domination, and his alliance with France and England in the war against Russia in 1855. After the close of that war he devoted his efforts to the liberation and unity of Italy, undismayed by the angry fulminations of the Vatican.

With the aid of the French emperor, he waged, in 1859, a war against Austria, which resulted in the annexation of Lombardy, Tuscany, Parma, and Módena to Sardinia. Cavour resigned in July, 1859, because he was displeased with the treaty of Villa-Franca. He resumed the place of premier in January, 1860, and, after the conquests of Garibaldi in Sicily and Naples, was the first minister of the kingdom of Italy. In the new parliament, which met about the beginning of 1861, his policy and ascendency were fully maintained. A serious disagreement occurred between Cavour and Garibaldi on the question of the attack on Venetia which the latter proposed; but they were reconciled by the mediation of Victor Emmanuel. Cavour died, after an illness of a few days, on the 6th of June, 1861. His death was generally deplored as an irreparable loss to Italy. On the next day after his death, Lord Palmerston, in the House of Commons, paid the following tribute to his memory: "The moral which is to be drawn from the life of Count Cavour is this,—that a man of transcendent talents, of indomitable energy, and inextinguishable patriotism, may, by the impulses which his own single mind may give to his countrymen, aiding a righteous cause, and seizing favourable opportunities, notwithstanding difficulties that at first sight appear insurmountable, confer on his country the greatest and most inestimable benefits." "His greatness," says the "Edinburgh Review" for July,1861, "wore the unassuming garb of common sense,—but a common sense of colossal proportions, exalted by perpetual direction to the pursuit of what was great and lofty." He was never married.

See "Reminiscences of the Life and Character of Cavour," translated from the French by EDWARD ROMILLY; "Cavour, a Memoir," by EDWARD DICEY; "Cavour, sein Leben und Wirken," in the "Jahrbuch zum Conversations-Lexikon" for 1859, (published by BROCKHAUS, Leipsic;) "London Quarterly Review," July, 1861.

Caw'thorne, (JAMES,) an English poet, born at Sheffield in 1719, became master of Tunbridge School about 1744. Among his poems is "The Perjured Lover." Died in 1761.

Caw'ton, (THOMAS,) an English Puritan divine and Orientalist, born in Norfolk in 1605. He assisted Walton in his "Polyglot Bible," and Castell in his "Lexicon." He preached for some time in London. Died in 1659.

His son THOMAS, born in Essex in 1637, was a clergyman, and was learned in Oriental languages. He wrote a "Dissertation on the Use of the Hebrew Tongue in Philosophy." Died in 1677.

See WOOD, "Athenæ Oxonienses."

Caxes or **Cajes,** kǎ'hês, (EUGENIO,) a Spanish painter, was born at Madrid in 1577. He obtained the title of painter to the king in 1612. Died in 1642.

Cax'ton, (WILLIAM,) an English scholar and printer, celebrated as the first who introduced printing into England, was born in Kent about 1412. He was a prominent merchant of London, and about 1442 visited the Low Countries as a commercial agent. In 1464 he was employed by Edward IV. to negotiate a treaty of commerce with the Duke of Burgundy. He received an appointment in the court of the Duchess of Burgundy in 1468,

---

ā, ē, ī, ō, ū, ȳ, *long;* ă, ĕ, ĭ, ŏ, ŭ, ў, *short;* ą, ȩ, į, ǫ, *obscure;* fär, fâll, fât; mĕt; nŏt; gŏŏd; mōōn;

and by her order translated from the French a " History of Troy," which he printed about 1474. This was the first book printed in the English language. The time of his return to England is supposed to have been between 1474 and 1476. He established a printing-office in Westminster Abbey, and printed sixty-four different books, many of which were translated by himself. An attempt was made by Richard Atkyns (1664) to deprive Caxton of the honour of being the first to introduce printing into England ; but the documents on which that writer relies to establish his point are, beyond all reasonable question, either erroneous or spurious. Died in 1492.

See J. LEWIS, "Life of Caxton," 1738 ; CHARLES KNIGHT, "W. Caxton : a Biography," 1844.

Cay. See CAIUS.

Cayet, kā′yȧ′, (PIERRE VICTOR PALMA,) a French theologian, born in Touraine about 1520. He was a Protestant in his youth, and was employed as chaplain by Catherine de Bourbon, who took him to court about 1590. He abjured Calvinism in 1595, and in the next year was chosen professor of Hebrew in the College of Navarre, Paris. He wrote many polemical and other works, among which is a "History of the War under Henry IV. from 1589 to 1598." Died in 1610.

See NICÉRON, "Mémoires ;" BAYLE, "Historical and Critical Dictionary."

Cayla, kȧ′lȧ′, (JEAN MAMERT,) a French *littérateur* and journalist, born at Vigan (Lot) in 1812. He published, among other works, a volume of "European Celebrities," and a "History of the City of Constantinople."

Cay′ley, (ARTHUR,) an English writer, published "The Life of Sir Walter Raleigh," (1805,) and a "Memoir of Sir Thomas More," (1808.)

Cayley, (ARTHUR,) an English mathematician, born at Richmond, Surrey, in 1821, became a Fellow of Trinity College, Cambridge. Having studied law, he was called to the bar in 1849, after which he devoted much time to pure mathematics. In 1852 he was chosen a Fellow of the Royal Society. Among his works is a treatise "On the Theory of Linear Transformations."

Cayley, (Sir GEORGE,) an English scientific writer, born about 1773. He wrote on aerial navigation, and other subjects. Died in 1857.

Caylus, de, deh kȧ′lüss′, (ANNE CLAUDE PHILIPPE de Tubières, (deh tü′be-aiR′,) de Grimoard, (gRe′moȧR′,) de Pestels, (pês′tĕl′,) de Lévi, (lȧ′ve′,) COUNT, Marquis of Esternay, (ês′tĕR′nȧ′,) a French author, born in Paris in 1692. He applied himself with success to the study of antiquities and fine arts, of which he was a liberal patron. In 1742 he was admitted into the Academy of Inscriptions, for which he wrote many valuable antiquarian treatises. Among his principal works are a "Collection of Egyptian, Etruscan, Greek, Roman, and Gallic Antiquities," (7 vols., 1752–67,) "Tableaux drawn from the Iliad, Odyssey, and Æneid," (1757,) and a "Collection of Ancient Paintings after the Designs of Bartoli," with beautiful coloured engravings. Some of his works are illustrated with fine plates engraved by himself. He wrote "Fairy Tales," and other works of fiction. Died in 1765.

See SERIEVS, "Souvenirs du Comte de Caylus," 1805 ; C. LE BEAU, "Éloge historique de M. le Comte de Caylus," 1766.

Caylus, de, (MARTHE MARGUERITE DE VILLETTE,) MARQUISE, an accomplished French lady, mother of the preceding, born in Poitou in 1673. She was educated at court as the protégée of her aunt, Madame de Maintenon, and in 1686 was married to the Marquis de Caylus, who died in 1704. She left a work, which was edited by Voltaire in 1770, entitled "Souvenirs de Madame de Caylus," in which she relates what she had witnessed, with great candour and *naïveté* and in an agreeable style. Died in 1729.

See SAINTE-BEUVE, "Causeries du Lundi ;" and a Notice prefixed to an edition of her "Souvenirs" by L. S. AUGER, 1803.

Cayot-Délandre, kȧ′yo′ dȧ′lôNdR′, (FRANÇOIS MARIE,) a French antiquary, born at Rennes in 1796. He wrote on French history and antiquities. Died in 1848.

Cayx, kȧ, (RÉMI JEAN BAPTISTE CHARLES,) a French historian, born at Cahors about 1795. He published a "History of France in the Middle Ages," (1835,) and an "Epitome of the History of Alexander's Successors,"

which were approved by the council of the university and used in colleges. About 1840 he was elected to the Chamber of Deputies, and in 1845 was appointed inspector-general of studies.

Cazal. See CASAL, (MANUEL AYRES.)

Cazalès, de, deh kȧ′zȧ′lês′, (EDMOND,) a French writer and ecclesiastic, son of Jacques Cazalès, noticed below, was born at Grenade-sur-Garonne in 1804. He became professor of history at Louvain in 1835, and a deputy to the National Assembly in 1848. He contributed articles on political history and literary criticism to the "Revue des Deux Mondes," and published "Historical Studies on Contemporary Germany," (1853.)

Cazalès, de, (JACQUES ANTOINE MARIE,) an eloquent French royalist, was born at Grenade-sur-Garonne in 1752. In 1789 he was deputed by the noblesse to the States-General, and soon became one of the ablest champions of monarchy. He had never made a public speech in his life until the chance which raised him upon the tribune disclosed to him that he was an orator. He refused to follow his order when it joined the Tiers-État in the National Assembly, but afterwards obeyed the command of that body to take part in its deliberations. His speech in defence of the clergy was one of his most brilliant efforts. "The character of his eloquence," says Lamartine, "was that of a desperate cause. He protested more than he debated ; he opposed to the violent triumphs of the Left (*gauche*) his ironical defiance, his bitter indignation." ("History of the Girondists.") He emigrated in 1792, travelled in Italy, England, etc., and returned to France in 1801. Died in 1805.

See M. CHARE, "Notice sur la Vie de Cazalès," prefixed to his speeches, 1821 ; THIERS, "History of the French Revolution ;" "Nouvelle Biographie Générale."

Cazalet, kȧ′zȧ′lȧ′, (JEAN ANDRÉ,) a French chemist, born in Médoc in 1750 ; died in 1821.

Caze, kȧz, (JEAN FRANÇOIS,) a French publicist, born at Montauban in 1781 ; died at Madrid in 1851.

Cazes, kȧz, (PIERRE JACQUES,) a French historical painter, born in Paris in 1676, was a pupil of Boullongne the elder. He was admitted into the Academy in 1704, and acquired a high reputation, though he did not attain the first rank. He adorned many of the churches of Paris with his works, among which are an "Adoration of the Magi," and "Tabitha raised from the Dead." His composition, design, and colouring are praised. Died in 1754.

See HEINECKEN, "Dictionnaire des Artistes."

Cazotte, kȧ′zot′, (JACQUES,) a French poet, born at Dijon in 1720. His principal works are "Ollivier," a poem, and the "Lord Impromptu," which were successful. His verses entitled "The English Brunette" were ascribed to Voltaire. As a royalist, he was executed by the terrorists in 1792.

See SAINTE-BEUVE, "Causeries du Lundi."

Cazweenee or **Cazwînî,** kâz-wee′nee, written also **Cazouyny, Cazwyny,** or **Caswini,** (ZACHARIA BEN MOHAM′MED,) an Arabian naturalist, born at Casbin, (or Cazwîn, whence he derived his name,) in Persia, is called "the Pliny of the Orientals." He wrote an important treatise entitled "The Wonders of Nature," designed to be a *résumé* or summing up of all the best previous works on natural science. This plan is executed in such a philosophic spirit that the work is preferred to the originals which treat of the same subjects. Died in 1283.

See HAJI-KHALFA, "Bibliographical Dictionary."

Cean-Bermudez, thă-ân′ bĕR-moo′Dĕth, (JUAN AUGUSTIN,) a Spanish writer on art, born at Gijon, in Asturias, in 1749. He became a resident of Madrid, and a student of architecture and design. Having devoted himself to the history of Spanish art, he published a "Dictionary of the most Eminent Professors of the Fine Arts in Spain," ("Diccionario Historico," etc., 6 vols., 1800,) a "Dialogue on the Art of Painting," "Notices of Spanish Architects and Architecture," (4 vols., 1829,) and other works. He founded an Academy of Painting at Seville. Died about 1830.

See SEBASTIAN DE MIÑANO, "Vie de Cean-Bermudez ;" TICKNOR, "History of Spanish Literature ;" "London Quarterly Review" for March, 1846.

Ceba, chā'bā, (ANSALDO,) an Italian writer, born at Genoa in 1565, published many mediocre works in prose and verse, and two popular tragedies, entitled "Alcippo" and "Gemelle Capuane." Died in 1623.

Çe'bēs, [Gr. Κέβης; Fr. CÉBÈS, så'bȧs',] sometimes written **Kebes,** a Greek philosopher, born at Thebes, was the disciple and friend of Socrates. He is introduced by Plato as one of the interlocutors in the "Phædon." He wrote several works, one of which is extant, namely, "Pinax," ("The Tablet," or "Picture,") a dialogue on human life, its trials, etc., and which has been often reprinted. Its spirit and style are said to be worthy of a disciple of Socrates.

See A. KNOLL, "Kebes des Thebaners Gemälde;" FLADE, "Ueber den Cebes."

Cecchi, chek'kee, (GIOVANNI MARIA,) an eminent Italian comic poet and lawyer, born at Florence in 1517. He wrote ten comedies, which were printed, and a multitude of dramas, (in manuscript.) Among his published plays are "Il Corredo," ("The Feast,") and "Il Donzello," ("The Bachelor.") Died in 1587. "This author," says Ginguené, "is worthy to be placed nearly in the same rank as Machiavel and Ariosto, for truth of character, vivacity of dialogue, and comic power."

See GINGUENÉ, "Histoire Littéraire d'Italie;" NEGRI, "Istoria degli Scrittori Fiorentini."

Cecchini, chĕk-kee'nee, (PIETRO MARIA,) an Italian comic author and actor, born at Ferrara, lived about 1620–50.

Cecco d'Ascoli, chek'ko dås'ko-lee, a learned Italian astrologer, originally named FRANCESCO STABILI, (stä'-be-lee,) was born at Ascoli. He taught astrology at Bologna, from which he removed to Florence in 1325. He wrote a Latin commentary on Sacrobosco's "Sphæra Mundi," and a poem called "Acerba," which passed through many editions. It treats of natural science, philosophy, astrology, etc. He was condemned as a heretic by the Inquisition, and was burnt alive in 1327.

See TIRABOSCHI, "Storia della Letteratura Italiana;" BERNINI, "Storie degli Eretici," 1707.

Cecil, sĕs'il or sĭs'il, (RICHARD,) an English clergyman, born in London in 1748, was ordained a priest in 1777. He became eminent as a preacher, and in 1780 accepted a call to Saint John's, in London. In 1800 he was presented to the livings of Chobham and Bisley, in Surrey. He wrote a "Life of the Rev. John Newton," one of "John Bacon the Sculptor," and a collection of sermons. Died in 1810.

Cecil, (ROBERT,) Earl of Salisbury, (saulz'ber-e,) an able English statesman, born about 1560, was the second son of Lord Burleigh, and first-cousin of Lord Bacon. He was appointed second secretary of state in 1596, after having been initiated in the mysteries of diplomacy and court intrigue. At the death of his father, in 1598, he succeeded him as prime minister. James I., who ascended the throne in 1603, retained Cecil as prime minister, and created him Viscount Cranborne in 1604, and Earl of Salisbury in 1605. In 1608 he succeeded Lord Dorset as lord treasurer of England. He was an adroit negotiator, and was regarded as one of the ablest statesmen of his time. His disposition is said to have been cold and selfish. He is censured for promoting the ruin of Raleigh and Essex, who were his rivals. He is charged with having received a pension from the Spanish government on the conclusion of the peace between England and Spain in 1604. He wrote the "State and Dignity of a Secretary of State." Died in 1612.

See MOTLEY, "History of the United Netherlands," vol. ii. chap. xviii. p. 359 et seq.; GARDNER, "History of England from 1603 to 1616," particularly chaps. ii. and x.

Cecil, (Lord ROBERT.) See CRANBORNE, LORD.

Cecil, (WILLIAM,) Baron Burleigh or Burghleigh, (bŭr'le,) an eminent English statesman, who was prime minister of England for about forty years, was born at Bourne, in Lincolnshire, in 1520. After graduating at Cambridge, he studied law at Gray's Inn, and married Mildred, daughter of Sir Anthony Cook, director of the king's studies. He was appointed master of requests in 1547, and secretary of state in 1548 by Lord-Protector Somerset. He refused to co-operate in the exclusion of Mary and Elizabeth from the throne, but signed as a

witness an instrument to that effect. On the accession of Mary in 1553 he retired from office and entered Parliament, where he opposed the measures of the court. When Elizabeth became queen, in 1558, she appointed Cecil secretary of state; and from that time until his death he was the principal director of the government. "Sir William Cecil," says Hume, "was the most vigilant, active, and prudent minister ever known in England; and, as he was governed by no views but the interests of his sovereign, his authority over her became every day more predominant." He was created Baron Burleigh in 1571, and lord treasurer in 1572. He died in 1598, leaving two sons, Thomas, Earl of Exeter, and Robert, Earl of Salisbury; also three hundred distinct landed estates. "Lord Burleigh," says Macaulay, "can hardly be called a great man. He was not one of those whose genius and energy change the fate of empires. Nothing that is recorded either of his words or actions indicates intellectual or moral elevation. But his talents, though not brilliant, were of an eminently useful kind. He had a cool temper, a sound judgment, great powers of application, and a constant eye to the main chance. He never deserted his friends until it was very inconvenient to stand by them, and was an excellent Protestant when it was not very advantageous to be a papist." In sagacity and foresight he seems to have been far inferior to Walsingham and other statesmen of that age. Lord Burleigh left numerous state papers, letters, etc., many of which have been published.

See MOTLEY, "History of the United Netherlands," especially chaps. vi., viii., and xviii.; FROUDE, "History of England," vol. v. chap. xxv.; ARTHUR COLLINS, "Life of William Cecil," 1732; EDWARD NARES, "Memoirs of the Life, etc. of W. Cecil," 3 vols., 1828–32; also HUME, "History of England."

Cécile. See CECILIA.

Ce-çil'ī-a, [Fr. CÉCILE, så'sèl',] SAINT, is supposed to have been a Roman virgin who suffered martyrdom in the second or third century. Fortunatus of Poitiers, the most ancient author that speaks of her, states that she died in Sicily about 180 A.D. She is regarded as the patroness of musicians, and is the subject of celebrated paintings by Raphael and Domenichino.

See BAILLET, "Vies des Saints;" MRS. JAMESON, "Sacred and Legendary Art."

Cecilianus. See DONATUS, BISHOP.

Cécilius. See CÆCILIUS.

Cécille, så'sèl', (JEAN BAPTISTE THOMAS MÉDÉE,) a French vice-admiral, born at Rouen in 1787. He was raised to the rank of senator in 1852.

Cécina. See CÆCINA.

Çe'crops or **Ke'krops,** [Gr. Κέκρωψ; Fr. CÉCROPS, så'krops',] a hero of the Pelasgian race, who, according to ancient legends, was the first king and legislator of Attica. He was regarded as the author of the earliest civilized customs and institutions of the Athenians, whom he instructed in marriage, agriculture, navigation, and the worship of Jupiter. The people of Attica were sometimes called Cecrop'idæ.

See THIRLWALL'S "History of Greece."

Cédmon. See CÆDMON.

Ce-dre'nus, (GEORGIUS,) [Γεώργιος ὁ Κεδρηνός,] a Greek monk, supposed to have been the author or compiler of a chronicle from the creation to 1057 A.D., entitled Σύνοψις ἱστορίων, "A Synopsis of History." It is written without judgment and in a barbarous style.

Cei, chā'ee, (FRANCESCO,) an Italian poet, was born at Florence. His contemporaries ranked him with Petrarch, but his fame has since declined. He wrote sonnets, canzone, etc. He died in or after 1523.

Ceillier, så'ye-ȧ', (RÉMI,) a French Benedictine monk, born at Bar-le-Duc in 1688. He became titular prior of Flavigny, and wrote a "History of Sacred and Ecclesiastic Authors," (23 vols., 1729–63,) which is esteemed for accuracy, and is more complete than that of Dupin. Died in 1761.

See QUÉRARD, "La France Littéraire."

Celakowsky, chä-lä-kov'skee, (FRANTISEK LADIS-LAW,) a Bohemian poet and philologist, born at Strakonice, or Strakonitz, in 1799. He became an enthusiastic student of the Slavonic languages, and in 1822 began to publish a collection of Slavonic national songs. A few years later he was professor of Bohemian literature in the University of Prague. About 1832 he was deprived of this place for having censured the Czar Nicholas in one of his writings. He translated some Russian national songs, and published popular original poems, one of which is "The Hundred-Leaved Rose." From 1842 to 1848 he was professor at Breslau. He died at Prague in 1852.

Ce′ler, a Roman architect of the first century, employed by Nero. Celer and Severus were the architects of the famous palace called the Golden House, built by order of Nero on Mounts Palatine and Esquiline. Its site was afterwards occupied by the Coliseum.

Céleste, så′låst′, or **Céleste-Elliot,** (MADAME,) a famous *danseuse* and actress, born in Paris about 1814. At the age of fifteen she made a successful *début* in the United States, where she was married to Mr. Elliot. She next visited England, and performed in London with applause. Since 1837 she has lived in London, and has taken a part in the dramas at Drury Lane and other theatres.

Celesti, chå-lês′tee, (ANDREA,) CAVALIERE, an eminent painter, born at Venice in 1637. He painted history, landscapes, and genre, (at Venice,) and excelled in richness of colouring and in design. Among his works are "The Pool of Bethesda," and an "Adoration of the Magi." His landscapes are highly prized. Died in 1706.

See LANZI, "History of Painting in Italy."

Célestin. See CELESTINE.

Cel′es-tīne or **Cel-es-tī′nus,** [Fr. CÉLESTIN, så′lês′-tåN′; It. CELESTINO, chå-lês-tee′no,] a Roman by birth, was chosen pope in 422 A.D. as successor to Boniface I. By his influence a council was called at Ephesus, and Nestorius was there deposed. He died in 432, and was succeeded by Sixtus III.

Celestine II., POPE, was originally called GUIDO DI CASTELLO, from his birthplace, Città di Castello, in Tuscany. He succeeded Innocent II. in September, 1143, and died in March, 1144.

Celestine III., (GIACINTO **Orsini**—or-see′nee,) successor of Clement III., was elected pope in 1191, at the age of eighty-five. He crowned the emperor Henry VI., stimulated the princes of Europe to join the crusade, and excommunicated Leopold, Duke of Austria, for detaining in prison Richard Cœur de Lion. Died in 1198.

Celestine IV., a native of Milan, was elected as successor to Gregory IX. in September, 1241, but died about three weeks later, before he had been crowned. His original name was GOFFREDO CASTIGLIONE, (gof-frå′do kås-têl-yo′nå.)

See ARTAUD DE MONTOR, "Histoire des souverains Pontifes."

Celestine V. (PIETRO **da Murrone** (då moor-ro′nå) or **Morone**) was born in Apulia in 1215. After the death of Nicholas IV. the cardinals failed to unite on a successor for twenty-seven months. In 1294 they chose an ignorant monk or hermit, who took the name of Celestine. A few months after his election, he abdicated his office, which was too heavy a burden for him. He was succeeded by Boniface VIII., who confined him in prison until he died, in 1296.

See V. SPINELLI, "Vita del S. Pietro del Morone Papa," 1664; L. MARINO, "Vita di S. Celestino V.," 1637.

Celestino or **Celestinus.** See CELESTINE.

Ce-les′tĭ-us, written also **Cœlestius** or **Cælestius,** a friend and coadjutor of Pelagius. He went from Rome to Carthage in 409 A.D., soon after which he was condemned by the Council of Carthage for denying the dogma of original sin, and other doctrines. He appealed to the pope, Zosimus, who at first recognized that his confession of faith was Catholic, but afterwards concurred with the Council of Carthage. He found a protector in Nestorius, at Constantinople, and presented himself at the Council of Ephesus in 430 A.D., but was not received. (See PELAGIUS.)

Celio Magno, chã′le-o mân′yo, an eminent Italian lyric poet, who flourished about 1600.

Célius. See CÆLIUS.

Cellamare, chêl-lå-må′rå, (ANTONIO GIUDICE,) Duke of Giovenazzo, (jo-vå-nåt′so,) Prince of Cellamare, a distinguished politician, born in Naples in 1657. In the war of the Spanish succession, which began in 1701, he fought for Philip V., and in 1712 was made a cabinet

minister. He was sent in 1715 as ambassador to France, where he was the master-spirit of a conspiracy against the regent Orléans. Having been detected, he was sent home in 1718, and became captain-general of Old Castile. Died in 1733.

See SAINT-SIMON, "Mémoires;" VATOUT, "La Conspiration de Cellamare, épisode de la Régence," 1832.

Cellarius, sêl-lå′re-ús, (ANDREAS,) a German geographer and mathematician, originally named KELLER, (kel′ler,) became rector of the College of Horn. He published "Military Architecture," (1656,) and a "Description of Poland," (1659.)

Cellarius, (CHRISTOPH,) an eminent German philologist and author, whose proper name was KELLER, (kel′ler,) born at Schmalkalden in 1638, was appointed rector of the College of Weimar in 1673, and professor of eloquence and history in the University of Halle in 1693. He published good editions of many Latin classics, and several original works. His "Antibarbarus Latinus," on the Latinity of the middle ages and subsequent period, appeared in 1695. His most celebrated work is "Ancient Geography," ("Notitia Orbis Antiqui," 1701,) which was more complete and extensive than any previous work on that subject. "The merit of this work," says Walckenaer, "does not respond to its celebrity." Died at Halle in 1707.

See AUGUST HERMANN FRANCKE, "Leichenpredigt auf C. Cellarium, nebst dessen Lebenslauf," 1708.

Cellarius, (JOHANN,) a German Protestant scholar, born at Kundstadt in 1496, was professor of Hebrew at Louvain, Tübingen, and Wittenberg. He became eminent as a preacher at Leipsic, and wrote several works on theology. Died at Dresden in 1542.

See JÖCHER, "Allgemeines Gelehrten-Lexikon."

Cellini, chêl-lee′nee, (BENVENUTO,) a celebrated Italian artist, born at Florence in 1500. He learned music in obedience to his father's will; but he preferred the arts of gold-worker, engraver, and sculptor, in which he excelled. Having wounded a man in a quarrel, he fled from Florence to Rome, and fought in defence of that city in 1527, when it was stormed by Constable Bourbon, whom he boasted of having killed on that occasion. He was employed by Pope Clement VII. as engraver to the mint, and he engraved medals with great success. He afterwards worked in Paris for Francis I., and in Florence for Cosimo de' Medici. Among his master-pieces is a bronze group of "Perseus and Medusa." He died at Florence in 1570, leaving an entertaining and curious autobiography, ("Vita di B. Cellini," 1720,) which was translated into German by Goethe, (1811,) into French by Farjasse, (1833,) and into English by Roscoe, (1822.)

See, also, B. GAMBA, "Raccordi di B. Cellini," 1831; ERSCH und GRUBER, "Allgemeine Encyklopaedie."

Celnart, sêl′når′, (ÉLISABETH FÉLICIE,) a French writer of educational works, born at Moulins in 1796.

Cels, sêl, (JACQUES MARTIN,) a French botanist, born at Versailles in 1743. He formed a fine botanic garden near Paris, which furnished Ventenat the subject of his book entitled "Jardin de Cels." He was a member of the Institute, had a large part in the preparation of the rural code, and published "Instructions" on agriculture. Died in 1806.

See SILVESTRE, "Notice sur Cels," 1806.

Celse. See CELSUS.

Celsius, sêl′se-us or sêl′she-us, (ANDERS,) a Swedish astronomer, a grandson of Magnus, noticed below, was born at Upsal in 1701. He was chosen professor of astronomy at Upsal in 1730. In 1736 he was selected by the French government to assist Maupertuis and others in the measurement of the length of a degree in Lapland. He afterwards erected an observatory at Upsal, where he extended his reputation by his observations and by his writings on astronomy. He was a Fellow of the Royal Society of London, and a member of other learned societies or institutions. Died in 1744.

See HOEPKEN, "Åminnelse-Tal öfver A. Celsius," 1745.

Celsius, (MAGNUS NILS,) a Swedish savant, born in Helsingland in 1621. He became professor of mathematics in Upsal, and wrote a treatise on Fish, and another on the Plants of Upsal. Died in 1679.

Celsius, (OLAUS,) a Swedish botanist and divine, born at Upsal in 1670, was the son of the preceding, and the father or uncle of Andrew, above noticed. He became professor of theology and Oriental languages in Upsal, and gained distinction by his researches to identify plants mentioned in the Bible. His capital work, "Sacred Botany," ("Hierobotanicon," 1745,) contains the results of those labours, and displays great erudition. He is regarded as the founder of natural history in Sweden, and had the honour of directing the early studies of Linnæus, whom he received into his family. He published a "Flora of Upsal," and several works on theology, antiquities, etc. Died in 1756.

See A. BAECK, "Åminnelse-Tal öfver O. Celsius," 1758.

Celso. See CELSUS.

Cel'sus, [Fr. CELSE, sĕls; It. CELSO, chĕl'so,] an Epicurean philosopher, who lived in the second century, in the reign of the Antonines, and was probably a Roman. He was a friend of Lucian. He is supposed to be the author of the attack on Christianity called "Λόγος ἀληθής," (a "True Discourse,") which was ably confuted by Origen, and which has not come down to us. Some have regretted that the early Christians in their zeal destroyed the work of Celsus, which might now be used to refute some arguments of infidels. He is said to have been the first pagan author that wrote against the Christian religion, and to have used the weapons of sophistry and irony with formidable power.

See ORIGEN, "Adversus Celsum;" NEANDER, "Geschichte der Christliche Kirche."

Celsus, (AURELIUS CORNELIUS,) a celebrated Latin writer on medicine, of whose history little is known. It is supposed that he lived in Rome in the reigns of Augustus and Tiberius. Of numerous works which he wrote on rhetoric, agriculture, medicine, etc., only one has been preserved,—namely, his excellent treatise "De Medicina," in eight books. His style is elegant, concise, clear, and equal in purity to that of the classic authors of the Augustan age. He adopts mostly the doctrines of Hippocrates and Asclepiades, (of Bithynia,) and treats impartially the prevailing sects of his time, the Empirics, Methodists, and Dogmatics. His treatise has been much used as a text-book in modern times. Fifteen editions were issued in the sixteenth century.

See C. KISSEL, "Celsus, eine historische Monographie," 1844; M. W. SCHILLING, "Quæstio A. C. Celsi Vita," 1824; F. VALORI, "Dissertatio de A. C. Celso," 1835; HALLER, "Bibliotheca Medica Practica."

Celsus, (MINOS,) [It. MINIO CELSI, mee'ne-o chel'see,] a learned Italian Protestant, was born at Sienna about 1500. He resided at Bâle as corrector of the press, and published a Latin treatise against the capital punishment of heresy, (1577.)

Celsus, (P. JUVENTIUS,) a Roman jurist of the second century, was the son of Juventius Celsus, who was also a jurist, mentioned by Ulpian. Celsus the Younger was a favourite of Nerva and of Trajan, and was consul the second time in 129 A.D. He wrote a work entitled "Digesta," fragments of which are preserved in the compilation of Justinian.

Celsus, (P. MARIUS,) a Roman general, who became consul in 62 A.D. In the year 68 he obtained command of an army under Galba, after whose death he gained the favour of Otho, whom he served with fidelity in the war against Vitellius. He was one of the generals defeated by Cæcina and Valens at Bedriacum in 69 A.D.

Cel'sus Al-bin-o-vā'nus, a Roman poet, was a friend of Horace, who addressed to him one of his Epistles.

Celtes, tsĕl'tĕs, (CONRAD,) a German poet and scholar, surnamed PROTUCIUS, (pro-tōōt'se-ús,) was born at Wipfeld in 1459. His family name was MEISSEL, (mīs'sĕl.) He received the title of imperial poet, or poet-laureate, about 1487. He was afterwards professor of eloquence in Vienna. He wrote the "Art of Making Verses," ("Ars Versificandi,") a volume of Odes, a poem on the customs of Germany, ("De Situ et Moribus Germaniæ,") and other works. Died in 1508.

See VOSSIUS, "De Historicis Latinis;" MELCHIOR ADAM, "Vitæ Eruditorum;" P. EKERMAN, "Dissertatio de C. Celte ejusque Sodalitate literaria," 1763; KLUEPFEL, "Programmata II. de Vita et Scriptis C. Celtis Protucii," 1827.

Cenci, chĕn'chee, (BEATRICE,) a Roman lady of patrician birth, famous for her beauty and tragical fate. Her father was an infamous person, who treated his family with such cruelty that several of them conspired and caused him to be assassinated. She was executed for that crime at Rome in 1599. Her story has been dramatized by Shelley.

See MURATORI, "Annales;" "Vita de B. Cenci tratta dal Manoscritto antico," Rome, 1849.

Cennini, chĕn-nee'nee, (BERNARDO,) a Florentine goldsmith, is reputed to have been the first who introduced the art of printing into Florence. A "Commentary of Servius on Virgil" (1471) is the only extant work printed by him.

See F. FANTOZZI, "Memorie biografiche di B. Cennini," 1839.

Cennini, (CENNINO,) an old Italian painter, born at Colle, in Tuscany, about 1360. He wrote an esteemed "Treatise on Painting," first printed in Rome in 1821. He was living in 1437.

Cen-so-rī'nus, a Latin grammarian, who lived in the reigns of Alexander Severus and Gordian, and wrote, about 238 A.D., a small work, entitled "On the Natal Day," ("De Die natali,") which is useful in chronology. It displays learning and good judgment.

Censorinus, (APPIUS CLAUDIUS,) was chosen by the army Emperor of Rome in 269 A.D., after having been twice consul. He was killed by his mutinous soldiers a few days after his elevation.

Censorinus, (C. MARCIUS,) a Roman general, was a partisan of Marius in the civil war. He killed the consul Octavius in 87 B.C., and commanded an army which was defeated by Pompey in the year 82, soon after which he was taken prisoner and killed.

Cen-tau'rī, [Eng. CEN'TAURS; Fr. CENTAURES, sŏn'tŏr'; Gr. Κένταυροι, supposed to be derived from κεντέω, to "pierce" or "goad," and ταῦρος, a "bull," in allusion, perhaps, to their driving off the cattle of the neighbouring districts,] a fabulous race of animals, half men and half horses, said to have been the offspring of Ixi'on and a cloud, (see IXION,) and to have lived in Thessaly. The battle of the Centaurs and the Lapithæ was a favourite subject with the ancient Greek artists. In the "Iliad" the Centaurs are called θῆρες, i.e. θῆρες, or "wild beasts:" the idea of their compound nature—of their being half men and half horse—was the invention of a later age. It has been conjectured that the fable of the Centaurs originated among a people who had never seen men on horseback, and who mistook the horse and rider for one animal. (See Palæphatus, "De Incredibilibus.")

Centenera, thĕn-tà-nā'rå, (MARTIN DEL BARCO,) a mediocre Spanish poet, born in Old Castile. He took part in a military expedition to South America in 1573, and wrote a description of the same in Spanish verse.

See TICKNOR, "History of Spanish Literature."

Centeno, thĕn-tā'no, (DIEGO,) a Spanish officer, born in Castile in 1505, obtained command of an army in Peru, and was defeated at Guarina (or Huarina) by Gonzalo in 1547. Died in 1549.

Centlivre, sent-liv'er or sent-lee'ver, (SUSANNA,) an English dramatic writer, born about 1675, was the daughter of Mr. Freeman, of Lincolnshire. She was thrice married, and her third husband was J. Centlivre, chief cook to Queen Anne. She wrote numerous successful comedies, among which were "The Busybody," "The Wonder," "A Bold Stroke for a Wife," also "The Perjured Husband," a tragedy. She was noted for wit and beauty. Died about 1723.

See CIBBER, "Lives of the Poets;" BAKER, "Biographia Dramatica;" "Memoirs of Eminent Englishwomen," by LOUISA S. COSTELLO, 1844.

Centofanti, chĕn-to-fän'tee, (SILVESTRO,) an Italian professor and writer, born at Calci, near Pisa. He published a poem "On Perfect Sovereignty," (1814,) in honour of Ferdinand III., "Œdipus," a tragedy, (1830,) "Stanzas on Dante," and other minor works. He acquired a high reputation as professor of history and philosophy in the University of Pisa from 1842 to 1848, and in the latter year was deprived of the chair on account of his liberal political principles.

Centorio degli Ortensi, chĕn-to're-o dàl'yee or-tĕn'see, (ASCAGNO,) an Italian writer, born at Rome,

ā, ē, ī, ō, ū, ȳ, long; à, è, ò, same, less prolonged; ă, ĕ, ĭ, ŏ, ŭ, ў, short; a, ę, į, ǫ, obscure; fär, fàll, fàt; mêt; nŏt; gōōd; mōōn;

served in the army many years with honour. He wrote a volume of verses, ("Amorose Rime,") and two esteemed works, entitled "Memoirs of the War of Transylvania," (1565,) and "Memoirs of the Affairs of Europe," (1569.)

See GINGUENÉ, "Histoire Littéraire d'Italie."

Ceo, do, do sā'o, [Fr. DU CIEL, dü se-êl',] (VIOLANTE,) a Portuguese poetess, born at Lisbon in 1601, was called "the Tenth Muse." She produced the "Portuguese Parnassus of Divine and Human Poetry," (" Parnaso Lusitaneo de divinos et humanos Versos,") and other admired poems. At the age of sixteen she entered a convent. Died in 1693.

See BOWRING, "Ancient Poetry and Romances of Spain ;" LONGFELLOW, "Poets and Poetry of Europe."

Ceolfrid, chol'frid, (?) or **Ceolfirth,** an Anglo-Saxon writer, born in Northumbria about 642 A.D.; died in 716.

Céphale. See CEPHALUS.

Ce-phā'lĭ-on or **Ceph-a-læ'on,** [Κεφαλίων or Κεφαλαίων,] a Greek historian, supposed to have lived in the second century. He wrote an epitome of general history from the time of Ninus to that of Alexander the Great.

Ceph'a-lus, [Gr. Κέφαλος; Fr. CÉPHALE, sȧ'fȧl',] a personage of the Greek mythology, was the husband of Procris. Incited by jealousy, she watched him when he was hunting, and he killed her by accident.

Cephalus, [Κέφαλος,] an eminent Athenian orator, who flourished about 400 B.C. and contributed largely to the overthrow of the Thirty Tyrants. According to some, he was the father of Lysias the orator.

Céphisodore. See CEPHISODORUS.

Ce-phis-o-do'rus, [Gr. Κηφισόδωρος; Fr. CÉPHISODORE, sȧ'fe'zo'doR',] an eminent Athenian orator, was a disciple of Isocrates, for whom he wrote an apology against Aristotle. He was perhaps the same with Cephisodorus, author of a "History of the Sacred War."

Cephisodorus, a celebrated Greek painter, mentioned by Pliny, is supposed to have lived about 420 B.C.

Céphisodote. See CEPHISODOTUS.

Ceph-ĭ-sod'o-tus, [Gr. Κηφισόδοτος; Fr. CÉPHISODOTE, sȧ'fe'zo'dot',] a celebrated Athenian sculptor, who flourished about 370 B.C. His sister was the wife of Phocion. Pliny speaks with admiration of his works, among which was a group of the nine Muses. His style was more graceful and less majestic than that of Phidias.

Cephisodotus, an Athenian general, whose talent for oratory is praised by Demosthenes. He was sent to negotiate a peace with Sparta about 370 B.C.

Cephisodotus THE YOUNGER, an excellent sculptor of Athens, son of the famous Praxiteles, lived about 300 B.C. In his youth he worked with his brother Timarchus in Athens and Thebes. His statues of Latona, Diana, and Venus were among his master-pieces. He was also distinguished in portrait-sculpture. His works are all lost ; but some critics consider the group of two wrestling youths at Florence an imitation of his "Symplegma."

See WINCKELMANN, "Geschichte der Kunst."

Ce-phis'o-phon, [Κηφισοφῶν,] a Greek actor, was a friend of Euripides, in whose dramas he performed important *rôles.* He is said to have aided Euripides in the composition of his works.

Ce'pĭ-o, [Fr. CÉPION, sȧ'pe'òN',] (QUINTUS SERVILIUS,) a Roman general, defeated by the Cimbri, 105 B.C.

Ceracchi, chä-räk'kee, (GIUSEPPE,) an Italian sculptor, born about 1760. When Bonaparte invaded Italy in 1796, he made a statue of the French general. In 1800, having formed, with Arena and others, a design to assassinate the First Consul, he proposed to make another statue ; but the plot was detected, and the conspirators were executed, in 1802.

See MONTANARI, "Elogio storico della Vita di G. Ceracchi," 1841.

Cerano. See CRESPI, (GIOVANNI BATTISTA.)

Cerasola. See CERESOLA.

Ceratinus, sȧ-rȧ-tee'nŭs, (JACOB,) a Dutch scholar and Hellenist, born at Hoorn, was professor of Greek at Tournay and Louvain, and wrote, besides other works, a "Lexicon Græco-Latinum," (1524.) Died in 1530.

Çer'ber-us, [Gr. Κέρβερος; Fr. CERBÈRE, sêR'baiR'; It. CERBERO, chêR'bȧ-ro,] the name of the triple-headed dog which guarded the entrance to Hades. (See PLUTO.)

Cerceau. See ANDROUET.

Cerceau, du, dü sêR'so', (JEAN ANTOINE,) a French poet and Jesuit, born in Paris in 1670. He produced successful dramas, among which were the "Prodigal Son," and the "Inconveniences of Greatness." He increased his reputation by epistles, fables, tales, and various poems. "These poems," says Voltaire, "are of a mediocre quality." His "Conspiracy of Rienzi" (in prose) is commended. He was killed by the accidental discharge of a gun in 1730.

See QUÉRARD, "La France Littéraire."

Cerda, de la, dà lä sêR'dä, (Dona BERNARDA Ferreira—fêr-rā'e-rä,) a Portuguese poetess, born at Oporto, was learned in languages, philosophy, etc., and music. Philip III. of Spain employed her to teach Latin to the princes Charles and Ferdinand. She wrote "Spain liberated," (" España libertada,") and other poems. Died about 1644.

See N. ANTONIO, "Bibliotheca Hispana Nova."

Cerda, de la, dà lä thêR'dä, (JUAN LUIS,) an eminent Spanish critic and Jesuit, born at Toledo about 1560, became professor of theology, logic, and eloquence at Toledo. He wrote a voluminous and learned commentary on Virgil, which has many defects. Among his best works is "Sacred Note-Books," ("Adversaria Sacra," 1626,) in which he explains many passages of Scripture. Died at Madrid in 1643.

See N. ANTONIO, "Bibliotheca Hispana Nova."

Cerda y Rico, thêR'dä e ree'ko, (Don FRANCISCO,) a Spanish scholar, born about 1730. He rendered a service to Spanish literature by making good editions of Lope de Vega, and other old authors. He was one of the principal compilers of the "Cronicas de Castilla." Died in 1792.

See TICKNOR, "History of Spanish Literature."

Cer'dic, a Saxon chief, invaded Britain, and, after gaining several victories over the natives, founded the kingdom of Wessex about 519 A.D. Died about 534.

Cer'don or **Cer'do,** [Gr. Κέρδων,] a heresiarch or dissenter of the second century, the master of Marcion, was a native of Syria. He is said to have rejected the Old Testament, and to have held other doctrines of the Marcionites. Saint Augustine regarded him as the precursor of the Manichæans.

Céré, sȧ'rȧ', (JEAN NICOLAS,) a meritorious French naturalist, born in the Ile de France in 1737, finished his studies in Paris. In 1775 he was chosen director of the royal botanic garden in his native isle, where he propagated the clove-, cinnamon-, and nutmeg-trees with success. He also widely extended the cultivation of these spices in other islands, and wrote scientific treatises which he sent to Buffon and others. Napoleon confirmed him in his office by a decree dated at Austerlitz, 1805. Died in 1810.

See JEAN COUDRAY, "Notice sur ᴍ. J. N. Céré," 1819.

Ce-re-ā'lis or **Ce-rĭ-ā'lis,** (PETILIUS,) a Roman general, a near relative of Vespasian, became a general in the army of that emperor in 69 A.D. In the year 70 he commanded the army sent against Civilis, the renowned chief of the Batavi, who were aided by the Germans. Cerealis defeated Civilis on the Moselle, and in another battle near Cologne, and soon suppressed the revolt. In 71 A.D. he was appointed governor or consular legate of Britain, where he gained several victories over the natives.

See TACITUS, "History."

Ce'rēs, [Fr. CÉRÈS, sȧ'rêss' or sȧ'rȧs',] the Roman name of the goddess of agriculture, and especially of corn or breadstuffs, was the reputed daughter of Cronos (Saturn) and Rhea. The Greeks called her Deme'ter, (Δημήτηρ.) She was the mother of Proserpine, (and, according to some authorities, of Dionysus.) The most remarkable of the myth of Ceres is the rape of her daughter by Pluto. (See PROSERPINE.)

See STOCKMANN, "Dissertatio de Cerere legifera," 1782; GUIGNIAUT, "Religions de l'Antiquité," Paris, 1825-29, vol. ii. book v. chap. ii.; KEIGHTLEY, "Mythology."

Ceresola, chä-rä-ṡo'lä, or **Cerasola,** chä-rä-ṡo'lä, (DOMENICO,) an Italian versifier, born at Bergamo in 1683, imitated with facility the style of Petrarch, and had an excellent talent for improvisation. Died in 1746.

є as *k;* ç as *s;* g̃ *hard;* ġ as *j;* G, H, K, *guttural;* N, *nasal;* R, *trilled;* ŝ as *z;* ᵺh as in *this.* (☞See Explanations, p. 23.)

Cerezo, thả-rā'tho, (MATEO,) a skilful Spanish painter, born at Burgos in 1635, was a pupil of Juan Carreño de Miranda, whom he imitated and perhaps equalled. He worked at Madrid, excelled in colour and design, and was distinguished for his facility. Among his master-pieces are a "Visitation of Saint Elizabeth," and the "Miracle at Emmaus." Died in 1685.

See QUILLIET, "Dictionnaire des Peintres Espagnols.'

Cerialis. See CEREALIS.

Cerini, chả-ree'nee, or **Cerrini,** chêr-ree'nee, (GIO-VANNI DOMENICO,) sometimes called IL CAVALIERE PERUGINO, (èl kả-vả-le-ā'rả pả-roo-jee'no,) an Italian painter, born at Perugia in 1606, was a pupil of Guido and Domenichino. Died in 1681.

Cerini, (GIUSEPPE,) an Italian poet and lawyer, born at Solferino in 1738. He became a resident of Milan, where in 1772 he produced "Clary," a drama, which was acted with brilliant success. His reputation was widely extended by a volume of lyric verses, displaying a gay and genial imagination. Died in 1779.

Cérinthe. See CERINTHUS.

Çe-rin'thus, [Gr. Κήρινθος; Fr. CÉRINTHE, sả'rånt',] a distinguished heretic of the first century, the founder of a sect called Cerinthians, lived mostly in Asia Minor or Syria. But little is known of his history. He taught that the world was created by angels, and that the presiding spirit among them was so inferior to the Supreme Being as to be ignorant of his character; that Jesus was the son of Joseph and Mary by ordinary generation, and selected to be the Messiah on account of his wisdom and piety; that the righteous would arise from the grave to inherit an earthly paradise or millennium. Irenæus considers him a thorough Gnostic, and states that Saint John wrote his Gospel for the purpose of counteracting the errors of Cerinthus.

See NEANDER, "History of the Church;" LARDNER, "History of Heretics;" PAULUS, "Historia Cerinthi," 1799; MATTER, "Histoire du Gnosticisme," 2d edition, 1838.

Cérisantes, sả're'zÒNt', (MARC DUNCAN,) a French officer and Latin poet, born at Saumur about 1600, was a son of Mark Duncan, a Scottish physician, noticed in this work. Having gained distinction by his Latin poems, he went to seek his fortune at the court of Sweden, and about 1642 was sent by Oxenstiern as envoy to the court of France. He was soon recalled for sending a challenge to the Duke of Candale. He fought for the Neapolitan insurgents under the Duke of Guise, and was killed in battle at Naples in 1648. His poetry is highly praised by the poet Rapin, who says, "his odes combine elevation and purity of style," ("il a joint dans ses odes élévation et pureté.")

See SISMONDI, "Histoire des Français."

Cerisier, seh-re'ze-À', (ANTOINE MARIE,) a French historian, who was born at Châtillon-les-Dombes in 1749. He was secretary of legation at the Hague, and afterwards published a "History of the United Provinces," (1778,) which is said to be the best French work on that subject. About 1790 he began to issue in Paris the "Gazette Universelle," of which he and Michaud were the editors. He was imprisoned in the reign of terror, and released on the 9th Thermidor, 1794. He wrote several political works, one of which was "The Destiny of America," (1782.) Died in 1828.

See QUÉRARD, "La France Littéraire."

Cerisiers, de, dẹh seh-re'ze-À', (RENÉ,) a French writer and Jesuit, born at Nantes about 1695, became almoner to Louis XIV. He wrote numerous historical and religious works, and a kind of spiritual romance, called "The Life of Saint Genevieve of Brabant," (1640.) Died about 1662.

Cérisy. See HABERT.

Cerito, chả-ree'to, (FRANCESCA,) a celebrated Italian opera-dancer, born at Naples in 1823.

Cermenati, de, dả chêr-mả-nả'tee, (GIOVANNI,) an Italian, who lived about 1310, and wrote a "History of Milan."

Cernitori, chêR-ne-to'ree, (GIUSEPPE,) an Italian bibliographer, born at Rome in 1746; died in 1816.

Ceroni, chả-ro'nee, (GIUSEPPE,) an Italian poet, born at Verona in 1773, wrote a poem "On the Capture of Tarragona," (1811.) Died in 1814.

Cerquozzi, chêR-kwot'see, (MICHELANGELO,) an Italian painter and engraver, born in Rome in 1602, was called MICHELANGELO DELLE BATTAGLIE, (" of battles.") He excelled in battle-pieces and in the familiar scenes called *bambochades.* He is said to have surpassed Laer in figures, and left some etchings, which are highly prized. Died at Rome in 1660.

See LANZI, "History of Painting in Italy."

Cerrato, chêr-rā'to, [Lat. CERRA'TUS,] (PAOLO,) a Latin poet, born in Montferrat, Italy, is said to equal Vida in majesty of style and purity of language. His poem "On Virginity" ("De Virginitate") is one of his principal works. Died about 1538.

Cerretti, chêr-ret'tee, or **Ceretti,** chả-ret'tee, (LUIGI,) a popular Italian poet, born at Módena in 1738, became professor of history and eloquence in his native city, where he lectured with brilliant success. He favoured the Cisalpine republic in 1796, and went to France in 1799. In 1804 he obtained the chair of eloquence in the University of Pavia. He wrote admired odes, epigrams, and satires, among which is an ode to Posterity, ("Alla Posterità.") Died in 1808.

See TIPALDO, " Biografia degli Italiani illustri;" FATTORI, "Elogio storico di L. Cerretti," 1808.

Cerrini. See CERINI, (GIOVANNI DOMENICO.)

Certon, sêr'tÒN', (SALOMON,) a French poet, born at Gien about 1550, became royal secretary. He produced in 1604 a poetical version of the "Odyssey" of Homer, which was favourably received. The Abbé Terrasson published a revised edition of it, with a version of the "Iliad," in 1615. Certon is supposed to have originated the verses called "lipograms," in which a certain letter of the alphabet is omitted by design. Died about 1610.

Ceruti, chả-roo'tee, (FREDERICO,) an Italian scholar and critic, born at Verona in 1541; died in 1579.

Cerutti, chả-root'tee, (GIUSEPPE ANTONIO GIOA-CHIMO,) an ingenious writer and Jesuit, born at Turin in 1738. He resided mostly in France, and wrote in French. About 1761 he wrote an anonymous essay on ancient and modern republics, which was ascribed to Rousseau, and an "Apology for the Order of the Jesuits," which attracted much notice. He was in Paris in 1789, and, having warmly espoused the popular cause, he was chosen a member of the Assembly in 1791. He was intimate with Mirabeau, whom he assisted in his political labours. He wrote "The Gardens of Betz," and other mediocre poems, and many prose works. Died in 1792.

See CUBIÈRES DE PALMEZEAUX, "Coup-d'œil rapide sur J. A. J. Cerutti," 1792; QUÉRARD, "La France Littéraire."

Cervantes, sẹr-van'tẽs, [Sp. pron. thêR-vȧn'tẽs,] or, more fully, **Cervantes Saavedra, de,** dả thêR-vȧn'tẽs sȧ-vȧ'DRȦ, (MIGUEL,) the celebrated author of "Don Quixote," was born at Alcalá de Henares, in Spain, on the 9th of October, 1547. He studied in the Universities of Salamanca and Madrid, and cultivated poetry in his youth without much success. About 1570 he entered as a volunteer the papal army under Marcantonio Colonna, and in 1571 he signalized his courage at the famous battle of Lepanto, where he was wounded. In 1575 he was taken by an Algerine corsair and carried as a slave to Algiers. After risking his life in gallant efforts to liberate his fellow-captives, and after terrible sufferings, he was ransomed in 1580 for five hundred ducats, and returned to Madrid. In 1584 he published "Galatea," a pastoral romance of some merit. The same year he married Catalina de Palacios Salazar y Vozmediano. He wrote numerous dramas, which, he informs us, were performed with success; but neither these nor his other earlier works sufficed to relieve him from poverty. At length, in 1605, he published the first part of the inimitable "Don Quixote de la Mancha," which soon became immensely popular, and ran through four editions in the first year. From this time he continued to reside in Madrid until his death. He produced in 1613 his "Novelas exemplares," ("Moral Tales,") which were much admired, and in 1614 his "Viaje al Parnaso," ("Journey to Parnassus,") a poem which some regard as a master-piece. The second part of "Don Quixote" appeared in 1615. Cervantes died on the same day as Shakspeare, April 23, 1616.

"'Don Quixote,'" says Hallam, "is the only book in the Spanish language which can now be said to possess much of a European reputation. . . . It is to Europe in general what Ariosto is to Italy, and Shakspeare to England,—the one book to which the slightest allusions may be made without affectation, but not missed without discredit. Numerous translations, and countless editions of them, in every language, bespeak its adaptation to mankind; and no critic has been found paradoxical enough to withhold his admiration. . . . Few books of moral philosophy display as deep an insight into the mechanism of the mind as 'Don Quixote.' And when we look also at the fertility of invention, the general probability of the events, and the great simplicity of the story, we shall think Cervantes fully deserving of the glory that attends this monument of his genius."

See T. Roscoe, "Life and Writings of Cervantes," 1839; Lockhart, "Life of Cervantes," 1822; Longfellow, "Poets and Poetry of Europe;" Prescott, "Miscellanies," article "Cervantes;" Pellicer, "Vida de Cervantes," 1800; Mayans y Ciscar, "Vida de Cervantes," 1750; Fern. de Navarete, "Vida de Cervantes," 1819; Mérimée, "Notice sur Cervantes," 1806; Viardot, "Notice sur la Vie de Cervantes;" Ticknor, "History of Spanish Literature," vol. ii. ; L. S. Auger, "Essai sur la Vie de Cervantes," 1825.

Cervantes de Salazar, thêR-vân'tês dà sâ-lâ-thaR', (Francisco,) a Spanish *littérateur,* for whose biography we have no materials. He wrote moral works, which were praised by A. Morales, and were published in 1546.

Cervetto, cheR-vêt'to, (Jacopo Bassevi,) a famous Italian musician, born about 1680, performed in London. Died in 1783.

Cervole or **Cervolle, de,** dçh sêR'vol', (Arnauld,) a famous French warrior, born in Périgord, was wounded at Poitiers in 1356. He became a chief of brigands, and sometimes fought for the dauphin. Died in 1366.

Cervolle. See Cervole.

Cervoni, chêR-vo'nee or sêR'vo'ne', (Jean Baptiste,) an able general in the French service, born in Sardinia in 1768. As general of brigade, he distinguished himself at Lodi in 1796, and in 1799 became a general of division. He was appointed chief of the staff of Marshal Lannes in 1809, and was killed at Eckmühl in that year.

See "Victoires et Conquêtes des Français."

Césaire. See Cæsarius.

Cesalpino, chà-sâl-pee'no, [Lat. Cæsalpi'nus ; Fr. Césalpin, sâ'zål'pån', often Anglicized as Cæsalpin or Cesalpine, sês-ål'pin,] (Andrea,) a distinguished Italian physiologist, was born at Arezzo, in Tuscany, in 1519. He applied himself particularly to the study of medicine, but was also learned in various sciences, and especially in the philosophy of Aristotle. After having been professor of medicine and botany at Pisa for many years, he became first physician to Pope Clement VIII., (about 1595.) He published "Quæstiones Peripateticæ," (1569,) a treatise on metaphysics, founded professedly on Aristotle's principles, with a tendency to pantheism, and several medical works, one of which is entitled "Ars Medica," (1601.) His most important service to science consists in an improved system of botany, which was developed in his great work "On Plants," ("De Plantis," 1583.) He was the first who attempted to establish a natural order of classification on philosophical principles. He founded it chiefly on the number, figure, and position of the organs of fructification. He announced several new ideas in physiology, including the circulation of the blood, the truth of which was not recognized until a long time afterwards. Died in 1603.

See Fuchs, "Andreas Cæsalpinus, de ejus Ingenio," etc., Marburg, 1798; Bayle, "Historical and Critical Dictionary;" Nicéron, "Mémoires;" Sprengel, "Historia Rei herbariæ."

César, the French of Cæsar, which see.

Cesare, the Italian of Cæsar, which see.

Cesare, di, dee chä'sâ-rà, (Giuseppe,) Cavaliere, an Italian historian, born in Naples in 1783. In 1837 he produced his chief work, "The History of Manfred, King of Sicily and Apulia," which had great success. He published "Roman Letters," an "Essay on the Philosophy of History," and many other works. Died in 1856.

Cesari, chä'sâ-ree, (Alessandro,) surnamed THE GREEK, a skilful Italian engraver, who lived about 1500-40. He worked in Rome, and was employed by several pontiffs to engrave medals and gems. Vasari considers the cameo representing the head of Phocion as his master-piece.

Cesari, (Antonio,) an able Italian critic and ecclesiastic, born at Verona about 1750. He published good editions of Dante's great poem, of the "Dictionary Della Crusca," and other works. His translations of the Odes of Horace and of the Letters of Cicero are admired. He also wrote popular tales or novels. Died in 1828.

See Manuzzi, "Cenni sulla Vita e sulle Opere di A. Cesari," 1829; G. Bonfanti, "Vita di A. Cesari," 1832; F. Villardi, "Vita del P. A. Cesari," 1832; F. Mordani, "Elogio del P. A. Cesari," 1842.

Cesari, (Giuseppe,) a celebrated Italian historical painter, sometimes called IL Cavaliere d'Arpino, (èl kä-vâ-le-â'rà daR-pee'no,) or Giuseppino, (joo-sêp-pee'-no,) and by the French LE Josépin, (lęh zho'zà'pån',) born at Arpino or Rome about 1565, (some say 1560.) He was patronized by Pope Gregory XIII. and by several of his successors, and was for many years the most fashionable painter of Rome. He is said to have neglected nature and skimmed the surface of art, thus promoting the depraved taste of the time. His works have an appearance of grandeur and animation in composition, but want correctness of design. He once challenged Annibal Caracci to fight; but that artist replied, "My weapon is the pencil, and not the sword." Among his works are frescos in the Capitol at Rome, representing events of ancient Roman history. Died in 1640.

See Lanzi, "History of Painting in Italy ;" Ticozzi, "Dizionario."

Cesarini, chà-sâ-ree'nee, (Giuliano,) an Italian cardinal and negotiator. Died in 1444.

Cesarini, [Lat. Cæsari'nus,] (Virginio,) an Italian poet, born probably at Rome in 1595. He was remarkable for the universality of his scholarship, and was an eloquent orator. Pope Urban VIII. gave him an office in the pontifical chamber. His Latin and Italian poems were published in 1662. Died in 1624.

See A. Favorinus, "Vita V. Cæsarini," 1677; Rycquius, "De Vita V. Cæsarini," 1629.

Césarion, the French of Cæsarion, which see.

Cesarotti, chà-sâ-rot'tee, (Melchior,) one of the most celebrated Italian poets and *littérateurs* of his time, was born at Padua in 1730. He became professor of rhetoric in Padua about 1750. In 1762 he removed to Venice, where he produced an admirable translation of Ossian into Italian verse, (1763,) and versions of several tragedies of Voltaire. He was chosen professor of Greek and Hebrew in the University of Padua in 1768. After this date he published a good translation of Demosthenes, and the "Death of Hector." He also made a literal prose version of Homer with notes, which is said to be one of the most complete and exact works by which that poet has been illustrated. Among his best critical works is an "Essay on the Philosophy of Language, applied to the Italian Language," (1785.) His style is remarkably spirited and powerful, but lacks purity and is marred by neologisms. The version of Ossian is regarded by some critics as his master-piece. Died in 1808.

See G. Barbieri, "Memorie sulla Vita e sugli Studj dell'Abbate M. Cesarotti," 1810.

Céséna, sà'zà'nà', (Sébastien **Gayet**—gâ'yà',) surnamed Rhéal, a French *littérateur,* born at Beaujeu in 1815. His most important work is a French translation of the complete works of Dante, (1843-53.)

Cesi, chä'see, (Bartolommeo,) an Italian painter, born at Bologna in 1557. He painted after nature, and acquired a high reputation at Bologna and Rome. His subjects were mostly scriptural. Died in 1629.

See Lanzi, "History of Painting in Italy."

Cesi, (Federigo,) Prince, Duke of Acqua-Sparta, an eminent Italian naturalist, born in Rome in 1585. At the age of eighteen he founded in Rome the renowned Lincean Academy for the promotion of natural history and philosophy. During his life he defrayed the expenses of this academy. He first discovered the spores of ferns. He wrote able scientific treatises, among which were "The Theatre of Nature," ("Naturæ Theatrum,") and an "Explanation of Natural Prodigies or Phenomena." Died in 1630.

See B. Odescalchi, "Memorie istorico-critiche dell'Accademia dei Lincei e del Principe F. Cesi," 1806; Tiraboschi, "Storia della Letteratura Italiana."

Cesio, chä'se-o, (Carlo,) an Italian painter and engraver, born near Rome in 1626, was a pupil of Pietro da Cortona. He painted frescos in several churches of Rome, and, in the gallery of the Quirinal, a picture of the "Judgment of Solomon." He was a correct designer and a skilful etcher. Among his works in this branch of art is the "Gallery of the Farnese Palace" at Rome. Died in 1686.

See LANZI, "History of Painting in Italy."

Cespedes, de, dä thĕs-pā'Dĕs, (PABLO,) an eminent Spanish painter, scholar, and writer on art, was born at Córdova in 1538. He was learned in Greek, Latin, Hebrew, and Arabic. Having studied art in Rome, he returned to Córdova about 1576, and adorned the churches of that city and of Seville with paintings. He excelled in colour, invention, and composition. A "Last Supper," at Córdova, is one of his most admired works. He wrote a poem on Painting, a "Comparison between Ancient and Modern Art," and a few other works. Died at Córdova in 1608.

See QUINTANA, "Tesoro del Parnaso Español."

Cessac, de. See LACUÉE, COUNT.

Cessart, de, dĕh sȧ'sär', (LOUIS ALEXANDRE,) a French engineer, born in Paris in 1719. In 1781 he was chosen to direct the great naval works at Cherbourg, where he invented a valuable process of hydraulic architecture. He wrote a treatise on hydraulic works, which is highly prized. Died in 1806.

Cessoles, de, dĕh sȧ'sol', (JACQUES,) a French monk and moralist, who lived about 1280, and wrote, in Latin, "The Game of Chess moralized," which was once very popular. An English version was printed by Caxton, (1474.)

Cesti, chĕs'tee, (MARCANTONIO,) one of the most celebrated musicians of his time, was born at Arezzo or Florence about 1620. He was a pupil of Carissimi, whose cantatas (composed for the church) he adapted or transplanted to the theatre. He produced on the theatre of Venice, between 1649 and 1669, "Titus Argenne," and six other operas, which were very successful. Died about 1680.

Cestoni, chĕs-to'nee, (GIACINTO,) an Italian naturalist, born in the March of Ancona in 1637. He wrote several treatises on natural history, which were the results of his own observations, and were printed with the works of his friend Vallisnieri. Died in 1718.

See SANGIORGIO, "Elogio di G. Cestoni," 1811.

Ce-the'gus, (CAIUS,) a Roman senator, and accomplice in Catiline's conspiracy, was a person of infamous character. Convicted on the evidence of his letter to the Allobröges, and of numerous deadly weapons found in his house, he was executed by Cicero in 690 A.U.C., (63 B.C.)

Cethegus, (MARCUS CORNELIUS,) a Roman general and orator, was chosen censor in 209 B.C., and consul in 204. In the next year, as proconsul, he commanded in Cisalpine Gaul, where, with the aid of Varus, he defeated Mago, the Carthaginian general. He had a high reputation for eloquence, and was called by Ennius "the Marrow of Persuasion," (" Suadæ Medulla.")

Cetina, de, dä thä-tee'nä, (GUTIERREZ,) a Spanish poet and ecclesiastic, born at Seville, wrote madrigals and anacreontic poems. He is praised by Velasquez and Herrera, the latter of whom compares him to Garcilasso for elegance. Many of his verses appear to have been lost.

Cetti, chet'tee, (FRANCESCO,) an Italian naturalist and Jesuit, born at Como in 1726. He published several treatises on the Quadrupeds, the Fish, and other Animals of Sardinia, (1774-77.) Died about 1780.

Cetti, (GIOVANNI,) an Italian *littérateur*, born at Lugano, made several translations from the Russian of Karamzin into Italian. Died in 1817.

Ceulen. See KEULEN.

Ceva, chā'vä, (GIOVANNI,) an Italian geometer, born probably at Milan. He published several Latin works of merit, entitled "Opuscula Mathematica," (1682,) "The Geometry of Motion," (" Geometria Motûs," 1692,) "Hydrostatica," (1728,) etc.

Ceva, (TOMMASO,) an Italian poet and distinguished geometer, brother of the preceding, was born at Milan in 1648, and entered the order of Jesuits in his youth. He invented an instrument to perform the trisection of

an angle, (1695,) and published mathematical writings, ("Opuscula Mathematica.") Among his Latin poems is "Philosophia novo-antiqua," which is extolled by Corniani. Died in 1736.

Cevallos, thä-väl'yös, (PEDRO,) a Spanish politician, born at Santander in 1764, became minister of foreign affairs under Charles IV. About 1808 he was sent to London on a political mission by the Junta, and published there a work which is said to have had great influence in exciting the Spaniards against Bonaparte. He was successively secretary of state and minister to Vienna between 1814 and 1820, after which he was excluded from political employment. Died about 1838.

See BROCKHAUS, "Conversations-Lexikon."

Cézelli, sȧ'zȧ'le', (CONSTANCE,) a French lady, noted for her heroic and successful defence of Leucate in 1590.

Chabannes, de. See PALICE, DE LA.

Chabannes, de, dĕh shȧ'bän', (ANTOINE,) Comte de Dammartin, (dĕh dȧ'mär'tän',) an able and successful French general, brother of Jacques, noticed below, born about 1410. He distinguished himself at the siege of Orléans in 1428, and fought under the banners of Joan of Arc in other battles. He became a favourite of Charles VII., who died in 1461; he was then disgraced and imprisoned by Louis XI. In 1468 he was pardoned, and gained the favour of Louis, who appointed him grand master *(grand-maître)* of France. He was commander-in-chief in the war against Charles the Bold in 1471. Died in 1488.

See DU PLESSIS, "Les Vies de Jacques et Antoine de Chabannes," 1612 ; "Nouvelle Biographie Générale."

Chabannes, de, (JACQUES,) Seigneur de la Palice, (dĕh lä pä'lèss',) a French general, brother of the preceding, born about 1400. He served with distinction in the wars against the English, and became grand master *(grand-maître)* of France, (1451.) He was mortally wounded at the battle of Castillon in 1453.

See DU PLESSIS, "Les Vies de Jacques et Antoine de Chabannes."

Chabannes, de, (JEAN,) Seigneur de Vandenesse, a brave general, was a nephew of the preceding, and a brother of Marshal de la Palice. (See PALICE.) He was a companion of Bayard, and was surnamed THE LITTLE LION. He contributed to the victory of Marignano in 1515, and commanded the artillery when he was killed with Bayard near the Sesia in 1524.

See BRANTÔME, "Vies des grands Capitaines."

Chabannes, de, (JEAN BAPTISTE MARIE,) MARQUIS, a French politician, born in 1770, was a descendant of Marshal de la Palice. He became a royalist emigrant about 1790. At the restoration in 1815 he was admitted into the Chamber of Peers. He published many political pamphlets, among which was "The Deceitful Beacon," (" Le Phare trompeur, ou la Chartomanie," 1821.) Died in 1835.

Chabannes-la-Palice, de, dĕh shȧ'bän' lä pä'lèss', (ALFRED JEAN EGINHARD,) COUNT, a French general, born in 1799. He served several campaigns in Algeria, was appointed aide-de-camp to the king about 1838, and a general of brigade in 1840. In 1848 he retired from the service, and went into exile with Louis Philippe.

Chabanon, de, dĕh shȧ'bȧ'nôn', (MICHEL PAUL GUI,) an able French writer, born in the island of Saint Domingo in 1730, became a resident of France. Among his best works are a "Life of Dante," (1773,) and a "Treatise on Music considered in itself and in its Relations with Language, Poetry, etc.," (1785.) His version of the Pythic Odes of Pindar was praised by Voltaire. He also made a good prose version of Theocritus, and left Memoirs of his own life, (1795.) Died in 1792.

See his Autobiography, entitled "Tableau de quelques Circonstances de ma Vie," 1795; FONTANES, "Notice sur Chabanon ;" QUÉRARD, "La France Littéraire."

Chabans, de, dĕh shȧ'bôn', (LOUIS du Maine—dü män,) BARON, a French writer on morals, lived about 1610. He was killed in a duel by the father of Ninon Lenclos.

Chabaud, shȧ'bō', (ANTOINE,) a French engineer, born at Nîmes in 1727. He projected a canal in Picardy, which was approved by Turgot, but, owing to the removal of that minister, it was not made. He published a "Memoir on Volcanoes and Earthquakes." Died in 1791.

Chabaud de la Tour, shả'bō' dẹh lả tooR, (AN-TOINE GEORGE FRANÇOIS,) BARON, a French Protestant legislator, son of the preceding, born in Paris in 1767, was an officer in the army when the Revolution began. He was chosen one of the Council of Five Hundred in 1797, a member of the Tribunat about 1800, and of the legislative body in 1807. From 1817 to 1828 he served with credit in the Chamber of Deputies. Died in 1832.

Chabaud-Latour, de, dẹh shả'bō' lả'tooR', (FRAN-ÇOIS ERNEST HENRI,) BARON, a French general, son of the preceding, was born at Nîmes in 1804. He chose the profession of military engineer, and became a captain in 1827. He was a member of the Chamber of Deputies from 1827 to 1848, and obtained the rank of general of brigade in 1853.

Chabert, shả'baiR', (J. XAVIER,) a French adventurer, known as "the Fire King," exhibited himself in London and the United States about 1830. He is said to have entered an oven heated to 380° Fahr.

Chabert, (THÉODORE,) a French general, born at Villefranche in 1758. He served in Germany and Italy, and in 1808 commanded the vanguard at Baylen, where the French, under Dupont, were defeated with dishonour by the Spaniards, for which he was dismissed from the service. In 1814 he took sides with Bonaparte, who made him a lieutenant-general. Died about 1830.

Chabert, de, dẹh shả'baiR', (JOSEPH BERNARD,) MARQUIS, an eminent French naval officer, savant, and hydrographer, born at Toulon in 1723. He entered the navy in his youth, and, after important services, became vice-admiral in 1792. His "Account of a Voyage made on the Coasts of North America in 1750" forms part of the records of the Academy of Sciences. He prepared charts of the coasts of the Mediterranean, and made other improvements in hydrography. He was an associate of nearly all the great Academies of Europe. He emigrated in the reign of terror, returned home in 1802, and was chosen a member of the bureau of longitudes in 1803. Died in 1805.

See "Nouvelle Biographie Générale."

Chabot, shả'bo', (FRANÇOIS,) a fanatical French Jacobin and demagogue, born in Rouergue in 1759, became a Capuchin monk noted for his vicious morals and shabby attire. About 1790 he was deputed to the Constituent Assembly, in which he acquired influence by his audacity and facility of speech. He was one of the instigators of the massacres of August and September, 1792. The adoption of the term "Montagnards" by his party is said to have been suggested by him. He became obnoxious to Robespierre, by whose orders he was executed in 1794.

See DE BARANTE, "Histoire de la Convention Nationale."

Chabot, (LOUIS FRANÇOIS JEAN,) a French general, born at Niort in 1757, served in Flanders and La Vendée, and became a general of division in 1794. Died in 1837.

See J. RICHARD, "Mémoire biographique sur le Général Chabot," 1844.

Chabot, de, dẹh shả'bo',(PHILIPPE,) Comte de Charni, (dẹh shảR'ne',) sometimes called "Admiral de Brion," a French general, born of a noble family of Poitou. He was a rival of Constable Montmorency, and the head of a party at court in the reign of Francis I. He was made prisoner at the battle of Pavia in 1525, and succeeded Bonnivet (who was killed in that action) as admiral of France. In 1535 he had the chief command in the war against the Duke of Savoy, and was so successful that Turin and nearly all Piedmont submitted. The colony of Canada was planted under his auspices by Cartier. Died in 1543.

See BRANTÔME, "Vies des grands Capitaines."

Chabot de l'Allier, shả'bo' dẹh lả'le-à', (GEORGES ANTOINE,) a French jurist, born at Montluçon in 1758. He became a member of the Convention in 1794, and of the Council of Elders in 1799. Being a member of the Tribunat when the treaty of Amiens was announced, in 1802, he moved that Bonaparte be appointed consul for life. He afterwards served in the legislative body, and was chosen a judge in the court of cassation in 1809. He wrote an esteemed work "On the Law of Successions," (1804.) Died in 1819.

See MOULIN, "Notice biographique sur Chabot."

Chabran, shả'bRŏN', (JOSEPH,) a French general, born at Cavaillon in 1763. He fought at Marengo in 1800, after which he had the command in Piedmont. He was created a count in December, 1814. Died in 1843.

Chabrée, shả'bRȁ', (DOMINIQUE,) a French botanist, born at Geneva, practised medicine at Yverdun about 1650. He supervised the publication of J. Bauhin's "History of Plants,"(1651,) which the author left in manuscript; and fifteen years later he published in his own name an abridgment of the same, "Stirpium icones et sciagraphia," (1666.) He is supposed to have died in 1667.

Chả'brī-as, [Χαβρίας,] an able Athenian general, who first appears in history as the commander of the army of Athens at Corinth in 392 B.C. He rendered efficient services to Evagoras of Cyprus against the Persians in 388. In a campaign against Agesilaus in 378 he acquired celebrity by the invention of a new manœuvre. He ordered his men to await the charge of the enemy with presented spears, and with the left knee supported against the shield. In 376 he gained a decisive naval victory over the Spartans at Naxos. In the Social war, which began in 357 B.C., he commanded a fleet co-operating with an army under Chares. Having exposed himself rashly at the siege of Chios, he was killed in the same year.

See CARL REHDANTZ, "Vitæ Iphicratis, Chabriæ et Timothei Atheniensium," 1845; PLUTARCH, "Life of Phocion;" CORNELIUS NEPOS, "Chabrias."

Chabrit, shả'bRe', (PIERRE,) a French jurist, born about 1740, was an advocate in the Parliament of Paris. He published a work "On the French Monarchy and Laws," (1783,) for which he received from the French Academy a prize founded by Valbelle for the most useful work. Died in 1785.

Chabrol de Crouzol, shả'bRol' dẹh kRoo'zol', (ANDRÉ JEAN,) COUNT, a French minister of state, born at Riom in 1771, was prefect of the Rhone, at Lyons, from 1814 to 1817. He was appointed minister of the marine in 1824, and was minister of finances from August, 1829, till May, 1830. Died in 1836.

See "Nouvelle Biographie Générale."

Chabrol de Volvic, shả'bRol' dẹh vol'vèk', (GILBERT JOSEPH GASPARD,) COUNT, a French civil officer, brother of the preceding, born at Riom in 1773. He accompanied the expedition to Egypt in 1798, as a member of the commission of arts and sciences. On his return he published a volume "On the Manners and Customs of the Modern Egyptians." He was appointed in 1812 prefect of the department of the Seine, and held that important office eighteen years, during which he constructed in Paris many bridges, markets, churches, schools, and the Bourse. Died in 1843.

See QUÉRARD, "La France Littéraire;" "Nouvelle Biographie Générale."

Chabroud, shả'bRoo', (CHARLES,) a French lawyer and republican, born at Vienne in 1750, was deputed to the States-General in 1789. He took an active part in the National Assembly, of which he was chosen president in April, 1791. From 1794 to 1797 he was a judge of the court of cassation in Paris. Died in 1816.

Chabry, shả'bRe', (MARC,) a French painter and sculptor, born at Lyons in 1660, worked with success in his native city. The king, after seeing his statue of Hercules, appointed him his sculptor at Lyons. Died in 1727.

Chacaton, shả'kả'tŏN', (JEAN NICOLAS HENRI,) a French painter of history and landscapes, born at Chézy in 1813. Among his productions are "The Prisoner of Chillon," (1835,) and "Souvenirs of Smyrna," admitted into the great Exposition of Paris in 1855.

Chacon, chả-kŏn', [It. CIACONE, chả-ko'nả; Lat. CIA-CO'NIUS,] (ALONZO,) a Spanish priest, born in the kingdom of Granada in 1540, was very learned in ecclesiastical history and antiquities. He lived some years in Rome, and was apostolic penitentiary under Gregory XIII. His principal work is a "History of the Popes and Cardinals," (1601.) Died in 1599.

See N. ANTONIO, "Bibliotheca Hispana Nova."

Chacon, [Lat. CIACO'NIUS,] (PEDRO,) a Spanish priest, eminent for his learning, and called "the Varro of his age," was born at Toledo in 1525. He became a resident of Rome, and was employed by Gregory XIII.

ɇ as k; ç as s; g̃ hard; g̃ as j; G, H, K, guttural; N, nasal; R, trilled; š as z; ŧh as in this. (☞See Explanations, p. 23.)

to revise the Bible and the Fathers. He annotated Isidore, Tertullian, Sallust, Varro, Pliny, etc., and wrote a treatise on the Roman manner of reclining at table, ("De Triclinio Romano,") and other works. His immense erudition was extolled by Vossius, De Thou, and Casaubon. Died in Rome in 1581.

See DUPIN, "Bibliothèque des Auteurs ecclésiastiques," etc.

Chad'er-ton, (LAWRENCE,) D.D., an English divine, born in Lancashire in 1546. In 1584 he was chosen first master of Emanuel College, Cambridge. He assisted in the version of the Bible made by order of James I., and wrote a "Treatise on Justification." Died in 1640.

See DILLINGHAM, "Vita L. Chadertoni," 1700.

Chadidscha. See KHADIJAH.

Chaduc, shả'dük', (LOUIS,) a French antiquary, born at Riom in 1560. He formed a collection of two thousand engraved gems. Died in 1638.

Chad'wick, (EDWIN,) an English reformer and statistician, whose life has been devoted to sanitary reform and the prevention of pauperism, was born in the environs of Manchester in 1801. He removed to London in his youth, and became a student in the Inner Temple. In 1828 he published in the "Westminster Review" an important article "On Life Assurance," and in 1829 in the "London Review" a paper "On Preventive Police," which procured him the friendship of Jeremy Bentham. He was appointed in 1834 secretary to the poor-law commission, and continued in that office until 1847. From masses of evidence collected for this commission he prepared a "Report on the Sanitary Condition of the Labouring Population of Great Britain," (1842,) which produced a great sensation. In consequence of this sanitary movement a public-health act was passed in 1848, and a general board of health was appointed, of which board Mr. Chadwick was a member from 1848 to 1854. "No public man of the present day," says the "North British Review," (1850,) "is more justly an object of general attention and interest than Edwin Chadwick. It would be difficult to mention another public man possessing so pre-eminently the passion and genius of rectification."

See "Brief Biographies," by SAMUEL SMILES; "North British Review" for May, 1850.

Chærea, kee're-ạ, (C. CASSIUS,) a Roman tribune of the prætorian cohort in the reign of Caligula. Having been insulted or ridiculed by that tyrant, and perhaps impelled by the love of liberty, he formed a conspiracy and assassinated Caligula in 41 A.D. Within a few days after this event he was executed by Claudius.

See TACITUS, "Annales."

Chæremon, kê-ree'mọn, [Gr. Χαιρήμων; Fr. CHÉRÉMON, kả'rả'môN',] an Athenian tragic poet, who is supposed to have flourished between 400 and 350 B.C. He imitated the defects of Euripides, and displayed the bad taste which belongs to an age of decadence. He excelled in the description of sensuous beauty. Fragments of his plays have come down to us.

See BARTSCH, "De Chæremone, Poeta tragico."

Chæremon, a Stoic philosopher and historian, lived in the first century of our era. He was librarian of the great Alexandrian Library, and afterwards a preceptor of Nero in Rome. His chief work was a "Sacred and Profane History of Egypt," of which only a fragment is extant.

See FABRICIUS, "Bibliotheca Græca."

Chærephon, kêr'e-fon, [Gr. Χαιρεφῶν; Fr. CHÉRÉPHON, kả'rả'fôN',] a Greek philosopher, born about 480 B.C., was a friend of Socrates, and is often noticed favourably in the works of Plato.

Chafei, (MOHAMMED-BEN-IDRYS.) See SHÂFEY-IBN-IDREES.

Chah. See SHAH.

Chahyn-Gherai. See SHAHEEN.

Chaillu. See DU CHAILLU.

Chais, shạ, (PIERRE,) a Swiss divine and pulpit orator, born at Geneva in 1701, became minister at the Hague in 1728. He founded a hospital or almshouse at the Hague, and published, besides other works, a "Commentary on the Old Testament," (7 vols.,) and "Theology of the Bible," (1752.) Died at the Hague in 1785.

Chaise, La. See LA CHAISE.

Chaix d'Est-Ange, shạ'dả'tôNzh',(VICTOR CHARLES,) an eloquent French advocate, born at Rheims in 1800, was elected to the Chamber of Deputies in 1831, 1837, and 1844. About the end of 1857 he became procureur-général at the imperial court of Paris.

Chalais, de, PRINCE. See TALLEYRAND, (HENRI DE.)

Chalbos, shả'bo', (FRANÇOIS,) a French general, born at Cubières; died in 1803.

Chal-çid'I-us, a Platonic philosopher, of whose nativity and life nothing is known. He is supposed to have lived between the beginning of the fourth and the end of the sixth century. He produced a Latin version of the first part of Plato's "Timæus," with a learned commentary on the same. It is doubtful whether he was a Christian or a pagan.

See CAVE, "Historia Literaria."

Chalcondylas. See CHALCONDYLES.

Chal-con'dy̆-las, [Fr. CHALCONDYLE, kȧl'kôN'dèl',] (DEMETRIUS,) a learned Greek, born at Athens about 1424. Invited by Lorenzo de' Medici, he went to Florence about 1480, and there taught Greek until the death of that prince in 1492. He then became professor of Greek in Milan, where he died about 1510. The first edition of Homer ever printed was edited by Chalcondylas in 1488.

See P. GIOVIO, "Elogia;" C. F. BÖRNER, "Programma de D. Chalcondylo," 1711.

Chalcondyle. See CHALCONDYLAS.

Chal-con'dy̆-lēs or **Chal-con'dy̆-las,** (LAON'ICUS or NICOLA'US,) [Gr. Λαόνικος or Νικόλαος Χαλκονδύλης,] an able Byzantine historian and statesman, was a native of Athens, and a relative of Demetrius, noticed above. In 1446 he was ambassador from John VII. Palæologus to Sultan Murad II. He wrote a "History of the Turks and of the Byzantine Empire from 1298 to 1463," which is an important work and considered reliable. His name is sometimes written CHALCOCONDYLES.

See FABRICIUS, "Bibliotheca Græca;" VON HAMMER, "Histoire de l'Empire Ottoman."

Chales. See CHALLES, (CLAUDE F. MILLET DE.)

Châles. See CHASLES.

Chalgrin, shả'grȧN', (JEAN FRANÇOIS THÉRÈSE,) an eminent French architect, born in Paris in 1739. Having gained the grand prize of the Academy, he went to Italy with a royal pension. Among his principal works are the College of France, many hôtels of Paris, the restoration of the Luxembourg Palace, and the "Arc de l'Étoile," a magnificent triumphal arch at Paris. He was a member of the Institute. Died in 1811.

See VIEL, "Notice sur J. F. T. Chalgrin," 1814.

Chalier, shả'le-ả', (MARIE JOSEPH,) a violent French Jacobin, born near Suza, Piedmont, in 1747. He was a merchant in Lyons when the Revolution began. He became the leader of the Jacobins of that city, and a fanatical admirer of Marat. A plot which he had formed to massacre the *aristocrats* having been detected, he was guillotined at Lyons in 1793.

See THIERS, "Histoire de la Révolution."

Chalkhill, chauk'il, (JOHN,) the supposed author of a pastoral poem published in 1683 by Izaak Walton, with the title of "Thealma and Clearchus." Some critics believe this work was written by Walton, as his statement respecting the authorship is not supported by other evidence.

Chalkley, chauk'le, (THOMAS,) a minister of the Society of Friends, born in London in 1675, removed to Pennsylvania about 1700. He resided at Frankford, near Philadelphia. While on a religious visit to the West Indies, he died in Tortola about 1742, leaving an interesting journal of his life, which was published in 1747.

Challamel, shả'lả'mèl', (JEAN BAPTISTE MARIE AUGUSTIN,) a French *littérateur*, born in Paris in 1818, published "A Summer in Spain," (1843,) a "Popular History of France, the Revolution, and Napoleon," (1851,) and other works.

Challan, shả'lôN',(ANTOINE DIDIER JEAN BAPTISTE,) a French lawyer, born at Meulan in 1754. He was elected to the Council of Five Hundred in 1798, was president of the Tribunat in 1802, and served in the legislative body from 1807 to 1814. He was the author

ā, ē, ī, ō, ū, ȳ, *long;* à, è, ò, same, less prolonged; ă, ĕ, ĭ, ŏ, ŭ, y̆, *short;* ạ, ẹ, ị, ọ, *obscure;* fär, fȧll, fȧt; mêt; nŏt; gŏŏd; mōŏn;

or *rédacteur* of the act by which the latter declared that Bonaparte was deposed in 1814. Died in 1831.

Challe, shăl, (CHARLES MICHEL ANGE,) a painter and architect, born in Paris in 1718. He became professor of perspective in the Academy, (1753,) and designer for the cabinet of the king. His fine taste and skill in antique monuments procured for him also the direction of public festivals. Died in 1778.

Challes, de, deh shăl, (CLAUDE FRANÇOIS MILLIET,) a French mathematician, born at Chambéry in 1621, was professor of mathematics in the Jesuits' College at Lyons. His principal work is a "Course of Mathematics," (1674,) which was highly prized at the time. Died in 1678.

See MORÉRI, "Dictionnaire Historique."

Chăl'lis, (Rev. JAMES,) an English divine, born in 1803, became professor of astronomy in the University of Cambridge about 1836. He published a work entitled "Creation in Plan and Progress," (1861.)

Chăl'lon-er, (RICHARD,) an English Catholic writer, born at Lewes, Sussex, in 1691. He was made coadjutor to Petre, the titular Bishop of London, in 1741, and succeeded him in 1758. He wrote a "Church History," the "Grounds of the Old Religion," and other works against the Protestants. Died in 1781.

See J. BARNARD, "Life of R. Challoner," 1784.

Chalmel, shăl'mĕl', (JEAN LOUIS,) a French republican and historian, born at Tours in 1756; died in 1829.

Chalmers, chăl'merz or chaw'merz, (ALEXANDER,) a British editor and critic, born at Aberdeen in 1759. About 1778 he came to London, where he wrote for literary periodicals, and edited the "Spectator," "Tatler," and various other works. His edition of Shakspeare (1809) is commended. He edited a "General Biographical Dictionary," (32 vols., 1812–17.) Died in 1834.

See "Gentleman's Magazine" for February, 1835; CHAMBERS, "Biographical Dictionary of Eminent Scotsmen," (Supplement.)

Chalmers, (GEORGE,) a Scottish writer and lawyer, born at Fochabers in 1742. He resided many years in London, and was a clerk of the board of trade from 1786 until his death. He wrote "Political Annals of the United Colonies," a "Life of Mary Queen of Scots," and various other works. He devoted many years to a great topographical and historical account of Great Britain, called "Caledonia," (1807–24,) which is said to be more elaborate and copious than any work on British history or antiquities which ever came from one author. ("London Quarterly Review" for November, 1810.) Died in 1825.

See CHAMBERS, "Biographical Dictionary of Eminent Scotsmen."

Chăl'mers, [Scottish pron. chaw'merz,] (Rev. THOMAS,) the most eminent Scottish divine of the present century, was born at Anstruther, in Fifeshire, on the 17th of March, 1780. He was a son of John Chalmers, a dyer, ship-owner, and general merchant. He entered the University of Saint Andrew's in 1791, and acquired great proficiency in mathematics, which was his favourite science. Even after he had been enrolled as a student of divinity, (1795,) he gave more attention to geometry than to theology. He was licensed as a minister of the Scottish Church in 1799; after which he passed two winters in attending the lectures of Dugald Stewart, Robison, Playfair, and Hope in Edinburgh. At this time his thirst for literary distinction was greater than his interest in vital religion. In the autumn of 1802 he became assistant professor of mathematics at Saint Andrew's, and "threw himself into the duties of the mathematical classes," says Mr. Hanna, "with all the fervour of an overflowing enthusiasm." He was ordained minister of Kilmany in 1803.

In 1807 he published an "Inquiry into the Extent and Stability of the National Resources," which was received with favour, and in 1809 became a contributor to the "Edinburgh Encyclopædia," for which he wrote an excellent article "On Christianity." About this time a great change was effected in his spiritual life, and in his religious principles, which had been anti-Evangelical. He married Miss Grace Pratt in 1812. Having acquired a wide reputation for eloquence and wisdom, he was elected minister of the Tron Church in Glasgow, to which he removed in 1815. In 1816 he delivered, on Astronomy in its Connection with Religion, a series of discourses, which were greatly admired. They were published in 1817, and ran through nine editions within the first year.

"To this day," says his biographer, "they command a larger sale than any other portion of Dr. Chalmers's writings." He became the most celebrated pulpit orator of Scotland, or probably of Great Britain, during the eight years which he passed in Glasgow. He appears to have wisely estimated the popular applause which he so largely shared, the dangers of which he thus described : "There is a far-sounding popularity, which is a most worthless article, . . . which, by elevating man above his fellows, places him in a region of desolation, where he stands a conspicuous mark for the shafts of malice, and envy, and detraction,—a popularity which, with its head among storms and its feet on the treacherous quicksands, has nothing to lull the agonies of its tottering existence but the hosannas of a drivelling generation." In 1819 he was translated to the parish of Saint John's, Glasgow. He accepted in 1823 the chair of moral philosophy at Saint Andrew's, where he remained about five years. From 1828 to 1843 he was professor of theology in the University of Edinburgh. During this period he produced many important works, among which are his "Political Economy," (1832,) and the Bridgewater treatise "On the Adaptation of External Nature to the Moral and Intellectual Constitution of Man," (1833.) Dr. Chalmers was the principal chief of the "Evangelical" party in the controversy which resulted in the disruption of the Church of Scotland in 1843. He and his friends then seceded from the Established Church, and organized what is known as the "Free Church." He was a corresponding member of the French Institute. Died in Edinburgh in May, 1847.

See "Memoirs of his Life and Writings," 4 vols., 1850–52, published by his son-in-law, Mr. HANNA, who has also edited his posthumous works; FRANCIS WAYLAND, "Memoirs of the Christian Labours of Thomas Chalmers;" "North British Review" for August, 1847, February, 1848, May, 1852, and November, 1856; "Edinburgh Review" for October, 1832; "London Quarterly Review" for October, 1852; "Blackwood's Magazine" for May, 1853; "Fraser's Magazine" for August, 1847, and July, 1852; REV. ROBERT STEEL, "Burning and Shining Lights."

Chăl'on, (ALFRED EDWARD,) an English portrait and historical painter of the present century. He painted the portrait of Lady Russell, and designed some of the figures of Finden's "Gallery of the Graces," (London, 1832.) He has also designed illustrations for the works of Sir Walter Scott.

Chal'on or **Char'lon,** (JOHN JAMES,) an English painter of genre, brother of the preceding, born about 1785; died in 1854.

Chăl'on-er, (EDWARD,) D.D., son of Sir Thomas, born at Chiswick in 1590, became chaplain to James I., and principal of Alban Hall, Oxford. Died in 1625.

Chaloner, (JAMES,) a brother of the preceding, wrote a "Description of the Isle of Man." He was a member of the Long Parliament, and one of the judges who tried Charles I. Died in 1661.

Chaloner, (THOMAS,) a brother of Edward and James, noticed above, became a member of the Long Parliament, and sat as judge in the trial of Charles I. At the restoration (1660) he was excepted as a regicide from the amnesty, and escaped to Holland, where he died, it is supposed, about 1662.

See WOOD, "Athenæ Oxonienses."

Chaloner, (Sir THOMAS,) an eminent English statesman and author, born in London about 1515. About 1541 he accompanied Charles V. in his disastrous expedition against Algiers, and nearly perished by shipwreck. For his gallant conduct at Musselburgh in 1547 he was knighted. Soon after the accession of Elizabeth (1558) he was employed with credit as ambassador to Ferdinand I. of Germany, and a few years later became minister at the court of Spain. He wrote, in Latin, a work "On the Right Ordering of the English Commonwealth," and some Latin verses. Died in 1565.

See "Biographia Britannica."

Chaloner, (Sir THOMAS,) a son of the preceding, and father of Edward, James, and Thomas, noticed above, was born in 1559. He became a favourite of James I., who appointed him, in 1603, director of the education and household of Prince Henry, which position he held until the death of Henry. He was author of a treatise on the virtue of Nitre. Died in 1615.

ɛ as *k*; ç as *s*; ḡ *hard*; ĝ as *j*; G, H, K, *guttural*; N, *nasal*; R, *trilled*; s as *z*; ᵗh as in *this*. (☞ See Explanations, p. 23.)

Chalotais, de la, dẹh lä shä'lo'tȧ', (LOUIS RENÉ de **Caradeuc,** dẹh kä'rä'dŭk',) a French lawyer and magistrate, born at Rennes in 1701, became attorney-general at that place. He contributed to the suppression of the Jesuits by a *compte-rendu* which he read before the parliament at Rennes in 1761. It produced much excitement. For his part in a quarrel between the court and parliament he was imprisoned in 1765, and, after a long and famous trial, was exiled to Saintes. He wrote an "Essay on National Education," which was praised by Voltaire and Grimm. Died in 1785.

Chalvet, shäl'vȧ', [Lat. CALVEN'TIUS,] (MATHIEU,) a French scholar, born in Auvergne in 1528, produced a translation of Seneca. Died in 1607.

Chalybaeus. See CHALYBÄUS.

Chalybäus or **Chalybaeus,** Kä-le-bä'ŭs, (HEINRICH MORITZ,) a German philosopher, born at Pfaffroda, in Saxony, in 1796. He published in 1836 a "History of the Development of Speculative Philosophy from Kant to Hegel," which was well received. In 1839 he became professor of philosophy in the University of Kiel. His principal work is a "System of Speculative Ethics, or Philosophy of the Family, of the State, and of Morality as connected with Religion," (1850, 2 vols.)

Cham. See HAM.

Chambard, shŏN'bär', (LOUIS LÉOPOLD,) a French sculptor, born at Saint-Amour (Jura) about 1812, gained the grand prize in 1837. Among his works are "A Girl listening to the Murmur of a Shell," and a "Cupid Chained," (1857.)

Chambarlhac, de, dẹh shŏN'bär'lȧk', (JEAN JACQUES VITAL,) a French general, born in 1754; died in 1826.

Chām'bẹr, (JOHN,) an English physician, who practised in London about 1520. He became physician to Henry VIII., and was one of the founders of the College of Physicians. Died in 1549.

Chamberet, shŏN'brả', (JEAN BAPTISTE,) a French medical writer, born at Limoges in 1779. He was one of the editors of the "Dictionary of Medical Sciences," and of the "Encyclopédie Méthodique."

Chamberlain. See CHAMBERLEN, (HUGH.)

Chamberlain or **Chamberlayne,** chäm'bẹr-lin, (ROBERT,) an English poet, wrote epigrams, comedies, pastorals, etc. Died in 1637.

Chamberlain or **Chamberlayne,** (WILLIAM,) an English poet and physician, born in Dorsetshire in 1619. He wrote "Love's Victory," a tragi-comedy, (1658,) and "Pharronida, a Heroic Poem," (1659.) Southey calls him "a poet who has told an interesting story in uncouth rhymes, and mingles sublimity of thought and beauty of expression with the quaintest conceits and most awkward inversions." Died in 1689.

See CAMPBELL, "Specimens of the British Poets."

Chamberlaine or **Chamberlayne,** chäm'bẹr-lin, (EDWARD,) an English writer, born in Gloucestershire in 1616, was tutor to the Duke of Grafton. He wrote, besides other works, "The Present State of England," (1668,) partly statistical, (often reprinted.) Died in 1703.

Chamberlaine, (JOHN,) F.R.S., a son of the preceding, was an excellent linguist. He translated several works from the Dutch and French, among others, "The Lives of French Philosophers," by Fontenelle; and he continued the publication of his father's work, above named. Died in 1723.

Chamberlayne. See CHAMBERLAIN and CHAMBERLAINE.

Chām'bẹr-len or **Chamberlain,** (HUGH,) an English physician, born in 1664, was the inventor of an obstetric forceps, and practised in London with success. He was noted for his skill as an accoucheur. He wrote several treatises, one of which is named "Practice of Physic." Died in 1728.

Chām'bẹrṣ, (DAVID,) a Scottish historian, born about 1530. He was an adherent of Queen Mary, who in 1564 created him a privy councillor and lord of session, with the title of Lord Ormond. About 1568 he was removed from office, and retired to France, where he published, in French, a "History of the Kings of France, England, and Scotland," and a few other works. Died in 1592.

See CHAMBERS, "Biographical Dictionary of Eminent Scotsmen."

Chām'bẹrṣ, (EPHRAIM,) the author of Chambers's "Cyclopædia," was born at Kendal, in England. He served an apprenticeship with Senex, a globe-maker of London. In 1728 he produced the first edition of his "Cyclopædia," in two volumes, which was very successful and speedily procured him a Fellowship in the Royal Society. It was the most complete and extensive work of the kind that had appeared, and suggested the idea of the great French "Encyclopédie" of Diderot. The most of the articles were written by the editor himself, who was a learned and very industrious compiler. The sixth edition was enlarged by Dr. Rees, (1785,) who also made Chambers's work the basis of a more extensive one, called "Rees's Cyclopædia." Died in 1740.

Chambers, (GEORGE,) an English painter, who excelled in marine views, was born at Whitby about 1780. Having learned the trade of house-painter, he went to London, where he worked seven years on Horner's Panorama of London. He painted battle-scenes, which were much admired, and was appointed marine painter to William IV. and to his queen. Among his works is the "Bombardment of Algiers in 1816." Died in 1840.

Chambers, (ROBERT,) LL.D., a well-known Scottish writer and publisher, born at Peebles in 1802. He became in his youth a bookseller in Edinburgh, and published, in 1824, "Traditions of Edinburgh," which was followed by several popular works on Scottish history. In 1832 he entered into partnership with his brother William in the publication of "The Edinburgh Journal," (published weekly,) which was very successful. (See CHAMBERS, WILLIAM, 2d.) They subsequently issued popular books, entitled "Information for the People," "Chambers's Miscellany," "Papers for the People," etc. Nearly two hundred thousand copies of "Information for the People" have been sold in England and the United States. Robert has published a valuable "Biographical Dictionary of Eminent Scotsmen," with portraits, (1835.) He was the principal editor of the "Cyclopædia of English Literature: Selections from the Works of English Authors, connected by a Critical and Biographical History," (1844,) which obtained a very large circulation.

Chambers, (Sir ROBERT,) an eminent English lawyer, born at Newcastle-on-Tyne in 1737. In 1762 he succeeded Sir William Blackstone as Vinerian professor of law at Oxford. He was appointed a judge of the supreme court of judicature in Bengal in 1774, and chief justice of the same in 1791. He returned home in 1799, and died in 1803.

Chambers, (Sir WILLIAM,) an eminent architect, of Scottish descent, born at Stockholm, Sweden, in 1726. At an early age he settled in London, where he was successful in his profession. George III., who had received lessons in drawing from Chambers, employed him to lay out the royal gardens at Kew. His principal works are Somerset House, in London, Milton Abbey in Dorsetshire, and the Marquis of Abercorn's mansion, near Edinburgh. The first of these, begun about 1775, is greatly admired. He published a "Treatise on Civil Architecture," (1759,) which, says Horace Walpole, "is the most sensible book ever written on that science," and a "Dissertation on Oriental Gardening," (1774.) Died in 1796.

See "Gentleman's Magazine," March, 1796.

Chambers, (Sir WILLIAM,) a Scottish editor, brother of Robert Chambers, noticed above, distinguished for successful enterprise in the publication of cheap and useful literature, was born at Peebles in 1800. In 1830 he produced "The Book of Scotland," a description of the customs, laws, and institutions of that country. In 1832 William and Robert Chambers began to edit "Chambers's Edinburgh Journal," which obtained a circulation of fifty thousand in 1834. Having entered into partnership, they established a publishing-house, which has become one of the most extensive in Scotland. They have compiled and published numerous works which are well adapted to the wants of the masses. (See CHAMBERS, ROBERT.) Among the most important of their recent publications is "Chambers's Encyclopædia for the People," begun in 1859 and completed in 1868. William is the author of a volume called "Things as they are in America." In 1865 he was made lord provost of Edinburgh.

ā, ē, ī, ō, ū, ȳ, *long;* ȧ, ė, ȯ, same, less prolonged; ă, ĕ, ĭ, ŏ, ŭ, ȳ, *short;* ạ, ẹ, ị, ọ, *obscure;* fär, fȧll, fȧt; mēt; nŏt; gōōd; mōōn;

Chambert, shŏN'baiR', (GERMAIN,) a French engraver, born in Languedoc in 1784 ; died in 1821.

Chambolle, shŏN'bol', (ADOLPHE,) a French journalist, born at La Châtaigneraye in 1802, was chief editor of the "Siècle" from 1837 to 1848. He was elected to the Chamber of Deputies in 1838, and to the Constituent and Legislative Assemblies of 1848. Having voted against President Napoleon, he was exiled for a few months in 1852.

Chambon, shŏN'bŏN', (ANTOINE BENOÎT,) a French republican, who was deputed from Corrèze to the Convention in 1792. He was one of the proscribed Girondists who escaped from the Convention on the 31st of May, 1793. Having been declared a traitor by the terrorists, he was arrested near Lubersac, and executed, in 1793.

Chambon de Montaux, shŏN'bŏN' deh mŏN'tō', (NICOLAS,) a French physician, and mayor of Paris, was born at Brevannes, in Champagne, in 1748. Before the Revolution he had been first physician of the army, and inspector-general of the military hospitals. Having become a politician, and a moderate partisan of the new régime, he was elected mayor of Paris in place of Pétion in the autumn of 1792. He resigned his office early in 1793. He published numerous medical treatises, and wrote articles for the "Encyclopédie Méthodique." Died in 1826.

See QUÉRARD, " La France Littéraire."

Chambord, COMTE. See BORDEAUX, DUC DE.

Chambray, de, deh shŏN'brȧ', (GEORGES,) MARQUIS, a French officer and historian, born in Paris in 1783, served in several campaigns in Germany, and in the Russian campaign of 1812, when he was taken prisoner at Wilna. He returned to France in 1815, and, having been made maréchal-de-camp, he retired from service about 1830. He published an important work, entitled a "History of the Expedition to Russia," (1833,) which was received with great favour in France and foreign countries. Died about 1850.

See RAYMOND-BORDEAUX, " Notice biographique sur le Général de Chambray," 1850.

Chambray, de, (JACQUES FRANÇOIS,) born at Évreux, in France, in 1687, became grand-cross of the order of Saint John, and commandant of the troops of Malta. He was one of the ablest naval officers of his time, and often fought against the Turks and Algerines. Died in 1756.

See HENNEQUIN, "Biographie maritime."

Chambray or Chambrai, de, (ROLAND FRÉARD,) SIEUR, a learned French artist and writer on art, born at Mans. He translated into French Palladio's work on Architecture, and published a "Comparison between Ancient and Modern Architecture," (1650,) which had great success. Died in 1676.

See BLONDEAU, "Les Hommes illustres de Maine."

Chambre, de la, (MARIN Cureau-kü'ro',) a French physician and philosophic writer, born at Mans in 1594. Having gained a brilliant reputation by his talents and attainments, he was chosen in 1635 a member of the French Academy. He was afterwards physician to Louis XIV., who often consulted him in physiognomy. He published, besides other works, a very successful one, called "The Characters of the Passions," (5 vols., 1640–62,) and another entitled "The Art of Judging Men," (1659.) Died about 1670.

Chambure, de, (AUGUSTE Lepelletier—leh-pêl'te-ȧ',) a French officer, noted for his daring actions, was born at Vitteaux in 1789 ; died in 1832.

Chamfort, shŏN'foR', (SÉBASTIEN ROCH NICOLAS,) a successful and satirical French author, born near Clermont in Auvergne in 1741, lived mostly in Paris. In 1769 his "Éloge" on Molière gained the prize of the French Academy. About 1776 he published a "Dramatic Dictionary," and a tragedy named "Mustapha and Zéangir," which was performed with applause before the court. His eulogy on La Fontaine gained a prize for which La Harpe competed. He was admitted into the French Academy in 1781, and soon after was appointed reader or secretary to Madame Elizabeth, the king's sister. He favoured the Revolution in its first stages, and was a personal and political friend of Mirabeau, who addressed a series of letters to him. In 1790 he commenced a large collection or book called "Tableaux of the Revolution,"

and was chosen librarian of the National Library. Having been arrested in the reign of terror, he died in 1794, after having failed in an attempt to commit suicide. His "Maxims and Thoughts" is part of an unfinished work which Ginguené thinks would have placed him among the great painters of manners. Mirabeau called him une tête électrique.

See GINGUENÉ, "Vie et Écrits de Chamfort," prefixed to an edition of his works, 4 vols., 1795; AUGUIS, "Notice sur la Vie de Chamfort," prefixed to his collected works, 5 vols., 1825; ARSÈNE HOUSSAYE, "Philosophers and Actresses," vol. ii. ; "Fraser's Magazine" for September, 1852.

Chamier, shă'me-ȧ', (DANIEL,) a French Protestant theologian, born at Montélimart about 1570, was a very learned and staunch champion of his creed. After preaching some years at Montpellier, he became professor of theology at Montauban in 1612. He was killed in the civil war at the siege of Montauban in 1621. He had written several polemical works, and, according to Varillas, was the chief rédacteur of the edict of Nantes. His learning excited the admiration of Scaliger.

See "Memoir of D. Chamier, Minister of the Reformed Church," etc., London, 1852; BAYLE, "Historical and Critical Dictionary;" MM. HAAG, "La France protestante."

Cham'ier, (FREDERICK,) an English novelist, born in London in 1796. He has written several popular novels, among which are "Ben Brace," (1835,) "The Arethusa," (1836,) and "Trevor Hastings," (1841.)

Chamillard, shă'me-yăR', (MICHEL,) a French minister of state, born in 1651. He was appointed controller-general of finances in 1699, when his modesty prompted him to decline the honour ; but Louis XIV. urged him, saying, "I will second you." In 1701 he became minister of war, probably through the influence of Madame de Maintenon. He proved to be incompetent for that office, and was driven by the force of public opinion to resign the ministry of finances in 1708, and that of war in 1709. Died in 1721.

See SAINT-SIMON, "Mémoires."

Chamillart, shă'me'yăR', or Chamillard,(ÉTIENNE,) a French Jesuit and antiquary, born at Bourges in 1656, edited Prudentius "ad usum Delphini." Died in 1730.

See MORÉRI, "Dictionnaire Historique."

Chamilly, de, deh shă'me'ye', (NOËL BOUTON,) MARQUIS, an able French general, born at Chamilly in 1636. After passing through all the grades, he greatly distinguished himself in 1675 by the defence of Grave, the siege of which lasted four months. He surrendered at last to the Prince of Orange. In 1703 he obtained a marshal's bâton. Certain love-letters addressed to him by a Portuguese nun added to his celebrity, and were often printed. (See ALCAFORADA.) Died in 1715.

His brother HÉRARD, Count de Chamilly, served under the Prince of Condé in many campaigns, and became lieutenant-general. Died in 1673.

See SAINT-SIMON, "Mémoires."

Chamisso, von, fon shă'me'so', (ADELBERT,) or more properly LOUIS CHARLES ADELAIDE DE CHAMISSO, a popular poet and naturalist, was born in Champagne, in France, in 1781. About 1790 he emigrated with the family to Berlin, where he became a page to the Queen of Prussia, and made himself master of the German language, in which his works are written. Having served several years in the Prussian army, he quitted the profession of arms about 1808, and applied himself to natural sciences. He wrote numerous popular lyric poems, and "Peter Schlemihl," (1814,) a singular and interesting story of a man who lost his shadow. In 1814 he was selected by Count Romanzoff to accompany, as naturalist, a scientific expedition round the world, of which he wrote a valuable account, "Observations during a Voyage round the World," (1827.) He was a member of the Academy of Sciences of Berlin, and author of a "Survey of the Plants of Northern Germany," (1827.) Died in 1838.

See J. E. HITZIG, "Leben und Briefe von A. v. Chamisso," 2 vols., 1839 ; AMPÈRE, article in the "Revue des Deux Mondes" for May 15, 1840 ; QUÉRARD, "La France Littéraire." (Supplément ;) LONGFELLOW, "Poets and Poetry of Europe ;" "Foreign Quarterly Review" for January, 1846.

Chamorin, shă'mo'răN', (VITAL JOACHIM,) BARON, a French general, born at Bonnelles (Seine-et-Oise) in 1773. He had two horses killed under him at Marengo in 1800. As major he made the campaigns of 1805, '06, and '07, and distinguished himself at Jena and Eylau. He became general of brigade in 1811, and was killed at Campo-Mayor, in Spain, the same year.

See "Notice historique sur le Général Chamorin," Paris, 1844.

Chamorro, chä-mor'ro, (Fruto,) a Central American statesman and general, born at Guatemala in 1806, was elected supreme director, or president, in 1853. Died in 1855.

Chamousset, de, deh shä′moo′să′, (Claude Humbert Piarron,) Chevalier, a Frenchman, noted for practical philanthropy, was born in Paris in 1717. He turned his house into a hospital for the poor, for whose benefit he employed physicians, and was instrumental in reforming the public hospital, (Hôtel-Dieu.) He wrote several humanitarian treatises, first proposed fire-insurance companies, and became intendant-general of the military hospitals. Died in 1773.

Champagne, shôn′pän′, (Jean Baptiste,) a Flemish painter, born at Brussels in 1643, was a nephew and pupil of Philippe, noticed below, whom he assisted in many works at Paris. He was employed by Louis XIV. at Versailles. Died in 1688.

See Descamps, "Vies des Peintres Flamands," etc.

Champagne, (Jean François,) a French professor, born at Semur in 1751. He was principal of the College of Louis le Grand, in Paris, for about fifteen years, beginning in 1791. A translation of Aristotle's "Politics" opened to him the Institute in 1797. Died in 1813.

Champagne, de, deh shôn′pän′, or **Champaigne,** shôn′pän′, (Philippe,) an eminent Flemish painter of history, born at Brussels in 1602, was a pupil of Fouquières. At the age of nineteen he went to Paris, where he was instructed by Nicholas Poussin, became painter to the queen, Anne of Austria, and acquired a high reputation. He worked with great facility, and adorned the royal palaces and the churches of Paris with many works, of which a "Mary Magdalene in the House of Simon the Pharisee" is one of the best. He made excellent portraits of Louis XIII., Cardinal Richelieu, Mazarin, and others. Died in 1674.

See Descamps, "Vies des Peintres Flamands," etc.; Félibien, "Entretiens sur les plus célèbres Peintres."

Champagne, de, (Thibaud.) See Thibaud.

Champagney, de, deh shôn′pän′yă′, (Frédéric Perrenot—pȧ′reh-no′,) a Flemish statesman, a younger brother of Cardinal Granvelle, was born about 1530. He was appointed Governor of Antwerp, and head of the Council of Finance in Flanders. Died in 1595.

See Motley, "United Netherlands," vol. i. chap. i. et seq.

Champagny, de, deh shôn′pän′ye′, (François Joseph Marie Thérèse,) Count, born at Vienna in 1804, was a son of the Duc de Cadore. He is, or was, attached to the political and religious school of Montalembert, and has contributed to the "Correspondant" and other periodicals. His chief work is a "History of the Cæsars," (1843.)

Champagny, de, (Jean Baptiste Nompère—nôn′paiR′,) Duc de Cadore, (kȧ′doR′,) a French courtier and negotiator, was born in 1756. He was deputed by the noblesse of Forez to the States-General in 1789, and, uniting with the Tiers-État, became a prominent and moderate member of the National Assembly. As chairman of the marine committee, he rendered valuable services in 1790 and 1791. Having passed several years in private, he became in 1800 councillor of state, and in 1801 ambassador to Vienna. He gained the favour of Napoleon by his address in negotiation and his pliability of character. In 1804 he was appointed minister of the interior, count of the empire, and grand officer of the legion of honour. He succeeded Talleyrand as minister of foreign affairs in 1807, and the next year was made Duc de Cadore. In the campaign of 1809 he attended Bonaparte in Austria, and negotiated the treaty of Vienna. He ceased to be foreign minister in 1811. During the absence of the emperor in 1812 and 1813, he was secretary of state. In 1819, after passing a few years in private life, he was restored to the Chamber of Peers, where he voted with the Right Centre. Died in 1834.

See his "Souvenirs," 1846; "Mémoires de Mirabeau;" "Nouvelle Biographie Générale."

Champaigne. See Champagne.

Champe, champ, (John,) an American officer, noted for his daring attempt to capture the traitor Arnold, was born in Loudon county, Virginia, about 1752. In 1780 he was sent by Washington to New York, in the guise of a deserter, for the purpose of bringing off Arnold in time, if possible, to save André. He formed a plan to seize him while walking in his garden, and drag him as a drunken soldier, between two men, to a boat on the Hudson. The plan failed in consequence of Arnold's moving his quarters the day preceding. Died about 1795.

Champeaux, de, deh shôn′po′, [Lat. Campellen′sis,] (Guillaume,) a celebrated French professor and scholastic philosopher, born at Champeaux. He taught rhetoric, logic, etc., in Paris, with great success, but was eclipsed by his pupil Abelard, who became his rival. In 1113 he became Bishop of Châlons-sur-Marne. He died in 1121, and left some works on theology.

See B. Hauréau, "De la Philosophie scolastique;" "Histoire Littéraire de France."

Champein, shôn′pän′, (Stanislas,) a French composer, born at Marseilles in 1753. He composed successful operas. Died in 1830.

Champfleury, shôn′fluh′re′, the assumed name of Jules Fleury, (zhül fluh′re′,) a French writer of fiction, born at Laon in 1821. He has published several dramas and many novels, among which we may name "Les Bourgeois de Molinchart."

Champier, shôn′pe-ă′, (Symphorien,) an eminent French physician, born in the Lyonnais in 1472. Having graduated as M.D., he settled at Lyons, where he founded a medical college and other useful institutions. He received or assumed the title of physician to Louis XII., and wrote many works on medicine and history, of which the former are the best, especially his "Hortus Gallicus." Died in 1539.

See Nicéron, "Mémoires;" "Biographie Médicale."

Champigny, de, deh shôn′pèn′ye′, (Jean,) a French littérateur, published a "History of England," (1777,) and several other historical works, and translated Schlegel's "History of Danish Kings." Died about 1787.

Champin, shôn′pän′, (Jean Jacques,) a French landscape-painter, born at Sceaux, near Paris, in 1796. He executed numerous fine lithographs, and paintings in water-colours. In conjunction with Regnier, he published "The Homes of Celebrated Persons," illustrated.

Cham′pi-on, (Anthony,) an English writer, born at Croydon in 1724-25. He was elected to Parliament in 1754, and again in 1761. A volume of his Miscellanies, in prose and verse, was published by his friend Lord Lyttleton in 1801. Died in 1801.

Champion, shôn′pe-ôn′, (Edme,) a French philanthropist, born in Yonne in 1764; died in 1852.

See C. L. Chassin, "La Légende historique du Petit Manteau Bleu," (i.e. E. Champion,) 1852.

Champion de Pontalier, shôn′pe-ôn′ deh pôn′tä′le-ă′, (François,) a French priest, born at Rennes in 1731, resided in Paris and Orléans. He wrote, besides other works, "Pious Readings, adapted to all States," (4 vols., 1804,) which is said to be excellent. Died in 1812. His brother, Charles François Champion de Nilon, (ne′lôn′,) born in 1724, was professor of theology at the Jesuits' College of La Flèche. He wrote an approved catechism, and a few other works. Died in 1794.

Championnet, shôn′pe-o′nă′, (Jean Étienne,) an able French general, born at Valence in 1762. About 1790 he obtained command of a battalion, and, having distinguished himself in the Palatinate in 1793, he was made general of division. From 1794 to 1797 he took part in the principal actions on the Lower Rhine. In 1798 he obtained the chief command of the army sent to defend the Roman republic against Naples. Having defeated General Mack, he entered Naples in triumph in January, 1799, and organized the Parthenopean republic. In August he succeeded Joubert as commander of the army of Italy, and was defeated by a superior force of Austrians at Genola in November. He died of an epidemic in December, 1799, or January, 1800.

See "Victoires et Conquêtes des Français;" Châteauneuf, "Histoire du Général Championnet," 1806; Henri Dourille, "Histoire de Championnet," 1839.

ā, ē, ī, ō, ū, ȳ, long; ă, ĕ, ŏ, same, less prolonged; ä, ĕ, ĭ, ŏ, ŭ, ȳ, short; a, ę, į, ǫ, obscure; fär, fȧll, fät; mēt; nŏt; gŏŏd; mŏŏn;

Championnière, shôN'pe'o'ne-aiʀ', (PAUL LUCAS,) a French jurist, born at Nantes in 1798; died in 1851.

Champlain, sham'plān', [Fr. pron. shôN'plåN',] (SAMUEL,) the founder of Quebec, and first Governor of Canada, was born at Brouage, in France. For his services in the navy in the war against the Spaniards he was pensioned by Henry IV., under whose auspices he made his first voyage to Canada in 1603. Renewing the enterprise in 1608, he ascended the Saint Lawrence to the site of Quebec, where he planted a colony. In 1610 he discovered the lake which bears his name, and spent several ensuing years in fostering the fur-trade and in exploring the region of the great lakes. In 1620 he was appointed Governor of Canada. The English captured Quebec about 1628, but restored it to the French soon after the treaty of peace which was made in 1629 or 1630. Champlain returned to Quebec in 1633, and died there in 1635. History represents him as brave, honourable, and capable. He wrote several narratives of his voyages and discoveries, which were published in 1632.

See "Nouvelle Biographie Générale;" CHARLEVOIX, "Histoire de la Nouvelle France."

Champmeslé, shôN'mȧ'lȧ', (MARIE Desmares— dȧ'måʀ',) a popular French actress, born at Rouen in 1644. She acted in Paris with great success from 1670 to 1698, and is said to have created many *rôles*, among which were Berenice, Iphigenia, Monimia, and Medea. Her features were radiant with sensibility, and her voice excelled in the expression of pathos. She was very intimate with the poet Racine. Died in 1698.

Champmeslé, de, deh shôN'mȧ'lȧ', (CHARLES Chevillet—shȩh've'lȧ',) SIEUR, the husband of Marie Desmares, noticed above, was an actor of moderate ability, and author of several dramas, of which "Crispin Chevalier" is called the best. Died in 1701.

Champollion, sham-pol'le-ǫn, [Fr. pron. shôN'po'-le-ôN',] (JEAN FRANÇOIS,) a French savant and linguist, celebrated as the interpreter of the symbols by which ancient Egypt sought to eternize its annals and its institutions, was born at Figeac, in the department of Lot, in December, 1791. In 1807 he went to Paris, where he studied Oriental languages and antiquities. He was appointed assistant professor of history in the Academy of Grenoble in 1809, and then began his researches into the history and language of ancient Egypt. In 1812 he became principal professor of history at Grenoble. He published in 1814 a "Geographical Description of Egypt under the Pharaohs." From the inscriptions of the famous Rosetta stone he derived a key to the hieroglyphic writing, and discovered that the symbols are occasionally used as phonetic signs, and each phonetic sign represents the initial sound of the object signified by the hieroglyphic. Thus, the mouth is the sign of *r*, because in Coptic the mouth is called *Ro.* Having obtained the equivalents of twenty-one letters of the Greek alphabet, he announced his discovery to the Academy of Inscriptions in 1822. It produced a great sensation, and its importance was highly appreciated. In 1824 he published a "Précis du Système hiéroglyphique des anciens Égyptiens," ("Summary of the Hieroglyphic System of the Ancient Egyptians,") in which he proves that the phonetic alphabet was used in the royal legends of all epochs and is the key to the whole hieroglyphic system. In 1826 he was appointed director of the Royal Egyptian Museum of Paris, and in 1828 was employed at the expense of the government in an expedition to Egypt, whose monuments he explored for sixteen months in company with Rosellini, who was sent by the Duke of Tuscany. He was admitted into the Institute (Academy of Inscriptions) in 1830, and a chair of Egyptian antiquities was founded for him in the College of France. He died in March, 1832, while preparing to publish the results of his researches in Egypt. This great work, in which Rosellini co-operated, has since appeared, with the title of "Monuments of Egypt and Nubia, considered in Relation to History, Religion, etc.," (1835-45.) Among his most important productions are an "Egyptian Grammar" and a "Hieroglyphic Dictionary," (published since his death,) which are said to place him in the highest rank of Egyptologists. But little progress has been made in this department of learning since

the death of Champollion. The English claim that his great discovery was anticipated by Dr. Young, but admit that the crude notions of Young were corrected by the French savant. Chevalier Bunsen has written in favour of Champollion, and calls his discovery of the Egyptian alphabet the greatest discovery of the century.

See SILVESTRE DE SACY, "Notice sur Champollion lue à la Séance publique de l'Institut," 1833; ROSELLINI, "Tributo di Riconoscenza alla Memoria di G. F. Champollion," 1832.

Champollion-Figeac, shôN'po'le-ôN' fe'zhȧk', (JEAN JACQUES,) a French linguist and antiquary, brother of the preceding, was born at Figeac in 1778. He became in his youth professor of Greek at Grenoble, and published, in 1807, "Antiquities of Grenoble." His "Annales des Lagides" ("Chronicles of the Greek Kings of Egypt") obtained a prize from the Institute in 1819. From 1828 to 1848 he was keeper of the manuscripts of the Royal Library, in Paris. He published a "Treatise on Archæology," (1843,) and various other works, and edited several posthumous works of his brother. From 1849 he was librarian to Napoleon III. Died in May, 1867.

See QUÉRARD, "La France Littéraire;" "Nouvelle Biographie Générale."

Champs. See DESCHAMPS.

Chancel. See LA GRANGE, (JOSEPH DE CHANCEL.)

Chan'cel-lǫr, (RICHARD,) an English navigator, who made an exploring voyage to the White Sea in 1553. He was drowned on the coast of Scotland in 1556.

Chandieu, shôN'de-uh', or **Sadeel,** sȧ'dȧl', (ANTOINE LA ROCHE,) an eminent Protestant minister, born in the Mâconnais, in France, about 1534. He began to preach in Paris at the age of twenty, and became noted for his zeal and eloquence. He officiated in the army of Henry IV. in 1587, and became professor of Hebrew at Geneva in 1589. Died in 1591.

See BAYLE, "Historical and Critical Dictionary;" J. LECTIUS, "Vita A. Sadeelis," prefixed to his works.

Chand'lẹr, (ABIEL,) a Boston merchant, born in Concord, New Hampshire, about 1778. He graduated at Harvard in 1806. Died in 1851. He bequeathed fifty thousand dollars to Dartmouth College for founding a scientific department of instruction, and the remainder of his estate to the New Hampshire Asylum for the Insane.

Chand'lẹr, (EDWARD,) D.D., an English bishop, born in Dublin. He was nominated to the see of Lichfield in 1717, and translated to Durham in 1730. He published a learned "Defence of Christianity from the Prophecies of the Old Testament," (1725.) Died in 1750.

Chandler, (ELIZABETH MARGARET,) an American poetess and philanthropist, born near Wilmington, Delaware, in 1807. She wrote "The Slave-Ship," and other poems on moral and religious subjects. Died in Michigan in 1834. A volume of her poems, with a memoir of her life, appeared in 1836.

See GRISWOLD's "Female Poets of America."

Chandler, (MARY,) an English poetess, born in Wiltshire in 1687, became a resident of Bath. She published a "Description of Bath," and other poems. Died in 1745.

See CIBBER's "Lives of the Poets," etc.

Chandler, (RICHARD,) D.D., an English antiquary and writer of travels, born at Elson, in Hampshire, in 1738. In 1764, as an agent of the Dilettanti Society, he visited and explored Asia Minor and Greece in company with the artists Revett and Pars. The results of their enterprise appeared in "Ionian Antiquities, or Ruins of Famous Buildings in Ionia," (1769.) He afterwards published "Travels in Asia Minor," (1775,) and "Travels in Greece," (1776,) which are highly esteemed, and other works. He became rector of Tylehurst in 1800, and died in 1810.

See WALCKENAER, "Vies de plusieurs Personnes célèbres;" ERSCH and GRUBER, "Allgemeine Encyklopaedie."

Chandler, (SAMUEL,) D.D., an eminent English dissenting minister, born at Hungerford in 1693. In 1716 he became pastor of a Presbyterian church at Peckham. He afterwards removed to London, where he preached many years at the Old Jewry, and gained a wide reputation by his religious writings. His "Critical History of the Life of David" (1766) is regarded by some as his best work. Died in 1766.

See "Biographia Britannica."

Chandler, (THOMAS BRADBURY,) an Episcopal clergyman and writer, born at Woodstock, Connecticut, in 1726, preached at Elizabethtown, New Jersey. Having joined the royalist party in the Revolution, he retired for safety to England in 1775, but returned to his former post in 1785. Died in 1790.

Chan'dos, (JOHN,) after the Black Prince, the most famous English captain of his time, was lieutenant-general of all the provinces of France which were subject to the English. In 1364 he gained a decisive victory over Du Guesclin at Auray. Chandos and the Black Prince defeated the same able general at Navarette in 1366. He was killed in battle at Leusac in 1369.

See SISMONDI, "Histoire des Français."

Chăn'drä, [common Hindoo pron. chŭn'dra or chŭn'der,] called also **So'ma,** in Hindoo mythology, the god or regent of the moon. He is usually represented as riding in a car drawn by antelopes, (or an antelope,) his head being adorned with a crescent.

See MOOR, "Hindu Pantheon;" COLEMAN, "Hindu Mythology."

Chandragupta or **Chandragoupta.** See SANDROCOTTUS.

Chanfary. See SHANFAREE.

Changarnier, shŏn'găr'ne-à', (NICOLAS ANNE THÉODULE,) a celebrated French general, was born at Autun in 1793. He distinguished himself as lieutenant in Spain in 1823, and joined the expedition to Algeria in 1830, with the rank of captain. After several remarkable exploits in Africa, he was made a colonel in 1838, and a maréchal-de-camp in 1840. He was wounded near Médeah in 1841, and for his important services in the expedition to the mountains of Ouarencenis he was raised to the rank of general of division in 1843. In 1847 he was appointed by the Duc d'Aumale commander of the division of Algiers. He returned to France soon after the revolution of 1848, and was nominated minister to Berlin, but was detained at Paris by the dangers that menaced the government, and in May went to Algeria as Governor-General in place of Cavaignac. Before the end of 1848 he was appointed commander-in-chief of the national guard of Paris, and of the first military division. He acquired great political influence, and strenuously supported the administration of Louis Napoleon in 1849 and 1850. He is said to have been opposed to the republican form of government, or, at least, to a French republic. In January, 1851, he was deprived of the command of the army by Napoleon, who appears to have regarded him as his rival. His efforts and designs to support the National Assembly were defeated by the *coup d'état* of December 2, 1851. He was arrested on that day, and exiled in January, 1852, since which he has resided mostly in Belgium.

See "Le Général Changarnier," Paris, 1848; LAMARTINE, "Histoire de la Révolution de 1848;" "Nouvelle Biographie Générale."

Changeux, shŏN'zhuh', (PIERRE JACQUES,) a French savant, born at Orléans in 1740. He cultivated the exact sciences, made improvements in the barometer, and wrote numerous works, of which the most remarkable is an ingenious "Treatise on Extremes, or Elements of the Science of Reality," (2 vols., 1767.) Died in 1800.

Chan'ning, (EDWARD TYRREL,) an American scholar and writer, born at Newport, Rhode Island, in 1790, graduated at Harvard. He studied law with his brother, Francis D. Channing. About 1815 he aided to found the "North American Review," which he edited for a short time in 1819 and to which he contributed many critical and biographical articles. He was appointed professor of rhetoric and oratory in Harvard University in the latter year, and continued to fill this position about thirty-two years, with much ability. Died in 1856.

Channing, (WALTER,) an American physician, brother of the preceding, born at Newport, Rhode Island, in 1786. He entered Harvard in 1804, graduated as M.D. in the University of Pennsylvania, studied afterwards in Edinburgh, and began to practise in Boston in 1812. He was professor of obstetrics and medical jurisprudence at Harvard from 1815 to 1854. He published "Etherization in Childbirth," (1848,) "Miscellaneous Poems," (1851,) and other works.

Channing, (WILLIAM ELLERY,) D.D., a distinguished Unitarian divine, and one of the most eloquent writers America has produced, was born at Newport, Rhode Island, April 7, 1780. Both his parents are said to have possessed rare moral worth as well as superior intellectual powers, and the early influences of his home appear to have been eminently favourable to the development of that delicacy, purity, and elevation of sentiment which formed perhaps the most striking feature of his character. Even as a child he was remarkable for a certain moral dignity which caused his playfellows always to look up to him with respect. Before he had completed his thirteenth year, his father died. The impression made upon his mind by this solemn event, strengthened as it was by the influence of a "revival" which occurred about the same time, may be said to mark the commencement of his religious life. In 1794 he entered Harvard, where he was distinguished for his varied acquirements as well as for the versatility of his powers. At his graduation, the English oration, regarded as the highest honour, was assigned to him. His effort on this occasion was brilliantly successful, and was received by the audience with enthusiastic and tumultuous acclamation.

The range of Channing's studies was very extensive. His mind, indeed, was powerfully attracted by every form of moral beauty or moral grandeur, wherever found, —whether in the stern virtue of the Stoics, the lofty and heroic morality of Fichte, or the divine purity and sublime simplicity of the teachings of the gospel. His favourite poets were Shakspeare and Wordsworth. He appears especially to have sympathized with the power of the latter poet to detect beauty in the simplest of Nature's works, and to recognize greatness under every disguise and in the lowliest situations.

Soon after leaving college, he accepted an invitation to become tutor in a family residing in Richmond, Virginia. He seems to have been very painfully impressed with what he saw of slavery, and declared in a letter that this alone would prevent him from ever settling in the South. During this period his views of the great importance of religion appear to have acquired additional distinctness and force; for he says, in one of his letters, "Religion is the only treasure worth pursuing. I consider the man who recommends it to society as more useful than the greatest sage and patriot who adorns the page of history." In the same letter he says, also, "I long most earnestly to be such a minister as Fénelon describes." The foregoing sentences seem clearly to indicate the purpose of his life. In July, 1800, he returned to Newport. The vessel in which he sailed was damp and leaky, and manned by a drunken captain and crew. From the exposure and hardships of that voyage may be dated that permanent physical derangement with which the remainder of his life was one long unceasing struggle. Having pursued his studies for more than a year at Newport, he removed in the beginning of 1802 to Cambridge. While here, he filled the office of regent in the college, carrying on at the same time his theological studies. He was installed in the Federal Street Church in Boston in 1803. At what time he definitely adopted the theological views which he subsequently taught, it is impossible to say: there is but little question, however, that they were developed gradually, through years of examination and reflection. On one point, indeed, we are not left in doubt; for he expressly tells us that he was "never in any sense a Trinitarian."

His first efforts as a preacher attracted much attention; and it was not long before he was generally acknowledged to be the most eloquent minister and most influential leader among the Unitarians. In 1814 he delivered a discourse on the fall of Napoleon, and "the goodness of God in delivering the Christian world from military despotism," which is regarded as among the most splendid of all his efforts as a pulpit orator. The same year he was married to Miss Gibbs, of Newport. In 1820 he received from Harvard College the degree of doctor of divinity. At the request of his friends, who were anxious that he should have some respite from his arduous and unremitting labours, he sailed for Europe in 1822; and after making in England many interesting acquaintances, among whom were Wordsworth and Coleridge, and visiting France, Switzerland, and Italy,

ā, ē, ī, ō, ū, ȳ, *long;* ă, ĕ, ŏ, same, less prolonged; ă, ĕ, ĭ, ŏ, ŭ, ȳ, *short;* a, e, i, o, *obscure;* fär, fäll, fät; mĕt; nŏt; gŏŏd; mŏŏn;

he returned home in the autumn of 1823. Coleridge said of him, " He has the love of wisdom, and the wisdom of love." Dr. Channing took a deep interest in every enterprise having for its object the relief of suffering or the promotion of knowledge and virtue among mankind. He gave his earnest sympathy and support to the peace-movement inaugurated by Noah (afterwards Doctor) Worcester, and in 1816 preached a sermon on war before the Convention of the Congregational ministers of Massachusetts. It was published and extensively circulated, and contributed much to prepare the way for the formation of peace societies in different parts of the United States. He did not, however, take the ground of absolute non-resistance ; he did not maintain that war could be wholly dispensed with, in the present condition of the world ; but he believed that by dissipating the false ideas of national glory which now prevail,—by enlightening and elevating the minds of the people,—wars must of necessity become less and less frequent as well as less cruel.

In 1828 he published, in the "Christian Examiner," " Remarks on the Life and Character of Napoleon Bonaparte." Probably none of his writings has contributed so much as this to spread his fame to every part of the civilized world. His lectures on "Self-Culture" and on the "Elevation of the Labouring Classes" had an extensive circulation, and were republished in England. Dr. Channing sympathized deeply with the temperance cause and with the anti-slavery movement. Having visited the West Indies for his health in the autumn of 1830, he remained there until the following spring, and during this period he commenced a work on slavery, which was published some years later. In 1837 he addressed a public letter to Henry Clay against the annexation of Texas, the acquisition of which was earnestly advocated by many Southern politicians on the ground that it would afford fresh territory for the extension of slavery. His last public address was delivered, August 1, 1842, at Lennox, Massachusetts, in commemoration of the abolition of slavery in the British West Indies. He died the 2d of October of the same year. He was buried at Mount Auburn, where his grave is marked by a monument designed by his friend Washington Allston.

As a writer, Dr. Channing's merits are of a very high order. His style, always clear, forcible, and elegant, not unfrequently rises into a strain of lofty and spirit-stirring eloquence. A critic in "Fraser's Magazine" remarks, " Channing is unquestionably the finest writer of the age. From his writings may be extracted some of the richest poetry and richest conceptions, clothed in language, unfortunately for our literature, too little studied in the day in which we live." Among his theological discourses, his lecture on the "Evidences of Christianity," delivered at Harvard in 1821, is perhaps the most remarkable. It would, we think, be difficult to point out anything more admirable on the same subject in the whole compass of English literature. Of his character as a man there can be among candid judges but one opinion. A writer, well qualified to form a just estimate of his rare qualities, observes, " Perhaps that which gives the highest idea of his character was the fact that he occupied a constantly growing place in your respect as you knew him more intimately. . . . His writings were not exceptions to his life, but the natural, unforced, and often incidental expression of his ordinary state of mind. His common conversation was more genial and varied, but it was pitched on the same moral key with his writings. . . . His life was a public one ; but he had no sensitiveness to public opinion so far as it affected himself. I do not believe there is a line in all his writings which ever received a different colouring from any thought of its influence on his own reputation. . . . He wrote, not for himself, but as one dedicated to truth." (See Letter from Dr. Peabody, in Sprague's "Annals of the American Pulpit," vol. viii. pp. 376–378.) One of the most beautiful and admirable traits in Dr. Channing's character was his anxiety not to allow the spirit of controversy or pride of opinion to hinder in any way the reception of new truth. For this reason he not only avoided controversy as much as possible, lest it might in some sense "commit" him to the support of certain opinions, but

he was most anxious to avoid that personal influence (whether arising from his acknowledged intellectual power, or from his superior power of expression) which might interfere with the perfect freedom of those with whom he conversed. He desired, *not that they should adopt his thoughts and convictions, but be true to their own.* So great was his sense of the sacredness of the human heart and conscience, that he would not willingly force them, even with the gentle force of irresistible persuasion. For illustrations of his extraordinary gentleness, fairness, and magnanimity towards those who were opposed to him, the reader is referred to the "Memoir," by his nephew, (vol. ii. pp. 88–90.)

In addition to his merits as a writer and orator, Dr. Channing is said to have possessed rare taste and judgment in regard to works of art. Washington Allston once said that he valued no one's opinions of his pictures so much as Dr. Channing's.

Channing's collected works have been published in six 12mo vols., (Boston, 1846,) and republished in London, in crown 8vo, (1855.) Several of his essays and other writings have been translated into French and German. A notice of Dr. Channing, from the eloquent pen of M. Laboulaye, appeared in the "Journal des Débats" in 1852.

See "Memoirs of William Ellery Channing, with Extracts from his Correspondence and Manuscripts," by his nephew, the Rev. WILLIAM H. CHANNING, Boston, 1848; SPRAGUE, "Annals of the American Unitarian Pulpit," 1 vol. 8vo, New York, 1865; also "North American Review" for October, 1835, (by ALEXANDER H. EVERETT;) "Fraser's Magazine" for May and September, 1838, (vols. xvii. and xviii.;) "Channing, sa Vie et ses Œuvres, avec une Préface de M. Charles de Rémusat," Paris, 1857 ; "Foreign Quarterly Review" for January, 1840; "Westminster Review" for January, 1849, vol. l. ; GRISWOLD, "Prose Writers of America."

Channing, (WILLIAM HENRY,) an eloquent Unitarian minister, a nephew of William Ellery Channing, and a son of Francis D. Channing, was born in Boston in 1810. He graduated at Harvard College in 1829, after which he studied divinity. He officiated as minister in New York City, Cincinnati, Boston, and Liverpool, England. He contributed articles to the "Christian Examiner," the "North American Review," and other periodicals. Among his works are a "Memoir of William Ellery Channing," (3 vols., 1848,) and a work "On the Christian Church and Social Reform."

Chantal, de, dẹh shŏn'tȧl', (JEANNE FRANÇOISE **Fremiot**—frẹh-me-o',) a French lady, and a saint of the Roman Church, born at Dijon in 1572, became the wife of Baron de Chantal. She founded and superintended many convents of the order of Visitation, between 1610 and 1630. Died in 1641. Her son was the father of Madame de Sévigné.

See BEAUFILS, "Vie de J. F. Fremiot de Chantal," 1752; MAUPAS DU TOUR, "Vie de J. F. Fremiot de Chantal," 1753; JANNART, "Abrégé de la Vie de Sainte-Chantal," 1752; MARSOLLIER, "Vie de la Mère de Chantal," 1715; WILLIAM H. COOMBES, "History of the Life of S. J. F. Chantal," 2 vols., 1830.

Chanteclair, de, dẹh shŏnt'klȧr', [Lat. CANTOCLA'-RUS,] (CHARLES,) a French jurist and distinguished Latin scholar, died in Paris in 1620.

Chantelauze, de, dẹh shŏnt'lōz', (JEAN CLAUDE BALTHAZAR VICTOR,) a French politician, born at Montbrison (Loire) in 1787. He was elected to the Chamber of Deputies in 1827, and in May, 1830, was appointed keeper of the seals, or minister of justice. Having shared with Polignac the responsibility of the measures which provoked the revolution of 1830, he was tried by the peers and sentenced to imprisonment for life. He was released by the king about 1838.

See LAMARTINE, "Histoire de la Restauration."

Chantereau-Lefebvre, shŏnt'rō' lẹh-fĕvr', (LOUIS,) a learned French antiquary, born in Paris in 1588, wrote on the genealogy of the house of Lorraine. Died in 1658.

Chantonay, de, dẹh shŏn'to'nȧ', (THOMAS PERRENOT,) a courtier, born at Besançon in 1514, was a son of Chancellor Granvelle. He was sent as ambassador by Philip II. of Spain to Paris, in order to watch the designs of Catherine de Médicis. Supported by the Guises, he assumed the part of a minister of state at the French court. Catherine requested that he should be recalled, (1563 ;) but he remained two years longer. Died in 1575.

See SISMONDI, "Histoire des Français."

€ as k; ç as s; ğ hard; ġ as j; G, H, K, *guttural;* N, *nasal;* R, *trilled;* s as z; th as in *this.*   (☞See Explanations, p. 23.)

Chantreau, shăn'trō', (PIERRE NICOLAS,) a French *littérateur,* born in Paris in 1741. Besides other works, he published a Spanish-French Grammar, and "The Science of History," (1803,) containing directions for the study of history. Died in 1808.

Chan'trey, (Sir FRANCIS,) an eminent English sculptor, born at Norton, Derbyshire, in 1782. Having learned the trade of carver in Sheffield, he went to London about 1804, and became a sculptor. Nollekens was among the first to recognize his merit and to promote his success, which soon became brilliant, especially in portraits and monumental sculpture. In 1816 he was chosen an associate, and in 1818 a member, of the Royal Academy. He visited Italy in 1819. He was knighted about 1836. Among his most admired works are a bronze statue of William Pitt, London; a statue of Bishop Heber, at Calcutta; of Canning, at Liverpool; of Washington, at Boston, Massachusetts; and "The Sleeping Children," in Lichfield Cathedral. His busts of eminent contemporaries are very numerous. He died in 1841, leaving a wife, but no children.

See GEORGE JONES, "Life of F. Chantrey," 1850; JOHN HOLLAND, "Memorials of Sir F. Chantrey," 1851; "Men I have known," by WILLIAM JERDAN, 1866; "Fraser's Magazine" for April, 1851.

Chanut, shä'nü', (PIERRE,) an able French diplomatist, born at Riom in 1600, was a friend of Descartes. Died in 1662.

Chanvalon, de, dęh shŏN'vȧ'lôN', (JEAN BAPTISTE THIBAUT,) a French savant, born at Martinique about 1725, was educated in Paris, by Jussieu, Réaumur, etc. He published in 1763 a description of his native island, entitled "Voyage à la Martinique." Died in 1785.

Chao-Hao. See SHAO-HAO.

Chao-Kang. See SHAO-KANG.

Cha'os, [Gr. Χάος,] a name originally applied to the infinite void which the ancients supposed to have existed before the creation of the world. Ovid represents it as a confused heterogeneous mass, containing the primitive elements out of which all the subsequent material creations were formed. According to Hesiod, Chaos was the parent of Erebus and Nox. Some of the poets personified Chaos as the monarch or ruler of the primeval void.

Chapelain, shăp'lâN', (ANDRÉ,) a French priest of the twelfth or thirteenth century, wrote "De Arte amatoria."

Chapelain, (JEAN,) a French poet and critic, born in Paris in 1595. He was one of a small company of literati who in 1635 organized themselves under the auspices of Richelieu with the title of the "French Academy." The Dictionary of the Academy was planned by him. He was regarded as an oracle in the literary world. His epic poem "La Pucelle" was extolled in advance as the greatest triumph of human genius; but its glory quickly faded under the sarcastic wit and ridicule of Boileau, and it sank into merited neglect. "He began by being the oracle of authors," says Voltaire, "and ended by being their shame." Died in 1674.

See VOLTAIRE, "Siècle de Louis XIV."

Chapelier, le, lęh shăp'le-à', (ISAAC RENÉ GUI,) an eminent French lawyer, born at Rennes in 1754, was deputed to the States-General in 1789. He was among the ablest orators of this body, in which he often presided. As a member and reporter of the committee on the first constitution, he drafted the decree which abolished nobility. His political affinities were with the Feuillants, or the friends of the constitution. He was condemned to death on a charge of having conspired in favour of royalty, and executed in 1794.

Chapelle, shä'pĕl', (CLAUDE EMMANUEL **Luillier**—lü-e'ye-à',) a witty French versifier, born at Chapelle, near Paris, in 1626. Gassendi, who frequented his father's house, gave him lessons in philosophy, to which Molière, the future dramatic poet, was admitted. Chapelle is said to have aided Molière, Racine, and Boileau in the composition of their poems. He wrote some pieces of verse which were much admired. He was one of a famous supper-party of Auteuil who, after copious potations, moralized so eloquently on the miseries of life that they resolved to take their quietus at the bottom of the river.

They were diverted from the instant execution of that purpose by Molière's suggestion that broad daylight should shine upon and witness so noble an action. Died in 1686.

See VOLTAIRE, "Siècle de Louis XIV;" D'ALEMBERT, "Éloge de Chapelle."

Chapelle, La. See LA CHAPELLE.

Chaperon, shăp'rôN', (NICOLAS,) a skilful French engraver, born at Châteaudun in 1596. He went to Rome, where he etched the pictures in the Vatican which are known by the name of the "Bible of Raphael." These engravings (fifty-two in number) were published in 1638, and are called good copies. He afterwards worked in Paris, where he died in 1647.

Cha'pin, (CALVIN,) D.D., an American divine, for upwards of thirty years secretary to the American Board of Missions, born at Springfield, Massachusetts, about 1764; died at Wethersfield, Connecticut, in 1851. He was a zealous advocate of temperance, and author of an essay recommending the substitution of water for wine in the Lord's Supper.

Chapin, (EDWIN HUBBELL,) D.D., an American Universalist divine and distinguished orator, was born in Washington county, New York, in 1814. He preached for several years at Charlestown, near Boston, and about 1848 removed to the city of New York. As a popular and eloquent preacher he is unrivalled among the ministers of his own denomination, and has few if any superiors among those of any class in our country. He has also the reputation of being one of the ablest and most attractive lecturers in the United States. He has published, besides several volumes of sermons and discourses, "The Crown of Thorns," and "Humanity in the City," (1854.)

See "Golden Age of American Oratory," by E. G. PARKER, Boston, 1857.

Chapin, (STEPHEN,) an American Baptist minister, born in Milford, Massachusetts, in 1778, graduated at Harvard in 1804. He was president of Columbian College, at Washington, from 1828 to 1841. Died in 1845.

Chapin, (WILLIAM,) an American teacher of the blind, born in Philadelphia in 1802. He became principal of the Pennsylvania Institution for the Blind in 1849.

Chap'lin, (JEREMIAH,) an American Baptist minister, born at Rowley, Massachusetts, in 1776. He was president of Waterville College, Maine, from 1820 till 1832. Died in 1841.

Chapman, chăp'măn, (?) (FREDERICK HENRY,) a Swedish vice-admiral and skilful naval architect, born in 1721. He published a "Treatise on Naval Architecture," (1775,) which was translated into many languages. Gustavus III. appointed him to direct the construction of vessels for his navy. Died in 1808.

See HALLSTROEM, "Minne öfver F. H. Chapman," 1817.

Chap'man, (GEORGE,) an English dramatic poet, and the earliest English translator of Homer, was born in 1557, at what place is not known. Having become a resident of London, and an author by profession, he enjoyed the society and friendship of Spenser and Shakspeare. His most memorable production is the translation of Homer into English verse. The "Iliad" appeared in 1598, the "Odyssey" in 1614. These versions were admired by Dr. Johnson, Pope, and Coleridge. "A daring, fiery spirit," says Pope, "animates his translation, which is something like what one might imagine Homer to have written before he had arrived at years of discretion." He wrote many comedies and tragedies, which are now forgotten. "The drama," says Campbell, "owes him very little." "His 'Bussy d'Amboise' is a piece of frigid atrocity." Died in London in 1634.

See CIBBER, "Lives of the Poets," etc.; "Minor Elizabethan Dramatists," in the "Atlantic Monthly" for December, 1867; "Retrospective Review" for 1821. vol. iv.

Chapman, (GEORGE,) a Scottish school-master, born at Alvah in 1723, taught in Dalkeith and Dumfries, and wrote a "Treatise on Education," which was often reprinted. Died in 1806.

See a "Sketch of the Life of G. Chapman," London, 1808.

Chapman, (JOHN,) a learned English divine, born in 1704. He published a work called "Eusebius," (1739,) in answer to Morgan and Tindal. In 1741 he became Archdeacon of Sudbury. He subsequently published numerous sermons, several antiquarian treatises, and a letter to Dr. Middleton, (1744,) in which he corrected some errors committed by that author in his "Life of Cicero." Died in 1784.

Chapman, (JOHN GADSBY,) an American painter, born in Alexandria, Virginia. He became a resident of Rome about 1848, before which date he had painted "The Baptism of Pocahontas" for the Rotunda of the Capitol at Washington. He has also published a "Drawing-Book" of great merit.

See TUCKERMAN, "Book of the Artists."

Chapman, (NATHANIEL,) an American physician, born in Fairfax county, Virginia, in 1780, graduated at the University of Pennsylvania in 1800. He began to practise in Philadelphia in 1804, and obtained the chair of materia medica in the University of Pennsylvania in 1813. In 1816 he was appointed professor of the theory and practice of medicine in the same institution. He published, besides other works, "Elements of Therapeutics and Materia Medica." He was president of the American Philosophical Society from 1846 until his death. He died January 1, 1853.

See S. D. GROSS, "American Medical Biography;" "Discourse commemorative of Nathaniel Chapman," by DR. S. JACKSON, 1854.

Chapman, (THOMAS,) an English scholar, born in Durham county in 1717, became master of Magdalen College, Cambridge, in 1746. He published an "Essay on the Roman Senate," (1750.) Died in 1760.

Chapone, sha-pōn', (HESTER,) an English authoress of great merit, born in Northamptonshire in 1727, was the daughter of Thomas Mulso. In 1760 she was married to Mr. Chapone, who died ten months after the union. She was the intimate friend of Elizabeth Carter and Mrs. Montague. She contributed to the "Adventurer" the story of "Fidelia," (1753,) and wrote an "Ode to Peace," and other admired poems. Her "Letters on the Improvement of the Mind" (1773) are highly esteemed. She also published "Miscellanies in Prose and Verse," and a few other works. Died in 1801.

See MRS. ELWOOD, "Memoirs of the Literary Ladies of England from the Commencement of the Last Century," 1843.

Chapour, (a king of Persia.) See SAPOR.

Chappe, shăp, (CLAUDE,) an inventor of a telegraph, born at Brûlon, in France, in 1763, was a nephew of Abbé Chappe d'Auteroche. In 1791 he conceived the project of communicating with his absent friends by means of signals. In 1792 he presented to the National Assembly a machine which he called a *telegraph*, which was tried with success between Paris and Lille, where a dispatch was transmitted through forty-eight leagues in thirteen minutes and forty seconds. The importance of the invention was immediately recognized, and the telegraph soon came into general use. Chappe is regarded as the first who operated successfully with the telegraph, although the idea did not originate with him. Died in 1805.

Chappe d'Auteroche, shăp dōt'rosh', (JEAN,) ABBÉ, a French astronomer, born at Mauriac in 1722. In 1760 the Academy of Sciences, of which he was a member, sent him to Tobolsk to observe the transit of Venus which occurred in June 6, 1761. On his return he published a "Narrative of his Journey in Siberia." He went to California to observe another transit of Venus, and died there in 1769.

Chap'pel, (WILLIAM,) a learned English divine, born in Nottinghamshire in 1582, became provost of Trinity College, Dublin, in 1637, and Bishop of Cork in 1638. He published "The Use of the Holy Scripture," (1653,) and other works, and was one of those to whom "The Whole Duty of Man" has been ascribed. Died in 1649.

See "Vita seipso conscripta," (Autobiography,) 1715.

Chap-pe'lōw, (LEONARD,) an eminent English Orientalist, born in 1683, became professor of Arabic at Cambridge in 1720, and promoted the study of Oriental literature in England. Among his works are "Elements of the Arabic Language," and a translation of the "Traveller," an Arabic poem. Died in 1768.

Chappuzeau, shăp'pü'zō', (SAMUEL,) a Swiss *littérateur,* born at Geneva about 1625; died in 1701.

Chapsal, shăp'sȧl', (C. P.,) a French grammarian, born about 1790, published "Lessons of Logical Analysis," (14th edit., 1842,) and a "New French Grammar," in which he was aided by M. Noël. The latter work is said to have made the fortune of the authors.

Chaptal, shăp'tăl', (JEAN ANTOINE,) Comte de Chanteloup, (shôN'loo',) a distinguished French chemist and statesman, born at Nogaret (Lozère) in June, 1756. Having graduated as a physician at Montpellier in 1777, he went to Paris, where he pursued the study of chemistry and other sciences. In 1781 he was appointed professor of chemistry at Montpellier, where he at the same time rendered valuable services to the state by the manufacture of certain chemicals for which France had previously been indebted to foreigners. He favoured the popular cause in the Revolution, but was imprisoned by the dominant party in 1793. After a brief detention, he was called to Paris by the government to superintend the manufacture of saltpetre, in which he was very successful. About 1796 he became a member of the Institute, just founded. Bonaparte appointed him a councillor of state in 1800, and minister of the interior in 1801. It is said that this department was never administered more efficiently for the prosperity of France than during the four years of Chaptal's ministry. In 1805 he was made grand officer of the legion of honour, and a senator. A few years later he became a count. He opposed the restoration of the Bourbons, and retired from public service in 1815, but was restored to the Chamber of Peers in 1819. In 1806 he had published "Chemistry applied to the Arts," ("La Chimie appliqué aux Arts,") an excellent work, which was translated into all the languages of Europe and is still much consulted. He also wrote "Elements of Chemistry," a "Treatise on the Culture of the Vine and the Art of making Wine," and other works. Died in Paris in 1832.

See FLOURENS, "Éloge historique de Chaptal," 1835; J. S. JULIA-FONTENELLE, "Éloge de J. A. Chaptal," 1833; THIERS, "Histoire du Consulat et de l'Empire;" "Nouvelle Biographie Générale."

Chapuis, shă'pü-e', (GABRIEL,) a French writer, born at Amboise in 1546. He succeeded Belleforest as historiographer of France, and in 1596 became Spanish interpreter to the king. He translated from the Spanish into French "Amadis de Gaul," and other works. Died in 1611.

Chapus, shă'püs', (EUGÈNE,) a French writer on hunting, horse-racing, etc., was born in Paris about 1800. Among his works are "The Turf," (1853,) and "Le Sport à Paris," (1854.)

Chapuys de Montlaville, shă'pü-e' deh môN'lă'vèl', (BENOÎT MARIE LOUIS,) a French writer, born at Tournus in 1801. He was a member of the Chamber of Deputies from 1832 to 1848, and was appointed a senator in 1853. He has written a "History of Dauphiny," (1827,) a "Life of Lamartine," (1843,) and other works.

Charas, shă'räs', (MOISE,) an eminent French physician and Protestant, born at Uzès in 1618. He taught chemistry for nine years in the Royal College of Paris. The revocation of the edict of Nantes (1685) forced him to emigrate. After practising in England and Holland, he went to Spain to attend Charles II., and was induced by the terrors of the Inquisition to turn Catholic. He returned to Paris about 1692, and died there in 1698. He had published in 1676 a "Pharmacopœia," which was extensively used. Voltaire says, "he was the first who wrote well on Pharmacy."

See ÉLOY, "Dictionnaire de la Médecine;" CAP, "Éloge de Moïse Charas," 1840.

Charbonnel, shăR'bo'nĕl', (JOSEPH CLAUDE MARGUERITE,) COUNT, a French general, born at Dijon in 1775. He displayed skill and courage at Jena in 1806, and in various actions in Prussia, Spain, and Russia. As general of division, he took part in the battles of Lutzen and Bautzen, (1813.) He became a peer of France in 1841. Died in 1846.

Charbonnet, shăR'bo'nȧ', (PIERRE MATTHIAS,) a French *littérateur,* born at Troyes in 1733. In August, 1792, he was intrusted with the surveillance of the royal family confined in the Temple. Died in 1815.

Charbonnières, de, deh shăR'bo'ne'aiR', (ALEXIS,) CHEVALIER, a French *littérateur,* born in Auvergne about

1778. He composed "The Battle of Austerlitz," a drama, a poem entitled an "Essay on the Sublime," and other works. Died in 1819.

Chardin, shăr′dăn′, (JEAN BAPTISTE SIMÉON,) a skilful French painter, born in Paris in 1699. He represented familiar scenes with admirable beauty and fidelity, and was employed to decorate the *salon* of the Louvre. Many of his works have been engraved. Died in 1779.

See CHARLES BLANC, "Histoire des Peintres."

Chardin, shar′din or shăr′dăn′, (Sir JOHN,) a celebrated traveller, born in Paris in 1643, was a jeweller by trade, and a Protestant. In 1664 he made a journey to India and Persia, partly on account of business, and remained six years at Ispahân, where he diligently studied the language, history, politics, customs, etc. of Persia. He was employed by the Persian king as an agent for the purchase of jewels. In 1670 he revisited Paris; but, finding that his religion was an insuperable obstacle to his preferment, he resolved in 1671 to return to the East. He passed the ensuing ten years mostly in Persia, and in 1681 became a resident of London. He was knighted by Charles II., chosen a Fellow of the Royal Society, and was sent on a diplomatic mission to Holland about 1682. In 1686 he published the first part of his "Travels in Persia and the East Indies," (3 vols. 4to, 1686–1711,) which, says Sir William Jones, "is the best account of Mohammedan nations ever published." "The faculty of seizing by a rapid and comprehensive glance the character of a country and people," says Sir James Mackintosh, "was possessed in the highest degree by Chardin, and secures him an undisputed supremacy in that department of literature." Died near London in 1713.

See LANGLÈS, "Voyage du Chevalier Chardin en Perse;" NICÉRON, "Mémoires;" "Nouvelle Biographie Générale."

Chardon de la Rochette, shăr′dŏN′ deh lä ro′shĕt′, (SIMON,) a French philologist and Hellenist, born in Gévaudan in 1753, was one of the principal contributors to the "Magasin Encyclopédique" of Milan, for which he wrote many able critical dissertations. His most important work is a "Greek Anthology," which cost the labour of twenty-five years and was left unfinished. Died in 1814.

Charenton, shȧ′rŏN′tŏN′,(JOSEPH NICOLAS,) a French writer and Jesuit, born at Blois in 1649. He was a missionary in Persia for fifteen years. By order of Philip V. of Spain, he made a good French translation of Mariana's "History of Spain," (1725,) with a supplement. His version was so successful that it prevented the publication of two others that were in progress. Died in Paris in 1735.

Chȧ′rēs, [Χάρης,] an Athenian general, whose extortions provoked the social war which began in 358 B.C. By party influence and corruption, he was chosen general-in-chief in this war, and besieged Chios without success.

Chares, a Greek statuary, born at Lindus, lived about 300 B.C., was a pupil of Lysippus, and the chief founder of the Rhodian school of sculpture. He constructed, near the port of Rhodes, the famous Colossus, one of the Seven Wonders of the World. It was a bronze statue of Apollo, seventy cubits in height, (about one hundred English feet,) and was thrown down by an earthquake about 224 B.C.,fifty-six years after its erection. The fragments remained on the spot more than nine hundred years.

Chares OF MITYLENE was master of ceremonies, or gentleman-usher, to Alexander the Great. He recorded facts and anecdotes in the life of that prince, in a work of which only small fragments are extant. In 340 he commanded an army sent to aid Byzantium against Philip of Macedon; but he failed to effect his object, and was superseded by Phocian. He was one of the commanders of the Athenians at the battle of Chæronæa, 338 B.C., the loss of which was ascribed to his incapacity. He survived that event five years or more. His character was extremely profligate and corrupt.

See PLUTARCH, "Phocion."

Charette de la Contrie, shȧ′rĕt′ deh lä kôN′tRe′, (ATHANASE,) a French royalist chief, nephew of François Athanase, noticed below, was born at Nantes in 1796. He fought for the Bourbons in the west of France in 1815. He went into exile with Charles X. in 1830, and

in 1832 raised an unsuccessful revolt in the west. He published a "Military Journal," (1842.) Died in 1848.

See LOUIS BLANC, "Histoire de dix Ans."

Charette de la Contrie, (FRANÇOIS ATHANASE,) a brave Vendean general, born in Bretagne in 1763. He was chosen as their leader by the insurgent peasants in 1793, and displayed remarkable talents for guerilla warfare. He gained several victories over the republicans in 1793–94, and maintained the contest after the other Vendean chiefs had fallen. "All the princes of Europe," says Alison, "looked to him as the only man capable of restoring the royal cause." In April, 1795, he signed a treaty of pacification, which he soon violated. "The renewal of hostilities," says Alison, "was owing to the delusive hopes held out by, and ill-judged assistance of, Great Britain." At the request of Count d'Artois, Charette resumed the command, but was unable to resist General Hoche, who is said to have offered him a million francs to leave the country in peace. He refused these terms, was taken prisoner, and shot in March, 1796.

See LE BOUVIER-DESMORTIERS, "Vie de Charette;" T. MURET, "Vie populaire de Charette," 1845.

Charidème. See CHARIDEMUS.

Chȧr-ĭ-dē′mus, [Χαρίδημος,] a Greek general, born in Eubœa about 400 B.C., became the leader of an army of mercenaries. He entered the service of Cotys, King of Thrace, and opposed the Athenians in their attempt to conquer Chersonesus. He obtained command of an Athenian army in 349 B.C.

Charidemus, [Fr. CHARIDÈME, kȧ′re′dȧm′,] an Athenian orator, born about 390 B.C., was a political friend of Demosthenes. He was ambassador to the court of Macedon when Philip was killed in the year 336, and was one of the eight orators whom Alexander required to be delivered to him after the reduction of Thebes. To escape this danger, he fled to Persia, where he was put to death by Darius in 333 B.C.

See THIRLWALL, "History of Greece."

Charis. See CHARITES.

Charisi. See CHARIZI.

Charisius, ka-rish′e-us, (AURELIUS ARCADIUS,) a Roman jurist, supposed to have lived about 350 A.D. He wrote "De Testibus," ("On Witnesses,") and other legal works, extracts of which are preserved in the "Digest."

Charisius, (FLAVIUS SOSIP′ATER,) a Latin grammarian, born in Campania, lived about the fifth century.

Chȧr′ĭ-tēs, singular **Chȧ′ris,** [Gr. Χάρις, Χάριτες; Fr. LES GRACES, lä grǎss; Lat. GRA′TIÆ,] the Graces of classic mythology, were the daughters of Jupiter. They were supposed to bestow grace, beauty, and refinement, and to preside over social enjoyments, dances, and festivals. They were also patrons of poetry and art. They were three in number,—namely, Aglaia, Euphrosyne, and Thalia.

See KEIGHTLEY's "Mythology."

Chȧr′ĭ-ton, [Gr. Χαρίτων,] author of a Greek romance entitled "The Loves of Chæreas and Callirrhoë," was a native of Aphrodisias, in Caria. His epoch is unknown; but he lived, it is supposed, in or after the fourth century of our era. The chief merit of his work is in the style.

Charizi, chȧ-ree′thee, (?) (JUDAH,) a Spanish poet and Jewish rabbi, born at Xeres; died about 1235.

Charke, chark, (CHARLOTTE,) an English actress, was a daughter of Colley Cibber. Died in 1760.

See "Narrative of the Life of Mrs. Charlotte Charke," by herself, London, 1827.

Charlemagne, shar′le-mān′, [Fr. pron. shȧRl′mȧñ′; Ger. CARL (or KARL) DER GROSSE, karl dĕR grōs′seh; It. CARLO MAGNO, kaR′lo mȧn′yo; Lat. CAR′OLUS MAG′NUS, *i.e.* "Charles the Great,"] or **Charles I,** King of France and Emperor of the West, born at the castle of Salzburg, in Bavaria, in 742 A.D., was the son of Pepin le Bref, King of the Franks. At the death of Pepin, in 768, Charlemagne became King of Austrasia, Neustria, etc., while his brother Carloman obtained the rest of his father's dominions. In 771 Carloman died, and Charlemagne became master of the whole. His kingdom then included France and a large part of Germany. He married Desirée or Desiderata, a daughter of Desiderius of Lombardy. In 772 he began a war against the Saxons, who, after a long and obstinate resistance, were finally subdued about

ā, ē, ī, ō, ū, ȳ, *long;* ȧ, ė, ȯ, same, less prolonged; ă, ĕ, ĭ, ŏ, ŭ, y̆, *short;* ạ, ẹ, ị, ọ, *obscure;* fär, fȧll, fȧt; mĕt; nŏt; gŏōd; mōōn;

thirty years later. Having defeated Desiderius, King of the Lombards, he was crowned King of Lombardy in 774. Having divorced his first wife, he married Hildegarde or Ildegerda. Returning from an invasion of Spain in 778, he suffered a reverse at Roncesvalles, where Roland and other famous paladins fell by the hands of the Saracens. The revolts of his subjects gave him many opportunities for the successful exercise of his military talents. In 800 he was crowned at Rome by Pope Leo III. as Emperor of the West, with the title of Cæsar Augustus. His son Pepin, whom he had made King of Italy, died in 810. In 813 he associated his son, Louis le Débonnaire, with himself in the empire. He died at Aix-la-Chapelle, his capital, in January, 814, leaving a great reputation as a statesman, legislator, and founder of the Germanic Empire. He established churches, monasteries, and schools, and promoted learning, arts, and civilization. He was the most powerful monarch of his time. His empire comprised all the region between the Elbe and the Ebro, extending eastward to Hungary and southward to Calabria. By his will, made in 806, he divided the empire between his three sons, Charles, Pepin, and Louis, the last of whom only survived Charlemagne, and became his successor. His descendants are denominated Carlovingians, constituting the second dynasty of French kings.

See HAURÉAU, "Charlemagne et sa Cour," 1854; GAILLARD, "Histoire de Charlemagne," 1782; ARN. SCHEUFFER, "Caroli Magni Vita togata;" G. P. R. JAMES, "Life of Charlemagne," 1832; DONATUS ACCIAJUOLI, "De Vita Caroli Magni Commentarius;" REINERUS REINECCIUS, "Annales de Gestis Caroli Magni;" EGINHARD, "Vita Caroli Magni," first published in 1521; CAPEFIGUE, "Charlemagne," 1840; THÉODORE NISARD, "Histoire de Charlemagne," 1843; HEINRICH C. VON GAGERN, "Carl der Grosse," 1845; BREDOW, "Carl der Grosse," 1814; SCHROEDER, "Geschichte Carls des Grossen," 1850; DIPPOLD, "Leben Kaiser Carl's des Grossen," 1810; SPORSCHIL, "Carl der Grosse, sein Reich und sein Haus," 1846.

Char'le-mont, (JAMES CAULFIELD,) EARL OF, a literary and patriotic Irish nobleman, born in Dublin in 1728, was the son of Viscount Charlemont, and a friend of Edmund Burke. He was president of the Royal Irish Academy, and author of a "History of Italian Poetry." He had great influence in the public affairs of Ireland. Died in 1799.

See FRANCIS HARDY, "Memoirs of the Political and Private Life of James Caulfield, Earl of Charlemont," 1810; "Edinburgh Review" for November, 1811; "London Quarterly Review," October, 1811.

☞ The following order has been adopted in regard to rulers or princes having the name of CHARLES: first, Emperors; secondly, Kings, (arranged according to the alphabetical order of their respective countries, England being placed first, France next, and so on;) thirdly, Archdukes; fourthly, Dukes.

Charles I., EMPEROR. See CHARLEMAGNE.

Charles II., EMPEROR. See CHARLES THE BALD, King of France.

Charles III., or THE FAT, [Fr. CHARLES LE GROS, shärl leh gro,] Emperor of the Franks, born about 832 A.D., was the third son of Louis II., (le Germanique,) and among the German emperors is reckoned Charles III. Louis II., at his death in 876, divided the empire among his sons, Carloman, Louis, and Charles. The first and second having died without lawful issue within six years ensuing, Charles inherited their portions. In 884 he became King or Regent of France, the legitimate heir of which was a minor. His dominions were much too large for his capacity, and his power was little more than nominal. He was unable to relieve Paris from the besieging Normans in 886, except by paying them to transfer their ravages to another part of France. He was deposed by his nephew, Arnulph or Arnolph, in 888, and died the same year.

Charles IV., of the house of Luxembourg, born in 1316, was a son of John de Luxembourg, King of Bohemia. He was elected Emperor of Germany in 1346, as successor to Louis V., whom the pope had excommunicated, and who died in 1347. He is reproached for his subservience to the pope. About 1356 he issued, at Nuremberg, the Golden Bull, which was the fundamental law of the empire for more than four hundred years. This Bull determined that the election of emperor should be made by seven electors, viz., four secular

princes and three ecclesiastics. He died in 1378, and was succeeded by his son Wenceslaus.

See PELZEL, "Geschichte Kaiser Karls IV.," 1780.

Charles V., [Ger. KARL (or CARL) DER FÜNFTE, karl dĕR fünf'teh; Fr. CHARLES QUINT, shärl kăn; It. CARLO QUINTO, kär'lo kwěn'to,] Don **Carlos I.** of Spain, afterwards Emperor of Germany, was the eldest son of the archduke Philip of Austria, and grandson of the emperor Maximilian I. and Mary, Duchess of Burgundy. His mother was Joanna, the daughter and sole heiress of Ferdinand and Isabella, the sovereigns of Aragon and Castile. He was born at Ghent in February, 1500, and educated in Flanders, under the care of William de Croy as governor and Adrien of Utrecht as preceptor. He inherited from his father, who died in 1506, the Low Countries and Franche-Comté. The death of Ferdinand of Spain in January, 1516, rendered Charles master of an empire more vast than any monarch had ruled since Charlemagne. He removed his court from Flanders to Spain in 1517, and dismissed Cardinal Ximenes from the regency. In 1519 Charles was elected Emperor of Germany, as successor to Maximilian, after a long contest with Francis I. of France. Having appointed Adrien of Utrecht Regent of Castile, he departed from Spain, and was crowned at Aix-la-Chapelle in October, 1520. In order to concert measures to check the progress of the Lutheran doctrines, he assembled a Diet at Worms in 1521. (See LUTHER, MARTIN.)

Foreseeing that a war was impending between himself and the French king, Charles made a secret alliance with Pope Leo X. and Henry VIII. of England. In his absence the people of Castile, led by Juan de Padilla, revolted against the regent, and were successful in several battles in 1520 and 1521. Charles returned to Spain in 1522, and by a wise moderation ended the civil war. In the mean time hostilities had commenced between the allies and the French, who were driven out from the Milanese in 1522 by Colonna. An imperialist army which invaded Provence in 1524 was repulsed by Francis, who again marched into Italy, and was defeated and made prisoner at the battle of Pavia in 1525. The war was suspended by the treaty of Madrid in 1526. (See FRANCIS I.) In 1526 he married Isabella of Portugal, a daughter of King Emmanuel. A league having been formed by Francis I. and the pope, Clement VII., against Charles, the war was renewed in 1527, when the imperial army, under Constable Bourbon, took Rome by assault, made the pope a prisoner, and committed great outrages on the citizens. This event excited general horror in Europe, and influenced Henry VIII. to join the league against the emperor. Peace was restored by the treaty of Cambrai in 1529.

In 1530 Charles attended the Diet of Augsburg, which he had appointed to oppose the progress of the Reformation, and which decreed that severe penalties should be enforced against the Protestants. The emperor, however, after the Protestant chiefs had united in the League of Schmalkalden for a common defence, granted them favourable terms of peace or compromise in 1531. In 1535 he acquired great renown by the defeat of Barbarossa and the conquest of Tunis, with a large armament which he commanded in person. He invaded France from the south in 1536, and besieged Marseilles; but, foiled by the cautious and defensive policy of Montmorenci, he was forced to retreat, after he had lost half of his army. A truce of ten years having been negotiated in 1538, Charles asked and received a safe-conduct to pass through France in 1539. In 1541 he conducted against Algiers an enterprise which, in consequence of a storm at sea, and disease in the army, resulted disastrously.

The truce between Charles and Francis having been broken in 1542, the former courted the favour of the Protestants, from whom he obtained material aid for the war. In 1544 the French gained a decisive victory at Cerisoles, soon after which Charles and Francis made a treaty of peace at Crespy, (Crépy,) and secretly agreed to exterminate heresy in their respective dominions. In 1546 he published the ban of the empire against the Elector of Saxony and the Landgrave of Hesse, the chiefs of the Protestant league, who promptly declared war against him. Their offer of battle having been declined by Charles, their armies were dispersed or disbanded in 1547. He then obtained an easy conquest, and subjected the Protestants to cruel oppression and exactions. Maurice of Saxony, who had hitherto fought for Charles, took the field against him in 1552, at the head of a powerful league and supported by Henry II. of France. Surprised by this sudden danger, and unable to resist, his army fled in confusion from Innspruck, and Charles, in August, 1552, signed the memorable treaty of Passau, "which," says Robertson, "overturned the vast fabric in erecting which Charles had employed so many years, and established the Protestant Church upon a firm and secure basis." To the great astonishment of Europe, he resigned with imposing ceremonies the sovereignty of the Netherlands, Spain, and his other hereditary dominions to his son Philip in the autumn of 1555. He assigned as his motive that his vigour was exhausted by an incurable distemper, the gout. He resigned the imperial crown to his brother Ferdinand, and retired to the monastery of Saint Yuste, near Plasencia, in Spain. " He was particularly curious," says Robertson, " with regard to the mechanism of clocks and watches; and having found, after repeated trials, that he could not bring any two of them to go exactly alike, he reflected, it is said, with a mixture of surprise and regret on his own folly in having bestowed so much time and labour on the more vain attempt of bringing mankind to a precise uniformity of sentiment concerning the profound and mysterious doctrines of religion." Unfortunately, this passage, so full of interest and instruction, rests upon no trustworthy foundation, and is inconsistent with the views which Charles is known to have held a little before his death. He died September 21, 1558.

See ROBERTSON, "History of the Reign of Charles V.," 1769; PRESCOTT, " History of Philip II., King of Spain," vol. i. chaps. i. and ix.; ULLOA, "Vita di Carolo V.," 1559; G. LETI, " Vita del Imperatore Carolo V.," 4 vols., 1700; LUIGI DOLCE, "Vita di Carolo V.," 1561; SANDOVAL, " Historia de la Vida de Carlos V.," 1606; MASENIUS, "Historia Caroli V.," 1672; A. PICHOT, "Charles Quint," 1854; STIRLING, "The Cloister Life of the Emperor Charles V.," 1852; French version of G. LETI's work, above noticed, 1704; JOHANN GUSTAV DROYSEN, "Zwei Verzeichnisse, Kaiser Karls V., seiner Laude und seiner grossen Einkünfte," etc., 1854; F. A. A. MIGNET, "Charles V; son Abdication, son Séjour et sa Mort au Monastère de Yuste," 1854; " London Quarterly Review" for January, 1853; " Edinburgh Review" for January, 1855; " Blackwood's Magazine" for July, 1857.

Charles VI, Emperor of Germany, born in 1685, was the second son of the emperor Leopold I. Leopold claimed a right to succeed Charles II. of Spain, who was his first-cousin, and who had no issue; but he waived his pretensions in favour of the subject of this article. By the will of the Spanish king, who died in 1700, the French Duke of Anjou was appointed his heir. In the war of the Spanish succession which followed, the claim of Charles was enforced by Austria, England, Portugal, etc., while the French and a majority of the Spaniards fought for his rival, Philip V. Charles entered Madrid with an army in 1706, but was soon driven out of that city. The French gained a decisive victory at Almanza in 1707, and Philip remained master of Spain. In 1711 he succeeded his brother, Joseph I., as Emperor of Germany and King of Hungary. He renounced his claim to Spain, by the treaty of Rastadt, in 1714. He was the last descendant in the male line of the house of Austria, (Hapsburg,) and had no issue except a daughter, Maria Theresa, for whom and her heirs he wished to secure his crowns. With this view, he promulgated in 1724 a new law of succession, the famous " Pragmatic Sanction." In the ensuing years of his reign, all the plans of his cabinet were directed to the settlement of the succession according to the Pragmatic Sanction. A war which Austria waged against France and Spain was terminated in 1735 by a treaty in which Charles ceded Naples to Don Carlos of Spain. He died in October, 1740, and was succeeded by Maria Theresa.

See SCHIRACH, " Biographie Kaiser Karls VI.," 1778; ZSCHACKWITZ, "Leben und Thaten Kaiser Caroli VI.," 1723; PIERRE MASSUET, " Histoire de l'Empereur Charles VI," 1742.

Charles VII, (**Charles Albert,**) Emperor of Germany, born at Brussels in 1697, was a son of Maximilian Emanuel, Elector of Bavaria. He married a daughter of the emperor Joseph I. in 1722, and succeeded his father as Elector of Bavaria in 1726. In 1740 he became a competitor of Maria Theresa for the throne of Austria, (or part of the dominions attached to it,) and was supported by France, Prussia, and other powers in the war of the Austrian succession. He was elected emperor in 1742. His armies were defeated by the Austrians, and he was driven from Bavaria for a time. He died in 1745, leaving a son, Maximilian Joseph, who succeeded him as Elector.

See J. J. MOSER, "Staatshistorie Deutschlands unter der Regierung Karls VII.," 2 vols., 1743.

Charles I, (**Charles Stuart,**) King of England, the third son of James I. and Anne of Denmark, was born at Dunfermline, Scotland, on the 19th of November, 1600. At the death of his elder brother Henry in 1612, he became heir-apparent to the crown, having previously been styled Duke of York and Cornwall. He succeeded his father March 27, 1625, and in the same year married Henrietta Maria, daughter of Henry IV. of France. His father's favourite, the unpopular and incompetent Buckingham, was retained as chief minister. and acquired an ascendency over Charles which involved him in a long series of errors and disasters. The growing spirit of liberty rendered it difficult to govern by the former arbitrary methods, to which the king adhered with fatal obstinacy. In the first year of his reign he was involved in a contest with Parliament, which resolved not to grant supplies without obtaining a redress of grievances, or concessions in favour of liberty. Between June, 1625, and March, 1629, three Parliaments were successively assembled and dissolved. He then resolved to govern without Parliaments, and resorted to new and tyrannical measures for raising money. Patents of monopoly were granted. The Petition of Rights, to which he had given his assent, was violated. The Puritans were imprisoned, whipped, and mutilated for their opinions. Buckingham having been assassinated in 1628, Laud and the Earl of Strafford became his chief advisers. A war with Spain, which had added nothing to British glory, was ended by peace in 1630. In 1637 John Hampden gained celebrity by his resistance to the illegal levy of ship-money. By his attempt to impose the Episcopal liturgy, etc. on the Scottish people, Charles provoked a rebellion and civil war in Scotland in 1638. A new Parliament was assembled in April, 1640, and was violently dissolved in the following May. In August, England was invaded by a victorious Scottish army. Defeat, financial distress, and general disorganization compelled the king to call another Parliament, which met in November, 1640, and became the famous Long Parliament. In 1641 Charles reluctantly consented to the execution of the Earl of Strafford, by which he made himself liable to the charge of ingratitude. In January, 1642, he failed in a rash attempt to seize five members of the Commons, which attempt was the proximate cause of the civil war. (See CROMWELL and HAMPDEN.) "From that moment," says Macaulay, "it must have been evident to every impartial observer, that, in the midst of professions, oaths, and smiles, the tyrant was constantly looking forward to an absolute sway and a bloody revenge." In the first and second years of the war the royalists gained numerous victories; but the tide was turned at Marston Moor in 1644, and the royal army was again defeated in 1645, at the decisive battle of Naseby, where Charles commanded in person. In 1646 he gave himself up to the Scottish army, which delivered him to the English Parliament in 1647. Having been subjected to a form of legal process by the Parliament, he was condemned, and beheaded on January 30, 1649. "It would be absurd to deny," says Macaulay, "that he was a scholar and a gentleman, a man of exquisite taste in the fine arts, a man of strict morals in private life. He was as good a writer and speaker as any modern sovereign has been."

See MACAULAY, Review of Hallam's " Constitutional History;" HUME, "History of England," chaps. l. to lix.; MACAULAY, "History of England," vol. i. chap. i.; PETER HEYLIN, " Life of Charles I.," 1658; WILLIAM HARRIS, "Life of Charles I.," 1758; DISRAELI, "Life and Character of Charles I.," 1828; SIR PHILIP WARWICK, "Memoirs of the Reign of Charles I.;" LUCY AIKIN, "Memoirs of the Court of King Charles I."

Charles II, King of England, the eldest surviving son of Charles I., was born on the 29th of May, 1630.

After the decisive triumph of the Parliament at Naseby, in June, 1645, he retired to Jersey, and the next year he joined his mother in Paris. In 1649 he was proclaimed king by the Scottish Parliament, "on condition of his good behaviour." Having received an invitation from the Covenanters and signed the Covenant, he landed in Scotland in June, 1650, and was crowned at Scone about the first of the next year. The austere religionists of Scotland required him to sign "articles of repentance," and treated him as a captive rather than a king. Cromwell having defeated the royalist army at Dunbar and reduced a great part of Scotland, Charles marched with his Scottish army into England, closely pursued by the enemy. His hopes that the English would rally to his standard were disappointed, and the enterprise terminated in his signal defeat at Worcester, September 3, 1651. Charles escaped by flight, and, after many adventures in various disguises, he embarked in October and found safety in France.

The restoration of Charles to the throne is ascribed to the loyalty and prudence of General Monk, seconded by the favour of the people and the law of reaction. Charles entered London in May, 1660, with ample demonstrations of popular joy. He appointed Hyde, Earl of Clarendon, prime minister. In 1662 he married Catherine of Braganza, daughter of the King of Portugal. Episcopacy was restored, and the Presbyterian clergy were ejected. In 1665 Charles declared war against the Dutch, who, after losing several naval battles, entered the Thames and burned some ships of war at Chatham. Peace was restored by the treaty of Breda in 1667. The next year, England, Holland, and Sweden formed against Louis XIV. of France a coalition, called the Triple Alliance, which was very popular with the English. The counsels of the ministry called the *Cabal* (a word which the initial letters of their names happened to compose) soon effected a change of policy and a secret treaty with Louis XIV., who supplied Charles with revenues, so that he might reign more absolutely and be independent of Parliaments. War was again declared against the Dutch in 1672, and several doubtful battles were fought at sea. Public opinion in England compelled the court to make peace in February, 1674.

The popularity with which Charles had begun his reign had long been expended. He was suspected of leaning towards popery, and he had actually in secret entered the Catholic communion, which he avowed at the hour of death. A rumoured popish plot in 1678 convulsed the nation with fear and furious excitement. The Parliament, which had existed since 1661, became so insubordinate that the king dissolved it in 1678. In 1679 the habeas-corpus act was passed. About this time the words whig and tory originated, and were applied respectively to the opponents and the partisans of the court. Charles died in February, 1685, without lawful issue, and was succeeded by his brother, James II. His reign was remarkable as an era of libertinism in morals and of servility in politics. He was sensual, indolent, unambitious, and good-tempered. "Honour and shame, to him," says Macaulay, "were scarcely more than light and darkness to the blind."

See Hume, "History of England," chaps. lxiii. to lxix.; Macaulay, "History of England," vol. i.; William Harris, "Life of Charles II.," 1765; Morley, "Character of King Charles II.," 1660; McCormick, "History of King Charles II.," 1740; Lord Halifax, "Character of Charles II.," 1750; Count Grammont, "Memoirs of the Court of Charles II.;" Armand Carrel, "Histoire de la Contre-révolution en Angleterre sous Charles II et James II," 1827; George Brodie, "History of the British Empire from the Accession of Charles I. to the Restoration of Charles II.," 1822.

Charles THE BALD, [Fr. LE CHAUVE, lĕh shŏv,] or **Charles I.**, King of France, the fourth son of Louis le Débonnaire, was born at Frankfort-on-the-Main in 823 A.D. His father died in 840, after dividing his empire among his sons, Lothaire, Louis, and Charles, the last of whom had all of France lying west of the Rhone. Lothaire having claimed the pre-eminence, the other two united against him, and defeated him at the great battle of Fontenai, in 842. In the reign of Charles the Bald, France was ravaged by the Normans, who took Paris, Rouen, and other cities. Charles, being unable to expel them by arms, was twice reduced to purchase peace from

them, in 845 and 861. On the death of Louis II. of Italy without issue, Charles invaded Italy in 875, and was crowned emperor by Pope John VIII., after defeating the army of his brother, Louis le Germanique. He was continually at war with his neighbours or subjects. His empire comprised Italy and all France except Lorraine, Alsace, and part of Burgundy. He died in 877, leaving the throne to his son, Louis le Bègue. As emperor, he is reckoned Charles II. ; as King of France, Charles I.

See Michelet, "Histoire de France ;" Sismondi, "Histoire des Français."

Charles III. of France, called THE SIMPLE, [Fr. LE SIMPLE, lĕh sǎmpl,] born in 879 A.D., was a younger son of Louis le Bègue, who died in that year. Two elder brothers having died before he had attained his majority, Eudes, Count of Paris, was chosen king by the nobles in 888. Charles was crowned by his partisans in 893, and at the death of Eudes, in 898, he became nominally sole king ; but his power was greatly restricted by the growing spirit of feudality. The remarkable event of his reign was the treaty by which Rollo, a Norman chief, acquired the sovereignty of Neustria, (Normandy.) About 920, Robert, Duke of France, aspired to the crown, and a civil war ensued, in which Robert was killed ; but his party gained the victory, and elected Raoul or Rodolph of Burgundy king in 923. Charles was treated as a captive until his death in 929. He left a son, Louis Outremer.

See Sismondi, "Histoire des Français ;" A. Borgnet, "Sur le Règne de Charles le Simple," 1843.

Charles IV. of France, surnamed LE BEL, (lĕh bĕl,) "the Handsome," was the third son of Philippe le Bel, and was Count de la Marche when, on the death of his brother, Philippe le Long, in 1322, he became king. He married Marie, daughter of the emperor Henry VII. He was involved in war with Edward II. of England, from whom he claimed homage for the duchy of Guienne. Edward's queen Isabella, who was the sister of Charles, went to France to negotiate the question, and there obtained the means by which her husband was deposed. The efforts of Charles to procure his election as Emperor of Germany were not successful. He died, without male issue, in 1328, and Philippe of Valois became king.

See Sismondi, "Histoire des Français ;" Michelet, "Histoire de France."

Charles V., called THE WISE, [Fr. LE SAGE, lĕh sǎzh,] King of France, born at Vincennes in 1337, was the son of John II., who was made prisoner by the Black Prince at Poitiers. He acted as regent while his father was a captive from 1356 to 1360, and at the death of his father, in 1364, became king. He frequently summoned the States-General to obtain subsidies for the war which he waged against the English invaders. This war, after a truce of several years, was renewed in 1370. Charles resolved not to lead his armies in person, and ordered his generals to avoid a general action. This policy was very successful. The French general Du Guesclin gained frequent advantages, and expelled the English from Poitou, Saintonge, and other provinces. Before his death, Charles had recovered nearly all the territory which had been conquered by Edward III., except Calais and Bordeaux. He had married Jeanne de Bourgogne, and had several sons, one of whom succeeded him as Charles VI. He patronized learning, and founded the Royal Library of Paris. Died in 1380.

See E. Roy, "Histoire de Charles V," 1849; Michelet, "Histoire de France ;" La Harpe, "Éloge de Charles V," 1767; Jean Sylvain Bailly, "Éloge de Charles V," 1770.

Charles VI., called THE WELL-BELOVED, [Fr. LE BIEN-AIMÉ, lĕh be'ǎN' ȧ'mȧ',] King of France, born at Paris in 1368, was the son of Charles V. He was the first French prince that bore the title of Dauphin, which he derived from the province of Dauphiné, given to him as an apanage. His reign nominally began in 1380, when his uncles, the Dukes of Anjou, Burgundy, and Berry, disputed with each other for the power of regent. Charles married Isabelle, daughter of the Duke of Bavaria, in 1385, and in the next year he fitted out a great armament against the English. The number of vessels of his fleet is stated at 1287. The designed invasion, however,

e as *k*; ç as *s*; g̃ hard; g̃ as *j*; G, H, K, *guttural*; N, *nasal*; R, *trilled*; s̄ as *z*; th as in *this*. (☞See Explanations, p. 23.)

was quickly abandoned. In 1388 he assumed the functions of royalty, which had before been shared by his uncles. Charles became deranged in 1392, and the prosperity of the kingdom was sacrificed to the rivalry of the Duke of Burgundy and the Duke of Orléans, the king's brother. The former had the ascendency for several years preceding his death, in 1404. His son Jean, inheriting his title and ambition, caused Orléans to be assassinated in 1407, and provoked a civil war which raged between the Burgundians and the Armagnacs. In 1413 the dauphin Louis seized, or attempted to seize, the throne. Henry V. of England, taking advantage of these intestine troubles, invaded France, and in October, 1415, won the great battle of Agincourt. The dauphin having died in 1415, his brother Charles, who favoured the Armagnac faction, became dauphin. The civil war still continued. The Burgundians, supported by Queen Isabelle, with a shameful disregard of the claims of their country, made, in 1420, a treaty with Henry V., which stipulated that he should be King of France on the death of Charles VI. The latter died in 1422.

See DUVAL-PINEU, "Histoire de France sous le Règne de Charles VI," 2 vols., 1842: JUVENAL DES URSINS, "Histoire de Charles VI," 1614; LE LABOUREUR, "Histoire de Charles VI," 1663; DE LUSSAN, (BAUDOT DE JUILLY,) "Histoire de Charles VI ;" SAINT-REMY, "Histoire de Charles VI," 1663.

Charles VII., THE VICTORIOUS, [Fr. LE VICTORIEUX, lęh vȇk'to're'uh',] born in 1403, was the son of Charles VI. He became dauphin in 1416, and king in October, 1422, when "malice domestic and foreign levy" grievously afflicted France. (See CHARLES VI.) Death had just removed his most formidable rival, Henry V. of England ; but the son of the latter was recognized by a powerful French faction, who were masters of the capital. In 1428 the English besieged Orléans, which was bravely defended by the citizens, who were loyal Armagnacs, and, after a long siege, was delivered in 1429 by the heroism of Joan of Arc, the "Maid of Orléans." The enthusiasm which she inspired into the French armies rendered them victorious in many succeeding encounters. Charles was crowned again at Rheims in 1429, made peace with the Duke of Burgundy in 1435, and entered Paris without opposition in 1436. Normandy was reconquered in 1450, and Guienne in 1451, and a few years later Calais was the only place in France which the English retained. In the early part of his reign he had married Marie of Anjou. He displayed much political ability in the various difficulties which beset his reign, and is reckoned among the kings to whom France owes great obligations. By the "Pragmatic Sanction" (1438) he protected the liberties of the Gallican Church against papal usurpation. He also made an important reform in the army, which before his time was a scourge to the citizens and peasants of France. He died in 1461, and was succeeded by his son, Louis XI.

See BAUDOT DE JUILLY, "Histoire de Charles VII," 1697 and 1754; P. CLÉMENT, "Jacques Cœur et Charles VII ; ou la France au XVe Siècle," 1853.

Charles VIII., King of France, surnamed THE AFFABLE, was the son of Louis XI. and Charlotte of Savoy, and was born at Amboise in June, 1470. He ascended the throne in 1483. During his minority his sister Anne of France was invested with the chief power. In 1491 he married Anne, Duchess of Brittany, who was previously affianced and married by proxy to Maximilian of Austria. The latter, resenting this affront, declared war, and formed a coalition with Henry VII. of England. Charles hastened to settle this difficulty by negotiation, in order that he might be at liberty to pursue his favourite design of the conquest of Naples, which was ruled by a prince of the house of Aragon. In 1494, with an army of 30,000 men, he marched into Italy, found an ally in Ludovico Sforza, and in February, 1495, took Naples without serious resistance. Ferdinand of Spain, the emperor, and several Italian powers, combined against Charles, who, after staying a few months in Naples, marched homeward with 8000 men, and defeated a much larger army of the allies at Fornovo. The small army which he had left in Naples was soon expelled by the Spaniards. Charles is represented as having been amiable and gracious in the highest degree.

He died in 1498 ; and, as he left no children, the crown passed to the Duke of Orléans, Louis XII.

See T. GODEFROY, "Histoire de Charles VIII ;" PHILIPPE DE SÉGUR, "Histoire de Charles VIII," 1835; ANTOINE VARILLAS, "Histoire de Charles VIII," 1691; PHILIPPE DE COMINES, "Mémoires."

Charles IX., King of France, the second son of Henry II. and Catherine de Médicis, was born at Saint-Germain-en-Laye in 1550. Succeeding his brother, Francis II., he ascended the throne in December, 1560. During his minority his mother was the master-spirit of the government, and Antoine de Bourbon, King of Navarre, was lieutenant-general. Before his accession the question of religious reform had arrayed against each other two powerful parties, the Catholics and the Huguenots, the latter of whom had been persecuted in the preceding reign and were determined to assert by force their religious liberty. The Duke of Guise was the leader of the Catholic party, which was supported by the court and the people of Paris. The Protestants, led by the Prince of Condé, by Coligni, etc., formed the majority in the south and west of France.

Catherine, who was jealous of the influence of the Guise family, adopted the subtle policy of holding the balance of power ; and her intrigues tended rather to foment the civil war, which began in 1562. The King of Navarre, who commanded the Catholic army, was killed at the siege of Rouen, in the same year. In February of the next year the Duke of Guise was assassinated while pressing the siege of Orléans ; and a few weeks later a treaty of peace was signed between the two factions. Charles was declared of age in 1563 ; but he remained under the control of his mother, who had infused into him her perfidious principles. The war was several times renewed, and suspended by treaties in which neither party had confidence. The Protestants were defeated at Saint-Denis, (1567,) and Jarnac, (1569,) where the Prince of Condé was killed.

In 1570 Charles married Elizabeth, the daughter of the emperor Maximilian II., and made overtures which resulted in a treaty of peace with the Huguenots. The terms were favourable to the latter ; but it is generally believed that the treaty was part of a scheme of deeply-meditated treachery, on the part of Catherine at least. If Charles was accessary to the plot, he must have acted the part of a consummate dissembler. He invited Coligni and the other chiefs of that party to court, treated them with favour and apparent cordiality, and succeeded in allaying their suspicions, especially after he had contracted a marriage between his sister Margaret and Henry of Navarre, which was celebrated in August, 1572. While the Protestant chiefs were sharing the nuptial festivities in Paris, on the night of August 24, ("Saint Bartholomew's Day,") the signal for the massacre was given. The fanatical populace of Paris, instigated by princes, nobles, and the high officers of the court, became willing agents in the murderous work. The massacre continued several days in Paris, where the number of victims was computed at about ten thousand ; and similar scenes were enacted in the provinces. Charles admitted that he had consented to this enormous crime, but sought to palliate it by affirming that a conspiracy against his life had been detected. His brother, the Duke of Anjou, appears to have been one of the prime managers of the plot. After suffering the agonies of remorse, Charles died, without issue, in 1574, and was succeeded by the Duke of Anjou as Henry III.

See VARILLAS, "Histoire de Charles IX," 1683; SISMONDI and H. MARTIN, "Histoire de France ;" WALTER ANDERSON, "History of France during the Reigns of Francis II. and Charles IX.," 5 vols., 1769-82.

Charles X., King of France, born at Versailles in October, 1757, was the son of the dauphin, (who was eldest son of Louis XV.,) and was the youngest brother of Louis XVI. He received at birth the name of Charles Philippe and the title of Comte d'Artois. In 1773 he married Maria Theresa of Savoy, daughter of the King of Sardinia, by whom he had two sons, the Duc d'Angoulême and the Duc de Berry. He constantly opposed all concessions to the Revolution from the first, and was one of the foremost to join in the royalist emigration of 1789. In the ensuing years he visited several courts of

ā, ē, ī, ō, ū, ȳ, *long;* à, è, ì, ò, same, less prolonged; ă, ĕ, ĭ, ŏ, ŭ, ў, *short;* a, ę, į, ǫ, *obscure;* fär, fàll, fàt; mêt; nŏt; gōōd; mōōn;

Europe, soliciting aid and levying war against the French republic. After the death of Louis XVI. he received the title of *Monsieur*. Having persuaded Charette, the Vendean chief, to renew the civil war, and having obtained an army in England, he commanded the expedition of Quiberon in 1795, which was a disastrous failure. Without landing on the soil of France, he returned to England ; and Charette wrote to Louis XVIII., "The cowardice of your brother has ruined all."

Bonaparte having ceased to reign, the Count d'Artois entered Paris with the allied army in April, 1814, and exclaimed, "There is nothing changed in France : there is only one Frenchman the more!"* He ascended the throne, September 16, 1824, under favourable circumstances, and his accession was attended with general rejoicing. Villèle and other ministers of the late king were retained ; but a conclave of ecclesiastics obtained an ascendency in the royal council, to which the misfortunes of his reign are ascribed. In 1825 the sacerdotal party procured the passage of a law against sacrilege, punishing with death the profanation of "sacred vases" and "holy wafers." This excited much indignation. In 1827 Charles disbanded the national guard, which had shown symptoms of disaffection. In January, 1828, the ministry of Villèle was superseded by that of M. de Martignac, which was formed by a compromise between the extreme royalists and the liberals, and did not enjoy the confidence of the king, who said to them, "Villèle's system was mine ; and I hope you will conform yourselves to it." The ministers having been defeated in the Chamber of Deputies, Charles dismissed them in August, 1829, and formed an extreme royalist ministry, at the head of which was the Prince de Polignac, who was also the confidant of the king. The Chamber, which met in March, 1830, voted an address hostile to the ministers, who, having appealed to the country by a new election, were defeated by a large majority. The king and cabinet then resolved on a *coup d'état*. On the 25th of July, 1830, they issued the ordinances which infringed the charter and caused an explosion of the monarchy. After a bloody contest of three days' duration in the streets of Paris, between the people and the army under Marmont, the revolution was completed, on the 30th of July, and the Bourbon dynasty ceased to reign. Charles abdicated in favour of his grandson, the Duc de Bordeaux, retired to England, and died at Göritz in October, 1836. The qualities of his heart are eulogized by Lamartine and others ; but his intellectual capacity was small. Lord Brougham represents him as a furious bigot and a declared enemy of liberty.

See VAULABELLE, "Histoire des deux Restaurations ;" MONTBEL, "Dernière Époque de l'Histoire de Charles X ;" LAMARTINE, "History of the Restoration ;" BAILLEUL, "La France sous le Règne de Charles X," 1824 ; LORIEUX, "Histoire du Règne de Charles X," 1834.

Charles I. OF ANJOU, King of Naples, Count of Anjou and Provence, born about 1220, was the youngest son of Louis VIII. of France. He married Beatrice, daughter of Raimond Berenger, Count of Provence, who appointed him the heir of his dominions. He joined his brother, Saint Louis of France, in a crusade against the Saracens of Egypt, about 1250. Instigated by Pope Urban IV. and his successor, Clement IV., he attacked Manfred, King of Naples, defeated him in 1266, and obtained his throne. (See MANFRED.) He was an able but tyrannical ruler, and was the head of the Guelph party. His cruelties or extortions provoked the people of Sicily, who revolted, and massacred several thousand Frenchmen at Palermo, on the 30th of March, 1282. This event is called "the Sicilian Vespers." He died in 1285, after he had failed to repress the rebellion in Sicily.

See SAINT-PRIEST, "Histoire de la Conquête de Naples par Charles d'Anjou."

Charles II., King of Naples, the son of the preceding, was born in 1248. He was more humane and just than his father. He married Mary, daughter of the King of Hungary ; and their eldest son, Charles Martel, obtained the crown of Hungary in 1290. Charles II. died in 1309, leaving the throne to his son Robert.

See SISMONDI, "Histoire des Français."

* This famous saying was the suggestion of Talleyrand.

Charles III., sometimes called DURAZZO, (doo-rât′so,) King of Naples, was a descendant of Charles II. In 1378 he commanded the army which Louis of Hungary sent against the Venetians. The pope, Urban, invited him to conquer Naples, which was then ruled by Joanna (or Joan) I. He entered Naples with an army in 1381, and, having put Joanna to death, made himself master of the kingdom. About 1385 a party in Hungary offered him the crown of that country, which he accepted. Soon after he had taken possession of his new kingdom, he was assassinated, in 1386.

Charles II., surnamed THE BAD, [Fr. LE MAUVAIS, leh mō′và′,] King of Navarre, born in 1332, was the son of Philip, third King of Navarre, and Jeanne of France, who was a daughter of Louis X. He became king in 1350, and married the daughter of King John. He was distinguished for talents, courage, and address. Having allied himself with the King of England, he waged war against Charles V. of France. His life was nearly all passed in wars and plots, which, though not successful, inflicted great calamities on France. Died in 1387.

See SECOUSSE, "Histoire de Charles le Mauvais."

Charles III., King of Navarre, surnamed THE NOBLE, born about 1360, was the son of Charles the Bad, whom he succeeded in 1387. In 1404 he signed a treaty with the French court, by which he renounced his claims to Champagne, Brie, and Évreux, and obtained Nemours, with the title of duke. Died in 1425.

Charles IV., King of Navarre, born in 1421, was a son of John II. His mother, Blanche, was a daughter of Charles III. He was a good scholar, and translated the "Ethics" of Aristotle into Spanish. Died in 1461.

Charles (Carlos) I. OF SPAIN. See CHARLES V.

Charles (or Carlos) II., King of Spain, the son of Philip IV., was born in November, 1661. He was proclaimed king in October, 1665, under the regency of his mother, Anne of Austria. A war between Spain and France was terminated by the treaty of Nymwegen in 1678, when Charles married Louise d'Orléans, a niece of Louis XIV. He was a feeble and indolent ruler, and left the direction of affairs to his ministers. In 1689 he joined a coalition of the great powers against Louis XIV., his brother-in-law. The peace of Ryswick in 1697 ended this war, in which the Spanish armies had been unfortunate. As he was childless, and as distempers of body and mind foreboded his early death, he became anxious about the succession to his crown. He made a will in favour of the Prince of Bavaria ; but the will had scarcely been signed when that prince died. The principal claimants now were Philip of France, Duke of Anjou, and the Archduke Charles of Austria. The court of Madrid was divided, and the dying king was distracted by a long contest between their partisans. At last he signed, in 1700, the memorable testament which recognized the claim of the Bourbon prince, who became Philip V., and caused the long European war of the Spanish succession. Died in November, 1700.

See MACAULAY, "History of England," vol. iv.; JOHN DUNLOP, "Memoirs of Spain during the Reigns of Philip IV. and Charles II.," 2 vols., 1834 ; "Spain under Charles II.: Extracts from the Correspondence of Alexander Stanhope," edited by PHILIP HENRY MAHON, 1840; "Leben S. M. Caroli II. Königs in Spanien," Leipsic, 1708.

Charles III., King of Spain, the second son of Philip V. and Elizabeth Farnese, was born in January, 1716. His father ceded to him the crown of the Two Sicilies in 1734. He married Amelia, a Saxon princess. His reign in Naples was rather prosperous and peaceful until he ascended the throne of Spain, left vacant by the death of his elder brother, Ferdinand VI., in August, 1759. He became the ally of France in the war against England in 1762, in accordance with the Family Compact which had been formed between the branches of the house of Bourbon. He directed his attention to the improvement of the condition of his subjects, by promoting industry, arts, and education, in which he was seconded by his ministers Florida, Blanca, and Campomanes. When his reforms excited a sedition among the populace of Madrid, Charles said, "My subjects are like infants, that cry when one goes to wash them." He restricted the power of the Inquisition, and expelled the Jesuits *en masse* from Spain and all his dominions, in 1767. In

1779 Charles declared war against England, which was then involved in a contest with France. The combined fleets and armies of France and Spain failed to capture Gibraltar, after a long siege; but Spain recovered Minorca and Florida from the English. He died in 1788, and was succeeded by his son, Charles IV. His reign appears to have been beneficial to Spain. He possessed a good disposition and sound judgment.

See BECCATINI, "Storia del Regno di Carlo III.," 1796; CABARRUS, "Elogio de Carlos III.," 1789; COXE, "Memoirs of the Kings of Spain of the House of Bourbon," 1813.

Charles IV., King of Spain, the second son of Charles III. and Maria Amelia of Saxony, was born in Naples in November, 1748. He followed his father to Spain in 1759, and then received the title of Prince of the Asturias. In 1765 he married his cousin, Maria Louisa Theresa of Parma, a woman of very vicious morals. He became king in December, 1788, and retained Florida Blanca as prime minister. In 1792 the latter was disgraced by the influence of the queen, and his place was supplied by her unworthy favourite, the upstart Godoy. In March, 1793, the French republic declared war against Charles, who had shown his hostility by expelling French residents from Spain. The French defeated the Spanish in many battles, and reduced them to sue for peace, which was concluded in July, 1795, when the French conquests in Spain were restored. Charles testified his joy at this result by creating Godoy Prince of Peace, generalissimo, etc. Through the influence of French diplomacy, the Spanish court declared war against England in 1796, and Charles gave up the direction of the government to the queen and her favourite. His son and heir, Ferdinand, in 1807, wrote to Bonaparte complaining of Godoy's misrule and asking protection. After scandalous dissensions in the royal family, Charles resigned the throne in favour of his son in March, 1808. Bonaparte then procured an interview with Charles and his son at Bayonne, and extorted from both a renunciation of the Spanish crown. Charles received a liberal pension, became a resident of Rome in 1811, and died in 1819.

See THIERS, "Histoire du Consulat et de l'Empire;" SCOTT, "Life of Napoleon Buonaparte."

Charles [Sw. KARL or CARL, karl] **VII.**, King of Sweden, ought perhaps to have been designated Charles the First. Historians generally agree that the first six Charleses, mentioned by Magnus, are imaginary personages; yet they have followed usage in recognizing their existence. Charles VII. was the son of Sverker I., King of Gothland. King Eric IX. having been assassinated in 1160, the Swedes elected Charles as his successor. He married Christina, a niece of the King of Denmark. Canute, a son of Eric IX., supported by a faction of Swedes, killed Charles in 1168 and reigned in his stead.

Charles VIII., King of Sweden, called CANUTSON or KNUTSON, (knoot'son,) was the son of Canute Bonde, and descended from Eric IX. At the age of twenty-seven he became marshal of the kingdom. Eric XIII. having been dethroned about 1438, Charles was chosen administrator of Sweden in 1440. On the death of Christopher, in 1448, he was elected his successor. Christian, King of Denmark, by the aid of his partisans in Sweden, expelled Charles in 1457, and usurped the throne. Charles was restored in 1467, and reigned until his death in 1470. His successor was Stenon Sture, his nephew.

See GEYER, "Histoire de la Suède."

Charles IX., King of Sweden, born in 1550, was the fourth son of Gustavus Vasa. About 1568 he co-operated with his brother John and other nobles in dethroning Eric XIV. When John died, in 1592, Charles became a competitor for the crown against Sigismund, (the son of John,) who was a Catholic and had been chosen King of Poland. In 1593 the legislature decreed that Lutheranism only should be tolerated in Sweden. Charles gained a victory over the army of Sigismund in 1598, and was soon after declared regent. In 1604 he was elected king by the States. He waged war against Russia with success, and founded Gothemburg and other cities. He died in 1611, leaving the throne to his son, Gustavus Adolphus.

See ANDERS FRYXELL, "Carl IX.," 1831.

Charles X.,(or **Charles Gusta'vus,**)King of Sweden, born at Nyköping in 1622, was the son of John Casimir, Prince of Deux-Ponts, and Catherine, a daughter of Charles IX. In his youth he learned the art of war under Torstenson, commander of the Swedish army. The Estates of the kingdom, in 1649, in accordance with the will of Christina, the queen-regnant, declared him the heir-apparent. On the abdication of Christina, in June, 1654, he began his enterprising and eventful reign. The genius of his uncle Gustavus Adolphus had raised Sweden to a high rank among European powers. The pretensions made by the King of Poland to the Swedish crown having provoked a war, Charles, in 1655, invaded Poland, took Warsaw, the capital, and in three months became master of the whole kingdom. While he was absent, the Danes attacked Sweden. He then made a rapid march against the new enemy, and, crossing the ice in January, 1658, dictated to the vanquished Danes a treaty of peace, by which he acquired Scania and other provinces. He died in February, 1660, and was succeeded by his son Charles, whose mother was Hedwige Eleonor of Holstein-Gottorp.

See S. PUFFENDORF, "De Rebus gestis Caroli Gustavi," 1696; LUNDBLAD, "Konung Carl X. Gustaf s Historia," 2 vols., 1823-29.

Charles XI., King of Sweden, the son of Charles X., was born in December, 1655. In 1660 a treaty of peace was made with the restored King of Poland, by which the Swedes retained their conquests on the east shore of the Baltic. Charles began to exercise royal power in 1672, and made an alliance with Louis XIV. of France, which in 1674 involved him in a war with Prussia and other powers. Charles defeated the Danes, who invaded Sweden in 1677, but suffered reverses in his German provinces. In 1679 he concluded a peace, and married Ulrica Eleonora, sister of the King of Denmark. He then resolved to observe neutrality in the wars of Europe, and the rest of his reign was peaceful and prosperous, though rather despotic. He promoted manufactures, commerce, sciences, and arts, subverted the power of the senate, and when he died, in 1697, left a flourishing kingdom to his son, Charles XII.

See JOHN ROBINSON, "Account of Sweden," 1717; E. PUFFENDORF, "Anecdotes de Suède."

Charles XII., King of Sweden, a celebrated conqueror, born at Stockholm, June 27, 1682, was the eldest son of Charles XI. and Ulrica Eleonora of Denmark. He was invincibly obstinate from childhood. The only way of moving his will was through the sentiment of honour. He made himself master of Latin, French, and German. He succeeded his father in April 15, 1697, and followed the counsels of Count Piper, who was in fact, though not in name, the prime minister. An opportunity to exert and develop his extraordinary martial genius was soon presented by the cupidity of three kings, who proposed to take advantage of his youth and to partition his dominions among themselves. These were Peter I. of Russia, Frederick IV. of Denmark, and Augustus, King of Poland, who, in 1700, formed a league against him. With intrepid alacrity he prepared for the unequal contest. He became extremely frugal in his dress, food, and mode of living. His body, by severe exercise, was made proof against fatigue. Denmark having begun the war by attacking the Duke of Holstein, Charles, at the head of his well-disciplined army, left Stockholm (to which he never returned) in May, 1700. Having effected a descent on the isle of Zealand, he besieged Copenhagen until the Danish king sued for peace, which was concluded in August, 1700. Without delay he marched with 20,000 Swedes against the Czar Peter, who, with about 80,000 men, was besieging Narva. Before the arrival of his main army, Charles began the attack with 8000 men, and gained in November, 1700, a complete victory, which filled his adversaries with consternation.

In the next campaign he invaded Poland, and, after several victories, formed the design of deposing Augustus, which, by the aid of a strong domestic faction, he easily effected. He designated for his successor Stanislas (or Stanislaus) Leczinski, who began to reign in 1704. Augustus having retired to Saxony, of which he was Elector, Charles invaded that country, fixed his camp near Leipsic, and in 1707 dictated conditions of peace

ā, ē, ī, ō, ū, ȳ, *long;* **ă, ĕ, ŏ,** same, less prolonged; **ă, ĕ, ĭ, ŏ, ŭ, ў,** *short;* **ạ, ẹ, į, ọ,** *obscure;* fär, fȧll, fȧt; mêt; nŏt; gōōd; mōōn;

to the Elector, who then renounced the crown of Poland. He received here the ambassadors of various powers, and among them the Duke of Marlborough, who came to sound his intentions. In September, 1707, with an army of 43,000 men, he marched towards Moscow to dethrone the Czar, whose armies, in the absence of Charles, had seized Ingria and invaded Poland. In June, 1708, he crossed the Berezina, the passage of which Peter disputed without success, and soon after gained some advantages over the Russians. About this time, according to Voltaire, Peter made overtures for peace, to which Charles answered, " I will treat with the Czar at Moscow."

At Smolensko he changed his course, and marched southward to the Ukraine, where he found an ally in Mazeppa, hetman of the Cossacks. In this march many of his men perished from cold and want of provisions. His operations were suspended in the winter of 1708-09, which was more severe than usual. In the spring his army was reduced to 18,000 Swedes and about as many Cossacks ; but he persisted in his design. While he was pressing the siege of Pultowa, and just after he had received a wound in the foot, the Czar, with 70,000 men, came to the relief of the city. In the decisive battle of Pultowa, July 8, 1709, Charles was defeated, with a loss of 9000 killed and 6600 prisoners. With a small body of men he retreated to Turkey, where he was received hospitably by the Sultan, who gave him an asylum at Bender. The agents of Russia urged the Sultan to drive him out of Turkey. When the Turks attempted to remove him, in February, 1713, he fought madly and desperately in resistance, was made prisoner, and taken to Demotica. There, feigning to be sick, he kept his bed about ten months. At last he quitted Turkey, and, passing through Hungary and Germany *incognito*, arrived with one attendant at Stralsund in November, 1714. The Danes, Prussians, and Russians besieged Stralsund, which Charles was forced to surrender in December, 1715. While Sweden was threatened with invasion by the allies, Charles invaded Norway, and was killed by a ball at the siege of Frederikshall on the 11th of December, 1718. He was never married. His sister, Ulrica Eleonora, the wife of Frederick of Hesse-Cassel, was chosen as his successor.

See Voltaire, "Life of Charles XII. ;" Adlerfeld, "Histoire de Charles XII," 1740; Nordberg, "Karls XII. Historia," 1740; Samuel Faber, "Ausführliche Lebensbeschreibung König Karls XII. von Schweden," 10 vols., 1705-19; Lundblad, " Konung Carls XII. Historia," 2 vols., 1830; Jacob le Long, "Leven van de heldhaftigen Karel XII.," 6 vols., 1722 ; Posselt, "Geschichte Carl's XII.," 1804 ; Frederick II. of Prussia, "Réflexions sur les Talents militaires et sur le Caractère de Charles XII," 1786.

Charles XIII, King of Sweden, born October 7, 1748, was the second son of King Adolphus Frederick and of Louisa Ulrica, who was a sister of Frederick the Great of Prussia. He was educated for the navy, having been made titular grand admiral in his infancy. In 1772 he seconded his brother, Gustavus III., in the revolution by which he depressed the aristocracy and initiated a more liberal constitution. For this service he was made Duke of Sudermania. He commanded the fleet in the war against Russia, 1788-90, and fought several indecisive battles. In 1792 he was chosen regent during the minority of his nephew, Gustavus IV. He favoured the French Revolution, and refused to join a coalition against France. In 1796 he resigned the government to Gustavus IV. By his insane and fanatical conduct the latter provoked the States of Sweden to dethrone him, and Charles was chosen king, June 5 or 6, 1809. As Charles had no heir, the Swedish Diet in 1810 designated as his successor the French general Marshal Bernadotte, who accepted the dignity of crown-prince and was adopted as a son by Charles XIII. In 1812 the King of Sweden acquired Norway by a treaty with Russia and with the assent of several other powers. Died in February, 1818.

See Geyer, "Histoire de Suède;" Lindgrén, "Memoria divi Caroli XIII.," 1818.

Charles XIV. Of Sweden. See Bernadotte.

Charles (or **Carl**) **XV.,** (Louis Eugene,) the son of Oscar I., King of Sweden and Norway, was born in 1826. He married Wilhelmina, a daughter of Prince Frederick of the Netherlands, in 1850, and succeeded his father in July, 1859.

Charles, (or **Karl**,) Archduke of Austria, a celebrated general, born at Florence in 1771, was a younger son of Leopold II., Emperor of Germany. He joined the army in 1793, fought against the French in Flanders, and commanded a wing at the battle of Neerwinde. In the spring of 1796 he was appointed commander-in-chief of the army of the Rhine. In this campaign he defeated the French under Jourdan at Wurtzburg and other places, and, by his skilful generalship, forced Moreau to repass the Rhine. He commanded the Austrians and their allies in Germany and Switzerland in 1799. In 1800 he retired from service on account of ill health. He was commanding in Italy when Bonaparte invaded Austria in 1805, and, on learning the successes of the French, marched his army of 80,000 men to cover Vienna, but did not arrive until after the capture of that city and after the battle of Austerlitz. In 1806 he became chief of the Aulic Council and generalissimo of the Austrian armies. In 1809 he invaded Bavaria, where he encountered Napoleon and was defeated at Eckmühl in April. He was compelled to retreat into Bohemia, while the French army entered Vienna in triumph. He commanded at the battle of Aspern, (May, 1809,) which, says Alison, "was the first great action in which Napoleon had been defeated." He maintained his reputation at the great battle of Wagram, (July, 1809,) where the loss was nearly equal, but the French remained masters of the field. Soon after that event he obtained an armistice from the victor, and resigned the command. He wrote two excellent works, namely, " Principles of Strategy," (1814,) and a "History of the Campaign in Germany and Switzerland in 1799," (1819.) Died in 1847. His son, Archduke Albert, has also distinguished himself as a general.

See Thiers, " Histoire du Consulat et de l'Empire ;" Eduard Duller, " Erzherzog Carl," 1845; Scott, " Life of Napoleon Buonaparte ;" Schneidawind, "Carl Erzherzog von Oesterreich," 1840; "Erzherzog Carl, sein Leben," etc., Berlin, 1847 ; " London Quarterly Review" for March, 1820.

Charles DE Blois, shȧrl deh blwȧ, or **de Chatillon,** deh shȧ'te'yôN', Duke of Bretagne, (breh-tȧn',) was a nephew of Philip of Valois, King of France. Having married Jeanne of Bretagne, he claimed the dukedom of Bretagne at the death of Duke Jean III., (1340.) This claim was disputed by Count de Montfort, a brother of the late duke, and occasioned a war of twenty-three years, in which De Montfort was aided by Edward III. of England. The army of Charles, commanded by Du Guesclin, was defeated in 1364, at the battle of Aurai, in which Charles was killed.

See Froissart, "Chronicles."

Charles, Duke of Brunswick. See Brunswick.

Charles the Bold, [Fr. Charles le Hardy, (or Hardi,) shȧrl leh hȧr'de' ; Ger. Karl (or Carl) der Kühne, kȧrl dēr kü'neh ; Lat. Car'olus Pug'nax, *i.e.* " Charles the Quarrelsome" or " Warlike,"] sometimes called **Charles the Rash,** [Fr. Charles le Téméraire, leh tȧ'mȧ'rȧr',] Duke of Burgundy, born at Dijon in 1433, was the son of Philippe "the Good" and Isabella of Portugal. He was styled Count de Charolais before the death of his father. In 1467 he succeeded his father, and the next year married Margaret, the sister of Edward IV. of England. His violence and ambition rendered him the scourge of adjoining nations. He waged war against Louis XI. of France, and René, Duke of Lorraine. Having invaded Lorraine, he was defeated and killed in battle near Nancy, in 1477, by René and his Swiss allies. His daughter Mary was the heiress of his dominions, (which included the Low Countries,) and became the wife of the emperor Maximilian I. She was a grandmother of the emperor Charles V.

See Kirk, " History of Charles the Bold," 1863; Comines, "Mémoires ;" Sismondi, " Histoire des Français ;" Jules Michelet, "Louis XI et Charles le Téméraire," 1853; Becker, "Karl der Kühne, Herzog von Burgund," 1792.

Charles (DE France,) shȧrl deh frôNss, Charles I. of Lorraine, (lo'rȧn',) second son of Louis IV. Outremer, was born in 953, and became Duke of Lorraine. He waged war with Hugh Capet for the throne of France, was made prisoner and confined until his death in 993.

Charles II., Duke of Lorraine, born at Toul about 1364, was the son of Jean I., whom he succeeded in 1390. About 1396 he fought for the Teutonic knights against the King of Prussia, whom he took prisoner. He fought at Agincourt in 1415, after which he was chosen Constable of France. He died in 1431. His daughter and heiress was married to René of Anjou.

Charles III., called THE GREAT, Duke of Lorraine, born at Nancy in 1543, was the son of Francis I., who died in 1545. He married Claude, the daughter of Henry II. of France, in 1559. He died in 1608, leaving the duchy to his son Henry.

Charles I., (or **Charles Frederick,**) Duke of Holstein-Gottorp, (hol'stīn got'torp,) born at Stockholm in 1700, was the son of Frederick IV., whom he succeeded in 1702. He married, in 1725, Anne of Russia, a daughter of Peter the Great. He lost Sleswick, which was conquered by the Danes. Died in 1739.

Charles OF ANJOU, Count of Maine (mận) and Duke of Calabria, a French prince of the fifteenth century, was the son of Charles, Count of Maine, and was a nephew of René, King of Sicily, by whose will, in 1480, he became Count of Provence. Charles died in 1481, and bequeathed Provence to Louis XI. of France.

Charles OF DENMARK, Count of Flanders, was the son of Canute, King of Denmark. At an early age he distinguished himself in the crusade against the Saracens of Palestine, and in 1119 became Count of Flanders, at the death of Baldwin, who chose him for his heir. His reputation for piety and virtue was such that the throne of Jerusalem was offered to him during the captivity of Baldwin II.; but he declined it. He was assassinated in 1127.

Charles OF LORRAINE. See LORRAINE.

Charles (Carlo) II., (LOUIS de Bourbon—dẹh boor'bôn',) Prince of Parma, etc., born in 1799, is a son of Louis, King of Etruria, and of Maria Louisa of Spain. He inherited the duchy of Lucca in 1824, and ceded the same to Tuscany in 1847. At the death of Maria Louisa (ex-Empress of France) in 1847, he became Archduke or Prince of Parma. He abdicated in favour of his son, Carlo III., in 1849.

Charles (Carlo) III., (FERDINAND JOSEPH VICTOR BALTHASAR DE BOURBON,) Duke of Parma, the son of the preceding, was born in 1823. He became duke in 1849, before which he had married a French princess, daughter of the Duc de Berry, and granddaughter of Charles X. He was assassinated in Parma in 1854.

Charles (Carlo) I., Duke of Sav'oy, born in 1458, succeeded his brother, Philibert I., about 1472. Died in 1489.

Charles (Carlo) II., a son of the preceding, born in 1489; died in 1497.

Charles (Carlo) III., Duke of Savoy, was born in Bugey in 1486, and succeeded his brother, Philibert II. He was an uncle of Francis I. of France. In 1521 he married Beatrix, a daughter of Emmanuel, King of Portugal. She was a sister of the queen of the emperor Charles V., and influenced her husband to become the ally of Charles in the war against Francis I. The army of the latter overran Savoy in 1535, and Geneva shook off the yoke of the duke, who thus lost the greater part of his dominions. Died in 1553. He was succeeded by his son, Emanuel Philibert.

See VINCENT, "Histoire de Savoie."

Charles, shǎrl, (CLAUDE,) a French painter, born at Nancy in 1661; died in 1747.

Charles, (JACQUES ALEXANDRE CÉSAR,) a French savant, noted for his experiments in electricity and ballooning, was born at Beaugency in 1746. He acquired a wide reputation by repeating Franklin's experiments which proved the identity of lightning with the electric fluid, and became a popular lecturer on physical science in Paris. He made a great improvement in the balloon which Montgolfier invented, by substituting hydrogen gas for heated air. He and M. Robert were the first persons who ventured to ascend in a balloon. They ascended from the Tuileries in December, 1783, to the height of 7000 feet, and came down safely nine leagues from the place of ascent. He was a member of the Institute, and was pensioned by Louis XVI. Died in 1823.

Charles, (ELIZABETH RUNDLE,) a popular English writer, the only child of the late John Rundle, formerly member of Parliament for Tavistock, Devonshire, was born about 1826. She was married about 1851 to Andrew

P. Charles, Esq., of London. She has published a number of fictitious works, which have enjoyed an extensive and deserved popularity. Among the most important of these are the "Chronicles of the Schönberg-Cotta Family," (1863,) and the "Diary of Mrs. Kitty Trevylyan," (1864.) She has also written "The Martyrs of Spain and Liberators of Holland," and other works.

Charles Al'bert, [It. CARLO ALBERTO, kar'lo âl-bĕR'-to,] King of Sardinia, born in 1798, was a son of Prince Charles Emanuel of Savoy-Carignan. He married in 1817 Maria Theresa, a daughter of the grand duke Ferdinand of Tuscany. In 1829 he was appointed Viceroy of the island of Sardinia. He succeeded Charles Felix as king in April, 1831, and made some liberal reforms in the government. About the time of the election of Pope Pius IX. he granted a constitution to his subjects, and rendered himself popular. He put himself at the head of the movement for Italian independence in the spring of 1848. After gaining several victories over the Austrians, his army was entirely defeated at Novara, March, 1849. He abdicated in favour of his son, Victor Emanuel, and died in July, 1849.

See ANDREOZZI, "Vita di Carlo Alberto," 1850; MARTINI, "Memorie intorno alla Vita del Rè Carlo Alberto," 1850.

Charles Au-gus'tus, (of Sleswick Holstein Sonderburg,) Prince-Royal of Sweden, and Prince of Augustenburg, was born about 1766. He commanded a Danish army against the Swedes in 1808, and gained the esteem of the latter. In 1809 he was adopted as son by Charles XIII., and designated as the heir to the throne by the States of Sweden. Died in 1810.

Charles d'Orléans, shǎrl doR'lä'ôn', Comte d'Angoulême, (dôn'goo'lêm',) born in Paris in 1391, was the son of Louis, Duke of Orléans, who was the brother of Charles VI. of France. In the civil war of the Armagnacs and Burgundians he was a leader of the former. At the battle of Agincourt, in 1415, he was made prisoner, and as such detained in England until 1440. He composed numerous verses admired for elegant simplicity, and is said to have been one of the best writers of his time. He died in 1465, leaving a son, who became King Louis XII.

Charles de Valois, shǎrl dẹh vǎ'lwǎ', Count of Maine and Anjou, born in 1270, was the third son of Philip III. of France. He was reputed one of the greatest captains of his time. He drove out of Florence the Ghibelines, including Dante, waged war against Frederick of Aragon, and conquered part of Sicily. He commanded with success against the English in Guienne a short time before his death, which occurred in 1325.

See SISMONDI, "Histoire des Français."

Charles Edward Stuart, called THE PRETENDER, born at Rome in 1720 or 1721, was a grandson of James II. of England. His father James having resigned his claim to the throne in favour of Charles Edward, the latter passed from France to Scotland, with a few attendants, in July, 1745. His standard was joined by a large body of Highlanders, and he entered Edinburgh on the 17th of September. A few days later they encountered at Preston Pans a royal army, which was seized with a panic and fled in disorder. The Pretender marched south as far as Derby, then retreated to Scotland, pursued by the Duke of Cumberland, who defeated the rebels at Culloden in April, 1746. Charles Edward concealed himself in the Western Isles, had many romantic adventures, and, by the aid of Flora Macdonald, escaped from his pursuers to France in September, 1746. He passed the latter part of his life at Rome, became intemperate, and died in 1788. His wife was afterwards married to Alfieri.

See AMÉDÉE PICHOT, "Histoire de Charles Édouard," etc.

Charles Eman'uel I., Duke of Sav'oy, surnamed THE GREAT, born in 1562, succeeded his father, Philibert Emanuel, in 1580. He married Catherine, the daughter of Philip II. of Spain. He was ambitious and warlike, and waged a long war against Henry IV. of France. Died in 1630.

His son, VICTOR AMADEUS I., succeeded him. Another son, THOMAS, Prince of Carignano, was a distinguished general.

See SISMONDI, "Histoire des Français."

ā, ē, ī, ō, ū, ȳ, *long;* ă, ĕ, ĭ, ŏ, ŭ, ў, *short;* ạ, ẹ, ị, ọ, *obscure;* fär, fâll, fât; mĕt; nŏt; gōŏd; mōōn;

Charles Emanuel II., Duke of Savoy, born about 1633, was the son of Victor Amadeus I., whom he succeeded in 1638. His reign was mostly pacific. Died in 1675.

Charles Emanuel III., King of Sardinia, the son of Victor Amadeus II., was born at Turin in 1701, and succeeded his father in September, 1730. In 1733 he joined France and Spain in a war against Austria, and, at the head of the allied armies, conquered the Milanese. In the general war which began in 1741 he declared for Maria Theresa of Austria, and fought against the French and Spaniards, who defeated him at Coni in 1744. He died in 1773, with the reputation of a wise and able ruler, and left the throne to his son, Victor Amadeus III.

See SEMERIA, "Storia del Rè di Sardegna Carlo Emmanuele," 2 vols., 1831.

Charles Emanuel IV., King of Sardinia, the eldest son of Victor Amadeus III., was born at Turin in May, 1751. In 1775 he married Marie Clotilde, a sister of Louis XVI. of France. In 1792 Savoy and Nice were conquered by the French, who, in 1796, dictated the terms of peace. Charles Emanuel became king in October, 1796, and found the kingdom in a miserable condition. His reign was disturbed by insurrections probably fomented by the French Directory. His fortresses, arsenals, etc. having been seized by French troops, he was compelled to abdicate in December, 1798, when he retired to the island of Sardinia. In 1802 he abdicated in favour of his brother, Victor Emanuel I. Died at Rome in 1819.

See BETTOLI, "Elogio storico di Sua Maesta Carlo Emmanuele," 1814.

Charles Fe′lix [It. CARLO FELICE, kaR′lo fȧ-lee′-chȧ] I., King of Sardinia, born at Turin in 1765, was the fourth son of Victor Amadeus III., and was styled Duc de Gênes, (or Genoa.) In 1807 he married Maria Christina, daughter of the King of Naples. When his brother, Victor Emanuel, recovered Piedmont in 1814, Charles Felix remained in the island of Sardinia as viceroy. In March, 1821, a revolution occurred in Piedmont, and Victor Emanuel, rather than accept the constitution offered by the insurgents, abdicated the crown, to which Charles Felix, as the lawful heir, succeeded. He suppressed the revolt by vigorous measures, and reigned in peace until his death in 1831. He left no issue, and was the last king of the elder branch of the house of Savoy. The crown then passed to Charles Albert, Prince of Carignano.

Charles Gustavus. See CHARLES X., King of Sweden.

Charles le Chauve. See CHARLES I. of France.

Charles le Gros. See CHARLES III., Emperor.

Charles le Hardy, (or **Hardi.**) See CHARLES THE BOLD, page 577.

Charles le Mauvais. See CHARLES THE BAD, King of Navarre.

Charles le Sage. See CHARLES V. of France.

Charles le Simple. See CHARLES III. of France.

Charles le Téméraire. See CHARLES THE BOLD.

Charles Mar′tel, [Fr. pron. shȧrl mȧr′tèl′,] King of the Franks, and grandfather of Charlemagne, was born about 694 A.D. He was the son of Pepin d'Heristal, Duke of Austrasia, and mayor of the palace under the last Merovingian kings. About 715 he succeeded his father as mayor of the palace, and king in reality, while Chilpéric II. was only the phantom of royalty. A large army of Saracens from Spain having invaded his kingdom, he gained an important victory over them near Poitiers in 732. He received his surname of MARTEL (hammer) in consequence of this victory, which gave a fatal blow to the power of the Saracens. He was successful in wars against the Saxons and other German tribes. He died in 741 A.D., and was succeeded by his sons Carloman and Pepin le Bref.

See EDUARD CAUER, "Dissertatio de Karolo Martello," 1848; SISMONDI, "Histoire des Français;" BARON DE NILINSE, "Charles Martel: Histoire des Maires du Palais," 1851.

Charles Martel of Hungary, was a son of Charles II. of Naples, and Mary, Princess of Hungary. He obtained the crown of Hungary in 1290, and died in 1295, leaving it to his son Charobert.

Charles Phil′ip, Duke of Suderma′nia, etc., born at Revel in 1601, was the son of Charles IX. and brother of Gustavus Adolphus. The Swedish army having conquered many provinces of Russia, the regency of Novogorod offered the throne to Charles Philip in 1611. After a long delay, he went to Viborg to accept the offer; but Michael Romanow was proclaimed king at Moscow. Charles formally renounced the crown in 1614, and died in 1622.

Charles Quint. See CHARLES V., Emperor of Germany.

Charles Robert. See CHAROBERT.

Charles the Rash. See CHARLES THE BOLD, Duke of Burgundy, page 577.

Charlet, shȧr′lȧ′, (NICOLAS TOUSSAINT,) a French painter, designer, and lithographer, born in Paris in 1792. His painting of an "Episode of the Russian Campaign" is highly praised. Died in 1845.

See JULES JANIN, "N. T. Charlet, Artiste," 1847.

Charle′ton, (LEWIS,) an English bishop, (of Hereford,) noted for learning. Died in 1369.

Charle′ton or **Charl′ton**, (ROBERT M.,) an American lawyer and poet, born at Savannah, Georgia, in 1807. He published a volume of poems in 1838, and was elected United States Senator in 1852. Died in 1854.

Charleton or **Charlton**, (WALTER,) F.R.S., an eminent and learned English physician, born at Shepton-Mallet in 1619. Having graduated in 1642, he became physician to Charles I., and practised some years in London. After the restoration (1660) he was physician-in-ordinary to Charles II. In 1689 he was chosen president of the College of Physicians. He wrote, besides professional works, "Epicurus his Morals," "Chorea Gigantum," a treatise on Stonehenge, and "Onomasticon Zoicon," a valuable work, in which he attempts to determine the class, order, genus, and species of animals vaguely designated by authors under diverse names. Died in 1707.

See NICÉRON, "Mémoires;" ÉLOY, "Dictionnaire de la Médecine."

Charleval, de, deh shȧrl′vȧl′, (CHARLES Faucon de Ris—fō′kòN′ deh re,) SEIGNEUR, a French versifier, born in Normandy about 1612. "He was one of those," says Voltaire, "who acquired celebrity by the delicacy of their wit, without devoting themselves (se livrer trop) to the public." He wrote fugitive poems, and the famous "Conversation of Marshal d'Hocquincourt with P. Canaye," printed in the works of Saint-Evremond. Died in 1693.

See FELLER, "Dictionnaire Historique."

Charlevoix, de, deh shȧr-leh-vwȧ′ or shȧrl′vwȧ′, (PIERRE FRANÇOIS XAVIER,) a French Jesuit and author, born at Saint-Quentin in 1682. He went to Canada as a missionary in 1720, explored Lakes Huron and Michigan, descended the Mississippi to its mouth, and returned to France by way of Saint Domingo in 1722. He wrote many years for the "Journal de Trévoux," and compiled a "History and Description of Japan," (1715,) and a "History of Canada," (3 vols., 1744,) the former containing a journal of his travels. These works are valuable, though not free from partiality and credulity. Died in 1761.

See FELLER, "Dictionnaire Historique."

Charlier, shȧr′le-ȧ′, (CHARLES,) a French Jacobin, born at Laon, was a member of the National Convention in 1792. Died in 1797.

Charlier, (JEAN.) See GERSON.

Charlotte (shar′lŏt) of Cyprus, was the daughter of John III. of Lusignan, King of Cyprus. She was married, in 1459, to Louis of Savoy. She failed in her attempt to obtain the throne of Cyprus, of which she was the legal heiress. Died in 1487.

See E. DE LUSIGNAN, "Histoire de Chypre."

Char′lotte Au-gus′ta, Princess of Wales, commonly known as Princess Charlotte, the daughter of George IV. of England and his queen Caroline, was born at Carlton House in 1796. When a final separation took place between the king and queen, she was regarded as the future queen of England. The English court favoured a marriage between Charlotte and the Prince of Orange; but she preferred Leopold of Saxe-Coburg, to whom she was married in 1816. She died in childbirth in November, 1817, universally regretted by the British people.

See "Memoir of the Life of the Princess Charlotte," by ROBERT HUISH, London, 1818; "Autobiography of Miss Cornelia Knight," London, 1861; "London Quarterly Review" for January, 1862.

Charlotte Elizabeth. See TONNA, MRS.

Charlton. See CHARLETON.

Charma, shȧʀ'mȧ', (ANTOINE,) a French writer, born in the department of Nièvre in 1801, became professor of philosophy at Caen about 1830. He published "Lessons of Social and Logical Philosophy," (1840,) an "Essay on Oriental Philosophy," (1842,) and other works.

Charmeil, shȧʀ'mȧl' or shȧʀ'mȧ'ye, (PIERRE MARIE JOSEPH,) a French surgeon, born in 1782; died in 1830.

Charmetton, shȧʀ'mȧ'tòn', (JEAN BAPTISTE,) a French surgeon, born at Lyons in 1710; died in 1781.

See FIGUET, "Vie de M. Charmetton," 1781.

Char'mĭ-dēs, [Χαρμίδης,] an Athenian philosopher, born about 450 B.C., was a maternal uncle of Plato, and first-cousin of Critias, one of the Thirty Tyrants. He was a pupil of Socrates. Having been appointed one of the ten tyrants whom Lysander established in the Piræus, he was killed in battle by the army of Thrasybu'lus about 404 B.C.

See PLATO, "Charmides;" XENOPHON, "Memorabilia."

Char'mis, a physician, born at Marseilles, settled at Rome in the reign of Nero. His favourite remedy was the cold bath.

Charnacé, de, dęh shȧʀ'nȧ'sȧ', (HERCULE GIRARD,) BARON, an able French diplomatist, born in Anjou or, according to some authorities, Bretagne. Through the influence of Richelieu, he was appointed ambassador to Sweden in 1628, and negotiated an important alliance with Gustavus Adolphus. He was killed at the siege of Breda, (1637,) where he fought, with the rank of colonel, for the Prince of Orange.

See BAYLE, "Historical and Critical Dictionary;" "Nouvelle Biographie Générale."

Charnage. See DUNOD.

Charnes, de, dęh shȧʀn, (JEAN ANTOINE,) a French abbé, born at Avignon in 1641, was preceptor of the son of Louvois in Paris. He published a "Life of Tasso," abridged from the Italian of G. B. Manso. Died in 1728.

Char'nock, (JOHN,) an English writer, born in 1756. After leaving Oxford, he studied naval and military tactics, and served some time in the navy. He wrote several esteemed works, viz., "Naval Biography," ("Biographia Navalis," 6 vols., 1796,) a "History of Marine Architecture," (1800,) and a "Life of Nelson," (1806.) Died in 1807.

Charnock, (STEPHEN,) an eminent English nonconformist divine, born in London in 1628. After preaching some time in Dublin, he was ejected for nonconformity in 1662. For about fifteen years he was a popular minister of a dissenting congregation in London. He wrote "Discourses on the Existence and Attributes of God," (1682,) a powerful and original work, highly commended by competent critics, and a "Discourse on the Salvation of Sinners." Two volumes of his sermons were published in 1682-83. His style is a model of sententious brevity. Died in 1680.

Charnois, de, dęh shȧʀ'nwȧ', (JEAN CHARLES Leva-cher—lęh-vȧ'shȧ',) a French journalist and littérateur, born in Paris about 1750. He was executed in September, 1792.

Charobert, shȧ'ro'baiʀ', **Caribert,** kȧ're'baiʀ', or **Charles Robert,** King of Hungary, was a son of King Charles Martel, and a grandson of Charles II., King of Naples. He began to reign in 1312, and raised Hungary to a high degree of power and splendour. He died in 1342, leaving the throne to his son, Louis I.

See ERSCH und GRUBER, "Allgemeine Encyklopaedie."

Charolais, COUNT DE. See CHARLES THE BOLD.

Chȧ'ron, [Gr. Χάρων,] the ferryman who conveyed the souls of the dead across the rivers of Hades. The poets represent him as the son of Erebus and Nox.

See VIRGIL's "Æneid," book vi.

Charon [Χάρων] of Lampsacus, an ancient Greek historian, who was anterior to Herodotus, and lived

probably about 500 B.C. He wrote a "History of Persia," and several other histories, of which only small fragments are extant.

Charon of Thebes was a prominent actor in the conspiracy or revolution which, under the direction of Pelopidas, subverted the power of the aristocratic party in Thebes in 379 B.C. Pelopidas, Charon, and Melon were then chosen chief magistrates of that state.

Charon, shȧ'ròn', (VIALA,) a French general and senator, born in Paris in 1794. He served in Algeria as officer of engineers with distinction from 1835 to 1845, and after the fall of Louis Philippe, in 1848, became general of division. He was afterwards chosen president of the committee of fortifications, and a senator.

Cha-ron'das, [Χαρώνδας,] an eminent Greek legislator, born at Catania, in Sicily, lived about 650 B.C. His laws, which were in verse, were adopted by the Athenians and other nations.

See ARISTOTLE, "Politica;" CICERO, "De Legibus."

Charost, de, dęh shȧ'ro', (ARMAND JOSEPH de Bé-thune—dęh bȧ'tün',) DUC, an opulent French philanthropist and economist, born at Versailles in 1728, was a descendant of the statesman Sully. He served in the army from 1745 to 1763, and became a lieutenant-general, He founded hospitals and other benevolent institutions. and made improvements in agriculture, on which he published several treatises. Louis XV. once said, pointing to him, "There is a man who vivifies three of my provinces." In the reign of terror he was imprisoned for six months, ending on the 9th Thermidor, 1794. Died in 1800.

See DE SAINT-AMAND, "Biographie du Duc de Béthune-Charost;" "Nouvelle Biographie Générale."

Charpentier, shȧʀ'pŏn'te-ȧ', (FRANÇOIS,) a French author, born in Paris in 1620. He became in 1651 a member of the French Academy, of which he was also perpetual director. He was one of the first members of the Academy of Inscriptions, and the principal designer of the medals struck in 1702 to commemorate the events of the reign of Louis XIV. Among his numerous works, which display talents and learning, are "A Life of Socrates," (1650,) "The Excellence of the French Language," (1695,) and "A Journey to the Tranquil Valley," a tale. Died in 1702. He warmly maintained that inscriptions on monuments in France should be in French rather than in Latin.

See QUÉRARD, "La France Littéraire."

Charpentier, (FRANÇOIS PHILIPPE,) an ingenious French mechanician, born at Blois in 1734, invented a process for making coloured engravings from paintings, which procured him the title of mechanician to the king; also, a fire-engine, which was generally used. Died in 1817.

Charpentier, (HENRI FRANÇOIS MARIE,) a French general, born at Soissons in 1769, entered the army in 1791. For his services at Marengo in 1800 he was made general of division. He made the campaign of Austria in 1809, and contributed to the victories of Lutzen and Bautzen in 1813. Soon after the restoration he was made a grand officer of the legion of honour. Died in 1831.

See DE COURCELLES, "Dictionnaire des Généraux Français."

Charpentier, [Lat. CARPENTA'RIUS,] (JACQUES,) a French physician, born at Clermont in 1524. He became professor of mathematics in the Collége Royal, Paris, in 1566, and physician to Charles IX. As a partisan of Aristotle, he wrote several discourses against Ramus. He published, in Latin, a "Description of Nature, after Aristotle," and other works. Died in 1574.

See MORÉRI, "Dictionnaire Historique;" JEAN PAPIRE MASSON, "Vita J. Carpentarii," 1574.

Charpentier, (JEAN PIERRE,) a learned and accomplished French critic, was born at Saint-Prest (Eure-et-Loire) in 1797. He was professor of eloquence in the Faculty of Paris for many years. He published, besides other works, an "Essay on the Literary History of the Middle Ages," ("Moyen Age,") (1833,) a "History of the Renaissance of Letters in Europe in the Fifteenth Century," (1843,) and a translation of Virgil's "Bucolics" and "Georgics."

Charpentier, (MARC ANTOINE,) an excellent French musician and composer, born in Paris in 1634. After he had gained a high reputation in Italy, he returned to Paris, where he became a rival of Lully, and director of the music of the Duke of Orléans. He composed the music of "Medea" and other operas. Died in 1702.

See Fétis, "Biographie Universelle des Musiciens."

Charpentier, [Lat. Carpenta′rius,] (Pierre,) a French jurist, born at Toulouse. He became a Calvinist, and lectured on law at Geneva. Having quarrelled with Beza, he removed to Paris just before the massacre of 1572, during which he found refuge in the house of Bellièvre. He published in 1572 an apology for the Massacre of Saint Bartholomew, and was rewarded with the office of royal advocate.

See De Thou, "Histoire."

Charras, shȧ′râs′, (Jean Baptiste Adolphe,) a French officer and military writer, born at Puy-de-Dôme in 1808. He was a republican member of the Constituent Assembly in 1848–49. He wrote a masterly strategic work—"Histoire de la Campagne de 1815—Waterloo," (2 vols. 8vo, 1858; 5th edition, 1863.) Died in 1865.

Charrier de la Roche, shȧ′re-à′ deh lȧ rosh, (Louis,) a French bishop, born at Lyons in 1738, was elected to the States-General in 1789. He became first almoner of Napoleon in 1804. Died in 1827.

Charrière, shȧ′re-âiR′, (Ernest,) a French littérateur, born at Grenoble in 1805, published "Saint Helena," a lyric poem, (1826,) and a work on political history, entitled "La Politique de l'Histoire," (1842.)

Charrière or **Charrières, de,** deh shȧ′re-âiR′, (Madame Saint-Hyacinthe,) a novelist, who was born in Holland about 1746. She married M. de Charrière, and settled near Neufchâtel, about 1766. She was a friend of Madame de Staël, and was highly gifted, morally and intellectually. She wrote several works of fiction, among which "Calliste" (1786) is said to be the most remarkable. Her pictures of life are faithful and very diversified. Died in 1805.

See Sainte-Beuve, "Portraits des Femmes," 1844.

Charrières. See Charrière.

Charrin, shȧ′rȧN′, (Pierre Joseph,) a French dramatist and littérateur, born at Lyons in 1784, wrote melodramas, songs, etc.

Charron, shȧ′rȯN′, (Pierre,) a French philosopher and Catholic priest, born in Paris in 1531. He became eminent as a preacher, and was successively théologal, or lecturer, at Lectoure, Agen, Bordeaux, Cahors, and Condom. He was an intimate friend of Montaigne, from whose Essays he has borrowed largely. In 1594 he published a religious book, called "Treatise on the Three Truths," ("Traité des trois Vérités.") His principal work is a "Treatise on Wisdom," ("Traité de la Sagesse," 1601,) which was censured as irreligious or skeptical by the Jesuits and others, but had great popularity. Died in Paris in 1603. "It becomes difficult," says Hallam, "to estimate the place of Charron as a philosopher, because we feel a good deal of uncertainty whether any passage be his own. He appears to be a man formed in the school of Montaigne,—not much less bold in pursuing the novel opinions of others, but less fertile in original thoughts, . . . with more reading than his model, with more disciplined habits, as well of arranging and distributing his subject as of observing the sequence of an argument; but, on the other hand, with far less of ingenuity in thinking and of sprightliness of language." ("Introduction to the Literature of Europe.")

See Nicéron, "Mémoires;" Luchet, "Analyse raisonnée de la Sagesse de Charron," 1763; Brucker, "Historia Philosophiæ."

Chartier, shȧR′te-à′, (Alain,) a French poet of great celebrity in his time, was born in Normandy about 1385. He was confidential secretary to Charles VI. and to Charles VII., and appears to have been idolized by cultivated men of that age. A majority of French critics agree that their language owes great obligations to him; and he appears to have contributed to the moral and political reformation of his country. Among his French poems are the "Breviary of the Nobles," and the "Book of the Four Ladies," ("Le Livre des quatre Dames.") He wrote "Le Curial," and other prose works. Died about 1455.

See G. Mancel, "Alain Chartier: Étude bibliographique," 1850; Longfellow, "Poets and Poetry of Europe."

Chartier, (Guillaume,) brother of the preceding, born at Bayeux about 1400, became Bishop of Paris in 1447. Died in 1472.

Chartier, (Jean,) a brother of the preceding, received from Charles VII. the title of historiographer. He published "Chronicles of France," and a "History of the Reign of Charles VII.," both of which are esteemed. Died in or after 1461.

Chartier, (Jean,) a son of René, noticed below, born in Paris in 1600, graduated in 1634, and became physician to the king. Died in 1662. Philippe, a younger brother of Jean, was also physician to the king, and professor in the Collége Royal. Died in 1669, aged thirty-six.

Chartier, (René,) [Lat. Rena′tus Charte′rius,] a French physician, born at Vendôme in 1572. He graduated at Paris in 1608, was appointed physician-in-ordinary to the king in 1613, and professor of surgery at the Collége Royal in 1617. He acquired a high reputation by an excellent edition, in Greek, of Hippocrates and Galen, with a Latin version and notes, (1639–79.) Died in 1654.

See "Nouvelle Biographie Générale."

Charton, shȧR′tȯN′, (Édouard,) a French littérateur, born at Sens in 1807. He established in 1833 the "Pictorial (Pittoresque) Magazine," which he conducted more than twenty years. In 1848 he was elected to the National Assembly. He contributed to several journals of Paris, and published, besides other works, "Ancient and Modern Voyagers," (1855.)

Chartran, shȧR′trȯN′, (J. H. S.,) a French general, born at Carcassonne in 1779. He was made a general of brigade for his services at Culm in 1813, and was put on half-pay by the Bourbons in 1814. He took the field for Bonaparte in 1815, and distinguished himself at Waterloo. He was tried by a military court, and executed in 1816.

Chartres, Duke of. Several French princes have borne this title. (See Louis Philippe; and Orléans, Philippe, Duke of.)

Chartres, de, deh shȧRtr, (Renaud or Reginald,) Archbishop of Rheims, was born about 1380. He was appointed chancellor of France in 1428, and acquired great influence with the king, Charles VII. He was jealous of Joan of Arc, whose bold and extraordinary measures did not accord with his mean and tortuous policy, and made no effort to prevent her tragical death. Died in 1444.

Chas, shâs, (J.,) a prolific French writer and compiler of history, biography, etc., was born at Nîmes about 1750; died about 1830.

Chase, (Irah,) D.D., a Baptist divine and theologian, born in Stratton, Vermont, in 1793. He was the principal founder, in 1825, of the Baptist Theological Seminary at Newton, Massachusetts, and professor in that institution until 1845. Died in 1864.

Chase, (Philander,) an American Episcopal bishop, born in Cornish, New Hampshire, in 1775, graduated at Dartmouth College in 1795. He became rector of a church at Hartford, Connecticut, about 1812, and in 1817 began to labour as a missionary in Ohio, where he planted the Episcopal Church. In 1819 he was elected Bishop of Ohio, and in 1835 became Bishop of Illinois. He founded Kenyon College, in Ohio, and Jubilee College, in Illinois. Died in 1852.

See "Reminiscences of Bishop Chase: an Autobiography."

Chase, (Salmon Portland,) an eminent American statesman, a nephew of the preceding, was born at Cornish, New Hampshire, on the 13th of January, 1808. He graduated at Dartmouth College in 1826, taught a classical school at Washington, District of Columbia, from 1826 to 1829, studied law under William Wirt, and settled at Cincinnati about 1830. He attained eminence as a lawyer, supported General Harrison in the Presidential election of 1840, and took a prominent part in the formation of the Liberty party about 1841. He was one of the chief promoters of the convention of Free-soilers which met at Buffalo in 1848 and nominated Martin Van Buren for the Presidency. He acted as counsel for the defence of several fugitive slaves.

In February, 1849, he was elected a Senator of the United States by the Democratic members of the legislature of Ohio. He made in the Senate a speech against the Compromise Bill in 1850. On the nomination of

---

e as k; ç as s; ḡ hard; ġ as j; G, H, K, guttural; N, nasal; R, trilled; s as z; th as in this. (☞See Explanations, p. 23.)

Mr. Pierce in 1852, he separated from the Democratic party, which was then committed to the support and extension of slavery. He opposed the Nebraska-Kansas Bill, by which the Missouri Compromise was repealed in 1854, and offered several amendments to the same. He proposed to add a clause that "the people of the territory, through their appropriate representatives, may, if they see fit, prohibit the existence of slavery therein." This amendment was rejected by a vote of ten yeas and thirty-six nays. He advocated the Homestead Bill, and maintained that the Federal Government should aid in the construction of a railroad to the Pacific.

He was elected Governor of Ohio for two years by the Republicans in October, 1855, and supported J. C. Fremont for the Presidency in 1856. In 1857 he was re-elected Governor. At the National Republican Convention which met in Chicago in May, 1860, Governor Chase received forty-nine votes for the office of President on the first ballot. Having been appointed a member of the Peace Conference which met at Washington in February, 1861, he there made a speech on the subject of fugitive slaves, and proposed that the Northern States should compensate their masters for them. "We cannot surrender [them,"] said he, "but we can compensate." He was appointed secretary of the treasury in the cabinet of Lincoln, March 4, 1861. In January, 1862, he recommended that the notes of the United States should be made a legal tender. When he accepted the office of secretary, the public credit was low, and the public revenue was scarcely sufficient to support the government even in a state of peace. He raised money by the issue of treasury notes, called "greenbacks," which bore no interest, and by loans which were taken at moderate rates, mostly by the people of the United States.

His services as a financier are eulogized by Horace Greeley in these terms: "Governor Chase had filled in the public service, through years of doubt, depression, and disaster, the second place in importance, and the first in the magnitude of its requirements, and had discharged its duties with pre-eminent ability, energy, and courage." ("American Conflict.") He resigned his office on the 30th of June, 1864, about which time his friends made a movement to procure his nomination as candidate for the Presidency, but without success. He was regarded with special favour by the radical Republicans. He supported the re-election of President Lincoln, who appointed him chief justice of the supreme court of the United States, in the place of Roger B. Taney, who died in October, 1864. In the controversy about the reconstruction of the seceded States he did not take a decided or prominent part; but in 1865, after the end of the civil war, he made a tour of observation in several of the Southern States, and made speeches to the freedmen. He identified himself with the Radicals on the question of impartial suffrage. He presided over the court of impeachment (March, 1868) for the trial of President Johnson. He is understood to have favoured the acquittal of the President, and by his course on that occasion gave much offence to the radical Republicans. He was an unsuccessful candidate for the Democratic nomination for President in July, 1868.

See MRS. STOWE'S "Men of our Times."

Chase, (SAMUEL,) an American judge and eloquent lawyer, born in Somerset county, Maryland, in 1741. He became a leader of the patriots of Maryland in the Revolution, was a delegate in Congress from 1774 to 1778, and signed the Declaration of Independence in 1776. In 1791 he was appointed chief justice of the general court of Maryland, and in 1796 was nominated an associate justice of the supreme court of the United States. He was impeached in 1804 for misdemeanour in relation to certain political trials. John Randolph of Roanoke instigated and conducted this impeachment, which resulted in the acquittal of Judge Chase in March, 1805. Died in 1811.

See "National Portrait-Gallery of Distinguished Americans," vol. iv. ; "Encyclopædia Americana."

Chasles or **Châles,** shâl, (LOUIS,) a French Jacobin and priest, born at Chartres in 1754, was a member of the Convention, (1792–95,) and voted for the death of the king. Died in 1826.

Chasles, (MICHEL,) an eminent French geometer, born at Épernon (Eure-et-Loire) in 1793. He entered the Polytechnic School in 1812. In 1837 he published a *résumé* of his previous works, in a volume entitled "Historical View *(Aperçu)* of the Origin and Development of Methods in Geometry," followed by a "Memoir on two General Principles of the Science, Duality and Homography." In this work he established the basis of a new theory of conic sections and of surfaces of the second order. He was appointed professor of astronomy and mechanics in the Polytechnic School in 1841. He was very successful in researches in pure geometry, several important theories of which he extended and simplified. In 1846 he obtained the chair of higher geometry in the Faculty of Sciences, Paris, and in 1852 published a "Treatise on Higher Geometry," ("Traité de Géométrie supérieure.") He was admitted into the Institute in 1851. By an ingenious algorithm he has introduced the principle of signs into pure geometry, and has created a new branch of mathematics, characterized by uniformity of method.

See "Nouvelle Biographie Générale."

Chasles, (VICTOR EUPHÉMION PHILARÈTE,) a successful French *littérateur,* a son of Louis Chasles, noticed above, was born near Chartres in 1799. He has been for more than twenty years an editor of the "Journal des Débats," and has contributed to the "Revue des Deux Mondes." His principal articles, written for these and other periodicals, have appeared under the general title of "Studies on Comparative Literature," (in 11 vols.,) among which are "Studies on Spain," "Studies on America," etc. He is, or was recently, professor of foreign languages and literature in the College of France. He has shown himself an able critic of English literature, and has reproduced for the "Revue Britannique" many articles from English reviews. He published, in 1862, "Galileo, sa Vie, son Procès et ses Contemporains."

See QUÉRARD, "La France Littéraire."

Chasles or **Challes, de,** deh shâl, (GRÉGOIRE,) a French writer, born in Paris in 1659. He was the author of "Illustrious Frenchwomen," ("Les illustres Françaises," 1713,) often reprinted. Died about 1720.

Chasles de la Touche, shâl deh lä toosh, (THÉODORE GASTON JOSEPH,) a French historical writer, born at Le Teil in 1787; died in 1848.

Chassaignac, shä'săn'yăk', (E . . . .,) a French physician, born at Nantes in 1805, published several works on anatomy.

Chassé, shä'sä', (DAVID HENDRIK,) BARON, a brave Dutch general, born at Thiel in 1765, entered the French service about 1790. He distinguished himself in the Prussian campaign of 1806, and displayed great bravery in Spain in 1808–09. He was created a baron about 1811, and became a general of division in 1814. He fought for the allies at the battle of Waterloo, (1815,) after which he became governor of Antwerp. His resolute defence of Antwerp against the French in 1832 was much admired. Died in 1849.

See CAMPO, "Life of Chassé."

Chassel, shä'sĕl', (CHARLES,) a French sculptor, born at Nancy in 1612, became a resident of Paris. He received the title of sculptor to Louis XIV., for whom he made a mimic army when that prince was a boy.

Chassel, (RÉMI FRANÇOIS,) a grandson of the preceding, born at Metz in 1666, worked at Nancy, and was successful in monumental sculpture. Died in 1752.

Chasseloup-Laubat, de, deh shäs'loo' lō'bä', (FRANÇOIS,) MARQUIS, a French general, born near Marennes in 1754. As chief engineer, he served with applause under Bonaparte in Italy in 1796 and 1797. In 1799 he was raised to the rank of general of division. He was employed for several years in fortifying Mantua, Alessandria, and other cities of Italy. In 1812 he obtained for the seventh time the chief command of the engineers of the grand army. After the restoration he received the title of Marquis. Died in 1833.

See "Victoires et Conquêtes des François."

Chasseloup-Laubat, de, (JUSTIN PRUDENT,) MARQUIS, a French general, son of the preceding, born in Paris in 1800. He became a captain of cavalry in 1830,

ā, ē, ī, ō, ū, ȳ, *long;* ă, ĕ, ŏ, same, less prolonged; ă, ĕ, ĭ, ŏ, ŭ, ў, *short;* ą, ę, į, ǫ, *obscure;* fär, fȧll, fät; mĕt; nŏt; gŏŏd; mōōn;

and a few years later accompanied General Maison as aide-de-camp in an embassy to Vienna. From 1837 to 1848 he was a member of the Chamber of Deputies. He was made a general of division in 1853.

His brother, Count JUSTIN NAPOLÉON, a lawyer and a Bonapartist politician, was born in 1805. He was a member of the Assembly in 1849, and afterwards of the Corps Législatif. In November, 1860, he was appointed minister of state for the marine and the colonies.

Chasseneux, shȧs'nŭh', (BARTHÉLEMI,) a learned French judge and legal writer, born near Autun in 1480. He was appointed president of the parliament of Provence in 1532. He wrote, among other works, "Consilia," and "Catalogus Gloriæ Mundi," a work designed to explain and determine questions of rank, precedence, etc. Died in 1541.

Chassériau, shā'sȧ're-ō', (THÉODORE,) a French painter, born at Samana, in Hayti, in 1819, worked in Paris, where he received several medals between 1836 and 1855. His works, among which is "The Supper of Macbeth," are said to display a fine imagination. Died in 1856.

Chassignet, de, deh shā'sèn'yȧ', (FRANÇOIS,) BARON, was born at Besançon, France, in 1651. Having entered the Austrian service, he quickly rose to a high rank in the army. He became the preceptor of the emperor Leopold's eldest son, (Joseph I.) In 1700 he was sent to Naples to manage a conspiracy against the Spanish government. He failed in this attempt, was arrested and confined in the French Bastille until 1714.

Chassiron, de, deh shā'se'rȯn', (PIERRE CHARLES MARTIN,) BARON, a French economist, noted for his improvements in agriculture, was born at La Rochelle in 1753. He wrote several esteemed letters on agriculture, and articles for Rozier's "Cours d'Agriculture." Died in 1825.

See SILVESTRE, "Notice sur le Baron Chassiron," 1826.

Chasteau, shā'tō', [It. CASTELLI, kâs-tel'lee,] (GUILLAUME,) a French engraver, born at Orléans in 1635. He studied and worked in Italy, and afterwards removed to Paris, where he was patronized by Colbert. He engraved after Poussin, Annibale Caracci, and other masters. Died in 1683.

See BASAN, "Dictionnaire des Graveurs."

Chastel. See CHÂTEL.

Chastel, shā'tĕl', (PIERRE LOUIS AIMÉ,) BARON, a French general, born at Vergi, in Chablais, in 1774. While serving in the army of Egypt, in 1798, he discovered the zodiac of Denderah. He displayed courage and capacity in the campaigns of Austerlitz and Jena, and, as general of division, distinguished himself at Borodino in 1812. After the campaign of 1815 in Belgium, he retired to private life. Died at Geneva in 1826.

See "Victoires et Conquêtes des Français."

Chastel, du. See DUCHÂTEL.

Chastelain, shāt'lȧN', (CLAUDE,) a French liturgist, born in Paris about 1640 ; died in 1712.

Chastelain, shāt'lȧN', (GEORGES,) a celebrated Flemish chronicler, born in Flanders in 1403. He lived at the court of Philip, Duke of Burgundy, and of his son, Charles the Bold. His chief work is a "General Chronicle of Events from 1420 to 1474." Died in 1475.

Chastelard, de, deh shāt'lȧR', (PIERRE de Boscosel—deh bos'ko'zĕl',) a French poet, born about 1540. He became enamoured of Mary Queen of Scots, concealed himself in her bedchamber, and was detected. Having repeated the offence, he was executed at Edinburgh in 1563.

See MIGNET, "Histoire de Marie Stuart ;" BRANTÔME, "Mémoires."

Chasteler, du, dü shȧt'lȧ', (JEAN GABRIEL,) MARQUIS, an eminent general in the Austrian service, born at Mons in 1763. He entered the army at the age of fifteen, and, after serving several campaigns in Flanders and Italy, was made quartermaster-general in 1799. In 1805 he was chief of the staff of the Archduke Charles in Italy. In 1808 he commanded in the Tyrol against the French, and in 1813 became general of artillery. About 1815 the emperor appointed him governor of Venice, where he died in 1825.

See "Nouvelle Biographie Générale."

Chastelet or **Châtelet, du,** dü shȧt'lȧ', (PAUL HAY,) SIEUR, an eloquent French lawyer, born in Bretagne in 1592, became attorney-general at Rennes, and councillor of state. He was the first secretary of the French Academy, and wrote, besides other works, a "Life of Du Guesclin." Died in 1636.

Chastellet, du, dü shā'tȧ'lȧ', or **Châtelet-Lomont, du,** dü shȧt'lȧ' lo'mȯn', (FLORENT LOUIS MARIE,) DUC, the son of the following, was born at Semur, France, in 1727. He served with distinction in the army, was created a duke in 1777, and afterwards became colonel of the French guards. In the States-General of 1789 he was a moderate royalist. He was proscribed in the reign of terror, and executed in December, 1793.

Chastellet, du, or **Châtelet,** shȧt'lȧ', (GABRIELLE EMILIE le **Tonnelier** de Breteuil—lĕh ton'le-ā' dĕh brĕh-tuI' or brĕh-tü'ye,) MARQUISE, a celebrated French savante, born in 1706. She was learned in mathematics and other sciences, and in Latin, English, and Italian. In 1740 she published a work on Physical Philosophy, entitled "Institutions de Physique." She afterwards made a good French translation of Newton's "Principia," which was revised by Clairaut. In early youth she was married to the Marquis du Chastellet-Lomont. She lived some years with Voltaire at Cirey between 1735 and 1747. Her *liaison* with Voltaire injured her reputation, and will probably be remembered after her writings are forgotten. Died in 1749.

Chastellux, de, deh shā'tȧ'lüks', (FRANÇOIS JEAN,) MARQUIS, a French general and author, born in Paris in 1734. He wrote an admired "Essay on Public Happiness," ("De la Félicité publique," 1772,) which Voltaire preferred to Montesquieu's "Spirit of Laws." In 1775 he was admitted into the French Academy. In 1780 he went to the United States, where he served with honour as major-general in the army of Rochambeau for three years. He published, among other works, "Travels in North America," (2 vols., 1786.) He was a personal friend of Washington. Died in 1788.

See GRIMM, "Correspondance Littéraire ;" ALFRED DE CHASTELLUX, "Notice sur le Marquis de Chastellux," 1822.

Chastillon. See CHÂTILLON.

Chastillon, deh shā'te'yȯn', (ALEXIS MADELEINE ROSALIE,) DUC, born in 1680, was a descendant of Gaucher, noticed below, and became maréchal-de-camp in 1719. As lieutenant-general, he commanded the cavalry at Guastalla in 1734. In 1735 he was appointed governor of the dauphin, the son of Louis XV. Died in 1754.

Chastillon, de, (EUDES.) See URBAN II., POPE.

Chastillon, de, (GAUCHER,) Count of Crecy, a French general, born in 1250, fought bravely at Courtray in 1302, and was made Constable of France in the same year. He gained a victory at Cassel in 1328. Died in 1329.

Château. See CHASTEAU, (GUILLAUME.)

Châteaubriand, de, deh shā'tō'bre'ȯn', (FRANÇOIS AUGUSTE,) VISCOUNT, the most celebrated of the French authors who wrote during the first empire, was born of a noble family, at Saint-Malo, in September, 1768. He was educated at Dol and at Rennes, where he made great progress in the ancient languages and in mathematics. His youth was passed mostly on the shore of the ocean, where his imagination was nourished by lonely reveries among the winds and waves. "A divine breath," says he, "passed over me. I began to lisp forth verses as if they had been my natural language. I wrote for a long time in verse before attempting prose." He was destined for the church, but preferred the army, which he entered as sub-lieutenant in 1786. He was in Paris and a spectator of the capture of the Bastille in 1789, but did not partake of the popular enthusiasm. "I had neither adopted nor rejected the new opinions," says he. "I wished neither to emigrate nor to follow the military profession. I retired." Impelled by a desire to travel, he sailed for the United States in 1791, ostensibly in search of a Northwest passage. He dined in Philadelphia with Washington, of whom he says, "There is virtue in the look of a great man. I felt myself warmed and refreshed by it during the rest of my life." Having traversed the primeval forests from Niagara to Florida, he returned

---

є as *k* ; ç as *s* ; g̃ *hard* ; g̃ as *j* ; G, H, K, *guttural* ; N, *nasal* ; R, *trilled* ; s̃ as *z* ; țh as in *this*. (☞See Explanations, p. 23.)

to France in 1792. He had not found a Northwest passage, but he had discovered the germs of a new and romantic literature. To please his sister, he married Mademoiselle de Lavigne, whom he appears not to have found a very congenial companion. In 1792 he joined the army of royalist emigrants, was wounded at Thionville, and left for dead in a ditch. From 1793 until 1800 he was an exile in England, where he was reduced to extreme poverty, and partly supported himself by translations for the booksellers.

Having been converted from skepticism by the death of his mother, in 1798, he began to compose his celebrated work, "The Genius of Christianity," ("Génie du Christianisme.") He returned to France in 1800, and published in 1801 his romance of "Atala," a picture of aboriginal American life, which extorted from Europe a general exclamation of surprise and admiration. In 1802 appeared his "Génie du Christianisme," to which "René," a romance, was attached as an episode. The publication of these brilliant works made a revolution in French literature, and caused him to be recognized as the literary glory of his age. He performed, in 1806 and 1807, a tour through Greece, Asia Minor, Palestine, and Spain, partly with a view to familiarize himself with the regions in which he proposed to lay the scene of a new work. This was a prose epic, entitled "The Martyrs, or the Triumph of the Christian Religion," which appeared in 1809.

In 1811 he was elected a member of the French Academy, and published his "Itinerary from Paris to Jerusalem." His long and implacable enmity to the emperor found utterance in his famous and eloquent pamphlet, "Bonaparte and the Bourbons," (1814.) Under the restoration, from 1814 to 1824, he showed himself an ultra-royalist. He was ambassador to Berlin in 1820, and to London in 1822, after he had fiercely and effectively opposed the Liberal minister Decazes, whose feet, he said, "had slipped in blood." He was appointed minister of foreign affairs in 1823, and dismissed by his rival, Villèle, in June, 1824, after which he became a formidable assailant of the ministry in the "Journal des Débats." In 1828 he was sent as ambassador to Rome by Martignac; but he resigned the embassy on the accession of Polignac as prime minister. After the revolution of 1830 he refused to take the oath to Louis Philippe, and defended the exiled Bourbons in several tracts, for which he was prosecuted and imprisoned a short time in 1832. His waywardness and inconsistency in politics were thus indicated in his own words: "I am a Bourbonist by honour, a royalist by reason and conviction, and a republican by taste and character." He died on the 4th of July, 1848, after seeing the advent of the second republic. He left posthumous memoirs, ("Mémoires d'Outre-Tombe,") 1849, which attracted general attention as a rare combination of genius and egotism. He had no children. His last years were passed in retirement and in a despondency which even the charming society and devoted attentions of Madame Récamier could not exhilarate.

See VILLEMAIN," M. de Châteaubriand, sa Vie, ses Écrits, son Influence," etc., 1858; COUNT DE MARCELLUS, "Châteaubriand et son Temps," 1859; L. DE LOMÉNIE, "Galerie des Contemporains illustres," tome i.; SCIPION MARIN, "Histoire de la Vie et des Ouvrages de Châteaubriand," 1833; CESARE CANTÙ, "Châteaubriand, Discorso," Milan, 1835; F. Z. COLLOMBET, "Châteaubriand, sa Vie et ses Écrits," 1851; ANCELOT, "Vie de Châteaubriand," 4to, 1853; SAINTE-BEUVE, "Causeries du Lundi," tomes i. and ii.; PRESCOTT, "Miscellanies;" "London Quarterly Review" for July, 1816; "Blackwood's Magazine" for June, 1837, September, 1849, and July, 1850; "Foreign Quarterly Review" for October, 1831, October, 1832, and April and January, 1837; "North British Review" for August, 1858; "Memoirs and Correspondence of Madame Récamier," translated from the French and edited by MISS LUYSTER, Boston, 1867.

Châteaubriant, de, dẹh shä'tō'bre'ŏn', (FRANÇOISE,) COUNTESS, a beautiful French lady, born in 1475, was the daughter of the Count de Foix, and sister of Marshal Lautrec. After her marriage with Seigneur de Châteaubriant, she became an ornament of the court of Francis I., who said that a court without ladies "is like a year without spring and a spring without roses." The current rumour that she was the mistress of Francis is denied by some writers. Died in 1537.

See VARILLAS, "Histoire de François I."

Châteaubrun, de, dẹh shä'tō'brŭn', (JEAN BAPTISTE VIVIEN,) a French dramatist, born at Angoulême in 1686. He composed dramas, which for many years he refused to present on the stage, through fear of displeasing the Duc d'Orléans, to whom he was attached as *maître-d'hôtel*, (steward.) He was received into the French Academy in 1753. The next year his tragedy "The Trojan Women" was performed, and was received with great favour. Died in 1775.

Châteauneuf, de, dẹh shä'tō'nŭf', (L'ÉPINE,) a French diplomatist, born about 1753, was a cousin of General Dumouriez. He was consul-general at Tunis in 1787, and minister to Geneva a short time about 1792. He translated the "Idyls" of Theocritus into French verse. Died in 1800.

Châteauneuf-Randon, de, dẹh shä'tō'nŭf' rŏn'dŏn', (ALEXANDRE,) COUNT, a French Jacobin and regicide, born probably in Gévaudan. In 1789 he was deputed by the noblesse of Mende to the States-General, and in 1792 to the Convention, in which he voted for the execution of the king. He made himself notorious for his cruelty and crimes at Lyons, whither he was sent by the Convention in 1793. Died in obscurity in 1816.

Château-Regnaud, de, dẹh shä'tō' rẹh-nŏ', also written **Château-Renaud** and **Château-Regnard,** (FRANÇOIS LOUIS DE ROUSSELET,) COUNT, a French vice-admiral and marshal, born in 1637. As *chef-d'escadre,* or commodore, he defeated the Dutch fleet under De Ruyter in 1673. In 1678 he gained a victory near Cadiz over Eversen, a Dutch admiral. He defeated the English in the Bay of Bantry, and was appointed lieutenant-general of the naval armies, in 1688. In 1701 Philip V. of Spain gave him the title of Captain-General of the Ocean. He received a marshal's bâton in 1703. Died in 1716.

Châteauroux, shä'tō'roo', (MARIE ANNE,) DUCHESS OF, was born of the noble family of Nesle. After the death of her husband, the Marquis de la Tournelle, she became the favourite of Louis XV. of France, who gave her the title of Duchess. She retained influence over him until her death in 1744.

Châtel. See DUCHÂTEL.

Châtel or **Chastel,** shä'tĕl', (JEAN,) a Frenchman, born in Paris about 1575. In December, 1594, he entered the Louvre and attempted to kill Henry IV. with a knife, but only inflicted a slight wound. He was arrested, and, when questioned respecting his motive, said that he had been taught at a college of Jesuits that it was lawful to kill a heretical king. He was executed, and the Jesuits were expelled from Paris.

See SISMONDI, "Histoire des Français."

Châtel, du, dü shä'tĕl', (FRANÇOIS,) a skilful Flemish historical painter, born at Brussels in 1626. He was a pupil of Teniers, whose style he imitated with success; and he excelled in design and colouring. A picture of the King of Spain receiving the Oath from the Estates of Flanders in 1666 is one of his most admired works. He often chose for his subject a festival, a social assembly, or a family group.

See DESCAMPS, "Vies des Peintres Flamands," etc.

Châtel, du, (TANGUY or TANNEGUY,) a French general, who served at Agincourt in 1415, and was chief of the Armagnac party. He was appointed Governor of Provence by Charles VII. in 1446. He died at the age of ninety.

Chatelain, shat'ẹh-lān', (?) (JOHN BAPTIST,) a skilful designer and engraver, born in London in 1710. He was reckoned among the best engravers of landscapes, many of which he executed after Gaspard Poussin, N. Poussin, and Cortona. He also engraved his own designs. Died in London in 1771.

See BASAN, "Dictionnaire des Graveurs."

Châtelain, (RENÉ THÉOPHILE,) a French writer, born at Saint-Quentin in 1790, served in the army from 1808 to 1815. In 1819 he became chief editor of the "Courrier Français," a paper of liberal politics, and acquired a high reputation as a journalist. His principal work is entitled "Letters of Sidi Mahmoud," (1825.) Died in 1838.

Châtelet. See CHASTELLET and CHASTELET.

Châtelet-Lomont. See CHASTELLET.

Chatham, chat'ạm, (JOHN PITT,) EARL OF, born in 1756, was the eldest son of the great Earl of Chatham. He was first lord of the admiralty in the ministry of his brother, William Pitt, and commanded the unfortunate expedition against Walcheren in 1809. He died, without issue, in 1835.

Chatham, LORD. See PITT, (WILLIAM.)

Chatillon. See CHASTILLON and CHARLES DE BLOIS.

Châtillon, shȧ'te'yòn', (ANDRÉ MARIE,) a French architect, born in Paris in 1782, gained the grand prize (de Rome) in 1809.

Châtillon or **Chastillon,** (NICOLAS CLAUDE,) born at Châlons, in Champagne, in 1547, was reputed one of the ablest engineers of France. He was employed as engineer by Henry IV. and Louis XIII. He built the Pont-Neuf (New Bridge) in Paris, and left a work entitled "French Topography," containing views of castles, cities, etc. Died in 1616.

Chat'tẹr-tọn, LADY, a British authoress of the present century. She has published "Rambles in the South of Ireland," (1838,) "A Good Match," a novel, (1839,) "The Reigning Beauty," (1858,) and other works.

Chatterton, (THOMAS,) an English poet, celebrated for his genius, precocity, and literary impostures, was born at Bristol in 1752. His father was sexton of Redcliffe Church. In childhood he was averse to study, and was pronounced by his teacher a dull boy. After he attained the age of eight, he made rapid progress, and became fond of antiquarian pursuits. About the age of twelve he wrote verses which evinced talent. In 1767 he was apprenticed to an attorney of Bristol. When the new bridge was opened in 1768, Chatterton published a "Description of the Friars first passing over the Old Bridge," which he professed to derive from ancient manuscripts found in the muniment-room of Redcliffe Church. He soon produced poems, which he ascribed to Rowley, a monk of the fifteenth century, and other ingenious fabrications, which excited among literary men no little sensation. A long and animated controversy ensued respecting the authenticity of the Rowleian poems, which the majority pronounced to be forgeries. In April, 1770, he went to London in search of literary employment, and was at first successful. He was employed by several booksellers, and, in letters to his mother, represented his prospects as extremely brilliant. He wrote sermons, songs, and political articles for the public journals. He soon became despondent, was reduced to a state of starvation, and in August, 1770, was found dead, probably by suicide. It appears that he had shown symptoms of insanity for some years before his death. His principal poems are "The Tragedy of Ella," "The Battle of Hastings," "Ode to Ella," "The Tournament," and a "Description of Canynge's Feast." "This youth," says T. Warton, "was a prodigy of genius, and would have proved the first of English poets had he reached a mature age." "No English poet," says Thomas Campbell, "ever equalled him at the same age. Tasso alone can be compared to him as a juvenile prodigy. His thirst for knowledge was that of a being taught by instinct to lay up materials for the exercise of great and undeveloped powers."

See WARTON, "History of English Poetry;" CAMPBELL, "Specimens of the British Poets;" JOHN DIX, "Life of T. Chatterton," 1837; GEORGE GREGORY, "Life of T. Chatterton," 1789; "Biographia Britannica;" H. PUETTMANN, "Chatterton," Barmen, 2 vols., 1840; CARY, "Lives of English Poets from Johnson to Kirke White;" "Edinburgh Review" for April, 1804, (by SIR WALTER SCOTT.)

Chau'cẹr, [Lat. CHAUCE'RUS,] (GEOFFREY,) the father of English poetry, was born in London in 1328. The Universities of Oxford and Cambridge both claim him as their alumnus. He enjoyed the favour of Edward III., and passed much time at court. About 1358 he served in the army which invaded France, where he was made prisoner. In 1373 he was employed on an embassy to Genoa, where perhaps occurred the interview with Petrarch which he mentions in his works. Soon after his return he was appointed comptroller of customs in London. He was elected a knight of the shire for Kent in 1386, and about that time is said to have been persecuted as a Wickliffite. He received an annual pension from 1367 until his death, excepting a few years when he was out of favour. In the latter part of his life

he wrote his principal work, the celebrated "Canterbury Tales," in a language so different from modern English that few persons can now enjoy their beauties. The plot is thought to be taken from the "Decameron" of Boccaccio; and the work purports to be a series of stories told by pilgrims travelling in company to Canterbury. Among his other poems are "The Court of Love," "The Legend of Good Women," "The House of Fame," and "Troilus and Cresseide." He died in 1400.

"Our greatest poet of the middle ages, beyond comparison," says Hallam, "was Chaucer; and I do not know that any other country except Italy produced one of equal variety in invention, acuteness of observation, or felicity of expression." ("Introduction to the Literature of Europe.") "I take unceasing delight in Chaucer," says Coleridge. "His manly cheerfulness is especially delicious to me in my old age. How exquisitely tender he is, yet how free from the least touch of sickly melancholy or morbid drooping!" "Chaucer stands in the first rank," says Southey, "with Spenser, Shakspeare, and Milton." He had a son, Sir Thomas, who became Speaker of the House of Commons, and a daughter Alice, who married the Duke of Suffolk. The poet himself had married Philippa Rouet, a maid of honour to the queen, and sister-in-law of John of Gaunt, Duke of Lancaster.

See W. GODWIN, "Life of Chaucer," 1804; TODD, "Lives of Gower and Chaucer," 1810; H. NICHOLAS, "Life of Chaucer," 1843; H. GOMONT, "G. Chaucer, Poëte Anglais," 1847; VILLEMAIN, "Cours de Littérature;" "Edinburgh Review" for June, 1815; "Retrospective Review," vol. ix., 1824, and vol. xiv., 1826; article on Chaucer (by SIR WALTER SCOTT) in the "Edinburgh Review" for January, 1804; "Fraser's Magazine" for April, 1856.

Chaucerus. See CHAUCER.

Chaudesaigues, shōd'zȧg', (CHARLES BARTHÉLEMI,) a French writer of songs, born in Paris in 1799.

Chaudet, shō'dạ', (ANTOINE DENIS,) an eminent French sculptor, born in Paris in 1763, was a pupil of Stouf. In 1784 he gained the grand prize of the Academy for a bas-relief of "Joseph sold by his Brethren." Having studied several years in Rome, he returned to Paris in 1789, and soon acquired the reputation of one of the first of modern sculptors. About 1805 he was chosen a member of the Institute, and one of the committee on the "Dictionary of the Language of the Fine Arts." Among his master-pieces are an "Œdipus," a statue of "Napoleon," "Paul and Virginia," and "Cincinnatus." He was also a skilful painter. Died in 1810.

See NAGLER, "Neues Allgemeines Künstler-Lexikon;" "Nouvelle Biographie Générale."

Chaudet, (JEANNE ÉLISABETH,) a French painter, wife of the preceding, born in 1767; died about 1830.

Chaudon, shō'dòn', (ESPRIT JOSEPH,) a French littérateur, born at Valensole (Lower Alps) in 1738. He became a priest of the Oratory, and taught in several colleges of that order. He published a useful work, called "The Library (Bibliothèque) of a Man of Taste, or Advice on the Choice of the Best Books in our Language," (1772,) and a "Dictionary of the Latin Names in Ancient and Modern Geography," (1778.) Died in 1800.

See QUÉRARD, "La France Littéraire."

Chaudon, (LOUIS **Maïeul**—mä'yul',) a brother of the preceding, born at Valensole, near Riez, in 1737, was eminent as a biographer. He was a monk of the fraternity of Cluny, and is usually called DON CHAUDON. In 1766 he produced a "New Historical Dictionary," which was superior to any work of that kind, and was very successful. The ninth edition, enlarged to twenty volumes, appeared about 1810. He afterwards published anonymously the "Anti-Philosophic Dictionary," (2 vols., 1769,) to refute the skeptical doctrines of Voltaire, "Lectures on History and Chronology," (2 vols., 1781,) and other works. He assisted his brother in the "Library of a Man of Taste," (1772.) Died in 1817.

See QUÉRARD, "La France Littéraire;" "Nouvelle Biographie Générale."

Chaudron-Rousseau, shō'dròn' roo'sō', (PIERRE GUILLAUME,) a French general, born in 1775, was killed at Chiclana in 1811.

Chaudruc de Crazannes, shō'drük' dẹh krȧ'zȧn', (JEAN CÉSAR MARIE,) a French antiquary, born near Saintes in 1782.

Chauffard, shō'fȧr', (MARIE DENIS ÉTIENNE,) a French medical writer, born at Avignon in 1796. He published "Works *(Œuvres)* of Practical Medicine," (3 vols., 1848,) which were received with favour.

Chauffepié, de, dẹh shōf'pe-ȧ', (JACQUES GEORGE,) a Dutch Protestant minister, of French descent, born at Leeuwarden in 1702. He preached at Flushing and Delft for some years. From 1743 until his death he was employed in Amsterdam. He published in 1750 "A New Historical and Critical Dictionary, supplementary to that of Bayle," (4 vols.,) a valuable work, in which he gives proof of much erudition. He translated, from the English, part of a "Universal History" (46 vols.) composed by a society of literary men. Died at Amsterdam in 1786.

See QUÉRARD, "La France Littéraire."

Chauliac, de, dẹh shō'le-ȧk', (GUI,) an eminent French surgeon, born at Chauliac. He lived in Avignon, where he was successively physician to Popes Clement VI., Innocent VI., and Urban V., between 1340 and 1370. He wrote, in Latin, an excellent treatise on Surgery, ("Inventarium Partis chirurgicalis Medicinæ," 1363,) which for about two centuries was considered a classic and standard work. A French writer, Chaumeton, says he did more than any one to render surgery a regular art. The great Haller observes that "his work may be regarded as an excellent historical sketch of surgery down to his epoch."

See ÉLOY, "Dictionnaire de la Médecine."

Chaulieu, de, dẹh shō'le-uh', (GUILLAUME AMFRYE,) a French lyric poet, was born at Fontenay, in Normandy, in 1639. He was patronized by the Dukes of Vendôme, who caused him to be appointed Abbé d'Aumale and procured him other rich benefices. He became distinguished for his wit, fine taste, and Epicurean morals, and was called the "Anacreon of the Temple." "Chaulieu," says Hallam, "was an original genius. His poetry is a happy mixture of a gentle and peaceable philosophy with a lively imagination. His verses flow from the soul, and, though often negligent through indolence, are never in bad taste or affected." ("Introduction to the Literature of Europe.") Voltaire praises him in his "Temple du Goût," the presiding genius of which advises Chaulieu not to estimate himself as the first of good poets, but the first of negligent poets, *(poètes négligés.)* He wrote an "Ode to Inconstancy," "Stanzas on the Solitude of Fontenay," "La Goutte," and other poems. Died in 1720.

See QUÉRARD, "La France Littéraire:" SAINTE-BEUVE, "Causeries du Lundi ;" VOLTAIRE, "Correspondance."

Chaulnes, de, dẹh shōn, (HONORÉ d'Albert—dȧl'-baïr',) DUC, a French general, a brother of Luynes, the favourite of Louis XIII., became a marshal of France in 1619, and was created Duc de Chaulnes in 1621. He was made Governor of Picardy in 1633, and commanded against the Spaniards in Artois in 1635. Died in 1649.

Chaulnes, de, (LOUIS AUGUSTE d'Albert d'Ailly —dȧl'baïr' dȧ'ye',) DUC, a French general, born in 1676, was the father of Michel Ferdinand, noticed below. Died in 1744.

Chaulnes, de, (MARIE JOSEPH LOUIS,) DUC, a French savant, son of Michel, noticed below, born in 1741, cultivated the physical sciences with success, and became a Fellow of the Royal Society of London. Died in 1793.

Chaulnes, de, (MICHEL FERDINAND D'ALBERT D'AILLY,) DUC, a French general, born in 1714. He was noted as a patron and votary of physical science, and spent a large revenue in constructing apparatus and forming collections. In 1743 he was chosen an honorary member of the Academy of Sciences. He wrote several ingenious treatises, which were published by that academy. Died in 1769.

Chaumeix, de, dẹh shō'mȧ', (ABRAHAM JOSEPH,) a French critic, born near Orléans about 1730, was noted for his zeal against the skeptical philosophers. He published a refutation of the "Encyclopédie," and was satirized by Voltaire in "The Poor Devil," ("Le pauvre Diable.") Died in 1790.

See QUÉRARD, "La France Littéraire."

Chaumeton, shōm'tôN', (FRANÇOIS PIERRE,) a French physician, eminent as a writer and a critic, born

at Chouzé, on the Loire, in 1775. He devoted much attention to the literary history of medicine, and wrote many able articles for the "Magasin Encyclopédique," the "Bibliothèque Médicale," and other scientific journals. For the "Biographie Universelle" he furnished notices of many eminent physicians. He undertook the "Medical Flora," of which he composed the text as far as the letter G. Died in 1819.

See VIREY, "Notice sur la Vie, etc. de Chaumeton."

Chaumette, shō'mĕt', (PIERRE GASPARD,) a French demagogue and Jacobin of infamous memory, born at Nevers in 1763. In 1789 he joined the Cordeliers Club in Paris, and acquired influence over the populace by his violent harangues. As procureur of the commune, (1792,) he was accessary to the worst crimes of that period. He was one of the chiefs of the atheistical faction called Hébertists, and was the author of the Festivals of Reason. As chief priest, he officiated at the profane orgies by which the worship of Reason as the only national religion was inaugurated in the cathedral of Notre-Dame, December, 1793. He was proscribed by Robespierre, and executed in 1794.

See THIERS, "History of the French Revolution."

Chaumonot, shō'mo'no', (PIERRE MARIE JOSEPH,) a French Jesuit, born in 1611, laboured as a missionary among the Indians of Canada. Died in 1693.

Chaumont, de, dẹh shō'môN',(CHARLES d'Amboise —dôN'bwȧz',) SEIGNEUR, a French general, nephew of the Cardinal d'Amboise, was born in 1473. He was appointed governor of Milan in 1500, and distinguished himself at the battle of Agnadello. In 1510 he invested Pope Julius II. in Bologna, and would have captured him if he had not resorted to negotiations. Died in 1511.

See SISMONDI, "Histoire des Républiques Italiennes."

Chaumont, de, (PAUL PHILIPPE,) a French ecclesiastic and author, succeeded his father as keeper of the books of the king's cabinet, (1667.) In 1654 he was admitted into the French Academy, and in 1671 became Bishop of Apt. He wrote an esteemed work entitled "Reflections on the Christianity taught in the Catholic Church," (1693.) Died in 1697.

See NICÉRON, "Mémoires."

Chauncey or **Chauncy,** chȧn'se or chawn'se, (CHARLES,) a distinguished lawyer, born at Durham, Connecticut, in 1747. He taught jurisprudence for many years, and became a judge of the superior court of Connecticut in 1789. Died in 1823.

Chauncey, (CHARLES,) an eminent American lawyer, a son of the preceding, was born at New Haven, Connecticut, in 1777. He removed about 1798 to Philadelphia, where he soon rose to distinction, although he had among his competitors several of the most accomplished lawyers in the United States. Died in 1849.

See an interesting notice of his character as a lawyer and a man, by HORACE BINNEY, in "Wallace's Reports," vol. ii., 1854, p. xii. *et seq.*

Chauncey, (ISAAC,) an American commodore, born in Connecticut about 1772. He obtained the rank of captain about 1806, and was appointed commander of the naval forces on the northern lakes in 1812. His squadron, aided by a land army under General Pike, took York (Toronto) in April, 1813. He defeated the British fleet on Lake Ontario in September, 1813, and gained a high reputation for ability. Died in 1840.

Chauncy, (CHARLES.) See CHAUNCEY, (CHARLES.)

Chauncy or **Chauncey,** chȧn'se or chawn'se, (CHARLES,) an English Puritan, born in Hertfordshire in 1592, became professor of Greek at Cambridge, and vicar of Ware. He emigrated to Massachusetts in 1638, preached some years at Scituate, and became president of Harvard College in 1654. Died in 1672.

Chauncy, (CHARLES,) a writer on theology, a descendant of the preceding, was born in 1705. He was minister of a church in Boston, Massachusetts, for many years. Died in 1787.

Chauncy, (Sir HENRY,) a British antiquary and lawyer, born in 1632, became reader and treasurer of the Middle Temple, and published "Historical Antiquities of Hertfordshire," (1700.) In 1688 he was made a Welsh judge. Died in 1719.

ā, ē, ī, ō, ū, ȳ, *long;* ȧ, ė, ȯ, same, less prolonged; ă, ĕ, ĭ, ŏ, ŭ, ў, *short;* ą, ę, į, ǫ, *obscure;* fär, fȧll, fȧt; mĕt; nŏt; gŏŏd; mŏŏn;

Chaupy, de, deh shō'pe', (CAPMARTIN BERTRAND,) a French antiquary and priest, born near Toulouse in 1720. In 1756 he removed to Rome, where he spent ten years in collecting materials for a "Description of Ancient Italy," a part of which was published. Died in 1798.

Chaussard, shō'säR', (PIERRE JEAN BAPTISTE,) an ingenious and prolific French writer, born in Paris in 1766. He was an ardent partisan of the Revolution, and obtained the important place of *chef des bureaux* of the committee of public safety about 1792. In 1805 he was appointed professor of literature at Nîmes, and two years later he was authorized by Fontanes to reside in Paris as director of classical studies, retaining his title and salary. He wrote an admired ode "On Industry and Arts," "Theory of Criminal Laws," (1789,) "Esprit de Mirabeau," (2 vols., 1797,) and various other works. In his youth he adopted the name of Publicola. Died in Paris in 1823.

See HÉREAU, "Notice sur Chaussard."

Chausse. See LA CHAUSSE.

Chausse, de la, deh lȧ shōss, (MICHEL ANGE,) a French antiquary, born in Paris about 1660, became a resident of Rome. He gained a high reputation by his antiquarian works, among which are "Romanum Museum," an illustrated treatise on ancient gems, images, insignia, etc., (1690.) Died after 1738.

Chaussée, de la, deh lȧ shō'sȧ', (PIERRE CLAUDE NIVELLE,) a French dramatic author, born in Paris in 1692. In 1732, in partnership with La Faye, he wrote an "Epistle from Clio," ("Epître de Clio,") in verse. His pathetic or sentimental comedy "Préjugé à la mode" ("Prejudice à la mode," in verse, 1735) obtained a triumph which time has confirmed. La Chaussée first introduced what the French call the *genre larmoyant*, (pathetic comedy.) He wrote other popular dramas, among which we may name "False Antipathy." He was a member of the French Academy. Died in 1754.

See LA HARPE, "Cours de Littérature."

Chaussier, shō'se-ȧ', (FRANÇOIS,) a celebrated French physician, was born at Dijon in 1746, and graduated in 1780. He had taught anatomy and chemistry at Dijon for some years, when the government called him to Paris, in 1794, to aid Fourcroy in reorganizing the medical institutions. The result was the "École de Santé," in which he obtained the chair of anatomy. In 1804 he became professor of chemistry in the Polytechnic School, where he lectured until 1815. He wrote many medical and scientific treatises, which were inserted in various periodicals, and rendered important services to legal medicine and physiology. Among his most useful works is a series of "Synoptical Tables on Zoonomy," (1799–1826.) Died in Paris in 1828.

See QUÉRARD, "La France Littéraire."

Chauveau, shō'vō', (ADOLPHE,) a French jurist, born about 1790, became professor of law in Toulouse in 1821. He published a "Theory of the Penal Code," (1834–43,) and a "General Formulary," (1853.) In the former work M. Hélie co-operated.

Chauveau, (FRANÇOIS,) a skilful French designer and engraver, born in Paris about 1620. He engraved works of Raphael, Poussin, Giulio Romano, etc. Died in 1676.

See HEINECKEN, "Dictionnaire des Artistes."

Chauveau, (RENÉ,) an ingenious French sculptor and architect, son of the preceding, was born in Paris in 1663. Louis XIV. employed him in various works for the decoration of his palaces. Died in 1722.

Chauveau-Lagarde, shō'vō' lȧ'gäRd',(CLAUDE FRANÇOIS,) an eloquent and courageous French lawyer, born at Chartres about 1760. After having gained reputation by defending Miranda and Brissot in times when the advocate shared the peril of the accused, he was designated by the judge to be counsel for Charlotte Corday. He was one of the counsel chosen by the queen Marie Antoinette, for whom he made an unavailing plea, in October, 1793. Soon after this date he was committed to prison, and detained until July, 1794. In the reign of Napoleon he was advocate of the Council of State. He published a "Narrative of the Trial of Marie Antoinette," (1816.) Died in 1841.

See LOUIS AIMÉ MARTIN, "Quelques Esquisses sur la Vie de Chauveau-Lagarde," 1841.

Chauvelin, shōv'lȧN', (HENRI PHILIPPE,) ABBÉ, a French lawyer, son of Germain Louis, noticed below, acquired reputation by his bold and successful attacks on the Jesuits, which resulted in the suppression of the order about 1762. He was canon of Notre-Dame, and a counsellor in the Parliament of Paris. Died in 1770, aged fifty-four.

Chauvelin, de, deh shōv'lȧN', (FRANÇOIS BERNARD,) an able French politician, born in 1766. He favoured the popular party in 1789, and in 1792 he was sent as ambassador to London in company with Talleyrand, who, though not formally accredited, was the real director of the negotiations. When the death of Louis XVI. became known in England, Chauvelin was ordered to leave the island within eight days. Under the régime of Bonaparte he served as member of the Tribunat and prefect of Lys, and received the title of Count. After the restoration (1816) he was for about ten years a prominent member and speaker in the Chamber of Deputies, in which he acted with the Liberals. Died in 1832.

See "Nouvelle Biographie Générale."

Chauvelin, de, (GERMAIN LOUIS,) an able French minister of state, born in 1685. In 1727 he became keeper of the seals and secretary of foreign affairs. He was thenceforth the second and confidant of Cardinal de Fleury, the prime minister, to whom he is said to have been superior in political talent. He was removed from office in 1737, and died in 1762.

Chauvin, shō'vȧN', (ÉTIENNE,) a learned French Protestant divine, born at Nîmes in 1640. He became an exile about 1685, and went to Rotterdam, where in 1688 he taught philosophy in place of Bayle during the long illness of the latter. He published the results of his studies in the history of philosophy, in a work called "Rational Lexicon, or Philosophical Treasury," ("Lexicon Rationale, sive Thesaurus Philosophicus," 1692.) In 1695 he obtained the chair of philosophy in the royal French College of Berlin. Died in Berlin in 1725.

See MM. HAAG, "La France protestante."

Chauvin, (JEAN.) See CALVIN.

Chavagnac, de, deh shȧ'vȧn'yȧk',(GASPARD,)COMTE, a French officer, born in 1624, published a volume of Memoirs, (1699.)

Chavée, shȧ'vȧ', (HONORÉ JOSEPH,) a Belgian linguist, born at Namur in 1815. He attempted to disprove the unity of the human race in his "Lexicologie Indo-Européenne," or Essay on the Knowledge of Sanscrit, Greek, Latin, French, and Russian Words, (1849.)

Chaves, de, deh shȧ'vĕs, (MANUEL de Silveyra Pinto de Fonseca—dȧ sĕl-vȧ'e-rȧ pĕn'to dȧ fon-sȧ'kȧ,) MARQUIS, and Count of Amarante, (ȧ-mȧ-rȧn'tȧ,) a Portuguese general, born at Villareal. He served in the Peninsular war from 1809 to 1814. In the civil war of 1823 he was a prominent partisan of Don Miguel and the absolutists, for whom he gained a victory. He again raised the standard of absolutism in 1827, and was defeated by Villaflor near Coimbra and Oporto. Died in 1830.

Chavignard. See CHAVIGNY.

Chavigny, shȧ'vĕn'ye', or **Chavignard**, shȧ'vĕn'yȧR', (THÉODORE,) a French diplomatist, and one of the most able negotiators of his time, born at Beaune, in Burgundy, was an uncle of Count de Vergennes. He represented France at the Congress of Ratisbon, and was minister to England in 1731. About 1745 he negotiated, at Frankfort, the treaty of alliance between the emperor Charles VII., the King of Prussia, and other powers. Died in 1771.

Chazal, shȧ'zȧl', (ANTOINE,) a French painter and designer, born in Paris in 1793, was one of the most eminent painters of the Museum of Natural History of Paris. He designed the plates for the "Flore Pittoresque," and for several scientific works.

Chazelles, de, deh shȧ'zĕl', (JEAN MATHIEU,) a French mathematician and hydrographer, born at Lyons in 1657, became, in 1685, professor of hydrography at Marseilles, where he made a chart of the coast of Provence. In 1693 he visited Greece and Egypt, where he measured the Pyramids and observed that the sides of one faced the cardinal points. In 1695 he became an Associate of the Academy of Sciences. Died in 1710.

€ as *k*; ç as *s*; ğ *hard*; ġ as *j*; G, H, K, *guttural*; N, *nasal*; R, *trilled*; s̄ as *z*; ᵺh as in *this*. (☞See Explanations, p. 23.)

Cheatham, cheet'ạm, (BENJAMIN F.,) an American general, born at Nashville, Tennessee. He took arms against the Union in 1861, commanded a division at Perryville, October, 1862, at Stone River, December 31, 1862, to January 2, 1863, and at Chickamauga, September 19 and 20, 1863.

Chedeaux, shẹh-dō', (PIERRE JOSEPH,) a French economist, born at Metz in 1767; died in 1832.

Chedel, shẹh'dĕl', (QUENTIN PIERRE,) a French engraver, born at Châlons, in Champagne, in 1705. He etched landscapes after the best Dutch painters. His works are numerous and much admired. Died in 1762.

See HEINECKEN, "Dictionnaire des Artistes."

Chee'vẹr, (EZEKIEL,) an eminent New England teacher, born in London in 1615. Having received a superior classical education, he came to America in 1638, and assisted in founding the colony in New Haven, of which he was a teacher for twelve years, and in 1646 was a representative in the General Assembly. He was subsequently for eleven years a teacher in Ipswich, Massachusetts, nine years in Charlestown, and thirty-eight years in Boston, where he died in 1708.

Cheever, (GEORGE B.,) an American author and preacher, born at Hallowell, Maine, in 1807, graduated at Bowdoin College in 1825. He was ordained minister of a Congregational church at Salem, Massachusetts, in 1832. About 1835 he wrote a satirical allegory called "Deacon Giles's Distillery," for which he was prosecuted on a charge of libel and sentenced to imprisonment for thirty days. He became a resident of New York City in 1839, and preached in the Allen Street Church. He published "Studies in Poetry," (1830,) "Lectures on Pilgrim's Progress," (1843,) "Wanderings of a Pilgrim in the Shadow of Mont Blanc," (1846,) and other works. Since 1846 he has been pastor of the Congregational Church of the Puritans, New York. He has particularly distinguished himself as an opponent of slavery and an advocate of temperance.

See GRISWOLD, "Prose Writers of America."

Cheever, (HENRY T.,) an author and Congregational minister, brother of the preceding, has published, besides other works, "The Island-World of the Pacific," (1851.)

Cheffontaines, de, dẹh shạ̀-fôN'tạ̀n', (CHRISTOPHE,) a French theologian, born in Brittany about 1532, became Archbishop of Cæsarea about 1586. He wrote, besides other works, a "Defence of the Faith of our Ancestors," (1570,) and a "Treatise against certain Dogmas of Scholastic Theology," (1586.) Died at Rome in 1595.

Chégaray, shà'gà'rà', (MICHEL CHARLES,) a French advocate and legislator, born at Bayonne in 1802. He became a judge of the court of cassation in 1853.

Cheiron. See CHIRON.

Cheke or **Cheeke,** (Sir JOHN,) an eminent English scholar and Hellenist, born at Cambridge in 1514. He became in 1540 the first professor of Greek in the university of that city. In 1544 he was appointed Latin tutor to Prince Edward. About 1550 he was knighted by his former pupil, Edward VI., and in 1553 was chosen secretary of state. As a zealous Protestant, he favoured the attempt to raise Lady Jane Grey to the throne. After the accession of Mary he retired to the continent, to escape persecution. In 1556, by order of Philip II. of Spain, he was arrested in Flanders and conveyed to the Tower of London. Being required to choose between death by fire and conversion to the Catholic faith, he accepted the latter. Remorse for this act hastened his death, which occurred in 1557. He had translated several religious works into elegant Latin, and contributed much to the revival of learning in England.

See STRYPE, "Life of Cheke," 1705.

Chelard, shẹh-lȁr', (HIPPOLYTE ANDRÉ JEAN BAPTISTE,) a French musician and composer, born in Paris in 1789. His opera "Macbeth" (with words by Rouget de Lisle) was very successful, and procured for him the place of chapel-master to the King of Bavaria. He produced other operas, cantatas, etc.

See FÉTIS, "Biographie Universelle des Musiciens."

Chelius, kā'le-ùs, (MAXIMILIAN JOSEPH,) a German physician, born at Manheim in 1794, was appointed professor of medicine in the University of Heidelberg in

1819, and privy councillor in 1826. His principal work is a "Manual of Surgery," which has been extensively used. The seventh edition appeared in 1851.

Chelmsford, chĕmz'fọrd, (Sir FREDERICK **Thesiger** —thês'e-jẹr,) LORD, an eminent English lawyer, born in London in 1794. He was returned to Parliament in 1840, after practising some years as leader of the home circuit, became solicitor-general in 1844, and attorney-general under Sir Robert Peel in 1845. He resigned his office in 1846, and was reappointed in 1852. On the accession of the Conservative party in 1858, he was appointed (by Lord Derby) lord chancellor of England, and was raised to the peerage as Lord Chelmsford. He resigned, in consequence of the defeat of the Derby ministry, in June, 1859, and was lord chancellor again from July, 1866, to February, 1868.

See FOSS, "The Judges of England," vol. ix.

Chel'sum, (JAMES,) an English clergyman, born in Westminster in 1740, published "Remarks on Gibbon's History," (1772.) Died in 1801.

Chemin, du, dü shẹh-mȁN', (CATHERINE,) a French flower-painter, born in Paris in 1630; died in 1698.

Cheminais de Montaigu, shẹh-me'nạ̀' dẹh môN'-tạ̀'gü', (TIMOLÉON,) a French Jesuit, distinguished as a pulpit orator, was born in Paris in 1652. He preached in several pulpits of Paris and Versailles until he was disabled by ill health, but for which he would probably have become one of the greatest orators of his age. Died in 1689. "Many persons," says Bayle, "esteem his sermons as highly as those of Bourdaloue."

Chemineau, shẹh-me'nō', (JEAN,) a French general, born in La Charente in 1775. He lost a leg at the battle of Lutzen in 1813, and in the same year became a general of division, and governor of Strasbourg. Died in 1852.

See GENERAL FOY, "Histoire de la Guerre de la Péninsule."

Chemnitius, (MARTIN.) See CHEMNITZ.

Chemnitz, kĕm'nits, (JOHANN JEROME,) of Magdeburg, a German naturalist and divine, born in 1730. He published, in German, several works which contributed to the progress of natural history, especially of conchology. His "Systematic Cabinet of Shell-Fish," (12 vols. 1776–1800,) says Du Petit-Thouars, "is one of the most beautiful and complete works of that kind." Died in 1800.

Chemnitz, [Lat. CHEMNIT'IUS,] (MARTIN,) an eminent German Protestant divine, born at Treuenbrietzen, in Brandenburg, in 1522. He studied mathematics, astronomy, and theology at Wittenberg, and about 1550 was chosen librarian to Duke Albert of Prussia. In 1554 he became minister of a church at Brunswick. He published in 1565 "Examen Concilii Tridentini," a sound and acute argument against the doctrines asserted by the Council of Trent. He took a prominent part in the formation of the doctrinal system of the Protestant Church. Chemnitz and Mörlin composed the "Corpus Doctrinæ Prutenicæ,"[*] (1566.) He was chosen superintendent at Brunswick in 1567, and wrote a confession of faith, which was adopted by the churches of Lower Saxony in 1571. His "Theological Topics" ("Loci Theologici," 1591) was esteemed high authority among his contemporaries, and regarded as superior to all similar works in learning and method. He died at Brunswick in 1586, leaving unfinished a "Harmonia Evangelica," which was published about 1600.

See BROCKHAUS, "Conversations-Lexikon;" JOHANN H. WOLFF, "Programma, M. Chemnitius ipsiusque in Ecclesiam Lutheranam Merita," 1719; JÖCHER, "Allgemeines Gelehrten-Lexikon."

Chemnitz, von, fon kĕm'nits, (PHILIPP **Bogislav**—bo'gis-lȁv,) a historian, grandson of the preceding, born at Stettin in 1605. He entered the service of Christina of Sweden, who ennobled him and gave him the office of councillor. He wrote, in German, a valuable history of the war waged by Gustavus Adolphus in Germany, (1648–52,) and a political work on the theory or method of government in the German Empire. Died in 1678.

Chemnitzer, kĕm'nit-sẹr, (IVAN IVANOVITCH,) a Russian fabulist, of German descent, born in Saint Petersburg in 1744. After serving for some time in the army, he retired about 1778 from the service, in order to indulge

---

[*] "Body of Prussian doctrine;" so called because it was prepared under the auspices of the Duke of Prussia.

his taste for literature, and then published a part of his fables, which the Russians compare to those of La Fontaine. He excels in vivacity of dialogue and *naïveté* of expression. He was appointed consul-general to Smyrna in 1782, and died there in 1784.

See OTTO, "Lehrbuch der Russischen Literatur."

Chemnizer. See CHEMNITZER.

Chenard, shĕh-nǎr′, (SIMON,) a French actor and singer, born at Auxerre in 1758; died in 1831.

Chenavard, shĕh-nǎ′vǎr′, (PAUL,) an eminent French painter of history, born at Lyons in 1808. He studied some years in Italy, and acquired a reputation by his picture of "Mirabeau replying to the Marquis de Dreux-Brezé." After the revolution of 1848 he received a commission to paint fifty large compositions for the decoration of the Pantheon. Among these are "The Deluge" and "The Passage of the Rubicon." The Pantheon having been restored to the Catholic worship, he was not permitted to finish the task.

See NAGLER, "Neues Allgemeines Künstler-Lexikon."

Chênedollé, de, dĕh shĕn′do′lǎ′, (CHARLES JULIEN Pioult—pe′oo′,) a French poet, born at Vire in 1769. He emigrated in 1791, served in the royalist army, and returned to France about 1800, before which date he had composed several odes. He became intimate with Fontanes and Châteaubriand. In 1807 he produced "The Genius of Man," ("Le Génie de l'Homme,") a poem, which is admired for elevated thought and brilliant style. He was appointed professor at Rouen in 1810. In 1820 he published a volume of his early odes, with some new poems, among which were "The Last Day of Harvest" and "Moonlight in May," containing fine descriptions of nature. He was chosen inspector-general of the university in 1830. Died in 1833.

See Louis BLANC, "Histoire de dix Ans;" CHÂTEAUBRIAND, "Mémoires d'Outre-Tombe;" LONGFELLOW, "Poets and Poetry of Europe;" SAINTE-BEUVE, "Revue des Deux Mondes" for June, 1849.

Chen′e-vix, (RICHARD,) an Irish writer, noted for versatility of talents. He was a Fellow of the Royal Societies of London and Edinburgh. He published various esteemed works, among which are "Chemical Nomenclature," (1802,) an "Essay on National Character," (published after his death,) and "Henry Seventh," a tragedy, (1812,) "which," says the "Edinburgh Review," "is the most successful imitation of the general style, taste, and diction of our elder dramatists, that has appeared in the present times." Died in 1830.

See "Edinburgh Review" for July, 1812.

Chénier, shǎ′ne-ā′, (MARIE JOSEPH,) a popular French poet and dramatist, born at Constantinople in 1764, was a brother of André Chénier. He was educated in Paris, where he also resided. He produced in 1789 "Charles IX.," a tragedy, which had prodigious success, especially with the popular party. In 1792 he became a prominent republican member of the Convention. He served the interests of liberty and order in the several Legislative Assemblies of the ensuing ten years. His tragedy of "Timoleon," in verse, (1794,) after being performed once with applause, was prohibited by the ruling powers. He composed other tragedies, and admirable odes, satires, and songs, in which he displayed a great variety of talent. His patriotic "Song of Departure" ("Chant du Départ," 1794) was said to be more popular than any other except the "Marseillaise." He wrote, besides other prose works, an excellent "Historical Treatise *(Tableau)* on the State and Progress of French Literature since 1789," (1808.) He was a member of the Institute. Died in 1811.

See LINGAY, "Éloge de M. J. Chénier;" ARNAULT, "Sur J. Chénier;" DAUNOU, "Notice sur M. J. Chénier," in his Complete Works, 8 vols., 1823–26; FÉLIX PYAT, "M. J. Chénier et le Prince des Critiques, (Jules Janin,)" 1844.

Chénier, de, dĕh shǎ′ne-ā′, (ANDRÉ,) an admirable French poet, born in Constantinople in October, 1762, was the son of Louis Chénier, noticed below. He was educated in Paris, and became an excellent classical scholar. He began his literary career by beautiful eclogues of antique simplicity, and elegies admired for sensibility. In 1787 he went to England as secretary of legation. In the Revolution he pursued a moderate course. Some letters which he published in the "Jour-

nal de Paris" rendered him obnoxious to the dominant party; and he was committed to prison as a Girondist. "There," says Lamartine, "his ideal reveries found their reality in Mademoiselle de Coigny, confined in the same prison. He addressed to her those immortal verses, 'The Young Captive,' ('La jeune Captive,') the most melodious sigh that ever issued from the crevices of a dungeon." He was executed in July, 1794, two days before the fall of Robespierre. He left unfinished poems, entitled "Hermes," and "America," and a completed poem, "L'Invention," which is praised by Villemain.

See H. de LATOUCHE, "Notice sur André Chénier;" BIBLIOPHILE JACOB, "Notice sur André Chénier;" SAINTE-BEUVE, "Causeries du Lundi," tome iv., and "Portraits contemporains," tome iii. (Sainte-Beuve estimates André Chénier as "the greatest French classic in verse since Racine and Boileau;") article by LEO JOUBERT, in the "Nouvelle Biographie Générale."

Chénier, de, (LOUIS,) a French historian, born at Montfort, in Languedoc, in 1723, was the father of the two poets André and M. J. Chénier. He was consul-general at Constantinople from 1753 to 1764. For several years preceding 1784 he was chargé-d'affaires at Morocco. He composed two works of merit,—viz., "Researches in the History of the Moors," and "Revolutions of the Ottoman Empire," (1789.) Died in 1796.

Chénier, de, (LOUIS JOSEPH GABRIEL,) a French military writer, a nephew of the poet André Chénier, was born in 1800. He published a "Manual for Councils of War," (1831,) and other works on the criminal legislation for the army.

Chenot, shĕh-no′, (CLAUDE BERNARD ADRIEN,) a French engineer, born at Bar-sur-Aube in 1803. In 1832 he invented an apparatus for the fabrication of metallic sponges. About ten years later he began a series of important researches relative to a new system of metallurgy, the first results of which appeared at the Industrial Exhibition of 1849. Died in 1855.

Chenu, shĕh-nü′, (JEAN CHARLES,) a French physician and naturalist, born at Metz in 1808. He published "An Essay on the Action of Mineral Waters," (1841,) "Illustrations of Conchology," (1842–45,) and an "Encyclopædia of Natural History," (14 vols., 1858.)

Che′ops, [Gr. Χέοψ,] King of Egypt, is supposed to have begun his reign about 1178 B.C. "He changed the government," says Herodotus, "into a despotism, and oppressed his subjects with forced labour in the construction of the great pyramid which bears his name." He was succeeded by his brother, Cephren or Chephren.

Cherbonneau, shĕR′bo′nŏ′, (JACQUES AUGUSTE,) a French Orientalist, born in Indre-et-Loire in 1813. He has published "The Fables of Lokmân," (1846,) and other works.

Cherbuliez, shĕR′bü′le-ā′, (VICTOR,) a French writer, born at Geneva in 1832, has produced several popular romances, among which are "Le Comte Kostia," "Le Prince Vitale," "Paul Méré," and "Le Roman d'une honnête Femme."

Chéréa, the French of CHÆREA, which see.

Chéreau, shǎ′rō′, (FRANÇOIS,) a skilful French engraver, born at Blois in 1680, executed portraits and historical subjects. He became engraver of the royal cabinet. Died in 1729.

Chérémon. See CHÆREMON.

Chéréphon. See CHÆREPHON.

Chérile. See CHŒRILUS.

Chérin, shǎ′rǎn′, (LOUIS NICOLAS HENRI,) a French general, born in Paris in 1762. He was appointed commander-in-chief of the guard of the Directory in September, 1797, and chief of the staff of the army of the Danube in 1799. He was killed at Zurich in that year.

See DE COURCELLES, "Dictionnaire des Généraux Français."

Cherler, shĕR′lĕr′, (JEAN HENRI,) a physician and botanist, was a citizen of Bâle. He married the daughter of J. Bauhin, the eminent botanist, whom he aided in the composition of his "General History of Plants," which appeared in 1650, some years after the death of Cherler.

See ÉLOY, "Dictionnaire de la Médecine."

Chéron, shǎ′rŏN′, (CHARLES,) a skilful French engraver, born at Lunéville in 1635. He was invited to Paris by Louis XIV., who gave him a pension, and employed him to engrave the medals which were struck to commemorate his actions. Died in 1698.

Chéron, (ÉLISABETH SOPHIE,) a skilful French artist and poet, born at Paris in 1648. She excelled in music, painting, and engraving, and wrote agreeable verses. She was very successful in portraits and in history. The exact likeness, it is said, was the least merit of her portraits. In 1672 she was admitted into the Academy of Painting. She executed a series of engravings called "Gems drawn from the Principal Cabinets of France." Died in 1711.

See FONTENAY, "Dictionnaire des Artistes;" FERMELHUIS, "Éloge de É. S. Chéron," 1712.

Chéron, (FRANÇOIS,) a French writer, born in Paris in 1764. He became director of the "Mercure" in 1815. He composed an ode entitled "Napoléon, ou le Corse dévoilé," ("The Corsican unveiled," 1814,) and a few other works. Died in 1828.

See QUÉRARD, "La France Littéraire."

Chéron, (LOUIS,) a French painter and engraver, brother of Élisabeth Sophie, noticed above, born in Paris in 1660. Compelled to leave France as a Protestant about 1690, he went to England, where he was successful as a painter of history and a designer. Died in 1723.

See HEINECKEN, "Dictionnaire des Artistes."

Chéron, (LOUIS CLAUDE,) a French writer of prose and verse, a brother of François, noticed above, was born in Paris in 1758. In 1791 he was elected to the Legislative Assembly, where he supported moderate measures. In 1805 he was chosen prefect of the department of Vienne. He produced, besides other dramas, an imitation of Sheridan's "School for Scandal," entitled "Le Tartufe des Mœurs," which was successful, and translated, from the English, Fielding's "Tom Jones." Died in 1807.

See QUÉRARD, "La France Littéraire."

Cherrier, de, dĕh shȧ′re-ā′, (CHARLES JOSEPH,) a French officer and writer, born at Neufchâteau (Vosges) in 1785. He published in 1841 a "History of the Contest between the Popes and the Emperors of the House of Suabia."

Chĕr′rŷ, (ANDREW,) an Irish actor and comic writer, born in 1762. He produced "The Soldier's Daughter," and other comedies. Died in 1812.

€her′sĭ-phron, [Gr. Χερσίφρων,] a famous Cretan architect, whose name is sometimes written **Ctesiphon,** flourished about 600 B.C. He was the first architect and designer of the temple of Diana at Ephesus, one of the Seven Wonders of the World. After his death, the unfinished work was directed by his son Metagenes, and others. This temple was adorned by one hundred and twenty-seven Ionic columns of solid marble, sixty feet high. Its length was four hundred and twenty-five Roman feet, and its breadth two hundred and twenty. It is said that two hundred years elapsed during its construction. The roof was burned by the agency of Erostratus in 356 B.C.; but the edifice was soon restored to its former splendor.

See HIRT, "Tempel der Diana von Ephesus," 1807.

Chérubin, shȧ′rü′bắN′, LE PÈRE, a Capuchin friar of Orléans, France, noted as a geometer and optician, lived in the reign of Louis XIV. He made an improvement in the binocular telescope, and wrote a valuable treatise on "Ocular Dioptrics," (1671.)

Cherubini, kȧ-roo-bee′nee, (MARIA LUIGI CARLO ZENOBI SALVADOR,) a celebrated Italian musical composer, born at Florence in 1760. He was instructed in music by the Felicis and by Bizzari and Sarti. About the age of fourteen he began to attract attention by his productions. He visited London in 1784, and there produced the successful operas "The Pretended Princess" ("La finta Principessa") and "Giulio Sabino." After 1786 he resided mostly in Paris, where his opera "Lodoiska" was performed with great applause in 1791. Soon after that date he produced "Élisa," "Médée," "Anacreon," etc. As a composer of sacred music he attained the highest rank. Among his best works in this department are his "Requiem," and his mass à trois voix. He was a member of the Royal Academy, and a professor in the Conservatory, of which he was director for twenty years. His last dramatic work was the opera "Ali Baba," (1833.) Died in 1842. Haydn

and Beethoven pronounced him the first dramatic composer of his time.

See LOUIS DE LOMÉNIE, "M. Cherubini, par un Homme de Rien," 1841; MIEL, "Notice sur la Vie de Cherubini," 1842; RAOUL-ROCHETTE, "Notice sur la Vie et les Ouvrages de Cherubini;" L. PICCHIANTI, "Notizie sulla Vita e sulle Opere di L. Cherubini," 1843; FÉTIS, "Biographie Universelle des Musiciens."

Chéruel, shȧ′rü′êl′, (AUGUSTE,) a French historian, born at Rouen in 1809, published a "History of Rouen," and a "Historical Dictionary of the Institutions, Manners, and Customs of France," (1855.)

Chervin, shĕR′vȧN′, (NICOLAS,) a French medical writer, born near Lyons in 1783; died in 1843.

Chéry, shȧ′re′, (PHILIPPE,) a skilful French painter of history, born in Paris in 1759, was a pupil of Vien. He was admitted into the Academy in 1791, when he exhibited the "Death of Alcibiades." In a concourse for the representation of the peace of Amiens, he obtained the prize in 1803. He was patronized by Napoleon, who charged him to paint a scene on the battle-field of Jena. Died in 1838.

Cheryf-Ed-Dyn-Aly. See SHEREEF-ED-DEEN.

Chéseaux, de, dĕh shȧ′zō′, (JEAN PHILIPPE LOYS,) a Swiss savant, born at Lausanne in 1718. He wrote "Essays on Physics," (1743,) "Treatises on Natural History," and several memoirs on astronomy, (1764.) Died in Paris in 1751.

See ERSCH und GRUBER, "Allgemeine Encyklopaedie."

Chesebro′, cheez′brọ, (CAROLINE,) an authoress, born at Canandaigua, New York. Among her works is "Dream-Land by Daylight," (1851,) and a novel entitled "Victoria, or the World Overcome," (1856.)

Chĕs′ẹl-dẹn, (WILLIAM,) an eminent English surgeon and anatomist, born in Leicestershire in 1688. He was a pupil of the great anatomist Cowper. About 1711 he began to lecture on anatomy in London, and was chosen a Fellow of the Royal Society before he was twenty-five, (one account says at thirty-three.) He published in 1713 "The Anatomy of the Human Body," which was generally used as a text-book for many years. After that date he was appointed chief surgeon of Saint Thomas's Hospital, consulting surgeon to Saint George's and to the Westminster Hospital, and surgeon to Queen Caroline. He was one of the most skilful operators of his time, and excelled especially in lithotomy. His fame was extended, in 1728, by an operation which restored sight to a young person, whose novel sensations afforded to Locke and Diderot a subject of metaphysical observations. He published in 1733 his "Anatomy of the Bones," a valuable work. Died at Bath in 1752. Pope, who was his intimate friend, says, "He is the most noted and most deserving man in the whole profession of chirurgery."

See HUTCHINSON, "Biographia Medica;" ÉLOY, "Dictionnaire historique de la Médecine."

Chesnaye-Desbois, de la, dĕh lắ shȧ′nắ′ dặ′bwȧ′, (FRANÇOIS ALEXANDRE AUBERT,) a French writer, born in Maine in 1699. Of all the compilers of the eighteenth century, he published the greatest number of dictionaries. Among these is a "Military Dictionary," and a "Genealogical and Historical Dictionary," (7 vols., 1757-65.) All his works are mediocre. He died in a hospital at Paris in 1784.

Chesne. See DUCHESNE.

Chĕs′ney, (FRANCIS RAWDON,) an officer distinguished for his explorations in the East, was born in Ireland in 1789. About 1830 he began to explore a route from Europe by the Red Sea to India. Having received aid from the government, and having been appointed commander of an expedition, he descended the Euphrates in a steamer, in 1836, from Beer (Bîr) to its mouth. In 1850 he published "The Expedition for the Survey of the Euphrates and Tigris," (4 vols.) He obtained the rank of major-general in 1855. He wrote a work on "The Russo-Turkish Campaigns of 1828-29."

Chessel. See CASELIUS.

Ches′tẹr-field, (PHILIP DORMER STANHOPE,) fourth EARL OF, an English courtier, orator, and wit, renowned as a model of politeness and an oracle of taste. He was born in London in September, 1694, and was the eldest son of Philip, third Earl of Chesterfield, and Elizabeth Saville, who was daughter of the Marquis of Halifax.

ā, ē, ī, ō, ū, ȳ, *long;* ȧ, ĕ, ŏ, same, less prolonged; ă, ĕ, ĭ, ŏ, ŭ, ў, *short;* ạ, ẹ, ị, ọ, *obscure;* fär, fȧll, fắt; mĕt; nŏt; gŏŏd; moͦon;

Having graduated at Cambridge, he made the tour of Europe in 1714, during which he contracted an inveterate passion for gaming. In 1715, through the influence of his uncle, General Stanhope, he was appointed a gentleman of the bedchamber to the Prince of Wales, and was elected to Parliament. He supported the party of the heir-apparent in the quarrel between the latter and his father, George I. He was one of the most brilliant and effective debaters of that period. Walpole says that on one occasion Chesterfield made "the finest oration he ever heard." On the death of his father, in 1726, he passed into the House of Lords, and in 1728 was ambassador to Holland. A few years later George II. appointed him lord steward of the household. "He was at the head of _ton_," says Macaulay, "in days when in order to be at the head of _ton_ it was not sufficient to be dull and supercilious." In 1733 he married Melusina Schulemburg, Countess of Walsingham. Though a Whig in politics, he was dismissed from office by Walpole in 1734, and joined the opposition. In 1745 he was lord lieutenant of Ireland, where his conduct was discreet and very popular. He accepted the office of principal secretary of state in April, 1746, which he resigned in 1748. He was intimate with Pope, Swift, Voltaire, Montesquieu, etc. His intercourse with Dr. Johnson was abruptly closed by a well-known indignant letter from the lexicographer. Chesterfield's fame as an author is founded chiefly on his "Letters to his Son," which appeared in 1774 and were admired for the beauty of the style and prized for the knowledge of the world which they teach. "Take out the immorality," says Dr. Johnson, "and it should be put into the hands of every gentleman." Lord Chesterfield wrote two numbers of "The World," and other brief productions, which were published under the title of "Miscellanies" in 1777. He died in 1773. His only son had died in 1768.

See MATY, "Life of the late Earl of Chesterfield," London, 2 vols., 1774; for a very interesting notice of Chesterfield, see "Blackwood's Magazine" for May, 1868; see also "Edinburgh Review" for October, 1845; "London Quarterly Review" for September, 1845.

Chétardie, de la, dẹh lả shả'tằr'de', (JOACHIM JACQUES TROTTI,) MARQUIS, a French diplomatist, born in 1705. He was sent as ambassador to Russia in 1739, and became the favourite of the empress Elizabeth. In 1744 she dismissed him abruptly and ordered him to leave the country. He afterwards had a command in the French army. Died in 1758.

See LÉVESQUE, "Histoire de Russie."

Chĕt'hạm, (HUMPHREY,) an English merchant, noted as the founder of a college and public library at Manchester, was born about 1580; died in 1653.

Chet'tle, (HENRY,) an English dramatist, who was a contemporary of Shakspeare, and flourished about 1600. He wrote numerous plays, of which only four have been preserved. One of these is "Hoffman," a tragedy.

Chĕt'wood, (KNIGHTLY,) born at Coventry in 1652, became Dean of Gloucester about 1707. He wrote several biographies and small poems. Died in 1720.

Chetwood, (WILLIAM RUFUS,) an English dramatist. Died in 1766.

Chĕt'wŷnd, (?) (JOHN,) an English divine, born in Somersetshire in 1623, published "Anthologia Historica," (1674.) Died in 1692.

Chevalier. See LECHEVALIER.

Chevalier, shẹh-vȧ'le-ȧ', almost shvȧ'le-ȧ', (ANTOINE RODOLPHE,) a noted French Protestant and Hebraist, born near Vire in 1507. While he was an exile in England he gave French lessons to Queen Elizabeth before her accession. He was afterwards professor of Hebrew at Geneva, and was employed by Calvin as interpreter of books in that language. He published a Hebrew Grammar. Died in 1572.

Chevalier, (CHARLES LOUIS,) a French optician, born in Paris in 1804. He invented and improved instruments used in optics and natural philosophy. Died in 1859.

Chevalier, (ÉTIENNE,) born about 1410, became treasurer of France in 1452. Died in 1474.

Chevalier, (MICHEL,) a celebrated French economist, born at Limoges in 1806. About 1833 he was sent by M. Thiers on a mission to the United States to examine the subject of railroads. In 1836 he published "Letters

on North America," which were highly commended. He produced in 1838 an important work "On the Material Interests of France," ("Des Intérêts matériels en France,") which was often reprinted. About 1840 he was chosen a councillor of state, professor of political economy in the College of France, and chief engineer of mines. His "History and Description of the Ways of Communication in the United States" appeared in 1840. He has greatly contributed to the triumph of free trade in France. In 1851 he was elected to the Institute, (class of moral and political sciences.)

See "Nouvelle Biographie Générale."

Chevalier, (NICOLAS,) a French antiquary and Protestant minister, born at Sedan, emigrated to Holland after the edict of Nantes was revoked in 1685. He was the author of a "History of William III. of England," and other works. Died about 1740.

Chevalier, (PAUL.) See GAVARNI.

Chevallier, shẹh'vȧ'le-ȧ, (JEAN BAPTISTE ALPHONSE,) a chemist, was born at Langres, in France, in 1793, and was for many years editor of the "Journal of Medical Chemistry." He has given special attention to questions relative to public hygiene, and has published a "Dictionary of Adulterations of Alimentary, Medicinal, and Commercial Substances," (1852.)

Chevanes, shẹh-vȧn', (JACQUES AUGUSTE,) a French jurisconsult, born at Dijon in 1624; died in 1690.

Chevert, de, dẹh shẹh-vair', (FRANÇOIS,) a successful French general, born at Verdun, on the Meuse, in 1695, distinguished himself at Prague in 1742, and was made lieutenant-general in 1748. The victory at Hastembeck, in 1757, was ascribed to him. Died in 1769.

Cheverus, shĕv'ẹ-rŭs, [Fr. DE CHEVERUS, dẹh shẹh-vrüs',] (JEAN LOUIS ANNE MADELEINE LEFEBVRE,) a French cardinal and philanthropist, born at Mayenne in 1768. He visited the United States as a missionary in 1795, and, having spent some time among the Indians of Maine, was made first Bishop of Boston by Pius VII. in 1808. During the prevalence of the yellow fever in Boston he was conspicuous for his efforts in behalf of the sufferers. He afterwards returned to France, and became Archbishop of Bordeaux in 1826, and a cardinal in 1836. He died the same year.

See HUEN-DUBOURG, "Vie du Cardinal de Cheverus," (1838,) and an English translation, by Mr. WALSH, Philadelphia, 1839.

Cheves, cheevz, (LANGDON,) an American statesman, born in Abbeville district, South Carolina, in 1776. He studied law, and became eminent in that profession. He was elected a member of Congress about 1811, and served two or more terms in that body. He was Speaker of the House of Representatives in the second session of the Thirteenth Congress, (1814–15,) and gave a casting vote against the re-charter of the United States Bank in 1815. The bank having been re-chartered in 1816, he afterwards became its president, which position he held for about three years. Died in 1857.

Chevillard, shẹh-ve'yằr', (FRANÇOIS,) a French poet, born at Orléans. He excelled in elegiac verse. Died in 1678.

Chevillier, shẹh-ve'ye-ȧ', (ANDRÉ,) a learned French ecclesiastic, born at Pontoise in 1636. He wrote a "Critical Dissertation on the Origin of Printing in Paris," (1694.) Died in 1700.

Chevreau, shẹh-vRŌ', (URBAIN,) an ingenious French writer, born at Loudun in 1613. He was versed in many languages and sciences, and travelled extensively. About 1652 he was secretary to Christina of Sweden, and afterwards was councillor to the Elector Palatine at Heidelberg. His "History of the World,"(1686,) poems, dramas, and "Chevræana," had a transient popularity. Died in 1701.

See NICÉRON, "Mémoires."

Chevret, shẹh-vRȧ', (JEAN,) a French moralist and writer, born at Meulan in 1747; died in 1820.

Chevreul, shẹh-vRUl', (MICHEL EUGÈNE,) an eminent French chemist, born at Angers in 1786, studied under Vauquelin in Paris. He became successively professor in the Collége Charlemagne, examiner at the Polytechnic School, and professor of special chemistry at the Gobelins. In 1823 he published an analytical treatise, called "Chemical Researches on Fat Substances of Animal

€ as _k_; ç as _s_; ḡ _hard_; ġ as _j_; G, H, K, _guttural_; N, _nasal_; R, _trilled_; ŝ as _z_; ₮h as in _this_. (☞See Explanations, p. 23.)

Origin," which established his reputation, and announced discoveries that produced important results in the arts. He was admitted into the Academy of Sciences in 1826, and succeeded Vauquelin as professor of applied chemistry in tne "Jardin des Plantes" in 1829. In 1831 he published "Lectures on Chemistry applied to the Art of Dyeing," and in 1839 a remarkable work "On the Law of the Simultaneous Contrast of Colours, and on the Distribution *(Assortiment)* of Coloured Objects," which is highly esteemed. He contributed many memoirs to the "Annales de Chimie," and to the collections of the Institute. In 1852 the Société d'Encouragement awarded him a prize of 12,000 francs for his work on "Fat Substances," ("Corps gras,") above noticed.

See " Nouvelle Biographie Générale."

Chevreuse, de, dẹh shẹh-vRuz', (MARIE de Rohan —dẹh ro'ôN',) DUCHESSE, a fascinating French lady, noted for her political ambition and influence, was born in 1600. She was married to Claude, Duke of Chevreuse, about 1622. Having intrigued against Richelieu, she was sent into exile, from which she returned at his death. During the troubles of the Fronde she acted with the enemies of Mazarin. Died in 1679.

See RETZ, "Mémoires."

Chevrier, shẹh-vRe-à', (FRANÇOIS ANTOINE,) a French writer, born about 1720 at Nancy. He removed to Paris in his youth, and indulged too freely his propensity to satire in several pamphlets, by which he made many enemies. He published a libellous book called "Le Colporteur," which had some success, and various other works. Died at Rotterdam in 1762.

See GRIMM, "Correspondance."

Cheyne, chän or cheen, (GEORGE,) an eminent Scottish physician, born about 1670, was a pupil of Dr. A. Pitcairn. About the year 1700 he settled in London. His treatise on Fluxions (1705) procured his election as Fellow of the Royal Society. He wrote a work called " Philosophical Principles of Natural Religion." In 1725 he produced his " Essay on Health and Long Life," which was successful, and was followed by a popular work on nervous diseases, entitled " The English Malady," (1733.) His writings are pervaded with a sincerely religious spirit. Died in 1742.

See his Autobiography, " Dr. Cheyne's own Account of Himself," 1743; " Biographia Britannica;" CHAMBERS, " Biographical Dictionary of Eminent Scotsmen."

Cheyne, (JAMES,) a learned Scottish philosopher, born in Aberdeenshire. He was professor of philosophy in the Catholic College of Douay, France, and author of several scientific works. Died in 1602.

Cheyne, (JOHN,) a Scottish physician, born at Leith in 1777. He settled in Dublin in 1809, and there practised with great success until 1830, when his health failed. From 1820 to 1830 his annual receipts amounted to about five thousand pounds. He published "Treatises on the Diseases of Children," (1801,) and other medical works. Died in 1836.

Chey'nell, (FRANCIS,) an English nonconformist divine, born at Oxford in 1608. He became rector of Petworth in 1643, and published " The Rise, Growth, and Danger of Socinianism," (1643,) in which he accused Chillingworth of heresy. He rendered himself notorious by his animosity towards Chillingworth, at whose funeral he made a violent speech. He also threw into the grave a book of the deceased author. Died in 1665.

See DR. JOHNSON'S Works.

Chézy, shà'ze', (ANTOINE,) an eminent French civil engineer, born at Châlons-sur-Marne in 1718. The canal of Burgundy was one of his works. Died in 1798.

Chézy, de, dẹh shà'ze', (ANTOINE LÉONARD,) son of the preceding, born at Neuilly in 1773, was an eminent Oriental scholar, and a pupil of De Sacy. He spoke Persian and Arabic with facility, and understood Hebrew, Syriac, Sanscrit, Greek, etc. A violent illness prevented him from accompanying the expedition to Egypt in 1798, which Bonaparte had invited him to join. Students of all European countries resorted to Paris to receive from him lessons in Sanscrit, which he esteemed the most beautiful and perfect language of the world. In 1815 a chair of Sanscrit was founded for him at Paris. W. Humboldt and A. Schlegel were among his pupils. He

published admirable translations of "Medjnoun and Leila," and of the Sanscrit poem " Sakoontala," by Calidasa, (1830.) He also left in manuscript an "Analysis of the Ramayana," a " Persian Anthology," a Sanscrit grammar, and other works. Died in 1832.

See SILVESTRE DE SACY, " Notice sur la Vie et les Ouvrages de M. de Chézy," 8vo, 1835; QUÉRARD, " La France Littéraire."

Chézy, von, fon shà'ze', (WILHELM,) a German author, born in 1806, wrote "The Travelling Student," (" Der fahrende Schüler," 1835,) and other novels.

Chézy, von, (WILHELMINE CHRISTINE,) a German authoress, born in Berlin in 1783, was the mother of the preceding. She was married to the French Orientalist above noticed, about 1803, and separated from him in 1811. She produced, in German, successful romances, tales, and lyric poems, among which were " Euryanthe," (1823,) and " Stundenblumen," (1824.)

Chiabrera, ke-ȧ-brā'rȧ, (GABRIELLO,) a celebrated lyric poet of Italy, born at Savona, near Genoa, June 8, 1552, was the founder of a new school of poetry. He was educated in Rome, where he resided some years, in the service of Cardinal Cornaro. His poetical genius was not developed early. An admiration of Pindar rendered him an imitator of that great model, after which he formed a style which distinguishes him from other Italian lyric poets. His sublime odes and canzoni soon extended his fame throughout Italy. After he became an author he resided chiefly in Florence and Genoa, and received many honours from several Italian rulers. In allusion to his innovations in style, he compared himself to Columbus, and said, " I resolved to discover a new world or perish in the attempt." He wrote much, and in many varieties of verse. Died at Savona in October, 1637. " He borrowed from Pindar," says Hallam, "that grandeur of sound, that pomp of epithets, that rich swell of imagery, that unvarying majesty of conception, which distinguish the odes of both poets." (" Introduction to the Literature of Europe.") He rivalled Anacreon in his lighter odes, which are exceedingly beautiful, graceful, and spirited.

See LARCHER, " Lives of Literary and Scientific Men of Italy ;" LONGFELLOW, " Poets and Poetry of Europe ;" " Lives of the Italian Poets," by REV. HENRY STEBBING, London, 1831; " Vita di G. Chiabrera," (written by himself,) Milan, 8vo, 1821; TIRABOSCHI, " Storia della Letteratura Italiana."

Chiaramonti, (B. LUIGI.) See PIUS VII.

Chiaramonti, ke-ȧ-rȧ-mon'te, (GIOVANNI BATTISTA,) an agreeable Italian writer, born at Brescia in 1731, published an " Essay on the Paternal Power of the Ancient Romans," (1754,) and other works. Died in 1796.

Chiaramonti, (SCIPIONE,) an Italian astronomer, born at Cesena in 1565, became professor of philosophy at Pisa. He wrote against Tycho Brahe a treatise on comets, entitled "Anti-Tycho," (1621,) a Latin " History of Cesena," (1641,) and other works. Died in 1652.

See NICÉRON, " Mémoires."

Chiari, ke-ȧ'ree, (FABRIZIO,) an Italian painter and engraver, born at Rome in 1621; died in 1695.

Chiari, (GIUSEPPE,) an Italian painter, born at Rome in 1654, was a pupil of Carlo Maratta, whose style he imitated successfully. Many of his easel-pictures are dispersed in Italy and England. His frescos in the Barberini palace and the Colonna Gallery at Rome are commended. Died in 1727.

See LANZI, " History of Painting in Italy."

Chiari, (PIETRO,) an Italian comic poet and priest, born at Brescia. He produced, in rivalry with Goldoni, many mediocre comedies, among which was "The Chinese Slave." Died about 1788.

Chiarini, ke-ȧ-ree'nee, (LUIGI,) an Italian ecclesiastic and philologist, born in Tuscany in 1789. He published a "Theory of Judaism applied to the Reform of the Israelites," etc. Died at Warsaw in 1832.

Chiaverini, ke-ȧ-vȧ-ree'nee, (LUIGI,) an Italian physician, born at Palena in 1777; died at Naples in 1834.

Chiavistelli, ke-ȧ-vès-tel'lee, (JACOPO,) an Italian painter, born at Florence in 1618; died in 1698.

Chichele or **Chichely,** chitch'ẹ-le, (HENRY,) an eminent English prelate, born about 1362, was noted as the founder of All Souls' College, Oxford. He performed several diplomatic missions to France. About 1414 he was chosen Archbishop of Canterbury. He opposed the growing pretensions of the court of Rome, and also the principles of Wickliffe. Died in 1443.

See ARTHUR DUCK, "Life of H. Chichele," 1699; O. L. SPENCER, "Life of H. Chichele," 1783; W. F. HOOK, "Lives of the Archbishops of Canterbury," vol. v. chap. xviii.

Chich'es-ter, (ARTHUR,) an English military officer, born near Barnstaple. He was appointed lord deputy of Ireland about 1604, and received the title of Baron of Belfast in 1612. Died in 1624 or 1625.

Chichester, EARL OF. See PELHAM, (THOMAS.)

Chick'er-ing, (JONAS,) an American manufacturer of piano-fortes, born at New Ipswich, New Hampshire, in 1798, lived in Boston; died in 1853.

Chicoyneau, she'kwä'nō', (FRANÇOIS,) a French physician and botanist, born at Montpellier in 1672, was a son-in-law of Pierre Chirac. He became a professor in his native city, and in 1720 was honoured for his services in Marseilles during the prevalence of the plague. He was first physician to the king from 1732 to 1752, and author of a work on the plague. Died in 1752.

Chicoyneau, (FRANÇOIS,) a son of the preceding, was born in 1699. He succeeded his father as professor of medicine at Montpellier. Died in 1740.

Chiesa, ke-ā'sä, (SILVESTRO,) an Italian painter, born at Genoa in 1625; died in 1657.

Chièvres, she'ȧvr', (GUILLAUME de Croy—dęh krwä,) LORD OF, a Flemish courtier and general, born about 1458. He distinguished himself under Charles VIII. and Louis XII. of France in the conquest of Naples and Milan. About 1508 he was appointed governor of the prince, afterwards Charles V. He gained the favour of his pupil, and was his prime minister from his accession, in 1516, until 1521. He offended the Spaniards by his avidity for money, and by the preference which he showed for the Flemings. He attended Charles V. to Germany in 1520, and died in 1521.

Chifflet, she'flä', (JEAN JACQUES,) a learned physician, born at Besançon, in France, in 1588. Having become eminent in his profession, he was invited to Spain by Philip IV., whom he attended as his first physician. He wrote a "History of Besançon," political tracts against France, a "Treatise on the Tomb of Childéric I.," discovered in 1653, and other works. He was the most eminent of a family which produced many learned men. Died in 1660.

Chifflet, (PHILIPPE,) a brother of the preceding, born at Besançon in 1597. He published "Notes on the Council of Trent," and translated "The Imitation of Christ" into French. Died about 1658.

Chifflet, (PIERRE FRANÇOIS,) a brother of the preceding, born in 1592, was professor of Hebrew, and keeper of the medals of the King of France. He wrote some religious works. Died in 1682.

Child, (Sir JOSIAH,) an English merchant, eminent as a writer on commerce and political economy, was born in London about 1630. He became very wealthy, and was one of the directors of the East India Company. In 1668 he published "Observations concerning Trade and the Interest of Money," in which he argues that the rate of interest should be reduced or kept low by legal restrictions. About that time he became chairman and autocrat of the East India Company. He afterwards wrote a "Treatise on the East India Trade," and a few other works. "Some of the principles advanced by Child," says McCulloch, "are so sound, and so forcibly and concisely expressed, that they assume the shape of maxims." Died in 1699. He left several children, who intermarried with various noble families of England.

Child, (Mrs. LYDIA MARIA,) a popular American writer, whose maiden name was FRANCIS, was born at Medford, Massachusetts, in 1802. Her first publication was "Hobomok, an Indian Story," (1824,) which was followed by "The Rebels: a Tale of the Revolution," (1825.) In 1826 she became editor of the "Juvenile Miscellany," which she conducted with ability and success for eight years. She was married in 1828 to Mr. David Lee Child, an able lawyer of Massachusetts. Soon after the commencement of the anti-slavery agitation she published an "Appeal in behalf of that Class of Americans called Africans," esteemed one of the most valuable works on that subject. She was editor

of the "National Anti-Slavery Standard" (New York) from 1841 to 1843, during which she wrote her "Letters from New York," (published in 2 vols., 1844.) Among her other productions may be named "The Mother's Book," "The Oasis," "Flowers for Children," "Fact and Fiction," and "Philothea: a Grecian Romance." She has also published "Progress of Religious Ideas," (3 vols. 8vo, 1855,) which, though giving proof of some learning and of great diligence, is a work of doubtful merit.*

See GRISWOLD's "Prose Writers of America;" "North American Review" for July, 1833, to January, 1837.

Child, (WILLIAM,) an English musical composer, born at Bristol in 1607; died in 1697.

See FÉTIS, "Biographie Universelle des Musiciens."

Chĭl'de-bert [Fr. pron. shĕl'dęh'baiR'] **I.,** King of the Franks, was the third son of Clovis and Clotilde. He inherited the kingdom of Paris, and began to reign in 511 A.D. In league with his brothers Clotaire and Clodomir, he conquered Sigismund, King of Burgundy. He died in 558; and, as he left no male issue, Clotaire became sole King of the Franks. This was the first precedent in French history of a custom or regulation which was afterwards recognized as the "Salic law."

See SISMONDI, "Histoire des Français."

Childebert II., King of Austrasia, born in 570 A.D., succeeded his father Sigebert in 575. His mother, Brunehaut, was regent during a part of his minority. By the will of his uncle Gontran, he acquired Orléans and Burgundy. He died in 596, leaving an infant heir, Thierri, whose kingdom was usurped by Clotaire II.

See MICHELET, "Histoire de la France."

Childebert III., the son of Thierri III., was born about 683 A.D. In 695 he succeeded his brother, Clovis III., as nominal King of France, the real power being exercised by the mayor of the palace, Pepin le Gros. He died in 711, leaving a son, Dagobert III., who was, like his father, one of the *rois fainéants,* (idle or mimic kings.)

Chĭl'de-brand, [Fr. pron. shĕl'dęh'bRŏN',] a Frankish prince, whose history is very obscure, and on whom much has been written by modern historians and genealogists. He is supposed to have been a son of Pepin le Gros, and a brother of Charles Martel, whom he accompanied in 737 A.D. in an expedition against the Saracens.

See SAINTE-MARTHE, "Histoire généalogique de la France."

Childéric, chil'dęr-ik, [Fr. pron. shĕl'dȧ'rĕk',] **I.,** King of the Franks, is reckoned the fourth king of the Merovingian race. He succeeded his father Mérovée (or Merovæus) in 458 A.D. We have little authentic history of his reign. He is said to have died about 480, leaving the kingdom to his son, Clovis I. His tomb, found near Tournai in 1653, contained his seal, medals, arms, etc., an account of which was published by J. J. Chifflet, (1655.)

Childéric II. was the second son of Clovis II. He inherited the kingdom of Austrasia, and began to reign in 660, at the age of seven. At the death of his elder brother, Clotaire III., he annexed to his realm Neustria and Burgundy. He was assassinated in 673, when his eldest son was also killed. His younger brother, Thierri, then became king.

See SISMONDI, "Histoire des Français."

Childéric III., the son of Chilpéric II., was the last King of France of the first race, (Merovingians.) He is called Childéric II. by some historians. He was per-

* The imaginative and philanthropic writings of Mrs. Child, uniting as they do with fine powers of delineation a most genial, kindly, and liberal spirit, command our heartfelt respect and sympathy. We regret all the more that she should have expended so much time and labour on a work affording little or no opportunity for the exercise of those gifts which have been the delight of so many readers, but demanding qualifications of a totally different kind. To render such a work as the "Progress of Religious Ideas" of any real value, the writer should possess not only accurate, profound, and varied learning, but also a sound critical judgment; because in such an undertaking it is no less important to reject what is false than to present what is true. The work, as we now have it, contains, along with a great deal of correct information, much that is totally untrustworthy; and this intermixture vitiates the whole. As the authorities on which the various statements rest are given only occasionally, the ordinary reader is without the means of forming any correct judgment as to their comparative value, and is quite as likely to accept the false as the true.

€ as *k;* ç as *s;* ḡ *hard;* ġ as *j;* G, H, K, *guttural;* N, *nasal;* R, *trilled;* š as *z;* th as in *this.* (☞See Explanations, p. 23.)

38

mitted, in 742 A.D., to assume the name and form of royalty by Pepin le Bref and Carloman, but was deposed by them about 750, and died in a monastery a few years later.

See AUGUSTIN THIERRY, "Récits des Temps Mérovingiens."

Chil′ders, (HUGH CULLING EARDLEY,) an English politician, born in London in 1827, graduated at Cambridge in 1850. He was returned to Parliament for Pontefract in 1860, and became a lord of the admiralty in 1864. From August, 1865, to June, 1866, he was financial secretary to the treasury, and in December, 1868, he was appointed first lord of the admiralty.

Chil′dren, (JOHN GEORGE,) an English chemist and electrician, born at Tunbridge in 1777. Having applied himself to chemistry, galvanism, and mineralogy, he was chosen a Fellow of the Royal Society in 1807. He constructed a galvanic battery, with plates of extraordinary size, (four feet long by two wide,) by which he demonstrated that the quantity of electricity is in proportion to the size of the plates, while its intensity depends on the number of plates. Among the results of his interesting experiments with the battery was the formation of steel by the combination of iron with diamond. Died in 1852.

Chil′drey, (JOSHUA,) an English clergyman and natural philosopher, born in 1623 ; died in 1670.

Chil′ling-worth, (WILLIAM,) a celebrated English writer and divine of the Arminian school of theology, was born at Oxford in October, 1602. His father, of the same name, was mayor of Oxford. At college he was noted for his subtlety and acuteness as a disputant in theology. About 1630 he was converted to the dogmas of the Roman Catholic Church by a Jesuit, John Fisher, alias John Perse, and entered the Jesuit College at Douay. But by the agency of Laud, then Bishop of London, he was restored to the Protestant communion, and he returned to Oxford in 1631. In 1637 he published his famous and principal work, "The Religion of Protestants a Safe Way to Salvation," in answer to a Jesuit named Knott. He maintained that all things necessary to be believed are clearly laid down in Scripture. Although he had scruples against some of the Thirty-Nine Articles, he was persuaded to subscribe to that creed as a bond of peace and union, and was appointed chancellor of Salisbury and prebendary of Brixworth. He was a zealous royalist in the civil war which began in 1642, and even acted as engineer at the siege of Gloucester in 1643. Soon after this event he was made prisoner, and, while thus detained, died, in January, 1644. After his death a collection of his sermons was published. Lord Mansfield esteemed Chillingworth "a perfect model of argumentation." Tillotson styled him "the incomparable Chillingworth, the glory of this age and nation." "His chief excellence," says Hallam, "is the close reasoning which avoids every dangerous admission," etc. "His work may be understood and appreciated without reference to any other,—the condition perhaps of real superiority in all productions of the mind." ("Introduction to the Literature of Europe.")

See DES MAIZEAUX, "Life of Chillingworth," 1725; DR. BIRCH, "Life of Chillingworth," prefixed to his works, 1742; "Retrospective Review," vol. vii., 1823; AUGUST NEANDER, "Erinnerung an den evangelischen Gottesgelehrten W. Chillingworth," Berlin, 4to, 1832; KIPPIS, "Biographia Britannica."

Chil′mead, (EDMUND,) an English scholar, born in Gloucestershire about 1610. He was chaplain of Christ Church, Oxford, from 1632 to 1648. He wrote a Latin treatise "On Ancient Greek Music," and translated several works from the French and Spanish into English. Died in 1653.

Chi′lo or **Chi′lon,** [Gr. Χίλων or Χείλων,] a Spartan, who is reckoned as one of the Seven Wise Men of Greece. He became one of the ephori of Sparta in 556 B.C., and died of joy caused by the victory of his son at the Olympic games. His recorded maxims justify his reputation for wisdom.

See DIOGENES LAERTIUS; J. F. BUDDEUS, "Dissertatio de Ethica Chilonis," Halle, 1699.

Chilpéric, chĭl′per-ik, [Fr. pron. shĕl′på′rĕk′,] **I.,** King of the Franks, was the youngest son of Clotaire I. After the death of his father he obtained the kingdom of Soissons in 561 A.D. He married the ambitious and wicked Frédégonde, and waged war with his brothers Sigebert and Gontran. Ancient writers called him the Nero and

Herod of his times. He was assassinated in 584, at the age of forty-five, and left an infant son, Clotaire II.

Chilpéric II., King of France, the son of Childéric II., was born about 670 A.D. After passing his youth in a monastery, he was proclaimed king in 715. He was defeated in battle in 718 by his rival, Charles Martel, who permitted him to act the part of *roi fainéant* until he died in 720. He left a son, who was Childéric III.

See AUGUSTIN THIERRY, "Récits des Temps Mérovingiens."

Chimæra, ke-mee′ra, [Gr. Χίμαιρα; Fr. CHIMÈRE, she′maiR′,] a fire-breathing monster of the Greek mythology, having the head of a lion, the body of a goat, and the tail of a dragon. According to Hesiod, she was a daughter of Typhon, and was killed by Bellerophon.

Chimay, de, (JEANNE MARIE IGNACE THÉRÈSE **de Cabarrus**—deh kå′bȧ′rüs′,) PRINCESS, born at Madrid or Saragossa in 1773, was the daughter of Count Cabarrus, noticed in this work. She was married in 1789 to the Marquis de Fontenay, a French lawyer. Having parted from him, she was going to Spain, to live with her father, in 1793, but at Bordeaux was imprisoned by the terrorists. There her dazzling beauty, her grace and wit, fascinated Tallien, the dreaded representative of the Convention, the arbiter of life and death. Her influence over him rescued many persons from the scaffold and the prisons. In 1794 she herself was imprisoned in Paris, where Josephine Beauharnais was her fellow-captive. Tallien, who then owned her as his wife, stimulated by her peril, conspired with success against Robespierre. On the fall of the latter she was released. Madame Tallien became the friend of Madame Bonaparte, and her *salon* was one of the most fashionable in Paris. She was divorced from Tallien in 1802, and married, in 1805, Count de Caraman, who soon after became Prince de Chimay. She had children by each of her husbands. Died in 1835.

See THIERS, "History of the French Revolution;" MADAME D'ABRANTÈS, "Mémoires."

Chimay, de, (JOSEPH PHILIPPE FRANÇOIS **Riquet de Caraman**—re′kȧ′ deh kå′rȧ′môn′,) PRINCE, a distinguished Belgian diplomatist,born in 1808.

Chimère. See CHIMÆRA.

Chiminello, ke-me-nel′lo, (VINCENZO,) an Italian natural philosopher, born at Marostica in 1741, lived at Padua. Died in 1815.

Chinard, she′näR′, (JOSEPH,) a French sculptor, born at Lyons in 1756, studied in Italy, and in 1786 won a prize offered at Rome for a "Perseus liberating Andromeda." He returned to Lyons about 1790. Among his works are admired busts of General Desaix, of Napoleon, etc. He had much facility, richness of imagination, and good taste. Died in 1813.

See JEAN BAPTISTE DUMAS, "Notice sur J. Chinard," 1814.

Chinchon, chĕn-chôn′, commonly but incorrectly written **Cinchon,** COUNTESS OF, was the wife of the Spanish Viceroy of Peru. On her return to Spain, in 1632, she introduced the Peruvian bark, which she had found to be efficacious in fevers. To perpetuate the remembrance of this important service, Linnæus gave to that plant the name of Cinchona.

See SEBASTIAN BADUS, "Anastasis Corticis Peruviani, seu Chinæ Defensio," Genoa, 1661.

Chingiz. See JENGIS.

Chiniac de la Bastide-Duclaux, she′ne′ȧk′ deh lä bȧs′tēd′ dü′klo′, (PIERRE,) a French writer and lawyer, born at Alassac in 1741. He published an "Essay on Moral Philosophy," (5 vols., 1802.) Died soon after 1800.

Chin-Koung. See SHIN-KOONG.

Chiocco, ke-ok′ko, (ANDREA,) an Italian physician, born at Verona, wrote a work on natural history, called "Museum Francisci Calceolarii Junioris," (1622,) and "Philosophical and Medical Inquiries." Died in 1624.

Chiodini. See CLAUDINI.

Chi′on, [Χίων,] a Greek philosopher of Heraclea, lived about 350 B.C., and was a disciple of Plato.

Chip′man, (DANIEL,) a jurist, born in Salisbury, Connecticut, in 1762. He wrote an "Essay on the Law of Contracts," (1822.) Died in 1850.

Chipman, (NATHANIEL,) a jurist, a brother of the preceding, was born in Salisbury, Connecticut, in 1752. He became chief justice of Vermont in 1789, judge of

ā, ē, ī, ō, ū, ȳ, *long;* ă, ĕ, ĭ, ŏ, ŭ, ў, *short;* ą, ę, į, ǫ, *obscure;* fär, fåll, fåt; mêt; nŏt; gōōd; mōōn, the District Court of the United States in 1791, and a Senator of the United States in 1797. He published "Principles of Government," 1833. Died in 1843.

See D. Chipman, "Life of N. Chipman," 1846.

Chirac, she'răk', (Pierre,) an eminent French physician, born at Conques in 1650, became a professor at Montpellier in 1687. In 1715 he was chosen first physician to the Duke of Orléans. He was made a free associate of the Academy of Sciences, and director of the royal garden about 1718. In 1731 he received the title of chief physician to Louis XV. Died in 1732. He left several medical works, of which the most remarkable is a "Treatise on Malignant Fevers," (1742.)

See Fontenelle, "Notice sur Chirac," in the "Mémoires de l'Académie des Sciences," 1732; "Nouvelle Biographie Générale."

Chirinos, de, dă che-ree'nŏs, (Juan,) a Spanish painter, born at Madrid about 1565; died in 1620.

Chi'ron or **Chei'ron,** [Gr. Χείρων,] the most celebrated of the Centaurs, said to be a son of Saturn, or Cronos. He was renowned for his skill in surgery, medicine, music, and hunting, and was the instructor of Achilles, Hercules, and Æsculapius.

Chischkof. See Shishkov.

Chisholm, chiz'ọm, (Mrs. Caroline,) a philanthropic Englishwoman, born in Northamptonshire in 1810. About 1830 she became the wife of Captain Chisholm, of the army, whom she accompanied to Madras and in 1838 to Australia. She devoted herself to the welfare of young women who arrived at Sydney in search of employment, established the "Female Immigrants' Home," and made journeys into the interior to provide places for them. About 1846 she visited England, and founded there "The Family Colonization Society," to encourage emigration by families. She returned with her husband to Australia in 1854.

See S. Smiles, "Brief Biographies."

Chisholm, chiz'ọm, (James,) an Episcopal clergyman, born in Salem, Massachusetts, in 1815. He graduated at Harvard in 1836, and in 1842 became rector of a parish in Berkeley county, Virginia. In 1850 he removed to Portsmouth, and during the terrible ravages of the yellow fever in 1855 his church was the only one kept open. While attending a funeral, he himself was attacked with the disease, of which he died in September, 1855.

Chis'hull, (Edmund,) an English antiquary, born in Bedfordshire. He was chaplain to the English factory at Smyrna from 1698 until 1702, and became rector of South Church, Essex, in 1731. He wrote, besides other works, "Asiatic Antiquities," (1728.) Died in 1733.

Chit'ten-den, (Martin,) a son of the following, was born in Connecticut in 1776. He was a member of Congress from 1803 to 1813, and was Governor of Vermont in 1813 and 1814. Died in 1840.

Chittenden, (Thomas,) an American statesman, born at East Guilford, Connecticut, in 1730. He removed to Vermont in 1774, and was one of the principal founders of that State, of which he was chosen the first Governor in 1778. He was re-elected several times, and held that office (except one year) until his death. He was a man of superior talents and virtues. Died in 1797.

Chit'ty, (Joseph,) an eminent English legal author and special pleader, born in 1776. He published numerous highly-esteemed legal works, among which are "Pleadings and Parties to Actions," (1808,) "Law of Nations relative to Belligerents and Neutrals," (1812,) a "Practical Treatise on the Criminal Law," (1818,) "Treatise on Medical Jurisprudence," (1834,) said to be an indispensable book, and "General Practice of the Law in all its Departments," (3d edition, 1837–42.) "The last," says Warren, "is well calculated to become a companion to Blackstone's 'Commentaries.'" He was called to the bar by the Society of the Middle Temple in 1816. Died in 1841.

Chiverny, de, dĕh she'vĕR'ne', (Philippe **Hurault** —hü'rō',) Count, a French statesman, born at Chiverny in 1528. Having rendered services to Henry IV. in the subjection of his revolted capital in 1594, he was rewarded with the office of chancellor, and enjoyed the constant favour of the king. He died in 1599, leaving memoirs, which were published in 1636, under the title of "Mémoires d'Estat," and often reprinted.

Chivot, she'vo', (Marie Antoine François,) a French linguist, born in Picardy in 1752. He became eminent as professor of humanities in Paris, and devoted his attention chiefly to the study of languages. He died prematurely in 1786, after he had commenced a work entitled "De l'Esprit ou de la Filiation des Langues."

Chladni, klăd'nee, (Ernst Florens Friedrich,) a distinguished philosopher and inventor, born at Wittenberg in 1756. He studied natural philosophy and mathematics, by the aid of which he perfected the theory of sound. He gained a wide reputation by his "Discoveries on the Theory of Sound," (1787,) and his "Treatise on Acoustics," (1802.) He also wrote a "Treatise on Fiery Meteors," (1819,) and other work. He invented the musical instruments called "euphone" and "clavicylinder." Died at Breslau in 1827.

See Fétis, "Biographie Universelle des Musiciens."

Chlapowski, klă-pov'skee, (Desiderius,) a Polish general, born in the duchy of Posen in 1788. He fought with distinction for Napoleon in Spain, Austria, and Russia. Having joined the Polish army in 1830 and obtained a high command, he gained some successes in Lithuania in 1831, and was received as a liberator by the people. Through the incapacity of Gielgud, who assumed the command, the Polish army was defeated, and Chlapowski retired to Prussia in 1831.

See "Nouvelle Biographie Générale."

Chlo'e, [Gr. Χλόη,] a surname given to Ceres by the Athenians, signifies "verdant, or blooming."

Chlopicki, klo-pits'kee, (Joseph,) a Polish general, born in Podolia in 1772. He entered the French army about 1796, and commanded four regiments in the Russian campaign of 1812. After the fall of Bonaparte he entered the Russian service (1814) as general of division, but resigned in 1818. At the beginning of the Polish Revolution, in December, 1830, he was chosen dictator. He preferred negotiation to active hostilities, was accounted deficient in zeal, and, on the approach of the Russian army, resigned the dictatorship in January, 1831. He was severely wounded in a battle in February, 1831, and then retired from the service. Died in 1854.

See "Nouvelle Biographie Générale."

Chlo'ris, [Χλωρίς,] the goddess of flowers in the Greek mythology, was identical with the Roman Flora. She was the wife of Zephyrus, (the west wind.) See Flora.

Chloris, a daughter of Amphi'on and Ni'obe, is said to have escaped when her brothers and sisters were massacred. Another Chloris was the mother of Nestor, the Pylian sage.

Chmel, kmĕl, (Joseph,) a German historian, born at Olmutz in 1798, was appointed first archivist of Vienna in 1840. He published "Materials for the History of Austria," (1832–40,) and a "History of Frederick IV.," (1843.) Died in 1858.

See Brockhaus, "Conversations-Lexikon."

Chmelnitzky, kmĕl-nits'kee, (Nicolaï Ivanovitch,) a Russian comic poet, born at Saint Petersburg in 1789. He was Governor of Smolensk, and afterwards of Archangel. He produced successful comedies, among which are "Castles in Spain" and "The Quarantine." Died in 1846.

See Brockhaus, "Conversations-Lexikon."

Chmielnicki, kme-ĕl-nits'kee, (Bogdan or Theophilus,) a Cossack chief, born in 1593, induced the Cossacks to revolt against the King of Poland. Died in 1657.

Choate, chōt, (Rufus,) the most eminent advocate of New England,—if we should say of America, perhaps the claim would not be disputed,—was born in what was then called Ipswich, (now Essex,) Massachusetts, October 1, 1799. Both his father and mother were noted for quickness of mind as well as for weight of character. Rufus was the second son, and the fourth of six children. As a boy, besides possessing unusual quickness, elasticity, and vigour, he was remarkable for a love of reading, and, before he was ten years old, had about exhausted the village library, though it contained some pretty ponderous works. He entered Dartmouth College in 1815, and soon took his place at the head of what proved to be an able and studious class. No one ever occupied such a position more free from the shafts of envy or with the more hearty votes of his classmates. After graduating, he spent a year at the college as tutor, and then entered upon the study of his profession in the law school at Cambridge, from which he went to the office of Mr. Wirt, then attorney-general of the United States, in Washington. He here enlarged his knowledge of public affairs and fixed his standard of professional excellence. He saw Marshall upon the bench, and heard Pinkney in the Senate and in the court.

After such preparation, he entered upon the practice of the law at Danvers, Massachusetts, from which he removed to Salem, and subsequently to Boston. Before leaving Salem, however, he was chosen to represent the Essex south district in Congress, which he did for one term and part of a second. On taking up his residence in Boston, he devoted himself assiduously to his profession, and soon gained the highest position as a powerful advocate. In 1841 he was chosen Senator in place of Mr. Webster, who had accepted the office of secretary of state under President Harrison. While in the Senate he spoke with great freedom and power on most of the important questions which came before that body. Among the most able of his speeches were those on the M'Leod case, the Fiscal Bank Bill, Oregon, the Tariff, and the Smithsonian Institution. On leaving the Senate in 1845, he returned again to his profession, and thenceforward resisted all temptations to public life. Often solicited, the pressure of his private business compelled him to decline office, though he always gave great attention and interest to questions affecting the country, and especially the welfare of the Union. After Mr. Webster's death, he was acknowledged to be the leader of the Massachusetts bar, and was regarded, especially by the younger members of the profession, with a love equal to their reverence.

During the year 1858 Mr. Choate's health became much impaired, and early the next year he was obliged to withdraw from active business. A voyage was advised by physicians, and he sailed for Europe, accompanied by his son. On reaching Halifax it became evident that he could proceed no farther. He therefore took lodgings, hoping to recover so far as to be able to return to Boston. He seemed to rally, was able to enjoy reading, and was hopeful of soon leaving for home, when he suddenly died, on the 13th of July.

In person, Mr. Choate was tall and commanding, with a countenance capable of uncommon power of expression. In speaking, his voice was rich, musical, and sympathetic, his action often intense, his gestures full of variety and force. Few men had a quicker insight into the character of those he addressed, or a more instinctive knowledge of the methods by which the mind is moved. His speech, often close and exact in argument, was marked by extraordinary amplitude, exuberance, and brilliancy, and was wonderfully persuasive. Whether he addressed a jury of twelve men, or a crowded audience, he seemed to bend their minds almost at will. Mr. Choate's studies were extensive and various. Literature in all its departments was his unfailing solace and delight. Political philosophy, especially as illustrated in history and in the unwritten annals of our own country, was the subject of his constant meditation. A high and unselfish patriotism, the love of the Union, the dangers to which he foresaw, a thorough belief in the future greatness of our national power, provided that passion could be kept obedient to reason and law, and a hope that conciliatory counsels might prevail till the sentiment of union should become so strong that nothing could destroy it,—these were the controlling ideas of his life, especially of the latter years of it. Of gracious and winning manners and a most affectionate temper, he drew to himself his associates with a strange attraction, and his death seemed to almost all who knew him like the loss of a personal friend. With his large and sound learning, his exuberant imagination, the magnetism of his address, his fertility and prodigious resources, there needed only the larger sphere, the graver and more exciting questions of civil commotions, to place him as an advocate and as an orator quite on a level with the most distinguished masters of modern eloquence. ***

See "Works of Rufus Choate, with a Memoir of his Life," by SAMUEL GILMAN BROWN, Boston, 1862; "Life of Rufus Choate;" "Golden Age of American Oratory," by E. G. PARKER, Boston, 1857; "North American Review" for January, 1863.

Chodowiecki, ĸo-do-ve-ĕts′kee, (DANIEL NIKOLAUS,) an excellent engraver and miniature-painter, born at Dantzic in 1726. He went to Berlin in 1743, and was employed some time as a tradesman's assistant. A few years later he studied design, and became one of the most skilful etchers of his time. He designed most of the figures of Lavater's "Physiognomy," and etched a great number of engravings, frontispieces, vignettes, etc. for the booksellers. His designs display great originality and a satirical genius, on account of which he has been called "the Hogarth of Germany." Died in Berlin in 1801.

See NAGLER, "Neues Allgemeines Künstler-Lexikon."

Chodzko, ĸodz′ko, (ALEXANDER,) a Polish Orientalist and poet, born at Krzywicze in 1804. He resided in Persia from 1829 to 1841, as consul and dragoman. He afterwards passed some years in France. He published "Specimens of the Popular Poetry of Persia," (translated by him into English, 1842,) "The Theatre in Persia," (in French, 1845,) and a "Persian Grammar," (1852.)

Chodzko, (JACQUES LÉONARD,) a Polish historian, who was born in 1800. He became a resident of Paris in 1826, and was an aide-de-camp of La Fayette in 1830. He was afterwards librarian of the ministry of public instruction. He has published, in French, several useful works, among which are "The Poles in Italy," (1829,) "Tableau of Poland, Ancient and Modern," (1830,) and "Poland, its History, Literature, Monuments, etc.," ("La Pologne, historique, littéraire, monumentale, pittoresque et illustrée," 1834-47.)

Chœrilus, kĕr′e-lus, [Gr. Χοιρίλος or Χοιρίλλος; Fr. CHÉRILE, kå′rĕl′,] an Athenian tragic poet, who flourished between 525 and 475 B.C. He gained the prize thirteen times, and composed one hundred and fifty dramas, none of which are extant. He was a competitor with Æschylus in a tragic contest, and is supposed to have been the first author of written tragedies.

See MEINEKE, "Fragmenta Comicorum Græcorum."

Chœrilus, a Greek bard of little merit, who followed Alexander the Great, and flattered him in bad verses, which Horace intimates were received with favour.

See BRUNCK, "Analecta."

Chœrilus of Samos, a Greek epic poet of high reputation, who lived about 450 B.C. He was an intimate friend of Herodotus, with whom he resided some time. His last days were spent at the court of Archelaus, King of Macedon. He wrote an epic poem on the wars of the Greeks against Xerxes and Darius, of which small fragments are extant.

See SUIDAS, "Chœrilus."

Choffard, sho′fȧr′, (PIERRE PHILIPPE,) a French artist, born in Paris in 1730, designed and engraved charming vignettes, etc. for the works of Rousseau, La Fontaine, and others, and wrote a "Historical Notice of the Art of Engraving," (1805.) Died in 1809.

Choffin, sho′făɴ′, (DAVID ÉTIENNE,) a French littérateur, born at Héricourt in 1703; died in 1773.

Choiseul, de, dęh shwȧ′zul′, (CÉSAR,) DUKE, Sieur du Plessis-Praslin, (dü plȧ′se′ prȧ̈s′lȧɴ′,) a French general, born in Paris in 1598, distinguished himself at the siege of Rochelle in 1628. After gaining several victories over the Spaniards in Italy and Spain, he was made a marshal of France in 1645. During the war of the Fronde he commanded the king's army, and defeated Turenne at Rethel about 1650. He was created duke in 1663. Died in 1675.

Choiseul, de, (CHARLES,) Count of Plessis-Praslin, an able French general, born in 1563, was the son of Ferri de Choiseul, and an uncle of the preceding. After fighting for the League, he was one of the first Catholic chiefs that recognized Henry IV., who made him captain of his guards in 1594. He became marshal of France in 1619, after which he commanded with success against the rebels. Died in 1626.

See BAZIN, "Histoire du Règne de Louis XIII."

Choiseul, de, (CLAUDE ANTOINE GABRIEL,) DUC, born in 1760, was a relative of the eminent statesman of that name. He became colonel of the royal dragoons in 1789, and in 1791 was chosen to guard the king in his escape to the frontier; but he did not arrive at Varennes

ā, ē, ī, ō, ū, ȳ, *long;* ȧ, ė, ŏ, same, less prolonged; ă, ĕ, ĭ, ŏ, ŭ, y̆, *short;* ą, ę, į, ǫ, *obscure;* fär, fȧll, fȧt; mĕt; nŏt; gṏd; mṏn;

until after the king was arrested. He emigrated about 1793, and returned to France about 1804. After the restoration of 1815 he entered the Chamber of Peers, in which he supported constitutional principles. Died in 1838.

See LAMARTINE, "History of the Restoration."

Choiseul, de, (ÉTIENNE FRANÇOIS,) Duc de Choiseul et d'Amboise, (dŏN'bwâz',) an eminent French statesman, born in 1719. In his youth he served in the army, and, before he left it, obtained the rank of lieutenant-general. He was appointed ambassador to Vienna in 1756, and minister of foreign affairs in 1758. By the influence of Madame de Pompadour, he soon became the favourite and chief minister of Louis XV., and was created a duke. In 1761 he negotiated with the Bourbon King of Spain a secret treaty called the "Family Compact," which was considered a master-piece of diplomacy. About 1762 he suppressed the order of Jesuits, who were banished from France. In the Seven Years' war (1756-63) the French fought for Maria Theresa against the King of Prussia. By the treaty of Paris, in 1763, he terminated a war with England, which had been disastrous to the French. Though he was popular with the nation, a party at court, aided by Madame du Barry, procured his dismissal from office in 1770. He died in 1785, and left no posterity. He was a liberal patron of literary men.

See "Mémoires de M. le Duc de Choiseul, écrites par lui-même," 2 vols., 1790; SOULAVIE, "Mémoires de M. le Duc de Choiseul;" VOLTAIRE, "Siècle de Louis XV;" PAULIN DE CHAMPROBERT, "Notice historique sur le Duc de Choiseul," 1836; SISMONDI, "Histoire des Français."

Choiseul, de, (GILBERT,) Bishop of Tournai, born in 1613, was a brother of César, noticed above. In 1682 he co-operated with Bossuet in the celebrated declaration of the clergy of France. Died in 1689.

Choiseul-d'Aillecourt, de, dẹh shwȃ'zul' dȃ'ye'-koor',(ANNE MAXIME URBAIN,)COUNT, a French writer, nephew of Choiseul-Gouffier, born about 1782. He published in 1809 a work "On the Influence of the Crusades on the Condition of European Nations." Died in 1854.

Choiseul-Francières,de, dẹh shwȃ'zul' frŏN'se-ȃR', (CLAUDE,) COUNT, a distinguished French general, born in 1632. Having served under Turenne and Condé in Flanders, he was made lieutenant-general in 1676. He commanded with success against the Elector of Bavaria in 1689, and was rewarded with a marshal's bâton in 1693. He died, without issue, in 1711.

See SISMONDI, "Histoire des Français."

Choiseul-Gouffier, de, dẹh shwȃ'zul' goo'fe-ȃ', (MARIE GABRIEL FLORENT AUGUSTE,) COUNT, a French scholar and traveller, born in Paris in 1752. Having married a rich heiress, he annexed her name (Gouffier) to his own family name. In 1776 he visited Greece and Asia Minor, and on his return published his magnificent work entitled "Picturesque Journey in Greece," (" Voyage pittoresque en Grèce," 1782,) elegantly illustrated. He was chosen a member of the Academy of Inscriptions in 1779, and of the French Academy, as successor to D'Alembert, in 1784. In the latter year he was appointed ambassador to Constantinople, and took with him several artists and savants and the poet Delille. He returned to France in 1802, and produced, a few years later, a second volume of his " Voyage pittoresque," which describes Greece and Asia Minor. After the restoration of 1816 he became a peer and a minister of state. Died in 1817.

See BON JOSEPH DACIER, "Notice historique sur la Vie de M. le Comte Choiseul-Gouffier," 1819.

Choisy, de, dẹh shwȃ'ze', (FRANÇOIS TIMOLÉON,) ABBÉ, a French priest and author, born in Paris in 1644. He published, in 1684, "Dialogues on the Immortality of the Soul," etc., which had much success. He afterwards went to Siam, and made an unsuccessful attempt to convert the king of that country. He published a "History of the Church," (11 vols., 1727.) He was Dean of the French Academy. Died in 1724.

See ABBÉ D'OLIVET, "Vie de M. l'Abbé de Choisy;" D'ALEMBERT, "Éloge de l'Abbé de Choisy;" SAINTE-BEUVE, "Causeries du Lundi."

Chokier, sho'ke-ȃ', (JOHN ERNEST,) a Flemish author and ecclesiastic, born at Liege in 1571, wrote "Treasury of Political Aphorisms," ("Thesaurus Aphorismorum Politicorum," 1610,) and other works. Died in 1650.

Chomel, sho'mĕl', (AUGUSTE FRANÇOIS,) a French physician, born about 1788. He became eminent as a practitioner in Paris, and in 1827 succeeded Laennec as professor in the École de Médecine. Among his works is a "Treatise on Fevers and Pestilential Diseases," (1821.) Died in 1858.

See "Biographie Médicale."

Chomel, (JACQUES FRANÇOIS,) a French physician and writer, born in Paris, lived between 1700 and 1750.

Chomel, (JEAN BAPTISTE LOUIS,) a French physician, born about 1700, was a son of Pierre Jean Baptiste, noticed below. He wrote several esteemed works, among which is a "Historical Essay on Medicine in France," (1762.) Died at Paris in 1765.

See "Biographie Médicale;" QUÉRARD, "La France Littéraire."

Chomel, (PIERRE JEAN BAPTISTE,) a French physician and botanist, born in Paris in 1671, was a pupil and friend of Tournefort. In order to assist the latter in a projected history of plants, Chomel in 1700 traversed Auvergne, Bourbonnais, etc. in search of new plants. In 1707 he was appointed by Louis XIV. *médecin de quartier.* His principal work is an " Abrégé de Plantes usuelles," (1712,) a popular treatise on medicinal plants, with directions for their use. He was chosen a member of the Academy of Sciences in 1720. Died in 1740.

See QUÉRARD, "La France Littéraire;" "Biographie Médicale."

Chomiakov or **Chomiakow.** See KHOMIAKOV.

Chompré, shŏN'prȃ', (NICOLAS MAURICE,) a French scientific writer, born in Paris in 1750. He composed "Elements of Arithmetic, Algebra, and Geometry," and other esteemed works. Died in 1825.

Chompré, (PIERRE,) a French teacher, born near Châlons-sur-Marne in 1698; died in 1760.

Chopart, sho'pȃR', (FRANÇOIS,) a French surgeon, born in Paris about 1750, and graduated in 1770. He and Desault published, in 1789, a "Treatise on Surgical Maladies." Died in 1795.

Chopin, ko'pin?(FREDERICK,) a distinguished Polish pianist and composer, born near Warsaw in 1810. He became a resident of Paris about 1832. He composed concertos, waltzes, mazurkas, etc., and was very popular as a performer. Died in Paris in 1849.

See FRANZ LISZT, "F. Chopin," 1852.

Chopin, sho'pȃN', (J. N.,) a French *littérateur,* brother of a distinguished painter who writes his name SCHOPIN, was born about 1800. He published, besides other works, one " On the Present State of Russia," (1822.)

Chopin or **Choppin,** sho'pȃN', (RENÉ,) an eminent French jurist, born near La Flèche in 1537. He united a solid judgment to a prodigious memory. In the reign of Henry III. he was an ardent partisan of the League ; but he changed sides when Henry IV. became master of Paris. Among his works are a "Commentary on the Common Law of Anjou," and a "Traité du Domaine." Died in 1606.

See J. PAPIRE MASSON, "R. Chopini Vita," 1606; NICÉRON, "Hommes illustres."

Choppin. See CHOPIN, (RENÉ.)

Choque, shok, (PIERRE,) called BRETAGNE, a French writer, flourished about 1500, and was chief herald and king-at-arms to Anne of Brittany.

Choricius, ko-rish'e-us, [Χορίκιος,] a Greek Sophist, born at Gaza, lived about 520 A.D. He composed orations, some of which were printed at Paris in 1846.

Chorier, sho're-ȃ', (NICOLAS,) a mediocre French writer, born at Vienne in 1609, wrote a "History of Dauphiné," (1661,) and other works. Died in 1692.

Choris, ko'ris, (LOUIS,) an eminent Russian painter and traveller, born at Ekaterinoslav in 1795. He accompanied as artist Count Romanzof's expedition under Captain Kotzebue, round the world, 1815-18. Chamisso the author was his companion in this voyage. After his return he worked some years in Paris, where he published, in French, his "Picturesque Voyage round the World," (1821.) It is accompanied with descriptions of mammifera by Cuvier, and illustrated with faithful pictures of human figures, landscapes, etc. by himself. He also published "Views and Landscapes of the Equinoctial Regions," (1826.) In 1827 he visited America. On the way from Vera Cruz to Mexico, he was killed by robbers in March, 1828.

See QUÉRARD, "La France Littéraire."

Chor'ley, (HENRY F.,) an English author of the present century. He has published, besides other works, "Music and Manners in France and Germany," (1841,) "Pomfret," (3 vols., 1845,) "Memorials of Mrs. Hemans," and "The Authors of England."

Chorluli Ali Pasha. See ALEE-CHORLEELEE.

Choron, sho'rŏN', (ALEXANDRE ÉTIENNE,) a French musician and writer on music, born at Caen in 1771. He made such progress in mathematics that Monge chose him in 1793 as assistant professor of descriptive geometry in the Normal School. In 1808 he produced his chief work, "Principles of Composition of the Schools of Italy." Died in 1834. Choron and Fayolle published a "Historical Dictionary of Musicians," (1810.)

See FÉTIS, "Biographie Universelle des Musiciens;" L. E. GAU-TIER, "Éloge d'A. E. Choron," Paris, 1846.

Chosroes. See KHOSROO.

Chouan, shoo'ŏN', a word signifying "owl," was applied as a surname or nickname to the family of COTTE-REAU, (kot'rŏ',) and adopted by the royalist insurgents of Maine, Bretagne, etc., after Jean Cottereau became their chief. He was a peasant, born in Mayenne in 1757, and became a smuggler. In 1792 he took arms against the French Convention, and was chosen as chief of the undisciplined rustics called "La Chouannerie." He united his troops with the Vendeans after the latter passed the Loire, and he shared their defeat at Mans, December, 1793. He was killed in a fight or retreat in July, 1794.

Choudieu, shoo'de-uh', (PIERRE,) a French regicide and Jacobin, born at Angers ; died in 1840.

Choudja-ed-Doulah. See SUJA-DOWLAH.

Chouet, shoo'ā', (JEAN ROBERT,) born at Geneva in 1642, became professor of philosophy in his native city in 1669, and was the first who taught the doctrines of Descartes in Switzerland. He wrote a "History of Geneva," and other works. Died in 1731.

Choul. See DUCHOUL.

Choulant, shoo'lŏN', (LUDWIG,) a distinguished German physician, born at Dresden in 1791. He was appointed professor of medicine at Dresden in 1828, and director of the Academy of Medicine in 1842. He was successful as a practitioner and professor, and published many approved works, among which are a "Manual of Special Pathology and Therapeutics," (1831,) and an "Introduction to Practical Surgery," (1836.)

See CALLISEN, "Medicinisches Schriftsteller-Lexikon," (Supplement.)

Choules, chōlz, (JOHN OVERTON,) a writer and Baptist minister, born at Bristol, England, in 1801. He came to the United States in 1824, and settled in New York City in 1841. He edited Neal's "History of the Puritans," and wrote several works. Died at New York in 1856.

Choumara, shoo'mä'rä', (PIERRE MARIE THÉODORE,) a French military writer, born in 1787, published "Memoirs on Fortifications," and other works.

Chouteau, shoo'tŏ', (AUGUSTE,) a citizen of New Orleans, who, in conjunction with his brother Pierre, founded the city of Saint Louis, in Missouri, (1764.) Auguste died in 1829, and Pierre in 1849. A son of P. Chouteau, of the same name, born in 1789, became a prominent merchant in the fur-trade at Saint Louis.

Chouvaloff. See SHOOVALOF.

Chrestien. See CHRÉTIEN.

Chrestien de Troyes, krȧ'te-ăN'deh tRwȧ, a French poet, wrote a number of romantic tales and poems, some of which are extant. Died about 1196.

Chrétien, krȧ'te-ăN', sometimes written **Chrestien,** (FLORENT,) a French poet, born at Orléans in 1541, was educated a Protestant. He learned Greek of Henry Estienne, and became the tutor of the Prince of Béarn, (Henry IV.) He wrote an "Ode on the Birthday of the Count de Soissons," the "Judgment of Paris," and part of the "Satire Ménippée." He translated into Latin verse Epigrams selected from the Greek Anthology and other Greek works. Died in 1596.

Chrétien, (GILLES LOUIS,) a French musician, born at Versailles in 1754 ; died in 1811.

See FÉTIS, "Biographie Universelle des Musiciens."

Christ, krῗst, (JOHANN FRIEDRICH,) a German scholar, born at Coburg in 1700. He became professor of history at Jena about 1730, and professor of poetry at Leipsic in 1740. He wrote able dissertations on philology, and other works. Died in 1756.

Christian, krῗs'che-ạn, or **Christiern,** krῗs'te-ĕRn', **I.,** King of Denmark, born in 1425, was the son of Theodoric, Count of Oldenburg, and Hedwige, who was heiress of Sleswick and Holstein. Christopher III. having died without issue in 1448, Christiern was chosen his successor. He attempted to acquire by force the crown of Sweden, from which he expelled his rival, Charles Canutson, in 1456. The latter was recalled by the Swedes about 1465, and, after a war of several years, Christiern renounced his claim to Sweden. Historians give him credit for liberality and humanity. He died in 1481, and was succeeded by his son John.

See HUITFELD, "Historiske Beskrivelse af Konung Christiern I.," 1599.

Christian (or **Christiern**) **II.,** King of Denmark, born in 1481, was the son of John, whom he succeeded in 1513. He married Isabella, sister of the emperor Charles V., in 1515. In 1520 he invaded Sweden, then distracted by intestine dissensions, and made himself master of that kingdom. He disgraced himself by the execution of numerous nobles and senators of Stockholm who were innocent, and by other acts of cruelty, for which he was called "the Nero of the North." Gustavus Vasa liberated Sweden about 1522. Near the close of that year the Danes deposed their tyrant, and elected as his successor his uncle, Frederick I. Christiern retired to Flanders in 1523. He returned with an army in 1531, and, having failed in an attempt to recover the throne, was taken prisoner, and kept in prison until his death in 1559.

See BEHRMANN, "Kong Christiern II. Historie," 1815; C. F. ALLEN, "Commentatio de Rebus Christiani II.," 1844.

Christian (or **Christiern**) **III.,** King of Denmark, the son of Frederick I., was born in 1503, and was educated as a Protestant. Soon after the death of his father, in 1533, he was proclaimed king. He adopted severe measures to suppress the Catholic religion. In 1543 he terminated a war with Charles V. by the treaty of Spire, after which he reigned in peace. He is regarded as a humane and wise ruler. He died in 1559, leaving his throne to his son, Frederick II.

See PONTANUS, "Vita Christiani III.," 1729.

Christian (or **Christiern**) **IV.,** King of Denmark, born in 1577, was the son of Frederick II., whom he succeeded in 1588. He was declared of age in 1596, and married Anne Catherine of Brandenburg in 1598. In 1611 he declared war against Sweden, with which he made peace in 1613. He was chosen, in 1625, commander of the army of the allies in a war against Austria. In 1626 he was defeated by the Austrians, under Tilly, at Lutter, and peace was restored in 1629. From 1641 to 1645 he waged war against Sweden, without decisive results. He displayed superior talents for war and civil affairs, and acquired the favour of his subjects in a high degree by his magnanimity and other qualities. Died in 1648. His son, Frederick III., was his successor.

See RASMUS NYERUP, "Charakteristik af Kong Christian IV.," 1816; NIELS SLANGE or SLANGEN, "Kong Christiern IV. Historie," 1749; H. NYERUP, "Kong Christiern IV. Dagboger," 1825; F. H. JAHN, "Christiern IV. Krigshistorie," 1822.

Christian (or **Christiern**) **V.,** King of Denmark and Norway, born in 1646, was the son of Frederick III., whom he succeeded in 1670. In 1673 he made a treaty of alliance with the Dutch against France and Sweden. After a war with Sweden, in which he was victorious in Pomerania and was defeated in Scania, peace was concluded in 1679. He published in 1693 a code which bears his name. He died in 1699, of a wound received in hunting, and was succeeded by his son, Frederick IV.

See FRIEDENREICH, "Kong Christiern V. Krigshistorie," 1758 to 1765.

Christian (or **Christiern**) **VI.,** King of Denmark and Norway, born in December, 1699, succeeded his father, Frederick IV., in 1730. In 1734 he made a defensive alliance with Sweden, which lasted many years. He improved the condition of the country, promoted industry and commerce, and by his zeal for Protestantism acquired the surname of Pious. Alarmed by the elevation of the house of Holstein-Gottorp on the thrones of Sweden and Russia, he formed in 1745 a defensive alliance with France. He died in 1746, leaving the throne to his son, Frederick V.

See RIEGELS, "Account of the Reign of Christian VI.," 1798.

Christian (or **Christiern**) **VII.**, King of Denmark, born in January, 1749, was the son of Frederick V., whom he succeeded in January, 1766. His mother was Louisa, daughter of George II. of England. He married in 1766 his cousin Caroline Matilda, a sister of George III. of England. His physician, Struensee, who acquired a paramount influence over him, became chief minister in 1770, but was deprived of power and life by a hostile party in 1772. The king, whose reason was impaired by disease, had no part in the government for many years before his death. In 1784 his son Frederick became regent. Christian died in 1808, and was succeeded by the son just named. (See STRUENSEE, and CAROLINE MATILDA.)

See G. L. BADEN, "Christiern VII. Regierings Aarbog," 1833; MYNSTER, "Sörgetale over Kong Christian VII.," 1814.

Christian (or **Christiern**) **VIII.**, King of Denmark, the son of the hereditary Prince Frederick, was born in 1786. About 1812 he was appointed Governor or Viceroy of Norway. The King of Denmark was obliged to cede Norway to Sweden in 1814; but the people of Norway protested against that act, and chose Prince Christian as their king. On the approach of Bernadotte with an army, he abdicated, in October, 1814. He succeeded his cousin, Frederick VI., in 1839, and took measures to prepare Denmark for the free institutions which were established in the next reign. He died in January, 1848, leaving the throne to his son, Frederick VII.

See "Nouvelle Biographie Générale."

Christian (or **Christiern**) **IX.**, King of Denmark, son of Duke Friedrich Wilhelm of Sleswick-Holstein, etc., was born in 1818. He ascended the throne in November, 1863. In the early part of 1864 he waged a very unequal war against Austria, Prussia, and other German powers which claimed Sleswick and Holstein as part of Germany. In August, 1864, he signed a treaty of peace, and ceded Sleswick, Holstein, and Lauenburg to the victors.

Christian, (ANDREW,) a Danish medical writer, born at Ripen in 1551; died in 1606.

Christian or **Christien Reisen**, (CHARLES,) an excellent engraver of gems, born in London, of Danish parents, about 1695. He is ranked among the first modern engravers of precious stones, and executed many works, which are in great request. Among them is a portrait of Charles XII. of Sweden. Died in 1725.

Chris'tian, (EDWARD,) professor of the laws of England in the University of Cambridge. He published an edition of "Blackstone's Commentaries," with notes, (1795,) "Origin of the Two Houses of Parliament," (1810,) "Bankrupt Laws," and other legal works. Died in 1823.

Christ'ian Augus'tus, [Ger. CHRISTIAN AUGUST, krĭs'te-ân ŏw'gŏŏst,] Duke of Sleswick-Holstein-Sonderburg-Augustenburg, was born at Copenhagen in 1798. He succeeded his father, Frederick Christian, in 1814, and became the chief of a party which attempted to separate Sleswick and Holstein from Denmark about 1848. After the victories of the Danes (1850) he was banished.

Christian von Hamle, KRIS'te-ân fon hâm'leh, a German minnesinger, who lived about 1250.

See LONGFELLOW'S "Poets and Poetry of Europe."

Christiani, kRĭs-te-â'nee, (WILLIAM ERNEST,) a Danish historian, born at Kiel in 1731. He was professor of eloquence and public law at Kiel, and author of a "History of Sleswick and Holstein," which is highly commended. Died in 1793.

Christie, krĭs'te, (JAMES,) an English antiquary and auctioneer of London. He published in 1806 a treatise on Etruscan Vases, and in 1815 an "Essay on the Earliest Species of Idolatry, the Worship of the Elements." Died in 1831.

Christie, (SAMUEL HUNTER,) F.R.S., an English magnetist, born in London in 1784. He became professor of mathematics in the Royal Military Academy, Woolwich, about 1838. He contributed many papers on magnetism to the "Philosophical Transactions." Died in 1865.

Christie, (THOMAS,) an ingenious Scottish writer, born at Montrose in 1761, lived in London and Paris. As an adversary of Burke, he wrote "Letters on the French Revolution," (1791.) He also published "Miscellanies, Philosophical, Medical, and Moral," and edited the "Analytic Review," founded by him in 1788. For commercial purposes, he went to Surinam, where he died in 1796.

Christiern. See CHRISTIAN, (of Denmark.)

Christin, krês'tăN', (CHARLES GABRIEL FRÉDÉRIC,) a French jurist, born at Saint-Claude in 1744; died in 1799.

Christina, Queen of Spain. See MARIA CHRISTINA.

Christina, krĭs-tee'nä, [Fr. CHRISTINE, krês'tĕn',] Queen of Sweden, born on the 8th of December, 1626, was the only surviving child of Gustavus Adolphus and Maria Eleonora, Princess of Brandenburg. She received a careful, solid, and masculine education. At the death of Gustavus, in 1632, she was proclaimed queen, and the regency was confided to Oxenstiern and four other dignitaries, who directed her education in accordance with the plan of her father. She learned Latin, Greek, Hebrew, history, politics, and other sciences, neglecting the usual feminine accomplishments. Her favourite recreations were horseback-riding and the chase. Her mind was strong, her character eccentric and impatient of the etiquette of courts. In 1644 she assumed the direction of the government, and, pursuing a pacific policy, took part in the important treaty of Westphalia in 1648, by which Sweden acquired Pomerania, Bremen, and Verden. Her subjects were proud of her, as the worthy daughter of a hero, and desired that she would choose a husband; but she evinced a constant aversion to the conjugal yoke. The States of Sweden, with the assent of Christina, in 1649 designated as her successor her cousin Charles Gustavus, who had aspired to her hand. Soon after this event she proposed to abdicate, but was induced by her ministers to change her purpose or postpone its execution. Her eccentricity appeared in the extravagant patronage of literary men, pedants, buffoons, artists, etc. Among the eminent persons whom she attracted to her court were Descartes, Grotius, Salmasius, Naudé, Vossius, and Bochart. In June, 1654, she gave, while still in the bloom of youth, a remarkable example of contempt for a throne, by a formal abdication, which is variously ascribed to vanity, levity, or magnanimity. According to Voltaire, "she preferred to live with men who think, rather than reign over men without learning or genius." Some suppose she was ambitious to make a sensation by an extraordinary act of self-denial. She abjured the Protestant for the Catholic religion, and, followed by a numerous suite, became a resident of Rome, where she busied herself in the promotion of arts and in political affairs. On the death of the King of Sweden in 1660, she visited Stockholm, and, it is said, wished to recover the crown; but, receiving no encouragement, she soon returned to Rome. She had reserved the power of life and death over the persons who remained in her service. Her memory is stained with the charge of cruelty to Monaldeschi, her grand-equerry, whom she accused of treason and caused to be put to death, in Paris, in 1656. She founded an academy in Rome, and made rich collections of medals and productions of art. Her superior mind and cultivation did not preserve her from chimerical projects and the vain dreams of astrology. She composed a volume of "Maxims and Sentences," and other works. Died in 1689.

See LACOMBE, "Histoire de Christine," 1762; CATTEAU-CALLEVILLE, "Histoire de Christine Reine de Suède," 1815; ARCHENHOLZ, "Memoirs of the Life of Christina," Stockholm, 4 vols., 1751, in French; JOHN BURBERY, "History of Christina, Queen of Swedeland," 1658; ANDERS FRYXELL, "Drottning Christinas förmyndare," 1838; HENRY WOODHEAD, "Memoirs of Christina of Sweden," 1863.

Christine de France, krês'tĕn' deh frŎNss, Duchess of Savoy, and daughter of Henry IV. of France, was married in 1619 to Victor Amadeus II. of Savoy. At his death, in 1637, she became regent and governess of the princes. The brothers of the late king rebelled, and drove her out of Turin, to which she was restored by the French in 1640. Died in 1663. She was a very accomplished lady.

Christine de Pisan, krĕs'tĕn' dĕh pe'zŏn', a poetess, born at Venice about 1363, was daughter of Thomas de Pisan, who was in the service of Charles V. of France as astronomer. She was educated at the French court, married Étienne du Castel, and lived mostly in France. She gained renown by her poems, ballads, lays, and rondeaux, and wrote some prose works.

See R. Thomassy, " Essai sur les Écrits politiques de Christine de Pisan;" Longfellow, "Poets and Poetry of Europe."

Chris'ti-son, (Robert,) a Scottish physician, son of Professor Alexander Christison, born at Edinburgh about 1798. He was appointed professor of medical jurisprudence in the University of Edinburgh about 1823, and professor of materia medica in the same in 1832. He attained a high reputation as a teacher of medicine and as a practitioner. In 1829 he published a "Treatise on Poisons," a standard work of the highest authority. He has also published a "Dispensatory," (1842,) and several other works.

Christman, krĭst'mån, (Jakob,) a learned German philologist and mathematician, born near Mentz in 1554. He was successively professor of Hebrew, of logic, and of Arabic in the College of Heidelberg between 1592 and 1613. He composed several treatises on Chronology, and other Latin works, among which were "Solar Observations," and a "Theory of the Moon," (1611.) Died in 1613.

See Vossius, "De Mathematicis;" M. Adam, "Vitæ Philosophorum Germanorum."

Christ'mas, (Rev. Henry,) an English writer, born in London in 1811. Among his various works are "Christian Politics," "Echoes of the Universe," and "Universal Mythology."

Christophe, the French of Christopher, which see.

Christophe, krĕs'tof', (Henri,) a negro king of Hayti, born in 1767. In the insurrection which began about 1790 he fought against the French, and by his courage and talents attracted the notice of Toussaint L'Ouverture, who made him a general of brigade. After Toussaint had been transported to France, Christophe fought under Dessalines, who assumed the title of emperor in 1804. When, in October, 1806, Dessalines was assassinated, Christophe became ruler of the northern part of the island. A rivalry between him and Péthion, who favoured a representative system, led to civil war. After several indecisive battles, Péthion retained the southwest part of the island, and Christophe in 1811 was crowned King of Hayti, as Henri I. He established the Catholic religion, and, in mimicry of European courts, created a nobility, with such titles as Duke of Marmalade and Count of Lemonade, these names having formerly been those of different plantations. In 1814, Louis XVIII. of France sent emissaries to Hayti with a design to recover that island, but without success. His cruelties having rendered him unpopular, Christophe was unable to suppress a revolt, and shot himself in October, 1820. Boyer then became President of Hayti.

See De Vastey, "Mémoires;" General P. La Croix, "Histoire de l'Expédition de Saint-Dominique."

Christophe, krĕs'tof', (Jean Baptiste,) a French historical writer, born at Amplepuis (Rhone) in 1809. He became curate of a parish near Lyons, and published in 1852 a "History of the Papacy during the Fourteenth Century," which is said to be a work of merit.

Christophe or **Christoph,** kris'tof, (Joseph,) a Dutch painter, born at Utrecht in 1498, was a pupil of Antonio Moro. He painted history and portraits with equal success, and excelled most artists of his time in perspective. He worked some time for John III. of Portugal, at Lisbon, where he died in 1557.

Chris'to-phẹr, Emperor of the East, was a son of Romanus Lecapenus, and a brother-in-law of Constantine Porphyrogenitus. He was associated with his father in the empire in 920 A.D. He died in 931, leaving a son, Michael, who became a priest.

Chris'to-phẹr, [Gr. Χριστοφόρος; Lat. Christoph'-orus; Fr. Christophe, krĕs'tof',] Saint, a native of Syria or Palestine, supposed to have suffered martyrdom in the third century.

See Siegmund Meyer, "Dissertatio de magno Christophoro," 1688; Mrs. Jameson, "Sacred and Legendary Art."

Chris'to-phẹr I., King of Denmark, was the son of Waldemar II. He began to reign about 1250, as successor to his brother Abel, and soon became involved in a contest with rebellious bishops, who owned allegiance to the pope alone. He died in 1259, leaving the kingdom to his son, Eric VII.

Christopher II., King of Denmark, born in 1276, was the son of Eric VI. He succeeded his elder brother, Eric VII., who died in 1319. His subjects revolted and dethroned him in 1326. After fighting for the throne several years against Gerhard of Rendsborg, he died in 1333. His son Waldemar became his successor.

Christopher III. of Denmark was the son of John, Duke of Bavaria, and Catherine, sister of Eric XIII., who reigned over Sweden, Denmark, and Norway. The latter having been deposed in 1439, Christopher was elected his successor in 1440 by the Danes, and soon afterwards by the Swedes and Norwegians. He chose Copenhagen as his capital. His reign was mostly peaceful. He published a code of laws which were in force in Sweden until the eighteenth century. He died, without issue, in 1448, and was succeeded by Christian I.

See Holberg, "Danemarks Riges Historie;" Mallet, "Histoire de Danemarck."

Chris'to-pher, [Ger. Christoph, kRĬs'tof,] Duke of Würtemberg, born in 1515, was a son of Duke Ulric, who was deprived of his dominions in 1519 or 1520. The efforts to restore Ulric were opposed by the emperor Charles V. with success, until the Austrians were defeated at Laufen by the Landgrave of Hesse in 1534. Christopher succeeded his father in 1550, and established the Protestant religion in the duchy about 1552. He is entitled to credit for appropriating the property of the old church to the support of schools and of the clergy, while other Protestant princes converted the church revenues to their own use. Died in 1568.

See J. C. Pfister, "Herzog Christoph zu Würtemberg," 2 vols., 1818-20; J. F. Roeslin, "Leben Herzogs Christoph von Würtemberg," 1739.

Chris'to-phẹr-son, (John,) an English bishop and scholar, translated into barbarous English the ecclesiastical histories of Eusebius, Socrates, Sozomen, etc. On the accession of Mary, in 1552, he became Bishop of Chichester. Died in 1558.

Christophorus, the Latin of Christopher, which see.

Christopoulos, krĕs-to-poo'los, (Athanasius,) a modern Greek lyric poet, born at Castoria about 1772. He published a "Grammar of Modern Greek" about 1805, and afterwards his popular lyric and erotic poems, which are his chief title to fame. He lived mostly in Constantinople and Moldavia. Died in 1847.

Christovão de Lisboa, krĕs-to-vŏwn' då lĕs-bo'å, (Frey,) a Portuguese ecclesiastic, who in 1623 went as a missionary to South America.

Christyn, krĭs-tîn' or krĕs'tån', (Jean Baptiste,) a Flemish jurist, born at Brussels in 1622, became a privy councillor of the King of Spain, whom he represented at the Congress of Nymwegen in 1678. He wrote able works on heraldry, one of which is called "Jurisprudentia heroica," and "Les Délices des Pays-Bas," (" The Delights of the Low Countries.") Died in 1690.

Christyn, (Jean Baptiste,) a Flemish jurist, born at Brussels in 1635; died in 1707.

Chronicle, krŏn'e-k'l, (William,) an American soldier of the Revolution, born in South Carolina in 1755, became a major in 1780, and was killed the same year at the battle of King's Mountain.

Chroscienski, kRo-she-ĕn'skee, written also **Chroscinsky,** (Adalbert Stanislas,) secretary of Prince James Sobieski, was reputed the best Polish poet of his time. He translated Lucan's "Pharsalia" into verse, and composed poems entitled "Esther," "Joseph Delivered," and "The Victory over the Turks at Vienna," (1684.) Died about 1737.

ā, ē, ī, ō, ū, ȳ, *long;* à, ė, ȯ, same, less prolonged; ă, ĕ, ĭ, ŏ, ŭ, ў, *short;* ạ, ẹ, ị, ọ, *obscure;* fär, fåll, fåt; mĕt; nŏt; gōŏd; mōŏn;

Chrysander, kRe-săn′der or kRe-zän′der, or **Gold-mann**, golt′măn, (WILHELM CHRISTIAN,) a German professor of Oriental languages, philosophy, etc., born at Halberstadt in 1718. Among his works is a poem on the "Memorable Events of 1740," ("Memorabilia Anni 1740.") Died in 1788.

Chrysippe. See CHRYSIPPUS.

Chrȳ-sip′pus [Gr. Χρυσίππος; Fr. CHRYSIPPE, kRe′-zĕp′] of Cnidos, a Greek physician, often quoted by Galen, lived in the fourth century B.C. He was a pupil of Eudoxus of Cnidos, and the teacher of Erasistratus.

Chrysippus, an eminent Stoic philosopher, born at Soli, in Cilicia, in 280 B.C., was a son of Apollonius of Tarsus, and was a pupil of Cleanthes. He was noted for his skill in dialectics and his subtlety as a reasoner, and used to say to Cleanthes, "Teach me only your doctrines, and I will find the arguments to defend them." There was a common saying "that, if the gods use any logic, it is doubtless that of Chrysippus." He was partial to the Sorites, which he is said to have invented. He wrote on various subjects several hundred volumes, none of which are extant. Chrysippus was the most eminent philosopher of his sect except Zeno, and was regarded as an oracle by the later Stoics. Died in 207 B.C.

See DIOGENES LAERTIUS; RITTER, "Geschichte der Philosophie;" J. F. RICHTER, "Dissertatio de Chrysippo Stoico," 1738; F. N. G. BAGUET, "Commentatio de Chrysippi Vita et Doctrina," 1822; C. PETERSEN, "Philosophiæ Chrysippeæ Fundamenta," 1827.

Chrȳs-o-coc′çĕs, (GEORGE,) [Gr. Γεώργιος ὁ Χρυσο-κόκκης,] a learned physician, who lived at Constantinople about the middle of the fourteenth century. He composed, in Greek, a treatise on the astronomy of the Persians, which exists in manuscript in the Imperial Library of Paris, and is a work of some value.

Chrysologue, kRe′zo′log′, (NOËL ANDRÉ,) a French friar and geographer, born in Franche-Comté in 1728. He published a "Celestial Planisphere," (1778,) which was approved by the Academy, and a very correct "Map of the World." In 1806 he produced "Researches on the Time and Agent of the Actual Arrangement of the Earth's Surface," commended by Cuvier. Died in 1808.

Chrȳs-o-lo′ras, (DEMETRIUS,) [Δεμήτριος ὁ Χρυσόλω-ρας,] a Greek theologian and philosopher of superior talents, was a native of Thessalonica, and flourished about 1400. He was employed by the emperor Manuel II. in important affairs of state, and was sent on several foreign embassies. One hundred letters from him to Manuel are extant in manuscript. He wrote several works on theology, among which is a "Treatise on the Procession of the Holy Spirit."

See FABRICIUS, "Bibliotheca Græca."

Chrysoloras, (EMANUEL or MANUEL,) a Greek scholar, memorable as the restorer of Greek literature in Italy, was born of a noble family in Constantinople. After having performed an embassy from the Byzantine emperor to the Western Powers, he became a public teacher of Greek in Florence about 1395. He also taught in Milan, Pavia, Venice, etc., and had many eminent pupils. His Greek grammar was for a long time the only one in use. Died in 1415.

His nephew JOHN, a professor of Greek, died in Constantinople about 1426.

See FABRICIUS, "Bibliotheca Græca."

Chrysostom, (DION.) See DION.

Chrȳs′os-tom, [Gr. Χρυσόστομος, (i.e. "Golden-mouthed;") Lat. CHRYSOS′TOMUS; Fr. CHRYSOSTOME, kRe′zos′tom′,] (JOHN,) a pre-eminent Greek Father of the Church, was born at Antioch, in Syria, about 350 A.D. His father, Secundus, was commander of the imperial army in Syria. He studied eloquence under the famous orator Libanius, whom he soon surpassed, and subsequently received lessons in philosophy at Athens. At an early age he devoted himself to religion, and in a monastery near Antioch inured himself to a severe ascetic discipline. It is said that he passed two years alone in a damp, unwholesome cavern in committing the Bible to memory.

In 381 he was ordained deacon by Meletius of Antioch, where he soon became noted as an eloquent preacher and writer. He was admitted to the station of priest in 386 by Bishop Flavian, who a few years later appointed him his vicar.

In 397 A.D. he was chosen Archbishop of Constantinople. There he founded hospitals, converted many pagans, and made zealous efforts to reform the morals of the clergy. Socrates the historian represents him as "temperate, sincere, and simple, but peevish, intolerant, and extremely ready to excommunicate." As the style of his preaching was declamatory, and the tenor of his theology practical, he made many enemies at court and among the higher classes. By the influence of the empress Eudoxia and Theophilus, Patriarch of Alexandria, a synod was assembled at Chalcedon in 403, and Chrysostom was deposed on trivial charges, one of which was that he favoured Origenism. He was exiled first to Nicæa and then to Cucusus. The common people, among whom he was very popular, raised a sedition on his account, and burned the church of Saint Sophia. He died at Comana in 407. His voluminous works consist of commentaries, homilies, epistles, and doctrinal treatises. He has great merit as an expositor of Scripture. His works are also prized for the light they shed on the manners and social condition of the times in which he lived. By Augustine and many others he was regarded as the most illustrious orator and doctor of the early Church. Among the ancient biographers of Chrysostom are Palladius, Photius, and Sozomen.

See, also, GODEFROI HERMANT, "Vie de Saint J. Chrysostome," 1664; J. A. W. NEANDER, "Life of Chrysostom," (in German, 2 vols., 1821;) MÉNARD, "Vie de Saint-Chrysostome," 1665; "Nouvelle Biographie Générale;" PERTHES, "Life of Chrysostom," 1854.

Chrysostome. See CHRYSOSTOM.

Chrysostomus. See CHRYSOSTOM.

Chrzanowski, kzhă-nov′skee, (ADALBERT,) a Polish general, born in the palatinate of Cracow in 1788, entered the Russian army about 1820. He rendered important services to the Poles in their revolt against Russia in 1830 and 1831. His retreat to and from Zamosc was regarded as a masterly movement, and procured him the rank of general of division in 1831. After the capture of Warsaw by the Russians in that year, he went into exile. He commanded the Sardinian army which was defeated by the Austrians at Novara in 1849. Died in 1861.

See "Nouvelle Biographie Générale."

Chubb, (THOMAS,) an English Unitarian writer and controversialist, born near Salisbury in 1679. Among his numerous works are "The Supremacy of the Father asserted," (1715,) "Discourse on Reason as a Guide in Religion," and "The True Gospel of Jesus asserted." He was for some time steward of Sir Joseph Jekyl in London. Died in 1746. His books were answered by Caleb Fleming and others.

See "Biographia Britannica."

Chudleigh, chŭd′le, (Lady MARY,) an English author-ess, whose maiden name was LEE, born in Devonshire in 1656, became the wife of Sir George Chudleigh. She published "Essays in Prose and Verse," (1710,) which are commended, and composed tragedies and other works which remain in manuscript. Died in 1710. Her writings indicate piety and good sense.

See BALLARD, "Learned Ladies;" CIBBER, "Lives of the Poets."

Chumacero, choo-mă-thă′ro, (JUAN,) a Spanish jurist, born in Estremadura about 1610, became president of the supreme council of Castile. Died in 1660.

Chum′nus, (NICEPHORUS,) a renowned Byzantine writer and statesman, held high offices under the emperor Andronicus Palæologus at Constantinople. He wrote several works on philosophy and religion, among which is "De Mundi Natura," ("On the Nature of the World,") and letters which possess historic interest. He is supposed to have died about 1330.

Chun. See SHUN.

Chun-Chi. See SHUN-TCHEE.

Chŭnd or **Chand**, a Hindoo poet, called the "Homer of the Rajpoots." The time when he lived is unknown.

Chundra or **Chundur.** See CHANDRA.

Chungiz. See JENGIS.

Chung-Ne, written also **Tchoung-Ni**, a name sometimes applied to CONFUCIUS, which see.

Church, (BENJAMIN,) an American soldier, born at Duxbury, Massachusetts, in 1639, served with distinction as an officer in the Indian wars. Died in 1718.

** є** as *k*; **ç** as *s*; **g̃** *hard*; **ġ** as *j*; G, H, K, *guttural*; N, *nasal*; R, *trilled*; **s̃** as z; th as in *this*.   (☞See Explanations, p. 23.)

Church, (BENJAMIN,) a physician and active Whig politician of Boston, was convicted of a treasonable correspondence with Governor Gage in 1775, and was imprisoned for that offence, but was released in 1776.

Church, (FREDERICK EDWIN,) an eminent American landscape-painter, born at Hartford, Connecticut, in 1826, was a pupil of Thomas Cole. His earliest productions were views of the Catskill Mountains, among which he resided, and a view of East Rock, near New Haven, which attracted very favourable notice. In 1853 he visited South America, and found in the magnificent scenery of that country materials for several of his most admired pictures. After his return he executed his "View of Niagara Falls from the Canadian Shore," regarded by many as the most successful representation of the great cataract. "In the rush of water, and the fine atmospheric effects," says a foreign critic, "it realizes the idea of sound as well as of motion." Among his other works are "The Heart of the Andes," "Cotopaxi," "Morning on the Cordilleras," "Under Niagara," "The Icebergs," and "Sunrise on Mount Desert Island."

See TUCKERMAN, "Book of the Artists."

Church, (JOHN HUBBARD,) an American Congregational divine, born at Rutland, Massachusetts, in 1772, preached at Pelham, New Hampshire. Died in 1840.

Church, (Sir RICHARD,) an English general, born about 1785, served in the British army in his youth. In 1827 he was chosen by the insurgent Greeks commander of their land army; but peace was made before he had performed any very important actions. He was ordered to leave Greece in 1830 by Capo d'Istrias, whose enmity he had incurred. After the death of Capo d'Istrias, in 1831, he was again for a short time at the head of the army. Died in 1850.

Church, (SAMUEL,) a jurist, born in Salisbury, Connecticut, in 1785. He became a judge of the superior court in 1833, and chief justice of Connecticut in 1847. Died in 1854.

Church, (THOMAS,) an English theologian, born in 1707; died in 1756.

Church'ill, (CHARLES,) a popular English poet and satirist, born at Westminster in 1731. At school he was the fellow-student and friend of William Cowper. He married a Miss Scott privately when he was about seventeen, and soon after applied for a studentship at Oxford, but was rejected. Against his own inclination, he unwisely adopted the profession of his father, who was a curate. In 1756 he was ordained priest, and began to officiate at Rainham. Two years later he succeeded his father as curate and lecturer of Saint John's, Westminster. It is usually stated that a sudden or total change occurred in his habits at this period, after which he became dissipated and licentious. Macaulay, who dissents from this opinion, thinks he never was or professed to be religious, and intimates that, "with violent recoil from the hypocrisies, he outraged the proprieties of life," because his youth had been misdirected to a profession from which his heart was estranged.

Resolving to abandon that profession, he produced, about 1760, two poems, "The Bard" and "The Conclave." His "Rosciad," a pungent satire on the performers and managers of the stage, appeared in 1761, and was successful beyond his most sanguine hopes. He vindicated himself against the malice of the "Critical Reviewers" by the "Apology," a poem, which is much admired. He became very intimate with John Wilkes, the profligate pseudo-patriot, whom he assisted in "The North Briton." In 1763 he produced "The Prophecy of Famine," a political satire on the Scotch, which was immensely popular. "The Conference," a poem, is one of his master-pieces. While on a visit to France, he died in 1764. "His vices were not so great as his virtues," says Macaulay. Besides the works already noticed, he wrote "The Author," "Gotham," and other poems. Cowper was a warm admirer of his poetry, and said that "he well deserved the name of 'the great Churchill.'"

See TOOKE, "Life of Churchill;" MACAULAY's Essay entitled "Charles Churchill," 1845: JOHN FORSTER, "Historical and Biographical Essays," vol. ii.; "Edinburgh Review" for January, 1845.

Churchill, (JOHN.) See MARLBOROUGH.

Church'ill, (SYLVESTER,) an American officer, born at Woodstock, Vermont, about 1783. He became inspector-general of the army about 1841.

Churchill, (Sir WINSTON,) born in Dorsetshire, England, in 1620, was the father of the Duke of Marlborough. He was a royalist in the civil war, and was knighted by Charles II. about 1662. He wrote a work of little merit on the lives of British kings, entitled "Divi Britannici." Died in 1688. He was a Fellow of the Royal Society.

Church'man, (WILLIAM H.,) a blind man, born in Baltimore in 1818, was educated in the Pennsylvania Institution for the Blind. He has been successively superintendent of similar institutions in Tennessee, Indiana, and Wisconsin.

Church'yard, (THOMAS,) an English versifier, born at Shrewsbury about 1520, became a domestic of the Earl of Surrey, after whose death he served in the army. He wrote a "Legend of Jane Shore," and other poems. Died in 1604.

See CIBBER, "Lives of the Poets;" DISRAELI, "Calamities of Authors."

Churruca y Elorza, de, då choor-roo′kå e å-loR′-thå, (C. DAMIAN,) an able and meritorious Spanish naval officer, was born in Guipuzcoa in 1761. He was employed in an expedition sent to survey the Straits of Magellan, and wrote a valuable "Diary of the Exploration of Terra del Fuego," which was published in 1793. He commanded an exploring expedition to the Gulf of Mexico in 1791, from which resulted numerous charts of the coasts. He was killed at the battle of Trafalgar, (1805.)

Chŭr′tọn, (EDWARD,) an English theologian and writer, son of Rev. Ralph Churton, born about 1800.

Churton, (RALPH,) an English clergyman, born in Cheshire in 1754. He was appointed Archdeacon of Saint David's in 1805, and published sermons, and several well-written biographies. Died in 1831.

Chyr-Shah. See SHER-SHAH.

Chyträus, Ke-trä′ŭs, [Fr. CHYTRÉE, she′trå′; Lat. CHYTRÆ′US,] (DAVID,) a German Protestant theologian and scholar, whose proper name was KOCHHAFF, (koK′-håf,) was born at Ingelfingen, Suabia, in 1530. He was a favourite disciple of Melanchthon, and became professor of divinity at Rostock in 1551. He published a large number of Latin works, among which are a "History of the Augsburg Confession," (1578,) and a "Chronicle of Saxony," (1593.) Died in 1600.

See ULRICH CHYTRÆUS, "Vita D. Chytræi," 1601.

Chyträus or **Chytræus,** (NATHAN,) a brother of the preceding, was born at Menzingen in 1543. He was professor of Latin and of poetry at Rostock, and author of "Iter Italicum et Gallicum," ("Journey to Italy and France,") and other poems in Latin. Died in 1598.

Ciacone and **Ciaconius.** See CHACON.

Cialderi, chål-då′ree, (GIROLAMO,) an Italian painter, born at Urbino in 1593.

Cialdini, chål-dee′nee, (ENRICO,) an able Italian general, born at Módena about 1814. He served in the campaign of 1848 against the Austrians, and fought by the side of Charles Albert at Novara in 1849. As general of division, he gained an advantage over the Austrians at Palaestro in June, 1859. He defeated the papal army under Lamoricière at Castelfidardo in 1860, and commanded the Sardinians at the siege of Gaeta, which he took in February, 1861. In June, 1861, he was appointed lieutenant-general of Naples, then disturbed by brigands and rebels. He commanded one of the armies operating against the Austrians in 1866, and became chief of the royal staff in August of that year.

Ciamberlani, châm-bêR-lå′nee, or **Ciamberlano,** châm-bêR-lå′no, (LUCA,) an Italian painter and skilful engraver, born at Urbino about 1580; died in 1641.

Ciampelli, châm-pel′lee, (AGOSTINO,) an Italian painter, born at Florence in 1578. He was employed by Clement VIII. in the Vatican, and was successful in fresco and oil. His style is noble and his design correct. Died at Rome in 1640.

See LANZI, "History of Painting in Italy."

Ciampi, châm′pee, (SEBASTIANO,) an Italian littérateur, born at Pistoia in 1769. Among his works are "Memoirs of Cino da Pistoia," and "Carteromaco." Died in 1847.

ā, ē, ī, ō ū, ȳ, *long;* ă, ĕ, ĭ, ŏ, *same, less prolonged;* ă, ĕ, ĭ, ŏ, ŭ, ў, *short;* ạ, ẹ, ị, ọ, *obscure;* fär, fåll, fåt; mêt; nŏt; gŏŏd; mŏŏn;

Ciampini, châm-pee′nee, (GIOVANNI GIUSTINO,) a learned Italian writer and antiquary, born at Rome in 1633. He obtained an office in the apostolic chancery. He studied sciences and belles-lettres with success, and, under the auspices of Christina of Sweden, founded at Rome, in 1677, an academy of natural and exact sciences. He composed several esteemed works, among which are "The Sacred Edifices built by Constantine," (1693,) and "Vetera Monumenta," a treatise on ancient buildings, mosaics, and rites. Died in 1698.

See NICÉRON, "Mémoires ;" FABIANI, "Vita di G. G. Ciampini."

Ciampoli, châm′po-lee, (GIOVANNI BATTISTA,) an Italian lyric poet, born at Florence in 1589. He studied philosophy under Galileo at Padua. His youthful essays in poetry procured for him the favour of Cardinal Barberini. Having removed to Rome, he was appointed secretary of briefs by Pope Gregory XV. His poems, which appeared in 1628, though marred by inflation and affectation, were received with applause. As an adherent of Galileo, he was disgraced and exiled from Rome in the pontificate of Urban VIII. Died in 1643.

See CRASSO, "Elogi d'Uomini letterati."

Cianchettini, chân-kĕt-tee′nee, (PIO,) a musical composer, of Italian extraction, born in London in 1799.

Cianci, chân′chee, (IGNAZIO,) a Neapolitan poet and theologian, lived about 1720–60.

Cianfanini, chân-fâ-nee′nee, (BENEDETTO,) an Italian painter, who was esteemed one of the best pupils of Fra Bartolommeo di San Marco.

Ciarpi, chaR′pee, (BACCIO, bât′cho,) an Italian painter, born at Florence in 1578 ; died in 1642.

Ciassi, châs′see, (GIOVANNI MARIA,) an Italian botanist, born at Treviso in 1654. He advanced some sound opinions on the phenomena of germination in his "Meditations on the Nature of Plants," ("Meditationes de Natura Plantarum," 1677.) Died in 1679.

Cib′ber, (CAIUS GABRIEL,) a successful sculptor, born in Holstein, (Denmark,) became a resident of London a short time before the restoration of 1660. He executed the bas-reliefs of the London Monument, and the two figures of Madness in Bethlehem Hospital. He was the father of Cibber the dramatist. Died about 1700.

Cib′ber, (COLLEY,) a witty English dramatic author and actor, son of the preceding, was born in London in 1671. He became a comic actor in 1689. In 1695 he produced his first play, "Love's Last Shift, or the Fool in Fashion," which was very successful. "The Careless Husband," which is considered his best production, was performed with great applause in 1704, Cibber himself enacting a principal *rôle*. His comedy the "Nonjuror," (1717,) an imitation of Molière's "Tartuffe," procured him a pension of £200 from George I. He was one of the managers of Drury Lane for many years. In 1730 he was chosen poet-laureate. He wrote an amusing "Apology for the Life of Colley Cibber," which Dr. Johnson pronounced "very well done." Cibber is a prominent hero of the "Dunciad." Died in 1757.

See POPE's "Dunciad," books i., ii., iii.; "Retrospective Review," vol. i., 1820.

Cibber, (SUSANNA MARIA,) a celebrated English actress, born probably in London in 1716, was the sister of Dr. Arne the musician. She became the wife of Theophilus Cibber in 1734. She made her *début* in 1736, and was very successful in tragedy. Died in 1766.

Cibber, (THEOPHILUS,) an English comedian, son of Colley Cibber, born in London in 1703. He was a successful actor, but a very immoral and prodigal man. He altered several plays from Shakspeare, and published in 1753 "Lives of the British Poets," said to have been chiefly written by Robert Shiels. Cibber perished by shipwreck in a voyage to Ireland in 1758.

See BAKER, "Biographia Dramatica."

Cibo. See CYBO.

Cibot, se′bo′, (FRANÇOIS BARTHÉLEMY MICHEL ÉDOUARD,) a French painter of history and genre, born in Paris in 1799. He obtained a first medal in 1843.

Cibot, (PIERRE MARTIAL,) a French missionary and Jesuit, born at Limoges in 1727, was learned in the sciences and languages. From 1760 to 1780 he was employed at Pekin, where he wrote valuable treatises on the arts, manners, etc. of the Chinese. Died in 1780.

Cibrario, che-bRâ′re-o, (LUIGI,) an Italian historian and jurist, born at Turin in 1802, was employed by King Charles Albert as a diplomatist. Among his works are a "History of the Princes of Savoy," (1825,) a "History of the Monarchy of Savoy," (1840,) and "Novels," ("Novelle," 1836.)

Ciccarelli, chĕk-kâ-rel′lee, (ALPHONSO,) an Italian physician, born at Bevagna. He was put to death for forgery in 1580.

Cicci, chĕt′chee, (MARIA LUISA,) an Italian poetess, born at Pisa in 1760 ; died in 1794.

See TIPALDO, "Biografia degli Italiani illustri."

Ciccione, chĕt-cho′nâ, (ANDREA,) an eminent Italian sculptor and architect, born at Naples ; died about 1440.

Ciceri, sès′re′, (PIERRE LUC CHARLES,) a French scene-painter of wide reputation, was born at Saint-Cloud in 1782. He worked in Paris and other places.

Cic′e-ro, [Gr. Κικέρων; It. CICERONE, che-châ-ro′nâ; Fr. CICÉRON, se′sà′rôn′; Ger. CICERO, tsits′ê-ro ; Sp. CICERON, the-thâ-rôn′,] (MARCUS TULLIUS,) often called **Tully** by English writers, an illustrious Roman orator, philosopher, and statesman, was born at Arpinum, (now Arpino,) about seventy miles east-southeast of Rome, on the 3d of January, 106 B.C., (647 A.U.C.) He was a son of Marcus Tullius Cicero, an opulent citizen of the equestrian order, who owned an estate near Arpinum and devoted much time to literary pursuits. His mother's name was Helvia. His early education was directed by Archias the Greek poet, Q. Ælius the grammarian, and other teachers, at Rome. During his minority he composed a number of poems, among which was "Pontius Glaucus," which is lost. His disposition was genial and amiable. He learned to speak Greek fluently, and was profoundly versed in Greek literature and philosophy. Having assumed the manly gown *(toga virilis)* in his sixteenth year, (91 B.C.,) he applied himself to the study of law under Mucius Scævola the Augur, an eminent jurist and statesman.

In the year 89 B.C. he served a campaign under Cneius Pompeius Strabo in the Social war, in obedience to the law which then required every citizen to perform military service. During the six ensuing years after this campaign he passed his life in studious retirement, and took no part in the bloody civil war between Marius and Sulla. He attended the lectures of the Greek philosopher Philo, the chief of the New Academy, studied logic with Diodotus the Stoic, and was instructed in rhetoric by Apollonius Molo of Rhodes. "He had," says Plutarch, "both the capacity and inclination to learn all the arts, nor was there any branch of science that he despised : yet he was most inclined to poetry. . . . In process of time he was looked upon as the best poet as well as the greatest orator in Rome. His reputation for oratory still remains ; . . . but, as many ingenious poets have appeared since his time, his poetry has lost its credit and is now neglected." In his admirable oration "Pro Archia," Cicero informs us that Archias the poet exerted great influence over the formation of his taste and the development and direction of his genius. Among his early productions was a heroic poem entitled "Marius," which is not extant : also a treatise on rhetoric, entitled "De Inventione Rhetoricâ."

Having laid a solid foundation for his fame by the severe and systematic discipline of his rare talents, and by assiduous efforts to perfect his elocution by the practice of declamation, he began, at the age of twenty-five, his career as a pleader in the Forum. An argument which he made in 81 B.C. for his client P. Quinctius, in a civil suit, is still extant. The first important criminal trial in which he was employed was that of Sextus Roscius Amerinus, who was accused of parricide by an agent of the dictator Sulla, the dread of whose power and cruelty was so great that all the other advocates declined to appear for the defence. Cicero defended him with success, denounced the malice and iniquity of the prosecutor, and gained great applause by his courage and eloquence. This event occurred in the twenty-seventh year of his age. His physical constitution in his youth was so delicate that his medical friends advised him to abandon the bar. "My body," says he, "was very weak and emaciated, my neck long and small, which is a habit thought liable to great risk of life, if engaged in any fatigue or labour of the lungs." He therefore resolved to improve his health by travel, and to finish his education by visits to the famous seats of learning and art in Greece and Asia. Having departed from Rome in 79 B.C., he spent about six months in Athens, where he pursued his favourite studies with Antiochus of Ascalon, Zeno the Epicurean, and Demetrius Syrus. He also enjoyed in Athens the society of Pomponius Atticus, with whom he formed a lasting and memorable friendship. He afterwards travelled extensively in Asia Minor. "He came back again to Italy," says Middleton, "after an excursion of two years, extremely improved, and changed, as it were, into a new man: the vehemence of his voice and action was moderated, the redundancy of his style and fancy corrected, his lungs strengthened, and his whole constitution confirmed."

In 76 B.C. he was elected quæstor (paymaster) by the unanimous suffrage of all the tribes. The quæstors were sent annually into the several provinces, one with every proconsul or governor, to whom he was next in authority. The office of quæstor was the first step in the gradation of public honours, and entitled him to an admission into the senate for life. He officiated as quæstor in Sicily, and performed his duties with such integrity, moderation, and humanity that he won, it is said, the love and admiration of all the Sicilians. As he was returning to Rome (74 B.C.) somewhat elated with his success, and entertaining the idea that the great capital was resounding with his praises, he met one of his acquaintances, a person of eminence, and inquired what they said and thought of his actions in Rome. The answer was, "Why, where have you been, then, Cicero, all this time?" He then perceived that the reports of his conduct and services had been lost in Rome, as in an immense sea, and had added little or nothing to his reputation. About 76 B.C. he married a rich heiress, named Terentia. The law prescribed that five years should elapse after his election to the quæstorship (or that he must attain the age of thirty-eight) before he could hold the office of ædile, which was the next in the ascending scale. The orations which he pronounced during this period have not been preserved. His principal rival in forensic eloquence was Hortensius, whom he soon surpassed. According to Plutarch, "it was not by slow and insensible degrees that he gained the palm of eloquence: his fame shot forth at once, and he was distinguished above all the orators of Rome." He excelled in sarcasm and witty repartees, with which he often seasoned his forensic arguments. All the resources of his genius, his art, his learning and influence were freely devoted to the defence of those whose lives or dignity or reputations were judicially assailed. He received no pay for his services as an advocate. He deviated from his general rule and practice of pleading for the defendant, in the case of the infamous Caius Verres, who in 70 B.C. was impeached by the Sicilians for atrocious acts of cruelty and rapine, but was supported by the most powerful families of Rome, including the Metelli. At the urgent request of the Sicilians, Cicero conducted the prosecution of Verres, who employed Hortensius to defend him; but the evidence against the accused was so overwhelming that his counsel declined to plead, or had nothing to say, the defence suddenly collapsed, and Verres himself, anticipating his sentence, went into exile. Cicero, therefore, actually spoke only two of his seven celebrated orations against Verres; but the others were published, and remain a noble and imperishable monument of his versatile and almost universal genius.

Having acquired great popularity, he was elected to the ædileship, in 70 B.C., by a majority of the voters of every tribe. As ædile, he had the care of the sacred edifices, and was required by law or usage to gratify the people with public games and shows and costly pageants, partly at his own expense. In the year 67 he offered himself as a candidate for the office of prætor, which was one grade higher than that of ædile, and next in dignity to the consulship. Although he had several eminent competitors, he was elected the first prætor urbanus by the suffrages of all the centuries. The duty of the prætors was to preside as judges in the highest courts, and their jurisdictions were assigned to them by lot, which decided that Cicero should judge in cases of extortion and rapine of which governors of provinces were accused. "As a president in the courts of justice, he acted with great integrity and honour." (Plutarch's "Life of Cicero.") While he held the office of prætor (66 B.C.) he made an important and famous political oration for the Manilian Law, ("Pro Lege Manilia,") the design of which was to appoint Pompey commander-in-chief in the war against Mithridates the Great. This was the first occasion on which Cicero ever mounted the rostrum. The Manilian Law, although strenuously opposed by the nobles, or optimates, and many powerful senators, was adopted. In the same year he defended A. Cluentius, (who was accused of poisoning his father-in-law,) in a plea which is still extant.

At the expiration of his prætorship, Cicero would not accept the government of a foreign province, which, says Middleton, "was the usual reward of that magistracy, and the chief fruit which the generality proposed from it. . . . The glory which he pursued was to shine in the eyes of the city as the guardian of its laws, and to teach the magistrates how to execute, the citizens how to obey them. But he was now preparing to sue for the consulship, the great object of all his hopes." The most formidable obstacle to his ambition was the jealousy of the nobles or aristocrats, who regarded the highest office as their birthright, and who would oppose the election of a "new man," (*novus homo,*) as they called all men whose ancestors were mere private citizens. He offered himself as a candidate for the consulship in his forty-third year, 64 B.C., with six competitors, among whom were P. Sulpicius Galba, C. Antonius, and L. Sergius Catilina. The last two formed a coalition against Cicero, and were favoured by Cæsar and Crassus. During the canvass Cicero uttered a severe invective on the habits and characters of Catiline and Antonius, in his oration "In Togâ Candidâ." The election resulted in the choice of Cicero and C. Antonius, the former of whom received the votes of all the centuries, and was the only "new man" that had been chosen consul in forty years. Among the events of this year was the birth of his only son. He had also a daughter, Tullia, who was born several years earlier and was the object of his warmest affection. She was a very amiable and accomplished woman.

He entered upon the office on the 1st of January, 63 B.C., and found the republic in a very critical and perilous condition, distracted by pestilent laws and seditious harangues and undermined by pervading corruption and traitorous conspiracies. The difficulty was increased by the fact that his colleague Antonius was a man of bad (though feeble) character and was opposed to the policy of Cicero. The latter, however, secured the co-operation, or at least the neutrality, of Antonius, by a bargain that he should have the best and most lucrative of the provinces which were to be assigned to the consuls at the expiration of their term. He promoted the cause of liberty and order by another capital stroke of policy when he induced the senators and the equites (knights) to form a political alliance and unite in a common party. "He was," says Middleton, "the only man in the city capable of effecting such a coalition, being now at the head of the senate, yet the darling of the knights." By an artful and powerful speech he persuaded the people to reject an agrarian law proposed by Rullus, a tribune of the people. According to Niebuhr, this was "one of the most brilliant achievements of eloquence." He defended Rabirius, (accused of the murder of L. Saturninus, who had been dead about forty years,) in an oration which is extant.

The most memorable part of his administration appears in the ability, courage, and elastic energy with which he detected and baffled the nefarious designs of Catiline and his accomplices. Catiline was a candidate for the consulship in the election of 63 B.C., and hired assassins to kill Cicero in the Campus Martius when he should come to preside at the election; but, as the consul came guarded by armed men, the plot failed, and Catiline was not elected. This second repulse rendered him furious. He conspired to seize the chief power by the burning of the city and a general massacre of the senators and the friends of order. His capacity and resources for such an enterprise were very great, and he was abetted by vast numbers of disaffected and desperate men, some of whom were of high rank and great influence. The leaders of this plot met on the 6th of November, and arranged the immediate execution of the same; but their plans were revealed to Cicero by Fulvia, the mistress of one of the conspirators, and when two of them went to his house next morning to assassinate the consul they found it well guarded. On the 8th of November, Cicero delivered in the senate the first of his famous orations against Catiline, who was present, and, at the end of that grand explosion of indignant eloquence, rose to speak; but his voice was drowned by cries of "Traitor!" and "Parricide!" Catiline hastily quitted Rome in the ensuing night, to join his army in Etruria, and Cicero on the next day addressed to the assembled people his second Oration "In Catilinam."

After he had delivered two more orations on the subject, Lentulus, Cethegus, and several other conspirators were condemned to death by the senate, and executed by the order of the consul, who was censured by many for putting citizens to death without a trial. During this perilous crisis, and before Catiline was defeated and killed, Cicero defended Murena against a charge of bribery, in an oration remarkable for wit and good-humoured raillery. For his preservation of the state from this conspiracy Cicero received unbounded honours. He was saluted as the father of his country by Catulus and Cato, and hailed as the saviour of Rome by the people:

"Roma Patrem Patriæ Ciceronem libera dixit."
JUVENAL, Sat. viii.

When he ceased to be consul at the end of the year, he declined the government of a province, and remained at Rome as a private senator. He now purchased an elegant mansion on the Palatine Hill. His favourite country residence was the Tusculan Villa, a few miles from Rome. He also owned villas near Arpinum, Formiæ, Cumæ, and other places.

When P. Clodius was tried for polluting the mysteries of the Bona Dea by his presence, Cicero appeared as a witness against him, and thus incurred his bitter enmity. Soon after this event, Cicero defended the poet Archias, his teacher, in an oration which is much admired. About the end of the year 60, Cæsar, Pompey, and Crassus united to form the first Triumvirate, which Cicero was urged to join by one or more of the parties; but he declined, as he regarded the coalition of the triumvirs as dangerous to the public liberty. He was on friendly terms with Pompey, who he hoped would prove loyal. Forsyth, who thinks that Cicero always distrusted Pompey, and that Pompey disliked Cicero, states that the latter "held aloof, determined to temporize." His enemy Clodius, who became tribune of the people in December, 59 B.C., and who was supported by Cæsar and Pompey, now manifested his vindictive malice against Cicero by a law which he proposed, "that whoever has put to death a Roman citizen without due form of trial shall be interdicted from fire and water." According to custom, Cicero put on mourning and appealed to the compassion of the people. It is said that 20,000 young nobles and equites expressed their sympathy with him by a change of dress; but, as the consuls were his enemies, he anticipated the passage of the law, and retired into exile in April, 58 B.C. Several writers censure him for the abject spirit which they say he now exhibited in adversity. He was banished by law, his property was confiscated, and his house on the Palatine Hill was burned by Clodius. He chose Greece as his place of exile, which he did not endure with the fortitude or apathy of a stoic; on the contrary, he appears from his letters of this period to have been extremely dejected. In a letter to his wife, Terentia, he wrote, "It is not my crimes, but my virtue that has crushed me."

The violence and excessive insolence of Clodius soon produced a reaction: the tribunes who entered office in the year 57 were mostly friends of Cicero, whose recall was demanded by the senate, by Pompey, and by the new consuls. In August a bill for his restoration was approved by the almost unanimous suffrage of the people of all Italy, voting by centuries. "There had never been known so numerous and solemn an assembly of the Roman people as this." (Middleton.) His return to Rome in September, 57 B.C., was like a triumphal progress, and was hailed with almost universal enthusiasm. That day, he said, seemed to him like immortality: "unus ille dies mihi quidem immortalitatis instar fuit, quo in patriam redii." ("Oratio in Pisonem.")

During the period of five years that followed his return, he pleaded a number of causes and wrote two important political works, entitled "De Republicâ," ("On the Republic, or the Principles of Government,") and "De Legibus," a philosophical treatise on the origin, principles, and perfection of law. The former of these treats on the best form of government and the duties of the citizen. This work, which was one of his greatest productions, is lost, except a large fragment discovered by Angelo Mai on a palimpsest about 1820. He also wrote, about 55 B.C., his "De Oratore," a systematic work on oratory, which is extant. In 52 B.C. he composed a celebrated oration in defence of T. Annius Milo, who was tried for killing P. Clodius; but this oration was not actually delivered in the court. He wrote a history of his consulship, in verse, which has not come down to us.

About the end of the year 52 Cicero was appointed proconsul or governor of Cilicia, Pisidia, etc. He accepted this office with reluctance, regarding it as a kind of honourable exile. He had under his command in his province an army of about fourteen thousand men, which he directed in successful operations against some predatory tribes, and was saluted by his soldiers with the title of "Imperator." His administration is extolled as a rare model of purity, moderation, and clemency. Having governed that province for one year, he returned to Rome about the end of 50 B.C., and found the country on the verge of civil war between the senate and Julius Cæsar. He offered himself as a mediator, advising the senate to make concessions to Cæsar; but after the latter had crossed the Rubicon he joined the army of Pompey and the senate, not without much hesitation. "He fluctuated greatly," says Plutarch, "and was in the utmost anxiety; for he says in his letters, 'Whither shall I turn? Pompey has the more honourable cause; but Cæsar manages his affairs with the greatest address, and is most able to save himself and his friends. In short, I know whom to avoid, but not whom to follow.'" When Pompey asked him, "Where is your son-in-law?" (Dolabella,) Cicero answered, "He is with your father-in-law." To one who reproached him for coming late to the camp of Pompey, he said, "By no means late; for I find nothing ready here." He wrote almost daily to Atticus, with whom he always corresponded frequently, (except when they lived at the same place,) and expressed his opinions without reserve.

After the battle of Pharsalia, (August, 48 B.C.,) in which he took no part, Cicero returned to Italy and submitted to the power of Cæsar, who treated him with much clemency and respect. He devoted himself to studious retirement and composition, and produced in the next four years numerous important works on philosophy and rhetoric, which demonstrate his immense intellectual activity and his vast learning, as well as the versatility of his mind. The following works are preserved entire: "De Finibus Libri v.," ("An Inquiry into the Supreme Good,") "Cato Major, seu De Senectute," ("Essay on Old Age,") "Brutus, seu De Claris Oratoribus," (a critical history of Roman orators, in the form of a dialogue,) "De Naturâ Deorum Libri iii.," ("On the Nature of the Gods,") "De Amicitiâ," ("A Dialogue on Friendship,") "Tusculanarum Disputationum Libri v.," (Discussions on various questions in Philosophy,) "Orator, seu de optimo Genere Dicendi," ("The Orator, or on the Best Manner of Speaking,") "De Partitione Oratoriâ," ("Analysis of Oratory," or Rhetorical Catechism,) "De optimo Genere Oratorum," "De Divinatione Libri ii.," ("On Divination,") and "De Officiis Libri iii.," ("On Duties,") an excellent treatise on ethics. He also wrote "Academicorum Libri iv.," and "De Fato," ("On Fate,") both of which remain in a mutilated state. His treatises "De Gloriâ" ("On Glory") and "De Virtutibus" ("On the Virtues") are lost, except small fragments. In philosophy he preferred the principles of the New Academy.

In the year 47 he uttered in the senate a beautiful oration for Marcus Marcellus, and in the next year he defended Ligarius with success before Cæsar, who is said to have trembled and changed colour as he heard this speech. Cicero divorced his wife Terentia in 46 B.C., and married a young lady named Publilia, who was his ward; but he repudiated her also in the year 45. He was not an accomplice in the assassination of Cæsar, (March, 44 B.C.;) but he afterwards applauded that action, which he had witnessed. He boldly denounced the ambitious and corrupt conduct of Mark Antony, in a series of fourteen orations, called Philippics, the first of which was spoken in the senate in September, 44, and is considered one of his master-pieces. The second Philippic was not inferior to the first, but it was not spoken. His favour was courted by young Octavius, with whom he co-operated after Antony had fled from the capital. Between the months of December, 44, and May, 43, B.C., he delivered the last twelve Philippics, which were greatly applauded. "His power at this time," says Plutarch, "was at its greatest height; he carried every point that he desired." The coalition of Octavius, Antony, and Lepidus, which was formed in November, rendered his patriotic efforts unavailing. He was proscribed by the triumvirs, and was killed by the soldiers of Antony, near his Formian villa, on the 7th of December, 43 B.C. It appears that he made little effort to escape, and met death with fortitude.

Cicero was tall in stature, with features regular and well formed. His gestures were natural and graceful, his presence manly and commanding. No greater master of composition and of the music of speech has ever appeared among men. He invented a style which adapts itself with rare felicity to every class of subjects, and which has been the model of succeeding ages. In his "Introduction to the Literature of Europe," Mr. Hallam expresses his admiration of the "consummate grace and richness which enchants every successive generation in the periods of Cicero." His orations display a profound knowledge of human nature, as well as a consummate art in the use of words. His diction is copious and flowing, his periods are sonorous, and the structure of his sentences is eminently ingenious and exact. He amplifies everything, and is more diffuse than Demosthenes. His chief foible was his vanity, manifested in a habit of self-laudation, which he indulged to an excessive degree. But there is a certain grace and charm even in these exhibitions of his vanity. "How shocking soever," says Addison, "this great man's talking of himself might have been to his contemporaries, I must confess I am never better pleased than when he is on this subject." ("Spectator," No. 562.) According to Niebuhr, "the predominant and most brilliant faculty of his mind was his wit. In what the French call esprit—light, unexpected, and inexhaustible wit—he is not excelled by any among the ancients." About fifty of his orations are extant, besides fragments of many others. The titles of those which have not been already named in this article are the following: "Pro Scamandro," "Pro C. Mustio," "In Q. Cæcilium," "Pro A. Cæcina," "De Lege Agrariâ," "Pro P. Cornelio Sullâ," "Pro Scipione Nasicâ," "Pro L. Valerio Flacco," "Post Reditum in Senatu," "Post Reditum ad Quirites," "Pro Domo Suâ," "Pro P. Sextio," "Pro M. Cœlio Rufo," "Pro L. Cornelio Balbo," "De Provinciis Consularibus," "In L. Pisonem," "Pro Cn. Plancio," and "Pro Rege Dejotaro." Among his extant works are more than eight hundred letters on politics, literature, domestic affairs, etc., which are considered as equal in value to any of his productions, and are rich in materials for a history of his time. They are also highly prized as models of exquisite Latinity, and as exhibiting a freshness and vivid reality which are seldom if ever found in a historical narrative. William Melmoth published an English version of about four hundred and twenty "Letters of Cicero to several of his Friends;" and his letters to Atticus have been translated by William Heberden, M.D. Among the best editions of his complete works are those of Ernesti, Halle, 5 vols. 8vo, 1774–77; Elzevir, Leyden, 10 vols., 1642; Olivet, Paris,

9 vols. 4to, 1742; Schütz, Leipsic, 20 vols. 8vo, 1814–23, and Orelli, Zurich, 9 vols. 8vo, 1826–37, which is said to surpass them all.

See CONYERS MIDDLETON, "History of the Life of Cicero," 1741; PLUTARCH, "Life of Cicero;" F. FABRICIUS, "Historia Ciceronis," 1563; FACCIOLATI, "Vita Ciceronis Literaria," 1760; MEIEROTTO, "Ciceronis Vita, ex ipsius ejus Scriptis excerpta," Berlin, 1783; ORELLI, "Onomasticum Tullianum;" PÉRICAUD, "Ciceroniana," 1812; DRUMANN, "Geschichte Roms;" NIEBUHR, "Roman History;" ABEKEN, "Cicero in seinen Briefen," 1835, (one of the best works on the subject:) English version of the same, 1854; WILLIAM FORSYTH, "Life of M. T. Cicero," 2 vols., 1864; MOMMSEN, "Römische Geschichte," 2 vols., 1854; J. MORABIN, "Histoire de Cicéron," 3 vols, 1745; DE QUINCEY, "Historical and Critical Essays," vol. i.; PETER EKERMAN, "Dissertatio de Cicerone," 1758; A. F. GAUTIER, "Cicéron et son Siècle," 1842; LINSÉN, "Momenta Vitæ M. T. Ciceronis," 1839; LAMARTINE, "Cicéron," 1852; HOLLINGS, "Life of Cicero," 1839; "Memoirs of Celebrated Characters," (1836,) by LAMARTINE; also the article "Cicéron" in the "Biographie Universelle," (from the masterly pen of M. VILLEMAIN;) "Westminster Review" for October, 1855.

Cicero, (MARCUS TULLIUS,) the only son of the great orator and Terentia, born in 65 B.C. He served in the army of Pompey in the year 49, after which he studied at Athens under Cratippus. After the death of Cæsar he was appointed military tribune by Brutus, and defeated C. Antonius. In the year 30 B.C. he became consul as colleague of Octavius. He is said to have been dissipated and intemperate.

Cicero, (QUINTUS TULLIUS,) a brother of the great Roman orator, was born about 100 B.C. He was elected prætor about the year 62, and obtained the government of Asia, which he held for three years. As legate or lieutenant, (legatus,) he accompanied Cæsar to Britain in 55. While commanding a legion in winter quarters (54 B.C.) he defended his camp with great courage and skill against the forces of the Gauls under Ambiorix until the arrival of Cæsar. (See Cæsar, "De Bello Gallico," lib. v.) In the year 51 he served as legate to his brother Marcus in Cilicia. He fought on the side of Pompey in the civil war, and made his peace with Cæsar in 47 B.C. Having been proscribed by the triumvirs, he was killed, by the orders of Antony, in 43 B.C. He had composed several tragedies, which are lost, and a few small poems.

Cicero, (Q. TULLIUS,) a son of the preceding, was born about 66 B.C. His mother was a sister of Pomponius Atticus. He served under his uncle, the great orator, in Cilicia, in the year 51. After the battle of Pharsalia (48 B.C.) he violently denounced his uncle, with the design, it is supposed, of courting the favour of the victor, by whom he was pardoned. Having joined the party of Brutus and Cassius, he was proscribed by Antony, and put to death in 43 B.C.

Cicogna, che-kôn'yȧ, (EMMANUEL ANTONIO,) an Italian littérateur, born at Venice in 1789. He published, besides other works, "Venetian Inscriptions," ("Iscrizioni Veneziani," 10 vols.)

Cicogna, (PASQUALE,) Doge of Venice, succeeded Nicholas da Ponte in 1585. In his reign Henry IV. of France was recognized king by the Venetians, the Rialto was built, and the superb edifices on the Piazza of Saint Mark were finished. Died in 1595.

See DARU, "Histoire de Venise."

Cicognara, da, dä che-kôn-yä'rä, (LEOPOLDO,) COUNT, an eminent Italian antiquary and writer on art, was born at Ferrara in 1767. He studied the fine arts in Rome, and settled at Módena about 1795. Between that date and 1808 he was minister from the Cisalpine republic to Turin, and councillor of state. He published in 1808 "Del Bello Ragionamenti," (a "Treatise on the Beautiful.") About this time he was appointed president of the Academy of Fine Arts at Venice, over which he presided many years. His capital work is a "History of Sculpture from the Renaissance of that Art to the Present Century," ("Storia della Scultura dal suo Risorgimento in Italia," 3 vols., 1813–18,) which procured him a European reputation. He afterwards produced two splendidly illustrated volumes of the "Remarkable Edifices of Venice," ("Le Fabbriche più conspicue di Venezia," 1815–20,) and other works. Died at Venice in 1834.

See TIPALDO, "Biografia degli Italiani illustri;" BECCHI, "Elogio del L. Cicognara," 1837; ZANETTI, "Cenni puramente biografici di L. Cicognara," 1834.

Cicognini, che-kôn-yee'nee, (JACOPO,) an Italian poet, born at Florence about 1610.

ā, ē, ī, ō, ū, ȳ, long; ă, ĕ, ĭ, ŏ, ŭ, ȳ, short; ạ, ẹ, ị, ọ, obscure; fär, fȧll, fȧt; mĕt; nŏt; gŏŏd; mŏŏn;

Cid, sĭd, [Sp. pron. thềD,] the Moorish appellation of a celebrated Castilian hero, who was born at Burgos about 1040, and whose proper name was **Rodrigo** or **Ruy Diaz de Bivar.** He was also surnamed CAMPEADOR, (the "Champion.") After he had fought with distinction under Sancho II. of Castile, he was excluded from the favour of his successor, Alphonso VI., who banished him from court. He gained a victory over five Moorish kings who invaded Rioja, and was recalled to court. He afterwards performed many martial exploits, which are celebrated in poems and chronicles and embellished by fabulous inventions. These have furnished Corneille the subject of an admired tragedy. A poem of which the Cid is the subject, composed by "the Homer of Spain," an author whose name is unknown, is thought to be the oldest poem in the Spanish language. Died in 1099.

See "Vie du Cid," 1837, translated from the Spanish of M. J. QUINTANA, whose original work is found in his "Vidas de Españoles celebres," 1807; BELORADO, "Coronica del famoso Cavallero Cid," 1498; ROBERT SOUTHEY, "Chronicles of the Cid," 1808; "London Quarterly Review" for February, 1807; TICKNOR, "History of Spanish Literature," vol. i. chap. ii.

Cieça de Leon. See CIEZA.

Ciel. See CEO.

Cienfuegos, the-ên-fwā'gồs, (ALVAREZ,) a Spanish Jesuit, born in Asturias in 1657. He was employed in negotiations by the emperors Joseph I. and Charles VI., and was made a cardinal in 1720. He wrote "The Life of Francis Borgia," and other works. Died in 1739.

Cienfuegos, (BERNARDO,) a Spanish botanist, born at Tarragona in the sixteenth century. He was a professor in the University of Alcalá, and left in manuscript a "History of Plants," with excellent figures.

Cienfuegos, de, dà the-ên-fwā'gồs, (NICASIO ALVAREZ,) a Spanish poet and dramatist of brilliant promise, was born at Madrid about 1764. He was a friend and imitator of Melendez. In 1798 he published a volume of poems, among which were odes, epistles, elegies, etc. His drama "Pitaco" was successful, and opened to him the Spanish Academy. He was editor of the official gazette in Madrid when Spain was invaded by the French in 1808; and, as he refused to comply with the directions of Murat, he was condemned to death. This sentence was commuted into transportation to France, where he died in 1809.

See TICKNOR, "History of Spanish Literature," vol. iii. chaps. v., vi.

Cieza or **Cieça de Leon,** the-ā'thồ dà lồ-ồn', (PEDRO,) a Spanish historian, born at Seville about 1520. He served under Pizarro in the West Indies, and resided many years in Peru. He was the author of a "Cronica del Peru," (1553,) which is commended by Prescott. It is said to be more geographical than historical.

See PRESCOTT, "Conquest of Peru," vols. i., ii.

Cifra, chee'frồ, (ANTONIO,) an Italian composer, born about 1575; was living in 1629.

Cigna, chên'yồ, (GIOVANNI FRANCESCO,) an eminent Italian physician and anatomist, born at Mondovi in 1734, was a nephew of Beccaria the jurist. In 1770 he became professor of anatomy at Turin. He published treatises on Electricity, Respiration, etc. Died in 1790.

Cignani, chên-yồ'nee, (CARLO,) COUNT, an eminent Italian painter, born at Bologna in 1628, was a pupil of Albano, whom in some respects he surpassed. He worked in fresco and oil at Bologna, Parma, and Forlì. In design he almost rivalled Correggio. He was a good colorist, and excelled in chiaroscuro. In 1708 he was chosen president of the Clementine Academy. His masterpiece is a large fresco at Forlì of the "Assumption of the Virgin." Died at Forlì in 1719.

See ZANETTI, "Vita del gran Pittore C. Cignani," 1722; ERSCH und GRUBER, "Allgemeine Encyklopaedie;" TARDINI, "Vita di C. Cignani," 1722.

Cignani, (FELICE,) an able painter of Bologna, a son of the preceding, was born about 1660; died in 1724.

Cignani, (PAOLO,) an Italian painter, nephew of Carlo, was born at Bologna in 1709; died in 1764.

Cignaroli, chên-yồ-ro'lee, (GIOVANNI BETTINO,) one of the most renowned Italian painters of his time, born near Verona in 1706, was a pupil of Balestra. He painted almost exclusively in oil. Among his master-pieces are a "Flight to Egypt," at Parma, and a "Transfiguration," at Verona. He declined the invitations of several sovereigns, and passed most of his life at Verona. He composed verses, and wrote short essays on art, which proved him to be a good critic and scholar. Died in 1770.

See BEVILACQUA, "Memorie della Vita di Cignaroli," 1771; LANZI, "History of Painting in Italy."

Cigoli, da, dà chee'go-lee, (LUDOVICO CARDI,) CAVALIERE, sometimes called **Civoli,** a celebrated painter, born at Cigoli, in Tuscany, in 1559. He was a pupil of Santo di Titi, and a successful imitator of Correggio. He worked at Florence, Rome, etc., and was patronized by the Grand Duke of Tuscany. As a colorist he ranks with Rubens and Van Dyck. His subjects are mostly scriptural. Among his most admired productions are "The Lame Man healed by Saint Peter," at Rome; an "Ecce Homo," and "The Martyrdom of Stephen," both at Florence. He was also an architect, and wrote a treatise on Perspective. He has been called "the Florentine Correggio." Died in 1613.

See LANZI, "History of Painting in Italy."

Cilano, da, dà se-lồ'no, (GEORGE CHRISTIAN MARTENUS,) a physician, born at Presburg, in Hungary, in 1696. He published Latin treatises on natural philosophy, Roman antiquities, etc. Died in 1773.

Cima, chee'mồ, (GIOVANNI BATTISTA,) an Italian painter, called LE CONEGLIANO, (là ko-nồl-yồ'no,) was born at Conegliano, in the March of Treviso, about 1460. He is said to have been a pupil of Bellini, whom he resembles in manner. Among his works are several Madonnas and saints at Venice, Milan, etc. He was living in 1517.

See LANZI, "History of Painting in Italy."

Cimabue, che-mồ-boo'à, (GIOVANNI,) a historical painter, celebrated as the restorer of painting in modern times, was born in Florence in 1240. He received his first lessons in design from two Greeks who worked at Florence. Having acquired reputation by his reforms, which tended to a natural style, he was employed to adorn the church of Saint Francis at Assisi. At Florence he painted a Madonna which excited general enthusiasm. He worked in fresco and distemper, and excelled in design and composition, but was ignorant of perspective. A few of his works are still extant. Giotto was his pupil. A noble style, a severe and correct design, and a natural expression are the chief merits of Cimabue. Died about 1300.

See VASARI, "Lives of the Painters;" LANZI, "History of Painting in Italy;" MRS. JAMESON, "Memoirs of Early Italian Painters."

Cimaline, che-mồ-lee'nà, (GIOVANNI,) a Florentine painter, who flourished about 1300.

Cimarosa, che-mồ-ro'sồ, (DOMENICO,) a celebrated Italian composer, born in Naples in 1755, was a pupil of Durante. Before he was twenty-five he had obtained many successes on the principal theatres of Italy. His comic operas are especially remarkable for verve and originality. "The Secret Marriage" ("Il Matrimonio segreto") is still popular. He also produced admired serious operas, among which are "The Horatii and Curiatii," and "L'Olimpiade." He passed several years at Saint Petersburg, whither he was invited by Catherine II. in 1787. Died at Venice in 1801.

See FÉTIS, "Biographie Universelle des Musiciens;" ARNOLD, "D. Cimarosa's kurze Biographie," 1809.

Cim'ber, (L. TILLIUS,) a Roman, who was a partisan of Cæsar in the civil war which began in 49 B.C. He entered into the conspiracy against the dictator, and gave the signal for his assassination by seizing Cæsar's robe.

Çi'mon or **Ki'mon,** [Κίμων,] an eminent Athenian general and statesman, born about 500 B.C., was the son of Miltiades the victor of Marathon, and Hegesipyle, a Thracian princess. He paid the fine imposed on his father, who died in prison about 489. He distinguished himself at the battle of Salamis. Cimon and Aristides commanded the forces which Athens sent to co-operate with other Greeks against the Persians, 476 B.C. These two Athenians were elected to the chief command by the allies in preference to Pausanias of Sparta; and, as Aristides soon returned to Athens, Cimon became sole general-in-chief. He defeated the Persians on the Strymon, and in 466

B.C. gained another great victory, at the mouth of the Eurymedon, in Pamphylia, where he sunk or captured two hundred ships. On the same day he defeated an army on land, and thus effectually humbled the power of Persia. At home he made a munificent use of his riches, and improved Athens by planting trees, building walls from the city to the Piræus, etc. He opposed the attempts of Themistocles and Pericles to increase the power of the people. In the year 461 he was exiled by ostracism for ten years, but was recalled in 456, with the concurrence of his rival Pericles. In 449 he obtained command of a large fleet destined for Egypt; but he first besieged Citium, in Cyprus, where he died in that year. According to most authors, he died a natural death. He was a liberal conservative in politics, and left the reputation of an honest and able statesman. His life has been written by Plutarch, who draws a comparison between him and Lucullus.

See, also, GROTE, "History of Greece;" THIRLWALL, "History of Greece;" CORNELIUS NEPOS, "Cimon;" DIODORUS SICULUS, books xi. and xii.; C. T. H. LUCAS, "Versuch einer Charakteristik Cimon's," 1835.

Çimon [Κίμων] of Cleonæ, a celebrated Greek painter, who lived about 700 B.C. Pliny attributes to him an invention which he calls "catagrapha," and which he explains by these words: "hoc est, obliquæ imagines." By this some understand foreshortening.

Çin'a-don, [Gr. Κινάδων,] the leader of a conspiracy against the Spartan oligarchy, was put to death by the ephori in 397 B.C.

Cinamus. See CINNAMUS.

Cinchon. See CHINCHON.

Cincinato. See CINCINNATO.

Cincinnato, chĕn-chĕn-nä'to, or **Cincinato,** chĕn-che-nä'to, (ROMULO or ROMOLO,) an Italian painter, born at Florence about 1525. He was employed many years by Philip II. of Spain, for whom he painted beautiful frescos in the Escurial. His "Circumcision," at Cuenca, is a celebrated picture. Died in Madrid about 1600.

His son, DIEGO ROMULO, was a successful portrait-painter. Died in Rome in 1626.

See LANZI, "History of Painting in Italy."

Çin-cin-nä'tus, (LUCIUS QUINTUS,) a celebrated Roman patriot, patrician, and dictator, born about 520 B.C. Having reduced himself to poverty by paying a fine for his son, he was cultivating with his own hands a small farm, when he was chosen consul in 457 B.C. He was a strenuous opponent of the plebeian party. At the end of his official term he returned to his former employment. The Romans, having been unfortunate in war with the Æqui, chose Cincinnatus dictator about the year 456 B.C. He gained a decisive victory, and then abdicated the dictatorship, which he had held only fifteen days. About the age of eighty he again reluctantly acted as dictator, on the occasion of the treason of Spurius Melius, who was promptly defeated and slain. Niebuhr is skeptical as to the cause of his poverty above assigned.

See LIVY, "History of Rome;" NIEBUHR, "History of Rome."

Cincius Alimentus, (LUCIUS.) See ALIMENTUS.

Çin'e-as, [Gr. Κινέας,] a Thessalian orator and negotiator, studied rhetoric under Demosthenes, and was renowned for eloquence. He visited Epirus, and became a favourite minister of King Pyrrhus, with whom he held a well-known conversation respecting his ambitious projects. After Pyrrhus had gained a victory over the Romans (280 B.C.) he sent Cineas to Rome to negotiate an alliance with them; but his art was baffled by Appius Claudius. On his return he reported to Pyrrhus that the senate appeared to him like an assembly of kings. He was living in 278 B.C., after which he is not mentioned in history.

See PLUTARCH, "Life of Pyrrhus."

Cinelli Calvoli, che-nel'lee käl-vo'lee, (GIOVANNI,) an Italian physician, born at Florence in 1625. Having free access to the library of the grand duke, he made researches in literary history, the results of which appeared in his "Biblioteca Volante," (1678–82,) which consists of the titles of rare and fugitive works, with notes by the editor. Died in 1706.

See CAGLIARDI, "Vita di G. Cinelli Calvoli," 1736.

Çi-ne'sĭ-as, [Κινησίας,] an Athenian dithyrambic poet, lived about 400 B.C.

Cingaroli, chĕn-gä ro'lee, (MARTINO,) an Italian painter, born at Verona in 1667, produced admirable landscapes with figures. Died in 1729.

Cin-ġet'o-rix, a chief of the Treviri, noticed in Cæsar's "Commentaries," (" Bello Gallico," lib. v.)

Cini, chee'nee, (GIOVANNI BATTISTA,) an Italian writer of dramas, poems, etc., born at Florence about 1530.

Cin'na, (C. HELVIUS,) a Roman poet, was a companion and friend of Catullus, who admired his poetry. He is supposed to be the Cinna favourably mentioned by Virgil in his ninth Eclogue. His chief work was an epic poem called "Smyrna," of which only a few lines are extant. We are not informed what the subject of this poem was. On the day of the funeral of Julius Cæsar, (44 B.C.,) Cinna, though a friend of the dictator, was killed by a Roman mob who met him in the street and mistook him for L. Cornelius Cinna, an accomplice of Brutus.

See SUETONIUS, "De illustribus Grammaticis;" APPIAN, "Bellum Civile;" AUGUST WEICHERT, "Commentationes II. de C. H. Cinna Poeta," 1822–23.

Cinna, (LUCIUS CORNELIUS,) a Roman demagogue of patrician rank, who, as the partisan of Marius, acted a prominent part in the civil war between the latter and Sulla. Having been elected consul (665 A.U.C.) in 86 or 87 B.C., he attempted to reinstate Marius, who was in exile. A fight between the two parties resulted in the expulsion of Cinna from the city. While Sulla was absent in Asia, Cinna raised an army and besieged Rome in concert with Marius, who had just returned from Africa. Having become masters of the city, they massacred a large number of the opposite party. Cinna was again chosen consul with Marius, and was about to lead an army against Sulla returning from the Mithridatic war, when he was killed by his mutinous soldiers in 668 A.U.C., or 84 B.C. His daughter Cornelia became the wife of Julius Cæsar.

See LIVY, "History of Rome;" PLUTARCH, "Pompey," "Marius," and "Sylla."

Cinna, (L. CORNELIUS,) a son of the preceding, was a brother-in-law of the dictator Cæsar, and a son-in-law of Pompey the Great. He was chosen prætor in 44 B.C., and was privy to the conspiracy against Cæsar in that year. His son Cn. Cornelius Cinna was a partisan of Antony in his contest with Octavius, but was pardoned by the latter, and was chosen consul in 5 B.C.

Çin'na-mus, written also **Cinamus** or **Sinnamus,** (JOANNES,) [Gr. Ἰωάννης Κίνναμος or Σίνναμος; Fr. CINNAME, se'nām',] an able Byzantine historian and statesman, who flourished between 1140 and 1180. He was an imperial notary of Manuel Comnenus, whom he accompanied in his military expeditions. As a historian he is considered to have surpassed all his contemporaries. His History (in Greek) comprises the reigns of Calo-Joannes and his successor, Manuel Comnenus, and the period from 1118 to 1176. It displays great political knowledge and considerable critical ability.

See FABRICIUS, "Bibliotheca Græca."

Cino da Pistoia, chee'no dä pĕs-to'yä, a noted Italian jurist and poet, whose family name was SINIBALDI, was born at Pistoia in 1270. He published in 1314 a commentary on the Code, which had a great reputation, and afterwards professed civil law at Perugia and Florence. He wrote verses in praise of a lady named Selvaggia, and was reputed one of the best poets of his time. He was a friend of Dante. Died about 1326.

See GINGUENÉ, "Histoire Littéraire d'Italie;" S. CIAMPI, "Memoria della Vita di Cino da Pistoja," 1808.

Cinq-Arbres or **Cinquarbres,** sănk'ărbr', (JEAN,) a French Orientalist, born at Aurillac. He translated some works of Avicenna into Latin, (2 vols., 1572,) and taught Hebrew in Paris. Died in 1587.

Cinq-Mars, de, dęh sănk'märss', (HENRY Coiffier de Ruzé—kwä'fe-â' dęh rü'zå',) MARQUIS, a French courtier, a son of Antoine, Marquis d'Effiat, (dà'fe'å',) born in 1620. He became a favourite of Louis XIII., and was made grand equerry of France at the age of nineteen. Richelieu, hoping to find in him a compliant instrument, favoured his promotion at first; but they soon became rivals and enemies. On a charge of complicity in the treasonable designs of Gaston, the king's brother, Cinq-Mars was executed in 1642.

See ALFRED DE VIGNY "Cinq-Mars, ou une Conjuration," 1826; CAPEFIGUE, "Richelieu, Mazarin, la Fronde," etc., 8 vols., 1836; "Blackwood's Magazine" for February, 1820.

Cinquarbres. See CINQ-ARBRES.

Cintra, de, då sèn'kå, (GONÇALO,) a Portuguese navigator, discovered the Bay of Cintra, on the coast of Africa. Died in 1445.

Ciofano, cho-fä'no, (ERCOLE,) an Italian poet and critic, born at Sulmona, wrote admired "Commentaries on the Works of Ovid," (1575,) and other short works.

Cionacci, cho-nät'chee, (FRANCESCO,) an Italian writer, born at Florence in 1633; died in 1714.

Cione, (ANDREA.) See ORCAGNA.

Cipelli. See EGNAZIO.

Cipierre, de, dęh se'pe-air', (PHILIBERT de Mar-silly—dęh mǎr'se'ye',) SEIGNEUR, a French general who served in the Catholic army in the civil war, (1562.) He was governor of the king's son, who became Charles IX. De Thou represents him as an able general and a good man. Died in 1566.

See DE THOU, "Histoire Universelle."

Cipriani, che-pRe-ä'nee, (GIOVANNI BATTISTA,) a skilful Italian artist, born at Florence about 1730. He removed to London about 1755, after which he devoted himself principally to engraving. He was one of the first members of the Royal Academy of London. His paintings are not numerous. His designs, engraved partly by himself and partly by Bartolozzi, are admired for correctness and grace. Among his engravings are "The Death of Cleopatra," after Cellini, and a "Descent from the Cross," after Van Dyck. Died in 1785.

See LANZI, "History of Painting in Italy."

Çir'çe, [Κίρκη,] a sorceress of the Greek mythology, celebrated for her skill in magic arts, was said to be a daughter of the Sun. She lived on the island Æoea, and tempted voyagers with a beverage which transformed those who drank it into swine. (See the "Odyssey," book x.)

Circignano, chèR-chèn-yä'no, or **Circignani,** chèR-chèn-yä'nee, (NICCOLÒ,) a painter, born at Pomerance, in Tuscany, in 1516, was called IL POMERANCIO. He painted some halls of the Vatican. His manner was grand, his design pure and correct. Died about 1590.

His son, ANTONIO, was an able painter. He worked at Rome with his father. Died about 1620.

Cirillo, che-rèl'lo, (DOMENICO,) an Italian physician and savant of great merit, born at Grugno in 1734. In his youth he accompanied Lady Walpole to England, and was chosen a Fellow of the Royal Society of London. On his return to Italy he became professor of medicine and an eminent practitioner in Naples. He published an excellent work on botanical philosophy, "Fundamenta Botanica," (1771,) which displays great knowledge of physiology; a Flora of the Kingdom of Naples, ("Plantarum rariorum Regni Neapolitani," 1788–93,) and several other scientific and medical treatises. In 1799 he was chosen a legislator in the new Parthenopean republic; but the royalists recovered power, and he was put to death in the same year. The king offered him his life if he would beg for pardon; but this he refused, saying that he did not fear death.

See "Nouvelle Biographie Générale."

Cirillo, (NICCOLÒ,) born in Naples in 1671, became professor of medicine in that city in 1706. He wrote a "Memoir on Earthquakes," published in the London "Philosophical Transactions." Died in 1734.

Ciro, the Italian of CYRUS, which see.

Ciro Ferri. See FERRI, (CIRO.)

Ciruelo, the-roo-ä'lo, (PEDRO,) a Spanish mathematician and writer, born in Aragon, was one of the preceptors of Philip II. Died about 1550.

Cisinge, de, dęh se'zånzh', (JEAN,) commonly called, in Latin, JA'NUS PANNO'NIUS, a Latin poet, born in Hungary in 1434. At the age of twenty-six he was chosen Bishop of Fünfkirchen. His poems have passed through many editions. Died in 1472.

Cisner, tsis'ner, (NICHOLAS,) a German historian, born at Morbach in 1529. He became professor of law at Heidelberg, and was afterwards councillor of the imperial court at Spire for fourteen years. He wrote good Latin verses, and published historical works, among which is an edition of Krantz's "History of Saxony." Died in 1583.

See NICÉRON, "Mémoires."

Cisneros. See XIMENES, CARDINAL.

Citois, se'twä', [Lat. CITO'SIUS,](FRANÇOIS,) a French medical writer, born at Poitiers in 1572; died in 1652.

Citolini, che-to-lee'nee, (ALESSANDRO,) an Italian poet, born at Seravalla about 1520.

Citri de la Guette, se'tRe' dęh lä gět, an author whose nationality is unknown, lived about 1680–1700. He published in Paris several esteemed works, viz., "History of the Conquest of Jerusalem by Saladin," (1679,) "History of the Two Triumvirates," (1681,) and "History of the Conquest of Mexico," translated from the Spanish, (1691.)

Cittadella. See LOMBARDI, (ALFONSO.)

Cittadella, chèt-tå-del'lå, (GIOVANNI,) COUNT, an Italian historian, born at Padua in 1806. His principal work is a "History of the Domination [of the family] of Carrara," ("Storia della Dominazione Carrarese," 1842.)

Cittadini, chèt-tå-dee'nee, (CELSO,) one of the most learned Italian writers of his time, born in Rome in 1553, published a "Treatise on the Origin and Progress of our Language," "Rime Platoniche del Celso Cittadini," ("Platonic Rhymes," etc.,) and other works. Died in 1627.

See "Vita di C. Cittadini," prefixed to his works by G. GIGLI, Rome, 1721.

Cittadini, (PIETRO FRANCESCO,) an Italian painter, born at Milan about 1615, and surnamed IL MILANESE, was a pupil of Guido. After painting a few historical pieces, which gave promise of high excellence, he renounced that branch of art, and confined himself to easel-pictures of animals, flowers, fruit, etc. Died in 1681.

See LANZI, "History of Painting in Italy."

Çiva. See SIVA.

Civerchio, che-vèR'ke-o, (VINCENZO,) an Italian painter and engraver, called IL VECCHIO DI CREMA, (èl vek'ke-o dee krä'må,) was born at Crema, and flourished about 1500–30. He worked mostly at Milan.

See VASARI, "Lives of the Painters."

Civiale, se've'äl', (JEAN,) a French physician, born at Thiézac (Cantal) in 1792. He distinguished himself by discoveries or improvements in the operation of lithotrity, and published several works on that specialty, among which is a "Treatise on the Calculous Disease," ("Traité de l'Affection calculeuse," 1838.) He was elected to the Institute in 1847. Died in June, 1867.

Ci-vi'lis, (CLAUDIUS,) a chief of the Batavi, who served twenty-five years in the Roman army, and was converted into an enemy of Rome by the unjust execution of his brother, Julius Paulus, and the ill treatment of himself. His remarkable heroism and exploits are elaborately described by Tacitus, who devotes to the subject a large part of the last two books of his history. While Vitellius and Vespasian contended for the empire of Rome, some partisans of the latter persuaded Civilis to make a show of insurrection, in order to detain in Gaul the Roman army, which was mostly favourable to Vitellius. Having raised a large force, 69 A.D., he rebelled in earnest, was joined by many Germans and Gauls, gained several victories, and was hailed as the liberator of his country. Vespasian sent another army, under Cerealis, who, after defeating Civilis in battle, induced him, by a promised amnesty, to desist from hostilities, in 70 A.D. The history of Tacitus ends abruptly in the midst of a speech of Civilis, in his interview with Cerealis, on a bridge across the Vahalis or Nabalia. "There is," says Motley, "more than a fanciful resemblance between Civilis and William the Silent,—two heroes of ancient German stock." ("Rise of the Dutch Republic," vol. i.)

See, also, "Levensgeschiedenis van C. Civilis," the Hague, 1841; J. MARCHAL, "Notice sur l'Insurrection de Civilis," 1846.

Civitali, che-ve-tå'lee, (MATTEO,) an eminent Italian sculptor, born at Lucca about 1435. He was a barber until he had attained the age of thirty, after which he became so skilful in art that his works were compared to those of Michael Angelo. He worked in Lucca and

є as k; ç as s; g̃ hard; ġ as j; G, H, K, guttural; N, nasal; R, trilled; s̃ as z; th as in this. (☞See Explanations, p. 23.)

39

Genoa, the cathedral of which contains several statues by him. Died about 1500.

See VASARI, "Lives of the Painters and Sculptors."

Civoli. See CIGOLI.

Claesson, klâs'son, (ARNOLD,) a Dutch painter, born at Leyden in 1498; died in 1564.

Clag'ett, (NICHOLAS,) D.D., an English divine, born in 1654, became Archdeacon of Sudbury in 1693. He published "Truth Defended," in answer to Whiston, and other works. Died in 1726.

Clagett, (WILLIAM,) D.D., born in 1646, wrote many theological works, chiefly controversial. Died in 1688.

Clag'gett, (JOHN THOMAS,) born in Prince George county, Maryland, in 1742, became in 1792 the first Episcopalian bishop in that State. Died in 1818.

Clai or **Clay,** klī, [Lat. CLA'JUS,] (JOHANN,) a German poet and philologist, born at Herzberg, Saxony, about 1533. He was professor of Latin, Greek, and Hebrew in several colleges in Saxony and Silesia. Among his chief works are a "Grammar of the German Language," the best that had then appeared, and "Alkumistica," (1586,) a poem against the alchemists, prized as a monument of early German poetry. Died in 1592.

See GOTTSCHED, "Kritische Beiträge."

Claiborne, klā'burn, (WILLIAM C. C.,) an American statesman, born in Virginia, became Governor of Mississippi Territory in 1801, and in 1803 Governor-General and Intendant of Louisiana. Died in 1817, aged forty-two.

See "National Portrait-Gallery of Distinguished Americans," vol. iv.

Clairac, de, deh klâ'ràk', (LOUIS ANDRÉ DE LA MARIE,) a French writer and engineer, born about 1690. He wrote a "History of the Revolutions of Persia," and a "Treatise on Fortification." Died in 1750.

Clairault. See CLAIRAUT.

Clairaut or **Clairault,** klâ'rō', (ALEXIS CLAUDE,) an eminent French geometer, born in Paris in 1713. About the age of ten he mastered L'Hôpital's analysis of "Infinitesimals," ("Infiniment Petits,") and in his thirteenth year presented to the Academy of Sciences a Memoir on Four Remarkable Curves. In 1731 he produced his "Researches on Curves of Double Curvature." Though under the regular age, he was admitted into the Academy of Sciences in the same year. He assisted Maupertuis in measuring a degree of the meridian in Lapland in 1735, and published in 1743 his "Theory of the Figure of the Earth." His "Theory of the Moon derived from the Simple Principle of Attraction" (1750) is another of his titles to celebrity as the successor of Newton. He was the first who applied the theory of Newton to estimate the perturbing influence of planets on the motions of comets. Aided by Lalande and others in his immense calculations of the action of Jupiter and Saturn, he predicted the return of Halley's comet in 1759, and missed the exact time by about twenty-two days,—part of this error being caused by the action of Uranus, then unknown. For this grand demonstration he had prepared the formulas with the simplicity and clearness which characterize all his works. He published in 1760 a "Theory of the Motion of Comets." In addition to the books which we have named, he published two admirable works, entitled "Elements of Geometry" and "Elements of Algebra." Died in 1765.

See QUÉRARD, "La France Littéraire;" "Biographie Universelle;" "Nouvelle Biographie Généra'e."

Clairé, klâ'rà', (MARTIN,) a French poet, born in 1612, wrote elegant Latin hymns. Died in 1690.

Clairfait. See CLERFAYT.

Clairfontaine, de, deh klâr'fôn'tàn', (PIERRE ANDRÉ Peloux—pèh-loo',) a French dramatist, born in Paris in 1727. He composed about 1750 the tragedy of "Hector," the style of which is admired. Died in 1788.

Clairon, klâ'rôn', (Mademoiselle CLAIRE JOSEPHE Leyris de la Tude,** là're' deh là tüd,) a famous French actress, born near Condé (Flanders) in 1723. She made her début at the Opera of Paris in 1743, and before the end of that year at the Comédie Française, where her success was complete. She retired from the stage in 1765, and died in 1803, leaving a volume of "Memoirs," (1799.)

See LEMONTEY, "Notice sur Mlle. Clairon," 1823; "Nouvelle Biographie Générale;" "Fraser's Magazine" for September, 1853.

Clairval, klâr'vàl', the assumed name of JEAN BAPTISTE **Guignard,** (zhôN bàp'tèst' gèn'yàR',) a popular French actor, born at Étampes in 1735. He performed in Paris from 1758 to 1792. Died in 1795.

Clairville, klâr'vèl', (LOUIS FRANÇOIS NICOLAIE,) a French dramatist, born at Lyons in 1811. He has produced a great number of successful farces, vaudevilles, etc., among which are "Clarissa Harlowe," (1846,) "The Bourgeois of Paris," (1850,) and "The Side-Scenes (Coulisses) of Life," (1852.)

Claissens, klâ'sôN', (ANTOINE,) a Flemish painter who lived about 1490, was a pupil of Quentin Matsys of Antwerp. He painted two pictures of the "Judgment of Cambyses." They were taken to the Museum of Paris in the reign of Napoleon I.

Clajus, the Latin of CLAI, which see.

Clamenges, de, deh klȁ'môNzh', or **Clémangis,** klȁ'môN'zhèss', (MATHIEU NICOLAS,) a French theologian, was born at Clamenges, near Châlons, about 1360. He was chosen rector of the University of Paris in 1393. Among his works (in Latin) is one "On the Corrupt State of the Church." He wrote an elegant style, and had as high a reputation as any writer of that age. Died about 1440.

See ADOLPHE MUNTZ, "N. de Clémangis; sa Vie et ses Écrits," 1846; CAVE, "Scriptorum ecclesiasticorum Literaria Historia."

Clam-Martinitz or **Clam-Martinico,** klȁm-màR-tee'nitz, (KARL JOSEPH,) COUNT, an Austrian general, born at Prague in 1792. He accompanied Napoleon to Elba in 1814, and was called to take part in the Congress of Vienna, (1815.) About 1824 he was sent on a diplomatic mission to St. Petersburg. He became first aide-de-camp to the Austrian emperor in 1835, and field-marshal-lieutenant in 1837. Died in 1840.

Clan'cy, (MICHAEL,) M.D., an Irish dramatist, wrote "The Sharpers," (1737,) and other plays. Died about 1760.

Clanricarde, klan're-kard, (ULICK,) MARQUIS OF, and Earl of Saint Alban's, born in London in 1604, was the chief of the noble family of Burgho or De Burgh. He was appointed governor of Galway in 1641. In the civil war he supported Charles I. and held a high command in Ireland. He died about 1658, leaving "Memoirs respecting the Rebellion in Ireland," (1737.)

Clap, (THOMAS,) a clergyman, born in Scituate, Massachusetts, in 1703. In 1739 he was elected president of Yale College, to which he rendered important services. Died in 1767.

Claparède, klȁ'pà'ràd', COUNT, a French general, born at Gignac (Hérault) in 1774. He commanded a brigade at Austerlitz, (1805,) and at Jena, (1806.) About 1808 he was made a general of division. He distinguished himself at Ebersberg, Essling, and Wagram, in 1809, and was wounded at the passage of the Berezina in 1812. He became inspector-general of infantry about 1816, and was raised to the peerage by Louis XVIII. Died in 1841 or 1842.

See DE COURCELLES, "Dictionnaire des Généraux Français;" "Notice sur le Général Claparède," 1843.

Clapisson, klȁ'pe'sôN', (LOUIS,) a French composer of successful operas, was born at Naples in 1809.

Clapp, (THEODORE,) an eloquent Unitarian minister, born in Easthampton, Massachusetts, in 1792, graduated at Yale College in 1814. In 1822 he became pastor of a church in New Orleans, where he preached about thirty-five years, during the prevalence of many fatal epidemics. He published, in 1858, "Autobiographical Sketches." Died in 1866.

Clapp, (WILLIAM W.,) JR., an American journalist, born in Boston in 1826, succeeded his father in 1847 as editor of the Boston "Saturday Evening Gazette."

Clap'per-ton, (HUGH,) CAPTAIN, a Scottish traveller and explorer of Africa, was born at Annan, Dumfriesshire, in 1788. He served some years in the British navy. In 1822, under the auspices of Lord Bathurst, he was associated with Dr. Oudney and Dixon Denham in an expedition to Timbuctoo. They arrived in February, 1823, at Lake Tchad, where Clapperton parted from Denham and pursued his journey until he reached Saccatoo. From that point he returned homeward by the same route, and arrived in England in 1825. (See DENHAM, DIXON.) In the same year he was raised to the

ă, ē, ī, ō, ū, ȳ, long; ă, ĕ, ĭ, ŏ, ŭ, ўु, same, less prolonged; ä, ĕ, ĭ, ŏ, ŭ, ў, short; ạ, ẹ, ị, ọ, obscure; fär, fäll, fât; mêt; nŏt; gŏŏd; mōōn;

rank of captain, and renewed the perilous enterprise with a more numerous party, among whom was his faithful servant, Richard Lander. Approaching this time from the west, he penetrated the Bight of Benin to Saccatoo in the spring of 1826. There he was detained about a year by the native prince; and he died of dysentery near that town in April, 1827. An interesting journal of his second expedition was published in 1829. Denham and Clapperton made important contributions to the geography of Africa, though they failed in the chief object of their expedition,—to discover the course and termination of the Niger.

See LANDER, "Records of Captain Clapperton," 1830; CHAMBERS, "Biographical Dictionary of Eminent Scotsmen."

Clarac, de, dẹh klả'rȧk', (CHARLES OTHON FRÉDÉRIC JEAN BAPTISTE,) COUNT, a French antiquary and artist, born in Paris in 1777. After a visit to South America, from which he brought many designs, he was appointed keeper of the Museum of Antiques in the Louvre about 1816. His most important work is called "Musée de Sculpture," (1826–52,) in which a vast number of antique statues, etc. are reproduced by engravings. Died in 1847.

See HÉRICART DE THURY, "Notice sur le Comte de Clarac," 1848.

Claramonte, de, dȧ klȧ-rȧ-mon'tȧ, (ANDRES,) a Spanish dramatist, whose reputation was founded chiefly on a comedy called "The Brave Negro in Flanders," ("El Negro valiente en Flandes.") Died at Murcia in 1610.

Clāre, (JOHN,) an English peasant and poet, born in Northamptonshire in 1793, was a son of a poor labourer. A "Sonnet to the Setting Sun" (1818) was the first of his works that attracted public attention. He published in 1820 "Poems descriptive of Rural Life and Scenery," which have considerable merit. A small annuity was settled on him by subscription; but he failed to support his increasing family, and fell into a state of despondency, followed by mental derangement. Died in 1864.

See SAMUEL SMILES, "Brief Biographies;" "London Quarterly Review" for May, 1820.

Clare, (JOHN HOLLIS,) EARL OF, a learned nobleman of the seventeenth century, was father-in-law of the famous Earl of Strafford. He wrote comments on Bacon's "Essay on Empire," and other works.

Clarence, DUKE OF. See WILLIAM IV. of England.

Clăr'en-dọn, (EDWARD HYDE,) first EARL OF, an eminent English historian and statesman, born at Dinton, Wiltshire, in 1608, was the third son of Henry Hyde, of that place. After leaving Oxford University he studied law, under the direction of his uncle, Nicholas Hyde, who was afterwards chief justice. In 1632 he married Frances Aylesbury, by whom he had several children. In his youth he made it a rule to associate only with persons eminent for rank, fortune, or other advantages. He was elected to Parliament in the spring of 1640, and again to the Long Parliament, which met near the end of that year. During the first year of his political course he acted with the popular party in their efforts for reform, and in the impeachment of Strafford; but in the great crisis of 1642 he espoused with zeal the royalist cause. He soon became one of the confidential advisers of the king, who requested him, with two others, to conduct his affairs in the House of Commons. He was the author of the able state papers issued by the king about the beginning of the civil war, (1642.) In 1643 he was appointed chancellor of the exchequer, and privy councillor. He was selected in 1645 as a counsellor to the Prince of Wales, whom he followed in his flight to Jersey in 1646. Remaining there when Prince Charles went to France, Hyde began his great work, the "History of the Rebellion and Civil Wars." After the execution of the king he received the title of lord chancellor, and was employed in the service of Charles II., and became his chief adviser while he was an exile in France, Holland, etc.

At the restoration of 1660 Hyde became prime minister of Charles II., lord chancellor of England, and in 1661 Earl of Clarendon. Soon after his promotion it was announced that his daughter, Anne Hyde, was recognized as the wife of the king's brother, the Duke of York. "For some time," says Hume, "no minister was ever possessed of more absolute authority, and all the counsels which he gave the king tended equally to promote the interest of prince and people." In the opinion of Macaulay, "the circumstance that he had long been an exile completely disqualified him for the supreme direction of affairs. . . . His virtues and vices alike contributed to his ruin." By opposing popery he lost the favour of Charles, and by various measures he ruined his popularity with the nation. He was deprived of the great seal in August, 1667, and was impeached by the Commons; but before the case was decided he retired to France, and was doomed by act of Parliament, December, 1767, to perpetual exile. After passing four years at Montpellier, he died at Rouen in December, 1674, leaving his title to his son Henry, noticed below. Two of his granddaughters, Mary and Anne Stuart, became queens of England. His celebrated History was published in 1702. "His majesty and eloquence," says Horace Walpole, "his power of painting characters, his knowledge of the subject, rank him in the first class of writers: yet he has both great and little faults." "His style is prolix and redundant," says Hume, "but it discovers imagination and sentiment, and it pleases us at the same time that we disapprove of it." "He was wise," says the "Edinburgh Review" for January, 1839, "neither for himself nor for his country. Belonging to the past rather than the future, he associated himself with causes which must fail and with parties whom he despised."

See "Life of Edward, Earl of Clarendon," by himself, 1759; T. H. LISTER, "Life of Lord Clarendon," 3 vols., 1838; MACAULAY, "History of England;" HUME, "History of England;" GEORGE A. ELLIS, "Historical Inquiries respecting the Character of Edward Hyde," etc.; CAMPBELL, "Lives of the Chancellors;" FOSS, "The Judges of England;" "Monk's Contemporaries," by GUIZOT.

Clarendon, (GEORGE WILLIAM FREDERICK VILLIERS,) fourth EARL OF, an eminent English statesman, the eldest son of the Hon. George Villiers, who was a younger son of the Earl of Clarendon, was born in January, 1800. He was minister plenipotentiary at the court of Madrid about five years, (1833–38.) In 1838 he succeeded, by the death of his uncle, to the title of Earl, and in 1840 was appointed lord privy seal in the Whig ministry. He married in 1839 a sister of the Earl of Verulam. He retired from office on the formation of a new ministry by Sir Robert Peel in 1841, and became president of the Board of Trade on the return of the Whigs to power in 1846. He was lord lieutenant of Ireland from May, 1847, until February, 1852. His administration of that country, then greatly agitated, displayed a union of moderation, energy, and prudence. In January, 1853, he accepted the office of secretary of foreign affairs in the ministry of Lord Aberdeen. He maintained his high reputation as a diplomatist in the negotiations which resulted in a coalition against Russia, and was retained in the foreign department when a new ministry was formed by Lord Palmerston in February, 1855. He was the principal negotiator on the part of Great Britain at the Congress of Paris by which peace was concluded between the allies and Russia in 1856. Lord Clarendon resigned office with Palmerston on the defeat of the latter in 1858. He succeeded Earl Russell as secretary of foreign affairs, November 3, 1865. In consequence of the defeat of the Reform Bill, he resigned, with his colleagues, in June, 1866, and refused to take office in the coalition ministry which Lord Derby attempted to form. He was appointed secretary of foreign affairs by Mr. Gladstone in December, 1868.

Clarendon, (HENRY HYDE,) second EARL OF, the eldest son of the historian, was born in 1638. After the banishment of his father, he opposed the court party. In 1685 his brother-in-law, James II., appointed him lord privy seal, and, a few months later, lord lieutenant of Ireland. His brother, the Earl of Rochester, was then prime minister; but because he refused to renounce his religion he was dismissed in 1687, and Clarendon, though a very obsequious courtier, was involved in his fall. "The dismission of the two brothers," says Macaulay, "is a great epoch in the reign of James." In December, 1688, he deserted James, and joined the party of the Prince of Orange. The next year he refused to take the oath to William III., and in 1690, for complicity in a Jacobite plot, was confined in the Tower about six months. He died in 1709, leaving a son Henry, who was Lord Cornbury. In 1828 was published "The

"Clarendon Papers," a work of great historical value, consisting of the correspondence of Henry Hyde with his brother, the Earl of Rochester.

See MACAULAY, "History of England," especially vols. ii. and iii. ; and "Monk's Contemporaries," by GUIZOT.

Claret de Fleurieu. See FLEURIEU.

Clari, klä′ree, (GIAN CARLO MARIA,) an Italian musician and composer, born at Pisa in 1669. He composed vocal duets and trios, published in 1720.

Clarici, klä′re-chee, (PAOLO BARTOLOMMEO,) an Italian botanist and priest, born at Ancona in 1664. He died at Padua in 1724, leaving unfinished works on history and geography, and a valuable treatise on botany, entitled "History and Culture of Plants which are most desirable for the Flowers," etc., (1726.)

Clär′idge, (RICHARD,) an eminent writer and minister of the Society of Friends, born at Farmborough, England, in 1649. Having graduated at Oxford, he took orders, and became rector of Peopleton in 1673. In 1697 he joined the Society of Friends, among whom he became an esteemed minister. He published several religious works, one of which was entitled "Gospel Light," ("Lux Evangelica.") Died in 1723.

See JOSEPH BESSE, "Life of R. Claridge," 1726.

Clarisse, klä-ris′sẹh, (JAN,) a Dutch theologian, born in 1770 ; died in 1846.

Cla′rĭ-us or **Clario,** klä′re-o, (ISIDORE,) a learned Italian, born near Brescia in 1495, was Bishop of Foligno. He distinguished himself by his talents and eloquence at the Council of Trent, (1546,) which followed his advice in recognizing the Vulgate version of Scripture as the most authentic. He published a revised edition of the Vulgate. Died in 1555.

See NICÉRON, "Mémoires ;" DE THOU, "Éloges."

Clark, (ABRAHAM,) an American patriot, born at Elizabethtown, New Jersey, in 1726. He was elected in 1776 a delegate to the Continental Congress, in which he signed the Declaration of Independence. He was re-elected to Congress several times. Died in 1794.

Clark, (ALVAN,) an American portrait-painter and mechanician, born in Ashfield, Massachusetts, in 1804. He distinguished himself as a fabricator of telescopes and achromatic object-glasses.

Clark, (DAVIS W.,) a Methodist minister, born on the island of Mount Desert, Maine, in 1812. He was elected editor of books at the "Methodist Book Concern" in Cincinnati in 1852. He wrote several works on theology, etc.

Clark or **Clarke,** (GEORGE ROGERS,) an American general, born probably in Virginia about 1752. He took a British fort and garrison at Vincennes in 1779, and built Fort Jefferson, on the Mississippi River. In 1780 he fought against Benedict Arnold in Virginia. He was raised to the rank of brigadier-general in 1781, and, after the end of the war, settled in Kentucky. He died in 1808, or, as some say, 1817.

See "National Portrait-Gallery of Distinguished Americans," vol. iv.

Clark, (Sir JAMES,) a distinguished British physician, born at Cullen, Banffshire, in 1788. He was educated at Aberdeen, Edinburgh, and London, practised eight years in Rome, between 1818 and 1826, and settled in London about 1828. In 1829 he published his valuable work "On the Sanative Influence of Climate," which is perhaps the most philosophical treatise on that subject. He was chosen a Fellow of the Royal Society in 1832, and became physician to the Duchess of Kent and the Princess Victoria in 1835. His "Treatise on Pulmonary Consumption and Scrofulous Diseases" (1835) is highly commended. On the accession of Victoria, in 1837, he was appointed her physician-in-ordinary. He was made a baronet in 1838.

Clark, (JOHN.) See CLARKE.

Clark, (JOHN,) a Scottish physician, born at Roxburgh in 1744. He was for some years surgeon in the service of the East India Company, and also practised at Newcastle. He published a "Treatise on Fevers," and other professional works. Died in 1805.

Clark, (JOHN,) an English critic and scholar, was master of a grammar-school at Hull. He published an "Essay on Study," and edited several Latin authors. Died in 1734.

Clark, (JONAS,) a patriotic clergyman, born at Newton, Massachusetts, in 1730. He preached for many years at Lexington, in that State. Died in 1805.

Clark, (LEWIS GAYLORD,) an American writer, born at Otisco, New York, in 1810. He became in 1834 editor of the "Knickerbocker Magazine," which he conducted many years with ability and success. He published, in 1852, "Knick-Knacks from an Editor's Table."

Clark, (SHELDON,) born at Oxford, Connecticut, in 1785. He gave to Yale College a large sum of money, with directions that twenty thousand dollars should be applied to found a professorship of moral philosophy. Died in 1840.

Clark, (WILLIAM,) an American general and explorer, born in Virginia in 1770, was a brother of George Rogers Clark. Captain M. Lewis and he were the leaders of an exploring expedition which by order of the government crossed the continent from Saint Louis to the mouth of the Columbia River in 1804. He was afterwards appointed a brigadier-general, and was Governor of Missouri Territory from 1813 to 1820. Died at Saint Louis in 1838.

See "London Quarterly Review" for January, 1815.

Clark, (WILLIAM TIERNEY,) F.R.S., an English civil engineer, born at Sion House, Somerset, in 1783. In 1811 he became engineer of West Middlesex Waterworks. He built a suspension bridge over the Thames at Hammersmith, finished about 1827. The principal monument of his skill is the suspension bridge across the Danube between Buda and Pesth, finished about 1850. Died in 1852.

Clark, (WILLIS GAYLORD,) an American poet, born at Otisco, New York, in 1810, was a twin-brother of Lewis Gaylord, noticed above. He produced in 1833 "The Spirit of Life," his longest poem, and about that time became associate editor of the "Columbian Star." He contributed to the "Knickerbocker Magazine" a series of amusing papers called "Ollapodiana." During the last years of his life he was editor and owner of the "Philadelphia Gazette." Died in 1841.

See GRISWOLD's "Poets and Poetry of America."

Clarke, (ADAM,) LL.D., an eminent Methodist minister, particularly distinguished as a biblical commentator, was born near Londonderry, Ireland, in 1762. He was educated in the principles of the Methodists, and, by the favour of John Wesley, was admitted into a school at Kingswood, near Bristol. In 1782 he became an itinerant preacher, and for more than twenty years he continued to preach with acceptance in various parts of England. About 1805 he settled in London, and began his principal work, a "Commentary on the Holy Bible," which was published between 1810 and 1826, and is a wonderful monument of his learning and industry. Some persons, however, think that he is too fond of innovations, and that many of his comments are exceptionable. He was the author of other esteemed works, among which are a "Bibliographical Dictionary," (1802,) "The Succession of Sacred Literature," (1807,) "Memoirs of the Wesley Family," and "The Eucharist." He had been from childhood eager in the pursuit of knowledge, and had acquired extensive Oriental learning, although he never had the advantage of a systematic or collegiate education. Died of cholera in London in 1832.

See J. B. CLARKE, "Religious and Literary Life of Adam Clarke," 1833; JAMES EVERETT, "Adam Clarke Portrayed," 3 vols., 1850.

Clarke, (ALURED,) an English clergyman, born in 1696, was Dean of Exeter. Died about 1740.

Clarke, (Sir ARTHUR,) an English or Irish medical writer and philanthropist, born in 1773. He wrote an "Essay on Bathing," "Diseases of the Skin," and other works. He founded a hospital in Dublin. Died in 1857.

Clarke, (EDWARD,) an English clergyman, born in 1730, became rector of Pepperharrow in 1758. Having visited Spain as chaplain to an embassy, he published "Letters concerning the Spanish Nation," (1765,) which treat of antiquities and literature. Died in 1786.

Clarke, (EDWARD DANIEL,) LL.D., a distinguished English traveller, son of the preceding, born at Willingdon, in Sussex, in 1769. In 1790 he became tutor to a nephew of the Duke of Dorset, with whom he made the tour of Great Britain. As companion to Lord Ber-

ā, ē, ī, ō, ū, ȳ, *long;* ă, ĕ, ĭ, ŏ, *same, less prolonged;* ă, ĕ, ĭ, ŏ, ŭ, ў, *short;* ạ, ẹ, ị, ọ, *obscure;* fär, fäll, fät; mēt; nŏt; gŏŏd; mŏŏn;

wick, he visited France, Switzerland, and Italy in 1792. About 1798 he was elected a Fellow of Jesus College, at Cambridge. In 1799, in company with Mr. Cripps, he started on the extensive tour by the description of which he has acquired such merited and durable celebrity. They were absent more than three years, during which they traversed Northern Europe, Asia Minor, Syria, Palestine, Egypt, Greece, Turkey, etc. He published in 1810 the first volume of his "Travels in Various Parts of Europe, Asia, and Africa," (6 vols.,) one of the most delightful and popular books of travel that have ever appeared. In 1808 Cambridge University founded for him a professorship of mineralogy, in which he was well versed, and on which he published a treatise, "The Mineral Kingdom." Having taken orders, he obtained the living of Yeldham about 1810. Died in 1822.

See WILLIAM OTTER, "Life and Remains of Edward Daniel Clarke," London, 1824; "London Quarterly Review" for August, 1810, and March, 1813; "Edinburgh Review" for August, 1810, and June, 1826.

Clarke, (ELIJAH,) an American general, born in North Carolina. He served in the Revolutionary war. Died about 1800.

Clarke, (GEORGE ROGERS.) See CLARK.

Clarke, klärk, (HENRI JACQUES GUILLAUME,) Duc de Feltre, (fĕltr,) an able French general and minister of state, was born at Landrecies in 1765. As lieutenant-colonel he served in the campaign of 1792, and had become general of brigade, when the Convention in 1793 deprived him of his command on account of his being a noble. In 1794, by the influence of Carnot, he was placed at the head of the topographical bureau in the ministry of war. For his important services in this office he was made general of division in 1795. The next year the Directory, alarmed at the success of Bonaparte in Italy, sent Clarke to negotiate with Austria, and to oversee or control the victorious general, who soon won him over to his interest. About 1804 Bonaparte appointed him councillor of state, and employed him in his cabinet as secretary. On the capture of Vienna by the French, (1805,) he was appointed governor of that city and of several Austrian provinces, which he ruled with probity and moderation. In 1806–07 he was governor of Berlin. From 1807 to 1814 he performed the functions of minister of war with such success that he received the title of Duc de Feltre in 1809. Having concurred in the deposition of Napoleon in 1814, he was created a peer by Louis XVIII., whom he served as minister of war in 1815 and 1816, and who made him a marshal of France. Died in 1818.

See "Victoires et Conquêtes des Français ;" "Nouvelle Biographie Générale."

Clarke, (HENRY,) an English mathematician, born at Salford, near Manchester, in 1745. After he had lectured on mathematics and natural philosophy at Manchester, he was chosen professor in the Royal Military College at Marlow about 1802. He published "The Summation of Series," "Practical Perspective," and other works. Died in 1818.

Clarke, (HENRY HYDE,) an English philologist and writer, born in London in 1815, became a civil engineer. He published in 1855 a "New Dictionary of the English Tongue," which is very complete. He has written various scientific works.

Clarke, (JAMES FREEMAN,) an American writer and Unitarian minister, born in 1810. He has preached for many years in Boston, and has distinguished himself as an opponent of slavery. Among his works are "The Christian Doctrine of Forgiveness," (1852,) and "The Christian Doctrine of Prayer," (1854,) also several poems.

Clarke, (JAMES STANIER,) an English writer, a brother of Edward D. Clarke, noticed above. He attended Lord Nelson as chaplain at Trafalgar, and was afterwards domestic chaplain of George IV., and canon of Windsor. He published "The Progress of Maritime Discovery," "The Life of James II.," and other works. He assisted Dr. McArthur in a "Life of Lord Nelson." Died in 1834.

Clarke, (JEREMIAH,) an English composer of church-music. He became organist of Saint Paul's Cathedral a few years before 1700. He published "Lessons for the Harpsichord," and composed the admired anthems

"I will love thee," and "Bow down thine ear." Having been unfortunate in love, he killed himself in 1707.

Clarke, (JOHN.) See CLARK, (JOHN.)

Clarke, (JOHN,) one of the founders of Rhode Island, was born in England. He emigrated to Rhode Island about 1638, and founded at Newport a Baptist church, of which he was pastor. In 1651 he was sent to England with Roger Williams as an agent of the colony, for which he procured a new charter. Died in 1676.

Clarke, (JOHN,) a Scottish engraver of portraits, born about 1650, worked in Edinburgh. Died in 1721.

Clarke, (JOHN,) D.D., an English divine, born at Norwich, was a brother of Dr. Samuel Clarke, (born in 1675.) He became chaplain-in-ordinary to the king, and finally Dean of Sarum. He published "Sermons at the Boyle Lecture," and translated into English Rohault's "Physics" and Grotius on the "Truth of the Christian Religion." Died in 1759.

Clarke, (JOHN,) an American officer, a son of Elijah, noticed above, was born in 1766. He served in the Revolutionary war, and became Governor of Georgia after 1816. Died in 1832.

Clarke, (MACDONALD,) an American writer, known for many years in New York as "the Mad Poet," was born in 1798. He published in 1820 his "Review of the Eve of Eternity, and other Poems," which was followed by "The Elixir of Moonshine : a Collection of Prose and Poetry, by the Mad Poet," in 1822. Died in 1842.

Clarke, (MARY COWDEN,) an English authoress, born in London in 1809, was a daughter of Vincent Novello, the composer. She was married in 1828 to Charles Cowden Clarke, the associate of Lamb, Keats, Shelley, etc., and soon after began "The Complete Concordance to Shakspeare," (1846.) This work, on which she spent the labour of sixteen years, was very successful. She also published "World-Noted Women," New York, 1858.

Clarke, (RICHARD,) an Episcopalian divine, born in England, became rector of Saint Philip's, Charleston, South Carolina, about 1750. He wrote several theological works.

Clarke, (SAMUEL,) an English theological writer, born at Woolston in 1599. He preached successively at Warwick, Alcester, and in London. In 1662 he was ejected for nonconformity, and thenceforward ceased to appear in the pulpit. He published a "Mirror for Saints and Sinners," (1645,) a "General Martyrology," (1651,) and "Lives of Sundry Eminent Persons," (1683,) which are considered valuable works. Died in 1682.

Clarke, (SAMUEL,) an English scholar and Orientalist, was born at Brackley in 1623. About 1655 he was made master of a boarding-school at Islington, and at the same time assisted Walton in his "Polyglot Bible." He published "Various Readings and Notes on the Chaldaic Paraphrase," and other works. Died in 1669.

Clarke, (SAMUEL,) an English divine, son of Samuel, (1599–1682,) born in 1626, was a Fellow of Pembroke Hall, Cambridge. He expended the labour of many years on "Annotations on the Scriptures," (1690,) a work which has been recommended by Owen, Baxter, Howe, and Calamy. Died about 1700.

Clarke, (Dr. SAMUEL,) a celebrated English philosopher, metaphysician, and divine, born at Norwich in October, 1675, was the son of Edward Clarke, alderman of that city. In 1691 he entered Caius College, Cambridge, where he made great progress in mathematics, and about the age of twenty-one, by an ingenious stratagem, substituted the Newtonian for the Cartesian philosophy. He effected this change by producing a more classical Latin version of Rohault's "Physics," (the text-book used at Cambridge,) with notes that virtually refuted the text. Having diligently studied theology and the ancient languages, and been ordained, he became chaplain to More, Bishop of Norwich, in 1698. The next year he published three essays on Confirmation, Baptism, and Repentance, which were followed by his "Paraphrase on the Four Gospels," (1701.) About this time he became rector of Drayton. In 1705 appeared his celebrated "Demonstration of the Being and Attributes of God," consisting of eight sermons preached at the Boyle Lecture, Oxford, and designed as a confutation of Hobbes and Spinoza by the argument a priori. The merit of this performance is variously estimated by orthodox divines ; and Pope thus alludes to it in the "Dunciad :"

"We nobly take the high priori road,
And reason downward till we doubt of God."

He translated Newton's "Optics" into Latin in 1706. Through the patronage of Bishop More, he became, about 1709, rector of Saint James's, London, and chaplain to Queen Anne. In 1712 he produced a good edition of Cæsar's "Commentaries," and "The Scripture Doctrine of the Trinity," which occasioned a long controversy and exposed him to the charge of Arianism. He wrote in defence of the Newtonian philosophy against Leibnitz, with whom he had a discussion on Philosophical Liberty and Necessity. In 1724 he was chosen master of Wigston Hospital, and published a volume of sermons. He contributed mathematical treatises to the "Philosophical Transactions" in 1728, and published in 1729 an edition of Homer, with a Latin version and notes, which long enjoyed a high reputation, and is still used by students of Homer. He died in May, 1729.

Addison calls Dr. Clarke "one of the most accurate, learned, and judicious writers this age has produced." Voltaire regarded him as a mere reasoning-machine, *(un moulin à raisonnement.)* "With a mind," says Dugald Stewart, "far inferior to that of Locke in comprehensiveness, originality, and fertility of invention, he was nevertheless the more wary and skilful disputant of the two."

See HOADLY, "Life of S. Clarke ;" WILLIAM WHISTON, "Historical Memoirs of Samuel Clarke," 1748 ; D. STEWART, "Preliminary Dissertation" in the "Encyclopædia Britannica."

Clarke, (SAMUEL,) D.D., a grandson of Dr. Samuel Clarke of Norwich, was pastor to a congregation of dissenters at Saint Alban's. He published a "Collection of the Promises of Scripture under their Proper Heads." Died in 1769.

Clarke, (SARAH J.) See LIPPINCOTT.

Clarke, (WILLIAM,) an English priest and antiquary, born in Shropshire in 1696. He became rector of Buxted in 1724, and prebendary of Chichester in 1738. He published "The Connexion of the Roman, Saxon, and English Coins." Died in 1771. EDWARD CLARKE, author of "Letters on the Spanish Nation," was his son.

Clark'son, (DAVID,) an eminent nonconformist divine, born at Bradford, England, in 1622. He was ejected from the living of Mortlake in 1662, and succeeded Dr. Owen in 1683. Baxter calls him "a divine of extraordinary worth." He published sermons and other theological treatises. Died in 1686.

Clarkson, (THOMAS,) an English philanthropist, whose name is memorably identified with the abolition of the slave-trade, was born at Wisbeach, Cambridgeshire, in 1760. He gained the first prize for a Latin dissertation in Saint John's College, Cambridge, in 1784. In the next year his interest was first excited in the question of slavery, when the vice-chancellor announced that the senior bachelors would compete for the prize by Latin essays on this subject : "Is involuntary servitude justifiable ?" He composed an essay, which was successful ; and he was so deeply impressed with the iniquity and miseries of the slave-trade that he continued to meditate on and investigate the subject, until, from a sense of duty, he resolved to devote himself entirely to the cause of the slaves. His essay led him into communion with William Dillwyn, George Harrison, and a few other "Friends" of Clarkson, who as early as 1783 had formed themselves into an anti-slavery committee. The Society of Friends had been the earliest pioneers in this reform, having in 1760 refused the privileges of fellowship to all who took part in the "guilty traffic." Clarkson collected and diffused information on the subject with unwearied zeal and diligence, and never quailed before the violence and threats of those whom self-interest made his enemies. He found a powerful coadjutor in Wilberforce, who in May, 1789, made an eloquent speech in the House of Commons against the traffic. In 1790 he spent several months in Paris, where he conferred with Mirabeau, who asked and received from him ample assistance in composing a speech on the subject. The immense efforts of Clarkson and his friends were often defeated in Parliament ; and the triumph of the cause was reserved to the ministry of Fox.

In March, 1807, the "Magna Charta of Africa was completed." In 1808 he published "The History of the Abolition of the Slave-Trade," (2 vols.) He was chosen in 1823 vice-president of the Anti-Slavery Society, just formed, and lived to witness the abolition of slavery in the West Indies in 1838. He was the author of a "Portraiture of Quakerism," and of "Memoirs of the Life of William Penn," (1813.) Died in 1846.

See THOMAS TAYLOR, "Life of T. Clarkson ;" "Thomas Clarkson : a Monograph," by JAMES ELMES, London, 1854.

Clarus, klä'rûs, (JOHANN CHRISTIAN AUGUST,) a German physician, born at Buch-am-Forst, in Franconia, in 1775. He was professor of medicine at the University of Leipsic for nearly forty years, beginning in 1810. He published "Views on the Progress of the Cholera," (1831,) and other works.

Clä'son, (ISAAC,) an American poet and actor, born in New York in 1789. He produced a continuation of Byron's "Don Juan," (1825,) and a collection of poems, entitled "Horace in New York," (1826.) He committed suicide in London in 1834.

See GRISWOLD, "Poets and Poetry of America."

Clauberg, klŏw'bĕRG, (JOHANN,) a Cartesian philosopher, born at Solingen, in Westphalia, in 1622. He taught at Herborn and Duisburg. He was one of the most profound disciples of Descartes. His works were published under the title of "Opera Philosophica," (2 vols., 1691.) Died in 1665.

See MORHOF, "Polyhistor Literarius."

Claude, the French of CLAUDIUS, which see.

Claude, klōd, (JEAN,) an eminent French Protestant minister, born at La Sauvetat, near Agen, in 1619. He preached at Nîmes and Montauban, and in 1666 became pastor of Charenton, near Paris. His eloquence and wisdom rendered him one of the most influential leaders of the Protestant cause in France. He had several disputes with Bossuet and Arnauld on theology. When the edict of Nantes was revoked, (1685,) he retired to the Hague, where he died in 1687. "Bossuet," says Hallam, "was the acknowledged champion of the Roman Church in France ; Claude was in equal pre-eminence on the other side." He was the author of a "Defence of the Reformation," (1673,) and many other works.

See ABEL RODOLPHE DE LADERIZE, "Abrégé de la Vie de M. Claude," 1687 ; BAYLE, "Historical and Critical Dictionary ;" NICÉRON, "Mémoires."

Claude, (JEAN JACQUES,) a grandson of the preceding, was born at the Hague in 1684. He became pastor of the French church in London in 1710, and died in 1712.

Claude de France, klōd deh fRŏNss, the daughter of Louis XII., was born at Romorantin in 1499. She was married to Francis I. in 1514. Historians praise her eminent virtues. Died in 1524.

Claude de Turin. See CLAUDIUS OF TURIN.

Claude Lorrain, * klaud (or klōd) lor-rän', [Fr. pron. klōd lo'râN',] the prince of landscape-painters, was born at the Château de Chamagne, in Lorraine, in 1600. His proper name was **Claude Gelée,** (zhĕh-lä'.) He went to Rome in early youth, and studied under G. Waals at Naples about two years. He then became a pupil of Agostino Tassi, a landscape-painter of Rome. There is a doubtful tradition that he served Tassi as cook, also that he was originally an apprentice to a pastry-cook. He observed with constant attention the Italian scenery, and the phenomena of nature as modified by the ever-changing hours and seasons. After a tour of two years in France and Germany, he returned to Rome in 1627, was patronized by Urban VIII., and rose rapidly to pre-eminence in his department of art. His works are not exact transcripts of real nature, but combinations of picturesque scenes, selected with taste and idealized with inimitable art. "Every period of the day, with all its elemental vicissitudes, has been successfully embodied by his magic pencil." His colouring is rich, delicate, and harmonious. His aerial perspective has probably never

* The last part of this name is often incorrectly written *Lorraine*. It should be remembered that it is an *adjective*, agreeing with Claude, in the masculine gender, which is always without the final *e*. The whole name signifies "Claude the Lorrainer." In case we should say Claude of Lorraine, it should then be written with the *e*, as reference is made to the province of Lorraine, which is feminine.

ā, ē, ī, ō, ū, ȳ, *long;* ă, ĕ, ĭ, ŏ, ŭ, ў, *short;* ą, ę, į, ǫ, *obscure;* fär, fåll, fåt; mêt; nŏt; gŏŏd; mōōn;

been equalled. Among his master-pieces are "Esther and Ahasuerus," "A Seaport at Sunset," and "The Embarkation of Saint Ursula." Died in Rome in 1682. In respect to the merit of Claude, Ruskin, the "Magnus Apollo" of art and prince of paradox, dissents from the great majority of critics. "Claude's capacities," says he, "were of the most limited kind; but he had tenderness of perception and sincerity of purpose, and he effected a revolution in art. This revolution consisted mainly in setting the sun in heaven. Till his time, no one had seriously thought of painting the sun but conventionally. . . . Claude made the sun his subject, and painted the effects of misty shadows cast by his rays over the landscape, and other delicate aerial transitions, as no one had ever done before, and, in some respects, as no one has done in oil-colour since. There was a certain foolish elegance in his work; but it resembled nothing that ever existed in the world." Reynolds used to say that "there would be another Raphael before there was another Claude."

See RUSKIN, "Modern Painters;" BRYAN, "Dictionary of Painters;" DUSSIEUX, "Les Artistes Français à l'Étranger."

Clauder, klŏw'der, (GABRIEL,) a German medical writer, born at Altenburg in 1633; died in 1691.

Clau'dĭ-ạ Gens, a patrician house of Rome, which produced many dictators, consuls, censors, etc., and from which the emperors Tiberius and Claudius were descended. The surnames of the patrician Claudii were Cæcus, Crassus, Pulcher, Sabinus, etc. They were distinguished for their pride and despotic character.

Clau'dĭ-ạn, [It. CLAUDIANO, klŏw-de-ä'no; Fr. CLAUDIEN, klŏ'de-ăn',] (CLAUDIUS CLAUDIANUS,) a distinguished Latin epic poet, born at Alexandria about 365 A.D. He became a resident of Rome, and a favourite of Stilicho, who was regent during the minority of Arcadius and Honorius. He acquired by his poems such celebrity that a statue was erected to him in the Forum of Trajan by the emperor and the senate. His principal works are "The Rape of Proserpine," a "Eulogy of Stilicho," ("De Laudibus Stilichonis,") "The War against the Getæ," ("De Bello Getico,") and satires against Eutropius and Rufinus. Some portions of these have been lost. He has a rich imagination, a picturesque style, and harmonious versification. In his religious opinions he appears to have been a pagan. The date of his death is unknown; but he was living in 408 A.D. He is regarded as the last of the Latin classic poets.

See T. MAZZO, "Vita di Claudiano," 1668; GIBBON, "Decline and Fall of the Roman Empire," chap. xxx.; ERSCH und GRUBER, "Allgemeine Encyklopaedie," and the prefatory remarks in J. M. GESNER's edition of Claudian's Works, 1759.

Claudiano. See CLAUDIAN.

Claudien. See CLAUDIAN.

Claudini, klŏw-dee'nee, or **Chiodini,** ke-o-dee'nee, (GIULIO CESARE,) an Italian physician, born at Bologna, won a high reputation by his writings, among which are "Crises and Critical Days," (1612,) and "Rational Practice," ("Empirica rationalis," 1653.) Died in 1618.

Clau'dĭ-us, [Fr. CLAUDE, klōd,] or more fully, **Tiberius Claudius Drusus Nero,** fourth Emperor of Rome, born at Lyons in 10 B.C., was the son of Drusus Nero by Antonia Minor, (who was a daughter of Mark Antony,) and was a nephew of the emperor Tiberius. Being feeble in mind and body, he took no part in public affairs during the reign of Tiberius. Caligula, who was his nephew, gave him the office of consul in 37 A.D. On the death of Caligula, in 41, Claudius was proclaimed emperor by the mutinous soldiers; and the senate, though they preferred a republic, acquiesced in the choice of the army. His accession, as usual, was signalized by acts of justice and clemency. He recalled exiles, diminished taxes, and built an aqueduct in Rome. The principal military event of his reign was his successful invasion of Britain in person. His wife, the infamous Messalina, acquired an ascendency over him, and caused senators and other innocent persons to be put to death. After she became so shameless as to marry Caius Silius, she was executed, by the order or permission of Claudius. He afterwards married his niece, Agrippina the Younger, who by a former husband had a son, L. Domitius. Having persuaded him to adopt this son, she

poisoned Claudius in 54 A.D., when her son, assuming the name of Nero, became emperor.

See SUETONIUS, "Claudius;" TACITUS, "Annales;" DION CASSIUS, "History."

Claudius, (APPIUS,) surnamed CRASSUS, a Roman decemvir of patrician rank, was elected consul in 451 B.C., soon after which he became one of the decemviri. He was notorious for his nefarious attempt to enslave and dishonour Virginia, who was rescued from his power by a tragical death. (See VIRGINIA.) Appius was imprisoned, and, according to Livy, committed suicide.

Claudius, (MARCUS AURELIUS,) surnamed GOTH'ICUS, an emperor of Rome, was born in Illyricum in 214 A.D. After having a high command under Valerian, he was proclaimed emperor by the army at the death of Gallienus, in 268. The senate confirmed this choice. The same year he defeated the rebel Aureolus in battle. In 269 he gained a decisive victory over the Goths or Scythians near Nissa, in Servia, and assumed the name of GOTHICUS. He died of an epidemic disease at Sirmium in 270, leaving a good reputation for virtue and talents. His brother, Quintilius, was proposed as his successor; but the army preferred Aurelian.

See TREBELLIUS POLLIO, "Claudius," in the "Historia Augusta;" TILLEMONT, "Histoire des Empereurs."

Claudius, klŏw'de-ŭs, (MATTHIAS,) surnamed ASMUS, and THE MESSENGER OF WANDSBECK, a popular German poet and prose writer, born at Rheinfeld, near Lubeck, in 1743. He was appointed controller (revisor) of the Bank of Altona in 1778, and resided mostly at Wandsbeck. His works consist of essays, fables, epigrams, humorous and serious poems, etc. He was the author of the famous "Rhine-Wine Song," ("Rheinweinlied.") Died at Hamburg in 1815.

See LONGFELLOW, "Poets and Poetry of Europe;" "Nouvelle Biographie Générale;" HENNINGS, "Asmus: Beiträg zur Geschichte der Literatur," etc., 1798.

Clau'dĭ-us OF TURIN [Lat. CLAU'DIUS TAURI'NUS; Fr. CLAUDE DE TURIN, klōd deh tü'råN'] was born in Spain towards the close of the eighth century. He became the chaplain of Louis le Débonnaire, who appointed him Bishop of Turin. He was very zealous in his efforts to reform the abuses which had gradually crept into the Church, and vehemently opposed the worship of images and of the cross; in consequence of which he has been styled "the Protestant of the ninth century." He was a man of great learning, and wrote commentaries on various portions of Scripture. He was publicly charged with heresy; but his death, which occurred about 840, saved him, probably, from a determined persecution.

See HODGSON, "Reformers and Martyrs before and after Luther," Philadelphia, 1867; NEANDER, "Church History."

Claudius Albinus. See ALBINUS.

Clau'dius Cæ'cus, (see'kus,) (APPIUS,) a Roman patrician, who was censor from 312 to 308 B.C. During this period he constructed the Appian Way from Rome to Capua. He was afterwards consul, and *interrex,* (or regent,) and became blind, as his surname indicates. He wrote a poem, and a legal work in prose.

Claudius Civilis. See CIVILIS.

Claudius Claudianus. See CLAUDIAN.

Claudius Herodes. See HERODES, (ATTICUS.)

Claudius Marius Victor. See VICTOR.

Claud'ĭ-us Pul'cher, (APPIUS,) a son of Publius Claudius Pulcher, was chosen prætor in 215 B.C., and in the next year was legate under Marcellus in Sicily. He was elected consul in 212, and commanded an army in the second Punic war. He was killed in a battle with Hannibal at Capua about 210 B.C.

Claudius Pulcher, (APPIUS,) a brother of the Clodius killed by Milo, was prætor in 57 B.C. and consul in 53, after which he misgoverned Cilicia about two years. On his return he was prosecuted by Dolabella, but was acquitted by the influence of Pompey and Hortensius. He became censor in the year 50, and in the exercise of that office expelled Sallust and others from the senate. Having taken the side of Pompey against Cæsar, he obtained command in Greece, where he died about 48 B.C.

Claudius Pulcher, (PUBLIUS,) a Roman general, son of Appius Claudius Cæcus, noticed above, was distinguished for his insolence and pride. He was elected consul in 249 B.C., during the first Punic war. He took command of the fleet, and, though the auspices were unfavourable, attacked the Carthaginians, who gained a decisive victory. Soon after this event he was deprived of office and disgraced.

Claudius Taurinus. See CLAUDIUS OF TURIN.

Claugh'ton, (Rev. THOMAS LEGH,) an English classical scholar, born about 1808. He was professor of poetry at Oxford from 1852 to 1857.

Clausade, de, děh klo͞'zȧd', (GEORGE JACQUES AMÉ-DÉE,) a French lawyer and writer, born in 1809. Among his works is a "Voyage to Stockholm." Died in 1847.

Clausberg, klo͞ws'běRG, (CHRISTLIEB,) a German mathematician, born in 1689, was preceptor of the prince-royal at Copenhagen, and published a "Treatise on the Law of Commerce," and an excellent "Demonstrative Arithmetic," (1732.) Died in 1751.

Clausel, klo͞'zĕl', (BERTRAND,) COUNT, a French marshal, born at Mirepoix (Ariége) in 1772. He became general of brigade in 1799, and general of division about 1804. He served with distinction in Austria in 1809, and commanded with *éclat* at Salamanca (where he was severely wounded) in 1812. Having fought for Napoleon during the Hundred Days, he was forced to fly for his life, and went to the United States in 1815. He returned to France in 1820, obtained command of the army in Africa in 1830, received a marshal's bâton in 1831, and became Governor-General of Algeria in 1835. For his ill success in an expedition against Constantine, he was recalled in 1837. Died in 1842.

See "Nouvelle Biographie Générale."

Clausel de Coussergues, klo͞'zĕl' děh koo͞'sȧRg', (JEAN CLAUDE,) a French politician, noted for intolerance, was born in Aveyron in 1759. He emigrated about 1790, and returned about 1800. After the restoration he became an ultra-royalist, and was chosen a judge of the court of cassation in 1815. Died in 1846.

Clausen, klo͞w'zĕn, (HENRIK GEORG,) an eminent Danish preacher, born in Sleswick in 1759. He became pastor of a church of Copenhagen in 1797, and continued to preach there about forty years. Died in 1840.

See ERSLEW, "Forfatter-Lexicon."

Clausen, (HENRIK NICOLAI,) a Danish theologian and statesman of great ability and influence, a son of the preceding, was born at Maribo, on the island of Laaland, in 1793. He became professor of theology in the University of Copenhagen in 1820, and developed his rationalistic doctrines in many works remarkable for learning and eloquence. Among them are "Augustin of Hippo the Interpreter of Scripture," ("Augustinus Hipponensis Sacræ Scripturæ Interpres," 1826,) "Popular Discourses on the Reformation," (1836,) and "The Augsburg Confession explained Historically and Dogmatically," (both in Danish, 1851.) In politics he is a champion of liberal principles and Danish nationality. He was elected a deputy to the States in 1840, and was the leader of the movement which resulted in the constitutional reform of 1848. About the end of that year he was appointed privy councillor and minister without a portfolio. He resigned office in 1851.

See ERSLEW, "Forfatter-Lexicon."

Clausewitz, von, fon klo͞w'zĕh-ŵits', (KARL,) a distinguished Prussian general and writer on war, born at Burg in 1780. He entered the service of Russia in 1812; served on the staff in the Russian army in 1813, and published in 1814 an "Account of the Campaign of 1813," which was favourably received. He was appointed director of the Military Academy *(allgemeine Kriegschule)* of Prussia in 1818, with the title of major-general. He died in 1831, after which appeared his "Posthumous Works," (10 vols., 1832–37.) Among these is a treatise entitled "On War," ("Vom Kriege,") which is said to be a work of extraordinary merit.

See BROCKHAUS, "Conversations-Lexikon."

Clavena, klȧ-vā'nȧ, (NICCOLÒ,) an Italian botanist, born at Belluno, lived about 1600.

Claver, klȧ-vaiR', (PEDRO,) a Spanish missionary, born about 1582. He laboured in the West Indies, and was noted for his kindness to the slaves. Died in 1654.

See SUAREZ, "Vida del P. P. Claver," 1657; FLEURIAU, "Vie du R. P. Claver," 1751.

Claveret, klȧv'rȧ', (JEAN,) a French dramatist, born at Orléans in 1590; died in 1666.

Claverhouse. See GRAHAM, (JOHN.)

Clavier, klȧ've-ȧ', (ÉTIENNE,) a French Hellenist and judge, was born at Lyons in 1762. He was judge of the criminal court in Paris under the Directory and under the empire until 1811. When the judges were urged to condemn Moreau to death, and were assured by Murat that the executive would pardon him, Clavier repelled the idea, saying, "But who will pardon us?" In 1809 he was admitted into the Institute. He contributed to the "Biographie Universelle," and published several works, among which is "Pausanias, Description de la Grèce," (6 vols.,) an edition of the Greek text, with a good French version. Died in 1817.

Clavière, klȧ've-aiR', (ÉTIENNE,) a Swiss financier and author, was born at Geneva in 1735. He removed to Paris, where, before the Revolution, he was engaged in banking. About 1789 he became a political associate of Mirabeau, who had a high opinion of his talents, and who availed himself of those talents in composing his speeches, essays, etc. In 1791 he was chosen deputy *suppléant* to the National Assembly, and was the Girondist minister of finance from March to June in 1792. Having been thrown into prison by the Jacobins, and doomed to die, he killed himself in December, 1793. He wrote treatises on Finance. "He was," says Dumont, "a man of superior intellect, and was the author of almost all Mirabeau's works on finance." ("Recollections of Mirabeau.")

See VILLAUMÉ, "Histoire de la Révolution."

Clavigero, klä-ve-hā'ro, (FRANCISCO SAVERIO,) a Mexican historian, born at Vera Cruz about 1720. He was employed about thirty years as a Jesuit missionary among the Indians of Mexico, whose history and traditions he diligently studied. In consequence of the suppression of the Jesuit order about 1767, he went to Europe, and found an asylum at Cesena, Italy, where he published, in Italian, his "Ancient History of Mexico," (1780.) It is the most complete account that has been written of the history, religion, customs, arts, and natural history of that country. Died in 1793.

See FELLER, "Biographie Universelle;" PRESCOTT, "Conquest of Mexico," vol. i. book i.

Clavijo, de, dȧ klä-vee'ho, (RUY GONZALEZ,) a Spaniard, who in 1403 was sent by Henry III. of Castile as ambassador to Tamerlane, whom he found at Samarcand. Having returned home in 1406, he published a "History of Tamerlane," with an account of the journey, which is said to be veracious and valuable.

See MARIANA, "Historia de España."

Clavijo y Fajardo or **Faxardo,** klä-vee'ho e fä-haR'do, (JOSÉ,) a Spanish writer, born in one of the Canary Islands in 1726. He published in Madrid a successful periodical, "The Thinker," ("El Pensador,") and was appointed officer or keeper of the archives in the department of state. It appears that about 1764 he was guilty of a breach of promise to Marie Caron, a French lady, whose brother, the famous Beaumarchais, appealing to the code of honour, obtained some revenge or satisfaction and published his version of the affair. This story has been dramatized by Goethe. Clavijo was editor of the "Mercurio," a political journal, from 1773 to 1793. Died in 1806.

See BEAUMARCHAIS, "Fragment de mon Voyage d'Espagne en 1764."

Clavius, klä've-ûs, (CHRISTOPH,) a learned German mathematician and Jesuit, born at Bamberg in 1537. Having visited Rome, he was employed in 1581 by Gregory XIII. to reform the calendar. He enjoyed a great reputation in his time; though he was criticised with much acrimony by Scaliger. He published many works, which were often reprinted, and among which were "Geometria Practica," (1604,) and an "Explanation of the Roman Calendar of Gregory XIII.," in Latin, (1603.) Died in 1612.

See BAILLY, "Histoire de l'Astronomie moderne;" BAYLE, "Historical and Critical Dictionary."

Clax'ton, (ALEXANDER,) a commodore in the United States navy, born in Maryland about 1790; died on the coast of Chili in 1841.

ā, ē, ī, ō, ū, ȳ, *long;* ȧ, ė, ȯ, same, less prolonged; ă, ĕ, ĭ, ŏ, ŭ, ў, *short;* ạ, ẹ, ị, ọ, *obscure;* fär, fȧll, fȧt; mĕt; nŏt; gо̄о̄d; mо̄о̄n;

Clay, (CASSIUS MARCELLUS,) an American statesman, a son of General Green Clay, noticed below, was born in Madison county, Kentucky, in 1810. He studied law, and was elected a member of the legislature of Kentucky several times between 1835 and 1841. His acknowledged abilities and rare force of character seemed to anticipate a distinguished political career; but his anti-slavery principles prevented the brilliant success he might otherwise have achieved. He raised his voice boldly against slavery, and opposed the annexation of Texas to the Union. He advocated the election of Henry Clay to the Presidency in 1844 by speeches in the Northern States. In 1845 he began to edit "The True American," an anti-slavery paper, published at Lexington, Kentucky. He encountered violent opposition, and defended himself courageously against the mob in several bloody conflicts. He served as captain in the Mexican war with distinction, (1846–47.) About 1850 he separated from the Whig party. He favoured the election of Abraham Lincoln to the Presidency in 1860, and received a commission as general of volunteers in 1861. In 1862 or 1863 he was appointed minister to Russia, which position he held until the spring of 1869, when Governor Curtin, of Pennsylvania, was appointed in his place. His writings and speeches were edited and published by Horace Greeley in 1848.

Clay, (CLEMENT C.,)an American lawyer and Senator, born in Halifax county, Virginia, in 1789, removed to Alabama about 1812. He was elected Governor of Alabama by the Democrats in 1835, and a Senator of the United States in 1837. Died in 1866.

Clay, (CLEMENT C.,) JR., a son of the preceding, born in Madison county, Alabama, in 1819. He practised law, was elected to the Senate of the United States in 1853 by the Democrats, and re-elected about 1857. He was a zealous disunionist in 1860–65.

Clay, (GREEN,) GENERAL, a pioneer and legislator, born in Powhatan county, Virginia, in 1757. He migrated to Kentucky about 1776, and served many years in the legislature of that State. In 1813 he defended Fort Meigs with success against a strong force of British and Indians. Died in 1826.

Clay, (HENRY,) an eminent American statesman and orator, born in a district called "the Slashes," in Hanover county, Virginia, on the 12th of April, 1777. He was a son of John Clay, a Baptist minister, who died about 1782, and who left but little property to his children. Having acquired the rudiments of education in a common school, Henry became, in 1792, a copying clerk in the court of chancery at Richmond, and there attracted the notice of the eminent judge George Wythe, from whose counsels and influence he derived much benefit. He studied law, was admitted to the bar in 1797, and removed in the same year to Lexington, Kentucky, where his practice was crowned with a rapid and brilliant success. In 1799 he married a daughter of Colonel Thomas Hart, of Lexington. When the people of Kentucky were about to adopt a State Constitution, in 1799, Mr. Clay, by his writings and speeches, advocated the gradual abolition of slavery. He began his political career as a Jeffersonian Democrat, was elected to the legislature of his State about 1804, and was sent in 1806 to fill for a short term a seat in the Senate of the United States, made vacant by the resignation of a Senator. Having been again chosen a Senator in 1809, he made a speech in favour of the protection of American manufactures, and one against the United States Bank. His term in the Senate having expired in 1811, he was then chosen a member of the House of Representatives, and was elected Speaker of the House in November of that year. He was a zealous advocate of the war of 1812, and probably contributed more than any other man to the success of the war party. He was re-elected Speaker of the House in May, 1813, resigned that office in January, 1814, and was then sent to Europe as a commissioner to treat for peace with Great Britain. The treaty of Ghent having been signed by Mr. Clay and his colleagues in December, 1814, he returned home in September, 1815. In December, 1815, (and thrice afterwards,) he was again elected Speaker of the House of Representatives. He supported in 1816 the bill to charter a Bank of the

United States, on which question he acknowledged that he had changed his opinions. In 1818 he made a great speech for the recognition of the South American republics. He was one of the most prominent supporters of the Missouri Compromise, by which, in 1821, after a long and exciting contest, Missouri was admitted into the Union with slavery, and slavery was prohibited in the territories north of 36° 30′ north latitude. Before this time he had acquired great popularity as a statesman and an orator. "At thirty," says Parton, "he was, to use the language of the stump, 'Kentucky's favourite son,' and incomparably the finest orator in the Western country. Kentucky had tried him, and found him perfectly to her mind. . . . In familiar conversation he used language of the most Western description; and he had a singularly careless, graceful way with him, that was in strong contrast with the vigour and dignity of his public efforts. During the thirteen years of his Speakership not one of his decisions had been reversed, and he had presided over the turbulent and restive House with that perfect blending of courtesy and firmness which at once restrains and charms."

Mr. Clay was one of the four candidates for the Presidency of the United States in 1824, and received thirty-seven electoral votes. When the election of President devolved on the House of Representatives, he preferred Mr. Adams to General Jackson, and his influence decided the result. He thus gave the partisans of Jackson some pretext for the calumnious charge of "bargain and corruption" which impaired his popularity for a time. In March, 1825, he was appointed secretary of state. In April, 1826, he fought a bloodless duel with John Randolph, who had spoken of the coalition of Mr. Adams and Mr. Clay as a "combination of the Puritan and the blackleg." He was elected a Senator of the United States for six years, 1831–37, and was the candidate of the anti-Jackson party in the Presidential election of 1832. He received the votes of only six States, viz., Massachusetts, Rhode Island, Connecticut, Delaware, Maryland, and Kentucky. Mr. Clay was the author of the Compromise Tariff of 1832–33, occasioned by the danger of a violent collision between the nullifiers of South Carolina and the Federal government. Although he was the favourite leader of the Whig party recently organized, he declined to be a candidate for the Presidency in 1836. About the end of that year he was re-elected a Senator of the United States. He supported General Harrison as a candidate for the office of President in 1840. In the Senate he advocated a national bank and the distribution of the proceeds of the public lands among the States. He resigned his seat in the Senate early in 1842, and retired to his residence at Ashland, near Lexington. The Whig National Convention of May, 1844, with great unanimity, nominated him for the Presidency. He opposed the annexation of Texas, (which was advocated by Mr. Polk, the Democratic candidate,) and declared that no earthly power should ever induce him to consent to the addition of one acre of slave territory to the United States. Mr. Clay received one hundred and five electoral votes, cast by Massachusetts, Connecticut, Rhode Island, Vermont, New Jersey, Delaware, Maryland, North Carolina, Ohio, Kentucky, and Tennessee; but he was not elected.

He joined the Protestant Episcopal Church in 1847. In December, 1848, he was again elected to the national Senate, in which he afterwards made numerous speeches, especially on the controversy occasioned by slavery. The Compromise of 1850, which postponed for ten years the conflict between freedom and slavery, was chiefly his work. In one of his speeches on the Compromise Bill he said, "I owe a paramount allegiance to the whole Union,—a subordinate one to my own State." He died at Washington, June 29, 1852. He had five sons and six daughters. "Take him for all in all," says Parton, "we must regard him as the first of American orators; but posterity will not assign him that rank, because posterity will not hear that matchless voice, will not see those large gestures, those striking attitudes, that grand manner, which gave to second-rate composition first-rate effect. . . . His speeches will long be interesting as the relics of a magnificent and dazzling personality, and for the light they cast upon the history of parties; but they

---

e as k; ç as s; g̃ hard; g̃ as j; G, H, K, guttural; N, nasal; R, trilled; s̃ as z; th as in this.　　(☞ See Explanations, p. 23.)

add scarcely anything to the intellectual property of the nation."

See PARTON, "Famous Americans of Recent Times," 1867; EPES SARGENT, "Life of Henry Clay," 1844; CALVIN COLTON, "Life of Henry Clay," 2 vols., 1846; "National Portrait-Gallery of Distinguished Americans," vol. i.; "North American Review" for October, 1827, October, 1831, (by A. H. EVERETT,) and January, 1866; "London Quarterly Review" for December, 1840; EDWARD G. PARKER, "Golden Age of American Oratory," Boston, 1857.

Clay, (JAMES B.,) a son of Henry Clay, was born in 1817. He joined the Democratic party, and was elected a member of Congress in 1857 to represent a district in Kentucky. He was a secessionist in 1861. Died in 1864.

Clay, (JOHANN.) See CLAI.

Clayborne, klā'bọrn, (WILLIAM,) an early settler and explorer of Virginia, occupied Kent Island, in Chesapeake Bay, about 1631. He was involved in disputes and violent conflicts with Lord Baltimore and Leonard Calvert. He became secretary of state about 1652.

Clay'tọn, (AUGUSTIN SMITH,) born at Fredericksburg, Virginia, in 1783, became a judge of the superior court of Georgia in 1819, and a member of Congress about 1832. Died in 1839.

Clay'tọn, (JOHN,) an English botanist, born in Kent about 1690. He emigrated in 1705 to Virginia, where he practised medicine and botanized extensively. He wrote articles on the natural history of Virginia, which were published by the Royal Society of London. In 1739 Linnæus and Gronovius published a "Flora of Virginia, exhibiting the Plants which J. Clayton has collected." A genus of herbaceous plants was named *Claytonia* in his honour by Gronovius. Died in 1773.

Clayton, (JOHN MIDDLETON,) an American statesman, born in Sussex county, Delaware, in 1796. He graduated at Yale College in 1815, and studied law, which he practised with success in Delaware. He gained a high reputation as a pleader. In 1829 he was elected a Senator of the United States for Delaware. Having joined the Whig party, he was re-elected to the Federal Senate in 1835. He was chief justice of Delaware from 1837 to 1839, and represented that State in the United States Senate from 1845 to 1849. In March, 1849, he was appointed secretary of state by President Taylor. He negotiated with the British government in 1850 the celebrated "Clayton-Bulwer treaty." He resigned office on the death of President Taylor, July, 1850, and was again elected a Senator of the United States for six years, 1851–57. He married in early life, and had several children, whom he survived. He died in November, 1856, leaving a fair reputation for ability and integrity.

Clay'tọn, (ROBERT,) F.R.S., a learned Irish divine, born in Dublin in 1695. He became Bishop of Killala in 1730, of Cork in 1735, and of Clogher in 1745. He published an "Introduction to the History of the Jews," and other works. His "Essay on Spirit" (1751) gave much offence to the Anglican Church by its advocacy of Arian or Unitarian doctrines. Died in 1758.

See "Biographia Britannica."

Cle-an'dẹr, [Gr. Κλείανδρος; Fr. CLÉANDRE, klä'-ŏNdR',] a corrupt prime minister of Commodus, Emperor of Rome, was originally a Phrygian slave. He was put to death about 189 A.D.

Cle-ā'nor, [Κλεάνωρ,] a Greek officer, born in Arcadia, lived about 400 B.C. He entered the service of Cyrus the Younger, and was one of the chiefs of that army of 10,000 whose famous retreat is described by Xenophon.

Cléanthe. See CLEANTHES.

Cle-an'thēs, [Gr. Κλέανθης; Fr. CLÉANTHE, klä'ŏNt',] a Greek Stoic philosopher, born at Assos, in Asia Minor, about 300 B.C. He became a resident of Athens, and a pupil of Zeno, with whom he studied many years, supporting himself by drawing water and other hard labour. At the death of Zeno, about 260 B.C., he became his successor as head of the Stoic school. He wrote many works, which are nearly all lost, except a hymn to Jupiter, remarkable for elevation and grandeur of thought. Chrysippus was his pupil and successor. The original occupation of Cleanthes was that of athlete. He was solid rather than brilliant, practical rather than speculative.

See DIOGENES LAERTIUS; W. T. KRUG, "Dissertatio de Cleanthe," 1819; CICERO, "De Natura Deorum."

Cle-ar'ehus, [Gr. Κλέαρχος; Fr. CLÉARQUE, klä'ȁRk',] a Spartan general, who, having been condemned to death for crimes committed while he commanded at Byzantium, escaped, and entered the service of Cyrus the Younger. He commanded a body of Greeks in the war between Cyrus and his brother Artaxerxes. After the battle of Cunaxa, in which Cyrus was killed, the King of Persia by treachery obtained possession of Clearchus and the other Grecian generals, and put them to death about 400 B.C. New generals were then chosen, under whose direction the Greeks successfully accomplished the famous retreat known as "the Retreat of the Ten Thousand."

See XENOPHON, "Anabasis."

Clearchus, tyrant of Heraclea, a Greek city of Pontus, had been a pupil of Plato at Athens. After he had reigned twelve years, and committed many acts of cruelty, he was assassinated by Chion and others, about 352 B.C.

Clearchus, an Athenian comic poet, lived probably in the third century B.C.

Clearchus, of Soli, a Greek philosopher, and a pupil of Aristotle, wrote on various subjects numerous works which have not come down to us. Among the titles were "On Friendship," ("Philia,") "On Paintings," "On Anatomy," and "On Sleep."

See FABRICIUS, "Bibliotheca Græca;" VOSSIUS, "De Historicis Græcis."

Cléarque. See CLEARCHUS.

Cleaveland, Cleveland, or **Clieveland,** kleev'land, (JOHN,) an English poet, born at Loughborough in 1613. He was once a tutor at a college in Cambridge. In the civil war he fought for the royal cause. He wrote the "Rustic Rampant," "The King's Disguise," and other poems, which were greatly admired by many in his own time, but are marred by perverse conceits, and are now neglected. Died in 1659.

See "Retrospective Review," vol. xii., 1825.

Cleaveland, kleev'land, (PARKER,) LL.D., an eminent American mineralogist, was born in Massachusetts in 1780. He graduated at Harvard in 1799, and from 1805 till his death was professor of chemistry, mineralogy, etc. in Bowdoin College, Maine. His work on "Mineralogy and Geology," (2 vols. 8vo,) issued in 1816, introduced him to the notice of Sir Humphry Davy, Cuvier, and other illustrious scientific men, with several of whom he corresponded. At his death he was an honorary member of the principal scientific associations in Europe. Died in 1858.

Cleaver, klee'vẹr, (WILLIAM,) an English divine, born in 1742, became successively Bishop of Chester, (1787,) of Bangor, (1800,) and of Saint Asaph, (1806.) He was editor of an Oxford edition of Homer, and published, besides other works, Sermons, and "De Rhythmo Græcorum Liber," (1789.) Died in 1815.

Cle'burn or **Cle'burne,** (PATRICK,) a general, born in Ireland about 1828. He was a lawyer in Arkansas before the civil war, in which he fought against the Union. He commanded a division at Stone River, December 31, 1862–January 2, 1863, and at Chickamauga, September, 1863. He was killed at the battle of Franklin, November 30, 1864. "The loss of Patrick Cleburne— the 'Stonewall Jackson of the West,'"—says Greeley, "would of itself have been a rebel disaster." ("American Conflict.")

Cleef, van, vän kläf, or **Cleeve,** klä'veh, (HENDRIK,) a skilful Flemish landscape-painter, born at Antwerp about 1510. He spent some years in Italy. Died in 1589. His brother MARTIN, born about 1520, was a historical painter of merit, and was employed by several landscape-painters to paint the figures of their works. The two brothers sometimes worked on the same piece of canvas.

See DESCAMPS, "Vies des Peintres Flamands," etc.

Cleef, van, (JAN,) an eminent Flemish painter, born at Venloo in 1646, was a pupil of Gaspar de Crayer. He became one of the most skilful Flemish artists of his time, and adorned the churches of Antwerp, Ghent, etc. He excelled many or all Flemish painters in the treatment of drapery. Among his master-pieces is "The Redemption of the Captives." Died in Ghent in 1716.

See DESCAMPS, "Vies des Peintres Flamands," etc.; "Nouvelle Biographie Générale."

ā, ē, ī, ō, ū, ȳ, *long;* ă, ĕ, ŏ, same, less prolonged; ă, ĕ, ĭ, ŏ, ŭ, ў, *short;* ạ, ẹ, į, ọ, *obscure;* fär, fȁll, fȁt; mêt; nŏt; gŏŏd; mŏŏn;

Cleef, van, (Joost,) a Flemish painter, born at Antwerp about 1490. He was an excellent colorist. In the latter part of his life he worked in Madrid, and is said to have become insane.

His father, Willem, was a skilful historical painter.

Cleeve. See Cleef.

Cleg'horn, (George,) an able Scottish physician, born in Edinburgh in 1716. Having passed thirteen years in Minorca, he published "The Diseases of Minorca," (1751,) which Dr. Fothergill calls "a just model for future writers." It treats on the botany, climate, etc. of that island. In 1751 he settled in Dublin, where he practised with success, and became professor of anatomy in the university. Died in 1787.

See Chambers, "Biographical Dictionary of Eminent Scotsmen."

Cleisthenes. See Clisthenes.

Cleitarchus. See Clitarchus.

Cleitus. See Clitus.

Cle'land, (John,) an English writer, born about 1710, was the son of Colonel Cleland, the original of the Spectator's "Will Honeycomb." In his youth he was consul at Smyrna. Besides other works, he wrote "The Man of Honour," and "The Way to Things by Words, and to Words by Things." Died in 1789.

See Nichols, "Literary Anecdotes," etc.

Cle'land, (Lieutenant-Colonel William,) a Scottish poet, born about 1660, was a zealous Covenanter. He was lieutenant-colonel of Lord Angus's regiment, and was killed in battle at Dunkeld in 1689. His poems were published in 1697.

See Macaulay's "History of England," vol. iii. chap. xiii.

Clemangis or **Clemangius.** See Clamenges.

Clémence Isaure, klā'mōnss' e'zōr', a French lady, who lived at Toulouse about 1470. She reanimated the literary spirit of her countrymen by instituting or endowing the Floral Games, *(Jeux floraux,)* which were held annually on the 1st of May at Toulouse. She bequeathed a fund, part of which was to be paid in prizes for the best poems. Her death is supposed to have occurred soon after 1500.

See Salvan, "C. Isaure, Étude historique," 1853; J. B. Noulet, "Dame Clémence Isaure," etc., 1852; Longfellow, "Poets and Poetry of Europe."

Clémencet, klā'mŏn'sā', (Charles,) a French Benedictine, born at Painblanc in 1703. He published, besides other works, a "History of Port-Royal," (10 vols., 1756,) and "The Art of Verifying Dates," (1750,) which displays great erudition. Died in 1778.

Clemencin, klā-měn-thěn', (Diego,) a Spanish statesman and author of merit, born at Murcia in 1765. Soon after he left college he was employed as tutor in the family of the Duke of Osuña, and became a resident of Madrid. He was editor of the Official Gazette in Madrid in 1808, and a member of the Cortes of Cadiz in 1812. When the Constitutional party, with which he was identified, prevailed in 1820, he was elected to the Cortes, of which he became president. In 1823 he was banished from Madrid by the Absolutists. About 1833 he was appointed librarian to the queen and was made a peer of the kingdom. Among his principal writings are a "Eulogy on Isabella of Castile," (1821,) which was then the best work on the subject, and an excellent "Commentary on Don Quixote," (1833.) Died in 1834.

Clemens, klā'měns, (Friedrich,) a German poet, born in Westphalia about 1800. Among his works are "The Eccentric People," and "The Manifesto of Reason," ("Manifest der Vernunft," 1836.)

Cle'mens, (T. Flavius,) a Roman consul, was a cousin-german of the emperor Domitian, and his colleague in the consulship, 95 A.D. He is reckoned among the Christian martyrs, having been put to death by order of Domitian on a charge of impiety towards the heathen gods.

Clemens Romanus. See Clement I.

Clem'ent [Lat. Cle'mens, or, more fully, Titus Flavius Clemens; Fr. Clément, klā'mŏn'] of Alexandria, an eminent Father of the Christian church, born about the middle of the second century. According to some writers, he was a native of Athens, and in his youth a disciple of the Platonic philosophy. After studying with various pagan teachers, he became a disciple of Pantænus, who was master of a Christian school in Alexandria. He succeeded Pantænus, and was ordained a presbyter in the church of that city. It is stated that in 202 A.D., to escape from persecution, he retired to Syria, and preached in Antioch and other cities. A few years later we find him again employed as teacher of catechumens in Alexandria. He died about the year 220. Eusebius, Chrysostom, and others extol his learning, wisdom, and virtue. Origen was the most eminent of his pupils. Clement left several esteemed works, written in Greek, which are still extant, and which afford various information on religion, history, and philosophy, viz., "Exhortation to the Greeks," "Pædagogus," and "Stromata," (Gr. Στρωματεῖς.) The last is a medley of Christian thoughts, maxims of philosophy, anecdotes, etc., without methodical arrangement. He is more addicted to speculation, and more favourable to the ancient Greek philosophy, than many of the other Christian Fathers.

See Eusebius, "Ecclesiastical History;" Kaye, "Account of the Writings, etc. of Clement of Alexandria," London, 1835; Matter, "Essai historique sur l'École d'Alexandrie;" Neander, "History of the Church;" Cave, "Historia Literaria;" Reinkens, "De Clemente Presbytero Alexandrino," 1851.

Clement I., (or **Cle'mens Roma'nus,**) a bishop of Rome, of whom we have little positive information. According to various authorities, he succeeded Linus in 67 A.D., or Anacletus in the year 91. He is supposed to be the Clement whom Saint Paul calls his fellow-labourer, (Philip. iv. 3.) Eusebius states that he died in 100 A.D., having been bishop nine years. He is reckoned among the martyrs; but there is some doubt whether he died a violent or a natural death. On the occasion of a dissension in the church of Corinth, Clement wrote to that church an excellent epistle, which is still extant, and is highly prized as a monument of antiquity and memorial of the primitive Church. It was often read publicly in the churches as late as the fourth century. Eusebius informs us that the other works ascribed to Clement are not genuine. His epistle is divided into more than fifty chapters. His authority tends to prove the genuineness of certain books of the New Testament which he quotes, viz., Matthew, Luke, and several epistles.

See Neander, "History of the Church;" Tillemont, "Mémoires."

Clement II., a native of Saxony, whose name was Suid'ger, was elected pope in 1046 as successor to Gregory VI. He crowned as emperor Henry III. in the same year, and died in October, 1047, when Benedict IX. was chosen pope.

Clement III., a Roman by birth, was elected pope at Pisa in December, 1187, after the death of Gregory VIII. Jerusalem having just fallen into the power of Saladin, Clement made successful efforts to enlist the Christians in another crusade against the Saracens, which was led by Richard I. of England and Philip of France. He died in March, 1191, and was succeeded by Celestine III.

Clement IV. (Guy Foulques, or Guido Fulcodi) was born at Saint-Gilles, in France. He had been secretary to Louis IX., whom he served many years in important affairs. In February, 1265, he succeeded Urban IV. He favoured Charles of Anjou in his conquest of Naples, which was then ruled by Manfred, and which the last pontiff had granted or given to Charles. He died in 1268, and was succeeded by Gregory X.

Clement V., Pope of Rome, succeeded Benedict XI. in June, 1305. He was a Frenchman, named Bertrand de Got. In 1299 he had been made Archbishop of Bordeaux. He was crowned as pope at Lyons, and to gratify his patron, Philippe le Bel, he chose Avignon as his residence and the capital of the popedom. This innovation caused great discontent, and was the origin of a long division in the Church. He co-operated with Philippe le Bel in his cruel persecution of the Templars. He is represented as immoral and venal. He died in 1314. John XXII. was chosen as his successor in 1316.

See De Guasco, "Histoire du Pape Clément V," 2 vols., 1756.

Clement VI., elected pope in 1342, succeeded Benedict XII. at Avignon. He was a native of Limousin, in France, and was named Pierre Roger, (ro'zhā'.) He purchased from Joanna of Naples the sovereignty of Avignon. During his pontificate the famous Rienzi attempted to effect a revolution in Rome, but failed. Clement ordained the celebration of a jubilee every fifty years. He died in 1352, and was succeeded by Innocent VI.

See ARTAUD DE MONTOR, "Histoire des souverains Pontifes."

Clement VII., (GIULIO DE' **Medici**—mêd'e-chee,) a natural son of Giuliano de' Medici, and a cousin of Leo X., succeeded Adrian VI. in November, 1523. In the pontificate of Leo X. he had been made Archbishop of Florence, and received a cardinal's hat. Alarmed at the growing power of Charles V., he made a league against him with the Venetians and Francis I. of France. The army of Charles V., commanded by Constable Bourbon, took Rome by assault in 1527, treated the citizens with great cruelty, and made the pope a prisoner. His dispute with Henry VIII. of England respecting the divorce of Queen Catherine produced results of great political importance. He issued a famous bull against Henry in 1534. He died in September of that year, and was succeeded by Paul III.

See GUICCIARDINI, "Historia d'Italia," 1564; RANKE, "History of the Popes."

Clement VIII. (IPPOLITO **Aldobrandini**—âl-do-brân-dee'nee) succeeded Innocent IX. in January, 1592. He was a native of Fano, in Italy, and became cardinal in 1585. He negotiated with Henry IV. of France with respect to his abjuration of Protestantism, which occurred in 1595. During his pontificate commenced the dispute on the doctrine of grace, which caused the long and angry controversy between the Molinists and the Jansenists in the seventeenth century. Clement appears to have been neutral in this question. He annexed the duchy of Ferrara to the Papal States. He died in 1605, and was succeeded by Leo XI.

See CICARELLA, "De Vita Clementis VIII.;" LUC WADDING, "Vita Clementis VIII.," 1723; DE THOU, "Historia sui Temporis."

Clement IX., elected pope in June, 1667, succeeded Alexander VII. He was born at Pistoia in 1600, and was originally named GIULIO DE ROSPIGLIOSI, (ros-pêl-yo'-see.) He was made a cardinal by Alexander VII. One of the principal events of his short pontificate was a compromise or transient peace which he made between the Jesuits and Jansenists of France. He died in December, 1669, regretted on account of his probity and other virtues. His successor was Clement X.

See ARTAUD DE MONTOR, "Histoire des souverains Pontifes."

Clement X. (EMILIO **Altieri**—âl-te-â'ree) succeeded Clement IX. in 1670, at the age of eighty. He was an Italian, and probably a native of Rome. He had been made a cardinal by the preceding pontiff. Cardinal Paluzzi Altieri had the chief control of affairs in this pontificate, the events of which were not very important. Clement died in 1676, and was succeeded by Innocent XI.

Clement XI. (GIAN FRANCESCO **Albani**—âl-bâ'-nee) was born at Pesaro, in Central Italy, in 1649. He was made a cardinal in 1690, and elected pope in November, 1700, after the death of Innocent XII. About 1707 he was involved in war with the Emperor of Austria, whose army entered the States of the Church and compelled the pope to sue for peace. In his pontificate the Jansenist controversy was renewed in France by the bull *Vineam Domini*, which denounced the Jansenist doctrines as heretical. In 1713 he raised a great commotion among the French religionists by the famous bull *Unigenitus*, which condemned one hundred and one propositions of a book, written by Père Quesnel, on Grace and Predestination. This bull was supported by the Jesuits and the court, and opposed by the Jansenists. The book of Quesnel had been approved by De Noailles, Archbishop of Paris. Clement assisted the Pretender in his attempt to obtain the British crown in 1715, and after his failure received him with regal honours at Rome. He died in March, 1721, leaving a fair reputation for morality and learning. He was a liberal patron of art and literature. His successor was Innocent XIII.

See ARTAUD DE MONTOR, "Histoire des souverains Pontifes;" LAFITAU, "Vie de Clément XI," 1752; BATTELLI, "Vita Clementis XI.," 1723.

Clement XII. (LORENZO **Corsini**—koR-see'nee) was born at Florence in 1652, and received a cardinal's

hat in 1706, before which he had been treasurer of the apostolic chamber. He succeeded Benedict XIII. in July, 1730. He failed in an attempt to make himself master of Parma and Piacenza. He died in 1740, and was succeeded by Benedict XIV.

See ARTAUD DE MONTOR, "Histoire des souverains Pontifes Romains;" A. FABRONI, "De Vita et Rebus gestis Clementis XII.," 1760.

Clement XIII. (CARLO **Rezzonico**—rêt-so-nee'-ko?) succeeded Benedict XIV., July, 1758. He was born in Venice in 1693, and became a cardinal in 1737. In 1762 he formally condemned Rousseau's "Emile" as heretical. By impolitic attempts to assert his prerogatives he provoked the hostility of France, Spain, and other powers. After the Jesuits had been proscribed in France and Spain, about 1767 he issued a bull in their favour and for their full justification. He was deprived of Avignon by the French and of Benevento by the King of Naples, and the papal authority in his reign was greatly reduced. His private character is said to have been virtuous. He died in 1769, and was succeeded by Clement XIV.

See ARTAUD DE MONTOR, "Histoire des souverains Pontifes."

Clement XIV. (GIOVANNI VINCENZO ANTONIO **Ganganelli**—gân-gâ-nel'lee) was born at Saint Arcangelo, near Rimini, in 1705. Having become eminent for his learning, he was made a cardinal by Clement XIII., whom he succeeded in May, 1769. The Catholic powers watched with great interest this election, which was protracted for several months by party intrigues. He took prompt measures to conciliate the various courts which Clement XIII. had offended, and adopted a more moderate policy. The most memorable act of his pontificate was the suppression of the order of the Jesuits, which, after weighing the subject in the "balance of the sanctuary" for several years, he formally decreed in July, 1773. He died so soon after this event, in September, 1774, that suspicion of poison was excited; but no evidence of the crime was discovered. He had respectable abilities, and was more liberal and enlightened than many of the popes. His habits were moral and simple. The Clementine Museum is an evidence of his munificence and taste for the arts.

See CARACCIOLI, "Vie de Clément XIV," 1775; THEINER, "Geschichte des Pontificats Clements XIV.," 3 vols., 1853, and French version of the same, "Histoire du Pontificat de Clément XIV;" "London Quarterly Review" for June, 1848.

Clement VII., ANTI-POPE, was elected by a party of cardinals, as a rival of Urban VI., about 1378.

Clement, a learned Irish ecclesiastic, was one of the scholars whom Charlemagne invited to his court and employed as a teacher. Died after 800 A.D.

Clément, klâ'môN', (AMBROISE,) a French economist, born in Paris in 1805. He published in 1846 a work entitled "Researches into the Causes of Indigence," which is highly commended. He was one of the chief authors or compilers of the "Dictionary of Political Economy," (1852–53.) Died in September, 1862.

Clement, klâ'ment, (DAVID,) a bibliographer of great erudition, was born at Hofgeismar, Hesse, in 1701. He became pastor of a church in Hanover in 1743. He published, in French, a work called "Catalogue *raisonné* of Books Difficult to Find," (9 vols., 1750–60.) Died in 1760.

See SAX, "Onomasticon."

Clément, (Dom FRANÇOIS,) a learned French Benedictine, born near Dijon in 1714. He was called by his superiors to Paris to work at the continuation of the "Literary History of France." He afterwards published the twelfth and thirteenth volumes of "The Collection of the Historians of France," and "The Art of Verifying Dates," which was very successful. In 1783–87 he produced an improved edition of the latter work, (in 3 vols.,) which Jourdain calls "the finest monument of erudition of the eighteenth century." He was a "free associate" of the Academy of Inscriptions. Died in 1793.

See "Nouvelle Biographie Générale."

Clément, (JACQUES,) a fanatical French monk and regicide, born at Sorbonne about 1566. When Henry III. was besieging Paris, then occupied by the forces of the Catholic League, Clement conceived a design to assassinate him, in which he was encouraged by his superiors and by the Duke of Mayenne. Having been admitted to the palace as the bearer of a letter to the king, he stabbed him with a knife, on August 1, 1589. The assassin was killed on the spot by the king's attendants.

See SISMONDI, "Histoire des Français;" DE THOU, "Histoire."

Clément, (JEAN MARIE BERNARD,) a French *littérateur* and critic, born at Dijon in 1742. He was noted for the severity of his criticisms and for his attacks on Voltaire, who surnamed him "Inclément." Among his best works are an "Essay on Tragedy," and an "Essay on the Manner of Translating Poets into Verse." He also wrote satires and poems. Died in 1812.

See GRIMM, "Correspondance."

Clem'ent, (JOHN,) a learned English physician, born about 1490. In 1529 he was sent by Henry VIII. to attend Cardinal Wolsey, who was then sick. He translated some Latin epigrams, and the "Letters of Gregory Nazianzen." Died in 1572.

Clément, (JULIEN,) a French surgeon and accoucheur, born at Arles, was patronized by Louis XIV. Died at Paris in 1729.

Clement, klä'měnt, (KNUT JUNGBOHN,) a Danish linguist, born in the isle of Amram in 1803, settled in 1835 at Kiel, where he lectured several years. Among his works are one "On the Origin of the Teutons," (1836,) a "Journey through Holland and Germany," (1847,) and "The French and their Language," (1848.)

Clement, (MARGARET,) an English lady and Latin scholar, born in 1508, was a niece of Sir Thomas More. Died in 1570.

Clément, (NICOLAS,) born at Toul, in France, in 1647, was assistant librarian in the Royal Library. Died in 1712.

Clément, klä'mŏN', (PIERRE,) a critic and dramatist, born at Geneva in 1707, was a preacher in Paris in his youth. In 1748 he began to issue a critical review, called "Nouvelles littéraires de France," which he continued about five years. His criticisms are said to be judicious and liberal. He was the author of "Mérope," a tragedy. Died in 1767.

See SENEBIER, "Histoire littéraire de Genève."

Clément, (PIERRE,) a French advocate of free trade, and a member of the Institute, was born in the department of Var in 1809. He published in 1846 a "History of the Life and Administration of Colbert," which was crowned by the French Academy and followed by other successful works on French history and finances.

Clementi, klà-měn'tee, (MUZIO,) a celebrated pianist and composer, born in Rome in 1752. At the age of nine or ten his skill was such that he obtained a place as organist in Rome. After this period he became a pupil of Santarelli and Carpini. About the age of thirteen he went to England with Mr. P. Beckford, who made to his father a generous offer in respect to his education. He learned ancient and modern languages and various sciences, without neglecting music. At the age of eighteen he surpassed all his contemporaries on the piano, and composed his "Opera 2," which is regarded as "the basis on which the whole fabric of modern sonatas for the piano has been founded." In 1780 and 1781 he performed with great applause in Paris and Vienna. He played alternately with Mozart before the Austrian emperor. In 1800 he became the head of a firm which was successful in the publication of music and the fabrication of pianos in London. He wrote "Practical Harmony" and "Gradus ad Parnassum," and composed one hundred and six Sonatas. Died in 1832.

See FÉTIS, "Biographie Universelle des Musiciens;" TIPALDO, "Biografia degli Italiani illustri."

Clementi, (PROSPERO,) an eminent Italian sculptor, born at Reggio. Several of the family were noted as sculptors before him. Many of his works are at Reggio, Parma, and Mantua. A monument to Bishop Andreassi is called his master-piece. Died in 1584. He was styled "the Correggio of Sculpture" by Algarotti.

See VASARI, "Lives of the Painters," etc.

Clementone. See BOCCIARDO.

Clénard, klä'nȧr', **Cleynaerts** or **Kleinarts,** klī'-nȧrts, (NICHOLAS,) a Flemish grammarian, born in Brabant in 1495. After he had been professor of Hebrew

and Greek in Louvain, he was employed by John III. of Portugal to finish the education of his brother, who was afterwards Henry I. Died in 1542. His Greek Grammar (1530) had great success.

Clen'nell, (LUKE,) an English painter and engraver, born near Morpeth in 1781, was a pupil of Bewick the engraver. He worked in London, and painted history, landscapes, etc. Died in a lunatic-asylum in 1840.

Cle'o-bis and **Bi'ton** [Gr. Κλέοβις and Βίτων] were sons of the priestess of Juno at Argos, and once drew her chariot to the temple. Their mother having prayed that the goddess would reward them with the greatest of blessings, they fell asleep and never awoke.

Cléobule. See CLEOBULUS.

Cle-o-bu'lus, [Gr. Κλεόβουλος; Fr. CLÉOBULE, klȧ'o'-bül',] one of the Seven Wise Men of Greece, was King of Lindus, in Rhodes, in the sixth century B.C. He claimed a descent from Hercules. His favourite maxim, Ἄριστον μέτρον, inculcates "Moderation in all things." Another of his sayings was, "Be swift to hear, and slow to speak." His daughter Cleobuline was celebrated for her skill in enigmas and in poetry.

See FABRICIUS, "Bibliotheca Græca."

Cléombrote. See CLEOMBROTUS.

Cle-om'bro-tus or **Kle-om'bro-tus,** [Gr. Κλεόμβροτος; Fr. CLÉOMBROTE, klȧ'ŏN'bROt',] the fourth son of Anaxandrides, King of Sparta, was the brother of Leonidas, the hero of Thermopylæ. He commanded the army after the death of Leonidas, 480 B.C. Pausanias, the victor at Platæa, was his son.

Cleombrotus I., King of Sparta, was the son of Pausanias, and grandson of the preceding. He ascended the throne at the death of his brother Agesipolis, 380 B.C. In 371 B.C. he commanded the Spartans at the battle of Leuctra, where he was defeated and killed by the Thebans under Epaminondas. He left two sons, Agesipolis II. and Cleomenes II.

Cleombrotus II. was the son-in-law of Leonidas II., King of Sparta. By the aid of Agis and Lysander, he succeeded in deposing Leonidas about 243 B.C., and reigned for a short time in his place. Leonidas was restored, and his rival was exiled, about 240.

Cleombrotus of Ambracia, a Greek Academic philosopher, drowned himself in the sea after reading the "Phædon" of Plato, in his eagerness to verify the doctrine of a future state.

Cléomède. See CLEOMEDES.

Cle-o-me'dēs, [Gr. Κλεομήδης; Fr. CLÉOMÈDE, klȧ'-o'mȧd',] a Greek astronomer, whose birthplace, residence, and era are unknown. He is the author of an interesting treatise on astronomy and cosmography, entitled "The Circular Theory of the Heavenly Bodies," ("Κυκλικὴ θεωρία μετεώρων.") He maintains that the form of the earth is spherical, that the number of the fixed stars is infinite, and that the moon's rotation on its axis is performed in the same time as its synodical revolution. The refraction of light is noticed in this work for the first time. He ridicules the physical theories of the Epicureans, and often quotes from Posidonius, who lived in the first century B.C. His work has been printed several times.

See DELAMBRE, "Histoire de l'Astronomie ancienne;" FABRICIUS, "Bibliotheca Græca;" "Nouvelle Biographie Générale."

Cléomène. See CLEOMENES.

Cle-om'e-nēs or **Kle-om'e-nēs** [Gr. Κλεομένης; Fr. CLÉOMÈNE, klȧ'o'măn'] **I.,** King of Sparta, was the son of Anaxandrides, whom he succeeded about 518 B.C. Demaratus at the same time reigned jointly with him. In 510 he liberated Athens from the rule of the Pisistratidæ, whom he expelled by arms; but he afterwards made an abortive attempt to restore Hippias. In 500 he refused a large bribe offered to induce him to aid the Ionians against Persia. About 491 the Spartans sent him to punish the people of Ægina for giving earth and water as signs of homage to Darius. By tampering with the priestess of Delphi, he caused Demaratus to be dethroned. Herodotus says that he killed himself, in a fit of insanity, in 489 B.C. His half-brother Leonidas succeeded him.

See HERODOTUS, "History;" GROTE, "History of Greece;" THIRLWALL, "History of Greece."

ɛ as *k*; ç as *s*; ḡ *hard*; ġ as *j*; G, H, K, *guttural*; N, *nasal*; R, *trilled*, ṣ as *z*; ṭh as in *this*. (☞ See Explanations, p. 23.)

Cleomenes II., King of Sparta, of the elder branch, succeeded his brother Agesipolis II. in 370 B.C. He died in 309 B.C., and left the throne to his grandson Areus.

Cleomenes III., King of Sparta, of the Agidæ line, succeeded his father Leonidas II. in 236 B.C. He had before married Agiatis, the widow of Agis IV., and daughter of Gylippus. Having formed a design to restore the ancient Spartan virtue and discipline, he declared war against the Achæan League, with the idea that war was conducive to his purpose. He gained a signal victory over Aratus near Megalopolis in 226 B.C. Finding the powers of the ephori an obstacle to his design, he put them all to death except Agesilaus, who escaped. He then made a new division of property or land, restored the old social system, abolished the office of ephorus, and made his brother Euclidas his partner in the throne. He afterwards defeated the Achæans in several battles, until the latter were reinforced by Antigonus, King of Macedon, who obtained a decisive victory over Cleomenes at Sellasia in 222 B.C. He then fled to Egypt, where he killed himself in the year 220. Plutarch extols his magnanimity, and says, "he showed himself in all respects the great man." He may be justly accounted the last great man of Sparta.

See PLUTARCH, "Cleomenes" and "Aratus;" FRANZ VAN CAPPELLE, "Dissertatio de Cleomene Lacedæmoniorum Rege," 1845; DROYSEN, "Geschichte der Hellenen."

Cleomenes, [Fr. CLÉOMÈNE,] a Greek sculptor, is mentioned by no ancient author except Pliny, who says the group of Muses placed by Pollio in his house in Rome was the work of Cleomenes. His name would perhaps have been forgotten if it had not been carved on that exquisite type of grace and beauty, the Venus de Medici, thus: ΚΑΕΟΜΕΝΗΣ ΑΠΟΛΛΟΔΩΡΟΥ ΑΘΗΝΑΙΟΣ ΕΠΩΙΗΣΕΝ, "Cleomenes, son of Apollodorus, an Athenian, made [this.]" He is supposed to have lived about 200 or 300 B.C.

See VISCONTI, "Notice critique sur les Sculpteurs Grecs qui ont porté le Nom de Cleomenes."

Cleomenes, a Greek of Naucratis, in Egypt, was appointed by Alexander the Great receiver-general of tribute in Egypt, and was notorious for his rapacity. He was also employed to superintend the building of Alexandria. He was put to death by King Ptolemy about 322 B.C.

Cle′on or **Kle′on,** [Κλέων,] an Athenian demagogue, noted for his insolence, venality, and facility of speech, first appears in history about 428 B.C. He was a favourite and leader of the popular party, or lower classes, while Nicias was the chief of the opposite party. He conducted a successful expedition against the Spartans at Pylos in 425, which raised his credit and filled him with presumption. Though he was ignorant of the military art, he again obtained command of an army sent against the Spartan general Brasidas, by whom he was defeated at Amphipolis in 422 B.C. Cleon and Brasidas both fell in this action.

See GROTE, "History of Greece;" THUCYDIDES, "History;" PLUTARCH, "Pericles" and "Nicias."

Cleon, a Greek sculptor, born at Sicyon, was a pupil of Antiphanes. He flourished about 388 B.C. Pliny speaks of a statue of Admetus as his master-piece. Cleon made two bronze statues of Jupiter for the temple at Olympia.

Cle′o-pas or **Cle′o-phas,** one of the primitive and immediate disciples of Christ. (See Luke xxiv. 18; John xix. 25.)

Cle-o-pā′tra, [Gr. Κλεοπάτρα,] the daughter of Philip of Macedon and Olympias, was the sister of Alexander the Great. In 336 B.C. she became the wife of Alexander, King of Epirus, her maternal uncle. After the death of her brother she was assassinated by order of Antigonus.

Cleopatra, the daughter of Antiochus the Great, was married to Ptolemy Epiphanes of Egypt in 193 B.C.

Cleopatra, an ambitious queen of Syria, was the daughter of Ptolemy Philometor. She was the wife of three successive kings of Syria,—Alexander Balas, Demetrius Nicator, and Antiochus Sidetes. It is said that she caused the second to be killed.

Cleopatra, Queen of Egypt, a daughter of Ptolemy Epiphanes, was married first to Ptolemy Philometor, and next to Ptolemy Physcon.

Cleopatra, Queen of Egypt, a daughter of the preceding, was married to Ptolemy Physcon. Died 89 B.C. She had a daughter Cleopatra, who became the queen of Ptolemy Lathyrus.

Cleopatra, [Gr. Κλεοπάτρα; Fr. CLÉOPÂTRE, klå′o′-pâtʀ′,] a queen of Egypt, celebrated for her personal charms, her various accomplishments, and her dramatic history, was the daughter of Ptolemy Auletes, and was born in 69 B.C. Her father died in the year 51, leaving the throne to her in partnership with her brother Ptolemy. She was richly endowed with mental qualities and captivating graces, and was mistress of many languages besides the Greek, her mother-tongue. In 48 B.C., Julius Cæsar, who had entered Egypt with a small army, having been caught "in her strong toils of grace," restored her to the throne, from which her brother had expelled her. War ensued between Cæsar and Ptolemy, who was defeated and killed. She then became the actual sovereign, though her young brother nominally shared the throne. She followed Cæsar to Rome in the year 46, and was an inmate of his palace until his death in 44 B.C., when she returned to Egypt. Her brother, above mentioned, was killed about this time,—it is said, by her order. In the year 41 she formed a *liaison* with the triumvir Mark Antony, who became her devoted admirer, and offered, as Plutarch says, at her shrine of luxury the sacrifice of his precious time. The great modern dramatist has described his infatuation and his dalliance with the voluptuous and dusky Egyptian while the empire of the world was passing into the hands of Octavius. Cleopatra was present at the naval battle of Actium, in 31 B.C., and was the first to order a retreat, in which Antony followed. After Antony had killed himself, she became the prisoner of Octavius, with whom she had an interview, and whose favour she failed to gain. Intending to lead her as a captive in his triumph in Rome, he took strict measures to secure her from suicide; but, according to Plutarch, she effected her purpose by means of an asp, which was conveyed to her in a basket of fruit, and died in 30 B.C., leaving a son, Cæsarion, (whose reputed father was Julius Cæsar,) besides several other children. She was the last of her dynasty that reigned in Egypt.

See PLUTARCH, "Antony;" CÆSAR, "Bellum Civile;" GIULIO LANDI, "Vita di Cleopatra," 1551; J. F. KINDERLING, "Hekuba und Cleopatra," 1804; DION CASSIUS, books xlii., xliii., xlviii., and xlix.

Cleopatra surnamed SELE′NE, the daughter of Mark Antony and Cleopatra, Queen of Egypt, was taken to Rome at the death of her parents, 30 B.C. She became the wife of Juba, King of Mauritania.

Cléopâtre. See CLEOPATRA.

Cle-o-phan′tus, [Κλεόφαντος,] a Corinthian, whom Greek tradition commemorates as the first who applied colour to designs. Respecting the time in which he lived we have nothing but conjecture.

Cle′o-phon or **Kle′o-phon,** [Κλεοφῶν,] an Athenian demagogue, who dissuaded the people from accepting the terms offered by the Lacedemonians after the battle of Arginusæ. He was condemned and executed by the senate in 405 B.C.

Cléostrate. See CLEOSTRATUS.

Cle-os′tra-tus or **Kle-os′tra-tus,** [Gr. Κλεόστρατος; Fr. CLÉOSTRATE, klå′o′strât′,] a Greek astronomer, born in Tenedos, is supposed to have lived about 500 B.C. He is said to have divided the zodiac into signs.

Clerc, klair, (NICOLAS GABRIEL,) a French physician, born in Franche-Comté in 1726. He became first physician of the French army in Germany in 1757. A few years later he went to Russia, where he had the title of chief physician to the grand duke. He published several medical works, one of which was very successful, namely, "Medicine restored to its First Simplicity," and a "History of Russia, Ancient and Modern," (6 vols., 1783-94,) which, says M. Weiss, (in the "Biographie Universelle,") "is still the most complete work we have on that subject." Died at Versailles in 1798.

See QUÉRARD, "La France Littéraire;" ÉLOY, "Dictionnaire de la Médecine."

Clerc de la Forrest, le, lẹh klair dẹh lä fo′rẹ′, (ANTOINE,) a French scholar, noted for his beneficence, was born at Auxerre in 1563. Among his works are "Letters and Maxims," (1644.) Died in 1628.

See his life, entitled "The Perfect Layman," (in French,) 1644.

ā, ē, ī, ō, ū, ȳ, *long;* à, è, ò, same, less prolonged; ă, ĕ, ĭ, ŏ, ŭ, ў, *short;* ạ, ẹ, ị, ọ, *obscure;* fär, fåll, fåt; mêt; nŏt; gō̆od; mōōn;

Clerc, Le. See LE CLERC.

Clerc, le, lĕh klair, (JEAN,) surnamed LE CHEVALIER, (lĕh shĕh-vă′le-à′,) a French painter, a pupil of Carlo Veneziano, was born at Nancy in 1587. He worked for many years at Venice. Died in 1633.

Clerck, klĕrk, (KARL,) a Swedish entomologist, and pupil of Linnæus, was the author of esteemed works, entitled "Swedish Spiders," ("Aranei Suecici," 1757,) and "Figures of Rare Insects," ("Icones Insectorum rariorum,") which was highly praised by Linnæus in a note to his "Systema Naturæ."

Clérembault, de, dĕh klà′rŏN′bŏ′, (PHILIPPE,) Count de Palluau, (pă′lü′ŏ′,) a marshal of France, born in 1606; died in 1665.

Clerfayt or **Clairfait, de,** pron. alike dĕh klĕR′fă′, (FRANÇOIS SEBASTIEN CHARLES JOSEPH de Croix—dĕh krwà,) COUNT, an eminent Austrian general, born near Binche, in Flanders, in 1733. He fought against the Prussians in the Seven Years' war, (1755–62,) and became general-major in 1773. For his victory over the Turks, near Korammeck, he was promoted to the rank of general of artillery in 1790. He commanded a division at the battle of Jemmapes, (November, 1792.) The victory of the Austrians at Neerwinden, (1793,) where he commanded the left wing, is attributed to him. He was defeated near Tournay in 1794. He received the bâton of field-marshal, with the command of the army of the Rhine, in 1795, forced Jourdan to repass the Rhine, and gained a victory over another French army at Mentz. In 1796 he was superseded by the Archduke Charles, and became a member of the council of war in Vienna. Died in 1798.

See JOMINI, "Histoire critique, etc. des Guerres de la Révolution."

Clérion, klà′re′ŏN′, (JACQUES,) a French sculptor, born near Aix in 1640. His principal works are in the park of Versailles. Died in 1714.

Clérisseau, klà′re′sŏ′, (CHARLES LOUIS,) a successful French painter and architect, born in 1720, built the Hôtel of the Government at Metz, and published "Antiquities of France." Died in 1820.

Clerjon, klĕr′zhŏN′, (PIERRE,) a French *littérateur*, born at Vienne in 1800, wrote a "History of Lyons," (1831,) and other works. Died in 1832.

Clerk, (JOHN,) a Scottish naval tactician, born at Eldin about 1730. He is the reputed inventor of the manœuvre in naval tactics called "breaking the line," which was first tried with success by Sir George Rodney in April, 1782, when he defeated De Grasse in the West Indies. He published, in 1782, an "Essay on Naval Tactics." Died in 1812.

See CHAMBERS, "Biographical Dictionary of Eminent Scotsmen."

Clerk, (JOHN,) Lord Eldin, a Scottish judge and eloquent advocate, son of the preceding, born about 1757. He lived in Edinburgh. Died in 1832.

Clerke, (CHARLES,) an able English navigator, born in 1741. He accompanied Captain Cook in his voyages around the world between 1768 and 1776, and upon the death of Cook he became commander of the expedition. He died at sea in 1779.

See COOK, "Voyages;" W. SMITH, "Voyages around the World."

Clermont, de, dĕh klĕR′mŏN′, (LOUIS de Bourbon Condé—dĕh booR′bŏN′ kŏN′dà′,) COMTE, a French prince, born in 1709. He displayed courage and ability in several campaigns between 1733 and 1750. About 1754 he was admitted into the French Academy. He commanded the army in Hanover in 1758, and was defeated at Crevelt. Died in 1770.

Clermont-Tonnerre, de, dĕh klĕR′mŏN′ to′naiR′, (AIMÉ MARIE GASPARD,) DUC, a French minister of state, born in Paris in 1780, was a son of Gaspard Paulin, and nephew of the cardinal. He entered the Chamber of Peers in 1815, was appointed minister of the marine in 1821, and was minister of war from 1823 until 1827.

Clermont-Tonnerre, de, (ANNE ANTOINE JULES,) CARDINAL, born in Paris in 1749, was a son of Jules Charles Henri, noticed below. He became Bishop of Châlons in 1782, and acted with the royalists in the States-General of 1789. In 1820 he was made Archbishop of Toulouse, and a cardinal in 1822. Died in 1830.

Clermont-Tonnerre, de, (FRANÇOIS,) a Frenchman, born in 1629, became Bishop and Count of Noyon. He was admitted into the French Academy in 1694, and

founded the annual prize of poetry offered by that institution. Died in 1701.

See SAINT-SIMON, "Mémoires."

Clermont-Tonnerre, de, (GASPARD,) MARQUIS, a French general, born in 1688. He commanded the left wing at Fontenoy, and had a prominent part in the battle of Laufeld in 1746. In the same year he was made marshal of France. Died in 1781.

. Clermont-Tonnerre, de, (STANISLAS,) COMTE, grandson of the preceding, was born in 1747. He was elected by the noblesse of Paris to the States-General in 1789. He was liberal in politics, and was one of those nobles who joined the Tiers-État. By his eloquence and other talents he acquired much influence in the Assembly, but was too moderate to please the party which became dominant. He advocated the absolute veto, and the civic equality of Protestants with all other Frenchmen. He perished in the massacre of August 10, 1792. "Clermont-Tonnerre and Malhouet," says Lamartine, "were statesmen rather than orators: their sure and deliberate speech impressed the reason only. They sought an equilibrium between liberty and monarchy, and believed they had found it in the English system of two chambers." ("History of the Girondists.")

Clerselier, klĕR′sà′le-à′, written also **Clersellier,** (CLAUDE,) a French metaphysician, born in 1614, was a partisan of the Cartesian philosophy. He edited the "Principles of Philosophy" and other works of Descartes. Bayle calls him the "ornament and pillar of Cartesianism." Died in 1684.

Cléry, klà′re′, (JEAN BAPTISTE CANT HANET,) the last servant of Louis XVI. of France, was born at Versailles in 1759. He served that king as valet-de-chambre in prison, and published a "Journal of the Captivity of Louis XVI. in the Temple." Died near Vienna in 1809.

See MADAME CAMPAN, "Mémoires;" VIGÉE LE BRUN, "Souvenirs."

Clesinger, klĕh-zăN′zhà′, (JEAN BAPTISTE AUGUSTE,) a successful French sculptor, born at Besançon about 1820. His statue of a "Woman bitten by a Serpent" (1847) is called one of his best works. About 1856 he exhibited in Paris an equestrian statue of Francis I.

Clève, van, văn klàv, (CORNELIUS,) a French sculptor, of Dutch extraction, born in Paris in 1645. After studying at Rome six years, he returned home in 1677, and worked in Paris with success. He was a member of the Royal Academy. Died in 1732.

Cleveland. See CLEAVELAND.

Cleveland, kleev′l*a*nd, (CHARLES DEXTER,) an American scholar and writer, born in Salem, Massachusetts, in 1802. He graduated at Dartmouth in 1827, and in 1830 was appointed Latin and Greek professor in Dickinson College, Pennsylvania. In 1834 he established a Young Ladies' Seminary in Philadelphia, which soon acquired a high reputation. He has published, besides other works, "A Compendium of Grecian Antiquities, with Maps and Illustrations;" "Compendium of English Literature from Sir John Mandeville to William Cowper," (1850;) "English Literature of the Nineteenth Century," (1851;) a critical edition of Milton's Poetical Works, (1853;) a "Compendium of American Literature," (1858;) and a "Compendium of Classical Literature," (1861.) All the last-named works have enjoyed an extensive and deserved popularity. Died in 1869.

Clev′en-ger, (SHOBAL L. VAIL,) an American sculptor, born at Middletown, Ohio, in 1812. He learned the trade of a stonecutter, which he followed in Cincinnati. Having attracted attention, he removed to Boston, where he made busts of Webster, Clay, and others, which were much admired. He afterwards studied for several years in Italy, and died at sea, while on his passage home, in September, 1843.

See TUCKERMAN, "Book of the Artists;" "Democratic Review" for February, 1844.

Clèves, de, dĕh klàv, (MARIE,) Duchess of Orléans, born in 1426, was a daughter of Adolphus IV., Duke of Clèves, and a niece of Philip the Good of Burgundy. She was married in 1440 to Charles d'Orléans the poet. She wrote ballads and other verses. Her son became Louis XII., King of France. Died in 1487.

See "Nouvelle Biographie Générale."

Cleyer, klī′ẹr, (ANDREAS,) a German botanist, born at Cassel, passed some years in Java, and enriched the science of botany with his observations and memoirs. Du Petit-Thouars says he visited China and Japan and returned to Europe about 1680.

Cleyn, klīn, (FRANZ,) a Danish painter, born at Rostock, worked in England, and received a pension from James I. Died in 1658.

Cleynaerts. See CLÉNARD.

Clichtove, klĭk′to′vẹh, (JOSSE,) a Flemish theologian, born at Nieuwpoort. He became professor of theology in Paris, and acquired a high reputation as a preacher and writer. His most popular work was an argument against Luther's doctrines, called "Anti-Lutherus," (1524.) His writings were commended by Erasmus as "uberrimus rerum optimarum fons," ("an abundant fountain of the best things.") Died in 1543.

Clicquot de Blervache, kle′ko′ dẹh blĕR′väsh′, (SIMON,) a meritorious French economist, born at Rheims in 1723, became inspector-general of commerce in 1765. He wrote an "Essay on the State of Commerce in France from Hugh Capet to Francis I.," (1756.) Died in 1796.

Clieveland. See CLEAVELAND.

Clifford. See CLIFFORT.

Clif′ford, (ANNE,) Countess of Dorset, an English lady, eminent for her virtue, intelligence, and high spirit, born at Skipton Castle in 1589, was the daughter of George Clifford, Earl of Cumberland. She was married first to the Earl of Dorset, and then to Philip Herbert, Earl of Pembroke. She built two hospitals and several churches. In the reign of Charles II. Sir Joseph Williamson nominated to her a candidate whom he wished to be returned to Parliament for Appleby. In reply she wrote this famous letter: "I have been bullied by an usurper, I have been neglected by a court, but I will not be dictated to by a subject: your man sha'n't stand." Died in 1676.

See "Autobiographic Memorials;" L. S. COSTELLO, "Memoirs of Eminent Englishwomen," London, 1844; HARTLEY COLERIDGE, "Lives of Distinguished Northerns," vol. ii.

Clifford, (ARTHUR,) an English writer, born of a noble family in 1778. He was author or editor of several works, among which are "Carmen Seculare,"and "State Papers and Letters of Sir Ralph Sadler." Died in 1830.

Clifford, (GEORGE,) third Earl of Cumberland, born in England in 1558, was famous for his gallantry. He was often the champion of Queen Elizabeth in tournaments. In 1588 he fought as captain against the Invincible Armada. He afterwards commanded several expeditions against the Spaniards. Died in 1605.

See J. BARROW, "Memoirs of the Naval Worthies of Queen Elizabeth's Reign," 1845; CAMPBELL, "Lives of the British Admirals."

Clifford, (JOHN,) LORD, called BLACK CLIFFORD, an English warrior, notorious for cruelty, fought for the house of Lancaster in the war of the Roses. He was killed in 1461. See Shakspeare's "Henry VI."

Clifford, (MARTIN,) an English writer, published "Observations on Human Reason," and other works. Died in 1677.

Clifford, (THOMAS,) eighth LORD, an English Lancastrian chief, performed an important part in the war of the Roses. He was the father of the "Black Clifford" noticed above. He was killed at the battle of Saint Alban's in 1455. (See Shakspeare's "Henry VI.")

Clifford, (THOMAS,) LORD, an English politician, born in 1630, became in 1660 a member of Parliament, in which he distinguished himself. In 1668 he was chosen a commissioner of the treasury, and in 1671 he with four others formed the notorious cabinet called the *Cabal* because the initial letters of their names happened to form that word. He was created Baron in 1672, and was lord treasurer for a short time, but resigned office in 1673. Macaulay calls him the most respectable member of the Cabal. Died in 1673.

See MACAULAY's "History of England."

Cliffort, klif′fọrt, or **Clifford,** (GEORGE,) a rich banker of Amsterdam, whose name is rendered memorable by his connection with Linnæus. Having a taste for natural history, he formed near Amsterdam a fine garden, with a rich collection of objects in natural history. When Linnæus was a poor student, he was employed to arrange and

direct this museum and garden, which he described in his "Hortus Cliffortianus," (1737,) a richly-illustrated work.

Clift, (WILLIAM,) F.R.S., an English naturalist, born near Bodmin in 1775, was employed as artist and clerk by the great John Hunter. He became conservator of the Hunterian Museum about 1800. Died in 1849.

Clif′tọn,(FRANCIS,) F.R.S., an English physician, practised in London with a high reputation, and became physician to the Prince of Wales. He translated several treatises of Hippocrates, and wrote "The State of Physic, Ancient and Modern," (1732.)

Clif′tọn, (WILLIAM,) an American poet, born in Philadelphia in 1772. He left an unfinished poem, called "The Chimeriad," a "Poetical Epistle to William Gifford," and other poems. Died in 1799.

See GRISWOLD's "Poets and Poetry of America."

Climaque. See CLIMACUS.

Clim′ạ-cus, (JOANNES,) [Gr. Ἰωάννης ὁ Κλίμακος; Fr. CLIMAQUE, kle′mȧk′,] a monk, noted for his learning and ascetic writings, was born about 525 A.D., and received the surname of SCHOLASTICUS. He passed many years as a hermit in the deserts of Sinai. In 600 he was chosen abbot of the monastery of Mount Sinai. He wrote (in Greek) several works, one of which is called "Climax, or the Ladder of Paradise," and has often been reprinted. Died in 605.

See FABRICIUS, "Bibliotheca Græca."

Clinchamp, klȧN′shŏN′, (FRANÇOIS ÉTIENNE VICTOR,) a French writer and historical painter, born at Toulon in 1787. He published a "Complete Course of Perspective, Linear and Aerial," (1840,) and "The Id:om of Painting," etc.

Cline, (HENRY,) an English surgeon, born in London about 1750, wrote an esteemed "Essay on the Form and Breeding of Domestic Animals," (1815.) Died in 1827.

Cling′mạn, (THOMAS L.,) born in Surry county, North Carolina, was elected a member of Congress in 1843, as a Whig, and was re-elected several times. Having joined the Democratic party, he was elected to the Senate of the United States in 1858.

Clin′I-as, the father of Alcibiades, was killed at the battle of Coronea in 447 B.C.

Clinias, a Pythagorean philosopher, and friend of Plato, born at Tarentum, lived about 400 B.C.

Clĭ-nom′ạ-ehus, [Gr. CLINOMAQUE, kle′no′măk′,] a philosopher of the school of Megara, was born at Thurium, and lived about 350 B.C.

Clin′tọn, (CHARLES,) COLONEL, the father of Governor George Clinton, was born in 1690 in Longford, Ireland. He emigrated to America in 1729, and settled in Ulster county, New York. He was judge of the county court, and a lieutenant under Bradstreet at the capture of Fort Frontenac. Died in 1773.

Clin′tọn, (CHARLES JOHN FYNES,) an English clergyman, born in 1799, edited or published "The Literary Remains of Henry Fynes Clinton," (1854.)

Clin′tọn, (DE WITT,) an eminent American statesman, born at Little Britain, Orange county, New York, March 2, 1769, was a son of General James Clinton and Mary De Witt. He was a nephew of George Clinton who was chosen Vice-President of the United States in 1804. He graduated at Columbia College, New York, in 1786, and studied law, but never practised it to much extent. About 1790 he became private secretary of his uncle, George Clinton, then Governor of New York. "The life of Clinton," says Renwick, "was from this moment one of political strife, into which he threw all the force of his ardent temperament and brilliant talents." He began his career as a Republican or Anti-Federalist. He married, about 1796, Maria Franklin, of New York City. In 1797 he was elected a member of the legislature, and in 1798 a Senator, of the State of New York. Among other pursuits, he applied himself with ardour to the study of natural history and other sciences.

Having become the most influential leader of the Democrats of New York, he was elected a Senator of the United States in 1801 or 1802. He made a powerful speech on the navigation of the Mississippi, and opposed a war against Spain, which disputed the right of the Americans to navigate that river. He possessed in high perfection the gift of commanding eloquence. According to Professor Renwick, "he was on all sides looked up to as the most rising man in the Union," when he was appointed mayor of the city of New York in 1803. This office was then more important than it is at the present time; for the mayor was also the president of the council and chief judge of the common pleas and of the criminal court. He continued to serve as mayor until 1807, was again appointed in 1809, and removed in 1810. He filled the same office from 1811 to 1814 inclusive, and by his wise and efficient administration contributed much to the prosperity of the city. Under his auspices the Historical Society and the Academy of Fine Arts were established. He also served as Lieutenant-Governor for two years, 1811–13. He was one of seven commissioners appointed in 1809 to examine and survey a route for a canal from the Hudson to the lakes.

De Witt Clinton and Aaron Burr were political rivals; and, after the latter fell into disgrace, Daniel D. Tompkins became a competitor for the leadership of the New York Democracy. Tompkins excelled in the art of gaining the favour of the people, while Clinton was deficient in popular arts and found it more difficult to ingratiate himself with strangers. His popularity was impaired by his disagreement with President Madison in relation to the war of 1812, for which he thought the country was not well prepared. He was nominated for the office of President of the United States in 1812, and received eighty-nine electoral votes, cast by New Hampshire, Massachusetts, Rhode Island, Connecticut, New York, New Jersey, Delaware, and Maryland, but was defeated by James Madison.

He was the first president of the Literary and Philosophical Society, founded about 1814. According to Mr. Renwick, "the charge of being opposed to a war with Great Britain, which has been so often urged against him, is devoid of foundation." In 1815 he gave a new impulse to internal improvement by an able memorial in favour of the immediate construction of the Erie Canal. The merit of this memorial, together with his subsequent services, was such as to entitle him to stand first in the list of the promoters of this vast and beneficent enterprise, on which his political prospects and reputation were staked. In the spring of 1817 a bill authorizing the construction of the Erie Canal passed the legislature. Mr. Clinton was almost unanimously elected Governor of New York about May, 1817; but his opponents soon formed against him a powerful party, called "Bucktails," who denounced the projected canal as visionary and impracticable. The canal policy was the chief point at issue in the election of 1820, and Governor Clinton was then re-elected in preference to his old rival, Daniel D. Tompkins; but the opponents of Clinton obtained majorities in both branches of the legislature.

He was pre-eminent among statesmen for his comprehensive views and his liberal patronage of learning and schools. In a message to the legislature he affirmed, "It cannot be too forcibly inculcated, nor too generally understood, that in promoting the great interests of moral and intellectual cultivation there can be no prodigality in the application of the public treasure." While he filled the office of Governor he was also president of the Board of Canal Commissioners. Having lost his first wife in 1818, he married Catherine Jones about 1820. He declined to be a candidate for Governor in 1822, and the election of that year resulted in the success of his adversaries, who removed him from the office of canal commissioner in 1824. This act excited the just indignation of the people, who elected him Governor in the autumn of 1824 by a majority of about 16,000, a greater majority than any candidate had ever received. The Erie Canal was completed in 1825, and Governor Clinton lived to witness the unexampled prosperity which it produced. The opening of the canal was celebrated with pomp in October, 1825, when the Governor was conveyed in a barge through a triumphal progress from Lake Erie to the city of New York. He was re-elected Governor for two years in 1826. In 1825 he declined the position of minister to England, offered to him by President Adams. He wrote several short treatises on natural history, which were published in the "Transactions" of the Literary and Philosophical Society, (of New York,) and

contributed to the Historical Society a valuable discourse on the history of the Indians of New York. He died at Albany in February, 1828, leaving several sons and daughters. His stature was tall, his person well formed, his manners dignified, and his presence majestic.

See JAMES RENWICK, "Life of De Witt Clinton," 1840; "National Portrait-Gallery of Distinguished Americans," vol. ii.; "Life of De Witt Clinton," by WILLIAM W. CAMPBELL, 1849; "Memoir of De Witt Clinton," by DAVID HOSACK, 1829; "North American Review" for October, 1829.

Clinton, (EDWARD.) See LINCOLN, EARL OF.

Clinton, (GEORGE,) fourth Vice-President of the United States, youngest son of Colonel Charles Clinton, was born in Ulster county, New York, in 1739. He practised law with success, and became the head of the Whig party in the Colonial Assembly of New York. Elected to the Continental Congress in 1775, he voted for the Declaration of Independence; but, being called shortly after to take command of a brigade of New York militia, his name does not appear among the signers of that instrument. Chosen Governor of New York at the first election under the State Constitution in 1777, he held the office, by successive re-elections, for eighteen years. In 1788 he was chosen president of the convention called to adopt or reject the Federal Constitution, which he opposed, as giving too much power to the central government and too little to the States. Governor Clinton was thenceforth the leader of the Republican party in New York, and at the close of Washington's first term, in 1792, received fifty electoral votes for Vice-President. He was again chosen Governor of New York in 1801, and in 1804 he was elected Vice-President of the United States, with Jefferson as President. In the national canvass of 1808 he was re-chosen Vice-President, James Madison being President. As President of the Senate by virtue of this office, he gave the casting vote against the re-charter of the United States Bank in 1811. Died at Washington in April, 1812.

See "Encyclopædia Americana."

Clinton, (Sir HENRY,) an English general, born about 1738, was a grandson of Francis Clinton, sixth Earl of Lincoln. He became a captain in the Guards in 1758, and had risen to the rank of major-general in 1775, when he took a prominent part in the battle of Bunker Hill. In January, 1778, he was appointed commander-in-chief instead of General Howe, who was recalled. He evacuated Philadelphia in June, and retired through Jersey to New York City. He sent an expedition against Savannah, which was successful, in 1779, and he led an army against Charleston, South Carolina, which he captured in May, 1780. In the same year he negotiated with General Arnold, and co-operated with him in his treasonable project. He was superseded by General Carleton in 1781, and returned to England in 1782. Died at Gibraltar in 1795.

See BANCROFT, "History of the United States;" "Encyclopædia Americana."

Clinton, (Sir HENRY,) an English general, born about 1765. In 1798 he acted as aide-de-camp of Lord Cornwallis in Ireland. He was made adjutant-general in 1802, and served in the East Indies until 1805. He obtained the rank of major-general in 1810, and served with distinction in several campaigns in the Peninsula under Wellington. As lieutenant-general, he commanded a division at Waterloo in 1815. For his conduct on this occasion he was rewarded with the title of knight of various orders. Died about 1830.

Clinton, (HENRY FYNES,) an eminent English classical scholar and writer, born at Gamston, Nottinghamshire, in 1781, was a descendant of the second Earl of Lincoln. He graduated at Oxford in 1805. He represented Aldborough in Parliament about twenty years previous to 1826. After long and close application to the study of Greek and Roman authors, he produced in 1834 an important work, entitled "Fasti Hellenici: the Civil and Literary Chronology of Greece," which is indispensable to students of ancient history. His "Chronology of Rome" ("Fasti Romani," 1845–50) is also highly prized. Died in 1852.

See "Literary Remains of H. F. Clinton," by C. J. F. CLINTON, 1854.

є as k; ç as s; g̃ hard; ğ as j; G, H, K, guttural; N, nasal; R, trilled; s̃ as z; th as in this. (☞ See Explanations, p. 23.)

Clinton, (HENRY PELHAM.) See NEWCASTLE, DUKE OF.

Clinton, (JAMES,) a distinguished officer in the American Revolution, fourth son of Colonel Charles Clinton, and father of De Witt Clinton, was born in Ulster county, New York, in 1736. He greatly distinguished himself in the English and French war, was appointed by Congress a colonel at the breaking out of the Revolution in 1775, and the same year accompanied Montgomery in his expedition to Canada. In 1777 he commanded, as brigadier-general, under his brother George, noticed above, at the defence of Fort Clinton against Sir Henry Clinton, with a force of 3000. He afterwards rendered valuable service in Sullivan's expedition against the Indians, and was for a long time stationed, in command of the Northern department, at Albany. In 1781 he assisted at the siege of Yorktown. After the war he filled various important civil offices in New York. Died in 1812.

See "Encyclopædia Americana."

Cli'o, [Gr. Κλειώ,] one of the nine Muses, presided over history, and was represented as holding in one hand a half-opened roll, and in the other a harp, (cithara.) See MUSÆ.

Clisson, de, dęh kle'sὸɴ', (OLIVIER,) a famous French captain, born in Bretagne about 1335. He became in 1370 a companion-in-arms of Du Guesclin, and in 1380 was made Constable of France. In 1382 he commanded the vanguard at the battle of Rosbecq. He was deprived of the command in 1391, and died in 1407, leaving a reputation tarnished by an unscrupulous avidity for money.

See LA FONTENELLE DE VAUXDORÉ, "Histoire d'Olivier de Clisson," 1825.

Clisthène. See CLISTHENES.

Clis'the-nēs, a tyrant of Sicyon, waged war against Argos, and prohibited his subjects from singing the poetry of Homer. Died about 580 B.C.

Clisthenes, Cleïs'the-nēs, or **Kleisthenes,** [Gr. Κλεισθένης; Fr. CLISTHÈNE, klès'tặn',] an Athenian statesman, who flourished about 500 B.C., was the grandfather of Pericles, and grandson of the preceding. He made important changes in the constitution, tending to increase the power of the commons, and thus became very popular. He changed the number of tribes of Attica from four to ten. After his rival Isagoras was exiled, Clisthenes was for some time the foremost man in the state. It is said that the mode of banishing by ostracism was instituted by him.

See HERODOTUS, "History," books v. and vi.; GROTE, "History of Greece;" THIRLWALL, "History of Greece."

Cli-tar'chus or **Cleï-tar'chus,** [Gr. Κλείταρχος; Fr. CLITARQUE, kle'tằrk',] a son of Dinon the historian, lived about 330 B.C. He followed Alexander the Great in his expedition to Asia, and wrote a history of the same, which has not come down to us. The veracity of this work is discredited by Quintilian and Cicero.

See VOSSIUS, "De Historicis Græcis."

Clitarque. See CLITARCHUS.

Cli-tom'a-chus, [Gr. Κλειτόμαχος,] a Carthaginian philosopher, who about 150 B.C. became a resident of Athens and a disciple of Carneades. At the death of the latter, in 130 B.C., he succeeded him as the head of the Academy. He wrote numerous works, which are not extant. Cicero often quotes him with respect.

See BRUCKER, "History of Philosophy."

Clit'o-phon, [Κλειτοφῶν,] a Greek historian of an uncertain epoch, was born at Rhodes. Plutarch quotes or borrows from several of his works.

Cli'tus or **Cleï'tus,** [Gr. Κλεῖτος,] a Macedonian officer, who accompanied Alexander in the invasion of Persia. He saved the life of that prince at the battle of the Grani'cus, (334 B.C.,) and afterwards obtained command of a division of the royal guards. In the year 328 he was appointed Satrap of Bactria. At a feast given in honour of the Dioscu'ri in that year, an angry dispute arose between Clitus and Alexander, who, being excited with wine, killed the former with a spear.

See PLUTARCH, "Alexander."

Clive, (CATHERINE,) an eminent English actress, born in 1711, made her *début* at Drury Lane about 1730. She performed in comedy for about thirty years, with distinguished success. She was married early to a Mr. Clive, from whom she soon separated. Died in 1785.

Clive, (ROBERT,) LORD, the founder of the British empire in India, an able and successful general and statesman, was born, of rather poor parents, near Market Drayton, Shropshire, in 1725. At school he made little progress in study, and was noted for his fiery passions and propensity to mischief. In his eighteenth year he went to Madras, as a writer in the service of the East India Company, then merely a trading corporation owning but a few acres of Indian ground. As his pay was small and his health was impaired by the climate, he became so weary of life that he attempted to kill himself; but his pistol twice missed fire. About that time war began between the English and French in India; and Clive entered the service of the Company as ensign in 1747. By his courage and sagacity he rose rapidly to distinction. The brilliant successes of the French governor Dupleix alarmed the English, and produced a crisis in the politics of India. Captain Clive, having obtained command of a few hundred men in 1750, turned the tide of fortune at Arcot, and gained several victories over the French and native armies combined. Having married Miss Maskelyne, a sister of the astronomer-royal, he returned to England for his health in 1753, and found himself an object of general favour and applause.

In 1755 the directors sent him back as governor of Fort Saint David. The next year Surajah Dowlah, Nabob of Bengal, captured the British garrison of Fort William, and smothered them in the "Black Hole" of Calcutta. Clive was sent to avenge this outrage. He recovered Calcutta, and compelled the nabob to sue for peace in 1757. But the war was quickly renewed, and in June, 1757, the fate of India was decided at the battle of Plassey, where Clive with 3000 men defeated about 60,000 of the enemy. Surajah was deposed, and was put to death by order of Meer Jaffier, who had been raised to the throne of Bengal in place of Surajah Dowlah. In the negotiations which preceded the battle of Plassey, Clive is censured for a breach of faith, which is not denied by his friends. The directors, on receiving news of his victory, appointed Clive Governor of Bengal. In 1759 he defeated a Dutch armament which had entered the Hoogly. In the next year he returned to England, immensely rich, and was raised to the Irish peerage as Lord Clive, Baron of Plassey. He was elected to Parliament, where he acquired great influence. In 1764 he was again sent to India, with supreme command, and remained about a year and a half. He returned home in ill health in 1767. His enemies arraigned his official conduct, and Burgoyne in 1773 accused him in the House of abusing his power in the acquisition of riches. The result of the inquest was that they "tempered a gentle censure with a liberal eulogy." From his youth he had been subject to fits of constitutional gloom, which were now aggravated by physical maladies. He resorted to the use of opium for relief, and gradually became enslaved by its insidious power. In November, 1774, he died by suicide. "His name," says Macaulay, in a strain of somewhat exaggerated eulogy, "stands high on the roll of conquerors. But it is found in a better list,—in the list of those who have done and suffered much for the happiness of mankind."

See MACAULAY, "Essays;" SIR JOHN MALCOLM, "Life of Lord Clive," 3 vols., 1836; G. R. GLEIG, "Life of Lord Clive," 1848; "Biographia Britannica;" C. CARACCIOLI, "Life of Lord Clive," 4 vols., 1776.

Clodion, klo'de'ὸɴ', (CLAUDE MICHEL,) a French sculptor, born at Nancy about 1745; died in 1814.

Clodius, klo'de-ûs, (CHRISTIAN AUGUST,) a German poet and professor, born at Annaberg, in Saxony, in 1738, was a son of Christian Clodius, who published several works in prose and verse. He obtained the chair of philosophy at Leipsic in 1764, and that of logic in 1778. He became professor of poetry in the same city in 1782. His writings display a brilliant imagination, good taste, and extensive knowledge of the ancients. Among his chief works are "Essays on Literature and Morality," (1769,) "Latin Poems," (1787,) and "New Miscellanies," ("Neue vermischte Schriften.") Died at Leipsic in 1784.

See ERNESTI, "Elogium C. A. Clodius;" MEUSEL, "Lexiko der vom Jahr 1750 bis 1800 verstorbenen Deutschen Schriftsteller."

ă, ē, ī, ō, ū, y̆, *iong;* à, è, ò, same, less prolonged; ă, ĕ, ĭ, ŏ, ŭ, y̆, *short;* ạ, ẹ, ị, ọ, *obscure;* fär, fȧll, fȧt; mĕt; nŏt; gŏŏd; mōŏn;

Clodius, (Johann Christian,) a German Orientalist, who became professor of Arabic at Leipsic in 1724. He published a work on the Arabic language, entitled "Theoria et Praxis Linguæ Arabicæ," and a "Hebrew Lexicon," (1744.) Died in 1745.

Clodius, (Juliana Stölzel,) the wife of Christian August, noticed above, born at Altenburg in 1755, was eminent for her literary talents and attainments. Died in 1805.

Clo'dĭ-us, (Licinius,) a Roman historian, who lived probably about 100 B.C., wrote a work called Ἔλεγχος Χρόνων, (" Trial of the Times.")

Clodius, (Publius,) surnamed Pul'cher, a Roman demagogue of very profligate character, was descended from the patrician house of Claudia, and was a brother of Appius Claudius Pulcher, noticed in this work. In his youth he served in Asia under Lucullus, his brother-in-law. In 62 B.C. he committed an act of sacrilege by procuring admission to the mysteries of Bona Dea in the disguise of a woman. For this he was tried, but acquitted by means of bribery; and he became a violent enemy of Cicero, who had appeared in evidence against him. He was chosen tribune of the people in 59, and in the next year caused Cicero to be proscribed and driven into exile. (See Cicero.) He raised several bloody riots against the friends of Cicero when they proposed and passed the decree for his restoration, 57 B.C. Milo, who succeeded Clodius as tribune, and was a partisan of Cicero, had several conflicts with the former. While Clodius was a candidate for the prætorship, and Milo for the consulship, they casually encountered each other with their armed retainers, and Clodius was killed, in the year 52 B.C.

See Cicero, "Oratio pro Milone;" Drumann, "Geschichte Roms."

Clo'dĭ-us Mä'cer, (Lucius,) a Roman general, who, on the death of Nero, raised the standard of revolt in Africa, and aspired to the power of emperor. He was put to death by order of Galba in 68 A.D.

Clo'do-mir, [Fr. pron. klo'do'mėR',] the second son of Clovis, King of the Franks, became King of Orléans in 511 A.D. He was killed in battle with the Burgundians in 524. He left three sons, two of whom were put to death by their uncles, and the third, Clodoald, (Saint-Cloud,) became a monk.

Clodovæus. See Clovis.

Clodwig. See Clovis.

Clonard, de, dĕh klo'nȁr', (Joseph Ernest,) a French dramatist, born in 1765, wrote numerous comedies. Died in 1816.

Clon-cŭr'rў, (Valentine Lawless,) Lord, an Irish politician, born at Dublin in 1773, was a member of the Society of United Irishmen, was a friend of Emmet and Grattan. He wrote "Thoughts on the Projected Union between Great Britain and Ireland," (1797.) Died in 1853.

See "Personal Recollections of the Life and Times of Lord Clon-curry."

Clootz, de, dĕh klōts, (Anacharsis,) Baron, a Prussian enthusiast, born near Cleves in 1755, was a nephew of Cornelius de Pauw. Having inherited a large fortune, he became a resident of Paris, and a fanatical partisan of the Revolution. Assuming the title of the "orator of the human race," he appeared at the bar of the Assembly in 1790, at the head of a pretended deputation from foreign nations. In 1792 he was elected to the Convention by the dominant party. He was proscribed by Robespierre, and executed in March, 1794.

See " Nouvelle Biographie Générale;" "Biographie Universelle."

Clopinel. See Meun.

Cloquet, klo'kȧ', (Hippolyte,) a distinguished professor of anatomy, was born in Paris in 1787. He wrote, besides other works, a "Treatise on Descriptive Anatomy," (1815.) Died about 1840.

Cloquet, (Jules Germain,) an eminent French physician and surgeon, a brother of the preceding, was born in Paris in 1790. He acquired a high reputation as professor, writer, and practitioner. In 1831 he was appointed professor of clinical surgery in the Faculty of Paris. He wrote "Human Anatomy," ("Anatomie de l'Homme," 5 vols., 1821–30,) and other professional works. He was elected a member of the Institute in 1855.

Clos. See Laclos.

Clōse, (Francis,) an eloquent English preacher, born about 1798, was for many years vicar of Cheltenham. He published "Discourses on Genesis," (1826,) several volumes of sermons, and other works, which maintain the doctrines of the Evangelical school. He was appointed to the deanery of Carlisle about 1856.

Closs, klos, or **Clossius, klos'se-ŭs,** (Johann Friedrich,) a German physician and poet, born at Marbach in 1735. He wrote several Latin poems on medical subjects. Died in 1787.

Closterman, klos'tẹr-mȧn', (Johann,) a German portrait-painter, born at Osnaburg in 1656, worked in England. Died in London in 1711.

Clostermann. See Klostermann.

Clot, klo, or **Clot-Bey, klo bȧ,** (Antoine,) a French physician, born near Marseilles about 1796. He became chief surgeon of Mehemet Ali, Viceroy of Egypt, about 1823, and founded a medical school in that country. He published "Observations on Egypt," (2 vols., 1840.) In 1849 he returned to France. Died in 1868.

See "Foreign Quarterly Review" for July, 1841.

Clot-Bey. See Clot, (Antoine.)

Clotaire, klo'tȁr', [Lat. Clota'rius,] **I.,** the fourth son of Clovis, King of the Franks, was born in 497 A.D. At the death of Clovis, in 511, he became King of Soissons. He extended his dominions by murdering his nephews, the heirs of the kingdoms of Orléans and Austrasia, and before his death he became ruler over all the territory which Clovis had divided among his sons. Paris was his capital after 558. He died about 560 A.D., leaving four sons,—Caribert, Gontran, Sigebert, and Chilpéric I.

See Jean Bouchet, "Histoire et Chronique de Clotaire I," 1584; Sismondi, "Histoire des Français."

Clotaire II., the son of Chilpéric I. and of Frédégonde, was an infant when he became heir to the kingdom of Soissons in 584 A.D. His mother was regent until her death in 597. By dethroning Brunehaut, Queen of Austrasia, whom, with her sons, he put to death, he made himself master of all France about 615. He was the first who conceded to the mayor of the palace a tenure of office for life. His abilities and success procured him the surname of "the Great." He died in 628, and was succeeded by his son Dagobert.

See Sismondi, "Histoire des Français."

Clotaire III., the eldest son of Clovis II., King of the Franks, was a minor when his father died, in 655 A.D.; and, the kingdom being divided into two portions, he inherited Neustria and Burgundy. He died, without issue, about the age of eighteen.

Clotaire IV., King of Austrasia, was raised to the throne in 717 A.D. by the policy of Charles Martel, but was only a nominal king. It is not known who was his father. Died in 720.

See Augustin Thierry, "Récits Mérovingiens."

Clotho. See Parcæ.

Clo-til'da, [Fr. Clotilde, klo'tēld',] Saint, Queen of France, the daughter of Chilpéric, King of Burgundy, became the wife of Clovis I. in 493 A.D. By her beauty and virtue she acquired much influence over Clovis, and was instrumental in converting him to the profession of Christianity. She adhered to the Catholic creed in opposition to Arianism, which was then very prevalent. Died in 545.

See Renaud de Rouvray, "Histoire de Sainte-Clotilde," 1840; J. Desmay, "Vie de Sainte-Clotilde," 1613; Madame de Renneville, "Vie de Sainte-Clotilde," 1809.

Clotilde. See Clotilda.

Clotilde de Vallon-Chalis. See Surville.

Clotz. See Klotz.

Cloud, kloo, or **Clo'do-ald,** Saint, youngest son of Clodomir, became an ecclesiastic, and founded a monastery at Nogent-sur-la-Rivière, since called by his name. Died about 560.

Clouet, kloo'ȧ', an able French chemist, born at Singly, near Mézières, in 1751, became professor of chemistry at Mézières. He discovered the important secret of making cast steel, which the English had found out before. Having gone to Cayenne to make some scientific inquiries, he died of fever in 1801.

e as k; ç as s; ğ *hard;* ġ as j; G, H, K, *guttural;* N, *nasal;* R, *trilled;* ŝ as z; ʇh as in *this.* (☞ See Explanations, p. 23.)

Clouet, (FRANÇOIS,) an eminent French painter, called Janet, (zhäʹnȧ́ʹ,) born about 1510, was valet-de-chambre and painter to the king. His works are extolled by Ronsard and other poets. Died about 1580. His portrait of Henry II. is regarded as a master-piece. His father, JEAN, (1485-1545,) was also distinguished as a painter.

Clouet, klŏwʹĕt, written also Clowet, Clouvet, klooʹvȧ́, or Clovet, (PETER,) a Flemish engraver, born at Antwerp in 1606. He engraved history, landscapes, and portraits with success, and worked mostly in his native city. The works of Rubens employed much of his time and talent, and the " Death of Saint Anthony" is called his master-piece. Died about 1670. His nephew, ALBERT, born at Antwerp in 1624, was a skilful engraver. He worked in Rome and Florence. Died in 1687.

See NAGLER, "Neues Allgemeines Künstler-Lexikon."

Clough, klŭf, (ARTHUR HUGH,) an English poet, born in Liverpool in 1819 or 1820. He was educated at Rugby and Oxford, and was a tutor in Oriel College. He produced in 1848 "Bothie of Tober-na-Vuolich : a Long Vacation Pastoral," (2 vols.,) which is much admired. Between 1849 and 1852 he was professor of English literature in University College, London. In 1852 he visited the United States, where he gained the friendship of Longfellow and other poets. Among his works are a version of Plutarch's "Lives," (Boston, 5 vols., 1859,) and poems called "Ambarvalia." Died at Florence in November, 1861. The "Long Vacation Pastoral," says the "Spectator," "belongs to a class of poems of which Goethe's 'Hermann and Dorothea' is perhaps the most perfect specimen; though in vigour and breadth of imagination Mr. Clough's pastoral is certainly not inferior. . . . Here we must close our notice of a truly noble poem—not without threads of unhealthy sentiment, but still broad, bright, buoyant, and tender."

See "Blackwood's Magazine" for November, 1862; "Fraser's Magazine" for January, 1849: "North American Review" for October, 1867.

Clouvet. See CLOUET.

Clovet. See CLOUET.

Clovio, kloʹve-o, (Don GIULIO,) an eminent Italian painter, born in Croatia in 1498, was a pupil of Giulio Romano. He is considered the most excellent miniature-painter that Italy has produced. He also painted some historical works, among which is a "Descent from the Cross." "His portraits," says Landon, "may be compared to those of Titian for vigour and naturel." Died in 1578.

See LANZI, "History of Painting in Italy."

Cloʹvis [Fr. pron. kloʹvèss'; Lat. CLODOVÆʹUS] I., called also Chlodwig and Hlodwig, (which is said to have become corrupted into Ludwig, Ludovicus, Louis, etc.,) King of the Franks, was born about 466 A.D., and educated as a pagan. In 481 he succeeded his father Childeric, who reigned over the Salian Franks at Tournay. By a victory over the Romans and Gauls in 486 he became master of Soissons, which he chose for his capital. In 493 he married Clotilda, a fair Christian princess, and in 496 he became a convert to her religion. This change induced the cities of Armorica to place themselves under his dominion and protection. In 507 he fixed his court at Paris. Alaric, King of the Visigoths, then possessed the region between the Loire and the Pyrenees. Clovis defeated and killed him in a great battle near Poitiers in 507, and added Aquitaine to his kingdom. He died in 511, leaving four sons, Thierri, Clodomir, Childeric, and Clotaire, among whom France was divided. "With the reign of Clovis," says Walckenaer, "commence the glory, empire, religion, laws, and usages of the French." His glory, however, was tarnished by many acts of cruelty. His descendants are called Merovingians, from Merovig, (in Latin, Merovæus,) the grandfather of Clovis.

See VIALLON, "Clovis le grand premier Roi chrétien," 3 vols., 1788; AUG. THIERRY, "Récits Mérovingiens;" SISMONDI, "Histoire des Français;" "Biographie Universelle;" "Nouvelle Biographie Générale."

Clovis II., the second son of Dagobert I., King of the Franks, was born about 633 A.D., and became King of Neustria and Burgundy in 638. Little is known of his reign, except that by revolts against the royal family of Austrasia he became sole ruler of the heritage of Clovis I. He died in 655, leaving two sons, Clotaire III. and Childeric II.

Clovis III., son of Thierri I., King of France, succeeded his father in 691 A.D., at the age of nine. Pepin le Gros in reality king, under the title of Mayor of the palace. Clovis died in 695, leaving the title to his brother, Childebert III.

See SISMONDI, "Histoire des Français."

Clowes, klouz, (JOHN,) an English Swedenborgian writer, born at Manchester in 1743. He was rector of Saint John's in Manchester about sixty years. He translated Swedenborg's "Celestia Arcana," and published several works, one of which is "Restoration of the Pure Religion." Died in 1831.

See DE QUINCEY, "Autobiographic Sketches," and "Literary Reminiscences," vol. i.

Clowes, (WILLIAM,) an eminent English surgeon, who practised in London between 1570 and 1600, and was for some years chief surgeon of Bartholomew's Hospital. He published several professional treatises, the principal of which is "The Approved Practice for all Young Surgeons," (1591.)

Clowes, (WILLIAM,) an enterprising English printer, born at Chichester in 1779. He became a master-printer in London about 1804, and twenty years later began to print by steam. His establishment eventually became, it is said, the largest and most complete in the world. Among the productions of his presses were the "Penny Magazine" and the "Penny Cyclopædia." He operated more than twenty steam-presses at once. Died in 1847.

Clowet. See CLOUET.

Clubbe, klŭb, (JOHN,) an English clergyman, born in 1703, was rector of Wheatfield. He published, besides other works, a "History and Antiquities of the Ancient Villa of Wheatfield or Whatfield," (1758,) an excellent piece of satire, directed against modern antiquaries. Died about 1772.

See NICHOLS, "Literary Anecdotes," etc.

Clubbe, (WILLIAM,) a son of the preceding, was vicar of Brandeston. He published a translation of six Satires of Horace, (1795,) "The Epistle of Horace on the Art of Poetry, translated into English Verse," (1797,) and other works. Died in 1814.

Clugny de Nuis, klün'ye' deh nü-e', (JEAN ÉTIENNE BERNARD,) a French financier, succeeded Turgot as controller-general of finances in April, 1776. He counteracted the policy of Turgot, and resorted to a royal lottery as a source of revenue. He died in office in October, 1776.

Cluʹnȳ, (ALEXANDER,) was the author of the "American Traveller," London, 1769, said to have been published under the auspices of Lord Chatham. It excited much interest in England and America at the time.

Cluseret, klü'zĕh-rȧ́', (GUSTAVE PAUL,) a French general, born in Paris in 1823. He served in the Crimean war, and gained the rank of captain. In 1859 he enlisted in the army of Garibaldi, under whom he fought with the rank of major. He offered his services to the United States, and became a colonel in the Union army about January, 1862. He commanded the advance of Fremont's army at Strasburg and Cross Keys, June, 1862.

Clusius. See LECLUSE.

Clutius. See CLUYT.

Clutʹter-buck, (ROBERT,) an eminent English antiquary, born in Hertfordshire in 1772. He published a complete "History and Antiquities of the County of Hertford," (1815-27,) with excellent plates. He resided mostly at Watford, his native place. Died in 1831.

Cluver, kloo-vairʹ, or Cluwer, [Fr. CLUVIER, klü'-ve-à'; Lat. CLUVEʹRIUS,] (PHILIP,) a learned linguist and geographer, was born at Dantzic in 1580. He visited England, France, Germany, and Italy in pursuit of information, and of materials for his works, among which are "Germania Antiqua" and "Italia Antiqua," (1624.) The latter is commended for accuracy. Died in 1623. "His works," says Hallam, "form a sort of epoch in ancient geography." ("Introduction to the Literature of Europe.")

See NICÉRON, "Mémoires;" DANIEL HEINSIUS, "Oratio in P. Cluverii Obitum," 1623.

ā, ē, ī, ō, ū, ȳ, long; ă, ĕ, ŏ, same, less prolonged; ä, ĕ, ɪ, ŏ, ŭ, ȳ, short; ạ, ẹ, ḭ, ǫ, obscure; fär, fȧll, fȧt; mĕt; nŏt; gōōd; mōōn;

Cluverius. See CLUVER.

Cluvier. See CLUVER.

Cluyt, kloit, (AUGER,) a Dutch botanist, a son of Theodore, noticed below, was born at Leyden about 1590. After making botanical researches in several countries, he became director of the botanical garden at Leyden. He wrote " Instructions for packing and conveying Trees, Plants, etc. to a Distance," (1631,) and a few other works.

See " Biographie Médicale."

Cluyt, [Lat. CLU′TIUS,] (THEODORE AUGER,) a Dutch botanist, was director of a public botanical garden founded at Leyden in 1577, which became, under his charge, one of the best that then existed. He wrote a " History of Bees," (1598.)

Clym′e-ne, [Gr. Κλυμένη; Fr. CLIMÈNE or CLYMÈNE, kle′mȧn′,] an ocean nymph, regarded as a daughter of Oceanus, the wife of Japetus, and the mother of Atlas, Prometheus, and Epimetheus.

Clȳ′mer, (GEORGE,) an American statesman, born in Philadelphia in 1739. He became about 1773 an active supporter of the popular cause, was chosen a member of Congress in 1776, and signed the Declaration of Independence. In 1780 he was re-elected to Congress. He was a member of the convention which framed the Federal Constitution in 1787, and was the founder of the Pennsylvania Agricultural Society. Died in 1813.

See GOODRICH, " Lives of the Signers to the Declaration of Independence."

Clȳt-em-nĕs′tra, [Gr. Κλυταιμνήστρα; Fr. CLYTEMNESTRE, kle′tĕm′nĕstr′,] the wife of Agamemnon, and the sister of Castor. Having formed a guilty connection with Ægisthus during the absence of her husband, she murdered the latter on his return from Troy. She was killed by her own Orestes.

Clytemnestre. See CLYTEMNESTRA.

Clȳt′ī-a or **Clȳt′ī-e,** [Gr. Κλυτία or Κλυτίη,] a nymph beloved by Apollo, (the sun :) having been deserted by her lover, she was changed into a heliotrope.

See OVID, " Metamorphoses," book iv.

Cnut. See CANUTE.

Cnutzen. See KNUTZEN.

Coad, kŏd, (JOHN,) an English carpenter, who was engaged in the rebellion of the Duke of Monmouth in 1685, for which he was transported to Jamaica. He wrote a curious narrative of his adventures.

See " Memorandum of the Wonderful Providences of God," etc., by JOHN COAD.

Cobad. See CABADES.

Cobb, (HOWELL,) an able American politician, born in Jefferson county, Georgia, in 1815. He was elected a member of Congress by the Democrats in 1843, and twice re-elected. In December, 1849, he was chosen Speaker of the House of Representatives. He was Governor of Georgia in 1851 and 1852, and was appointed secretary of the treasury by President Buchanan in March, 1857. He resigned before the end of 1860, was president of the Congress of secessionists which met in February, 1861, and became a major-general in the Confederate service. Died in 1868.

Cobb, (HOWELL,) an American lawyer, born at Savannah, Georgia, in 1795. He published, in 1845, a work on legal forms.

Cobb, (JAMES,) an English dramatic poet, born in 1756. He was employed as clerk or secretary by the East India Company about 1772. He composed " The Humorist," " The Strangers at Home," (1786,) and other dramas. Died in 1813.

See BAKER, " Biographia Dramatica."

Cobb, (JOSEPH BECKHAM,) son of Thomas W., noticed below, was born in Oglethorpe county, Georgia, in 1819. He was a contributor to the " American Review," and wrote, among other works, a novel entitled " The Creole." Died in 1858.

Cobb, (NATHANIEL R.,) a philanthropic merchant of Boston, was born in Falmouth, Maine, in 1798 ; died in 1834.

Cobb, (SAMUEL,) an English poet, who graduated at Cambridge in 1702. He published a volume of poems, (1707,) " The Oak and Brier," a tale, and the " Female Reign." Died in 1713.

Cobb, (THOMAS R. R.,) a lawyer, born in Jefferson county, Georgia, in 1820, published in 1851 a " Digest of the Laws of Georgia." He became a general in the Confederate service, and was killed at Fredericksburg in December, 1862.

Cobb, (THOMAS W.,) born in Columbia county, Georgia, in 1784. He was elected to Congress in 1816, and became a Senator of the United States in 1824. In 1828 he was made a judge of the superior court. Died in 1830.

Cobbe, kob, (FRANCES POWER,) a rationalistic writer on religion and morals, a descendant of Charles Cobbe, Archbishop of Dublin, was born in that city in 1822. In early youth Miss Cobbe seems to have been left very much to herself. She read not only the Bible and " Pilgrim's Progress," but also some books of a very different character. Shelley appears to have been a special favourite with her. We need not be surprised that, with such companions for her solitude, her mind should sometimes become a prey to universal doubt. As she was one day musing on the great problem of existence, she said to herself that, although she knew nothing of God, or of any law beyond her own soul, she would at least be true to that and merit the approbation of her own conscience. This resolution, we are told, brought almost immediately a renewed faith in God,—" a sense that somehow such an effort must be pleasing to her Creator, who had given her that inner law." From that hour she was a theist. Meeting not long afterwards with some of Theodore Parker's writings, she read them with great avidity and delight. Her mother's death having vividly presented to her mind the great question of a future life, she wrote to Mr. Parker, asking him why he believed in immortality. His " Sermon of the Immortal Life" was his reply. (See PARKER, THEODORE.)

Among the most important of Miss Cobbe's productions are her " Intuitive Morals," (London, 1855,) and her " Religious Duty," both of which works evince strong powers of reasoning, joined with great earnestness of character. Miss Cobbe has been pronounced the best interpreter of the views of Theodore Parker ; and " since his death," says Mr. Chadwick, " no one has done more to perpetuate his influence and increase his fame."

See " Christian Examiner" for November, 1867.

Cob′bett, (JOHN MORGAN,) a son of William Cobbett, noticed below. He published a selection of his father's political works, in 6 volumes, (1842.) In 1852 he was elected a Liberal member of Parliament for Oldham.

Cobbett, (WILLIAM,) a popular and vigorous political writer, born at Farnham, England, in 1762. He was the son of a farmer, and was self-educated. About 1784 he enlisted in the army, and served with honour in North America until 1791. Having left the service, he emigrated to the United States in 1792, and became a resident of Philadelphia, where he issued " Peter Porcupine's Gazette," a Federalist paper. He was fined $5000 for a libel on Dr. Rush. In 1800 he returned to England, and established in London " The Weekly Political Register," which at first was a Tory paper; but after the lapse of several years he became a strenuous opponent of Pitt and of the Tories. For his political libels or satires on members of government he was several times fined heavily, and in 1810 was sentenced to imprisonment for two years. He continued to issue the " Register" for thirty-three years. After two unsuccessful attempts to enter Parliament for Oldham, he was finally returned in 1832, and again in 1834. He died in 1835. He was the author of many successful works, among which are " The Emigrant's Guide," " Cottage Economy," " Advice to Young Men and Women," and " Rural Rides." His style is described as " the perfection of the rough Saxon English." He was remarkable for his mastery of the weapons of sarcasm and the resources of common sense, and had great powers of observation and description. " Cobbett," says Hazlitt, " is a very honest man, with a total want of principle. I mean, he is in downright earnest in the part he takes at the time ; but in taking that part he is led entirely by headstrong obstinacy, caprice, novelty, pique, or personal motive of some sort. He has no comfort in fixed principles. As soon as anything is settled in his own mind, he quarrels with it. If nobody else can argue against him, he is a very good match for himself."

See the piquant but not ill-natured article on Cobbett, in HAZLITT's "Miscellaneous Works," vol. v.; "Life of William Cobbett," Philadelphia, 1831; "Edinburgh Review" for July, 1807, and February, 1823; "Blackwood's Magazine" for September, 1823; "Fraser's Magazine" for August and October, 1835; "Westminster Review" for October, 1835; SIR H. L. BULWER, "Historical Characters," London, 1868.

Cob′den, (EDWARD,) D.D., an English divine, who became prebendary of Saint Paul's, and obtained several livings in London. He published Sermons, Poems, and Essays. Died in 1764.

Cobden, (RICHARD,) an eminent English Liberal statesman and economist, was born at Dunford, near Midhurst, Sussex, in June, 1804. He was the son of a farmer who owned a small estate in land. After having been initiated in business in the warehouse of his uncle in London, he removed to Manchester and established a manufactory of fine cotton goods, (prints,) in which he was successful. Between 1834 and 1838 he visited Egypt, Greece, the United States, France, and Germany. He published, about 1836, a pamphlet entitled "England, Ireland, and America," and another on Russia. He became in 1838 a prominent advocate of the free importation of bread-stuffs, and was soon known as the principal champion and orator of the National Anti-Corn-Law League, a powerful political organization, formed in 1839. In 1841 he was elected member of Parliament for Stockport. On this new arena he acquired great influence by his extensive information, oratorical talents, and indomitable energy. He also addressed many public meetings of the Anti-Corn-Law League, until the contest ended in the repeal of the Corn-Laws in June, 1846. On this occasion Sir Robert Peel made a remarkable speech, in which he generously declared that the merit of this important reform belonged to Mr. Cobden more than to any other man. After the close of the session he performed an extensive journey on the continent, and during his absence (1847) was returned to Parliament for the West Riding of Yorkshire, including Leeds and Sheffield. He was an active member of the Peace Congress of Paris in 1849, and of that held at Frankfort in 1850.

Mr. Cobden and John Bright were the leaders of the Manchester party or school, which holds an independent position with respect to the Whigs and Tories. He was in favour of the vote by ballot, of electoral reform, of the French alliance, of a pacific foreign policy, and of non-intervention in foreign quarrels. He opposed the war against Russia, (1854,) and the Chinese policy of Palmerston in 1857, with such a loss of popularity that he was defeated at the election of 1857 as candidate for Huddersfield. He was, however, elected by the voters of Rochdale in 1859. While he was absent on a visit to the United States, in 1859, a new ministry was formed by Lord Palmerston, who offered him a seat in the cabinet, (as president of the Board of Trade,) which he declined. As British commissioner, he negotiated, in 1860, an important commercial treaty with the French, which has greatly increased the trade between England and France. Referring to this treaty, Mr. Gladstone (August, 1866) said, "I don't believe that the man breathed upon earth at that epoch, or now breathes upon earth, that could have effected that great measure, with the single exception of Mr. Cobden." He was one of the few British statesmen who cordially favoured the cause of liberty and humanity in the United States during the civil war. Died April 2, 1865.

See LOUIS DE LOMÉNIE, "R. Cobden, par un Homme de Rien," 1844; "Life of Richard Cobden," by J. McGILCHRIST, 1865; JOSEPH GARNIER, "R. Cobden, les Ligueurs et la Ligue," 1846; "Brief Biographies," by SAMUEL SMILES: "British Quarterly Review" for January, 1866; "North British Review" for March, 1867.

Cobenzl, von, fon ko-bĕnt′sl, or **Cobentzel,** ko-bĕnt′sel, (JOHANN PHILIPP,) COUNT, a diplomatist, born at Laybach in 1741; died in 1810.

Cobenzl or **Cobentzel, von,** (KARL,) COUNT, an Austrian diplomatist, born at Laybach in 1712. He was placed in 1753 at the head of the government of the Austrian Netherlands. Died in 1770.

Cobenzl or **Cobentzel, von,** (LOUIS,) COUNT, an Austrian diplomatist, son of the preceding, was born at Brussels in 1753. He was ambassador to Russia in 1780,

and signed the treaty of Campo Formio in 1797. In 1801 he negotiated the treaty of Lunéville with the French, and became a minister of state at Vienna. Died in 1808.

See SÉGUR, "Mémoires."

Cobham, kob′ạm, (Sir JOHN OLDCASTLE,) LORD, an English nobleman, was the head of the sect of Lollards, whom the Catholics stigmatized as heretics. "His high character, and his zeal for the new sect," says Hume, "pointed him out as the proper victim of ecclesiastical severity." He was condemned to the flames in 1413, but escaped, and instigated his friends to an open rebellion. Hume states that he designed to seize the king at Eltham. The insurgent Lollards were overpowered in 1414; but Cobham escaped until 1418, when he was hanged. (See LOLLARD.)

See T. GAPSEY, "Life and Times of the Good Lord Cobham," London, 1844.

Cobo, ko′bo, (BARNABÉ,) a Spanish missionary, born at Lopera in 1582, passed fifty years in Peru, Mexico, etc. He wrote a work on the natural history of those countries, (still in manuscript.) Died in 1657.

Cobo, (JUAN,) a Spanish monk and missionary, born near Toledo. He went to Manilla in 1586, learned the Chinese language, and compiled a dictionary of the same. In 1592 he was sent on a mission to Japan, with the ruler of which he negotiated a treaty favourable to the Spaniards. On his return the ship was wrecked at Formosa, and he was massacred by the natives, in 1592.

Cobourg. See COBURG.

Co′bŭrg, written also **Cobourg,**[Ger.pron. ko′bōōRG,] (JOSIAS,) PRINCE, an Austrian general, born in 1737. He commanded the Austrian army which, with the aid of Suwarrow, defeated the Turks in 1789. In the spring of 1793 he was appointed generalissimo of the army of the allies, and gained a victory over the French at Neerwinden. He invaded France the same year, and took Condé and Valenciennes. Having been defeated by Jourdan at Wattignies in October, 1793, he resigned the command. Died in 1815. "He belonged," says Alison, "to the old methodical school of Lacey, and was destitute of either decision or character." ("History of Europe.")

Coccaie, (MERLIN.) See FOLENGO.

Coccapani, kok-kȧ-pä′nee, (SIGISMONDO,) an Italian painter and architect, born at Florence in 1585. He was one of the architects employed on the façade of the Duomo of Florence. Died in 1642.

Cocceius. See COCCEJUS, (JOHN.)

Coc-çē′ius, (kok-see′yŭs,) (NER′VA,) an eminent Roman jurisconsult, who was chosen consul in 22 A.D. He was the grandfather of the emperor Nerva. He obtained the favour and confidence of Tiberius, whose measures, it seems, he did not approve. His legal learning is highly extolled by Tacitus, and he is often cited in the Digest. He died by voluntary starvation about 33 A.D. His son, of the same name, was a distinguished jurist, the author of several treatises, and is supposed to have been the father of the emperor Nerva.

Cocceji. See COCCEJUS.

Coccejus, von, fon kot-sā′yŭs, or **Cocceji,** kot-sā′-yee, (HEINRICH,) BARON, a German jurist,born at Bremen in 1644. He was professor of law at Heidelberg and at Utrecht, and wrote, besides other works, a commentary on Grotius "De Jure Belli et Pacis," published by his son, (1744-48.) Died in 1719.

See LUCANUS, "Lebensbeschreibung des H. von Cocceji," 1741.

Coccejus, Cocceius, or **Cock,** (JOHN,) an eminent theologian, born at Bremen in 1603. He became professor of Hebrew at Franeker in 1636, and from 1649 to 1669 was professor of theology at Leyden. He was the founder of a school of theologians which became numerous in the United Provinces under the name of "Coccejans." He carried the system of figurative interpretation to the extreme. His fundamental rule of interpretation was that we should understand the words and phrases of Scripture in all the senses of which they are susceptible, and that almost every passage, in addition to its literal meaning, had a figurative signification. "Two natives of Holland," says Hallam, "opposite in character, in spirit, and principles of reasoning, and consequently the founders of opposite schools of dis-

ciples, stand out from the rest,—Grotius and Coccejus."
("Introduction to the Literature of Europe.") He published "Summa Doctrinæ de Fœdere et Testamento,"
(1648,) and other works. Died in 1669.

See JONCOURT, "Entretiens sur les Coccéiens;" NICÉRON, "Mémoires;" MOSHEIM, "Ecclesiastical History."

Coccejus or **Cocceji**, (SAMUEL,) a German jurist, a
son of Heinrich, noticed above, was born at Heidelberg
in 1679. He was appointed by the King of Prussia minister of state and of war in 1727, and grand chancellor
in 1746. His reputation is founded chiefly on the new
code of laws which he composed, by order of Frederick
the Great, about 1746. Died in 1755.

See MEUSEL, "Lexikon der verstorbenen Gelehrten."

Cocchi, kok'kee, (ANTONIO,) a learned Italian physician, born at Benevento in 1695, was professor of
medicine at Pisa, and subsequently of philosophy at
Florence. He published several works on medicine
and other subjects. Died in 1758. He had been a
regular correspondent with Sir Isaac Newton.

See FABRONI, "Vitæ Italorum doctrina excellentium."

Coccia, kot'chå, (CARLO,) an Italian composer, born
at Naples in 1789. Among his most popular works are
the operas "Clotilde" and "Maria Stuart."

Coccopani, kok-ko-på'nee, (GIOVANNI,) an Italian
artist, born at Florence in 1582, was versed in many
sciences and arts. In 1622 he was invited to Vienna
by the emperor, who employed him as a military engineer. He afterwards designed the palace called Villa
Imperiale at Florence. Died in 1649.

Cochard, ko'shăr', (NICOLAS FRANÇOIS,) a French
littérateur, born near Lyons in 1763; died in 1834.

Cochereau, kosh'ro', (MATHIEU,) a French painter
of genre, born at Montigny, became a pupil of David in
1807. He died at the age of twenty-seven.

Cochet, ko'shå', (JEAN,) born at Faverges, in Savoy,
became professor of philosophy in the Collége Mazarin
of Paris. He wrote, besides other works, a treatise on
Logic, said to have been the best elementary work on
that subject that had appeared in French. Died in 1771.

Cochin, ko'shăn', (CHARLES NICOLAS,) a skilful
French artist, born in Paris in 1688. He engraved with
the burin and point his own designs, and some works
of Lemoine, Coypel, and Watteau. Died in 1754.

Cochin, (CHARLES NICOLAS,) an eminent French
designer and engraver, born in Paris in 1715, was the
son and pupil of the preceding. He was chosen keeper
of the designs of the king's cabinet in 1752. In 1756
he published an excellent work, entitled "Picturesque
Journey in Italy," ("Voyage pittoresque d'Italie,")
which was often reprinted. Louis XV. granted to him
letters of nobility. Cochin etched a great number of
his own designs, and some works of Vernet and other
masters. The number of his designs and engravings
is about fifteen hundred. Died in 1790.

See BASAN, "Dictionnaire des Graveurs."

Cochin, (HENRI,) an eminent French advocate and
orator, born in Paris in 1687, was admitted to the bar in
1706. Though very eloquent in public, he was taciturn
and timid in conversation. Several volumes of his pleas
have been published. Died in 1747.

See C. LENORMAND, "Éloge de Cochin," 1825.

Cochin, (JACQUES DENIS,) a French priest, writer,
and founder of the hospital which bears his name, was
born in Paris in 1726; died in 1783.

Cochlæus. See COCHLÄUS.

Cochläus, kok-lä'us, [Fr. COCHLÉE, kok'lå'; Lat.
COCHLÆ'US,] (JOHANN,) a German theologian and controversialist, born near Nuremberg in 1479. He became
a canon of Worms, Mentz, and Breslau. He was a zealous opponent of the Protestant Reformation, and wrote
"Remarks (Commentaria) on the Actions and Writings
of Luther," (1549,) and other works. Died in 1552.

See SECKENDORF, "Historia Lutheranismi;" BAYLE, "Historical
and Critical Dictionary;" DE THOU, "History."

Cochlée. See COCHLÄUS.

Cochon de Lapparent, ko'shòn' deh lä'pä'ròn',
(Count CHARLES,) a French politician, born in 1749.
He was a deputy from Poitiers to the States-General
in 1789, and afterwards a prominent republican member
of the Convention. He was appointed prefect at Antwerp in 1804, and a member of the senate in 1809.
Died in 1825.

Cochran, (WILLIAM,) a Scottish painter of history
and portraits, born at Strathaven in 1738; died at Glasgow in 1785.

Cochrane. See DUNDONALD, EARL OF.

Cochrane, kok'ran, (ALEXANDER DUNDAS BAILLIE,)
a British writer, son of Admiral Sir Thomas John Cochrane, born in 1814, became a member of Parliament in
1841. He published "The Morea, with Remarks on
Greece," (1841,) "Young Italy," (1850,) and "Ernest
Vane," a novel.

Cochrane, (Sir ALEXANDER INGLIS,) a British admiral, brother of Archibald, noticed below, born in 1758.
He was made a post-captain in 1782, and rear-admiral
in 1804. For his services in a battle against the French
in 1806, near Hayti, he was knighted. In 1809 he
obtained the rank of vice-admiral, and in 1815 assisted
the British land-forces in the attack on New Orleans.
He became admiral of the blue in 1819. Died in 1832.

Cochrane, (ARCHIBALD,) Earl of Dundonald, a British chemist, born in 1749, was the son of Thomas, Earl
of Dundonald, whom he succeeded in 1778. He published a "Treatise on Coal-Tar," a "Treatise on the
Connexion of Agriculture and Chemistry," (1795,) and
a valuable work on "The Application of Chemistry
to Agriculture." Died in 1831. His son was a distinguished admiral, Lord Cochrane. (See DUNDONALD,
EARL OF.)

See CHAMBERS, "Biographical Dictionary of Eminent Scotsmen."

Cochrane, (JOHN,) an American general, born in
Montgomery county, New York, about 1813. He was
elected a member of Congress by the voters of New
York City in 1856 and 1858. He was appointed a brigadier-general about July, 1862.

Cochrane, (JOHN DUNDAS,) CAPTAIN, an eccentric
British naval officer, surnamed "the Pedestrian Traveller," was born about 1780. In 1820 he resolved to perform a journey around the world on foot, in pursuance
of which design he traversed Russia and Siberia as far
as Kamtchatka. Having married a native of that region,
he changed his mind, and returned by way of Russia
to England in 1823. Of this journey he published a
narrative, which is said to be curious and amusing. Died
in South America in 1825.

Cochrane, (Sir THOMAS JOHN,) a British admiral,
son of Admiral Sir Alexander Inglis Cochrane, born
about 1790, served as captain under his father in the war
against the United States in 1814. He was elected to
Parliament in 1837. Having been made a rear-admiral, he commanded on the East India station from 1842
to 1846, and became a vice-admiral about 1850.

Cock, kok, (JEROME,) a Flemish engraver and dealer
in prints, was born at Antwerp about 1510. He published several collections of his engravings, among which
are many portraits of historical personages. Some of
his works are highly prized. Died in 1570.

Cock, (JOHN.) See COCCEJUS.

Cock or **Cocke**, (MATTHEW,) a landscape-painter
of Antwerp, born about 1500, was a brother of Jerome,
noticed above. He was one of the first Flemish painters
that abandoned the Gothic style. Died in 1554.

Cockaine. See COKAINE.

Cockburn, ko'bern, (CATHERINE,) an English dramatic writer, whose maiden name was TROTTER, was
born in London in 1679. She became in 1708 the wife
of the Rev. Patrick Cockburn. She composed successful tragedies, entitled "Agnes de' Castro," "Fatal
Friendship," etc. In 1747 she produced "Remarks
on the Nature and Obligations of Virtue," which was
praised by Warburton. Died in 1749.

See CIBBER, "Lives of the Poets."

Cockburn, ko'bern, (Sir GEORGE,) G.C.B., a British
admiral, born about 1772, was a relative of Lord Cockburn, noticed below. He entered the navy in early youth,
and about 1812 obtained the rank of rear-admiral. He
took part in the capture of Washington City in 1814, and
conveyed Napoleon to Saint Helena in 1815. He was
a lord of the admiralty from 1818 to 1828, and sat in
Parliament for many years. Died in 1853.

Cockburn, (HENRY THOMAS,) LORD, an able Scottish judge, born in 1779. He was appointed solicitor-general for Scotland in 1830, and became one of the Lords of Session in 1834. He wrote articles for the "Edinburgh Review," and published "The Life and Correspondence of Lord Jeffrey," (1852.) Died in 1854.

See "North British Review" for November, 1856; "London Quarterly Review" for July, 1852; "Edinburgh Review" for January, 1857; "Blackwood's Magazine" for September and October, 1852.

Cockburn, (PATRICK,) a Scottish linguist, born at Langton, was for some years professor of Hebrew and Syriac in the University of Paris. Having become a Protestant, he returned to Scotland, and preached at Haddington. He was reckoned one of the first scholars of his time, and wrote several religious works in Latin, one of which is "The Utility and Excellence of the Word of God." Died in 1559.

Cockburn or Cockburne, (WILLIAM,) an English medical writer, born about 1650; died about 1736.

Cocke, kok, (PHILIP SAINT GEORGE,) a general, born in Virginia about 1808, graduated at West Point in 1832. He took arms against the Union, and became a brigadier-general in 1861. He killed himself in December of the same year.

Cock'er, (EDWARD,) an English teacher and educational writer, born in 1632, was a resident of London. His "Arithmetic" obtained a very large circulation, and passed through fifty-five editions between 1677 and 1758. Died about 1677.

Cock'er-ell, (CHARLES ROBERT,) an eminent English architect, born in London in 1788. He was elected a Royal Academician in 1836, and became professor of architecture in the Royal Academy in 1840. He designed the New Library at Cambridge in 1840, the University Galleries at Oxford, the College of Lampeter, and other public edifices. He was for some years chief architect of the Bank of England, in which he made considerable alterations. Mr. Cockerell was partial to the classic style of architecture. He was a foreign associate of the Institute of France. Died in 1863.

Cock'er-ill, (JOHN,) a Belgian engineer and machinist, noted for his enterprise and talents, was born of English parents in 1790. He fabricated steam-engines, etc. at the great iron-foundry of Seraing, in which King William of Holland was once a partner. Died in 1840.

See "Nouvelle Biographie Générale."

Cock'son, (THOMAS,) an English engraver of portraits, flourished about 1620-30.

Cock'ton, (HENRY,) an English writer, born about 1808. He published, besides other works, "The Ventriloquist: being the Life and Adventures of Valentine Vox," (1840.) Died in 1853.

Co'clēs, (HORATIUS,) a Roman hero, who acquired renown, about 500 B.C., by the defence of the Sublician bridge against the army of Porsena while the Romans were cutting off the communication with the opposite shore. When the bridge had been made impassable, he plunged into the river and saved himself by swimming. This legend forms the basis of Macaulay's spirited ballad in his "Lays of Ancient Rome."

See NIEBUHR, "History of Rome."

Coco, ko'ko, (VINCENZO,) an Italian writer, born at Campomarano in 1770, lived mostly in Naples. He published a philosophic romance called "Plato in Italy," (3 vols., 1806,) which was very successful, and a "History of the Revolution of Naples." Died at Naples in 1823.

See TIPALDO, "Biografia degli Italiani illustri."

Cocoli, kok'o-lee, (DOMENICO,) an Italian geometer, born at Brescia in 1747, was for thirty years professor of natural philosophy and mathematics in his native city. He published "Elements of Geometry and Trigonometry," and other works. Died in 1812.

Cocquard, ko'kǎr', (FRANÇOIS BERNARD,) a French poet and prose-writer, born at Dijon in 1700; died in 1772.

Coda, ko'dä, (BENEDETTO,) an Italian painter, born at Ferrara about 1460; died about 1520.

His son, BARTOLOMMEO, born at Ferrara, was a painter of good reputation. He was living in 1558.

Codagora, ko-dä-go'rä, (VIVIANO,) an Italian painter, who lived about 1650, excelled in perspective and in pictures of ruined buildings.

Codazzi, ko-dät'see, (AGOSTINO,) an Italian engineer and geographer, born at Lugo in 1792. He emigrated to Santa Fé de Bogotá, in South America, about 1826, and was afterwards employed in the survey of Venezuela. The results of his labours were published in a work on the "Geography of Venezuela," with maps, ("Resúmen de la Geografía de Venezuela," 1841.)

Cod'ding-ton, (WILLIAM,) the founder of the colony of Rhode Island, was born in Lincolnshire, England, in 1601. He emigrated to Massachusetts in 1630, and, in consequence of a disagreement with Governor Winthrop on religious subjects, removed with a party of settlers to Rhode Island in 1638. In 1640 he was chosen governor of that colony, which position he held for seven years. He was a member of the Society of Friends. Died in 1678.

Co-dī'nus, (GEORGIUS,) [Γεώργιος Κώδινος ὁ Κυροπαλάτης,] surnamed CUROPALA'TES, a Greek compiler, who lived at Constantinople about 1450. He compiled two works, which treat of the public offices in church and state, and of the antiquities of Constantinople.

Codomannus. See DARIUS III.

Co-drā'tus, [Κόδρατος,] a Greek physician and Christian martyr, born at Corinth, was put to death about 258 A.D.

Cod'ring-ton, (CHRISTOPHER,) a British officer, born at Barbadoes in 1668, wrote some Latin verses, and gave £10,000 to form a library at Oxford. Died in 1710.

Codrington, (Sir EDWARD,) G.C.B., an English admiral, born in 1770. He was made a captain in 1794, and received a medal for his conduct at Trafalgar in 1805. He was raised to the rank of rear-admiral in 1814, and served at the battle of New Orleans in 1815. In 1821 he became vice-admiral. He commanded the fleet of the English, French, and Russians which defeated the Turks at Navarino in 1827. He obtained the rank of full admiral in 1837. Died in 1851.

See CAMPBELL's "Lives of British Admirals."

Codrington, (ROBERT,) an English writer, born in 1602, wrote a "Life of Robert, Earl of Essex," and made translations from the Latin and French. Died in 1665.

Codrington, (Sir WILLIAM JOHN,) K.C.B., an English general, son of Admiral Sir Edward Codrington, born in 1800, entered the army in 1821, became colonel in the Coldstream Guards in 1846, and major-general in June, 1854. He distinguished himself at the Alma and at Inkerman, (1854,) and was promoted to the command of the light division. He directed the attack on the Redan of Sevastopol in September, 1855. In November of the same year he succeeded General Simpson as commander-in-chief of the British army in the Crimea, and was appointed governor of Gibraltar in 1859.

Codronchi, ko-dRon'kee, (BATTISTA,) an eminent Italian physician and writer, born at Imola about 1550.

Co'drus or Ko'drus, [Κόδρος,] the last king of Athens, is supposed to have reigned about 1060 B.C. An oracle having declared that the Dorians would be victorious in war against the Athenians provided they spared the life of the Athenian king, Codrus went in disguise to the Dorian camp and provoked a quarrel, in which he was killed. His son, Medon, became archon of Athens.

Codrus, a Roman poet, was a contemporary of Virgil, who mentions him in his seventh Eclogue.

Coeberger. See KOEBERGER.

Coeck, (PETER.) See KOECK.

Coëffeteau, ko'ěf'tō', (NICOLAS,) a French Dominican and theologian, born in Maine in 1574. Henry IV. gave him the title of his preacher. At the request of Gregory XV., he wrote a work to refute A. de Dominis, who attacked the papal power. In 1617 he became titular Bishop of Dardania. His version of the history of Florus was highly praised as a master-piece of French style. Died in 1623.

See NICÉRON, "Hommes illustres."

Coehorn or Cohorn, ko'horn, [Fr. pron. ko'oRN',] (LOUIS,) a French general, born at Strasburg in 1771, was a relative of Menno van Coehorn, noticed below. He was made a general of brigade in 1807, and displayed great bravery at Friedland, and took part in the battles of Aspern, Wagram, and Lutzen, and was mortally wounded at Leipsic in 1814.

ā, ē, ī, ō, ū, ȳ, *long;* à, è, ò, same, less prolonged; ă, ĕ, ĭ, ŏ, ŭ, ў, *short;* ạ, ẹ, ị, ọ, *obscure;* fär; fàll, fàt; mêt; nŏt; gŏŏd; mōōn;

Coehorn, van, vặn koo'horn, written also **Cohorn,** (MENNO or MENNON,) BARON, a famous Dutch engineer and general, born in Friesland in 1632, or, as some say, in 1641. Having acquired skill in mathematics, he entered the army as captain at an early age, and served with distinction in the campaigns of 1673 and 1674. At the siege of Namur, (1692,) which city he had fortified, he was opposed to the French engineer Vauban. Three years later he was employed as engineer in the recapture of Namur. Among his master-pieces are the fortresses of Nymwegen, Breda, Namur, and Bergen-op-Zoom. He became lieutenant-general in 1703, and published his "New Method of Fortification," an excellent work. According to some biographers, this was published in 1685. Died at the Hague in 1704.

See ERSCH und GRUBER, "Allgemeine Encyklopaedie;" MACAULAY, "History of England," vol. iv.; NICOLAUS YPEY, "Narratio de Rebus gestis Mennonis Cohorni," 1771; Dutch version of the same, 1772.

Cœlestinus, POPE. See CELESTINE.

Cœlestius. See CELESTIUS.

Cœlius. See RUFUS CŒLIUS.

Cœ'li-us or **Cæ'li-us** (see'le-us) **An-tip'ạ-tẹr,** (LUCIUS,) a Roman historian and jurist, who wrote, about 125 B.C., a "History of the Second Punic War," which was highly esteemed until it was surpassed by Livy. Only fragments of it are extant. Cœlius was the first Roman historian that aimed at the ornaments of style. Marcus Brutus valued his work so highly that he made an abridgment of it.

Coello, ko-êl'yo, (ALONZO SANCHEZ,) a skilful Spanish painter, born in 1515. He studied at Rome in the school of Raphael, and was afterwards employed by Philip II. of Spain to adorn the Escurial. He also painted portraits of that king and his courtiers. Died in 1590.

See NAGLER, "Neues Allgemeines Künstler-Lexikon."

Coello, (CLAUDIO,) a celebrated Spanish painter, born at Madrid in 1621. He was a pupil of Ricci. About 1680 he was chosen painter to the king, (Charles II.) His master-piece is the "Collocation of the Host," which adorns the sacristy of the Escurial, and which is sufficient to immortalize his name. He is said to equal Cano in design, Murillo in colour, and Velasquez in effect. Died at Madrid in 1693.

See QUILLIET, "Dictionnaire des Peintres Espagnols."

Coelmans, kool'mǎns, (JACQUES,) a Flemish engraver, born at Antwerp in 1670; died at Aix, France, in 1735.

Coeln. See CÖLN.

Cœlus. See URANUS.

Coen, koon, (JOHN PETERSON or PIETERZON,) a Dutch colonial governor, born at Hoorn about 1587. He founded Batavia in 1619, and was chosen president of Bantam. Died in 1629.

Coenrads. See CONRAD, (ABRAHAM.)

Çœnus, see'nus, [Gr. Κοῖνος,] an able Macedonian general, a son-in-law of Parmenio, accompanied Alexander the Great in the invasion of Persia, 334 B.C. He distinguished himself at the battle of Issus, and, when Alexander proposed to march beyond the Hyphasis, he insisted on returning. He died in India in 327 B.C.

Coëssin, ko'ạ'sǎN', (F. G.,) a French ultramontane religionist, born at Lisieux in 1782, was noted for his eccentric mysticism. Died about 1842.

Coëtlogon, de, dẹh ko'êt'lo'gôN', (ALAIN EMMANUEL,) MARQUIS, a French admiral and marshal, born in 1646; died in 1730.

Coëtlogon, de, (JEAN BAPTISTE FÉLICITÉ,) COUNT, a French poet, born at Versailles in 1773. He wrote an epic poem, entitled "David," (1820,) which the royal council of instruction judged worthy to be given as a prize to students. Died in 1827.

Coëtlosquet, de, dẹh ko'êt'los'kǎ', (JEAN GILLES,) a French priest, born at Saint-Pol-de-Leon in 1700. He became Bishop of Limoges in 1739, and preceptor of the Duke of Burgundy in 1758. He was also preceptor of the Duke of Berry, afterwards Louis XVI., and a member of the French Academy. Died in 1784.

Cœur, kUR, (JACQUES,) a French merchant and able financier, born at Bourges, acquired an immense fortune. Charles VII. appointed him director of his finances. In 1448 he lent that king 200,000 crowns of gold. It is stated that he transacted more commerce than all the other merchants of France. He was falsely accused of various crimes, and in 1453 was fined 400,000 crowns and banished. He went to Rome, and received from Calixtus III. the command of part of a fleet which he sent against the Turks. He died at Scio about 1456.

See BARON TROUVÉ, "Histoire de Jacques Cœur," 1840; LOUISA S. COSTELLO, "Jacques Cœur, the French Argonaut, and his Times."

Cœur, (PIERRE LOUIS,) a French bishop and eloquent preacher, born at Tarare (Rhône) in 1805. He removed to Paris in 1835, and became a fashionable pulpit orator. He was appointed Bishop of Troyes in 1848. His sermons are compared to those of Massillon.

Cœur de Lion. See RICHARD I.

Coffin, ko'fǎN', (CHARLES,) a French scholar and poet, born at Buzancy in 1676. He succeeded Rollin in the College of Beauvais, at Paris, in 1712, and was chosen rector of the University of Paris in 1718. His "Ode on the Wine of Champagne" was admired. He gained much reputation by the hymns which he composed for the Breviary of Paris. Died in 1749.

See LENGLET, "Éloge de Coffin," prefixed to his works.

Cof'fin, (Sir ISAAC,) an English admiral, was born at Boston, Massachusetts, in 1759. He was raised to the rank of admiral about 1814. Died in 1839.

Coffin, (ROBERT S.,) a printer and poet, called "the Boston Bard," born at Brunswick, Maine, in 1797. He served as a sailor in the war of 1812. Died in 1827.

Coffinhal, ko'fe'nǎl', (JEAN BAPTISTE,) a French Jacobin, born at Aurillac in 1754. He became a judge of the Revolutionary Tribunal in Paris in 1793, and a partisan of Robespierre. He was a party to many acts of cruelty, and fought resolutely for Robespierre on the 9th Thermidor, 1794. A few days later he was executed.

See THIERS, "Histoire de la Révolution Française."

Co'gan, (THOMAS,) an English physician, born in Somersetshire. He practised at Manchester, and wrote "The Haven of Health," and a few other treatises. Died in 1607.

Cogan, (THOMAS,) an English physician and writer, born at Rowell in 1736. He practised in Leyden, Amsterdam, and London. About 1774 he and Dr. Hawes instituted the Humane Society of London. He published, besides other works, "The Rhine, a Journey from Utrecht to Frankfort," (1794,) a "Philosophical Treatise on the Passions," (1800,) and an "Ethical Treatise on the Passions," (1807,) which are works of considerable merit. Died in 1818.

Cogels, ko'zhêl',(JOSEPH CHARLES,) a Belgian painter, born at Brussels in 1785; died in 1831.

Coggeshalle, kogz'ạl, ? (RALPH,) an English monk, who was wounded at Jerusalem when that city was besieged by Saladin. He wrote a "History of the Holy Land," and several other works. Died about 1228.

Coghetti, ko-ğet'tee, (FRANCESCO,) an Italian painter, born at Bergamo in 1804. He painted at Rome, for Prince Torlonia, several pictures, among which is "The Parnassus of Illustrious Men of all Ages." His fresco which decorates the Basilica of Savona is much admired.

Coglioni. See COLEONI.

Cognatus, the Latin of COUSIN, which see.

Cogniet, kon'ye-à', (LÉON,) a French painter of history and portraits, was born at Paris in 1794. He was elected a member of the Institute in 1849.

Cogs'well, (WILLIAM,) an American divine, born in New Hampshire in 1789. He became professor of history in Dartmouth College, of which he was a graduate, in 1841, and professor of theology at Gilmanton in 1844. Died in 1850.

Cohausen, ko'hŏw'zen, (JOHANN HEINRICH,) a German physician, born at Hildesheim about 1670. He wrote several professional works, among which was "Hermippus Redivivus," (1742.) Died in 1750.

Cohen, ko'ÔN', (ANNE JEAN PHILIPPE LOUIS,) a French littérateur, of Dutch descent, was born at Amersfoort in 1781. Among his works are a "Life of Chevalier Bayard," (2d edition, 1825,) and "Jacqueline de Bavière," (4 vols., 1821.) He translated several works of Washington Irving, Bulwer, and other English authors. Died in 1848.

See QUÉRARD, "La France Littéraire."

Cohen Atthar. See KOHEN ATTÂR.

Cohon, ko′ôN′, (ANTHYME DENIS,) born at Craon, in France, in 1594, became Bishop of Nîmes. Died in 1670.

Cohorn. See COEHORN.

Coictier. See COITIER.

Coignard, kwân′yår′, (LOUIS,) a French painter of landscapes, born at Mayenne about 1812. He obtained a first medal in 1848.

Coignet, kwân′yâ′, (GILLES,) a Flemish painter, born at Antwerp in 1530. He studied in Italy, and returned to Antwerp, where he painted landscapes and figures with success. Died at Hamburg in 1600.

See DESCAMPS, "Vie des Peintres Flamands," etc.

Coigny, de, dęh kwân′ye′,(FRANÇOIS de Franquetot —dęh fRôNk′to′,) DUKE, a French marshal, born in 1670, gained in 1734 a decisive victory over the Austrians at Parma, and another at Guastalla. In the next year he commanded in Germany, where his adversary, Prince Eugene, would not risk a battle; and the campaign was closed by a treaty of peace. He was created marshal of France in 1741. Died in 1759.

See "La Campagne de Maréchal de Coigny en Allemagne en 1743," Amsterdam, 1761.

Coigny, de, (MARIE FRANÇOIS HENRI DE FRANQUE-TOT,) DUKE, a French general, grandson of the preceding, was born in Paris in 1737. Having entered the service of Portugal in 1791, he attained the rank of captain-general. He returned to France in 1814, and was made marshal of France in 1816. Died in 1821.

Coimbra, ko-êm′bRâ, (Don PEDRO,) DUKE OF, a Portuguese prince and poet, born in 1392, was a younger son of King John I. His mother was a daughter of the English Duke of Lancaster, John of Gaunt. He travelled in Palestine and in many other foreign countries, and was chosen Regent of Portugal in 1449. He was killed in battle against Alphonso V. in 1449, and left a number of admired poems.

See BARBOSA MACHADO, "Bibliotheca Lusitana;" H. SCHOEFFER, "Histoire de Portugal."

Coin-Delisle, kwân dęh-lèl′,(JEAN BAPTISTE CÉSAR,) a French jurist, born in Paris in 1789.

Coindet, kwân′dâ′, (JEAN FRANÇOIS,) a Swiss physician, born at Geneva in 1774. For his discovery of the action of iodine on the goître (1820) he received a prize of 3000 francs from the Academy of Sciences at Paris. Died in 1834.

Cointe, Le, lęh kwânt, (CHARLES,) a French historian and priest of the Oratory, born at Troyes in 1611. As chaplain to the French ambassador, he passed several years at Münster, and rendered important services in preparing the treaty of Westphalia in 1648. He afterwards became a resident of Paris, and published his "Ecclesiastical Annals of France," (8 vols., 1665–80,) a work of much erudition. Died in 1681.

See NICÉRON, "Mémoires."

Cointre. See LECOINTRE.

Coiny, kwâ′ne′, (JACQUES JOSEPH,) a French engraver, born at Versailles in 1761; died in 1809.

Coislin, de, dęh kwâ′lâN′, (HENRI CHARLES de Camboust—dęh kôN′boo′,) DUKE, a French theologian, born in Paris in 1664. He became Bishop of Metz in 1698, chief almoner of the king, and a member of the French Academy. Died in 1732.

Coiter, koi′tęr, (VOLCHER,) an eminent Dutch anatomist, born at Groningen in 1534. He studied in Italy under Fallopius and Eustachio, and was for some years surgeon or physician in the French army. He was called one of the creators of pathologic anatomy, and made improvements in osteology and myology. He published several professional treatises. Died about 1600.

See M. ADAM, "Vitæ Eruditorum;" ÉLOY, "Dictionnaire de la Médecine."

Coitier or **Coictier,** kwâ′te-à′, (JACQUES,) a French physician, born at Poligny, became first physician to Louis XI., over whom he is said to have had great influence. Died about 1505.

Cokaine or **Cokayn,** ko-kān′, written also **Cockaine,** (Sir ASTON,) an English Catholic, born in Derbyshire in 1608, was a royalist in the civil war. He composed some worthless plays and doggerel poems, which

are only worthy of notice on account of the anecdotes which they furnish of contemporary authors or actors. Died in 1684.

See CIBBER, "Lives of the Poets."

Cokayn. See COKAINE.

Coke or **Cook,** [always pronounced kŏŏk in his own time, and at present by the members of the English bar,] (Sir EDWARD,) one of the most eminent of English judges and jurists, was born at Mileham, in Norfolk, in 1552. After graduating at Cambridge, he studied law in the Inner Temple, London, and was called to the bar in 1578. He rapidly acquired a very extensive practice, was appointed solicitor-general in 1592, and attorney-general in 1594, although the Earl of Essex strenuously urged the appointment of Francis Bacon to the last office. In 1593 he was chosen Speaker of the House of Commons. He is justly censured for his insolence to Raleigh at the trial of the latter in 1603, and for his cruelty in applying torture to persons charged with crimes. In 1606 he was appointed chief justice of the common pleas, and in 1613 chief justice of the king's bench. From this office he was removed in 1616, because he was not sufficiently obsequious to the court or king. In 1622 he was confined in the Tower many months for his opposition to the court party. He was elected to Parliament in 1625, and again in 1628, when he zealously opposed the arbitrary measures of the court, and was one of the leaders of the popular party. About 1628 he produced his celebrated work called "Coke upon Littleton," or the "First Institute," being the first part of the "Institutes of the Laws of England." It is a work of the highest authority on English law, and a rich mine of legal learning. "He hath thrown together," says Blackstone, "an infinite treasure of learning in a loose desultory order." Died in 1633.

See CHARLES W. JOHNSON, "Life of Sir Edward Coke," 2 vols., 1837; E. FOSS, "The Judges of England;" BRIDGEMAN, "Legal Biography;" GARDINER, "History of England from the Accession of James I. to the Disgrace of Chief-Justice Coke," 2 vols. 8vo, London, 1863; "Retrospective Review," vol. viii., 1823; "Edinburgh Review" for July, 1838.

Coke, (THOMAS,) a zealous Wesleyan missionary, born at Brecon, South Wales, in 1747. About 1780 he was appointed by John Wesley superintendent of the London district, and a few years later was ordained a bishop of the Methodist Episcopal Church. He made nine voyages to North America between 1784 and 1814, and incurred danger of violence by preaching against slavery. He died at sea, on a voyage to Ceylon, in 1814. His principal work is a "Commentary on the Old and New Testaments."

See S. DREW, "Life of the Rev. Thomas Coke;" REV. ROBERT STEEL, "Burning and Shining Lights," London, 1864.

Coke, (THOMAS WILLIAM.) See LEICESTER, EARL OF.

Cola, di, de ko′là, (GENNARO,) an Italian painter, born in the kingdom of Naples in 1320; died about 1370.

Colalto, ko-lâl′to, or **Collalto,** kol-lâl′to, (ANTONIO Mattiuzzi—mât-te-oot′see,) an Italian actor and dramatic author, born at Vicenza about 1717. His comedy of the "Three Venetian Twins" (1773) was very successful at Paris. Died at Paris in 1778.

Colantonio, di, dee ko-lân-to′ne-o, (MARZIO,) an Italian painter, born at Rome in 1662; died in 1701.

Colardeau, ko′lâr′do′, (CHARLES PIERRE,) a French poet, born at Janville in 1732. In 1758 he produced his "Letter from Heloise to Abelard," imitated from Pope, which was very successful. Among his best works are "The Men of Prometheus," "Epistle to M. Duhamel," and "Astarbé," a tragedy. He was admitted into the French Academy in 1776. His merit consists in the charm and harmony of his versification, rather than in the force or originality of his thoughts. Died in 1776.

See "Nouvelle Biographie Générale;" "Biographie Universelle."

Colardeau, (JULIEN,) a French poet, born in Poitou about 1590, wrote a poem on the victories of Louis XIII.

Colas de Rienzi. See RIENZI.

Colaud, ko′lô′, (CLAUDE SILVESTRE,) COUNT, a French general, born at Briançon in 1754. In 1801 he was made a senator by the First Consul, on account of his military services. Died in 1819.

Colbert, kol′bair′, (AUGUSTE MARIE FRANÇOIS,) a French general, born in Paris in 1777. He went to Egypt as aide-de-camp of Murat in 1798, and, returning with

Desaix, distinguished himself at Marengo in 1800. For his conduct at Austerlitz in 1805 he was made general of brigade, and was employed to carry to the emperor Alexander the ultimatum of the victor. He was killed in a battle near Astorga, Spain, in 1809.

See "Victoires et Conquêtes des Français."

Colbert, (CHARLES,) Marquis de Croissy, (krwǎ'se',) brother of the great Colbert, was born in Paris in 1629. He was successively councillor of state, first president of the parliament of Metz, and ambassador to England. He had a prominent part in the treaty of Aix-la-Chapelle in 1668, and was afterwards secretary of state. Died in 1696.

Colbert, (JEAN BAPTISTE,) an eminent French statesman and financier, born at Rheims on the 29th of August, 1619, was the son of Nicolas Colbert, a person of moderate fortune. In his youth he travelled through many provinces of France, giving special attention to the state of commerce and the means of improving it. In 1648 he was introduced to Cardinal Mazarin, who, discerning his merit, took him into his service and confidence, as intendant of his estate. He became a councillor of state at the age of twenty-nine, and secretary to the queen in 1654. In 1661 Mazarin died, commending Colbert to the confidence of Louis XIV. Fouquet, superintendent of the finances, aspired to succeed Mazarin as prime minister; but the king, resolving to be the actual ruler, suppressed the office of prime minister, and that of superintendent. Colbert, having given him proof that the finances were verging to a state of ruin and chaos, was appointed controller-general of finances in 1661. He reduced the *taille,* (land- and income-tax,) and established strict order and economy in all the branches of the revenue and public expenses. Though the people paid more than eighty millions annually, in 1660 only thirty-two millions were received into the treasury ; but at the death of Colbert eighty-three millions were received out of a total revenue of one hundred and fifteen millions. Under his auspices the commerce and manufactures of France were so efficiently promoted, and acquired so great prosperity, that, as Voltaire says, "he may be regarded as the founder of commerce and protector of all the arts." He formed a chamber of commerce, opened canals, chartered two companies to trade in the East and West Indies, and planted colonies in Canada, etc. In 1669 he was appointed minister of the marine, in which he made great reforms. The manufactures of glass, silk, woollen stuffs, and other commodities were either originated or much enlarged by him. He also patronized letters and science by founding the Academy of Inscriptions, the Academy of Sciences, (1666,) the Observatory, and other institutions. He was a member of the French Academy. He opposed without success the system of loans proposed by Louvois during the war which began in 1672, and constantly favoured the toleration of Protestants. His austere probity found little sympathy at the court of Louis XIV.; and he was at last supplanted (at least partially) by the more obsequious Louvois, who was minister of war. He died, however, in office in September, 1683, leaving several sons, noticed in this work. His manners were rather cold and reserved, his morals regular. Louis XIV. said he always retained at court the tone and manners of a bourgeois. Probably no minister ever rendered so great services to France as Colbert.

See D'AUVIGNY, "Vie de Colbert;" NECKER, "Éloge de J. B. Colbert ;" PIERRE CLÉMENT, "Histoire de Colbert," 1846 ; A. DE SERVIEZ, "Histoire de Colbert," 1842 ; VOLTAIRE, "Siècle de Louis XIV ;" CHARLES PERRAULT, "Mémoires ;" W. SEELIG, "Dissertatio de Colberti Administratione Aerarii," 1844.

Colbert, (JEAN BAPTISTE,) Marquis de Seignelay, (sǎn'yĕh-lǎ',) the eldest son of the great financier, was born in Paris in 1651. He inherited a good share of his father's talents and firmness. In 1676 he was appointed secretary of the navy, or minister of the marine, which, under his direction, became one of the most powerful in the world. He was chosen a minister of state in 1689, and died in 1690. His brother, JACQUES NICOLAS, born in Paris in 1654, became Archbishop of Rouen. He was admitted into the French Academy in 1678. He left a fair reputation for talents and conduct. Died in 1707.

See SISMONDI, "Histoire des Français."

Colbert,(JEAN BAPTISTE,) Marquis de Torcy,(toR'se',) a French negotiator, son of the Marquis de Croissy, born in Paris in 1665. About the age of twenty he was sent on a mission to Denmark, and in 1687 performed another to London. Between 1690 and 1700 he was appointed secretary for foreign affairs. He negotiated a separate peace with England about 1712, and took part in the general pacification of Utrecht in 1713. About 1715 he retired from office. He was a member of the Academy of Sciences, and wrote a treatise on the negotiations from the treaty of Ryswick to the peace of Utrecht. Died in 1746.

Colbert, (JULES ARMAND,) a French general, a son of the eminent statesman, was mortally wounded at the battle of Blenheim in 1704.

Colbert, (PIERRE DAVID,) a French general, born in Paris in 1774. He made the campaign of Austerlitz (1805) as aide-de-camp to Berthier, and became a general of division in 1813. He fought for Napoleon at Waterloo, but entered the service of Louis XVIII. in 1816. In 1838 he was made a peer of France. Died in 1853.

See "Victoires et Conquêtes des Francais."

Colborne, (Sir JOHN.) See SEATON, LORD.

Cŏl'burn, (WARREN,) a mathematician, born at Dedham, Massachusetts, in 1793, graduated at Harvard in 1820. He became a school-teacher in Boston, and published in 1821 his "Mental Arithmetic," which had an immense circulation in Europe as well as in the United States. He also published a Sequel to the above work. Died in 1833.

Colburn, (ZERAH,) a mathematical prodigy, born at Cabot, Vermont, in 1804. Before he was seven years old he displayed such wonderful expertness in mental arithmetic that his father began, in 1810, to exhibit him in public. He could solve with accuracy and rapidity the most difficult questions in involution, evolution, etc., without the use of figures. Being asked the number of seconds in 1813 years, 7 months, and 27 days, he quickly answered, 57,234,384,000. About 1825 he became a Methodist preacher. He lost his faculty of computation as he grew up to manhood. Died in 1840.

See his "Autobiography," 1833.

Cŏl'bў, (or kŏl'be,) (THOMAS,) an English engineer, was born at Rochester in 1784. In 1802 he was appointed assistant in the Ordnance Survey, with which his history is inseparably connected. He was raised to the rank of captain in 1807. He evinced great energy and endurance in the survey of Scotland, 1813-17. In 1820 he was chosen a Fellow of the Royal Society, a member of the Board of Longitude, and succeeded General Mudge as superintendent of the survey. He next pursued the same task in Ireland, where he used with advantage the "compensation-bars" invented by himself. The maps engraved under his direction are said to be more accurate than any previously made. He was raised to the rank of major-general in 1846. Died in 1852.

Col'chĕs-tĕr, (CHARLES ABBOT,) LORD, an English peer and vice-admiral, born in 1798, was postmaster-general during the ministry of Lord Derby in 1858-59.

Colchester, LORD. See ABBOT, (CHARLES.)

Cŏl'dĕn, (CADWALLADER,) a physician, born at Dunse, Scotland, in 1688, emigrated to America about 1708. He wrote a "History of the Five Indian Nations of Canada." He was a correspondent of Linnæus, to whom he sent several hundred American plants. He was lieutenant-governor of New York from 1761 until his death in 1776.

Colden, (CADWALLADER D.,) a grandson of the preceding, was born in Queen's county, Long Island, in 1769. He practised law in New York, was elected mayor of that city in 1818, and a member of Congress in 1822. He wrote a "Life of Robert Fulton." Died in 1834.

Coldoré, kol'do'rā', a French engraver of precious stones, appears to have been the same as JULIEN DE FONTENAY, whom Henry IV., in his letters-patent of 1608, entitles his valet-de-chambre and engraver of gems. His portraits of Henry and others are prized almost as highly as antique gems. He engraved a portrait of Queen Elizabeth, which she preferred to all others.

Cōle, (CHARLES NELSON,) an English legal antiquary, born in 1722 ; died in 1804.

Cole, (Sir GALBRAITH LOWRY,) an officer of the British army, born in 1772, was a son of the Earl of Enniskillen.

є as *k;* **ç** as *s;* **g̃** *hard;* **g̃** as *j;* G, H, K, *guttural;* N, *nasal;* R, *trilled;* s̄ as *z;* th as in *this.* (☞See Explanations, p. 23.)

He became colonel in 1801, and served with distinction in the Peninsular war, (1808–14.) Died in 1842.

Cole, (HENRY,) an English Catholic theologian, became Fellow of New College, Oxford, in 1523. He was chosen provost of Eton in 1554, and had a disputation with Cranmer in that year. He wrote "Letters to Bishop Jewel," and a few other works. Died in 1579.

Cole, (HENRY,) C.B., an English art-critic and editor, noted as the promoter of "Art-Manufactures," was born at Bath in 1808. In his youth he became assistant keeper of the public records, and by his writings caused the establishment of a general record office. He was one of the executive committee of the Exhibition of the Crystal Palace in 1851, the success of which is in great measure ascribed to him. Mr. Cole was the British commissioner for the Universal Exposition of Paris in 1855.

Cole, (THOMAS,) an eminent landscape-painter, born in Lancashire, England, in 1801, at an early age accompanied his parents to Ohio. Having had no instructions in art except what he received from an itinerant portrait-painter, he set out in 1822 to seek his fortune. After a short sojourn in Western Pennsylvania and Philadelphia, he arrived in New York City, where his works soon attracted the notice of artists and connoisseurs. His reputation was now established, his landscapes, including views of the Catskills and the White Mountains, were eagerly sought for, and he was soon enabled to visit Europe. He set out in 1829, and, after a residence of two years in London, repaired to Florence and Rome. He returned to New York in 1832, bringing with him a number of Italian landscapes, which, though perhaps no improvement on the style of his previous works, are highly esteemed by many amateurs. Cole, who in one of his letters had said, "Neither the Alps nor the Apennines, nor even Etna itself, have dimmed in my eyes the beauty of our own Catskills," now again devoted himself to his favourite subjects. The result of these labours were his "Cross in the Wilderness," "The Hunter's Return," "Home in the Woods," "Mountain Ford," and other admirable illustrations of American scenery. His great allegorical series (in four pictures) of "The Voyage of Life" is ranked among his master-pieces. Among his other pictures may be named "The Course of Empire," (in 5 parts,) "View of Mount Etna, taken from Taormina," "Kenilworth Castle," and "Dream of Arcadia." Died in 1848.

See L. NOBLE, "Life of T. Cole;" TUCKERMAN, "Book of the Artists;" "North American Review" for October, 1853; "Oration on the Death of Thomas Cole," by W. C. BRYANT, New York, 1848.

Cole, (Rev. THOMAS,) an English dissenter and religious writer, was one of the teachers of John Locke. Died in 1697.

Cole, (WILLIAM,) an English botanist, born at Adderbury in 1626. His works are "The Art of Simpling," and "Adam in Eden." Died in 1662.

Cole, (WILLIAM,) an English physician, who graduated in 1666, and practised at Bristol. He published treatises on Fevers, on Animal Secretions, etc.

Cole, (WILLIAM,) an English antiquary and divine, born in Cambridgeshire in 1714. He became rector of Bletchley in 1767, and vicar of Burnham in 1774. He contributed to the antiquarian works of Grose, Ducarel, Gough, etc., and collected manuscripts for an account of Cambridge scholars in imitation of Wood's "Athenæ." Died in 1782.

See NICHOLS, "Literary Anecdotes," etc.

Colebrooke, kōl′brŏŏk, (HENRY THOMAS,) an eminent Oriental scholar, born in England in 1765. He went to India in 1782, and held several high positions in the service of the East India Company. He published a "Grammar" and a "Dictionary of the Sanscrit Language," (1808,) and "Remarks on the Husbandry and Internal Commerce of Bengal," which, says McCulloch, "is by far the best and most trustworthy work on the subject." He was chosen professor of Sanscrit at the College of Fort William soon after the same was founded, and was at one time a member of the supreme council of Bengal. He wrote valuable treatises, which were inserted in the Transactions of the Asiatic Society. He returned to England before his death, which occurred in 1837.

See WALCKENAER, "Notice sur la Vie et les Ouvrages de Colebrooke."

Cōle′man, (WILLIAM,) an American journalist and lawyer, born in Boston in 1766. He settled in New York about 1794, and became in 1801 editor of the "Evening Post," the organ of the Federalists, which he edited with ability for about twenty years. He was intimate with Alexander Hamilton. Died in 1829.

Co-len′so, (JOHN WILLIAM,) an English theologian, born in 1814, graduated at Cambridge in 1836. He became Bishop of Natal, in South Africa, in 1854. He published, besides other works, "The Pentateuch and Book of Joshua critically examined," (1862,) which was condemned by both houses of Convocation of the province of Canterbury in 1864. He denies the inspiration and historical accuracy of several books of the Old Testament.

See "London Quarterly Review" for April, 1863; "Westminster Review" for January, 1863; "British Quarterly Review" for January, 1863.

Coleoni, ko-là-o′nee, or **Coglioni,** kŏl-yo′nee, (BARTOLOMMEO,) an Italian general, born near Bergamo in 1400. In the war between the Venetians and Milanese he fought for and betrayed both by turns. He was generalissimo of the Venetian state from 1454 until his death in 1475. He passed for the best tactician of that age.

See SISMONDI, "Histoire des Républiques Italiennes."

Co′ler, (JOHANN CHRISTOPH,) a German theologian, born near Langensalza in 1691, published a journal called "Auserlesene theologik Bibliothek," (1724–36,) in which he gave an analysis of recent works on theology. Died in 1736.

See JÖCHER, "Allgemeines Gelehrten-Lexikon."

Coleridge, kōl′rij, (Rev. DERWENT,) a son of the celebrated poet S. T. Coleridge, was born at Keswick in 1800, and educated at Cambridge. He was ordained about 1826, and became a prebendary of Saint Paul's, London. In 1839 he published "The Scriptural Character of the English Church considered." He succeeded his sister (Sara H.) as editor of his father's unpublished works. His "Memoir of Hartley Coleridge" is highly praised. He is, or was recently, principal of Saint Mark's College, Chelsea.

Coleridge, (HARTLEY,) an English poet and prodigy, born at Clevedon, near Bristol, in 1796, was the eldest son of the eminent poet. In 1800 his father removed to Keswick, in the Lake region. Hartley was a deep thinker in childhood, and was in all periods of his life dreamy, wayward, and fantastic. While he was a "baby in his mother's arms," he exclaimed, on seeing the lamps of London, "Oh, now I know what the stars are : they are the lamps that have been good on earth and have gone up to heaven." When he was six years old, Wordsworth addressed to him these lines :

"O thou ! whose fancies from afar are brought,
Who of thy words dost make a mock apparel,
And fittest to unutterable thought
The breeze-like motion and the self-born carol," etc.

He graduated at Oxford with honour in 1818, and was elected a Fellow of Oriel College. About a year after that event he forfeited the Fellowship by intemperance, which became habitual. The formation of this habit is partly ascribed to physical deformity and a morbid sensitiveness on that subject. His personal appearance is said to have been very grotesque, and his conversational powers most extraordinary. The latter half of his life was passed at Grasmere and Rydal Water, with no occupation but literary pursuits. He wrote articles for "Blackwood's Magazine," and "The Worthies of Yorkshire and Lancashire," which is highly esteemed. A volume of his poems, published in 1833, contains Sonnets which are greatly admired. He also left Essays on various subjects. Southey in one of his letters wrote, "It is impossible to give you any adequate idea of his oddities ; for he is the oddest of all God's creatures, and grows quainter every day." Died in 1849.

See a "Memoir of Hartley Coleridge," prefixed to his "Poems," by his brother, REV. D. COLERIDGE; "Brief Biographies," by SAMUEL SMILES, 1860; "Edinburgh Review" for July, 1851; "Fraser's Magazine" for June, 1851.

Coleridge, (HENRY NELSON,) an English lawyer and distinguished scholar, born about 1800, was the son of Colonel Coleridge, and a nephew of the celebrated poet. He was a graduate of King's College, Cambridge. In

1825 he made a voyage to Barbadoes with his uncle, Bishop Coleridge, and published "Six Months in the West Indies," which was favourably received. Having been called to the bar in 1826, he acquired extensive practice. In 1830 he published an "Introduction to the Study of the Greek Classic Poets," which was followed by the "Table-Talk of Samuel T. Coleridge." He rendered valuable services to the public as editor of his uncle's writings, viz., "Literary Remains of S. T. Coleridge," (1836,) "The Friend," "Biographia Literaria," etc. Died in 1843.

Coleridge, (JOHN DUKE,) an English orator, son of Sir John T. Coleridge, noticed below. As a Liberal member of Parliament for Exeter, he made an able speech for the Reform Bill in April, 1866. In December, 1868, he became solicitor-general.

Coleridge, (Sir JOHN TAYLOR,) an English lawyer, a nephew of the eminent poet S. T. Coleridge, was born at Tiverton in 1790. He published an edition of "Blackstone's Commentaries" in 1825, and was appointed a judge of the court of king's bench in 1835. In 1858 he was admitted to the privy council.

See Foss, "The Judges of England," vol. ix.

Coleridge, (SAMUEL TAYLOR,) an eminent English poet, critic, and speculative genius, was born at Ottery Saint Mary, in Devonshire, on the 21st of October, 1772. He was the youngest among many children of John Coleridge, vicar of that parish, and did not inherit the favours of fortune. Before he was fifteen he was deeply interested in metaphysics. He entered Jesus College, Cambridge, in 1791, gained high distinction by his classical attainments, but abruptly left the university without a degree in 1793, in consequence of the rejection of his addresses by a young lady of Cambridge. In a reckless state of mind, and with an empty purse, he enlisted in a regiment of dragoons, under the assumed name of Silas Tomken Comberback; but his friends soon procured his discharge. In 1794 he became intimate with Robert Southey, whose politics and creed were then, like his own, democratic and Socinian. They resolved to emigrate to America and to found on the Susquehanna a Utopian republic or pantisocracy, with a community of goods, the idea of which originated with Coleridge. This romantic reverie, however, was never realized, as they had not sufficient capital even for the outfit.

Coleridge had already begun to write poetry, and to display his marvellous aptitude and passion for lecturing in all places and on all occasions. In 1794 he sold to his generous friend Mr. Cottle, of Bristol, for thirty guineas in advance, the first volume of his poems, which were printed in 1796. Early in 1795 he gave lectures on political and moral subjects at Bristol, and was warmly applauded. In the same year he married Sarah Fricker, a sister of Southey's wife, and took a cottage at Clevedon, whence, after a few months, he removed to Bristol. He formed many literary projects, among which was "The Watchman," a weekly periodical, of which he issued ten numbers in 1796, but it did not pay expenses. For two or three years he lived at Nether Stowey, where he wrote the "Ancient Mariner," a poem, and "Osorio, or Remorse," a tragedy, both of which are greatly admired; also "Lyrical Ballads," in conjunction with Wordsworth, and other poems. He made some essays in preaching for the Unitarians; but his absence of mind, instability, and want of punctuality disqualified him for the regular duties of the pulpit. In 1798 he visited Germany with Wordsworth, and studied German literature, etc. at Göttingen. In 1800 he removed to Keswick, in the Lake district, where Southey and Wordsworth also resided, and from which charming locality the three friends received the appellation of "Lake Poets." About 1805 he renounced Unitarianism for the creed of the Anglican Church. He lectured on Shakspeare and the Fine Arts at the Royal Institution in 1808, and in 1809 published a periodical entitled "The Friend." About 1810, leaving his wife and daughter dependent on Southey, he departed from Keswick, and resumed his wandering habits. Between 1816 and 1825 he produced "Christabel," a "Lay Sermon," (1817,) "Zapoyla," a drama, (1818,) "Biographia Literaria," and "Aids to Reflection," (1825.) His health having failed, he contracted

a habit of using opium in excess, (a pint of laudanum per day,) which increased his natural infirmities and caused much remorse. Some years before his death he was enabled to overcome that pernicious habit. In 1816 he was kindly received in the house of Mr. Gillman, a physician of London, with whom his last years were passed. He died in 1834, after which appeared his "Literary Remains," "Table-Talk," and other works. "Born alike poet and orator, he might in either walk, or in both, have left a fame of the highest rank, but for the disease implanted in his fabric, and an indulgence which operated until the day was far spent in tarnishing the rightful glory of his gifts and acquisitions." ("London Quarterly Review.") "He displays," says John Foster, "more of what we mean by the term genius than any mortal I ever saw." The eloquence and affluence of his conversation, or rather monologues, have perhaps never been equalled. As a poet he was one of the most imaginative of modern times, and as a critic his merits are of the highest order.

See JOSEPH COTTLE, "Reminiscences of Coleridge and Southey," 1847; JAMES GILLMAN, "Life of S. T. Coleridge," 1838; LORD JEFFREY, critique on Coleridge's "Biographia Literaria," in the "Edinburgh Review" for August, 1817; and "Edinburgh Review" for April, 1848, on Coleridge and Southey; "Quarterly Review" for July, 1868; DE QUINCEY, "Literary Reminiscences," vol. i.

Coleridge, (SARA HENRY,) the only daughter of the preceding, whose genius she inherited, was born at Keswick in 1803. Her early years were passed in the home of her uncle, Robert Southey, at Keswick, where she enjoyed the society of Wordsworth the poet. In 1822 she produced an excellent version of Dobrizhoffer's Latin work on the Abipones, an equestrian people of Paraguay. She was married in 1829 to her cousin, Henry N. Coleridge, whom she assisted in editing her father's works. She was sole editor of the "Aids to Reflection," and a few others. Her imaginative faculty is displayed in her "Phantasmion," a tale, which is much admired, and has all the charms of a beautiful poem except the form and colour of verse. Died in 1852.

Coleridge, (WILLIAM HART,) D.D., an uncle of Henry Nelson, noticed above, was born in 1790. He was appointed, in 1824, Bishop of Barbadoes, which office he resigned in 1841. He published sermons, and charges to the clergy. Died in 1850.

Coles, (Captain COWPER PHIPPS,) an English naval officer, born in 1819. He is noted as the inventor of shot-proof rafts or floating batteries, and claims the invention of the turret system first used in the American Monitor.

Coles, (ELISHA,) an English teacher, born in Northamptonshire about 1640. He taught school in London, and published, besides other educational works, one on "Short-Hand," an "English Dictionary," and a "Dictionary English-Latin, Latin-English," which passed through eighteen editions between 1677 and 1772.

Col'et, (JOHN,) an eminent scholar, born in London in 1466, and educated at Oxford. He became rector of Dennington in 1485, and Dean of Saint Paul's in 1505. His lectures are said to have contributed to the Reformation, which occurred in the following generation. A few years before his death he founded and endowed Saint Paul's School, London. He published "Daily Devotions," a "Latin Grammar," and other works. Colet was an intimate friend of Erasmus, and was persecuted for his liberal opinions. Died in 1519.

See SAMUEL KNIGHT, "Life of Colet," 1724; "Biographia Britannica."

Colet, ko'lå', (LOUISE,) a popular French poetess, born at Aix, in Provence, in 1815. Her maiden name was RÉVOIL. She gained three prizes at the Académie Française for three poems, "Le Musée de Versailles," (1839,) "The Monument of Molière," (1843,) and "The Acropolis of Athens," (1854.) Among her chief productions is a poem on Woman, ("Le Poëme de la Femme,") designed to develop the various phases of the life of woman, in six parts. The first of these, called "La Paysanne," appeared in 1853.

See CUVILLIER-FLEURY, "Études historiques et littéraires."

Coletti, ko-let'tee, (GIOVANNI DOMENICO,) an Italian Jesuit, born in 1727, published a "Geographical Dictionary of South America," (2 vols., 1771,) and other works. Died in 1797.

ᴇ as *k*; ç as *s*; ḡ *hard*; ḡ as *j*; G, H, K, *guttural*; N, *nasal*; R, *trilled*; ṣ as *z*; ŧh as in *this*. (☞See Explanations, p. 23.)

Cŏl′fax, (SCHUYLER,) an American statesman, born in the city of New York on the 23d of March, 1823, a short time after the death of his father. He was a grandson of General William Colfax, who commanded General Washington's life-guards throughout the Revolutionary war. Owing to the limited circumstances of his widowed mother, he had scarcely any opportunities for obtaining a school education. In 1836 he removed with his mother to Northern Indiana. Not long after he was appointed deputy auditor for Saint Joseph county. He employed his leisure hours in reading law, in which he made great proficiency, although he appears not to have taken up the study with any view of adopting it as a profession. About 1845 he established at South Bend, Indiana, a weekly paper, called the "Saint Joseph Valley Register," which he edited for many years, and which was an able organ of the Whig party. He was secretary of the National Convention which nominated General Taylor for the Presidency in 1848. As a member of the Convention which framed the Constitution of Indiana in 1850, he opposed the clause which prohibited free coloured men from settling in that State. He was the Whig candidate for Congress in 1851, but was defeated by a small majority. In 1854 he was elected a member of Congress by the voters of the ninth district of Indiana, which he represented until he entered upon his duties as Vice-President. Soon after his entrance into Congress he made an eloquent speech on the Kansas question, of which, according to the New York "Tribune," five hundred thousand copies were printed and circulated.

He was elected Speaker of the House of Representatives by the Republicans in December, 1863; and he was afterwards twice re-elected to the same position, each time with an increased majority. In 1867 he was chosen Speaker of the Fortieth Congress. During the civil war he was an intimate friend and confidential adviser of President Lincoln. In 1865 he made an excursion across the continent to California.

"As a presiding officer," says "Putnam's Magazine," "Mr. Colfax is the most popular the House has had since Henry Clay. . . . He is eminently representative. A glance at his broad, well-balanced, practical brain indicates that his leading faculty is the sum of all the faculties,—judgment. His talents are administrative and executive rather than deliberative. He would make a better President, or Speaker of the House, than Senator." (See "Putnam's Magazine" for June, 1868.) In person he is not above middle stature. His hair is brown, and his eyes blue. His moral character is represented as irreproachable. On the 21st of May, 1868, he was nominated as the Republican candidate for the office of Vice-President of the United States, General Grant being the nominee for President. They were triumphantly elected, receiving 214 electoral votes against 80 which were given to Seymour and Blair. His peculiar fitness for the office and rare popularity induced the Convention to disregard those geographical considerations which usually require that the President and Vice-President shall not be taken from the same section of the country.

See HARRIET BEECHER STOWE, "Men of our Times," 1868; MOORE, "Life of Schuyler Colfax," 1868; "Life and Public Services of Schuyler Colfax," by E. M. MARTIN, 1868; "Grant and Colfax," by C. A. PHELPS.

Coli, ko′lee, (GIOVANNI,) an Italian painter, born at Lucca in 1634, was a pupil of P. Cortona. Died in 1681.

Coligni, (FRANÇOIS.) See DANDELOT.

Coligni or **Coligny, de,** dẹh ko′lěn′ye′, (FRANÇOIS,) a son of the admiral, born in 1557. Having escaped the massacre in which his father perished, he took refuge in Geneva in 1572. Two years later he returned, and took part in the war which was renewed between Catholics and Protestants. He was chosen colonel-general by Henry IV. while the latter was fighting against the League. Died in 1591.

Coligni or **Coligny, de,** (GASPARD,) a French general, the father of Admiral Coligni. After the battle of Marignan, (1515,) where he commanded a corps, he was made marshal of France. He married Louise, a sister of the Constable Montmorenci. He had just been appointed commander of the army sent against Spain, when he died, in 1522.

See SISMONDI, "Histoire des Français."

Coligni, ko-leen′ye or ko′lěn′ye′, or **Coligny, de,** [Lat. COLIN′IUS,] (GASPARD,) a renowned Huguenot chief and French admiral, son of the preceding, was born at Châtillon-sur-Loing, February 16, 1517. He served first in the campaign of 1543, and was knighted by Condé on the field of Cerisoles in 1544. A few years later he was appointed colonel-general of infantry, and in 1552 admiral of France. He was taken prisoner by the Spaniards at Saint-Quentin in 1557. Soon after this date he was converted to the Reformed religion. When the civil war began in 1562, Coligni was chosen second in command of the Protestant army under the Prince of Condé. He succeeded to the chief command at Jarnac in 1569, after Condé had been killed, and was defeated at Moncontour in the same year. In 1570 the court granted the Protestants peace on terms so favourable that they suspected it to be treacherous. These suspicions, however, were artfully dispelled, and Coligni went to Paris to attend the marriage of Henry of Navarre with the king's sister, in August, 1572. After he had been warmly caressed by the king, he was wounded in the arm, as he passed along the street, by a partisan of the Duke of Guise. Two days later occurred the Massacre of Saint Bartholomew, in which Coligni was killed in his chamber in the presence of the Duke of Guise. (See CHARLES IX.) Though not fortunate as a general, his prudence, firmness, and ability rendered him formidable even after defeat.

See BRANTÔME, "Discours sur l'Amiral de Châtillon;" PÉRAULT, "Vie de Coligni;" DE LA PONNERAYE, "Histoire de l'Amiral de Coligni," 1830; JEAN DE SERRES, "Gasparis Colinii Vita," 1575; SISMONDI, "Histoire des Français;" DUFFY, "Coligny, Histoire Française," 4 vols., 1824; "Nouvelle Biographie Générale."

Coligni, de, (GASPARD,) a French general, called Marshal de Châtillon, a son of François, noticed above, was born in 1584. He obtained at an early age the rank of colonel-general of infantry. He became a marshal in 1622, and gained several victories over the Spaniards in Flanders and Piedmont between 1630 and 1640. Died in 1646.

See MORÉRI, "Dictionnaire Historique."

Coligni, de, (HENRIETTE,) Countess de la Suze, (dẹh lä süz,) a French poetess, daughter of the preceding, was born in 1618. She became the wife of the Count de la Suze, from whom she was divorced in 1653. She acquired considerable renown by her elegies, odes, songs, etc., and was admired for her personal and mental graces. Died in 1673.

Coligni, de, (ODET,) Cardinal de Châtillon, (shä′te′-yŏn′,) a brother of the admiral, born in 1515, became a cardinal in 1533. About 1560 he made an open profession of the Reformed religion. After the battle of Saint-Denis (1567) he retired to England, where he died in 1571.

See BRANTÔME, "Mémoires."

Colignon, ko′lěn′yŏn′, (FRANÇOIS,) a distinguished French engraver, born at Nancy about 1621; died in 1671.

Coligny. See COLIGNI.

Colin, kol′in or ko′lăn′, (ALEXANDER,) an eminent Flemish sculptor, born at Mechlin in 1526. Invited by Ferdinand I., he went to Innspruck in 1563, and executed a magnificent monument to the emperor Maximilian I. It is composed of numerous marble figures in alto-relievo, and is a very admirable specimen of art. He was appointed sculptor to the emperor Ferdinand I., and executed other monuments in Innspruck. Died in 1612.

Colin, ko′lăn′, (JACQUES,) a French poet, born at Auxerre, was secretary to Francis I. He composed verses in Latin and French. His "Dialogue between Venus and Cupid" is an ingenious poem, in French. Died in 1547.

Colines, de, dẹh ko′lěn′, (SIMON,) an eminent French printer of the sixteenth century. He became a partner in Paris of Henry Estienne, whose widow he subsequently married. He published many editions remarkable for correctness and elegance. Died about 1546.

Colini. See COLLINI.

Colinius. See COLIGNI.

Colins, ko′lăn′, (PIERRE,) Lord of Heetvelde, a Flemish soldier and historian, born at Enghien in 1560, served under Alexander Farnese from 1581 to 1583. He wrote a "History of the most Memorable Events from 1130 to the Present Time," (1634.) Died in 1646.

ā, ē, ī, ō, ū, ȳ, *long;* à, ė, ō, same, less prolonged; ă, ĕ, ĭ, ŏ, ŭ, ў, *short;* ạ, ẹ, ị, ọ, *obscure;* fär, fäll, fät; mêt; nŏt; gōōd; mōōn;

Collado, kol-yä'DO, (DIEGO,) a Spanish missionary, born in Estremadura, went to Japan in 1619, and preached there many years. He published in Rome a valuable "Japanese Grammar" and a "Dictionary of the Japanese Language." Died at sea in 1638.

Collado, (LUIS,) a skilful Spanish anatomist, born at Valencia, lived about 1550. He made discoveries in the structure of the ear, and wrote several professional works.

Collado, (LUIS,) a Spanish military engineer of the first part of the sixteenth century, was the author of a "Practical Manual of Artillery," (1586.)

Colladon, kol'lä'dôN', (THÉODORE,) a Genevese physician and medical writer, lived about 1610–40.

Collaert, kol'lärt', (ADRIAN,) an eminent Flemish engraver, born at Antwerp about 1520. He studied in Italy, where he formed the grand manner which characterizes his works. He published many engravings designed by himself, and others, among which is "The Annunciation." Died at Antwerp in 1567.

His son JOHN, born about 1545, was a skilful engraver, and worked with his father. He executed many admired engravings after Rubens and other masters.

Collalto, kol-läl'to, (ANTONIO,) an Italian mathematician, born at Venice about 1750. He obtained the first chair of mathematics at Padua about 1808. He published a work on "Analytic Geometry," (1802.) Died in 1820.

Collalto, (ANTONIO MATTIUZZI.) See COLALTO.

Col'la-mer, (JACOB,) LL.D., an American statesman and Senator, son of Samuel Collamer, a patriot of the Revolution, was born in Troy, New York, in 1792. At an early age he accompanied his father to Burlington, Vermont, and graduated at the university in that town in 1810. He served as a lieutenant in the first campaign of the second war with Great Britain, was admitted to the bar in 1813, and rose to eminence in his profession. He was from 1833 to 1841 judge of the supreme court of Vermont. Elected to Congress in 1842, he was re-elected in 1844, and again in 1846, and in March, 1849, was appointed by President Taylor postmaster-general of the United States. On the death of the President, in July, 1850, Judge Collamer resigned, with the other members of the cabinet, and in the following autumn was again elected judge of the supreme court of Vermont, to which office he was annually re-elected till chosen United States Senator in 1854. He was re-elected to the Senate in 1860. Died in 1865.

Collanges, de, dẹh kol'lôNzh', (GABRIEL,) a French mathematician, born in Auvergne in 1521. He was valet-de-chambre to Charles IX., and, though a Catholic, was killed in the Massacre of Saint Bartholomew in 1572. He published a work on cabalistic writing.

Collantes, kol-yän'tĕs, (FRANCISCO,) a skilful Spanish painter of landscape and history, was born in Madrid in 1599. He composed with great facility. Among his chief productions are a "Saint Jerome" and a "Resurrection." Died in 1656.

Collard. See ROYER-COLLARD.

Collas, ko'läs', (ACHILLE,) born in Paris in 1795, invented about 1836 a machine by which statues can be copied or reproduced on a smaller scale. Died in 1859.

Collas, LE PÈRE, a French Jesuit, born at Thionville about 1730, was well versed in the exact sciences. In 1767 he went as missionary to Pekin, where he was employed by the emperor as mathematician. Died in Pekin in 1781.

Col-la-ti'nus, [Fr. COLLATIN, ko'lä-tăN',] (L. TARQUINIUS,) was a relative of Tarquin, the last King of Rome, and was the husband of Lucretia, whose tragical fate occasioned a revolution in 509 B.C. Collatinus and J. Brutus were the first consuls of the new Roman state. Before the end of the year he resigned, or was deposed.

See LIVY, books i. and ii. ; NIEBUHR, "Commentary on the Story of the Last Tarquinius," in his "History of Rome."

Col-la'tius, (PETRUS APOLLONIUS,) or **Collazio,** kol-lät'se-o, (PIETRO APOLLONIO,) an Italian poet, born at Novara in the fifteenth century. He wrote a poem "On the Destruction of Jerusalem," ("De Eversione Urbis Jerusalem," 1481,) and several other works.

Collé, ko'lä', (CHARLES,) a French comic poet, born in Paris in 1709. He became reader to the Duke of Orléans, and received a pension for his song on the capture of Port Mahon. In 1763 he produced the comedy "Dupuis et Desronais," which was very successful. His "Hunting-Party of Henry IV.," and "Truth in Wine," were much admired. He wrote other dramas and songs. Died in 1783.

See his "Journal Historique," 3 vols., 1805-07; "Nouvelle Biographie Générale."

Colle, kol'lä, (GIOVANNI,) an Italian physician, born at Belluno in 1558. He practised with success in Venice, and lectured at Padua, where he died in 1630, leaving several able Latin treatises on medicine.

Colle, kol'lẹh, or **Colli,** kol'lee, (HIPPOLYTE,) written also **Collibus,** a Swiss jurist, born at Zurich in 1561, was professor of law at Heidelberg. Died in 1612.

Colle, kol, (JEAN THÉODORE,) a French general, born in the department of Meurthe in 1734, served in the Seven Years' war, and subsequently in several campaigns of the Revolution. Died in 1807.

Colle, dal, dăl kol'lä, (RAFFAELLINO or RAPHAEL,) an eminent Italian painter, born at Colle, in Tuscany, about 1490. He was a pupil of Raphael and of Giulio Romano. The latter had so high an opinion of his skill that he employed his pencil on his own works. Colle's style was noble, his design correct, and his colouring warm and brilliant. He painted frescos in the Vatican, where he is said to have worked under the direction of Raphael. Among his master-pieces is a picture of the Deluge. Died in 1530.

Collenuccio, kol-lä-noot'cho, (PANDOLPH or PANDOLFO,) a learned Italian historian and jurist, born at Pesaro in the fifteenth century. He was chosen podesta of several towns, and was employed with honour as a negotiator. His principal work is a "History of the Kingdom of Naples," (1539.) He was strangled in prison by John Sforza about 1500.

Colleoni or **Colleone,** (BARTOLOMMEO.) See COLEONI.

Colleoni, kol-lä-o'nee, (GERONIMO,) an Italian writer, born at Correggio in 1742, was learned in languages, history, and philosophy. He was employed in several high offices, and wrote "Notices of the Authors who were Natives of Correggio," (1776.) Died in 1777.

Colleoni, (GIROLAMO,) an Italian painter, born at Bergamo about 1490, went to Madrid, and was patronized by the king.

Colles, kol'lis, (CHRISTOPHER,) a philosophic Irish inventor and projector, born about 1738. He emigrated to Pennsylvania before the Revolution, and devised various plans and projects for the public welfare, but never obtained much success. It is stated that he was the first person who proposed to connect the Hudson River with the lakes by a canal. Died in 1821.

Collet. See COLET.

Col'let, (JOHN,) an English humorous painter, born in London about 1725 ; died in 1780.

Collet, ko'lä', (JOSEPH,) born in the Isle of Bourbon in 1768, entered the French navy, and distinguished himself at the siege of Antwerp in 1814. He was made rear-admiral in 1828, and died the same year.

Collet, (PHILIBERT,) a French writer, born at Châtillon-les-Dombes in 1643. He became an advocate at the parliament of Burgundy, and was author of works on various subjects, among which are a "History of Reason," (in Latin,) and an "Essay on Botany." Died in 1718.

Collet, (PIERRE,) a French theologian, born near Montoire in 1693, wrote, besides other works, a "Treatise on the Holy Mysteries," (1768.) Died in 1770.

Colletet, kol'tä', (GUILLAUME,) one of the first members of the French Academy, was born in Paris in 1598. Richelieu having persuaded him to write for the theatre, he produced "Cyminde," a tragi-comedy. He composed some admired epigrams, an able "Essay on the Epigram," (1653,) a "Treatise on Pastoral Poetry," (1658,) and other works. He was a royal advocate. Died in 1659.

His son FRANÇOIS, born in Paris in 1628, was a poet of inferior merit, whom Boileau ridiculed in his satires. He wrote, besides other works, "La Muse coquette," and a "Treatise on Foreign Languages."

Col'le-ton, (JAMES,) Governor of South Carolina from 1686 to 1690, came from the Barbadoes, and in 1687 procured a change in the fundamental laws of the colony. His unpopular measures resulted in his final expulsion from the office of Governor.

Colletta, kol-lêt'tä, (PIETRO,) an Italian historian and general, born in Naples in 1775. He was appointed a general in 1812, and director-in-chief of the military engineers in 1813. He was a warm partisan of the French régime. The revolution of 1820 raised him for a short time to the post of minister of war. Having been exiled in 1821, he retired to Florence, and wrote a "History of the Kingdom of Naples," (from Charles VII. to Ferdinand IV.,) (1834,) which passed through four or more editions. Died in 1833.

See "Foreign Quarterly Review" for October, 1835.

Colli, kol'lee, BARON, a Piedmontese general, born at Alessandria in 1760, was made a lieutenant-general in 1792, and gained a victory over the French in 1793. In 1794 he obtained the chief command of the Sardinian army. He was defeated at Mondovi by Napoleon in 1796. Died in 1812. His wife was a sister of the poet Alfieri.

Collier, kol'yer, (ARTHUR,) an English philosopher, born near Sarum, in Wiltshire, in 1680. He obtained the living of Langdorf-Magna about 1704. His reputation is founded on a metaphysical work called "Clavis Universalis, or a New Inquiry after Truth," (1713,) in which he proposes to demonstrate the non-existence of the material world. Died in 1732.

Collier, (HENRY WATKINS,) an American jurist, born in Virginia in 1801. He rose to eminence as a lawyer in Tuscaloosa, Alabama, was many years chief justice of that State, and Governor from 1849 to 1853.

Collier, (JEREMY,) a famous English theologian and non-juring bishop, born at Stow-Quy, in Cambridgeshire, in 1650. He was educated at Cambridge, and ordained a priest in 1677. In 1685 he obtained the office of lecturer at Gray's Inn, London. His talents and attainments were of a high order. In politics he was an ultra-Tory ; his religious opinions were nearly identical with modern Puseyism. In 1688 he was so zealous a Jacobite that he renounced his preferments rather than take the oaths to William III. ; and he wrote several works against the new régime. In 1696 he gave absolution to Freind and Parkins, as they were about to be executed for treason and attempt to murder. To escape prosecution for this, he absconded, and was outlawed, but continued to reside in London and to write with impunity. In 1698 he published his celebrated work, a "Short View of the Profaneness and Immorality of the English Stage," which, says Macaulay, "threw the whole literary world into commotion. . . . There is hardly any book of that time from which it would be possible to select specimens of writing so excellent and so various. He was complete master of the rhetoric of honest indignation. The spirit of the book is truly heroic." Congreve appeared in defence of the stage, but his answer was a complete failure ; and a great reform in the English drama was the result of Collier's work. Between 1697 and 1705 he published, in 3 vols., "Essays on Several Moral Subjects," which have great merit. He also translated Moréri's "Historical Dictionary." In 1713 he was consecrated as a bishop by Dr. Hickes, a non-juror. Died in 1726. Respecting Collier's character Macaulay says, "We believe him to have been as honest and courageous a man as ever lived."

See "Comic Dramatists of the Restoration," in MACAULAY's "Essays."

Collier, (JOHN PAYNE,) an eminent English critic and antiquary, born in London in 1789. He produced in 1820 "The Poetical Decameron, or Ten Conversations on English Poets and Poetry," which is highly prized. In 1831 he published an excellent "History of English Dramatic Poetry to the Time of Shakspeare, and Annals of the Stage to the Restoration," (3 vols.,) and in 1844 an edition of "The Works of Shakspeare, the Text formed from a New Collation of the Old Editions," (8 vols.) His collection entitled "Shakspeare's Library" (1848) is accounted valuable. Great excitement was produced among critics and antiquaries by the publication, in 1852, of his "Notes and Emendations to

the Text of Shakspeare's Plays." These Emendations he had found in the margin of a copy of Shakspeare printed in 1632.

See "Blackwood's Magazine" for August, September, and October, 1853 ; "London Quarterly Review" for April, 1856.

Collier, (Sir ROBERT PORRETT,) an English lawyer, born in 1817, was called to the bar in 1843. He was returned to Parliament for Plymouth in 1852, was solicitor-general from October, 1863, to July, 1866, and was appointed attorney-general in December, 1868.

Collin, kol-leen', (HEINRICH JOSEPH,) a German physician, born at Vienna in 1731, was the father of the poet Heinrich Joseph von Collin, noticed below. He was chief physician of the hospital of Vienna, and wrote several medical works. Died in 1784.

Collin, kol'lin, (JONAS,) a distinguished Danish statesman and economist, born at Copenhagen in 1776. He became chief secretary or first commissioner of the treasury in 1841. He took a prominent part in many public affairs and benevolent institutions, and wrote discourses on rural economy, geography, and statistics, one of which is entitled "For Historie og Statistik især Fædrelandets," (1825.)

Collin, (MATTHÄUS,) a poet and critic, born at Vienna in 1779, was a brother of Heinrich Joseph von Collin, noticed below. He became professor of æsthetics at Cracow in 1808, and, when that city was taken by the Russians, he obtained a chair of philosophy in Vienna. He was chosen preceptor of the Duke of Reichstadt (son of Napoleon I.) in 1815. He wrote "Marius," and other dramas. Died in 1824.

Collin, ko'lăN', (NICOLAS,) a French theologian, born in the early part of the eighteenth century. He wrote a number of religious works. Died in 1788.

Collin, von, fon kol-leen', (HEINRICH JOSEPH,) a German dramatic poet, born at Vienna in 1772. After filling several civil offices with credit, he became aulic councillor, and held a high position in the ministry of finances. He produced six tragedies in verse, among which are "Regulus," (1802,) "Coriolanus," and "Balboa." He also composed several patriotic war-songs, which were much admired. Died in 1811.

Collin d'Ambly, ko'lăN' dŏm'ble', (FRANÇOIS,) a French writer, born at Ambly-sur-Meuse in 1759, was the author of many educational works. Died about 1830.

Collin de Bar, ko'lăN' deh băR, (ALEXIS GUILLAUME HENRI,) a French historical writer, born at Pondicherry, India, in 1768, was president of the superior court at the capture of that place in 1803, and then removed to France. He wrote a "History of Ancient and Modern India," (1814,) a work of some merit. Died in 1820.

Collin de Plancy, ko'lăN' deh plŏN'se', originally **Collin Danton,** (dŏN'tŏN',) (JACQUES ALBIN SIMON,) a French littérateur, a nephew of the famous Danton, was born at Plancy in 1793. Having written several heretical works, among which was "The Infernal Dictionary," he changed his course about 1837, and produced "Legends of the Holy Virgin," "Legends of the Wandering Jew," and other books of a so-called religious character.

Collin-Harleville, ko'lăN' haRl'vêl', (JEAN FRANÇOIS,) a French comic poet, born at Maintenon, near Chartres, in 1755. He produced in 1786 his first drama (in verse,) the "Inconstant," ("Inconstant Lover,") which obtained great success. His master-piece is the "Old Bachelor," which was received in 1792 with general applause. He was admitted into the second class of the Institute. La Harpe thought his "Optimiste" superior to the "Inconstant." Died in Paris in 1806.

Col'lings or **Collinges,** (JOHN,) an English nonconformist minister, born in 1623. His sermons and other theological works are highly commended by Cotton Mather and Calamy. Died in 1690.

Col'ling-wood, (CUTHBERT,) ADMIRAL LORD, an eminent English admiral, born at Newcastle-upon-Tyne in 1750. Having entered the navy in 1761, he served at Bunker Hill in 1775, and was made a post-captain in 1780. He contributed to Lord Howe's victory over the French, June 1, 1794, and displayed great skill and courage in the action off Cape Saint Vincent in 1797. In 1799 he obtained the rank of rear-admiral, and in 1804 that of vice-admiral. He was second in command

ā, ē, ī, ō, ū, ȳ, *long;* à, ê, ò, same, less prolonged; ă, ĕ, ĭ, ŏ, ŭ, ў, *short;* a, e, i, o, *obscure;* fär, fåll, fåt; mêt; nŏt; gōōd; mōōn;

at the battle of Trafalgar, (1805,) and when Nelson was killed he succeeded to the chief command. Soon after this event he was raised to the peerage. He commanded for several years with honour in the Mediterranean, and died at sea near Port Mahon in 1810. He was greatly distinguished as a naval tactician. The memoir of his life published by G. L. N. Collingwood is highly esteemed.

See, also, CAMPBELL, "Lives of the British Admirals;" "Edinburgh Review" for May, 1828.

Collingwood, (THOMAS,) an English physician, noted for his learning and versatile talents, was born near Berwick-on-Tweed in 1751. He practised in Norham, Sunderland, and London. He published "The Hermit," and other poems, and left in manuscript some mathematical works, etc. Died in 1831.

Collini, kol-lee'nee, (COSIMO ALESSANDRO,) an Italian writer, born at Florence in 1727. About 1750 he went to Berlin, where he met Voltaire, whom he served as secretary from 1752 to 1756. In 1759 he became secretary of the Elector Palatine, and director of the Cabinet of Natural History at Manheim. He wrote "My Residence with Voltaire," (1807, in French,) and several historical and scientific treatises. Died in 1806.

See VOLTAIRE, "Correspondance."

Col'lins, (ANTHONY,) an English writer on theology, born of a rich family at Heston, in Middlesex, in 1676, was an intimate friend of John Locke. He studied law, but did not practise it. He published an "Essay on Reason," (1707,) "Priestcraft in Perfection," (1709,) a "Vindication of the Divine Attributes," and a "Discourse on Free-Thinking," (1713.) These works gave offence to the orthodox, and were attacked by several able divines, among whom was Bentley. In 1718 he was chosen treasurer of the county of Essex. His "Discourse on the Grounds and Reasons of the Christian Religion" (1724) excited great commotion among the clergy, some of whom treated him as an infidel. He was a subtle disputant, and a writer of much ability. Died in 1729.

See "Biographia Britannica;" THORSCHMIDT, "Kritische Lebensgeschichte A. Collins," 1755; "Nouvelle Biographie Générale."

Collins, (ARTHUR,) an English antiquary, born in 1682. He published, besides other works, the "Peerage of England," (3 vols., 1709,) "English Baronage," and "The Life of Lord Burleigh," (1732.) The first work, augmented by Sir E. Brydges to nine volumes, (1812,) is highly prized. Died in 1760.

Collins, (DAVID,) a grandson of the preceding, was born in 1756. He became an officer in the British army, and Governor of Van Diemen's Land. He wrote a curious and interesting "Account of the English Colony of New South Wales," (1798–1802.) Died in 1810.

Col'lins, (ISAAC,) an American publisher, born in Delaware in 1746, lived at Burlington, New Jersey, at Trenton, and New York. He published an octavo Bible, the text of which was very correctly printed. Died in 1817.

See "Memoir of Isaac Collins of Burlington," 1848.

Collins, (JOHN,) an eminent English mathematician, born at Wood Eaton, near Oxford, in 1624. He published good elementary works on geometry, arithmetic, and navigation, and contributed papers to the Royal Society, of which he was chosen a Fellow in 1667. He was a correspondent of Sir Isaac Newton. Died in 1683.

See WOOD, "Athenæ Oxonienses."

Collins, (SAMUEL,) an English physician, who graduated at Oxford in 1659. Soon after that date he went to Russia, and practised nine years at the court of the Czar. He published in London, in 1671, "The Present State of Russia," and a "Treatise on Anatomy, Physiology, etc.," (1685.) He became physician to the queen, and died about 1700.

See WOOD, "Athenæ Oxonienses."

Collins, (WILLIAM,) an eminent English lyric poet, born at Chichester in 1720. Having graduated at Oxford, he went to London about 1744, with little resources except his poetical genius. There he became the friend of Dr. Johnson, who speaks well of his character, and adds that "his great fault was irresolution." His excellent odes on "The Passions," "To Mercy," "To Evening," etc. appeared in 1747, but were treated with unmerited neglect. In 1749 he received a legacy of £2000 from his uncle, Colonel Martin. The latter part of his short life was darkened by melancholy, and he was for some time an inmate of a lunatic-asylum. He died in 1756. Besides the above-named pieces, he wrote "The Dirge in Cymbeline," and a few other short poems. T. Campbell, comparing them with Milton's early works, remarks, "If they have rather less exuberant wealth of genius, they have more exquisite touches of pathos."

See JOHNSON, "Lives of the Poets;" MRS. BARBAULD, "Essay on Collins;" DRAKE, "Literary Hours;" CAMPBELL, "Specimens of the British Poets."

Collins, (WILLIAM,) an English landscape-painter, born in London in 1787, was a pupil of Morland. He was elected a Royal Academician in 1820, and visited Italy in 1836. He represented homely rural scenery and views on the sea-coast with great success, and acquired an extensive reputation. Among his most admired pictures are "Cromer Sands," "Prawn-Fishers," and a "Frost Scene," the last of which he sold for five hundred guineas. His works are finely finished, and are admired for fidelity to nature. (See a "Memoir" published by his son, W. Wilkie Collins, 1848.) Died in 1847. His son, CHARLES ALSTON, born about 1828, is also a painter.

See "Blackwood's Magazine" for February, 1850.

Collins, (WILLIAM WILKIE,) an English novelist, born in London in 1824 or 1825, is a son of the landscape-painter above noticed. He published a well-written "Life of William Collins," (his own father, 1848,) "Rambles beyond Railways," (1851,) and several successful novels, among which are "Antonina," (2d edition, 1850,) "Basil," (1852,) "The Dead Secret," (1857,) and "The Woman in White," published in "All the Year Round," (1859–60.)

Col'lin-son, (JOHN,) an English writer, published, in 1791, the "History and Antiquities of the County of Somerset." Died in 1793.

Collinson, (PETER,) an English merchant and naturalist, who rendered great services to science, especially to botany, was born in Westmoreland in 1693. He lived in London, and availed himself of his mercantile connections to procure seeds and plants from foreign lands. He was a member of the Royal Society, for which he wrote several memoirs, and was a liberal patron of the Philadelphia Library, whose commissions he executed gratis for thirty years. "He was the means," says Southey, "of procuring national advantages for his country, and possessed an influence which wealth cannot purchase. Franklin's first essays on electricity were originally communicated to this good man. They were read in the Royal Society, 'where they were not thought worth so much notice as to be printed in their Transactions;' and his paper in which the sameness of lightning with electricity was first asserted, was laughed at by the connoisseurs." (See FRANKLIN, BENJAMIN.) Collinson was a member of the Society of Friends. Linnæus named the genus Collinsonia in honour of him. Died in 1768.

See "Biographia Britannica;" FOTHERGILL and COLLINSON, "Account of the Late Peter Collinson;" and "Tribute to the Memory of Peter Collinson," by WILLIAM DILLINGHAM.

Col'li-us, (FRANCESCO,) an Italian theologian, born near Milan about 1590, was the author of two learned works, remarkable for singularity of opinions, one of which is entitled "On the Souls of the Heathens," ("De Animabus Paganorum.") He decides adversely to the salvation of Aristotle. Died in 1640.

Cölln or **Ccelln, von,** fon köln, (DANIEL GEORG CONRAD,) a German rationalistic theologian, born in Lippe-Detmold in 1788; died in 1833.

Collombet, ko'lôn'bà', (FRANÇOIS ZÉNON,) a French Catholic writer, born at Sièges (Jura) in 1808, published a "History of Saint Jerome," (1844,) and other works. Died in 1853.

Colloredo, kol-lo-rā'do, (FRANZ G.,) born in 1731, was Austrian ambassador to Spain in 1767, and became vice-chancellor of the empire in 1789. Died in 1807.

Colloredo, (RUDOLPH,) Count of Waldsee, a general of the Imperialist army, born in 1585, distinguished himself in the Thirty Years' war, and in 1648 defended Prague with success against the Swedes. Died in 1657.

є as k; ç as s; g *hard;* ġ as j; G, H, K, *guttural;* N, *nasal;* R, *trilled;* s as z; th as in *this.* (☞See Explanations, p. 23.)

41

Collot, ko′lo′, (JEAN FRANÇOIS HENRI,) a French writer, born near Charleville in 1716, was a contributor to the "Encyclopédie" of Diderot, and published other works. Died in 1804.

Collot. See COLOT.

Collot-d'Herbois, ko′lo′ dêR′bwȧ′, (JEAN MARIE,) a notorious French Jacobin, born about 1750, was a strolling player before the Revolution, and author of several comedies. He was deputed by the people of Paris to the Convention in 1792, became a partisan of Robespierre, and was one of the Committee of Public Safety in 1793. He rendered himself infamous by his cruelties at Lyons, where many hundred persons perished by his order, in 1793. In this he is said to have been actuated by revenge, having once been hissed on the stage of Lyons. He presided over the Convention on the 9th Thermidor, 1794, and contributed to the ruin of Robespierre. In 1795 he was transported to Cayenne, where he died miserably in 1796.

See THIERS, "History of the French Revolution;" "Nouvelle Biographie Générale;" "Biographie Universelle."

Collucio. See COLUCCIO.

Collyer, (JOSEPH,) an English engraver, born in London in 1748, was a son of Mary Collyer, the successful translator of Gesner's "Death of Abel." He excelled in the stippled style of engraving. Died in 1827.

Collyer, (WILLIAM BENGO,) an English divine, was minister of the Independent Chapel, Peckham. He published several volumes of lectures "On Scripture Facts," "On Scripture Prophecy," "On Scripture Doctrine," etc., (1807-22.) Died in 1854.

Colman, (BENJAMIN,) an American clergyman, born in Boston in 1673. He became pastor of a church in his native city about 1700, and published sermons, poems, etc. Died in 1747.

Colman, (GEORGE,) an eminent English dramatic author, was born about 1733 at Florence, where his father was British minister. He was a graduate of Oxford. In 1760 he produced "Polly Honeycomb," a drama, which was warmly applauded, and in 1761 "The Jealous Wife," which was also very popular. He made an excellent translation of Terence into verse in 1764. Between 1767 and 1775 he was acting manager of Covent Garden Theatre, and was afterwards proprietor of the Haymarket Theatre. He published a translation of Horace's "Art of Poetry," and several other works. In 1789 he lost his reason. Died in 1794.

See BAKER, "Biographia Dramatica."

Colman, (GEORGE,) "the Younger," a son of the preceding, was born in 1762. He inherited his father's dramatic taste and talent, and succeeded him as director of the Haymarket Theatre in 1785. He wrote many popular comedies and farces, among which are "The Iron Chest," (1796,) "John Bull," "Inkle and Yarico," and "Heir at Law." For "John Bull" he received the largest sum that had ever been paid for any drama. He also composed comic tales, called "Broad Grins" and "Poetic Vagaries," (1812,) and memoirs of his own life, entitled "Random Recollections," (2 vols., 1830.) Died in 1836.

See BAKER, "Biographia Dramatica;" R. B. PEAKE, "Memoirs of the Colman Family;" "Edinburgh Review" for July, 1841.

Colman, (HENRY,) a Unitarian minister, and writer on agriculture, born in Boston, Massachusetts, in 1785. He was pastor at Salem from 1825 to 1831, after which he was appointed agricultural commissioner for the State of Massachusetts. He went to Europe in 1842, and published "European Agriculture and Rural Economy," and other works. Died in London in 1849.

Colman, (SAMUEL,) an American landscape-painter of the present century. Among his best works are "Lake George," "Barges on the Hudson," and an "Autumn Landscape."

See TUCKERMAN, "Book of the Artists."

Colmar, kol′mȧR, (JOHANN,) a German educational writer, born at Nuremberg in 1684; died in 1737.

Colmeiro, kol-mā′e-ro, (MANUEL,) a Spanish writer on political economy, was born at Santiago de Galicia in 1818. He became professor of political economy at Madrid in 1847.

Colmenar, de, dȧ kol-mȧ-naR′, (JUAN ALVAREZ,) a historian and compiler, who was the reputed author of

two esteemed French works, viz., "Annals of Spain and Portugal," (1741,) and a "Description of Spain and Portugal," (5 vols., 1707.) It is suspected that J. A. de Colmenar was an assumed name of the French compiler.

Colmenares, de, dȧ kol-mȧ-nä′rês, (DIEGO,) born at Segovia, in Spain, in 1586, wrote a "History of Segovia and Compendium of the Histories of Castile," (1634.) Died in 1651.

Cöln or **Coeln, von,** fon köln, (WILHELM,) called MEISTER WILHELM, an excellent German painter, lived at Cologne about 1370. He painted religious subjects in distemper.

Colnet, de, dęh kol′nạ′, (CHARLES JOSEPH AUGUSTE MAXIMILIEN,) often called **Colnet de Ravel,** a French satirical poet and journalist, born in Picardy in 1768. He became a bookseller at Paris in 1797. In 1810 he produced an ingenious poem, entitled "The Art of Dining Out, *(en ville,)* for the Use of Authors." He wrote editorials for the "Journal de Paris" and the "Gazette de France" between 1811 and 1832. Died in 1832.

See "Nouvelle Biographie Générale."

Colocci, ko-lot′chee, [Lat. COLO′TIUS,] (ANGELO,) an Italian poet, born near Ancona in 1467, became a resident of Rome and secretary of Leo X. He lived in grand style, and had a fine library, which was burned when Rome was sacked in 1527. He gained a temporary reputation by his Latin poems. Died in 1549.

Colocotroni. See KOLOCOTRONI.

Cologne, de, dęh ko′loñ′, (PETER,) a Protestant divine, was a native of Ghent. Died in 1558.

Coloma, ko-lo′mä, (Don CARLOS,) a Spanish general and historian, born at Alicante in 1573. He rose to the highest rank in the army, and became Governor of the Milanese. He received from Philip IV. the title of Marquis of Espina, and wrote a history of the war in Flanders from 1588 to 1599, ("Las Guerras de los Estados Baxos," 1625,) a work of considerable merit. Died in 1637.

Colomb. See COLUMBUS.

Colomb, ko′lòn′, written also **Columb,** (MICHEL,) a French sculptor, born in Bretagne in the fifteenth century. His master-piece is the tomb of Francis II. (Duke of Bretagne) at Nantes, which is much admired.

Colomba. See COLUMBA.

Colomban. See COLUMBAN.

Colombe, ko′lòmb′, (MARIE THÉRÈSE,) a famous actress, born at Venice in 1757, made a successful *début* in Paris in 1772. She retired from the stage in 1788, and died in 1837.

Colombel, ko′lòn′bêl′, (NICOLAS,) a French painter of history, born near Rouen in 1646, was the most eminent pupil of Le Sueur. He studied in Rome, and afterwards worked in Paris with success. Died in 1717.

Colombier, ko′lòn′be-ȧ′, (JEAN,) an able French physician, born at Toul in 1736, became inspector-general of the hospitals of the kingdom in 1780, and of the military hospitals a few years later. He died in 1789, leaving, besides other medical treatises, one entitled "Precepts on the Health of Soldiers, or Military Hygiene," (1775.)

Colombière, de la, dęh lä ko′lòn′be-aiR′, (CLAUDE,) a French Jesuit, born near Lyons in 1641; died in 1682.

Colombière, de la, (VULSON.) See VULSON.

Colombo, ko-lom′bo, (DOMENICO,) an Italian pastoral poet, born at Gabiano in 1749. He published pastoral Poems, and an "Essay on the Drama and Tragedy of Italy," (1794.) Died in 1813.

Colombo, (REALDO,) [Lat. REAL′DUS COLUM′BUS,] a distinguished Italian anatomist, born at Cremona, succeeded Vesalius, in 1544, as professor at Padua. He afterwards taught in the Universities of Pisa and of Rome. He is said to have first discovered the pulmonary circulation. His reputation is founded on his work "De Re Anatomica," (1559,) a most important contribution to anatomy for that period. Died about 1576.

See HALLER, "Bibliotheca Anatomica;" SPRENGEL, "Geschichte der Arzneikunde."

Colomby, de, dęh ko′lòn′be′, (FRANÇOIS Cauvigny —kō′vèn′ye′,) SIEUR, a French writer, born at Caen about 1588. He was one of the first members of the French Academy, and published a translation of Justin's "History." Died about 1648.

Colomiès, ko'lo'me-ês', (PAUL,) a French Protestant writer on biography, theology, etc., was born at Rochelle in 1638. He removed to England in 1681, and became librarian to Archbishop Sancroft at Lambeth. He published, besides many other learned works, "Eastern Gaul," ("Gallia Orientalis," 1665,) "Protestant Rome," ("Rome protestante," 1675,) and "Historical Miscellanies," (" Mélanges historiques,") reprinted with the title "Colomesiana." Died in 1692.

See BAYLE, "Historical and Critical Dictionary;" NICÉRON, "Mémoires."

Coloni, ko-lo'nee, (ADAM,) THE OLD, a Dutch painter, born at Rotterdam in 1634, worked in London. He painted landscapes and rural subjects. Died in 1685.

Coloni, (HENRY ADRIAN,) called THE YOUNG, a painter, son of the preceding, born in 1668; died in 1701.

Colonia, de, dęh ko'lo'ne'å', (DOMINIQUE,) a French Jesuit, born at Aix in 1660, became professor of rhetoric and theology in Lyons. He composed a "Literary History of Lyons," and several tragedies. Died in 1741.

Colonna, ko-lon'nå, the name of an illustrious Roman family, which acquired distinction as early as the twelfth century. They were adherents of the Ghibeline party, and rivals of the Orsini. GIOVANNI COLONNA was made a cardinal in 1216, and took part in the fifth crusade. Died in 1245. His nephew, of the same name, became Archbishop of Messina in 1255. He wrote a "Chronicle, or History of the World," to the time of Louis IX. of France. Cardinal GIACOMO COLONNA was chief councillor of the court of Rome during the pontificate of Nicholas IV., which ended about 1292. He died in 1318. SCIARRA COLONNA was one of the chiefs of a successful conspiracy against Boniface VIII. in 1303. He died in exile about 1328. STEPHEN, a brother of Sciarra, was created Count of Romagna about 1290, and was for many years chief of the Guelphs at Rome. In a conflict with Rienzi he was killed about 1350. OTHO COLONNA was elected pope in 1417. (See MARTIN V.) ANTONIO, a nephew and favourite of Martin V., was made Prince of Salerno and Duke of Amalfi in 1419. In 1431 Pope Eugene IV. declared war against Antonio and his brothers, who had seized the treasury of the late pontiff. Antonio was the father of PROSPER COLONNA.

See SISMONDI, "Histoire des Républiques Italiennes;" O. DI AGOSTINO, "Istoria della Famiglia Colonna."

Colonna, (ANGELO MICHELE,) an Italian painter, born at Ravenna in 1600, was invited to Spain by Philip IV., for whom he painted in the Escurial. Among his master-pieces are "Fortune" and "Prometheus." He died at Bologna in 1687.

See LANZI, "History of Painting in Italy."

Colonna, (ASCAGNO,) an Italian cardinal, born about 1560, became Viceroy of Aragon. He wrote, in Latin, a treatise "On the Sicilian Monarchy." Died in 1608.

Colonna, (EGIDIO,) [Lat. ÆGID'IUS ROMA'NUS; Fr. GILLES DE COLONNE, zhèl dęh ko'lon',] a theologian and writer, born at Rome, studied under Thomas Aquinas in Paris. He became preceptor to the Dauphin of France, Philippe le Bel, for whom he wrote a treatise entitled "De Regimine Principis." Died in 1316.

See ANGELO ROCCHA, " Vita Ægidii," prefixed to Colonna's work called "Defensorium," Naples, 1644.

Colonna, (FABIO.) See COLUMNA.

Colonna, (FABRIZIO,) an Italian general, was first-cousin to Prospero, and son of Edoardo, Duke of Amalfi. He served successively Frederick, King of Naples, and Ferdinand the Catholic, who in 1507 appointed him grand constable of the kingdom of Naples. Having passed into the service of the pope, Julius II., he was taken prisoner by the French at Ravenna in 1512. Died in 1520.

See SISMONDI, "Histoire des Républiques Italiennes."

Colonna, (Fra FRANCESCO,) an Italian writer, born at Venice about 1435, or, according to another account, in 1449. He became a Dominican monk, and professor of theology at Padua. He acquired celebrity by a fantastic and singular work, entitled "Hypnerotomachia Poliphili," (Venice, 1499,) in which he teaches that all human passions are but dreams. (For a more particular account of this strange production, see "Nouvelle Biographie Générale.") The language is a mixture of Italian,

Greek, Latin, Hebrew, etc. Tiraboschi designates the work "a confused mélange of fables, history, architecture, and antiquities." Died in 1527.

Colonna, (FRANCESCO MARIA POMPEO,) an Italian alchemist, born about 1650. He lived many years in Paris, and published numerous works, among which was a "Natural History of the Universe," (1734.) He perished by a fire which consumed his lodgings in Paris in 1726.

See F. HOEFER, "Histoire de la Chimie."

Colonna, (GIOVANNI PAOLO,) one of the most eminent Italian composers of his time, was born at Brescia. He composed only sacred music. His science was profound and his style brilliant. Died in 1695.

See FÉTIS, "Biographie Universelle des Musiciens."

Colonna, (MARCANTONIO,) Duke of Palliano, an Italian general, who obtained in 1570 command of the twelve galleys which the pope sent to aid the Venetians in defence of Cyprus. The chief command of the allies was claimed by Colonna, Doria, and Zeno, neither of whom would yield. To obviate the difficulty and danger arising from this dispute, Philip of Spain gave the command of his ships to Don John of Austria, from whom Colonna consented to receive orders ; and they defeated the Turks at Lepanto in October, 1571. "He had the fortune," says Sismondi, "to attach his name to the greatest exploit of the sixteenth century, the battle of Lepanto." He was afterwards appointed Viceroy of Sicily by Philip II. Died in 1584.

See SISMONDI, "Histoire des Républiques Italiennes."

Colonna, (POMPEO,) an Italian prelate, nephew of Prosper Colonna, noticed below. He was a turbulent and violent character, and was hostile to Leo X., by whom he had been made a cardinal. After having decided the election in favour of Clement VII., he quarrelled with him, and attempted to seize him with a troop of soldiers. But he served the same pope efficiently when the latter was held in durance by the army of Constable Bourbon. Died in 1532.

See AUBERY, " Histoire des Cardinaux."

Colonna, (PROSPER or PROSPERO,) the son of Antonio, above noticed, was one of the greatest generals that Italy has produced. In 1494 he fought for the French king Charles VIII. in his invasion of Naples. After the expulsion of the French he served under Gonsalvo de Córdova against France. In 1513 he won for Ferdinand of Spain a great victory over the Venetians near Vicenza. He was taken prisoner by the French at Villa Franca by a surprise in 1515. He took Milan in 1521, and defeated Lautrec, a French general, at Bicoque in 1522. Died in 1523.

See BRANTÔME, "Grands Capitaines ;" SISMONDI, "Histoire des Républiques Italiennes."

Colonna, (VITTORIA,) daughter of Fabrizio, above noticed, was illustrious as a poetess and as a woman. She was born in 1490, and was married in 1507 to the Marquis of Pescara, who became a celebrated general. She was extolled as the most eminent of her sex in Italy for beauty, virtue, and talents. After the death of her husband, in 1525, she wrote poetical laments on that subject, and also religious verses. In 1541 she retired into a convent, first at Orvieto and then at Viterbo. She is reputed one of the most successful imitators of Petrarch. "The rare virtues and consummate talents of this lady," says Hallam, "were the theme of all Italy in that brilliant age of her literature." ("Introduction to the Literature of Europe.") Died in 1547.

See LONGFELLOW, "Poets and Poetry of Europe ;" MRS. HENRY ROSCOE, "Vittoria Colonna : her Life and Poems," 1868 ; "Lives of the Italian Poets," by REV. H. STEBBING, London, 1831.

Colonne, de, (GILLES.) See COLONNA, (EGIDIO.)

Colot, ko'lo', or **Collot,** the name of several French lithotomists. GERMAIN COLOT, a French surgeon, who lived about 1480, was the first of his countrymen who practised lithotomy. LAURENT settled in Paris in 1556, and was patronized by Henry II. PHILIPPE, a descendant of Laurent, born in 1593, had a high reputation, and was employed at court. Died in 1656. FRANÇOIS, a son or grandson of Philippe, lived about 1690. His reputation attracted patients from foreign countries. He left a "Treatise on Lithotomy."

ɛ as k; ç as s; g hard; g as j; G, H, K, guttural; N, nasal; R, trilled; ś as z; th as in this. (☞ See Explanations, p. 23.)

Co-lo'tēs, [Κολώτης,] a Greek sculptor, a native of Paros, lived about 450 B.C. He assisted Phidias in the colossal statue of Jupiter at Olympia. His master-piece was an ivory statue of Æsculapius.

Colpani, kol-pâ'nee, (GIUSEPPE,) an Italian poet, born at Brescia in 1738; died in 1822.

Colquhoun, ko-hoon', ? (Lady JANET,) an Irish authoress, born in 1781, was the daughter of Sir John Sinclair of Ulster, and the wife of Sir James Colquhoun. Besides other religious works, she wrote "Impression of the Heart," (1825,) and "The World's Religion contrasted with Christianity," (1839.) Died in 1846.

See JAMES HAMILTON, "Memoirs of Lady Colquhoun," 1849.

Colquhoun, ko-hoon', (PATRICK,) a Scottish political economist and practical reformer, born at Dumbarton in 1745. He became a Glasgow merchant about 1768, and lord provost of Glasgow in 1782. He promoted the fabrication of muslin in Scotland, and developed other resources. In 1789 he removed to London, where he initiated reforms in the police. He published a valuable "Treatise on the Police of the Metropolis," (1796,) a "Treatise on the Population, Power, and Resources of the British Empire," (1814,) and other works on manufactures, trade, and education. Died in 1820.

See CHAMBERS, "Biographical Dictionary of Eminent Scotsmen."

Col'quitt, (WALTER T.,) an American lawyer and Senator, born in Halifax county, Virginia, in 1799. He settled in Georgia, and was elected a member of Congress in 1838 and in 1840. In 1842 he was elected to the Senate of the United States by the Democrats. Died in 1855.

Col'rane, (HENRY HARE,) LORD, an English scholar and collector of prints, books, and antiquities, born in Surrey in 1693; died in 1749.

Colson, kol'sòn', (GUILLAUME FRANÇOIS,) a French historical painter, born in Paris in 1785, was a pupil of David.

Colson, (JEAN FRANÇOIS GILLE,) a French painter and architect, born at Dijon in 1733; died in 1803.

Cŏl'sǫn, (JOHN,) an English mathematician, who was chosen professor of mathematics in Cambridge in 1739, before which he taught school at Rochester. He translated from the Latin Newton's "Fluxions." Died in 1760.

Cŏl'stǫn, (EDWARD,) an opulent English merchant and philanthropist, born at Bristol in 1636, was noted for his munificence. He founded and endowed a number of charitable institutions in Bristol. Died in 1721. ·

Cŏlt, (SAMUEL,) an American inventor, born at Hartford, Connecticut, in 1814. He went to sea as a sailor-boy about the age of fifteen. In 1835 he took out a patent for a pistol, called a revolver, which he had invented. About 1848 he began to manufacture revolvers on a large scale at Hartford, where he built one of the most extensive armories in the world. His revolvers have a high reputation in every part of the world. Died in 1862.

Coltellini, kol-tĕl-lee'nee, (AGOSTINO,) an Italian poet, born at Florence in 1613. He founded in his own house, in 1631, the celebrated academy of Apatisti at Florence. Died in 1693.

Cŏl'tǫn, (CALEB C.,) an English clergyman, vicar of Kew and Petersham. He wrote "Hypocrisy," a Poem, (1812,) and other works, the most remarkable of which was "Lacon,"(1820,) an excellent collection of apothegms and sententious precepts. In consequence of his addiction to the vice of gaming, he absconded to America in 1828. He killed himself at Fontainebleau in 1832.

Cŏl'tǫn, (CALVIN,)an Episcopal clergyman and writer, born in Longmeadow, Massachusetts, in 1789, graduated at Yale College in 1812. He published, besides other works, "Four Years in Great Britain," and a "Life of Henry Clay," (3 vols., 1844.) He also wrote "Junius Tracts" in support of the Whig party about 1840–44. Died in 1857.

Colton, (GEORGE HOOKER,) a son of the preceding, was born in Otsego county, New York, in 1818. He wrote a poem entitled "Tecumseh, or the West Thirty Years Since," (1842.) In 1845 he became editor of the "American Whig Review." Died in 1847.

Colton, (WALTER,) an American clergyman and writer, born in Rutland, Vermont, in 1797. He became a chaplain in the navy in 1831, and published, besides other works, "Ship and Shore in Madeira, Lisbon, etc.," (1835,) "Deck and Port," (1850,) and "Three Years in California," (1850.) He established the first newspaper in California, now called the "Alta California." Died in 1851.

See GRISWOLD'S "Poets and Poetry of America."

Coluccio, ko-loot'cho, (SALUTÀTO,) an Italian writer and friend of Petrarch, born at Stignano in 1330. He became secretary to Pope Urban V. and to the republic of Florence. He acquired renown as a Latin poet, and translated part of Dante's "Divina Commedia" into Latin verse. Died in 1406.

See TIRABOSCHI, "Storia della Letteratura Italiana."

Columb. See COLOMB.

Co-lum'ba, SAINT, called "the Apostle of the Highlanders," was born in Ireland about 520 A.D. He is regarded as the first who preached Christianity in Scotland, which he visited about 565. He founded in Iona, one of the Hebrides, an abbey and college, which became a renowned seat of learning. Died in 597 A.D.

See BURTON'S "History of Scotland," vol. i. chap. vii. ; BUTLER, "Lives of the Saints ;" DR. JOHNSON, "Journey to the Hebrides."

Co-lum'ban, written also **Colomban,** [Lat. COLUMBA'NUS,] SAINT, an eminent Irish monk, born in Leinster about 540 A.D. He preached in France, founded a monastery at Luxeuil, near Besançon, and acquired celebrity as the teacher and author of a monastic rule. "He was the man," says Montalembert, "who gave the greatest impulse to the monasticism of the seventh century." Died in Italy in 615 A.D.

See A. GIANELLI, "Vita di S. Colombano," Turin, 1844.

Columbanus. See COLUMBAN, SAINT.

Co-lum'bus, (Don BARTHOLOMEW,) a younger brother of the great navigator, who in 1488 sent him to solicit the patronage of Henry VII. of England. In 1493 he accompanied his brother in the second voyage to America, and was appointed adelantado, or governor, of Hispaniola. On this island he founded, in 1496, the town of Saint Domingo. He displayed much ability in subduing the revolts of the natives. (See COLUMBUS, CHRISTOPHER.) "He united in a singular degree," says Irving, "the sailor, the soldier, and the legislator. His portrait has been suffered to remain too much in the shade : it is worthy of being brought into the light as a companion to that of his illustrious brother." He died in Saint Domingo in 1514.

See IRVING, "Life of C. Columbus."

Columbus, (CHRISTOPHER,) [Lat. CHRISTOPH'ORUS COLUM'BUS ; It. CRISTOF'ORO COLOM'BO ; Sp. CRISTOVAL COLON, krès-to'vâl ko-lòn'; Fr. CHRISTOPHE COLOMB, krès'tof' ko'lòN'; Ger. CHRISTOPH COLUMBUS, kris'tof ko-lōōm'bùs,] the most illustrious of navigators and discoverers, was born of poor parents, at Genoa, about 1440. His birth is variously dated between 1435 and 1445, (Irving prefers 1435,) and his early history is involved in obscurity. The family name Colombo was Latinized into Columbus by the subject of this article, who afterwards adopted the Spanish form, Cristoval Colon. At an early age he evinced a fondness for geography, and a strong attraction towards the sea and the mysterious regions which his imagination suggested beyond its horizon. At the University of Pavía he pursued for a short time the congenial studies of geometry, astronomy, navigation, etc. According to his own statement, he entered on a nautical life at the age of fourteen. During many years he was employed in the Mediterranean, sometimes in commercial adventures and sometimes in warlike enterprises.

About 1470 he removed to Lisbon, which, under the auspices of Prince Henry, was then the chief seat of nautical science, and there married a lady of Italian extraction,—Felipa Moñis de Palestrello. He sailed with several Portuguese expeditions to the west coast of Africa, and when on shore supported his family by the construction of maps and charts. Amidst a general excitement about maritime discovery, attended with various fanciful theories and fabulous rumours, he gradually matured the idea of his own sublime enterprise. A lofty and religious enthusiasm sustained him in surmounting the difficulties and repulses which he was destined to meet. He expected

ā, ē, ī, ō, ū, ȳ, *long;* à, è, ò, same, less prolonged; ă, ĕ, ĭ, ŏ, ŭ, ў, *short;* ạ, ẹ, ị, ọ, *obscure;* fär, fåll, fåt; mêt; nŏt; gŏŏd; mōōn;

that by sailing westward he would reach Cipango, (Japan,) or the eastern part of Asia, after a voyage of moderate length. According to Irving, he meditated the discovery of a western route to India as early as the year 1474. He made a northern voyage, of which we have no memorial except this passage in one of his letters : " In 1477 I navigated one hundred leagues beyond Thule," (supposed to be Içeland.) .

Soon after the opportune application of the astrolabe to navigation, he solicited the patronage of John II. of Portugal in the execution of his favourite project. That king, while he protracted the negotiation, secretly sent a vessel to explore the Atlantic ; but the timid pilots, after a voyage of a few days, returned to Lisbon. Indignant at this treatment, Columbus left Portugal in 1484, and applied to the court of Spain for assistance. He was then so poor that he begged some bread at the convent near Palos while he was on his way to the court. His project was referred to a council, and by them disapproved. Although tantalized, neglected, and repulsed by the minions of office, he continued to urge his claims with ardour and eloquence. At length, after the capture of Granada, which he witnessed, in 1492, Queen Isabella was induced to furnish him with two small vessels : a third was added by himself or his friends. On the 3d of August, 1492, he sailed from Palos with one hundred and twenty men, in the Santa Maria, the Pinta, and the Niña.

After passing the Canaries, the propitious trade-wind wafted them swiftly over a tranquil sea for many days. The variation of the needle, then first observed, alarmed his crew, who were also dismayed by the idea of being lost in a shoreless ocean. About the 20th of September they were cheered by the visits of several birds of song ; but the farther they advanced the more their impatience increased. Their heroic chief, however, was resolute in "pursuing his dim and perilous way." A few days before the discovery of land his crew became openly mutinous, and talked of throwing him overboard. On the morning of October 12, 1492, his voyage was crowned with triumph by the discovery of San Salvador, (or Cat Island,) one of the Bahama Isles, which he found inhabited. Supposing it to be on the coast of India, he called the natives Indians ; and they received their visitants as citizens and messengers of heaven. Having visited Cuba and Hayti, (Hispaniola,) he sailed homeward, and arrived at Palos in March, 1493. In his progress through Spain he was received with rapturous demonstrations and more than regal homage. In accordance with a previous contract, he obtained the titles of Admiral and Viceroy of the New World. "Thus honoured by the sovereigns," says Irving, "and idolized by the people, Columbus for a time drank the honeyed draught of popularity." "His discovery burst with such sudden splendour upon the world as to dazzle envy itself."

In the autumn of 1493 he made a second voyage across the Atlantic, with seventeen ships, and, after the discovery of Jamaica, Porto Rico, etc., returned to Spain in June, 1496. He sailed again in May, 1498, with six vessels, and discovered Terra Firma at the mouth of the Orinoco. Envy and malice had at last produced an ebb in the tide of his popularity, so that in 1500 Ferdinand appointed Francisco de Bobadilla governor in place of Columbus, who was sent to Spain in chains. It has been questioned whether the king had authorized the infamous conduct of Bobadilla ; for he pretended to disavow it, after the indignation of the Spanish public had been loudly expressed. Columbus was received with smiles and favour by the king and queen, but was not reinstated in his high office. In May, 1502, he sailed on his fourth voyage, hoping to find a more direct passage to India than that just discovered by Vasco da Gama. He explored the coasts of Honduras, Costa Rica, etc., and, after suffering from famine, mutiny, and other disasters, he returned to Spain in 1504. He died in poverty and neglect, at Valladolid, in 1506.

Columbus was tall in stature, with blue eyes, and an aquiline nose. He possessed a commanding presence and a fluent elocution. His temper was impetuous, though benevolent, and his mind was highly imaginative and poetical. He left two sons, noticed below. He died in ignorance of the real grandeur of his discovery, sup-

posing that Cuba, Terra Firma, etc. were only remote parts of Asia.

See IRVING, "Life of Columbus ;" PRESCOTT, "Ferdinand and Isabella," chaps. xvi. and xviii. of Part First, and viii. and xviii. of Part Second ; FERNANDO COLON, "Historia del Almirante ;" HERRERA, "Historia de las Indias Occidentales ;" NAVARRETE, "Coleccion de Viages ;" OVIEDO, "History of the Indies ;" BERNALDEZ, "Reyes Católicos ;" MUÑOZ, "Historia del Nuevo Mundo ;" BENZONI, "Novi Orbis Historia ;" BOSSI, "Vita di Colombo," 1818; FORESTER, "Christoph Columbus," (in German,) 1842; RETA, "Vita di Colombo," 1846 ; ARTHUR HELPS, "Life of Columbus," 1869; A. DE LAMARTINE, "C. Colomb," 1853 ; H. ROSCOE SAINT-JOHN, "Life of Columbus," 1850; BONNAFOUX, "Vie de C. Colomb," 1853 ; SCHNEIDAWIND, "C. Columbus America's Entdecker," 1843 ; A. SANGUINETTI, "Vita di C. Colombo," 1846.

Columbus, (DIEGO or GIACOMO,) was a priest, and a brother of the great navigator. He governed Saint Domingo for a short time in 1500, and soon after that date was sent to Spain, with his brother, in chains. In 1509 he embarked again for the New World with his nephew Diego.

Columbus, (Don DIEGO,) the eldest son of the great admiral, was born probably at Lisbon about 1472. He was in early youth a page in the court of Ferdinand and Isabella. At the death of his father he urged his claim to the office of viceroy which was promised to Christopher Columbus and his heirs, and about 1509 he obtained the office of Governor of the West Indies. He had married Doña Maria de Toledo, whose father and uncle were the most powerful grandees of Spain. Charles V., about 1520, recognized his right to the office of viceroy. He died in Spain in 1526, leaving two sons. "He appears to have been," says Irving, "a man of great integrity, of respectable talents, and of a generous nature."

See IRVING, "Life of Christopher Columbus."

Columbus, (FERNANDO,) born at Córdova about 1488, was the son of Christopher Columbus and Beatriz Enriquez. He was educated at the court of Isabella of Castile, whom he served as a page. In 1502 he accompanied his father in his fourth voyage to America. He resided some years at Seville, where he formed a rich library and devoted himself to study and authorship. His most important work is a "History of Admiral C. Columbus," ("Vida y Hechos del Almirante D. C. Colon," Madrid, 1530.) Died in 1539.

See IRVING, "Life of C. Columbus ;" "Nouvelle Biographie Générale."

Columbus, (REALDUS.) See COLOMBO.

Col-u-mel'la, [Fr. COLUMELLE, ko'lü'mêl',] (LUCIUS JUNIUS MODERATUS,) the author of the most important Latin work on ancient agriculture, was born probably at Cadiz, (Gades,) and wrote in the first half of the first century. He resided at or near Rome, after having travelled over many parts of the Roman empire. He was the owner of a large estate, and was a practical cultivator. His work entitled "De Re Rusticâ" is a voluminous and systematic treatise on rural affairs, in twelve books, of which the tenth is in verse. His Latinity is nearly as pure as that of the Augustan age, and his precepts have much intrinsic value. He is cited by Seneca and eulogized by Pliny.

See FABRICIUS, "Bibliotheca Latina ;" SCHOELL, "Histoire de la Littérature Romaine ;" ERSCH und GRUBER, "Allgemeine Encyklopaedie."

Columelle. See COLUMELLA.

Co-lum'na, (FABIUS,) [It. FABIO COLONNA, fä'be-o ko-lon'nä,] one of the greatest botanists of his time, was born of a noble family at Naples in 1567. He received a classical education, and attained skill in music, design, painting, etc. From early childhood he manifested a taste for botany. His first work, "Touchstone of Plants," ("Phytobasanos," 1592,) was remarkable for the accuracy of the descriptions and the correctness and beauty of the figures. He was the first to use copper plates to delineate plants. In 1606 he produced the first part of his "Ecphrasis," a history of rare plants, in which he laid down the true basis of the science by recognizing and employing the distinction of genera. About 1616 he went to Rome, and assisted in founding the Academy of Lyncei, which had great influence on the revival of natural philosophy. In his notes to the work of Hernandez he still further developed the principles of botany with great clearness. He appears to have been the only botanist of his time who appreciated the lumi-

---

ɇ as *k*; **ç** as *s*; **ḡ** *hard*; **ġ** as *j*; G, H, K, *guttural*; N, *nasal*; R, *trilled*; ś as *z*; ŧh as in *this*. (☞See Explanations, p. 23.)

nous ideas which Cesalpino had previously presented. Died in Naples in 1650.

See ERSCH und GRUBER, "Allgemeine Encyklopaedie;" ÉLOY, "Dictionnaire de la Médecine;" "Biographie Universelle."

Columna, de, (GUIDO,) or **Guido de Columnis,** the name of a celebrated Italian chronicler. See GUIDO DELLE COLONNE.

Co-lu'thus, [Κόλουθος,] a Greek poet, who lived about the end of the fifth century, was born at Lycopolis, in Egypt. His works are all lost except "The Abduction of Helen," a small poem of little merit.

Col'ville, (Sir CHARLES,) a British general, a younger son of Lord Colville, born in 1770, served in Spain for several years, and was wounded at Vittoria. He commanded a division at Waterloo in 1815, and was made a general in 1837. Died in 1843.

Colville, (JOHN,) a Scottish politician, became master of requests about 1580. In 1591 and 1592 he was an adherent of the Earl of Bothwell in an unsuccessful rebellion against the king. He published, in 1600, "The Palinode," and, having become a Catholic, he wrote several treatises against Protestantism. Died in 1607.

Col'vï-us, (ANDREW,) a learned Dutch divine, born at Dort in 1594. He was a friend of Paul Sarpi, whose "History of the Inquisition" he translated into Latin.

Cöl'well, (STEPHEN,) an American writer on trade and finance, born in Brooke county, Virginia, in 1800. He practised law several years, and afterwards became a merchant of Philadelphia.

Comazzi, ko-mät'see, (GIOVANNI BATTISTA,) an Italian moralist, of whom nothing is known except that he wrote an able essay "On the Morals of Princes." An English version appeared in 1729.

Combalot, kôn'bä'lo', (THÉODORE,) a French abbé and eloquent preacher, was born at Châtenay (Isère) in 1798. From 1830 to 1840 he was the principal rival of Lacordaire in the pulpits of Paris. He published "The Dogma of the Incarnation regarded as the Final Reason of all that Exists," (1841,) and other works.

Combalusier, kôn'bä'lü ze-à', (FRANÇOIS DE PAULE,) a French physician, born in Vivarais in 1713. He published "Pneumatic Pathology," (1747,) and other works. Died in 1762.

Combe, koom, (ANDREW,) M.D., an eminent Scottish writer, born in Edinburgh in 1797. He began to practise medicine in that city in 1823, having previously become a believer in phrenology. He acquired distinction as a writer on physiology and other scientific subjects. His "Principles of Physiology applied to the Preservation of Health" (1834) has been very successful, having passed through about sixteen editions. In 1836 he was appointed consulting physician to the King of Belgium. Among his principal works are "Observations on Mental Derangements" and "The Physiology of Digestion." Died in 1847. He was a brother of George Combe.

See "Life of Andrew Combe," by G. COMBE, 1850; CHAMBERS, "Biographical Dictionary of Eminent Scotsmen;" SMILES, "Brief Biographies," 1860; "Westminster Review" for July, 1850.

Combe, koom or kōm, (CHARLES,) M.D., an English antiquary, born in London in 1743. He published a "Description of the Ancient Medals in the Cabinet of Dr. William Hunter," and another work on numismatics. Died in 1817.

Combe, (GEORGE,) an eminent phrenologist, born in Edinburgh, Scotland, in 1788, was a brother of Andrew, noticed above. He studied law, and practised in his native place about twenty-five years. In 1816 he heard Spurzheim on the subject of phrenology, in which he soon became a firm believer. He published in 1819 "Essays on Phrenology," a later edition of which was entitled "System of Phrenology." His principal work, "The Constitution of Man considered in Relation to External Objects," (1828,) passed through eight or more editions. He married a daughter of the actress Mrs. Siddons in 1833, and about that time delivered in several places "Lectures on Popular Education," which were published, (3d edition, 1848.) In 1838 he visited the United States, in which he passed two or three years and gave many lectures on phrenology. He afterwards published "Notes on the United States of America," (1841,) and other works. Died in 1858. George Combe

has been called the ablest writer that ever advocated the peculiar doctrines of Phrenology.

See "Edinburgh Review" for September, 1826; "North British Review" for May, 1852; "Fraser's Magazine" for November, 1840.

Combe, kôn, (MICHEL,) COLONEL, a brave French officer, born at Feurs in 1787. He was killed at Constantine, in Africa, where he led an assault, in 1837.

Combe, (TAYLOR,) an English antiquary, son of Charles Combe, noticed above, born in 1774. He was chosen keeper of the antiquities and coins of the British Museum in 1807, and published, besides other works, "Ancient Marbles in the British Museum," (7 vols., 1812–35.) Died in 1826.

Combe, La. See LACOMBE.

Combefis, kômb'fe' or kôn'bĕh-fe', (FRANÇOIS,) a French Dominican friar and Hellenist, born at Marmande in 1605. He undertook to restore the text of the Fathers to its purity, and spent nearly fifty years in this task. He published many learned works. Died in 1679.

See NICÉRON, "Mémoires."

Combelle, kôn'bĕl', (JEAN ANTOINE FRANÇOIS,) a French general, born at Pouzat in 1774, served with distinction in Syria and Spain. He was killed at Dresden in September, 1813.

Comber, kŭm'bẽr, ? (THOMAS,) D.D., a learned English theologian, born in Kent in 1644. He obtained the living of Thornton in 1678, and was chosen Dean of Durham in 1691. He wrote a "Companion to the Temple," (3 vols., 1672–75,) and other esteemed works. Died in 1699.

Comber, (THOMAS,) a grandson of the preceding, became rector of Morborne and Buckworth. He wrote a "Vindication of the Revolution of 1688," and a few other works. Died in 1778.

Com'bẽr-mere, (STAPLETON COTTON,) VISCOUNT, an English general, born in 1773, was a son of Sir R. S. Cotton. He served several campaigns in India, joined the army in Spain in 1808, and distinguished himself in many actions. He was second in command at the battle of Salamanca, (1812,) where he was severely wounded. He was appointed commander-in-chief of the army in India in 1822, and received the title of Viscount for his services in that country about 1825. In 1855 he was made a field-marshal. Died in 1865.

See "Memoirs and Correspondence of Viscount Combermere," by LADY COMBERMERE and CAPTAIN W. W. KNOLLYS, London, 1866; "Fraser's Magazine" for November, 1866.

Combes, kômb, (CHARLES PIERRE MATHIEU,) a French engineer, born in 1801. He became a member of the Institute, and inspector-general and professor in the École des Mines. He published a "Treatise on the Exploitation of Mines," (3 vols.,) and other works.

Comella, ko-mĕl'yä, (LUCIANO FRANCISCO,) a popular Spanish dramatic poet, born in 1716; died in 1779.

Comenius, ko-mā'ne-ŭs, (JOHN AMOS,) an eminent German philologist, born at Komna, in Moravia, in 1592. His family name is lost, having been superseded by the above name, derived from Komna or Comna. He became a minister of the Moravan sect at Fulnek, whence he was driven by persecution in 1621. He retired to Lesna, in Poland, where he taught school, and published, in Latin and Bohemian, his "Janua Linguarum reserata," ("The Gate of Languages Unlocked, or a New Method of Learning Languages," 1631,) which procured for him a great reputation and was soon translated into twelve or more languages. He was invited to several foreign countries for the purpose of reforming the methods of public instruction. He went to England in 1638, and to Sweden about 1642. In 1648 he returned to Lesna, which was pillaged and burnt in 1657, when he lost his books and manuscripts. He then settled in Amsterdam, and published "Opera Didactica," (1657,) and "Orbis Sensualium Pictus," (1658,) a kind of encyclopædia with woodcuts. He was author of other works. Died in 1671.

See BAYLE, "Historical and Critical Dictionary;" ERSCH und GRUBER, "Allgemeine Encyklopaedie;" ADELUNG, "Geschichte der menschlichen Narrheit."

Comes Natalis. See CONTI, (NOËL.)

Co-mes'tor, [Fr. pron. ko'mĕs'tor',] (or DEVOURER,) (PIERRE,) (thus surnamed because he *devoured* many books,) a French theologian, born at Troyes, became master of the school of theology in Paris in 1164, and wrote "Scholastica Historia." It was received with great favour, and was for about three centuries esteemed an excellent body of positive theology. Died in 1178 or 1185.

Comet, ko'mǎ', (CHARLES JEAN BAPTISTE,) a French physician, born in Paris in 1796, published many medical works.

Co-me'tas, called SCHOLAS'TICUS, a poet, who lived probably in the ninth century, was the author of six epigrams in the Greek Anthology.

Comiers, ko'me-à', (CLAUDE,) a French priest, born at Embrun, was professor of mathematics in Paris for some years, and an editor of the "Journal des Savants" in 1676-78. He wrote treatises on astronomy, theology, language, etc. Died in 1693.

Comines, de, dęh ko'měn', (PHILIPPE,) Lord of Argenton, an eminent historian, was born near Menin, in Flanders, in 1445. He became a confidential adviser of Charles the Bold, Duke of Burgundy, and acquitted himself with ability in negotiations. In 1472 he passed into the service of Charles's rival, Louis XI. of France, who loaded him with favours and made him Seneschal of Poitou. After the death of Louis, Comines favoured the party of the Duke of Orléans, and in 1488 was sentenced to banishment. He attended Charles VIII. in his invasion of Italy in 1494, and served him in a diplomatic capacity. Soon after that date he began to write his "Memoirs," which narrate the historical events from 1464 to 1498. This work, which was printed in 1523, is highly prized for its fidelity, candour, sound judgment, agreeable style, and deep insight into men and things. "Comines," says Macaulay, "was one of the most enlightened statesmen of his time." Died in 1509.

See MACAULAY, "History of England," vol. i.; VILLEMAIN, "Essais de Littérature;" SAINTE-BEUVE, "Causeries du Lundi;" FÉLIX VAN HULST, "P. de Comines," Liège, 1845: "Nouvelle Biographie Générale;" "Retrospective Review," vol. vii., 1823.

Comitolo, ko-me-to'lo, (PAOLO,) an Italian Jesuit and casuist, born at Perugia in 1545; died in 1626.

Commandine. See COMMANDINO.

Commandino, kom-mân-dee'no, written also **Commandine** or **Commandin,** (FEDERIGO,) an eminent Italian mathematician, born at Urbino in 1509. In 1535 he went to Padua, where he studied medicine; but the latter part of his life was passed at Verona, where he taught mathematics to the Duke of Urbino. He published good editions and Latin translations of many ancient geometers, including Euclid and Archimedes. Montucla calls him the model of commentators for the pertinence and sufficiency of his notes. Died in 1575.

See MONTUCLA, "Histoire des Mathématiques;" BAYLE, "Historical and Critical Dictionary."

Commelin. See COMMELYN.

Commelin, kom'lâN', written also **Commelyn,** (JÉRÔME,) a French printer, born at Douai. Having become a Protestant, he removed to Geneva. Some years later he was chosen librarian to the Elector Palatine at Heidelberg. There he published Greek and Latin editions which were noted for correctness. Scaliger and Casaubon praise him highly. Died in 1598.

Commelyn, kom'męh-lïn', written also **Commelin,** (CASPAR,) a Dutch botanist, born at Amsterdam in 1667, was the nephew of John, noticed below. He became professor of botany in his native city, and developed a great knowledge of that science in several works. He published, with fine plates, the second volume of his uncle's work on the "Plants of the Botanic Garden of Amsterdam," and a Flora of Malabar, (1696.) The genus Commelina was named in honour of these botanists. Died in 1731.

See HALLER, "Bibliotheca Botanica."

Commelyn or **Commelin,** [Lat. COMMELI'NUS,] (ISAAC,) a Dutch historical writer, born in Amsterdam in 1598. He published a "History of the Dutch East India Company," a "Life of William I.," and other works. Died in 1676.

See MORÉRI, "Dictionnaire Historique."

Commelyn or **Commelin,** (JOHN,) an eminent botanist, born in Amsterdam in 1629, was the son of the preceding. He contributed to the advancement of botany as professor in the botanic garden of his native city, and as author of several treatises, among which are a "Catalogue of the Indigenous Plants of Holland," (1683,) and a "Description of the Plants of the Botanic Garden of Amsterdam," (1697.) Died in 1692.

See HALLER, "Bibliotheca Botanica."

Commendoni, kom-měn-do'nee, [Fr. COMMENDON, ko'môN'dôN',] (GIAN FRANCESCO,) CARDINAL, born at Venice in 1524, was an able negotiator, and was sent by the pope on a secret mission to England in 1553. About 1561 he was employed as nuncio in Germany in order to check the progress and defeat the designs of the Protestants. He persuaded the King of Poland to accept the decrees of the Council of Trent, and was made a cardinal in 1565. Died in 1584.

See FLÉCHIER, "Vie du Cardinal Commendon," 1671; A. M. GRAZIANI, "De Vita J. F. Commendoni Cardinalis," 1609.

Commerson, ko'měR'sôN', (PHILIBERT,) an excellent French botanist, born at Châtillon-les-Dombes in 1727. He formed a rich botanic garden at his native place. In 1764 he removed to Paris, and soon after that date was chosen naturalist of the exploring expedition of Bougainville, which sailed in 1767. Having visited South America, and many islands of the South Sea, he explored the Isle of France and Madagascar, where he remained a long time. He died in the Isle of France in 1773, before he was ready to publish the results of his researches. "Commerson," says Cuvier, "was a man of profound science. If he had published his observations, he would hold one of the foremost ranks among naturalists." His manuscripts and collections were deposited in the Jardin des Plantes.

See CUVIER, "Histoire des Sciences naturelles;" "Nouvelle Biographie Générale."

Commire, ko'měR', (JEAN,) a modern Latin poet and Jesuit, born at Amboise, in France, in 1625. He was for many years professor of theology, and gained distinction by his Latin poems, consisting of odes, fables, epigrams, etc., published collectively in 1678. They are remarkable for elegance and correctness of style. Died in Paris in 1702.

Commode. See COMMODUS.

Commodi, (ANDREA.) See COMMODO.

Com-mo-dī-ā'nus, [Fr. COMMODIEN, ko'mo'de-âN',] (GAZÆUS, ga-zee'us,) a Christian poet, who lived probably in the third or fourth century. The place of his birth is not known. He wrote a Latin poem entitled "Instructions against the Gods of the Gentiles," (1650.)

See CAVE, "Historia Literaria."

Commodien. See COMMODIANUS.

Commodo, kom'mo-do, or **Comodi,** kom'o-dee, (ANDREA,) an Italian painter, born at Florence in 1560. He had a remarkable talent for copying the most beautiful paintings with such fidelity that it was almost impossible to distinguish the original from the copy. He worked in Florence. The "General Judgment" is called his master-piece. Died in 1638.

Com'mo-dus, [Fr. COMMODE, ko'mod',] (LUCIUS ÆLIUS AURELIUS,) a Roman emperor, born in 161 A.D., was the son of Marcus Aurelius and Faustina. He succeeded his father in 180, and found the empire prosperous. Though he had been carefully educated, he soon exhibited a character which inspires unmixed detestation. He resigned the direction of the government to his favourites Perennis and others, and indulged his cruel temper and evil passions without restraint. He ordered his wife Crispina to be put to death, and took a concubine named Marcia. His subjects were required to offer homage to him as Hercules. Many senators and others were doomed to death by his cruelty. His officers Lætus and Eclectus having conspired with Marcia against him, he was poisoned and strangled in 192 A.D., and Pertinax then became emperor.

See TILLEMONT, "Histoire des Empereurs;" DION CASSIUS, "History of Rome;" LAMPRIDIUS, "Commodus."

Comnène. See COMNENUS.

Com-ne'nus, [Gr. Κομνηνός; Fr. COMNÈNE, kom'-nậN'.] the name of an illustrious Byzantine family of Italian origin, which first acquired historical importance in the tenth century, and from which descended six emperors of the East, all the emperors of Trebizond, and many generals, statesmen, etc. (See ALEXIS I., ANDRO-

NICUS I., DAVID COMNENUS, ISAAC I., MANUEL I., and ANNA COMNENA.)

Comnenus, (DEMETRIUS,) born in Corsica about 1750, claimed to be a descendant of David, the last emperor of Trebizond. He was a captain in the French service, and emigrated as a royalist about 1792. He returned to France about 1800, and died in 1820.

Comodi. See COMMODO, (ANDREA.)

Comonfort, ko'mon-foRt' or kom'on-fort', (IGNACIO,) a Mexican general and President, was born at Puebla about 1810. He served in several civil wars in his youth, was elected a member of the Mexican Congress in 1842, and a senator about 1848. In 1854 he joined Alvarez in a revolutionary movement against Santa Anna, who was forced to abdicate in 1855. Alvarez having retired or abdicated in December, 1855, Comonfort then obtained the chief power as provisional President. The clergy and conservatives raised a revolt, which was suppressed by an army in March, 1856, soon after which he issued a decree to confiscate the property of the Church. In December, 1857, he was declared constitutional President. The disaffection of the army and the hostility of the clergy rendered his position untenable. The capital was taken by the rebels in January, 1858, and Comonfort went into exile. In 1863 he commanded an army which fought for the Liberal cause against the French. He was murdered by bandits in November of that year.

Comontes, de, då ko-mon'tĕs, (FRANCISCO,) a Spanish painter, born at Toledo ; died in 1564.

Compagni. See DOMENICO DEGLI CAMEI.

Compagni, kom-pån'yee, (DINO,) an Italian magistrate, born at Florence, wrote a "History of Florence from 1270 to 1312," which is praised for veracity and elegance. He held the office of prior of Florence in 1289 and in 1301.

Compagnon, kòn'pån'yòn', a French traveller, who in 1716 was factor of the French company at Senegal. He ascended the Senegal, and explored Galam and Bambook, which had not then been visited by Europeans. The narrative of his journey was published by Labat. He died in Paris about 1750.

Compagnoni, kom-pån-yo'nee, (GIUSEPPE,) an able Italian *littérateur*, born at Lugo in 1754, lived at Venice, Milan, etc. He published an "Essay on the Hebrews and Greeks," "The Evenings of Tasso," (" Le Veglie del Tasso,") a "History of America," and various other works. He was a republican, and held several high offices under the French régime, among which was that of councillor of state at Milan. Died in 1834.

See his Autobiography, "Vita letteraria di G. Compagnoni," 1834; TIPALDO, "Biografia degli Italiani illustri."

Compans, kòn'pòn', (JEAN DOMINIQUE,) COUNT, a French general, born at Salies (Haut-Garonne) in 1769. He served several campaigns among the Alps and in Italy during the republic. He was chief of the staff of Lannes at Austerlitz in 1805, and became a general of division in 1806. In the campaign of Saxony, 1813, his conduct was highly praised by Napoleon. He was taken prisoner at Waterloo, 1815. Died in 1845.

Comparetti, kom-på-ret'tee, (ANDREA,) an eminent Italian naturalist and physician, born in Friuli in 1746. He was for many years professor of medicine in the University of Padua. In 1787 he published, in Latin, "Observations on the Refraction of Light," and in 1789 "Observations on the Anatomy of the Ear," which is much esteemed. He produced a celebrated work entitled "Medical Comparisons or Collations of Masked Periodical Fevers," (" Riscontri medici delle Febbri larvate periodiche," 1795,) and an Italian treatise "On the Animal Dynamics of Insects," (1800,) which Cuvier designates as "very curious, instructive, and full of new views on the organs of locomotion." Died in 1801.

See D. PALMAROLI, "Saggio sopra la Vita, etc. di Andrea Comparetti," 1802 ; "Biographie Médicale."

Compte, Le. See LECOMPTE.

Comp'ton, (HENRY,) an eminent English prelate, born at Compton in 1632, was the youngest son of Spencer Compton, Earl of Northampton. He became Bishop of Oxford in 1674, and of London in 1675. Charles II. confided to him the education of his nieces Mary and Anne. For his zeal against popery he was

suspended from the episcopal office in 1686. On the accession of William III. (at whose coronation he supplied the place of the primate Sancroft) he was restored to the bishopric and admitted to the privy council. He wrote a "Treatise on the Communion," "Letters to the Clergy," and other works, and made great efforts to unite the Dissenters with the Anglican Church. Died in 1713.

See BURNET, "History of his Own Times ;" MACAULAY, "History of England;" "Life of Dr. Compton, Lord Bishop of London," London, 1716.

Compton, (SPENCER,) second Earl of Northampton, the son of William Compton, the first Earl, was born in 1601. He attended Prince Charles to Spain in 1622 as master of his robes. In the civil war which began in 1642 he fought for the king, and was killed in 1643 at Hopton Heath, refusing to give or take quarter.

Comstock, kŭm'stok, (JOHN LEE,) M.D., a compiler of school-books, born in Lyme, Connecticut, in 1789. He published, besides other works, a "System of Natural Philosophy," (1831,) and "Elements of Chemistry," which had a large circulation. Died in 1858.

Comte, kòNt, (ACHILLE JOSEPH,) a French naturalist, born at Grenoble in 1802, became professor of natural history in the Collége Charlemagne. He published several popular educational works, among which are "Physiology for Colleges," (1834,) and a "Complete Treatise on Natural History," (1844–48.) His wife ARABELLA, formerly MADAME LAYA, has written "Julien," (1841,) a comedy called "Veuvage," (" Widowhood,") and several other works.

See QUÉRARD, "La France Littéraire."

Comte, (AUGUSTE,) a French philosopher, the founder of the system called *Positivisme*, or Positive Philosophy, was born at Montpellier in January, 1798. His father was a treasurer of taxes. He entered the Polytechnic School in 1814, and gave much attention to mathematics and the physical sciences. About 1818 he became a disciple and coadjutor of Saint-Simon, whose doctrines he undertook to expound in a work entitled "System of Positive Politics," (" Système de Politique positive," 1822.) His connection with Saint-Simon continued about six years, and they separated in 1824, mutually disgusted and completely estranged. Before 1824 he had discovered his law of Social Evolution. He formed a new system, which is described as a combination of the doctrines of Fourier, Saint-Simon, and Hegel, and was developed in his "Cours de Philosophie positive," (6 vols., 1830–42,) a work which exhibits intellectual powers of a high order.

He married in 1825 ; but the union proved to be unhappy. Soon after this event he was seized with an acute attack of insanity, and attempted to commit suicide by drowning ; but he was rescued by a soldier. He rapidly recovered, and was entirely restored to sanity before the end of 1827. His new system of philosophy attracted great attention and was adopted by numerous disciples. In 1832 he was appointed a professor or tutor in the Polytechnic School of Paris. About 1842 he was finally separated from his wife, and two years later he formed a "passionate friendship" with Clotilde de Vaux. He speaks of her as "having inspired him with a happiness of which he had always dreamed, but which he had never hitherto experienced."

He published, besides other works, "Discours sur l'Esprit positive," (1844,) a "Philosophic Treatise on Popular Astronomy," (1844,) "Catéchisme positiviste, ou Sommaire Exposition de la Religion universelle," (1852,) and "Système de Politique positive, ou Traité de Sociologie, instituant la Religion de l'Humanité," (4 vols., 1851–54.) According to Comte, all the knowledge which man can possibly acquire is comprised in six pure sciences, viz., mathematics, astronomy, physics, chemistry, biology or physiology, and sociology or social science. He proposed to introduce and propagate a new religion,—the worship of humanity,—and assumed the title of chief priest of that religion. "To himself and a few followers," says the "Edinburgh Review" for April, 1868, "he appeared the philosopher of the age, who had summed up the course of past thought, the legislator of a new era, the author and chief minister of a new religion, which was to supersede all religions. . . . No one who has studied his great work can be insensible to his services. His undoubted influence lies in certain great conceptions with which he has enriched and illuminated the modern mind. . . . He not only took up the Baconian method, but he purified and extended it. He has at once given it a wider application than any previous thinker, and far more clearly understood its import." Died in Paris in September, 1857.

See GEORGE H. LEWES, "Comte's Philosophy of the Sciences," 1853; HARRIET MARTINEAU, "The Positive Philosophy of Auguste Comte," freely translated and condensed, 2 vols., 1854; JOHN STUART MILL, "Auguste Comte and Positivism," 1865; E. LITTRÉ, "Auguste Comte et la Philosophie positive," 1863; "Edinburgh Review" for July, 1838; "Westminster Review" for 1865; "British Quarterly Review" for July, 1866; "North British Review" for May, 1854.

Comte, (FRANÇOIS CHARLES LOUIS,) a French publicist, born in the department of Lozère in 1782. He published, in 1826, a "Treatise on Legislation," for which he received the Montyon prize of the Institute. In 1831 he was elected to the Chamber of Deputies. He was perpetual secretary of the Academy of Moral and Political Sciences. Died in 1837.

See F. A. A. MIGNET, "Notice historique sur la Vie de M. Comte," 1846.

Comyns, kŭm′ins, ? (Sir JOHN,) a British jurist, who became lord chief baron of the exchequer, and was author of a "Digest of the Laws of England," (1762–67,) which is considered high authority. Died about 1740.

Conæus, the Latin of CONE, which see.

Co′nant, (HANNAH O'BRIEN CHAPLIN,) an American linguist and writer, born ·at Danvers, Massachusetts, about 1811. She married Thomas J. Conant, a Hebraist, about 1833. She translated some of Neander's commentaries, and published, besides other works, a "History of the English Bible," (1859.) Died in Brooklyn in 1865.

Co′nant, (JOHN,) an English divine, born in Devonshire in 1608. He became professor of divinity at Oxford in 1654, Archdeacon of Norwich in 1676, and prebendary of Worcester in 1681. Several volumes of his sermons were published. Died in 1693.

Conant, (THOMAS J.,) D.D., an eminent biblical scholar, born in Vermont in 1802. He graduated at Middlebury, Vermont, in 1823, and has since filled professorships in Waterville College, Maine, and in the Baptist Theological Seminaries at Hamilton and Rochester, New York. For many years he has been engaged on a translation of the Bible, of which the book of Job was published by the American Bible Union in 1857. His "Gesenius's Hebrew Grammar" is one of the most popular text-books of the kind in use.

Conca, kon′kȧ, (SEBASTIANO,) a skilful Italian painter in oil and fresco, was born at Gaeta about 1678. He studied under Solimena of Naples for sixteen years, and then removed to Rome, where he worked with great success. Clement XI. employed him to adorn the church of Saint Clement. His renown extended beyond the limits of Italy; but modern critics think his merit was overrated. Among his master-pieces is a "Piscina Probatica," ("Pool of Bethesda,") at Sienna. Died in 1764.

See LANZI, "History of Painting in Italy."

Conc′a-nen, (MATTHEW,) an Irish writer, who came to London in his youth. He published a volume of poems in 1724. In a public journal he attacked Pope, who took revenge in the "Dunciad." In 1732 he was appointed attorney-general of Jamaica. Died in 1749.

Concha, de la, dȧ lȧ kon′chȧ, (Don JOSÉ,) a Spanish general, born in Madrid about 1800, served against the Carlists in several campaigns of the civil war. He was twice appointed Captain-General of the island of Cuba. In 1862 he was sent as minister to France. He was appointed nominal prime minister by the queen just after the revolution broke out in Spain, in September, 1868.

Concha, de la, (MANUEL,) a Spanish general, brother of the preceding, was born in Madrid in 1794. He served with the rank of general against Don Carlos, (1834–40.) In 1844 he was appointed Captain-General of Catalonia. He was banished for political reasons in January, 1854, but on the return of Espartero to power, in July of the same year, he was restored, and promoted to the rank of marshal.

Conchillos-Falco, kon-chēl′yȯs fȧl′ko, (JUAN,) a Spanish painter, born at Valencia in 1641; died in 1711.

Conchylius. See COQUILLE.

Concina, kon-chee′nȧ, (DANIELE,) an Italian theologian, born in Friuli about 1686, entered the Dominican order. He gained eminence as a preacher and as author of several works, (in Latin,) one of which is called "Christian Theology, Doctrinal and Practical," (1749.) Died in 1756.

See "Vita di D. Concini," 1768.

Concini. See ANCRE, D', MARSHAL.

Condamine, La, lȧ kȯN′dȧ′mĕn′, (CHARLES MARIE,) an eminent French savant and author, born in Paris in 1701. He travelled in the Levant in his youth. Under the auspices of the Academy of Sciences, he went in 1736 with Bouguer to Peru, to determine the size and figure of the earth. He returned in 1745, and published an "Account of a Journey in South America," (1745,) "The Figure of the Earth Determined," (1749,) "Journal of an Expedition made by Order of the King to the Equator," (1751,) and other works. In 1760 he was admitted into the French Academy, in consideration of his high reputation as a traveller and of his literary merit. He was a Fellow of the Royal Society of London. His gayety, courage, and curiosity were said to have never failed. M. Biot praises the elegant facility of his style. Died in Paris in 1774.

See CONDORCET, "Éloge de La Condamine;" VOLTAIRE, "Dictionnaire Philosophique," article "Curiosité;" L. BRIGHTWELL, "By-Paths of Biography."

Conde, kon′dȧ, (ANTONIO JOSÉ,) a Spanish historian and Orientalist, born about 1760. He gave special attention to Hebrew and Arabic, and collected many historical documents in Arabic. He was for many years one of the keepers of the Royal Library, and during the reign of Joseph Bonaparte was chief librarian. In 1814 he became an exile in France. It appears that he returned to Madrid about 1818, and died in 1820 or 1821. His principal work, a "History of the Dominion of the Arabs in Spain," ("Historia de la Dominacion de los Arabes en España," 3 vols., 1820–21,) has acquired a European reputation.

See PRESCOTT, "History of Ferdinand and Isabella," vol. i. part i.

Condé, de, dĕh kȯn′dȧ′, (HENRI I. de Bourbon—dĕh boor′bȯN′,) PRINCE, the son and heir of Louis I., Prince of Condé, was born in 1552. He escaped the massacre of August, 1572, (Saint Bartholomew,) by a promise to abjure Calvinism, and fled to Germany. He afterwards joined the Protestant army, was excommunicated (with his cousin, Henry of Navarre) by the pope in 1585, and died by poison, administered by his domestics, in 1588. "He was," says Brantôme, "a liberal, gracious, and eloquent prince, and promised to be as great a captain as his father." ("Vies des Hommes illustres.")

Condé, de, (HENRI II. DE BOURBON,) PRINCE, born at Saint-Jean-d'Angély in 1588, was a son of the preceding, and father of "the great" Condé. He was the first prince of the blood, and was educated at court as a Catholic. During the minority of Louis XIII. he put himself at the head of the malcontents, for which he was arrested by the regent and imprisoned three years at Vincennes. He afterwards obtained command of an army, and took several places from the Spaniards. Died in 1646.

See RENAUDOT, "Abrégé de la Vie du Prince de Condé," 1647; SISMONDI, "Histoire des Français."

Condé, de, (HENRI JULES DE BOURBON,) PRINCE, the only son of the great Condé, was born in 1643. He distinguished himself at the siege of Tournay in 1665, and in 1674 took part in the battle of Seneffe, where he is said to have saved his father's life. Saint-Simon gives an unfavourable view of his character. Died in 1709.

See SAINT-SIMON, "Mémoires."

Condé, de, (LOUIS I. DE BOURBON,) PRINCE, a famous French general, born at Vendôme in 1530, was the youngest son of Charles de Bourbon, Duc de Vendôme, and uncle of Henry IV. His promotion was retarded by the enmity of the Guises. About 1560 he openly avowed himself a Calvinist, and soon became the general-in-chief of the Protestant army in the civil war. He was defeated and made prisoner at Dreux in 1562, and released the next year. After the war had been suspended a few years, Condé fought, in 1567, the indecisive battle of Saint-Denis, where his army was greatly inferior in number to that of the enemy. At Jarnac, in 1569, he lost another battle, was wounded, and then killed after he had surrendered.

See DE THOU, "Histoire Universelle ;" DESORMEAUX, "Histoire de la Maison de Condé."

Condé, de, (LOUIS II. DE BOURBON,) PRINCE, styled "the great Condé," a celebrated French general, born in Paris on the 8th of September, 1621, was the first prince of the blood, and the son of Henri II., above noticed, and Charlotte de Montmorenci. He made his first campaign at the age of seventeen, with the title of Duc d'Enghien. In 1641 he married Claire Clémence de Maillé-Brézé, a niece of Cardinal Richelieu. In May, 1643, he gained a great victory over the Spaniards at Rocroi, and in 1645 defeated the Germans, commanded by Mercy, at Nordlingen. He was equally successful at Lens in 1648, where the once invincible Spanish infantry was ruined. During the civil war of the Fronde he commanded the royalists at first, (1649;) but he was arrested by the queen or Mazarin in January, 1650, and imprisoned one year. Burning for revenge, he raised an army and attacked the royalists under Turenne, at Paris, in 1652. Having been sentenced to death in 1653, he entered the service of Spain, and commanded in several campaigns in Flanders, where he was opposed by Turenne, and was far less successful than he had been when he fought for his own country. The treaty between France and Spain in 1659 procured an amnesty for his offences, and he returned to France. In 1672 he received command of an army against Holland, and in 1674 he defeated William of Orange at Seneffe. The next year he retired from the service on account of the gout. " He was born a general," says Voltaire : " the art of war seemed in him a natural instinct." Died in 1686. He possessed an ardent temperament, an admirable *coup-d'œil*, and abundant resources. His education is said to have been brilliant and complete. His funeral oration was pronounced by Bossuet.

See MACAULAY, "History of England," vol. ii. ; DESORMEAUX, "Histoire de Louis Prince de Condé," 4 vols., 1768 ; " Mémoires du Cardinal de Retz ;" " Mémoires du Comte de Grammont ;" " Mémoires de La Rochefoucauld ;" COUSIN, " Histoire de Madame de Longueville ;" LORD MAHON, " Life of the Prince of Condé," 1840 ; COSTE, "Histoire de Louis Prince de Condé," 1693 ; VOLTAIRE, "Siècle de Louis XIV ;" ADRIEN LEMERCIER, " Histoire du grand Condé," 1844 ; VOIVREUIL, " Histoire du grand Condé," 1847 ; " Lives of the Warriors of the Civil Wars of France and England," by SIR EDWARD CUST, London, 1867.

Condé, de, (LOUIS HENRI JOSEPH,) styled Duke of Bourbon and Prince of Condé, born in 1756, was the last of the line of Condé. He fought in several campaigns against the French Republic between 1792 and 1800. After the restoration, his chief occupation was the chase. He was found dead in 1830, with circumstances that indicated either suicide or assassination. He was the father of the Duc d'Enghien executed in 1804.

See ALBERT DE CALVIMONT, "Le dernier des Condé," 1832.

Condé, de, (LOUIS JOSEPH DE BOURBON,) PRINCE, born in Paris in 1736, was the only son of the Duke of Bourbon who became prime minister about 1724. In the Seven Years' war he signalized his courage at Hastembeck in 1757, and was successful at Johannisberg in October, 1762. Having become obnoxious to the popular party in 1789, he emigrated, and became commander of the emigrants who took arms against the new régime in 1792. He gained a victory at Berstheim in 1793, and shared the defeats of the Austrians in 1796 and 1799. In 1801 he disbanded his corps and retired to England. He returned to France in 1814, and died in 1818, leaving a son, Louis Henri Joseph.

See CHAMBELLAND, " Vie du Prince de Condé," 3 vols., 1820.

Con'der, (JOHN,) an English dissenting minister, who was born in 1714, and preached in London. He published an " Essay on the Ministerial Character," and several sermons between 1755 and 1768. Died in 1781.

Conder, (JOSIAH,) an English author, born in London in 1789, became a bookseller in that city. From 1814 to 1837 he edited the "Eclectic Review," to which Robert Hall, Dr. Chalmers, and other eminent writers contributed. He published many learned works, among which are "The Modern Traveller," (33 vols.,) a "History of Italy," and a "View of All Religions." In the latter part of his life he edited "The Patriot," the organ of the Baptists and Congregationalists. Died in 1855.

See E. R. CONDER, " Life of Josiah Conder," 1857.

Condillac, de, dęh kôn'de'yăk', (ÉTIENNE **Bonnot** —bo'no',) Abbé de Mureaux, (mü'rō',) an eminent French philosopher and metaphysician, born at Grenoble in 1715. In his youth he was intimate with J. J. Rousseau and Diderot ; but this friendship declined or ceased in his mature years. In 1746 appeared his first work, an "Essay on the Origin of Human Knowledge," ("Sur l'Origine des Connaissances humaines,") in which he advanced new and ingenious ideas. He produced in 1749 his "Treatise on Systems," ("Traité des Systèmes,") and in 1754 his "Treatise on Sensations," ("Traité des Sensations,") a luminous and admirable work, which extended his celebrity throughout Europe. Soon after this date he was chosen preceptor of the Duke of Parma, for whose use he composed "The Art of Writing," "The Art of Thinking," and other works, forming a series entitled "Cours d'Études." He was admitted into the French Academy in 1768. He has been much praised for his discoveries in relation to the progress and influence of language. According to him, man owes the development of his faculties to the use of signs, and we are able to reflect only because we are able to speak. He was a brother of the Abbé de Mably. Died near Beaugency in 1780. His moral character was virtuous and discreet,—at least according to the French standard. An edition of his works, in 32 vols. 12mo, was published in 1803.

See LA HARPE, "Cours de Littérature ;" TENNEMANN, "Geschichte der Philosophie ;" SACCHI, " Elogio di Condillac," 1819; " Nouvelle Biographie Générale."

Condivi, kon-dee'vee, (ASCANIO,) an Italian painter, born in the March of Ancona about 1520, was a pupil of Michael Angelo, whom, it is said, he never quitted. He wrote a "Life of Michael Angelo," (1553,) which is accounted valuable.

See LANZI, "History of Painting in Italy."

Condorcet, de, dęh kôn'dor'să', (MARIE JEAN ANTOINE NICOLAS **Caritat**—kă're'tă',) MARQUIS, a celebrated French mathematician and philosopher, born at Ribemont, in Picardy, on the 17th of September, 1743. His parents were noble, but not rich. After leaving the College of Navarre he became a resident of Paris in 1762. His "Essay on the Integral Calculus," and that on the "Problem of Three Bodies," opened to him in 1769 the Academy of Sciences, of which a few years later he was chosen perpetual secretary. He was an intimate friend of D'Alembert, and an admirer of Voltaire. In 1782 he was elected a member of the French Academy in preference to Bailly. He wrote in favour of American independence, and sowed in his works the germ of republican principles. He embraced with ardour the popular cause in 1789, published many able political treatises, and was deputed by Paris to the Legislative Assembly in 1791. In the Convention he was one of the most popular and prominent members, and voted generally with the Girondists, but did not vote for the death of Louis XVI.

He was chosen a member of the Committee of Public Safety in 1792. Proscribed as a Girondist in May, 1793, he remained secreted in the house of Madame Vernet, in Paris, for eight months, during which he wrote his treatise "On Human Perfectibility," in which he was a believer. Impelled by a longing to enjoy the open air and the vernal season, he imprudently departed from his asylum in April, 1794. In a few days he was arrested on suspicion, and thrown into prison at Bourg-la-Reine, where he ended his life by poison. His wife was a sister of General Grouchy. (See following article.) As a geometer he stands high in the second rank. He composed admired eulogies on Buffon, D'Alembert, Franklin, and others. His "Historical Sketch of the Progress of the Human Mind" ("Esquisse d'un Tableau historique des Progrès de l'Esprit humain," 1795) is

ā, ē, ī, ō, ū, ȳ, *long;* ă, ĕ, ŏ, same, less prolonged; ă, ĕ, ĭ, ŏ, ŭ, ў, *short;* ą, ę, į, ǫ, *obscure;* fär, făll, făt; mĕt; nŏt; gōōd; mōōn;

called his greatest work. His character was noble and benevolent. "Thus died," says Lamartine, "this Seneca of the modern school. Placed between two camps to combat the old world and moderate the new, he perished in the shock without regret. The day of recognition *(reconnaissance)* has not come for him; but it will come, and will exculpate his memory from reproach." The best edition of his works is that published in Paris, in 12 vols., 1847-49.

See ARAGO, "Notice sur Condorcet," read before the Academy of Sciences in December, 1841; LAMARTINE, "History of the Girondists;" "Quarterly Review" for July, 1850, vol. lxxxvii.; D. F. ARAGO, "Biographie de M. J. A. N. C. de Condorcet," 4to, 1849; S. F. LACROIX, "Notice historique sur la Vie de Condorcet," 8vo, 1813; ISAMBERT, Notice in the "Nouvelle Biographie Générale;" "Lives of the Most Eminent French Writers," by Mrs. SHELLEY; "London Quarterly Review" for September, 1855, vol. xcvii.

Condorcet, de, (SOPHIE de Grouchy—dẹh gROO′-she′,) MARQUISE, born in 1765, was a sister of Marshal Grouchy, and was one of the most beautiful women of her time. In 1786 she became the wife of the Marquis de Condorcet. In the first years of the new régime she shared with Madame de Staël the homage of the Parisian *salons.* She made a good French translation of Adam Smith's "Theory of Moral Sentiments." Died in 1822. Her daughter married General O'Connor.

See "Nouvelle Biographie Générale."

Condren, de, dẹh kòn′dRŏn′, (CHARLES,) an eminent French ecclesiastic, born near Soissons in 1588. He entered the society of the Oratory in 1617, and was elected general of the same in 1629. He modestly refused the rank of cardinal and archbishop. When he died, (1641,) the king exclaimed, "The most holy and disinterested man in the realm is dead." He left a few religious treatises.

See AMELOTTE, "Vie du Père Condren," 1643.

Cōne or **Cōwne,** [Lat. CONÆ′US,] sometimes written **Conei,** (GEORGE,) a Scottish Roman Catholic writer, resided at Rome. He wrote a "Life of Mary Stuart, Queen of Scots," (1624.) Died in 1640.

Cōne, (SPENCER HOUGHTON,) an eloquent Baptist minister, born at Princeton, New Jersey, in 1785. He was in early life a popular play-actor, and began to preach about 1814. He was pastor of a Baptist church in the city of New York from 1823 till 1841, and was the principal founder of the American Bible Union. Died in 1855.

See "Life of S. H. Cone," by his sons, 1856.

Conecte or **Connecte,** ko′nĕkt′, (THOMAS,) a French Carmelite monk and popular preacher, born at Rennes. He declaimed against the disorders of the clergy, and maintained that they should be permitted to marry. He was condemned as a heretic at Rome, and was burnt to death in 1434.

Conegliano. See CIMA.

Conegliano, DUC DE. See MONCEY.

Conei. See CONE.

Co′ney, (JOHN,) an English engraver, born in London in 1786. He published "Ancient Cathedrals of France, Holland, and Germany," with fine engravings, "English Ecclesiastic Edifices of the Olden Time," and other works. Died about 1833.

Conflans, de, dẹh kòn′flŏn′, (HUBERT de Brienne—dẹh bRe′ĕn′,) COUNT, a French marshal, born about 1690. He was made a captain in 1734, lieutenant-general in 1752, and vice-admiral in 1756, and afterwards obtained the rank of marshal of France. In 1759 he was defeated with great loss by the English near Quiberon. Died in 1777.

Conflans, de, (LOUIS DE BRIENNE,) Marquis d'Armentières, (dȧR′mŏN′te′aiR′,) a French general, born in 1711, was made marshal of France in 1768. Died in 1774.

Confucius, kon-fu′she-us, [the Latinized form of KONG-FOO-TSE or KONG-FU-TSE, kong′foot′sẹh′ or kong-foot′sŭh′, or KHOONG-FOO-TSE,* written also KOUNG-

FOU-TSE, KUNG-FOO-TSZE, and KHOUNG-FOU-TSEU, k'hōōng-fŏō′tsŭh′, sometimes simply KHOONG-TSE or KHOUNG-TSEU. Khoong-Foo-tsze signifies "the master Khoong," Khoong or K'ung being the name of the family: he was also called NE, (or NI,) and CHUNG-NE, (or TCHOUNG-NI,)] the most illustrious of Chinese philosophers, was born, according to the best authorities, 551 B.C., in the kingdom or state of Loo, (included in the modern province of Shan-toong.) His father, Shuh-Liang-Heih, (in French, Chou-liang-hé,) a soldier of extraordinary strength as well as bravery, was descended from a long line of illustrious ancestors. He had had by his first wife nine daughters, but no son. Having become a widower, he married in his old age a young lady of rare virtues, whose only son, the subject of this notice, was destined to acquire a renown scarcely paralleled in the history of the human race. It is related among the legends concerning Confucius that just before his birth the *Ki-lin,* a supernatural being, who never appeared among men except to announce some extraordinary event, left in the garden of the house of Shuh-Liang-Heih a piece of precious stone, on which was written, "A child is about to be born, pure as the crystal wave : he shall be a king, but without any [territorial] domain." The young Confucius was commonly called Kew, or K'ew, (in French, Kieou,) because, as Pauthier informs us, his mother soon after her marriage visited a neighbouring hill, (called Ne-Kew, or Ni-Kieou,—that is, the "hill Ne,") in order to offer her prayers to Heaven that she might be blessed with children. Hence also, as it appears, the sage was called Ne, (or Ni.)* "The venerable Ne" was a title often applied to him after his death.

As a child, Confucius was remarkable for his entire obedience to his mother, for the respect which he always showed to elderly people, and especially for a careful observance of all the requisite ceremonies in honour of the living and the dead. While other children found their diversion in childish sports, it was his favourite pastime, the Chinese historians tell us, to go through all the various forms of politeness observed among persons of high education. At school he was distinguished for his obedience, gentleness, and modesty, as well as for a marvellous quickness of intellect. He acquitted himself with particular credit as a monitor ; (for the monitorial system of instruction, commonly supposed to be a modern invention, appears to have been practised in China from a very early period.) At the age of nineteen he married, and about this time he was made a mandarin, though of a subordinate grade. In fulfilling the duties of his office he exhibited extraordinary industry, faithfulness, and intelligence. He superintended the public markets, and took care that nothing should be sold as food that was injurious to the health of the people, and that the poor should not have to pay an unreasonable price for the necessaries of life. He was afterwards put in charge of the public fields and lands, with the care of the sheep and cattle. Through his diligence and sagacity the most extraordinary improvements in agriculture were introduced, so that in a few years the face of the country presented a totally different appearance. Scarcity was followed by abundance, penury by affluence, among the cultivators of the soil.

When about twenty-two, Confucius came forward for the first as a public teacher. He never refused his instruction, however small the fee his pupils were able to pay him. All he required was an earnest desire to learn, joined to a respectable capacity. After he had shown his pupils the paths which lead to wisdom, he expected them to pursue the same, without continually looking to him for further instruction. "When I have presented," he said, "one corner of a subject to any one, and he cannot from it learn the other three, I do not repeat my lesson." When he was only twenty-four years of age, his mother died. After the appropriate ceremonies were performed, he caused her remains to be buried by those of his father, observing that "those who had been united in life should not be parted after death." Following the

---

* The initial letter of this name (K) is followed by something similar to the aspirate which occurs so frequently in Hindoo words, as *Ghora,* a "horse," (pronounced almost g'ho′ra, but in *two* syllables only.) To indicate this peculiar sound, some writers use an apostrophe after the K,—K′ung. The *tseu* in the French spelling, KHOUNG-FOU-TSEU, is used to indicate a sound expressed by the Germans with *tse,* that is, tsuh or tsüh. See remarks on Chinese pronunciation in the Introduction.

* According to Pauthier, the name of Tchoung-Ni was given in allusion to the hill Ni, (visited by his mother after her marriage,) and to the fact of his being the heir (or eldest son) of his father. See Legge's "Life and Teachings of Confucius,' chap. v. p. 58.

---

usag‘ of his country, he mourned for his mother three years, during which time he filled no public office. When in his thirtieth year, he is said to have taken lessons in music under the celebrated master Siang, (or Seang.) The following story will serve to give us some idea of the estimation in which music was held by Confucius and the Chinese of that age, as well as to show us the enthusiastic wonder with which his talents were regarded by his followers. Siang spoke to Confucius of music as the most precious gift conferred by Heaven upon men, on account of its power not only to calm the tumultuous passions, but also to purify and exalt the nobler sentiments of the heart. The master played a piece composed by a former Chinese musician of marvellous skill. Confucius listened as if his very soul would pass into the instrument. Some days afterwards the teacher repeated the same lesson, and his pupil continued to study it with unremitting application. At length Siang told Confucius that, as he had already attained in that particular piece a skill equal to his master's, he had better pass on to something new. But Confucius begged that he might be allowed to study the same lesson a few days longer. At last he told his teacher why he desired to dwell so long on that one piece. After playing it a number of times, he had caught, as he believed, a glimpse of the design and spirit of the composer. As he continued to play, he seemed to be penetrated with the same spirit as that which inspired the author while composing it. At length he seemed not only to hear the voice, but to see the person, of the gifted but unknown musician. Confucius then described his general figure, the expression of his eyes, and even his very features. He was not mistaken. It was the celebrated Wen-Wang, an illustrious sage as well as musician. Siang, astonished beyond measure at his pupil's marvellous powers, prostrated himself before him, saying that he could teach him no longer, but that he himself must in future become the pupil of Confucius. (See Pauthier's "Chine," pp. 128–9.)

Passing over some of the less important events of his life, we find Confucius in 499 B.C. one of the chief ministers of the King or Prince of Loo. The forces of the neighbouring King of Tsi (or Ts'e) had upon some frivolous pretext taken possession of three frontier towns belonging to the King of Loo. In order to settle the dispute, it was agreed between the two princes that they should have a friendly interview on the common frontier of their respective states. Confucius, who is described as possessing a wonderful power of reading the characters of men, suspected the King of Tsi of a design to seize the person of the King of Loo. He therefore ordered that a very strong military force should advance and occupy a position where it would be out of sight and yet within signalling-distance of the place appointed for the interview. The result showed a deep-laid scheme of treachery on the part of the King of Tsi and his ministers; but the foresight, vigilance, and resolute courage of Confucius baffled all their plans, and they were fain to restore the disputed towns to their lawful ruler. (For a particular account of this extraordinary interview, see Pauthier's "Chine," pp. 152, 153, and 154.)

Confucius held for some time the office of minister of crime. A father having brought an accusation against his son, Confucius kept them both in prison for three months. One of the chief men objected that the minister did not act consistently with his own teachings, for he had always taught that filial duty was among the first of human obligations. Confucius replied, "When superiors fail in their duty, and yet go to put their inferiors to death, they are not just. This father has not taught his son to be filial: to listen to his charge would be to slay the guiltless."* After the three months had elapsed, the minister called both father and son before him. The father acknowledged his fault. Confucius said to him, kindly, "Go, and instruct your son in his duties." To the young man he said, "Do not forget that filial piety is the first of all your obligations."

* It appears that, according to the old Chinese law, every serious offence against a parent was punishable with death. Even at the present day, to strike a parent is a capital crime.

But the King of Loo found the precepts of the sage too high and difficult for his feeble virtue; and Confucius, perceiving that his services had ceased to be in request, retired from public life, and spent his time in travelling and study. The following passage may serve to show his manner of making any remarkable occurrence the occasion of imparting instruction to those around him. "As he was journeying, one day, he saw a woman weeping and wailing by a grave. Confucius inquired the cause of her grief. 'You weep as if you had experienced sorrow upon sorrow,' said one of the attendants of the sage. The woman answered, 'It is so: my husband's father was killed here by a tiger, and my husband also; and now my son has met the same fate.' 'Why do you not remove from the place?' asked Confucius. On her replying, 'There is here no oppressive government,' he turned to his disciples, and said, 'My children, remember this:—Oppressive government is more cruel than a tiger.'"

After leaving the service of the King of Loo, he appears to have spent the greater part of his time in disseminating his doctrines while travelling from one province to another, on which occasions he was always attended by some of his disciples. On one of these journeys their provisions became exhausted, and they were unable to procure a fresh supply. The disciples were overcome with hunger; and one of them said to the master, "Must the superior man indeed suffer in this way?" The sage replied, "The superior man may indeed have to suffer want; but the mean man, when he is in want, gives way to unbridled license." The last five years of his life were passed in Loo, his native state, in teaching, and in finishing the works which he had before commenced.

Among the pupils of Confucius there were a number who gave promise of becoming distinguished lights of philosophy; but all the warmest affections and fondest hopes of the Chinese sage appear to have been centred in his favourite and gifted disciple, Yen-Hoei, (or Hwuy,) to whom he looked, when he himself should be no more, to uphold and extend those lofty principles of wisdom and virtue which had constituted the one supreme object of his life-long pursuit. All these bright hopes were, however, destined to be crushed by the death of his beloved pupil, cut off in the very flower of his life. In the anguish of this unutterable sorrow, he could only exclaim, from time to time, "Heaven has destroyed me! Heaven has destroyed me!" On this occasion some of his disciples said to him, "Master, your grief is excessive." "Is it excessive?" said he. "If I am not to mourn bitterly for this man, for whom should I mourn?"

The great stress laid by Confucius upon the external forms of politeness and propriety might naturally suggest the idea that he was deficient in the spontaneous affections of the heart. But we have sufficient evidence that this was not the case. He appears, indeed, to have considered the observance of external forms to be not only directly beneficial to society, but also indirectly useful, through their influence upon the minds of those who practised them, on the same general principle that the practice of outward acts of morality tends to give strength and vitality to our moral convictions. We have just seen, in the case of Yen-Hoei, that his affections were so strong that he found the greatest difficulty in conforming his conduct to those principles of propriety which he had always so strongly inculcated. The following anecdote may show how his views of propriety were sometimes modified by the feelings of his heart. Once, as he passed by a house where he had formerly been lodged, learning that the master was dead, he went in to condole with the family. On coming out, he told a disciple to take one of the horses from his carriage and give it as a contribution towards the expenses of the funeral. The disciple remonstrated that the gift was too great for the occasion. The sage replied that, when he entered, his presence caused a fresh burst of grief from the chief mourner, with whose tears he mingled his own. "I dislike," he said, "the thought of my tears not being followed by anything. Do it, my child." (Legge's "Confucius," chap. v. sect. i.)

As he drew near the close of his career, he appears to

have felt at times bitterly disappointed that, after all his earnest efforts to reform abuses and exalt the standard of virtue, so little had been accomplished. He seemed to leave society in much the same condition as he found it. Everywhere the rulers and higher dignitaries were devoted to the pursuits of pleasure or ambition, paying little or no regard to the rights or happiness of the people. He once expressed this feeling of disappointment to Yen-Hoei, but modestly suggested that the fault might be in himself, and that perhaps his gifted disciple might be more successful than he had been. In one respect Confucius was more fortunate than many other great benefactors of the human race. Although he frequently experienced ingratitude and neglect, he appears never to have suffered from persecution. It is related that a few days before his death he chanted, sorrowfully,—

"The great mountain must crumble,
The strong trees must break, (or fall,)
The wise man must wither away like a plant." . . .

He died 478 B.C., or about eight years before the birth of Socrates.

Confucius had one son, named Pé-yu, (or Pih-yu,) commonly called Le, (or Li,) from the name of a fish which the King of Loo sent the sage as a congratulatory present on the birth of his child. Le died before his father, leaving one son, K'ung Keih, called also Tse-sse, (or Tsze-sze,) who was a distinguished philosopher, and was the author of a celebrated work called "Chung-Yung," (for an account of which see Legge's "Life and Teachings of Confucius," chap. iv.)

If to exert a great and permanent influence on millions of intelligent minds* through many successive ages is a proof of greatness, we can scarcely deny to the Chinese sage the name of great. If extent of renown constitutes greatness, he was the greatest of the human race; for of all the men that ever lived upon the earth he has enjoyed the widest fame and received the greatest honours. Even the fame of Alexander the Great has not been sounded in the ears of so many millions as that of Confucius. Amid all the changes of dynasty that have taken place in the Celestial Empire, whether caused by foreign conquest or domestic rebellion, his posterity have always been treated with a peculiar respect; and they constitute at this day the only hereditary nobility† in China. His male descendants at the present time number more than eleven thousand persons. Ever since the days of Confucius his writings have formed the chief object of study in all the schools of China. "In many school-rooms," says Dr. Legge, "there is a tablet or inscription on the wall, sacred to the sage; and every pupil is required, on coming to school on the morning of the first and fifteenth of every month, to bow before it the first thing, as an act of worship."

In all that Confucius did or taught, the useful and practical (using these words in an extended sense) formed the sole object of his labours and his thoughts. The end and scope of his philosophy were limited to the present world. There is none of his recorded sayings, either uttered near the close of his life or at any previous time, indicating that he had any distinct belief in a state of existence after death. Dr. Legge inclines to the opinion that, in regard to the belief in a God, Confucius came short of the faith of the older sages. The term *Shang-Te* (*i.e.* "supreme divine Ruler") was anciently used as the name of the Divine Being. Confucius preferred to speak of Heaven. His influence, according to the view of the above writer, has been unfavourable to the development of true religious feeling among the Chinese. (See Legge's "Life and Teachings of Confucius," p. 100.)

The most valuable and trustworthy source of information respecting the character and genius of the Chinese sage is to be found in his "Analects," called in Chinese *Lun-Yu,*—that is, the "digested conversations" of Confucius. The whole of the "Analects" are well worthy of a perusal by every one who wishes to understand the

spirit and scope of the Confucian philosophy.* They seem fully to justify the high eulogiums that have been pronounced upon the wisdom of Confucius. It may well be doubted whether among all the pagan writers of the Western nations anything can be found superior, or even equal, to many of these sayings, in respect either to practical wisdom or high morality.

The following are some of his remarkable sayings:

"He who exercises government by means of his virtue may be compared to the north polar star, which keeps its place, and all the [other] stars turn towards it." "In the book of poetry are three hundred pieces; but the design of them all may be embraced in that one sentence, '*Have no depraved thoughts.*' " "Learning without thought is labour lost; thought without learning (or knowledge) is perilous." Which perhaps may be para phrased thus: The knowledge of facts, without the intellect necessary to apply them wisely, is useless; on the other hand, speculation or thought, however powerful, without a basis of positive knowledge to rest on, or without facts to serve as landmarks to direct its course, is in imminent danger of going astray. "I do not know how a man without truthfulness is to get on." "He who offends against Heaven has none to whom he can pray." "When we see men of worth, we should think of equalling them; when we see men of a contrary character, we should turn inwards and examine ourselves." "Good government obtains when those who are near are made happy and those who are far off are attracted." Being asked what were the essential requisites of government, he replied, "Sufficiency of food, military equipment, and confidence of the people in their ruler." When asked which, in case of necessity, could best be dispensed with, he answered, "The military equipment." When again asked which of the remaining two might best be dispensed with, he said, "Part with the food: from of old, death has been the lot of all men; but if the people have no faith in their rulers there is no standing for the state."

We have in one place a negative statement of the golden rule: "What you do not like when done to yourself, do not do to others." In another place he says, "The man of perfect virtue, wishing to be established himself, seeks also to establish others; wishing to be enlarged himself, he seeks also to enlarge others. To be able to judge of others by what is *nigh*, [*i.e. in ourselves,*] this may be called the art of virtue." "I am not concerned that I have no place, (or office;) I am concerned how I may fit myself for one. I am not concerned that I am not known; I seek to be worthy to be known." "When the accomplishments and solid qualities are equally blended, we then have the man of complete virtue." "The superior man thinks of virtue; the small man thinks of comfort. The superior man thinks of the sanctions of law; the small man thinks of the favours which he may receive." "The superior man is affable, but not adulatory; the mean man is adulatory, but not affable."

One of the disciples of Confucius said of him, "There were four things from which the master was entirely free. He had no foregone conclusions, no arbitrary predeterminations, no obstinacy, and no egoism." He appears to have held that mankind are naturally good, or, at least, that under favourable circumstances they readily become good. (See MENCIUS.) He taught that if rulers were virtuous the people would be virtuous as a matter of course. He said, "If good men were to govern a country for a hundred years, they would be able to transform the violently bad, and dispense with capital punishment." Again, "If a superior man love righteousness, the people will not dare to refuse to submit to his example. If he love good faith, the people will not dare to be insincere." Confucius was very bold in reproving men in power. To a usurping ruler who complained of the multitude of thieves, he said, "If you, sir, were not covetous, although you should reward them to do it, they would not steal." He justly attached great importance to the power of example; but his own later experience

<hr>

* In regard to the high intellectual character of the Chinese, and the peculiarity of their civilization, see some excellent remarks in Whitney's "Lectures on Language," pp. 332–334.

† The descendants of Mencius should perhaps form an exception to this statement: they do not, however, rank with the posterity of Confucius. (See LEGGE's "Chinese Classics," vol. ii* p. 40.)

* These have been presented to the English reader in a convenient form in the excellent version made by the accomplished Chinese scholar, Dr. James Legge, published by Trübner & Co., London, 1867.

might have convinced him that he overestimated its influence. As we have already seen, he bitterly lamented, near the close of his life, that all his teachings, though enforced—if we may trust the unvarying testimony of Chinese writers—by an admirable example, had availed so little towards promoting true virtue among his countrymen. He once said, doubtless in a moment of great discouragement, "I have not seen a person who loved virtue, or one who hated what was not virtuous."

There is a total difference in kind between the philosophy of Confucius and the philosophies of Plato, Aristotle, Bacon, and Locke. The Chinese sage did not aim to investigate the mysteries of the universe, or even the hidden laws of nature or of the human mind. His great object was to lay down such rules as would best promote the happiness and virtue of the community at large. And it must be acknowledged that in the practical wisdom of his precepts, both to rulers and subjects, he has never been surpassed by any philosopher of any age or nation. That wise and beautiful thought which is the basis of Chinese government—that the ruler or officer should be as a father, and the people as children—dates, there is reason to believe, from a very remote antiquity. Confucius did not originate this idea; but he did everything in his power to give it practical efficacy.

But if, on the one hand, he never wasted his thoughts on subjects too high or too profound for the human intellect, it must, on the other, be confessed that his maxims are often deficient in depth and comprehensiveness. While his writings everywhere abound with admirable practical precepts, they rarely contain the statement of any profound principle. He did not pretend or aim to improve upon the wisdom of the ancient Chinese sages, —to attempt which he would have deemed the height of folly and presumption,—but only to. expound and enforce those maxims and doctrines which, with the lapse of ages, had become neglected or misunderstood. In explaining and enforcing the teachings of antiquity, he was indeed admirable. In the clearness, simplicity, power, and poetic beauty of his expressions, as well as in the practical wisdom of his views, he excelled all his countrymen, either before or since his time. The great defect of his philosophy is that it does not contain within itself any elements of progress or expansion: hence it is not only immeasurably inferior, even as a practical system, to Christianity, but is in the point above referred to far below most of the philosophies of the Western nations. His moral precepts, having no root in any definite religious faith, are wanting in vitality and power. Confucius was undoubtedly great and noble in his way, —far superior to his system. We need not hesitate to admit what his disciples claimed for him, that "from the birth of mankind till now there has never been [among the Chinese] one like our master." But his intellect appears to have been sagacious and penetrating, rather than comprehensive or profound in the highest sense of these terms. He did not shed any new light upon the great problems respecting the condition and destiny of man. "He did not," says Dr. Legge, "speculate on the creation of things or the end of them. He was not troubled to account for the origin of man, nor did he seek to know about his hereafter. He meddled neither with physics nor metaphysics." (Legge's "Confucius," p. 99.) He was content to follow in the wake of the sages of antiquity: he sought neither to rise above nor to change the course of their teachings. It appears to have never once occurred to him to call in question the wisdom of his ancestors. If he modified at all any of the doctrines or precepts handed down to him, he seems to have done so unintentionally. Even his very virtues— his reverence and humility—contributed, it would seem, to mislead him. Otherwise a man of his rare sagacity and insight could scarcely have failed to see the insufficiency and poverty of that stereotyped conservatism which durst not advance one step beyond the teaching of a remote antiquity, but which required the wheels of civilization to run for all time in the well-worn grooves of the past. A very little force, as is well known, is sufficient to keep a train of cars in motion on a smooth and level or descending track. This may suggest one of the essential points of difference between the system

of Confucius and Christianity. The one never ran counter to, nor ever rose much above, the general tendency of the national character. The other, beginning at a period which was confessedly one of the darkest and most corrupt known in history, moving, not in accordance with, but against, the most cherished prejudices of the people among whom it rose, instead of finding a track ready made and rendered smooth by the attrition of ages, had to make its own way, ever upwards, and over countless obstacles, any one of which would have been insuperable to anything less than divine power.

The influence that Confucius has exerted upon nearly one-third of the human race, during so many successive centuries, in addition to his own inherent greatness, and the fact that, since the opening of the ports of the Celestial Empire to an intercourse with other countries, a new and more general interest in all that relates to China is felt among the nations of the West, must constitute our apology—if any apology be needed—for extending this notice to so great a length.

See, in addition to the works referred to in the foregoing article, P. REGIS, "Antiquissimus Sinarum Liber," Stuttgart, 1839; MEDHURST'S translation of the "Shoo-King;" COLLIE'S translation of the Chinese classical works commonly called "The Four Books," Malacca, 1828; "Mencius et Confucius; Les quatre Livres de Philosophie morale et politique de la Chine," translated from the Chinese by G. PAUTHIER, Paris, 1851; RÉMUSAT, "L'invariable Milieu," Paris, 1817; AMIOT, "Mémoires concernant les Chinois;" "Confucius and the Chinese Classics," by REV. A. W. LOOMIS," San Francisco, 1867; OLOF CELSIUS, "Exercitatio historica Confucium Sinarum Philosophum adumbrans," 1710; CORTIN, "Disputatio de Confucio," 1743; DRESSLER, "Compendium Confucii Sinensium Philosophi principis Vitæ et Doctrinæ," 1701; "Edinburgh Review" for April, 1869.

Congleton, kŏng'gl-tǫn, (HENRY BROOKE PARNELL,) LORD, a British statesman, son of Sir John Parnell, born in 1776. He married Lady Dawson, a granddaughter of the Earl of Bute. In 1806 he became lord treasurer of Ireland. When the Whig party obtained power in 1831, he was appointed secretary at war. From 1835 to 1841 he was paymaster of the forces. He published several treatises on currency, exchange, trade, etc. His principal work is entitled "On Financial Reform," (1830.) Died in 1842.

Congreve, kŏng'grēv, (WILLIAM,) a popular, witty, and original English dramatic poet, was born near Leeds in 1670. On leaving college he entered the Middle Temple as a student of law, but devoted himself to literature and society. He produced in 1693 "The Old Bachelor," which was performed with brilliant success, and the next year the "Double-Dealer," which was highly extolled by Dryden. "Love for Love," (1695,) and "The Mourning Bride," a tragedy, (1697,) were received with great applause, and rendered Congreve the most popular dramatist of his time. "We believe," says Macaulay, "that no English writer, except Lord Byron, has at so early an age stood so high in the estimation of his contemporaries." Montagu, a member of the ministry, bestowed on him several lucrative offices. For the licentiousness and immorality of his works he received a severe and merited castigation in Collier's "View of the Profaneness, etc. of the English Stage," (1698,) which produced an immense effect. Congreve's defence was admitted to be a complete failure. In 1700 he produced "The Way of the World," which, though brilliantly written, was so coldly received that he renounced the drama in disgust. In 1714 he was appointed secretary of Jamaica. Pope dedicated to him his "Iliad," about 1715,—an evidence that he was still held in high estimation. Johnson praises the magnanimity of Pope in thus preferring Congreve to peers and statesmen, who would have been proud of the honour. Congreve's ambition to pass for a man of fashion caused him to disclaim the character of poet, saying that his plays were trifles produced in an idle hour. "The peculiar excellence of Congreve," says Hallam, "is his wit, incessantly sparkling from the lips of almost every character." ("Introduction to the Literature of Europe.") Died in 1729.

See JOHNSON, "Lives of the English Poets;" MACAULAY, "Essay on the Comic Dramatists of the Restoration;" "Biographia Britannica;" ERSCH und GRUBER, "Allgemeine Encyklopaedie;" CIBBER, "Lives of the English Poets;" CHARLES WILSON, "Memoirs of the Life of W. Congreve," 1730; "Lives of British Dramatists," by CAMPBELL, GIFFORD, etc.

Congreve, (Sir WILLIAM,) an English officer and engineer, born in Middlesex in 1772, inherited a baronetcy from his father, of the same name, who was a general. He rose in the army to the rank of lieutenant-colonel, and distinguished himself in 1808 by the invention of the rocket which bears his name. He was elected to Parliament several times. In 1816 he was selected to attend the grand duke Nicholas of Russia in a tour through England. He published a "Treatise on the Mounting of Naval Ordnance," (1812,) and other works. Died at Toulouse in 1828.

See "Nouvelle Biographie Générale."

Coninck, ko′nink, (SOLOMON,) a Dutch painter of history and portraits, born at Amsterdam in 1609. Among his works, which are highly prized, is "David and Bathsheba."

Coninck, de, deh ko′nink, (DAVID,) a skilful Flemish painter of animals, flowers, and fruit, born at Antwerp in 1636; died in Rome in 1689.

Coningsloo. See COONINXLOO.

Co′ning-ton, (JOHN,) an English classical scholar, born at Boston in 1825, was educated at Oxford. He became professor of Latin at Oxford in 1854. He made a poetical version of Horace's "Odes" in 1863, and translated Homer's "Iliad" into verse, (1866.) Died in 1869.

See "Blackwood's Magazine" for January, 1867; "North British Review" for December, 1866.

Cŏnk′ling, (ROSCOE,) an American Senator and lawyer, son of Judge Alfred Conkling, was born at Albany in 1828. He settled at Utica about 1846, was elected a member of Congress by the Republicans of Oneida county in 1858, and was re-elected in 1860. He represents the State of New York in the Senate of the United States for the term extending from 1867 to 1873. He is distinguished as a debater.

Conneau, ko′nō′, (HENRI,) a French physician, born at Milan about 1802. He removed to Marseilles about 1832, and subsequently became the physician of Hortense Bonaparte, who obtained from him a promise that he would never abandon her son, Louis Napoleon. In 1840 he followed the latter to the prison of Ham, and shared his captivity until 1846, when the prince escaped. He has continued in the service of Louis Napoleon, and in 1852 received the title of first physician to the emperor.

Connecte. See CONECTE.

Con′ner, (DAVID,) an American naval officer, born in Mifflin county, Pennsylvania, about 1792. He served with distinction as lieutenant in the war against England, 1812–14, and became a captain about 1835. Died in 1856.

Connor. See O'CONNOR.

Con′nor, (BERNARD,) F.R.S., an Irish physician, born in Kerry in 1666. He became physician to King John Sobieski of Poland about 1694, and returned to England in 1695. He lectured with success at Oxford and Cambridge, and published, besides other works, "Evangelium Medici," (1697,) an effort to explain on natural principles the miraculous cures performed by Christ. Died in 1698.

Co′non or **Ko′non,** [Κόνων,] an eminent Athenian general, the son of Timotheus. He first appears in history in 413 B.C., when he commanded a fleet. In 407 he was chosen one of the ten generals, and in 405 was defeated by Lysander at Ægospotami. He then took refuge with Evagoras in Cyprus. Having obtained command of a fleet of allied Persians and Athenians, he defeated the Spartans near Cnidos in 394 B.C., with important results, among which was that Sparta lost the empire of the sea. On his return to Athens he rebuilt the long walls, and afterwards went as ambassador to Persia, where he was imprisoned. Historians differ about the time and manner of his death.

See PLUTARCH, "Artaxerxes;" XENOPHON, "Hellenica;" CORNELIUS NEPOS, "Conon;" DIODORUS SICULUS, books xiii. and xiv.

Conon, born in Eastern Europe, was elected pope in 686 A.D., as successor to John V. He died in 688, and was succeeded by Sergius II.

Conon OF SAMOS, a celebrated Greek geometer and astronomer, who lived at Alexandria about 250 B.C., and was a friend of Archimedes. The latter expresses in one of his works a high admiration of his sagacity and attain-

ments. The works of Conon are entirely lost. He was the inventor of the curve called the "Spiral of Archimedes." Seneca informs us that he collected the observations of solar eclipses made in Egypt; and Virgil mentions him in his third Eclogue. His name is commemorated in the ode of Callimachus "De Coma Berenices."

See DELAMBRE, "Histoire de l'Astronomie ancienne."

Cŏn′rad [Ger. pron. kon′råt ; Fr. pron. kǒN′råd′; Lat. CONRA′DUS ; It. CORRADO, kor-rä′do] **I.,** Emperor of Germany, was elected to the imperial throne in 911, before which date he was Count of Franconia. He waged war against Henry the Fowler, Charles the Simple, and Arnulf of Bavaria. He was killed in battle in 918, and was succeeded by Henry the Fowler.

See SCHWARTZ, "König Conrad I. der Franke," 1850.

Conrad II., called THE SAL′IC, was a son of Henry, Duke of Franconia. He was elected King of Germany in 1024, after which he marched into Italy, and was crowned as emperor by the pope at Rome in 1027. He became master of Burgundy at the death of Rodolph, who was an uncle of Conrad's wife. Conrad is regarded as the author of the written feudal law of Germany. He died in 1039, and was succeeded by his son, Henry III.

See LUDEN, "Histoire de l'Allemagne ;" VENNINGEN, "Dissertatio de Conrado Salico," 1783.

Conrad III. of Germany, born in 1093, was a son of Frederick of Hohenstaufen. His mother was a daughter of Henry IV. He was elected emperor in 1138; but his title was disputed by Henry the Proud, Duke of Saxony. A civil war ensued between these competitors. Welf, a brother of Henry the Proud, commanded one of the armies in the battle of Weinsberg, which is memorable as the origin of the party names of Guelph and Ghibeline. The battle-cry of the Saxons was *Welf,* and that of Conrad's men was *Weiblingen,* a town connected with the origin of the Hohenstaufen family. Ghibeline is the Italian version or modification of Weiblingen. Conrad gained a victory at Weinsberg, (1140,) and the war then ended. In 1147 he conducted a large army of crusaders to Palestine. He besieged Damascus, but failed to take it, and returned in 1149. He died in 1152, and was succeeded by Frederick Barbarossa.

See MASCOVIUS, "Commentarius de Rebus Imperii sub Conrado III." 1753; LUDEN, "Histoire de l'Allemagne ;" GUNDLING, "Geschichte und Thaten Kayser Conrads III.," 1720.

Conrad IV. born in Apulia in 1228, was a son of Frederick II., Emperor of Germany and King of Italy. He was crowned King of the Romans in 1237. At the death of his father, in 1250, he took the title of emperor, which was also claimed by William of Holland. The latter was favoured by the Guelphs and by Pope Innocent IV., who excommunicated Conrad, the chief of the Ghibelines. Conrad led an army into Italy in 1251, and took Naples and other places. He died in 1254, leaving a son, Conrad V., or Conradin.

See VON RAUMER, "Geschichte der Hohenstaufen ;" GUNDLING, "Geschichte und Thaten Conrads IV.," 1719.

Conrad V., or **Con′ra-din,** [Lat. CONRADI′NUS ; It. CONRADINO, kon-rä-dee′no,] born in 1252, was the son and heir of Conrad IV. The kingdom of Naples was usurped by his uncle Manfred, and was offered by the pope to Charles of Anjou, who defeated Manfred in 1265 and made himself master of Naples and Sicily. Conradin attempted to enforce his rights, but was defeated at Tagliacozzo in 1268, taken prisoner, and put to death.

See VON RAUMER, "Geschichte der Hohenstaufen ;" W. JAEGER, "Geschichte Conradins II. Königs beider Sicilien," 1785; C. M. RICCIO, "Alcuni Studii storici intorno a Manfredi e Conradino," 1850.

Conrad, Marquis of Tyre and Montferrat, was a famous captain of the crusaders. He defended Tyre against Saladin about 1188, and compelled him to raise the siege. He had just been elected King of Jerusalem, when he was assassinated, at Tyre, in 1192.

Conrad of Kirchberg, a German minnesinger, was a native of Suabia, and lived about 1150–90.

See LONGFELLOW, "Poets and Poetry of Europe."

Conrad of Wurtzburg, an eminent German minnesinger or troubadour, of whose life little is known. He wrote, besides other works, an epic poem on the Trojan war. Died in 1287.

See GRÆVINUS, "Geschichte der Altdeutschen Poesie;" LONGFELLOW, "Poets and Poetry of Europe."

ɛ as *k;* ç as *s;* ğ *hard;* ġ as *j;* G, H, K, *guttural;* N, *nasal;* R, *trilled;* ŝ as *z;* th as in *this.* (☞See Explanations, p. 23.)

Conrad, kon′rắt, or **Coenrads,** koon′rắts, (ABRA-HAM,) a skilful Dutch designer and engraver, flourished about 1650. His works are mostly portraits.

Con′rad, (CHARLES M.,) a lawyer, born at Winchester, Virginia, about 1804, removed in his youth to Louisiana. He was appointed secretary of war by President Fillmore in August, 1850, and held that office till March, 1853. He was a member of the Confederate Congress in 1862–64.

Conrad, (ROBERT T.,) an American dramatist, orator, and judge, born in Philadelphia about 1809. He produced two tragedies, entitled "Conrad of Naples," and "Aylmere," which were performed with success. About 1840 he became a judge of the court of general sessions in Philadelphia. He published a volume of poems in 1852. In 1854 he was elected mayor of Philadelphia by the American party. "His 'Aylmere,'" says R. W. Griswold, "has proved the most successful American drama yet written." Died in 1858.

See GRISWOLD's "Poets and Poetry of America."

Conrad, (TIMOTHY ABBOTT,) an American conchologist and palæontologist, born in New Jersey about 1804. He published, besides other works, "Fossil Shells of the Tertiary Formations of North America," (1832,) and "Palæontology of the State of New York," (1838–40.) He was one of the naturalists employed by the State of New York about 1838. He is a member of the Imperial Society of Natural History of Moscow, and of other learned societies.

Conradi, kon-rä′dee,(JOHANN WILHELM HEINRICH,) a German physician, born at Marburg in 1780, became in 1837 professor of medicine at Göttingen. He wrote a "Manual of General Therapeutics," (1833,) and other medical works.

Conrart, kôn′rắr′, (VALENTIN,) born in Paris in 1603, was one of the founders of the French Academy, which first met in his house, and which was chartered in 1635. He was then chosen its perpetual secretary. He was a councillor and secretary to the king. Died in 1675.

Conring, kon′ring, (ELISA SOPHIA,) a German poetess, was a daughter of Hermann Conring, noticed below, and wife of the Baron von Reichenbach. She translated into German verse the "Wisdom of Solomon," and wrote other poetry. Died in 1718.

Her sister, MARIA SOPHIA, was also a poetess.

Conring, kon′ring, [Lat. CONRIN′GIUS,] (HERMANN,) a very learned writer on history, law, medicine, etc., was born at Norden, in East Friesland, in 1606. He was chosen professor of natural philosophy at Helmstedt in 1632. In 1650 he received the title of Physician to Christina of Sweden. He was soon after appointed professor of law at Helmstedt, and by his lectures and writings acquired such renown that he was consulted by several kings on important questions. He published, in Latin, many excellent works, among which are a "Commentary on the Origin of German Law," (1643,) "On the Causes of the Physical Constitution *(corporis habitâ)* of the Ancient and Modern Germans," (1645,) and "On the Limits of the German Empire." Died in 1681.

See A. FROELING, "Leichenpredigt auf H. Conringium nebst seinem Lebenslauf," 1682; ERSCH und GRUBER, "Allgemeine Encyklopaedie;" NICÉRON, "Mémoires."

Conringius. See CONRING.

Con′rў, written also **Conroy,** [Lat. CON′RIUS,] (FLORENCE,) an Irish theologian, born at Galway in 1560. He became Roman Catholic Archbishop of Tuam, and published a "Compendium of the Doctrines of Saint Augustine," (1634.) Died at Madrid in 1629.

Consalvi, kon-sâl′vee, (ERCOLE,) CARDINAL, an eminent Italian statesman, born in Rome in 1757. At an early age he obtained the office of *auditor de Rota,* a member of the highest civil court. In 1800 he was appointed secretary of state, or first minister, of Pius VII., and in 1801 negotiated the Concordat with Bonaparte in Paris. In compliance with the wish of the French emperor, he was dismissed from office in 1806, and exiled from Rome about 1810. From 1814, when he was reinstated in the office of secretary, to 1823, the Papal States experienced the benefits of his liberal and humane policy. Capital punishment for heresy, and the torture, were abolished, and new codes of law were enacted. Died in 1824.

See EARTHOLDI, "Züge aus dem Leben des Cardinal Consalvi," 1825; "Cenni biografici sul Cardinale Consalvi," Venice, 1824.

Consbruch, kons′brook, (GEORG WILHELM CHRISTOPH,) a German medical writer, born in Westphalia in 1764.

Conscience, kôn′se′ônss′, (HENRI or HENDRIK,) a popular Flemish novelist, born at Antwerp in 1812. He entered the army in 1830, but retired from that service a few years later, after composing some popular songs. In 1837 he produced, in Flemish, a successful romance, "The Year of Miracles, 1566," ("In het Vonderjaer,") and another entitled "Phantasia." His reputation was confirmed by "The Lion of Flanders," (1838.) He was appointed a professor in the University of Ghent in 1845. Among his numerous works are a "History of Belgium," (1845,) "Pages from the Book of Nature," (1846,) and "The Poor Gentleman," (1851.)

See BROCKHAUS, "Conversations-Lexikon."

Consentius, kon-sen′she-us, a Greek grammarian, lived at Constantinople in the fifth century.

Consetti, kon-set′tee, (ANTONIO,) an Italian painter, born at Módena in 1686; died in 1766.

Considérant, kôn′se′dằ′rôN′, (VICTOR,) a French socialist, born at Salins in 1805. He became a disciple of Fourier about 1831, and on the death of the latter, in 1837, was recognized as the chief apostle of Fourierism. In 1845 he began to issue in Paris the "Démocratie Pacifique," a daily political journal. After the revolution of 1848 he was elected to the Assembly, in which he acted with the party called the "Mountain." About 1854 he founded a colony in Texas. He wrote, besides other works, "Destinée sociale," (3 vols., 1834–44.)

See BLANQUI, "Histoire de l'Économie politique."

Con′sta-ble, (kŭn′stȧ-b'l,) (ARCHIBALD,) an eminent Scottish publisher, born at Kellie in 1776. He opened a shop in Edinburgh in 1795, and in 1802 began to publish the "Edinburgh Review," which he managed twenty-four years. He published Scott's first original work in 1805, and gave that author one thousand pounds for "Marmion" in 1807. Constable & Company also published Scott's prose works, (1813–26.) In consequence partly of his generosity and want of prudence, he failed in 1825 for about £250,000, in which failure Sir Walter Scott was largely involved. Died in 1826.

See CHAMBERS, "Biographical Dictionary of Eminent Scotsmen."

Con′sta-ble, (HENRY,) an English poet, who graduated at Cambridge about 1580. He published a volume of sonnets, which were commended by Ben Jonson and others.

See WARTON, "History of English Poetry."

Constable, (JOHN,) an eminent English landscape-painter, born at East Bergholt, Suffolk, in 1776, was the son of a miller. His early love of art was encouraged by Sir George Beaumont. In 1799 he became a student in the Royal Academy. He exhibited in 1819 a large picture of a "Scene on the River Stour," usually called "The White Horse," which is among his best works. The public and the artists were slow to appreciate his simplicity of style, fidelity to nature, and contempt of conventionalities. He was elected a Royal Academician in 1829. Among his master-pieces are "The Corn-Field," (1826,) and "The Valley Farm," (1835.) Died in 1837. "His early associations," says Ruskin, "induced in him a morbid preference of subjects of a lower order. His works are eminently wanting in both rest and refinement. Yet, with all these deductions, they are to be deeply respected as thoroughly original, honest, free from affectation, and manly in manner." ("Modern Painters.")

See C. R. LESLIE, "Life of John Constable."

Constance. See CONSTANTIUS.

Con′stance, Empress of Germany, was a daughter of Roger, King of the Two Sicilies, and was born in 1155. She was married in 1185 to the emperor Henry VI., and became the mother of Frederick II. In 1194 she inherited the throne of her father. Died in 1198.

See MURATORI, "Annali d'Italia."

Constance, Queen of Sicily, was the daughter of King Manfred. She became the wife of Pedro of Aragon in 1261. She reigned in the island of Sicily from 1283 until her death, in 1298.

See SISMONDI, "Histoire des Républiques Italiennes."

î, ē, ī, ō, ū, ŷ, *long;* ȧ, ė, ȯ, *same, less prolonged;* ă, ĕ, ĭ, ŏ, ŭ, ў, *short;* ą, ę, į, ǫ, *obscure;* fär, fȧll, fât; mêt; nŏt; gŏŏd; mōōn;

Con'stance, (FAULCON, FAULKON, or PHAULKON,) an ambitious Greek adventurer, whose proper name was **Con'stan-tin,** was born in Cephalonia about 1648. After having been a trader in the East Indies, he went to Siam, where about 1680 he became prime minister. He made an alliance with Louis XIV. of France, who sent a body of troops to Siam. Having attempted to establish there the Roman Catholic religion and the French domination, he was killed by some natives, who conspired against him, about 1688.

See P. d'ORLÉANS, "Vie de M. Constance;" "Biographie Universelle;" "Nouvelle Biographie Générale."

Constance Chlore. See CONSTANTIUS I.

Constancio, kon-stân'se-o, (FRANCISCO SOLANO,) a Portuguese physician and writer on science, born at Lisbon in 1777. From 1820 to 1829 he was minister from Portugal to the United States. Died in Paris in 1846.

Con'stans [Fr. CONSTANT, kôN'stôN'] **I.,** (FLAVIUS JULIUS,) the third son of the emperor Constantine the Great and Fausta, was born about 320 A.D. At the death of his father, in 337, he inherited the sovereignty of Italy, Africa, and Western Illyricum. His brother Constantine, having invaded his dominions, was defeated and killed in battle in 340, when the victor became master of the whole Western Empire. He was indolent, weak, and depraved. He favoured Athanasius, who had been proscribed by the Arians. Magnentius having revolted in Gaul, Constans fled towards Spain, but was overtaken near the Pyrenees, and killed, in 350 A.D.

See GIBBON, "Decline and Fall of the Roman Empire;" LE BEAU, "Histoire du Bas-Empire."

Constans II., (FLAVIUS HERACLIUS,) born at Constantinople in 630 A.D., was the son of Constantine III., Emperor of the East, whom he succeeded in 641. He waged unsuccessful war against the Saracens, who conquered Egypt and Rhodes from him. He favoured the Monothelites, and issued an edict which prohibited the discussion of religious questions. In 655 he was signally defeated by the Arabs at sea. His cruelty, avarice, etc. rendered him generally detested. He was assassinated at Syracuse in 668, and was succeeded by his son, Constantine IV., (Pogonatus.)

See GIBBON, "Decline and Fall of the Roman Empire;" ABOOLFEDA, "Annales;" LE BEAU, "Histoire du Bas-Empire."

Constant. See CONSTANS.

Constant de Rebecque, kôN'stôN' deh reh-bêk', (BENJAMIN,) commonly called simply BENJAMIN CONSTANT, a French publicist, orator, and politician, was born of French Protestant parents at Lausanne in 1767. He was a fellow-student of Erskine and Mackintosh at Edinburgh. In 1795 he entered Paris as a protégé of Madame de Staël, (of whom he was a life-long admirer,) and in 1799 became a member of the Tribunate. His opposition to the First Consul resulted in his removal and banishment in 1801. He visited several courts of Europe during the ensuing years. In 1813 he composed his celebrated pamphlet "On the Spirit of Conquest and Usurpation," which procured him the favour of the allied powers. As an editor of the "Journal des Débats," he denounced Napoleon in 1815, but was persuaded to accept a place in his council during the Hundred Days. After the second restoration he became a popular chief of the opposition, and in 1819 was chosen a deputy for La Sarthe. He was one of the most powerful and witty debaters of that period, and was for some time the leader and moderator of the Liberal party. Just after the revolution of 1830, in which he was not an actor, he was appointed president of the council of state. He died in Paris in December, 1830, leaving, besides many political works, a treatise "On Religion, considered in its Source, its Forms, and its Developments," (5 vols., 1823–31.) He had great facility in composition. His letters are models of grace and *finesse*, but seem very deficient in heart. He has been called a second Voltaire, and was reputed the most brilliant converser among the men of his age. Though a professor of the Protestant religion, he appears to have been profoundly skeptical.

See LAMARTINE, "History of the Restoration;" LOUIS BLANC, "Histoire de dix Ans;" SAINTE-BEUVE, articles in the "Revue des Deux Mondes" for 1844 and 1845; DE CORMENIN, "Le Livre des Orateurs;" J. PHARAON, "Notice sur B. Constant," 1830; LOUIS DE LOMÉNIE, "B. Constant," 1841; "Nouvelle Biographie Générale."

Constant de Rebecque, (DAVID,) great-grandfather of Benjamin Constant, was born in 1638. He was a Protestant minister, and lived in Geneva and Lausanne. He wrote an "Epitome of Politics," and edited some of the works of Cicero, Florus, and Erasmus. Died in 1733.

Constant-Prévost. See PRÉVOST.

Constantia, kon-stan'she-a, (FLAVIA VALERIA,) a half-sister of Constantine the Great, born about 300 A.D., was married in 313 to the emperor Licinius. The mutual attachment between her and Constantine appears to have continued even after Licinius was killed by his order. She used her influence in favour of the Arian creed. Died about 330.

Constantin. See CONSTANTINE.

Constantin, kôN'stôN'tÅN', (ABRAHAM,) a skilful Swiss painter on porcelain, born at Geneva in 1785, worked in Paris. He copied some pictures of Raphael on porcelain.

Constantin, kôN'stôN'tÅN', (ROBERT,) a French scholar and eminent linguist, born at Caen. He graduated as a physician in 1564, and practised at Montauban. For the sake of religious freedom he retired to Germany, where he died in 1605. He had compiled a "Lexicon Græco-Latinum," (1562,) which was highly esteemed.

See NICÉRON, "Mémoires."

Con'stan-tine, [Lat. CONSTANTI'NUS; Gr. Κωνσταν-τῖνος; Fr. CONSTANTIN, kôN'stôN'tÅN'; Ger. CONSTANTIN, kon-stân-teen'; It. CONSTANTINO, kon-stân-tee'no; Dutch, KONSTANTIJN, kon-stân-tÅn',] (FLAVIUS VALERIUS AURELIUS,) surnamed THE GREAT, the first Christian emperor of Rome, born in 272 A.D., was the son of the emperor Constantius Chlorus and his wife Helena. Before his accession, his talents, courage, and martial services had rendered him a favourite of the army, and an object of jealousy to Galerius, one of the two emperors then reigning. He was at York when his father died there, in July, 306, and was proclaimed emperor by the legions under his command. Galerius accorded to him only the title of Cæsar, and conferred the rank of Augustus on his own son, Severus. At Rome, Maxentius and his father Maximian, in the absence of Galerius, raised a successful revolt, (307,) after which six emperors and Cæsars at one time ruled the provinces of Rome. About 307 Constantine married Fausta, daughter of Maximian; but a war soon ensued between these emperors, and Maximian, having been defeated, was put to death in 309. Galerius died in 311, after which Licinius and Maximin remained masters of the provinces east of Italy. In 312, Constantine, who reigned in Gaul, marched against Maxentius, who was defeated and killed near Rome in that year. About this time, according to tradition, he was converted to Christianity by a miraculous vision, in which he saw in the heavens the sign of a cross, with this inscription, "Thou shalt conquer by this sign," ("In hoc signo vinces.")

Having obtained undisputed supremacy over the West, including Italy and Africa, he began to favour more openly the Christians, and displayed wisdom in the promotion of order and prosperity among his subjects. In 314 he fought in Thrace an indecisive battle against Licinius, his only remaining rival, with then made a peace, which lasted nine years. During this period he was employed in political reforms, and adopted a more humane code of laws, by which Christianity was recognized as the religion of the state, but the pagan worship was still tolerated.

In 323 he gained a complete victory over Licinius near Adrianople, and another opposite Byzantium, after which he was the sole emperor. He assembled at Nicæa in 325 the first general council, in which Arianism was condemned and a famous Catholic creed was adopted. In the next year he was guilty of an act which has left a deep stain on his memory, the execution of his eldest son, Crispus, falsely accused of a crime by Fausta, who was his step-mother. About 328 he transferred his court to Byzantium, which he enlarged, and the name of which he changed to Constantinople,—"City of Constantine." The duration of the Eastern Empire so many centuries after the fall of the Western seems to approve the wisdom of his policy in this affair. A few years before his death he favoured the Arians, and recalled some banished

ε as *k*; ç as *s*; ḡ *hard*; ġ as *j*; G, H, K, *guttural*; N, *nasal*; R, *trilled*; š as *z*; ᵗh as in *this*. (☞See Explanations, p. 23.)

42

bishops of that party. He died at Nicomedia in 337 A.D., having divided the empire between his three sons, Constantine, Constantius, and Constans. His character is variously estimated; but it is admitted that he had many of the qualities of a great statesman and general. He was far from being a saint, and in the opinion of Niebuhr was not even a Christian, though he permitted himself to be baptized just before his death.

See GIBBON, "Decline and Fall of the Roman Empire;" EUSE-BIUS, "Vita Constantini;" VOGT, "Historia Constantini Magni," 1720; TILLEMONT, "Histoire des Empereurs;" JOSEPH FLETCHER, "Life of Constantine the Great," 1852; J. C. F. MANSO, "Leben Constantin's des Grossen," 1817; JAKOB BURCKHARDT, "Die Zeit Constantin's des Grossen," 1853.

Constantine (or **Constantinus**) **II.**, (FLAVIUS CLAUDIUS,) a Roman emperor, the eldest surviving son of the preceding, was born at Arelatum (now Arles) in 312 A.D. In 335 he was intrusted with the administration of Gaul, Britain, and Spain, and at the death of his father, in 337, inherited the sovereignty of the same provinces, with a part of Africa. Having invaded the dominions of his brother Constans, he was defeated and killed in battle near Aquileia in 340. He left no issue.

See EUSEBIUS, "Vita Constantini;" GIBBON, "Decline and Fall of the Roman Empire."

Constantine (or **Constantinus**) **III.**, (FLAVIUS HERACLIUS,) called NO'VUS, Emperor of the East, born in 612 A.D., was the son of the emperor Heraclius and Eudoxia. At the death of his father, in 641, he became a partner in the empire with his half-brother Heracleonas. After a reign of three months, he died, or was poisoned by Martina, his step-mother. He left a son, Constans II.

See GIBBON, "Decline and Fall of the Roman Empire."

Constantine (or **Constantinus**) **IV.**, surnamed POGONA'TUS, a Roman emperor of the East, succeeded his father, Constans II., in 668 A.D. A powerful Arabian fleet in 672 blockaded Constantinople, his capital, which was defended by the Greek fire newly invented. After fighting several years, the Arabs purchased peace by the payment of an annual tribute. In 680 he assembled a council at Constantinople, by which the Monothelites were condemned. He died in 685, and left the throne to his son, Justinian II.

See LE BEAU, "Histoire du Bas-Empire."

Constantine (or **Constantinus**) **V.**, surnamed CO-PRON'YMUS, [ὁ Κοπρώνυμος,] Emperor of the East, born in 719 A.D., was the son of Leo III., (Isaurus,) whom he succeeded in 741. In 743 he defeated Artavasdes, who had rebelled and had made himself master of the capital. He was a zealous iconoclast and a persecutor of the orthodox. In 754 he assembled a council which condemned the worship of images. He appears to have been unprincipled and superstitious. He died in 775, and was succeeded by his son, Leo IV.

See CEDRENUS, "Compendium;" GIBBON, "Decline and Fall of the Roman Empire."

Constantine (or **Constantinus**) **VI.**, (FLAVIUS,) born in 771 A.D., was the son of Leo IV. At the death of his father, in 780, he became emperor at Constantinople, under the regency of his mother, the ambitious Irene. (See IRENE.) A council held at Nicæa in 787 restored the worship of images. After the end of his minority, Irene, who still wished to rule, was kept in confinement. In 797 she conspired against him with success, and injuries were inflicted on him which caused his death. Irene then became his successor.

See LE BEAU, "Histoire du Bas-Empire."

Constantine (or **Constantinus**) **VII.**, Emperor of the East, surnamed PORPHYROGEN'ITUS, [Gr. ὁ Πορφυρο-γέννητος, i.e. "Born in Purple,"] the son of the emperor Leo VI., was born in 905 A.D. His father died in 911, soon after which Romanus Lecapenus usurped the government and ruled as emperor until 944. The popular favour then restored Constantine, who in his long seclusion from public life had cultivated learning and science with success. He gained the affection of his subjects by his humanity and love of justice, and composed several valuable works, among which is a "Treatise on the Government of the Empire." He was poisoned in 959 by his son and successor, Romanus II.

See LEICHIUS, "De Vita et Rebus gestis Constantini Porphyro-geniti," 1746; FABRICIUS, "Bibliotheca Græca."

Constantine (or **Constantinus**) **VIII.** was the son of Romanus Lecapenus the usurper. He and his brother Stephen reigned a few months between the deposition of Romanus Lecapenus and the restoration of Constantine VII., 944 A.D. Died about 946.

Constantine (or **Constantinus**) **IX.**, Emperor of the East, born in 961 A.D., was the second son of Romanus II. In 976 his brother Basil II. and he were proclaimed emperors. He took no part in the affairs of state until the death of Basil, in 1025. His reign was disgraced by cruelty and other vices. He died in 1028, without male heir, and was succeeded by Romanus Argyrus.

Constantine (or **Constantinus**) **X.**, surnamed MO-NOM'ACHUS, [ὁ Μονομάχος,] became Emperor of the East in 1042 by marriage with Zoe, the daughter of Constantine IX. His surname was given on account of his courage in war. A memorable event of his reign was the schism between the Greek and Roman Churches, which began in 1054 and has continued to the present time. Died, without issue, in 1054.

Constantine (or **Constantinus**) **XI.**, surnamed DU'CAS, [Gr. ὁ Δοῦκας,] Emperor of the East, was chosen as his successor by Isaac Comnenus, who abdicated in 1059 A.D. He had obtained a high reputation as a general, but proved rather incompetent as a ruler. He died in 1067, leaving three minor sons, Michael, Androni'cus, and Constantine; but Romanus Diogenes was his successor. The youngest of the three sons was styled **Constantine XII.**, about 1071; but his reign was only nominal.

Constantine (or **Constantinus**) **XIII.**, surnamed PALÆOLOGUS, (pa-le-ol'o-gus,) the last Emperor of Constantinople, was the fourth son of Manuel II., and was born in 1394. He succeeded his brother, John VII., in 1448. By the encroachments of the Turks the empire had been reduced within a very small compass. In 1453 Mahomet II. besieged the capital with 250,000 men, and, after an obstinate contest of several weeks, took it by storm. Constantine was killed in the fight just as the Turks entered the walls.

See GIBBON, "Decline and Fall of the Roman Empire;" VON HAMMER, "Geschichte des Osmanischen Reichs."

Constantine, (or **Constantinus,**) surnamed THE AFRICAN, was a native of Carthage, and was one of the most learned men of his time. He studied at Babylon, visited India, and afterwards lived at Salerno. He published works on medicine and other sciences, and translated into Latin some of the best Greek and Arabic books. Died in 1087.

See MORÉRI, "Dictionnaire Historique."

Constantine, (or **Constantinus,**) POPE, a native of Syria, succeeded Sisinnius in 708 A.D. He is said to have approved the worship of images, in opposition to the Patriarch of Constantinople. He died in 714, and was succeeded by Gregory II.

Con'stan-tine, (NIKOLAEVITCH,) Grand Duke of Russia, the second son of the emperor Nicholas, was born September 21, 1827. During his childhood he received the title of Grand Admiral of the Fleet. Under the instructions of Admiral Lütke, he acquired great proficiency in naval science. His talents and disposition rendered him a favourite, especially with the old Russian party. He married the Princess Alexandra of Saxe-Altenburg in 1848. He was a strenuous supporter of the late war against France and England, and commanded the fleet in the Baltic in 1854-55. By his cautious defensive operations he prevented the British from gaining any decisive victories over his fleet. He was appointed Viceroy of Poland in the spring of 1862.

Constantine, (PAVLOVITCH,) GRAND DUKE, the second son of the emperor Paul of Russia, was born at Saint Petersburg in 1779. In 1796 he married Juliana, Princess of Saxe-Coburg, an aunt of Queen Victoria. His martial conduct was applauded at Austerlitz, (1805,) where he commanded a corps. In several ensuing campaigns he maintained his reputation for courage. He was appointed generalissimo of Poland in 1814. In 1820, having obtained a divorce from his first wife, he married a Polish lady named Grudzinska, by which he appears to have injured his prospects or forfeited his claim as heir-

---

ā, ē, ī, ō, ū, ȳ, *long;* ă, ĕ, ĭ, ŏ, ŭ, ў, *same, less prolonged;* ă, ĕ, ῐ, ŏ, ŭ, ў, *short;* ạ, ẹ, ị, ọ, *obscure;* fär, fåll, fât; mêt; nŏt; gōōd; mōōn;

presumptive to the throne. At the death of Alexander without issue in 1825, Constantine renounced his right in favour of his younger brother Nicholas, who had offered to acknowledge him as Czar. He became Viceroy of Poland, where his tyranny provoked a revolt in 1830. In the war which ensued he acted an inferior part, and died of cholera in 1831.

See HARRO HARRING, "Der Grossfürst Constantin wie er war," 1832.

Constantine Manasses. See MANASSES.

Constantino, the Italian of CONSTANTINE, which see.

Constantino, kon-stân-tee'no, (MANOEL,) a Portuguese historian, born at Funchal, in Madeira, became professor of theology in Rome, and wrote a "History of the Kings of Portugal," (1601.) Died in 1614.

Constantinus, the Latin of CONSTANTINE, which see.

Con-stan-tī'nus, a Greek or Roman jurist, was one of those whom Justinian selected, in 528 A.D., to frame the first Code.

Constantinus, (JULIUS CELSUS,) the author of a well-written commentary on the "Life of Cæsar," which first appeared as an appendage to "Cæsar's Commentaries" in 1473. Walckenaer has endeavoured to prove that he wrote in the tenth century and lived in Constantinople.

Con-stan'tĭ-us (kon-stan'she-us) **I.,** commonly called **Constantius Chlo'rus,** [Fr. CONSTANCE CHLORE, kôn'stôns' klor,] (FLAVIUS VALERIUS,) a Roman emperor, born about 250 A.D., was the son of Eutropius, and father of Constantine the Great. In 292, Diocletian and Maximian, in order to divide the labours of the administration, chose Galerius and Constantius, each of whom received the title of Cæsar. Gaul, Spain, and Britain were allotted to the latter, who was required to repudiate Helena and marry Theodora, the daughter of Maximian. He became emperor in 305, on the abdication of Diocletian, and died at York in 306, leaving the reputation of a just and humane ruler. His son Constantine was his successor.

See EUTROPIUS; AURELIUS VICTOR, "Cæsares."

Constantius [Fr. CONSTANCE, kôn'stôns'] **II.,** (FLAVIUS JULIUS,) the third son of Constantine I., Emperor of Rome, was born at Sirmium in 317 A.D. By his father's will he inherited the Asiatic provinces and Egypt in 337. It is said that he ordered or permitted the massacre of his father's nephews, brother, etc. at the time of his accession. During nearly all his reign he was at war with the Persians, by whom he was often defeated. In 350 the revolt of Magnentius resulted in the death of Constans, Emperor of the West. Constantius turned his arms against Magnentius, whom he defeated at Mursa, on the Drave, in 351, and in Gaul in 353, after which he was master of the whole empire. In 355 he appointed his cousin Julian, Cæsar and commander in Gaul, and in 357 visited Rome for the first time. He favoured the Arians, and banished the orthodox bishops. Julian having been proclaimed emperor by his army in Gaul, Constantius was marching to attack him, when he died near Tarsus in 361, and was succeeded by Julian. His reputation is not high either for talents or for virtue.

See EUSEBIUS, "Vita Constantii;" TILLEMONT, "Histoire des Empereurs;" GIBBON, "Decline and Fall of the Roman Empire."

Constantius III., Emperor of the West, a native of Illyria. His merit had raised him to the rank of general in 411 A.D. He married Placidia, sister of Honorius, who in 421 gave him the title of Augustus and received him as a partner in the empire. He died in 421, leaving a son, who became Valentinian III.

See TILLEMONT, "Histoire des Empereurs;" LE BEAU, "Histoire du Bas-Empire."

Constanzo, (ANGELO.) See COSTANZO, DI.

Contades, de, dẹh kôn'tăd', (LOUIS GEORGE ÉRASME,) MARQUIS, born in 1704, became a marshal in 1758, and commanded in Germany, where he took several fortified towns, but was defeated at Minden in 1759, and was soon recalled. Died in 1795.

See DE COURCELLES, "Dictionnaire des Généraux Français."

Contamine, deh, dẹh kôn'tă'mèn', (THÉODORE,) VI-COMTE, a French general, born at Givet (Ardennes) in 1773. He took part in the battle of Trafalgar, (1805.) Died in 1845.

Contant, kôn'tôn', (PAUL,) a French botanist and poet, born about 1570, established a botanic garden at Poitiers. He described the plants and animals which he had collected, in a poem called "Jardin et Cabinet poétique," (1609.) Died in 1632.

Contant d'Ivry, kôn'tôn' dèv're', (PIERRE,) an eminent French architect, born at Ivry-sur Seine in 1698, studied design under Watteau. He designed the church of Condé in Flanders, that of Saint-Waast at Arras, and the greater part of the Palais Royal of Paris. His plans for the church of the Madeleine were adopted; but he died before it was finished, in 1777.

Contant d'Orville, kôn'tôn' doR'vèl', (ANDRÉ GUIL-LAUME,) a French littérateur, born in Paris about 1730. He published an "Account of the Different Nations," etc., (6 vols., 1772,) and other works. Died about 1800.

Contarini, kon-tâ-ree'nee, a noble family of Venice, which has produced many doges, senators, etc. DO-MENICO was doge from 1043 to 1071. GIACOMO was doge from 1275 to 1280. ANDREA CONTARINI was chosen to that office in 1367. About 1380 the Genoese, having taken Chiozza, threatened the existence of the Venetian state, which Contarini saved in that year by a decisive victory. He died in 1382, aged about eighty. DOMENICO II. became doge in 1659, when the republic was at war with the Turks for the possession of Candia. The celebrated siege of Candia ended in the capitulation of the Venetians in 1667, after the Turks had lost 100,000 men. Died in 1674.

See DARU, "Histoire de Venise;" SISMONDI, "Histoire des Républiques Italiennes."

Contarini, (AMBROGIO,) a Venetian senator and traveller, was sent in 1473 as ambassador to the King of Persia. Passing through Poland, Russia, etc., he found the king at Ispahân and made a treaty with him. Having returned to Venice in 1477, he published a curious journal of his mission.

Contarini, (GASPARO,) CARDINAL, born of a noble family at Venice in 1483. He was employed as negotiator in important missions, and was made a cardinal in 1535. He wrote treatises on the "Immortality of the Soul," and other works. Died in 1542.

See DARU, "Histoire de Venise;" L. BECCATELLI, "Vita de Cardinale G. Contarini," 1746.

Contarini, (GIOVANNI,) an Italian painter of history and portraits, born at Venice in 1549, was an imitator of Titian. He excelled in the adornment of arches and ceilings. He worked in Germany for the emperor Rodolph II. Died in 1605.

See LANZI, "History of Painting in Italy."

Contarini, (VINCENZO,) born at Venice in 1577, became professor of eloquence at Padua at the age of twenty-six. He published a volume of "Various Readings of Classic Authors," and a few other works. Died in 1617.

Contat, kôn'tă', (LOUISE,) a popular French actress, born in Paris in 1760; died in 1813.

Conte. See LECONTE.

Conté, kôn'tà', (NICOLAS JACQUES,) a French painter, chemist, and mechanician, born in Normandy in 1755. In 1798 he followed the French army to Egypt, where he rendered great services, as artist and savant, in the invention or fabrication of arms, tools, machines, etc. Having returned to France, he was selected to direct the execution of the great work on Egypt published by the Egyptian Commission. He invented a machine by which he engraved with surprising facility. Died in 1803.

See E. F. JOMARD, "Vie, Travaux et Services de N. J. Conté," 1852; "Nouvelle Biographie Générale."

Conte, del, dèl kon'tà, (JACOPINO,) a skilful portrait-painter, born at Florence in 1502, worked in Rome, where he painted several popes and princes. Died in 1598.

See LANZI, "History of Painting in Italy."

Contessa, kon-tes'sâ, (KARL WILHELM SALICE,) a German novelist, born at Hirschberg in 1777, wrote, besides other novels, "The Talisman," (1810.) Died in 1825.

His brother CHRISTIAN, born in 1767, was the author of several tales and dramas in verse. He died in Berlin in 1825.

---

e as k; ç as s; ğ hard; ġ as j; G, H, K, guttural; N, nasal; R, trilled; s as z; th as in this. (☞See Explanations, p. 23.)

Conti, kon'tee, (ANTONIO SCHINELLA,) ABBÉ, an Italian poet and philosopher, born at Padua in 1677, removed to Venice in 1699, and became a priest. In 1715 he was admitted, through the influence of Newton, into the Royal Society of London. He studied sciences and philosophy in Paris for several years. He was one of the Italian authors who contributed most to impress a philosophic character on the literature of his country. In 1739 he published the first volume of his works, which were designed to form a grand treatise on the Beautiful, conformed to the doctrine of Plato. It comprised a philosophic poem, entitled "The Sphere of Venus," ("Il Globo di Venere.") Died at Padua in 1749.

See MAZZUCHELLI, "Biografia degli Uomini illustri;" "Nouvelle Biographie Générale."

Conti, (GIOVANNI FRANCESCO,) sometimes called, in Latin, QUINTIA'NUS STO'A, an Italian author, born at Quinzano, near Brescia, in 1486. He wrote many and various works. Died in 1557.

See COSSANDO, "Vitæ Quintiani Stoæ," 1694; NICÉRON, "Mémoires."

Conti, (M. ANTONIO.) See MAJORAGIO.

Conti, [Lat. DE COMIT'IBUS,] (NICCOLÒ,) an Italian traveller, born in Venice, travelled twenty-five years, between 1419 and 1444, in India, China, and the Asiatic islands. The narrative of his travels in Ramusio's collection is commended.

Conti, (NOËL,) [Lat. NATA'LIS CO'MES,] a learned Italian writer, born at Milan, lived in Venice. He was the author of Latin odes and epigrams, a "Treatise on Mythology," and a general history of his own time. Died about 1582.

Conti, de, dẹh kôN'te', (ARMAND de Bourbon—dẹh boor'bôN',) PRINCE, a brother of the great Condé, was born in Paris in 1629. In the frivolous civil war of the Fronde he commanded an army in opposition to Condé. He married a niece of Cardinal Mazarin. In 1654 he commanded in Guienne, and took two towns from the Spaniards. He wrote a tract against stage-plays. "He ought rather," says Voltaire, "to have written against civil wars." Died in 1666.

See CARDINAL DE RETZ, "Mémoires;" LA ROCHEFOUCAULD, "Mémoires."

Conti, de, (FRANÇOIS LOUIS DE BOURBON,) PRINCE, a French general, son of the preceding, was born in Paris in 1664. He became so renowned for his courage and his admirable personal and mental endowments that he was elected King of Poland in 1697; but Augustus of Saxony, chosen by another party, obtained possession. He distinguished himself at Steenkerke in 1698. In consequence of the jealousy or prejudice of the king, he did not obtain command of an army until 1709. He died in the same year, as he was about to open the campaign in Flanders. Saint-Simon, who is sparing of praise, represents him as "the delight of the world and the court, the idol of the soldiers, and the hero of the officers."

See VOLTAIRE, "Siècle de Louis XIV;" SAINT-SIMON, "Mémoires;" "Journal de Dangeau."

Conti, de, (LOUISE MARGUERITE de Lorraine—dẹh lo'rằn',) PRINCESS, a French lady, distinguished for her wit and talents, born in 1577. She was a daughter of Henry, Duke of Guise, and became the wife of a Prince of Conti, after whose death (1614) she was married secretly to Marshal Bassompierre. She wrote a "History of the Amours of Henry IV." Died in 1631.

See BASSOMPIERRE, "Journal;" TALLEMANT DES RÉAUX, "Historiettes de la Princesse de Conti."

Conti, de', dà kon'tee, (GIUSTO,) an Italian poet and orator, surnamed DA VAL MONTONE, (dà vâl mon-to'nà,) from the place of his birth, near Rome, is considered one of the most faithful imitators of Petrarch. Died in 1449. A volume of his poems, entitled "The Beautiful Hand," ("La bella Mano,") in honour of the beautiful hand of the lady whose praises the poet sang, was published in 1472.

See GINGUENÉ, "Histoire Littéraire d'Italie."

Contile, kon-tee'là, (LUCA,) an Italian writer, born at Cetone, near Sienna, in 1506. He published a volume of poems, ("Rime," 1560,) several comedies in prose, and other works. Died in 1574.

Contreras, de, dà kon-trā'ràs, (HIERONIMO,) a Spanish poet and novelist, born in Andalusia, lived about 1600. He was appointed historiographer by Philip II. Among his works is "Selva de Aventuras."

See LONGFELLOW's "Poets and Poetry of Europe."

Contri, kon'tree, (ANTONIO,) an Italian painter of landscapes and flowers, born at Ferrara about 1680, settled at Cremona. He is the reputed inventor of the art of transferring frescos to canvas. Died in 1732.

Contucci, kon-toot'chee, (ANDREA,) called also **Sansovino,** (sân-so-vee'no,) an eminent Italian sculptor and architect, born at Sansovino, in Tuscany, in 1460. He worked at Florence and Rome, and became one of the first sculptors of his age. His figures of the Virgin and Child, in Rome, were much admired. He built a palace for the King of Portugal, and other edifices. Died in 1529.

See VASARI, "Lives of the Painters, Sculptors," etc.

Con'way, (HENRY SEYMOUR,) FIELD-MARSHAL, an English general and statesman, second son of the first Lord Conway, was born in 1720. He was aide-de-camp to the Duke of Cumberland at Culloden in 1746. As lieutenant-general, he commanded in Germany in 1761. From 1765 to 1768 he was secretary of state in the Whig cabinet. In 1782 he became commander-in-chief of the army, and made in Parliament a motion to terminate hostilities against the United States, in allusion to which Burke remarked, "All England, all America, joined in his applause." "He was," says Macaulay, "versed in the learning of his profession, and personally courageous, but wanted vigour and capacity." Died in 1795. Mrs. Damer the artist was his only child. His state papers have been published.

Con'way, (THOMAS,) a native of Ireland, removed in 1777 to America, and served a short time in the republican army. He was a partisan of General Gates, and a secret enemy of Washington.

Conybeare, kŭn'e-bair, (JOHN,) an eminent English theologian, born near Exeter in 1692. He became Dean of Christ Church in 1732, and Bishop of Bristol in 1750. He published an admired "Defence of Revealed Religion," in answer to Tindal, and a number of sermons, which had a high reputation. Died in 1755.

See "Biographia Britannica."

Conybeare, (JOHN JOSIAS,) an English antiquary and clergyman, born in London in 1779. He obtained the professorship of Anglo-Saxon at Oxford in 1807, and that of poetry in 1812. He was a canon in the cathedral of York. He published "Illustrations of Anglo-Saxon Poetry," and other learned works. Died in 1824.

Conybeare, (Rev. WILLIAM DANIEL,) Dean of Llandaff, a distinguished English geologist and divine, born near London in 1787. He graduated at Oxford in 1811, and was chosen a Fellow of the Royal Society in 1819. He discovered the Plesiosaurus, an antediluvian monster, and rendered important services to the science of geology by his writings on the coal-fields and other strata of Britain. He published, in conjunction with W. Phillips, "Outlines of the Geology of England and Wales." In 1839 he preached the Bampton Lectures. He was appointed Dean of Llandaff in 1845. Died in 1857.

Conybeare, (Rev. W. J.,) a son of the preceding, was a Fellow of Trinity College, Cambridge, and principal of the Collegiate Institution, Liverpool. In 1850–54 he and J. S. Howson produced the "Life and Epistles of Saint Paul," which is highly esteemed. He is said to have translated nearly all the Epistles in this book. He also published some Essays, and Sermons preached in the Chapel Royal, Whitehall, in 1844. Died in 1857.

See "North British Review" for February, 1854.

Conz or **Konz,** konts, (KARL PHILIPP,) a German poet, born in Würtemberg in 1762, was professor at Tübingen. Among his works is "Conradin," a tragedy. Died in 1827.

Cooghen or **Kooghen, van der,** vän dẹr kō'Hẹn, (LEONARD,) a Dutch painter and engraver, born at Haarlem in 1610; died in 1681.

Cook, kŏŏk, (CHARLES,) a British missionary in France who laboured with great zeal and success, and became president of the French Wesleyan Conference. Died in 1858.

Cook, (ELIZA,) a popular English poetess, born in Southwark, London, in 1817. At an early age she became a contributor to the "New Monthly Magazine" and other periodicals. A volume of her poems and songs published in 1840 was received with favour. In 1849 she began to publish "Eliza Cook's Journal," which was continued several years. Among her popular productions are "The Old Arm-Chair" and "Home in the Heart."

Cook, (GEORGE,) a Scottish historical writer and theologian, born at Saint Andrew's about 1780, published a "History of the Reformation in Scotland," (3 vols., 1811,) a "History of the Church of Scotland," (3 vols., 1815,) and other works. Died in 1845.

Cook, (Captain JAMES,) a celebrated English circumnavigator, born of poor parents at Marton, Yorkshire, in 1728. He followed the sea, in the coal-trade, for several years, and had attained the position of mate, when in 1755 he entered the royal navy as a volunteer. He served as master of a sloop at the capture of Quebec by Wolfe in 1759, and displayed great skill in the formation of a chart of the river from Quebec to the sea. In 1764 he was chosen marine surveyor of Newfoundland. Four years later he was selected to command a vessel sent by government to the South Pacific to observe the transit of Venus and make discoveries in geography and other sciences. He sailed in August, 1768, stopped at Tahiti to observe the transit, explored the east coast of Australia, and, returning by the Cape of Good Hope, reached home in June, 1771, having performed his mission with ability and success. In 1772 he was again sent, in the Resolution and Adventure, to search for a Southern continent. He circumnavigated the globe in high southern latitudes without finding the *Terra Australis;* but he discovered a large island, which he named New Caledonia. The most southern point he reached was 71°, where his progress was arrested by ice. He arrived at Portsmouth in July, 1775, and published a Journal of his voyage, (2 vols., 1777,) which is a model of simplicity and precision. He had given proof of remarkable courage, sagacity, and nautical skill in this enterprise. In 1776 he was chosen Fellow of the Royal Society, which gave him the Copley Medal for his services in preserving the health of his crew. He sailed the same year on a third voyage, in search of a northern passage between the Atlantic and Pacific. In 1778 he discovered the Sandwich Islands, explored Behring Strait, and advanced northward as far as the 70th degree. He returned to winter in the Sandwich Islands. One of the ship's boats having been stolen by the natives of Hawaii, Captain Cook went ashore with a few of his men to recover it. The violent resistance of the natives caused him to retreat towards his boat; and, after firing in self-defence, he and four of his men were killed on the shore, February 14, 1779.

See A. KIPPIS, "Life of Captain James Cook," 1788; GEORGE YOUNG, "Life and Voyages of Captain J. Cook," 1836; HARTLEY COLERIDGE, "Lives of Distinguished Northerns," vol. iii.; VAN TENAC, "Histoire générale de la Marine;" J. H. WIEDMANN, "Leben und Schicksale des Capitäns J. Cook," 2 vols., 1789–90.

Cook, (JOHN,) an American officer, born in Saint Clair county, Illinois, in 1825. He commanded a brigade at Fort Donelson, and became a brigadier-general in 1862.

Cooke, kŏŏk, (Sir ANTHONY,) an English scholar, grandfather of Lord Bacon, born about 1506, was eminent for learning and virtue. He was appointed tutor of Edward VI. As a Protestant, he was exiled during the reign of Mary, and returned home about 1558. Died in 1576. His daughters were noted for their classical acquirements. Mildred was married to Lord Burleigh, Anne to Sir Nicholas Bacon, the father of Lord Bacon, and Elizabeth to the son of the Earl of Bedford.

Cooke, (BENJAMIN,) an English musical composer and organist, born in London in 1739, was a pupil of Pepusch. From 1752 to 1789 he was conductor of the Academy of Ancient Music. In 1762 he was appointed organist of Westminster Abbey. He composed anthems and other admired pieces of sacred music, and several popular glees, among which are "How Sleep the Brave," "In the Merry Month of May," etc. Died in 1793.

Cooke, (ELIZABETH.) See RUSSELL, LADY.

Cooke, (GEORGE,) a skilful English engraver, born in London in 1781. He engraved numerous landscapes and scenes on the coast of England, and in partnership with his brother, William B., published several illustrated works, among which is "The Southern Coast of England." Died in 1834.

Cooke, (Sir GEORGE,) a British officer, born in 1767, served in the Peninsula in 1811, 1812, and 1813, and became a major-general. He commanded a division of the Guards at Waterloo, where he lost his right arm. Died in 1837.

Cooke, (GEORGE FREDERICK,) a popular English actor, was born in Westminster in 1755. He made his *début* at the Haymarket, in London, in 1778, soon after which he went to Dublin, where he performed with great success for many years. In 1800 he returned to London, and acted Richard III., Iago, etc. with great applause. For several years Cooke and J. Kemble were the chief favourites of the London stage. In 1810 he crossed the ocean to New York, where he died in 1812. His death was hastened by intemperance.

See "Memoirs of the Life of George Frederick Cooke," by WILLIAM DUNLAP, 1813.

Cooke, (GEORGE WINGROVE,) a British lawyer and writer, born in 1814, edited a "Life of Lord Shaftesbury," (1836,) and wrote "Memoirs of Lord Bolingbroke," (2 vols., 1835,) a "History of Party," (2d edition, 1840,) which is commended, and several legal treatises, (1844–52.) After a visit to China in 1857, he published "China and Lower Bengal." Died in 1865.

Cooke or **Cook,** (HENRY,) an English painter, born in 1642, was a pupil of Salvator Rosa. He was employed by the king to restore the cartoons of Raphael. Died in 1700.

See WALPOLE, "Anecdotes of Painting in England."

Cooke, kŏŏk, (JOHN ESTEN,) a novelist and lawyer, son of John Rodgers Cooke, noticed below, was born at Winchester, Virginia, in 1830. He contributed to several periodicals, and published, besides other works, "Leather Stocking and Silk," (1854,) "The Virginia Comedians," (1854,) and "The Last of the Foresters," (1856.)

Cooke, (JOHN RODGERS,) an American lawyer, born in Bermuda in 1788. He practised with distinction in Virginia for many years. In 1829 he was associated with John Marshall and Ex-President Madison in the committee which drafted the Constitution of Virginia. Died in 1854.

Cooke, (PHILIP PENDLETON,) an American poet, son of the preceding, was born at Martinsburg, Virginia, in 1816. He graduated at Princeton, New Jersey, and studied law. He wrote, besides other poems, "Florence Vane," "Rosa Lee," and "Chevalier Merlin." He contributed to the "Southern Literary Messenger." Died in 1850.

Cooke, (PHILIP SAINT GEORGE,) an officer, a brother of John Rodgers, noticed above, was born in Virginia in 1809. He defeated the Comanches in New Mexico in 1855, and had a high command in Kansas about 1857. He afterwards served in the expedition against the Mormons.

Cooke, (THOMAS,) an English poet, born at Braintree about 1705. He composed the "Battle of the Poets," a poem, and translated Hesiod and Plautus. Pope, whom he had offended in his writings, avenged himself on him in the "Dunciad." Died in 1756.

See J. MAWBEY, "Life of Thomas Cooke."

Cooke, (WILLIAM,) a poet of considerable merit, born at Cork, became a resident of London and adopted the profession of author. His poem entitled the "Art of Living in London" was received with favour, and was followed by a prose "Essay on the Elements of Dramatic Criticism." In 1796 he produced an admired didactic poem, entitled "Conversation," which is his principal work. Died in 1824.

Cooke, (WILLIAM,) an eminent English lawyer and writer on law, born in London in 1757. About 1786 he published a "System of Bankrupt Laws," which was long the standard upon the subject, but is now obsolete. Died in 1832.

Cooke, (WILLIAM FOTHERGILL,) an Englishman, born in Middlesex in 1806, was a partner of Professor Wheatstone, and constructed the first magnetic telegraph in England, in 1838–39.

Cookesley, kŏŏks'le, (Rev. WILLIAM GIFFORD,) an English classical scholar, born in Kent in 1802. He edited Pindar, (1842–49,) and published some essays.

Cookman, kŏŏk′man, (GEORGE G.,) an eloquent Methodist divine, born in Kingston-upon-Hull, England, in 1800, came to America in 1821. He was twice elected chaplain to Congress. In March, 1841, he embarked for Europe in the ocean-steamer President, which was never afterwards heard of.

Cookson, kŏŏk′sọn, (GEORGE,) an English general, born in Hampshire in 1760. He directed the artillery at the siege of Aboukir about 1798, and took part in the Walcheren expedition in 1809. In 1830 he was promoted to the rank of lieutenant-general. Died in 1835.

Coo′ley, (THOMAS,) an Irish architect, born in 1740. He designed the Royal Exchange of Dublin, one of the noblest edifices of that city, erected about 1770. He was the first architect of the "Four Courts," which he did not live to finish. Died in 1784.

Coolhaas, kōl′hȧss, (CASPAR,) a German Protestant theologian, born at Cologne in 1536; died in 1615.

Coomans, ko′mȧns or ko′mŏN′, (JEAN BAPTISTE NICOLAS,) a Belgian writer, born at Brussels in 1813. He edited the "Journal of Brussels" from 1841 to 1845, and the "Courier of Antwerp" from 1845 to 1848. He published a "History of Belgium," (1836,) and other works. His brother, PIERRE OLIVIER JOSEPH, born in 1816, gained distinction as a painter of history, genre, etc.

Coombe, koom, (WILLIAM,) an ingenious English writer, born at Bristol in 1741. Having spent a handsome fortune in fashionable dissipation, he was reduced to the necessity of writing for a subsistence. He excelled in humour and satire, and published several successful works, namely, "The Diaboliad," a poem, "The Dance of Life," "Tour of Dr. Syntax in Search of the Picturesque," and "Tour of Dr. Syntax in Search of a Wife." The last two are in verse. Died in 1822.

See R. HAWKER, "Life of William Coombe," 1802.

Cooninxloo, de, deh kō′ninks-lō′, written also **Conigsloo** and **Coningsloo,** (GILLES,) an eminent Flemish landscape-painter, born at Antwerp in 1544. After working some years in Paris, he settled in Antwerp, and was patronized by the King of Spain and the emperor. "He was," says the "Biographie Universelle," "the greatest landscape-painter of his time."

See DESCAMPS, "Vies des Peintres Flamands," etc.

Cooper, (ANTHONY ASHLEY.) See SHAFTESBURY, EARL OF.

Coo′per, (Sir ASTLEY PASTON,) a celebrated English surgeon, was born at Brooke, in Norfolk, in 1768. He went in 1784 to London, where he studied under Mr. Cline, who in 1791 employed him as assistant in his lectures. In 1792 he attended lectures in Paris. He was chosen surgeon of Guy's Hospital in 1800, and a Fellow of the Royal Society in 1805. His reputation was greatly extended by the publication of his work on Hernia, (1804-07,) and a few years later he had acquired an immense practice. His annual income is said to have amounted to £21,000. He was employed by George IV. in 1820, and was made a baronet in 1821. In 1822 he published an important work "On Dislocations and Fractures." He was appointed surgeon to the king in 1828. He published the "Anatomy and Diseases of the Breast," and other works. Died in 1841.

See B. B. COOPER, "Life of Sir Astley P. Cooper," 1843; "London Quarterly Review" for March, 1843; "Blackwood's Magazine" for April, 1849; G. COEN, "Biografia scientifica di Sir A. Cooper," Venice, 1841; "Nouvelle Biographie Générale."

Cooper, (BRANSBY B.,) a nephew of the preceding, born about 1792, was for many years surgeon to Guy's Hospital. He published "Lectures on Anatomy," and "The Principles and Practice of Surgery," (1851,) and a "Life of Sir Astley P. Cooper," (1843.) Died in 1853.

Coo′per, (JAMES,) an American general and Senator, born in Frederick county, Maryland, about 1810. He studied law, settled in Pennsylvania, and was elected to Congress as a Whig about 1840. He represented Pennsylvania in the Senate of the United States from 1849 to 1855. He became a brigadier-general of the Union army in 1861, and served in several actions. He died at Columbus, Ohio, in March, 1863.

Cooper, (JAMES FENIMORE,) a popular American novelist, born at Burlington, New Jersey, in September, 1789, was a son of Judge William Cooper. His mother's maiden name was Fenimore. About 1790 his father settled at Cooperstown, which he founded on the shore of Lake Otsego, New York, where he owned a large tract of land, then covered with forests and lying on the frontier of civilization. He entered Yale College in 1802, remained there about three years, and became a midshipman in the navy in 1806. Having retired from the navy in 1811, he married Susan De Lancey, of New York, a sister of Bishop De Lancey. His first literary production was "Precaution," a novel, (1819,) which was inferior to his later works. He published next "The Spy, a Tale of the Neutral Ground," founded on incidents connected with the Revolutionary war, which was very successful and was republished in many parts of Europe. It was translated into several languages. "He has the high praise," says the "North American Review," "and will have, we may add, the future glory, of having struck into a new path,—of having opened a mine of exhaustless wealth. In a word, he has laid the foundations of American romance." In 1823 he produced "The Pioneers" and "The Pilot," which were also very popular. His next novels were "Lionel Lincoln" and "The Last of the Mohicans," (1826,) in which Indian life and character were well represented. During a visit to Europe he published "The Prairie," (1827,) "The Red Rover," (1827,) "The Wept of Wish-ton-Wish," (1829,) "The Bravo," (1831,) and other works. Alluding to his admirable delineations of life at sea in the "Pilot" and the "Red Rover," the "Edinburgh Review" says, "The empire of the sea has been conceded to him by acclamation." He satirized the foibles of his own countrymen in "The Monikins," (1835,) "Homeward Bound," (1838,) and "Home as Found," (1838,) which were not so popular as his former works. In 1839 he published a "History of the Navy of the United States," which is a work of much labour and some merit. Among his later works are "The Pathfinder," (1840,) "The Deerslayer," (1841,) "Wing and Wing," (1842,) "Wyandotte," (1843,) "Afloat and Ashore," (1844,) "The Chain-Bearer," (1845,) "Oak Openings," (1848,) and "The Ways of the Hour," (1850.) He died at Cooperstown in September, 1851. "His writings," says William H. Prescott, "are instinct with the spirit of nationality. In his productions every American must take an honest pride. For surely no one has succeeded like Cooper in the portraiture of American character, or has given such glowing and eminently truthful pictures of American scenery." "The same sort of magical authority over the spirit of romance," says the "North American Review" for July, 1826, "which belongs in common to Scott, Radcliffe, Walpole, and our countryman Brown, is, for us at least, possessed by this writer in an eminent degree." "We consider Mr. Cooper," says the same authority, (April, 1831,) "as possessing in a very high degree the first qualification to which we have adverted,—that of power in description. . . . It is, however, most strikingly displayed in one department, in which nobody has preceded him or has yet attempted to become his rival. Whatever opinion may be entertained of his success in other respects, all will agree that his boldest and most triumphant march is on the mountain wave. He treads the deck with the same conscious pride with which the Highland outlaw stood upon his native heath." "He wrote for mankind at large," says W. C. Bryant: "hence it is that he has earned a fame wider than any [American] author of modern times. The creations of his genius shall survive through centuries to come, and only perish with our language."

See GRISWOLD, "Prose Writers of America;" "London Quarterly Review" for October, 1816 and 1837; "North American Review" for July, 1822, July, 1826, July, 1828, January, 1838, January, 1852, and October, 1859; "National Portrait-Gallery of Distinguished Americans," vol. i.; ALLIBONE's "Dictionary of Authors;" "Atlantic Monthly," January, 1862.

Cooper, (JOHN GILBERT,) an English writer, born in Nottinghamshire in 1723, was educated at Cambridge. His principal works are "The Power of Harmony," a poem, (1745,) a "Life of Socrates," (1749,) and "Letters on Taste," (1754,) which are commended for splendour of style and imagery. Died in 1769.

Cooper, (PETER,) a benevolent and enterprising American manufacturer, born in the city of New York in 1791. He conducted with success various industrial

ā, ē, ī, ō, ū, ȳ, *long;* à, ė, ȯ, *same, less prolonged;* ă, ĕ, ĭ, ŏ, ŭ, ў, *short;* ạ, ẹ, ị, ọ, *obscure;* fär, fȧll, făt; mĕt; nŏt; gŏŏd; mōōn;

enterprises on a large scale. He founded in his native city the "Cooper Institute," devoted to the instruction and improvement of the working-classes, at a cost of $500,000 or more.

Cooper, (RICHARD,) a painter, called "the British Poussin," studied in Italy, and excelled in landscapes. Died after 1806.

Cooper, (RICHARD,) an English designer and engraver, born in 1730, studied in Paris under Le Bas. Among his works is a "View of Saint Peter's, at Rome." Died about 1820.

Cooper, (SAMUEL,) an eminent English miniature-painter, born in London in 1609. He was a pupil of his uncle, John Hoskins. He surpassed all the artists in his line during the Commonwealth and the reign of Charles II., and painted an admirable portrait of Cromwell, which was engraved by Vertue. He visited France, where he painted many celebrated men. His works are still highly prized. Died in 1672.

See WALPOLE, "Anecdotes of Painting."

Cooper,(SAMUEL,) D.D., an eminent American divine, born in Boston in 1725, graduated at Harvard in 1743, and in 1746 succeeded his father as pastor of the church in Brattle Street, Boston. He soon became known as one of the most accomplished orators and scholars in New England. He was intimate with Franklin and Adams, and an influential patriot in the Revolution. He was active in establishing in Boston the American Academy of Arts and Sciences, of which he was chosen the first vice-president in 1780. Died in 1783.

Cooper, (SAMUEL,) an American general, born in the State of New York about 1795, graduated at West Point in 1815. He obtained the rank of captain in 1836, and served in the Mexican war as assistant adjutant-general, 1846–47. In 1852 he became adjutant-general, with the rank of colonel. He resigned his commission in March, 1861, and offered his services to Jefferson Davis, who appointed him adjutant-general. He held throughout the civil war the rank of full general,—the highest in the Confederate army.

See "Southern Generals," (anonymous,) New York, 1865.

Cooper, (SAMUEL,) a distinguished surgeon and medical writer of London, was born about 1780. He published, in 1807, "First Lines of the Practice of Surgery," which passed through seven or more editions. He afterwards produced a "Dictionary of Practical Surgery," (1809,) and other professional works. Died in 1848.

Cooper, (SUSAN FENIMORE,) an American authoress, a daughter of James Fenimore Cooper, was born about 1825. In 1850 she published an attractive and popular work entitled "Rural Hours." Among her other productions is "Rhyme and Reason of Country Life," (1854.)

Cooper or **Cou'per,** (THOMAS,) a learned English divine and eminent preacher, born at Oxford about 1517, became Bishop of Lincoln in 1570, and of Winchester in 1584. He published some sermons, an "Epitome of Chronicles," and a valuable "Latin Dictionary." Died in 1594.

Cooper, (THOMAS,) a natural philosopher and lawyer, born in London in 1759, emigrated with his friend Dr. Priestley to America about 1792. He was a zealous and active Democrat, and wrote political essays, etc. In 1820 he became president of Columbia College, South Carolina, where he was also professor of chemistry. Died in 1840.

Cooper, (THOMAS ABTHORPE,) an English tragedian, born in 1776, performed with success in England and America. Died in Pennsylvania in 1849.

Cooper, (THOMAS SIDNEY,) an English painter of animals, was born at Canterbury in 1803. He rose from a humble position, and acquired the art of drawing almost without the aid of masters. About 1820 he began to paint scenery for the theatre of Canterbury. Having studied the works of the Dutch and Flemish schools, he devoted himself to animal-painting with great success. His favourite subjects are cattle and sheep, in the representation of which he is perhaps unrivalled by any British artist. He was chosen an associate of the Royal Academy in 1845.

See "Autobiographic Memoir" in the "Art Journal" for November, 1849.

Coopmans, kōp'mǎns, (GADSO,) a Dutch physician, son of George, noticed below, born in 1746, was professor at Franeker, Kiel, and Copenhagen. He wrote a Latin poem of merit on the small-pox, "Varis, sive Carmen de Variolis." Died at Amsterdam in 1810.

Coopmans, (GEORGE,) a distinguished Dutch physician, born at Makkum in 1717, published a work entitled "Neurologia," (1789.) Died in 1800.

Coornhert. See CORNHERT.

Coote, kōōt, (Sir CHARLES,) an Irish judge, who promoted the restoration of Charles II. in 1660, and was made Earl of Montrath. Died in 1661.

Coote, (Sir EYRE,) a British general, born in Ireland in 1726. He distinguished himself at the battle of Plassey, in India, in 1757. Returning to England in 1762, he was thanked by the Commons for the capture of Pondicherry. In 1780 he was appointed a member of the supreme council, and commander-in-chief of the army in Bengal. In that year he completely defeated Hyder Ali at Porto Novo. Died near Madras in 1783.

Cootwyk, kōt'wīk, sometimes written **Cootwich,** (JOHN,) a Dutch traveller, born at Utrecht. He travelled in France, Italy, Syria, Palestine, etc., and published in 1619 an account of those countries.

Cop, kop, (GUILLAUME,) a Swiss physician, born at Bâle, finished his studies in Paris, and graduated in 1495. He was successively chief physician of Louis XII. and of Francis I. Though he published no original work, he rendered great services to medical science by his translations of Hippocrates, and of Galen's "Treatise on the Causes and Differences of Diseases and Symptoms." Died in 1532.

See M. ADAM, "Vitæ Eruditorum."

Cōpe, (Sir ANTHONY,) an English scholar, was the author of a "History of Annibal and Scipio," (1544.) Died in 1551.

Cope, (CHARLES WEST,) an English historical painter, born at Leeds about 1812, was the son of a drawing-master. He studied in the Royal Academy, in which he began to exhibit in 1831. His cartoon of "The First Trial by Jury" gained a prize of three hundred pounds awarded by the Royal Commission of the Fine Arts in 1843. After that date he painted with success several frescos in the House of Lords. Among his chief oil-paintings are "Lear and Cordelia," (1850,) and "Othello relating his Adventures," (1853.) He was elected Royal Academician in 1848.

Cope, (HENRY,) an Irish physician, who lived about 1690–1740, studied under Boerhaave at Leyden, and practised with success in Dublin.

Cope, (Sir JOHN,) a British general, the time and place of whose birth are unknown. He was commander-in-chief of the army in Scotland when the rebellion of 1745 began. At the first approach of the Pretender's army, Cope retired from the Highlands southward. The rebels took Edinburgh, and a few days later routed the king's army at Prestonpans, September, 1745. General Cope was much censured for his conduct on this occasion, and was superseded in the command. Died in 1760.

Cōpe, (THOMAS PYM,) a distinguished merchant of Philadelphia, born in Lancaster county, Pennsylvania, August 26, 1768. His parents were "Friends," and he was educated in the principles of that society. He commenced business in Philadelphia in 1790. In 1807 he built his first ship, which he named in honour of his native county, Lancaster. In 1821 he established the first regular line of packet-ships between Philadelphia and Liverpool. This line, we may remark in passing, was sustained through all those adverse circumstances which for a time threatened the destruction of the foreign commerce of Philadelphia, and continued in full vigour until the breaking out of the civil war. When Thomas P. Cope retired from business, it passed into the hands of his sons, (Henry and Alfred Cope,) and afterwards into those of the Cope Brothers, (Francis and Thomas P., sons of Henry Cope.)

To the foresight, liberality, and indefatigable energy of Thomas P. Cope, Philadelphia was principally indebted for her first abundant supply of pure water from the Schuylkill, before her increasing population rendered the present extensive water-works a necessity. The water was pumped from the river by means of a steam-engine, and conveyed to a reservoir in a building at the intersection of Broad and High Streets, whence it was distributed by pipes to different parts of the city. This plan was first carried into operation in 1801. Mr. Cope was for many years president of the Board of Trade of Philadelphia; he was also one of the originators and principal promoters of the Mercantile Library, of which he was president for more than a quarter of a century. He closed his long and useful life November 22, 1854, leaving a high character for spotless integrity as well as for commercial ability. EDWARD D. COPE, an eminent naturalist, author of the "Origin of Genera," "Extinct Batrachia and Reptilia of North America," etc., is a grandson of Thomas P. Cope, and a son of Alfred Cope.

See HUNT's "Lives of American Merchants," vol. i.

Copeland, kōp'land, (THOMAS,) an English surgeon, born about 1780, practised in London, and published several professional works. Died in 1855.

Copernic. See COPERNICUS.

Co-per'ni-cus or **Koper'nicus**, the Latinized form of **Kopernik** or **Copernic**, [Fr. pron. ko'pěr'nĕk',] written also **Zepernic** and **Zopernic**, (NICHOLAS,) a celebrated astronomer, the author of the Copernican System, was born, according to the best authorities, at Thorn, in Prussia, in February, 1473. After learning Greek and Latin at home, he pursued his studies at Cracow, where he gave attention to philosophy, medicine, mathematics, design, and astronomy. At the age of twenty-three he visited Italy, formed an intimacy with Regiomontanus, and obtained at Rome a chair of mathematics, which he filled with high reputation for a few years. Having returned to his native land, he was appointed canon of Frauenburg by his uncle, the Bishop of Warmia. Thenceforth his time was spent in his religious services, in astronomical studies, and in gratuitous visits to the poor who required medical aid.

Observing the complexity and discordance of the systems of astronomy then received, he began to compare them with each other and with the celestial processes of nature, in order to found a system more simple, symmetrical, and stable. He knew that the Pythagoreans favoured the theory that the sun was the centre of the system, and that Philolaus had given the earth a rotation on its axis in addition to its motion around the sun; but these sublime paradoxes were combated by ancient prejudices, and were apparently negatived by the dictates of common sense. After he had adopted his own system, he spent many years in proving it by observations and calculations, and he then expounded his beautiful theory and discoveries, in a work entitled "The Revolutions of the Celestial Orbs," ("De Orbium Celestium Revolutionibus,") which appears to have been finished about 1530. Although he was assured that he had solved the grandest problem which pertains to astronomy, he delayed to publish his work, probably from a presentiment of the persecution which is reserved for great reformers and innovators. His theory, which he was careful to propound as a hypothesis, was accepted as true by several astronomers, and, after much persuasion on the part of his friends, he consented to print the work in 1543, with a dedication to the pope. While it was in the press at Nuremberg, he approached the end of his career; and he died on the same day that he received the first copy, (May 24, 1543,) having only strength sufficient to touch it with his hand. The progress of his system, even among astronomers, was extremely slow, and the clergy and the masses were generally hostile to it. "The whole weight of Aristotle's name," says Hallam, "which in the sixteenth century not only biassed the judgment but engaged the passions, connected as it was with general orthodoxy and preservation of established systems, was thrown into the scale against Copernicus. It must be confessed that the strongest presumptions in favour of his system were not discovered by himself. One of the most remarkable passages in Copernicus is his conjecture that gravitation was not a central tendency, but an attraction common to matter, and probably extending to the heavenly bodies." ("Introduction to the Literature of Europe.") It is proper to observe that the system which bears his name has received important modifications since his time by the genius of Galileo, Newton, etc.

See GASSENDI, "Vita Copernici," 1654; PERCY, "Notice biographique sur Copernic," 1824; SNIADECKI, "Discours sur N. Copernik," Warsaw, 1803; D. SZULE, "Biographie de Kopernik," 1855; L. PROWE, "Zur Biographie von N. Copernicus," 1853: WEST-PHAL, "N. Copernicus," Constance, 1822; CZYNSKI, "Kopernik et ses Travaux," 1846; F. ARAGO, "Éloge de Copernic."

Cop'land, (JAMES,) an eminent Scottish physician, born at Deerness, in one of the Orkney Isles, in 1792, settled in London about 1818. He published, besides other works, an excellent "Dictionary of Practical Medicine," (3 vols., 1833–58,) a work of great labour and research.

Copleston, kop'el-ston, (EDWARD,) D.D., an English bishop, born in Devonshire in 1776. He became a Fellow of Oriel College, Oxford, in 1795, and professor of poetry in the university in 1802. In 1813 he published, in elegant Latin, his "Academic Lectures," ("Prælectiones Academicæ,") which were much admired. He wrote an "Enquiry into the Doctrines of Predestination," (1821.) In 1827 he was appointed Bishop of Llandaff, and Dean of Saint Paul's, London. Died in 1849.

See WILLIAM JAMES COPLESTON, "Memoirs of E. Copleston, with Selections from his Diary," etc., 1851; RICHARD WHATELY, "Remains of the late Edward Copleston," etc., 1854; "Fraser's Magazine" for September, 1851; "North British Review" for February, 1852.

Cop'ley, (JOHN SINGLETON,) an eminent historical painter, born at Boston, Massachusetts, in 1737. He is said to have had no instructor except nature. He exhibited at the Royal Academy of London, in 1760, a picture of a "Boy and Tame Squirrel," which was greatly admired. In 1774 he visited Italy, and in the next year became a resident of London, where he painted portraits and historical subjects with success. He was elected a member of the Royal Academy in 1783. "The Death of Lord Chatham" is one of his chief productions. He died in 1815, leaving a son, who became Lord Lyndhurst, and chancellor of England.

See TUCKERMAN, "Book of the Artists."

Copley, (JOHN S.) See LYNDHURST.

Coppetta. See BECCUTI.

Coq. See LECOQ.

Coqueau or **Cocqueau**, ko'kō', (CLAUDE PHILIBERT,) a French architect, born at Dijon in 1755. He was guillotined in 1794.

Coquebert de Montbret, kok'baiR' děh mòN'bRâ', (CHARLES ÉTIENNE,) BARON, a French mineralogist and botanist, born in Paris in 1755; died in 1831.

See SILVESTRE, "Notice sur le Baron Coquebert de Montbret," 1832.

Coquelin, kok'lǎN', (CHARLES,) a French economist, born at Dunkirk in 1803, wrote, besides other works, one on "Credit and Banks," (1848.) Died in 1852.

See MOLINARI, "Notice sur C. Coquelin," 1853.

Coquereau, kok'ro', (FÉLIX,) a popular French preacher, born in 1808, published "Souvenirs of Saint Helena."

Coquerel, kok'rěl', (ATHANASE LAURENT CHARLES,) a French Protestant divine, born in Paris in 1795. He began to preach in Paris about 1830, and became eminent as a pulpit orator. He was elected in 1848 to the Constituent Assembly, in which he voted with the moderate republicans. His religious opinions were liberal. He published, besides other works, "Sacred Biography," (1837,) "Modern Orthodoxy," (1842,) and many volumes of sermons. Died in 1868.

See QUÉRARD, "La France Littéraire;" "Blackwood's Magazine" for May, 1838.

Coquerel, (CHARLES AUGUSTIN,) a brother of the preceding, born in Paris in 1797. He was one of the founders of the "Revue Britannique," and wrote a "History of English Literature," (1828.) Died in 1851.

Coques, kok, (GONZALES,) a Flemish miniature-painter, born at Antwerp in 1618. He imitated Van Dyck with success, and acquired a high reputation by his portraits. He was employed by Charles I. of England, and other princes. Died about 1684.

See DESCAMPS, "Vies des Peintres Flamands," etc.

Coquille, ko'kēl' or ko'ke'ye, [Lat. CONCHYL'IUS,] (GUI,) Sieur de Romenay, a meritorious French jurist,

ā, ē, ī, ō, ū, ȳ, *long;* à, ê, ò, same, less prolonged; ă, ĕ, ĭ, ŏ, ŭ, ȳ, *short;* a, e, i, o, *obscure;* fär, fàll, fàt; mêt; nŏt; gŏŏd; mōŏn;

born at Decize about 1524. He advocated civil and religious liberty in his writings, among which are a "Treatise on the Liberties of the Gallican Church," and several Latin poems. He was a friend of Lord Bacon and of Brantôme. Died in 1603.

See TAISAND, "Vies des Jurisconsultes."

Co'ram, (THOMAS,) a benevolent Englishman, born about 1668, was bred to the sea, and became captain of a merchant-vessel trading to the West Indies. He founded in 1740 a "Hospital for Exposed and Deserted Children." In 1756 Parliament voted £10,000 to the institution. The result was a great increase of the number of infants exposed. Died in 1751.

Corancez, de, deh ko'rŏN'să', (LOUIS ALEXANDRE OLIVIER,) a French *littérateur* and savant, born in Paris in 1770, was sent in 1802 as consul-general to Aleppo. He published a "Description of the Northern Part of Syria," and other esteemed works. Died in 1832.

Coras, de, deh ko'râs', (JACQUES,) a French poet, born at Toulouse in 1630, wrote "Jonas, or the Repentance of Nineveh," (1663.) Died in 1677.

Coras, de, (JEAN,) an eminent French jurist, born at Toulouse or Réalmont in 1513. He became chancellor to the Queen of Navarre, and judge in the parliament of Toulouse. Having joined the Protestants, he was killed at the Massacre of Saint Bartholomew in 1572. Among his works is one entitled "Miscellanies of Civil Law," ("Miscellanea Juris Civilis.")

Co'rax, [Gr. Κόραξ,] a famous Sicilian orator, who flourished about 470 B.C. He was called the creator of the rhetorical art, and wrote a treatise on that subject, (not extant.)

Coray, ko'râ', written also **Koray,** and **Korais,** (DIAMANT,) [Gr. Ἀδαμάντιος Κοραῆς,] an eminent modern Greek philologist and patriot, born at Smyrna in 1748. He made himself master of Greek and other languages. In 1782 he began to study medicine in Montpellier, and six years later removed to Paris. Resolving to devote himself to the freedom and regeneration of Greece by means of education, he published good editions of old Greek authors, with notes and translations, and some original political tracts. About 1802 the First Consul employed him to translate Strabo's "Geography." He died in 1833, with the reputation of one of the best Hellenists of his time, and one of the influential restorers of Greek nationality. (See his "Autobiography," entitled "Βίος Ἀδαμαντίου Κοραῆ παρὰ τοῦ ἰδίου," Paris, 1833.)

Corazzi, ko-rât'see, (ERCOLE,) an Italian mathematician and scientific writer, born at Bologna in 1689. He was professor of mathematics in Turin. Died in 1726.

Corbaux, kor-bō', (FANNY,) an English painter and author, born in 1812. She became a self-taught artist, with a view to support her parents, and painted portraits and historical subjects with success. In 1830 she received the gold medal for a miniature portrait. She has written dissertations on Hebrew archæology or Biblical literature.

Corbeil, (GILLES.) See ÆGIDIUS CORBOLIENSIS.

Cor'bet, (JOHN,) an English nonconformist minister, born at Gloucester in 1620; died in 1680.

Corbet, (RICHARD,) an English poet and pulpit orator, born in Surrey in 1582, became a chaplain of James I. He was appointed Bishop of Oxford in 1629, and of Norwich in 1632. Though he was a partisan of the High Church, and required by Laud to act against the Puritans, he was respected for his moderation. He composed humorous poems, among which were a "Journey to France" and "Farewell to the Fairies." Died in 1635.

See "Retrospective Review," vol. xii., 1825.

Corbet, (WILLIAM,) a general, born in Ireland in 1781, served some years in the French army. He went to Greece in 1828, fought against the Turks, and obtained command of the Greek army. Died in 1842.

Corbière, koR'be-air', (ÉDOUARD,) a French novelist, born at Brest in 1793, was a naval officer in his youth. He published "The Banian," (1835,) "The Slaver," and other marine stories.

Corbière, de, deh koR'be-air', (JACQUES JOSEPH GUILLAUME PIERRE,) COUNT, a French politician, born near Rennes about 1767. In 1820 he was appointed a minister of state, and in December, 1821, minister of the interior. He retired from office with Villèle in January, 1828. Died in 1853.

See LAMARTINE, "History of the Restoration."

Corbiere, di, de koR-be-ā'râ, (PIETRO,) an Italian priest, who, by the authority of the emperor Louis of Bavaria, was elected anti-pope in 1328 as a rival to John XXII. He assumed the title of Nicholas V. Failing to obtain popular support, he abjured his usurpation in 1330, was imprisoned, and died in 1336.

Corbineau, koR'be'nō', (CLAUDE LOUIS,) a French general, born at Laval in 1772, became a general of brigade in 1806, and was killed at Eylau in 1807.

Corbineau, (JEAN BAPTISTE JUVENAL,) a French general, brother of the preceding, born at Marchiennes in 1776. For his services in Russia in 1812 he was made aide-de-camp général to Bonaparte. He became general of division in 1813, and is said to have saved the life of Napoleon at Montmirail, 1814. He directed the arrest of Louis Napoleon at Boulogne in 1840. Died in 1848.

See "Victoires et Conquêtes des Français."

Corbinelli, koR-be-nel'lee, (JEAN,) a French writer, of Italian descent, born about 1615, became secretary to Queen Marie de Médicis. He published "The Old Latin Historians reduced to Maxims," and a few other works. Died in 1716.

Corbould, kor'bōld, (EDWARD HENRY,) an English painter in water-colours, born in London in 1815. His subjects are mostly historical. His "Plague of London" (1843) obtained a prize of £100. Among his best productions are "The Fair Rosamond," and "The Eglinton Tournament," (1839.)

Cor'bu-lo, [Fr. CORBULON, koR'bü'lôN',] (CN. DOMITIUS,) a celebrated Roman commander, who flourished under Claudius and Nero. He commanded with success in a war against the Parthians under Tiridates, and excited the jealousy of Nero, who ordered him to be put to death in 67 A.D. He was reputed the ablest general of his time.

See PLINY, "Natural History," books ii., vi., and vii.; TACITUS, "Annales," books iii. and ix.

Corbulon. See CORBULO.

Cor'co-ran, (MICHAEL,) an officer in the United States army, born in Ireland in 1827. Having acquired distinction in the campaign of 1861, in Virginia, he was made a brigadier-general in 1862. Died in 1863.

Cordaire. See LACORDAIRE.

Cordara, kor-dâ'râ, (GIULIO CESARE,) an Italian Jesuit, born in Piedmont in 1704. He was chosen to continue Orlandini's "History of the Jesuits," of which he published one volume, (Rome, 1750.) The style of this work (in Latin) is pure and elegant. He wrote also Latin and Italian poems. Died in 1784.

See TIPALDO, "Biografia degli Italiani illustri."

Corday d'Armans, de, deh koR'dä' dăR'môN', (MARIE ANNE CHARLOTTE,) usually called simply CHARLOTTE CORDAY, born of a noble family, in Normandy, in 1768, was a descendant of the celebrated poet Corneille. She passed several years in a convent at Caen, where, says Lamartine, "she was a model of piety." Her disposition was thoughtful and imaginative. In person she was tall, her face serenely beautiful, her air dignified and commanding. She adopted with enthusiasm the principles of the new régime, and sympathized deeply with the Girondists proscribed in May, 1793. The infamous Marat being then at the zenith of his political influence, she formed a secret resolution to sacrifice herself for the liberties of her country. Once, in spite of the watchful reserve under which she veiled a deep and terrible purpose, a few tears chanced to escape from her. To her aunt, who inquired the cause, she said, "I weep for my country. . . . So long as Marat lives, no one's life is secure for a single day." Soon after, her aunt, accidentally entering Charlotte's chamber, found a Bible open at the tenth chapter of the apocryphal book of Judith, and the passage marked which contains the prayer of the ancients of the city that God would prosper the enterprise of Judith for the deliverance of Israel. Confirmed in her resolution by such meditations, she came to Paris. But Marat, suspicious of attempts against his life, could not readily be approached. She therefore, though with extreme reluctance, resorted to a stratagem, pretending that she was the bearer of important information from the provinces. He received her while in his bath; and, as he was foretelling to her the speedy doom of the surviving Girondists, she stabbed him to the heart, with a knife which she had concealed in her bosom. In prison she wrote an eloquent letter to Barbaroux, manifesting in every line that courageous and lofty spirit which never left her, even on the scaffold. She was executed in July, 1793. "There are deeds," says Lamartine, "so mingled with pure intentions and culpable means, that we know not whether to pronounce them criminal or virtuous." "In beholding her act of assassination, history dares not applaud; nor yet, while contemplating her sublime self-devotion, can it stigmatize or condemn."

See CHÉRON DE VILLIERS, "M. A. Charlotte de Corday d'Armans, sa Vie, son Temps, ses Écrits," etc., Paris, 1865; LAMARTINE, "History of the Girondists," book xliv.; and the article "Corday" in the "Biographie Universelle."

Cordeiro or **Cordeyro**, koR-dā'e-ro, (ANTONIO,) a Portuguese historian and priest, born in the isle of Terceira in 1641. He wrote a "History of Madeira, Terceira," etc., (1717,) which is commended. Died in 1740.

Cordemoy, de, dęh koRd'mwȃ', (GÉRAUD,) a French historian, born in Paris, became a member of the French Academy. Bossuet employed him as reader to the dauphin, and persuaded him to write a "History of Charlemagne," which is a work of merit, though not attractive in style. He left a few other minor essays. Died in 1684.

See NICÉRON, "Mémoires."

Corder, koR'der, or **Cordier,** koR'de-ȃ', [Lat. CORDE'-RIUS,] (BALTHASAR,) a Flemish Jesuit, theologian, and Hellenist, born at Antwerp in 1592, became a professor of theology at Vienna. He published several works. Died in 1650.

Corderius, (BALTHASAR.) See CORDER.

Cor-de'rĭ-us, [Fr. CORDIER, koR'de-ȃ',](MATHURIN,) a celebrated Protestant school-teacher, born in France in 1479. He was the preceptor of Calvin, who dedicated to him one of his works; and he published several popular school-books, among which is "Scholastic Colloquies," ("Colloquia scholastica," 1564,) a work which was long very extensively used. He lived some years in Geneva. Died in 1564.

See BAYLE, "Historical and Critical Dictionary;" "Nouvelle Biographie Générale."

Cordes, koRd, or **Cor-de'sĭ-us,** (JEAN,) a learned French ecclesiastic, born at Limoges in 1570, collected a library of 8300 volumes. Died in 1642.

Cordeyro. See CORDEIRO.

Cordier, (BALTHASAR.) See CORDER.

Cordier, (MATHURIN.) See CORDERIUS.

Cordier, koR'de-ȃ', (NICOLAS,) a French sculptor of high reputation, born in Lorraine in 1561, worked in Rome. He made a bronze statue of Henry IV. for the church of Saint John de Lateran. Died in 1612.

Cordier, (PIERRE LOUIS ANTOINE,) a French geologist and mineralogist, born at Abbeville in 1777. As engineer, he accompanied the expedition to Egypt in 1798, and obtained the grade of engineer-in-chief in 1808. In 1819 he was chosen professor of geology in the Museum of Natural History at Paris, and in 1822 was admitted into the Institute in place of Haüy. He published an able "Essay on the Internal Temperature of the Earth," (1827,) and other scientific memoirs. He was made a peer about 1840. Died in March, 1861.

See "Nouvelle Biographie Générale."

Cor'dĭ-nęr, (CHARLES,) a British antiquary and topographer, born about 1746; died in 1794.

Cordova. See GONSALVO.

Cordova, koR'do-vȃ, (JOSÉ,) a South American general, born at Antioquía, New Granada, in 1797. He fought under Bolivar about 1820, and contributed to the victory of Ayacucho, (1824,) after which he was made general of division. In 1829 he revolted against Bolivar, but was defeated and killed the same year.

Cordova, de, dȃ koR'do-vȃ, (ADRIANO,) a Spanish historical painter and monk; died about 1630.

Cordova, de, (FERNANDO FERNANDEZ,) a Spanish general, born in Madrid in 1792. He opposed Espartero in 1841, and afterwards joined the moderate *Progresistas.* In 1850 he was appointed Captain-General of New Castile, and in 1851 Captain-General of Cuba. He was driven into exile by the revolution of July, 1854, and returned to Spain in 1856, on the fall of Espartero.

Cordova, de, (FRANCISCO HERNANDEZ,) a Spanish navigator, commanded a small expedition which sailed from Havana in 1517, discovered Yucatan, and, in returning, touched at Florida. He died in Cuba, a few days after his return, in 1518.

Cordova, de, (LUIS FERNANDEZ,) a Spanish general, a brother of Fernando Fernandez, noticed above, was born at Cadiz in 1799. He was a favourite of Ferdinand VII., and was sent as ambassador to Berlin about 1828. In the civil war which began in 1833 he was a partisan of Isabella. Having been an unsuccessful rival of Espartero, he retired to Portugal about 1838, and died in 1840.

Cor'dus, (AULUS CREMUTIUS,) a Roman historian, who wrote a "History of the Civil War of Rome and of the Reign of Augustus," (not extant.) He was accused of treason by Sejanus because he had praised Brutus and Cassius in his history. Being assured that his death was resolved on, he ended his life by starvation in 25 A.D.

See TACITUS, "Annales," book iv.; SENECA, "Suasoria."

Cordus, koR'dûs, (EURICH or EURICIUS,) a German poet and physician, born at Simtshausen, in Hesse, about 1480. He became professor of medicine at Marburg about 1527. He corresponded with the most distinguished men of his time, and composed Latin poems (1614) and prose works, among which is "Botanologicon, a Dialogue on Plants," (1534.) Died in 1535.

See KAHLER, "Vita E. Cordi," 1744; ERSCH und GRUBER, "Allgemeine Encyklopaedie;" NICÉRON, "Mémoires."

Cordus, (VALERIUS,) an eminent botanist, son of the preceding, born at Simtshausen in 1515. He explored the botanical riches of Germany, and proved himself a good observer. In 1535 he published a valuable "Dispensatory," ("Dispensatorium Pharmacorum,") and in 1542 visited Italy on a botanical excursion. He died prematurely, in Rome, in 1544. The results of his labours appeared in 1561, in a work which was edited by Conrad Gesner and entitled a "History or Description of Plants," etc., ("Historiæ Stirpium Libri quatuor a Conrado Gesnero collectæ.") His merit as a botanist is highly eulogized by Gesner.

See ERSCH und GRUBER, "Allgemeine Encyklopaedie;" NICÉRON, "Mémoires."

Coreal, ko-rȃ-ȃl', (FRANCISCO,) a Spanish traveller, born at Cartagena in 1648. He spent about thirty years in the West Indies and South America between 1666 and 1697, and left an interesting narrative, which was published in French, in 3 vols. 1722. This purported to be a translation from the Spanish.

Corella, de, dȃ ko-rȇl'yȃ, (ALFONZO,) a Spanish medical writer, born at Corella, Navarre, lived about 1550.

Corelli, ko-rel'lee, (ARCANGELO,) a famous Italian musical composer and performer, born at Fusignano, near Imola, in 1653. He published in Rome, in 1683, his first work, "Twelve Sonatas for two Violins and a Bass." In 1686 he was leader of an orchestra of one hundred and fifty musicians in an opera performed at Rome under the auspices of Christina of Sweden. His reputation had then extended over Europe. He was patronized by Cardinal Ottoboni, who appointed him director of his music. Among his most popular productions is "Concerti Grossi," (1712.) Died in 1713.

See FÉTIS, "Biographie Universelle des Musiciens;" FAYOLLE, "Notices sur Corelli, Tartini," etc., 1810.

Corenzio, ko-rȇn'ze-o, (BELISARIO,) a skilful painter, born in Greece, was a pupil of Tintoretto, and settled in Naples about 1590. He was noted for his invention and facility of execution, and worked mostly in fresco. Among his chief productions is "The Feeding of the Five Thousand." His memory is branded with the charge of tyrannical treatment of Guido and other foreign artists at Naples. Died in 1643.

See LANZI, "History of Painting in Italy."

Corilla, ko-rȇl'lȃ, (MARIA MADDALENA FERNANDEZ,) an Italian improvisatrice, born in 1740. She was publicly crowned at Rome about 1775. Died in 1800.

ā, ē, ī, ō, ū, ȳ, *long;* ȧ, ė, ȯ, same, less prolonged; ă, ĕ, ĭ, ŏ, ŭ, ў, *short;* ą, ę, į, ǫ, *obscure;* fär; fȧll, fȧt; mêt; nŏt; gōōd; mōōn;

Co-rin'na, [Gr. Κόριννα; Fr. Corinne, ko'rèn',] a celebrated Greek lyric poetess, born at Tanagra, in Bœotia, lived about 500 B.C. Contemporary with Pindar, she is said to have instructed him in poetry, and was five times victorious in competition with him. Pausanias ascribes her triumph partly to her beauty. She was surnamed Μύια, ("The Fly.") Only a few fragments of her poems are now extant.

See Suidas, "Corinna;" Fabricius, "Bibliotheca Græca;" J. B. Schupp, "Corinna die ehrbare und scheinbare Hure," 1660.

Corinne. See Corinna.

Corio, ko're-o, (Bernardino,) an Italian historian, born at Milan in 1459. Under the patronage of Ludovico Sforza, he wrote, in Italian, the "History of Milan," (1503.) Died in 1519.

Coriolan. See Coriolano and Coriolanus.

Coriolano, ko-re-o-lä'no, or **Coriolan,** ko-re-o-lân', (Bartolommeo,) Cavaliere, a skilful Italian designer and engraver, son of Cristoforo, noticed below, was born at Bologna in 1590. He was a pupil of Guido. He dedicated to Pope Urban VIII. many wood-cuts in chiaroscuro, after Guido and the Caracci. Died in 1654.

See Huber, "Manuel du Graveur."

Coriolano, ko-re-o-lä'no, [Fr. Coriolan, ko're'o'lôn',] (Cristoforo,) an eminent wood-engraver, born at Nuremberg about 1550. His original name was Lederer, (lä'der-er.) He removed to Venice, where he engraved, besides other works, the portraits of Vasari's biographical work. Died at Bologna about 1600.

Coriolano, (Giambattista,) a son of the preceding, born at Bologna in 1595, was a painter, and engraver on copper and wood. He engraved many pictures by Guido, the Caracci, and other masters. Died in 1649.

Co-ri-o-lā'nus, [Fr. Coriolan, ko're'o'lôn'; Ger. Coriolan, ko-re-o-lân', or Coriolanus, ko-re-o-lä'nŭs,] (Caius (or Cneius) Marcius,) the hero of an early Roman legend, was said to be a descendant of King Ancus Marcius. According to the poetical traditions on the subject, he obtained the surname Coriolanus for his victory over the Volscians at Corioli about 490 B.C. During a famine he advised that corn should not be distributed gratis to the commons unless they gave up their tribunes. For this offence he was banished; and, having obtained command of a Volscian army, he besieged Rome. The Romans were unable to resist him or to avert his anger, until his stern purpose yielded to the tears of Veturia his mother and of Volumnia his wife, who led a deputation of Roman matrons to his tent. He is supposed to have passed the rest of his life among the Volsci, (Smith's "Dictionary of Greek and Roman Biography;") but, according to the popular tradition, he was killed by the Volsci immediately after he abandoned his purpose of taking Rome. This legend is the subject of Shakspeare's drama of "Coriolanus."

See Plutarch's "Lives;" Niebuhr, "History of Rome;" Fr. Rochlitz, "Helden des alten Roms und des neuen Frankreichs, Coriolan und Dumouriez," 1796.

Coriolis, ko're'o'lèss', (Gaspard Gustave,) a French mechanician, born in Paris in 1792; died in 1843.

Co-rip'pus, (Flavius Cresconius,) a Latin poet of the sixth century, who is supposed to have been born in Africa and to have been a bishop. He wrote several works, which have some merit and are still extant. Among them is an epic poem called "Johanneis," and a panegyric on the emperor Justin, ("De Laudibus Justini minoris.")

See Fabricius, "Bibliotheca Latina;" "Nouvelle Biographie Générale."

Cork, Earl of. See Boyle, (Richard.)

Cormenin, de, deh korm'năn', (Louis,) Baron, a French journalist, son of Louis Marie, noticed below, born in Paris in 1826. In 1852 he supported the government, and obtained the direction of the "Moniteur Officiel."

Cormenin, de, (Louis Marie de la Haye—deh lä hä,) Vicomte, an eminent French political writer and jurist, born in Paris in January, 1788. He was appointed auditor of the council of state in 1810, and master of requests (by Louis XVIII.) in 1815. In 1828 he was elected deputy for Orléans. He was often re-elected by the Liberal party, became a popular pamphleteer, and exercised great influence on political affairs. His pamph-

lets appeared under the pseudomyn of "Timon." He opposed the government of Louis Philippe. In 1838 he published a work called "Studies on Parliamentary Orators," ("Études sur les Orateurs parlementaires," 17th edition, 1854.) He was president of the committee which framed a new constitution in 1848. After the coup d'état of December, 1851, he deserted the Liberal party and became a member of Louis Napoleon's council of state. He was admitted into the Institute in 1855. Among his important works are his "Administrative Law," ("Droit administratif," 1822,) and "Letters on the Civil List," (1831,) which passed through twenty-five editions. M. Cormenin also distinguished himself as a practical philanthropist, and took part in founding numerous charitable institutions. Died in May, 1868.

See Loménie, "Galerie des Contemporains;" "Nouvelle Biographie Générale;" Chapuis-Montlaville, "Étude sur Timon," 1848.

Cormontaingne, de, deh koR'môn'tânñ', (Louis,) an eminent French military engineer, born about 1695. Between 1734 and 1745 he directed the sieges of Menin, Ypres, Tournay, etc. The great works added in the reign of Louis XV. to the fortifications of Metz and Thionville were constructed on his plans. He obtained the rank of maréchal-de-camp. He made improvements in the art of fortification, on which he also wrote several esteemed treatises. Died in 1752.

Cornacchini, koR-näk-kee'nee, (Marco,) an Italian medical writer, flourished at Pisa about 1610. His father, Tommaso, was professor of medicine at Pisa, and author of "Tabulæ Medicæ," 1605.

Cornarius. See Cornarus.

Cornaro, (Angelo.) See Gregory XII.

Cornaro, koR-nä'ro, (Caterina,) Queen of Cyprus, was born in Venice about 1454. She became the wife of James de Lusignan, King of Cyprus, and was adopted as daughter of Saint Mark by the senate of Venice. At the death of the king, in 1473, she ascended the throne, which she abdicated in 1489, when the Venetians became masters of Cyprus. Died in 1510.

See Daru, "Histoire de Venise."

Cornaro, or **Cornelio,** koR-nä'le-o, sometimes written **Corner,** (Flaminio,) a Venetian senator, eminent for learning, born in Venice in 1693. He published a "History of the Churches of Venice," (1758,) and several religious works. Died in 1778.

Cornaro, (Giovanni I.,) Doge of Venice, succeeded Francis Contarini in 1625. He waged a war against Austria, which he left unfinished when he died in 1629.

Cornaro, (Giovanni II.,) was elected Doge of Venice in 1709. During his administration the Turks made war on Venice, and took the Morea about 1715. He obtained peace in 1718. Died in 1722.

See Daru, "Histoire de Venise."

Cornaro, (Luigi,) a Venetian gentleman, born about 1463, gained distinction by his successful experiments on diet and by his writings on the preservation of health. In his youth, by intemperance and sensuality, he ruined his health, which was naturally delicate. About the age of forty he reformed his habits, became very abstemious, and found the results of his change highly satisfactory. After he was eighty years old he published a "Treatise on a Temperate Life," which had a wide circulation, and was translated into English and French. He died, it is said, in his 103d year. Addison, in his "Spectator," No. 195, says Cornaro passed his hundredth year, and commends the good sense and cheerful spirit of his book.

See "Biographie Médicale."

Cornaro-Piscopia, koR-nä'ro pès-ko'pe-â, (Elena Lucrezia,) an illustrious Italian scholar and writer, born at Venice in 1646, was a relative of the preceding. Her attainments in languages, philosophy, etc. spread her fame throughout Europe. She made a vow of celibacy, and observed the rules of a monastic order. She composed admired verses and academic discourses. Died in 1684.

See Nicéron, "Mémoires;" M. Deeza, "Vita di E. L. Cornaro-Piscopia," 1686; Antonio Lupis, "L'Eroina Veneta, ovvero la Vita di E. L. Cornaro-Piscopia," 1689.

Cornaros, koR-nä'ros, (Vincent,) a Greek poet of the sixteenth century, born in the island of Crete. His life is involved in obscurity. He is styled "the Homer of modern Greece," and wrote a poem in rhymes entitled "Erotocritos," which is admired, and is an interesting monument for the history of the Greek language.

See BRANDIS, "Mittheilungen über Griechenland."

Cor-na'rus or **Cornarius**, koR-nä're-ŭs, the Latinized name of JOHANN HAGENBUTT, (hä'gĕn-bŏŏt,) a German physician, born at Zwickau, Saxony, in 1500. He practised at Frankfort and Zwickau, and was professor of medicine at Marburg and Jena. He gained a wide reputation by his Greek edition of Hippocrates, (1538,) and a Latin version of the same, (1546.) He translated some works of Plato, Saint Basil, and other Greek writers into Latin, and wrote several medical treatises. Died in 1558.

See M. ADAM, "Vitæ Eruditorum ;" ÉLOY, "Dictionnaire de la Médecine."

Cornazzani, koR-nät-sä'nee, or **Cornazzano**, koR-nät-sä'no, (ANTONIO,) an Italian poet, born at Piacenza or Ferrara, lived about 1500. He wrote lyric poems (printed in 1502) and some prose works.

Cornbury, korn'bĕr-e, (EDWARD HYDE,) LORD, son of the second Earl of Clarendon, was one of the first of James II.'s officers to desert his standard in 1688 and go over to the Prince of Orange, (afterwards William III.,) who in return for this service appointed him Governor of New York, where he arrived in 1702. His avarice, despotic measures, and frivolous character soon drew upon him the execration of the people, and in 1708 procured his removal from office. Died in 1723.

Cornbury, (HENRY HYDE,) LORD, eldest son of the Earl of Clarendon, wrote a comedy called "The Mistakes, or the Happy Resentment," which was printed in 1758. He was killed by a fall from a horse in France in 1753.

Corne, koRn, (HYACINTHE,) a French publicist, born at Arras in 1802, was elected to the Chamber of Deputies in 1837. He wrote, besides other works, a "Treatise on Civil Courage."

Corneille, koR'nål' or koR'nå'ye, (JEAN BAPTISTE,) a French historical painter and engraver, born in Paris in 1646, was a son of Michel, noticed below. He received the grand prize in 1668. Died in 1695.

Corneille, (MICHEL,) a French painter and engraver, born at Orléans in 1601, was a pupil of Vouet. He painted religious subjects, and was one of the first members of the Academy of Paris. Died in 1664.

Corneille, (MICHEL,) a skilful French painter, son of the preceding, born in Paris in 1642. He studied in Italy, and on his return, in 1663, was received into the Royal Academy. He was employed by the king, and adorned several churches of Paris with his works. Died in 1708.

Corneille, koR'nål', [Fr. pron. koR'nål' or koR'nå'ye,] (PIERRE,) a celebrated French dramatic author, the founder of the French drama, and the writer who has perhaps contributed most to the development of the national genius, was born at Rouen on the 6th of June, 1606. He studied law, which he practised a few years without success. His first work, a comedy called "Mélite," (1629,) and others which quickly followed, were performed with applause, which they owed partly to the vicious taste of the public. His "Medea" (1635) gave a new tone of grandeur and dignity to the French tragedy, though it contained much bombast and vain declamation. In 1636 he astonished and enraptured the public with the tragedy of "The Cid," (an imitation of a Spanish drama of that name,) which, by nervous eloquence and mastery of dramatic resources, eclipsed everything that had hitherto appeared on the French stage. To silence his detractors, who called him a mere imitator, he produced, in 1639, "Les Horaces," and "Cinna," which were admired for invention and style. Many persons consider "Cinna" as his master-piece ; while others prefer "Polyeucte." "A deeper interest," says Hallam, "belongs to 'Polyeucte ;' and this is his only tragedy wherein he affects the heart. The beautiful character of Pauline would redeem much greater defects than can be ascribed to this tragedy. It is the noblest, perhaps, on the French stage, and conceived with admirable delicacy and dignity." ("Introduction to the Literature of Europe.") His "Menteur" ("Liar," 1642) was the first comedy of character and intrigue which was

an honour to France. His subsequent efforts indicate a decline of his power ; but his opera called the "Golden Fleece" ("Toison d'Or") was performed with success in 1661. He had been admitted into the French Academy in 1647. He died in Paris in October, 1684, leaving several children. The French call him the "grand Corneille," not only to distinguish him from his brother Thomas, but from the rest of mankind. Fontenelle, who was his nephew, preferred him as a poet to Racine ; but Voltaire, La Harpe, and other critics reverse that judgment. It is generally admitted that in impressive declamation, in dignity, in sublime thoughts, in condensed and noble style, he has not been equalled by any succeeding dramatist. In private life his manners were simple and his conversation rather dull. He is represented as a man of pure morals and amiable character. "It is difficult," says a recent French critic, "to draw the portrait of Corneille and to do justice to the subject. His most magnificent eulogy is perhaps in this verse of Voltaire :

" ' Le grand Condé pleurant aux vers du grand Corneille.' "*

" When the Academy was endeavouring to correct the language which Pascal was destined to fix and Racine to polish, Corneille formed and created it, by giving it force and precision in reasoning, energy and profoundness in discourse, elevation and sublimity in sentiment, dignity and majesty in the utterances of kings and heroes." ("Nouvelle Biographie Générale.")

See FONTENELLE, "Éloge de Corneille ;" SAINTE-BEUVE, "Portraits littéraires," tome i. ; GUIZOT, "Corneille et son Temps," 1852 ; TASCHEREAU, "Histoire de la Vie et des Ouvrages de Corneille," 1829 ; JEAN SYLVAIN BAILLY, "Éloge de Corneille," 1768 ; M. J. J. VICTORIN-FABRE, "Éloge de Corneille," 1808 ; LOUIS SIMON AUGER, "Éloge de Corneille," 1808 : "Biographie Universelle ;" LONGFELLOW, "Poets and Poetry of Europe ;" "Lives of the Most Eminent French Writers," by MRS. SHELLEY, London, 1840 ; "Blackwood's Magazine" for October, 1852.

Corneille, (THOMAS,) a popular French dramatist, brother of the preceding, was born at Rouen in 1625. On leaving college he became a resident of Paris. His first play, "Engagements du Hasard," appeared in 1647. In the ensuing eight years he produced several other comedies. In 1656 he composed "Timocrate," a tragedy, which was very popular, and was performed eighty times in six months. It was followed by "Darius," " Stilicon," and many other tragedies, which had a transient success. His tragedies "Ariane" and "Earl of Essex" obtained more durable favour, and still keep their place on the stage. He succeeded his brother in the French Academy in 1685. "He was," says Voltaire, "a man of great merit and of vast learning ; and, if we except Racine, he was the only French author of his time worthy to be ranked next to his brother." Died in 1709.

See NICÉRON, "Mémoires ;" LA HARPE, "Cours de Littérature."

Cornejo, koR-nä'ho, (PEDRO,) a Spanish historian, who lived about 1550–80, wrote, among other works, a "Summary of the Civil Wars in Flanders," (1577.)

Cor-ne'lĭ-a, [Fr. CORNÉLIE, koR'nå'le' ; It. CORNIGLIA, koR-nèl'yä,] a noble Roman matron, the daughter of P. Scipio Africanus, and the wife of T. Sempronius Gracchus. She was eminent for virtue and mental cultivation. After the death of her husband she refused an offer of marriage from Ptolemy, King of Egypt. As the daughter of Scipio and the mother of the Gracchi, she had as high a position as any woman in Roman history. A Campanian dame, having displayed to her the jewels with which she was adorned, expressed her curiosity to see those of Cornelia. The latter, pointing to her sons, Tiberius and Caius, exclaimed, "These are my jewels and ornaments."

See PLUTARCH, "T. Gracchus" and "Caius Gracchus ;" L. MERCKLIN, "Programma de Corneliæ, Gracchorum Matris, Vita, Moribus et Epistolis," 1844.

Cornelia, the daughter of Cinna, was the first wife of Julius Cæsar the dictator, to whom she was married in 83 B.C. She died young, leaving a daughter, Julia, who became the wife of Pompey the Great.

Cor-ne'lĭ-a Gens, a patrician family or tribe, which produced more illustrious men than any other in Rome. Among them were the Cinnas, Lentulus, Rufinus, the Scipios, and Sulla.

Cornélie. See CORNELIA.

* "The great Condé weeping at the verses of the great Corneille."

ā, ē, ī, ō, ū, ȳ, *long*; à, è, ò, same, less prolonged; ă, ĕ, ĭ, ŏ, ŭ, ў, *short*; a, e, i, o, *obscure*; fär, fåll, fât; mêt; nŏt; gŏŏd; mŏŏn;

Cornelio, (FLAMINIO.) See CORNARO.

Cornelis, koR-nā'lis, [Fr. CORNEILLE, koR-nål', (or koR-nå'ye,) or CORNILLE; Ger. CORNELIUS, koR-nā'le-ûs,] a famous Dutch painter of history and portraits, was born at Haarlem in 1562. He studied under Porbus and Coignet at Antwerp, and settled in Haarlem. He excelled in design and colouring, and imitated nature with fidelity. Among his master-pieces is a large picture of "The Deluge." Died in 1638. His brother, HENRY, was a sculptor and painter. He was most successful in landscapes and marine views.

See DESCAMPS, "Vies des Peintres Flamands," etc.

Cornelisz, koR-nā'lis, (JACOB,) a Dutch painter of history, born at Oost-Sanen about 1471, worked at Amsterdam, where he died in 1567.

Cornelisz, (LUCAS,) a Dutch painter, born at Leyden about 1492, removed to England, and was patronized by Henry VIII. Died in 1552.

Cor-ne'lĭ-us, Bishop of Rome, succeeded Fabianus in 251 A.D. He was a Roman by birth. Novatian, having refused to recognize him, was chosen Bishop of Rome by his partisans ; and thus arose the schism of the Novatians. Cornelius was banished to Città Vecchia by Gallus in 252, and died the same year.

Cor-ne'lĭ-us, (ELIAS,) an American clergyman, born in 1795. He became secretary of the American Education Society in 1826. Died in 1832.

Cornelius Nepos. See NEPOS.

Cor-ne'lĭ-us Se-ve'rus, (PUBLIUS,) a Latin epic poet, of whose life but little is known. He lived in the reign of Augustus, and died prematurely, leaving unfinished a poem called "The Sicilian War," ("Bellum Siculum,") which is praised by Quintilian. A beautiful fragment on the death of Cicero has been preserved.

Cornelius, von, fon koR-nā'le-ûs, (PETER,) the greatest German painter of his time, born at Dusseldorf on the 16th of September, 1787, was a son of the inspector of the Dusseldorf gallery of paintings. At the age of nineteen his genius revealed itself in painting the cupola of the old church of Neuss. From 1811 to 1819 he studied and worked in Rome, where he formed an intimate friendship with the artist Overbeck, who sympathized with his enthusiasm for the old Italian masters. About 1814 he finished his "Illustrations of Faust," one of his most remarkable productions. His original genius was also displayed in a series of designs illustrating the "Niebelungen-Lied." After the completion of these he devoted himself to fresco-painting, which had been long neglected. He is considered the restorer of this art among the Germans. In 1819 he removed from Rome to Munich, whither he had been invited by the crown-prince, (afterwards King Ludwig,) and was appointed director of the Academy of Dusseldorf. He was commissioned by Prince Ludwig to adorn the Glyptothek of Munich with frescos. In the Hall of Heroes of that edifice he painted on a large scale a series of subjects from the "Iliad" of Homer. Among his grandest productions is a picture of the "Last Judgment," in the church of Saint Louis, in Munich. It is about sixty feet high, and more than thirty feet wide. In the Pinakothek of Munich he illustrated, in a series of frescos, the "History of Painting," with that profoundness of conception which characterizes his genius. At the invitation of the King of Prussia, he went to Berlin in 1841, and painted in the Campo Santo several frescos, among which are "The Four Horsemen of the Apocalypse." Died at Berlin in 1867.

See BROCKHAUS, "Conversations-Lexikon ;" "Nouvelle Biographie Générale."

Corner. See CORNARO, (FLAMINIO.)

Cor'ner, (JULIA,) an English authoress, born about 1815. She published "The Baronet," a novel, (1835,) "Edward Castleton," "Questions on the History of Europe," and several useful books for children.

Cornet, de, deh koR'nå', (MATHIEU AUGUSTIN,) COUNT, a French politician, born at Nantes in 1750. He promoted the revolution of the 18th Brumaire, 1799, was made a senator the same year, and in 1804 received the title of count. Under the restoration he entered the Chamber of Peers. Died in 1832.

See THIERS, "History of the French Revolution."

Cornhert, koRn'hĕRt, written also **Coornhert,** (DIE-DRIK,) a Dutch author and Reformer of great merit, born at Amsterdam in 1522. He was a zealous promoter of the Protestant Reformation, although he was never a sectarian, and dissented from the doctrines of Calvin. He rendered important services to the Prince of Orange in his contest with Spain. He composed, besides other works, a poem "On the Use and Abuse of Fortune," and a "Treatise against the Capital Punishment of Heretics." The national air of "William of Nassau," which was very popular with several generations, is commonly attributed to him ; though Motley and some other writers ascribe it to Marnix de Saint Aldegonde. He sometimes supported himself, at Antwerp and Cleves, by his skill as an engraver. In 1572 he was appointed secretary of state in Holland. "He formed with Spiegel and Visscher," says the "Biographie Universelle," "the triumvirate that restored the Dutch language and poetry." Died at Gouda in 1590.

See BAYLE, "Historical and Critical Dictionary ;" "Nouvelle Biographie Générale ;" "Fraser's Magazine" for February, 1854.

Corniani, koR-ne-â'nee, (GIOVANNI BATTISTA,) an eminent Italian *littérateur*, born at Orzi-Nuovi in February, 1742, obtained an office in the magistracy. He wrote, besides various other works, an "Analysis of Taste and Morality," (1790,) and a "History of Italian Literature," (9 vols., 1804–13.) The latter contains critical notices of authors who wrote between the eleventh century and the middle of the eighteenth, and is a work of high reputation. "His erudition appears to me considerable," says Hallam, "and his judgments generally reasonable." ("Introduction to the Literature of Europe.") Died at Brescia in November, 1813.

See TIPALDO, "Biografia degli Italiani illustri ;" G. LABUS, "Notizie intorno alla Vita di G. B. Corniani," 1814 ; CAMILLO UGONI, "Elogio storico di G. B. Corniani," 1818.

Cornic-Duchêne, koR'nĕk' dü'shĕn', (CHARLES,) a French naval officer, born at Morlaix in 1731; died in 1809.

Cornificius, koR-ne-fish'e-us, (QUINTUS,) a Latin poet, who lived about 50 B.C., was a friend of Catullus.

Cornificius, (QUINTUS,) a Roman who supported the party of Cæsar in the civil war, and became governor of Syria. Died about 40 B.C.

Corniglia, the Italian of CORNELIA, which see.

Cornille. See CORNELIS.

Cornille, kor-neel', or **Corneille,** otherwise called **Cornelius Engelbrechtsen,** (ĕng'hĕl-brĕkt'sĕn,) a Dutch painter, born at Leyden in 1468. He painted in oil and fresco with success. The famous Lucas van Leyden was his pupil.

His son, CORNILLE KUNST, born at Leyden, inherited his father's talent for painting. He worked at Leyden and at Bruges. Among his best works is a "Descent from the Cross." He died in 1544, aged fifty-one.

Cornu, koR'nü', (SÉBASTIEN MELCHIOR,) a French painter, born at Lyons in 1804, obtained at Paris a medal of the first class in 1845.

Cornuole, delle, del'lå koR-noo-o'lå, or **Carniole,** kaR-ne-o'lå, (GIOVANNI,) an Italian engraver of gems, who worked in Florence about 1580. His productions compare favourably with those of the ancient Greeks. His portrait of Savonarola was celebrated.

Cornut. See CORNUTI.

Cornuti, koR'nü'te', or **Cornut,** koR'nü', (JACQUES PHILIPPE,) a French botanist and physician, born in Paris. He published a "Description of the Plants of Canada," (1635,) with numerous figures. Died in 1651.

Cor-nu'tus, (LUCIUS ANNÆUS,) a Roman philosopher, born at Leptis, in Africa. He taught the Stoic philosophy in Rome, and counted among his pupils the poets Lucan and Persius. Nero banished him about 68 A.D. He wrote, in Greek, a commentary on Aristotle and other philosophical works.

See SUIDAS, "Cornutus ;" FABRICIUS, "Bibliotheca Græca ;" G J. DE MARTINI, "Disputatio de L. A. Cornuto," 1825.

Cornwall, (BARRY.) See PROCTER, (BRYAN W.)

Cornwallis, korn-wŏl'lis, (CAROLINE FRANCES,) an English writer on philosophy, religion, etc., was born in 1786. She produced anonymously a series of twenty-two essays, entitled "Small Books on Great Subjects," the last of which, "The State of Man subsequent to the Promulgation of Christianity," was published in 1854. These works are highly esteemed. Died in 1858. A volume of her letters and poems was published in 1864.

See "Selections from the Letters of Caroline F. Cornwallis."

Cornwallis, (CHARLES,) EARL and MARQUIS, a British general, commonly known as LORD CORNWALLIS, born in 1738, was the eldest son of the first earl, before whose death he was styled Lord Brome or Broome. He served on the continent as aide-de-camp of the Marquis of Granby in 1761, and inherited his father's earldom in 1762. Though he was an aide-de-camp and favourite of the king, he opposed the measures which caused the American war. He joined the army in 1776, and, as major-general, took part in the battles of Brandywine and Germantown in 1777, after being foiled at Trenton by Washington. In 1780 he commanded an army in Carolina, and defeated General Gates at Camden. The next year he gained an unimportant advantage over General Greene at Guilford, and invaded Virginia. He marched to Yorktown, intending to embark there, but was prevented by a French fleet, while the army of Washington attacked him by land. He surrendered, with about 8000 men, on the 19th of October, 1781. In 1786 he was appointed Governor-General of Bengal, and commander-in-chief of the army in India. The principal event of his administration was the war against Tippoo Saib. Cornwallis in person took Bungalore in 1791, and defeated the enemy at Seringapatam in 1792. Tippoo then obtained peace by ceding half of his dominions to the British and their allies. Lord Cornwallis, having returned to England in 1793, was made a marquis, and appointed master-general of the ordnance. In 1798 he became lord lieutenant of Ireland, which was then in rebellion, and which he pacified by a moderate policy. He negotiated the treaty of Amiens in 1802. In 1805 he was again appointed Governor-General of India, and died the same year at Ghazapore. Without brilliant talents, he filled with credit a prominent place on conspicuous stages in several trying epochs of British history. He is generally admitted to have been by far the ablest British general who took part in the war of the American Revolution.

See ADOLPHUS and BISSETT, "History of the Reign of George III.;" J. W. KAYE, "Lives of Indian Officers," 1867; "London Quarterly Review" for January, 1859.

Cornwallis, (Sir CHARLES,) an English gentleman, whom James I. sent as ambassador to Spain. He wrote the Life of Henry, Prince of Wales. Died about 1630.

His son, Sir WILLIAM, published "Discourses upon Seneca," and essays on various subjects, (1600–32.)

Cornwallis, (FREDERICK,) a son of the Earl of Cornwallis, became Bishop of Lichfield and Coventry in 1749, and Archbishop of Canterbury in 1768. He published several volumes of sermons. Died in 1783.

Cornwallis, (WILLIAM,) an English admiral, brother of Lord Cornwallis, born in 1744. After serving in the American war, he commanded a squadron in the East Indies from 1789 to 1793, and was made vice-admiral in 1795. In that year he received the thanks of Parliament for his conduct in an action with the French. From 1801 to 1806 he was commander-in-chief of the Channel fleet. He died in 1819, with a fair reputation for talents and courage.

See "Annual Register."

Corona, ko-ro'nä, (LEONARDO,) an Italian painter of the Venetian school, was born at Murano in 1561. His manner is said to resemble that of Tintoretto. Among his admired works is a "Crucifixion." Died in 1605.

See LANZI, "History of Painting in Italy."

Coronado. See VASQUEZ.

Coronelli, ko-ro-nel'lee,(MARCO VINCENZO,) a learned Italian geographer and monk, born at Venice about 1650. He passed some years in Paris, where he made globes twelve feet in diameter, (1683.) In 1685 he was chosen cosmographer of the Venetian state. He published many maps and volumes on geography, among which were a "Description of the Morea," (1685,) and "Ancient and Modern Rome," (1716.) Died in 1718.

See TIRABOSCHI, "Storia della Letteratura Italiana."

Coronini-Cronberg, von, fon ko-ro-nee'nee kRon'-bĕRG, (JOHANN,) COUNT, an Austrian general, born at Göritz in 1794. He was chosen preceptor to Francis Joseph (the present emperor) in 1836, and obtained the rank of field-marshal in 1849. In 1854 he was appointed commander of the army which occupied the Danubian principalities.

Corot, ko'ro', (JEAN BAPTISTE CAMILLE,) a successful French landscape-painter, born in Paris in 1796. Among his works are "The Roman Campagna," (1827,) a "Souvenir of the Environs of Florence," (1839,) "Homer and the Shepherds," (1845,) and a "Sunset Scene," (1857.)

Corr, (ERIN,) a Belgian engraver of high reputation, born at Brussels in 1803, was a son of an Irishman. He engraved "The Descent from the Cross," after Rubens, and several works of Van Dyck and Da Vinci. Died in Paris in 1862.

Corradi. See GHIRLANDAIO.

Corradi, kor-rä'dee, (OTTAVIO,) an Italian painter, born at Bologna. He copied the works of great masters with success. Died in 1643.

Corradini, kor-rä-dee'nee, (PIETRO MARCELLINO,) an Italian antiquary and jurist, born at Sezza in 1658. He was made a cardinal in 1712. Among his works is "Ancient Latium, Sacred and Profane," ("Vetus Latium profanum et sacrum," 1704.) Died in 1743.

See TIPALDO, "Biografia degli Italiani illustri."

Corrado, the Italian of CONRAD, which see.

Corrado, kor-rä'do, (CARLO,) an Italian painter, born in Naples in 1693, was employed for some years by the King of Spain at Madrid. Died in 1768.

Corrado, (SEBASTIANO,) an Italian scholar and writer, born in the duchy of Módena. He became professor of eloquence at Reggio in 1540, and professor of Greek and Latin in the University of Bologna in 1545. He published in 1537 an interesting work, entitled "Quæstura," in which the life of Cicero is related, and his character vindicated from unjust charges. Died in 1556.

See FILIPPO RE, "Elogio di S. Corrado," 1812; A. FAPPANI, "Elogio di S. Corrado," 1820;" "Nouvelle Biographie Générale."

Correa, kor-rä'ä, (D. PAYO PEREZ,) a renowned Portuguese general, was chosen grand master of the order of Santiago in 1242. He gained many victories over the Moors, and was reputed the greatest captain of his time. The old Spanish writers assert that he once arrested the course of the sun, like Joshua. Died in 1275.

See LACLÈDE, "Histoire de Portugal."

Correa, (GASPAR,) a Portuguese historian, served in several expeditions in the East Indies, and wrote a valuable "History of India," ("Historia da India," in manuscript.) Died at Goa about 1560.

Correa, (THOMÉ,) an eloquent Portuguese orator, poet, and grammarian, born at Coimbra in 1537. He professed rhetoric at Rome and Bologna with great success, and wrote treatises on eloquence, grammar, etc., among which was a commentary on Horace's "Art of Poetry." Died in 1595.

Correa de Saa, kor-rä'ä dà sä, (SALVADOR,) a distinguished Portuguese admiral, born about 1594. He was for many years Governor of Brazil, where, between 1625 and 1640, he gained several victories over the Dutch. In 1648 he commanded an expedition to Africa, and conquered Benguela and Angola. Died in 1680.

Correa de Serra, kor-rä'ä dà sĕr'rä, (JOSÉ FRANCISCO,) a distinguished Portuguese botanist and savant, born at Serpa in 1750. He was chosen perpetual secretary of the Academy of Sciences of Lisbon about 1780. To escape persecution for religion, he retired to France in 1786 and to England in 1795. About 1814 he supplied the place of Mr. Barton as professor of botany in Philadelphia. From 1816 to 1821 he was minister from Portugal to the United States. He was the author of some treatises on vegetable physiology and other subjects, and wrote several articles for the "Biographie Universelle." Died in 1823.

See "Nouvelle Biographie Générale."

Correa Garção, kor-rä'ä gaR-sŏwn', (PEDRO ANTONIO,) a Portuguese poet, born about 1750, was the author of lyric poems which are in style excellent imitations of

ă, ē, ī, ō, ū, ȳ, *long;* à, è, ò, same, less prolonged; ă, ĕ, ĭ, ŏ, ŭ, ȳ, *short;* ą, ę, į, ǫ, *obscure;* fär, fåll, fåt; mĕt; nŏt; gŏŏd; mōōn;

Horace. "No one," says Longfellow, "since Ferreira had approached so near the ancient prototype."

See LONGFELLOW's "Poets and Poetry of Europe."

Correggio, da, dä kor-rĕd'jo, [Fr. LE CORRÈGE, lĕh koʀ'ʀȧzh': it may be observed that in French he is nearly always called LE CORRÈGE, in Italian IL CORREGGIO, *i.e.* "the Correggio,"] (ANTONIO **Allegri**—äl-lȧ'gʀee,) an illustrious Italian painter, the founder of a new and original style of art, was born at Correggio (whence his surname) in 1494. We have little positive information respecting him. Vasari and others state that his origin was humble and that his life was passed in poverty; but there is good reason to believe that he enjoyed a comfortable subsistence. Among his supposed teachers in art were his uncle, Lorenzo Allegri, and Francesco Bianchi; but he was the sole former of his own style. He probably never saw Rome or Venice. He worked at his native city and at Parma. He died in 1534. Correggio not only surpassed all former artists in the magic of the chiaroscuro, but he was also distinguished by his admirable skill in foreshortening. His forms are exquisitely soft and beautiful; his colours are as pure and as delicate as those of Titian. The art which Angelo exalted to sublimity, which Titian enriched with the magic of colouring, and which Raphael inspired with the soul of expression and grace, may be said to have received its complement of perfection in the softness, tenderness, and harmony of Correggio. One of his masterpieces is the Assumption of the Virgin,—a fresco in the Cathedral of Parma. Among his admired oil-paintings are a Holy Family, known as "La Vierge au Panier;" an "Ecce Homo;" a picture of the Nativity, at Dresden, called "Notte," or "Night;" and a Saint Jerome, which Annibal Caracci preferred to Raphael's Saint Cecilia, One of his most remarkable productions is a "Penitent Magdalen," in the gallery at Dresden: for this picture, only about eighteen inches square, one of the Saxon kings is said to have paid 6000 louis-d'ors, (30,000 dollars.) His representations of women and children are especially admirable. Many of his female countenances possess an ineffable and almost divine beauty. Correggio is said to have been remarkably modest. After gazing on a production of Raphael, he exclaimed, exultingly, *Anch'io son' pittore!* ("I also am a painter!") "The harmony of Correggio," says Fuseli, "though assisted by exquisite hues, was entirely independent of colour: his great organ was *chiaro oscuro* in its most extensive sense. The bland light of a globe gliding through lucid demi-tints into rich reflected shades, composes the spell which pervades all his performances." The celebrated Danish poet Oehlenschläger has made Correggio the subject of one of his most successful tragedies.

See "Memorie istoriche di A. Allegri detto il Correggio," Parma, 1817; VASARI, "Lives of the Painters," etc.; "Lives of Correggio and Parmegiano," London, 1823; "Biographie Universelle;" "Nouvelle Biographie Générale."

Correggio, kor-rä'jo, (GIBERTO,) an able chief of the Guelph party, who in 1303 obtained the sovereignty of Parma. He was expelled in 1316. Died in 1321.

Cor're-us, a chief of the Bellovaci, a tribe of Gaul, who, at the head of an army, encountered Cæsar, and, after a brave resistance, was killed.

Cor'rie, (DANIEL,) an English clergyman, born about 1776, became Bishop of Madras in 1834. He translated part of the Bible into Hindostanee. Died in 1837.

See "Memoirs of Daniel Corrie," by his brothers, 1847.

Corrodi, kor-ro'dee, (HENRY,) a learned Swiss writer, born at Zurich in 1752. He published (in German) a number of works on philosophy and theology, among which is a "History of Millenarism,"(1781.) Died in 1793.

See L. MEISTER, "Lebensbeschreibung H. Corrodi's," 1793.

Corse, (JOHN M.,) an American general, who, in October, 1864, defended Allatoona with success against a superior force of Confederate troops, while General Sherman, from the top of Kenesaw Mountain, signalled that he should hold out to the last. He commanded a division of Sherman's army in its march through Georgia and Carolina.

Corsetti, koR-set'tee, (FRANCESCO,) an Italian poet, born at Sienna about 1700; died in 1774.

Corsignani, koR-sèn-yȧ'nee, (PIETRO ANTONIO,) an Italian historian, born at Celano in 1686; died in 1751.

Corsini, koR-see'nee, (ANDREA,) born at Florence in 1302, was renowned for his piety and ascetic life. He became Bishop of Fiesole about 1360. Died in 1373.

See F. VENTURI, "Vita di S. A. Corsini," 1620; ANGULO, "Vida di S. A. Corsini," 1630.

Corsini, (EDOARDO,) an eminent Italian antiquary and monk, born at Fanano in 1702. In 1735 he became professor of logic, and in 1746 of moral philosophy, at Pisa. He published "Fasti Attici," (1744-56, 4 vols.,) a capital work on Grecian chronology and history, and other antiquarian treatises. Died at Pisa in 1765.

See TIPALDO, "Biografia degli Italiani illustri."

Corsini, (LORENZO.) See CLEMENT XII.

Cort, koRt, (CORNELIUS,) a skilful Dutch designer and engraver, born at Horn about 1530. After visiting Venice about 1566, and engraving some works of Titian, he settled in Rome, where he opened a school of engraving. He produced many prints after various masters, among which is "The Transfiguration of Raphael." Died in Rome in 1578.

See NAGLER, "Neues Allgemeines Künstler-Lexikon."

Cort, (HENRY,) an English mechanician, who effected great improvements in the manufacture of iron, was born at Lancaster in 1740; died in 1800.

See SMILES, "Industrial Biography."

Cortambert, koR'tôN'baiR', (PIERRE FRANÇOIS EUGÈNE,) a French geographer and writer, born at Toulouse in 1805.

Corte, (CESARE and VALERIO.) See CORTI.

Corte, de la, dä la koR'tä, (JUAN,) a skilful Spanish painter of landscapes and battles, born at Madrid in 1597; died in 1660. His son, GABRIEL, (1648-94,) was a painter of flowers.

Corte-Murari, della, del'lä koR'tä moo-rä'ree, (GIROLAMO,) COUNT, an Italian poet, born at Mantua in 1747; died in 1832.

Cortenaer or **Cortenaar,** koR'teh-nȧR', (EGBERT,) a famous Dutch admiral. He distinguished himself as captain in a battle against the Swedes in 1658, and was killed near Lestoff in 1665.

Cortenovis, koR-tä-no'vèss, (ANGELO MARIA,) an Italian antiquary, born at Bergamo in 1727, wrote a treatise "On the Purple of the Ancients." Died in 1801.

Corte-Real or **Cortereal,** koR-tä-rä-äl', (GASPAR,) a Portuguese navigator, commanded in 1500 an exploring expedition to the region since called Canada. In 1501 he again sailed from Lisbon towards the Arctic regions, and was never afterwards heard of.

See "Nouvelle Biographie Générale."

Corte-Real, (JERONYMO,) a Portuguese poet, composed several admired poems, of which the "Shipwreck of Sepulveda" (1594) is the most popular. Died in 1593.

See SISMONDI, "Histoire de la Littérature du Midi de l'Europe."

Cortés. See CORTEZ.

Cortés, (DONOSO.) See DONOSO CORTÉS.

Cortés, koR-tĕs', (MARTIN,) a Spanish geographer, who lived at Cadiz, published in 1561 an excellent work on geography and navigation, called "Breve Compendio de la Esfera y de la Arte de navegar."

Cortese. See CORTEZ.

Cortese, koR-tä'sȧ, (GIULIO CESARE,) an Italian poet, born in the kingdom of Naples about 1570. He wrote several facetious and satirical poems, one of which, called the "Vajasseide," (1604,) passed through sixteen editions in fourteen years.

See GINGUENÉ, "Histoire Littéraire d'Italie."

Cortesi. See COURTOIS, (JACQUES.)

Cortesius. See CORTEZ.

Cor'tez, [Sp. CORTÉS, koR-tĕs'; It. CORTESE, koR-tä'sȧ; Lat. CORTE'SIUS,] (HERNANDO (or HERNAN) or FERNANDO,) the conqueror of Mexico, was born at Medellin, a village of Estremadura, in Spain, in 1485. Resolving to seek his fortune in the New World, he sailed to Hispaniola in 1504, and became a planter. He displayed courage and ability in the conquest of Cuba, which Velasquez began in 1511, and was rewarded with an estate in that island. In 1518 he was appointed by Velasquez commander of an expedition sent against Mexico, which had just been discovered, and which presented a most brilliant theatre for ambition and enterprise. The armada, which consisted of eleven vessels, ten cannon, and about seven hundred men, sailed from Cuba in February, 1519, its primary ostensible object being the conversion of the infidels. This process he initiated by a battle at Tabasco, where he defeated a native army. He next landed on the site of the present Vera Cruz, where he made friendly demonstrations and learned that he had entered the wide empire of Montezuma. The Aztec artists by their picture-writing informed the monarch of the arrival of the Spaniards. Having destroyed his ships, in order that his soldiers might be forced to conquer or perish, Cortez marched to Mexico, or Tenochtitlan, the capital of Anahuac, which, after several bloody victories over the Tlascalans, he entered in November, 1519, without resistance. Montezuma, after receiving them with due hospitality, was made prisoner by his audacious guests in his own palace. He was induced to swear allegiance to the emperor Charles V., and to pay an immense tribute in gold and silver; but he refused to profess the creed of the Spaniards. In the mean time, Velasquez, jealous of the success of Cortez, whom he regarded as a rival or rebel, sent against him an army of about 1000 men, under Narvaez, who arrived in Vera Cruz in April, 1520. Leaving a small garrison in the capital, Cortez marched with about 250 men against Narvaez, whom he defeated and took prisoner near Zempoalla in 1520. Having persuaded the soldiers of Narvaez to join his standard, Cortez returned to Mexico, which he found in revolt against him. After several days of severe fighting, in which Montezuma was mortally wounded by the natives, the Spaniards were expelled from the city of Mexico, with a loss of several hundred men. The great victory at Otumba in July, 1520, restored the ascendency of Cortez, and in 1521 he again became master of the capital, where he committed acts of infamous atrocity, and the conquest of Mexico was completed. In 1522 he was appointed by the Spanish court Governor and Captain-General of New Spain, (Mexico.) In 1525 he executed Guatemozin, the last emperor of the Aztecs. To vindicate himself from the accusations of his enemies, he returned in 1528 to Spain, where he was graciously received by Charles V.; but when he went again to Mexico, in 1530, he no longer had the supremacy there. An exploring expedition which he fitted out discovered California in 1535. He revisited Spain in 1540, and took part in the disastrous invasion of Algiers in 1541. Died at Seville in 1547. His virtues and vices are thus summed up by Prescott: "He was avaricious, yet liberal; bold to desperation, yet cautious and calculating in his plans; magnanimous, yet very cunning; lax in his notions of morality, yet a sad bigot. The great feature in his character was constancy of purpose."

See Robertson, "History of America;" Prescott, "History of the Conquest of Mexico;" "Despatches of Hernando Cortes," New York, 1843; Antonio de Solis y Ribadeneyra, "Historia de la Conquista del Mexico," 1684; English version of the same, by Thomas Townsend, 1724; Gomara, "Historia de F. Cortez," Rome, 1556; Carl Curths, "F. Cortez der Eroberer Mexiko's," 1818; "Lives of Nuñez de Balboa, Hernan Cortes, and Francis Pizarro," 1847.

Corti, kor'tee, or **Corte,** kor'tà, (Cesare,) a painter of portraits and history, was born at Genoa about 1554; died about 1612.

Corti, [Lat. Cur'tius,] (Matteo,) an Italian medical writer, born at Pavia in 1475; died in 1542.

Corti or **Corte,** (Valerio,) an Italian portrait-painter of merit, born at Venice in 1530, was a pupil of Titian. Died at Genoa about 1580. His son Marcantonio was an excellent designer.

Corticelli, kor-te-chel'lee, (Salvadore,) an eminent Italian philologist, born at Piacenza in 1690. He produced an excellent Italian grammar, (1745,) which, says Roquefort, "is the best in the language." Died in 1758.

See Tipaldo, "Biografia degli Italiani illustri."

Cortona, da, dà kor-to'nà, (Pietro Berrettini,)[Fr. Pierre de Cortone, pe-aiR' deh koR'ton',] an eminent Italian painter, born at Cortona about 1600. He painted some pictures in the Pitti palace, Florence, and afterwards settled in Rome, where he worked with success. He excelled in composition, and had a certain freedom and facility of style. Mengs, however, says that he neglected the study of principles founded on reason, and aimed

only to gratify the eye of the spectator. He was also architect of several Roman edifices. Died in Rome in 1669. Among his oil-paintings is "The Conversion of Saint Paul." The Barberini palace, Rome, contains one of his principal frescos.

See Lanzi, "History of Painting in Italy;" Bryan, "Dictionary of Painters."

Cortone, de. See Cortona.

Cortot, kor'to', (Jean Pierre,) a French sculptor, born in Paris in 1787, won the first prize of the Institute in 1809. Among his finest works are "The Soldier of Marathon" and the bas-relief which adorns the Chamber of Deputies. Died in 1843.

Cortusi, koR-too'see, (Giacomo Antonio,) an Italian botanist, and director of the botanic garden at Padua. He published a description of the plants growing in that garden, (1591.) Died in 1593.

Cor-un-cā'nǐ-us, (Tiberius,) an eminent Roman jurist and senator, was elected consul in 280 B.C., and pontifex maximus about 254. He was the first plebeian who attained the latter dignity. His talents and virtues are highly praised by Cicero. He was appointed dictator in 246 B.C., soon after which he died.

See Cicero, "De Legibus," and "De Oratore;" Wuerffel, "Commentatio de T. Coruncanio," 1740.

Corvetto, di, de koR-vet'to, (Luigi Emmanuele,) Count, a financier, born at Genoa in 1756. In 1805 he became a member of Bonaparte's council of state. From 1815 to 1818 he was minister of finance in France. Died in 1822.

See Solari, "Elogio storico del Conte L. E. di Corvetto," 1824.

Corvi, koR'vee, (Domenico,) an Italian painter, born at Viterbo in 1623, excelled in nocturnal scenes. Died in 1703.

Corvin. See Corvinus.

Corvinus, koR-vee'nûs, (Johann August,) a German engraver, born about 1682, worked for booksellers of Augsburg. Died in 1738.

Cor-vi'nus, [Fr. Corvin, koR'vǎn',] (Matthias,) King of Hungary, born at Klausenburg in 1443, was the son of John Huniades. He was elected king in 1458. His reign was marked by a series of wars with the emperor Ferdinand III., the Turks, and the Kings of Poland and Bohemia. In the intervals of peace he promoted the arts and sciences. He was eminent for military talents, and made himself master of Austria and Vienna in 1485. He died at Vienna in 1490, leaving the reputation of a wise ruler. Vladislaus, King of Bohemia, was his successor.

See Turotz, "Chronica Hungaria;" Galeottus Martius, "De Dictis et Factis Regis Matthiæ;" Fessler, "Matthias König von Hungarn," 1793; Wenzel, "Matthias Corvinus," 1810.

Corvisart-Desmarets, kor've'zǎR' dà'mǎ'rà', (Jean Nicolas,) an eminent French physician, born in Champagne in 1755. Having attended the lectures of Petit, Desault, and others, he was received as docteur-régent of the faculty in 1782. In 1788 he was chosen professor of clinic at the hospital La Charité, and in 1797 professor of practical medicine in the College of France. He was very successful as a lecturer, and had a rare sagacity in diagnosis. About 1800 he was appointed chief physician to Bonaparte, and a few years later received the title of Baron. He published an "Essay on the Diseases and Organic Lesions of the Heart," (1808,) and other works. Bonaparte once said he "was an honest and able man, but rather blunt," (brusque.) Died in 1821.

See Ferrus, "Notice sur Corvisart," 1821; "Biographie Médicale;" "Nouvelle Biographie Générale."

Cor'vus, (M. Valerius,) a famous Roman general, born about 370 B.C. He was chosen consul in 348, and was re-elected five times. In 343 he gained two important victories over the Samnites near Gaurus and Suessula. He was chosen dictator in 342. Again summoned to the dictatorship in 301 B.C., he defeated the Marsi and Etruscans. He was elected consul the sixth time in 299. Died about 270 B.C.

See Valerius Maximus; Niebuhr, "History of Rome."

Cor'win, (Thomas,) an American statesman and orator, born in Bourbon county, Kentucky, in July, 1794. His parents removed to Ohio while he was a boy. He studied law, was admitted to the bar about 1818, and soon acquired celebrity as a lawyer and an orator. He supported John Quincy Adams for the Presidency in 1828, was elected a member of Congress by the voters of the Warren district in 1830, and acted with the Whig party. In 1840 he advocated the election of General Harrison by numerous speeches at mass-meetings, for which his popular style of oratory was especially adapted. He was elected Governor of Ohio for two years in October, 1840, and represented that State in the Senate of the United States from 1845 to 1850. He opposed the Mexican war, on which he made an able speech in 1846. In July, 1850, he was appointed secretary of the treasury by President Fillmore. On his retirement from office, March, 1853, he resumed the practice of law at Lebanon, Ohio. He was elected a member of Congress for the seventh district of Ohio in October, 1858, and again in 1860; but soon after the latter date (in 1861) he was sent as minister to Mexico. He returned home in 1864, and died at Washington in December, 1865.

Cor′ў-ạt or **Cor′ў-ạte,** (GEORGE,) an English clergyman, noted as a writer of Latin verse, became rector of Odcombe about 1570. Died in 1606.

Coryat or **Coryate,** (THOMAS,) an eccentric Englishman, a son of the preceding, was born at Odcombe rectory in 1577. In 1608 he traversed France, Italy, and Germany on foot, and published, in 1611, "Crudities hastily gobbled up in Five Months' Travel, etc." This work was accompanied by numerous pieces of humorous or ironical verse by Jonson, Drayton, Chapman, and many other poets. In his youth he appears to have officiated as court jester, or king's fool, in the service of Henry, Prince of Wales. Between 1612 and 1617 he journeyed on foot through Palestine and Persia to Hindostan. Died at Surat in 1617.

See "Retrospective Review," vol. vi., 1822.

Cor-ў-ban′tēs, [Gr. Κορύβαντες,] the priests of Cybele, sometimes called also GALLI. They celebrated the festivals of Cybele with orgiastic dances and loud cries, beating on timbrels, clashing cymbals, and cutting their flesh with knives.

Cosa, de la, dà lä ko′sä, (JUAN,) a Spanish navigator, who served Columbus as pilot in his second voyage to America. He was skilful in the construction of maps or charts. He was killed by some natives at Tabasco in 1509.

Cosimo, koš′e-mo, (JACOPO or GIACOMO,) a celebrated engraver of gems and cameos, was born at Trezzo, in the Milanese. He worked at Madrid for Philip II.

Cosimo, (PIETRO,) an Italian painter of high reputation, also called ROSSELLI, was born at Florence in 1441. He excelled in bacchanalian scenes. Died about 1525.

Cosimo de′ Medici. See MEDICI.

Cosin or **Cozen,** kuz′ẹn, (JOHN,) an English divine, born at Norwich in 1594. He became Dean of Peterborough in 1640. During the civil war he retired to Paris, where he preached several years. About 1660 he returned, and was appointed Bishop of Durham. He published "A Scholastic History of the Canon of Holy Scripture," and other works. Died in 1672.

Cosini, ko-šee′nee, (SILVIO,) an able sculptor, a pupil of Michael Angelo, born near Florence, lived about 1550.

Cos′mas, [Gr. Κοσμᾶς,] an Egyptian geographer, surnamed INDICOPLEUS′TES, ("Indian navigator,") lived about 540 A.D. In his youth he was a merchant, and made voyages to India and other countries. He afterwards became a monk at Alexandria, and wrote, in Greek, several works, one of which, entitled "Christian Topography," (Τοπογραφία Χριστιανική,) is still extant. He argues that the earth is not spherical.

See FABRICIUS, "Bibliotheca Græca;" MANNERT, "Géographie des Anciens."

Cosmas OF JERUSALEM, a poet and monk of the eighth century, wrote thirteen Greek hymns, which are extant.

Cosmas [Fr. COSME, kŏm] OF PRAGUE, born in 1045, was the earliest historian of Bohemia whose work has come down to us. He was a priest, and secretary to Henry IV. of Germany. About 1125 he finished his "Bohemian Chronicle," ("Chronicon Bohemorum.") Died in 1126.

Cosme OF PRAGUE. See COSMAS.

Cosme, kŏm, (JEAN BASEILHAC,) called FRÈRE COSME, a French surgeon, born in the diocese of Tarbes in 1703,

lived mostly in Paris. He was reputed one of the first lithotomists of his time in France, and invented an instrument used in lithotomy. Died in 1781.

Cosmico, kos′me-ko, (NICCOLÒ HELIO,) a Latin poet, born at Padua about 1440; died in 1489.

Cosmo (or **Cosimo**) **de′ Medici.** See MEDICI.

Cosnac, de, dẹh kos′nȧk′, (DANIEL,) a French bishop, noted for his address, vivacity, and talent for intrigue, was born in Limousin about 1630. He became Archbishop of Aix in 1687. Died in 1708. He left "Mémoires," which were published in 1852.

See ABBÉ CHOISY, "Mémoires," liv. viii.; SAINT-SIMON, "Mémoires;" SAINTE-BEUVE, "Causeries du Lundi," tome vi.; "Nouvelle Biographie Générale."

Cospéan, de, dẹh kos′pȧ′ŏn′, sometimes incorrectly written **Cospeau,** (PHILIPPE,) a Flemish prelate, born in Hainaut in 1568, was eminent as a preacher. Moréri gives him credit for purging the pulpit of quotations from profane authors. He became Bishop of Nantes in 1622. Died in 1646.

See RENÉ LEMÉE, "Le Prélat accompli, ou la Vie de P. de Cospéan," 1646; R. BORDEAUX, "Notice relative à P. Cospeau," 1852.

Cospeau. See COSPÉAN.

Cosroes. See KHOSROO.

Cossa. See JOHN XXIII., (Pope.)

Cossale, kos-sä′lä, or **Cozzale,** kot-sä′lä, (ORAZIO,) an Italian painter, lived at Brescia about 1600.

Cossali, kos-sä′lee, (PIETRO,) an Italian geometer and Theatin friar, born at Verona in 1748, was professor of natural philosophy and astronomy at Parma, and afterwards of mathematics at Padua. He wrote, besides other works, a "Critical History of Algebra," (2 vols., 1779,) which was highly prized. Died in 1815.

See TIPALDO, "Biografia degli Italiani illustri."

Cossart, ko′sȧr′, (GABRIEL,) a learned French Jesuit, born at Pontoise in 1615; died in 1674.

Cossé, de, dẹh ko′sȧ′, (ARTHUR or ARTUS,) Comte de Secondigny, (sẹh-kòn′dèn′ye′,) a French general, born about 1512. He became a marshal of France in 1567, after which he served in the civil wars against the Calvinists. Died in 1582.

See BRANTÔME, "Vies des grands Capitaines."

Cossé, de, (CHARLES,) Comte de Brissac, (bRe′sȧk′,) an able French general, brother of the preceding, born in Anjou about 1505. Having served in several campaigns in Italy and Flanders, he was made grand master of artillery in 1547. In 1550 he became a marshal of France, after which he fought successfully in Piedmont against the Spaniards. He died about 1564, with the reputation of one of the greatest captains of his age.

See DE THOU, "Mémoires;" BRANTÔME, "Vies des grands Capitaines."

Cossé, de, (CHARLES,) Duc de Brissac, a son of the preceding, was a partisan of the League against Henry III., and was the first who employed the Barricades in Paris, (1588.) He was appointed by the Duke of Mayenne governor of Paris, which he surrendered to Henry IV. in 1594. He was afterwards made a marshal and a duke. Died in 1621.

See PÉRÉFIXE, "Vie de Henri IV."

Cossé, de, (LOUIS HERCULE TIMOLÉON,) Duc de Brissac, a French royalist, born in 1734. He was appointed commandant of the royal guard in 1791, and was massacred in September, 1792.

Cossiers, ko′se-à′, (JEAN,) a Flemish historical painter, born at Antwerp in 1603, was patronized by the King of Spain. Among his best works is a "Presentation in the Temple." Died in 1652.

Cossigny de Palma, ko′sèn′ye′ dẹh pȧl′mȧ′, (JOSEPH′ FRANÇOIS,) a French naturalist, born at Palma, in the Isle of France, in 1730. He published a "Treatise on the Fabrication of Indigo," (1779,) and other esteemed scientific works. Died in Paris in 1809.

Cossin, ko′sȧn′, (LOUIS,) a French engraver, born at Troyes in 1633; died at Paris in 1682.

Cos′sus, (AULUS CORNELIUS,) a patrician Roman general, who was appointed dictator in 385 B.C., during the Volscian war. He gained a decisive victory over the Volscians soon after that date, and on his return to Rome committed Manlius Capitolinus to prison.

See LIVY, "History of Rome."

є as *k;* ç as *s;* ḡ *hard;* ġ as *j;* G, H, K, *guttural;* N, *nasal;* R, *trilled;* s̄ as *z;* th as in *this.* (☞ See Explanations, p. 23.)

43

Cossus, (SERVIUS CORNELIUS,) a Roman warrior, who killed in single combat Lar Tolumnius, King of the Veii, about 437 B.C. He was the second person among the Romans that obtained the *spolia opima*. He was chosen consul in 428 B.C.

See NIEBUHR, "History of Rome."

Cossutius, kos-su'she-us, a Roman architect of high reputation, lived about 170 B.C. He was the first Roman who built in the Greek manner. He rebuilt the grand temple of Jupiter Olympius at Athens.

See PLINY, "Natural History," book xxxvi.; FÉLIBIEN, "Vies des plus célèbres Architectes."

Costa, kos'tä, (LORENZO,) THE ELDER, an Italian painter, born at Ferrara about 1450; died about 1530.

Costa, (MICHELE,) an Italian composer, born in Naples in 1810. Among his chief works are "Don Carlos," an opera, and "Eli," an oratorio.

Costa, (PAOLO,) an Italian writer, born at Ravenna in 1771, was one of the editors of the "Great Dictionary of the Italian Language," (1819-26.) He published two editions of Dante, (1819 and 1830,) and wrote various works, among which is a novel called "Demetrio di Modone." Died in 1836.

See RAMBELLI, "Elogio di P. Costa," 1837; FILIPPO MORDANI, "Biografia di P. Costa," 1840.

Costa, da. See DA COSTA.

Costa, da, dä kos'tä, (ANTONIO RODRIGUEZ,) a Portuguese historian, born at Setuval in 1656; died in 1732.

Costa, da, dä kos'tä, (CLAUDIO MANOEL,) a Brazilian poet, born in 1729. He was educated at Coimbra, and returned to Brazil. He wrote "Villarica," and other poems, which are commended. Died in 1789.

Costa-Cabral, da, dä kos'tä kä-bräl', (ANTONIO BERNARDO,) Count de Thomar, (to-maR',) a Portuguese politician, born in 1803, was several times prime minister between 1838 and 1851.

Costa de Beauregard, de, deh kos'tä' deh bor'gäR', (JOSEPH HENRI,) MARQUIS, a general and historian, born in Savoy in 1752, was educated at Paris. He fought against the French between 1792 and 1800. He published (in French) "Historical Memoirs of the House of Savoy." Died in 1824.

Costa e Sylva, da, dä kos'tä ä sèl'vä, (JOZÉ MARIA,) a Portuguese poet and critic, born in 1788. He wrote "The Sepulchre of Mary," and other poems. His principal work is a "Biographical and Critical Essay on the Best Portuguese Poets," ("Ensaio biographico-critico sobre os melhores Poetas Portuguezas," 7 vols., 1850-54,) which he did not live to finish. Died in 1854.

See "Nouvelle Biographie Générale."

Costanzi, kos-tän'zee, (CARLO,) a skilful engraver on precious stones, born in Naples in 1703, worked in Rome. He copied antique gems with great success, and engraved on diamonds a Leda, and a head of Antinoüs. "Few artists," says the "Biographie Universelle," "have received from their contemporaries so many testimonials of admiration."

See NAGLER, "Neues Allgemeines Künstler-Lexikon."

Costanzi, (PLACIDO,) an Italian painter, born at Rome in 1688; died in 1759.

Costanzo, di, de kos-tän'zo, (ANGELO,) a popular Italian historian and lyric poet, born at Naples about 1507. He published in 1582 a "History of the Kingdom of Naples from 1250 to 1489," which, says Ginguené, "is regarded as one of the best works on that subject." As a poet he held a high rank among his contemporaries. The Academy of Arcadians, near the close of the seventeenth century, selected him as the best model for imitation. Died about 1590.

See TIRABOSCHI, "Storia della Letteratura Italiana;" LONGFELLOW, "Poets and Poetry of Europe."

Cos'tard, (GEORGE,) an English clergyman, noted as an Oriental and classical scholar, was born in 1710. He became Fellow and tutor of Wadham College, Oxford, about 1733, and vicar of Twickenham in 1764. His principal work is a "History of Astronomy," (1767,) which obtained a wide reputation. Died in 1782.

Coste. See LACOSTE.

Coste, kost, (JEAN FRANÇOIS,) an eminent French physician, born at Ville (Ain) in 1741. He was chief physician of the French army which fought for the United States in 1778-83. In 1790 he displayed courage and firmness as mayor of Versailles. He was physician-in-chief of the grand army in the campaigns of Austerlitz, Jena, and Eylau, (1805-09.) He published a treatise on "Military Hospitals," and other able works. Died in 1819.

See "Biographie Médicale;" "Nouvelle Biographie Générale;" REGNAULT, "Notice sur J. F. Coste," 1819.

Coste, (JEAN JACQUES CYPRIEN VICTOR,) a French naturalist, born at Castries in 1807, was professor of embryology (*embryogénie*) in Paris, and became a member of the Academy of Sciences in 1851. He published a "Voyage of Exploration on the Coasts of France and Italy," (1855,) and other works.

Coste, (PIERRE,) a French *littérateur* and Protestant, born at Uzès in 1668, took refuge in England about 1700. He translated into French Locke's great work, and Newton's "Optics," and edited several French authors. Died in Paris in 1747.

Coste, kost, (XAVIER PASCAL,) a French architect, born at Marseilles in 1787, was employed by the Viceroy of Egypt from 1818 to 1827. He published a magnificent work entitled "Arabian Architecture, or Monuments of Cairo," (1827.)

Costello, (LOUISA STUART,) a popular authoress, was born in Ireland in 1815. She wrote, among other works, "Summer amongst the Bocages and Vines," (1840) a "Pilgrimage to Auvergne," (1842,) "Memoirs of Eminent Englishwomen," (4 vols., 1844,) and "The Rose Garden of Persia," an admired translation from the Persian poets, (1845.)

Costeo, kos-tä'o, [Lat. COSTÆ'US,] (GIOVANNI,) an Italian physician and writer, born at Lodi; died at Bologna in 1603.

Cos'ter, [Lat. COSTE'RUS,] (BERNARD,) a Dutch historical writer, born at Woerden in 1645; died in 1735.

Coster, kos'tä', (JOSEPH FRANÇOIS,) a meritorious French economist and financier, born at Nancy in 1729, filled the position of chief clerk (*premier commis*) of the finances under eleven successive ministers. He wrote an "Éloge de Colbert," and other works. Died in 1813.

See "Nouvelle Biographie Générale;" BLAU, "Éloge de M. Coster," 1808.

Coster or **Costar,** (LAURENT JANSZOON.) See KOSTER.

Coster, (SAMUEL,) M.D., an eminent Dutch dramatic poet, called the founder of the theatre of Amsterdam, was born about 1580 or 1590. He produced five comedies and six tragedies between 1615 and 1644. His "Iphigenia," a tragedy, (1626,) was perhaps the most popular of his works. "His characters," says the "Biographie Universelle," "are well sustained, and his style is often noble and energetic."

See JÖCHER, "Allgemeines Gelehrten-Lexikon."

Costha-Ben-Louka. See KOSTA-IBN-LOOKA.

Cos'way, (RICHARD,) a successful English painter, born at Tiverton in 1740, was a pupil of Hudson. He had great skill in miniature-painting, in which he was employed by persons of the highest rank. Died in 1821. His wife, Maria Hadfield, was an excellent portrait-painter and musician. Her musical parties in London were frequented by the noble and fashionable, attracted partly by the paintings and other works of art with which the house was profusely adorned.

Cota, ko'tä, (RODERIGO,) a Spanish poet, born at Toledo; died in 1470. He was the reputed author of the famous tragi-comedy "Calisto and Melibea," (sometimes called "Celestina,") and of "Mingo Rebulgo," a satire.

See TICKNOR, "History of Spanish Literature."

Cotan, ko-tän', (JUAN SANCHEZ,) a Spanish painter of flowers and fruit, born at Alcázar de San Juan in 1561; died in 1627.

Cotelerius. See COTELIER.

Cotelier, kot'le-à', [Lat. COTELE'RIUS,] (JEAN BAPTISTE,) a French Hellenist of great merit, born at Nîmes in 1627. As professor of Greek in the Royal College of Paris, he officiated with great distinction. He published "Monuments of the Greek Church," (3 vols., 1677-86,) and other works. Died in 1686.

See NICÉRON, "Mémoires."

ā, ē, ī, ō, ū, ȳ, *long;* ă, ĕ, ĭ, ŏ, ŭ, ў, *same, less prolonged;* ă, ĕ, ĭ, ŏ, ŭ, ў, *short;* ạ, ẹ, ị, ọ, *obscure;* fär, fäll, fät; mēt; nŏt; gŏŏd; mōōn;

Cōtes, (FRANCIS,) an English artist, born in London in 1725, was one of the founders of the Royal Academy. He was very successful as a portrait-painter, both in oil and in crayon. Died in 1770.

Cotes, (ROGER,) an eminent English mathematician, born at Burbage in 1682. He became Fellow of Trinity College, Cambridge, in 1705, and Plumian professor of astronomy in 1706. In 1713 he took orders, and published the second edition of Newton's "Principia," with a preface which was greatly admired. His premature death, in 1716, was deeply lamented by the learned. Newton exclaimed, "If Cotes had lived, we should have known something." He left a mathematical work,— "Harmonia Mensurarum," ("Harmony of Measures.")

Cotignola, da, dä ko-tên-yo'lä, (FRANCESCO,) an Italian painter, lived at Parma about 1520.

See VASARI, "Lives of the Painters."

Cotin, ko'tăN', (CHARLES,) a French author, born in Paris in 1604, owed the publicity of his name in a great measure to the satires of Boileau and Molière. He was almoner to the king, and a member of the French Academy. He was author of a volume of verses and of several prose works. Died in 1682.

See "Ménagiana."

Cot'man, (JOHN SELL,) an able English artist, born at Norwich in 1780. He gained a high reputation in engraving and architectural drawing. He published "Architectural Antiquities of Norfolk," (1812,) "Architectural Antiquities of Normandy," (1820,) and other works. His etchings are highly prized. Died in 1843.

Cotolendi, ko'to'lôN'de', (CHARLES,) a French littérateur, born at Aix or Avignon ; died about 1710. He wrote a "Life of Saint Francis de Sales," (1689,) and other works.

Coton. See COTTON.

Cotta, kot'tä, (BERNHARD,) a distinguished German geologist, born in Thuringia in 1808. He became professor in the school of mines at Freiberg in 1842. He wrote, besides other works, "Letters on the Cosmos of Humboldt," (1848–51,) and "Geological Letters from the Alps," (1850.) His theory of the production of organic bodies may be regarded as a refined and improved exhibition of Epicurean philosophy. He maintains that the higher organisms are developed from the lower.

Cot'ta, (CAIUS AURELIUS,) a Roman general, noted for his strict discipline, became consul in 252 B.C. He commanded with success against the Carthaginians in Sicily, and was elected consul again in 248.

Cotta, (CAIUS AURELIUS,) a Roman orator, born about 125 B.C. He obtained the consulship in 75 B.C., and the province of Gaul was allotted to him in the year 74. He was one of the most eminent orators of his time, and was one of the interlocutors in Cicero's "De Oratore." Died about 70 B.C.

Cotta, kot'tä, (GIOVANNI,) an Italian poet, born near Verona about 1480. He was for some time in the service of the Venetian general Alviano. "He acquired," says Ginguené, "by a small number of verses (in Latin) a high and merited reputation." Died in 1510. His "Carmina" were published with the poems of Sannazar in 1527.

See TIRABOSCHI, "Storia della Letteratura Italiana."

Cotta, (GIOVANNI BATTISTA,) an Italian poet and pulpit orator, born at Tende, near Nice, in 1668. He became professor of logic at Florence in 1693, and composed sonnets, hymns, and other poems. Died in 1738.

See LONGFELLOW, "Poets and Poetry of Europe;" GIACINTO DELLA TORRE, "Elogio storico di G. B. Cotta," 1738.

Cotta, (HEINRICH,) a German naturalist, father of Bernhard, noticed above, was born in 1763. He published "Principles of the Science of Forests," (1832,) and other scientific treatises. Died in 1844.

Cotta, (JOHANN FRIEDRICH,) an eminent German theologian, born at Tübingen in 1701. He was professor of Oriental languages at Göttingen, and subsequently of theology at Tübingen, (1740.) He wrote many works, among which was "Plan of a Complete Church History," ("Entwurf einer ausführlichen Kirchenhistorie," 1768,) and published an edition of Gerhard's "Loci Theologici," (1762–77.) Died in 1779.

See MEUSEL, "Gelehrtes Deutschland."

Cotta, (JOHANN FRIEDRICH,) Baron von Cottendorf, (kot'ten-dorf,) a distinguished publisher, born at Stuttgart in 1764, was a grandson of the preceding. In 1793 he founded at Tübingen the "Allgemeine Zeitung," an important daily journal, since published at Augsburg He became intimate with Goethe and Schiller, whose works he published, and with many other authors, of whom he was a liberal patron. He established a steampress at Augsburg in 1824, and introduced steam-navigation on the Rhine about 1825. Died in 1832.

See "Nouvelle Biographie Générale."

Cotta, (L. AURELIUS,) a brother of C. Aurelius, noticed above, became prætor in 70 B.C., and then procured the passage of the "lex Aurelia," which deprived the senate of the exclusive right to dispense justice. He was consul in the year 65, and supported Cicero against Catiline in 63. Cotta made the first motion in the senate for the recall of Cicero from exile. He sided with Cæsar in the civil war, 49 B.C.

See CICERO, "In Pisonem," Philippic II.

Cotta, (L. AURUNCULEIUS,) a Roman officer, who distinguished himself in Gaul as legate of Julius Cæsar. In 54 B.C. he and Sabinus commanded a body of troops encamped for the winter among the Eburones. He was killed during that winter, in a fight with the Gauls, who attacked his camp.

Cotta, (MARCUS AURELIUS,) a Roman general, was a brother of Caius Aurelius Cotta the orator. He became consul with L. Lucullus in 74 B.C., and obtained for his province Bithynia, then the seat of war against Mithridates, by whom he was defeated with great loss at Chalcedon.

Cotte, kot, (LOUIS,) an eminent French meteorologist, born at Laon in 1740. He was one of the first in France who made and recorded observations on the weather three times a day ; and he began to publish the results in 1765. He wrote a "Treatise on Meteorology," (1774,) and other works. Died in 1815.

See "Nouvelle Biographie Générale."

Cotte, de, deh kot, (ROBERT,) a French architect, born in Paris in 1656. He was appointed first architect of the king in 1708. Among his works are the colonnade of the Grand Trianon, and the gallery of the Hôtel de la Vrillière, now the Bank of France. Died in 1735.

See PINGERON, "Vies des Architectes."

Cottenham, kot'ten-am, (CHARLES CHRISTOPHER PEPYS,) EARL OF, an English statesman, born in 1781. He was appointed solicitor-general in 1833, and lord chancellor in the Whig ministry in 1836. Having been superseded in 1841, he again obtained the same office in August, 1846. He was raised to the peerage, as Baron Cottenham, in 1836, and created an earl in 1850, when he retired from office. Died in 1851.

See LORD CAMPBELL, "Lives of the Lord Chancellors;" Foss, "The Judges of England," vol. ix.

Cottereau, (JEAN,) See CHOUAN.

Cot'ter-el, (Sir CHARLES,) an English scholar, was master of requests to Charles II. He translated from the French La Calprenède's romance of "Cassandra," and from the Italian Davila's "History of the Civil Wars of France," (1647.)

See WOOD, "Athenæ Oxonienses."

Cottin, ko'tăN', (SOPHIE RISTAUD,) a Protestant French authoress, born at Tonneins in 1773. She was married at the age of seventeen to M. Cottin, a banker of Paris, and was left a widow after the lapse of three years. Gifted with a vivid imagination, she amused her solitude with composition, without aspiring to literary fame. Her first production was a romance named "Claire d'Albe," which was much admired. She afterwards wrote "Malvina," (1800,) "Amélie Mansfield," (1802,) and other popular novels, of which the best-known is "Elizabeth, or the Exiles of Siberia." Died in 1807.

See AUGUIS, "Notice historique sur la Vie, etc. de Madame Cottin ;" A. PETITOT, "Notice sur la Vie de Madame Cottin," 1817 ; "Edinburgh Review" for January, 1808 ; SAINTE-BEUVE, "Biographie portative des Contemporains."

Cot'tle, (AMOS,) an English poet, brother of Joseph Cottle, noticed below, translated the Icelandic "Edda" into English verse, and wrote some original poetry. Died in 1800.

ē as k; ç as s; g̃ hard; g̃ as j; G, H, K, guttural; N, nasal; R, trilled; s̃ as z; th as in this. (☞ See Explanations, p. 23.)

Cottle, (JOSEPH,) an English poet, born in 1770 or 1774, was a kind friend to Coleridge and Southey in their early adversities,—

"When friends were few, and fortune frowned."

In his youth he was a bookseller and publisher in Bristol. He published the first poems of the authors just named, in 1796. Southey, many years later, expressed his gratitude and esteem for his benefactor. Cottle was the author of "Malvern Hills," "Alfred," "The Fall of Cambria," and other poems, also of interesting "Reminiscences of Coleridge and Southey," (1847.) Died in 1853.

Cot′ṭọn, (CHARLES,) an English translator and humorous poet, born in Staffordshire in 1630, was an adopted son of Izaak Walton. He wrote an addition to the "Complete Angler," made an approved translation of Montaigne's "Essays," and composed several poems, among which are "The Wonders of the Peak," a "Voyage to Ireland," and "Virgil Travestie." The latter is a coarse and disgusting parody. Died in 1687.

See SIR J. HAWKINS, "Life of Cotton;" CIBBER, "Lives of the Poets;" "Biographia Britannica."

Cotton, (GEORGE,) an English divine of the present century, became Bishop of Calcutta in 1858. He was conspicuous for his zeal in discharging the duties of his office, and for his exertions in the cause of education. He was drowned in the Ganges in 1867.

See "British Quarterly Review" for January, 1867.

Cotton, (JOHN,) a learned English Puritan minister, born at Derby in 1585. He became vicar of a church at Boston (England) about 1612, and emigrated to Massachusetts in 1633. He afterwards preached at Boston, where he acquired great influence, and was an antagonist of Roger Williams, in reply to whom he asserted the right of magistrates to interfere in religion. Died in 1652.

See NORTON and MATHER, "Life of J. Cotton."

Cotton, (NATHANIEL,) an English poet and physician, born in 1707, was noted for his skill in the treatment of insanity. The poet Cowper, who was an inmate of his private lunatic-asylum at Saint Alban's, afterwards spoke of him in very favourable terms. He wrote "Marriage, a Vision," and other works, in prose and verse. Died in 1788.

See CAMPBELL, "Specimens of the British Poets."

Cotton, ko′tôN′, or **Coton,** (PIERRE,) an eminent French Jesuit, born at Néronde in 1564, became a popular preacher, and is said to have converted many Protestants. He was confessor of Henry IV. for some years before the death of that king, whose favour he enjoyed in a high degree. Somebody remarked that Henry "had *cotton* in his ears." He officiated as confessor to Louis XIII. from 1610 to 1617. Died in 1626.

See PÈRE D'ORLÉANS, "Vie de Cotton," 1688.

Cotton, (Sir ROBERT BRUCE,) an eminent English antiquary, the founder of the Cottonian Library, born at Denton, in Huntingdopshire, in 1570, graduated at Cambridge in 1585. He gave special attention to antiquarian researches, and to the collection of historical records and documents. At the accession of James I. (1603) he was knighted. He was often consulted and employed by the king and ministers, by whom he was regarded as an oracle. In 1628 he was a member of Parliament. He died in 1631, leaving to his heirs his valuable library, which was increased by his son, Sir Thomas, and was deposited in the British Museum about 1755. Sir Robert wrote a "Life of Henry III. of England," and many political and historical treatises.

See "Biographia Britannica;" "Life of Sir R. Cotton," prefixed to Dr. Smith's Catalogue of Cotton's Library, 1696.

Cotton, (STAPLETON.) See COMBERMERE.

Cotton, (Sir SYDNEY,) an English general, born in 1792, served in India during the mutiny of 1857–58, and was knighted for his services in that crisis.

Cottret, ko′trả′, (PIERRE MARIE,) a French bishop and writer, born at Argenteuil in 1768; died in 1841.

Cotugno, ko-toon′yo, (DOMENICO,) an eminent anatomist, born at Ruvo, in the kingdom of Naples, in 1736. He became surgeon of the Hospital of Incurables in Naples in 1754, and professor of anatomy in the University in 1766. He was afterwards employed by the royal family. Among his most important works are a "Treat-ise on the Anatomy of the Internal Ear," (1761,) and one on "Sciatica," (1765.) He made some discoveries in anatomy. Died at Naples in 1822.

See "Biographie Médicale;" FOLINEA, "Elogio del Cavaliere D. Cotugno," 1823.

Co′tỹs, [Gr. Κότυς,] a king of Thrace, waged war against the Athenians. Died about 356 B.C.

Couailhac, koo′ȧ′lȧk′, (LOUIS,) a French dramatist and journalist, born at Cahors in 1810.

Couch, (DARIUS N.,) an American general, born in Putnam county, New York, about 1822, graduated at West Point in 1846. He was appointed a brigadier-general of volunteers about August, 1861. He commanded a division at Fair Oaks, May 31–June 1, became a major-general in July, 1862, and directed a corps at Chancellorsville, May 3–5, 1863. He commanded the Department of the Susquehanna from June, 1863, to December, 1864.

Couch, (RICHARD QUILLAR,) an English naturalist and surgeon, born in Cornwall in 1816. He practised at Penzance, and wrote a number of essays on marine animals, and on the geology of Cornwall. Died in 1863.

Coucke, kŏw′keh, (JEAN,) a Belgian landscape-painter of the present century, was born at Ghent. His works are dated from 1808 to 1834.

Coucy, de, deh koo′se′, (RAOUL or RENAUD,) a French minstrel, who went to Palestine as a crusader, and was killed in battle in 1192. He wrote a number of songs, which were once popular.

See LA BORDE, "Mémoires historiques sur Raoul de Coucy," etc., Paris, 1781.

Coucy, de, (ROBERT,) a famous French architect, born at Rheims (or Coucy, according to some authorities.) He was chief architect of the cathedral of Rheims, a master-piece of the Gothic style, and of the church of Saint-Nicaise, in the same city, both of which had been begun by Libergier. Died in 1311.

See D. MARLOT, "Histoire de la Ville de Reims," 1846.

Couder, koo′daiʀ′, (LOUIS CHARLES AUGUSTE,) a French historical painter, born in Paris about 1790, was a pupil of David. He established his reputation by the "Levite of Ephraim," (1817.) His "Soldier of Marathon" is admired for grandeur of style. Among his later productions are "The Battle of Laufeld," (1836,) and "The Oath at the Tennis-Court," (1848.) He was admitted into the Institute in 1839.

Coudray, du. See TRONÇON.

Coudrette, koo′dʀĕt′, (CHRISTOPHE,) a French priest, born in Paris in 1701. He became an adversary of the order of Jesuits, and wrote, besides other works, a "History of the Rise and Progress of the Jesuits," (1761.) Died in 1774.

Coulanges, koo′lôNzh′, (MARIE ANGÉLIQUE **du Gué Bagnoles**—dü gà băn′yol′,) a French lady, born in 1641, became the wife of the Marquis de Coulanges, noticed below. She was a friend of Madame de Sévigné, and author of letters which were published. Died in 1723.

Coulanges, de, deh koo′lôNzh′, (PHILIPPE EMANUEL,) MARQUIS, a French song-writer, born in Paris in 1631, was noted for his wit and bon-mots. He was cousin-german to Madame de Sévigné. Died in 1716.

See MADAME DE SÉVIGNÉ, "Lettres."

Coulet, koo′lả′, (ANNE PHILIBERTE,) a French engraver, born in Paris in 1736. She engraved after Vernet and other masters.

Coulomb, de, deh koo′lôn′, (CHARLES AUGUSTIN,) a French savant, eminent for his discoveries in experimental physics and electricity, was born at Angoulême in 1736. His "Theory of Simple Machines" (1779) gained the prize offered by the Academy of Sciences, and opened to him the doors of that Institution. In 1784 he was appointed intendant of the waters and springs of France. At an early stage of the Revolution he retired from public service. He wrote for the Academy many able treatises on mechanics, electricity, etc. He invented the Torsion Balance, which he used in successful experiments on the laws of magnetic and electric attraction and repulsion. By the same means he determined the laws of the distribution of electricity on the surface of bodies, and of magnetism in the interior. He was admitted into the Institute about 1796. Died in 1806. M. Biot remarks that the labours of Poisson have illustrated the admirable sagacity of Coulomb as an observer, as well as the accuracy of his experiments.

See QUÉRARD, "La France Littéraire;" "Nouvelle Biographie Générale."

Coulon, koo'lôn', (LOUIS,) a French geographer, born at Poitiers in 1605. He published a "Treatise on the Rivers of France," (2 vols., 1644,) and several historical compilations. Died in 1664.

Coulon de Thévenot, koo'lôn' dĕh tăv'no', (A.,) the inventor of French *tachygraphie*, or short-hand, was born about 1754. In 1792 he served La Fayette in the army as chief secretary. He published "The Art of Writing as rapidly as One speaks," (1794.) Died in 1814.

See QUÉRARD, "La France Littéraire."

Coupé, koo'pâ', (JEAN MARIE LOUIS,) a French *littérateur*, born at Péronne in 1732. Among his works are "Literary Evenings," ("Soirées littéraires," 20 vols., 1795-1801,) and "Œuvres d'Hésiode." Died in 1818.

Couperin, koop'răn', (FRANÇOIS,) a French organist and composer, called "le Grand," was born in Paris in 1668; died in 1733.

Couplet, koo'plâ', (PHILIPPE,) a Flemish missionary, born at Malines about 1628. He went to China in 1659, and became deeply versed in the language and history of that empire. He and several of his colleagues published a Latin version of the works of Confucius. Died at sea in 1692.

Courayer, le, lĕh koo'râ'yà', or **Courayer,** (PIERRE FRANÇOIS,) a French Catholic priest, born at Rouen in 1681. He published in 1723 a work in favour of the validity of ordinations in the Anglican Church. In consequence of the persecution to which this subjected him, he retired to England, where he died in 1776, without having renounced the Roman Catholic communion. He left a good French version of Sarpi's "History of the Council of Trent," (2 vols., 1736,) and other works.

See "London Quarterly Review" for December, 1811.

Courbes, de, dĕh koorB, (JEAN,) a French engraver, born about 1592, engraved a portrait of Sir Philip Sidney.

Courbet, koor'bâ', (GUSTAVE,) a French painter, born at Ornans (Doubs) in 1819. His works are chiefly landscapes and portraits.

Courbière, de, dĕh koor'be-air', (WILHELM RENÉ,) Baron de Homme, a Prussian general, born at Groningen in 1733; died in 1811.

Courbon, de, dĕh koor'bôn', MARQUIS, a French officer, noted for his ability and romantic adventures, was born in 1650. He obtained a high rank in the Venetian army, and was killed at Negropont in 1688.

See AIMAR, "Vie du Marquis de Courbon," 1692.

Courcelles, de, dĕh koor'sêl', [Lat. CURCELLÆ'US,] (ÉTIENNE,) an eminent Protestant divine, born at Geneva in 1586. After preaching at Amiens, he removed to Amsterdam, where he succeeded Simon Episcopius as professor of theology. He translated into Latin the Philosophy of Descartes, and published several theological works. Died about 1660.

See MORÉRI, "Dictionnaire Historique."

Courcelles, de, dĕh koor'sêl', (ÉTIENNE CHARDON,) a French physician, born at Rheims in 1705. He wrote, besides other works, a "Manual of Surgical Operations," (1756.) Died in 1775.

Courcelles, de, (JEAN BAPTISTE PIERRE JULIEN,) CHEVALIER, a French writer, born at Orléans in 1759. He was the author of a "Historical Dictionary of French Generals since the Eleventh Century," (Paris, 1820-23,) a "Genealogical History of the Peers of France," etc., (1830,) and other works. Died in 1834.

See QUÉRARD, "La France Littéraire."

Courcelles, de, (THOMAS,) a French theologian, born in 1400, was one of the judges who condemned Joan of Arc to death. Died in 1469.

Courcillon. See DANGEAU.

Couret de Villeneuve, koo'râ' dĕh vêl'nuv', (LOUIS PIERRE,) a French *littérateur* and printer, born at Orléans in 1749. He wrote and translated many works, in prose and verse. He was drowned in the Lys in 1806.

Courier, koo're-à', (or **Courier de Méré**—dĕh mâ'rà,') (PAUL LOUIS,) an ingenious and popular French author and pamphleteer, born in Paris in 1772 or 1773, was liberally educated, and was an excellent Greek scholar. He entered the army as engineer in 1792, became a captain in 1795, and fought in the campaign of Rome in 1798. In 1803 he obtained the brevet of chef d'escadron, (major.) During the intervals when active service was suspended, he pursued his literary studies and translated from Cicero, Isocrates, etc. His last campaign was that of Austria in 1809, after which he resigned his commission. He published an excellent edition and version of Longus, (1810,) and translated Xenophon "On the Command of Cavalry," and other classics. (See LONGUS.) In 1814 he married a daughter of Étienne Clavier. He produced numerous political pamphlets and letters which display much humour and satirical power. In politics he was liberal or independent. He was assassinated by one or two of his servants on his own estate in Touraine in 1825. "The merits of his works," says Lord Brougham, "are of a very high order. They abound in strong masculine sense, illustrated with classical allusions and seasoned with wit more brilliant than is almost anywhere else to be found ; for it has the keen edge of Swift's satire, and the easy playfulness of Voltaire, without his pertness and flippancy. He is truly a writer of extraordinary powers ; and nothing could have prevented him from attaining a very eminent place among the literary men of his age, but his never having composed a work of considerable magnitude on a subject of permanent importance." ("Edinburgh Review.") Armand Carrel pronounced his "Pamphlet des Pamphlets" (1824) "the most finished work in respect to taste, and the most wonderful in respect to art, in the language."

See A. CARREL, "Essai sur la Vie et les Œuvres de P. L. Courier," 1838 ; SAINTE-BEUVE, "Causeries du Lundi;" QUÉRARD, "La France Littéraire;" "Nouvelle Biographie Générale;" "Edinburgh Review" for March, 1829; "Westminster Review" for April, 1866.

Cournot, koor'no', (ANTOINE AUGUSTIN,) a French mathematician, born in 1801. He published, besides other works, an "Exposition of the Theory of Chances and Probabilities," (1843,) and a French version of Sir J. Herschel's "Treatise on Astronomy."

Courrayer. See COURAYER.

Courson, de, dĕh koor'sôn', (AURÉLIEN,) a French historian, born at Port Louis, Ile de France, in 1811, became librarian of the Louvre, Paris. Among his works is a "History of the Breton Peoples of Gaul and the British Isles," (1846.)

Court, koor, (ANTOINE,) a French Protestant divine, born in Vivarais in 1696. He laboured with success to reorganize the Protestant churches after the civil war, and discouraged a factious resistance to the government. He was president of a theological seminary at Lausanne from 1730 to 1760, and wrote a "History of the War of the Camisards." Died in 1760.

See DE FALIAC, "Histoire des Protestants de France ;" "Nouvelle Biographie Générale."

Court, (JOSEPH DÉSIRÉ,) a French historical painter, born at Rouen in 1797, won the grand prize in 1821. His reputation was established by the "Death of Cæsar," (1827,) which is placed in the Luxembourg Gallery.

Court de Gébelin, koor dĕh zhâb'lân', (ANTOINE,) a French scholar and Protestant, son of Antoine Court, noticed above, was born at Nimes in 1725. He became a resident of Paris about 1760, and devoted much time to the study of antiquity, mythology, the filiation of languages, etc. Between 1773 and 1784 he published nine volumes of his "Primitive World Analyzed and Compared with the Modern," a work of great learning, which was never completed. The French Academy twice awarded to him the annual prize founded for the most useful work. He co-operated with Dr. B. Franklin and others in editing a periodical called "The Affairs of England and America," (15 vols., Paris, 1776 *et seq.*) Died in 1784.

See RABAUD SAINT-ÉTIENNE, "Lettres sur la Vie, etc. de Court de Gébelin," 1784 ; THÉODORE FOURNIER, "Notice sur A. Court de Gébelin," 1848 ; "Nouvelle Biographie Générale."

Courtais, de, dĕh koor'tâ', (AMABLE GASPARD HENRI,) a French general, born at Moulins in 1786, was elected to the Chamber of Deputies in 1842. Soon after the revolution of 1848 he was appointed commander of the national guard of Paris. He was censured and removed because he failed to prevent the invasion of the Chamber by the mob in May, 1848.

Courtanvaux, de, dẹh koor'tǒṉ'vō', (FRANÇOIS CÉSAR **Letellier**—lẹh-tä'le-ä',) MARQUIS, a French savant, was born in Paris in 1718. He was admitted in 1764 to the Academy of Sciences, for which he wrote memoirs on chemistry, etc. Died in 1781.

Cour'ten, kŭr'ten, ? (WILLIAM,) an English naturalist, born in London in 1642. He made a rich collection of medals, etc. Died in 1702.

Courten, (Sir WILLIAM,) an eminent merchant of London, of Flemish descent, born about 1570, made large loans to James I. and Charles I. Died in 1636.

Courtenay or **Courtnay,** kŭrt'ne, (JOHN,) an Irish politician and writer, born about 1740. He was elected in 1780 to the British Parliament, in which he sat many years, and voted with the Whigs. In 1806 he was appointed commissioner of the treasury, and a few months later retired from the public service. He wrote tracts on the French Revolution, "Manners, Arts, and Politics of France and Italy," in verse, and a few other works. Died in 1816.

Courtenay, de, dẹh koort'nặ', (PIERRE,) a French count, who succeeded his father in 1183, was one of the most powerful princes of his time. He joined a crusade to Palestine in 1190. In 1216 he was chosen Emperor of Constantinople. He was defeated, made prisoner, and put to death about 1220, by Theodore, a Greek prince.

See MICHAUD, "Histoire des Croisades."

Courtenay, (Hon. THOMAS PEREGRINE,) M.P., an English scholar and writer of the present century, of whose life we have no details. He published a "Life of Sir William Temple," (1836,) which Macaulay commends for "diligence, good sense, and impartiality."

See MACAULAY's Essay on "Sir William Temple."

Courtilz de Sandras, de, dẹh koor'tĕlz' dẹh sǒṉ'-drặs', (GATIEN,) a French littérateur, born in Paris in 1644. He published, anonymously, a "Life of Coligny," a "History of the War in Holland," (1672–77,) and many mediocre works, which purport to be memoirs, historical or biographical, but contain much fiction or falsehood. He was imprisoned in the Bastille nine years, (1702–11.) His style is praised by Bayle. Died in 1712.

See NICÉRON, "Mémoires."

Courtin, koor'tăṉ', (ANTOINE,) a French negotiator and moralist, born at Riom in 1622. He became private secretary of Christina of Sweden in 1651, and after her abdication was ambassador from Sweden to France. About 1662 he was employed by Louis XIV. in a negotiation with England. He published a number of moral essays. Died in 1685.

See QUÉRARD, "La France Littéraire."

Courtin, (EUSTACHE MARIE PIERRE,) a French lawyer and editor, born at Lisieux in 1768, became advocate-general in the imperial court, Paris, in 1811. Between 1824 and 1832 he published the "Encyclopédie Moderne," (24 vols.,) a work of merit. Died in 1839.

Courtivron, de, dẹh koor'tė'vRǒṉ', (GASPARD le Compasseur de Créqui-Montfort—lẹh kǒṉ'pặ'sur' dẹh krä'ke' mǒṉ'foR',) MARQUIS, a French scientific writer, born in Burgundy in 1715. He became an officer in the army, and saved the life of Marshal Saxe in 1742. He wrote a "Treatise on Optics," (1752,) and other works. Died in 1785.

See CONDORCET, "Éloge de M. le Marquis de Courtivron."

Courtnay. See COURTENAY.

Courtney or **Courtenay,** kŭrt'ne, the name of a noble English family, to which the Earls of Devonshire belong, and which came from Normandy with William the Conqueror. One of this name was made Earl of Devonshire by Queen Mary about 1554. He was "nearly allied to the crown," says Hume, and received overtures of marriage with the queen, which he neglected, from his partiality to her sister Elizabeth. (See DEVONSHIRE, EARL OF.)

Courtney, (WILLIAM,) a younger son of Hugh Courtney, Earl of Devonshire, born about 1340, became chancellor of England and Archbishop of Canterbury in 1381. He persecuted the disciples of Wickliffe. Died in 1396. His mother, Margaret, was a daughter of Edward I.

See W. F. HOOK, "Lives of the Archbishops of Canterbury," vol. iv. chap. xvi.

Courtois, koor'twä', (EDME BONAVENTURE,) a French politician, born at Arcis-sur-Aube about 1755, became a member of the National Convention in 1792, and a political friend of Danton. He favoured the triumph of Bonaparte in November, 1799, and became a member of the Tribunate. Died in 1816.

See QUÉRARD, "La France Littéraire."

Courtois, [It. CORTESI, kor-tä'see,] (GUILLAUME,) a distinguished French painter, born in 1628, was a pupil of Pietro da Cortona. He worked mostly in Rome, and was patronized by Pope Alexander VI. "The Miracle of Joshua suspending the Motion of the Sun" is one of his master-pieces. He aided his brother Jacques in some of his works. Died in Rome in 1679.

Courtois or **Curtois,** (JACQUES,) [It. JACOPO CORTESI, yä'ko-po koR-tä'see,] an eminent painter of battles and history, often called IL BORGOGNONE, (èl boR-gon-yo'nà,) or LE BOURGUIGNON, (lẹh booR'gěn'yòN',) born at Saint-Hippolyte, in Franche-Comté, in 1621, was a brother of the preceding. He studied with Guido at Bologna, and worked some time in Florence. About 1658 he became a Jesuit or monk, and settled in Rome, where he painted many works, among which are the "Battle of Arbela," and some sacred subjects. He excelled in freedom of design, facility of execution, and in the disposition, variety, and movement of the figures. Died in Rome in 1676.

See BRYAN, "Dictionary of Painters;" NAGLER, "Neues Allgemeines Künstler-Lexikon."

Courtois, koor'twä', (RICHARD JOSEPH,) a Belgian naturalist, born at Verviers in 1806, was the author of a "Compendium Floræ Belgicæ," (3 vols., 1827–36.) Died in 1835.

Courtonne, koor'ton', (JEAN,) a French architect, born in Paris about 1670; died about 1740.

Courvoisier, koor'vwä'ze-à', (JEAN BAPTISTE,) a French jurist, born at Arbois in 1749; died in 1803.

Courvoisier, (JEAN JOSEPH ANTOINE,) a French lawyer and politician, son of the preceding, born at Besançon in 1775. He emigrated as a royalist about 1790, and became minister of justice in 1829. He resigned in May, 1830, and died in 1835.

See LAMARTINE, "History of the Restoration."

Cousin, koo'zăṉ', [Lat. COGNA'TUS,] (GILBERT,) a classical scholar and writer, born at Nozeroy, in Franche-Comté, in 1506. He lived about five years with Erasmus, who employed him as secretary or amanuensis and treated him as a companion and friend. He afterwards opened a school in his native place. Conrad Gesner states that he was the first who caused learning to flourish in Burgundy. Cousin wrote notes on Lucian, Aristotle, Ovid, etc., and Latin works on theology and other subjects. Suspected of Protestantism, he was imprisoned, and during his trial died at Besançon in 1567.

See NICÉRON, "Mémoires;" MORÉRI, "Dictionnaire Historique."

Cousin, (JACQUES ANTOINE JOSEPH,) a French geometer, born in Paris in 1739. He was for many years professor of physics in the College of France. In 1795 he became a member of the Institute, and senator in 1799. He published a "Treatise on the Differential and Integral Calculus," and other works. Died in 1800.

See QUÉRARD, "La France Littéraire."

Cousin, (JEAN,) an eminent French painter and sculptor, born at Souci, near Sens, about 1500, worked many years in Paris. He is regarded as the first Frenchman who gained distinction by painting history. The most celebrated of his works was "The Last Judgment," a large oil-painting. His correctness of design was his chief merit. He painted on glass more than in oil. He also wrote able treatises on perspective, geometry, and the proportions of the human body. Died about 1590.

See FÉLIBIEN, "Entretiens sur les Vies des Peintres."

Cousin, (LOUIS,) a French lawyer and learned translator, born in Paris in 1627, became president of the court des monnaies. In 1697 he was admitted into the French Academy. He published a "History of the Church," (1675,) a "History of the Empire of the West," (1683,) and other works, all of which are translations from Greek and Latin authors. Died in 1707.

See NICÉRON, "Mémoires."

ā, ē, ī, ō, ū, ȳ, long; ă, ĕ, ĭ, ŏ, ŭ, ў, short; ạ, ẹ, ị, ọ, obscure; fär, fȧll, fȧt; mĕt; nŏt; gŏŏd; mōōn;

Cousin, (VICTOR,) a celebrated French philosopher and metaphysician, born in Paris on the 28th of November, 1792, was the son of a clockmaker. He gained the first prize of honour at the Lycée Charlemagne in 1810, after which he attended Laromiguière's lectures on philosophy. In 1815 he succeeded Royer-Collard as substitute professor of philosophy at the Sorbonne, where he delivered eloquent and popular lectures on the history of philosophy. He was deprived of the professorship by the government in 1820 or 1821 for his liberal principles, and then commenced a translation of Plato. He published in 1826 an edition of Descartes, in eleven volumes, and "Philosophic Fragments," ("Fragments philosophiques,") an important original work. After being imprisoned six months in Berlin on suspicion of liberalism, he was again appointed professor of philosophy at the Sorbonne in 1828. His lectures displayed an admirable combination of sensibility, imagination, and reason, and he shared with his colleagues, Guizot and Villemain, an immense popularity. The revolution of 1830 opened to him a new career. Retiring from the chair of philosophy, he became councillor of state, and a member of the council of public instruction. He was elected to the French Academy in 1830 in place of Fourier, and was made a peer of France in 1832. M. Cousin was minister of public instruction about eight months in the cabinet formed by M. Thiers in March, 1840. He displayed superior oratorical powers in his speeches in the Chamber of Peers. After the revolution of 1848 he took no part in public affairs. Among his principal works are an excellent French translation of Plato, (13 vols., 1825-40,) a "Treatise on the Metaphysics of Aristotle," (1838,) a "Course of Moral Philosophy" ("Cours de Philosophie morale") from 1816 to 1820, (5 vols., 1840,) a new series of "Philosophic Fragments," (1838-40,) "Lectures on the Philosophy of Kant," (1842,) a "Biography of Jacqueline Pascal," (1845,) and "The True, the Beautiful, and the Good," ("Du Vrai, du Beau et du Bien," 1853.) He published a collective edition of his works, in 22 vols. 18mo, (1847.) His system of philosophy may be briefly characterized as eclecticism, or a union of sensualism and idealism. He is regarded as one of the first philosophical writers of his time. Died in January, 1867.

See MARBACH, "Schelling, Hegel und Cousin;" C. FUCHS, "Die Philosophie von Victor Cousin," 1847; SAINTE-BEUVE, "Causeries du Lundi;" SIR WILLIAM HAMILTON, critique in the "Edinburgh Review," vol. l.; LOUIS DE LOMÉNIE, "M. V. Cousin, par un Homme de Rien," 1842; "Nouvelle Biographie Générale;" "North British Review" for March, 1867.

Cousin d'Avallon, koo'zǎN' dǎ'vǎ'lôN', (CHARLES YVES,) a French compiler, born in 1769, published many collections of anecdotes with titles ending in *ana*. His "Pironiana" ran through eleven editions. Died about 1840.

Cousin-Despréaux, koo'zǎN' dǎ'prǎ'ō', (LOUIS,) a French writer, born at Dieppe in 1743, published two esteemed works, viz., a "History of Greece," (16 vols., 1780-89,) and "Lessons on Nature," (1802.) Died in 1818.

Cousinéry, koo'ze'nǎ're', (ESPRIT MARIE,) a Frenchman noted for his skill in medals, born at Marseilles in 1747, wrote "Letters on the Rosetta Stone," "Travels in Macedonia," (1831,) and several treatises on medals. He was a member of the Institute. Died after 1830.

Cousinet, koo'ze'nǎ', (ÉLISABETH,) a French engraver, born about 1726.

Cousinot, koo'ze'no', (GUILLAUME,) a French poet and historian, born about 1400; died about 1484.

Coussemaker, de, dęh koos'mǎ'kaiR', (CHARLES EDMOND HENRI,) a French antiquary, born at Bailleul (Nord) in 1805. He wrote a prize essay "On the Harmony of the Middle Ages."

Coustant, koo'stôN', (PIERRE,) a French Benedictine monk, born at Compiègne in 1654. He aided in revising and editing the works of Augustine, and published an edition of Saint-Hilaire, (1693,) in which he showed much critical judgment. Died in Paris in 1721.

Coustou, koos'too', (GUILLAUME,) an able French sculptor, born at Lyons in 1678, was a pupil of his uncle Coysevox. After studying in Rome, he settled in Paris. Among his best productions are two groups, each of which is composed of a horse prancing and a groom,

a bronze figure of the river Rhone, and the bas-relief which adorns the entrance of the Hôtel des Invalides. Died in 1746.

His son GUILLAUME, born in Paris in 1716, was also a skilful sculptor. He became in 1746 a professor in the Academy of Arts, of which he was afterwards rector. He made statues of Mars and Venus for the King of Prussia. Died in 1777.

See D'ARGENVILLE, "Vies des Architectes et des Sculpteurs;" NAGLER, "Neues Allgemeines Künstler-Lexikon."

Coustou, (NICOLAS,) an eminent sculptor, a brother of Guillaume the elder, was born at Lyons in 1658. Having gained the grand prize, he went to Rome with a pension about 1682. He afterwards settled in Paris, where he was patronized by Louis XIV. Among his most admired works are a group of the junction of the Seine and Marne, the "Berger Chasseur," ("Shepherd Huntsman,") and a "Descent from the Cross." Died in 1733.

See COUSIN DE CONTAMINE, "Éloge historique de N. Coustu l'Aîné," 1837; "Nouvelle Biographie Générale."

Cousturier or **Couturier,** koo'tü're-à', (PIERRE,) [Lat. PE'TRUS SU'TOR,] a French monk, who had a dispute with Erasmus respecting the version of the New Testament published by the latter. Died in 1537.

Coutan, koo'tôN', (AMABLE PAUL,) a French painter of history, born in Paris in 1792. He gained the first prize in 1827. Died in 1837.

Coutelle, koo'têl', (JEAN MARIE JOSEPH,) a French engineer and balloonist, born at Mans in 1748; died in 1835.

Couthon, koo'tôN', (GEORGES,) a French Jacobin, born at Orsay, in Auvergne, in 1756. He was a lawyer before the Revolution, and entered the Convention in 1792. He voted for the death of the king, and became a partisan of Robespierre. He has been accused of the crimes and cruelties committed at Lyons, whither he was sent as commissioner in 1793; but Lamartine asserts that he restrained the excesses of his party on that occasion. After the committee of public safety was divided into two parties, Robespierre, Couthon, and Saint-Just formed a triumvirate, which for some time controlled the government. He was involved in the fall of Robespierre on the 9th Thermidor, and was guillotined July 28, 1794.

See DE BARANTE, "Histoire de la Convention Nationale."

Coutinho, kō-tèn'yo, (Dom FRANCISCO,) Count of Redondo, a Portuguese officer, was appointed Viceroy of India in 1561. He was a friend of Camoens, who commemorated, in verse, his virtues and benefactions. Died in 1564.

See LACLÈDE, "Histoire de Portugal."

Couto, de, dà kō'to, (DIOGO or DIEGO,) a Portuguese historian, born in Lisbon in 1542. He went to India about 1556, served in the army several years, and settled at Goa. He received from Philip II. of Spain the title of historiographer of India, and between 1602 and 1616 published a continuation of Barros's valuable work entitled "Decades of Asia," ("Decadas da Asia,") containing an account of the discoveries and conquests of the Portuguese in the East. Died at Goa in 1616.

See S. DE FARIA, "Vida de Diogo de Couto;" "Nouvelle Biographie Générale."

Couto-Pestana, do, do kō'to pês-tä'nä, (JOZÉ,) a Portuguese poet, born in Lisbon in 1678. He became controller of the treasury at Lisbon, and wrote a poem entitled "Quitería la Santa." Died in 1735.

Coutts, koots, (ANGELA GEORGIANA BURDETT,) an English lady noted for wealth and munificence, a daughter of Sir Francis Burdett, was born in 1814. Having become the heiress of a vast fortune left by her grandfather, Thomas Coutts, a banker, she assumed his name. She has given large donations to benevolent and religious societies, and built a fine church in Westminster, (1847.)

Coutts, (THOMAS,) an eminent banker of London, born at Dundee about 1733, acquired a very large fortune. Died in 1821 or 1822. He left three daughters, Frances, married to the Marquis of Bute, Sophia, married to Sir Francis Burdett, and Susan, married to the Earl of Guilford.

See CHAMBERS, "Biographical Dictionary of Eminent Scotsmen."

Couture, koo'tür', (GUILLAUME,) a French architect, born at Rouen in 1732. He was chief architect of the church de la Madeleine, Paris, which he left unfinished at his death, in 1799. It has since been completed, with some variations from his design.

Couture, (JEAN BAPTISTE,) a French writer, born at Saint-Aubin in 1651. He was professor of eloquence in Paris, and a member of the Academy of Inscriptions. He wrote an "Abridged History of the Assyrian, Persian, Macedonian, and Roman Empires," (1699,) and some minor works. Died in 1728.

Couture, (THOMAS,) a French painter of history and genre, was born at Senlis in 1815. He produced "The Love of Gold" in 1844, and in 1847 a picture of "The Romans of the Decadence," which obtained the gold medal at the *Salon.*

Coutures, des, dā koo'tür', (JACQUES **Parrain—** pä'rĂn',) BARON, a French translator, born at Avranches. He published a French version of Lucretius, (1685,) with notes, and several other works. Died in 1702.

Couvay, koo'vā', (JEAN,) a skilful French artist, born at Arles in 1622. He engraved after Raphael, Guido, Poussin, and other masters. "The Martyrdom of Saint Bartholomew," after Poussin, is his *chef-d'œuvre.*

Couvreur. See LE COUVREUR.

Covarrubias, ko-vär-roo've-âs, or **Covarrubias,** (Don ANTONIO,) an eminent Spanish jurist and Hellenist, born in 1524. He was professor of law at Salamanca, and member of the royal council of Castile. He wrote a "Commentary on the Politics of Aristotle." Lipsius calls him "Hispaniæ magnum lumen." Died in 1602.

See N. ANTONIO, "Bibliotheca Hispana Nova."

Covarrubias y Horozco, ko-vär-roo've-âs e o-roth'-ko, (Don JUAN,) a nephew of the preceding, was born at Toledo. He became Canon of Seville, and afterwards Bishop of Girgenti, Sicily, where he established a printing-press. He was author of "Moral Emblems," (1591,) "Christian Paradoxes," (1592,) and other works, (in Spanish.) Died in 1608.

See TICKNOR, "History of Spanish Literature."

Covarrubias y Leyva, ko-vär-roo've-âs e lā'e-vâ, (DIEGO,) a brother of Antonio, noticed above, was born at Toledo in 1512. He became Bishop of Segovia in 1565, president of the council of Castile in 1572, and of the council of state in 1574. He was reputed one of the first jurists or canonists of his time, and wrote several legal works. Died in 1577.

See N. ANTONIO, "Bibliotheca Hispana Nova."

Co'vel or **Co'vell,** (JOHN,) an English divine, born in Suffolk in 1638, wrote an "Account of the Greek Church," (1722.) Died in 1722.

Covelli, ko-vel'lee, (NICCOLÒ,) an Italian chemist and mineralogist, born at Cajazzo in 1790. He investigated the phenomena of Vesuvius by chemical analysis, and published, besides other works, "Prodromo della Mineralogia Vesuviana," (1825.) Died in 1829.

See TIPALDO, "Biografia degli Italiani illustri."

Coventry, kŭv'en-tre, (HENRY,) an English scholar, a Fellow of Magdalene College, was one of the authors of the "Athenian Letters." (See YORKE, CHARLES.) He published "Letters of Philemon to Hydaspes," (on "False Religion,") 1736–44. Died in 1752.

Coventry, (THOMAS,) an English lawyer, born in Worcestershire in 1578. He became attorney-general in 1621, and lord keeper of the great seal in 1625. He was also made a baron, with the title of Lord Coventry. Died in 1640.

Coventry, (Sir WILLIAM,) M.P., the youngest son of the preceding, was born in 1626. He filled several civil offices with credit, and published "England's Appeal from the Cabal, etc." The "Character of a Trimmer," commonly attributed to Lord Halifax, is by some ascribed to Coventry. Died in 1686.

Cov'er-dāle, (MILES,) an English bishop and Reformer, was born in Yorkshire in 1487. He became an Augustine monk, and entered holy orders in 1514. He was one of the first Englishmen that embraced the Reformed religion, which he zealously promoted. In 1535 he published, with the royal sanction, the first entire Bible which appeared in the English language,

translated by himself. He also edited the Cranmer or "Great Bible," in 1539. He was appointed Bishop of Exeter in 1551. In the reign of Mary he was imprisoned two years and then exiled. He returned about 1558, but was not reinstated in the bishopric. Died about 1568.

See "Memorials of the Right Rev. Myles Coverdale, Bishop of Exeter."

Covilham or **Covilhão, da,** dä ko-vèl-yŏwn', (Don PEDRO,) a Portuguese explorer, was born about 1450. He was sent by John II. in 1487 to search for Prester John and to explore a route to India. He visited India, and obtained about commerce and geography important information, which he sent home. About 1492 he visited Abyssinia, the prince of which induced or constrained him to remain in his service. He was living there in 1525.

See JOÃO DE BARROS, "Asia," vol. i.; "Nouvelle Biographie Générale."

Covilhão. See COVILHAM.

Covillard, ko'vè'yĂr', written also **Couillard,** (JOSEPH,) a French surgeon, born in Dauphiné, was noted for his skill in lithotomy. He lived about 1630.

Cow'ard, (WILLIAM,) an English physician, born in 1656, published, besides some medical works, "Second Thoughts concerning the Human Soul," (1702,) which favoured materialism and excited much indignation. It was burned by order of Parliament. Died in 1725.

See "Biographia Britannica."

Cow'din, (ROBERT,) an American officer, born at Jamaica, Vermont, in 1805. He fought in the campaigns of 1861, and became a brigadier-general of volunteers in 1862.

Cow'ell, (JOHN,) an English jurist, born in Devonshire in 1554, wrote "The Interpreter." Died in 1611.

Cŏw'ley, [formerly pronounced and sometimes written Coo'ley,] (ABRAHAM,) a celebrated English poet, was born in London in 1618. At the age of fifteen he published a volume of poems, called "Poetic Blossoms," and in 1636 entered Trinity College, Cambridge, from which he was ejected as a royalist in 1643. In 1646 he went to Paris with the queen, and was employed as agent of a correspondence in cipher between her and Charles I. He produced in 1647 "The Mistress," a series of poems replete with frigid conceits which then passed for wit. "It is the most celebrated performance," says Hallam, "of the miscalled metaphysical poets." Having returned to England about 1656, he published an edition of poems, including "Pindaric Odes," "Miscellanies," and "The Davideis," an epic. By his contemporaries he was more admired than any other poet of his age. At the restoration he failed to receive the expected reward of his loyalty, and, retiring from the world in disgust, settled at Chertsey as a farmer in 1665. He died in 1667. "His 'Pindaric Odes,'" says Hallam, "contain very beautiful lines; but his sensibility and good sense—nor has any poet more—are choked by false taste. Cowley, perhaps, on the whole, has had a reputation more above his deserts than any English poet." "It may be affirmed," says Dr. Johnson, "that he brought to his poetic labours a mind replete with learning, and that his pages are embellished with all the ornaments which books can supply; that he was the first who imparted to English numbers the enthusiasm of the greater ode and the gayety of the less; and that he was equally qualified for sprightly sallies and for lofty flights." His prose essays are perspicuous and unaffected in style, and are among the earliest English models of good writing.

See JOHNSON, "Lives of the English Poets;" DR. SPRAT, "Life of A. Cowley," 1700; "Biographia Britannica;" CAMPBELL, "Specimens of the British Poets;" "North British Review" for February, 1847; "Retrospective Review," vol. i., 2d Series, 1827.

Cowley, (Mrs. HANNAH,) whose maiden name was PARKHOUSE, an English dramatist, born at Tiverton in 1743, was married to Captain Cowley, an officer of the East India Company. She composed, besides other plays, two successful comedies, called "The Runaway" and "The Belle's Stratagem." She also wrote "The Maid of Aragon," and other poems. Died in 1809.

See BAKER, "Biographia Dramatica;" "Gentleman's Magazine," 1809.

Cowley, (HENRY RICHARD WELLESLEY,) LORD, a British diplomatist, eldest son of Sir Henry Wellesley,

ā, ē, ī, ō, ū, ȳ, *long;* ă, ĕ, ŏ, *same, less prolonged;* ă, ĕ, ĭ, ŏ, ŭ, ў, *short;* a, e, i, o, *obscure;* fär, fâll, fät; mĕt; nŏt; gŏŏd; mōōn;

fiist Lord Cowley, and nephew of the Duke of Wellington, was born in 1804. He was appointed secretary of legation to Constantinople in 1831, minister to Switzerland in 1848, and ambassador to Paris in 1852. Lords Clarendon and Cowley represented England in the Congress of Paris which in 1856 concluded peace with Russia.

Cowley, (HENRY WELLESLEY,) the first LORD, an English diplomatist, born in 1773, was a brother of the Duke of Wellington. He was ambassador at Paris and other courts for many years. Died in 1847.

Cow'per, (EDWARD,) an Englishman distinguished as an inventor and improver of printing-machinery, was born in 1790. We have little information respecting his life. He was for some time a partner in an extensive printing-office in London. In his later years he was professor of mechanics, etc. in King's College, London, where his lectures were highly popular. He contributed to the "Penny Cyclopædia." Died in 1852.

Cowper, (SPENCER,) an English lawyer, was a younger brother of the first Earl Cowper, (1664–1723,) and grandfather of the great poet. After being tried for the murder of Sarah Stout, and acquitted, he became a judge in the court of common pleas, and a member of Parliament.

See MACAULAY, "History of England," vol. v.; "Blackwood's Magazine" for July, 1861.

Cowper, (WILLIAM,) a British divine, born in 1566. He preached about twenty years at Perth, after which he became Bishop of Galloway. He published Sermons, and other works on theology, which are commended. Died in 1619.

Cowper, (WILLIAM,) an eminent English surgeon and anatomist, born in Hampshire in 1666. He settled in London, and became a Fellow of the Royal Society. He published a treatise on Muscles, entitled "Myotomia Reformata," (1694,) and the "Anatomy of the Human Body." His name has been applied to certain glands of the urethra. Died in 1709.

See THOMPSON, "History of the Royal Society."

Cowper, (WILLIAM,) LORD, an eminent English judge and orator, born in the castle of Hertford in 1664, was the son of Sir William Cowper, and a great-uncle of the poet of that name. He entered the Middle Temple in his eighteenth year, and was called to the bar in 1688. Few men have had finer endowments for that profession; and it appears that in a short time he was the leader of the home circuit. In 1695 he was elected to Parliament, where he acted with the Whig party. "The younger Cowper," says Lord Campbell, "like the younger Pitt, is a rare instance of a member of the House of Commons being considered from his maiden speech a consummate debater." He was appointed king's counsel, and became the leader of the Whig party in the House of Commons. He was made lord chancellor, or keeper of the great seal, in 1705, and was raised to the peerage, as Baron Cowper, in 1706. The Tories having come into power in 1710, he resigned the great seal, which was again confided to him on the accession of George I. in 1714. For some years he was the king's chief adviser in political affairs, in which capacity he appears to have acted with wisdom and moderation. He resigned the office of chancellor in 1718, and was created an earl. He died in 1723, leaving several sons. He had a high reputation for integrity.

See LORD CAMPBELL, "Lives of the Lord Chancellors;" Foss, "The Judges of England."

Cowper, (WILLIAM,) an English clergyman and geometer, born in London in 1713, became Dean of Durham. He was a younger son of Earl Cowper. Died in 1772.

Cow'per, (or koo'per,) (WILLIAM,) one of the most eminent and popular of English poets, was born at Great Berkhamstead, in Hertfordshire, on the 26th of November, 1731. His father, John Cowper, a nephew of Earl Cowper, was rector of that parish, and chaplain to George II. Having lost his mother, whose maiden name was Donne, at the age of six years, he was then placed at the boarding-school of Dr. Pitman at Market Street, on the line between Bedford and Hertford counties. Here his sensitive spirit and delicate organization suffered much from the cruelty of a larger boy. Between the ages of ten and eighteen he was a student of Westminster School, and became a good classical scholar.

He entered the Middle Temple about 1752, and was called to the bar in 1754, but had little if any practice. While he was a student in the Temple, "he was struck," he says, "with such a dejection of spirits, as none but they who have felt the same can have the least conception of. To this moment I had felt no concern of a spiritual kind. Ignorant of original sin, insensible of the guilt of actual transgression, I understood neither the law nor the gospel." Thus it appears that religion was not, as some assert, the original cause of his terrible mental malady. He was tenderly attached to his cousin, Theodora Cowper, who favoured his suit, but whose parents forbade their union,—

"With a little hoard of maxims preaching down a daughter's heart."

In 1763, when his funds were nearly exhausted, he accepted the offer of the place of clerk of the journals of the House of Lords; but, when required to pass an examination before the bar of that House, his morbid nervousness was such that he could not endure the ordeal. After vain and agonizing efforts to brace himself for the trial, he made abortive attempts to commit suicide, and his miseries produced insanity, which, he says, he had ardently wished for, and during which his dominant idea was despair of his salvation. Under the skilful treatment of Dr. Cotton, at Saint Alban's, he recovered in 1765, and became an inmate in the family of the Unwins at Huntingdon. After the death of Mr. Unwin, in 1767, Cowper and Mrs. Unwin removed to Olney, than which it would be difficult to select a worse locality for an invalid. The adjacent land was low, damp, and miasmatic, and there was no genial society within their reach. Then came a nervous fever, followed by a renewal of his insanity or delusion, which began about 1773, abated in 1776, but did not cease entirely until several years later. He was nursed in this period, as in other times of need, by his constant friend, Mary Unwin. About 1780 his friends persuaded him to cultivate his poetical powers. "Encompassed by the midnight of absolute despair," says he, "I first commenced as an author." In 1782 he published a volume of didactic poems, entitled "Truth," "Table-Talk," "Hope," "Charity," "Conversation," etc. At the suggestion of Lady Austen, he wrote "John Gilpin," and "The Task," which appeared in 1785 and speedily obtained great and universal favour. It was more popular than any other poem of equal length in the language. He spent about a year in its composition. In 1784 he began the translation of Homer into blank verse,—a labour of six years which were among the happiest of his life. In 1786 he was visited by his cousin, Lady Hesketh, with whom he had corresponded many years, and removed to Weston, a pleasant village about two miles from Olney. Lady Hesketh and others were very assiduous in providing for his comfort. But the last six years of his life were passed in a state of hopeless dejection. He died April 25, 1800. "His familiar letters sparkle with playful humour. They are the pleasantest and most genial ever written." ("North British Review.") "I have always considered the letters of Cowper," says Robert Hall, "as the finest specimen of the epistolary style in our language. To an air of inimitable ease and carelessness they unite a high degree of correctness, such as could result only from the clearest intellect combined with the most finished taste." His version of Homer, considered with respect to fidelity to the original, is perhaps the best that has appeared in English. Besides the works above named, he composed numerous minor poems, and some of the "Olney Hymns," of which his friend John Newton was the principal author. His "Lines on his Mother's Portrait" are exquisitely beautiful and touching. The chief characteristics of his poetry are originality, good sense, simplicity, piety, and warmth of heart. He was emphatically a Christian poet. No English poet, except Shakspeare, is more frequently quoted. "The great merit of this writer," says Lord Jeffrey, "appears to us to consist in the boldness and originality of his composition, and in the fortunate audacity with which he has carried the dominion of poetry into regions that had been considered as inaccessible to her ambition. . . . The great variety and truth of his descriptions, the minute and correct paintings of those home scenes and private feelings with which every one is internally familiar, the sterling weight and sense of most of his observations, and, above all, the great appearance of facility with which everything is executed, and the happy use he has so often made of the most common and ordinary language, all concur to stamp upon his poems the character of original genius, and remind us of the merits that have secured immortality to Shakspeare." ("Edinburgh Review" for April, 1803.)

See T. S. GRIMSHAW, "Life of Cowper," 1835; SOUTHEY, "Life of W. Cowper," 2 vols., 1838; HAYLEY, "Life of W. Cowper," 4 vols., 1803–09; THOMAS TAYLOR, "Life of W. Cowper," 1833; "Edinburgh Review" for July, 1804.

Cowper, (WILLIAM FRANCIS,) M.P., an English politician, a younger son of the fifth Earl Cowper, was born in Hertfordshire in 1811. He became a lord of the treasury in 1837, and served under Lord John Russell as lord of the admiralty from 1846 to 1852. He was a step-son of Lord Palmerston, who appointed him president of the Board of Health in 1855, and vice-president of the Board of Trade in 1859.

Cox, (DAVID,) an English landscape-painter, born at Birmingham in 1793. He has attained distinction in painting in water-colours, chiefly British scenery. His works, though rather rough and not minutely finished, represent the phenomena of nature and of the weather with eminent success. He published a "Treatise on Painting in Water-Colours," (1814.) Ruskin praises "the purity and felicity of some of the careless, melting, water-colour skies of Cox," and says, "His foliage is altogether exquisite in colour, in its impressions of coolness, shade, and mass." ("Modern Painters.")

Cox, (FRANCIS AUGUSTUS,) D.D., an English theologian, born about 1783, published, besides other works, a "Life of Melanchthon," (1815,) and "Our Young Men," a prize essay, (1838.) Died in 1853.

Cox, (JACOB D.,) an American general, born at Montreal about 1828, was a lawyer before the civil war. He was appointed a brigadier-general in May, 1861, soon after which he commanded a force in Western Virginia. In the autumn of 1862 he became a major-general. He served under General Sherman in the campaign against Atlanta, May–September, 1864, and commanded a division at the battle of Nashville in December of that year. He was elected Governor of Ohio by the Republicans in October, 1865, and appointed by President Grant secretary of the interior, in March, 1869.

Cox, (JOHN EDMUND,) an English clergyman, born at Norwich in 1812, wrote a "Life of Cranmer," a "Life of Luther," and other works.

Cox, (LEONARD,) an English classical scholar, who wrote several works in Greek and Latin. Died in 1549.

Cox, (RICHARD,) an English prelate, born in the county of Bucks in 1499. He was employed as tutor to Prince Edward, after whose accession as Edward VI. he was almoner to the king, and Dean of Westminster. In 1559 he became Bishop of Ely. He translated for the "Bishops' Bible" the four Gospels, the Acts, and the Epistle to the Romans. Died in 1581.

Cox, (Sir RICHARD,) an Irish writer, born in the county of Cork in 1650. He was made lord chancellor of Ireland in 1703. He published a "History of Ireland," and a few other works. Died in 1733.

See CROKER, "Researches in the South of Ireland."

Cox, (SAMUEL HANSON,) D.D., a Presbyterian theologian, born at Leesville, New Jersey, in 1793. He was pastor of a church in Brooklyn, New York, from 1837 to 1854. He wrote "Quakerism not Christianity," and other works.

Cox, (WILLIAM SANDS,) F.R.S., an eminent English surgeon and writer, born at Birmingham in 1802. He founded Queen's College, and the Queen's Hospital, both in Birmingham.

Coxcie. See COXIE.

Coxe, koks, (ARTHUR CLEVELAND,) an American Episcopal clergyman, a son of Dr. S. H. Cox, noticed above, was born at Mendham, New Jersey, in 1818. He published, besides other works, "Christian Ballads," (1840,) "Saul, a Mystery," and "Impressions of England," (1856.) In 1859 he became rector of Grace Church, in the city of New York, and in 1865 became Bishop of Western New York.

See GRISWOLD's "Poets and Poetry of America."

Coxe, koks, (RICHARD CHARLES,) an English theologian and poet, born in 1799, was Archdeacon of Lindisfarne. Died in 1865.

Coxe, (TENCH,) an American writer on political economy, commerce, manufactures, etc., was born in 1756; died in 1824.

Coxe, (WILLIAM,) a successful English historian and writer of travels, born in London in 1747. He became curate of Denham in 1771, after which he travelled on the continent as tutor of the Marquis of Blandford and other young members of the nobility. He published "Travels in Russia, Poland, Sweden, and Denmark," (1784,) which are highly prized and interesting, and "Travels in Switzerland," (1789.) He was appointed chaplain to the Tower about 1796, and Archdeacon of Wilts in 1805. Among his most important works are a "History of the House of Austria," (1792,) "Memoirs of Sir Robert Walpole," (3 vols., 1798,) "Memoirs of the Kings of Spain of the House of Bourbon, 1700–1788," (3 vols., 1813,) and "Memoirs of the Duke of Marlborough," (1817–19.) Died in 1828.

See article on the "Life and Works of Archdeacon Coxe," in the "London Quarterly Review" for October, 1833; "Edinburgh Review" for April, 1808.

Cox'e-ter, (THOMAS,) an English critic and collector of rare books, was born in Gloucestershire in 1689. He assisted Ames in his "Typographical Antiquities," and Warton in his "History of English Poetry." He was making a collection of old English poets for publication when he died in 1747.

Coxie or **Coxcie,** kok'see, (MICHAEL,) a celebrated Flemish painter, born at Mechlin in 1497, was a pupil of Van Orley. After studying the works of Raphael in Rome, he returned home, and acquired a large fortune by his art. He had a fertile invention, a correct design, and a brilliant colouring. Among his best-known works is a copy of Van Eyck's "Adoration of the Lamb," which Coxie made for Philip II. of Spain. He was killed by a fall in 1592.

See DESCAMPS, "Vies des Peintres Flamands," etc.

Coyer, kwä'yȧ', (GABRIEL FRANÇOIS,) ABBÉ, a French writer, born in Franche-Comté in 1707, published "Moral Bagatelles," a "History of John Sobieski," "The Commercial Noblesse," and other works. Died in 1782.

Coyne, koin, (JOSEPH STERLING,) a dramatist, born in King's county, Ireland, in 1805, produced many successful farces. Died in 1868.

Coypel, kwä'pêl', (ANTOINE,) an eminent French painter, born in Paris in 1661, was the son and pupil of Noël Coypel, with whom he studied in Rome. About 1680 he returned to Paris, where he acquired a high reputation. In 1715 he received the title of first painter to the king. His style, though affected and artificial, was much admired by his contemporaries. He was a skilful engraver. Died in 1722.

His son CHARLES, born in 1694, though an inferior artist, became first painter to the king. Died in 1752.

See BRYAN, "Dictionary of Painters."

Coypel, (NOËL,) a successful French painter, born in Paris in 1628. In 1655 he was employed by the king to adorn the Louvre and other edifices, and was received into the Royal Academy in 1663. Louis XIV. appointed him director of the Academy at Rome in 1672. His *ordonnance* and colouring are admired. To distinguish him from his sons Antoine and Noël Nicolas, he was sometimes called "Coypel le Poussin." Died in 1707.

Coypel, (NOËL NICOLAS,) the son and pupil of the preceding, was born in Paris in 1688. He obtained a high reputation as a historical painter, but his works are now less prized than in his own time. Died in 1734.

Coysevox, kwȧz'voks', (ANTOINE,) an eminent French sculptor, of Spanish origin, born at Lyons in 1640. He studied under Lérambert in Paris, of which he became a resident, and was admitted into the Academy in 1676. Among his celebrated works are two statues of Louis XIV., the tomb of Colbert, and two winged horses surmounted by Fame and Mercury, at the Tuileries. He excelled in busts and portraits. Died in 1720.

Cozen. See COSIN.

Cozza, kot'sä, (FRANCESCO,) an Italian painter, born in Calabria in 1605; died in 1682.

ā, ē, ī, ō, ū, ȳ, *long;* ȧ, ė, ȯ, same, less prolonged; ă, ĕ, ĭ, ŏ, ŭ, ў, *short;* ạ, ẹ, ị, ọ, *obscure;* fär, fȧll, fȧt; mȇt; nŏt; gŏŏd; mŏŏn;

Cozza, (GIOVANNI BATTISTA,) an Italian painter, born at Milan in 1676 ; died in 1742.

Cozzens, kŭz'enz, (FREDERICK SWARTWOUT,) an American writer, born in New York in 1818. A volume entitled "Prismatics," made up of his contributions to the "Knickerbocker Magazine," appeared in 1853. He published, also, "Sparrowgrass Papers," in 1856, (originally contributed to "Putnam's Magazine,") besides other works in prose and verse. Died in 1869.

Craanen, krä'nen, (DIEDRIK,) a Dutch medical writer, lived at Leyden ; died in 1688.

Crabb, (GEORGE,) an English philologist, born about 1778, was a graduate of Oxford. He published a number of useful works, among which are "English Synonymes," (1816 ; 10th edition, 1852,) a "Universal Historical Dictionary," (1825,) and "Mythology of All Nations," (1847.) Died in 1854. "As an etymologist, Mr. Crabb seems to have some dictionary knowledge of many languages, but to be unacquainted with the philosophy, or history even, of language in general." ("London Quarterly Review," vol. xxv.)

Crabbe, krab, (GEORGE,) a popular English poet, born at Aldborough, in Suffolk, in 1754. His father filled the humble office of collector of salt-duties. He learned the profession of surgeon, which, however, he abandoned at an early age. Conscious of talents above the common order, he resolved to seek his fortune as an author, and in 1780 went to London with five pounds which he had borrowed. After his first productions had been rejected by the booksellers, he published, on his own account, "The Candidate," a poem, which brought him neither fame nor profit. In great pecuniary distress, he asked and received the generous patronage of Edmund Burke, who gave him a room in his own house, introduced him to Fox, Thurlow, and others, and enabled him, in 1781, to publish "The Library," which was received with favour. He was ordained a priest in 1782, and soon after became chaplain to the Duke of Rutland at Belvoir Castle. He published in 1783 "The Village," which confirmed his reputation as a powerful and original poet. At this period he married Sarah Elmy, the object of his early affections. Between 1785 and 1813 he officiated as curate or rector successively at Strathern, Muston, and Parham. After an interval of more than twenty years since his last appearance as a poet, he produced "The Parish Register," (1807,) "The Borough," (1810,) and "Tales in Verse," (1812.) In 1813 he was presented to the living of Trowbridge, Wiltshire, where he passed his last years. About 1819 he received £3000 for his "Tales of the Hall," and for the unexpired term of former copyrights. Died in 1832. His moral character was amiable and excellent. As a poet he is remarkable for vigour, truth in description, and a "Chinese accuracy" of observation. "Mr. Crabbe," says Lord Jeffrey, "is the greatest *mannerist*, perhaps, of all our living poets. The homely, quaint, prosaic style, the eternal full-lengths of low and worthless characters, with their accustomed garnishing of sly jokes and familiar moralizing, are all on the surface of his writings. . . . An unrivalled and almost magical power of observation,—an anatomy of character and feeling not less exquisite and searching, . . . are interspersed by fits and strangely interwoven with the most minute and humble of his details. Add to all this the sure and profound sagacity of the remarks with which he every now and then startles us ; the weight and terseness of the maxims which he drops like oracular responses ; and that sweet and seldom-sounded chord of lyrical inspiration, the lightest touch of which instantly charms away all harshness from his numbers and all harshness from his themes."

See "Life of George Crabbe," by his son, 1838, new edition, 1847 ; JEFFREY, "Miscellanies ;" "Quarterly Review" for November, 1810 ; "Edinburgh Review" for April, 1810, and November, 1812 ; "Blackwood's Magazine" for July, 1819.

Crabet. See CRABETH.

Crabeth or **Crabet**, krä'bet, (THIERRY or DIRK and VAUTIER,) excellent Dutch painters on glass, are supposed to have been born in Gouda. They were brothers. They executed (between 1560 and 1570) on the glass windows of the church of Gouda pictures which were considered inimitable. Dirk died in 1601.

See DESCAMPS, "Vies des Peintres Flamands," etc.

Crab'tree, (WILLIAM,) an English astronomer, who was associated with Jeremiah Horrox in scientific pursuits. His observations were printed by Wallis in 1672. He died at an early age in 1641.

Cradock, (JOHN FRANCIS.) See HOWDEN, BARON.

Crad'ock, (JOSEPH,) an English gentleman and author, born at Leicester in 1742, inherited an easy fortune, and lived in London. He published "Village Memoirs," a work of fiction, "Zobeide," (1771,) a tragedy, which was performed with success, "Literary Memoirs," (4 vols., 1826,) and other works. Died in 1826.

Cradock, (LUKE,) an English painter of birds, etc. Died in 1717.

Cradock, (SAMUEL,) an English nonconformist divine, born in 1620. He became rector of North Cadbury, from which he was ejected in 1662. Besides other works, he published "Knowledge and Practice," "The Harmony of the Four Evangelists," and "Apostolical History," which were highly esteemed. Died in 1706.

Cradock, (ZACHARY,) a brother of Samuel, noticed above, was born probably in England in 1633. He left two sermons which have been greatly admired, the subjects of which are Providence and the Design of Christianity. Died in 1695.

Craesbeke, van, văn krăs'bă'keh or krăs'băk', (JOSEPH,) a skilful Flemish painter, born at Brussels in 1608, was a pupil of Brauwer, whom he imitated. He preferred low and sordid subjects, such as drunken brawls and parties of smokers. Died in 1668.

See DESCAMPS, "Vies des Peintres Flamands," etc.

Craft. See CRATO.

Crafts, (SAMUEL C.,) born at Woodstock, Connecticut, in 1768, was a member of Congress from 1816 to 1824, and was chosen Governor of Vermont in 1828, 1829, and 1830. Died in 1853.

Crafts, (WILLIAM,) a lawyer and poet, born at Charleston, South Carolina, in 1787 ; died in 1826.

See S. GILMAN, "Memoir of W. Crafts," 1828.

Craggs, (JAMES,) an English politician, was a friend of Addison, whom he succeeded as secretary of state in 1718. "He was a young man," says Macaulay, "whose natural parts were quick and showy, whose graceful person and winning manners had made him generally acceptable in society, and who if he had lived would probably have been the most formidable of all the rivals of Walpole." ("Essay on the Life and Writings of Addison.") Died in 1720.

Cragius. See CRAIG, (NICHOLAS.)

Craig, (JAMES,) a Scottish divine, born in East Lothian in 1682, became one of the most popular preachers of Edinburgh. He published several volumes of sermons and religious poems. Died in 1744.

See CHAMBERS, "Biographical Dictionary of Eminent Scotsmen."

Craig, (JAMES,) an American officer, born in Pennsylvania about 1820, served in the Mexican war, and was made a brigadier-general of volunteers in 1862.

Craig, (JOHN,) a Scottish Reformer, born about 1512, was a monk in early life. He visited Italy, where he was employed as teacher and rector in a school. Having been converted to the Protestant faith and made an open profession, he was sentenced at Rome to die by fire ; but in consequence of the death of the pope his prison was broken open by a mob, and he escaped from that doom, and returned to Scotland. He became a prominent coadjutor in the work of reformation in Scotland, and was chosen minister of Aberdeen in 1574. In 1577 he removed to Edinburgh, was appointed chaplain to James VI., and in 1580 composed the "National Covenant." Died in 1600.

See CHAMBERS, "Biographical Dictionary of Eminent Scotsmen."

Craig, (JOHN,) a Scottish mathematician, the dates of whose birth and death are unknown. He contributed to the "Philosophical Transactions," (1698–1712,) and published a work on fluxions, entitled "De Calculo Fluentium," (1718,) and a few other treatises. He first made known in England the differential calculus discovered by Leibnitz.

See CHAMBERS, "Biographical Dictionary of Eminent Scotsmen."

Craig, krăg, [Lat. CRA'GIUS,] (NICHOLAS,) a Danish writer, probably of British extraction, born at Ripen in

1549, became professor of Greek in Copenhagen, and rector of the university. He published a book on the Republic of Sparta, (1593,) which was highly esteemed, and a few other Latin works. In 1598 he was sent on a political mission to England. He was a friend of Scaliger. Died in 1602.

See KRAFT og NYERUP, "Litteraturlexicon."

Craig, (Sir THOMAS,) of Riccarton, an eminent Scottish lawyer and antiquary, born in Edinburgh about 1540, was a relative of John Craig, (1512–1600.) After pursuing his studies in Paris, he passed advocate in Edinburgh in 1563, and became a judge (justice depute) in 1564. He wrote several admired Latin poems, one of which is on the birth of James VI. In 1603 he completed his celebrated work on "Feudal Law," (" Jus Feudale,") which was not published until 1655, and which is regarded as an authority all over Europe. He was eminent for modesty and other virtues. Died in 1608.

See P. F. TYTLER, "Life of Sir Thomas Craig," 1823; CHAMBERS, "Biographical Dictionary of Eminent Scotsmen."

Craig, (WILLIAM,) a Scottish minister, born at Glasgow in 1709; died in 1784.

Craig, (WILLIAM,) a literary Scottish judge, born in 1745, succeeded Lord Hailes as judge in 1792. He contributed numerous papers to the "Mirror." Died in 1813.

See CHAMBERS, "Biographical Dictionary of Eminent Scotsmen."

Craik, (GEORGE LILLIE,) an able historical and critical writer and editor, born in Fifeshire, Scotland, in 1799. He became a resident of London about 1824, and produced "The Pursuit of Knowledge under Difficulties," (1831.) He contributed many historical and biographical articles to the "Penny Cyclopædia." Mr. Craik and C. Macfarlane were the principal editors or authors of the "Pictorial History of England" published by Knight, (1840–49.) He wrote the chapters on religion, commerce, industry, and literature in that work, and other useful works, among which are "Bacon : his Writings and his Philosophy," (3 vols., 1846,) "Romance of the Peerage," (1848–50, 4 vols.,) and a "History of English Literature," (2 vols.) In 1849 he was chosen professor of English literature in Queen's College, Belfast. Died in June, 1866.

See "Gentleman's Magazine" for August, 1866.

Craik, (JAMES,) a physician, born in Scotland in 1731. He accompanied Washington in an expedition against the French and Indians in 1754, and served as physician under General Braddock in 1755. After the Revolutionary war he settled near Mount Vernon, and became the family physician of Washington. Died in 1814.

Craik, MRS. See MULOCH.

Crak'an-thorp or Crakanthorpe, (RICHARD,) an English divine, born in Westmoreland in 1567. He was an eloquent Puritan preacher, and author of several works, among which is "Defence of the English Church," (" Defensio Ecclesiæ Anglicanæ.") Died in 1624.

Cramail, de, dęh krȧ′mȧl′ or krȧ′mȧ′yę, (ADRIEN DE Montluc—môN′lük′,) COUNT, a French writer, born in 1568, was a grandson of Marshal de Montluc. He was imprisoned in the Bastille from 1630 to 1642 for alleged intrigues against Richelieu. His farce called "La Comédie des Proverbes" (1616) was much admired. Died in 1646.

Cramer, krȧ′męr, (ANDREAS WILHELM,) a Danish professor, son of J. Andreas Cramer, the eminent poet, was born at Copenhagen in 1760. He became professor of law in his native city, and wrote several esteemed treatises on law and philology. Died in 1833.

See NIETZSCH, "Memoria A. W. Crameri."

Cramer, krȧ′męr, (CARL FRIEDRICH,) a littérateur, born at Kiel about 1750, was a son of Johann Andreas, noticed below. He was for some time professor of ancient literature in Copenhagen, and removed to Paris about 1795. He translated Schiller's "Joan of Arc," and other German works, into French, and published a good German-French Dictionary, (1805.) Died in Paris in 1808.

See "Conversations-Lexikon;" QUÉRARD, "La France Littéraire."

Cramer, krȧ′męr, (DANIEL,) a German Protestant theologian, born at Reetz in 1568. He was professor at Wittenberg and Stettin, and author of several works,

among which is "Schola Prophetica," (1606–12.) Died in 1637.

Cramer, (FRANZ,) a German composer of instrumental music, born at Munich in 1772; died in 1848.

Cramer, krȧ′męr, (GABRIEL,) an eminent Swiss geometer, born at Geneva in 1704. He cultivated many sciences with success, and in 1750 was appointed professor of philosophy in his native city. He was a Fellow of the Royal Society of London. One of his most important works is "An Analysis of Algebraic Curves." Died in 1752.

See SENEBIER, "Histoire littéraire de Genève."

Cramer, (JEAN JACQUES,) a Swiss Protestant professor of Hebrew and theology, was born near Zurich in 1673. He wrote, in Latin, "Theology of Israel," (1705.) Died in 1702.

Cramer, (JOHANN ANDREAS,) a German mineralogist, born at Quedlinburg in 1710, made important discoveries in metallurgy. He published, in Latin, "Elements of the Docimastic Art," (1739,) and in German, "Principles of Metallurgy," (1774–77,) both valuable works. Died in 1777.

See ADELUNG, Supplement to JÖCHER, "Allgemeines Gelehrten-Lexikon."

Cramer, (JOHANN ANDREAS,) an eminent German poet and prose-writer, born at Jöhstadt, in Saxony, in 1723. He was invited to Copenhagen by Frederick V., and appointed preacher to the court in 1754. In 1765 he became professor of theology in the university of that city. He translated Bossuet's "Universal History" into German, published "The Northern Spectator," (1759 -70,) a series of essays which was successful, and three volumes of poems, "Sämmtliche Gedichte," (1783.) The Germans reckon him among their best lyric poets. In 1774 he obtained the chair of theology at Kiel. Died in 1788.

See CHRISTIANI, "Oration (Gedächtnissrede) in Honour of J. A. Cramer," 1788; HIRSCHING, "Historisch-literarisches Handbuch."

Cramer, (JOHANN BAPTIST,) an excellent German composer and pianist, was born at Manheim in 1771, and taken to London in infancy. He passed most of his life in England. His "Studies for the Piano" are said to be unsurpassed in richness and harmony. Died in 1858.

See "Nouvelle Biographie Générale."

Cramer, (JOHANN FRIEDRICH,) a German jurist, was preceptor of the prince-royal of Prussia. Died in 1715.

Cramer, (JOHANN RUDOLPH,) a Swiss theologian and Hebraist, born near Zurich in 1678; died in 1737.

See J. ZIMMERMANN, " Vie de J. R. Cramer."

Cra′mer, (JOHN ANTONY,) an eminent scholar, born at Mitlödi, Switzerland, in 1793, removed to England in his youth. He became pastor of Binsey in 1822, and professor of modern history at Oxford in 1842. He published a "Description of Ancient Italy," (1826,) a "Description of Asia Minor," (1832,) "Anecdota Græca," (1837,) and other able works. Died in 1848.

Cramer, krȧ′męr, (NICOLAAS,) a Dutch portrait-painter, born at Leyden in 1670, was a pupil and imitator of Karel Moor. Died in 1710.

Cramp′tǫn, (Sir PHILIP,) a naturalist and physician, born in Dublin in 1777. He wrote several professional treatises. Died in 1858.

Cranach or Kranach, von, fon kran′ȧk or krȧ′nȧk, (LUCAS,) a celebrated German painter and engraver, born at Cranach, near Bamberg, in 1472. His family name was SUNDER. He painted history and portraits, and worked about fifty years at Wittenberg in the service of three Electors of Saxony, the last of whom was John Frederick. He was an intimate friend of Luther and Melanchthon, whose portraits he painted and engraved. Among his master-pieces are "The Preaching of John the Baptist," and a "Crucifixion." His works are said to be more admirable for thought or invention than for execution. He was a good colorist, but very deficient in design. Died at Weimar in 1553.

See SCHUCHARDT, "L. Kranachs des Aeltern Leben und Werke," 1851; HELLER, "Versuch über das Leben, etc. L. Cranachs," Bamberg, 1821.

Cranach, von, (LUCAS,) a son of the preceding, born in 1515, was also an eminent painter. He was a burgomaster of Wittenberg. Died in 1586.

Cran'borne or **Cran'bourne**, (ROBERT ARTHUR TALBOT GASCOIGNE CECIL,) LORD, a younger son of the Marquis of Salisbury, born in 1830. He was formerly called LORD ROBERT CECIL. In 1853 he was elected to Parliament by the voters of Stamford, which he represented for many years. He is one of the foremost debaters of the Conservative party. He became secretary for India in the cabinet of Lord Derby in July, 1866, and resigned in March, 1867. He inherited the title of Marquis of Salisbury in the spring of 1868, and then passed into the House of Lords.

Cranbourne. See CRANBORNE.

Cranch, (CHRISTOPHER P.,) a poet and landscape-painter, a son of William Cranch, noticed below, was born at Alexandria, Virginia, in 1813. He visited Italy about 1848, after which he resided many years in Paris. He wrote "The Last of the Huggermuggers," (1856.)

See GRISWOLD, "Poets and Poetry of America;" TUCKERMAN, "Book of the Artists."

Cranch, (WILLIAM,) LL.D., an eminent American jurist, born at Weymouth, Massachusetts, in 1769, graduated at Harvard in 1787. In 1801 he was appointed by President Adams an associate judge of the United States circuit court for the District of Columbia, of which he was made chief justice by Jefferson in 1805. The duties of these two positions Judge Cranch discharged with unwearied assiduity until his death; and, during this period of more than half a century, it is said that only two of all his decisions were overruled by the United States supreme court and sent back for amendment. His legal attainments were varied and profound, and his industry and powers of application were extraordinary. He made careful reports of cases decided in the circuit court for the District of Columbia from 1801 to 1841, published in 6 octavo vols., and, as reporter to the supreme court of the United States, issued 9 vols. from 1801 to 1815, and others in 1835. Died in September, 1855.

Cräne, (THOMAS,) an English nonconformist minister of Lancashire, wrote a "Prospect of Divine Providence," (1672.) Died in 1714.

Cräne, (WILLIAM M.,) an American commodore, born at Elizabethtown, New Jersey, in 1776. He served with distinction in the war of 1812. In 1827 he was appointed commander of a squadron in the Mediterranean, and in 1842 became chief of the bureau of ordnance. Died in 1846.

Cran'mer, (THOMAS,) Archbishop of Canterbury, an English statesman, divine, and Reformer, was born at Aslacton, in Nottinghamshire, in 1489. He became a Fellow of Jesus College, Cambridge, and was learned in Greek, Hebrew, and theology. In 1529 he obtained the favour of Henry VIII. by proposing that the question of his divorce should be referred to the universities. The king appointed him his chaplain, and sent him to Rome to procure the assent of the pope to the divorce. Having failed in this mission, he returned home in 1530, and infringed the rule of his church by marriage with a niece of Osiander. He was appointed Archbishop of Canterbury in 1533, and became Henry's favourite adviser, or prime minister. He had secretly adopted the principles of the Reformers, and he used his influence to subvert the power of the pope in England and to abolish the monasteries. A few years after his elevation to the primacy he openly favoured the Reformation, assisted in compiling the "Bishops' Book," and in 1538 opposed without success the law of the Six Articles, or "Bloody Statutes." Though he resisted the royal will on this and other occasions, he was protected by Henry when the Catholic courtiers conspired to ruin him in 1544. In 1547 he was chosen one of the regency during the minority of Edward VI. He was the head of a commission which composed the English Liturgy in 1548.

"The man who took the chief part," says Macaulay, "in settling the conditions of the alliance which produced the Anglican Church, was Thomas Cranmer. He was the representative of both the parties which at that time needed each other's assistance. In his character of divine, he was ready to go as far in the way of change as any Swiss or Scottish Reformer. In his character of statesman, he was desirous to preserve that organization which

had served the purposes of the bishops of Rome and might be expected to serve equally well the purposes of the English kings and their ministers. His temper and his understanding eminently fitted him to act as mediator." Notwithstanding his general moderation, he went so far as to condemn two persons to death for heresy. By the entreaties of King Edward VI. he was induced in 1553 to sign the patent which settled the crown on Lady Jane Grey, and in the same year was committed to the Tower for treason against Queen Mary. His enemies, in order to subject him to a more cruel punishment, withdrew the charge of treason, and prosecuted him for heresy. He was excommunicated in 1555. Tempted with the hopes of life, and overcome by the fear of torture, he agreed to subscribe to the doctrines of the papal supremacy and the real presence. Repenting of this lapse, which would not have saved him from the stake, he suffered with fortitude martyrdom by fire in 1556.

"He was undoubtedly," says Hume, "a man of merit; possessed of learning and capacity, and adorned with candour, sincerity, and all those virtues which were fitted to render him useful and amiable in society. His moral qualities procured him universal respect, and the courage of his martyrdom made him the hero of the Protestant party." Others, including Macaulay, form a less favourable estimate, and call him an unscrupulous time-server. For Froude's view of the character of Cranmer, formed, as it appears, from a very careful examination of his life and acts, see the first six volumes of his "History of England," but more particularly chap. xxxiii. Cranmer was author of many theological treatises.

See ARCHDEACON TODD, "Life of Cranmer," 1831; STRYPE, "Memorials of Cranmer;" "Lives of Eminent British Statesmen," in "Lardner's Cabinet Cyclopædia;" MACAULAY, "History of England," vol. i.; LINGARD, "History of England;" W. F. HOOK, "Lives of the Archbishops of Canterbury;" A. VAN DEINSE, "Leven van T. Cranmer," Amsterdam, 1847; SHAKSPEARE's "Henry VIII."

Cran'tor, [Κράντωρ,] a Greek Academic philosopher, born at Soli, or Soles, in Cilicia, lived about 300 B.C. After he had become distinguished in his own country, he went to Athens, and studied in the school of Xenocrates. He is cited by Horace as an eminent moralist. He wrote, besides other works, a "Treatise on Affliction," (Περὶ Πένθους,) which was highly praised, and from which Cicero borrowed largely in his "Consolatio."

See DIOGENES LAERTIUS; KAYSER, "Dissertatio de Crantore Academico," 1841.

Crantz, (ALBERT.) See KRANTZ.

Crantz, kränts, (HEINRICH JOHANN NEPOMUCENUS,) a German botanist, born in 1722, was a professor of medicine at Vienna.

Cran'worth, (ROBERT MONSEY ROLFE,) BARON, an English judge, born at Cranworth, in Norfolk, in 1790. He was elected to Parliament by the Liberals in 1832, appointed solicitor-general in 1834, and a baron of the exchequer in 1839. In 1850 he became vice-chancellor, and was raised to the peerage, as Baron Cranworth. On the formation of a ministry by Lord Aberdeen in December, 1852, he was appointed lord chancellor of England. He retired from office when Lord Derby came into power, in February, 1858, was again appointed lord chancellor in July, 1865, and resigned with his colleagues in June, 1866. Died in July, 1868.

See FOSS, "The Judges of England," vol. ix.

Cranz, kränts, (DAVID,) a Moravian missionary and historian, born at Neugarten, Pomerania, in 1723. He became secretary of Count Zinzendorf in 1747, after which he laboured in Greenland. He wrote a "History of Greenland," (1765,) and a "History of the Moravians," (1771.) Died in Silesia in 1777.

Crapelet, kråp'lậ', (GEORGES ADRIEN,) a French publisher and writer, born at Paris in 1789. He translated into French verse "The Marriage of Thetis and Peleus," by Catullus, (1809,) and wrote "Souvenirs of London," (1817.) Died in 1842.

Crapone, de, deh krȧ'pon', (ADAM,) a French engineer, born at Salon in 1519, was skilled in hydraulic architecture. He constructed the most ancient canal in France, called the "Canal of Crapone," finished about 1560. Died in 1559.

Cras, kräs, (HENDRIK CONSTANTIN,) a Dutch jurist, born at Wageningen in 1739; died in 1820.

See M. KEMPER, "Memoria H. C. Cras," 1825.

Crash'aw, (RICHARD,) an English poet and priest, born in London. He became a Fellow of Peterhouse, Cambridge, in 1637, before which he had published some Latin poems in one of which occurs this much-admired line on the miracle at Cana :

"*Lympha pudica Deum vidit et erubuit.*"[*]

He was ejected from the university in 1644 for refusing to take the Covenant, and went to France, where he was converted to the Roman Catholic faith. In 1646 he published "Steps to the Temple," "Sacred Poems," etc., which display a rich imagination. He was a canon of the church of Loretto, Italy, when he died about 1650.

See "*Retrospective Review,*" vol. i., 1820.

Crasset, krȧ'sȧ', (JEAN,) a French Jesuit, born at Dieppe in 1618, lived many years in Paris. He published several ascetic works, and a "History of the Church of Japan," (1689.) Died in 1692.

Crasso, krȧs'so, (FRANCESCO,) an Italian jurist of high reputation, lived at Milan in the sixteenth century.

Crasso, (LORENZO,) an Italian author, of whose life we have no details, was born at Naples. His works, in prose and verse, display talent, but are marred by the bad taste of that time. Among the principal of them are "Heroic Epistles," (1655,) and "Eulogies on Literary Men," (1656.)

Crasso, (NICCOLÒ,) a Venetian historian, born in the sixteenth century, wrote, besides other Latin works, "Eulogies of Illustrious Venetians,"(1612,) and a treatise "On the Form of the Venetian Government," ("De Forma Reipublicæ Venetæ.")

Cras'sus, (LUCIUS LICINIUS,) a famous Roman orator and lawyer, born about 140 B.C., (612 A.U.C.) He was elected consul in 95 B.C., and censor about two years later. He was considered the most excellent orator of his time, and was highly praised by Cicero, who assigned to Crassus a part of the dialogue in his treatise "De Oratore." His orations are not extant. Died in 90 or 91 B.C.

See CICERO, "Brutus" and "De Oratore;" DRUMANN, "Geschichte Roms;" MEYER, "Oratorum Romanorum Fragmenta."

Crassus, (MARCUS LICINIUS,) a Roman triumvir, noted for his great wealth, was born about 108 B.C. He was chosen prætor in 74 B.C., (680 A.U.C.,) and defeated Spartacus, the leader of a servile revolt. In the year 71 he was chosen consul with Pompey, and a few years later he united with Pompey and Cæsar to form the first triumvirate, which ruined the power of the senate. Crassus and Pompey were elected consuls in 56 B.C., and, while Cæsar commanded in Gaul, Crassus obtained command of Syria for five years. He is said to have manifested extravagant joy at the prospect of increasing his fortune in the East. Having resolved to invade Parthia, he crossed the Euphrates, and, after taking a town in the year 54, returned to Syria, where he passed the winter. The next season he entered Mesopotamia, and was defeated with great loss by the Parthian general Surena near Carrhæ, (the Haran of the Bible.) He was then compelled by his mutinous troops to meet in conference with Surena, who had made overtures for peace, and was there treacherously killed in 53 B.C. His ruling passion was avarice. He was a man of great industry, a keen speculator, and a large dealer in slaves.

See PLUTARCH, "Crassus;" DRUMANN, "Geschichte Roms;" "Nouvelle Biographie Générale."

Crassus, (PUBLIUS,) a son of the triumvir Crassus, served as legate of Cæsar in Gaul in 58 B.C. He fought bravely against the Parthians, and was killed at the battle near Carrhæ in 53 B.C.

Crassus, (P. LICINIUS,) a Roman general, who was chosen pontifex maximus in 212 B.C. In 205 he became consul with Scipio Africanus, and gave proof of military talents in the war against Hannibal. Died in 183 B.C.

Crastoni, krȧs-to'nee, or **Crestoni,** krȧs-to'nee, (GIOVANNI,) an Italian Hellenist and monk, born at Piacenza, is said to have compiled the first Greek-Latin Dictionary, printed about 1478.

Cratère. See CRATERUS.

Crat'e-rus, [Gr. Κρατερός; Fr. CRATÈRE, krȧ'tair',] one of the most eminent of the generals and successors of Alexander the Great, whom he followed in the invasion of Persia. He was a rival of Hephæstion in the royal favour. His character is said to have been noble and highly esteemed by the king. In 324 B.C. he was selected to conduct the veterans back to Macedonia. At the death of Alexander (323) he was associated with Antipater in the government of Macedonia and Greece. He commanded an army in Cappadocia, where he was defeated by Eumenes, and killed in battle, in 321 B.C.

See PLUTARCH, "Alexander," and "Phocion."

Cra'tes [Κράτης] of Athens, an excellent Greek comic poet, who flourished about 450 B.C. In his youth he was the principal actor in the plays of Cratinus. He indulged in personalities less than other writers of the old comedy. Among the titles of his plays are "The Neighbours," (Γείτονες,) and "The Games," (Παιδιαί.) The fragments of his works which have come down to us are admired for purity and elegance of style.

See FABRICIUS, "Bibliotheca Græca;" MEINEKE, "Quæstiones Scenicæ," and his "Fragmenta Comicorum Græcorum."

Crates of Athens, a philosopher of the old Academy, flourished about 280 B.C. He was a pupil and intimate friend of Polemo, whom he succeeded in the chair of the Academy. His writings are lost.

Crates of Thebes, a famous Cynic philosopher, was a son of Ascondas. He became a disciple of Diogenes, at Athens, probably about 330 B.C., and was highly esteemed for his probity and wisdom. He was noted for his self-control, abstinence, and preference of poverty to riches. He wrote essays on philosophy, tragedies, which were praised by Diogenes Laertius, and small poems, all of which are lost. Crates was living in 307 B.C.

See BRUCKER, "Historia Philosophiæ;" POSTHUMUS, "Dissertatio de Cratete Cynico," 1823; FABRICIUS, "Bibliotheca Græca."

Crates, an eminent grammarian and Stoic, born at Mallus, in Cilicia, left, besides many other works, a corrected or annotated edition of Homer, fragments of which are extant. He lived at Pergamos, and about 156 B.C. was sent by the king of that country as ambassador to Rome, where he gave lectures on grammar. He founded a flourishing school of grammar at Pergamos.

See FABRICIUS, "Bibliotheca Græca;" SUETONIUS, "De illustribus Grammaticis."

Cra-te'vas, [Κρατεύας,] a Greek botanist, who lived about 80 B.C., is often quoted by Pliny and Dioscorides. He wrote on Materia Medica.

Cra-ti'nus, [Κρατῖνος,] a celebrated Athenian poet of the old comedy, born about 519 B.C., was a son of Callimedes, and a rival of Aristophanes. He was the first comic writer who made the drama an instrument of personal satire, and was noted for the audacity of his sarcasms. Pericles was often the object of his unsparing invective. He produced numerous plays, nine of which gained prizes. None of his works exist in a complete state. In 423 B.C. he obtained a triumph over Aristophanes for his "Wine-Flask." He died in 422, aged about ninety-six. The extant fragments of Cratinus were edited by Runkel, 1827.

See MEINEKE, "Historia Critica," and "Fragmenta Comicorum Græcorum;" C. W. LUCAS, "Cratinus et Eupolis," 1826.

Cratippe. See CRATIPPUS.

Cra-tip'pus, [Κράτιππος,] a Greek historian, who lived about 400 B.C., and continued the work of Thucydides.

Cratippus, [Gr. Κράτιππος; Fr. CRATIPPE, krȧ'tèp',] a Greek Peripatetic philosopher of Mitylene. He was a teacher and friend of Cicero, who estimated him as the first philosopher of that age. When Pompey, retreating from Pharsalia, passed through Mitylene, Cratippus conversed with him on Providence. About 48 B.C. he opened a school at Athens, to which Cicero sent his son Marcus. Brutus attended his lectures at Athens in 44 B.C. Cratippus appears to have left only one work, a "Treatise on Divination by Dreams." The date of his death is unknown.

See CICERO, "De Officiis" and "De Divinatione;" PLUTARCH, "Pompey" and "Cicero;" BAYLE, "Historical and Critical Dictionary."

Crato, krȧ'to, or **Craton,** krȧ'ton, (JOHANN,) a German physician, originally named CRAFT or CRAFFT, was born at Breslau in 1519. He studied under Luther and Melanchthon at Wittenberg, and was the favourite pupil of Montano in medicine. He practised many years at

---

[*] "The modest water saw its God and blushed."

á, ē, ī, ō, ū, ȳ, *long;* ȧ, ė, ȯ, same, less prolonged; ă, ĕ, ῐ, ŏ, ŭ, y̆, *short;* ą, ę, į, ǫ, *obscure;* fär, fåll, fät; mët; nŏt; gōōd; mōōn;

Augsburg, and became chief physician of the emperors Ferdinand I. and Maximilian II. He published "Introduction to Medicine," ("Isagoge Medicinæ," 1560,) and other medical works. Died in 1585.

See NICÉRON, "Mémoires:" ADAM, "Vitæ Germanorum Medicorum;" MORÉRI, "Dictionnaire Historique."

Crat′y̆-lus, [Κρατυλος,] a Greek philosopher, who lived in the fifth century B.C., and professed the doctrines of Heraclitus. He was one of the teachers of Plato.

Crauford. See CRAWFORD and CRAUFURD.

Crau′furd or **Craw′furd,** (JOHN,) a British officer and writer of the present era, published several valuable works on Oriental affairs, among which are a "History of the Indian Archipelago," (1820,) "Siam and Cochin China," (1828,) and a "Grammar and Dictionary of the Malay Language," (1852.)

Craufurd, Crau′ford, or **Craw′ford,** (QUINTIN,) a Scottish author, born in Ayrshire in 1743, went to India in his youth, served the Company as military and civil officer, and about 1780 returned to Europe with an easy fortune. He lived some years in Paris, where he had intimate relations with the queen Marie Antoinette and the empress Josephine. He published "Sketches of the History, Religion, and Manners of the Hindoos," (1790,) "Mélanges of History and Literature," (1809,) and other works, which are commended. Died in 1819.

Crause. See KRAUSE.

Cră′ven, (CHARLES,) became Governor of South Carolina in 1712. He successfully defended the colony against the Yemassee Indians in 1715.

Craven, (THOMAS T.,) an American rear-admiral, born in the District of Columbia, entered the service in 1822. He distinguished himself as commander of the Brooklyn in the victory by which Farragut captured New Orleans in April, 1862.

Craven, (TUNIS AUGUSTUS,) an American naval officer, born in New Hampshire, entered the navy about 1829. He became a lieutenant in 1841, and afterwards a captain. He was captain of the iron-clad Tecumseh, and was drowned when it was sunk by a torpedo in the attack on the defences of Mobile, August 5, 1864.

Cră′ven, (WILLIAM,) an English clergyman, born in 1731, was professor of Arabic in Cambridge, and published "Sermons on a Future State," and "Discourses in Answer to Hume," (1802.) Died in 1815.

Craveta, krä-vä′tä, (AIMONE,) an Italian jurist, born in Piedmont in 1504; died in 1569.

Craw′ford, (ADAIR,) F.R.S., an eminent British chemist and physician, born in 1749. He was professor of chemistry at Woolwich, and a member of the Philosophical Society of Philadelphia. He acquired reputation by an ingenious work entitled "Experiments and Observations on Animal Heat," (1779.) Died in 1795.

Crawford, EARL OF. See LINDSAY, (JOHN.)

Craw′ford, Crau′ford, or **Craw′furd,** (DAVID,) a Scottish historian, born in 1665. He was appointed historiographer royal for Scotland by Queen Anne, and in 1706 published "Memoirs of the Affairs of Scotland, 1566–81," which is charged with partiality. Died in 1726.

See CHAMBERS, "Biographical Dictionary of Eminent Scotsmen."

Craw′ford, (GEORGE W.,) an American lawyer, born in Columbia county, Georgia, in 1798. He was elected Governor of Georgia in 1843, and re-elected in 1845. He was appointed secretary of war by President Taylor in March, 1849, and resigned, in consequence of the death of the President, in July, 1850.

Crawford, (NATHANIEL MACON,) an American Baptist minister, born near Lexington, Georgia, in 1811, was a son of William H. Crawford, noticed below. He was chosen president of Mercer University, Georgia, in 1854, resigned in 1856, and was re-elected about 1858. He is distinguished as a pulpit orator.

Crawford, (QUINTIN.) See CRAUFURD.

Crawford, (ROBERT,) a Scottish poet, acquired reputation by the admired lyrics of "Tweedside," and "The Bush aboon Traquair." Died in 1733.

Crawford, (SAMUEL W.,) an American general, born in Franklin county, Pennsylvania, in 1829. He became a surgeon in the army about 1851, and was one of the garrison of Fort Sumter in April, 1861. In the spring of 1862 he was appointed a brigadier-general of volunteers.

He commanded a division at Antietam, September 17, 1862, and at Gettysburg, July 1–3, 1863.

Crawford, (THOMAS,) an eminent American sculptor, born in New York in 1814. He visited Italy about 1835, and studied under Thorwaldsen at Rome, where he worked many years. About 1840 he produced a statue of "Orpheus," which was much admired. He received in 1849 a commission from the State of Virginia to execute a colossal equestrian statue of Washington, which is at Richmond. Among his numerous works are several religious and mythological subjects, and a colossal statue of the Genius of America for the Capitol at Washington. Died in London in 1857.

See TUCKERMAN, "Book of the Artists:" "Democratic Review" for May, 1843; "Atlantic Monthly" for July, 1869.

Crawford, (WILLIAM,) a Scottish divine, born at Kelso in 1676, wrote a work entitled "Dying Thoughts." Died in 1742.

Crawford, (WILLIAM HARRIS,) an American statesman, born in Amherst county, Virginia, in 1772, removed with his father to Georgia in his childhood. He studied law, was admitted to the bar in 1798, and settled at Lexington, Georgia. In 1807 he was elected a Senator of the United States by the Democrats, and in 1813 he was appointed minister to France. He became secretary of war in 1815, and secretary of the treasury in 1816. He continued to hold this position throughout the administration of President Monroe, which ended in March, 1825. In 1824 he was nominated for the Presidency by the Congressional caucus, the right of which to select a candidate was disowned by the majority of the party. His competitors were General Jackson, John Quincy Adams, and Henry Clay. Crawford received only forty-one electoral votes. He was afterwards a circuit judge in Georgia. Died in 1834.

See "National Portrait-Gallery of Distinguished Americans," vol. iv.

Crawfurd, (DAVID.) See CRAWFORD.

Craw′furd, (GEORGE,) a British historian, of whose life we have no details, born probably in Scotland. He published an esteemed "History of the Family of the Stuarts," (1710,) and the "Peerage of Scotland," (1716.)

Crawfurd, (JOHN.) See CRAUFURD.

Crayer, de, deh kri′yer or krā′yä′, (CASPAR or GASPARD,) a celebrated Flemish historical painter, was born at Antwerp in 1582. He worked for a time at Brussels, and afterwards for many years at Ghent. He adorned the cities of Flanders with many large altar-pieces and other pictures. His design is generally correct, and his colouring good. He nearly equalled Van Dyck in portraits. Among his master-pieces are "Saint Catherine passing up to Heaven," and the "Martyrdom of Saint Blaise," painted in his eighty-sixth year. Died at Ghent in 1669.

See BRYAN, "Dictionary of Painters;" DESCAMPS, "Vies des Peintres Flamands," etc.

Crayon, (GEOFFREY.) See IRVING, (WASHINGTON.)

Crea′sy̆, (Sir EDWARD SHEPHERD,) an English historian and lawyer, born at Bexley, in Kent, in 1812. He was called to the bar about 1837, and appointed professor of history in University College, London, in 1850. He published in 1852 "Fifteen Decisive Battles of the World," which has passed through nine or more editions, and in 1856 "The Rise and Progress of the English Constitution," which is commended. In 1860 he was appointed chief justice of Ceylon. The first volume of his "History of England" (in 5 vols.) appeared in 1869.

Crébillon, de, deh krā′be′yòn′, (CLAUDE PROSPER Jolyot—zho′le-o′,) a French novelist, son of Prosper Jolyot, noticed below, was born in Paris in 1707. He wrote several licentious novels which were once in vogue. His own conduct is said to have been strictly moral. Died in 1777.

See GRIMM, "Correspondance;" ABBÉ DE VOISENON, "Anecdotes littéraires et critiques," etc.

Crébillon, de, (PROSPER JOLYOT,) an eminent French dramatic poet, born at Dijon in 1674. He was sent to Paris to study law with a M. Prieur, an amateur of the theatre, who persuaded him to compose tragedies. His "Idoménée" was successful in 1705, and his "Atrée" ("Atreus," 1707) added to his reputation. In 1711 he produced his "Rhadamiste," which is pronounced by

La Harpe and others not only his master-piece, but one of the finest tragedies which have appeared on the French stage. His "Pyrrhus" (1726) was much admired. During the twenty-two years which followed, he wrote nothing. In 1731 he was admitted into the French Academy, on which occasion he pronounced a poetical address, in which occurs this applauded line :

"Aucun fiel n'a jamais empoisonné ma plume."*

He produced in 1749 his "Catilina," which had been long expected, and in reference to which the public exclaimed, with Cicero, "How long, O Catiline, wilt thou abuse our patience?" It was performed with immense applause; though critics think it betrays a decline in power. He died in 1762, having won a place among the dramatists of the first order next to Corneille and Racine. He preferred to live in liberty and poverty rather than cringe for favour at the feet of power.

See D'ALEMBERT, "Éloge de Crébillon ;" LA HARPE, "Lycée ;" ABBÉ DE LA PORTE, "Biographie de Crébillon ;" "Nouvelle Biographie Générale ;" AMANTON, "Révélations sur les deux Crébillon," 1835 ; "Fraser's Magazine" for September, 1851.

Credi, di, de .krä′dee, (LORENZO **Sciarpelloni**—shaR-pĕl-lo′nee,) an excellent Italian painter, born at Florence in 1453. He imitated with success Leonardo da Vinci, his fellow-pupil. A "Nativity" at Florence, and a "Madonna and Child" in the Louvre, are reckoned among his best productions. He died at Florence about 1535. His name is sometimes written LORENZO ANDREA DI CREDI.

See VASARI, "Lives of the Painters."

Credner, krĕd′ner or krĕt′ner, (KARL AUGUST,) a German theologian, born near Gotha in 1797, became professor of theology at Giessen in 1832. Among his works are an "Introduction to Biblical Studies," (1832–38,) and a "History of the New Testament," (1852.)

Creech, (Rev. THOMAS,) an English scholar, eminent as a translator, was born at Blandford, Dorsetshire, in 1659. He was educated at Oxford, and became a Fellow of All Souls' College. In 1682 he published his translation of Lucretius, in verse, which is much admired. He also translated Horace, Theocritus, and portions of other classic authors. He committed suicide in 1701. "Creech is a much better translator," says Dr. Warton, "than he is usually supposed to be. He is a nervous and vigorous writer."

See "Biographia Britannica."

Creech, (WILLIAM,) a Scottish bookseller of Edinburgh, noted for his facetious talents and penuriousness, was born in 1745 ; died in 1815.

See CHAMBERS, "Biographical Dictionary of Eminent Scotsmen."

Cregut, krä′gŏŏt, (FRIEDRICH CHRISTIAN,) a German medical writer, born at Hanau in 1675 ; died in 1758.

Creighton, krā′ton, ? or **Creichton,** (JOHN,) an Irishman, who was born in 1648, fought against the Scottish Covenanters, and wrote "Memoirs" (1731) of events which he witnessed. Died in 1733.

Creighton, krā′ton, (JOHN ORDE,) an American commodore, born in New York City ; died in 1846.

Creighton or Crighton, krī′ton, (ROBERT,) Bishop of Bath and Wells, was born at Dunkeld in 1593. He was chaplain to Charles II. during his exile. Died in 1672.

Creighton, (ROBERT,) an English clergyman, son of the preceding, born in 1639. He had great skill in church-music, and composed the admired anthem for four voices, "I will arise and go to my Father." Died in 1736.

Crell, krĕl, (CHRISTOPH LUDWIG,) a distinguished German jurist, born at Leipsic in 1703. He was professor of law at Wittenberg, and wrote many legal dissertations. Died in 1758.

See SPERBACH, "Merita et Memoria C. L. Crellii," 1758.

Crell, (JOHANN.) See CRELLIUS.

Crell, (LUDWIG CHRISTIAN,) a German classical scholar, father of Christoph Ludwig, noticed above, was born at Neustadt in 1671. He became professor of philosophy at Leipsic. Died in 1733.

See MORÉRI, "Dictionnaire Historique."

Crell, (NIKOLAUS,) born in Leipsic about 1550, became prime minister of Christian I., Elector of Saxony.

* " I ne'er in gall dipt my envenomed pen."

He was imprisoned and put to death by order of Frederick William, the successor of Christian, in 1601.

Crelle, kRel′leh,(AUGUST LEOPOLD,) a German mathematician, born at Eichenwerder, Prussia, in 1780. In 1828 he was chosen a member of the Academy of Sciences of Berlin. Among his works are an "Essay on a General Theory of Analytic Functions," (1826,) and a "Manual of Geometry," (1827.) He edited the "Journal of Mathematics," (Berlin, 1826–51.)

See BROCKHAUS, "Conversations-Lexikon."

Crellius, kRel′le-ûs, or **Crell,** kRĕl, (JOHANN,) a German Socinian theologian, born near Nuremberg in 1590. He became rector of a Socinian school at Cracow, where he died in 1633. His most important work is a "Vindication of Religious Liberty," (" Vindiciæ pro Religionis Libertate," 1637.)

See J. F. MAYER, "Programma de J. Crellio," 1706.

Crémieux, krā′me-uh′, (ISAAC ADOLPHE,) a French politician and eloquent advocate, was born at Nîmes in 1796. He removed to Paris about 1830, and became advocate to the court of cassation. In 1842 he was elected to the Chamber of Deputies, in which he acted with the radical party, (extrème gauche.) On the abdication of Louis Philippe, February, 1848, he declared in favour of a republic, and became minister of justice in the provisional government. He retired from office June 7, 1848, and favoured the election of Louis Napoleon to the Presidency. In 1849 and 1850 he was an orator of the opposition in the Assembly. Since the coup d'état of December, 1851, he has lived as a private citizen.

See LAMARTINE, " Histoire de la Révolution de Février."

Cremonese dei Paesi. See BASSI, (FRANCESCO.)

Cremonini, krà-mo-nee′nee, (CESARE,) an Italian Peripatetic philosopher, born at Cento in 1550. For forty years he taught philosophy in the University of Padua, and was one of the chiefs of the rigid Aristotelians. He was widely renowned in his day, but his works are now neglected. Died in 1631.

See GINGUENÉ, "Histoire Littéraire d'Italie ;" BAYLE, "Historical and Critical Dictionary ;" RITTER, "History of Philosophy."

Cremonini, (GIOVANNI BATTISTA,) an Italian painter of perspective and of sacred history, born at Cento about 1560, worked at Bologna, and was the master of Guercino. Died in 1610.

Cremutius. See CORDUS.

Crenius, krā′ne-ûs,(THOMAS,) a German writer, whose proper name was **Crusius,** (kRoo′ze-ûs,) was born in Brandenburg in 1648. He was employed as corrector of the press at Leyden, and published several mediocre Latin works, among which was "Historical and Critical Dissertations," (10 vols., 1691.) Died in 1728.

See MORÉRI, "Dictionnaire Historique."

Cre′on, [Gr. Κρέων,] a fabulous king of Thebes, was a brother of Jocasta. He succeeded Laius, and gave the throne to Œdipus to reward him for liberating Thebes from the Sphinx. He became king again after Œdipus went into exile.

See SOPHOCLES. "Œdipus" and "Antigone."

Cre-o-phȳ′lus, [Κρεώφυλος,] an ancient Greek epic poet, who is supposed to have been a contemporary and friend of Homer.

Crépin, krā′pän′, (LOUIS PHILIPPE,) a French painter of marine views, born in Paris in 1772 ; died about 1845.

Crepu, kReh-pü′, (NICOLAS,) a Flemish painter, born at Brussels in 1680. He painted flowers, camps, and other subjects with success, in Brussels. Died in 1761.

See DESCAMPS, "Vies des Peintres Flamands," etc.

Créqui, de, deh krà′ke′, (ANTOINE,) Seigneur de Pont de Rémi, (pòn deh rà′me′,) a famous French captain, who for a time defended Thérouane against Henry VIII. of England, (1513.) He was killed about 1525.

Créqui, de, (FRANÇOIS DE BONNE,) Duc de Lesdiguières, (là′de′ge′aiR′,) an able French general, born about 1624, was made a marshal of France in 1668. After Turenne died, in 1675, Créqui was the senior of the marshals. He gained victories over the Duke of Lorraine, in Lorraine and Alsace, in 1677 and 1678. Died in 1687. "He had the reputation," said Voltaire, "of one who was destined to supply the place of Turenne."

See SISMONDI, "Histoire des Français ;" VOLTAIRE, "Siècle de Louis XIV."

ā, ē, ī, ō, ū, ȳ, long; à, è, ò, same, less prolonged; ă, ĕ, ĭ, ŏ, ŭ, ў, short; a, e, i, o, obscure; fär, fäll, fät; mĕt; nŏt; gŏŏd; mōōn;

Créqui de Blanchefort, de, dẹh krȧ′ke′ dẹh blôNsh′-foR′, (CHARLES,) MARQUIS, afterwards Duc de Lesdiguières, a French general, who became marshal of France in 1622. He defeated the Duke of Feria in Piedmont in 1625. He was killed at the siege of Brema in 1638.

See N. CHORIER, "Histoire de la Vie de C. de Créqui," 1683; SISMONDI, "Histoire des Français."

Créqui de Blanchefort, de, (CHARLES,) DUC, a French general, brother of François, noticed above, born about 1624. He served in several battles in Flanders, and was sent as ambassador to Rome, where he was insulted by the papal guards in 1662. Louis XIV. forced the court of Rome to apologize for this insult. Died in 1687.

Crescence. See CRESCENTIUS.

Crescentini, krȧ-shĕn-tee′nee, (GIROLAMO,) a famous Italian singer, born at Urbania in 1769, made his *début* at Naples in 1788. In 1809 Napoleon appointed him first singer of his court. Died in 1846.

See FÉTIS, "Biographie Universelle des Musiciens."

Crescentius, kres-sen′she-us, [Fr. CRESCENCE, krȧ′-sôNss′,] a Roman chief, who obtained the title of consul in Rome in 980 A.D. He attempted, says Sismondi, to restore to Rome its liberty and former glory. His designs, however, were thwarted by Pope Gregory V. and the emperor Otho III., who entered Rome with an army in 998. Crescentius, having capitulated to Otho, was put to death.

See SISMONDI, "Histoire des Républiques Italiennes."

Crescenzi, (BARTOLOMMEO.) See CAVARAZZI.

Crescenzi, krȧ-shĕn′zee, (GIOVANNI BATTISTA,) a skilful Italian painter and architect, born in Rome about 1595. He went to Spain in 1617, and was employed by Philip III., for whom he designed the beautiful Pantheon of the Escurial, begun about 1620. He received from Philip IV. the title of Marquis de la Torre. Died at Madrid in 1660.

See NAGLER, "Neues Allgemeines Künstler-Lexikon."

Crescenzi, Crescenzo, krȧ-shĕn′zo, or **Crescenzio,** krȧ-shĕn′ze-o, (NICCOLÒ,) a physician of Naples, lived about 1700, and wrote some valuable medical works.

Crescenzi, de′, dȧ krȧ-shĕn′zee, (PIETRO,) an Italian senator, called "the restorer of agriculture," was born at Bologna in 1230. He wrote, in Latin, a "Treatise on Rural Economy," ("Opus ruralium commodorum,") —a remarkable monument, says Du Petit-Thouars, "in the history of agriculture." It obtained a great circulation, and was translated into many languages. He became a senator at the age of seventy. Died about 1320.

See GINGUENÉ, "Histoire Littéraire d'Italie;" FILIPPO RE, "Elogio storico di P. de' Crescenzi," 1812.

Crescimbeni, krȧ-shĕm-bā′nee, (GIOVANNI MARIA,) a distinguished Italian poet and critic, born at Macerata, in the March of Ancona, in 1663. He was received as doctor of law at the age of sixteen, and in 1681 began to practise law in Rome. He founded there in 1690 the celebrated Academy of Arcadians. After composing a number of lyric poems, he published in 1698 a "History of National Poetry," ("Istoria della volgar Poesia,") a learned and valuable work. In 1719 he took orders, and received several benefices in Rome. Died in 1728. "Crescimbeni," says Hallam, "has made an honourable name by his exertions to purify the national taste." ("Introduction to the Literature of Europe.")

See TIRABOSCHI, "Storia della Letteratura Italiana;" F. M. MANCURTI, "Vita di G. M. Crescimbeni," 1729; NICÉRON, "Mémoires."

Cresconius. See CORIPPUS.

Cres′Ï-las, [Κρεσίλας,] an Athenian sculptor, spoken of by Pliny, was a contemporary of Phidias. The name is sometimes improperly written CTESILAS or CTESILAUS.

Crespi, krĕs′pee, (DANIELE,) a historical painter, born in the Milanese about 1590. His works are admired for expression and vigour of colour. He painted at Milan, in fresco, "The Resurrection of Saint Bruno," which is called his master-piece. Died at Milan in 1630.

Crespi, (GIOVANNI BATTISTA,) called IL CERANO, (èl chȧ-rȧ′no,) an Italian painter and architect, born at Cerano in 1557. He worked at Milan, and was president of the Academy of that city. Died in 1633.

Crespi, (GIUSEPPE MARIA,) CAVALIERE, a skilful Italian painter and engraver, born at Bologna in 1665,

was a pupil of Cignani. He was surnamed SPAGNUOLO, (spȧn-yoo-o′lo,) (the "Spaniard,") on account of the magnificence of his dress. He imitated Correggio and the Caracci with success, and had great facility of execution. Among his admired works are an "Ecce Homo," and "Seven Sacraments." He was a capricious artist, and produced many bizarre compositions. Died in 1747. His sons LUIGI and ANTONIO were painters of a different style. Luigi was a writer on Art. Among his works is the "Lives of Bolognese Painters." Died in 1779.

See LANZI, "History of Painting in Italy."

Crespin, krĕs′pän′, or **Crispin,** krĕs′pän′, (DANIEL,) a Swiss philologist, who lived at Lausanne about 1690. He edited Sallust and Ovid (1681) "ad usum Delphini."

Crespin, (JEAN,) a French Protestant writer, born at Arras. He removed to Geneva in 1548 with Theodore de Beza, and established there a printing-press, from which many excellent editions were issued. He was author of "The Book of Martyrs," ("Le Livre des Martyrs," 1554.) Died in 1572.

See BAYLE, "Historical and Critical Dictionary;" M. ADAM, "Vitæ Eruditorum."

Cres′sey or **Cres′sȳ, de,** (HUGH PAULIN,) an English Catholic writer, born at Wakefield in 1605. He was chaplain to Lord Wentworth and to Lord Falkland. During a visit to Rome in 1646 he became a Roman Catholic, and afterwards changed his name to SERENUS DE CRESSEY. After the restoration of 1660 he was chaplain to the Queen of England. He wrote a "Church History of England," (unfinished,) and several treatises in defence of the Roman Church. Died in 1674.

See WOOD, "Athenæ Oxonienses."

Cres′sọn, (ELLIOTT,) president of the Pennsylvania Colonization Society, was born in 1796; died in 1854.

Cress′well or **Cres′well,** (JOHN A. J.,) an American lawyer and Senator, born at Port Deposit, Maryland, in 1828. He was elected a member of Congress in 1862, and a Senator of the United States for a short term in 1865. He supported the Radical policy. In March, 1869, he was appointed postmaster-general of the United States.

Cressy. See CRESSEY.

Cresti. See PASSIGNANO.

Crestoni. See CRASTONI.

Crésus. See CRŒSUS.

Creswell. See CRESSWELL.

Cres′wick, (THOMAS,) an eminent English landscape-painter, born at Sheffield in 1811. He became a student of the Royal Academy, London, in 1828, and an associate of the same in 1842, and afterwards exhibited many admired views of British scenery. Among his principal works are a "London Road a Hundred Years ago," (1847,) "The Weald of Kent," "Home by the Sands," (1848,) a "Shady Glen," and "Wind on Shore," (1850,) His pictures are mostly faithful transcripts of nature. Died January 1, 1870.

Crétet, krȧ′tȧ′, (EMMANUEL,) Comte de Champmol, (shôN′mol′,) born in Dauphiné, France, in 1747, was minister of the interior from 1807 to 1809. Died in 1809.

Creti, krȧ′tee, (DONATO,) an Italian painter, born at Cremona in 1671. His master-piece is a Saint Vincent. Died in 1749.

Crétin or **Chrestin,** krȧ′tăN′, (GUILLAUME,) a French poet, whose proper name was DUBOIS. Died about 1525.

Crétineau-Joly, krȧ′te′nō′ zho′le′, (JACQUES,) a French historian, born at Fontenay-Vendée in 1803. Among his works is a "History of the Jesuits," (6 vols., 1844-46.)

Crettè de Palluel, krȧ′tȧ′ dẹh pȧ′lü′êl′, (FRANÇOIS,) a French writer on agriculture, born near Paris in 1741. He invented several farming-implements. Died in 1798.

Cre-u′sạ, [Gr. Κρέουσα; Fr. CRÉUSE, krȧ′üz′,] a daughter of Priam, and wife of Æneas. When Troy was captured by the Greeks, she fled with her husband by night, but was separated from him in the confusion, and mysteriously disappeared.

See VIRGIL'S "Æneid," book ii. 738-794.

Créuse. See CREUSA.

Creutz, (F. K. C.) See CREUZ.

Creutz, krẽ′ŏŏts, (GUSTAVUS PHILIP,) COUNT OF, a Swedish poet and statesman, born in Finland in 1726.

e as k; ç as s; g̃ hard; ğ as j; G, H, K, guttural; N, nasal; R, trilled; ŝ as z; ᵗh as in *this*.   (☞See Explanations, p. 23.)

44

He wrote two admired poems, "Atys and Camilla," and an "Epistle to Daphne." For twenty years he resided as minister at Paris, where he was intimate with Dr. Franklin, with whom he negotiated a treaty in 1783. In that year he became minister of foreign affairs in Sweden. Died in 1785.

See SCHROEDERHEIM, " Åminnelse-Tal öfver Riks Radet Grefve Creutz," 1787 ; MARMONTEL, "Mémoires."

Creutzfelder, kROits'fêl'dẹr,(JOHANN GEORG,) a German portrait-painter, born at Nuremberg in 1570 ; died in 1633.

Creutziger, kROit'siG-ẹr, [Lat. CRU'CIGER,] (GASPARD,) a German theologian, born at Leipsic in 1504. He became a professor at Wittenberg, and aided Luther in his translation of the Bible into German. He wrote (in Latin) "On the Dignity of Theological Studies," and a few other treatises. Died in 1548.

Creuz or **Creutz,** kROits, (FRIEDRICH KARL CASIMIR,) a German didactic poet, born at Homburg-vorder-Höhe in 1724. His reputation is founded chiefly on "The Tombs," (" Die Gräber," 1760,) a philosophic poem, which is much esteemed. He wrote "Essays on Man," and other prose works. He contributed to the reformation of the style of German literature. Died in 1770.

See " Nouvelle Biographie Générale."

Creuzé de Lesser, kRuh'zȧ' dẹh lȧ'sȧ', (AUGUSTE FRANÇOIS,) BARON, a French poet and dramatist, born in Paris in 1771. He was a member of the legislative body for six years, (1800–06,) and after the restoration was prefect of Hérault. He published poems entitled "The Knights of the Round Table," (1812,) "Roland," (1814,) and "The Last Man," (1832,) and also several dramas, among which is "The Revenge," (1815.) His "Travels in Italy" (1806) passed through three editions. Died in 1839.

Creuzer, kROit'sẹr, (GEORG FRIEDRICH,) a learned and ingenious German philologist and antiquary, was born at Marburg in 1771. He became professor of philology and ancient history at Heidelberg in 1804. He acquired a European reputation by his "Symbolism and Mythology of Ancient Peoples, especially the Greeks," (" Symbolik und Mythologie der alten Völker, besonders der Griechen," 1810–12, 4 vols. 8vo ; 2d edition, 6 vols., 1820–23.) The opinions and method of this work were attacked by G. Hermann in "Letters on Homer and Hesiod," and by other critics. In 1826 he was appointed privy councillor to the Grand Duke of Baden, and in 1848 he resigned his chair at Heidelberg. He was the author of numerous antiquarian treatises. Died in 1858. A masterly French translation of his "Symbolik" was published by J. D. Guigniaut, 1825–36.

See his Autobiography, "Aus dem Leben eines alten Professors," 1847 ; "Nouvelle Biographie Générale."

Crèvecœur, de, dẹh kRȧv'kuR', (HECTOR SAINT-JEAN,) a French writer, born at Caen in 1731. He emigrated to America in 1754, and settled on a farm near New York. In 1782 he published a flattering description of the United States, in "Letters of an American Farmer," and was appointed consul for France at New York. He enjoyed the friendship of Washington and Franklin. Died in France in 1813.

Crèvecœur, de, (PHILIPPE,) an able French general in the service of Louis XI., commanded the French at the battle of Guinegate (or battle of the Spurs) in 1479. He became marshal of France in 1492. Died in 1494.

See COMINES, "Mémoires."

Crévier, krȧ've-ȧ', (JEAN BAPTISTE,) a French historian, born in Paris in 1693, was a pupil of Rollin. He filled the chair of rhetoric in the College of Beauvais for twenty years with success. He wrote eight volumes in continuation of Rollin's "Roman History." Besides other works, he published a "History of the Roman Emperors down to Constantine." He has merit ; but his style is less agreeable than that of Rollin. Died in 1765.

Crew or **Crewe,** kRu, (NATHANIEL,) an English divine, born at Stean in 1633, became Bishop of Durham, and an abettor of the arbitrary policy of James II. Died in 1721.

Crichna. See KRISHNA.

Crichton, kRī'tọn, (JAMES,) commonly styled "the Admirable Crichton," a Scottish prodigy, born at the castle of Cluny, Perthshire, about 1560, was the son of Robert Crichton, lord advocate of Scotland. At the age of fourteen he graduated as A.M. in the University of Saint Andrew's, and before he was twenty could speak ten languages. · He was handsome in form and feature, and excelled in drawing, fencing, dancing, music, and other accomplishments. In the course of a continental tour, about 1580, he challenged the doctors and scholars of Paris to dispute with him, at an appointed time, on any question and in any one of twelve specified languages. Having by this means assembled a numerous company of professors and others, he acquitted himself to the general admiration. Proceeding thence to Italy, he repeated his exhibition, and obtained similar triumphs in Rome, Venice, and Padua. Aldus Manutius describes the *éclat* with which he sustained for three days a contest in philosophy and mathematics at Padua. The Duke of Mantua employed Crichton as tutor to his son Vincenzo, a dissolute youth. One night, about 1582, he was attacked by six persons in masks, whom he repulsed. Having disarmed one of them and found it was his pupil, he returned the sword to Vincenzo, who plunged it into the heart of Crichton. He left four short Latin poems, which, says Dr. Kippis, "will not stand the test of a rigid examination." "He was a man of very wonderful genius," says Scaliger, "more worthy of admiration than esteem. He had something of the coxcomb about him, and only wanted a little common sense."

See P. F. TYTLER, "Life of the Admirable Crichton," 1823 ; F. DOUGLAS, "The Life of J. Crichton," 1760 ; D. IRVING, "Lives of the Scottish Writers," 1839 ; SIR THOMAS URQUHART, "Life of J. Crichton ;" CHAMBERS, "Biographical Dictionary of Eminent Scotsmen."

Crillon, de, dẹh kRe'yọ̀N', (LOUIS ATHANASE **des Balbes de Berton**—dạ̈' bȧlb dẹh bêR'tọ̀N',) a brother of the Duc de Crillon-Mahon, was born in 1726. He became a priest, and wrote "Philosophic Memoirs of the Baron de * * *," (2 vols., 1779,) said to be a work of merit. Died at Avignon in 1789.

Crillon, de, (LOUIS DES BALBES (or BALBIS) DE BERTON,) a famous French warrior, born in Provence in 1541. He fought against the Protestants in the civil wars, signalized his courage at Lepanto in 1571, and had a high command in the army of Henry III. during the war of the League, (1580–89.) After the death of that king, he entered the service of Henry IV., who called him the "bravest of the brave." He took part in the battle of Ivry, and commanded in Savoy in 1600. The king wished to make him a marshal, but was dissuaded by the Duchess de Beaufort. Died in 1615.

See MADEMOISELLE DE LUSSAN, "Vie de Balbes de Crillon," 1757 ; SERVIEZ, "Histoire du brave Crillon," 1844 ; MONTROND, "Histoire du brave Crillon," 1845 ; ABBÉ DE CRILLON, "Vie de L. de Balbis de Berton de Crillon," 3 vols., 1826 ; DE THOU, "Historia sui Temporis."

Crillon-Mahon, de, dẹh kRe'yọ̀N' mä'ọ̀N', (LOUIS ANTOINE FRANÇOIS **de Paul**—dẹh pōl,) DUC, a Spanish general, the grandson of the following, born in Paris in 1775. He obtained command of a division in 1801, and was chosen Captain-General of Guipuscoa, Alava, and Biscay in 1808. Soon after this he took an oath to Joseph Bonaparte, who appointed him lieutenant-general, and Viceroy of Navarre. Died in 1832.

See FOY, "Histoire des Guerres de la Péninsule."

Crillon-Mahon, de, (LOUIS DE BERTON DES BALBES de Quiers—dẹh ke'aiR',) DUC, a French general, born in 1718, contributed to the victory of Fontenoy in 1745. Having obtained the rank of lieutenant-general in the Seven Years' war, (1755–62,) he passed into the service of Spain. He took Minorca in 1782, was made Captain-General of Spain, and received the title of Duke of Mahon. He commanded without success in the famous siege of Gibraltar, about 1782. Died in 1796.

See VOLTAIRE, "Siècle de Louis XV."

Crī-nag'o-ras, [Κριναγόρας,] a Greek poet, who was born at Mitylene and lived in the reign of Augustus.

Crinesius, kri-nee'she-us or kRe-nā'ze-ús, (CHRISTOPHER,) born in Bohemia in 1584, became professor of Oriental languages at Wittenberg and Altdorf. He published "Gymnasium Syriacum," (1611,) a work on the Syriac language, a "Syriac Lexicon," (1612,) and a "Treatise on the Confusion of Tongues," ("De Confusione Linguarum," 1629.) Died in 1629.

Crinito, kRe-nee'to, [Lat. CRINI'TUS,] (PIETRO,) an Italian *littérateur*, born at Florence about 1465. He wrote Latin verses, which approach the elegance of Politian, and two popular prose works, "De honesta Disciplina," ("On Honest (or Honourable) Instruction," 1500,) and "Vitæ Poetarum Latinorum," ("Lives of the Latin Poets.") Died about 1504.

See TIRABOSCHI, "Storia della Letteratura Italiana."

Crinitus. See CRINITO.

Crishna. See KRISHNA.

Crisp, (STEPHEN,) an eminent minister of the Society of Friends, born at Colchester about 1628. He was converted to the principles of the Friends in 1655. As a minister of the gospel, he travelled many years in Great Britain, Holland, and Germany. He published a "Plain Pathway Opened," "A Faithful Warning to Friends," several Epistles, and other works. Died in 1692.

See SAMUEL TUKE, "Memoirs of the Life of S. Crisp," 1824.

Crisp, (TOBIAS,) an English theologian, noted as a chief of the Antinomians, was born in London in 1600. He became rector of Brinkworth in 1627. In 1642 he was engaged in a great controversy, on the subject of free grace, with fifty-two opponents. His sermons have been published. Died in 1642.

Crispin. See CRESPIN.

Cris'pin, (GILBERT,) a Norman of noble rank, was Abbot of Westminster. Died about 1115.

Crispo, kRès'po, [Lat. CRIS'PUS,] (ANTONIO,) an Italian medical writer, born at Trapani, in Sicily, in 1600 ; died in 1688.

Crispo, (GIOVANNI BATTISTA,) an Italian writer and priest, born at Gallipoli, (Naples,) was a friend of Tasso and Annibal Caro. Among his works is a "Life of Sannazaro," (1583.) Died in 1595.

Cris'pus, (FLAVIUS JULIUS,) the eldest son of the Roman emperor Constantine I., was born about 300 A.D. He served in the wars against the Franks and against Licinius, and gave proof of courage and abilities. Being falsely accused by his step-mother Fausta of an attempt to seduce her, he was put to death, by his father's order, in 326 A.D.

Cristiani, kRès-te-ä'nee, (BERTRANDO,) COUNT OF, an Italian statesman of high reputation, born at Genoa in 1702. He was appointed by the empress Maria Theresa grand chancellor of the Milanese. Died in 1758.

Cristofori, kRès-tof'o-ree, (PIETRO PAOLO,) a celebrated Italian painter in mosaic, adorned the church of Saint Peter at Rome. Died at an advanced age in 1740.

Critias, krish'e-as, [Κριτίας,] or **Critios,** krish'e-os, a celebrated Athenian statuary, who flourished about 470 B.C. Among his master-pieces were statues of Harmodius and Aristogi'ton.

Critias, an Athenian orator and poet, and one of the Thirty Tyrants, was a relative of Plato and a pupil of Socrates. Having been exiled from Athens for an unknown cause about 406 B.C., he returned with the Spartan general Lysander in 404, and became one of the thirty who tyrannized over the state. He put Theramenes and others to death. He was killed in battle when Thrasybu'lus liberated Athens in 404 B.C. His eloquence was highly praised by Cicero. He wrote elegies and other works.

See W. E. WEBER, "Dissertatio de Critia Tyranno," 1824; PLUTARCH, "Alcibiades ;" BAYLE, "Historical and Critical Dictionary ;" GROTE, "History of Greece ;" XENOPHON, "Hellenica."

Critios. See CRITIAS.

Crito. See CRITON.

Crit-o-lā'us, [Κριτόλαος,] a Greek philosopher, was a native of Phaselis, in Lycia. He studied at Athens under Ariston of Ceos, became after his death the head of the Peripatetic school in Athens, and acquired a high reputation as a philosopher and orator. About 155 B.C. he was sent to Rome on an important embassy with Carneades and Diogenes. He wrote a treatise to prove the eternity of matter.

See FABRICIUS, "Bibliotheca Græca ;" VOSSIUS, "De Historicis Græcis."

Critola'us, an Achæan general and demagogue, was one of the chief authors of the war against Rome which resulted in the destruction of Corinth and the subjugation of Greece. In 146 B.C. he was defeated by Metellus in Locris. As he was never heard of after this action, it was supposed he died by poison.

Cri'ton or **Crito** [Κρίτων] of Athens, was a friend and disciple of Socrates. He tried to persuade Socrates to escape from prison, and attended him in his last hour. He wrote seventeen dialogues on philosophy, which are not extant. Plato gave the name of Criton to one of his books.

See HERMANN, "Geschichte und System der Platonischen Philosophie."

Criton, a Roman physician, who attended the emperor Trajan. He wrote a book "On Cosmetics."

Crit'ten-den, (GEORGE B.,) an American general in the Confederate service, a son of John J. Crittenden, noticed below. He commanded as major-general at the battle of Somerset in 1862, where he was defeated by General Thomas.

Crittenden, (JOHN JAY,) an American statesman, born in Woodford county, Kentucky, in 1786. He studied law, gained distinction as an advocate, and was elected to the Senate of the United States in 1817. His term having expired in 1819, he practised law at Frankfort from that time until 1835, when he was again elected to the Senate for six years by the Whigs. He was a warm friend of Henry Clay, and a constant supporter of his principal measures. He was appointed attorney-general of the United States by President Harrison in March, 1841 ; but he resigned in the ensuing September because he disapproved the policy of Tyler. In 1843 he was re-elected to the national Senate, and in 1848 was chosen Governor of Kentucky. He was attorney-general in the cabinet of President Fillmore from July, 1850, until March, 1853, after which he was in the Senate of the United States from 1855 to 1861. On the dissolution of the Whig party he joined the American party. He opposed the repeal of the Missouri Compromise in 1854, and the disunion movement of 1860. In the session of 1860–61 he performed a prominent part as a mediator and as the mover of a series of resolutions called the Crittenden Compromise, which were not adopted. Died in 1863.

Crittenden, (THOMAS L.,) an American general, a son of the preceding, was born at Russellville, Kentucky, about 1819. He became a brigadier-general of volunteers in the Union army in 1861, commanded a division at Shiloh, April, 1862, and was promoted to the rank of major-general in the summer of the same year. He commanded a corps at the battle of Stone River, which ended January 2, 1863, and at Chickamauga, in September of that year.

Crittenden, (THOMAS T.,) an American general, a nephew of John J. Crittenden, noticed above, was born in Alabama about 1828. He lived in Indiana before the civil war. He was appointed a brigadier-general of volunteers in the Union army about April, 1862.

Crivellari, kRe-vĕl-lä'ree, (BARTOLOMMEO,) an able Italian engraver, born at Venice in 1725 ; died in 1777.

Crivelli, kRe-vel'lee, (ANGELO MARIA,) sometimes called "Il Crivellone," an Italian painter of animals and hunting-scenes, was born at Milan. Died about 1730.

Crivelli, (CARLO,) a Venetian painter of the fifteenth century, was living in 1475.

Croce, kRO'chà,(BALDASSARE,) an Italian painter, born at Bologna in 1553, worked in Rome. Died in 1628.

Croce, della, del'lä kRO'chà, [Lat. CRU'CIUS,] (VINCENZO ALSARIO,) an Italian physician and medical writer, born near Genoa about 1570, lived at Rome.

Crocifissajo. See MACCHIETTI, (GIROLAMO.)

Crock'ett, (DAVID,) an American hunter, noted for his adventures and eccentric habits, was born in Tennessee in 1786. He was elected a member of Congress in 1827, 1829, and 1831, and began his public life as a friend of General Jackson ; but he changed sides about 1830. Having joined the Texans in their revolt against Mexico, he was taken prisoner at Fort Alamo, and massacred, by Santa Anna, in 1836.

See his "Autobiography," 1834.

Crocus. See CROKE, (RICHARD.)

---

c as *k*; ç as *s*; g *hard*; ġ as *j*; G, H, K, *guttural*; N, *nasal*; R, *trilled*; s as z; th as in *this*. (☞See Explanations, p. 23.)

Croese, kroo′seh, (GERARD,) a Dutch clergyman, born at Amsterdam in 1642, was the author of a "History of the Quakers," ("Historia Quakeriana," 1695,) and other works. Died in 1710.

Croeser, kroo′ser, (JACQUES HENRI,) a Flemish physician, born at Grave in 1691; died in 1753.

Crœsus, kree′sus, [Gr. Κροῖσος; Fr. CRÉSUS, krâ′züss′,] a king of Lydia, proverbial for his great wealth, born about 590 B.C., succeeded his father Alyattes in 560. He subjugated the Æolians, Ionians, and other peoples of Asia Minor, and about 554 formed an alliance with the Spartans and the King of Egypt against Cyrus of Persia. In the year 546 Crœsus was defeated by Cyrus near Sardis, his capital, and taken prisoner. According to Herodotus, whose story is discredited by some, he was doomed to be burned alive, but was saved by his recalling a saying of Solon, which Cyrus desired him to explain, and afterwards not only delivered him from death, but bestowed upon him distinguished marks of favour.

See "History of Crœsus, King of Lydia," London, 1756; CLINTON, "Fasti Hellenici;" HERODOTUS, "History;" DIODORUS SICULUS, books ix. and xvi.

Croft, (HERBERT,) an English prelate, born in Oxfordshire in 1603, was educated as a Catholic. He was converted to the Anglican Church in 1622, and became Dean of Hereford in 1644, and Bishop of Hereford in 1661. He published "The Naked Truth, or the True State of the Primitive Church," (1675,) which tended to a union of the Protestants and produced much sensation. Died in 1691.

Croft, (Sir HERBERT,) an English writer, of the same family as the preceding, born in 1751. He took orders in 1782, after which he succeeded to a baronetcy. He published "Love and Madness," and other works, and wrote the Life of Young for Dr. Johnson's "Lives of the Poets." About 1792 he issued a prospectus of an improved edition of Johnson's Dictionary, which was never completed. Died in 1816.

Croft, (Sir JAMES,) an English statesman, born about 1530, was appointed lord deputy of Ireland by Edward VI. in 1551. Under the reign of Elizabeth he became comptroller to the household. Died in 1591.

See "Retrospective Review," vol. i., 2d Series, 1827.

Croft, (WILLIAM,) a celebrated composer of cathedral music, born in Warwickshire in 1677. He became composer to the Chapel Royal and organist of Westminster Abbey in 1708. He published "Divine Harmony," (1712,) and his admirable "Musica Sacra" in 1724. Died in 1727.

See FÉTIS, "Biographie Universelle des Musiciens."

Crof′ton, (ZACHARY,) an English nonconformist minister of London. Died about 1672.

Croghan, kro′gan, (Colonel GEORGE,) an American officer, born near Louisville, Kentucky, in 1791. He became inspector-general in 1825, and served in the Mexican war, (1846–47.) Died in 1849.

Croï, de, deh kro′e′, [Lat. CROI′US,] (JEAN,) a French Protestant minister, born at Uzès. He preached at Béziers and Uzès, and wrote, besides other works, "Notes on Origen, Irenæus, and Tertullian," (in Latin, 1652.) Bayle represents him as well versed in languages, criticism, and ecclesiastic antiquities. Died in 1659.

See BAYLE, "Historical and Critical Dictionary."

Croiset, krwä′zâ′, (JEAN,) a French Jesuit and popular writer, born at Marseilles about 1650, published "The Christian Year," ("Année Chrétienne," 18 vols.,) and "Meditations," 4 vols., both often reprinted. Died in 1738.

Croius. See CROÏ.

Croix. See LACROIX, CRUZ, and CROCE.

Croix, (FRANÇOIS PÉTIS.) See PÉTIS DE LA CROIX.

Croix, (JUAN.) See CRUZ.

Croix du Maine. See LA CROIX DU MAINE.

Croke, krōōk, ? (Sir ALEXANDER,) an English civilian and miscellaneous writer, born at Aylesbury in 1800; died in 1842.

Croke, krōōk, or **Crook,** (Sir GEORGE,) an English judge, born in the county of Bucks in 1559. He was appointed justice of the king's bench in 1628, and took side with Hampden in the Ship-money case in 1636. His "Reports of Select Cases" acquired a high and durable reputation. Died in 1641.

See FOSS, "The Judges of England."

Croke, [Lat. CRO′CUS,] (RICHARD,) an English scholar, born in London, taught Greek at Oxford about 1520. His Latin orations have been published. Died in 1558.

Cro′ker, (Rt. Hon. JOHN WILSON,) an author, critic, and politician, was born in Galway, Ireland, in 1780. He was educated at Trinity College, Dublin, and chose the profession of the law. He was elected to Parliament in 1807, and appointed secretary to the admiralty in 1809. In this year Scott, Croker, and others founded the "London Quarterly Review." He gained literary distinction by a satire called "An Intercepted Letter from Canton," (1807,) "The Songs of Trafalgar," a poem on the battle of Talavera, and other works. His talent for satire and sarcasm was displayed in the "Quarterly Review," to which he frequently contributed for about thirty years or more. He became a member of the privy council in 1828. He opposed the Reform Bill in several able speeches, declared he would never sit in a Reformed House of Commons, and, after the passage of the bill in 1832 retired from Parliament. His most important work is his edition of Boswell's "Life of Johnson," (5 vols., 1831,) which is praised by many critics, but was severely criticized by Macaulay, ("Edinburgh Review," 1831,) who exposes many instances of his "scandalous inaccuracy." Died in 1857.

Croker, (THOMAS CROFTON,) a popular Irish writer, born at Cork in 1798. Having served an apprenticeship to a merchant of Cork, he obtained a clerkship in the admiralty about the age of twenty-one. He published "Researches in the South of Ireland," (1824,) "Fairy Legends," "Legends of the Lakes, or Sayings and Doings at Killarney," (1829,) and other works. He was a frequent contributor to "Fraser's Magazine," and was for about thirty years a clerk in the admiralty. Died in 1854.

Croll, krōl, (OSWALD,) a German alchemist, born at Wetter, in Hesse. He became physician to Prince Christian of Anhalt, and a partisan of Paracelsus. He published a curious work, called "Basilica Chymica," (1609,) which was often reprinted. Died in 1609.

See F. HOEFER, "Histoire de la Chimie."

Cro′lȳ, (GEORGE,) a popular poet and voluminous author, born in Dublin in 1780. He was for many years, beginning in 1835, rector of Saint Stephen's, Wallbrook, London, and was eminent as a pulpit orator. Besides numerous sermons, he published "The Angel of the World," a tale, (1820,) "Salathiel, a Story of the Past, the Present, and the Future," (1827,) which is admired by many, "Poetical Works," (2 vols., 1830,) a "Personal History of George IV.," (1830,) "Catiline," a tragedy, a "Life of Edmund Burke," (1840,) "Marston," a novel, (1846,) "Scenes from Scripture, with other Poems," (1851,) and various other works. "There can be no doubt that his 'Catiline,' whether considered as a poem or a drama, is a splendid performance." ("Blackwood's Magazine," vol. xi.) Died in 1860.

Cromarty, EARL OF. See MACKENZIE, (GEORGE.)

Crome, (JOHN,) an English landscape-painter, born at Norwich in 1769; died in 1821.

Cro′mer, (MARTIN,) born at Biecz, in Poland, in 1512, held a distinguished place among the historians of his time. His principal work, a Latin "History of Poland," (1558,) was highly esteemed for style and other merits. He became Bishop of Warmia in 1579. Died in 1589.

Cromp′ton, (SAMUEL,) an English artisan, born in Lancashire in 1753, was the inventor of the spinning-jenny or mule which was brought into use about 1778. Died in 1827.

See G. FRENCH, "Life, etc. of Samuel Crompton," London, 1859; HENRY HOWE, "Lives of Eminent American and European Mechanics," 1847.

Cromvele or **Cromuelos.** See CROMWELL,(OLIVER.)

Crom′well, (or krŭm′wel,) (HENRY,) a younger son of Oliver, was born at Huntingdon in 1627, and entered the army at the age of twenty. In 1649, with the rank of colonel, he accompanied his father to Ireland, where he displayed courage in several actions. He was chosen a member of Parliament in 1653. In 1657 he was appointed lord deputy of Ireland, where he became popular by his moderate policy. Soon after his brother Richard ceased to be Protector, April, 1659, Henry resigned his office, and lived as a private citizen in England. Died in 1674.

ā, ē, ī, ō, ū, ȳ, *long;* à, è, ò, same, less prolonged; ă, ĕ, ĭ, ŏ, ŭ, ȳ, *short;* a, e, i, o, *obscure;* fär, fàll, fât; mêt; nŏt; gŏŏd; mōōn;

Cromwell, krŭm′wel or krŏm′wel, (formerly almost universally called krŭm′ĕl,) [It. CROMVELE, kʀom-vā′là; Sp. CROMUELOS, kʀom-wā′lôs,] (OLIVER,) one of the most extraordinary men that ever lived, was born at Huntingdon, England, on the 25th of April, 1599. He was the eldest surviving son of Robert Cromwell and Elizabeth Steward. Robert was the son of Sir Henry Cromwell, had sat in Parliament, and owned an estate in land, which Oliver inherited. On April 23, 1616, the day of Shakspeare's death, Oliver entered Sidney College, Cambridge, where he remained until his father's death, in June, 1617. It appears that he studied law in London; but we have no authentic record of this part of his career. In 1620 he married Elizabeth Bouchier, with whom he settled on the hereditary estate in Huntingdon, and passed several years employed in farming and social duties. During this period he lived in intimate fellowship with the Puritans, who were very numerous among the various ranks of society, and he appears to have given his serious and earnest attention to the great questions of religion. In 1628 Oliver represented the borough of Huntingdon in Parliament, which, after passing the Petition of Right, was dissolved in March, 1629, and the leaders of the popular party were committed to prison. In this session he made his first speech against Popery, which was significant of the great idea of his public life. This was the last Parliament that met in England for eleven years, during which period the measures of the government seemed to become every day more arbitrary and tyrannical. In 1637 Cromwell and his cousin Hampden, the great Commoner, resolved to leave their native land, and had actually embarked for North America; but the ship, when about to sail, was arrested by an order of council. They therefore remained in England; and "with them remained," to use the language of Macaulay, "the evil genius of the House of Stuart." In the next Parliament, which met in April, 1640, Cromwell, who then resided at Ely, represented the town of Cambridge, and also in the famous Long Parliament, which met near the end of that year. Sir Philip Warwick describes his first impressions of Cromwell, whom he saw at this period in the House, and whom, judging by his unfashionable dress and rusticity, he was inclined to regard with contempt. "But," he adds, "I lived to see this gentleman, by multiplied successes and by more converse with good company, appear in my own eye of a comely presence and a great and majestic deportment." One day, as he rose to address the House, Lord Digby asked Hampden who the "sloven" then speaking was. Hampden replied that it was Oliver Cromwell, adding, "That sloven whom you see before you has no ornament in his speech; but, if we should ever come to a breach with the king, that sloven, I say, will be the greatest man in England." On November 22, 1641, after a stormy debate, the Grand Remonstrance passed the House, by a small majority of the popular party.

In January, 1642, Charles I. having failed in an attempt to arrest five members of the House, affairs came to a crisis, and both sides appealed to arms. Cromwell entered the army as captain of cavalry, and soon distinguished himself by his strict discipline, his military talents, and his invincible courage. After the affair at Edgehill he perceived the necessity of having men of high principle, or enthusiasm of some kind, to contend against men of honour such as the Cavaliers; and he used his personal influence in enlisting numerous companies of yeomen among the Puritans of the Eastern counties. Although when he entered the army he was over forty, he never lost a battle; and his victories were always decisive, even when the enemy had a great superiority in numbers. On July 2, 1644, he commanded the left wing at the battle of Marston Moor, which was won chiefly by the irresistible charge of Cromwell's Ironsides. In 1645, as lieutenant-general under Fairfax, he led the right wing at the decisive victory of Naseby, where the king lost his artillery, his private papers, and about 5000 men.

There were two parties among the Parliamentarians, which became more and more widely divergent as the royal cause declined,—namely, the Presbyterians, who had a majority in the Parliament, and the Independents, who controlled the army and owned Cromwell as their leader. At length, in 1647, these came to an open rupture. On June 2, one of Cromwell's officers seized the person of the king and transferred him from the custody of Parliament to that of the army. In August, 1648, at the battle of Preston, Cromwell, with about 8000 men, defeated the royal forces under the Duke of Hamilton, consisting of about 20,000, most of whom were Scotch. Near the close of this year, the majority of the House seeming inclined to treat with the king and restore him to the throne, forty-one members were picked out as they were entering the House, and placed under arrest by the agency of Colonel Pride, one of Cromwell's officers. Cromwell was a member of the court which tried the king in January, 1649, and signed the warrant for his execution. The part taken by Cromwell in the death of Charles has left a shadow on his fame which must always remain unless it can be clearly shown that such an act of severity was necessary to the safety of the cause of liberty. "The murder of the king," says Hume, "the most atrocious of all his actions, was to him covered under a mighty cloud of republican and fanatical illusions." Having been sent as lord lieutenant to Ireland, which was then in a state of riot and anarchy, he defeated the royalists at Drogheda and Wexford, and in less than a year the enemy were generally subdued, though not without the exercise of extreme and perhaps indefensible severity.

In 1650, the Scotch having raised an army with a view to restore Charles II. to the throne, and having induced him to co-operate with them, Cromwell was appointed commander-in-chief, *vice* Lord Fairfax, who resigned his commission. The armies met at Dunbar on September 3, where the Scotch were totally defeated and 10,000 of them taken prisoners. Charles, having recruited his army, marched into England, and was followed by Cromwell to Worcester, where, September 3, 1651, a battle was fought which resulted in the complete overthrow of the royal cause and rendered the victorious general virtually dictator. And who could be more competent for a crisis so difficult, which required the greatest resolution, vigour, and sagacity? At this period there was observed a change in his manner,—"an indescribable kind of exaltation." Clarendon remarks "that his parts seemed to be raised, as if he had concealed his faculties till he had occasion to use them." In 1653 he entered the House of Commons, now reduced to a small remnant, and dissolved it *vi et armis*, exclaiming, "You are no longer a Parliament." At a council of the army in the early part of 1654 he was formally proclaimed Protector of the Commonwealth. The government of the Protector commanded the respect of foreign powers, many of whom vied with each other in courting his alliance. He made liberty of conscience one of the fundamental principles of his policy, and defended the Protestant cause in foreign countries. When Spain solicited his alliance, he required two conditions, one of which was the suppression of the Inquisition. He employed Milton, who had previously served the Parliament in the same capacity, as his Latin secretary. In 1656 a new Parliament was assembled, which voted supplies for the war with Spain and offered the crown to Cromwell; but, though urged by various parties to accept the insignia of royalty, he persisted in refusing it.

Southey, though a Tory, admits that Cromwell's "good sense and good nature would have led him to govern equitably, to promote literature, to cherish the arts, to pour wine and oil in the wounds of the nation;" but the mutinous spirit of his opponents partially frustrated these designs. It is usually affirmed that he became very suspicious near the end of his career, and took extreme precautions against assassination. He died of fever on September 3, 1658, the anniversary of his greatest victories, those of Dunbar and Worcester. He left two sons, Richard and Henry, and four daughters.

It is admitted by all that Cromwell, as a statesman, as a reformer, and as a military leader, displayed abilities of the very highest order. His memory has been subjected to a severe ordeal by the enmity of two opposite parties whose policy he frustrated, one of which denounced him as unfaithful to liberty, and the other found him guilty of treason against the divine right of kings. Many, while admitting his intellectual ability, impeach the sincerity of his motives and deny his claim to any noble or estimable moral qualities. But, after the lapse of two centuries, an impartial public begins to appreciate his meritorious services and moral integrity, as well as his political wisdom and invincible valour. It is acknowledged that under his direction England was prosperous, powerful, and well governed, that his foreign policy was enlightened, magnanimous, and successful. Macaulay has remarked that, "though constantly attacked and scarcely ever defended, the character of Cromwell had yet always continued popular with the great body of his countrymen." Again he says, "Cromwell was emphatically a man. Never was any ruler so conspicuously born for sovereignty. The cup which has intoxicated almost all others sobered him. His spirit, restless, from its buoyancy, in a lower sphere, reposed in majestic placidity as soon as it had reached the level congenial to it. Rapidly as his fortunes grew, his mind expanded more rapidly still. Insignificant as a private citizen, he was a great general ; he was a still greater prince."

See CARLYLE, "Letters and Speeches of Cromwell ;" JOHN FORSTER, "Life of Cromwell," in his "Statesmen of the Commonwealth of England," 7 vols., 1840; ROBERT SOUTHEY, "Life of O. Cromwell," 1844; VILLEMAIN, "Histoire de Cromwell," 1819; GUIZOT, "Histoire de la Révolution d'Angleterre," and his "Histoire de la République d'Angleterre et de Cromwell," 1854; (and English version of the same ;) J. H. MERLE D'AUBIGNÉ, "The Protector: a Vindication," New York, 1848; PHILARÈTE CHASLES, "O. Cromwell ; sa Vie privée," etc., 1847; GREGORIO LETI, "Historia e Memorie recondite sopra la Vita di O. Cromvele," 1692; WILLIAM HARRIS, "Historical and Critical Account of the Life of O. Cromwell," 1762 ; KARL SEBALD, "Leben O. Cromwells," 1815; DANIEL WILSON, "O. Cromwell and the Protectorate," 1848; J. T. HEADLEY," Life of O. Cromwell," 1848; MACAULAY, "Essays," (Review of "Hallam's Constitutional History ;") CLARENDON," History of the Rebellion ;" HUME, "History of England ;" NOBLE, "Memoirs of the Protectorate House of Cromwell," 2 vols., 1784; LAMARTINE, "Memoirs of Celebrated Characters," vol. ii., 1856: "London Quarterly Review" for July, 1821: "Fraser's Magazine" for December, 1847 ; "Edinburgh Review" for January, 1856.

Cromwell, (OLIVER,) said to be the last male descendant of the Protector, was the author of "Memoirs of Oliver Cromwell, and of his Sons Richard and Henry," published in 1820.

Cromwell, (RICHARD,) the eldest surviving son of the Protector Oliver, was born at Huntingdon in 1626. He was admitted into Lincoln's Inn in 1647, but appears to have been an indolent student. In 1649 he married Dorothy Major, with whom he passed several years in rural retirement at Hursley, Hampshire. He had a mild, virtuous, and unambitious character, and inherited little or nothing of his father's mental power. In 1654 Oliver brought him to court and appointed him first lord of trade and navigation, privy councillor, etc. He succeeded his father, September 3, 1658, without open opposition, and was proclaimed Protector by General Monk and the army. A general disaffection, however, was soon apparent, and the republicans and royalists united in hostility to his power. Fleetwood, Lambert, Desborow, and other officers, having formed a cabal against him, demanded the dissolution of Parliament, which was effected in April, 1659. "By the same act," says Hume, "he was considered as effectually dethroned. Soon after, he signed his demission in form." "Thus fell, suddenly and from an enormous height, but, by a rare fortune, without any hurt or injury, the family of the Cromwells." About 1660 he retired to the continent, and resided some years in Paris and Geneva. He returned to England in 1680, and passed the rest of his life in obscurity and peace. Died in 1712.

See HUME, "History of England ;" LINGARD, "History of England ;" VILLEMAIN, "Histoire de Cromwell."

Cromwell, (THOMAS,) Earl of Essex, an ambitious English courtier and minister of state, born of humble parentage at Putney about 1490. In early life he was a servant or agent of Cardinal Wolsey, whom he defended with spirit and honour in the House of Commons in 1629. A few years later he entered the service of the king, whose confidence he gained, and by whom he was rapidly promoted. He had become an adherent of the Reformation, when, about 1535, he was appointed principal secretary of state and keeper of the privy seal. In 1536

the king's supremacy over the Church was delegated to Cromwell, with the title of Vicar-General. Many monasteries were suppressed, and other reforms were effected, by his agency and that of Cranmer, who was his friend. He was made Earl of Essex in 1539 or 1540, and obtained precedency over all the officers of state. His sudden fall was hastened by his agency in the marriage of Henry VIII. to Anne of Cleves, whom the king quickly resolved to divorce. After a trial for treason and heresy, he was beheaded in July, 1540. "He was," says Hume, "a man of prudence, industry, and abilities, worthy of a better master and of a better fate." Froude gives Cromwell a very high character both for ability and honesty of purpose ; but some other historians, including Lingard, accuse him of rapacity, servility, and selfish ambition.

See FROUDE, "History of England," chaps. vi.-xvii. ; LINGARD, "History of England," vol. iv. chaps. viii. et seq.; MICHAEL DRAYTON, "Historie of the Life and Death of Lord Cromwell," London, 1609; also SHAKSPEARE, "Henry VIII.," Act Third.

Cronaca, Il, èl kRo'nä-kä or kRon'ä-kä, the surname of **Simone Pollaiolo** (pol-lī-o'lo) or **Pollajuolo,** an Italian architect, born at Florence in 1454. He acquired celebrity by his design of the Strozzi palace, one of the most magnificent edifices of Florence, and of the church of Saint Francis. He was a zealous partisan or disciple of Savonarola. Died in 1509.

Cronegk, von, fon kRo'něk, (JOHANN FRIEDRICH,) BARON, an excellent German poet, born at Anspach in 1731. He was versed in many languages, and had travelled in France and Italy. He wrote elegies, odes, didactic poems, hymns, and several dramas in verse, which display a fine imagination. His tragedy of "Codrus" (1758) abounds in beauties of the first order, and is called his master-piece. He died prematurely in 1758.

See BROCKHAUS, "Conversations-Lexikon."

Cronholm, kRon'holm, (ABRAHAM,) a Swedish historian, born at Landscrona in 1809. Among his works are "Memorials of the Ancient North," (2 vols., 1835,) and "Political History of Scania," (2 vols., 1846-51.)

Cro'nos, [Κρόνος,] a god of the Greek mythology, represented as the son of Uranus, and the father of Jupiter, Neptune, Ceres, and Juno. He was identified with the Saturn of the Romans.

Cronstedt, kRon'stět, (AXEL FREDRICK,) a Swedish mineralogist, born in Sudermania in 1722. He discovered about 1754 a new metal, which he named "nickel," and published a valuable "Essay on Mineralogy, or on the Classification of the Mineral Kingdom," (1758,) which was translated into German by Werner. Died in 1765.

See GEZELIUS, "Biographiskt-Lexicon."

Crook. See CROKE.

Crook, krook, (GEORGE,) an American general, born near Dayton, Ohio, about 1828, graduated at West Point in 1852. He became a captain in 1861, and a brigadier-general of volunteers about September, 1862. He commanded a corps of Sheridan's army at the battle of Winchester or Opequan Creek, September 19, 1864, and at that of Cedar Creek, October 19 of the same year. He was commander of the department of West Virginia from August, 1864, to February, 1865.

Crooks, (GEORGE R.,) an American Methodist preacher, born in Philadelphia in 1822. He became adjunct professor of ancient languages in Dickinson College in 1846. In conjunction with Professor Schem, he published a "Latin-English Lexicon," (1858.)

Croon or **Croune,** kroon, (WILLIAM,) M.D., an English scholar, born in London, was the founder of the Croonian Lectures. He became professor of rhetoric in Gresham College, and founded a course of lectures on algebra at Cambridge. He published a "Treatise on Muscular Motion." Died in 1684.

Crop'sey, (JASPER FRANK,) an American landscape-painter, was born at Westfield, Richmond county, New York, in 1823, and became a resident of England in 1856. Among his works are "The Sibyl's Temple," "Peace" and "War," and "Niagara Falls."

See TUCKERMAN, "Book of the Artists."

Cros'by, (BRASS,) an English politician, born at Stockport-on-Tees in 1725. He was elected lord mayor of

ā, ē, ī, ō, ū, ȳ, long; ă, ĕ, ĭ, ŏ, ŭ, ў, short; ą, ę, į, ǫ, obscure; fär, fäll, făt; mēt; nŏt; gŏŏd; mōōn;

London in 1770, and opposed the ministry, who confined him in the Tower. Died in 1793.

Crosby, (THOMAS,) was author of a " History of English Baptists from the Reformation to the Reign of George I.," (1740,) said to be the best work on that subject. He was a Baptist minister of London.

Cros'land, MRS., whose maiden name was CAMILLA TOULMIN, an English authoress, born in London about 1814. She published a volume of poems, "Stratagems, a Tale," "Toil and Trial," (1849,) "Lydia, a Woman's Book," (1852,) and other works of fiction, which are praised for their moral tendency.

Cross, (JOSEPH,) a Methodist minister, born in Somersetshire, England, in 1813, removed to the United States about 1825. He published, besides other works, " Headlands of Faith."

Cross or **de la Crux,** (MICHAEL,) an English painter, flourished between 1640 and 1680. He was patronized by Charles I.

Crosse, kross, (ANDREW,) an English gentleman, noted for his successful experiments in electricity, was born near Taunton, in Somersetshire, in 1784. He inherited an easy fortune, and lived in retirement. He gave special attention to the formation of crystals by means of a voltaic battery, and spent many years in search of new facts and phenomena, without regard to theories. He obtained numerous mineral crystals similar in form to those produced by nature ; also a subsulphate of copper which was entirely new. About 1816 he predicted that, by electrical agency, human thought would be conveyed instantaneously to the farthest parts of the earth. His discoveries were not made public until he explained them before the British Association for the Advancement of Science, in 1836. On introducing him to the Association, Dr. Buckland said, "This gentleman has actually made no less than twenty-four minerals, and even crystalline quartz. He [Dr. Buckland] did not know how he had made them, but he pronounced them discoveries of the highest order." A great sensation was excited in England in 1836 by the apparent generation of insects during his experiments with voltaic action, —a strange phenomenon, which has not yet been satisfactorily explained. Died in 1855.

See " Memorials of Andrew Crosse," 1857, (containing a number of his poems and letters,) by his wife.

Cros'well, (EDWIN,) an American politician and journalist, born at Catskill, New York, about 1795. He became, about 1824, editor of the "Albany Argus," a Democratic journal of great influence, which he continued to edit until 1854. He was a prominent member of the Albany Regency.

Croswell, (HARRY,) an American journalist and clergyman, an uncle of the preceding, was born at West Hartford, Connecticut, in 1778. He edited several Federalist papers. Died in 1858.

Croswell, (WILLIAM,) an Episcopalian clergyman and poet, a son of the preceding, was born at Hudson, New York, in 1804. He was settled in Boston from about 1844 until his death in 1851.

See "Memoir of the Rev. William Croswell," 1854 ; "North American Review" for April, 1854 ; GRISWOLD, "Poets and Poetry of America."

Crotch, (WILLIAM,) a skilful English musical composer, born at Norwich in 1775. He played on the harpsichord marvellously when he was about three years old. In 1797 he was chosen professor of music in the University of Oxford. He published "Styles of Music of all Ages," and composed music for the organ and piano, and for the ode entitled "Mona on Snowdon calls." Died in 1847.

Croune. See CROON, (W.)

Crousaz, de, deh kroo'zȧ',(JEAN PIERRE,) a prolific and mediocre Swiss writer, born at Lausanne in 1663. He was professor of philosophy, etc. at Lausanne and Groningen, and published an "Essay on Logic," (1712,) a "Treatise on Pyrrhonism, Ancient and Modern," (1733,) and other works. Died in 1750.

Crouzet, kroo'zȧ', (PIERRE,) a French poet and professor of rhetoric, born in Picardy in 1753 ; died in 1811.

Crōwe, (Mrs. CATHERINE,) an English authoress, whose maiden name was STEVENS, was born at Borough Green, Kent, about 1802. She became the wife of Lieu-

tenant-Colonel Crowe in 1822. She produced in 1847 " Lillie Dawson," a novel. Her "Night Side of Nature" (1848) treats of the spiritual or supernatural world. Among her later works is "Light and Darkness, or the Mysteries of Life," (1850.)

See " Blackwood's Magazine" for September, 1850.

Crowe, (EYRE EVANS,) an English writer of the present century, published a "History of France," (in 5 vols., 1858-68,) and other works. Died in March, 1868.

Crōw'ley, (ROBERT,) an English Protestant divine and poet, became a Fellow of Magdalene College in 1542. He composed many epigrams, and was the first editor of "Piers Plowman's Vision." In 1558 he became prebendary of Saint Paul's, London. Died in 1588.

Crȯwne, (JOHN,) an English dramatist of inferior order, born in Nova Scotia. He removed to England, wrote several successful plays, and obtained some favour at the court of Charles II. Among his works are "City Politiques," (1675,) and "Sir Courtly Nice," a comedy.

See CIBBER, " Lives of the Poets."

Crowquill. See FORRESTER.

Crox'all, (SAMUEL,) an English writer, born at Walton-upon-Thames. He became prebendary of Hereford and Archdeacon of Salop, and published, besides other works, "Scripture Politics," (1735,) and a popular English version of "Æsop's Fables." Died in 1752.

Croy, de, deh krwȧ, (EMMANUEL,) DUKE, and Prince de Solre, a French general, born at Condé in 1718, was made marshal of France in 1782. Died in 1784.

Croy, de, (GUILLAUME.) See CHIÈVRES.

Crozat, kro'zȧ', (LOUIS FRANÇOIS,) Marquis du Châtel, a French general, born in 1695 ; died in 1750.

Croze. See LA CROZE.

Crozier, kro'zhęr, (Captain FRANCIS RAWDON MOIRA,) F.R.S., the second officer of Sir John Franklin's last expedition, born at Banbridge, Ireland, about 1795. In 1845 he sailed with Franklin in search of a Northwest passage, after which nothing was heard of the party until 1859, when Captain McClintock found on King William's Island a record, dated April 25, 1848, signed by Captain Crozier, stating that the ships had just been abandoned, and that the crews, under command of Crozier, were about to start for Great Fish River. (See FRANKLIN, Sir JOHN.)

Cruciger, the Latin of CREUTZIGER, which see.

Cruciger, krōŏt'siG-ęr, (GEORG,) a German philologist, born in 1575. He was professor of philosophy at Marburg, and wrote " Harmony of Languages," (" Harmonia Linguarum.") Died in 1636.

Crucius. See CROCE, DELLA.

Crucy, de, deh krü'se', (MATHURIN,) a French architect, born at Nantes in 1748, gained the grand prize in 1774. He was a member of the Institute. Died in 1826.

Cru'den, (ALEXANDER,) an eccentric Scottish bookseller, born at Aberdeen in 1700. He studied for the church ; but symptoms of insanity prevented his ordination. In 1732 he became a resident of London, where he opened a bookstore and received the title of bookseller to the queen. He styled himself "Alexander the Corrector," imagining that he had a mission to reform the manners of the age. In 1737 he published his "Concordance of the Old and New Testaments," the result of his unassisted industry. It was the most complete Concordance that had appeared, and is still esteemed indispensable to biblical scholars. His mental disease manifested itself in whimsical and extravagant actions and writings. He showed his zeal for good morals by effacing with a sponge indecent inscriptions in public places. Died in 1770.

See " Retrospective Review," vol. x., 1824.

Cruger. See KRUGER.

Cru'ger, (JOHN HARRIS,) born in New York in 1738, became mayor of that city in 1764. In the Revolutionary war he fought on the side of the royalists. Died in London in 1807.

Cruikshank, krŏŏk'shank, (GEORGE,) an English artist, distinguished for his comic humour and skill in caricature, was born in London about 1794. He acquired popularity about 1820 by designs for William

Hone's satirical works, among which is the "Political House that Jack built." His humorous genius and fertile imagination were displayed in illustrations of "Peter Schlemihl," "The Comic Almanac," "Oliver Twist," "My Sketch-Book," and many other books. His series of plates called "The Bottle," in which he illustrated the miseries of intemperance, had great success.

See "Blackwood's Magazine" for August, 1863; "Westminster Review" for June, 1840.

Cruik'shank, (WILLIAM,) F.R.S., an eminent Scottish anatomist, born in Edinburgh in 1745. At an early age he went to London, where he was successively the assistant and partner of Dr. William Hunter. He acquired reputation by his lectures, and by his work on "The Anatomy of the Absorbent Vessels," (1786.) Died in 1800.

See CHAMBERS, "Biographical Dictionary of Eminent Scotsmen."

Crumpe, krŭmp, (SAMUEL,) a physician, born in 1766, practised at Limerick, in Ireland. He wrote an able "Treatise on the Properties and Use of Opium," and a prize "Essay on the Means of Providing Employment for the People." Died in 1796.

Cruquius. See CRUSQUE, DE.

Crusenstolpe, kroo'zẹn-stol'pẹh, (MAGNUS JAKOB,) a popular Swedish novelist and political writer, born at Jonköping in 1795. He published a "Historical Picture of the First Years of Gustavus IV.," (1837,) and a political work called "Ställningar och Förhållanden," ("Positions and Relations,") for which he was imprisoned three years, (1838-40.) His historical romance of "Morianen" (6 vols., 1840-44) was very popular. He also wrote an interesting romance entitled "Charles John [Bernadotte] and the Swedes," (1845,) and other works.

Crusius. See CRENIUS.

Crusius, kroo'ze-ŭs or kroo'zhe-ŭs, (CHRISTIAN AUGUST,) a German philosopher, born at or near Merseburg about 1714. He became professor of theology at Leipsic, and published many works, among which is "Logic, or the Way to Certainty and Confidence respecting Human Knowledge," (1747.) He zealously opposed the philosophy of Wolf. Died in 1775.

See TENNEMANN, "Grundriss der Geschichte der Philosophie;" BUHLE, "Lehrbuch der Geschichte der Philosophie;" "Nouvelle Biographie Générale."

Crusius, (MARTIN,) a German philologist and historian, born near Bamberg in 1526, became in 1559 professor of Greek at Tübingen. He published valuable works, among which are a "History of Suabia," ("Annales Suevici," 1594,) and a "Commentary on Homer's Iliad," (1612.) Died in 1607.

See MÜLLER, "Oratio de Vita et Obitu M. Crusii," 1608 ; MORÉRI, "Dictionnaire Historique."

Crusque, de, dẹh krüsk or krŭsk, [Lat. CRU'QUIUS,] (JAMES,) a Flemish scholar, born near Ypres, became professor of Greek and Latin in Bruges in 1544, and published a valuable edition of Horace, with notes, (1578.)

Crut'well, (CLEMENT,) an English divine, born in Berkshire about 1745. He published, besides other works, an elaborate and valuable "Scripture Harmony, or Concordance of Parallels," (1790.) Died in 1808.

Cruveilhier, krü'vȧ'le-ȧ', (JEAN,) a distinguished French anatomist, born at Limoges about 1790, became professor of anatomy in Paris in 1825. In 1835 he obtained the chair of pathological anatomy founded by Dupuytren. His principal works are his "System of Anatomy," (American edition, 1844,) and "Pathologic Anatomy of the Human Body," (1829-40.)

Cruvelli, kroo-vel'lee, (SOPHIE,) a German vocalist, originally named **Cruwell,** born at Bielefeld in 1830. She was married in 1856 to Baron Vigier.

Cruyl, kroil, (LEVINUS,) a Flemish designer and engraver, born at Ghent about 1640, produced views of Roman scenery.

Cruz. See LA CRUZ and DINIZ DA CRUZ.

Cruz, da, dä krooz, (AGOSTINHO,) a Portuguese poet and monk, born at Ponte da Barca in 1540, was a brother of the poet Diogo Bernardes. His family name was PIMENTA. He wrote elegies, odes, and religious poems, which were first printed in 1771. They are ranked among the Portuguese classics. Died in 1619.

See LONGFELLOW's "Poets and Poetry of Europe."

Cruz, da, (GASPAR,) a Portuguese missionary, born at Evora, is stated to have been the first monk that preached the Catholic faith in China, which he visited in 1556. After his return to Portugal he published an account of his voyage. Died in 1570.

Cruz, da, (MARCOS,) an eminent Portuguese painter, born about 1649; died about 1678.

Cruz, de la, (JUAN.) See PANTOJA.

Cruz, de la, dä lä krooth, [Fr. DE LA CROIX, dẹh lä krwä,] (JUAN,) a Carmelite friar and ascetic writer, born in Old Castile in 1542. He founded several monasteries, and wrote, among other works, the "Dark Night of the Soul," ("Noche obscura del Alma.") Died in 1591.

See DOSITHÉE DE SAINT-ALEXIS, "Vie de Saint Jean de la Croix."

Csányi, chän'yee, (LASZLO,) a Hungarian statesman, born in 1790, took an active part in the revolution of 1848. He was executed in 1849, by order of the Austrian government.

Csaplovics, chŏp'lo-vitch, (JÁNOS,) a Hungarian writer, born about 1780, published "Topographical and Statistical Archives of the Kingdom of Hungary," (1821.)

Csokonai, cho'ko-ni', (MIHÁLY VITEZ,) a Hungarian poet, born at Debreczin in 1773. At the age of twenty he became professor of poetry at his native place, but was expelled two years later for his irregular habits. He wrote popular love-poems, and other works, mostly comic. He passed his life in poverty. Died in 1805.

Csoma, cho'mŏ, (ALEXANDER,) of Körös, an eminent Hungarian traveller and Orientalist, born at Körös about 1790. In early youth it became the cherished purpose of his life to discover the origin of his race, the Magyars, who were generally supposed to have come from Asia. He visited Thibet about 1822, and studied the Thibetan language for four years (1827-30) at Kanam. He went to Calcutta in 1830, and published an excellent Thibetan-English Dictionary (1834) and a Thibetan Grammar. Having undertaken another journey to Thibet, he died at Darjeeling in 1842, without having solved the question of the origin of the Magyars.

Ctesias, tee'she-as, [Κτησίας,] a Greek historian and physician, who flourished about 400 B.C., was a native of Cnidos, in Caria. He was for many years physician to Artaxerxes Mnemon, King of Persia, and afterwards returned to his native place. He wrote Περσικά, (a "History of Persia,") and a "Description of India." Of these works we have only abridgments in Photius, and extracts preserved by other writers. His accuracy and veracity have been questioned by ancient and modern critics.

See FABRICIUS, "Bibliotheca Græca ;" PLUTARCH, "Artaxerxes ;" SUIDAS, "Ctesias :" RETTIG, "Ctesiæ Vita," 1827 ; K. L. BLUM, "Herodotus und Ctesias," 1836.

Ctesibius, te-sib'e-us, [Κτησίβιος,] a famous Greek mechanician, who lived in Alexandria about 130 B.C. He invented the clepsydra, a pump, and other machines. Pliny and Vitruvius express admiration for his talents and works. Hero the Elder was his pupil.

Ctesidemus, tês-e-dee'mus, [Fr. CTÉSIDÈME, tȧ'ze'dȧm',] a Greek painter, lived about 350 B.C.

Ctesilas. See CRESILAS.

Ctesiphon. See CHERSIPHRON.

Ctesiphon, tês'e-phon, [Κτησιφῶν,] an Athenian, who obtained a notice in history by proposing that a crown of gold should be decreed to Demosthenes for his public services. For this he was prosecuted by Æschines, and successfully defended by Demosthenes in his famous oration "On the Crown," 330 B.C.

Ctesiphon, a Greek historian of an uncertain epoch, wrote a "History of Bœotia."

Cubero, koo-bā'ro, (PEDRO,) a Spanish priest, born near Calatayud in 1645. He is said to have been the first who made the tour of the world from west to east, and in part by land, (1670-79.) He published a short account of his voyage, (1680.)

Cubières, de, dẹh kü'be-air', (AMÉDÉE LOUIS Despans—dȧ'pŏN',) a French general and peer, born in Paris in 1786, was a son of Simon Louis Pierre, noticed below. He fought at Austerlitz, (1805,) and at Essling and Wagram, (1809.) He became a colonel in 1813, maréchal-de-camp in 1829, and lieutenant-general in 1835. He was made a peer in 1839, and was for a short time minister of war in 1839-40. Died in 1853.

ā, ē, ī, ō, ū, ȳ, *long;* ȧ, ė, ȯ, same, less prolonged; ă, ĕ, ĭ, ŏ, ŭ, ў, *short;* ạ, ẹ, ị, ọ, *obscure;* fär, fȧll, fȧt; mĕt; nŏt; gōōd; mōōn;

Cubières, de, (MARIE AGLAÉ **Buffaut**—büf'fō',) the wife of the preceding, born in 1794, wrote "Léonore de Biran," and other novels. The French Academy awarded the Montyon prize to her "Trois Soufflets," (1838.)

Cubières, de, (SIMON LOUIS PIERRE,) MARQUIS, a French naturalist, born at Roquemaure in 1747. Attached to the person of the king as equerry, he served him at the risk of his life in the Revolution. He published a "Description of Shell-Fish and their Habits," and other treatises on natural history. Died in 1821.

See CHALLAN, "Notice sur la Vie du Marquis de Cubières," 1822.

Cubillo, koo-Bēl'yo, (ALVARO DE ARAGON,) a Spanish dramatic poet, born at Granada about 1590.

Cu'bitt, (THOMAS,) an eminent English architect, born at Buxton, Norfolk, in 1788. He was chief architect of Belgravia, and erected several fine buildings in London and other places. He was employed by the queen to rebuild Osborne on the Isle of Wight, and took an active part in the sanitary improvement of London. Died in 1855.

See "Men I have known," by WILLIAM JERDAN, London, 1866.

Cubitt, (Sir WILLIAM,) an English civil engineer, distinguished as an inventor of machinery, was born at Dilham, Norfolk, in 1785. He invented a treadmill for prisons, and removed to London about 1826, after which he was engineer of the South-Eastern Railway. He superintended the erection of the Crystal Palace of Hyde Park in 1851. Died in October, 1861.

See "Gentleman's Magazine" for November, 1861.

Cucheval-Clarigny, küsh'vãl' klä'rĕn'ye', (NARCISSE,) a French journalist, born at Rennes in 1820, became an editor of the "Constitutionnel" in 1845.

Çuddhôdana, (Suddhodana.) See GAUTAMA.

Čudena, koo-Dā'nä, (PEDRO,) a Spanish traveller, who lived about 1630, wrote a "Description of Brazil."

Cŭd'worth, (RALPH,) an eminent English philosopher and Arminian divine, born at Aller, in Somersetshire, in 1617, was a graduate of Cambridge. He became master of Clare Hall in 1644, professor of Hebrew in 1645, master of Christ College in 1654, and prebendary of Gloucester in 1678. He was one of the chiefs of those who were called "Latitudinarians" in divinity. In 1678 he produced the first part of his celebrated work, "The True Intellectual System of the Universe," which he left unfinished. "By this," says Hallam, "he placed himself between the declining and rising schools of philosophy,—more independent of authority and more close, perhaps, in argument than the former, but more prodigal of learning and less conversant with analytical and inductive processes of reasoning than the latter. . . . Hobbes is the adversary with whom he most grapples." "The Intellectual System," says Dugald Stewart, "will forever remain a precious mine of information to those whose curiosity may lead them to study the spirit of the ancient theories." "The Intellectual System, his great production," says Mackintosh, "is directed against the atheistical opinions of Hobbes : it touches ethical questions but occasionally and incidentally. It is a work of stupendous erudition, of much more acuteness than at first appears ; . . . and it is distinguished, perhaps, beyond any other volume of controversy, by that best proof of the deepest conviction of the truth of a man's principles,—a fearless statement of the most formidable objections to them ; a fairness rarely practised but by him who is conscious of his power to answer them." He left several manuscripts, one of which, entitled a "Treatise concerning Eternal and Immutable Morality," has been published. His daughter was the well-known Lady Masham, the friend of John Locke. Died in 1688.

See JANNET, "De Cudworthii Doctrinâ," 1849; MACKINTOSH, "View of the Progress of Ethical Philosophy;" ALLIBONE, "Dictionary of Authors :" "Retrospective Review," vol. vi., 1822.

Cuellar, kwĕl-yaR', (GERONIMO,) a Spanish dramatic poet, born in 1608 ; died in 1669.

Cuerenhert, van, vän kü'rĕn-hĕrt, (THEODORE,) a Dutch engraver and writer, born at Amsterdam in 1522 ; died in 1590.

Cuesta, de la, dä lä kwĕs'tä, (GREGORIO GARCIA,) a Spanish general, born in Old Castile in 1740, was defeated by the French, near Medellin, about 1809. He afterwards became Captain-General of Old Castile, and united his force to that of Wellington. He resigned his command about 1810, and died in 1812.

Cueva, de la, (ALFONSO.) See BEDMAR.

Cueva, de la, dä lä kwä'vä, (BELTRAM,) a Spanish grandee, who passed for the most gallant and handsome man in Spain. In consequence of the favouritism shown to him by Henry IV., many of the nobles revolted against that prince. Cueva commanded for Henry at the indecisive battle of Medina del Campo, (1464,) soon after which peace was restored. He embraced the party of Isabella about 1475, and fought against Joanna, who was supposed to be his natural daughter. Died in 1492.

Cueva, de la, (JUAN,) an eminent Spanish poet, born at Seville about 1550. He composed dramas, lyric poems, and an epic poem called "Betica," (1603,) which Ticknor regards as a failure. A volume of his poems was published in 1582. His "Egemplar Poetico" (1605) was the earliest didactic poem of Spain. "The Spaniards place him," says Villenave, "in the first rank of their poets."

See TICKNOR, "History of Spanish Literature ;" N. ANTONIO, "Bibliotheca Hispana Nova."

Cuevas, de las, dä läs kwä'väs, (EUGENIO,) a Spanish portrait-painter, born at Madrid in 1613 ; died in 1667.

Cŭff, (HENRY,) an English scholar, born about 1560. He became professor of Greek in the University of Oxford, and afterwards secretary to the Earl of Essex. During the trial of Essex for treason, he accused Cuff of having been the first adviser of his rash measures. Cuff was executed in 1601. He left a work called "The Difference of the Ages of Man's Life," (1607.)

See WOOD, "Athenæ Oxonienses ;" FULLER, "Worthies."

Cŭf'fee, (PAUL,) a negro philanthropist, a member of the Society of Friends, was born near New Bedford, Massachusetts, in 1759. He accumulated a fortune as a sea-captain, commanded his own vessel, and had a crew composed entirely of negroes. In the latter part of his life he took a deep interest in the subject of African colonization, corresponded with prominent friends of the enterprise in Great Britain, and in 1811 visited Sierra Leone. Died in 1818.

Cugnet de Montarlot, kün'yà' dĕh mÒN'täR'lo', (CLAUDE FRANÇOIS,) a French politician and journalist, born in Franche-Comté in 1778 ; died in Spain in 1824.

Cugnières, kün'ye-aiR', written also **Gugnières** or **Congnières,** (PIERRE DE,) a French jurist, became royal advocate under Philip VI. about 1325.

Cugnot, kün'yo', (NICOLAS JOSEPH,) a French engineer, born in Lorraine in 1725 ; died in 1804.

Cujacius. See CUJAS.

Cujas, kü'zhäs', [Lat. CUJA'CIUS,] (JACQUES,) a French jurist of pre-eminent merit, was born at Toulouse in 1520. Having learned Latin and Greek without a teacher, he studied law in Toulouse, and in 1555 became professor at Bourges, the chief seminary of Roman law in France. About 1567 he removed to Valence, where his lectures were extremely popular. After several changes, he returned in 1577 to Bourges, where he passed the rest of his life. His lectures were attended by students from all nations of Europe. His works, published in 1577, made an epoch in the annals of jurisprudence. He was loyal to Henry IV., and took no part in the civil or religious discords of the times. Died in 1590. "This greatest of all civil lawyers," says Hallam, "pursued the track that Alciat had so successfully opened, avoiding all scholastic subtleties of interpretation, for which he substituted a general erudition that rendered the science more intelligible and attractive." ("Introduction to the Literature of Europe.") Among his numerous works are commentaries on Justinian's Institutes, on the Pandects and Decretals, and "Observationes et Emendationes."

See "Vie de Cujas," by PAPIRE-MASSON, 1590; BERNARDI, "Éloge de Cujas," 1775; J. BERRIAT SAINT-PRIX, "Histoire de Cujas," (in his "Histoire du Droit Romain,") 1821; TAISAND, "Vies des Jurisconsultes," 1721; BRUNQUELL, "Historia Juris," 1738; NICÉRON, "Mémoires;" SPANGENBERG, "J. Cujas und seine Zeitgenossen," 1822; "Nouvelle Biographie Générale."

Culant, de, dĕh kü'lÒN', (PHILIPPE,) a French general, esteemed one of the first captains of his time. He became a marshal in 1441, and took a prominent part in the reduction of Normandy and the expulsion of the English from France. Died in 1453.

є as k; ç as s; g̃ hard; g̃ as j; G, H, K, guttural; N, nasal; R, trilled; s as z; th as in this. (☞See Explanations, p. 23.)

Cŭl′len, (PAUL,) a Roman Catholic prelate, born in Ireland about 1805. He became Archbishop of Armagh and Primate of Ireland in 1850. A few years ago he was translated to the diocese of Dublin. He is the reputed author of a treatise designed to prove that the earth does not move.

Cŭl′len, (WILLIAM,) one of the most celebrated physicians of the eighteenth century, was born in Lanarkshire, in Scotland, in 1712. Having studied surgery and pharmacy at Glasgow, he went to London in 1729, and sailed thence to the West Indies as surgeon of a merchant-vessel. About 1732 he returned to Scotland, and pursued his medical and literary studies in Edinburgh. In 1736 he began to practise at Hamilton, where he formed a friendship and partnership with William Hunter, the eminent surgeon. The course of events soon dissolved their partnership; but they continued to be friends for life. In 1741 he married Anna Johnstone, and removed to Glasgow in 1745. He became professor of chemistry in the Glasgow University in 1746, and of medicine in 1751. There he developed a remarkable talent for giving science an attractive form, and for treating abstract subjects clearly. In 1756 he obtained the chair of chemistry in Edinburgh. "He claims," says Dr. Thomson, "a conspicuous place (in the history of chemistry) as the true commencer of the study of scientific chemistry in Great Britain." He became professor of theoretical medicine in 1766, and of practical medicine in 1773. He raised the medical celebrity of that university to a great height, and founded a new and ingenious system, which was promptly and generally adopted. His most important works are "First Lines of the Practice of Physic," (1777,) "Synopsis of Methodical Nosology," ("Synopsis Nosologiæ Methodicæ," 2 vols., 1785,) and a "Treatise of the Materia Medica," (2 vols., 1789.) Died in 1790.

See JOHN THOMSON, "Life and Writings of William Cullen," 1832; "Lives of British Physicians," London, 1857; "Edinburgh Review" for July, 1832; CHAMBERS, "Biographical Dictionary of Eminent Scotsmen;" SPRENGEL, "Geschichte der Arzneikunde."

Cŭl′lum, (GEORGE W.,) an American general and engineer, born in the city of New York about 1812, graduated at West Point in 1833. He superintended the construction of many forts before the civil war, and became chief of staff to General Halleck about November, 1861. He published a "Biographical Register of the Graduates of West Point," (2 vols., 1868.)

Cŭl′lum, (Rev. Sir JOHN,) an English antiquary, born in 1733, published "The Antiquities of Hawstead and Hardwick," (2d edition, 1813.) Died in 1785.

Cŭl′pep-pẹr, (JOHN,) a surveyor-general and popular leader in the provinces of North and South Carolina, was the head of an insurrection which, in 1678, deposed and imprisoned the royal president and deputies in North Carolina and established a new government.

Cŭl′pep-pẹr, (NICHOLAS,) an English astrologer, born in 1616, published, besides other works, "The English Physician," (1652,) which passed through many editions. Died in 1654.

Culpepper, (THOMAS,) LORD, Governor of Virginia from 1680 to 1683, was one of the persons to whom King Charles II. granted the territory of Virginia about 1673. He was noted for covetousness. Died in 1719.

Cul′vert, (GEORGE,) a Choctaw Indian chief, born in 1744. He served under Washington in the Revolutionary war, and under General Jackson in the Seminole war in 1814, when he became a colonel.

Cumberland, DUKE OF. See ERNEST AUGUSTUS of Hanover.

Cum′bẹr-lạnd, (RICHARD,) an eminent English moral philosopher, born in London in 1632. Having graduated at Cambridge, he became rector of Brampton in 1658, and obtained the living of Allhallows, Stamford, in 1667. In 1672 he published, in Latin, a work designed as a refutation of the system of Hobbes, and entitled a "Philosophic Inquiry into the Laws of Nature," ("De Legibus Naturæ Disquisitio Philosophica.") "This was of great importance," says Hallam, "in the annals of ethical philosophy, and was, if not a text-book in either of the universities, the basis of the system therein taught, and of the books which had most influence in this country. . . . He seems to have been the first

Christian writer who sought to establish systematically the principles of moral right independently of revelation." ("Introduction to the Literature of Europe.") He afterwards produced "Origines Gentium Antiquissimæ," or "Attempts for discovering the Times of the First Planting of Nations," and other works. He was appointed Bishop of Peterborough in 1691. Died in 1718.

See S. PAYNE, "Life and Writings of R. Cumberland," 1720; "Biographia Britannica."

Cumberland, (RICHARD,) an eminent English dramatic author and essayist, born at Cambridge in 1732, was the great-grandson of the preceding, and grandson of Bentley, the renowned critic. He was chosen a Fellow of Trinity College about 1750, and became private secretary to the Earl of Halifax, in whose service he remained many years. About 1776 he was appointed secretary to the board of trade, and in 1780 was sent on a secret mission to Madrid. After his return he devoted himself to literary pursuits, and produced a great variety of works, in prose and verse, among which are several popular comedies, including "The West Indian," "The Wheel of Fortune," etc. In 1785 he published a series of essays under the title of "The Observer," which, says Dr. Drake, "in literary interest and fertility of invention may be classed with the 'Spectator' and 'Adventurer.' . . . I consider it as superior in its powers of attraction to every other periodical composition except those papers just mentioned." Died in 1811.

See "Memoirs of Richard Cumberland," by himself, 2 vols., 1806; SIR WALTER SCOTT, "Miscellaneous Prose Works;" "Edinburgh Review" for April, 1806.

Cumberland, (WILLIAM AUGUSTUS,) DUKE OF, the third son of George II., King of England, was born in 1721. He commanded the English and allies at the great battle of Fontenoy in 1745, where he was defeated by the French. At the end of this campaign he was recalled to England to resist the Pretender, whom he defeated at Culloden in 1746. He was justly reproached for his cruelty on that occasion, when not only the flying troops of the Pretender, but many spectators, were mercilessly slaughtered; and he became in consequence extremely unpopular. In the Seven Years' war he took command of the English army on the continent, and, after losing a battle at Hastembeck in 1757, disbanded his army and retired from the service. In 1765, at the request of the king, he formed a new Whig ministry, of which he was the main support, when he died suddenly the same year. "With great courage," says Macaulay, "he had the virtues which are akin to courage. He spoke the truth, was open in enmity and friendship, and upright in all his dealings; but his nature was hard, and what seemed to him justice was rarely tempered with mercy."

See "Historical Memoirs of his Royal Highness William Augustus, Duke of Cumberland," 1767; ANDREW HENDERSON, "Life of the Duke of Cumberland," 1766.

Cŭm′ing, (HUGH,) an English naturalist, born in Devonshire in 1791. He passed many years on the coasts of South America and among the islands of the Pacific, where he obtained a rich collection of shells and of plants. Died in London in 1865.

See "Gentleman's Magazine" for October, 1865.

Cum′ming, (JOHN,) D.D., a popular British preacher and theological writer, was born in Aberdeenshire, Scotland, in 1810. In 1832 he became minister of the Scottish church in Crown Court, Covent Garden, London. He has distinguished himself as an adversary of the Roman Catholic Church, and as an opponent of the party which under Dr. Chalmers established the Free Church in 1843. Among his numerous works are "Lectures on the Parables," "The Great Sacrifice," "Discourses on the Revelations," and "The Great Tribulation," (1860.)

Cumming, (ROUALEYN GORDON,) of Altyre, a Scottish sportsman, born about 1820. Between 1843 and 1849 he spent about five years in South Africa, where his principal employment was hunting lions, elephants, etc. He published in 1850 a "Hunter's Life in South Africa." "We give entire credit to the truthfulness of the book, which is assuredly one of extraordinary interest after its kind. . . . In fact, the narrative has the charm of vivid romance; and the professed novelist may study with envy the native spring of his sinewy style." ("London Quarterly Review" for January, 1851.) Died in 1866.

Cum'mings, (JOSEPH,) a Methodist minister, born at Falmouth, Maine, in 1817. He became president of the Wesleyan University of Middletown, Connecticut.

Cummings, (MARIA,) an American authoress of the present age. She produced "The Lamplighter," (1854,) of which about 70,000 copies were issued in the first year, and "Mabel Vaughan," a novel, (1857.) Died in 1866.

Cunæus, ku-nā'ůs, or **Van der Kun**, vân dẹr kůn, (PETRUS,) a Dutch scholar, born at Flushing in 1586, was reckoned among the most learned men of his time, and was the associate of Grotius and Scaliger. In 1611 he was appointed professor of Latin at Leyden, and he afterwards obtained the chair of law in addition. He wrote, in Latin, a "Treatise on the Hebrew Republic," (1617,) which was often reprinted, a number of able orations, and other works. Died at Leyden in 1638.

See MORÉRI, "Dictionnaire Historique;" BURMANN, "Trajectum Eruditum;" A. VORSTIUS, "Oratio Funebris recitata in Exequiis P. Cunæi," 1638.

Cunc-ta'tor, a surname of Q. FABIUS MAXIMUS, the Roman general. (See FABIUS.)

Cunego, koo-nā'go, (DOMENICO,) an excellent Italian engraver, born at Verona in 1727. He worked in Rome the greater part of his life, and engraved many of the productions of Michael Angelo and Raphael, including "The Last Judgment" and "La Fornarina." Gavin Hamilton's "Schola Italica" contains twenty-two engravings of Cunego, after the Italian masters. He worked in Berlin four years, from 1785 to 1789. Died in 1794.

Cu'ne-gonde, [Ger. KUNIGUNDE, koo'ne-gŏŏn'dẹh,] SAINT, was the wife of Henry II., Emperor of Germany. According to the legend, she was delivered from a suspicion of conjugal infidelity by passing unhurt through an ordeal of fire. Died in 1040.

See J. RION, "Leben und Thaten des heiligen Heinrichs und der heiligen Kunigunde," 1832.

Cunha, da, dâ koon'yâ, (JOZÉ ANASTASIO,) a Portuguese, born at Lisbon in 1744, became professor of mathematics at Coimbra in 1774. Died in 1787.

See SISMONDI, "Littérature du Midi de l'Europe."

Cunha, da, (NUNO,) a Portuguese, born in 1487, was appointed Governor-General of India in 1528. After several successful enterprises, he was removed from office about 1538, and died at sea during the voyage homeward. His exploits have been sung by Camoëns.

Cunha, da, (Dom RODRIGO,) a patriotic Portuguese prelate, born in Lisbon in 1577. He became Archbishop of Braga and of Lisbon in 1635. He contributed greatly to the success of the revolution of 1640, and wrote Histories of the Churches of Braga and of Lisbon. Died in 1643.

See BARBOSA MACHADO, "Bibliotheca Lusitana."

Cunha, da, (TRISTAM,) a Portuguese navigator, the father of Nuno, noticed above, commanded a fleet sent in 1508 to make explorations and conquests. He discovered in the South Sea three small islands, one of which bears his name, and gained a victory over the King of Calicut. In 1515 he was ambassador at Rome.

Cunha Barbosa, da, dâ koon'yâ baR-bo'sâ, (JANUARIO,) a Brazilian priest and journalist, born in 1780. He founded the "Reverbero Constitucional," a journal which, about 1821, advocated the independence of Brazil. He became canon of the imperial chapel in 1824, and afterwards director of the national library. He founded the Geographical and Historical Institute of Rio Janeiro. Died in 1846.

See "Nouvelle Biographie Générale."

Cunha Mattos, da, dâ koon'yâ mât'tos, (RAYMUNDO JOZÉ,) a Portuguese general, born at Faro in 1776. About 1820 he became commandant of the province of Goyaz, and afterwards obtained the highest rank in the army. He published a valuable work, called "Itinerary from Rio Janeiro to Pará and Maranham," etc., (1836.) Died in 1840.

See "Nouvelle Biographie Générale."

Cunich, koo'nik, (RAIMONDO,) a Jesuit, noted as a Latin poet, was born at Ragusa in 1719; died at Rome in 1794.

Cunin-Gridaine, kü'nâN' gre'dân', (LAURENT,) born at Sedan, in France, in 1778, was minister of commerce in several cabinets between 1837 and 1848. Died in 1859.

Cunitia. See CUNITZ.

Cunitz, koo'nits, or **Cunitia**, (MARIA,) a learned German lady, born at Schweidnitz, in Silesia. After learning several languages, she gave special attention to astronomy. She was married in 1630 to M. Lewen. Having undertaken to render the tables of Kepler more convenient in practice, she published, in 1650, astronomical tables, under the title of "Urania Propitia." Died in 1664.

Cunningham, kun'ning-am, (ALEXANDER,) a Scottish historian, born near Selkirk in 1654. From 1715 to 1720 he was British envoy to Venice. He wrote, in Latin, a "History of Great Britain from 1688 to 1714," which is said to be valuable, and has been translated into English. Died about 1737.

See "Biographia Britannica;" CHAMBERS, "Biographical Dictionary of Eminent Scotsmen."

Cunningham, (ALEXANDER,) a Scottish classical scholar, born about 1650. He became professor of law in Edinburgh, and afterwards removed to the Hague, where he published an edition of Horace, (1721,) which is much esteemed. Died about 1730.

Cunningham, (ALLAN,) a successful Scottish author and critic, born at Blackwood, Dumfriesshire, in 1785. In early youth he was apprenticed to a stone-mason. In 1810 he went to London, where he was employed as reporter for newspapers. From 1814 to 1841 he held the desirable position of clerk or foreman of Sir F. Chantrey's studio. He published an admired dramatic poem, "Sir Marmaduke Maxwell," (1822,) and the popular romances "Lord Roldan" and "Paul Jones." In 1829-33 he produced a valuable work entitled "Lives of the Most Eminent British Painters, Sculptors, and Architects." He also composed several songs, and a "Critical History of the Literature of the Last Fifty Years." Died in 1842. Sir Walter Scott, who was his friend, described him as a "man of genius, who only requires the tact of knowing when and where to stop, to attain the universal praise that ought to follow it."

See CHAMBERS, "Biographical Dictionary of Eminent Scotsmen," (Supplement;) DE QUINCEY, "Literary Reminiscences," vol. ii.; "Edinburgh Review" for January, 1828; "Fraser's Magazine" for September, 1832, (with a portrait.)

Cunningham, (EDWARD FRANCIS,) a distinguished Scottish painter, born at Kelso about 1742. After studying in Rome, he worked with success in London, Paris, Saint Petersburg, and Berlin. He painted portraits of several royal personages, and other admired works. His habits were very dissipated. Died in 1793.

Cunningham, kun'ning-am, (GEORGE GODFREY,) an English historian, published a "Biographical History of England, or a History of England in the Lives of Englishmen," (8 vols., 1853.)

Cunningham, (JOHN,) an Irish actor and poet, born in Dublin in 1729. He performed some years in Edinburgh and the north of England, and composed pastoral and other poems, which were received with favour. Died in 1773.

Cunningham, (JOHN WILLIAM,) Vicar of Harrow, an English writer, born about 1780, published "The Velvet Cushion," (1814,) which passed through many editions, "De Rance," (a poem,) and other works. Died in 1861.

Cunningham, (PETER,) an English author and critic, a son of Allan Cunningham, the poet, was born in Pimlico, London, in 1816. He became chief clerk in the Audit Office in 1854, and published a "Life of Inigo Jones," (1848,) and a good edition of Oliver Goldsmith's Works, (1854.) He also edited Johnson's "Lives of the Poets," (1854.)

See "London Quarterly Review" for April and October, 1854.

Cunningham, (WILLIAM,) an English engraver and physician, born at Norwich about 1520; died in 1577.

Cunningham, (WILLIAM,) D.D., a Scottish minister of the Free Church, was born at Hamilton in 1805. He succeeded Dr. Chalmers as principal of the New College, Edinburgh, in 1847. Died in 1861.

Cuno, koo'no, (JOHANN CHRISTIAN,) a German poet and botanist, born at Berlin in 1708. He wrote, in German, an "Ode on his Garden," (1750,) and "Letters on Moral Subjects," (in verse; 3d edition, 1766.) Linnæus named the genus Cunonia in honour of him. Died about 1780.

See ADELUNG, Supplement to JÖCHER, "Allgemeines Gelehrten-Lexikon."

Cup, kŭp, (WILLEM,) a Dutch jurist, born at Bommel in 1604; died in 1667.

Cupani, koo-pä'nee, (FRANCESCO,) an Italian botanist, born in Sicily in 1657. He became a monk in 1681, after which he published two catalogues of the rare or newly-found plants of Sicily. At his death in Palermo, in 1711, he was about to publish an extensive work, called "Description of All the Plants of Sicily," ("Panphytum Siculum.") In 1715 Bonani, who became possessor of his papers, published a volume of this work and claimed it as his own.

See MONGITORE, "Bibliotheca Sicula."

Cuper, kü'per, [Lat. CUPE'RUS,] (GISBERT,) a Dutch critic and philologist, born at Hemmendem in 1644. He was for many years professor of history at Deventer, and published several valuable works, among which are "Observations in which many Passages of Authors are Explained," (1670,) and a "History of the Three Gordians," (Emperors of Rome,) (1697.) Died in 1716.

See NICÉRON, "Mémoires;" BOSSCHA, "Oratio de G. Cupero," 1816.

Cu'pid, [Lat. CUPI'DO, (or A'MOR;) Fr. CUPIDON, kü'pe'dôN'; It. CUPIDINE, koo-pee'de-nâ,] the name of the god of love in the Roman mythology, corresponding exactly to the E'ROS ['Eρως] of the Greeks. He is usually regarded as the son of Venus; though respecting his parentage there is considerable diversity among the ancient authors. He is represented as a winged boy armed with a bow and arrows. He is often pictured with a bandage over his eyes, to indicate the blindness or unreasonableness of love. The corresponding Hindoo deity is called KÂMADÊVA or KÂMADÊO, which see.

See KEIGHTLEY's "Mythology."

Cupidon or **Cupido.** See CUPID.

Curadi. See GHIRLANDAIO.

Curæus. See CURÄUS.

Curaudau, kü'rō'dō', (FRANÇOIS RENÉ,) a French practical chemist and inventor, born at Séez in 1765. He improved the processes of tanning leather, of making soap, beet-sugar, invented stoves, etc. Died in 1813.

Curäus or **Curæus,** koo-rä'ŭs, (JOACHIM,) a German historian and physician, born at Freystadt, in Silesia, in 1532, was a friend of Melanchthon. He published, besides several theological treatises, an important work on the "History of Silesia," ("Annales Silesiæ ab Origine Genti," 1571.) Died in 1573.

Curcellæus, (STEPHEN.) See COURCELLES, (ÉTIENNE DE.)

Cureau. See CHAMBRE.

Curée, kü'râ', (JEAN FRANÇOIS,) a French politician, born near Lodève in 1756. He was elected to the Convention in 1792. As a member of the Tribunate in 1804, he first proposed to declare Napoleon emperor. He afterwards obtained the office of senator and the title of Count. Died in 1835.

Curio, koo're-o, [Fr. CURION, kü're'ôN',] (CŒLIUS SECUNDUS,) a Protestant theologian, born in Piedmont in 1503. He was professor of belles-lettres at Bâle from 1547 to 1569, and published, besides other works in Latin, "The Amplitude of the Kingdom of Heaven," (1554,) and "Pasquillus Ecstaticus," an ingenious and satirical work of a controversial character. About 1540 he was confined in various prisons of Italy by the Inquisition, but he escaped by stratagem. Died in 1569.

See BAYLE, "Historical and Critical Dictionary;" NICÉRON, "Mémoires;" STUPANI, "Oratio de C. S. Curionis Vita," 1570.

Cu'rĭ-o, [Fr. CURION, kü're'ôN',] (CAIUS SCRIBONIUS,) a Roman general, a friend of Cicero, was a son of an orator of the same name. He became tribune of the people in 90 B.C., prætor in 82, and consul in 76. He afterwards commanded in Macedonia, and defeated the Dardanians and Mœsians. In 57 B.C. he was chosen pontifex maximus. Died in 53 B.C.

Curio, (CAIUS SCRIBONIUS,) a son of the preceding, was a profligate politician. He had great natural talents for oratory. He became tribune in 50 B.C., soon after which he deserted the cause of the senate and became a

partisan of Cæsar. He is considered as one of the principal instigators of the civil war between Pompey and Cæsar. In the year 49 he obtained command in Sicily, from which he expelled the troops of Pompey. Having led an army into Africa, he was defeated by Juba and killed in battle about 48 B.C.

See ORELLI, "Onomasticon Tullianum;" APPIAN, "Bellum Civile;" TACITUS, "De Claris Oratoribus."

Curion. See CURIO.

Curius Dentatus. See DENTATUS.

Curl or **Curll,** (EDMUND,) an English bookseller of London, to whom Pope has given notoriety in his "Dunciad." He lost his ears by publishing licentious books. Died in 1748.

Curne, La. See SAINTE-PALAYE.

Curopalates. See CODINUS.

Curradi. See CURRADO and GHIRLANDAIO.

Currado, koor-rä'do, or **Curradi,** koor-rä'dee,(FRANCESCO,) CAVALIERE, a skilful Italian painter, born at Florence in 1570, was a pupil of B. Naldini. Among his works, which are mostly of small dimensions, is "The Three Marys." Died in 1661.

See LANZI, "History of Painting in Italy."

Cur'ran, (JOHN PHILPOT,) a famous Irish orator and barrister, born of Protestant parents at Newmarket, near Cork, in 1750. His mother, whose name was Philpot, was witty and highly gifted. In 1769 he entered Trinity College, Dublin, where he acquired an extensive knowledge of the classics. He began the study of law in the Middle Temple, London, in 1773, and was called to the Irish bar in 1775. His eloquence, humour, and mastery of sarcasm soon procured him a large practice. In cross-examination he was inimitable: "he argued, he cajoled, he ridiculed, he mimicked, he played off the various artillery of his talent upon the witness." In 1783 he entered Parliament, where he acted with the opposition, of which Grattan was the leader; but he was not so successful there as in the forum. "He had all the qualities," says Phillips, "by which his countrymen are attracted. His imagination was wonderful, his eloquence copious, rapid, and ornate, his powers of mimicry beyond all description. . . . He had another quality, apart from intellect, which the times demanded,—indomitable courage." Among his greatest efforts was the defence of Rowan, indicted for a seditious libel in 1794. He was counsel for Theobald Wolfe Tone and other persons implicated in the rebellion of 1798. He strenuously opposed the union of Ireland and England, which was effected in 1800. On the formation of a Whig ministry in 1806, Curran was appointed master of the rolls in Ireland, a position for which he was not well adapted, and which was quite repugnant to his habits. In his latter years he was subject to great and habitual dejection of spirits. Died in 1817. Among many recorded instances of his ready wit is this anecdote: When a tobacconist desired a Latin motto for his new carriage, Curran proposed "Quid Rides."*

See "Life of J. P. Curran," by his son, W. H. CURRAN, 1819; CHARLES PHILLIPS, "Curran and his Contemporaries," 1850; W. O. REGAN, "Life of Curran," 1817; T. DAVIS, "Life of Curran," 1846; "Edinburgh Review" for May, 1820.

Currer Bell. See BRONTÉ, (CHARLOTTE.)

Cur'rie or **Cur'ry,** (JAMES,) a Scottish physician, born in Dumfriesshire in May, 1756. Having passed a few years in Virginia in mercantile pursuits, he returned home in 1776, and studied medicine. In 1780 he settled in Liverpool, where he practised with success. His principal professional work is "Medical Reports on the Effects of Water, Cold and Warm, as a Remedy for Fever," (1797.) He acquired literary reputation by an edition of Burns's Works, with a memoir of his life. Died in 1805.

See "Life and Writings of James Currie," by his son, W. W. CURRIE, 1831; "Edinburgh Review" for October, 1805, January, 1814, and April, 1832; CHAMBERS, "Biographical Dictionary of Eminent Scotsmen."

Cur'ry, (DANIEL,) an American writer and Methodist minister, born at Peekskill, New York, in 1809. He wrote, besides other works, a "Life of Wycliffe."

Curry, (JAMES.) See CURRIE.

Cursor. See PAPIRIUS CURSOR.

* *I.e.* "Why do you laugh?" (See Horace's First Satire, l. 69.)

ā, ē, ī, ō, ū, ȳ, *long;* å, ė, ȯ, same, less prolonged; ă, ĕ, ĭ, ŏ, ŭ, ў, *short;* a, e, i, o, *obscure;* fär, fåll, fåt; mêt; nŏt; gŏŏd; mŏŏn;

Cur'teis, (THOMAS,) an English divine and poet, born about 1690, wrote essays and sermons. Died in 1747.

Curti, kooʀ'tee, (FRANCESCO,) an Italian painter and engraver, born at Bologna in 1603.

Curti, (GIROLAMO.) See DENTONE, (GIROLAMO.)

Cur'tin, (ANDREW G.,) an American politician, born at Bellefonte, Centre county, Pennsylvania, in 1817. He studied law, became an active supporter of the Whig party, and was appointed secretary of state in 1855. He was elected Governor of Pennsylvania by the Republicans in October, 1860. In 1863 he was again elected Governor of the same State for a term of three years. He was appointed minister to Russia in April, 1869.

Cur'tis, (BENJAMIN R.,) an American lawyer, born in Watertown, Massachusetts, about 1810. He was admitted to the bar in 1832, soon after which he began to practise in Boston. He was appointed a judge of the supreme court of the United States in 1851, and resigned in 1857. He was one of the counsel that defended President Johnson in his trial before the Senate in April, 1868. He published "Reports of Cases in the Circuit Courts of the United States," 1854.

Curtis, (GEORGE TICKNOR,) an American lawyer and eminent legal writer, brother of the preceding, was born at Watertown, Massachusetts, in 1812. He graduated at Harvard in 1832. His "Treatise on the Rights and Duties of Merchant Seamen," (1841,) says Judge Story, "is written with great ability, accuracy, and learning." Among his other works may be mentioned his valuable treatise on the law of Copyright, (1847,) and his "Commentaries on the Jurisdiction, Practice, etc. of the Courts of the United States," (2 vols., 1854.)

Curtis, (GEORGE WILLIAM,) a popular American author and lecturer, born at Providence, Rhode Island, in 1824. He visited Europe about 1846, studied for some time in the University of Berlin, and made an extensive tour in the Levant, after which he returned home in 1850. He published in 1851 an attractive work entitled "Nile Notes of a Howadji," and in 1852 "The Howadji in Syria." He acquired a high reputation as an orator and lecturer on various subjects. In 1856 he advocated, in numerous public speeches, the election of John C. Fremont to the Presidency. Among his works are "Lotus-Eating," (1852,) and "The Potiphar Papers," reprinted from "Putnam's Monthly Magazine," (1854.)

See CLEVELAND'S "Compendium of American Literature."

Curtis, (SAMUEL R.,) an American general, born in Ohio about 1807, graduated at West Point in 1831. He served as colonel in the Mexican war, (1846-47,) after which he settled in Iowa. He represented the first district of Iowa in Congress, 1856-61, and voted with the Republicans. In May, 1861, he became a brigadier-general of volunteers. He gained an important victory at Pea Ridge, Arkansas, March 7 and 8, 1862. He was speedily promoted to the rank of major-general, and took command of the district of Missouri in September, 1862. Died in December, 1866.

Curtis, (WILLIAM,) an English botanist, born at Alton, Hampshire, in 1746, was proprietor of botanic gardens at Bermondsey, Lambeth Marsh, and Brompton. In 1777 he began to publish a splendid "Flora Londinensis," with coloured plates, which was continued by Sir W. J. Hooker, (1835.) He originated the "Botanical Magazine," and was author of a useful work entitled "Observations on British Grasses," (1790.) He also left two treatises on insects. Died in 1799.

Curtius. See CURTZ.

Curtius, kooʀt'se-ùs, (ERNST,) a German antiquary, born at Lubeck in 1814. He visited Athens in 1837, and became preceptor of Prince Friedrich Wilhelm of Prussia about 1844. He published "The Acropolis of Athens," (1844,) "Peloponnesus," (1852,) and other works on Greece. He was appointed professor of Greek and Latin at Göttingen in 1856.

Curtius, kur'she-ns, (LANCINUS,) a mediocre Latin poet, born at Milan; died in 1511.

Curtius, kur'she-us, (MARCUS,) a Roman youth, celebrated for his patriotic devotion. According to tradition, a gulf opened in the Forum of Rome about 360 B.C., and the soothsayers declared it could not be filled except by the sacrifice of the principal strength of the

Roman people. Curtius asked his fellow-citizens if their courage and arms were not the most worthy offerings. Then, having devoted himself to the Dii Manes, he mounted his horse and plunged into the abyss, which immediately closed up.

See LIVY, "History of Rome ;" PLUTARCH, "Romulus."

Curtius, (MATTHEW.) See CORTI, (MATTEO.)

Curtius, (METIUS,) a Sabine hero, who fought against the Romans in the war caused by the abduction of the Sabine women, and killed Hostus Hostilius in single combat. Having been attacked by Romulus, he took refuge in a marsh which occupied the site of the future Forum of Rome, and which was called Lacus Curtius in memory of that event.

See LIVY, "History of Rome ;" PLUTARCH, "Romulus."

Curtius, (MICHAEL CONRAD,) a German historian, born in Mecklenburg in 1724, was professor of history at Marburg. He wrote (in Latin) a good "Commentary on the Roman Senate under the Emperors," (1768.) Died in 1802.

See G. F. CREUZER, "Memoria M. C. Curtii," 1802.

Curtius, (QUINTUS.) See QUINTUS CURTIUS.

Curtois. See COURTOIS.

Curvo, kooʀ'vo, (JOÃO SEMMEDO,) a Portuguese physician and medical writer, born in 1635; died in 1719.

Curtz or **Kurtz,** kooʀts, [Lat. CUR'TIUS,] (ALBRECHT,) a German astronomer, born at Munich in 1600; died in 1671.

Cur'wen, (JOHN C.,) an English agriculturist, who represented Cumberland in Parliament for many years. He made improvements in agriculture, and published "Observations on the State of Ireland," (1818.) Died in 1828.

Curzon, de, deh kür'zòn', (PAUL ALFRED,) a French landscape-painter, born near Poitiers in 1820. He obtained a second medal in 1857.

Cusa. See CUSANUS.

Cu-sa'nus, or **de Cu'sa,** written also **Cuss** and **Cusel,** (NICHOLAS,) à pious and learned prelate, born at Cusa, in the diocese of Treves, in 1401. His family name was KREBS. He was one of the most liberal men of his time, and was at the head of the progressive movements in religion and science. About 1448 he was made a cardinal. He wrote a work in favour of a reform in the Church, and others on mathematics and astronomy. He is said to have been the first modern who favoured the theory of the earth's motion. Died in 1464.

See HARTZHEIM, "N. Cusæ Vita," 1730; F. J. CLEMENS, "Giordano Bruno und Nicol. von Cusa," 1847; "Nouvelle Biographie Générale ;" RITTER, "History of Philosophy ;" R. ZIMMERMANN, "Der Cardinal N. Cusanus als Vorläufer Leibnitzens," 1852.

Cusel. See CUSANUS.

Cushing, koosh'ing, (CALEB,) a distinguished American jurist, politician, and scholar, was born in Essex county, Massachusetts, in 1800. Having graduated at Harvard College, he studied law at Cambridge. He was elected to the State Senate in 1826, and in 1829 visited Europe. He published, soon after, "Reminiscences of Spain," and a "Historical and Political Review of the Revolution in France," (1830.) He represented the North Essex district in Congress for four terms, 1835-43. He acted with the Whigs until 1841, when he united with President Tyler in his hostility to the Whig measures, and went over to the Democratic party. He was nominated by the President in 1843 as secretary of the treasury ; but he was not confirmed by the Senate. He was soon after appointed commissioner to China, and in 1844 negotiated the first treaty of the United States with the government of that country. On his return he became an advocate of the Mexican war, then in progress, and equipped a regiment of volunteers at his own expense. As colonel of this regiment, he went to Mexico in 1847, and was appointed brigadier-general. During his absence he was nominated by the Democratic party as their candidate for Governor ; but he was not elected. He was appointed in 1852 a justice of the supreme court of Massachusetts, and was attorney-general of the United States from March, 1853, to March, 1857.

See LIVINGSTON'S "Portraits of Eminent Americans, 1854."

Cushing, (LUTHER STEARNS,) an American jurist, born in Lunenburg, Massachusetts, in 1803. He was reporter to the supreme court of his State, and published 8 vols. of Reports. Among his works is "The Law and Practice of Legislative Assemblies in the United States," (1855.) Died in 1856.

Cushing, (THOMAS,) an American patriot, born in Boston in 1725. He was a member of the first and second Congress, and was afterwards for several years Lieutenant-Governor of Massachusetts. Died in 1788.

Cushing, (WILLIAM,) a jurist, born in Scituate, Massachusetts, in 1733. He became chief justice of the superior court of Massachusetts in 1777, and a justice of the supreme court of the United States in 1789. Died in 1810.

Cushing, (WILLIAM B.,) a brave naval officer, born in Wisconsin about 1842. He performed several daring exploits in the civil war. Among these was the destruction of the iron-clad ram Albemarle in the Roanoke River, on a dark night of October, 1864. Aided by thirteen men, he exploded a torpedo-boat under the Albemarle, while the enemy poured a destructive fire into his little craft. All of his party, except one besides himself, were either killed or captured. He jumped into the river, swam to the shore, and escaped. He was promoted to the rank of commander. "No man in our navy," says J. T. Headley, "at his age has ever won so brilliant a reputation."

See HEADLEY, "Farragut and our Naval Commanders," 1867.

Cushman, kōōsh'man, (CHARLOTTE S.,) a distinguished American actress, born in Boston about 1816. She made her *début* about 1835, and performed tragic parts with success in New York and other cities of the Union. In 1845 she went to England, where she performed with success for several years. Her sister SUSAN was also a popular actress.

Cushman, (ROBERT,) one of the founders of Plymouth colony, was born in England about 1580. He emigrated to Plymouth in 1621, before which year he had acted as agent of the colony. He preached, in December, 1621, the first sermon that was printed in America. Died in 1625 or 1626.

Cushman, (THOMAS,) a son of the preceding, was born about 1608. He became in 1649 an elder of the Church of Plymouth. Died in 1691.

Cuspinian, koos-pee'ne-ân, [Lat. CUSPINIA'NUS ; Fr. CUSPINIEN, küs'pee'ne'ân',] (JOHANN,) a German writer, born in Franconia in 1473. His German name was SPIESHAMMER, (speess'häm-mer.) He was privy councillor to Maximilian I., and wrote, besides other works, a valuable "History *(Commentarius)* of the Emperors from Julius Cæsar to Maximilian I.," (1540.) Died in 1529.

See GERBELIUS, "Vita J. Cuspiniani," 1540; M. ADAM, "Vitæ Eruditorum ;" P. GIOVIO, "Elogia."

Cuspinianus. See CUSPINIAN.

Cuspinien. See CUSPINIAN.

Cuss. See CUSA.

Cusson, kü'sôn', (PIERRE,) M.D., a skilful French botanist, born at Montpellier in 1727. He was employed in Spain as a botanist by B. de Jussieu in 1754, after which he practised medicine in Montpellier. He wrote a treatise on the family of Umbelliferæ, which was his speciality, but did not live to publish it. Died in 1783.

Cust, (Sir EDWARD,) an English general, born in London in 1794, served under Wellington, and was afterwards a member of Parliament. He published "Lives of the Warriors of the Civil Wars of France and England," (1867,) and other works.

Cust'er, (GEORGE A.,) an American general, born in Harrison county, Ohio, in 1839, graduated at West Point in 1861. He commanded a brigade of cavalry in Northern Virginia in May, 1864, and a division of the army of General Sheridan in the spring of 1865. He took part in the pursuit and capture of General Lee's army, April, 1865.

Custine, de, deh küs'tèn', (ADAM PHILIPPE,) COUNT, an eminent French general, born of a noble family at Metz in 1740. He entered the army very young, and became a colonel about 1760. For his conduct at Yorktown, Virginia, in 1781, he was made maréchal-de-camp. In 1789 he was deputed to the States-General, in which he advocated with ardour the cause of reform. Having command of an army on the Rhine in 1792, he

conducted bold and successful expeditions against Spire, Mentz, and Frankfort, which he took almost without resistance, and suddenly obtained great popularity. In the campaign of 1793 he failed in an attempt to relieve Mentz, which was recovered by the allies. He was then denounced by the violent Jacobins as a counter-revolutionist, was arrested at the head of his army by a member of the Convention, and taken to Paris, in the beginning of the reign of terror. The popularity acquired by his success, his eloquence and affable manners, excited the jealousy of the Jacobin chiefs. Accordingly, he was condemned and executed in August, 1793.

See LAMARTINE's "History of the Girondists," book xlvi.; "Biographie Universelle."

Custine, de, (ASTOLPHE,) MARQUIS, a French traveller and writer, grandson of the preceding, was born in Paris in 1793. Between 1811 and 1822 he travelled in England, Switzerland, and other countries. He published an account of this tour, entitled "Mémoires et Voyages," (1830,) a successful work called "Russia in 1839," and several novels.

Custine, de, (RENAUD PHILIPPE,) a son of Adam Philippe, noticed above, was born in 1760. For his intimacy with Condorcet, and his spirited conduct during his father's trial, he was proscribed by Robespierre, and suffered death in January, 1794.

See THIERS, "Histoire de la Révolution."

Cus'tis, (GEORGE WASHINGTON PARKE,) an adopted son of General Washington, was born in Maryland in 1781. He was a grandson of Mrs. Martha Washington and her first husband. He was the author of several plays and orations. Died in 1857.

Cüs'tos, (DOMINIC,) a Flemish engraver, born at Antwerp in 1560, was a son of a painter named Battens. He settled in Augsburg, and published several series of portraits engraved by himself. Died in 1612.

Cüth'bert, SAINT, an English or Anglo-Saxon monk of the seventh century. He was prior of the monastery of Lindisfarne or Holy Isle, near Berwick, and for some time was Bishop of Durham. His memory was greatly venerated, and marvellous legends of his miracles were circulated. He is sometimes styled the "Thaumaturgus of Britain." Died about 686 A.D.

Another CUTHBERT, Archbishop of Canterbury, was a disciple of Bede, of whose life and death he wrote an account. Died about 760.

Cut'ler, (MANASSEH,) an American botanist and preacher, born at Killingly, Connecticut, in 1744. He examined and described three hundred and fifty species of plants of New England, and was called the pioneer of botany in that region. He was a leader of a party which settled at Marietta, Ohio, in 1788. Died in 1823.

Cutler, (TIMOTHY,) an American clergyman, born in Massachusetts in 1685. He was chosen president of Yale College in 1719, joined the Episcopal Church in 1722, and became rector of a church in Boston about 1724. Died in 1765.

Cutts, (Lord JOHN,) a brave English general, born in Essex. His gallantry at Buda in 1686 was applauded by Addison in a Latin poem. He served with distinction under William III. at the battle of the Boyne and at the siege of Namur, (1695.) Before the latter date he was rewarded with an Irish peerage and made a major-general. He sat in several Parliaments between 1695 and 1707, and wrote a poem on the death of Queen Mary. Died in 1707.

Cuvelier de Trye, küv'le-â' deh tre, (JEAN GUILLAUME ANTOINE,) a mediocre French dramatist, born at Boulogne-sur-Mer in 1766 ; died in 1824.

Cuvera. See KUVERA.

Cuvier, kü've-â', (CLÉMENTINE,) was a daughter of the celebrated Baron Cuvier. She died in 1828, aged about twenty-two.

Cuvier, (FRÉDÉRIC,) a French naturalist, born at Montbéliard in 1773, was a brother of the celebrated Cuvier. He removed to Paris about 1797, and devoted himself to the study of natural history. A few years later he became director of the menagerie at the Jardin des Plantes, and professor of comparative anatomy. He published an able treatise on the teeth of Mammalia, (1822.) His most popular and extensive work is a "Natu-

ā, ē, ī, ō, ū, ȳ, *long;* à, ė, ò, same, less prolonged; ă, ĕ, ĭ, ŏ, ŭ, ў, *short;* a, ę, į, ǫ, *obscure;* fär, fåll, fät; mĕt; nŏt; gōōd; mōōn;

ral History of the Mammals," ("Histoire naturelle des Mammifères," (1824,) in which he gives a graphic description of the habits and instincts of those animals, with many curious anecdotes. Died at Strasburg in 1838.

See FLOURENS, "Éloge de F. Cuvier."

Cuvier, kü've-à′ or kü′ve-ęr, (GEORGE CHRÉTIEN LÉOPOLD FRÉDÉRIC DAGOBERT,) BARON, an illustrious philosopher, statesman, and author, and one of the greatest naturalists of modern times, was born on the 23d of August, 1769, at Montbéliard, then a part of the German Empire, now in Doubs, a department of France. His parents were Protestants, of French origin, who were driven from their native land by religious persecution. His father was an officer in the French service. His early training was directed by an accomplished mother. The favourite amusement of his childhood was to copy and colour the figures of animals in Buffon's works. He was educated at the Academia Carolina of Stuttgart, which he left in 1788 with a very extensive general instruction and the reputation of a prodigious memory. He then became tutor to the son of Count d'Héricy, of Caen, in the vicinity of which he passed in peaceful studies the stormy period of the Revolution. His early essays on natural history attracted the notice of Jussieu and Geoffroy; and when he arrived in Paris in March, 1795, he was looked upon as one destined to give a new impulse to science. He read to the Society of Natural History an essay on the formation and use of methods, and a memoir on the organization of white-blooded animals. On the formation of the central schools he was chosen professor of natural history in Paris, and in July, 1795, became assistant professor of comparative anatomy in the Museum of Natural History. He immediately began to form his great cabinet of comparative anatomy. In December, 1795, he was chosen a member of the Institute, then just founded. In 1798 Cuvier published his "Tableau élémentaire des Animaux," in which he began to apply his principles on the subordination of characters, and to display his genius for classification. He succeeded Daubenton as professor of natural history in the College of France in 1800, and then commenced the publication of his "Lectures on Comparative Anatomy," which proved very successful.

About 1802 he was chosen perpetual secretary of the Academy of Sciences, and married Madame Duvaucel, the widow of a farmer-general. He contributed to the "Annales du Muséum" a series of memoirs on fossil bones, with plates skilfully designed and engraved by himself. In 1808 he was appointed councillor to the Imperial University, and in several ensuing years presided over commissions charged to visit and organize academies or colleges in Italy, Holland, etc. He published in 1812 a collection of his treatises on fossil bones, with an admirable preliminary "Discourse on the Revolutions of the Surface of the Globe." In this important work he propounds the theory of the correlation of forms in organized beings, and arrives at the following conclusions : that the career of man on this planet began about five or six thousand years ago ; that no vestiges of the human species are found among fossil remains ; that the present form of the continents was produced by a great revolution which occurred before the origin of existing animal species. Cuvier was appointed by Napoleon master of requests in 1813, and councillor of state in 1814.

He produced in 1817 his celebrated "Animal Kingdom," ("Règne animal distribué d'après son Organisation," in 4 vols.,) by which he made a new arrangement of animals into four divisions, the Vertebrata, the Mollusca, the Articulata, and the Radiata. This work immediately took the highest rank among books of the kind, and became generally the basis or guide of zoological studies throughout Europe. The introduction is a rapid and profound summary of the animal functions, and a clear exposé of the natural method which he first applied to zoology. He was admitted into the French Academy in 1818, and received the title of Baron in 1820. In 1822, as a member of the Lutheran Church, he was appointed superintendent of the Faculties of Protestant Theology. In 1823 he began the publication of his splendid "Natural History of Fishes," of which eight volumes were finished during his life. He wrote many

admirable notices of scientific men for the "Biographie Universelle." From 1819 until his death he was president of the committee of the interior, and rendered important civil services to the state. He was made a peer of France in 1831. His great activity was unabated by age, and he died peacefully in May, 1832. He is considered the founder of the science of comparative anatomy, in which he attained such skill that, with a small fragment of a characteristic part of an animal, he could determine the class, order, and even genus to which it belonged. Cuvier also made great improvements in geology. He left unfinished a philosophic work of high order on the history of the natural sciences, which he began in 1830 to develop in a course of lectures in the College of France. As a professor he equalled or surpassed his predecessors in facility of elocution, in clearness of ideas, and in the art of sustaining the attention in philosophic or historical digressions, which revealed the great variety and extent of his attainments. In respect to this almost universal aptitude and excellence, he has been compared to Aristotle ; and the comparison would have been more remarkable if the fall of Napoleon had not frustrated a design to confide to Cuvier the direction of the education of the heir of the empire. His head was large, his features regular, and his expression noble and dignified, and indicative of great force. His disposition was social and amiable, and his moral character eminently high-toned.

See PARISOT, "Éloge de Cuvier ;" A. DE CANDOLLE, "Notice sur la Vie et les Ouvrages de G. Cuvier ;" R. LEE, "Memoir of Baron Cuvier," 1833; DUVERNOY, "Notice historique sur les Ouvrages et la Vie de G. Cuvier," 1833 ; LOUIS DE LOMÉNIE, "G. Cuvier, par un Homme de Rien," 1841 : FLOURENS, "Cuvier, Histoire de ses Travaux," 1845 ; "Edinburgh Review" for May, 1811–January, 1836 ; "Foreign Quarterly Review" for December, 1834–October, 1838.

Cuvillier-Fleury. See FLEURY.

Cuyp or **Kuyp,** koip, (ALBERT,) a celebrated Dutch landscape-painter, born at Dort in 1606, was the son and pupil of Jacob Gerritse Cuyp, a painter of much merit. He painted with great success landscapes, cattle, views of rivers, moonlight-scenes, frost-pieces, flowers, etc. No painter perhaps has surpassed him in harmony of colour and in the purity of his aerial tint. He represented by the appropriate tone the different periods of the day, and gave his productions the merit of fidelity to nature. His works are highly prized in England, where as much as two thousand guineas have frequently been paid for one of them. He is said to have lived as late as 1683. Ruskin calls him the principal master of pastoral landscape, and says, "Cuyp can indeed paint sunlight, the best that Holland's sun can show. He is a man of large natural gifts, and sees broadly, nay, even seriously, finds out that there are reflections in water. A brewer by trade, he feels the quiet of a summer afternoon, and his work will make you marvellously drowsy. It is good for nothing else that I know of." ("Modern Painters.")

See DESCAMPS, "Vies des Peintres Flamands," etc. ; BRYAN, "Dictionary of Painters."

Cuyp or **Kuyp,** (JACOB GERRITSE,) THE OLD, a Dutch landscape-painter, father of the preceding, born at Dort about 1575, was a pupil of A. Bloemaert. Died about 1650.

Cyaxare. See CYAXARES.

Çȳ-ax′ạ-rēš,[Gr. Κυαξάρης; Fr. CYAXARE, se′áks′ȧr′,] a warlike king of the Medes, the son of Phraortes, ascended the throne about 634 B.C. According to Herodotus, he was defeated by the Scythians, and became tributary to them for many years. A war which he waged for five years against the King of Lydia was terminated about 610 by the terror caused by a total eclipse of the sun, predicted by Thales. The Scythians were driven out of Media in 607 B.C. About 606 he took Nineveh, with the aid of the King of Babylon. He died in 594 B.C., leaving the throne to his son Astyages.

See VOLNEY, "Nouvelles Récherches sur l'Histoire ancienne."

Cyaxares II., King of the Medes, was the son of Astyages, and uncle of Cyrus the Great. According to Xenophon, he became king about 560 B.C. ; but Herodotus does not mention him. He is probably identical with Darius the Mede of the Scriptures, who succeeded Belshazzar on the throne of Babylon by conquest about 538 B.C. (See Daniel vi.) He was succeeded by Cyrus.

Cybebe. See CYBELE.

Çўb′e-le or **Çȳ-be′le,*** [Gr. Κυβέλη or Κυβήλη; Fr. CYBÈLE, (se′bạl′,)] called also **Çy-be′be** [Gr. Κυβήβη] and **Rhe′a,** [Gr. Ῥέα, Ῥέα, or Ῥείη; Fr. RÉE, rȧ,] a goddess of classic mythology, supposed to be the daughter of Uranus and Terra, (Ge,) was distinguished by the appellation of "Mother of the Gods," or "Great Mother." She was the wife of Saturn, (Cronos,) and mother of Jupiter and the other principal gods. One of the chief places of her worship was Pessinus, a town of Galatia, above which rose Mount Dindymus, whence her surname of DINDYME′NE. She was also called "Berecynthia," or "Berecynthia Mater," (the "Berecynthian Mother,") from the hill Berecynthus, where she had a temple. She is often represented as riding in a chariot drawn by lions, and always has a crown of towers on her head. Her priests were called Corybantes.

See KEIGHTLEY's "Mythology."

Cybo or **Cibo,** chee′bo, (ARANO or AARON,) the ancestor of a noble Genoese family, was born of Greek origin at Rhodes in 1377. He was Viceroy of Naples about 1442, and died in 1457, leaving a son, who became Pope Innocent VIII. in 1485. INNOCENT CYBO was a grandson of that pope, a nephew of Clement VII. and of Leo X. At the age of twenty-two he was made a cardinal, and he afterwards obtained four archbishoprics. His merit is extolled by historians. Died in 1550. AL-BERICO CYBO MALASPINA inherited the sovereignty of Massa and Carrara in 1553, and died about 1620.

Cyclopes. See CYCLOPS.

Çȳ′clops, [Gr. Κύκλωψ,] plural, **Çȳ-clo′pēs,** a fabulous race of giants, having each one eye in the middle of the forehead. According to the theogony of Hesiod, they were the sons of Uranus and Gæa, and were named Brontes, Steropes, and Arges, and their business was to forge thunderbolts for Jupiter. Homer represents them as a gigantic and lawless race of shepherds and cannibals who lived in Sicily. According to a later tradition, they were assistants of Vulcan, in whose workshop they fabricated armour for gods and heroes.

See the "Odyssey," book ix., and VIRGIL's "Æneid," book iii. 617–681, and book viii. 370–448.

Çȳc′nus, [Gr. Κύκνος,] a son of Neptune, and the father of Tenes. He fought against the Greeks in the Trojan war, and, though invulnerable by iron, was choked to death by Achilles, and changed into a swan.

Çȳd′i-as, [Gr. Κυδίας,] a Greek painter, born in the isle of Cythnus, lived about 360 B.C.

Çȳ′don, a Greek sculptor, mentioned by Pliny, lived in the time of Phidias.

Cygne, du, dü sēn, (MARTIN,) a Flemish scholar and writer, born at Saint-Omer in 1619. He taught rhetoric in various colleges with much celebrity. He published "The Art of Rhetoric," ("Ars Rhetorica," 1659,) "The Art of Poetry," ("Ars Poetica,") and other works, which were often reprinted. Died in 1669.

Çyl-le′nï-us, a surname of MERCURY, which see.

Çyna. See CYNANE.

Cynægeirus, sin-ee-ji′rus, [Κυναίγειρος,] an Athenian, remarkable for his courage, was the brother of Æschylus the poet. At the battle of Marathon, 490 B.C., he pursued the Persians to the sea, and seized a ship with his hand, "which," says Herodotus, "was cut off." Other writers add that, having lost both hands, he seized the vessel with his teeth.

Cynæthus or **Cinæthus,** se-nee′thus, [Κίναιθος or Κίναιθος,] a Greek rhapsodist, born at Chios (Scio) at a date which is not ascertained. He was the reputed author of the "Hymn to Apollo" sometimes attributed to Homer. According to Eustathius, he was the first who collected and arranged the poems of Homer.

---

* The best scholars seem to be agreed that the penultimate vowel in Cybele ought to be short; although the fact that CYBEBE, another form of the same name, always has the penultima long, might well suggest the strong probability that the ancients themselves were not uniform in their pronunciation of the vowel. Byron, who is generally extremely accurate in the accentuation of ancient as well as modern names, taking advantage doubtless of this uncertainty, has adopted the more euphonious pronunciation—Cybe′le. Speaking of Venice, he says:

"She looks a sea Cybele, fresh from ocean,
 Rising with her tiara of proud towers."
                Childe Harold, canto iv. stanza 2.

Çў-nā′ne̦, Çȳn′na, or **Çȳ′na̦,** [Gr. Κυνάνη, Κίννα, or Κίνα,] a daughter of Philip of Macedon, and half-sister of Alexander the Great. She was married to her cousin Amyntas, who died in 336 B.C. About 322 B.C. she was put to death by order of Perdiccas.

Cynna. See CYNANE.

Çȳn-o-su′ra̦, [Gr. Κυνοσουρά; Fr. CYNOSURE, se′no′-zür′; Eng. ÇYN′OSURE,] a nymph of Ida, said to have been one of the nurses of Jupiter, who placed her among the stars. The name is applied to Ursa Minor, which includes the North Star.

Cynosure. See CYNOSURA.

Çȳn′thï-a̦, [Gr. Κυνθία,] a surname of DIANA.

Çȳn′thï-us, [Gr. Κύνθιος,] a surname of APOLLO.

Çȳp′rï-an, [Lat. CYPRIA′NUS; Fr. CYPRIEN, se′-pRE-ăN′,] SAINT, Bishop of Carthage, an eminent Latin Father, who was often called **Thas′cius Cæcil′ius Cypria′nus,** was probably born at Carthage about 200 A.D. In early life he gained distinction as a teacher of rhetoric. He had been converted only a few years when he was chosen Bishop of Carthage, in 248 A.D. About 250 the emperor Decius commenced a persecution, during which Cyprian retired from Carthage and remained in concealment, for which he was censured. In 251 A.D. he assembled a council on the question of reinstating apostates who had lapsed under the pressure of persecution, and he favoured a moderate course. His decision, that baptism performed by heretics and schismatics is null and void, caused a violent controversy between him and the pope, Stephen. He suffered martyrdom under Valerian in 258 A.D. Cyprian was eminent for learning, eloquence, and ascetic zeal, and has left numerous epistles and tracts, which are extant, and afford valuable information on the views and discipline of the early Church. Among them are treatises "On the Unity of the Church," "On Mortality," and "On the Grace of God."

See GERVAISE, "Vie de Saint-Cyprien," 1717; POOLE, "Life and Times of Saint Cyprian," 1840; CAVE, "Scriptorum Ecclesiasticorum Historia;" F. W. RETTBERG, "C. Cyprianus, dargestellt nach seinem Leben," etc., 1831.

Cypriani. See CIPRIANI.

Cyprianus or **Cyprien.** See CYPRIAN.

Çȳp′se-lus, [Gr. Κύψελος,] tyrant of Corinth, a semi-fabulous person, who is supposed to have reigned thirty years, and to have died about 625 B.C.

Cyrano. See BERGERAC.

Çy-re′ne̦, [Gr. Κυρήνη,] a mythical nymph, beloved by Apollo, by whom she became the mother of Aristæus.

See VIRGIL, "Georgica," book iv. 321–548.

Çȳr′il or **Çy-ril′lus,** [Gr. Κύριλλος; Fr. CYRILLE, se′rĕl′,] SAINT, Bishop of Jerusalem, is supposed to have been born in that city in 315 A.D. He was chosen Bishop or Patriarch of Jerusalem in 351. In that year, it is reported, a great luminous cross appeared in the sky over Golgotha. He had a controversy with Acacius, an Arian bishop of Cæsarea, who caused him to be deposed in 358. After this he was twice banished, and finally restored about 380 A.D. He predicted the failure of Julian's attempt to rebuild the Temple at Jerusalem in 363, which attempt was frustrated by eruptions of fire, etc., as stated by Ammianus Marcellinus. Died in 386 A.D. His works consist chiefly of eighteen catecheses, or lectures to catechumens, which have great value and interest in the eyes of theologians and antiquaries.

See SOCRATES, "Historia Ecclesiastica;" CEILLIER, "Histoire des Auteurs sacrés;" FABRICIUS, "Bibliotheca Græca;" CAVE, "Scriptorum Ecclesiasticorum Historia."

Cyril or **Cyrillus,** SAINT, an arrogant and turbulent prelate, born in Alexandria, Egypt, became Archbishop of that place in 412 A.D. He manifested his fanatical zeal by driving the Jews out of the city, and quarrelled with Orestes, the governor. He instigated his monks or partisans to murder the celebrated and accomplished Hypatia, whose influence perhaps excited his envy. On the subject of the Incarnation he maintained a long controversy with Nestorius, and presided in 431 over the Council of Ephesus, by which Nestorius was condemned as a heretic. A council convoked by the Patriarch of Antioch that year excommunicated Cyril. He wrote, in Greek, numerous works, chiefly controversial, which are still extant. Died in 444 A.D.

See FABRICIUS, "Bibliotheca Græca;" CAVE, "Scriptorum Ecclesiasticorum Historia;" TILLEMONT, "Mémoires ecclésiastiques."

ā, ē, ī, ō, ū, ȳ, *long;* ȧ, ė, ȯ, *same, less prolonged;* ă, ĕ, ĭ, ŏ, ŭ, ў, *short;* a̦, e̦, i̦, o̦, *obscure;* fär, fäll, fȧt; mêt; nŏt; gŏŏd; mōŏn;

Cyril, SAINT, also called CONSTANTINE, was born at Thessalonica. About 848 A.D. he propagated the gospel among the Slaves and Bulgarians with great success. He had a brother, Method (or Methud) or Methodius, who co-operated with him. He invented the Slavonian alphabet, and translated the Bible, or part of it, into that language. Died about 868 A.D.

See J. DOBROWSKY, "Cyrill und Methud der Slawen Apostel," 1823; JAN HOLY, "Cyrillo-Methodiada," 1837.

Cȳr'il-Lu'car, [Fr. CYRILLE-LUCAR, se'rêl' lü'kǎr'; Lat. CYRIL'LUS LUCA'RIS,] a Greek Protestant prelate, born in Candia in 1572. In his youth he visited Germany, and adopted, or at least studied, the Reformed doctrines. Having been chosen Patriarch of Constantinople in 1621, he made an effort to spread Protestant principles in the Greek Church, but was deposed and exiled to Rhodes. He recovered his see, was again expelled, and was strangled, it is said, about 1637.

See MORÉRI, "Dictionnaire Historique;" J. AYMON, "Lettres anecdotiques de Cyrille-Lucar," etc.

Cyrille, the French of CYRIL, which see.

Cyrillo. See CIRILLO.

Cyrillus. See CYRIL.

Çy-næ'us, (PIETRO,) an Italian historian, born in Corsica in 1474, wrote a "History of Corsica," (1506.)

Çȳ'rus, [Gr. Κῦρος* or Κῦρος ὁ παλαιός or ἀρχαῖος, (i.e. "Cyrus the ancient" or "elder;")] It. CIRO, chee'ro; Persian, KAI-KHOSRŌ or -KHOSRÛ,] surnamed THE GREAT, the second prince of the Kaianian dynasty, the founder of the Persian empire, and the greatest of the Persian kings and heroes, was the son of Cambyses, a Persian nobleman, and Mandane, the daughter of Astyages, King of Media. His history is supposed to be much embellished with fabulous tales. Herodotus informs us that in his time there were three different versions of that history. According to the account which Herodotus adopted, Astyages, being warned in a dream that his daughter's son would become king, commanded an officer, named Harpagus, to kill the infant. Harpagus, however, ordered one of the herdsmen of Astyages to expose the child on the mountains; but he spared its life, and the future hero was educated as a shepherd. Cyrus was afterwards restored to his parents, and, having incited the Persians to revolt, defeated Astyages, and ascended the throne in 559 B.C. According to Xenophon, he succeeded Cyaxares, his mother's brother. Ecbatana was one of his capitals. He extended his dominions by the conquest of Crœsus, King of Lydia, in 546, and of several princes or states. He marched with a large army against Babylon, the capital of Assyria, whose king was the Belshazzar of the prophet Daniel. Having diverted the course of the Euphrates, after a long siege, he entered the city by the dry channel of the river, while the impious king and court were feasting, in 538 B.C. The capture of Babylon is the epoch at which sacred and profane history form their first connection. (See Daniel v., and Ezra i.-vi.) It was foretold in the remarkable prophecy of Isaiah xlv. 1, "Thus saith the Lord to his anointed, to Cyrus, whose right hand I have holden, to subdue nations before him," etc. (See also Isaiah xlvi. and xlvii.) About 536 Cyrus issued an edict that the Jewish captives of Babylon should return home and rebuild the temple of their holy city, and proclaimed, "The Lord God of heaven hath given me all the kingdoms of the earth; and he hath charged me to build him an house at Jerusalem," etc. His next important enterprise appears to have been the invasion of the country of the Massagetæ, a Scythian nation who lived north of the Araxes (Arras) and were ruled by Queen Tomyris. After gaining several battles, (says Herodotus,) he was drawn into an ambush, defeated, and killed, in 529 B.C. According to Xenophon and Ctesias, Cyrus died a natural death at Pasargadæ. He was succeeded by his son, Cambyses.

See XENOPHON, "Cyropædia;" DIODORUS SICULUS, books ii., ix., x., xvii., and xxxi.; SCHUBART, "Programma de Cyro," 1743; F. HANSEN, "Disputatio de Cyro majore," 1781; WETZKE, "Cyrus der Gründer des Persischen Reiches," 1849; GERHARD, "Dissertatio de Cyro primo Persarum Monarcha," 1653; ARRHENIUS, "Dissertatio de Cyro Monarcha," 1693; J. L. FREY, "Dissertatio historica de Cyro," etc., 1706.

* This name is said to be derived from *Kohr*, a Persian word signifying "sun."

Cyrus THE YOUNGER was the second son of Darius Nothus, King of Persia, and of Parysatis. During the reign of his father he was appointed (in 407 B.C.) Satrap of Lydia, Phrygia, etc. At the death of Darius, in 404, the eldest son, Artaxerxes Mnemon, succeeded to the throne. Cyrus, having formed a design to dethrone his brother, employed Clearchus, a Spartan, to raise a large body of Greek mercenaries. In the year 401 B.C. he marched from Sardis with an army who were at first kept ignorant of their destination. At Cunaxa, in the province of Babylon, he met the immense army of Artaxerxes. The Greeks of Cyrus gained the advantage in the first attack, until Cyrus, who rashly exposed himself in the front rank, was killed, after wounding his rival. His character is highly praised by Xenophon, who accompanied the army of Cyrus, and who ascribes to him great generosity, and other qualities adapted to win the popular favour.

See GROTE, "History of Greece;" THIRLWALL, "History of Greece;" XENOPHON, "Hellenica," and "Anabasis;" PLUTARCH, "Lysander" and "Artaxerxes;" JAMES RENNELL, "Illustrations of the History of the Expedition of Cyrus the Younger from Sardis to Babylon," etc., 1816.

Cyrus, (FLAVIUS,) a Greek or Byzantine poet, born at Panopolis, in Egypt, flourished about 450 A.D.

Cysat, se-sât' or se'zǎ', [Lat. CYSA'TUS,] (JEAN BAPTISTE,) a Swiss astronomer, born at Lucerne in 1588; died in 1657.

Çȳ-the'ra, Cȳth-e-re'a, Cytherei'a, or **Çȳ-the'-rī-as,** [Gr. Κυθῆρα, Κυθέρεια, or Κυθηρίας,] a surname of the goddess VENUS, which see.

Czacki, châts'kee, (THADDEUS,) COUNT, a patriotic Polish statesman and writer, born in Volhynia in 1765. He was for many years a professor in the University of Cracow, and was appointed a member of several commissions by Stanislas Augustus. About 1800 the Czar of Russia made him a privy councillor. He zealously promoted education, by opening primary schools, and other means. He published, besides other works, one on "The Laws of Poland and Lithuania," (1801.) Died in 1813.

See ALOIS OSINSKI, "Histoire de la Vie de T. Czacki," 1816; "Nouvelle Biographie Générale."

Czajkowski, chī-kov'skee, written also **Czaykowski,** (MICHAEL,) a Polish novelist and general, born in Podolia about 1808. He fought against Russia in 1831, and a few years later removed to Constantinople. To avoid being given up on demand of the Russian court, he adopted the Moslem religion, (1851,) and assumed the name of MOHAMMED SADIK. During the war against Russia (1853-55) he had the rank of pasha, and commanded an army.

Czarniecki, chârn-yĕts'kee, (STEPHEN,) a famous Polish general, born in 1599. He performed many daring and successful exploits in the war against Charles X. of Sweden between 1655 and 1660, and was saluted as the liberator of Poland. Polish writers compare him to the French Du Guesclin. He also defeated the Cossacks, (1661,) and had attained the highest rank in the army when he died in 1665.

See M. KRAIEWSKI, "Histoire de Czarniecki."

Czartoryski, chär-to-ris'kee, (ADAM CASIMIR,) PRINCE, a Polish nobleman, born at Dantzic in 1731, was the first-cousin of King Stanislas. His rank, fortune, and talents gave him great influence in the affairs of Poland. He became starost-general of Podolia, and afterwards marshal or master of the ordnance in the Austrian army. In 1812 he was president or marshal of the Diet which met to establish a new confederation. Died in 1823.

See CHODZKO, "La Pologne illustrée;" LOMÉNIE, "Galerie des Contemporains."

Czartoryski, (ADAM GEORGE,) PRINCE, an eminent Polish statesman, son of the preceding, was born at Warsaw in 1770. Having fought against Russia in 1792, he was taken to Saint Petersburg as a hostage, and acquired the favour of the grand duke Alexander, who, soon after his accession to the throne, (about 1802,) appointed him minister of foreign affairs. He attended the Czar at the battle of Austerlitz in 1805, and retired from office about 1808. From 1803 to 1821 he was curator of the University of Wilna. He supported the popular cause in the revolution of 1830, and in January, 1831, was elected

ɛ as *k*; ç as *s*; ḡ *hard*; ġ as *j*; G, H, K, *guttural*; N, *nasal*; R, *trilled*; s̄ as *z*; th as in *this*. (☞ See Explanations, p. 23).

45

president of the new government, which he directed with ability, until the victories of the Russians compelled him to resign, in August, 1831. He then became an exile, and resided in Paris until his death, in July, 1861.

See J. B. Ostrowski, "A. G. Prince Czartoryski," Paris, 1845; "Gentleman's Magazine" for August, 1861.

Czartoryski, (Isabella or Elizabeth,) the daughter of Count Flemming of Saxony, born in 1743, became the wife of Adam Casimir Czartoryski, noticed above. She gained celebrity and much political influence by her beauty and mental endowments. Died in 1835.

Czartoryski, (Michael Frederick,) a noble Pole, born about 1695. By his wealth, energy, and talents, he acquired great political power, and in 1752 was chosen grand chancellor of Lithuania. In his efforts to reform the constitution of Poland, he applied for assistance to the Russian court, and thus unintentionally contributed to the partition of the kingdom which followed in 1772. Died in 1775.

See Ferrand, "Histoire des trois Démembrements de la Pologne."

Czaykowski. See Czajkowski.

Czechowicz, chĕk′o-vitch,(Simon,) a Polish painter, born at Cracow in 1689; died in 1775.

Czecz, tsĕts, (János,) a Hungarian general, born in 1822, served in the battles of 1848, and published in 1850 an account of the campaign of Bem in Transylvania.

Czelakowski, (a Bohemian poet.) See Cēlakowski.

Czerni-(chĕR′nee) **George,**or **Kara-**(kä-rä′) **George,** (*i.e.* "Black George,") a Servian chief, born about 1766, was originally a peasant. Having distinguished himself by his courage, he was chosen leader of the Servians in a revolt against the Turks, from whom he liberated Servia in 1807. He ruled that province with rigour until 1813, when, abandoned by his ally the Czar, he was compelled by a Turkish army to fly from Servia. He returned in 1817, was arrested, and put to death.

Czoernig. See Czörnig.

Czörnig or **Czoernig,** chör′nig, (Karl,) Baron, a statistician, born at Czernhausen, Bohemia, in 1804. In 1840 he was chosen director of the bureau of statistics in Vienna, and afterwards became an imperial councillor. In 1852 he published his "Ethnographic Chart of the Austrian Monarchy," with several volumes of text.

Czuczor, tsoot′soR′, (George,) a popular Hungarian poet and prose-writer, born at Andód, in the county of Neutra, in 1800. In his youth he was a Benedictine monk. He expressed liberal and national ideas in epic poems entitled "The Battle of Augsburg" (1824) and "John Huniade," and other poems, which exposed him to persecution from his ecclesiastical superiors. In 1844 the Hungarian Academy confided to him the important task of compiling a national dictionary,—not yet finished, (1870.) Having united with Kossuth in the revolution of 1848, he was confined in prison until 1850.

D.

Daa, dau, (Ludvig Kristensen,) a Norwegian writer, born in Saltdalen, Nordland, in 1809. Among his works is a "Swedish-Norwegian Hand-Dictionary," ("Svensk-Norsk Haandordbog," 2 vols., 1841.)

Dach, dȧk, (Johann,) a German painter, born at Cologne about 1560. He was patronized by the emperor Rudolph II., who sent him to Italy to design antique models. He afterwards worked in Vienna, where he painted many fine pictures for the court. Died about 1650.

See Descamps, "Vie des Peintres Flamands," etc.

Dach, (Simon,) a German poet, born at Memel in 1605, became professor of poetry at Königsberg about 1638. His hymns were for a long time popular. He also wrote odes and other poems. Died in 1659.

See Longfellow, "Poets and Poetry of Europe;" Gebauer, "S. Dach und seine Freunde als Kirchenlieder-Dichter," 1828.

Daciano, dä-chä′no, (Giuseppe,) an Italian physician, born in Friuli in 1520; died in 1576.

Dacier, dȧ′se-ȧ′, (André,) an eminent French scholar and critic, born at Castres in 1651, was the husband of Madame Dacier, still more famous as a classical scholar. He studied at Saumur under Tannegui-Lefèvre, father of the lady just named. Having removed to Paris, he was employed as one of the collaborators on the editions of the classics for the use of the dauphin. He edited Pomponius Festus, (1681,) Horace, (1689,) and the "Reflections of M. Antoninus," and translated into French Aristotle's "Poetica," Plutarch's "Lives," (1721,) and other works. He was a member of the French Academy and of the Academy of Inscriptions, and librarian to the king. Died in 1722.

See Nicéron, "Mémoires."

Dacier, (Anne Lefèvre,) universally known as Madame Dacier, the wife of the preceding, born at Saumur in 1654, was instructed by her father, and was a fellow-student with M. Dacier. It is related that while still a child she used to overhear the lessons given to her brother while she was engaged in embroidering, and that even under these disadvantages she greatly surpassed him in learning. One day, as she whispered to him the answer (which he was unable to give) to a question that had been put to him, her father first discovered her extraordinary aptitude for learning, and from that time afforded her the fullest opportunity for cultivating her mind. In 1672, when she was about eighteen, she went to Paris with such a reputation for learning that she was engaged by the Duke of Montausier to edit, for the educa-tion of the dauphin, the following Latin authors: Aurelius Victor, Florus, (1674,) and Eutropius, (1683.) She was married in 1683. In 1685 her husband and herself renounced the Protestant for the Catholic religion. She made French versions of Anacreon, (1681,) of Terence, Plautus, Homer's "Iliad," (1699,) and of the "Odyssey," (1708.) Her essays in defence of Homer against La Mothe and Hardouin display an enthusiasm which some thought extravagant; but her zeal for the ancient classics was seconded by Boileau, who took a prominent part in that famous controversy which she began, and who estimated her as a critic far higher than her husband. She was designated to succeed M. Dacier as librarian to the king in case she survived him; but this contingency was not realized, as she died in 1720. She appears to have maintained her fidelity to domestic duties, and the modesty indispensable to her sex, amidst all the homage and celebrity which she merited and won. Although the editions and versions of the Daciers have since been surpassed, they must ever be entitled to honour and gratitude as the first who enriched the French literature with the immortal productions of Greek and Roman genius. Voltaire, who calls her one of the prodigies of that age, says, "No woman has ever rendered greater services to literature."

See Burette, "Éloge de Madame Dacier;" "Nouvelle Biographie Générale;" Sainte-Beuve, "Causeries du Lundi."

Dacier, (Bon Joseph,) a French savant, born at Valogne, in Normandy, in 1742, went to Paris in early youth. He became a member of the Academy of Inscriptions in 1772, and in 1782 was chosen perpetual secretary of that institution, which he enriched with numerous historical dissertations. Though he favoured the cause of the Revolution, Louis XVI. offered him about 1791 the portfolio of finance, which he declined. At the creation of the Institute, in 1795, he was chosen a member of the class of moral and political sciences. He was a useful member of the Tribunate from 1802 until its suppression. In 1822 he was admitted to the French Academy. Dacier composed eulogies on one hundred and fifty Academicians from 1782 to 1826, and translated the "Cyropædia" of Xenophon. Died in 1833.

See Silvestre de Sacy, "Notice sur Dacier," 1834; Quérard, "La France Littéraire."

Da Costa, (Claudio Manoel.) See Costa, da.

Da Costa, dä kos′tạ, (Emanuel Mendez,) was foreign secretary of the Royal Society of London, and author of a "Natural History of Fossils," (1757,) and other scien-tific works. Died about 1788.

ā, ē, ī, ō, ū, ȳ, *long;* ȧ, ė, ȯ, same, less prolonged; ă, ĕ, ĭ, ŏ, ŭ, ў, *short;* ạ, ẹ, ị, ọ, *obscure;* fär, fȧll, fȧt; mĕt; nŏt; gōŏd; mōŏn,

Da Cunha, dä koon′yä, (J. A.,) a Portuguese mathematician and poet, lived about 1790.

See LONGFELLOW's "Poets and Poetry of Europe."

Daddi, däd′dee, (BERNARDO,) an Italian painter, born at Arezzo ; died in 1380.

Daddi, (COSIMO,) a painter of the Florentine school, lived about 1600.

Dadin or **Dadine.** See HAUTE-SERRE.

Dadouville, dä′doo′vèl′, (JACQUES,) a satirical and facetious French poet of the sixteenth century,

Dædalus, dĕd′ạ-lus, [Gr. Δαίδαλος; Fr. DÉDALE, dä′däl′,] an artist and inventor, celebrated in the Greek mythology, is said to have excelled in sculpture and in architecture, and may be regarded as a personification of artistic ingenuity. Tradition ascribes to him the Labyrinth of Crete, and the invention of the saw, auger, etc. It is said that he made wings, by which he was enabled to fly from Crete to Sicily, and that his son Icarus, who was his companion in this aerial voyage, fell into that sea which has since been named the Icarian Sea.

See PAUSANIAS, i., ii., iii., v., vii., viii., ix.; HYGINUS, "Fabulæ."

Dael, van, vän däl, (JOHN FRANCIS,) a Flemish painter, born at Antwerp in 1764 ; died in 1840.

Daele, van, vän dä′lĕh, (JOHN,) a Flemish landscape-painter, flourished about 1560.

Daendels, dän′dĕls, (HERMANN WILLEM,) an able Dutch general, born at Hattem in 1762. He entered the French army about 1792, and as general of brigade served under Pichegru in Holland in 1794. He became a general of division in the service of the Batavian republic about 1796, and exercised great influence in the state until 1803, when he resigned. He was restored to his rank by King Louis, who made him marshal of Holland in 1807. From 1808 to 1811 he was Governor-General of the Dutch colonies in the East Indies, which he ruled with ability. He commanded a division in Russia in 1812. Died in 1818.

See "Nouvelle Biographie Générale ;" RAFFLES, "History of Java," 1817.

Dagar, dä′gäR′, (JACQUES,) a French painter, born in Paris in 1640 ; died in Denmark in 1715.

Dag′gett, (DAVID,) LL.D., an eminent American lawyer and judge, born at Attleborough, Massachusetts, in 1764, graduated at Yale College in 1783. He was United States Senator from 1813 to 1819. He became instructor in the law school of Yale College in 1824, and was appointed Kent professor of law in 1826. In 1832 he was made chief justice of the State. Died in 1851.

Daggett, (NAPHTALI,) an American theologian, born at Attleborough, Massachusetts, in 1727. He was appointed professor of theology at Yale College in 1755, and was president of the same *pro tempore* in 1766. Died in 1780.

D'Agincourt, dä′zhăn′kooR′, (JEAN BAPTISTE LOUIS SEROUX,) a French antiquary, born at Beauvais in 1730, obtained the office of farmer-general. In pursuing the study of archæology, he visited various countries of Europe, and at length settled in Rome, where he employed his time in composing an extensive and valuable work, entitled "History of Art by Monuments from its Decadence in the Fourth Century to its Restoration in the Sixteenth," (6 vols. folio, 325 plates.) The last volume appeared in 1823. Died at Rome in 1814.

Dagnan, dän′yôN′, (ISIDORE,) a skilful French landscape-painter, born at Marseilles in 1794, won a gold medal of the first class at Paris in 1831. Among his works are a "View of Lake Geneva," and "The Bridge of Nice," (1843.)

Dagobert. See DAIMBERT.

Dag′o-bert (or dä′go′baiR′) [Lat. DAGOBER′TUS] **I.,** King of the Franks, born about 602 A.D., was the son of Clotaire II., whom he succeeded in 628. He died in 638, leaving two minor sons, Sigebert, King of Austrasia, and Clovis II., King of Neustria.

Dagobert II., King of Austrasia, was the son and heir of Sigebert II., who died in 656 A.D. Grimoald, mayor of the palace, sent the infant Dagobert to Scotland, reported that he was dead, and proclaimed his own son as king. Dagobert returned in 674, and recovered the kingdom, but was assassinated in 679.

See SISMONDI, "Histoire des Français."

Dagobert III., King of the Franks, succeeded his father, Childebert III., in 711 A.D. Like several of his predecessors, he had only the name of king, the real power being usurped by Pepin, mayor of the palace, who died in 714. Dagobert died in 715, leaving an infant son, Thierry IV., whom Charles Martel invested with the form of royalty.

See BERAIN, "Mémoires historiques sur le Règne des trois Dagobert," 1717; SISMONDI, "Histoire des Français."

Dagobert, dä′go′baiR′, (LUC SIMÉON AUGUSTE,) a French general, born at or near Saint-Lo in 1736. He distinguished himself in the campaign of Italy in 1792, and in 1793 was appointed general-in-chief of the army of the Pyrenees. He defeated the Spaniards near Olette, and took Urgel after a decisive victory, in which he was mortally wounded, in 1794.

See "Victoires et Conquêtes des Français."

Dagoty. See GAUTHIER.

Dagoumer, dä′goo′mȧ′, (GUILLAUME,) a French philosopher, born at Pont-Audemer, was the author of a "Course of Philosophy," (in Latin, 1701–03.) Died in 1745.

Daguerre, dä′gaiR′, (LOUIS JACQUES MANDÉ,) a French artist, whose name has been rendered memorable by the invention of the Daguerrotype,—a picture formed on a metallic plate by the chemical action of light,—was born at Cormeilles in 1789. After acquiring great skill as a scene-painter in Paris, he co-operated with Bouton in the invention of the diorama, about 1822, which they exhibited with decided success in Paris and London until 1839, when their building and its contents were destroyed by fire. About 1830 he began to make researches and experiments in photography in conjunction with Niepce, who died in 1833. His patience and ingenuity at length perfected the grand desideratum of rendering indelible the authentic image and signature of nature. The invention announced by Arago in the Academy of Sciences, in 1839, produced a profound sensation. A pension of 6000 francs was granted by the Chamber of Deputies to Daguerre, on condition that the process should be made public. Talbot, in England, also, by independent experiments, obtained photographic pictures by a different process; but the honour of priority is conceded to M. Daguerre. He continued to make improvements in the art as long as he lived, and published two short treatises on the subject. Died in 1851.

See LEREBOURS, "Traité de Photographie ;" A. GAUDIN, "Traité pratique de Photographie ;" "Nouvelle Biographie Générale ;" "British Quarterly Review" for July and October, 1866.

Daguesseau. See AGUESSEAU.

Dahl, däl, (JOHN CHRISTIAN CLAUSEN,) a Norwegian landscape-painter, born at Bergen about 1780, settled in Dresden in 1818, and acquired a high reputation. He chose the subjects of his master-pieces among the grand and sombre scenery of Northern Europe. His marine views are much admired. Died in 1857.

See BROCKHAUS, "Conversations-Lexikon."

Dahl, däl, (MIKAEL,) a Swedish portrait-painter, born at Stockholm in 1656, studied in Paris and in Italy, and settled in London in 1688. He became a fashionable artist, and was patronized by the royal family. Died in 1743.

Dahl, däl, (VLADIMIR IVANOVITCH,) a popular Russian novelist of the present century, was born at Saint Petersburg. He has published, under the name of "Kosak Luganski," several novels, among which is "The Dream and the Awaking." He served some years in the army, from which he retired about 1835. He excels in the delineation of the characters and manners of the lower classes.

Dahlberg, däl′bĕRg, (ERIC,) an eminent Swedish engineer and general, born in 1625, became director-general of all the fortresses. He planned the successful expedition of Charles Gustavus when the latter marched over the ice against the Danes in 1658. In the reign of Charles XI. he was made Governor-General of Livonia, field-marshal, and count. He formed the plan and drew the designs of the work entitled "Ancient and Modern Sweden," ("Suecia antiqua et hodierna," 1700.) Died in 1703.

€ as *k*; ç as *s*; ḡ *hard*; ġ as *j*; G, H, K, *guttural*; N, *nasal*; R, *trilled*; s̄ as *z*; ᵗh as in *this*. (☞See Explanations, p. 23.)

Dahlbom, dȧl′bom, (ANDERS GUSTAF,) a distinguished Swedish entomologist, born at Forssa, in East Gothland, in 1806. He is the author of numerous Latin works on insects, among which is "The Hymenoptera of Northern Europe," (" Hymenoptera Europea præcipue Borealia," 2 vols., 1845-52.) He became professor of natural history at Lund about 1844.

Dahlgren, dȧl′grĕn, (JOHN A.,) a rear-admiral, of Swedish extraction, born in Philadelphia in 1809. He became a lieutenant about 1838. He devoted several years to experiments under the direction of the bureau of ordnance, made important changes in naval armament, and invented the shell-gun which bears his name. In 1855 he obtained the rank of commander. He took command of the navy-yard at Washington in May, 1861, and was appointed chief of the bureau of ordnance in July, 1862. In June, 1863, he became commander of the South Atlantic squadron, employed in the siege of Charleston. He attacked Fort Sumter by night in September, 1863, and attempted to take it by storm, but was not successful.

Dahlgren, dȧl′grĕn, (KARL JOHAN,) a Swedish poet, born near Norrkjöping in 1791, was minister of a church in Stockholm. He published "Juvenile Writings," ("Ungdomskrifter," 1829,) and "Collected Writings or Works," (" Samlade Skrifter," 1834.) Died in 1844. A complete edition of his works appeared in 1849.

See BROCKHAUS. "Conversations-Lexikon."

Dahlgren, (Colonel ULRIC,) an American officer, born in 1842, was a son of Rear-Admiral Dahlgren, noticed above. He became aide-de-camp successively to Generals Sigel, Burnside, and Hooker, and distinguished himself by heroic courage in several actions. In July, 1863, he led a charge at Hagerstown, where he lost a leg. He commanded a body of cavalry in a raid against Richmond, the outer works of which he assaulted, but was repulsed. He was killed in his retreat, March 4, 1864.

Dahlmann, dȧl′mȧn, (FRIEDRICH CHRISTOPH,) a German historian, born at Wismar, in Mecklenburg, in 1785. He became professor of political science at Göttingen in 1829, and published an important work called "Original Documents for German History," (" Quellenkunde der Deutschen Geschichte," 1830.) Having protested boldly against the subversion of the constitution of Hanover in 1837, he was deprived of his chair at Göttingen. In 1840-43 he published his excellent "History of Denmark," (3 vols.) He was appointed professor of history and political science at Bonn in 1842. In 1848 he was elected to the Parliament of Frankfort.

See BROCKHAUS, "Conversations-Lexikon."

Dahm, dȧm, (JOHANN MICHAEL,) a German jurist, who was professor at Mentz. Died about 1772.

Daignan, dȧn′yôN′, (GUILLAUME,) a French physician, born at Lille in 1732. Under the republican régime he became first physician to the armies. He published many able medical works. Died in 1812.

Daigue, dȧg, (ÉTIENNE,) a French naturalist, born about 1490, wrote on Tortoises, Frogs, Snails, etc. Died about 1560.

Daillé, dȧ′yà′, [Lat. DALLÆ′US,] (JEAN,) an eminent French Protestant divine, born at Châtellerault in 1594. From 1626 to 1670 he ministered at the church of Charenton, near Paris. He was one of the most learned and eloquent Protestants of his time, and published several works on theology, among which are a celebrated "Treatise on the Right Use of the Fathers in Deciding Religious Disputes," (1628,) and an "Apology for the Reformed Churches," (1633.) The former is called by Hallam "a well-timed and important book." "He was the first who boldly attacked the new school of historical theology in their stronghold." Died in 1670.

See "Abrégé de la Vie de Daillé," by his son ANDRÉ, prefixed to a volume of his Sermons, 1670.

Daillon, dȧ′yôN′, (JACQUES,) a French Protestant minister, born at Anjou in 1645 ; died in London in 1726.

Dailly. See AILLY.

Daimbert, dȧN′baiR′, or **Dagobert,** dȧ′go′baiR′, commanded the Pisan and Genoese army in the first crusade, and arrived in Palestine soon after the conquest of Jerusalem, (1098,) of which he became the first Latin patriarch. He aspired to the throne at the death

of Godfrey ; but his rival, Baldwin I., was preferred. Died in Sicily in 1107.

See MICHAUD, "Histoire des Croisades."

Daire, dȧr, (LOUIS FRANÇOIS,) a French writer and monk, born at Amiens in 1713, wrote a "History of Amiens," and other works. Died in 1792.

Dairval. See BAUDELOT.

Daityă, dīt′yạ, (English plural, DAITYAS,) in Hindoo mythology, the sons of DITI, (which see.) They are regarded as evil beings or demons, and, according to some writers, are the same as the Asuras.

See MOOR, "Hindu Pantheon."

Da′kins, (WILLIAM,) one of the English translators of the Bible in the time of James I., was employed on the Epistles of Paul, and other Epistles. Died in 1607.

Dăk′shă, [common Hindoo pron. dŭk′shạ,] a Hindoo deity, usually regarded as an avatar (but by some as a son) of Brahma. Daksha having offended Siva, the latter killed him by cutting off his head : he afterwards restored him to life, but the head, having accidentally been burnt up, was replaced by that of a goat. This explains why Daksha is usually represented with a goat's head.

See MOOR, "Hindu Pantheon ;" COLEMAN, "Mythology of the Hindus."

Dalayrac, dȧ′lȧ′rȧk′, (NICOLAS,) a skilful French musician and composer, born at Muret in 1753, went to Paris in 1774, and worked twenty-eight years for the Comic Opera. He was very successful in various kinds of music. Among his master-pieces are "The Little Savoyards," "Camille," and "Nina." Died in 1809.

See FÉTIS, "Biographie Universelle des Musiciens."

Dalberg, (JOHANN FRIEDRICH HUGO,) a canon at Worms, wrote on music, and a work on Oriental religions, called a "History of a Druse Family." Died in 1812.

Dalberg, dȧl′bĕRG, (NILS,) a Swedish physician, president of the Academy of Sciences at Stockholm. The genus Dalbergia was named in honour of him by Linnæus. Died in 1820, aged about eighty.

Dalberg, von, fon dȧl′bĕRG, (EMERIC JOSEPH,) DUKE, a German diplomatist, born at Mentz in 1773, was a son of Wolfgang Heribert. He was made a peer of France and councillor of state by Napoleon in 1810. Died in 1833.

Dalberg, von, (JOHANN CAMERER,) a German bishop, was born at Oppenheim in 1445. He became Bishop of Worms in 1482, two years before which he founded at Heidelberg the most ancient academy of Germany, called "Societas Literaria Rhenana." He contributed much to the progress of learning among the Germans. Died in 1503.

Dalberg, von, (KARL THEODOR ANTON MARIA,) an eminent German author and prelate, was born of a noble family at Herrnsheim in 1744. He was appointed governor of Erfurt by the Elector of Mentz in 1772. In 1802 he became Archbishop of Mentz, and arch-chancellor of the empire. He received from Napoleon the titles of Prince Primate of the Confederation of the Rhine, (1806,) and Grand Duke of Frankfort in 1810. On the fall of Napoleon he was deprived of these dignities, but retained the archbishopric of Ratisbon. He was author of several popular works, among which are "Contemplations on the Universe," ("Betrachtung über das Universum," 1777,) and "The Influence of the Sciences and Fine Arts on the Public Tranquillity," (1793.) Died in 1817.

See ZAPF, "Dalberg Grossherzog von Frankfurt," 1810; CRAMER, "Karl Theodor von Dalberg," 1821; BROCKHAUS, "Conversations-Lexikon ;" "Nouvelle Biographie Générale."

Dalberg, von, (WOLFGANG HERIBERT,) BARON, a German poet, born in 1750, was a brother of the preceding. He was a liberal patron of arts and sciences. He wrote dramas entitled "Cora," (1780,) and "Montesquieu," (1787,) and others translated or imitated from Shakspeare. Died in 1806.

Dalborgo, dȧl-boR′go, (FLAMINIO,) an Italian jurist and historian, born at Pisa in 1706, was for many years professor of Roman law in the university of that city. His principal work is a volume of "Essays on the History of Pisa." Died in 1768.

D'Albret. See ALBRET.

Dȧl′bў, (ISAAC,) an English mathematician, born in Gloucestershire in 1744, received a very defective education, and is numbered among the self-taught men who have attained eminence under great disadvantages. He went to London in 1772, and engaged as a teacher in Archbishop Tenison's school. From 1787 to 1790 he assisted General Roy in a trigonometrical survey for the purpose of connecting the meridians of Greenwich and Paris. He was appointed professor of mathematics in the Royal College of High Wycombe in 1799. He published a valuable "Course of Mathematics," (2 vols., 1805.) Died in 1824.

Dale. See VAN DALE.

Dāle, (DAVID,) a Scottish philanthropist, born at Stewarton in 1739, was the first proprietor of the Lanark Mills, well known as the scene of experiments in social economy, made by Robert Owen, who married the daughter of Mr. Dale. The latter was noted for his benevolence to his operatives. Died in 1806.

See CHAMBERS, "Biographical Dictionary of Eminent Scotsmen," vol. v.

Dāle, (RICHARD,) an American commodore, born near Norfolk, Virginia, in 1756. He served with distinction in the Revolutionary war, and obtained the rank of captain in 1794. He resigned his commission in 1802. Died in 1826.

See "National Portrait-Gallery of Distinguished Americans," vol. iii.

Dāle, (SAMUEL,) F.R.S., an English physician and botanist, born in 1659, practised medicine at Bocking. He published a work on "Materia Medica," (1693,) the "Antiquities of Harwich and Dover Court," (1730,) and treatises on botany, etc. Died in 1739.

Dale, (THOMAS,) an English divine and poet, born in London in 1797. He produced in 1818 "The Widow of Nain," and in 1824 a version of Sophocles. He became canon of Saint Paul's in 1843, and vicar of Saint Pancras, London, in 1846. Several volumes of his sermons, which are highly esteemed, have been published. He is author of other popular religious works, among which is the "Sabbath Companion," (2d Series, 1844.)

See "London Quarterly Review" for December, 1824; "Blackwood's Magazine" for November, 1820.

Dale, (Sir THOMAS,) an English magistrate, who was sent to Virginia in 1611 with a number of colonists, and founded the town of Henrico, on the James River.

Dalechamps, däl'shŏn', (JACQUES,) a learned French physician and botanist, born at Caen in 1513. In 1552 he settled at Lyons, where he practised with success until his death. He formed a project to unite in a single work all previous acquisitions in botanical science, and, after expending thirty years on it, left the completion of it to Desmoulins. The result was a "General History of Plants," (1586,) a work of much merit, containing 2731 figures. He also published editions of Pliny and Athenæus, and several medical treatises. Died in 1588.

See SPRENGEL, "Historia Botanica;" HALLER, "Bibliotheca Botanica."

D'Alembert. See ALEMBERT, D'.

Dal-e-mi'lus, written also **Dalemile,** was born at Mezritsch, in Bohemia, and wrote in verse a history of his country, which was finished in 1314, and is said to be the oldest monument of the Bohemian language.

Dalen, van, văn dä'len, (CORNELIS,) a skilful Dutch engraver, born at Haarlem in 1640. He engraved historical pictures after Rubens and other masters, and portraits of eminent persons.

Dalens, van, văn dä'lĕns, (DIRCK or THIERRY,) a Dutch painter, born at Amsterdam in 1659, painted landscapes with success. Died in 1688.

Dal-gar'no, (GEORGE,) born at Aberdeen about 1626, taught a private grammar-school in Oxford for about thirty years. In 1661 he published his "Art of Signs," ("Ars Signorum," etc.,) from which, it appears, Bishop Wilkins derived the idea of his "Essay toward a Real Character." He wrote also "The Deaf and Dumb Man's Tutor," (1680,) and has the credit of inventing the first manual alphabet. Died in 1687.

See CHAMBERS, "Biographical Dictionary of Eminent Scotsmen;" "Edinburgh Review" for July, 1835.

Dalgas, däl'gås, (CARL FREDERIC ISAAC,) a Danish writer on agriculture, born at Fridericia in 1787.

Dalhousie, EARL OF. See PANMURE, LORD.

Dalhousie, dăl-hoo'ze, (GEORGE RAMSAY,) ninth EARL OF, a Scottish general, born in 1770, was a son of the Earl of Dalhousie. He fought under Wellington in the Peninsular war, was made a major-general in 1813, and distinguished himself at Waterloo. He was appointed Governor-General of Canada in 1819, and commanded the army in India from 1829 to 1832. Died in 1838.

Dalhousie, (JAMES ANDREW RAMSAY,) first MARQUIS OF, a British statesman, son of the preceding, was born near Edinburgh in 1812. He was returned to Parliament for Haddington in 1837. On the death of his father, in 1838, he became tenth Earl of Dalhousie, and entered the House of Lords. His political principles were designated as Liberal-Tory. About 1845 he was appointed, by Sir Robert Peel, president of the Board of Trade, in which department he displayed so much practical ability that when a new Whig ministry was formed, in 1846, he was retained in office. He was appointed Governor-General of India in 1847. His administration appears to have been generally approved by the British. He waged a successful war against the Sikhs, annexed the Punjâb, Pegu, Oude, etc. to the British dominions, and developed the resources of Hindostan. In 1849 he was created Marquis Dalhousie. He constructed railroads, promoted manufactures, and made various public improvements. He returned to England in 1856, and died, without male issue, in December, 1860. His cousin, Lord Panmure, succeeded to the earldom of Dalhousie.

See "Edinburgh Review" for January, 1863; "Blackwood's Magazine" for August, 1856; "Fraser's Magazine" for August, 1855.

Dalibard, dä'le'bäR', (THOMAS FRANÇOIS,) a French botanist, born at Crannes about 1703. He published in 1749 a work on the plants growing near Paris,—"Floræ Parisiensis Prodromus,"—and was the first botanical writer of France that adopted the system of Linnæus, who named in honour of him the *Rubus Dalibarda*. He was the first Frenchman who employed the lightning-rod, the idea of which he obtained from Franklin's writings. He erected at Marly an iron rod, with which he drew the electric fluid from the sky in May, 1752, one month before Franklin's experiment with the kite. Died in Paris in 1779.

See B. HAURÉAU, "Histoire littéraire du Maine;" "Biographie Médicale."

Dalibray or **Dalibraí,** dä'le'bRä', (CHARLES VION,) SIEUR, a French poet, born in Paris about 1590. He made poetical versions of Tasso's "Aminta" and "Torismena," and of other Italian and Spanish works. He also wrote some other verses. Died in 1654.

Dalin, von, fon dä'lin, (OLOF,) an eminent Swedish historian and poet, born at Winberga in 1708. He became librarian to the king in 1737, and acquired reputation by a poem on Swedish liberty in 1743. He was soon after employed by the Diet to write a history of Sweden, which was issued from 1747 to 1762 and was received with favour. About 1750 he was appointed preceptor to the heir of the crown, afterwards Gustavus III. He received a title of nobility and the order of the Polar Star, and in 1763 was appointed chancellor of the court. His writings, among which are several odes, and a tragedy named "Brunehilde," form a new era in Swedish literature, which before his time was almost uncultivated. Died in 1763.

See BROCKHAUS, "Conversations-Lexikon;" OLOF CELSIUS, "Åminnelse-Tal öfver O. af Dalin," 1764.

Dallæus. See DAILLÉ.

Dallamano, däl-lä-mä'no, (GIUSEPPE,) an Italian painter, born at Módena in 1679; died in 1758.

Dal'lans, (RALPH,) an English organ-builder; died about 1672.

Dăl'las, (ALEXANDER JAMES,) an American statesman and lawyer, born in the island of Jamaica in 1759. He emigrated to Philadelphia in 1783, acquired distinction as a lawyer, and became an active supporter of the Republican party. In 1801 he was appointed district attorney of the United States by President Jefferson. He became secretary of the treasury in the cabinet of Madison in October, 1814, when, in consequence of the war against Great Britain, the financial condition of the country was extremely depressed. Mr. Dallas at once recommended to Congress, in a report which is still regarded as one of the ablest ever issued from the treasury department, the establishment of a national bank. The energy which he brought to his branch of the public service enabled him in a few months to procure a loan on favourable terms, and in January, 1815, United States treasury notes were negotiable at par with interest added. In March he undertook the additional trust of secretary of war. In November, 1816, Mr. Dallas retired from public life, and resumed his profession in Philadelphia. Died in 1817. He edited for some time the "Columbian Magazine," and in 1790 published "Reports of Cases in the Courts of the United States and Pennsylvania," (4 vols. 8vo,) which, says Lord Mansfield, "do credit to the court, the bar, and the reporter." He also published the "Laws of Pennsylvania from 1700 to 1801," (4 vols. 8vo,) "Exposition of the Causes and Character of the Late War," (1815,) and various other works.

Dăl'lạs, (ALEXANDER ROBERT CHARLES,) an English clergyman, first-cousin of George M. Dallas, and a son of Robert Charles, noticed below. After serving as an officer in the army for some years, he became a priest of the Anglican Church at Wonston. He published, besides other works, "The Pastor's Assistant," (1842,) and "The Cottager's Guide to the New Testament," (6 vols., 1839-45.) He distinguished himself as a missionary in the west of Ireland between 1844 and 1852.

Dallas, (Sir GEORGE,) M.P., an English political writer, brother of Sir Robert, noticed below, was born in London in 1758. About 1776 he went to India as a clerk in the service of the East India Company, where he published the "India Guide," a poem. Having returned home, he wrote a pamphlet in defence of Warren Hastings, (1789,) and "Remarks on the Policy of a War with France," (1793.) His "Letters to Lord Moira on Ireland," published in the "Anti-Jacobin," attracted much attention, and were approved by Mr. Pitt. He was knighted in 1798. Died in 1833.

Dallas, (GEORGE MIFFLIN,) an American statesman, a son of Alexander J. Dallas, was born in Philadelphia in July, 1792. He graduated at Princeton College in 1810, studied law, and was admitted to the bar in 1813. In 1831 he was elected by the Democrats to the Senate of the United States, in which he advocated a protective tariff and the recharter of the United States Bank. In 1837 he was appointed minister to Russia, from which he returned in 1839. He was elected Vice-President of the United States when James K. Polk was chosen President in 1844. In 1846 he gave in the Senate a casting vote for a new tariff-bill, which was obnoxious to the protectionists and was designed merely for revenue. In February, 1856, he was appointed minister to England, and was recalled in 1861. Died in December, 1864.

See "Democratic Review" for February, 1842; "Letters from London," by G. M. DALLAS, Philadelphia, 1869.

Dallas, (Sir JAMES,) M.P., an English judge, was the eldest son of Robert Dallas of Kensington. Having gained reputation as a lawyer, he was employed as counsel for Warren Hastings in 1785. He was first returned to Parliament in 1802, and appointed president of the court of common pleas in 1818. Died in 1824.

See Foss, "The Judges of England."

Dallas, (ROBERT CHARLES,) a brother of A. J. Dallas, noticed above, a British author, born in Jamaica in 1754, was educated in London. He eventually settled in England, where he published many able works on various subjects, among which are "Miscellaneous Writings," (1797,) a "History of the Maroons," (1804,) "Percival, a Novel," and "Recollections of the Life of Lord Byron." He was intimate with Byron, (whose uncle had married a sister of Mr. Dallas,) and is said to have persuaded him to expunge some offensive passages of "Childe Harold." He was the father of A. R. C. Dallas, noticed above. Died in 1824.

Dăl'lạ-way, (JAMES,) an English divine and author, born at Bristol in 1763, became vicar of Leatherhead in 1801. He published an essay on the "Origin and Progress of Heraldry," (1793.) Having accompanied an embassy to Turkey as chaplain, he produced, on his return, "Constantinople, Ancient and Modern," (1797.) He wrote an esteemed work on "English Architecture," a "Treatise on Ancient Sculpture," (1816,) and other antiquarian works. Died in 1834.

Dallemagne, (dȧl'mȧn', (CLAUDE,) BARON, a French general, born at Périeux in 1754, served in the United States about 1778–82. He subsequently distinguished himself at Castiglione and Roveredo, and in 1798 took command of the army of Rome. Died in 1813.

Dallery, (dȧl're', (CHARLES,) a French organ-builder, born at Amiens in 1710; died in 1780.

His nephew, PIERRE DALLERY, born in 1735, was an eminent organ-builder. Among his works was the organ of Notre-Dame, Paris. Died in 1800.

Dallery, (THOMAS CHARLES AUGUSTE,) an ingenious French mechanician, son of Charles, noticed above, was born at Amiens in 1754. He constructed a steamboat in 1803, and ruined his fortune by experiments in steam navigation. Died in 1835.

Dăl'ling-tọn, (Sir ROBERT,) an English writer, born at Geddington about 1560, became secretary to the Earl of Rutland. He wrote a "Survey of Tuscany," (1604,) a "Method for Travel," and other works. Fuller, in his "Worthies," says "he had an excellent wit and judgment; witness his most accurate aphorisms on Tacitus." Died in 1637.

Dalloz, dȧ'loz', (VICTOR ALEXIS DÉSIRÉ,) a French advocate and jurist, born at Septmoncel (Jura) in 1795, practised with *éclat* at the bar of Paris. He published an important "Methodical and Alphabetical Repertory of General Jurisprudence," (2d edition, 40 vols., 1845,) which has been translated into other languages.

Dalmasio, dȧl-mȧ'se-o, (LIPPO,) an Italian painter, who worked at Bologna between 1376 and 1410.

Dalmatia, DUKE OF. See SOULT, MARSHAL.

Dalmatin, dȧl-mȧ-teen', ? (GEORGE,) born in Slavonia, became a Lutheran minister at Laybach. He made a Slavonian translation of the Bible, which the Archduke Charles in 1580 forbade him to publish in the Austrian dominions; but it was printed at Wittenberg in 1584. He was exiled for his religion in 1598.

Dalmatius, dal-mȧ'she-ụs, (FLAVIUS JULIUS,) a Roman prince, born in Gaul, was the nephew of the emperor Constantine, who invested him with the title of Cæsar in 335 A.D. Soon after this date he commanded in Thrace and Macedonia. He was killed in 338 by his soldiers, who, it is said, were instigated by Constantius.

Dal'rȳm-ple, (dȧl'rim-pl,) (ALEXANDER,) F.R.S., an eminent Scottish hydrographer, born at New Hailes in 1737, was a brother of Lord Hailes, and seventh son of Sir James Dalrymple. He entered the service of the East India Company at Madras, as writer, at the age of sixteen. In 1759 he resigned his clerkship, made a voyage of observation from Madras to the Eastern Archipelago for the promotion of commerce, and returned to England in 1765, after which he published charts of the Eastern seas. In 1779 he was appointed hydrographer to the East India Company, and in 1795 obtained a similar office from the admiralty. He published an "Account of the Discoveries in the Southern Ocean," (1767,) and other valuable works on navigation and geography. Died in 1808.

See CHAMBERS, "Biographical Dictionary of Eminent Scotsmen."

Dalrymple, (Sir DAVID,) a Scottish lawyer, the youngest son of Viscount Stair, was created a baronet in 1700. He was appointed lord advocate of Scotland in 1709, and died in 1721, leaving a son James, who was the father of David, (Lord Hailes.)

Dalrymple, (Sir DAVID,) afterwards Lord Hailes, an eminent British judge and antiquary, born in Edinburgh in 1726, was the son of Sir James, and a great-grandson of the first Viscount Stair. He was admitted as an advocate at the Scottish bar in 1748, and became a judge of the court of session in 1766, when the title of Lord Hailes was conferred on him. Ten years later he was appointed a lord of justiciary. He published a number of able works on history and antiquities, of which the most important and popular is his "Annals of Scotland," (1779,) a "book which," says Dr. Johnson, "will always sell; it has such a stability of dates, such a certainty of facts, and such punctuality of citation." His "Remains of Christian Antiquity," a work of great erudition, was also admired. He left no issue, except two daughters. Died in 1792.

See CHAMBERS, "Biographical Dictionary of Eminent Scotsmen;" "Encyclopædia Britannica."

ā, ē, ī, ō, ū, ȳ, *long;* ă, ĕ, ĭ, ŏ, ŭ, ў, *short;* ạ, ẹ, ị, ọ, *obscure;* fär, fäll, fåt; mêt; nŏt; gōōd; mōōn;

Dalrymple, (Sir Hew,) a Scottish judge, born in 1652, was the third son of the first Viscount Stair. He was admitted an advocate in 1677, and was appointed president of the court of session in 1698. Died in 1737.

His son, Hew Dalrymple, was made a lord of session in 1726, with the title of Lord Drummore. Died in 1755.

Dalrymple, (Sir Hew Whiteford,) of Highmark, a British general, born in 1750, was a descendant of Sir Hew Dalrymple, noticed above. After several campaigns in the war against France, he was appointed in 1808 to command the British army in Portugal, where he entered into the convention of Cintra with Junot. He was made a general in 1812, and a baronet about 1815. He wrote a Memoir of his proceedings in Portugal. Died in 1830.

Dalrymple, (James,) first Viscount Stair, an eminent Scottish statesman and jurist, born at Drummurchie, Ayrshire, in 1619, was the son of James Dalrymple of Stair, and was the ancestor of many distinguished men. In 1641 he obtained a chair of philosophy in the University of Glasgow. He studied law, was admitted an advocate in 1648, and became eminent in the profession. In 1657 Cromwell appointed him a judge of the court of session, and in 1661 Charles II. made him one of the lords of session. He was president of the court of session from 1671 to 1681. In the latter year he published "Institutions of the Law of Scotland," an excellent and authoritative work, which is still the great text-book of Scottish lawyers. In consequence of his refusal to take the test-oath in 1681, he was deprived of office, and suffered so much persecution that he preferred exile, and retired to Holland in 1682. Returning with the Prince of Orange in 1688, he again became president of the court, and in 1690 was raised to the peerage, as Viscount Stair. He died in 1695, leaving four sons,—John, James, Hew, and David.

See Chambers, "Biographical Dictionary of Eminent Scotsmen;" Macaulay, "History of England," vol. iii. chap. xiii.; "Encyclopædia Britannica."

Dalrymple, (John,) first Earl of Stair, a son of the preceding, born in 1644, was admitted an advocate in 1672, and appointed lord advocate of Scotland in 1685. After the lapse of a year he exchanged this office for that of lord of session, but in 1690 resumed the former function. From 1691 to 1695 he was secretary of state, and incurred great odium by his complicity in the massacre of Glencoe, of which he was regarded as the chief author. He inherited his father's title in 1695, and was made an earl in 1703. He died in 1707, leaving a son, John, the great general.

Respecting the guilt of the Earl of Stair in relation to Glencoe, see Macaulay, "History of England," vol. iv. chap. xviii.; "London Quarterly Review" for April, 1868; J. Paget, "New Examen," London, 1861.

Dalrymple, (John,) second Earl of Stair, an able general, a son of the preceding, born in Edinburgh in 1673, entered the army in 1692. In 1702 he served as aide-de-camp to the Duke of Marlborough in Flanders. He inherited his father's title in 1707, and was chosen one of the representative peers in the first British Parliament. He commanded the Scottish Greys at the battles of Oudenarde, Malplaquet, (1709,) and Ramillies, where his conduct was much applauded. On the accession of George I. (1715) he was made a privy councillor, and was appointed commander-in-chief in Scotland. He performed with credit a diplomatic mission to Paris, whence he returned in 1720 and lived many years in retirement. In 1743 he was appointed commander-in-chief of the forces in Great Britain. He died without issue in 1747, when a son of his brother William became heir to the earldom.

See Andrew Henderson, "Life of John, Earl of Stair," 1748; Chambers, "Biographical Dictionary of Eminent Scotsmen."

Dalrymple, (Sir John,) of Cranston, a Scottish lawyer and author, born in 1726, was a great-grandson of Viscount Stair. He was a baron of exchequer in Scotland from 1776 to 1807. He gained much reputation as a historian by his "Essay towards a General History of Feudal Property," (1757,) and his admirable "Memoirs of Great Britain and Ireland from 1681 to the Battle off La Hogue," (1771.) From the records of the French foreign office he obtained evidence which convinced him

that Algernon Sidney and other Whigs were in the pay of Louis XIV. Died in 1810. He had a son who became Earl of Stair.

Dal'rym-ple, (John,) an English surgeon and oculist, born at Norwich in 1804, began to practise his profession in London in 1827. He published in 1834 an excellent treatise on the "Anatomy of the Human Eye," and in his later years gave his attention chiefly to ocular surgery. He wrote a treatise on the "Eye of Fishes," and other papers on natural history, which procured his election as F.R.S. in 1850. Died in 1852.

Dal'ton, (John,) an English divine, born in Cumberland in 1709, became prebendary of Worcester and rector of Saint Mary-at-Hill, London. He adapted Milton's "Comus" for the stage, and wrote a number of sermons, (1745–55,) and some short poems. Died in 1763.

Dalton, (John,) an English chemical philosopher, celebrated as the author of the atomic theory, was born at Eaglesfield, near Cockermouth, September 5, 1766. He was the son of Joseph Dalton, a farmer. From 1781 to 1793 he was employed as usher in a school at Kendal, where he was assisted in his scientific studies by Mr. Gough, a blind philosopher. Through the influence of this friend he obtained in 1793 the chair of mathematics in New College, Manchester, which thenceforth was his permanent residence. He devoted his leisure to observations and experiments in various branches of physics, published "Meteorological Essays," (1793,) and an account of a singular defect in his vision, in consequence of which certain colours—red, blue, and green—appeared to him alike. This peculiarity of vision has since been termed "Daltonism." After the New College was removed to York, (1799,) Dalton taught mathematics and philosophy in private schools, and gave public lectures on physical science at Manchester, London, and other cities. In 1802 he propounded his important theory of "The Constitution of Mixed Gases," (in a contribution to the "Transactions of the Manchester Society,") which is now universally adopted. In 1803 he began to develop the most important and fundamental principles of chemical philosophy, in connection with the atomic theory, which he announced in a lecture in London in 1804, and explained in the first volume of his "New System of Chemical Philosophy," (1808.) This discovery contributed immensely to perfect the processes of chemical analysis and synthesis, which have since attained almost mathematical precision. From this theory, which supposes that each body is composed of atoms of definite size and weight, he deduced the following laws of combination: 1, each compound consists invariably of the same constituents; 2, the elements of every compound unite in definite and constant proportions; 3, when elements combine in more proportions than one, those proportions are multiples, etc. About 1821 Dalton was elected Fellow of the Royal Society; and in 1826 that body unanimously awarded him one of two gold medals which the king ordered to be given to those who had most distinguished themselves by discoveries in science. He was a foreign associate of the French Institute. An annual pension of £300 was settled on him in 1836. In 1827 he published the third volume of his "System of Chemical Philosophy." Besides the works above mentioned, he wrote many which were inserted in the "Philosophical Transactions," "Nicholson's Journal," etc. He died in July, 1844. He excelled in generalization, and had an extraordinary sagacity in tracing the relations of natural phenomena. His moral character was excellent, his disposition unassuming and rather reserved. He never married. He was a member of the Society of Friends, whose meetings he constantly attended. The citizens of Manchester testified their high estimate of his merit by a magnificent public funeral. "Dalton," says the "Edinburgh Review," "first gave clear declaration to the principle [of definite proportions] and illustrated its applications, mighty in their universality, with a simple sagacity belonging to the genius and habits of the man."

See Dr. Henry, "Life of Dalton," 1854; Ersch und Gruber, "Allgemeine Encyclopaedie;" "Edinburgh Review" for July, 1858; "Quarterly Review" for January, 1855; "Fraser's Magazine" for November, 1854; "London Quarterly Review" for December, 1854; "North British Review" for October, 1857; "Westminster Review" for March, 1846.

Dâl'tọn, (JOHN C.,) a distinguished American physiologist, born at Chelmsford, Massachusetts, February 2, 1825, graduated at Harvard in 1844, and in 1847 took the degree of M.D. in the medical department of that university. His "Essay on the Corpus Luteum," &c. (1851) won the prize of the American Medical Association. His "Treatise on Human Physiology" (1st edition, 1859; 4th edition, revised and enlarged, 1867) placed him at once in the first rank of American physiologists. He has since written, besides other works, a "Treatise on Physiology and Hygiene for Schools, Families, and Colleges," (1868.)

Dalton, (MICHAEL,) M.P., an English lawyer, born in 1554, was chiefly noted as the author of "The County Justice," a standard legal work. Died about 1620.

Dalton, (RICHARD,) an English artist, was a brother of the Rev. John Dalton, (1709–63.) He studied painting in Rome, travelled in the Levant, and, on his return, became keeper of the medals and pictures of George III. He published "Antiquities and Scenery in Greece and Egypt," (1791.) Died in 1791.

Dalyell, då-êl', ? (Sir JOHN GRAHAM,) a Scottish naturalist and author, born in 1777. He published, besides other works, "Fragments of Scottish History," (1798,) "Monastic Antiquities," (1809,) and "Rare and Remarkable Animals of Scotland," (1847.) The last is highly commended. Died in 1851.

See CHAMBERS, "Biographical Dictionary of Eminent Scotsmen," (Supplement.)

Dalzell, då-êl', (ANDREW,) F.R.S., a Scottish professor, eminent as a Greek scholar, born at Ratho, near Edinburgh, about 1750. He was professor of Greek in the Edinburgh University, and secretary of the Royal Society of that city. He published selections from Greek authors, with the titles of "Analecta Græca Minora" and "Collectanea Græca Majora," (1802,) which were, and still are, extensively used in schools. He also translated Chevalier's "Plains of Troy," (1791.) Died in 1806.

See CHAMBERS, "Biographical Dictionary of Eminent Scotsmen;" "London Quarterly Review" for October, 1822.

Damain, då'mâN', (JACQUES,) a French Catholic priest, born at Orléans about 1530, wrote an "Account of the Events at Orléans during the Massacre of Saint Bartholomew" in 1572. His humanity was conspicuous in that dreadful crisis. Died in 1596.

Damas, då'mås', (ANGE HYACINTHE MAXENCE,) BARON, a French general and statesman, born in Paris in 1785, was minister of war in 1823, and afterwards of foreign affairs from 1824 to January, 1828. Died in 1862.

Damas, (FRANÇOIS ÉTIENNE,) a French general, born in Paris in 1764. As general of brigade, he distinguished himself at the passage of the Rhine in 1795. He served as chief of the staff of Kleber in Egypt in 1798–99, and as general of division at the battle of Heliopolis. He returned to France in 1801, and was appointed military commandant of the grand duchy of Berg in 1807. He maintained his reputation in the Russian campaign of 1812, and after the restoration of 1815 was employed as inspector in the army. Died in 1828.

See "Victoires et Conquêtes des Français."

Damas, de, dẹh då'mås', (JOSEPH FRANÇOIS LOUIS CHARLES CÉSAR,) DUC, a French peer, born in 1758. As colonel of dragoons, he was charged with the important duty of expediting the passage of the royal family in their attempt to escape to the frontier in 1791. On this occasion he was deficient in energy and presence of mind. He emigrated about 1792, and became aide-de-camp of the Count d'Artois, (Charles X.) After the restoration, Louis XVIII. made him a peer and lieutenant-general. Died in 1829.

See CHASTELLUX, "Éloge du Général de Damas," 1829.

Damas, de, (ROGER,) COMTE, a brother of the preceding, born in 1765. As France was at peace with all nations, he indulged his martial passion in the service of Russia against the Turks. He fought with the royalists against the French republic from 1793 to 1797. In 1798 he entered the service of the King of Naples, and obtained command of a division. In 1814 he returned to France, and recovered his titles. Died in 1823.

Damascène. See DAMASCENUS.

Dam-as-çe'nus, (JOANNES,) [Gr. Ἰωάννης Δαμασκηνός; Fr. JEAN DAMASCÈNE, då'mås'sản', or DE DAMAS, dẹh då'mås',] a noted theologian, born in Damascus about 700. He succeeded his father in the office of councillor to the caliph. In the prime of life he retired to the monastery of Saint Saba, near Jerusalem, where he became well versed in dialectics, philosophy, and theology, and gained a great reputation by his writings, of which the principal is entitled "Summary of the Orthodox Faith." This served as a model to several generations of Schoolmen. He also wrote a treatise against Iconoclasts. He first applied to scholasticism the philosophy of Aristotle. Died about 760, though some say 780 A.D.

See CAVE, "Historia Literaria."

Damascenus, (NICOLAUS,) [Νικόλαος Δαμασκηνός,] a Greek historian and philosopher, born in Damascus in 74 B.C., was a contemporary of the emperor Augustus, and a friend of Herod, King of Judea, at whose court he lived. He wrote a "Universal History," of which fragments are extant, and other works, including poems. His History is praised for its style and other merits.

Damascius, dạ-mash'e-us, [Gr. Δαμάσκιος,] a pagan philosopher, born in Damascus about 480 A.D. He studied under Isidorus and others, at Athens, where he afterwards taught the Neo-Platonic philosophy. Justinian having in 529 prohibited the pagans from teaching, Damascius retired to the court of Chosroes, King of Persia. He wrote a work called "Doubts and Solutions of the First Principles," which is still extant, and is accounted an important contribution to the history of philosophy.

See PHOTIUS, "Bibliotheca;" RITTER, "History of Philosophy."

Damase. See DAMASUS.

Damas-Hinard, då'mås' he'når', (JEAN JOSEPH STANISLAS,) a French littérateur, born at Madrid in 1805, produced French versions of Calderon, (1841–44,) of Lope de Vega, (1842,) and of "Don Quixote," (1847.) He became private secretary of the empress Eugenie in 1853.

Dạ-mas'tēs [Δαμάστης] OF SIGÆUM, a Greek historian, who lived in the fifth century B.C.

See VOSSIUS, "De Historicis Græcis."

Dam'ạ-sus [Fr. DAMASE, då'måz'] I., a Spaniard by birth, was elected Bishop of Rome, as successor to Liberius, in 366 A.D. A competitor named Ursinus was also chosen by a party of the clergy; and this double election gave rise to violent tumults, in which many persons were killed. Damasus was recognized by the bishops and by the emperor Valentinian, who exiled Ursinus. He called councils at different times to oppose the Arians and other schismatics. Saint Jerome, who was his secretary, speaks favourably of his character. He died in 384, and was succeeded by Siricius.

See CAVE, "Scriptorum Ecclesiasticorum Historia;" TILLEMONT, "Mémoires ecclésiastiques."

Damasus II., POPPO or POPPON, Bishop of Brixen, was elected pope in 1048 in place of Benedict IX. He died about three weeks after his election.

See ARTAUD DE MONTOR, "Histoire des souverains Pontifes."

Damase de Raymond, då'måz' dẹh rå'môN', a French journalist, born at Agen in 1770; died in 1813.

Dambourney, dôN'boor'nả', (LOUIS AUGUSTE,) a French chemist and botanist, born at Rouen in 1722, was intendant of the botanic garden of that place. He made useful experiments and discoveries in vegetable dyes, and wrote a treatise on the "Colours which Indigenous Plants of France impart to Wool," which was printed at the expense of the state, (1789.) Died in 1795.

Dambray, dôN'brả', (CHARLES HENRI,) chancellor of France, born at Rouen in 1760, removed to Paris in 1779. Having acquired distinction as an eloquent advocate, he was appointed in 1788 attorney-general in the Parliament of Paris. He favoured the royalist cause, and during the reign of terror lived in retirement. In 1814 he was appointed chancellor of France by Louis XVIII., and was raised to the rank of a peer. The seals were taken from him in 1815, after which he was president of the Chamber of Peers for some years. His character is represented as excellent. Died in 1829.

See DE LAPORTE-LALANNE, "Notice sur Charles Henri Dambray, etc.," Paris, 1830; LAMARTINE, "History of the Restoration."

Dã'me-as, [Δαμέας,] written also Damias, a Greek statuary, born in Arcadia, lived about 410 B.C.

Dã'mẹr, (ANNE SEYMOUR,) an English lady, eminent as a sculptor, born in 1748, was the daughter of General

Conway, and the friend of David Hume and Horace Walpole. In 1767 she became the wife of Hon. John Damer, who killed himself in 1776. She then devoted her time to sculpture, and produced a statue of George III., a bust of Nelson, and other works. Died in 1828.
See CUNNINGHAM's "Lives of Painters, Sculptors," etc.

Damer, Hon. MRS., an English writer of the present age, and a descendant of Lady Mary Wortley Montagu, published an interesting "Diary of her Tour in Greece, Turkey, and the Holy Land," (1841.)

Damery, dăm're', (WALTER,) a Flemish painter, born at Liege in 1614. His "Translation of Elijah" is highly commended. Died in 1678.

Damesme, dă'mĕm', (ÉDOUARD ADOLPHE MARIE,) a French general, born in 1807, was killed in June, 1848.

Damiani, dă-me-ă'nee, (FELICE,) called FELICE DA GUBBIO, (goob'be-o,) a painter of the Roman school, born at Gubbio about 1550; died after 1606. His picture of the "Decapitation of Saint Paul" is highly praised.

Damiani, dă-me-ă'nee, (JÁNOS,) of Tuhegli, a Hungarian Catholic theologian, born at Tuhegli in 1710. He published "Doctrine of the True Church of Christ," ("Doctrina veræ Christi Ecclesiæ," 1762.) Died in 1768.

Damiani, [Fr. DAMIEN, dă'me'ăN',] (PIETRO,) an Italian prelate, born at Ravenna about 988 A.D. In 1057 the pope appointed him Cardinal Bishop of Ostia. He made zealous efforts to reform the evil practices of the clergy, especially simony, and, as legate of the pope, performed several missions with success, and had great influence in the Church. He wrote several religious works. Died in 1072.
See MORÉRI, "Dictionnaire Historique;" BARONIUS, "Annales;" LADERCHI, "Vita S. P. Damiani," 3 vols., 1702.

Damianics or **Damjanics,** dăm-yă'nitch, (JÁNOS,) a Hungarian general, born in 1804. In the insurrection of 1848 he obtained a command, and gained several victories. Having been raised to the rank of general, he distinguished himself at Nagy Sarlo and Comorn in April, 1849. He surrendered to the Russians at Arad, and was hung by the Austrians in August, 1849.
See BALLEYDIER, "Histoire de la Guerre de Hongrie."

Da-mĭ-ā'nus, [Gr. Δαμιανός,] a celebrated rhetorician of Ephesus, lived about 200 A.D., and was a pupil of Ælius Aristides.
See SUIDAS, "Damianus."

Damianus, a physician, said to have been born in Arabia. In company with his brother Cosmas, he suffered martyrdom about 310 A.D.

Damien, the French of DAMIANI, which see.

Damiens, dă'me'ăN', [Anglicized pron. dā'me-ęnz,] (ROBERT FRANÇOIS,) a French fanatic, born in the diocese of Arras about 1714, became a domestic in Paris. He was repeatedly dismissed by his employers for vicious conduct. He became violently excited on the subject of a controversy between the pope and the Jansenists, which then distracted the Church. In January, 1757, as Louis XV. was entering a coach, Damiens darted through the guards and wounded him slightly with a knife. He was seized and put to the torture, but persisted in denying that he had any accomplice. On his trial he said he did not wish to kill the king, but to induce him to do right. He was condemned to be broken alive by horses, which doom was carried into effect.
See "Vie de R. F. Damiens," 1757; VOLTAIRE, "Siècle de Louis XV."

Damilaville, dă'me'lā'vèl',(ÉTIENNE NOËL,) a French infidel writer, born about 1721, was a correspondent of Voltaire. He wrote "Christianity Unveiled," which provoked even the censure of Voltaire, who called it "Impiety Unveiled." Died in 1768.
See VOLTAIRE, "Correspondance."

Damini. See DAMINO, (PIETRO.)

Damino, dă-mee'no, or **Damini,** dă-mee'nee, (GIORGIO,) an Italian portrait-painter, was a brother of Pietro, noticed below. Died about 1630.

Damino or **Damini,** (PIETRO,) a Venetian painter and self-taught artist, born at Castel-Franco in 1592. He worked in Padua and Venice, and acquired a wide reputation, but died prematurely in 1631. His "Crucifixion," in a church of Padua, is considered his master-piece.
See LANZI, "History of Painting in Italy."

Damiron, dă'me'rôN', (JEAN PHILIBERT,) a French philosopher, born at Belleville (Rhône) in 1794, studied in Paris under Cousin. About 1830 he became professor of philosophy in the Faculty of Letters, Paris. He was chosen a member of the Institute in 1836. He published an "Essay on the History of Philosophy in France in the Nineteenth Century," (1828,) and an "Essay on the History of Philosophy in France in the Seventeenth Century," (2 vols., 1846.) Died in Paris in 1862.
See LOUANDRE and BOURQUELOT, "Littérature Française;" "Nouvelle Biographie Générale."

Damjanics. See DAMIANICS.

Damm, dăm, (CHRISTIAN TOBIAS,) a German scholar, born near Leipsic in 1699. He was rector of the gymnasium of Berlin for about twenty years, ending in 1764. He published a valuable Greek Lexicon, (1765,) and translated into German the poems of Homer, (1769–71,) and other classics. Died in 1778.
See MEUSEL, "Gelehrtes Deutschland."

Dammartin. See CHABANNES, DE, (ANTOINE.)

Dā'mo, [Gr. Δαμώ,] a daughter of Pythagoras, to whom he intrusted the writings containing the secrets of his philosophy. Though suffering from extreme poverty and tempted with liberal offers of money, she adhered to her father's injunctions, and handed down the precious documents inviolate to her daughter Bistalia.

Dam'o-clēs, [Gr. Δαμοκλῆς,] a Syracusan courtier, whose admiration of the luxury and pomp of royalty is said to have been cured by Dionysius, who invited him to a sumptuous repast, over which a sword was suspended by a hair. This anecdote is related by Cicero.

Dạ-moc'rạ-tēs or **De-moc'rạ-tēs,** [Gr. Δαμοκράτης or Δημοκράτης,] a Greek physician, who lived at Rome about 50 A.D., was commended by Pliny.

Damoiseau, dă'mwă'zō', (MARIE CHARLES THÉODORE,) a French astronomer, born at Besançon in 1768. He was a member of the Academy of Sciences, and wrote on the Lunar theory. Died in 1846.

Dā'mon [Δάμων] of Athens, an eminent Greek musician, was the teacher of Pericles and Socrates, both of whom respected him highly. His penetration and finesse are praised by Plato in his "Republic." Plutarch intimates that he was a "politician who, under the pretence of teaching music, concealed his great abilities from the vulgar." He was ostracised in the latter part of his career, from jealousy of his political influence.
See PLUTARCH, "Pericles;" DIOGENES LAERTIUS.

Damon and **Pȳth'ĭ-as** or **Phin'tĭ-as** were two Syracusans, and disciples of Pythagoras, who exhibited a remarkable instance of faithful friendship. It is said that Pythias was condemned to death by Dionysius, and obtained leave to go and settle his affairs, while Damon remained as a hostage for his return. Pythias, having returned punctually, was pardoned by the astonished king, who desired to be admitted into their friendship.
See DIODORUS SICULUS; JAMBLICHUS, "Vita Pythagoræ."

Da-moph'ĭ-lus [Gr. Δαμόφιλος; Fr. DAMOPHILE, dă'mo'fèl'] or **De-moph'ĭ-lus,** a Greek painter and sculptor of uncertain date, who adorned the temple of Ceres, in Rome.

Dam'o-phon, [Δαμοφῶν,] a Greek sculptor, born in Messenia or Messene, flourished probably between 300 and 400 B.C. He was the only famous sculptor that Messenia produced. After he had gained a high reputation, he was chosen to restore or repair the ivory statue of Jupiter which was the master-piece of Phidias.
See PAUSANIAS, iv. and viii.

Damoreau, dă'mo'rō', (LAURE CINTHIE,) originally named **Montalant,** (môN'tă'lôN',) a French vocalist, called in Italian MADEMOISELLE CINTI, (chèn'tee,) born in Paris in 1801, became a public favourite about 1822.
See FÉTIS, "Biographie Universelle des Musiciens."

Damours, dă'moor', (LOUIS,) a French jurist, born at Lude about 1720; died in 1788.

Dampe, dăm'pęh, (JACOB JACOBSON,) a Danish philosopher, born at Copenhagen in 1790. He became principal of a school in his native city, and wrote, besides other works, one "On the Harmony of Liberty with the Spirit of Christianity," (1819.) He was imprisoned for his liberal doctrines from 1821 to 1841. Died in 1850.
See ERSLEW, "Forfatter-Lexicon."

Dăm′pier, (WILLIAM,) an enterprising English navigator, born in Somersetshire in 1652, served in the navy in the war with Holland about 1673. He afterwards sailed with an expedition to Campeachy to cut logwood, and in 1678 returned to London with a journal of his observations. In 1679 he joined a party of filibusters, who cruised about the Isthmus of Darien and infested the Spanish settlements for several years. About 1685 he made a voyage to the East Indies, in which he had some perilous adventures. Returning to England in 1691, he published an interesting narrative of his "Voyage round the World." In 1699 the admiralty gave him command of a vessel, and sent him to make discoveries in the South Sea. He explored the western coast of Australia, the coasts of New Guinea and other islands, and passed through the straits which bear his name. He returned home in 1701, and published the results of his voyage. He went to sea again, but not in the service of government. A remarkable faculty for observation and description renders his writings valuable and attractive.

See "Nouvelle Biographie Générale;" "Retrospective Review," vol. ix., 1824.

Dampierre, dŏN′pe-aiR′, (JEAN,) a French poet, born at Blois ; died in 1550.

Dampierre, de, deh dŏN′pe-aiR′, (AUGUSTE HENRI MARIE PICOT,) a French general, born in Paris in 1756. In 1791 he was aide-de-camp to Marshal Rochambeau. He commanded a division at Jemmapes, (1792,) the victory of which was attributed partly to his bravery and skill. He distinguished himself in several other actions under Dumouriez. When he learned the defection of that general, (April, 1793,) he decided in favour of the republic, and was made commander-in-chief in place of Dumouriez. He was killed in battle near Vicogne in May, 1793.

See THIERS, "History of the French Revolution;" DE COURCELLES, "Dictionnaire des Généraux Français."

Dampierre, de, (GUI,) Count of Flanders, was born in 1225, and began to reign in 1280. He became involved in war with Philip V. of France, who conquered Flanders about 1300 and kept Gui in prison. The Flemings revolted, and gained a victory at Courtrai in 1302. Gui died in prison in 1305.

See SISMONDI, "Histoire des Français."

Dampmartin, de, deh dŏN′mäR′tåN′, (ANNE HENRI,) a French *littérateur,* born at Uzès in 1755, served in the army as colonel before the Revolution. He returned from the emigration about 1800, and in 1810 was appointed imperial censor of books. In 1813 he was a deputy to the legislative body, and in 1814 was reinstated in the office of censor by Louis XVIII. He wrote a "History of the Rivalry between Carthage and Rome," (1789,) essays on education, and other works. Died in 1825.

See "Nouvelle Biographie Générale."

Damrémont. See DANRÉMONT.

Dan, [Heb. ן׳ד.] a son of the Hebrew patriarch Jacob, was born, it is supposed, about 1788 B.C.

See Genesis, chaps. xxx., xxxv., and xlix.

Dan, a prince who, according to Malte-Brun, founded the kingdom of Denmark about the end of the third century, and from whose name are derived the words "Dane" and "Danemark," (*i.e.* country of Dan.)

See MALLET, "Histoire de Danemarck."

Dā′na, (FRANCIS,) LL.D., an American statesman and jurist, son of Judge Richard Dana,was born at Cambridge, Massachusetts, in 1743. He graduated at Harvard in 1762, was admitted to the bar in 1767, and was engaged as counsel in many of the most important trials of that stirring period. As a member of the "Sons of Liberty," he took a prominent part in the discussions on the Stamp Act and other aggressive measures that produced the Revolution. He served in the first provincial Congress of Massachusetts in 1774. From 1776 to 1780 he was a member of the Massachusetts council, at that time the supreme authority in the State. He was a delegate in the Congress which formed the Confederation in 1777, and in the Congress of 1778 was chairman of the committee charged with the responsible duty of reorganizing the army. In November, 1779, he embarked for Europe as secretary to John Adams in his embassy to negotiate a treaty of peace and commerce with Great Britain. Having been appointed minister to Russia, Mr. Dana,

in July, 1781, proceeded to Saint Petersburg ; but, failing to obtain a recognition of the claims of America, he returned to Boston in 1783. He was again a delegate to Congress in 1784. In January, 1785, he was appointed by Governor Hancock judge of the supreme court of Massachusetts, and from 1791 to 1806 was chief justice of the State. Mr. Dana was in the National Convention which met at Annapolis in 1786, and was chosen a delegate to the convention that framed the Federal Constitution in 1787 ; but ill health and judicial duties prevented his attendance. He served in the Massachusetts convention for ratifying the Federal Constitution in 1788, and was among its most prominent supporters. Died at Cambridge in 1811. Judge Dana combined eminent talents with thorough attainments and rare excellence of character. He was throughout a zealous Federalist.

Dana, (JAMES DWIGHT,) a distinguished American naturalist, born at Utica, New York, in February, 1813, graduated at Yale College in 1833. He was appointed the geologist and mineralogist of the exploring expedition sent out by the United States government about 1838 under Captain Wilkes. In 1837 he published a " System of Mineralogy," (5th edition, 1858. In 1868 appeared the first volume of a new and greatly improved edition of this work.) He married a daughter of Professor Benjamin Silliman about 1845. Since 1846 he has been one of the editors of the "American Journal of Science," and has resided at New Haven. In connection with the exploring expedition above mentioned, he wrote a "Report on Zoophytes," (1846,) a "Report on the Geology of the Pacific," (1849,) etc. He was elected to the chair of natural history and geology at Yale College about 1850, but did not enter immediately upon the duties of that position. One of his most important works, and that on which his reputation chiefly rests, is his excellent "Manual of Geology," (1862.) Professor Dana combines with the faculty of close and accurate observation so necessary to every student of nature, intellectual powers which place him in the very highest rank of philosophic naturalists. He is a member of the Academy of Sciences of Berlin, and of other learned societies.

See "North American Review" for October, 1863.

Dana, (JAMES FREEMAN,) an American chemist, born at Exeter, New Hampshire, in 1793, was a son of Luther Dana, a naval officer. He studied medicine, and was appointed professor of chemistry at Dartmouth College about 1819. He published an "Epitome of Chemical Philosophy," (1825.) Died at New York in 1827.

Dana, (NAPOLEON J. T.,) an American general, born in Maine in 1822, graduated at West Point in 1842. He became a brigadier-general about February, 1862, and served in several battles near Richmond in June of that year. He was wounded at the battle of Antietam, September 17, 1862, and disabled. In July and August, 1863, he commanded the defences of Philadelphia. He resigned in May, 1865.

Dana, (RICHARD,) an able American lawyer, the father of Francis Dana, noticed above, was born at Cambridge, Massachusetts, in 1699. He practised law with great distinction at Boston, and, as a supporter of the cause of liberty, took a prominent part in the movements which preceded the Revolution. Died in 1772.

Dana, (RICHARD HENRY,) an American poet and essayist, born at Cambridge, Massachusetts, in November, 1787, was a son of Chief-Justice Francis Dana. He was educated at Harvard College, which he left without a degree in 1807, after which he studied law, and was admitted to the bar of Boston in 1811. In 1814 he began to contribute to the " North American Review," of which he became associate editor in 1818. He produced the "Dying Raven," a poem, (1821,) and " The Buccaneer," (1827,) which was highly commended by Professor Wilson in "Blackwood's Magazine" of 1835. "We pronounce it," says he, "by far the most powerful and original of American poetical compositions. The power is Mr. Dana's own ; but the style—though he has made it his own too—is coloured by that of Crabbe, of Wordsworth, and of Coleridge. He is no servile follower of those great masters, but his genius has been inspired by theirs, and he almost places himself on a level with them by this extraordinary story,—we mean on the level on which they stand in such poems as the 'Old Grimes' of Crabbe, the 'Peter Bell' of Wordsworth, and the 'Ancient Mariner' of Coleridge." In 1833 he published an edition of his poems and prose writings, including "The Buccaneer," with some new poems and essays, which originally appeared in "The Idle Man," a periodical issued in 1821–22. "The Idle Man," says W. C. Bryant, "notwithstanding the cold reception it met with from the public, we look upon as holding a place among the first productions of American literature." ("North American Review" for January, 1828.) He delivered a course of ten lectures on Shakspeare in Boston, New York, and Philadelphia in the winter of 1839–40.

See GRISWOLD, "Poets of America," and "Prose Writers of America;" ALLIBONE, "Dictionary of Authors;" DUYCKINCK, "Cyclopædia of American Literature;" "North American Review" for January, 1851.

Dana, (RICHARD HENRY,) JR., an American lawyer and author, a son of the preceding, was born at Cambridge, Massachusetts, in August, 1815. He was educated at Harvard, which he entered in 1832. Having been compelled to suspend his studies by an affection of the eyes in 1834, he performed as a common sailor a voyage to California, of which he wrote an admirable narrative in his "Two Years before the Mast," (1840,) which obtained a wide celebrity. He graduated at Harvard in 1837, studied law under Judge Story, and was admitted to the bar of Boston in 1840. He has since attained eminence as an advocate. In 1841 he published "The Seaman's Friend, containing a Treatise on Practical Seamanship, etc." Mr. Dana was one of the founders of the "Free-Soil party," and acted with the Republicans in the Presidential election of 1856.

Dana, (SAMUEL LUTHER,) an American chemist and writer on agriculture, born at Amherst, New Hampshire, in 1795. He became chemist of the Merrimac Print Works at Lowell in 1833, and invented a mode of bleaching cotton goods, which was generally adopted. He acquired distinction as a writer on agriculture, and discovered that phosphate of soda has the property of fixing mordants. Died in March, 1868.

See "American Journal of Science," May, 1868.

Dan'a-e, [Gr. Δανάη,] a daughter of Acrisius, King of Argos, who confined her in a brazen tower or cell because an oracle had declared her son would kill her father. In spite of his precaution, she became the mother of Perseus by Jupiter, who is fabled to have obtained access to her apartment in the form of a golden shower.

Danæus. See DANEAU.

Da-na'ï-dēs, [Gr. Δαναΐδες,] the fifty daughters of Danaus, were married to their cousins, the sons of Ægyptus. By the order of their father, each of them killed, on the wedding-night, her bridegroom, except Hypermnestra, who spared her husband, Lynceus. (See next article.)

Dan'a-us, a son of Belus, after his father's death reigned conjointly with his brother Ægyptus on the throne of Egypt. Jealous of the power of the fifty sons of Ægyptus, or, as some say, terrified by an oracle, he gave his fifty daughters in marriage to the sons of his brother, with a secret command that they should kill their husbands on the wedding-night. (See DANAIDES.) Danaus is said to have reigned fifty years.

See KEIGHTLEY, "Mythology."

Dânăvă, dâ'nạ-vạ, (Hindoo Myth.,) a demon or evil spirit, one of the children of Danu.

Danby, EARL OF. See DANVERS.

Dan'bỹ, (FRANCIS,) an eminent landscape-painter, born near Wexford, Ireland, in 1793. He became a resident of England in his youth, and about 1824 produced a "Sunset at Sea after a Storm," which was much admired. Between 1825 and 1829 he gained a high reputation by historical landscapes, among which was the "Embarkation of Cleopatra on the Cydnus," (1827.) Among his later works are "The Deluge," "Departure of Ulysses from Ithaca," and "Caius Marius amidst the Ruins of Carthage," (1848.) He is regarded by some as unrivalled in historical or poetic landscapes among the English artists.

His son THOMAS is a successful landscape-painter.

Dan'bỹ, (THOMAS OSBORNE,) EARL OF, Marquis of Caermarthen, Duke of Leeds, an English statesman, born in 1631. He entered Parliament about 1660, supported the measures of the court, and acquired the favour of the king. In 1673 he obtained the chief direction of affairs, as lord treasurer, and in 1674 was created Earl of Danby. Having been accused of treason, he was committed to the Tower by the Commons in 1678, and was detained there five years. In 1689 he was appointed president of the council by William III. "In practical ability and official experience," says Macaulay, "he had no superior among his contemporaries. . . . Yet the Whigs regarded him with unconquerable distrust and aversion. Even in becoming a rebel he had not ceased to be a Tory." ("History of England," vol. iii. chaps. xi., xv., and xvi.) He was made Duke of Leeds in 1694. Died in 1712.

Dancarville. See HANCARVILLE.

Dance, (GEORGE,) an English architect, who held the office of city surveyor of London. He was the architect of the Mansion House, built about 1740, and of several churches in London. Died in 1768.

Dance, (GEORGE,) JR., an English architect, son of the preceding, born probably in London in 1740, succeeded his father as city surveyor. He was one of the first members of the Royal Academy, in which he was professor of architecture. His reputation is founded chiefly on the erection of Newgate prison, which was begun in 1770. He also designed the front of Guildhall, and other buildings in London. Died in 1825.

Dance, (Sir NATHANIEL,) an English painter, brother of the preceding, was born in 1729. After acquiring some reputation as a painter, he married a rich Mrs. Dunmer, and assumed the name of Holland. He was made a baronet in 1800. Died in 1811.

Dan'çẹr, (DANIEL,) a notorious English miser, born about 1715, subjected himself to extreme privations while he had large sums of money hoarded. Died in 1774.

See "Memoirs of Celebrated Misers."

Danchet, dôN'shạ', (ANTOINE,) a French dramatic poet, born at Riom in 1671, studied in Paris, where he resided after 1696. He wrote four tragedies, one of which is entitled "Cyrus," and numerous operas, which were more successful, especially "Hésione," which is ranked by La Harpe above those of Duché and Fontenelle. Danchet was a member of the French Academy and of the Academy of Inscriptions. Died in 1748

See SABATIER, "Les trois Siècles de la Littérature."

Danckelmann. See DANKELMANN.

Danckert, dânk'kert, almost dänk'kert, or **Danckerts,** dânk'kerts, (CORNELIS,) a Dutch engraver, born in Amsterdam in 1561, treated with success portraits, landscapes, and history. He settled in Antwerp as a dealer in engravings, and was the head of a family who were long eminent in the same art.

Danckert, (PETER,) a son of the preceding, born in Antwerp in 1600, surpassed his father as an engraver, and used the burin and the etching-point together. He engraved after Berghem and Wouwerman, and also his own designs. Died about 1660. Peter left two sons, Henry and John, who were skilful artists, and settled first in Amsterdam. John afterwards went to England, where he engraved in partnership with Hollar.

See NAGLER, "Neues Allgemeines Künstler-Lexikon;" BASAN, "Dictionnaire des Graveurs."

Danckerts. See DANCKERT.

Danckerts de Ry. See DANKERS.

Dancks or **Danks,** dânks, almost dänks, (FRANCIS,) a Dutch painter of history and portraits, born at Amsterdam in 1650; died about 1700.

Dancourt, dôN'kooR', (FLORENT CARTON,) a popular French comic author, born at Fontainebleau in 1661. He chose the profession of law, in which he acquired some reputation, but, falling in love with an actress, La Thorillière, he exchanged the bar for the stage in 1685, as one of the king's comedians. He was successful both as an actor and an author. Having a mind fertile in invention, he produced "Le Chevalier à la Mode," and about sixty other plays,—chiefly farces, in which the dialogue is spirited, humorous, and piquant. Voltaire observed, "What Regnard was in respect to Molière in the high comedy, Dancourt was in the farce." Died in 1726.

See GRIMM, "Correspondance;" HIPPOLYTE LUCAS, "Molière et Dancourt;" "Nouvelle Biographie Générale."

ɛ as k; ç as s; g̃ hard; g̃ as j; G, H, K, guttural; N, nasal; R, trilled; s̃ as z; ŧh as in this. (☞See Explanations, p. 23.)

Dandelin, dŏnd′lăN′, (GERMINAL PIERRE,) a French engineer and scientific writer, born near Paris in 1794, became a citizen of Belgium in 1816. Died in 1847.

Dandelot, dŏnd′lo′, (FRANÇOIS de Coligny—ko′-lĕn′ye′,) an able French general, born at Châtillon-sur-Loing in 1521, was a brother of the admiral Coligny. For his conduct at Cérisoles he was knighted on the field. As general of infantry he took a prominent part in the battle of Saint-Quentin in 1557. He was a warm adherent of the Reformed Church, and in the civil war between Protestants and Catholics which began about 1562, he fought at Dreux, at Chartres, and at Jarnac, (1569,) a few days after which battle he died of fever.

See SISMONDI, "Histoire des Français."

Dandini, dăn-dee′nee, (CESARE,) a painter, born at Florence about 1595; died in 1658.

Dandini, (ERCOLE FRANCESCO,) an Italian jurist and legal writer, born at Ancona in 1695, became professor of law at Padua, where he died in 1747.

See FABRONI, "Vitæ Italorum doctrina excellentium."

Dandini, (GIROLAMO,) an Italian Jesuit, born at Cesena in 1554, professed philosophy in Paris, and theology at Padua. In 1596 he was sent by the pope on a mission to the Maronites of Mount Lebanon, of which he published an account. Died in 1634.

See BAYLE, "Historical and Critical Dictionary."

Dandini, (PIETRO,) a skilful Italian painter, born at Florence in 1647, was the son of Vincenzo. He painted with equal success in fresco and in oil, (at Florence,) and acquired distinction by the brilliancy of his colouring and the richness of his composition. Died in 1712.

Dandini, (VINCENZO,) a successful painter, born at Florence about 1607, was a pupil of Cortona, and a brother of Cesare, noticed above. He was patronized by the Grand Duke of Tuscany. Died in 1675.

See LANZI, "History of Painting in Italy."

Dandolo, dăn′do-lo, (ANDREA,) a Venetian historian and doge, born about 1306. Having acquired a high reputation for ability and virtue, he was elected doge in 1342. He was a friend of Petrarch, and was author of a valuable Latin Chronicle of Venice, terminating in the year 1339. He waged war against the Genoese for several years between 1348 and 1354. Died in 1354.

See MARINO SANUTO, "Vite de' Duchi."

Dandolo, (ENRICO,) a renowned Venetian statesman and general, who greatly increased the maritime power of Venice, was born about 1105. He was elected doge in 1192, before which he had become nearly blind. At this period the Venetian state was the greatest commercial and naval power in the world. In 1201 the leaders of the fourth crusade applied for means of transport to the Venetians, who, through the influence of the doge, furnished ships and made an alliance with the crusaders. Their combined forces, commanded by Dandolo, reduced Zara, which had revolted against Venice, and next attacked Constantinople, which was ruled by a usurper. That city was taken by storm in 1204, and the throne was offered to Dandolo, who declined it, but accepted the office of despot of Romania. He obtained the cession of several islands and ports of the Levant to the Venetian state. He died in 1205. Byron calls him

> "blind old Dandolo,
> Th' octogenarian chief, Byzantium's conquering foe."
> *Childe Harold*, canto iv.

See MICHAUD, "Histoire des Croisades;" DARU, "Histoire de Venise;" MARINO SANUTO, "Vite de' Duchi;" A. DANDOLO, "Chronicon," in the "Collection" of MURATORI.

Dandolo, (FRANCESCO,) was Doge of Venice from 1328 to 1339. During his administration the Venetians extended their dominion over the adjacent terra firma, by annexing Treviso, etc.

Dandolo, (GIOVANNI,) was Doge of Venice from 1280 to 1289, during which period the cities of Pirano and Isola were added to the republic, and Trieste shook off its allegiance.

See DARU, "Histoire de Venise."

Dandolo, (VINCENZO,) COUNT, an Italian chemist and economist, born in Venice in 1758. He united and digested the recent discoveries of French chemists, in a work called "Fondamenti della Fisico chimica," etc., ("Principles of Physical Chemistry," 1796.) When Venice

was annexed to Austria (1797) he removed to Milan, and was there appointed a member of the grand council. From 1804 to 1809 he was governor or *proveditor* of Dalmatia under Napoleon. He wrote valuable treatises on the production of wine, wool, and silk, and on other subjects of rural economy. Died in Venice in 1819.

See ERSCH und GRUBER, "Allgemeine Encyclopaedie;" M. BONAFOUS, "Éloge historique de V. Dandolo," 1839; "Nouvelle Biographie Générale."

D'Andrada. See ANDRADA, D'.

Dandré, dŏN′drA′, (ANTOINE BALTHASAR JOSEPH,) born at Aix in 1759, was appointed in 1814 by Louis XVIII. director of the police and steward *(intendant)* of his domains. Died in 1827.

See VAULABELLE, "Histoire des deux Restaurations."

Dandré-Bardon, dŏN′drA′ băR′dŏN′,(MICHEL FRANÇOIS,) a French painter and writer on art, born at Aix in 1700, founded an academy of painting at Marseilles. He published a "Treatise on Painting and Sculpture, with a Catalogue Raisonné of the Most Famous Artists of the French School," also an illustrated work on the costumes of ancient nations. Died in 1783.

Dāne, (NATHAN,) an American jurist, born in Ipswich, Massachusetts, in 1752, graduated at Harvard in 1778. He was one of the most eminent lawyers in New England. He was a member of the Continental Congress in 1785–87. In the last-named year he framed the important ordinance for the government and organization of the Northwest Territory, and inserted a clause prohibiting slavery. He published "An Abridgment and Digest of American Law," (9 vols., 1823–29.) Died in 1835.

Daneau, dȧ′nō′, [Lat. DANÆ′US,] (LAMBERT,) a French Calvinistic divine, born at Beaugency in 1530, preached at Geneva, Castres, and other places. He published many treatises on theology, which were once esteemed. Died at Castres in 1596.

See MELCHIOR ADAM, "Vitæ Theologorum Exterorum;" NICÉRON, "Mémoires;" HAAG, "La France protestante."

Danedi, dȧ-nā′dee, (GIOVANNI STEFANO,) an Italian historical painter, called MONTALTO, born at Treviglio in 1608. He adorned many edifices of Milan with his works, which display a rich imagination. Died in 1689.

Danedi, (GIUSEPPE,) brother of the preceding, born in 1618, was also a skilful painter, and a pupil of Guido. He worked in Milan and Turin, sometimes in company with Giovanni Stefano, his brother. Died in 1689.

See LANZI, "History of Painting in Italy."

Danès, dȧ′nès′, (PIERRE,) a French scholar, born in Paris in 1497. In 1530 Francis I. appointed him first professor of Greek in the Royal College, and in 1545 ambassador to the Council of Trent. In the reign of Henry II. he was preceptor to the dauphin, afterwards Francis II., and in 1557 he was made Bishop of Lavaur. He published an edition of Pliny, a few letters, etc. Died in 1577.

See DE THOU, "Éloges, avec les Additions de Teissier;" P. H. DANÈS, "Vie de P. Danès," 1731.

Danet, dȧ′nȧ′, (PIERRE,) a learned French priest, born in Paris about 1650. The Duke of Montausier selected him, with others, to edit classic authors for the use of the dauphin, and assigned Phædrus to him. He gained more reputation by his "Latin and French Dictionary, for the Use of the Dauphin," (1685.) Died in 1709.

See FELLER, "Biographie Universelle."

Dangeau, de, deh dŏN′zhō′, (LOUIS de Courcillon —deh kooR′se′yòN′,) ABBÉ, a brother of the Marquis of Dangeau, noticed below, was born in Paris in 1643. Descended from Du Plessis-Mornay, he was educated a Protestant, but was converted by Bossuet. He was employed as reader to Louis XIV. from 1671 to 1687, and was admitted into the French Academy in 1682. "He was," says Voltaire, "an excellent academician." He was a candidate for the office of preceptor to the Duke of Burgundy; but Fénelon was preferred. He wrote several treatises on grammar, and some other works. Died in 1723.

See D'ALEMBERT, "Éloges;" SAINT-SIMON, "Mémoires."

Dangeau, de, (PHILIPPE DE COURCILLON,) MARQUIS, an accomplished French courtier and officer, born in 1638.

He became a favourite of Louis XIV., and colonel of the king's regiment in 1655. In 1667 he was governor of Touraine. He afterwards attended the king as aide-de-camp in several campaigns. He was elected to the French Academy in 1668, partly in consideration of his facility in composing verses, (*vers de société.*) He died in 1720, leaving in manuscript a voluminous "Journal of the Court of Louis XIV.," (comprising the period from 1684 to 1720,) said to contain much important and curious matter. It has since been published, (1854.)

See SAINT-SIMON, "Mémoires;" MADAME DE GENLIS, "Abrégé du Journal de M. de Dangeau," 4 vols., 1817; VOLTAIRE, "Journal de la Cour;" SAINTE-BEUVE, "Causeries du Lundi;" "Edinburgh Review" for January, 1864.

Danger, dŏN'zhȧ', (E. P.,) a French chemist, born about 1800, has gained distinction by experiments on arsenic and mercury.

Dangeville, dȯNzh'vĕl', (MARIE ANNE BOTOT,) a French actress, born in Paris in 1714; died in 1796.

Danhaver, dȧn'hȧ'ver, a German portrait-painter of great merit, born in Suabia, settled in Saint Petersburg, where he was patronized by Peter the Great. He died in Saint Petersburg about 1735.

See DESCAMPS, "Vies des Peintres Flamands," etc.

Danhawer or **Danhower.** See DANNHAUER.

Danican, dȧ'ne'kȯN', (FRANÇOIS ANDRÉ,) surnamed PHIL'IDOR, a French composer and famous chess-player, born at Dreux in 1727. In early youth he was a chorister in the chapel of Louis XV. He wrote for the Comic Opera of Paris with success. About 1777 he visited London, where he published a "Treatise on the Game of Chess," to which in his later years he was almost exclusively addicted. He found no equal in the chess-clubs of Paris and London, and was the victor in three simultaneous games which he played blindfolded against skilful opponents. Died in 1795.

See FÉTIS, "Biographie Universelle des Musiciens;" GEORGE ALLEN, "Life of Philidor," 1866.

Daniel, dan'yel, [Heb. דָּנִיֵּאל,] one of the four greater Hebrew prophets, was a member of the tribe of Judah. In his childhood, about 605 B.C., he was carried captive to Babylon, where he was educated at the court of Nebuchadnezzar and became proficient in learning and wisdom. (See Daniel i. 17.) Having by divine inspiration interpreted an important dream of the king, he was promoted to be ruler of the province of Babylon and chief of the Magi. About 580 he interpreted another dream of Nebuchadnezzar. The next event recorded of Daniel is that he read and explained the handwriting on the wall at Belshazzar's feast, (chap. v.,) about 538 B.C. Shortly after that date he obtained the favour of Darius the Mede, (Cyaxares,) and became the first of three presidents who had authority over the one hundred and twenty princes or satraps of the empire. For an account of his miraculous preservation in the lions' den, see Daniel, chap. vi. After the death of Darius, Daniel "prospered in the reign of Cyrus the Persian," (chap. vi. 28,) and saw his last recorded vision in 534 B.C. He is generally believed to have been the author of the book which bears his name, and which has been designated "the last form of prophecy and the first philosophy of history." His high character as a prophet appears to be attested by the Saviour, in Matthew xxiv. 15.

See, also, Ezekiel xiv. 14, and xxviii. 3; BITTELMAIER, "Disputatio de Vita Danielis," 1676.

Daniel, dȧ'ne-êl, (CHRISTIAN FRIEDRICH,) a German physician, born at Halle in 1753, published several medical works. Died in 1798.

Daniel, dȧ'ne'êl', (GABRIEL,) a French author and Jesuit, born at Rouen in 1649, lived in Paris, and obtained from Louis XIV. a pension of 2000 francs, with the title of historiographer of France. He wrote a "Reply to Pascal's Provincial Letters," which was admired by the Jesuits, and many other works, of which the most important is his "History of France," (1713.) Walckenaer thinks this is justly celebrated; but he admits that there is some foundation for the severe criticisms of Voltaire and others, who charge him with being partial and inaccurate. Died in 1728.

See LAMBERT, "Histoire littéraire du Règne de Louis XIV;" JOLY, "Éloges de quelques Auteurs Français."

Daniel, dan'yel, (GEORGE,) an English poet and antiquary, born about 1790. He published "The Modern Dunciad and other Poems," (1835,) and "Merry England in the Olden Time," (2 vols., 1842.) Died in 1864.

Daniel, (JOSEPH HENRI,) a French sculptor, born at Nantes in 1804. He obtained several gold medals for his works, among which are a marble statue of Cleopatra, (1847,) and a group representing Music, ordered for the Louvre.

Daniel, dan'yel, (PETER V.,) a lawyer, born in Stafford county, Virginia, about 1785. He was a member of the privy council from 1812 to 1830, and became an associate justice of the supreme court of the United States in 1840.

Daniel, (PIERRE,) a French antiquary and scholar, born at Orléans in 1530; died in 1603.

Daniel, (SAMUEL,) a meritorious but neglected English poet, born at Taunton in 1562, was educated at Oxford. He became tutor to Anne Clifford, who was afterwards the Countess of Pembroke, and he lived some years in London, where he associated with Shakspeare, Marlowe, and other poets. The report that he succeeded Spenser as poet-laureate is doubted by some; but it is evident that he was highly appreciated by his contemporaries. He wrote "The Tragedy of Cleopatra," (1594,) a "History of England," (1613–18,) a historical poem on "The Civil Wars of York and Lancaster," (1595,) "Musophilus," (1599,) and other poems. "Though very rarely sublime," says Headley, "he has skill in the pathetic; and his pages are disgraced by neither pedantry nor conceit." Hallam thinks "his English is eminently pure, free from affectation and pedantic innovation, with very little that is now obsolete." ("Introduction to the Literature of Europe.") Died in 1619.

See BAKER, "Biographia Dramatica;" FULLER, "Worthies of England;" "Life of S. Daniel," prefixed to his "Poetical Works," 2 vols., 1718; HEADLEY, "Beauties of Ancient English Poetry;" "Retrospective Review," vol. viii., 1823.

Daniel, (WILLIAM BARKER,) an English clergyman and writer, produced a work on "Rural Sports, or Treatises on Hunting," etc., (2 vols., 1801.) Died in 1833.

Daniel de Volterra. See VOLTERRA.

Daniele, dȧ-ne-ā'lȧ, or **Danieli,** dȧ-ne-ā'lee, (FRANCESCO,) a Neapolitan antiquary, born near Caserta in 1740. Having written a work called "Codice Fredericiano," he was appointed historiographer royal in 1778. In 1787 he became perpetual secretary of the Herculanean (or Ercolanese) Academy, founded for the publication of discoveries made at Herculaneum and Pompeii. He was chosen Fellow of the Royal Society of London. Among his works are a "Dissertation on the Caudine Forks," (1778,) and one on the "Ancient Coins of Capua," (1802.) Died in 1812.

See CASTALDI, "Vita di Francesco Daniele," 1812; CIAMPITTI, "De Vita F. Danielis Commentarius," 1818.

Danieli. See DANIELE.

Dan'iell, (JOHN FREDERICK,) an eminent English natural philosopher, born in London in 1790. He was elected Fellow of the Royal Society in 1814. In 1816 he was associated with Professor Brande as joint editor of the "Quarterly Journal of Science," twenty volumes of which were edited by them. He produced an important work entitled "Meteorological Essays," (1823,) and an "Essay on Artificial Climate," (1824.) He was professor of chemistry in King's College from 1831 until his death. For his invention of the pyrometer, the Royal Society in 1832 awarded him the Rumford medal, and in 1837 he received the Copley medal for an improvement in the Voltaic battery. In 1839 he published his admirable "Introduction to Chemical Philosophy." He wrote several smaller treatises on chemistry and other sciences, and obtained in 1842 another royal medal. He is said to be the only person who has ever received all the three medals in the gift of the Royal Society. Died in 1845.

Daniell, (SAMUEL,) an English artist, born in 1777. He spent a few years at the Cape of Good Hope, and after his return home published "African Scenery and Animals," (1808.) He also visited Ceylon, and illustrated its scenery and animals. Died in Ceylon in 1811.

Daniell, (THOMAS,) R.A., an eminent landscape-painter and engraver, born about 1750, was an uncle of

William Daniell, noticed below. He was a Fellow of the Royal Society and of the Antiquarian Society. Died in 1840. (See next article.)

Daniell, (WILLIAM,) R.A., an English landscape-painter and engraver, born in 1769, went to India with his uncle Thomas in 1784, and spent ten years in sketching the magnificent scenery of that region. They engraved a great number of views, which were published in several volumes, entitled "Oriental Scenery," (1808.) He also painted in oil several Indian landscapes. From 1814 to 1825 he was employed in drawing and engraving views for a great work entitled "Voyage round Great Britain." Died in 1837.

Daniello, dä-ne-el′lo, (BERNARDINO,) an Italian critic, who wrote "La Poetica," (1536,) translated Virgil's "Georgics" into verse, (1556,) and wrote a "Commentary on Dante," (1568.) Died in 1565.

Danilevski, dä-ne-lĕv′skee, (MIKHAELOVSKI,) a Russian general, served in several campaigns against the French, and against the Poles in 1831. He wrote "An Account of the Campaigns of 1812," (1834,) and other similar works. Died in 1848.

See "Foreign Quarterly Review" for July, 1839.

Dânishwâr or **Dânischvâr,** dä′nish-vâr′, a Persian poet and historian, born about 600 A.D., was celebrated as the compiler or author of poetical traditions connected with Persian history.

Dankelmann, dänk′ĕl-mân, or **Danckelmann,** dänk′kĕl-mân, (ERHARD CHRISTOPH BALTHASAR,) a Prussian minister of state, born in Lingen in 1643. He became in 1663 preceptor to Prince Frederick, son of the Elector. His pupil, having ascended the throne in 1688, appointed Dankelmann prime minister. He founded the Academy of Sciences at Berlin, and the University of Halle. By the intrigues of the courtiers, he was dismissed in 1697, and unjustly imprisoned until 1713. Died in 1722.

See ERSCH und GRUBER, "Allgemeine Encyklopaedie."

Dankers (dänk′ers) or **Danckerts** (or **Danckaerts**) **de Ry,** dänk′keRts deh rī, (CORNELIS,) a Dutch architect, born at Amsterdam in 1561. He held for forty years the office of architect of his native city, where he erected many public buildings. The most remarkable of these is the Exchange, finished in 1613. Died in 1634.

See PINGERON, "Vies des Architectes."

Dancks. See DANCKS.

Danloux, dôN′loo′, (PIERRE,) a French historical painter, born in Paris in 1745. During the Revolution he retired to England, where he painted history and portraits, among which is a portrait of the poet Delille, who complimented him in his poem on "Pity." Died in Paris in 1809.

Dannecker, von, fon dän′nĕk-ker, (JOHANN HEINRICH,) a celebrated German sculptor, born at or near Stuttgart in 1758. He was educated in the school of design at Ludwigsburg with Schiller, who became his friend. About 1780 he was appointed sculptor to the Duke of Würtemberg. He studied in Paris under Pajou in 1783 and 1784. In 1785 he visited Rome, where he remained about five years and associated with Goethe, Herder, and Canova. On his return to Stuttgart in 1790 he was chosen professor of plastic arts in the Academy of that place. He made admirable busts of Schiller, Lavater, Gluck, and others. In 1809 he commenced a statue of Ariadne, which is highly commended. Among his greatest works are a colossal statue of Christ, finished in 1824, and a statue of John the Baptist. Died in 1841.

See "Life of Dannecker," published at Hamburg in 1841; NAGLER, "Allgemeines Künstler-Lexikon;" "Nouvelle Biographie Générale;" MRS. L. M. CHILD's "Looking towards Sunset," p. 279.

Dannemayer, dän′neh-mī′er, (MATTHÄUS,) a German theologian, born in Suabia in 1741; died in 1805.

Dannhauer, dän′hŏw′er, written also **Danhawer** or **Danhower,** (JOHANN CONRAD,) a German Lutheran divine, born at Kendring in 1603. He was professor of eloquence and theology at Strasburg. Died in 1666.

Danrémont, de, deh dôN′rā′môN′, (CHARLES MARIE DENIS,) COUNT, a French general, born at Chaumont (Haute-Marne) in 1783. He entered the army in 1804, became a lieutenant-general in 1830, and was made a peer of France in 1835. In February, 1837, he was appointed

Governor-General of Algeria. He was killed in October of that year, at the siege of Constantine, where he was commander-in-chief.

See "Revue des Deux Mondes" for August 15, 1845.

Dansse. See VILLOISON.

Dantal, dôN′tâl′, (PIERRE,) a French grammarian, born at La Souchère in 1781; died in 1820.

Dantan, dôN′tôN′, (ANTOINE LAURENT,) a French statuary, born at Saint-Cloud in 1798. Having gained the first prize in 1828, he went to Rome as a pensioner. He returned in 1833, and worked in Paris with success. Among his works are a bas-relief of Silene, and a bust of Josephine of France.

Dantan, (JEAN PIERRE,) a distinguished sculptor, brother of the preceding, was born in Paris in 1800. He displayed a remarkable talent for caricature in grotesque figures of celebrated contemporaries, and attained pre-eminence in this novel branch of art. He has produced busts of Cherubini, (1847,) Maine de Biran, (1850,) Rosa Bonheur, and other persons, which are good likenesses without caricature.

Dän′te, [It. pron. dän′tà; Fr. DANTE, dôNt or dânt,[*]] or, more fully, **Durante[†] Allighieri,** (or **Alighieri,**) doo-rân′tà â-le-ge-ā′ree, [Lat. DAN′TES ALIGE′RIUS,] an illustrious Italian poet, regarded as the greatest poetical genius that flourished between the Augustan and the Elizabethan age, was born in Florence in May, 1265. He was instructed in liberal studies and arts by Brunetto Latini and other eminent scholars, and became well versed in Latin, philosophy, and theology. He also acquired skill in music, painting, and other accomplishments. He is said to have studied at Padua, Bologna, and Paris. In early youth (1274) his spiritual life and imaginative faculty were awakened by his love for Beatrice Portinari. This passion inspired his first poetic efforts, and exerted on his mind a profound and lasting influence. In his "Vita Nuova," a beautiful reverie, written about 1290 in alternate prose and verse, he has commemorated this tender passion, which, it appears, was not unrequited, though, for some unknown reason, they were not united. The tradition that she married another is not confirmed by any passage in his writings. After her death (in 1290) his friends persuaded him to marry Gemma Donati, a lady of a noble family; but the parties were so uncongenial that they finally separated. She complained of his unsocial habits.

Florence and Italy were then distracted by the implacable feuds of the Guelphs and Ghibelines. Dante's family being Guelphs, he espoused their cause with characteristic ardour, and fought for it at Campaldino, in 1289, with signal bravery. His eloquence and address were displayed in several political missions to foreign courts. In 1300 he was elected to the high office of Prior of Florence, where the Guelph party was divided between two factions, called Bianchi and Neri, (Whites and Blacks.) The Donati were the leaders of the Neri, and Dante favoured the Bianchi. The Neri prevailed, and in 1302 condemned Dante, with many others, to perpetual banishment, and the confiscation of his estate, on a charge of peculation. From this time he wandered without a home, and suffered much from poverty in addition to his other afflictions. It appears that his wife and children did not follow him in exile.

The events of his life subsequent to his banishment are mostly involved in uncertainty. Like his fellow-exiles, he joined the Ghibeline party, and made unsuccessful attempts to recover his rights. Among the princes whose hospitality he enjoyed in his exile were Cane Grande de la Scala, of Verona, and Guido Novello, of Ravenna, to the former of whom he dedicated his "Paradiso." About 1316 the privilege of returning to Florence was offered to him, on condition that he would pay a fine and confess his guilt. This offer he rejected with indignation; though he expressed a desire to be restored on any terms "consistent with the fame and honour of Dante." He died at Ravenna, September 14, 1321. The

* Chaucer has DAUNT or DAUNTE, (Wyf of Bathes Tale,) which seems to be merely an English representation of the French pronunciation.

† Durante, his original name, was contracted in popular parlance into Dante.

ā, ē, ī, ō, ū, ȳ, *long;* ä, ĕ, ĭ, ŏ, ŭ, ў, *short;* a, e, i, o, *obscure;* fär, fäll, fât; mĕt; nôt; gŏŏd; mŏŏn;

following lines inscribed on his tomb are supposed to be his own composition :

"Hic claudor Dantes patriis extorris ab oris,
Quem genuit parvi Florentia mater amoris."*

Soon after his death appeared his sublime and unique poem, the "Divina Commedia," which is supposed to have been written during his exile; but the time and place of its origin are not ascertained. It was first printed in 1472. The subject of this poem is the author's own experience, real or imaginary, and the scene is laid in the infernal regions, purgatory, and paradise. It is certainly a surprising phenomenon to appear in that dark period of transition between ancient and modern literature.

"Dante," says Hallam, "is among the very few who have created the national poetry of their country. Of all writers he is the most unquestionably original. . . . No poet ever excelled him in conciseness and in the rare talent of finishing his pictures by a few bold touches,— the merit of Pindar in his better hours. . . . The great characteristic excellence of Dante is elevation of sentiment, to which his compressed diction and the emphatic cadences of his measure admirably correspond." ("Introduction to the Literature of Europe.")

"I suppose," says Ruskin, "that the powers of the imagination may always be tested by accompanying tenderness of emotion ; and thus (as Byron said) there is no tenderness like Dante's, neither any intensity nor seriousness like his,—such seriousness that it is incapable of perceiving that which is commonplace or ridiculous, but fuses all down into its white-hot fire."

"Ah, from what agonies of heart and brain,
What exultations trampling on despair,
What tenderness, what tears, what hate of wrong,
What passionate outcry of a soul in pain,
Uprose this poem of the earth and air,
This medieval miracle of song !"
LONGFELLOW's "Divina Commedia."

Dante was taciturn, inclined to solitude, and familiar with but few. Voltaire, who did not appreciate his genius, wittily says, "His reputation will go on increasing, because scarcely anybody reads him." To this it may be replied that he is read, if not by ordinary readers, at least by all those who can appreciate originality and power in the expression of human passion. Dante wrote, in Latin prose, a political work "On Monarchy," ("De Monarchia,") and "De Vulgari Eloquio," a treatise on the structure of the Italian language ; also, in Italian prose, "Il Convito," a mystical commentary on three of his odes. The style of his prose is pure, elegant, and nervous ; that of his verse is still more admirable. Two of his sons, Pietro and Jacopo, had literary tastes, and wrote valuable commentaries on their father's poem. Cary's translation of the "Commedia" into English blank verse is highly commended. We have also an excellent English version of the "Divina Commedia" by Longfellow, remarkable for its literalness.

See BOCCACCIO, "Vita di Dante," 1544; CHABANON, "Vie de Dante," 1773; FABRONI, "Elogj di Dante, di Poliziano," etc., 1800; ARTAUD DE MONTOR, "Histoire de Dante," 1841 ; R. DE VERICOUR, "Life and Times of Dante," 1858 ; LONGFELLOW, "Poets and Poetry of Europe;" FAURIEL, "Dante et les Origines de la Langue et la Littérature Italiennes," 2 vols., 1854; AMPÈRE, "Voyage Dantesque" in the "Revue des Deux Mondes," 1839 ; MACAULAY, "Essay on Milton;" F. X. WEGELE, "Dante's Leben und Werke," 1852 ; CESARE BALBO, "Vita nuova di Dante," 1839; English version of the same, by BUNYAN, 1852 ; MISSIRINI, "Vita di Dante Alighieri," 1840; EMIL RUTH, "Studien über Dante Alighieri," 1853 ; UGO FOSCOLO, "Discorso sul Testo di Dante," 1825; REV. HENRY STEBBING, "Lives of the Italian Poets," London, 1831.

Dante, dån'tà, (GIOVANNI BATTISTA,) an Italian mathematician, born at Perugia, lived about 1500. He attempted to fly with artificial wings, but fell, and broke his leg.

Dante or **Danti,** dån'tee, (GIROLAMO,) a Venetian painter of the sixteenth century, was a pupil of Titian.

Dante or **Danti,** (IGNAZIO,) an Italian geometer, born at Perugia in 1537, entered the Dominican order. Cosimo I. invited him to Florence to teach mathematics. In 1583 he was made Bishop of Alatri. He wrote several treatises on astronomy and mathematics, and was the first modern who made a gnomon by which the equinoxes and solstices could be determined. His "Mathematical

* Literally, "Here [I] Dante, whom Florence, a mother of little love, bore, am enclosed, an exile from my native country."

Science reduced to Tables" is a work of great erudition. Died in 1586.

Dante or **Danti,** (PIETRO VINCENZO,) an Italian poet and mathematician, born at Perugia, wrote a commentary on the Sphere of Sacrobosco, (1544,) and verses in imitation of the great poet Dante. Died in 1512.

Dante or **Danti,** (VINCENZO,) an eminent Italian architect and sculptor, born at Perugia in 1530, was employed by the grand duke Cosimo de' Medici. His statue of Julius III. at Perugia is esteemed a masterpiece. He was a near relative of Ignazio, noticed above. He made for the Escurial designs which Cosimo I. sent to Philip II. of Spain. Died in 1576.

See VASARI, "Lives of the Painters," etc.

Dantes Aligerius. See DANTE.

Danti. See DANTE.

Dantine, dôN'tèN', or **D'Antine,** (FRANÇOIS,) a French Benedictine monk, born in the diocese of Liege in 1688, lived some years in Paris. He was one of the editors of Du Cange's "Glossary," (1733,) and the first principal editor of the "Art of Verifying Dates," a valuable work on chronology. Died in 1746.

Danton, dan'ton or dôN'tôN', (GEORGES JACQUES,) an arch-demagogue of the French Revolution, born at Arcissur-Aube in 1759, was a lawyer by profession. With a large, muscular frame, a passionate temperament, an audacious spirit, and the voice of a Stentor, he was well constituted for a political agitator. "Nature has given me," said he, "the athletic form and the harsh expression of liberty." He instituted the club of Cordeliers, perhaps even more intemperately radical than that of the Jacobins, and became the chief orator of the Parisian populace. He instigated and directed the sanguinary insurrection of the 10th of August, 1792, which subverted the French monarchy. The supreme power then fell into the hands of Danton, Marat, and Robespierre, the first of whom, obtaining the office of minister of justice, had the chief control of the capital.

In the alarm caused by the invasion of France by the Prussians, he spoke with confidence, and urged the adoption of a bold and resolute policy. He appears to have been responsible for the massacre of the imprisoned royalists in September, 1792, as he made little or no effort to protect them. On his election to the Convention he resigned the office of minister of justice, became the leader of the Mountain, and voted for the death of the king. His power soon declined, as his crimes disgusted the honest republicans and his success excited the jealousy of Robespierre. He used to say, "All will go well as long as men say, 'Robespierre and Danton ;' but woe to me if ever they should say, 'Danton and Robespierre.'" In 1793 he was chosen a member of the committee of public safety. At the crisis of his struggle with Robespierre, Danton's decision failed. Though he knew his death was resolved on, he declined to fly or to strike the first blow. In March, 1794, he was arrested with Lacroix and others, and taken before the fatal tribunal which he had himself instituted. Little formality was observed at his trial,—or rather his condemnation ; for the judges refused to hear his defence. When the judge asked him his name, residence, etc., he answered, "My name is Danton ; my dwelling will soon be in annihilation; but my name will live in the Pantheon of history." He maintained his usual assurance and lofty bearing at the scaffold, where he perished April 5, 1794. According to Lamartine, "Nothing was wanting to make Danton a great man, except virtue."

See THIERS, "History of the French Revolution ;" LAMARTINE, "History of the Girondists ;" MICHELET, "Histoire de la Révolution Française ;" VILLAUMÉ, "Histoire de la Révolution ;" LORD BROUGHAM, "Statesmen of the Time of George III. ;" BARANTE, "Histoire de la Convention ;" DES JARDINS, "Vie de Danton," 1851 ; "Encyclopædia Britannica ;" "Blackwood's Magazine" for February, 1823; "Foreign Quarterly" for April, 1844; "British Quarterly" for April, 1866.

Danton, (JOSEPH ARSÈNE,) a French editor, nephew of the preceding, was born at Plancy (Aube) in 1814. In 1840 he was employed by M. Villemain, minister of public instruction, as chef de cabinet. He edited in 1839 "Cousin's Lectures on Philosophy delivered in 1819-20."

Dantz or **Danz,** dånts, (JOHANN ANDREAS,) a German Orientalist, born near Gotha in 1654, was professor of

e as k; ç as s; g hard; ġ as j; G, H, K, guttural; N, nasal; R, trilled; ṣ as z; th as in this.   (☞See Explanations, p. 23.)

Oriental languages, and afterwards of theology, at Jena. He published grammars of the Hebrew and Syriac languages, and many works on the history and antiquities of the Jews. Died in 1727.

Dantzic, Duke of. See Lefebvre, (François Joseph.)

Dănu, [Hindoo pron. dŭn′ŏŏ,] in Hindoo mythology, a daughter of Daksha, and the mother of the Dânavas. (See Danava.)

Dan′vẹrs, (Henry,) Earl of Danby, an English officer and courtier, born in Wiltshire in 1573, served as captain in the army which Elizabeth sent to aid Henry IV. of France, and was knighted for his conduct in that war. He was afterwards major-general under the Earl of Essex in Ireland. Charles I. created him Earl of Danby and a member of the privy council. He founded a botanic garden for the University of Oxford. Died in 1644.

Danville. See Anville, d′.

Danz. See Dantz.

Danz, dânts, (Ferdinand Georg,) a German physician, born in the duchy of Darmstadt in 1761, published several useful medical works. He was professor at Giessen, where he died in 1793.

Danzer, dânt′sẹr, (Jakob,) a German Catholic theologian, born at Langenfeld in 1743; died in 1796.

Danzi, dânt′see, (Franz,) a German composer of operas and church-music, was born at Manheim in 1763; died in 1826.

Dɔph′ne, [Gr. Δάφνη,] a nymph of classic mythology, beloved by Apollo. According to the poetical legend, she fled from Apollo, who pursued her, and was transformed into a laurel-tree, which was afterwards sacred to Apollo.

Daph′nis, [Gr. Δαφνίς,] a shepherd and hero of Sicily, the reputed inventor of pastoral poetry, was called a son of Mercury. The poets relate that he was the favoured lover of a Naiad, who punished him with blindness for his infidelity to her.

See the First Idyl of Theocritus and the Fifth Eclogue of Virgil.

Da Ponte, dâ pon′tà, (Lorenzo,) an Italian poet, born at Ceneda in 1749. Having been banished from Venice for some satirical verses, he went to Vienna, where he became Latin secretary to Joseph II. Here he wrote several operas for the Italian theatre. After the death of Joseph II. he passed some years in London, whence, in 1805, he emigrated to New York. About 1829 he was appointed professor of Italian in Columbia College. He wrote "Don Giovanni" (or "Don Juan") and other dramas, and sonnets.

Da Ponte, (Lorenzo,) a son of the preceding, born in London in 1805, became professor of belles-lettres in the University of New York. He wrote a "History of the Florentine Republic," (1833.) Died in 1841.

Dapper, dâp′pẹr, (Oliver or Olfert,) a Dutch physician and geographer, published several extensive and interesting works, among which are a "Description of Africa," (1668,) a "Description of the Chinese Empire," and a "Description of Asia." His works contain many maps and excellent plates. Died in 1690.

Daquin or **D'Aquin.** See Aquin, d′.

Daquin, dǎ′kăn′, (Joseph,) a noted physician, born at Chambéry in 1757, wrote, besides other works, "La Philosophie de la Folie," ("The Philosophy of Insanity," 2d ed., 1804.) Died in 1815.

Dârâ or **Dârâb,** the Persian of Darius, which see.

Dârâ-Shikôh, dâ′râ shï-kôh′, written also **Dara-Chékouh,** a Hindoo prince, born in 1616, was the favourite son of Shâh Jehân. He was defeated in battle by his brother Aurung-Zeb, and put to death by his order in 1643.

Daran, dâ′rôn′, (Jacques,) a skilful French surgeon, born at Saint-Frajon in 1701, practised with success in Milan, Turin, and Messina. At the last place he gained credit by his professional services and humanity during the plague. He was settled at Marseilles, when the fame of his skill in disorders of the urethra induced the king to invite him to Paris, where he resided until his death. The king granted him letters of noblesse in 1755. Daran invented the bougies which bear his name, and wrote a few professional works. Died in 1784.

See "Biographie Médicale."

D'Arblay, dar′blä or dǎr′blȧ′, Madame, (originally Frances Bur′ney,) a celebrated English novelist, born at Lynn-Regis in 1752, was the daughter of Dr. Charles Burney, an eminent musician and author of the "History of Music." She was a shy and silent child, and at the age of eight did not know her letters. Her mother having died when Frances was about ten, no teacher or governess was provided for her; but her fond father's negligence was compensated by her own efforts in self-education. In 1760 Mr. Burney removed to London, where he gained admission into the highest literary society, and his house was frequented by Johnson, Burke, Garrick, and many others. His concerts, at which the greatest Italian vocalists performed gratis, attracted a throng of the most noble as well as the most fashionable of the metropolis. By such social influences, rather than by books and schools, was her mind trained and matured; though she seldom performed any part on this scene but that of a silent and diffident observer. About 1776 her novel "Evelina"—commenced some years before—was ready for the press. Observing a strict secrecy respecting the authorship of the book, she sent the manuscript to Dodsley without her name; but he refused to publish it on such conditions. After much delay, it was sold for twenty pounds, and appeared anonymously in 1778. The admiration and applause with which it was received were much increased when the secret transpired that the author was a reserved, obscure young woman. Her book was warmly eulogized by Burke, Johnson, Gibbon, and Sheridan, the first of whom sat up all night to read it, and the second pronounced her superior to Fielding. "She found herself," says Macaulay, "on the highest pinnacle of fame." Her second book, "Cecilia," (1782,) did not disappoint the high expectations of the public. "It was placed," says Macaulay, "by general acclamation, among the classical novels of England." In 1786 she had the misfortune to be appointed second keeper of the robes to Queen Charlotte, with a salary of two hundred pounds. This situation was peculiarly and extremely irksome to a person of her fine sensibility, as she was debarred from all congenial society and subject to the constant restraints of despotic etiquette. For five years, in deference to her father's wishes, she sacrificed her health and domestic happiness for the privilege of standing in the presence of royalty. In 1793 she married Count D'Arblay, an amiable and estimable French officer, then an exile. From 1802 to 1816 she resided with her husband in France. She died at Bath in 1840. Besides the above-named works, she wrote "Camilla," and other fictions. Her "Diary and Letters" (7 vols., 1842–46) is a work of rare interest.

See Macaulay, "Essay on Madame D'Arblay."

Dar′bў, (William,) an American geographer, born in Pennsylvania. He published a valuable and interesting work, entitled a "View of the United States," with a particular account of the various river-basins, and other information. Died in 1854.

Darc, (Joan.) See Joan of Arc.

Darcet, dâr′să′, (Jean,) a distinguished French chemist and physician, born at Doazit, in Guienne, in 1727. About 1742 he acquired the friendship of Montesquieu, who employed him as tutor to his son in Paris. After the death of that patron, Darcet devoted himself to chemical researches in concert with Count de Laugarais. He made successful experiments in the fabrication and improvement of porcelain, the components of which he discovered by analysis about 1766. At the death of Macquer (1784) he was chosen in his place a member of the Academy of Sciences, and director of the manufactory of Sèvres. He was also inspector-general of the assay-office, and a professor in the College of France. He demonstrated that the diamond is combustible, and invented the metallic alloy which bears his name, and which is fusible at the temperature of boiling water. He was the author of several chemical treatises. Died in 1801.

See J. J. Dizé, "Précis historique sur la Vie de J. Darcet," 1802; "Nouvelle Biographie Générale."

Darcet, (Jean Pierre Joseph,) an eminent chemist, son of the preceding, was born in Paris in 1777. He was appointed assayer of the mint in 1801, and afterwards founded or directed several manufactories of chemical products which he improved, and among which were soda and soap. In 1823 he succeeded Berthollet as chemist in the Academy of Sciences. He wrote many useful treatises on sanitary and economical questions, one of which is "On the Principal Salt-Mines of Europe," (1824.) Died in 1844.

See "Notice sur J. P. J. Darcet," Paris, 1844.

Darçon. See ARÇON, D'.

D'Ar'cy, (PATRICK,) COUNT, an Irish engineer and scientific author, born at Galloway in 1725, removed to France in early youth, and served in the French army in 1744. He was skilled in mechanics and other sciences, and wrote an "Essay on Artillery," a "Memoir on the Duration of the Sensation of Sight," and other works. Condorcet composed his eulogy in the Academy of Sciences. Died in Paris in 1779.

Dar'da-nus, [Gr. Δάρδανος,] a mythical or semi-fabulous personage, who is represented as a son of Jupiter and Electra, and the ancestor of the Trojans. Homer reckons five generations between Dardanus and Priam.

Dardel, dăR'dĕl', (ROBERT GUILLAUME,) a French sculptor, born in Paris in 1749; died in 1821.

Dardi, daR'dee, (BEMBO,) an Italian Hellenist, born at Venice about 1560, translated the works of Plato into Italian. Died about 1640.

Dareau, dă'rō', (FRANÇOIS,) a French jurist, born near Guévet in 1736; died about 1783.

Daremberg, dă'rôN'baiR', (CHARLES VICTOR,) a French physician, born at Dijon in 1817. He published (in French) "Select Works of Hippocrates," (1843,) an edition of Galen, (1854,) and other works. In 1849 he became librarian of the Mazarin Library.

Dā'rēs [Gr. Δάρης; Fr. DARÈS, dă'rĕs'] of Phrygia, a priest of Vulcan, is mentioned in the "Iliad" of Homer, who praises his wisdom. He is supposed to have been present at the siege of Troy. There existed in the early ages a history of the destruction of Troy, which was regarded as the work of Dares, and as older than Homer's "Iliad." A prose work in barbarous Latin has come down to us which purports to be a version of that of Dares. It was popular in the fifteenth century, and was often printed with the work of Dictys Cretensis.

See J. G. ECK, "Dissertatio de Darete Phrygio," 1768.

Dareste, dă'rĕst', (ANTOINE ÉLISABETH CLÉOPHAS,) a French. historical writer, born in Paris in 1820.

Daret, dă'rȧ', (PIERRE,) a French engraver, born in Paris in 1610, published a collection of the portraits of eminent persons of the sixteenth and seventeenth centuries, which was highly prized, also a "Life of Raphael," translated from the Italian," (1651.) Died in 1675.

Dar'gan, (WILLIAM,) an eminent Irish engineer and contractor, born in Carlow county about 1800. He superintended the construction of several railways and canals in Ireland. He was the chief promoter of the Dublin Exhibition of 1853, on which he expended many thousand pounds of his own money.

Dargaud, dăR'gō', (J. M.,) a French writer, a friend and imitator of Lamartine, born at Paray-le-Monial in 1800, published, among other works, "Solitude," (1838,) a "History of [Queen] Mary Stuart," (1850,) and poetical versions of Job and the Psalms of David.

See SAINTE-BEUVE, "Causeries du Lundi."

D'Argenson. See ARGENSON, D'.

D'Argental. See ARGENTAL, D'.

D'Argentré. See ARGENTRÉ, D'.

D'Argenville. See DEZALLIER.

D'Argonne. See ARGONNE, D'.

Daries, dă're-ês, or **Darjes,** daR'yĕs, (JOACHIM GEORG,) a German jurist and philosopher, born at Güstrow in 1714. He began in 1738 to teach philosophy at Jena, and in 1763 was appointed by Frederick the Great professor of law at Frankfort-on-the-Oder, with the title of privy councillor. He published many able works, among which are "The First Principles of Finance," (in German, 1756,) and "Institutes of Universal Jurisprudence," (in Latin, 1766.) Died in 1791.

See J. H. FICHTE, "Beiträge zur Charakteristik der Neueren Philosophen;" C. R. HAUSEN, "J. G. Daries als academischer Lehrer geschildert," 1791.

Da-rī'us* [Gr. Δαρεῖος; It. DARIO, dä-ree'o; Persian, DARA, dă'rä, or DARAB, dä-räb'] I, or **Da-rī'us Hȳs-tas'pis,** (known as GUSHTÂSP (gōosh-tâsp') in the legendary history of Persia,) King of Persia, was the son of Hystaspes, a member of the noble family of Achæmenidæ. In 521 B.C., having killed the usurper Smerdis, he ascended the throne recently vacated by the death of Cambyses. He first organized the extensive empire which Cyrus and Cambyses had acquired by conquest, and divided it into twenty grand satrapies. After suppressing a revolt of the Babylonians, he led a great expedition against the nomadic Scythians of Europe, which was not successful. To chastise the Athenians for aiding some Ionian insurgents, he sent Datis and Artaphernes with a large army, which was completely routed at Marathon in 490 B.C. He was preparing to renew the contest, when he died in 485, and was succeeded by his son Xerxes. Darius was a ruler of superior ability.

See HERODOTUS; GROTE, "History of Greece;" THIRLWALL, "History of Greece;" CARL L STRUVE, "Feldzug des Darius gegen die Scythen," 1812; JUSTIN, books i., ii., and vii.

Darius II., called **Da-rī'us O'chus** or **No'thus,** was the natural son of Artaxerxes Longimanus, who gave him in marriage his daughter Parysatis. Having deposed Sogdianus, who had killed Xerxes II., the lawful heir, he became king in 424 B.C. He died in 405, leaving two sons, Artaxerxes Mnemon and Cyrus the Younger, the former of whom was his successor.

See XENOPHON, "Hellenica" and "Anabasis."

Darius III. or **Cod-o-man'nus,** the last king of the ancient Persian monarchy, was a descendant of Darius Nothus. He began to reign at the death of Arses, in 336 B.C. In the second year of his reign Persia was invaded by Alexander of Macedon, who gained a victory at the river Grani'cus. Darius, having taken command of his army, was defeated at Issus in 333, and at Arbela in 331 B.C. He then retreated towards Bactriana, pursued by the Macedonians, who were on the point of taking him prisoner, when he was killed by Bessus, one of his own satraps, in 330. With his expiring breath he expressed his thanks to the victor for his humane treatment of the royal captives, his wife and daughters. Alexander married his daughter Statira.

See the Histories of ARRIAN, JUSTIN, and QUINTUS CURTIUS.

Darius Hystaspes. See DARIUS I.

Darius Ochus. See DARIUS II.

Darius the Mede, of the Bible, is supposed to be the Cyaxares II. of profane history.

See Daniel vi.

Darjes. See DARIES.

Darke, dark, (WILLIAM,) an American officer, born in Pennsylvania in 1736. He served with distinction in the Revolutionary war. Died in 1801.

Dar'ley, (FELIX O. C.,) an eminent American designer, born in Philadelphia in 1822. He removed to New York about 1848. He has illustrated Irving's "Sketch-Book," "Knickerbocker's New York," "Rip van Winkle," and other humorous works, with success; also the novels of J. Fenimore Cooper, and the works of Dickens. His outline illustrations of Judd's "Margaret" are greatly and justly admired.

See TUCKERMAN, "Book of the Artists."

Dar'ley, (GEORGE,) a poet and mathematician, born in Dublin in 1785, removed to London in 1825. He gained distinction by his critical contributions to the "Literary Gazette" and "Athenæum," and wrote several poems, one of which is called "Sylvia, or the May Queen," (1827,) and treatises on geometry and algebra. Died in 1849.

Dar'ling, (GRACE,) an English heroine, born at Bamborough in 1815, was the daughter of the keeper of the Longstone light-house, on one of the Farne Islands. The Forfarshire steamer having been wrecked in that vicinity, September 6, 1838, she went out in a small boat, at the imminent peril of her life, and rescued nine persons who were clinging to a rock. A public subscription of about £700 was raised by the people of the United Kingdom as a testimonial to her heroic conduct. Died in 1842.

* Darius, in Persian Dârâ or Dârâb, and in Hebrew Daryavesh, signifies "prince," or "lord:" hence Darius Hystaspis would signify the "lord or king [son of] Hystaspes or Gushtâsp." (See GUSHTÂSP.)

€ as k; ç as s; ḡ hard; ġ as j; G, H, K, guttural; N, nasal; R, trilled; ŝ as z; ᵵh as in this. (☞ See Explanations, p. 23.

Darling, (JAMES,) an English bibliographer, born in 1797, was for many years a bookseller in London. He published (1852–57) a valuable work, entitled "Cyclopædia Bibliographica: a Library Manual of Theological and General Literature," (2 vols.) Died in 1862.

Dar'ling-ton, (WILLIAM,) M.D., an eminent American botanist, born in Birmingham, Chester county, Pennsylvania, in 1782. He practised medicine at West Chester, and was elected a member of Congress in 1814 by the voters of his native county, which he also represented for two other terms, (1819–23.) He published a valuable work on the plants of Chester county, entitled "Flora Cestrica," (1837,) which was commended by eminent botanists of Europe; also, "Memorials of John Bartram and Humphrey Marshall," (1849.) Died in 1863.

See "Obituary Notice of William Darlington," read before the American Philosophical Society, February 19, 1864, by T. P. JAMES.

Darluc, dăr'lük', (MICHEL,) a French physician and naturalist, born at Grimaud in 1707 or 1717, obtained the chair of botany in the University of Aix. He wrote the "Natural History of Provence," (3 vols., 1782–86,) and several medical works. Died in 1783.

Darmagnac, dăr'măn'yăk', (JEAN BARTHÉLEMI,) VICOMTE, a French general, born at Toulouse in 1766, distinguished himself at Austerlitz in 1805, and, as general of division, rendered important services at Vittoria (June, 1813) and Toulouse, (1814.) Died in 1855.

Darmaing, dăr'mǎN', (JEAN JÉRÔME ACHILLE,) a French journalist, born at Pamiers in 1794, began in 1825 to publish the "Gazette des Tribunaux," which was very successful. About 1832 he became chief editor of the "Constitutionnel." Died in 1836.

Darnau, dăr'nō', (JACQUES,) BARON, a French general, born in Loiret in 1768; died in 1830.

Darn'ley, (HENRY STUART,) LORD, a Scottish noble, born in England about 1545, was the son of the Earl of Lenox and Margaret Douglas, a niece of Henry VIII. of England. His father was descended from the house of Stuart, and his mother was a half-sister of James V. His relation to the royal family and his comely person caused him to be selected in 1565 as the husband of Queen Mary. She treated him at first with much kindness, but was soon disgusted by his stupidity, insolence, and profligacy. He instigated the murder of Rizzio, which she deeply resented and resolved to revenge. During a fit of illness Darnley lodged in an isolated house called the Kirk in the Field, which was blown up by gunpowder, Darnley being killed, February 9, 1567. Respecting the responsibility of this crime, see MARY STUART.

See BURTON, "History of Scotland," vol. iv. chaps. xliii.–xlviii.; ROBERTSON, "History of Scotland;" FROUDE, "History of England," vol. viii., chaps. viii., ix., x.; MIGNET, "Histoire de Marie Stuart."

Darondeau, dă'rôN'dō',(STANISLAS,) a French painter of genre and religious subjects, born about 1800; died in 1842.

Darquier de Pellepoix, dăr'ke-â' dĕh pĕl'pwâ', (AUGUSTIN,) a French astronomer, born at Toulouse in 1718, had an observatory at his own house, and hired persons to calculate. He wrote a "Uranography," (1771,) which Lalande commended, "Astronomical Observations," (1777–82,) and a few other scientific works. He was an associate of the Institute. Died in 1802.

Darracq, dă'răk', (FRANÇOIS BALTHASAR,) a French legislator, born at Mont-de-Marsan about 1750, was a member of the Council of Five Hundred, (1795–99.) Died about 1808.

Darrigol, dă're'gol', (JEAN PIERRE,) a French priest, born in 1790. He wrote an able "Critical Dissertation on the Basque Language." In 1829 he won a prize from the French Academy for his "Analysis Raisonnée of the Grammatical System of the Basque Language," when William Humboldt was a competitor. Died in 1829.

Darriule, dă're'ül', (JEAN,) BARON, a French general, born at Arudy in 1774; died in 1850.

Dart, (JOHN,) an English antiquary, flourished about 1725, and wrote "Antiquities of Westminster Abbey," (2 vols., 1723.)

Darthé, dăr'tà', (AUGUSTIN A. J.,) a French Jacobin, born at Saint-Pol in 1769. He was executed as an accomplice of Babeuf in 1797.

Dartmouth, LORD. See LEGGE, (GEORGE.)

Dartois de Bournonville, dăr'twâ' dĕh booR'nôN'-vèl', (FRANÇOIS VICTOR ARMAND,) a French dramatist, born at Beauvais in 1788, wrote many vaudevilles.

Daru, dă'rü', (MARTIAL NOËL PIERRE,) BARON, born in Paris in 1774, was a brother of Count Pierre Antoine Noël. He was commissary of war during the republic, and gained distinction as an able administrator under Napoleon I., who appointed him intendant of Vienna in 1809, and intendant of the crown at Rome in 1811. He left in manuscript an unfinished "History of Rome during the French Occupation." Died in Paris in 1827.

Daru, (NAPOLÉON,) COUNT, a son of the statesman noticed below, was born in Paris about 1804. He entered the army, and served as captain in Algeria. In 1832 he became a member of the Chamber of Peers. He acted with the moderate republicans in the Assembly of 1848–49.

Daru, (PIERRE ANTOINE NOËL BRUNO,) COUNT, an eminent French statesman and author, born at Montpellier in 1767. About 1790 he wrote "Washington," an epic poem. He favoured the Revolution, and in 1791 became a commissary in the army of Brittany. While imprisoned during the reign of terror, he translated into French verse the Odes and Epistles of Horace. About 1800 he was appointed secretary of war, and in 1802 a member of the Tribunate, in which he advocated the cause of public instruction. Between 1804 and 1806 Bonaparte made him a councillor of state, a count of the empire, and intendant-general of the imperial household. In the campaigns of 1806 and the ensuing years he accompanied Bonaparte, who had much confidence in his ability and employed him as commissary-general, financier, and negotiator. Having become chief minister of state in 1811, he opposed the Russian expedition, but, when other counsels prevailed, made extraordinary exertions to meet its exigencies. In 1815 he was chosen president of the French Academy, an office for which he was well adapted by his dignity, his good taste, his sonorous voice and lucid diction. As an author his merit is conspicuous. His "History of Venice" (1819) is esteemed the best work on that subject, and his poems and eulogies on Volney and others are admired. Died in 1829.

See SAINTE-BEUVE, "Causeries du Lundi;" LAMARTINE, "Éloge du Comte Daru;" VIENNET, "Notice sur Daru," prefixed to his "Histoire de Venise;" ARMAND MARRAST, "Notice sur M. Daru," 1829; "London Quarterly Review" for March, 1825.

Darvieux. See ARVIEUX.

Dar'win, (CHARLES,) a son of Erasmus Darwin the poet, was born at Lichfield in 1758. While a student of medicine at Edinburgh, he gained a first-prize medal. Died in 1778.

Darwin, (CHARLES,) F.R.S., an eminent English naturalist and geologist, a grandson of the poet Dr. Darwin, was born at Shrewsbury, February 12, 1809. He accompanied Captain Fitzroy in the Beagle in a voyage of exploration, 1831–36, and recorded his observations respecting geology, etc. in his "Voyage of a Naturalist round the World," which obtained great popularity. "The author," says the "London Quarterly Review" for December, 1839, "is a first-rate landscape-painter with the pen, and the dreariest solitudes are made to teem with interest." In 1839 he published a "Journal of Researches into the Geology and Natural History of Countries visited by H.M.S. Beagle." His "Monograph of the Family Cirripedia," (which includes the Barnacle,) published in 1851–53, is a remarkable and excellent work. He produced arguments against the immutability of species, in a work entitled "The Origin of Species by means of Natural Selection," (1859,) "which," says the "Edinburgh Review" for April, 1860, "was perused with avidity not only by professional naturalists, but by the far wider intellectual class which now takes interest in the higher generalizations of all the sciences. The same pleasing style which marked his earliest work, and a certain artistic disposition and sequence of arguments, have recalled the attention of thinking men to the hypothesis of the inconstancy and transmutation of species." Among his works are a treatise "On the Fertilization of Orchids," (1862,) and "The Variation of Animals and Plants under Domestication," (1868.)

See "London Quarterly Review" for July, 1860; "Westminster Review" for April, 1860; "Darwin and his Reviewers," in "Atlantic Monthly," October, 1860.

ā, ē, ī, ō, ū, ȳ, *long;* ă, ĕ, ŏ, same, less prolonged; ă, ĕ, ĭ, ŏ, ŭ, ў, *short;* ą, ę, į, ǫ, *obscure;* fär, fǎll, fǎt; mĕt; nŏt; gōŏd; mōŏn;

Darwin, (ERASMUS,) M.D., an ingenious English poet and physiologist, born at Elton, near Newark, in 1731. Having graduated at Cambridge, he settled at Lichfield, where he married, and practised with success until 1781, when he removed to Derby. His principal poem, "The Botanic Garden," (1791,) had a great popularity among his contemporaries, which has since rather declined. It was composed on an original plan, and displayed great powers of description ; but the style is too ornate. His "Phytologia" (1800) presented many novel ideas and analogies in physiology, some of which are now received as true. He also wrote "Zoonomia, or the Laws of Organic Life," "The Temple of Nature," a poem, and other works. A writer in the "Edinburgh Review" for 1803 says of the " Botanic Garden," "The novelty of its plan, an imposing air of boldness and originality in his poetical and philosophical speculations, and a striking display of command over the sources of poetical embellishment, were sufficient to secure him the approbation of even fastidious readers." Died in 1802.

See ANNE SEWARD, "Memoirs of the Life of Dr. Darwin ;" CARY, "Lives of English Poets from Johnson to Kirke White ;" "Edinburgh Review" for July, 1803, and April, 1804.

Darwin, (ROBERT WARING,) an English physician, brother of the preceding. He published "Principia Botanica, or an Introduction to the Sexual System of Linnæus," (3d edition, 1810.)

Daschkow or **Daschkoff.** See DASHKOF.

Dä'sent, (GEORGE WEBBE,) a British writer, born about 1818, published "The Norsemen in Ireland,"(1855,) "Popular Tales from the Norse," (1859,) and other similar works.

See "Blackwood's Magazine" for March, 1859; "Edinburgh Review" for October, 1861.

Dashkof or **Daschkow,** dåsh'kof, written also **Dashkov,** (EKATERINA ROMANOVNA,) a Russian princess, eminent for her talents and achievements, born in 1744, was the daughter of Count Roman Woronzof. About the age of sixteen she was married to Prince Dashkof. In 1762 she was the master-spirit of the conspiracy which dethroned Peter III. and made his wife autocrat as Catherine II. Having lost the favour of the empress, she travelled several years in foreign countries, and returned in 1782, when she was appointed president of the Academy of Sciences at Saint Petersburg. Under her auspices was founded the Russian Academy, (literary,) of which she became the first president in 1784. She planned and in part compiled the Dictionary published by this academy, and wrote several plays, etc. On the accession of the emperor Paul, in 1796, she was deprived of her offices and banished from the capital. Died in 1810. She left "Memoirs of her Life," which were published (in English) in 1840.

See OTTO, "Lehrbuch der Russischen Literatur ;" VOLTAIRE, "Correspondance."

Dassdorf, dås'dorf, (CARL WILHELM,) a German scholar, born at Staubitz, Saxony, in 1750; died in 1812.

Dassier, då'se-å', (JOHN,) a Swiss engraver of medals, was born at Geneva in 1677. The medals which he executed of many eminent persons in the age of Louis XIV. have been used as models by other artists. Died in 1763.

His son, JACOB ANTHONY, born at Geneva in 1715, was also a skilful engraver, and was employed about 1740 in the London Mint as second engraver. He then removed to Saint Petersburg, where he worked for some time. He engraved medals of the most illustrious men of science, which are highly prized. Died in 1759.

Dassouci, då'soo'se', (CHARLES COYPEAU,) a French burlesque poet and musician, born in Paris about 1604 ; died after 1675.

Dat'a-mēs, [Gr. Δατάμης ; Fr. DATAME, då'tåm',] a Persian general, distinguished for his military talents, revolted against Artaxerxes Mnemon, and was killed about 362 B.C.

See CORNELIUS NEPOS, "Lives of Eminent Commanders."

Dathe, då'teh, [Lat. DA'THIUS,] (JOHANN AUGUST,) an able German Orientalist and theologian, born at Weissenfels, Saxony, in 1731, obtained the chair of Oriental languages at Leipsic in 1762. His capital work is a Latin version of the Old Testament, (published in separate parts from 1773 to 1789,) which is commended for fidelity and for elegance of style. Died in 1791.

See AUGUST W. ERNESTI, "Elogium J. A. Dathii," 1792.

Datheen, då-tän', [Lat. DATHE'NUS,] (PETER,) a Dutch poet, born at Ypres, became a Protestant minister at Frankfort in 1555, and returned to the Low Countries about 1566. He acquired great celebrity as a preacher, and composed a Dutch poetical version of the Psalms, which was used in the churches of Holland for about two centuries. In consequence of his seditious speeches against the Prince of Orange, he exiled himself, took the name of P. Montanus, and practised medicine with success at Stade and Elbing from 1585 until his death in 1590.

See MOTLEY, "Rise of the Dutch Republic," vol. i. ; DE VRIES, "Histoire de la Poésie Hollandaise."

Dati, då'tee, (AGOSTINO,) an eminent Italian orator and writer, was born at Sienna in 1420. He opened a school of rhetoric in that city, and was often chosen to make public orations in Latin by his fellow-citizens, who also raised him to high offices in the republic. He wrote, in Latin, a "History of Sienna," and other works, historical and religious, among which is a "Treatise on the Immortality of the Soul." Died in 1478.

See N. BANDIERA, "De Augustino Datho," Rome, 1733 ; NICÉRON, "Mémoires ;" MORÉRI, "Dictionnaire Historique."

Dati, (CARLO ROBERTO,) usually called simply CARLO DATI, an eminent Italian scholar, born at Florence in 1619, was a descendant of Goro Dati. He studied geometry under Galileo. In 1638 he formed an intimate friendship with Milton, who visited Florence in that year, and who has commemorated their friendship in Latin epistles. Dati was one of the most learned of Italian philologists. He was appointed professor of Greek and Latin literature at Florence in 1648. He published, besides other works, a "Discourse on the Necessity of Speaking one's own Language correctly," (1657,) and "The Lives of Ancient Painters," ("Vite de' Pittori antichi," 1 vol., 1667,) "which," says Ginguené, "is one of the best works on ancient painting." Died in 1676.

See G. NEGRI, "Istoria degli Scrittori Fiorentini ;" NICÉRON, "Mémoires ;" "Nouvelle Biographie Générale ;" F. FONTANI, "Elogio di C. R. Dati," 1794.

Dati, (GIULIANO,) an Italian writer, born at Florence in 1445 ; died in 1524.

Dati, (GIULIO,) an Italian poet, born at Florence about 1560, wrote "La Contessa di Parione," (1596.) Died about 1630.

Dati, (GORO DI STAGGIO,) a noble Florentine, born in 1363, was one of the priors of the republic in 1425, and gonfalonier in 1428. He wrote, in Latin, a "History of Visconti, First Duke of Milan," which was not printed until 1735. Died in 1436.

Dati, (LEONARDO,) an Italian ecclesiastic of high reputation, brother of the preceding, was born at Florence about 1360. He was employed by the republic of Florence as ambassador to various courts between 1409 and 1422. Died in 1425.

Dä'tis, [Gr. Δᾶτις,] a Persian general, who, in conjunction with Artaphernes, commanded the army which was defeated at Marathon, 490 B.C.

D'Attaignant. See ATTAIGNANT.

Daub, dowp, (KARL,) a German theologian, born at Cassel in 1765, became professor of theology at Heidelberg about 1795. He published volumes of lectures entitled "Daub's Vorlesungen," (1838,) "Prolegomena to Moral Theology and the Principles of Ethics," (1839,) and "The System of Christian Dogmatics," (1841,) and other works. Died in 1836.

See ROSENKRANZ, "Erinnerungen an C. Daub," 1837

Daubanton, do'bôn'tôn', (ANTOINE GRÉGOIRE,) a French judge and jurist, born in Paris in 1752, wrote a "Dictionary of the Civil Law," a "Dictionary of the Commercial Code," and other legal works. Died in 1813.

Daubasse, do'båss', (ARMAND,) a French poet, born in Quercy in 1664. His works were all improvised. Died in 1727.

Daubenton, do'bôn'tôn', (GUILLAUME,) a French Jesuit, born at Auxerre in 1648. About 1700 Louis XIV. appointed him confessor to his grandson, Philip V. of Spain, over whom he acquired a great influence. According to Voltaire, Daubenton revealed, in a letter to the French regent, the secret of Philip's intended abdication, and the regent sent the letter to Philip. The latter then showed it to his confessor, who fainted, and soon after expired, in 1723.

See VOLTAIRE, "Siècle de Louis XV."

Daubenton, (LOUIS JEAN MARIE,) a celebrated French naturalist, born at Montbar on the 29th of May, 1716, was sent to Paris by his father to study theology; but he preferred medicine. Having graduated as M.D. in 1741, he returned home with the intention to practise. Buffon, who was also a native of Montbar, and his former schoolmate, having been chosen intendant of the Jardin du Roi at Paris, (now Jardin des Plantes,) engaged Daubenton in 1742 to assist him in his projected scientific works. By his sound judgment, invincible patience, and unerring accuracy, he was admirably qualified for such a task. In 1745 he was appointed curator and demonstrator of the cabinet of natural history. He enriched Buffon's "Natural History" with an immense number of facts and descriptions, cautiously avoiding the bold hypotheses to which Buffon was rather prone. In 1778 he obtained a chair of natural history in the College of France. He wrote many articles on that science for the first "Encyclopédie," and for the "Memoirs of the Academy of Sciences." He made great improvements in the cabinet of natural history, of which he had charge fifty years. About 1794 the Jardin du Roi was converted into a school, styled the Museum of Natural History, in which he was appointed professor of mineralogy. He merited public favour by promoting the propagation of Spanish sheep, and wrote several popular treatises on the subject, one of which is entitled "Instruction for Shepherds." In 1799 he was elected a senator. He died January 1, 1800.

See CUVIER, "Notice sur la Vie et les Ouvrages de Daubenton," in the "Mémoires de l'Institut," tome iii. ; LACÉPÈDE, "Éloge historique de Daubenton," 1790 ; "Nouvelle Biographie Générale."

Daubenton, (MARGUERITE,) cousin and wife of the preceding, born at Montbar in 1720, was married in 1749. Her romance of "Zélie in the Desert" is written in a natural style, and was received with favour. Madame Buffon was her niece. Died in 1818.

Daubeny, dŏb'ne or dawb'ne, (CHARLES,) D.D., an English divine, born in 1744, became prebendary of Salisbury in 1784, and Archdeacon of Sarum in 1804. He published a "Guide to the Church," and other works on theology. Died in 1827.

Daubeny, (CHARLES GILES BRIDLE,) an English chemist and naturalist, born at Stratton in 1795, was for many years professor of botany and rural economy in the University of Oxford. In 1824 he published an "Essay on the Geology and Chemical Phenomena of Volcanoes." He wrote an important work called "Description of the Active and Extinct Volcanoes, with Remarks on their Origin," (1826,) treatises on the Geology of North America and Italy, and several memoirs on chemistry. He was president of the British Association in 1856. Died in December, 1867.

D'Aubigné, dŏ'bĕn'yȧ', (JEAN HENRI MERLE,) a Swiss divine and popular historian, was born at or near Geneva in 1794. His father, Louis Merle, was descended from the French Calvinist family of D'Aubigné. He was educated for the church, and was pastor of a French church in Hamburg for five years. Between 1823 and 1830 he preached at Brussels. About 1830 he became professor of Church history in a college at Geneva. He published in 1835 the first volume of his capital work, a "History of the Reformation in the Sixteenth Century," (" Histoire de la Réformation au seizième Siècle,") which obtained a great popularity, especially in England and the United States. Among his other works are "The Protector, (Cromwell,) a Vindication," (1848,) and "Germany, England, and Scotland," (1848.)

See HAAG, "La France protestante ;" CHARLES DE RÉMUSAT, "Mélanges de Littérature et Philosophique."

D'Aubigné, (THÉODORE AGRIPPA.) See AUBIGNÉ, D'.

Daubigny, dŏ'bĕn'ye',(CHARLES FRANÇOIS,) a French landscape-painter, born in Paris in 1817. He has produced many pictures of French scenery, some of which have been purchased by the emperor and the ministers

of state. Among his works are a "View of the Seine at Charenton," and a "Sunset," (1851.)

Daubigny, (PIERRE,) a French painter in miniature, an uncle of the preceding, was born in Paris in 1793.

Daubrée, dŏ'brȧ', (GABRIEL AUGUSTE,) a French geologist, born at Metz in 1814.

Daubus, dŏ'büs', written also **Daubuz,** (CHARLES,) a French Protestant, born at Auxerre, lived about 1625, and was for a long time minister at Nérac. He published "L'Échelle de Jacob," ("Jacob's Ladder," 1626,) and "Bellarmin reformé," ("Bellarmin Reformed," 1631.)

Daubuz. See DAUBUS.

Daubuz, dŏ'büz', (CHARLES,) a French Protestant divine, born about 1670, removed to England on the revocation of the edict of Nantes, (1685,) and became vicar of Brotherton. He was author of a "Commentary on Revelation," (1712,) which is much esteemed. Died about 1740.

Daucourt, dŏ'koor', (BONAVENTURE,) a French geologist, who lived about 1630, and wrote a treatise on volcanoes, deluges, etc.

Daude, dŏw'dĕh, (ADRIAN,) a German historian, born in Franconia, wrote a "Universal History," (4 vols., 1748–58.) Died in 1755.

Daudé, dŏ'dȧ', (PIERRE,) a French Protestant minister and writer, born in 1681 ; died in England in 1754.

Daudet, dŏ'dȧ', (ROBERT,) a French engraver, born at Lyons in 1737; died in 1824.

Daudiguier. See AUDIGUIER, D'.

Daudin, dŏ'dăN', (FRANÇOIS MARIE,) a French naturalist, born in Paris about 1774, was in childhood afflicted with an infirmity which almost entirely deprived him of the use of his legs. His wife assisted him in the composition of his works, for which she designed the figures. His principal works are a "Treatise on Ornithology," (1800,) which was never finished, and a "Natural History of Reptiles," (1802.) The latter, according to Cuvier, was the most complete work on that class of animals which had then appeared. Died in 1804.

Daugier, dŏ'zhe-ȧ', (FRANÇOIS HENRI EUGÈNE,) COUNT, a noted French admiral, born at Courtezon in 1764. He commanded one of the four grand corps of the flotilla destined for the invasion of England in 1804, and distinguished himself at the battle of Baylen in 1808. Died in 1834.

Daullé, dŏ'lȧ', (JEAN,) a skilful French engraver with the burin, born at Abbeville about 1705. He removed to Paris, and engraved portraits and history with a high reputation. Among his master-pieces are a portrait of the Countess of Feuquières, and a "Magdalene," after Correggio. Died in 1763.

Daum, dŏwm, [Lat. DAU'MIUS,] (CHRISTIAN,) an eminent German teacher, born at Zwickau, Saxony, in 1612. He became regent of the College of Zwickau in 1642, and rector of the same in 1662. He published editions of several Latin authors, and left, in manuscript, unfinished works, among which was a "History of the Poets." Died in 1687.

See WINTER, "C. Daumii Poetæ clarissimi," etc., 1688 ; LOESCHER, "Memoria C. Daumii renovata," 1701 ; NICÉRON, "Mémoires."

D'Aumale. See AUMALE, D'.

Daumas, dŏ'mȧs', (MELCHIOR JOSEPH EUGÈNE,) a French general and writer, born in 1803. He went to Algeria in 1835, and learned the Arabic language. About 1841 he was placed by General Bugeaud at the head of the political affairs (affaires indigènes) of Algeria, which he managed with credit. He published an "Exposé of the Actual State of Arab Society and Government,"(1845,) "Manners and Customs of Algeria," and other works of merit. In 1850 he was chosen director of affairs of Algeria in the ministry of war. He obtained the rank of general of division in 1853.

Daumat. See DOMAT.

Daumer, dŏw'mer, (GEORG FRIEDRICH,) a German pantheist, born at Nuremberg in 1800. He was professor at Nuremberg a few years between 1822 and 1830. He published a "System of Speculative Philosophy," (1831,) "Philosophy, Religion, and Antiquity," (1833,) translations from the Persian poet Háfiz, (1846,) and other works. His system resembles the pantheism of Hegel.

ā, ē, ī, ō, ū, ȳ, *long;* ă, ĕ, ŏ, same, less prolonged; ă, ĕ, ĭ, ŏ, ŭ, ȳ, *short;* a̤, e̤, i̤, o̤, *obscure;* fär, fâll, fät; mĕt; nŏt; gōōd; mōōn;

Daumesnil, dō'mȧ'nĕl', (PIERRE,) a brave French general, born at Périgueux in 1777, served in Italy and Egypt from 1795 to 1800, and became chef d'escadron about 1806. He lost a leg at Wagram in 1809. In 1812 he was made general of brigade and governor of Vincennes castle, which he defended obstinately against the allies in 1814 and 1815. He obtained the rank of lieutenant-general in 1831. Died in 1832.

See "Vie du Général Daumesnil," Paris, 1832.

Daumont. See AUMONT, D'.

Daun, von, fon dŏwn, (LEOPOLD JOSEPH MARIA,) COUNT, an able Austrian general, born at Vienna in 1705. He made his first campaign against the Turks. About 1748 he obtained the rank of field-marshal. He commanded at the battle of Kolin, June 18, 1757, where Frederick the Great was defeated with great loss. In the same year the Austrians, under Charles of Lorraine and Daun, lost a great battle at Leuthen. Having surprised the Prussian king at Hochkirchen, (1758,) Daun gained a victory, for which he was rewarded with 300,000 florins, a sword from the pope, and many honours. He was defeated in turn by Frederick at Torgau in 1761. After the peace of 1763 he became president of the Aulic Council, and enjoyed great favour at court until his death in 1766.

See ARCHENHOLZ, "History of the Seven Years' War," 1793; "Memoirs of Count Von Daun," by A. HENDERSON, London, 1757.

Daunou, dō'noo', (PIERRE CLAUDE FRANÇOIS,) a meritorious French statesman and author, born at Boulogne in 1761, entered the order of Oratorians. In 1792 he was elected to the National Convention, in which he supported moderate measures, opposed the proscription of the Girondists, and was one of the framers of the constitution of the year III., (1795.) He was the first president of the Council of Five Hundred, and a member of the committee appointed to frame the constitution of the year VIII., (1800.) In 1807 he was chosen keeper of the archives of France. He was chief editor of the "Journal des Savants" from 1816 to 1838, and about 1818 obtained a chair of history in the College of France. He contributed many articles to the "Biographie Universelle." In 1838 he was chosen perpetual secretary of the Academy of Inscriptions, and in 1839 was created a peer. Among his numerous useful works are an "Essay on the Temporal Power of the Pope," (1810,) and a "Course of Historical Studies," in 20 vols., the first of which was published in 1842. Died in 1840. "He was so simple, so modest, so firm and consistent," says Villenave, "that envy was compelled to pause, and criticism reduced to silence, before the renown of his talents and his virtues."

See A. H. TAILLANDIER, "Documents biographiques sur Daunou," 1841; VICTOR LECLERC, "Notice sur Daunou;" SAINTE-BEUVE, "Portraits contemporains;" "Nouvelle Biographie Générale;" WALCKENAER, "Notice sur la Vie, etc. de M. Daunou," 1841.

Daunt or **Daunte.** See DANTE.

Dauphin, dō'fǎN', (AUGUSTIN ANNE,) a mediocre French poet, born at Niort about 1759; died in 1822.

Daurat. See DORAT.

Dausque, dōsk, (CLAUDE,) a learned French Jesuit, born at Saint-Omer in 1566; died in 1644.

Dauvergne. See AUVERGNE, D'.

Dauvigny. See AUVIGNY, D'.

Dauxiron. See AUXIRON, D'.

Dauz, dŏwts, (JOHANN ANDREAS,) a German Orientalist, born near Gotha in 1654, is known as the author of a system of Hebrew grammar. Died in 1727.

Dauzats, dō'zǎ', (ADRIEN,) a French painter and lithographer, born at Bordeaux in 1808. As a painter of genre, he obtained medals of the first class in 1835, 1848, and 1855.

Daval, dạ-vǎl', ? (PETER,) an English mathematician, was a Fellow of the Royal Society. Died in 1763.

Davanzati Bostichi, dä-vän-zä'tee bos-tee'kee,(BERNARDO,) an Italian writer and merchant, born at Florence in 1529. He cultivated literature with success, and filled several civil offices with credit. The perfection of the Tuscan language was his favourite pursuit. His most remarkable work is an Italian version of Tacitus, (1658,) which, says Ginguené, "is a master-piece of purity of style, of vigour, precision, and elegance." It is said to

be more concise than the original. He also wrote a treatise on "The Tuscan Cultivation of the Vine and other Trees," (1600.) Died in 1606.

See G. NEGRI, "Istoria degli Scrittori Fiorentini ;" TIRABOSCHI, "Storia della Letteratura Italiana."

Dav'en-ạnt, (CHARLES,) LL.D., an English writer on finance and political economy, a son of Sir William Davenant, was born in 1656. In 1685 he was returned to Parliament, and appointed inspector of plays. In 1695 he gained reputation by his "Essays on the Ways and Means of Supplying the War," which was followed by several treatises on the revenues, trades, etc., the merit of which was variously estimated. In 1703 he was appointed inspector-general of exports and imports. Died in 1714.

See MACAULAY, "History of England," vol. i. chap. iii. ; "Biographia Britannica."

Davenant, (JOHN,) an English prelate, born in London in 1576. In 1618 James I. sent him to attend the Synod of Dort, and in 1621 appointed him Bishop of Salisbury. He had previously been professor of divinity in Cambridge University. He published an excellent "Exposition of Paul's Epistles," (in Latin, 1627,) and several other works. Died in 1641.

Davenant, (Sir WILLIAM,) an English dramatic poet, born at Oxford in 1605. Having written "Albovine" and another tragedy, he was chosen poet-laureate in 1637 as successor to Ben Jonson. He was a royalist in the civil war, and was knighted by Charles I. in 1643. He was confined in the Tower about two years for political reasons, and owed his safety to Milton. His principal production is "Gondibert," an unfinished epic poem, which was much admired by Cowley, Waller, and others, but is now neglected. He was associated with Dryden in an alteration of Shakspeare's "Tempest." He died in 1668, and was buried in Westminster Abbey.

See SOUTHEY, "British Poets ;" CAMPBELL, "Specimens of the British Poets ;" "Retrospective Review," vol. ii., 1820.

Davenant, (WILLIAM,) a son of the preceding, translated La Mothe le Vayer's work on the Greek and Latin historians. He was drowned near Paris in 1681.

Dav'en-pōrt, (CHRISTOPHER,) an English Catholic friar, born at Coventry in 1598, assumed the name of Sancta Clara, and was chaplain to Queen Henrietta. He wrote several theological works. Died in 1680.

Davenport, (JOHN,) an English Puritan, born at Coventry in 1598, emigrated to Massachusetts in 1637. He was the first minister of New Haven, Connecticut, where he preached about thirty years, and had much influence in the civil affairs of the colony. Died in 1670.

Davenport, (RICHARD ALFRED,) an English editor and biographer, born about 1780, published, besides other works, a "Dictionary of Biography," (1 vol. 12mo, 1831.) Died about 1852.

Daverhoult, dä'ver-hŏwlt', [Fr. pron. dä'vĕR'hoo',] (JEAN ANTOINE,) a native of Holland, was a member of the French Legislative Assembly in 1791–92. He was one of the founders of the club of Feuillants. Died in 1792.

Dā'vid, [Heb. דוד or דויד; Gr. Δαβίδ or Δαυίδ; Arabic, Dâood or Dâûd, dä'ōōd',] a celebrated Hebrew poet, prophet, and king, a son of Jesse, was born at Bethlehem about 1090 B.C. He was a shepherd in his youth, and an excellent musician. About the age of twenty-two he entered the service of King Saul, whose morbid spirit he soothed by playing on the harp, and he was anointed by the prophet Samuel as king in the place of Saul. Soon after this event he killed, in single combat, Goliath, a Philistine giant, and married Michal, a daughter of Saul. The king, however, regarded him with jealous malignity, and made several attempts against his life. David, therefore, fled for safety to Achish, King of Gath, where he feigned insanity. After many perilous adventures, he ascended the throne about 1055 B.C. He reigned seven years at Hebron as King of Judah, and on the death of Saul's son was recognized as king by all the tribes of Israel. By victories over the Philistines, the Moabites, the Syrians, the Edomites, etc., he greatly extended the boundaries of his kingdom, which, under his rule, attained a high degree of prosperity and power. His reign was disturbed by a rebellion of his son Absalom, and by

e as k; ç as s; g̅ hard; g̅ as j; G, H, K, guttural; N, nasal; R, trilled; s̅ as z; th as in this. (☞ See Explanations, p. 23.)

conspiracies of other sons. He died about 1015, and was succeeded by his son Solomon. David was the author of many of the Psalms which bear his name, and which give proof of poetical genius of the highest order. Though not without human infirmities, by which he was more than once betrayed into great sins, he was, on the whole, distinguished for magnanimity and a tenderness of heart rare in one so constantly engaged in the pursuits of war. (See I. Samuel xxvi. 7–12, and I. Chronicles xi. 13, 14.)

See also I. Samuel, chap. xv. ; II. Samuel, *passim*; I. Chronicles, chaps. xi.–xxix. ; CHANDLER, "History of the Life of David," 1758; EWALD, "Geschichte des Volkes Israel;" DROSTE, "Leven van Koning David," 1716; HANSER, "Historia Davidis," 1780; DELANY, "Life and Reign of David, King of Israel," 3 vols., 1742.

Dā'vid, a Christian emperor of Abyssinia, born about 1500, succeeded his father Nahu in 1507. His realm was invaded and partly conquered about 1514 by the Turkish Sultan Selim I. David formed an alliance with Portugal about 1520. Died about 1540.

See "Nouvelle Biographie Générale."

Dā'vid III., a celebrated king of Georgia, was the son of George II., whom he succeeded in 1089. The Turks had subjected the greater part of Georgia, and even Teflis, the capital, was in their power. David raised an army, defeated the Turks, and recovered Teflis in 1121. Several battles were fought afterwards, in which the Georgians were victors. He died in 1124, and left the throne to his son, Demetrius II.

See SAINT-MARTIN, "Mémoires sur l'Arménie."

David, King of Eastern Armenia, began to reign about 980 A.D. He defeated the Sultan Togrul and other Mussulman chiefs. Died in 1046.

David, an Armenian philosopher. See DAVID OF NERKEN.

Dā'vid I., King of Scotland, sixth son of Malcolm III., succeeded his brother, Alexander I., in 1124. Before this event he had married Maud, the great-niece of William the Conqueror, and obtained Northumberland as her dowry. Having refused to acknowledge Stephen as King of England, and supported the claim of Matilda, who was his niece, he was involved in war with that prince. In 1137 David invaded England, and was defeated at Northallerton. He died in 1153, and was succeeded by his grandson, Malcolm IV.

See BURTON, "History of Scotland," vol. ii. chap. xiii.; BUCHANAN, "History of Scotland."

David II. or **David Bruce,** King of Scotland, was the son of Robert Bruce, and was a minor when his father died in 1329. In 1332 Edward Baliol invaded Scotland, defeated an army commanded by the regent Mar, and was crowned at Scone. David then took refuge in France. His subjects maintained the contest against Baliol and his English ally, and in 1342 he recovered the throne. In 1346 he invaded England, was defeated and taken prisoner, and did not obtain his liberty until 1357. Died in 1371, and was succeeded by his nephew, Robert Stuart, or Robert II.

See BURTON, "History of Scotland," vol. iii. chap. xxv.

David, dȁ'vēd', (CHARLES,) a French engraver, born in Paris about 1600; died about 1660.

His brother JÉRÔME was a skilful etcher with aquafortis.

David, dȁ'vid, (CHRISTIAN GEORG NATHAN,) a popular Danish journalist and statesman, born at Copenhagen in 1793. He wrote some successful works on political economy, became a leader of the Liberal party, and was a member of the Diet from 1848 to 1853.

See J. B. SCHICK, "Professor David und sein Vaterland," 1835.

David, (FÉLICIEN,) a French musical composer, born at Cadenet (Vaucluse) in 1810. He became in 1830 a pupil of Lesueur, Fétis, and Reber, in the Conservatoire of Paris. In 1831 he quitted the Conservatoire and joined the Saint-Simonians, by whom he was employed to set hymns to music. On the dispersion of that society he visited the Levant, where he collected popular melodies, etc., and returned to Paris in 1835. He produced "The Rebel Angel," "The Swallows," and other melodies, which failed to render him famous. His "ode-symphonie" called "The Desert," performed in 1844, first revealed to the public his superior talent, and procured for him a European reputation. In 1847 he produced "Chris-topher Columbus," an "ode-symphonie," which was very successful.

See SYLVAIN SAINT-ÉTIENNE, "Biographie de Félicien David;" "Nouvelle Biographie Générale."

David, dȁ'vit, (FERDINAND,) a German composer and violinist, born at Hamburg in 1810. He became concertmeister at Leipsic about 1836.

David, (FRANÇOIS ANNE,) a French engraver, born in Paris in 1741, was a pupil of Le Bas. In youth he became engraver of the cabinet of Monsieur, (Louis XVIII.) He published "The Antiquities of Herculaneum," and illustrated works on the history of England and other nations. Died in 1824.

David, dȁ'vēd' or dā'vid, (JACQUES LOUIS,) a celebrated French historical painter, born in Paris in 1748, was a pupil of Vien. Having obtained the grand prize of the Academy for his "Antiochus and Stratonice," in 1775, he went to Rome with Vien, and was affected to tears by the superiority of the classical antique style, and the conviction that he must begin anew the study of his art. When Vien saw his "Triumph of Paulus Æmilius," he exclaimed, "You are destined to ruin or regenerate the school." He returned to Paris in 1780, composed his "Belisarius," and was received as academician in the Royal Academy, with the title of painter to the king, in 1783. The next year he again visited Rome, where he produced the "Horatii," which was highly applauded and made a great sensation among the Parisians. He had become the chief of the French painters when the Revolution began. Elected to the Convention in 1792, he voted for the death of the king, and disgraced himself by complicity in the crimes of Robespierre. On the fall of this leader, (1794,) David was imprisoned several months. He was the chief manager of the great national festivals and spectacles of the republic. About 1795 he produced his "Rape of the Sabines," which is called his master-piece, and was sold for 60,000 francs. Napoleon patronized him, and appointed him his first painter. At the restoration he was exiled as a regicide, and lived in Brussels until his death, in 1825. He was a member of the Institute. He had a vivid imagination, an ardent and susceptible temperament, and was not devoid of magnanimity. As an artist he was deficient in colouring, but attained the highest rank by his design, which, in the opinion of his admirers, is inimitably beautiful and true.

See MIETTE DE VILLARS, "Mémoires de David Peintre," etc., 1850; COUPIN, "Essai sur Jacques Louis David," 1827; MIEL, "Notice sur J. L. David," 1834; DELÉCLUZE, "David et son École," 1855; NAGLER, "Allgemeines Künstler-Lexikon;" ANTOINE THOMÉ, "Vie de David," 1826.

David, (JEAN PIERRE,) a French surgeon, born at Gex in 1737. He obtained prizes for several treatises, one of which was "On the Mechanism of Respiration," (1766.) He shared the labours of the surgeon Lecat, who chose him as his successor. Died in 1784.

David, (MAXIME,) a French miniature-painter, born at Châlons-sur-Marne in 1798. He obtained a medal of the first class in 1841.

David, (PIERRE,) a French poet and diplomatist, born near Falaise in 1771. As consul at Smyrna, he saved the lives of many Greeks during an insurrection. Among his poems is "The Siege of Athens," (1827.) Died in 1846.

David, (PIERRE JEAN,) an eminent French sculptor, born at Angers in 1789. He went to Paris in 1808, and, having won the first prize (with a pension) in 1811, was enabled to pursue his studies in Rome. About 1824 he established his reputation by a statue of the Prince of Condé. He was elected to the Institute in 1826, and in 1831 was ordered by the government to adorn the Pantheon with sculptures. He preferred to exercise his talent on republican subjects and on persons who have been useful to society. Among his works are busts of Washington, La Fayette, Lamartine, Arago, Lamennais, and Goethe. He produced statues of Jefferson, (at New York,) Cuvier, Racine, and many others. He was a republican member of the Assembly in 1848. Died in 1856.

See GUSTAVE PLANCHE, "Portraits d'Artistes;" ADRIEN MAILLARD, "Étude sur la Vie et les Ouvrages de David d'Angers," 1839.

Dā'vid, SAINT, the patron of Wales, born in Cardiganshire about 490 A.D., founded several monasteries, for which he composed rules. He was the author of Homilies, and other works. Died in 544.

ā, ē, ī, ō, ū, ȳ, *long;* ȧ, ė, ȯ, same, less prolonged; ă, ĕ, ĭ, ŏ, ŭ, y̆, *short;* ą, ę, į, ǫ, *obscure;* fär, fȧll, fȧt; mēt; nŏt; gŏŏd; mōōn;

Dā'vid ap Gwil'lum, a famous Welsh bard of the fourteenth century, is said to have courted the favour of the fair Morvid in one hundred and forty-seven poems. Notwithstanding these demonstrations, or perhaps in consequence of them, she married another.

David Bruce. See DAVID II.

Dā'vid Com-ne'nus, the last emperor of Trebizond, usurped the throne at the death of his brother John. When his capital was attacked by Mahomet II. in 1461, he surrendered on condition that this Sultan should marry his daughter Anna. David and his sons were reduced to choose between death and the Moslem religion, and preferred the former, in 1462.

Dā'vid de Po'mis, a Jewish rabbi and physician, born at Spoleto, in Italy, in 1525. He produced a Hebrew Lexicon, (1587.) Died about 1600.

David de Saint-George, dȧ'vĕd' deh sȧN'zhoRzh', (JEAN JOSEPH ALEXIS,) a French philologist, born in Franche-Comté in 1759. He produced a version of Ossian. Died in 1809.

Dā'vid-George, a noted fanatic and impostor, born at Delft about 1500, had some natural eloquence and cunning. After associating with the Anabaptists, he formed a new sect, called Davidists, and, according to some accounts, professed that he was the Messiah. To escape persecution, he fled about 1542 to Bâle, where he lived in disguise eleven years. In 1553 he endeavoured to save Servetus, and wrote in favour of toleration. He published a "Wonderbook," and other works. Mosheim thinks he had more virtue than his opponents give him credit for. Died in 1556.

David of Nerken, an eminent Armenian philosopher of the Platonist school, lived about 460–490 A.D. He studied at Athens under Syrianus, the master of Proclus, and wrote a number of works, among which is "The Foundations of Philosophy." He is said to have translated into Armenian the works of Plato and Aristotle.

See FR. NEUMANN, "Mémoire sur la Vie de David," 1829.

David Rubeni, dā'vid roo-bā'nee, a Jewish fanatic, lived towards the end of the fifteenth century, and predicted that the Messiah would come in 1500. He pretended that he had a mission to conduct the Jews of Europe to Palestine.

Davide, dā've-dȧ,(LUIGI ANTONIO,)an Italian painter, born at Lugano in 1648; died about 1730.

Dav'ĭ-dis, (FRANZ,) a Socinian minister, born in Hungary about 1510; died in 1579.

Davidof, Davydow, or **Davuidof,** dȧv-wee'dof, (DENIS VASILIEVITCH,) a Russian general and poet, born at Moscow in 1784; died in 1839.

Dā'vids, (ARTHUR LUMLEY,) an English Orientalist, born in Hampshire in 1811. He published a Turkish Grammar, (1832.) Died in 1832.

Dā'vid-son, (JOHN,) an English traveller, born in London. He was killed in Northern Africa by some natives in 1836.

Da'vid-son, (JOHN W.,) an American general, born in Fairfax county, Virginia, about 1824. He graduated at West Point in 1845, became a captain in 1855, and a brigadier-general of Union volunteers early in 1862. He served in Missouri and Arkansas in 1862 and 1863.

Davidson, (LUCRETIA MARIA,) an American poetess, born at Plattsburg, New York, in 1808. She wrote verses before she was six years old, and composed with great facility. It is stated that she wrote two hundred and seventy-eight poems, besides many which were destroyed. Died in August, 1825. A collection of her poems was published, with a Memoir by S. F. B. Morse, in 1829.

See a "Life of L. M. Davidson," by CATHERINE SEDGWICK, 1843, and a review of her poems, by ROBERT SOUTHEY, in the "London Quarterly Review" for 1829, vol. xli.; DUYCKINCK, "Cyclopædia of American Literature."

Davidson, (MARGARET MILLER,) a sister of the preceding, born in 1823, was also a poetess, and a child of equal precocity. Her poems were praised by Washington Irving, who wrote a biography of her about 1843. She is said to have been "angelic" in her disposition. Died in 1838.

See GRISWOLD'S "Female Poets of America;" DUYCKINCK, "Cyclopædia of American Literature."

Dā'vid-son, (Rev. SAMUEL,) an Irish dissenter and biblical critic, born at Ballymena about 1808. He pub-lished, besides other works, "Sacred Hermeneutics Developed," (1843,) and "Biblical Criticism," (2 vols., 1852.)

See "London Quarterly Review" for April, 1863; "Westminster Review" for July, 1862.

Davidson, (WILLIAM,) an American general, born in Pennsylvania in 1746. He was killed in battle at Cowan's Ford, in North Carolina, in 1781.

Dā'vie, (WILLIAM RICHARDSON,) born in England in 1756, came to America about 1762. He served as colonel under Generals Greene and Sumter in the Revolutionary war, was a member of the convention which formed the Federal Constitution in 1787, and was chosen Governor of North Carolina in 1799. He was sent as envoy to France in 1799 or 1800. Died in 1820.

See SPARKS, "American Biography," vol. xv., Second Series; "National Portrait-Gallery of Distinguished Americans," vol. iii.

Daviel, dȧ've'ĕl', (JACQUES,) a skilful French oculist, born in Normandy in 1696. He settled in Paris in 1746, and received the title of oculist to the king in 1749. He invented a method to cure cataract by extraction, which was successful. Died in 1762.

Davies, dā'vĕz, (CHARLES,) an American mathematician, born in Litchfield county, Connecticut, in 1798. He became professor of mathematics at West Point about 1824. He published "Elementary Algebra," (1839,) "Elementary Geometry and Trigonometry," (1840,) "Practical Mathematics," (1852,) and other works, which have been extensively used as text-books in colleges and academies. Having resigned his chair at West Point, about 1837, he visited Europe, and subsequently was appointed a professor in Columbia College, New York.

Dā'vieš, (EDWARD,) a Welsh divine, born in 1756, was rector of Bishopston and chancellor of Brecon. He wrote, besides other works, "Celtic Researches, or the Origin, Traditions, and Language of the Ancient Britons," (1804,) and a treatise on Druidism, which is commended. Died in 1831.

Dā'vieš, (Lady ELEANOR,) born in 1603, was the daughter of the Earl of Castlehaven, and wife of Sir John Davies. She gained notoriety as a prophetess, and published some strange predictions in 1649. Died in 1652.

Davies, (JOHN,) a learned Welsh divine, who graduated at Oxford in 1593, and became a canon of Saint Asaph's. He was well versed in the antiquities of his nation, and published a work on "Ancient British Languages." Died in 1644.

Davies, (JOHN,) a Welsh writer, born in 1625, translated several works from the French. Died in 1693.

Davies, (JOHN,) D.D., an English philologist, born in London in 1679, was appointed prebendary of Ely in 1711. He edited the works of Cicero, Cæsar, and other Latin authors. Died in 1732.

Davies, (Sir JOHN,) an eminent English poet and judge, born in Wiltshire in 1570, graduated at Oxford. In 1599 he acquired reputation by his poem entitled "Nosce Teipsum," ("Know Thyself.") In 1603 he was appointed solicitor-general of Ireland, and soon after attorney-general. He was knighted in 1607. In 1612 he published an excellent work on the political state of Ireland. He was returned to the English Parliament in 1621, and obtained the dignity of lord chief justice in 1626, but died suddenly the same year. In reference to the poem above noticed, Hallam remarks, "Perhaps no language can produce a poem, extending to so great a length, of more condensation of thought, or in which fewer languid verses will be found."

See JOHNSON, "Lives of the English Poets;" G. CHALMERS, "Life of Davies;" FOSS, "The Judges of England;" "Biographia Britannica;" "Retrospective Review," vol. v., 1822.

Davies, (MYLES,) a Welsh writer or compiler, lived about 1715. He published "Athenæ Britannicæ," (3 vols., 1716.)

Davies, (ROBERT,) a Welsh poet, born in 1770, was the author of a good Welsh grammar, and of some admired poems. Died in 1836.

Davies, (SAMUEL,) D.D., an American divine and distinguished pulpit orator, born at New Castle, Delaware, in 1724. He was instrumental in founding the College of New Jersey, and in 1758 succeeded Jonathan Edwards as president of that institution. Died in 1761, leaving several volumes of sermons, which have passed through many editions, both in America and England.

Davies, (SNEYD,) Archdeacon of Derby, an English poet, wrote some imitations of Horace in Duncombe's edition, (1767,) and poems in Dodsley's collection. Died in 1769.

Davies, (THOMAS,) an English actor and bookseller, born about 1712. He made his *début* on the stage about 1736, and soon after opened a bookstore in London, where he acquired the friendship of Dr. Johnson. Returning again to the stage, he married Miss Yarrow, a beautiful actress. The satire of Churchill in the "Rosciad" induced him to quit the theatre and resume the book-trade. He wrote a "Life of Garrick," (1780,) which procured for him both fortune and reputation, and was author of several other biographies. Died in 1785. Johnson and Boswell met for the first time in his house.
See BOSWELL's "Life of Johnson."

Davies, (THOMAS ALFRED,) born in Saint Lawrence county, New York, in 1809, served in the campaigns of 1861, and was made brigadier-general of volunteers in 1862.

Davies, (Rev. WALTER,) a British author, born in 1761, wrote an esteemed treatise on the "Agriculture and Domestic Economy of Wales," (1811,) and other works. Died about 1848.

Daviess, dā'vis, (JOSEPH HAMILTON,) U. S. attorney for Kentucky, volunteered in an expedition against the Indians in 1811, and was killed at the battle of Tippecanoe, November 7 of that year. His wife was a sister of Chief-Justice Marshall.

Davila. See AVILA.

Davila, dä've-lä, (FRANCISCO,) a Spanish theologian, born at Avila, was a Dominican. Died in 1604.

Davila, dä've-lä, (ENRICO CATERINO,) a celebrated Italian historian, born at Sacco, near Padua, in 1576, was the son of Antonio Davila, who, like several of his ancestors, had been Constable of Cyprus. About the age of seven he was taken to Paris, where he was educated, and became a page at the French court. From 1594 to 1598 he served with distinction in the army of Henry IV., and collected materials for his history. In 1599 he returned to Padua. About 1606 he engaged in the service of the Venetian senate, and commanded several military expeditions with success. In 1630 he produced his "History of the Civil Wars of France from 1559 to 1598," ("Historia delle Guerre civili," etc.,) which is unanimously regarded as authentic, and generally impartial, excepting his favouritism towards Catherine de Médicis, to whom his family was indebted. His style is graphic, spirited, and concise, and free from the prevalent defects of his time. The narration is remarkably varied and picturesque. In 1631 Davila was appointed governor of Crema. As he was performing the journey thither, he was involved in a dispute with an insolent official, who refused to furnish accommodations that Davila had a right to demand. Davila was shot dead by this person, who was instantly killed by the son of the historian.
See "Life of Davila," prefixed to an edition of his works published by APOSTOLO ZENO, Venice, 1733; GINGUENÉ, "Histoire Littéraire d'Italie;" TIRABOSCHI, "Storia della Letteratura Italiana."

Davila, (Don PEDRO FRANCO,) a Spanish naturalist, born at Guayaquil, removed about 1748 to Paris, where he formed an extensive cabinet. In 1767 he sold this for 800,000 reals, and in 1769 went to Madrid, and was chosen perpetual director of the cabinet of natural history, which he made one of the richest in Europe. Died in 1785.

Davila y Padilla, dä've-lä e pä-Dèl'yä, (AUGUSTIN,) a Spanish or Mexican monk, became Bishop of Saint Domingo. He wrote a "History of the Province of Santiago de Mexico," (1596.) Died in 1604.

Davin, dä'vǎN', (FÉLIX,) a French novelist, born at Saint-Quentin in 1807; died in 1836.

Da Vinci. See VINCI.

Davini, dä-vee'nee, (GIOVANNI BATTISTA,) an Italian physician, born at Camporgiano in 1562; died in 1633.

Dā'vis, (ANDREW JACKSON,) a clairvoyant and spiritualist, born in Orange county, New York, in 1826, published "Principles of Nature, her Divine Revelations," etc., (1845,) and several other works, including "The Great Harmonia," (in 4 vols.,) advocating the doctrines of Spiritualism.
See "The Magic Staff: an Autobiography of A. J. Davis;" "Fraser's Magazine" for February, 1848.

Davis, (CHARLES HENRY,) an American naval commander, born in Boston in 1807. He entered the navy in 1823, was appointed superintendent of the "Ephemeris" and "Nautical Almanac" about 1850, and gained the rank of commander in 1854. He served as chief of staff and captain of the fleet at the capture of Port Royal by Dupont in November, 1861. In May, 1862, he took command of the Mississippi flotilla. He gained a victory over the ram Louisiana and several gunboats on the 10th of May, and another near Memphis in June. He was raised to the rank of rear-admiral in February, 1863, and was appointed superintendent of the National Observatory in May, 1865. His services in relation to the "Nautical Almanac" are highly commended.

Dā'vis, (DAVID,) a skilful physician, born in South Wales about 1777, practised in London. He published "Elements of Obstetric Medicine," (new edition, 1842.) Died in 1842.

Dā'vis, (EDWARD,) an English buccaneer, was a companion of Dampier. He became the chief of a band of filibusters who plundered the Spanish colonies in Peru about 1684.

Davis, (EDWARD,) an English painter and engraver, born in Wales in 1640. His engraved portraits are highly praised.

Davis, (EDWIN HAMILTON,) M.D., an American physician and archæologist, for many years professor of materia medica and therapeutics in the New York Medical College, was born in Ross county, Ohio, in 1811. His principal work is his "Monuments of the Mississippi Valley," published by the Smithsonian Institution.

Davis, (HENRY,) D.D., an American divine and scholar, born at East Hampton, New York, in 1770. He graduated at Yale College in 1796, was appointed professor of Greek in Union College in 1806, and in 1809 was chosen president of Middlebury College, Vermont. He was president of Hamilton College, New York, from 1817 to 1833. Died in 1852.

Davis, (Rev. HENRY EDWARDS,) an English clergyman, born at Windsor in 1756, became a Fellow and tutor of Baliol College, Oxford. At the age of twenty-one he published an Examination of Gibbon's History, charging him with misrepresentation. Gibbon published a Vindication against this charge. Died in 1784.

Davis, (HENRY WINTER,) an eloquent American statesman, born at Annapolis, Maryland, about 1817, graduated at Hampden-Sidney College. He was elected a member of Congress for the third district of Maryland (*i.e.* a part of Baltimore) in 1854, and again in 1856. After the dissolution of the Whig party he joined the "American" party. He was re-elected to Congress in 1858. In the crisis of 1861 he gave proof of ardent loyalty to the Union, and became a radical Republican. He represented a part of Baltimore in the thirty-eighth Congress, (1863-65,) in which he served as chairman of the Committee on Foreign Affairs. In the summer of 1865 he made a public speech at Chicago in favour of negro suffrage. His intellect was keen, inventive, and capable of long-continued effort. Died in December, 1865.

Davis, (JEFFERSON,) an American statesman and military leader, born in Christian county, Kentucky, in 1808. He studied at Transylvania College, and subsequently at the Military Academy of West Point, where he graduated in 1828. He served in the Black Hawk war on the Northwest frontier, 1831–32, and in the campaigns against the Pawnees and other Indian tribes, 1833 to 1835. Having settled in Mississippi, he was elected to Congress by the Democratic party in 1845. On the breaking out of the Mexican war in 1846, he resigned his seat in Congress, and as colonel of a regiment of volunteers joined General Taylor on the Rio Grande. He took a prominent part in the engagements of Monterey and Buena Vista, and his conduct on the latter occasion was noticed in General Taylor's dispatch of March 6 in high terms of commendation. He was appointed to fill a vacancy in the United States Senate in 1847, and in 1848 elected to the same office for the remainder of the term. It is said that John Quincy Adams, on hearing Mr. Davis's first speech in the Senate, observed to his friends, "That young man, gentlemen, is no ordinary man : he will make his mark yet." While in the Senate he was one of the most prominent among the advocates of slavery and State rights. As Democratic candidate for Governor of Mississippi in 1851 he was defeated by H. S. Foote, the Union candidate. He was secretary of war during Mr. Pierce's administration, from March, 1853, till March, 1857. At the latter date he again became a Senator of the United States. Having taken a prominent part in the secession movement in 1860–61, he resigned his seat in the Senate of the United States in February of the latter year, and was soon after elected President of the provisional government formed by the secessionists. In November, 1861, he was elected without opposition President (for six years) of the Confederate States, and was inaugurated February 22, 1862. There seems no reason to doubt that the Southern leaders made a wise selection in placing Davis at the head of their perilous, not to say wild and desperate, enterprise; and he appears to have done all that any man in his position could do to bring it to a successful issue. The war was at last terminated by the capture of Richmond by General Grant in April, 1865, after which event President Davis retreated southward. He was taken prisoner in Southern Georgia in May, 1865, was confined in Fortress Monroe two years, and was then released on bail. He was included in the general amnesty of December 25, 1868.

See E. A. Pollard, "Life of Jefferson Davis;" Livingston, "Portraits of Eminent Americans;" Dr. J. J. Craven, "Prison-Life of Jefferson Davis," 1866; "Life and Imprisonment of Jefferson Davis, with the Life and Military Career of Stonewall Jackson," New York, 1866; "Life of Jefferson Davis," by F. H. Alfriend, 1868.

Davis, (Jefferson C.,) an American general, born in Clarke county, Indiana, in 1828. He served in the Mexican war, 1846–47. He was one of the garrison of Fort Sumter when it was bombarded by the rebels in April, 1861. He served at Pea Ridge, March, 1862, and commanded a division at the battle of Stone River, December 31, 1862–January 2, 1863, and at the battle of Chickamauga, September 19 and 20, 1863. He led a corps of the army of Sherman in the march from Atlanta to the sea, in December, 1864.

Davis, (John.) See Davies, (John.)

Davis, (John,) an eminent English navigator, born at Sandridge, in Devonshire. Between 1585 and 1587 he made three voyages for the discovery of a Northwest passage, in which he discovered the strait that bears his name, and advanced as far as the 72d degree of north latitude. In 1591 he served as captain in Cavendish's expedition to the South Sea, and afterwards made five voyages to the East Indies. He was killed by the Japanese in 1605. He had published an account of his Northwestern discoveries, and a work entitled "The World's Hydrographical Description," 1595.

See Hakluyt, "Navigations;" A. Saint John, "Lives of Celebrated Travellers;" J. Barrow, "Memoirs of the Naval Worthies of Queen Elizabeth's Reign," 1845.

Davis, (John,) an American jurist, born at Plymouth, Massachusetts, in 1761, graduated at Harvard in 1781. He was appointed comptroller of the treasury of the United States in 1795, and in 1801 a judge of the district court, which office he held for forty years. Died in 1847.

Davis, (John,) an American Senator, born in Northborough, Massachusetts, in 1787, graduated at Yale College. He was elected a member of Congress in 1824, and re-elected several times. In 1834 he was chosen Governor of Massachusetts. He represented his State in the United States Senate from 1835 to 1841. He acted with the Whig party, and was a prominent advocate of a protective tariff. He became Governor of Massachusetts again in 1841 or 1842. His reputation for integrity was such that he was commonly called "Honest John Davis." He was again elected a Senator of the United States about 1845. Died at Worcester in April, 1854.

Davis, (John A. G.,) professor of law in the University of Virginia, was born in Middlesex county, in that State, in 1801. He was educated at William and Mary College. He was the author of a "Guide to Justices of the Peace," and other legal works. Died in 1840.

Davis, (Sir John Francis,) an English officer and writer on China, was born in London in 1795. He was attached to Lord Amherst's embassy to China in 1816, and afterwards became chief superintendent at Canton. He is one of the few Europeans who have mastered the language and literature of China. On his return to England he published "The Chinese: a General Description of China and its Inhabitants," (1836, 2 vols.,) which is one of the best English works on that subject. He was governor of Hong-Kong from 1841 to 1847. In 1841 he produced "Sketches of China."

Davis, (Matthew L.,) an American writer, born in 1766, was an intimate friend of Aaron Burr. He wrote, besides other works, "Memoirs of the Life of Aaron Burr," (2 vols., 1836–37.) Died in 1850.

Da'vis, (Thomas,) an Irish poet and political writer, born at Mallow in 1814. He was a leader of the party called "Young Ireland," and in favour of a repeal of the Act of Union. Died in 1845.

Dā'vĭ-sǫn, (Francis,) an English poet, son of William, noticed below. He published in 1602 "The Poetical Rhapsody," which contains, besides his own verses, selections from the writings of contemporary poets.

Davison, (William,) an English statesman in the service of Queen Elizabeth. After having performed embassies to Holland and Scotland, he was appointed privy councillor, and one of the principal secretaries of state, about 1586. Hume says, "He was a man of parts, but easy to be imposed on, and who for that very reason had been made secretary." The queen ordered him privately to draw a warrant for the execution of Mary Stuart, which she signed. After the execution (1587) she disowned the act, and threw the odium on Davison, who was confined in the Tower a number of years.

See Sir N. H. Nicholas, "Life of William Davison," 1823; Motley, "History of the United Netherlands," vol. i. chap. iii.

Davout or **Davout,** dȧ'voo', (Louis Alexandre Edme François,) Baron, a French officer, brother of Marshal Davout, was born at Étivey (Yonne) in 1773. He served at the battles of Saint-Jean-d'Acre and of the Pyramids, and became aide-de-camp to his brother in 1800. For his services at Austerlitz, Jena, and Wagram he was made a baron in 1809, and general of brigade in 1811. Died in 1820.

See "Victoires et Conquêtes des Français."

Davout, more correctly **Davout,** pronounced alike dȧ'voo', (Louis Nicolas,) Duke of Auerstadt and Prince of Eckmühl, an able and successful French marshal, born near Noyers (Yonne) in 1770, was a fellow-student with Bonaparte at Brienne. In 1791 he became a colonel, or chef-de-bataillon, in the republican army, and in 1793 made a daring attempt to seize Dumouriez, the general-in-chief. In the same year he obtained the rank of general of brigade. He accompanied Bonaparte to Egypt in 1798, fought several battles under Desaix, and contributed to the victory of Aboukir, 1799. The next year he returned to France, and was promoted to the grade of general of division by Bonaparte, of whom he was an ardent admirer. He commanded the cavalry of the army of Italy in 1800. In 1804 he was made major-general of the imperial guard, and marshal of the empire. He led the right wing of the army at Austerlitz in 1805, where his services were very conspicuous, and defeated the Prussians at the great battle of Auerstadt, which was fought on the same day as that of Jena, October 14, 1806. "This last success," says Alison, "put the keystone to the arch of Marshal Davout's fame." He was created Prince of Eckmühl in 1809 for his success at the village of that name. After taking part in the Russian campaign, 1812, and being wounded at Borodino, he defended Hamburg against the allies for several months, and excited loud complaints by his extortions and severity to the inhabitants. He was Napoleon's minister of war during the Hundred Days, 1815, and after the battle of Waterloo was appointed by the provisional government general-in-chief of the French armies; but he retired from the command in the same year. In 1819 he was a member of the Chamber of Peers. Died in 1823.

See Chénier, "Vie du Maréchal Davout," 1866; "Davoust des Tyrannen, Leben und Thaten," Leipsic, 1815; Jourdan, "Éloge funèbre de M. le Maréchal Davoust," 1823; Thiers, "Histoire du Consulat et de l'Empire."

Davout. See Davoust.

D'Avrigny. See Avrigny.

Dā'vȳ, (Sir Humphry,) one of the most eminent chemists that Great Britain has produced, was born at Penzance, in Cornwall, December 17, 1778. His father was a carver of wood. Endowed by nature with an ardent and fertile imagination, he early manifested a decided taste for works of fiction, and especially for poetry. It is stated that when about eleven years old he commenced an epic poem, of which Diomede, the son of Tydeus, was the hero : whether the work was ever fully completed, we are not informed ; but enough, at least, was written to prove the soaring fancy and inexhaustible invention of the youthful poet. He appears subsequently to have limited his efforts to fugitive poetry, of which he has left some very respectable and interesting specimens. When he was sixteen (1795) he lost his father. Not long after, Gregory Watt, son of the celebrated James Watt, visiting the west of England for his health, became a lodger in the house of Mrs. Davy, the mother of Humphry. A warm friendship, the result of congenial tastes, sprang up between the young men, and appears to have had an important influence in directing the studies and determining the subsequent career of Davy. But the cause of science is especially indebted to Mr. Davies Gilbert for the early encouragement which he afforded to Davy, and afterwards for introducing him to the notice of the Royal Institution in London. In 1798 he became associated with Dr. Beddoes in the "Pneumatic Institution" which the latter had founded at Bristol. In the following year the young chemist gave to the world his first contributions to science,—viz., "Essays on Heat and Light, with a New Theory of Respiration," etc., (these essays forming part of a volume published by Dr. Beddoes.) His "Researches, Chemical and Philosophical, chiefly concerning Nitrous Oxide and its Respiration," appeared in 1800, and attracted great attention in the scientific world. He was not only the first to discover and make known the peculiar exhilarating or intoxicating properties of nitrous oxide gas, but his "Researches" contain also the results of a number of most interesting though hazardous experiments on the respiration of carburetted hydrogen, nitrogen, hydrogen, carbonic acid, and nitrous gases. In 1801 he gave his first lecture before the Royal Institution, (London,) in which he was the following year appointed professor. As a lecturer he was eminently successful. "His youth, his simplicity, his natural eloquence, his chemical knowledge, his happy illustrations and well-conducted experiments, excited universal attention and unbounded applause." (" Life of Sir Humphry Davy," by Dr. Paris, p. 90.) In his second Bakerian lecture before the Royal Society in 1807, he announced his great achievement,—the decomposition by galvanism of the fixed alkalies,—whereby he demonstrated that these alkalies are simply metallic oxides. Davy's account of this grand discovery has been justly pronounced the most important contribution made to the "Philosophical Transactions" (of the Royal Society) since the time of Sir Isaac Newton. It is to be regretted that one possessing such rare intellectual endowments should not have been proof against the intoxication of success. It is, however, too true that, after his sudden rise to distinction, Davy occasionally betrayed a spirit of arrogance, especially towards younger aspirants to fame, unworthy of a great man, and certainly not to have been expected in one who had himself owed so much to the generous patronage of men of science. In 1812, Davy was knighted ; and shortly afterwards he married Mrs. Apreece,—a widow who possessed, with many accomplishments, a considerable fortune. He was made in 1818 a baronet, in consideration of the great services which he had rendered his country and mankind,— among which one of the most important was his invention of the safety-lamp. In 1820 he was chosen president of the Royal Society, and for seven successive years was elected to the same office,—which, however, in 1827 he was compelled to resign on account of his health. He died at Geneva in May, 1829.

Our limits will permit us to mention only a very few of Davy's numerous and important publications. Among the principal are his " Elements of Chemical Philosophy" (1812) and his " Elements of Agricultural Chemistry," (1813 ;) to which may be added his papers relating to "Fire-Damp," etc., and those giving an account of his researches concerning "Oxymuriatic Acid" (chlorine) and "Fluoric Compounds." His "Consolations in Travel," published after his death, consists principally of speculations and reflections on religious subjects.

Davy has been styled by Dumas "the greatest chemical genius that ever appeared." He seems, indeed, to have possessed in the largest measure all the endowments requisite for a profound and successful investigator of nature. To an intellect in the highest degree penetrating and comprehensive, he joined an invention inexhaustible in resources, and an enthusiasm for science which no difficulties or discouragements could repress. "Davy," says Cuvier, "when not yet thirty-two years old, occupied, in the opinion of all those who could judge of such labours, the first rank among the chemists of this or any other age." A writer in the " Edinburgh Review" for April, 1836, observes that, "since the age of Sir Isaac Newton, the history of British science has recorded no discoveries of equal importance with those of Sir Humphry Davy."

See "Life of Sir Humphry Davy," by DR. J. A. PARIS," 1831; "Memoirs of the Life of Sir Humphry Davy," by his brother, DR. JOHN DAVY, 1836; J. AYRTON, "Life of Sir H. Davy," 2 vols., 1831; H. C. VAN DER BOON MESCH, "Redevoering over H. Davy," 1837; KIRÉEVSKY, "Histoire des Législateurs-chimistes: Lavoisier —Berthollet—H. Davy," 1845; "Edinburgh Review" for January, 1814, and April, 1836; "London Quarterly Review" for September, 1812.

Davy, (JOHN,) an English musician and composer, born near Exeter about 1770 ; died in 1824.

Davy, (JOHN,) M.D., an English chemist and physiologist, was a younger brother of Sir Humphry Davy. He served as surgeon in the army for many years in the East Indies, etc. In 1821 he published in London an excellent "Account of the Interior of Ceylon." He wrote numerous able works on various subjects, among which are "Researches, Physiological and Anatomical," (1839,) a "Life of Sir Humphry Davy," (1840,) "Notes and Observations on the Ionian Islands and Malta," (1842,) and "Lectures on the Study of Chemistry," etc., (1849.) Died in 1868.

Davydow or **Davuidof.** See DAVIDOF.

Dawe, dau, (GEORGE,) an eminent English portrait-painter, born about 1775, acquired a European reputation. The Royal Academy received him as associate about 1809, and as academician in 1814. In 1819 the emperor Alexander invited him to Saint Petersburg, where he passed ten years, with the title of first painter. He executed portraits of nearly all the sovereigns of Europe. His "Andromache" proves that he was also skilful as a historical painter. He wrote a "Life of George Morland." Charles Lamb, who was his friend, mentions him in his "Essays." Died in London in 1829.

Dawes, dauz, (HENRY L.,) a lawyer, born in Hampshire county, Massachusetts, in 1816. He represented a district of Massachusetts in Congress from 1857 to 1869, acting with the Republicans. He is also a member of the forty-first Congress, (1869-71.)

Dawes, dauz, (MANASSEH,) an English writer on law, morals, and political economy. Died in 1829.

Dawes, (RICHARD,) an English critic, eminent as a Greek scholar, born at Market Bosworth in 1708, became a Fellow of Emanuel College, Cambridge. From 1738 to 1749 he was master of a grammar-school in Newcastle. In 1745 he published " Miscellanea Critica," which was at one time a high authority. Porson thought it "second only to Bentley's 'Phalaris.'" Died in 1766.

Dawes, (RUFUS,) an American poet, born in Boston in 1803, studied law, but never practised it. In 1839 he published "Geraldine, Athenia of Damascus, and Miscellaneous Poems."

See GRISWOLD's " Poets and Poetry of America."

Dawes, (Sir WILLIAM,) an English prelate, born near Braintree, Essex, in 1671, was the son of Sir John Dawes, and was educated at Oxford. He was chaplain to William III. about 1698, and to Queen Anne some years later, and had great popularity as a preacher. He was appointed Bishop of Chester in 1707, and Archbishop of York in 1714. He wrote the "Anatomy of Atheism," a poem, and published several sermons. Died in 1724.

See "Biographia Britannica."

Dawison, dä've-son, ? (BOGUMIL,) a popular actor, born at Warsaw in 1818. In 1866 he came to the United States.

Daw'son, (GEORGE,) an English writer on law, published "The Origin of Laws," ("Origo Legum," 1694.) Died in 1700.

Daxenberger, dåk'sen-bĕrg'er, (SEBASTIAN FRANZ,) a German poet, born at Munich in 1809, assumed the name of KARL FERNAU.

Day, (JEREMIAH,) president of Yale College, was born in New Preston, Connecticut, in 1773. He graduated at Yale College in 1795, studied theology, and became in 1801 professor of mathematics and natural philosophy at that college. He succeeded Dr. Dwight as president in 1817, and continued to hold that position until 1846. He published, besides other works, "An Introduction to Algebra," (1814,) and "Navigation and Surveying," (1817,) which were highly esteemed. Died in 1867.

Day or **Daye,** (JOHN,) an English printer, born at Dunwich in 1522, established a printing-office in London in 1544. He perfected the Greek types, and was the first who printed with Saxon characters in England. By his editions of the Bible and other books he promoted the Reformation. Died in 1584.

See AMES and DIBDIN, "Typographical Antiquities of Great Britain."

Day or **Daye,** (JOHN,) son of the preceding, born in 1566, became a popular preacher, and published numerous sermons and lectures. Died in 1627.

Day, (JOHN,) an English poet and comedian, lived about 1600-20. Among his works is "The Isle of Guls," (1606.)

Day, (STEPHEN,) an English printer, born in 1611, removed to Massachusetts in 1638, and established at Cambridge the first printing-press in New England. Died in 1668.

Day, (THOMAS,) an English author and philanthropist, born in London in 1748, inherited an ample fortune. He studied law, but did not practise at the bar. In 1773 he attacked the slave-trade in a poem entitled "The Dying Negro." He expressed his sympathy with the American patriots by two poems, "The Devoted Legions," and "The Desolation of America," (1777.) The following may serve to illustrate his eccentric habits and peculiar opinions on education. He selected from a foundling-hospital two girls about twelve years old, with the intention of educating them rationally on the system of Rousseau and taking one of them as his wife. But the experiment did not succeed; and he married Miss Milnes in 1778. One of his protégées, however, did honour to his system of education, and became the wife of his friend Bicknell. His most popular work is "Sandford and Merton," (1783,) a juvenile tale, of which Leigh Hunt says, "The pool of mercenary and time-serving ethics was first blown over by the fresh country breeze of 'Sandford and Merton,' a production that I shall ever be grateful for." He wrote several other minor works. He was killed by a kick from a horse in 1789.

See "An Account of the Life and Writings of Thomas Day," by himself; "Biographia Britannica;" J. BLACKMAN, "Life of T. Day;" TIMAEUS, "T. Day's Leben," 1798.

Daye. See DAY.

Day'ton, (ELIAS,) an American officer, born in 1737, was a native of New Jersey. He fought in the American Revolution, obtained the rank of colonel in 1778, and afterwards became a general. Died in 1807.

Dayton, (JOHN,) born about 1760, was elected Governor of South Carolina in 1800, and again in 1808. He afterwards became judge of the United States district court of that State. He was author of "A View of South Carolina," "Memoirs of the Revolution," etc. Died in 1822.

Dayton, (JONATHAN,) an American statesman, born at Elizabethtown, in New Jersey, in 1760. He was a member of the convention which framed the Federal Constitution in 1787, and was elected to Congress by the Federalists of New Jersey in 1791. He was Speaker of the House of Representatives for two terms between 1793 and 1797, and was elected to the Senate of the United States in 1799. Died in 1824.

Dayton, (WILLIAM LEWIS,) an American statesman, born at Baskingridge, Somerset county, New Jersey, in 1807. He was liberally educated, studied law, and was admitted to the bar about 1830. He was appointed in 1842 a Senator of the United States by the Governor of New Jersey, to fill a vacancy. He also represented New Jersey in the national Senate for a full term of six years, (1845-51,) during which he acted with the Whig party and opposed the extension of slavery. He also disapproved of the Fugitive Slave bill. In 1851 he returned to the practice of law at Trenton. In 1856 he was nominated as Republican candidate for Vice-President by the convention which nominated J. C. Fremont for the Presidency. They received the votes of the New England States, and of New York, Ohio, Michigan, Wisconsin, and Iowa. In 1857 he became attorney-general of New Jersey. He was appointed minister to France in the spring of 1861. He died in Paris in December, 1864.

Dazille, då'zĕl' or då'ze'ye, (JEAN BARTHÉLEMY,) a French physician, became honorary physician to the king in Saint Domingo in 1776. He wrote a "Treatise on the Diseases of Warm Climates," and other valuable medical works. Died in Paris in 1812.

Dazzi, dåt'see, (ANDREA,) born in Florence about 1470, was professor of ancient literature in his native city, and wrote a number of Latin poems. Died in 1548.

Deageant, då'zhŏn', a French courtier and writer, born at Saint-Marcellan, was author of historical "Mémoires," printed in 1668. Died in 1639.

Deák, då åk', (FRANCIS,) a Hungarian orator and statesman, born at Kehida in 1803. He was elected to the Diet about 1830, and became a leader of the moderately liberal party. In 1848 he was appointed minister of justice; but he retired from that office when Kossuth obtained the ascendency in September, 1848. On the approach of General Windischgrätz in 1849, Deák was selected to negotiate with him. The important address or manifesto of the Diet in answer to the imperial rescript in the summer of 1861 was drawn by Deák. He is said to be the most popular man in Hungary.

Deane, deen, (JAMES,) M.D., an American physician and naturalist, and one of the first discoverers of the fossil footprints in the valley of the Connecticut, was born in Coleraine, Massachusetts, in 1801; died in 1858. He was author of numerous papers on fossil footprints and other scientific subjects.

Deane, (SILAS,) an American diplomatist, born at Groton, Connecticut. He was a member of Congress in 1774, and was sent to France as a political and financial agent in 1776. He deviated from his instructions, and by profuse promises induced so many French officers to enter the service of the United States, that Congress was dissatisfied with his conduct, and recalled him in 1777. Died in England in 1789.

Deani, då-å'nee, (MARCANTONIO,) a popular Italian preacher, commonly called "Padre Pacifico," born at Brescia in 1775; died in 1824.

See GAMBARA, "Elogio storico del P. Pacifico," 1825.

Dear'born, (HENRY,) an American general, born in Hampton, New Hampshire, in 1751. He served as captain at the battle of Bunker Hill, and as major at the capture of the army of Burgoyne in 1777. In 1781 he took part in the capture of the British army at Yorktown. He was secretary of war for eight years, (1801-09.) In the spring of 1813 he captured Yorktown, in Canada. He was sent as minister to Portugal in 1822, and returned in 1824. Died in 1829.

Dearing. See DERING, (EDWARD.)

Debacq, deh-båk', (CHARLES ALEXANDRE,) a French painter of history and portraits, was born in Paris in 1804. Among his works are "Mary Stuart departing from France," and "The Death of Molière." Died in 1850.

Debay, deh-bå', (AUGUSTE HYACINTHE,) a French painter and sculptor, born at Nantes in 1804. He gained the first prize for painting in 1823, since which he has won several medals of the first class. Among his paintings is "Lucretia in the Forum of Collatia," (1831.) As a sculptor he has produced an admired group called "The Primitive Cradle, or Eve and her Two Infants."

Debay, (JEAN BAPTISTE JOSEPH,) the father of the preceding, born at Malines in 1779, was a skilful sculptor. He worked at Nantes and Paris. Among his works are a group of the "Three Parcæ," (1828,) and a statue of Pericles, (1833.)

Debay, (JEAN BAPTISTE JOSEPH,) a French sculptor, a son of the preceding, was born at Nantes in 1802. He gained the first prize in 1819. He produced a statue of Cambronne, (1846,) and other works.

Debelle. See BELLE, DE.

Debelloy. See BELLOY, DE.

Débonnaire, då'bo'når', (LOUIS,) a French theological writer, born at Ramerupt-sur-Aube; died in 1752.

Deb'o-rah, [Heb. דבורה,] a Hebrew prophetess and judge, who lived in the thirteenth century before Christ. She was instrumental in delivering the people from Jabin, King of Canaan, and his captain Sisera. (See Judges, chap. iv.) She is supposed to have been the author of the sublime hymn or lyric poem which forms the fifth chapter of Judges.

De Bōw, (JAMES DUNWOODY BROWNSON,) an American writer and statistician, born at Charleston in 1820. He graduated at Charleston College in 1843, was admitted to the bar in 1844, and the same year took charge of the "Southern Quarterly Review," published at Charleston. Near the close of 1845 he removed to New Orleans, and established "De Bow's Commercial Review," of which he was for many years the editor and proprietor. He was chosen professor of political economy and statistics in the University of Louisiana in 1847. In 1853 appeared his "Industrial Resources of the South and West," (3 vols. 8vo.) Died in 1867.

Debraux, dẹh-brō', (PAUL ÉMILE,) a popular French song-writer, born at Ancerville in 1798, published "La Colonne," "Prince Eugène," and other songs, which had great success. Died in 1831.

Debret, dẹh-brä', (JEAN BAPTISTE,) a French painter, born in Paris in 1768, removed to Rio Janeiro some time after 1815, and received the title of first painter to the imperial family of Brazil, for whom he painted several historical pieces and portraits. Died in Paris about 1845.

De Brosses. See BROSSES, DE.

Debry, dẹh-bre', (JEAN ANTOINE JOSEPH,) a French lawyer, born at Vervins about 1760, was elected to the Legislative Assembly in 1791, and was a prominent supporter of the moderate republican party. He was one of the committee of public safety in 1793, and became a member of the Council of Five Hundred in 1796. In 1798 he was sent, with two others, as minister plenipotentiary to Rastadt. As they were departing from that place, in 1799, on their return home, a party of Austrian soldiers massacred his colleagues; but he escaped by favour of the darkness. He was prefect of Doubs from 1801 till 1814. Died in 1834.

See THIERS, "History of the French Revolution;" "Nouvelle Biographie Générale."

Debure, dẹh-bür', written also **De Bure,** (GUILLAUME,) a French publisher and bibliographer, born in Paris in 1734; died in 1820.

Debure, (GUILLAUME FRANÇOIS,) a French bookseller and bibliographer, born in Paris in 1731. He published a "Bibliographie Instructive," (7 vols., 1763-68,) which was the most important work on the subject of rare books that had then appeared. Died in 1782.

Decaen, dẹh-kôn', written also **De Caen,** (CHARLES MATHIEU ISIDORE,) a French count, born near Caen in 1769, became general of brigade in 1796. As general of division, he contributed to the victory of Hohenlinden in 1800. In 1802 he was appointed captain-general of the French possessions in India. He defended with ability the Isles of France and of Bourbon against the English for eight years, and returned home in 1811. For his success against the Spaniards he was created count in 1813. In 1815 he commanded at Bordeaux for Louis XVIII., but joined the army of Napoleon when he returned from Elba. After the restoration of 1815 he was excluded from the service. Died in 1832.

See M. L. E. GAUTIER, "Biographie du Général Decaen," 1850.

Decaisne, dẹh-kản', (HENRI,) a historical painter of much merit, born at Brussels in 1799. Many of his works are in the Musée of Versailles, and in various public buildings of Paris. Died about 1852.

Decaisne, (JOSEPH,) an eminent botanist and horticulturist, a brother of the preceding, was born at Brussels in 1808. He removed to Paris in his youth, and in 1830 became aide-naturaliste under Adrien de Jussieu in the Museum of Natural History. In 1850 he succeeded Mirbel as professor of culture and director of the

famous botanical garden of Paris. He wrote treatises on Madder, the Chinese Yam, Rice, etc., and published a valuable work entitled "Asiatic Plants collected by V. Jacquemont." He is a member of the Institute.

Decamps, dẹh-kôn', (ALEXANDRE GABRIEL,) an eminent French painter of landscapes, history, and genre, was born in Paris in 1803. He studied nature in Italy and in the Levant. His style is regarded as original. Among his principal works are "The Defeat of the Cimbri," a "Souvenir of Turkey in Asia," and other pictures of Oriental scenes and customs. At the Exposition in Paris in 1855 he divided the public favour with Vernet and Delacroix. His pictures display great vigour of colouring and mastery of the effects of light.

Decamps, (FRANÇOIS.) See CAMPS, DE.

Decamps, (J. B.) See DESCAMPS, (J. B.)

De Candolle. See CANDOLLE, DE.

De Castro. See CASTRO, DE.

De-cā'tur, (STEPHEN,) a celebrated American commodore, born at Sinnepuxent, Maryland, in January, 1779. He entered the navy in 1798, and obtained the rank of lieutenant in 1799. In February, 1804, he commanded a small party which entered the harbour of Tripoli and burned the American frigate Philadelphia, which had been captured. For this daring exploit he was promoted to the rank of captain. At the beginning of the war of 1812 he commanded the frigate United States, forty-four guns, with which he captured the British frigate Macedonian in October of that year. He was blockaded by a superior force in the harbour of New London for several months, 1813-14. In January, 1815, he sailed from New York in the President, which, after being injured by striking a bar, was pursued by four British vessels and forced to surrender. In May, 1815, he took command of a squadron sent against the Algerines, who had committed hostile acts on the commerce of the United States. He captured two Algerine war-vessels, and dictated a treaty of peace to the Dey of Algiers, in June, 1815. He was renowned for extraordinary resolution and cool intrepidity. He was killed in a duel near Bladensburg, Maryland, by Commodore James Barron, in March, 1820.

See "Life of S. Decatur," in SPARKS's "American Biography," vol. ii., second series; S. PUTNAM WALDO, "Life and Character of S. Decatur," 1821, 2d edition; "National Portrait-Gallery of Distinguished Americans," vol. iii.; "Encyclopædia Americana."

Decazes, dẹh-kåz', (ÉLIE,) a French statesman and peer, born at or near Libourne (Gironde) in 1780. He became a resident of Paris under the régime of Napoleon, and was banished thence because he was a royalist during the Hundred Days. On the restoration of 1815 he was appointed minister of police instead of Fouché. By his address and tact he was well qualified for that office, which was highly important in those critical times. He gained the confidence of the king, so that when the ministers resigned, in December, 1818, and the king resolved to have a Liberal ministry, he consulted Decazes, by whose advice General Dessolles was appointed premier; and the subject of this article became minister of the interior. In the next year he became prime minister. In February, 1820, he resigned in consequence of calumnies which had obtained currency and which charged him with complicity in the death of the Duke of Berry. The king, whose favourite he remained to the last, then gave him the title of duke, and appointed him ambassador to London. "M. Decazes," says Lamartine, "won his political fortune by his courage, confirmed it by his urbanity, merited it by the sagacity of his views, and lost it finally by a tragical event of which he was innocent. He was the statesman of concord, of impartiality, and of the charter." In 1834 he was chosen grand referendary of the Chamber of Peers. Died in October, 1860.

See LAMARTINE, "History of the Restoration;" "Nouvelle Biographie Générale;" LOUIS DE LOMÉNIE, "M. Decazes, par un Homme de Rien," 1844.

Dèce, the French of DECIUS, which see.

Décébale. See DECEBALUS.

De-çeb'a-lus, [Gr. Δεκέβαλος; Fr. DÉCÉBALE, då'sà'bål',] King of the Dacians, born in the first century, was for a long time a formidable enemy of the Romans. He waged a successful war against the emperor Domitian, who was compelled to become tributary to him about 90.

When Trajan became master of the empire, (98 A.D.,) he refused to pay tribute, and in the war which ensued Decebalus was defeated. He killed himself in 105 A.D.

See TILLEMONT, "Histoire des Empereurs."

Decembrio, dà-chêm'bRE-o, (ANGELO,) an Italian writer, born in the duchy of Milan; died about 1500.

Decembrio, (PIETRO CANDIDO,) an Italian writer, born at Pavía in 1399, was a brother of Angelo. He was elected president of the Milanese republic in 1447. When Milan had been conquered by Francis Sforza, he went to Rome, where Pope Nicholas V. made him apostolic secretary. He wrote numerous works, among which are a "Life of Francis Sforza" and a "Life of Petrarch," and translated some of the works of Plato, Aristotle, and others. Died in 1477.

See TIRABOSCHI, "Storia della Letteratura Italiana."

Dechalles or **Dechasles**. See CHALLES, DE.

Dechamps, dęh-shŏN', (ADOLPHE,) a Belgian statesman and orator, born at Melle in 1807. In 1845 he became minister of foreign affairs. He was removed from office in 1847, after which he united himself with the Catholic opposition.

De Charmes, de charmz, (RICHARD,) an American author and Swedenborgian minister, born in Philadelphia in 1796. He graduated at Yale College in 1826. His principal publications are the "New Churchman Extra," devoted to polemics and church history, and several volumes of sermons.

Dechazelles. See CHAZELLES, DE.

Decio, dā'cho, [Lat. DE'CIUS,] (FILIPPO,) an eminent Italian jurist, born at Milan in 1454. He professed civil and canon law with great reputation at Pisa, Pavía, Sienna, and Rome. Having been excommunicated by Julius II., he went to France, and was chosen professor at Valence. After Leo X. became pope, Decio returned to Italy, and died in 1535. He wrote a legal work entitled "Consilia."

See BAYLE, "Historical and Critical Dictionary;" P. GIOVIO, "Elogia."

Decius. See DECIO.

Decius, dee'she-us, [Fr. DÈCE, dạs,] (CAIUS MESSIUS QUINTUS TRAJANUS,) a Roman emperor, born in Pannonia about 200 A.D. He was Governor of Mœsia, under Philip, when his army proclaimed him emperor. A battle followed between the two rivals, in which Philip was defeated and killed, 249 A.D. Decius persecuted the Christians with great cruelty. In a battle with the Goths, who had invaded his dominions, he was killed in 251.

See GIBBON, "Decline and Fall of the Roman Empire."

De'cius Ju-bel'lĭ-us, a general sent by the Roman senate to guard the city of Rhegium during the invasion of Italy by Pyrrhus. He treacherously massacred the male citizens of that city, and revolted against the Roman republic. Died about 270 B.C.

De'cius Mus, (PUBLIUS,) a Roman consul, celebrated for his patriotic devotion. In a battle against the Latins, 337 B.C., he devoted himself formally to the Dii Manes, then, rushing into the midst of the enemy, was instantly killed. His son, P. Decius Mus, also a consul, imitated his example in 296 B.C.

Decker, dĕk'ķer, **Dekker**, or **Deckers**, dĕk'ķers, (JOHN,) a Dutch chronologist and theologian, born at Haasbroek about 1555; died in 1619.

Decker, (Sir MATTHEW,) a writer on political economy, born in Amsterdam. In 1702 he settled in London, where he became an eminent merchant, was made a baronet in 1716, and elected to Parliament in 1719. He published "Serious Considerations on the Several High Duties which the Nation labours under," (1743.) A work on the "Causes of the Decline of the Foreign Trade" is by some ascribed to him. Died in 1749.

Deck'er, **Dek'ķar**, or **Dek'ķer**, (THOMAS,) an English dramatist, who lived in the reign of James I. He wrote several plays in partnership with Ford, Rowley, and others. Among the works which he composed alone are "Fortunatus, or the Wishing-Cap," and "The Gull's Horn-Book," the latter of which presents a curious picture of the manners of his time. Died about 1638.

See DIBDIN, "History of the English Stage;" "Minor Elizabethan Dramatists," in the "Atlantic Monthly" for December, 1867.

Decker, van. See DEKKER, DE.

Decker, von, fon dĕk'ķer, (KARL,) a German writer on war and tactics, was born in Berlin in 1784. He served some years in the Prussian army, and rose to the rank of general-major, (1842.) He wrote many works, among which are "Bonaparte's Campaigns in Italy," and "Tactics," etc., (1834.) Died in 1844.

De Columnis. See GUIDO DELLE COLONNE.

Decomberousse, dęh'kŏN'bRooss',(FRANÇOIS-ISAAC HYACINTHE,) a French dramatist, born at Vienne in 1786. He wrote a successful comedy, called "The Present of the Prince," (1821,) and "Judith," a tragedy, in verse, (1825,) which is commended. Died in 1856.

Decrès, dęh-kRà', (DENIS,) DUC, a French naval officer, born at Chaumont, in Champagne, in 1761, entered the navy at the age of seventeen, and obtained the rank of rear-admiral in 1798. For his conduct in a fight with the English near Malta in 1800, he received a sabre of honour from the First Consul. In 1801 he was appointed minister of the marine, which he directed with ability for thirteen years. In 1815 he retired from the service. In 1820 he was killed by his valet, who designed to rob him.

See "Nouvelle Biographie Générale."

Dédale, the French of DÆDALUS, which see.

Dedecker, dā'dĕk'ķer, (PIERRE JACQUES FRANÇOIS,) a leader of the Catholic or clerical party in Belgium, was born at Zele in 1812. He entered the Chamber of Deputies in 1839, and was one of the chief editors of the "Revue de Bruxelles" from 1837 to 1851. In 1855 he formed a new ministry, which was dissolved in 1857.

Dedekind, dā'dęh-kĭnt', (CONSTANTINE CHRISTIAN,) a German poet, born at Rheinsdorf, wrote dramas on scriptural subjects, and other works. Died in 1713.

Dedekind, (FRIEDRICH,) a German poet, born at Neustadt about 1530. He was inspector of the Protestant churches of the diocese of Lubeck. He wrote, besides other works, a humorous satire in Latin verse, entitled "Grobianus, de Morum Simplicitate," (1549,) which is often reprinted. An English version appeared, with the title of "Grobianus, or the Compleat Booby." Died in 1598.

See HEGEL, "Geschichte der komischen Literatur."

Dedelay. See DE DELLEY.

De Delley, dęh-dạ'là', written also **Dedelay**,(CLAUDE PIERRE,) a meritorious French economist, born at Romans (Dauphiné) in 1750. He wrote valuable treatises on agriculture and the public revenue, and founded a hospital and free school. He became a senator in 1800, and was made a count under the empire. Died in 1827.

De Dominis. See DOMINIS.

Dee, (ARTHUR,) M.D., an English alchemist, son of John Dee, noticed below, born at Mortlake in 1579, became physician to Charles I., and wrote a treatise on alchemy, called "Fasciculus Chymicus," (1631.) Died in 1651.

Dee, (JOHN,) a famous English astrologer and mathematician, remarkable for his versatile talents and learning, was born in London in 1527. He was educated at Cambridge, where he made great progress in astronomy and other sciences. About 1550 he lectured on geometry in Paris or Rheims, and returned to London in 1551. In the reign of Mary he was imprisoned on a charge of magic. He was patronized by Queen Elizabeth, who is said to have employed him as her secret agent or "intelligencer." In 1564 he produced his "Monas Hieroglyphica," and some years later wrote an able treatise on the reformation of the calendar. Having associated with himself Edward Kelley and a Polish noble named Laski, for the purpose of conversing with spirits, they passed some years in Bohemia and Poland. In 1595 the queen appointed him warden of Manchester College. He died in 1608, leaving many curious works, some of which are still in manuscript.

See DISRAELI, "Amenities of Literature;" DIBDIN, "Bibliomania;" THOMAS SMITH, "Vita J. Dee," London, 1707.

Deering, deer'ing or dā'ring, (KARL,) a German physician and botanist, born in Saxony, emigrated to England. He published a catalogue of the plants growing near Nottingham. Died about 1750.

Defermon des Chapelières, dęh-fěR'mŏN' dạ shăp-le-aiR', (JOSEPH,) COUNT, an able French minister of state, born at Rennes in 1756, was educated for the law. As a member of the National Assembly, he favoured a moderate reform, and was chosen president of that body in 1791. In the Convention he voted against the death of the king, and in 1795 passed into the Council of Five Hundred. Bonaparte appointed him councillor of state in 1800, and minister of state in 1807. Soon after this date he was made a count of the empire, and one of the directors of the finances. Died in 1831.

See "Nouvelle Biographie Générale."

Deffand or **Deffant, du,** dü dạ'fôN', (MARIE de Vichy-Chamroud—dẹh ve'she'shôN'roo',) MARQUISE, a literary French lady, born in 1697. She became at an early age the wife of the Marquis du Deffand, from whom she soon separated. Though intelligent, witty, beautiful, and accomplished, she was much disposed to ennui. Her house in Paris for fifty years was frequented by authors and statesmen of the highest eminence, and the most noble and fashionable were attracted to her parties. She corresponded many years with Horace Walpole, D'Alembert, and Voltaire. She became nearly blind at the age of fifty-four. She was inclined to skepticism, and was remarkable for egotism. Her letters are much admired for literary merit and soundness of criticism. (See her "Letters to Walpole and Voltaire," published in 4 vols., 1810.) Died in 1780. (See ESPINASSE, MADEMOISELLE.)

See MARMONTEL, "Mémoires;" VOLTAIRE, "Correspondance;" GRIMM, "Correspondance;" "Edinburgh Review" for January, 1810, February, 1811, and October, 1859.

Deffant. See DEFFAND.

De Foe or **Defoe,** (DANIEL,) a popular English author and original genius, born in London in 1661, was the son of James Foe, a butcher. The particle De was prefixed to the name by Daniel himself. He was educated for the ministry among the dissenters, but did not pursue that vocation. In 1685 he enlisted in the service of the Duke of Monmouth in rebellion against James II., and on the failure of that attempt became a merchant or tradesman. He produced an "Essay on Projects" in 1697, and a poetical satire entitled "The True-Born Englishman," (about 1700,) which had a very large sale and procured him the favour of the king. For the publication of his ironical pamphlet entitled "The Shortest Way with the Dissenters," (1702,) he was condemned by the House of Commons to be fined, pilloried, and imprisoned two years. During his confinement and after his release he produced works on various subjects with great industry and rapidity. In 1706 he was sent to Scotland by the queen's ministers to promote the Union, and in 1709 published his admired "History of the Union." His political works, in which he defended the principles of the Whigs and dissenters, exposed him to much suffering and pecuniary loss, which he summed up in this couplet:

"No man has tasted differing fortunes more;
And thirteen times I have been rich and poor."

The number of his works amounts to about two hundred and ten, among which the principal are "Adventures of Robinson Crusoe," (1719,) "Memoirs of a Cavalier," "The History of the Plague of 1665," "The Fortunes of Moll Flanders," "Religious Courtship," (1722,) "Adventures of Roxana," "Captain Singleton," a "Treatise on Apparitions," and a "Plan of English Commerce." The above are chiefly fictitious, but produce a lively impression of truth and reality. De Foe was a pithy writer, an accurate observer of social phenomena, and was remarkable for his versatility of mind and fertility of invention. "Perhaps there exists no work in the English language," says Sir Walter Scott, "which has been more generally read and more universally admired than the Adventures of Robinson Crusoe." Died in 1731.

See "Life of Defoe," by WALTER WILSON, 1830; J. FORSTER, "Essay on Defoe;" SIR WALTER SCOTT, "Biography" prefixed to De Foe's Works; W. HAZLITT, "Memoirs of De Foe," 1843; GEORGE CHALMERS, "Life of Defoe," London, 1790; WILLIAM LEE, "Life of Daniel Defoe," 3 vols., 1869, including a portion of his unpublished writings; "Edinburgh Review" for October, 1845; "Retrospective Review," vols. iii. and vi., 1821–22; also, an elaborate article on "Defoe," in the "British Quarterly" for October, 1869.

Deforis, dẹh-fo'rẹss', (JEAN PIERRE,) a French priest, born at Montbrison in 1732, wrote in 1762 a Refutation of Rousseau's "Émile," and published an edition of Bossuet's works. He was guillotined in 1794.

Defrémery, dẹh-frȧm're', (CHARLES,) a French Orientalist, born at Cambrai in 1822.

Degen, dā'gẹn, (CARL FERDINAND,) a Danish mathematician, born at Brunswick in 1766; died in 1825.

Degenfeld, von, fon dā'gẹn-fĕlt', (CHRISTOPH MARTIN,) BARON, a German general, fought for Gustavus Adolphus, and for the Venetians against Pope Urban VIII. Died in 1653.

Deger, dā'ger, (ERNST,) an eminent German historical painter of the Dusseldorf school, born near Hildesheim in 1809. His subjects are mostly scriptural.

De Gerando. See GERANDO.

Degrave. See GRAVE.

De Grey and Rip'on, (GEORGE FREDERICK SAMUEL ROB'INSON,) EARL, a British statesman, the eldest son of the first Earl of Ripon, was born in London about 1827. Before the death of his father in 1859 he was called LORD GODERICH. He represented the West Riding of Yorkshire from 1857 to 1859. In April, 1863, he succeeded Sir George Cornewall Lewis as secretary of war. In the ministry formed or reconstructed by Earl Russell he was appointed secretary for India in February, 1866. He resigned this office with the other members of the cabinet in June of the same year, and became lord president of the council in December, 1868.

Deguerle, dẹh-gârl', (JEAN NICOLAS MARIE,) a French *littérateur*, born at Issoudun in 1766, became professor of eloquence at Paris in 1809. He translated the "Æneid" into prose, and wrote several admired poems. Died in 1824.

De Hā'vẹn, (EDWIN J.,) an American naval officer, born in Pennsylvania in 1819. He commanded an expedition sent out from New York in search of Sir John Franklin in 1850. Died in 1865.

Deheem, dẹh-hām', (JOHN DAVID,) a Dutch painter of flowers, fruit, etc., born at Utrecht about 1604; died in 1674.

Dehn, dān, (SIEGFRIED WILHELM,) a German writer on music, born at Altona in 1799.

Deianira or **Deianeira.** See DEJANIRA.

Deidier, dạ'de-ȧ', ABBÉ, a French mathematician, was born at Marseilles in 1696. He published in 1739 "New Elements of Mathematics," and "The Theory and Practice of Geometry," both of which are praised for clearness and precision. Died in 1746.

Deidier, (ANTOINE,) a French physician, born at Montpellier. He became professor of chemistry in that city in 1696. In 1732 he removed to Marseilles. He published many works on medicine, chemistry, and physiology, abounding in paradoxical ideas. Died in 1746.

Deiman, di'mȧn, or **Deimann,** (JOHN RODOLPH,) a Dutch physician and chemist, born in 1743. He was the soul of the reunion known as "the Dutch Chemists," by whom the olefiant gas was discovered. The academic collections of Holland are filled with memoirs on chemistry, etc. which attest the extent and soundness of his knowledge. About 1806 he became physician to the king, Louis Bonaparte. Among his works is a "Treatise on Medical Electricity." Died in 1808.

See JEROME DE BOSCH, "Lofrede op J. R. Deiman," 1808; DOORNIK, "J. R. Deiman gedacht in eene Redevoering," 1808; ERSCH und GRUBER, "Allgemeine Encyklopaedie."

Deimier, de, dẹh dạ'me-ȧ', (PIERRE,) a French *littérateur* and critic, was born at Avignon about 1570; died about 1618.

Deinarchus. See DINARCHUS.

Deinhardstein, dīn'hȧrt-stīn', (JOHANN LUDWIG,) a German dramatist, born in Vienna in 1794. He was professor of æsthetics in the University of Vienna in 1827 –32. His dramas "Floretta," "Hans Sachs," and others were received with favour. He published a volume of Poems, (1844,) and two volumes entitled "Dramas of Artists," ("Künstlerdramen," 1845.)

Deinocrates. See DINOCRATES.

De-I-ot'ạ-rus or **De-jot'ạ-rus,** [Gr. Δηϊόταρος,] King of Galatia, was the ally of the Romans in their war against Mithridates, and was involved in the vicissitudes of the civil wars which followed. He fought for Pompey at the battle of Pharsalia, 48 B.C., and was successfully defended by Cicero in an oration ("Pro Rege Deiotaro") against the charge of a design to assassinate Cæsar. In the civil

ȧ, ē, ī, ō, ū, ȳ, *long;* ȧ, ė, ò, same, less prolonged; ă, ĕ, ĭ, ŏ, ŭ, ў, *short;* ạ, ẹ, ị, ọ, *obscure;* fȧr, fȧll, fȧt; mĕt; nŏt; gōōd; mōōn;

war between Octavius and Antony, Deiotarus aided the former. He lived to a great age; but the year of his death is not known.

See APPIAN, "Bellum Civile;" DION CASSIUS, "History of Rome;" LUCAN, "Pharsalia."

Dej-a-ni′ra, Deianira, or **Deianeira,** [Gr. Δηιάνειρα or Δηιάνειρα; Fr. DÉJANIRE, dâ′zhâ′nĕR′,] a daughter of Œneus, King of Ætolia, and the wife of Hercules. She was persuaded by the dying centaur Nessus to preserve some of his blood as a love-charm, and applied it to a tunic of Hercules, who was fatally poisoned by it.

Déjanire. See DEJANIRA.

Dejaure, dĕh-zhōR′, (JEAN ÉLIE BEDENC,) a French dramatist, born in 1761. He composed several successful comedies and operas, among which are "The Shade (*Ombre*) of Mirabeau," (1791,) "Lodoïska," an opera, (1791,) and "Montano and Stéphanie," an opera, (1799.) Died in 1799.

Dejazet, dĕh-zhâ′zạ′, (MARIE VIRGINIE,) a popular French actress, born in Paris in 1797.

Dejean, dĕh-zhôN′, (JEAN FRANÇOIS AIMÉ,) COUNT, a French general, born at Castelnaudary in 1749. In 1800 he became a councillor of state, and performed a mission to Genoa with ability. He was chosen minister of war in 1802, and first inspector-general of engineers in 1808. In 1814 he was created by the Bourbons a peer of France, and governor of the Polytechnic School. In 1815 he served Napoleon as aide-de-camp. Died in 1824.

See HAXO, "Notice historique sur le Comte Dejean," 1824.

Dejean, (PIERRE FRANÇOIS AUGUSTE,) COUNT, a son of the preceding, was born at Amiens in 1780. He became general of division in 1814, and distinguished himself at Waterloo in 1815. He acquired distinction as an entomologist, and published a "History of Coleoptera," (7 vols., 1825–39.) Died in 1845.

Dej′o-çēs̄, [Gr. Δηιόκης,] the first king of the Medes, reigned about 700 or 650 B.C. He is said to have been a wise and just ruler.

Dejotarus. See DEIOTARUS.

Dejoux, dĕh-zhoo′, (CLAUDE,) an eminent French sculptor, born near Arbois (Jura) in 1731, was apprenticed to a carpenter. About 1756 he went to Paris, and became the pupil of G. Coustou the younger. After studying at Rome from 1768 to 1774, he returned to Paris, where he executed admired statues of Catinat, Desaix, Achilles, and others. He was chosen a member of the Institute about 1796. Died in 1816.

De Kalb, (JOHN,) BARON, a German general, born in Alsace about 1732, became an officer in the French service. He came to America with La Fayette in 1777, was appointed a major-general by Congress in the same year, and served in the army of Washington in Pennsylvania and New Jersey. In 1780 he was second in command under General Gates in Carolina. He was killed at the battle of Camden, August, 1780.

De Kay, (JAMES E.,) an American physician and naturalist, born about 1792. Having made a tour of Europe in 1831–32, he published on his return "Sketches in Turkey." He also wrote the five volumes of the "Natural History of New York" devoted to Zoology. Died in 1851.

Deken, dā′ken, (AGATHA,) a popular Dutch authoress, born near Amsterdam in 1741. She associated herself in literary pursuits with Marie Bosch, and afterwards with Madame Wolff, *née* Bekker. They exercised much influence on the national character by the publication of popular works, among which are "Letters on Various Subjects," (1780,) "Sara Burgerhart," a romance, (1782,) "History of William Leevend," (8 vols., 1784,) and "Promenades in Burgundy," in verse, (1789.) A. Deken also wrote "Songs for Country-people," ("Liederen voor den Boerenstand.") Died in 1804.

See JAN KONIJNENBURG, "Lofrede op E. Wolff en A. Deken," 1805; "Fraser's Magazine" for July, 1854.

Dekkar, (THOMAS.) See DECKER.

Dekker. See DECKER.

Dekker, de, dĕh dĕk′ker, or **Van Decker,** vän dĕk′ker, (JEREMIAS,) an eminent Dutch poet, born at Dort about 1610, passed his life in mercantile pursuits in his native city, and wrote poetry for recreation. In 1656 a collection of his verses was published, among which are numerous epigrams, "Good Friday," and "The Morning Dawn." His style is pure, and his sentiments devout. "The Praise of Avarice," a satire which is compared to Erasmus's "Praise of Folly," is one of his last and principal productions. It is much admired, and indicates great knowledge of human nature. Died in 1666.

See LONGFELLOW, "Poets and Poetry of Europe;" JERONIMO DE VRIES, "J. de Dekker als Mensch en als Dichter," 1807.

De la Beche, dĕh lã bāsh, (Sir HENRY THOMAS,) F.R.S., an eminent English geologist, born near London in 1796. In 1817 he became a member of the Geological Society, of which he was chosen president about 1847. He explored the geology of Wales, Devonshire, and Jamaica, on which he produced several works. He published a "Geological Manual," (1832,) and "How to Observe Geology," (1835.) He was appointed chief director of the geological survey of England ordered by the government, and president of the Museum of Practical Geology, now the School of Mines. He was knighted in 1848, and became a correspondent of the Institute of France in 1853. Died in 1855.

Delaborde. See LABORDE.

Delaborde or **De Laborde,** d′lã′boRd′ or dĕh lã′boRd′, (HENRI,) a French historical painter, son of Henri François, noticed below, was born at Rennes in 1811. He obtained a medal of the first class in 1847. Among his works is "Hagar in the Desert."

Delaborde, (HENRI FRANÇOIS,) COUNT, a French general, born at Dijon in 1764, was made a peer by Bonaparte during the Hundred Days. Died in 1833.

Delacépède. See LACÉPÈDE.

Delacour, dĕl-a-koor′, (JAMES,) an Irish poet, born near Blarney in 1709, studied for the clerical profession. He wrote "Abelard and Eloïsa," a poem in imitation of Pope, and "The Prospect of Poetry," (1733.) Died in 1781.

Delacroix. See LACROIX.

Delacroix or **De Lacroix,** d′lã′kRwã′ or dĕh lã′kRwã′, (FERDINAND VICTOR EUGÈNE,) a celebrated French historical painter, born at Charenton, near Paris, in 1799. He was a son of Charles Delacroix, a republican member of the Convention, and minister of foreign affairs in 1797. He was a pupil of P. Guérin, but soon renounced the principles of the classic school taught by that artist. In 1822 he exhibited a picture of "Dante and Virgil," which produced a great sensation and was severely criticised. His reputation was increased by the "Massacre of Scio," (1824,) after which he was regarded as the chief of the romantic school. He displayed original genius and energy in "Mephistopheles appearing to Faust," "Sardanapalus Dying," "The Prisoner of Chillon," (1835,) and "Medea," (1838.) Among his master-pieces is the "Women of Algiers," (1834,) which procured him a high reputation as a colorist; but his colouring is powerful rather than harmonious. He has decorated one of the halls of the Palais Bourbon, and some interior portions of the Louvre, the Luxembourg, and other public buildings. He was admitted into the Institute in 1857. Died in 1863.

See L. DE LOMÉNIE, "Galerie des Contemporains;" GUSTAVE PLANCHE, "Portraits des Artistes contemporains."

Delacroix, (JACQUES VINCENT,) a distinguished French lawyer and voluminous writer, born in Paris in 1743. He revived the "Spectateur Français," founded by Marivaux, of which he issued many volumes, (1771–1820.) During the Revolution he was professor of public law in the Lycée, and published a successful work on the "Constitutions of Europe," (1790.) He wrote political tracts and moral essays, and a "History of France from Clovis to Louis XIV.," (3 vols., 1813.) Died in 1832.

See QUÉRARD, "La France Littéraire."

Delacroix, (NICOLAS,) a French antiquary and deputy, born in Meuse in 1785. He wrote a work called "Statistics of the Department of Drôme," which gained the Montyon prize medal in 1835. Died in 1843.

Delafosse. See LAFOSSE.

Delafosse, d′lã′fos′, (GABRIEL,) a French naturalist, a member of the Institute, born about 1795, has written several scientific works.

Delahaye, d′lã′hạ′, (GUILLAUME NICOLAS,) a French map-engraver, born in Paris in 1725, engraved all the works of D'Anville. Died in 1802.

Delaistre, dẹh-lȧtr', (LOUIS JEAN DÉSIRÉ,) a successful French engraver of history and portraits, born in Paris in 1800.

Delalande. See LALANDE.

Delalande, d'lȧ'lȯNd', (PIERRE ANTOINE,) a French naturalist, born at Versailles in 1787. He accompanied Geoffroy Saint-Hilaire as assistant in his journey to Portugal in 1808, and in 1816 went to Brazil, where he collected rare objects of natural history. From 1818 to 1821 he explored the country of the Hottentots and Caffres, and returned home with an immense zoological collection. He published in 1822 a brief "Account of his Voyage to the Cape of Good Hope," and was prevented by his early death from finishing a more complete work on the subject. Died in 1823.

See "Nouvelle Biographie Générale."

Delamalle, d'lȧ'mȧl', (GASPARD GILBERT,) a French advocate and orator, born in Paris in 1752. As an opponent of the Revolution, he was proscribed and imprisoned in 1793. He was appointed by Bonaparte counsellor to the University in 1808, and councillor of state in 1811. He retained these offices under the Bourbons. In 1820 he obtained the prize offered by the French Academy for an essay on eloquence. He wrote a work on Oratory, entitled "Essai d'Institutions oratoires," (1816,) and other works. Died in 1834.

See RICHOMME, "Éloge de M. Delamalle," 1834.

Delamarche, d'lȧ'mȧrsh', (C. F.,) a French geographer, born at Paris in 1740; died in 1817.

Delambre, dẹh-lȯMbr' or dẹh-lȯN'b'R, (JEAN BAPTISTE JOSEPH,) a celebrated French astronomer and author, born at Amiens on the 19th of September, 1749, was a pupil of the poet Delille, at the College of Amiens. Having gained the highest prizes, and attained great proficiency in the classics, he pursued the study of rhetoric and philosophy in Paris. When he left college he was destitute of resources, and suffered much privation. He supported himself for several years by teaching, and employed his leisure in the study of Greek and mathematics, which he had neglected at college. Having acquired command of the resources of ancient and modern learning, he began, about 1780, to devote himself to astronomy, and received lessons from Lalande, who became his friend and soon employed him as an assistant. In 1787 he resolved to calculate the observations of Jupiter and Saturn, and two years later produced tables of those planets, which were remarkable for precision. His "Tables of the Orbit of Uranus" were crowned by the Academy in 1790, and have since been used for half a century. In 1792 he was elected to the Academy of Sciences, which in the same year awarded him a prize for his "Tables of Jupiter's Satellites," respecting which La Place had just offered a new theory. Between 1792 and 1799 Delambre and Méchain were employed to measure the arc of the meridian from Dunkirk to Barcelona; and the former published the results in his "Basis of the Decimal System of Measure." On presenting this work to Bonaparte, the latter said, "Conquests pass away, but these operations remain." He was admitted into the Institute at its formation in 1795, and was chosen perpetual secretary of the Academy of Sciences in 1803. His eulogies on departed members were admired for an elegant simplicity of style. He married Madame Pommard in 1804. In 1807 he succeeded Lalande as professor of astronomy in the College of France. He wrote for the "Biographie Universelle" the articles on Hipparchus, Kepler, and other great astronomers. In 1814 he produced an important work, entitled "Theoretical and Practical Astronomy," ("Astronomie théorique et pratique," 3 vols.) After the immense labours of thirty years devoted to observations and calculations, he began to write the "History of Astronomy" from the earliest times, of which he completed five volumes. This excellent work was issued in three parts, viz.: "History of Ancient Astronomy," (1817,) "History of Mediæval Astronomy," (1819,) and "History of Modern Astronomy," (1821.) His character was virtuous, sincere, and disinterested. He presents a remarkable instance of the union of high literary attainments with an extraordinary capacity for the abstract sciences. Died in Paris in

August, 1822. The celebrated naturalist Cuvier pronounced a discourse over his tomb.

See FOURIER, "Éloge de Delambre;" CH. DUPIN, "Notice sur Delambre," in the "Revue Encyclopédique;" V. J. F. WARMÉ, "Éloge historique de M. Delambre," 1824; "Nouvelle Biographie Générale."

Delamet. See LAMET.

De Lan'cey, (WILLIAM HEATHCOTE,) an American Episcopalian bishop, born in Westchester county, New York, in 1797. He was ordained a priest in 1822, was provost of the University of Pennsylvania from 1828 to 1833, and became rector of Saint Peter's Church in Philadelphia about 1836. In 1838 he was chosen Bishop of the diocese of Western New York. Died in 1865.

Delandine, d'lȯN'dĕn', (ANTOINE FRANÇOIS,) a French littérateur, born in Lyons in 1756, was a royalist member of the Constituent Assembly in 1790–91, and was imprisoned during the reign of terror. In 1803 he was chosen keeper of the Library of Lyons. He published, in conjunction with Chaudon, the eighth edition of the "New Historical Dictionary," improved and enlarged, (1804,) and wrote numerous works, among which are "Academic Crowns," and a "History of the National Assemblies of France," (1788.) Died in 1820.

See J. B. DUMAS, "Notice historique sur la Vie de Delandine," 1820.

De-lane', (JOHN T.,) an English lawyer, editor of the London "Times," was born about 1818. He was educated at Oxford. In 1841 he became manager or chief editor of what has been called the leading journal of Europe.

Delane, (WILLIAM AUGUSTUS FREDERICK,) an English journalist, father of the preceding, born about 1795, was for many years the chief editor or manager of the London "Times." It is said that he wrote but little himself, but displayed judgment in directing the talents of others, and was an able and successful administrator. Died in 1857.

Delangle, d'lȯNgl, (CLAUDE ALPHONSE,) a French advocate and senator, born at Varzy (Nièvre) in 1797. He became advocate-general in the court of cassation in 1840, and attorney-general in the cour royale in 1847. After the revolution of 1848 he supported Louis Napoleon, who appointed him in 1852 first president of the imperial court of Paris, and added the dignity of senator. He wrote a "Treatise on Commercial Companies," (les Sociétés commerciales,) and became minister of the interior in 1858, and minister of justice in 1859. Died in 1869.

See "Biographie des Sénateurs."

Del'a̤-no, (AMASA,) an American traveller, born at Duxbury, Massachusetts, in 1763. He died in 1817, leaving a "Narrative of Voyages and Travels in the Northern and Southern Hemispheres, comprising Three Voyages around the World," etc., (Boston, 1817.)

De-la'ny̆, (MARY,) originally GRANVILLE, an English lady, born in Wiltshire in 1700, was the daughter of Lord Lansdowne. She was married to Alexander Pendarves, who died in 1724, and afterwards to Dr. Delany, noticed below. She corresponded with several eminent literary persons, and her published letters were much admired. Died in 1788.

See "Life of Mary Delany," by herself and Lady LLANOVER, 1862; MRS. ELWOOD, "Memoirs of the Literary Ladies of England," etc., vol. i., 1843; "Blackwood's Magazine" for April, 1862; "Westminster Review" for April, 1862.

De-la'ny̆, (PATRICK,) a learned Irish divine, born about 1686, was a Fellow of Trinity College, Dublin, and in 1744 became Dean of Down. He was an intimate friend of Dean Swift. In 1743 he married Mary, daughter of Lord Lansdowne. He published, besides other works, "Revelation examined with Candour," (3 vols., 1732–63,) which is commended by Adam Clarke, and a "Life of David, King of Israel," (3 vols., 1740–42.) Died in 1768.

See "Biographia Britannica."

Delaram, (FRANCIS,) a skilful engraver, born in London about 1590. He engraved portraits of many eminent persons of the time, among which is "John, Bishop of Lincoln." Died in 1627.

Delarbre, d'lȧRbR, (ANTOINE,) a French botanist, born at Clermont about 1724; died about 1810.

Delaroche or **De Laroche,** d'lȧ'rosh', (PAUL,) an excellent French historical painter, born in Paris in 1797.

He was a pupil of Baron Gros, and formed for himself a mixed style between the classic and the romantic. In 1824 he produced "Joan of Arc interrogated in Prison," and in 1826 "The Death of Queen Elizabeth." He acquired great popularity in the early part of his career, and became the recognized chief of a school called the Eclectic. In 1832 he was elected to the Institute. His "Cromwell gazing on the Corpse of Charles I." (1832) is greatly admired. In 1837 he was ordered to decorate the hemicycle of the Palais des Beaux-Arts, where he represented the artists of all ages, in a large and admirable composition. Among his other master-pieces are "The Death of the Duke of Guise," (1835,) "Napoleon at Fontainebleau," (1840,) "Bonaparte at Saint-Bernard,"(1850,) and "The Girondists in Prison," (1855.) His colouring is brilliant and harmonious, and his design correct. He married a daughter of Horace Vernet. Died in 1856.

See L. DE LOMÉNIE, "Galerie des Contemporains."

Delarue, d'lä′rü′, (GERVAIS,) ABBÉ, an eminent French antiquary, born at Caen in 1751. Having been driven into exile in 1793, he went to London, and made extensive researches in the literary history of the middle ages. In 1808 he became professor of history at Caen. He published in 1834 "Historical Essays on the Norman Bards and Trouvères," (3 vols.) Died in 1835.

Delatour. See LATOUR.

Delatour, d'lä′tooR′, (LOUIS FRANÇOIS,) a French writer, born in Paris in 1727, published "Essays on the Architecture of the Chinese, their Gardens, Manners, Customs, etc.," (1803.) Died in 1807.

Delaudun, d'lō′dŭN′, (PIERRE,) a French poet and critic, born at Uzès in 1575; died in 1629.

Delaulne, d'lōn, (ÉTIENNE,) a French designer and engraver, born at Orléans in 1520; died about 1595.

Delaunay. See LAUNAY.

Delaunay, d'lō′nā′, (CHARLES,) a French mathematician, and member of the Institute, born at Lusigny (Aube) in 1816.

Delaunay, (LOUIS,) a mineralogist and advocate, born about 1740, practised in the courts of Brussels. He was living in 1805.

De-lâune′, (THOMAS,) an English theologian, wrote "A Plea for Nonconformists," (1684,) and other works. He was punished for his writings by the loss of his ears, and died in prison.

Delauney. See ENTRAIGUES, COMTE D', and LAUNEY.

Del-a-vāl′, (EDWARD HUSSEY,) an English chemist and philosopher, born in 1729, was a Fellow of the Royal Society. He wrote an "Experimental Inquiry into the Cause of the Change of Colour in Opaque and Coloured Bodies," (1744,) and several other treatises. Died in 1814.

Delaval, d'lä′vål′, (PIERRE LOUIS,) a French historical painter, born in Paris in 1790, won a gold medal in 1817, when he exhibited "Clotilde exhorting Clovis." Among his works are "Saint Louis carrying the Oriflamme," (1840,) and a portrait of Châteaubriand.

Delavigne or **De Lavigne,** d'lä′vēñ′, (GERMAIN,) a French dramatist, brother of the poet noticed below, was born at Giverny (Eure) in 1790. He assisted Scribe in many successful plays and operas. Among these are "The Somnambulist," (1819,) "The Old Bachelor," (1822,) and "The Diplomate," (1827.) Died in 1868.

Delavigne, (JEAN FRANÇOIS CASIMIR,) a popular French poet and dramatist, born at Havre on the 4th of April, 1793, was the son of a merchant, and was educated at Paris. In 1811 he wrote a poem on the birth of Napoleon's son, which procured him the patronage of François de Nantes. Soon after the restoration of 1815 he successfully invoked the spirit of French nationality by his admirable *Messéniennes,**—the general title of several poems, one of which was on the subject of Waterloo. The government appointed him librarian of the chancery, although his political opinions were those of the liberal opposition. His next performance was an elegy on Joan of Arc. In 1819 he produced "The Sicilian Vespers," a drama, which was performed with great applause. In 1825 he was elected a member of the French Academy, and refused the offer of a pension of

* Named in allusion to the verses in which the people of ancient Messenia deplored the disasters of their country.

1200 francs. On the occasion of the revolution of 1830 he wrote a song, "La Parisienne," which was received with extraordinary favour. Besides the above-named, he is the author of numerous dramas, of which the most important are "The School of Old Men," ("L'École des Vieillards," 1823,) "Marino Faliero," (1829,) and "Louis XI.," (1832.) He died at Lyons in December, 1843.

See LONGFELLOW, "Poets and Poetry of Europe;" "Notice sur C. Delavigne," prefixed to his works by his brother GERMAIN; LOUIS DE LOMÉNIE, "M. C. Delavigne, par un Homme de Rien," 1841; GIACOMO CALVI, "C. Delavigne, Notizia bibliografico-necrologica," 1844; G. VERENET, "Éloge de C. Delavigne," 1844; KRUSE, "Ueber C. Delavigne als Vermittier, etc.," 1847.

Delbene, dĕl-bā′nà or dĕl′bản′, (ALPHONSE,) a French historian and bishop, born about 1540; died in 1608.

Delbene, dĕl-bā′nà, (BENEDETTO,) an Italian savant, born at Verona in 1749. He wrote essays on the "Culture of Olives," on the "Manufacture of Wine," etc., and translated Columella, Virgil's "Georgics," and other Latin works. Died in 1825.

Delbrück, dĕl′brük, (JOHANN FRIEDRICH FERDINAND,) a German philosophic writer, born at Magdeburg in 1772. He became counsellor of the regency and professor of eloquence at Königsberg in 1809. In 1818 he was appointed to similar functions at Bonn. Among his principal works are "Xenophon, a Defence of his Reputation against Niebuhr," (1829,) and "Discourses," ("Reden," 1831.) Died in 1848.

See NICOLOVIUS, "J. F. F. Delbrück's Leben," 1848.

Delbrück, (JOHANN FRIEDRICH GOTTLIEB,) a brother of the preceding, born at Magdeburg in 1768, became professor of theology in Magdeburg. Between 1800 and 1809 he superintended the education of the two princes of Prussia, sons of Frederick William III. Died in 1830.

Deleau, d'lō, (NICOLAS,) a French physician, born at Vézelise in 1797. He published "Researches on the Diseases of the Ear," etc., (1834,) and other works.

Delécluse, d'lä′klüz′, (ÉTIENNE JEAN,) an able French *littérateur,* born in Paris in 1781. He wrote editorial articles on art for the "Moniteur" and the "Journal des Débats" for many years, and published, besides several novels, a "Treatise on Painting," (1828,) and "Roland, or Chivalry," ("Roland, ou la Chevalerie," 2 vols., 1845.)

See LOUANDRE, "La Littérature contemporaine."

Delen, van, vàn dā′lẹn, (DIRCK or THIERRY,) a Dutch painter, born at Heusden in 1635, was a pupil of F. Hals. He preferred to paint churches, public edifices, and interiors, and excelled in perspective and colouring. Among his works is a "Game of Foot-Ball," in the Louvre. Died at Arnemuyden about 1700.

See DESCAMPS, "Vies des Peintres Flamands," etc.

Delessert, d'lä′saiR′, (BENJAMIN,) a French financier and philanthropist, born in Lyons in 1773. He was chosen regent of the Bank of France about 1802. Soon after that date he established a model spinning-mill for the fabrication of cotton stuffs. He founded saving-funds, and contributed largely to other provident institutions. Having cultivated botany and collected 86,000 species, he associated with De Candolle in the publication of "Select Figures of Plants," ("Icones selectæ Plantarum," 5 vols., 1820–46.) He sat in the Chamber of Deputies *(centre gauche)* from 1827 to 1843. Died in 1847.

See ALPHONSE DECANDOLLE, "Notice sur B. Delessert," 1847; CHARLES DUPIN, "Travaux et Bienfaits de B. Delessert," 1848; "Nouvelle Biographie Générale."

Delessert, (FRANÇOIS,) a brother of the preceding, born in 1780, was an eminent banker, regent of the Bank of France, a member of the Institute, and a liberal patron of arts and sciences.

Deleuze, d'luz, (JOSEPH PHILIPPE FRANÇOIS,) a French naturalist, born at Sisteron in 1753. He was chosen aide-naturaliste to the Museum of Natural History in 1795, and librarian to the same in 1828. He translated Thomson's "Seasons" into French, and wrote several other works. Died in 1835.

Deleyre, d'lăR, (ALEXANDRE,) a French writer, born near Bordeaux in 1726. On the suppression of the order of Jesuits, with which he was connected, he went to Paris, where he associated with Diderot, Rousseau, etc. He published an "Analysis of Bacon's Philosophy," (1755,) which is said to be written with ability, and was

€ as k; ç as s; ğ hard; ġ as j; G, H, K, *guttural;* N, *nasal;* R, *trilled;* ś as z; th as in *this.* (☞See Explanations, p. 23.)

47

one of the editors of the "Encyclopédie." He was one of the first members of the Institute. In 1793 he was a republican member of the Convention, and voted for the death of the king. Died in 1797.

See J. LEBRETON, "Notice sur la Vie d'A. Deleyre," 1797.

Delfau, dĕl'fō', (Dom FRANÇOIS,) a French Benedictine monk, born in Auvergne in 1637, was charged by his order to edit the works of Saint Augustine. Died in 1676.

Delfico, dĕl'fe-ko, (MELCHIOR,) an Italian statesman and able writer on political economy, born in the Abruzzo in 1744. During the political troubles that followed the French Revolution he found refuge in the republic of San Marino. From 1806 to 1815 he was councillor of state at Naples, and acquired a high reputation for ability and integrity. The restored king Ferdinand in 1815 made him president of the commission of the archives of the kingdom. His most important works are a "History of San Marino," "Researches into the True Character of Roman Jurisprudence," (1791,) and "Thoughts on the Uncertainty and Inutility of History," etc., ("Pensieri su' la Storia e su' la Incertezza ed Inutilità della medesima," 1806.) He also wrote an Essay in favour of Free Trade. Died at Teramo in 1835.

See TIPALDO, "Biografia degli Italiani illustri;" F. MOZZETTI, "Ricordanza degli Studii e delle Opere di M. Delfico," 1835; F. RANALLI, "Elogio di M. Delfico," 1836; G. F. DELFICO, "Della Vita e delle Opere di M. Delfico," libri ii., 1836.

Delfino, dĕl-fee'no, (GIOVANNI,) Doge of Venice, elected in 1356, was previously procurator of Saint Mark. He found the republic at war with Louis, King of Hungary, who obtained the advantage and imposed the conditions of peace in 1358. Died in 1361.

Delfino, (GIOVANNI,) an Italian cardinal and poet, born about 1618 of a patrician family in Venice. He wrote "Cleopatra," and other tragedies, in verse, the style of which is praised by Ginguené. Died in 1699.

Delfosse, dĕl'foss', (NOËL JOSEPH AUGUSTE,) a Belgian advocate, born at Liege about 1810, was president of the Chamber from 1852 to April, 1855.

Delft, (GILLES DE.) See DELPHUS.

Delft, dĕlft, or **Delff,** dĕlf, (JACOB WILLEM,) a Dutch portrait-painter, lived at Delft; died in 1601.

Delft, (JACOB WILLEMSZOON,) a skilful Dutch portrait-painter, a grandson of the preceding, was born at Delft in 1619; died in 1661.

Delgado, dĕl-gä'Do, (JUAN PINTO,) a Spanish Jew and poet, wrote poems on Ruth and Esther, (1627.)

De l'Huys. See DROUYN DE L'HUYS.

Delia, a name of DIANA, which see.

Deliberatore, dà-le-bà-rà-to'rà, (NICCOLÒ,) an Italian painter, born at Foligno, flourished about 1460.

Delille or **De Lille,** deh-lèl' or d'lèl, (JACQUES,) L'ABBÉ, an eminent French didactic poet, born at Aigueperse, near Clermont in Auvergne, in 1738, was educated in Paris. Soon after leaving college he became professor of humanities at Amiens, where he began his translation of the "Georgics" of Virgil, which he published in 1769. It was deemed a wonderful performance in respect to the magnitude of the difficulties that had been overcome; and the French were enraptured to learn that their language was so capable of reproducing the grace, harmony, and variety of Virgil. Voltaire was so well pleased with the work that he wrote to the Academy in favour of the election of Delille. He was received into the French Academy in 1774, in the place of Condamine. In 1780 he produced "The Gardens," ("Les Jardins,") a poem abounding with picturesque descriptions: it was received with great favour, and translated into many languages. For several years before the Revolution he was professor of belles-lettres in the University of Paris, and of Latin poetry in the College of France. To escape from the anarchy of the new régime, he retired in 1794 to Saint-Dié, and afterwards to Switzerland, where he found the calm seclusion most congenial to the spirit of poetry. During this period of absence, part of which was passed in London, he meditated or matured several poems worthy of his high reputation. Returning to Paris in 1801, he published in rapid succession a poem on Pity, (1803,) "Virgil's Eneid translated into French Verse," (1804,) a poetical version of "Paradise Lost," (1805,) and "Imagination," a poem, (1806.) The last three are

among the most successful of his works. His version of the "Eneid" is regarded as the best in the language. "No French work," says the "Biographie Universelle," "presents a greater number of rich and beautiful images, or more harmonious and ingenious verses, than his poem on the Imagination." He had a perfect mastery of the art of ennobling words by their application, of giving a brilliant colour to thoughts and a sustained harmony to language. Died in Paris in May, 1813.

See LINGAY, "Éloge de Delille," 1814; CAMPENON, "Éloge de Delille," 1813; BERVILLE, "Éloge de J. Delille," 1817; FILIPPO MORDANI, "Elogio storico di G. Delille," 1845; "Nouvelle Biographie Générale;" "Edinburgh Review" for April, 1806.

Deliniers, deh-le'ne-air', (JACQUES ANTOINE MARIE,) Viceroy of Buenos Ayres, was born at Niort, France, in 1756. He entered the French navy, became a captain, and was sent on a mission to South America. Having taken command of a Spanish army, he captured Buenos Ayres from the British in 1807, gained great popularity, and became viceroy. About 1809 the Junta of Spain sent Cisneros to supersede him. In a revolutionary movement which followed, Deliniers supported the royalist cause, was made prisoner, and shot in 1810.

See F. DENIS, "Buenos Ayres et le Paraguay."

Delisle or **De Lisle,** deh-lèl' or d'lèl, (CLAUDE,) a French writer on history and geography, born at Vaucouleurs in 1644. After practising law some years, he removed to Paris, where he gave lectures on history. He published a "Historic Relation of Siam," an "Introduction to Geography," and a few other works. Several of his sons became eminent in science. Died in 1720.

Delisle, deh-lèl', [sometimes anglicized in pronunciation de-lïl',] (GUILLAUME,) a French geographer of great celebrity, born in Paris in 1675, was the son of the preceding. In early youth he conceived the project of reforming the system of geography; and, having accomplished this difficult task, he published, in 1700, a map of the world, celestial and terrestrial globes, and other valuable works, which procured his admission into the Academy of Sciences. According to Walckenaer, he is the principal author of the modern system of geography. He published afterwards numerous maps, ancient and modern, which obtained a European reputation; and he wrote many memoirs of geography, which were inserted in the Collection of the Academy. Louis XV. received lessons from Delisle, and rewarded him with the title of first geographer to the king. He died in 1726, and Fontenelle composed his eulogy.

See NICÉRON, "Mémoires;" "Biographie Universelle."

Delisle, (JOSEPH NICOLAS,) an eminent French astronomer, born in Paris in 1688, was the son of Claude, noticed above. In 1710 he obtained permission to occupy the dome of the Luxembourg, which he used as an observatory. Received into the Academy of Sciences in 1714, he communicated to it his observations. In 1724 he visited London, and by the influence of Newton was chosen a Fellow of the Royal Society. About 1725, at the solicitation of the empress Catherine, he went to Saint Petersburg to found a school of astronomy, and wrote several elementary treatises for his pupils. He returned to Paris in 1747, and resumed his observations. Among his principal works is a "Historical Essay on the Progress of Astronomy and Geography," (1738.) Died in 1768.

See LALANDE, "Notice sur De Lisle," in the "Nécrologe et Bibliographie Astronomique;" "Nouvelle Biographie Générale;" "Biographie Universelle."

Delisle, (LOUIS,) a brother of the preceding, was an astronomer and a member of the Academy of Sciences. He accompanied his brother Joseph to Saint Petersburg in 1725. Having traversed Siberia, he embarked in 1741 with Captain Behring on an exploring voyage, but died the same year. He had written a "Treatise on the Proper Motion of the Fixed Stars," and other works.

De Lisle, (ROUGET.) See ROUGET DE LISLE.

Delisle de la Drévetière, deh-lèl' deh lä dRäv'-te-air', (LOUIS FRANÇOIS,) a French dramatic author, born in Dauphiné; died in 1756.

Delitzsch, dä'litsh, (FRANZ,) a German theologian, born at Leipsic in 1813, published a "History of Jewish Poetry," (1836,) and other works.

Delius, a name of APOLLO, which see.

Delius, dä′le-ûs, (CHRISTOPH TRAUGOTT,) a German mineralogist, born in Saxony about 1730, became counsellor for the department of mines and of the mint in Vienna. He published "Directions for the Working of Mines," (1773.) Died in 1779.

Delius, (HEINRICH FRIEDRICH,) a German physician and naturalist, born at Wernigerode, Saxony, in 1720; died in 1791.

See "Nouvelle Biographie Générale."

Dell, (WILLIAM,) an English nonconformist minister, who became master of Caius College, Cambridge. In 1662 he was ejected for nonconformity.

See HODGSON, "Reformers and Martyrs," Philadelphia, 1867.

Della Maria, del′lä mä-ree′ä, (DOMINIQUE,) a composer of operatic music, was born at Marseilles in 1768; died in Paris in 1800.

Delling or **Dellingr.** See NÖRVI.

Dello, del′lo, a Florentine painter, born in 1372, resided for some time in Spain, where he obtained a high reputation. Died in 1421.

See VASARI, "Lives of the Painters," etc.; LANZI, "History of Painting in Italy."

Dellon, dä′lôN′, (C.,) a French physician and traveller, born about 1650, made a voyage to the East Indies in 1668. He was persecuted and imprisoned for two years by the Inquisition at Goa. He returned home in 1677, and published a "Narrative of his Voyage," (1685,) a work of some merit.

Delmas, dĕl′mäs′, (ANTOINE GUILLAUME,) an able French general, born near Tulle in 1768. He became general of brigade in 1793, and took command of a division, with which he obtained several successes in 1794. He served a few years in Italy, where he was the second in command under Joubert in 1799. In 1802 he offended the First Consul, and was dismissed from service. The cause of this disgrace was supposed to be a reply which he made when Bonaparte asked him what he thought of the ceremony performed in honour of the Concordat. "A piece of mummery," *(capucinade,)* said Delmas: "nothing is wanting but the million of men who have perished in order to overthrow what you have now re-established." In 1813 he again commanded a division, and was killed at the battle of Leipsic.

See "Victoires et Conquêtes des Français."

Delmas, (JEAN FRANÇOIS BERTRAND,) a French Jacobin, born near Toulouse in 1754, entered the Legislative Assembly in 1791. In the Convention he voted for the death of the king, (1792,) and for the destruction of Robespierre in 1794. He was afterwards chosen president of the Jacobins. Died in 1798.

Delmas, PÈRE, a French priest and poet, born in Rouergue in 1733, professed rhetoric, etc. in the College of Toulouse. He published an admired Latin poem on the pastoral office, entitled "Art of Arts," etc., ("Ars Artium," etc.) Died in 1790.

Delmatius, [Fr. DELMACE.] See DALMATIUS.

Delminio. See CAMILLO.

Delmont, dĕl′môN′, (DEODAT,) a Flemish historical painter, born at Saint-Tron in 1581, is said to have been a pupil and friend of Rubens. Descamps praises his design, composition, and colouring. Among his works is an "Adoration of the Kings." Died at Antwerp in 1634.

See DESCAMPS, "Vies des Peintres Flamands," etc.

Delmotte, dĕl′mot′, (HENRI FLORENT,) a Belgian *littérateur,* born at Mons in 1779, was a member of the Academy of Brussels, and author of a great number of works on different subjects. Died in 1836.

See HENNEBERT, "Notice sur la Vie de H. F. Delmotte," 1837.

De Lolme, deh-lolm′, (JOHN LOUIS,) a Swiss lawyer and author, born at Geneva in 1740. Having offended the government by a political pamphlet, he consulted his safety by emigrating to England, where he lived many years. He became very indigent, and received aid from the literary fund. In 1771 he published "The Constitution of England," originally written in French, which was much celebrated, and often reprinted. A few years later he published an English edition of this work. It was commended by Lord Chatham and Chief-Justice Story. The author of "Junius" called it "a performance

deep, solid, and ingenious." De Lolme wrote a few other minor works. Died in Switzerland in 1806.

See CHARLES COOTE, "Notice of De Lolme," prefixed to his work, "The Constitution of England," 1807.

Delord, d'loR, (TAXILE,) a French editor, born at Avignon in 1815. He became chief editor of the "Charivari," a satirical paper of Paris, in 1842. He also contributed to the "Siècle" and other journals.

Delorme, d'loRm, (CHARLES,) born at Moulins, France, in 1584, succeeded his father, Jean, as physician to Louis XIII., and was very eminent in his profession. He acquired the friendship of Richelieu and Chancellor Seguier, who granted him a pension. Died in 1678.

Delorme, (JEAN,) a French physician, born at Moulins in 1547, was the father of the preceding. He was for some time professor at Montpellier. He became physician to Henry IV. in 1606, and afterwards to his successor, Louis XIII. He resigned his office in 1626, and died in 1637.

Delorme, (MARION,) a famous French beauty and courtesan, born at Châlons, in Champagne, about 1612. She is said to have been extremely witty and intelligent. Her salon was the rendezvous of princes, courtiers, etc., including Richelieu, De Grammont, and Saint-Evremond. Died in 1650.

See GRAMMONT, "Mémoires;" "Vie de M. Delorme," Paris, 1805.

Delorme, (PHILIBERT,) an eminent French architect, born at Lyons about 1518, studied art in Rome, and returned home in 1536. After erecting several fine edifices in Lyons, he went to Paris, where he was patronized by Catherine de Médicis, for whom, about 1564, he designed the palace of the Tuileries, which is regarded as his best production. She appointed him almoner to the king, and gave him several benefices in the church. He was architect of the Château de Meudon and the Château d'Anet, which were much admired. He published a work on architecture, and a treatise entitled "New Inventions for Building well at Little Expense," (1561.) "He divested his art of Gothic habiliments," says Milizia, "and arrayed it in those of ancient Greece." Died in 1577.

See MILIZIA, "Mémoires sur les Architectes;" PINGERON, "Vies des Architectes anciens et modernes;" COLLET, "Notice sur P. Delorme;" FLACHERON, "Éloge de P. Delorme."

Delorme, (PIERRE CLAUDE FRANÇOIS,) a French historical painter, born in Paris in 1783. Among his works are "The Death of Hero and Leander," (1814,) "Eve Plucking the Forbidden Fruit," (1834,) and a "Repose in Egypt," (1850.)

Delort, d'loR, (JACQUES ANTOINE ADRIEN,) BARON, a French general, born at Arbois in 1773. He commanded with *éclat* in 1812 at the battle of Castalla, and became general of division in February, 1814. He distinguished himself at Waterloo in 1815, and in 1837 was made a peer. Died in 1846.

Delort, (JOSEPH,) a French historian, born at Mirande (Gers) in 1789. Among his works is a "History of the Man in the Iron Mask," (1825.)

Deloy, d'lwä, (JEAN BAPTISTE AIMÉ,) a French poet, born near Lure in 1798; died in 1834.

See SAINTE-BEUVE, "Portraits contemporains."

Delpech, dĕl′pâsh′, (FRANÇOIS SÉRAPHIN,) a skilful French designer, born in Paris in 1778; died in 1825.

Delpech, (JACQUES MATHIEU,) a French physician and skilful surgeon, born at Toulouse about 1775. He was chosen professor of clinical surgery in the faculty of Montpellier, (1812,) where he lectured with success, and published several treatises on surgery, among which is an important work, entitled "Summary of Diseases called Surgical," ("Précis des Maladies réputées chirurgicales," 1815.) He was murdered in 1832 by a man named Duceptos.

See F. BUISSON, "Parallèle de Delpech et Dupuytren," 1841; "Nouvelle Biographie Générale."

Delphinus. See DELFINO.

Del′phus, (ÆGIDIUS,) sometimes called **Gilles de Delft,** was professor of theology in Paris in 1507. Erasmus praised his talent for Latin poetry. Among his works are a Latin poetical version of Saint Paul's Epistle to the Romans, and a commentary on Ovid's "De Remedio Amoris."

Delpon de Livernon, dĕl′pŏN′ deh le′vĕR′nŏN′, (JACQUES ANTOINE,) a French writer and antiquary, born in 1778, wrote an "Essay on Liberty of Worship," and other works. Died in 1833.

Delporte, dĕl′poRT′, (FRANÇOIS,) a French agriculturist, born at Boulogne-sur-Mer in 1746; died in 1819.

Delrieu, dĕl′re-u̲h′, (ÉTIENNE JOSEPH BERNARD,) a French dramatic author, born in 1761, was for a long time regent of rhetoric at Versailles. He wrote numerous dramas, which had a moderate success, and gained a durable reputation by his tragedy of "Artaxerxes," (1808,) which procured him a pension of two thousand francs. Died in 1836.

See QUÉRARD, " La France Littéraire."

Delrio, dĕl-ree′o,(MARTIN ANTOINE,) a learned Jesuit, born at Antwerp in 1551, was master of ten or more languages. He became procureur-général of Brabant in 1578, removed to Valladolid in 1580, and obtained the chair of philosophy at Douay in 1589. He wrote "Notes on Claudian's Poems," and other critical works. His "Essay on Magic" (1599) was once popular. Died in 1608.

See NICÉRON, "Mémoires."

Delta. See MOIR, (DAVID MACBETH.)

Deluc, d'lük, (GUILLAUME ANTOINE,) a brother of the celebrated geologist noticed below, born at Geneva in 1729, was associated with his brother in his geological excursions and other scientific labours. He wrote numerous treatises on mineralogy and geology, which were inserted in the "Journal de Physique" and other periodicals. They indicate accurate observation and a philosophic mind. Died in 1812.

Deluc or **De Luc,** deh-look′, [Fr. pron. d'lük,] (JEAN ANDRÉ,) an eminent natural philosopher, born at Geneva in 1727. In early life he was engaged in commerce, and employed his leisure in the study of geology and other sciences. He improved the thermometer, and measured the height of mountains more exactly than any one had previously done, by means of the portable barometer which he invented. In 1772 he published his "Researches on the Modifications of the Atmosphere," an excellent work, which was then the most complete on that subject. About 1773 he visited England, and was chosen Fellow of the Royal Society, and reader to the queen, who gave him a lodging in Windsor Castle. In 1778 he produced his great work on geology, "Letters, Physical and Moral, on the History of the Earth and of Man," in which he maintains the accordance of the Mosaic history with the facts of geology. The theories advanced in this excited much opposition, but were supported at one time by Cuvier. He ascribed the formation of the present continents to causes no longer operative, to a great and sudden revolution which occurred four or five thousand years ago. His "Letters to Blumenbach on the Physical History of the Earth" (1798) increased his reputation as a geologist. He wrote a large number of works, (in French,) among which are a "Summary of Bacon's Philosophy," and "Geological Journeys in Northern Europe," (1810.) Died at Windsor in 1817.

See SENEBIER, "Histoire littéraire de Genève," tome iii.; QUÉRARD, "La France Littéraire."

Delvaux, dĕl′vŏ′, [Lat. VALLEN′SIS,] (ANDRÉ,) a Belgian jurist and canonist, born in 1569; died in 1636.

Delvig, dĕl′viG, a Russian poet, born in 1798; died in 1831.

Delvincourt, dĕl′vǎN′kooR′, (CLAUDE ÉTIENNE,) a French jurist, born in Paris in 1762. When the schools of law were reorganized, in 1805, he obtained a chair in the capital, and began the first public course on the new civil code. In 1810 he became dean of the faculty in the University. At the restoration in 1814 he retained this place, and was chosen royal censor. He published in 1808 "Institutes of French Law," which is highly commended. Died in 1831.

See DE PORTETS, "Notice sur la Vie, etc. de M. Delvincourt," 1832.

Delzons, dĕl′zŏN′, (ALEXIS JOSEPH,) a brave French general, born at Aurillac in 1775, joined the expedition to Egypt, (1798,) where he obtained the rank of general of brigade in 1801. As general of division, he commanded the army of Illyria in 1811. In 1812 he fought at Boro-

dino, and was killed in battle during the retreat from Moscow in the same year.

See SÉGUR, "Campagne de la Russie."

Demabuse. See MABUSE, DE.

Demachy, d'mǎ′she′, (JACQUES FRANÇOIS,) a French chemist, born in Paris in 1728. He wrote, among other works, "Elements of Chemistry," (2 vols., 1766,) and refused to adopt the theories of Lavoisier. Died in 1803.

Démade. See DEMADES.

De-mā′dēs, [Gr. Δημάδης; Fr. DÉMADE, dǎ′mǎd′,] an Athenian orator and demagogue, noted for his witticisms, venality, and profligacy. He entered public life about 350 B.C., became an opponent or enemy of Demosthenes, and acquired great influence by his eloquence, wit, and other talents. He usually spoke extempore. After the battle of Chæronea he acted with the party of the King of Macedon, by whom he was bribed; and he was one of the chief authors of the peace between Philip and the Athenians. He was convicted of receiving a bribe from Harpalus, and for a subsequent offence was sentenced to exclusion from political functions; but a few years later he was sent on an embassy to Antipater. He was put to death by the order of Antipater, (or, according to Plutarch, of Cassander,) in 318 B.C.

See DIODORUS SICULUS, books xvi., xvii., and xviii.; PLUTARCH, "Demosthenes;" SUIDAS, Δημάδης; RUHNKEN, "Historia critica Oratorum Græcorum;" FREYTAG, "De Demade," 1752; H. LHARDY, "Dissertatio de Demade Oratore," Berlin, 1834.

De Maistre. See MAISTRE.

Demante, deh-mŏNt′, (ANTOINE MARIE,) a French jurist, and professor of civil law at Paris, was born in that city in 1789. He published an excellent work entitled "Programme du Cours de Droit civil Français," (3 vols., 1830.) Died in 1856.

Démarate. See DEMARATUS.

Dem-a-rā′tus, [Gr. Δημάρατος,] a native of Corinth, emigrated to Etruria about 650 B.C., and became a prince. He was the father of Aruns and Lucumo.

Demaratus, [Fr. DÉMARATE, dǎ′mǎ′rǎt′,] King of Sparta, began to reign jointly with Cleomenes about 510 B.C. He quarrelled with his colleague, who caused him to be deposed about 491, on the ground that he was not a son of the late king Ariston. He retired to Persia, where he was favourably received by Darius I. He gave wise counsels to Xerxes on the invasion of Greece, and is said to have secretly informed the Spartans that such an event was impending.

See HERODOTUS, books v., vi., vii.; XENOPHON, "Hellenica."

Dembarrère, dŏN′bǎ′raiR′, (JEAN,) COUNT, a French general and engineer, born at Tarbes in 1747, became a general of division in 1794, and obtained the chief command of the engineers in Italy. In 1805 he was chosen a senator, and retired from the army. Died in 1828.

Dembinski, dĕm-bin′skee, (HENRY,) a Polish general, born in the palatinate of Cracow in 1791. In 1830 he took arms for Polish independence, obtained command of a brigade, and distinguished himself in several actions. He made a masterly retreat from Lithuania in July, 1831, and went into exile in the autumn of that year. In February, 1849, he was appointed by Kossuth commander-in-chief of the Hungarian army; but in consequence of the refusal of Görgei, and other officers, to serve under a Pole, he was soon superseded. He accepted the post of quartermaster-general under Meszaros, and commanded at Temesvar, (August, 1849,) where the Hungarians were finally defeated. Died in 1864.

Dembowski, dĕm-bov′skee, (EDWARD,) a Polish writer, born in Plock about 1810; died in 1846.

Dembowski, (LOUIS MATHIEU,) BARON, a general in the French army, born at Gora in 1769; died in 1812.

Demeste, deh-mêst′, (JEAN,) a Flemish surgeon and chemist, born in 1743, lived at Liege; died in 1783.

De-me′ter, [Δημήτηρ,] the name of one of the principal Greek divinities, identified with the Ceres of the Roman mythology. (See CERES.)

De-me′tri-us, [Δημήτριος,] an Athenian poet of the old comedy, lived in the fifth century B.C.

Demetrius, a Greek sculptor, flourished about 350 B.C. Among his chief works was a statue of Minerva, called "Musica," because the motion of the serpents on the Gorgon's head produced a musical sound.

ā, ē, ī, ō, ū, ȳ, long; ă, ĕ, ĭ, ŏ, ŭ, y̆, short; ạ, ẹ, ị, ọ, obscure; fär, fǎll, fǎt; mĕt; nŏt; gōōd; mōōn;

Demetrius I. See DEMETRIUS POLIORCETES.

Demetrius II., son of Antigonus Gonatas, became King of Macedon in 243 B.C., as successor to his father. He married first a daughter of Antiochus Theos, and then Phthia, a daughter of the King of Epirus. After a reign of ten years, he died, and left the throne to his son, Philip III.

Demetrius, a Macedonian prince, grandson of the preceding, born in 207 B.C., was the second son of Philip III., and brother of Perseus, (Perses.) When Philip was defeated by the Romans, Demetrius was delivered to the victors as a hostage. Having returned home, he was sent as an ambassador by Philip to defend him against certain charges before the Roman senate, whose favour he gained by his ingenuous modesty. Perseus, by false accusations, induced his father to put Demetrius to death about 180 B.C.

See POLYBIUS, "History," books xviii., xx., xxiii., and xxiv.

Demetrius I. and II., (Kings of Syria.) See DEME-TRIUS SOTER, and DEMETRIUS NICATOR.

De-me'trĭ-us II., King of Georgia, succeeded his father, David III., in 1126. He waged a long war with the Turks, who fought for the possession of Armenia and sometimes invaded Georgia. He died in 1158, and left the throne to his son, David IV.

Demetrius III., King of Georgia, the son and successor of David V., reigned from 1272 to 1289, and was succeeded by his son, David VI.

De-me'trĭ-us, [Russ. DMITRI, dmee'tRee,] Czar of Russia, usually styled "the False Demetrius," claimed to be the son of Ivan IV. The latter, at his death, left a minor son, who was reported to have died, or to have been killed, in 1591. During the reign of Boris in Russia, about 1603, Demetrius raised an army of Poles, invaded Russia, and fought several battles with various success, until Boris died, in 1605, when Demetrius obtained the throne without further opposition. His subjects, offended by his partiality to foreign customs, and by the insolence of his Polish soldiers, revolted and put him to death in 1606. Prince Shuisky (or Schuiskoi) was then proclaimed Czar, as Basil III.

See DE THOU, "Histoire Universelle ;" KARAMZIN, "Histoire de l'Empire de Russie ;" PROSPER MÉRIMÉE, "Épisode de l'Histoire de Russie ; les faux Démétrius," 1852.

Demetrius, [Russ. DMITRI,] THE FALSE, the second of that name who made pretensions to the Russian crown. Soon after the accession of Shuisky, this person asserted that he was the Czar Demetrius. He found many partisans, was recognized by the wife of the late Czar, and was enabled to besiege Moscow with an army, but was killed in 1610 by some Tartars who served in his guard. Schiller and Pushkin have dramatized the story of these impostors.

See PROSPER MÉRIMÉE, "Épisode de l'Histoire de Russie ; les faux Démétrius," 1852.

Demetrius of Alexandria, a Peripatetic philosopher, lived about 150 B.C.

Demetrius of Apamea, a Greek physician of unknown date, who is often cited by Cœlius Aurelianus.

Demetrius of Byzantium, a Greek historian, lived about 280 B.C.

Demetrius of Magnesia, a Greek grammarian, who flourished about 60 B.C. He was author of an important critical and historical work which treated of authors that bore the same name, ("Peri homonymōn Poietōn kai suggraphëon.")

Demetrius of Scepsis, a Greek grammarian, who lived about 150 B.C.

Demetrius of Sunium, a Greek Cynic philosopher, who acquired celebrity as a teacher in the first century. He lived some time at Corinth, visited Rome in the reign of Nero, and was banished from Italy by Vespasian. He is eulogized by Seneca, who quotes his maxims.

De-me'trĭ-us Çў-do'nĭ-us, a Greek or Byzantine theologian and writer, held high offices under John Cantacuzene. He entered a cloister in 1355.

De-me'trĭ-us Mos'chus, a Greek poet, who lived about 1450, and wrote a poem on the "Marriage of Paris and Helen," printed in 1510.

De-me'trĭ-us Nĭ-cā'tor, [Νικάτωρ,] King of Syria, was the son of Demetrius Soter, and ascended the throne in 146 B.C., after defeating the usurper Balas. He mar-ried Cleopatra, an Egyptian princess. In a war with the Parthians he was taken prisoner, and in his absence his brother, Antiochus Sidetes, usurped the throne. On his release from captivity, he again obtained the kingdom ; but his misgovernment provoked a general revolt of his subjects, and he was assassinated at Tyre in 126 B.C.

See JUSTIN, books xxxv., xxxvi., and xxxviii.

De-me'trĭ-us Pep-ạ-gom'e-nus, [Δημήτριος Πεπαγό-μενος,] a Greek physician, who lived in the thirteenth century, composed a work on the gout, which has some merit. It was printed in Greek in 1558. He was physician to the emperor Michael Palæologus, who reigned from 1260 to 1282.

De-me'trĭ-us Pha-le'reũs, (or fa-lee're-us,) [Fr. DÉMÉTRIUS DE PHALÈRE, dắ'mắ'tRe'ŭs' dẹh fắ'laiR',] a distinguished Grecian orator and philosopher, born at Phale'rum, in Attica, about 345 B.C., was a pupil of Theophrastus in philosophy. It is said that he was condemned to death with Phocion, but saved himself by flight. About 316 B.C. Cassander appointed him governor of Athens, which for ten years enjoyed prosperity under his wise and popular administration. Three hundred and sixty statues were erected to him by the Athenians. When Athens was taken by Demetrius Poliorcetes, in 306, he retired to the court of Ptolemy, King of Egypt. He died in Egypt about 284 B.C. He wrote historical and philosophical works, which are all lost. Cicero and other ancient writers extol his merit as an orator and a statesman.

See DIOGENES LAERTIUS ; CICERO, "Brutus," and "De Oratore ;" H. DOHRN, "De Vita et Rebus Démetrii Phalerei," 1825 ; BONAMY, "Vie de Démétrius de Phalère," in the "Mémoires de l'Académie des Inscriptions," tome viii.

De-me'trĭ-us Pol-ĭ-or-çe'tēs, [Gr. Δημήτριος Πολιορ-κητής ; Fr. DÉMÉTRIUS POLIORCÈTE, dắ'mắ'tRe'ŭs' po'le'-oR'sằt',] born about 335 B.C., was the son of Antigonus, one of Alexander's generals and successors. From his great success as a commander, he was surnamed POLIORCETES, or "taker of cities." He delivered Athens from the dominion of Cassander, and commanded his father's army in the war against Ptolemy. About 306 he gained a great naval victory over Ptolemy, and took Cyprus. At the siege of Rhodes he displayed great skill as engineer, but was baffled in his attempt to take the city. After his father was killed at the battle of Ipsus, (299 B.C.,) he formed an alliance with Seleucus, and again made himself master of Athens. Having been invited to mediate in a dispute between two claimants to the throne of Macedon, he killed one, and usurped the throne himself, in 294. Pyrrhus and Lysimachus declared war against him, and expelled him from Macedon. He died about 283, leaving a son, Antigonus Gonatas. Demetrius possessed military talents of a high order. Plutarch draws a parallel between him and Mark Antony.

See PLUTARCH, "Demetrius," and "Pyrrhus ;" APPIAN, passim ; ROLLIN, "Ancient History ;" DIODORUS SICULUS, books xix., xx., and xxi. ; JUSTIN, books xv. and xvi. ; J. C. DE WIT, "Dissertatio de Demetrio Poliorcete," 1840.

De-me'trĭ-us So'tẹr, [Δημήτριος Σωτήρ,] King of Syria, was the son of Seleucus Philopator, and was born about 185 B.C. At the age of ten he was sent to Rome as a hostage, where he was detained many years, while his uncle Antiochus Epiphanes obtained the throne at the death of Seleucus in 175 B.C. In 161 Demetrius escaped from Rome, and was proclaimed king by the Syrians. The Maccabees bravely and successfully maintained the cause of the Jews against the army of this prince. Alexander Balas, pretending to be the son of Antiochus, entered Syria with an army, and, in a battle that followed, Demetrius was killed, 150 B.C. His son, Demetrius Nicator, became king a few years afterwards.

See POLYBIUS, "History," books xxxi., xxxii., and xxxiii. ; AP-PIAN, "Syriaca ;" JUSTIN, book xxxv.

Demetz, dẹh-mắs', (FRÉDÉRIC AUGUSTE,) a French philanthropist, born in 1796, became a judge in Paris. In 1836 he visited the United States with De Tocqueville, to examine the prisons of that country. He founded about 1840, at Mettray, near Tours, an institution for the reformation of juvenile offenders, which has been very successful and has become the model after which others are formed. His system is very popular in England, where it has been tried near London.

Demeulemeester, dẹh-muh′lẹh-mās′tẹr,? (JOSEPH CHARLES,) a Belgian engraver, born at Bruges in 1771. He engraved some frescos of biblical subjects painted by Raphael in the Vatican. Died in 1836.

Démeunier, dắ′muh′nẹ-ȧ′, or **Desmeunier,** dắ′-muh′nẹ-ȧ′, (JEAN NICOLAS,) an able French writer, born at Nozeroy in 1751. He was secretary of Monsieur (afterwards Louis XVIII.) when the Revolution began, was elected to the States-General in 1789, and became a senator in 1802. He translated several histories and voyages of discovery from the English, and wrote, besides other works, an "Essay on the United States," (of North America,) (1786,) and a "Treatise on the Customs of Various Nations, ("Esprit des Usages," etc., 1776,) which induced Voltaire to write him a flattering letter. Died in 1814.

Demidof, dĕm-e-dof′ or dĕm′e-dof, **Demidov,** or **Demidow,** the founder of the noble and wealthy Russian family of Demidof, was a native of Toola, (Tula.) He became skilful in the manufacture of arms, and gained the favour of Peter the Great. He established the first iron-foundry in Siberia. His descendants, about 1725, discovered the gold-mines of Kolyvan.

Demidof, Demidov, or **Demidow,** (ANATOLI,) COUNT, a rich Russian capitalist, a son of Count Nikolai, noticed below, was distinguished as a patron of science and literature. He was born at Florence about 1812. In 1839 he published, in French, "Travels in Southern Russia and the Crimea, through Hungary," etc., the result of an exploring expedition performed by him in company with several artists and savants. He married in 1840 Mathilde, a daughter of Jerome Bonaparte.

Demidof, Demidov, or **Demidow,** (NIKOLAI,) COUNT, a learned Russian noble, noted for benevolence, born near Saint Petersburg in 1774, inherited from his father a fortune in mines and forges. He studied the sciences, and travelled in pursuit of knowledge, which he applied in the promotion of the industrial arts. He made great improvements in the processes of mining and in the manufacture of iron, and established for his vassals an academy of fine arts. He died at Florence in 1828, leaving two sons, Paul and Anatoli. He had been chosen a privy councillor by the emperor Paul I.

See V. MÜLLER, "Notice sur la Vie privée de N. Demidof," 1830.

Demidof, Demidov, or **Demidow,** (PAUL,) of the same family as the preceding, was born at Revel about 1738. He cultivated natural history, and made a rich collection of specimens, which he presented to the University of Moscow. He founded the Demidof Lyceum at Yaroslav about 1800. Died in 1826.

Demidof, Demidov, or **Demidow,** (PROKOP,) born in Moscow about 1730, was the proprietor of gold-mines in the Ural Mountains, the product of which, it is said, made him the richest subject of Russia. He was the uncle of Count Nikolai, noticed above.

Demidov or **Demidow.** See DEMIDOF.

De Missy, dẹ-mis′see, (CÆSAR,) a learned German divine, born in Berlin in 1703, removed about 1731 to London, where he preached in a French chapel. Died in 1775.

Demme, dĕm′mẹh, (HERMANN CHRISTOPH GOTTFRIED,) a popular German moralist and novelist, born at Mühlhausen in 1760. His *nom-de-plume* was KARL STILLE, (stil′lẹh.) He became superintendent-general at Altenburg in 1801. Among his works are "The Farmer Martin and his Father," (2 vols., 1793,) and "Abendstunden," (2 vols., 1804.) Died in 1822.

Démocède. See DEMOCEDES.

Dem-o-çe′dēš, [Gr. Δημοκήδης; Fr. DÉMOCÈDE, dắ′-mo′sȧd′,] an eminent Greek physician of Crotona, born about 550 B.C. He was taken prisoner at Samos by the Persians, and carried to Darius Hystaspes, whose favour he gained by his medical skill. The king rewarded him richly, but refused him permission to return home. The queen Atossa, who had been cured by him, promised to aid him in escaping from captivity, and persuaded Darius to send him with a small party of Persians to explore the coasts of Greece with hostile designs. When they arrived at Tarentum, the Persians were arrested, and Democedes escaped to Crotona.

See HERODOTUS, book iii.

De-moch′a-rēš, [Gr. Δημοχάρης; Fr. DÉMOCHARÈS, dắ′mo′kȧ′rès′,] an Athenian orator, was a nephew of Demosthenes. His public career began about 322 B.C., soon after which he became one of the leaders of the anti-Macedonian party. After the restoration of democracy in Athens by Demetrius Poliorcetes in 307, Demochares was the chief of the patriotic party. He was exiled about 295, but returned in 287 or 286 B.C., and managed the finances with ability and success. He was living in 280 B.C. He left a history of his own time, which has not come down to us.

See PLUTARCH, "Demosthenes" and "Demetrius;" "Vitæ Decem Oratorum;" DROYSEN, "Geschichte der Nachfolger Alexanders."

Démocrate. See DEMOCRATES.

De-moc′ra-tēš, [Gr. Δημοκράτης; Fr. DÉMOCRATE, dắ′mo′krȧt′,] an Athenian orator, who lived about 350 B.C., was a contemporary of Demosthenes. Aristotle has preserved one of his orations.

Démocrite or **Democrito.** See DEMOCRITUS.

De-moc′rī-tus, [Gr. Δημόκριτος; Fr. DÉMOCRITE, dắ′mo′krèt′; It. and Sp. DEMOCRITO, dȧ-mok′re-to,] a celebrated Greek philosopher, born at Abdera, in Thrace, was the son of a man of large fortune. The date of his birth is variously given between 490 and 460 B.C. He received early lessons from some Chaldean Magi left by Xerxes in his invasion of Greece, and is thought to have been a disciple of Leucippus. Having inherited one hundred talents upon the division of his father's estate, he travelled in Egypt, Greece, Persia, and India, in pursuit of knowledge. When his patrimony was spent, he returned to Abdera, and read in public one of his works, which, according to Diogenes Laertius, procured him a large present of money and great honours from the people. His love of study and of solitude induced him to decline the political pre-eminence which the citizens of Abdera offered to him. There is a prevalent tradition that he was habitually laughing at the follies of mankind.

Democritus possessed a profound and original genius for philosophy. He was versed in geometry, logic, physics, natural history, and ethics, and wrote many works on these subjects; but none of them has come down to us. Cicero informs us that his style was as charming as that of Plato. His atomic philosophy presents in some respects a great analogy to that which prevails in the present time. He supposed that the universe is composed of empty space and of indivisible atoms, which are infinite in number, and which by their different motions and affinities produce the various phenomena of nature. He taught that matter is eternal, and that the mind or soul is the motion of round fiery atoms. He ascribed sensation to images or emanations flowing from its objects. Many of his theories were adopted by Epicurus, and illustrated by Lucretius in his poem "De Rerum Natura." Democritus lived to the age of one hundred years or more. He is not mentioned in any work of Plato, who was his contemporary.

See RITTER, "History of Philosophy;" G. H. LEWES, "Biographical History of Philosophy;" DIOGENES LAERTIUS; TENNEMANN, "Geschichte der Philosophie;" FABRICIUS, "Bibliotheca Græca;" BURCHARD, "Commentatio critica de Democriti de Sensibus Philosophia," 1830; F. G. A. MULLACH, "Democriti Operum Fragmenta," or "De Philosophi Vita Scriptis et Placitis," 1843; JENICHEN, "Programma de Democrito Philosopho," 1720.

Demoivre, dẹh-mwȧvr′, (ABRAHAM,) an eminent mathematician, born at Vitry (Champagne) in 1667, was the son of Protestant parents. In consequence of the revocation of the edict of Nantes, 1685, he emigrated to London, where he taught mathematics, and acquired the friendship of Newton. He was a Fellow of the Royal Society, and an Associate of the Academy of Sciences in Paris. His reputation was so high that he was one of a committee appointed to decide on the claims of Newton and Leibnitz to the invention of the method of fluxions. He published in 1730 "Analytical Miscellanies," ("Miscellanea Analytica," etc,) which presented ingenious and original ideas on the subject, also "The Doctrine of Chances," and "Annuities on Lives." Died in 1754.

See MATY, "Mémoire sur la Vie de Abraham Demoivre;" MONTUCLA, "Histoire des Mathématiques."

Demolombe, dẹh-mo′lômb′, (JEAN CHARLES FLORENT,) a French jurist, born in 1804.

De'mon, [Δήμων,] an Athenian orator, who lived about 330 B.C., was a nephew of Demosthenes.

De-mo'nax, [Δημώναξ,] a Cynic philosopher, born in Cyprus, lived at Athens about 150 A.D., and was intimate with Lucian. The latter esteemed him as one of the best or wisest philosophers of that time.

Démons, dȧ'môn', (CLAUDE,) a French poet, born at Amiens in 1591 ; died after 1628.

Demont, dẹh-môn', COUNT, a French general, born at Courbevoie. He obtained the rank of general of division for his conduct at Austerlitz. Died in 1826.

De-moph'ạ-nēs, [Gr. Δημοφάνης ; Fr. DÉMOPHANE, dȧ'mo'fȧn',] a Greek Platonic philosopher of Megalopolis, aided Aratus to restore liberty to Sicyon.

Demophilus. See DAMOPHILUS.

De-moph'ĭ-lus, [Δημόφιλος,] a Greek historian, lived about 320 B.C. He wrote a continuation of the history of Ephorus, who was his father.

Demophilus, [Fr. DÉMOPHILE, dȧ'mo'fêl',] a Pythagorean philosopher of uncertain epoch. He left a work on morality called "Βίου Θεράπεια," of which fragments are extant.

Demophon. See DAMOPHON.

Dem'o-phon or **De-moph'o-on,** [Gr. Δημοφῶν or Δημοφόων,] a son of Theseus and Phædra, was betrothed to Phyllis. (See PHYLLIS.) Having become King of Athens, he aided the Heraclidæ in war against Eurystheus.

Demophoon. See DEMOPHON.

De Mor'gan, (AUGUSTUS,) an English mathematician, born in the isle of Madura, near Java, in 1806. About 1828 he became professor of mathematics in the University of London, (now University College, London.) He contributed largely to the "Penny Cyclopædia," the "North British Review," and other periodicals, and has obtained a high reputation by many mathematical works, among which are "Elements of Algebra," an "Essay on Probabilities," (1838,) "Formal Logic, or the Calculus of Inference Necessary and Probable," (1847,) and "Arithmetical Books from the Invention of Printing to the Present Time," (1847.)

Demostene or **Démosthène.** See DEMOSTHENES.

Demosthenes, de-mos'the-nêz, [Gr. Δημοσθένης ; Lat. DEMOS'THENES ; Fr. DÉMOSTHÈNE, dȧ'mos'tain' ; It. DEMOSTENE, dȧ-mos'tȧ-nȧ ; Sp. DEMOSTENES, dȧ-mos'tȧ-nês,] regarded by almost universal consent as the greatest orator that ever lived, was born in the *demos* ("district") of Pæania, near Athens, in Greece, about 382, or, according to some authorities, 385 B.C. His father, whose name was also Demosthenes, was a cutler and cabinet-maker : he died when his son was seven years old, leaving a fortune of fifteen talents (above 15,000 dollars) to be shared between him and his sister. His guardians converted to their own use a large part of his property, and neglected to improve the remainder. Demosthenes studied rhetoric with Isæus, and, according to some accounts, received lessons in philosophy from Plato. Cicero states that Demosthenes was the pupil of the orator Isocrates ; but this is discredited by many critics.

When about eighteen years old, Demosthenes prosecuted his unfaithful guardians, and pleaded his own cause. The case was decided in his favour ; but he recovered only a part of his just claim. Some years previously, it is said, his emulation had been excited by the forensic triumphs of Callistratus, and he resolved to devote all his energies to the study of eloquence, although he laboured under great physical disadvantages. His constitution was delicate, his breath short, his voice feeble and stammering. It is said that he remedied these defects by running up-hill and speaking with pebbles in his mouth ; that he declaimed on the sea-shore, in order to accustom himself to the noise and tumult of popular assemblies ; and that he usually spoke his orations before a mirror, in order to discover and correct any awkwardness of gesture. According to Plutarch, his first address before a popular assembly was a failure. The people laughed at his ungraceful gestures, his confused periods, and his defective elocution. But Satyrus the actor encouraged him, and gave a proper direction to his indomitable resolution, by showing him the importance of appropriate action and of a distinct and well-modu-

lated utterance. Demosthenes then shut himself up in a subterranean study, and laboured with unremitting diligence in order to perfect himself as an orator. He is said to have shaved one side of his head, that he might be absolutely prevented from going into society. He improved his style by transcribing Thucydides, the concentrated thought and energy of whose writings were the objects of his especial emulation. Some writers state that he copied the history of Thucydides no less than eight times.

At the age of about twenty-seven (355 B.C.) he again came forward to compete for the palm of eloquence in his oration against Leptines, and was completely successful. Soon afterwards he appeared on a more conspicuous stage, and became one of the principal actors in the history of that period. "He had a glorious subject for his political ambition," says Plutarch,—"to defend the cause of Greece against Philip. He soon gained great reputation both for eloquence and for the bold truths which he spoke." Amidst the general venality of the Grecian orators, Demosthenes alone was proof against the seductions of Macedonian gold ; and his political foresight was not inferior to his integrity or patriotism. Had the watchful sagacity with which he penetrated the deep-laid schemes of Philip been ably seconded by the other Athenian leaders, and had their armies been led by competent generals, the liberties of Greece would, in all probability, never have succumbed to the arts or arms of the King of Macedon. Between the years 352 and 340 B.C. Demosthenes pronounced his eleven (or, as some say, twelve) celebrated orations against Philip. Four of these are especially denominated "Philippics." In 338 B.C. Demosthenes was one of the fugitives from the disastrous battle of Chæronea ; but he still preserved his controlling influence in the state ; and Ctesiphon proposed that the people should confer upon him a crown of gold as the reward of his eminent public services. This measure caused between him and his rival Æschines a contest which, after the lapse of several years, resulted in the triumph of Demosthenes in 330 B.C., when he made his famous speech "On the Crown," (Περὶ Στεφάνου,) regarded by many critics as the greatest of all his achievements as an orator.

When Harpalus, the unfaithful steward of Alexander, sought refuge in Athens, Demosthenes was accused by his enemies of having received a bribe from the Macedonian, and was condemned to pay a heavy fine. In the opinion of the best historical critics, however, his guilt is very far from having been established. Unable to pay the penalty imposed, he retired to Ægina. He remained in exile till the death of Alexander, when he returned in triumph to Athens. His last efforts for liberty having failed, and his death having been decreed by the victorious Antipater, he took poison and died in 322 B.C.

Sixty orations and about sixty-five introductions (*i.e.* exordial fragments of speeches) ascribed to Demosthenes have been preserved ; but of these several are considered to be spurious. There is no reason to suppose that all the orations were spoken in the exact form in which they have come down to us : it is, indeed, probable that many of them were revised after they were delivered. Demosthenes seldom spoke in public without careful preparation ; and he appears to have been extremely averse to extemporaneous speaking, although, according to some authorities, his unpremeditated speeches were superior in spirit and boldness to his more elaborate efforts. The extraordinary success of his oratory was due in no small measure to the steadfastness with which he kept the attention of his hearers riveted on the one great object which he had in view. Nothing superfluous, nothing which did not contribute to that object, was admitted into his discourse. There was no striving after ornament, no effort at mere display. "He uses language," says Fénelon, "as a modest man uses his dress,—simply to cover him. We think not of his words : we think only of the things which he says. He lightens, he thunders, he is a torrent which sweeps everything before it. We can neither criticise nor admire, because we have not the command of our own faculties." "His style," observes Hume, "is rapid harmony exactly adjusted to the sense ; it is vehement reasoning without any appearance of art; it is disdain, anger, boldness, freedom, involved in a continued stream of argument; and of all human productions his orations present the models which approach the nearest to perfection." "Such was the first of orators," says Lord Brougham : "at the head of all the mighty masters of speech, the adoration of ages has consecrated his place, and the loss of the noble instrument* with which he forged and launched his thunders, is sure to maintain it unapproachable forever."

See GROTE, "History of Greece," vol. xi. chap. lxxxvii.; THIRLWALL, "History of Greece;" PLUTARCH, "Lives;" FÉNELON, "Letter to the French Academy on Rhetoric, Poetry," etc.; HUME, "Essay on Eloquence;"† BROUGHAM, "Dissertation on the Eloquence of the Ancients;" CICERO, "De Oratore," iii.; H. WOLF, "Vita Demosthenis et Æschinis," 1572; AIMÉ BOULLÉE, "Vie de Démosthène," 1834; F. THEREMIN, "Demosthenes und Massillon," 1845; P. EKERMAN, "Demosthenes Oratorum Princeps," 1740; RENÉ RAPIN, "Comparaison de Démosthène et de Cicéron," 1676; E. PISTOR, "Demosthenes als Staatsbürger, Redner, etc.," 1830; FABRICIUS, "Bibliotheca Græca;" "Edinburgh Review" for January, 1820, and February, 1822; "Nouvelle Biographie Générale."

Demosthenes, an able Athenian general, who was a conspicuous actor in the Peloponnesian war. In 425 B.C. he defended Pylos against the Spartans with skill and success, and compelled the enemy to capitulate; but Cleon, who had assumed the command, claimed the honour of this exploit. In the year 413 he and Eurymedon commanded the army sent to reinforce Nicias at Syracuse. Demosthenes disapproved the dilatory conduct of Nicias, and attacked the heights of Epipolæ by night, but was repulsed with loss. After another defeat in the harbour, the Athenians raised the siege, and retreated by land; but they were compelled to surrender, and Demosthenes was put to death, 413 B.C.

See THUCYDIDES, books v., vi., and vii.; GROTE, "History of Greece;" THIRLWALL, "History of Greece;" PLUTARCH, "Alcibiades," and "Nicias."

De-mos'the-nēs Phil-a-le'thēs, a Greek physician, who lived probably about the beginning of the Christian era, and was a skilful oculist.

Demours, deh-moor' or d'moor, (ANTOINE PIERRE,) a French surgeon, son of Pierre, noticed below, was born in Paris in 1762. He directed his attention chiefly to ocular surgery, in which he became very expert. He received the title of oculist to the king from Louis XVIII. and from Charles X. In 1818 he published the results of his multiplied researches and long experience, in a "Treatise on Diseases of the Eyes," (3 vols.,) which was the most complete work that had appeared on this subject. Died in 1836.

See QUÉRARD, "La France Littéraire."

Demours, (PIERRE,) a French oculist, born at Marseilles in 1702. In 1730 he obtained the place of demonstrator and curator of the cabinet of natural history in the Royal Garden. He assisted Antoine Petit in his anatomical researches, and acquired skill in diseases of the eye. He was a Fellow of the Royal Society of London, of the Academy of Sciences of Paris, royal censor, and oculist to the king. He wrote a few treatises on ocular surgery. Died in 1795.

See QUÉRARD, "La France Littéraire."

Demoustier, deh-moos'te-à', (CHARLES ALBERT,) a French writer, born at Villers-Cotterets in 1760, was descended by his father from Racine, and by his mother from La Fontaine. His "Letters to Emilia on Mythology" (1786) had a great temporary popularity; but the style is pretentious and offends against good taste. He wrote several comedies and operas, which were successful, but are now neglected. Among these are "Alceste," and "Les Femmes," ("Women,") both comedies in verse. Died in 1801.

Demp'ster, (GEORGE,) a Scottish lawyer, born at Dundee in 1736, was a member of Parliament from 1762 to 1790, and was a political friend of Fox. He published the "Magnetic Mountains of Cannay," "Letters on Agriculture," and a few other works. Died in 1818.

See CHAMBERS, "Biographical Dictionary of Eminent Scotsmen."

Dempster, (THOMAS,) a Scottish writer, noted for his learning and violent temper, was born at Muiresk in

---

1579, and studied at Paris and Rome. It is said that he was regent of the College of Navarre in Paris at the age of seventeen; he was afterwards professor of law and belles-lettres at Toulouse, Nîmes, Pisa, and Bologna. His quarrelsome temper often involved him in scenes of armed violence. He wrote numerous works, of which the best-known is "Historia Gentis Scotorum," which is a biographical dictionary of Scottish authors. Baillet accuses him of literary forgery. Died in 1625.

See CHAMBERS, "Biographical Dictionary of Eminent Scotsmen;" "Encyclopædia Britannica."

Denesle, deh-nĕl', a mediocre French author, born at Meaux; died in 1767.

Deneux, deh-nuh', (LOUIS CHARLES,) a French medical writer, born at Heilly (Somme) in 1767; died in 1846.

Denham, dĕn'am, (Colonel DIXON,) a British officer and traveller, born in London in 1786, served in the Peninsular war in 1811, and in Belgium in 1815. In 1821 he accompanied Clapperton and Oudney in an expedition to Timbuctoo. In February, 1823, they arrived at Kouka, on Lake Tchad, where they were kindly received. There Denham parted from his companions, and joined a party of natives on an expedition to Mandara, in which he met with perilous adventures. Returning homeward, he arrived in England in June, 1825, and published a valuable narrative of the enterprise, in which he had displayed great energy and courage. This narrative was written chiefly by Denham, and contained some small contributions from Clapperton. Having been appointed Governor of Sierra Leone, he died there in 1828.

Denham, dĕn'am, (Sir JOHN,) a British poet, born in Dublin in 1615, was the only son of Sir John Denham, baron of the exchequer, who brought him to London while in his infancy. He studied law; but his success was hindered by an extravagant passion for gaming. In 1641 he produced "The Sophy," a tragedy, which was very successful, and which drew from Waller the following expression,—"He broke out like the Irish rebellion, threescore thousand strong, when nobody was aware or in the least suspected it." His reputation was increased by his poem of "Cooper's Hill," (1643,) which was praised by Dryden and Pope. Dr. Johnson says, "Denham is deservedly considered as one of the fathers of English poetry. Denham and Waller, according to Prior, improved our versification, and Dryden perfected it." He died in 1668, and was buried in Westminster Abbey.

See JOHNSON, "Lives of the Poets;" WOOD, "Athenæ Oxonienses;" CHALMERS, "General Biographical Dictionary;" "Nouvelle Biographie Générale."

Denina, dà-nee'nà, (GIACOMMARIA CARLO,) an eminent Italian historian and priest, born at Revello, in Piedmont, in 1731. Having written an approved work on the "Study of Theology," about 1758, he was chosen professor of humanities and rhetoric in the Superior College of Turin. In 1769 he published the first volume of his "History of the Revolutions of Italy," ("Istoria delle Rivoluzioni d'Italia,") which was received with favour and is his principal work. Two other volumes of it appeared soon after. In 1782 he went to Berlin, by invitation from Frederick II., and there wrote numerous works on history, etc. In 1804 he was appointed librarian to the emperor Napoleon, and resided in Paris from that time until his death. In 1809 he produced a "History of Western Italy." He was author of an important work entitled "The Vicissitudes of Literature," ("Vicende della Letteratura," 1760, 1 vol.; 2d ed., 1785, in 2 vols.; 3d ed., 1811, in 4 vols.) Died in 1813.

See TIPALDO, "Biografia degli Italiani illustri;" SCARRONE, "Memorie intorno alla Vita dell'Abate Denina," 1798; CARLO G. REINA, "Vita di C. Denina," 1820.

Denis, (King of Portugal.) See DINIZ.

Denis, deh-ne' or d'nĕ, (FERDINAND,) a French *littérateur*, born in Paris in 1798. He made a voyage to Brazil, and on his return published "Brazil, or the History, Manners, and Customs of the Inhabitants of that Region," (1822, 6 vols.) He also wrote "A Compendium of the Literary History of Portugal and Brazil," (1826,) "The Travelling Brahmin, or Popular Wisdom of all Nations," (1832,) and many other works. He has contributed to the "Nouvelle Biographie Générale" most of the notices of eminent Portuguese.

See "Nouvelle Biographie Générale."

---

* The Greek language.
† The passage above cited is found only in the later editions of Hume's "Essays."

ā, ē, ī, ō, ū, ȳ, *long;* à, è, ò, same, less prolonged; ă, ĕ, ĭ, ŏ, ŭ, ў, *short;* a, e, i, o, *obscure;* fär, fàll, fàt; mêt; nôt; gŏŏd; mōŏn;

Denis, (JEAN BAPTISTE,) a French physician, born in Paris, obtained the title of consulting physician to Louis XIV. In 1673 he was invited by Charles II. to England, where he remained but a short time. He published in 1672 a "Collection of Memoirs and Conferences on the Arts and Sciences presented to the Dauphin." He practised the transfusion of blood. Died in 1704.

See ÉLOY, "Dictionnaire de la Médecine."

Denis, dā'nis, (JOHANN MICHAEL COSMUS,) a German poet and bibliographer, born at Schärding, Bavaria, in 1729. He published a learned "Introduction to the Knowledge of Books," comprising bibliography and literary history, (1777.) In 1791 he was appointed chief librarian of the Imperial Library, Vienna. He rendered important services by his efforts to reform and polish the German language and poetry, and took Ossian and the Northern bards as his models. He wrote, in German verse, an "Epistle to Klopstock," (1764,) odes on public events, Souvenirs, (1794,) and other admired poems, among which is a version of Ossian. Died in 1800.

See "M. Denisii Commentariorum de Vita sua libri v.," in German, 1802; CARL ANTON VON GRUBER, "Sineds Tod," Vienna, 1800.

Denis, (LOUIS,) a French geographer and engraver, published, among other works, a "Physical, Political, and Mathematical Map of the World," (1764.)

Denis, (NICOLAS.) See DENYS.

Denis, SAINT, (POPE.) See DIONYSIUS.

Denis or **Denys,** SAINT, the patron saint of France, and the first bishop of Paris, was sent from Rome about the middle of the third century to evangelize the Gauls. It is said that he converted numerous idolaters, and built a church in Paris. He suffered martyrdom during the persecution of Valerian, about 272 A.D.

See VERCELLY, "Vie de S. Denis, premier Évêque de Paris," 1854; TILLEMONT, "Mémoires ecclésiastiques;" MRS. JAMESON, "History of Sacred and Legendary Art."

Den'i-son, (JOHN EVELYN,) an English legislator, and a member of the Liberal party, born in 1800. He has represented Newcastle, Hastings, and Malton in Parliament. He was elected Speaker of the House of Commons in 1857, in 1859, in 1866, and in 1868.

Den'is-toun or **Den'nis-toun,** (JAMES,) a Scottish biographer and writer on art, born about 1802. He published, besides other works, "Memoirs of the Dukes of Urbino," (London, 1850.) Died in 1855.

See "Edinburgh Review" for October, 1851.

Den'man, (THOMAS,) an English physician, born in Derbyshire in 1733, was a surgeon in the royal navy, and afterwards practised with success in London. He published, besides other able treatises on obstetrics, an "Introduction to the Practice of Midwifery." Died in 1818.

Denman, (THOMAS,) first Lord Denman, an English judge, born in London in 1779, was the son of the preceding. He was educated at Cambridge, and was called to the bar in 1806. Having attained eminence in his profession, he was returned to Parliament for Wareham in 1818. From 1820 to 1831 he represented Nottingham, and supported electoral reform and other liberal measures. In 1820 he was employed as solicitor-general for Queen Caroline, and was associated with Brougham in her defence. He became attorney-general in 1830, and chief justice of the king's bench in 1832. In 1834 he was raised to the peerage, and in the upper house advocated the abolition of slavery. Having discharged the duties of judge with credit, he resigned his office in 1850, and died in 1854.

See FOSS, "The Judges of England."

Denne, dĕn, (JOHN,) an English divine and antiquary, born at Littlebourne, in Kent, in 1693, became Archdeacon of Rochester in 1728, and rector of Lambeth in 1731. He contributed to Lewis's "Life of Wicklif," and published a volume of sermons. Died in 1767.

Denne, (SAMUEL,) a son of the preceding, born at Westminster in 1730, became vicar of Darent in 1767. He wrote the "History and Antiquities of Rochester," and other antiquarian treatises. Died in 1799.

Denne-Baron, dĕn'bȧ'rôN', (PIERRE JACQUES RENÉ,) a French poet, born in Paris in 1780, wrote "Hero and Leander," an epic poem, (1806,) and made translations from other languages. Died in 1854.

Denne-Baron, (RENÉ DIEUDONNÉ,) a musical composer, son of the preceding, was born in Paris in 1804. He has contributed to Didot's "Nouvelle Biographie Générale" most of the notices of musicians, and has been engaged on a history of music in France.

Denner, dĕn'ner, (BALTHASAR,) an eminent German portrait-painter, born at Hamburg in 1685. He worked in several countries, gained a brilliant reputation, and painted many portraits of kings and princes. His works are chiefly remarkable for extreme minuteness of finish. Died in 1747.

See ERSCH und GRUBER, "Allgemeine Encyklopaedie."

Denner, (JOHANN CHRISTOPH,) a maker of musical instruments, born at Leipsic in 1655. He made flutes of superior quality, and is said to have invented the clarionet. Died in 1707.

Dennery, dĕn're', (ADOLPHE PHILIPPE,) a French dramatist, born in Paris in 1812, composed successful dramas, vaudevilles, and comic operas, among which are "The Market of London," (1845,) and "The Bohemians of Paris."

Den'nie, (JOSEPH,) an American critic, author, and journalist, born in Boston in 1768. He studied law, but did not practise it. He edited "The Farmers' Museum" at Walpole, New Hampshire, 1795-98, and wrote the "Lay Preacher" in that periodical. He removed to Philadelphia in 1799, and founded "The Portfolio," a literary magazine, which he edited from 1801 till 1812. He had a high reputation as a writer among his contemporaries. Moore, the poet, in a note to one of his "Poems relating to America," speaks in terms of high commendation of Dennie's taste and literary attainments. Died in Philadelphia in 1812.

See DUYCKINCK, "Cyclopædia of American Literature," vol. i.

Den'nie, (WILLIAM HENRY,) a British officer, who served with distinction in the Burmese war (1826-27) and in the Afghan war. He was killed at Jellalabad in April, 1842.

Denniée, dȧ'ne-ā', (ANTOINE,) BARON, a French officer, born at Versailles in 1754. Under the empire he was made secretary of the war department. Died in 1829.

Dennis. See DINIZ.

Den'nis, (JOHN,) an English writer and critic, born in London in 1657, acquired notoriety as a politician, pamphleteer, and dramatist. His habits were improvident, and his temper quarrelsome, if not malevolent. He made many enemies by his defamatory or satirical attacks on authors and public functionaries. The most successful of his dramas were "Liberty Asserted," and "A Plot and No Plot." He published some offensive criticisms on Pope, who took his revenge in the "Dunciad." His vanity and hatred of the French caused him to imagine that the French king would not make peace with England except on the condition that the latter power should deliver him up to the former. The proverbial expression of "stealing one's thunder" is said to owe its origin to Dennis. Having invented a new artificial thunder for one of his own plays, he found the managers of Drury Lane employing it in "Macbeth," when he exclaimed, "These rascals have stolen my thunder!" Died in 1734.

See DISRAELI, "Calamities of Authors;" "Biographia Britannica;" EDMUND CURLL, "Life of J. Dennis," 1734; "Retrospective Review," vol. i., 1820.

Dennistoun. See DENISTOUN.

Den'ny̆, (Sir ANTHONY,) an English courtier and favourite of Henry VIII., who appointed him a privy councillor and one of the executors of his will. Died in 1550. Sir John Cheke honoured his memory by a poem.

Denon, deh-nôN', (DOMINIQUE VIVANT,) an eminent French artist and author, remarkable for his various accomplishments, was born at Châlons-sur-Saône in 1747. In early youth he obtained a place in the retinue of the ambassador to Russia. About 1774 he was patronized by the Count de Vergennes, minister of state, who employed him on a mission to Switzerland. On his way thither he visited Voltaire at Ferney, and drew his portrait. From 1782 to 1787 he was chargé-d'affaires at Naples, and after the latter date exchanged diplomacy for the arts of design. He became a member of the

---

Є as k; ç as s; g hard; ġ as j; G, H, K, guttural; N, nasal; R, trilled; s̈ as z; ṭh as in this. (☞ See Explanations, p. 23.)

Royal Academy in 1787, and during the Revolution received from Robespierre a commission to design republican costumes. In 1798 he was invited by Bonaparte to join the expedition to Egypt, and eagerly embraced an opportunity which afforded him so rich a field for artistic studies. He made drawings of the monuments and other objects of interest in that country. He was one of the favourite attendants whom Bonaparte selected when he returned to France, and was the first to gratify the public curiosity by a description of what he had witnessed, which appeared in 1802 with the most flattering success. About 1802 he was appointed director-general of the museums. He accompanied Bonaparte in several of his campaigns, displayed intrepidity by making designs in the midst of battles, and had great influence in deciding questions relative to works of art and public monuments. Denon was made a baron, an officer of the legion of honour, and member of the Institute. The title of his principal work, above referred to, is "Travels in Upper and Lower Egypt during the Campaigns of General Bonaparte," ("Voyage dans la haute et la basse Égypte pendant les Campagnes du Général Bonaparte.") He also contributed to the great work published by the Commission of Egypt. Died in 1825.

See "Nouvelle Biographie Générale;" COUPIN, "Notice sur Denon," 8vo, 1825; AMÉDÉE DE PASTORET, "Éloge historique de M. le Baron Denon," 1851.

Denores. See NORES.

Dens, dĕns or dŏn, (PETER,) a Flemish Roman Catholic theologian, born near Antwerp about 1690. He published several religious works. Died in 1775.

Dent, (JOHN H.,) a naval officer, born in Maryland, entered the United States navy in 1798. He commanded a vessel of the squadron under Commodore Preble in the war with Tripoli in 1804, and became a captain in 1811. Died in 1823.

Den-tā'tus, (LUCIUS SICINIUS,) a Roman tribune, noted for his bravery and extraordinary services. He took part in one hundred and twenty battles, received about forty wounds in the breast, and obtained fourteen civic crowns, besides other honours. Appius Claudius the decemvir, whom he had offended, caused him to be assassinated about 450 B.C.

Dentatus, (MANIUS CURIUS,) a Roman consul, renowned for his military exploits and frugal mode of life. He was surnamed DENTATUS, it is said, because he was born with teeth. He was consul in 290 B.C., and terminated a long war against the Samnites by a signal victory. In 275 B.C. he gained a decisive victory over Pyrrhus near Beneventum. He was consul for the third time in 274, and, after the expiration of his term, retired to his farm, where he once proved his integrity by refusing rich presents from a Samnite embassy. While holding the office of censor, in 272, he supplied Rome with water from the Anio by an aqueduct. Died about 270 B.C.

See ROLLIN, "Roman History;" NIEBUHR, "History of Rome;" POLYBIUS, book ii.

Den'tọn, (JOHN,) an English nonconformist minister and writer, born in 1625, became prebendary of York. Died in 1708.

Denton, (THOMAS,) an English clergyman, born in Cumberland in 1724, published two poems in imitation of Spenser, viz., "Immortality," and "The House of Superstition," (1762.) Died in 1777.

Denton, (WILLIAM,) an English physician, born at Stowe, in Bucks, in 1605. He was appointed physician to Charles I. in 1636, and after the restoration served Charles II. in the same capacity. He wrote a few discourses against the Catholics. Died in 1691.

Dentone, dĕn-to'nà, (ANTONIO,) an Italian sculptor, lived in Venice about 1470.

Dentone, Il, ĕl dĕn-to'nà, (GIROLAMO **Curti**—kooR'-tee,) an Italian painter, born at Bologna in 1576. He was skilful in vertical perspective, and was distinguished as a painter of theatrical decorations. His works were adorned with figures by Antonio Caracci and Guercino. Died in 1631.

See MALVASIA, "Felsina pittrice."

Dentrecolles, dŏNtr'kol', (FRANÇOIS XAVIER,) a French Jesuit, born at Lyons in 1664, went as missionary to China, where he laboured many years, became superior-general of the mission, and published many religious books in the Chinese language. Died in Pekin in 1741.

Denuelle, dĕh-nü'ĕl', (DOMINIQUE ALEXANDRE,) a French painter, born in Paris in 1818.

Den'vẹr, (JAMES W.,) an American general, born at Winchester, Virginia, in 1818. He emigrated to California about 1850, was elected a member of Congress in 1854, and was Governor of Kansas from December, 1857, to August or November, 1858. He was appointed a brigadier-general in 1861.

Denys. See DENIS and DIONYSIUS.

Denys, dĕh-ne', (JACQUES,) a Flemish painter, born at Antwerp about 1645. He studied in Rome and Venice, and acquired the noble style of the Italian masters. He painted historical pictures, at Mantua, for the Duke of Mantua, and was successful in portraits. After a residence of fourteen years in Italy, he returned to Antwerp, where he soon after died. Among his works, which are nearly all in Italy, is an "Ecce Homo."

See DESCAMPS, "Vies des Peintres Flamands," etc.; NAGLER, "Neues Allgemeines Künstler-Lexikon."

Denys or **Denis,** dĕh-ne', (NICOLAS,) a Frenchman, born at Tours, was appointed Governor of Canada and Acadia in 1632. He wrote a "Description of the Coasts of North America," etc., (2 vols., 1672.)

Denys, SAINT. See DENIS, (SAINT.)

Denys d'Halicarnasse. See DIONYSIUS OF HALICARNASSUS.

Denys l'Ancien. See DIONYSIUS THE ELDER.

Denys le Jeune. See DIONYSIUS THE YOUNGER.

Denys le Périégète. See DIONYSIUS PERIEGETES.

Deodati. See DIODATI.

D'Éon. See ÉON, D', (CHEVALIER.)

Déparcieux, dà'pȧR'se̤-uh', sometimes written **De Parcieux,** (ANTOINE,) an able French mathematician, born near Nîmes in 1703, went to Paris, where he supported himself by tracing sun-dials, in which he was very skilful. He had much mechanical talent, and invented several useful machines. He became royal censor, and a member of the Academy of Sciences, to which he contributed sixteen treatises. By his zeal for the public good he merited the title of citizen-philosopher which Voltaire gave him. He published an "Essay on the Probability of the Duration of Human Life," (1746,) "Astronomical Tables," and other works. Died in 1768.

See GRANDJEAN DE FOUCHY, "Éloge de A. Déparcieux."

Déparcieux or **De Parcieux,** (ANTOINE,) a nephew of the preceding, born at Cessoux-le-Vieux in 1753, acquired distinction as a writer and lecturer on mathematics and physical sciences. On the formation of the central schools he was chosen professor of chemistry and physics at the Pantheon. He published a "Treatise on Annuities," (1781,) and left in manuscript an able work called a "Complete Course of Physics and Chemistry," in which he demonstrated the intimate connection of chemistry with other sciences. Died in 1799.

See MAHÉRAULT, "Notice sur la Vie du Citoyen Déparcieux," 1800.

Depaulis, dĕh-po'lĕss', (ALEXIS JOSEPH,) a French engraver of medals, born in Paris in 1792, received a medal of the first class in 1831.

Deperthes, dĕh-pȧrt', (JEAN BAPTISTE,) a French artist and writer on art, born at Rheims in 1761, lived in Paris. In 1818 he published his "Theory of Landscape-Painting," ("Théorie du Paysage,") which was followed by a "History of the Art of Landscape-Painting from the Renaissance of Art to the Eighteenth Century." Both of these works are highly appreciated. Died in 1833.

De Peyster, de pīs'tẹr, (ABRAHAM,) an eminent New York merchant, son of Johannes de Peyster, was born in 1658. He was mayor of New York, chief justice of the province, and president of the king's council, in which capacity he officiated as governor in 1691. Died in 1728.

De Peyster, (A. SCHUYLER,) grandson of the preceding, was born in New York in 1736. He served in the French war of 1755 under his uncle, Colonel Peter Schuyler, and held various commands in the royal army during the Revolution. It was largely through his efforts that the Indians were detached from the American cause and allied with the British. Died in 1832.

ā, ē, ī, ō, ū, ȳ, *long;* ȧ, ė, ȯ, same, less prolonged; ă, ĕ, ĭ, ŏ, ŭ, ȳ, *short;* ạ, ẹ, ị, ọ, *obscure;* fär, fåll, fåt; mêt; nŏt; gŏŏd; mōōn;

De Peyster, (JOHANNES,) one of the early settlers of New York, was born at Haarlem, in Holland. He became mayor of New York after it had passed into the power of the English. Died in 1685.

Deplace, dẹh-plås', (GUY MARIE,) a French writer, born at Roanne (Loire) in 1772; died in 1843.

See COLLOMBET, "Notice sur G. M. Deplace," 1843; SAINTE-REUVE, "Portraits littéraires," vol. ii.

Deponthon, dẹh-pôN'tôN', (CHARLES FRANÇOIS,) BARON, a French general, born at Éclaron in 1777, served at the battles of Moskwa, Lutzen, and Bautzen, (1813.) He became a peer of France in 1846. Died in 1849.

Dep'ping, (GEORGE BERNARD,) an eminent scholar and *littérateur*, born at Münster in 1784, became a resident of Paris about 1803, and was afterwards naturalized. He pursued the vocation of author and translator with industry and success, and produced some popular juvenile works, among which is "Les Soirées d'Hiver," or "Evening Entertainments," (3d edition, 1832.) He obtained the prize offered by the Institute for his excellent work on "The Maritime Expeditions of the Normans in the Tenth Century," (1826,) which was followed by a "History of Normandy," (1835,) and other historical works. He wrote several important articles for the "Biographie Universelle," and was associated with Malte-Brun in the "Annales des Voyages." Died in 1853.

See DEPPING's Autobiography, entitled "Erinnerungen aus dem Leben eines Deutschen in Paris," 1832; ALFRED MAURY, "Notice sur la Vie et les Travaux de G. B. Depping," 1854.

Deprès. See DESPRÈS, (JOSQUIN.)

De Quin'cey, (THOMAS,) an eminent English author, sometimes called "The English Opium-Eater," was born in a suburb of Manchester on the 15th of August, 1785. He was a younger son of a rich merchant, who died about 1792, leaving to his widow and six children a clear fortune of £1600 a year. His childhood was passed in rustic solitude. He thanked Providence that "his infant feelings were moulded by the gentlest of sisters, instead of horrid pugilistic brothers." About the age of twelve he was sent to the grammar-school of Bath, where he attained such proficiency in Greek that his teacher said he could harangue an Athenian mob. In July, 1802, he eloped from the Manchester Grammar-School, and, after a pedestrian tour in Wales, went to London, resolving to hide himself from his guardians until they should cease to have any control over his actions. He passed several months in London in abject poverty and strange adventures, of which he has given an almost incredible narrative in his "Confessions of an English Opium-Eater." "It is probable," says the "London Quarterly Review" of July, 1861, "that the story, as we now have it, represents the exaggerated shape in which his reminiscences came back upon him under the influence of the favourite drug." He entered in 1803 the University of Oxford, (Worcester College,) where he remained about five years, during which he contracted a habit of eating opium. He was noted at this period for his rare conversational powers and for his vast and varied stock of information. In 1808 or 1809 he formed an intimate acquaintance with Coleridge, Wordsworth, and Southey, and took up his abode at Grasmere Cottage, recently vacated by Wordsworth. He relieved the embarrassments of Coleridge by a present of £500. He continued to reside at Grasmere about twenty years, married in 1816, and devoted his time to literary pursuits. He produced good translations from Lessing and Jean Paul Richter, and contributed many articles on biography, philosophy, and metaphysics to several periodicals, including "Blackwood's" and "Tait's Magazine." After he had indulged in the excessive use of opium for many years, he overcame the habit, by a desperate and long-continued effort, about 1820. In 1821 he produced a great sensation by the "Confessions of an English Opium-Eater," which purports to be an autobiography. After he quitted Grasmere he resided in Glasgow and Edinburgh, in which city he passed the latter years of his life.

De Quincey, though a voluminous writer, published few books under his own name. He projected a great work to be entitled "On the Improvement of the Human Intellect," ("De Emendatione Humani Intellectus,") which he never finished. "He himself," says the "Lon-don Quarterly Review," "never finished anything except his sentences, which are models of elaborate workmanship. But many of his essays are literally fragments. . . . He left us his most precious ideas in the condition of the Sibyl's leaves after they had been scattered by the wind. Hence those who approach him with any serious purpose are only too likely to come away disappointed. . . . It is in the region of pure speculation that he is most at home. . . . The authors about whom he has written most are Milton, Pope, Wordsworth, and Coleridge. Of the first, third, and fourth he was a devoted admirer and champion. But the second seemed to him the very incarnation of the worst epoch of our literature." According to the same critic, "We might search in vain for a writer who, with equal powers, has made an equally slight impression upon the general public. His style is superb, his powers of reasoning unsurpassed, his imagination is warm and brilliant, and his humour both masculine and delicate. Yet, with this singular combination of gifts, he is comparatively little known outside of that small circle of men who love literature for its own sake." (See "Quarterly Review" for July, 1861.)

The first edition of his collected works was that published in Boston by Ticknor & Fields, (18 or 20 vols., 1851–58.) Volume I. contains "Confessions of an English Opium-Eater" and "Suspiria de Profundis;" II., "Biographical Essays on Shakspeare, Pope, Lamb, Göthe, and Schiller;" III., "Miscellaneous Essays;" IV., "The Cæsars;" V., "Life and Manners," "Early Days," "London," "Ireland," "Premature Manhood," etc.; VI. and VII., "Literary Reminiscences;" VIII. and IX., "Narrative and Miscellaneous Papers;" X., "Essays on the English Poets;" XI. and XII., "Historical and Critical Essays on the Philosophy of Roman History, the Essenes, Plato's Republic, Cicero," etc.; XIII. and XIV., "Essays on Philosophical Writers and other Men of Letters;" XV., "Letters to a Young Man whose Education had been neglected;" XVI. and XVII., "Theological Essays, and other Papers;" XVIII., "The Note-Book of an English Opium-Eater." It is stated that this edition of his works was published with the concurrence of the author, who also began about 1855 to issue another edition or selection in Great Britain. He died in Edinburgh on the 8th of December, 1859.

See the excellent article on De Quincey in the "London Quarterly Review" for July, 1861; "Westminster Review" for April, 1854; "Fraser's Magazine" for April, 1852, and January, 1861; "British Quarterly" for July, 1863; and "Atlantic Monthly" for September, 1863.

Dẹr'bỹ, (or dar'be,) (CHARLES STANLEY,) EARL OF, the son of James, the seventh earl, was Lord of Man and of the Isles. He wrote a work entitled "The Protestant Religion is a Sure Foundation of a True Christian and a Good Subject," etc., (1669.)

Derby, (EDWARD GEOFFREY SMITH STANLEY,) fourteenth EARL OF, an eminent British statesman and orator, the eldest son of Edward, Lord Stanley, (afterwards the thirteenth Earl of Derby,) was born in Lancashire in March, 1799. He was educated at Oxford, and in 1820 was elected to Parliament, in which he soon attained great eminence as a debater, and represented successively Stockbridge, Preston, Windsor, and North Lancashire. He married, in 1825, Emma Caroline, a daughter of Lord Skelmersdale. From 1830 to 1833 he was chief secretary for Ireland, with a seat in the cabinet of Lord Grey. On the succession of his father to the earldom, in 1834, he received the title of Lord Stanley. Having served as colonial secretary a short time, he retired from office in 1834, and joined the Tory or Conservative party. On the accession of Sir Robert Peel to power, in 1841, Lord Stanley was appointed secretary for the colonies. He was created Baron Stanley, and entered the House of Lords, in 1844. He resigned in the autumn of 1845, because he would not support Sir Robert in the repeal of the Corn-Laws; and when the Conservative party was divided into two parts—the Peelites and the Protectionists—about 1846, he became the leader of the latter, and directed the opposition to the ministry of Russell, 1846–51. On the death of his father, in June, 1851, he succeeded to the earldom. After the defeat of Russell in the House, in February, 1852, Lord Derby formed a ministry, in which he was first lord of the treasury;

but, failing to obtain the support of a majority for his financial measures, he resigned in December, 1852, and was succeeded by Lord Aberdeen. He was "sent for" by the queen, in 1855, to construct a Conservative ministry; but he declined, thinking probably that he could not command a sufficient number of votes in the House of Commons. He maintained a general opposition to the ministry of Palmerston, who was compelled to resign in February, 1858. Lord Derby then accepted the place of premier. Among the important measures of his administration was the reorganization of the government of India. He manifested more sympathy with Austria in the Italian question than was conducive to his popularity. The agitation of the question of electoral reform also tended to make his position untenable, and, by a combination of Liberals, Peelites, and the Manchester party, he was driven from power in June, 1859. (See DISRAELI.) In June, 1866, the Liberal ministry resigned, because the Reform bill was rejected by the House of Commons, and Lord Derby again became prime minister. He attempted to form a coalition with certain Whig leaders, among whom was Lord Clarendon ; but his overtures were coldly received, and he was compelled to appoint an exclusively Tory cabinet. During his administration a Reform bill, giving the right of suffrage to all householders in boroughs, became a law, and was signed by the queen in August, 1867. He resigned on the 25th of February, 1868, and was succeeded by Disraeli. Lord Derby produced a translation of Homer's "Iliad" in blank verse, (1865.) This version, says the "Edinburgh Review," "is far more closely allied to the original, and superior to any that has yet been attempted in the blank verse of our language." Died in October, 1869.

See "Edinburgh Review" for January, 1865 : "Blackwood's Magazine" for April, 1865.

Der′by, (ELIAS HASKET,) an American merchant, born at Salem, Massachusetts, in 1739, made important improvements in shipbuilding. At the commencement of the Revolution he loaned to the government a large portion of the supplies for the army, and took a conspicuous part in equipping the 158 private armed ships fitted out at Salem during the war. Died in 1799.

See HUNT's "Lives of American Merchants," 1858.

Derby, (HENRY,) EARL OF, the title of Henry IV. of England in his early life. (See HENRY IV.)

Derby, (JAMES STANLEY,) seventh EARL OF, an English nobleman, born about 1600, was the nephew of the fifth earl, and son of William Stanley. He fought for Charles I. in the civil war, and was eminent for bravery as well as loyalty. After the ruin of the royal cause he retired to the Isle of Man, of which he was proprietor. He afterwards joined the standard of Charles II., was taken prisoner at the battle of Worcester, and executed in October, 1651. His wife, Charlotte de Tremouille, was the last person in the three kingdoms who submitted to the Parliament. She died about 1660.

See HUME, "History of England;" HARTLEY COLERIDGE, "Lives of Distinguished Northerns."

Der′çe-to, Der′ke-to, or **Der′çe-tis,** a Syrian goddess, supposed to be the same as ASTARTE, (which see.) She was worshipped under the form of a fish.

See PIERER, "Universal-Lexikon."

Der-çȳl′lĭ-das, [Δερκυλλίδας,] a Spartan general, who in 399 B.C. was appointed commander of an army employed to protect the Asiatic Greeks against the Persians. He took nine cities of Æolia in eight days, and reduced Atarneus in 398. He was recalled in 396 B.C.

Der-çȳl′lus or **Der′çȳ-lus,** [Gr. Δέρκυλλος or Δερκύλος,] an Athenian orator, was one of the ten ambassadors sent in 347 B.C. to negotiate a peace with King Philip.

Derfflinger, von, fon dĕRf′fling-ẹr, or **Dörfling,** doR′fling, (GEORG,) a German general, born in Bohemia in 1606. He served in the army of Gustavus Adolphus, after whose death he entered the service of the Elector of Brandenburg. He commanded with success against the Swedes about 1675-78. Died in 1695.

Derham, dẹr′am or dŭr′ŭm, (SAMUEL,) an English physician, born in Gloucestershire in 1655 ; died in 1689.

Derham, (WILLIAM,) D.D., an eminent English divine and philosopher, born near Worcester in 1657, became rector of Upminster in 1689, and canon of Wind-

sor in 1716. He was a Fellow of the Royal Society, to which he contributed several able scientific treatises. His principal works are "Physico-Theology," (1713,) "Astro-Theology," (1714,) and "Christo-Theology," (1730,) (consisting of sermons which he had delivered at the Boyle Lecture,) which are highly commended, and have been translated into other languages. He edited the works of Ray the naturalist, and published the philosophical experiments of Robert Hook. Died in 1735.

Derick, dĕR′ik, sometimes written **Deryck,** (PETER CORNELIS,) a skilful Dutch landscape-painter, born at Delft in 1568 ; died in 1630.

De′ring or **Dear′ing,** (EDWARD,) an English Puritan divine, eminent for his eloquence, born in Kent, became professor of divinity at Cambridge in 1567. He obtained the rectory of Pluckley in 1569. In 1573 he was suspended from the ministry for his opposition to episcopacy. He published "Lectures on the Epistle to the Hebrews." Died in 1576.

Dering, (Sir EDWARD,) an English politician, born in Kent about 1598. He became about 1640 a member of the Long Parliament, in which he acted at first with the popular party, but in the civil war he was a royalist. Died in 1644.

Deriot, dẹh-re′o′, (ALBERT FRANÇOIS,) BARON, a French general, born in 1766, was appointed chamberlain to Napoleon in 1813. Died in 1836.

Derivaux, dẹh-re′vō′, (ACHILLE,) a French general, born at Senones in 1776 ; died in 1843.

Derjavine. See DERZHAVIN.

Dẹr′mo-dȳ, (THOMAS,) an Irish poet, born at Ennis in 1775, wrote poems about the age of twelve, which were printed in 1792. When young, he enlisted in the army ; but his promotion was hindered by intemperance. He published two volumes of poems about 1802, also "The Battle of the Bards," a poem. Died in 1802.

See J. G. RAYMOND, "Life of T. Dermody," 2 vols., 1806.

Derodon, dẹh-ro′dôN′, (DAVID,) a French writer, born in Dauphiné about 1600, was eminent for his skill in dialectics. He taught philosophy at Orange, Nîmes, and Geneva, and was a zealous opponent of the doctrines of Descartes. In 1630 he was converted from Calvinism to the Catholic faith, and afterwards returned to Calvinism. He wrote treatises on "Metaphysics," "Logic," "Philosophy," and other subjects. His "Tombeau de la Messe" (1654) caused his banishment, and was often reprinted. Died in 1664.

See HAAG, "La France protestante ;" DE GERANDO, "Histoire de la Philosophie moderne ;" BAYLE, "Historical and Critical Dictionary."

Derosne, dẹh-rōn′, (CHARLES,) a French chemist, born at Paris in 1780 ; died in 1846.

Derossi, dȧ-ros′see, (GIOVANNI GHERARDO,) an Italian poet, born in Rome in 1754. He wrote a "Treatise on the Dramatic Art," "Memoirs on the Fine Arts," (1792,) and numerous comedies, fables, and epigrams. He was chosen a correspondent of the French Institute in 1812. Died in 1827.

Deroy, dẹh-rwȧ′, (BERNARD ERASMUS,) a German general, born at Manheim in 1743. He commanded a corps of Bavarians in the service of Napoleon I., and was killed at Potolsk in August, 1812.

See "Erinnerungen an den General von Deroy," Augsburg, 1852.

Derrand, dȧ′rôN′, (FRANÇOIS,) a French Jesuit and architect, born in 1588, designed the church of Saint-Louis, Paris. Died in 1644.

Der′rick, (SAMUEL,) an Irish author, born in 1724, came to London about 1751. In 1761 he succeeded Beau Nash as master of ceremonies at Bath and Tunbridge. His habits were extravagant and dissolute. He wrote "A View of the Stage," and other works. Died in 1769.

Derschawin. See DERZHAVIN.

De Ruyter. See RUYTER.

Dẹr′went-wâ-tẹr, (JAMES RADCLIFFE,) EARL OF, an English Catholic, born in Northumberland in 1689, inherited his title from his father. He was a zealous adherent of the house of Stuart, and a leader of those who fought for the Pretender in 1715. With a small army of insurgents under the command of Forster, he marched to Preston, where they were defeated and taken prisoners. After trial for treason, he was executed in March, 1716.

See his "Life," by SYDNEY GIBSON.

ā, ē, ī, ō, ū, ȳ, *long;* à, ė, ò, same, less prolonged; ă, ĕ, ĭ, ŏ, ŭ, ȳ, *short;* ạ, ẹ, ị, ọ, *obscure;* fär, fàll, fàt; mĕt; nŏt; gŏŏd; mŏŏn;

Derzavin. See Derzhavin.

Derzhavin, dĕr-zhä'vin, written also **Derzavin,** **Derjavine,** or **Derschawin,**(Gabriel Romanovitch,) a celebrated lyric poet of Russia, born at Kazan in 1743. He entered the army as engineer in 1760, and became a colonel about 1778. In 1784 he was made a councillor of state, and in 1791 secretary of state. He was successively advanced to the dignity of senator in 1793, imperial treasurer in 1800, and minister of justice in 1802. Before this date he had produced a number of admirable odes, one of which is an "Ode to the Deity," ("Oda Bog°-.") This sublime and original poem has been translated into Latin and Chinese. Four volumes of his works were published in 1810. He also wrote an excellent treatise on lyric poetry, and a few other prose works. Died in 1816.

See Otto, "Lehrbuch der Russischen Literatur."

De Sacy. See Sacy.

Desaguliers, dä'zä'gü'le-ā', (John Theophilus,) an eminent natural philosopher, born at Rochelle, France, in 1683, was the son of a Protestant who emigrated to London about 1685. Having studied at Oxford, and entered into orders, he settled in London, and began about 1712 a course of lectures on natural philosophy, which, on account of their novelty and other merits, were very successful. In 1714 he was elected a Fellow of the Royal Society. He obtained the living of Edgeware, and was for some time chaplain of the Prince of Wales. He wrote a "System of Experimental Philosophy," (1719,) besides other works. Died in 1744.

See Weiss, "Histoire des Réfugiés Français."

Desaix* de Veygoux, deh-sā' deh vā'goo', commonly called simply **Desaix,** (Louis Charles Antoine,) an eminent and gallant French general, born of a noble family at Saint-Hilaire-d'Ayat, near Riom, in Auvergne, in 1768, entered the army at the age of fifteen. He favoured the Revolution, but not the crimes which its more violent partisans committed. In 1792 he was chosen aide-de-camp by General Victor de Broglie. During the reign of terror he was imprisoned, and narrowly escaped death. His military talents were displayed in several campaigns on the Rhine, and procured for him a rapid promotion. As general of division, he contributed to the good order of the famous retreat made by Moreau in 1796. In 1798 he was quartermaster-general or chief of the staff under Bonaparte when the latter proposed the invasion of England. Having received command of a division in the expedition to Egypt, he pursued Mourad Bey into Upper Egypt, and gained a decisive victory at Sidiman, October 7, 1798. He governed that conquered province with such wisdom and moderation that the natives gave him the title of "the Just Sultan." When Bonaparte embarked on his homeward voyage, he left orders that Desaix should follow him; and the latter arrived at the army in Italy in June, 1800, a few days before the battle of Marengo. The French were retiring in disorder at four o'clock, when Desaix brought up his reserve, and by an impetuous charge converted defeat into a signal victory. In this charge he received a mortal wound, and almost instantly expired. One account, which is rather apocryphal, represents him as saying, "Tell the First Consul that my only regret in dying is to have perished before having done enough to live in the recollection of posterity." His grave was made at Saint-Bernard, near the summit of the Alps, and two monuments were erected to his memory in Paris. "The tomb of Desaix," said Napoleon, "shall have the Alps for its pedestal, and the monks of Saint-Bernard for its guardians."

See Thiers, "Histoire du Consulat;" De Courcelles, "Dictionnaire des Généraux Français;" J. Lavallée, "Éloge historique du Général Desaix," 1801; Cousin d'Avallon, "Histoire des Généraux Kléber et Desaix," 1801; Allemand, "Essai sur le Général Desaix," 1845; Becker, Comte de Mons, "Le Général Desaix, Étude historique," 1852: "Nouvelle Biographie Générale."

Desani, dä-sä'nee, (Pietro,) an Italian painter, born at Bologna in 1595; died in 1657.

Desargues, deh-zäRg', (Gaspard,) an able French geometer, born in Lyons in 1593. He fought at the siege

* In Scott's "Life of Napoleon" this name is everywhere erroneously spelled Dessaix.

of Rochelle, where he formed a friendship with Descartes. After the peace he quitted the army, and resided in Paris, where he associated with Gassendi and Pascal. He was the author of a "Treatise on Perspective," (1636,) and a "Treatise on Conic Sections," (1639.) Died in 1662.

Désaugiers, dä'zō'zhe-ā', (Marc Antoine,) a French composer of songs, born at Fréjus in 1752; died in 1793.

Désaugiers, (Marc Antoine Madeleine,) a French song-writer, son of the preceding, was born at Fréjus in 1772. He composed, besides many popular songs, successful theatrical pieces or vaudevilles. He was for a long time the foremost among French chansonniers, until Béranger appeared. He died, greatly regretted, in 1827.

See Décour, "Notice sur M. A. M. Désaugiers," 1827.

Desault, deh-sō', (Pierre,) a French physician, born in Béarn in 1675; died about 1740.

Desault, (Pierre Joseph,) an eminent French surgeon, born near Lure, in Franche-Comté, in 1744. After passing a few years in the military hospital of Béfort, he went to Paris in 1764, and received lessons from Antoine Petit. He gained a high reputation by his lectures on anatomy, and made improvements in surgery, before he was admitted into the College of Surgery in 1776. In 1782 he was chosen chief surgeon of the hospital La Charité. On the appointment of chief surgeon of the Hôtel-Dieu, in 1788, he was preferred to many eminent competitors. His reputation and practice increased, until he had the treatment of almost all the important cases in the capital. He continued to lecture, and the school founded by him was frequented by students from many foreign countries. In 1794 he was appointed professor of clinic surgery in the École de Santé, then just instituted. The French estimate him the most skilful surgeon of his time. Bichat published "Surgical Works" which contain the doctrines of Desault. Died in 1795.

See Petit, "Éloge de Desault," 1795; Caillau, "Notice sur la Vie et les Écrits de Desault," 1800; Bichat, "Notice sur Desault," in the "Magasin Encyclopédique."

De Saussure. See Saussure, de.

Desbarreaux. See Barreaux, des.

Desbarres, dä-bäR', ? (Joseph Frederick,) an English hydrographer, of French descent, born in 1722. He rose to the rank of colonel in the army, was aide-de-camp to General Wolfe at Quebec, and was made governor of Prince Edward's and Cape Breton Islands about 1784. He published, at the expense of the government, "The Atlantic Neptune," (1777,) which is said to be the finest collection of charts, plans, and views ever issued. He taught navigation to Captain Cook. Died in 1824, aged one hundred and two years.

Desbillons, dä'be'yôn', (François Joseph Terrasse,) a French Jesuit, born in Berry in 1711, excelled in Latin poetry. He professed rhetoric at Nevers, Caen, and La Flèche, and wrote (in Latin verse) numerous fables, ("Fabulæ Æsopicæ,") the "Art of being Well," (or "Art of Preserving Health,") ("Ars bene Valendi,") and other poems. After the dissolution of his order he retired to Manheim. Died in 1789.

See Quérard, "La France Littéraire;" Feller, "Dictionnaire Historique."

Desbœufs, dä'buf', (Antoine,) a French sculptor and engraver on gems, born in Paris in 1795, was a pupil of Cartellier. He obtained a medal of the first class in 1843. He produced statues of History and Science for the Chamber of Peers, one of Voltaire, and other works.

Desbois. See Chesnaye.

Desbois de Rochefort, dä'bwä' deh rosh'foR', (Louis,) born in Paris in 1750, became physician to the hospital La Charité, where he lectured to a large class with eminent ability. He left a work on "Materia Medica," (1789,) which was for a long time the best on that subject. Died in 1786.

Desbordes-Valmore, dä'boRd' väl'moR', (Madame Marceline,) a popular French writer, born at Douai in 1787; died in 1859. She has left romances, and several beautiful poems indicating true poetic feeling and deep religious sentiment.

Desborough. See Desborow.

Desborow or **Desborough,** dez'bur-uh, an ∙English republican general in the time of Charles I., was a brother-in-law of Oliver Cromwell. He strenuously opposed the project to make the Protector king, in 1657.

Soon after the death of Oliver, he joined the cabal of the Wallingford House, and by threats induced Richard Cromwell to dissolve the Parliament in 1659. The succeeding Parliament cashiered him soon after that date.

Desbrosses, dậ′bross′, (MARIE,) a French comic actress, born in Paris in 1764; died after 1855.

Desbureaux, dậ′bü′rō′, (CHARLES FRANÇOIS,) a French general, born at Rheims in 1755; died in 1835.

Descamps, dậ′kôN′, (JEAN BAPTISTE,) a French painter and writer, born at Dunkirk in 1714. He was chosen director and professor of a free school of design at Rouen, and a member of the Royal Academy of Paris. He was moderately successful as a painter of familiar scenes, but derives his reputation chiefly from a work entitled "Lives of Flemish, German, and Dutch Painters," ("Vies des Peintres Flamands, Hollandais, et Allemands," 4 vols., 1753–63,) which, however, is incomplete and often inaccurate. He also published a "Picturesque Journey in Flanders and Brabant," (1 vol., 1769.) Died at Rouen in 1791.

See DESCAMPS, "Notice sur J. B. Descamps, Peintre du Roi," 1807.

Descartes, dậ′kȧRt′, (RENÉ,) [Lat. RENA′TUS CAR-TE′SIUS,] an illustrious French philosopher and mathematician, born at La Haye, in Touraine, March 31, 1596. He was educated at the College of La Flèche, where he formed a lasting friendship with Mersenne, and cherished a partiality for mathematical science, in which he was destined to make most important dis-coveries. On leaving college, at the age of nineteen, his first step was to renounce all his books, to efface from his mind all scholastic dogmas and prejudices, and then to admit nothing that could not bear the test of reason and experiment. It is difficult to realize at the present day how bold was such an attempt, how arduous such a task, at a time when the philosophy of Aristotle still maintained despotic sway, and when to question his decisions was generally deemed by learned men the height of arrogance. To perfect his education, he re-solved to travel; and, as it was usual in that age to make the military profession subservient to such a design, he entered the Dutch army in 1616, and passed into the service of the Duke of Bavaria in 1619. He gave proof of courage at the battle of Prague in 1620, but soon after renounced a profession that was not congenial to his favourite studies. He continued his travels for several years in France, Italy, etc., and in 1629 settled in Holland, (where he hoped to find more freedom and seclusion than in France,) to meditate on metaphysics, chemistry, mathematics, and astronomy. Some years passed before he published any extensive work on mathematics; but his genius for this science had often been manifested by the facility with which he resolved the most difficult questions. In 1637 he produced his celebrated "Discourse on the Method of Reasoning well, and of investigating Scientific Truth," ("Discours sur la Méthode pour bien conduire sa Raison, et chercher la Vérité dans les Sciences,") which contains treatises on metaphysics, dioptrics, and geometry. The last treatise announced important discoveries in algebra and geometry, among which are the employment of algebraic formulæ in the construction of curves, and the application of the notation of indices to algebraic powers. "One man," says Hallam, "the pride of France and wonder of his contemporaries, was destined to flash light upon the labours of the analyst and point out what those symbols, so darkly and painfully traced, might represent and explain. The theory developed by Descartes in this short treatise displays a most consummate felicity of genius." ("Introduction to the Literature of Europe.") His treatise on Dioptrics affords ingenious geometric applications, and announces the first discovery of the law of the refraction of light. His style is so admirably pure, clear, and concise that he is entitled to a high rank among the creators and reformers of the French language.

In 1641 he published, in Latin, his great metaphysical work, "Meditationes de Prima Philosophia," the speculations of which gave a wonderful impulse to philosophical inquiry in his own and succeeding times. They manifest an original, daring, and independent genius, endowed with great force and subtlety of thought. He performed the same service in the philosophy of mind

that Bacon performed in natural science. Taking his departure from universal doubt, he found the basis of all positive knowledge in self-consciousness expressed by this enthymem, "Cogito; ergo sum," "I think; therefore I exist." His bold innovations and brilliant paradoxes excited much hostility as well as admiration. His book was condemned by the College of Cardinals at Rome; and Voet, a professor of Utrecht, accusing Descartes of atheism, instigated the civil power to persecute him, but his malice was partially frustrated. Cartesianism became modified by his admirers into systems quite dissimilar or opposite. Thus, Spinoza derived from it his pantheism, and Berkeley his pure idealism.

He published in 1644 "Principles of Philosophy," ("Principia Philosophiæ,") in which he propounds his theory of the world, and the doctrine of Vortices. He supposed that the sun is the centre of a vortex of an all-pervading ethereal fluid, whose whirling motion produces the revolution of the planets. In 1647 the French court granted him a pension of 3000 livres. Soon after this date Christina, Queen of Sweden, offered him an asylum at her court, which he accepted. There he was treated with much honour; but the change in his habits, together with the rigour of the climate, was too much for his constitution, which was always delicate. He died at Stockholm in February, 1650. He was never married. His works, including some not named above, were published in nine volumes, (1690,) with the title of "Opera Omnia." His influence, which was almost universal in the seventeenth century, has declined since Gassendi reformed the philosophy of mind and Newton demonstrated his more simple physical principles. But he still has just and various claims to celebrity, in the noble thoughts, the precious truths, the wise maxims, which, along with some brilliant errors, he has transmitted to posterity. "He worked a more important change in speculative philosophy," says Hallam, "than any who had preceded him since the revival of learning; for there could be no comparison in that age between the celebrity and effect of his writings and those of Lord Bacon." ("Introduction to the Literature of Europe.")

See BRUCKER, "Historia Philosophiæ;" G. H. LEWES, "Biographical History of Philosophy;" MERCIER, "Éloge de Descartes;" THOMAS, "Éloge de Descartes;" 1765; ADRIEN BAILLET, "Vie de Descartes," 2 vols., 1691; PIERRE BOREL, "Vitæ Ren. Cartesii Compendium," Paris, 1656; G. H. GAILLARD, "Éloge de Descartes," 1765; BORDAS-DUMOULIN, "Le Cartésianisme," 2 vols., 1843; BOUILLIER, "Sur la Philosophie Cartésienne," 2 vols., 1854; GARNIER, "Descartes;" D. NIZARD, "Descartes et son Influence," etc., in the "Revue des Deux Mondes," December 1, 1844; CARL F. HOCK, "Cartesius und seine Gegner," 1835; "Edinburgh Review" for January, 1852.

Descemet, dậs′mả′ or dậ′seh′mả′, (JEAN,) a learned French physician and anatomist, born in Paris in 1732, discovered the internal lamina of the cornea. He practised medicine with success. Died in 1810.

Deschamps, dậ′shôN′, (ANTOINE,) a French poet, brother of Émile, noticed below, was born in Paris in 1800. He published a translation of Dante's "Divina Commedia," (1829,) and several volumes of poems.

Deschamps, (CLAUDE FRANÇOIS,) a French priest, born at Orléans in 1745, devoted his talents and fortune to the instruction of deaf-mutes, in which he followed the system of Pereira. He published an "Elementary Course of Education for Deaf-Mutes," (1779,) and a few other treatises on that subject. Died in 1791.

Deschamps, (ÉMILE,) a popular French poet and dramatist, born at Bourges in 1791. He produced in 1818 two comedies, called "Selmours et Florian," and "Le Tour de Faveur," both of which had great success. With Victor Hugo and others, he founded the "Muse Française" in 1827. He published a collection of poems entitled "French and Foreign Studies," ("Études françaises et étrangères," 1828,) which contains some translations, and a volume of "Poésies complètes," (1840,) which were received with favour. In prose he has written several tales and critical articles for the journals.

Deschamps, (EUSTACHE,) sometimes called **Morel,** a French poet, born about 1320. Among his works is the "Miroir du Mariage." Died about 1400.

Deschamps, (JEAN MARIE,) a French *littérateur*, born in Paris in 1750, was secretary to the empress Josephine, and remained in her service until her death, (1814.) He was the author of "Piron with his Friends," and other dramatic pieces, and published a translation, in verse, of Monti's "Bard of the Black Forest." Died in 1826.

Deschamps, (JOSEPH FRANÇOIS LOUIS,) a French physician, born at Chartres in 1740. He succeeded Desault as surgeon-in-chief of the hospital La Charité in 1788. When Corvisart became first physician to Napoleon, Deschamps was chosen one of his consulting surgeons. In 1811 he became a member of the Institute. He published a "Treatise on Cystotomy." Died in 1824.
See "Biographie Médicale."

Deschizeaux, dậ'she'zō', (PIERRE,) a French botanist, born at Mâcon in 1687; died about 1730.

Deseine, deh-sản', (FRANÇOIS,) a French bookseller and writer, born in Paris, became a resident of Rome. He was author of a work entitled "Rome, Ancient and Modern," (10 vols., 1713,) which is prized for its accuracy. Died at Rome in 1715.

Deseine, (LOUIS PIERRE,) a French sculptor, born in Paris in 1750; died in 1827.

Desenne, deh-sěn', (ALEXANDRE JOSEPH,) an eminent French designer, born in Paris in 1783. After the death of Moreau, in 1814, he occupied perhaps the first place in his art. He embellished the works of Rousseau, Delille, Boileau, Voltaire, etc. Died in 1827.

Desericius. See DESERIZ.

Deseriz or **Deseritz,** dā'zeh-rits, [Lat. DESERIÇ'IUS,] (JOSEPH INNOCENT,) a Hungarian cardinal, born at Nitra in 1702, was the author of several works, of which the principal treats on the origin and early history of the Hungarians, "De Initiis ac Majoribus Hungarorum," (1748.) Died in 1765.
See HORANYI, "Memoria Hungarorum."

Desessarts, dậ'zậ'sắR', (NICOLAS Lemoyne—leh'-mwản',) a French *littérateur,* born at Coutances in 1744, lived in Paris. He published, besides other works, "Celebrated Trials," ("Causes célèbres," 196 vols., 1773–89,) and a "Dictionary, Historical and Critical, of all French Writers to the End of the Eighteenth Century," ("Siècles littéraires de la France, ou Nouveau Dictionnaire historique, critique et bibliographique," etc., 6 vols. 8vo, 1800.) Died in 1810.
See QUÉRARD, "La France Littéraire."

Desèze. See SÈZE, DE.

Desfaucherets, dậ'fōsh'Rậ', (JEAN LOUIS BROUSSE,) a French dramatic writer, born in 1742; died in 1808.

Desfontaines, dậ'fôN'tận', (GUILLAUME FRANÇOIS FOUQUES DESHAYES,) a French dramatist, born at Caen in 1733, became librarian of Monsieur, (Louis XVIII.) He produced numerous successful comedies, among which were "The Marriage of Scarron," and the "Traveller Incog.," ("Le Voyageur inconnu.") Died in 1825.

Desfontaines, (PIERRE FRANÇOIS GUYOT,) ABBÉ, a French critic, born in Rouen in 1685. In 1724 he was invited to Paris to write for the "Journal des Savants," to which he imparted new vitality. Devoting his pen to polemic criticism, he issued successively several periodicals, such as "Le Nouvelliste du Parnasse," (1731,) and "Judgments on New Works," (1745.) His critiques involved him in a quarrel with Voltaire, which was prosecuted with much rancour. Desfontaines published a "Neologic Dictionary," (1726,) and other works. His version of the "Æneid" (1743) is said to be the best prose version in the French language. Died in 1745.
See DE LA PORTE, "L'Esprit de l'Abbé Desfontaines," 4 vols., 1757; CHARLES NISARD, "Les Ennemis de Voltaire: Desfontaines, Fréron et Beaumelle," 1853.

Desfontaines, (RENÉ LOUICHE,) an eminent French botanist, born at Tremblay, in Bretagne, about 1752. He studied medicine in Paris, and made such progress in botany that he was received into the Academy of Sciences in 1783. Through the influence of Lemonnier, the government furnished him with means to make a botanical excursion in Barbary, from which, after two years' absence, he returned in 1785. He was appointed by Buffon professor of botany in the Jardin des Plantes in 1786. About 1795 he was admitted into the Institute. In 1798 he published his most important work, the result of his researches in Africa, entitled "Flora Atlantica," (2 vols. 4to.) Vegetable physiology is indebted to him for the valuable discovery of the difference in the growth and

structure of monocotyledons and dicotyledons. He published "Lectures on Botany," a "Description of the Trees and Shrubs of France," (1809,) and numerous treatises on new genera which he discovered. Died in November, 1833.
See "Biographie des Naturalistes," in the "Dictionnaire universelle des Sciences naturelles;" A. P. DE CANDOLLE, "Notice historique sur la Vie et les Travaux de M. Desfontaines," 1834; PIERRE FLOURENS, "Éloge historique de R. L. Desfontaines," 1837; "Nouvelle Biographie Générale."

Desforges, dậ'forzh', (PIERRE JEAN BAPTISTE CHOUDARD,) a French dramatic writer, born in Paris in 1746, was a comic actor in his youth. He retired from the stage in 1782, and then produced "Tom Jones at London," a comedy in verse, of which La Harpe says, "The situations are interesting, the dialogue is rapid and animated, and the style ingenious and easy." He was author of many other comedies, and of successful operas, among which is "Joconde." Died in 1806.
See "Nouvelle Biographie Générale."

Desfourneaux, dậ'fooR'nō',(EDME ÉTIENNE BORNE,) a French general, born in 1767, commanded an expedition to Saint Domingo, from which he expelled the British in 1796 or 1797. In 1802 he was sent back to that island, though not as general-in-chief, and gained some advantages over the negro insurgents. Died in 1849.

Desgallards, dậ'gậ'lẳR', (NICOLAS,) a Protestant theologian, born about 1520, became minister in Geneva about 1552, and planted a French church in London in 1560. He was much esteemed by Calvin, and was appointed preacher to the Queen of Navarre in 1571. He translated several of Calvin's works into French, and published an edition of Saint Irenæus, (1570.)

Desgenettes, dậzh'nět' or dậ'zheh-nět', (NICOLAS RENÉ DUFRICHE,) BARON, an eminent French physician, born at Alençon in 1762. He became chief physician of the army of Italy about 1794, and in 1798 served in the same capacity in Egypt, where he displayed great skill and courage. He attended the grand army during the empire, and at Waterloo in 1815. On the restoration of Louis XVIII. he lost his position in the army, and in 1823 he was dismissed from a chair of medicine which he had obtained in Paris about 1800. He was chosen chief physician of the Invalides in 1832. He published, besides other medical works, "The Medical History of the Army of the East," (1802,) and wrote articles for the "Biographie Universelle." Died in 1837.
See PARISET, "Éloge du Baron R. Desgenettes," 8vo, 1838; DESGENETTES, "Souvenirs de la Fin du 18me Siècle et des Commencements du 19me, ou Mémoires de R. D. G.," 2 vols., 1836; "Nouvelle Biographie Générale."

Desgodets, dậ'go'dậ', (ANTOINE,) a French architect, born in Paris in 1653, was chosen pensioner of the king at the Academy of Rome in 1674. On his return he published, by order of Colbert and at the public expense, "The Ancient Edifices of Rome, designed and measured accurately," a work of considerable merit. Died in 1728.

Desgoffe, dậ'gof', (ALEXANDRE,) a French historical and landscape painter, born in Paris in 1805. Among his works are "The Roman Campagna," and "The Sleep of Orestes," (1857.)

Desgranges, dậ'grŏNzh', (JEAN BAPTISTE,) a French medical writer, born at Mâcon in 1751; died in 1831.

Deshauterayes, dậ'zōt'Rậ', (MICHEL ANGE ANDRÉ LE ROUX,) a French linguist, born near Pontoise in 1724, was a nephew and pupil of Étienne Fourmont, who taught him Hebrew, Arabic, Chinese, etc. From 1752 to 1784 he was professor of Arabic in the Collége Royal, Paris. He wrote a "Life of Fourmont," and published some letters on Oriental languages. Died in 1795.

Deshayes, dậ'zậ' or dậ'hậ', (LOUIS,) Baron of Courmemin, a French diplomatist, born about 1590. He was sent by Louis XIII. on a mission to the Levant in 1621, and on his return published a "Journey to the Levant," an interesting and valuable work. Having joined in some intrigues against Richelieu, he was beheaded in 1632.

Deshays, dậ'zậ', (JEAN BAPTISTE,) an eminent French historical painter, born at Rouen in 1729. He studied under Vanloo, and afterwards visited Rome. In 1758 he was admitted to the Royal Academy of Paris, on which occasion he exhibited his "Venus embalming the Body of Hector." This established his reputation as one of the best painters of his time. His "Saint Benedict Dying" is also much admired. Died in 1765.

See C. N. COCHIN, "Lettres sur la Vie de Deshays," 1765.

Deshoulières, dạ′zoo′le-aìR′, MADAME, (née ANTOINETTE du Ligier de la Garde—dü le′zhe-ạ′ d′lä gärd,) a French poetess, born in Paris about 1634. She was beautiful, graceful, and learned. In 1651 she became the wife of Seigneur Deshoulières, an officer in the army. She was much caressed and complimented by the poets, who called her the tenth Muse. Voltaire said that "she was the most successful of all the French ladies who have cultivated poetry." Her idyls, one of which is entitled "Les Moutons," are said to be the best in the language, and are more admired than her other poems, among which are eclogues, odes, elegies, etc. Her "Moral Reflections" are also much esteemed. A pension of two thousand francs was granted her in 1688. Her works were often read in the public sessions of the French Academy. She was a faithful wife and mother, and did not sacrifice her domestic duties to literary fame. She wrote a tragedy, "Genseric," which was so unsuccessful that some one, alluding to her pastoral above named, applied to her the popular proverb, "Retournez à vos moutons," ("Return to your sheep.") Died in 1694.

See VOLTAIRE, "Siècle de Louis XIV," and "Le Temple du Gout:" A. PÉRICAUD, "Les deux Deshoulières," 1853: P. É. LEMONTEY, "Notice sur Madame Lafayette et Mesdemoiselles Deshoulières," 1822.

Deshoulières, (ANTOINETTE THÉRÈSE,) the daughter of the above, born in Paris in 1662, was also a poetess. In 1687 she gained the prize of the French Academy for her ode on the following subject : "The Care which the King bestows on the Education of the Nobility." M. Caze, her accepted lover, having been killed in battle in 1692, she composed elegiac verses to his memory. She also wrote songs and epistles. Died in 1718.

Desideri, dà-se-dā′ree, (IPPOLITO,) an Italian missionary, born at Pistoia in 1684, went to Thibet about 1715, and passed ten years in Lassa. He translated into Latin the "Kangiar," the sacred book of Thibet. Died at Rome in 1733.

Desiderio da Settignano, dà-se-dā′re-o dà sêt-tên-yä′no, an eminent Italian sculptor, born in Tuscany in 1457. Among his works is a mausoleum of Carlo Marsuppini in the Santa Croce at Florence. Died in 1485.

See VASARI, "Lives of the Painters:" TICOZZI, "Dizionario."

Des-ï-de′rï-us, [Fr. DIDIER, de′de-ạ′,] the last king of the Lombards, was Duke of Istria at the death of Astolph, whom he succeeded in 757 A.D. In 770 Charlemagne married his daughter ; but he repudiated her the next year. In 772 Desiderius was involved in war with Pope Adrian, in whose defence Charlemagne marched an army into Italy and besieged Desiderius in Pavia. The latter surrendered in 774, and was confined in a monastery, where he ended his days.

See MURATORI, "Annali d'Italia;" SISMONDI, "Histoire des Français."

Desjardins, dạ′zhäR′dăN′, (JACQUES,) a French general, born at Angers in 1757. He served as general of division in 1794 under Pichegru in Holland. He was mortally wounded at Eylau in 1807.

Desjardins, [Lat. HORTEN′SIUS,] (JEAN,) born near Laon, in France, became one of the physicians of Francis I., and had so great a reputation that it was believed he could cure all diseases, provided the fatal hour had not arrived. Some punster applied to him this proverb : "Contra vim mortis, non est medicamen in hortis." Died in 1549.

Desjardins, dạ′zhäR′dăN′, (MARTIN VAN DEN Bogaert—bo′gärt,) a skilful Dutch sculptor, born at Breda in 1640, removed to Paris, where he made a colossal group in honour of Louis XIV., which was destroyed in the Revolution. Died in 1694.

Deslandes, dạ′lôNd′, (ANDRÉ FRANÇOIS Boureau—boo′rō′,) a skeptical French writer, born at Pondicherry, in India, in 1690, came to France in his youth. His "Critical History of Philosophy" (1737) had great success. Voltaire criticised the style of this, and called the author "un vieux écolier précieux, un bel-esprit provinciel," ("an affected pedant, a provincial witling.")

Deslandes also wrote "Reflections on Great Men who have died jestingly," and other works. Died in 1757.

See QUÉRARD, "La France Littéraire."

Deslyons, dạ′le-ôN′, (JEAN,) a French theologian, born at Pontoise in 1615 ; died at Senlis in 1700.

Deslys, dạ′lèss′, (CHARLES,) a French littérateur, born in Paris about 1820.

Desmahis, dạ′mä′e′, (JOSEPH FRANÇOIS ÉDOUARD de Corsembleu—dęh koR′sôN′bluh′,) a French poet, born at Sully-sur-Loire in 1722. At the age of eighteen he went to Paris, and by the favour of Voltaire obtained access to the society of the élite. He wrote "Le Voyage de Saint-Germain," and other fugitive poems, which had considerable popularity, and several comedies, one of which, "The Impertinent," (1750,) was performed with success. "It sparkles with wit," says La Harpe, "but at the expense of naturalness," (naturel.) Died in 1761.

See DESESSARTS, "Siècles littéraires."

Desmaiseaux, dạ′mạ′zō′, (PIERRE,) a learned writer, born in Auvergne, France, in 1666, emigrated to England in his youth, and there associated with eminent authors. He was chosen Fellow of the Royal Society. He wrote, in English, a "Life of Boileau," (1712,) and a "Life of Bayle," (1722,) and translated into English Bayle's "Dictionary," Fénelon's "Telemachus," and other works. His writings are said to be valuable for literary history. Little is known of the events of his life. Died in London in 1745.

See MORÉRI, "Dictionnaire Historique."

Desmarais. See REGNIER-DESMARAIS.

Desmares. See CHAMPMESLÉ.

Desmares, dạ′mär′, (TOUSSAINT GUI JOSEPH,) a French Jansenist preacher and writer, born at Vire in 1599 ; died in 1687.

Desmarets. See MAILLEBOIS, MARSHAL DE.

Desmarets or **Desmarais,** (FRANÇOIS SÉRAPHIN REGNIER.) See REGNIER-DESMARAIS.

Desmarets, dạ′mä′rạ′, (NICOLAS,) a French statesman and financier, was the nephew and pupil of Colbert. He became director of finances in 1702. The resources of France were exhausted by long wars, and the financial fabric raised by the skill of Colbert was falling to ruin, when Desmarets was appointed controller-general in 1708. His administration was wise, honest, and partially successful. On the death of Louis XIV., in 1715, he was deprived of office. Died in 1721. His son became distinguished as the Marshal de Maillebois.

See VOLTAIRE, "Siècle de Louis XIV;" SAINT-SIMON, "Mémoires."

Desmarets, (NICOLAS,) a French natural philosopher and geologist, born at Soulaines in 1725. In 1753 he wrote a prize essay on the ancient junction of Great Britain with the continent. He was admitted to the Academy of Sciences in 1771. He was one of the editors of the "Encyclopédie Méthodique." His "Treatise on the Origin and Nature of Basalt," in the opinion of Cuvier, who wrote his eulogy, should secure for him a durable reputation. Died in 1815.

Desmarets, [Lat. MARE′SIUS,] (ROLAND,) born in Paris in 1594, was a brother of Jean Desmarets de Saint-Sorlin. He wrote "Latin Letters" in verse, (1625,) often reprinted. Died in 1653.

Desmarets, (SAMUEL,) a French Protestant divine, born at Oisemont in 1599, preached at Laon, Sedan, Bois-le-Duc, Groningen, etc. He wrote many works on theology, which are praised by Bayle. Died in 1673.

Desmarets de Saint-Sorlin, dạ′mä′rạ′ dęh săN′-soR′lăN′, (JEAN,) a French poet, born in Paris in 1595, was one of the first members of the French Academy. He wrote successful dramas, entitled "Aspasia," and "The Visionaries ;" and "Clovis," an epic poem, (1657,) which was justly ridiculed by Boileau. Desmarets was prominent in the party that studiously depreciated the ancients, and was a fanatical opponent of the Jansenists. He pretended to be inspired, and wrote some visionary devotional works. Died in 1676.

See BAYLE, "Historical and Critical Dictionary;" NICÉRON, "Mémoires."

Desmars, dạ′mär′, a French writer on medical topography and natural history, lived at Boulogne-sur-Mer. Died in 1767.

Desmasures, dạ̈'mä'züʀ', (LOUIS,) a mediocre French poet, born at Tournay about 1516, made a translation of the "Æneid" into French verse. Died about 1580.

Desmeunier. See DÉMEUNIER.

Desmichels, dạ̈'me'shĕl', (LOUIS ALEXIS,) BARON, a French general, born at Digne in 1779, fought as captain at Austerlitz, (1805,) and as colonel at Waterloo, (1815.) He became lieutenant-general in 1835, and was afterwards Governor of Corsica. Died in 1845.

Desmichels, (OVIDE CHRYSANTHE,) a French historian, born in the department of Var in 1793, was professor of history in Paris from 1818 to 1831. His "History of the Middle Ages" (1825; 12th edition, 1846) is regarded as a classic work.

Desmolets, dạ̈'mo'lȧ', (PIERRE NICOLAS,) a learned French compiler, born in Paris in 1678, became a priest of the Oratoire. He was employed as editor or compiler of many useful works, among which were a new and improved edition of Lami's "Apparatus Biblicus," (1723,) and "The Continuation of Memorials of History and Literature, by Sallengre," (11 vols., 1726–31.) Died in 1760.

See QUÉRARD, "La France Littéraire."

Desmonceaux, dạ̈'môn's̄ō', ABBÉ, a French oculist, born in Paris in 1734, wrote a "Treatise on Diseases of the Eyes and Ears," and other works. Died in 1806.

Dĕs'mọnd, (CATHERINE FITZGERALD,) COUNTESS OF, an Irish lady, the wife of James XIV., Earl of Desmond, was born in the county of Waterford. She was presented at the court of Edward IV., danced with his brother, Richard III., and lived through five subsequent reigns. It is said that she reached the age of one hundred and forty, and died after the accession of James I., (1603.)

See "Memoirs of Eminent Englishwomen," by LOUISA S. COSTELLO, London, 1844; "London Quarterly Review" for March, 1853.

Desmoulins, dạ̈'moo'lăn', (ANTOINE,) a French naturalist, born at Rouen in 1796. He wrote a "Natural History of the Human Races of Northern Europe and Asia," etc., (1826,) and published in a short treatise the results of researches in the nervous system, (1824.) Died in 1828.

Desmoulins, (CAMILLE,) a prominent French democrat and political writer, born at Guise, in Picardy, in 1762, was educated in Paris, where Robespierre was his schoolmate. An enthusiastic partisan of the Revolution, he took an active part in the storming of the Bastille, became a devoted follower of Danton, and acquired distinction by his pamphlets, which were written with great ability. He assumed or received the title of "Attorney-General of the Lamp-post," for his share in the death of those who were hung by the mob in the street. He had an impediment of speech, which prevented his success as an orator. In 1791 he married an amiable lady named Lucile Duplessis. Some writers accuse him of complicity in the massacre of September, 1792, but add that on that occasion he saved the lives of several worthy persons. He was elected to the Convention in 1792, and voted for the death of the king and the destruction of the Girondists, but subsequently advocated milder measures, for the promotion of which he began to issue the "Vieux Cordelier," a periodical which had much celebrity and is still admired for its literary merit. He incurred the implacable enmity of the fanatical Saint-Just by saying that this demagogue "carried his head like the holy sacrament," and was involved in the proscription of his friend Danton, with whom he was executed, April 5, 1794. His wife soon after shared the same fate. "The talent which he displayed as a writer," says Lord Brougham, "may not be of the highest order, were we considering the merit of one who was a mere author. But he also played a great part among the actors in the scenes of the time, and of those he stands certainly highest as a master of composition." "No one," says Lamartine, "could so well personify the populace, with its tumultuous movements, its mobility, its inconstancy, and its quick transitions from fury to pity for its victims. A man at once so ardent and so volatile, so trivial and so inspired, so undecided between blood and tears, must have influence over an insurgent people in proportion as his nature is congenial with theirs." ("History of the Girondists.") "A fellow of endless wit and soft lambent

brilliancy," says Carlyle; "a man for whom art, fortune, or himself would never do much, but to whom Nature had been very kind."

See THIERS, "History of the French Revolution;" CARLYLE, "French Revolution;" E. FLEURY, "Biographie de C. Desmoulins," 1850, and enlarged edition, entitled "Études révolutionnaires," etc., 2 vols., 1851; CARLYLE, "Miscellanies;" BROUGHAM, "Statesmen of the Time of George III."

Desnoiresterres, dạ̈'nwȧʀ'taiʀ', (GUSTAVE le Brisoys—lẹh bʀe'zwȧ',) a French novelist and critic, born at Bayeux in 1817. He wrote several novels, one of which is entitled "Entre deux Amours," (1845.)

See "Nouvelle Biographie Générale."

Desnoyer, dạ̈'nwȧ'yȧ', (LOUIS FRANÇOIS CHARLES,) a prolific French dramatist, born at Amiens in 1806; died in 1858.

Desnoyers, dạ̈'nwȧ'yȧ', (AUGUSTE GASPARD LOUIS BOUCHER,) BARON, a celebrated French engraver and designer, was born in Paris in 1779. He studied under Lethière and Darcis, and gained distinction by a copper-plate engraving of "La belle Jardinière" of Raphael, (1804,) which he afterwards surpassed in works after various masters. He produced in 1808 a portrait of Napoleon, by Gérard, and in 1814 one of Raphael's Madonnas, ("Vierge à la Chaise.") In 1816 he was elected to the Institute. He afterwards devoted his burin chiefly to the works of Raphael, with a success which perhaps has never been surpassed. Among his master-pieces is "The Transfiguration," (1840.) He received the title of baron in 1828. Died in 1857.

See "Nouvelle Biographie Générale;" "Archives des Musées Impériaux."

Desnoyers, (JULES PIERRE FRANÇOIS STANISLAS,) a French geologist and antiquary, born at Nogent-le-Rotrou (Eure-et-Loir) in 1800. He was chosen librarian of the Museum of Natural History at Paris in 1834. He has written, besides other works, "Observations on the Tertiary Formations of the West of France," (1832,) and "Ecclesiastic Topography of France," (1853.)

See "Nouvelle Biographie Générale."

Desnoyers, (LOUIS CLAUDE JOSEPH,) a French littérateur, born at Replonges (Ain) in 1805. He founded in 1832 the "Charivari," which he edited with success until 1836, in which year he became one of the proprietors of the "Siècle" in Paris. He also wrote several popular tales, among which are "The Adventures of Jean P. Choppart," (1836,) and "Gabrielle, or Every Road leads to Rome," (1846.)

Desorgues, dạ̈'zoʀg', (JOSEPH THÉODORE,) a satirical French poet, born at Aix in 1764; died in 1808.

Desormeaux, dạ̈'zoʀ'mō', (JOSEPH LOUIS RIPAULT,) a French historian, born at Orléans in 1724, lived in Paris. He wrote a "History of Spain and Portugal," (1758,) and a "Life of the Marshal de Luxembourg," (1764,) which were very successful. He was admitted into the Academy of Inscriptions in 1771. Died in 1793. (See DINGÉ, ANTOINE.)

See QUÉRARD, "La France Littéraire."

Desormeaux, (MARIE ALEXANDRE,) a French physician and professor of obstetrics, born in Paris in 1778; died in 1830.

De Soto, dȧ so'to, (HERNANDO or FERNANDO,) a Spanish explorer, born in Estremadura about 1500, served with distinction under Pizarro in Peru. He conducted an expedition from Spain to Florida in 1539, discovered the Mississippi River, and died in Louisiana in 1542.

See LAMBERT A. WILMER, "Life, Travels, and Adventures of Ferdinand de Soto," Philadelphia, 1858; BANCROFT, "History of the United States," vol. i.

Des'pạrd, ? (EDWARD MARCUS,) an Irish conspirator, born in Queen's county. He became a colonel in the British army, but was afterwards suspended or disgraced. He formed a conspiracy to kill the king, for which he was executed in 1803.

Despars or **Desparts,** dạ̈'pȧʀ', (JACQUES,) a French physician, born at Tournay, graduated in Paris in 1409, and practised there with great reputation. He became first physician to Charles VII., founded and endowed a medical school in Paris, and wrote a "Commentary on Avicenna." Died in 1457.

Desparts. See DESPARS.

€ as k; ç as s; ḡ hard; ğ as j; G, H, K, guttural; N, nasal; R, trilled; s̄ as z; ᵗh as in this. (☞See Explanations, p. 23.)

48

Despautère, dȧ′pō′taiʀ′, (JEAN,) a noted Flemish grammarian, born at Ninove about 1460, was the author of a Latin work on grammar, ("Commentarii Grammatici,") which was very popular, and was used in the schools of France. "Too long," says Boinvilliers, "it caused the despair of youth, who shed many tears over its obscurities." His Flemish name was VAN PAUTEREN. Died in 1520.

Despaze, dȧ′pȧz′, (JOSEPH,) a French satirical poet, born at Bordeaux in 1776, lived in Paris. Died in 1814.

Despeisses, dȧ′pȧss′, (ANTOINE,) an eminent French jurisconsult, born near Alais in 1594, was one of the authors of a "Treatise on Successions." Died in 1658.

See MORÉRI, "Dictionnaire Historique."

Despence. See ESPENCE, D′.

Despencer, le, (HUGH.) See SPENSER.

Desperiers, dȧ′pȩh-re-ȧ′, or **Desperriers,** dȧ′pȧ′-re-ȧ′, (BONAVENTURE,) a French skeptic, born at Arnayle-Duc, was valet-de-chambre of Marguerite, sister of Francis I. He wrote, in French, a work called "Cymbal of the World," ("Cymbalum Mundi,") the object of which was to throw ridicule on revealed religion. He also wrote poems and tales—"New Recreations," ("Nouvelles Récréations")—which were admired. Died in 1544.

See "Les vieux Conteurs Français," 1840; BAYLE, "Historical and Critical Dictionary;" CHARLES NODIER, "B. Desperriers et Cyrano de Bergerac," 1841; "Nouvelle Biographie Générale."

Desperriers. See DESPERIERS.

Desplaces, dȧ′plȧss′, (LOUIS,) a skilful French engraver, born in Paris in 1682. He engraved after Rubens, Paul Veronese, and other Italian masters. Died in 1739.

Despois, dȧ′pwȧ′, (EUGÈNE,) a French *littérateur*, born in Paris in 1818. He contributed able articles to the "Revue des Deux Mondes."

Desport, dȧ′poʀ′, (FRANÇOIS,) a French surgeon, born about 1700. Having practised with success in the army for several years, he was chosen surgeon-in-chief of the army of Corsica in 1738. He passes for one of the greatest military surgeons that France has produced. He wrote a "Treatise on Gun-Shot Wounds," (1749,) which was then the most complete on the subject. Died about 1760.

Desportes, dȧ′poʀt′, (AUGUSTE,) a French poet, born at Aubenas (Ardèche) in 1798. He made a good poetical version of the "Satires" of Persius, (1841,) and wrote "Molière at Chambord," a comedy, (1843.)

Desportes, (CHARLES ÉDOUARD **Boscheron**—bosh′rōṉ′,) a French lawyer and *littérateur*, born in Paris in 1753. He embraced the royal cause in the Revolution, for which he suffered in prison and in exile. In 1814 he became president of the imperial court of Orléans. Died in 1832.

See BUZONNIÈRE, "Notice sur C. E. Boscheron Desportes," 1832.

Desportes, (CLAUDE FRANÇOIS,) a French painter, a son of the following, whom he imitated, died in 1774.

Desportes, (FRANÇOIS,) an eminent French painter, born in Champagne in 1661, resided in Paris. He was received into the Royal Academy in 1699, when the king gave him a pension. He painted portraits with skill; but he excelled in representing dogs and other animals. He executed many works of this kind for Louis XIV. and for his successor. Died in 1743.

Desportes, (JEAN BAPTISTE POUPÉE,) a French physician, born in Bretagne in 1704, practised in Saint Domingo. He wrote a "History of the Diseases of Saint Domingo," in 3 vols., (1770,) one of which is devoted to botany. Died in 1748.

Desportes, (PHILIPPE,) a French poet, born at Chartres in 1545 or 1546, was an uncle of the satirist Regnier. He enjoyed the favour of Henry III., who gave him rich benefices and chose him for reader in his cabinet. He wrote elegies and erotic poems, and excelled in Anacreontic verse. "Desportes wrote more purely than Ronsard," says La Harpe, "and removed the rust which covered our versification." "He rejected," says Hallam, "the pedantry and affectation of his predecessors, and gave a tenderness and grace to the poetry of love." ("Introduction to the Literature of Europe.") Died in 1606.

See SAINTE-BEUVE, "Tableau de la Poésie Française au seizième Siècle;" LONGFELLOW, "Poets and Poetry of Europe."

Despréaux. See BOILEAU.

Despréaux, dȧ′pʀȧ′ō′, (JEAN ÉTIENNE,) a popular French dramatist and song-writer, born in Paris in 1748; died in 1820.

Despréménil. See ESPRÉMESNIL.

Després, dȧ′pʀȧ′, (JEAN BAPTISTE DENIS,) an accomplished French writer, born at Dijon in 1752. In 1805 he became secretary of Louis, King of Holland, who made him a councillor of state. About 1810 he was chosen a member of the council of the University of Paris. He wrote several dramas, among which are the "Alarmiste" and the "Satiric Poet." Died in 1832. Després and Campenon made an elegant version of Horace.

See "Nouvelle Biographie Générale."

Desprès, dȧ′pʀȧ′, or **Deprès,** written also **Desprez,** dȧ′pʀȧ′, (JOSQUIN,) a famous Flemish musician, born in Hainault about 1450 or 1460. He was a singer in the pontifical chapel under Pope Sixtus IV., after whose death he was attached to the court of Louis XII. of France. He composed masses, motets, and songs. Died about 1530. "Many poems and epitaphs," says Denne-Baron, "attest the regret caused by the death of this musician, whom all Europe proclaimed the greatest composer of his time."

See FÉTIS, "Biographie Universelle des Musiciens."

Despretz, dȧ′pʀȧ′, (CÉSAR MANSUÈTE,) a French savant, born at Lessines (Hainault) in 1792. He taught physical sciences in the Collége Henri IV., Paris, and was appointed professor in the Sorbonne about 1837. He published an "Elementary Treatise on Physics," (1825,) which was adopted by the Council of Public Instruction, and "Elements of Chemistry," (1830.) He produced from carbon or charcoal minute black crystals, said to be a good substitute for diamond-dust in polishing precious stones. Died in 1863.

Desprez, (JOSQUIN.) See DESPRÈS.

Desprez, dȧ′pʀȧ′, (LOUIS,) a French sculptor, born in Paris in 1799. He obtained the grand prize in 1828 for "The Death of Orion." Among his other works are a statue of General Foy and a bronze statue of Diana, (1845.)

Desprez, (LOUIS JEAN,) a French artist, born in Lyons about 1745, was appointed painter and architect to Gustavus III. of Sweden. He displayed a rich imagination as a painter. The "Battle of Suenskund" is one of his master-pieces. Died in 1804.

Desprez de Boissy. See BOISSY.

Desrenaudes, dȧ′rȩh-nōd′, (MARTIAL BORYE,) an able French *littérateur*, born at Tulle in 1755, became grand vicar of the Bishop of Autun, (Talleyrand,) whom he served as secretary. He is the reputed author of the famous report on public instruction presented by Talleyrand in 1791. He was imperial censor under Napoleon I. Died in 1825.

Desrochers, dȧ′ro′shȧ′, (ÉTIENNE **Jehandier**—zhōṉ′de-ȧ′,) a French engraver of portraits, was born at Lyons; died in Paris in 1741.

Desroches, dȧ′rosh′, (JEAN,) a learned historian of Belgium, born at the Hague in 1740. In 1783 he published a well-written Latin "Epitome of Belgian History," (2 vols.,) and left (unfinished) an "Ancient History of the Austrian Netherlands," (1787.) Died in 1787.

Desroches de Parthenay, dȧ′rosh′ dȩh pȧʀt′nȧ′, (J. B.,) a French historian, born at La Rochelle, published, besides other works, a "History of Denmark," (6 vols., 1730,) and a "History of Poland under Augustus II.," (4 vols., 1734.) Died in 1766.

Desrotours, dȧ′ro′tooʀ′, (NOËL FRANÇOIS MATHIEU **Angot**—ōṉ′gō′,) a French numismatist and writer, born at Falaise in 1739, was chief clerk of the administration of the mint before the Revolution. Died in 1821.

Dessaix, dȧ′sȧ′, (JOSEPH MARIE,) a French general, born at Thonon, Savoy, in 1764. As major he served in Italy in 1796, was a deputy to the Council of Five Hundred in 1798, and became a general of division in 1809. For his conduct at Wagram (1809) he was made a count of the empire. He was chosen grand officer of the legion of honour in 1811. He joined the army of Napoleon in March, 1815, and was in consequence excluded from office after the restoration. Died in 1834.

See DE COURCELLES, "Dictionnaire des Généraux Français."

ā, ē, ī, ō, ū, ȳ, *long;* ȧ, ȩ, ȯ, same, less prolonged; ă, ĕ, ĭ, ŏ, ŭ, ў, *short;* ạ, ẹ, ị, ọ, *obscure;* fär, fȧll, fȧt; mĕt; nŏt; gŏŏd; mōŏn;

Dessaix, (de Veygoux.) See DESAIX.

Dessalines, dā'sā'lĕn', (JEAN JACQUES,) a negro emperor of Hayti, born in or near Guinea about 1760, was brought to Hayti as a slave. In the servile war which followed the French Revolution he was distinguished for his courage and cruelty, and became first lieutenant of Toussaint L'Ouverture. He massacred all the whites and mulattoes who fell into his power. In 1802 he made a desperate resistance to the French army under Leclerc, especially at Saint-Marc. After Toussaint was transported to France, Dessalines became general-in-chief of the blacks, and expelled the French from the island in 1803. He ordered a general massacre of the white residents, who had remained under a promise of protection. In October, 1804, he assumed the title and power of emperor. Two of his officers, Christophe and Pétion, conspired against him and assassinated him in 1806, when the former became President of Hayti.

See LOUIS DUBROCA, "Vie de J. J. Dessalines," 1804.

Dessalles, dā'sāl', (JEAN LÉON,) a French philologist, born at Le Bugue (Dordogne) in 1803.

Dessau, dĕs'sŏw, (Prince LEOPOLD ANHALT,) a German general, born in 1676, distinguished himself in the war of the Spanish succession, and was made field-marshal in 1712. He obtained command of an army of Frederick II. of Prussia, with which he invaded Silesia in 1744 and repulsed the Austrians in 1745. He afterwards defeated the Saxons near Dresden. Died in 1747.

Dessen van Cronenburg. See DESSENIUS.

Des-sē'nĭ-us, [Ger. pron. dĕs-sā'ne-ùs,] or **Dessen van Cronenburg,** dĕs'sĕn vän kRo'nĕn-bŭRG, (BERNARD,) a skilful Dutch physician, born at Amsterdam in 1510, practised at Cologne. He published a work "On the Compounding of Medicines," ("De Compositione Medicamentorum," 1555,) and another on the Plague. Died in 1574.

Dessolles, dā'sol', (JEAN JOSEPH PAUL AUGUSTIN,) MARQUIS, an able French general and statesman, born at Auch in 1767, served several campaigns under Bonaparte in Italy between 1793 and 1797, and in 1799 became general of division. He served under Moreau in 1800, and contributed to the victory of Hohenlinden, (1801.) In this year he was made councillor of state and secretary of war. From 1808 to 1810 he commanded a division in Spain. In 1814 he was appointed by the provisional government general-in-chief of the national guard of Paris, with command of the first military division. On the first restoration of Louis XVIII. he became minister of state and a peer of France. He was appointed minister of foreign affairs and president of the council, or premier, on the formation of the Liberal ministry in December, 1819. The ultra-royalists, whose policy he opposed, procured his dismissal from power in 1820. Died in 1828.

See LAMARTINE, "History of the Restoration;" DE COURCELLES, "Dictionnaire des Généraux Français;" "Nouvelle Biographie Générale."

De Staël. See STAËL, DE.

D'Estaing. See ESTAING, D'.

Destaing, dā'tăN', (JACQUES,) a French general, born at Aurillac in 1764, commanded the light infantry at the battle of Aboukir, and was made a general of division in 1801. He returned to France, and was killed in a duel by General Reynier in 1802.

Destandoux. See CAILHAVA.

Destouches, dā'toosh', (PHILIPPE Néricault—nā're'kō',) a popular French dramatic writer, born at Tours in 1680, is said to have been an actor in his youth. His comedy "Le Curieux impertinent" was performed in 1710 with success. He was sent on a mission to England in 1717, and married an English lady. In 1723 he was received into the French Academy. He gained great eminence among comic authors by his "Married Philosopher," (1727,) which is his master-piece, "The Boaster," ("Le Glorieux,") and many other comedies. Died in 1754.

See VILLEMAIN, "Tableau de la Littérature au dix-huitième Siècle;" D'ALEMBERT, "Éloge de Destouches," 1755; "Nouvelle Biographie Générale."

D'Estrées. See ESTRÉES, D'.

Destutt de Tracy. See TRACY.

Des Vergers. See NOËL DES VERGERS.

Desvignoles, dā'vèn'yol', (ALPHONSE,) a French Protestant minister, born in Languedoc in 1649, preached at Lausanne, Berne, Berlin, and Brandenburg. He became a member of the Royal Society of Berlin in 1701, and one of the editors of the "Bibliothèque Germanique" in 1711. In 1738 he published a "Chronology of Sacred History," which was esteemed one of the best works on that subject. Died in 1744.

See HAAG, "La France protestante."

Desyveteaux or **Des Yveteaux,** dā'zèv'tō', (NICOLAS **Vauquelin**—vōk'lăN',) SEIGNEUR, a Frenchman, born near Falaise about 1560, was preceptor to the Duke of Vendôme, and to the dauphin, (Louis XIII.,) for the former of whom he wrote a poem called "The Education of a Prince." In 1611 he was dismissed from court on account of his immoral habits. Died in 1649.

See RATHERY, "Vauquelin des Yveteaux," 1854; J. TRAVERS, "Addition à la Vie et aux Œuvres de V. des Yveteaux," 1856; "Nouvelle Biographie Générale."

Detharding, dĕt'haR'ding, [Lat. DETHARDIN'GIUS,] (GEORG,) a learned German physician, born at Stralsund in 1671. He became professor of medicine at Rostock in 1697, and at Copenhagen in 1732. He gave evidence of a philosophic and ingenious mind in numerous works, (in Latin,) among which are a "Guide to Long Life," ("Dissertatio de Manuductione ad Vitam longam," 1724,) "Principles of Semiology," (1740,) and "Principles of the System or Art of Healing," ("Fundamenta Methodi Medendi," 1743.) Died in 1747.

See KÄMPFER, "Publicum Virtutis et Eruditionis Monumentum G. Dethardingio erectum."

Detharding, (GEORG CHRISTOPH,) a son of the preceding, born at Rostock in 1699, was professor of medicine at Copenhagen from 1747 to 1760. He wrote many dissertations on medicine. Died in 1784.

See "Biographie Médicale."

Detmold, dĕt'molt, (JOHANN HERMANN,) a German statesman, born at Hanover in 1807, was elected to the National Assembly in 1848, and was in 1849 for a short time minister of justice and of the interior for the empire. He wrote several satirical works.

See BROCKHAUS, "Conversations-Lexikon."

De Tocqueville. See TOCQUEVILLE, DE.

Detroy, dĕh-trwä', (FRANÇOIS,) a French portrait-painter, born at Toulouse in 1645, worked in Paris. Died in 1730.

Deü-cā'lĭ-on, [Gr. Δευκαλίων,] a personage of the Greek mythology, was said to be a son of Prometheus. According to popular tradition, he escaped in a ship with his wife Pyrrha from a general deluge, and landed on Parnassus; after which they threw stones behind them, which were transformed into men and women.

See OVID'S "Metamorphoses," book i.

Deurhoff, duR'hof, (WILLEM,) a Dutch writer on theology, born at Amsterdam in 1650; died in 1717.

Deusdedit. See DIEUDONNÉ.

Deusing, doi'zing, (ANTON,) a learned German physician, born at Meurs, in Westphalia, in 1612. He was versed in Oriental languages, philosophy, etc. In 1646 he became first professor of medicine at Groningen. He published, in Latin, "The Universal Theatre of Nature," (1645,) a "Synopsis of Medicine," (1649,) "The Economy of the Animal System," (1660,) and other works. Died in 1666.

See NICÉRON, "Mémoires;" SAMUEL MARESIUS, "Oratio in Obitum A. Deusingii," 1666; "Biographie Médicale."

Deusing, (HERMANN,) born in 1654, was a son of the preceding, and a partisan and admirer of Cocceius. He wrote an "Allegorical History of the Bible," (1690,) and other works on theology. Died in 1722.

Deutsch, doitsh, (NICOLAS EMANUEL,) a Swiss painter and engraver, born at Berne in 1484. His engravings are more prized than his paintings, and both are rare. His most remarkable work is a series of six engravings representing the Wise and Foolish Virgins. Died in 1530.

His son, JEAN RODOLPHE, produced engravings which are valued as showing the picturesque state of the great cities of Europe in the sixteenth century.

є as k; ç as s; g̃ hard; g̃ as j; G, H, K, guttural; N, nasal; R, trilled; ŝ as z; ŧh as in this.　(☞ See Explanations, p. 23.)

DEVA, dā'va,* a Sanscrit word signifying "god," and forming part of several compound names in the Hindoo mythology, as Kâmadêva, the "god of love," Mahâdêva, the "great god," (one of the many names applied to Siva,) etc. The feminine of Dêva is Dêvî, (dā'vee,) which signifies simply a "goddess," but is more usually applied to Pârvatî, the consort of Siva.

Devaines, dęh-vằn', (JEAN,) a French *littérateur,* born before 1750, was chief clerk of the treasury under Turgot. Died in 1803.

Devaris, dă-vă'ris, or **Devarius,** dă-vă're-ůs, (MATTHEW,) a Greek scholar, born in Corfu, lived about 1540, and became, under Paul III., corrector of Greek manuscripts in the Vatican. His chief work is a "Treatise on the Particles of the Greek Language," (1588.)

Devarius. See DEVARIS.

Devaux. See VAUX, DE.

Devaux, dęh-vō', (FRANÇOIS ANTOINE,) a French *littérateur,* born at Lunéville in 1712, enjoyed the constant friendship of Voltaire. In 1752 he produced a successful comedy, "Rash Promises," ("Engagements indiscrets.") Died in 1796.

See VOLTAIRE, "Correspondance de 1739 à 1761;" "Nouvelle Biographie Générale."

Devaux, (GABRIEL PIERRE FRANÇOIS **Moisson—**mwă'sòn',) a French botanist, born at Caen in 1742, formed near Bayeux a garden which became well known as the "Jardin Devaux." Died in 1802.

See LAIR, "Notice historique sur Moisson-Devaux," 1803.

Devaux, (JEAN,) a skilful French surgeon, born in Paris in 1649, practised in that city for sixty years with a high reputation. He was author of a popular treatise on the "Art of Preserving Health by Instinct," (1682,) and other able professional works. He also translated several foreign medical books. Died in 1729.

See SUE, "Éloge historique de Devaux," etc., Amsterdam, 1772.

Devaux, dęh-vō', (PAUL LOUIS ISIDORE,) a Belgian statesman, born at Bruges in 1801. He was one of the leaders of the party called "Doctrinaire" before the revolution of 1830. In the congress which met soon after that event, he took an important part in framing the constitution of Belgium, and promoted the election of Leopold. He exercised great influence as editor of the "Revue Nationale."

Devaux, (PIERRE,) BARON, a French general, born at Vierzon in 1762. He distinguished himself at Lutzen in 1813. Died in 1814.

Dev'ęnā, (CHARLES,) an American officer, born at Charlestown, Massachusetts, in 1820, distinguished himself at the battle of Ball's Bluff, and became brigadier-general of volunteers in 1862.

Deventer, van, vȧn dêv'ęn-tęr or dā'vēn-tęr, (HENDRIK,) an eminent Dutch physician, born at Deventer in the second half of the seventeenth century. He was repeatedly called to attend the King of Denmark, Christian V. He published some esteemed works on obstetrics. Died in 1739.

See ÉLOY, "Dictionnaire de la Médecine."

De Vere, dę veer, (AUBREY,) an English poet and dramatist. He published "The Song of Faith," (1842,) "The Waldenses," (1842,) "Mary Tudor," a drama, (1847,) and other works. Died in 1846.

See "London Quarterly Review" for May, 1843.

De Vere, (EDWARD.) See VERE.

De Vere, (MAXIMILIAN SCHELE,) a writer and scholar, born in Sweden in 1820. He came to the United States, and in 1844 was appointed professor of modern languages and belles-lettres in the University of Virginia. His principal works are his "Outlines of Comparative Philology," and "Stray Leaves from the Book of Nature."

Devereux. See ESSEX, EARL OF.

Devergie, dęh-vȇR'zhe', (MARIE GUILLAUME ALPHONSE,) an eminent French physician, born in Paris in 1798, became professor of chemistry, etc. in 1825. His most important work is "Legal Medicine, Theoretical and Practical," (3 vols., 1836.)

Devéria, dęh-vằ're'ằ', (EUGÈNE FRANÇOIS MARIE JOSEPH,) a French historical painter, born in Paris in 1805. Among his works are "Marco Bozzaris at Missolonghi," (1827,) and "The Flight into Egypt," (1838.)

Devéria, (JACQUES JEAN MARIE ACHILLE,) a French painter and lithographer, brother of the preceding, was born in Paris in 1800. He produced, among other historical paintings, a "Repose of the Holy Family," and a "Visitation." About 1849 he became keeper of engravings in the Imperial Library. Died in 1857.

Devèze, dęh-vằz', (JEAN,) a French physician, born at Rabastens in 1753, went to Hayti in 1775. He escaped from massacre in 1793 by going to Philadelphia, where he had charge of a hospital during the prevalence of the yellow fever. Returning to France, he became physician-in-ordinary to the king. Died in 1829. He wrote able "Treatises on the Yellow Fever."

Dêvî, dā'vee, [the feminine form of the Sanscrit Dêvă, a "god,"] a common Hindoo word, signifying "goddess," but usually applied to Pârvatî (or Kâlî) *par excellence.* (See PÂRVATÎ.)

Devienne, dęh-ve'ên', (FRANÇOIS,) a French musician and composer, born at Joinville in 1759 ; died in 1803.

De Vigny. See VIGNY.

Deville, dęh-vèl', (ANTOINE,) an eminent French engineer, born at Toulouse in 1596, passed some years in the service of the Duke of Savoy. He wrote an important treatise on fortifications. Died about 1656.

Devillers, dęh-ve'yằ', (CHARLES,) a French naturalist, born in 1724, lived at Lyons. His chief production is an edition of Linnæus's "Entomology." Died in 1809.

Dev'is, (ARTHUR WILLIAM,) an English historical painter, born in 1762 ; died in 1822.

Devonshire, first DUKE OF. See CAVENDISH, WILLIAM.

Dev'ǫn-shire, (EDWARD COURTNEY or COURTENAY,) EARL OF, an accomplished English nobleman, born about 1526, was the son of Henry Courtenay, Earl of Devonshire, whose mother was a daughter of Edward IV. He was confined in the Tower from 1538 till 1553, for fear that he might avenge his father, who had been unjustly executed. Queen Mary released him and restored to him the earldom. According to several historians, she was inclined to marry him, but he treated her advances with indifference, because he was attached to her sister Elizabeth. He was again confined for a short time in the Tower during Mary's reign, and then obtained leave to go abroad. He died at Padua in 1556.

Devonshire, (ELIZABETH HERVEY,) DUCHESS OF, a beautiful and accomplished English lady, born in 1759, was the daughter of the Earl of Bristol. She married as her second husband W. Cavendish, Duke of Devonshire, who died in 1814. After this event she resided in Italy, and published an elegant edition of the Fifth Satire of Horace, and other works. Died at Rome in 1824.

Devonshire, (GEORGIANA,) DUCHESS OF, an English lady, eminent for her beauty, talents, and accomplishments, born in 1757, was the daughter of Earl Spencer. In 1774 she was married to William Cavendish, Duke of Devonshire. She wrote some admired poetical effusions, one of which is "The Passage of Mount Saint Gothard." She was a personal and political friend of Charles James Fox, for whom, it is said, she purchased votes by granting electors the privilege of kissing her. Died in 1806.

Devonshire, (WILLIAM SPENCER CAVENDISH,) sixth DUKE OF, born in 1790, was the only son of the fifth duke and Georgiana Spencer. He was styled Marquis of Hartington before the death of his father, in 1811. He favoured the Whig party, and was sent as ambassador to Russia in 1826. Died in 1858.

See ERSCH und GRUBER, "Allgemeine Encyklopaedie."

Devos or **De Vos,** dęh-vos', or **Van Vos,** vȧn vos, (MARTIN,) a skilful Flemish painter, born at Antwerp about 1534. He studied at Rome and Venice, and co-operated with Tintoretto, who employed him to paint the landscapes of his pictures. He returned to Antwerp about 1559, and produced historical paintings and portraits of great merit. Among his works is a picture of the great rivers of Asia and Africa. Died in 1604.

See NAGLER, "Neues Allgemeines Künstler-Lexikon."

---

* This word is etymologically related to the Latin *Deus* and *Divus;* in some of the popular dialects it is changed to *Deo:* hence we have Kamadeo and Mahadeo, instead of Kamadeva, Mahadeva, etc.

ā, ē, ī, ō, ū, ȳ, *long;* ă, ĕ, ĭ, ŏ, ŭ, ў, *short;* ạ, ẹ, ị, ọ, *obscure;* fär, fȧll, fȧt; mêt; nŏt; gŏŏd; mŏŏn;

Devosges, dĕh-vozh', (FRANÇOIS,) a French designer, born at Gray in 1732. He founded at Dijon a free school of design, which was successful with aid from the government. "He ought to share with Vien," says M. Weiss, "the honour of contributing to the study of the antique and the imitation of nature." Died in 1811.

Devoti, dà-vo'tee, (GIOVANNI,) an Italian prelate, born in Rome in 1744, became eminent as professor of canon law in the college di Sapienza. About 1804 he was made Bishop of Carthage. He published a work on canon law, ("Institutiones Canonicæ.") Died in 1820. See TIPALDO, "Biografia degli Italiani illustri."

Devrient, dĕv're-ŏN', (GUSTAV EMIL,) an eminent German actor, of French extraction, nephew of Ludwig Devrient, was born in Berlin in 1803. He made his *début* at an early age, and performed in Berlin and other cities of Germany with great success, both in tragedy and comedy.

Devrient, (KARL AUGUST,) born in 1798, made his *début* in 1819, and became a popular comic actor. He married the famous singer Wilhelmine Schroeder, from whom he was divorced in 1828.

Devrient, (LUDWIG,) a popular German actor, uncle of the preceding, born in Berlin in 1784. He became the chief favourite of the public of Berlin, where he first performed in 1815, and received the surname of "the German Garrick." He excelled both in tragedy and comedy, and performed many parts in the tragedies of Shakspeare. Died in 1832.

See H. SCHMIDT, "L. Devrient, eine Denkschrift," 1833; CARL F. KUNZ, "Aus dem Leben zweier Schauspieler; Ifflands und Devrients," 1838.

Devrient, (PHILIPP EDUARD,) an actor and dramatic writer, brother of Gustav Emil, noticed above, was born in Berlin in 1801. Among his works are the comedies of "The Little Gray Man" and "The Favour of the Moment," ("Die Gunst des Augenblicks,") and a "History of the Dramatic Art in Germany," (1848–51.)

Devrient, (WILHELMINE.) See SCHROEDER.

Devuez, dĕh-vü'à', (ARNOULD,) an excellent painter of history, born near Saint-Omer in 1642. He worked in Rome, and afterwards in Paris, where he was patronized by Louvois. "His compositions are in the manner of Raphael," says the "Biographie Universelle," "and his design is correct." Died at Lille in 1724.

Dew, (THOMAS R.,) an American writer, born in Virginia in 1802, became professor of political economy, history, and metaphysics in William and Mary College in 1827, and president of that institution in 1836. His principal works are "The Policy of the Government," (1829,) an "Essay in Favour of Slavery," (about 1833,) and a "Digest of the Laws, Customs, etc. of Ancient and Modern Nations." Died in 1846.

Dewaal. See WAEL, DE.

Dewailly. See WAILLY, DE.

Dę-weeš', (WILLIAM POTTS,) an American physician, born at Pottsgrove, Pennsylvania, in 1768. He practised in Philadelphia for many years, and was chosen professor of obstetrics in the University of Pennsylvania in 1834. He published a "System of Midwifery," and other works. Died in 1841.

D'Ewes, düz, (Sir SYMONDS,) an English antiquary, born at Coxden in 1602, was elected to Parliament in 1640, and was made a baronet in 1641. In the civil war he was a moderate opponent of the royal cause, and was one of the members who were expelled from Parliament by Colonel Pride's "purge" in 1648. He was a laborious collector of historical records, medals, etc., and compiled a useful work, entitled "Journals of all the Parliaments during the Reign of Elizabeth," which was published after his death. Died in 1650. His "Autobiography and Correspondence" was published in 1845 by J. O. Halliwell.

De Wette. See WETTE, DE.

Dewey, dü'e, (CHESTER,) an American botanist, born at Sheffield, Massachusetts, in October, 1784. He was professor of mathematics and natural philosophy at Williams College for seventeen years, and became in 1836 principal of the Collegiate Institute at Rochester, New York. He was eminently successful as a teacher. He contributed to the "American Journal of Science" a series of papers on Caricography, (or the Carices of North America,) which was continued, with few interruptions, for forty-two years. Died in December, 1867.

Dewey, (ORVILLE,) D.D., a distinguished Unitarian divine, born in Sheffield, Massachusetts, in 1794, graduated at Williams College in 1814. He became an assistant of Dr. Channing, in whose pulpit he preached about two years, was pastor at New Bedford from 1823 to 1833, and in the city of New York from 1835 to 1848. In 1858 he became pastor of the New South Church, Boston. Among his writings are "Discourses on Human Life," and "The Unitarian Belief." He has contributed to the "North American Review" and "The Christian Examiner." Dr. Dewey is a strong and original thinker.

Dewez, dĕh-vå', (LOUIS DIEUDONNÉ JOSEPH,) a Belgian writer, born at Namur in 1760. In 1821 he was chosen perpetual secretary of the Academy of Brussels. He wrote a "General History of Belgium," (1805–07,) and other historical works. Died in 1834.

De Winter. See WINTER, DE.

De Witt, dę wit, (CORNELIUS or KORNELIS,) a Dutch naval officer and statesman, born at Dort, was an elder brother of John de Witt. At an early age he was chosen burgomaster of Dort and governor of Putten. In 1666 he held a high command under De Ruyter when the latter burned the English shipping in the Thames. He displayed skill and courage in the great naval battle of Solebay in 1672, soon after which he returned home, sick. A man of infamous character accused him of attempting to bribe him to poison the Prince of Orange. Though no proof was found to convict him, the judges condemned him to banishment. The populace then assembled round his prison, and he fell a victim to their rage. (See DE WITT, JOHN.)

See JOSSELIN, "Eer en Leer van wijlen den Heer C. de Witt verdedigt," 1774; J. A. OOSTKAMP, "Leven voornaamste haden en lotgevallen van C. de Witt," 1831.

De Witt, (EMANUEL,) a Dutch painter, born at Alkmaar in 1607, excelled in perspective and architectural views. Died in 1692.

De Witt or **Wit,** (JAKOB,) a Dutch painter of history, born at Amsterdam in 1695; died in 1744.

De Witt, (JOHN,) one of the most eminent statesmen that the Dutch nation has produced, was born at Dort in 1625. His father, Jacob, was a burgomaster of Dort and a deputy to the States of Holland. At the age of twenty-three he wrote a "Treatise on Curve Lines," which evinced his profound knowledge of mathematics. About 1650 he was chosen pensionary of Dort. His political principles were republican, and hostile to the encroachments of the house of Orange. He opposed without success the war against the English which began in 1652. The great losses of the Dutch in this war rendered his pacific policy so popular that in 1653 he was elected (for a term of five years) Grand Pensionary of Holland, by virtue of which office he became the president or most influential member of the States-General. He was now the leader of the republican or anti-Orange party, and had the chief direction of the government in the United Provinces. The Stadtholder had died, and his heir (William III.) was then an infant. In 1654 De Witt negotiated a treaty of peace with Cromwell, which contained a secret article that no member of the Orange family should ever be made Stadtholder. At the expiration of his term of office he was re-elected in 1658, and again unanimously in 1663. Having failed in his efforts to prevent the renewal of war with England in 1664, he conducted it with energy and ability. When the Dutch admiral Opdam was defeated and killed, De Witt took command of the fleet, and gave proof of great capacity for naval affairs. In 1666 the Dutch fleet under De Ruyter entered the Thames and burned several English ships of war, soon after which peace was restored. About this time the young Prince of Orange placed himself under the tuition of De Witt. When Louis XIV. in 1667 began to assert his claim to Flanders, De Witt formed an alliance with England and Sweden to resist him. But the French king, having seduced Charles II. to favour his design, invaded Holland in 1672 with a large army, which the Dutch could not effectually resist, and several towns were taken by the invaders. The fickle populace imputed the blame of these disasters to De Witt, and William of Orange was chosen captain-general of the army, and Stadtholder. The pensionary thereupon resigned his office.

His brother Cornelius, charged with a conspiracy against the life of the Prince of Orange, had been acquitted. The pensionary visited him in his prison, on which occasion the infuriated mob, probably instigated by the dominant party, burst into the prison and murdered them both, August 20, 1672. Hume represents John de Witt as "a minister equally eminent for greatness of mind, for capacity, and for integrity."

See MACAULAY, "History of England," vol. i. chap. ii.; PIETER SIMON, " J. de Witt en zijn Tijd," 3 vols., 1832–35; F. A. VAN HALL, "Lofrede op J. de Witt," 1827; R. VAN DER HOEVEN, "Leven bedrijf en Dood der doorglugtigte Heeren Gebroeders C. en J. de Witt," 1705; French version of the same, by ZOUTELANDT, 1709.

De Witte, (PIETER.) See CANDIDO.

Dews'bur-y̆, (WILLIAM,) an eminent English minister of the Society of Friends, was born at Allerthorpe, in Yorkshire, probably about 1620. In order to obtain relief from spiritual conflicts, and actuated by a zeal for religious liberty, he entered the army of the Parliament in 1642, but soon, from a sense of duty, renounced the use of carnal weapons. In 1651 he met George Fox, whose doctrines he recognized as the true gospel which had been already revealed to himself, and of which he soon became a powerful preacher. He was imprisoned in Warwick jail nearly eight years, ending in 1671, and again in the same place from 1678 to 1685 on the charge of being a Jesuit. "I entered prisons," said he, "as joyfully as palaces, telling my enemies to hold me there as long as they could." In 1688 he preached in London an impressive sermon, which is preserved in Sewel's "History of the Quakers." Died in 1688.

See EDWARD SMITH, "Life of W. Dewsbury," 1836; and the same reprinted in "Friends' Library," Philadelphia, vol. ii., 1838.

Dex-ip'pus or **Di-ox-ip'pus,** [Gr. Δέξιππος or Διώξιππος; Fr. DEXIPPE, děk'sèp', or DIOXIPPE, de'ok'sèp',] a Greek physician of Cos, lived in the fourth century B.C., and was a disciple of Hippocrates.

Dexippus, [Δέξιππος,] a Greek philosophic writer of the fourth century of our era. He composed a commentary on the "Categories" of Aristotle, which is extant, and is said to be interesting.

Dexippus, (PUBLIUS HERENNIUS,) a Greek historian, born in Attica, flourished in the third century of our era. He wrote "Chronike Historia," a history from the fabulous times to Claudius Gothicus, and " Σκυθικά," a history of the invasion of the Scythians or Goths, fragments of which are extant. Died about 280 A.D.

See FABRICIUS, "Bibliotheca Græca."

Dex'ter, (SAMUEL,) an American jurist, born in Boston in 1761, graduated at Harvard in 1781, and was admitted to the bar in 1784. He joined the Federalist party, and was chosen a Senator of the United States in 1798. He was appointed secretary of war in 1800, and secretary of the treasury about January, 1801. In 1801 or 1802 he retired from political life, and resumed the practice of law in Boston. He was highly distinguished as a lawyer and as an advocate before the supreme court at Washington. In 1812 he supported the war against Great Britain, disagreeing with the Federalists on that question. Died in 1816.

Deyeux, dȧ'yuh', (NICOLAS,) a French chemist and apothecary, born in Paris in 1753; died in 1837.

Deyling, di'ling, (SALOMON,) a German Orientalist, born at Weida in 1677. He wrote "Observationes Sacræ," (4 vols., 1708–36.) Died in 1755.

See ERSCH und GRUBER, "Allgemeine Encyklopaedie."

Deyns. See DENYS, (JACQUES.)

Deynum, van, vȧn di'nŭm, (JEAN BAPTISTE,) a Flemish miniature-painter, born at Antwerp in 1620.

Deyster, di'ster, (ANNE,) a painter, born at Bruges, was a daughter of Louis de Deyster, whose works she copied skilfully. Died in 1746.

Deyster, de, deh di'ster, (LOUIS,) a Flemish historical painter, born at Bruges in 1656. He studied in Rome and Venice, and worked in his native place, painting mostly scriptural subjects, among which is "The Apparition of Christ to the three Marys." This is praised by

Descamps, who considered Deyster as equal to the great Flemish masters in chiaroscuro. Died in 1711.

See DESCAMPS, "Vies des Peintres Flamands," etc.

Deyverdun, dȧ'vêr'duN', (GEORGE,) a Swiss writer, born at Lausanne about 1735. He was a friend of the historian Gibbon, whom he assisted in his literary labours. He wrote "Literary Memoirs of Great Britain for the Years 1767 and 1768." Died in 1789.

Dezallier d'Argenville, deh-zȧ'le-ȧ' dȧR'zhôN'vèl', (ANTOINE JOSEPH,) a mediocre French writer, born in Paris in 1680, published a "Treatise on Gardening," another on "Conchology," and "The Lives of Celebrated Painters," with portraits, (1745.) This contains the lives of one hundred and eighty painters. He was a Fellow of the Royal Society of London. Died in 1765.

His son, ANTOINE NICOLAS, published "Lives of Architects and Sculptors," (1787,) which is said to be incomplete and inexact. Died in 1794.

Dezobry, deh-zo'bRe', (CHARLES LOUIS,) a French writer, born at Saint-Denis (Seine) in 1798. He published in 1835 a historical and antiquarian work called "Rome in the Augustan Age, or A Journey of a Gaul to Rome," (4 vols.,) which is accounted a very successful representation of the life and manners of the ancient Romans. He edited a "General Dictionary of Biography and History," (2 vols., 1857.)

Dezoteux, deh-zo'tuh', (FRANÇOIS,) a French physician and surgeon, born at Boulogne-sur-Mer in 1724. He was a zealous promoter of inoculation. He wrote with Valentin an able "Historical Treatise on Inoculation." Died in 1803.

Dhaher, dȧ'her, a famous Arab sheik of Palestine, who at first possessed only the little town of Safed, to which he added Tiberias and Acre. For thirty years he waged war against various parties, and extended his power by courage and policy. In 1771 Dhaher and Ali Bey defeated the Turkish pasha of Damascus. He was afterwards defeated and killed about 1775.

See VOLNEY, "Voyage en Égypte et en Syrie."

Dharmasoka, Dharmaçoka, or **Dharmashoka** See ASOKA.

D'Hilliers. See HILLIERS, D'.

D'Hozier, do'ze-ȧ', (CHARLES RENÉ,) a son of Pierre, noticed below, was born in 1640. He was well versed in heraldry, and wrote several works by order of Louis XIV. Died in 1732.

D'Hozier, (PIERRE,) a French genealogist, born at Marseilles in 1592, was noted for his knowledge of heraldry. He was appointed judge of arms of France in 1641, steward of the king's household in 1642, and councillor of state in 1654. He wrote "The Genealogy of the Principal Families of France," (in 150 vols.,) and several other works. Died in 1660. Boileau wrote a few verses under his portrait, one of which is,

"Ses talents surprendront tous les ages suivants."*

D'Huxatime, dük'să'tèm', a French poet, born in Dauphiné, lived about 1470.

See LONGFELLOW's "Poets and Poetry of Europe."

Di-a-du-me-nI-ā'nus, [Fr. DIADUMÉNIEN, de'ȧ'dü'mȧ'ne'âN', or DIADUMÈNE, de'ȧ'dü'mȧn',] (MARCUS OPILIUS ANTONINUS,) was the son of the Roman emperor Macrinus, who began to reign in 217 A.D., and then conferred the title of Cæsar on the subject of this article, at Antioch. After a reign of about a year, Macrinus was defeated by Elagabalus, and the son, who was still a minor, was put to death in 218. He is sometimes reckoned among the emperors, as some of his medals bear the title of Augustus.

Diago, de-ȧ'go, (FRANCISCO,) a Spanish historian and friar, born at Bibel, in Valencia. He received from Philip III. the title of historiographer, and wrote, besides other histories, "Annals of the Kingdom of Valencia," (1613.) Died in 1615.

Di-ag'o-ras, [Διαγόρας,] a Greek poet and philosopher, born in the island of Melos, lived about 420 B.C. He is said to have been a disciple of Democritus of Abdera, and was commonly stigmatized as an atheist, because he dissented from the popular notions about the gods. He

* "His talents (or attainments) will surprise all succeeding ages."

ā, ē, ī, ō, ū, y̆, *long;* ȧ, ė, ŏ, same, less prolonged; ă, ĕ, ĭ, ŏ, ŭ, y̆, *short;* a, e, i, o, *obscure;* fär, fäll, fåt; mêt; nŏt; gōōd; mōōn;

fled from Athens about 411 B.C., to avoid prosecution for impiety, and a reward was offered to any one who should kill him. His moral character appears to have been good. His works are not extant.

See FABRICIUS, "Bibliotheca Græca;" REUTHEN, "De Atheismo Diagoræ," 1812: BAYLE, "Historical and Critical Dictionary;" J. L. MOUNIER, "Dissertatio de Diagora Melio," 1838.

Diamante, de-â-mân'tâ, an Italian painter and Carmelite monk, born at Prato, in Tuscany, was a pupil of Filippo Lippi. He was esteemed a good artist by his contemporaries, and promoted the renaissance of art in Italy. Died about 1440.

See LANZI, "History of Painting in Italy."

Diamante, de-â-mân'tâ, (JUAN BAUTISTA,) a popular Spanish dramatist, lived about 1640. Among his works are "The Siege of Zamora," ("El Cerco de Zamora,") and "The Jewess of Toledo," ("La Judia de Toledo.")

See TICKNOR's "History of Spanish Literature."

Diamantini, de-â-mân-tee'nee,(GIOVANNI GIUSEPPE,) an Italian painter and engraver, born in the Romagna about 1650. He settled in Venice, where he painted many works, among which is an "Adoration of the Magi." He left many fine engravings after his own designs. He died about 1715.

Dī'an, a poetical form of DIANA. See DIANE.

Dī-an'a, [Fr. DIANE, de'ân',] the Roman name of the goddess of the chase, corresponding to the **Ar'te-mis** [Ἄρτεμις] of the Greeks. She is often called Delia, from the island Delos, her birthplace. She was represented as the daughter of Jupiter and Latona, and the counterpart of her brother Apollo, like whom she appeared armed with a bow and arrows. She was also the goddess of the moon, in which character she is called Phœbe, Cynthia, and other names. She was regarded as the patroness of chastity; and all her attendants were virgins. There was at Ephesus a magnificent temple of Diana, which was regarded as one of the wonders of the world.

See GUIGNIAUT, "Religions de l'Antiquité," Paris, 1825-29, vol. ii. book iv. chap. iv.; ARNOLDI, "Commentatio de Diana Ephesia," 1708; MEVEN, "Dissertatio de Diana Taurica et Anaitide," 1835; KEIGHTLEY, "Mythology."

Diana, de-â'nâ, (BENEDETTO,) a painter of the Venetian school, lived in the fifteenth century.

Dī-an'a of France, [Fr. DIANE DE FRANCE, de'ân' deh fRÔNss',] a daughter of Henry II. and Philippa Duc, was born in 1538, and became in 1557 the wife of François de Montmorency, afterwards marshal. She had much influence with her brother, Henry III., and in 1558 mediated successfully between him and the King of Navarre, who was then recognized as the heir to the French crown. Davila praises her prudence and political ability. Died in 1619.

See DE THOU, "Historia sui Temporis."

Diane, (Anglicized as DĪ'AN.) See DIANA.

Diane de France. See DIANA OF FRANCE.

Diane de Poitiers, de'ân' deh pwâ'te-à', a beautiful French lady, born in 1499. Having been left a widow in 1531, she soon after gained the affection of the king's son, who in 1547 ascended the throne as Henry II. and gave her the title of Duchess of Valentinois. She had a complete ascendency over the king, who allowed her to exercise royal power and to control even the foreign policy of the government. De Thou attributes to her the misfortunes of Henry's reign and the persecution of the Protestants. By her graces and talents she retained her influence over Henry until his death in 1559. Died in 1566.

See DE THOU, "Historia sui Temporis;" BRANTÔME, "Femmes galantes."

Dias. See DIAZ.

Dias Gomes, dee'âs go'mês, (FRANCISCO,) a Portuguese poet, born in Lisbon in 1745, wrote odes, elegies, tragedies, etc., some of which are commended for correctness and classic taste. Died in 1795.

Diaz, dee'âz or dee'âs, or **Dias,** (A. GONÇALVEZ,) a Brazilian poet, born in the province of Maranham in 1823. He published a volume of poems in 1846, and "Segundos Cantos" in 1848.

Diaz, dee'âs or dee'âz, or **Dias,** (BALTHAZAR,) a Portuguese poet, born in the island of Madeira, lived about 1550. He wrote plays called "Autos sacramentales."

Diaz or **Dias,** (BARTOLOMEU,) a Portuguese navigator, was sent in 1486 to explore the west coast of Africa, and, sailing southward, was driven by violent winds as far as Great Fish River, without being aware that he had doubled the cape of which he was in search. On his return he discovered in 1487 this cape, which he named Tormentoso; but this was subsequently changed to Cabo de boa Esperança, (or "Cape of Good Hope.") In 1500 he sailed for India, as captain of a ship, in the fleet commanded by Cabral, and perished by shipwreck during the voyage the same year.

See JOÃO DE BARROS, "Asia, Decada I.;" RAMUSIO, "Voyages;" "Nouvelle Biographie Générale."

Diaz, dee'ath, or **Dias,** dee'âs, (DIEGO VALENTIN,) a Spanish painter, born at Valladolid; died in 1660.

Diaz or **Dias,** (FRANCISCO,) a Spanish missionary, born in Old Castile, went to the Philippine Isles in 1632. He afterwards preached in China, and was killed in 1646.

Diaz, (GASPAR,) a Portuguese painter, who flourished about 1530, was a pupil of Raphael. But little information can be found respecting him. He was called "the Portuguese Raphael." In the estimation of Boissonade, he was a great painter and expressed the passions admirably. His subjects were mostly religious.

Diaz or **Dias,** (JUAN MARTIN,) a Spanish general, surnamed EL EMPECINADO, êl êm-pâ-the-nâ'DO, (a word which literally signifies "covered with pitch" or "shoemaker's wax,"—supposed to have been applied to him because most of the inhabitants of his native village were shoemakers,) was born at Castrillo in 1775. He became in 1808 the leader of a band of guerillas, and fought against the French invaders with such success that he obtained the rank of general under the regency. In 1814 he was deprived of his command by Ferdinand. He favoured the Constitution of the Cortes in 1820, for which he fought against the absolutists. He commanded a division of the army of Placencia in 1823. After the triumph of the absolutists, he was executed for treason, in 1825.

See "Military Exploits, etc. of Don Juan Martin Diaz," London, 1823; "Nouvelle Biographie Générale."

Diaz or **Dias,** (MIGUEL,) a Spanish captain, born in Aragon, was a companion of Columbus. He discovered a gold-mine in Hayti. Died about 1514.

Diaz or **Dias,** (PEDRO,) a Spanish missionary, born near Toledo in 1546; died at Mexico in 1618.

See MACHADO, "Vida del P. P. Diaz," 1632.

Diaz de Bivar. See CID.

Diaz de la Peña, dee'âth dâ lâ pân'yâ, (NARCISSE,) a French historical painter, of Spanish extraction, born at Bordeaux in 1809, gained the first medal in 1848. Among his works are "The Nymphs of Calypso," (1840,) and "The Dream," (1841.)

Diaz de Lugo, dee'âth dâ loo'go, (JUAN BERNARDO,) a Spanish jurist, born at Seville, was appointed a member of the grand council of the Indies by Charles V., and became Bishop of Calahorra. Died in 1556.

Diaz (or **Dias**) **de Novaes,** dee'âs dâ no-vâ'ês, (PAULO,) a Portuguese general, was a grandson of Bartolomeu, and commanded an expedition sent in 1574 to Angola, where he planted a colony. Died in 1589.

Diaz del Castillo. See CASTILLO.

Dib'din, (CHARLES,) an English bard, actor, and dramatist, born at Southampton in 1745, went to London about the age of sixteen. His essays as a performer on the stage were not successful. About 1778 he became musical manager of Covent Garden Theatre. In 1789 he began to give musical entertainments in which he was the sole performer, and which were accompanied by popular songs of his composition. The success of this enterprise enabled him to open the Sans-Souci Theatre in 1796. His fame is derived chiefly from his songs, which amount to one thousand or more. His sea-songs especially have obtained durable popularity, and "have been the solace of sailors in long voyages, storms, and battles." "Tom Bowling" and "Poor Jack" are two of his most popular ballads. Died in 1814.

See "The Professional Life of C. Dibdin," by himself, 4 vols., 1803; WILLIAM JERDAN, "Men I have known," London, 1866.

Dibdin, (THOMAS,) son of the preceding, born in 1771, was also an actor and a dramatic writer. About 1791 he joined a company of strolling players, and after the lapse of several years returned to London. He then performed in Covent Garden, and wrote numerous comedies, farces, etc., some of which were successful. In 1828 he published "Reminiscences," (of the Theatre.) Died in 1841.

Dibdin, (THOMAS FROGNALL,) D.D., an eminent English bibliographer, born in Calcutta in 1776, was the nephew of Charles Dibdin, noticed above. He was educated at Oxford, and entered the priesthood in 1804. In 1809 he produced his amusing work entitled "Bibliomania," which was favourably received. The next year he began to issue a new and improved edition of "Ames's Typographical Antiquities of Great Britain," which is perhaps his most important performance. He instituted in 1812 the Roxburghe Club, devoted to bibliography, of which he was chosen vice-president. In 1817 appeared his "Bibliographical Decameron, or Ten Days' Pleasant Discourse on Illuminated MSS.," which is greatly admired by amateurs. Another admirable and costly specimen of typography was furnished by his "Bibliographic, Antiquarian, and Picturesque Tour in France and Germany." Died in 1847.

See DIBDIN'S "Reminiscences of a Literary Life," 2 vols., 1836; "Quarterly Review," vol. xxxii.; WILLIAM JERDAN, "Men I have known," London, 1866.

Dĭ-bu'ta̤-dēs [Fr. DIBUTADE, de'bü'täd'] of Sicyon, a Greek artist of uncertain epoch, is said to have invented the art of modelling bas-reliefs.

Dicæarchus, di-sē-ar'kus, [Gr. Δικαίαρχος; Fr. DICÉARQUE, de'sȧ'ȧrk',] an eminent Greek Peripatetic philosopher and writer, born at Messina, in Sicily, was a disciple of Aristotle, and lived about 300 B.C. He wrote numerous works on geography, history, etc., which are lost except small fragments. It is said he denied the immortality or existence of the soul. Cicero highly praises him as a sage, an excellent citizen, a great man, an able historian, and one of the most eloquent disciples of Aristotle. Among his principal works was a treatise on Greek geography, history, institutions, and politics, entitled "The Life of Greece," ("Ἑλλάδος βίος.")

See VOSSIUS, "De Historicis Græcis;" BRUCKER, "Historia Philosophiæ."

Dicéarque. See DICÆARCHUS.

Diç'e-to, de, (RALPH,) an English historian, was Dean of Saint Paul's, London. He wrote, in Latin, a "History of the Kings of Britain." Died in 1283.

Dick, (Sir ALEXANDER,) a Scottish physician, born in 1703, wrote a treatise on Epilepsy, ("De Epilepsia," 1725.) Died in 1785.

See CHAMBERS, "Biographical Dictionary of Eminent Scotsmen."

Dick, (JOHN,) D.D., a Scottish divine, born at Aberdeen in 1764, was a minister of the United Secession Church. He wrote an esteemed work on the "Inspiration of the Scriptures," "Lectures on Theology," and other religious books. Died in 1833.

See CHAMBERS, "Biographical Dictionary of Eminent Scotsmen."

Dick, (THOMAS,) LL.D., a Scottish author, born near Dundee in 1772, was in early life a minister of the Secession Church at Stirling. He exchanged this avocation for that of a school-teacher, which he pursued at Perth for a number of years. He devoted much attention to physical sciences, and wrote many popular scientific and religious works, viz.: "The Christian Philosopher," "The Philosophy of Religion," "The Philosophy of a Future State," "Celestial Scenery," "The Solar System," and other works. Died in 1857.

Dick'ens, (CHARLES,) one of the most popular of English novelists, born at Landport, Portsmouth, in February, 1812, was a son of John Dickens, who served in the navy pay department and afterwards became a reporter of Parliamentary debates. Young Dickens was designed for the profession of the law, and was placed in the office of an attorney, after he had studied in a college near Rochester. Finding the pursuit of law uncongenial to his taste, he soon abandoned it, and became a reporter for the daily press of London. He began his literary career by "Sketches of Life and Character," which first appeared in the "Morning Chronicle," and were published collectively as "Sketches by Boz," (2 vols., 1836.) These exhibit great acuteness of observation, and were received by the public with much favour.

In 1837 he produced a work called "The Posthumous Papers of the Pickwick Club," which in a certain department of humour is probably unrivalled by anything in the English language. The success of this work was almost without example; and it is still perhaps the most popular of all Mr. Dickens's productions. In 1838 he married a daughter of George Hogarth, a musical critic. He published in rapid succession "Oliver Twist," a novel, (3 vols., 1838,) "The Life and Adventures of Nicholas Nickleby," (3 vols., 1839,) "Master Humphrey's Clock," (1840–41,) and "Barnaby Rudge," (2 vols., 1841.) Having visited the United States in 1841, he published in 1842 "American Notes for General Circulation." His next work was the "Life and Adventures of Martin Chuzzlewit," (3 vols., 1843–44.) About the end of 1845 he became the chief editor of the "Daily News" of London, a Liberal paper, then just founded; but he held this position for a short time only. Among his later works (most of which were first issued in a serial form) are "Dombey and Son," (1847–48,) "The Personal History of David Copperfield," (4 vols., 1850,) "Bleak House," (1852,) "Hard Times," (1854,) "Little Dorrit," (1857,) "A Tale of Two Cities," (1860,) "Great Expectations," (1862,) and "Our Mutual Friend," (1864–65.)

In 1850 he began to issue, weekly, a periodical called "Household Words," which had a large circulation. Since 1859 he has published "All the Year Round," a weekly literary paper. He revisited the United States in 1867, and met with a cordial and flattering reception. In many large cities of the Union he gave public readings, which attracted crowded audiences.

"One of the qualities we most admire in him," says the "Edinburgh Review" for October, 1838, "is his comprehensive spirit of humanity. The tendency of his writings is to make us practically benevolent,—to excite our sympathy in behalf of the aggrieved and suffering in all classes, and especially in those who are most removed from observation. . . . We think him a very original writer, well entitled to his popularity, and not likely to lose it, and the truest and most spirited delineator of English life, amongst the middle and lower classes, since the days of Smollett and Fielding."

The following strictures, however, are not without justice, at least as regards many of the actors in Mr. Dickens's works: "The good characters of Mr. Dickens's novels," says the "North British Review," (vol. iv.,) "do not seem to have a wholesome moral tendency. The reason is that many of them—all the author's favourites—exhibit an excellence flowing from constitution and temperament, and not from the influence of moral or religious motive. They act from impulse, not from principle."

"He [Dickens] has revived," says Mr. Whipple, "the novel of genuine practical life, as it existed in the works of Fielding, Smollett, and Goldsmith; but at the same time he has given to his materials an individual colouring and expression peculiarly his own. . . . Dickens's eye for the forms of things is as accurate as Fielding's, and his range of vision more extended; but he does not probe so profoundly into the heart of what he sees, and he is more led away from the simplicity of truth by a tricksy spirit of fantastic exaggeration." ("North American Review" for October, 1849.)

See "London Quarterly" for October, 1837; "Edinburgh Review" for October, 1838, June, 1839, and March, 1843; "Blackwood's Magazine" for April, 1855; "British Quarterly" for July, 1862; "Westminster Review" for October, 1864; "Atlantic Monthly" for May, 1867.

Dick'in-son, (ANNA,) an American female orator, born in Philadelphia, October 28, 1842, was originally a member of the Society of Friends. She gained great distinction during the civil war by her public speeches against slavery and disunion. She is one of the most popular public lecturers in the United States. She is author of a novel entitled "What Answer?" (1868.)

See "Eminent Women of the Age," 1868.

Dickinson, (DANIEL STEVENS,) an American Senator, born in Goshen, Connecticut, in September, 1800. He was educated in Central New York, whither his parents removed when he was a child. He studied law, became an active Democrat, and in 1836 was elected to the Senate of New York. In 1842 he was chosen Lieutenant-Governor of New York for two years. He represented that State in the Senate of the United States from December, 1844, to March, 1851, during which period he voted with the Democratic party on the Wilmot proviso, the slavery question, etc. He gained distinction as a debater, and was recognized as the leader of the "Hunker" Democrats in New York. He resided at Binghamton in the latter part of his life. In 1861 he was elected attorney-general of the State of New York. During the civil war he cordially supported the Federal government in its efforts to suppress the rebellion, and acted with the Union Republican party. He was appointed district attorney for the southern district of New York by President Lincoln about March, 1865. Died in April, 1866.

See "Speeches, Correspondence, etc. of Daniel S. Dickinson, with a Biographical Sketch," by his brother, JOHN R. DICKINSON, 2 vols., 1867.

Dick'in-son, (EDMUND,) an eminent English physician, born at Appleton in 1624, gained reputation by the publication of "Delphi Phœnizicantes;" but it appears that the real author was Henry Jacob. He settled in London in 1684, practised there many years, and became physician to Charles II. and James II. Died in 1707.

See "Account of the Life, etc. of Edmund Dickinson," London, 1739.

Dickinson, (JOHN,) an English author, born about 1554. Among his works is "Speculum Tragicum." Died in 1606.

Dickinson, (JOHN,) an American statesman and lawyer, born in Maryland in 1732. He was chosen a member of the Continental Congress in 1774, and wrote several important state papers issued by that body. In June, 1776, he opposed the Declaration of Independence, which he thought premature. Having declined to sign that declaration, he impaired his popularity, and lost his election to the next Congress. He afterwards served as a private soldier against the British. In 1779 he was again elected to Congress from Delaware. He was President of Pennsylvania about three years, 1782-85. He was an able debater, and distinguished for his elegant manners and superior culture. Died in 1808.

See "National Portrait-Gallery of Distinguished Americans," vol. iii.; BANCROFT, "History of the United States," vol. viii.

Dickinson, (JONATHAN,) a Presbyterian minister, born in Hatfield, Massachusetts, in 1688, graduated at Yale College in 1706. He preached for many years at Elizabethtown, New Jersey, and acquired distinction as a writer on theology. He was elected president of the College of New Jersey in 1746. Died in 1747.

Dickinson, (PHILEMON,) a patriot of the American Revolution, was born in New Jersey about 1740. He took an active part in the struggle for independence, and at the battle of Monmouth displayed great spirit and gallantry in command of the New Jersey militia. He was a delegate to the Continental Congress in 1782 and 1783, and a United States Senator from 1790 to 1793. Died in 1809.

Dick'ons, MRS., an English singer, whose maiden name was POOLE. Died in 1833.

Dick'son, (ADAM,) a Scottish clergyman, born in East Lothian. From 1750 to 1770 he was minister of Dunse, and wrote a valuable "Treatise on Agriculture," and "The Husbandry of the Ancients," (1788,) which, says McCulloch, "is the best work on the subject in the English language." Died in 1776.

Dickson, (DAVID,) an eloquent Scottish preacher, born at Glasgow in 1583, became professor of divinity at Glasgow in 1643, and afterwards in the University of Edinburgh. He published an "Exposition of all the Epistles," an "Exposition of the Gospel of Saint Matthew," and other works, which were received with favour. Died in 1663.

See CHAMBERS, "Biographical Dictionary of Eminent Scotsmen."

Dick'son, (JAMES,) an English botanist, born in 1738. He published, besides other works, a "Collection of Dried Plants," (1788.) Died in 1822.

Dick'son, (SAMUEL HENRY,) an American physician and writer, born at Charleston, South Carolina, in 1798, graduated in the University of Pennsylvania in 1819. In 1858 he was appointed professor of the practice of medicine in the Jefferson Medical College in Philadelphia.

See ALLIBONE's "Dictionary of Authors."

Dicquemare, dĕk'mȧr', (JACQUES FRANÇOIS,) a French naturalist and priest, born at Havre in 1733, became professor of natural history in that city. He made discoveries in the nature and habits of Radiata and other marine animals, on which he wrote many treatises inserted in the "Journal de Physique." He also published "The Knowledge of Astronomy rendered Easy." Died in 1789.

Dic'tys Cre-ten'sis, [Fr. DICTYS DE CRÈTE, dĕk'tèss' deh krȧt,] a Greek, who is said to have followed Idomeneus to the siege of Troy, and to have written a narrative of the same. There exists in Latin prose a "History of the Trojan War," which purports to be a version of the work of Dictys, and has little literary merit. The works of Dictys and Dares were the chief channels through which the heroic legends of the Greeks and Trojans passed into the literature of the middle ages, and were often printed in the fifteenth century.

See PERIZONIUS, "Dissertatio" prefixed to Smids's edition of the poem of Dictys Cretensis, 1702.

Dictys de Crète. See DICTYS CRETENSIS.

Dic'uil, an Irish monk and geographer, wrote, about 825 A.D., a treatise "On the Measurement of the Earth," ("De Mensura Orbis Terræ,") which was published by Walckenaer in 1807.

Diday, de'dȧ', (FRANÇOIS,) a Swiss painter, born at Geneva in 1812, has exhibited several Alpine landscapes. He obtained a medal of the first class in 1841.

Diderot, dĕd'ro', (DENIS,) an eminent French philosopher and savant, born at Langres, in Champagne, in 1712 or 1713, was the son of a cutler, who gave him a good education. Having quitted the study of law in disgust, he went to Paris in his youth, with a ruling passion for literary pursuits. He was obliged to support himself by teaching and translating, and passed many years in poverty and obscurity, but contented in his ample intellectual resources. About the age of thirty he married a Miss Annette Champion. In 1746 he published "Philosophic Thoughts," ("Pensées philosophiques,") which produced considerable sensation. The book was condemned to the fire by Parliament, its doctrines being thought unsound. A few years before this period he had formed a friendship with J. J. Rousseau and with D'Alembert. He was imprisoned a few months in 1749 for the publication of his "Letter on the Blind, for the Use of those who see."

In partnership with D'Alembert, he commenced the great work on which his reputation is founded, the "Encyclopédie, ou Dictionnaire raisonné des Sciences, des Arts et Métiers." The project was one of immense labour and difficulty, and was accomplished chiefly by the ardent zeal and resolution of Diderot. He wrote the articles on ancient philosophy and on the arts and trades, (arts et métiers,) and, in conjunction with D'Alembert, supervised the other parts of the work. The first volume was issued in 1751, and attracted great attention. Its publication was suspended several times by government, and D'Alembert retired from the enterprise in 1759; but it was completed about 1765. Much complaint was made, and not without reason, of the infidel tendency of the work, and its partiality to the new philosophy. It has also other defects, arising from the incompetence and haste of some of the contributors. Catherine II. of Russia settled a handsome pension on Diderot in 1765, and invited him to her capital, which he visited in 1773; but he soon returned to Paris. He is the author of numerous works, among which are two novels, "The Nun," and "James the Fatalist," ("Jacques le Fataliste,") and two dramas, entitled "The Father of a Family," and "The Natural Son."

His "Essay on the Reigns of Claudius and Nero," chiefly devoted to the vindication—or rather eulogy—of Seneca, is esteemed by some as one of his ablest productions. He also contributed largely to some of the most popular French works of his time, such as Raynal's "Philosophic History," "L'Esprit," by Helvetius, and "The System of Nature," by D'Holbach. As a writer he displays talent and eloquence, but is deficient in judgment and taste. "He has written fine passages," says Marmontel, "but could not produce a good book." Grimm thought "he had perhaps the most encyclopedical head that ever existed." He is regarded as the chief of the skeptical school known as Encyclopedists; and it is asserted that he was a professed atheist. But F. Genin ("Nouvelle Biographie Générale") defends him from this charge. It is said that he taught his daughter to read the Bible. In reference to this fact, Voltaire wrote, in 1767, "I am displeased with 'Tonpla,'" (anagram of *Platon*, (Plato:)) "they say he permits his daughter to be educated in the principles which he detests." The doors of the Academy were kept closed against him, although Voltaire solicited his election. He died in Paris in July, 1784.

See DE VANDEUL, "Notice sur Diderot;" NAIGEON, "Mémoires sur Diderot," 1821; GRIMM, "Correspondance;" "Vie de Diderot," prefixed to his "Select Works," ("Œuvres choisies," 2 vols.;) CARLYLE, "Essay on Diderot;" DAMIRON, "Mémoire sur Diderot," 1852; "Foreign Quarterly Review" for January, 1833.

Didier, (King of the Lombards.) See DESIDERIUS.

Didier, de'de-ả', (CHARLES,) a French writer and traveller, was born at Geneva in 1805. He has published, besides other works, "Helvetian Melodies," (1830,) and "Subterranean Rome," ("Rome souterraine," 1833; 10 editions in France.)

Did'I-us, (JULIANUS SEVERUS,) a Roman emperor, born at Milan in 133 A.D., was the son of Petronius Didius Severus. He served in the army with distinction, and was made consul with Pertinax. After the murder of this emperor, in 193, the Prætorians offered the empire at public auction to the highest bidder. The chief competitors were Sulpitianus and Didius, who was immensely rich. The latter made the highest bid, (6250 drachmas for each soldier,) and was proclaimed emperor. But Septimius Severus and other generals refused to recognize him, and, after a reign of about two months, he was killed by the soldiers in his palace. Severus was his successor.

See DION CASSIUS, "History of Rome;" TILLEMONT, "Histoire des Empereurs."

Didius, (TITUS,) a Roman general, was consul in 98 B.C., after which he gained some victories in Spain.

Di'do, [Gr. Διδώ; Fr. DIDON, de'dòN',] called also **E-lis'sạ** or **E-lī'sạ,** [Fr. ÉLISE, ả'lèz',] a Phœnician princess, celebrated as the founder and queen of Carthage. Her story forms a beautiful episode in the "Æneid" of Virgil, who commits an anachronism when he represents her as a contemporary of Æneas. Tradition teaches that she was a sister of Pygmalion, King of Tyre, who put to death her husband, Acerbas or Sichæus. After this event she embarked secretly with a party of friends, and founded Carthage, in the ninth century before Christ.

See VIRGIL, "Æneid," books i., ii., and iv.

Didon. See DIDO.

Didot, de'do', (AMBROISE FIRMIN,) a son of Firmin, noticed below, was born in Paris in 1790. He was a printer, engraver, and type-founder, and became in 1827 the head of the great publishing-house of Firmin Didot Frères. He published many important works, among which are the "Dictionary of the French Academy," Estienne's "Thesaurus Linguæ Græcæ," (improved,) and a "New General Biography," ("Nouvelle Biographie Générale," 46 vols., 1857–66.) The processes and specimens of this house obtained the first medal in many annual expositions.

See ERSCH und GRUBER, "Allgemeine Encyklopaedie;" "Nouvelle Biographie Générale."

Didot, (FIRMIN,) a celebrated French publisher, typographer, and engraver of types, son of François Ambroise, noticed below, was born in Paris in 1764. In 1794 he invented or improved the process of stereotype printing, which differs from that now used. He issued beautiful editions of Virgil and of Horace, and many other works, and translated into French verse the "Bucolics" of Virgil and the "Idyls" of Theocritus. These versions have considerable merit. He was a chevalier of the legion of honour, and became a member of the Chamber of Deputies in 1827. He was for some time in partnership with his elder brother Pierre. His sons Ambroise, Firmin, and Hyacinthe are celebrated printers and publishers of Paris. Died in 1836.

See ERSCH und GRUBER, "Allgemeine Encyklopaedie."

Didot, (FRANÇOIS AMBROISE,) an eminent French printer and type-founder, born in Paris in 1730, was the son of François Didot, the first printer of this name. He brought the art of printing to a high degree of perfection, and produced correct and elegant editions of various works. Louis XVI. employed him to print a series of French classics for the dauphin. He was succeeded in his business by his sons Pierre and Firmin. Died in 1804.

Didot, (PIERRE,) a son of François Ambroise, born in 1760. He published magnificent editions of the Latin classics, called "du Louvre," ("of the Louvre.") His "Racine" was pronounced by a jury "the most perfect typographic production of all ages." He translated into verse the fourth book of Virgil's epic, and the first book of the Odes of Horace. Died in 1853.

Didron, de'drŏN', (ADOLPHE NAPOLÉON,) an eminent French archæologist, born at Hautvillers (Marne) in 1806. He began in 1844 to issue a periodical devoted to mediæval art and antiquities, with the title of "Annales archéologiques." His most important work is "Christian Iconography," ("Iconographie chrétienne," 1843,) which is highly prized.

Didyme. See DIDYMUS.

Did'y-mus, [Gr. Δίδυμος; Fr. DIDYME, de'dèm',] a celebrated grammarian of Alexandria, surnamed CHALCEN'TERUS, born about 62 B.C., was remarkable for his fecundity as a writer. According to Seneca, he wrote four thousand treatises on various subjects, mostly frivolous, among which were inquiries respecting the native place of Homer, the mother of Æneas, and the morals of Anacreon. None of his works are extant. There were several other ancients of this name, one of whom was an Academic philosopher who wrote a work on the "Solution of Probabilities."

See SUIDAS, "Didymus;" W. M. SCHMIDT, "De Didumo Chalcentero," 1852.

Didymus OF ALEXANDRIA, [Fr. DIDYME D'ALEXANDRIE, de'dèm' dả'lĕk'sŏN'dre',] a teacher of the Alexandrian Church, born about 308 A.D., lost his sight in childhood, but became eminent for his attainments in theology, philosophy, and in various sciences, and numbered among his disciples Saint Jerome, Isidore, and Rufinus. He was the author of numerous works, of which four have been preserved, viz.: "On the Trinity," "On the Holy Spirit," "Against the Manicheans," and "On the Canonical Epistles." Died about 395.

See SOCRATES, "Historia Ecclesiastica;" CAVE, "Scriptorum Ecclesiasticorum Historia;" FABRICIUS, "Bibliotheca Græca."

Diebitsch, dee'bitch, or, more fully, **Diebitsch-Sabalkanski,** dee'bitch sả-bål-kån'skee, (HANS KARL FRIEDRICH ANTON,) a Russian count and field-marshal, born at Grossleippe, in Silesia, in 1785, was the son of a major-general in the Russian service, which he also entered at an early age. In 1805 he was wounded at the battle of Austerlitz. Attached to the staff of Count Wittgenstein in 1812, he performed important services, and was raised to the rank of major-general. He gave proof of skill at the battles of Dresden and Leipsic, and was made a lieutenant-general at the age of twenty-eight. In 1814 he urged the advance of the allies to Paris. About 1820 he was appointed chief of the imperial staff, and was a constant attendant on the emperor in his journeys until the death of the latter in 1825. He took Varna from the Turks in 1828, and in the next year, being appointed general-in-chief, gained several victories, and performed the famous passage of the Balkan, which procured him the title SABALKANSKI ("Trans-Balkanian") and the rank of field-marshal. A treaty of peace was soon after signed at Adrianople. In January, 1831, he commanded the army sent to subdue the revolted Poles, with whom he fought indecisive battles near Praga and Ostrolenka. His success was hindered by bad weather, sickness, etc.; and he died of cholera in June, 1831.

See SCHUEMBERG, "Graf Diebitsch-Sabalkanski," Dresden, 1830; STURMER, "Der Tod des Grafen Diebitsch," 1832.

Diebolt, de'ả'bol', ? (GEORGES,) a French statuary, born at Dijon in 1816, gained the grand prize at Paris in 1841. Died in 1861.

Diecman, deek'mȧn, (JOHANN,) a German divine and philologist, born at Stade in 1647, was professor of theology at Kiel. He wrote good prefaces to five

ā, ē, ī, ō, ū, ȳ, *long;* ȧ, ė, ị, ȯ, same, less prolonged; ă, ĕ, ĭ, ŏ, ŭ, ў, *short;* ạ, ẹ, ị, ọ, *obscure;* fȧr, fȧll, fȧt; mĕt; nŏt; gōōd; mōōn;

editions of Luther's version of the Bible, and many dissertations, one of which is "On Naturalism," ("De Naturalismo," 1683.) Died in 1720.

Diederichs, dee'deh-riks',(JOHANN CHRISTIAN WILHELM,) a distinguished German Orientalist, born at Pyrmont in 1750, became professor of Oriental languages at Königsberg in 1780. He published a Hebrew grammar, and other works. Died in 1781.

See ERSCH und GRUBER, "Allgemeine Encyklopaedie."

Diedo, de-ā'do, (GIACOMO,) an Italian historian, born in Venice in 1684, published a "History of the Republic of Venice," (1751,) which is esteemed for its style and just reflections. Died in 1748.

Diefenbach, dee'fen-bâk', (LORENZ,) a German philologist, born at Ostheim (Hesse) in 1806, published works entitled "On Life, History, and Language," (1835,) "Celtica," (5 vols., 1839–42,) a "Comparative Lexicon of the Indo-Germanic Languages," (1846–51,) and several small poems.

Dieffenbach, deef'fen-bâk', (ERNST,) a German naturalist, born at Giessen in 1811, visited New Zealand, and wrote "Travels in New Zealand," (1843.)

Dieffenbach, (JOHANN FRIEDRICH,) a skilful Prussian surgeon, born at Königsberg in 1792. He graduated in 1822, and settled in Berlin, where he practised surgery and soon acquired a wide reputation. About 1832 he became professor in the University of Berlin. He was very skilful in the formation of artificial noses, lips, etc., and in the cure of strabismus. His chief work is "Operative Surgery," ("Die operative Chirurgie," 1844–48.) Died in 1847.

See BROCKHAUS, "Conversations-Lexikon."

Diego de Yepes, de-ā'go dà yā'pês, a Spanish historian and prelate, born near Toledo in 1531, was confessor to Philip II. Died in 1614.

Diel, deel, (AUGUST FRIEDRICH ADRIAN,) a German pomologist and physician, born at Gladenbach in 1756. He wrote a "Systematic Nomenclature or Description of the Finest (vorzüglichsten) Fruits of Germany," (1818,) and other works on pomology. Died in 1833.

Diel du Parquet, (JACQUES.) See DUPARQUET.

Dielhelm, deel'hêlm, (JOHANN HERMANN,) a German antiquary, born at Frankfort-on-the-Main. He published "The Antiquary of the Rhine," (1739,) and a "Dictionary of all the Rivers of Germany," (1741.) Died in 1764.

Diemen, van, vän dee'men, (ANTHONY,) a Dutch officer, born at Kuilenburg in 1593, went to India as a cadet, and rose rapidly from grade to grade. In 1631, as admiral, he conducted the fleet to Holland, and in 1636 was appointed Governor-General of the Dutch East Indies, which he governed with ability until his death. In 1642 he sent out an exploring expedition under Abel Tasman, who discovered the island of Van Diemen. Died at Batavia in 1645.

See "Nouvelle Biographie Générale."

Diemerbroeck, van, vän dee'mer-brōōk',(ISBRAND,) a skilful Dutch physician, born at Montfort in 1609, became professor of medicine and anatomy in the University of Utrecht, of which he was twice chosen rector. He published able treatises on Anatomy, on the Plague, and other diseases. His "Anatome Corporis Humani" appeared in 1672, and was often reprinted. Died in 1674.

See "Biographie Médicale."

Dien, de'âN', (CLAUDE MARIE FRANÇOIS,) a French engraver, born in Paris in 1787, obtained the first medals in 1838 and 1848. Among his works are a "Holy Family," after Raphael, and a "Madonna," after Murillo.

Diepenbeck, van, vän dee'pen-bêk', written also **Diepenbeke,** (ABRAHAM,) an eminent Dutch historical painter, born at Bois-le-Duc about 1606, was one of the best scholars of Rubens. He was chosen director of the Academy of Antwerp in 1641, and acquired a high reputation by his skill in composition and colouring. He also excelled in painting on glass, and made many designs for the booksellers. Among his chief works is a series of fifty-eight designs, called "The Temple of the Muses," a "Life of Saint Paul," on glass, at Antwerp, and a "Virgin and Child," in oil, at Berlin. Died in 1675.

See DESCAMPS, "Vies des Peintres Flamands," etc.

Diepenbeke. See DIEPENBECK.

Dièreville, de-aiR'vêl', a French traveller, born in Normandy, made a voyage in 1699 to Acadia, (Nova Scotia,) and, after his return in 1700, published a Description of that region. Tournefort, the botanist, named the genus Dierevilla in honour of him.

Dieringer, dee'ring-er, (FRANZ XAVER,) a German Catholic theologian, born at Rangendingen in 1811, became professor of theology at Bonn about 1843.

Dies, deess, (ALBRECHT,) a German landscape-painter, born at Hanover in 1755, studied in Rome, and settled in Vienna. Died in 1822.

Dies, (GASPAR.) See DIAZ.

Diesbach, von, fon dees'bâk, (JOHANN FRIEDRICH,) an Austrian general, born at Freyburg in 1677, was made a field-marshal in 1723. Died in 1751.

See ERSCH und GRUBER, "Allgemeine Encyklopaedie."

Diesbach, von, (NICHOLAS,) an able Swiss statesman, born at Berne in 1430, was employed about 1470 to negotiate with Louis XI. of France. Died in 1475.

Dieskau, von, fon dees'kŏw, (LUDWIG AUGUST,) a German officer in the French service, went in 1755 to Quebec as maréchal-de-camp. He was wounded and taken prisoner by the British and colonial troops near Fort Edward, in Washington county, New York. Died near Paris in 1767.

Di-es'pi-ter, a surname of JUPITER, which see.

Diest, deest, (HEINRICH,) a German theologian and Hebrew scholar, born at Altena in 1595; died in 1673.

Diest, van, vän deest, (ADRIAN,) a Dutch landscape-painter, born at the Hague in 1655, worked in England. Died in 1704.

Diesterweg, dees'ter-wêG', (FRIEDRICH ADOLPH WILHELM,) a German teacher, born at Siegen in 1790, taught at Berlin, and wrote many educational works.

Dieterich. See DIETRICH.

Dieterichs, dee'teh-riks', (JOACHIM FRIEDRICH CHRISTIAN,) a German writer on veterinary science, born at Stendal in 1792.

Dieterici, dee'teh-reet'see, (KARL FRIEDRICH WILHELM,) a Prussian economist and statistician, born in Berlin in 1790. He entered the civil administration about 1815, and became a privy councillor in 1831. In 1834 he obtained a chair of political economy in Berlin, and in 1844 was appointed director of the national bureau of statistics. He published, among other works, "Statistics of the Principal Objects of Commerce and Consumption in Prussia," etc., (1842–51,) and a work called "Public Welfare in the Prussian States," ("Der Volkswohlstand im Preussischen Staate," 1846.)

Dietmar, deet'mâR, or **Dietmar von Ast,** deet'mâR fon âst, a German minnesinger of great merit, lived about 1180.

See LONGFELLOW's "Poets and Poetry of Europe."

Dietrich, dee'tRiK, (ALBRECHT,) a German botanist of the present age, became professor of botany in the University of Berlin. He published a "Flora of the Kingdom of Prussia," ("Flora Regni Borussici," 1833–44.)

Dietrich, written also **Ditrich** and **Dietricy,** detreet'see, (CHRISTIAN WILHELM ERNST or JOHANN WILHELM ERNST,) an excellent German painter, born at Weimar in 1712. He was a pupil of Alexander Thiele, and was patronized in the early part of his career by Augustus, King of Poland, who enabled him to visit Rome about 1744. Having returned to Dresden, he gained a high reputation by his skill in imitating various masters in history and landscape. His touch is broad and mellow, and the verdure of his landscapes rivals that of Claude. Among his finest works is an "Adoration of the Magi." He also produced many etchings of historical subjects. He was chosen professor in the Academy of Dresden in 1763. Died at Dresden in 1774.

See NAGLER, "Neues Allgemeines Künstler-Lexikon;" J. F. LINCK, "Monographie der von dem vormals königlich Polnischen Hofmaler, C. W. E. Dietrich," etc., Berlin, 1846.

Dietrich, (DAVID NATHANAEL FRIEDRICH,) a German botanist, and director of the botanic garden of Jena, was born near Jena in 1800. Among his works are a "Flora of Germany," (7 vols., 1833–51,) and an "Encyclopædia of Plants," with engravings, (1841–51.)

Dietrich, (FRIEDRICH GOTTLIEB,) a German horticulturist, born in 1768. He published a "Dictionary of

Botany and Gardening," (10 vols., 1802–10,) and other works. Died at Eisenach in 1850.

Dietrich or **Dieterich,** dee'tẹh-RĬK, (JOHANN CONRAD,) a German philologist and historian, eminent for learning, was born at Butzbach in 1612. He became professor of Greek at Giessen in 1653, and was author of numerous Latin works, among which are a "History of the German Emperors of Saxon Race," (1666,) and "Greece in Exile," ("Græcia exulans.") Died in 1669.

Dietrich, de, dẹh dee'trĬK, (PHILIPPE FRÉDÉRIC,) BARON, a mineralogist, born at Strasburg in 1748, held several civil offices, among which was that of mayor of his native city. He translated into French Scheele's chemical treatise on air and fire, and wrote a valuable "Description of the Deposits of Ore and the Forges of France," (3 vols., 1786–1800.) He was guillotined at Paris by the Jacobins in 1793. Rouget de Lisle lodged in the house of Dietrich when he wrote the "Marseillaise" hymn.

See QUÉRARD, "La France Littéraire."

Dietrichstein, von, fon dee'trĬK-stīn', (ADAM,) a German diplomatist, born in 1527, was employed by the emperor Maximilian. Died in 1590.

Dietrichstein, von, (FRANZ,) PRINCE, a son of the preceding, was born at Madrid in 1570. He became a cardinal, and president of the council of state of the Emperor of Germany. Died in 1636.

See his Life, by VOIGT, 1792; ERSCH and GRUBER, "Allgemeine Encyklopaedie."

Dietricy. See DIETRICH.

Dietzsch, deetsh, (JOHANN CHRISTOPH,) a German landscape-painter, born at Nuremberg in 1710; died in 1769.

Dieu, de, dẹh de-uh', (LOUIS,) a Dutch Protestant minister and Orientalist, born at Flushing in 1590. In 1619 he became assistant professor in the Walloon College, Leyden. He wrote a "Grammar of the Hebrew, Syriac, and Chaldaic Languages," (1628,) "Rudiments of the Persian Tongue," (1639,) and several commentaries on Scripture, ("Critica Sacra," 1693.) His Persian Grammar was for a long time the only one existing in Europe. Died in 1642. His father, DANIEL, was an eloquent minister of Brussels and Flushing, and a good linguist.

See BAYLE, "Historical and Critical Dictionary;" POLYANDER, "L. de Dieu Oratio funebris," 1643.

Dieu, de, dẹh de-uh', ? (SAINT-JEAN,) a devout Portuguese, born at Monte-Major-el-Novo in 1495, was a shepherd at the age of forty, when he consecrated himself to works of charity. In 1540 he opened a house in Granada for the reception of the indigent sick, which was the origin of the order of charity since widely propagated. He died in 1550, and was canonized by the pope in 1690.

Dieudonné, de-uh'do'nȧ', [Lat. A DE'O DA'TUS or DE'US DE'DIT,] I, was elected pope in 614 A.D. as successor to Boniface IV. He was a native of Rome. He died in 618 or 617, and was succeeded by Boniface V.

Dieudonné II., elected pope in 672, was a Roman by birth. He died in 677.

Dieudonné, de-uh'do'nȧ', (JACQUES AUGUSTIN,) a French sculptor and engraver of medals, born in Paris in 1795.

Dieulafoy, de-uh'lȧ'fwȧ', (JOSEPH MARIE ARMAND,) a French dramatist, born at Toulouse in 1762, wrote successful comedies, etc. Died in 1823.

Dieve, van, vȧn dee'vẹh, (PETER,) a Flemish historian, born at Louvain in 1536; died in 1591.

Diez, deets, (FRIEDRICH CHRISTIAN,) a German professor, regarded as the founder of Romance (Romanisch) philology, was born at Giessen in 1794. He produced in 1825 a work on Provençal poetry, "Beiträge zur Kenntniss der Romantischen Poesie," and in 1829 "The Life and Works of the Troubadours." He was appointed professor of modern literature in Bonn in 1830, and published a "Grammar of the Romance Language," ("Grammatik der Romanischen Sprachen," 1842.)

Diezel or **Diez.** See TETZEL.

Dig'by, (Sir EVERARD,) an English Catholic, born in 1581, inherited a fortune from his father, Everard Digby, who was author of "Theoria Analytica" and other learned

works. The son was knighted in 1603. Hume says "he was as highly esteemed and beloved as any man in England." In 1605 he was induced by mistaken zeal to become an accomplice in the Gunpowder Plot, to which he contributed largely in money, arms, etc. For this crime he was tried and executed in 1606.

See HUME's "History of England."

Digby, (GEORGE,) Earl of Bristol, son of John Digby, noticed below, was born in Madrid in 1612. He was remarkable for his inconsistency in politics. At the trial of Strafford he deserted from the popular party to that of the court. As a royalist he was exiled, and went to France and Spain, where he became a Catholic. After the restoration he returned home, and sat in the House of Lords, having inherited his father's title of earl. Among his rash and violent actions was his impeachment of Lord Clarendon, in 1663, which impaired his own credit. He published several letters, and "Elvira," a comedy. Died in 1676. Horace Walpole speaks of him as "a singular person, whose life was contradiction."

See WOOD, "Athenæ Oxonienses."

Digby, (Sir HENRY,) an English admiral, born about 1770; died in 1843.

Digby, (JOHN,) Earl of Bristol, born in 1580, was descended from a Warwickshire family. He was knighted in 1606, sent as ambassador to Spain in 1611, and to the Emperor of Germany in 1621. The next year he was employed by James I. to negotiate a marriage between the king's son Charles and the Infanta of Spain, and was created Earl of Bristol. His efforts for the Spanish match were frustrated by the Duke of Buckingham. Hume represents Digby as an able negotiator. He was the author of several minor poems. He favoured the cause of Charles I. in the civil war, was exiled, and died in Paris in 1653.

See HUME, "History of England;" GARDINER, "History of England from 1603 to 1616," chaps. x., xi.

Digby, (Sir KENELM,) F.R.S., an English courtier and author, son of Sir Everard, noticed above, was born in Buckinghamshire in 1603. In the reign of Charles I. he was gentleman of the bedchamber, and filled other high offices. He married the famous beauty Venetia Anastasia Stanley. In the civil war he favoured the royalist cause, and retired to France, where he associated with Descartes and other learned men. He was reputed to be versed in occult philosophy, on which and other subjects he wrote numerous treatises. Among these are a "Treatise on the Nature of Bodies," (1644,) "Institutiones Peripateticæ," (1651,) "The Body and Soul of Man," and "Chemical Secrets." "He possessed," says Lord Clarendon, "all the advantages which nature and art and an excellent education could give him." After the restoration he returned to England, where he died in 1665.

See "Private Memoirs of Sir Kenelm Digby," by himself, 1827; "Biographia Britannica."

Digeon, de'zhŏN',(ALEXANDRE ÉLISABETH MICHEL,) a French general and viscount, born in Paris in 1771. For his conduct at Austerlitz he received the badge of the legion of honour in 1805. As general of brigade he was sent to Spain in 1808, and in 1812 was appointed commandant of Córdova and Jaen. He became a general of division in 1813. Died in 1826.

Digges, digz, (Sir DUDLEY,) a son of Sir Thomas Digges, born in 1583, was eminent as a politician and a writer. He went as ambassador to Russia in 1618, and in 1621 was elected to Parliament, where he displayed talents and zeal for the rights of the people. He wrote a "Defence of the East India Trade," (1615,) "Political Discourses," and "The Complete Ambassador," (1655,) a collection of diplomatic letters respecting the marriage between Elizabeth and the Duke of Anjou. Died in 1639.

Digges, (DUDLEY,) a son of the preceding, born about 1612, wrote a tract on "The Unlawfulness of Subjects taking Arms against their Sovereign." Died in 1643.

See WOOD, "Athenæ Oxonienses."

Digges, (LEONARD,) an eminent English mathematician, born at Barham, Kent, was educated at Oxford. He wrote "Tectonicum," (a work on mensuration, 1556,)

ā, ē, ī, ō, ū, ȳ, *long;* ȧ, ė, ȯ, same, less prolonged; ă, ĕ, ĭ, ŏ, ŭ, ў, *short;* ạ, ẹ, ị, ọ, *obscure;* fär, fȧll, fȧt; mĕt; nŏt; gŏŏd; mo͞on;

a military treatise named "Stratioticos," and a few other ingenious works. Died about 1574.

See Wood, "Athenæ Oxonienses."

Digges, (LEONARD,) grandson of the preceding, and son of Thomas Digges, born in 1588, translated from the Latin Claudian's "Rape of Proserpine," and from the Spanish a work named "Gerardo." The author of "Athenæ Oxonienses" says he was "a great master of the English language, a good poet, and no mean orator." Died in 1635.

Digges, (THOMAS,) the son of Leonard, (the first of that name,) and father of Sir Dudley Digges, was one of the greatest geometers of his time. After graduating at Oxford, he was appointed commissary-general of the troops sent by Queen Elizabeth to aid the Dutch. He edited his father's works, and wrote several original treatises, viz., a "Description of the Celestial Orbs," (1592,) a "Treatise on Military Arithmetic," (1599,) and "England's Defence." Died in 1595.

See Wood, "Athenæ Oxonienses."

Dilherr, dil'hĕr, (JOHANN MICHAEL,) a German philologist and Protestant divine, born at Themar (Saxe-Meiningen) in 1604. He wrote many learned works on sacred philology and ethics. Died in 1669.

Dilke, dilk, (CHARLES WENTWORTH,) an English editor and critic, born in 1789. He edited in 1814 a collection of old English plays, (6 vols.) About 1830 he purchased the "Athenæum," of which he became editor, and which he rendered a flourishing and able literary journal. He retired from that position in 1846, and was manager of the "Daily News" until 1849. Died in 1864.

Dilke, (CHARLES WENTWORTH,) a son of the preceding, born in 1810. As a member of the executive committee, he rendered important services in the Great Exhibition of 1851. Died in May, 1869. His son, CHARLES WENTWORTH, wrote a valuable work entitled "Greater Britain," (1868.)

Dilkes, dilks, (WILLIAM THOMAS,) a British general, born in 1765; died in 1841.

Dil'len, [Lat. DILLE'NIUS,] (JOHANN JAKOB,) an eminent botanist, born at Darmstadt in 1687, was a graduate in medicine. In 1719 he gained a wide reputation by his "Catalogue of Plants growing near Giessen," with plates. Having been invited by William Sherard, a rich amateur of botany, he went to London in 1721, and prepared a new edition of Ray's "Synopsis of British Plants," which appeared in 1724. In 1732 he produced his "Hortus Elthamensis," with figures drawn and engraved by himself. This was one of the most excellent botanical works that had then appeared, both in respect to the text and the figures, and was highly commended by Linnæus. His reputation was raised still higher by his "History of Mosses," (1741,) which, says Du Petit-Thouars, "is a fundamental work, and will always be consulted." Dillen obtained the chair of botany in Oxford, founded by his friend Sherard, about 1728. Died in 1747. Linnæus gave the name Dillenia to a genus of Indian trees.

See "Vie de Linnée," Paris, 1832; "Nouvelle Biographie Générale."

Dillen, (PHILIPP EVERHARD,) a German physician, born at Darmstadt in 1644, was the father of Johann Jakob, noticed above. Died in 1720.

Dillenius. See DILLEN.

Dillens, dil'lens, (HENRI,) a Belgian painter of history and genre, born at Ghent in 1812.

Dillis, von, fon dil'lis, (GEORG,) a German artist, born in Upper Bavaria in 1759, became teacher of landscape-painting in the Academy at Munich, (1805.) Died in 1841.

Dil'lon, (ARTHUR,) COUNT, born in Roscommon county, Ireland, in 1670, was the third son of Theobald, Lord Dillon, who fought for James II. in the civil war of 1688. He entered the service of Louis XIV. of France, as colonel, at the age of twenty, gained a rapid promotion by his brilliant conduct, and became a lieutenant-general at thirty-six. He was employed under Marshal Villars in 1708, and under Marshal Berwick in 1709. In the last year he commanded in chief a corps, and gained a victory near Briançon. He died in 1733.

His son JAMES was killed at the battle of Fontenoy in 1745. Another son, EDWARD, fell at Laufeld. ARTHUR

RICHARD, the youngest, became Archbishop of Toulouse, and then of Narbonne, and was twice president of the General Assembly of the French clergy.

See "Nouvelle Biographie Générale."

Dillon, de'lòn', (ARTHUR,) COUNT, a French general, born in 1750, was the grandson of Count Arthur, noticed above. He commanded a regiment in the West Indies in 1777, and took part in the capture of Grenada, Tobago, and Saint Christopher. He was governor of Tobago when he was chosen a deputy to the States-General in 1789. In 1792 he was appointed to the command of a corps-d'armée under Dumouriez, and, although he was disaffected towards the new régime, he consented to defend France from foreign invasion, and obtained some successes in the forest of Argonne. He was recalled in 1793, imprisoned, and perished on the scaffold in April, 1794.

See DE COURCELLES, "Dictionnaire des Généraux Français."

Dillon, (JACQUES VINCENT MARIE DE LACROIX,) born at Capua, in Italy, in 1760, was of Irish descent. Having studied engineering, he was appointed professor of arts and trades in Paris. He displayed his skill as an engineer in the construction of the Pont des Arts, the first iron bridge made in France, and was chosen chief engineer of bridges and roads. Died in 1807.

Dil'lon, (JOHN TALBOT,) an English traveller, resided many years in Vienna, where he was created a baron of the empire. He wrote "Travels through Spain," (1780.) Died in 1806.

Dil'lon, (PETER,) a British navigator, who, in 1827, visited Vanikoro and found evidence that La Pérouse was wrecked there. Died in 1847.

See "Nouvelle Biographie Générale."

Dillon, (ROGER HENRI,) ABBÉ, born at Bordeaux in 1762, was a brother of Arthur, noticed above. He published a "Universal History," (10 vols., 1822,) and other works. Died in 1829.

Dillon, de, deh de'lòn', (THÉOBALD,) COUNT, a brother of Arthur Dillon, was born in Dublin about 1744. He entered the French army at an early age, and obtained the grade of maréchal-de-camp in 1783. He favoured the popular cause in the Revolution, and served under Rochambeau on the frontier of Flanders. While moving his division from Lille to Tournay, in April, 1792, he met a division of the enemy, and, in obedience to the orders of his superiors, declined a battle. A panic seized his soldiers, who ascribed his conduct to treachery and fled in confusion to Lille, abandoning their cannon. During this retreat, or on the arrival at Lille, he was massacred by his own mutinous troops.

See DE COURCELLES, "Dictionnaire des Généraux Français."

Dillon Wentworth. See ROSCOMMON, EARL OF.

Dill'wyn, (LEWIS W.,) an English naturalist, born in 1778. He published a "Synopsis of British Confervæ," (1802–09,) and (with D. Turner) "The Botanist's Guide through England and Wales." Died in 1855.

Dil'worth, (THOMAS,) an English school-teacher of Wapping, published several popular school-books, among which were an "Arithmetic" and a "Spelling-Book." Died in 1780.

Dims'dale, (THOMAS,) M.D. and F.R.S., an eminent English physician, born in Essex in 1712, practised at Hertford. Having gained distinction by inoculation for the small-pox, he was invited to Russia about 1768 by the empress Catherine, who rewarded his professional services to her by the titles of baron and first physician and a pension of £500 per annum. He returned to England, and published, in 1776, a treatise on "Inoculation." He afterwards became a London banker, and a member of Parliament. Died in 1800.

See "Biographie Médicale."

Di-nar'chus or **Dei-nar'chus,** [Gr. Δείναρχος; Fr. DINARQUE, de'nărk',] a Greek orator, born at Corinth about 360 B.C. About the year 335 he removed to Athens, and connected himself with the Macedonian party and Demetrius Phalereus. He gained a high reputation for eloquence by writing arguments, especially when Demosthenes and other orators were in exile. Accused in 307 of an attempt to subject Athens to the Macedonian yoke, he fled to Chalcis, where he remained fifteen years, and then returned to Athens, 292 B.C. He is reckoned the last of the ten Athenian orators. Three only of his orations are extant, of which one is against Demosthenes for his transactions with Harpalus.

See FABRICIUS, "Bibliotheca Græca;" PLUTARCH, "Vitæ Decem Oratorum;" J. G. ADLER, "Dissertatio de Dinarchi Oratoris Vita et Dictione."

Dinarque. See DINARCHUS.

Dinaux, de'nō', (ARTHUR MARTIN,) a French antiquary and writer, born at Valenciennes in 1795. He published, among other works, "The Trouvères, Jugglers, and Minstrels of the North of France," (1833–43,) and furnished articles for Michaud's "Biographie Universelle."

Dindorf, din'dorf, (LUDWIG,) a German philologist, born in 1805. He published good editions of Xenophon, Diodorus Siculus, and other Greek authors. He assisted his brother Wilhelm as editor of the series of Greek classics published by Firmin Didot, Paris.

Dindorf, (WILHELM,) a distinguished German philologist, born at Leipsic in 1802, was a son of a professor of Oriental languages. From 1828 to 1833 he was professor of literary history in Leipsic, after which he was associated with his brother Ludwig and M. Hase in the renovation of Stephanus's Greek "Thesaurus." He produced an excellent edition of Demosthenes for the University of Oxford, (1849,) and commentaries on Æschylus, Sophocles, and Euripides.

See BROCKHAUS, "Conversations-Lexikon."

Dinez da Cruz. See DINIZ DA CRUZ.

Dingé, dăN'zhă', (ANTOINE,) a French *littérateur* of great learning, born at Orléans in 1759. According to Villenave, he was the author of several popular works which appeared under the name of J. R. Désormeaux, viz., "History of the House of Bourbon," "Life of Condé," etc. He published several poems, one of which is called "Henry IV. on the Pont-Neuf," (1818.) He left voluminous manuscripts, among which are a "Universal Biography," numerous poems, and various other works. Died in 1832.

Dingelstedt, ding'el-stĕt', (FRANZ,) a German poet, born at Halsdorf, in Hesse, in 1814. He acquired much popularity among the German Liberals by his political poems called "Lieder eines kosmopolitischen Nachtwächters," ("Songs of a Cosmopolitan Night-Watch," 1840.) In 1843 he received from the King of Würtemberg the title of councillor, and the office of librarian at Stuttgart. He published several novels, one of which is called "Heptameron," (1841,) and a successful tragedy, entitled "The House of Barneveldt," (1850.) Among his later poems is "Night and Morning," (1851.)

See LONGFELLOW, "Poets and Poetry of Europe;" WEBER, "Geschichte der Deutschen Literatur."

Ding'ley, (ROBERT,) an English writer and Puritan minister, born about 1620; died in 1659.

Dini, dee'nee, (PIETRO,) an Italian scholar and prelate, born at Florence about 1570; died in 1625.

Diniz, de-nĕz', anglicized as **Den'nis** or **Den'is I.,** King of Portugal, born in 1261, was the son of Alfonzo III. He ascended the throne at the age of eighteen, and married Elizabeth of Aragon in 1282. The kingdom prospered under his wise government. In 1290 he founded the University of Lisbon. He built many cities and fortresses, and planted the forest of Leiría, which, two centuries later, furnished materials for the naval power of Portugal. He was reputed the most liberal and magnificent prince of his time. He died in 1325, and was succeeded by his son, Alfonzo IV.

See FARIA Y SOUZA, "Europa Portugueza;" SCHOEFFER, "History of Portugal," (in German,) 5 vols.

Diniz (de-nĕz') or **Dinez da Cruz,** de-nĕz' dă KROOZ, (ANTONIO,) a Portuguese lyric poet and lawyer, born at Castello de Vide in 1730. He was a good classical scholar, and associated himself with some friends to form the Society of Arcadians in Lisbon, which made successful efforts to improve the language and literary taste of the nation. In 1759 he composed an admired ode on the subject of an attempt against the life of the king. He afterwards wrote epistles, sonnets, idyls, and a mock-heroic poem entitled "Goupillon." Some critics estimate him the greatest Portuguese poet of the eighteenth

century. He was a member of the supreme council of the colonies. He died at Rio de Janeiro about 1798.

See LONGFELLOW's "Poets and Poetry of Europe."

Din'nies, (ANNA PEYRE,) an American poetess, a daughter of Judge Shackleford, of South Carolina, was married in 1830 to J. C. Dinnies. She published a volume of poems called "The Floral Year," (1846.) Her *nom-de-plume* was "Moina."

See GRISWOLD's "Female Poets of America."

Dino, dee'no, [Lat. DI'NUS,] a famous Italian jurist, born at Mugello. He was professor of law in Bologna, and was employed by Boniface VIII. in the compilation of the sixth book of "Decretals." Died in 1303.

Dinocourt, de'no'koor', (PIERRE THÉOPHILE ROBERT,) a French writer, was born at Doullens in 1791. His "Cours de Morale sociale" ("Lectures on Social Morality") obtained the Montyon prize in 1840. Died in 1862.

Dinocrate. See DINOCRATES.

Dī-noc'ra̤-tēs or **Deī-noc'ra̤-tēs,** [Gr. Δεινοκρατης; Fr. DINOCRATE, de'no'krăt',] an eminent Greek architect, who lived in the time of Alexander the Great, and proposed to cut Mount Athos into a statue of that prince which should hold in one hand a large city. Alexander employed him in the building of Alexandria, about 332 B.C. It is said that he rebuilt the temple of Ephesus, burnt by Erostratus.

See PLUTARCH, "Alexander."

Dinocrates, a profligate Messenian politician, was an enemy of Philopœmen, for whose death he was chiefly responsible. He killed himself in 182 B.C.

Dī'non, [Δεινων or Δίνων,] a Greek historian, lived in the fourth century B.C. He wrote a "History of Persia."

Di-nos'tra̤-tus, [Gr. Δεινόστρατος; Fr. DINOSTRATE, de'no'străt',] a Greek geometer, who lived about 400 B.C. His works are all lost. According to Proclus, he was a pupil of Plato.

Dinoth, de'not', (RICHARD,) a French Protestant historian, born at Coutances, wrote "De Bello Civili Gallico," (1582.) Died about 1590.

Dinouart, dee'noo-ăr', (JOSEPH ANTOINE TOUSSAINT,) a mediocre French compiler and translator, born at Amiens in 1716; died in 1786.

Dinter, din'ter, (GUSTAV FRIEDRICH,) a meritorious German teacher and writer on education, was born at Borna, in Saxony, in 1760. He became minister of a church at Görnitz in 1807, and professor of theology in Königsberg in 1822. He laboured zealously to promote reforms in popular instruction, and published many popular books, among which are "Malvina, a Book for Mothers," (1819,) and a "Bible for the Use of Schoolmasters," ("Schullehrerbibel," 1825–28.) Died in 1831.

See his Autobiography, "G. F. Dinter's Leben," 1829.

Dinus. See DINO.

Din-wid'die, (ROBERT,) born in Scotland about 1690, was Governor of Virginia from 1752 to 1758. He was incompetent and unpopular. Died in 1770.

Dio Cassius. See DION CASSIUS.

Dī'o-clēs, [Διοκλῆς,] a Syracusan, celebrated for his code of laws, lived about 410 B.C., and was a leader of the democratic party of Syracuse.

Diocles, a Greek poet of the old comedy, lived in the fifth century B.C.

Diocles, a Greek geometer, of whom nothing is known except that he solved the problem of the duplication of the cube. Eutocius has preserved this solution, which consists in describing in a circle a curve called the "cissoid."

Dī'o-clēs Ca-rys'tĭ-us, [Διοκλῆς ὁ Καρύστιος,] an eminent Greek physician, born in Eubœa, lived in the third century before Christ, and belonged to the sect of Dogmatics. He was ranked by the ancients next to Hippocrates. He wrote several works, of which some fragments are extant.

See FABRICIUS, "Bibliotheca Græca;" A. RIVINUS, "Programma de Diocle Carystio," 1655.

Diocletian, dī-o-kle'she-an, [Lat. DIOCLETIA'NUS; Fr. DIOCLÉTIEN, de'o'klå'te-ăN',] or, more fully, **Cai'us Vale'rius Aure'lius Diocletia'nus,** a Roman emperor, was born of obscure parents at Dioclea, in Dalmatia, about 245 A.D. He entered the army young, served under Aurelian, and obtained a high command under Probus. He accompanied Carus in his expedition against Persia, and at the death of that prince, in 283, he became commander of the imperial guards of his successor, Numerianus. The latter having been assassinated by Aper, the army at Chalcedon proclaimed Diocletian emperor in 284. In 286 he adopted Maximian as his colleague in the empire, and gave him the title of Augustus. They were successful in suppressing revolts in Gaul and other parts of the empire. About 292 they nominated two Cæsars to divide the labours of the administration,—namely, Galerius and Constantius Chlorus. Diocletian reserved to himself Asia and Egypt, and fixed his court at Nicomedia. He assigned Italy and Africa to Maximian, Gaul and Spain to Constantius, and Thrace and Illyricum to Galerius. The supremacy of Diocletian was recognized by the other three, and general prosperity resulted from this arrangement. One design of this policy was to prevent the revolt of the armies in favour of their commanders, by which so many emperors had been ruined. After this division the Roman arms were successful in Egypt, Persia, and Britain. In 297 a peace was made with Persia, which was maintained forty years. The Christians had enjoyed the favour and protection of Diocletian; but in 303 Galerius, by false accusations, persuaded him to issue an edict against them. This persecution, to which he unwillingly assented, is the chief error of a reign otherwise honourable and happy. In 304 he had a long attack of sickness, and in the next year he abdicated in favour of Galerius, and retired to Salona, where he turned his attention to the cultivation of a vegetable-garden, and died in 313. His political talents were superior, and entitle him to a place among the most eminent Roman emperors.

See TILLEMONT, "Histoire des Empereurs;" GIBBON, "Decline and Fall of the Roman Empire;" AURELIUS VICTOR, "De Cæsaribus;" J. C. SICKEL, "Diocletianus et Maximinus," 1792.

Dioclétien. See DIOCLETIAN.

Diodati, de-o-dȃ′tee, or **Deodati,** (CHARLES,) born in London about 1608, was of Italian extraction, and a nephew of John Diodati. He was Milton's most intimate companion at school, and his correspondent in later years. He became a physician, and practised in Cheshire. On hearing of his death, in 1608, Milton wrote, in Latin, "Epitaphium Damonis."

Diodati, de-o-dȃ′tee, (DOMENICO,) an Italian antiquary, born at Naples in 1736. His principal work is an ingenious essay, "De Christo Græce loquente," (1767,) in which he endeavoured to prove that Greek was the vernacular language of Christ and the apostles. Died in 1801.

See "Vita di D. Diodati," Naples, 1815; TIPALDO, "Biografia degli Italiani illustri."

Diodati, de-o-dȃ′tee, (JOHN,) a Protestant theologian, of Italian extraction, born at Geneva in 1576. He made so great progress in the study of ancient languages that Beza thought him qualified, at the age of twenty-one, to fill the chair of Hebrew in the University of Geneva. In 1609 he was chosen professor of theology, and in 1618 was deputed by the Church of Geneva to the Synod of Dort, in which he performed an important part. He made Italian and French translations of the Bible, (1644,) and a French version of Sarpi's "History of the Council of Trent," (1621.) He also wrote several treatises against the doctrines of the Roman Church, and "Annotations on the Bible," (1607.) Died in 1649.

See BRANDT, "History of the Reformation;" SENEBIER, "Histoire littéraire de Genève;" LIPENIUS, "Bibliotheca Theologica," 1685; SCHOTEL, "J. Diodati," 1844.

Diodore de Sicile. See DIODORUS SICULUS.

Dï-o-do′rus [Gr. Διόδωρος; Fr. DIODORE, de′o′doR′] of Antioch, a Christian bishop and writer of high reputation, was appointed to the see of Tarsus about 375 A.D. He wrote commentaries on the Scriptures, and other works, which are all lost.

Diodorus surnamed PERIEGE′TES, a Greek historian, lived about 320 B.C. He wrote "Περὶ δήμων."

Diodorus of Sinope, an Athenian poet of the new comedy, lived about 350 B.C.

Diodorus of Tyre, a Peripatetic philosopher, flourished about 130 B.C. He succeeded Critolaus as the head of the Peripatetic school at Athens.

Dï-o-do′rus Cro′nus, a Greek logician and philosopher of the school of Megara, lived about 300 B.C., and was one of the masters of Zeno the Stoic. His skill in dialectics is praised by Cicero. He was the reputed author of a famous sophism against motion.

Dï-o-do′rus Sic′u-lus, [Fr. DIODORE DE SICILE, de′o′doR′ dȩh se′sȇl′,] often called simply **Diodorus,** an eminent historian, was born at Agyrium, in Sicily, and lived in the first century B.C. He travelled many years in Europe and Asia to collect materials for a universal history, and then settled in Rome, where he produced his "Historical Library," in Greek, (" Βιβλιοθήκη ἱστορική,") which contained, in forty books, the history of the world from the earliest times to 60 B.C. Only fifteen of these books have been preserved entire. He is supposed to have finished this history about 10 B.C. His merit as a historian is not estimated very highly, but his work supplies many important facts which would otherwise have been lost to posterity. He is very deficient in criticism and judgment.

See FABRICIUS, "Bibliotheca Græca;" SCHOELL, "Histoire de la Littérature Grecque;" HEYNE, "De Fontibus Historiarum Diodori," 1782; DAUNOU, article on "Diodorus Siculus" in the "Nouvelle Biographie Générale."

Dï-od′o-tus, [Gr. Διόδοτος; Fr. DIODOTE, de′o′dot′,] a Stoic philosopher, lived at Rome, and taught dialectics to Cicero. Died in 59 B.C.

Diogène. See DIOGENES.

Diogène d'Apollonie. See DIOGENES OF APOLLONIA.

Diogène Laerce. See DIOGENES LAERTIUS.

Dï-oḡ′e-nȇȇ, [Gr. Διογένης; Fr. DIOGÈNE, de′o′zhạn′; It. DIOGENE, de-o′jȃ-nȃ,] a Cynic philosopher, born at Sinope, in Asia Minor, lived for some time at Athens, where he was a disciple of Antisthenes. He affected an extravagant contempt for the comforts of life and for the customs of society, and inured himself to severe privations, relying on alms for the supply of his simple wants. It is said that he lodged in a cask or tub. He was noted for witty and sarcastic sayings. When Alexander the Great visited him, and inquired, "What can I do for you?" Diogenes replied, "Stand from between me and the sun." Alluding to this interview, Juvenal thus moralizes:

"Sensit Alexander testa quum vidit in illa,
Magnum habitatorem, quanto felicior hic qui
Nil cuperet, quam qui totum sibi posceret orbem."*
                                    Sat. xiv.

Plato having defined man as a featherless biped, the Cynic plucked a fowl, and exclaimed, "Behold the man of Plato!" It is stated that he was taken by pirates and exposed for sale in the market of Crete, and, being asked what he could do, he replied, "I can govern men: therefore sell me to some one who needs a master." He was purchased by Xeniades, a rich citizen of Corinth, by whom he was kindly treated. He is said to have died in 323 B.C., aged about ninety. If he wrote any works, as some assert, they have not been preserved.

See LUCIAN, "Cynicus," and "Dialogues of the Dead;" GRIMALDI, "La Vita di Diogene Cinico," 1777; RITTER, "History of Philosophy;" G. H. LEWES, "Biographical History of Philosophy."

Diogenes OF APOLLONIA, [Fr. DIOGÈNE D'APOLLONIE, de′o′zhạn′ dȃ′po′lo′ne′,] a Greek philosopher, born in Crete, was a disciple of Anaximenes, and was probably born about 500 B.C. He taught philosophy at Athens, and wrote a work on cosmology, of which Diogenes Laertius has preserved a fragment. Like his teacher, he considered air as the first principle of all things.

See G. H. LEWES, "Biographical History of Philosophy;" RITTER, "History of Philosophy."

Diogenes THE BABYLONIAN, an eminent Stoic philosopher, was a native of Seleucia. He studied under Chrysippus at Athens, and became the master of the Stoic school in that city. He was associated with Carneades in a memorable embassy to Rome in 155 B.C. He wrote on various subjects, but his works are not extant.

See C. F. THIERRI, "Dissertatio de Diogene Babylonico," 1830.

---

* Literally, "When Alexander beheld the noble dweller in that tub, [i.e. the tub of Diogenes,] he perceived (or felt) how much happier [was] he who desired nothing, than he who demanded for himself the whole world."

Diogenes of Tarsus, a Greek Epicurean philosopher, is supposed to have lived in the first or second century before Christ. His works are lost.

Dī-og'ẹ-nĕs̄ La-er'tĭ-us, (la-er'she̠-us,) [Gr. Διογένης ὁ Λαέρτιος; Fr. DIOGÈNE LAERCE, de'o˜zhȧn' lȧ'ȧrss',] a Greek author, who was so called because he was born at Laërtes, in Cilicia. Some suppose that he lived in the reign of Severus or Caracalla, 211–235 A.D.; but nothing is known of his history, except that he wrote a very important work on the lives and doctrines of the ancient philosophers. He evidently lacked the critical ability and judgment to do justice to such an enterprise; but at the same time he has collected and preserved valuable contributions to the history of philosophy. The title of it is "Βίοι καὶ Γνῶμαι τῶν ἐν Φιλοσοφίᾳ εὐδοκιμησάντων." He appears to have been a mere compiler, who knew little about the principles of philosophy. His work is neither well planned nor well digested; but it contains valuable extracts from works which are lost.

See FABRICIUS, "Bibliotheca Græca;" KLIPPEL, "De Diogenis Laërtii Vita et Scriptis," 1831; "Nouvelle Biographie Générale."

Diogo Bernardes. See BERNARDES.

Diomed and **Diomède.** See DIOMEDES.

Dī-o-me'dĕs̄, often anglicized **Dī'o-mēde** and **Dī'-o-med,** [Gr. Διομήδης; Fr. DIOMÈDE, de'o'mȧd',] a hero of the early Grecian legends, was a son of Tydeus, and is hence called TYDI'DES. He became King of Argos, and acted a prominent part in the siege of Troy. He was accounted the bravest of the Grecian chiefs next to Achilles, and was a favourite of Minerva. According to Homer, he was so audacious as to attack Mars himself. His adventures after the capture of Troy are variously related.

Diomedes, [Eng. DI'OMEDE,] a king of the Bistones, in Thrace, is said to have fed his horses on human flesh. He was killed by Hercules.

Dī-om'e-don, [Διομέδων,] an able Athenian general, who appears first in history in 412 B.C. He then commanded a fleet which defeated the Chians and recovered Lesbos. In 411 he declared for the democracy, and promoted the recall of Alcibiades from exile. He was one of the ten generals appointed in place of Alcibiades in 407, and contributed to the victory at Arginusæ. Soon after this event he was unjustly put to death, in 405 B.C.

See XENOPHON, "Hellenica."

Dī'on [Gr. Δίων] of Syracuse, an eminent statesman and patriot, born about 410 B.C., inherited from his father Hipparinus an immense fortune. His sister Aristomache having become the wife of King Dionysius, Dion through this connection and his own merit acquired much influence at court. The lessons of Plato, who was then teaching in Syracuse, made so deep an impression on him that he became an intimate friend and one of the most eminent disciples of that philosopher. Soon after the accession of Dionysius the Younger, Dion persuaded him to invite Plato up to the Syracusan court. The courtiers of the young king, the companions of his vicious pleasures, who were jealous of Dion's influence and were reproved by his pure example, prevailed on their master to banish him. Dion retired to Athens, where he was received with the greatest honour. When he learned that Dionysius had confiscated his estate and forced his wife to marry another man, he resolved to avenge himself and to liberate Syracuse by an appeal to arms. In 357, against the advice of Plato, he led a small body of soldiers to Syracuse, which he entered without resistance, seconded by the popular favour. By the intrigues of Heraclides, an unscrupulous demagogue, Dion was again expelled for a time; but he was soon recalled. He was assassinated by Calippus about 354 B.C. Plutarch has thought him worthy to be the subject of a comparison with Marcus Brutus, the noble Roman.

See GROTE, "History of Greece," part ii. chap. lxxxiv.; PLUTARCH, "Lives;" CORNELIUS NEPOS, "Dion;" DIODORUS SICULUS, books xv. and xvi.

Dion or **Dio** surnamed CHRYS'OSTOM, ("Golden-mouthed,") born at Prusa, in Bithynia, about the middle of the first century, was a Greek sophist or rhetorician. He was living in Moldavia when Domitian was killed, and by his eloquent harangue persuaded the army to remain loyal to the senate. This act procured for him the favour of Nerva and Trajan, the latter of whom gave him a seat in his chariot when he made a triumphal entry into Rome. About eighty of his orations are extant, the chief merit of which is beauty and simplicity of style.

See L. ÉTIENNE, "Dio Philosophus," 1849; BRECQUIGNY, "Vies des Orateurs Grecs;" FABRICIUS, "Bibliotheca Græca;" PHILOSTRATUS, "Vitæ Philosophorum."

Dī'on Cas'sĭ-us (kash'e̠-us) or **Dio Cassius,** or, more fully, **Cas'sius Dī'on Cocceia'nus,** (kok-se-yā'nus,) an eminent historian, born at Nicæa, in Bithynia, about 155 A.D., was the son of a Roman senator, and descended by his mother from Dion Chrysostom. He lived in Rome, was a senator in the reign of Commodus, and governor of Smyrna and Pergamos under Macrinus. By the favour of Alexander Seve'rus, he was elected consul with that emperor in 229 A.D. He wrote in Greek several works, the principal of which is his "History of Rome" ("Ῥωμαϊκὴ Ἱστορία") from the arrival of Æneas in Italy to the year 229 A.D., in eighty books, of which the first thirty-five are lost except fragments, and the last twenty exist only in the abridgment of Xiphilinus. As a historian he is esteemed for elegance of style, accuracy in dates, and diligence in search of the truth, for which his official position afforded him facilities. His work is a rich collection of documents on the later years of the republic and the first ages of the empire. His knowledge of Roman institutions was more exact and extensive than that of previous historians.

See FABRICIUS, "Bibliotheca Græca;" REIMARUS, "De Vita et Scriptis Cassii Dionis," 1752; SCHLOSSER, "Dissertation on Dion Cassius," prefixed to LORENZ's German version of Dion, 1826; NIEBUHR, "Lectures on Roman History."

Dī-o'ne, [Gr. Διώνη,] a female Titan, according to some authorities a daughter of Uranus, according to others of Oceanus or Æther. The poets feigned that she was beloved by Jupiter, by whom she became the mother of Venus.

Dionigi, de-o-nee'jee, (MARIANNA,) an Italian artist, born in Rome in 1756. She acquired skill in painting, and gave much attention to archæology, especially to the researches of Cyclopean walls. She wrote a successful work, entitled "On the Five Cities of Latium said to have been founded by Saturn," ("Sulle cinque Città del Lazio che diconsi fondate da Saturno.") Died in 1826.

Dionis, de'o'nèss', (PIERRE,) an eminent French surgeon, born in Paris, became first surgeon to the queen Maria Theresa and the dauphin. Louis XIV. appointed him professor of anatomy in the Jardin des Plantes. He possessed great learning, and wrote several excellent works, among which are a "Treatise on Operations," and a Treatise on Anatomy, ("Anatomie de l'Homme, suivant la Circulation du Sang," 1690.) Died in 1718.

See ÉLOY, "Dictionnaire de la Médecine."

Dionis du Séjour, de'o'nèss' dü sȧ'zhoor', (ACHILLE PIERRE,) a French geometer, born in Paris in 1734. In 1765 he was admitted to the Academy of Sciences, which he enriched with many treatises on eclipses, comets, on Saturn's ring, etc. He afterwards published these collectively, with the title of "Analytical Treatise on the Apparent Motions of the Heavenly Bodies," (1786,) "which," says Nicollet, "is a monument raised to the glory of astronomy, and will form an epoch in the history of that science." Died in 1794.

See "Nouvelle Biographie Générale."

Dionisi, de-o-nee'see, (FILIPPO LORENZO,) an Italian antiquary and priest, born at Rome in 1712; died in 1789.

Dionisi, (GIOVANNI GIACOMO,) an Italian philologist, born at Verona in 1724. He published an edition of Dante's "Divina Commedia," 1795.) Died in 1808.

Dionysius, dī-o-nish'e̠-us, [Gr. Διονύσιος,] THE ELDER, [Fr. DENYS L'ANCIEN, deh-ne' lȯN'se'ȧN',] a celebrated tyrant of Syracuse, was born about 430 B.C. The Carthaginians having invaded Sicily and threatened Syracuse, (which was then a republic,) he was appointed one of the generals; and in 405, by his artful policy, he persuaded the people to invest him with the supreme direction of the government. He confirmed his power by increasing the pay of the troops, suppressed several revolts, and in 397 declared war against Carthage, which held some cities in Sicily. The fleet of Dionysius was defeated, and the victorious army of Himilco or Imilkon encamped under the walls of Syracuse ; but a pestilence broke out in the besieging army, and a successful attack from the Syracusans completed their ruin. Dionysius then subjected several towns of Sicily, made some conquests on the Italian peninsula, and became one of the most powerful princes of his time. Many anecdotes are related to show how suspicious he was, and what precautions he observed against personal danger, as that his bedchamber was surrounded by a wide ditch crossed by a drawbridge. His brother-in-law, Dion, persuaded him to invite Plato to his court; but the king was so offended by the philosopher's lectures that he soon sent him away, directing the captain of the ship to sell him as a slave in the first port which he should enter. Ambitious of literary fame, he sent some verses to the Olympic games; but his offerings were rejected with contempt. One of his tragedies, however, gained a prize at Athens, by which he was much elated; and, during a feast which he gave on the occasion, he died suddenly, in 367. His death was ascribed by some to intemperance, by others to poison.

See GROTE, "History of Greece," part ii. chaps. lxxxi.–lxxxiii. ; DIODORUS SICULUS; THORKIL BADEN, "Res gestæ Dionysii Syracusii recognitæ," 1795; F. W. ROLOFF, "Dissertationes de Dionysiis Siciliæ Tyrannis," 1736.

Dionysius THE YOUNGER, [Fr. DENYS LE JEUNE, deh-ne′ leh zhuN′,] a son of the preceding, succeeded him without opposition in 367 B.C. He was inferior to his father in political ability, and was early addicted to licentious habits, from which Dion endeavoured to reclaim him. Dion also prevailed on Plato to exert his eloquence for this purpose. The latter was received with honour, and for a time seemed to exercise a beneficial influence ; but evil counsels effected the banishment of Dion, and Plato soon followed him. The capricious prince, it is said, induced Plato to return to Syracuse, on condition that his friend should be restored from exile ; but this promise was not fulfilled. In 357 Dion led a successful expedition against Dionysius, who, not being supported by his subjects, was expelled from Syracuse and retired to Locri. (See DION.) After tyrannizing over the Locrians several years, he recovered possession of Syracuse about 346. To assist them in expelling Dionysius and in repelling a threatened invasion of the Carthaginians, the Syracusans invoked the aid of the Corinthians, who sent Timoleon with an army in the year 344. Dionysius was again deposed, and banished to Corinth, where, it is said, he employed himself in teaching school.

See GROTE, "History of Greece," part ii. chaps. lxxxiv.–lxxxv. ; PLUTARCH, "Life of Dion ;" DIODORUS SICULUS, books xv., xvi. ; P. EKERMAN, "Dissertatio de Tyrannide Dionysii utriusque Syracusani," Upsal, 1757.

Dionysius THE AREOPAGITE is said to have been a judge of the Areopagus in Athens when the Apostle Paul appeared before that tribunal. (See Acts xvii. 19.) He was converted to Christianity by Paul, (Acts xvii. 34.) Tradition adds that he was appointed first Bishop of Athens, and that he suffered martyrdom about 95 A.D.

See RITTER, "History of Christian Philosophy ;" BAUMGARTEN-CRUSIUS, "Programma de Dionysio Areopagita," Jena, 1823; ÉTIENNE BINET, "Vie de S. Denys l'Aréopagite," 1624.

Dionysius OF BYZANTIUM, a Greek writer, of whom little is known. He is supposed to have lived before 200 A.D., and is mentioned by Suidas as the author of the "Voyage of the Bosphorus," ("Ἀνάπλους Βοσπόρου.")

Dionysius [Fr. DENYS] **THE CARTHUSIAN,** a monk, born near Liege, was eminent for learning. He entered a monastery at Ruremonde in 1423, and wrote a large number of works. His "Mirror of the Conversion of a Sinner" (1473) is said to be the first book printed in Belgium with a date. Died in 1471.

Dionysius surnamed CHAL′CUS, [ὁ Χαλκοῦς,] an ancient Attic poet and orator, flourished about 450 B.C. He was surnamed Chalcus because he advised the Athenians to coin brass money. His poems (including elegies) are quoted or noticed by Aristotle and other critics.

Dionysius OF COLOPHON, a celebrated Greek painter of the age of Pericles, lived about 450 B.C. He excelled

in portraits, and imitated the style of his contemporary Polygnotus with success. "Polygnotus," says Aristotle, "painted portraits more beautiful than the originals, Pauson made them worse, and Dionysius painted exact likenesses." Another Dionysius flourished as a painter at Rome in the first century before Christ, and is favourably mentioned by Pliny.

Dionysius OF HALICARNASSUS, [Gr. Διονύσιος ὁ Ἁλικαρνασσεύς; Lat. DIONYS′IUS HALICARNAS′SEUS or HALICARNASSEN′SIS ; Fr. DENYS D'HALICARNASSE, deh-ne′ dä′le′kär′nåss′,] a Greek historian and critic of high reputation, born at Halicarnassus, in Caria, about 70 B.C. All our knowledge of him is derived from his writings, which inform us that he came to Rome in 30 B.C. and spent more than twenty years there in studying Latin and composing his history (in Greek) entitled "Roman Antiquities," ("Ῥωμαϊκὴ Ἀρχαιολογία.") It embraces the period from the origin of Rome to the year 265 B.C. The greater part of this work is extant. He is accused of partiality to the Greeks, and is not esteemed a high authority as a historian. He also wrote a "Treatise on Rhetoric," another on the eloquence of Demosthenes, a "Criticism on the Style (ἰδιωμάτων) of Thucydides," and other critical works, which are highly appreciated. Some persons assign him a place in the first rank of ancient critics.

See article by JACOBS, in ERSCH und GRUBER's "Allgemeine Encyklopaedie ;" NIEBUHR, "Lectures on Roman History ;" C. J. WEISMANN, "De Dionysii Halicarnassensi Vita," 1837; BUSSE, "De Dionysii Halicarnassensis Vita," 1848; P. F. SCHULIN, "De Dionysio Halicarnassensi historico," 1821; F. MATTHÄI, "De Dionysio Halicarnassensi," 1779.

Dionysius OF HERACLEA, [Fr. DENYS D'HÉRACLÉE, deh-ne′ dä′rä′klä′,] a Greek philosopher, lived about the end of the third century B.C. He was a Stoic in his youth, and afterwards an Epicurean.

Dionysius surnamed IAM′BUS, a Greek poet, lived about 300 B.C.

Dionysius OF MILETUS, an early Greek historian, who wrote about 500 B.C. Among his principal works, which are all lost, was a "History of Darius I. of Persia."

Dionysius, [Fr. DENYS,] SAINT, a disciple of Origen, was a native of Alexandria, and in the year 248 A.D. was made patriarch of that city. During the persecution of the Christians by Valerian in 257 he was exiled to Libya, whence he was restored in 260. He wrote numerous letters and treatises against various errors in doctrine, that prevailed ; but they have not been preserved. Died in 265 A.D.

Dionysius surnamed THRAX, or "the Thracian," an eminent Greek grammarian, was a disciple of Aristarchus. He taught rhetoric at Rome with great distinction about 80 B.C., and composed many works on grammar, etc. His "Τέχνη γραμματική," ("Art of Grammar,") which has come down to us, was a standard work for centuries, and served as a basis to many other treatises.

Dionysius Cato. See CATO, (DIONYSIUS.)

Di-o-nȳs′ĭ-us (dĭ-o-nish′e-us) **Pe-rī-ē-ḡe′tēs** [Fr. DENYS LE PÉRIÉGÈTE, deh-ne′ leh pä′re′ä′zhåt′] is the author of a Greek poem entitled "Περιήγησις τῆς Γῆς," ("Journey round the Earth.") Nothing is known respecting the time and place of his birth ; but he probably lived between the Augustan age and the fourth century. His poem was once popular, and has been often reprinted and translated.

See FABRICIUS, "Bibliotheca Græca ;" UKERT, "Geographie der Griechen ;" MATTHÆI, "De Dionysio Periegeta," 1788.

Di-o-nȳ′sus, [Διόννυσος or Διώννσος,] the original name in Greek mythology of the god of wine, afterwards called BACCHUS, which see.

Di-oph′a-nēs, [Gr. Διοφάνης ; Fr. DIOPHANE, de′o′-fån′,] a Greek orator, born at Mitylene. He taught at Rome, where Tiberius Gracchus was his pupil.

Diophante. See DIOPHANTUS.

Di-o-phan′tus [Gr. Διόφαντος ; Fr. DIOPHANTE, de′-o′fôNt′] OF ALEXANDRIA is the author of the most ancient treatise on algebra which is extant. The time in which he lived is very uncertain. The question has been much discussed whether he was the inventor of algebra, or whether he derived it from the Hindoos. Lagrange favoured the former opinion. Hypatia, who lived about 400 A.D., wrote a commentary on Diophantus. Of the

є as k; ç as s; ḡ hard; ġ as j; G, H, K, guttural; N, nasal; R, trilled; ŝ as z; ŧh as in this. (☞See Explanations, p. 23.)

49

thirteen books which composed his remarkable work, seven have been lost.

See MONTUCLA, "Histoire des Mathématiques."

Diophantus, an Athenian orator, a contemporary of Demosthenes, lived about 350 B.C.

Dĭ-o-pī′thēs, [Διοπείθης,] an Athenian general. the father of the poet Menander, lived about 344 B.C.

Dioscore. See DIOSCORUS.

Dioscoride. See DIOSCORIDES.

Dioscorides, (a Greek artist.) See DIOSCURIDES.

Dĭ-os-cor′Ĭ-dēs, [Fr. DIOSCORIDE, de′os′ko′rēd′,] a Greek historian, a disciple of Isocrates, lived in the fourth century B.C. He wrote "Οἱ παρ′ Ὁμήρῳ νόμοι," a treatise on the customs and laws recognized in the Homeric poems.

Dioscorides of Alexandria, a Greek poet of an unknown epoch. He is author of numerous epigrams preserved in the Greek Anthology.

Dĭ-os-cor′Ĭ-dēs Pe-dā′nĭ-us, [Διοσκουρίδης Πεδάνιος,] a Greek botanist, born at Anazarbus, in Cilicia, lived about the first century A.D., and is the author of a celebrated Greek work on Materia Medica, in which more than five hundred plants are described or named. A passage of his book informs us that he traversed Asia Minor, Greece, and a part of Italy, to qualify himself for such a task. For sixteen centuries this book was considered the highest authority, and was universally studied by medical students and botanists. It is composed without regard to order in the arrangement of the matter, and is defective in other respects, but is still highly prized as a memorial of the state of science in that age. Galen speaks of Dioscorides in very high terms, and says that he surpassed all who wrote before him on plants. His work became the basis of modern treatises on botany, which science derives nearly all its nomenclature from him.

See FABRICIUS, "Bibliotheca Græca;" SPRENGEL, "Geschichte der Botanik;" HALLER, "Bibliotheca Botanica."

Dĭ-os′co-rus [Gr. Διόσκορος; Fr. DIOSCORE, de′os′koR′] was chosen Patriarch of Alexandria in 444 A.D., as successor to Cyril. Having sided with Eutyches, who was deposed for heresy by Flavian of Constantinople, he obtained the convocation of a council at Ephesus in 449. Dioscorus was president of this council, by which Flavian was condemned, and which was conducted with such violence that it was stigmatized as a scene of robbery, *(Latrocinium Ephesinum.)* A schism resulted, and Pope Leo decided against Dioscorus, who was exiled in 451, and died in 454 A.D.

Dĭ-os-cu′rĭ, [Gr. Διόσκουροι; Fr. DIOSCURES, de′o′-skür′,] *i.e.* "sons of Jupiter," a name applied to CASTOR and POLLUX, which see.

Dĭ-os-cu′rĭ-dēs or **Dĭ-os-cor′Ĭ-dēs,** a Greek artist, who lived at Rome in the reign of Augustus, was reputed the greatest gem-engraver of ancient times. He engraved the portrait of Augustus, which was one of his master-pieces.

Diotallevi, de-o-tâl-lā′vee, (ALESSANDRO,) an Italian pulpit orator and religious writer, born at Rimini in 1648; died in 1721.

Dĭ-o-ti′mus, [Gr. Διότιμος; Fr. DIOTIME, de′o′tēm′,] a Greek poet of uncertain epoch, author of numerous epigrams preserved in the Greek Anthology.

Diotisalvi, de-o-te-sâl′vee, a celebrated Italian architect, designed the beautiful baptistery of Pisa, commenced about 1152 and finished in 1161. It is one of the earliest examples of the renaissance of the art in Italy.

Diphile. See DIPHILUS.

Diph′Ĭ-lus, [Gr. Δίφιλος; Fr. DIPHILE, de′fēl′,] an eminent Athenian comic poet of the new comedy, was a native of Sinope, and flourished about 300 B.C. He produced about one hundred comedies, of which some fragments remain. His style is admired for simplicity and elegance.

Diplovatazio, de-plo-vâ-tât′se-o, (TOMMASO,) a jurist, born at Corfu in 1468. He published "Synopsis Juris Græci," and other works. Died at Pesaro in 1541.

Dippel, dip′pẹl, (JOHANN CONRAD,) a German alchemist, noted for his aberrations and vagaries, was born near Darmstadt in 1673. He studied medicine, and professed to be an adept in the hermetic arts. He was ad-

dicted to wandering habits and to theological controversy, and was imprisoned at various places. By accident he discovered the valuable pigment prussiate of potash, or Prussian blue. About 1710, to escape the power of the law, he took refuge in Holland, and practised medicine for several years. After many adventures in Denmark, Sweden, etc., he died in 1734.

See "Biographie Médicale;" HOFFMANN, "Leben und Meinungen J. C. Dippel's," 1783.

Diræ. See EUMENIDES.

Dirichlet, de′rēsh′lạ′, (GUSTAV LEJEUNE or PETER GUSTAV,) an eminent German geometer, born at Düren, in Rhenish Prussia, in 1805. He became professor of mathematics in Berlin in 1828, and a member of the Academy of Sciences in 1832. He wrote dissertations on the most difficult parts of mathematics, and was esteemed one of the first mathematicians of the age. In 1855 he succeeded Gauss as professor at Göttingen. Died in May, 1859.

Dirk or **Dirck,** (dirk,) a Dutch painter, born at Haarlem, was living in 1462. He was one of the ablest artists of his time.

Diroys, de′rwä′, (FRANÇOIS,) a French theologian, born in 1620, became canon of Avranches. He wrote "Proofs and Presentiments *(Préjugés)* in favour of the Christian and Catholic Religion," (1683.) Died in 1691.

Discepoli, de-shẹp′o-lee or de-shä′po-lee, (GIOVANNI BATTISTA,) an Italian painter, born at Lugano in 1590; died in 1660.

Disdier, de′de-à′, (HENRI FRANÇOIS MICHEL,) a skilful French surgeon, professor of anatomy, and writer, was born at Grenoble in 1708; died in 1781.

Dĭś′ney, (JOHN,) a learned English divine, born at Lincoln in 1677, studied law, and for many years discharged the duties of magistrate with great credit. In 1719 he was ordained a priest of the Anglican Church, and in 1722 became Vicar of Saint Mary, Nottingham. He wrote "Essays on Laws against Immorality and Profaneness," and other works. Died in 1730.

Disraeli, diz-rā′ẹl-e, (BENJAMIN,) a distinguished English statesman and author, a son of Isaac, noticed below, was born in London in December, 1805. He produced in 1826 his first work, "Vivian Grey," a fashionable novel, which was received with great favour : it was followed by "The Young Duke," (1830,) and "Contarini Fleming," (1832.) In 1829 and 1830 he visited Greece, Egypt, Syria, and other parts of the Levant. He commenced his political life as a radical, and was an unsuccessful candidate for Parliament in 1831. Having become a Tory candidate for Taunton, he was again defeated in 1835 ; but he was returned by the Conservatives of Maidstone in 1837. His ambitious or pretentious maiden speech was a complete failure, and excited the ridicule of the House. On this occasion he exclaimed, "I shall sit down now, but the time will come when you will hear me !" In 1839 he married the rich widow of Wyndham Lewis. He has represented Buckinghamshire in Parliament since 1847. He gradually attained success as a parliamentary debater, and about 1841 became the leader of the "Young England" party. Among his most brilliant efforts were his speeches against the Free-Trade measures of Sir Robert Peel in 1845 and 1846, in which he displayed great powers of invective and sarcasm. In 1844 he published "Coningsby, or the New Generation," a political novel, which was very successful. He became about 1848 the recognized leader of the Protectionist party in the House of Commons. He was chancellor of the exchequer in the Tory ministry of Lord Derby, which lasted from March to December of 1852. On the defeat of Palmerston in February, 1858, power passed into the hands of the Tories, and Disraeli again became chancellor of the exchequer in the Derby-Disraeli ministry. (See DERBY, EARL OF.) He introduced an electoral Reform bill, which was rejected by the House in March, 1859, and resigned with his colleagues in June of that year. A Tory writer in the "London Quarterly Review" for April, 1860, ascribes to Disraeli "unrivalled powers for conducting his party into the ditch," and adds, his Reform bill "had that fatal and damning defect, that the complication of its details exposed it to the suspicion of stratagem and finesse. It

---

ă, ē, ĭ, ō, ū, ȳ, *long;* à, ė, ò, same, less prolonged; ă, ĕ, ĭ, ŏ, ŭ, ў, *short;* ą, ę, į, ǫ, *obscure;* fär, fåll, fåt; mēt; nŏt; gōōd; mōōn;

was not statesmanlike: it was only ingenious." He is said to have annoyed his party by voting for the admission of Jews into the House of Commons. "Gradually, almost imperceptibly," says the London "Times," "Mr. Disraeli has weaned his party from their most flagrant errors. He has taught them to profess, at any rate, and probably to feel, a sympathy for the great body of their countrymen." He opposed the bill for electoral reform which Russell and Gladstone introduced, and which was defeated in June, 1866. In consequence of this defeat the Liberal ministers resigned, and Disraeli again became chancellor of the exchequer. Derby and Disraeli then exhibited a surprising change of front on the subject of electoral reform, and supported a more liberal or radical bill than that which they opposed in 1866. As leader of the House of Commons, Disraeli was the chief author and manager of the Reform bill of 1867, which extends the right of suffrage to every householder in a borough, every forty-shilling freeholder, etc. This bill was signed by the queen, August 15, 1867.

Much admiration has been expressed at the dexterity with which he induced his party to abandon their prejudices or principles in the support of this measure. "His triumph," says Goldwin Smith, "is a triumph over public morality and over the self-respect of the nation." He became premier about February 25, 1868. He and his party opposed the resolutions which Mr. Gladstone moved to abolish or disendow the Irish Church as a state establishment. On this important question he was defeated in the House by a majority of fifty-six votes, April 3, 1868, and again on the 1st of May by a majority of sixty-four. It was expected that he would resign or appeal to the country; but, after a visit to the queen at Osborne, he and his colleagues made statements which resolved themselves into the simple proposition that they had determined neither to resign nor to dissolve Parliament. The Liberal party having gained a decisive victory in the general election of November, Disraeli and his colleagues resigned on the 2d of December, 1868.

See "Edinburgh Review" for April, 1853; "Blackwood's Magazine" for March, 1854; "Fraser's Magazine" for January and February, 1847, and February, 1852; "Westminster Review" for September, 1844; SAMUEL SMILES, "Brief Biographies."

Disraeli, (ISAAC,) an English *littérateur*, born at Enfield, near London, in 1766, was the son of a Venetian merchant of Jewish extraction, who left him a large fortune. He preferred literature to all other professions or pursuits, and, directing his attention to literary history and anecdotes, he produced in 1790 the first volume of "Curiosities of Literature," which was received with favour and followed by several other volumes of the same work. He published "Calamities of Authors," (1812,) "Quarrels of Authors," (1814,) "The Life and Reign of King Charles I.," (1828,) "Amenities of Literature," (1841,) and a few other works. "The numerous editions which have been printed of the 'Curiosities of Literature,'" says T. H. Horne, "amply attest the value of this instructive and amusing work." Lord Byron denominates him "that most entertaining and searching writer, whose works in general I have read oftener than perhaps those of any other English writer whatever." Died in 1848. He was the father of the eminent statesman Benjamin Disraeli.

See B. DISRAELI, "Notice of I. Disraeli," prefixed to his "Curiosities of Literature," Boston, 4 vols., 1858; "London Quarterly Review" for September, 1812.

Dissen, dis'sen, (GEORG LUDOLF,) a distinguished German philologist, born near Göttingen in 1784, studied philology under Heyne, and became professor of classical literature at Göttingen in 1813. He published good editions of Pindar (1830) and of Tibullus, (1835.) He gave especial attention to the philosophy of the ancients, and wrote a work on the moral philosophy of Socrates, as handed down to us in the writings of Xenophon. Died in 1837.

Distelmeyer, dis'tel-mī'er, (LAMBERT,) a German jurist, born at Leipsic in 1522, was appointed chancellor by the Elector of Brandenburg in 1558. Died in 1588.

See GUNDLING, "Distelmeyer's Leben," 1722.

Dithmar or **Ditmar,** dit'mär, a German chronicler, born about 978, was chosen Bishop of Merseburg in 1009.

He wrote a Latin chronicle of the reigns of the emperors Henry I., Otho I., Otho II., Otho III., and Henry II., which was edited by Leibnitz, who calls it a valuable work. Died in 1018.

See ERSCH und GRUBER, "Allgemeine Encyklopaedie."

Dithmar or **Ditmar,** (JUSTUS CHRISTOPH,) a German historical writer, born at Rottenburg (Hesse) in 1677, became successively professor of history and of natural law at Frankfort-on-the-Oder. He published a "Life of Pope Gregory VII.," (1710,) "Tacitus's Germany, with a Commentary," (1725,) and other works. Died in 1737.

Diti, dīt'ĭ, in the Hindoo mythology, the mother of the Daityas, or demons. She was one of the wives of Kâsyapa, (or Kâçyapa,) and would seem to be opposed to Aditi, whose children, the Adityas or Suras, are in eternal antagonism to the Daityas or Asuras.

See MOOR's "Hindu Pantheon."

Ditmar. See DITHMAR.

Ditmar, dit'mär, (THEODOR JAKOB,) a Prussian historian, born in Berlin in 1734, was professor of history in his native city, and wrote a "Method of Teaching Universal History," and other works. Died in 1791.

Ditmer, dit'mer, or **Ditmar,** (JAN,) a Dutch engraver, born about 1538; died in 1603.

Ditrich. See DIETRICH.

Ditters von Dittersdorf, dit'ters fon dit'ters-dorf', (KARL,) a celebrated German composer, born in Vienna in 1739. He formed a friendship with Metastasio, and composed the music of four oratorios of that poet, viz., "Isaac," "David," "Job," and "Esther." He composed many successful operas, symphonies, etc. His masterpieces are "Esther," an oratorio, (1785,) and "The Doctor and Apothecary," (1786,) a comic opera. Died in 1799.

See his Autobiography, ("Selbstbiographie,") 1801; FÉTIS, "Biographie Universelle des Musiciens."

Ditt'mer, (or dèt'mair',) (ADOLPHE,) a French *littérateur*, born in London in 1795. He wrote, with M. Cavé, "Les Soirées de Neuilly," dramatic and historic sketches, (1827,) which had great success. Died in 1846.

Dit'ton, (HUMPHREY,) an eminent English mathematician, born at Salisbury in 1675, became minister of a dissenting church at Tunbridge. Having attained great proficiency in mathematics, he attracted the notice of Sir Isaac Newton, by whose influence he was chosen mathematical master of Christ's Hospital. He gained a high reputation by his writings, among which are "Laws of Nature and Motion," (1705,) a "Treatise on Fluxions," (1706,) "Synopsis Algebraica," (1709,) a "Treatise on Perspective," (1712,) and a "Discourse on the Resurrection of Christ." Died in 1715.

See "Biographia Britannica;" WHISTON, "Memoirs."

Divini, de-vee'nee, (EUSTACHIO,) an Italian optician, born at San Severino about 1620, excelled in the fabrication of telescopes.

Divino, El. See MORALES, (LUIS.)

Divitiac. See DIVITIACUS.

Div-ĭ-ti'a-cus, [Fr. DIVITIAC, de've'te'åk',] a chief of the Ædui, a tribe of Gaul, was the friend of Cæsar, and the brother of Dumnorix. His tribe, being attacked by the Germans, sent him to Rome to solicit aid. He rendered services to Cæsar in his war against Ariovistus and against the Belgæ.

See CÆSAR, "De Bello Gallico;" A. THIERRY, "Histoire des Gaulois."

Dix, (DOROTHEA L.,) an American philanthropist, was born in Worcester, Massachusetts. In her youth she supported herself by teaching school, but about 1830 inherited sufficient property from a relative to relieve her from the necessity of daily toil. Previous to this she had become deeply interested in the condition of criminals, lunatics, and paupers. She has visited almost every State in the Union in her efforts to relieve the unfortunate and the wretched. Her exertions have contributed largely towards the establishment of lunatic-asylums in New York, Pennsylvania, North Carolina, and several other States; and, by her heroic persistency in memorializing Congress, a bill was finally passed in 1854, appropriating 10,000,000 acres of the public lands to endow hospitals for the indigent insane. But the bill was vetoed by President Pierce. Besides tracts for prisoners, memorials to legislatures, etc., she has published several works anonymously, among which may be mentioned the "Garland of Flora," issued in 1829, "Evening Hours," etc.

Dix, (JOHN A.,) an American general and statesman, born at Boscawen, New Hampshire, in 1798. He became a lawyer, and a resident of Cooperstown, New York. Having joined the Democratic party, he was elected secretary of state in 1833, and represented the State of New York in the Senate of the United States from 1845 to March, 1849. From December, 1860, to March, 1861, he held the position of United States secretary of the treasury. In May, 1861, he was appointed a major-general, and took command at Fortress Monroe in July, 1862. In June, 1863, he moved an army up the York River, threatened Richmond, and cut Lee's communications. He commanded the department of the East in 1864. He was sent as minister to France early in 1867. General Dix is the author of two works of travel,—"A Winter in Madeira," (1851,) and "A Summer in Spain and Florence," (1855.)

Dixmerie, de la, dęh lä dĕz'mĕh-re', (NICOLAS BRICAIRE,) a French *littérateur,* born in Champagne in 1730, resided in Paris. He was the author of "The Two Ages of Taste and Genius under Louis XIV. and Louis XV.," (1769,) and other works. Died in 1791.

Dix'on, (ARCHIBALD,) an American lawyer, born in North Carolina in 1802. Having removed to Kentucky, he was in 1843 elected by the Whig party Lieutenant-Governor. On the resignation of Mr. Clay, in 1852, he was chosen to fill the vacancy. He afterwards became a pro-slavery Democrat.

See LIVINGSTON's "Portraits of Eminent Americans."

Dix'on, (GEORGE,) CAPTAIN, a British navigator, who discovered a number of small islands near the northwest coast of America, and a strait called Dixon's Entrance. He published a "Voyage round the World, 1785–88." Died about 1800.

See F. DENIS, "Génie de la Navigation."

Dix'on, (JAMES,) an English Methodist minister of the present century. He wrote, about 1842, "Methodism, its Origin, Economy, and Present Position," and other works.

Dixon, (WILLIAM HEP'WORTH,) an able and popular English writer and critic, born in the West Riding of Yorkshire in 1821. He became a resident of London about 1845, and published a "Life of John Howard," (1850; 5th edition, 1854,) a work of decided merit. "William Penn, a Historical Biography," in which Penn is ably and successfully defended against the charges of Macaulay, appeared in 1851. "His style is good and easy," says the "Edinburgh Review:" "there is life in his narrative and vigour in his descriptions." Since 1853 he has been chief editor of the "Athenæum." In addition to the works mentioned above, Mr. Dixon has written a "Personal History of Lord Bacon," (1861,) "The Holy Land," (1865,) "New America," (1867,) "Spiritual Wives," (1868,) and "The Tower of London," (1869.) "Mr. Dixon," says the London "Star," referring to "Spiritual Wives:" "has, on the whole, treated a very difficult and delicate subject with great refinement and judgment." It has been objected to his "New America" by some critics, and not altogether without reason, that a reader who had little acquaintance with the condition of society in the United States would be apt to suppose many things to be of common occurrence in this country which are in fact so rare as to be unknown even to the most intelligent and best-informed Americans, except a few who have made them the subject of especial investigation.

Dix'well, (JOHN,) COLONEL, an English republican, born in 1608. He was one of the judges of Charles I. When his party lost power, he escaped to New England and changed his name. Died in 1689.

Diziani, dĕt-ze-ä'nee, (GASPARO,) an Italian painter, born at Belluno in the seventeenth century ; died in 1767.

Djaafar or **Djafar.** See MANSOOR.

Djami or **Djamy.** See JÂMEE.

Djannaby. See JANNABEE.

Djayadeva. See JAYADEVA.

Djehan-Guir, (or **-Guyr.**) See JAHÂN-GEER.

Djehan-Guire. See JAHÂN-GEER.

Djelal-Eddin-Roumi. See JELÂL-ED-DEEN.

Djem. See JEM.

Djemchyd or **Djemchid.** See JEMSHEED.

Djémlah. See JUMLAH.

Djemschid or **Djemschyd.** See JEMSHEED.

Djenghiz or **Djenghis.** See JENGIS KHAN.

Djenguiz or **Djenguyz.** See JENGIS KHAN.

Djerir. See JEREER.

Djévhéry. See JEVHERY.

Djezzar. See JEZZAR.

Djihanguire. See JAHÂN-GEER.

Djihan-Guyr, (or **-Guir.**) See JAHÂN-GEER.

Djordjani. See JORJÂNEE.

Dlugosz, dloo'gosh, [Lat. LONGI'NUS,] (JAN,) an eminent Polish historian, born at Brzesnica in 1415. He was employed by Casimir IV. as ambassador to several foreign courts, and as preceptor of his sons. He opened a new era in Polish historical literature by his Latin "History of Poland," a work of much merit, which consists in the matter rather than the style. It was not all printed until 1711. He died in 1480, soon after he had been chosen Archbishop of Lemberg.

See ISLEMBIOWSKI, "Les Historiens Polonais," 1826; "Nouvelle Biographie Générale."

Dmitri. See DEMETRIUS, Czar of Russia.

Dmitrief or **Dmitriev,** dmee'tre-ĕf, (IVAN IVANOVITCH,) a Russian poet, born in Simbeersk (Simbirsk) in 1760, served some years in the army, and passed into the civil service. In the reign of Alexander he became minister of justice and privy councillor. He cultivated literature in the intervals of his public employments, and produced popular odes, poetical tales, satires, and fables. His fables are among the best in the language. Died at Moscow in 1837.

See OTTO, "Lehrbuch der Russischen Literatur."

Dmochowski, dmo-Kov'skee, (FRANCIS XAVIER,) a Polish poet and historian, born in 1762. He translated the "Iliad" and "Paradise Lost" into Polish. Died in 1808.

Doane, dōn, (GEORGE WASHINGTON,) an American poet and ecclesiastic, born at Trenton, New Jersey, in 1799. He was ordained an Episcopalian priest in 1821, and preached for several years in New York City and Boston. In 1832 he was elected Bishop of New Jersey. He founded Burlington College in 1846. He published several theological works, and a volume of poems, (1824.) Died in 1859.

See GRISWOLD's "Poets and Poetry of America."

Dob'bin, (JAMES COCHRANE,) an American statesman of the Democratic party, born in Fayetteville, North Carolina, in 1814. He graduated at the University of North Carolina, and in 1845 represented the Raleigh district in Congress. He was a delegate to the Baltimore Convention in 1852, and was active in promoting the nomination of Franklin Pierce, who in 1853 appointed him secretary of the navy. Died in 1857.

See LIVINGSTON's "Portraits of Eminent Americans."

Dob'bin, (THOMAS,) a native of Ireland, who removed to Baltimore in 1790 and published the Baltimore "Telegraph," the first daily newspaper of that city.

Do-bell', (SYDNEY,) an English poet, born in Kent, or in a suburb of London, in 1824, was first known as SYDNEY YENDYS. He was employed for some years in the counting-house of his father, who was a wine-merchant at Cheltenham. He produced in 1850 "The Roman," a poem, and in 1854 "Balder," which were admired by some and censured as spasmodic by others. Mr. Dobell and Alexander Smith published in 1855 a volume entitled "Sonnets on the War." Among his other poems is "England in Time of War," (1856.)

Döbereiner or **Doebereiner,** dö'bęh-rī'nęr,(JOHANN WOLFGANG,) an eminent German chemist, born at Hof, in Bavaria, in 1780. He became professor of chemistry at Jena in 1810, and, aided by Goethe, made some useful and curious discoveries, among which is the property of spongiform platinum to inflame hydrogen. He published, besides other works, "Essays on Physical Chemistry," (1824–36,) and "Principles of General Chemistry," (3d edition, 1826.) Died in 1849.

See AUGUST VOGEL, "Denkrede auf J. W. Döbereiner," 1849.

Dobner, dob'nęr, (FELIX JOB, otherwise called GELASE,) a Bohemian historian and monk, born at Prague in 1719. He taught in the colleges of his order in Vienna, Prague, etc., and left works on the history of Bohemia and Moravia which are prized for extensive research and judicious criticism. The most important of these is "Historical Monuments of Bohemia," ("Monumenta historica Bohemiæ," 6 vols., 1764–86.) Died in 1790.

See ERSCH und GRUBER, "Allgemeine Encyklopaedie."

Do-bree', (PETER PAUL,) an English critic, born in Guernsey in 1782, was a Fellow of Trinity College, Cambridge, and a friend of Porson. He superintended the publication of the notes on some Greek authors, which Porson left at his death, and became professor of Greek at Cambridge about 1823. He left an edition of Demosthenes unfinished at his death in 1825.

Döbrentei, do'bren-tà', or **Döbrentey**, do'bren-ti', (GÁBOR,) an eminent Hungarian author, born at Nagy Szöllös in 1786, became about 1820 a resident of Pesth, where he held several public offices. He edited a valuable magazine called the "Transylvanian Museum," ("Erdélyi Muzéum,") wrote odes, elegies, and other poems, and translated several of Shakspeare's dramas. His principal work, "Ancient Monuments of the Magyar Language," is highly commended. Four volumes of it were published between 1825 and 1850. He was engaged on this work when he died in 1851.

Döbrentey. See DÖBRENTEI.

Dobrizhoffer, do'brits-hof'fer, (MARTIN,) a Jesuit missionary, born at Grätz, in Styria, in 1717. He went to Paraguay in 1749, and laboured about eighteen years among the natives, one tribe of whom were called Abipones. In 1784 he published at Vienna, in Latin, a "History of the Abipones, an Equestrian and Warlike Nation," (3 vols.,) a work of some interest for history and geography. It was translated into English by Sara Coleridge. Died in 1791.

See "Nouvelle Biographie Générale."

Dobrowski, do-brov'skee, (JOSEPH,) an eminent Bohemian author and philologist, born near Raab in 1753, was the most learned of those who have cultivated Bohemian literature. He was educated at Prague, and joined the Jesuits. He assisted Pelzel in his "Biographies of Bohemian Authors and Artists," and gained distinction by his researches into the language and literature of the Slavonic nations. He wrote numerous works, of which the most important are a "Grammar of the Bohemian Language," a "History of the Bohemian Language and Literature," (1792,) a "German and Bohemian Dictionary," and "Principles of the Old Slavic Dialect," ("Institutiones Linguæ Slavicæ Dialecti Veteris," 1822,) which is highly prized by the Russians. He was subject to frequent attacks of insanity, and in 1801 was in a lunatic-asylum. Died in 1829.

See BROCKHAUS, "Conversations-Lexikon;" F. PALACKY, "J. Dobrowski's Leben und Wirken," 1833.

Dob'son, (MATTHEW,) F.R.S., an English physician, who practised at Liverpool and Bath. He wrote a "Medical Commentary on Fixed Air," and some other scientific treatises. Died in 1784.

Dob'son, (THOMAS,) a bookseller and writer of Philadelphia, republished the "Encyclopædia Britannica," (21 vols. 4to, 1798–1803,) and wrote "Letters on the Character of the Deity, and the Moral State of Man." Died in 1823.

Dobson, (WILLIAM,) a successful English painter of portraits and history, born in London in 1610, was apprenticed to a picture-dealer. Van Dyck introduced him to Charles I., whose portrait he painted. After the death of Van Dyck, Dobson succeeded him as court painter, and was considered the most excellent English portrait-painter of his time. Died in 1646.

Docampo, do-käm'po, (FLORIAN,) a Spanish historian, born at Zamora in 1513, became canon of the metropolitan church of Granada. At the request of Charles V., he undertook to write a history of Spain, and published in 1578 "The First Five Books of a General Chronicle of Spain," which throws much light on the origin and antiquities of that nation. It appears that he left the work unfinished when he died in 1590.

See N. ANTONIO, "Bibliotheca Hispana Nova."

Doccum, van, vän dok'küm, or **Doccom**, (JAN,) a Dutch jurist, born at Doccum; died in 1540.

Doche, dosh, (JOSEPH DENIS,) a French composer of airs, etc., born in Paris in 1766; died in 1825.

Dod, (ALBERT BALDWIN,) D.D., an American divine, son of Daniel Dod, noticed below, was born in Mendham, New Jersey, in 1805. He graduated at Princeton in 1822, and became tutor in that college in 1827, and professor of mathematics in 1830. Died at Princeton in 1845. Dr. Dod was an eloquent preacher, and one of the ablest contributors to the "Biblical Repertory and Princeton Review." A collection of his writings has been published.

Dod, (CHARLES ROGER,) an English journalist, born in 1793. For about twenty years he was connected with the London "Times," for which he wrote notices of eminent men who died in that period, and reported debates in Parliament. He published an annual called "The Peerage, Baronetage, and Knightage of Great Britain," (1840–56.) Died in 1855.

Dod, (DANIEL,) an American machinist, born in Virginia in 1788. He built the engine for the Savannah, which in 1819 made the first voyage across the Atlantic ever accomplished by steam. He was killed by a boiler-explosion on the East River, New York, in 1823.

Dod, (JOHN,) an English Puritan divine, born at Shotledge, in Cheshire, in 1547, ministered at Hanwell for about twenty years, and was suspended for nonconformity about 1598. He excelled in the knowledge of Hebrew, and is often called "the Decalogist," from his "Commentaries on the Decalogue," (1606.) In 1624 he became rector of Fawesley. Fuller, in his "Worthies," says, "John Dod was by nature a witty, by industry a learned, and by grace a godly divine." Died in 1645.

Dodart, do'där', (CLAUDE JEAN BAPTISTE,) a son of Denis, noticed below, was chosen first physician to Louis XV. in 1718, and died in 1730, aged sixty-six.

Dodart, (DENIS,) an eminent French physician, born in Paris in 1634, became physician to Louis XIV. He was chosen a professor of pharmacy in 1666, and was admitted into the Academy of Sciences in 1673. He contributed to this institution several treatises on natural history, medicine, etc., and made many experiments on insensible perspiration, the results of which were published in a work called "Statica Medicina Gallica," (1725.) He wrote the preface of a work which the Academy published on the "History of Plants." Died in 1707.

See FONTENELLE, "Éloge de Dodart," 1707.

Dodd, (CHARLES,) the assumed name of an English Catholic priest, who resided at Harvington and wrote "The Church History of England, 1500–1688," said to be rare and curious. It was intended as an antidote to Burnet. Died about 1745.

Dodd, (RALPH,) an English engineer, born in Northumberland about 1756, resided in London. He was the first projector of the Thames Tunnel, which, however, was not made in his time. He also planned the Surrey Canal, Vauxhall Bridge, and other works of public utility, and wrote an "Account of the Principal Canals in the World." Died in 1822.

Dodd, (ROBERT,) a skilful English painter of marine views, born in 1748. Among his works is "The Storm which sunk the Jamaica Fleet in 1782." Died about 1810.

Dodd, (WILLIAM,) D.D., an English clergyman, born at Bourne, in Lincolnshire, in 1729, was ordained in 1753, and became an eloquent and fashionable preacher of London. He was appointed chaplain to the king and preceptor to Philip Stanhope (Earl of Chesterfield) about 1764. He gained reputation by his writings, among which are "Reflections on Death," "The Visitor," "Sermons," "The Beauties of Shakspeare," and "Commentaries on Scripture." In 1777 he was convicted of forging the signature of Lord Chesterfield to a bond for £4000, for which he was executed. While confined for this offence, he wrote a poem entitled "Thoughts in Prison."

See "Memoirs of Dodd," prefixed to his "Thoughts in Prison;" GEORG FORSTER, "Leben Dr. W. Dodd's," Berlin, 1779.

Dodd'ridge, written also **Doderidge**, (Sir JOHN,) an eminent English lawyer, born at Barnstaple in 1555. He was appointed the king's principal sergeant-at-law in 1607. From 1613 until his death he was a judge of the court of king's bench. He was a good scholar and a learned antiquary, and author of several works, among which are "The Lawyer's Light," "The English Lawyer," and "The Laws of Nobility." Died in 1628.

See Foss, "The Judges of England."

Doddridge, (PHILIP,) an eminent English dissenting minister, born in London in 1702, was a relative of the preceding, and was the twentieth child of a London merchant. After finishing his studies in a theological seminary at Kibworth, he began to preach at the same place in 1722. In 1729 he opened an academy for the education of candidates for the ministry at Northampton, where he was also employed as the minister of a dissenting church from that date until his death. He married a Miss Maris in 1730. As a minister, he was remarkable for his earnestness, fidelity, and fervent devotion. He wrote a large number of excellent and popular religious works, of which the most important are "The Rise and Progress of Religion in the Soul," (1744,) and "The Family Expositor," (3 vols., 1738,) which is an exposition of the Bible. These have been translated into many languages. The Rev. Robert Hall, in one of his letters, says, "Doddridge is now my prime favourite among divines." His work on the "Evidences of Christianity" has long been used as a text-book at Cambridge, England. He composed some of the best hymns which are used in the dissenting churches. In 1751 he visited Lisbon for his health; he died there the same year.

See "Memoirs of the Life and Writings of P. Doddridge," by JOB ORTON; "Life of Doddridge," by REV. DR. KIPPIS; D. A. HARSHA, "Life of Philip Doddridge;" SCHMIDT, "Leben des Dr. P. Doddridge," 1830.

Dodd'ridge, (PHILIP,) an American lawyer, born in Brooke county, Virginia, in 1772. He acquired distinction as an advocate in trials by jury. In the Constitutional Convention of 1829-30 he represented several counties of western Virginia, and was the leader of the party which preferred a white basis of representation. Died in 1832.

Doderidge. See DODDRIDGE.

Döderlein, dö'der-lïn', (JOHANN ALEXANDER,) a German historian and antiquary, born in Franconia in 1675; died in 1745.

See ERSCH und GRUBER, "Allgemeine Encyklopaedie."

Döderlein or **Doederlein,** (JOHANN CHRISTOPH,) an eminent German Protestant divine and critic, born at Windsheim, in Bavaria, about 1746, was versed in the Oriental languages. He was chosen professor of theology at Altdorf in 1772. He made from the Hebrew text a Latin version of Isaiah, with notes, (1775,) which, says Silvestre de Sacy, "is written in an elegant style." Among his chief works are a "Summary of the Instruction of a Christian Theologian," ("Summa Institutionis Theologi Christiani," 1782,) and (in German)" The Christian Doctrine adapted to the Wants of our Time," (1785.) He contributed to introduce a new theological system opposed to the doctrines of the first Reformers. In 1782 he became professor of theology at Jena. Died in 1792.

Döderlein or **Doederlein,** (LUDWIG,) a son of the preceding, born at Jena in 1791, was a distinguished philologist. He became professor of philology at Erlangen in 1827. He published "Latin Synonyms and Etymologies," (6 vols., 1826-38,) a "Manual of Latin Synonymy," (1839,) an edition of "Tacitus," (1847,) and other works. Died in 1863.

Dodge, (GRENVILLE M.,) an American general, born at Danvers, Massachusetts, in 1831. He commanded a brigade at Pea Ridge, March, 1862, and a corps in the army of General Sherman in the campaign against Atlanta, May to September, 1864.

Dodge, (MARY ABIGAIL,) a popular and piquant American writer, born in Hamilton, Massachusetts, about 1838. She has written on a variety of subjects under the pseudonym of GAIL HAMILTON, (composed of the last syllable of her Christian name and the name of her birthplace.) Among her works may be mentioned "Country Living and Country Thinking," (1862,) "Gala Days," (1863,) "A New Atmosphere," (1864,) and "Woman's Wrongs: a Counter-Irritant," (1868.) No inconsiderable portion of her writings originally appeared as contributions to the "Atlantic Monthly."

Dod'ing-ton, (GEORGE BUBB,) Lord Melcombe, an English courtier and politician, born in 1691. He was elected to Parliament in 1715, and sent as ambassador to Spain. In 1720 he inherited a large fortune from his uncle, George Dodington, whose name he then assumed. In 1724 he became a lord of the treasury and a partisan of Walpole, whom he deserted in 1740. In 1761 he was raised to the peerage, as Lord Melcombe. He wrote some poetical pieces, and left a Diary, which gives an insight into the cabals and intrigues of his time, together with a candid exposure of his own venality and egotism. He was the patron of Young, Thomson, and Fielding. Died in 1762.

Dodoens, do-doons', [Lat. DODONÆ'US; Fr. DODONÉE, do'do'nà',] (REMBERT,) an eminent botanist and physician, was born at Malines, or, according to some authorities, in Friesland, about 1518. He was one of those who contributed most to the progress of botany in the sixteenth century. He became physician to the emperor Maximilian II. in 1570, and to Rodolph II. in 1576. About 1580 he was chosen professor of medicine at Leyden. Before that date he had published several works on botany, with fine figures. The plates of some of these were lent to him by L'Écluse. In 1583 he summed up his previous labours in a "History of Plants," ("Stirpium Historiæ Pemptades,") a work of great erudition, illustrated with 1300 engravings. He was author of "Praxis Medica," and other works. Died in 1585.

See FOPPENS, "Bibliotheca Belgica;" NICÉRON, "Mémoires;" VAN MEERBECK, "Recherches sur la Vie et les Ouvrages de Dodoens," 1841; AVOINE, "Éloge de R. Dodoëns."

Do-do-næ'us, a surname of JUPITER, which see.

Dodonée or **Dodonæus.** See DODOENS.

Dods'ley, (ROBERT,) a noted English bookseller and author, born near Mansfield in 1709, lived in London. He was a footman in early life, and in 1732 published a volume of verses entitled "The Footman's Miscellany." His drama "The Toyshop" gained him the friendship of Pope, and was performed with great success in 1735. He then opened a bookstore in Pall Mall, which was much frequented by authors and literary amateurs. He prospered in business, and became one of the principal booksellers in London. In 1737 he produced the farce of "The King and the Miller of Mansfield," which was greatly applauded. The popular and ingenious "Economy of Human Life," which appeared anonymously in 1750, is generally ascribed to him. His tragedy of "Cleone" was performed in 1758 with complete success. Dr. Johnson said, "If Otway had written it, no other of his pieces would have been remembered." He published a "Select Collection of Old Plays," which is highly prized. He purchased Dr. Johnson's poem of "London" (1738) for ten guineas, and his "Vanity of Human Wishes" for fifteen guineas. Dodsley was the author of other works, not named above, and was the projector of literary enterprises in which the most eminent talents of the time were enlisted. Died in 1764.

See "Biographia Britannica;" JOHNSON, "Lives of the English Poets."

Dod'son, (JAMES,) an English mathematician, published various works on mathematics. Died in 1757.

Dods'worth, (ROGER,) an English antiquary, born in Yorkshire in 1585, wrote 122 volumes on antiquities, which remain as manuscripts in the Bodleian Library. He co-operated with Dugdale in the "Monasticon Anglicanum." Died in 1654. He was patronized by General Lord Fairfax, who bequeathed the above-mentioned manuscripts to the Bodleian Library.

Dodvens. See DOUDYNS.

Dod'well, (Colonel EDWARD,) a British antiquary and artist, produced in 1818 a "Classical and Topographical Tour through Greece," richly illustrated, which is esteemed one of the best works on that subject. It was followed by a costly volume, entitled "Thirty Views in Greece," (1821.) From 1800, when he left college, until his death, he passed the most of his time on the continent. He died in Rome in 1832, leaving drawings of "Cyclopean or Pelasgic Remains in Greece and Italy," which have since been published.

Dodwell, (HENRY,) a theologian and chronologist, born in Dublin about 1642, settled in London in 1674, and adopted the profession of author and critic, in which he displayed great learning and industry. In 1688 he was chosen Camden professor of history at Oxford; but, refusing to take the oath of allegiance to William III., he was removed about 1691. He wrote several works on theology and chronology, among which are "Annals of Thucydides and Xenophon," (1696,) "Annotations on the Greek Geographers," "Dissertations on the Ancient Cycles of the Greeks and Romans," etc., (1701,) and a discourse proving that the soul is naturally mortal, and that the bishops have the power of giving immortality, (1706.) The last work excited much controversy, and naturally gave especial offence to the dissenters. Died in 1711.

See Brokesby, "Life of Henry Dodwell," 1715; Macaulay, "History of England," vol. iii.

Dodwell, (William,) a son of the preceding, born in 1709, became prebendary of Salisbury and Archdeacon of Berks. He published sermons and treatises on theology, among which is "The Sick Man's Companion." Died in 1785.

Doebereiner. See Döbereiner.
Doederlein. See Döderlein.
Doellinger. See Döllinger.
Doenniges. See Dönniges.
Doerfel. See Dörfel.
Doerflinger or **Doerfling.** See Derfflinger.
Doeringk. See Döringk.
Does, van der. See Dousa.

Does, van der, vän der doos, (Antoon,) a Dutch engraver, born at the Hague in 1610; died about 1680.

Does, van der, (Jacob,) called the Elder, a Dutch landscape-painter, born at Amsterdam about 1620, was a pupil of N. Moyaert. He finished his studies in Rome, and settled at the Hague. He imitated Van der Laer with success, and painted animals and figures with skill. Died in 1673 at Amsterdam.

See Descamps, "Vies des Peintres Flamands, Hollandais," etc.

Does, van der, (Jacob,) the Younger, a Dutch painter of history, son of the preceding, was born at Amsterdam in 1654. He studied under Dujardin and Lairesse. Died in Paris in 1693.

Does, van der, (Peter,) a Dutch admiral, who acted a brilliant part in the war which liberated the Dutch from Spanish domination. About 1598 he obtained command of a large fleet, with which he attacked the coast of Spain and pillaged several colonies. Died in the island of Saint Thomas, in the West Indies, in 1599.

See Van der Aa, "Biographisch Woordenboek der Nederlanden."

Does, van der, (Simon,) a son of Jacob the elder, born at Amsterdam in 1653, was a skilful landscape-painter. He worked at the Hague, Antwerp, and other places. His works have found their way into the cabinets of various foreign countries. Died about 1700.

See Descamps, "Vies des Peintres Flamands," etc

Doeveren, van, vän doo'ver-en, (Wouter,) a Dutch medical writer, born in Zealand in 1730, became professor of medicine at Leyden in 1771. Died in 1783.

Dog'gett or **Dog'get,** (Thomas,) an Irish actor, born in Dublin; died in 1721.

Dogiel, dŏg'yĕl, (Matthew,) a Polish historian, born about 1715, became rector of a college at Wilna. He wrote an important work on Polish diplomacy, "Codex Diplomaticus Regni Poloniæ," (1758.) Died in 1760.

Doglioni, dŏl-yo'nee, (Giovanni Niccolò,) a Venetian historical writer, born at Udine, published in 1598 a "History of Venice from its Origin to 1597."

Dohm, dōm, (Christian Wilhelm,) a German diplomatist and historical writer, born at Lemgo in 1751. He entered the civil service of Prussia about 1778, became privy councillor in 1783, and was employed in several missions. He represented Prussia in the Congress of Rastadt in 1797. In 1807 he entered the council of state of Jerome Bonaparte. He wrote, besides other works, "Memoirs of my Time," (1814–19, 5 vols.,) which is regarded as an important work. Died in 1820.

See Gronau, "Dohms Biographie," 1824; Ersch und Gruber, "Allgemeine Encyklopaedie."

Dohna, von, fon dō'nä, (Alexander,) Count, a Prussian general, born in 1661, was governor of the prince Frederick William who became King of Prussia. He was afterwards appointed first minister of Frederick I. and Frederick William II. Died in 1728.

See Ersch und Gruber, "Allgemeine Encyklopaedie."

Dohna, von, (Christoph,) born in Prussia in 1702, was made lieutenant-general in 1751, and served with distinction in the Seven Years' war. He commanded the right wing at the battle of Zorndorf, and defeated Haddik in 1758. Died in 1762.

See Ersch und Gruber, "Allgemeine Encyklopaedie."

Doig, (David,) a Scottish writer and classical scholar, born in 1719, taught school at Stirling. He contributed several articles to the "Encyclopædia Britannica," and addressed to Lord Kames two "Letters on the Savage State," (1792.) Died in 1800.

See Chambers, "Biographical Dictionary of Eminent Scotsmen."

Doigny du Ponceau, dwän'ye' dü pòn'sō', a French poet, born in Maine about 1750; died in 1830.

Doissin, dwä'sĂN', (Louis,) a French Jesuit, born in America in 1721, excelled in Latin poetry. He wrote, besides other works, "Sculptura, Carmen," (1752,) a poem on sculpture, and "Scalptura," a poem on engraving. Died in Paris in 1753.

Dökkalfar. See Elves.

Dol-a-bel'la, (Publius Cornelius,) a Roman of patrician rank and profligate habits, born about 70 B.C. He married Cicero's daughter Tullia. He was an adherent of Cæsar in the civil war, and fought for him at Pharsalia. He obtained the consulship soon after the death of Cæsar, 44 B.C. At first he favoured the senate against Antony; but he soon went over to the interest of the latter, who probably gave him a large bribe. He commanded an expedition to Syria, where he was defeated by Cassius, and, being besieged in Laodicea, committed suicide, 43 B.C.

See Plutarch, "Antony;" Dion Cassius, "History of Rome."

Dolabella, do-lä-bel'lä, (Tommaso,) an Italian painter, born at Belluno in 1570, worked in Cracow. Died in 1650.

Dol'ben, (John,) an English prelate, born at Stanwick in 1625. He fought for the king at Marston Moor and at York in the civil war. In 1656 he was ordained, and officiated at Oxford several years. He was rewarded with several benefices at the restoration, (1660,) became Bishop of Rochester in 1666, lord high almoner in 1675, and Archbishop of York in 1683. A few of his sermons were printed. Died in 1686.

Dolce, dol'chà, or **Dolci,** dol'chee, (Carlo,) an eminent Italian painter, born at Florence in 1616, was a pupil of Jacopo Vignali. He confined his talents to religious subjects, except a few portraits. The Emperor of Germany invited him to his court, where he painted several portraits of the imperial family. Among his master-pieces are "Christ on Mount Olivet," and a "Holy Family." His works have an exquisite finish, a soft and harmonious colouring, and are remarkable for a tender and sentimental expression. His pictures are prized as ornaments in many well-chosen collections. Died at Florence in 1686. "Three pen-strokes of Raffaelle," says Ruskin, "are a greater and better picture than the most finished work that ever Carlo Dolci polished into inanity."

See Lanzi, "History of Painting in Italy."

Dolce, (Luigi,) an Italian littérateur, born in Venice in 1508. He translated Cicero's Orations, and other ancient authors, and wrote, among other works, "Jocasta," a tragedy, (1549,) a "Life of Charles V.," (1551,) and a Dialogue on Painting, called "Aretino," (1557.) Died about 1568.

See Tiraboschi, "Storia della Letteratura Italiana."

Dolci. See Dolce, (Carlo.)

Dolendo, do-lĕn'do, (Bartholomeus,) a Dutch engraver, born at Leyden about 1560. He was a pupil of Goltzius.

Dolendo, (Zacharias,) an able engraver, born at Leyden, was a pupil of Jacob von Ghein. He was living in 1590.

Dolet, do'lĂ', (Étienne,) a learned Frenchman, born at Orléans in 1509, gained a wide reputation by his writings on theology, literature, etc., which also exposed him to persecution. He lived for some time at Lyons, where he established a printing-press and published some of his own works, for which he was imprisoned. In 1543 the Parliament condemned his books to be burned, as too favourable to the new doctrines. About

1546 the author himself, on a false charge of atheism, suffered death by fire. Among his works, in Latin, are a "Dialogue on the Imitation of Cicero," written against Erasmus, a "Commentary on the Latin Language," (1536,) and "Summary of the Acts of Francis I.," (1540.) He was a friend of Bonaventure Desperiers. "The French language," says A. F. Didot, "owes him much for his treatises, translations, [from Cicero and Plato,] and poesies."

See BAYLE, "Historical and Critical Dictionary;" A. F. DIDOT, "Essai sur la Typographie."

Dolgorouki. See DOLGORUKI.

Dolgoruki or **Dolgorouki,** dol'go-roo'kee, (IVAN MIKHAILOVITCH,) PRINCE, a Russian poet, born at Moscow about 1760, attained high dignities in the public service. From 1802 to 1812 he was Governor of Vladimir. He wrote many articles for literary journals, and gained a high reputation by his poetical epistles and satires. Died in 1823.

See OTTO, "Lehrbuch der Russischen Literatur."

Dolgoruki, (VASSILI VLADIMIROVITCH,) a Russian prince and field-marshal, born in 1667. He was sent as ambassador to France and Germany by Peter the Great. In 1726 Catherine I. appointed him ambassador, and sent him on an expedition against Persia. Peter II. raised him to the rank of field-marshal in 1728. Soon after this date he lost the favour of the court, and was imprisoned, but was restored in 1741. Died in 1746.

Dolgoruki, (YAKOF FEODOROVITCH,) a Russian prince, born in 1639. He distinguished himself in the campaigns of 1696 and 1697 against the Turks, and obtained the rank of general. In 1700 he was made prisoner at Narva by the Swedes, who detained him ten years. He was made a senator by Peter I. Died in 1720.

Doligny, do'lèn'ye', (LOUISE ADELAÏDE,) afterwards MADAME **Dudoyer de Gastels,** dü'dwä'yà' deh gås'-těl', a French comic actress, born in Paris in 1746; died in 1823.

Dolivar, do-le-vaR', (JUAN,) a Spanish engraver, born at Saragossa in 1641; died in Paris in 1701.

Döll or **Doell,** döl, (FRIEDRICH WILHELM,) a German sculptor, born at Hildburghausen in 1750; died in 1816.

Döllinger or **Doellinger,** döl'ling'ẹr, (IGNAZ,) a German physiologist, born at Bamberg in 1770. In 1826 he became professor of anatomy at Munich. Among his principal works are "Elements of Physiology," (1835,) and "On the Importance of Comparative Anatomy." Died in 1841.

See P. F. VON WALTHER, "Rede zum Andenken an Dr. I. Döllinger," 1841.

Döllinger or **Doellinger,** (JOHANN JOSEPH IGNAZ,) a learned Catholic theologian, son of the preceding, born at Bamberg in 1799. He became professor of ecclesiastical history and canon law at Munich in 1826. He has published a "Treatise on the History of the Church," (1838,) "Origin of Christianity," and other works.

See "Edinburgh Review" for July, 1862; "British Quarterly Review" for July, 1862.

Dol'lọnd, (JOHN,) an eminent English optician, born in London in 1706, was descended from French refugees. He learned the trade of a silk-weaver, and followed the same for many years, improving his leisure in the study of sciences and languages. He thus became a profound mathematician and a good linguist. About 1752 John Dollond retired from the trade of weaver, and became a practical optician in partnership with his son. They made improvements in the art, and became celebrated for the fabrication of telescopes. About 1757 he made an important discovery respecting the dispersion (or aberration) of light, and wrote a treatise on the subject, for which the Royal Society awarded him the Copley medal. The result of this discovery was the achromatic telescope. In 1761 he was chosen a Fellow of the Royal Society, and became optician to the king. Died about 1761.

See JOHN KELLY, "Life of J. Dollond."

Dollond, (PETER,) a son of the preceding, born about 1730, was a worthy successor of his father, under whose tuition he attained great proficiency in mathematics. From 1766 until 1804 he and his brother John were partners, and maintained a high reputation by their skill as opticians. In 1804 John died, and Peter took as a partner his nephew, George Huggins, who then changed his name to Dollond. Peter died in 1820. George died in 1832. The former had improved Hadley's quadrant, and written a treatise on telescopes.

Dolomieu, de, deh do'lo'me-ụh',(DÉODAT GUI SYLVAIN TANCRÈDE DE **Gratet**—grȁ'tȁ',) a celebrated French geologist and mineralogist, born at Dolomieu, in Dauphiné, in 1750, was the son of the Marquis of Dolomieu. He was admitted into the order of Malta, in which he remained until about 1770, when he killed one of his companions in a duel. While confined for this offence, he became a student of the natural sciences. After his release he formed a friendship with La Rochefoucauld, by whose influence he was chosen a correspondent of the Academy of Sciences. About 1777 he returned to Malta, where he was promoted to some offices in the order. From Malta he made scientific excursions to Sicily and Italy for several years, during which he wrote treatises on volcanoes. He returned to France in 1791, composed some important articles on geology for the "Journal de Physique," and traversed on foot all parts of that country, with the geologist's hammer in his hand. In 1796 he was appointed professor in the School of Mines, and was chosen a member of the Institute. He was one of the savants selected to attend Bonaparte in his expedition to Egypt in 1798, and was delighted with such an opportunity to pursue his favourite studies in a new field of inquiry. After a hasty survey of a part of Lower Egypt, he sailed for France in March, 1799, and was taken prisoner by the Neapolitans, (then at war with the French,) who kept him in a dungeon and treated him with great cruelty. Efforts were vainly made by several sovereign powers for his release, which could not be obtained until the victory of Marengo compelled Naples to make a treaty in which his liberation was positively stipulated. He arrived at Paris in March, 1801, and found that he had been appointed professor of mineralogy in the Museum of Natural History. He delivered one course of lectures, then made a journey to the Alps, and died in November, 1801. "Dolomieu," says Cuvier, "seemed to be born for geology. To a decided passion for that study he joined all the physical and moral faculties requisite for success." Though adverse fortunes did not permit him to fully develop his powers as the author of any system of geology, yet the science is much indebted to his treatises. During his imprisonment, though deprived of pen and ink, he wrote a "Treatise on Mineralogical Philosophy" and a "Memoir on Mineral Species," using the smoke of his lamp as a substitute for ink.

See notice, by CUVIER, in the "Biographie Universelle;" LACÉPÈDE, "Notice historique sur la Vie de Dolomieu;" 1802; "Edinburgh Review" for July, 1804.

Dolscius, dols'tse-ŭs, (PAUL,) a German Hellenist, born at Plauen in 1526, was a friend of Melanchthon. Died in 1589.

Domairon, do'mạ̈'rôN', (LOUIS,) a French Jesuit, born at Béziers in 1745, wrote "The General Principles of Belles-Lettres," (1785,) and other works. Died in 1807.

Domard, do'mȁR', (JOSEPH FRANÇOIS,) a French engraver of medals and gems, born in Paris in 1792; died in 1858.

Domat, do'mȁ', or **Daumat,** dō'mȁ', (JEAN,) an eminent French jurist, born at Clermont in Auvergne in 1625. He had intimate relations with the recluses of Port-Royal, especially with Pascal, who at his death intrusted to him his private papers. The details of his virtuous and useful life have not been recorded. His reputation is founded on a great systematic work entitled "The Civil Laws in their Natural Order," (1689.) Many persons had attempted to systematize the confused and ill-digested materials of Roman law; but no one succeeded so perfectly as Domat, who is considered the most eminent jurist of his age. He received a pension from Louis XIV. D'Aguesseau, a most competent judge, spoke of him with profound respect. Domat was for many years king's advocate in the presidial court of Clermont. Died in Paris in 1695.

See EUGÈNE CAUCHY, "Études sur Domat," 1852; VICTOR COUSIN's article in the "Journal des Savants," 1843; SAINTE-BEUVE, "Port-Royal;" CARRÉ, "Notice historique sur Domat," prefixed to his works, Paris, 1822.

ā, ē, ī, ō, ū, ȳ, *long;* à, è, ò, same, less prolonged; ă, ĕ, ĭ, ŏ, ŭ, ў, *short;* ạ, ẹ, ị, ọ, *obscure;* fär, fȁll, fȁt; mët; nŏt; gŏŏd; mŏŏn;

Dombay, von, fon dom'bī, (Franz,) an Austrian Orientalist, born in Vienna in 1758, was appointed interpreter to the court for Oriental languages in 1792. He published "Geschichte der Scherifen," a "History of the Shereefs," (princes of Morocco,) (1801,) a "Persian Grammar," (1804,) and other works, which are commended by Silvestre de Sacy. Died in 1810.

Dombey, dôN'bȧ', (Joseph,) a French botanist and physician, born at Mâcon in 1742, studied botany at Paris under Jussieu. He received a commission from Turgot, the prime minister, to visit South America and collect such useful plants as could be profitably cultivated in France, and arrived at Callao in 1778. He traversed Peru, Chili, etc., discovered mines of gold and quicksilver, and had many romantic adventures. Returning home, he landed at Cadiz in 1785 with an immense collection, of which, it is stated, the Spanish officials confiscated half and damaged the other half. Buffon procured for him a pension of six thousand livres. Dombey was living at Lyons when it was besieged in 1793, after which he obtained a mission to the United States. On the voyage thither he was taken by privateers, and imprisoned in Montserrat, where he died about 1794. The French regard him as one of the most enterprising and successful explorers of the domain of botany in the eighteenth century. As he was unable to defray the expense of publishing the results of his researches in Peru, he placed his herbal in the hands of L'Héritier, who prepared a Flora of Peru, which he left in manuscript.

See Deleuze, "Notice sur Dombey," in the "Annales du Muséum d'Histoire naturelle;" "Nouvelle Biographie Générale."

Dombrowski, dom-brov'skee, (John Henry,) an able Polish general, born in the palatinate of Cracow in 1755. In the effort for independence which the Poles began about 1791, he took a prominent part, and obtained the rank of general. He was compelled to surrender to Suwarrow in November, 1794, when his nation ceased to exist. In 1797 he entered the service of the Cisalpine Republic, for which he formed and commanded a Polish legion. He displayed great valour and ability at Trebbia, (1799,) where he commanded a wing of the French army. After the battle of Jena (1806) Bonaparte called him to Poland, where he raised an army of 30,000 Poles. As general of division, Dombrowski gained victories at Dirschau and at Bromberg in 1809. He was wounded at Berezina in 1812, but continued to fight for Bonaparte until 1814. Died in 1818.

See L. Chodzko, "Histoire des Légions Polonaises en Italie," 1829; "Nouvelle Biographie Générale."

Domenichi, do-mĕn'e-kee or do-mā'ne-kee, (Luigi,) an Italian *littérateur*, born at Piacenza, lived at Venice and at Florence, where he was patronized by Duke Cosimo I. He translated into Italian Plutarch's "Lives," (1555,) Pliny's "Natural History," (1561,) and other works. He also wrote several original works, among which are "The Nobility of Women," ("La Nobilità delle Donne,") and "The Court Lady," ("La Donna di Corte.") Died in 1564.

See Tiraboschi, "Storia della Letteratura Italiana."

Domenichi, da, dä do-mĕn'e-kee or do-mā'ne-kee, (Domenico,) a learned prelate, born in Venice in 1416, lived many years in Rome. He was made referendary by Calixtus III., nuncio by another pope, and Bishop of Brescia by Paul II. He wrote a "Treatise on the Episcopal Dignity," and many other works on theology. Died in 1478.

Domenichino, do-mĕn-e-kee'no, [Fr. Dominiquin, do'me'ne'kȧN',] an eminent Italian painter, whose proper name was Domenico Zampieri, do-mĕn'e-ko dzäm-pe-ā'ree, was born at Bologna in 1581. He studied under Annibal Caracci in Rome, where he remained some years and was patronized as a painter and architect by Gregory XV. He afterwards worked in Naples, where he died in 1641. He painted in oil and in fresco, was a good colorist, and excelled both in history and landscapes. Among his master-pieces are "The Martyrdom of Saint Agnes," and the "Communion of Saint Jerome," finished about 1612, which is to be seen in the Vatican opposite Raphael's "Transfiguration." Some judges, as Caracci and N. Poussin, estimate him as scarcely inferior to any painter except Raphael, Correggio, and Titian.

See Lanzi, "History of Painting in Italy;" Malvasia, "Felsina Pittrice;" Bolognini-Amorini, "Vita di Domenico Zampieri," 1839; Bellori, "Vite de' Pittori;" Nagler, "Neues Allgemeines Künstler-Lexikon;" Lecarpentier, "Notice sur D. Zampieri," 1812.

Domenici, do-mĕn'e-chee or do-mā'ne-chee, (Francesco,) an Italian painter, born at Treviso, lived about 1530, and died at the age of thirty-five. He is called one of the best pupils of Titian.

Domenico. See Dominic, Saint.

Domenico, do-mĕn'e-ko, (Alexis,) [Fr. Dominique le Grec, do'me'nĕk' lĕh grĕk,] called il Greco, (ĕl grā'ko,) an artist, born in the Greek Archipelago about 1547, was a pupil of Titian in Venice. He excelled in painting, sculpture, and architecture, and imitated the manner of Titian with success. In his later years he worked in Toledo and other cities of Spain, where he produced many admired paintings and formed some able pupils. He designed a church in Toledo, and adorned it with sculptures and pictures. Died in 1625.

See Nagler, "Neues Allgemeines Künstler-Lexikon."

Domenico d'Asciano. See Bartolo, (Domenico.)

Domenico de' Barbieri, do-mĕn'e-ko dä baR-be-ā'ree, or **Domenico Fiorentino**, (fe-o-rĕn-tee'no,) a painter, sculptor, and engraver, born at Florence in 1506; died in 1560.

Domenico degli Camei, do-mĕn'e-ko dâl'yee kä-mā'ee, an Italian artist, born at Milan, derived his surname from his skill in engraving gems in relief, or cameos. His family name was Compagni. Vasari speaks with admiration of his portraits of Ludovico Sforza and other princes, which are among the most precious monuments of modern iconography. Died about 1490.

Domenico Veneziano, do-mĕn'e-ko vå-nĕt-se-ā'no, or Domenico of Venice, an Italian painter, born about 1408, is said to have been the first who painted in oil at Florence. He was assassinated by Castagno, the painter, about 1462. (See Castagno.)

See Vasari, "Lives of the Painters."

Domergue, do'mȧRg', (François Urbain,) a French grammarian, born at Aubagne in 1745, settled in Paris about 1790, and a few years later was chosen a member of the Institute. He was the author of "Orthographic Exercises," and other grammatical works. Died in 1810.

Dom'ett, written also **Domott**, (Sir William,) an English admiral, born in Devonshire about 1754, served under Rodney and Nelson against the French. Died in 1828.

Domingo, do-mĕng'go, (Luis,) a Spanish painter and sculptor, born at Valencia in 1718; died in 1767.

Domingo de Guzman. See Dominic, Saint.

Dom'ĭ-nic, [Sp. Domingo de Guzman, do-mĕng'go dä gooth-mân'; Fr. Dominique, do'me'nĕk'; It. Domenico, do-mĕn'e-ko,] Saint, the founder of the order of Dominicans, was born at Calahorra, in Old Castile, in 1170. Having become noted for his zeal and eloquence as a preacher, he was admitted in 1198 into the chapter of the Bishop of Osma, whom he assisted in his efforts to convert the Albigenses in France. According to the Catholics, he performed many miracles, and offered to sell himself as a slave in order to raise money for charitable purposes. He appears to have been one of the instigators of the crusade against the Albigenses about 1212, in which many thousands of those people perished. In 1215 he founded the order of Preaching Friars, or Dominicans, which was approved by the pope in 1216 and was rapidly multiplied in Christendom. Their rules exact rigorous fasting and total abstinence from flesh. The design of the founder was to make the conversion of heretics their special pursuit. In France they were often called Jacobins. Dominic became the first general of the order. The pope created in his favour the office of Master of the Sacred Palace, which is always filled by a Dominican. He died in 1221, and was canonized by Gregory IX. in 1234.

See Touron, "Vie de Saint-Dominique," 1739; Castillo, "Historia del Santo Domingo," 1612–22; Lacordaire, "Vie de Saint-Dominique," 1840; Bottoni, "Vita di San Domenico," 3 vols., 1789.

Dominici, da, dä do-mee'ne-chee, (Bernardo,) a Neapolitan artist, published "The Lives of Neapolitan Painters, Sculptors, and Architects," (3 vols., 1742–45.)

ɛ as *k*; ç as *s*; g̃ *hard*; g̃ as *j*; g, h, k, *guttural*; n, *nasal*; R, *trilled*; ŝ as *z*; ŧh as in *this*. (☞See Explanations, p. 23.)

Dominikus, do-mee'ne-kŭs, (JAKOB,) a German historian, born at Rheinbergen in 1764. Among his works, which are highly commended, are "Ferdinand, Duke of Alva," (1796,) and "Henry IV. of France," (2 vols., 1797.)

Dominique. See DOMENICO and DOMINIC, SAINT.

Dominique Barrière, do'me'nĕk' bǎ're-aiR', a French engraver, born at Marseilles in 1622, worked in Rome.

Dominique le Grec. See DOMENICO, (ALEXIS.)

Dominiquin. See DOMENICHINO.

Dominis, de, dà dom'e-nĕss, (MARCANTONIO,) an Italian theologian, born in the isle of Arba, near Dalmatia, in 1566. He gained early distinction as professor of philosophy and mathematics at Padua, and became Archbishop of Spalatro. Before this promotion he wrote a curious treatise on light, "On the Rays of Light and Vision in Perspective Glasses and in the Rainbow," ("De Radiis Visus et Lucis in Vitris perspectivis et Iride," 1611,) in which the phenomenon of the rainbow was explained for the first time. About 1615 he removed to England, turned Protestant, and was appointed Dean of Windsor by James I. He published arguments against Popery in his work "On the Ecclesiastical Republic," ("De Republica Ecclesiastica," 1617.) He returned to Italy in 1622, and abjured the doctrines of that work. On a suspicion that he was about to recant again, he was imprisoned at Rome, and died in prison in 1624.

See VOLTAIRE, "Lettres philosophiques;" LIMBORCH, "Historia Inquisitionis."

Domitian, do-mish'e-an, [Lat. DOMITIA'NUS; Fr. DOMITIEN, do'me'se'ǎN',] or, more fully, **Ti'tus Fla'vius Domitia'nus,** a Roman emperor, the second son of Vespasian, born in 51 A.D., succeeded his brother Titus in 81. Though his character was depraved and cruel, he at first affected a zeal for public virtue and justice. He was defeated by the Dacians, and made a disgraceful treaty, by which he bound himself to pay them tribute. His armies were generally unsuccessful, except in Britain, which was conquered by Agricola. He married Domitia Longina, to whom he gave the title of Augusta. Many innocent persons fell victims to his suspicions, his cruelty, or his rapacity. He banished the philosophers and literati, among whom was Epictetus. One of his favourite pastimes was hunting and killing flies. A conspiracy was formed among his guards and courtiers, and he was killed in his palace in 96 A.D., when the senate chose Nerva as his successor.

See TACITUS, "Historia;" SUETONIUS, "Domitianus;" NIEBUHR, "Römische Geschichte," vol. ii.; J. ARRHENIUS, "Vita Imperatoris Domitiani," 1696.

Domitianus. See DOMITIAN.

Domitianus, do-mish-e-ā'nus, (LUCIUS DOMITIUS,) a Roman general, who assumed the title of emperor in the reign of Diocletian. He was put to death in 288 A.D.

Dom-ĭ-til'la or **Domitia,** do-mĭsh'e-a, the wife of the emperor Vespasian, was the mother of Titus and Domitian. She died before the accession of Vespasian.

Domitius Afer. See AFER.

Domitius Ahenobarbus. See AHENOBARBUS.

Dommartin, do'mǎR'tǎN', (ELZÉARD AUGUSTE,) a French general, born in 1768, distinguished himself at the battle of the Pyramids and at El Arish. He was killed at Rosetta in 1799.

Domnus. See DONUS.

Don, (DAVID,) a Scottish botanist, born at Forfar in 1800. He went to London in 1819, and gained reputation by a "Monograph on the Genus Saxifraga." In 1822 he was appointed librarian of the Linnæan Society, to which he contributed several able botanical treatises. In 1825 he produced a valuable work on the plants of Nepaul, "Prodromus Floræ Nepalensis." He became professor of botany in King's College, London, in 1836. Died in 1840.

Don, (GEORGE,) father of the preceding, born about 1770, was proprietor of a nursery and botanic garden at Forfar, and was a good botanist. Died in 1814.

Don, (Sir GEORGE,) a British general, born in 1756; died in 1832.

Don, (GEORGE,) a botanist, born in 1798, was a brother of David Don, noticed above. He made scientific ex-

cursions to Africa and South America, and published an excellent "System of Gardening and Botany," (4 vols., 1831–38.) Died in 1856.

Don'ald I., King of Scotland, is said to have been the first Christian king of that country. Died about 216 A.D.

Donald II., King of Scotland, reigned about four years, and died about 864 A.D.

Donald IV. or **VI.,** King of Scotland, reigned from 892 to 904 A.D.

Donald VII. See DUNCAN.

Donald VIII., sometimes called **Donald Bane,** usurped the throne of Scotland in 1093. He was deposed by Edgar Atheling in 1098.

Don'ald-son, (JOHN,) a skilful Scottish portrait-painter, born in Edinburgh in 1737, lived some years in London. He published an "Essay on the Elements of Beauty," and a volume of poems. He was a very successful artist, especially in miniature. Died in 1801.

See CHAMBERS, "Biographical Dictionary of Eminent Scotsmen."

Don'ald-son, (Professor JOHN,) an eminent British agriculturist of the present age. He published a "Treatise on Manures and Grasses," (1842,) "Cultivated Plants of the Farm," (1847,) and "Agricultural Biography," (London, 1854,) which is said to be an excellent work.

Don'ald-son, (Rev. JOHN WILLIAM,) an English philologist, born in 1812, published Greek, Latin, and Hebrew grammars, and other works. Died about 1861.

Donaldson, (THOMAS LEVERTON,) an English architect, born in London about 1795. He published a "Collection of Doorways from Ancient and Modern Buildings in Greece and Italy," (1833.) In 1843 he became professor of architecture in University College, London. He was architect of All-Saints Church, London, and of other churches in or near that city.

Donaldson, (WALTER,) a Scottish writer, born at Aberdeen about 1575, published "Synopsis Œconomica."

Donat. See DONATUS.

Donatello, do-nä-tel'lo, (DONATO DI BELTO DI BARDO,) an eminent sculptor, born in Florence in 1383, worked in Florence, Venice, Rome, and Padua, and was highly successful. He was patronized by the famous Cosimo de' Medici. Among his best productions are bronze figures of Saint George, of Saint Mark, and of "Judith holding the Head of Holofernes." He excelled in the representation of historical events by bas-reliefs. His character was noble and liberal. Died in 1466. His works are commended for correctness of form, for propriety of attitude, and for power and truth of expression, sometimes reaching the pathetic and sublime.

See ANDREA FRANCIONI, "Elogio di Donatello," 1837; NAGLER, "Neues Allgemeines Künstler-Lexikon."

Donatello, (SIMONE,) a Florentine sculptor, brother of the preceding. He was invited to Rome in 1431 by Pope Eugene, and spent about twelve years in adorning one of the doors of Saint Peter's with bas-reliefs.

Donati, do-nä'tee, a noble and powerful Guelph family of Florence, which flourished about the end of the thirteenth century. Gemma Donati, the wife of Dante, was a member of this family.

Donati, (ALESSANDRO,) an Italian Jesuit, poet, and antiquary, born at Sienna in 1584, professed rhetoric in Rome with distinction. He wrote, in Latin, a poem on the "Poetic Art," an epic poem named "Constantinus," (1640,) and an excellent work on the edifices of Rome, ("Roma vetus et recens," 1633,) which was perhaps superior to anything previously written on the antiquities of that city. Died in 1640.

Donati, (ANTONIO,) a Venetian naturalist, born in 1606; died in 1659.

Donati, do-nä'tee, (BINDO,) an Italian poet, born at Florence, wrote in the Tuscan language. He was ranked by Crescimbeni among the first writers of his time. Died about 1300.

Donati, (CORSO,) a Florentine noble, who was a leader of the Guelphs. By his talents and rank he acquired great influence in public affairs. About 1300 the people of Florence were divided into two factions, the Neri and Bianchi, (Blacks and Whites.) Corso Donati was the chief of the former party, which, by the aid of foreign troops under Charles de Valois, obtained power in 1301, when they banished or killed their principal rivals, of whom Dante was one. Donati soon lost his influence with his own party, was accused of tyrannical designs, and, failing to appear at the trial, was condemned in 1308, and destroyed himself.

See SISMONDI, "Histoire des Républiques Italiennes."

Donati or **Donato**, do-nä′to, (MARCELLO,) Count di Ponzano, (de pon-zä′no,) an Italian physician, born at Correggio in 1538. He wrote "De Medica Historia mirabili," (1586.) Died in 1602.

See CASTELLANI, "Vita del celebre Medico M. Donati," 1788.

Donati, (VITALIANO,) an Italian physician, eminent as a naturalist, was born at Padua in 1713. Prompted by a passion for botany and other natural sciences, he traversed Italy for about eight years, and was employed by Pope Benedict XIV. to make collections for his college. He then explored Illyria, and undertook a description of the productions of the Adriatic. In 1750 an outline of his intended work on the "Natural History of the Adriatic" was published. He also visited Syria and Egypt for scientific purposes, and sent home many objects of natural history. On his voyage homeward he perished by shipwreck in 1763.

See GENNARI, "Elogio di V. Donati," 1839.

Donato. See DONATELLO.

Donato, do-nä′to, (BERNARDINO,) an Italian philologist, was born at Zano, near Verona. He was professor of Greek at Padua about 1532. He translated Xenophon's book "On Economy," and other Greek works. He was the first editor of "Chrysostom on Saint Paul" in Greek. Died about 1550.

Donato, (FRANCESCO,) Doge of Venice, was elected in 1545, and died in 1553, leaving a good reputation for eloquence and wisdom. He maintained the neutrality of Venice in the war between Charles V. and Henry II. of France.

See DARU, "Histoire de Venise."

Donato or **Donati**, (GERONIMO,) a Venetian statesman, negotiated a peace between the pope and Venice in 1510. His abilities were extolled by Erasmus. Died in 1513.

Donato, (LEONARDO,) was Doge of Venice from 1606 to 1612. He firmly resisted Pope Paul V., who wished to deprive the republic of its jurisdiction over the clergy, and who laid the state under an interdict in 1606. This was finally removed without any concession on the part of Venice. Died in 1612.

See ANDREA MOROSINI, "Vita Leonardi Donati," 1628; PIERRE MARCEL, "Vitæ Donatorum."

Donato, (NICCOLÒ,) a Venetian diplomatist, born in 1705. He wrote "L'Uomo di Governo," ("The Statesman,") which was translated into French by Robinet, (1767.) Died in 1765.

Donato, (ZENO,) an Italian painter, born at Verona, flourished about 1500.

See VASARI, "Lives of the Painters," etc.

Do-nā′tus, [Fr. DONAT, do′nä′,] Bishop of Casæ Nigræ, in Numidia, the chief author of the schism of Donatists, which began about 305 A.D., disturbed the church for more than a century, and filled Africa with dire calamities. With an affected zeal for discipline, he formed a party against Cecilianus, Bishop of Carthage, as being identified with some who, through fear of persecution, had given up the sacred books and were hence called "Traditores." He taught that the Church was not infallible; but it does not appear that he made innovations in doctrine. This party became very numerous in Africa, and, it is said, burned the churches of the Catholics and massacred the members of that party. At the Council of Arles, in 314, the question was decided in favour of Cecilianus. The Donatists, however, increased until 410, when the emperor Honorius convinced a council at Carthage, which condemned them as heretics. This result is ascribed chiefly to the efforts of Saint Augustine. They became divided into several sects, and about the sixth century had sunk into insignificance.

See SAINT AUGUSTINE, "De Hæreticis;" TILLEMONT, "Mémoires;" "Nouvelle Biographie Générale."

Donatus, the second of this name, was elected Bishop of Carthage in 316 A.D. by the Donatists, of whom he became the master-spirit. He is said to have been learned and eloquent, but haughty. His partisans gave him the surname of MAGNUS, (the "Great.") He died in exile about 355. The Donatists in his time were nearly as numerous in Africa as the Catholics.

See PLUQUET, "Dictionnaire des Hérésies."

Donatus, [Fr. DONAT, do′nä′,] (ÆLIUS,) a celebrated Latin grammarian, born about 333 A.D. He taught rhetoric in Rome, and was a teacher of Saint Jerome, who speaks highly of his talents. His "Elements of Grammar" ("Ars Grammatica") served as the basis of nearly all subsequent elementary works on that subject, and was generally used in the schools of the middle ages. He also wrote an able commentary on Terence, which is extant.

See L. SCHOPFEN, "De Terentio et Donato," 1824.

Donckers. See DONKERS.

Dondi, don′dee, (GIACOMO,) born at Padua, was eminent as a philosopher and physician. He wrote "Storehouse of Medicine," ("Promptuarium Medicinæ,") and made a famous clock in Padua in 1344.

Dondi, (GIOVANNI,) a son of the preceding, born in 1318, was a physician and mathematician, and the friend of Petrarch, who addressed to him several letters. He invented a celebrated clock, which was placed in Pavia and procured for him and his descendants the surname of HOROLOGIUS, or DALL' OROLOGIO. Died in 1389.

See TIRABOSCHI, "Storia della Letteratura Italiana."

Dondi dall' Orologio, don′dee däl-lo-ro-lo′jo, (CARLO ANTONIO,) MARQUIS, an Italian naturalist, was born of a noble family of Padua about 1750. He devoted his life chiefly to natural history and chemistry. He wrote an "Introduction to the Natural History of the Euganean Hills," (1780,) and a few other scientific works. Died in 1801.

Dondini, don-dee′nee, (GUGLIELMO,) an Italian poet and Jesuit, born at Ancona in 1606, was professor of eloquence in Rome for many years. Among his works are a Latin poem "On the Birth of the Dauphin of France," (1639,) and a "History of the Actions, in France, of Farnese, Prince of Parma," (1673.)

Donducci, don-doot′chee, (GIOVANNI ANDREA,) an Italian painter, surnamed IL MASTELLETTA, èl mâs-tel-let′tä, was born at Bologna in 1575. "He had a rich imagination," says Auguis, "a pure design, and vigorous colour." His reputation was high in his own time, but has since declined. He died in 1637, or, according to another account, in 1655.

See LANZI, "History of Painting in Italy."

Doneau, do′nō′, [Lat. DONEL′LUS,] (HUGUES,) an able French jurist and Protestant, born at Châlons-sur-Saône in 1527. He was teaching jurisprudence at Bourges in 1572, when, by the aid of his scholars, he escaped the Massacre of Saint Bartholomew and fled from France. He afterwards professed law at Heidelberg, Leyden, and Altorf, where he died in 1591. He is the author of voluminous and esteemed commentaries on civil law.

See TAISAND, "Vies des Jurisconsultes;" MORÉRI, "Dictionnaire Historique;" ZEIDLER, "Spicilegium Observationum Vitam H. Donelli illustrantium," 1766.

Donellus. See DONEAU.

Don′el-lў, (Sir ROSS,) a British admiral, who entered the navy at an early age. He fought with distinction under Lord Howe in June, 1794, and commanded the squadron before Toulon in 1803. For his conduct at Montevideo in 1807 he received the thanks of Parliament. He was made rear-admiral in 1814, and full admiral in 1838. Died in 1841.

Dongelberge, de, deh dong′ęl-bĕRG′ęh, (HENRI CHARLES,) a Belgian historian, born probably at Brussels in 1593; died in 1660.

Dongois, dôN′gwä′, (NICOLAS,) a French jurist, born in Paris about 1634, was a nephew of the poet Boileau, and an acquaintance of Voltaire. Died in 1717.

Doni, do′nee, (ADONE,) an able painter of the Roman school, born at Assisi, worked about 1540. He is reputed the greatest painter that Assisi ever produced.

Doni, (ANTONIO FRANCESCO,) an Italian *littérateur*, born at Florence about 1508. He lived a wandering life, and gained a scanty subsistence by his writings, some of which were facetious, humorous, or satirical, and had a temporary vogue. Among his works is a treatise on painting and sculpture, entitled "Disegno partito in più Ragionamenti," "The Gourd," ("La Zucca," 1551,) "The Marbles of Doni," (1552,) and "La Libraria del Doni," (1550,) a bibliographical work, which passed through many editions, but is very defective. Died in 1574.

See TIRABOSCHI, "Storia della Letteratura Italiana;" NEGRI, "Istoria de' Fiorentini Scrittori;" NICÉRON, "Mémoires."

Doni, (GIOVANNI BATTISTA,) an eminent Italian scholar and antiquary, born in Florence in 1593. The study of antiquities became his ruling passion, and he made an immense collection of rare objects. In 1623 he removed to Rome, where he was patronized by Cardinal Barberini and was made secretary of the Sacred College. He returned to Florence in 1640, and was chosen professor of eloquence. He wrote several Latin poems, ("Carmina," 1628,) and treatises on ancient music, one of which is named "Lyra Barberina," (1773.) Died in 1646.

See BANDINI, "De Vita et Scriptis J. B. Donii," 1755.

Doni d'Attichi, do'ne' dắ'te'she', ? (LOUIS,) a French bishop and biographer, born in 1596; died in 1664.

Donini, do-nee'nee, (GIROLAMO,) a skilful Italian painter, born at Correggio in 1681, was a pupil of Carlo Cignani, and worked at Bologna. He excelled in design and colour, and is said to have finished his works with greater care and delicacy than any eminent painter except Carlo Dolce. Died about 1740.

See LANZI, "History of Painting in Italy."

Donis, do'nis, (NIKOLAUS,) a German monk and geographer, lived in the monastery of Reichenbach about 1450. He produced a Latin version of Ptolemy's Geography, to which he added graduated maps, and an original treatise (in Latin) "On the Wonders of the World." He presented a copy of this work to the pope in 1471.

Donizetti, don-e-zet'tee or do-nid-zet'tee, (GAETANO,) an excellent Italian musical composer, born at Bergamo in 1798, studied music under Mattei at Bologna. He served several years in the army, which he quitted about 1822. After many essays, he produced in 1830, at Milan, his opera "Anna Bolena," which was much admired. It was followed by many other operas, which were very successful and still retain their popularity, among which are "Lucrezia Borgia," (1833,) "Lucia di Lammermoor," (1835,) and "Linda di Chamouni," (1842.) In the latter part of his life he was professor of counterpoint in the Royal College of Naples, and chapel-master and composer to the court of Vienna. Died at Bergamo in 1848.

See A. DE LAFAGE, "Notice sur Donizetti;" SCUDO, "Donizetti et l'École Italienne depuis Rossini;" FÉTIS, "Biographie Universelle des Musiciens."

Donkers, donk'ẹrs, or **Donkers,** (JAN or PIETER,) a Dutch painter, born at Gouda about 1610, died prematurely. His works are highly praised.

Donkers, Donckers, or **Doncker,** (PIETER,) a Dutch painter of history and portraits, born at Gouda about 1612. He worked at Rome. Died in 1668.

Donn or **Donne,** don, (ABRAHAM,) an English mathematician, born at Bideford in 1718; died in 1746.

Donnadieu, do'nǎ'de-uh', (GABRIEL,) a French general, born at Nîmes in 1777; died in 1849.

Donné, do'nà', (ALPHONSE,) a French savant, born at Noyon in 1806. He wrote treatises on the physiology of milk, blood, mucus, and saliva.

Donne, don, or **Donn,** (BENJAMIN,) an English mathematician of Bideford, born in 1729, published several treatises. Died in 1798.

Donne, (JOHN,) an eminent English poet and divine, born in London in 1573, was educated in the Catholic religion, which he renounced in favour of the Church of England. He was secretary to Lord-Chancellor Egerton, when he privately married a niece of that nobleman and consequently lost his office. In 1610 he wrote the "Pseudo-Martyr," which procured him the favour of James I., who persuaded him to take holy orders about 1614, and made him one of his chaplains. He gained celebrity for his eloquence as a preacher, and in 1621 was appointed Dean of Saint Paul's. Donne was the first and Cowley the second of the school which Johnson denominates "metaphysical poets," who laboured after conceits and novel turns of thought. "Donne," says

Hallam, "is the most inharmonious of our versifiers. Of his earlier poems many are very licentious; the later are chiefly devout. Few are good for much; the conceits have not even the merit of being intelligible." Dryden styles him "the greatest wit, though not the greatest poet, of our nation." He wrote satires, elegies, and other poems. His Sermons, published in 1640, are much admired for learning and subtlety. He died in 1631. His life was written by Izaak Walton, (1640.)

See, also, H. ALFORD, "Life of Donne," 1839; "Retrospective Review," vol. viii., 1823.

Donneau de Vizé, do'nō' dẹh ve'zà', (JEAN,) a French critic and journalist, born in Paris in 1640. He wrote several successful comedies, and founded about 1680 the "Mercure galante," a monthly review, in which he attacked Racine and Molière and published news of the court, etc. This was probably the earliest French journal or newspaper. Died in 1710.

Donner, don'nẹr, (GEORG RAPHAEL,) a skilful German sculptor, born at Essling in 1695; died in 1741.

Donnet, do'nà', (FERDINAND FRANÇOIS AUGUSTE,) a French prelate, born at Bourg Argental in 1795, became Archishop of Bordeaux in 1837, and a cardinal in 1852.

Dönniges or **Doenniges,** dön'niG-ẹs, (WILHELM,) a German publicist, born near Stettin in 1814. He wrote, besides other works, a "History of the German Empire in the Fourteenth Century," (1842.)

Donnino, don-nee'no, (AGNOLO,) a painter, born at Florence, lived about 1500. He is praised by Vasari.

Donnissan, de, dẹh do'ne'sŏN', MARQUIS, a French royalist officer, who took a prominent part in the civil war of La Vendée in 1793. He died on the scaffold about the end of 1793.

Dono, (PAOLO DI.) See UCCELLO, (PAOLO.)

Donoli, do-no'lee, (ALFONSO FRANCESCO,) an Italian medical writer, born in Tuscany in 1635; died in 1724.

Donoso, do-no'so, (JOSÉ,) a Spanish painter, born in New Castile in 1628, worked in Madrid, several churches of which he adorned with paintings. His manner is said to resemble that of Paul Veronese. Died in 1686.

Donoso Cortés, do-no'so koR-tês', (JUAN,) Marquis de Valdegamas, (vàl-dà-gä'mäs,) a Spanish statesman and writer, born in Estremadura in 1809. He was a classical scholar, and displayed poetical talents at an early age. He at first favoured the Liberal party in politics. At the death of Ferdinand VII. (1833) he supported the cause of Isabella and her mother, Christina, against Carlos. About 1840 he was secretary to the queen-mother Christina, then an exile in France. In 1844 he was chosen secretary to the queen Isabella, and was made Marquis of Valdegamas. In his later years he became conservative, and wrote political works which are admired for their literary merit. In his "Essay on Catholicism, Liberalism, and Socialism" (1851) he appears as a zealous champion of the Catholic Church. He was sent as minister to Berlin in 1848, and was Spanish minister at Paris when he died in 1853.

See "Nouvelle Biographie Générale."

Donoughmore. See HUTCHINSON, (RICHARD HELY.)

Don'ọ-vạn, (EDWARD,) an English naturalist, author of an esteemed "Natural History of British Insects," (16 vols., 1792–1816.) About 1797 he produced a "Natural History of British Birds." Between 1798 and 1805 he issued a series of works on the insects of China, India, and other parts of Asia, which were favourably received. "A great number of species," says Swainson, "are here delineated for the first time." He also wrote "Descriptive Excursions through South Wales," and edited a periodical called "The Naturalist's Repository." Died in 1837.

Do'nus I., or **Dom'nus,** a native of Rome, was chosen pope in 677 A.D., as successor to Dieudonné II., (Adeodat.) Died in 678.

Donus II., or **Domnus,** elected pope in 974, according to some authorities was the successor of Benedict VI. He is supposed to have died in December, 975.

Dony, do'ne', (JEAN JACQUES DANIEL,) a Belgian metallurgist, born at Liege in 1759; died in 1819.

Donzelli, don-zel'lee, (IPPOLITO and PIETRO,) Italian painters, who were brothers, and worked at Naples about 1460–90.

ā, ē, ī, ō, ū, ȳ, *long;* ă, ĕ, ĭ, ŏ, ŭ, ў, same, less prolonged; ă, ĕ, ĭ, ŏ, ŭ, ў, *short;* ạ, ẹ, ị, ọ, *obscure;* fär, fàll, fàt; mêt; nŏt; gŏŏd; mŏŏn;

Donzellini, don-zĕl-lee'nee, (GIROLAMO,) an Italian medical writer, born in the province of Brescia; died at Venice about 1560.

Donzello. See DONZELLI.

Doo, (GEORGE THOMAS,) an eminent English historical engraver, was born in Surrey in 1800. He was elected Royal Academician about 1857, having previously received the title of historical engraver to the queen. Among his works, which are mostly line engravings, are the "Ecce Homo," after Correggio, the "Infant Christ," after Raphael, and "Italian Pilgrims coming in Sight of Rome," after Eastlake.

Doo'dy, (SAMUEL,) an English botanist, born in Staffordshire, was director of a botanic garden at Chelsea. He made discoveries in cryptogamous plants, and contributed to the "Synopsis" of Ray, who was his friend. Died in 1706.

Doo'lit-tle, (THOMAS,) an English nonconformist minister, was born at Kidderminster in 1630. He wrote "The Complete Body of Practical Divinity," and other approved works. Died in 1707.

Doo'ly, (JOHN MITCHELL,) an American judge, was born in Georgia about 1772. He embraced the profession of law, and became judge of the Western Circuit of Georgia in 1816. He was afterwards twice elected judge of the Northern Circuit of Georgia. Died in 1827. Judge Dooly was a noted wit and humorist.

Doorree, Dourri, or **Durri** (door're) EFFENDI, (AHMED,) a Turkish diplomatist and writer, born in Erzroom, was sent as ambassador to Persia in 1720. Died in 1722.

See VON HAMMER, "Geschichte des Osmanischen Reichs."

Doppelmayr, dop'pĕl-mīr', written also **Doppelmaier** and **Doppelmayer,** (JOHANN GABRIEL,) a German mathematician, born at Nuremberg in 1671. He was professor of mathematics at Nuremberg from 1704 until 1750. In 1713 he was chosen Fellow of the Royal Society of London. He was skilful in polishing mirrors and grinding lenses for telescopes. Among his principal works are an "Introduction to Geography," (1714,) a "Celestial Atlas," in Latin, (1742,) and "Electric Phenomena recently discovered," (1744.) Near the end of his life he distinguished himself by his electrical experiments. Died in 1750.

See "Nouvelle Biographie Générale."

Doppert, dop'pĕRt, (JOHANN,) a German scholar, born at Frankfort-on-the-Main in 1671; died in 1735.

Doppet, do'pĕ', (FRANÇOIS AMÉDÉE,) a physician and general, born at Chambéry in 1753. He entered the army of the French republic about 1792, became general-in-chief of the army of the Alps, and directed the siege of Lyons in 1793. He exerted his power to prevent carnage and pillage at the capture of this city, and afterwards commanded in Spain. On account of ill health, he retired from service in 1794. He wrote medical and political treatises, romances, and memoirs of his own life. The last is his best work. Died about 1800.

See LAMARTINE, "History of the Girondists;" "Nouvelle Biographie Générale."

Dop'ping, (ANTHONY,) Bishop of Meath, was born in Dublin about 1642; died in 1697.

Doppler, dop'plĕr, (CHRISTIAN,) a German mathematician, born at Salzburg in 1803, became professor of experimental physics at Vienna in 1851.

Do'ran, (JOHN,) an English author, born in London in 1807. He was tutor of several young members of the English nobility, and passed some years in France. In 1822 he produced "The Wandering Jew," a melodrama. He contributed many articles in prose and verse to the periodicals, and wrote, among other works, "Table Traits," (1854,) "Habits and Men," "Knights and their Days," and "Monarchs Retired from Business," (1857,) which were favourably received.

See "Fraser's Magazine" for August, 1855.

Dorange, do'rŏNzh', (JACQUES NICOLAS PIERRE,) a French poet, born at Marseilles in 1786; died in 1811.

Dorat, do'rĕ', (CLAUDE JOSEPH,) a French poet, born in Paris in 1734, inherited an easy fortune, and had no profession but that of author. He wrote "Zulica," and other tragedies, some of which were moderately successful, several comedies, and numerous odes, poetical tales, and fugitive verses, which were favourably received. His "Theatrical Declamation" is considered his best poem. He was severely criticised by contemporary writers for his mannerism and *persiflage.* Died in 1780.

See GRIMM, "Correspondance;" MADAME DE GENLIS, "Mémoires:" LONGFELLOW, "Poets and Poetry of Europe."

Dorat or **Daurat,** do'rĕ', [Lat. AURA'TUS,] (JEAN,) a French poet, born at Limoges, in Limousin, about 1500. In 1560 he was appointed professor of Greek in the Royal College at Paris. Scaliger thought him a judicious critic. Dorat was one of the celebrated poetic "Pléiade," *i.e.* one of the seven most admired poets of the age. He wrote, in Latin, epigrams, odes, anagrams, etc. Charles IX. gave him the title of poet-royal. Died in 1588.

See "Ménagiana;" J. B. VITRAC, "Éloge de J. Dorat," 1775.

Dorat, (MADELEINE,) a daughter of the preceding, born in 1548, was versed in Greek, Latin, and other languages. Died in 1636.

Dorbay, doR'bĕ', (FRANÇOIS,) a French architect, born in Paris, was a pupil of L. Levau. He directed the execution of his master's designs for the College of Quatre-Nations, and was employed as architect on the Louvre and the Tuileries. He also gave the designs of several churches of Paris. Died in 1697.

Dordoni, doR-do'nee, (ANTONIO,) an Italian artist, born at Busseto, near Parma, in 1528, was one of the most excellent gem-engravers of his time. His works are very rare. Died in Rome in 1584.

Doré, do'rĕ', (GUSTAVE,) a French engraver and designer, born at Strasbourg about 1833, has acquired great popularity as an illustrator of the Bible and other works, among which are Tennyson's "Idylls," "Don Quixote," Dante's "Inferno," Rabelais, La Fontaine's "Fables," and "Paradise Lost." Doré is remarkable for the power and richness of his imagination, but is, generally speaking, more distinguished for the strength than for the delicacy or refinement of his conceptions.

See "North British Review" for September, 1867.

Doré, (PIERRE,) [Lat. PE'TRUS AURA'TUS,] a French theologian, born at Orléans about 1500, was a violent adversary of Protestantism. Died in 1559.

Doreid. See IBN-DOREID.

Dörfel or **Doerfel,** dör'fĕl, (GEORG SAMUEL,) a German astronomer of the latter half of the seventeenth century, was minister at Plauen, in Saxony. He wrote "Observations on the Comet of 1680," and discovered that the orbit of each comet is a parabola, of which the sun occupies the focus.

Dorfeuille, doR'fuI' or doR'fuh'ye, (ANTOINE,) a French Jacobin, born about 1750, rendered himself infamous by the massacre of a multitude of people at Lyons in 1793. He was killed in 1795.

Dörfling. See DERFFLINGER.

Dörfling or **Doerfling, von,** fon dör'fling, (GEORG,) a German general, born at Dorf, in Bohemia, in 1606. He fought for the Elector of Brandenburg, distinguished himself in many campaigns against the Poles, Swedes, and French, and was raised to the rank of field-marshal in 1670. Died in 1695.

Doria, do're-ă, one of the four most noble and powerful families of Genoa. The Dorias and Spinolas were Ghibelines, and the Grimaldi and Fieschi were Guelphs. The family of Doria was distinguished in the twelfth century. In 1339 these four families, which had long disturbed the state by their rivalry, were all exiled, and the nobles were excluded from power.

LAMBA DORIA was admiral of the Genoese fleet in 1298, when he gained a decisive victory over the Venetians near Corzola.

PAGANINO DORIA, a famous admiral, commanded in the third war against Venice. In 1352 a great naval battle was fought near Constantinople, between Admiral Doria and the Venetian admiral Pisani, in which the former was the victor. Doria gained another victory over Pisani in 1354.

PIETRO DORIA commanded the fleet in 1379, when he attempted to take Venice, but was defeated and killed in January, 1380.

Doria, (ANDREA,) known in English Histories as ANDREW DORIA, the restorer of Genoese liberty, born at Oneglia in 1468, was of the same family as the preceding. After serving several years in the armies of France and Naples, he entered the French navy about 1490, and soon acquired the reputation of the first admiral of his time. He commanded the fleet of Francis I. in his war with Charles V., and gained an advantage over the Imperialists at Marseilles. In 1528, suspecting the French court of treacherous designs against his country and himself, he made a treaty with Charles V., and stipulated for the liberation of Genoa, which was subject to the misrule of two rival factions,—the Adorni and Fregosi. He entered Genoa, was received with joy by the citizens, and gave them a free constitution, which has lasted, without any important change, until the present century. The senate voted to him the title of "Father of his Country." He declined the office of doge, that he might serve Charles V. as admiral against the Turks. In 1541 he commanded the fleet in Charles's unfortunate expedition against Algiers. That emperor rewarded him with the order of the Golden Fleece, and the titles of Prince of Melfi and Marquis of Tursi. At the age of eighty-five he conducted his fleet to the relief of Corsica, invaded by the French, from whom he took the sea-port of San Fiorenzo. He died, without issue, at Genoa, in November, 1560.

See CAPELLONI, "Vita del Principe Doria," 1565; CARLO SIGONIO, "De Vita et Gestis Andreæ Doriæ," 1586: ANDRÉ RICHER, "Vie d'André Doria," 1789; J. B. GIRALDI, "De Gestis Andreæ Doriæ," 1696; ANTONIO BIANCHINI, "Elogio del Principe Andrea Doria," 1781.

Doria, (ANTONIO,) a Genoese officer, who served with distinction under Charles V. He wrote an account of events which occurred in his time, "Compendio d'A. Doria," (1571.)

Doria, (OBERTO,) a Genoese admiral, commanded the fleet which gained a decisive victory over the naval force of Pisa in 1284.

Doria, (PAOLO MATTEO,) a philosopher, born at Naples in 1675, wrote, besides other works, "The Idea of a Perfect Republic," (suppressed by government.) Died in 1743.

Dorigny or **Dorigni,** do'rēn'ye', (LOUIS,) a French painter and engraver, born in Paris in 1654, was the son of Michel, noticed below, and was a pupil of Le Brun. He studied in Rome, and painted with success in Venice and Verona. In 1711 he was invited to Vienna, where he adorned the palace of Prince Eugene. His frescos in the cathedral of Trent are much admired. Died about 1742.

Dorigny or **Dorigni,** (MICHEL,) a painter and engraver, born at Saint-Quentin in 1617, was the pupil and son-in-law of Simon Vouet. He engraved with aqua-fortis, after Vouet and other masters. He died in 1663, leaving two sons, Louis and Nicolas, who were artists.

Dorigny, (Sir NICOLAS,) an eminent French engraver, born in Paris in 1657, was the son of the preceding. He studied his art in Rome, where he remained twenty-eight years and engraved many master-pieces, among which are "The Transfiguration," by Raphael, and "The Martyrdom of Saint Sebastian," by Domenichino. In 1711 he was invited to England, where he engraved the Cartoons of Raphael in Hampton Court, and was knighted by George I. In 1725 he was chosen a member and professor of the Academy of Painting in Paris. Died in 1746. He was perhaps second only to G. Audran among French engravers of history. He is praised as a "noble artist" in Addison's "Spectator," No. 226.

See BASAN, "Dictionnaire des Graveurs."

Dorimon, do're'mŏn', a French comic author and actor, flourished between 1650 and 1690.

Döring or **Doering,** dö'ring, (GEORG CHRISTIAN WILHELM ASMUS,) a German novelist, born at Cassel in 1789; died in 1833.

Döringk or **Doeringk,** written also **Döring** and **Dörink,** dö'rink, (MATTHÄUS,) a German theologian, born in Thuringia. He wrote a Chronicle of Misnia and Thuringia. Died about 1464.

Doriole or **Doriolle,** do're'ol', (PIERRE,) a French statesman, born at La Rochelle in 1407, was employed by Louis XI. in important missions. He became chancellor of France in 1472. Died in 1485.

Doriolle. See DORIOLE.

Dorion, do're'ŏN', (CLAUDE AUGUSTE,) a French poet, born at Nantes about 1770. He produced in 1809 "The Battle of Hastings," an epic poem, which obtained an honourable mention in the report on the decennial

prizes. He also wrote "The Conquest of Palmyra," a poem, and several odes and idyls. Died in 1829.

Do'ris, [Gr. Δωρίς,] a goddess of the sea, was a daughter of Oceanus and Tethys, and the wife of Nereus. The name was sometimes applied by the poets to the sea itself.

Dorislaus, do'ris-lā'ŭs, (ISAAC,) a Dutch lawyer, who removed to England and in the civil war acted with the republicans. He was employed by them at the trial of Charles I., and in 1649 was sent as minister to Holland. Soon after his arrival at the Hague he was murdered by some English royalists, in 1650.

Dorival, do're'vȧl', (CLAUDE FRANÇOIS,) surnamed PLUME D'OR, (plüm doR,) a French jurist, born at Besançon in 1656; died in 1733.

Dorléans, doR'lā'ŏN', or **D'Orléans,** (LOUIS,) a Frenchman, born in Paris in 1542, was a partisan of the League, and wrote libels against Henry IV. Died in 1629.

Dorléans or **D'Orléans,** (PIERRE JOSEPH,) a French historian, born at Bourges in 1644. He professed belles-lettres in various colleges of the Jesuits, and was employed in preaching. Voltaire has remarked that he was the first historian who chose revolutions as his special subject. He produced in 1693 a "History of the Revolutions of England," which was esteemed even by fastidious critics, and was followed by a "History of the Revolutions of Spain." He had the art of discerning what events were most worthy of notice, and of narrating them in an agreeable manner. Died in 1698.

Dorléans de la Mothe, doR'lā'ŏN' deh lȧ mot, (LOUIS FRANÇOIS GABRIEL,) Bishop of Amiens, was born at Carpentras in 1683; died in 1774.

Dormans, de, deh doR'mŏN', (JEAN,) a French cardinal, born at Dormans. He was Bishop of Beauvais when Charles V., about 1364, appointed him chancellor of France and keeper of the seals. In 1368 he was made a cardinal. He founded the College of Beauvais at Paris in 1370. Died in 1373.

Dorn, doRn, (JOHANN CHRISTOPH,) a German bibliographer, born at Schleusingen. He published "Bibliotheca theologico-critica," (2 vols., 1721.) Died in 1752.

Dornau, doR'now, (CASPAR,) a German physician and writer, born in Thuringia in 1577; died in 1632.

Dorner, doR'ner, (ISAAC AUGUST,) a German Protestant theologian, born at Neuhausen-ob-Eck, in Würtemberg, in 1809, became in 1849 professor of theology at Bonn. He wrote a "History of the Development of the Doctrine of the Person of Christ," (1839,) an excellent and exhaustive work, and a "History of Protestant Theology, particularly in Germany," ("Geschichte der Protestantischen Theologie, besonders in Deutschland," etc., 1867,) which displays not only profound learning, but great critical ability.

Dornmeyer, doRn'mi'er, (ANDREAS JULIUS,) a German critic and philologist, born at Lauenstadt in 1674. His chief work is "Philologia Sacra." Died in 1717.

Dor-o-the'a, [Fr. DOROTHÉE, do'ro'tā',] SAINT, a Christian virgin of Alexandria, lived about 310 A.D. She is said by some writers to have suffered martyrdom; but Eusebius states that she was deprived of her property and banished. Her life has furnished the subject of Massinger's drama of "The Virgin Martyr."

See EUSEBIUS, "Ecclesiastical History;" MRS. JAMESON, "History of Sacred and Legendary Art."

Dorothée. See DOROTHEA and DOROTHEUS.

Do-ro'the-us, [Gr. Δωρόθεος; Fr. DOROTHÉE, do'ro'tā',] a Greek author, of whom little is known. He wrote a "History of Alexander the Great," which is quoted by Athenæus.

Dorotheus, an eminent jurist, lived at Ber'ytus, and was one of the compilers of Justinian's "Digest." He flourished about 533 A.D.

Dorotheus OF SIDON, a Greek poet, lived probably before the Christian era.

Dorow, do'ro, (WILHELM,) a German antiquary, born at Königsberg in 1790. He visited Italy in 1827, and made a large collection of Etruscan antiquities, which are now in the museum of Berlin. He published "Monuments of Ancient Art and Language," (1824,) "Etruria and the Orient," (1829,) and other works. Died in 1846.

Dorpius, doR'pe-ŭs, (MARTIN,) a Dutch scholar, born at Naeldwyck about 1480. He professed eloquence and philosophy at Lille, and was the head of a college in Louvain when he died in 1525. He was highly esteemed by Erasmus, who wrote his epitaph. Dorpius left a discourse in praise of Aristotle, and a few other small works.

See FOPPENS, "Bibliotheca Belgica."

Dorr, (THOMAS W.,) an American politician, born at Providence, Rhode Island, in 1805. He became the leader of the suffrage party, which in 1841 framed a new Constitution, under which he was elected Governor. These movements were treated as seditious by the government acting under the old charter, and both parties appealed to arms, (1842.) Dorr was arrested, convicted of treason, and sentenced to imprisonment for life. He was pardoned in 1847. Died in 1854.

. See "Democratic Review" for August, 1842.

Dorsanne, doR'săn', (ANTOINE,) a French priest, born at Issoudun, was a friend of Cardinal De Noailles, Archbishop of Paris, who appointed him a canon of his church. He took a prominent part against the Jesuits and the bull Unigenitus, and was employed by Cardinal de Noailles in the negotiations with which he amused the court of Rome and France. Dorsanne left a "Journal of what passed at Rome and in France on the Subject of the Bull Unigenitus." Died in 1728.

Dorsch, doRSH, (EVERARD,) a German engraver of gems, born at Nuremberg in 1649; died in 1712.

Dorsch, (JOHANN CHRISTOPH,) a German gem-engraver, son of the preceding, born in 1676; died in 1732.

Dorsenne, doR'sĕn', (JEAN MARIE FRANÇOIS,) a French officer, born at Ardres (Pas-de-Calais) in 1773. In 1809 he became a general of division, and in 1811 commanded an army in the north of Spain. Died in 1812.

Dor'set, (CHARLES SACKVILLE,) sixth EARL OF, son of Richard, Earl of Dorset, born in 1637, was a distinguished courtier, wit, and patron of letters. In youth he bore the title of Lord Buckhurst, and was a decided libertine; but his courage, good nature, and other redeeming qualities rendered him a general favourite. He had too little ambition, or too much indolence, to raise himself to the highest political positions to which his talents were adequate. "He became," says Macaulay, "an intellectual voluptuary, and a master of all those pleasing branches of knowledge which can be acquired without severe application. . . . Such a patron of letters England had never seen. His bounty was bestowed with equal judgment and liberality. Dryden owned that he had been saved from ruin by his princely generosity." In 1665 he served as volunteer in the naval war against the Dutch, during which he wrote the admired song beginning "To all you ladies now on land." He became Earl of Dorset at the death of his father in 1677, after which he married the daughter of the Earl of Northampton. At the accession of William III. (1689) he accepted the office of lord chamberlain, which he resigned in 1697. Died in 1706. He was the author of a few songs and satires, which, says Macaulay, "sparkle with wit as splendid as that of Butler." Pope wrote his epitaph, which contains these lines,—

"Bless'd courtier, who could king and country please,
Yet sacred keep his friendships and his ease."

See MACAULAY, "History of England," vol. ii. chap. viii., vol. iii. chap. i., and vol. iv. chap. xxii.

Dorset, (EDWARD SACKVILLE,) fourth EARL OF, born in 1590, was the grandson of the first earl. He was sent on an embassy to France in 1621. In 1624, by the death of his brother Richard, he became Earl of Dorset. He was chosen president of the council in 1641. In the civil war he was a royalist, and fought bravely at Edgehill. He died in 1652, leaving his title to his son Richard. A number of his speeches were published between 1620 and 1644. He was an excellent master of speech and composition. Clarendon says "his wit was pleasant, sparkling, and sublime." ("History of the Rebellion.")

See, also, ERSCH und GRUBER, "Allgemeine Encyklopaedie."

Dorset, (RICHARD SACKVILLE,) third EARL OF, the eldest son of Robert, Earl of Dorset, was born in London in 1589. In 1609 he married Anne Clifford, who was eminent for her noble spirit, attainments, and munificence, and was afterwards known as the Countess of Dorset and Pembroke. (See CLIFFORD, ANNE.) He died in 1624, when the title passed to his brother Edward.

Dorset, (RICHARD SACKVILLE,) fifth EARL OF, born in 1622, was the father of Charles, the celebrated courtier and patron, and the son of Edward, Earl of Dorset, noticed above. He wrote a "Poetical Address to the Memory of Ben Jonson." Died in 1677.

Dorset, (THOMAS SACKVILLE,) first EARL OF, an English statesman and poet, born at Buckhurst in 1536, was the son of Sir Richard Sackville. He was a graduate of Cambridge, and a lawyer by profession. In his youth he cultivated poetry with success. He wrote the much-admired "Induction to the Mirror for Magistrates," (see BALDWIN, WILLIAM,) and the tragedy of "Gorboduc, or Ferrer and Porrex," (1565,) which, says Sir Philip Sidney, "is full of stately speeches and well-sounding phrases, climbing to the height of Seneca's style, and as full of notable morality." It was the first regular or respectable tragedy that appeared in the English language. He was created Lord Buckhurst in 1566, and was minister to France in 1570. In 1587 he was sent to the Netherlands to inquire into the difficulties between the States and Leicester, the governor-general. He fulfilled this mission with great sagacity and impartiality; but, having expressed a judgment unfavourable to Leicester, he was banished from court and imprisoned in his own house till the death of that favourite. (See Motley's "United Netherlands," chaps. xv. and xvi.) In 1598 he succeeded Lord Burleigh as lord treasurer of England, which office he retained with honour until his death, in 1608. He had been created Earl of Dorset by James I., and left the title to his son Robert.

See "Biographia Britannica."

Dor'sey, (JOHN SYNG,) M.D., an eminent physician and surgeon of Philadelphia, was born in that city in 1783. He studied in London, where he attended the lectures of Humphry Davy, the distinguished chemist; he afterwards attended the medical schools of Paris. In 1813 he was appointed to the chair of materia medica in the University of Pennsylvania, and in 1818 succeeded Wistar as professor of anatomy, but died the same year. His "Elements of Surgery" (1813) had a European reputation, and was long popular in this country. Dr. Dorsey was a nephew of the celebrated Dr. Physick.

See S. D. GROSS, "American Medical Biography."

Dorsten, doR'stĕn, (JOHANN DANIEL,) a German medical writer, born at Marburg in 1643; died in 1706.

Dorthes, doRT, (JACQUES ANSELME,) a French entomologist, born at Nîmes in 1759; died in 1794.

Dortoman, doR'to-mân', (NICOLAAS,) a physician, born at Arnheim, in Holland, became professor of medicine at Montpellier, and afterwards physician-in-ordinary to Henry IV. of France. Died in 1596.

Dortous. See MAIRAN.

Do'rus, [Gr. Δῶρος,] a mythical person, from whom the Dorians claimed their descent. He was commonly regarded as a son of Hellen.

Dorval, doR'văl', (MARIE AMÉLIE THOMAS DELAUNAY,) MADAME, a popular French actress, born at Lorient in 1801; died in 1849.

Dorvigny, doR'vĕn'ye', (LOUIS,) a French comic writer, born at Versailles in 1743. His comedy of "Janot, ou les Battus payent l'Amende," (1779,) obtained great success. Died in 1812.

Dorville. See CONTANT D'ORVILLE.

Dorvo, doR'vo', (HYACINTHE,) a French poet and dramatic writer, born at Rennes in 1769. He wrote many popular comedies. Died in 1851.

Dosi, do'see, (GIROLAMO,) an eminent Italian architect, born at Carpi in 1695, was a pupil of Fontana. He went to Rome, and became the architect of Pope Clement XII. He displayed his talents on the Villa Cibo, the Lazaretto of Ancona, the basilica of Santa Maria Maggiore, and other edifices. Died in 1775.

Do-sī'a-das OF RHODES, a Greek poetaster of an unknown epoch, is mentioned by Lucian. He wrote a poem in the figure of an altar, which is extant.

Dosio, do'se-o, (GIOVANNI ANTONIO,) an Italian sculptor, born in 1533. He made statues and bas-reliefs for the Belvedere palace, Rome. Died about 1600.

Do-sith'e-us OF COLONE, a Greek geometer, lived about 220 B.C. Archimedes dedicated to him several treatises.

Dositheus, [Fr. DOSITHÉE, do'ze'tǎ',] a Jewish impostor or magician of Samaria, lived in the first century. He pretended to be the Messiah.

Dositheus surnamed MAGIS'TER, a Greek grammarian, lived about 300 A.D.

See SMITH's "Dictionary of Greek and Roman Biography and Mythology."

Dosma-Delgado, dos'mǎ dĕl-gǎ'DO, (RODRIGO,) a Spanish theologian and linguist, born at Badajos in 1533 ; died in 1607.

D'Ossat. See OSSAT.

Dossi, dos'see, (DOSSO,) an Italian painter, born at or near Ferrara in 1474, was the friend of Ariosto, who has commemorated him among the eminent artists of that age. He painted an admirable portrait of Ariosto. He had a brother Giobattista, who worked with him in Ferrara and was an excellent landscape-painter. As Dosso excelled in the human figure, they were often employed on the same picture. Dosso died in 1558. Among their master-pieces is an oil-painting of the four Fathers Ambrose, Augustine, Gregory, and Jerome consulting together.

See NAGLER, "Neues Allgemeines Künstler-Lexikon."

Dos'sie, (ROBERT,) an English apothecary or chemist, who lived in London, published "Institutes of Experimental Chemistry." Died in 1777.

Dost- (dŏst) **Mo-ham'med,** Emir of Cabool, an Affghan chief, was born about 1798. He began to reign at Cabool about 1826, was expelled by a British army in 1840, and was restored in 1843. He was an ambitious and warlike ruler. Died about 1857.

See MOHUN LAL, "Life of Dost-Mohammed," 2 vols., 1846.

Dotteville, dot'vĕl', (JEAN HENRI,) a French translator, born at Palaiseau in 1716, produced a translation of Sallust, (1749,) which is commended, and a version of the "Annals" of Tacitus, (1774.) Died in 1807.

Dotti, dot'tee, (BARTOLOMMEO,) an Italian satirical poet, born at Valcanonico in 1642, lived some years in Venice. His personal satires gave great offence. He published a volume of verses called "Rime e Sonnetti," ("Verses and Sonnets,") and wrote "The Carnival" and other satires. He was assassinated in 1712.

Dottori, di, de dot-to'ree, (CARLO,) COUNT, an Italian poet, born at Padua in 1624, wrote "Aristodemo," a tragedy, often reprinted, and other poems. Died in 1686.

Dou, (GERARD.) See DOW.

Douaren, doo'ǎ'rŏN', or **Duaren,** dü'ǎ'rŏN', [Lat. DOUARE'NUS,] (FRANÇOIS,) a French jurist, born in Bretagne about 1509. He professed law at Bourges for some years, and in 1548 began to practise in Paris. He was reputed one of the most learned jurists of his time, particularly in civil law, and published many legal works. He also wrote a curious treatise on Plagiaries. Died at Bourges in 1559.

See ZEIDLER, "Vita Douareni," 1768; BAYLE, "Historical and Critical Dictionary."

Double, doobl, (FRANÇOIS·JOSEPH,) a French physician, born at Verdun-sur-Garonne in 1776, practised in Paris with success. He had a share in the discovery and application of quinine by Pelletier, his brother-in-law. Died in 1842.

Doub'le-day, (dŭb'l'dā,) (ABNER,) an American general, born in Saratoga county, New York, about 1820, graduated at West Point in 1842. He was a captain before the civil war, and was one of the garrison of Fort Sumter, April, 1861. He commanded a division at the battle of Antietam, September 17, 1862, and a corps at Gettysburg, July 2 and 3, 1863. In September, 1867, he obtained the rank of colonel in the regular army.

Doub'le-day, (EDWARD,) an English naturalist, born in 1810. He visited the United States for scientific purposes. After his return home he was one of the curators of the British Museum, where he gave much attention to the study of insects. His principal work is "On the Genera of Diurnal Lepidoptera," which he continued to issue in parts until his death. He also published a treatise on the "Nomenclature of British Birds," and other works. Died in London in 1849.

Doublet, doo'blǎ', (FRANÇOIS,) a French physician, born at Chartres in 1751. In 1794 he was appointed professor of pathology in the École de Santé, Paris. He

wrote medical articles for the "Encyclopédie Méthodique," a treatise on "Reform in Prisons," and one on "Puerperal Fever." Died in 1795.

See DOUBLET DE BOISTHIBAULT, "Notice sur la Vie de F. Doublet," 1826.

Douce, dŏwss, (FRANCIS,) an English antiquary, born in 1762. He was a diligent collector of rare and curious books, prints, coins, etc., was a Fellow of the Antiquarian Society, and at one time keeper of the manuscripts in the British Museum. He wrote several papers for the "Archæologia," and published "Illustrations of Shakspeare," (1807.) Died in 1834.

See WILLIAM JERDAN, "Men I have known," London, 1866.

Doucet, doo'sǎ', (CHARLES CAMILLE,) a French dramatist, born in Paris in 1812.

Doucin, doo'sǎN', (LOUIS,) a French Jesuit, born at Vernon in 1652. He gained a reputation by his writings, among which are a "History of Nestorianism," (1693,) and a "History of Origenism," (1700.) These are said to be interesting and well written. He took a prominent part as the supporter of the bull "Unigenitus" against Jansenism. Died in 1726.

Doudeauville, de, dĕh doo'dō'vĕl', (AMBROISE POLYCARPE **de la Rochefoucauld,** dĕh lǎ rosh'foo'kō', Duc, a philanthropic nobleman, born in Paris in 1765; died in 1841.

Doudyns, dŏw'dïns, or **Dodvens,** (WILLEM,) a Dutch painter, born at the Hague in 1650. He studied in Rome for twelve years, after which he returned to the Hague and worked with great success. Descamps praises his composition, design, and colour. One of his works represents "Time, which discovers Truth and Deception." Died in 1697.

See DESCAMPS, "Vies des Peintres Flamands, Hollandais," etc.

Doueli-al-Basri. See DUALI-AL-BASREE.

Douffet or **Douffeit.** See DUFFET.

Dougados, doo'gǎ'dos', (JEAN FRANÇOIS,) a French poet, born at Carcassonne in 1763. In his youth he turned monk, and assumed the name of PÈRE VENANCE. He entered the army in 1791, rose to the rank of adjutant-general, and was executed by the Jacobins in 1794. He was author of a "Christmas Hymn," and of other verses.

Doughty, dŏw'te, (THOMAS,) an American landscape-painter, born in Philadelphia in 1793. He learned the trade of a tanner and currier, but relinquished that business about 1820 for landscape-painting, which he followed many years in the United States, and afterwards in London and Paris. Died in New York in 1856.

See TUCKERMAN, "Book of the Artists."

Douglas, dug'lass, an ancient noble family of Scotland, which traces its ancestry as far back as the twelfth century. The Earls of Douglas, the Earls of Angus, and the Earls of Morton belonged to this family. Sir James Douglas, surnamed THE GOOD, was the founder of their fame and grandeur. He commanded the left wing at Bannockburn in 1314, and was killed by the Saracens in Spain about 1330, in a pilgrimage to Palestine, whither he was going to deposit the heart of Robert Bruce. As he left no lawful issue, he was succeeded by his brothers Hugh and Archibald. The latter, who was killed at the battle of Halidon Hill in 1333, left a son William, who became the first Earl of Douglas and married for his third wife the heiress of the Earl of Angus. He died in 1384, leaving two sons, James, second Earl of Douglas, and George, Earl of Angus. James, second Earl, married Margaret, a daughter of King Robert II. He was a famous warrior, and was killed at the battle of Otterburn in 1388. As he left no male issue, the earldom passed to Archibald the Grim, third Earl, who fought for the French at Poitiers and died about 1400. He was succeeded by his son Archibald, fourth Earl, who married a daughter of King Robert III. He displayed great courage at the battle of Shrewsbury, (1403,) where he fought against Henry IV., and rendered important military services to Charles VII. of France, who rewarded him with the duchy of Touraine. He was killed at the battle of Verneuil, in France, in 1424. His son Archibald, the fifth Earl of Douglas, was chosen a member of the regency at the death of James I., (1437.) He died in 1438, leaving his title to his son William, the sixth Earl, who was born about 1425. William, charged with ambitious designs or contempt for the authority of the infant king, was beheaded in 1440, or, as some say, in 1437. The earldom of Douglas then passed to James, an uncle or grand-uncle of William. James was succeeded by William, eighth Earl. (See separate article.)

See ROBERTSON, "History of Scotland."

Douglas, (ARCHIBALD,) fifth Earl of Angus, grandson of George, above named, was lord chancellor about the end of the fifteenth century. He was a powerful, ambitious, and lawless subject. He was called "the Great Earl of Angus," and also surnamed "Bell-the-Cat." He had several sons, one of whom was Gavin, the poet and bishop. (See separate notice below.) Died about 1514. Archibald VI., grandson of the fifth Earl of Angus, and son of George, was lord chancellor about 1527. He married in 1514 Margaret, queen-dowager of James IV. and sister of Henry VIII. He died in 1567, leaving a daughter, who was the mother of Lord Darnley. George, a nephew of the sixth Earl, inherited his title, and had a younger brother, who became Earl of Morton, afterwards Regent Morton in the time of Queen Mary Stuart. William, the son of the tenth Earl of Angus, in 1633 was created Marquis of Douglas, and his son Archibald was created Earl of Ormond by Charles II.

Douglas, (Sir CHARLES,) a Scottish naval officer, the father of General Sir Howard Douglas. He commanded a squadron in the Gulf of Saint Lawrence in 1775. In 1781 he was appointed first captain to Admiral Rodney, and contributed to the victory gained by him over the French in the West Indies, April 12 of that year. In 1787 he was made rear-admiral. Died in 1789.

See CHAMBERS, "Biographical Dictionary of Eminent Scotsmen."

Douglas, (DAVID,) an eminent Scottish botanist, born at Scone, in Perthshire, in 1798. He served an apprenticeship as a gardener, and worked in the botanic garden of the University of Glasgow. About 1823–24 he was employed by the London Horticultural Society as a botanical collector in the United States, and extended his researches as far as Oregon and California. He returned in 1827 with many valuable acquisitions for English flower-gardens. A few years later he sailed for America on a similar mission, and visited the Sandwich Islands, where he was killed, in 1834, by a wild bull which had been entrapped in a pit, he himself having soon after accidentally fallen into the same pit.

See CHAMBERS, "Biographical Dictionary of Eminent Scotsmen," (Supplement.)

Douglas, dŭg′lạss, (FREDERICK,) a distinguished American orator, originally a mulatto slave, born in Talbot county, Maryland, about 1817. He escaped from his master in 1838, and went to New Bedford, Massachusetts. About 1841 he began to deliver lectures against slavery, which attracted much attention throughout the Northern States. He published his Autobiography in 1845, after which he visited England, where he made anti-slavery speeches and drew large audiences by his earnest and brilliant eloquence. He edited at Rochester, New York, a paper called "The North Star." "His glow and fervour," says Mr. T. W. Higginson, "are extraordinary, and so is his dramatic power; and he surpasses in his perception of the finer felicities of the English language all other self-made men whom I have ever known."

See "My Bondage and my Freedom," by FREDERICK DOUGLAS.

Douglas, (GAVIN or GAWIN,) a Scottish poet, born about 1474, was the third son of Archibald, fifth Earl of Angus. He finished his education in the University of Paris, and entered the Church. In 1515 he was appointed bishop of Dunkeld. His reputation as a poet is founded chiefly on his translation of Virgil's "Æneid" into Scottish verse, (1513,) which was the first version of a classic into any British language. "This translation," says Warton, "is executed with equal spirit and fidelity. The several books are introduced with metrical prologues, which are often highly poetical." His principal original poem is "The Palace of Honour." Died in 1522.

See IRVING, "Lives of the Scottish Poets;" CHAMBERS, "Biographical Dictionary of Eminent Scotsmen."

Douglas. See MORTON, EARL OF, and ORMOND, EARL OF.

Douglas, dŭg′lạss, (Sir HOWARD,) a British general, born at Gosport, in Hampshire, in 1776, was a son of Admiral Sir Charles Douglas. He served in the Peninsula from 1808 to 1812, and published an "Essay on Military Bridges," (1816.) His "Treatise on Naval Gunnery," approved by the admiralty, was published in 1819, (4th edition, 1855.) He was Governor of New Brunswick from 1823 to 1829, was elected to Parliament in 1842, and obtained the rank of general in 1851. Died in November, 1861.

See "Blackwood's Magazine" for May, 1863.

Douglas, (JAMES,) ninth and last EARL OF, a brother of William the eighth Earl, raised an army against the king, but was taken prisoner, and confined until his death in 1488.

Douglas, (JAMES,) M.D., an eminent Scottish anatomist, born in 1675, resided and practised in London. He gained a high reputation as a surgeon and a writer on anatomy, and became physician to the king. He lectured many years on anatomy and surgery. Haller, who visited him, calls him a "learned and skilful person." He published a "Description of the Peritonæum," "Myographiæ comparatæ Specimen," (1707,) and other works. Died in 1742.

See CHAMBERS, "Biographical Dictionary of Eminent Scotsmen."

Douglas, (JOHN,) a brother of the preceding, was surgeon to the Westminster Infirmary. He was distinguished as a lithotomist, and was the author of several professional works, among which is a "Treatise on the Utility of Bark as a Remedy for Mortification."

See CHAMBERS, "Biographical Dictionary of Eminent Scotsmen."

Douglas, (JOHN,) F.R.S., a Scottish bishop, born in Fifeshire in 1721. He was eminent for learning and literary ability. In 1750 he published a "Vindication of Milton from Lauder's Charge of Plagiarism," and in 1754 "The Criterion of Miracles," in which he refuted the sophistries of Hume. He was appointed one of the king's chaplains in 1761, Bishop of Carlisle in 1787, and of Salisbury in 1791. As a member of Dr. Johnson's Club, he is noticed in Goldsmith's "Retaliation" in these terms :

"Here Douglas retires, from his toils to relax,
The scourge of impostors, the terror of quacks."

Died in 1807.

See a "Memoir of Bishop Douglas," prefixed to his Select Works, by W. MACDONALD, 1820.

Douglas, (STEPHEN ARNOLD,) an American politician, born at Brandon, Rutland county, Vermont, in April, 1813. He studied in an academy at Canandaigua, New York, from 1830 to 1833. He adopted the profession of law, removed to Illinois in 1833, and began to practise at Jacksonville. He soon became an active politician and a popular orator of the Democratic party, who, in allusion to his small stature, gave him the name of "the Little Giant." He was nominated for Congress in 1838, but was defeated by a small majority. In the canvass for President in 1840 he distinguished himself as a "stump speaker." He was elected a judge of the supreme court of Illinois in February, 1841. In 1843 he was elected a member of Congress, in which he advocated the annexation of Texas to the Union. He represented Illinois in the Senate of the United States from March, 1847, to 1853, during which term he was chairman of the committee on territories. He married a Miss Martin in 1847.

He supported Clay's "Compromise measures" of 1850, and in relation to the extension of slavery in the territories maintained that Congress should not interfere, but that the people of each territory should be permitted to decide whether it should be a free State or a slave State. This was called the doctrine of "Popular Sovereignty," of which Douglas was the reputed author. He was re-elected a Senator of the United States for a term of six years, 1853–59. In January, 1854, he reported from the committee on territories an important bill to organize the territories of Nebraska and Kansas. This bill, which was afterwards passed, and by which the Missouri Compromise was repealed, produced a great excitement, and was denounced by many Northern Democrats, who on this account separated from their party.

In the National Democratic Convention of 1856, Buchanan and Douglas were rival candidates for the nomina-

ϵ as k; ç as s; g hard; g as j; G, H, K, guttural; N, nasal; R, trilled; s as z; th as in this. (☞ See Explanations, p. 23.)

tion, which the former obtained. Douglas opposed the admission of Kansas in 1857 under the Lecompton Constitution, and was thus involved in a controversy with President Buchanan and a majority of his party in the Senate. This affair caused a division in the Democratic party, and those who acted with Douglas were styled Anti-Lecompton Democrats. Henceforth Buchanan and Douglas were bitter enemies. In 1858 Illinois was the arena of a memorable contest between Douglas and Abraham Lincoln, who were competitors for the office of Senator of the United States, and canvassed the State in joint discussions at various places. (See LINCOLN, ABRAHAM.) Douglas gained his election as Senator, receiving 54 votes out of 100.

He was supported by a majority of Northern Democrats as candidate for President at the National Convention which met at Charleston in April, 1860. This convention adopted a platform which was in accordance with his policy and was not satisfactory to the extreme Southern politicians. The delegations of Alabama, Mississippi, South Carolina, Georgia, Louisiana, Arkansas, and Florida then withdrew from the convention. On the first ballot Douglas received 145 votes, and no other candidate received more than 42. Having taken more than fifty ballots without effecting a nomination, the convention adjourned, to meet in Baltimore in June. He received 181 votes at Baltimore, and was declared the regular nominee. The seceders nominated John C. Breckinridge, and thus rendered the election of Douglas almost hopeless. The latter, however, advocated his cause by many public speeches in the Northern and Southern States. At the end of the contest Douglas received only twelve electoral votes. After the rebellion began, he supported the government in efforts to suppress it. On the 25th of April, 1861, he made a patriotic speech at Springfield, Illinois, before the legislature. He died at Chicago in June, 1861, leaving several children.

See J. W. SHEAHAN, "Life of Stephen A. Douglas," 1860.

Douglas, (SYLVESTER,) Lord Glenbervie, a Scottish lawyer, born at Ellon in 1743, lived in England. He attained eminence in his profession, and published "Reports in King's Bench," which are high authority. He was appointed secretary for Ireland in 1793, was made Lord Glenbervie in 1800, and held several high civil offices. His wife was a daughter of the celebrated Lord North. He was repeatedly elected to Parliament. Died in 1823.

Douglas, (WILLIAM,) Lord of Nithsdale, called "the Black Douglas," was a formidable enemy to the English. He was assassinated by Lord Clifford, about 1390.

Douglas, (WILLIAM,) eighth EARL OF, was an imperious and turbulent person. Having defied the royal authority, he was killed by King James II. during a conference in 1452.

Douglas, (WILLIAM,) first MARQUIS OF, the son of the tenth Earl of Angus, was created a marquis in 1633. His son Archibald became Earl of Ormond; his second son, William, was made Earl of Selkirk, and, after his marriage with the Duchess of Hamilton, obtained the title of Duke of Hamilton. (See HAMILTON.) The third Marquis of Douglas was made Duke of Douglas, and died in 1761, when the dukedom became extinct, and the marquisate devolved on the seventh Duke of Hamilton. The Dukes of Queensberry are also a branch of the house of Douglas.

Douglas, (Sir WILLIAM,) Knight of Liddesdale, was a natural son of "the good Sir James," and was called "England's scourge and Scotland's bulwark." He was assassinated in 1353.

See CHAMBERS, "Biographical Dictionary of Eminent Scotsmen," (Supplement.)

Douglas, (Sir WILLIAM,) of Glenbervie, a son of Archibald "Bell-the-Cat," was killed at the battle of Flodden, (1513.) His brother GEORGE, Master of Angus, was also killed in the same battle.

Douglass, dŭg′lass, (DAVID BATES,) LL.D., an American engineer, born in Pompton, New Jersey, in 1790. He was for many years professor of natural philosophy, engineering, etc. at West Point. He was chief engineer in projecting the New York Croton Aqueduct in 1833 –34, and president of Kenyon College, Ohio, from 1840 to 1844. Died in 1849.

Doujat, doo′zhă′, (JEAN,) an eminent French scholar and jurist, born at Toulouse in 1606. In 1650 he was received in the French Academy, and in 1655 was appointed doctor-regent of the Faculty of Law in Paris, and afterwards historiographer of France. He wrote a "History of Canon Law," (1677,) and other works, and edited Livy "ad usum Delphini." Died in 1688.

See TAISAND, "Vies des Jurisconsultes."

Doulcet. See PONTÉCOULANT.

Doulet-Shâh or **Douletschah,** dŏw′let-shâh′, a Persian of the fifteenth century, who wrote "Memoirs of Persian and Arabian Poets," (1487.)

Doultreman. See OULTREMAN, D'.

Dounot, doo′no′, a French mathematician and jurist, born at Bar-le-Duc, produced the first complete French version of "Euclid," (1610.) He was highly esteemed by Descartes. Died in 1640.

Dourga. See DURGA.

Douri, doo′re′, (FRÉMIN,) a French scholar and poet, born in Normandy in 1512; died in 1578.

Dourri. See DOORREE.

Dousa, dŏw′să, (GEORG,) a Dutch scholar, son of Jan Dousa, noticed below, was born about 1574. He wrote verses in Greek and Latin, and translated a work of Codinus. In 1597 he visited Constantinople, where he collected old manuscripts and inscriptions. After his return he published a "Letter on a Journey to Constantinople." Died about 1600.

Two younger brothers of the preceding, FRANCIS and THEODORE, were literary men, and editors of several works.

Dousa, or **Van der Does,** vǎn der doos, written also **Douza,** (JAN,) Lord of Noordwyck, a distinguished Dutch Protestant statesman and scholar, born at Noordwyk in 1545. He concurred in the efforts to liberate Holland from Philip II. of Spain, and was governor of Leyden in 1574 when it was besieged by the Spaniards. He displayed wisdom and firmness in this memorable siege. After the siege was raised, the University of Leyden was founded by his agency, and he was chosen first curator. In 1585 he was appointed keeper of the archives of Holland. Dousa and his son John wrote the "Annals of Holland," in Latin verse and prose, (1601,) which added to his high reputation. He was a diligent student of history, and wrote Latin odes for recreation. He also published notes on Horace and other classics. Died in 1604.

See MOTLEY, "Rise of the Dutch Republic," part iv. chap. ii.; DANIEL HEINSIUS, "Laudatio J. Dousæ," 1605.

Dousa, (JAN,) a son of the preceding, born in 1571, was proficient in the languages and sciences. He was chosen librarian of the University of Leyden in 1591, assisted his father in the "Annals of Holland," and wrote the first part of an admired Latin poem on astronomy, ("Rerum Cœlestium Liber,") which was not finished when he died prematurely in 1596. Joseph J. Scaliger lamented his death in an "Epicedium."

See VERUEL, "Redevoeringen over J. Dousa en over J. Bellamy," 1791; M. SIEGENBEEK, "Laudatio J. Dousæ," 1812.

Doussin-Dubreuil, doo′săN′ dü′brŭl′ or dü′brŭh′ye, (JACQUES LOUIS,) a French physician, born at Saintes in 1762; died at Paris in 1831.

Douven, dŏw′ven or doo′ven, (JOHN FRANCIS,) a skilful portrait-painter, born at Roermont, near Cleves, in 1656. He removed to Dusseldorf about 1684, and afterwards worked in Vienna, Denmark, and Florence. He received the title of first painter to the emperor Leopold, and is said to have painted three emperors, five kings, and seven queens. Died at Prague in 1710.

See DESCAMPS, "Vies des Peintres Flamands," etc.

Douville, doo′vêl′, (JEAN BAPTISTE,) a French traveller, born in Manche in 1794. He returned to France in 1831, after an absence of some years, with an account of pretended discoveries in Congo, and published a book called "Travels in Congo," (1832,) which was at first received with favour by the learned, who were soon convinced that they had been deceived. He visited in 1833 the valley of the Amazon, where he is supposed to have been killed.

See DOUVILLE, "Trente Mois de ma Vie," etc., 1833; "Foreign Quarterly Review" for August, 1832.

Douvre, de, dĕh doo′vẹr, (THOMAS,) born in 1027, became Archbishop of York in 1070. Died in 1100.

Douw. See DOW.

Douza. See DOUSA.

Dovalle, do′vȧl′, (CHARLES,) a distinguished French poet, born at Montreuil-Bellay in 1807, was the author of an admired poem, entitled "L'Oratoire du Jardin," and a song on Liberty, which was commended by Béranger. He was killed in a duel by M. Mira in 1829.

See "Nouvelle Biographie Générale."

Dove, do′vẹh, (HEINRICH WILHELM,) an eminent German meteorologist, born at Liegnitz, in Silesia, in 1803, became professor of physics in the University of Berlin in 1829. He made extensive observations and researches into the laws of climate and atmospheric phenomena, and published many works, among which are "Meteorological Researches," (1837,) a "Treatise on the Electricity of Induction," (1843,) and "On Electricity," (1848.)

Dover, LORD. See ELLIS, (GEORGE J. WELLBORE AGAR.)

Dovizi or **Dovizio.** See BIBBIENA.

Dŏw, (ALEXANDER,) COLONEL, a Scottish writer, born at Crieff, became secretary to the Governor of Bencoolen. He published a "History of Hindostan," (1767,) from the Persian of Ferishta, preceded by an "Inquiry into the State of Bengal," and an "Essay on the Origin and Nature of Despotism in Hindostan," which are works of merit and display much acquaintance with Oriental literature. Died in 1779.

Dow or **Douw,** dŏw, (GERARD,) a celebrated Dutch painter, was born at Leyden in 1613. In the school of Rembrandt he made himself expert in colouring and chiaroscuro. He sought the ideal perfection in minute precision and exquisite delicacy of finish, which he bestowed on all the most trivial accessories of the picture. It is said that he spent three days in finishing a broom-handle. It is only by the aid of a microscope that one can appreciate his exact imitation of nature in all its minutiæ. His works are marvels of technical skill, but not of inventive genius. He chose his subjects from the scenes of common life. Among his master-pieces are "The Dutch Cook," "The Dropsical Woman," "The Charlatan," and "The Village Grocer." His paintings, though of small dimensions, command high prices. Mieris was his most noted pupil. Dow resembled Rembrandt in harmony of colour, and is said to have obtained Rembrandtesque effects notwithstanding his excessive elaboration. Died at Leyden in 1680.

See CHARLES BLANC, "Histoire des Peintres."

Dŏw, (LORENZO,) an eccentric Methodist preacher, born in Coventry, Connecticut, in 1777. He preached in many parts of the United States and in England. He was noted for his earnestness and courage, as well as for some singularities of dress and expression. He died in 1834, leaving a journal of his life and travels.

Dow, (NEAL,) the originator of the celebrated "Maine Law," was born at Portland, Maine, about 1803. He was elected a member of the legislature of Maine, in which he procured the passage of a law to prohibit the sale of ardent spirits. He was twice mayor of Portland. He became a brigadier-general of volunteers about April, 1862, and served under General Butler in Louisiana.

Dŏwd′all, (GEORGE,) was appointed Archbishop of Armagh by Henry VIII. in 1543. The pope refused to confirm this nomination; but Dowdall occupied the see for some years. Died in 1558.

Dŏw′land, (JOHN,) an English musician, born in or near London in 1562, was a friend of Shakspeare. He composed songs, airs, etc., and wrote several treatises on music. Died after 1625.

Dŏw′lẹr, (BENNET,) an American physician, born in Ohio county, Virginia, in 1797, graduated in the University of Maryland in 1827. He settled in New Orleans about 1835, and by his numerous experiments on the human body soon after death, made discoveries in relation to muscular contractility, capillary circulation, etc.

Downame. See DOWNHAM.

Downe, dŏwn, (JOHN,) an eminent English divine, was a nephew of Bishop Jewel. He published sermons, (1633,) and other works.

Downes, dŏwnz, [Lat. DUNÆ′US,](ANDREW,) an English scholar, born in Shropshire about 1550, became professor of Greek at Cambridge in 1586, and was one of the translators of the Bible. He published "Prelections on Lysias," (1593.) Died in 1627.

Downes, dŏwnz, (JOHN,) an American naval officer, born at Canton, Massachusetts, in 1786. He served as lieutenant in the Essex, under Captain Porter, in the war against Great Britain, (1812–14,) after which he fought with distinction against the Algerines. About 1817 he became a captain. He obtained in 1832 command of a squadron in the Pacific Ocean, and destroyed Quallah Batoo, in Sumatra, in retaliation for an outrage committed on an American vessel. Died in 1855.

Downham, dŏwn′am, or **Down′ame,** (GEORGE,) an English theologian, born at Chester. He professed logic at Cambridge, was chaplain to James I., and was appointed Bishop of Derry in 1616. He wrote "The Pope the Antichrist," ("Papa Antichristus," 1603,) a "Treatise on Justification," (1623,) and other works. Died in 1634.

Downham, (JOHN,) a brother of the preceding, was a clergyman, and author of several approved religious works, one of which is "The Christian Warfare," (1609–18.) Died in 1644.

Dŏwn′ing, (ANDREW JACKSON,) a distinguished American landscape-gardener and pomologist, born at Newburg, New York, in October, 1815. He was the son of a nurseryman, and his tastes early led him to the study of botany, rural architecture, and kindred pursuits. About 1841 he published an excellent "Treatise on the Theory and Practice of Landscape-Gardening," which was received as a standard work on the subject of which it treats. His "Fruits and Fruit-Trees of America" (1845) was very successful, and had passed through fourteen editions in 1852. He also produced a work called "Cottage Residences," and was editor of "The Horticulturist," a monthly published at Albany, from 1846 until his death. He was a passenger on the North River steamboat Henry Clay on the 28th of July, 1852, and was drowned while attempting to escape from the burning vessel. In 1854 a collection of his "Rural Essays" was published, with a Memoir of the author by George W. Curtis. As a landscape-gardener Mr. Downing stood pre-eminent among his countrymen; and he probably had few superiors in this department even in Europe. His writings have contributed greatly to the introduction and diffusion of a taste for rural architecture and other rural improvements in America.

Dŏwn′man, (HUGH,) M.D., an English poet, born near Exeter in 1740. He was a graduate of Baliol College, and practised medicine at Exeter. He wrote several dramas, and "Infancy, a Poem," (1774–88,) which ran through seven editions in his lifetime. Died in 1809.

Dowse, douz, (THOMAS,) an American book-collector, born at Charlestown, Massachusetts, in 1772. He was a leather-dresser by trade, and enjoyed few advantages of education. He became the owner of a library of 5000 volumes, which, a short time before his death, he presented to the Massachusetts Historical Society. He also obtained by lottery a choice collection of engravings after the old masters, which he gave to the Boston Athenæum. Died in 1856.

Doyen, dwȧ′yôN′, (GABRIEL FRANÇOIS,) a French historical painter, born in Paris in 1726, was a pupil of Vanloo. He gained the grand prize of painting in 1746, studied in Rome about seven years, and returned to Paris, where he produced a successful picture of the "Death of Virginia," and was admitted into the Academy in 1758. His reputation was increased by the picture of "Sainte-Geneviève des Ardents," which is called his master-piece. About 1790 he went to Saint Petersburg, where the empress Catherine employed him to adorn her palaces. Died in Saint Petersburg in 1806.

See CHARLES BLANC, "Histoire des Peintres."

Doyère, dwȧ′yaiR′, (LOUIS,) a French naturalist, born in Calvados in 1811, has written on anatomy and physiology.

Doyle, doil, (Sir CHARLES WILLIAM,) a general, born in Ireland, entered the British army about 1793. He distinguished himself in Spain between 1808 and 1812, and obtained the rank of general in the Spanish army. For his conduct at Valenciennes and Lannois he was made a knight-commander of the Guelph in 1819. He became a major-general in 1815, and lieutenant-general in 1837. Died in 1843.

Doyle, (JAMES,) a learned Irish Catholic priest, born about 1786, was appointed Bishop of Kildare in 1819. He wrote a "Letter to Daniel O'Connell on the Poor-Laws of Ireland," a "Vindication of the Religious and Civil Principles of the Irish Catholics," (1823,) and several polemical treatises. Died in 1834.

See W. J. FITZPATRICK, "Life of Bishop Doyle," 1862.

Doyle, (Sir JOHN,) a British general, born in Dublin about 1756. He made several campaigns in America. In 1796 he was made a colonel, and soon after was secretary-at-war in Ireland. He served as brigadier-general in Egypt in 1800. He was made a lieutenant-general in 1808, and obtained the rank of full general several years later. Died in 1834.

Doyle, (RICHARD,) an English artist, distinguished in caricature, was born in London in 1826. He is a son of Mr. Doyle, an artist, whose political sketches, signed "H. B.," obtained much popularity. He contributed humorous and satirical designs to the London "Punch" for some years. His skill in design, and his moral tendency, are highly praised.

D'Oyly, doi'le, (GEORGE,) D.D., an English clergyman, born in 1778. He became rector of Buxted in 1815, of Lambeth and Sundridge in 1820. He contributed to the "London Quarterly Review," and published several volumes of sermons. Dr. D'Oyly and the Rev. R. Mant prepared an annotated Bible, published in 1814 by the Society for Promoting Christian Knowledge, which had a large sale. Died in 1846.

Dozy, do'ze, ? (REINHART,) a Dutch Orientalist, born at Leyden in 1820. He became professor of history at Leyden in 1850, and wrote several works which attest his extensive attainments and critical judgment. Among these is "Researches into the Political and Literary History of Spain during the Middle Ages," (1849.)

Drabicius, drä-bit'se-ùs, (NIKOLAUS,) a German visionary or impostor, born in Moravia in 1587, pretended to be a prophet. He was executed at Presburg in 1671.

Drä'co or **Drä'con,** [Gr. Δράκων; Fr. DRACON, drä'-kôN',] an Athenian legislator, celebrated for his sanguinary penal code, was archon in the 39th Olympiad, about 624 B.C. He was the author of the first written laws among the Athenians, and made even the least theft a capital crime, so that, as Demades remarked, "his laws seemed to be written with blood instead of ink."

See GROTE, "History of Greece;" THIRLWALL, "History of Greece;" CARL F. HERMANN, "Disputatio de Dracone Legislatore Attico," 1849.

Dracon. See DRACO.

Draconites, drä-ko-nee'tês, (JOHANN,) a German Lutheran divine, born at Carlstadt in 1494; died in 1566.

Dracontius, dra-kon'she-us, a Latin poet of Spain, wrote a poem called "Hexaemeron," describing the creation of the world. Died about 450 A.D.

Draeseke. See DRÄSEKE.

Draexler-Manfred, drëks'ler mân'frêt, (CARL FERDINAND,) a German novelist and poet, born at Lemberg in 1806. Among his novels is "Gruppen und Puppen,"(1836.)

Draghi, drä'gee, (ANTONIO,) an Italian composer of dramatic music, born at Ferrara in 1642, was noted for prolific talent. Died in 1707.

Draghi, (GIOVANNI BATTISTA,) an Italian painter, born at Genoa; died in 1712.

Dragoncino, drä-gon-chee'no,(GIOVANNI BATTISTA,) an Italian poet, flourished about 1500.

Dragonetti, drä-go-net'tee, (LUIGI,) an Italian literary journalist, born at Aquila about 1800.

Dragut, drä'gut, a Turkish corsair, born in Natolia, rose to high command in the navy under Barbarossa. He committed many piracies against the Spaniards and Italians, and was once taken prisoner by the Genoese admiral Doria, but was liberated after a few years' detention. He gained a victory over the Spaniards at Gerbes in 1560, and was killed at the siege of Malta in 1565.

See VON HAMMER, "Geschichte des Osmanischen Reichs;" BRANTÔME, "Vie de Dragut;" PRESCOTT, "History of Philip II.," vol. ii.

Drāke, (DANIEL,) M.D., an American physician and author, was born at Plainfield, New Jersey, in 1785. He took the degree of M.D. at the University of Pennsylvania in 1816. He was connected at different periods with the schools of medicine in Cincinnati, Lexington, Louisville, and Philadelphia. It was chiefly through his efforts that the Medical College of Ohio was founded at Cincinnati in 1819. Dr. Drake was distinguished as a lecturer. He edited for many years the "Western Journal of Medical Science," published at Cincinnati. He was also author of various medical and other works, the most important of which is his "Systematic Treatise on the Principal Diseases of the Interior Valley of North America, as they appear in the Caucasian, African, Indian, and Esquimaux," (2 vols. 8vo, 1850–54.) Died at Cincinnati in 1852.

See E. D. MANSFIELD, "Life of D. Drake," 1855; S. D. GROSS, "American Medical Biography."

Drāke, (Sir FRANCIS,) a celebrated English navigator and naval hero, born in Devonshire about 1540. After learning navigation in the coasting-trade, he commanded a vessel in Sir John Hawkins's disastrous expedition to the Spanish Main in 1567, in which he lost all his property. In 1570, with a commission from the queen, he cruised with some success against the Spaniards in the West Indies. In 1572 he sailed with two vessels on a marauding expedition against the Spanish shipping and settlements of America, from which he returned next year with prizes of great value. From the Isthmus of Darien he had obtained a view of the Pacific Ocean. With five small vessels, in December, 1577, he embarked on a buccaneering enterprise to the Pacific through the Straits of Magellan. He obtained immense treasures by plunder on the coast of Chili and Peru, and, in the hope of finding a passage to the Atlantic, sailed northward as far as 48 degrees north. Failing in this design, he returned to San Francisco, and thence steered across the ocean to the Moluccas, and came home by the Cape of Good Hope in 1579, having circumnavigated the globe. Drake was knighted by Queen Elizabeth, who dined on board his vessel at Deptford and directed the ship to be preserved as a monument of his memorable achievement. He was appointed commander of a fleet in 1587, and sent to "singe the King of Spain's beard,"—that is, to burn his ships in the Spanish harbours. In the port of Cadiz he burnt, sunk, or captured one hundred vessels destined for the invasion of England. In the next year, as vice-admiral, he contributed to the victory of the English over the Invincible Armada. He was elected to Parliament in 1592. In 1595 an expedition was fitted out against the West Indies, and the command was divided between Drake and Hawkins, who disagreed and consequently failed. After losing many men by disease, Drake died near Puerto Bello in 1595.

See BARROW, "Life, Voyages, etc. of Sir Francis Drake," 1843; SAMUEL CLARKE, "Life of Sir Francis Drake," 1671; CAMPBELL, "Lives of British Admirals;" MOTLEY, "United Netherlands," vol. ii. chap. xi.; SAMUEL JOHNSON, "Life of Sir Francis Drake," London, 1767; J. BARROW, "Memoirs of the Naval Worthies of Queen Elizabeth's Reign;" "Edinburgh Review" for October, 1844.

Drake, (FRANCIS,) an English surgeon and antiquary of York. He published "The History and Antiquity of the City of York," (1736.) Died in 1770.

Drake, drä'kēh, (FRIEDRICH,) a celebrated German sculptor, born at Pyrmont in 1805. He became a pupil of Rauch in Berlin. One of his early works, a "Madonna and Child," was purchased by the Empress of Russia. His reputation was increased by his allegorical group of the "Eight Provinces of Prussia," (1844,) and by marble statues, busts, and statuettes of eminent Germans, among which are the Humboldts, Rauch, Oken, and Frederick William III.

Drake, (JAMES,) M.D., an English physician and political writer, born at Cambridge in 1667. He published in 1702 "The History of the Last Parliament," and soon after "Historia Anglo-Scotica," which gave great offence to the Scots and was burnt by the hangman. He wrote several other works in favour of Toryism; also a "New System of Anatomy," a work of merit. Died in 1707.

Drake, (JOSEPH RODMAN,) an American poet, born in the city of New York in August, 1795, was educated at Columbia College. He studied medicine, and mar-

ā, ē, ī, ō, ū, ȳ, *long;* à, è, ò, same, less prolonged; ǎ, ě, ǐ, ǒ, ǔ, ȳ, *short;* a, e, i, o, *obscure;* fär, fâll, fât; mêt; nôt; gōōd; mōōn;

ried Sarah Eckford about 1816. In 1819 he wrote humorous and satirical verses which were published in the "Evening Post" under the signature of "Croaker." He was an intimate friend of Fitz-Greene Halleck. His principal works are "The Culprit Fay," a beautiful imaginative poem, and the much-admired verses on "The American Flag,"* (1819.) He died prematurely in September, 1820, in New York, leaving one daughter, who afterwards became the wife of Commodore De Kay. Halleck wrote a poetical tribute to his memory.

See GRISWOLD, "Poets and Poetry of America;" DUYCKINCK, "Cyclopædia of American Literature."

Drake, (NATHAN,) M.D., an English critic and essayist, born at York in 1766. From 1792 until his death he practised medicine at Hadleigh, in Suffolk, and produced numerous excellent literary works, among which are "Literary Hours," (1798,) "Essays illustrative of the Tatler, Spectator, and Guardian," (1805,) and "Shakspeare and his Times," (1817.) Of the last, Archdeacon Nares says, "No work has hitherto appeared in which so much of agreeable and well-digested information on this subject will be found, as in this masterly production. It may be considered as a magnificent temple dedicated to the genius of Shakspeare." He published some professional treatises. Died in 1836.

Drake, (SAMUEL GARDNER,) an American writer, born at Pittsfield, New Hampshire, in 1798, became a bookseller in Boston. He published "Indian Biography," (1832,) "The Book of the Indians, or History and Biography of the Indians of North America," (1833,) and other works.

Drakenberg, DRÄ'kĕn-bĕRg', (CHRISTIAN JACOBSEN,) a Norwegian, remarkable for longevity and strength, born at Blomsholm in 1626. He served as a common sailor about fifty years, and was held as a slave by the Algerines and others about sixteen years. At the age of one hundred and ten he married, and several years later was able to perform long journeys on foot. Died in 1772, aged one.hundred and forty-five.

Drakenborch, DRÄ'kĕn-boRk',(ARNOLD,) an eminent Dutch scholar, born at Utrecht in 1684. He was educated at Utrecht and Leyden. In 1704 he wrote "De Præfectis Urbis," a treatise on the office of prefect in Rome, by which he gained a high reputation. In 1716 he became professor of history and eloquence in Utrecht, where he remained till his death. He published an edition of Silius Italicus, and one of Livy, which is a master-piece of accuracy and erudition. Died in 1747.

See ERSCH und GRUBER, "Allgemeine Encyklopaedie."

Dran, Le. See LEDRAN.

Drant, (THOMAS,) D.D., an English divine, known as the first English metrical translator of Horace, in 1567. He published sermons and other works. Died about 1578.

Draparnaud, DRÄ'pÄR'nŏ', (JACQUES PHILIPPE RAYMOND,) a French naturalist and linguist, born at Montpellier in 1772. He was professor of natural history at Montpellier, and wrote many scientific memoirs, some of which were commended by the Institute of France. Among his principal works is "The Natural History of Mollusks." Died in 1805.

See "Biographie Médicale;" JACQUES POITEVIN, "Notice sur la Vie de M. Draparnaud," 1805.

Drā'per, (ELIZA,) MRS., an English lady, was a friend and correspondent of Laurence Sterne, who addressed to her the "Letters of Yorick to Eliza."

Drā'per, (JOHN WILLIAM,) M.D., a distinguished chemist and physiologist, was born in Liverpool, England, in 1811. He came to America in 1833, and in 1836 graduated at the medical department of the University of Pennsylvania. In 1839 he accepted the chair of chemistry in the University of New York. He took a prominent part in establishing the medical department of the New York University in 1841, and has since been a professor in that institution. Professor Draper has devoted much attention to the chemical action of light, and written able treatises on this subject. He has made numerous contributions to the "Edinburgh Scientific Journal." Among his most important works are his "Human

Physiology, Statistical and Dynamical, or the Conditions and Course of Life in Man," (8vo, 1856,) and his "History of the Intellectual Development of Europe," (1863,) a work which has attracted much attention, having been as warmly praised by some as it has been severely criticised by others. He has also written "Thoughts on the Future Civil Policy of America," (1865,) and a "History of the American Civil War," (2 vols., 1867–68.)

See "North American Review" for October, 1867.

Draper, (Sir WILLIAM,) a British officer, born at Bristol in 1721, commanded as colonel at the capture of Manilla from the Spaniards in 1763. He is best known by his controversy with Junius, against whom he undertook to defend the Marquis of Granby in 1769. Four of the letters of Junius were addressed to Draper, who, being foiled by the keen wit and sarcasm of his opponent, endeavoured to provoke him to a duel. The intemperate and somewhat scurrilous letters of Draper are published with those of his antagonist. Died in 1787.

Drapiez, DRÄ'pe-â', (AUGUSTE,) a Belgian savant, born at Brussels in 1790, published several works on mineralogy and other sciences.

Dräseke or **Draeseke,** DRÄ'zĕh-kĕh, (JOHANN HEINRICH BERNHARD,) a distinguished German pulpit orator, born at Brunswick in 1774. He became first preacher of the cathedral of Magdeburg in 1832. He published numerous sermons, and "Faith, Love, and Hope," (1813; 6th edition, 1834.) Died in 1849.

Draud, dRŏwt, (GEORG,) a German bibliographer, born at Dauernheim in 1573, published "Bibliotheca Classica," (1611,) the most complete and methodical bibliography of printed books that had then appeared. Died about 1630.

Drāy'ton, (MICHAEL,) an English poet, born at Hartshill, in Warwickshire, in 1563. The events of his early life are nearly all unknown. He was patronized in youth by Sir Walter Aston, and in the decline of life he found a comfortable home at the seat of the Earl of Dorset. About 1596 he published historical poems, entitled "The Barons' Wars" and "England's Heroical Epistles." His principal production, "The Poly-Olbion," (1613,) is greatly admired, and is regarded as good authority in reference to English antiquities. It is a poetical description of all the rivers, tracts, mountains, forests, etc. of Great Britain, with notices of traditions and stories connected with them. "Drayton is a sweet poet," says Coleridge, "and Selden's notes to the earlier part of the 'Poly-Olbion' are well worth your perusal." He received the title of poet-laureate in 1626. The next year he published several short poems, among which is his admirable "Nymphidia," a fairy poem. Died in 1631.

"There is probably," says Hallam, "no poem of this kind in any other language comparable together in extent and excellence to the 'Poly-Olbion;' nor can any one read a portion of it without admiration for its learned and highly-gifted author." ("Introduction to the Literature of Europe.")

See JOHNSON, "Lives of the English Poets;" SIR S. E. BRYDGES, "Imaginative Biography;" DISRAELI, "Amenities of Literature;" CAMPBELL, "Specimens of the British Poets."

Drāy'ton, (PERCIVAL,) an American naval officer, born in South Carolina about 1812, entered the navy about 1828. He obtained the rank of commander in 1855, and maintained his loyalty to the Union in the civil war. He was promoted to the rank of captain in 1862, and commanded the monitor Passaic in the attack on Fort Sumter in April, 1863. He was highly esteemed by Admiral Farragut, who selected him to command his flag-ship in his operations against the defences of Mobile Bay, August, 1864. Died in August, 1865.

Drayton, (WILLIAM,) a judge, born in South Carolina in 1733. He became, after the Revolution, an associate justice of his native State, and a judge under the Federal government. Died in 1790.

Drayton, (WILLIAM,) an American politician, born in South Carolina. He was from 1825 to 1833 a representative in Congress. Originally a Federalist, he was the leader of the Union party in the nullification movement of South Carolina in 1830. He succeeded Nicholas Biddle as president of the United States Bank in 1839. Died in 1846.

---

* The last four lines of "The American Flag" were written by Fitz-Greene Halleck.

€ as k; ç as s; ğ hard; ğ as j; G, H, K, guttural; N, nasal; R, trilled; ŝ as z; th as in this. (☞ See Explanations, p. 23.)

Drayton, (WILLIAM HENRY,) an American patriot and judge, born on Ashley River, in South Carolina, in 1742. He became chief justice of South Carolina in 1776, and delivered to the grand jury an able charge, which gave an impulse to the popular cause. He was an active and prominent member of Congress, when he died suddenly in Philadelphia in 1779, in the thirty-sixth year of his age, and left historical memoirs of the Revolution, published by his son, (in 2 vols., 1821.)

See "Encyclopædia Americana."

Drebbel, van, vän dRĕb'bĕl, (CORNELIS,) a Dutch philosopher, born at Alkmaar in 1572. The latter part of his life was passed in England, where he was patronized by James I. and is said to have invented an air thermometer and some curious machines. He published, in Dutch, a work "On the Nature of the Elements," and one on "Quintessence." He pretended that he had discovered a perpetual motion. Died in 1634.

See F. HOEFER, "Histoire de la Chimie."

Drelincourt, dRĕh'lȧN'kooR', (CHARLES,) an eminent French Protestant minister, born at Sedan in 1595. He became minister of Charenton, near Paris, in 1620, and acquired great popularity as a preacher. He wrote against the Church of Rome a number of polemical treatises, which had great influence in confirming his fellow-professors. His work entitled "Consolations against the Fear of Death" (1651) was translated into English and German, and often reprinted. He also published "Charitable Visits," etc., ("Les Visites charitables pour toutes Sortes de Personnes affligées," 5 vols., 1669.) His sermons were especially remarkable for their unction. Died in Paris in 1669.

See HAAG, "La France protestante."

Drelincourt, (CHARLES,) a son of the preceding, born in Paris in 1633, was a physician and author of high reputation. He took his degree as doctor in 1654, soon after which he was appointed first physician to the army of Turenne. In 1663 he became physician-in-ordinary to Louis XIV., and in 1668 obtained the chair of medicine at Leyden. He was an eloquent and learned writer. Among his works are "Præludium Anatomicum," (1670,) and "Homericus Achilles," (1693.) He was employed as physician by William Prince of Orange, and was the precepter of Boerhaave. He died in 1697, leaving a son CHARLES, who was a physician.

See BAYLE, "Historical and Critical Dictionary;" NICÉRON, "Mémoires;" "Nouvelle Biographie Générale."

Drelincourt, (LAURENT,) a brother of the preceding, born in Paris in 1626, became minister at Rochelle and Niort, and was distinguished as a preacher. He published Sermons, and "Christian Sonnets." Died in 1680.

Drennan, (WILLIAM,) M.D., an Irish poet and political writer, born at Belfast in 1754; died in 1820.

Dre-pā'nĭ-us, (LATI'NUS PACA'TUS,) a poet and orator, born at Bordeaux or Agen, in France, was deputed to Rome, in 388 A.D., to congratulate Theodosius on his victory over Maximus, and then pronounced a panegyric on that emperor, which is still extant. His poems, which are praised by Ausonius, have not been preserved.

Drepanius Florus. See FLORUS.

Dresig, dRā'ziG, (SIGISMOND FRIEDRICH,) a German scholar and writer, born in 1700, lived at Leipsic; died in 1742.

Dres'ser, [Lat. DRESSE'RUS,] (MATTHÄUS,) a learned German professor, born at Erfurt in 1536, was a disciple of Luther, and studied at Wittenberg. He succeeded Justus Lipsius as professor of history at Jena in 1574. In 1581 he became professor of humanities at Leipsic, where by his influence the Confession of Augsburg was adopted in the University. He wrote, besides other Latin works, a "Treatise on Rhetoric," (1585,) and a "Life of Luther," (1598.) Died in 1607.

See BAYLE, "Historical and Critical Dictionary."

Dresserus. See DRESSER.

Dressler, dRĕs'lĕr, (ERNST CHRISTOPH,) a German musician and writer of songs, was born at Greussen in 1734; died in 1779.

Dreux du Radier, dRuh dü rȧ'de-ȧ', (JEAN FRANÇOIS,) a French lawyer and writer, born at Châteauneuf-en-Thymerais in 1714. He wrote a "Historical and Critical Library of Poitou," (1754,) which is regarded as an excellent work, "Historical and Critical Memoirs and Anecdotes of France," (1764,) and "Recreations, Historical, Critical, and Moral," (1767.) Died in 1780.

See ERSCH, "La France Littéraire," 5 vols., 1797-1806; LASTIC-SAINT-JAL, "Notice sur la Vie et les Ouvrages de J. F. Dreux du Radier," 1842.

Dreux et de Brézé, de, dĕh dRuh ā dĕh bRā'zà', (HENRI EVRARD,) MARQUIS, was grand master of ceremonies when the States-General met in 1789. An order which he conveyed from the king, that this body should disperse, provoked a famous reply from Mirabeau. Died in 1829.

Drevet, dRĕh-vȧ', (PIERRE,) an excellent French engraver, born in Lyons in 1664. After receiving lessons from Germain Audran, he went to Paris, where he devoted his talents to portraits. Among his best works are portraits of Louis XIV., Cardinal Fleury, the dauphin, and Boileau. He was perhaps unrivalled by any engraver of his time except his son, who surpassed him. Died in 1739.

See BASAN, "Dictionnaire des Graveurs."

Drevet, (PIERRE,) a son and pupil of the preceding, born in Paris in 1697. He engraved a number of portraits, which are master-pieces, and treated subjects of history with nearly equal success. His portrait of Bossuet, after Rigaud, (1733,) is called his best work. It is said that he was able to imitate articles of dress and furniture so that the various colours, textures, and other qualities of those accessories can be recognized by the least practised eyes. He was a member of the Academy of Painting. Died in 1739.

See BASAN, "Dictionnaire des Graveurs."

Drew, (SAMUEL,) an English writer, born in Cornwall in 1765, was a shoemaker, and supplied the defects of his education by studying in the intervals of labour. He was converted from infidelity in early life, and joined the Methodist Church. He published "The Immateriality and Immortality of the Soul," (1802,) which is highly praised, and other religious works. He became editor of the "Imperial Magazine" in 1819. Died in 1833.

See "Life, Character, and Literary Labours of Samuel Drew," by his son, 1834.

Drex-e'lĭ-us, [Ger. pron. dRĕk-sā'le-ŭs,] (JEREMIAS,) a German Jesuit and pulpit orator, born at Augsburg in 1581, wrote some ascetic works. Died in 1638.

See ERSCH und GRUBER, "Allgemeine Encyklopaedie."

Dreyer, dRī'ĕr, (JOHANN MATTHIAS,) a German poet, born at Hamburg in 1716; died in 1769.

Dreyschock, dRī'shok, (ALEXANDER,) a celebrated pianist, born in Bohemia in 1818. He has acquired distinction by his concerts in the principal capitals of Europe.

Dreyse, von, fon dRī'zĕh, (JOHANN NIKOLAUS,) the inventor of the celebrated "needle-gun," was born at Sömmerda, in Prussia, November 20, 1787. He was the son of a locksmith, and he himself followed the same trade. His attention having been directed to the extraordinary clumsiness of the muskets used by the Prussians at the battle of Jena, he was convinced that, until she was provided with better arms, his country could never become a first-rate military power. His invention was made in the early part of 1828, but was not put to the proof until the war of 1866. The great improvement of his gun is his new contrivance for igniting the cartridge, which is still a secret. Died December 9, 1867.

See "London Examiner" for September 8, 1866.

Driander. See DRYANDER.

Dridoens. See DRIEDO.

Driedo, dRe'do', or **Dridoens,** dRee'doons, (JAN,) a Flemish theologian and prominent adversary of Lutheranism. He was a canon of the church of Louvain, and wrote several works, one of which is "On the Writings and Doctrines of the Church," ("De Scripturis et Dogmatibus ecclesiasticis.") Died in 1535.

See POSSEVIN, "Apparatus Sacer."

Driesche. See DRUSIUS.

Drink'er, (ANNA,) an American poetess, who wrote under the assumed name of EDITH MAY, was born in Pennsylvania. She published a volume of poems, (1851,) which were commended by N. P. Willis.

See GRISWOLD's "Female Poets of America."

ā, ē, ī, ō, ū, ȳ, *long;* à, ė, ȯ, same, less prolonged; ă, ĕ, ĭ, ŏ, ŭ, ў, *short;* ạ, ẹ, ị, ọ, *obscure;* fär, fȧll, fȧt; mĕt; nŏt; gŏŏd; mōōn;

Drivère, dRe'vaiR', [Lat. THRIVE'RUS,] (JEREMIAS,) born at Braeckel, in Flanders, in 1504, became professor of medicine at Louvain. He wrote many medical works, besides commentaries on Hippocrates. Died in 1554.

See P. J. HAAN, "Notice sur la Vie de H. Thriverus," 1846; NICÉRON, "Mémoires."

Drobisch, dRo'bish, (MORITZ WILHELM,) a German philosopher, born in 1802 at Leipsic, where he became professor of mathematics in 1842.

Drolling, dRO'lâN' or dRol'ling, (MARTIN,) a French painter, born at Oberbergheim (Haut-Rhin) in 1752. He painted familiar scenes, interiors, etc. with success, and was a good colorist. Died in 1817.

Drolling, (MICHEL MARTIN,) a skilful historical painter, son of the preceding, born in Paris in 1786. He gained the first prize in 1810 for a picture of "The Wrath of Achilles." Among his best productions is "Orpheus losing Eurydice," (1817.) He also painted many portraits. Died in 1851.

See SAINT-MAURICE-CABANY, "M. M. Drolling, Peintre," 1851.

Drollinger, dRol'ling-er, (KARL FRIEDRICH,) a German poet, was born at Durlach in 1688. His odes on "The Immortality of the Soul," and "On Divine Providence," were much admired. Died in 1742.

See BUXTORF, "Brevis Historia Vitæ et Obitus C. F. Drollingeri," 1742; ADELUNG, Supplement to JÖCHER's "Allgemeines Gelehrten-Lexikon."

Dro'mon, [Δρομῶν,] an Athenian comic poet, lived in the fourth century B.C.

Drooch-Sloot, dRŌK'slōt, (J. C.,) a Dutch painter, born at Gorcum about 1600. Among his works are views of Holland and of village festivals.

Drossander, dRos-sän'der, (ANDERS,) a Swedish physician and philosopher, born at Upsal in 1648. He wrote several scientific works. Died in 1696.

See "Biographie Médicale."

Drost, dRost, a skilful Flemish painter, and a pupil of Rembrandt, was living in 1670.

Droste-Hülshoff, von, fon dRos'teh hüls'hof, (ANNETTE ELISABETH,) a German lyric poetess, born near Münster in 1798; died in 1848.

Droste zu Vischering, von, fon dRos'teh tsoo fish'er-ing, (CLEMENS AUGUST,) FREIHERR, a German Catholic prelate, born near Münster in 1773. He became Archbishop of Cologne in 1835. Died in 1845.

See STOEVEKEN, "C. A. Droste zu Vischering in seinem Leben," etc., 1846.

Drouais, dRoo'â', (HUBERT,) a French painter, born in Normandy in 1699, was a grandfather of Jean Germain, noticed below. He excelled in portraits. Died at Paris in 1767.

Drouais, (JEAN GERMAIN,) an eminent French painter, born in Paris in 1763, was the son of Henri Drouais, a portrait-painter, who died in 1775. In 1780 he became a pupil of David. About the age of twenty-one he gained by a unanimous vote the grand prize of the Academy by his picture of the "Woman of Canaan at the Feet of Christ," which established his reputation. He then went to Rome, where he painted "Marius at Minturnæ," and died prematurely in 1788. Goethe, in one of his works, expresses his admiration of the last-named picture.

See CHAUSSARD, "Notice sur Drouais;" NAGLER, "Neues Allgemeines Künstler-Lexikon."

Drouet, dRoo'â', (ÉTIENNE,) a French editor and compiler, born in Paris in 1715. He published the last and best edition of Moreri's Dictionary, (10 vols., 1759,) and a new edition of Lenglet-Dufresnoy's "Method for the Study of History," (15 vols., 1772.) Died in 1779.

Drouet, (JEAN BAPTISTE,) a French revolutionist, born at Sainte-Menehould in 1763, was the son of the postmaster of that town. He acquired notoriety by his agency in the arrest of Louis XVI. at Varennes in 1791. In 1792 he was elected a member of the Convention, in which he voted for the death of the king and the destruction of the Girondists. Soon after Bonaparte obtained the chief power, Drouet was appointed sub-prefect of Sainté-Menehould. In 1807, as he gave him the cross of the legion of honour, the emperor said to him, "You have changed the face of the world." Died in 1824.

See THIERS, "History of the French Revolution."

Drouet de Maupertuy, dRoo'â' deh mō'pêR'tü-e', (JEAN BAPTISTE,) a French writer and priest, born in Paris in 1650; died in 1730.

Drouet d'Erlon, dRoo'â' dêR'lôN', (JEAN BAPTISTE,) COUNT, and Marshal of France, born at Rheims in 1765. He entered the army as a private in 1782, served under Hoche in 1797, and was made a general of brigade in 1799. He became a general of division in 1800, and contributed by a skilful movement to the victory at Jena, (1806.) In March, 1815, he was arrested on a charge of being an accomplice of Lefèbvre-Desnouettes in his design to seize the Bourbon family, and in the ensuing June he was created a peer by Napoleon, for whom he commanded a corps at Waterloo. He passed ten years in exile, returned to France in 1825, and was restored to his rank in the army in 1830. He was chosen Governor-General of Algeria in 1834, and obtained the rank of marshal in 1843. Died in 1844.

See "Notice sur la Vie militaire de Drouet d'Erlon," by himself, 1844; "Nouvelle Biographie Générale."

Drouineau, dRoo'e'nō', (GUSTAVE,) a French dramatist and novelist, born at La Rochelle in 1800. He produced "Rienzi," (1826,) a tragedy, and "Ernest," (1829,) a novel, both of which were popular. About 1830 he became one of the editors of the "Constitutionnel." He was author of other dramas and tales. Died in 1835.

Drouot, dRoo'o', (ANTOINE,) COUNT, an able French general of artillery, born at Nancy in 1774. He fought as captain at Hohenlinden in 1800, and gave proof of courage and skill at Wagram, (1809,) and at Borodino, (1812.) For his conduct at Lutzen and Bautzen, (1813,) where he commanded the artillery of the imperial guard, he was made a general of division and aide-de-camp to Napoleon, whom he followed to Elba, of which he was chosen governor. He was at the side of Napoleon at the battle of Waterloo, June, 1815, soon after which he was commandant of the imperial guard at Paris. After the restoration he lived as a private citizen. Died in 1847. "France was astonished in 1814 to learn," says C. Héquet, "that she had possessed for a long time the best officer of artillery in Europe." ("Nouvelle Biographie Générale.") He was surnamed by Napoleon "the sage of the grand army," ("le sage de la grande armée.")

See J. NOLLET-FABERT, "Biographie du Général Drouot," 1850; HENRI LE PAGE, "Le Général Drouot," 1847; LACORDAIRE, "Éoge du Général Drouot," 1847.

Drouyn de Lhuys, dRoo' âN' deh lü-e', (ÉDOUARD,) a French diplomatist and minister of state, was born in Paris in 1805. He became in 1833 chargé-d'affaires at the Hague, where he gave proof of high diplomatic ability. In 1840 he was appointed director of commercial affairs in the ministry of foreign affairs. He was brought into frequent contact with Guizot, whose policy he disapproved. As a member of the Chamber of Deputies, he voted against the ministry in 1845, and was dismissed from office. He was elected to the National Assembly in 1848, and became minister of foreign affairs in the first cabinet of President Louis Napoleon. In June, 1849, he was sent as ambassador to London. He was a conservative member of the National Assembly in 1851, and again became foreign minister in July, 1852. His diplomatic letters on the occasion of the establishment of the empire added to his reputation. He represented France at the Conference of Vienna in 1855, at the close of which he retired from office because he differed from his colleagues on the Eastern question. In October, 1862, he was again appointed minister of foreign affairs. He was removed from this office about September, 1866.

See "Nouvelle Biographie Générale."

Drovetti, dRō-vet'tee, (BERNARDINO,) an Italian antiquary, born at Leghorn in 1775. He was consul in Egypt, where he formed two rich collections of antique objects. The King of France purchased one of these collections for 250,000 francs. Died in 1852.

Droysen, dRoi'zen, (JOHANN GUSTAV,) a German historian, born at Treptow, in Pomerania, in 1808. He obtained the chair of history at Kiel in 1840, before which he had been professor in Berlin. In 1851 he became professor of history at Jena. His "History of Prussian Politics" ("Geschichte der Preussischen Politik," 2 vols.,

1855) is called his most important work. He has also published a "History of Alexander the Great," (1833,) a "History of Hellenism," ("Hellenismus," 2 vols., 1836-43,) and a "Life of Field-Marshal Graf York von Wartenburg," (1851.)

See BROCKHAUS, "Conversations-Lexikon."

Droz, dRO, (FRANÇOIS XAVIER JOSEPH,) a French writer and moralist, born at Besançon in 1773. He served in the republican army from 1792 to 1796, and became a resident of Paris in 1803. After several unsuccessful attempts as an author, he published in 1806 an "Essay on Happiness," ("Essai sur l'Art d'être heureux,") which was received with more favour. He became a contributor to several journals. In 1824 he gained the Montyon prize for his treatise "On Moral Philosophy," and in the next year was admitted to the French Academy. His "History of the Reign of Louis XVI." (3 vols., 1839-42) is esteemed his most important work. "A mild solemnity of tone," says Sainte-Beuve, "was the habitual rhythm of his thoughts." In conjunction with Picard, he wrote "Memoirs of Jacques Fauvel," (1823,) which is represented as a Gil Blas less witty but more moral than that of Le Sage. He became in 1832 a member of the class of Moral and Political Sciences in the Institute. Died in 1850.

See F. A. MIGNET, "Notice historique sur la Vie de M. Droz," 1852; SAINTE-BEUVE, "Causeries du Lundi."

Droz, dRO, (HENRI LOUIS,) a son of Pierre Jacquet, noticed below, born in 1752, inherited his mechanical and inventive talent. He produced an automaton in the form of a girl, which played tunes on the harpsichord and at the end of the performance would rise and salute the company. He also made artificial hands. He lived some years at Geneva, where he was much esteemed for his character as well as his talents. Died in 1791.

Droz, (JULES ANTOINE,) a sculptor, a son of Pierre Jean, noticed below, was born in Paris in 1807. Among his works are the marble statues of Winter and Summer which adorn the palace of the Luxembourg.

Droz, (PIERRE JACQUET,) a skilful mechanician and watchmaker, born in Neufchâtel in 1721. He improved the pendulum by using two metals of unequal expansibility, and made a writing automaton which displayed great ingenuity. Died in 1790.

Droz, (PIERRE JEAN,) a Swiss engraver of coins and medals, born at Chaux-de-Fond in 1746. He settled in Paris in 1766, and invented a method to engrave stamps for the coinage of money with celerity. About 1790 Watt and Boulton took him into their service, and his skill was exercised in the fabrication of English coins. He returned to France, and during the empire was the chief engraver of public medals and coins. His portraits of Napoleon are praised. Died in 1823.

Druey, drü'å', (CHARLES,) a Swiss politician, born about 1800, was a leader of the radicals, or the party of progress. In 1845 he was chosen president of the provisional government formed after the resignation of the council of state. Under the new constitution adopted in 1848, he was one of the chiefs of the executive power. Died in 1855.

Drumann, dRoo'mån, (KARL WILHELM,) a German historian and philologist, born near Halberstadt in 1786, became professor of philology at Königsberg in 1817. His capital work is a "History of Rome," ("Geschichte Roms," 6 vols., 1834-44,) which is highly commended. Died in 1861.

Drümel or **Druemel,** drü'mel, (JOHANN HEINRICH,) a German writer, born at Nuremberg in 1707; died in 1770.

Drum'mond, (ALEXANDER,) a British traveller, who was consul at Aleppo in 1744, and published "Travels in Germany, Greece, and Asia," (1754.) Died in 1769.

Drum'mond, (GEORGE,) a Scottish officer, noted for public spirit, was born in 1687. He fought against the Pretender at Sheriffmuir in 1715. He was chosen lord provost of Edinburgh in 1725 and at several subsequent periods. The Royal Infirmary of Edinburgh was founded chiefly by his efforts in 1736. Died in 1766.

See CHAMBERS, "Biographical Dictionary of Eminent Scotsmen."

Drum'mond, (HENRY,) M.P., an English writer on theology and politics, born in 1786. He was a disciple of Edward Irving.

Drummond, (JAMES,) Earl of Perth, was appointed lord chancellor of Scotland in 1684. He was a cruel persecutor of the Covenanters. On the expulsion of James II. from the throne he was exiled. Died in 1716.

Drummond, (MAURICE,) the ancestor of the Scottish family of that name, was a grandson of Andrew, King of Hungary. He was a resident of England at the Norman conquest, (1066,) and he followed Edgar Atheling to Scotland about 1068, and was made seneschal of Lennox. Annabella Drummond, his descendant, was married to Robert III., King of Scotland.

Drummond, (ROBERT HAY,) a British prelate, born in London in 1711, was the second son of the Earl of Kinnoul, and a grandson of Harley, Earl of Oxford. In 1737 he was appointed chaplain-in-ordinary to George II. He became Bishop of Saint Asaph in 1748, of Salisbury in 1761, and Archbishop of York in the same year. Some of his sermons have been published. Died in 1776. His son ROBERT became ninth Earl of Kinnoul.

See CHAMBERS, "Biographical Dictionary of Eminent Scotsmen."

Drummond, (THOMAS,) CAPTAIN, known as the inventor of the "Drummond Light," was born in Edinburgh in 1797. In 1813 he entered, as cadet, Woolwich Military Academy, where he displayed superior talents for mathematics and mechanics. He became one of the royal engineers, and was employed in the trigonometrical survey of Scotland about 1824, when he conceived the idea of using the incandescence of lime, instead of the argand lamp, for rendering distant stations visible. The experiment was very successful. In 1825 he invented the heliostat, and, through the influence of Lord Brougham, received a pension of £300 a year. In 1835 he was made under-secretary for Ireland. Died in 1840.

See CHAMBERS, "Biographical Dictionary of Eminent Scotsmen," (Supplement.)

Drummond, (WILLIAM,) of Hawthornden, an eminent Scottish poet, born of a noble family in 1585. He studied civil law at Bourges, in France, but soon renounced that profession for literature. In 1610 his father, Sir John, died, and left him his beautiful seat at Hawthornden, remarkable for picturesque scenery. He was of a melancholy temperament, and inclined to retirement. In 1619 Ben Jonson performed a journey of several hundred miles for the purpose of visiting Drummond, who has preserved some curious and famous notes of the conversation which passed between them. These were published after his death, and are perhaps more known and read than any of his works. Drummond has been censured for leaving these notes and betraying the confidence of his guest; but his friends say he did not intend them for publication. Southey represents Drummond as the first Scottish poet who wrote well in English. Among his most admired productions are "The River Forth Feasting," "The Praise of a Solitary Life," and his sonnets. "The sonnets of Drummond," says Hallam, "are polished and elegant, free from conceit and bad taste, in pure, unblemished English." In his forty-fifth year he married Elizabeth Logan. Died in December, 1649.

See P. CUNNINGHAM, "Life of W. Drummond;" CHAMBERS, "Biographical Dictionary of Eminent Scotsmen;" CAMPBELL, "Specimens of the British Poets;" "Retrospective Review," vol. ix., 1824; "Encyclopædia Britannica."

Drummond, (Sir WILLIAM,) of Logie Almond, a British scholar and ingenious writer, was returned to Parliament for Saint Mawes in 1795, and a few years later was minister to Naples. About 1802 he was ambassador to the Ottoman Porte. He published, besides other works, a good translation of Persius's Satires, (1798,) "Academical Questions," (1805,) "Odin," a poem, and "Origines, or Remarks on the Origin of Several Empires, States, and Cities," (4 vols., 1824-29,) a critical work of considerable merit. Died at Rome in 1828.

See CHAMBERS, "Biographical Dictionary of Eminent Scotsmen;" "Edinburgh Review" for October, 1805; "Encyclopædia Britannica."

Drum'mond de Mel'fort, (LOUIS HECTOR,) COUNT OF, born in 1726, was the descendant of Maurice Drummond, noticed above. He served with distinction in the French armies as colonel, inspector-general, and lieutenant-general. He published in 1776 a valuable "Treatise on Cavalry." Died in 1788.

Dru'ry, (DREW,) an English naturalist, published a work on entomology called "Illustrations of Natural

History," (1770,) which was commended by Linnæus and others. "The exquisite work of Drury," says Sir James Edward Smith, "displays the complete insect in a degree of perfection that leaves nothing to be desired." Died in 1804.

Drury, (Rev. Joseph,) an English scholar, born in London in 1750, was head-master of Harrow from 1785 to 1805. Lord Byron, who was his pupil, has expressed in his works gratitude and respect for him. Died in 1834.

Drury, (Robert,) an English sailor, born about 1687. He was shipwrecked in 1702 on the coast of Madagascar, where he was kept a captive fifteen years. He returned to England and published (1722) a journal of his adventures, and an account of Madagascar, regarded as authentic.

Dru-sil'la, a daughter of Herod Agrippa, King of Judea, became the wife of Felix, the Roman governor of Judea. She was present when Saint Paul preached before Felix, in 60 A.D. (See Acts xxiv. 24.) Tacitus says that Drusilla the wife of Felix was a granddaughter of the famous Cleopatra.

Drusilla, (Livia.) See Livia Drusilla.

Drusius, drü'se-ŭs, (Jan,) a Flemish Protestant scholar and eminent biblical critic, whose proper name was Van den Drifsche, (dRees'keh,) was born at Oudenarde in 1550. He professed Oriental languages at Oxford, in England, from 1572 to 1576, and obtained a similar chair at Leyden in 1577. He was professor of Hebrew at Franeker from 1585 until his death, in 1616. He wrote commentaries on Scripture, and several treatises on grammar, one of which is a Hebrew Grammar, entitled "Grammatica Linguæ sanctæ nova."

See Abel Curiander, "Vita J. Drusii," 1618; Bayle, "Historical and Critical Dictionary."

Drusius, (Jan,) a son of the preceding, born at Leyden in 1588, was a prodigy of learning and of precocity. At the age of nine he could read Hebrew without points, and at seventeen he addressed the King of England in a Latin oration. Scaliger thought he excelled his father in Hebrew. Died in 1609.

Dru'sus, a Roman prince, was the second son of Germanicus and Agrippina, and a brother of the emperor Caligula. His disposition, according to Tacitus, was violent and unruly. He appears to have been a victim of the ambitious intrigues of Sejanus. Having been condemned to death by the senate, he was confined by Tiberius, who permitted him to die by starvation in 33 A.D.

Drusus, (Claudius Nero,) a Roman general, born 38 B.C., was the son of Tiberius Claudius Nero and Livia, whose second husband was the emperor Augustus. He married Antonia, the daughter of Mark Antony. In the year 13 B.C. he commanded an army on the Rhine, and defeated several German tribes. Horace composed an admired ode in honour of this victory, (lib. iv. 4.) In the ensuing campaigns he extended his conquests as far as the Elbe, after which the senate gave him the surname Germanicus. He died at the age of thirty, leaving a fair reputation for talents and virtue. The emperor Tiberius was his brother. It is said that Augustus intended to give a portion of the empire to Drusus, who was born a few months after the marriage of the former with Livia. Drusus left two sons, Germanicus, and Claudius who became emperor.

See Dion Cassius, books xlviii. and liv.; Tacitus, "Annals;" Ersch und Gruber, "Allgemeine Encyklopaedie."

Drusus, (Marcus Livius,) a Roman tribune, was a colleague of Caius Gracchus in the tribuneship in 122 B.C. The senate, alarmed at the innovations of Gracchus, procured the election of Drusus because he was popular and eloquent, in order to undermine the influence of Gracchus. Drusus founded many colonies, and courted the popular favour with success, at the same time promoting the interests of the optimates. He was chosen consul for 112 B.C., obtained Macedonia as his province, and defeated the Thracian Scordisci.

See Plutarch, "Caius Gracchus;" Livy, "Epitome," book lxiii.; Niebuhr, "History of Rome."

Drusus, (Marcus Livius,) a son of the preceding, and uncle of Cato Uticensis, was called Drusus Junior. He was an ambitious politician, and a champion or

patronus of the senate, which at that period was involved in a contest with the equites respecting the judicial power. In 91 B.C. he was chosen tribune of the people, whose favour he gained by largesses and agrarian laws. The consul Philippus was arrested by his order, and the senate voted that the laws of Drusus were null. He became the leader of a conspiracy or party which designed to give the right of citizenship to the Italiotes and to make other changes. He was assassinated by an unknown hand in 91 or 90 B.C.

See Niebuhr, "History of Rome ;" Cicero, "Brutus," "De Officiis," and "Pro Milone ;" Appian, "De Bello Civili;" Bemmel, "Dissertatio de M. L. Drusis Patre et Filio," 1826.

Dru'sus Cæ'sar, (see'zar,) sometimes called Drusus Junior, a son of the emperor Tiberius, married Livia, a sister of Germanicus. His character was depraved by cruelty and other vices. Died in 23 A.D., from poison.

See Tacitus, "Annals."

Drŭth'mar' or dRoot'mǎr', (Christian,) a monk and grammarian, who lived at Corbie, France, about 850 A.D.

Drȳ'ad, [Gr. δρυάς, plural δρυάδες, (from δρῦς, an "oak" or any "tree ;") Lat. Dry'ades ; Fr. Dryades, dRe'ǎd'.] The dryads, in classic mythology, were nymphs or goddesses presiding over woods and groves. The Ham'a-dry'ads [from the Greek ἅμα, "together with"] were supposed to be attached to some particular tree, with which they lived and died.

See "Biographie Universelle," (Partie mythologique.)

Dryades. See Dryad.

Dryander, dRe-än'der, (Johann,) or **Eichmann,** īk'-mǎn, a German astronomer, born at Wetteren, in Hesse. He published esteemed works, among which are "De Cylindro" and "The Terrestrial Globe." Died in 1560.

Dryander, dRe-än'der, (Jonas,) a Swedish naturalist, born in 1748, was a pupil of Linnæus. About 1780 he removed to England, where he made an excellent Catalogue of Sir Joseph Banks's Library, (1798.) He wrote some botanical treatises, and was one of the founders of the Linnæan Society. Died in London in 1810.

See Ersch und Gruber, "Allgemeine Encyklopaedie."

Drȳ'den, (Charles,) the eldest son of the great poet, was educated as a Catholic. In 1692 he obtained an office in the palace of Pope Clement XI., but resigned it to his brother John, and returned to England. He was the author of some fugitive poems. He was drowned, while swimming in the Thames, in 1704.

Dryden, (John,) a celebrated English poet, born at Aldwinckle, in Northamptonshire, on the 9th of August, 1631. He was the eldest son of Erasmus Driden, a rigid Puritan of gentle birth. After passing under the discipline of Dr. Busby at Westminster, he entered Trinity College, Cambridge, in 1650. He left college in 1657, and became a citizen of London. One of his first poetic essays was "Heroic Stanzas on the Death of Cromwell," (1658,) of whom he was at that time an admirer. He hailed with alacrity the restoration of 1660, in a poem named "Astræa Redux." In 1662 he produced his first drama, "The Wild Gallant," which did not make much impression on the public mind. About 1663 he married Lady Howard, the daughter of the Earl of Berkshire. In 1667 appeared his "Annus Mirabilis," or "Year of Wonders," and a tragi-comedy entitled "The Indian Emperor." He succeeded Davenant as poet-laureate in 1668, and published his excellent prose "Essay on Dramatic Poesy," which entitled him, as Dr. Johnson observed, to be considered the father of English criticism. He afterwards produced many successful comedies and tragedies, among which are "Marriage à-la-Mode," "All for Love," (1678,) "Aurengzebe," and "Don Sebastian," (1690.) His dramas are eminent examples of genius perverted, and abound in passages of disgusting indecency. He also acquired great celebrity in satire and in lyric poetry. His "Absalom and Achitophel" (1681) is a poetical satire against the party of which Lord Shaftesbury was the master-spirit and the Duke of Monmouth the nominal head. It had a prodigious success. In reference to this poem, Hallam remarks, "The spontaneous ease of expression, the rapid transitions, the general elasticity and movement, have never been excelled." About 1686 he avowed himself a convert to the Roman Catholic Church, which was then favoured at court, and wrote

"The Hind and the Panther," an allegory in verse. The subject is the controversy between the Romish Church (the Hind) and the Church of England, represented by the Spotted Panther.

In the latter part of his life he gradually ceased to write for the stage, and acquired with a purer taste a more natural style. "He had turned his powers in a new direction," says Macaulay, "with success the most splendid and decisive. His taste had gradually awakened his creative faculties. The first rank in poetry was beyond his reach, but he secured the most honourable place in the second. . . . His command of language was immense. With him died the secret of the old poetical diction of England,—the art of producing rich effects by familiar words. . . . Dryden was an incomparable reasoner in verse."

Among his later productions are translations of Juvenal and Virgil, (1697,) and the celebrated "Ode for Saint Cecilia's Day," (about 1700,) which Macaulay pronounces "his greatest work, and a master-piece of the second class of poetry." Some critics esteem it the finest ode in the language. "His translation of Virgil," says Pope, "is the most noble and spirited translation I know in any language." Brougham speaks of his prose as "the matchless prose of Dryden, rich, various, natural, animated, pointed," etc. He died on the 1st of May, 1700, and was buried in Westminster Abbey.

See JOHNSON, "Lives of the Poets;" SIR WALTER SCOTT, "Life of Dryden," prefixed to an edition of Dryden's works, 18 vols., 1808; MACAULAY, "Essays," articles "Dryden" and "Comic Dramatists of the Restoration;" also, "History of England," vol. ii. chap. vii. and vol. iv. chap. xx.; MALONE, "Life of Dryden;" VILLEMAIN, "Tableau de la Littérature au dix-huitième Siècle;" PROF. JOHN WILSON, "Critique on Dryden," in "Blackwood's Magazine" for February, March, and April, 1845; "Edinburgh Review" for July, 1855; "Retrospective Review," vol. i., 1820; "Fraser's Magazine" for August, 1854, and August, 1865; "Westminster Review" for April, 1855.

Dryden, (JOHN,) son of the preceding, born about 1668. He translated the 14th Satire for his father's version of Juvenal, and wrote a comedy, "The Husband his own Cuckold," (1696.) Died at Rome in 1701.

ERASMUS HENRY, the third son of the great poet, inherited the title of baronet from a kinsman of his father, and died in 1710.

Drys̆'dale, (JOHN,) D.D., a Scottish divine and eloquent preacher, born at Kirkaldy in 1718. In 1766 he was appointed one of the ministers of the Tron Church in Edinburgh. Died in 1788. His sermons were published in 1793.

See CHAMBERS, "Biographical Dictionary of Eminent Scotsmen."

Dschafer or **Dschaafar.** See MANSOOR.

Dschami. See JÂMEE.

Dschehan- or **Dschahan-Ghir.** See JAHÂN-GEER.

Dschelal-Eddin. See JELÂL-ED-DEEN.

Dschemschid. See JEMSHEED.

Dschengis. See JENGIS KHAN.

Dschihan-Ghir. See JAHÂN-GEER.

Dschingis. See JENGIS KHAN.

Duali- (or **Douali-**) **al-Easree,** (or **-Basrî,**) dŏ̄-âl'e âl bâs'ree, written also **Dueli-** (**Doueli-**) and **Duwali-el-Basrî,** (**Abool-** (or **Abû-l-**) **Aswed-Zâlim-** (or **Sâlim-**) **Ibn-Amroo-Ibn-Sofyân,** â'bŏ̄l âs'wed zâ'lim Ib'n âm'rŏ̄ Ib'n so-fe-ân',) an eminent Arabian grammarian and miser, born at Bassora (Basra) about 600 A.D., (or 630, according to some authorities ;) died at the age of eighty-two.

See HAMMER-PURGSTALL, "Literaturgeschichte der Araber;" IBN-KHALLIKAN, "Biographical Dictionary."

Du-âne', (WILLIAM,) an American politician, born near Lake Champlain, New York, in 1760. He learned the trade of printer, and went to India about 1784. He afterwards passed several years in England. Having returned to the United States about 1795, he became editor of "The Aurora," a Democratic paper which was published at Philadelphia, and acquired much influence. He edited "The Aurora" for many years. Died in 1835. Parton, in his "Life of Jackson," says that "Jackson formed a very high idea of his character and talents."

Du-âne', (WILLIAM J.,) an eminent lawyer and statesman, born at Clonmel, Ireland, in 1780, was a son of the preceding. He was admitted to the bar in 1803, and practised in Philadelphia. About 1821 he represented that city in the legislature of Pennsylvania. He was the legal adviser of Stephen Girard, whose last will he wrote in 1831. He was appointed secretary of the treasury in January or June, 1833, and was ordered by President Jackson to remove the deposits of public money from the Bank of the United States. Having refused to comply with this order, he was removed from office in September, 1833. He passed the rest of his life as a private citizen. He published "The Law of Nations Investigated in a Popular Manner," (1809.) Died in Philadelphia in 1865.

Duaren. See DOUAREN.

Duarte I., King of Portugal. See EDWARD.

Duault, dü'ō', (FRANÇOIS MARIE GUILLAUME,) a French poet, born at Saint-Malo in 1757, translated "The Vicar of Wakefield," and wrote elegiac poems which are commended. Died in 1833.

Duban, dü'bôN', (FÉLIX LOUIS JACQUES,) a French architect, and member of the Institute, born in Paris about 1798. He finished the Palace of Fine Arts, commenced by Debret, and was chosen architect of the Louvre in 1848.

Du Bartas. See BARTAS.

Dubayet. See AUBERT DU BAYET.

Dubellay. See BELLAY,

Dubeux, dü'buh', (LOUIS,) an Orientalist, born of French parents in Lisbon about 1795. He wrote a work entitled "Persia," ("La Perse," 1841,) and became professor of Turkish in Paris in 1848.

Dübner or **Duebner,** düb'něr, (FRIEDRICH,) a German philologist, born in 1802, published an edition of Justin, (1831.) He afterwards edited for Firmin Didot's "Bibliotheca Græca" several authors, among whom are Arrian and Maximus of Tyre.

Duboccage. See BOCCAGE.

Dubois, dü'bwâ', (ANTOINE,) an eminent French surgeon and physician, born at Gramat (Lot) in 1756. He was chosen royal professor in the School of Surgery in Paris in 1790, and in 1802 surgeon-in-chief of the hospital which bears his name, the Hospice Dubois. He possessed rare sagacity and dexterity, and was regarded by the French as one of the first physicians of Europe. He attended the empress Maria Louisa on the occasion of the birth of her son. His medical principles have been published by several of his pupils. Died in 1837.

See "Nouvelle Biographie Générale."

Dubois, du-bois' or dü'bwâ', (EDWARD,) an English satirical writer, born about 1775, published, besides other works, "The Wreath," (1799,) an edition of Boccaccio's "Decameron," (in English, 1804,) and "My Pocket-Book," a satire, (1807.) Died in 1850.

Dubois, (FRANÇOIS,) a French painter of history, born in Paris in 1790. He gained the grand prize in 1819, and a first-class medal in 1831.

Dubois, (FRANÇOIS NOËL,) a French botanist, born at Orléans in 1752; died in 1824.

Dubois, (FRÉDÉRIC,) an able French medical writer, born at Amiens about 1796, succeeded Pariset in 1847 as perpetual secretary of the Academy of Medicine, Paris. Among his works is a "Treatise on General Pathology," (2 vols., 1837.)

Dubois, (FRÉDÉRIC,) a Swiss naturalist and traveller, born in 1798, published "Travels in the Crimea, Colchis, and Georgia," and became professor of archæology at Neufchâtel in 1843. Died in 1849.

Dubois, (GIRARD,) a French priest, born at Orléans in 1628, wrote, in Latin, a "History of the Church of Paris." Died in 1696.

Dubois, (GUILLAUME,) a French troubadour, surnamed CRETIN, wrote a "History of France" in French verse, (still in manuscript.) A collection of his songs, etc. was published in 1527. Died in 1525.

See LONGFELLOW's "Poets and Poetry of Europe."

Dubois, (GUILLAUME,) a French cardinal and minister of state, born at Brive-la-Gaillarde, in Limousin, in 1656. In the reign of Louis XIV. he was appointed preceptor to the Duc de Chartres, (afterwards Duke of Orléans and Regent of France,) whose favour he gained by pandering to his baser passions and appetites. The appointment of his pupil to the regency in 1715 favoured the ambitious designs of Dubois, who was then made a councillor of state, although the regent's mother entreated him not to employ one whom she stigmatized as a most arrant knave. He displayed great address and astuteness in political intrigues, and had an important part in the triple alliance of 1717. Soon after this he became minister of foreign affairs, and, in spite of his scandalous life, Archbishop of Cambray. After much opposition, he obtained a cardinal's hat in 1721, and was made prime minister the next year. He exiled all who resisted his will, and he retained power until his death in 1725.

See SAINT-SIMON, "Mémoires;" DUCLOS, "Mémoires secrets sur les Règnes de Louis XIV et XV;" PAUL LACROIX, "Mémoires du Cardinal Dubois," 4 vols., 1829.

Dubois, [Lat. SYL′VIUS,] (JACQUES,) a learned French physician, born at Amiens in 1478. He lectured on medicine in Paris, and in 1550 became a professor of medicine in the Collége Royal. He wrote several able professional treatises. Died in 1555.

See RENÉ MOREAU, "Vita Sylvii," prefixed to an edition of his works; BAYLE, "Historical and Critical Dictionary."

Dubois, (JEAN,) a Flemish or French medical writer, born at Lille; died at Douai in 1576.

Dubois, (JEAN,) a French sculptor, born at Dijon in 1626, was a grandfather of the poet Alexis Piron. Died at Dijon in 1694.

Dubois, (JEAN ANTOINE,) ABBÉ, a French missionary, who laboured many years in Hindostan, was born in Ardèche in 1765. He wrote, in English, "The Character, Manners, Customs, and Institutions of the People of India," which was published by the East India Company in 1816. It is said to be one of the best works on that subject. Died in Paris in 1848.

Dubois, (JEAN BAPTISTE,) a French writer, born in Burgundy in 1753, resided for a time in Poland, where he became a councillor at court. Having returned to Paris, he became the friend and assistant of Malesherbes. After the reign of terror he held a high office in the ministry of the interior. He wrote a "Notice of the Life and Labours of Malesherbes," and other works. Died in 1808.

Dubois, (LOUIS FRANÇOIS,) a French *littérateur*, born at Lisieux in 1773, published a voluminous treatise on Agriculture, entitled "Cours complet d'Agriculture," (1825-32,) and a French version of Orderic Vital's "History of Normandy," (1827.) Died in 1855.

Dubois, (PAUL,) a French surgeon, son of Antoine, noticed above, was born in Paris in 1795. He published in 1849 the first part of a "Complete Treatise on the Art of Accouchements." He was accoucheur to the empress Eugénie. Died in October, 1860.

Dubois, (PAUL ALEXIS,) a French general, born about 1754, was killed at Alla, in the Tyrol, in 1796.

Dubois, (PAUL FRANÇOIS,) a French journalist and professor, born at Rennes in 1795. He was one of the editors of the "Globe," a liberal daily journal of Paris, for several years, ending in 1830, and sat in the Chamber of Deputies from 1831 to 1848. He became professor of French literature in the Polytechnic School in 1834, and succeeded Victor Cousin as director of the Normal School in 1840.

See "Nouvelle Biographie Générale."

Dubois, (PHILIPPE **Goibaud**,) a French writer, born at Poitiers in 1626, was tutor of the Duc de Guise, (Louis Joseph.) He made translations of the works of Saint Augustine, and of Cicero "De Officiis," "De Senectute," etc., which procured his admission into the French Academy in 1693. Died in 1694.

Dubois, dü′bwȧ′, (SIMON,) a Flemish painter of portraits and animals, born in Antwerp after 1622, worked in England. Died in 1708.

Dubois-Crancé. See DUBOIS DE CRANCÉ.

Dubois de Crancé, dü′bwȧ′ deh krôn′sȧ′, or **Dubois-Crancé,** (EDMOND LOUIS ALEXIS,) a French general and Jacobin, born at Charleville in 1747. He was elected to the Convention in 1792, became a partisan of Danton, and was one of the first members of the committee of public safety. He directed the siege of Lyons, from which he was recalled by the Convention on the charge of *modérantisme* in 1793. He was inspector-general and minister of war in 1799, but lost all his offices when Bonaparte obtained power. Died in 1814.

Dubois de Jancigny, dü′bwȧ′ deh zhôn′sèn′ye′, (ADOLPHE PHILIBERT,) a French writer, a son of Jean Baptiste Dubois, noticed above, was born in Paris in 1795. He spent many years in British India, and was sent on a mission to China in 1841. He wrote several books on India, China, etc. Two of these, namely, "India," (1845,) and "China and the Birman Empire," (1850,) form part of Firmin Didot's series entitled "L'Univers."

Dubois [Lat. SYL′VIUS] **de la Boë,** dü′bwȧ′ deh lä bo′ä′, (FRANCISCUS,) a German or Dutch physician, of French extraction, eminent for learning and eloquence, was born at Hanau in 1614. He practised about fifteen years at Amsterdam, and obtained the chair of practical medicine at Leyden in 1658. He gave an impulse to the study of chemistry by his zeal and eloquence. "It is to Dubois," says Fournier, "that we owe the first idea of clinic instruction and the initiative in the study of pathologic anatomy." He published several works, among which is "Disputationum Medicarum decas," (1663.) Died in 1672.

See ÉLOY, "Dictionnaire historique de la Médecine."

Dubois-Fontanelle, dü′bwȧ′ fôn′tä′nêl′, (JEAN GASPARD,) a French dramatist and *littérateur*, born at Grenoble in 1737; died in 1812. His drama of "Éricie," against monastic vows, was prohibited by the censor.

See "Nouvelle Biographie Générale."

Dubos, dü′bo′, (CHARLES FRANÇOIS,) a French ecclesiastic and writer, born in 1661; died at Luçon in 1724.

Dubos, (JEAN BAPTISTE,) a French writer and negotiator, born at Beauvais in 1670. He studied public law, and was employed in many important and secret negotiations with foreign courts by De Torcy and Dubois. He wrote, besides other works, the "History of the League of Cambray," (1712,) which Voltaire said was "profound, politic, and interesting," and "Critical Reflections on Poetry and Painting," (1719,) which the same critic praised as "the most valuable book ever written on those subjects in any nation of Europe." He was chosen in 1722 perpetual secretary of the French Academy, into which he had been admitted in 1720. Died in 1742.

See QUÉRARD, "La France Littéraire;" AUGUSTE MOREL, "Étude sur l'Abbé Dubos," 1851; V. TREMBLAY, "Notice sur l'Abbé Dubos," 1848.

Dubosc. See BOSC, DU.

Duboscq, dü′bosk′, (JULES,) a French optician, born in 1817, invented or improved several instruments, among which is the stereoscope.

Duboulay. See BOULAY, DU.

Dubouloz, dü′boo′lo′, or **Dubouleau,** dü′boo′lo′, (JEAN AUGUSTE,) a French painter of history, born in Paris in 1800.

Dubourcq, dü′boork′, (PIETER LODEWIJK,) a Dutch painter of landscapes and genre, born at Amsterdam in 1815.

Dubourg-Butler, dü′boor′ büt′laiR′, (FRÉDÉRIC,) a French general, born in Paris in 1778. He took an active part against Charles X. in July, 1830. Died in 1850.

Duboury, dü′boo′re′, (LODEWIJK FABRICIUS,) a skilful Dutch painter and engraver, born at Amsterdam in 1691. His *tableaux de boudoir* are highly prized. Died in 1775.

Dubraw, doo′bRäv, (JOHANN,) a Bohemian historian, born at Pilsen. His family name was SKALA. He became Bishop of Olmutz, and wrote, in Latin, a "History of Bohemia," (1552,) which is accounted accurate. Died in 1553.

Dubreton, dü′bReh-tôn′, (JEAN LOUIS,) BARON, a French general, born in Bretagne in 1773; died in 1855.

Dubreuil, dü′bRul′ or dü′bruh′ye′, (ALPHONSE,) a French horticulturist, born at Rouen in 1811. He founded at Rouen the *École d'Arbres fruitiers*, the first of the kind. In 1846 he published a work on the culture of trees, entitled "Cours d'Arboriculture," (2 vols.,) which has been often reprinted and translated.

Dubreul, dü′bRul′, (JACQUES,) a French antiquary, born in Paris in 1528, wrote on the Antiquities of Paris. Died in 1614.

Dubufe, dü′büf′, (CLAUDE MARIE,) a French painter of history and portraits, born in Paris in 1790. He was a fashionable portrait-painter for many years. Died in 1864.

Dubufe, (ÉDOUARD,) a successful French portrait-painter, son of the preceding, born in Paris about 1818.

Dubuisson, dü'bü-e'sŏN', (FRANÇOIS RENÉ ANDRÉ,) a French naturalist, born at Nantes in 1763. He became in 1810 director of the Museum of Natural History at Nantes, where he made a rich collection of minerals. He published an "Essay of a Geological Method," (1819.) Died in 1836.

Dubuisson, (PAUL ULRICH,) a mediocre French writer of dramas, etc., was born at Laval in 1746. He was guillotined in 1794.

Duby, dü'be', (PIERRE **Ancher Tobiesen**—ŏN'-shaiR' to'be'zŏN',) a Swiss linguist and medallist, born in the canton of Soleure in 1721, received the title of interpreter to the Royal Library of Paris. He wrote a treatise on Medals relating to Sieges, entitled "Recueil de Pièces obsidionales." Died in 1782.

Duc. See LEDUC and DUCQ.

Duc, dük, (JOSEPH LOUIS,) a French architect, born in Paris in 1802, gained the grand prize in 1825. In 1854 he was selected to enlarge the Palais de Justice.

Duc, du, dü dük, (FRONTON,) a French Jesuit, born at Bordeaux in 1558, was professor of theology at the College of Clermont in Paris. He published a good edition of the works of Chrysostom, (1609-24,) edited the works of some other Fathers, and wrote a curious book on the Maid of Orleans, entitled "The Tragical History of the Pucelle de Domremy, newly divided into Acts and represented by Personages," (1581.) Died in 1624.

See NICÉRON, "Mémoires."

Duca, del, dĕl doo'kä, (GIACOMO,) an Italian architect of the sixteenth century, born in Sicily, was a pupil of Michael Angelo. Among his works are the Palazzo Panfili, Palazzo Strozzi, and the Villa Mattei, all at Rome.

Du Camp or **Ducamp,** dü'kŏN', (MAXIME,) a French writer and artist, a son of Théodore J., noticed below, was born in Paris in 1822. Having twice visited Asia Minor, Greece, etc., he published "Souvenirs et Paysages d'Orient," and an elegant work entitled "Egypt, Nubia, Palestine, and Syria," (1852,) with photographic illustrations.

Du Camp, (THÉODORE JOSEPH,) a skilful French surgeon, born at Bordeaux in 1793, improved the method of treating diseases of the urinary organs. Died in 1824.

Ducancel, dü'kŏN'sêl', (CHARLES PIERRE,) a French dramatist and lawyer, born in 1766; died in 1835.

Du Cange or **Ducange,** dü'kŏNzh', (CHARLES **du Fresne**—dü'fRĕn',) Sieur du Cange, a French historical writer, born at Amiens in 1610. He was educated for the law, but did not practise it long. He was learned in the languages, history, geography, law, antiquities, etc., and wrote a great number of works, among which are a "History of the Empire of Constantinople under the French Emperors," "Byzantine History Illustrated," and "Glossary of Latin Words used in the Dark and Middle Ages," ("Glossarium ad Scriptores mediæ et infimæ Latinitatis,") which is highly prized. He left many manuscripts on various subjects. In 1668 he became a resident of Paris. "One is appalled," says Voltaire, "at the immensity of his learning and his labours." Died in 1688.

See DUFRESNE D'AUBIGNY, "Mémoires historiques pour servir à l'Histoire de C. du Fresne du Cange;" HARDOUIN, "Essai sur la Vie, etc. de Du Cange;" "Nouvelle Biographie Générale."

Ducange or **Du Cange** (VICTOR HENRI JOSEPH **Brahain**—bRä'ăN',) a French novelist and dramatist, born at the Hague in 1783. For the liberal political opinions expressed in his novel of "Valentine," (1821,) he was imprisoned six months. He wrote, among other works, two novels, entitled "Léonide" (1823) and "La Luthérienne," (1825,) and many dramas. Died in 1833.

See QUÉRARD, "La France Littéraire."

Ducarel, dü'ka-rêl' or dü'kä'rêl', (ANDRÉ **Coltée**—kol'tà',) a learned antiquary, born at Caen, in Normandy, about 1714. He passed his mature life in England, and was appointed commissary of Saint Catherine's and commissary of Canterbury about 1755. He was a Fellow of the Royal Society. Besides other works, he wrote a "Treatise on the Anglo-Gallic Medals of the Ancient Kings of England," (1757,) and "Anglo-Norman Antiquities," (1767,) which is esteemed valuable. Died in London in 1785.

See "Biographia Britannica."

Ducarla-Bonifas, dü'kăR'lä' bo'ne'fäs', (MARC,) a French physicist, born at Vabre in 1738; died in 1816.

Du Cart, dü kăRt, or **Ducart,** (IZAAK,) a Dutch painter of flowers, born at Amsterdam in 1630. He painted flowers on satin and vellum with a fidelity at that time unequalled. His productions are still prized by amateurs. Died in 1694.

Ducas. See CONSTANTINE DUCAS.

Du'cas, (MICHAEL,) [Μιχαὴλ ὁ Δούκας,] a Greek historian, who was descended from the imperial family of Ducas, and flourished about 1450. He wrote a "History of the Decadence of the Byzantine Empire, 1355 to 1453," which forms part of the collection called "Historia Byzantina." It is esteemed judicious and impartial, but is written in a barbarous style. He was living at Lesbos in 1462.

See VON HAMMER, "Geschichte des Osmanischen Reichs."

Ducasse, dü'kăss', (FRANÇOIS,) a French doctor of theology, eminent as a canonist; died in 1706.

Ducasse, (JEAN BAPTISTE,) a successful French naval officer, born in Béarn. He was a captain in the marine when he was appointed Governor of Saint Domingo in 1691. He defended that island against the English and Spaniards, and defeated Admiral Benbow in 1702, near Sainte-Marthe. In 1703 he was made chief of a squadron, and retired from the office of governor. He was raised to the grade of lieutenant-general, and commanded the fleet which invested Barcelona in 1714. Died in 1715.

See VAN TENAC, "Histoire de la Marine;" "Nouvelle Biographie Générale."

Ducasse, (JEAN MARIE AUGUSTE,) a skilful French physician and writer, born at Toulouse in 1786.

Ducaurroy de la Croix, dü'kō'rwä' dĕh lä kRwä, (ADOLPHE MARIE,) a French jurist, born in Normandy in 1788. He published "The Institutes of Justinian newly explained," (4 vols., 1835; 8th edition,1851,) which had a great and durable success. Died in 1850.

Duccio di Buoninsegna, doot'cho de boo-ŏn-ĕn-sän'yä, an eminent Italian painter, born in or near Sienna, flourished between 1280 and 1340. He was a pupil of Segna or Boninsegna, and was one of the most famous artists of his time. About 1310 he produced his great work, the altar-piece of the Sienna cathedral, which represents the Virgin and many saints.

See VASARI, "Lives of the Painters," etc.; LANZI, "History of Painting in Italy."

Ducerceau. See ANDROUET DU CERCEAU.

Du Chaillu, dü shä'yü', (PAUL,) a French traveller, born about 1830, became a citizen of the United States. He travelled in the interior of Africa in 1855-56, and published in 1861 his "Explorations and Adventures in Equatorial Africa." His veracity has been questioned by some critics. He was the first European that discovered and described the gorilla.

See "Edinburgh Review" for July, 1861.

Duchal, du-shal', ? (JAMES,) an Irish Protestant writer on theology, born at Antrim in 1697; died in 1761.

Duchalais, dü'shä'lä', (ADOLPHE,) a French antiquary and numismatist, born at Beaugency in 1814; died in 1854.

Duchange, dü'shŏNzh', (GASPARD,) a skilful French engraver, born in Paris in 1662, was a pupil of Jean Audran. He was especially successful in reproducing the works of Correggio, after whom he engraved "Leda" and "Danaë." Died in 1756.

Duchanoy, dü'shä'nwä', (CLAUDE FRANÇOIS,) a French physician and writer, born at Vauvilliers in 1742; died in 1827.

Duchat, Le, lĕh dü'shä', (JACOB,) a French critic and editor, born at Metz in 1658. He became a Protestant exile in 1700, and retired to Berlin, where he was appointed a judge. He published valuable editions of the works of Rabelais, (1711,) of the "Apology for Herodotus" by Stephanus, (1735,) and of other old French works. Died in 1735.

See J. H. S. FORMEY, "Ducatiana," 2 vols., 1738; NICÉRON, "Mémoires."

Duchâtel, dü'shä'tĕl', (CHARLES MARIE **Tanneguy**—tän'ge',) COMTE, a French minister of state, born in Paris in 1803, was a son of a peer of France. In September, 1836, he became minister of finance; and in April,

1837, retired with Guizot, whose political opinions he approved. He was minister of the interior from October, 1840, until the revolution of 1848.

Duchâtel, (FRANCOIS.) See CHÂTEL, DU.

Duchâtel, (GASPARD,) a French Girondist, born in 1766, was a deputy from Poitou to the National Convention in 1792. In the trial of the king he voted for banishment, as the most practicable mode of saving his life. He was one of the twenty-two Girondists proscribed by the Jacobins and executed in 1793.

Duchâtel, [Lat. CASTELLA'NUS,] (PIERRE,) a French bishop and scholar, born at Arc, in the diocese of Langres. In his youth he worked with Erasmus on editions of Greek authors. Curiosity led him to visit Egypt, Palestine, and Syria. On his return he became reader to Francis I., who said, "He is the only man of letters that I have never exhausted in discourse." He was appointed Bishop of Mâcon in 1544, grand almoner in 1547, and Bishop of Orléans in 1551. He died in 1552, leaving the reputation of a virtuous and tolerant prelate and one of the most learned and eloquent men of his age. He opposed the persecution of the Vaudois and Protestants.

See GALLAND, "Vita Castellani," 1674: BAYLE, "Historical and Critical Dictionary;" "Nouvelle Biographie Générale."

Duchâtel, (TANNEGUY.) See CHÂTEL, DU.

Du Châtelet. See CHASTELLET,(GABRIELLE ÉMILIE.)

Duché, du-shā', (JACOB,) D.D., an Episcopal clergyman, distinguished for his talents and eloquence, was born in Philadelphia about 1739. He graduated at the College of Philadelphia in 1757. On the assembling of the first Continental Congress, in 1774, he was elected chaplain ; and his opening prayer was remarkable for its earnestness and pathos, and contributed much towards reconciling the discordant elements of that body. He was subsequently chosen chaplain of several successive Congresses. Yet, when the British had taken Philadelphia, he not only made his peace with England, but wrote a letter to Washington urging him to follow his example. This letter Washington laid before Congress. Duché was declared a traitor, and fled to England. He afterwards returned to Philadelphia, and died in 1798.

Duché de Vancy, dü'shà' deh vŏn'se',(JOSEPH FRANÇOIS,) a French dramatist, born in Paris in 1668. He was a member of the Academy of Inscriptions, and a friend of Jean Baptiste Rousseau. Among his best productions are the tragedy of "Absalom," which La Harpe pronounced a work of merit, and the opera "Iphigenia in Tauris," of which Voltaire said, "It recalls a grand idea of what was most excellent in the Greek tragedy." Died in December, 1704.

Duchemin. See DUCLOS.

Duchenius. See DUCHESNE.

Duchesne, dü'shĕn', [Lat. DUCHE'NIUS or QUERCETA'NUS,] (ANDRÉ,) one of the most learned historians of France, was born in Touraine in 1584. After finishing his studies in Paris, he became geographer and historiographer to the king. His numerous and valuable works have procured for him the title of "the father of French history." Among them are "The Antiquities and Researches of the Grandeur of the Kings of France," (1609,) "Ancient Historians of the Normans," in Latin, (1619,) and "Contemporary Writers of the History of the Franks," ("Historiæ Francorum Scriptores coetanei," 1636–49.) He was run over by a carriage and killed, near Paris, in 1640.

See NICÉRON, "Mémoires;" LELONG, "Bibliothèque Historique."

Duchesne, (ANTOINE NICOLAS,) a learned French naturalist, born at Versailles in 1747, wrote a "Manual of Botany," (1764,) and other works. Died in 1827.

Duchesne, (FRANÇOIS,) a son of André, noticed above, born in Paris in 1616, cultivated history with zeal, and obtained the title of historiographer. He wrote a "History of the Chancellors of France," (1680,) and published editions of several works of his father, viz. : "The Antiquities of the Cities and Castles of France," (1647,) and "The History of the Popes," (1653.) Died in 1693.

Duchesne, (HENRI GABRIEL,) a French naturalist, born in Paris in 1739, published, conjointly with M. Macquer, a "Naturalist's Manual," (1771,) and a "Dictionary of Industry," (3 vols., 1776.) Died in 1822.

Duchesne, (JOSEPH,) a French physician and chemist, born in Armagnac about 1544. In 1593 he went to Paris, where he became physician-in-ordinary to Henry IV. He published "Pharmacopœia dogmaticorum restituta," and other medical works. Died in 1609.

See ÉLOY, "Dictionnaire de la Médecine."

Duchesne de Gisors, dü'shĕn' deh zhe'zoR', (JEAN BAPTISTE JOSEPH,) a French miniature-painter, born at Gisors (Eure) in 1770. He became court painter during the restoration, and painted on ivory the portraits of the royal family. In 1840 he was employed to continue for the Louvre a collection of enamels begun by Petitot. Among his master-pieces are miniatures of Napoleon I. and of the Duchess of Berry. Died in 1856.

Duchesnois, dü'shà'nwä', (CATHERINE JOSEPHINE,) a popular French tragic actress, whose proper name was RAFIN, was born near Valenciennes in 1777. She made her *début* at the Théâtre Français in 1803, with complete success, and continued to be a favourite actress until she retired in 1820. Died in 1835.

See A. DINAUX, "Notice biographique sur Mademoiselle Duchesnois," 1836.

Duchoul, dü'shool', [Lat. CAU'LIUS,] (GUILLAUME,) a French antiquary, born at Lyons, lived about 1550. He wrote a "Discourse on the Religion of the Ancient Romans," (1555.) His son JEAN was a naturalist, and published several treatises.

Ducis, dü'sèss', (JEAN FRANÇOIS,) an eminent French dramatic poet, born at Versailles in August, 1733. He produced in 1769 a version of Shakspeare's "Hamlet," which was very successful. His "Romeo and Juliet" (1772) was received with equal favour. He succeeded Voltaire in the French Academy in 1778, after which he produced imitations of "King Lear" and "Macbeth," (1784.) He favoured the Revolution of 1789, but took no active part in it. His "Othello" was performed by Talma with great success in 1792. In 1795 he composed an original drama, "Abufar, or the Arab Family," which is called his master-piece. He refused a pension offered to him by Bonaparte. "Ducis," says Villemain, "was one of those men most adapted to impress the imagination and to leave a long remembrance. Amidst that sort of uniformity which involves the secondary minds of an epoch, he had something rare and original. . . . He meddled not with the petty affairs of the world, nor was his life infested with petty ambitions. A distinctive trait in his character was a noble independence. He submitted to no yoke, not even to that of his age ; for in that skeptical age he was very religious. His taste and solitary choice was the reading of the Bible and Homer. This explains how he resisted the influence of the eighteenth century, and was an original thinker compared with his contemporaries." Died at Versailles in March, 1816.

See VILLEMAIN, "Cours de Littérature ;" M. O. LEROY, "Études sur Ducis," 1832; CAMPENON, "Essais de Mémoires, ou Lettres sur la Vie et les Ecrits de J. F. Ducis," 1824 ; "Nouvelle Biographie Générale."

Ducis, (LOUIS,) a French historical painter, nephew of the preceding, was born in 1775. He was a pupil of David, and was one of the artists employed in 1814 to restore pictures in the palace of Versailles. About 1817 he produced "Francis I. knighted by Bayard," which is in the palace of Compiègne, and "The Death of Tasso." He painted portraits of Napoleon I., Talma, and many others. His uncle once said to him, "I have sought to be a painter in verse ; I see with pleasure that you aim to be a poet on canvas." Died in 1847.

See GUYOT DE FÈRE, "Biographie des Artistes Français."

Duck, (ARTHUR,) an eminent English civilian, born near Exeter in 1580. He became chancellor of London, and master of requests. In the civil war he adhered to the royal cause. He wrote a treatise on the Civil Law of the Romans. Died in 1649.

See WOOD, "Athenæ Oxonienses."

Duck, (STEPHEN,) an English peasant-poet, born at Charlton, in Wiltshire. He was self-taught, became a clergyman, and published rude specimens of poetry. In a fit of insanity, he drowned himself in the Thames in 1756.

See JOSEPH SPENCE, "Life of S. Duck."

Ducker. See DUKER.

Duckwitz, dook′wits, (ARNOLD,) a German political economist, born at Bremen in 1802, has written on the commerce and customs of Germany.

Duck′worth, (Sir JOHN THOMAS,) an English admiral, born at Leatherhead, in Surrey, in 1748. He entered the navy in 1759, and became post-captain in 1780. In June, 1794, he won great distinction by his skill and courage in Lord Howe's victory over the French. About 1800 he was made rear-admiral, and two years later was commander-in-chief at Jamaica. In 1806 he defeated the French near Saint Domingo, for which Parliament voted him thanks and a large pension. As vice-admiral, he performed a daring exploit by entering the Dardanelles in 1807. He was knighted in 1813. Died in 1817.

See THIERS, "Histoire du Consulat et de l'Empire;" VAN TENAC, "Histoire générale de la Marine;" "Nouvelle Biographie Générale."

Duclerc, dü′klaiR′, (CHARLES THÉODORE EUGÈNE,) a French financier and writer on political economy, was born in Hautes-Pyrénées in 1812.

Duclercq, dü′klaiR′, (JACQUES,) a French chronicler, born in 1420, wrote on the events of his own time. Died after 1467.

Duclos, dü′klo′, (CHARLES **Pineau**—pe′nō′,) a witty and ingenious French writer, born at Dinan in 1704, was liberally educated in Paris. He acquired reputation by his romances "The Baroness of Luz," (1741,) and "Confessions of Count * * *," a series of tableaux and satirical portraits. He was admitted into the Academy of Inscriptions in 1739, and into the French Academy in 1747, and was chosen perpetual secretary of the latter in 1755. His most admired work is a series of moral essays, entitled "Considérations sur les Mœurs de ce Siècle," (1750.) He wrote a "History of Louis XI.," (about 1744,) and obtained the title of historiographer of France. D'Alembert said of him, "He has more wit in a given time than any man I know." Rousseau designated him as one who was at the same time *droit et adroit*, ("upright and adroit.") His "Secret Memoirs of the Reigns of Louis XIV. and Louis XV." are highly praised. Died in 1772.

See AUGER, "Notice sur Duclos;" VILLENAVE, "Notice sur Duclos," prefixed to his works, published by BELIN, 1821 ; SAINTE-BEUVE, "Causeries du Lundi," tome ix. ; "Mémoires sur la Vie de Duclos, écrites par lui-même;" ROUSSEAU, "Confessions."

Duclos, (JEAN FRANÇOIS,) a French poet, born at Toulouse in 1705, wrote an ode on Enthusiasm, and translated portions of Tibullus and Horace into verse. Died in 1752.

Duclos, afterwards **Duchemin,** dü′sheh-mǎN′, (MARIE ANNE,) a French actress, born in 1664. She married an actor named Duchemin. Died in 1748.

Duclos, (SAMUEL **Cotreau**—kot′rō′,) a French physician, born in Paris, was chosen a member of the Academy of Sciences in 1666, and was at one time physician-in-ordinary to the king. He wrote "Observations on the Mineral Waters of France." Died in 1715.

Ducloz-Dufresnoy, dü′klo′ dü′frǎ′nwǎ′, (CHARLES NICOLAS,) a French financier, born at Montcornet in 1734. He was elected alternate deputy to the States-General by the citizens of Paris in 1789. He wrote several able treatises on the public finances, (1790.) He perished on the scaffold in 1794. He was the putative father of the savant Walckenaer, who wrote an article on him in the "Biographie Universelle."

Ducornet, dü′koR′nǎ′, (LOUIS CÉSAR JOSEPH,) a French painter, born at Lille in 1806. Having been born without arms, he learned to paint with his feet, and received a pension of 1200 francs in 1824. Among his works, which have gained several prizes, are "The Parting of Hector and Andromache," and "Saint Louis dispensing Justice."

Ducos, dü′ko′, (JEAN FRANÇOIS,) a French republican, born at Bordeaux in 1765. He was a deputy to the Convention from the department of Gironde in 1792, and voted for the death of the king. When the Girondist leaders were proscribed in May, 1793, he was at first omitted from the list ; but, having bravely asserted their innocence in the Convention, he was consigned to the same prison with them. He suffered death, with his brother-in-law Fonfrède and others, in October, 1793.

See LAMARTINE, "History of the Girondists."

Ducos, (NICOLAS,) a French general, brother of Roger Ducos, noticed below, was born at Dax in 1756. He fought bravely at Arcola, etc. in 1796, and obtained the rank of general of brigade in 1802. He served with *éclat* in the campaigns from 1805 to 1808. Died in 1823.

Ducos, (ROGER,) a French lawyer and politician, born at Dax about 1750. Deputed to the Convention by the department of Landes in 1792, he was a moderate partisan of the new régime, and sat with the members of the Plain. He voted, however, for the death of the king. In 1796 he was elected to the Council of Elders, and in 1799 was chosen a member of the Directory. He appears to have favoured Siéyès in his intrigues against their colleague Barras, and he co-operated with Bonaparte in the *coup d'état* of the 18th Brumaire, (November 9,) 1799, after which Ducos became Third Consul ; but he soon resigned this office, and was made a senator. He was exiled as a regicide in 1816, and died the same year.

See THIERS, "History of the French Revolution;" "Nouvelle Biographie Générale."

Ducos, (THÉODORE,) a French minister of state, a nephew of the preceding, born at Bordeaux in 1801. He was elected in 1834 to the Chamber of Deputies, in which he acted with the opposition. In the Constituent Assembly of 1848 he opposed socialism, and caused to be inserted in the constitution this phrase : "The republic is based on the family, property, and public order." He supported Louis Napoleon, and was minister of marine from December, 1851, until his death in April, 1855.

See "Nouvelle Biographie Générale."

Ducq or **Duc, Le,** leh dük or dük, (JAN,) a Dutch painter and engraver, born at the Hague in 1636, was a pupil and imitator of Paul Potter. His subjects are mostly animals, robbers, and guard-rooms. In 1671 he became director of the Academy at the Hague. Died about 1695.

See BASAN, "Dictionnaire des Graveurs."

Ducq, dük or dük, (JOSEPH FRANÇOIS,) a Belgian painter, born at Ledeghem in 1762. He gained several prizes at the expositions of Paris, where he lived many years. In 1815 he became court painter to the King of the Netherlands. Among his master-pieces is "Venus rising from the Sea." Died at Bruges in 1829.

Ducray-Duminil, dü′kră′ dü′me′nèl′, (FRANÇOIS GUILLAUME,) a popular French novelist, born in Paris in 1761 ; died in 1819.

Ducrest, dü′kră′, (CHARLES LOUIS,) born near Autun in 1747, was a brother of Madame de Genlis. He became a colonel in the army, and wrote on political economy. Died in 1824.

Ducrest de Villeneuve, dü′kră′ deh vèl′nuv′, (ALEXANDRE LOUIS,) a French admiral, born near Vitré in 1777 ; died in 1852.

See SALVANDY, "Notice sur Ducrest de Villeneuve," 1852.

Ducreux, dü′kRuh′, (FRANÇOIS,) a French historian, born at Saintes in 1596, wrote a "History of Canada," ("Historia Canadensis," 1664.) Died in 1666.

Ducreux, (GABRIEL MARIN,) a French priest, born at Orléans in 1743, wrote a history of Christianity, entitled "Siècles chrétiens," (10 vols., 1767.) Died in 1790.

Ducreux, (JOSEPH,) a French portrait-painter, born at Nancy in 1737 ; died in 1802.

Ducros, dü′kRo′, (PIERRE,) a Swiss painter and engraver, born in 1745. He removed to Rome, where, with the assistance of Volpato, he produced fine views of Roman scenery and monuments. In partnership with Montagnani, he published admirable views of Sicily and Malta. Died in 1810.

Du Deffand. See DEFFAND, DU.

Dudevant, Madame. See SAND, (GEORGE.)

Dudinck, dü′dink, (JOSSE,) a learned Dutchman, published a work on bibliography, entitled "Palatium Apollinis et Palladis," ("The Palace of Apollo and Minerva.")

Dudith, doo-deet′, (ANDREW,) a Hungarian Reformer, born at Buda in 1533. About 1560, Ferdinand II. gave him the bishopric of Tina. In 1562 he was sent by that emperor and the clergy of Hungary to the Council of Trent, in which he spoke eloquently in favour of the marriage of priests and other reforms. He married Reyna Strazzi, resigned his bishopric, was excommunicated, and

ā, ē, ī, ō, ū, ȳ, *long;* ă, ĕ, ĭ, ŏ, ŭ, ў, *short;* ạ, ẹ, ị, ọ, *obscure;* fär, fåll, fåt; mĕt; nŏt; gōŏd; mōŏn·

became an avowed Protestant. He was learned in languages and sciences, and wrote numerous Latin works on theology, etc. Among them are a treatise on comets, and several poems. He translated Dionysius of Halicarnassus into Latin. Died at Breslau in 1589.

See REUTER, "Vita Dudithi," prefixed to his *Orations*, 1610; SAMUELFY, "Dissertatio de Vita et Scriptis A. Dudithi," 1743; NICÉRON, "Memoires."

Dud'ley, (AMBROSE,) Earl of Warwick, a son of the Duke of Northumberland, was born about 1530. He was condemned to death as an accomplice in his father's treason in 1553, but was pardoned. In 1557 he fought with distinction for the Spaniards at Saint-Quentin. After the accession of Elizabeth he was created Earl of Warwick, and held several high offices. Died in 1589.

Dud'ley, (BENJAMIN WINSLOW,) M.D., an American surgeon, born in Virginia in 1785. He took the degree of M.D. at the University of Pennsylvania in 1806, and afterwards pursued his professional studies in London and in Paris. On his return to America, in 1814, he established himself as a surgeon in Lexington, Kentucky. He has been successful in a multitude of difficult operations in surgery, and has contributed various essays to medical journals.

Dudley, (CHARLES EDWARD,) a Senator of the United States, born in Staffordshire, England, in 1780. He became a resident of Albany, New York, about 1812, and represented New York in the Federal Senate from 1828 to 1833. He erected at Albany the Dudley Observatory, to which his widow gave seventy thousand dollars or more. He died in 1841.

Dudley, (EDMUND,) an English lawyer, notorious as the minister employed by Henry VII. in extorting money from his subjects, was born in 1462. He was chosen Speaker of the Commons in 1504. Soon after the accession of Henry VIII., Dudley and Empson were tried on a charge of treason, and, to appease the popular clamour, were executed in 1510. His son JOHN became Duke of Northumberland.

Dudley, (Lord GUILFORD,) the fourth son of the Duke of Northumberland, married Lady Jane Grey in 1553. He was beheaded, with his wife, in February, 1554.

Dudley, (Sir HENRY BATE,) an English clergyman, eminent as a magistrate and journalist, born at Fenny Compton in 1745. He established the "Morning Post," (1775,) and the "Morning Herald," (1780,) and wrote "The Rival Candidates," (1775,) and other plays. He became rector of Willingham in 1812, and prebendary of Ely in 1816. In 1812 he was rewarded for his services as magistrate by a baronetcy. Died in 1824.

Dudley, (Lady JANE.) See GREY.

Dudley, (JOHN,) Duke of Northumberland, born in 1502, was the son of Edmund Dudley, noticed above. He was created Viscount Lisle in 1542, and was afterwards appointed by Henry VIII. lord high admiral of England. On the accession of Edward VI. (1547) he became Earl of Warwick. Two years later he formed a successful conspiracy against the Protector Somerset, obtained the chief control of the government, and was made Duke of Northumberland in 1551. He persuaded Edward VI. to appoint Lady Jane Grey successor to the crown. At the death of Edward (1553) he vainly resisted the accession of Mary, and was executed for treason. Robert, Earl of Leicester, was his son.

See FROUDE, "History of England," vols. v. and vi.; also HUME's and LINGARD's Histories of England.

Dudley, (JOHN WILLIAM WARD,) a son of Viscount Dudley Ward, was born about 1781. He was elected to the House of Commons in 1802, and distinguished himself by his talents for business. At the death of his father, in 1823, he entered the House of Lords. He was secretary of state for a few months in the ministry of Canning formed in April, 1827. He was a friend of the poet Byron, and author of a "Life of Horne Tooke." Died in 1833.

Dudley, (JOSEPH,) born in Massachusetts in 1647, was a son of Thomas, noticed below. He became chief justice of Massachusetts in 1686, chief justice of New York in 1690, and was governor of his native province from 1702 to 1715. Died in 1720.

Dudley, (PAUL,) F.R.S., chief justice of Massachusetts, a son of the preceding, was born in 1675. He

graduated at Harvard College in 1690, and, having completed his law studies at the Temple in London, was attorney-general of Massachusetts from 1702 to 1718. In 1745 he was appointed chief justice of Massachusetts. Died in 1751. He was a man of eminent talents and powerful eloquence. Upon a bequest of his was founded the Dudleian Lecture at Harvard.

Dudley, (ROBERT,) Earl of Leicester, a son of John Dudley, noticed above, was born about 1532. He married Amy Robsart about 1550. Soon after the accession of Queen Elizabeth, 1558, he became her chief favourite. This partiality is attributed to his handsome person, polite address, and skill in the arts of a courtier. She made him Earl of Leicester and privy councillor, and bestowed on him titles and estates with a lavish hand. His wife died in 1560, not without the strongest suspicions that she perished by violence and that Leicester was privy to her murder. (See ROBSART.) In 1578 he married the widow of the first Earl of Essex, by which act he excited the violent anger of the queen. He was suspected by many of having hastened the death of Essex. In 1585 the Earl of Leicester commanded an army sent to aid the Low Countries, which gave him the title of Governor. His operations there were not successful, and proved his incapacity as a general. When England was threatened by the Spanish Armada, in 1588, he was appointed lieutenant-general. He died in the same year. According to Hume, "he was proud, insolent, ambitious, without honour, without generosity, without humanity, and atoned not for these bad qualities by such abilities or courage as could fit him for that high trust and confidence with which she [the queen] had honoured him." Motley, while admitting that Leicester was vain, arrogant, and often unjust, says he was "always generous as the sun."

See MOTLEY's "United Netherlands," chaps. vi. to xvi., particularly chap. vi. vol. i., and chap. x. vol. ii.; also FROUDE's "History of England," vols. vii., viii., ix., x.

Dudley, (Sir ROBERT,) born in Surrey in 1573, was the illegitimate son of the Earl of Leicester and Lady Douglas Sheffield. He was knighted for his conduct at the capture of Cadiz in 1596. Having been outlawed for the abduction of Miss Southwell, he settled at Florence, where he lived in grand style, assumed the title of Earl of Warwick, and was made a duke of the Holy Roman Empire. He wrote a treatise on navigation, entitled "Dell' Arcano del Mare," and a few other works, and improved the harbour of Leghorn. Died in 1639, or, according to some authorities, in 1649.

See CAMPBELL's "Lives of British Admirals."

Dudley, (THOMAS,) one of the early governors of Massachusetts, was born in Northampton, England, in 1576. He served for some time in the army, but, having joined the nonconformists, came to America in 1630 as deputy-governor of Massachusetts. He was zealous in promoting the temporal and religious interests of the colony, and was governor from 1634 to 1640, and again from 1645 to 1650. Died in 1652.

Dudoyer. See DOLIGNY.

Duebner. See DÜBNER.

Duelli, doo-el'lee, (RAIMOND,) a German priest and antiquary, born about 1670, published, besides other works, a "History of the Teutonic Knights Hospitalers of Jerusalem," (1727.) Died in 1740.

Duentzer. See DÜNTZER.

Du'er, (JOHN,) LL.D., an eminent American jurist and legal writer, born at Albany, New York, in 1782. His father, Colonel William Duer, was a soldier of the Revolution. After serving two years in the army, he embraced the profession of law, and commenced practice in Orange county, but removed to New York City about 1820. He was appointed one of the commissioners to revise the statutes of the State in 1825. In 1849 he was elected judge of the superior court of the city of New York, and in 1857 succeeded Chief-Justice Oakley as presiding judge. Died August 8, 1858. His "Law and Practice of Marine Insurance," (2 vols. 8vo,) published in 1845–46, says the "London Magazine and Quarterly Review of Jurisprudence," "so far as it has gone, is the most complete and able treatise on the subject which has ever appeared in our language." He was also author of other legal works.

є as *k*; ç as *s*; g̃ *hard*; ğ as *j*; G, H, K, *guttural*; N, *nasal*; R, *trilled*; s̃ as *z*; ŧh as in *this*.   (☞See Explanations, p. 23.)

Duer, (WILLIAM ALEXANDER,) a jurist, brother of the preceding, was born in Dutchess county, New York, in 1780. He was admitted to the bar in 1802, became a judge of the supreme court of New York in 1822, and was elected president of Columbia College in 1829. He wrote a "Treatise on the Constitutional Jurisprudence of the United States," (1856.) Died in 1858.

Duernhoffer. See DÜRNHOFFER.

Du Fail, dü′fîl′ or dü′fî′ye, (NOËL,) a French writer of tales, lived about 1550.

Dufau, dü′fō′, (FORTUNÉ,) a French historical painter, born in Saint Domingo. He became a pupil of David in Paris, and a partisan of the Revolution. Among his most admired works is "Ugolino in Prison." Died in 1821.

Dufau, (PIERRE ARMAND,) a French author, born at Bordeaux in 1795. He wrote, with Guadet, a "History of France from Charles IX. to Henry IV.," (7 vols., 1821,) and other historical works. He also published a "Treatise on Statistics," which was crowned by the Academy of Sciences in 1841, and several works on political economy. From 1840 to 1855 he was director of the Royal Institution for the education of the blind in Paris.

Dufaure, dü′fōR′, (JULES ARMAND STANISLAS,) a French orator and minister of state, born at Saujon (Charente-Inférieure) in 1798. He practised law in Bordeaux, and in 1834 was elected to the Chamber of Deputies, in which he acted with the opposition. In 1839 he became minister of public works in the coalition ministry of Soult, which was dissolved in March, 1840. He afterwards exerted much influence in the Chamber as the chief of a third party. Under the republic of 1848 he was a leader of the moderate democrats, became minister of the interior in October, and resigned in December of that year. He filled the same office for five months in 1849. Since the *coup d'état* of December, 1851, he has not held office, but has attained great eminence at the bar.

See VICOMTE DE CORMENIN, (TIMON,) "Études sur les Orateurs parlementaires."

Dufay, dü′fî′, (CHARLES FRANÇOIS de Cisternay—dĕh sĕs′tĕR′nā′,) a French savant, born in Paris in 1698, served for a time in the army. Having been admitted into the Academy of Sciences, he retired from the service, and wrote treatises on chemistry and five other sciences, which the Academy thought worthy to be published. He originated the theory of two kinds of electricity, namely, vitreous and resinous. About 1732 he was chosen director of the Jardin des Plantes, which he greatly enlarged and rendered the finest in Europe. Died in 1739.

See FONTENELLE, "Éloge de Dufay."

Dufay, (GUILLAUME,) a French or Flemish composer, lived about 1400, and made important improvements in the art of music.

Duff, (ALEXANDER,) D.D., a Scottish Presbyterian missionary, born in Perthshire about 1806. In the service of the Church of Scotland he went to India in 1830, and laboured zealously as a missionary. He published, besides other essays, a volume entitled "On India and India Missions," (1839,) which is highly esteemed. He adhered to the Free Church, organized in 1843, since which he has been the chief agent of the mission sustained by that church at Calcutta, where he laboured as a missionary for many years with devoted zeal and eminent success. He visited the United States in 1854, sailed a second time for India in 1855, and returned to England in 1863.

Duff, (MOUNTSTUART ELPHINSTONE GRANT,) called GRANT DUFF, a British politician, born in 1829. He published "Studies in European Politics." In 1857 he was elected to Parliament, as a Liberal, for Elgin. He was appointed under-secretary for India in December, 1868.

Duffer-in, LADY, a granddaughter of Richard Brinsley Sheridan, and a sister of Mrs. Norton. Her maiden name was SELINA SHERIDAN. She composed a number of popular ballads, among which is "The Irish Emigrant's Lament." She was married in 1825 to Baron Dufferin, (Price Blackwood,) who died in 1841.

Dufferin, (FREDERICK TEMPLE BLACKWOOD,) LORD, a British peer, author, and scholar, only son of the preceding, was born at Florence about 1826. He published,

in 1856, "Letters from High Latitudes, being some Account of a Voyage to Iceland and Spitzbergen," which is highly praised.

Duffet, dü′fā′, **Douffet,** or **Douffeit,** doo′fā′, (GERARD,) an eminent Flemish painter of history and portraits, born at Liege about 1600. He studied and worked some years in Rome, and returned to Liege, where he acquired a high reputation. Among his master-pieces are a "Discovery of the Holy Cross," (at Dusseldorf,) and a picture of himself and B. Flemael employed in painting each other's portraits. His works are admired for originality of composition, boldness of design, beauty of colour, and variety of expression. Died about 1660.

See "Nouvelle Biographie Générale."

Duf′fy, (CHARLES GAVAN,) an Irish journalist, and a leader of Young Ireland, was born in Ulster in 1816. In 1842 he founded in Dublin a journal called "The Nation," which supported the policy of O'Connell.

Dufieu, dü′fe-uh′, (JEAN **Ferapied**—frā-pe-ā′,) a French writer on physiology, born at Tence in 1737; died in 1769.

Duflos, dü′flo′, (CLAUDE,) a French engraver with the burin, born in Paris in 1678, was the most skilful rival of François Poilly. His works, after various Italian and French masters, are engraved with great neatness. Among them is "The Pilgrims of Emmaus," after Paul Veronese. Died in 1747.

Du Fossé. See FOSSÉ.

Dufouart, dü′foo′âR′, (PIERRE,) a skilful French surgeon, born in the department of Bigorre in 1737, was chosen in 1791 inspector-general of the hospitals of Paris. He published an excellent treatise on gun-shot wounds, entitled "Analyse des Blessures d'Armes-à-feu, et de leur Traitement," (1801.) Died in 1813.

See "Biographie Médicale."

Dufour, dü′foor′, (GABRIEL MICHEL,) a French jurist, born at Moulins (Allier) in 1811. His "Treatise on Administrative Law Applied" (4 vols., 1844) is said to be the most complete on that subject.

Dufour, (GEORGES JOSEPH,) a French general, born in Burgundy in 1758; died in 1820.

Dufour, dü′foor′, (GUILLAUME HENRI,) a Swiss general, born at Constance in 1787, entered the French army in 1809. He wrote a "Manual of Tactics," (1842,) and other military works. The unity and integrity of the Swiss republic having been menaced by the Sonderbund, a Catholic faction, he was appointed in 1847 commander-in-chief of the Swiss federal army. He quickly suppressed the rebellion, after giving proof of his moderation as well as military skill.

Dufour, (LÉON,) a French naturalist, born about 1782, practised medicine at Saint-Sever. He published "Anatomical and Physiological Researches on the Hemiptera," (1833,) and other works.

Dufour, (LOUIS.) See LONGUERUE.

Dufour, (PHILIPPE,) a French Protestant antiquary, born at Manosque in 1622. His family name was SYLVESTRE, which he exchanged for DUFOUR, his mother's name. He formed a cabinet of medals, and corresponded with many eminent literati. He wrote, among other works, "Moral Instructions of a Father for his Son," (often reprinted.) Died in 1687.

Dufrénoy, dü′frā′nwā′, (ADELAÏDE,) an eminent French poetess, whose maiden name was GILLETTE-BILLET, born in Paris in 1765. She lived mostly in Paris, where her soirées were frequented by Condorcet, La Harpe, etc. Her husband having lost his fortune, she resorted to authorship for a living, and wrote several poems which entitle her to a place in the first rank of the female poets of France. Her poem "The Last Moments of Bayard" was crowned by the Institute in 1815. Among her works are odes, elegies, tales, dramas, etc., whose merit consists in the genuine expression of a loving and suffering heart. Died in 1825.

See "Nouvelle Biographie Générale."

Dufrénoy, (CHARLES ALPHONSE.) See DUFRESNOY.

Dufrénoy, (PIERRE ARMAND,) an eminent French geologist, a son of Adelaïde, born at Sevran (Seine-et-Oise) in 1792. In conjunction with Élie de Beaumont, he was ordered in 1823 to make a geological survey of France, the important result of which was a large geological map, with three volumes of explanatory text, (1841.) This text develops the theories of the two authors, which are entirely accordant. He published, besides other works, an excellent "Treatise on Mineralogy," (4 vols., 1847.) A new theory propounded in his memoir "On the Volcanic Formations of the Vicinity of Naples" has become one of the laws of geology. He was a member of the Institute, inspector-general of mines, and for many years professor of mineralogy in the Museum of Natural History. Died in March, 1857.

See "Nouvelle Biographie Générale."

Dufresne. See FRANCHEVILLE and QUINAULT.

Dufresne, dü'frĕn', (BERTRAND,) a French financier, born in Béarn in 1736. He was chief clerk of finance under Necker, who made him director of the public treasury about 1790. During the reign of térror he was imprisoned by the Jacobins. He was elected to the Council of Five Hundred in 1795, and in 1800 was appointed director-general of the treasury, which prospered under his skilful management. Died in 1801.

Dufresnoy. See DUFRESNY.

Dufresnoy. See LENGLET-DUFRESNOY and DUCLOZ.

Dufresnoy, dü'frȧ'nwȧ', (ANDRÉ IGNACE JOSEPH,) a French physician, born at Valenciennes in 1733. He was appointed physician-in-chief of the army of the North in 1793, but was soon discharged for an act of humanity to a royalist. He was the first who cultivated in France the *Rhus radicans*, and in one of his letters he expressed his impatience to see his dear *rhus*. This letter was intercepted by certain officious patriots, who denounced him to the Tribunal for a traitorous correspondence with the Russians. He was arrested on this charge, but was released from danger by the revolution of the 9th Thermidor. Died in 1801.

See "Biographie Médicale."

Dufresnoy, written also **Dufrénoy,** (CHARLES ALPHONSE,) a French historical painter and poet, born in Paris in 1611, was the son of an apothecary. Having received lessons from Perrier and Vouet, he visited Rome and studied the works of Raphael. He went to Venice in 1653, and returned to France in 1656. He had a fair reputation for correctness of design, and was a good colorist. He wrote, in Latin verse, a critical treatise on painting, "De Arte Graphicâ," which was much admired, and was translated into English by Dryden. Died in 1665.

See QUÉRARD, "La France Littéraire;" LECARPENTIER, "Notice sur A. Dufresnoy," 1812.

Dufresny, dü'frȧ'ne', or **Dufresnoy,** dü'frȧ'nwȧ', (CHARLES RIVIÈRE,) a witty French dramatist and artist, born in Paris in 1648, was a great-grandson of Henry IV., and a valet-de-chambre of Louis XIV. He had a natural talent for music and painting, excelled in landscape-gardening, and was appointed controller of the royal gardens. He wrote several successful comedies, among which are "The Spirit of Contradiction," in prose, (1700,) "The Village Coquette," in verse, (1715,) and "Le Faux-sincère." "He sparkles with wit," says La Harpe, "and his wit is perfectly original." ("Cours de Littérature.") Died in 1724.

See VOLTAIRE, "Écrivains du Siècle de Louis XIV.;" QUÉRARD, "La France Littéraire;" "Nouvelle Biographie Générale."

Dufresse, dü'frȧss', (SIMON CAMILLE,) BARON, a French general, born at La Rochelle in 1762 ; died in 1833.

Dufriche-Valazé. See VALAZÉ.

Dufrische. See FRISCHE.

Duganne, du-gan', (AUGUSTINE JOSEPH HICKEY,) an American poet and *littérateur*, born in Boston in 1823, published, among other works, a "Comprehensive Summary of General Philosophy," (1845,) and "Class-Book of Governments and Civil Society," (1859.) His principal poetical works are "Home Poems," (1844,) "The Iron Harp," (1847,) and "The Lydian Queen," a tragedy.

Du-gard', (WILLIAM,) an eminent English teacher, born in Worcestershire in 1605, became master of the Merchant-Tailors' School, London, about 1642. He published a Greek grammar, a "Lexicon Græci Testamenti," and other school-books. Died in 1662.

Dugas-Montbel, dü'gâs' môn'bĕl', (JEAN BAPTISTE,) an excellent French Hellenist, born at Saint-Chamond in 1776, was a merchant of Lyons in early life. At the

age of thirty he began to study Greek, and settled in Paris in 1810. He produced a translation of Homer, (1815-18,) which is regarded as the best prose version in the French language. A copious commentary accompanies it. He was a free associate of the Academy of Inscriptions. He represented Lyons in the Chamber of Deputies in 1831-33. Died in 1834.

See J. B. DUMAS, "Éloge de Dugas-Montbel," 1835; "Nouvelle Biographie Générale."

Dugazon, dü'gȧ'zòN', (JEAN BAPTISTE HENRI **Gourgault**—gooR'gō',) a popular French comedian, born at Marseilles in 1743 ; died in 1809.

His wife, LOUISE LEFÈVRE, born at Berlin in 1755, was a successful actress. Died in 1821.

Dug'dale, (Sir WILLIAM,) an eminent English antiquary, born at Shustoke, in Warwickshire, in 1605. He became a resident of London in 1638, and was appointed a pursuivant-at-arms, by the name of Blanch Lyon. In 1640 he was made rouge-croix pursuivant-in-ordinary. He was a royalist in the civil war. In 1655 Dugdale and Dodsworth published the first volume of their great and celebrated work on English monasteries, "Monasticon Anglicanum," (3 vols., 1655-73.) This contains a record of the history and descent of the greater part of the landed property of England. He wrote several other valuable works, among which are "The Antiquities of Warwickshire," (1656,) "Origines Juridiciales," (1666,) and "The Baronage of England," (1675.) In the reign of Charles II. he was knighted, and obtained the office of Norroy king-at-arms. Died in 1686.

See "Life, Diary, and Correspondence of W. Dugdale," edited by HAMPER, 1827; "Biographia Britannica."

Dugès, dü'zhȧ', (ANTOINE LOUIS,) an eminent French physician, born at Mézières (Ardennes) in 1797. He became professor of pathology and operative medicine at Montpellier about 1825, and published, besides other works, a "Manual of Obstetrics," (1826,) and an able "Treatise on the Comparative Physiology of Man and Animals," (3 vols., 1838.) He was a member of the Academy of Sciences. Died in 1838.

See QUÉRARD, "La France Littéraire;" "Nouvelle Biographie Générale."

Dughet, dü'gȧ', (GASPARD,) a distinguished landscape-painter, sometimes called LE GUASPRE, (lĕh gȧspR,) or GASPRE POUSSIN, (poo'săN',) was born of a French family at Rome in 1613. He was a pupil of the famous Nicolas Poussin, who married his sister. It is stated that he hired four houses at the same time near Rome and Tivoli, that he might observe a great diversity of scenes. He had great executive facility, and a vague, agreeable manner. His works present a great variety of composition and of effects. He painted many real scenes in the vicinity of Rome, enriched with details of his own invention. He excelled in the treatment of clouds and the foliage of trees, which he represented in their characteristic forms. Among his master-pieces is "Abraham and Isaac going to the Sacrifice." Died in Rome in 1675.

See PASCOLI, "Vite de' Pittori e Scultori moderni," 1730-36; BRYAN, "Dictionary of Painters;" "Nouvelle Biographie Générale."

Dughet, (GIOVANNI,) a younger brother of the preceding, born about 1615, was also a pupil of N. Poussin. He renounced painting at an early age, and devoted himself to engraving with the burin and point. He worked in Rome, and engraved many works of N. Poussin, among which is "The Seven Sacraments."

Dugommier, dü'go'me-ȧ', (JEAN FRANÇOIS **Coquille**—ko'ke'yĕ,) a French general, born in the isle of Guadeloupe in 1736. He favoured the popular cause in the Revolution, and went to Paris in 1792. As general of division, he commanded at the successful siege of Toulon in 1793, where Bonaparte acted under his orders. The next year he was appointed to command the army of the Eastern Pyrenees, and gained advantages over the Spaniards at Saint-Elme and other places. He was killed in November, 1794, at the battle of Sierra Negra, near Figuières, where the Spaniards were defeated. Bonaparte mentioned him in his last will, *honoris causâ*, and left a legacy to his son.

See LAMARTINE, "History of the Girondists."

Dugua, dü'gü'ȧ', (CHARLES FRANÇOIS JOSEPH,) a French general, born at Valenciennes in 1744. For his

ɛ as *k;* ç as *s;* g̃ *hard;* g̃ as *j;* G, H, K, *guttural;* N, *nasal;* R, *trilled;* š as *z;* th as in *this.* (☞ See Explanations, p. 23.)

51

services at the siege of Toulon in 1793 he was made a general of division. In 1798 he accompanied Bonaparte to Egypt. In the absence of Kleber, who had been wounded, Dugua commanded his division at the battle of the Pyramids. He went to Saint Domingo in 1801 as chief of the staff of Leclerc, and died there in 1802.

See A. DUMÈGE, "Mémoires du Général Dugua," 4 vols., 1838.

Duguay-Trouin, dü′gà′ troo′ǎN′, (RENÉ,) a brave and successful French admiral, born at Saint-Malo in 1673. Having obtained command of a privateer frigate in 1691, he performed several daring exploits, and took many prizes from the English. In 1694 he was taken prisoner by an English squadron and carried into port, but soon escaped, and returned to France. He entered the royal marine in 1697, and displayed great skill and prudence as captain in the war of the Spanish succession, which began in 1702. Between 1703 and 1705 he cruised on the coasts of England, defeated a Dutch fleet, and captured several ships. In 1707 his squadron, united to that of Forbin, intercepted a large English convoy and took three of the ships of war by which it was escorted. He gained great glory by the capture of Rio Janeiro in 1711. In 1715 he was appointed vice-admiral, and lieutenant-general in 1728. His disposition was modest and generous. He died in 1736, leaving Memoirs of his life, which were published in 1740 and translated into English in 1742.

See, also, M. DE LA LANDELLE, "Histoire de Duguay-Trouin," 1844; ADRIEN RICHER, "Vie de R. Duguay-Trouin," 1784 and 1835; ANTOINE THOMAS, "Éloge de Duguay-Trouin," 1761; "Nouvelle Biographie Générale."

Duguernier, dü′gĕR′ne-à′, (LOUIS,) a French portrait-painter, born about 1550, acquired celebrity in miniatures, which he painted on vellum. He painted the portraits of the most distinguished personages of his time.

Duguernier, (LOUIS,) a son of the preceding, was a skilful portrait-painter, and worked in Paris. Nagler states that he was exiled on the revocation of the edict of Nantes, (1685;) but, according to another account, he died in Paris in 1659. He left three sons who were painters, one of whom, named Pierre, was reputed the best painter on enamel of his time.

See NAGLER, "Neues Allgemeines Künstler-Lexikon."

Du Guesclin or **Duguesclin,** dü′gà′klǎN′, (BERTRAND,) a famous French captain, born near Rennes about 1314. He distinguished himself in fighting against the English, who then held many places in France. In 1356 he defeated the Duke of Lancaster at Rennes, and forced him to raise the siege. About 1364 Charles V. gave him command of an army, with which he defeated the King of Navarre. The next year he led a large army against Pedro the Cruel of Castile, who was unable to resist him until the English Black Prince came to his assistance. In a battle that followed in 1367 the Black Prince was the victor, and took Du Guesclin prisoner, but soon released him. In 1369, when the war was renewed between the French and the English, he was appointed Constable of France. After he took the command the English ceased to conquer, and in 1374 he had expelled them from nearly every province of France. Died in 1380. "He seems to have been," says Hume, "the first consummate general that had yet appeared in Europe."

See FROISSART, "Chronicles;" CLAUDE MENARD, "Histoire de B. Duguesclin," 1618; GUYARD DE BERVILLE, "Vie de Duguesclin," 1767; JAMISON, "Life of Duguesclin," 1864; FRÉMINVILLE, "Histoire de Bertrand Duguesclin," 1841.

Duguet, dü′gà′, (JACQUES JOSEPH,) a French theologian, born at Montbrison in 1649. He became a priest of the Oratory in 1667, and was attached to the principles of the Jansenists. He published many esteemed works on religion and morality, among which are "Conduct of a Christian Lady," (1725,) "The Work of Six Days," (1732,) and a "Treatise on the Principles of the Christian Faith," (1736.) Died in 1733.

See ANDRÉ, "L'Esprit de J. J. Duguet," etc., Paris, 1764.

Du Haillan. See HAILLAN, D'.

Duhalde, dü′hǎld′, (JEAN BAPTISTE,) a French Jesuit, born in Paris in 1674. He was employed by his superiors to digest and edit the letters received from the foreign missionaries of the Society. The result of his

labours is a work entitled "Lettres édifiantes et curieuses écrites des Missions étrangères," which contains much interesting and valuable information. In 1735 he published a "Historical, Geographical, and Physical Description of the Chinese Empire," the first work in which China had been described with such detail and exactness by a European. Died in 1743.

See MORÉRI, "Dictionnaire Historique."

Duhamel or **Du Hamel,** dü′hǎ′mĕl′, (JEAN BAPTISTE,) a French philosopher and savant, born at Vire in 1624, became curate of Neuilly-sur-Marne. He was a diligent student of natural philosophy and other sciences, and gained reputation in 1660 by a treatise on Astronomy, ("Astronomia Physica.") At the formation of the Academy of Sciences (1666) he was chosen perpetual secretary. He published an interesting "History of the Royal Academy of Sciences," (1698,) a "Treatise on the Old and New Philosophy," for the use of colleges, (1678,) and other scientific works, which were once highly prized, but are not much read at present. Died in 1706. The above-named works are all in Latin, which he wrote with great purity and elegance.

See NICÉRON, "Mémoires;" FONTENELLE, "Eloges des Académiciens;" "Nouvelle Biographie Générale."

Du Hamel, (JEAN MARIE CONSTANT,) a French mathematician, born in 1797, became in 1851 professor in the Faculty of Sciences. He succeeded Poisson as member of the Institute in 1840. He wrote a work on analysis, ("Cours d'Analyse de l'École Polytechnique," 1841.)

Duhamel or **Du Hamel,** (JEAN PIERRE FRANÇOIS Guillot — ge′yo′,) a French savant and metallurgist, born at Nicorps in 1730. He made improvements in the art of mining and working metals; and, when the School of Mines was founded, about 1787, he was chosen professor of metallurgy, etc. In 1786 he was received into the Academy of Sciences. About 1795 he was chosen a member of the Institute and inspector-general of mines. He was a savant of the old school,—profound, practical, unassuming. He wrote, besides other works, a manual for miners, entitled "Subterranean Geometry," (1788,) "which," says Cuvier, "is an indispensable work, and is at the present time the manual of all who practise the art of mining in France." Died in 1816.

See CUVIER, "Éloges historiques," tome iii.; "Nouvelle Biographie Générale."

Duhamel du Monceau, dü′hǎ′mĕl′ dü mÖN′sō′, (HENRI LOUIS,) an eminent economist and botanist, born in Paris in 1700, was one of the most remarkable French savants of the eighteenth century, in respect to the extent, variety, and utility of his researches in botany, physiology, agriculture, etc. He was admitted into the Academy of Sciences in 1728, after which he wrote more than sixty memoirs, nearly all on important subjects. He published, besides other works, a "Treatise on the Culture of Land," (1751,) a "Treatise on the Trees and Shrubs which grow in France in the Open Ground," (1755,) and one entitled "De la Physique des Arbres," (1758,) treating of the structure, anatomy, and physiology of plants. This is regarded as his most important work.

See CUVIER, "Histoire des Sciences naturelles;" "Biographie Universelle;" "Nouvelle Biographie Générale;" "Encyclopædia Britannica."

Duhan, dü′hŏN′, (CHARLES GILLES,) a French Protestant, born in Champagne in 1685, removed to Berlin, where he became preceptor to the prince-royal, (Frederick the Great.) After the accession of that prince (1740) Duhan was made a privy councillor. Died in 1746.

Duhan, (LAURENT,) a French philosopher, born at Chartres about 1656, published "Philosophus in utramque Partem," (1694.) Died in 1726.

Duhem, dü′ŏN′ or dü-hêm′, (PIERRE JOSEPH,) a French Jacobin, born at Lille in 1760, was a member of the Convention, 1792–95. Died in 1807.

Duhesme, dü′hêm′, (PHILIPPE GUILLAUME,) COUNT, a French general, born in Burgundy in 1766. He was made general of division in 1794 for his services at Granjean and Maestricht. His passage of the Rhine at Diersheim, in 1797, was much applauded. He afterwards commanded in Italy and Spain, where he gained several victories, and received the title of count in 1814. In the Hundred Days he took arms for Napoleon, and was wounded and taken prisoner at Waterloo, where he was massacred by a Prussian soldier, June 18, 1815.

See "Nouvelle Biographie Générale."

Duigenan, dōōg′e-nąn, (PATRICK,) an Irish civilian, born in 1735, in the county of Leitrim. He was a judge, privy councillor, and member of Parliament, and wrote several political pamphlets. He promoted the Union, and opposed Catholic emancipation. Died in 1816.

Du-il′i-us or **Du-il′li-us,** (CAIUS,) a Roman general, elected consul in 261 B.C., is noted as the first Roman who obtained a naval victory over the Carthaginians. In the first Punic war he built a number of ships after the model of one captured from the enemy. This fleet under his command defeated that of Carthage, near the Lipari Islands, in 260, on which occasion the Romans used with great advantage the new invention of grappling-irons, and boarded the ships of the enemy. He afterwards commanded the land-army, and defeated the Carthaginians in Sicily.

See POLYBIUS, book i.; DIODORUS SICULUS, book xxiii.

Duilius, (MARCUS,) a Roman tribune, who, about 450 B.C., persuaded the people to assume an attitude of determined hostility to the decemvirs by withdrawing to Mons Sacer.

Duisburg, doo′is-bŏōRG, written also **Duisbourg,** (PETER,) a German chronicler, lived about 1320. He wrote a "History of Prussia."

Duiven, doi′ven, (JAN,) a Dutch portrait-painter, born at Gouda in 1610; died in 1640.

Dujardin, dü′zhăR′dăN′, (BÉNIGNE,) a French author who assumed the name of BOISPRÉAUX, (bwä′pRä′ō′,) flourished about 1740.

Dujardin, (FÉLIX,) a French naturalist, born at Tours in 1801. He cultivated geology, botany, and zoology, and became professor of mineralogy at Toulouse in 1839. Among his chief works are a "Natural History of Infusoria," (1841,) and a "Manual of the Observer with the Microscope," (1843.) Died in April, 1860.

Dujardin, dü′zhăR′dăN′, sometimes written **De Jardyn,** (KAREL,) an eminent Dutch painter, was born in Amsterdam about 1640. He is called the most excellent pupil of Berghem. He studied and worked in Rome, and returned to his native place, where he was very successful. He painted history, animals, pastoral scenes, and other familiar subjects. He excelled in colour, expression, and chiaroscuro. Some of his works are regarded as master-pieces, and bring high prices. His "Charlatan" is said to be one of the most highly-prized tableaux of that kind which the gallery of the Louvre contains. Having visited Italy a second time, he died at Venice in 1678.

See DESCAMPS, "Vies des Peintres Flamands," etc.

Duke, (RICHARD,) an English clergyman, born in Devonshire, was a Fellow of Trinity College, Cambridge, and prebendary of Gloucester. He wrote several mediocre poems, and published sermons which are commended. He co-operated with others in the translation of Ovid and Juvenal. Died in 1711.

Duker, doo′ker, (KARL ANDREAS,) a German scholar, born at Unna, Prussia, in 1670. He studied under Perizonius at Franeker. In 1716 he was associated with Drakenborch in the chair of history and eloquence at Utrecht vacated by Burmann. His principal work is an edition of Thucydides, (1731,) which attests his profound knowledge of Greek and was for a long time the best edition of that author. He also edited Florus, (1722.) He resigned his chair in 1734. Died at Mydrecht in 1752.

See ERSCH und GRUBER, "Allgemeine Encyklopaedie;" C. SAXIUS, "Laudatio C. A. Dukeri," 8vo, 1788.

Duker, doo′ker, (KARL GUSTAVUS,) a Swedish general, distinguished in the wars of Charles XII. He fought at Pultowa in 1709, when he was made prisoner. In 1712, as lieutenant-general, he commanded a corps in the isle of Rügen, and surrendered Stralsund after a brave defence in 1715. He was afterwards made a field-marshal, senator, and count. Died in 1732.

See ERSCH und GRUBER, "Allgemeine Encyklopaedie;" VOLTAIRE, "Histoire de Charles XII."

Dulac. See ALLÉON.

Dulard, dü′lăR′, (PAUL ALEXANDRE,) a French poet, born at Marseilles in 1696; died in 1760.

Dulauloy. See RANDON.

Dulaure, dü′lōR′, (JACQUES ANTOINE,) a French republican, known as an able and prolific writer, was born at Clermont-Ferrand in 1755. In 1788 he published the first volumes of a "Description of France." Elected to the Convention in 1792, he voted for the death of the king. He wrote many political pamphlets, was proscribed as a Girondist in 1793, and saved his life by flight. He was one of the Council of Five Hundred in 1796–98. He produced a "History of Paris from the Earliest Times," (10 vols., 1821,) and "Historical Sketches of the Revolution," (6 vols., 1825.) Died in 1835.

See "Nouvelle Biographie Générale:" TAILLANDIER, "Notice sur J. A. Dulaure."

Du Laurens or **Dulaurens,** dü′lō′rŏN′, (ANDRÉ,) a learned French physician, born at Arles about 1550, became first physician to Henry IV. in 1606. He published several professional works in Latin, one of which was very successful, viz., "Anatomical Description of the Human Body," (1595.) Renauldin praises the elegance of its style. Died in 1609.

See H. RODRIGUES, "Notice sur Dulaurens," etc., Montpellier, 1842.

Dulaurens, (HENRI JOSEPH,) a French writer and abbé, born at Douai in 1719. Among his works are a "Satire against the Jesuits," (1761,) and "The Evangile of Reason." In 1767 he was sentenced to perpetual imprisonment as author of anti-religious works. Died in 1797.

Dulaurier, dü′lō′re-ă′, (ÉDOUARD,) a French Orientalist, born at Toulouse in 1807, became professor of the Javanese and Malay languages at Paris in 1841.

Dulcino, dool-chee′no, [Lat. DULCI′NUS,] an Italian theologian, and leader of a sect called Dulcinists, was born at Novara. He was put to death in 1307.

Dulcis, dül′sèss′, (CATHERIN,) a Protestant noted as a linguist, was born in Savoy in 1540. He was professor of modern languages at Wittenberg and at Cassel, and wrote "Principles of the Italian Languages," and other works.

Dulin, dü′lăN′, (PIERRE,) a French painter of history, born in Paris in 1670, gained the grand prize in 1696, and died in 1748.

Du Lis, dü lèss, or **Dulis,** (CHARLES,) a Frenchman descended from a brother of Joan of Arc, was born about 1560. He was a privy councillor of Henry IV. He wrote a valuable notice of the genealogy, actions, and arms of Joan of Arc, (1610.) Died about 1632.

Dulk, dŏŏlk, (FRIEDRICH PHILIPP,) a German chemist, born at Schirwindt, in Prussia, in 1788, became professor of chemistry at Königsberg. He published a "Manual of Chemistry," (1834,) and other works.

Dullaert, dül′lăRt, (HEYMAN,) a skilful Dutch painter of history and portraits, born at Rotterdam in 1636. He was a pupil of Rembrandt, whose manner he imitated with such success as to puzzle Houbraken and other connoisseurs. His "Hermit Kneeling" is an instance of this imitation. In consequence of feeble health, he did not produce a great number of pictures. He was skilled in many languages, wrote verses with facility, and translated Tasso's epic poem. Died in 1684.

See DESCAMPS, "Vies des Peintres Flamands," etc

Duller, dŏŏl′ler, (EDUARD,) a popular German poet and historian, born in Vienna in 1809. He produced a successful drama, "Master Pilgrim," (1828,) and "The Prince of Love," a poem, (1842.) He settled in Mentz (Mayence) in 1849, after which he devoted himself to history. Among his works are a "History of the German People," (2 vols., 1840,) and a continuation of Schiller's "History of the Revolt of the Netherlands," (3 vols., 1841.) He published a volume of poems, "Gesammelte Gedichte," (1845.) Died in 1853.

See BROCKHAUS, "Conversations-Lexikon;" WEBER, "Geschichte der Deutschen Literatur."

Dulon, doo′lon, (LUDWIG,) a Prussian performer on the flute, born in 1769, became blind in infancy. He composed music for the flute. Died in 1826.

€ as *k*; ç as *s*; ḡ *hard*; ġ as *j*; G, H, K, *guttural*; N, *nasal*; R, *trilled*; š as *z*; ŧh as in *this*. (☞ See Explanations, p. 23.)

Dulong, dü'lôN', (PIERRE LOUIS,) a French chemist and natural philosopher, born at Rouen in 1785. He studied chemistry with Berthollet, and discovered the chloride of nitrogen in 1812. In co-operation with Berzelius, he analyzed water, and made researches in the animal heat produced by respiration and the combustion of carbon in the lungs. He succeeded Petit as professor of physique in the Polytechnic School, and in 1823 was admitted into the Academy of Sciences, for which he wrote memoirs on the theory of heat, the elastic force of steam, etc. Died in Paris in 1838.

See ÉTIENNE ARAGO, "Dictionnaire de la Conversation;" "Nouvelle Biographie Générale."

Dulong de Rosnay, dü'lôN' deh ro'nậ', (LOUIS HENRI,) COMTE, a French general, born in Champagne in 1780; died in 1828.

Du Lorens, dü lo'rôN', (JACQUES,) a French satirical poet, born at Châteauneuf in 1583; died about 1650.

Dumaniant, dü'mǎ'ne'ôN',(ANTOINE JEAN,) a French comic author, whose family name was BOURLIN, (booR'-lăN',) born at Clermont in Auvergne, or Clermont-Ferrand, in 1754. He lived in Paris, where for some time he performed on the stage. He wrote many comedies, some of which were successful, especially his "Open War, or Ruse against Ruse," (1786.) Died in 1828.

Dumanoir, dü'mǎ'nwăR',(PHILIPPE,) a French dramatist, born in Guadeloupe in 1808.

Dumanoir le Pelley, du'mǎ'nwăR' leh pǎ'lậ', (PIERRE ÉTIENNE RENÉ MARIE,) COUNT, a French admiral, born at Granville in 1770. As chef-de-division he conducted the convoy attached to the army which invaded Egypt in 1798. The next year he commanded one of the two ships which escorted Bonaparte back to France, and was made a rear-admiral. At the battle of Trafalgar in 1805 he commanded the vanguard, and escaped with four ships, which were taken a few days later. He was made a count in 1814, and vice-admiral in 1819. Died in 1829.

See "Nouvelle Biographie Générale."

Dumaresq, du-mǎ-rěsk', (HENRY,) a brave British officer, born in 1792, served in the Peninsula, was severely wounded at Waterloo, and obtained the rank of lieutenant-colonel in 1817. Died in 1838.

Dumarest, dü'mǎ'rậ', (RAMBERT,) a skilful French engraver of medals, born at Saint-Étienne, in Forez, in 1750. He resided in Paris, and became a member of the Institute. About the time of the Revolution his medal of J. J. Rousseau gained the first prize. He engraved the medal which the Institute gives to each of its members, and one for the Peace of Amiens. Died in 1806.

Dumarsais, dü'mǎR'sậ', (CÉSAR CHESNEAU,) an eminent French grammarian, born at Marseilles in 1676, became a citizen of Paris about 1702. His works are more highly appreciated by posterity than they were by his contemporaries, and his "Treatise on Tropes or Figures" is especially commended. He also wrote a "Treatise on Logic," and "Principles of Grammar." "He was," says Voltaire, "one of those obscure sages who judge soundly of all," etc. Died in 1756.

See DE GERANDO, "Eloge de Du Marsais," 1805; D'ALEMBERT, "Éloge de Du Marsais," in the "Encyclopédie," tome vii.

Dumas, dü'mǎ', (ADOLPHE,) a French poet, cousin of Alexandre, noticed below, born at Bompas (Vaucluse) in 1806; died in 1861.

Dumas, (ALEXANDRE,) a celebrated French novelist and dramatist, born at Villers-Cotterets (Aisne) in 1803. His early education was very defective. At the age of twenty he went to Paris to seek his fortune, and by the favour of General Foy obtained a clerkship in the bureau of the Duke of Orléans. He produced in 1828 "Henri III," a drama, the great success of which was a triumph of the new romantic school over the classic. He wrote many other successful dramas, among which are "Antony," a tragedy," (1831,) and "Mdlle. de Belle Isle," a comedy, (1837.) The immorality of "Antony" was pronounced scandalous even by the French. He excels in the construction of plots, and exhibits a marvellous example of literary fecundity. Dumas also obtained great popularity as a novelist. Among his principal romances are "The Three Musketeers," ("Les trois Mousquetaires," 1844-45, 30 vols.,) and "The Count of Monte-Christo," ("Le Comte de Monte-Christo," 1845, 12 vols.) These are greatly admired by the French for the *verve* and faculty of improvisation which they display. It is stated that he makes a very free use of the assistance of other writers in the composition of his works.

See L. DE LOMÉNIE, "Notice sur M. A. Dumas," 1845; ALEXANDRE DUMAS, "Mémoires," Paris, 10 vols., 1850-52; EUGÈNE DE MIRECOURT, "Fabrique de Romans: Maison A. Dumas et Compagnie," 1846; CHARLES ROBIN, "Notice sur A. Dumas," 1848.

Dumas, (ALEXANDRE,) a son of the preceding, was born in Paris in 1824, and is widely known as a romancer and comic author. Among his romances are "Césarine," (1848,) and "Trois Hommes forts," (4 vols., 1850.) He produced in 1852 "La Dame aux Camélias," a comedy, which was highly applauded. His comedy "Demi-Monde" (1855) was also very successful. His works are censured as immoral.

Dumas, (ALEXANDRE DAVY DE LA Pailleterie—pǎ'yeh-tre',) a French general, born at Jérémie in 1762, was the father of Alexandre, noticed above. His mother was a negress, named Dumas. He was made a general of brigade in July, 1793, and general of division in September of that year. He defeated Wurmser at Mantua in 1796, and for his services in the Tyrol in 1797 was saluted by Bonaparte with the title of "the Horatius Cocles of the Tyrol." In 1798 he commanded the cavalry in Egypt, and was at the battle of the Pyramids. He died in 1806, having been disabled by ill health for several years.

See "Victoires et Conquêtes des Français;" "Nouvelle Biographie Générale."

Dumas, (CHARLES LOUIS,) an eminent French physician, born in Lyons in 1765, graduated at Montpellier. In 1795 he obtained the chair of anatomy and physiology in that city. He was afterwards chosen professor of clinic medicine, dean of the Faculty, a corresponding member of the Institute, member of the legion of honour, etc. He wrote many learned works, of which the most important are "Principles of Physiology," (4 vols., 1800,) "The Future Progress of the Science of Man," (1804,) and "Doctrine of Chronic Diseases," (1812.) The last is highly praised. Died at Montpellier in April, 1813.

See PRUNELLE, "Éloge de C. L. Dumas," 1814; "Nouvelle Biographie Générale."

Dumas, (JEAN BAPTISTE,) an eminent French chemist and senator, born at Alais (Gard) in July, 1800. He went about 1814 to Geneva, where he studied chemistry and botany and became the scientific associate of Prévost. Having removed to Paris in 1821, he was chosen tutor of chemistry in the Polytechnic School in 1823. He married the daughter of the celebrated chemist A. Brongniart. He acquired a wide reputation by his researches on isomerism, the law of substitutions, the atomic weights of elements, and other parts of chemical philosophy. His labours have contributed greatly to simplify the study of organic chemistry. He was elected to the Institute in 1832, and became professor of organic chemistry in the School of Medicine in 1834. He published many important works, among which are a "Treatise on Chemistry applied to the Arts," (8 vols., 1828-45,) and "Lectures on Chemical Philosophy," ("Leçons sur la Philosophie chimique,"(1837.) His works are remarkable for elegance of style. From October, 1849, to January, 1851, he was minister of agriculture and commerce. He was nominated senator and vice-president of the council of public instruction about the end of 1851. France is indebted to him for the organization of a system of instruction in agriculture, and the institution of a European sanitary congress.

See "Galerie historique des Membres du Sénat;" "Nouvelle Biographie Générale."

Dumas, (LOUIS,) a French musician, born at Nîmes in 1676. He wrote "The Art of Music, taught and practised by the Method of the Typographic Bureau," and "La Bibliothèque des Enfants." He was tutor of the Marquis de Montcalm who fell at Quebec. Died in 1744.

Dumas, (MATHIEU,) COUNT, a French general and historian, born at Montpellier in 1753. He was aide-de-camp of Count de Rochambeau in the United States, where he served three campaigns, 1780-82. In the revolution of 1789 he was identified with the party of La

Fayette, and was charged with several important missions. In 1791 Colonel Dumas commanded the troops which guarded Louis XVI. on his return from Varennes, and was raised to the rank of maréchal-de-camp. He was a moderate member of the Legislative Assembly in 1791 and 1792, and was condemned to death in the reign of terror, but escaped to Switzerland. About 1800 he obtained the rank of general of brigade, and was appointed councillor of state. He became a general of division in 1805, and, as aide-major-général of Napoleon, made the campaigns of Ulm and Austerlitz, and that of Austria in 1809. He accompanied the grand army to Moscow (1812) as intendant-général of the administrative service. In 1814 he entered the service of Louis XVIII., and in the Hundred Days accepted a command from Napoleon. He published a narrative of the French campaigns from 1798 to 1807, entitled "Précis des Evénements militaires," (19 vols., 1816-26,) which is highly prized. He co-operated with La Fayette in the revolution of 1830, after which he was created a peer of France. Died in Paris in October, 1837.

See his autobiographic memoirs, entitled "Souvenirs," 3 vols., 1839, and English version of the same; "Histoire des Généraux Français;" "Nouvelle Biographie Générale."

Dumas, (RENÉ FRANÇOIS,) a French Jacobin, born at Lons-le-Saulnier in 1757, was notorious for cruelty as president of the Revolutionary Tribunal in 1793. As a partisan of Robespierre, he was guillotined, July 28, 1794.

Dumay, düʹmäʹ, (LOUIS,) a French publicist, born in the first part of the seventeenth century. He published, besides other works, "The Science of Princes, or Considerations on Coups d'État by Naudé, with Reflections," (1673,) which was greatly esteemed. Died in 1681.

Dumay, (PAUL,) a French poet, born at Dijon in 1626, associated or corresponded with the most eminent scholars, and wrote admired Latin verses. His poem in honour of the Duc d'Enghien, entitled "Enguinneis," (1643,) was praised by Gronovius. Died in 1711.

Dumée, düʹmäʹ, (JEANNE,) a French astronomer, born in Paris in the seventeenth century. She published a "Discourse on the Opinion of Copernicus respecting the Mobility of the Earth," which has some merit.

Dumerbion, düʹmĕrʹbeʹŏnʹ, (PIERRE J.,) a French general, born at Montmeillant in 1734; died in 1797.

Duméril, düʹmäʹrĕlʹ, (ANDRÉ MARIE CONSTANT,) a French physician and naturalist of high reputation, born at Amiens on the 1st of January, 1774, was a pupil of Cuvier. He was chosen professor of anatomy à la faculté in Paris in 1800, and admitted into the Institute about 1815. For four years he supplied the place of Cuvier as professor of natural history in the École Centrale. In 1822 he exchanged his chair of anatomy for that of physiology, and in 1825 succeeded Lacépède as professor at the Jardin des Plantes. He published in 1803 a "Treatise on Natural History," a fourth edition of which was entitled "Eléments des Sciences naturelles," (2 vols., 1846.) His greatest work is a "Natural History of Reptiles," ("Erpétologie générale," 9 vols., 1834-54,) in which Bibron co-operated. About 1830 he became professor of medical pathology in the Faculty of Medicine at Paris.

Dumesnil, (JEAN BAPTISTE.) See GARDIN-DUMESNIL.

Dumesnil, düʹmäʹnĕlʹ, (LOUIS ALEXIS LEMAÎTRE,) a French littérateur, born at Caen in 1783, wrote a "History of Philip II. of Spain," (1822,) and other historical works. Died in 1858.

Dumesnil, (MARIE FRANÇOISE,) a celebrated French actress, born near Alençon in 1711. She made her début in Paris in 1737. She was most successful in tragedy, and in the expression of fierce or sublime passions. It has been said that she created the rôle of Mérope in Voltaire's tragedy of that name. Voltaire, La Harpe, and other poets have paid tributes of admiration to this actress. Dorat, in his poem "Theatrical Declamation," speaks of her in high terms. She retired from the stage in 1776, and died about 1802.

See VOLTAIRE, "Correspondance;" MARMONTEL, "Mémoires."

Dum'mer, (JEREMIAH,) an American writer, born in Boston about 1680. He was sent to England as an agent of Massachusetts, and became a friend of Lord Boling-

broke. He wrote an able defence of the charters of New England, (1721,) and other works. Died in 1739.

Dum'no-rix, an ambitious chieftain of the Ædui, a nation of Gaul, was the brother of Divitiacus. He figures largely in the "Commentaries" of Cæsar, who, for the sake of Divitiacus, once pardoned Dumnorix for a conspiracy against the Romans. Having subsequently disobeyed the order to follow Cæsar in the invasion of Britain, he was killed by Cæsar's soldiers about 59 B.C., exclaiming, with his latest breath, "I am a free citizen of a free state."

See CÆSAR, "De Bello Gallico."

Dumolard, düʹmoʹlärʹ, (JOSEPH VINCENT,) a French politician, born in Dauphiné in 1766; died in 1820.

Dumolin. See DUMOULIN.

Dumolinet, düʹmoʹleʹnäʹ, (CLAUDE,) a French priest and antiquary, born at Châlons-sur-Marne in 1620, wrote a "History of the Popes by their Medals," and dissertations on several points of antiquity. Died in 1687.

Dumon, düʹmŏnʹ, (PIERRE SYLVAIN,) a French statesman, born at Agen in 1797, became minister of finance in 1847.

Dumonceau, düʹmŏnʹsōʹ, (JEAN BAPTISTE,) a French general, born at Brussels in 1760. He entered the French army in 1792, and in 1794 fought in Holland under Pichegru, who gave him command of the Hague. He became general-in-chief in the service of the Batavian republic in 1805, obtained a marshal's bâton in 1806 or 1807, and repulsed the English at Walcheren in 1809. In 1813 he gained a victory over the Russians at Pirna. Died in 1821.

See "Victoires et Conquêtes des Français."

Dumont, düʹmŏnʹ, (ANDRÉ,) a French Jacobin, born in Picardy in 1764, was a member of the Convention, 1792-95. He took side against Robespierre on the 9th Thermidor. Died in 1836.

Dumont, (AUGUSTIN ALEXANDRE,) a French sculptor, born in Paris in 1801. He gained the grand prize in 1823, and went to Rome with a pension. He executed marble statues of Poussin, (for the Institute,) Saint Louis, (for the Luxembourg,) and of several other Frenchmen. In 1838 he was chosen a member of the Institute. Among his later works are figures of Glory and Immortality, for the new Louvre, (1857.)

See "Nouvelle Biographie Générale."

Dumont, (CHARLES HENRI FRÉDÉRIC,) a French writer, born near Abbeville in 1758, was the author of a "Manual for Mayors," a "Dictionary of Forests," ("Dictionnaire forestier," 1802,) and other useful works. Died in 1830.

Dumont, COMTE DE GAGES. See GAGES.

Du-mŏnt', (EBENEZER,) an American general, born at Vevay, in Southern Indiana, about 1815, was a lawyer before the civil war. He became a brigadier-general about September, 1861, and gained a victory at Lebanon, Kentucky, in May, 1862. He represented the sixth district of Indiana in Congress in 1863-65, having been elected by the Republicans.

Dumont, (FRANÇOIS,) a sculptor, born in Paris in 1688. He gained the first prize of the Academy at an early age, and was received as a member of the same in 1712, when he produced in marble his "Thunderstruck Titan," ("Titan foudroyé.") Died in 1726.

Dumont, (GABRIEL,) a learned Protestant minister and Orientalist, born in Dauphiné in 1680; died in 1748.

Dumont, (GABRIEL MARTIN,) a French architect, born in Paris about 1720. He was living in 1790.

Dumont, (GEORGE,) a statistical writer, born in Paris in 1725; died in 1798.

Dumont, (JACQUES EDME,) a French sculptor, born in Paris in 1761, was a grandson of François Dumont, noticed above, and the father of Augustin Alexandre. He adorned the Louvre, Luxembourg, and other public edifices with statues and bas-reliefs, among which are statues of Marceau, Colbert, (1808,) and Malesherbes, (1829.) Died in 1844.

Dumont, (JEAN,) a historian, born in France about 1650, became a resident of Vienna. The Emperor of Germany appointed him historiographer, and gave him the title of baron. He wrote a "History of the Treaties of Peace of the Seventeenth Century," ("Corps universel diplomatique du Droit des Gens," 8 vols., 1726,) a

"Collection of Treaties made from the Time of Charlemagne to the Present Time," and other works. Died in 1726.

Dumont, (JEAN,) a French historical painter, called "the Roman," was born in Paris in 1700, and studied in Rome. "His talent," says Auguis, "was not equal to his reputation." He was admitted into the Academy of Paris in 1728. Died in 1781.

Dumont, dü'môn', (PIERRE ÉTIENNE LOUIS,) an eminent Swiss author, born of a French family at Geneva in 1759. He was ordained minister of a Protestant church in Geneva in 1781. In consequence of the defeat of the Liberal party in the Swiss state, he emigrated about 1782, and went to Saint Petersburg. There he gained reputation as an eloquent preacher; but, after a residence of eighteen months, he accepted an invitation from London to become the tutor of the sons of Lord Shelburne. He became intimate with Bentham and Romilly. In 1789 and 1790 he was in Paris, where he was patronized by Mirabeau, whom he assisted in composing his speeches and reports. About 1792 he returned to England, and, as secretary or coadjutor of Bentham, he began the important task of polishing and popularizing his great works on legislation, which were then in a rude and confused state. "M. Dumont was admirably qualified," says Macaulay, "to supply what was wanting in Mr. Bentham. In the qualities in which the French writers surpass those of all other nations,—neatness, clearness, precision, condensation,—he surpassed all French writers." Among the works of Bentham edited by Dumont (in French) are "Traités de Législation," (1802,) and "Théorie des Peines et des Récompenses," (1810.) From 1814 until 1829 he lived in Geneva, where he became a member of the representative council. He died in Milan in 1829, leaving "Recollections of Mirabeau," ("Souvenirs sur Mirabeau,") since published, which, remarks Macaulay, "is a very amusing and instructive book, and a relic of a wise and virtuous man."

See MACAULAY, Review of Dumont's "Recollections of Mirabeau;" A. P. DECANDOLLE, "Notice sur la Vie et les Écrits de M. Dumont," 1829; SIMONDE DE SISMONDI, "Notice nécrologique sur M. Dumont," 1829; "Encyclopædia Britannica."

Dumont de Courset, dü'môn' deh koor-sâ', (GEORGES LOUIS MARIE,) BARON, a French botanist, born near Boulogne in 1746. At his château De Courset he formed gardens famous for their extent and beauty. He wrote a successful work entitled "Le Botaniste-Cultivateur," (1798, 5 vols.,) containing a description of 8700 foreign and indigenous plants. Died in 1824.

Dumont d'Urville, dü'môn' dür'vèl', (JULES SÉBASTIEN CÉSAR,) a celebrated French navigator and botanist, born at Condé-sur-Noireau, Normandy, in 1790, entered the navy in 1807. Having been raised to the rank of captain, he commanded the corvette Astrolabe, which was sent in 1826 to obtain tidings of La Pérouse and to make hydrographic observations. In this voyage he made coast-surveys of New Zealand, New Guinea, New Britain, etc., and found evidence that La Pérouse had been wrecked on one of the Solomon Islands named Vanikoro. The results of the expedition, which made rich contributions to natural history, were published under the title of "Voyage de Découvertes autour du Monde," (22 vols., 1832–34.) In 1837 he sailed with the Astrolabe and Zélée on a voyage of Antarctic discovery. In January, 1840, he discovered land, which he named Terre Adélie, situated in latitude 66° 30′ south and longitude 138° 21′ east. On his return in November, 1840, he was made a rear-admiral, and began the publication of his "Voyage au Pôle sud et dans l'Océanie," (24 vols., 1841–54. Eleven volumes of this work were written by the other naturalists of the expedition. He was killed by a railway-accident near Versailles in May, 1842.

See DE BARINS, "Vie et Voyages de l'Amiral Dumont d'Urville," 1844; LESSON, "Notice historique sur Dumont d'Urville," 1846; ISIDORE LEBRUN, "Biographie de Dumont d'Urville," in the "Annales maritimes."

Dumortier, dü'moR'te-â', (BARTHÉLEMY CHARLES,) a Belgian botanist, was born at Tournay in 1797.

Dumoulin, dü'moo'lâN', or **Dumolin,** dü'mo'lâN', [Lat. MOLINÆ'US,] (CHARLES,) an eminent French jurist, born in Paris in 1500, was a relative of Queen Anne Boleyn. He embraced the Protestant religion, for which he was often persecuted and was once driven out of France by violence. He resided at Paris, Orléans, Lyons, etc. In 1564 he published a work against the acts of the Council of Trent, which made a great sensation. The French estimate him as one of the greatest jurisconsults and most learned men of his time. "His name," says De Thou, "was venerated not only for his solid judgment and profound learning, but also for his probity and purity of character." He died in December, 1566, leaving several volumes of legal works.

See BRODEAU, "Vie de Dumoulin," prefixed to his works, dated 1681, 5 vols. folio; notice by DUPIN aîné in "Encyclopédie des Gens du Monde;" HENRION DE PANSEY, "Éloge de C. Dumoulin," 1769; NICÉRON, "Mémoires;" HELLO, "Essai sur la Vie et les Ouvrages de C. Dumoulin," 1839; "Nouvelle Biographie Générale."

Dumoulin, (ÉVARISTE,) a French journalist, born in the Gironde in 1776, favoured the popular cause in the Revolution. In 1815 he removed to Paris and became one of the editors of the "Constitutionnel," a new journal which opposed the government. His articles contributed greatly to the popularity of this journal. Next to Thiers he took the most prominent part in the protest of the journalists against the ordinances of July, 1830. Died in 1833.

Dumoulin, (PIERRE.) See MOULIN.

Dumouriez, dü'moo're-â', (ANNE FRANÇOIS Dupérier — dü'pâ're-â',) a French poet, born in Paris in 1707. He was appointed commissary of war in 1732, and intendant of the army of De Broglie in 1759. He wrote "Richardet," a poem in imitation of Forteguerri, (1766,) and other poems. Died in 1769.

Dumouriez, (CHARLES FRANÇOIS,) a celebrated French general and statesman, born at Cambrai in 1739, was a son of the preceding. In early youth he was initiated in the arts of diplomacy by an uncle who was in the foreign office. At the close of the Seven Years' war (1763) he had obtained the rank of captain and received twenty-two wounds. He served with distinction as quartermaster-general in the expedition against Corsica in 1768. About 1770 the Duke of Choiseul sent him on a secret political mission to Poland, whence he was soon recalled in consequence of the dismissal of that minister. He was then confined nearly a year in the Bastille for some political reasons or pretexts, and was released in 1774. Before the Revolution he was for more than ten years commandant of Cherbourg, where he ably directed the construction of the port and the great naval works which he had planned.

In 1790 he favoured the moderate or constitutional party, and became intimate with the Girondist leaders, who discerned in him a rare combination of the qualities requisite for those critical times, both as a general and a diplomatist. His mind was at once powerful, flexible, and resolute. He possessed, besides, a spontaneous, direct, and captivating eloquence. In March, 1792, he was appointed minister of foreign affairs, and became the master-spirit of the government. He gained the confidence of the king, to whom he appears to have been loyal. A few weeks after Dumouriez became minister, war was declared against Austria. In June, 1792, he resigned his office, and in August of the same year became general-in-chief of the army in place of La Fayette. He defended the passes of the forest of Argonne against a superior Prussian force which was marching in triumph towards Paris. It is now admitted that the dilatory movements of the Prussian general were caused by secret negotiations pending between him and Dumouriez for the restoration of Louis XVI.

The Prussians having abandoned the invasion of France in October, Dumouriez undertook a campaign against Flanders with about 100,000 men. In November, 1792, he defeated the Austrians at the battle of Jemmapes, (the first pitched battle that had been gained by the republican army,) which was followed by the speedy conquest of Belgium. At this period, as Lamartine says, Dumouriez "was the virtual dictator of all parties," and such he might have continued if he had not striven against the tide which impelled him on to fortune. But, from loyalty to the Bourbons, hostility to the Jacobins, or some other cause, he paused in the career of victory, and plotted a counter-revolution in concert with the Austrians. Rumours of his defection having reached

---

ā, ē, ī, ō, ū, ȳ, *long;* ă, ĕ, ŏ, same, less prolonged; ă, ĕ, ĭ, ŏ, ŭ, ў, *short;* a, ę, į, o, *obscure;* fär, fall, fât; mêt; nŏt; gōōd; mōōn;

Paris, the Convention sent four commissioners, in April, 1793, to summon him to their bar. On his refusal to obey this summons, they ordered his soldiers to arrest him. "This is too much!" exclaimed Dumouriez. "It is time to resist such audacity!" and the deputies were instantly seized by his hussars and taken as prisoners to the Austrian camp. His army, however, refusing to join in his designs, he was compelled to escape with a few adherents, and passed the rest of his life in exile. He was pensioned by England, and died near Henley-on-Thames, in Buckinghamshire, in 1823, leaving memoirs of his life and several political treatises.

See "Mémoires de Dumouriez," written by himself, 2 vols., 1794, and an English translation of the same, by JOHN FENWICK; also, LEDIEU, "Dumouriez et la Révolution Française," 1826; THIERS, "History of the French Revolution;" "Nouvelle Biographie Générale."

Dumoustier, dü′moos′te-à′, (PIERRE,) COUNT, a French general, who was born at Saint-Quentin in 1771. For his conduct at Pultusk he was made general of brigade about 1806. After he had served several campaigns in Spain, he became general of division in 1811. He took part in the battle of Lutzen, (1813.) Died in 1831.

Dumoutier, dü′moo′te-à′, (DANIEL,) a skilful French portrait-painter, was born in Paris about 1550. He holds a high rank among the early French artists, and has left portraits of several kings, from Henry II. to Louis XIII. Died in 1631.

Dun, LORD. See ERSKINE, (DAVID.)

Dunæus, the Latin of DOWNES, which see.

Dŭn-bar′, (GEORGE,) a Scottish scholar, born in 1774. He was professor of Greek in the University of Edinburgh from 1805 until 1851. He published several useful educational works, of which the most important is an excellent "Greek and English Lexicon," (1840.) Died in 1857.

Dunbar, (WILLIAM,) one of the greatest of the early Scottish poets, was born at Salton about 1465. He became a Franciscan friar and itinerant preacher. He was afterwards employed by James IV., probably as clerk or secretary of embassy, and in 1500 he received the grant of a small pension, which was eventually increased to £80. In 1503 he produced "The Thistle and the Rose," an allegory in honour of the marriage of James IV., which is one of his best works. He excels in allegory and in didactic and humorous poetry. Sir Walter Scott thought him "unrivalled by any poet that Scotland had yet produced." Among his principal poems are "The Golden Terge or Targe," "The Merle and Nightingale," and "The Jousts between the Tailor and Souter." Died about 1530.

See WARTON, "History of English Poetry;" ELLIS, "Specimens of Early English Poetry;" CHAMBERS, "Biographical Dictionary of Eminent Scotsmen;" CAMPBELL, "Specimens of the British Poets;" "Encyclopædia Britannica."

Dŭnc′an I., King of Scotland, was the son of Beatrix, who was a daughter of King Malcolm II. After a reign of a few years' duration, he was murdered at Elgin about 1040 by Macbeth, whose story has been dramatized by Shakspeare. Duncan's son, Malcolm III., became king.

Dŭnc′an, (ADAM,) Viscount of Camperdown, an able British admiral, born at Dundee in 1731. He entered the navy about 1746, and was made a post-captain in 1761. He distinguished himself at Cape Saint Vincent in 1780, and was made a rear-admiral in 1789, and vice-admiral in 1795, when he commanded in the North Sea. During the war against the Dutch, an alarming mutiny broke out in the English navy in 1797, and Duncan was deserted by nearly all his ships. The mutineers having returned to their duty, he gained a decisive victory over the Dutch near Camperdown in October, 1797, for which he was created Viscount Duncan of Camperdown. Died in 1804. He had married the daughter of Lord-President Dundas, and left two sons.

See CAMPBELL, "Lives of the British Admirals;" CHAMBERS, "Biographical Dictionary of Eminent Scotsmen;" "Encyclopædia Britannica."

Duncan, (ANDREW,) a Scottish physician, born in Edinburgh in 1745. He delivered clinical lectures in the University of Edinburgh from 1773 to 1776, and wrote some medical treatises. Died in 1828.

See CHAMBERS, "Biographical Dictionary of Eminent Scotsmen."

Dŭnc′an, [Fr. pron. dŭN′kôN′,] (DANIEL,) an eminent French physician, of Scottish descent, born at Montauban in 1649. After graduating about 1673, he lived some years in Paris. In 1685, to escape persecution as a Protestant, he retired to Geneva, and thence to Berne, where he was professor of anatomy. He practised a number of years at the Hague, and about 1714 settled in London, where he died in 1735. He was author of "La Chimie naturelle," (1680,) and of several other works.

Duncan, (HENRY,) D.D., a Scottish minister and author, born near Dumfries in 1774, was presented to the church of Ruthwell in 1799. He was the founder of savings-banks, and author of several works, among which are "The Cottage Fireside," and "The Sacred Philosophy of the Seasons," (4 vols., 1836.) Died in 1846.

See a "Memoir of Dr. Duncan," published by his son in 1848; CHAMBERS, "Biographical Dictionary of Eminent Scotsmen."

Duncan, (JOHN,) D.D., grandson of Daniel, noticed above, was born in 1720. He published an "Essay on Happiness," a poem, and other works. Died in 1808.

Dŭnc′an, (JOHNSON K.,) an American general, born in Pennsylvania, graduated at West Point in 1849. He took arms against the Union, and commanded Forts Jackson and Saint Philip, below New Orleans. He surrendered those forts about April 29, 1862, after the Union fleet had passed them. Died in 1863, aged about thirty-six years.

Duncan, (JOSEPH,) an American general and politician, born in Kentucky about 1790. He served with credit in the second war with Great Britain, and at its close settled in Illinois. While in the legislature of that State, he was chiefly instrumental in the passage of the law establishing common schools. He was afterwards Governor of Illinois, and from 1827 to 1835 a representative in Congress. Died in 1844.

Duncan, (MARK,) a Scottish physician, was the ancestor of Daniel, noticed above. He became principal of the Calvinist college at Saumur, France, and wrote a treatise on Logic, ("Institutiones Logicæ," 1612.) Died in 1640.

His son MARK was a distinguished poet and soldier. (See CERISANTES.)

Duncan, (PHILIP BURY,) an English scholar and philanthropist, born in South Warnborough in 1772. He lived mostly at Oxford and Bath, was a Fellow of New College, Oxford, and keeper of the Ashmolean Museum. He contributed largely to charitable purposes. He wrote "Essays on Various Subjects," and other works. Died near Bath in 1863.

Duncan, (THOMAS,) a Scottish artist, born in Perthshire in 1807. He painted subjects of Scottish history. Died in Edinburgh in 1845.

Duncan, (WILLIAM,) a Scottish writer, born at Aberdeen in 1717. He became a resident of London about 1740. His translation of Cicero's "Select Orations," with notes, and his "Elements of Logic," (1748,) were esteemed and often reprinted. In 1752 he was chosen professor of philosophy in Marischal College, Aberdeen. Died in 1760.

See CHAMBERS, "Biographical Dictionary of Eminent Scotsmen."

Duncker, dŏönk′ker, or **Dunker,** (BALTHASAR ANTOINE,) a painter and engraver, born at Saal, in Pomerania, in 1746. He studied and worked some years in Paris, where he painted history and landscapes. He also made etchings of paintings in the cabinet of the Duc de Choiseul. Died at Berne in 1807.

Duncker, (MAXIMILIAN WOLFGANG,) a German historian, born in Berlin in 1812. He became professor of history at Halle about 1840, and was a prominent member of the National Assembly of Frankfort in 1848. He has published "Origines Germanicæ," (1840,) a "History of Antiquity," ("Geschichte des Alterthums," 1852,) and other works.

Dun′combe, (Rev. JOHN,) an English writer, born in 1730, became vicar of Herne. He published a few sermons, "The Feminead," a poem, and a version of the emperor Julian's works. Under the signature of "Crito," he contributed to the "Gentleman's Magazine" for many years. Died in 1785.

Duncombe, (THOMAS SLINGSBY,) an English radical legislator, born in 1796. He was elected to Parliament a 1826, and represented Finsbury (London) from 1834 until his death. He was a witty and fluent speaker, and very popular with the voters. No man ever sat so long for any metropolitan borough. He constantly advocated the vote by ballot, extended suffrage, and other reforms. In 1858 he carried an important motion, which resulted in the relief of the Jews from political disabilities. Died in November, 1861.

See a "Life of Thomas S. Duncombe," by his son THOMAS, 2 vols., 1868.

Duncombe, (WILLIAM,) an English writer, father of the Rev. John Duncombe, noticed above, was born in London in 1690. He published several successful works, among which are a translation of Racine's "Athalie," a poetical version of Horace, (in which he was assisted by his son,) and "L. J. Brutus," a tragedy. Died in 1769.

Dŭn-dăs', (Sir DAVID,) a British general, born in or near Edinburgh about 1735. He entered the army in 1752, was aide-de-camp to General Elliott in 1761, and obtained the rank of colonel in 1781. In 1788, after studying tactics in Prussia, he wrote "Principles of Military Movements," which were adopted as rules for the royal army. He obtained the grade of major-general in 1790, and distinguished himself at Tournay in 1794. In 1804 he was made governor of Chelsea Hospital and knight of the Bath, and in 1809 he succeeded the Duke of York as commander-in-chief of the British army. Died in 1820.

See CHAMBERS, "Biographical Dictionary of Eminent Scotsmen."

Dundas, (HENRY,) Lord Melville, a Scottish lawyer and statesman, born about 1740. He was appointed lord advocate of Scotland in 1775, and treasurer of the British navy in 1783. He was one of Pitt's most useful and steadfast supporters. He became a member of the cabinet as secretary of state for the home department in 1791, and a few years later exchanged that office for the place of secretary at war. Having resigned this office at the dissolution of Pitt's ministry, he was raised to the peerage, as Viscount Melville, in 1802. Lord Brougham says "he was an admirable man of business, and a skilful debater." In 1804 he was appointed first lord of the admiralty. The next year the Commons impeached him for misapplication of the public money, for which he was tried by the Lords and acquitted. Died in 1811, leaving the title to his son, Robert Saunders.

See CHAMBERS, "Biographical Dictionary of Eminent Scotsmen;" BROUGHAM, "Statesmen of the Time of George III."

Dundas, (Sir JAMES WHITLEY DEANS,) a British admiral, born in 1785, was a son of Dr. James Deans. He assumed the name of Dundas about 1808. He became rear-admiral in 1841, and commanded the fleet which operated against Russia in the Black Sea in 1854, but did not perform any important action. He resigned, or was recalled, about the end of 1854, and Sir E. Lyons succeeded to the command. Died in 1862.

Dundas, (RICHARD SAUNDERS,) a British admiral, born at Melville Castle, Scotland, in 1802, was a son of the third Viscount Melville. He entered the navy in 1817, and became a post-captain in 1824. About 1840 he served with distinction in the Chinese war. He obtained the rank of rear-admiral in 1853, and the command of the fleet in the Baltic, *vice* Sir Charles Napier, in February, 1855. His principal exploit was the very effective bombardment of Sweaborg in 1855. He was made a vice-admiral in 1858. Died in 1861.

Dundas, (ROBERT,) an eminent Scottish lawyer, born in 1685, was the father of Lord Melville. He was appointed lord advocate of Scotland in 1720, and lord president of the court of session in 1748. Died in 1753.

See CHAMBERS, "Biographical Dictionary of Eminent Scotsmen."

Dundas, (ROBERT,) a Scottish lawyer, son of the preceding, was born in 1713. After filling other high offices, he was appointed president of the court of session in 1760. Died in 1787.

Dundee. See GRAHAM, (JOHN.)

Dundonald, EARL OF. See COCHRANE, (ARCHIBALD.)

Dun-don'ald, (THOMAS COCHRANE,) tenth EARL OF, a distinguished British admiral, born in 1775, was the eldest son of Archibald, Earl of Dundonald. (See COCHRANE, ARCHIBALD.) He entered the navy in 1793, and obtained the rank of post-captain in 1801, after capturing many prizes from the French. In 1809 he commanded the fire-ships that destroyed the French fleet in the Basque Roads, and was rewarded with knighthood for that daring and successful exploit. About this time he was elected by the Whigs to Parliament, where he was an active opponent of the ministry. In 1814 he was accused of spreading a false report of Napoleon's death, which caused a great rise in the funds, and by the influence of party spirit was convicted, fined £1000, sentenced to imprisonment for one year, and dismissed from the naval service. Before the expiration of his term of imprisonment, his constituents, believing him to be innocent, re-elected him to Parliament. The injustice of his condemnation was recognized many years before his death. He commanded the fleet of Chili from 1818 to 1822, and that of Brazil in 1822 and 1823. In 1827 he distinguished himself as admiral of the Greeks in their revolt against Turkey. He inherited the earldom in 1831, and was restored to his rank in the navy in 1833. He was made vice-admiral of the white in 1851, and full admiral about 1854. Died in 1860. His "Autobiography of a Seaman" has since appeared. "He performed greater actions with smaller means," says the "North British Review" for February, 1861, "than any other captain or commander recorded in history. He combined the chivalrous audacity of Sir Sydney Smith and the calculated dash of Nelson, with an originality of conception to which neither of them so much as approximated."

See, also, "Blackwood's Magazine" for February, 1860.

Dunfermline, BARON. See ABERCROMBY, (JAMES.)

Dungal, dŭn-gaul', a scholar and teacher, supposed to have been a native of Ireland, became a resident of France. Charlemagne having consulted him respecting an eclipse of the sun which occurred in 810, he answered in a long letter, which is extant.

Dunglison, dŭng'glĭ-son, (ROBLEY,) M.D., a physician and author, distinguished for his profound and varied learning, as well as for his numerous valuable contributions to medical literature, was born at Keswick, county of Cumberland, England, January 4, 1798. His medical education, begun at Keswick, was carried on in London. He subsequently attended a course of lectures at the University of Edinburgh, and also a course at the École de Médecine of Paris. He graduated in medicine in 1823 at the University of Erlangen, in Germany. In 1824 he was engaged by the University of Virginia, then newly established, to fill a chair of medicine (including anatomy and physiology) in that institution, and, in accordance with this arrangement, he came to America in the autumn of the same year. He held this position until October, 1833, when he accepted the professorship of materia medica, therapeutics, etc. in the University of Maryland. In the summer of 1836 he was appointed professor of the institutes of medicine in the Jefferson College of Philadelphia, that chair having been newly created for him. He continued to fulfil the duties of this position with the highest credit to himself and to the institution until within a year of his death. It was owing in a great measure to his talents, reputation, and personal influence that the Jefferson College rose rapidly, from the inferior position which it had held before his accession to its faculty, to the very first rank among the medical schools of America. He died the 1st of April, 1869.

Dr. Dunglison enjoyed the friendship and confidence of the ex-Presidents Jefferson and Madison, both of whom he attended in the capacity of medical adviser. To Mr. Madison he dedicated his first important work,— his "Human Physiology." Although assiduous in the cultivation of the sciences more immediately connected with his profession, he found time to give a share of his attention to a great variety of subjects, including philology and general literature. Among the many objects of his benevolence, he took a particular and deep interest in the Philadelphia Institution for the Blind, and gave liberally of his time and services, that he might lighten the privations and enhance the enjoyments of that unfortunate class for whose sake it had been established.

As a man, Dr. Dunglison was distinguished for his freedom from prejudice, for a dispassionate fairness in all his judgments of men and things, as well as for a liberal and kindly spirit which constantly prompted him to acts of courtesy and beneficence. His character commanded the universal respect, esteem, and confidence of that large circle who enjoyed the privilege of his friendship.

Among his numerous works we may name·his "Human Physiology," (2 vols. 8vo, 1832; 8th edition, 1856,) his "Dictionary of Medical Science," of which the first edition appeared in 1833, "Elements of Hygiene," (1835; 2d edition, published under the title of "Human Health," 1844,) "General Therapeutics, or Principles of Medical Practice," (1836; 6th edition, 1857,) "New Remedies," (1839; 7th edition, 1856,) "Medical Student," (1837; 2d edition, 1844,) and his "Practice of Medicine," (2 vols., 1842; 3d edition, 1848.)

He made numerous contributions not only to the principal medical and surgical journals published in the United States, but also wrote articles for several of the scientific and literary periodicals of Great Britain. Of all his works his "Medical Dictionary" is probably the most widely known: its success has scarcely had a parallel in this department of literature. The number of copies sold, from the date of its first publication up to the present time, (1869,) has reached nearly 60,000. (For a particular account of Dr. Dunglison's various publications, the reader is referred to Allibone's "Dictionary of Authors.")

See the notice of Dr. Dunglison in the "American Journal of the Medical Sciences" for July, 1869, by DR. S. H. DICKSON: and "Memoir of Dr. Robley Dunglison," by his son, DR. R. J. DUNGLISON, 1870.

Dunham, dŭn′ạm, (S. ASTLEY,) LL.D., an English author of the present century. He wrote the following able works: "History of Poland," (1830,) "History of Spain and Portugal," (1832,) "History of Europe during the Middle Ages," and "History of the Germanic Empire," (1837.) Died in 1858.

Duni, doo′nee, (EGIDIO,) a Neapolitan composer, born at Matera in 1709. He settled in Paris, and composed successful operas. Died in 1775.

Dunker. See DUNCKER.

Dŭnk′in, (Rev. WILLIAM,) an Irish poet, was a friend of Dean Swift. He published a volume of Epistles in 1741. After his death his Poetical Works were published in 2 vols., (1774.)

Dŭn′lap, (WILLIAM,) an American painter and author, was born at Perth Amboy, New Jersey, in 1766. He was a pupil of Sir Benjamin West in London. On his return to America he devoted himself to portrait-painting and dramatic composition in New York, and was manager of the Park Theatre from 1798 till 1805. Thenceforth his efforts were variously directed to his profession as an artist, to literature, to the career of a theatrical manager, etc. In 1821, when Dunlap was in his fifty-fifth year, appeared his first great painting, "Christ Rejected," (18 feet by 12,) after the plan of West's picture on the same subject, and in 1828 he painted "Calvary," (18 feet by 14,) both of which were exhibited with success in the principal cities of the United States. His "History of the American Theatre" was published in 1833, and his "History of the Rise and Progress of the Arts of Design in the United States" appeared in 1834. He also wrote a "Life of Charles Brockden Brown." Died in 1839.

Dŭn′lop, (ALEXANDER,) a distinguished scholar, of Scottish extraction, born in 1684. He was appointed professor of Greek in the University of Glasgow in 1720. His Greek Grammar was long used in the Universities of Scotland. Died in 1742.

Dunlop, (JOHN,) a British author, born probably in Scotland. He published a "History of Fiction," (London, 1814,) which passed through several editions, a "History of Roman Literature," and "Memoirs of Spain during the Reigns of Philip IV. and Charles II.," (1834,) said to be a work of merit.

See "Edinburgh Review" for November, 1814; "Quarterly Review" for July, 1815.

Dunlop, (WILLIAM,) a brother of Alexander, noticed above, was born at Glasgow in 1692. He was an eloquent preacher, and became professor of divinity in the University of Edinburgh in 1716. He published a valuable

"Collection of Confessions of Faith, Catechisms, Books of Discipline," etc. Died in 1720.

See CHAMBERS, "Biographical Dictionary of Eminent Scotsmen."

Dŭnn, (SAMUEL,) an English mathematician, born at Crediton. He taught mathematics at Crediton and Chelsea, and published several works on astronomy and navigation, (1759–93.) Died in 1792.

Dun′ning, (JOHN,) Lord Ashburton, an eminent English lawyer, born at Ashburton in 1731. He was called to the bar in 1756, and a few years later was recorder of Bristol. In 1767 he was appointed solicitor-general, and soon after was returned, by the borough of Calne, to Parliament, in which he acted with the Whigs. He was very successful in his profession, and was regarded by many as the first advocate in England at that time. His style of oratory was brilliant, witty, and sarcastic; but his gestures were not graceful, and his person was the reverse of imposing. In 1780 he married Elizabeth Baring. He was raised to the peerage, as Baron Ashburton, in 1782, and was appointed chancellor of the duchy of Lancaster. Died at Exmouth in 1783.

See SIR WILLIAM JONES's Eulogy on Dunning, in his Works, vol. iv.

Dunod, dü′no′, (PIERRE JOSEPH,) a French antiquary, born near Saint-Claude in 1657; died in 1725.

Dunod de Charnage, dü′no′ dĕh shăr′năzh′, (FRANÇOIS IGNACE,) a French jurist, born at Saint-Claude in 1679. He was appointed professor of law at Besançon in 1720. He wrote a "History of Burgundy," (1735,) which was much esteemed, and several able legal works. Died in 1752.

Dunod de Charnage, (SOPHIE ÉDOUARD,) a French administrator, born at Besançon in 1783; died in 1826.

Dunois, dü′nwä′, (JEAN,) the "Bastard of Orléans," a famous French captain, born in Paris in 1402, was a natural son of Louis, Duke of Orléans, who was a brother of the king, Charles VI. He defeated the English at Montargis in 1427, and shared with Joan of Arc the honour of raising the siege of Orléans in 1429. In 1436 he made himself master of Paris. Having obtained the chief command, with the title of lieutenant-general, he conquered Normandy from the English about 1448, and expelled the same enemy from Guienne in 1453. In reward for these services, Charles VII. declared him a prince of the blood, with the title of Count of Orléans. Dunois is one of the most popular names among the national heroes of France. Died in 1468.

He left a son FRANÇOIS, Count of Dunois and Longueville, ancestor of the celebrated Duc de Longueville.

See AIMÉ-CHAMPOLLION, "Louis et Charles d'Orléans;" ANSELME, "Histoire généalogique;" "Nouvelle Biographie Générale."

Dunoyer, dü′nwä′yä′, (ANNE MARGUERITE PETIT,) MADAME, a French writer of fiction, born at Nîmes about 1663, was a Protestant, and became an exile. She wrote "Lettres historiques et galantes," (7 vols., 1704.) Died in 1720.

Dunoyer, (CHARLES BARTHÉLEMI PIERRE,) a French economist, born at Carennac (Lot) in 1786. During the restoration he edited (with Charles Comte) the "Censeur," an able and liberal periodical. He was admitted into the Institute in 1832, and was prefect of La Somme from 1833–37. His chief work is "On the Liberty of Labour," (3 vols., 1845.)

Duns Escoto. See DUNS SCOTUS.

Duns-Scot. See DUNS SCOTUS.

Dŭns Sco′tus, [Fr. DUNS-SCOT, dŭn′sko′; It. DUNS ESCOTO, doons ĕs-ko′to,] (JOHN,) surnamed THE SUBTLE DOCTOR, a famous theologian and metaphysician, supposed to have been born about 1265 at Dunse, in Scotland. The Irish and English, however, claim him as their countryman. He was a Fellow of Merton College, Oxford, and a Franciscan friar. In 1301 he was chosen professor of theology at Oxford, where he is said to have lectured to an immense class. About 1307 he professed theology in Paris. He wrote many works on metaphysics, theology, etc., and was reputed one of the greatest doctors of his time. He founded a new school, the Scotists, which for several centuries maintained a rivalry with the Thomists, or disciples of Aquinas. Died at Cologne in 1308. "The greatest of the Schoolmen," says Hallam, "were Thomas Aquinas and Duns Scotus. They were founders of rival sects, which wrangled with each other for two or three centuries." ("Introduction to the Literature of Europe.")

See J. COLGAN, "Tractatus de Vita Joannis Scoti," 1655; CHAMBERS, "Biographical Dictionary of Eminent Scotsmen;" ALONZO DE GUZMAN, "Vida de J. Duns Scoto," 1671; LUCAS WADDING, "Vita J. Duns Scoti," Lyons, 1644.

Dunstable, dŭn′stạ-b'l, or **Dunstaple,** (JOHN,) an English musical composer, born at Dunstable about 1400; died in 1458.

Dŭn′stạn, SAINT, an eminent and ambitious English prelate and statesman, born at Glastonbury in 925 A.D. He became noted for monkish austerity, and obtained the chief power in the reign of Edred, which began in 946. King Edgar made him Bishop of London, and in 959 Archbishop of Canterbury. Dunstan exerted his paramount influence in this and the next reign to secure the papal supremacy. He exalted and enriched the monks at the expense of the secular clergy, who were expelled from their livings. On the accession of Ethelred II., in 978, Dunstan lost his political power. Died in 988.

See W. ROBINSON, "Life of Saint Dunstan," 1844; EADMER, "Life of Dunstan;" WILLIAM OF MALMESBURY, "History;" W. F. HOOK, "Lives of the Archbishops of Canterbury," vol. i. chap. vii.

Dŭn′stẹr, (CHARLES,) an English clergyman, was for many years rector of Petworth. He published "Notes on Paradise Regained," and other works. Died about 1816.

Dunster, (HENRY,) an English divine, who on his arrival in Massachusetts in 1640 was chosen the first president of Harvard College. He was an excellent Oriental scholar, but was compelled to resign in 1654 for preaching against infant baptism. Died in 1659.

Dŭn′tọn, (JOHN,) an eccentric English author and bookseller, born at Graffham in 1659. Having served an apprenticeship to a London bookseller, he opened a shop of his own in London about 1685. He married an aunt of the celebrated John Wesley. He failed in business once, or oftener. He wrote a great number and variety of curious books, among which are "The Athenian Mercury," (20 vols., 1690–96,) "The Dublin Scuffle," (1699,) and "The Life and Errors of John Dunton, with the Lives and Characters of a Thousand Persons," (1705.) He was a dissenter, a supporter of the Whig party, and a person of great fertility in projects. Died in 1733.

Düntzer, dŭnt′sẹr, or **Duentzer,** (JOHANN HEINRICH JOSEPH,) a German writer and philologist, born at Cologne in 1813. Among his numerous works are "The Faust of Goethe," (2 vols., 1836,) "Homer and the Epic Cycle," (1839,) and a "Commentary on the Poems of Horace," (5 vols., 1840–44.)

Dunz, dŏŏnts, (JOHANN,) a skilful Swiss painter of portraits and flowers, was born at Berne in 1645; died in 1736.

Dupain-Montesson, dü′păN′ môn′tạ′sôN′, a French geometer and writer on military tactics, born about 1720; died about 1790.

Du Pan. See MALLET DU PAN.

Dupanloup, dü′pôN′loo′, (FÉLIX ANTOINE PHILIBERT,) a distinguished French bishop, born at Saint-Félix, Savoy, in 1802. He was naturalized in 1833, and made Bishop of Orléans in 1849. In 1854 he was elected to the French Academy. Among his works is a popular treatise on Education,("De l'Éducation," 3 vols.,1855–57.)

See LAVEDAN, "Monseigneur Dupanloup," 1849; "Nouvelle Biographie Générale."

Duparquet, dü′păr′kạ′, (JACQUES DIEL,) a French officer, was appointed Governor of Martinique in 1638. In 1650 he planted a colony in Grenada, and soon after purchased those two islands, together with Saint Lucia, from the King of France, who gave him the title of lieutenant-general. He is praised for his kind and generous treatment of the aborigines. Died in 1658.

Dupasquier, dü′păs′ke-ạ′, (GASPARD ALFONSE,) a French chemist, born at Chassy (Rhône) in 1793; died in 1848.

Dupaty, dü′pä′te′, (CHARLES MARGUERITE JEAN BAPTISTE MERCIER,) a French littérateur and magistrate, born at Rochelle in 1746. He was successively advocate-general and president à mortier in the parliament of Bordeaux. He wrote a valuable work called "Historical Reflections on the Criminal Laws," (1788,) and

"Letters on Italy," (1788,) which had a brilliant success and were often reprinted. La Harpe designated the latter as "a mélange of good sense and false wit." Died in 1788. Two of his sons became eminent, one as sculptor and the other as author.

See VOLTAIRE, "Correspondance."

Dupaty, (CHARLES MERCIER,) an eminent French sculptor, born at Bordeaux in 1771, was a son of the preceding. He was a pupil of Lemot in Paris, where in 1799 he gained the grand prize for sculpture for his "Pericles visiting Anaxagoras." He studied several years at Rome, and adopted the antique style with great success. In 1816 he was chosen a member of the Institute. He was patronized by the government, for which he executed a statue of Louis XIII. His "Ajax pursued by Neptune" is considered his principal work. Died in November, 1825.

See COUPIN, "Notice sur Charles Dupaty," 1825; "Nouvelle Biographie Générale."

Dupaty, (LOUIS EMMANUEL CHARLES MERCIER,) a French poet, brother of the preceding, was born in the Gironde in 1775. He produced a successful comedy, "The Military Prison," (1803,) several comic operas, and a poem entitled the "Informers," ("Délateurs," 1819.) He was elected to the French Academy in 1835. Died in 1851.

Dupérac, dü′pă′răk′, (ÉTIENNE,) a French architect and painter, born in Paris, published a work "On the Antiquities of Rome," which is highly prized. Died in 1601.

Duperche, dü′pȧrsh′, (J. J. M.,) a French dramatist and able translator, born about 1775. He produced many successful dramas and novels. Died in 1829.

Dupérier, dü′pȧ′re-ȧ′, (CHARLES,) a French poet, born at Aix, in Provence, became a resident of Paris. His verses in honour of the king gained the prizes of the Academy in 1681 and 1683, and he acquired still higher reputation by his Latin poems. He excelled most in the ode. Ménage calls him the prince of the lyric poets of his age. Died in 1692.

See "Ménagiana."

Duperray, dü′pȧ′rȧ′, (MICHEL,) a French jurist and advocate of high reputation, born at Mans about 1640; died in 1730.

Duperré, dü′pȧ′rȧ′, (VICTOR GUY,) BARON, an able French admiral, born at La Rochelle in 1775. He was made captain of a frigate in 1806, and in 1808 defended himself with success against two English ships near L'Orient. In 1809 he was sent to India with one frigate, and captured several vessels of the enemy. He became baron and rear-admiral in 1810, and vice-admiral in 1826. He commanded the fleet of one hundred and three vessels of war which Charles X. sent in 1830 to attack Algiers. (See BOURMONT.) For his services in the capture of Algiers he was raised to the peerage and to the rank of admiral in 1830. Died in 1846.

See F. CHASSERIAU, "Vie de l'Amiral Duperré;" L. DE LOMÉNIE, "Galerie des Contemporains;" "Nouvelle Biographie Générale."

Duperret, dü′pȧ′rȧ′, (CLAUDE ROMAIN LAUS,) a French republican, born about 1746. In the Convention of 1792 he acted with the Girondists, and voted for the banishment of the king. He was elected as deputy, says Lamartine, as the most honest man, against his own wish. He shared the proscription of his party, and was executed in October, 1793.

Duperrey, dü′pȧ′rȧ′, (LOUIS ISIDORE,) a French navigator and savant, born in Paris in 1786. He served as hydrographer in the Uranie, under De Freycinet, who made explorations in the North Pacific, 1817–20. He commanded an expedition sent out in 1822 to explore the hydrography and natural history of the islands in the Pacific. He surveyed parts of Australia, New Zealand, New Guinea, etc., discovered several groups of islands, one of which received the name of Duperrey, and returned, without the loss of a man, in April, 1825. His "Voyage around the World in the Corvette La Coquille" (1826–30) is considered a very valuable contribution to the sciences. Duperrey wrote the historical part of this work, and the volumes on hydrography and physical science. He was elected to the Institute in 1842.

See "Nouvelle Biographie Générale;" "Notice sur les Travaux de M. L. I. Duperrey," etc., Paris, 1842.

ā, ē, ī, ō, ū, ȳ, *long;* à, ê, ò, same, less prolonged; ă, ĕ, ĭ, ŏ, ŭ, ў, *short;* ạ, ẹ, ị, ọ, *obscure;* fär, fåll, fåt; mêt; nôt; gŏŏd; moon;

Duperron. See ANISSON-DUPERRON.

Duperron. See ANQUETIL-DUPERRON.

Duperron, dü′pạ′rὸn′, (JACQUES DAVY,) a learned and eloquent French cardinal, was born at Saint-Lo, in Normandy, (or, as some assert, near Berne, in Switzerland,) in 1556. He was educated as a Protestant, but became a Catholic in his youth. He acquired the favour of Henry IV., who appointed him Bishop of Evreux in 1591; and he was the chief agent in the conversion of that king to the Roman communion. He was very skilful in disputation, and in 1600 gained an advantage over Du Plessis-Mornay in a famous conference. (See MORNAY.) He obtained a cardinal's hat in 1604, and died in Paris in 1618, leaving several theological works and short poems.

See PELLETIER, "Vie du Cardinal Duperron," 1618; "Perroniana," by C. DUPUY, 1669; SULLY, "Mémoires;" LÉVESQUE DE BURIGNY, "Vie du Cardinal Duperron," 1768; SISMONDI, "Histoire des Français."

Dupetit-Thouars, dü′peh-te′ too′ȧr′, (ABEL Aubert—o′baıʀ′,) a French admiral, born about 1792. In 1837 he commanded the Venus, sent on a voyage of circumnavigation, at the end of which in 1839 he was made a rear-admiral. He obtained command of the naval forces in the Pacific Ocean. Having received some provocation from the natives of Tahiti, he seized that island in 1842, but he was recalled by Guizot, who disavowed his act. He afterwards published a "Voyage round the World in the Frigate Venus," (10 vols.) He was appointed a member of the board of admiralty in 1848.

See "L'Amiral Dupetit-Thouars," Paris, 1844.

Dupetit-Thouars, (ARISTIDE AUBERT,) a French naval officer, born near Saumur in 1760. In 1792 he commanded a vessel sent out in search of La Pérouse, but was taken prisoner by the Portuguese, and the enterprise failed. He passed about three years in the United States, (1794-97.) In Bonaparte's expedition to Egypt he was captain of the Tonnant, which carried his friend Dolomieu the geologist. He displayed heroic courage at the battle of the Nile, in which he was killed, August 1, 1798. His character is said to have been very noble.

See J. DE LA GRAVIÈRE, "Guerres maritimes de la République," etc.; "Nouvelle Biographie Générale."

Dupetit-Thouars, (LOUIS MARIE AUBERT,) an eminent French botanist, brother of the preceding, was born at Saumur, in Anjou, about 1756. In 1792 he made a botanical excursion to the Isle of France, where he expected to join his brother, but was disappointed. He remained there and in Bourbon about nine years, and returned home with his collections in 1802. He was elected a member of the Institute about 1820, and lived mostly in Paris. Among his publications are a "History of Plants collected in the Isles of France, Bourbon, and Madagascar," (1804,) "The French Orchard," a treatise on the culture of fruit-trees, a "Flora of the Southern Isles of Africa," and "Mélanges of Botany and Travels," (1811.) He wrote for the "Biographie Universelle" many articles on botanists and physicians. Died in May, 1831. He was author of an "Essay on the Organization of Plants," (1805,) and other treatises on vegetable physiology. He originated a new and ingenious theory of the formation of annual layers of wood, and of the production of buds.

See P. FLOURENS, "Éloge historique de A. Dupetit-Thouars," 1845; "Nouvelle Biographie Générale."

Duphot, dü′fo′, (LÉONARD,) a French general, born at Lyons about 1770. He accompanied Joseph Bonaparte in an embassy to Rome in 1797, and was killed the same year, in a conflict between the papal soldiers and some Roman citizens who favoured a revolution.

Dupin, dü′pȧn′, (ANDRÉ MARIE JEAN JACQUES,) an eminent French lawyer, orator, and legislator, born at Varzy (Nièvre) in February, 1783. He was one of the counsel for Marshal Ney in 1815, and signalized his courage and eloquence in the defence of many persons tried for political offences, among whom was Béranger, (1821.) In 1826 he was elected to the Chamber of Deputies, in which he continued to sit for many years. He was the reporter (rapporteur) of the famous address of the two hundred and twenty-one deputies in March, 1830, and firmly opposed the ordinances which caused the revolution of 1830. He was appointed procureur-général of the court of cassation, and a member of the first cabinet of Louis Philippe, to whose elevation he contributed perhaps more than any other man. Between 1832 and 1848 he was chosen president of the Chamber eight times. On the 24th of February, 1848, he presented the infant Count of Paris to the deputies and proposed that he should be recognized as successor to the throne just abdicated. He acquiesced, however, in the republic, and in the Constituent Assembly he took a prominent part in defending social order, and was president of the committee of legislation. He displayed great firmness and coolness as president of the Assembly in the stormy period of 1849-50. M. Dupin retired from public life in 1852. He had been elected to the French Academy, in place of Cuvier, in 1832. He was author of many legal and political works, among which are "Principia Juris Civilis," (5 vols., 1806,) and "Mémoires et Plaidoyers," (20 vols., 1806-30.) "He is the greatest reviser of trials," says an anonymous French biographer, "the greatest redresser of wrongs, in the world. . . . If he be not the most eloquent he is certainly the most original of our orators. At times his bonmots have created a majority or upset a cabinet." He was reappointed procureur-général of France in 1857. He died in November, 1865.

See L. DE LOMÉNIE, "Galerie des Contemporains;" ORTOLAN, "Notice sur Dupin," 1840; "Nouvelle Biographie Générale."

Dupin, (CLAUDE,) a French economist, born at Châteauroux probably about 1700. He wrote "Œconomiques," (3 vols., 1745,) and several other works. He died at an advanced age in 1769.

His second wife, née MADEMOISELLE FONTAINE, was distinguished for wit and beauty. Her house in Paris was the resort of Fontenelle, Marivaux, and other authors. She employed J. J. Rousseau, when he was yet unknown to fame, as the preceptor of her son; but she was so little aware of his talents that she never invited him to her assemblies. Died about 1800.

The authoress Madame Dudevant (George Sand) is a descendant of Claude Dupin.

See J. J. ROUSSEAU, "Confessions;" GEORGE SAND, "Histoire de ma Vie."

Dupin, (CLAUDE FRANÇOIS ÉTIENNE,) BARON, a French writer, born at Metz in 1767, was the author of several able works on the Statistics of the Department of Deux-Sèvres. He married the widow of Danton in 1796. Died in 1828.

Dupin, (FRANÇOIS PIERRE CHARLES,) BARON, a distinguished French geometer and senator, brother of André, noticed above, was born at Varzy (Nièvre) in 1784. He entered the navy as an engineer in 1803. In 1813 he founded the Maritime Museum at Toulon. He volunteered to defend his friend Carnot by his pen and voice in 1815; but his client avoided the trial by going into exile. In 1816 he obtained leave to visit England in order to examine the public works and military resources of that country. He published the results of these observations in an important work entitled "Travels in Great Britain between 1816 and 1821," (6 vols., 1820-24,) which was received with great favour on both sides of the Channel. He was admitted into the Academy of Sciences in 1818, and became professor of mechanics in the Conservatoire des Arts et Métiers about 1820. His lectures were published (in 1825-26) in three works, entitled "Geometry applied to the Arts," "Mechanics applied to the Arts," and "La Dynamie," or "Science of Force," which were very successful.

M. Dupin made an application of statistics to moral and political questions in his work "On the Productive and Commercial Power of France," ("Sur les Forces productives et commerciales de la France," 2 vols., 1827,) which was popular with the Liberal party. He was elected to the Chamber of Deputies in 1828, and acquired distinction as a speaker. In 1831 he became a councillor of state, and in 1834 was minister of marine for the space of three days. He was created a peer of France in 1837. In the Assembly of 1848 and 1849 he voted with the majority, and in 1852 he was appointed a senator.

See "Notice historique sur M. le Baron C. Dupin," Paris, 1837; "Nouvelle Biographie Générale."

Dupin, (LOUIS ELLIES,) a French theologian and historian of great merit, was born in Paris in 1657. He became a doctor of the Sorbonne, and professor of philosophy in the Royal College. He composed, besides other works, a complete history of theological literature, —at least within the limits of the Church,—entitled "Bibliothèque universelle des Auteurs ecclésiastiques," (58 vols., 1686–1704.) "It is unquestionably," says Hallam, "the most standard work of that kind extant. The immense erudition requisite for such an undertaking may have rendered it inevitable to fall into some errors. . . . Integrity, love of truth, and moderation distinguish this history perhaps beyond any other." ("Introduction to the Literature of Europe.") The pope, in a letter to Louis XIV., called Dupin, who had written against the papal supremacy, "a man of pernicious doctrine." He was a Jansenist. Died in Paris in June, 1719.

See NICÉRON, "Mémoires ;" MORÉRI, "Dictionnaire Historique ;" "Nouvelle Biographie Générale."

Dupin, MADAME. See DUPIN, (CLAUDE.)

Dupin, (PHILIPPE,) born at Varzy in 1795, was an able lawyer. He practised in Paris many years, and was elected a deputy in 1830 and in 1842. He was a brother of the celebrated lawyer and legislator. Died at Nice in 1846.

Dupin de Francueil, dü′pǎN′ deh fRÕN′kuI′ or fRÕN′-kuh′ye, (MARIE AURORE,) a French lady, born in 1750, was the daughter of the famous Marshal Maurice de Saxe. After the death of her first husband, Count de Horn, she was married to Dupin de Francueil, the son of Claude Dupin, noticed above. The issue of this marriage was Maurice Dupin, the father of the well-known authoress Madame Dudevant, (George Sand.) The latter in her infancy was under the care of the subject of this article, who died in 1821.

Dupinet, dü′pe′nǎ′, (ANTOINE,) a French Protestant, lived in Lyons and Paris. He made a French version of Pliny's "Natural History," (1542,) which was highly praised by Bayle, and wrote "The Conformity of the Reformed Church of France with the Primitive Church," (1565,) besides a few other works. Died in 1584.

Duplanil, dü′plǎ′nèl′, (J. D.,) a French medical writer, born in 1740 ; died in 1802.

Dupleix, dü′plǎ′, (JOSEPH,) MARQUIS, an enterprising Frenchman, born about 1695, was the son of a director of the East India Company. Having received a liberal education and made great progress in the exact sciences, he was appointed in 1720 a member of the council at Pondicherry. Ten years later he became director of the factory at Chandernagore, in Bengal, which speedily prospered under his management. He made a large fortune by commercial operations. In 1742 he was appointed Governor of Pondicherry and of all the French possessions in India. His aspiring and capacious mind was the first that formed the project of founding a European empire on the ruins of the Mogul monarchy. By intrigues with native princes and a few battles he became master of the Carnatic, and about 1750 was the greatest potentate in India. The English, alarmed at his success, resolved to counteract him by force, and gave the command of their troops to Captain Clive, who gained several victories over the French and their allies. Dupleix was not supported by his employers in France, who disapproved his policy. Having been superseded in 1754, he returned to Paris, where he died poor in 1763. He had spent his own fortune in the service of the Company, who refused to repay him. About 1748 he had been rewarded with the title of Marquis for his able defence of Pondicherry against the English fleet under Boscawen.

See MILL, "History of British India ;" COLLIN DE BAR, "Histoire de l'Inde ancienne et moderne," 1814 ; CLAUDE NOËL LE FÈVRE, "Éloge de Dupleix," 1818.

Dupleix, (SCIPION,) a French historian, born at Condom in 1569. About 1619 Louis XIII. gave him the title of historiographer, and charged him to write a general history of France. He produced a voluminous work on that subject, (1621–43,) which was soon supplanted by better histories. Died in 1661.

Duplessis. See RICHELIEU, CARDINAL.

Duplessis, dü′plǎ′se′, (JOSEPH Siffrein, se′frǎN′,) a skilful French portrait-painter, born at Carpentras in

1725. He studied several years in Rome under Subleyras, and settled in Paris in 1752, where he painted with success. He was admitted into the Royal Academy in 1774. Among his best works are portraits of Dr. Franklin, Necker, and Marmontel. Died in 1802.

Duplessis, (MICHEL TOUSSAINT CHRÉTIEN,) a French monk and historian, born in 1689, was an inmate of the abbey of Saint-Germain-des-Prés. He wrote a "Historical Notice of Upper Normandy," (1740,) and other works. Died in 1767.

Duplessis, (PIERRE ALEXANDRE **Gratet**—grǎ′tǎ′,) a French scholar and bibliographer, born at Janville in 1792, was professor in several colleges. He published "The Flower of French Proverbs," (1851,) and a good edition of La Rochefoucauld's "Reflections and Maxims." Died in 1853.

Duplessis-Mornay. See MORNAY.

Duplessis-Praslin. See CHOISEUL.

Duponceau, du-pon′sõ, [Fr. pron. dü′pŎN′sõ′,] (PETER S.,) a lawyer and scholar, born in the Isle of Rhé, on the coast of France, in 1760, came to America in 1777 with Baron Steuben, whom he served as secretary and aide-de-camp. He quitted the army in 1780, on account of ill health, and studied law, which he practised in Philadelphia, and became eminent in his profession. Besides treatises on philology and essays on various subjects, he published a "Dissertation on the Nature and Extent of the Jurisdiction of the Courts of the United States," (1824.) He received a prize of the French Institute for a "Memoir on the Indian Languages of North America," (1835.) He was for some years president of the American Philosophical Society. Died in Philadelphia in 1844.

See "Discourse in Commemoration of Peter S. Duponceau," by R. DUNGLISON, M.D., Philadelphia, 1844.

Dupont, dü′pŎN′, or, more fully, **Dupont de L'Eure,** dü′pŎN′ deh lur, (JACQUES CHARLES,) a French Liberal legislator, born at Neubourg (L'Eure) in 1767. He was a judge under the first republic and the empire, and became president of the imperial court at Rouen in 1811. From 1817 to 1848 he constantly represented his native department in the Chamber of Deputies. He was appointed minister of justice in August, 1830, but resigned about the end of that year, after which he sat with the opposition in the Chamber. His long services and his high character for integrity caused him to be chosen president of the provisional government formed in February, 1848. He retired from public life in 1849, and died in 1855. He was respected by all parties.

See LOUIS BLANC, "Histoire de dix Ans."

Dupont, (PIERRE,) a popular French song-writer, born at Lyons in 1821. He produced about 1842 a poem entitled "The Two Angels," which was crowned by the French Academy. Among his popular productions are the "Song of Bread" and the "Song of the Workers." In many of his songs he manifests republican or socialistic tendencies.

See C. BAUDELAIRE, "Notice sur P. Dupont," 1849 ; E. DE MIRECOURT, "P. Dupont," 1854.

Dupont, or, more fully, **Dupont de l'Étang,** dü′pŎN′ deh lǎ′tôN′, (PIERRE,) a French general, born at Chabannais in 1765. He became a general of division in 1797. About 1801 he defeated the Austrians under Belle-garde near the Mincio. He rendered important services at Jena in 1806, and at Friedland. In 1808 he commanded an army in Spain, and obtained some successes ; but in July of that year he was defeated at Baylen, where he surrendered about 18,000 men as prisoners of war. For this disaster he was disgraced by Napoleon and condemned to an indefinite imprisonment. He was minister of war under Louis XVIII. from April to December, 1814. "In the whole French army," says Alison, "there was not a general of division who bore a higher character than Dupont," [before his Spanish campaign.] ("History of Europe.") Died in 1838.

See "Nouvelle Biographie Générale ;" VEDEL, "Précis des Opérations militaires en Espagne."

Dupont, or, more fully, **Dupont de Nemours,** dü′-pŎN′ deh neh-moor′, (PIERRE SAMUEL,) a French author and economist, born in Paris in 1739. As a disciple of Quesnay, he applied himself to the study of commerce and political economy, and gained reputation by his writings on those subjects. The prime ministers Turgot and Vergennes enlisted his talents in the public service. During the ministry of Calonne he was made councillor of state, and in 1787 he was secretary of the Assembly of the Notables. He was a member of the National Assembly in 1790, of which he was twice chosen president, and defended the king at the peril of his own life in the insurrection of August 10, 1792. He was chosen one of the Council of Elders, and a member of the Institute about 1796. From 1798 to 1802 he resided in New Jersey, United States, whither he retired to escape from persecution. He refused all the public offices that Napoleon offered him. Having emigrated in 1815 to Delaware, he died there in 1817. He had composed for the Institute many treatises on public economy, natural history, etc., and published "Philosophie de l'Univers," (1796.) His sons were proprietors of the powder-mills near Wilmington, Delaware.

See DACIER, "Éloge de Dupont de Nemours," in "Recueil de l'Académie des Inscriptions;" AIMÉ BOULLÉE, "Notice biographique sur P. Poivre et Dupont de Nemours," 1835; "Nouvelle Biographie Générale."

Du-pŏnt′, (SAMUEL FRANCIS,) an able American rear-admiral, born at Bergen Point, New Jersey, in 1803, was a grandson of the preceding. He entered the navy at an early age, and gained the rank of commander in 1845. In the summer of 1861 he obtained command of the Atlantic blockading squadron. He commanded the large naval expedition which gained possession of Port Royal harbour, South Carolina, by a victory over two forts at the entrance, in November, 1861. In July, 1862, he was promoted to the rank of rear-admiral. He commanded the fleet of iron-clad vessels which attacked Fort Sumter in April, 1863, and was defeated, with the loss of the monitor Keokuk sunk. Four other monitors were disabled. The flag-ship of Dupont in this battle was the Ironsides. He was relieved of the command in June, 1863, and died in June, 1865. Dupont was a man of imposing presence and great personal dignity.

See J. T. HEADLEY, "Farragut and our Naval Commanders," 1867.

Duport, dü′pōr′, (ADRIEN,) an eminent French lawyer, born about 1758. He was deputed by the noblesse of Paris to the States-General in 1789, and was a prominent partisan of the new régime in the first years of the Revolution. In the National Assembly Barnave and Duport were leaders of the popular party for a time ; but after the arrest of the king at Varennes, June, 1791, they became decided royalists. It is stated that he was chiefly instrumental in introducing the trial by jury into French legislation. Duport was president of the Criminal Tribunal of Paris when the insurrection of August 10, 1792, forced him to fly. He died in exile, at Appenzel, in 1798. His speech against capital punishment in 1791 is highly praised by Lamartine for its profound logic.

See LAMARTINE, "Histoire des Constituants;" THIERS, "History of the French Revolution."

Du-pŏrt′, (JAMES,) D.D., born at Cambridge, England, in 1606. He became eminent as a Greek scholar, and was chosen regius professor of Greek at Cambridge in 1632. After the restoration he was chaplain to Charles II., and Dean of Peterborough. He published "Gnomologia Homeri," Sermons, and other works. Died in 1679.

Duport, (PAUL,) a French dramatist, born in Paris in 1798, wrote popular comedies and vaudevilles.

Duport-Dutertre, dü′pōr′ dü′tȧrtr′, (MARGUERITE LOUIS FRANÇOIS,) a minister of state, born at Paris in 1754. In the constitutional ministry formed in November, 1790, he was minister of justice. He was attached to the party or principles of Barnave and Adrien Duport. Removed from office in March, 1792, and proscribed by the dominant party, he escaped by flight until the next year. He was condemned by the Revolutionary Tribunal and executed in 1793.

See LAMARTINE, "History of the Girondists."

Duportail, dü′pōr′tāl′ or dü′pōr′tȧ′ye, (LEBÈGUE, leh-bȧg′,) a French officer, who served with distinction in the United States under La Fayette, with whose political opinions he agreed. By the influence of La Fayette

he was appointed minister of war in November, 1790. The hostility and violence of the Assembly induced him to resign in December, 1791. In the reign of terror he escaped death by exile to America about 1794. He embarked for France in 1802, but died during the passage.

Dup′pą, (BRIAN,) an English divine, born at Lewisham in 1588. He was appointed chaplain to Charles I. in 1634, and tutor to the Prince of Wales in 1638. He became Bishop of Salisbury in 1641, and of Winchester about 1660. He published sermons and other religious works. Died in 1662.

Duppa, (RICHARD,) an English lawyer and writer, born about 1766. He published several books of travels in Europe, "The Life and Works of Michael Angelo," (1806,) "The Life of Raphael," (1816,) a "Translation of Virgil's Bucolics," and other works. Died in 1831.

Duprat, dü′prȧ′, (ANTOINE,) a cardinal and chancellor of France, born at Issoire in 1463. He became first president of the Parliament of Paris in 1507, and chancellor in 1515. As the favourite minister of Francis I., he rendered himself the object of the popular odium by subverting civil and religious liberty. He procured the passage of atrocious laws against the Reformers. In 1527 he obtained a cardinal's hat. Died in 1535.

See DE THOU, "Histoire Universelle."

Duprat, (JEAN,) a French merchant of Avignon, was a Girondist member of the Convention, in which he voted for the death of the king in 1792. He was condemned by the Jacobins, and executed with the leaders of his party, in October, 1793, aged about thirty-six.

Duprat, (PARDOUX, pȧr′doo′,) an eminent French jurist, born at Aubusson about 1520. He resided some years in Lyons, and wrote esteemed works on Roman law. Died in or before 1570.

Duprat, (PASCAL,) a French republican journalist, born in the department of Landes in 1812. Soon after the revolution of 1848 he co-operated with Lamennais in founding the journal entitled "Le Peuple Constituant," and was elected to the National Assembly. He was one of the chiefs of the party which made Cavaignac dictator in 1848, and was banished about 1852.

Dupré d'Aulnay, dü′prȧ′ dō′nȧ′, (LOUIS,) a French writer of fiction, born in Paris about 1670 ; died in 1758.

Dupré de Saint-Maur, dü′prȧ′ deh sȧN′mōr′, (NICOLAS FRANÇOIS,) a French writer, who promoted a taste for English literature in France, was born in Paris in 1695. The success of his version of "Paradise Lost" opened for him the doors of the Academy in 1733. He afterwards produced a useful work, entitled "Essay on Money, or Reflections on the Relations between Money and Articles of Food," (1746,) and "Tables of Mortality," which Buffon praised and inserted in his works. Died in 1774.

Duprez, dü′prȧ′, (GILBERT LOUIS,) a French tenor singer of great celebrity, was born in Paris in 1806. After performing in Italy for some years, he made a successful *début* in Paris in 1837. He became the chief favourite of the Parisians, and was especially admired in the opera of "William Tell."

Dupuis, dü′pü-e′, almost dü′pwe′, (CHARLES,) born in Paris in 1685, was esteemed one of the best engravers of his time. He worked some years in England, and returned to Paris. The "Marriage of the Virgin," after Vanloo, is called his master-piece. Died in 1742.

Dupuis, (CHARLES FRANÇOIS,) a distinguished French philosopher and savant, born at Trie-le-Château (Oise) in 1742. He was educated in Paris, and in 1766 became professor of rhetoric in the College of Lisieux. For several years he attended the astronomical lectures of Lalande, with whom he was very intimate. He directed his researches to the origin of the figures or symbols which represent the constellations of the zodiac. The new theory which he formed was explained in a volume entitled "Memoir on the Origin of the Constellations, and on the Explanation of Mythology by Astronomy," (1781.) This work attracted much attention among the learned. A few years later he was appointed professor of Latin eloquence in the College of France, and in 1788 was admitted to the Academy of Inscriptions. He was a member of the Convention, 1792–95, he acted and spoke with moderation. In 1794 he produced his celebrated "Origin of all *Cultes*, or Universal Religion," which excited much controversy by the novelty and boldness of its speculations. It is stated that the interest excited by this work caused the appointment of the scientific commission which accompanied Bonaparte to Egypt. Dupuis was one of the first members of the Institute. In Bonaparte's consulate he was president of the legislative body. Among his later works is a "Memoir on the Zodiac of Tentyra," to which he assigns a date anterior by many centuries to the first historical period. The researches of Champollion, however, appear to have fully disproved this opinion. Died near Dijon in 1809.

See DACIER, "Notice sur Dupuis," 1812; "Notice sur la Vie de Dupuis," by his widow, 1813; "Nouvelle Biographie Générale."

Dupuis, (NICOLAS GABRIEL,) a French engraver, brother of Charles, noticed above, and a pupil of Duchange, was born in Paris in 1695. His style is pure and correct. Among his admired works are "Æneas saving his Father from Burning Troy," after Vanloo, and "The Adoration of the Kings," after Paul Veronese. Died in 1771.

See BASAN, "Dictionnaire des Graveurs."

Dupuis, du-pwee', (THOMAS SAUNDERS,) a musical composer, born in London in 1733. He was an excellent performer on the organ. In 1779 he was appointed organist and composer of the royal chapel. He died in 1796, after which his select works were published by John Spencer, nephew of the Duke of Marlborough.

Dupuy, dü'pü-e', [Dutch, VAN DE PUTTE, vän der püt'teh,] (HENRY,) [Lat. ENRI'CUS PUTEA'NUS,] a Dutch scholar, was born at Venloo in 1574. He succeeded his teacher, Justus Lipsius, in the chair of belles-lettres at Louvain, which he filled from 1606 to 1646. He wrote many learned works on history, philosophy, etc., among which are "Historia Insubrica," and "Belli et Pacis Statera," (1633.) Died in 1646.

Dupuy, dü'pü-e', (LOUIS,) a French scholar of great learning, born in Le Bugey in 1709. He became principal editor of the "Journal des Savans," which he directed for thirty years with much critical ability. In 1756 he was admitted into the Academy of Inscriptions, of which he was made perpetual secretary in 1773, and to which he contributed many treatises. He wrote "Observations on Infinitesimals, and the Metaphysical Principles of Geometry," and other mathematical works. Died in 1795.

See DESESSARTS, "Les Siècles littéraires."

Dupuy, (PIERRE,) a French historical writer, born at Agen in 1582, became successively councillor and librarian to the king. He wrote a "Treatise on the Rights and Liberties of the Gallican Church," (1639,) a "History of the Most Illustrious Favourites, Ancient and Modern," and other works. Died in 1651.

His brother JACQUES was also royal librarian, and aided in some of the productions of Pierre. Died in 1656.

See N. RIGAULT, "Vita Petri Puteani," in the "Vitæ Selectorum aliquot Virorum," London, 1681.

Dupuy-Demportes, dü'pü-e' dôN'poRt', (JEAN BAPTISTE,) a French *littérateur.* Died in 1770.

Dupuy des Islets, dü'pü-e' dä'ze'lä', CHEVALIER, a French poet, born in Hayti about 1770; died in 1831.

Dupuy-Montbrun. See MONTBRUN.

Dupuytren, dü'pü-e'trôN', (GUILLAUME,) BARON, a celebrated French surgeon and anatomist, born at Pierre-Buffière, near Limoges, in 1777. He was educated in Paris, where, in 1803, he obtained the place of second surgeon of the Hôtel-Dieu. He was appointed inspector-general to the University in 1808, professor of surgery in 1811, and chief surgeon of the Hôtel-Dieu about 1816. On the accession of Charles X. he became first surgeon to the king. His practice was very lucrative, and his reputation more extensive than that of any French surgeon of his time. He made improvements in surgical operations, invented some valuable instruments, and was an eloquent and popular lecturer. He did not publish any extensive work, but his lectures were printed in the medical periodicals, and his opinions were reported in the works of Royer-Collard, Sanson, etc. Dupuytren was a member of the Academy of Sciences. His contribu-

tions to the knowledge of morbid anatomy form perhaps his chief title to a durable reputation. Died in Paris in February, 1835.

See VIDAL DE CASSIS, "Essai historique sur Dupuytren," 1835; PARISET, "Éloge de Dupuytren," 1836; CRUVEILHIER, "Vie de Dupuytren," 1841; BARDINET, "Notice sur Dupuytren," 1853; ISIDORE BOURDON, "Illustres Médecins et Naturalistes;" "Nouvelle Biographie Générale."

Duquerie. See CALLARD DE LA DUQUERIE.

Duquesne, dü'kèn', (ABRAHAM,) a French naval hero, born at Dieppe in 1610. He had acquired a reputation for courage and talents when, in 1637, he was chosen to command a ship in the war with Spain. He rendered important services at Tarragona in 1641, and at the Cape de Gates in 1643. A few years later, as vice-admiral of the Swedish fleet, he gained several victories over the Danes. About 1650 he was made a commodore. He fought under D'Estrées against the Dutch under De Ruyter in May, 1673. Having obtained the rank of lieutenant-general, he defeated the Dutch near Catanea in 1676, where the admiral De Ruyter was killed. The king once avowed to Duquesne that his religion (Protestantism) was an obstacle to his promotion. For this reason he never received a marshal's bâton, though he was the most able and successful admiral that France had then produced. He was, however, created a marquis, and was excepted from the operation of the decree which revoked the edict of Nantes. Died in 1688.

See E. SUE, "Histoire de la Marine;" ANDRÉ RICHER, "Vie du Marquis Duquesne," 1783; FERET, "Esquisse de la Vie de Duquesne," 1844; "Nouvelle Biographie Générale."

Duquesne, (ABRAHAM,) a son of the preceding, was an able seaman. In 1690 he commanded an expedition to the East Indies, of which Challes published an account, (3 vols., 1721.)

Duquesne, (ARNAUD BERNARD d'Icard—de'kär',) a French priest, writer, and doctor of the Sorbonne, born in Paris about 1732; died in 1791.

Duquesne, (HENRI,) a son of Abraham, (the first of the name,) was born in 1652, and became a captain in the navy in 1675. He served with distinction at the battle near Catanea in 1676. When the edict of Nantes was revoked, (1685,) he withdrew to Switzerland. He wrote "Reflections on the Eucharist," (1718.) Died in 1722.

Duquesnoy, dü'kå'nwå', (ADRIEN,) a French lawyer, born in 1759, was deputed to the States-General by Bar-le-Duc in 1789, and acquitted himself with credit. He edited a journal called "The Friend of the Patriots," which was issued until August 10, 1792. In the reign of terror he was arrested, but was saved by the fall of Robespierre. Died in 1808.

Duquesnoy, dü'kå'nwå', (FRANÇOIS,) an excellent Flemish sculptor, born at Brussels in 1594, was better known by the name of FRANÇOIS FLAMAND. About 1619 he went to Rome, where he became an intimate friend of Nicolas Poussin and worked there many years. He excelled in the representation of infants, and was considered by some as the best sculptor of his time. Among his master-pieces are statues of Saint Susanna (in Rome) and of Saint Andrew, (in the basilica of Saint Peter's.) He was on his way to Paris, whither he had been invited by Richelieu, when he died at Leghorn in 1646.

See CICOGNARA, "Storia della Scultura."

Duquesnoy, (JÉRÔME,) a skilful sculptor, brother of the preceding, was born at Brussels in 1612. He worked some years at Rome, and was appointed sculptor to Philip IV. of Spain in 1645. He was executed for some alleged crime at Ghent in 1654.

Duræus. See DURY.

Duram or **Durão,** doo-röwn', (ANTONIO Figueira—fe-gä'e-rä,) a Portuguese Latin poet, born in Lisbon about 1617; died in 1642.

Duram or **Durão,** doo-röwn', (JOZÉ DE SANTA RITA,) a Brazilian epic poet, born near Mariana in 1737. He was educated in Portugal, where he resided nearly all his life, and became a monk. He wrote a popular and national epic poem, entitled "Caramurú, or the Discovery of Bahia," (1781.) Died in Lisbon in 1783.

See ADOLFO DE VARNHAGEN, "Epicos Brazileiros," 1845; PEREIRA DA SYLVA, "Plutarco Brazileiro."

Duramano, doo-rä-mä'no, (FRANCESCO,) a Venetian painter of flowers, flourished about 1750.

ā, ē, ī, ō, ū, ȳ, *long*; ă, ĕ, ŏ, same, less prolonged; ă, ĕ, ĭ, ŏ, ŭ, ў, *short*; ạ, ẹ, ị, ọ, *obscure*; fär, fäll, fät; mět; nŏt; gōōd; mōōn;

Durameau, dü'rä'mō', (LOUIS JEAN JACQUES,) a French historical painter, born in Paris in 1733. His "Continence of Bayard" and "Saint Louis washing the Feet of the Poor" are admired. Died in 1796.

Duran, doo-rân', (Don AUGUSTIN,) an eminent Spanish author and critic, born in Madrid about 1794. He obtained an office in the department of public instruction in 1821, but was removed in 1823 for his liberal opinions. In 1828 he published an "Essay on the Influence which Modern Criticism has exercised on the Decline of the Old Drama," *(teatro antiguo,)* which produced a revolution in favour of the romantic school. His "Romancero de Romances Moriscos," (5 vols., 1828–32,) (a collection of old ballads,) had great success. About 1835 he was appointed secretary or librarian in the National Library of Madrid. He has recently written an important history and bibliography of the Spanish drama, which perhaps is not yet printed.

Durand, dü'rŏn', a learned French Benedictine, born at Neubourg about 1012, acquired much influence, and was consulted by William the Conqueror. He promoted a taste for religious music. Died in 1089.

Du-rand', (ASHER BROWN,) an eminent American painter and engraver, born at Jefferson, New Jersey, in 1796. He engraved Trumbull's "Declaration of Independence," a number of portraits for "The National Portrait-Gallery," and other works. About 1835 he began to devote himself exclusively to painting. He became an excellent landscape-painter, and produced many pictures of American mountain-scenery. Among his paintings are "The Capture of Major André," "Primeval Forest," and "Franconia Mountains."

See H. T. TUCKERMAN, "Book of the Artists," 1867; DUNLAP, "Rise and Progress of the Arts of Design in America."

Durand, (CATHERINE **Bédacier**—bâ'dä'se-à',) a French novelist and poetess, wrote the "Comtesse de Mortane," (1699,) and other works. Died in Paris in 1736.

Durand, (CHARLES ÉTIENNE,) a French architect, born at Montpellier in 1762. He restored the ancient temple at Nîmes called "Maison carrée." Died in 1840.

Durand, (DAVID,) a learned French Protestant writer, born in Languedoc about 1680. After being chaplain to a French regiment in Spain, he went about 1714 to London, where he preached about fifty years. He wrote "The Religion of Mohammed," (1721,) a "History of the Sixteenth Century," (6 vols., 1725–29,) and other works. Died in London in 1763.

See A. A. BARBIER, "Notice sur la Vie et les Écrits de D. Durand," 1809; MM. HAAG, "La France protestante;" "Nouvelle Biographie Générale."

Durand, (FRANÇOIS JACQUES,) an eloquent French Protestant preacher, born near Alençon in 1727. He became professor of history at Lausanne, and published Sermons, a "Treatise on the Statistics of Switzerland," an "Epitome of Sciences and Arts," (1762,) which had great success, and other works. Died in 1816.

See A. DELILLE, "Notice sur la Vie de F. J. Durand," 1805.

Durand or **Duranti,** doo-rân'tee, (GUILLAUME,) a French jurist, born at Puymisson about 1230, was surnamed the "Spéculateur." In 1287 he became Bishop of Mende. He wrote a work on canon law, called "Speculum Judiciale." Died in 1296.

See S. MAIOLO, "Duranti Vita."

Durand, (JACQUES,) a French historical painter, born at Nancy in 1699; died in 1767.

Durand, (JEAN NICOLAS LOUIS,) a French architect, born in Paris in 1760. Having received lessons from l'anseron, he became draughtsman to Boulée, the king's architect. In 1780 he gained a prize in the Royal Academy. He also obtained several of the prizes offered by the Convention in 1793 for public structures. About 1794 he was appointed professor of architecture in the Polytechnic School, for the use of which he published an important work, entitled "A Collection and Comparison of Edifices of all Kinds, Ancient and Modern," (1800,) and "Lectures on Architecture," (2 vols., 1802,) also an excellent performance. Died in 1834.

See RONDELET, "Notice historique sur la Vie de J. N. L. Durand," 1835.

Durand, (Dom LÉOPOLD,) a French architect and monk, born in Lorraine in 1666; died in 1749.

Durand, (PIERRE BERNARD,) a French botanist, born in Calvados in 1814; died in 1853.

Durand-Brager, dü'rŏn' brä'zhà', (JEAN BAPTISTE HENRI,) a distinguished French marine and landscape painter, born near Dol (Ile-et-Vilaine) in 1814. In 1840 he went to Saint Helena on the staff of Prince de Joinville, and after his return published a "Description of Saint Helena," richly illustrated, (1844.) He produced a Panorama of Rio Janeiro, and received a commission to paint the principal actions and scenes of the campaign against Morocco, in which he took part about 1845. He has published several other successful works.

Durand de Maillane, dü'rŏn' deh mä'yän', (PIERRE TOUSSAINT,) a French lawyer, born at Saint-Remi in 1729. Elected to the States-General in 1789, he was one of the committee who framed the civil constitution of the clergy. In the Convention of 1792 he opposed the execution of the king, and voted for his banishment. During the reign of Bonaparte he was a judge at Tarascon and Aix until 1809. He was author of several esteemed treatises on canon law. Died in 1814.

See "Notice sur Durand de Maillane," prefixed to his "Histoire de la Convention Nationale."

Durand de Saint-Pourçain, dü'rŏn' deh sáN'poor'-sáN', (GUILLAUME,) a French scholastic doctor and bishop, born in Auvergne; died in 1334.

Durande, dü'rŏnd', (JEAN FRANÇOIS,) a French botanist, born at Dijon, became professor of botany in that city. Died in 1794.

Durandi, doo-rân'dee, (JACOPO,) an Italian poet and antiquary, born near Vercelli in 1739. He wrote numerous operas, some of which were performed with success at Turin; "Arianna," an admired pastoral; and several works on history and geography. Died in 1817.

See DE GREGORI, "Vita di J. Durandi," 1817.

Durando, doo-rân'do, (GIACOMO,) an Italian general, born at Mondovì in 1807. He was minister of war at Turin during the Crimean war, 1854–55, commanded a division at Solferino, June, 1859, and became minister of foreign affairs in the cabinet of Ratazzi in March, 1861.

Durando, (GIOVANNI,) a brother of the preceding, and an eminent Italian general of the present age, commanded the first corps-d'armée against the Austrians, and was wounded at Custozza in June, 1866.

Durant, dü'rŏN', (GILLES,) a French poet and advocate, was born at Clermont about 1550, and settled near Paris. He is supposed to have written part of the "Satire Ménippée," which promoted the cause of Henry IV. by ridiculing the League. His works, which were much admired, consist of odes, sonnets, songs, etc. Died in 1615.

See MORÉRI, "Dictionnaire Historique."

Durante, doo-rân'tà, (CASTORE,) an Italian botanist, born at Gualdo, became physician to Pope Sixtus V., and wrote many works, which were once esteemed. Died at Viterbo in 1590.

Durante, (FRANCESCO,) one of the most celebrated Italian composers, was born in Naples in 1693. He was the pupil of Scarlatti, and is regarded as the founder of the modern school which produced Sacchini, Pergolesi, etc. His style was severe, his harmony pure, and his modulations natural. He confined himself mostly to sacred music. Died in Naples in 1755.

See FÉTIS, "Biographie Universelle des Musiciens."

Durante Alighieri. See DANTE.

Durante da Gualda, doo-rân'tà dä goo-äl'dä, (PIETRO,) an Italian poet, born about 1460.

Duranti. See DURAND, (GUILLAUME.)

Duranti, doo-ran'tee, (DURANTE,) COUNT, a popular Italian poet and orator, was born of a noble family at Brescia in 1718. His memory was such that he could repeat a poem which he had read or heard but once. He imitated Ariosto in satirical epistles with success, and wrote lyric verses which were celebrated through all Italy. In the latter part of his life he resided at the court of the King of Sardinia, as gentleman of the chamber. Among his principal works is a satirical poem entitled "Custom," or "Fashion," ("Uso," 1778.) Several of his orations were printed. His moral character is said to have been pure. Died in 1780.

See TIPALDO, "Biografia degli Italiani illustri."

Duranti, dü´rŏN´te´, (JEAN ÉTIENNE,) a French judge, born at Toulouse about 1534, became first president of the parliament of Toulouse in 1581. For his fidelity to the king he was massacred by a mob of furious partisans of the Catholic League in 1589. He was author of a book "On the Rites of the Catholic Church," (" De Ritibus Ecclesiæ," 1581.)

See PONSARD, "Éloge de J. Étienne Duranti," 1770; DE THOU, "Histoire."

Duranton, dü´rŏN´tôN´, (ALEXANDRE,) a French jurist, born at Cusset (Bourbonnais) in 1782, was the author of a "Course of French Law," (4th edition, 22 vols., 1844.)

Durão. See DURAM.

Duras. See DURFORT, (GUI ALPHONSE and LOUIS.)

Duras, de, dĕh dü´râs´, (CLAIRE Lechat de Kersaint—lĕh-shǎ´ dĕh kĕR´sâN´,) DUCHESS, a French authoress, born at Brest in 1778, was a daughter of the Count de Kersaint, who was a member of the Convention and executed in 1793. She became the wife of the Duc de Duras, and the friend of Madame de Staël. After the restoration she was one of the ornaments of the French court. She produced two novels, "Ourika," (1823,) and "Édouard," which had prodigious success. Died in 1828.

See SAINTE-BEUVE, "Portraits des Femmes;" BARANTE, "Notice sur Madame la Duchesse de Duras," 1828; "Nouvelle Biographie Générale."

Duras, de, (JACQUES HENRI de Durfort—dĕh dür´foR´,) DUKE, a French marshal, born of a noble family of Guienne about 1624, was a nephew of the famous Turenne. He fought at the battle of Nordlingen and the capture of Landau. As lieutenant-general, he served with distinction in Italy and Flanders. He was created a marshal of France in 1675, and a duke in 1689. Died in 1704.

Duras, de, (JEAN BAPTISTE,) DUKE, a son of the preceding, was born in 1684. He rendered important services in the war of the Spanish succession, (1701-12,) and was made lieutenant-general in 1720. He afterwards became marshal of France, and in 1745 defeated the enemy at Etlingen. Died in 1770.

Durazzo, doo-rât´so, a noble family of Genoa, which furnished many doges to the republic, and several cardinals to the Church, in the sixteenth and seventeenth centuries.

Durbach, (ANNE LOUISE.) See KARSCHIN.

Dur´bin, (JOHN PRICE,) an American Methodist minister, born in Bourbon county, Kentucky, in 1800, graduated at the Cincinnati College in 1825. He was elected chaplain of the Senate of the United States in 1831, and president of Dickinson College, in Pennsylvania, in 1834. After a visit to Europe, he published "Observations in Europe, principally in France and Great Britain," (2 vols., 1844,) and "Observations in Egypt, Palestine, Syria, etc.," (2 vols., 1845.) He resigned the presidency of Dickinson College in 1845. Since 1851 he has been secretary of the Missionary Society of the Methodist Episcopal Church. He is now (1869) in the fiftieth year of his pastoral services.

Durdent, dür´dôN´, (RENÉ JEAN,) a prolific French writer, born at Rouen about 1776. He had great facility in composition, and wrote for the booksellers mediocre works of fiction, history, criticism, etc., which had a temporary success. Died in 1819.

Dureau de la Malle, (or **de Lamalle,**) dü´rō´ dĕh lă măl, (ADOLPHE JULES CÉSAR AUGUSTE,) a learned French poet and antiquary, born in Paris in 1777. He produced in 1807 a poem entitled "The Pyrenees," and in 1811 a poetical version of the "Argonautica" of Valerius Flaccus. In 1818 he was elected to the Academy of Inscriptions, which he enriched with many antiquarian treatises. Among his principal works are "Bayard, or the Conquest of the Milanese," a poem, (2 vols., 1823,) and "The Political Economy of the Romans," (2 vols., 1840.) Died in 1857.

See LOUANDRE et BOURQUELOT, "La Littérature Française;" "Nouvelle Biographie Générale."

Dureau de la Malle, (or **de Lamalle,**) (JEAN BAPTISTE JOSEPH RENÉ,) a French scholar and eminent translator, father of the preceding, was born in Saint Domingo in 1742. He was educated in Paris, where he afterwards resided. His house was the resort of the most eminent authors, namely, Delille, D'Alembert, Marmontel, and La Harpe. In 1790 he produced an admired version of Tacitus, superior to any previously made in French. He was also successful in translating Sallust, and began a version of Livy, which, interrupted by his death, was finished by M. Noël. He was chosen a member of the legislative body in 1802, and of the French Academy in 1804. Died in 1807.

See " Nouvelle Biographie Générale."

Durel, (DAVID.) See DURELL.

Du-rel´, (JOHN,) D.D., a learned English theologian, born in the isle of Jersey in 1626, was an adversary of the Puritans. He passed many years in France during the English civil war and the Commonwealth. About 1660 he became preacher at the French Church in London. He was appointed Canon of Windsor in 1663 or 1664, and Dean of Windsor in 1677. He wrote, besides other theological works, a "Defence of the Church of England," (1669.) Died in 1683.

Du-rell´ or **Durel,** (DAVID,) D.D., an English biblical critic, born in the isle of Jersey in 1728. He became a Fellow of Hertford College, (Oxford,) and principal of the same in 1757. His "Critical Remarks on Job, Psalms, Proverbs," etc. (1772) are commended. He also published "The Hebrew Text of the Parallel Prophecies of Jacob and Moses relating to the Twelve Tribes," (1764.) Died in 1775.

Dürer or **Duerer,** dü´rẹr, (ALBERT or ALBRECHT,) a celebrated German painter and engraver, born at Nuremberg on the 20th of May, 1471, was the son of a goldsmith, who designed that he should learn the same occupation. He became in 1486 a pupil of Michael Wohlgemuth, a painter of Nuremberg. In 1490 he began a tour, in the course of which he visited various countries of Germany. He returned to Nuremberg in 1494, and, to please his father, entered into an ill-assorted marriage. Soon after his return he produced a drawing of "Orpheus," which was much admired. In 1505 he visited Venice, where he remained eight months, and painted the "Martyrdom of Saint Bartholomew," and other works, for which "he received," says Ruskin, "the rarest of all rewards granted to a good workman, and for once in his life was understood." During his visit to Italy he formed a friendship with Raphael. About 1508 he was appointed court painter to Maximilian I., for whom he painted "The Virgin with many Angels," and other historical pictures. He was also patronized by Charles V. as court painter.

Dürer surpassed all the painters and engravers of Germany in exuberance of imagination and in sublimity and correctness of design. He was successful in history, portraits, and landscapes. Vasari expresses the opinion that he would have equalled the great masters of Italy if he had been a native of Tuscany and had studied in Rome. Some critics regret the absence of the ideal in his works. Among his master-pieces in painting are a "Crucifixion," (1511,) "Adam and Eve," an "Adoration of the Magi," and portraits of Raphael, Erasmus, and Melanchthon, who were his friends. He is the reputed inventor of the art of etching and the art of printing wood-cuts in two colours. His engravings (on copper) of "Adam and Eve," "The Knight and Death," and the "Revelation of Saint John" (on wood) are very celebrated. All his engravings are after his own designs, and are finished with great neatness and refinement. He wrote several works on geometry and perspective, and contributed to polish and purify the German language, in which those works are written. It appears that he favoured the doctrines of the Reformation. He died at Nuremberg in April, 1528. His death is said to have been hastened by domestic misery. His wife, covetous, insatiable, and imperious, would neither permit him to work in peace and quietness nor to recreate himself in the society of his friends. His gentle disposition and delicate sensibility rendered him especially liable to be thus victimized. "This artist," says Michiels, "has become the symbol of his epoch. An inexhaustible imagination, an intelligence which could observe life in its most delicate shades, a profound sentiment of grace, *naïveté,* and sublimity, and an earnest spirit joined to the

courage required for protracted studies, were the qualities which distinguished him."

See J. Heller, "Das Leben und die Werke A. Dürers," 1827–
31; Nagler, "Neues Allgemeines Künstler-Lexikon;" Ersch und
Gruber, "Allgemeine Encyklopaedie;" A. Michiels, "Études sur
l'Allemagne;" Leopold Schefer, "An Artist's Married Life;"
G. C. Nagler, "A. Dürer und seine Kunst," 1837; Roth, "Leben
A. Dürers," 1791; "Foreign Quarterly Review" for January, 1833;
"Edinburgh Review" for July, 1861.

Duret, dü'râ', (Claude,) a French naturalist and linguist, born at Moulins; died in 1611.

Duret, (Francisque,) an eminent French sculptor,
born in Paris about 1805. He studied in Rome, and
about 1831 gained a prize by his statue of "Mercury."
He adorned several churches and public edifices of Paris
with statues, among which are those of Molière, (in the
Hall of the Institute,) Richelieu, and Châteaubriand.
At the Exposition of 1855 he received a grand medal.
He is a member of the Institute.

Duret, (Jean,) born in Paris in 1563, was a skilful
physician, and a bitter partisan of the League against
Henry of Navarre. He succeeded his father as professor of medicine in the Royal College, and became
physician to the queen Marie in 1610, after the death
of Henry IV. Died in 1629.

Duret, (Louis,) an eminent French physician, father
of the preceding, was born at Bagé in 1527. He came
to Paris in youth, and graduated in 1552. From 1568 to
1586 he was a professor in the Royal College, and was
successively physician to Charles IX. and Henry III.
His most important work is a commentary on Hippocrates, (1588,) which Boerhaave called "an inestimable
book." Died in 1586.

See Chomel, "Éloge de L. Duret, Médecin célèbre," 1765; Nicéron, "Mémoires;" "Biographie Médicale."

Duret, (Noël,) a French astronomer, born at Montbrison in 1590, was a professor of mathematics in Paris,
and obtained the title of cosmographer to the king. He
wrote a "New Theory of the Planets," (1635,) and other
works. Died about 1650.

Dur'fee, (Job,) an American jurist, born at Tiverton,
Rhode Island, in 1790. He was elected a member of
Congress in 1820, and became chief justice of Rhode
Island in 1835. He wrote a poem, entitled "What
Cheer?" (1832,) on the adventures of Roger Williams.
Died in 1847.

D'Urfey, dur'fe, (Thomas,) an English dramatist and
wit, born at Exeter, in Devonshire. He was a favourite
at the court of Charles II., and author of several successful and licentious dramas. He wrote popular songs and
odes, which were published with the title "Laugh and be
Fat." According to Addison, his ode entitled "Joy to
Great Cæsar" "gave the Whigs such a blow as they were
not able to recover that whole reign." Died in 1723.

See Baker, "Biographia Dramatica;" Cibber, "Lives of the
Poets."

Durfort, de, deh dür'foR', (Gui Alphonse,) Duke of
Lorges, (loRzh,) a French marshal, born in 1628, was a
younger brother of the first Duke of Duras. He served
as lieutenant-general in the army of his uncle Turenne,
whose talents in a great measure he inherited. In 1692
he gained the battle of Pfortzheim. He had received a
marshal's bâton in 1676. Died in 1703.

See Voltaire, "Siècle de Louis XIV;" Saint-Simon, "Mémoires."

Durfort, de, (Louis,) sometimes called **Durfort-
Duras,** (dü'râs',) Count, the youngest brother of the
preceding, emigrated to England, where Charles II. gave
him the title of Baron Duras. At the time of the peace
of Nymwegen (1678) he was ambassador at the court of
France. He was created Earl of Feversham, and became general-in-chief of the army of James II., which
defeated the Duke of Monmouth in 1685 at Sedgemoor.

Durfort-Duras. See Duras.

Durfort-Duras, de, deh dür'foR' dü'râs',(Emmanuel
Félicité,) Duc, born in 1715, inherited the title of duke
from his father, Jean Baptiste. He became first gentleman of the chamber, a knight of the Golden Fleece, one
of the forty members of the French Academy, and marshal of France. As lieutenant-general, he made all the
campaigns of the Seven Years' war. He was a finished
model of a courtier. Died in 1789.

Durgâ, dōōr'gâ, a Sanscrit word signifying "difficult
of access," "impregnable," and forming the name of
Siva's consort in her character of active virtue. (See
Pârvatî.)

Durham, dŭr'am, (James,) an eminent Scottish divine,
born in 1622. He became minister of Blackfriars' Church,
Glasgow, about 1647, and was a very popular preacher.
In 1650 he was appointed professor of divinity in the
College of Glasgow. He was chaplain to Charles II.
about 1650, and in 1651 preached a sermon before Cromwell, who rebuked him for meddling with political affairs
in the pulpit. He wrote "Commentaries on Revelation," (1660,) often reprinted, "Expositions of the Ten
Commandments," (1675,) and several religious treatises.
His works were highly esteemed. Died in 1658.

See Chambers, "Biographical Dictionary of Eminent Scotsmen."

Durham, dŭr'am, (John George Lambton,) Earl
of, an able English statesman, born at Lambton Castle,
Durham, in 1792, was a son of William Henry Lambton.
He married Miss Cholmondeley in 1812, and the daughter of Earl Grey in 1816. In 1813 he was returned to
Parliament, where he acted with the Whig party, of
which he was one of the most liberal members. He
was raised to the peerage, as Baron Durham, in 1828. In
1830 he became lord privy seal in the cabinet of Lord
Grey, and was one of the four persons who prepared the
Reform bill of the ensuing year. He made an eloquent
speech in favour of the second Reform bill. He resigned
his place in the ministry in 1833, and was then created
Earl of Durham. He was sent on a special mission to
Russia in 1833, and was appointed ambassador to Russia
in 1836. In 1838 he was sent as Governor-General to
Canada, with extraordinary powers, to restore peace and
order in that province, then disturbed by rebellion. He
returned suddenly in December, 1839, in consequence of
his disagreement with the ministry at home. He died
in July, 1840, and was succeeded by his son, George
Frederick, born about 1828. Lord Durham was a great
favourite with the advanced Liberals.

See "Nouvelle Biographie Générale."

Durham, (Joseph,) an English sculptor, born in London in 1822. Among his works are a bust of Jenny
Lind, and "Paul and Virginia," (1857.)

Durham, (Sir Philip Charles Calderwood,) a
British admiral, born in Fifeshire in 1763; died in 1845.

See A. Murray, "Life of Admiral Durham," 1846.

Duringer, doo'ring-er, (Melchior,) professor of ecclesiastical history at Berne, was born about 1647; died
in 1723.

Düringsfeld, von, (Ida.) See Reinsberg.

Du'ris [Δοῦρις] of Samos, a Greek historian, a brother
of Lynceus, was born about 350 B.C. His most important
work was a history of Greece, entitled "Macedonica and
Hellenica," or "ἡ τῶν Ἑλληνικῶν Ἱστορία," of which fragments are extant. He became chief ruler of Samos.
Died after 280 B.C.

Durival, dü're'vâl', (Jean,) a French writer, brother
of Nicolas L., noticed below, was born at Saint-Aubin
in 1725. He was minister to Holland in 1777. About
this date he assisted Mirabeau in translating Watson's
"Philip II." into French. Died in 1810.

Durival, (Nicolas Luton—lü'tôN',) a French writer,
born at Commercy in 1733, published a "Description
of Lorraine," (4 vols., 1778–83,) which is regarded as a
model for works of that kind. Died in 1795.

Durivier, dü're've-â', (Jean,) a French engraver of
medals, born at Liege in 1687. He settled in Paris, received the title of engraver to the king, and was admitted
to the Academy. Died in Paris in 1761.

Dürnhoffer or **Duernhoffer,** dürn'hof'fer,(Lorenzo,)
a German poet and pastor, born at Nuremberg in 1532,
was a friend of Melanchthon. Died in 1594.

Duroc, dü'rok', (Gérard Christophe Michel,)
Duke of Friuli, a favourite officer of the court and
camp of Bonaparte, was born at Pont-à-Mousson in 1772.
In the early wars of the republic he was aide-de-camp
of General Lespinasse; and in 1796 he became aide-de-
camp of Bonaparte, whom he followed to Egypt in 1798.
During the consulate and the empire he was employed
on important missions, and was sent successively to the
courts of Berlin, Vienna, and Saint Petersburg. In these

ê as k; ç as s; ḡ hard; ġ as j; G, H, K, guttural; N, nasal; R, trilled; s̄ as z; th as in this. (☞See Explanations, p. 23.)

52

difficult affairs he acquitted himself to the satisfaction of Napoleon, who ever treated him with confidence, and who made him marshal of his palace and Duke of Friuli. "Duroc loved Napoleon for himself," says Alison, "and possessed perhaps a larger share of his confidence than any of his other generals." He accompanied the emperor in the campaigns of 1805–06 and 1807, and was killed by his side at Mackersdorf, in Saxony, May, 1813. Bonaparte wept as he pressed the hand of the dying man, and said, "Duroc, there is another world, where we shall meet again."

See "Memorial de Saint-Hélène;" ALISON, "History of Europe;" "Nouvelle Biographie Générale."

Durocher. See GUÉRIN DU ROCHER.

Duroi. See DUROY.

Duroi, dü'rwȧ', (JOHANN PHILIPP,) a German botanist, born in 1741 ; died in 1786.

Durosnel, dü'ro'nĕl', (ANTOINE JEAN AUGUSTE HENRI,) born in Paris in 1771, became in 1809 a general of division, and aide-de-camp to Napoleon. During the Hundred Days he was second in command of the national guard of Paris. He was aide-de-camp to Louis Philippe in 1832, and was made a peer in 1837. Died in 1849.

See "Victoires et Conquêtes des Français."

Duroy, dü'rwȧ', or **Deroy,** [Lat. REGIUS,] (HENDRIK,) a Dutch physician, born in 1598 at Utrecht, where he was professor of medicine for forty years, ending at his death. He wrote, in Latin, works on Physiology, (1641,) Natural Philosophy, (1651,) and Medicine. He was involved in a quarrel with Descartes, who charged him with plagiarism. Died in 1679.

See ÉLOY, "Dictionnaire de la Médecine."

Du Rozoir, dü ro'zwȧr', (CHARLES,) a French editor and historical writer, born in Paris in 1790, became professor of history in the college Louis-le-Grand in 1818. He was one of the editors of Michaud's "Biographie Universelle," and of other valuable works. He published a "Programme of Roman History." Died in 1844.

Durri. See DOORREE.

Durrieu, dü're-uh', (ANTOINE SIMON,) BARON, a French general, born at Grenade (Landes) in 1775 ; died in 1862.

Durrius, dōōr're-ús, (JOHANN CONRAD,) a German author, born at Nuremberg in 1625, wrote, besides other works, a "Compendium of Moral Theology," which was often reprinted. Died in 1677.

Duruflé, dü'rü'flȧ',(LOUIS ROBERT Parfait—pȧR'fȧ',) a French poet, born at Elbeuf in 1742 ; died in 1793.

Durutte, dü'rüt', (JOSEPH FRANÇOIS,) a French general, born at Douai in 1767 ; died in 1827 or 1837.

See "Victoires et Conquêtes des Français."

Duruy, dü'rü-e', (VICTOR,) a French historical writer, born in Paris in 1811, became professor of history at the Lycée Napoléon, and published, for the use of schools, many popular historical works, among which are a "History of the Romans," (1844,) and a "History of France," (1852.)

Durvâsas, dōōr-vȧ'sas, an irascible and famous Hindoo sage, who was, in his own estimation, "a very mine of penitential merit." Sakoontalâ, the heroine of Kâlidâsa's drama "The Lost Ring," having failed, through absence of mind, to show him the respect he deemed his due, he cursed her; and on this curse the plot of the story turns.

See "Sakoontalâ," translated by PROFESSOR M. WILLIAMS, of Oxford, 1856.

Durville. See DUMONT D'URVILLE.

Du'rÿ, [Lat. DURÆ'US,] (JOHN,) a Scottish clergyman, who laboured and travelled many years to effect a union between the Lutherans and the Calvinists. He wrote "An Earnest Plea for Gospel Communion," (1654,) and other works. Died after 1674.

Duryee, dur-yȧ', (ABRAM,) an American officer, born in New York City in 1815. He commanded a regiment of zouaves at the battle of Great Bethel in 1861, and was made brigadier-general of volunteers the same year.

Duryer or **Du Ryer,** dü're-ȧ', (ANDRÉ,) a French scholar, born at Marcigny, in Burgundy, lived about 1640. He was consul at Alexandria, and lived many years in the East. He published a translation of the "Gulistan" of Saadi, (1634,) and one of the Koran, (1647,) which was very successful.

See BAYLE, "Historical and Critical Dictionary," edition of Desmaiseaux.

Duryer, (PIERRE,) a French dramatist and *littérateur*, born in Paris in 1605. He was admitted into the French Academy in 1646, when the celebrated Corneille was his competitor. Before that year he had produced several successful tragedies, and in 1647 appeared the tragedy of "Scévole," which is esteemed his best work. He published bad versions of the works of Cicero and of other Latin authors. Died about 1658.

See NICÉRON, "Mémoires."

Dusart, dü'sART', (CORNELIS,) a Dutch painter, born at Haarlem in 1665. He was a pupil and successful imitator of Van Ostade. His favourite subjects were the life, actions, and manners of villagers and peasants. Died in 1704.

See BASAN, "Dictionnaire des Graveurs."

Dusaulchoy de Bergemont, dü'zō'shwȧ'dĕh bȧRzh'-mòN', (JOSEPH FRANÇOIS NICOLAS,) a French *littérateur*, born at Toul in 1761. He edited several journals between 1790 and 1800, and was imprisoned in the reign of terror. He wrote spirited songs and other agreeable verses, among which are "The Victories of the French Armies," (1808,) and "The Poetic Nights," (1825.) Among his prose works is "The Censor," (2 vols., 1818.) Died in 1835.

Dusaulx. See DUSSAULX.

Dusch, dōōsh, (JOHANN JAKOB,) a German poet, born at Zelle, Hanover, in 1725. He became in 1766 director of a college in Altona, where he taught philosophy and mathematics. He excelled in didactic poetry, and in the art of enlivening dry themes of morality and philosophy by the charms of his diction. His chief poem is entitled "The Sciences," ("Die Wissenschaften.") His "Letters on the Formation of Taste" ("Moralische Briefe zur Bildung des Geschmacks," 6 vols., 1764) is called an excellent work. Died at Altona in December, 1787.

Duseigneur, dü'sȧn'yuR', (JEAN BERNARD,) a distinguished French sculptor, born in Paris in 1808. Among his successful works is "Roland Furieux," or "Orlando Furioso," (1831.)

Du Séjour. See DIONIS.

Dush-yän'tä, [modern Hindoo pron. dōōsh-yŭn'ta,] a celebrated king of India, the hero of Kâlidâsa's drama of "Sakoontalâ, or the Lost Ring."

See "Sakoontalâ," translated by PROFESSOR M. WILLIAMS, of Oxford, 1856.

Du Sommerard, dü som'rȧR', (ALEXANDRE,) a French antiquary, born at Bar-sur-Aube in 1779. He was appointed a member of the *cour des comptes* in 1807, and *conseiller référendaire* of the same in 1823. He devoted much time to the study and search of monuments of mediæval arts, and made a rich collection of manuscripts, arms, costumes, etc., which he deposited in the Hôtel de Cluny, now a public museum. He published, besides other minor works, "The Arts of the Middle Ages," ("Les Arts au Moyen Age," 5 vols., 1839–43,) which is highly commended. Died in 1842.

See LOUANDRE et BOURQUELOT, "La Littérature Française."

Dussault, dü'sō', (JEAN JOSEPH,) an able French journalist and critic, born in Paris in 1769. He was a tutor in the college Du Plessis until the Revolution deprived him of that place. During the first republic he wrote for Fréron's "Orator of the People." In 1800 he became one of the editors of the "Journal des Débats," then just established, which position he held until 1817. Died in 1824.

Dussaulx or **Dusaulx,** dü'sō', (JEAN,) a French *littérateur*, born at Chartres in 1728. Having published a good prose version of Juvenal, he was admitted into the Academy of Inscriptions in 1776. He adopted the principles of the Revolution, and as a member of the Convention acted with moderation and opposed the execution of the king. In 1796 and 1797 he was one of the Council of Elders. He wrote several "Essays on the Passion for Gaming," and other works. Died in 1799.

See "Mémoires sur la Vie de Dussaulx," by his widow, 1801 ; "Nouvelle Biographie Générale."

ă, ē, ī, ō, ū, ÿ, *long;* ȧ, ė, ȯ, same, less prolonged; ă, ĕ, ĭ, ŏ, ŭ, ÿ, *short;* ą, ę, į, ǫ, *obscure;* fär, fȧll, făt; mēt; nŏt; gōŏd; mōŏn;

Dussek, dōŏs'sĕk, (JOHANN LUDWIG,) an eminent German composer and pianist, was born at Czaslau, in Bohemia, about 1760. He performed in Paris, London, and other cities, and composed for the piano numerous concertos, symphonies, sonatas, etc., some of which were very popular. From 1806 until his death in 1812 he was in the service of Prince Talleyrand as director of music.
See Fétis, "Biographie Universelle des Musiciens."

Dussieux, dü'se-uh', (ÉTIENNE LOUIS,) a French writer, born in Paris in 1815, published "Historical Geography of France," (1844,) "Essay on the Invasion of Europe by the Huns," *(Hongrois,)* and other works.

Dutems, dü'tŏN', (JEAN FRANÇOIS HUGUES,) better known as ABBÉ DUTEMS, born in Franche-Comté in 1745, became a doctor of the Sorbonne. He wrote a "Historical Picture of the Archbishops, Bishops, etc. of France," (4 vols., 1775,) and a "Life of the Duke of Marlborough," (3 vols., 1808.) Died in 1811.

Dutens, dü'tŏN', (JOSEPH MICHEL,) a French political economist, nephew of Louis, noticed below, was born at Tours in 1765. He was sent to England in 1818 by the government, to examine the inland navigation of that country, and published, in 1819, "Memoirs on the Public Works of England." His most important work is "The Philosophy of Political Economy," (2 vols., 1835,) which was severely criticised by the disciples of Adam Smith. He agrees with Quesnay in the opinion that the riches of a nation proceed from agriculture rather than from manufactures or trade. Died in 1848.
See "Nouvelle Biographie Générale."

Dutens, (LOUIS,) a French Protestant writer, born at Tours in 1730. In his youth, for the sake of religious liberty, he emigrated to London. He learned Greek and several Oriental languages. About 1760 he became chargé-d'affaires at the court of Turin, where he wrote "Researches on the Origin of Discoveries attributed to the Moderns," (1766,) which was received with favour. About this time he was presented to the rich living of Elsdon. He was a Fellow of the Royal Society of London, and of the Academy of Inscriptions at Paris. He published many valuable works, among which are a "Treatise on Greek and Phoenician Medals," (1773,) and "Journal of Travels to the Principal Cities of Europe," (1775.) Died in London in 1812.
See his "Mémoires d'un Voyageur qui se repose," 2 vols., 1806; "Edinburgh Review" for July, 1806.

Dutertre. See DUPONT-DUTERTRE.

Dutertre, dü'tąRtR', (JEAN BAPTISTE,) a French Dominican, born at Calais in 1610. He was sent in 1640 as missionary to the Antilles, where he laboured eighteen years, and composed a "General History of the Antilles inhabited by the French." Died in Paris in 1687.

Dutheil de la Porte, dü'tąl' (dü'tą'ye) deh lå poRt, (or **Laporte du Theil,**) (FRANÇOIS JEAN GABRIEL,) a French Hellenist, son of Jean Gabriel, noticed below, was born in Paris in 1742. He was admitted into the Academy of Inscriptions in 1770, and published translations of Callimachus (1775) and Æschylus, (2 vols., 1794.) In conjunction with Coray and Gosselin, he was employed by the government to translate the Geography of Strabo, which was half finished when he died in 1815.
See Silvestre de Sacy, "Notice abrégé sur la Vie de M. de Laporte-Dutheil," 1816.

Dutheil de la Porte, (JEAN GABRIEL,) a French diplomatist, father of the preceding, was born about 1683. In 1735 he was minister to Vienna, and in 1748 he was ambassador extraordinary to the Congress of Aix-la-Chapelle. Died in 1755.

Duthillœul, dü'te'yul', (HIPPOLYTE ROMAIN JOSEPH,) a French bibliographer, born at Douai in 1788, wrote several biographies, and other works.

Dutillet, (JEAN.) See TILLET.

Dutour, dü'tooR', (ÉTIENNE FRANÇOIS,) a French savant, born at Riom in 1711, was a correspondent of the Academy of Sciences, and author of treatises on Magnetism, Electricity, the Diffraction of Light, etc. Died at Riom in 1784.

Du Tramblay. See DUTREMBLAY.

Dutremblay or **Du Tramblay,** dü'trŏN'blå', (ANTOINE PIERRE,) BARON, a French writer, born in Paris in 1745, was the author of numerous fables. Died in 1819.

Dutrochet, dü'tro'shå', (RENÉ JOACHIM HENRI,) a French physiologist•and natural philosopher, born at the château de Néon, Poitou, in 1776. He graduated as M.D. in 1806, and became military physician to Joseph Bonaparte in Spain in 1808, but returned to France in 1809. He published a series of essays on physiology, which present new ideas, and among which are "Observations on the Structure of Feathers," (1819,) and "Researches in Endosmosis and Exosmosis," (1828.) His former works appeared revised in a collection called "Mémoires pour servir à l'Histoire anatomique et physiologique des Végétaux et Animaux," (1837.) Died in Paris in 1847.
See Quérard, "La France Littéraire;" Adolphe Brongniart, "Notice sur H. Dutrochet," 1852; "Nouvelle Biographie Générale."

Duvair, dü'văR', (GUILLAUME,) a French writer and moralist, distinguished for learning and probity, was born in Paris in 1556. He opposed the League, and became first president of the parliament of Provence in 1599. In 1616 he was chosen keeper of the seals. He made a French version of Epictetus, and wrote several excellent treatises on philosophy and other subjects, among which is one on "French Eloquence." He was regarded as one of the best writers of his time. Died in 1621.
See C. A. Sapey, "Essai sur la Vie, etc. de Du Vair," 1847.

Duval. See Espréménil.

Duval, dü'văl', (ALEXANDRE VINCENT **Pineu**—pe'-nuh',) a popular French dramatist, born at Rennes in 1767. He produced in 1802 "Edward in Scotland," a political drama, which was warmly applauded. He excelled in invention, in dialogue, and in variety of effects. His works are numerous, and consist chiefly of comedies and comic operas. He was elected to the French Academy in 1812 in the place of Legouvé. Died in 1842. His brother, HENRI CHARLES, born in 1770, wrote a "History of France in the Reign of Charles VI.," (1842,) and a few other works. Died in 1847.
See "Nouvelle Biographie Générale;" Ballanche, "Discours de Reception à l'Académie Française."

Duval, (AMAURY PINEU,) a French *littérateur,* brother of the preceding, was born at Rennes in 1760. He was chosen a member of the Institute in 1811. In 1816 he was selected by the Academy of Inscriptions to replace Ginguené in the commission of the "Histoire Littéraire de France," for which work he wrote many articles. Died in 1839.
See "Nouvelle Biographie Générale."

Duval, (CHARLES,) a French architect, born at Beauvais in 1800.

Duval, (EUGÈNE EMMANUEL AMAURY,) a French painter of history and portraits, son of Amaury Pineu, noticed above, was born near Paris in 1808.

Duval, (JEAN PIERRE,) a French legislator and advocate, who, elected to the Convention in 1792, opposed the execution of the king, was proscribed as a Girondist, and escaped by concealment. When the Convention was dissolved, in 1795, he passed into the Council of Five Hundred. Died in 1819.

Duval, dü'văl', (NICOLAAS,) a Dutch painter, born at the Hague in 1644. He was employed at Loo by William III. of England. Died in 1732.

Duval, (PIERRE,) a nephew of Nicolas Sanson, was born at Abbeville, France, in 1618. He cultivated and taught geography with success, and received the title of royal geographer. Among his numerous works are "The World, or Universal Geography," and a "Description of France," (1691.) Died in 1683.

Duval, (VALENTINE **Jameray**—zhăm'rå',) was born of poor parents in Champagne in 1695. In early youth he became a servant of certain hermits near Lunéville, and contracted a passion for study. The Duke of Lorraine (Leopold) sent him to college, and founded for him a chair of history at Lunéville, where Duval lectured with success. About 1730 he became librarian to Francis, Grand Duke of Tuscany, and in 1748 he was appointed director of the imperial cabinet at Vienna. He wrote two treatises on medals and coins. Died in 1775.
See "Vie de Duval," 1788; L. Brightwell, "Bypaths of Biography;" Carl Dielitz, "V. J. Duvals höchst merkwürdige Lebensgeschichte," 1839.

Duval, (VINCENT,) a French physician, skilled in the treatment of deformed feet, was born in Eure in 1796.

Duval le Camus, dü'vȧl' lĕh kä'müss', (PIERRE,) a skilful French painter, born at Lisieux (Calvados) in 1790. He painted portraits, genre, landscapes, and familiar scenes. Among his works are "L'Ennui," (1827,) and "The Passage of the Ford," (1837.) Died in 1854.

Duval Leroy, (or le Roy,) dü'vȧl' lĕh-ʀwȧ', (NICO-LAS CLAUDE,) a French mathematician, born at Bayeux about 1730, published "Elements of Navigation," and other works. Died in 1810.

Duvau, dü'vō', (AUGUSTE,) a French botanist and *littérateur*, born at Tours in 1771, contributed to the "Biographie Universelle" the articles on Tournefort, Schiller, Lessing, Wieland, Wallenstein, and many others. Died in 1831.

Duvaucel, dü'vō'sĕl', (ALFRED,) an able French naturalist, born in Paris in 1792, was a step-son and pupil of the illustrious Cuvier. He had a great facility in acquiring languages, and made extensive attainments in natural history. In 1817 he went, with the title of naturalist to the king, on a scientific excursion to India, which he explored about six years with M. Diard. They made rich collections of animals, minerals, etc. for the Museum of Paris. He died at or near Madras in 1824.

See CUVIER, "Notice sur les Voyages de M. Duvaucel," in the "Mémoires de l'Académie des Sciences."

Duvaucel, (CHARLES,) a French astronomer, born in Paris in 1734; died in 1820.

Duvenède, van, vän dü'vĕh-nȧd', (MARC,) a Flemish painter, born at Bruges about 1674, was a pupil of Carlo Maratta in Rome. He returned to Bruges, and painted pictures for churches. His "Martyrdom of Saint Lawrence" is praised by Descamps. Died in 1729.

See DESCAMPS, "Vies des Peintres Flamands," etc.

Duverdier, dü'vĕʀ'de-ȧ', (ANTOINE,) a French bibliographer, was born at Montbrison in 1544. He was counsellor to the king, and gentleman of the chamber. He is chiefly known by his "Bibliothèque de A. Duverdier," (1585,) a catalogue of French authors. Died in 1600.

Duverdier, (GILBERT Saulnier—sō'ne-ȧ',) a French historian, who died in Paris in 1686.

Duvergier, dü'vĕʀ'zhe-ȧ', (JEAN BAPTISTE MARIE,) a French jurist, born at Bordeaux in 1792, published a "Complete Collection of Laws, Decrees, etc.," (24 vols., 1824–28.) In 1855 he became a councillor of state.

Duvergier de Hauranne, dü'vĕʀ'zhe-ȧ' dĕh hō'rȧn', Abbé of Saint-Cyran, (se'ʀ̂ON',) a noted French Jansenist theologian, was born at Bayonne in 1581. He formed a friendship with Jansenius at Louvain, and afterwards became a resident of Paris. He acquired great distinction and influence by his ascetic life and his zeal for reforms. In 1620 he was chosen Abbé of Saint-Cyran. Among his friends or disciples were Arnauld and other recluses of Port-Royal. He published several tracts against the Jesuit Garasse. In 1638 he was imprisoned by Richelieu at Vincennes. He was released in 1642, and died in 1643.

See LANCELOT, "Mémoires touchant la Vie de Monsieur de Saint-Cyran;" RACINE, "Histoire de Port-Royal;" SAINTE-BEUVE, "Histoire de Port-Royal."

Duvergier de Hauranne, (JEAN MARIE,) a French legislator, born at Rouen in 1771. He was a member of the Chamber of Deputies from September, 1815, until 1823, and supported liberal principles. He wrote several legal works. Died in 1831.

Duvergier de Hauranne, (PROSPER,) an eminent French statesman, a son of the preceding, was born at Rouen in 1798. He was identified with the Doctrinaires in politics, and in 1831 entered the Chamber of Deputies, in which he acquired much influence. He was one of the master-spirits of the coalition formed by several shades of opposition in 1837, and maintained the maxim "The king reigns, but does not govern." He was one of the chief agitators of electoral reform in 1846 and 1847, and in the Assembly of 1848 acted with the conservatives. Having opposed the *coup d'état* of December, 1851, he was exiled for a few months. He wrote a "History of Parliamentary Government in France," (2 vols., 1857.)

See LOUIS BLANC, "Histoire de dix Ans."

Duvernet, dü'vĕʀ'nȧ', (THÉOPHILE,) ABBÉ, a French writer, born at Ambert in 1730, wrote a "Life of Voltaire," which had a large sale, but has not much merit. Died in 1796.

See VOLTAIRE, "Correspondance."

Duverney, dü'vĕʀ'nȧ', (JOSEPH Guichard—gĕ'-shȧʀ',) an eminent French anatomist, born at Feurs, in Forez, in August, 1648. He went to Paris in his youth, and soon became distinguished as an eloquent lecturer on anatomy. His elocution was so graceful and impressive that famous actors attended his course to receive instruction in their art. He was received into the Academy of Sciences in 1676, and was appointed professor of anatomy in the Jardin du Roi in 1679. He wrote an excellent treatise "On the Organ of Hearing," (1683,) and other anatomical works. Died in 1730.

See "Biographie Médicale;" FONTENELLE, "Éloges des Académiciens."

Duvernoy, dü'vĕʀ'nwȧ', (GEORGES LOUIS,) an eminent French zoologist and anatomist, born at Montbéliard in 1777. About 1802 he was employed by Cuvier as editor of his "Lectures on Comparative Anatomy," and he published the last three volumes of that work in 1805. He practised medicine at Montbéliard nearly twenty years, and became professor of natural history at Strasbourg in 1827. In 1837 he succeeded Cuvier as professor in the College of France, and in 1850 he exchanged that place for the chair of comparative anatomy. He wrote numerous and important works on anatomy and zoology, among which is "Lectures on the History of Organized Bodies," (1842,) and contributed to the "Dictionary of Natural Sciences." Died in Paris in 1855.

See QUÉRARD, "La France Littéraire."

Duvernoy, (JEAN GEORGES,) a French anatomist and writer, born at Montbéliard in 1691. He became professor of medicine at Tübingen in 1715, and in 1725 obtained the chair of anatomy and surgery in the Academy of Saint Petersburg, which he filled until 1746. Died in 1759.

Duveyrier, dü'vȧ're-ȧ', (ANNE HONORÉ JOSEPH,) a French dramatist, born in Paris in 1788. He wrote, under the assumed name of MÉLESVILLE, many successful comedies and vaudevilles.

Duveyrier, (CHARLES,) a brother of the preceding, born in Paris in 1803, wrote "La Marquise de Senneterre," (1837,) and other popular comedies.

Duviquet, dü've'kȧ', (PIERRE,) a French critic, born at Clamecy in 1766. In the Revolution he acted with the popular party, and in 1798 was one of the Council of Five Hundred. From 1814 to 1830 he was employed as editor of the "Journal des Débats," for which he wrote able critiques on the drama. Died in 1835.

See "Nouvelle Biographie Générale."

Duvivier, dü've've-ȧ', (FRANCIADE FLEURUS, fʀ̂ON'-se'ȧd' fluh'rüss',) a French general, born at Rouen in 1794, served with distinction in Algeria from 1830 to 1840. On the formation of the republic, in 1848, he became a general of division. He was mortally wounded in a fight with the insurgents of Paris in June, 1848. He wrote several military works.

See "Nouvelle Biographie Générale."

Duvoisin, dü'vwȧ'zȧN', (JEAN BAPTISTE,) a French bishop, born at Langres in 1744. He was a professor in the schools of the Sorbonne before the Revolution, and was an exile from 1792 till 1802. About the latter date he became Bishop of Nantes. He was one of the four bishops chosen to reside with the pope during his captivity in France. Besides other works, he published "Evangelical Demonstration," and "Defence of Social Order against the Principles of the French Revolution," (1798.) Died in 1813.

See QUÉRARD, "La France Littéraire."

Duyckinck, dī'kĭnk, (EVERT AUGUSTUS,) an American essayist and critic, born in the city of New York in 1816. He founded the "Literary World" in 1847, and edited it for several years. In conjunction with his brother GEORGE L., he published a valuable work entitled "Cyclopædia of American Literature, embracing Personal and Critical Notices of Authors," (2 vols., 1856; new edition, with Supplement, 1866.)

ā, ē, ī, ō, ū, ȳ, *long;* ă, ĕ, ĭ, ŏ, ŭ, ў, *short;* ạ, ẹ, ị, ọ, *obscure;* fär, fȧll, fȧt; mĕt; nŏt; gōōd; mōōn;

Duyckinck, (George Long,) an essayist and scholar, brother of the preceding, was born in New York in 1822 or 1823. He contributed to the "Literary World" and the "Cyclopædia of American Literature," and wrote a "Life of George Herbert," (1858.) Died in March, 1863.

Duyse, van, văn doi'zĕh, (Prudens,) a Dutch antiquary and poet, born at Dendermonde in 1805.

Duzi, doot'see, or **Ducci,** doot'chee, (Virgilio,) an Italian painter, born at Città di Castello, lived about 1600.

Dwapâyana. See Vyâsa.

Dwight, dwīt, (Edmund,) an American merchant and patron of learning, born at Springfield, Massachusetts, in 1780, graduated at Yale College in 1799. He was a partner of the firm which established large cotton-mills at Chicopee Falls and Holyoke. He is said to have been the first who proposed to establish normal schools in Massachusetts, and he subsequently gave ten thousand dollars towards their support. Died in 1849.

Dwight, (Harrison Gray Otis,) an American missionary, born about 1803. He published "Christianity Revived in the East," (1850.) Died in 1862.

Dwight, (Sereno Edwards,) D.D., an American divine, son of President Dwight, was born at Greenfield Hill, Connecticut, in 1786. He graduated at Yale in 1803. After practising law for nearly ten years, he studied divinity, and was several years pastor of Park Street Church, but afterwards taught school in New Haven and Boston. From 1833 to 1836 he was president of Hamilton College, New York. Died in 1850. Dr. Dwight edited the works of his great-grandfather, Jonathan Edwards, (10 vols. 8vo,) to which he added a life of the author. A volume of his discourses, with a memoir of his life, has been published by W. T. Dwight.

Dwight, (Theodore,) an able American journalist, born at Northampton, Massachusetts, in 1765, was a brother of Timothy Dwight, noticed below. He gained distinction as a lawyer, and was a prominent leader of the Federal party. He edited "The Hartford Mirror," an organ of the Federalists, was secretary of the Hartford Convention in 1814, and founded, about 1817, the "New York Daily Advertiser," which he edited with great ability until 1836. Died in 1846.

Dwight, (Timothy,) an eminent American divine and scholar, born at Northampton, Massachusetts, on the 14th of May, 1752, was a son of Timothy Dwight, a merchant. His mother, Mary Edwards, a daughter of the celebrated Jonathan Edwards, was a woman of talents and rare worth. In 1765 he entered Yale College, where he graduated in 1769. He acted as tutor in that college for six years, from 1771 to 1777. In 1774 he finished "The Conquest of Canaan," an epic poem, (printed in 1785.) He married a lady named Woolsey in 1777, was licensed to preach, and became a chaplain in the army the same year. Having left the army in October, 1778, he worked on a farm in Northampton for five years, during which he aided to support his mother, and preached occasionally at several adjacent villages. In 1783 he was ordained minister of the Congregational church of Greenfield, Connecticut. His salary being insufficient for the support of his family, he opened an academy, (at Greenfield,) which had a high reputation.

He was chosen president of Yale College in 1795, and was annually appointed professor of theology there for ten years. This appointment was made permanent in 1805. He also performed the functions of preacher at the chapel of the college. He published "Greenfield Hill," a poem, (1794,) and a number of occasional sermons at different times. He continued to preside over Yale College until his death, and rendered important services as a teacher of youth, for which he was eminently qualified. His principal works are "Theology Explained and Defended in a Series of One Hundred and Seventy-three Sermons," (5 vols., 1818,) which is highly esteemed, and "Travels in New England and New York," (4 vols., 1821.) "This work," says Southey, "though the humblest in its pretences, is the most important of his writings, and will derive additional value from time. . . . The remarks upon natural history are those of an observant and sagacious man who makes no pretences to science : they are more interesting, therefore, than those of a merely scientific traveller." ("London

Quarterly Review," vol. xxx., October, 1823.) He died at New Haven in January, 1817.

See his Life in Sparks's "American Biography," vol. iv., second series, by William B. Sprague; "Life of Dr. Dwight," by his son, Sereno E. Dwight; Griswold, "Poets and Poetry of America," and "Prose Writers of America;" "National Portrait-Gallery of Distinguished Americans," vol. i.; Duyckinck, "Cyclopædia of American Literature," vol. i.; Sprague, "Annals of the American Pulpit."

Dwight, (Wilder,) Lieutenant-Colonel, a brave American officer, born at Springfield, Massachusetts, in 1833, was a brother of General William Dwight. He died of wounds received at the battle of Antietam, September 17, 1862.

See "Life and Letters of Wilder Dwight," 1868.

Dwight, (William,) an American general, born in Massachusetts. He served in Louisiana in May, 1863, and took part in the battle of Pleasant Hill, under General Banks, April, 1864.

Dȳce, (Rev. Alexander,) a British editor and critic, born in Edinburgh about 1798. He became a resident of London in 1827, after which he gave proof of his critical ability in editions of Webster, Middleton, Beaumont and Fletcher, Marlowe, and other old dramatists. In 1858 he published an excellent edition of Shakspeare, in 6 vols., "which is," says the Athenæum, "the most perfect text now to be obtained, with brief annotations sufficient for all practical purposes." He wrote the lives of Shakspeare, Pope, and Akenside in a collection called the "Aldine Poets." Died in May, 1869.

See "London Quarterly Review" for January, 1859.

Dyce, (William,) R.A., a painter of history, was born at Aberdeen, in Scotland, about 1806. He began to exhibit in the Royal Academy in 1827. His picture of "Joash shooting the Arrow of Deliverance" (1844) procured him a high reputation and admission into the Royal Academy as associate. He was one of the artists employed to decorate the new Houses of Parliament, and painted in the House of Lords a fresco of the "Baptism of Ethelbert," which is much admired. Among his oil-paintings are a "Madonna and Child," (1846,) and "The Meeting of Jacob and Rachel," (1850.) Died in 1864.

Dȳche, (Thomas,) an English teacher and educational writer. Died in 1750.

Dyck, van, (Anthony.) See Van Dyck.

Dyck, van, văn dīk, (Floris,) born in Haarlem in 1577, was a skilful painter of history and of fruits. The Museum of the Louvre contains two of his works, representing scenes in the life of Hagar.

See Descamps, "Vies des Peintres Flamands," etc.

Dyck, van, (Philip,) an excellent painter, born in Amsterdam in 1680, is regarded by the Dutch as the last of their great painters. He was a pupil of Arnold Boonen. In 1710 he settled at Middelburg, where he gained a high reputation, and imitated Gerard Dow with success. He afterwards worked at the Hague, and was employed as painter by the States of Holland. He painted portraits, history, and cabinet pictures, imitated nature with fidelity, and finished his work with care. Among his works are "Susanna and the Elders," and a portrait of the Prince of Orange. Died in 1752.

See Descamps, "Vies des Peintres Flamands," etc.

Dȳ'er, (Sir Edward,) an English poet, born about 1540. He was employed in several embassies by Queen Elizabeth, who knighted him. He associated with the famous Dr. Dee, and was reputed a Rosicrucian. His works consist of pastoral odes and madrigals.

See Ellis, "Specimens of the Early English Poets."

Dyer, (George,) an English scholar, antiquary, and divine, born in London in 1755. Having officiated as a Baptist minister at Oxford, he became a resident of London in 1792, and applied himself with success to literary pursuits. He wrote a "History of the University of Cambridge," and edited the Greek Testament, and several plays of Euripides. He contributed the original portions (except the preface) of "Valpy's Classics," (141 vols.,) on which he was employed from 1819 to 1830, and published some poems and other works. Charles Lamb, who was his friend, has commemorated his merit as an author and a man, in his Essays. Died in 1841.

Dyer or **Deyer,** (Sir James,) an English jurist, born at Roundhill in 1511. He became eminent in his profession, and in 1552 was elected Speaker of the House of Commons. From 1560 until his death, in 1582, he was chief justice of the common pleas. His Reports were recommended to students by Lord Coke.

See Foss, "The Judges of England."

Dyer, (JOHN,) a British poet, born in 1700, was the son of a Welsh solicitor. In his youth he was an itinerant painter. In 1727 he produced his "Grongar Hill," which is regarded as his best poem. "The scenes which it displays," says Dr. Johnson, "are so pleasing, the images which they raise are so welcome to the mind, that when it is once read it will be read again." He went to Italy to study painting, and wrote there "The Ruins of Rome," a poem, which was much admired. After his return he took orders, married Miss Ensor, and obtained the livings of Calthorpe, Coningsby, Bedford, and Kirkby. In 1757 he published his longest poem, "The Fleece," which was unfavourably criticised by Johnson. Dr. Drake, on the other hand, thinks "it contains a vast variety of landscapes, drawn and coloured in the most spirited and fascinating style." Dyer was a man of pure morality and amiable temper. Died in 1758.

See JOHNSON's "Lives of the English Poets."

Dyer, (MARY,) a member of the Society of Friends, or Quakers, who suffered death for her religion. She was hanged on Boston Common in 1660.

See HILDRETH's "History of the United States," vol. i. chap. xii.

Dyer, (SAMUEL,) an English scholar, born about 1725, was noted for his wit and convivial habits. He was a member of the literary club composed of Dr. Johnson and his friends. About 1758 he revised the English edition of Plutarch's "Lives," for which he made new translations of the lives of Pericles and Demetrius. Died in 1772.

Dyer, (WILLIAM,) an English clergyman, who, in 1662, was ejected from Cholesbury, in Buckingham-shire, for nonconformity. His Sermons, printed in 1663-66, are said to resemble the style of Bunyan. He afterwards joined the Society of Friends. Died in 1696, aged sixty.

Dȳke, (DANIEL,) an eminent English Puritan divine, who wrote a treatise "On Repentance," (1631,) and Sermons, which were highly praised by Bishop Wilkins. Died about 1614.

Dȳ′mọnd, (JONATHAN,) an eminent English moralist and writer, born at Exeter in 1796, was a member of the Society of Friends. He became a linen-draper in his native city. He advocated the principles of peace in an able work entitled an "Inquiry into the Accordancy of War with the Principles of Christianity," (1823.) He also wrote "Essays on the Principles of Morality, and on the Private and Political Rights and Obligations of Mankind," (1829,) which has passed through numerous editions. Commenting on this work, Professor George Bush remarks, "Whether we regard the soundness and lucidness of his reasonings, the temper, candour, and wisdom of his conclusions, the elegance of his style, the felicity of his illustrations, or the singularly excellent spirit which pervades the whole, the Essays of Dymond are entitled to rank high in the highest class of ethical productions." (See Preface to the American edition of Dymond's "Essays," New York, 1834.) Died in 1828.

See a Review of Dymond's Essays, by ROBERT SOUTHEY, in the "London Quarterly Review" for January, 1831, vol. xliv.; "Christian Examiner," vol. xviii.; ALLIBONE, "Dictionary of Authors."

Dzahabi, dzȧh′hạ-bee, or **Dzehebi,** (**Ahmed,** ȧh′med,) a famous Arabian historian and jurist, born at Damascus in 1275; died in 1347.

Dzatee or **Dzati,** dzȧ′tee, surnamed ROUMI, (roo′-mee,) a Turkish poet, born at Carasi; died in 1546.

Dzondi, dzon′dee, (CARL HEINRICH,) a German medical writer, born in Saxony in 1770; died in 1835.

E.

Eachard. See ECHARD.

Eachard, ĕtch′ạrd, (JOHN,) D.D., an English clergyman, born in Suffolk in 1636. He became a Fellow of Catherine Hall, Cambridge, in 1658, and Master of the same in 1675. He displayed a talent for ridicule in his works, among which were "The Ground and Occasions of the Contempt of the Clergy and Religion inquired into," (1670,) and a "Dialogue on Hobbes's State of Nature," (1672.) "I have known men happy enough at ridicule," says Dean Swift, "who upon grave subjects were perfectly stupid; of which Dr. Eachard was a great instance." Died in 1697.

See THOMAS DAVIES, "Life of J. Eachard;" "Biographia Britannica."

Eadgar. See EDGAR.

Eadie, ee′de, (JOHN,) a Scottish Presbyterian divine and biblical critic, born at Alva, in the county of Stirling, about 1814. He has published several popular works, among which are the "Biblical Cyclopædia," (6th edition, 1857,) a "Life of Dr. Kitto," and a "Condensed Concordance to the Scriptures," (20th edition, 1860.) He succeeded Dr. Mitchell as professor of biblical literature to the United Presbyterian Church in 1843. He is, or was recently, pastor of a congregation in Glasgow.

Eadmer, ĕd′mẹr, or **Edmer,** an English historian and monk, was the friend and companion of Bishop Anselm. He wrote the "Historia Novorum," or "History of his own Times" from 1066 to 1122, which contains valuable information, and the "Life of Anselm." He was elected Bishop of St. Andrew's in 1120. Died about 1124.

Eadmund. See EDMUND.

Eadred. See EDRED.

Eadward. See EDWARD.

Eadwig. See EDWIG.

Eagles, ee′glz, (Rev. JOHN,) an English writer and artist, born at Bristol about 1784. He contributed to "Blackwood's Magazine" and other periodicals. A volume of his contributions to Blackwood was published, under the title of "The Sketcher," in 1856. Died in 1855.

See "Blackwood's Magazine" for December, 1855.

Eames, eemz, ? (JOHN,) an English savant, wrote papers on "Natural Philosophy," etc. for the "Philosophical Transactions" from 1726 to 1742, and was associated with J. Martyn in publishing an Abridgment of the said Transactions, (1719–33.) Died in 1744.

Eandi, ȧ-ân′dee, (GIUSEPPE ANTONIO FRANCESCO GIROLAMO,) born at Saluces, Piedmont, in 1735, became professor of natural philosophy in the University of Turin in 1788. He wrote "Elements of Geometry and Physics," (1793,) and other works. Died in 1799.

Eaque, the French of ÆACUS, which see.

Eardley, ẹrd′le, (Sir CULLING,) an English publicist, born at Hatfield in 1805. He was noted for his zealous assertion of Protestantism. Died in 1863.

Earle, ẹrl, (JAMES,) an American portrait-painter, born in Massachusetts, studied in London. Died in Charleston, South Carolina, in 1796. He held a high rank among American artists of his time.

Earle, ẹrl, (JOHN,) an English bishop, born at York in 1601, graduated at Oxford in 1624, and became chaplain and tutor to Prince Charles, (afterwards Charles II.,) whom he followed into exile. In 1662 he was appointed Bishop of Worcester, and in 1663 transferred to the see of Salisbury. He wrote a popular work entitled "Microcosmography," a delineation of character and manners, and translated into Latin the "Eikon Basilike." His character was excellent. Burnet says, "Earle was the man of all the clergy for whom the king had the greatest esteem." Died in 1665.

See WOOD, "Athenæ Oxonienses."

Earle, (PLINY,) an American inventor, born at Leicester, Massachusetts, in 1762. He invented a machine for making cards which are used in carding wool and cotton. Died in 1832.

Earle, (THOMAS,) an American writer and philanthropist, son of the preceding, was born at Leicester, Massachusetts, in 1791. He practised law in Philadelphia for many years. He was one of the most influential members of the State Constitutional Convention of 1837,

---

ā, ē, ī, ō, ū, ȳ, *long;* ă, ĕ, ĭ, ŏ, ŭ, ў, *short;* ạ, ẹ, ị, ọ, *obscure;* fâr, fâll, fȧt; mĕt; nŏt; gōōd; mōōn;

and in 1840 was the candidate of the Liberty party for the Vice-Presidency. Died in 1849. Among his works are treatises on penal law and on States' rights.

His brother PLINY, a physician, born in 1809, published in 1841 a work on the asylums for the insane in Europe.

Earlom, ęr'lǫm, (RICHARD,) one of the most eminent English engravers of his time, was born in London about 1742, or, as some say, in 1728. He has probably never been surpassed as a mezzotinto engraver. Among his master-pieces is "The Royal Academy." He engraved the works of many Italian and Flemish painters; he also left fruit- and flower-pieces, after Huysum, and a collection of prints after Claude Lorrain, entitled "Liber Veritatis," (3 vols., 1777–1804.) Died in 1822.

Early, ęr'le, (JOHN,) an eminent American divine, Bishop of the Methodist Episcopal Church, South, was born in Virginia in 1785. At an early age he became an itinerant preacher, and was chosen bishop in 1854.

Early, (JUBAL A.,) an American general, born in Virginia about 1818, graduated at West Point in 1837. He commanded a division of General Lee's army at Gettysburg, July 2–3, 1863. In July, 1864, he invaded Maryland, and sent a body of cavalry on a raid to Chambersburg, which they burned. Having moved his army back to the Shenandoah Valley, he was defeated by Sheridan on the Opequan Creek and at Fisher's Hill on the 19th and 20th of September. On the 19th of October, 1864, he surprised the Union army at Cedar Creek, in the absence of General Sheridan; but the latter, having arrived in the afternoon, gained a decisive victory, General Early losing the greater part of his artillery and trains.

East, (Sir EDWARD HYDE,) an English jurist, born about 1764, published "King's Bench Reports, 1800–1812," which are highly commended, and another excellent legal production, entitled "Pleas of the Crown," (1803.) Died in 1847.

East'burn, (JAMES WALLIS,) a poet and Episcopal clergyman, born in England in 1797. He became in 1818 rector of a church in Accomac county, Virginia. In conjunction with Robert C. Sands, he wrote "Yamoyden," a romantic poem founded on the history of the Indian king Philip. Died in 1819.

See "North American Review" for April, 1821.

Eastburn, (MANTON,) D.D., a bishop, brother of the preceding, was born in England in 1801. Having been brought by his parents to New York, he graduated at Columbia College in 1817. He received holy orders in 1822, and was for many years pastor of the Church of the Ascension in New York. He was appointed Bishop of Massachusetts in 1843.

East'lake, (Sir CHARLES LOCK,) an eminent English historical painter, born at Plymouth in 1793. He became a pupil of Fuseli in the Royal Academy, and visited Italy and Greece about 1818, after which he passed some years in Rome. In 1828 he produced a remarkable picture of "Pilgrims to Rome first coming in Sight of the Holy City." He was elected a Royal Academician in 1830, and president of the Royal Academy in 1850. His picture of "Christ Weeping over Jerusalem" was greatly admired for a union of refinement with earnest religious feeling. He has enriched the literature of art with valuable works, among which are a version of Goethe's "Theory of Colours," (1840,) and "Materials for a History of Oil-Painting," (1847.) Died about the end of 1865.

See NAGLER, "Neues Allgemeines Künstler-Lexikon;" "London Quarterly Review" for March, 1848; "Gentleman's Magazine" for February, 1866.

Eastlake, (ELIZABETH RIGBY,) LADY, wife of the preceding, to whom she was married in 1849. Among her works are "Letters from the Shores of the Baltic," (1841,) and "Livonian Tales."

East'man, (CHARLES G.,) an American poet and journalist, born in Oxford county, Maine, in 1816. He became about 1846 editor of the "Vermont Patriot," published at Montpelier, and produced a volume of poems in 1848.

Eastman, (MARY HENDERSON,) an American writer, born at Warrenton, Virginia, about 1818. She published, besides other works, "Romance of Indian Life," (1852,) and "Aunt Phillis's Cabin," designed as a reply to "Uncle Tom's Cabin."

East'wick, (EDWARD B.,) an English Orientalist, born in Berkshire in 1814. He was employed in India as interpreter in the service of the East India Company. About 1845 he became professor of Oriental languages in the College of Haileybury. He has published, besides other works, "Dry Leaves from Young Egypt," (1849,) a version of "Gulistan," from the Persian, (1852,) "Lights of Canopus," (1854,) and a version of "The Four Dervishes," a Persian tale.

Eaton, ee'ton, (AMOS,) a distinguished American naturalist, born in 1777, graduated at Williams College, studied law in early life, and was admitted to the bar. On the organization of the Rensselaer Institute, about 1828, at Troy, New York, he was appointed principal and senior professor, which position he held till his death in 1842. He published a text-book on botany, which passed through numerous editions, an "Index to the Geology of the Northern States," and other scientific works. By his writings and zeal in the cause of natural science he did much to promote the study of natural history in the United States in the early part of the present century.

Eaton, ee'ton, (JOHN,) an English clergyman, born in 1575, preached at Wickham Market, and wrote Antinomian treatises on Faith and Justification. Died in 1641.

Eaton, (HORACE,) born in Windsor county, Vermont, in 1804, was elected Governor of Vermont in 1846, and was for several years State superintendent of common schools. Died in 1855.

Eaton, (WILLIAM,) an American soldier, born in Woodstock, Connecticut, in 1764. He was sent as consul to Tunis in 1798, and was involved in a series of negotiations and disputes, which he conducted with great ability and courage. After hostilities had begun between the United States and Tripoli in 1801, he made an attempt to revolutionize Tripoli by means of an army which he commanded; but a treaty of peace in 1805 rendered his attempt abortive. Died in 1811.

See a "Life of W. Eaton" in SPARKS's "American Biography," vol. ix., 1st series, by C. C. FELTON.

Ebben, ěb'bęn, or **Ebbon,** ěb'bǫn, a German monk of the twelfth century, wrote a "Life of Otho, Bishop of Bamberg."

Ebbesen, ěb'bęh-sen, (NIELS, or NICHOLAS,) a Danish patriot, who took arms against Count Gerard, a petty tyrant, whom he killed. He afterwards defeated the army of Gerard, but lost his life in the action, in 1340.

Eb'bon, [Fr. pron. ą'bôn',] a French ecclesiastic, born about 775 A.D. He became Bishop of Rheims in 816, and aided Lothaire in rebellion against Louis le Débonnaire. Died in 851.

E'bed Je'su, a Syrian writer, who became Nestorian Bishop of Nisibis about 1290. Died in 1318. Among his numerous works is "The Book of the Pearl," a treatise on the truth of the Christian religion.

Ebel, ā'bęl, (JOHANN GOTTFRIED,) a German geologist, born at Züllichau in 1764. He wrote a popular "Guide to Travellers in Switzerland," (1793,) an able treatise on the geology of the Alps, ("Ueber den Bau der Erde in den Alpen-Gebirgen," 1808,) and other works. Died in 1830.

Ebel, (JOHANN PHILIPP,) a German writer, born in 1592; died in 1627.

Ebeling, ā'bęh-ling', (CHRISTOPH DANIEL,) a German historian and scholar, born in Hildesheim, Hanover, in 1741, was for many years professor of history and of Greek at Hamburg. His principal work is a valuable "History and Geography of North America," (7 vols., 1796–1816.) Died in 1817.

Ebelmen, ą'běl'môn', (JACQUES JOSEPH,) an eminent French chemist, born at Beaume-les-Dames in 1814. He became professor of docimacy in the École des Mines in 1845. In 1847 he was appointed an engineer of the first class, and director of the porcelain manufactory at Sèvres, the products of which he raised to a higher state of perfection. He wrote for the "Annales des Mines" and "Annales de Physique et de Chimie" many treatises, among which was one "On the Decomposition of Rocks," (1848.) He died in 1852, a few days after he had been appointed engineer-in-chief of mines.

See M. CHEVREUL, "Notice sur Ebelmen," 1855; "Nouvelle Biographie Générale."

Eber, ä′bĕr, [Lat. Ebe′rus,] (Paul,) a German Protestant theologian, born at Ritzingen in 1511, was a friend of Melanchthon, with whom he attended the Conference of Worms in 1541. He became professor of Hebrew at Wittenberg in 1556, and wrote, among other works, (in Latin,) an "Exposition of the Gospels," and a "History of the Jews," (1561.) Died in 1569.

See M. Adam, "Vitæ Eruditorum;" Balthasar Menz, "Oratio de Vita et Rebus gestis P. Eberi," 1581; G. H. Sixt, "P. Eber, der Schüler, Freund und Amtsgenosse der Reformatoren," 1843.

Eb′er-ard, a son-in-law of the emperor Lothaire, obtained about 845 A.D. the duchy of Friuli, then one of the most important fiefs of Italy. He was the father of Berenger, King of Italy.

Eberhard, ä′bĕr-haRt′ or ĕb′ĕr-haRt′, (August Gottlob,) a German savant and writer, born at Belzig, Prussia, in 1769. Among his prose works are stories entitled "Ferdinand Werner," (1802,) and "Hannchen and the Chickens," which had a great success. His poem "The First Man and the Earth" ("Der erste Mensch und die Erde," 1828) is praised for its noble style. Died in 1845.

See Brockhaus, "Conversations-Lexikon."

Eberhard, (Christoph,) a German natural philosopher, born in 1655; died in 1730.

Eberhard, (Johann August,) a German philosopher and elegant writer, born at Halberstadt in 1739. He published in 1772 an "Apology for Socrates," which exercised great influence in the propagation of that theological system popularly known as neology or rationalism. This work was severely criticised by Lessing and others, and hindered Eberhard's advancement in the Church. He was appointed professor of history at Halle in 1778. In philosophy he was a staunch partisan of Leibnitz, and an adversary of Kantism. He wrote, among other works, a "History of Philosophy," (1788,) and a "Dictionary of German Synonyms," (6 vols., 1793–1802,) which was universally admired. Died in 1809.

See F. Nicolai, "Gedächtnissschrift auf J. A. Eberhard," Berlin, 1810; "Nouvelle Biographie Générale."

Eberhard, (Johann Heinrich,) a German jurist, born at Hochstädt in 1743; died in 1772.

Eberhard, (Johann Peter,) a German medical writer, born at Altona in 1727; died in 1779.

Eberhard, (Konrad,) a distinguished German sculptor, born at Hindelang in 1768. He became professor of sculpture in the Academy of Munich in 1816. Among his works are "Leda and the Swan," and a statue of Saint Michael.

See Nagler, "Neues Allgemeines Künstler-Lexikon."

Eb′er-hard or **Evrard de Bethune,** a Flemish grammarian of the twelfth century, wrote a Latin Grammar.

Eberle, ä′bĕr-lĕh, (Adam,) a German painter, born at Aix-la-Chapelle in 1805; died at Rome in 1832.

Eb′er-le, (John,) an American medical writer, born in Lancaster county, Pennsylvania, in 1788, graduated in the University of Pennsylvania in 1809. He published about 1822 a "Treatise on Therapeutics," took a prominent part in establishing the Jefferson Medical College in Philadelphia, and became a professor in that institution. Died in 1838.

See S. D. Gross, "American Medical Biography."

Eberlin, ä′bĕr-leen′, (Daniel,) a German musician, born at Nuremberg about 1630. He became successively soldier, chapel-master, and banker. Died at Cassel in 1685.

Ebers, ä′bĕrs, (Emil,) a German painter, distinguished for humour and comic talent, was born at Breslau in 1807. Among his subjects are smugglers, outlaws, etc.

Ebersberger, ä′bĕrs-bĕRG′ĕr, or **Ebersperger,** ä′bĕrs-pĕRG′ĕr, (Johann Georg,) a German engraver of maps, born at Lichtenau in 1695; died in 1760.

Eberstein, von, fon ä′bĕr-stīn′, (Wilhelm Ludwig,) Baron, a German metaphysical philosopher, born in 1762; died in 1805.

Ebert, ä′bĕRt, (Friedrich Adolph,) a distinguished German bibliographer, born at Taucha, near Leipsic, in 1791. He was appointed director of the Royal Library of Dresden in 1828. Among his principal works are a "Life of Napoleon," (1817,) and a "Universal Bibliographic Dictionary," (2 vols., 1820–30.) Died in 1834.

Ebert, (Johann Arnold,) a German poet, born at Hamburg in 1723. He was for a long time professor in the Carolinum of Brunswick. His German version of Young's "Night Thoughts" (1790–95) is praised by Guizot. He translated other English works, and wrote lyric verses of some merit. Died in 1795.

See Ersch und Gruber, "Allgemeine Encyklopaedie."

Ebert, (Johann Jakob,) a German philosopher, born at Breslau in 1737, became professor of mathematics at Wittenberg. He published "Principles of Practical Philosophy," (1784,) and other works for the instruction of youth. Died in 1805.

Ebert, (Theodor,) a German Hebraist, who was professor of Hebrew at Frankfort-on-the-Oder. He published several works. Died in 1630.

Eberus, (Paul.) See Eber.

Eberwein. See Ebroin.

E′bĭ-on, the supposed founder of the E′bionites, a sect of heretics who existed in the East in the first century. They rejected the New Testament and observed the Mosaic law, but professed to be Christians. Origen and some others, however, derive the name of Ebionites from a Hebrew word signifying "poor."

See Matter, "Histoire du Gnosticisme."

Eblé, ĕb′lä′, (Jean Baptiste,) an eminent French general, born in Lorraine in 1758. As general of brigade, he directed the sieges of Ypres, Nieuwpoort, Bois-le-Duc, etc. He was made a general of division in 1793. In 1795 he made the campaign of the Palatinate, under Moreau, and in 1800 commanded the artillery at the victory of Hohenlinden. In the Russian campaign of 1812 he was chief commandant of the pontoon-train, and rendered great services at the passage of the Berezina, where it is said Bonaparte was saved by his energy and skill. He died from the effects of cold and exposure on this occasion, just as he was appointed inspector-general and commander-in-chief of the artillery of the grand army.

See De Courcelles, "Dictionnaire des Généraux Français."

Ebn. See Ibn.

Ebn-Koteybah. See Ibn-Koteybah.

Ebner, ĕb′nĕr, (Erasmus,) a German poet, born at Nuremberg in 1511, was a pupil of Melanchthon. He wrote Latin epigrams which were printed with those of Melanchthon, and discovered that cadmium and copper fused together produce brass. Died in 1577.

Eboli, ĕb′o-lee or ä′bo-lee, (Aña de Mendoza—dä mĕn-do′thä,) Princess of, a Spanish lady, born about 1535 or 1540, became the wife of Ruy Gomez de Sylva, Prince of Eboli. She was, it is said, the mistress of Philip II., and was suspected of being an accomplice of Antonio Perez in the assassination of Escovedo. She was arrested in 1579 and imprisoned, but was soon released.

See Mignet, "Antonio Perez et Philippe II."

Ebrard, ä′bRäRt, (Johann Heinrich August,) a prominent German Protestant theologian, born at Erlangen in 1818. He became professor of theology at Erlangen in 1847. He edited a review called "The Future of the Church," (1845–47,) and wrote, besides other works, "Christian Dogmatics," (2 vols., 1852,) and "The Divine and Human (*Gottmenschlichkeit*) in Christianity," (1844.) Many of his sermons have been published. He is, or was recently, preacher and councillor of the Consistory at Spire.

Eb′re-mar, written also **Evermer,** third Patriarch of Jerusalem, was born near Thérouanne. He was raised to the dignity of patriarch in 1103. Died after 1122.

E′broin, [Lat. Ebroi′nus,] written also **Eberwein,** a powerful and ambitious Frank, was mayor of the palace under Clotaire III. (King of Neustria) and under Theodoric III. He was killed in 681 A.D.

See Sismondi, "Histoire des Français."

Ebu. See Aboo.

Ebu-Beker. See Aboo-Bekr.

Eb′ur-ȳ, (Robert Grosvenor,) Lord, an English peer, a son of the second Earl Grosvenor, was born in 1801. He was a member of the House of Commons from 1822 to 1857, and was then raised to the peerage. He supported several bills for the promotion of civil and religious liberty.

Ebu-Thalib. See Aboo-Tâlib.

Ecatarina. See CATHERINE, Empress of Russia.

Ecbert. See EGBERT.

Eccard. See ECKHART.

Eccelino da Romano. See ROMANO.

Ecchelensis. See ECHELLENSIS.

Eccius. See ECK.

Eccles, êk'klz, (AMBROSE,) an Irish critic, published editions of "Cymbeline," "King Lear," and the "Merchant of Venice," with copious notes and critical essays on these dramas by himself and others. Died in 1809.

Eccles, êk'klz, (JOHN,) an excellent English musical composer, set some of Congreve's songs to music, with a success that gained great applause. Died in 1735.

Eccles, (SOLOMON,) an English musician, father of the preceding, lived about 1680.

Ecgberht or **Ecgbert.** See EGBERT.

Echard, ḣ'shǎr',(JACQUES,) a French Dominican friar, born at Rouen in 1644, wrote a work on the authors who had been members of his order, entitled "Scriptores Ordinis Prædicatorum recensiti," (1721,) which is highly commended. Died in 1724.

Echard, etch'ḁrd, (Rev. LAWRENCE,) an English historian, born in Suffolk about 1670, obtained Alford and other livings in Suffolk. He is the author of a "General Ecclesiastical History," (1702,) and of a "History of England to 1688," (3 vols., 1707-18,) which was once quite popular, but has ceased to be read since the publication of Rapin. Died in 1730.

Ech-el-len'sis, (ABRAHAM,) a learned Maronite, born at Eckel, Syria. After professing Syriac and Arabic at Rome, he came to Paris about 1630 to assist in the edition of Le Jay's Polyglot Bible, and received the title of interpreter to the king. He returned to Rome in 1653. He wrote an "Oriental Chronicle," and translated several works from the Arabic. Died in 1664.

Echeverri, de, dà êtch-ê-vêr-ree', sometimes written **Etcheverri,** (JUAN,) the most famous of the Basque poets, born at Tafalla, in Navarre, about 1550, wrote the "Mysteries of the Faith," and other religious poems.

E-chid'na, [Gr. Ἔχιδνα,] in the Greek mythology, a daughter of Tartarus, represented as a monster, half woman and half serpent, was the mother of the Chimæra, Cerberus, the Sphinx, and other monsters.

Echinus, (SEBASTIAN.) See ERIZZO.

E-chi'on, [ʼEχίων,] a Greek painter and statuary, who lived about 350 B.C., is ranked by Pliny among the great painters, and is praised by Cicero.

E'cho, [Gr. ʼHχώ,] a nymph of classic mythology, and an attendant of Juno, was called a daughter of the Air. The poets feigned that Juno, offended by her unruly tongue, changed her into an echo, and ordained that she should not be able to speak until another had spoken, nor be silent after another had spoken to her. She was disappointed in her love of Narcissus, and pined away until nothing remained of her but her voice.

Eck, êk, **Eckius,** êk'ke-ûs, or **Eccius, Echius,** ā'ke-ûs, (JOHANN,) a German theologian, famous as an able antagonist of Luther, was born at Eck, in Suabia, in 1486. He became a professor in the University of Ingolstadt. In 1519 he disputed against Luther at Leipsic, and in 1530 was chosen, with others, to controvert the Lutheran Confession of Faith at the Diet of Augsburg. He wrote a "Manual of Controversy," and other works. Died in 1543.

See ARNOLD, "Kirchen- und Ketzer-Historie."

Eck or **Eckius,** (LEONARD,) a German jurist, born in 1480, acquired a great reputation as a lawyer, and was employed by Charles V. Died at Munich in 1550.

Eck, van, vǎn êk, (CORNELIS,) a Dutch jurist, born at Arnheim. He became professor of civil and modern law at Utrecht in 1692. He wrote "Principles of Civil Law," ("Principia Juris Civilis," 1689,) and other works. Died in 1732.

Eckard. See ECKHARD and ECKHART.

Eckard, êk'kǎrt, (GEORG LUDWIG,) a German portrait-painter of high reputation, born at Hamburg in 1769 ; died in 1794.

Eckart, (DIETRICH GOTTHARD,) a German jurist, born at Eilenburg in 1696 ; died in 1760.

Eckartshausen, von, fon êk'kǎrts-hŏw'zęn, (KARL,) a German writer, born in Bavaria in 1752, became aulic

councillor at Munich. He wrote, besides other works, "God is the Purest Love," ("Gott ist die reinste Liebe," 1784,) which had great success. Died in 1803.

Eckerbrecht, êk'kęr-bręKt', (PHILIPP,) a German astronomer, born at Nuremberg in 1594, was a pupil or friend of Kepler. Died in 1667.

Eckermann, êk'kęr-mân', (JOHANN PETER,) a German littérateur, born at Winsen, Hanover, in 1792. He published in 1821 a volume of poems, which procured for him the friendship of Goethe, and he co-operated with that author in the complete edition of his works at Weimar. In 1832-33 he published the posthumous works of Goethe, in accordance with his last will. His "Conversations with Goethe" ("Gespräche mit Göthe," 3 vols., 1836-48) has been translated into various languages. Died in 1854.

See "Foreign Quarterly Review" for October, 1836 ; BROCKHAUS, "Conversations-Lexikon."

Eckersberg, êk'kęrs-bêRG', (CHRISTOPH WILHELM,) an eminent Danish painter, born in Holstein about 1782, studied in Paris and Italy. He painted history, portraits, and marine pieces with great success. Among his works is "The Death of Balder." Died in 1853.

Eck'ford, (HENRY,) a distinguished naval architect, born in Scotland in 1775. He served an apprenticeship to a shipbuilder in Quebec, and in 1796 established himself in business in New York. He was soon distinguished for the superiority of his vessels in strength and speed, and in the second war with Great Britain was employed by the government to furnish fleets for the lakes. He afterwards built many vessels of war for foreign nations, established a professorship of naval architecture at Columbia College, and in 1831 accepted the appointment of naval constructor for the Ottoman Empire. Died at Constantinople, November 12, 1832.

See HENRY HOWE, "Lives of Eminent American Mechanics," etc., 1847.

Eckhard, êk'hâRt, (JOHANN FRIEDRICH,) a German philologist, born at Quedlinburg in 1723, wrote many literary treatises. Died in 1794.

Eckhard, (JOHANN GEORG.) See ECKHART.

Eckhard, (TOBIAS,) a German Hellenist, born at Delitzsch in 1558 ; died in 1652.

Eckhard, (TOBIAS,) a distinguished German philologist, born at Jüterbock, Saxony, in 1662. He was rector of the Academy of Quedlinburg. He published (in Latin) a treatise on logic, "Ars Rationis," (1714,) "Technica Sacra," (1716,) a treatise on philosophy, (1717,) "Testimonies to Christ by those who were not Christians," (1725,) and other works. Died in 1737.

See C. H. ECKHARD, "Vita T. Eckhardi," 1739.

Eckhart or **Eckhard, von,** fon êk'hâRt, written also **Eccard** and **Eckard,** (JOHANN GEORG,) a German historian, born at Duingen in 1674. Through the influence of Leibnitz he obtained a chair of history at Helmstedt in 1706. He succeeded Leibnitz as librarian at Hanover. To escape his creditors he retired to Cologne, where he joined the Roman Catholic Church. He afterwards became librarian and counsellor to the Bishop of Würtzburg. He was author of several Latin histories, which are valued for research and criticism, viz., a "History of the Princes of Upper Saxony," (1722,) "History of the Middle Ages," ("Corpus historicum medii Ævi," 1723,) and a work "On the Origin of the Germans," ("De Origine Germanorum," 1750.) Died in 1730.

Eckhel, êk'hęl, (JOSEPH HILARY,) a pre-eminent Austrian numismatist, born at Enzersfeld in 1737, entered the order of Jesuits. Having made extensive researches in Italy and attained great proficiency in the knowledge of medals, he was appointed, in 1774, director of the imperial cabinet of medals at Vienna, and professor of antiquities. In 1775 he published an excellent work on medals, entitled "Numi Veteres." His capital work is "Doctrina Numorum Veterum," (8 vols., 1792-98,) a systematic treatise on the science of numismatics, which the perfection of the plan, the extent of the researches, and the soundness of the criticism render perhaps the best work, on the whole, which is to be found on that subject. Died in 1798.

See ERSCH und GRUBER, "Allgemeine Encyklopaedie ;" AUBIN LOUIS MILLIN, "Notice historique sur J. H. Eckhel," Paris, 1798 ; "Nouvelle Biographie Générale."

ɇ as ḳ, ç as s; ḡ hard; ġ as j; G, H, K, guttural; N, nasal; R, trilled; ṣ as z; ṭh as in this.   (☞See Explanations, p. 23.)

Eckhof, ĕk′hof, (CONRAD,) one of the most celebrated German actors, was born at Hamburg in 1720. He excelled in tragedy, and was called "the Garrick of Germany." He produced "The Desert Isle," and other comedies. Died in 1778.

Eckhout. See EECKHOUT.

Eckmühl, PRINCE OF. See DAVOUST.

Eckstein, von, fon ĕk′stīn, (FERDINAND,) BARON, a publicist, born at Copenhagen in 1790, was converted to Roman Catholicism. He removed to France, and edited the "Catholique," (1826-29,) in which he advocated the doctrines of De Maistre.

Écluse. See LÉCLUSE.

Écluse des Loges, de l', dĕh lä′klüz′ dą lozh, (PIERRE MATHURIN,) born at Falaise, France, in 1715, was a doctor of the Sorbonne. His reputation rests chiefly on his edition of Sully's "Memoirs." Died about 1783.

Écolampade. See ŒCOLAMPADIUS.

Ec-phan′tĭ-dēs,['Εκφαντίδης,]an Athenian comic poet, who lived about 450 B.C. His works are not extant.

Ecquevilly, d', dĕk′vel′ye′, (ARMAND FRANÇOIS,) COUNT and MARQUIS, a French general, was born of a noble family of Champagne in 1747. He emigrated in 1791, and served under the Prince of Condé, as quartermaster-general of cavalry, in 1794. Returning to France with the king, he was made lieutenant-general in 1814, and marquis in 1820. Died in 1830.

Edebali, ed-eb′ă-lee, SHEIK, a Mussulman, noted for devotion and learning, born in Caramania about 1210, founded a monastery which was much frequented. Othmân, the founder of the Turkish Empire, married the daughter of Edebali. Died in 1326.

Edelinck, ā′dĕh-link, (CASPAR,) a Flemish engraver, was a brother and pupil of Gerard, noticed below.

His brother JOHN, born about 1630, was also an engraver, and worked some time with Gerard.

Edelinck, ĕd′ĕl-ink or ā′dĕh-link′, (GERARD,) a celebrated Flemish engraver, born in Antwerp in 1649, removed to Paris at an early age, and received the title of engraver to the cabinet of Louis XIV. Among his master-pieces are "The Holy Family," after Raphael, the "Crucifixion," after Lebrun, the "Virgin," after Guido, "The Combat of Cavalry," after Leonardo da Vinci, and portraits of many eminent men. His works are highly finished, and are characterized by freedom of touch, fidelity of design, and perfect harmony of execution. Died in 1707. He is reckoned among the engravers of the first class. "No one but Audran," says Ponce, "can be placed on a par with him."

His son NICOLAS engraved at Venice a "Madonna and Child," after Correggio, and other subjects. Died in 1730.

See BASAN, "Dictionnaire des Graveurs."

Edelmann, ā′dĕl-mân′ or ā′dĕl′môN′, (JEAN FRÉDÉRIC,) a musical composer, born at Strasburg in 1749, was a violent revolutionist. He was guillotined in 1794, after he had procured the death of several persons.

Edelmann, ā′dĕl-mân′, (JOHANN CHRISTIAN,) a German deist, born in Saxony in 1698. He wrote "The Divinity of Reason," (1742.) Guizot calls him a *fameux esprit-fort.* Died in 1767.

See WILHELM ELSTER, "Erinnerung an J. C. Edelmann," 1839; Edelmann's Autobiography, ("Selbstbiographie,") published by CARL R. W. KLOSE, Berlin, 1849.

Edema, ā′dĕh-mâ, (GERARD,) a Dutch landscape-painter, born in Friesland about 1655, is said to have travelled in America for artistic purposes, and finally settled in England. Died about 1700.

See BRYAN, "Dictionary of Painters."

E′den, (Sir FREDERICK MORTON,) an English diplomatist and writer on political economy, published in 1797 "The State of England," which, says McCulloch, "is the grand storehouse of information respecting the labouring classes of England." He also wrote "Friendly Societies," "Maritime Rights of Great Britain," and other works. From 1792 to 1796 he was ambassador to Berlin, Vienna, and Madrid. Died in 1809.

Eden, (GEORGE.) See AUCKLAND, LORD.

Eden, (Sir MORTON,) an English diplomatist, who was ambassador to several continental courts in the eighteenth century. He was raised to the peerage as Lord Henley, and died in 1802.

Eden, (RICHARD,) an Englishman, who was the first to publish collectively the results of maritime enterprise which followed the discovery of America. He translated, from the Latin, "Decade of Voyages," by Vertomanus, (1576,) and other works on navigation and geography. His "History of Travel in the West and East Indies" is partly original and partly translated. He is by some considered as superior to Hakluyt.

Eden, (WILLIAM.) See AUCKLAND, LORD.

E-de′nĭ-us, (JORDAN,) a Swedish savant, born in 1624, was chosen professor of theology at Upsal in 1659. He wrote an "Epitome of Ecclesiastical History," and other works. Died in 1666.

Eder, ā′der, (GEORG,) a German Catholic theologian, born at Freysingen in 1524. He was rector of the University of Vienna, and a councillor of the emperor Ferdinand. He wrote "Economy of the Scriptures," ("Economia Bibliorum," 1568,) often reprinted, and other works, mostly polemical. Died in 1586.

Ed′gar or **Eadgar,** a Saxon king of England, surnamed THE PEACEABLE, was the son of Edmund I. and Elgiva, and was born in 943 A.D. He ascended the throne at the death of his brother Edwy, in 959. Dunstan, Bishop of London, and afterwards primate, early acquired an ascendency over Edgar, and retained during the whole reign the chief control of affairs, which he directed to the aggrandizement of the church and clergy. Consequently, Edgar is pompously eulogized by the monkish chroniclers, though his morals were depraved. He married first Elfleda and then Elfrida, and founded many monasteries. It is usually said that he extirpated the wolves from England. He died in 975, and was succeeded by his son, Edward the Martyr.

See HUME's "History of England," chap. ii.

Edgar or **Eadgar Atheling,** a Saxon prince, was a grandson of King Edmund Ironside. His father Edward was exiled by Canute in 1017, and went to Hungary, where Edgar was born. At the death of Edward the Confessor, in 1066, Edgar was the nearest heir to the throne, and was proclaimed at London just after the battle of Hastings; but he submitted to William the Conqueror, who deprived him in consideration of his feeble character. He was induced to engage in several unsuccessful revolts against the Norman king, and took refuge in Scotland at the court of Malcolm, who had married his sister. About 1091 he was received in peace at the court of William Rufus. Died about 1120.

Ed′gar, King of Scotland, was the nephew of the preceding, and was the son of Malcolm III., who died in 1093. Donald Bane then usurped the throne, until Edgar Atheling raised an army and deposed him, in 1097, when Edgar became king. His sister Matilda became the wife of Henry I. of England. Edgar, after a peaceful reign, died in 1107, and was succeeded by his brother, Alexander I.

Edgeworth, (ABBÉ.) See FIRMONT.

Edgeworth, ĕj′worth, (MARIA,) a popular English authoress, born near Reading, Berkshire, January 1, 1767, was the daughter of Richard Lovell Edgeworth (see below) and his first wife, Miss Elers. In 1782 she removed with her father to his paternal estate at Edgeworthstown, in Ireland, where she continued to reside nearly all the remainder of her life. She was associated with her father in several literary labours, the first result of which was a "Treatise on Practical Education," in 1798, followed by an "Essay on Irish Bulls," (1802,) which was very successful. In 1801 she began to issue a series of novels of superior merit and of good moral tendency, which were received with general and lasting favour, viz., "Castle Rackrent," "Belinda," (1801,) "Patronage," (1814,) "Ormond," (1817,) "Helen," etc., (1834.) In 1823 she made a visit to Abbotsford, the home of Sir Walter Scott, who greatly admired her writings, and once said, "If I could but hit Miss Edgeworth's wonderful power of vivifying all her persons and making them live as beings in your mind, I should not be afraid." Besides the above-named works, she published several volumes, respectively entitled "Moral Tales," (1801,) "Popular Tales," (1804,) and "Tales of Fashionable Life," (1809-12,) and co-operated with her father in the "Parent's Assistant" and "Early Lessons." "The

ā, ē, ī, ō, ū, ȳ, *long;* ă, ĕ, ĭ, ŏ, ŭ, ў, *same, less prolonged;* ä, ĕ, ĭ, ŏ, *obscure;* fär, fàll, fàt; mĕt; nŏt; gōŏd; mōōn;

writings of Miss Edgeworth," says Lord Jeffrey, "exhibit a singular union of sober sense and inexhaustible invention, and a minute knowledge of all that distinguishes manners or touches on happiness in every condition of human fortune." Died in May, 1849.

See "Edinburgh Review," July, 1809, (vol. xiv.,) July, 1812, (vol. xx.,) and August, 1817, (vol. xxviii.;) Sir Walter Scott's critique in the "Edinburgh Review," January, 1814, (vol. xxii.;) also "Edinburgh Review" for October, 1867; "London Quarterly Review" for October, 1811.

Edgeworth, (Richard Lovell,) an ingenious English author and philosopher, born at Bath in 1744, was the father of Maria Edgeworth, the popular novelist. Much of his childhood was passed at Edgeworthstown, Ireland, where his father's estate was situated. While a student at Oxford, when he was only about nineteen, he married Miss Elers, with whom he resided for some time in Berkshire, where he formed an intimacy with Thomas Day and Dr. Darwin. He was distinguished by his genial character, versatile talents, and mechanical ingenuity. In 1780 he was chosen Fellow of the Royal Society. In 1782 he fixed his residence permanently at Edgeworthstown, where he was actively engaged in the education of his numerous children and in the duties of magistrate, legislator, and author. Besides the works in which his daughter co-operated, (see Edgeworth, Maria,) he wrote "Professional Education," "Letter on the Telegraph," and Memoirs of himself, and contributed to the "Philosophical Transactions" treatises on mechanics and natural philosophy. In the course of his life he married four wives, two of whom were sisters, named Sneyd. Died in 1817.

See "Memoirs of R. L. Edgeworth," by himself, and concluded by his daughter; "Edinburgh Review" for October, 1809, August, 1820; "London Quarterly Review" for July, 1820.

Edgeworth, (Roger,) an English Catholic divine, was chancellor of Wells in 1554. He published a volume of sermons. Died about 1560.

Ed-ğī'va or **Ogive,** Queen of France, was a daughter of Edward, King of the West Saxons, and a granddaughter of Alfred the Great. She was married to Charles the Simple of France in 919. Louis d'Outre-Mer was her son,

Edinburgh, Duke or See Alfred, (Ernest Albert.)

Edith. See Editha.

Ed'ī-tha, Saint, daughter of Edgar, King of England, and Wilfrida, took the monastic vows at the age of fifteen, and died about 984 A.D., aged twenty-three.

Editha or **E'dith,** an Anglo-Saxon queen, was a daughter of Earl Godwin, and was married in 1044 to King Edward the Confessor. Her virtues and accomplishments have been highly celebrated by historians and poets. King Edward is said to have treated her with neglect and severity.

Edmer. See Eadmer.

Edmondes, êd'münz, or **Ed'monds,** (Sir Clement,) an English writer, born in 1566, obtained some places at court. He wrote "Observations on the Commentaries of Cæsar," (1600–1609.) Died in 1622.

Edmondes or **Edmonds,** (Sir Thomas,) an English statesman, born at Plymouth in 1563, was employed with success in negotiations with several European courts in the reigns of Elizabeth and James I. In 1616 he was chosen privy councillor. His letters and papers were published by Dr. Birch. Died in 1639.

Edmonds. See Edmondes.

Ed'monds, (John W.,) an American painter, born in Hudson, New York, in 1806. In 1835 he commenced sending paintings in oil to the exhibitions of the Academy. Among these were "Sparking," "The City and Country Beaux," "Dominie Sampson," etc. In 1840 he embarked for Europe, and spent the subsequent winter and spring in Rome. Since his return he has followed his profession in New York.

See Tuckerman's "Book of the Artists."

Edmonds, (John Worth,) an American jurist and advocate of spiritualism, born at Hudson, New York, in 1799. He graduated at Union College, and subsequently practised law in New York. Being appointed, in 1843, one of the inspectors of State prisons, he effected an important reform in prison-discipline. He became one of the circuit judges of the State in 1845. He pub-

lished in 1853 his principal work, entitled "Spiritualism," (2 vols.)

See Livingston's "Portraits of Eminent Americans."

Ed'mond-son, (Henry,) an English scholar, born in 1607, wrote "Lingua Linguarum," (1655,) and a work on Latin Homonyms and Synonyms. Died in 1659.

Edmondson, (Joseph,) an English writer and antiquary, was appointed Mowbray herald-extraordinary in 1764. He wrote a "Companion to the Peerage," (1776,) a "Complete Body of Heraldry," (1780,) and several other esteemed works. Died in 1786.

Edmonstone, (Sir Archibald,) a British writer, born in 1795, published a "Journey to Two of the Oases of Upper Egypt," (1822,) "The Progress of Religion," a poem, (1842,) and other works.

Ed'mund the Martyr, King of the East Angles, born in 840 A.D., began to reign in 855. In 870 he was defeated in battle by the Danes under Hinguar and Hubba, who took him prisoner and put him to death.

Edmund or **Eadmund I.,** King of the Anglo-Saxons, born about 922, was the son of Edward the Elder and Edgiva his wife, and grandson of Alfred the Great. He succeeded his half-brother, Athelstane, in 941, and married Elgiva. His brief reign gave evidence of his courage, prudence, and other kingly qualifications. He was assassinated by Liof, an outlaw, at a feast in 946. He left two infant sons, Edwy and Edgar, and was succeeded by his brother Edred.

See Hume's "History of England," chap. ii.

Edmund or **Eadmund II.,** surnamed Ironside, a king of England of the Saxon dynasty, born in 989 A.D., was the son of Ethelred II., who died in 1016. Before this event, Edmund had signalized his valour in battle against the Danish invaders under Canute, and at his accession he found the greater part of the kingdom in the power of that enemy. After the Danes gained a victory at Assandun, Edmund and Canute agreed by a treaty to divide the kingdom, of which the former received the southern and the latter the northern part. Edmund survived this treaty about a month, and, as Hume thinks, was murdered in 1016, when Canute became master of the whole kingdom. Edmund's half-brother, Edward the Confessor, afterwards became king. Freeman calls Edmund "a true king of men, a hero worthy to wield the sword of Ælfred [Alfred] and Æthelstan."

See Freeman, "History of the Norman Conquest," vol. i. chap. v., p. 419; Hume, "History of England," chap. iii.; Turner, "History of the Anglo-Saxons."

Edmund of Langley, Duke of York, born in 1341, was the fifth son of Edward III. of England, and was the head of the house of York, famous in the war of the Roses. He married Isabella of Castile, and left two sons, Edward and Richard. Died in 1402.

Edmund, Saint, an English prelate, sometimes called Edmund Rich and Edmund of Pontigny, born at Abingdon, became Archbishop of Canterbury in 1234. He is said to have been the first who taught logic at Oxford. He died in 1242, and was canonized by Innocent IV. in 1249.

See W. F. Hook, "Lives of the Archbishops of Canterbury," vol. iii. chap. iii.

Ed'mund Plan-tağ'ę-net, Earl of Kent, the son of Edward I. of England, was born in 1301. In the reign of Edward II. he aided the queen, Isabella, to depose the king and to crown the young prince Edward III. He was executed on a charge of treason in 1330.

Edom, a name of Esau, the son of Isaac. See Esau.

Ed'red or **Eadred,** King of the Anglo-Saxons, was the younger son of Edward the Elder, and brother of Edmund I., whom he succeeded in 946 A.D. In this reign the ambitious Dunstan acquired the ascendency which he maintained through several ensuing reigns. He died in 955, and was succeeded by his nephew Edwy.

See Hume, "History of England," chap. ii.

Edrees or **Edrîs,** ed-rees', I., a descendant of Alee, son-in-law of Mohammed, was the founder of the dynasty of the Edrisites or Edrisides, which reigned in Africa nearly two hundred years. When his party was defeated by the Abbassides in 784 A.D., he fled to Barbary, or Mauritania, where he was recognized as imam, or chief, about

789. He was poisoned in 793 by an emissary of Haroun-al-Raschid.

Edrees or **Edrîs II.**, a son of the preceding, born in 793, succeeded to the throne, and is represented as a learned, wise, and just ruler. He founded the city of Fez, and reigned in peace. He died in 828, and was succeeded by his son Mohammed.

See IBN-KHALDOUN, "Histoire des Berbères," translated by SLANE, 1854.

Edreesee or **Edrîsî**, ed-ree'see, an eminent Arabian geographer, born at Ceuta, Africa, about 1100, was a descendant of the dynasty above named, which ceased to reign in 919. He lived at the court of Roger II. of Sicily, for whom he made a silver terrestrial globe and wrote his celebrated treatise on Geography, (1154.) In 1619 Gabriel Sionita and J. Hesronita published a Latin version of an abridgment of Edreesee's Geography; and since that time the manuscript of the entire work has been found and translated into French by M. Jaubert, (1836-40.)

See HAJI-KHALFA, "Lexicon Bibliographicum;" CASIRI, "Bibliotheca Arabico-Hispana."

Ed'ric, Duke of Mercia, was a treacherous minister of Ethelred II. When England was invaded by the Danes, he deserted, and fought against the Anglo-Saxon king. He was put to death by Canute.

Ed'ridge, (HENRY,) an English painter of landscapes and miniatures, born at Paddington in 1768; died in 1821.

Edrîs. See EDREES.

Edrîsî. See EDREESEE.

Ed'ward or **Eadward I.**, surnamed THE ELDER, King of the Anglo-Saxons, was the third son of Alfred the Great and Alswitha. At the death of Alfred, in 901 A.D., he was acknowledged as his successor by the Wittena-gemote. He inherited his father's military talents, and found abundant occasion to exercise them. He defeated his cousin Ethelwald, who raised an army to contest his title to the throne, and waged a successful war against the Northumbrians and Danes. He married two or three wives, the last of whom was Elgiva, and left three sons, Athelstane, Edmund, and Edred, who all reigned successively. Died in 925.

See HUME's "History of England," chap. ii.

Edward or **Eadward II.**, surnamed THE MARTYR, King of the Anglo-Saxons, was the eldest son of Edgar, and great-grandson of the preceding. He was born about 960 A.D., and succeeded his father in 975. His step-mother, Elfrida, took measures to obtain the crown for her son Ethelred; but she was defeated by Saint Dunstan, the primate of England. A council having been assembled during this reign at Calne to decide between the secular clergy and the monks of Saint Dunstan, the part of the floor on which the former sat suddenly gave way. The monks claimed this as a miracle in their favour, and consequently prevailed. Edward was assassinated by order of Elfrida in 978, and was succeeded by his half-brother, Ethelred II.

See HUME's "History of England," chap. ii.

Edward or **Eadward III.**, surnamed THE CONFESSOR, King of the Anglo-Saxons, was the son of Ethelred II., (by his second wife, Emma of Normandy,) and was half-brother of Edmund Ironside. He was born at Islip about 1004. When England was invaded by the victorious Danes, Edward and his mother found refuge with the Duke of Normandy, and remained there till 1040. Canute, having conquered England, married Edward's mother, Emma, in 1017. When Hardicanute died, in 1042, Edward, who was the half-brother of the late king, was proclaimed his successor. In 1044 he married Editha, daughter of Earl Godwin, but with the express condition that she should not share his bed: hence he was canonized with the title of "Confessor." He showed partiality to the Normans, and in his reign a powerful Norman party was formed in the island. He died, without issue, in January, 1066, and was succeeded by his wife's brother, Harold, whose title was disputed by the Duke of Normandy. Edward was the last of the Saxon line that reigned in England.

See HUME, "History of England," chap. iii.; JEROME PORTER, "Life of Saint Edward, King and Confessor," 1710.

Edward I., King of England, surnamed LONGSHANKS, born at Westminster in 1239, was the eldest son of Henry III. and Eleanor, daughter of the Count of Provence. He was married in early youth to Eleanor of Castile. In 1263 he took a prominent part in the civil war between his father and the barons under the Earl of Leicester, who took him prisoner in 1264. Having escaped from custody in 1265, he gained a complete victory over Leicester at Evesham. After the end of this civil war, his next important enterprise was a crusade to the Holy Land in 1271, where he maintained his reputation for prowess. On his homeward journey he found that his father had died, in 1272, and he was crowned soon after his arrival, in 1274. He began the conquest of Wales in 1277, and completed it in 1282, when Llewellyn, prince of that country, was slain in battle. In 1291, the numerous competitors for the throne of Scotland, then vacant, having referred their claims to Edward as lord paramount, he decided in favour of John Baliol, and received from him the oath of fealty, thus paving the way to the conquest of that kingdom. The Scotch in 1294 took arms to regain their independence; but Edward speedily overpowered them, dethroned Baliol, and seized the kingdom. The celebrated and heroic William Wallace renewed the contest in 1297, gained a victory at Stirling, and expelled the English troops from all the Scotch fortresses. The war was alternately suspended by truce and feebly prosecuted until 1303, when Edward invaded Scotland with a large army and effected its temporary subjection. Wallace was taken, and hanged in London in 1305. Edward died in 1307, while on his march to Scotland, where Robert Bruce had again raised the national standard against him. He was one of the most able, ambitious, and politic princes that ever filled the English throne; but his character was deeply disgraced by his vindictive treatment of Wallace and by other acts of injustice. His reign is rendered memorable by the confirmation of the Great Charter, the institution of the House of Commons, and great improvement in common law.

See HUME, "History of England," chaps. xiii. and xiv.; also, the character of Edward I. in GARDINER's "History of England from 1603 to 1616," pp. 15 and 16; BURTON, "History of Scotland," vol. ii. chaps. xviii.-xxii.

Edward II., King of England, the eldest surviving son of the preceding, was born at Caernarvon, Wales, in 1284. In his minority he became subject to the pernicious influence of his favourite, Piers Gaveston, who was banished in 1300 by Edward I. In 1301 Edward was created Prince of Wales, and in July, 1307, he became king. One of his first acts was to recall Gaveston from exile and create him Earl of Cornwall. In 1308 he married Isabella, daughter of Philip V. of France, a corrupt and ambitious woman. The insolence of Gaveston, who had acquired a complete ascendency over his imbecile king, provoked the barons to form a league against that favourite, who was executed in 1312. In 1314 Edward invaded Scotland with a large army, which in the same year was routed with great loss by Bruce at Bannockburn, and Scottish independence was thus secured. The king's new favourite, Hugh Spencer or Despencer, involved him in another quarrel with his barons. The queen, who hated the favourite and despised her consort, put herself at the head of a powerful party, who took arms in 1326 with the avowed purpose of removing Spencer from power. The king being generally deserted, the queen's party easily prevailed; Spencer was executed, and Edward was dethroned and confined in prison. The king's son, a minor, was proclaimed in Parliament as Edward III., under the regency of Isabella and her favourite, Roger de Mortimer, the latter of whom is charged with causing the murder of the deposed king, which was perpetrated, with circumstances of great atrocity, in Berkeley Castle in 1327.

See HUME, "History of England," chap. xiv.; FALKLAND, (HENRY CARY,) "History of King Edward II.," 1680.

Edward III., King of England, born at Windsor in 1312, was the eldest son of Edward II. and Isabella of France. He was proclaimed king on January 25, 1327, under the nominal regency of twelve nobles and bishops, while the queen and Mortimer exercised the power in reality. In 1328 Edward married Philippa of Hainault, and concluded a treaty of peace with Robert Bruce, King

ā, ē, ī, ō, ū, ȳ, *long;* ă, ĕ, ŏ, same, less prolonged; ă, ĕ, ĭ, ŏ, ŭ, ў, *short;* a, e, i, o, *obscure;* fär, fȧll, fât; mêt; nŏt; gŏŏd; mŏŏn;

of Scotland. In 1330 the young king ordered the arrest of Mortimer, who after trial was put to death. The queen-mother was at the same time confined to her own house, and ceased to exercise political power. After the death of King Robert, Edward, in violation of the treaty, supported Edward Baliol in his pretensions to the Scottish throne, and in 1333 defeated the Scotch at Halidon Hill, when Baliol became for a time master of Scotland. But repeated invasions by the English were required in the ensuing years to prevent his expulsion ; for the Scotch detested him as a vassal and partisan of the English king.

The attention of Edward was diverted from Scotland by a new and important project, namely, the conquest of France, the crown of which he claimed by inheritance, as nephew of the late king, Charles IV., (who left no male issue,) while Philip VI. was recognized as the lawful heir by the French people. Hostilities began in 1340 by a sea-fight in which the English were victorious, after which a long truce was concluded. Renewing the war in 1346, Edward, with his son the Black Prince, invaded France and gained a great victory at Crécy. After a long siege, Calais was surrendered to the English king, (1347,) who was prevented from a disgraceful act of vengeance against six citizens, who offered their lives as a sacrifice for the city, only by the entreaties of Queen Philippa. A truce of about eight years followed the reduction of Calais.

In September, 1356, the Black Prince gained a complete victory at Poitiers, where the French king John was taken prisoner. In 1360 a treaty of peace was made, by which Edward retained several French provinces. Charles V., having become King of France, renewed the war in 1370, and in a few years recovered nearly all that the English had conquered. The Black Prince died in 1376, and King Edward in 1377, leaving the crown to his grandson, Richard II. The reign of Edward, though arbitrary, was very popular with his subjects, elated with the glory which attended his military enterprises, and favoured with domestic peace and prosperity.

See HUME, "History of England," chaps. xv. and xvi. ; ROBERT HOWARD, "History of the Reigns of Edward III. and Richard II.," 1690 ; WILLIAM LONGMAN, "Life and Times of Edward III.," 2 vols., 1869 ; VIDALIN, "Édouard III et la Régence, ou Essai sur les Mœurs du XIVe Siècle," Paris, 1843.

Edward IV., King of England, born at Rouen in 1441, was the son of Richard, Duke of York, who was a grandson of Edmund of York, a younger son of Edward III. This Richard also inherited from his mother the title of Earl of March, and with that title all the right to the throne transmitted by Lionel of Clarence, another son of Edward III. The subject of this article, then styled the Earl of March, first appears on the scene of the civil wars of York and Lancaster in 1460, when his army defeated the Lancastrians near Northampton, and took the king (Henry VI.) a prisoner. In the same year his father, the Duke of York, was defeated and killed in the battle of Wakefield, at which Edward was not present. Having gained a battle at Mortimer's Cross, he entered London, was received with favour and acclamation, and was proclaimed king, March 4, 1461. His bravery, personal beauty, affability, and other popular qualities contributed much to his success.

But Margaret of Anjou, the ambitious and indomitable queen of Henry VI., soon raised another army to renew the contest. At Towton, in 1461, the Lancastrians were defeated with great loss, and Margaret escaped to Scotland. In 1464 the Lancastrian army was again defeated, at Hexham, Henry VI. was made prisoner, hostilities were suspended for several years, and the war appeared to be terminated. In 1464 Edward married Elizabeth Woodville, a person of rather obscure condition, by which he gave great offence to the nobility, especially to the Earl of Warwick, "the King-Maker," a great leader of the Yorkist party. This nobleman, conspiring with Queen Margaret, compelled Edward to retire to Holland in 1470, when Henry VI. was released from the Tower to assume again the form of royalty. The next year Edward returned with an army, gained a victory at Barnet, where Warwick was slain, and recovered the throne. At the great battle of Tewkesbury, May, 1471, the Lan-

castrians were finally defeated, and Margaret, with her son, fell into the hands of the victor. She was confined in the Tower, and her son was murdered in Edward's presence. Such was the tragical end of the War of the Roses, in which the old nobility of England was almost annihilated. The subsequent events of this reign were unimportant. Edward died in 1483, leaving the crown to his son, Edward V.

Edward IV. is described by Hume as "a prince more splendid and showy than either prudent or virtuous ; brave, though cruel; addicted to pleasure, though capable of activity in great emergencies." He forms a prominent character in Bulwer's "Last of the Barons."

See HUME, "History of England," chap. xxii. ; WILLIAM HABINGTON, "History of King Edward IV.," 1640.

Edward V., King of England, the eldest son of Edward IV. and Elizabeth Woodville, was born in Westminster in 1470, and succeeded his father on the 9th of April, 1483. His uncle, Richard, Duke of Gloucester, by the will of the late king, became regent during the minority. This wicked and crafty usurper, aspiring to wear the crown himself, obtained possession of the young king and his brother, whom he secretly ordered to be put to death. They disappeared in June, 1483 ; and it is generally reported and believed that they were suffocated with pillows in the Tower of London.

See HUME, "History of England," chap. xxiii. ; MISS STRICKLAND, "Lives of the Bachelor Kings of England," 1861 ; W. HEPWORTH DIXON, "Her Majesty's Tower," 1869.

Edward VI., King of England, born at Hampton Court, October 12, 1537, was the only surviving son of Henry VIII. and Jane Seymour. He succeeded his father January 28, 1547, the government during his minority being confided, by the will of Henry VIII., to sixteen executors, who elected for their president the young king's uncle, Edward Seymour, Earl of Hertford. The latter, who was created Duke of Somerset and assumed the title of lord protector, led an army against the Scotch in order to compel the fulfilment of a certain treaty by the marriage of Edward VI. with Mary Stuart. The English gained a victory at Pinkie in 1547, but did not effect their purpose. Somerset favoured the Protestant religion, and used effectual measures to establish it. The "Bloody Statute," and other acts, of the former reign were repealed in Parliament, images were removed from the churches, and the Book of Common Prayer was ordered to be used, (1548.) About 1550 the Protector was supplanted by John Dudley, Earl of Warwick and Duke of Northumberland, whose son married Lady Jane Grey, a member of the royal family of Tudor. When the death of the young king was evidently at hand, he was induced by Northumberland to settle the succession in favour of Lady Jane Grey. Died in 1553.

See HUME, "History of England," chaps. xxxiv. and xxxv. ; MISS STRICKLAND, "Lives of the Bachelor Kings of England," 1861 ; SHARON TURNER, "History of the Reigns of Edward VI., Mary, and Elizabeth," 1829 ; VAN DER HOLK, "Leven van Edward de Seste," 1690.

Ed'wạrd [Port. DUARTE, doo-aR'tả] **I.,** King of Portugal, was a son of John I., whom he succeeded in 1433. His mother was an English princess, Philippa of Lancaster. He is said to have been a moderate, wise, and enlightened prince ; but his reign was not prosperous. He died young, in 1438, leaving the throne to his son, Alfonzo V.

See LOPEZ, "Elogios dos Reys de Portugal."

Edward, Prince of Wales, surnamed THE BLACK PRINCE, (so called from the colour of his armour,) a heroic and idolized representative of the spirit of chivalry, was the eldest son of Edward III. and Philippa of Hainault. He was born at Woodstock in 1330, and at the age of fifteen accompanied his father in the invasion of France. He commanded the main body of the English at the victory of Crécy, the glory of which was ascribed to him, and then adopted the motto *Ich dien*, ("I serve,") which is still worn by his successors. In 1356 he alone commanded at the battle of Poitiers, where he won applause both by his military skill and his humanity to the vanquished. He married his cousin Joanna, daughter of the Earl of Kent, in 1361, and, being created Prince of Aquitaine, held his court at Bordeaux. On account of his declining health, he returned to England in 1371, and died in 1376. His son became King Richard II.

See HUME, "History of England," chap. xvi.; ARTHUR COLLINS, "Life of Edward, Prince of Wales," 1740; G. P. R. JAMES, "History of the Life of Edward the Black Prince," 1839.

Edward [Port. DUARTE] OF BRAGANZA, a Portuguese prince, born in 1605, was brother of John IV., who became King of Portugal in 1640. At this time Edward was lieutenant-general in the army of the emperor Ferdinand III. The Spanish court, jealous of his military talents, persuaded the emperor to deliver him into their power. He was imprisoned at Milan in 1641, and died in 1649.

See GOUVEA, "Perfidia de Alemania y de Castilla en la Prision y Proceso de Don Duarte," 1652.

Edward, (CHARLES,) THE PRETENDER. See CHARLES EDWARD.

Ed'ward Plan-tag'e-net, born in 1475, was a son of George, Duke of Clarence, and was styled Earl of Warwick. He was confined in the Tower by Henry VII. in 1485, and executed, as an accomplice of Perkin Warbeck, in 1499.

Edwardes, éd'wardz, (Sir HERBERT BENJAMIN,) a distinguished English officer, born in Shropshire in 1819 or 1820. He entered the army of the East India Company in 1840, and fought at Moodkee and Sobraon in 1845. Having obtained the rank of lieutenant, he gained a decisive victory over the Dewan Moolraj, near the Chenab, in 1848. For this service he was made an extra Companion of the Bath. He published in 1851 "A Year on the Punjaub Frontier in 1848–9." He was appointed commissioner of Peshawur in 1853, and knighted in 1866. Died in December, 1868.

Ed'wards, (BELA BATES,) an American theologian, born in Southampton, Massachusetts, in 1802, graduated at Amherst College in 1824. He founded the "American Quarterly Observer" in 1833, edited the "Biblical Repository" from 1835 to 1838, and the "Bibliotheca Sacra" from 1844 to 1852. In 1837 he became professor of Hebrew, and in 1848 professor of biblical literature, at Andover Seminary. Died in 1852.

See "Writings of Bela B. Edwards, with a Memoir," by E. A. PARK, (Boston, 1853.)

Ed'wards, (BRYAN,) M.P., an English writer, born at Westbury in 1743, removed in 1759 to Jamaica, where he remained many years and became a wealthy planter. He published in 1793 a "History of the British Colonies in the West Indies," an interesting and well-written work, which acquired great popularity. He also wrote a "History of Saint Domingo." Returning to England, he was elected to Parliament in 1796, and died in 1800.

Edwards, (EDWARD,) an English artist, born in London in 1738, was an excellent draughtsman. He became an associate of the Royal Academy in 1773, and teacher of perspective at that institution in 1788. He wrote a "Treatise on Perspective," (1803,) and "Anecdotes of English Painters," (1808.) Died in 1806.

Edwards, (EDWARD,) an English bibliographer, born in London in 1812, published about 1860 a valuable work entitled "Memoirs of Libraries, together with a Practical Hand-Book of Library Economy." He has written many other works on public libraries.

Edwards, (GEORGE,) an eminent English naturalist and artist, born at Westham or Stratford, Essex, about 1693. Having travelled on the continent, he applied himself after his return to the study of natural history, supporting himself by drawing and colouring figures of animals. In 1743 he began to issue his excellent "Natural History of Birds," with coloured plates, which was received with favour and procured his admission to the Royal Society in 1757. He wrote, also, "Gleanings of Natural History," (1763.) Died in 1773.

See "Memoirs of the Life, etc. of G. Edwards," London, 1776.

Edwards, (GEORGE,) M.D., an English writer on politics and political economy, born in 1751, lived in London. Among his numerous productions are "Political Interests of Great Britain," and "Means adequate to the Present Crisis." Died in 1823.

Edwards, (GUILLAUME FRÉDÉRIC,) M.D., a brother of Milne-Edwards, born in Jamaica in 1777, was a distinguished physiologist and ethnologist. He lived in Bruges and in Paris. His "Physiological Characters of Human Races considered in Relation with History" (1839) placed him in the first rank of French ethnologists. He became a member of the Institute in 1832. He wrote (in French) "On the Influence of Physical Agents on Life," (1824,) and other scientific works. Died near Paris in 1842.

Edwards, (HENRY MILNE.) See MILNE-EDWARDS.

Edwards, (JOHN,) D.D., a learned English Calvinistic divine, born at Hertford in 1637, was a son of Thomas Edwards, author of "Gangræna." He became minister of Trinity College Church, Cambridge, in 1664. He wrote, besides many other works, "The Authority, Style, and Perfection of the Books of the Old and New Testaments," (3 vols., 1693–96,) and "Theologia Reformata," (2 vols., 1713.) Died in 1716.

Edwards, (JONATHAN,) D.D., an English divine, born at Wrexham in 1629, became rector of Hinton in 1681. He wrote a "Preservative against Socinianism," (1698–1703.) Died in 1712.

Edwards, (JONATHAN,) the greatest metaphysician that America has produced, and one of the greatest that ever lived, was born at East Windsor, Connecticut, the 5th of October, 1703. His father, Timothy Edwards, was the minister at East Windsor, and was a man of rare learning for those times. Jonathan was the only son out of thirteen children. He began the study of Latin when he was but six years old. At a very early age he wrote essays and other compositions, indicating an inquiring mind and reasoning powers of an uncommon order for one so young. When he was ten, he wrote a paper ridiculing the idea, which some one had advanced, of the materiality of the soul. While still a child, he was the subject of deep and earnest religious impressions. In a letter written at the age of twelve, he speaks of "a very remarkable outpouring of the Spirit of God" in his native place, in which event he evidently felt a deep interest. He entered Yale College in 1716, and before leaving that institution as a graduate, in 1720, he is said to have completely reasoned out for himself his great doctrine of the freedom of the will. After his conversion, which, according to his view of the subject, did not take place until his seventeenth year, the whole universe seemed changed in his sight ; God's excellency, wisdom, purity, and love were revealed to him "in the sun, moon, and stars, in the clouds and blue sky, and in the grass, flowers, and trees, in the water and in all nature." After taking his degree, he remained two years in New Haven, studying for the ministry ; and before he had completed his nineteenth year he began to preach to a Presbyterian congregation in the city of New York. In less than a year he returned to New Haven, and in September, 1723, took his degree of master of arts. In 1724 he became a tutor in Yale College, where he remained about two years. In February, 1727, he became pastor of a church at Northampton, and not long after was married to Miss Sarah Pierrepont, of New Haven, who in her unaffected and fervent piety, in the purity, sweetness, and elevation of her character, and in her entire devotion to what she felt to be right, may be said to have been his perfect counterpart. After many years of comparative happiness,—not that happiness which results from the enjoyment of indolent ease, but from duties laboriously, conscientiously, and faithfully performed,—his faith and virtue were destined to undergo a great trial. A lax custom had crept into the Church of admitting to the communion-table all those professing with the congregation, without inquiring whether they were truly regenerate, and without regard to the spiritual consistency of their life or character. Edwards believed it to be required of him to insist on a purer and higher standard. At length, after years of opposition, he was driven forth, like Calvin, (whose religious views and entire devotion to duty he so ably represented,) from his chosen field of gospel labour, not knowing whither he should go, and without any outward means of support for his numerous family. He was soon after offered the situation of missionary to the Housatonnuck Indians at Stockbridge. His friends in Scotland sent it, it is said, a considerable contribution for the support of his family, and his scanty income was eked out by the industry of his wife and daughters, whose delicate handiwork was sent to Boston to be sold. It was during this period of his life that he elaborated and wrote out his celebrated work on the Freedom of the Will. In this work he exhibits a power of close and subtile reasoning which perhaps has never been equalled by any other writer. Whatever we may think of his doctrine that philosophic necessity is compatible with freedom of the will, rightly defined, and with human responsibility, we may safely assume that, as the ultimate interests of truth are necessarily promoted by all true philosophic investigation, they must be best promoted by that investigation which is the most thorough and exhaustive. In the reasoning of Edwards we see what the perfection of human logic can accomplish, and are thus enabled to discern more clearly its just limitations and necessary deficiencies.

About the close of 1757 Edwards left his field of labour among the Indians, and reluctantly accepted the position of president of Princeton College, in New Jersey. He died there, of the smallpox, in March, 1758.

In person, Edwards was tall (above six feet) and slender. He is said to have been, in middle life, much emaciated by intense and constant application to study. "He had," says his grandson, "a high, broad, bold forehead, and an eye unusually piercing and luminous; and on his whole countenance the features of his mind —perspicacity, sincerity, and benevolence—were so strongly impressed, that no one could behold it without at once discovering the clearest indications of great intellectual and moral elevation." (See "Life," by Sereno E. Dwight.)

He left a great number of miscellaneous writings. The titles of his principal works are the following : "A Treatise concerning the Religious Affections," (published in 1746;) "An Inquiry into the Qualifications for Full Communion in the Church," (1749;) "An Inquiry into the Modern Prevailing Notions respecting that Freedom of the Will which is supposed to be essential to Moral Agency," etc., (1754;) (this is his most celebrated work, of which we have spoken above;) "The Great Christian Doctrine of Original Sin Defended," (about 1757;) "The History of Redemption," (1774;) "A Dissertation concerning the End for which God created the World," (1789;) and "A Dissertation concerning the True Nature of Christian Virtue," (1788.)

See EDWARDS DWIGHT, "Life of Jonathan Edwards," 1830; SAMUEL HOPKINS, "Life of Jonathan Edwards ;" SAMUEL MILLER, "Life of Jonathan Edwards," in SPARKS'S "American Biography," vol. viii.; ALLIBONE, "Dictionary of Authors ;" GRISWOLD, "Prose Writers of America ;" DUYCKINCK, "Cyclopædia of American Literature," vol. i.

Edwards, (JONATHAN,) an eminent minister, born at Northampton, Massachusetts, in 1745, was a son of the preceding. He graduated at the College of New Jersey in 1765, and was tutor at Princeton College for two years, (1767-68.) In 1769 he became pastor of the church at White Haven, near New Haven, Connecticut, where he remained until 1795, when he was dismissed on account of his religious opinions. He was appointed president of Union College, Schenectady, in 1799. He was a man of superior talents and great penetration. He published a number of sermons and treatises on theology. Died at Schenectady in August, 1801.

See a "Memoir of J. Edwards," by TRYON EDWARDS, his grandson; SPRAGUE, "Annals of the American Pulpit."

Edwards, (JONATHAN W.,) an eminent American lawyer, grandson of the celebrated Jonathan Edwards, was born in New Haven, Connecticut, in 1772. He graduated at Yale, with distinguished honours, in 1789. On taking his second degree, in 1791, he attacked with so much ability the law granting a double portion of an estate to the eldest son (if the father died intestate) as to cause its repeal. He practised at Hartford. Died in 1831.

Edwards, (JUSTIN,) D.D., an American divine and author, born in Westhampton, Massachusetts, in 1787. He graduated at Williams College in 1810, and was afterwards for fifteen years pastor at Andover, and two years in Boston, when he resigned his ministerial charge and devoted himself to the cause of temperance, the observance of the Sabbath, and to educational and literary labours. He was for six years president of the theological seminary at Andover. As secretary of the American Temperance Society, he prepared the "Tem-

perance Manual," of which about two hundred thousand copies have been printed. He was also one of the founders of the Boston Tract Society. Died in 1853.

Edwards, (NINIAN,) an American judge and Senator, born in Montgomery county, Maryland, in 1775. He became chief justice of Kentucky, and Governor of Illinois in 1809. He represented Illinois in the Senate of the United States from 1818 to 1824, and became Governor of that State in 1826. Died in 1833.

Edwards, (RICHARD,) an English dramatic poet, born in Somersetshire in 1523, was a Fellow of one of the Oxford Colleges. He was the principal contributor to the "Paradise of Dainty Devises," and author of "Damon and Pythias," a tragedy, acted in 1566. His poems were once popular. Died about 1566.

Edwards, (THOMAS,) an English Presbyterian theologian, was a violent opponent of the Independents, against whom he wrote his "Gangræna," (1646,) a very vituperative work. He also wrote a "Treatise against Toleration," (1647.) He was driven out of the country, and died in Holland in 1647.

Edwards, (THOMAS,) an English critic, born in or near London in 1699, was a student of law, but did not practise. He gained distinction by his "Canons of Criticism," (1747; 7th edition, 1765,) in which he amused the public at the expense of Warburton on the subject of an edition of Shakspeare published by the latter. Died in 1757.

See "Biographia Britannica."

Edwards, (THOMAS,) an English divine, born at Coventry in 1729, became rector of a church in that place in 1758, and vicar of Nuneaton about 1770. He published, besides other works, a "New English Translation of the Psalms from the Original Hebrew," (1755,) and "Selecta Theocriti Idyllia," (1779.) Died in 1785.

Edwards, (TRYON,) an American theologian, a son of Jonathan W., noticed above, was born at Hartford, Connecticut, in 1809. He graduated at Yale College in 1828, and became pastor of a church at New London, Connecticut, in 1845. He published several religious works.

Edwards, (WILLIAM,) an English engineer and architect, noted as a builder of bridges, was born in Glamorganshire in 1719; died in 1789.

See "Pursuit of Knowledge under Difficulties," vol. ii., 1839.

Ed'win, King of Northumbria, was the son of King Ella, who died about 590 A.D. He began to reign in 617, and became one of the most powerful princes of the island. In his reign Christianity became the established religion. He was defeated in battle and slain by Penda, King of the Mercians, in 633 A.D.

See HUME'S "History of England," chap. i.

Ed'win, (JOHN,) an excellent English comedian, born in London in 1749, first appeared on the public stage in 1765. He performed many years with success, especially in ludicrous characters. Died in 1794.

See J. WILLIAMS, "Eccentricities of John Edwin," London, 1781.

Ed'wy̆, written also **Eadwig,** King of the Anglo-Saxons, born about 938 A.D., was the eldest son of Edmund I., who died in 946. Edwy became king at the death of his uncle Edred in 955. He appears to have incurred the enmity of Dunstan and the monks by marrying Elgiva, who was rather nearly related to him by blood. Edwy banished Dunstan, and the friends of the latter retaliated by murdering Elgiva and instigating a successful rebellion in favour of the king's brother, Edgar. Died or was killed in 958.

See HUME'S "History of England," chap. ii.

Edzardi, êt-saR'dee, (ESDRAS,) a German Orientalist, born in 1629 at Hamburg, where he taught Hebrew with a high reputation. Died in 1708.

His son GEORG ELEAZAR (1661-1727) was an eminent professor of Oriental languages at Hamburg.

Edzardi, (SEBASTIAN,) a German theologian, brother of the preceding, born at Hamburg in 1673; died in 1736.

Eeckhout, van den, vän den āk'höwt, written also **Eckhout,** (ANTON,) a Flemish painter of flowers and fruit, born at Bruges about 1656. He went with Louis de Deyster to Italy, where he produced many pictures, the figures of which were painted by Deyster. He afterwards worked with success in Lisbon, where he was assassinated in 1695. The author of the deed was never discovered. His works present an immense variety of flowers, and are highly prized.

See DESCAMPS, "Vies des Peintres Flamands," etc.

Eeckhout, van den, (GERBRAND,) an excellent Dutch painter, born at Amsterdam in 1621. He was a pupil and successful imitator of Rembrandt, and excelled both in history and portraits. His compositions, in the opinion of Descamps, are rich and judicious. He had a rare and superior talent for expressing the character in the countenances of his portraits. Among his master-pieces are "Christ in the midst of the Doctors," "Abraham dismissing Hagar," and a portrait of his own father. Died in 1674.

See DESCAMPS, "Vies des Peintres Flamands," etc.

Eelkhanian. See ILKHANIAN.

Eète, the French of ÆETES, which see.

Effen, van, văn ĕf'fen, (JUSTUS,) a popular Dutch *littérateur,* born at Utrecht in 1684. In 1711 he began to issue, weekly, in imitation of Addison's "Spectator," "The Misanthrope," in French, which was continued to the end of 1712. He was chief editor of the "Literary Journal," an able review, published in French at the Hague, (1715-18.) He was employed as secretary of embassy to London in 1715, and again about 1727, and made successful French translations of "Robinson Crusoe" and the "Tale of a Tub." From 1731 to 1735 he issued, in Dutch, the "Hollandsche Spectator," another happy imitation of the model English essayist, which obtained more permanent popularity than his other works. The most of his publications were anonymous. Died in 1735.

See MORÉRI, "Dictionnaire Historique;" "Nouvelle Biographie Générale;" "Fraser's Magazine" for July, 1854.

Effiat, (HENRI COIFFIER.) See CINQ-MARS.

Effiat, d', dầ'fe-ậ', (ANTOINE Coiffier—kwã'fe-ậ',) MARQUIS, a French general and statesman, born in 1581. After serving several years in the army, he was sent as ambassador to London in 1624, and was appointed superintendent of finances in 1626. As lieutenant-general, he commanded in Piedmont in 1630, and was made marshal of France the next year. He was a friend of Lord Bacon, who left him a legacy. He died in 1632, leaving a high reputation for civil and military talents. He had three sons, one of whom was Henry, Marquis of Cinq-Mars.

See SISMONDI, "Histoire des Français," chap. xxiii.

Ef'fing-ham, LORD, an English nobleman, who resigned his commission in the British army, about 1775, rather than fight against the cause of American liberty.

Eg'bert, Ec'bert, or **Ecgbert,** an Anglo-Saxon prelate, born about 678 A.D., was a brother of the King of Northumberland. He became Archbishop of York in 732. Died in 766.

Egbert or **Ecgbert,** surnamed THE GREAT, King of the West Saxons, (Wessex,) was a descendant of Cerdic, the first king of Wessex. After passing some years at the court of Charlemagne, he became king in 800 A.D. In 823 he defeated the Mercians at Ellendune, and in a few years completed the conquest of Mercia and Northumbria. By his prudent policy and military success all the states of the Heptarchy were first united into one kingdom, whose limits were nearly identical with those of England proper. This occurred in 827. In 835 an army of Danes invaded the island and were defeated by Egbert. He died in 836, or, according to Hume, in 838, leaving the throne to his son, Ethelwulf.

See HUME's "History of England," chaps. i. and ii.; FREEMAN's "Norman Conquest."

Egede, ěg'eh-deh, (HANS,) the founder of the Danish missions of Greenland, was born at Harstad, in Norway, in 1686, and was ordained pastor of Vaagen in 1707. Having for many years cherished the desire of converting the Greenlanders, he obtained the assistance of the king, Frederick IV., and a trading-company was formed to co-operate with the mission. In 1721 Egede sailed with one ship and forty-five persons. They were kindly received by the natives, many of whom were converted. The Danes were unable to subsist without frequent supplies from the mother-country, and the trading-company

was dissolved in 1727. Egede pursued his purpose with constancy through great hardships and privations, until the death of his wife in 1735. Some Moravian missionaries having arrived to continue the work, he then returned to Copenhagen, where he became superintendent of a seminary for the Greenland mission, with the title of bishop, and wrote a narrative of his enterprise. Died in 1758.

See HOST, "Literary History of Denmark under Christian VII.," (in German;) LUND, "Biskop H. Egedes Levnet," 1778; BODEMANN, "H. Egede der Apostel der Grönländer," 1853; ERSCH und GRUBER, "Allgemeine Encyklopaedie."

Egede, (PAUL,) a son of the preceding, born in 1708, was a fellow-labourer in the mission above named, and remained in Greenland until 1740. He then returned to Copenhagen, was chosen a member of the College of Missions in 1775, and Bishop of Greenland in 1776. Died in 1789.

Egée, the French of ÆGEUS, which see.

Egenod, ĕzh'no', (HENRI FRANÇOIS,) a French jurist, born at Orgelet in 1697; died in 1783.

Egéon, the French of ÆGÆON, which see.

E-ǵe'rĭ-ą, sometimes, but very rarely, written **Ægeria,** [Fr. EGÉRIE, ả'zhả're',] a nymph in Roman mythology, and one of the Camenæ, was regarded as a prophetic divinity, from whom Numa derived inspiration or instruction in relation to religion and forms of worship. According to tradition, Numa had interviews with her in a grove, and when he died she melted away in tears into a fountain.

Egérie. See EGERIA.

Egerton, (FRANCIS HENRY.) See BRIDGEWATER, EARL OF.

Eg'er-ton, (FRANCIS LEVESON GOWER,) Earl of Ellesmere, an English nobleman and author, born in London, January 1, 1800, was the second son of the first Duke of Sutherland. His family name was GOWER. He assumed the name of Francis Egerton, instead of his patronymic Francis Leveson Gower, in 1833, on becoming heir to part of the estates of the last Duke of Bridgewater. He became a lord of the treasury in 1827, secretary for Ireland in 1828, and secretary at war in 1830. He gained literary distinction by translations of "Faust" and of several poems of Schiller and Körner, and published admired original poems, among which are the "Camp of Wallenstein" and "The Pilgrimage." His gallery of paintings in London was one of the richest owned by any individual in the kingdom. In 1846 he was created Earl of Ellesmere and Viscount Brackley. Besides the poems and translations above named, he wrote "Mediterranean Sketches," (1843,) and other works. Died in 1857.

His wife, LADY FRANCES, accompanied him in a voyage up the Mediterranean in 1840, and published a "Tour in the Holy Land."

See article on Lord Ellesmere in "Fraser's Magazine" for June, 1847.

Egerton, (JOHN,) an excellent English prelate, born in London in 1721, was the son of Henry Egerton, Bishop of Hereford, and a descendant of Lord Ellesmere the chancellor. He was appointed Bishop of Bangor in 1756, of Lichfield in 1768, and of Durham in 1771. Died in 1787. He was the father of the Earl of Bridgewater, the patron or originator of the "Bridgewater treatises."

See F. H. EGERTON, "Life of Thomas Egerton, Lord Ellesmere, with a Sketch of John Egerton, Bishop of Durham," etc.

Egerton, (SCROOP,) first Duke of Bridgewater, an English nobleman, born in the seventeenth century, was a descendant of Lord-Chancellor Egerton. By inheritance he was the fourth Earl of Bridgewater, and in 1720 he was raised to the rank of duke. His son FRANCIS, who inherited his title, became eminent for his services in inland navigation.

See ERSCH und GRUBER, "Allgemeine Encyklopaedie."

Egerton, (THOMAS,) Lord Ellesmere, lord chancellor of England, born in Cheshire in 1540, was the son of Sir Richard Egerton. Having become eminent in his profession, he was chosen solicitor-general in 1581, and attorney-general in 1592. After holding several other high offices, he attained the dignity of keeper of the great seal in 1596. He enjoyed a high degree of favour with Queen Elizabeth to the end of her reign. After the accession of James I., in 1603, he was created Baron of Ellesmere and lord high chancellor. He was made Viscount Brackley in 1616. In 1617 he resigned the great seal, and was succeeded by Lord Bacon. He was esteemed an excellent judge and a great orator, "especially when he was provoked." During his last illness the king offered him the title of Earl of Bridgewater, with a pension; but he declined both, saying, "These things were now to him but vanities." Died in 1617. His son JOHN became the first Earl of Bridgewater.

See LORD CAMPBELL, "Lives of the Lord Chancellors;" FOSS, "The Judges of England;" F. H. EGERTON, "Life, etc. of Thomas Egerton, Lord Ellesmere."

Egg, (AUGUSTUS,) A.R.A., an English painter, born in London in 1816. He has illustrated with success comic scenes from the works of Shakspeare, Le Sage, and others. Among his works are "Peter the Great sees Catherine, his Empress, for the First Time," and the "Life and Death of Buckingham," (1855.) Died in 1863.

Egg, êk, (JOHN CASPAR,) a Swiss economist, born at Ellikon in 1738; died in 1794.

Eggeling, ĕg'ġeh-ling' or ĕk'eh-ling, (JOHANN HEIN-RICH,) a German antiquary, born at Bremen in 1639, became professor of history in his native city. His principal work is a "Treatise on Various German Antiquities," ("De Miscellaneis Germaniæ Antiquitatibus," 1694–1700.) Died in 1713.

Egger, ặ'kaiR' or êg'zhaiR', (ÉMILE,) a French linguist, born in Paris in 1813. He published editions of Varro, Longinus, and other classics, and wrote, besides other works, "Elementary Notions of Comparative Grammar," which reached the fifth edition in 1854 and is highly commended. In 1855 he was chosen professor of Greek at the Faculté des Lettres, Paris.

Eggers, eg'ġers, (JACOB,) a Swedish or Livonian engineer and military officer, born at Dorpat in 1704. He published a military lexicon of engineering, artillery, etc., entitled "Kriegs-Ingenieur-Artillerie-See- und Ritter-Lexikon," (2 vols., 1757.) Died in 1773.

Eggestein, eg'ġes-tīn', (HENRI,) an eminent printer, worked at Strasburg in 1471.

Egidio Antonini. See GILES DE VITERBO.

Egidius. See GILLES, GILES, and ÆGIDIUS.

Eg'il, an Icelandic poet and warrior of the tenth century, who was captured by Eric, King of Norway, and saved his own life by improvising an ode on the exploits of that king, which Malte-Brun says is still extant.

Eg'ill, a Scandinavian warrior of the seventh or eighth century, who is said to have performed, at the command of a tyrant, a feat of archery exactly like the celebrated exploit of William Tell.

See P. SALANUS, "Historia Egilli et Asmundi," Upsal, 1693.

Eginard. See EGINHARD.

Egineta or **Egina,** PAUL OF. See PAULUS ÆGINETA.

Eg'in-hard, written also **Eginard, Einhardt,** and **Einhard,** ān'hard, an eminent French historian of the ninth century, was born in Austrasia, or East France. He was a pupil of Alcuin, and was appointed secretary to Charlemagne. The romantic story of his courtship and marriage of Charlemagne's daughter Emma is now discredited. (See EMMA.) After the death of that king he passed into the service of his successor, Louis le Débonnaire, and spent many of his last years in a monastery. He wrote the "Life of Charlemagne," "Annals of the French Kings from 741 to 829," and numerous Letters. Died about 844.

See SMINCKIUS, "De Vita et Scriptis Eginhardi," 1711; TEULET, "Notice sur Eginhardt," prefixed to an edition of his works, 1840; J. FRESE, "De Einhardi Vita et Scriptis Specimen," 1846.

Eginhardt. See EGINHARD.

Eg'in-ton, (FRANCIS,) an English artist, born about 1737, was distinguished for his skill in painting on glass, and made improvements in that art. He executed many admired historical works in the English cathedrals. Died in 1805.

Égisthe, the French of ÆGISTHUS, which see.

Egizio, ȧ-jèt'se-o, (MATTEO,) COUNT, an Italian savant, born in Naples in 1674, was well versed in law and antiquities. In 1735 he was secretary of embassy in Paris, and on his return to Naples was chosen keeper of the Royal Library. He wrote a few antiquarian treatises. Died in 1745.

Eglantine. See FABRE D'EGLANTINE.

Eglinger, êG'ling'ẹr, (NICHOLAS,) a Swiss medical writer, born at Bâle in 1645; died in 1711.

Eglinger, (SAMUEL,) a Swiss medical writer, born at Bâle in 1638; died in 1673.

Eg'lin-ton and Win'ton, (ARCHIBALD WILLIAM MONTGOMERIE,) fifteenth EARL OF, a British peer, born at Palermo in 1812, succeeded to the earldom in 1819. He produced a great sensation by a famous tournament at Eglinton Castle, Ayrshire, in 1839, in which Louis Napoleon took part, with many of the British nobility. He was lord lieutenant of Ireland during the short administration of Lord Derby, 1852–53, and again in 1858 –59. In politics he acted with the Conservatives. Died in 1861.

Egloff, êG'lof, (LOUISE,) a Swiss poetess, born at Baden in 1803, was either born blind or became so in infancy. A volume of her poems was published in 1823. Died in 1834.

See ERSCH und GRUBER, "Allgemeine Encyklopaedie."

Egloffstein, von, fon êG'lof-stīn', (KARL AUGUST,) a German general, born at Egloffstein in 1771. He entered the French army in his youth, and served with distinction in Germany and Spain. He commanded a brigade in the Russian campaign of 1812. Died in 1834.

See ERSCH und GRUBER, "Allgemeine Encyklopaedie."

Égly, d', dȧ'gle', (CHARLES PHILIPPE **Monthénault** —mòn'tǎ'nō',) born in Paris in 1696, wrote a History of Naples. Died in 1749.

Egmond. See EGMONT, (LAMORAL and PHILIP.)

Egmond, van, vǎn êg'mònt, (JUSTUS,) a Dutch historical painter of high reputation, born at Leyden in 1602. He worked in France, and was patronized by Louis XIV. Died at Antwerp in 1674.

Eg'mŏnd or **Eg'mŏnt, van,** [Dutch pron. vǎn êg'-mònt; Fr. D'EGMOND, dêg'mòn',] (KAREL,) a Dutch prince, born at Gâvre in 1467, was the son of Adolph, Duke of Gelderland. He began to rule that duchy in 1492, and defended it successfully against Maximilian of Germany. In 1507 he invaded Brabant, and took several cities; but his progress was arrested by the treaty of Cambrai. Nearly all his life was spent in war against the Austrians, which he conducted with great ability, and ended in 1528 by rendering homage to Charles V. Died in 1538.

See PONTANUS, "Historia Geldricæ;" DUJARDIN, "Histoire des Provinces unies."

Egmond, van, (MAXIMILIAN,) Count of Buren, an able general of Charles V., was born probably in Flanders. He commanded an imperial army in 1536 against Francis I., and took Saint-Pol. "He was," says De Thou, "great in war and great in peace." He died in 1548, leaving no issue but a daughter, who was the first wife of William, Prince of Orange.

See DE THOU, "Histoire," vol. v.

Egmont, EARL OF. See PERCEVAL, (JOHN.)

Eg'mŏnt, (JOHN,) COUNT OF, and Duke of Gelderland, formed a conspiracy against the Count of Holland about 1415, and was condemned to death, but escaped by flight. Died in 1452.

See ERSCH und GRUBER, "Allgemeine Encyklopaedie."

Egmont or **Egmond,** [Fr. pron. êg'mòn',] (LAMO-RAI, lǎ'mo'rǎl',) COUNT OF, Prince de Gâvre, and Baron of Fiennes, one of the most illustrious nobles of the Low Countries, was born in Amsterdam in 1522. He was a descendant of the Dukes of Gelderland. In 1546 Charles V. conferred on him the order of the Golden Fleece. He married at an early age Sabina, Duchess of Bavaria. Appointed commander of cavalry in the Spanish army, he defeated the French at Saint-Quentin in 1557, and the next year gained the important victory of Gravelines. Though he continued constant in his support of the Catholic Church, he used his great influence in favour of peace and moderate measures in the contest between the Spanish court and the Reformers. This conduct, together with his extraordinary popularity, provoked the vindictive jealousy of Philip II., who sent to Flanders, with vice-regal power, the Duke of Alva, Egmont's personal enemy. Egmont was arrested, with Count Horn, tried for treason, and executed, in 1568, after several

---

e as k; ç as s; ġ hard; ġ as j; G, H, K, guttural; N, nasal; R, trilled; ʒ as z; ŧh as in this. (☞See Explanations, p. 23.)

German princes had made earnest efforts to save his life. His death became the signal of a general revolt against Philip II., which resulted in the independence of the United Provinces. It is also the subject of an admired tragedy by Goethe. Motley, who has had access to the most various and ample sources of information, takes a less favourable view of Egmont's character than most other historians. (See "Rise of the Dutch Republic," more especially the remarks on Egmont's character near the end of chap. ii. Part iii.)

See BERCHT, "Geschichte des Grafen Egmond," 1810; P. J. BRUNELLE, "Éloge du Comte d'Egmont," 1820; PRESCOTT, "History of Philip II.," vols. i. and ii.

Egmont, (PHILIP,) COUNT OF, son of the preceding, born in 1558, served in the army of Philip II., who sent him at the head of a small force to fight for the League against Henry IV. of France. When in Paris a certain official made to him a public address and began to eulogize his father, Egmont checked him by saying, "Say no more of that rebel: he deserved his fate." He was killed at the battle of Ivry in 1590.

His brother CHARLES, Count of Egmont, married Marie of Lens, Baroness of Aubignies, became a chevalier of the Golden Fleece, and was constantly attached to the cause of the Prince of Orange. He died at the Hague in 1620. The posterity of Lamoral became extinct in the person of Procope François, Count of Egmont, a general in the French army, who died in 1707, aged thirty-eight.

Egnatius. See EGNAZIO.

Egnazio, ên-yät'se-o, [Lat. EGNA'TIUS,] the assumed name of GIOVANNI BATTISTA Cipelli, (che-pel'lee,) an Italian orator and author, born at Venice about 1475. He was professor of eloquence in Venice about thirty years, (1520–50.) His lectures were very popular, and are said to have attracted a class of five hundred students. He edited the poems of Ovid, and wrote, in Latin, several works, including an "Epitome of the Lives of the Roman Emperors," which has some merit. Died in 1553.

See VOSSIUS, "De Historicis Latinis;" ERSCH und GRUBER, "Allgemeine Encyklopaedie."

Eg're-mont, (GEORGE O'BRIEN WYNDHAM,) EARL OF, an English nobleman, born in 1751, inherited that title at the age of twelve. He was eminent for his public spirit and his liberality as a patron of native artists. Died in 1837.

Eguia, de, dà à-gee'à, (FRANCISCO RAMON,) a Spanish general, born at Durango in 1750; died in 1827.

Egyptus, the French of ÆGYPTUS, which see.

Ehingen, von, fon ä'ing-ẹn, (GEORGE,) a German traveller and knight-errant, born about 1435. He fought with distinction against the Moors in Spain and Portugal. He wrote a narrative of his travels in Europe, Palestine, etc., (1600.)

Ehinger, ä'ing-ẹr, (ELIAS,) a German theologian, born in 1573, was professor and rector at Augsburg, and published several theological works. Died in 1653.

See JACOB BRUCKER, "Commentatio de Vita et Scriptis E. Ehingeri," 1724.

Ehlers, ä'lẹrs, (MARTIN,) a German novelist, born in Holstein in 1732, became professor of philosophy at Kiel in 1776. His chief work is "Considerations on the Morality of our Enjoyments and Pleasures," (2 vols., 1790.) "All his thoughts," says Guizot, "are those of a wise man. He presents a number of important truths with clearness and simplicity." ("Biographie Universelle.") Died in 1800.

See MEUSEL, "Lexikon der vom Jahr 1750–1800 verstorbenen Deutschen Schriftsteller."

Ehninger, en'ing-ẹr,? (JOHN W.,) an American painter, born in the city of New York in 1827, studied in Paris. His forte is genre. Among his works are "The Foray," "Ars celare Artem," "Lady Jane Grey," and familiar rural scenes.

See H. T. TUCKERMAN, "Book of the Artists."

Ehrenberg, ä'rẹn-bêRG', (CHRISTIAN GOTTFRIED,) a German naturalist, celebrated for his microscopic researches, was born at Delitzsch, in Prussian Saxony, in 1795. He studied medicine at Leipsic, and took his degree in 1818. His first writings were treatises on fungi and other cryptogamous plants. At the expense of the Berlin Academy, he made with Dr. Hemprich a scientific excursion to Egypt, Arabia, and Syria, in which they spent about six years, (1820–26.) On his return to Berlin he was appointed adjunct professor of the Faculty of Medicine. He published his observations in "Scientific Travels through Northern Africa and Western Asia," (1828,) and in several special treatises entitled "Physical Symbols of Birds, Insects," etc., ("Symbolæ physicæ Avium, Insectorum," etc., 1828–34.) In 1829 he accompanied Humboldt in an excursion to the Ural and Altai Mountains. Having turned his attention to the study of animalcula, he made remarkable discoveries with the microscope. He published in 1838 a description of the structure and habits of infusoria, in his great work "The Infusoria as Perfect Organisms," ("Die Infusionsthierchen als vollkommene Organismen.") He wrote other works, in which he announced that cretaceous and calcareous strata and large portions of mountains are composed of the skeletons of infusoria or microscopic organisms. His "Mikro-Geologie," (1854–56,) treating of this department of geology, is among his most important works.

See BROCKHAUS, "Conversations-Lexikon;" "Nouvelle Biographie Générale."

Ehrenberg, (FRIEDRICH,) a German theologian, born at Elberfeld in 1776, became court preacher in 1834.

Ehrenheim, ä'rẹn-hīm', (FREDRICK WILHELM,) BARON OF, a Swedish statesman, born at Broby in 1753. In 1794 he was minister at the court of Denmark, and a few years later he obtained the portfolio of foreign affairs. When Gustavus IV. was dethroned, in 1809, Ehrenheim retired from the public service. He wrote an excellent treatise on "General Physics and Meteorology," and a few other works. Died in 1828.

Ehrenmalm, ä'rẹn-mälm', (ARVID,) a Swedish traveller, who published in 1742 a "Journey through Nordland and Lapland," etc.

Ehrenpreus, ä'rẹn-prê-ŏŏs, (CARL,) a Swedish statesman, born at Œrebro in 1692. He was employed by Charles XII. as secretary at Bender about 1710, and after his return to Sweden was made a senator and a count. Died in 1760.

See ERSCH und GRUBER, "Allgemeine Encyklopaedie."

Ehrenschild, ä'rẹn-shĭlt', (CONRAD BIERMAN,) a Danish statesman, born in 1629; died in 1698.

Ehrenschöld or **Ehrenschoeld,** ä'ren-shölt', or **Ehrenskjold,** ä'rẹns-chòlt', (NILS,) a Swedish admiral, born in 1674. In 1714 or 1715 he commanded the Swedish fleet which was defeated in the Gulf of Finland by a superior Russian fleet, in which Peter the Great served as rear-admiral. Died in 1728.

Ehrensteen. See EHRENSTEN.

Ehrensten, ä'rẹn-stên', written also **Ehrensteen** (EDUARD,) a Swedish statesman and author, born at Locknevid in 1620, was the son of Philip Bononius. In 1653 he became secretary of the king, Charles Gustavus, and, having subsequently received letters of nobility, he took the name of Ehrensten. He was appointed secretary of state in 1659, and chancellor of the court in 1671. He wrote "De Forma Substantiali," (1642,) and other works, which are commended. Died in 1686.

See ERSCH und GRUBER, "Allgemeine Encyklopaedie."

Ehrenstral, ä'rẹn-strål', (DAVID CLÖCKER,) a painter of history and portraits, born at Hamburg in 1629, studied in Italy. In 1661 he was appointed painter to the court of Sweden. Died in 1698.

Ehrensvärd. See EHRENSWÄRD.

Ehrenswaerd. See EHRENSWÄRD.

Ehrenswärd or **Ehrenswaerd,** ä'rẹn-swêRd', (AUGUST,) COUNT OF, a Swedish field-marshal, born in 1710, made himself famous by devising and organizing a new plan of national defence,—a fleet of transport-vessels and gun-boats,—which was employed with success on several occasions. He also planned the fortifications of Sveaborg. Died in 1773.

See GEYER, "History of Sweden;" AXEL M. ARBIN, "Åminnelse-Tal öfver A. Ehrenswaerd," 1774.

Ehrenswärd or **Ehrenswaerd,** (CARL AUGUST,) a Swedish admiral and artist, a son of the preceding, was born about 1745. He visited Italy about 1780, and after

ā, ē, ī, ō, ū, ȳ, *long;* à, ê, ô, same, less prolonged; ă, ĕ, ĭ, ŏ, ŭ, ў, *short;* ạ, ẹ, ị, ọ, *obscure;* fär, fàll, fât; mêt; nŏt; gŏŏd; mŏŏn;

his return published an account of his travels, illustrated with fine engravings by himself. He was admiral of the fleet in 1789, and fought against the Russians. Died in 1800.

Ehret, ā′rĕt, (GEORG D.,) a German artist, distinguished for his skill in drawing and painting plants, was born in Baden in 1710. He worked some time in Bâle, from which he removed to Paris, where he was employed by Bernard de Jussieu. He became intimate with Linnæus in Holland, and designed the figures of his beautiful "Hortus Cliffortianus," (1737.) In 1740 he went to England, where he worked for the Royal Society and published a series of engravings of plants, (1748–59.) Died in 1770.

See NAGLER, "Neues Allgemeines Künstler-Lexikon."

Ehrhardt, āR′haRt, (SIGISMOND JUST,) a German historian and preacher, born in 1733. He wrote on the early history of Lower Saxony, and "On the Origin and Antiquities of Schmalkalden." Died in 1793.

See ERSCH und GRUBER, "Allgemeine Encyklopaedie."

Ehrhart, āR′haRt, (BALTHASAR,) a German botanist, was born at Memmingen. His chief work is an "Economical History of Plants," of which five volumes had appeared at his death in 1756. It was continued and completed by P. F. Gmelin.

Ehrhart, (FREDERICK,) a Swiss botanist, born at Holdarbanc about 1745, learned the trade of apothecary, and in the study of botany was a pupil of Linnæus at Upsal. From 1787 to 1792 he issued "Fragments of Natural History," in 7 vols. He received in 1787 the diploma of botanist to his Britannic Majesty. Died in 1795.

See ERSCH und GRUBER, "Allgemeine Encyklopaedie."

Ehrmann, ĕR′mŏN′ or āR′mân, (FRÉDÉRIC LOUIS,) a French writer, born about 1740, published "Elements of Physics," (1779.) Died in 1800.

Ehrmann, āR′mân, (JOHANN CHRISTIAN,) a German medical writer, born at Strasburg in 1740; died about 1800.

Ehrmann, āR′mân, (MARIANNE,) a Swiss authoress, whose maiden name was BRENTANO, (brĕn-tä′no,) born at Rapperschwyl in 1755. She was married to T. F. Ehrmann, a geographer. She wrote works for the instruction of women, among which were "Amelia, a True Story," (1787,) and "The Solitary of the Alps," (1794.) "Her style is clear and easy," says Guizot; "her reflections are always just, and often new. All her writings are pervaded by an excellent morality." Died in 1795.

See ERSCH und GRUBER, "Allgemeine Encyklopaedie."

Eichendorff, von, fon ī′ḳen-doRf′, (JOSEPH,) BARON, a popular German poet and novelist, born at Lubowitz, near Ratibor, in 1788. He became *referendar* of the government at Breslau in 1816, and afterwards councillor *(regierungsrath)* at Königsberg and Berlin. He wrote several tragedies and novels, some of which are considered master-pieces. Among the latter are "Presentiment and Reality," (1815,) and "Aus dem Leben eines Taugenichts," ("From the Life of a Good-for-Nothing," 1824: translated into English by C. G. Leland in 1866.) His songs are admired for melody and tenderness. Died in 1857.

See BROCKHAUS, "Conversations-Lexikon."

Eichens, ī′ḳens, (FRIEDRICH EDUARD,) an eminent German engraver, born in Berlin in 1804. He pursued his studies in Paris and Italy, where he acquired reputation by engravings of "The Daughter of Titian" and Raphael's "Vision of Ezekiel." He returned to Berlin about 1832, and was admitted into the Royal Academy. His "Adoration of the Magi," after Raphael, is admired.

Eichhoff, ā′kof′, (FRÉDÉRIC GUSTAVE,) a French philologist, born at Havre in 1799. He studied Sanscrit and other Oriental languages, and wrote, among other works, a "Comparison of the Languages of Europe with those of India," (1836.) In 1855 he was chosen inspector-general of the classes of living languages in the lyceums *(lycées)* of France.

Eichhorn, īḳ′hoRn, (HEINRICH,) a German medical writer, graduated in 1822; died in 1832.

Eichhorn, (JOHANN ALBRECHT FRIEDRICH,) born in Prussia in 1779, was minister of public instruction and worship from 1840 to 1848. Died in 1856.

Eichhorn, (JOHANN CONRAD,) a German naturalist, born at Dantzic in 1718, wrote on aquatic animals. Died in 1790.

See ERSCH und GRUBER, "Allgemeine Er.cyklopaedie."

Eichhorn, (JOHANN GOTTFRIED,) an excellent German scholar and biblical critic, born at Dörenzimmern, Hohenlohe-Oehringen, on the 16th of October, 1752. He was professor of Oriental languages at Jena from 1775 to 1788. In the latter year he obtained the chair of Oriental and biblical literature at Göttingen, where he taught until his death. He edited a periodical called a "General Repository of Biblical Literature," (10 vols., 1787–1801,) and published many important works, among which are an "Introduction to the Old Testament," (3 vols., 1783,) and an "Introduction to the New Testament," (2 vols., 1804–10.) His "Primitive History" ("Urgeschichte," 3 vols., 1790–93) is admired for style and erudition. He left a "Universal History," (5 vols., 1799,) a "History of Literature from its Origin to the Most Recent Times," (6 vols., 1806–12,) "The Primitive History of the House of Guelph," (1817,) and other historical works. As a biblical critic he favours rationalism or philosophic skepticism. Died in 1827.

See ERSCH und GRUBER, "Allgemeine Encyklopaedie;" T. C. TYCHSEN, "Memoria J. G. Eichhorn," 1828; "Nouvelle Biographie Générale."

Eichhorn, (KARL FRIEDRICH,) an eminent Prussian jurisconsult and historian, born at Jena in 1781, was a son of the preceding. He became professor of German law at Berlin in 1811, and at Göttingen in 1817. In 1828 he resigned his chair on account of ill health. About 1833 he was appointed a member of the council of state at Berlin, and of the commission of legislation. Among his principal works is a "History of the States and Law of Germany," (4 vols.,1808–18,) which has passed through eight editions, and an "Introduction to German Civil Law," *(Privatrecht.)* Died at Cologne in 1854.

Eichler, īḳ′ler, (GOTTFRIED,) a German painter of portraits and history, was born at Augsburg about 1675. He studied under Carlo Maratta in Rome, and returned to Augsburg, where he received the title of court painter. Died in 1757.

Eichler, (GOTTFRIED,) a son of the preceding, born in 1715, was a skilful designer and engraver on copper. Died in 1770.

Eichler, (MATTHIAS GOTTFRIED,) a son of the preceding, born in 1748, lived at Berne. He engraved "The Deluge," after Poussin, and many other historical pieces and landscapes. Died about 1818.

See NAGLER, "Neues Allgemeines Künstler-Lexikon."

Eichmann. See DRYANDER, (JOHANN.)

Eichner, īḳ′ner, (ERNST,) a German musician and composer, born at Manheim in 1740 ; died in 1777.

Eichstad, īḳ′stät, (LORENZ,) a German medical writer, born at Stettin ; died in 1660.

Eichstädt, īḳ′stät, (HEINRICH KARL ABRAHAM,) a German philologer, born at Oschatz in 1772. He was professor of eloquence at Jena, edited the "Literary Gazette," and published "Questiones Philologicæ," (1796,) and an edition of Lucretius, (1801.) Died in 1848.

Eichwald, īḳ′wâlt, (EDWARD,) a Russian naturalist, of German extraction, born at Mittau in 1795. He was appointed professor of zoology and obstetrics at Kazan in 1823, after which he made an excursion to the Caspian Sea and Persia. About 1838 he became professor of mineralogy and zoology in Saint Petersburg ; he afterwards explored the scientific resources of parts of Russia and Italy. He wrote a treatise, in German, "On the Natural History of Lithuania, Volhynia, and Podolia," (1830,) a "Fauna Caspio-Caucasia," (1841,) "The Primitive World of Russia," ("Die Urwelt Russlands," 4 vols., 1840–47,) and other works.

See BROCKHAUS, "Conversations-Lexikon."

Eimmart, īm′mäRt, or **Eimart,** ī′mäRt, (GEORG CHRISTOPH,) a German painter, born in 1597 ; died at Ratisbon in 1660.

Eimmart, (GEORG CHRISTOPH,) an ingenious German artist and astronomer, born at Ratisbon in 1638. He painted portraits and history with success at Nuremberg, where he settled in 1660. He made astronomical observations, and left many volumes of manuscripts on astronomy, meteorology, etc. Died in 1705.

Einari, i-nä're, (GISSUR,) the first Protestant Bishop of Skalholt, Iceland, received lessons from Luther at Wittenberg, and, returning home, became the leader of the Reformation in that island.

Einari, written also **Einarson,** (HALFDAN,) an Icelandic savant, became in 1755 rector of the Latin School at Holum. His most important work is "Sciagraphia," or "Sketch of the Literary History of Iceland," in which he notices four hundred and five writers. Died in 1784.
See KRAFT og NYERUP, "Litteraturlexicon."

Einarson. See EINARI.

Einem, von, fon i'nem, (JOHANN JUSTUS,) a German writer and teacher, published a "Sketch of the Life of Luther," (1730,) and other works.

Einhard. See EGINHARD.

Einheriar, in-hä're-ar, or **Einherjar,** [from _einn,_ "one," "single," hence "singled out" or "chosen," and _heri,_ (allied to the German _Herr,_) "lord," "hero,"] in the Norse mythology, the name given to the chosen heroes who are admitted to Valhalla. (See ODIN and VALKYRIA.)

Einsiedel, von, fon in'see-del, (FRIEDRICH HILDEBRAND,) a German writer and politician, born at Leipsic in 1750; died in 1828.

Eioub or **Eiub.** See AIYOOB.

Eira, i'rä, or **Eir,** ir, [etymology unknown,] in the Norse mythology, the goddess of medicine,

Eirene, i-ree'ne, [Gr. Εἰρήνη; Lat. PAX; Fr. LA PAIX, lä pȧ,] the goddess of peace, in classic mythology, was called a daughter of Jupiter and Themis. Altars and statues were raised in her honour at Athens, and a magnificent temple was erected to her in Rome by Vespasian.

Eiselen, i'zeh-len, (JOHANN FRIEDRICH,) a German publicist, born at Rothemburg in 1785, became professor of law at Halle in 1829. He wrote a "Theory of Political Economy," (1843.)

Eisen, ȧ'zŏN', (CHARLES,) a French painter and engraver, born in Paris in 1721; died in 1778.

Eisen von Schwarzenberg, i'zen von shwȧrt'sen-bĕRG', (JOHANN GEORG,) a German physician and writer on theology, etc., was born at Bolsingen in 1717. He promoted the abolition of serfdom in Livonia. Died in 1779.

Eisengrein, i'zen-grin', (MARTIN,) a German theologian, born in 1535, lived at Ingolstadt. Died in 1578.

Eisenhart, i'zen-hart', (JOHANN FRIEDRICH,) a distinguished German jurist, born at Spire in 1720. He published "Institutes of German Private Law," ("Institutiones Juris Germanici privati," 1753,) and other legal works. "His style is clear and precise," says Guizot, "his discussions are animated, and give proof of equal sagacity and judgment." ("Biographie Universelle.") Died in 1783.
See J. C. WERNSDORF, "Memoria J. F. Eisenharti," 1783; HIRSCHING, "Historisch-literarisches Handbuch."

Eisenmann, i'zen-mȧn', (GOTTFRIED,) a German medical writer and liberal politician, born at Würtzburg in 1795. He was imprisoned for political reasons from 1832 to 1841. Among his works is a treatise "On Rheumatism," (3 vols., 1841–43.)

Eisenmenger, i'zen-mĕng'er, (JOHANN ANDREAS,) a German philologist and Hebraist, born at Manheim in 1654. He became professor of Oriental languages at Heidelberg in 1700, and published "Judaism Unveiled," (1700,) which is regarded as a libellous work by the Jews and others. Died in 1704.
See A. T. HARTMANN, "J. A. Eisenmenger und seine jüdischen Gegner," 1834.

Eisenschmid, i'zen-shmit', (JOHANN KASPAR,) a skilful mathematician, born at Strasburg in 1656, was chosen in 1699 an associate of the Academy of Sciences at Paris. He wrote a treatise on "The Figure of the Earth," and several other works. Died in 1712.

Eisinga, i'sing-hä, (EISE,) born in Holland in 1744, was a councillor of state, and noted as the inventor and maker of a remarkable planetarium. He died at Franeker in 1828.

Eiyub. See AIYOOB.

Ekama, ä'kä-mä, (CORNELIS,) a Dutch mathematician, born in Friesland in 1773; died in 1826.

Ekber. See AKBAR.

Ekeberg, ĕk'eh-bĕRg', (ANDERS GUSTAF,) an eminent Swedish chemist, born at Stockholm in 1767. He made some chemical discoveries, and taught chemistry at Upsal. Died in 1813.

Ekeberg, (CARL GUSTAF,) a Swedish captain and savant, born in 1716, made several voyages to India and China, and gained distinction by his useful observations. He published an "Account of the Rural Economy of the Chinese," (1754,) and a "Voyage to India in 1770–71." For his treatise on Inoculation he received medals and pensions from several foreign powers. Died in 1784.
See A. SPARRMAN, "Åminnelse-Tal öfver C. G. Ekeberg," 1791.

Ekeblad, ek'eh-blåd', (CLAUDIUS,) COUNT OF, a Swedish statesman, born about 1700, was chosen in 1761 minister of foreign affairs. His opponents, styled the party of Caps, prevailed in 1766, and he lost his place, but recovered it in 1769, when the Hats, or French party, were in the ascendant. Died in 1771.
See HOEPKEN, "Åminnelse-Tal öfver C. Ekeblad," 1773.

Ek'ins, (JEFFERY,) an English parson, born in Cheshire. He translated from the Greek "The Loves of Medea and Jason," by Apollonius of Rhodes. Died in 1791.

Ekström or **Ekstroem,** ĕk'ström, (DANIEL,) a Swedish mechanician and mathematician, born at Ekesog in 1711. He made excellent mathematical instruments. Died in 1755.
See ERSCH und GRUBER, "Allgemeine Encyklopaedie;" P. WARGENTEN, "Gedächtniss auf Daniel Ekstroem."

Elagabale. See ELAGABALUS.

El-a-ga-ba'lus or **El-a-gab'a-lus,** or **He-lī-o-ga-ba'lus,** [Fr. ÉLAGABALE, ȧ'lȧ'gȧ'bȧl', or HÉLIOGABALE, ȧ'le'o'gȧ'bȧl',] (MARCUS AURELIUS ANTONINUS,) a Roman emperor, born at Antioch in 204 A.D., was supposed to be the natural son of Caracalla. His original name was Varius Avitus Bassianus; but, having become a priest in the Temple of the Sun, (the Syrian Elagabal,) he adopted the name of that idol. In 218 he was proclaimed by the army as successor to Caracalla, and, having defeated his rival Macrinus, he assumed the name of M. A. Antoninus. His reign was short, and was disgraced by cruelty, extravagance, and infamous vices. He was assassinated by his soldiers in 222, and was succeeded by Alexander Severus.
See TILLEMONT, "Histoire des Empereurs;" GIBBON, "Decline and Fall of the Roman Empire;" LAMPRIDIUS, "Elagabalus;" "Nouvelle Biographie Générale."

Elbée, d', dĕl'bȧ', (GIGOT, zhe'go',) a Vendean general-in-chief, born of a French family at Dresden in 1752. He resided in France when the Revolution began, and put himself at the head of a body of royalists in March, 1793. His army joined that of Cathelineau and defeated the republicans at Fontenay and Saumur. On the death of Cathelineau, in June, Elbée was chosen general-in-chief. He was defeated at Luçon, and gained a decisive victory over Marceau at Chantonnay. He lost a great battle and was desperately wounded at Chollet, in October. Having been taken prisoner, he was shot, by order of a court-martial, in January, 1794.
See THIERS, "History of the French Revolution;" DE COURCELLES, "Histoire des Généraux Français."

Elbene. See DELBENE.

El'bert, (SAMUEL,) an American officer, born in South Carolina in 1743, served with distinction as colonel in the Revolutionary war, and was chosen Governor of Georgia in 1785. Died in 1788.

Elbeuf or **Elbœuf, d',** dĕl'buf', (CHARLES,) DUKE, born about 1556, was a son of René de Lorraine, noticed below. Died in 1605.

Elbeuf, d', (CHARLES,) a son of the preceding, born in 1596, became Duke of Elbeuf, and married in 1619 an illegitimate daughter of Henry IV. Died in 1657.

Elbeuf, d', (EMMANUEL MAURICE,) PRINCE, a grandson of the preceding, born in 1677, entered the service of the Emperor of Germany. He became owner of a villa at Portici, and there ordered some excavations which resulted in the discovery of Herculaneum. Died in 1763.

Elbeuf, d', (RENÉ de Lorraine—deh lo'rȧN',) MARQUIS, a son of Claude, Duc de Guise. Died in 1566.

Elbœuf. See ELBEUF.

ā, ē, ī, ō, ū, ȳ, _long;_ ȧ, ė, ȯ, _same, less prolonged;_ ă, ĕ, ĭ, ŏ, ŭ, ў, _short;_ ą, ę, į, ǫ, _obscure;_ fär, fȧll, fȧt; mēt; nŏt; gŏŏd; mŏŏn;

Elburcht, van, vän êl'bürkt, (JAN,) a Dutch painter, born at Elburg about 1550, worked at Antwerp. He painted landscapes, storms at sea, and scriptural subjects.

Elchingen, DUKE OF. See NEY.

El'cho, (FRANCIS WEMYS CHARTERIS,) LORD, a Scottish politician, born in Edinburgh in 1818. He has been for many years a member of Parliament, and is called Liberal Consèrvative.

Elci, êl'chee, (ANGELO,) COUNT, an eminent Italian philologist, born of a noble family in Florence in 1764. He published a fine edition of Lucan's "Pharsalia," and some satires of his own. Died in 1824.

El'dad the Danite, a Jewish traveller, lived in Arabia in the ninth century. He travelled in China, Persia, and other countries, and wrote a narrative of his travels.

El'don, (JOHN SCOTT,) EARL OF, lord chancellor of England, was born at Newcastle in 1751. His father, William Scott, was a prosperous "coal-fitter," or dealer in coal. John Scott was educated at Oxford, where in 1771 he gained a prize of £20 for a prose essay on the "Advantages and Disadvantages of Foreign Travel." In 1772 he ran away with and married Elizabeth Surtees, a lady of exquisite beauty. He began the study of law in the Middle Temple in 1773, where, by the most intense application, he laid the foundation of the unrivalled reputation which he acquired as a judge. In 1776 he was called to the bar, and practised in London and on the northern circuit. His great excellence as a lawyer was publicly recognized in 1780 in the case of Acroyd vs. Smithson before Lord Thurlow. From this time his success was rapid and uninterrupted. In 1783 he was returned to Parliament, in which he took a prominent part as a supporter of the ministry of Pitt. Though not a brilliant orator, he often spoke with great effect. In 1786 he warmly defended Warren Hastings in the House.

In 1788 he was appointed solicitor-general, and received the title of baronet. From 1793 until 1799 he officiated as attorney-general amidst the excitement of the French Revolution. He prosecuted Hardy, Horne Tooke, and others for treason, who were defended by Erskine and acquitted. In 1799 he obtained the office of chief justice of the common pleas, and was raised to the peerage under the title derived from a manor in the county of Durham. Lord Kenyon congratulated the profession on this appointment, and predicted that Eldon would prove to be "the most consummate judge that ever sat in judgment." It is admitted that he performed the duties of this station admirably.

In April, 1801, on the accession of Addington as prime minister, Lord Eldon was raised to the dignity of lord chancellor, which he ascribed to the favour of the king. The latter, having sent for Eldon, drew the seals out from his bosom, saying, "I give them to you from my heart!" He retained the great seal for the period of twenty-six years, excepting an interval of about a year in 1806-07, when Erskine succeeded him. He possessed great influence in the cabinet and in the Upper House. It may, however, be mentioned as his reproach that he constantly supported the Conservative party, that he opposed the abolition of the slave-trade, the Reform bill, and nearly every other change, whether of useful reform or useless innovation. When Canning became prime minister, in 1827, Eldon was superseded by Lord Lyndhurst, and retired from public life. A few years before this he had been created Viscount Encombe and Earl of Eldon. Died in 1838.

See "The Public and Private Life of Lord Eldon," by HORACE TWISS, 3 vols., 1844; LORD CAMPBELL, "Lives of the Lord Chancellors;" FOSS, "The Judges of England," vol. ix.; "London Quarterly Review" for December and June, 1844; "Westminster Review" for December, 1844; "Fraser's Magazine" for August, 1844.

Eleanor, êl'a-nor, [Sp. LEONORA, lä-o-no'rä,] OF ARAGON, Queen of Portugal, was a daughter of Ferdinand of Aragon. She was married in 1428 to a Portuguese prince, who became in 1433 King Edward I. He died in 1438, leaving her guardian of her minor son, Alfonso V., and regent. Died in 1445.

Eleanor, [Fr. ÉLÉONORE, à'lä'o'noR'] OF AUSTRIA, a sister of the emperor Charles V., was born at Louvain in 1498, and was married in 1519 to Emanuel, King of Portugal, who died about two years later. In 1530 she

became the consort of Francis I. of France, in accordance with the first clause of the treaty of Cambrai. She had two children, who were the issue of her first marriage. She survived Francis, and died in Spain in 1558.

See SISMONDI, "Histoire des Français."

Eleanor OF CASTILE, a daughter of Ferdinand III. of Castile, was married in 1254 to the Prince of Wales, who became Edward I. of England. Died in 1290.

Eleanor [Fr. ÉLÉONORE, à'lä'o'noR'] OF GUIENNE, Queen of France, and afterwards Queen of England, was born about 1122. She was daughter and heiress of the last Duke of Aquitaine. In 1137 she married Louis VII. of France, whom she followed on a crusade in 1147. Having been divorced in 1152, she married Henry II. of England. In order to revenge his infidelity to her, she is said to have instigated the king's sons to rebel, for which she was imprisoned about fifteen years. She was regent while her son, Richard I., was absent on a crusade. Died in 1203.

See SISMONDI, "Histoire des Français."

Eleanor or Ellinor [Port. ELEONORA, or, more fully, ELEONORA TELLEZ, à-la-o-no'rä tel'lêz] OF PORTUGAL, a beautiful Portuguese lady, born about 1350. She became the queen of Ferdinand I. of Portugal. She was artful and unscrupulous, and is said to have caused the death of her sister. Died in 1405.

See LACLÈDE, "Histoire de Portugal."

Eleanor OF PROVENCE, Queen of England, was a daughter of Raimond Berenger IV., and was married to Henry III. of England in 1236. She was mother of Edward I. Died in 1291.

E-le-ā'zar, [Heb. אֶלְעָזָר,] a high-priest of the Hebrew church, was a son of Aaron, whom he succeeded in the high-priesthood about 1452 B.C.

See Exodus xxviii. 1; Numbers xx. 28, xxxi. 6; Joshua xxiv. 33.

Eleazar, a Jewish high-priest, who about 277 B.C. sent to Ptolemy, King of Egypt, (in compliance with his request,) seventy-two wise men to translate the Mosaic law into Greek.

Eleazar, a Jewish warrior, was a brother of Judas Maccabæus. He was killed in battle in 163 B.C.

Eleazar, an eminent Jewish scribe, who resisted the tyrannical orders of Antiochus Epiphanes, and was put to death in 167 B.C.

Eleazar, a son of Ananias, a fanatical Jew, instigated his countrymen to revolt against the Romans. During the siege of Jerusalem by Titus (70 A.D.) he was the leader of one of the hostile factions of that city.

See JOSEPHUS, "History."

Eleazar, a Jewish warrior, noted for his obstinate defence of Massada against the Romans in 70 A.D. When resistance was no longer practicable, to avoid capture he and his men killed themselves.

Eleazar or Eliezer of Garmiza or of Worms, an eminent Hebrew rabbi, lived about 1240.

E-lec'tra, [Gr. Ἠλέκτρα,] one of the Pleiades, was regarded as the daughter of Atlas and Pleione, and the mother of Dardanus.

Electra, [Gr. Ἠλέκτρα; Fr. ÉLECTRE, à'lâktR'; It. ELETTRA, à-lêt'trä,] a daughter of Agamemnon, and a sister of Orestes, was sometimes called Laodice. Her story has been dramatized by Æschylus, Sophocles, and Euripides.

Électre. See ELECTRA.

E-lec'try-on, [Gr. Ἠλεκτρύων,] a son of Perseus and Andromeda, was King of Mycenæ, (or, as some say, of Argos,) and father of Alcmena. Returning victorious from war, he was accidentally killed by Amphitryon, who was betrothed to his daughter Alcmena.

Eleonora Tellez. See ELEANOR OF PORTUGAL.

Elettra. See ELECTRA.

E-leū'sis, [Gr. Ἐλευσίς,] a mythical person, called a son of Mercury or of Ogyges. The town of Eleusis in Attica is supposed to have derived its name from him.

E-leū-the'rĭ-us or E-leū'the-ros, [Fr. ÉLEUTHÈRE, à'luh'taiR',] a native of Nicopolis or Epirus, in Greece, was elected pope or bishop of Rome in 177 A.D. He died in 192, and was succeeded by Victor I.

El-fle'da or Eth'el-fle'da, daughter of Alfred the Great of England, and sister of Edward the Elder, inherited some of her father's royal qualities. She became about 890 the wife of Ethelred, Count of Mercia, after whose death she defended her dominions against the Danes with courage and ability. Died in 922.

Elfric. See ALFRIC.

El-fri′dạ, queen of Edgar, King of the Anglo-Saxons, was the mother of Ethelred II., and was a woman of infamous character.

Elger. See ELLIGER, (OTMAR.)

El′gin, (JAMES BRUCE,) EARL OF, son of Thomas, noticed below, a distinguished British statesman, was born in 1811, and educated at Oxford. In 1841 he succeeded his father in the earldom of Elgin and Kincardine. From 1842 to 1846 he was Governor of Jamaica, and in the latter year he was appointed Governor-General of Canada. In this position his policy was liberal, and his administration obtained the general approbation of the colonists and of the central government. In 1849 he was created an English peer. He left Canada in 1854, and was sent in 1857 to China on a special mission, which he performed with ability and success, and after the capture of Canton negotiated the treaty of Tien-Tsien or Tientsin, (1858.) In June, 1859, he became postmaster-general in the cabinet of Palmerston. He went as ambassador to China in 1860, and, after the success of the British army, entered Pekin in triumph. He returned home in the spring of 1861, and was appointed Governor-General of India. Died in 1863.

See "Gentleman's Magazine" for January, 1864.

Elgin, (THOMAS BRUCE,) EARL OF, seventh Earl of Elgin and Kincardine, born in Scotland in 1777, was descended from King Robert Bruce. He succeeded to the peerage in childhood, entered the army at an early age, and rose to the rank of general. In 1795 he was appointed envoy extraordinary to Berlin, and in 1799 was sent in the same capacity to Constantinople. While engaged in the latter mission, he availed himself of the opportunity to procure, with great labour and expense, at Athens, a large collection of statues, bas-reliefs, medals, monuments, and other remains of ancient art, which were purchased by the government in 1816, and now form part of the British Museum, under the name of the "Elgin Marbles." The government paid him £35,000 for these treasures, for removing which he was severely satirized by Lord Byron. Died in 1841.

See ERSCH und GRUBER, "Allgemeine Encyklopaedie;" "Quarterly Review" for January, 1816; "Edinburgh Review" for January, 1860.

El-ḡi′vạ, ? Queen of Edmund I., King of the Anglo-Saxons, and mother of Edgar.

E′lī, [Heb. עֵלִי,] a Hebrew high-priest and judge, who flourished about 1170 B.C. He judged Israel forty years, and was succeeded by Samuel.

See I. Samuel i., ii., iii., and iv.

Elia. See LAMB, (CHARLES.)

Elian. See ÆLIAN.

Elias, (of Scripture.) See ELIJAH.

Elias, à-lee′ȧs, (MATTHÄUS,) a German painter, born near Cassel in 1658, worked at Paris. Among his works is a "Transfiguration." Died in 1741.

E-li′as Le-vi′tạ, a Jewish rabbi, born probably in Italy in 1472, was one of the most celebrated writers and skilful grammarians among the modern Jews. He taught Hebrew in Rome and Venice, and published many works, among which were a "Hebrew Grammar" and a "Chaldaic, Talmudic, and Rabbinical Lexicon." His critical notes on the text of Scripture, entitled "Massorah," (1538,) are highly prized. Died at Venice in 1549.

See BASNAGE, "Histoire des Juifs."

Elichmann, ā′lĭk-mȧn′, (JOHANN,) a German Orientalist and physician, born in Silesia, practised at Leyden, where he died in 1639. In the opinion of Salmasius, he understood Persian better than any European of his time.

Elie, the French of ELIJAH, which see.

Élie de Beaumont, à′le′ dĕh bō′mŏN′,(ANNE LOUISE Morin-Dumesnil—mo′rȧN′ dü′mȧ′nĕl′,) an authoress, born at Caen in 1729, was the wife of Jean Baptiste Jacques, noticed below. She wrote a novel entitled "Letters of the Marquis de Roselle," (2 vols., 1764.) Died in 1783.

Élie de Beaumont, (JEAN BAPTISTE ARMAND LOUIS LÉONCÉ,) a French geologist, born at Canon (Calvados) in 1798. He studied in the École Polytechnique and the École des Mines. In 1823 he was sent with M. Dufrénoy on a scientific excursion to Great Britain. He afterwards co-operated in a great geological map of France. (See DUFRÉNOY, P. A.) He became professor of geology in the College of France in 1832, chief engineer of mines in 1833, and a member of the Institute in 1835. Though not a politician, he was appointed a senator in 1852. He succeeded Arago in 1853 as perpetual secretary of the Academy of Sciences. Among his principal works are a "Glance at Mines," ("Coup-d'Œil sur les Mines," 1824,) "Researches in some of the Revolutions of the Surface of the Globe," (1829,) and "Lectures on Geology," (3 vols., 1845 et seq.)

See "Galerie historique des Membres du Sénat."

Élie de Beaumont, (JEAN BAPTISTE JACQUES,) a French lawyer, grandfather of the preceding, was born at Carentan in 1732. He acquired a European reputation by his judicial "Mémoires." In reference to his memoir of "les Calas," Voltaire pronounced him a true philosopher. He died in 1786.

Élie de la Poterie, ȧ′le′ dĕh lȧ pot′re′, (JEAN ANTOINE,) a French physician, brother of the preceding, was born about 1731. He died in 1794, leaving a few able treatises on mesmerism, pharmacy, etc.

Élien, the French of ÆLIAN, which see.

Eliezer. See ELEAZAR.

E-lī-e′zẹr, a Jewish rabbi and writer, surnamed THE GREAT, lived in Palestine about 100 A.D.

Eligius. See ELOI.

Eligoum. See ELIKOUM.

E-lī′jah [Heb. אֵלִיָּהוּ or אֵלִיָּה] THE TISHBITE, an eminent Hebrew prophet, whose name is written ELIAS in the New Testament, [Fr. ÉLIE, ȧ′le′.] He was a native of Thisbe. The first recorded fact in his history is that he predicted to Ahab a great drought. (I. Kings xvii. I.) He made zealous efforts to convert the people from idolatry, and was the honoured instrument in the most signal manifestations of miraculous power. Finally, favoured with an exemption from the common doom of mortality, he was translated to heaven about 895 B.C.

See I. Kings xviii., xix., xx., xxi.; II. Kings i., ii.; Matthew xi. 14, xvii. 3; Luke i. 17; also, F. KORN, "Der Prophet Elias; ein Sonnen-Mythus," 1837; KRUMMACHER, "Elijah the Tishbite."

Elikoom or **Elikoum** (el-e-koom′) I., written also **Eligoum,** a Christian prince of the Orpelian race in Georgia. About 1168 he entered the service of the Sultan of Azerbaijân, who made him governor of Ispahan and other cities and in 1172 ceded to him part of Armenia. He had one son, Libarid, who succeeded him.

Elio, ā′le-o, (FRANCISCO XAVIER,) a Spanish general, born at Pampeluna in 1769. In 1805 he took Buenos Ayres from the English, and in 1811 defended the royalist cause against the insurgents of Montevideo. Recalled to Spain about 1812, he was appointed general of an army, fought against the French, aided to restore Ferdinand VII., and was made Captain-General of Valencia and Murcia in 1814. He was imprisoned by the insurgents in 1820, and executed at Valencia in 1822.

See SOUTHEY's "History of the Peninsular War."

Eliot, (GEORGE.) See EVANS, (MARIAN C.)

El′ī-ọt, (JARED,) an American preacher and botanist, born in Connecticut in 1685, was a grandson of John Eliot, the Apostle of the Indians. Died in 1763.

Eliot, (JOHN,) called "the Apostle of the Indians," was born in England in 1604, and was educated at Cambridge. He emigrated to Boston in 1631, and soon became minister of the church of Roxbury. He learned the language of the Indians, and began about 1646 to preach to the aborigines of Massachusetts in their own tongue. In the prosecution of his missionary work he travelled extensively, amidst great privations and dangers, and acquired great influence over the Indians, many of whom were converted by him. He translated the Bible into the Indian language, (1661-63.) Died in 1690.

See a "Life of John Eliot," by CONVERS FRANCIS, in SPARKS's "American Biography," vol. v., 1st series.

Eliot, (JOHN,) an American biographer and minister, born in Boston in 1754, was one of the founders of the

ā, ē, ī, ō, ū, ȳ, long; ȧ, ė, ȯ, same, less prolonged; ă, ĕ, ĭ, ŏ, ŭ, ў, short; ạ, ẹ, ị, ọ, obscure; fär, fȧll, fȧt; mĕt; nŏt; gŏŏd; mōōn;

Massachusetts Historical Society. He published the "New England Biographical Dictionary," (1809,) and other works. Died in 1813.

El'ĭ-ot, (Sir JOHN,) an eminent English statesman and orator, born at Port Eliot, in Cornwall, in April, 1590, was educated at Exeter College, Oxford. He left college in 1610, soon after which he travelled in France and Italy. In 1623 he was elected a member of Parliament, in which he became a leader of the popular party and an eloquent debater. "For quickness and completeness of classical allusion," says Forster, "Eliot had no rival in Parliament." In the second Parliament of Charles I. he made a great speech on grievances. He was the chief author of the impeachment of the Duke of Buckingham, against whom he uttered a powerful philippic, (1626.) For this speech he was committed to the Tower, from which, however, he was released about ten days later. "He had in great perfection," says Forster, "some of the highest qualities of an orator,—singular power of statement, clearness and facility in handling details, pointed classical allusion, keen and logical argument, forcible and rich declamation." In 1629 Eliot again offended the king by his remonstrance against arbitrary impositions, tonnage and poundage. The Parliament was suddenly dissolved by the king, and Eliot, with many other patriots, was committed to prison. As he refused to make dishonourable concessions, he was confined in a dark and cheerless apartment and treated with a severity that ruined his health. He died in the Tower in November, 1632. During this imprisonment he wrote a philosophical work entitled "The Monarchy of Man," (unpublished,) which is highly commended.

See JOHN FORSTER, "Sir John Eliot: a Biography," 2 vols., 1864; "Edinburgh Review" for July, 1864; "London Quarterly Review" for June, 1865.

Eliot, (SAMUEL,) an American historian, born in Boston, December 22, 1821. He graduated at Harvard with the highest honours of his class in 1839, and afterwards spent several years in Europe. While in Rome, in 1845, he formed the plan of writing "The History of Liberty," of which two volumes appeared in New York and London, in 1849, under the title of "The Liberty of Rome." Part II., entitled "The Early Christians," (2 vols. 8vo,) was published in 1858. In 1856 he published "A Manual of United States History from 1492 to 1850." He was chosen president of Trinity College, Hartford, in 1860.

Eliott. See ELLIOT.

Elisabetta, the Italian of ELIZABETH, which see.

Elisæus, el-e-see'us, [Fr. ÉLISÉ, à'le'zà',] an eminent Armenian historian, was secretary of Vartan, general of the Armenian and Georgian armies. In 449 he became a bishop. He wrote a history of the war of Vartan against Persia, a work of superior merit, which has been often reprinted and translated into English, French, and Italian. Died in 480 A.D.

Élisée, the French of ELISHA, which see,

Élisée, à'le'zà', (JEAN JACQUES COPEL,) known as FATHER ÉLISÉE, a noted French pulpit orator, born at Besançon in 1726, preached in the fashionable churches of Paris. His sermons were published and much admired. Died in 1783.

Élisée, (MARIE VINCENT Talachon—tă'lä'shòn',) a French surgeon, born at Lagny in 1753. He emigrated in 1792, and became chief surgeon of the royalist army. In 1797 Louis XVIII. chose him as his first surgeon. Died in 1817.

El-lī'sha, [Heb. אֱלִישָׁע; Fr. ÉLISÉE, à'le'zà',] the son of Shaphat, an eminent Hebrew prophet, was a disciple of Elijah, whose mantle he inherited and by whom he was anointed. (See I. Kings xix. 16–21.) He performed many miracles between 890 and 840 B.C.

See II. Kings ii., iii., iv., v., vi., vii., viii., and xiii.

Elisio, à-lee'se-o, [Lat. ELYS'IUS,] (GIOVANNI,) a Neapolitan physician, who lived about 1550.

Elissa. See DIDO.

E-liz'a-beth or E-lis'a-beth, of Scripture, was the wife of Zacharias and the mother of John the Baptist.

See Luke i. 5 to 57.

Eliz'abeth or Isabeau (e'zä'bō') OF ANGOULÊME was a daughter of Aimar, Count of Angoulême. She was married in 1200 to King John of England. Died in 1245.

Eliz'abeth [Ger. ELISABETH, à-lee'zä-bĕt] OF AUSTRIA, Queen of France, born in 1554, was a daughter of the emperor Maximilian II., and a granddaughter of Charles V. She was married in 1570 to Charles IX. of France, and had one child, a daughter, who died young. She expressed abhorrence of the Massacre of Saint Bartholomew. It is stated that after the death of Charles IX. she declined an offer of marriage from Philip II. of Spain. Died in Vienna in 1592.

See CLARY DARLEM, "Élisabeth d'Autriche, Reine de France," 1847; ALFRED DE MARTONNE, "Isabelle d'Autriche," 1848.

Eliz'abeth OF BOSNIA was the wife of Louis the Great, King of Hungary and Poland, who, dying in 1382, left her regent during the minority of his daughter Maria. She was put to death by Giornard of Croatia in 1386.

Eliz'abeth of ENGLAND, or OF YORK, a daughter of Edward IV. and Elizabeth Woodville, was born in 1466. She was married to Henry VII. in 1486, and became the mother of Arthur and Henry VIII.

Elizabeth, [Sp. ISABEL, e-sä-bĕl'; It. ELISABETTA, à-le-sä-bet'tä,] Queen of England, the daughter of Henry VIII. and of Anne Boleyn, was born at Greenwich on the 7th of September, 1533. In 1535 her father opened a negotiation for a marriage between Elizabeth and the Duke of Angoulême, son of Francis I. of France; but the alliance was not effected. In 1548 she was addressed by the ambitious Lord Seymour, with whom she indulged in a brief flirtation. She was endowed with superior mental powers, which were diligently improved by study, and, under the tuition of Roger Ascham, she attained a proficiency in classical learning. Before the age of seventeen she was mistress of the Latin, French, and Italian languages, and had read several Greek works. She was attached by her education to the Protestant Church. Her sister, Queen Mary, who regarded her with jealousy, committed her to the Tower in 1554, on the pretext that she was concerned in Wyatt's rebellion. Much apprehension was felt by the people that attempts might be made upon her life; but she was released from the Tower after the lapse of a few months, and removed to Woodstock. In 1558 she declined an offer of marriage from Eric, King of Sweden.

On the 17th of November, 1558, Mary died, and Elizabeth, with the general approbation, was proclaimed queen. Her popularity was doubtless increased by the contrast between her and the late sovereign. She acted with politic caution in her design of restoring the Protestant religion, retaining a number of Romanists in her privy council. She appointed William Cecil secretary of state, and Nicholas Bacon keeper of the great seal. She began the religious reform by ordering that a large part of the service should be read in English, and forbade the host to be elevated in her presence. The Catholic bishops refused to officiate at her coronation, excepting the Bishop of Carlisle, who, it seems, acted his part reluctantly. When Parliament met in 1559, a bill was passed which vested in the crown the supremacy claimed by the pope; the mass was abolished, and the liturgy of Edward VI. restored. "Thus," says Hume, "in one session, without any violence or tumult, was the whole system of religion altered by the will of a young woman." At her accession Elizabeth found England at war with France and in alliance with Philip of Spain, who made her an offer of marriage, which she declined. In 1559 Francis II. (King of France) having assumed the arms and title of England in right of his wife, Mary Stuart, Elizabeth retaliated by sending an army to Scotland, which drove the French out of that kingdom. In 1562 she supported with money and troops the French Huguenots, who were then engaged in civil war with the Catholics. The next year the Parliament, anxious respecting the succession, voted an address to the queen, in which they entreated her to choose a husband; but she returned an evasive answer, and was equally averse to decide in favour of any claimant to the succession or of any suitor for her hand. Besides the suitors already named, she gave encouragement to the Archduke Charles of Austria, the Duke of Anjou, and Robert Dudley, Earl of Leicester, the last of whom was the chief favourite from the early part of her reign until his death in 1588.

After the treaty with the French in 1564, England was at peace with foreign nations for more than twenty years,—a period of national prosperity and progress, in which commerce flourished and the naval power of the kingdom was greatly increased. Cecil, Lord Burleigh, was Elizabeth's prime minister and adviser during the greater part of her reign. For an account of her rivalry with the Queen of Scots, who was executed in 1587, see MARY STUART.

As the representatives of opposite interests in religion, Elizabeth and Philip of Spain had long felt a mutual hostility, which in 1588 resulted in the famous enterprise of the Invincible Armada, fitted out by Philip for the invasion of England. This armament, which consisted of more than 130 vessels and about 30,000 men, was commanded by the Duke of Medina Sidonia. The English harassed the Armada in the Channel by partial attacks, and defeated the Spaniards in a general action on the 8th of August. The Spanish admiral then retreated northward, intending to sail home by that circuitous route ; but, a violent storm having arisen near the Orkney Isles, more than fifty of the ships were wrecked and their crews perished. The Spanish loss was probably not less than 20,000 men. (Motley.) About this time Elizabeth began to show a decided partiality for the Earl of Essex. (See ESSEX.) Hostilities still continued between the English and Spaniards ; and, while Philip subsidized the French Catholics, Elizabeth sent an army to aid Henry IV. in 1590 and in several ensuing years. The reign of Elizabeth was considered eminently beneficial and glorious to the nation. It was illustrated by such names as Spenser, Shakspeare, Sidney, Bacon, and Raleigh. Her personal character was deformed by selfishness, inconstancy, deceit, heartlessness, and other unwomanly faults ; but she has generally been regarded as a ruler of eminent ability as well as courage. She died in 1603, after signifying her will that King James of Scotland should succeed her. (For a more particular account of Elizabeth's character, both as a woman and a queen, see Froude's "History of England," vols. vii. to x., and Motley's "United Netherlands," chaps. vi., vii., viii. *et seq.*)

See, also, DR. THOMAS BIRCH, "Memoirs of the Reign of Queen Elizabeth," 1754 ; CAMDEN, "History of Queen Elizabeth," ("Annales Rerum Anglicanarum," etc., 1625 ;) LUCY AIKIN, "Memoirs of the Court of Queen Elizabeth," 1818 ; HUME, "History of England," chaps. xxxviii. to xlix. ; GREGORIO LETI, "Historia ovvero Vita di Elisabetta, Regina d'Inghilterra," 1693 ; FR. VON RAUMER, "Die Königinnen Elisabeth von England und Maria von Scotland," 1836 ; ROBERT NAUTON, "Fragmenta Regalia, or Observations on the Late Queen Elizabeth," 1642 ; also an article entitled "Elizabeth and Mary," in "Blackwood's Magazine" for April, 1867 ; "London Quarterly Review" for July, 1854, and October, 1863 ; "Fraser's Magazine" for October and November, 1853.

Eliz′abeth (or **Élisabeth**) or **Isabelle**, e′zȧ′bėl′, OF FRANCE, born in Paris in 1389, was a daughter of Charles VI., and became the consort of Richard II. of England. Died in 1409.

Elizabeth OF FRANCE, daughter of Henry IV., was born in 1602, and was married to Philip IV. of Spain in 1615. Died in 1644.

Eliz′abeth, SAINT, OF HUNGARY, born at Presburg in 1207, was a daughter of Andrew (András) II., King of Hungary. She was married to Louis, Landgrave of Thuringia, in 1221, and was eminent for her fervent piety and ascetic life. Died in 1231.

See "History of Saint Elizabeth of Hungary," London, 1632 ; SCHOPPE, "Leben Elisabeth's der heiligen," 1834 ; CHARLES DE MONTALEMBERT, "Vie de S. Élisabeth de Hongrie," 1836.

Elizabeth, (**Élisabeth**,) (PHILIPPINE MARIE HÉLÈNE,) a French princess, usually called MADAME ÉLISABETH, a sister of Louis XVI., was born at Versailles in 1764. During the reign of terror she shared the dangers and adversities of the king with fortitude, was imprisoned in August, 1792, and executed in May, 1794.

See PARISOT, "Vie de Madame Élisabeth de France," 1814.

Elizabeth, daughter of the King of Poland, married Charobert, King of Hungary, in 1319. She was mother of three sons, one of whom, Louis, inherited his father's throne. By her intrigues and influence over her brother, Casimir of Poland, she procured for Louis also the throne of Poland in 1370. She was Regent of Poland from 1370 to 1378. Died in 1381.

Elizabeth OF VALOIS, a daughter of Henry II. of France, was born in 1545, and married to Philip II. of Spain in 1559. She died at Madrid in 1568.

Elizabeth, (CHARLOTTE.) See TONNA, MRS.

Elizabeth, PRINCESS PALATINE, the daughter of Frederick V. of Bohemia and Elizabeth Stuart of England, was born in 1618. She received lessons in philosophy from Descartes, who is reported to have said that he "found none, except her, who thoroughly understood his works." She was instructed in religion by William Penn, whose friendship she highly valued. Having declined an offer of marriage from the King of Poland, she retired to Hervorden, where she died in 1680. The famous Prince Rupert was her brother, and George I. of England was her sister's son.

See PRUDHOMME, "Biographie des Femmes célèbres."

Eliz′abeth Alexiev′na, (â-lěks-e-êv′nâ,) Empress of Russia, born in 1779, was a princess of Baden, whose original name was LOUISA MARIA AUGUSTA. In 1793 she became the consort of Alexander I., then grand duke. Her character is represented as very amiable. Died in 1826.

Elizabeth (**Elisabeth**) **Christi′na** or **Christi′ne**, (κris-tee′nȧ,) Queen of Prussia, born at Brunswick in 1715, was a daughter of Ferdinand Albert, Duke of Brunswick-Wolfenbüttel. In 1732 or 1733 she was married to Frederick the Great. She had a literary taste, and was distinguished for modesty, piety, and many virtues. She translated several religious works into French. Died in 1797.

See VON HAHNKE, "Elisabeth Christine, Königin von Preussen," Berlin, 1848.

Elizabeth Christina or **Christine**, Empress of Germany, born in 1691, was a daughter of the Duke of Brunswick-Wolfenbüttel. She was the wife of Charles VI., Emperor of Germany, and the mother of Maria Theresa. Died in 1750.

Eliz′abeth Farnese, (far-neez′; It. pron. faR-nā′sȧ,) a daughter of Odouard II., Prince of Parma, was born in 1692. She was married in 1714 to Philip V. of Spain, and, being crafty and ambitious, soon acquired a complete ascendency over that indolent, timid, and uxorious king. (See PHILIP V.) Charles III. was her son. Died in 1766.

See "Memoirs of Elizabeth Farnese," London, 4 vols., 1746.

Eliz′abeth Petrovna, (or **Petrow′na**,) pȧ-trov′nâ, Empress of Russia, the daughter of Peter the Great and Catherine I., was born in 1709. In 1740 Ivan, the infant son of the Duke of Brunswick, was proclaimed emperor, in accordance with the will of the late empress Anna. By a successful conspiracy of Elizabeth's partisans, of whom her surgeon, Lestocq, was the leader, she obtained the throne in 1741. In the Seven Years' war, which began in 1756, she co-operated with the enemies of Frederick the Great so successfully that her army entered Berlin in 1760 ; and he was probably saved from ruin only by her death. She was indolent and dissolute, but inclined to clemency. Though never married, she had several children. She founded the University of Moscow and the Academy of Fine Arts at Petersburg. She died in the winter of 1761–62, and was succeeded by her nephew, Peter III.

See LECLERC, "Histoire de la Russie moderne ;" LOMONOSOF, "Panegyricus Elizabethæ Imperatricis," 1749 ; WIEDEMEYER, "Die Regierung der Kaiserin Elisabeth Petrowna," 2 vols., 1834.

Eliz′abeth Stu′art, Queen of Bohemia, born in 1596, was the daughter of James I. of England and Anne of Denmark. She was distinguished for beauty and captivating manners. In 1613 she became the wife of the Elector Palatine Frederick V. In 1619 she prevailed on him to accept the offered crown of Bohemia. This step involved him in war ; he was defeated in 1620, and lost even his hereditary state. Among her numerous children was Prince Rupert, the famous Cavalier. Died in England in 1662.

See MISS BENGER, "Memoirs of Elizabeth Stuart," 1825 ; GARDINER, "History of England," vol. ii. chap. x.

Eliz′abeth Wood′ville, a daughter of Sir Richard Woodville, was distinguished for her personal beauty. She was married to Sir John Gray, and after his death to Edward IV. in 1464. She was the mother of Edward V. and of Elizabeth, the queen of Henry VII. Died in 1488.

ā, ē, ī, ō, ū, ȳ, *long ;* à, ė, ò, same, less prolonged ; ă, ĕ, ĭ, ŏ, ŭ, ў, *short ;* ą, ę, į, ǫ, *obscure ;* fär, fäll, fät ; mêt ; nŏt ; gōŏd ; mōŏn ;

Ellain, ȧ'lȧN', (NICOLAS,) a French physician and poet, born in Paris in 1534; died in 1621.

Ellenborough, el'len-bŭr'ruh, (EDWARD LAW,) LORD, an eminent English lawyer, born at Great Salkeld, Cumberland, in 1750, was a son of Edmund Law, Bishop of Carlisle. After practising some years with success, and becoming the leader of the northern circuit, he was employed in 1785 as leading counsel for the defence in the trial of Warren Hastings, after Erskine had refused to act on that side. Although he could not compete with Burke or Fox in eloquent declamation or in logical argument, he managed the case with a certain skill and success. In 1801 Law was appointed attorney-general. On the death of Lord Kenyon, in 1802, he became lord chief justice of the king's bench, and was created Baron Ellenborough. In the House of Lords he opposed all measures for the relief of Catholics, and voted for the impeachment of Lord Melville in 1806. He is said to have been extremely grieved by the acquittal of William Hone, the popular author, in 1818, at whose trial he presided. He died in 1818, and left his title to his son, the present Earl of Ellenborough. As a judge, Lord Brougham says, "no one could accuse him of partiality. He despatched business with great celerity, and for the most part with success."

See LORD CAMPBELL, "Lives of the Chief Justices;" Foss, "The Judges of England;" BROUGHAM, "Statesmen of the Time of George III."

Ellenborough, (EDWARD LAW,) first EARL OF, a Tory statesman, and a son of the preceding, was born in 1790. He inherited the title of baron in 1818, and was appointed lord privy seal in 1828. During the brief ministry of Sir Robert Peel in 1835 he was president of the Board of Control. He was appointed Governor-General of India in 1842, and, having annexed Scinde and Gwalior by conquest, was recalled in 1844 and raised to the rank of earl. He was first lord of the admiralty in 1845 and 1846. On the accession of the Derby-Disraeli ministry, in February, 1858, he became president of the Board of Control. The publication of a despatch in which he condemned Lord Canning's conduct in India, gave so much offence that Ellenborough resigned a few months after his appointment. The House of Lords, by a majority of nine, rejected a motion to censure him for his conduct in this affair.

See "Foreign Quarterly Review" for January, 1845.

Ellenrieder, el'len-ree'der, (MARIA,) a German painter of history and genre, was born at Constance in 1791. She visited Italy, and lived at Munich and Carlsruhe. She is considered by the Germans the most skilful female artist of her time. Among her works is a picture of "Faith, Hope, and Charity."

Eller, el'ler, (JOHANN THEODOR,) a German physician and chemist, born at Pleskau in 1689. He was physician to Frederick the Great, who made him a privy councillor in 1755. He wrote "Observationes de Cognoscendis et Curandis Morbis," (" Observations on the Diagnosis and Cure of Diseases," 1762,) and other medical works. Died in 1760.

See ADELUNG, Supplement to JÖCHER, "Allgemeines Gelehrten-Lexikon."

El'ler-y̆, (WILLIAM,) an American patriot, born at Newport, Rhode Island, in 1727, was educated at Harvard College. He was engaged in mercantile pursuits in his native city for some years, and began the practice of the law in 1770. Having established a character for integrity, good sense, and firm attachment to public welfare and liberty, he was chosen a delegate to the memorable Congress of 1776, in which he signed the Declaration of Independence. Placing himself by the side of Secretary Thompson, he observed the expression and manner of each member in the act of signing his name, and was convinced that the men were equal to the crisis. He continued to serve in Congress (with the exception of two years) until the end of 1785, being rather eminent for his talents for business than for his powers as a debater. Retiring from public service in 1785, he found himself reduced in fortune by his patriotism, as his dwelling had been burnt by the enemy. In 1790 he was appointed to the office of collector of customs in Newport, which he retained to the end of his life.

His political sympathies were with the Federal party. Died in 1820.

See a "Life of W. Ellery," in SPARKS's "American Biography,' by his son-in-law, E. T. CHANNING, vol. vi., 1st series ; GOODRICH, "Lives of the Signers to the Declaration of Independence."

Ellesmere, EARL OF. See EGERTON, (FRANCIS LEVESON GOWER.)

Ellesmere, LORD. See EGERTON, (THOMAS.)

El'let, (CHARLES,) an American engineer, born at Penn's Manor, Bucks county, Pennsylvania, in 1810. He constructed the wire suspension bridge at Fairmount, Philadelphia, (the first made in America,) and that which crosses the Niagara River below the Falls. He was employed as engineer of several railroads. After the civil war began, he became a colonel of engineers, and converted several steamers into rams for military operations on the Mississippi River. He received in a naval battle near Memphis a wound, of which he died in June, 1862.

Ellet, (ELIZABETH FRIES,)an authoress, whose maiden name was LUMMIS, was born at Sodus Point, New York, in 1818. She published, besides other works, a volume of poems, (1835,) " Women of the American Revolution," (1848,) and "Summer Rambles in the West," (1853.)

See GRISWOLD's "Female Poets of America."

Ellet, (WILLIAM HENRY,) M.D., an American chemist, born in New York about 1804, became professor of chemistry, etc. in South Carolina College about 1835. He discovered a method of preparing gun-cotton. The poetess Elizabeth F. Ellet was his wife. Died in New York in 1859.

Elleviou, êl've'oo', (PIERRE JEAN BAPTISTE FRANÇOIS,) a French singer and composer, born at Rennes in 1769 ; died in 1842.

El'lIce, (EDWARD,) an English politician of the Whig party, born about 1786, was a merchant of London, and for many years an influential member of Parliament. In 1830 he became secretary of the treasury, and was secretary of war from April, 1833, to December, 1834. His wife was a sister of the first Earl Grey. Died in 1863.

Ellicot. See ELLICOTT.

El'lI-cott, (ANDREW,) surveyor-general of the United States, born in Bucks county, Pennsylvania, in 1754, served as an officer in the Revolution, and throughout the greater part of his life filled important positions under the Federal and State governments. In 1790 he laid out the Federal metropolis. He was appointed surveyor-general in 1792 ; from 1796 to 1801 he acted as commissioner in settling the southern boundary of the United States, and from 1812 till his death, in 1820, was professor of mathematics, engineering, etc. at West Point. He made valuable contributions to the Transactions of philosophical societies of Europe.

El'lI-cott or **El'lI-cot,** (CHARLES JOHN,) an English theologian, born near Stamford about 1820. He became professor of divinity in King's College, London, in 1858, and Bishop of Gloucester and Bristol in 1863. He published, besides other works, "Commentaries on the Epistles of Saint Paul to the Galatians, Ephesians, Philippians, Colossians," etc.

Ellies-Dupin. See DUPIN, (LOUIS.)

Elliger, el'le-ger,(OTTOMAR,) a skilful Swedish painter, born at Gottenburg in 1633. He became painter to the Elector Frederick William at Berlin.

Elliger, (OTTOMAR,) son of the above, a skilful historical painter, born at Hamburg in 1666, was a pupil of Lairesse, and worked in Amsterdam. He excelled in architectural pictures. Among his best works are "The Feast of the Gods," and the "Nuptials of Thetis and Peleus." Died in 1732.

See DESCAMPS, "Vies des Peintres Flamands," etc.

Ellinger, el'ling-er, (ANDREAS,) a German physician, born in Thuringia in 1526, was professor at Leipsic. He wrote "Hippocratis Aphorismi," in Latin verse, (1579.) Died in 1582.

El'lI-ot, (GEORGE,) an English admiral, born in 1784, commanded the fleet which operated against the Chinese in 1840, and became vice-admiral in 1847.

El'lI-ot or **El'I-ott,** (GEORGE AUGUSTUS,) Lord Heathfield, born at Stobbs, in Scotland, in 1718, entered the army at an early age. From 1740 to 1748 he served in Germany as lieutenant-colonel and aide-de-camp of George II. He was second in command at the capture of Havana. In 1775, having obtained the rank of lieutenant-general, he was appointed Governor of Gibraltar, the defence of which was his last and most memorable achievement. During the siege, which commenced in 1779 and continued more than three years, he successfully resisted the combined armaments of France and Spain, displaying great prudence and humanity, as well as high military talents. After peace was restored, he was raised to the peerage, with the title of Lord Heathfield of Gibraltar. Died in 1790.

See CHAMBERS, "Biographical Dictionary of Eminent Scotsmen."

Elliot, (Sir GILBERT,) sometimes styled LORD MINTO, was a Scottish judge, who lived in the early part of the eighteenth century. He became lord justice clerk, and was distinguished for his patriotic efforts in favour of the Protestant succession.

Elliot (Sir GILBERT) of Minto, a British orator, son of the preceding, was the father of the first Earl of Minto, and was eminent as a parliamentary speaker. He wrote an admired pastoral beginning thus:

"My sheep I neglected, I broke my sheep-hook,
And all the gay haunts of my youth I forsook."

Died in 1777.

Elliot, (Sir GILBERT,) the first Earl of Minto, an eminent Scottish statesman, born in Edinburgh in 1751, was the son of the preceding. In 1774 he was returned to Parliament for Morpeth. In 1777 he married the daughter of Sir George Aymand. He acted with the party of Mr. Fox for several years, but about 1790 he changed sides and supported the ministry. In 1793 he was sent, with two other commissioners, to protect the Bourbon interest in Toulon and Corsica. In 1796 he was raised to the peerage, as Baron Minto. He was appointed Governor-General of India in 1806, and, after an able and successful administration, returned home in 1814. He died in June of that year. He had been created Earl of Minto in 1813.

See CHAMBERS, "Biographical Dictionary of Eminent Scotsmen."

Elliot, (GILBERT ELLIOT MURRAY KYNINMOUND,) second Earl of Minto, a son of the preceding, was born in 1782. He was elected to Parliament in 1806, and entered the House of Lords in 1814. He was sent as ambassador to Berlin in 1832, and was appointed first lord of the admiralty, under the Whig ministry, in 1835. From 1846 to 1852 he was lord privy seal in the cabinet of Lord John Russell, who was his son-in-law. He died in 1859, leaving several sons.

Elliot, (Miss JANE,) a sister of Sir Gilbert Elliot of Minto, wrote an admired dirge for the slain at the battle of Flodden, entitled "The Flowers of the Forest."

Elliot, (WILLIAM,) an English designer and engraver, born at Hampton Court in 1717. He excelled in landscapes. Died in 1766.

El-lĭ-ŏt-sŏn, (JOHN,) F.R.S., an eminent English physician, born in London about 1795. He became physician to Saint Thomas's Hospital in 1822. By new prescriptions of prussic acid and creosote, and other innovations in medical practice, he excited much hostility among a portion of the medical profession. He was chosen professor of medical science in University College, London, in 1831, and afterwards became president of the Royal Medical and Chirurgical Society. He was the author of valuable works entitled "Principles and Practice of Medicine," (1839,) and "Human Physiology," (1840.) Died in August, 1868.

Elliott. See ELIOT, ELIOTT, and ELYOT.

El-lĭ-ŏtt, (CHARLES,) a Methodist minister, born in the county of Donegal, Ireland, in 1792, emigrated to Ohio about 1818, and edited the "Western Christian Advocate" for many years. He wrote several religious works.

Elliott, (CHARLES LORING,) an American portrait-painter, born in Scipio, New York, in 1812. He lived many years in New York City, and painted portraits of many eminent persons. His works are remarkable for fidelity of likeness and vigorous colouring. Died in August, 1868.

See H. T. TUCKERMAN's "Book of the Artists," 1867.

Elliott, (CHARLES WYLLYS,) an American author, a descendant of John Eliot, "the Apostle of the Indians," was born in Guilford, Connecticut, in 1817. He has published a "History of New England from the Discovery of the Continent by the Northmen, in 986, to 1776."

El-lĭ-ŏtt, (EBENEZER,) an English poet, called "the Corn-Law Rhymer," was born at Masborough, near Rotherham, Yorkshire, on the 17th of March, 1781. His father was a clerk in an iron-foundry, with a small salary, and was a strict Calvinist. The son, after having made small progress at school, where he passed for a very dull boy, was set to work in the foundry above mentioned, in which he was employed many years. A love of nature and of books counteracted the tendency to intemperance and other vices usual among his associates. In his seventeenth year he began to write verses, the first of which were the "Vernal Walk," and "Night." In 1821 he removed to Sheffield, where he gained a competence in the iron-trade. Soon after this change of residence he wrote his most popular poem, the "Corn-Law Rhymes," urging the repeal of duties on corn, which excited general admiration. He wrote also "The Village Patriarch," (1829,) "Byron and Napoleon," (1831,) "Love," and a few other poems. The poet Montgomery says, "I am quite willing to hazard my critical credit by avowing my persuasion that in originality and power he might have measured heads beside Byron in tremendous energy, Crabbe in graphic description, and Coleridge in effusions of domestic tenderness; while in intense sympathy with the poor, in whatever he deemed their wrongs or their sufferings, he excelled them all." Died in 1849.

See J. SERLE, "Life, Character, and Genius of Ebenezer Elliott," 1850; "Brief Biographies," by SAMUEL SMILES, 1860; JOHN WATKINS, "Life, Poetry, and Letters of E. Elliott," 1850; "Edinburgh Review" for July, 1832, and October, 1834; "Westminster Review" for January and April, 1850.

Elliott, (JESSE DUNCAN,) an American naval officer, born in Maryland in 1782. He was second in command under Commodore Perry at the battle of Lake Erie, September, 1813, and was raised to the rank of captain in 1818. Died in 1845.

Elliott, (STEPHEN,) an American naturalist, born at Beaufort, South Carolina, in 1771, graduated at Yale College in 1791. He became president of the Literary Society and of the Philosophical Society of South Carolina, and professor of natural history at Charleston. He was the author of a valuable work entitled "The Botany of South Carolina and Georgia," (2 vols., 1821-24.) Died in 1830.

Elliott, (STEPHEN,) D.D., son of the preceding, was born at Beaufort, South Carolina, in 1806. He became professor of sacred literature in South Carolina College. He was ordained in 1835, and was constituted Bishop of Georgia in 1841.

Elliott, (WILLIAM,) a politician and writer, born at Beaufort, South Carolina, in 1788. He opposed nullification in 1832, and afterwards wrote against secession, (1851.) Among his works are "Fiesco," a tragedy, (1850,) and several short poems.

El'lis, (CLEMENT,) an English divine, born in Cumberland in 1630, was appointed prebendary of Southwell in 1693. He was the author of several approved works on theology. Died in 1700.

See JOHN VENEER, "Life of Clement Ellis," 1738.

Ellis, (GEORGE,) F.R.S., a witty and accomplished English writer, born in 1745. During the French Revolution he gained distinction as one of the authors of the "Rolliad," (a political satire against Pitt and his ministry,) for which he wrote the "Birth-Day Ode" and the "Ode on Dundas." In 1790 he published "Specimens of the Early English Poets," which is thought to have rendered an essential service to the national literature. Ellis was distinguished for his refined taste as well as for his literary attainments. In 1800 he became the friend of Sir Walter Scott, who addressed to him the fifth canto of "Marmion," and who is reported to have said "he was one of the most accomplished scholars and delightful companions he had ever known." In 1797-98 he wrote many articles for "The Anti-Jacobin," a weekly paper under the auspices of Canning. Died in 1815.

ā, ē, ī, ō, ū, ȳ, *long;* ă, ĕ, ĭ, ŏ, ŭ, ў, *short;* ą, ę, į, ǫ, *obscure;* fär, fȧll, fȧt; mĕt; nŏt; gōōd; mōōn;

El'lis, (GEORGE EDWARD,) D.D., a distinguished Unitarian divine and author, born in Boston in 1815. He graduated at Harvard in 1833, and about 1838 was ordained pastor at Charlestown. In 1857 he was appointed professor of theology in the Divinity School at Cambridge, a position which he held for five years. He wrote several memoirs for Sparks's "American Biography," and a "Half-Century of the Unitarian Controversy," (1857.) In 1864 he gave a course of Lowell Lectures on the "Evidences of Christianity."

Ellis, (GEORGE JAMES WELBORE AGAR,) Lord Dover, an English author, born in 1797, was educated at Oxford. He was elected to Parliament in 1818 and at several subsequent periods. In 1831 he was raised to the peerage as Baron Dover, and the next year was chosen president of the Royal Society of Literature. Among his principal works are "Life of Frederick II. of Prussia," (1831,) and "The Ellis Correspondence, illustrative of the Revolution of 1688." He also contributed to the Edinburgh and London Quarterly Reviews. Died in 1833.

Ellis, (HENRY,) an English navigator, born in 1721. He accompanied an expedition which sailed from England in 1746 in search of a Northwest passage. Captains Moore and Smith commanded this expedition, Ellis being employed as naturalist and agent of the committee which sent it out. He published a narrative of his voyage, (1748,) and was afterwards Governor of New York and Georgia. Died in 1806.

See ERSCH und GRUBER, "Allgemeine Encyklopaedie."

Ellis, (Sir HENRY,) an English antiquary, born in London in 1777. He became assistant librarian of the British Museum in 1805. In 1823 he published the first series of "Original Letters illustrative of English History," (3 vols., second series, 1827; third series, 1846, 4 vols.) He was principal librarian of the British Museum from 1827 to 1856. Among his valuable works are "Elgin Marbles of the Classic Ages," (2 vols., 1847,) and "The Townley Gallery of Sculpture," (1847.) Died in January, 1869.

Ellis, (Sir HENRY,) K.C.B., an English officer, who in 1816 accompanied Lord Amherst as secretary of embassy to China with dormant credentials as minister plenipotentiary, and published an interesting Journal of the Embassy, with Observations on China and the Chinese. Died in 1855.

Ellis, (JOHN,) a literary scrivener, born in London in 1698, was a particular favourite of Dr. Johnson, who said, "The most literary conversation that I ever enjoyed was at the table of Jack Ellis the money-scrivener, with whom, at one period, I used to dine generally once a week." He wrote "The South Sea Dream," (1720,) a poem, and often exercised his talent in poetical squibs. He also translated Ovid's "Epistles," and other Latin poems. Died about 1791.

Ellis, (JOHN,) F.R.S., an eminent English naturalist, born in London about 1710, was a merchant in early life. In 1754 he published an "Essay towards the Natural History of Corallines," in which the opinion was first advanced that they are of animal origin. He also wrote treatises on "Coffee," the "Bread-Fruit Tree," and other subjects. Died in 1776.

See ERSCH und GRUBER, "Allgemeine Encyklopaedie."

Ellis, (SIR RICHARD.) See ELLYS.

Ellis, (ROBERT LESLIE,) an English philosopher and mathematician of Cambridge, was born in 1817. He edited, in conjunction with James Spedding and D. Denon Heath, "The Philosophical Works of Lord Bacon," (5 vols., 1857-58.) Died in 1859.

Ellis, (SARAH,) a popular English authoress, whose maiden name was STICKNEY, was born about 1812. She was married to William Ellis, author of "Polynesian Researches," in 1837, before which she had published a successful work, "The Poetry of Life." She rendered important services to female education by numerous works, among which are "The Women of England," (1838,) "The Daughters of England," (1842,) "The Wives of England," (1843,) "The Mothers of England," (1843,) "Family Secrets," (1841-43,) and "Pictures of Private Life," (3 vols., 1844.)

Ellis, (WILLIAM,) an English surgeon, who accompanied Captain Cook in his third voyage, (1776-79,) and published a well-written narrative of that voyage, (2 vols., 1782.) Died at Ostend in 1785.

Ellis, (Rev. WILLIAM,) an eminent English missionary and author. He was sent by the London Missionary Society to the South Sea Islands in 1816, and returned home in 1825. In 1829 he published his very interesting "Polynesian Researches," (2 vols. 8vo,) and in 1838 a "History of Madagascar," (2 vols.) "Here is a work as copious, as comprehensive, as minute, and, as far as we can judge, as accurate, as it would be possible to produce." ("London Eclectic Review.") He married Sarah Ellis, noticed above, in 1837.

Ellis, (WILLIAM,) an English economist and writer on social science, was born near London in 1800. He distinguished himself by successful efforts to introduce the study of political economy into schools. He wrote "Outlines of Social Economy," "Phenomena of Industrial Life," "Progressive Lessons in Social Science," and other works.

Ellisen. See ELLISSEN.

Ellissen, el'lis-sen, or Ellisen, (ADOLF,) a German critic and historian, born at Gartow, Lüneburg, in 1815, was a moderate democratic member of the parliament of Frankfort in 1848. He translated Montesquieu's "Esprit des Lois," (1844.) Among his works are an "Essay of a Polyglot of European Poetry," ("Versuch einer Polyglotte der Europäischen Poesie," 1846,) and one "On the History of Athens since the Loss of its Liberty," (1848.)

Ell'is-ton, (ROBERT WILLIAM,) a celebrated English actor, born in London in 1774, ran away from school, and appeared on the stage for the first time at Bath in 1791. After obtaining success in the provinces, he made his début at the Haymarket in 1796. In 1803 he was principal actor and acting manager of that theatre, where he acquired great popularity. When Drury Lane was rebuilt after the fire, Elliston became one of its leading performers. He was the lessee of the theatre last named from 1819 to 1826, when he became insolvent. He was very successful in a great variety of characters; and he is generally regarded as the most excellent comedian that the English nation has produced. Died in 1831.

See G. RAYMOND, "Memoirs of Elliston," 1846.

Ells'worth, (EPHRAIM ELMER,) a brave American patriot, born at Mechanicsville, Saratoga county, New York, in 1837. He removed to Chicago before he was of age, and studied law. He organized about 1859 a zouave corps which became noted for the excellence of its discipline. In March, 1861, he accompanied President Lincoln to Washington, and in April he went to New York City, where he organized a zouave regiment of firemen, of which he became the colonel. He was ordered to Alexandria, where he saw a rebel flag floating over a hotel. He ascended to the roof and took down the flag, for which act Jackson, the keeper of the hotel, immediately shot him dead, in May, 1861. Jackson was instantly afterwards killed by one of the soldiers of Ellsworth.

Ellsworth, (OLIVER,) Chief Justice of the United States, was born in Windsor, Connecticut, April 29, 1745. He graduated at Princeton, New Jersey, in 1766, was admitted to the bar in 1771, and chosen a delegate to the Continental Congress in 1777. He was a member of the Convention which in 1787 formed the Federal Constitution, and was elected in 1789 to the Senate of the United States. He acquired distinction as a debater, and acted with the Federal party. According to John Adams, "he was the firmest pillar of Washington's whole administration in that body." He was appointed chief justice of the United States by Washington in 1796. His official conduct in this position was generally approved. He was sent to Paris in 1799 as envoy extraordinary, and, with his colleagues Davie and Murray, negotiated a treaty with France. He died in 1807, leaving a high reputation for ability and integrity.

See "National Portrait-Gallery of Distinguished Americans," vol. iv.: "Encyclopædia Americana."

Ell'wood, (THOMAS,) an English author, born at Crowell, in Oxfordshire, in 1639, adopted at an early age the religion of the "Friends," or Quakers, among whom he became a prominent member and a public minister. In 1662, having a desire to improve himself in learning, he procured, by the mediation of Isaac Penington and Dr. Paget, the place of reader to the poet Milton, who was then blind and resided in London. Ellwood says, "he kept always a man to read to him, which usually was the son of some gentleman, whom in kindness he took to improve in his learning. . . . I went every day in the afternoon, (except on the first days of the week,) and, sitting by him in his dining-room, read to him in such books in the Latin tongue as he pleased to hear." Thus they went on pleasantly together for six weeks, when ill health compelled Ellwood to leave London. The world is indebted to his suggestion for Milton's second epic poem, "Paradise Regained." In 1665 Ellwood paid a visit to Milton at Giles-Chalfont, where, says he, "after some common discourse had passed between us, he called for a manuscript of his, which he delivered to me, bidding me take it home with me and read it at my leisure, and, when I had done so, return it to him with my judgment thereon." He found it was "Paradise Lost," and, when he returned it, was asked by the author how he liked it and what he thought of it. Ellwood "modestly and freely" answered this question, and added, "Thou hast said much here of Paradise Lost; but what hast thou to say of Paradise Found?" "He made no answer, but sat some time in a muse." Ellwood published a "Sacred History," (1705,) and a poem called "Davideis," (1712.) He died in 1713, leaving interesting "Memoirs of his own Life," (1714.)

See, also, "The Penns and Peningtons," by MARIA WEBB, London, 1867; "Retrospective Review," vol. xiii., 1826.

El'lys, (ANTHONY,) an English divine, born in 1693, became Bishop of Saint David's in 1752. He wrote "Tracts on the Liberty, Spiritual and Temporal, of Subjects in England," and a few other works. Died in 1761.

Ellys or **El'lis,** (Sir RICHARD,) a grandson of the English patriot Hampden, was a member of Parliament from 1715 to 1734. He excelled in Hebrew, Greek, and biblical criticism, on which he published a work called "Fortuita Sacra," (1728.) Died in 1742.

Elmacîn, êl-mâ-seen', (GEORGE,) [Lat. GEOR'GIUS ELMACI'NUS,] written also **Elmakin** (êl-mâ-keen') and **Almakin,** an Oriental historian and Christian, born in Egypt in 1223, became secretary to the court of the Sultans of Egypt. He wrote, in Arabic, a history of the world from the creation to 1118 A.D., which obtained European celebrity, and part of which was translated by Erpenius about 1625. Died in 1273.

See HOTTINGER, "Bibliotheca Orientalis."

Elmacinus, (GEORGIUS.) See ELMACÎN.

Elmakin. See ELMACÎN.

Elmenhorst, êl'men-horst', (GEVERHARD, GERHARD, or GERHART,) a distinguished German critic, born at Hamburg, published notes on Arnobius, (1603,) Minucius Felix, and other old authors. Died in 1621.

See BAYLE, "Historical and Critical Dictionary."

Elmenhorst, (HEINRICH,) a German poet and pastor, born at Parchim in 1632, wrote "Spiritual Songs," and "Dramatologia antiquo-hodierna," (1688.) Died in 1704.

Elmer. See AYLMER.

Elmes, êlmz, (HARVEY LONSDALE,) an eminent English architect, born near Chichester about 1814, was the son of James Elmes, noticed below, with whom he entered into partnership in London. His reputation as an architect is chiefly founded on the erection of Saint George's Hall, Liverpool, his design for which was preferred to those of about eighty competitors. This edifice, which is esteemed the principal ornament of Liverpool, and one of the finest specimens of the Corinthian order in England, was finished about 1855. It is 490 feet long by 165 feet wide. Before its completion Mr. Elmes's health failed; he died in Jamaica in 1847.

Elmes, (JAMES,) the father of the preceding, was born in London in 1782. He was architect of several public and private buildings of London, and acquired distinction as a writer. He published "The Life and Works of Sir Christopher Wren," (1823,) "School of the Fine Arts," (3 vols., 1825,) "Ecclesiastical and Civil Dilapidations," (3d edition, 1829,) "Thomas Clarkson, a Monograph," (1854,) and other works. Died in 1862.

El'more, (ALFRED,) an Irish historical painter, born at Clonakilty, county of Cork, about 1816. He became a student in London, where he worked with success. Among his chief productions are "Rienzi in the Forum," (1844,) "The Fainting of Hero," (1846,) "The Inventor of the Stocking-Loom," (1847,) and "The Emperor Charles V. at Yuste," (1856.)

El'more, (FRANKLIN HARPER,) an American financier and politician, was born in Laurens district, South Carolina, in 1799. He was a member of Congress in 1837–39, and was president of the Bank of the State of South Carolina from 1840 to 1850. In this year he was chosen to fill a vacancy in the Senate of the United States caused by the death of John C. Calhoun. Died in May, 1850.

Elms'ley, (PETER,) an eminent English critic, and one of the first Greek scholars of his time, was born in 1773. He wrote articles for the early numbers of the "Edinburgh Review" about 1802. In 1819 he was chosen to assist Sir Humphry Davy in unrolling the Herculanean manuscripts. After this date he lived chiefly at Oxford, where, in 1823, he became professor of history. He published excellent editions of several dramas by Euripides and Sophocles, which gained him a European fame. Southey, speaking of the Edinburgh Reviewers, said, "Elmsley has more knowledge and a sounder mind than any or all of them." Died in 1825.

Éloi, â'lwâ', [Lat. ELIG'IUS,] a French benefactor, born near Limoges in 588 A.D., became a favourite minister of King Dagobert, and founded monasteries and hospitals. He was appointed Bishop of Noyon in 640. Died in 659.

See SAINT-OUEN, "Vita Eligii;" BARTHÉLEMY, "Vie de Saint-Eloi."

Elorza. See CHURRUCA Y ELORZA.

Éloy, â'lwâ', (NICOLAS FRANÇOIS JOSEPH,) a Flemish physician, born at Mons in 1714, was employed professionally by Prince Charles of Lorraine. He wrote a "Historical Dictionary of Medicine, Ancient and Modern," (4 vols., 1778.) Died in 1788.

Elphege, êl'fe-ge, ? written also **Alphege,** an English prelate, born in 954 A.D., became Archbishop of Canterbury in 1006. He was killed by the Danish pirates in 1011.

See W. F. HOOK, "Lives of the Archbishops of Canterbury," vol. i., 1860.

El'phin-ston, (ARTHUR,) Lord Balmerino, a Scottish Jacobite, born in 1688. On the accession of George I. he took arms for the Stuart cause, and fought at Sheriffmuir. He was taken prisoner at the battle of Culloden in 1745, and, after trial, was executed in 1746.

Elphinston, (JAMES,) an eccentric Scottish grammarian, born in Edinburgh in 1721, was for many years principal of a successful school at Kensington, near London. He associated with Dr. Johnson, by whom he was highly esteemed, and he made versions of certain Latin mottoes of the "Rambler," which were adopted by the editor of that work. He published, among other works, "Education," a poem, (1763,) "Propriety ascertained in her Picture," and "English Grammar reduced to Analogy," (1765,) in which he advocated a reform of orthography on phonetic principles. Died in 1809.

See CHAMBERS, "Biographical Dictionary of Eminent Scotsmen."

Elphinston, (JOHN,) an able naval officer, born in the Highlands of Scotland in 1720. In 1768 his government placed him at the disposal of Catherine, Empress of Russia, who employed him as admiral of the fleet sent against the Turks in 1770. After fighting one battle near Scio, and burning a Turkish fleet, he quarrelled with Orloff, the Russian general-in-chief, and left the service. Died in 1774.

See RULHIÈRES, "Histoire de l'Anarchie de Pologne."

El'phin-stone, (GEORGE KEITH,) Viscount Keith, a distinguished British admiral, born in Scotland in 1746, was the son of Viscount Elphinstone. As post-captain he served in America about 1776. In 1795 he obtained the rank of vice-admiral, and captured Cape Town. In 1800 he was commander-in-chief in the Mediterranean, where he took Malta and Genoa. For his services in Egypt he was raised to the British peerage, as Baron Keith, (1801,) and obtained the rank of admiral. In 1814 he was created a viscount of the United Kingdom. He died in 1823.

See CHAMBERS, "Biographical Dictionary of Eminent Scotsmen."

Elphinstone, (GEORGE WILLIAM KEITH,) C.B., a British general, born about 1782, was descended from the noble Scottish family of Elphinstone. After serving in many campaigns, he became lieutenant-colonel in 1813, and gained distinction at Waterloo. In 1837 he was promoted to the rank of major-general. He commanded the army which was defeated in Afghanistan, a short time before his death, which occurred in 1842.

Elphinstone, (Hon. MOUNTSTUART,) a British historian and statesman, born in 1779, was the fourth son of the eleventh Lord Elphinstone. He entered the civil service of the East India Company in 1795, became secretary to Sir Arthur Wellesley in 1803, and ambassador to the court of Cabool in 1808. He published in 1815 an "Account of the Kingdom of Cabool," a standard historical work of great merit. From 1810 to 1817 he was resident at the court of Poona. He was appointed commissioner of that province in 1817, and Governor of Bombay in 1819. "His policy, so far as India is concerned," says Bishop Heber, "appeared to me peculiarly wise and liberal." The same writer adds, "Mr. Elphinstone is in every respect an extraordinary man, possessing great activity of mind and body, remarkable talent for and application to public business," etc. He resigned his office in November, 1827, and returned to England in 1829. In 1836 he declined the offer of the Governor-Generalship of India, on account of his health. His "History of India : the Hindoo and Mohammedan Periods" (2 vols., 1841) is highly commended. He was never married. He died in November, 1859.

See "Journal of the Royal Asiatic Society," vol. xviii. part ii. p. 221 ; J. W. KAYE, "Lives of Indian Officers ;" "London Quarterly Review" for October, 1815, and September, 1841.

Elphinstone or **Elphinston,** (WILLIAM,) an eminent Scottish statesman and prelate, founder of King's College, Aberdeen, was born at Glasgow about 1435. He studied law in France, and became professor of that science in Paris. Having returned home about 1470, he obtained several high civil offices, and in 1484 was chosen Bishop of Aberdeen. Soon after this he was employed with honour as negotiator at several foreign courts. In 1492 he accepted the office of lord privy seal, which he appears to have retained until his death. In 1494 he obtained a papal bull for the foundation of a university which was built in 1506. He wrote a book of canons and a "History of Scotland." Died in 1514.

See CHAMBERS, "Biographical Dictionary of Eminent Scotsmen."

El′ring-ton, (THOMAS,) D.D., a skilful Irish mathematician, born near Dublin about 1760. He became professor of mathematics in Dublin University in 1795, provost of Trinity College in 1811, Bishop of Limerick in 1820, and was translated to the see of Leighlin and Ferns in 1822. He published an edition of Euclid which is used as a text-book in Dublin University, and an edition of Juvenal. Died in 1835.

Elsasser, (FRIEDRICH AUGUST,) a German landscape-painter, born at Berlin in 1810 ; died at Rome in 1845. Among his works is the "Grotto of Sirens" at Tivoli.

Elsevier. See ELZEVIR.

Elsheimer, ĕlss′hī′mer, or **Elzheimer,** ĕlts′hī′mer, (ADAM,) an excellent German landscape-painter, born at Frankfort-on-the-Main in 1574, was known among the Italians by the name of IL TEDESCO, (*i.e.* "the German.") He worked mostly in Rome, where he acquired a high reputation by his good taste and his fidelity in the imitation of nature. He excelled in colour and chiaroscuro. His works are of small dimensions and very highly finished. Besides many landscapes, he painted a "Flight into Egypt," which is much admired, "Ceres in Search of her Daughter," and other historical and mythological pieces. Died in Rome in 1620.

See BRYAN, "Dictionary of Painters and Engravers ;" J. D. PASSAVANT, "A. Elsheimer, Maler aus Frankfurt," 1847.

Elshoecht, ĕl′so′ĕkt′, or **Elshoëct,** (CARLE,) a skilful French statuary, born at Dunkirk in 1797, was a pupil of Bosio. He gained a gold medal for his statue of "Innocence," (1825.) He adorned several buildings of Paris

with busts of Mirabeau, Molière, Poussin, and Claude Lorrain, and the Tuileries with a group representing the Genius of Asia. Died in 1856.

See "Nouvelle Biographie Générale."

Elshoëct. See ELSHOECHT.

Elsholtz. See ELSHOLZ.

Elsholz, von, or **Elsholtz,** fon ĕls′holts, (FRANZ,) a German comic poet, born in Berlin in 1791, obtained in early life an office of secretary in the public service at Cologne. He produced "The New Achilles," and a successful drama called "Come here," ("Komm her," 1824.) His comedy "The Lady at Court" ("Die Hofdame") attracted much attention.

Elsholz or **Elsholtz,** (JOHANN SIGISMUND,) a German botanist, born at Frankfort-on-the-Oder in 1623. He became physician to the Elector of Brandenburg in 1656, and lived in Berlin. He published, besides other works, "Flora Marchica," (1663.) Died in 1688.

See ERSCH und GRUBER, "Allgemeine Encyklopaedie ;" BOEDIKER, "Ehrengedächtniss J. S. Elsholzen's," 1688.

Elsner, ĕlss′ner, (CHRISTOPH FRIEDRICH,) a German medical writer, born at Königsberg in 1749 ; died in 1820.

Elsner, (JAKOB,) a learned German Protestant theologian, born at Saalfeld, in Prussia, in 1692. He became in 1722 rector of the College of Joachimsthal, in Berlin, and afterwards first preacher to the court. He published, besides other works, a commentary on the New Testament, ("Observationes sacræ in Novi Fœderis Libros," 2 vols., 1720–28.) Died in 1750.

See ADELUNG's Supplement to JÖCHER, "Allgemeines Gelehrten-Lexikon."

Elsner, (JOHANN GOTTFRIED,) a meritorious German economist, born at Gottesburg, in Silesia, in 1784. He was a practical farmer, and studied rural economy in various countries. He published many works, among which are a "Manual for the Propagation of Merino Sheep," (1832,) and a "Shepherd's Catechism," (1841.)

Elss′ler, (FANNY,) a German danseuse, born in Vienna in 1811. She performed with great applause in Vienna, Berlin, Paris, and London. In 1841 she visited the United States.

El′stob, (ELIZABETH,) an English linguist, sister of William, noticed below, was born at Newcastle in 1683. She was noted for her knowledge of the Saxon language. She translated Scudéry's "Essay on Glory," and published a "Saxon Grammar," (1715,) and "Saxon Homilies." From 1739 to 1756 she was governess to the children of the Duchess of Portland. Died in 1756.

Elstob, (WILLIAM,) an English antiquary, born at Newcastle in 1673, was a Fellow of one of the Oxford colleges, and an excellent Saxon scholar. He became rector of Saint Swithin, London, in 1702. He published an edition of "Ascham's Latin Letters," "An Essay on the Affinity, etc. between the two Professions of Law and Divinity," and began an edition of Saxon laws, which was finished after his death by Wilkins. Died in 1714.

Elsynge, ĕl′sinj, ? (HENRY,) an English civil officer and writer, born at Battersea, Surrey, in 1598. After leaving college and travelling a few years, he obtained the office of clerk of the House of Commons, which he kept during the Long Parliament, and resigned in 1648. "Mr. Elsynge," says Whitelocke, "was the best I ever knew to take the sense of the House and put it into apt terms." He published a much-esteemed work on the "Manner of Holding Parliaments in England." Died in 1654.

See WOOD, "Athenæ Oxonienses."

El′ton, (Sir ARTHUR HALLAM,) an English writer, son of Charles Abraham, noticed below, and a nephew of Henry Hallam the historian, was born in 1818. He wrote a tale entitled "Below the Surface."

Elton, (CHARLES ABRAHAM,) an English poet, born in 1778, published a volume of poems in 1804, and a poetical version of the remains of Hesiod, (1809,) which is highly praised by the "Edinburgh Review." In 1814 he published "Specimens of the Classic Poets from Homer to Tryphiodorus, translated into English Verse," (3 vols.,) in which there are many brilliant and spirited passages. Died in 1853.

See "Edinburgh Review" for October, 1809.

Elvenich, ĕl′vĕh-niK′, (PETER JOSEPH,) a German Catholic philosopher, born at Embken in 1796, is called the chief of Hermesianism, on which he wrote several treatises.

Elves, [Norse, ALFAR, ȧl′fạr, in the singular, ALFI, signifying " Spirit,"] the name given in the Norse mythology to a class of subordinate beings or deities who are supposed to inhabit that part of the atmosphere which is nearest the earth's surface and the interior of the earth. The former are aerial beings, and are called light-elves, (Ljosalfar :) they preside over the plants on the surface of the earth. The latter dwell in the bowels of the earth, and are distinguished as dark-elves, (Dökkalfar or Svartalfar :) they have charge of the ores and minerals lying within the earth, and are skilful workers in metal. The Dwarfs (Dwergar) nearly resemble the dark-elves : they work in the interior of the earth, and possess magic or supernatural powers.

See THORPE's " Northern Mythology," vols. i. and ii., more particularly pp. 56 and 57.

Elvius, ĕl′ve-ûs, (PEHR,) the Elder, a Swedish writer and savant, lived in the first half of the eighteenth century.

Elvius, (PEHR,) a scientific Swedish traveller, son of the preceding, was born at Upsal in 1710. He was employed in the survey and exploration of Sweden about 1745, of which he wrote an account. Died in 1749.

See OLOF CELSIUS, "Åminnelse-Tal öfver P. Elvius," 1749; OLOF DALIN, "Åminnelse-Tal öfver P. Elvius," 1750.

Elwart, ĕl′vȧr′, (ANTOINE,) a French composer of operas, symphonies, etc., born in Paris in 1808, gained the grand prize of the Institute in 1834.

El′wes, (JOHN MEGGOT,) an English miser, born in London in 1714, became member of Parliament about 1774. He is said to have left more than £500,000. Died in 1789.

See E. TOPHAM, "Life of J. Elwes," 1790; "Retrospective Review," vol. ix., 1824.

Elye, ee′lī or ȧ′le′, (ELIAS,) a Swiss philologist, born at Laufen about 1400, was the first who introduced the printing-press into Switzerland. Died about 1475.

El′y̆-ọt, (Sir THOMAS,) an English diplomatist and author, eminent for his profound learning, was sent by Henry VIII. on a mission to Rome about 1532, and to the court of Charles V. a few years later. He composed admired works entitled "The Governor," (1531,) and "The Castle of Health," (1534.) His "Latin Dictionary" (1538) passed through many editions. Died in 1546.

El′y̆s or **El′lis,** (Rev. EDMUND,) an English poet and nonjuror, published "Divine Poems," (1658.) Died after 1693.

Elysium, or **Elysian Fields.** See PLUTO.

Elzevier. See ELZEVIR.

Elzevir, ĕl′zẹh-vir, [Dutch, ELZEVIER or ELSEVIER, ĕl′zẹh-veer′,] the name of a family of Dutch printers and publishers, who were celebrated for the beauty of their typography, and rendered great services to literature by the publication of classic authors. The most distinguished are the following :

Elzevir, (LEWIS, or LODEWIJK,) the first eminent member of the family, was born about 1540, and settled at Leyden. Some of his publications are dated 1592. He died about 1617, leaving four sons, Matthew, Lewis, Gilles, and Bonaventure, who were publishers. Matthew died in 1640, and left sons named Isaac, Abraham, and Bonaventure. The last two were partners, and published at Leyden the master-pieces of typography which rendered the name of Elzevir famous. Among these are the works of Virgil, Pliny, Livy, and Cicero. They both died between 1650 and 1660.

LEWIS III., a son of Lewis II., established a press at Amsterdam in 1638, and produced fine editions of many authors. He died about 1670.

DANIEL, a son of Abraham, (or, as others say, of Bonaventure,) was the last of the family that excelled in the art of printing. He lived at Leyden, and died in 1680.

See A. DE REUME, " Recherches historiques, etc. sur les Elsevier," Brussels, 1847; DODT VAN FLENSBURG, "Over de Elzeviers, Lodewijk den Vader," etc., 1851.

El′zey, (ARNOLD,) an American general, was born in Maryland about 1815. He served in the Mexican war, and, on the breaking out of the rebellion of 1861, entered the Confederate army. He was made brigadier-general in 1862.

Elzheimer. See ELSHEIMER.

Emâdee or **Emâdi,** ẹ-mâ′dee, a celebrated Persian poet, surnamed SHEHERIARI, because he resided in Sheheriar, lived in the reign of Malek II., one of the Seljukides. He published a divan, or a collection of four thousand verses, and died in 1177.

See D'HERBELOT, " Bibliothèque Orientale."

Emanuel. See EMMANUEL and MANUEL.

Eman′uel ben Sol′omon, a famous Hebrew poet, a native of Rome, lived in that city about the end of the thirteenth century. He was the author of a poem called "Mechabberoth" or "Mechaberoth," (" Poetic Compositions,") and of several commentaries on the Scriptures. He is called by some rabbis "the Voltaire of the Hebrews," and is reputed the most elegant poet that his nation has produced since their dispersion.

Emanuele, ȧ-mȧ-noo-ā′là, (surnamed FRA COMO, from the place of his birth,) an Italian painter, born at Como in 1625; died in 1701.

Embury, ĕm′bẹr-e, (EMMA CATHERINE,) an American writer, daughter of Dr. James R. Manley, of New York, was married to Daniel Embury, Esq., of Brooklyn, in 1828. She published "Guido, and other Poems," "Constance Latimer, or the Blind Girl," and "Nature's Gems, or American Wild-Flowers." Died in 1863.

See GRISWOLD's " Female Poets of America."

Emelraet, ā′mẹl-rȧt′, a Flemish landscape-painter, born at Brussels about 1612. He passed some years in Rome, and afterwards settled in Antwerp. He worked principally for the churches, painted often the landscape for the pictures of other artists, and was regarded as one of the best landscape-painters of Flanders.

See DESCAMPS, " Vies des Peintres Flamands," etc.

Emeri. See EMERY.

Émeriau, ȧm′re′ō′, (MAURICE JULIEN,) a French admiral, born in Bretagne in 1762. He commanded a ship at Aboukir in 1798, where he was wounded and made prisoner. He became a rear-admiral in 1802, a count in 1810, and a vice-admiral in 1811. About 1812-15 he was commander-in-chief of the fleet in the Mediterranean, and resisted the English with success. He was placed on the retired list in 1816. Died in 1845.

See " Nouvelle Biographie Générale."

Emeric. See EYMERIC.

Émeric-David, ȧm′rĕk′ dȧ′vĕd′, (TOUSSAINT BERNARD,) a French archæologist and writer on art, was born at Aix (Provence) in 1755. He practised law at Aix in his youth, and sat in the legislative body from 1809 to 1814. In 1815 he was elected to the Academy of Inscriptions, for which he wrote memoirs on Greek mythology, etc. He was author of a "Historical Discourse on Modern Painting," (1807,) of a "History of Painting in the Middle Ages," (1842,) and of many articles in the "Biographie Universelle." Died in 1839.

See FAURIEL, in the " Histoire littéraire de France," tome xx. ; "Nouvelle Biographie Générale."

Émerigon, ȧm′re′gŏN′,(BALTHASAR MARIE,) a French jurist, born about 1714, published an excellent "Treatise on Assurances (or Sureties) and Contracts," etc., (1784,) and other works. Died in 1785.

Em′ẹr-sọn, (GEORGE B.,) a distinguished American teacher and writer on education, was born in York county, Maine, in 1797. He taught in Boston for many years, and was president of the Boston Society of Natural History. He wrote "Lectures on Education," and a "Report of the Trees and Shrubs growing naturally in the Forests of Massachusetts," (1846.)

Emerson, (RALPH WALDO,) an American essayist, poet, and speculative philosopher, was born in Boston in 1803. He entered Harvard in 1817, and took the degree of A.B. in 1821. While at college he is said to have spent much of his time in the library, and, although not distinguished for his proficiency in the regular studies of the curriculum, he was superior to most of his classmates in his knowledge of general literature. His health failing about 1827, he spent the ensuing winter in Florida. In 1829 he was ordained at the Second Unitarian Church of Boston, as colleague of Henry Ware ; but he resigned this position in 1832, because he could not accept the views of his Church in regard to the

Lord's Supper. In December of the same year he sailed for Europe, and returned to his native land in the autumn of 1833. Soon after, he commenced his career as lecturer, his discourses embracing almost every variety of topic, from simple "Water" to "Milton," "Human Culture," and universal "Nature." A volume of his "Essays" appeared in 1841, and, by its freshness and originality of thought and sparkling beauty of expression, excited much attention. In 1840, on the establishment of the "Dial," (the organ of the New England Transcendentalists,) he became one of the contributors to that periodical, and was afterwards its editor from 1842 to 1844. A second volume (or series) of "Essays" made its appearance in 1844. It was characterized by the same striking peculiarities of thought and expression that had previously attracted so many readers, and soon procured for him a multitude of admirers on both sides of the Atlantic. A collection of his poems was published in 1846. In the following year he visited England, in order to fulfil an engagement which he had made to deliver a series of lectures before various institutes and societies in that country. In 1850 he issued a small volume, entitled "Representative Men," one of the most important of all his publications: it is doubtless that upon which his permanent reputation as a thinker will principally rest. It consists of a series of characters or mental portraits, each of which is designed to represent a class: 1. Plato, or the Philosopher; 2. Swedenborg, or the Mystic; 3. Montaigne, or the Skeptic; 4. Shakspeare, or the Poet; 5. Napoleon, or the Man of the World; 6. Goethe, or the Writer. It is scarcely necessary to say that the judgments formed of Mr. Emerson's writings, and more especially of the last-named work, must vary according to the habits of thought and prepossessions of the critic; the more so as our author does not attempt to establish his positions by any process of reasoning; he simply announces his views, leaving his reader to accept them or not, as he may have the capacity to do so, in accordance with the scriptural saying, "He that is able to receive it, let him receive it." In his philosophical or metaphysical views he may be said to approximate the celebrated German transcendentalist Fichte. Mr. Emerson's "English Traits" (1856) is one of his most popular and attractive books, although many of the remarks and statements contained in it require to be received with liberal qualifications.

Mr. Emerson is distinguished for originality, as well as for subtlety of intellect. One cannot, however, help suspecting that, in his love of originality and his anxiety to shake himself wholly free from the trammels of the past, he sometimes runs into errors in the opposite direction, from which his good sense and rare sagacity might otherwise have preserved him. "As a writer," observes an accomplished critic, "Mr. Emerson is distinguished for a singular union of poetic imagination with practical acuteness. . . . The brilliant transcendentalist is evidently a man not easy to be deceived in matters pertaining to the ordinary course of human affairs. . . . His observations on society, on manners, on character, on institutions, are stamped with rare sagacity. . . . His style is in the nicest harmony with the character of his thought. It is condensed almost to abruptness. Occasionally he purchases compression at the expense of clearness."* "There never was," says Mr. Alger, "a bolder champion of mental freedom for himself and for all men. His rich and vigorous freshness has been an invaluable tonic to his contemporaries." But the same writer justly observes that "the emphasis of his statements is often fatal to the needful qualifications; but that requires his readers to be thinkers too, and not passive recipients of his thinking." ("Christian Examiner" for May, 1868.) As a poet, Mr. Emerson's merits are of a high order, although his poetry is not of a kind to be popular with the generality of readers. A number of his more recent poems have appeared as contributions to the "Atlantic Monthly."

See "Blackwood's Magazine" for December, 1847; "Westminster Review" for March, 1840, and October, 1856; "Fraser's Magazine" for May, 1867; "Christian Examiner," vols. xxx. and xxxviii.; ALLIBONE, "Dictionary of Authors;" GRISWOLD, "Prose Writers of America;" DUYCKINCK, "Cyclopædia of American Literature," vol. ii.

* See Mr. WHIPPLE'S article on Emerson, in the "New American Cyclopædia."

Em'er-son, (WILLIAM,) an eminent English mathematician, born at Hurworth, near Darlington, in 1701. He was educated at home by his father, who was a schoolteacher. At his father's death, he conducted the school a short time, and then retired from all business except writing on mathematics. Among his numerous works (which for some time were probably the best mathematical works in the language, except those of Simpson) are "Doctrine of Fluxions," (1748,) "Principles of Mechanics," (1754,) and "Method of Increments." He was eccentric in his habits. Died in 1782.

See "Biographia Britannica."

Émery, àm're', (ÉDOUARD FÉLIX ÉTIENNE,) a French medical writer, born in Dauphiné in 1788, practised in Paris. Died in 1856.

Émery, (JACQUES ANDRÉ,) a French Catholic divine, born at Gex in 1732, entered the community of Saint-Sulpice, Paris, about 1750. In 1782 he was chosen superior-general of his order. He is commended for his wise, firm, and moderate conduct during the reign of terror, in which he was twice imprisoned. He wrote "The Spirit of Leibnitz," (1772,) the "Christianity *(Christianisme)* of Lord Bacon," (1799,) and other learned works. Died in 1811.

See PICOT, "Notice sur la Vie de J. A. Émery," 1811.

Em'er-ў, (JOHN,) an English comic actor, born at Sunderland in 1777; died in 1822.

Émery, d', dàm're', (MICHEL **Particelli**—păr'te'sà'-le',) SIEUR, a French financier, of Italian descent, born at Lyons; died in 1650.

Émile or Emili, (PAUL.) See EMILIO.

Emilian. See ÆMILIAN.

Émilien, the French of ÆMILIAN, which see.

Emilio, à-mee'le-o, (PAOLO,) or **Emili,** à-mee'lee, (PAUL,) [Lat. PAU'LUS ÆMIL'IUS; Fr. PAUL ÉMILE, pôl à'mèl',] an Italian historian, born at Verona, removed to Paris about 1495, and, by the order of the king, wrote a Latin "History of France," ("De Rebus gestis Francorum," 1516-19,) which was admired and often reprinted. The style is pure and concise. Erasmus expressed a high opinion of Emilio's learning. Died in Paris in 1529.

See TIRABOSCHI, "Storia della Letteratura Italiana."

Emilius. See ÆMILIUS, and PAULUS.

Emilius Macer. See MACER.

Emin, à-meen', ? (FEODOR ALEXANDROVITCH,) a Russian historian and novelist, born about 1735. His chief work is a "History of Russia to 1213," (1767.) Died in 1770.

Em'lуn, (HENRY,) an English architect, born about 1730; died in 1815.

Emlyn, (THOMAS,) an English Unitarian minister, born at Stamford in 1663. In 1691 he settled in Dublin, where he preached a number of years. He was fined and imprisoned about two years for his doctrines. He wrote a "Life of Dr. Samuel Clarke," (1731,) and several controversial works. Died in 1743.

See "Life of Thomas Emlyn," by his son.

Em'ma, a daughter of Charlemagne, who, according to a doubtful legend, was married to Eginhard. It is reported that before their marriage she once carried Eginhard from the palace, lest his traces in the snow might betray the secret of his visit. Died in 837 A.D.

See J. C. DAHL, "Ueber Eginhard und Emma," 1817; EGINHARD, "Vita Caroli Magni."

Em'ma, Queen of England, was a daughter of Richard I., Duke of Normandy. She was married first to Ethelred II., and became mother of Edward the Confessor. About 1017 she was married to Canute the Great, by whom she had a son, Hardicanute. Died in 1046.

Em-man'u-el, [Port. MANOEL, mâ-no-êl',] surnamed THE GREAT, King of Portugal, born at Alconcheta in 1469, was the son of Ferdinand, Duke of Viseu, a younger branch of the reigning family. Upon the death of John II., in 1495, he succeeded to the throne. He married the widow of the late prince-royal, Alonzo or Alphonso, Isabella of Castile, whose consent he obtained only on the condition that he should banish the Moors and Jews from the kingdom, which was repugnant to his own more liberal principles. During his reign the glory and power of Portugal attained their greatest height by the discoveries and victorious expeditions of Vasco da Gama, Almeida, Albuquerque, and Alvares de Cabral. From 1497 to 1520 these famous captains maintained the ascendency of the Portuguese arms in India and Brazil. In 1519 Emmanuel married Eleonore, sister of the emperor Charles V. He died in 1521, and was succeeded by his son, John III.

See A. DE VARNHAGEN, "Retratos e Elogios des Personagens ilustres de Portugal," 1842; LACLÈDE, "Histoire générale de Portugal;" H. OSORIO, "De Rebus Emmanuelis Regis Lusitaniæ gestis," 1571; translated into English by JAMES GIBBS, 1752.

Em-man'u-el Phil'I-bert, surnamed TÊTE DE FER, têt dẹh fair, (i.e. "Iron-headed,") Duke of Savoy, an Italian general of great ability, born at Chambéry in 1528, was a son of Charles III. of Savoy. He entered the service of the emperor Charles V. in 1548, and in 1553 obtained the chief command of the imperial army in the war against the French. He gained a great victory over them at Saint-Quentin in 1557. In 1559 he married Margaret, a sister of Henry II. of France, and recovered part of his paternal dominions, which had been seized by the French. In 1574 he obtained from Henry III. the evacuation of all Piedmont, the condition of which was greatly improved by his wise statesmanship. Died in 1580. He was succeeded by his son, Charles Emmanuel.

See G. TOSI, "Vita Emmanuelis Philiberti," 1596; BRUSLÉ DE MONTPLAINCHAMP, "Histoire de Emmanuel Philibert," 1692; DE THOU, "Historia."

Emmerich, êm'mẹh-riҡ, (GEORG,) a German physician, born at Königsberg in 1672, wrote several able treatises. Died in 1727.

Emmery, êm're', (JEAN LOUIS CLAUDE,) Count of Grozyeulx, a learned French lawyer and legislator, born at Metz in 1752, was a member of the National Assembly in 1790. He became a senator in 1802. Died in 1823.

Em'met, (ROBERT,) an eloquent Irish enthusiast, born in Cork in 1780, was a brother of Thomas Addis Emmet. He was an ardent but misguided partisan of Irish independence, and appears to have been a sincere patriot. Like his brother, he was one of the chiefs of the "United Irishmen." In July, 1803, he rashly put himself at the head of a party of insurgents consisting of the rabble of Dublin, who murdered the chief justice, Lord Kilwarden, and others, but were quickly dispersed by the military. Emmet was arrested, was tried, and, after an eloquent and impassioned speech in vindication of his course, suffered with intrepid courage a felon's death, September, 1803. The poet Moore commemorated his tragic fate and his attachment to Miss Curran in two of his "Irish Melodies."

See MADDEN, "United Irishmen," vol. iii.; JOHN W. BURKE, "Life of Robert Emmet."

Emmet, (THOMAS ADDIS,) an eloquent Irish lawyer, a brother of the preceding, was born at Cork in 1764. He was liberally educated, was called to the bar in 1790, and became a leader of the "United Irishmen." He was arrested in 1798, and imprisoned in a dungeon for about three years. In 1804 he emigrated to New York, where he practised law with great success, and became attorney-general of the State of New York in 1812. He died in 1827. "That he had great qualities as an orator," says Judge Story, "cannot be doubted by any one who has heard him. His mind possessed a good deal of the fervour which characterizes his countrymen. It was quick, vigorous, searching, and buoyant." He wrote pieces of Irish history illustrative of the condition of the Catholics of Ireland, (1807.)

See "Memoirs of Thomas Addis Emmet," by CHARLES GLIDDEN HAYNES, 1829; a sketch of Emmet's character in the Miscellaneous Works of JOSEPH STORY; T. MCGEE, "O'Connell and his Friends."

Emmius, êm'me-ŭs, (UBBO,) a Dutch scholar and historian, born in 1547, was eminent for his knowledge of ancient languages and history, and for modesty and other virtues. After teaching many years in Norden and Leer, he was chosen in 1614 professor of history and Greek in the University of Groningen, of which he was also rector. He wrote a "History of Friesland," (1596,) a "General Chronology," (1619,) "Ancient Greece Illustrated," ("Vetus Græcia illustrata," 1626,) a valuable

work on the history and topography of Greece, and a few other works. Died in 1625.

See FOPPENS, "Bibliotheca Belgica;" N. MULERIUS, "Elogium U. Emmii," 1628; NICÉRON, "Mémoires."

Em'mọns, (EBENEZER,) M.D., an American geologist, born in Middlefield, Berkshire county, Massachusetts, in 1798, became professor of natural history in Williams College in 1833. When the geological survey of New York was ordered by the government, he was appointed one of the geologists-in-chief. Several volumes of his Reports were published in the "Natural History of New York." He advanced the novel opinion that beneath the oldest member of the Silurian system there is a series of fossiliferous rocks, to which he applied the term "Taconic." He died in North Carolina in October, 1863.

Emmons, (NATHANIEL,) an American theologian, born in East Haddam, Connecticut, in 1745, preached for many years at Franklin, Massachusetts. He wrote several works on theology. Died in 1840.

Emo, ā'mo, (ANGELO,) an able Venetian statesman and admiral, born in 1731. Having served with success against the Algerine pirates, he was made vice-admiral in 1765, and compelled the Dey of Algiers to sign a treaty favourable to Venice. He then obtained the rank of captain-general and admiral of all the maritime forces. In 1772 he was appointed a senator, and about 1780 a member of the Council of Ten. He afterwards held other high offices with credit. Died in 1792.

See MENEGHELLI, "Di A. Emo e delle sue Gesta," 1836.

Em'o-rỹ, (JOHN,) an American Methodist bishop, born in Queen Ann county, Maryland, in 1789. He was elected a bishop about 1832. He wrote several controversial treatises. Died in 1835.

See a "Life of Bishop Emory," by his son ROBERT.

Emory, (ROBERT,) a Methodist minister, a son of the preceding, was born in Philadelphia in 1814. He wrote a "History of the Discipline of the Methodist Episcopal Church," (1843.) Died in 1848.

Emory, (WILLIAM H.,) an American general, born in Maryland about 1812, graduated at West Point in 1831. He became a lieutenant of topographical engineers about 1839, and gained the rank of captain in 1851. He was appointed a brigadier-general of volunteers early in 1862, and commanded a division under General Banks in Louisiana in 1863, and a corps in 1864. He repulsed the enemy at Pleasant Hill, April 7 of that year. He fought with distinction at Opequan Creek, September 19, and Cedar Creek, October 19, 1864.

Empecinado. See DIAZ, (JUAN MARTIN.)

Empedocle. See EMPEDOCLES.

Em-ped'o-cleͅs, [Gr. Ἐμπεδοκλῆς; Fr. EMPÉDOCLE, ȯN'pā'doҡl'; It. EMPEDOCLE, êm-pā'do-klà,] a celebrated Greek philosopher, born at Agrigentum, Sicily, flourished about 450 B.C. It is not known who were his teachers. He excelled in medicine and poetry as well as philosophy. By these merits he acquired great influence in his native state, which he is said to have transformed into a republic, after refusing to accept the offer of royalty. He originated or adopted the theory that nature consists of four elements,—fire, air, earth, and water. He appears to have taught the Hindoo philosophy that the soul has been banished into the body in order to punish it, and that it migrates through animal and vegetable bodies until it shall be entirely purified. The popular tradition that he threw himself into the crater of Mount Etna to immortalize his name is probably fabulous. His greatest work was a poem on the "Nature and Principles of Things," of which fragments are extant. Lucretius, in his great poem, "De Rerum Naturâ," expresses his admiration of Empedocles.

See RITTER, "History of Philosophy;" G. H. LEWES, "Biographical History of Philosophy;" DIOGENES LAERTIUS; SCINA, "Memorie sulla Vita de Empedocle," 2 vols., 1813; J. G. NEWMANN, "Programma de Empedocle Philosopho," 1690; HEINRICH STEIN, "Dissertatio de Empedoclis Scriptis," 1851.

Empereur, L', lȯN'pẹh'rur', (CONSTANTIJN,) a Dutch Orientalist, born at Oppyck, was one of the most eminent pupils of Erpenius. He obtained the chair of Hebrew in Leyden in 1627, and became councillor to Maurice of Nassau in 1639. He translated portions of the Talmud and other Jewish writings, and published, besides other works, a "Treatise on the Forensic Laws of the Hebrews," and a "Key to the Talmud," ("Clavis Talmudica," 1634.) Died in 1648.

See TRIGLAND, "Oratio in Obitum C. L'Empereur," 1648.

Empiricus Sextus. See SEXTUS.

Empis, ŏɴ′pe′, (ADOLPHE,) a French dramatist, born in Paris in 1790. He produced successful comedies and operas, which in 1847 opened to him the doors of the French Academy. Among his works are "Joan of Arc," an opera, (1822,) and "A Change in the Ministry," a comedy, (1831.)

Empoli, ĕm′po-lee, (JACOPO CHIMENTI,) an Italian painter in oil, usually called L'EMPOLI, was born at Empoli in 1554. He worked mostly in Florence, the churches of which contain many of his pictures. Among his chief productions are "Saint Yves," "The Virgin with Saint Nicholas," and an "Annunciation." His design and colour are commended. He also painted portraits with success. Died in 1640.

See LANZI, "History of Painting in Italy."

Empoli, d', dĕm′po-lee, (GIOVANNI,) a Florentine, who lived about the year 1500, in the service of the Portuguese king, sailed with Albuquerque to India in 1503, and wrote a brief account of the voyage.

See LAFITEAU, "Histoire des Conquêtes des Portugais."

Em-po′rĭ-us, a Latin grammarian, who lived in the fifth or sixth century, left some extant works on rhetoric.

Empson, (RICHARD.) See DUDLEY, (EDMUND.)

Emp′son, (WILLIAM,) an English editor and writer on various subjects, born about 1790. He was for several years editor of the "Edinburgh Review," to which he contributed many articles between 1823 and 1850. Died in 1852.

Emser, ĕm′ser, (HIERONYMUS,) a German Catholic theologian, noted as an adversary of Luther, was born at Ulm in 1477. He became secretary of Duke George of Saxony, who gave him a benefice in Dresden. In 1523 he published a criticism on Luther's version of the New Testament. He also made a German translation of the New Testament, (1527,) which was adopted by the Catholics. Died in 1527.

See WALDAU, "Nachricht von H. Emser's Leben," 1783.

Énambuc, d', dā′nŏɴ′bük′, (PIERRE **Vandrosque Diel**—vŏɴ′drosk′ de′ĕl′,) an able French mariner and colonial governor, who, with the permission of Richelieu, planted a colony in the isle of Saint Christopher in 1625. He also formed the first settlement in the isle of Martinique, in 1635. He died in 1636, and was succeeded as governor by his nephew, Diel Duparquet.

Encélade. See ENCELADUS.

En-çel′a-dus, [Gr. Ἐγκέλαδος; Fr. ENCÉLADE, ŏɴ′-sȧ′lȧd′,] a son of Tartarus, and one of the giants that rebelled against Jupiter. According to one tradition, he was buried under the island of Sicily or Mount Ætna, and his struggles caused earthquakes.

Encina. See ENZINA, (JUAN DE LA.)

Encinas or Enzinas, ĕn-thee′nȧs, often called **Dry-ander,** (FRANCISCO,) a Spanish Reformer, born at Burgos about 1520. Having been converted to Lutheranism, he went to Wittenberg about 1541, and acquired the friendship of Luther and Melanchthon. He produced a Spanish translation of the New Testament, (1543,) which he presented to Charles V. at Brussels. For this offence he was imprisoned about a year. Having escaped from prison, he went to England. Died in 1552.

See BAYLE, "Historical and Critical Dictionary:" N. ANTONIO, "Bibliotheca Hispana Nova;" MRS. CHARLES, "Martyrs of Spain," etc., 1865.

Encinas, (JUAN,) a brother of the preceding, born at Burgos, was also a Protestant. He went to Rome, or was sent thither by his father. There he openly avowed his principles, and suffered death by fire in 1545.

See MRS. CHARLES, "Martyrs of Spain," etc.

Enciso, de, dā ĕn-thee′so, (DIEGO XIMENES,) a Spanish dramatic poet, born at Seville, lived about 1620–40. He wrote "El Principe Don Carlos," and other dramas, which display superior talents.

Enciso, de, (Don MARTIN FERNANDEZ,) a Spanish geographer, accompanied the expeditions to Central America, and published "Suma de Geografia," (1519.)

Encke, ĕnk′keh, (JOHANN FRANZ,) an eminent German astronomer, born at Hamburg in 1791. He gained distinction by his determination of the orbit of the comet of 1680, and of the distance of the earth from the sun, and published "The Distance of the Sun," ("Die Entfernung der Sonne," 2 vols., 1822–24.) He afterwards made important and successful investigations into the orbit and period of the comet of Pons, since known as Encke's comet. About 1825 he became director of the Royal Observatory of Berlin, and secretary of the Academy of Sciences. After 1830 he published the "Astronomische Jahrbücher," and other works. Died in 1865.

See G. HAGEN, "Memoir of Encke," in the "Smithsonian Report" for 1868.

Encontre, ŏɴ′kŏɴtʀ′, (DANIEL,) a French Protestant divine, eminent for talents and learning, born at Nîmes in 1762, was ordained, but was unable to preach, on account of a defect in the vocal organs. He became in 1808 professor of sciences in the Academy of Montpellier, and in 1814 he accepted the chair of theology at Montauban. He wrote an "Essay on the Theory of Probabilities," "Elements of Plane Geometry," a "Dissertation on the True System of the World," (1807,) and many other works. Died in 1818.

See JUILLERAT-CHASSEUR, "Notice sur la Vie, etc. de Daniel Encontre," 1821.

Ende, von, fon ĕn′deh, (FRIEDRICH ALBRECHT,) BARON, a German general, born at Celle in 1765 ; died in 1829.

Ender, ĕn′der, (JOHANN,) a German painter, born in Vienna in 1793. He went to Rome as imperial pensioner in 1820, and afterwards worked in Vienna with success in portraits and history. Died in 1854.

Ender, (THOMAS,) a landscape-painter, brother of the preceding, was born in Vienna about 1794. He went about 1817 with a scientific expedition to Brazil, from which he brought home many designs. He accompanied Metternich to Italy, where he worked some years. His landscapes are admired for the vigorous effects of light which they display.

En′der-bĭe, (PERCY,) a British author, published a mediocre history of Wales, (1661.)

En′dĭ-cott, (JOHN,) one of the first colonial Governors of Massachusetts, born at Dorchester, England, in 1589. In 1636 he conducted an expedition against the Pequot Indians. He was several times Deputy-Governor of Massachusetts, and in 1644 was chosen Governor. He was again Governor in 1649, and, with the exception of 1650 and 1654, was regularly re-elected to the same office till his death in 1665. Governor Endicott was a zealous Puritan, and was especially severe in executing the laws against those who differed from the prevailing religion.

Endlicher, ĕnt′lik-er, (STEPHEN LADISLAUS,) an eminent botanist and linguist, born at Presburg, in Hungary, in 1804. Having studied Oriental languages and natural sciences, he was appointed director of the Imperial Library, Vienna, in 1828, and professor of botany in the University of Vienna in 1840. He liberally expended his fortune in the promotion of science, and was one of the founders of the Academy of Vienna. He published, in Latin, many works on botany, the most important of which is his "Genera of Plants arranged in the Natural Order," (1836–40,) and "Rudiments of Chinese Grammar," (1845,) with various other well-written works. He sympathized with the people in the insurrection of 1848. Died in 1849.

See BROCKHAUS, "Conversations-Lexikon;" "Nouvelle Biographie Générale."

En-dym′ĭ-on, [Gr. Ἐνδυμίων,] in the Greek mythology, was represented as a beautiful youth, a darling of Diana, (Selene,) and a perpetual sleeper. One of the various traditions announces him as a king of Elis. His eternal sleep is ascribed to different causes.

See SMITH'S "Dictionary of Greek and Roman Biography and Mythology."

Enea, the Italian of ÆNEAS, which see.

Eneas. See ÆNEAS.

Eneas Sylvius. See PIUS II.

Enée, the French of ÆNEAS, which see.

Enemann, ĕn′eh-mȧn′, (MIKAEL,) a Swedish Orientalist, born at Enköping in 1676; died in 1714.

Enfant, L'. See L'ENFANT.

ɛ as k; ç as s; ḡ hard; ǧ as j; G, H, K, guttural; N, nasal; R, trilled; s̄ as z; th as in this. (☞See Explanations, p. 23.)

54

Enfantin, ŏN'fŏN'tăN', (BARTHÉLEMI PROSPER,) a French arch-socialist, born in Paris in 1796, is called one of the founders of Saint-Simonism. He began to propagate the doctrines of Saint-Simon about 1825, and in 1830 had united numerous followers into an association founded on community of property. A disagreement between him and Bazard resulted in a schism, after which Enfantin assumed the name of "the Living Law and the Messiah." Charged with corruption of public morals, he was condemned to imprisonment for one year in 1832. After that event his disciples were dispersed, and he was employed as director of the Paris and Lyons Railway. Died in 1864.

See "Nouvelle Biographie Générale."

En'field, (WILLIAM,) LL.D., an English author and dissenting minister, born at Sudbury in 1741, officiated successively in the Unitarian churches of Liverpool, Warrington, and Norwich. He published several volumes of popular sermons, a "Preacher's Directory," which was highly esteemed, and said to be the best work of the kind, and largely assisted Dr. Aikin in his "General Biographical Dictionary." Besides several educational works, he published in 1791 a "History of Philosophy from the Earliest Periods to the Present Century," abridged from Brucker's History. Died in 1797.

See AIKIN, "Memoirs of Enfield," prefixed to his "Sermons."

Engau, ĕng'gŏw, (JOHANN RUDOLF,) a German jurisconsult, born at Jena in 1708. He became professor of law in the University of Jena in 1740, and councillor of the court of Saxe-Weimar in 1748. "His numerous writings," says Guizot, "attest his vast knowledge, and are highly esteemed in Germany." Among them are (in Latin) "Elements of German Civil Law," (1736,) and "Elements of Criminal Law," (1738.) Died in 1755.

See "Biographie Universelle;" HIRSCHING, "Historisch-literarisches Handbuch."

Engel, ĕng'ĕl, (JOHANN,) a German astronomer, born in Bavaria; died in 1512.

Engel, (JOHANN JAKOB,) an excellent German author, born at Parchim (Mecklenburg) in 1741. He was professor of belles-lettres in Berlin from 1776 to 1787, and was preceptor of the prince Frederick William, who ascended the throne in 1787. His comedy "The Grateful Son" (1770) was very successful. In 1775 he published "The Philosopher for the World," ("Der Philosoph für die Welt," 2 vols.,) which is admired for great clearness, facility, and elegance. He afterwards produced "Lorenz Stark," (1795,) a romance, which was very popular, and a "Mirror for Princes," ("Fürstenspiegel.") His works are characterized by an excellent judgment, and by a refinement of taste and purity of diction which are rare among the Germans. Died in 1802.

See F. NICOLAI, "Gedächtnissschrift auf J. J. Engel," 1806; "Nouvelle Biographie Générale."

Engel, (KARL CHRISTIAN,) a dramatist, brother of the preceding, was born at Parchim in 1752. He wrote "Biondetta," a comedy, and a metaphysical essay, entitled "Nous nous reverrons," ("We shall see each other again," 1787,) which caused a great sensation. Died in 1801.

See ERSCH und GRUBER, "Allgemeine Encyklopaedie."

Engel, ĕng'ĕl, (SAMUEL,) a Swiss geographer and economist, born at Berne in 1702, wrote an "Essay on the Question, 'When and how was America peopled?'" (1767,) and several works on rural economy. Died in 1784.

En-ǵel-ber'ga, sometimes written **Engelberta** and **Angilberga,** Empress of Germany, was married in 856 A.D. to Lewis II. of Germany. Having been accused of conjugal infidelity by two courtiers, she was about to be subjected to the ordeal of fire and water, when Boson, Count of Arles, came forward as her champion. He defeated her accusers in single combat, and forced them to retract. Died in 890 A.D.

Engelbert, ĕng'ĕl-bĕrt', a German historian, born in the thirteenth century. He wrote, in Latin, a "History of the Roman Empire." Died in 1331.

Engelbert, SAINT, Archbishop of Cologne, became tutor to Henry, a son of the emperor Frederick II., about 1220. He was assassinated by his cousin in 1225.

Engelberta or **Engelberda.** See ENGELBERGA.

Engelbrecht, ĕng'ǵel-bRĕKt', (ENGELBRECHTSON, ĕng'ǵel-bRĕKt'son,) a Swedish statesman and general, was born in Dalecarlia about 1390. When Eric XIII. was deposed, Engelbrecht was selected to administer the government jointly with Charles Canutson; but the former was soon after assassinated by Magnus Bengtson, in 1436.

See J. J. PALM, "Dissertatio de Meritis Engelbrechti," 1802.

Engelbrecht, ĕng'ĕl-bRĕKt', (JOHANN,) a German visionary and fanatical religionist, born at Brunswick in 1599; died in 1642.

Engelbrechtsen or **Enghelbrechtsen,** ĕng'hĕl-bRĕKt'sĕn, (CORNELIS,) a Dutch painter, born at Leyden in 1468, was the first of his nation who used oil-colours. He is considered one of the ablest painters of his time. Among his master-pieces are a "Descent from the Cross," (in Paris,) "The Lamb of the Apocalypse," (at Utrecht,) and "The Sacrifice of Abraham," (in Paris.) Died in 1533.

See DESCAMPS, "Vies des Peintres Flamands," etc.

Engelgrave, ĕng'ĕl-gRä'vĕh, (HENDRIK,) a learned Jesuit and preacher, born at Antwerp in 1610. He became rector of colleges at Cassel, Bruges, and Antwerp. His sermons were often reprinted, under the title of "Gospel Light," ("Lux Evangelica," 1648.) Died in 1670.

Engelhardt, ĕng'ĕl-haRt, (JOHANN GEORG VEIT,) a German theologian, born at Neustadt (an-der-Aisch) in 1791. He became professor of theology at Erlangen in 1822. Among his principal works is a "History of Dogmas," ("Dogmengeschichte," 1839.) Died in 1855.

Engelhardt, (KARL AUGUST,) a German writer, born at Dresden in 1768. He published "The Friend of Children," ("Der Kinderfreund," 12 vols., 1797–1814,) "Poems," ("Gedichte," 3 vols., 1820–23,) and other works. Died in 1834.

Engelmann, ŏN'zhĕl'mŏN' or ĕng'ĕl-mân', (GODE-FROY,) one of the inventors or improvers of lithography, was born at Mulhouse, (Haut-Rhin,) in France, in 1788. In 1816 he founded the first important and successful lithographic establishment in Paris, in which he was aided by Vernet, Girodet, Isabey, and other artists. He published a "Treatise on Lithography,"(1839.) Died in 1839.

See G. PEIGNOT, "Essai historique sur la Lithographie."

Engelschall, ĕng'ĕl-shâl', (JOSEPH FRIEDRICH,) a German poet, born at Marburg in 1739. He wrote short lyric poems, epistles, epigrams, and prose essays, which, in the opinion of Schoell, entitle him to a prominent place among German authors of the second rank. Died in 1797.

Engelstoft, ĕng'ĕls-toft', (CHRISTIAN THORNING,) a learned Danish theologian, born at Næsberg in 1805. He became professor of theology at Copenhagen in 1845, and Bishop of Funen in 1851. He has written on church history, etc.

Engelstroem. See ENGESTRÖM.

Engenio, d', dĕn-jä'nĕ-o, (CESARE Caracciolo—kä-rät-she-o'lo,) an Italian historian, flourished about 1600. He wrote a "Description of the Kingdom of Naples," (1618.)

Engeström or **Engestroem,** ĕng'ǵĕh-stRöm', written also **Engelstroem,** (GUSTAF,) a Swedish savant, born at Lund in 1738. He was president of the Academy of Sciences at Stockholm, and wrote several treatises on chemistry and mineralogy. Died in 1815.

Engeström or **Engestroem,** (LARS,) a Swedish statesman, brother of the preceding, was born at Stockholm in 1751, and entered the civil service in 1770. Appointed secretary of foreign affairs in 1776, he displayed superior diplomatic talents, and was sent as ambassador to London, Berlin, and other courts, between 1788 and 1798. In 1809 he became minister of foreign affairs, and received the title of baron. In 1816 he was raised to the rank of count. Died in 1826.

See "Nouvelle Biographie Générale."

Enghelbrechtsen. See ENGELBRECHTSEN.

Enghelrams, ĕng'hĕl-râms', (CORNELIS,) an able Flemish painter, born at Malines in 1527. Among his works is "The Conversion of Saint Paul," at Hamburg. Died in 1583.

ā, ē, ī, ō, ū, ȳ, *long;* ă, ĕ, ĭ, ŏ, ŭ, ў, *short;* ą, ę, į, ǫ, *obscure;* fär, fäll, fät; mĕt; nŏt; gŏŏd; mŏŏn;

Enghien, d', dôN'ge̥-ȧN', (LOUIS ANTOINE HENRI de Bourbon—deh book bón',) DUC, a French prince, born at Chantilly in 1772, was the son of the Duke of Bourbon, and related to the royal family. He emigrated in 1789, and, after travelling a few years, entered the army under his grandfather, the Prince of Condé, and fought bravely against the republic from 1793 until 1801, when the army was disbanded. He then retired to Ettenheim, in Baden, where he was arrested, though on neutral territory, in 1804, on suspicion of conspiracy, and taken to the castle of Vincennes, near Paris. After a hurried trial before a military tribunal, he was sentenced and shot in March, 1804. This deed excited general and deep indignation against Bonaparte, and is commonly regarded as one of the worst crimes by which his memory is stained. (See BONAPARTE, NAPOLEON.)

See THIERS, "Histoire du Consulat et de l'Empire;" FIRMAS-PERIÈS, "Notice historique sur L. A. Duc d'Enghien," 1814.

Engilbert. See ANGILBERT.

England, ing'gla̤nd, (JOHN,) a Catholic theologian, born at Cork, Ireland, in 1786. He was in 1820 appointed the first Bishop of Charleston, South Carolina, where he founded an academy and the "Charleston Catholic Miscellany." He wrote many treatises on theology, etc. Died in 1842.

England, ing'gla̤nd, (Sir RICHARD,) a British general, born in Canada in 1793. He was sent to India in 1842, and distinguished himself in the Afghan war. He commanded a division at the Alma and at Inkerman, etc., (1854-55.)

En'gle-field, (Sir HENRY CHARLES,) M.P., an English antiquary and astronomer, born in 1752, was a person of extensive and accurate attainments in science. In 1788 he was elected a Fellow of the Royal Society. He wrote a treatise on the Orbits of Comets, a "Walk through Southampton," (1801,) and "Beauties, Antiquities, etc. of the Isle of Wight," (1816.) Died in 1822.

English, ing'glish, (GEORGE BETHUNE,) an American adventurer and linguist, born in Boston in 1789. About 1820 he entered the army of the Pasha of Egypt, and served as an officer in an expedition against Sennaar. He wrote several works on theology, etc. Died in 1828.

English, (THOMAS DUNN,) an American poet and novelist, born in Philadelphia in 1819. He published a collection of poems in 1855.

Engramelle, ôN'gra̤'mĕl', (MARIE DOMINIQUE JOSEPH,) a French naturalist and musician, born in Artois in 1727. He published "The Butterflies of Europe," (8 vols., 1779-93.) Died in 1781.

See FÉTIS, "Biographie Universelle des Musiciens."

Engström or Engstroem, ĕng'strŏm, (JOHAN,) a Swedish poet and novelist, born in 1794. He published "The Æolian Harp," (1830,) and other poems.

Enjedin, ĕn'yeh-deen', or Enyedin, [Lat. ENJE'DIUS,] (GEORGE,) a noted Unitarian writer, born at Enyed, in Transylvania, was superintendent of the churches in the province above named. Died in 1597.

Enjedius. See ENJEDIN.

Ennebel, ĕn'neh-bĕl', (LOUIS,) a Belgian theologian and canonist, born at Louvain in 1652; died in 1720.

Ennemoser, ĕn'neh-mo'zer, (JOSEPH,) an eminent German physician and writer on magnetism and physiology, born in the Tyrol in 1787. He was professor at Bonn from 1820 to 1841, after which he practised at Munich. Among his works are "Magnetism in its Relations to Nature and Religion," (1842,) and "Der Magnetismus," (1844,) which was translated into English by William Howitt, ("History of Magic," 1854.) Died in 1854.

Ennery, (ADOLPHE.) See DENNERY.

Ennery, d', dĕn're', (MICHELET,) a French antiquary, born at Metz in 1709, made a large collection of medals and coins. His cabinet at Paris, which contained over twenty thousand medals, was sold and dispersed after his death. Died in 1788.

En'nĭ-us, (QUINTUS,) a Roman epic poet of great celebrity, born of a Greek family at Rudiæ, in Calabria, about 239 B.C. In early life he became a citizen of Rome, where he obtained the patronage and friendship of Cato, Scipio, and others. He contributed perhaps more than any other early Latin writer towards forming the national literature of Rome. His principal work, called the "Annals," a historical epic, was for a long time the most popular poem in the language. He also wrote several tragedies and comedies. He is said to have first introduced from the Greek the heroic hexameter into Latin poetry. His works are all lost, except some fragments quoted by Cicero and others. "He stands out prominently in that early time," says Professor Sellar, "as a man of true genius and of a great and original character. . . . Whatever in the later poets is most truly Roman in sentiment and morality, appears to be conceived in the spirit of Ennius. . . . The variety and extent of his works bear witness to remarkable learning as well as a strong productive energy." He was a great favourite of Cicero, who often quotes him, and he was highly eulogized by Lucretius, Propertius, Aulus Gellius, and Ovid. Died in 169 B.C.

See SELLAR, "Roman Poets of the Republic," chap. iv.; VOSSIUS, "De Poetis Latinis;" SAGITTARIUS, "De Vita et Scriptis L. Andronici, Ennii," etc.; H. FORELIUS, "De Ennio Diatriba," Upsal, 1707.

En-no'dĭ-us, (MAGNUS FELIX,) SAINT, one of the Fathers of the Latin Church, and a distinguished writer, born at Arles about 473 A.D. He obtained the bishopric of Pavía (Papia) about 511. He wrote a "Panegyric on King Theodoric," an "Apology for Pope Symmachus," "The Fourth Council of Rome," and a "Life of Saint Epiphanius of Pavía." He was sent to Constantinople by the pope in 515 and again in 517 to negotiate a union between the Eastern and Western Churches, but did not succeed in effecting that object. Died in 521.

See SIRMOND, "Vita Ennodii," prefixed to his edition of the works of Saint Ennodius.

Enobarbus. See AHENOBARBUS.

E'noch, [Heb. חנוך; Ger. ENOCH, ā'noK, or HENOCH, hā'noK,] an antediluvian patriarch, born in the year 3378 B.C., was the son of Jared, and father of Methuselah. He was pre-eminently favoured by a holy life and immunity from death. At the age of three hundred and sixty-five he "was translated that he should not see death." (Hebrews xi. 5; Genesis v. 24.) The book of Enoch, quoted in the Epistle of Jude, was extant in the time of the primitive Christians, but was rejected as apocryphal by the Fathers and by the Church.

Énoch, ä'nok', (LOUIS,) a French Hellenist and grammarian, born at Issoudun, became principal of the College of Geneva in 1556. Died about 1570.

His son ENOCH was a poet. Died about 1590.

Enrico OF PORTUGAL. See HENRY.

Enriquez Gomez, ĕn-ree'kĕth go'mĕth, (ANTONIO,) or ENRIQUEZ DE PAZ, (dȧ pȧth,) a Spanish poet and writer of fiction, lived about 1650. Among his works is "The Pythagorean Age."

Ens, ĕns, (JAN,) a Dutch theologian and writer, born in 1682, preached at Utrecht. Died in 1732.

Ens, ĕnss, (KASPAR,) a prolific and mediocre German writer in Latin, born about 1570.

Ense. See VARNHAGEN VON ENSE.

Ensenada, de, dȧ ĕn-sȧ-nä'dä, (ZENON SILVA,) MARQUIS, a Spanish statesman, born near Valladolid in 1690. He was appointed first minister of state by Ferdinand VI., who began to reign in 1746, and at the same time was created a marquis. The administration of Ensenada was wise and economical, and improved the condition of Spain. Died in 1762.

En'sor, (GEORGE,) an Irish writer, born in Dublin about 1769. He published, besides other works, "The Independent Man," (1806,) and "Defects of the English Laws and Tribunals," (1812.) Died in 1843.

Ent, (Sir GEORGE,) an eminent English physician, born in Kent in 1604, acquired a large practice, and was knighted by Charles II. He wrote a defence of Harvey's theory of the circulation of the blood. Died in 1689.

En-tel'lus, a celebrated athlete and a friend of Æneas, is mentioned in Virgil's "Æneid" (book v.) as having conquered Dares in the funeral games of Anchises.

En'tick or En'tinck, (JOHN,) an English writer, born in 1713, was employed by the booksellers to compile several histories and other works. His Latin and English Dictionary was successful, and has been reprinted. Died in 1773.

Entinck. See ENTICK.

En-tin'o-pus, an architect, born in the island of Candia, is noted as the founder of Venice. It is reported that he built the first house there, in 405 A.D.

See DARU, "Histoire de Venise."

Entius. See ENZIO.

Entraigues or **Antraigues, d',** dôN'trȧg', (EMMANUEL LOUIS HENRI de Launey—deh lō'nȧ',) COUNT, a French politician, born in Vivarais. He published in 1788 an eloquent "Memoir on the States-General," which was extremely revolutionary. Having been deputed by the noblesse to the States-General in 1789, he changed his course, and acted with the royalists. He emigrated about 1790, and was assassinated near London by one of his servants in 1812.

Entrecasteaux, d', dôNtR'kȧs'tō', (JOSEPH ANTOINE Bruni—brü'ne',) a French navigator, born at Aix about 1740, entered the navy young, and soon distinguished himself by his talents and steady courage. In 1785 he was appointed commander of the naval forces in India, and in 1791 was sent, with the rank of rear-admiral, in search of the lost navigator La Pérouse. Although he failed in this object, he made important discoveries on the coasts of Australia, Van Diemen's Land, etc. He died at sea, near Java, in 1793. The narrative of the voyage was published in 1808 by Rossel, one of his officers.

See DE ROSSEL, "Voyage de D'Entrecasteaux," etc.

Entrecolles. See DENTRECOLLES.

E-ny'o, ['Evvώ,] the Greek name of the goddess of war. (See BELLONA.)

Enzina or **Encina, de la,** dȧ lȧ ên-thee'nȧ, (JUAN,) a popular Spanish poet, born in Old Castile about 1468, is regarded as the founder of the Spanish theatre. He was patronized by Ferdinand the Catholic. He published in 1496 the first edition of his works, comprising odes, comedies, and a poem called "A Vision of the Temple of Fame." His "Art of Making Verses" ("Arte de Trovar") was received with favour, and his "Placida y Victoriano" is called a master-piece of dramatic art. His works are characterized by purity of style, brilliant ideas, and natural imagery. He was also distinguished as a musician, and became musical director to Pope Leo X. He went as a pilgrim to Palestine in 1519. Died about 1534.

See TICKNOR, "History of Spanish Literature;" LONGFELLOW, "Poets and Poetry of Europe."

Enzinas. See ENCINAS, (FRANCISCO.)

Enzio, ên'ze-o, or **Enzo,** ên'zo, [Lat. EN'TIUS,] a nominal king of Sardinia, born about 1224, was a natural son of the emperor Frederick II. He distinguished himself in the war which his father waged against the pope and the Guelphs. He gained a great naval victory over the Genoese in 1241. In 1249 he was made prisoner at Fossalto by the Guelphs, who kept him in prison until his death, in 1272.

See SISMONDI, "Histoire des Républiques Italiennes."

Enzo. See ENZIO.

Eoban, ā'o-bân, (HELIUS,) [Lat. EOBA'NUS HES'SIUS,] a German poet, born at Bockendorf, in Hesse, in 1488. He was professor of rhetoric and poetry at Nuremberg seven years, between 1526 and 1533, after which he obtained a similar position at Erfurt and Marburg. He translated into Latin verse Homer's "Iliad" and the Idyls of Theocritus, and wrote Latin eclogues, and other poems. His "Iliad" was often reprinted. Died in 1540.

See LOSSIUS, "H. Eoban und seine Zeitgenossen;" M. ADAM, "Vitæ Germanorum Philosophorum."

Eobanus. See EOBAN.

Eoetvoes. See EÖTVÖS.

Éole, the French of ÆOLUS, which see.

Éon de Beaumont,d', dȧ'ôN' deh bō'môN',(CHARLES GENEVIÈVE LOUISE AUGUSTE ANDRÉ TIMOTHÉE,)styled CHEVALIER D'ÉON, a famous French diplomatist, born at Tonnerre in 1728. Having gained reputation by writing an Essay on the Finances of France, he was employed about 1755 on a mission to the court of Russia, with which he negotiated an advantageous treaty. In 1759 he served with credit as captain in the French army in Germany. A few years later he was minister plenipotentiary to London, but was superseded soon after his appointment. On his return to France, about 1777, the government, for some mysterious reason, required him

to assume the female dress, which he wore for the rest of his life. Being reduced to poverty, he supported himself in his later years by giving lessons in the art of fencing. He was author of many historical and political essays. Died in 1810.

See "Mémoires du Chevalier D'Éon," by F. GAILLARDET; GRIMM, "Correspondance;" BACHAUMONT, "Mémoires."

E'os, [Gr. 'Hώς,] of the Greek mythology, corresponds to the Latin Aurora, the goddess of morning. She was supposed to be a daughter of Hyperion, a sister of Diana or Selene, and the wife of Tithonus.

Eosander, à-o-zân'der, (JOHANN FRIEDRICH,) an eminent German architect, of Swedish origin, born towards the end of the seventeenth century, was employed by the Elector Frederick on a palace in Berlin, and on other edifices. That prince also sent him as ambassador to Charles XII. of Sweden. Among his works is the palace of Schönhausen, Berlin. Died at Dresden in 1729.

See HIRSCHING, "Historisch-literarisches Handbuch."

Eötvös or **Eoetvoes,** à-öt-vösh', (JOSEPH,) a popular Hungarian author and statesman, born at Buda (or Ofen) in 1813. He produced about 1833 "The Critics," a comedy, and "The Revenge," a tragedy. His reputation was increased by "The Carthusian," a novel, (1838–41.) He defended Kossuth in a pamphlet, (1841,) which proved that he possessed polemical abilities of a high order. He was afterwards one of the chief orators of the popular party in the Diet. His political novel "The Village Notary" (1844–46) had great popularity, and was translated into English and German. In 1848 he was for a short time minister of public instruction.

E-pam-i-non'das, [Gr.'Επαμεινώνδας or 'Επαμνώνδας,] an illustrious Theban statesman and general, a son of Polymnis, was born about the year 412 B.C. He received instruction from Lysis of Tarentum, a Pythagorean philosopher. He first distinguished himself on the field of Mantinea, where he and his friend Pelopidas performed prodigies of valour, under the standard of Sparta, (385.) In youth he loved retirement and study, and, it is said, preferred poverty from principle. The aristocrats of Thebes, aided by Spartan soldiery, gained the ascendency, and banished Pelopidas and other popular chiefs; but Epaminondas, being regarded as a speculative philosopher, was not included in the proscription. When he was about forty years of age, at a congress of deputies from the Grecian states he spoke eloquently against the encroachments of the Spartan power, and acquired the reputation of one of the best orators of Greece. When, soon after this, Sparta declared war against Thebes, Epaminondas was nominated commander-in-chief of the Theban army, consisting of 6000 foot and 500 horse, to which Sparta opposed 10,000 foot and 1000 horse. The armies met at Leuctra, where the Spartans were totally routed, with a loss of 4000 men, in 372 B.C. This battle was a fatal blow to the supremacy of Sparta, and became forever memorable for the profound and skilful combinations in the military art of which Epaminondas gave the first example. He invaded Peloponnesus in 369, and threatened Sparta, which was defended with firmness and success by Agesilaus. He commanded the Thebans at the battle of Mantinea, (July 4, 363,) and had just achieved a glorious victory, when he received a mortal wound. Some writers date this event in 362 B.C. Cicero maintains that Epaminondas was the greatest man that Greece has produced; and all parties admit that he was one of the most perfect models of the statesman, warrior, patriot, and sage.

See PLUTARCH, "Pelopidas;" GROTE, "History of Greece," chaps. lxviii., lxix., lxxx.; SERAN DE LA TOUR, "Histoire d'Epaminondas," 1739; A. G. MEISSNER, "Epaminondas," (in German, 1801;) CORNELIUS NEPOS, "Epaminondas;" DIODORUS SICULUS, book xv.; E. BAUCH, "Epaminondas und Theben's Kampf um die Hegemonie," 1834.

Ep'a-phras, a primitive Christian minister of Colosse, was a fellow-prisoner with the Apostle Paul in Rome about 66 A.D.

See Colossians i. 7, iv. 12; Philemon, 23d verse.

E-paph-ro-di'tus, [Fr. ÉPAPHRODITE, à'pt'fro'dèt',] one of the primitive Christians, was a companion and "fellow-soldier" of the Apostle Paul.

See Philippians ii. 25 and iv. 18.

ā, ē, ī, ō, ū, ȳ, *long;* ȧ, ė, ȯ, same, less prolonged; ă, ĕ, ĭ, ŏ, ŭ, ў, *short;* ą, ę, į, ǫ, *obscure;* fär, fȧll, fȧt; mĕt; nŏt; gŏŏd; mŏŏn;

Épée, de l', děh lǎ'pà', (CHARLES MICHEL,) a French abbé, born at Versailles in 1712, was distinguished for his successful devotion to the instruction of the deaf and dumb. He refused, as a Jansenist, to sign a formulary, and thus hindered his success in the church at Paris; but he afterwards obtained a canonicate in the church of Troyes. He had inherited an income of seven thousand francs, when, casually meeting with two sisters who were deaf-mutes, he thenceforth devoted his life and fortune to the gratuitous instruction of that class. His institution acquired a wide reputation, and at his death passed into the hands of Abbé Sicard. He wrote several treatises on the subject of his pursuits. He has the credit of being the first who used natural signs or gestures in the instruction of the deaf and dumb. Died in 1789.

See J. VALETTE, "Vie de l'Abbé de l'Épée," 1857; BÉBIAN, "Éloge de C. M. de l'Épée;" E. MOREL, "Notice sur l'Abbé de l'Épée," 1833; F. BERTHIER, "L'Abbé de l'Épée, sa Vie, son Apostolat, etc.," 1852.

Épernon, d', dǎ'pěR'nŏN', written also **Espernon,** (JEAN LOUIS DE **Nogaret de la Vallette**—no'gǎ'rǎ' děh lǎ vǎ'lět',) DUC, sometimes called CAUMONT, a noted French courtier, born in Languedoc in 1554. He was a favourite of Henry III., who created him Duke of Espernon and in 1587 appointed him admiral of France. In the next two reigns he also held high offices. He was in the carriage of Henry IV. when that king was assassinated, and was suspected of complicity in the crime. Died in 1642.

See G. GIRARD, "Histoire de la Vie du Duc d'Espernon," 1655, translated into English by CHARLES COTTON, 1670.

Éphialte. See EPHIALTES.

E-phī-al'tēs, [Gr. Ἐφιάλτης; Fr. ÉPHIALTE, ả'fe'ǎlt',] in the Greek mythology, a giant, supposed to be the son of Neptune and Iphimedi'a. He and his brother Otus are said to have grown nine inches every month. When only nine years old, they attempted to scale the heavens by piling Mount Ossa on Olympus and Pelion upon Ossa; but they were slain by Apollo, (or, as one account says, by Diana.) (See IPHIMEDIA.)

Ephialtes, an Athenian orator, lived about 350 B.C. He was one of the ten orators whom Alexander the Great required to be delivered to him. They were saved by the intervention of Demades.

Ephialtes, a Greek traitor, who, while Leonidas was defending the pass of Thermopylæ, guided the Persian invaders through a defile, by which they turned the position of the Greeks.

Ephialtes, an Athenian statesman and general, was a political friend of Pericles. He was the principal author of a law which diminished the power of the Areopagus and changed the government into an unmixed democracy. Several ancient historians commend his integrity and other virtues. He was assassinated by the aristocrats in 456 B.C.

See GROTE, "History of Greece;" THIRLWALL, "History of Greece;" PLUTARCH, "Pericles;" CICERO, "De Republica."

E-phip'pus, [Ἔφιππος,] an Athenian poet of the middle comedy, lived about 340 B.C. The titles of some of his plays have been preserved by Athenæus.

Ephippus of Olynthus, a Greek historian who wrote an account of Alexander the Great, which is lost.

Ephore. See EPHORUS.

Eph'o-rus, [Gr. Ἔφορος; Fr. ÉPHORE, ả'foR',] an eminent Greek historian, born probably about 400 B.C. He studied rhetoric with Isocrates, who persuaded him to devote himself to history in preference to oratory. His principal work was a general history of Greece and of the Barbarians from the siege of Troy to 340 B.C., only a few fragments of which have not come down to us. He has a good reputation for sincerity and veracity as a historian. His style is clear and elegant, but rather feeble and diffuse. He is supposed to have died about 330 B.C.

See PLUTARCH, "Lives of the Ten Orators;" C. MÜLLER, "De Ephoro," in his "Fragmenta Historicorum Græcorum."

E'phra-em or **E'phra-im,** [Lat. EPHRÆ'MUS,] written also **Ephrem,** THE SYRIAN, an eminent ecclesiastical writer of the fourth century, born at Nisibis. In youth he adopted the monastic life in a cave near Edessa, where he improved his time in study and writing. He zealously opposed Arianism with his voice and pen. The

bishopric of Edessa was offered to him, but was declined. According to some accounts, he renounced his solitary way of life many years before his death. He was venerated as a prophet by his contemporaries. He wrote, in Syriac, numerous sermons, hymns, commentaries, etc., which were very popular, and are still extant. Died about 378 A.D. Gerard Voss published a Latin version of his works, (1586–97.) An edition of his works in Syriac and Greek was published by the Assemani at Rome, (6 vols., 1732–46.)

See VILLEMAIN, "Tableau de l'Éloquence chrétienne au quatrième Siècle;" CAVE, "Scriptorum Ecclesiasticorum Historia;" LENGERKE, "Commentatio critica de Ephraemo Syro," 1828.

E'phra-im, [Heb. אֶפְרַיִם,] one of the Hebrew patriarchs, was the second son of Joseph, and a favourite grandson of Jacob.

See Genesis, chap. xlviii.

Éphraïm [Fr. pron. ả'frǎ'ǎN'] DE NEVERS, a French monk, who was sent as missionary to India about 1645, and laboured many years at Madras. He was confined in prison by the Inquisitors of Goa, and liberated by the King of Golconda about 1650.

Ephrem. See EPHRAEM.

Épicharme. See EPICHARMUS.

Ep-ĭ-char'mus, [Gr. Ἐπίχαρμος; Fr. ÉPICHARME, ả'pe'shǎRm',] a Greek poet and philosopher, born in the island of Cos, passed the greater part of his life at Syracuse, to which he removed about 485 B.C. He was a disciple of Pythagoras, and is called by Aristotle the inventor of comedy. Plato designates him as the first of comic writers. His productions, of which scarcely anything remains but the titles, were partly political dramas, and partly parodies of mythological subjects. He was an elegant and original writer. He wrote also treatises on philosophy and morality. He died about 450 B.C., aged ninety or more. Some of his philosophical ideas were adopted by Plato.

See O. MÜLLER, "The Dorians;" DIOGENES LAERTIUS; H. HARLESS, "De Epicharmo," 1822; GRYSAR, "De Doriensium Comœdia," 1828.

E-pic'ra-tēs, [Gr. Ἐπικράτης,] an Athenian orator, who lived about 390 B.C., belonged to the democratic party.

Epicrates, an Athenian comic poet of the middle comedy, flourished about 360 B.C. Fragments of his plays are extant.

Épictète. See EPICTETUS.

Ep-ic-te'tus, [Gr. Ἐπίκτητος; Fr. ÉPICTÈTE, ả'pěk'tǎt'; Ger. EPIKTET, ȧ-pik-tāt'; It. EPITETTO, ȧ-pe-tet'to,] a celebrated Stoic philosopher, was born at Hierapolis, in Phrygia, about 60 A.D. He was a freedman of Epaphroditus, a favourite servant of Nero. He retired from Rome to Nicopolis, in Epirus, in consequence of an edict by which Domitian banished the philosophers, in 89 A.D. Few other events of his life are known. He acquired a great reputation as a teacher of philosophy, which he made subservient to practical morality. His life was an example of temperance, moderation, and other virtues. His temper and principles were less austere, and more allied to the spirit of the gospel, than those of the early Stoics. He left no written works; but his doctrines were recorded by his disciple Arrian in eight books, four of which have come down to us. No heathen philosopher taught a higher or purer system of morality. "The maxim *suffer and abstain* (from evil)," says Professor Brandis, "which he followed throughout his life, was based with him on the firm belief in a wise and benevolent government of Providence; and in this respect he approaches the Christian doctrine more than any of the earlier Stoics, though there is not a trace in the *Epictetea* to show that he was acquainted with Christianity." (Smith's "Dictionary of Greek and Roman Biography and Mythology.") His "Enchiridion," or "Manual," has been translated into English by Mrs. E. Carter.

See RITTER, "History of Philosophy;" FABRICIUS, "Bibliotheca Græca;" J. F. BEYER, "Ueber Epiktet und sein Handbuch der Stoischen Moral," 1795; G. BOILEAU, "Vie d'Épictète et sa Philosophie," 1655, and English version of the same, by J. DAVIES, 1670.

Épicure and **Epicuro.** See EPICURUS.

Ep-ĭ-cu'rus, [Gr. Ἐπίκουρος; Fr. ÉPICURE, ả'pe'küR'; It. EPICURO, ȧ-pe-koo'ro; Ger. EPIKUR, ȧ-pe-kooR',| an eminent Greek philosopher, the founder of the Epicurean sect, was born in the island of Samos about 340 B.C. He was the son of Neocles, an Athenian; he studied under Pamphilus in Samos, and under Xenocrates in Athens, which he visited at the age of eighteen; but he professed to be self-taught, *(autodidactos.)* He then travelled in Ionia, and spent several years in Mitylene and Lampsacus. Here he began to teach new doctrines, and made numerous disciples. In the year 309 he removed to Athens, where he bought a garden, and founded a new school of philosophy, which bears his name. His school became very popular, and exerted an important influence on many succeeding ages. Diogenes Laertius says that Epicurus "had so many friends that even whole cities could not contain them." It is said that he objected to a community of property, as tending to excite mutual distrust. Gassendi has ably defended Epicurus against the accusations of the Stoics and the prejudices of the Schoolmen with respect to his doctrines and his private life; though he recognizes a mixture of error in his system.

His principles are the reverse of Stoicism, and form a system of materialism founded on utility. (See ZENO.) He taught that the gods live forever, far remote from human affairs, in a state of passionless repose, indifferent alike to the virtues and the crimes of mankind. Cicero supposes that Epicurus had no belief whatever in any gods, but that he nominally acknowledged their existence that he might not offend the prejudices of the Athenians. (See his "De Natura Deorum," i. 30.) When he proposed pleasure or happiness as the supreme good, he qualified this doctrine by the maxim that temperance is necessary in order to enjoy the noble and durable pleasures which are proper to human nature. Chrysippus, an opponent, admits the purity of his moral character, but insinuates that it was owing to his insensibility. He took no part in political affairs, seeking in self-reliance and internal resources a compensation for the loss of national liberty.

He derived the basis of his philosophy, both his psychology and his physics, from Democritus, who taught that the universe consists of space (or vacuum) and of matter, which is composed of eternal indivisible atoms of various kinds; and that everything—the soul as well as the body—is formed by the fortuitous concurrence of these atoms; that all our knowledge is derived from sensations; that sensation is produced by images or emanations flowing from external objects. Lucretius was a follower of the Epicurean philosophy, which is fully explained in his admirable poem "De Rerum Naturâ." (See LUCRETIUS.) Of the voluminous writings of Epicurus nothing now remains but a few letters preserved in the works of Diogenes Laertius, and fragments of his treatise on Nature found at Herculaneum. Died in 270 B.C.

See GASSENDI, "De Vita et Moribus Epicuri," 1647; and "Syntagma Philosophiæ Epicuri," 1659; RONDEL, "La Vie d'Épicure," 1679; RITTER, "History of Philosophy;" G. H. LEWES, "Biographical History of Philosophy;" MACKINTOSH, "Progress of Ethical Philosophy;" DIOGENES LAERTIUS; ERSCH und GRUBER, "Allgemeine Encyklopaedie;" C. MALLET, "Épicure," in his "Études philosophiques," 1843.

Ep-ĭ-çȳ'dēs, [Gr. Ἐπικύδης,] a Syracusan general, who served with distinction under Hannibal in Italy. In 214 B.C. he and his brother Hippocrates took Syracuse, of which they had command when it was besieged by Marcellus, 213 B.C.

Épigène. See EPIGENES.

E-pig'e-nēs, [Ἐπιγένης,] an Athenian poet of the middle comedy, lived probably about 375 B.C.

Epigenes, [Fr. ÉPIGÈNE, à'pe'zhǎn',] a Greek astronomer, who is supposed to have lived before the Christian era. He is mentioned by Seneca and Pliny.

Épigones. See EPIGONI.

E-pig'o-nī, [Gr. Ἐπίγονοι; Fr. ÉPIGONES, à'pe'gon',] a term which signifies "heirs" or "descendants," was applied to the sons of the seven chiefs who conducted an expedition against Thebes to restore Polyni'ces, and who were all killed except Adrastus. Ten years later, the Epigoni—namely, Alcmæon, Thersander, Diomedes, Ægialeus, Promachus, Sthenelus, and Euryalus —renewed the enterprise and took Thebes. The war

of the Epigoni was celebrated by several ancient epic and dramatic poets.

Epiktet, the German of EPICTETUS, which see.

Epikur. See EPICURUS.

Ep-ĭ-men'ĭ-dēs, [Gr. Ἐπιμενίδης; Fr. ÉPIMÉNIDE, à'pe'mà'nèd',] an eminent Greek poet and prophet, born in Crete, is supposed to have lived about 600 B.C. By some writers he was reckoned among the seven wise men of Greece. A tradition was current that in early youth he fell asleep in a cave, and remained in that state more than fifty years, after which he was reputed to be an inspired prophet, and was noted for his skill in medicine. About 596 B.C. he accepted the invitation of the Athenians to come and purify their city, then visited by the plague. He wrote a poem on the Argonautic expedition, which is not extant. Other works were ascribed to him by the ancients.

See C. F. HEINRICH, "Epimenides aus Creta," 1801; GRABENER, "Dissertatio de Epimenide," 1742.

Épiméthée. See EPIMETHEUS.

Ep-ĭ-me'theūs, [Gr. Ἐπιμηθεύς; Fr. ÉPIMÉTHÉE, à'pe'mà'tà',] a mythical personage, said to be a son of Iapetus, a brother of Prometheus, and the husband of Pandora. (See PROMETHEUS.) His name signifies "after-thought."

Épinac or **Espinac, d',** dȧ'pe'nȧk',(PIERRE,) a French prelate, born at the château d'Épinac in 1540, was made Archbishop of Lyons in 1574. He was a violent partisan and instigator of the Catholic League against Henry III. and Henry IV. Died in 1599.

Épinat, à'pe'nȧ', (FLEURY,) a French landscape-painter, born at Montbrison in 1764, was a pupil of David. Among his works is "The Lady of the Lake." Died in 1830.

Épinay, d', dȧ'pe'nȧ', (LOUISE FLORENCE **Pétronille** de la Live—pȧ'tʀo'nèl' dĕh lȧ lèv,) MADAME, a French authoress, born about 1725. She was married in youth to M. d'Épinay, who deserted her. She afterwards formed *liaisons* with Grimm and with J. J. Rousseau, for whom she built the hermitage at Montmorenci about 1755. She wrote a work on education, called "Conversations of Emilie," (1783,) which was crowned by the French Academy. Died in 1783. Her autobiographic Memoirs were published in 1818, (3 vols.)

See ROUSSEAU, "Confessions;" SAINTE-BEUVE, "Causeries du Lundi;" "Edinburgh Review" for December, 1818.

Épiphane. See EPIPHANIUS.

Ep-ĭ-phā'nĭ-us, [Gr. Ἐπιφάνιος,] a Greek philosopher and founder of a sect, was a son of Carpocrates, noticed in this work, and lived between 150 and 200 A.D.

Epiphanius OF ALEXANDRIA, a Greek mathematician, who lived about the second century of our era.

Epiphanius, [Fr. ÉPIPHANE, à'pe'fàn',] SAINT, a dogmatical bishop, born near Eleutheropolis, in Palestine, about 310 A.D., passed a part of his youth in Egypt, where he imbibed ascetic notions. Returning to Palestine, he became a disciple of Hilarion. About 368 he was chosen Bishop of Constantia, formerly called Salamis, in the island of Cyprus. He exhibited a rather violent zeal against Origen and the Arians, which involved him in many contentions, and he took a prominent part in the deposition of Chrysostom. He wrote "Panarium," a treatise against heresies, and several other works, in Greek. They contain many errors, but are valued for passages quoted from other authors whose works are lost. Died in 402 A.D.

See NEANDER, "History of the Church;" CAVE, "Historia Literaria."

Ep-ĭ-phā'nĭ-us Scho-las'tĭ-cus lived about 510 A.D., and was a friend of Cassiodorus. He translated into Latin the Ecclesiastical Histories of Sozomen, Socrates, and Theodoret, and other Greek works.

Ep-is-co'pĭ-us, (SIMON,) a Dutch divine, whose proper name was BISSCHOP, (bis'ᴋop,) born in Amsterdam in 1583. He was eminent for his learning, charity, and liberality, and became the principal pillar of the Arminian party, or Remonstrants. He was professor of theology in the University of Leyden from 1612 until 1618, when the Synod of Dort banished him from Holland for his opinions. Having passed some years in France, he returned to his native land in 1626, and in 1634 became rector of a college in Amsterdam. He wrote the "Confession of the Remonstrants," a treatise on Predestination, and other theological works. Died in 1643.

See J. KONIJNENBURG, "Laudatio Simonis Episcopii," 1791; BAYLE, "Historical and Critical Dictionary;" P. VAN LIMBORCH, "Leven van S. Episcopius," Amsterdam, 1693; FREDERICK CALDER, "Memoirs of Simon Episcopius."

Epitetto, the Italian of EPICTETUS, which see.

Epo or **Epona.** See HIPPONA.

Ep-o-ni'na, a woman of Gaul, noted for her conjugal devotion, was the wife of Julius Sabinus, a chief of the Lingones, who revolted against Vespasian. She was put to death, with her husband, in 78 A.D.

Eppendorf, von, fon ĕp'pen-dorf', (HEINRICH,) a German writer, an adversary of Erasmus, was born in Misnia. Died about 1554.

Épréménil. See ESPRÉMESNIL.

Equicola, à-kwee'ko-lä, (MARIO,) an Italian historian and philosopher, born at Alveto about 1460. His principal works are a "History of Mantua," (1521,) and a curious philosophic treatise on "Love," ("Della Natura d'Amore," 1525.) Died in 1539.

Eraclito, the Italian of HERACLITUS, which see.

E-ra'clī-us, a Roman painter of the tenth or eleventh century, wrote an essay on the "Arts of the Romans," in which he treats of painting in oil and on glass.

Érard. See ERRARD.

Érard, à'rǎr', (JEAN BAPTISTE ORPHÉE PIERRE,) a nephew of the following, was born in Paris in 1794. He repaired in 1850 the organ of the Tuileries, which had been damaged by the populace in 1830. Died in 1855.

Érard, (SÉBASTIEN,) a French inventor of musical instruments, born at Strasburg in 1752. In 1780 he began, in Paris, the manufacture of pianos, (then almost unknown,) in which he made improvements. His piano-factory, in which his brother John Baptist was a partner, became the most celebrated in Europe. His harp with double action, invented about 1811, had a great sale. In 1823 he produced the grand piano with repeating movement, *(à double échappement.)* He finished in 1830 an organ for the chapel of the Tuileries, which is his master-piece. Died in 1831.

See FÉTIS, "Biographie Universelle des Musiciens."

Érasistrate. See ERASISTRATUS.

Er-a-sis'tra-tus, [Gr. Ἐρασίστρατος; Fr. ÉRASISTRATE, à'rå'ze'strǎt',] a celebrated Greek physician and anatomist, supposed to have beèn born at Iulis, in the island of Ceos. He was, according to Pliny, a grandson of Aristotle, and lived between 300 and 250 B.C. He gained much credit at the court of Seleucus Nicator by discerning and remedying the secret malady of his son Antiochus, who pined with a hopeless passion for Stratonice, his own step-mother. He practised chiefly in Alexandria, with a high reputation as a teacher of anatomy and medicine, and was regarded as the first anatomist of his time. His most important discoveries were those of the *viæ lacteæ,* and the functions of the brain and nervous system. For blood-letting and cathartics he substituted dieting, bathing, and exercise. His writings are not extant.

See HALLER, "Bibliotheca Anatomica;" LECLERC, "Histoire de la Médecine."

Érasme, (DIDIER.) See ERASMUS, (DESIDERIUS.)

E-ras'mus, (DESIDERIUS,) [Fr. DIDIER (or DÉSIRÉ, dā'ze'rā') ÉRASME, de'de-à' à'rǎsm',] surnamed ROTERDA'MUS or ROTERDAMEN'SIS, a celebrated Dutch scholar and philosopher, pre-eminent as a restorer of learning, was born at Rotterdam on the 28th of October, 1465, or, according to some authorities, in 1467. He was a natural son of Gerard Praet, a resident of Gouda, who by a false report of the death of Margaret (the mother of Erasmus) was induced to enter the priesthood.

The subject of this article, at first named GERHARDUS GERHARDI, or Gerard son of Gerard, was educated at Utrecht and Deventer. He studied at Deventer about six years, and made rapid progress under the tuition of Alexander Hegius. Having become an orphan about the age of thirteen, he was urged by his guardians (who defrauded him of his patrimony) to enter a monastery; but he felt a decided aversion to that mode of life. At length he was enticed or compelled, in 1486, to become a monk and an inmate of the convent of Stein. Here he

pursued the study of the classics and acquired a reputation as a Latin scholar. He was employed as secretary by the Bishop of Cambray for five years, 1492–96, and at the latter date obtained permission to go to Paris, where he passed some time in the Collége de Montaigu. He earned a subsistence in Paris by acting as tutor. It is related that while in the French capital, being almost in rags, he wrote to a friend, "As soon as I get money I will buy, first Greek books, and then clothes."

In 1498 he visited England, where he formed friendships with Sir Thomas More and John Colet, and studied Greek at Oxford. He returned to the continent in 1499, and in 1506 went to Italy, where he associated with the most eminent scholars, passed several years in travel and in the study of Greek, and obtained from the pope a dispensation from his monastic vows. He accepted in 1510 an invitation to visit England, and was employed for a few years as professor of divinity and of Greek at the University of Cambridge. In 1510 he produced and dedicated to Sir Thomas More his "Praise of Folly," ("Encomium Moriæ,") a witty satire against all professions, but especially against the mendicant monks. It met with a rapid sale, and was received with almost universal applause.

Erasmus was now at the head of the literary world, and made zealous efforts to dispel the inveterate ignorance and prejudices which then prevailed. The greatest monarchs solicited the honour of his presence in their capitals. About 1515 the Archduke Charles, (afterwards Charles V.,) whose court was at Brussels, gave Erasmus the title of royal councillor, with a pension of 400 florins, which enabled him to gratify his inclination to travel. It appears that he never remained long in one place. Among his remarkable works is a collection of proverbs, etc., entitled "Adagia," which was published about 1500, and is a monument of his immense and multifarious learning.

In 1516 he published an excellent edition of the Greek Testament, with Latin version and notes,—the first edition ever printed,—a work for which he was eminently qualified. By his witty and satirical writings against the abuses and corruptions of the Roman Church he contributed greatly to the success of the Reformation; and at one time he was favourable to the Protestants. But he was offended at the radical course of Luther, some of whose tenets he did not approve, and the timidity or moderation of his character prevented his open revolt against the pope and the Church of Rome. His "passionless moderation" and neutral position in the latter part of his life exposed him to annoyance from the zealots of both parties, who considered him lukewarm or heretical. In 1521 he removed to Bâle, where, the next year, appeared his celebrated "Colloquies," professedly intended for the instruction of youth in Latin and morals, but aiming many hard blows against the Roman Church. In one year twenty-four thousand copies of this work were printed, all of which were sold. His alienation from the Reformers, however, increased, and he engaged in 1524 in a dispute on Free Will with Luther, who denounced him in severe language. He died at Bâle on the 12th of July, 1536.

His epistles are very voluminous, and contain rich stores of materials for literary history. He is considered the greatest wit and most eminent scholar of the age in which he lived, and one of the most conspicuous and successful among those who have laboured to restore classical learning and sound philosophy. His views on the subject of war appear to have been perfectly accordant with those of Penn and Barclay. His complete works were published in nine volumes (1541) by Beatus Rhenanus.

See BURIGNY, "Vie d'Érasme," 1757; Lives of Erasmus, by ADOLPH MÜLLER, (in German, 1828,) and JORTIN, (in English, 1758;) KNIGHT, "Life of Erasmus," 1726, and notice in BAYLE's "Dictionary;" also, CHARLES BUTLER, "Life of Erasmus," 1825; MERULA, "Vita D. Erasmi," 1607; "London Quarterly Review" for July, 1859; "Retrospective Review," vol. v., 1822.

E-ras'mus Jo-an'nis, [Fr. ÉRASME DE JEAN, à'rǎsm' deh zhŏN,] a Dutch theologian and Unitarian of the sixteenth century. He had a dispute with Socinus at Cracow. Died after 1593.

Eraso, à-rä'so, (Don BENITO,) a Spanish general, born in Navarre in 1789, was a colonel in the army at the death of Ferdinand VII., (1833.) He then took arms in favour of Don Carlos, obtained the rank of general, and commanded in several engagements during the civil war. Died in 1835.

Erasth. See ERASTUS.

E-ras′tus or **Erasth**, à-râst′, (THOMAS,) a Swiss physician, whose family name was LIEBER, (lee′ber,) born at Baden in 1524. He was a skilful practitioner of medicine, on which he wrote several treatises. For many years he was professor of medicine at Heidelberg, with the title of physician to the Elector, Frederick III. In 1580 he removed to Bâle, where he obtained the chair of moral philosophy. His name is identified with certain opinions on the relation of church and state, since called Erastianism. His "Theses on Excommunication," published after his death, became the subject of much disputation. He proposed that offences against morality should be punished by the civil power, rather than by the church. Died in 1583.

See "Biographia Britannica;" MORÉRI, "Dictionnaire Historique;" WORDSWORTH, "Ecclesiastical Biography."

Erath, ā′rât, (ANTON ULRICH,) a German historian, born at Brunswick in 1709, wrote a "History of Brunswick," (in Latin, 1745.) Died in 1773.

Erath, von, fon ā′rât, (AUGUSTIN,) a German theologian, born in Suabia in 1648, published the "Noble Order of the Golden Fleece," ("Augustus Velleris Aurei Ordo," 1694,) and other works. Died in 1719.

Er′a-to, [Ἐρατώ,] in Greek mythology, was one of the nine Muses, and presided over erotic poetry and pantomimic performances. She was represented with a lyre in her hand.

Eratosthène. See ERATOSTHENES.

Er-a-tos′the-nēs, [Gr. Ἐρατοσθένης; Fr. ÉRATOSTHÈNE, à′rä′tos′tản′,] a famous Greek geometer and astronomer, born at Cyrene in 276 B.C., was a pupil of Ariston of Chios, and of Callimachus the poet. He was for many years superintendent of the great library of Alexandria in the reigns of Ptolemy Evergetes and his successor. He acquired durable celebrity by his astronomical labours, and is recognized by Delambre as the first founder of genuine astronomy. Among his remarkable operations was the measurement of the obliquity of the ecliptic, which he computed to be 23° 51′ 20″. He also made a memorable attempt to ascertain the dimensions of the earth by a method which has been used with success in modern times, and which was invented by him. He rendered important services to the science of geography, and wrote works on philosophy, grammar, etc., which are not extant. Died about 196 B.C.

See FABRICIUS, "Bibliotheca Græca;" DELAMBRE, "Histoire de l'Astronomie ancienne."

Erauso, d', dà-rŏw′so, (CATALINA,) a Spanish heroine, surnamed LA MONJA ALFEREZ, (lä mon′HÄ âl-fä′rĕth,) ("the Ensign Nun,") was born at Saint Sebastian, in Biscay, in 1592. She was placed when an infant in the convent of her native town, from which she effected her escape at the age of fifteen. Disguised as a man, she embarked for South America, and, after various romantic adventures, entered the army and acquired a high reputation for courage. On her return to Spain, in 1624, she obtained a pension from Philip III., and was received with great favour by Pope Urban VIII. The time of her death is not known. Her Memoirs, by herself, were published by Don J. M. Ferrer, (Paris, 1829.)

See, also, DE QUINCEY's account of the Spanish Nun, in "Narrative and Miscellaneous Papers," vol. i.

Er′chem-bert [Lat. ERCHEMBER′TUS] or **Er′chempert**, a monk and historian, lived about 860–900 A.D. He wrote a "Chronicle of the Lombards," of which a part is extant.

Er-chin′o-ald was elected mayor of the palace of Neustria in 640 A.D., in the reign of Clovis II., and governed the kingdom for many years. Died about 660.

Ercilla y Arteaga, de, dà ĕR-thĕl′yä e aR-tà-ä′gä, (FORTUNIO GARCÍA,) a Spanish jurist, who flourished about 1550, was the father of the following.

Ercilla y Zuñiga, ĕR-thĕl′yä e thoon-yee′gä, (ALONSO,) the first epic poet of Spain, born at Bermeo about 1530, was the son of Fortunio Garcia, Lord of Ercilla. In early youth he was a page of Philip II. of Spain, whom

he attended in a voyage to England in 1554. In the same year he enlisted as a volunteer in an expedition against the Araucanians, a brave native tribe of South America. Amidst the tumults and dangers of this war, in which he performed a conspicuous part, he composed his "Araucana," which is thought to be the best heroic poem that Spain has produced, and is at the same time a historical record of events that the author witnessed. It was first printed in 1577, and has acquired a European reputation. He died in obscurity and poverty in Spain about 1600.

See VOLTAIRE, "Essai sur la Poésie épique;" LONGFELLOW, "Poets and Poetry of Europe;" TICKNOR, "History of Spanish Literature."

Erckmann-Chatrian, ĕRk′mŏn′ shä′tre′ŏn′, the name of a literary partnership which has become celebrated as the source from which has proceeded a series of interesting works on the customs of the Germans, and on the history and romance of the wars of the French Revolution and Empire. Among the most popular of these works are "Stories of the Borders of the Rhine," ("Contes des Bords du Rhin,") "La Maison forestière," "The Conscript of 1813," "The Invasion," and "Waterloo." Of this partnership ÉMILE ERCKMANN was born at Phalsbourg, in France, in 1825; ALEXANDRE CHATRIAN was born in 1826.

Ercolanetti, ĕR-ko-lä-net′tee, (ERCOLANO,) an Italian painter, born at Perugia in 1615; died in 1687.

Ercolani, ĕR-ko-lä′nee, (GIUSEPPE MARIA,) an Italian poet and prelate, born at Sinigaglia about 1690. He wrote two admired poems, entitled "Maria," (1725,) and "La Sulamitide;" also a treatise on architecture, (1744.) Died at Rome about 1760.

Erdélyi, ĕR-dāl-yee, (JÁNOS,) a Hungarian poet, born in 1814. He gained distinction by a volume of lyric poems, published in 1844, and "Legends and Popular Tales of Hungary," (5 vols., 1845–48.)

Erdl, ĕRtl, (MICHAEL PIUS,) a skilful German anatomist and physiologist, born in 1815, was professor of physiology and comparative anatomy at Munich. He wrote a treatise on the Eye, "On the Circulation of Infusoria," (1841,) "The Development of Man and of the Chick in the Egg," (1846,) and other works. Died in 1848.

Erdmann, ĕRt′mân, (JOHANN EDUARD,) a German philosopher and disciple of Hegel, born at Volmar, in Livonia, in 1805. He became professor of philosophy at Halle about 1836. Among his principal works are an "Essay of a Scientific Exposition (Darstellung) of the History of Modern Philosophy," (4 vols., 1834–51,) "Nature and Creation," (1840,) "Elements of Psychology," (3d edition, 1847,) and "On Ennui," ("Ueber die Langweile," 1852.)

Erdmann, (OTTO Linné—lin-nā′,) a German chemist, born at Dresden in 1804, published a valuable "Manual of Chemistry," (1828,) and a treatise on drugs.

Erdt, ĕRt, (PAULIN,) a German monk, born at Wertach in 1737, published a "Literary History of Theology," ("Historia literaria Theologiæ," 1785.) Died in 1800.

Érèbe. See EREBUS.

Er′e-bus, [Gr. Ἔρεβος; Fr. ÉRÈBE, à′rĕb′,] in classic mythology, was represented as a son of Chaos. The name was also applied to the dark and gloomy region or space under the earth. (See PLUTO.)

Érechthée. See ERECHTHEUS.

E-rech′the̅ūs, [Gr. Ἐρεχθεύς; Fr. ÉRECHTHÉE, à′rĕk′tà′,] a fabulous or semi-fabulous hero, supposed to have been a son of Vulcan and the father of Cecrops. According to another tradition, he was a son of Pandíon. He is considered by many critics as the same as Erichthonius. Homer mentions him as a king of Athens. The Erechtheum, a temple of Minerva on the Acropolis, is said to have been built by him.

Eredia, d', dà-rà-dee′ä, (LUIGI,) a Sicilian poet, born at Palermo; died in 1604.

Eremita. See ERMITE, (DANIEL L'.)

Erevantsi, ĕR-e-vânt′see, (MELCHISEDEC,) an eminent Armenian doctor and monk, born in 1550, wrote an "Analysis of Aristotle's Philosophy." Died in 1631.

Erhard, ĕR′hârt, (HEINRICH AUGUST,) a German archæologist, born at Erfurt in 1793. He practised medicine in early life, and became archivist at Magdeburg in 1824. In 1831 he obtained a similar office at Münster. Among his works are a "History of the Revival of Literature in Germany down to the Reformation," (1827–32,) and a "History of Münster," (1837.) Died in 1851.

Erhard, (JOHANN BENJAMIN,) a German philosopher and physician, born at Nuremberg in 1766; died in 1827.

See VARNHAGEN VON ENSE, "Denkwürdigkeiten des Philosophen und Arztes J. B. Erhard," 1830.

Erhardt, êR'hÄRt, (SIMON,) a German philosopher, born at Ulm in 1776, wrote "The Idea and Object of Philosophy," (1817,) and other works. Died in 1829.

Er'ī-bęrt, [Lat. ERIBER'TUS,] an ambitious Italian prelate, obtained in 1018 the archbishopric of Milan, and the highest rank among the princes of Italy. He procured the crown of Italy for Conrad the Salic, who in return made him Lieutenant of Lombardy. In 1035 Eribert was involved in a civil war against the Vavasseurs, with whom Conrad united. An important result of this war was the edict of Conrad which rendered fiefs hereditary and settled the public law of Europe. Died in 1045.

See SISMONDI, "Histoire des Républiques Italiennes."

Er'ic or **Er'ik I.,** surnamed THE GOOD, King of Denmark, began to reign about 1095. It was by his request that the pope gave Denmark an archbishop. He was noted for piety, and undertook a pilgrimage to Jerusalem, but died on the way, in the island of Cyprus, in 1103. His brother, Nicholas, obtained the throne in 1105. Eric I. left three sons, Harold, Canute, and Eric.

Eric II., King of Denmark, who was probably a son of Eric I., succeeded to the throne about the year 1135. He was involved in a war with the Vandals, occasioned by their piratical habits. He was assassinated in 1137, and was succeeded by his son, Eric III.

Eric III., King of Denmark, surnamed THE LAMB, a son or nephew of the preceding, began to reign about 1138. He retired into a monastery at Odensee, where he died in 1147.

Eric IV., V., and **VI.,** Kings of Denmark in the thirteenth century, reigned during a period fruitful in revolutions and disorders. Powerful vassals aspired to independence, and the clergy admitted no supremacy but that of the pope. Eric IV. began to reign in 1241, and died by violence in 1250. Eric V. succeeded his father, Christopher I., in 1259, and was assassinated in 1286. His son, Eric VI., began to reign in 1286, waged war against Norway, and died in 1319, leaving the throne to his brother, Christopher II.

Eric VII. and **VIII.** of Denmark. See ERIC XIII. of Sweden.

Er'ic or **Er'ik I.** to **VIII.,** the name of a series of kings who reigned in Sweden during the ninth and tenth centuries, of whose history little is known. Eric VIII. ascended the throne about 954 A.D. It is said that he instituted the rank and title of earl among the Swedes.

Eric IX., surnamed SAINT, was elected King of Sweden in 1152. Being animated with zeal for the conversion of infidels, he conducted a crusade against the Finns, who made a successful resistance. Soon after his return he was killed by Magnus, a Danish prince, who invaded Sweden with an army about 1160. He left a son, Canute, (Knut,) who became king in 1168.

Eric X., King of Sweden, grandson of the preceding, reigned from 1210 to 1216. He was son of Knut, or Canute, and is regarded as the first king of Sweden who was solemnly crowned. He was succeeded by John I.

Eric XI. of Sweden, son of Eric X., ascended the throne in 1222, and died, without issue, in 1250, when the throne passed to the house of Folkungar.

Eric XII., King of Sweden, was the son of King Magnus and Blanche of Namur. In 1344 he was declared a colleague of his father by a powerful party of clergy and nobles. A civil war that followed was terminated by a partition of the country between Magnus and Eric. Died in 1359.

See GEYER, "Histoire de la Suède."

Eric XIII., King of Sweden, reckoned Eric VII. or VIII. of Denmark, was born in 1382. He was the son of the Duke of Pomerania, and grand-nephew of Queen Margaret of Waldemar, who had united the crowns of Denmark and Sweden. After her death, in 1412, he succeeded to the throne. He married Philippa, daughter of Henry IV. of England. By his oppressive measures

and lack of kingly qualities he alienated his subjects, who revolted and drove him from the kingdom about 1438. He retired to the island of Rügen, where he died about 1450.

Eric XIV., King of Sweden, son of Gustavus Vasa, was born about 1535, and succeeded his father in 1560. He patronized science, and founded literary institutions. His proposal of marriage to Queen Elizabeth of England having been declined, he resolved to wed Catherine Mansdoter, the daughter of a corporal, and gave her the title of queen. His violent character and misgovernment rendered him so unpopular that his brothers, with other nobles, conspired against him, and in 1568 he was deposed from the throne and confined in prison, where he died, or was killed, in 1577. His brother John was his successor.

See ERSCH und GRUBER, "Allgemeine Encyklopaedie;" OLOF CELSIUS, "Konung Eriks Historia," 1774, (translated into French by GENEST, 1777.)

Eric the Red, a Scandinavian navigator, the reputed discoverer of North America. He emigrated to Iceland about 982 A.D., after which he discovered Greenland, where he planted a colony. He sent out, about 1000 A.D., an exploring party under his son Lief, who discovered a continent, part of which they called Markland, and another part Vinland, (supposed to correspond to the southern portion of New England.) Tradition adds that he or his son formed a settlement in Vinland.

Eric Olai, êr'ik o-lā'e, or **Eric** of UPSAL, a Swedish historian of the fifteenth century, was a doctor of theology in Upsal. He composed, by order of Charles VIII., a Latin history of Sweden.

Ericeira or **Ericeyra,** à-re-sā'e-rä, (FERNANDO de Menezes—dà mà-nā'zĕs,) COUNT OF, an eminent Portuguese author and statesman, born at Lisbon in 1614, was distinguished for his learning and for his civil and military services. He wrote a "History of Tangier," a "History of Portugal," and other esteemed works. Died in 1699.

Ericeira or **Ericeyra,** (FRANCISCO XAVIER DE MENEZES,) COUNT, a Portuguese general and author, born at Lisbon in 1673, was the son of Luiz, noticed below. The Portuguese rank him among their most eminent men as a writer and public functionary. He was a Fellow of the Royal Society of London. He wrote an epic poem entitled "Henriqueida," (1741,) and many occasional poems; he also made a translation of Boileau's "Art of Poetry," which was admired by the author of the original. Died in 1743.

See J. BARBOZA, "Elogio do I. Conde da Ericeira," 1785.

Ericeira or **Ericeyra,** (LUIZ DE MENEZES,) COUNT, the father of the preceding, was born at Lisbon in 1632. He gained distinction as a statesman, general, and author. He wrote an esteemed "History of Portugal" (in Latin) from 1640 to 1668, and various other works. In a fit of insanity he committed suicide in 1690.

Ericeyra. See ERICEIRA.

Erichsen, êr'ik-sęn, (JOHN,) an eminent English surgeon of the present age, published an important work entitled "The Science and Art of Surgery," (1853,) which has been reprinted in the United States. He was for some time professor of surgery in University College, London.

Er-ich-tho'nī-us, [Gr. Ἐριχθόνιος,] a fabulous king of Athens, called a son of Vulcan, was regarded by some writers as identical with ERECHTHEUS, (which see.) According to tradition, he was the successor of Amphictyon, and the father of Pandi'on.

Ericius. See ERIZZO, (SEBASTIANO.)

Er'ics-sǫn, (JOHN,) an eminent Swedish engineer, inventor of the caloric engine, was born in the province of Vermeland in 1803. After he had served several years in the army, he removed to England about 1826, and made unsuccessful experiments with an engine which he proposed to run without steam. He produced in 1829 a locomotive which ran fifty miles per hour on the Liverpool and Manchester Railway. About 1833 he exhibited in England a caloric engine, which attracted much attention among scientific men. He also invented the important application of the screw or propeller to steam navigation, and about 1840 came to the United

---

ϵ as k; ç as s; g̃ hard; g̃ as j; G, H, K, guttural; N, nasal; R, trilled; s̃ as z; th as in this.   (☞See Explanations, p. 23.)

States, where he received aid from government in reducing his inventions to practice. He built the iron-clad steamer Monitor, which successfully opposed the Merrimac in Hampton Roads, March 9, 1862.

See "Ericsson and his Inventions," in the "Atlantic Monthly," July, 1862.

E-rig′e-na, (JOANNES SCOTUS,) [Fr. JEAN SCOT ÉRIGÈNE, zhŏN sko tă′re′zhăn′,] a philosopher and intellectual giant, was a native of Ireland, or Erin, as his name indicates, and lived about 850 A.D. He passed the most of his mature life in France, at the court of Charles the Bald, who liberally patronized him. He was celebrated for classical learning and subtlety as a disputant in scholastic theology. Hallam thinks "he was, in a literary and philosophical sense, the most remarkable man of the dark ages: no one else had his boldness and subtlety in threading the labyrinths of metaphysical speculations." His writings on theology were considered heterodox by the Roman Church. He translated from the Greek the works of Dionysius Areopagita, and wrote a "Treatise on Predestination." His principal production is entitled "On the Division of Nature," (" De Divisione Naturæ,") and treats of theology, metaphysics, etc. It was printed at Oxford in 1681. He is supposed to have died about 875 A.D.

See S. RENÉ TAILLANDIER, "Jean Scot Érigène et la Philosophie scolastique;" CHAMBERS, "Biographical Dictionary of Eminent Scotsmen."

Érigène. See ERIGENA.

E-rig′o-ne, [Gr. Ἠριγόνη,] a daughter of Icarius, beloved by Bacchus. It was fabled that she killed herself from grief for the death of her father, and was placed among the stars as the constellation Virgo.

Erik. See ERIC.

E-rin′na, [Gr. Ἤριννα ; Fr. ÉRINNE, ă′rèn′,] a Greek poetess, who lived about 600 B.C., was a contemporary and friend of Sappho, and a native of Rhodes or Telos. She died unmarried at the age of nineteen, leaving a poem, called "The Distaff," in three hundred hexameter verses, few of which are extant. Some ancient critics thought her verses compared favourably with those of Homer.

See RICHTER, "Sappho und Erinna;" BODE, "Geschichte der Hellenischen Dichtkunst."

Érinne. See ERINNA.

E-rin′nȳs, plural **E-rin′nȳ-es,** [Gr. Ἐρινννς, Ἐρίννυες,] a name applied to the Furies, or Eumenides, personifications of the avenging spirit. (See EUMENIDES.)

E-riph′I-le, sister of Adrastus, King of Argos, and wife of Amphiaraus. She was bribed by Polynices to discover the hiding-place of her husband, who was unwilling to accompany the Argives in their expedition against Thebes. Amphiaraus, before his departure, charged his son Alcmæon to murder his mother, which order was obeyed.

E′ris, [Gr. Ἔρις ; Lat. DISCOR′DIA ; Fr. ÉRIS, ă′rèss′, or DISCORDE, dès′kord′,] the goddess of discord, in classic mythology, was called a daughter of Night.

Erizzo, à-rèt′so, (FRANCESCO,) a Venetian general and doge, born about 1570. After he had obtained the rank of commander-in-chief, he was elected doge in 1632. In 1645 the senate gave him supreme command of a large armament which they prepared to resist the victorious progress of the Turks in Candia ; but just as he was ready to sail he died, in January, 1646.

See M. TREVISANO, "Vita di F. Erizzo," 1651; DARU, "Histoire de Venise."

Erizzo, [Lat. ERIÇ′IUS or ECHI′NUS,] (SEBASTIANO,) a noble Italian, born in Venice in 1525, was eminent as an antiquary, author, and senator. He was an excellent classical scholar, and had a remarkable memory. His "Discourse on Ancient Medals" (1559) had such success that three editions were issued in one year, and it opened a new era in the science of numismatics. He wrote other works, and translated several Dialogues of Plato. Died in 1585.

See NANI, "Storia Veneta."

Erlach, ĕʀ′lăk′, [Ger. pron. ĕʀ′lăk,] or **D'Erlach,** dĕʀ′lăk′, (CHARLES LOUIS,) a Swiss general, born at Berne in 1746 ; died in 1798.

See ERSCH und GRUBER, "Allgemeine Encyklopaedie."

Erlach, d', (JEAN LOUIS,) a successful Swiss general, born at Berne in 1595. After making several campaigns in Germany, he entered the service of Gustavus Adolphus, who made him quartermaster of his army and in 1632 appointed him a councillor. At the death of the Duke of Weimar, Erlach became commander of his army, and passed into the service of the French king. In 1648 he fought at the battle of Lens under the Prince of Condé, who, on presenting him to Louis XIV. after the action, said, "Sire, behold the man to whom you owe the victory of Lens." On the defection of Turenne, the king gave to Erlach the chief command, and soon after a marshal's bâton. He survived this promotion only a few days, and died in 1650.

See SISMONDI, "Histoire des Français;" A. d'ERLACH, "Mémoires concernant le Général J. L. d'Erlach," 1784.

Erlach, d', (JEAN LOUIS,) an able admiral in the Danish service, born at Berne in 1648, became commodore in 1672, and vice-admiral in 1678. He was employed in the war which Denmark and France waged against the Swedes in 1678. Died in 1680.

Erlach, d', (JÉRÔME,) a skilful Swiss general, born in 1667, entered the service of the emperor Leopold in 1702, and was employed in the wars of the Spanish succession. In 1712 he was created a count of the German Empire. Died in 1748.

Erlach, d', (SIGISMUND,) a Swiss general, born at or near Berne in 1614, served in the French army under his uncle Jean Louis, noticed above, (the first of the name.) He obtained the rank of maréchal-de-camp in 1650, and was afterwards general of the Helvetic army. Died in 1699.

See SISMONDI, "Histoire des Français."

Erle, ĕrl, (Sir WILLIAM,) an English judge, born in Dorsetshire in 1793. He was appointed chief justice of the court of common pleas in 1859.

Erlon. See DROUET D'ERLON.

Erman, ĕʀ′mân, (GEORG ADOLF,) a German natural philosopher, born in Berlin in 1806. He performed (1828–30) a voyage around the world, and made a series of magnetic observations which served as the basis of Gauss's theory of terrestrial magnetism. He published, in German, a " Voyage around the World through Northern Asia and the Two Oceans," (5 vols., 1833–42,) and was afterwards professor of physics in Berlin.

Erman, (JOHANN PETER,) a German writer, the father of Paul, noticed below, was born at Berlin in 1733. He became principal of the French College in his native city, and a member of the Academy of Sciences. He wrote "Historical Memoirs of the French Refugees in Prussia," (9 vols., 1782–94.) Died in 1814.

See P. BUTTMANN, "Denkschrift auf Herrn Erman, Vater," 1814.

Erman, (PAUL,) the father of Georg Adolf, noticed above, was born in Berlin in 1764. He was professor of physical science in the University of Berlin, and a secretary of the Academy of Sciences, for which he wrote treatises on galvanism and other subjects. Died in 1851.

Ermenald. See ERMOLDUS.

Ermengarde, ĕr′mĕn-gard, or **Hermengarde,** Queen of Provence, was a daughter of Louis II., Emperor of Germany, and Engelberga. She was born in 855, and was married in 877 A.D. to Boson, brother-in-law of Charles the Bald of France, who gave Boson the government of Provence. She persuaded her husband to assume the title of King of Arles. Her ambition involved Boson in a disastrous war with Louis III. of France. After the death of her husband (888) she governed Provence as guardian of her minor son Louis.

See SISMONDI, "Histoire des Français."

Er′mens, [Fr. ĕʀ′mŏN′,] (JOSEPH,) born at Brussels in 1736, left in manuscript a " Bibliography of the Low Countries," or "Catalogue Raisonné" of all books which treat of the history of that country. Died in 1805.

Er′me-ric [Lat. ERMERI′CUS] or **Her′menric,** King of the Suevi, invaded Spain, and obtained Galicia by conquest in the reign of Honorius. He repulsed an attack of Gonderic the Vandal in 419 A.D. Died in 440.

Ermite, l', lĕʀ′mèt′, [Lat. EREMI′TA,] (DANIEL,) a Flemish writer, born at Antwerp about 1584, was a friend or protégé of Scaliger. He entered the service of Cosimo

ă, ē, ī, ō, ū, ȳ, *long;* à, ė, ò, same, less prolonged; ă, ĕ, ĭ, ŏ, ŭ, ȳ, *short;* a, ę, į, ǫ, *obscure;* fär, fåll, fåt; mêt; nŏt; gōōd; mōōn;

de' Medici, who employed him as secretary and sent him on missions to several courts. He wrote "Iter Germanicum," (a "Journey to Germany," 1637,) and an essay on "Court Life and Civil Life," ("Aulicæ Vitæ ac civilis Libri IV.,") which is praised for style and other merits. It was published by Grævius in 1701. Died at Leghorn in 1613.

Er-mol′dus or **Er′me-nald,** (NIGEL′LUS,) a French monk and writer of the ninth century, composed a Latin poem on the military and other acts of Louis le Débonnaire, (826,) which is valued for the historical facts which it records.

Ernest, ẽr′nest, [Ger. ERNST, ễRNST,] Prince of Anhalt, born at Amber in 1608, was mortally wounded at Lutzen, where he fought for Gustavus Adolphus, in 1632.

See ERSCH and GRUBER, "Allgemeine Encyklopaedie."

Ernest, (Ernst,) Archduke of Austria, born at Vienna in 1533, was a son of Maximilian II. In 1592 he was appointed Governor of the Low Countries by Philip II. He was generally considered an incapable governor. Died in 1595.

See PRESCOTT, "Philip II."

Ernest, (Ernst,) Duke of Austria, born in 1378, was the third son of Leopold V. He ruled over Carinthia, Styria, and Carniola. Died in 1424.

See ERSCH und GRUBER, "Allgemeine Encyklopaedie."

Ernest, (Ernst,) Margrave of Austria, was a son of Albert the Victorious. He took arms against the emperor Henry IV. as an ally of Otho of Bavaria, and was killed in battle in 1075.

See ERSCH und GRUBER, "Allgemeine Encyklopaedie."

Ernest, (Ernst,) Duke of Bavaria, succeeded his father, John, in 1397. Died in 1438.

See ERSCH und GRUBER, "Allgemeine Encyklopaedie."

Ernest (Ernst) of Bavaria, Archbishop of Cologne, born in 1554, was a younger son of Albert V. of Bavaria. He became Archbishop of Cologne, and Elector in 1583. Died in 1612.

See ERSCH und GRUBER, "Allgemeine Encyklopaedie."

Ernest, (Ernst,) Prince of Holstein-Schauenburg, was born in 1569 ; died in 1622.

Ernest, (Ernst,) Archbishop of Magdeburg, son of the Elector of Saxony, was born in 1466. He was elected archbishop in 1476. Died in 1513.

Ernest (Ernst) OF MANSFELD. See MANSFELD.

Ernest, (Ernst,) Duke of Saxe-Coburg, the eldest brother of Albert, consort of Queen Victoria, was born in 1818. He began to reign in 1844, and showed himself favourable to reform and the unity of Germany.

Ernest, (Ernst,) surnamed THE PIOUS, Duke of Saxe-Gotha, born in 1601, was a brother of Bernard of Saxe-Weimar. He fought for Gustavus Adolphus in the Thirty Years' war. At the battle of Lutzen, after Gustavus fell, Ernest defeated Pappenheim. He obtained the duchy of Gotha in 1640, and became the founder of the house of Saxe-Gotha. He had a good reputation for ability and virtue. Died in 1675.

See A. TEISSIER, "Vie d'Ernest le Pieux," 1707 ; REDENBACHER, "Ernst der Fromme, Herzog von Gotha," 1851.

Ernest, (Ernst,) Duke of Saxe-Gotha, born about 1745, began to reign in 1772. He was a distinguished astronomer, and founded an observatory at Seeberg, near Gotha. The measurement of an arc of the meridian by Zach was made under his auspices. Died in 1804.

Ernest, (Ernst,) Elector of Saxony, and head of the branch called Ernestine, was born in 1441, and was the eldest son of Frederick II., whom he succeeded in 1464. He inherited Thuringia at the death of his uncle in 1482. Died in 1486, and was succeeded by his son, Frederick III.

Ernest (Ernst) I. of Zell, Duke of Brunswick-Lüneburg, born at Ultzen in 1497, was one of the first proselytes of Luther. He abolished the Romish worship in his duchy, and signed in 1529 the famous protest against the decree of the Diet of Spire. He joined the league of Schmalkalden about 1532, and rendered great services to his party in the wars that followed. Died in 1546.

See MORÉRI, "Dictionnaire Historique."

Er′nest Au-gus′tus, [Ger. ERNST AUGUST, ễRNST ŏw′gŏŏst,] the first Elector of Hanover, born in 1629,

was a son of George, Duke of Brunswick-Lüneburg. He married Sophia, a daughter of Frederick, King of Bohemia, and had a son who became George I. of England. He joined the coalition against Louis XIV. of France, and distinguished himself in several battles between 1675 and 1690. He obtained the dignity of Elector in 1692. Died in 1698.

Ernest Augustus, King of Hanover, born in 1771, was a younger son of George III. of England. He was styled the Duke of Cumberland before his accession to the throne, and obtained the rank of field-marshal in the British army. He married in 1815 Frederica of Mecklenburg-Strelitz. On the death of William IV., in 1837, he succeeded to the throne of Hanover. He died in 1851, and left the throne to his son, George V.

Er′nest Cas′i-mir, [Ger. ERNST KASIMIR, ễRNST kă′ze-mễễR,] Count of Nassau, born at Dillenburg in 1573, was a son of John, Count of Nassau. In 1597 he entered the service of the United Provinces as captain. He fought against the Spaniards in many sieges and battles, was raised to the rank of general, and gained several victories. He was killed at Roermonde in 1632.

See ERSCH und GRUBER, "Allgemeine Encyklopaedie."

Ernesti, ễR-nês′tee, (AUGUST WILHELM,) a philologist, born at Frohndorf (Thuringia) in 1733, was a nephew of the celebrated J. A. Ernesti. He succeeded his uncle as professor of eloquence at Leipsic in 1770. He spoke and wrote Latin with elegance and facility, and filled the chair above-named with great distinction. His most important work is an edition of Livy, (3 vols., 1769.) Died in 1801.

See ERSCH und GRUBER, "Allgemeine Encyklopaedie."

Ernesti, (JACOB DANIEL,) a German Lutheran theologian, born at Rochlitz in 1640 ; died in 1707.

Ernesti, (JOHANN AUGUST,) one of the most celebrated critics that Germany has produced, was born at Tennstedt, in Thuringia, in August, 1707. He was a son of Johann Christoph, pastor of Tennstedt, and was educated at Wittenberg and Leipsic. In 1734 he became rector of the school of Saint Thomas, in Leipsic. He was chosen professor of ancient literature in the university of that city in 1742, after he had published an excellent edition of the works of Cicero, (in 5 vols., 1737-39,) which is his principal title to celebrity. In the same university he obtained the chair of eloquence in 1756, to which the chair of theology was added in 1758. He edited the works of Homer, (1759-65,) Polybius, and Tacitus, (1752.) He developed a new system of biblical criticism in his "Institutes of an Interpreter of the New Testament," ("Institutio Interpretis Novi Testamenti," 1761,) which is regarded as a work of great merit. In theology he belonged to the rationalistic school. Ernesti imitated the style of Cicero with success, and was considered by many judges the first Latinist of his time. He was author of other theological and philological works. Died in 1781.

See J. VAN VOORST, "Oratio de J. A. Ernesto," Leyden, 1804 ; "J. A. Ernesti's Verdienste in Theologie und Religion," Berlin, 1783 ; E. F. VOGEL, "Oratio de J. A. Ernesti Meritis in Jurisprudentiam," 1829 ; AUGUST W. ERNESTI, "Memoria J. A. Ernesti," 1781.

Ernesti, (JOHANN CHRISTIAN GOTTLOB,) a German scholar and critic, born at Arnstadt in 1756, was a nephew of the preceding, and cousin of August Wilhelm. He became professor of philosophy at Leipsic in 1782, and published, among other works, a good edition of Silius Italicus, (1791,) a valuable "Lexicon of Greek Rhetorical Technology," (1795,) and an elegant German version of Cicero's best works, "Spirit and Art of Cicero," ("Ciceros Geist und Kunst," 1799-1802.) Died in 1802.

See MEUSEL, "Gelehrtes Deutschland."

Ernesti, (JOHANN HEINRICH,) a German scholar, brother of Jacob Daniel, noticed above, was born in 1652. He wrote a "Compendium of Profane Hermeneutics," (1699,) and other works. Died in 1729.

Ernouf, ễR′noof′, (JEAN AUGUSTIN,) BARON, a French general, born at Alençon in 1753. He became a general of division in 1793, and distinguished himself at Fleurus and Novi. Died in 1827.

Ernst, the German of ERNEST, which see.

€ as *k; ç* as *s;* ğ *hard;* ğ as *j;* G, H, K, *guttural;* N, *nasal;* R, *trilled;* ŝ as *z;* ꜩh as in *this.* (☞ See Explanations, p. 23.)

Ernst, êRnst, [Lat. ERN′STIUS,] (HEINRICH,) a learned Danish jurist, born at Helmstedt in 1603, wrote, in Latin, many able works on law, religion, and other subjects, among which are "Sabbatismos," and "Introduction to the True Life," (1643.) Died in 1665.

See KRAFT og NYERUP, "Litteraturlexicon."

Ernst, (HEINRICH WILHELM,) a German violinist, born at Brünn in 1814; died in 1865.

Ernst August. See ERNEST AUGUSTUS.

Ernst Kasimir. See ERNEST CASIMIR.

Ernsting, êRn′sting, (ARTHUR CONRAD,) a German botanist, born at Sachsenhagen in 1709, published a "Description of the Families of Plants," (1762,) and other works. Died in 1768.

Ernstius. See ERNST.

Ernulph. See ARNULPH.

Erolés, de, dà à-ro-lês′, BARON, a Spanish general, noted for energy and audacity, born in Catalonia in 1785, took an active part in the guerilla war against the French in 1809-10. He was a partisan of the royalists in 1820, and in 1822 a member of the Supreme Regency, formed during the king's captivity. In the same year he commanded at two battles, in which the royalists were totally defeated by Mina. Died in 1825.

Erope, the French of ÆROPE, which see.

E′ros, [Ἔρως,] the Greek name of the god of love, corresponding to the Cupido of the Romans. He was generally regarded as a son of Aphrodite, (Venus,) and was personified as a beautiful boy with wings and armed with a bow and arrows. (See CUPID.)

Erostratus. See HEROSTRATUS.

Erotianus, e-ro-she-ā′nus, [Ἐρωτιανός,] a Greek writer, who lived in the first century of our era, in the reign of Nero, is sometimes called HERODIANUS. He wrote, in Greek, a glossary of Hippocrates, which explains some obscure terms found in that writer. It was first printed in Paris in 1564.

Er′o-vant II., King of Armenia, occupied the highest rank among the Armenian generals in the reign of Sanadrook, (Sanadrouk.) At the death of that prince, 68 A.D., he usurped the throne. In 78 he founded a new and splendid capital, which he named Erovantaschad. Ardasches II., the son of Sanadrook, having raised an army in Persia, came back to recover his throne. In the battle that followed, Erovant was defeated and killed in the year 88.

Er-pe′nĭ-us, or **Van Erpen,** vän êR′pẹn, (THOMAS,) a celebrated Orientalist, born at Gorkum, in Holland, in 1584, graduated at Leyden in 1608, and afterwards pursued his favourite studies in England, France, Italy, etc. In 1613 he was chosen professor of Arabic and other Oriental languages, except Hebrew, in the University of Leyden. In 1619 a second chair of Hebrew was founded in his favour. He kept an Arabic press in his own house. His labours have rendered important services to Oriental learning, and have scarcely been surpassed in the same department, although his career was closed by a premature death. His most important works are an "Arabic Grammar," (1613,) the first composed in Europe, a "Collection of Lokmân's Arabic Proverbs," translated into Latin, an Arabic version of the New Testament, and "Historia Saracenica," an edition of Elmacin's history, with Latin version, (1625.) Died in 1624.

See P. SCRIVARIUS, "Manes Erpinianæ," 1625: G. J. VOSSIUS, "Oratio in Obitum T. Erpenii," 1625; "Nouvelle Biographie Générale."

Errante, êr-rän′tà, (GIUSEPPE,) a skilful Italian historical painter, born at Trapani in 1760, passed the greater part of his life in Milan. Among his works are "Endymion" and "Psyche." Died in 1821.

Errard. See ÉRARD.

Errard, ḁ′rȧR′, (CHARLES,) a French painter, born at Bressuire about 1570. He received the title of painter to the king. Died about 1635.

Errard, (CHARLES,) a French painter and architect, a son and pupil of the preceding, was born at Nantes in 1606. He painted historical subjects, among which is "Saint Paul restored to Sight." In 1646 he began to decorate the Palais Royal for Louis XIV. He afterwards adorned the Louvre, Tuileries, the château of Versailles, and other palaces. He was one of the twelve artists who founded the Academy of Painting at Paris in 1648. He had the principal part in the foundation of the French Academy of Art in Rome in 1666, and was director of that institution until 1683. He published (with Chambray) a "Comparison of Ancient with Modern Architecture," (1666.) Died at Rome in 1689.

See MILIZIA, "Memorie degli Architetti," etc.

Errard or **Érard,** ḁ′rȧR′, (JEAN,) a French military engineer, born at Bar-le-Duc, was employed by Henry IV., who called him the first of engineers. He wrote an able treatise on Fortification, (1594.) Died about 1620.

Er-Rasheed or **Er-Rashîd.** See AR-RASHEED and HAROUN-AL-RASCHID.

Erri, degli, dàl′yee êr′ree, (PELLEGRINO,) an Italian Orientalist, born at Módena in 1511, produced an Italian version of the Psalms of David, (1573.) Died in 1575.

Errico, êr-ree′ko, or **Enrico,** ên-ree′ko, (SCIPIONE,) a popular Italian poet and priest, born in 1592 at Messina, where he obtained the chair of moral philosophy and the title of poet-laureate. He wrote "The Wars of Parnassus," (a history of literary quarrels, 1643,) "Deidamia," a drama, (1644,) and other works. Died in 1670.

See MONGITORE, "Bibliotheca Sicula."

Ersch, êRsh, (JOHANN SAMUEL,) an eminent encyclopædist, and founder of German bibliography, was born at Gross Glogau, in Silesia, in 1766. He published between 1793 and 1809 a "General Repertory of Literature," (8 vols.,) and a work entitled "Literary France," ("Das gelehrte Frankreich," 5 vols., 1797-1806.) About 1800 he was chosen librarian of the University of Jena, and in 1803 professor of geography at Halle. His principal work is the great "Encyclopædia of Sciences and Arts," ("Allgemeine Encyklopaedie der Wissenschaften und Künste,") by Ersch and Gruber, of which he edited 17 vols., (1818-28.) After the death of Ersch (1828) it was continued by Gruber and others.

See ERSCH und GRUBER, "Allgemeine Encyklopaedie;" "Nouvelle Biographie Générale."

Erskine, ẹr′skin, (DAVID,) Lord Dun, an eminent Scottish lawyer, born at Dun in 1670, became lord of session in 1711, and was a commissioner in the court of justiciary from 1713 to 1750. He published a valuable work, styled "Lord Dun's Advices." Died in 1755.

See CHAMBERS, "Biographical Dictionary of Eminent Scotsmen."

Erskine, (DAVID STEWART,) Earl of Buchan, and Lord Cardross, a literary Scottish nobleman and antiquary, born in 1742, was the eldest son of Henry David, tenth Earl of Buchan, and was a brother of Lord-Chancellor Erskine. About 1766 he was elected a Fellow of the Royal Society and appointed secretary to the British embassy in Spain. In 1780 he took the principal part in founding the Society of Scottish Antiquaries, and in 1791 instituted an annual festive commemoration of the poet Thomson. He wrote several antiquarian treatises. Died in 1829.

See CHAMBERS, "Biographical Dictionary of Eminent Scotsmen."

Erskine, (EBENEZER,) the founder of a sect in Scotland designated as Seceders, born in 1680, was a son of Henry Erskine, noticed below. From 1703 to 1731 he ministered at Portmoak, in Kinross, where he became eminent and popular as a theologian, preacher, and writer. In 1731 he accepted a call from the church of Stirling. About 1732 a controversy arose in the Church of Scotland respecting lay patronage, on which subject Mr. Erskine opposed the action of the General Assembly, and was suspended from the ministry. In 1736 Erskine and his friends organized the "Secession Church." His sermons and other writings have been often reprinted, and are much admired. Died in 1754. The Secession Church in 1847 formed a union with the Relief Synod, and took the name of the United Presbyterian Church.

See CHAMBERS, "Biographical Dictionary of Eminent Scotsmen."

Erskine, (HENRY,) a Scottish clergyman, father of the preceding, was born in 1624. He became pastor at Cornhill, was ejected in 1662, and banished about 1682. He was imprisoned in 1685. Died in 1696.

Erskine, (HENRY,) an eminent Scottish patriot, born about 1650. He was third Lord Cardross, eldest son of the second Lord Cardross, and ancestor of Lord-Chancellor Erskine. Having been persecuted by fine and imprisonment on account of his religion, he emigrated about 1680 to South Carolina, whence he was driven by the Spaniards. He next went to Holland, enlisted in the service of the Prince of Orange, and returned with him to England in 1688. He was restored to his estates and made a privy councillor. Died in 1693.

See CHAMBERS, "Biographical Dictionary of Eminent Scotsmen."

Erskine, (Hon. HENRY,) an able Scottish lawyer, born in Edinburgh in 1746, was the second son of David, tenth Earl of Buchan, and brother of the lord chancellor. He was called to the bar in 1768, and appointed lord advocate of Scotland in 1782. On the accession of Pitt as premier he was removed, but obtained the same high office in 1806 under the Whig ministry, and was elected to Parliament. He was an eloquent and witty advocate, and for some years was considered the leader and brightest ornament of the Scottish bar. Probably none of his competitors equalled him in professional tact, in suavity of temper, or in fascination of manner. As a statesman he constantly supported the Whig or Liberal party. He died in 1817, leaving two sons, Henry and George, the former of whom is the present Earl of Buchan. "In his long and splendid career at the bar," says Lord Jeffrey, "he was distinguished not only by the peculiar brilliancy of his wit and the gracefulness and vivacity of his eloquence, but by the still rarer power of keeping those seducing qualities in perfect subordination to his judgment."

See CHAMBERS, "Biographical Dictionary of Eminent Scotsmen."

Erskine, (JOHN,) Baron of Dun, an eminent Scottish Reformer, born near Montrose about 1508. At an early age he became one of the leaders of the Protestants in Scotland. He first introduced, it is said, the study of the Greek language into the schools of Scotland, about 1534. In 1557 he was appointed a commissioner to attend the marriage of Queen Mary in France. About 1560 he was ordained as a minister. He assisted in compiling the Second Book of Discipline in 1577. Died in 1591.

See CHAMBERS, "Biographical Dictionary of Eminent Scotsmen."

Erskine, (JOHN,) COLONEL, a Scottish officer, born in 1661, was the third son of Lord Cardross. Having served in Holland under the Prince of Orange, he was appointed in 1688 lieutenant-governor of Stirling Castle, and afterwards governor of Dumbarton Castle. In 1707 he was elected to the British Parliament. His son JOHN was an eminent jurist. Died in 1743.

Erskine, (JOHN,) eighteenth Lord Erskine, and eleventh Earl of Mar, an ambitious and corrupt Scottish politician, born at Alloa in 1675, was the son of Charles, tenth Earl of Mar. At the accession of Queen Anne, in 1702, he joined the Tories, and in 1708 was chosen secretary for Scotland, and became one of the most powerful leaders of the Jacobites. In September, 1715, he raised the standard of the Pretender, and, though destitute of military skill, assumed the command of the insurgents, amounting to 12,000 men. He was defeated by Argyle at Dunblane in November, and soon after escaped with his master to the continent, where he continued to plot for several years, and died in 1732.

See CHAMBERS, "Biographical Dictionary of Eminent Scotsmen."

Erskine, (JOHN) of Carnoch, an eminent Scottish jurist, born in 1695, was the son of Colonel John Erskine, and a cousin of Lord-Chancellor Erskine. In 1737 he was chosen professor of Scottish law in the University of Edinburgh, and in 1754 published "Principles of the Law of Scotland," which became a leading authority in the courts. He retired from his chair in the university in 1765, and died at his estate of Cardross in 1768. He left an extension of the above work, which appeared in 1773, entitled "An Institute of the Law of Scotland." It is a standard work of great merit, whose authority is as unquestionable as "Coke upon Littleton."

See CHAMBERS, "Biographical Dictionary of Eminent Scotsmen."

Erskine, (JOHN,) D.D., an eminent Scottish divine, son of the preceding, was born in 1721. In 1744 he was ordained minister of Kirkintilloch, near Glasgow. From 1753 to 1758 he preached at Culross, and in the latter year removed to the New Grey-Friars', a church of Edinburgh. He was for many years the leader of the

popular or orthodox party in the Church,—the same which in 1843 seceded and formed the "Free Church." In 1767 he became a colleague of Dr. Robertson in the Old Grey-Friars' Church, Edinburgh. Among his writings on theology—which are numerous and highly prized—are "Theological Dissertations," (1765,) and "Sketches and Hints of Church History," (1790.) Died in 1803.

See Sir H. MONCRIEFF WELLWOOD, "Life of John Erskine," 1818; CHAMBERS, "Biographical Dictionary of Eminent Scotsmen."

Erskine, (RALPH,) an eminent Scottish divine, born at Monilaws in 1685, was the brother of Ebenezer Erskine, noticed above. He was ordained in 1711 as minister of Dunfermline, and acquired a high reputation as a preacher and writer on theology. About 1736 he co-operated with his brother, and joined the Seceders. (See ERSKINE, EBENEZER.) He published sermons and "Gospel Sonnets." Died in 1752.

See CHAMBERS, "Biographical Dictionary of Eminent Scotsmen."

Erskine, (THOMAS,) LORD, an illustrious British orator and advocate, born in Edinburgh in January, 1750, was the youngest son of Henry David, Earl of Buchan. He received his education at the high-schools of Edinburgh and of Saint Andrew's. As his father could not afford to defray the expense of preparing him for a learned profession, he entered the navy in 1764 as midshipman. After the lapse of four years, being disappointed in his hope of promotion, he purchased an ensign's commission in the army. In 1770 he married the daughter of Daniel Moore, M.P., with whom he lived in uninterrupted harmony. The same year his regiment was ordered to Minorca, where he spent two years profitably in the systematic study of English literature. Returning home in 1772, he passed several months in London, where he produced a sensation in the higher circles by his graceful volubility, his genial temper, and his charming social qualities. Rendered restless by the consciousness of grand dormant powers and faculties, he happened one day, in 1774, to enter court, in which Lord Mansfield, the presiding judge, invited him to sit by his side. Thinking that he could make a better speech than any that he heard in that trial, he resolved to study law. In 1775 he was admitted a student of Lincoln's Inn, and in 1776 was matriculated at Cambridge, as the degree of A.M. would shorten the term required to qualify him for the bar,—to which he was called in 1778.

The first cause in which he was engaged was that of Captain Baillie, tried for a libel on the Earl of Sandwich, a member of the cabinet. "Then was exhibited," says Lord Campbell, "the most remarkable scene ever witnessed in Westminster Hall. It was the *début* of a barrister, wholly unpractised in public speaking, before a court crowded with the men of the greatest distinction, belonging to all parties in the state. And I must own that, all the circumstances considered, it is the most wonderful forensic effort of which we have any account in our annals." The impression made on the audience was such that before he left the court a large number of retainers were presented to him by the attorneys who flocked around him. He had risen at one bound to the highest rank in his profession. In 1781 he made a great and successful plea in defence of Lord George Gordon, indicted for treason, in which logic and passion were combined with consummate art.

In 1783, by the influence of the Whig leaders, Erskine obtained a seat in the House of Commons, where his success was not equal to the high expectations that had been raised. In the election of 1784 he lost his seat. He could not adapt himself to the tenor of parliamentary debate with the same success that attended him in the forum. In 1789, in the trial of Stockdale, he vindicated the freedom of the press by another triumph of eloquence. In 1790 he was again returned to Parliament for Portsmouth, and continued to support the principles of Fox, even in the crisis of the French Revolution, by which the Whigs were divided. In 1794 Erskine appeared as the champion of public liberty in the state trials, when the ministry attempted to put down the friends of reform by the law of "constructive treason." He spoke seven hours in defence of Hardy, who was acquitted, amidst the rapturous applause of the popular party. Next came the case of John Horne Tooke, which had a similar result. In 1802 he was made chancellor of the duchy of Cornwall. On the formation of the Grenville ministry, in January, 1806,he became lord chancellor, and was raised to the peerage, as Baron Erskine of Restormel Castle. In consequence of a change in the ministry, he retired from office in 1807. Lord Campbell, late chancellor of England, gives it as his opinion that "as an advocate in the forum he is without an equal in ancient or modern times." He did not aim at wit or ornament in his speeches, though his diction was pure, simple, and full of variety. "But he spoke as his clients respectively would have spoken, being endowed with his genius; and those who heard him seemed to be inspired with a new, ethereal existence." Died in November,1823. His principal publications are "Armata," a political romance, and a "View of the Causes and Consequences of the War with France," which ran through forty-eight editions. He left several daughters, and three sons, of whom the eldest, David Montague, inherited the title of Lord Erskine.

See LORD CAMPBELL, "Lives of the Lord Chancellors;" FOSS, "The Judges of England," vol. ix.; LORD BROUGHAM, "Speeches of Lord Erskine, with a Prefatory Memoir;" "London Quarterly Review" for April, 1858.

Erskine, (THOMAS,) of Linlethan, a member of the Scottish bar, distinguished as a biblical scholar, wrote "Remarks on the Internal Evidence for the Truth of Revealed Religion," (3d edition, 1821,) an "Essay on Faith," and "The Doctrine of Election Illustrated," (1837.)

Erskine, (THOMAS ALEXANDER,) sixth Earl of Kellie, a musical composer, born in 1732, was the son of the fifth Earl of Kellie. He devoted his attention chiefly to music, studied with Stamitz at Manheim, and gained distinction as a composer and performer. Died in 1781.

Erslev. See ERSLEW.

Erslew or **Erslev,** ĕR'slĕv, (THOMAS HAN'SEN,) a Danish bibliographer, born at Randers in 1803. He was appointed director of the archives of the ministry of worship in 1849. His most important work is a "General Dictionary of the Authors of Denmark," ("Almindeligt Forfatter-Lexicon for Danmark," etc., 3 vols., 1841–53,) to which he has added a supplement.

Ertborn, van, vän ĕRt'boRn, (JOSEPH CHARLES EMMANUEL,) BARON, a Belgian linguist and writer on art and literature, born at Antwerp in 1778, wrote "Historical Researches on the Academy of Antwerp and the Artists which it produced," (1806.) Died in 1823.

Ertinger, ĕR'tăN'zhằ', (FRANÇOIS,) a French engraver, born at Colmar in 1640, engraved after Rubens and Poussin.

Ertogrul, ĕR'to-gRŏŏl, a Turkish chief, son of Soliman Shah, and father of Othmân, the founder of the Ottoman Empire. He ruled a tribe of Carismians, on the Sangara River, near the Black Sea, for the space of fifty years, and preached the Moslem religion with a sword in his hand. He took the city of Kutaia from the Greeks in 1281, and died soon after that date.

See VON HAMMER, "Geschichte des Osmanischen Reichs."

Erwin, ĕR'win, (JOHN,) a German architect, who succeeded his father, Erwin von Steinbach, as architect of the cathedral of Strasburg. Died in 1339.

Erwin von Steinbach, ĕR'win fon stīn'bằK, a German architect, born at Steinbach, near Bühl. He was the chief architect of the doorway and tower of the Strasburg cathedral, one of the most imposing and admirable specimens of the modern Gothic style. He commenced this tower in 1275, and died in 1318, after which it was continued by his son John, who died in 1339. It has a greater altitude than any other structure in Europe, being about 436 French feet, or more than 465 English feet, in height.

See MILIZIA, "Memorie degli Architetti;" PINGERON, "Vies des Architectes anciens et modernes;" JOSEPH BADER, "Meister Erwin von Steinbach und seine Heimath," 1844.

Erxleben, ĕRks'lā-bĕn, (JOHANN CHRISTIAN POLYCARP,) an eminent German naturalist, born at Quedlinburg, Saxony, in 1744. He was chosen professor of philosophy at Göttingen in 1771. He gained a high reputation by his works, some of which are said to be models of accuracy. He published "Elements of Natural His-

tory," (1768,) "Elements of Natural Philosophy," ("Naturlehre," 1772,) and "Systema Regni Animalis per Classes, Ordines, Genera, Species, Varietates, cum Historiâ Animalium; Classis I., Mammalia," ("System of the Animal Kingdom by Classes, Orders, Genera," etc., 1777.) "There exists not in zoology," says the "Biographie Universelle," "a more exact and complete treatise than this history of the mammalia." Died in 1777.

His mother, DOROTHY LEPORIN, born in 1715, was eminent for her attainments in medical science. She received a diploma from the University of Halle in 1754, and practised medicine. Died in 1762.

See "Biographie Médicale."

Eryceira. See ERICEIRA.

Er-ÿ-çï'na, [Fr. ÉRYCINE, â're-sĕn',] a surname of Venus, derived from Mount Eryx, in Sicily, where she had a temple.

Erycine. See ERYCINA.

E'rÿx, [Gr. Ἔρυξ,] a son of Butes and Venus, killed by Hercules in a combat with the cestus. (See Virgil's "Æneid," book v., lines 402-12.) A mountain in Sicily, near Drepanum, was named Eryx, from his having been buried there.

Erzilla. See ERCILLA.

Es, van, vän ĕs, (JACOB,) a Flemish painter, born at Antwerp about 1570, excelled in the imitation of shells, flowers, and fruits. He is praised by Descamps.

See DESCAMPS, "Vies des Peintres Flamands," etc.

Esaias. See ISAIAH.

E-sā'ï-as of Egypt, a monk, who lived in Egypt in the fourth century, and wrote, in Greek, a number of works, some of which were published in 1684.

E'sau, [Heb. עֵשָׂו,] the eldest son of Isaac and Rebecca, born about 1836 B.C., lived in Mount Seir or Edom. He was sometimes called EDOM, which signifies "red," and was the ancestor of the Edomites.

See Genesis xxv. 25; xxvii., xxxii., xxxiii., and xxxvi.

Escalante, ĕs-kä-län'tà, (JUAN ANTONIO,) a Spanish historical painter, born at Córdova in 1630, lived in Madrid, and adorned the churches of that city with his works, among which is "The Life of Saint Gerard." He imitated Tintoret and Titian with moderate success. Died in 1670.

Escalante, d', dĕs-kä-län'tà, (JUAN,) was one of Cortez's principal officers when he undertook, in 1518, the conquest of Mexico. He received from Cortez the command of the colony or town founded by him at Vera Cruz. He was killed in a battle against a Mexican chief in 1519.

See PRESCOTT's "Conquest of Mexico."

Escale. See SCALA.

Escarbot. See LESCARBOT.

Eschasseriaux, à'shäs're'ō', (JOSEPH,) BARON, a French Jacobin, born near Saintes in 1753. He was an active member of the Convention, 1792–95, and of the Tribunate, 1800–04. Died in 1823.

Eschasseriaux, (RENÉ,) a brother of the preceding, born in 1754, was an able and moderate member of the Convention, and of various legislative assemblies in succession. In 1798 he made an important report on the subject of supplying horses for the cavalry. Died in 1831.

Eschels-Kroon, ĕsh'ĕls-kRōn',(ADOLPHUS,)a Danish traveller, born in 1736, passed many years in the East Indies, where he was agent of Denmark from 1782 to 1784. He wrote a "Description of Sumatra," (1782,) and other works. Died in 1793.

See ERSCH und GRUBER, "Allgemeine Encyklopaedie."

Eschenbach, ĕsh'en-bằK', (ANDREAS CHRISTIAN,) a learned German writer, born in 1663 at Nuremberg, where he became professor of Greek in 1695. He published an edition of the works of Orpheus, (1689,) "Epigenes on Orphic Poetry," ("Epigenes de Poesi Orphicâ," 1702,) "Dissertationes Academicæ," (1705,) and other works. Died in 1705.

Eschenbach,(CHRISTIAN **Ehrenfried**--â'ren-freet',) a German physician, born at Rostock in 1712, wrote "Elements of Surgery," (1745,) "Medicina Legalis," (1746,) and other professional works. Died in 1788.

ā, ē, ī, ō, ū, ȳ, *long;* ă, ĕ, ĭ, ŏ, ŭ, ў, *short;* ạ, ẹ, ị, ọ, *obscure;* fär, fàll, fàt; mĕt; nŏt; gŏŏd; mōŏn;

Eschenbach, von, fon êsh'ẹn-bȧk', (WOLFRAM,) a famous German poet or minnesinger, was born in Bavaria, and flourished about 1200. According to the custom of the mediæval bards, he wandered from castle to castle, and found a welcome at the courts of several princes. His principal poems are entitled "Titurel" and "Parcival." He is generally admitted to have been the greatest German poet anterior to the revival of German literature.

See GERVINUS, "Geschichte der poetischen National-Literatur," 1837; SAN MARTE, "Wolfram von Eschenbach," Magdeburg, 2 vols., 1841; "Nouvelle Biographie Générale."

Eschenburg, êsh'ẹn-bŏŏRG', (JOHANN JOACHIM,) a German littérateur, born at Hamburg in 1743. He was professor in a college of Brunswick, and aulic councillor. He produced good German prose versions of Shakspeare's Dramatic Works, (14 vols., 1775–87,) and of other foreign works; he also wrote a "Life of Handel," (1785.) His "Manual of Classical Literature" reached the eighth edition in 1837. Died in 1820.

Eschenmayer, êsh'ẹn-mī'ẹr, (KARL ADOLF,) a German philosopher, metaphysician, and mystic, born at Neuenberg, in Würtemberg, in 1768. He became in 1811 professor of philosophy and medicine at Tübingen. From 1818 to 1836 he filled the chair of practical philosophy in the same university. Among his chief works are a "System of Moral Philosophy," (1818,) and "Philosophy of Religion," (3 vols., 1818–24.) Died in 1854.

See RITTER, "History of Philosophy;" "Nouvelle Biographie Générale."

Escher, êsh'ẹr, (F. A.,) a German scholar, known as the translator of Horace, was born in 1777; died in 1802.

Escher, êsh'ẹr, (HENRY,) a Swiss statesman, born at Zurich in 1626, acquired by his talents and virtues great influence in the state. Died in 1710.

Escher, (JEAN HENRI ALFRED,) a prominent Swiss statesman, born at Zurich in 1819, acted with the Liberals against the Jesuits and the Sonderbund. In 1847 he was president of the grand council, and advocated a reform of the federal system, tending to a greater centralization. He was chosen president of the new council of regency in 1848, and vice-president of the national council in 1856.

Escher, (JOHANN CASPAR,) a Swiss magistrate, born at Zurich in 1678. He was employed in various important negotiations. Died in 1762.

See ERSCH und GRUBER, "Allgemeine Encyklopaedie;" DAVID WYSS, "Lebensgeschichte J. C. Eschers," 1790.

Escher, (JOHANN CONRAD,) surnamed VON DER LINTH, (fon dêr lînt,) a Swiss geologist, born at Zurich in 1768, gained much credit by the improvement of the channel of the river Linth, whence his surname is derived. He published "Geological Observations on the Alps," (1795,) and "The Formation of the Great Chain of the Jura," (1820.) Died in 1823.

See JOHANN J. HOTTINGER, "H. C. Escher von der Linth; Charakterbild eines Republikaners," 1852.

Escherny, d', dȧ'shêʀ'ne', (FRANÇOIS LOUIS,) COUNT, a French littérateur, born at Neufchâtel in 1733. He went to Paris in 1762, and became intimate with Diderot, D'Alembert, and Rousseau. His principal works are an "Essay on Equality," and "Lacunæ of Philosophy," (1783.) Died in 1815.

Eschil. See ESKIL.

Eschine, the French of ÆSCHINES, which see.

Eschines. See ÆSCHINES.

Eschius, ês'ke-ŭs, or **Van Esche,** vȧn ês'Kẹh, (NICOLAAS,) a Dutch Catholic priest and writer, born near Bois-le-Duc in 1507; died in 1578.

Eschricht, êsh'ʀiKt, (DANIEL FREDERIK,) a Danish physician and physiologist, born at Copenhagen in 1798. He became professor of medicine in the University of Copenhagen in 1836, and published several valuable works on physiology, zoology, etc.

Eschscholtz, êsh'sholts, (JOHANN FRIEDRICH,) a German naturalist and traveller, born at Dorpat in 1793. He accompanied Kotzebue as physician in his voyage of discovery, 1815–18, and in a second voyage about 1823. He wrote a description of two thousand animals, which was published with Kotzebue's narrative in 1830, and published "Entomographien," (1823,) and a "Zoological

Atlas," (1829-33.) Died in 1831. The genus Eschscholtzia was named in honour of him by Chamisso.

Eschyle, the French for ÆSCHYLUS, which see.

Eschylus. See ÆSCHYLUS.

Esclava, de, dȧ ês-klȧ'vȧ, (ANTONIO,) a Spanish writer of romances, born in Aragon about 1570.

Escobar, de, dȧ ês-ko-bȧʀ', (ANTONIO,) a Portuguese littérateur, born at Coimbra, wrote many and various works. Died in 1681.

Escobar, de, dȧ ês-ko-bȧʀ', (BARTOLOMÉ,) a Spanish missionary and writer, born at Seville in 1562, preached in the West Indies and at Lima. Died at Lima in 1624.

Escobar, de, (FRANCISCO,) a Spanish Hellenist and writer, born at Valencia; died after 1557.

Escobar, de, (MARIA,) a Spanish lady, born at Truxillo, was the wife of Diego de Chaves, who followed Pizarro to the conquest of Peru, about 1540. She was the first who carried wheat to Peru.

Escobar y Mendoza, ês-ko-bȧʀ' e mên-do'thȧ, (ANTONIO,) a famous casuist and Jesuit, born at Valladolid, in Spain, in 1589. He was a popular preacher, and a learned writer on theology, but was severely censured by Pascal and others for teaching a lax morality. He wrote, in Latin, "Moral Theology," (1646,) a "Treatise on Justice and Law," and another on "Cases of Conscience," ("Summula Casuum Conscientiæ," 1626.) It was to refute the doctrines and sophisms broached in the last work that Pascal wrote the fifth and sixth of his admirable "Provincial Letters." Died in 1669. In the dictionary of the French Academy ESCOBAR is a synonym for an "adroit hypocrite."

See TICKNOR, "History of Spanish Literature;" N. ANTONIO, "Bibliotheca Hispana Nova."

Escoiquiz, ês-ko-e-kêth', sometimes written **Escoiquitz,** (Don JUAN,) a Spanish priest and courtier, born in Navarre in 1762, was appointed preceptor of the king's son, afterwards Ferdinand VII. The latter employed him in secret negotiations with Napoleon, and when he became king, in 1808, made him a councillor of state. He had a paramount influence with Ferdinand, whom he accompanied to France; and he was his principal agent or adviser in the conferences at Bayonne, which resulted in his forced abdication. Escoiquiz returned to Spain with Ferdinand in 1814, and was appointed minister; but he was dismissed the same year, and exiled from court. He wrote an epic poem of little merit, entitled "The Conquest of Mexico," (1802,) and translated Milton's "Paradise Lost" into Spanish. Died in 1820.

See SOUTHEY, "History of the Peninsular War;" "Nouvelle Biographie Générale."

Escosura, de la, dȧ lȧ ês-ko-soo'rȧ, (Don PATRICIO,) a Spanish author and politician, born at Madrid in 1807. He became secretary of state about 1843, after which he was a member of the Narvaez ministry. He retired from office in 1846, and was minister of the interior in 1854–55. Among his works are romances entitled "El Conde de Candespina," (1832,) and "Ni Rey ni Roque," (1835,) several dramas, a "Manual of Mythology," (1843,) and the text of "Artistic and Monumental Spain."

Escousse, ês'kooss', (VICTOR,) a French poet, born in Paris in 1813. He produced "Farruck the Moor," ("Farruck le Maure,") a drama, (1831,) which was applauded, and some songs. He committed suicide in February, 1832, in company with his friend Lebras.

Esculape, the French of ÆSCULAPIUS, which see.

Esculapius. See ÆSCULAPIUS.

Esdras of Scripture. See EZRA.

Es'dras, an Armenian, was chosen Patriarch of Armenia in 628 A.D. In concert with Heraclius, the Greek emperor, he called a council in 629, approving the reunion of the Armenian and Greek Churches; but the bishops of Persian Armenia opposed the measure. Died in 639.

Esiodo, the Italian of HESIOD, which see.

Es'kil, written also **Eschil** or **Eskild,** an ambitious Swedish prelate, became in 1138 Archbishop of Lund and Primate of Denmark. He founded several monasteries, took part in political contests, and was sometimes in open war with the king. He performed a pilgrimage to the Holy Land, and wrote a work on Ecclesiastical Law. Died in 1187 or 1181.

See KRAFT og NYERUP, "Litteraturlexicon."

€ as k; ç as s; g̱ hard; ġ as j; G, H, K, guttural; N, nasal; R, trilled; š as z; ŧh as in this. (☞See Explanations, p. 23.)

Eskild. See ESKIL.

Esmark, ês′mӓʀk, or **Esmarch,** (JENS,) a Danish geologist and mineralogist, born in 1763, published several works on mineralogy. He became professor of metallurgy at Christiania in 1814. Died about 1838.

See "Biografi öfver J. Esmark," Stockholm, 1839.

Esmenard, ês′mҽh-nӓʀ′, (JEAN BAPTISTE,) born in Provence, in France, in 1772, served many years in the army, and became lieutenant-colonel. During the restoration he resigned his commission, and rendered important services to the republic of Colombia. He afterwards became an editor of the "Gazette de France," "Journal des Débats," and "Mercure." Died in 1842.

Esmenard, (JOSEPH ALPHONSE,) a French didactic poet, born at Pélissanne (Bouches-du-Rhône) in 1769, was a brother of the preceding. He emigrated as a royalist in 1792, returned to Paris about the end of 1799, and associated himself with La Harpe and Fontanes as an editor of the "Mercure de France." About 1801 he accompanied General Leclerc as secretary in the expedition to Hayti. He published in 1805 "La Navigation," a poem, which was composed at sea and is admired for the fidelity of its descriptions and the harmony of its versification. His opera of "Trajan" was performed with applause in 1808. He was elected to the Institute (class of French literature) in 1810. He was thrown out of his coach and killed near Naples in June, 1811.

See "Nouvelle Biographie Générale."

Éson, the French of ÆSON, which see.

Esop. See ÆSOP.

Ésope, the French of ÆSOP, which see.

Espagnac, d′, dês′pӓn′yӓk′, (JEAN BAPTISTE JOSEPH **Damazit de Sahuguet**—dӓ′mӓ′ze′ dҽh sӓ′ü′gӓ′,) BARON, a French general, born at Brive-la-Gaillarde in 1713. He served several campaigns in Germany, became aide-major-général under Marshal Saxe, and obtained the grade of lieutenant-general in 1780. He wrote a "Life of Marshal Saxe," and an "Essay on the Science of War," (1751.) Died in 1783.

Espagnandel, L′, lês′pӓn′yŏn′dêl′, (MATHIEU,) a French sculptor, born in 1610, adorned several churches of Paris with his works. Died in 1689.

Espagne, d′, (Don CARLOS.) See ESPAÑA.

Espagne, d′, dês′pӓñ′, (CHARLES,) a valiant French warrior, was made Constable of France in 1350, and became a great favourite with the king. He was assassinated in 1354 by Charles, King of Navarre.

Espagne, d′, (JEAN,) a French Protestant theologian, born in Dauphiny in 1591. He preached in Holland, and afterwards settled in London, where he was pastor of a French church. He published many works, which were often reprinted, the best-known of which is "Popular Errors in the Knowledge of Religion," (1648.) Died in London in 1659.

Espagne, d′, (JEAN LOUIS BRIGITTE,) COMTE, a French general of division, born at Auch (Armagnac) in 1766. He defeated the Austrians at San Michele, in Italy, and distinguished himself at Heilsberg in 1807. He was killed at the battle of Essling, in 1809.

Espagne, d′, [Sp. DE ESPAÑA, dӓ ês-pӓn′yӓ,] or **De la Cerda,** dӓ lӓ thêʀ′dӓ, (LOUIS,) was a grandson of Ferdinand de la Cerda, a Spanish prince, and a brother of Charles, noticed above. He became admiral of France in 1341, and fought for Charles de Blois in the war for the succession of Brittany.

Espagnet, d′, dês′pӓn′yӓ′, (JEAN,) a French alchemist of Bordeaux, lived about 1610-40. He wrote two Latin works which were regarded as classic, viz., "Secret of the Hermetic Philosophy," ("Arcanum Philosophiæ Hermeticæ," 1623,) and a "Manual of the Restored Philosophy," (1633.)

Espagnoletto. See SPAGNOLETTO.

España. See ESPAGNE, D′, (LOUIS.)

España, de, dӓ ês-pӓn′yӓ, [Fr. D'ESPAGNE, dês′pӓñ′,] (Don CARLOS,) COUNT, a Spanish general, born in France in 1775. He fought against the French in the war which began in 1808, and rendered important services at Badajoz, Albuera, Salamanca, etc., for which he was rewarded with the place of Captain-General of Aragon. He was assassinated in 1839.

Esparbès. See AUBETERRE.

Espartero, ês-paʀ-tā′ro, (Don BALDOMERO,) Duke de la Vittoria, (dӓ lӓ vêt-to′re-ӓ,) a Spanish statesman and general, born at Granatula, La Mancha, in 1792 or 1793, was the son of a mechanic. He enlisted in the army in 1808, and went in 1815 to South America, where he fought against Bolivar, and became a colonel in 1822. He returned to Spain in 1825, with the rank of brigadier. When the civil war began, in 1833, he took arms for the young queen Isabella, and was appointed commandant-general of Biscay. He became a lieutenant-general in 1835, and commander-in-chief of the army of the North in 1836. In 1837 he defended Madrid from an attack of the Carlist army, which he drove back across the Ebro. He gained victories at Burgos and other places in 1838 and 1839, for which he was made a grandee of the first class, as Duke de la Vittoria y Morella. The war terminated by the submission of the Carlists in 1840. In May, 1841, Espartero was appointed by the Cortes Regent of Spain during the minority of Isabella. He acted at first with energy in the suppression of revolts at Barcelona, but was unable to resist a coalition of *progresistas* and *moderados*. An army of insurgents under Narvaez having entered Madrid in July, 1843, Espartero was exiled, and passed several years in England. He was permitted to return to Spain in 1847 or 1848. By another revolution, Narvaez, the leader of the absolutists, was driven from power, July, 1854, and Espartero again became prime minister of a cabinet in which O'Donnell, his political enemy, was minister of war. This rivalry resulted in a dissolution of the ministry in July, 1856, and in the triumph of O'Donnell.

See "Espartero; Historia de su Vida," etc., by JOSÉ SEGUNDO FLOREZ, 3 vols., 1844; L. DE LOMÉNIE, "Galerie des Contemporains," (republished in 12mo, 1844;) "Foreign Quarterly Review" for October, 1843.

Espejo, -ês-pā′HO, (ANTONIO,) a Spanish traveller, born at Córdova, was the leader of a small expedition which in 1582 explored the regions north of Mexico and discovered New Mexico. The account of his journey is preserved in Hakluyt's collection.

See A. VON HUMBOLDT, "Essai sur la Nouvelle Espagne."

Espen, van, vӓn ês′pҽn, (ZEGER BERNARD,) a Flemish casuist and priest, born at Louvain in 1646, was eminent for skill in canon law. He obtained in the University of Louvain a chair of law, which he filled many years. His connection with the party of Port-Royal caused him to lose this place about 1728. He published several works, of which the most important is his "Universal Ecclesiastical Law." Died in 1728.

See DE BELLEGARDE, "Vie de Van Espen," 1767; BAVAY, "Van Espen, Jurisconsulte et Canoniste Belge," 1846.

Espencæus. See ESPENCE, D′.

Espence, d′, dês′pŏnss′, [Latin, ESPENCÆ′US,] (CLAUDE,) a French priest, born near Châlons-sur-Marne in 1511, became a doctor of the Sorbonne, and rector of the University of Paris. Dupin expresses a favourable opinion of him. He wrote many and various works, among which is the "Education of a Christian Prince," (1548.) Died in 1571.

Esper, ês′pҽr, (EUGEN JOHANN CHRISTOPH,) a German entomologist, born at Wunsiedel, Bavaria, in 1742, became professor of philosophy at Erlangen in 1782. He published "The Butterflies of Europe, figured after Nature," (1777-1807,) and a work on Zoophytes, ("Die Pflanzenthiere in Abbildungen nach Natur," 1788-1809.) Died in 1810.

See ERSCH und GRUBER, "Allgemeine Encyklopaedie."

Esper, (JOHANN FRIEDRICH,) a German naturalist, brother of the preceding, was born at Drossenfeld in 1732. He wrote "The Marvellous Adventures of many Travellers," (2 vols., 1762,) and other works. Died in 1781.

Espercieux, ês′pêʀ′se-uh′, (JEAN JOSEPH,) a skilful French sculptor, born at Marseilles in 1758, worked in Paris. Among his works are statues of Molière, Racine, Napoleon, (1810,) and Voltaire, (1814.) Died in 1840.

Esperiente. See CALLIMACHUS.

Espernon. See ÉPERNON.

Espiard, ês′pe-ӓʀ′, (FRANÇOIS IGNACE DE LA BORDE,) born at Besançon in 1707, wrote an "Essay on the Genius and Character of Nations," (1743.) Died in 1777.

Espic, ês′pêk′, (JEAN BARTHÉLEMY,) a French poet and teacher, born in Languedoc in 1767; died in 1844.

ӓ, ē, ī, ō, ū, ȳ, *long;* ӑ, ĕ, ĭ, ŏ, ŭ, ў, *short;* ӓ, ҽ, į, ǫ, *obscure;* fӓr, fӓll, fӓt; mêt; nŏt; gōōd; mōōn;

Espinac. See ÉPINAC.

Espinasse, ês'pe'näss', (ESPRIT CHARLES MARIE,) a French general, born at Saissac, in Aude, in 1815, became aide-de-camp to Napoleon III. about 1852. In the Crimean war, in 1855, he served with distinction at the Tchernaya and other places, and was made general of division. In 1858 he acted for a few months as minister of the interior. He was killed at the battle of Magenta, June, 1859.

Espinasse, de l', dęh lês'pe'näss', (AUGUSTIN,) COUNT, a French general, born at Pouilly-sur-Loire in 1736, commanded the artillery, under Bonaparte, at the siege of Mantua, and at Arcola in 1796. Died in 1816.

Espinasse, de l', (CLAIRE FRANÇOISE or JULIE JEANNE ÉLÉONORE,) a French lady, remarkable for her talents, imagination, and sensibility, was born in 1732. In 1752 she became the protégée of the witty Madame du Deffand, with whom she lived in Paris about ten years, until her patroness was induced by jealousy to dissolve the connection. Having gained the special favour of D'Alembert, she formed a brilliant literary circle in her own *salon*, which was the resort of the élite of Paris. Her death was hastened by her excessive sensibility and unhappy attachments. She died in 1776, "leaving on the minds of almost all the eminent men of France," says Lord Jeffrey, "an impression of talent and of ardour of imagination which seems to have been considered as without example." Her letters to M. de Guibert (2 vols., 1809) are admirable in style and spirit.

See D'ALEMBERT, "Aux Manes de Mlle. Lespinasse;" SAINTE-BEUVE, "Causeries du Lundi;" MARMONTEL, "Mémoires;" VOL-TAIRE, "Correspondance;" and critique, by LORD JEFFREY, in the "Edinburgh Review" for January, 1810.

Espinel, ês-pe-nĕl', (VINCENTE,) a popular Spanish poet, born at Ronda about 1544, was ordained a priest, but, never receiving any valuable preferment, passed his life in great poverty. He was thoroughly versed in the ancient and modern languages. He acquired a high reputation, and was considered one of the best poets of his age for purity of style and fertility of imagination. He translated into Spanish verse Horace's "Art of Poetry" and Odes, and wrote "The House of Memory," ("La Casa de Memoria,") and numerous songs. Died in 1634. His novel "Marcos de Obregon" (1618) is said to be seasoned with fine pleasantry. Le Sage derived from the last-named work some materials for his "Gil Blas."

See TICKNOR, "History of Spanish Literature;" LONGFELLOW, "Poets and Poetry of Europe;" N. ANTONIO, "Bibliotheca Hispana Nova."

Espinosa, ês-pe-no'sâ, (JACINTO GERONIMO,) an excellent Spanish painter, born at Cocentayna, in Valencia, in 1600. He excelled in chiaroscuro, in correctness of design, and in the expression of his figures. He worked mostly in Valencia, the churches of which he adorned with many pictures. Among his works are a "Mary Magdalene," a "Nativity of the Saviour," and a "Holy Family." Died at Valencia in 1680.

See BERMUDEZ, "Diccionario Historico."

Espinosa, (JOSÉ,) a Spanish painter and engraver, born at Valencia in 1721; died in 1784.

Espinosa, (JUAN,) a Spanish poet and soldier, born at Bellovado about 1540, became secretary of Gonzales de Mendoza, Captain-General of Sicily. He wrote, besides other works, a poem on "The Praise of Women," (1580,) which contains beautiful passages and was received with favour. Died about 1595.

Espinosa, (NICOLAS,) a Spanish poet, born at Valencia about 1520, wrote a continuation of Ariosto's "Orlando Furioso," (1555.)

Espinosa, (PEDRO,) a Spanish poet and critic, born at Antequera about 1582. He became almoner to the Duke of Medina-Sidonia. He displayed his taste in a collection of specimens of Spanish poets, "Tesoro de Poesias," (1605,) on which his reputation chiefly rests. He wrote the "Concealed Treasure," ("Tesoro escondido," 1644,) and other poems. Died in 1650.

See N. ANTONIO, "Bibliotheca Hispana Nova;" TICKNOR, "History of Spanish Literature."

Espinosa, de, dâ ês-pe-no'sâ, (Don DIEGO,) an eminent Spanish statesman and cardinal, born in Old Castile in 1502. His ability and fame as a lawyer insured

his rapid promotion to the highest dignities and to the favour of Philip II., who made him president of the royal council (the highest place in the kingdom) and Inquisitor-General. In 1568 he was created a cardinal. He was an intolerant and relentless enemy of religious liberty and reform. For a few years he exercised almost unbounded influence over the king; but he lost the royal favour by his arrogance. Philip announced to him his disgrace by saying, "Cardinal, remember that I am the president." Espinosa died shortly after this blow, in 1572. The death of the king's son, Don Carlos, is imputed to him by some writers.

See AUBERY, "Histoire des Cardinaux;" PRESCOTT, "History of Philip II.," vol. iii. book vi. chap. i.; MOTLEY, "Rise of the Dutch Republic," vol. ii.

Espremesnil, d', (or **Épréménil, d',**) dâ'prâ'mâ'nĕl', (JACQUES DUVAL,) a French economist, a son-in-law of the famous Dupleix, became chief of the supreme council of Madras about 1746. Died in France in 1767.

Esprémesnil, d', (or **Épréménil, d',**) (JEAN JACQUES DUVAL,) a French advocate, a son of the preceding, was born at Pondicherry, in India, in 1746. He was richly endowed with personal and mental advantages. In 1787 he was one of the most eloquent and prominent members of the Parliament of Paris, and in 1789 he was one of the chief agitators of the popular party. In a contest between the court and the Parliament he asserted the rights of the latter so boldly that he was committed to custody. Having been deputed to the States-General by the noblesse of Paris, he changed his course, and in 1790 defended bravely the royal cause in the Assembly. He retired from that body in 1791. He was condemned by the Revolutionary Tribunal, and executed in 1794.

See LAMARTINE, "History of the Girondists;" "Nouvelle Biographie Générale."

Esprit, ês'prE', (JACQUES,) usually called the ABBÉ ESPRIT, born at Béziers, in France, in 1611. By his agreeable manners and conversation he gained the favour of Seguier and the Prince of Conti, who each gave him a large pension. Although only a mediocre writer, he was in 1639 admitted into the French Academy. The work called "Falsity of Human Virtues" is supposed to have been written by him. Died in 1678.

See NICÉRON, "Mémoires;" TALLEMANT, "Historiettes."

Espronceda, de, dâ ês-pRon-thā'Dâ, (JOSÉ,) a popular Spanish poet and politician, born near Almendralejo, in Estremadura, in 1810. In early youth he devoted himself to poetry and politics, and became so obnoxious to government by his radical principles, or his connection with a secret society, that he was imprisoned about the age of fifteen, and banished a few years later. He passed several years in London. In 1830 he fought with the popular party at the barricades of Paris. On the death of the Spanish king, in 1833, he returned to Madrid and entered the queen's body-guards. Again banished to Cuellar for a too free expression of his opinions, he there wrote his popular novel "Sancho Saldaña, or the Castellan of Cuellar," (1834.) A new régime having succeeded, he obtained his liberty, and returned to Madrid about 1835. He took an active part in the revolutionary contests of 1835–36. In 1841 he was appointed secretary of embassy to the Hague, and was elected a member of the Cortes, but died prematurely in 1842. The Spanish critics highly extol his "Hymn to the Sun," "Pirate," "Executioner," and "The Devil World," ("El Diablo-Mundo,") which was left unfinished. His poetry has some characteristics of the Byronic school. Among his works are poems entitled "El Pelayo," and "The Student of Salamanca."

See KENNEDY's "Modern Poets and Poetry of Spain."

Es'py, (JAMES P.,) an American meteorologist, born in Washington county, Pennsylvania, in 1785. He published "The Philosophy of Storms," (1841,) and, among other opinions, maintained that rain might be produced by human agency in all kinds of weather. Died in 1860.

Esquirol, ês'ke'rol', (JEAN ÉTIENNE DOMINIQUE,) a French physician, born at Toulouse in 1772. He founded at Paris in 1799 an asylum for the insane, which became a model institution. In 1817 he commenced a course of clinical lectures for mental maladies. He

€ as *k*; ç as *s*; ğ *hard*; ġ as *j*: G, H, K, *guttural*; N, *nasal*; R, *trilled*; ŝ as *z*; th as in *this*. (☞See Explanations, p. 23.)

55

appears to have rendered important services to humanity, and to have promoted a reform in the harsh régime to which the insane were subjected. He was chosen chief physician of the asylum at Charenton in 1826. In 1838 he published a work on insanity, "Des Maladies mentales," (2 vols.,) which is highly esteemed. Died in 1840.

See QUÉRARD, "La France Littéraire;" PARISET, "Histoire des Membres de l'Académie de Médecine;" LEURET, "Notice sur M. Esquirol," 1841.

Esquiros, ĕs'ke'ros', (HENRI ALPHONSE,) a French socialist, poet, and novelist, born in Paris in 1814. He published "Charlotte Corday," a novel, (1840,) "The Evangel of the People," "Songs of a Prisoner," (1841,) and a "History of the Mountain," (*Montagnards*,) (1847.) He was exiled for his political radicalism about December 2, 1851.

Esquivel de Alava. See ALAVA.

Esra. See EZRA.

Ess, van, vän ĕs, (KARL,) a Catholic theologian and Benedictine monk, born at Warburg, in Westphalia, in 1770. In co-operation with his cousin, Leander van Ess, he published a German version of the New Testament, (1807,) which was often reprinted. Died in 1824.

See ERSCH und GRUBER, "Allgemeine Encyklopaedie."

Ess, van, (LEANDER,) a theologian, born at Warburg in 1772; died about 1846.

Essarts, des, dā zā'sắr', (CHARLOTTE,) Countess of Romorentin, (ro'mo'rŏN'tắN'.) After being the mistress of Henry IV. of France, she became, in 1630, the wife of Marshal L'Hôpital. Died in 1651.

Essarts, des, (PIERRE,) a French politician, born about 1360, became provost of Paris in 1408, and superintendent of finances. He deserted the Duke of Burgundy, and joined the faction of Orléans. He was executed in 1413.

Essé, d', dā'sā', (ANDRÉ de Montalembert—dẹh mŏN'tắ'lŏN'baiR',) one of the most valiant French captains of his time, was born in Poitou in 1483. He served in the Italian campaigns with such distinction that Francis I. chose him as his comrade in the tournament of 1520. In 1543 he defended Landrecy with success against Charles V., and in 1548 commanded in Scotland, where he gained some advantages over the English. He was killed at the siege of Thérouanne in 1558.

See BRANTÔME, "Vies des grands Capitaines;" "Nouvelle Biographie Générale."

Essen, ĕs'sẹn, (HANS HENRIK,) COUNT OF, a Swedish field-marshal, born in West Gothland in 1755. He was made governor of Stockholm about 1796, and grand equerry in 1800. He defended Stralsund against the French in 1807. Charles XIII., who came to the throne in 1809, appointed him a councillor of state, with the title of count, and sent him on an embassy to Paris. For his success against the Norwegians in 1814 he was made a field-marshal, and Governor of Norway. He was reputed one of the greatest Swedish generals of his time. Died in 1824.

See THIERS, "Histoire de l'Empire."

Essenius, ĕs-sā'ne-ŭs, (ANDREAS,) a Dutch divine, born at Bommel in 1618. He became professor of theology at Utrecht in 1653, and wrote, among many works, "Systema Theologicum," (1659.) Died in 1677.

Essex. See CAPEL, (ARTHUR,) and CROMWELL, (THOMAS.)

Es'sex, (JAMES,) an English architect, born at Cambridge in 1723, was educated at King's College. He acquired distinction by his skill in Gothic architecture, and by restoring the chapel of King's College. He also repaired other colleges in Cambridge, and the cathedrals of Ely and Lincoln. He wrote several approved works on Architecture. Died in 1784.

Essex, (ROBERT DEVEREUX,) second EARL OF, born at Netherwood in 1567, was the eldest son of Walter, the first Earl. He was educated at Cambridge. In 1587 he served as captain-general of cavalry in the army commanded by his stepfather, the Earl of Leicester. On the death of the latter, in 1588, Essex, whose person and manners were very agreeable, and who was endowed with many virtues, became the special favourite of the queen, and the rival of Raleigh. In 1590 he married a daughter of Sir Francis Walsingham, and widow of Sir Philip Sid-

ney. He displayed courage and capacity in the victorious expedition against Cadiz in 1596, of which he commanded the land-forces, and Lord Effingham the navy. The next year he was named earl marshal of England. In 1598 he quarrelled with the queen, and, receiving from her a box on the ear, he indulged his pride and resentment so far as to withdraw from court for several months. In 1599 he was unsuccessful in an expedition against the Irish rebels, and again incurred the displeasure of the queen, who ordered him to be confined, intending to correct rather than ruin him. Having been examined before the privy council, he was suspended from office. Trusting to his general popularity, and led by his impetuous temper, he attempted to compel the queen by force to dismiss his enemies. For this purpose he marched with about two hundred retainers into London, and vainly invoked the aid of the citizens; he was arrested, convicted of treason, and executed in 1601. Elizabeth signed the warrant for his execution very reluctantly, and was inconsolable for his loss. He is admitted to have been by nature noble and generous; but his vanity, ambition, and imprudence rendered these advantages of no avail.

See W. B. DEVEREUX, "Lives and Letters of the Earls of Essex," etc.; HUME, "History of England;" CLARENDON, (EDWARD HYDE,) "The Characters of Robert, Earl of Essex, and George, Duke of Buckingham," 1700; "Edinburgh Review" for July, 1853.

Essex, (ROBERT DEVEREUX,) third EARL OF, son of the preceding, was born in London in 1592, and restored to his father's rank and titles by James I. In 1605 he married Lady Frances Howard, who was, only thirteen years of age. She indulged a passion for Lord Rochester, and procured a divorce from Essex, whom she hated. After several years spent in retirement at his country mansion, in 1620 he served in the army of the Elector Palatine in Holland, where he gave proof of military talents. Having inherited a share of his father's noble qualities, he became a popular favourite, and, in the troubles of Charles I.'s reign, encouraged the opposition. The king, however, in 1641 appointed him lord chamberlain, and lieutenant-general of a part of the army. When Charles fled from London, he ordered Essex to follow him; but the earl refused to do so, and was deprived of his commission. He was now the most popular leader of the Presbyterian party.

In 1642 the Parliament gave him the chief command of the army. The same year he fought the indecisive battle of Edgehill, and in 1643 besieged and took the fortified town of Reading. After suffering reverses in Cornwall, the army of Essex defeated the royalists at Newbury in 1644. He was considered too slow and vacillating by the more zealous republicans, who thought he was averse to a decisive triumph of their cause. They therefore passed the "Self-denying Ordinance," by which members of both Houses were excluded from command in the army, and Essex resigned in 1644. A pension of £10,000 was settled on him. At his death the title became extinct. Died in 1647.

See HUME, "History of England;" R. CODRINGTON, "Life of Robert, Earl of Essex," 1646; "Lives of the Warriors of the Civil Wars of France and England," by SIR EDWARD CUST, London, 1867.

Essex, (THOMAS CROMWELL,) EARL OF. See CROMWELL.

Essex, (WALTER DEVEREUX,) first EARL OF, an English statesman and commander of superior ability, born in Caermarthenshire about 1540. He inherited, at the age of nineteen, the title of Viscount Hereford, and married Lettice Knollys or Knolles. To reward his military services against the "rebellion of the north" in 1569, he was created Earl of Essex in 1572. He became a great favourite with Queen Elizabeth, and was appointed commander of an army sent in 1573 to subdue the insurgents in Ulster. His success in this enterprise was hindered by the intrigues of his rival Leicester, or by the acts of the lord deputy. He resigned his command in 1575, but was persuaded to return with the title of earl marshal of Ireland. He died at Dublin in 1576. His widow Lettice married the Earl of Leicester.

See HUME, "History of England."

Essling, PRINCE OF. See MASSENA.

Estaço, ĕs-tä'so, (ACHILLE,) [Lat. ACHIL'LES STA'-TIUS,] a Portuguese poet and scholar, born at Vidigueira in 1524. He studied at Louvain and Paris, became eminent for learning, and obtained a chair in the college di Sapienza, at Rome. About 1562 Pope Pius IV. appointed him secretary of the Council of Trent. He also acted as Latin secretary to Pius V. He published a collection of elegant Latin verses, ("Sylvæ aliquot," 1549,) and notes on Horace's "Art of Poetry," on Catullus, Cicero, and other classic authors. Died in 1581.

See GASPAR ESTAÇO, "Familia dos Estaços;" DE THOU, "Historia sui Temporis."

Estaing, ĕs'tȧN', [It. STAGNO, stȧn'yo,] an ancient and noble family of Rouergue, in France. CHEVALIER D'ESTAING in 1214 saved Philip Augustus from imminent peril at the battle of Bouvines. FRANÇOIS, born in 1460, became Bishop of Rhodez in 1501, and died in 1529. JOACHIM, Count d'Estaing, born about 1617, was noted for military talents. He wrote a "Genealogical Account" of his family. Died in 1688.

Estaing, d', dĕs'tȧN', (CHARLES HECTOR,) COUNT, a French admiral, was born in Auvergne in 1729. He served in India under De Lally about 1758. In 1763 he was chosen lieutenant-general of the naval armies, though his experience was gained in the land-service. In 1778, as vice-admiral, he commanded the fleet sent to aid the American republic. Just as this fleet met that of Lord Howe, near Rhode Island, in August, 1778, a violent storm separated them, with much damage to the French. Having captured the isle of Grenada, in 1779, he returned to France in 1780, and, as commandant of the national guard of Versailles in 1790–91, co-operated with La Fayette in efforts to save the lives of the king and queen. He was guillotined in April, 1794.

See LEBOUCHER, "Histoire de la Guerre de l'Independance des États-Unis;" "Nouvelle Biographie Générale."

Estampes. See ÉTAMPES.

Estampes-Valençay. See ÉTAMPES-VALENÇAY.

Estancelin, ȧs'tŏNs'lȧN', (LOUIS,) a French writer on commerce, navigation, etc., born at Eu in 1777.

Est'cŏurt, (RICHARD,) an English actor, born at Tewkesbury in 1668, performed in London with success as a comedian, and excelled in mimicry. He was purveyor of the Beefsteak Club, and is favourably mentioned in the "Tatler" and "Spectator." He wrote "The Fair Example," a comedy. Died in 1713.

See BAKER, "Biographia Dramatica."

Este, ĕs'te or ĕs'tȧ, one of the most illustrious sovereign houses of Italy, and perhaps the most ancient among those which have preserved their power and titles to the present time. The following are a few of the prominent persons who have inherited the marquisate of Este, or the duchies of Ferrara and Módena. Among the first who appears on record is OBERTO I., who possessed fiefs in Tuscany and Lunigiana, and married the daughter of Otho, King of Italy. He died about 972, and left a son, OBERTO II., who ruled Lunigiana and Obertenga. ALBERTAZZO II., who succeeded about 1020, added to the above the fiefs of Este, Rovigo, and other small towns of Lombardy, and married a princess of the great German house of Guelph or Welf. Their son, styled GUELPH IV., was invested in 1071 with the duchy of Bavaria, and is the ancestor of the royal line of Brunswick and Hanover. OBIZZO, who began to reign in 1137, was the first who assumed the title Marquis of Este. In 1208 the citizens of Ferrara, then a republic, elected AZZO VI., Marquis of Este, as their sovereign. During the civil war which raged between the Guelphs and Ghibelines in the thirteenth century, the Marquis of Este, AZZO VII., was the chief of the former faction. He reigned with glory from 1215 to 1264. OBIZZO II. succeeded in 1264 to the titles of Marquis of Este and Lord of Ferrara. In 1288 a deputation from Módena offered to him the perpetual sovereignty of their city,— an example which was followed by Reggio. Died in 1293. ALFONZO I., Duke of Ferrara and of Módena, a son of Ercole I., was an able statesman and warrior. He reigned from 1505 to 1534, and married the famous Lucretia Borgia. He was involved in war with the pope Julius II., who took from him Módena and Reggio; but Charles V. in 1531 confirmed his rights over those cities. His son, ERCOLE (or HERCULES) II., succeeded him in 1534, and married Renée, daughter of Louis XII. of France. He died in 1559. Cardinal IPPOLITO, a brother

of Alfonzo I., was accounted the greatest patron of learning in his time. Died in 1520. ALFONZO II., who succeeded his father in 1559, tarnished his fame by the imprisonment of Tasso, who had been an ornament of his court. Having died without issue in 1597, and named his cousin Cesare as heir, the pope claimed Ferrara as devolved to the see of Rome, by which it has since been held. CESARE, Duke of Módena, transferred the court from Ferrara to Módena. He died in 1628, and was succeeded by his son, ALFONZO III., who, after a short reign, abdicated and turned monk. FRANCIS I., son of Alfonzo III., succeeded in 1629, and died in 1658, leaving the duchy to his son, ALFONZO IV. The latter had a daughter, Mary, who was married to James II. of England, and a son, FRANCIS II., who succeeded in 1662. He died without issue in 1694, when his uncle, Cardinal RINALDO, became the heir. By the marriage of the latter with Charlotte, daughter of the Duke of Brunswick, two branches of the house of Este, which had been separated since 1070, were reunited. He died in 1737. His son, FRANCIS III., Duke of Módena, etc., born in 1698, commanded the Spanish armies in Italy in the war of the Austrian succession. Died in 1780. ERCOLE III., (1727 –1803,) a son of the preceding, married the Duchess of Massa-Carrara, and left an only child, Maria Beatrice, who became the wife of Ferdinand, Archduke of Austria. In 1797 the duchy of Módena was annexed to the Cisalpine republic by the treaty of Campo Formio. By the peace of Paris, (1814,) FRANCIS IV., son of Maria Beatrice, recovered his dominions, which he left at his death, in 1846, to his son, FRANCIS V. (See FRANCIS V.)

See SISMONDI, "Histoire des Républiques Italiennes;" POMPEO LITTA, "Famiglie celebri Italiane;" CRAWFURD, "History of the House of Este," London, 1681.

Este, ĕs'te, (Rev. CHARLES,) an English writer, born in 1753, was ordained in 1777, and became one of the chaplains at Whitehall. He was one of the editors of "The World," a daily journal, and published a "Journey through Flanders, Germany," etc., (1795.) Died in 1829.

Este, d', dĕs'tȧ, (Cardinal IPPOLITO,) an Italian prelate, born in 1479, was a brother of Alfonzo I., Duke of Módena, and was noted as a patron of learned men. Ariosto passed a long time in his service. Died in 1520.

See MURATORI, "Annali d'Italia."

Esterhazy or **Eszterházy,** ĕs-ter-hä'ze, a noble family of Hungary, which traces its origin to Paul d'Esteras, who lived in the tenth century, and has produced in the space of eight hundred years many eminent men. The most celebrated of these was PAUL ESTERHAZY DE GALANTHA, son of Nicholas, born at Kis-Martony (or Eisenstadt) in 1635. He displayed literary talents at a very early age, and served in the Austrian army with such success that he was made a field-marshal before he was thirty years old. In 1681 Count Esterhazy was elected Governor-General or Palatine of Hungary, and in 1686 took Buda from the Turks. He co-operated with the Austrian court in the subversion of civil and religious liberty. He was created a prince of the Holy Roman Empire in 1687. He used his great wealth in the liberal patronage of art and literature. Died in 1713.

Esterhazy or **Eszterhazy,** (NICHOLAS JOSEPH,) grandson of Paul, born in 1714, succeeded in 1762 to his titles and estates. He was a knight of the Golden Fleece, privy councillor, and field-marshal-general. In 1783 the dignity of prince, which was previously confined to the eldest son of the family, was extended to all his descendants. He patronized literature and the arts, especially music, and collected at his palace of Eisenstadt the first musicians of his time. Died in 1790.

Esterhazy de Galantha, ĕs-ter-hä'ze dȧ gȧ-lȧn'tȧ, (NICHOLAS,) PRINCE, a magnate of Hungary, born in 1765, was a son of the preceding. He married in 1783 the Princess of Lichtenstein. In 1792, as ambassador to the election of Francis II., he displayed extraordinary magnificence. For his alacrity in defending the Austrian throne against the French, about 1797, he was made a field-marshal and privy councillor, and was employed in diplomatic missions to Paris, London, and Saint Petersburg from 1801 to 1816. His immense revenues enabled him to support a liberal, or rather a prodigal, expenditure. Died in 1833.

Esterhazy de Galantha, (PAUL ANTONY,) a son of the preceding, was born in 1786. He represented Austria at the court of London from 1815 to 1818 and from 1830 to 1838. He favoured the national and liberal movement which preceded the revolution of 1848, and held office for a short time in the Batthyányi ministry, but resigned before the war began. He owns larger estates in land than any other subject of Austria.

Esther, ĕs'tẹr, [Heb. אסתר,] a Jewess, whose original name was HADAS'SAH, (or, according to some writers, EDISSA,) and who is supposed to have lived about 450 B.C. at Susa, (Shushan,) the capital of Persia. She was a cousin and adopted daughter of Mordecai, and on account of her beauty was selected as the queen of Ahasuerus, King of Persia, who is supposed to be the Artaxerxes Longimanus of profane history. She has the honour of giving her name to a canonical book of the Bible. The authorship of this book is not ascertained.

See A. NICCOLAI, "L'Ester, Dissertazione," Florence, 1765.

Estienne. See ÉTIENNE.

Es'tĭ-us or **van Est,** vän ĕst, (WILLEM,) a Dutch Catholic divine, born at Gorkum in 1542, was a professor of theology in Douay. He wrote commentaries on the Epistles, and other theological works. Died in 1613.

Estocart, L', lês'to'kǎR', (CHARLES,) a French sculptor, who worked in Paris about 1650.

Estocq. See LESTOCQ.

Estoile. See ÉTOILE, DE L'.

Estor, ĕs'toR, (JOHANN GEORG,) a German jurist and legal writer, born in Hesse in 1699, became professor of law at Jena in 1735. Died in 1773.

Estourmel, d', dĕs'tooR'mĕl', (ALEXANDRE CÉSAR LOUIS,) COMTE, a French legislator, born in Paris in 1780. He was one of the twenty-nine deputies who gave the influence of their names to the insurgents who dethroned Charles X. In 1833 he was sent on a mission to the United States, from which he soon returned.

Estourmel, d', (FRANÇOIS DE SALES MARIA JOSEPH LOUIS,) COMTE, a French traveller, brother of the preceding, born in 1783; died in 1852.

Estourmel, d', (LOUIS MARIE,) MARQUIS, born in Picardy, France, in 1744. As a member of the Constituent Assembly, he opposed the Revolution. He afterwards served in the army of the Rhine, and became a general of division. In 1805 and in 1811 he was chosen a member of the legislative body. Died in 1823.

Estouteville, d', dĕs'toot'vĕl',(GUILLAUME,)a French prelate, born in 1403. He obtained successively six bishoprics, some of which were in Italy, and was at the same time Archbishop of Rouen. He built the towers of the cathedral of Rouen. Died in 1483.

Estrada, de, dà ĕs-tRä'Dä, (BARTOLOMÉ RUIZ,) a Spanish pilot, who served under Pizarro in South America. He conducted Pizarro and Almagro to the Rio Peru about 1525.

Estrades, d', dĕs'tRăd', (GODEFROI,) COMTE, an able French general and negotiator, born at Agen in 1607, was employed in several foreign missions from 1637 to 1647. As lieutenant-general, he commanded at the siege of Dunkirk in 1652, and at Rochelle in 1653. He was sent as ambassador to England in 1661, and obtained the cession of Dunkirk to France. For his military services in Holland from 1672 to 1675 he was created marshal of France. He negotiated on the part of France the peace of Nymwegen in 1678, and was chosen governor of the Duke of Chartres in 1685. He was reputed one of the ablest negotiators of his time. Died in 1686.

See MIGNET, "Négociations relatives à la Succession d'Espagne;" "Nouvelle Biographie Générale;" and his "Lettres, Mémoires," etc., published by J. AYMON, 5 vols., 1709.

Estrées, d', dĕs'tRä', (ANTOINE,) a son of Jean, (the first of that name,) noticed below, was at one time grand master of artillery, and defended Noyon against the Duke of Mayenne in 1593. Henry IV. for this service appointed him Governor of the Isle of France.

Estrées, d', (CÉSAR,) CARDINAL, a son of François Annibal, and grandson of the preceding, was born in 1628. Soon after graduating in the Sorbonne, he was appointed Bishop of Laon. Having been made a cardinal, he was sent as minister to Rome, where he con-

curred in the election of Innocent XI. in 1676. He was a member of the French Academy. Died in 1714.

See D'ALEMBERT, "Histoire des Membres de l'Académie."

Estrées, d', (FRANÇOIS ANNIBAL,) a French general and peer, born in 1573, was the son of Antoine, and brother of Gabrielle. He was for a short time Bishop of Noyon, but exchanged the church for the army, in which his talents and services procured for him a marshal's bâton in 1626. Richelieu sent him to Rome as envoy extraordinary in 1636. He officiated as constable at the coronation of Louis XIV., who soon after created him Duke of Estrées. Died in 1670.

See BAZIN, "Histoire de Louis XIII;" J. CHASSEBRAS, "Éloge de F. A. Duc d'Estrées," 1687.

Estrées, d', (GABRIELLE,) a beautiful French lady, born about 1571, was the daughter of Antoine, and a sister of the preceding, the first Duke of Estrées. She became the mistress of Henry IV., who designed to marry her and raise her to the throne; but she died suddenly in 1599. It is said that he was more attached to her than to any other woman, and that his partiality was merited by her amiable qualities.

See TALLEMANT DES RÉAUX, "Historiettes;" SAINTE-BEUVE, "Causeries du Lundi;" LAMOTHE-LANGON, "Mémoires de G. d'Estrées," 2 vols., 1829.

Estrées, d', (JEAN,) a skilful French officer, born in 1486 of a noble family in Picardy. He followed Francis I. to the battles of Marignao, (1515,) Pavia, (1525,) and Cerisoles, (1544.) In 1550 he was chosen grand master and captain-general of the artillery. He embraced the Reformed doctrines, and became attached to the cause of Henry of Navarre. Died in 1571.

See BRANTÔME, "Vies des grands Capitaines;" MORÉRI, "Dictionnaire Historique."

Estrées, d', (JEAN,) COMTE, a French marshal, a son of François Annibal, was born in 1624. As lieutenant-general, he commanded a corps-d'armée at Valenciennes in 1655. Having entered into the marine service, he became a vice-admiral in 1670, and commanded the French fleet at Solebay against De Ruyter in 1672. He gained advantages over the Dutch at Cayenne and To-bago in 1676-77, and was made a marshal of France in 1681, being the first naval officer who ever obtained that rank. Died in 1707, leaving a son, Victor Marie.

See LÉON GUÉRIN, "Les Marins illustres de la France;" "Nouvelle Biographie Générale."

Estrées, d', (JEAN,) a French courtier and priest, nephew of Cardinal d'Estrées, was born in Paris in 1666. He was ambassador to Spain in 1703, and succeeded Boileau in the French Academy in 1711. The king appointed him in 1716 successor to Fénelon as Archbishop of Cambray; but he died before his consecration, in 1718.

Estrées, d', (LOUIS CÉSAR **Letellier**—lẹh-tà'lẹ-à',) COMTE, born in 1697, was a nephew (sister's son) of Victor Marie, and was styled in youth CHEVALIER DE LOUVOIS. He was a grandson of the famous minister Louvois. In 1739 he assumed the name of Comte d'Estrées. As lieutenant-general, he served with distinction in Flanders from 1744 to 1748. In 1756 he became a marshal of France, received the chief command of the army in Germany, and defeated the Duke of Cumberland near Hastenbeck in 1757. He died, without issue, in 1771.

See "Nouvelle Biographie Générale."

Estrées, d', (VICTOR MARIE,) DUC, an admiral, the son of Jean, noticed above, was born in Paris in 1660. He obtained in 1684 the reversion of the vice-admiralty possessed by his father. At the death of his uncle, in 1687, he inherited the title of duke. In 1690 he destroyed the fleet of the English admiral Torrington. In the war of the Spanish succession he commanded the fleet sent to aid Philip V. of Spain. He was made a marshal of France in 1703, and a member of the French Academy about 1714. He was a good scholar and a patron of learning. Died in 1737.

See L. GUÉRIN, "Les Marins illustres de la France;" HENNE-QUIN, "Biographie maritime;" RENÉ BIET, "Éloge de M. le Maréchal d'Estrées," 1739.

Estrella, ĕs-tRĕl'yä, (JUAN CRISTOVAL **Calvete**—käl-vā'tà,) a Spaniard, who wrote a "Narrative of the Voyage of Philip of Spain to Flanders in 1549."

ā, ē, ī, ō, ū, ȳ, *long;* ă, ĕ, ĭ, ŏ, ŭ, ў, *short;* ạ, ẹ, ị, ọ, *obscure;* fär, fàll, fàt; mĕt; nŏt; gōŏd; mōŏn;

Estrup, ês′trŏŏp, (HEKTOR FREDERIK JANSON,) a Danish writer, born about 1794 ; died in 1846.

Eszterhazy. See ESTERHAZY.

Étampes, ă′tŏMp′, or **Estampes,** ă′tŏMp′, (ANNE,) DUCHESS OF, called at first MADEMOISELLE DE HEILLY, a French lady, born in 1508. She was a mistress of Francis I., over whom her beauty and talents acquired great influence. She was complimented as "the fairest among the learned, and the most learned among the fair." Died about 1576.

Étampes or **Estampes,** d′, (JACQUES,) Marquis de Ferté-Imbaut, a French general, born in 1590. He displayed skill and courage in many campaigns in Flanders, and was lieutenant-general at the battle of Lens in 1648. He became a marshal of France in 1651. Died in 1668.

Étampes or **Estampes-Valençay,** d′, dă′tŏMp′ vȧ′lôN′sȧ′, (HENRI,) a naval officer, born in Paris in 1603, commanded the French squadron which blockaded Rochelle under the orders of Richelieu. In 1652 he was sent as ambassador to Rome by Louis XIV., and in 1670 was chosen grand prior of France. Died in 1678.

See MORÉRI, "Dictionnaire Historique."

Etchegoyen, ă′chă′go′e′ĕn′, a French philosopher, born near Pau (Béarn) about 1786. He published a work entitled "On Unity, or a Philosophic Treatise on the Identity of the Principles of Mathematics, General Grammar, and the Christian Religion," (4 vols., 1836-42,) which is highly commended. Died in 1843.

Etcheverri. See ECHÉVERRI.

Étéocle. See ETEOCLES.

E-te′o-clēs, [Gr. Ἐτεοκλῆς; Fr. ÉTÉOCLE, ă′tȧ′okl′,] a son of Œdipus, after whose death he and his brother Polynices agreed to reign alternately at Thebes. Eteocles having usurped the sole power, his brother fled to Adrastus, who espoused his cause and led the expedition of the Seven against Thebes. Eteocles was killed by Polynices in a single combat.

Étex, ă′tĕks′, (ANTOINE,) a successful French sculptor, born in Paris in 1808. Among his works are statues of Charlemagne at the Luxembourg, Saint Augustine at the Madeleine, busts of Châteaubriand and Cavaignac, and two colossal groups which decorate the Arc de l'Étoile.

Eth′el-bâld, King of Mercia, who began to reign in 716 A.D., was one of the most eminent princes who ruled this part of the Heptarchy. He was defeated by Cuthred, King of Wessex, in 754 and in 757, and soon after was killed by Beornred, one of his officers.

Ethelbald, King of Wessex, or of the Anglo-Saxons, was the eldest surviving son of Ethelwolf, and brother of Alfred the Great. While his father was absent from the kingdom in 855, Ethelbald aspired to the throne with such success that Ethelwolf, for the sake of peace, ceded to him the kingdom of Wessex. He married his father's widow, Judith of France. Died in 860, and was succeeded by his brother Ethelbert.

Eth′el-bęrt, King of Kent, son of Hermenric, began to reign about 560 A.D. By a victory over Ceaulin, King of Wessex, he obtained the ascendency in the Heptarchy. Before the death of his father he married Bertha of Paris, a French princess, who was a zealous Christian and gained great influence over the king and people. The conversion of Ethelbert, with many of his subjects, was completed by the agency of a Roman monk, Augustine, who arrived in 597. Under Ethelbert's wise reign the kingdom was prosperous. He was the author of the first written laws among the Anglo-Saxons. Died in 616.

See LINGARD's "History of England."

Ethelbert, King of the Anglo-Saxons, a son of Ethelwolf, succeeded his brother Ethelbald in 860 A.D. During the life of his father, in 852, he had been made king or regent of Kent, Essex, and Sussex, to which Wessex was added at the death of Ethelbald. The kingdom was infested by the Danes during his reign. He died in 865 or 866, and left the throne to his brother, Ethelred.

Ethelfleda. See ELFLEDA.

Eth′el-frid or **A′dęl-frid,** King of Northumbria, began to reign in 593 A.D. He was killed in battle fighting against Redwald in 617.

Eth-el-ḡi′vạ, an ambitious concubine of Edwy, King of the Anglo-Saxons. Her influence over Edwy excited

the jealousy of his subjects, who put her to death in 958 A.D.

Ethelnoth. See AGELNOTH.

Eth′ęl-red I., written also Æthelred, King of Wessex, and head of the Saxon Heptarchy, the fourth son of Ethelwolf, became king in 866 A.D. In the same year a large army of Danes invaded the island, and in a few years had conquered about half of the kingdom. In 870 the English under Alfred defeated the Danes at Ash-Tree Hill. The next year the Danes defeated the English at Merton, where Ethelred received a mortal wound. His brother, Alfred the Great, was his successor.

Ethelred II., written also Æthelred, surnamed THE UNREADY, King of the Anglo-Saxons, was the son of Edgar and Elfrida. He was born about 968 A.D., and succeeded his half-brother, Edward the Martyr, in 978. The crimes of Elfrida rendered the people disaffected to her son, who was accepted only because there was no other heir. His reign was perhaps the most disastrous and inglorious in English history. The kingdom was repeatedly ravaged by the Danes, who, after extorting large sums of money as the price of peace, soon returned for more, and demanded each time a larger tribute. In 1002 Ethelred ordered a general massacre of the Danish settlers in his realm, which was avenged by Sweyn, King of the Danes, who took London in 1014. Ethelred then fled to the court of the Duke of Normandy, whose sister Emma he had married. He died in 1016, leaving two sons, Edmund Ironside and Edward the Confessor, who became kings.

See HUME, "History of England," vol. i. chap. ii. ; FREEMAN, "Norman Conquest," vol. i. chap. v.

Eth′ęl-werd or **Eth′ęl-ward,** an Anglo-Saxon writer of the eleventh century, wrote a "History of the Anglo-Saxons," in Latin.

Eth′ęl-wold, a learned Anglo-Saxon prelate, born about 925, was a friend of Dunstan. He became Bishop of Winchester in 963, founded several monasteries, and made a reform in the monastic orders by the expulsion of married priests. Died in 984.

Eth′ęl-wolf, (eth′el-wōŏlf,) King of Wessex, or of the Saxon Heptarchy, the eldest son of Egbert, began to reign in 836 A.D. The country in this reign was harassed by frequent invasions of the Danes, who in 851 plundered London. Soon after this they were defeated with great loss at Okeley by Ethelwolf. He had five sons, Ethelstan, (who died before his father,) Ethelbald, Ethelbert, Ethelred, and Alfred the Great. In 856 he married Judith of France, daughter of Charles the Bald, and resigned Wessex to Ethelbald. Died in 858.

See WILLIAM OF MALMESBURY, "De Gestis Regum Anglorum."

Ethelwolf, an Anglo-Saxon monk of the eighth and ninth centuries, born before 770, wrote a metrical history of the Abbots, etc. of the monastery of Lindisfarne, which is of some historical value, and has some interest as the only specimen of Anglo-Latin poetry of that period.

Eth′er-eġe or **Etheridge,** (Sir GEORGE,) an English wit and dramatic author, born about 1636, wrote several licentious and successful comedies, among which are "Love in a Tub," and "Sir Fopling Flutter, or the Man of Mode." James II. sent him as minister to Ratisbon about 1687. Died about 1690.

See BAKER, "Biographia Dramatica."

Etheridge. See ETHEREGE.

Ethicus. See ÆTHICUS.

Éthra, the French of ÆTHRA, which see.

Eth′rўḡ, written also **Etheridge,** [Lat. EDRY′CUS,] (GEORGE,) was professor of Greek at Oxford in 1553. He published a Latin version of Justin Martyr, and several other works. He was a zealous Catholic.

Étienne, ă′te′ĕn′, written also **Estienne,** (ANTOINE,) son of Paul, noticed below, was born in Geneva in 1594. In 1614 he obtained the title of printer to the King of France, with a pension of 500 livres, and published many valuable editions of ancient authors. Died in 1674.

Étienne, ă′te′ĕn′, or **Estienne,** (CHARLES,) a scholar and physician, born in Paris about 1504. In 1551 he engaged in printing in Paris, and was appointed printer to the king. His editions were models of typography and accuracy. He compiled several dictionaries, a "Thesaurus Ciceronis," (1557,) and other works. Died in 1564.

€ as k; ç as s; ḡ hard; ġ as j; G, H, K, guttural; N, nasal; R, trilled; š as z; th as in this. (☞See Explanations, p. 23.)

Étienne, (CHARLES GUILLAUME,) a French dramatic poet, born at Chamouilly in 1778. He produced in 1807 the successful comedy of "Brueys et Palaprat." His comedy of "Two Sons-in-Law" ("Deux Gendres") opened to him the French Academy in 1811. After the restoration he became editor of the "Constitutionnel," which he rendered one of the most popular of the liberal organs of Paris. His "Letters on Paris," which appeared in the "Minerve," were read with avidity. He sat in the Chamber of Deputies from 1822 to 1839, when he was raised to the peerage. He was author of numerous comedies and operas. Died in 1845.

See SAINTE-BEUVE, "Causeries du Lundi;" LÉON THIESSÉ, "M. Étienne; Essai biographique et littéraire," 1853; "Nouvelle Biographie Générale."

Étienne or Estienne, [Eng. STE′PHENS; Lat. STEPH′-ANUS,] (HENRY I.,) born in Paris about 1470 or 1460, was the head of a remarkable family of printers and scholars, who greatly promoted the progress of learning by the issue of good editions of classic authors. He began to print books about 1503, and chose the device "Plus olei quam vini," ("More oil than wine.") His publications were chiefly scientific or theological. He died in 1520, leaving three sons, Francis, Robert, and Charles. Simon de Colines married his widow, and continued the business in partnership with Francis.

Étienne or Estienne, (HENRY II.,) son of Robert Étienne, (the first of that name,) born in Paris in 1528, is considered by some the most eminent of the whole family. In childhood he showed a remarkable aptitude in acquiring the Latin and Greek languages, and about the age of eighteen he began to assist his father in his business. In 1547 he visited Italy, where he passed three years in the search of ancient literary treasures. He established a press in Paris about 1556, and adopted as his emblem the olive-tree. At the death of his father, in 1559, Henry appears to have removed to Geneva and to have taken charge of his father's establishment. The number of works which he printed and edited is immense. His celebrated Greek "Thesaurus," or "Dictionary," (1572,) would alone insure him an enduring reputation. The learned bestowed on this the highest eulogies; but the sale of it was retarded by its great price, (especially after an abridgment was published by Scapula,) and the author was involved in pecuniary difficulties. He published, among others, editions of Herodotus, Æschylus, Plato, Horace, Virgil, Pliny, and Plutarch. In the latter part of his time he led a wandering life, passing several years in Paris, and in other parts of France. He professed the Reformed religion, and was one of the most learned men that have ever lived. He died in Lyons in 1598, leaving one son, Paul, and a daughter, who was the wife of Isaac Casaubon.

See MAITTAIRE, "Stephanorum Historia," 1709; RENOUARD, "Annales des Estienne," 1843; FIRMIN DIDOT, "Observations sur Henri Estienne," 1826; LÉON FEUGÈRE, "Essai sur la Vie et les Ouvrages de H. Estienne," 1853; "London Quarterly Review" for April, 1865; also AMBROSE FIRMIN DIDOT's notice in the "Nouvelle Biographie Générale."

Étienne or Estienne, (HENRY III.,) son of Robert, (the second of that name,) became treasurer of the French royal palaces. He had a son Henry, who had some reputation as a poet, and was the author of the "Art of making Devices" and "The Triumphs of Louis the Just," (1649.)

Étienne or Estienne, (PAUL,) son of Henry Étienne, (the second of that name,) born at Geneva in 1566, applied himself to the same pursuits in which his ancestors had acquired such fame. After travelling for several years in various countries of Europe, he returned to Geneva, and became successor to his father in 1599. He produced fine editions of Euripides, Sophocles, and other classic authors. Died about 1627.

Étienne or Estienne, (ROBERT I.,) born in Paris in 1503, was one of the most celebrated printers of this family, and one of the most excellent scholars of his time. He was well versed in Latin, Greek, and Hebrew. In 1526 he established a press, from which he issued editions of the classics that were superior to all former editions and in many cases were enriched with notes and prefaces by himself. In 1532 he published an edition of the Bible in Latin, and in the same year an important

original work, "Thesaurus Linguæ Latinæ," which has often been reprinted. In 1539 he was appointed printer to the king. As Étienne was a Protestant, this favour excited the jealousy of the doctors of the Sorbonne, who instigated a charge of heresy against him; but he was protected by Francis I. as long as the latter lived. After the accession of Henry II., (1547,) the vexations to which he was subjected by the Catholics, who wished to stop the sale of his Bible, induced him to remove to Geneva in 1552. He compiled the first "Latin-French Dictionary," (1543,) which was much esteemed. His contemporaries ranked him among the greatest scholars that ever lived. He died in 1559, leaving three sons, Henry, Robert, and Francis.

See MAITTAIRE, "Stephanorum Historia," 1709; NICÉRON, "Mémoires;" A. F. DIDOT's article in the "Nouvelle Biographie Générale;" also "Essai sur la Typographie;" also "London Quarterly Review" for April, 1865.

Étienne or Estienne, (ROBERT II.,) son of the preceding, born in Paris about 1530. As he preferred the old religion, he refused to follow his father to Geneva, and opened a printing-office in Paris about 1556. In 1561 he received the title of printer to the king. Died in 1571, leaving two sons, Robert and Henry.

Étienne or Estienne, (ROBERT III.,) son of the preceding, was born in Paris, and commenced business as a printer in 1572. He was a man of talents and cultivation, and author of several poetical pieces. He translated the "Rhetoric" of Aristotle into French. Died about 1630.

See GRESWELL, "Parisian Greek Press;" A. A. RENOUARD, "Annales des Estienne," 1843; DIDOT, "Essai sur la Typographie."

Étienne de Blois. See STEPHEN, King of England.

Étienne de Tournay, ā′te-ĕn′ deh toor′nā′, a French prelate, born at Orléans in 1132; died in 1203.

Étoile or Estoile, de l', dĕh lā′twâl′, (CLAUDE,) born in Paris about 1597, was the son of Pierre, noticed below. He was one of the first members of the French Academy, and enjoyed the favour of Cardinal Richelieu. His principal productions were "The Fair Slave," a tragi-comedy, and some fugitive poems. Died in 1651.

Étoile or Estoile, de l', (PIERRE,) a French chronicler, born in Paris about 1544, was a crier (grand audien-cier) of the chancery. He left a promiscuous journal of events, anecdotes, manners, customs, etc. during the reigns of Henry III. and Henry IV., (1574–1610,) which was published, the first part in 1621 and the second part in 1719. It is highly prized by antiquaries and students of history, and appears to have been written with candour. Died in 1611.

See MORÉRI, "Dictionnaire Historique."

Ettmüller, ĕt′mül′ler, (ERNST MORITZ LUDWIG,) a German philologist, born at Gersdorf, near Löbau, in 1802. He is distinguished for his researches in ancient German literature. In 1833 he became professor of German at Zurich. He published, besides editions of old German poets, several epic poems, among which is "The Chiefs of the Royal German Houses," ("Deutsche Stammkönige," 1844,) also an "Anglo-Saxon Lexicon," (1852.)

Ettmüller, (MICHAEL,) an eminent German physician, born at Leipsic in 1644. He graduated in 1668, and became a member of the Faculty of Medicine in 1676. He acquired great popularity as professor of botany and surgery in Leipsic. His works were often reprinted, with the title of "Opera Omnia." Died in 1683.

See ERSCH und GRUBER, "Allgemeine Encyklopaedie."

Ettmüller, (MICHAEL ERNST,) a son of the preceding, was born at Leipsic in 1673. He practised in Leipsic, and was successively professor of anatomy, physiology and medicine in the university of that city. Died in 1732.

See ERSCH und GRUBER, "Allgemeine Encyklopaedie."

Et′tȳ, (WILLIAM,) an eminent English historical painter, born at York in 1787, was a pupil of Sir Thomas Lawrence. He visited Italy in 1816, and again in 1822, and copied with rapidity many of the old masters. His picture of "Cleopatra arriving in Cilicia," exhibited in the Academy in 1821, was very successful. In 1824 he was elected an associate of the Royal Academy. His favourite subjects were nude female figures. He attained a high rank among English painters, and is considered

ā, ē, ī, ō, ū, ȳ, long; ă, ĕ, ŏ, same, less prolonged; ă, ĕ, ĭ, ŏ, ŭ, ȳ, short; ạ, ẹ, ị, ọ, obscure; fär, fâll, fät; mĕt; nŏt; gŏŏd; mŏŏn;

unrivalled as a colorist. Among his best productions are "Pandora crowned by the Seasons," (1824,) "The Combat: Woman pleading for the Vanquished," (1825,) "Joan of Arc," "Ulysses and the Sirens," and "The Judgment of Paris," (1826.) In 1848 a collection of one hundred and thirty of his pictures was exhibited in London. Died in 1849.

See his "Autobiography;" A. GILCHRIST, "Life of William Etty," 1855; "Fraser's Magazine" for August, 1855.

Eubœus, ū-bee′us, [Εὔβοιος,] OF PAROS, a celebrated Greek writer of parodies, lived about 350 B.C. His works are not extant.

Eubulide. See EUBULIDES.

Eū-bu′lī-dēṣ, [Gr. Εὐβουλίδης; Fr. EUBULIDE, uh′bü′-lèd′,] a Greek philosopher of the Megaric school, was a native of Miletus and an adversary of Aristotle. He flourished probably about 350 B.C. He was the reputed author of several sophistical syllogisms, among which was the *sorites,* and was one of the successors of Euclid in the school of Megara.

See MALLET, "Histoire de l'École de Mégare."

Eubulides, [Εὐβουλίδης,] a Greek statuary of uncertain date. He made a group of statues of Apollo, Athena, Zeus, and the Muses, which he dedicated in a temple at Athens. This group was found in 1837.

Eū-bu′lus, [Εὔβουλος,] an eminent Greek comic poet of the middle comedy, lived at Athens about 375 B.C. He composed many comedies on mythological subjects, and in simple, elegant language. Small fragments of his works are extant.

See CLINTON, "Fasti Hellenici."

Eu-ehe′rĭ-us, [Fr. EUCHER, uh′shaiR′,] a native of Gaul, became Bishop of Lyons about 434 A.D. He wrote several religious works, which are extant. Died about 450 A.D.

Eucleides or **Euclides.** See EUCLID.

Eū′clid, Eū-cli′dēs, Eū-klī′dēs or **Eū-clei′dēs,** [Gr. Εὐκλείδης; Fr. EUCLIDE, uh′klèd′,] OF ALEXANDRIA, a celebrated Greek geometer, whose name is nearly synonymous with geometry, but of whose life we have only scanty information. He taught mathematics in the capital of Egypt in the reign of the first Ptolemy, (323 –283 B.C.,) and appears to have been a disciple of the Platonic philosophy. Having been asked by Ptolemy if geometry could be mastered by some easier method than the ordinary one, he returned the witty and celebrated answer, "There is no royal road to geometry." He was the editor or author of the most ancient systems of geometry which are extant, and surpassed all competitors in the luminous exposition of his theorems and the rigorous order of his demonstrations. For about two thousand years no improvement was made on his labours, and his Elements were considered an almost perfect standard.

See DELAMBRE, "Histoire de l'Astronomie ancienne;" MONTUCLA, "Histoire des Mathématiques;" SMITH, "Dictionary of Greek and Roman Biography and Mythology."

Euclid, Euclides, Euklides, or **Eucleides,** [Gr. Εὐκλείδης; Fr. EUCLIDE,] OF MEG′ARA, a Greek philosopher, an eminent disciple of Socrates, flourished about 400 B.C. He also derived some of his doctrines from the Eleatic school. On the death of Socrates, 399 B.C., he removed to Megara, where he founded the school called Megaric or Dialectic. He appears to have combined in his system the ethics of Socrates with the ontology or metaphysics of the Eleatics. In the fifteenth century he was often confounded with Euclid the great geometer.

See MALLET, "Histoire de l'École de Mégare;" G. H. LEWES, "Biographical History of Philosophy;" "Dictionnaire des Sciences philosophiques."

Euclide. See EUCLID and EUCLIDES.

Eū-cli′dēs or **Eū-clei′dēs** [Gr. Εὐκλείδης; Fr. EUCLIDE, uh′klèd′] was archon of Athens in 403 B.C. During his archonship the ancient laws of Solon were restored.

Euclides, an Athenian sculptor, mentioned by Pausanias, lived about 372 B.C.

Euclides, a Spartan general, a brother of Cleomenes III., was killed at the battle of Sellasia, 223 B.C.

Euclides, (the geometrician.) See EUCLID OF ALEXANDRIA.

Euclides, (the philosopher.) See EUCLID OF MEGARA.

Eū′cra-tēs, [Gr. Εὐκράτης; Fr. EUCRATE, uh′kRȁt′,] an Athenian general, a brother of Nicias, lived about 420 B.C. He was put to death by the Thirty Tyrants.

Eucratide. See EUCRATIDES.

Eū-crat′ĭ-dēs, [Gr. Εὐκρατίδης; Fr. EUCRATIDE, uh′-kRȁ′tèd′,] a powerful king of Bactria, reigned probably between 180 and 150 B.C., and was contemporary with Mithridates I. of Parthia. He waged war against Demetrius, King of India, and made extensive conquests in the northern part of that empire. He was assassinated by his own son.

Eūc-te′mon, [Εὐκτήμων,] an Athenian astronomer, who lived about 432 B.C., was a friend and associate of Meton, the inventor of the cycle of nineteen years. He corrected the time assigned by Hesiod for the heliacal setting of the Pleiades.

Eudæmon, ū-dee′mon, (JOHANNES ANDREAS,) born in the isle of Candia about 1560, came to Rome in his youth, and joined the Jesuits in 1581. He was a professor of philosophy and rector of the Greek College in Rome. He wrote an apology for Henry Garnet, an English Jesuit, which was answered by Isaac Casaubon, and he was the reputed author of a libel against Louis XIII. of France, "Ad Ludovicum XIII. Admonitio," (1625.) Died in 1625.

Eū-dam′ĭ-das, [Εὐδαμίδας,] a Spartan general, who lived between 400 and 375 B.C.

Eudamidas, a king of Sparta, a son of Archidamus III., began to reign about 330 B.C.

Eudème. See EUDEMUS.

Eū-de′mus [Gr. Εὐδημος; Fr. EUDÈME, uh′dȁm′] of Rhodes, a Greek Peripatetic philosopher, who flourished about 330 B.C. He was one of the principal disciples of Aristotle, and rendered important services as editor and commentator of the works of his master. Several modern critics ascribe to Eudemus certain works which others suppose to have been written by Aristotle himself. He was the author of a "History of Geometry and Astronomy," which is not extant.

See FABRICIUS, "Bibliotheca Græca;" DIOGENES LAERTIUS.

Eudemus, [Gr. Εὐδημος; Fr. EUDÈME,] a general of Alexander the Great. He obtained command of the army left in India, and, after the death of Alexander, conquered the dominions of Porus, whom he killed by insidious means. He joined Eumenes in a war against Antigonus, by whom he was put to death about 316 B.C.

Eudemus, a celebrated Greek anatomist, who lived probably in the third century B.C. According to Galen, he was a contemporary of Erasistratus.

Eudes. See EUDO.

Eū′dēs, ? [Fr. pron. ud,] Count of Paris, was the eldest son of Robert, Duke of France. In 885 A.D. he ably defended Paris against the Normans for nearly a year. At the death of Charles le Gros, in 888, Eudes was elected King of France by many of the nobles. The throne being contested by Charles III., Eudes made peace by ceding to him the country between the Seine and the Rhine. Died in 898.

Eudes I., Duke of Burgundy, succeeded his brother, Hugh (Hugues) I., in 1078. He once attacked Anselm, Archbishop of Canterbury, with the design to rob him, but was so affected by his venerable aspect that he changed his mind. He afterwards departed on a crusade to Palestine, and died in Cilicia in 1103.

Eudes II., Duke of Burgundy, was the son of Hugh II., whom he succeeded in 1142. In 1143 he compelled Thibaut of Champagne to render homage for the county of Troyes and other fiefs. Died in 1162, and left the duchy to Hugues III.

Eudes III., grandson of Eudes II., became Duke of Burgundy in 1190. He refused the chief command of the crusaders in 1201, and remained at home. In 1214 he commanded a wing of the French army at the battle of Bouvines. Died in 1218. His son, Hugh IV., was his heir.

Eudes IV., Duke of Burgundy, was the son of Robert II., and succeeded his brother, Hugh V., in 1315. He married in 1318 the daughter of Philip, King of France. In a long and prosperous reign he was a powerful support to the throne of Charles the Fair, who was his nephew, and of Philip of Valois, who married Eudes's sister. Died in 1350.

Eudes, Count of Champagne, was an ambitious and warlike baron, and one of the most powerful feudatories of the kingdom. In an attempt to make himself master of Lorraine, he was defeated and killed in 1037.

Eudes, ud, (JEAN,) a French priest, born at Ry, near Argentan, in 1601, was a brother of Mézeray the historian. About 1645 he founded for the promotion of missions a new community called Eudistes, which was dissolved at the Revolution. He wrote several devotional works. Died in 1680.

Eudes de Mézeray. See MÉZERAY.

Eū′do [Fr. EUDON, uh′dòN′] or **Eudes,** Duke of Aquitaine and Vasconie, (Gascony,) born in 665 A.D., succeeded his father Boggison about 681. He added to his dominions large tracts obtained by conquest from the Kings of Austrasia and Neustria. In 720 a large army of Saracens invaded his dominions, and were signally defeated near Toulouse, the capital of Eudo. About 732 Aquitaine was invaded by Abderrahman the Saracen, who defeated Eudo. The latter then solicited the aid of his former enemy, Charles Martel, who gained an important victory over the Saracens at Poitiers. Died in 735 A.D.

Eudocia, ū-do′she-a, [Gr. Εὐδοκία; Fr. EUDOCIE, uh′do′se′,] sometimes called **Eudoxia,** a Roman empress, distinguished for her beauty and talents, the wife of Theodosius II., was born at Athens about 394 A.D., and was called ATHENAÏS before her conversion to Christianity. She was married in 421 A.D. Theodosius became jealous, and banished her in 449 to Palestine, where she died in 460 or 461. She wrote several poems, among which was a Paraphrase of the first Eight Books of the Old Testament.

See GIBBON, "History of the Decline and Fall of the Roman Empire."

Eudocia. See EUDOXIA.
Eudocie. See EUDOCIA.
Eudokia. See EUDOCIA.
Eudon. See EUDO.

Eū-do′rus, [Gr. Εὐδωρος; Fr. EUDORE, uh′doR′,] a Greek philosopher, who lived probably before the Christian era, and was a commentator on Aristotle's "Metaphysics."

Eudoxe. See EUDOXUS.
Eudoxia. See EUDOCIA.

Eu-dox′ĭ-ạ, [Gr. Εὐδοξία; Fr. EUDOXIE, uh′dok′se′,] sometimes called **Eudocia,** Empress of the East, was of French origin, and was married to Arcadius in 395 A.D. She acquired a complete ascendency over that feeble prince, and procured the exile of Chrysostom, Patriarch of Constantinople. Her son reigned as Theodosius II.

Eudoxia or **Eudocia,** a Roman empress, daughter of Theodosius II. and Eudocia, noticed above, became the wife of Valentinian III. Petronius Maximus, having assassinated the emperor and usurped the throne, (455 A.D.,) compelled Eudoxia to be his wife. She avenged herself by inviting Genseric the Vandal, who sacked Rome and carried her to Africa.

See GIBBON, "History of the Decline and Fall of the Roman Empire."

Eudoxia or **Eudocia** was the wife of Constantine Ducas, who became Emperor of Constantinople in 1059. He died in 1067, leaving three minor sons, Constantine, Michael, and Andronicus, under the tutelage of their mother. She married Romanus Diogenes in 1068, and three years later was forced to resign the royal power to her son Michael. She was the author of a learned work, entitled "Ionia," on the genealogy and metamorphoses of gods, heroes, and heroines.

Eudoxie. See EUDOXIA.

Eū-dox′ĭ-us, a native of Armenia. He embraced the doctrines of Arius in their full extent, and was chosen Bishop of Antioch about 356, and Patriarch of Constantinople in 360. Died in 370.

Eudoxius, surnamed HEROS, or THE HERO, a Roman jurist, who lived about the fifth century.

Eū-dox′us, [Gr. Εὐδοξυς; Fr. EUDOXE, uh′doks′,] a celebrated Greek astronomer, born at Cnidus, in Caria, lived about 370 B.C. He was a pupil of Archytas, and a friend or disciple of Plato. He opened a school in Athens, which was very flourishing. Pliny informs us that he approximately determined the length of the year

at 365¼ days. Eudoxus is also said to have originated the doctrine of the concentric solid crystalline spheres, by which the apparent motions of the sun, moon, and planets were explained. Cicero thought him the greatest astronomer that had ever lived. His works are not extant.

See DELAMBRE, "Histoire de l'Astronomie ancienne."

Eudoxus, an Athenian comic poet of the new comedy, is supposed to have lived in the third century B.C.

Eudoxus OF CYZICUS, a Greek navigator, who lived about 130 B.C., and was sent by Ptolemy Evergetes on an exploring or trading expedition to India, from which he returned with success. It is supposed he afterwards attempted to reach India by sailing round Africa, but that he failed in that enterprise. He made no important discoveries.

See FABRICIUS, "Bibliotheca Græca;" BOEHMER, "Dissertatio de Eudoxo," 1715; "Nouvelle Biographie Générale."

Eū-gạ-le′nus, (SEVERIN,) a Dutch physician, born at Dokkum, wrote a "Treatise on the Scurvy," (1588,) which was often reprinted.

Eū′gạ-mon, [Εὐγάμων,] a Greek epic poet of Cyrene, lived probably about 560 B.C. He wrote a poem called "Telegonia," which was designed as a continuation of the "Odyssey:" it is not extant.

Eugen, the German of EUGENIUS and EUGENE, which see.

Eugène, the French of EUGENIUS, which see.

Eū-gēne′, [Fr. EUGÈNE, uh′zhẹn′; Ger. EUGEN, oi-gān′,] PRINCE, (or, more fully, FRANÇOIS EUGÈNE de Savoy—dẹh sä′vwä′,) one of the most celebrated generals of modern times, born in Paris in 1663, was the grandson of the Duke of Savoy. His father was Eugene Maurice, Count de Soissons, and his mother Olympia Mancini, a niece of Cardinal Mazarin. He was destined for the church, but, disliking the study of theology, he applied to Louis XIV. for the command of a regiment, which was refused. Deeply resenting this refusal, he offered his services, in 1683, to the Emperor of Austria, by whom he was so rapidly promoted in the war against the Turks that he was général-major at the siege of Belgrade, in 1688. In 1691 he was appointed to command the Imperial army in Piedmont, where he gained advantages over the French, and received the commission of field-marshal.

About 1694 he rejected the offer of a marshal's bâton, with a large pension, which Louis XIV. proposed to him as an inducement to return to the French service. He received the command of the Austrian army of Hungary, and in 1697 gained a decisive victory over the Turks at Zenta. The war of the Spanish succession soon called him to a more arduous and brilliant career. In 1701 he commanded in Italy, where he outgeneralled the able French marshal Catinat, and, by an act of successful audacity, surprised Villeroi in Cremona and made him a prisoner. Vendôme, having taken the command, proved himself a more equal match for Eugene, who at the indecisive battle of Luzara, in 1702, lost the best part of his army. At the end of this campaign he was made president of the council of war in Vienna. Eugene and the Duke of Marlborough being associated in the command of the allies, their congenial qualities and hearty co-operation contributed greatly to their success. On the 13th of August, 1704, they defeated the French at the famous battle of Blenheim. To check the victorious French army, he was again sent to Italy in 1705, and, engaging with the Duke of Vendôme, was wounded and defeated at the battle of Cassano. But in 1706 he gained a complete victory at Turin, and drove the French out of Italy. He returned to Vienna in 1707, and was received with great applause. Appointed to command the Imperial army in Flanders, he co-operated with Marlborough in the victory of Oudenarde, (1708,) and in the great battle of Malplaquet, (1709,) which the allies claimed as a victory, although they lost 25,000 men. Eugene, who advised the attack against the opinion of the Dutch deputies, was censured for temerity in this affair.

In 1712 he performed a diplomatic mission to London, but did not succeed in preventing the defection of the English from the alliance against France, or in restoring Marlborough to the command from which he had just been dismissed. He returned to the army in Flanders in 1712, and, having made another campaign with little success, began to think of peace. In March, 1714, he signed with Marshal Villars a treaty of peace at Rastadt. In 1716 and 1717 he gained great victories at Peterwaradin and Belgrade over the Turks, who were vastly superior in number. After the end of this war he was employed many years in civil affairs, and was treated with great honour and confidence by Charles VI. of Germany. He died, having never been married, in 1736. He was regarded by some as the greatest general of his time, though he made no remarkable improvements in the art of war. His success was due not so much to skill in strategy as to his audacity and decision, the admirable rapidity of his *coup-d'œil*, and his promptitude to perceive and rectify his errors.

See JOHN CAMPBELL, "Military History of Prince Eugene and the Duke of Marlborough," 2 vols., 1736; "Histoire du Prince Eugène," by MAUVILLON, 5 vols., 1740; DUMONT and ROUSSET, "Histoire militaire du Prince Eugène," 1729-43; FERRARI, "De Rebus gestis Eugenii," 1747; PRINCE DE LIGNE, "Vie du Prince Eugène," 1809; MAJOR-GENERAL J. MITCHELL, "Biographies of Eminent Soldiers of the Last Four Centuries," 1865; F. VON KAUSLER, "Leben des Prinzen Eugen von Savoyen," 2 vols., 1838-39; "Edinburgh Review" for November, 1810.

Eugène de Beauharnais. See BEAUHARNAIS.

Eū-ġen'ĭ-cus, an eloquent Greek theologian, became Archbishop of Ephesus in 1436 A.D. He opposed the union of the Greek with the Latin Church, with great eloquence and vehemence, at the Council of Florence, (1438.) Died in 1447.

Eugénie, uh'zhǎ'ne', (or, more fully, EUGÉNIE MARIE de Montijo—deh môn'te'zho',) Empress of France, a daughter of the Count of Montijo, a Spanish grandee, was born at Granada, Spain, on the 5th of May, 1826. Her mother, Maria Manuela Kirkpatrick, was of Scottish extraction. Eugenie received the title of Countess of Teba, and was educated in France and England. In 1851 she appeared at the festivals of L'Elysée, Paris, where her beauty and graces attracted the notice of Louis Napoleon, to whom she was married in January, 1853.

See "Notice sur l'Impératrice des Français" etc., Paris, 1853; VAPEREAU, "Dictionnaire universel des Contemporains," 1858; "Eminent Women of the Age," 1868.

Eugenios Bulgaris. See EUGENIUS BULGARIS.

Eū-ġe'nĭ-us, a Greek physician, mentioned by Galen, lived probably about the first century.

Eugenius, a Gaul, who was noted for his rhetorical talents, and was proclaimed emperor about 392 A.D. He was defeated by Theodosius and put to death in 394.

Eugenius [Fr. EUGÈNE, uh'zhǎn'; Ger. EUGEN, oi-gān'] I., a native of Rome, was elected pope in 654 as successor to Martin I., who was banished by the emperor Constans II. Died in 658.

Eugenius II., a Roman by birth, was elected pope in 824 A.D. in place of Pascal I. He held a council at Rome in 826 for the reformation of the clergy. This council issued an injunction that the believers should learn to read and write. He died in 827, and was succeeded by Valentinus.

Eugenius III., (BERNARD OF PISA,) elected pope in 1145, as successor to Lucius II., was a native of Pisa, and a disciple of Saint Bernard. At this period the Roman senate and people, excited by the preaching of Arnaldo da Brescia, were in a state of revolt against the papal power. The pope, therefore, retired to Viterbo, and then to France, where he favoured the second crusade by the offer of indulgences. He returned to Rome about 1152, and died in 1153. Anastasius IV. succeeded him.

Eugenius IV., (GABRIELE CONDOLMERO,) born at Venice about 1383, was chosen pope in 1431. He was soon involved in a contest with the Council of Bâle, which had been convoked by the late pope, Martin V., for the reformation of the Church, and which refused to own his supremacy. Having failed in an attempt to dissolve this council, he ordered them to transfer their sessions to Ferrara. They summoned him to appear before the council in sixty days; and he answered by a bull declaring the council dissolved, and calling another at Ferrara in 1437. The council then deposed the pope for contumacy, (1438,) and elected in his stead Amadeus of Savoy, who assumed the name of Felix V. Eugenius, however, persisted in his course, and anathematized the bishops who remained at Bâle. Thus a great schism in the Church was produced, which continued until the

death of Eugenius. A formal but insincere convention was signed in 1439 by Eugenius and John Palæologus for the reunion of the Latin and Greek Churches. He waged war against the Duke of Milan and the King of Aragon, and instigated the Kings of Poland and Hungary to violate their treaty with the Turks. He died in 1447, when Nicholas V. was chosen his successor, and Felix V. resigned.

See PLATINA, "Vitæ Pontificum;" ARTAUD DE MONTOR. "Histoire des souverains Pontifes;" GIBBON, "History of the Decline and Fall of the Roman Empire," chap. lxvi.

Eugenius, SAINT, [Fr. SAINT-EUGÈNE, sân'tuh'zhân'; Ger. SANKT EUGEN, sânkt oi-gān',] was chosen Bishop of Carthage about 480 A.D., when the church was divided between the Catholics and the Arians, the latter of whom were favoured by the Vandal king Huneric. A few years later the Arians persecuted their opponents, and exiled Eugenius. He wrote an "Exposition of the Catholic Faith," and other works. Died in 505 A.D.

Eū-ġe'nĭ-us or **Eū-ġe'nĭ-os Bul-ġā'ris,** a Greek prelate, born at Corfù in 1716. He taught philosophy at Corfu, Yánina, and Constantinople. His reputation having spread to the court of Russia, the empress Catherine, in 1775, made him Archbishop of Slavonia and Cherson. His writings, which are in Greek, have contributed much to the revival of learning and science in Greece. , He published a "Treatise on Logic," (1766,) and a poetical Greek version of Virgil, (1786-94.) It is stated that his scientific works are written in ancient Greek, and the others in modern. Died in 1806.

Eū'ġe-on OF SAMOS, an ancient Greek historian, lived about 500 B.C.

Euhemerus. See EVEMERUS.

Euklides. See EUCLID and EUCLIDES.

Eū-lā'lĭ-a, [Fr. EULALIE, uh'lǎ'le',] SAINT, a Christian martyr, born at Merida, in Spain, about 290 A.D. She perished at the stake under the reign of Maximian, aged about fourteen.

See TILLEMONT, "Mémoires ecclésiastiques."

Euler, yoo'ler, [Ger. pron. oi'ler,] (CHRISTOPH,) a son of Leonard, born in 1743, became a major in the Russian army, and cultivated astronomy with success. He was selected with others by the Academy of Saint Petersburg to observe the transit of Venus in 1769.

See ERSCH und GRUBER, "Allgemeine Encyklopaedie."

Euler, (JOHANN ALBRECHT,) the eldest son of Leonard Euler, born in Saint Petersburg in 1734, inherited a good share of his father's taste for mathematics. Having resided some years in Berlin, he returned to Saint Petersburg about 1766, and obtained a chair of philosophy. He afterwards served as secretary of the Imperial Academy, and councillor of state. In 1762 he shared with Clairaut the prize proposed by the Academy of Saint Petersburg on the theory of comets. He assisted his father in a treatise on the theory of the moon, which obtained the prize of the Academy of Paris in 1770. He wrote many other treatises on astronomy, optics, and physics. Died in Saint Petersburg in 1800.

See ERSCH und GRUBER, "Allgemeine Encyklopaedie."

Euler, (KARL,) second son of the great geometer, born in Saint Petersburg in 1740, graduated at Halle. Returning to Saint Petersburg in 1766, he was appointed physician to the court and to the Imperial Academy. He gained the prize proposed by the Academy of Paris in 1760 for a treatise on the Mean Velocity of the Planets.

See ERSCH und GRUBER, "Allgemeine Encyklopaedie."

Euler, (LEONARD,) a celebrated Swiss geometer, born at Bâle on the 15th of April, 1707, was the pupil of John Bernoulli in his native city. About 1727 he accompanied Nicholas and Daniel Bernoulli to Saint Petersburg, whither they had been invited to teach in the new Academy, in which he obtained a place as assistant professor. In 1733 he succeeded Daniel as professor of mathematics. Here he composed an immense number of memoirs, which display a profound, inventive genius and an extraordinary fecundity of mind. It is stated that he wrote more than half of the forty-six volumes published by the Academy of Saint Petersburg from 1727 to 1783. From 1741 to 1766 he lived in Berlin, having been invited by Frederick the Great to assist in the formation of the Berlin Academy, which he enriched with his writings. In 1755 he was chosen an associate of the Academy of Sciences of Paris, which awarded him several prizes. Returning to Saint Petersburg, he published, in French, his popular work on physical philosophy, "Letters to a German Princess," (1768.) He greatly improved the integral calculus, the indeterminate analysis, and the science of mechanics by analysis, and is reckoned one of the greatest mathematicians of the eighteenth century. Among his principal works are "Mechanics; or the Science of Motion analytically explained," ("Mechanica; sive Motus Scientia analyticé exposita," 2 vols., 1736,) "Introduction to the Analysis of Infinites," ("Introductio in Analysin Infinitorum," 1748,) a "Treatise on Naval Science," (1749,) a Treatise on the Integral Calculus, ("Institutiones Calculi Integralis," 1768,) a "Treatise on Dioptrics," (1771,) and a "Theory of the Moon's Motion," (1772.) He was blind during the last sixteen years of his life. He died in September, 1783. He left several sons, who became eminent in science. "His genius," says Condorcet, "was equally capable of the greatest efforts and of the most continuous labour. He multiplied his productions marvellously, and yet was original in each. His brain was always active, and his soul always calm." Euler's memory was so extraordinary that he knew, it is said, the "Æneid" by heart. He was a man of deep and earnest religious convictions, and had family worship daily in his own house.

See CONDORCET, "Éloge de L. Euler;" NICHOLAS VON FUSS, "Éloge de L. Euler;" "Nouvelle Biographie Générale," article "Euler."

Eumathius or **Eumathe**. See EUSTATHIUS.

Eumèle. See EUMELUS.

Eū-me'lus, [Gr. Εὔμηλος; Fr. EUMÈLE, uh'mạl',] a son of Admetus and Alcestis, was one of the chiefs of the Greek army which besieged Troy. His horses were distinguished for fleetness.

Eumelus [Εὔμηλος] of Corinth, a very ancient Greek epic poet, flourished about 750 B.C. His works are lost.

Eumelus, a Greek painter, who lived probably about 200 A.D. His picture of Helen was placed in the Forum at Rome.

Eumène. See EUMENES.

Eū'mẹ-nēs, [Gr. Εὐμένης; Fr. EUMÈNE, uh-mạn',] a favourite officer and confidential secretary of Alexander the Great, was born at Cardia, in the Thracian Chersonesus, about 360 B.C. He attended Alexander in his expedition against Persia about 330 B.C., commanded a division of the army, and was highly esteemed by that prince for his bravery and military talents. When the conquests of their departed chief were divided among the Macedonian generals, Eumenes received Cappadocia, Pontus, and Paphlagonia. He was an ally of Perdiccas in the war between the latter and Ptolemy, and gained a complete victory over Craterus in the year 321. In this action Craterus was killed. After the death of Perdiccas (321) Antipater and Antigonus combined against Eumenes, who defended himself for several years. The Macedonians were jealous of Eumenes because he was an alien. At length, by means of treachery, Antigonus took him prisoner and put him to death in 317 or 316 B.C. He was one of the few among Alexander's officers who continued loyal to the royal family.

See "Life of Eumenes," in PLUTARCH, who compares him with Sertorius; CORNELIUS NEPOS, "Eumenes;" ARRIAN, "Anabasis;" B. GEER, "Specimen historicum de Eumene Cardiano," 1838; THIRLWALL, "History of Greece."

Eumenes [Fr. EUMÈNE] **I.**, King or Governor of Pergamus. He began to reign about 262 B.C., defeated Antiochus Soter near Sardis, and died about 240 B.C. He was succeeded by his cousin, Attalus I.

Eumenes II., King of Pergamus, a son of Attalus I., began to reign in 197 B.C. He was a faithful and efficient ally of the Romans in their war against Antiochus the Great about 190, and was rewarded by the addition to his kingdom of Mysia, Lydia, and Phrygia. By his political sagacity he greatly increased the importance of his kingdom, which prospered in a long peace. He patronized the arts and sciences, and founded at Pergamus a celebrated library, which became a rival to that of Alexandria. He died about 159 B.C.

See POLYBIUS, "History;" APPIAN, "Syriaca;" LIVY, "History of Rome."

Eū-men'ĭ-dēs [Gr. Εὐμενίδης; Ger. EUMENIDEN, oi'meh-nee'den] or **E-rin'nȳ-ēs**, often called, in Latin, **Fu'rĭ-æ** and **Di'ræ**, the Greek name of the Furies, or goddesses who punished crimes in this world and after death, and pursued the guilty with burning torches. Some writers limit the number of Furies to three, namely, Tisiphone, Alecto, and Megæra.

Eū-me'nĭ-us, a Latin grammarian and rhetorician, born at Autun about 260 A.D. He taught rhetoric in Rome, and then in Autun. Four of his discourses are extant, one of which is a panegyric on Constantine, spoken in his presence.

Eumolpus. See EUMOLPUS.

Eū-mol'pus, [Gr. Εὔμολπος; Fr. EUMOLPE, uh'-molp',] a Thracian, who was regarded as a priestly bard and founder of the Eleusinian mysteries, was called a son of Neptune and Chione. According to one tradition, he fought for the people of Eleusis against the Athenians, and was killed in battle.

Eunape. See EUNAPIUS.

Eū-nā'pĭ-us, [Gr. Εὐνάπιος; Fr. EUNAPE, uh'năp',] a heathen Sophist and physician, born at Sardis, in Lydia, about 347 A.D. He lived at Athens, was a Neoplatonist, and a violent opponent of Christianity. He wrote, in Greek, a work entitled "Lives of Philosophers and Sophists," which is extant. "It is of great importance for literary and philosophic history," says Boissonade, "as without it there would be an immense void in the history of Eclecticism." He left a continuation of Dexippus's history from 270 to 404 A.D., which has not come down to us.

See FABRICIUS, "Bibliotheca Græca."

Eū-ni'cus, [Εὔνικος,] an Athenian comic poet, who lived in the fifth century B.C.

Eunome. See EUNOMUS.

Eū-no'mĭ-us, [Gr. Εὐνόμιος,] the founder of an Arian sect called Eunomians, was born at Dacora, in Cappadocia, and was a man of superior talents. About 360 A.D., Eudoxius, Bishop of Antioch, ordained him Bishop of Cyzicus, but afterwards deposed him for heresy. He was an ultra-Arian, and opposed the worship of martyrs and relics. He was several times banished by successive emperors, and suffered persecution with firmness and constancy. His writings are nearly all lost, except a "Confession of Faith." Saint Basil, and Saint Gregory of Nyssa, wrote books to refute his doctrines. Died in 394 A.D.

See RITTER, "History of Christian Philosophy."

Eū'no-mus, [Gr. Εὔνομος; Fr. EUNOME, uh'nom',] one of the early kings of Sparta, supposed to have lived nine hundred years or more B.C. According to some writers, he was the father of Lycurgus. Simonides calls him a brother of Lycurgus.

Eū'nus, a native of Syria, was the leader of the insurgents in the servile war which broke out in Sicily in 135 B.C. He defeated several Roman armies in succession, but was captured about 133 B.C., and died in prison soon afterwards.

Euphante. See EUPHANTUS.

Eū-phan'tus [Gr. Εὔφαντος; Fr. EUPHANTE, uh'-fănt'] of Olynthus, a Greek poet and Pythagorean philosopher, who wrote about 330 B.C. He was a preceptor of Antigonus I. of Macedonia, to whom he dedicated a work, Περὶ Βασιλείας, ("On Royalty,") which was highly commended. He composed also numerous tragedies.

Eū-phe'mĭ-ạ, (FLAVIA ÆLIA MARCIA,) an empress of the East, was originally a slave named Lupicina, and was married to a Thracian of obscure condition, who in 518 ascended the throne of Constantinople as Justin I.

Euphorbe. See EUPHORBUS.

Eu-phor'bus, [Gr. Εὔφορβος; Fr. EUPHORBE, uh'-forb',] a brave Trojan warrior, killed by Menelaus. Pythagoras professed that his soul was the same which had animated Euphorbus.

Euphorbus, a physician, who lived at Rome in the reign of Augustus, was a brother of Antonius Musa. He was employed professionally by King Juba, who in honour of him named a certain plant Euphorbia, which is still the name of a numerous genus.

Eū-pho'rĭ-on, [Εὐφορίων,] a tragic poet of Athens, was the son of Æschylus. He is said to have gained the prize four times with his father's posthumous tragedies. He wrote several of his own, one of which was crowned in competition with Sophocles and Euripides.

Euphorion, an eminent Greek poet and grammarian, born at Chalcis, in Eubœa, about 275 B.C. He lived some years at Athens, and became librarian to Antiochus the Great about 220 B.C. He wrote epic poems entitled "Hesiodos," "Mopsopia," and "Chiliades," (Χιλιάδες;) also several epigrams. His poems were very popular among the Romans of the Augustan age; but his style was censured by Cicero and others as affectedly obscure. He was author of a celebrated treatise on grammar, and of other prose works. Only small fragments of his writings are extant.

See Vossius, "De Historicis Græcis;" Fabricius, "Bibliotheca Græca;" A. Meineke, "Dissertatio de Euphorionis Vita et Scriptis," 1823.

Euphorion, a Greek statuary, whose works were not extant in the time of Pliny, by whom he is mentioned.

Euphræus, u-free'us, or **Eū-phrā'tēs,** [Gr. Εὔφραιος or Εὐφράτης,] a native of Oreus, in Eubœa, was a disciple of Plato, and became a favourite of Perdiccas, King of Macedonia. After the death of the latter he returned to Oreus and opposed the party of Philip of Macedon.

Eū-phrā'nor, [Εὐφράνωρ,] a celebrated Greek painter and sculptor, born in Corinth, flourished between 365 and 325 B.C. He was pupil of Ariston, and a contemporary of Apelles and Praxiteles. It appears that he worked in Athens, as Pliny ranks him among Athenian artists. He was the first artist who represented heroes with proper dignity. He painted in encaustic and worked in marble and bronze, and was equally successful in painting and sculpture. Pliny and Plutarch highly applaud his productions. Among his master-pieces in painting are "The Twelve Gods," "The Battle of Mantinea," and the "Feigned Insanity of Ulysses;" and in sculpture, a statue of Paris, and colossal statues of "Valor" and "Greece."

See Pliny, "Natural History."

Euphrate. See EUPHRATES.

Euphrates. See EUPHRÆUS.

Eū-phrā'tēs, [Gr. Εὐφράτης; Fr. EUPHRATE, uh'frȧt',] an eminent Stoic philosopher, lived in the reign of Hadrian, in the second century. He was a native of Syria or Egypt, and a friend of Pliny the Younger, who eulogizes his virtues and talents, (Epist. i. 10.)

Euphrates, a heretic, who, in the second century, founded the sect of Ophites.

Eū'phron, an Athenian comic poet of the new comedy, lived about 300 B.C.

Eū-phros'y̆-ne, [Gr. Εὐφροσύνη,] one of the Three Graces, (in Greek, "Charites,") supposed to be the offspring of Venus. The Greeks personified in her the genius of Mirth or Joy. (See CHARITES.)

Euphrosyne, an empress, was the wife of Alexis III., who in 1195 obtained the throne of Constantinople by a conspiracy of which she was a chief instigator. By her courage and talents she acquired a nearly absolute ascendency over Alexis, but exposed herself to public contempt by her immoral excesses. She died in exile about 1215.

Eū'po-lis, [Εὔπολις,] an excellent Athenian comic poet of the old comedy, was born about 446 B.C., and was a rival of Aristophanes. Several of his plays obtained the honour of a triumph. He is ranked by Horace with Cratinus and Aristophanes, (see Satires, book i. iv. 1,) and in the opinion of some critics he surpassed Aristophanes in the graces of diction. He often chose political subjects, and severely satirized the persons and conduct of eminent men then living. Only small fragments of his works are extant. He is supposed to have died about 410 B.C. According to one account, he was killed in a naval action.

See Clinton, "Fasti Hellenici;" Fabricius, "Bibliotheca Græca;" Suidas, "Eupolis;" C. W. Lucas, "Cratinus et Eupolis," Bonn, 1826; Stevenart, "Étude sur le Poète Eupolis," 1850.

Eupompe. See EUPOMPUS.

Eu-pom'pus [Gr. Εὔπομπος; Fr. EUPOMPE, uh'pômp'] of Sicyon, a celebrated Greek painter, a contemporary of Zeuxis, lived about 350-370 B.C., and was the master of Pamphilus. He is called the founder of a new school, the Sicyonian. In answer to the young sculptor Lysippus, who consulted him on the choice of a model, he said, "Follow nature."

Eū'ric [Lat. EURI'CUS] or **Ev'a̧-ric,** [Lat. EVARI'CUS,] an able and warlike king of the Visigoths, began to reign in 466 A.D. He enlarged his dominions by conquest until they extended from the Loire to the Pyrenees and from the Rhone to the ocean. His alliance was courted by Franks, Romans, Vandals, and other nations. Died in 484.

See Gibbon, "History of the Decline and Fall of the Roman Empire."

Euripide. See EURIPIDES.

Eū-rip'ĭ-dēs, [Gr. Εὐριπίδης; Fr. EURIPIDE, uh're'pĕd',] one of the three great tragic poets of Greece, was born at Salamis in 480 B.C. According to a popular tradition, he was born on the day of the battle of Salamis. His parents, Mnesarchus and Clito, were Athenians who sought refuge at Salamis from the Persian invaders. He studied rhetoric under Prodicus, and philosophy or physics under Anaxagoras. About the age of twenty-five he produced his "Peliades," the first of his dramas which was performed. He maintained an animated rivalry with Sophocles, (who was his senior,) and gained the first prize in several dramatic contests. He was a friend of Socrates, who, it is said, seldom went to the theatre except when the tragedies of Euripides were performed. Euripides composed seventy-five — or, as some say, ninety-two — tragedies, of which eighteen are still extant. Among his most admired works are "Hecuba," "Ion," "Alcestis," "Medea," "Helena," "Iphigenia in Aulis," "Hippolytus," and "Bacchæ." His other extant dramas are "Heraclidæ," "The Suppliants," ("Supplices,") "Hercules Furens," "Orestes," "Troades," "Electra," "Andromache," "Iphigenia in Tauris," "Rhesus," and "Phœnissæ." His style is distinguished by elegance, perspicuity, and harmony. Cicero and Milton were great admirers of Euripides, and Aristotle calls him "the most tragic of poets." "When we look only at the highest excellences of Euripides," says Hallam, "there is perhaps a depth of pathos and an intensity of dramatic effect which Racine himself has not attained." ("Introduction to the Literature of Europe.") About the year 408 he retired from Athens, where a violent and unscrupulous faction was arrayed against him, and found repose at the court of Archelaüs, King of Macedon, who treated him with much favour. According to a prevalent but doubtful tradition, he was killed by a pack of hounds in 406 B.C.

See C. Hasse, "De Euripide Poeta," 1833; Jodrell, "Illustrations of Euripides," 3 vols.; 1781; F. Jacobs, "Animadversiones in Euripidis Tragœdias," 1790; Zirndorfer, "De Chronologia Fabularum Euripidearum," Marburg, 1839; Hartung, "Euripides Restitutus," 2 vols., 1844; Fabricius, "Bibliotheca Græca;" Bouterwek, "De Philosophia Euripidis," 1819; J. Lapaume, "De Euripidis Vita et Fabulis Dissertatio," 1848; Reuter, "Dissertatio de Æschylo, Sophocle et Euripide," 1831; "Blackwood's Magazine" for September, 1838; "Foreign Quarterly Review" for January, 1840.

Eū-ro'pa̧, [Gr. Εὐρώπη; Fr. EUROPE, uh'rop',] in classic mythology, a daughter of Agenor, King of Phœnicia, and a sister of Cadmus. The poets feigned that she was carried off by Jupiter, who previously assumed the form of a bull. She became the mother of Minos and Rhadamanthus.

Europe. See EUROPA.

Euryale. See EURYALUS.

Eū-ry̆'a̧-lus, [Gr. Εὐρύαλος; Fr. EURYALE, uh're'ȧl',] a son of Mecisteus, was one of the ARGONAUTÆ, and one of the EPIGONI, (which see.) He was distinguished for his bravery at the siege of Troy, where he was a companion of Diomede.

Euryalus, a beautiful young Trojan mentioned by Virgil. (See "Æneid," books v. and ix.)

Eū-ry̆-cli'das, [Εὐρυκλείδας,] an Athenian orator, lived about 220 B.C.

Eū-ry̆d'ĭ-çe, [Gr. Εὐρυδίκη,] the wife of Orpheus, was bitten by a serpent as she fled from Aristæus, and died. The poets feigned that Orpheus descended to the lower regions and persuaded Pluto to restore her to life on condition that she should walk behind her husband and he should not look back until they had arrived in the upper world. But Orpheus, unable to resist his longing to see her again, turned back, and thus lost her forever. (See ORPHEUS.)

See Virgil's "Georgics," book iv. 454-527.

Eurydice, [Εὐρυδίκη,] the wife of Amyntas, King of Macedonia, was the mother of Alexander, Perdiccas, and Philip, all of whom became kings; the last was the father of Alexander the Great. She is charged with attempting the life of her husband, and with taking the life of her eldest son, about 365 B.C.

Eurydice, a Macedonian princess, a daughter of Antipater, became the queen of Ptolemy, son of Lagus, about 320 B.C., and mother of Ptolemy Ceraunus. Her niece Berenice having gained her husband's affections, Eurydice retired to the court of Seleucus, King of Syria.

Eurydice, sometimes called **Ade′a,** a daughter of Amyntas III. of Macedonia. Her mother was Cynane, a half-sister of Alexander the Great. About 322 B.C. she was married to Arrhidæus, a son of King Philip. She was a rival competitor for the regency with Olympias, by whose order she was put to death, 316 B.C.

Eū-rȳl′o-ehus, [Εὐρύλοχος,] a Spartan general, who was defeated and killed in battle by the Athenians about 426 B.C.

Eū-rȳm′e-don, [Εὐρυμέδων,] an Athenian general, who took part in the Peloponnesian war. He and Sophocles commanded an army and fleet sent against Sicily in 425 B.C.; but their operations were arrested soon after their arrival by a peace or truce negotiated by Hermocrates. In conjunction with Demosthenes, Eurymedon commanded an armament sent against Syracuse in 414. He was killed in a naval battle in the harbour of that city in 413 B.C.

See PLUTARCH, "Nicias."

Eū′rȳ-phon, [Εὐρυφῶν,] an eminent Greek physician of Cnidos, said to have lived in the time of Hippocrates, about 350 B.C. He is quoted by Galen.

Eurysthée. See EURYSTHEUS.

Eurysthène. See EURYSTHENES.

Eū-rȳs′thẹ-nēs, [Gr. Εὐρυσθένης; Fr. EURYSTHÈNE, uh′rès′tàn′,] a son of Aristodemus, King of Sparta, had a twin-brother, Procles. As their mother refused to say which was the eldest, the oracle of Delphi decided that they should reign jointly. After their death the throne continued to be shared between two kings, one of whom was descended from Eurysthenes and the other from Procles.

See CLINTON, "Fasti Hellenici;" MÜLLER, "The Dorians."

Eū-rȳs′theūs, [Gr. Εὐρυσθεύς; Fr. EURYSTHÉE, uh′rès′tà′,] a fabulous king of Argos and Mycenæ, was a son of Sthenelus. Juno hastened his birth that he might have the advantage over Hercules, as the younger of the two was ordained by Jupiter to serve the other. He was a severe taskmaster, and imposed on Hercules the well-known twelve labours. (See HERCULES.) He was slain by Hyllus, a son of Hercules.

Eūs′dẹn, (Rev. LAWRENCE,) an English poet and clergyman, was born in Spotsworth, Yorkshire. Having written an epithalamium on the marriage of the Duke of Newcastle, the latter procured his appointment as poet-laureate in 1718. He wrote a few articles for the "Spectator," and some occasional poems, and was noticed in Pope's "Dunciad." Died in 1730. His version of Claudian's "Court of Venus" was highly praised by one of the editors of the "Guardian," in which it was inserted. (See "Guardian," Nos. 127 and 164.)

Eusèbe, the French for EUSEBIUS, which see.

Eū-se′bĭ-ạ, (AURELIA,) a Roman empress, was married to Constantius about 353 A.D. She patronized learning, and is charged with favouring Arianism. She died childless in 360.

Eū-se′bĭ-us, [Gr. Εὐσέβιος; Fr. EUSÈBE, uh′zầb′,] Bishop of Emesa, in Phœnicia, was born near Edessa about 300 A.D. He refused the bishopric of Alexandria, from which Athanasius was deposed in 341, and soon afterwards became Bishop of Emesa. He is said to have favoured the doctrines of the Semi-Arians. His numerous works were once admired for learning and eloquence, but are nearly all lost. Died about 360.

Eusebius OF DORYLÆUM, [Fr. EUSÈBE DE DORYLÉE, uh-zầb′ dẹh do′re′là′,] a Greek theologian of the fifth century. He became Bishop of Dorylæum, and a zealous opponent of Eutyches.

Eusebius OF NICOMEDIA, [Fr. EUSÈBE DE NICO-MÉDIE, uh′zầb′ dẹh ne′ko′mà′de′,] an eminent and am-

bitious Arian prelate, was a friend of Eusebius Pamphili. He became Bishop of Berytus and of Nicomedia. At the Council of Nice, 325 A.D., he refused to sign the condemnation of Arius, and was consequently banished; but, finding a powerful patron in Constantia, sister of the emperor, he was restored to his see. Having acquired paramount influence at court, he assembled a council at Tyre in 334, by which Athanasius was condemned. He also procured the restoration of Arius, and, after his death, became the chief of the Arian party, who were also called Eusebians. In 339 he obtained the bishopric of Constantinople. His name is identified with a modified form of Arianism, (i.e. the Homoiousian doctrine.) Died in 342 A.D.

See TILLEMONT, "Mémoires ecclésiastiques;" NEANDER, "History of the Church;" CAVE, "Historia Literaria."

Eusebius PAM′PHILI, [Fr. EUSÈBE PAMPHILE, uh′zầb′ pŏN′fèl′,] an eminent writer and theologian, called "the Father of Ecclesiastical History," was born in Palestine, probably at Cæsarea, about 266 A.D. He assumed the surname PAMPHILI in memory of his friend Pamphilus the Martyr. He was appointed Bishop of Cæsarea about 314, and retained that dignity until his death. At the Council of Nice, summoned in 325 to condemn Arius, he was selected by the emperor Constantine to deliver the opening address; but he objected to some of the terms of the creed therein adopted. He was afterwards charged with favouring Arianism, and actually used his influence to reinstate Arius. At the Council of Tyre, in 334, he was one of the bishops who censured Athanasius, the orthodox leader, and was chosen by his colleagues to defend their decision before the emperor, who was his friend. He was a man of superior talents and of great learning. His most important works (which are written in Greek) are an "Ecclesiastical History" from the Christian era to 324 A.D., a "Universal History or Chronicle," a "Life of Constantine," "Gospel Preparation," ("Preparatio Evangelica,") and a work "On the Proof or Demonstration of the Gospel," ("De Demonstratione Evangelica." He wrote many other works, which have not been preserved. His History is written in a moderate and impartial spirit, and is highly prized; but his merit as a man and a Christian is variously estimated. Jerome calls him the "Prince of the Arians." The manuscript of his "Universal History" was found at Constantinople about 1818. Died about 340.

See TILLEMONT, "Mémoires ecclésiastiques;" CAVE, "Historia Literaria;" NEANDER, "History of the Church;" GIBBON, "History of the Decline and Fall of the Roman Empire;" "Biographie Universelle;" "Nouvelle Biographie Générale."

Eusebius of Samosata, an eminent orthodox prelate, so named from the place of his birth, (the modern Sumeisat,) on the Euphrates. He was bishop of his native place in 361 A.D., and perhaps before that date. Having been intrusted with the documents which proved the election of Meletius as Bishop of Antioch, he firmly refused to give them up to the Arians, who wished to annul the election, although their wish was seconded by the order of the emperor. He was banished by Valens about 371, and restored to his see in 378 A.D. About 379 he was killed by an Arian who threw a stone on his head from the roof of a house.

See CEILLIER, "Histoire des Auteurs sacrés," etc.

Eusebius, POPE, succeeded Marcellus I. in 310 A.D., and died after a pontificate of a few months. He was a Greek by birth.

Eusebius, Bishop of Vercelli, born in Sardinia in the fourth century, was noted for his zeal against Arianism. Soon after the Council of Milan, 355 A.D., he was banished to Palestine by Constantius; but on the accession of Julian, in 361, he was relieved from persecution. He co-operated with Athanasius in the Council of Alexandria in 362. Two of his pastoral letters are extant. Died about 370.

See CEILLIER, "Histoire des Auteurs sacrés," etc.

Eustace or **Eustache.** See EUSTASIUS.

Eūs′tạce, (JOHN CHETWODE,) an English writer and Roman Catholic priest, born about 1765. He published, besides other works, "An Elegy to Burke," (1797,) and a "Classical Tour through Italy," (2 vols., 1813,) which was received with favour, but is said to be inaccurate.

ā, ē, ī, ō, ū, ȳ, *long;* à, ė, ȯ, same, less prolonged; ă, ĕ, ĭ, ŏ, ŭ, y̆, *short;* ạ, ẹ, ị, ọ, *obscure;* fâr, fâll, fât; mêt; nŏt; gŏŏd; mōōn;

The sixth edition was published in 4 vols., 1821. A supplement to this work was published by R. Colt Hoare in 1819. Eustace died at Naples in 1815.

See "London Quarterly Review" for October, 1813.

Eustache, uh'stȧsh', (DAVID,) a French Protestant minister, born in Dauphiné. He published numerous sermons and controversial works. Died about 1660.

Eustachi or **Eustachio.** See EUSTACHIUS.

Eū-stä'chī-us, [It. EUSTACHIO, ĕ-oo-stä'ke-o, or EŪ-STACHI, ĕ-oo-stä'kee,] (BARTOLOMMEO,) a pre-eminent Italian anatomist, was born at San Severino, in the March of Ancona. He studied medicine in Rome, where he also settled as a practitioner, and was professor in the college di Sapienza in 1562. But, though patronized by Cardinal Borromeo and widely celebrated as an anatomist, he did not obtain pecuniary success, and died, as he lived, in poverty. He was perhaps the greatest anatomist of his time; and probably no other anatomist, ancient or modern, has made so many discoveries. His most important work, "On the Controversies of Anatomists," ("De Anatomicorum Controversiis,") was announced by him as ready for the press, but was not published, and is not now extant. His anatomical plates, about forty in number, engraved in 1552, after having been lost a century and a half, were published in 1712, being a valuable acquisition to science, as well as a most interesting relic of their illustrious author. He also published an edition of Erotianus's Lexicon, and several treatises collected with the title "Opuscula Anatomica." A part of the ear derives from him the name of "the Eustachian tube." Died in 1574.

See HALLER, "Bibliotheca Anatomica;" CUVIER, "Histoire des Sciences naturelles;" G. C. GENTILI, "Elogio di B. Eustachio," 1837; SPRENGEL, "Geschichte der Arzeneikunde."

Eū-stä'sī-us (ū-stä'she-us) or **Eu-stä'chī-us,** [Fr. EUSTACE, us'tȧss', or EUSTACHE, us'tȧsh',] Abbé of Luxeu, (now Luxeuil,) was born in Burgundy about 560 A.D. He was employed by Saint Columbanus as teacher or director of his school at Luxeu. Died in 625.

Eustathe. See EUSTATHIUS.

Eū-stä'thī-us [Gr. Εὐστάθιος; Fr. EUSTATHE, uh'stȧt'] of Cappadocia, a Neoplatonic philosopher, was a pupil of Jamblichus, and lived about 350 A.D. He was celebrated for his eloquence.

Eustathius, Archbishop of Thessalonica, celebrated as a commentator on Homer, lived at Constantinople. He was one of the most learned men of his time. He became Bishop of Myra, in Lycia, about 1175, and afterwards Archbishop. His voluminous commentary on Homer's "Iliad" and "Odyssey" is an immense and valuable store of ancient erudition, consisting chiefly of extracts from the earlier scholiasts, as Apion, Porphyry, and Demosthenes of Thrace. It was first printed in 1542. He also wrote a commentary on Dionysius Periegetes, which is extant, and one on Pindar, which has been lost. Died about 1200.

See FABRICIUS, "Bibliotheca Græca."

Eustathius, sometimes written **Eumathius,** a Greek novelist, who is supposed to have lived in the twelfth century. His name appears as author of a licentious work in Greek called "The Drama of Hysmine and Hysminias."

Eustathius, [Gr. Εὐστάθιος; Fr. EUSTATHE,] SAINT, born at Sida, in Pamphylia, became Bishop of Berea, from which he was translated to the see of Antioch. He opposed with zeal the doctrine of Arius, and spoke eloquently on the subject at the Council of Nice, 325 A.D. Eusebius, the Arian leader, caused him to be deposed and exiled about 330. His writings are lost. Died about 337, or, according to some, in 360 A.D.

See CEILLIER, "Histoire des Auteurs sacrés," etc.

Eū-stä'thī-us Ro-mä'nus, a celebrated Byzantine jurist, who flourished at Constantinople between 950 and 1000 A.D.

Eūs'tis, (WILLIAM,) an American physician and politician, born in Cambridge, Massachusetts, in 1753. He served as a surgeon in the army during the Revolutionary war, and was elected a member of Congress in 1800. He was appointed secretary of war by President Madison in 1809, resigned in 1812, and was sent as minister to Holland in 1814. In 1823 he was elected Governor of Massachusetts. Died in 1825.

Eū-sto'chī-um, (JULIA,) a pious Roman lady, was a disciple of Saint Jerome, who dedicated to her his commentary on Isaiah. She became an inmate of a convent in Palestine in 385 A.D. Died in 419.

Eustratius, ū-strä'she-us, Bishop of Nice, lived in the twelfth century, and wrote a commentary on Aristotle.

Eū-ter'pe, [Gr. Εὐτέρπη,] a name given by the ancient Greeks to one of the nine Muses. She presided over lyric poetry, and was represented with a flute.

Euthycrate. See EUTHYCRATES.

Eū-thȳc'rạ-tēṣ, [Gr. Εὐθυκράτης; Fr. EUTHYCRATE, uh'te'krȧt',] a Greek sculptor, who lived about 300 B.C., was a son and pupil of Lysippus. His works were more remarkable for correctness and severity than for grace.

Euthydème. See EUTHYDEMUS.

Eū-thȳ-de'mus, [Gr. Εὐθύδημος; Fr. EUTHYDÈME, uh'te'dȧm',] a Greek sophist, whom Xenophon mentions as an opponent in argument of Socrates. He afterwards became a disciple of that philosopher, by whose wisdom he had been confounded.

Euthydemus, an Athenian general, who had a high command in the army which besieged Syracuse in 413 B.C.

Euthydemus, a powerful king of Bactria, formed an alliance with Antiochus the Great about 210 B.C. Silver coins of this king (with Greek inscriptions) have been found at Bokhara and Balk.

Euthyme. See EUTHYMIUS.

Eū-thȳm'ī-us, [Fr. EUTHYME, uh'tèm',] SAINT, an Armenian priest, born in 377 A.D., lived in Palestine, built several monasteries, and converted the empress Eudocia. Died in 473.

Eū-thȳm'ī-us Zig-ạ-be'nus, a Byzantine monk, lived about 1100. He wrote, in Greek, a work in defence of the orthodox faith, which was printed in 1536.

Eutocius, ū-to'she-us, [Gr. Εὐτόκιος,] a Greek geometer of Ascalon, in Palestine, lived about 550 A.D., and was the pupil of Isidorus the architect. The only extant works of this author are Commentaries on Apollonius and Archimedes. His comments on Archimedes's "Treatise on the Sphere and Cylinder" are interesting and valuable. He gives various modes for solving the problem of the duplication of the cube.

Eutrope. See EUTROPIUS.

Eū-tro'pī-us, [Fr. EUTROPE, uh'trOp',] sometimes called **Fla'vius Eutro'pius,** a Latin historian of the fourth century. He was secretary to the emperors Constantine and Julian, the latter of whom he attended in his expedition against the Parthians. He wrote an "Epitome of Roman History" ("Breviarium Rerum Romanorum") from the foundation of the city to the time of Valens, which has been popular for many centuries and extensively used as a school-book in modern times. The language is pure, and the style clear and simple. Little is known of the author's life.

See SUIDAS, "Eutropius;" GENNADIUS, "De Viris illustribus;" MOLLER, "Disputatio de Eutropio," 1685.

Eū'tȳ-chēṣ, [Gr. Εὐτύχης,] the founder or head of a heretical sect called Eutychians, born about 375 A.D., became noted for his piety and ascetic zeal, and was superior of a monastery near Constantinople. In warmly opposing a doctrine ascribed to Nestorius, he erred in the opposite extreme, teaching that there is only one nature in Christ,—that is, the divine. For this he was condemned by the Council of Constantinople in 448. His opinion, however, was adopted by the empress Eudocia and others in high station, and Theodosius II. assembled in 449 a council at Ephesus, which reversed the former decision. The Œcumenical Council of Chalcedon in 451 annulled the acts of the Council of Ephesus. This sect became numerous in the East, and received the name of Monophysites.

See PLUQUET, "Dictionnaire des Hérésies;" ALTHUSIUS, "Historia Eutychiana," 1659; "Nouvelle Biographie Générale."

Eutyches or **Eū-tȳch'ī-us,** a Latin grammarian, a disciple of Priscian, lived in the sixth century.

Eū-tȳch-ī-ā'nus, [Fr. EUTYCHIEN, uh'te'ke-ȧn',] Pope or Bishop of Rome, was a native of Tuscany. He succeeded Felix I. in 275 A.D., and died in 283.

Eū-tўҽh'ĭ-dēs [Εὐτυχίδης] OF SICYON, a Greek sculptor, who lived about 300 B.C., was a pupil of Lysippus. He made a statue of the Eurotas, which is mentioned by Pliny, "in quo artem ipso amne liquidiorem plurimi dixere," ("in which many said the art showed itself more liquid than the river itself.")

Eutychien. See EUTYCHIANUS.

Eū-tўҽh'ĭ-us, [Gr. Εὐτύχιος,] born at Fostât, in Egypt, in 876 A.D., became Patriarch of Alexandria in 933. He was learned in theology, history, and medicine, on which he wrote several works. His "Universal History" acquired a high reputation among the Orientals. J. Selden published a part of this, with a Latin version. Died about 940.

E-vag'o-ras, [Gr. Εὐαγόρας; Fr. ÉVAGORE, ȧ'vä'goR',] King of Salamis, in Cyprus, was descended from Teucer, son of Telamon. He reigned from 410 to 375 B.C. Aided by the Athenians and the King of Egypt, he carried on a war ten years against the King of Persia, whose army invaded Cyprus, and he obtained peace on not unfavourable terms in 376. He was assassinated in 374, and left the throne to his son Nicocles. Isocrates the orator describes Evagoras as an able ruler. EVAGORAS II., supposed to have been a son of the preceding, became King of Salamis after the death of Nicocles, and was dethroned by Protagoras.

See XENOPHON, "Hellenica."

Évagore. See EVAGORAS.

Évagre. See EVAGRIUS.

E-vā'grĭ-us [Fr. ÉVAGRE, ȧ'văgR'] OF ANTIOCH. During a schism in the Church, Evagrius and Flavian were respectively elected to the dignity of Patriarch of Antioch by the two different parties in 388 A.D. Evagrius translated into Latin a "Life of Saint Anthony" by Athanasius. Died after 392.

Evagrius, [Gr. Εὐάγριος,] surnamed PON'TICUS, [Fr. ÉVAGRE DE PONT, ȧ'văgR' deh pòn,] a monk, born near the Euxine Sea, in the fourth century, was noted for piety and learning. He removed to Egypt, and passed many years in the monastery of Nitria. He wrote, besides other works, "Monachus" and "Gnosticus." Died about 400.

See TILLEMONT, "Mémoires ecclésiastiques."

Evagrius, surnamed THE SCHOLASTIC, born at Epiphania, in Syria, in the sixth century, became an eminent advocate of Antioch, and obtained the dignity of quæstor. He wrote, in Greek, an ecclesiastical history from 431 A.D. to 593, which is a respectable work in point of authenticity and style.

Evald. See EWALD.

Evald or Ewald, ā'wȧlt, (JOHANNES,) the most eminent Danish poet of the eighteenth century, was born in Copenhagen in 1743. He was educated for the church; but, finding such studies uncongenial to his romantic and ambitious ideas, he furtively enlisted in the Prussian service about the age of sixteen. Failing to obtain a more eligible rank than that of a private in the infantry, he soon deserted to the Austrian standard, under which he fought several battles in the Seven Years' war. Disenchanted from his youthful illusions of military glory, he returned home to study theology; but a disappointment in love soon diverted him from this pursuit and rendered him weary of life. He appears to have been unconscious of his poetical genius until he was employed to write a poem on the death of Frederick V., (1766,) which excited general admiration. His reputation was increased by his "Temple of Fortune," his tragedy of "Rolf" or "Rollo," (1770,) and the "Death of Balder," a drama, (1773.) The last is considered his masterpiece, and was superior to any Danish drama which had then appeared. He also wrote "Harlequin Patriot," a satirical comedy, "The Fisherman," an opera, (1778,) a beautiful elegy, entitled "Hope and Memory," and several other works. His writings are pervaded by a high moral tone. He suffered much in his later years from a chronic malady, and received a rather sparing pecuniary aid from government. Died in 1781.

See LONGFELLOW, "Poets and Poetry of Europe;" HOWITT, "Literature and Romance of Northern Europe," vol. i. chap. ii.; ERSCH und GRUBER, "Allgemeine Encyklopaedie;" C. MOLBECH, "J. Ewalds Levnet med Bidrag til hans digtervaerkers Historie," 1831.

E-van'der, [Gr. Εὔανδρος; Fr. ÉVANDRE, ȧ'vȯndR',] a semi-fabulous Grecian hero, supposed to have been a son of Hermes. He emigrated from Arcadia to Italy, where he founded Pallantium and became an ally of Æneas against Turnus. He was the father of Pallas. (See Virgil's "Æneid.")

E-van'der Au-lĭ-ā'nus, an Athenian sculptor, who worked at Rome about 40 B.C.

Évandre. See EVANDER.

Evangeli, ȧ-vän'jȧ-lee, (ANTONIO,) an Italian poet and linguist, born at Cividale in 1742, filled for thirty years the chair of belles-lettres in Padua. He made a Latin version of Gray's "Elegy," ("Elegia in rusticum Sepulchretum," 1772,) wrote a poem entitled "Musical Love," ("Amor musico,") and turned some poetry of the Bible into Italian verse. Died in 1805.

Evangelista, ȧ-vän-jȧ-lès'tä, of Canobio, an Italian canonist and civilian, born in 1511; died in 1595.

Ev'ans,[*] (ABEL,) an English wit, was a graduate of Oxford in 1699, and had a great reputation as an epigrammatist. He wrote "Vertumnus," "The Apparition," and other small poems. His name occurs in the following couplet:

"Alma novem genuit celebres Rhedycina poetas,
Bubb, Stubb, Cobb, Crabb, Young, Carey, Tickell, Evans."

Evans, (CALEB,) D.D., an English Baptist minister, born at Bristol in 1737, preached in his native city. He published several sermons, and a letter to John Wesley in which he defends the rights of the American colonies. Died in 1791.

Ev'ans, (Sir DE LACY,) K.C.B., a general of the British army, born at Moig, Ireland, in 1787. He fought as a commissioned officer in the Peninsula from 1810 to 1813, and against the Americans at Baltimore, Washington, and New Orleans in 1814. He took part in the battle of Waterloo, 1815. In 1831 he was elected to Parliament, in which he acted with the Liberal party. He obtained command in 1835 of a legion of 10,000 men raised to suppress the Carlist rebellion in Spain. He defeated the Carlists in several actions in 1836 and 1837. In 1846 he became a major-general, and in 1854, as lieutenant-general, obtained command of a division of the army in the East. He distinguished himself at the Alma and Inkerman, 1854.

Ev'ans, (EVAN,) a Welsh poet and clergyman, born in Cardiganshire in 1730. He published "Love of our Country," a poem, and "Specimens of Welsh Poetry," with an English version and notes. Died in 1790.

See OWEN, "Cambrian Biography."

Evans, (JOHN,) D.D., an English dissenting divine, born at Wrexham in 1680, became successor to Daniel Williams in London. His "Discourses on Christian Temper" (4th edition, 1729) were highly commended by Dr. Watts, Dr. Doddridge, and others, and have often been reprinted. Died in 1730.

See "Life of John Evans," by DR. JOHN ERSKINE.

Evans, (JOHN,) LL.D., born at Usk, in Monmouthshire, in 1767, was minister of a General Baptist congregation in London from 1792 to 1827. He wrote a "Brief Sketch of the Different Denominations of Christians," (1794,) which passed through eighteen editions and was translated into several languages. He sold the copyright for ten pounds. Died in 1827.

Evans, (JOHN HARRINGTON,) an English Baptist minister, born at Salisbury in 1785, preached in John Street Chapel, London, about thirty years. He published Letters, Sermons, and other religious works. Died in 1849.

See "Memoirs of J. H. Evans," by his son, 1852.

Ev'ans, (LEWIS,) an American geographer, born about 1700. He published a Map of New York, New Jersey, and other colonies in 1749. Died in 1756.

Evans, (MARIAN C.,) an English novelist, born in the north of England about 1820. She published, under the assumed name of GEORGE ELIOT, popular novels, entitled "Adam Bede," (1858,) "The Mill on the Floss," (1859,) "Scenes of Clerical Life," "Romola," (1863,) and "Felix Holt the Radical," (1866;) also a poem, entitled "The Spanish Gypsy," (1868.) Miss Evans was married, a

* The name EVANS is variously pronounced, both in England and America,—often iv'anz, but perhaps still more frequently ĕv'anz.

ā, ē, ī, ō, ū, ȳ, long; ȧ, ė, ȯ, same, less prolonged; ă, ĕ, ĭ, ŏ, ŭ, ў, short; ạ, ẹ, ị, ọ, obscure; fär, fȧll, fät; mět; nȯt; gōōd; mōōn;

few years since, to the distinguished writer, G. H. Lewes, Esq.

See "London Quarterly Review" for October, 1860; "Edinburgh Review" for July, 1859; "Blackwood's Magazine" for April, 1859, and May, 1860; "British Quarterly Review" for October, 1863, and October, 1868; "Westminster Review" for April, 1859; "Novels of George Eliot," in the "Atlantic Monthly" for October, 1866.

Evans, (NATHAN G.,) an American general, born in South Carolina about 1828, graduated at West Point in 1848. He commanded the insurgents at Ball's Bluff, October, 1861.

Evans, (OLIVER,) an American inventor and mechanist, born at Newport, Delaware, in 1755. He is said to have invented the first steam-engine constructed on the high-pressure system, the drawings and specifications of which he sent to England about 1795. He projected a railroad to connect New York and Philadelphia, but lacked the means to realize it. Died in 1819.

Evans, (ROBERT WILSON,) an English author, born at Shrewsbury about 1790, was vicar of Heversham. He published several esteemed works, among which is "The Rectory of Valehead," (15th edition, 1852.)

Evans, iv'anz, (THOMAS,) an eminent controversial writer and minister of the Society of Friends, or Quakers, born in Philadelphia in 1798. In 1827 and 1828 he opposed the Unitarian views of Elias Hicks, in a series of able papers in "The Friend." He also published (1828) an "Exposition of the Faith of the Religious Society of Friends," etc., which is probably the most complete exhibition extant of the doctrines of the early Quakers in relation to the divinity and offices of Christ. In 1837 he narrowly escaped shipwreck on a voyage to Charleston, South Carolina, when by over-exertion at the pumps (and other efforts to save the sinking vessel) his health sustained a serious and irreparable injury. From 1837 to 1854 he edited, in conjunction with his brother, William Evans, "The Friends' Library," a collection of the standard religious writings of the Society, in fourteen volumes. He died May 25, 1868. He was distinguished for rare acuteness as well as comprehensiveness of intellect, for a most kindly and benevolent spirit, and for an unquenchable zeal in defence of what he believed to be the principles of truth.

See notice in the Philadelphia "North American and United States Gazette" of June 22, 1868, which was afterwards reprinted in pamphlet form.

Ev'an-son, (EDWARD,) an English clergyman, born in 1731, became vicar of South Mimms in 1768, and rector of Tewkesbury in 1770. He was prosecuted for altering the liturgy and preaching unsound doctrine, but was acquitted. In 1778 he resigned his livings, and opened a school at Mitcham. He published several tracts against the Trinity and other doctrines of evangelical religion. Died in 1805.

Evaric. See EURIC.

Évariste. See EVARISTUS.

Ev-a-ris'tus, [Fr. ÉVARISTE, à'vȧ'rèst',] SAINT, a Greek by birth, was chosen Bishop of Rome in 100 A.D. as successor to Saint Clement. He suffered in Trajan's persecution, and is honoured as a martyr by the Church, though history does not inform us of the manner of his death, which occurred in 109 A.D.

See ARTAUD DE MONTOR, "Histoire des souverains Pontifes."

Ev'arts, (JEREMIAH,) an American editor, born in Sunderland, Vermont, in 1781, studied law. He became editor of "The Panoplist," a religious paper of Boston, about 1810, and of the "Missionary Herald" in 1820. In 1821 he was chosen corresponding secretary of the Board of Commissioners for Foreign Missions. Died in 1831.

See E. C. TRACY, "Memoirs of J. Evarts," 1845.

Evarts, (WILLIAM M.,) an eminent American lawyer, a son of the preceding, was born in Boston, Massachusetts, in 1818. He graduated at Yale College in 1837, studied law at Harvard University, and began to practise in the city of New York about 1840. He became an active member of the Republican party. In the trial of President Johnson, in the spring of 1868, he was the principal counsel for the respondent, who nominated him attorney-general of the United States about July 1 of that year.

Eve, eev, [Heb. חוה, *Hevah* or *Chavah*; Arab. HAWA, hȧ'wȧ; Gr. Εὔα; Lat. E'VA,] the wife of Adam, and the original mother of the human race.

See Genesis ii., iii., and iv.; II. Corinthians xi. 3; I. Timothy ii. 13.

Éveillon, à'vȧ'yòN', (JACQUES,) a French priest, born at Angers in 1572, was learned in canon law, and wrote several theological works. Died in 1651.

Ev'e-lyn, (JOHN,) an English author and gentleman, eminent for his accomplishments, public services, and honourable life, was born at Wotton, in Surrey, on the 31st of October, 1620, and educated at Oxford. In 1644 he visited the continent, where he passed seven years in travel and in the diligent study of natural philosophy and the fine arts. Returning to England in 1652, he settled at Say's Court, near Deptford, with his wife, whose maiden name was Browne. After the restoration he was employed in important public services, as member of the Board of Trade, commissioner for the rebuilding of Saint Paul's, etc. He was one of the first members of the Royal Society, formed in 1662. In 1664 he published his most important and popular work, "Sylva, or a Discourse on Forest-Trees," which widely diffused a taste for rural occupations, and gave an effectual impulse to the propagation of timber. "Evelyn's 'Sylva,'" says Scott, "is still the manual of British planters, and his life, manners, and principles, as illustrated in his Memoirs, ought equally to be the manual of English gentlemen." Sir Walter here refers to his Diary from 1641 to 1705, a work of great historical interest and value. Evelyn also wrote "Sculptura, a History of the Art of Engraving," (1662,) a "Treatise on Architecture," (1664,) several treatises on Horticulture, and various other works. His "Sylva" was the first book printed by order of the Royal Society. Died in February, 1706.

See "Biographia Britannica;" EVELYN's "Diary;" "London Quarterly Review" for April, 1818; "Blackwood's Magazine" for July, 1854.

Evelyn, (JOHN,) a son of the preceding, born at Say's Court about 1655, was an elegant scholar. He translated Plutarch's Life of Alexander the Great, and wrote some original verses. Died in 1698.

Évémère. See EVEMERUS.

E-vem'e-rus or **Eū-hem'e-rus,** [Gr. Εὐήμερος; Fr. ÉVÉMÈRE, à'vȧ'maiR',] a Greek philosopher, who lived about 300 B.C., and was a friend of Cassander, King of Macedonia. He wrote a Sacred History, (Ἱερὰ Ἀναγραφή,) in which he expressed his dissent from the established polytheism, and aimed to prove that the pagan deities were mortals. This work was very popular with the Epicureans, and was translated into Latin by Ennius. The original and version are both lost.

E-ve'nor, [Εὐήνωρ,] a Greek painter, was the father and master of Parrhasius. He lived about 420 B.C.

E-ve'nus, [Εὔηνος,] a Greek poet of Paros, who wrote about 450 B.C., and from whom Socrates is said to have taken lessons in poetry. He is supposed to have been the author of numerous epigrams found in the Greek Anthology.

Everaerts. See EVERARD.

Everard. See EVERARDI, (ANGELO.)

Everard, ā'veh-raRt', or **Everaerts,** ā'veh-rȧRts,(EGIDIUS,) a Dutch physician, born at Berg-op-Zoom, practised at Antwerp, where he published in 1583 a treatise "On the Marvellous Virtues of the Peruvian Weed called Tobacco."

Everard, (JOANNES SECUNDUS,) a popular poet, son of Nicolaas, noticed below, was born at the Hague in 1511. He studied law, and about 1533 went to Spain, where he became Latin secretary to the emperor Charles V. He gained an extensive reputation by his Latin poem entitled "Basia." Died in 1536.

Everard or **Everardi,** à'veh-raR'dee, (NICOLAAS,) an eminent Dutch jurist, born at Grypskerk in 1473, was a friend of Erasmus. He was president of the supreme court, or grand council, of Holland, at the Hague, from 1509 to 1527, and was eminent for learning and probity. He published "Topica Juris," (1516.) Died in 1532.

See FOPPENS, "Bibliotheca Belgica."

Everard, (NICOLAAS GRUDIUS,) a Latin poet, son of the preceding, was born at Louvain about 1515. He was a councillor to Philip II., and secretary of the order of the Golden Fleece. He wrote admired poems called "Negotia, sive Poemata Sacra," (1566,) and "Otia, sive Poemata Profana," (1612.) Died at Venice in 1571.

His brother, ADRIAN MARIUS, also gained distinction as a Latin poet. His verses were printed in 1612 with those of Nicolaas and Joannes. Died in 1568.

Everardi. See EVERARD.

Everardi, à-và-raR'dee, [Fr. ÉVERARD, â'veh-rȧR',] (ANGELO,) an Italian painter, born at Brescia in 1647, died prematurely in 1678.

See LANZI, "History of Painting in Italy."

Everdingen, van, vȧn ĕv'er-ding'en or ā'ver-ding'-Hen, (ALBERT,) an excellent Dutch landscape-painter and engraver, born at Alkmaar in 1621, studied with Savery and Peter Molyn, both of whom he surpassed. He travelled in Norway, the wild, rugged, and picturesque scenery of which afforded many subjects for his art. He excelled also in marine views and storms, and executed admirable engravings in aqua-fortis. Died at his native place in 1675.

His brother CÆSAR, born at Alkmaar in 1606, was a skilful painter of history and portraits, and an able architect. Died at Alkmaar in 1679.

See DESCAMPS, "Vies des Peintres Flamands," etc.

Ev'er-ett, (ALEXANDER HILL,) an American scholar and diplomatist, born in Boston in 1792, was a brother of Edward Everett, noticed below. He graduated at Harvard University in 1806, and studied law under John Q. Adams, whom he accompanied to Russia as secretary of legation about 1809. He published in 1821 a work entitled "Europe, or a General Survey of the Principal Powers," etc. In 1825 he was appointed minister to the court of Spain, where he remained several years. He published "America, or a General Survey of the Political Situation of the Several Powers of the Western Continent." Having returned home about 1830, he became editor of the "North American Review," to which he contributed many literary and political articles. He conducted this review for about five years with great ability. He became an adherent of the Democratic party and a political friend of General Jackson about 1832, after which he was nominated several times as a candidate for Congress, but was not elected. In 1845 he published a volume of poems. He was appointed commissioner to China in 1845, and died at Canton in May, 1847. He had married Lucretia Peabody about 1816.

See GRISWOLD, "Prose Writers of America;" ALLIBONE, "Dictionary of Authors."

Everett, (EDWARD,) a distinguished American orator, scholar, and statesman, was born in Dorchester, Norfolk county, Massachusetts, on the 11th of April, 1794. His father, the Rev. Oliver Everett, was for a number of years the minister of the New South Church, in Boston, and in 1799 was appointed judge of the circuit court. While preparing for college, Edward Everett attended a school kept by Ezekiel Webster, brother of the celebrated Daniel Webster, who on one occasion, during Ezekiel's absence, took charge of the school for a week. It was thus that the acquaintance began between two individuals who were afterwards destined to act together a distinguished part in their country's history. Edward Everett entered Harvard in the summer of 1807, and graduated, with the highest honours of his class, in 1811. He immediately commenced the study of divinity under President Kirkland. In February, 1814, he was ordained as minister of Brattle Street Church, Boston. In 1815 he was called to the chair of the Greek professorship at Harvard ; but, in order more fully to qualify himself for the position, he visited Germany, and went through a course of study at the University of Göttingen. He afterwards made the tour of Europe. Returning, after an absence of four years, to his native country, in 1819, he entered upon the duties of his professorship, and gave to the study of Greek literature an impulse the influence of which is still felt in America. In 1822 he married the daughter of the Hon. Peter Chardon Brooks. In 1824 he was elected to Congress, and took his seat in the House of Representatives, in 1825, as a supporter of John Quincy Adams. He continued in

Congress ten years. In 1835 he was elected Governor of Massachusetts. During the four years of his official term the Board of Education was organized, the normal schools founded, and other important public measures adopted or carried on. In the gubernatorial election of 1839, Mr. Everett failed to be re-elected by a single vote only. Thus released from public duty, he visited Europe the second time in the summer of 1840, and passed the winter in Italy. On the election of General Harrison to the Presidential chair, Webster became secretary of state, and, chiefly through his influence, Everett was appointed minister at the court of Saint James. Several important questions, including that of the northeastern boundary, were then agitated between the two countries. Mr. Everett performed his difficult diplomatic duties in a manner that reflected the highest credit upon himself and distinguished honour upon the administration with which he was connected. Having returned home in 1845, he was soon after elected president of Harvard University. He resigned this position in 1849. In 1852 Mr. Everett was called by President Fillmore to the office of secretary of state, left vacant by the death of Daniel Webster ; he held this place, however, only four months,—that is, until the inauguration of Franklin Pierce, March 4, 1853. Previously to his retiring from the cabinet he had been elected, by the legislature of Massachusetts, to the Senate of the United States. Although in feeble health, he applied himself assiduously, during that exciting period, to the discharge of his public duties. In May, 1854, in compliance with the earnest recommendation of his physician, he resigned his seat in Congress, and withdrew to private life. As soon as his health was somewhat restored, he commenced his labours in behalf of the Mount Vernon Fund, the object of which was to purchase the home and burial-place of the immortal Washington, (then in the possession of his nephew, Bushrod Washington,) in order that it might for all future time belong to the American people as a place of public resort and pilgrimage. The sum collected for this noble purpose by the efforts of Mr. Everett (as the result of his lectures, writings, etc.) amounted to scarcely less than one hundred thousand dollars.

Mr. Everett was by temperament and mental constitution strongly conservative. This tendency was perhaps strengthened by the obvious consideration that, without a measure of the spirit of conciliation and mutual concession, the government of a free people, spread over a vast extent of territory and having a great diversity of interests, would necessarily be exposed to continual jars, if not fatal collisions. His tastes and his principles alike made him averse to all discord and violence ; and, like many others, he was led to hope that, by a moderate and conciliatory policy on the part of the North, the spirit of Southern slavery—that great source of peril to the nation —might be rendered more mild and less aggressive. When at length the assault committed by Brooks upon Mr. Sumner in the Senate, and the subsequent outrages of the pro-slavery party in Missouri and Kansas, had excited deep and general indignation among the people of the non-slaveholding States, Mr. Everett's anxiety seemed to increase, with the increasing danger, to avert, if possible, the dreadful scourge of civil war from his hitherto prosperous and happy country. With this view, he allowed his name to go before the people as a representative of the party of conciliation and compromise, by which party he was chosen in the summer of 1860 a candidate for the Vice-Presidency, John Bell, of Tennessee, being the nominee for President. In the ensuing election they received only thirty-nine electoral votes, and Mr. Lincoln was chosen President by a large majority. The events of the next few months showed that the Southern leaders had for many years been making preparations for a separation from the Union, and that the election of Mr. Lincoln merely furnished them with a plausible pretext before the people for carrying their schemes into effect. When Mr. Everett perceived that war was inevitable, and that the nation could only be preserved by putting down the rebellion by force of arms, he gave all his energies and influence towards the support of the Federal government. He died of an affection of the lungs, terminating in apoplexy, on the 15th of January, 1865.

ā, ē, ī, ō, ū, ȳ, *long;* ă, ĕ, ŏ, same, less prolonged; ă, ĕ, ĭ, ŏ, ŭ, ȳ, *short;* ą, ę, į, ǫ, *obscure;* fär, fȧll, fȧt; mĕt; nŏt; gōͦd; mōͦn;

Edward Everett affords a remarkable example of an almost universal culture,—of the successful prosecution of the most diversified pursuits, combined with rare accuracy and thoroughness in those departments of learning to which he more especially devoted himself. His literary productions consist chiefly of his elaborate public speeches and addresses delivered on various occasions. He also contributed several important articles to the "North American Review." Among these we would call especial attention to one which most ably discussed the doctrine of nullification, (then rife in South Carolina,) published in October, 1830. His published speeches and addresses are perhaps not surpassed in value by those of any other American orator, if, in addition to the grace and elegance of the style, we take into consideration the correct and valuable information which they contain.

For some excellent remarks on the character of Mr. Everett, both as a gentleman and a scholar, see "Character and Characteristic Men," by E. P. WHIPPLE, pp. 243–252; see. also, "A Memoir of Edward Everett," Boston, 1865; "Christian Examiner" for November, 1850; GRISWOLD'S "Prose Writers of America;" "National Portrait-Gallery of Distinguished Americans," vol. iv.; "Golden Age of American Oratory," by EDWARD G. PARKER, Boston, 1857; "North American Review" for April, 1825, January, 1837, and October, 1850; "London Quarterly Review" for December, 1840.

Evermer. See EBREMAR.

Evers, à-vair′, (CHARLES JOSEPH,) BARON, a Belgian general in the French service, born at Brussels in 1773; died in 1818.

Ev′ers-ley, (CHARLES SHAW LEFEVRE,) VISCOUNT, an English legislator, born in London in 1794. His family name was SHAW. He was elected to Parliament as a Whig in 1830, and became Speaker of the House of Commons in 1839. He was re-elected to that office in 1841, in 1847, and in 1852, and ceased to be Speaker in 1857, when he was raised to the peerage, as Viscount Eversley. His official conduct was highly approved by both parties. He was remarkable for dignity of manner.

Everts, (NICOLAAS.) See EVERARD.

Evertsen, ĕv′ert-sĕn, a Dutch family which produced several distinguished naval officers, of whom five were brothers. Cornelius, a vice-admiral, was killed in battle with the English, July, 1666. His brother John, holding the same rank in the navy, was killed in the ensuing month. Cornelius, the son of John, attained the rank of vice-admiral, and died in 1679.

See J. C. DE JONGE, "Vie des Amiraux de Zélande J. et C. Evertsen," 1817.

Évesque. See LÉVESQUE.

Evliya or **Evleea,** ĕv-lee′â, (EFFENDI,) a noted Turkish traveller, born in Constantinople in 1611, passed the greater part of his mature life in travel through Asia and Europe. He often accompanied military expeditions or diplomatic missions as secretary. He wrote several volumes of Travels, which, although they display more credulity than judgment, are well adapted to give an insight into the Turkish character and mode of thought. Died about 1680.

See VON HAMMER, "Notice of Evlya Effendi," in his "Histoire de l'Empire Ottoman."

E-vo′dĭ-us, an intimate friend of Saint Augustine, was born at Ṭagaste, (Africa.) He became Bishop of Uzalis, near Utica, about 396 A.D. He wrote letters to Saint Augustine, which are extant.

Evremond, ăvr′môn′, (CHARLES **de** Saint-Denis —dĕh săn′dĕh-ne′,) Seigneur de Saint-Évremond, a French courtier, wit, and *littérateur,* born at Saint-Denys-le-Guast, near Coutances, in 1613. He entered the army at an early age, and, by his bravery, wit, and polite accomplishments, attracted the notice of Turenne and Condé, with the latter of whom he became intimate. In the war of the Fronde, about 1650, he supported the royal cause, and was promoted by the king. For some political offence, Louis XIV. ordered him to be confined in the Bastille in 1661; but he escaped to England in 1662, was received with great favour at court, and never returned to France. Charles II. granted him a pension of £300. His letters, essays, dramas, etc. (in French) gained him much temporary reputation; but they are mostly of a trifling character, and have little merit except the natural and graceful style. Died in 1703.

See P. DESMAISEAUX, "Vie du Sieur de Saint-Évremond," 1705; C. COTOLENDI, "Saint-Évremontiana," Amsterdam, 1701.

Ewald, ä′wält, (GEORG HEINRICH AUGUST,) an eminent German Orientalist and biblical critic, was born at Göttingen in 1803. He became professor of philosophy at Göttingen about 1827, and of Oriental languages in the same university in 1835. He published a good Hebrew grammar, (1835.) From 1837 to 1848 he was professor of theology at Tübingen. In 1848 he resumed his former functions at Göttingen. Among his principal works are "The Poetical Books of the Old Testament," (1835–37,) a "History of the People of Israel until the Advent of Christ," (3 vols., 1843–50,) and "The Prophets of the Old Testament," ("Die Propheten des alten Bundes," 2 vols., 1840.) In his religious views he inclined towards rationalism.

See BROCKHAUS, "Conversations-Lexikon;" E. RENAN, in the "Revue des Deux Mondes," November 15, 1855; CARL WEX, "Professor Ewald als Punier gewurdigt," Rostock, 1843; "Nouvelle Biographie Générale."

Ewald, (JOHANN LUDWIG,) a German Protestant theologian and writer, born in Hesse-Darmstadt in 1748. After he had preached rationalism some years at Offenbach, he avowed his conversion to evangelical doctrines. In 1781 he became court preacher at Detmold. In 1796 he removed to Bremen, and to Heidelberg in 1805. He published many works. Died in 1822.

See ERSCH und GRUBER, "Allgemeine Encyklopaedie."

Ewald, (JOHANNES.) See EVALD.

Ewald, ä′vält, or **Evald,** (JOHN,) a Danish general, born at Cassel in 1744. He fought for the British in the United States in 1776–82, and entered the Danish service in 1788. Having risen to the rank of general, he distinguished himself in defence of the neutrality of Denmark about 1806. He was author of an able and very successful treatise, "Instructions in War," ("Belehrungen über den Krieg," 1798.) Died in 1813. Malte-Brun represents him as a brother of the poet Evald.

See ERSCH und GRUBER, "Allgemeine Encyklopaedie."

Ew′art, (yoo′ạrt,) (WILLIAM,) an English Liberal legislator, born in Liverpool in 1798, was educated for the law. He represented the burghs of Dumfries district in Parliament for many years, beginning in 1841. About 1850 he procured the passage of an act to establish free public libraries, and laboured for the abolition of capital punishment. Died in 1869.

Ew′bank, (THOMAS,) a writer on practical mechanics, was born in the county of Durham, England, in 1792. He emigrated to New York about 1820, and was appointed commissioner of patents in 1849. Among his works are a "Descriptive and Historical Account of Hydraulic and other Machines, Ancient and Modern," (1842,) and "Thoughts on Matter and Force," (1858.)

Ew′ell, (yoo′el,) (RICHARD STODDARD,) an American general, born in the District of Columbia about 1818, graduated at West Point in 1840. He became a captain about 1849, resigned his commission in 1861, and took arms against the Union. He commanded a division in several battles near Richmond in June, 1862, and lost a leg in August near Bull Run. Having been raised to the rank of lieutenant-general, he commanded a corps of Lee's army at Gettysburg, July, 1863. He took part in the battles of the Wilderness and Spottsylvania Court-House, May, 1864. He was taken prisoner near the Appomattox River, April 6, 1865.

See "Southern Generals," anonymous, New York, 1865.

Ewers, ä′wẹrs, (JOHANN PHILIPP GUSTAV,) a German historian, born in the diocese of Corbie in 1781. He became professor of history at Dorpat in 1810, and published several works on the history and statistics of Russia. Died in 1830.

See ERSCH und GRUBER, "Allgemeine Encyklopaedie."

Ew′ing, (yoo′ing,) (Rev. GREVILLE,) a Scottish theologian, born in Edinburgh in 1767, was for many years pastor of an Independent church in Glasgow. He gained distinction as an expositor of Scripture, and published a "Greek and English Lexicon," (1802,) "Letters to the Jews," and several religious treatises. Died in 1841.

Ew′ing, (yoo′ing,) (JOHN,) an American Presbyterian minister, born in Maryland in 1732. He became pastor of a church in Philadelphia in 1759, and provost of the University of Pennsylvania in 1779. He contributed to the

e as k: ç as s; ḡ *hard;* ğ as j; G, H, K, *guttural;* N, *nasal;* R, *trilled;* ŝ as z; th as in *this.* (☞See Explanations, p. 2c

56

Transactions of the American Philosophical Society. Died in 1802.

Ewing, (THOMAS,) an American statesman, born in Ohio county, Virginia, in December, 1789. He was taken to the State of Ohio about 1792 by his father, who was not able to give him much education at school. After he was twenty-one years of age, he entered the Ohio University at Athens. He studied law, was admitted to the bar in 1816, and practised with success in the courts of Ohio and in the supreme court of the United States. He represented Ohio in the Senate of the United States from March, 1831, to March, 1837, during which period he acted with the Whig party. He supported General Harrison for the Presidency in 1840, and became secretary of the treasury in March, 1841. In September, 1841, he resigned because President Tyler vetoed a bill for a national bank (for the regulation of exchanges) of which Mr. Ewing was in part the author. He was secretary of the interior from March, 1849, until the death of President Taylor, July, 1850. In the latter part of 1850 he was appointed a Senator of the United States, to fill a vacancy caused by the removal of Thomas Corwin to a seat in the cabinet. He opposed Clay's Compromise bill and the Fugitive Slave bill. After his retirement from the Senate, March, 1851, he resumed the practice of law at Lancaster, Ohio. He is the father-in-law of General William T. Sherman.

Exauvillez, d', dĕk'sō've'yȧ', (PHILIPPE IRÉNÉE Boistel—bwȧs'tĕl',) a French Catholic, born at Amiens in 1786, wrote "The Good Curate," (1827,) and other popular religious works. He made a French version of Sir Walter Scott's works, from which he omitted all passages contrary to Roman Catholicism.

Excelmans, ĕk'sĕl'mŏN', or **Exelmans,** (RÉMI JOSEPH ISIDORE,) BARON, an eminent French general, was born at Bar-le-Duc in 1775. He entered the army young, and became aide-de-camp to Murat in 1801. For his gallant conduct at Austerlitz, in 1805, he was made a colonel. He served with distinction at Eylau, where he won the rank of general of brigade, and at Friedland, in 1807. In 1811 he was grand equerry of Murat, then King of Naples; but in 1812 he returned to France, was created a baron, and commanded a division in the campaign of Russia. He displayed great courage and skill at Borodino, and in the campaign of 1814 in France. At Waterloo he commanded a corps of cavalry of the reserve. After an exile of four years, he returned to France in 1819. He was restored to his rank as a peer in 1831, and became a marshal of France about 1850. Died in 1851 or 1852.

See J. NOLLET-FABERT, "Notice sur M. le Maréchal Exelmans," 1851; "Victoires et Conquêtes des Français."

Exelmans. See EXCELMANS.

Exeter, BISHOP OF. See PHILLPOTTS, (HENRY.)

Eximeno, ĕk-se-mā'no, (Don ANTONIO,) a learned Spanish Jesuit and ingenious author, born at Balbastro, in Aragon, in 1732. On the suppression of his order he removed to Rome. He wrote the "Military History of Spain," (1769,) the style of which is admired, and a treatise on the "Origin and Principles of Music, with a History of its Progress," etc., (1774,) which is his chief production. Died in Rome in 1798.

Exmouth, ĕks'mŭth, (EDWARD PELLEW,) VISCOUNT, an eminent English admiral, born at Dover in 1757, entered the navy in 1770. He took a conspicuous part in the battle of Lake Champlain in 1776, and became a post-captain in 1782. During the war against France he captured a number of the enemy's ships, for which service he was knighted about 1794. He was elected member of Parliament in 1802, and obtained the rank of rear-admiral in 1804, with a command in the East Indies. As vice-admiral, he was appointed commander-in-chief in the Mediterranean in 1810. In 1814 he was created Baron Exmouth and promoted to the rank of full admiral. In 1816 Lord Exmouth commanded a perilous expedition against the Algerines, who had violated a treaty for the abolition of Christian slavery. The English and Dutch fleets attacked Algiers on the 26th of August, and directed their fire with such skill and effect that the Dey, after an obstinate resistance, was compelled to submit on the same day, and about twelve hundred captives

were liberated. In this action the admiral's coat was torn by a cannon-ball. On his return to England, Lord Exmouth was received with unbounded applause, and was raised to the rank of viscount. He retired from public service in 1821, and died in 1833.

See EDWARD OSLER, "Life of Admiral Exmouth," 1835; "London Quarterly Review" for December, 1835.

Exner, ĕks'ner, (FRANZ,) a German philosopher, born in Vienna in 1802, was professor of philosophy at Prague from 1831 to 1848. He wrote, among other works, one "On Nominalism and Realism," (1841,) and the "Doctrine of the Unity of Thought and Existence," (1845.)

Expilly, ĕks'pe'le', (CLAUDE,) a French lawyer and councillor of state, born at Voiron in 1561. He was employed by Henry IV. and Louis XIII. as negotiator in Piedmont and Savoy, and became president of the Parliament of Grenoble. He wrote a "Life of Chevalier Bayard," (1650.) Died in 1636.

See J. C. MARTIN, "Histoire et Vie de Claude Expilly," 1803.

Expilly, (JEAN JOSEPH,) ABBÉ, a French geographer, born at Saint-Remi, Provence, in 1719, performed many journeys in the public service, and others, for the purpose of collecting materials for his works. He was a prolific and accurate writer, and published, between 1750 and 1770, treatises on geography, which were among the best of that period. Among these is a "Geographical and Historical Dictionary of Gaul and of France," (6 vols., 1762-70.) Died in 1793.

Expilly, (LOUIS ALEXANDRE,) a French priest and revolutionist, born at Brest in 1742, became a deputy to the States-General in 1789, and was one of the framers of the civil constitution of the clergy. In 1790 he was chosen constitutional Bishop of Finisterre. He was condemned on a charge of Federalism, and executed in 1794.

Ex-u-pe'rĭ-us, [Fr. EXUPÈRE, ĕk'sü'paiR',] Bishop of Toulouse, lived about 400 A.D., and was eminent for charity.

Byb, von, fon īp, (ALBRECHT,) a German ecclesiastic of high reputation, born about 1420, became chamberlain to Pope Pius II. He published a compilation from ancient authors, entitled "The Poetic Pearl," ("Margarita poetica," 1472,) often reprinted. Died about 1478.

Eyck, van, vȧn īk, (HUBERT,) a famous Flemish painter, born in 1366, was a brother of Jan, with whom he worked in partnership at Bruges and Ghent. They sometimes painted together on the same picture,—for example, the altar-piece of a church in Ghent representing the Adoration of the Lamb, which is called their master-piece. To these brothers is ascribed the invention of oil-painting, or, more properly, an improved method of preparing the pigments. (See EYCK, JAN VAN.) Died in 1426.

See DÉSCAMPS, "Vies des Peintres Flamands," etc.

Eyck, van, (JAN,) a celebrated Flemish painter, sometimes called JOHN OF BRUGES, was born at or near Maaseyck about 1390, and was a pupil of Hubert, his brother. He worked mostly at Ghent and Bruges. About 1425 he obtained the favour of Philip the Good, Duke of Burgundy, who employed him as an artist and ambassador. He had received from nature the qualities requisite for a great painter. He and his brother were the first who attained to great success in oil-painting, having discovered a new vehicle of colour, composed of siccative oils and resins. His pictures preserve to the present time an admirable freshness and brilliancy of colour. "His colour," says Émeric-David, in the "Biographie Universelle," "though inferior in harmony to that of modern master-pieces, has more vivacity." Among his works are "The Adoration of the Magi," a "Virgin and Child," and a "Saint Jerome." Died about 1440.

See A. MICHIELS, "Histoire de la Peinture Flamande;" CARTON, "Les trois Frères Van Eyck," etc., 1848.

Eyck, van, (KASPAR,) a Flemish painter, born at Antwerp, lived in the second half of the seventeenth century. He painted marine views with skill.

Eyck, van, (MARGARET,) a sister of Hubert and Jan, was a successful painter. She refused an offer (or offers) of marriage because she preferred to devote herself to art. She probably worked with her brothers in Bruges and Ghent.

ā, ē, ī, ō, ū, ȳ, *long;* ȧ, ė, ȯ, same, less prolonged; ă, ĕ, ĭ, ŏ, ŭ, ў, *short;* ạ, ẹ, ị, ọ, *obscure;* fär, fȧll, fât; mêt; nŏt; gōōd; mōōn;

Eyck, van, (NICOLAAS,) a Flemish painter, born in Antwerp about 1630, acquired a great reputation for battle-pieces. The particulars of his life are not known.

See DESCAMPS, "Vies des Peintres Flamands," etc.

Eyckens. See EYKENS.

Eyer. See AYRER, (JAKOB.)

Eyke de Rebkow. See REBKOW.

Eykens, ī'kẹns, or **Eyckens,** īk'kẹns, (JAN,) a son of Pieter, noticed below, was a skilful painter of flowers and fruits. Died in 1669.

Eykens or **Eyckens,** (PIETER,) called THE ELDER, a skilful Flemish historical painter, born in Antwerp about 1600. He worked in his native city, the churches of which contain the most of his paintings. Among them are a "Last Supper," a "Saint Catherine Disputing," and "Elijah Ascending in a Chariot of Fire." His design, colour, and expression are praised by Descamps. He sometimes painted figures for the works of landscape-painters.

See DESCAMPS, "Vies des Peintres Flamands," etc.

Eymar, à'mǎR',(CLAUDE,) a literary French merchant, born in Marseilles in 1744. He wrote commentaries on Rousseau's works, and essays on various subjects. Died in 1822.

Eymar, d', dà'mǎR', (ANGE MARIE,) COMTE, a French *littérateur,* born at Marseilles about 1740; died at Geneva in 1803.

Eymer. See HYMIR.

Eymeric, à-mặ-rèk', (NICOLAS,) a native of Gerona, in Spain, born about 1320, entered the Dominican order, and was accounted the greatest canonist of his time. He was made Inquisitor-General in 1356, and wrote "The Inquisitor's Directory," the atrocious maxims of which became the guide of Torquemada. Died in 1399.

Eynard, à'nǎR', (J. G.,) a merchant, born at Lyons in 1775, removed to Geneva in his youth. About 1824 he devoted himself to the cause of Greek nationality, and in 1829 he loaned or advanced 700,000 francs to the Greek treasury.

Eynde, van den, vǎn den īn'dẹh, [Lat. EYN'DIUS,] (JAKOB,) a Dutch writer, born at Delft about 1575, published a volume of Latin poems,(1611,) and a "Chronicle of Zealand," (1634.) Died in 1614.

Eynden, van, vǎn īn'dẹn, (JACOB,) a Dutch painter of animals, flowers, etc., born at Nymwegen in 1733; died about 1800.

Eynden, van, (ROLAND,) a Dutch writer and painter, born at Dort in 1748, published, in conjunction with Vander Villigen, a "History of the Painters of the Low Countries," from the middle of the eighteenth century, which is esteemed valuable. Died in 1819.

Eyndius. See EYNDE, VAN DEN.

Eyre, air, (EDWARD JOHN,) an Englishman, distinguished as an explorer of Australia, was born about 1818. He published in 1845 "Discoveries in Central Australia." In 1864 he was appointed Governor of Jamaica. He was censured for the severity with which he suppressed an insurrection in October, 1865, and was removed soon after that date.

Eyre, (Sir JAMES,) an English judge, born in Wiltshire in 1734. After practising law in London, he became recorder of that city in 1762. He was appointed a baron of the exchequer in 1772, and first commissioner of the great seal in 1792. He held the office of lord chief justice of the court of common pleas from 1793 until his death in 1799.

See FOSS, "The Judges of England."

Eyriès, à're-ès', (JEAN BAPTISTE BENOÎT,) a French geographer and translator, born at Marseilles in 1767.

He translated from the English and German many works on geography and narratives of voyages, was one of the founders of the Geographical Society of Paris, and editor of the "Annales des Voyages." He wrote many articles for Michaud's "Biographie Universelle," and published with Pinkerton an "Abridgment of Modern Geography," (2 vols., 1827.) Died in 1846.

Eysel, ī'zẹl, (JOHANN PHILIPP,) a German physician and writer, born at Erfurt in 1652; died in 1717.

Eytelwein, ī'tẹl-wīn', (JOHANN ALBRECHT,) a Prussian engineer born at Frankfort in 1764. He published a "Manual of the Mechanics of Solid Bodies and Hydraulics," (1801,) a "Manual of Perspective," (1810,) and other works. Died about 1840.

Eytzing, von, fon īt'sing, (MICHAEL,) a German historian of the sixteenth century, published a history of events in the Low Countries from 1559 to 1583, entitled "On the Belgic Lion," ("De Leone Belgico," etc., 1583.)

Ezéchias, the French of HEZEKIAH, which see.

Ézéchiel. See EZEKIEL.

Ez-ed-deen or **Ez-ed-dîn,** ĕz-ed-deen', an Arabian poet, born in 1181; died in 1261.

E-ze'kǐ-el, [Heb. יְחֶזְקֵאל; Fr. ÉZÉCHIEL, à'zà'she'êl' or à'zà'ke-êl'; Ger. EZECHIEL, êt-sā'ke-êl,] one of the four greater prophets, was a contemporary of Daniel. During the first Babylonian captivity he was removed, with other captives, about 600 B.C., to the river Chebar, an affluent of the Euphrates. He began to prophesy and to proclaim the judgments of God against idolatry and other sins in 595 B.C. His prophecies are generally considered obscure, but are remarkable for bold and magnificent imagery. Many critics concede to him considerable poetical genius and great energy of character. The data of his external life are very deficient. The only important event of his personal history noticed in his writings is the death of his wife, (chap. xxiv. 18.) The New Testament contains no mention of Ezekiel, nor any quotation from the book which bears his name.

See C. F. BOERNER, "Dissertatio de Ezechiele Propheta," 1719.

Ezekiel, a Jewish poet, who lived at Alexandria, and wrote, in Greek, a drama on the Exodus from Egypt.

E-ze'kǐ-el, an Armenian astronomer, born about 673 A.D. After travelling in Greece, he opened in his native place in 710 a school, which became flourishing. He wrote a "Treatise on the Zodiac," and other works. Died in 727.

Ezengatsi, êz-en-gât'see, written also **Ezenkantsi,** (HOVAN, *i.e.* JOHN,) an eminent Armenian writer and priest. Died about 1325.

Ez'nig, Ez'nag, or **Ez'nik,** an Armenian writer and theologian, born in 397 A.D.; died in 478.

Eznik. See EZNIG.

Ezquerra, êth-ker'rä, or **Esquerra,** ês-ker'rä, a Spanish poet and priest, born in Biscay about 1568. His reputation is founded on his "Epistle to Bartholomew Argensola," the style of which is a model of elegance, purity, and grace. Died in 1641.

Ez'ra, [Heb. עֶזְרָא; Lat. ES'DRAS; Fr. ESDRAS, ês'-drâs'; Ger. ES'RA or ES'DRAS,] an eminent Jewish scribe and reformer, was the author of the canonical book which bears his name, and perhaps of the two books of Chronicles. He was probably born in Babylon. After the temple had been rebuilt at Jerusalem, Ezra received authority from the King of Persia, about 458 B.C., to lead a large number of captive Jews back to their fatherland. (See Ezra vii., viii., ix., and x., and Nehemiah viii.) He was Governor of Judea until 445 B.C. He is called the "Restorer of the Scriptures," which he appears to have revised.

Ezzelino, (da **Romano.**) See ROMANO.

€ as *k;* ç as *s;* ğ *hard;* ġ as *j;* G, H, K, *guttural;* N, *nasal;* R, *trilled;* s̄ as *z;* th as in *this.* (☞ See Explanations, p. 23.)

F.

Fabbra, della, dĕl′lä fäb′brä, (LUIGI,) a distinguished professor of medicine in the University of Ferrara, born in that city in 1655; died in 1723.

Fabbrici, de′, dä fäb-brĕt′see, (LUIGI CINZIO,) an Italian writer, born in Venice about 1450, published "Origine de' volgari Proverbi," (1526.) Died about 1526.

See TIRABOSCHI, "Storia della Letteratura Italiana."

Fabbroni. See FABRONI.

Faber. See FABRE, LE FÈVRE, and FÈVRE.

Faber, (ANTOINE and CLAUDE.) See FAVRE.

Faber, fä′bĕr, (BASIL,) a German scholar and Protestant writer, born at Sora, or Sorau, in 1520. His chief work is "Treasury of Scholastic Learning," ("Thesaurus Eruditionis scholasticæ," 1571,) often reprinted. Died about 1575.

Faber, (FELIX,) an author and itinerant preacher, whose original name was SCHMIDT, born at Zurich about 1442; died at Ulm in 1502.

Fä′bĕr, (FREDERICK WILLIAM,) a Roman Catholic priest and writer, nephew of George Stanley Faber, noticed below, was born in England in 1815. Died in 1863.

See BOWDEN, "Life of F. W. Faber," 1869.

Faber, (GEORGE STANLEY,) an eminent English theologian, born near Bradford, in Yorkshire, in 1773. He studied at University College, Oxford. Having graduated in 1803, he rose through several preferments to be a prebendary in the cathedral of Salisbury in 1831. Among his principal works we may name his "View of the Mosaical Records," ("Horæ Mosaicæ," 1801,) "On the Mysteries of the Cabyri, or the Great Gods of Phœnicia," (1803,) "Difficulties of Infidelity," (1824,) (a masterly production,) "Difficulties of Romanism," (1826,) "View of the Prophecies relating to Judah and Israel," and "The Sacred Calendar of Prophecy," (3 vols., 1828.) His productions evince great learning and research and a spirit of fervent piety, and are regarded by competent critics as among the most valuable that have been written on those subjects. Died in 1854.

See "Gentleman's Magazine" for May, 1854; ALLIBONE, "Dictionary of Authors."

Faber, fä′bä′, **Fabre,** fäbR, or **Le Fèvre,** lĕh fĕvR, (JEAN,) a celebrated French lawyer and jurist, born in Angoulême; died in 1340.

Faber, fä′bĕr, (JOHANN,) surnamed THE HAMMER OF HERETICS, a German theologian and zealous adversary of Luther, was born at Leutkirch, in Suabia, about 1475. He became a Dominican monk. He published, besides other polemical works against the Protestants, the "Hammer of Heretics," ("Malleus Hæreticorum," 1524.) In 1531 he became Bishop of Vienna. Died in 1541.

See KETTNER, "Dissertatio de J. Fabri Vita et Scriptis," 1737.

Faber, (JOHANN,) a German Catholic theologian and controversialist, born at Heilbronn about 1500; died about 1560.

Faber, (JOHANN,) a German botanist and physician, born at Bamberg about 1570, practised in Rome, and was physician to Pope Urban VIII.

Faber, (JOHANN ERNST,) a German Orientalist and writer, born at Simmerthausen in 1745; died in 1774.

Faber, (PIERRE,) a French classical scholar, born in Auvergne about 1530; died about 1615. He wrote commentaries on Cicero, (1601.)

Faber, (SAMUEL,) a Swiss writer, born at Altorf in 1657. His chief work is "The World in a Nutshell," ("Orbis Terrarum in Nuce.") Died in 1716.

Faber Stapulensis. See LEFÈVRE D'ESTAPLES.

Fabert, fä′bĕrt or fä′bair′, (ABRAHAM,) a noted ornamental printer, born at Metz about 1560; died in 1638.

Fabert, (ABRAHAM,) a famous French general, a son of the preceding, was born at Metz in 1599. After having distinguished himself in several battles, he was created marshal of France by Louis XIV. in 1658, and at the same time was appointed governor of Sedan, at which place he died in 1662. His exploits and good fortune

were so extraordinary that they were by many ascribed to magic.

See COURTILZ DE SANDRAS, "Vie du Maréchal Fabert," 1697; J. DE LA BARRE, "Vie du Maréchal Fabert," 1752; VOLTAIRE, "Siècle de Louis XIV;" BÉGIN, "Éloge du Maréchal Fabert," 1837.

Fä′bĭ-an or **Fabyan,** (ROBERT,) a noted merchant and sheriff of London, born about 1450, was the author of "Concordance of Histories," or "Fabian's Chronicle," (1516,) which treats of English history. Died in 1512.

See DIBDIN, "Typographical Antiquities."

Fä′bĭ-ạn, [Lat. FABIA′NUS; Fr. FABIEN, fȧ′be-ăN′,] SAINT, was elected pope in 236 A.D., and suffered martyrdom under the emperor Decius in 250.

Fa-bĭ-ā′nus, (PAPIR′IUS,) a Roman philosopher of the first century, wrote numerous treatises on philosophy. The two Senecas expressed a high opinion of his works.

Fabii, fä′be-ī, a powerful patrician house of ancient Rome, which became conspicuous soon after the establishment of the republic. Three brothers named Fabius obtained seven successive consulships between 486 and 479 B.C.

Fa-bĭ-o′la, SAINT, a Roman lady of the illustrious house of Fabius, was celebrated for her piety and benevolence, and was the founder of hospitals in Italy. Died about 400 A.D.

See BAILLET, "Vies des Saints."

Fä′bĭ-us Am-bus′tus, (MARCUS,) a general, was consul in 360, in 356, and in 354 B.C., and afterwards dictator of Rome about 351 B.C. He was the father of Fabius Maximus Rullianus, noticed below. He defeated the Hernici and Tarquinians.

Fä′bĭ-us Max′ĭ-mus, (QUINTUS,) a son of the following, and grandson by adoption of Paulus Æmilius, was chosen consul 122 B.C. Having the department of Transalpine Gaul, he carried on a successful war against the Arverni and the Allobroges. On one occasion he defeated the enemy, who lost 120,000 men, while the loss of the Romans was very small. For this victory he received the surname of ALLOBROGICUS.

Fä′bĭ-us Max′ĭ-mus Æ-mil-ĭ-ā′nus, (QUINTUS,) son of the consul Paulus Æmilius, passed by adoption into the house of Fabius. He was elected consul of Rome 147 B.C. He carried on a successful war in Spain against Viriathus, a famous general commanding the Lusitanians. Like the great Fabius Cunctator, he pursued in his wars the defensive policy.

Fä′bĭ-us Max′ĭ-mus Gur′gĕs, (QUINTUS,) a son of Fabius Maximus Rullianus, was consul in 292 B.C., and again in 276. He was the grandfather of the great Fabius Cunctator.

Fä′bĭ-us Max′ĭ-mus Rul-lĭ-ā′nus, (QUINTUS,) a famous general, was five times consul (322-295 B.C.) and twice dictator of Rome. He also held many other high offices. He gained victories over the Samnites in 325, in 322, and in 296 B.C. He was reputed the greatest Roman general of his time.

See NIEBUHR, "History of Rome;" LIVY, "History of Rome;" VALERIUS MAXIMUS, "History of Rome;" AURELIUS VICTOR, "Viri illustres."

Fä′bĭ-us Max′ĭ-mus Vĕr-ru-co′sus, (QUINTUS,) surnamed CUNCTA′TOR, the greatest of the Fabian line, was consul for the first time in 233 B.C., when he conquered the Ligurians and had the honour of a triumph. After the Carthaginians had taken Saguntum, the Romans sent Fabius to Carthage at the head of their ambassadors. After the defeat of the Roman armies at Thrasymene in 217, a dictator being thought necessary, Fabius was chosen to that office. He marched against Hannibal, and firmly adhered to the policy of carrying on only a defensive war, in which he was so successful that the Carthaginian general was unable to obtain any advantage over him. Minucius, master of the Roman cavalry, at one time obtaining command of part of the army, engaged with Hannibal, and would have been entirely defeated if Fabius had not hastened to assist him, after

---

ī, ē, ī, ō, ū, ȳ, *long*; ă, ĕ, ŏ, same, less prolonged; ă, ĕ, ĭ, ŏ, ŭ, ȳ, *short*; ạ, ẹ, ị, ọ, *obscure*; fär, fȧll, fȧt; mĕt; nŏt; gōōd; mōōn;

which Minucius gave up his command to Fabius. The dictatorship of Fabius having expired, Paulus Æmilius and Terentius Varro were appointed consuls, and, pursuing a different method, were totally defeated at the battle of Cannæ, in 216 B.C., after which the Romans returned to the defensive policy of Fabius. He was chosen consul for the fifth time in 209 B.C. His uniform success against the most formidable enemy of Rome justly won for him the name of Maximus. Ennius spoke of him as one "qui nobis cunctando restituit rem." Died about 203 B.C.

See PLUTARCH, "Lives;" LIVY, "History of Rome," books xx.-xxiv. and xxvi.-xxx.; NIEBUHR, "History of Rome;" POLYBIUS, book iii.; "Nouvelle Biographie Générale."

Fā'bĭ-us Pic'tor, (CAIUS,) a Roman painter, was the grandfather of the historian Fabius Pictor. He painted the temple of Salus ("Safety") about 304 B.C.

Fabius Pictor (QUINTUS) was the first Roman historian, and is sometimes called "the father of Latin history." His works were known as the "Annals of Fabius Pictor." He lived at the time of the second Punic war, and died after 216 B.C. His History, which was highly esteemed by the ancients, is lost, except small fragments.

See WHISTE, "De Fabio Pictore cæterisque Fabiis historicis," 1832; MÖLLER, "De Q. Fabio Pictore," 1690.

Fabius Planciades Fulgentius. See FULGENTIUS.

Fā'bĭ-us Vib-u-lā'nus, (KÆSO,) a Roman commander, was chosen consul in 484, in 481, and in 479 B.C. He rendered himself very popular with the plebeians, and gained victories over the Veientes and Æqui. During his third consulship the Fabian family volunteered to make a campaign against the Veientes without the aid of other citizens. Kæso led out three hundred and six Fabii, (among whom was his brother Marcus,) attended by their clients or servants, and occupied a fortified post on the Cremera, which enters the Tiber near Rome. They gained several victories, but at length were surprised and all killed in 477 B.C.

See NIEBUHR, "History of Rome;" LIVY, "History of Rome;" "Nouvelle Biographie Générale."

Fabius Vibulanus, (MARCUS,) a Roman general, was a brother of the preceding. He was consul in 483 and 480 B.C. He was killed at Cremera in 477. (See preceding article.)

Fabius Vibulanus, (QUINTUS,) a son of Marcus, was the only one of the Fabii who escaped from being massacred at Cremera by the Veientes in 477 B.C. The different branches of the great Fabian house were descended from him. He was consul in 467, 465, and 459 B.C., and defeated the Volsci. Appius Claudius and Q. Fabius Vibulanus were the chiefs of the decemvirate formed in 450, and were exiled for their tyrannical acts.

Fabre, (fȧbR, (ANTOINE FRANÇOIS HIPPOLYTE,) a French medical writer, born at Marseilles in 1797. He edited the "Lancette Française," and won a medal of the Institute in 1833 for a work on cholera. Died in 1853.

Fabre, (DENIS,) a French advocate, born at Montpellier, was a member of the Convention in 1792, and voted for the death of the king. He was killed in a battle against the Spaniards in January, 1794.

Fabre, (FRANÇOIS XAVIER PASCAL,) an able French painter, born at Montpellier in 1766, was a pupil of David. He worked many years at Rome and Florence. Among his best works are "The Judgment of Paris," "The Preaching of John the Baptist," and a portrait of Alfieri. He died at Montpellier in 1837.

Fabre, (JEAN CLAUDE,) a French ecclesiastic and writer, born in Paris in 1668. He wrote a continuation of Fleury's "Ecclesiastic History," (16 vols., 1734,) and other works. Died in 1753.

Fabré, (JEAN RAYMOND AUGUSTE,) a French poet, born at Jaujac in 1792, was a brother of Marie Joseph Victorin. He wrote, besides other works, a poem called "Calédonie," (1823,) which was received with favour, and "Irène," a tragedy, (1825.) Died in 1839.

See SABBATIER, "Vies de Victorin et d'Auguste Fabre."

Fabre, (MARIE JOSEPH VICTORIN,) a distinguished French poet and orator, born at Jaujac in 1785. He produced in 1808 a "Eulogy on Corneille," (in prose,) which was crowned by the Institute. Among his finest works are "The Death of Henry IV.," a poem, (1808,) an "Ode on Tasso," a "Eulogy on Montaigne," (1812,) and "Literary History of France in the Eighteenth Century," ("Tableau littéraire de la France au dix-huitième Siècle," 1810.) Died in 1831.

See SABBATIER, "Vies de Victorin et d'Auguste Fabre," 1832; "Nouvelle Biographie Générale."

Fabre de l'Aude, fȧbR deh lōd, (JEAN PIERRE,) a French statesman, born at Carcassonne in 1755. He was proscribed during the reign of terror, but in 1795 was named deputy to the Council of Five Hundred, and became commissioner of finance. At the coronation of Bonaparte, Fabre, as president of the tribunes, delivered a congratulatory address to the emperor. He was appointed senator in 1807, and received the title of count of the empire. He was afterwards chosen a member of the grand council of administration of the senate. Died in 1832.

Fabre d'Églantine, fȧbR dȧ'glŏN'tĕn', (PHILIPPE FRANÇOIS NAZAIRE,) one of the leading French Jacobins, born at Carcassonne in 1755. At the commencement of the Revolution he leagued himself with Danton, La Croix, and Camille Desmoulins, and participated in all the excesses of this party. He was chosen as deputy from Paris to the National Convention. He voted for the death of Louis XVI. without appeal, and was elected a member of the committee of public safety. He was one of the instigators of the decree which ordered that no English or Hanoverian prisoners should be made. He was accused of royalist principles, or *modérantisme*, and, with Danton, was executed in 1794. He had written numerous comedies.

See LAMARTINE, "History of the Girondists;" "Nouvelle Biographie Générale;" "Biographie Universelle."

Fabre d'Olivet, fȧbR do'le'vȧ', (M.,) a French philologist and fanciful *littérateur*, born at Ganges (Languedoc) in 1768. He produced numerous plays, poems, treatises on philology, history, etc. He found, it is said, allegories or mystic meanings in every word, syllable, and figure. Died in 1825.

Fabretti, fȧ-bret'tee, (RAFAEL,) an excellent Italian antiquary, born at Urbino about 1615. He was secretary to Pope Alexander VIII., and in the pontificate of Innocent XII. was appointed keeper of the archives in the castle of Saint Angelo. His principal works are "De Columna Trajani," ("On the Column of Trajan," 1683,) and "Inscriptionum Antiquarum Explicatio," ("Explanation of Ancient Inscriptions," 1699.) Died at Rome in 1700.

See FABRONI, "Vitæ Italorum doctrina excellentium."

Fabri. See PEIRESC, (FABRI DE.)

Fabri, fȧ'bree, (ALESSANDRO,) a noted scholar and author, born near Bologna in 1691. He wrote with great elegance, both in Latin and Italian. Died in 1768.

Fabri, fȧ'bre', (HONORÉ,) a learned French Jesuit, born about 1607, wrote numerous works, among which are a "Treatise on Plants and the Generation of Animals," (1666,) and "Synopsis Optica," (1667.) Died in 1688.

Fabri de Hilden. See FABRICE DE HILDEN.

Fabriani, fȧ-bre-ȧ'nee, (SEVERINO,) an Italian author and philanthropist, born in the duchy of Módena in 1792. He assisted Baraldi in his "Memoirs on Religion, Literature," etc., and published several biographies. He devoted much time to the instruction of the deaf and dumb. Died in 1849.

Fabriano, da, dȧ fȧ-bre-ȧ'no, (GENTILE,) a skilful painter of the Roman school, born at Fabriano, in the March of Ancona, about 1370. He worked at Venice and in Rome, where he painted the history of Saint John in the church of San Giovanni Laterano. He is called one of the best painters of his time. Died in 1450.

See VASARI, "Lives of the Painters;" LANZI, "History of Painting in Italy;" BALDINUCCI, "Notizie;" P. BENEDETTI, "Memorie delle Opere di Maestro Gentile da Fabriano," 1830.

Fabrice. See FABRIZIO.

Fabrice de Hilden, fȧ'brĕss' deh hil'dĕn, [Lat. FABRIÇ'IUS HILDA'NUS,] called also **Fabri** (fȧ'bree) de **Hilden,** (WILHELM,) a skilful surgeon and writer, derived his surname from a village near Cologne, where he was born in 1560. Died in 1634.

Fabricius, fȧ-bʀee'se-us, (ANDREAS,) a Roman Catholic divine, born near Liege in 1520. He wrote "Harmony of the Augustinian Confession," ("Harmonia Confessionis Augustinianæ," 1573.) Died in 1581.

Fabricius, fȧ-bʀit'se-ùs, (DAVID,) a German astronomer, born at Essen in 1564. He is said to have discovered spots in the sun. Among his works are "Letters to Kepler." Died in 1617.

See ERSCH und GRUBER, "Allgemeine Encyklopaedie."

Fabricius, (FRANZ,) a theological writer, called also LEFÈVRE, born in Rhenish Prussia in 1524; died in 1573.

Fabricius, fȧ-bʀit'se-ùs, (FREDERICK ERNEST,) a German or Swedish nobleman, who was a companion or attendant of Charles XII. at Bender. He wrote "Anecdotes of the Residence of the King of Sweden at Bender," ("Anecdotes du Séjour du Roi à Bender," 1760.) Died after 1727.

Fabricius, or **Goldschmidt,** (GEORG,) a German philologist and Latin poet, born at Chemnitz in 1516. He was president of the College of Meissen from 1553 to 1571. Among his works are a "Description of Rome," (1550,) and "Res Germaniæ et Saxoniæ memorabiles," (1609.) Died in 1571.

See BAUMGARTEN-CRUSIUS, "Programma de G. Fabricii Vita," 1839.

Fabricius, (JAKOB,) a German physician and mathematician, born at Rostock in 1577. He was physician to the King of Denmark. Died at Copenhagen in 1652.

Fabricius, (JEAN LOUIS,) a Swiss theological writer, born at Schaffhausen in 1632; died in 1696.

Fabricius, (JOHANN,) a German astronomer, son of David, noticed above, wrote a treatise on the spots of the sun, ("De Maculis in Sole observatis," 1611.) Died in 1625.

Fabricius, (JOHANN,) a German Orientalist, born at Dantzic in 1608, was professor of Hebrew at Rostock, and published "Specimen Arabicum," (1638.) Died in 1653.

Fabricius, (JOHANN,) a German Protestant writer and professor of theology, born at Altorf in 1644. Among his works is "Amœnitates theologicæ," (1699.) He taught theology at Altorf for many years. Died in 1729.

See ERSCH und GRUBER, "Allgemeine Encyklopaedie."

Fabricius, (JOHANN ALBRECHT,) a German scholar and writer, eminent for his profound and various learning, born at Leipsic on the 11th of November, 1668, was a son of Werner the composer. He became professor of eloquence and philosophy at Hamburg about 1700. He published numerous and excellent works, among which are "Bibliotheca Latina, sive Notitia Scriptorum Veterum Latinorum," (3 vols., 1697,) "Bibliotheca Græca," (14 vols. 4to, 1705-28,) containing notices of all the Greek authors who lived before the subversion of the Eastern Empire; "Bibliographia Antiquaria," (1713,) and "Bibliotheca Latina Ecclesiastica," (1718.) He passed the greater part of his mature life at Hamburg, where he died in April, 1736.

See REIMAR, "De Vita et Scriptis J. A. Fabricii Commentarius," 1737; NICÉRON, "Mémoires."

Fabricius, (JOHANN ANDREAS,) a German scholar and teacher, born at Dodendorf in 1696, published an "Abridgment of General Literary History," (3 vols., 1752-54.) Died in 1769.

See ERSCH und GRUBER, "Allgemeine Encyklopaedie."

Fabricius, (JOHANN CHRISTIAN,) the most eminent entomologist of his time, born at Tondern, in the duchy of Sleswick, in January, 1743, studied under Linnæus at Upsal. In 1775 he was appointed professor of natural history at Kiel, and about the same time published his "Systema Entomologiæ." In this work, at the suggestion of Linnæus, he made an arrangement of insects according to the organs of the mouth. Besides the treatise mentioned above, he wrote "Philosophia Entomologia," (1778,) "Supplementum Entomologiæ," (1797,) and others of a similar nature. Died at Kiel in 1807.

See "Biographie Médicale;" "Nouvelle Biographie Générale."

Fabricius, (KAREL,) a Dutch painter, born at Delft in 1624, excelled in perspective and portraits. Died in 1654.

Fabricius, (THEODOR,) a German Reformer and theologian, born at Anholt in 1501, wrote several religious

works. He taught Hebrew at Wittenberg, and acquired the friendship of Luther. Died in 1570.

See ERSCH und GRUBER, "Allgemeine Encyklopaedie."

Fabricius, (THEODOSIUS,) a Lutheran theologian, and nephew of the preceding, born at Nordhausen in 1560, was professor of theology at Göttingen. His work entitled "Harmony of the Four Evangelists" was published in the Latin, Greek, Hebrew, and German languages. Died in 1597.

Fabricius, (VINCENZ,) a German physician, jurist, and Latin poet, born at Hamburg in 1612; died in 1667.

Fabricius, (WERNER,) a composer and musician, born in Holstein in 1633, was the father of Johann Albrecht, noticed above. He lived at Leipsic. Died in 1679.

Fabricius Hildanus. See FABRICE DE HILDEN.

Fa-briç'ī-us (fạ-brish'e-us) **Lus-çī'nus,** (CAIUS,) a Roman statesman, celebrated for his great integrity and simplicity of life, became consul 282 B.C. About 280 he was sent on an embassy to Pyrrhus, who was encamped with an army near Tarentum. His conduct on this occasion was a celebrated theme of ancient historians and poets. He refused the rich presents or bribes which Pyrrhus offered him. According to tradition, the physician of Pyrrhus proposed to poison his master, expecting a reward from the Romans, but Fabricius not only rejected his offer, but exposed his treachery to Pyrrhus. Fabricius gained victories over the Samnites, the Bruttii, and other allies of Pyrrhus, about 277 B.C.

See NIEBUHR, "History of Rome;" PLINY, "Natural History," book xxxiv.

Fa-briç'ī-us Vei-en'to, a Latin author. Having written a satirical work entitled "Codicilli," which was supposed to be directed against the senators and priests, he was banished by Nero in 62 A.D. After Nero's death he returned to Rome, and was received with great favour by Domitian.

Fabrini, fȧ-bʀee'nee, (GIOVANNI,) an Italian grammarian, born in Tuscany in 1516; died about 1580.

Fabris, fȧ'bʀèss, (NICCOLÒ,) an ingenious Italian mechanician, born at Chioggia in 1739; died in 1801.

Fabrizio, fȧ-bʀèt'se-o, (GERONIMO,) [Lat. HIERON'YMUS FABRIÇ'IUS AB ACQUAPENDEN'TE; Fr. FABRICE, fȧ'bʀèss',] an eminent Italian anatomist and surgeon, was born at Acquapendente, near Orvieto, in 1537. He was a pupil of Fallopius, whom he succeeded in 1562 as professor at Padua. He wrote many short treatises on anatomy and surgery. Among his pupils was the celebrated Dr. Harvey, whose great discovery was perhaps suggested by some new observations which Fabrizio made on the valves of the veins. He obtained great success and celebrity as a teacher of anatomy. Died in 1619.

See THUILIUS, "Memoria H. Fabricii ab Acquapendente," 1619; CUVIER, "Histoire des Sciences naturelles;" SALVADORI, "Notitiæ de H. Fabricio," 1837.

Fabrizzi, fȧ-bʀèt'see, (ANTONIO MARIA,) an Italian painter, born at Perugia in 1594, was a pupil of Annibal Caracci. Died in 1649.

Fabroni, fȧ-bʀo'nee, or **Fabbroni,** fȧb-bʀo'nee, (ANGELO,) an eminent Italian biographer and Latin scholar, born at Marradi in September, 1732. He produced in 1766 the first volume of the "Lives of Italians eminent for Learning who flourished in the Seventeenth and Eighteenth Centuries," ("Vitæ Italorum doctrina excellentium qui Sæculis XVII. et XVIII. floruerunt," 20 vols.,) which is his principal work. In 1767 he was appointed prior or president of the church of San Lorenzo, Florence. He is sometimes called "the Plutarch of Modern Italy." Died at Pisa in 1803.

See TIPALDO, "Biografia degli Italiani illustri;" FABRONI, "Vitæ Italorum," etc., vol. xix.

Fabroni or **Fabbroni,** (GIOVANNI VALENTINO,) an Italian naturalist and writer on physical science, was born at Florence on the 13th of February, 1752. He applied various physical sciences to objects of general utility. He was director of the Museum of Florence, and wrote many useful treatises on botany, chemistry, rural economy, etc. Cuvier characterized him as a "living encyclopædia." Died in December, 1822.

See CUVIER, "Éloges historiques," tome iii.; TIPALDO, "Biografia degli Italiani illustri;" G. FABRONI PELLI, "Biografia del Cavaliere G. Fabroni," 1837.

ā, ē, ī, ō, ū, ȳ, *long;* ă, ĕ, ŏ, same, less prolonged; ă, ĕ, ĭ, ŏ, ŭ, ў, *short;* ạ, ẹ, į, ọ, *obscure;* fär, fȧll, fȧt; mêt; nŏt; gŏŏd; mŏŏn;

Fabrot, fȧ′bʀo′, [Lat. Fabro′tus,] (Charles Anni-bal,) a celebrated French jurist, born at Aix in 1580. ·He was professor in the University of Aix, and the au-thor of several legal treatises, one of which is entitled "Basilicon." Died in Paris in 1659.

See C. Giraud, "Notice sur la Vie de C. A. Fabrot," 1833.

Fabry, fȧ′bʀe′, (Jean Baptiste Germain,) a French writer, born at Cornus in 1780. He was editor of the "Spectateur Français," (12 vols., 1805–12,) and wrote a history of the Hundred Days, entitled "Itinéraire de Bonaparte de l'Isle d'Elbe à Sainte-Hélène," ("Account of the Journey of Bonaparte from Elba to Saint Helena," 1817.) Died in 1821.

Fabvier, fȧ′ve-ȧ′, (Charles Nicolas,) Baron, a French general, born at Pont-à-Mousson in 1782. He served with distinction in Germany and Spain, and was severely wounded at Moscow in 1812. In 1814 he signed with Colonel Davis the capitulation of Paris. In 1823 he went to the assistance of the Greeks, and rendered essential service in organizing an army. After his return he was created in 1839 lieutenant-general, and in 1845 a peer of France. He was the author of several military and historical treatises. Died in 1855.

Fabyan. See Fabian.

Facchetti, fȧk-ket′tee, (Pietro,) an Italian portrait-painter, born at Mantua in 1535; died in Rome in 1613.

Facciardi, fȧt-chȧʀ′dee, (Cristoforo,) an Italian Capuchin and eloquent preacher, born near Rimini, lived about 1570–90.

Faccini, fȧt-chee′nee, (Bartolommeo,) an Italian painter of architecture, born at or near Ferrara about 1520; died in 1577.

Faccio. See Fatio.

Facciolati, fȧt-cho-lȧ′tee, or **Facciolato,** fȧt-cho-lȧ′to, [Lat. Facciola′tus,](Giacomo,) an eminent Italian philologist, born at Torreglia, near Padua, in 1682. He was a professor of logic or classical literature in the University of Padua. He published an improved edition of a dic-tionary called "Calepino," (1731,) wrote several works on grammar and logic, and commenced an excellent Latin Lexicon, which was finished by his pupil Forcel-lini, (which see.) Died at Padua in 1769.

See Fabroni, "Vitæ Italorum doctrina excellentium;" G. B. Ferrari, "Vita J. Facciolati," 1799; Giuseppe Gennari, "Vita di J. Facciolati," Padua, 1818.

Facini, fȧ-chee′nee, or **Faccini,** fȧt-chee′nee, (Pie-tro,) an able Italian painter, born at Bologna about 1560, was a pupil and afterwards a rival of Annibal Caracci. His chief merits were a vivacity of attitude, and skill in colouring, especially in carnation. Died in 1602.

See Lanzi, "History of Painting in Italy."

Fa-cun′dus, a Latin theologian and bishop, who lived in Africa about 550 A.D. He defended the decision of the Council of Chalcedon against the decree of the emperor Justinian.

Fadhl-Ibn-Yahya-Al-Barmakee, (-Barmakî or **-Barmekî,)** fȧd′l Ib'n yȧh′he-ȧ ȧl baʀ′mek-ee, vizier of Haroun-al-Raschid, was born about 762 A.D. He was a brother of Jaafar, and one of the Barmecides, which see. Died about 807 A.D.

See Aboolfeda, "Annales Moslemici."

Fadlalla or **Fadlallah,** fȧd-lȧl′lah, a Persian his-torian, born at Hamadan, lived about 1290. He wrote a "History of the Moguls."

Fadl-Ibn-Rabee, (-**Rabî,)** fȧd′l Ib'n rȧb′ee, became vizier of Haroun-al-Raschid about 803 A.D., which posi-tion he continued to hold until the death of that sove-reign. In the contest between the caliph's sons Ameen and Mâmoon, Fadl sided with the former, and was con-sequently obliged to fly when Mâmoon ascended the throne. Died about 824 A.D.

See Ibn-Khallikan, "Biographical Dictionary."

Fadl-Ibn-Sahal, (or -**Sahl,)** fȧd′l Ib'n sȧh′hạl, (or sȧh′l,) a descendant of the ancient kings of Persia, and vizier of the celebrated caliph Mâmoon, was clothed with absolute power by this prince. He was assassi-nated by an opposite faction in 818 A.D.

See Elmacin, "Historia Saracenica."

Faed, fȧd, (Thomas,) a Scottish painter, born at Burley-Mill in 1826. He settled in London about 1852. Among

his works are "Walter Scott and his Friends at Abbots-ford," "Home and the Homeless," "Highland Mary," and "Sunday in the Backwoods."

Faenza, da, dȧ fȧ-ên′zȧ, (Giambattista Bertucci—bêR-toot′chee,) an Italian painter of the Bolognese school, flourished about 1500.

Faerna, fȧ-êR′nȧ, or **Faerno,** fȧ-êR′no, [Fr. Faerne, fȧ′êRn′,] (Gabriele,) a celebrated modern Latin poet, born at Cremona, in Italy. His most important work was his Collection of a Hundred Fables in Latin verse, (1564,) the subjects of which were taken from Æsop or Phædrus. He was patronized by Pope Pius IV. Died in 1561.

See Jan Hendrik Kroon, "Commentatio de Fabulis G. Faërni," 1824; Tiraboschi, "Storia della Letteratura Italiana."

Fagan, fȧ′gŏn′, (Christophe Barthélemi,) a French writer of comedies, born at Paris in 1702; died in 1755.

Fage, fȧzh, (Durand,) a French Protestant, called "the Prophet of the Cévennes," born at Aubais in 1681, was one of the Camisards.

Fage, La. See La Fage, (Raimond.)

Fagel, fȧ′hẹl, (Frans Nicolaas,) nephew of Kaspar, noticed below, was a distinguished military commander. He was successively general of infantry in the service of the States-General, and lieutenant-field-marshal to the Emperor of Germany. His greatest exploits were at the battle of Fleurus in 1690, the defence of Mons, the siege of Namur, the capture of Bonn in 1703, and several other battles in Flanders. Died in 1718.

Fagel, (Hendrik,) a Dutch politician, born in 1706, was an adherent of the Prince of Orange. A transla-tion of Lady Montagu's Letters (published in 1764) was ascribed to him. Died in 1790.

Fagel, (Hendrik,) a Dutch diplomatist, born at the Hague, was an adherent of the house of Orange. Having been sent as minister to London, he signed a treaty between Holland and Great Britain in 1814. He became secretary of state in 1824. Died in 1834.

Fagel, (Kaspar,) a celebrated Dutch statesman, born at Haarlem in 1629. In 1670 he was elected master of the rolls of the States-General, and in 1672 was created grand pensionary. It was partly by his influence that William III. was placed upon the throne of England. In 1682 Count d'Avaux, ambassador of France in Hol-land, made great efforts to win Fagel to the French interests, and even offered a large bribe, which was nobly refused. Died in 1688.

See Ersch und Gruber, "Allgemeine Encyklopaedie;" Macau-lay, "History of England," vol. v.; Lenting, "Specimen historico-politicum de G. Fagelio," 1849.

Faggiuola, fȧd-joo-o′lȧ,(Uguccione, oo-goot-cho′nȧ,) a celebrated Italian general, chief of the Ghibelines, and Lord of Pisa. He won several battles over the Neapoli-tans and Florentines; and in August, 1315, he gained the memorable victory of Monte-Catini. He, however, made himself so odious to the Pisans by his severity that he was driven from Pisa and from Lucca. He died at the siege of Padua in 1319.

See Leo and Botta, "Histoire d'Italie."

Faggot, fȧg′got, (Jakob,) a distinguished engineer and metallurgist, born in the province of Upland, in Sweden, in 1699, was secretary of the Academy of Sciences, and published a valuable work on rural economy. Died in 1778.

See H. Nicander, "Åminnelse-Tal öfver J. Faggot," 1778.

Fagiuoli, fȧ-joo-o′lee, (Giambattista,) a celebrated comic and burlesque poet, born at Florence in 1660. His works were very voluminous. Died in 1742.

Fagius, fȧ′je-us or fȧ′ge-ŭs, (Paul,) a learned Prot-estant theologian and Hebraist, born in the Palatinate in 1504. His family name was Bücher, (Beech,) which, according to the custom of that age, he changed into its Latin equivalent. He studied at Heidelberg under the celebrated Wolfgang Capito, whom he succeeded in 1544 as professor of Hebrew at Strasburg. In 1549, on the solicitation of Cranmer, Archbishop of Canterbury, he visited England, where he was appointed to the chair of theology at Cambridge; but his sudden death pre-vented him from performing the duties of that office. Eight years after his death his body was burnt, by the order of Queen Mary. Fagius was the author of numerous classical and critical works. Died about 1550.

See "De Vita, Obitu et Combustione Buceri et P. Fagii," 1562; FEUERLEIN and SEYFRIED, "Tentamen historicum de Vita P. Fagii," 1736.

Fagnan, făn'yŏN', (MARIE ANTOINETTE,) a French romancer, born in Paris, wrote "The Mirror of Oriental Princesses," (1755,) and other tales. Died about 1770.

Fagnani, făn-yä'nee, (GIOVANNI MARCO,) an Italian poet and scholar, born at Milan in 1524; died in 1609.

Fagnani or **Fagnano,** făn-yä'no, (GIULIO CARLO,) Marquis of Toschi, an eminent Italian mathematician, born at Sinigaglia in 1682, or, as some say, in 1690. He published a collection of mathematical treatises, ("Produzioni matematiche," 2 vols., 1750.) Died in 1766.

See MANCINI, "Elogi storici di F. Commandino, G. C. Fagnani," etc., 1828; TIPALDO, "Biografia degli Italiani illustri."

Fagnani, (PROSPERO,) an eminent Italian canonist, born in 1598, wrote a "Commentary on the Decretals," (1661.) Died in 1678.

Fagon, fȧ'gŏN', (GUI CRESCENT,) a distinguished French physician and botanist, born in Paris in 1638. He became first physician to Louis XIV. in 1693. Died in 1718.

See FONTENELLE, "Éloges des Académiciens;" ÉLOY, "Dictionnaire de la Médecine;" ANTOINE DE JUSSIEU, "Éloge de M. Fagan," 1718.

Fahie, fā,? (Sir WILLIAM CHARLES,) a British admiral, born in 1763; died in 1833.

Fahlcranz, fȧl'krȧnts, (CARL JOHANN,) a celebrated Swedish landscape-painter, born in the province of Falun in 1774. He painted many excellent pictures of the wild and mountainous scenery of Sweden and Norway.

Fahlcranz, (CHRISTIAN ERIK,) a Swedish poet and ecclesiastic, brother of the preceding, born in 1790. He is the author of a witty piece entitled "Noah's Ark," and "Ansgarius," an epic poem. He became Bishop of Westerås, and in 1839 associate editor of the "Ecclesiastic Journal," ("Ecclesiastik Tidskrift.")

Fah-le'nï-us, (ERIC,) a noted Swedish scholar, lived about 1700. He was professor of Oriental languages at Pernau, in Livonia.

Fahrenheit, fär'ĕn-hīt' or fä'rĕn-hīt', (GABRIEL DANIEL,) an eminent German natural philosopher and maker of philosophical instruments, was born at Dantzic about 1690. He became a resident of Amsterdam, and invented the thermometer which bears his name. He is said to have been the first who used mercury in the construction of thermometers. He fixed the zero of his scale at the point to which the mercury sank in the winter of 1709, and reproduced the same degree of cold by a mixture of sal-ammoniac, common salt, and snow. Died in 1740.

See ERSCH und GRUBER, "Allgemeine Encyklopaedie."

Faider, fi'der, [Fr. pron. fȧ'dair',] (CHARLES,) a Belgian jurist and writer, born about 1805. He was appointed minister of justice in 1852.

Faidit. See FAYDIT.

Faiguet de Villeneuve, fȧ'gȧ' deh vèl'nuv', (JOACHIM,) one of the earliest French writers on political economy, born at Moncontour, in Brittany, in 1703. Died about 1780.

Faille, de la, deh lȧ fȧl or fä'ye, (GERMAIN,) a French historian, born at Castelnaudary in 1616; died in 1711. He wrote "Annals of Toulouse," (2 vols., 1687–1701.)

Fain, făn, (AGATHON JEAN FRANÇOIS,) BARON, a French historian, born in Paris in 1778. He attended Napoleon I. in his campaigns in the capacity of secretary, *(secrétaire-archiviste.)* He wrote "Historical Memoirs of the Last Three Years of the Reign of Napoleon," (1823–27.) Died in 1837.

Faini, fä-ee'nee, (Madame DIAMANTE,) an Italian poetess, who wrote in Latin and French with great elegance and purity of diction. She died at Salo in 1770.

See G. PONTARA, "Vita della Signora Faini," 1774; A. BROGNOLI, "Elogio storico di D. Faini," 1785.

Faipoult. See FAYPOULT.

Fairbairn, (WILLIAM,) F.R.S., a British civil engineer and mechanician, born at Kelso, on the Tweed, in 1789. He is distinguished for the introduction of iron water-wheels and other iron machinery, and as one of the first constructors of iron ships, which he began to

build about 1835. He is author of several works, one of which is entitled "Mills and Mill-Work," and has made important contributions to the Philosophical Transactions and the Transactions of the Philosophical Society of Manchester. Among his works are numerous iron bridges.

See SAMUEL SMILES, "Industrial Biography," 1864; "North British Review" for August, 1850.

Fairbanks, (ERASTUS,) born at Brimfield, Massachusetts, in 1792, was an extensive manufacturer of platform scales. He was chosen Governor of Vermont in 1860. Died in 1864.

Fairclough. See FEATLEY.

Fairfax, (EDWARD,) a celebrated English poet, son of Sir Thomas Fairfax, was born at Denton, in Yorkshire, in the latter part of the sixteenth century. His principal work is a translation of Tasso's "Jerusalem Delivered," (1600,) which he rendered, verse for verse, with a fidelity and facility rarely equalled. King James placed this translation above all other works of English poetry. Waller recognizes him as his master in the art of verse; and Dryden, in comparing him to Spenser, gave the preference to Fairfax on the score of harmony. He also wrote a "History of Edward the Black Prince," in verse, and a treatise on "Demonology." His version of Tasso has often been reprinted in England, and once in the United States, (1855.) Died in 1632.

See Preface to FAIRFAX's Tasso, 1749; "Biographia Britannica;" CAMPBELL, "Specimens of the British Poets."

Fairfax, (ROBERT,) an English musician and composer, flourished about 1510–20.

Fairfax, (THOMAS,) LORD, one of the most conspicuous actors in the rebellion against Charles I. of England, and general of the parliamentary forces, was born at Denton, in Yorkshire, in January, 1611. He was the son of Ferdinando, Lord Fairfax, and Mary, daughter of Edmund Sheffield, Lord Mulgrave. Having strong inclinations for a military life, he went to Holland, and served as a volunteer under Horace, Lord Vere, whose daughter he afterwards married. When Charles endeavoured to form a body-guard at York, the people, fearing that he would raise an army, deputized Fairfax to present a petition to him entreating him not to do it. Although the king tried to shun him, Fairfax succeeded in presenting the petition, in the presence of about one hundred thousand persons. When the civil war broke out, (1642,) the father of Lord Fairfax received from Parliament the commission of commander-in-chief of the Northern forces, and he himself that of general of cavalry. He distinguished himself in this war by his activity and bravery, particularly at Marston Moor, where he commanded the right wing and where the king's army was totally defeated, (July 2, 1644,) and at the capture of York. Fairfax was appointed commander-in-chief of the parliamentary forces early in 1645, with Cromwell as his lieutenant-general. On the 14th of June the battle of Naseby was fought, on which occasion Lord Fairfax gained a decided victory. On the 16th he besieged Leicester, which surrendered on the 18th. He afterwards defeated Lord Goring, took Bridgewater by assault, and made himself master of several other places. On the 10th of September he forced Bristol to surrender. In September, 1646, he captured Oxford, the last stronghold of the king, who fled for protection to Scotland. Lord Fairfax then went to London, where he was complimented and thanked by both Houses of Parliament, and was immediately sent with two hundred thousand pounds to Scotland to obtain the king, the Scotch having agreed to deliver him up for that sum. Soon after this he yielded to the superior genius of Cromwell, and when on his father's death, which took place about March, 1648, he succeeded to all his titles, he still continued to fight for Cromwell. He was nominated one of the judges of the king; but he refused to serve in that trial. In the spring of 1649 he was appointed commander of all the forces in England and Ireland. He resigned his commission in June, 1650. About the end of 1659 he joined General Monk against Lambert, was appointed councillor of state, and also chairman of the committee delegated by the Chamber of Commons to go to the Hague and persuade Charles II. to return and take the royal functions. He was received by that prince, whose restoration to the throne was partially owing to the sincere efforts of Lord Fairfax. After these events, he retired to his estates, where he died of a fever in February, 1671, at the age of sixty years.

See HUME, "History of England;" VILLEMAIN, "Histoire de Cromwell;" GUIZOT, "Histoire de la Révolution d'Angleterre;" "Monk's Contemporaries," by GUIZOT, London, 1865; HARTLEY COLERIDGE, "Lives of Distinguished Northerns;" RICHARD BELL, "Fairfax Correspondence—Memorials of the Civil War," etc., 2 vols., 1849; SIR EDWARD CUST, "Lives of the Warriors of the Civil Wars of France and England," London, 1867.

Fair′fax, (THOMAS,) LORD, of the same family as the preceding, was born about 1691. Owning large estates in Virginia, he left England and settled in that colony, in the county of Frederick. He was a patron and friend of General Washington in his younger days; and in the Revolutionary war the hospitality and noble qualities of Lord Fairfax caused him to be held in so much veneration that his property was equally respected by the Americans and the English. Died in 1782.

Fair′field, (SUMNER LINCOLN,) an American poet, born at Warwick, Massachusetts, in 1803. He published in 1830 "Abaddon, the Spirit of Destruction, and other Poems." In "The Last Night of Pompeii" he claimed to have suggested the leading ideas in Bulwer's famous novel of "The Last Days of Pompeii," which appeared about two years later. Died in 1844.

See a Memoir of his Life, by his widow, 1846; GRISWOLD, "Poets and Poetry of America;" DUYCKINCK, "Cyclopædia of American Literature."

Fair′hōlt, (FREDERICK WILLIAM,) a British artist and writer, published in 1854 a "Dictionary of Terms in Art."

Faistenberger, fī′stẹn-bêR′ğẹr, (ANTON,) a Tyrolese landscape-painter, born at Innspruck in 1678, was a pupil of Gaspard Poussin at Rome. Died in Vienna in 1721.

See ERSCH und GRUBER, "Allgemeine Encyklopaedie."

Fai′thorne, (WILLIAM,) an English engraver, born in London about 1616. He was an adherent of the royalists, and was for a time imprisoned in London. Having refused, after his release, to take the oath of obedience to Cromwell, he was banished from England, and went to France, where he studied engraving under Champagne. About 1650 he returned to England, where he died in 1691. His engravings of "Christ at Prayer in the Garden of Olives," and of the "Marriage of Cana in Galilee," were among his principal works. He was also the author of a "Treatise on the Art of Engraving."

See STRUTT, "Dictionary of Engravers."

Faithorne, (WILLIAM,) a son of the preceding, engraved portraits in mezzotint. He died about 1686.

Fakhr-Eddaulah. See FAKHR-ED-DOWLAH.

Fakhr-ed-Deen or **Fakhr-ed-Dîn,** (or -Dyn,) fâk′r ed-deen, (i.e. the "Glory of the Religion.") There have been many Moslem doctors of this name, the most celebrated of whom is the Imâm Fakhr-ed-Deen-Razee, (or -Razy,) who was born at Rei, a city of Persia, about 1150 A.D. He is esteemed one of the ablest Mohammedan doctors that ever lived. He composed numerous works on theology, philosophy, and mathematics. Died in 1210.

See ABOOLFARAJ, "Historia Dynastiarum," translated by POCOCK; ABOOLFEDA, "Annales."

Fakhr-ed-Deen, better known as **Facardin Ameer,** (or **Amîr,**) Prince of the Druzes, born in 1574, was conquered by Amurath IV. and taken to Constantinople, where he was put to death in 1635.

Fakhr-ed-Deen Binakeetee, or **Fakhr-ed-Dîn Binakiti,** fâk′r ed-deen bin-ạ-kee′tee, (ABOO SOLYMÂN DÂOOD,) a Persian historian, born at Binakeet (Binakît) in 1329.

Fakhr-ed-Dowlah or **-Eddaulah,** fâk′r ed-dŏw′lạh, (ALEE,) a prince who ruled over part of Persia towards the close of the tenth century. Died in 997 A.D.

Falaize, fȧ′lȧz′, (CAROLINE PHILIBERTE,) originally named JACQUEMAIN, (zhăk′mân′,) a French authoress, born at Châteauroux in 1792; died in 1852.

Falbaire, de, dẹh fȧl′bȧr′, (CHARLES GEORGE Fenouillot— fẹh-noo′yo′,) a French dramatist, born at Salins in 1727. Among his most successful plays were "The Honest Criminal" and "The Two Misers." Died in 1800.

Falcand, fȧl′kôn′, [Lat. FALCAN′DUS,] (HUGO,) a historian of the twelfth century, supposed to have been born in Normandy, wrote, in Latin, a "History of Sicily" from 1146 to 1169. Falcand witnessed the events which he has recorded. His work is highly commended by Gibbon.

See GIBBON, "History of the Decline and Fall of the Roman Empire," chap. lvi.; VOSSIUS, "De Historicis Latinis."

Falcieri, fȧl-che-ā′ree, (BIAGIO,) a skilful painter of the Venetian school, born at San Ambrogio in 1628. Among his master-pieces is "The Council of Trent." Died in 1703.

Falck, fâlk, (ANTOON REINHARD,) a distinguished Dutch statesman, born at Utrecht in 1776. He became secretary of state in 1814, after the fall of Napoleon. In 1818 he was appointed minister of public instruction, and in 1832 received the title of minister of state. He wrote a treatise "On the Influence of Dutch Civilization on the Nations of Northern Europe." Died in 1843.

See QUETELET, "Hommage à la Mémoire d'A. R. Falck," 1844.

Falck, fâlk, (JEREMIAS,) a German engraver of history and portraits, born at Dantzic in 1629, worked in Holland and Sweden. Died about 1710.

Falck, (JOHN PETER.) See FALK.

Falck or **Falk,** fâlk, (NIELS,) a Danish jurist, born near Tondern in 1784, was elected president of the Diet in Sleswick-Holstein in 1838. He published a treatise "On the Duchy of Sleswick in its Present Relations to Denmark and Holstein." Died in 1850.

Falckenstein, fâl′kẹn-stīn′, (JOHANN HEINRICH,) the author of numerous historical and antiquarian works, is supposed to have been born in Silesia in 1682; died in 1760.

Falco. See CONCHILLOS-FALCO.

Falco, di, de fâl′ko, (BENEDETTO,) a learned Italian writer, born at Naples, lived about 1530.

Fal′con-berg or **Fal′con-bridge,** (fau′kọn-brij,) (MARY,) COUNTESS of, a daughter of Oliver Cromwell, born about 1636, became the wife of Viscount Falconberg. She was a person of superior talents. Died in 1712.

Falconbridge, fau′kọn-brij, (ALEXANDER,) an English traveller who visited Africa, was the author of a treatise "On the Slave-Trade of the African Coast," (1789.) Died in 1792.

His wife, ANNA MARIA, who accompanied him, wrote "Two Voyages to Sierra Leone," (1791.)

Falcone, fâl-ko′nà, (ANIELLO or ANGELO,) an Italian painter, born at Naples in 1600, excelled in painting battles. He was the master of Salvator Rosa. Died in 1680.

Falcone, di, de fâl-ko′nà, (BENEDETTO,) an Italian chronicler, born at Benevento, lived in the twelfth century.

Falconer, faw′kọn-ẹr, or fawk′nẹr, (Sir DAVID,) a Scottish jurist, born in 1639, was lord president of Scotland, and author of "Decisions of the Lords of Council," (1701.) Died in 1685.

Falconer, (HUGH,) M.D., a British naturalist and palæontologist, born at Forres, Scotland, about 1808. He was a surgeon in the service of the East India Company, and discovered numerous fossils in the Sivalik Hills, which are described in the "Fauna antiqua Sivalonis," (1846,) of which Falconer and T. Proby Cautley were joint authors. Died in January, 1865.

See a biographical notice prefixed to the "Palæontological Memoirs of Hugh Falconer," 2 vols., London, 1868.

Falconer, faw′kọn-ẹr, (THOMAS,) an English scholar, brother of Dr. William Falconer, noticed below, was born at Chester in 1736. He edited Strabo, and wrote several works. Died in 1792.

Falconer, (THOMAS,) an English lawyer and able writer, a grandson of Dr. William Falconer, was called to the bar about 1830, and was appointed a judge of county courts in Wales in 1851.

Falconer, (WILLIAM,) a Scottish poet, born at Edinburgh about the year 1735. He early became an orphan, and, owing to the narrowness of his resources, passed but little time at school. He afterwards went to sea as a common sailor,—a position which was little calculated to develop his poetical genius. At the age of eighteen he embarked as boatswain on the ship Britannia, which was wrecked on the passage from Alexandria to Venice.

Falconer and two of his companions were the only ones who were saved. This disaster furnished him with the subject of a poem, called "The Shipwreck," which he published in London in 1762, and which at once acquired for him a high reputation as a poet. Falconer returned to Scotland after the publication of his peom, and remained some time at Gladsmuir, with his relation the celebrated historian Robertson. In 1769 he embarked as treasurer in the frigate Aurora for the East Indies, and is supposed to have been shipwrecked ; for nothing was heard from the vessel after it left the Cape of Good Hope. Besides the work previously mentioned, Falconer wrote a "Nautical Dictionary," a poem "Upon the Death of Frederick, Prince of Wales," and an ode entitled "The Demagogue," a political satire.

See J. MITFORD, "Memoir of Falconer," prefixed to an edition of his poems, 1836; CHAMBERS, "Biographical Dictionary of Eminent Scotsmen;" CAMPBELL, "Specimens of the British Poets."

Falconer, (WILLIAM,) an eminent English physician, born at Chester about 1743. He was the author of an "Essay upon the Waters of Bath," "Observations" relating to the Gout, "Remarks on the Influence of Climate, Situation, etc. on the Disposition and Temper, Manners, Laws, and Customs, Government and Religion, of Mankind," (1781,) and a "Dissertation on the Influence of the Passions on the Disorders of the Body," (1788.) He resided many years at Bath. Died in 1824. He left an only son, the Rev. THOMAS FALCONER, born in 1772 ; died in 1839.

See notice of W. Falconer in the "Allgemeine Encyklopaedie" of ERSCH und GRUBER.

Falconet, fȧl'ko'nạ́', (ANDRÉ,) a distinguished French physician, born at Roanne in 1611 or 1612. He was medical counsellor to the King of France, and the author of a work on the treatment of scurvy. Died in 1691.

Falconet, (CAMILLE,) a distinguished physician and medical writer, son of Noël, noticed below, was born at Lyons in 1671. He was a member of the Academy of Inscriptions and Belles-Lettres, to which he contributed several dissertations. Died in Paris in 1762.

See QUÉRARD, "La France Littéraire."

Falconet, (ÉTIENNE MAURICE,) a distinguished French sculptor, born at Paris in 1716, was a pupil of Lemoine. His statue of Milo of Crotona opened to him the Academy of Paris in 1745. Having been invited by the empress Catherine II., he went to Saint Petersburg in 1766, and spent about twelve years on a colossal bronze equestrian statue of Peter the Great, which is his principal work and is generally admired. He returned to France in 1778. He wrote a Commentary on the books of Pliny which treat on sculpture and painting, and several treatises on art. Died in Paris in 1791.

See CICOGNARA, "Storia della Scultura;" L. BRIGHTWELL, "Bypaths of Biography."

Falconet, (NOËL,) a noted physician and medical writer, son of André, noticed above, was born at Lyons in 1644. He was appointed consulting physician to the king. Died at Paris in 1734.

Falconetto, fȧl-ko-net'to, (GIOVANNI ANTONIO,) a painter of the Venetian school, born at Verona, flourished about 1500.

Falconetto, (GIOVANNI MARIA,) an Italian architect, brother of the preceding, born at Verona in 1458, built the Rotunda of Padua, and other admired edifices in that city. His master-piece is the palace of Louis Cornaro, his intimate friend, with whom he resided many years. Died in 1534.

See VASARI, "Lives of the Painters," etc.

Fal-co'nĭ-a, (PROBA,) a Latin poetess, who lived in the latter part of the fourth century. She composed a poem upon the "Civil Wars of Rome," which is lost, and a "Cento Virgilianus," which is extant. The subject of the latter is sacred history.

Falconieri, fȧl-ko-ne-ā'ree, (OTTAVIO,) an Italian antiquary, born at Florence in 1646 ; died in 1676.

Falcucci, fȧl-koot'chee, (NICCOLÒ,) or **Nicholas of Florence,** a celebrated Italian physician, supposed to have been born about 1350. His medical skill procured for him the title of "the Divine." Died in 1411.

See TIRABOSCHI, "Storia della Letteratura Italiana."

Falda, fȧl'dȧ, (GIOVANNI BATTISTA,) a skilful Italian engraver, born in the Milanese about 1640. He engraved some monuments at Rome. Died about 1700.

Faldoni, fȧl-do'nee, (GIOVANNI ANTONIO,) an Italian painter of landscapes, and an excellent engraver, was born in the March of Treviso about 1690.

Faleiro, fȧ-lā'e-ro, or **Falero,** fȧ-lā'ro, (RUY,) a Portuguese geographer and mathematician. Having formed an agreement with Magellan in a project to discover a new route to the Moluccas, he offered his services to Charles V. in 1518. His offer was accepted; but a difficulty arose between Faleiro and Magellan, who departed without him. Died in 1523.

Faletti, fȧ-let'tee, or **Falletti,** fȧl-let'tee, (GERONIMO,) Count of Trino, an Italian writer, born at Trino, in Montferrat, about 1518. He was the author of an "Account of the War in Germany in the Time of Charles V.," (1552,) in verse, and other historical works. Died in 1564.

Falgani, fȧl-gȧ'nee, (GASPARE,) an Italian landscape-painter, born at Florence about 1620.

Falieri, fȧ-le-ā'ree, or **Faliero,** fȧ-le-ā'ro, (MARINO,) became Doge of Venice in 1354. He incited the plebeians to a conspiracy against the nobles, in which the latter were to have been massacred ; but, the plot being revealed, Falieri was tried for his crime and beheaded in April, 1355. This event forms the subject of Byron's well-known drama "Marino Faliero." In the hall of the Grand Council of Venice the portraits of the doges are placed, but instead of that of Falieri there is represented a ducal throne covered with a pall, with this inscription : "Here is the place of Marino Falieri, beheaded for his crimes." He was about eighty years old.

See MARINO SANUTO, "Vite de' Duchi de Venezia;" "Nouvelle Biographie Générale;" "Biographie Universelle."

Falieri or **Faliero,** (VITALE,) became Doge of Venice about 1084. He increased the power and commercial prosperity of the republic. Died about 1096.

Faliero, fȧ-le-ā'ro, (ANGELO,) an eminent Venetian senator, who persuaded his fellow-citizens to reject the proposition made by the doge Pietro Ziani, in 1225, to remove the seat of government to Constantinople.

Faliero, (ORDELAFO,) a Venetian general, who was elected doge in 1102. In the same year he conducted a fleet to aid Baldwin I. and the Crusaders in the conquest of Palestine. He was killed at the siege of Zara in 1117.

Falk, fȧlk, (JOHANN DANIEL,) a German *littérateur* and philanthropist, born at Dantzic in 1770. He founded at Weimar an institution for the education of destitute children, known as Falk's Institute. Among his works we may cite a satire in verse, entitled "Men and Heroes," (1796,) and his dramatic poem "Prometheus," (1804.) Died in 1826.

See GERVINUS, "Geschichte der poetischen National-Literatur," etc.; A. WAGNER, "Falk's Liebe, Leben, und Leiden in Gott," 1818; "Falkiana," Hamburg, 1811.

Falk, fȧlk, (JOHAN PEHR,) a Swedish physician and distinguished botanist, born in 1727. He was employed by Linnæus as tutor to his son, and became, about 1765, professor of botany or pharmacy in Saint Petersburg. He was one of the naturalists appointed in 1768 to make a scientific exploration of Russia, and wrote "Memoirs on the Topography of the Russian Empire," (3 vols., 1784–86.) In a fit of hypochondria, he killed himself in 1774.

See "Biographie Médicale."

Falkland, fauk'lạnd, (HENRY LUCIUS CARY,) third VISCOUNT, a son of the second Lord Falkland, is represented as a young man of great promise. He wrote a play called "The Marriage-Night," (1664.) He died in the prime of life in 1663.

Falkland, (LUCIUS CARY,) second VISCOUNT, eldest son of Henry, Viscount Falkland, is supposed to have been born at Burford, in the county of Oxford, in 1610. He studied at Dublin, and afterwards at Cambridge. Possessing a good memory, great talents, and a passionate love of literature, he progressed so rapidly in the study of the classics that, besides the Greek historians, he had read all the Greek and Latin poets before he had arrived at the age of twenty-three. In 1633, at the death of his father, he became gentleman of the cham-

ā, ē, ī, ō, ū, ȳ, *long;* ȧ, ė, ȯ, same, less prolonged; ă, ĕ, ĭ, ŏ, ŭ, y̆, *short;* ạ, ẹ, į, ọ, *obscure;* fär, fȧll, fȧt; mēt; nŏt; gōŏd; mōŏn;

ber of the king, and in 1639, although he was disappointed in the hope which had been held out to him of a command in the army sent against the Scotch, he went as a volunteer. In 1640 Lord Falkland was chosen member of Parliament, in which capacity he distinguished himself by his efficiency. In the contest between Charles I. and the people, he at first acted with the latter, and favoured the prosecution of the Earl of Strafford; but, becoming convinced that the popular party were going too far, he attached himself to the interests of the king, to whom he afterwards adhered with exemplary fidelity, and by whom he was appointed secretary of state. After the battle of Edgehill, where the royal army was victorious, Lord Falkland exposed himself to imminent danger in saving the lives of his enemies who had laid down their arms. He was killed at the battle of Newbury, on the 20th of September, 1643, where, having insisted on going in the first rank of Lord Byron's cavalry, he was shot at the first charge: his body was not found until the next day. He was the author of a work entitled "A Discourse on the Infallibility of the Church of Rome," and is supposed to have assisted Chillingworth in his "History of Protestantism."

See CLARENDON, "History of the Rebellion;" MACAULAY, "History of England," vol. v.; WALPOLE, "Royal and Noble Authors."

Falkner, fauk'nẹr, (THOMAS,) an English missionary, born at Manchester, studied surgery in London and Cadiz, where he was persuaded to become a Jesuit and to go to South America. He exercised his ministry in the vice-royalty of Buenos Ayres and as far south as the Rio de la Plata, where his great ability as a physician and surgeon was very useful to him. After remaining forty years in that country, he returned to England, where he published a work in 1774, entitled "Descriptions of Patagonia and the Adjoining Countries." Died in 1780.

See QUÉRARD, "La France Littéraire."

Fallaro, fäl-lä'ro, (GIACOMO,) a painter of the Venetian school, flourished about 1530. He is praised by Vasari.

Fallati, fäl-lä'tee, (JOHANN,) a German writer, of Italian extraction, born at Hamburg in 1809, published an "Introduction to the Science of Statistics," (1843,) and other treatises. Died in 1854.

Falle, faul or fäl, (PHILIP,) born in the isle of Jersey in 1655, was the author of a learned work entitled "An Account of the Island of Jersey." Died in 1742.

Fallet, fä'lẹ', (NICOLAS,) a French dramatist and poet, born at Langres in 1753; died in 1801.

Falletti. See FALETTI.

Fallmerayer, fäl'mẹh-rī'ẹr, (PHILIPP JACOB,) a distinguished German linguist and historian, born in the Tyrol in 1791. He performed several journeys to Palestine, Egypt, Greece, etc. Among his works are a "History of the Morea in the Middle Ages," (1830-36,) and "Fragments from the East," (1845.) Died in April, 1862.

Falloppio, fäl-lop'pe-o, sometimes written Fallopio, [Lat. FALLO'PIUS; Fr. FALLOPE, fä'lop',] (GABRIELLO,) a celebrated Italian surgeon and anatomist, born at Modena about 1523. He at first studied at Ferrara under Antonio Musa Brasavola, and afterwards at Padua. About 1550 he became professor of surgery and anatomy at Padua, where he succeeded Vesalius. He was the author of several valuable anatomical works, of which only his "Anatomical Observations" (1561) was published before his death. He was one of the three anatomists who, according to Cuvier, restored, or rather created, the science of anatomy in the sixteenth century. Died at Padua in 1562. He was an excellent teacher and a skilful operator. He discovered or first described several parts of the human body which bear his name. "No one," says Hallam, "had understood that delicate part of the human structure, the organ of hearing, so well as Fallopius; though even he left much for others." ("Introduction to the Literature of Europe.")

See NICÉRON, "Mémoires;" ÉLOY, "Dictionnaire de la Médecine."

Falloux, de, dẹh fä'loo',(FRÉDÉRIC ALFRED PIERRE,) VICOMTE, a French statesman and able writer, born at Angers in May, 1811. He published a "History of Louis XVI." in 1840, and favoured the formation of a republic

in 1848. He was minister of public instruction from December 20, 1848, to October, 1849. Since the latter date he has not been in public office. He became a member of the French Academy in 1857.

See "Nouvelle Biographie Générale."

Fäl'lōwṣ, (FEARON,) born about 1790, became astronomer-royal at the Cape of Good Hope in 1821. Died in 1831.

Falret, fäl'rä', (JEAN PIERRE,) a French physician, born in 1794, wrote on mental maladies.

Fals, fäls, (RAYMOND,) a Swedish engraver of medals, born at Stockholm in 1658; died in 1703.

Falsen, fäl'sẹn, (CHRISTIAN MAGNUS,) a Norwegian historian and jurist, born near Christiania in 1782, wrote a "History of Norway under Harold Haarfager and his Male Descendants." Died in 1830.

Fäl'staf, Fas'tolff, or **Falstolf,** (Sir JOHN,) a famous English captain, born in Norfolk about 1377. He distinguished himself at the battle of Agincourt, (1415,) and other actions in France. After the death of Henry V. he was Governor of Anjou and Maine. Died in 1459.

Falster, fäl'ster, (CHRISTIAN,) a Danish critic and poet, born about 1690, lived at Flensburg. He produced a number of satires, which were favourably received; also "Amœnitates Philologicæ," (3 vols., 1729-32,) and other works. Died in 1752.

See JENS HANSEN, "Programmata II. de Vita et Rebus gestis C. Falsteri," 1769-71.

Famin, fä'mäN', (STANISLAS MARIE CÉSAR,) a French historical writer, born at Marseilles in 1799. Among his works, which are highly commended, are "A History of the Invasion of Italy by the Saracens in the Seventh, Eighth, Ninth, and Tenth Centuries," (1843,) and "Histoire monétaire du Portugal," (in manuscript.) Died in 1853.

See "Nouvelle Biographie Générale."

Fanachen. See ACHEN.

Fancelli, fän-chel'lee, (JACOPO ANTONIO,) an Italian sculptor, born at Rome about 1630.

Fancelli, (PIETRO,) an eminent Italian historical painter, born at Bologna in 1764; died in 1850.

See MASSINI, "Cenno biografico di P. Fancelli," 1850.

Fan'cọurt, (SAMUEL,) an English dissenting minister of Salisbury, born about 1678, commenced in London the first circulating library that was established in England. Died in 1768.

Fane, (Sir HENRY,) a British general, born in 1778, commanded a brigade of cavalry at Talavera (1810) and other battles in the Peninsula. He became commander-in-chief in India about 1835. Died in 1840.

Fanelli, fä-nĕl'lee, (FRANCESCO,) an Italian advocate, born at Venice, wrote a "History of Athens," (1707.)

Fanelli, (VIRGILIO,) a Florentine sculptor, who died at Toledo, in Spain, in 1678.

Faneuil, popularly pronounced fŭn'el,(PETER,) founder of Faneuil Hall, Boston, was born in New Rochelle, New York, in 1700. About 1740 he erected for the town, at his own expense, the building which has since been famous as the scene of the most memorable public meetings held in Boston. Died in 1743.

Fangé, fôN'zhä', (AUGUSTIN,) a French Benedictine, born near Verdun about 1720; died about 1791.

Fan'nin, (JAMES W.,) COLONEL, an officer in the Texan war of independence, a native of North Carolina, was one of the three hundred and fifty-seven massacred at Goliad by order of Santa Anna, March 27, 1836.

Fan'ning, (DAVID,) an American Tory and outlaw, notorious for his daring exploits and for his barbarity, was born in North Carolina about 1756. He became the leader of a band during the Revolution. Died in 1825.

Fan'nĭ-us, (CAIUS,) surnamed STRABO, a Roman consul, during whose administration (161 B.C.) a law, called from him "Lex Fannia," was passed, to restrain the luxury of the people.

Fannius, (CAIUS,) son of the preceding, and a friend of Scipio Africanus, was elected consul 122 B.C. He was one of the most celebrated orators of his age.

Fannius, (CAIUS,) a Latin historian and orator, and a friend of Pliny the Younger. He commenced a work entitled "Exitus occisorum aut relegatorum a Nero,"

ɛ as k; ç as s; ḡ hard; ġ as j; G, H, K, guttural; N, nasal; R, trilled; ś as z; ᵵh as in this. (☞ See Explanations, p. 23.)

but died after he had completed only three volumes. A few fragments of his writings remain.

Fan'nĭ-us Ce'pĭ-o, one of a party who conspired against the emperor Augustus; but his design was detected, and he was put to death. He forms the subject of one of Martial's epigrams.

Fan'nĭ-us Quad-rā'tus, a Latin poet, whose bust and works were placed in the library founded by Augustus, and who was the subject of the fourth satire of Horace.

Fano, da, dä fä'no, (BARTOLOMMEO,) a painter of the Roman school, born about 1460; died after 1534. His son POMPEO was a painter.

Fanoli, fä'no-lee, (MICHELE,) an Italian painter and lithographer, born near Venice in 1807.

Fansaga, fän-sä'gä, (COSIMO,) an Italian architect and sculptor, born in 1591; died at Naples in 1678.

Fan'shawe, (ANNE HARRISON,) wife of Sir Richard Fanshawe, noticed below, was born in 1625. She was distinguished for her talents and accomplishments, and left interesting autobiographic "Memoirs," (1829.) Died in 1680.

See "Edinburgh Review" for October, 1829.

Fanshawe, (CATHERINE,) a literary English lady of the nineteenth century. She associated with Scott, Southey, Joanna Baillie, and other authors, and wrote verses, among which is an enigma on the letter H.

Fanshawe or **Fanshaw,** (Sir RICHARD,) an English diplomatist and poet, born in Hertfordshire in 1608, studied at Cambridge. He was sent as minister-resident to the court of Spain by Charles I. At the commencement of the revolution he joined the king's party, and was taken prisoner in 1651 at the battle of Worcester, and detained in confinement for several years. After the restoration he was made privy councillor for Ireland, then envoy extraordinary, and afterwards ambassador to Portugal, where he negotiated the marriage of Charles II. with the princess Catherine. In 1664 he was sent as ambassador to Spain, where he died in 1666. Notwithstanding the cares of office and the troubles of that period, Fanshawe found time for literary pursuits. He was the author of several translations into English poetry, among which were the "Pastor Fido" of Guarini, and the "Lusiad" of Camoens.

See "Biographia Britannica;" "Westminster Review" for October, 1829.

Fant, fänt, (ERIK MICHAEL,) a Swedish historian, born in Sudermanland in 1754. He became professor of history at Upsal in 1781, and made a collection of materials for Swedish history. He commenced a work entitled "Mediæval Writers of Swedish History," ("Scriptores Rerum Suecicarum Medii Ævi,") the first volume of which was published in 1818. Died in 1817.

Fantetti, fän-tet'tee, (CESARE,) a Florentine engraver, born about 1660, engraved, at Rome, thirty-seven of Raphael's subjects from the Bible.

Fantin des Odoards, fôN'tăN' dä'zo'do'ǎr', (ANTOINE ÉTIENNE NICOLAS,) a French historian, born at Pont-de-Beauvoisin in 1738. Among his works is a "History of the French Revolution," (6th edition, 1817.) Died in 1820.

See "Nouvelle Biographie Générale."

Fantoni, fän-to'nee, (GIOVANNI,) an Italian physician, son of Giovanni Battista, noticed below, born at Turin in 1675. He was professor of anatomy in his native city, and wrote many anatomical works, which are remarkable for their pure and elegant Latin style. Died in 1758.

Fantoni, (GIOVANNI,) an eminent Italian lyric poet, born at Fivizzano, Tuscany, in 1755. He was a man of unstable character, and was successively a monk, a captain in the French army, and professor of eloquence at Pisa. He produced "Horatian and Anacreontic Odes," ("Odi Oraziane ed Anacreontiche," 1785,) and other works. Died in 1807.

See "Autobiographic Memoirs," prefixed to an edition of his Poems, 3 vols., 1823; TIPALDO, "Biografia degli Italiani illustri," vol. i.; "Nouvelle Biographie Générale."

Fantoni, (GIOVANNI BATTISTA,) a medical writer, born in Piedmont in 1654, became professor of medicine at Turin. Died in 1692.

Fantosme, fan'tǫm, ? (JORDAN,) a poet and historian, lived in England in the twelfth century. He wrote, in verse, a history of the wars and events which he witnessed in 1173 and 1174. It was published about 1840.

Fantucci, fän-toot'chee, or **Fantuzzi,** fän-toot'see, (MARCO,) COUNT, an Italian *littérateur* and antiquary, born at Ravenna in 1745. He published "Monuments of Ravenna," etc., ("Monumenti Ravennati de' Secoli di mezzo," 6 vols., 1801-04,) and "On Honest People," ("De Gente honesta.") Died in 1806.

Fantuzzi, fän-toot'see, a family of Bologna, which produced several distinguished writers. GIOVANNI BATTISTA published a work on the Peripatetic Philosophy in 1536. GIOVANNI FANTUZZI, born at Bologna, lived about 1780. He contributed much to the literature of Bologna by his work entitled "Notices of the Bolognese Authors," ("Notizie degli Scrittori Bolognesi," 9 vols. fol., 1781-94.)

Fantuzzi, fän-toot'see, (ANTONIO,) sometimes called ANTONIO DA TRENTO, an Italian painter and skilful engraver, born at Trent, worked at Fontainebleau with Primaticcio. Died about 1550.

See TICOZZI, "Dizionario."

Fanucci, fä-noot'chee, (GIOVANNI BATTISTA,) an Italian historian, born at Pisa in 1756, wrote a "History of the Three Great Maritime Nations of Italy, the Venetians, Genoese, and Pisans," (4 vols., 1817-22.) Died in 1834.

Fanzoni, fän-zo'nee, or **Fenzoni,** fĕn-zo'nee, (FERRAU,) called also FERRAU DA FAENZA, a skilful painter of the Bolognese school, was born at Faenza in 1562; died in 1645.

See LANZI, "History of Painting in Italy."

Fa Presto. See GIORDANO, (LUCA.)

Făr'ą-day, (MICHAEL,) F.R.S., an English chemist and natural philosopher of great eminence, was born at Newington, in the county of Surrey, in 1791. He was the son of a blacksmith, by whom he was apprenticed to a bookbinder and stationer at an early age. His education, consequently, was not very liberal. During his apprenticeship he employed his leisure time in the construction of an electric machine and other apparatus. Having attended four lectures on chemistry delivered by Sir H. Davy, and taken notes of them, he wrote a letter to that great chemist, enclosing a copy of the notes, and soliciting his patronage in order to obtain scientific employment. This occurred in December, 1812. In 1813, by the influence of Davy, he obtained the position of assistant in the laboratory of the Royal Institution. In the same year he accompanied Sir H. Davy in a journey on the continent. The celebrity of Faraday is chiefly founded on his discoveries in electricity and electro-magnetism. He discovered the rotation of a magnet on itself produced by an electric current properly directed. As Ampère had made magnets by electricity, so Faraday produced electrical phenomena by magnets. He is considered as the founder of the science of magneto-electricity. In 1831 he commenced a series of memoirs on these subjects, which appeared first in the "Philosophical Transactions," and have since been collected in three volumes, entitled "Experimental Researches in Electricity," (1839-1844-1855.) He received the Rumford medal and royal medal in 1846 for his discovery of dia-magnetism. Among the results of his chemical experiments are the condensation into a solid form of carbonic acid gas and other gases, and the production of excellent optical glass. His researches and writings have contributed to establish the theory that electricity, caloric, and light are modifications of the same power or principle and are convertible into each other. These speculations conducted him to the surprising discovery of the action of electricity on light.

From 1827 until his death, Faraday delivered annual lectures on chemistry, etc. at the Royal Institution, in which he was appointed professor of chemistry in 1835. His lectures were rendered very attractive and popular by his graceful elocution and his admirable tact as an experimenter, joined with his genius as an interpreter of nature. "Nothing," says Professor de la Rive, "can give a notion of the charm which he imparted to these improvised lectures, in which he knew how to combine animated and often eloquent language with a judgment and art in his experiments which added to the clearness and elegance of his exposition. He exerted an actual fascination upon his auditors; and when, after having initiated them into the mysteries of science, he terminated his lecture, as he was in the habit of doing, by rising into regions far above matter, space, and time, the emotion which he experienced did not fail to communicate itself to those who listened to him, and their enthusiasm had no longer any bounds.

"Faraday was, in fact, thoroughly religious; and it would be a very imperfect sketch of his life which did not insist upon this peculiar feature which characterized him. His Christian convictions occupied a great place in the whole of his being; and he showed their power and sincerity by the conformity of his life to his principles. It was not in arguments derived from science that he sought the evidences of his faith. He found them in the revealed truths at which he saw that the human mind could not arrive by itself alone, even though they are in such great harmony with that which is taught by the study of nature and the marvels of creation. Faraday had long and justly perceived that scientific data, so movable and variable, cannot suffice to give to man a solid and impregnable basis for his religious convictions; but he at the same time showed by his example that the best answer which the man of science can give to those who assert that the progress of science is incompatible with these convictions, is to say to them, 'And yet I am a Christian.'" (See "Annual Report of the Smithsonian Institution" for 1867, pp. 227–245.) He was one of the eight foreign members of the Academy of Sciences of Paris, an honour reserved exclusively for savants of the highest rank and merit. English and foreign writers concur in ascribing to him an honourable character, free from jealousy, and animated with a disinterested love of science. Among his later works is "Experimental Researches in Chemistry and Physics," (1859.) Died in August, 1867.

See JOHN TYNDALL, "M. Faraday as a Discoverer," 1868; "Quarterly Review" for December, 1846; "British Quarterly Review" for April, 1868.

Faraj or **Faradj,** fär′aj, written also **Farage** and **Ferruj,** became Sultan of Egypt about 1399. His army was defeated by Taimoor near Haleb (Aleppo) in 1400. He was assassinated in Damascus in 1412.

Farcy, făr′se′, (FRANÇOIS CHARLES,) a French writer, born in Paris in 1792, was chief editor of the "Journal des Artistes" from 1827 to 1835.

Farcy, (JEAN GEORGES,) a French poet and prosewriter, born in 1800, was a friend of M. Cousin, who dedicated to him his translation of the laws of Plato. He left a volume of *mélanges* in prose and verse, which are highly commended. He was killed in Paris, fighting for the popular cause, in July, 1830.

See SAINTE-BEUVE, "Critiques et Portraits littéraires."

Fardella, faR-del′lä, (GIOVANNI BATTISTA,) an Italian general, born in 1762; died in 1836.

Fardella, (MICHELANGELO,) an Italian philosopher, professor of theology and geometry at Rome, and of astronomy and medicine at Padua, was born at Trapani, in Sicily, in 1650. He left some valuable mathematical and philosophical works. Died in 1718.

See NICÉRON, "Mémoires;" MANCUSO, "Elogio del Cavaliere M. Fardella," 1839; "Nouvelle Biographie Générale."

Far′dulf or **Far-dul′fus,** a favourite of Desiderius, the last king of the Lombards, was appointed by Charlemagne abbot of Saint-Denis in 790.

Fare, de la, deh lä fäR, (CHARLES AUGUSTE,) MARQUIS, a French soldier and writer, born in Ardèche in 1644, was the author of a work entitled "Memoirs of the Principal Events of the Reign of Louis XIV." Died in 1712.

Farel, fä′rĕl′, (GUILLAUME,) one of the most distinguished Protestant Reformers in France, was born near Gap in 1489. He studied in Paris under Lefèvre d'Étaples, and in 1524 publicly maintained at Bâle a number of theses on controverted points. He afterwards visited successively the principal towns of Switzerland, where his impetuous and fervent eloquence made numerous converts to the Protestant cause. He was chiefly instrumental in establishing the Reformed religion at Geneva about 1532; and through his influence Calvin was induced to remain in that city. Farel had a share in the confession of faith and plan of ecclesiastical discipline drawn up by Calvin in 1537. The following year, however, they were compelled to leave Geneva, and Farel repaired to Neufchâtel, where he organized a church. (See CALVIN.) He died in 1565, leaving a number of religious works. He was more eminent as a preacher than as a writer.

See D. ANCILLON, "Vie de G. Farel," 1691; CHOUPART, "Histoire de Guillaume Farel;" VON KIRCHHOFER, "Das Leben W. Farels," Zurich, 1831; C. SCHMIDT, "Études sur Farel," 1834; REV. WILLIAM M. BLACKBURN, "William Farel and the Story of the Swiss Reform," Philadelphia, 1865; BAYLE, "Historical and Critical Dictionary;" HAAG, "La France protestante;" G. GOGUEL, "Vie de G. Farel Réformateur," 1841.

Farelli, fä-rel′lee, (GIACOMO,) a painter of the Neapolitan school, born in 1624; died in 1706.

Faret, fä′rą′, (NICOLAS,) a French *littérateur,* born at Bourg-en-Bresse about 1600. He was one of the first members of the French Academy, and author of several works in prose and verse. "He had," says Pelisson, "much purity and neatness in style, and much genius for language and eloquence." Died in 1646.

See PELISSON, "Histoire de l'Académie."

Fä′rey, (JOHN,) an English geologist and surveyor, born at Woburn in 1766. He wrote a "General View of the Agriculture and Minerals of Derbyshire," (2 vols., 1811.) Died in 1826.

Farey, (JOHN,) an English civil engineer and draughtsman, son of the preceding, was born at Lambeth in 1791. He received a gold medal for the invention of a machine for drawing ellipses. Died in 1851.

Farge. See LA FARGE, (MADAME.)

Faria, de, dä fä-ree′ä, (MANOEL SEVERIM,) a Portuguese antiquary and theologian, born at Lisbon in 1581 or 1582, was the author of some able historical and political works, among which are "The Lives of João de Barros and Luiz de Camoens," (1624,) and "Noticias de Portugal," (1655.) Died in 1655.

Faria, de, (THOMÉ,) a Portuguese Carmelite, born at Lisbon, made a translation of the "Lusiad" of Camoens into Latin poetry, which has been much admired for its elegance and purity. Died in 1628.

Faria y Souza, (or **Sousa,**) de, dä fä-ree′ä e sō′zä, (MANOEL,) a distinguished Portuguese historian and poet, born at Pombeiro or Souto in 1590. He became secretary of the Spanish embassy at Rome about 1630, and returned to Spain in 1634, after which he resided at Madrid. His histories are written in the Spanish language. Among his numerous works are a "Commentary on the Lusiad of Camoens," (2 vols., 1639,) "Asia Portuguesa," (3 vols., 1666,) a History of Portugal to 1557, ("La Europa Portuguesa," 3 vols., 1667,) and "Various Poems," or "Fuente de Aganippe." As a poet, he belongs to the school of Gongora. Died in 1649.

See his life, in Portuguese, by F. MORENO PORCEL, 1733; LONGFELLOW, "Poets and Poetry of Europe;" N. ANTONIO, "Bibliotheca Hispana Nova;" "Nouvelle Biographie Générale."

Farina. See LA FARINA.

Farina, fä-ree′nä, (FABRIZIO,) a Tuscan sculptor, who flourished about 1600, and worked in porphyry.

Farinacci, fä-re-nät′chee, or **Farinaccio,** fä-re-nät′cho, (PROSPERO,) an Italian lawyer, celebrated for his talents and his vices, was born at Rome in 1544 or 1554. Died in 1618. His numerous legal writings were collected and published at Antwerp in 1620.

See TAISAND, "Vies des plus célèbres Jurisconsultes."

Farinato, fä-re-nä′to, (ORAZIO,) a skilful painter and engraver, born at Verona about 1500.

Farinato, (PAOLO,) an eminent Italian painter, son of the preceding, born at Verona about 1525, was a pupil or imitator of Titian and Giorgione. He painted in oil and fresco, and excelled in design. Among his best works is "The Miracle of the Loaves and Fishes." Died in 1606.

See LANZI, "History of Painting in Italy."

Farinelli, fä-re-nel′lee, (CARLO,) a celebrated Italian soprano singer, whose proper name was CARLO BROSCHI, was born at Naples in 1705. He was a pupil of Porpora. He performed with great applause in London in 1734 and 1735. About 1737, invited by the Queen of Spain, he went to Madrid, in order to soothe the nervous agitation or melancholy spirit of King Philip V. He succeeded in this effort, and became the favourite attendant and adviser of the king. It is said that he never abused his great influence at court, and that he gave a good example of integrity and benevolence. He enjoyed equal favour with Philip's successor, Ferdinand VI. Died at Bologna in 1782.

See GIOVENALE SACCHI, "Vita di Carlo Broschi detti Farinelli," 1784: FÉTIS, "Biographie Universelle des Musiciens."

Făr'ing-dọn or **Făr'in-dọn**, (ANTHONY,) an eloquent preacher of the Anglican Church, born at Sunning, Berkshire, in 1596. He became vicar of Bray in 1634, was ejected during the rebellion, and was subsequently pastor of Saint Mary Magdalene, London. He published a volume of Sermons, (1647,) which are highly esteemed. Died in 1658.

Făr'ing-tọn, (GEORGE,) an English painter, born in Lancashire in 1754, was a pupil of West. Died in India in 1788. His brother JOSEPH, a landscape-painter, died in 1818.

Farini, fä-ree'nee, (CARLO LUIGI,) a popular Italian statesman, historian, and orator, born at Russi, in the Roman States, in October, 1822. He studied medicine, and wrote several medical treatises. About 1842 he was proscribed for his political opinions, (which, however, were moderate rather than radical,) and went into exile. He was elected a member of Parliament for Faenza in 1848, and was minister of public instruction in Piedmont about nine months in 1850. In 1859 he was dictator at Módena after the expulsion of the duke. He was minister of commerce in the last cabinet of Cavour, and president of the council (prime minister) from December, 1862, to March 24, 1863, when he resigned on account of ill health. His chief works are "Il Stato Romano," (a History of Rome from 1815 to 1850,) and a continuation of Botta's "History of Italy." Died in 1866. The Hon. W. E. Gladstone published a translation of his "Il Stato Romano," in 2 vols., (1851.)

See "Quarterly Review" for January, 1852; "Edinburgh Review" for April, 1852.

Farini, (GIOVANNI,) an Italian mathematician, born near Ravenna in 1778; died in 1822.

Farjat, făr'zhȁ', (BENOÎT,) a French engraver, born at Lyons in 1646, worked in Rome. Among his best works are the "Baptism of Jesus Christ," and the "Communion of Saint Jerome."

Farlati, faR-lä'tee, (DANIELE,) an Italian monk and historian, born at Friuli in 1690; died in 1773.

Far'mer, (HUGH,) an eminent English dissenting minister and eloquent preacher, was born near Shrewsbury in 1714. He preached in London, and published, besides other works, a "Treatise on Miracles," (1771,) an "Essay on the Demoniacs of the New Testament," (1775,) and "Worship of Human Spirits in the Ancient Heathen Nations," (1783.) Died in 1787.

See MICHAEL DODSON, "Life of H. Farmer," 1804.

Far'mer, (JOHN,) an American genealogist, born in Chelmsford, Massachusetts, in 1789. He published a "Genealogical Register of the First Settlers of New England," (1829.) Died in 1838.

Farmer, (RICHARD,) a learned and ingenious English author and critic, born at Leicester in 1735. His principal work was his "Essay upon the Learning of Shakspeare," (1766,) in which he maintains that Shakspeare derived his knowledge of classic authors from translations. He became prebendary of Canterbury in 1782, and canon of Saint Paul's in 1788. Died in 1797.

See NICHOLS, "Literary Anecdotes of the Eighteenth Century."

Far'nạ-bỹ or **Far'nạ-bie**, (THOMAS,) a grammarian, born in London about 1575, obtained a high reputation and great success as a teacher, and was the author of several critical and grammatical works. Died in 1647. According to Anthony Wood, "he was the chief grammarian, poet, Latinist, and Grecian of his time, and his school was so much frequented that more churchmen and statesmen issued thence than from any school taught by one man in England."

See WOOD, "Athenæ Oxonienses."

Farn'bọr-ọugh, (CHARLES LONG,) LORD, an English politician, born in 1761, became postmaster-general. He was a friend of William Pitt. Died in 1838.

Farnese, faR-nā'sȁ, (ALESSANDRO,) an Italian diplomatist, born in 1520, was a grandson of Pope Paul III. He became Bishop of Parma, and was employed by Paul III. in missions to France and Germany. Died in 1589.

Farnese, far-neez', [It. pron. faR-nā'sȁ; Lat. FARNE'-SIUS,] (ALEXANDER,) Duke of Parma, a celebrated general, born in 1546, was a nephew of Philip II. of Spain, and the eldest son of Ottavio Farnese and Margaret of Austria. In 1565 he married Mary, niece of King John of Portugal. When his mother was made Regent of Flanders, he accompanied her to that country; he afterwards fought under Don John of Austria, and distinguished himself by his great courage and presence of mind, particularly at the naval battle of Lepanto, (1571.) Upon the death of Don John, (1578,) Farnese was invested with the government of the Low Countries, where he gained many important victories. He was appointed to the command of the Invincible Armada in 1588; but, being shut up in Antwerp by the Dutch fleet, he was unable to take any part in the action which resulted so disastrously to Spain. During the civil war in France he marched against Henry IV. and compelled him to raise the siege of Paris, (1590.) After this he successfully opposed, at the same time, two of the greatest generals of that period, Henry IV. of France, and Maurice of Nassau. He received a wound in December, 1592, of which he died in Arras at the age of forty-seven. While in the midst of his military career, upon receiving information of the death of his father, he asked permission of Philip II. to return to Italy, in order to take possession of his dukedom; but, as his services were invaluable to that monarch, his request was not granted, so that he never entered his provinces after he became their sovereign. "He possessed," says Motley, comparing him with Don John of Austria, "far greater power for governing men, whether in camp or cabinet. . . . Cool, incisive, fearless, artful, he united the unscrupulous audacity of a *condottiere* with the wily patience of a Jesuit."

See MOTLEY, "Rise of the Dutch Republic," part vi. chaps. i.-vii.; DE THOU, "Historia sui Temporis;" STRADA, "De Bello Belgico;" G. DONDINI, "De Rebus in Gallia gestis ab Alexandro Farnesio," 1671.

Farnese, (ODOARDO,) a son of Ranuccio, noticed below, succeeded him in authority in 1622. He took part with France in a war against Spain, and afterwards fought against Pope Urban VIII. He died in 1646, and was succeeded by his son, RANUCCIO II., who was born about 1630 and reigned from 1646 until 1694. FRANCESCO succeeded his father, Ranuccio II.; on the death of this prince, in 1727, his brother ANTONIO followed him as the eighth Duke of Parma and Piacenza. Died in 1731. Antonio was the last of the family of Farnese who occupied the ducal throne.

Farnese, (OTTAVIO,) a son of Pietro Luigi, noticed below, was born about 1520. He married Margaret of Austria, natural daughter of Charles V., and became the second Duke of Parma and Piacenza upon the death of his father. He appears to have governed with as much mildness and discretion as his father did with despotism. Died in 1586.

Farnese, (PIETRO LUIGI,) was created first Duke of Parma and Piacenza in 1545 by his father, Pope Paul III. He was notorious for his vices and tyranny. He was assassinated in 1547.

See SISMONDI, "Histoire des Républiques Italiennes;" POMPEO LITTA, "Vita di Pier Luigi Farnese," 1821.

Farnese, (RANUCCIO,) a son of Alexander, the celebrated Duke of Parma, noticed above, was born in 1569, and began to reign in 1592. He was notorious for tyranny and cruelty. Died in 1622.

Farnesius. See FARNESE, (ALEXANDER.)

Farnes'worth or **Farne'worth**, (ELLIS,) an English divine of the eighteenth century, born in Derbyshire. He translated into English, from the Italian, Davila's "History of the Civil Wars in France," and the works of Machiavel. Died in 1763.

Farn'ham, (ELIZA W.,) (originally MISS WOODSON,) an American authoress and philanthropist, born in Rensselaerville, New York, in 1815. In 1836 she was married to Thomas J. Farnham, noticed below. She was for four years matron of the female department of the State prison at Sing Sing, and was highly successful in

---

ā, ē, ī, ō, ū, ȳ, *long;* ȧ, ė, ȯ, *same, less prolonged;* ă, ĕ, ĭ, ŏ, ŭ, ў, *short;* ạ, ẹ, ị, ọ, *obscure;* fär, fȧll, fȁt; mĕt; nŏt; gōōd; mōōn;

her efforts to govern by kindness. She published "Life in Prairie-Land," "California Indoors and Out," and "My Early Days." She died in 1864.

Farnham, (THOMAS J.,) an American traveller and writer, born in Vermont in 1804, published "Travels in Oregon Territory," (1842,) and "Travels in California and Scenes in the Pacific," (1845.) Died in California in 1848.

Farochon, fȧ'ro'shòN', (JEAN BAPTISTE EUGÈNE,) a French statuary and engraver of medals, born in Paris in 1807.

Farquhar, far'kȧr, (GEORGE,) a distinguished dramatic writer, born at Londonderry, in Ireland, in 1678, was educated at the University of Dublin, and afterwards settled in London. Among his principal productions were "Love and a Bottle," (1698,) "Twin Rivals," (1703,) and "The Beaux Stratagem," (1707.) Died in London in 1707.

See a notice of his life, by LEIGH HUNT, prefixed to Farquhar's Works, 1849; "Lives of the British Dramatists," by CAMPBELL, LEIGH HUNT, etc.

Farr, (SAMUEL,) an English physician, born at Taunton in 1741. He wrote, besides other works, "Elements of Medical Jurisprudence," (1788.) Died in 1795.

Farr, (WILLIAM,) M.D., F.R.S., an English writer on statistics and public health, born at Kenley, in Shropshire, in 1807. He promoted sanitary reform by a number of works, among which are "Vital Statistics," (1837,) and "Statistical Nosology."

Fär'ra-gut, (DAVID GLAS'COE,) a celebrated American admiral, born near Knoxville, Tennessee, on the 5th of July, 1801. His father was a Spaniard, a native of Minorca, who fought for the United States in the Revolution and attained the rank of major. He entered the navy in 1812, became a lieutenant in 1821, and was assigned to duty at Norfolk navy-yard in 1824. He remained there until 1833, and married Virginia Loyall, of Norfolk. In 1841 he received a commission as commander. Besides being well versed in naval science, he spoke fluently, it is said, several modern languages. He was appointed commander of the navy-yard at Mare Island, California, about 1854, and obtained the rank of captain in 1855. In April, 1861, he went to Washington and offered his services to fight for the Union; but the government had no ship for him to command, as Toucey, the late secretary of the navy, had scattered the navy over distant parts of the world. He was employed for some time as a member of the naval retiring board.

In January, 1862, the government fitted out for the capture of New Orleans an armament, of which Farragut was appointed commander. He sailed from Hampton Roads about the 3d of February to Ship Island, which was used as a rendezvous. The expedition was accompanied by a land-army under General B. F. Butler. New Orleans was defended against attacks from the Gulf by Fort Jackson and Fort Saint Philip, about seventy miles below the city, and by many gunboats and steam-rams. On the 18th of April, Farragut, who had selected the Hartford as his flag-ship, and whose fleet consisted of wooden steamers and bomb-vessels or mortar-boats, began to bombard Fort Jackson. The sides of some of his vessels were protected by an armour of heavy chain cables. He bombarded the fort for six days without success, and then resolved to try the perilous experiment of running past the forts in the darkness. Before daylight on the 24th, his fleet advanced in two columns, one of which was composed of the Hartford, Brooklyn, Richmond, Scioto, Iroquois, Itasca, etc.; the other of the Cayuga, Pensacola, Mississippi, and five others. A grand and terrific spectacle was then exhibited when the guns of both the forts opened on the Union fleet, which was also assailed by the iron-clad ram Manassas, and by a number of gun-boats and fire-rafts rushing down the river. Of the seventeen Union vessels engaged in this action, thirteen passed the forts safely, and sunk or burned the fleet of the enemy, including the Manassas. Farragut lost in this battle, which lasted about one hour and a half, 36 killed and 135 wounded. Captain Craven, of the Brooklyn, silenced Fort Saint Philip as he passed it. "The passing of the forts Jackson and Saint Philip," says Farragut, "was one of the most awful sights and events I ever saw or expect to experience. The smoke was so dense that it was only now and then you could see any thing but the flash of the cannon and the fire-ships or rafts, one of which was pushed down upon us (the Hartford) by the ram Manassas, and in my effort to avoid it it ran the ship on shore, and then the fire-raft was pushed alongside, and in a moment the ship was one blaze all along the port side. But, thanks to the good organization of the fire-department by Lieutenant Thornton, the flames were extinguished, and at the same time we backed off and got clear of the raft." (Letter to G. V. Fox, dated April 27, 1862.) He moved up to New Orleans, which, being entirely indefensible against the guns of the fleet, was evacuated by the rebel army. According to the "Rebellion Record" and other authorities, the city surrendered on the 25th; but Farragut, in the letter just cited, says, "I demanded the surrender of the city yesterday of the mayor. His reply was that the city was under martial law, and he would consult General Lovell. His lordship said he would surrender nothing, but at the same time he would retire and leave the mayor unembarrassed." The capture of New Orleans was one of the most important victories of the war.

Farragut was promoted to the rank of rear-admiral in July, 1862, having previously obtained command of the Western Gulf blockading squadron. About the end of June he attacked the batteries at Vicksburg, which were found to be impregnable to an attack on the river-front. Having been ordered to co-operate with General Grant against Vicksburg, he attempted, in March, 1863, to pass the batteries of Port Hudson. The Hartford and Albatross, which were lashed together, succeeded, after a desperate contest; but the Richmond and others were disabled, and dropped down the river. His next great enterprise was directed against the defences of Mobile, the port of which the government desired to close against the ingress of blockade-runners. The entrance to Mobile Bay was defended by Fort Morgan and Fort Gaines, and the insurgents had in the bay a powerful iron-clad ram, called the Tennessee, besides three gunboats. Co-operating with a land-army under Generals Canby and Granger, the fleet of Farragut, consisting of fourteen wooden steamers and gunboats and four iron-clad monitors, passed Fort Morgan on the 5th of August, 1864, and entered the bay. The admiral lashed himself near the maintop of the Hartford, (according to one account,) in order that he might be able to overlook the whole scene. He states in his report that he "had an elevated position in the main rigging, near the top." In the early part of the action the monitor Tecumseh was sunk by a torpedo. Just after his fleet passed the forts, it encountered the Tennessee; and "then began," says Farragut, "one of the fiercest naval combats on record." The monitors, and such of the wooden vessels as I thought best adapted for the purpose, were immediately ordered to attack the ram, not only with their guns, but bows on at full speed." The Tennessee was "sore beset," and never fired a gun from the time the Hartford struck her until her surrender. A few days after this victory the Union forces took Fort Gaines and Fort Morgan, with their garrisons, and rendered the access of blockade-runners to Mobile impossible. The Congress which met in December, 1864, recognized the obligations of the country to Farragut by creating for him the grade of vice-admiral. His character is described by the "United States Service Magazine" for January, 1865, in the following terms: "The stainless honour, the straightforward frankness, the vivacity of manner and conversation, the gentleness, the flow of good humour, the cheerful, ever-buoyant spirit of the true man,—these will be added to the complete education, the thorough seamanship, the devotion to duty, and, lastly, the restless energy, the disdain of obstacles, the impatience of delay or hesitation, the disregard of danger, that stand forth in such prominence in the portrait, deeply engraven on the loyal American heart, of the GREAT ADMIRAL." He was promoted to the rank of admiral July 25, 1866, and held a higher rank than any other officer of the United States navy. Died at Portland, Maine, in August, 1870.

See J. T. HEADLEY, "Farragut and our Naval Commanders," 1867.

Far'rant, (RICHARD,) an English composer of church music, was a gentleman of the Chapel Royal. His anthems are regarded as master-pieces. Died about 1585.

Far'rar, (JOHN,) an American mathematician, born in Lincoln, Massachusetts, in 1779, graduated at Harvard in 1803. He became professor of mathematics and natural philosophy in that college in 1807. He translated Lacroix's "Elements of Algebra," and other French works, and contributed some articles to the "North American Review." Died in 1853.

Far'ren, (ELIZA,) a popular English actress, and Countess of Derby, born in 1759, was the daughter of a surgeon of Cork. She performed with great applause at the theatres of Liverpool and London. In 1797 she was married to Lord Derby. Died in 1829.

Farsetti, far-set'tee, a noble Italian family, one branch of which settled at Florence and another at Venice. GIUSEPPE TOMMASO FARSETTI, a chevalier of the order of Malta, was the author of numerous miscellaneous works. He collected a large number of poems in Latin and Italian of great taste and elegance, by requesting all the poets of his time to compose and send one or more pieces of the best quality for the collection. Died about 1775.

Farsetti, (FILIPPO,) an Italian antiquary, born at Venice in 1705; died in 1774.

Farulli, fä-rool'lee, (GIORGIO ANGELO,) a voluminous Italian historical writer; died at Florence in 1728.

Farwharson, far'hwar-son, a Scottish mathematician, whom Peter the Great, when he visited England in 1698, induced to return with him to Moscow. In 1701 he founded in that city the first Russian school of marine, and in 1716 became professor of mathematics at Saint Petersburg. Farwharson is said to have been the first to introduce the Arabic figures into Russia. Died in 1739.

Fasch, fåsh, (AUGUSTIN HEINRICH,) a German medical writer, born in Thuringia in 1639; died in 1690.

Fasch, (KARL FRIEDRICH CHRISTIAN,) a German musical composer, born at Zerbst, in Anhalt-Dessau, in 1736. His "Kyrie and Gloria" for sixteen voices is esteemed one of the most exquisite productions of its kind. Fasch was the founder of the Academy of Singing at Berlin, *(Berliner Singakademie.)* Died in 1800.

See KARL F. ZELTER, "Biographie von C. F. Fasch," 1801.

Fäsch or **Faesch,** fêsh, (SEBASTIAN,) a Swiss antiquary, born at Bâle in 1647; died in 1712.

Fascitelli, fä-she-tel'lee, (ONORIO,) a Latin poet, born at Isernia, Naples, in 1502; died in 1564.

Fasel, fä'zel, (JOHANN FRIEDRICH,) a German physician, and professor of medicine at Jena, born in the duchy of Weimar in 1721; died in 1767.

Fasolato, fä-so-lä'to, (AGOSTINO,) a Venetian sculptor, lived about 1700, and made a famous group of "The Fall of Rebellious Angels" at Padua.

Fasolo, fä'so-lo, (BERNARDINO,) an Italian painter, a pupil of Leonardo da Vinci, born at Pavía, lived about 1540.

Fasolo or **Fassolo,** fäs'so-lo, (GIOVANNI ANTONIO,) an Italian painter, pupil of Paul Veronese, was born at Vicenza in 1528; died in 1572.

Fassin, de, deh fä'säN', (NICOLAS HENRI JOSEPH,) a skilful Belgian landscape-painter, born at Liege in 1728, worked at Geneva, Brussels, and Liege. Died in 1811.

See F. VAN HULST, "Biographie de N. H. J. de Fassin," 1837.

Fassolo. See FASOLO.

Fastolf. See FALSTAF.

Fatah- (or **Fat'h-**) **Abu-Nâsr.** See ALFATH.

Fateh-Alee- (or **Alî-**) **Shâh,** fät'eh ä'lee shâh, written also **Futteh-Aly-Shah** and **Feth-Ali-Shah,** (called, before his accession to the throne, **Bâbâ-Khân,** bä'bä kän,) King of Persia, born about 1762, began to reign in 1798. About 1802 war broke out between Persia and Russia, who fought for the possession of Georgia. This war was ended in 1813 by a treaty in which Fateh-Alee-Shah ceded Georgia to Russia. A dispute about boundaries occasioned a renewal of the war in 1826, when the Persians were again defeated. Peace was restored in 1828. Died in 1834.

See MALCOLM, "History of Persia;" W. G. OUSELEY, "Travels in Various Countries of the East," 1823; "Nouvelle Biographie Générale."

Fathime. See FATIMAH.

Fathimites. See FATIMITES.

Fâtimah, fä'te-mah, [Fr. FATHIME, fä'tèm'; Ger. FATIME, fä-tee'meh,] written also **Fathimet,** the only daughter of Mohammed, was born at Mecca before her father assumed the character of a religious teacher. While still very young, she was married to her cousin Alee, who was surnamed the "Lion of God." Fâtimah died about six months after her father.

See ABOOLFEDA, "Vie de Mahomet."

Fatime. See FÂTIMAH.

Fatimides or **Fatimiden.** See FATIMITES.

Fät'I-mites, sing. **Fät'I-mite,** [Fr. pron. fä'te'mèt'; Ger. FATIMIDEN, fä-te-mee'den; Lat. FATIM'IDÆ or FATIMI'TÆ,] the name of a celebrated Moslem dynasty, the rulers of which claimed to be descended from Fâtimah, the daughter of Mohammed. The Fatimite caliphs ruled in Egypt about two hundred years,—that is, from about 970 to 1170. The founder of this dynasty was the Sheeite Al-Mahdee-Aboo-Mohammed Obeydallah, (often called simply Obeydallah,) who about 910 overthrew the dynasty of the Benee-Aghlab (the seat of whose power was at Tunis) and conquered a large part of Eastern Africa. He died in 934. One of his descendants, Moez or Mōōiz, nearly forty years later, subdued Egypt and Western Africa, and established his throne at Cairo. Al-Adhed, the fourteenth and last caliph of this dynasty, was dethroned by the celebrated Saladin (Sala-ed-Deen) the Aiyoobite. From Al-Mahdee's name of Obeydallah his successors are often called Obeydites.

Fatio (or **Faccio**) **de Duillers,** fä'te-o (or fät'cho) de dwee'yä, (NICOLAS,) a celebrated mathematician, astronomer, and religious enthusiast, was born at Bâle in 1664. He became a Fellow of the Royal Society of London in 1688. Among his discoveries were a method for forming glasses for telescopes, one for measuring the velocity of vessels, and one for the perfect regulation of watches. He was the author of numerous mathematical works. Died in England in 1753. He pretended to be able to work miracles.

See SÉNEBIER, "Histoire littéraire de Genève."

Fatouville, de, deh fä'too'vèl', a French dramatic writer of Normandy, lived about 1670.

Fattore, Il. See PENNI.

Faucci, fôwt'chee, (CARLO,) an Italian engraver, born at Florence in 1729, settled in London.

Fauchard, fo'shär', (PIERRE,) a celebrated dentist, born in Brittany about 1680, is regarded as the founder of the art of dentistry. He wrote a valuable work entitled "The Surgeon-Dentist; or, Treatise on the Teeth," (1728.) Died in Paris in 1761.

Fauche-Borel, fôsh bo'rèl', (LOUIS,) born at Neufchâtel in 1762, was a zealous adherent of the royal family during the Revolution. After the accession of Napoleon he was engaged in several attempts to restore the Bourbons. Died in 1829.

See LOUIS FAUCHE-BOREL, "Mémoires," 4 vols., 1828.

Faucher, fo'shä', (CÉSAR and CONSTANTIN,) French generals, born at La Réole in 1759, were twin brothers. They served with distinction in the army of the republic in La Vendée in 1793, fighting side by side. During the empire they were engaged in civil pursuits; but in March, 1815, they accepted office under Napoleon. Having been falsely accused of treason, they were shot at Bordeaux in September, 1815.

Faucher, (JEAN,) a French Protestant minister and polemical writer; died at Nîmes in 1628.

Faucher, (LÉON,) a French minister of state and able writer on political economy and finance, was born at Limoges in September, 1803. He contributed many articles to the "Courrier Français" and the "Revue des Deux Mondes." In the Chamber of Deputies, to which he was elected in 1846, he acted with the *gauche*. He was minister of the interior from December, 1848, to May, 1849, and from April to October, 1851. He was liberal in politics, but not a republican. Among his works are "Studies on England," (1845,) and "Miscellanies of Political Economy and Finance," ("Mélanges d'Économie politique et de Finances," 2 vols., 1856.) Died at Marseilles in December, 1854. He resolutely declined to hold any office under Louis Napoleon after the latter had usurped imperial power.

Alluding to the conduct of Faucher on this occasion, a writer in the "Edinburgh Review" remarks, "We do not remember an example in political history of greater sacrifices made by an ambitious and ardent man to his sense of public duty and personal dignity."

See LAVERGNE, "Biographie de Léon Faucher," in the "Revue des Deux Mondes," January 1, 1855; LÉON FAUCHER, "Correspondance. Vie parlementaire," 2 vols., 1868; and article on "Léon Faucher" in the "Edinburgh Review" for July, 1868.

Fauchet, fō'shȧ', (CLAUDE,) a French historical writer, born in Paris about 1530, published "Gallic and French Antiquities," (1579,) and "Origin of Dignities and Magistrates in France." Died in 1601.

Fauchet, (CLAUDE,) a French ecclesiastic, born in Nivernais in 1744. He joined the revolutionary party in 1789, and delivered in favour of their cause his "Discourse upon the National Religion," and "Civic Eulogy on Franklin." He became constitutional Bishop of Calvados in 1791. He was opposed to the death of the king, and showed great courage in condemning those who favoured it. Having been accused as an accomplice of Charlotte Corday, he was condemned and executed as a Girondist in October, 1793.

See ABBÉ VALMERON, (JARRY,) "Vie de l'Abbé Fauchet."

Faucheur, Le, lęh fō'shŭr', (MICHEL,) an eloquent French Protestant minister; died in Paris in 1657.

Faugère, fō'zhair', (ARNAUD PROSPER,) a French littérateur, born at Bergerac in 1810. He gained, three times, the prize of eloquence offered by the French Academy. One of these prizes was awarded for his "Eulogy on Pascal," (1842.) He also edited the works of Pascal, "Pensées, Fragments et Lettres de Blaise Pascal," (2 vols., 1844.) This is said to have been the first correct and complete edition of Pascal's "Thoughts." In 1864 he published a revised edition of the "Memoirs of Madame Roland."

See "Nouvelle Biographie Générale."

Faujas de Saint-Fond, fō'zhȧs' dęh sȧN'fôN', (BARTHÉLEMY,) an eminent French geologist and traveller, born at Montélimart in 1741. He was a friend of Buffon, by whose influence he obtained the place of adjoint-naturaliste in the Museum of Paris, and that of commissioner of mines. He explored France, England, Germany, Italy, etc. In 1793 he became professor of geology in the Jardin des Plantes. Among his numerous works are "Mineralogy of Volcanoes,"(1784,) "Travels in England and Scotland," (1797,) and an "Essay on Geology, or Memoirs subservient to the Natural History of the Globe," (2 vols., 1803-09.) Died in 1819.

See QUÉRARD, "La France Littéraire;" LOUIS DE FREYCINET, "Essai sur la Vie, etc. de B. Faujas de Saint-Fond," 1820; "Nouvelle Biographie Générale."

Faulcon, fō'kôN', (MARIE FÉLIX,) a French politician and jurist, born at Poitiers in 1758; died in 1843.

Faulhaber, fŏwl'hä'ber, (CHRISTOPH ERHARDT,) a German mathematician, born at Ulm in 1708; died in 1781.

Faulhaber, (JOHANN,) a German mathematician and engineer, born at Ulm in 1580, was the author of "Inventions for the Delineations of Redoubts and Fortifications," and other treatises. Died in 1635.

See MONTUCLA, "Histoire des Mathématiques."

Faulkner, fauk'ner, (GEORGE,) the first Irish printer of any note, born about 1700, was apprenticed to the celebrated Bowyer, and established himself in Dublin in 1727. He enjoyed the friendship and patronage of Dean Swift, Lord Chesterfield, and other celebrated men of the time. Died in 1775.

Fau'na, a goddess of ancient Italy or Latium, said to be a daughter of Picus, and wife of Faunus. She was sometimes identified with the Bona Dea and with Ops.

Fau'ni, [Eng. FAUNS; Fr. FAUNES, fōn,] mythical beings whom the ancient Romans represented as having human bodies with the legs and feet of the goat. They were sportive and frolicsome, and presented some analogy to the Satyrs of the Greek mythology.

Faun'tle-roy, (THOMAS T.,) an American officer, born in Virginia, served in the Confederate army in 1861, and was made a brigadier-general.

Fau'nus, [Fr. FAUNE, fōn,] a rural divinity and king of the ancient Latins, was supposed to be the son of Picus and the father of Latinus. He was worshipped as the god of fields and shepherds, and was considered as one of the founders of the religion of Latium. He was sometimes identified with the Arcadian Pan of the Greeks.

Fauques, fōk, (MARIANNE AGNÈS,) a French authoress, born at Avignon about 1720. Having visited London, she became a teacher of the French language, and numbered among her pupils the celebrated linguist Sir William Jones. She wrote numerous works in French and English, among which are "The Triumph of Friendship," (1751,) and "The Viziers, or the Enchanted Labyrinth." She was living in 1777.

See PRUDHOMME, "Biographie des Femmes célèbres."

Faur, du, (GUI.) See PIBRAC.

Faure, fōr, (FRANÇOIS,) Bishop of Amiens, in France, and one of the preceptors of Louis XIV., was born near Angoulême in 1612; died in 1687.

Faure, (JOSEPH DÉSIRÉ FÉLIX,) a French judge, and afterwards a peer, born at Grenoble in 1780.

Faure, (LOUIS JOSEPH,) a French statesman under Bonaparte and Louis XVIII., born in 1760; died in 1837.

Fauriel, fō're-ĕl', (CLAUDE CHARLES,) an eminent French philologist and historian, born at Saint-Étienne in 1772, was a nephew of the Abbé Siéyès. He was intimate with Guizot, Manzoni, and Madame de Staël, who characterized him as "inexhaustible in knowledge and kindness." Among his principal works are a "History of Southern Gaul under the Rule of the German Conquerors," (1836,) and "History of Provençal Literature," (1846.) A chair of foreign literature was founded for him in Paris in 1830. His "Popular Songs of Modern Greece" (with a French version, 1825) had great success. In the opinion of E. Renan, "Fauriel is without contradiction the man of our age who has put into circulation the most ideas." Died in Paris in July, 1844.

See SAINTE-BEUVE, "Étude sur Fauriel," in the "Revue des Deux Mondes" for May 15 and June 1, 1845; RENAN, notice in the "Revue des Deux Mondes," December, 1855; "Nouvelle Biographie Générale."

Fauris de Saint-Vincens, fō'rèss' dęh sȧN'vȧN'sôN', (ALEXANDRE JULES ANTOINE,) a French antiquary, born at Aix in 1750; died in 1819. His father, JULES FRANÇOIS PAUL, born in 1718, wrote on numismatics; died in 1798.

Faust, fŏwst, or **Fust,** fŏost, (JOHANN,) a wealthy citizen of Mentz, supposed to have shared in the invention of printing. Having, after his law-suit with Gutenberg, gained possession of his printing-apparatus, he carried on the business with his son-in-law, Peter Schöffer, who made important improvements in the art. (See GUTENBERG.) Died in 1460.

Faust, fŏwst, or **Faus'tus,** (Dr. JOHN,) a famous magician and astrologer, born in Würtemberg in the latter part of the fifteenth century. The German tradition is, that, after spending a large fortune in his astrological studies, he made a league for twenty-four years with the devil, who gave him a spirit named Mephistopheles for his servant. Having lived luxuriously through the appointed time, and astonished the world by his wonderful performances, he was destroyed by the fiend at midnight. It is the general opinion that Dr. Faust really existed, and, by his jugglery and magical arts, deluded people into the belief that he was leagued with evil spirits. This legend has formed the subject of numerous dramas, romances, and poems: the most celebrated of these are Goethe's "Faust," Lessing's poetical fragment entitled "Faust and the Seven Spirits," and Marlowe's tragedy "The Life and Death of Dr. Faustus."

See DÜNTZER, "Die Sage von Dr. Faust untersucht;" H. HEINE, "La Légende de Faust," in the "Revue des Deux Mondes," February, 1852; MEYER, "Studien zu Göthe's Faust," 1847.

Faus'ta, (FLAVIA MAXIMIANA,) a Roman empress, the daughter of Maximian, became the wife of Constantine the Great in 307 A.D. She is said to have procured the death of Crispus, her step-son, by a false accusation. His innocence having become evident, she was put to death in 326.

Faus'ta Cor-ne'lǐ-a, a daughter of the Roman dictator Sulla, was born about 88 B.C. She was married about 55 to T. Annius Milo, and was notorious for her conjugal infidelity.

e as k; ç as s; ğ hard; ġ as j; G, H, K, guttural; N, nasal; R, trilled; s as z; th as in this. (☞See Explanations, p. 23.)

57

Faus-ti′na, (AN′NIA,) daughter of the following, and wife of Marcus Aurelius. The infamy of her conduct even surpassed that of her mother. Died in Cappadocia in 176 A.D.

Faustina, [Fr. FAUSTINE, fōs′tĕn′,] (ANNIA GALE-RIA,) a daughter of Antoninus Verus, one of the Roman consuls, was born in 105 A.D. She became the wife of the emperor Antoninus, and was notorious for her licentiousness. She died in the third year of her husband's reign, 141 A.D.

Faustina Bordoni, fōw-stee′nä boR-do′nee, (or **Bordone,** boR-do′nä,) an Italian singer, born in 1702, was married in 1730 to Jean Adolphe Hasse. Died in 1783.

Fausto, fōws′to, (SEBASTIANO,) surnamed DA LONGI-ANO, a learned Italian author, who lived in the sixteenth century. He made numerous translations from the Latin and Greek.

Faus′tus OF BYZANTIUM, Bishop of Cappadocia, born at Constantinople about 320 A.D. His principal work, entitled "Byzantine History," is written in Armenian. His style was far from elegant ; but his history contains valuable information not to be found elsewhere.

Faus′tus, surnamed REIENSIS or REGENSIS, a monk, born in Bretagne, became Bishop of Riez about 470 A.D. He was a chief of the Semi-Pelagians. Died about 490.

Fauveau, fō′vō′, [Lat. FUL′VIUS,] (PIERRE,) born in Poitou, was the author of Latin poems, which were published in the "Deliciæ Poetarum Gallorum." Died in 1562.

Fauveau, de, deh fō′vō′, (FÉLICIE,) a sculptor, born at Florence, of French parents, about 1802. Among her works is a monument of Dante and a statue of Sainte-Geneviève.

Fauvel, fō′vĕl′, a French antiquary, born in 1753 ; died in 1838.

Fava, fä′vä, (PIETRO ERCOLE,) COUNT, an Italian painter, born at Bologna in 1669 ; died in 1744.

Favard de Langlade, fä′väR′ deh lôn′gläd′, (GUIL-LAUME JEAN,) a French jurist, born in 1762 ; died in 1831.

Favart, fä′väR′, (ANTOINE PIERRE CHARLES,) a French dramatist and painter, born in Paris in 1784.

Favart, (CHARLES SIMON,) a popular French dramatist and voluminous writer, born in Paris in 1710, was the grandfather of the preceding. Among his best works is his comedy of "Solomon II., or the Three Sultans." Died in 1792. His Memoirs and Correspondence were published in 1809, in 3 volumes.

Favart, (MARIE JUSTINE BENOÎTE **Duronceray—** dü′rŏNss′rä′,) wife of Charles Simon, noticed above, and one of the most celebrated actresses of her time, was born at Avignon, in France, in 1727. In her plays she was distinguished by her grace and versatility of power. She is supposed to have been the authoress of three works which appeared under her husband's name, viz., "Annette and Lubin," " Bastien and Bastienne," and the "Fête of Love." Died in 1772.

See "Mémoires de C. S. Favart," 1809.

Favart d'Herbigny, fä′väR′ dĕR′bĕn′ye′, (NICOLAS RÉMI,) a French military engineer, and general in the corps of engineers, born at Rheims in 1735. He distinguished himself in the defence of Belle-Isle against the British in 1761, and wrote a valuable book, entitled "Memoirs on the Defence of Coasts and upon Military Reconnoissances." Died in 1800.

Favé, fä′vä′, (ALPHONSE,) a French officer and writer on military tactics, born at Dreux in 1812.

Favelet, fäv′lä′, (JEAN,) a Flemish physician, and medical professor in the University of Louvain, born near Antwerp in 1674 ; died in 1743.

Favereau, fäv′RŌ′, (JACQUES,) a French advocate and poet, born at Cognac in 1590. He was the author of a number of small poems which won for him a considerable reputation. Died in 1638. " La Milliade," a satire in verse against Richelieu, was ascribed to him.

Favier, fä′ve-ä′, (JEAN LOUIS,) a celebrated French writer on civil law and politics, born at Toulouse about 1720. He published a "Historical and Political Essay upon the Government of Holland," (2 vols., 1748,) and other works. Died in 1784.

Fa-vo′lǐ-us or **Favoli,** fä-vo′lee, (HUGO,) a Dutch physician, of Italian extraction, born at Middelburg in 1523. He visited Turkey and Greece, and published an account of his travels, entitled " Hodoeporicon Byzantium," (1563,) written in Latin hexameter verse. Died in 1585.

Fa-vo′nǐ-us, (MARCUS,) a Roman senator, was a partisan of the Optimates, a friend of Cato Uticensis, and an opponent of Pompey. He was elected prætor in 49 B.C., and fought against Cæsar in the civil war. He was nicknamed " the ape of Cato," whom he took as his model. Having joined the army of Brutus and Cassius, he was taken prisoner at Philippi and put to death in 42 B.C.

Fav-o-rī′nus or **Phavori′nus,** [Φαβωρῖνος,] a Greek writer, a native of Arles, in Gaul, removed to Rome, where he became celebrated under the reigns of Trajan and Adrian for his learning and literary productions. Of his numerous works but a few fragments are now extant. Favorinus was a friend of Plutarch, from whom he received the dedication of a work.

See PHILOSTRATUS, "Vitæ Sophistarum ;" DIOGENES LAER-TIUS ; MARRES, "Dissertatio de Favorini Vita," 1853.

Favorinus, known also as **Va-ri′nus** or **Guarino,** gwä-ree′no, Bishop of Nocera, born near Camerino, in Italy. He was noted for his learning, and as the preceptor of Giovanni de' Medici, afterwards Pope Leo X. Died in 1537.

Favoriti, fä-vo-ree′tee, (AGOSTINO,) an Italian priest and Latin poet, born at Lucca in 1624 ; died in 1682.

Favras, de, deh fäv′räs′, (THOMAS **Mahi—**mä′e′,) MARQUIS, born at Blois in 1745. He entered the French army, and became lieutenant in the Swiss body-guards of the Count of Provence. He afterwards had the command of a legion in Holland. In 1789 he was accused by the revolutionary party of conspiracy, and crimes of which he was innocent. He was condemned to death and executed in 1790.

Favrat, fäv′rät, (FRANZ ANDREAS,) a Prussian general, noted for his physical strength, born in 1730 ; died in 1804.

Favre, fävR, [Lat. FA′BER,] (ANTOINE,) an eminent French jurist, born at Bourg-en-Bresse in 1557, was for many years a judge and senator at Chambéry. He published several valuable works. Died in 1624.

Favre, (CLAUDE DE.) See VAUGELAS.

Favre, (JULES GABRIEL CLAUDE,) an eloquent French republican and orator, born at Lyons in 1809, became an advocate in Paris. On the formation of the republic, in February, 1848, he became secretary-general in the ministry of the interior. He was a member of the Constituent Assembly of 1848. Since Napoleon III. obtained the chief power, M. Favre has been a leader of the opposition. He is distinguished for his radical opinions and independence or audacity of character. He was elected a member of the corps législatif in 1858 and in 1869, and admitted into the French Academy in 1868.

See "Nouvelle Biographie Générale."

Favre, (PIERRE,) a learned Jesuit, born in the diocese of Geneva in 1506. He was the companion of Loyola, to whom he rendered important aid in establishing the order of the latter through Europe. Many stories are told of his great piety and miraculous performances. Died in 1546.

Favyn, fä′văN′, (ANDRÉ,) a French historical writer, born in Paris between 1550 and 1590. Among his works were a "History of Navarre," (1612,) and a "History of the Military Orders of Christian Kings and Princes."

Faw′cet, (Sir WILLIAM,) an English general and writer, born in Yorkshire in 1728. He served with distinction on the continent during the Seven Years' war. He translated from the French the "Reveries" of Count de Saxe, (1757,) and from the German "Rules for the Prussian Cavalry and Infantry," (1759.) Died in 1804.

Faw′cett, (JOHN,) an English Baptist minister and religious writer, born near Bradford in 1740 ; died in 1817.

Fawkes, fauks, (FRANCIS,) an English poet and *littérateur,* born in Yorkshire about 1725. He was the author of "Bramham Park," and other poems, and made good translations from Anacreon, Sappho, Theocritus, and Musæus. Died in 1777.

See NICHOLS, "Literary Anecdotes," etc.

Fawkes, (GUY or GUIDO,) one of the chief conspirators in the Gunpowder Plot in the reign of James I., was a Catholic, and a native of Yorkshire. In 1604, Robert Catesby, Thomas Percy, Guy Fawkes, and others conspired to blow up, with gunpowder, the House of Parliament and kill the king, with the Lords and Commons, their motive being a fanatical zeal against the Protestants. They hired a vault under the House of Lords, placed in it thirty-six barrels of gunpowder, and arranged that Fawkes should explode it on the 5th of November, 1605. Before that time arrived, Lord Mounteagle, a Catholic peer, received an anonymous letter advising him to absent himself from Parliament and intimating that a great catastrophe was impending over that body. This excited the suspicion of the king and others, who searched the cellars in the vicinity and found Fawkes with matches and a dark lantern about midnight, November 4. He was tried and executed in January, 1606.

See HUME, "History of England;" GARDINER, "History of England from 1603 to 1616," chap. v.

Faxardo. See SAAVEDRA.

Fay. See DUFAY.

Fáy, fī or fâ'e, (ANDRÁS,) a Hungarian novelist, poet, and dramatic writer, born at Kohany in 1786. As a prose writer he may be ranked among the best his country has produced.

Fay, (THEODORE SEDGWICK,) an American writer, born in New York in 1807. He produced, besides other works, "Norman Leslie," a novel, (1835,) a poem entitled "Ulric, or the Voices," (1851,) and a "History of Switzerland." He was sent as minister-resident to Switzerland in 1853.

See GRISWOLD, "Prose Writers of America;" DUYCKINCK, "Cyclopædia of American Literature," vol. ii.

Fayderbe or **Fay-d'Herbe,** fã'dàRb', (LUCAS,) an able Flemish sculptor and architect, born at Malines in 1617, was a pupil of Rubens. Died in 1694.

See G. A. VANDERPOEL, "Notice sur la Vie, etc. de L. Fayd'Herbe," 1854.

Faydit or **Faidit,** fã'de', (ANSELME or GANCELM,) a French troubadour, born in Limousin. After he had led for some time the strolling life of a buffoon, and juggler, he found a patron in Richard Cœur-de-Lion, whom he accompanied in his crusade to the Holy Land. Died in 1220.

See "Histoire littéraire des Troubadours;" LONGFELLOW, "Poets and Poetry of Europe."

Faydit, (PIERRE,) a French priest and theological writer, born in Auvergne. He is particularly noted for the part he took in the dispute between France and Pope Innocent XI., on which occasion he preached against the pontiff with great boldness. Died in 1709.

Faye. See LAFAYE.

Faye, fã'yêh, (ANDREAS,) a Norwegian preacher and writer, born at Drammen in 1802, published a "History of Norway," (1831,) and several educational works.

Faye, fã, (HERVÉ AUGUSTE ÉTIENNE ALBANS,) a French astronomer and writer, born in the department of Indre in 1814. He became a member of the Institute. He discovered in 1843 a new comet, which bears his name.

Faye, (JACQUES,) Lord of Espeisses, a jurist, born in Paris in 1542. When the Duke of Anjou was elected King of Poland, he accompanied that prince to Warsaw, and rendered him efficient service in conciliating some of the principal inhabitants. Upon the death of Charles IX., when the Duke of Anjou mounted the throne of France as Henry III., Faye still retained his confidence, and held many stations of importance under him. Upon the death of this prince he joined Henry IV. He greatly distinguished himself at the siege of Paris, but died soon after, in 1590, of a fever. He was the author of some political works.

See DE THOU, "Historia sui Temporis;" TAISAND, "Vies des plus célèbres Jurisconsultes."

Fayette, de la, dçh lã fã'êt', (GILBERT Motier—mo'te-à',) was appointed marshal of France in 1428 by the regent, afterwards Charles VII. Died in 1464.

Fayette, de la, (MARIE MADELÈNE **Pioche de la Vergne**—pe'osh' dçh lã vàRñ,) COUNTESS, a distinguished French writer of romances, born in 1632. The most important of her works were "Zaïde" and "The Princess of Cleves." She also wrote a historical romance,

entitled "History of Henrietta of England." Died in 1693.

See SAINTE-BEUVE, "Portraits of Celebrated Women."

Fayette, La, GENERAL. See LA FAYETTE.

Fayolle, fã'yol', (FRANÇOIS JOSEPH MARIE,) a French littérateur, musician, and critic, born in Paris in 1774, wrote, besides other works in prose and verse, "The Four Seasons of Parnassus," (16 vols., 1805-09,) and a French version of Gerber's "Dictionary of Musicians," (1810-12.) Died in Paris in 1852.

See "Nouvelle Biographie Générale;" FÉTIS, "Biographie Universelle des Musiciens."

Fayot, fã'yo', (ALFRED CHARLES FRÉDÉRIC,) a French historian, born in Paris in 1797. Among his works is a."History of France from 1793 to the Accession of Charles X.," (16 vols., 1830.) Died in 1861.

Faypoult de Maisoncelle, fã'poo' dçh mã'zôN'sêl', (GUILLAUME CHARLES,) an able French statesman, born in Champagne in 1752, became minister of finance in 1795, and minister plenipotentiary at Genoa in 1796. His services here were recognized by a medal which the Genoese senate ordered to be struck in honour of Bonaparte and Faypoult. He was minister of finance in Spain under Joseph Bonaparte about 1810-13. Died in 1817.

See "Nouvelle Biographie Générale."

Fazaree or **Fazary, Al,** ål fã-zâ'ree, or **Fezari,** (MOHAMMED IBN IBRÂHEEM,) a Moslem astronomer of the eighth century, translated some important Indian mathematical tables into Arabic.

Fazelli, fåd-zel'lee, (TOMMASO,) an Italian historian, and professor of philosophy at Palermo, born at Sacca, in Sicily, in 1498. His chief work is his "History of Sicily," (1558,) esteemed for its accuracy and elegance of style. Died in 1570.

Fazio, fåt'se-o, (BARTOLOMMEO,) a distinguished Latin scholar and historian, born in the republic of Genoa. He was patronized by Alfonso of Aragon, King of Naples, whose history he wrote. His most important work was a "History of the Illustrious Men of his own Time," ("De Viris Ævi sui illustribus Liber," 1745.) Died in 1457.

See VOSSIUS, "De Historicis Latinis."

Fazio degli Uberti, fåt'se-o dål'yee oo-bêR'tee, a famous Italian poet, born at Florence in the fourteenth century, was an ardent Ghibeline. He wrote a long descriptive poem entitled "Ditta Mundi," or "Il Dittamondo," in which he proposed to imitate or rival Dante. It was printed in 1474. Died in 1367.

Fazy, fã'ze', (JEAN JACQUES,) a Swiss statesman and journalist, born at Geneva in 1796. He edited several liberal journals at Paris between 1826 and 1835. Having returned to Geneva, he became the leader of the democratic party, which triumphed in the revolution of 1846. He was afterwards president of the council of state of his canton, and had the chief control of its affairs for many years. He published various works.

Fazzini, fåt-see'nee, (LORENZO,) an Italian natural philosopher, born in 1787; died in 1837.

Fea, fã'å, (CARLO,) an Italian antiquary, born at Pigna, in Piedmont, in 1753. Among his works we may name the "Philological, Critical, and Antiquarian Miscellany," (1790,) and "Descrizione de Roma e dei Contorni con vedute," (3 vols., 1824,) which are said to have great merit. Died about 1834.

See TIPALDO, "Biografia degli Italiani illustri."

Fearn, fern, (JOHN,) an English metaphysician, published a "Review of Berkeley, Reid, and Stewart," (1813,) "Primary Vision," (1815,) and a work on "The Human Mind."

Fearne, fern, (CHARLES,) an English jurist and writer of high reputation, born in London in 1749. His chief work is an "Essay on Contingent Remainders," (1772; 4th edition, enlarged, 1791.) Died in 1791. "It was reserved for Mr. Fearne," says Judge Story, "to honour the profession by a treatise so profound and accurate that it became the guide of the ablest lawyers, yet so luminous in method and explanations that it is level to the capacity of every attentive student. He has in fact exhausted the subject, and this chef-d'œuvre will forever remain a monument of his skill, acuteness, and research."

€ as k; ç as s; g hard; g as j; G, H, K, guttural; N, nasal; R, trilled; s as z; th as in this. (☞See Explanations, p. 23.)

Fearnley, fẽrn′le, (THOMAS,) a Norwegian landscape-painter, born at Frederickshall in 1802. Among his master-pieces are "The Glacier of Grindenwald," and 'A Scene in Norway," which was purchased by Thorwaldsen. Died in 1842.

Featherstonehaugh, feth′er-stọn-hau′, (GEORGE W.,) an American traveller, published a "Geological Report of the Elevated Country between the Missouri and Red Rivers," (1835,) and other works. Died September 28, 1866.

Featly, feet′le, or **Fair′clough,** (DANIEL,) a learned English theologian and controversialist, born at Charlton, in Oxfordshire, in 1582. His "Ancilla Pietatis" (1626) was very popular. He also wrote "Clavis Mystica," (1636,) and a treatise against the Anabaptists, entitled "The Dippers Dipt," (1647.) Died in 1645.

Febre or **Febvre, Le,** lẹh fẽvR, (VALENTINE,) a skilful Flemish painter and engraver, born at Brussels in 1642 or 1643. He worked mostly in Venice, and imitated Paul Veronese. He engraved numerous works of Titian and Paul Veronese. Died about 1700.

Fébure, fâ′büR′, or **Fèvre,** (MICHEL,) a French missionary and Orientalist, lived about 1650–80. Among his works are "The Present State of Turkey," (1674,) and a "Treatise on the Manners and Customs of the Ottomans," etc.

Fechner, fĕk′nẹr, (GUSTAV THEODOR,) a German natural philosopher and poet, born near Muskau in 1801. He obtained the chair of physics at Leipsic in 1834, and distinguished himself by researches in galvanism. He published a number of able works on organic chemistry, anthropology, etc., also humorous essays, which were very popular.

Fecht, fĕkt, (JOHANN,) a learned Lutheran theologian, writer, and professor of Hebrew, theology, and metaphysics, was born at Saltzburg in 1636; died at Rostock in 1716.

See ERSCH und GRUBER, "Allgemeine Encyklopaedie."

Feck′ẹn-ham, de, (JOHN,) an English Catholic theologian, whose original name was HOW′MAN, born in Worcestershire about 1516. He was appointed chaplain to Bonner, Bishop of London, and when that prelate was deprived of his bishopric, under Edward VI., he was sent to the Tower. Upon the accession of Mary to the throne, (1553,) Feckenham was appointed her chaplain, and was sent to Lady Jane Grey a short time before her death, to endeavour to reclaim her to the Catholic faith; but without success. During the bloody persecutions that followed, he used all his influence in favour of moderation towards the suffering Protestants. He even went so far as to intercede with the queen for her sister, the princess Elizabeth, who, when she became queen, offered him the archbishopric of Canterbury if he would conform to the rules of the Episcopal Church, — which, however, he refused to do. After having opposed the Reformation in the House of Lords, where he was the last mitred abbot, he was imprisoned in 1560. He died in prison in the island of Ely in 1585.

See WOOD, "Athenæ Oxonienses."

Fedele, fâ-dā′là, (CASSANDRA,) an Italian lady, celebrated for her great learning and accomplishments, was born in Venice in 1465. She possessed the friendship of Pope Leo X., Louis XII. of France, and Ferdinand and Isabella of Spain: the latter tried to draw her to the court of Castile, but without success. Died about 1558.

See F. TOMASINI, "Vita della Signora C. Fedele," 1636.

Fedelissimi, fâ-dà-lès′se-mee, (GIOVANNI BATTISTA,) an Italian poet and physician, born at Pistoia, lived about 1620.

Feder, fā′dẹr, (JOHANN GEORG HEINRICH,) a learned German, who was professor of philosophy at Göttingen, born near Bayreuth in 1740; died in 1821.

See his "Autobiography," ("J. G. H. Feders Leben," 1825;) OERTEL, "De Vita et Fatis J. G. H. Federi," 1789.

Federici, fâ-dà-ree′chee, (CAMILLO,) originally **Giovanni Battista Viassolo,**(ve-âs′so-lo,) one of the most popular Italian dramatists of recent times, born in Piedmont in April, 1749. He is regarded as the founder of a new dramatic school in Italy, and his plays are distinguished by a higher moral tone than those of his predecessors. Among his best pieces are comedies called "The Sculptor and the Blind Man," "Henry IV. at the Passage of the Marne," and "I falsi Galantuomini." Died at Padua in December, 1802.

See TIPALDO, "Biografia degli Italiani illustri;" UGONI, "Della Letteratura Italiana."

Federici, (CESARE.) See FEDRICI.

Federici, (FRANCESCO,) an Italian republican general, born at Naples in 1748. He obtained the chief command at Naples in 1799. Having surrendered to the royalists as a prisoner of war, he was treacherously put to death in 1799.

Federici, (LUIGI,) an Italian poet and jurist, born at Brescia about 1540; died about 1607.

Federmann, fā′dẹr-mân′, (NIKOLAUS,) a German, born at Ulm, commanded an expedition which explored New Granada about 1537.

Fedrici, fâ-dRee′chee, or **Federici,** fâ-dà-ree′chee, (CESARE,) a Venetian merchant and traveller, spent many years in the East Indies. He published, on his return, an interesting book, entitled "Voyage to the East Indies," etc., (1587.)

Fedrigotti, fâ-dRee-got′tee, (GERONIMO,) an Italian lyric poet of superior merit, born in 1742; died in 1776.

Fée, fâ, (ANTOINE LAURENT APOLLINAIRE,) a French physician and eminent botanist, and first professor at the military hospital of Strasbourg, was born in 1789. He published a "Flora of Virgil," or "Critical Nomenclature of the Plants, Fruits, etc. mentioned by Virgil," (1822,) "Méthode lichénographique," (1824,) being a description of lichens, (regarded as the best work on this subject,) and other scientific works; also, a "Life of Linnæus," (1832.)

See QUÉRARD, "La France Littéraire;" "Nouvelle Biographie Générale."

Fehling, fā′ling, (HEINRICH CHRISTOPH,) a German painter, born at Sangerhausen in 1653; died in 1725.

Fehr, fāR, (JOHANN MICHAEL,) a learned German physician, born in Franconia in 1610, became imperial physician to Leopold I. Died in 1688.

Fehrmann, fāR′mân, (DANIEL,) a Swedish engraver of medals, born in Stockholm in 1710; died in 1780.

Fei, fā′ee, (ALESSANDRO,) an Italian historical painter, called DEL BARBIERE, was born in Florence in 1543.

Feijou. See FEYJOU.

Fein, fīn, (EDUARD,) a German jurist and legal writer, born at Brunswick in 1813, became professor of Roman law at Jena in 1845. He published, among other works, a continuation of Glück's "Complete Explanation of the Pandects," (44th vol., 1851.) He became professor of law at Tübingen in 1852. Died in 1857.

Fein, (GEORG,) a German democrat and revolutionist, brother of the preceding, was born at Helmstedt in 1803. He was connected with secret political societies, and was often banished and expelled from various states in which he sought refuge.

Feitama, fī′tâ-mâ, (SIBRAND,) a Dutch dramatic writer, born in Amsterdam in 1694. Among his works are two tragedies, "Fabricius," and the "Triumph of Poetry and Painting." He made excellent translations of Fénelon's "Télémaque" and Voltaire's "Henriade" into Dutch verse, and of several plays of Lamotte, Corneille, and other French writers. Died in 1758.

See JAN DE KRUYFF, "Leven van S. Feitama," Leyden, 1782.

Feith, fīt, [Lat. FEI′THIUS,] (EVERARD,) a distinguished Dutch scholar, born at Elburg about 1597. Among his principal works are "Athenian Antiquities" and "Antiquities of Homer," (1677,) the latter of which was highly esteemed. The death of Feith is enveloped in mystery. As he was walking one day in Rochelle, a citizen invited him to enter his house. He entered, and was never seen or heard of afterwards, notwithstanding the thorough search of the magistrates. He was young when he disappeared.

See BAYLE, "Historical and Critical Dictionary."

Feith, (RHIJNVIS or RHYNVIS,) one of the most eminent Dutch poets of modern times, born at Zwolle, in Overyssel, in 1753. He studied law at Leyden, where he graduated in 1770. Among his best productions are his didactic poem "The Grave," ("Het Graf," 1792,) the tragedies of "Inez de Castro," (1793,) "Thirza," and

"Johanna Gray," and numerous hymns and odes of great beauty. His "Letters on Various Subjects" ("Brieven over verscheiden Onderwerpen," 6 vols., 1784–94) are among his most admired prose writings. Died in 1824. His son PETER RUTGER was also a poet.

See "Gedenkzuil voor Mr. R. Feith," 1825; CORNELIS LOOTS, "Hulde aan de Nagedachtenis van Mr. R. Feith;" "Nouvelle Biographie Générale."

Feizee or **Feizi,** fī'zee, written also **Fyzee** and **Feyazi,** (**Abool-Feiz-Hindee,**) an eminent poet, born at Agra, in India, in 1547, was a brother of the famous Abool-Fazl. He wrote in Persian. Died in 1595.

Fejer, fā-yār, (GYÖRGY,) a distinguished Hungarian writer, born at Keszthely in 1766. His chief production is entitled "Codex diplomaticus Hungariæ ecclesiasticus ac civilis." This valuable work is composed of twenty-eight (or twelve) large volumes relating to the history of Hungary, published in 1829–44. He became librarian of the University of Pesth and Buda in 1824.

Feldbausch, fĕlt'bŏwsh, (FELIX SEBASTIAN,) a German scholar and educational writer, born at Manheim in 1795.

Feldmann, fĕlt'mân, (LEOPOLD,) a German dramatist, of Jewish extraction, born at Munich in 1803, was the author of several popular comedies.

Felekee or **Feleki,** fĕl'e-kee, a distinguished Persian poet, whose true name was **Abool-Nizâm-Mohammed;** but, having devoted himself to astronomy and astrology, he received the title of Felekee, ("Celestial.") Died in 1182.

See VON HAMMER, "Geschichte der schönen Redekünste Persiens."

Féletz, de, dĕh fā'lås', (CHARLES MARIE DORIMOND,) ABBÉ, a French critic, born near Brives-la-Gaillarde in 1767. He contributed a number of learned and elegant essays to the "Journal des Débats" and the "Mercure de France." He was chosen a member of the French Academy in 1827, and was also director of that institution. Among his works is "Mélanges de Philosophie et Littérature," (6 vols., 1828.) He wrote for the "Journal des Débats" about twenty-five years, and defended the classical against the romantic school. Died in 1850.

See M. DELPIT, "Notice sur M. de Féletz," 1852; VILLEMAIN, "De M. de Féletz et de quelques Salons de son Temps," 1852; "Nouvelle Biographie Générale."

Félibien, fā'le'be̯-ăn', (ANDRÉ,) a French architect and able writer on art, born at Chartres in 1619. He was one of the first eight members of the Academy of Inscriptions, and in 1673 became keeper of the Royal Cabinet of Antiquities. He wrote, besides other works, "Conversations on the Lives and Works of the Most Excellent Painters, Ancient and Modern," ("Entretiens sur les Vies et sur les Ouvrages des plus excellents Peintres," etc., 5 vols., 1666–88,) which was translated into various languages. Died in 1695.

See NICÉRON, "Mémoires;" "Nouvelle Biographie Générale."

Félibien, (JACQUES,) a Roman Catholic theologian and writer, brother of the preceding, was born at Chartres in 1636; died in 1716.

Félibien, (JEAN FRANÇOIS,) an architect, son of André, noticed above, was born about 1658. He possessed his father's taste for the fine arts, and left several works on the subject, the principal of which is entitled "Historical Collection of the Life and Works of the Most Celebrated Architects," (1687.) Died in 1733.

Félibien, (MICHEL,) a Dominican, brother of the preceding, was born at Chartres in 1666. He wrote a "History of the Royal Abbey of Saint-Denis in France," and a "History of the City of Paris." Died in 1719.

Felice, fā-lee'chå, (COSTANZO,) [Lat. CONSTAN'TIUS FELIÇ'IUS,] an Italian of the sixteenth century, born near Ancona, wrote, besides other works, a "History of the Conspiracy of Catiline."

Felice, (FORTUNATO BARTOLOMMEO,) a celebrated Italian author, and professor of philosophy at Naples, was born at Rome in 1725. He published in 1770 his greatest work, entitled "Encyclopædia, or an Accurate Universal Dictionary of Human Knowledge," (42 vols.,) in which he was assisted by several eminent savants, including Haller. Died in 1789.

See FELLER, "Biographie Universelle," edited by WEISS.

Feliciano, fā-le-chä'no, (FELICE,) surnamed ANTIQUARIO, an Italian antiquary, born at Verona about 1420. He collected inscriptions, medals, and other antiquities, and wrote a number of epigrams.

Feliciano, (GIOVANNI BERNARDINO,) an Italian scholar and physician, born at Verona about 1490. He translated a number of medical and philosophical works from the Greek and Latin. He was living in 1550.

Feliciano, or **Feliciani,** fā-le-chä'nee, (PORFIRIO,) an Italian bishop and Latin poet, born in Vaud in 1562; died in 1632.

Fe-liç'i̇-tas, SAINT, a Roman lady and Christian martyr of noble birth, lived under the reign of Marcus Aurelius Antoninus. She suffered martyrdom in 164 A.D., having previously witnessed the death of her seven sons.

See MRS. JAMESON, "Poetry of Sacred and Legendary Art."

Felino, de, dĕh fā-lee'no, (GUILLAUME LÉON du Tillot—düi te'yo',) MARQUIS, born at Bayonne, in France, in 1711. Being appointed in 1759 prime minister of Parma, he commenced a series of reformations which added greatly to the prosperity of the country. He expelled the Jesuits, founded a university, and liberally patronized education. In 1765 he was created Marquis of Felino. Died at Paris in 1774.

Felinski, fā-lin'skee, (ALOYS,) a Polish poet and political essayist, born at Ossow in 1773, was secretary of Kosciusko about 1794. In 1809 he was appointed professor of poetry and rhetoric at Krzemicniec. Died in 1822 or 1820.

Fe'lix, (ANTONIUS,) a profligate Roman officer, a freedman of the emperor Claudius, became Governor of Judea about 60 A.D. According to Tacitus, "he exercised the sovereign power with the character of a slave." He was removed from office in 62 A.D.

See Acts xxiii. 24, and xxiv. 24, 27.

Fe'lix I., SAINT, was elected pope in 269. At this time the Christians suffered persecutions under the emperor Aurelian, and Saint Felix himself was condemned to death. He died, however, in prison, in 274.

Felix II., POPE, or, as some say, ANTIPOPE, was chosen by the Arians, or the emperor Constantius, in 355, to succeed Liberius, who had been banished. Upon the return of Liberius, in 358, Felix was driven from the city. Died in 365. He was canonized as a saint of the Roman Church.

Felix II. or **III.,** a native of Rome, was chosen pope in 483. He is said to have been a great-grandfather of Gregory the Great. In 484 or 485 he condemned Acacius, Patriarch of Constantinople, who was accused of heresy but was protected by the emperor. This act of Felix occasioned the first schism between the Eastern and the Western Church. Died in 492.

Felix III. or **IV.,** became pope in 526. He was appointed by Theodoric, King of the Goths, against the wishes of the clergy and people of Rome. Died in 530.

See ARTAUD DE MONTOR, "Histoire des souverains Pontifes."

Felix V., POPE or ANTIPOPE. See AMADEUS VIII. of Savoy.

Fe'lix, Bishop of Urgel, in Catalonia, lived in the eighth century. He advanced the doctrine that our Saviour, according to the human nature, was only the adopted Son of God. This doctrine was condemned in several councils, and Felix was sent to Rome, where he abjured it before Pope Adrian; but when he returned to his diocese he relapsed into his former opinion. He was deposed and banished about 800. His doctrine was called Adoptionism. Died about 818.

See EGINHARD, "Annales;" BARONIUS, "Annales."

Félix. See RACHEL, (MADEMOISELLE.)
Felix, (CASSIUS.) See CASSIUS FELIX.
Felix, (MINUCIUS.) See MINUCIUS.

Felix, surnamed PRATENSIS, a native of Tuscany, and son of a Jewish rabbi, became a Christian, and translated the Hebrew Psalms and other books of the Old Testament into Latin. Died in 1557.

Félix, SAINT, a French prelate, born about 512 A.D., became Bishop of Nantes in 549. He is said to have displayed much political ability, and to have constructed useful public works. Died about 583.

€ as k; ç as s; ğ hard; ğ as j; G, H, K, guttural; N, nasal; R, trilled; ŝ as z; ᵗh as in this. (☞See Explanations, p. 23.)

Felix, SAINT, Bishop of Ravenna, incited the people of that city to revolt against Justinian II., who punished him with the loss of his eyes. Died in 716 A.D.

Félix de Tassy, fā'lèss' dĕh tă'se', (CHARLES FRANÇOIS,) a skilful French surgeon, born in Paris, was appointed first surgeon to Louis XIV. Died in 1703.

Fell, (JOHN,) an English prelate, born at Longworth, in Berkshire, in 1625, was a son of Samuel Fell, noticed below. He became Dean of Christ Church, Oxford, about 1660, and Bishop of Oxford in 1676. He wrote a number of works, including a "Life of Henry Hammond," (1660,) and an edition of the New Testament in Greek, (1675,) which was favourably received. Died in 1686.

See "Biographia Britannica;" WOOD, "Athenæ Oxonienses."

Fell, (JOHN,) an English dissenting theologian, born at Cockermouth, in Cumberland, in 1735. Among his works we may mention his "Genuine Protestantism, or the Inalienable Rights of Conscience defended," (1773.) Died in 1797.

Fell, (SAMUEL,) an English clergyman, born in London in 1594, was the father of John Fell, Bishop of Oxford. He became Margaret professor of divinity at Oxford in 1626, and Dean of Christ Church in 1638. Died in 1648.

Felle, fĕl, (GUILLAUME,) a French traveller and Dominican monk, born at Dieppe in 1639 ; died in 1710.

Fel'len-berg, von, [Ger. pron. fon fel'len-bĕRG',] (PHILIP EMANUEL,) a celebrated Swiss philanthropist, was born at Berne in June, 1771. His mother was a descendant of the Dutch admiral Van Tromp. He travelled in his youth for the purpose of obtaining information. About 1799 he founded at Hofwyl, near Berne, an institution designed to supply a practical education to poor children by means of a model farm, a manual-labour school, and a normal school. His institution acquired a high reputation, and, together with his writings, exercised an extensive influence. He was the author of many works on agriculture and education. Died in November, 1844.

See HAMM, "Fellenbergs Leben und Wirken," 1845 ; E. ROCHHOLZ, "Gespräche über E. von Fellenberg und seine Zeit," 1834 ; "Nouvelle Biographie Générale ;" "Edinburgh Review" for December, 1818.

Feller, fel'ler, (JOACHIM,) a German scholar, born at Zwickau in 1628. He wrote a number of Latin poems, and contributed to the "Acta Eruditorum." Died in 1691.

See JÖCHER, "Allgemeines Gelehrten-Lexikon."

Feller, (JOACHIM FRIEDRICH,) son of the preceding, born at Leipsic in 1673, was the author of several valuable historical works, and assisted in Leibnitz's "History of the House of Brunswick." Died in 1726.

Feller, de, fel'ler or fā'lair', (FRANÇOIS XAVIER,) a learned Jesuit, born at Brussels in 1735, was the author, among other works, of a "Historical Dictionary," in French, which passed through numerous editions. This was written with a view to serve the Roman Catholic Church, and is censured for lack of impartiality. Died in 1802.

See DESDOYARTS, "Notice sur la Vie de M. Feller," 1802.

Fellon, fā'lòN', (THOMAS BERNARD,) a French Jesuit and Latin poet, born at Avignon in 1672, published funeral orations on Louis XIV., Louis, Dauphin of France, and others. Died in 1759.

Fel'lowes, (Sir CHARLES,) an English traveller and antiquary, born in Nottingham in 1799. He explored in 1838 various parts of Asia Minor, and discovered the ruins of Xanthus, the capital of ancient Lycia. In 1839 he published his "Journal written during an Excursion in Asia Minor." As an agent of the British Museum, he visited Lycia again in 1839, and discovered many other ruined cities with beautiful sculptures, which he described in "An Account of Discoveries in Lycia," (1841.) Having obtained from the Sultan of Turkey a firman permitting him to remove works of art, he conducted a party of explorers to the valley of the Xanthus in 1841, and brought home a collection of Xanthian marbles, which are now in the British Museum. Died in 1860.

See "Gentleman's Magazine" for January, 1861.

Fellowes, (Rev. ROBERT,) an English writer on theology, born in Norfolk in 1770, was a friend of the famous Dr. Parr. He published, besides other works,

"Christian Philosophy,"(1798,) a "Guide to Immortality," (3 vols., 1804,) and a "Body of Theology," (2 vols., 1807.) He withdrew from the Anglican Church, of which he had been ordained a priest, and became editor of the "London Critical Review." Died in 1847.

Felsing, fĕl'sing, (JAKOB,) an excellent German engraver, born at Darmstadt in 1802. He studied and worked for about ten years in Italy, and returned in 1832 to Darmstadt, where he obtained the title of engraver to the court. Among his master-pieces are "The Marriage of Saint Catherine," after Correggio ; a "Holy Family," after Overbeck ; and a "Violin-Player," after Raphael.

Fel'tham or **Fell'tham**, (OWEN,) a learned English writer under the reign of James I., was born about 1608. He was a zealous royalist in the civil war. He is chiefly celebrated as the author of a work entitled "Resolves, Divine, Moral, and Political," (2d edition, 1628.) Died about 1678. "He is one of our worst writers in point of style," says Hallam, who thinks him "not only a laboured and artificial, but a shallow, writer." ("Introduction to the Literature of Europe.")

See, also, "Retrospective Review," vol. x., 1824.

Fel'ton, (CORNELIUS CONWAY,) LL.D., a distinguished American scholar and author, was born at West Newbury, Massachusetts, in 1807. He graduated at Harvard with high honours in 1827. He was appointed Latin tutor in that institution in 1829, Greek tutor in 1830, and professor of Greek in 1832. In 1834 he was selected to fill the chair of Eliot professor of Greek literature, which position he held until 1860, when he succeeded Dr. Walker as president of the university. He contributed many articles to "The North American Review," "The Christian Examiner," "Bibliotheca Sacra," and other leading reviews and journals of the country. Of his numerous classical works, his "Iliad" of Homer, issued in 1833, "Greek Reader," (1840,) "Panegyricus" of Isocrates, (1847,) "Agamemnon" of Æschylus, (1847,) "The Clouds" of Aristophanes, and "The Birds" of Aristophanes, have each passed through several editions, and the two last have been reprinted in England. Among his most important works is "Greece, Ancient and Modern : Lectures delivered before the Lowell Institute," (2 vols., 1867.) Died in 1862.

Fel'ton, (HENRY,) an English divine, born in London in 1679. He became rector of Whitewell, Derbyshire, in 1711, and principal of Edmund Hall, Oxford, in 1722. He published, besides a number of sermons, a "Dissertation on reading the Classics and forming a Just Style," (1711.) Died in 1740.

See WILLIAM FELTON, "Life of Henry Felton," 1748.

Felton, (JOHN,) a native of Ireland, notorious for having assassinated, in 1628, George Villiers, Duke of Buckingham, the favourite of James I.

See HUME, "History of England."

Felton, (NICHOLAS,) an English divine, born at Yarmouth about 1563, was appointed Bishop of Bristol in 1617, and translated to the see of Ely in 1619. He was one of the persons employed by James I. in the translation of the Bible. Died in 1626.

Feltre, DUKE OF. See CLARKE.

Feltrino, fĕl-tRee'no, (ANDREA,) a painter of the Florentine school, born about 1490 ; died about 1554.

Feltro, da, dā fĕl'tRo, (MORTO,) a Venetian painter of arabesques, born at Feltre about 1474, had a high reputation as a decorative painter, and was an assistant of Giorgione. He was killed in battle near Zara about 1519.

See VASARI, "Lives of the Painters."

Fenaroli, fā-nā-ro'lee, (CAMILLA Solar d'Asti—solaR' dās'tee,) an Italian poetess, born at Brescia about 1705 ; died in 1769.

Fenaroli or **Feneroli**, fā-nā-ro'lee, (FEDELE,) an Italian composer, born at Lanciano, in the Abruzzi, in 1732, was professor of music at Naples. Died in 1818.

Fenaruolo, fā-nā-roo-o'lo, (GERONIMO,) an Italian poet, a native of Venice, died about 1570.

Fendi, fĕn'dee, (PETER,) an eminent German painter of history and portraits, born at Vienna in 1796, was also an engraver. He painted many subjects of German history, and the portraits of the eminent numismatists of Europe. Died in 1842.

Fénel, fȧ'nĕl', (JEAN BAPTISTE PASCAL,) a French abbot, born in Paris in 1695, was the author of several historical and antiquarian essays. Died in 1753.

Fénelon, fĕn'ĕh-lọn or făn'lôn', (FRANÇOIS **de Salignac de la Mothe,** (or **la Motte)**—dẹh săʹlĕn'yăk' dẹh lă mot,) Archbishop of Cambray, an illustrious French prelate and author, born at the château de Fénelon, in Périgord, August 6, 1651. He was sent about the age of twelve to the College of Cahors, from which he passed to the college Du Plessis in Paris, and devoted himself to the study of philosophy and theology. At the age of fifteen he preached his first sermon, which elicited so much applause that his uncle, the Marquis de Fénelon, fearing it would have a bad effect on one so young, sent him to the seminary of Saint-Sulpice. He was ordained as a priest about 1675, after which he was employed for ten years in Paris as superior of a community called "Nouvelles Catholiques," founded for the instruction of new converts. Among his earliest publications was an argument against the Protestant religion, entitled "Traité du Ministère des Pasteurs." Soon after the edict of Nantes was revoked, (1685,) Louis XIV. sent Fénelon to convert the Protestants of Poitou. In this mission he employed mildness and persuasion in preference to military power.

In 1689 Fénelon was appointed preceptor to the Duke of Burgundy, a grandson of Louis XIV., and the presumptive heir to the throne, a prince of violent and irascible temper. He performed the duties of this highly responsible position with great ability, and, it appears, effected a decided improvement in the temper and conduct of his pupil, for whom he composed "Dialogues of the Dead," and other works. He gained the favour and confidence of Madame de Maintenon. In 1693 he was admitted into the French Academy. He was appointed Archbishop of Cambray in February, 1695, and accepted the office on condition that he should reside for nine months of the year in his diocese and devote three months to the instruction of the Duke of Anjou and the Duke of Berry, grandsons of the king. Fénelon excited general admiration at court by his ready and brilliant wit and the graceful amenity of a character in which, it has been remarked, "the apostle and the great lord seemed to be strangely united."

About this time great excitement was produced in the religious world of France by the mystical sentiments and writings of Madame Guyon, of whom Fénelon was an intimate friend. His sympathy with her involved him in a long controversy with Bossuet, who condemned the quietism of Madame Guyon and somewhat arrogantly insisted that Fénelon should define his position on the subject. The latter accordingly wrote his "Explication des Maximes des Saints," (1697,) which was regarded as an indirect apology for Guyonism. Fénelon was denounced by Bossuet to the king, and was dismissed from court in disgrace. He appealed to the judgment of the pope, who, after long hesitation, yielding to the imperious will of Louis XIV. and the menaces of his agents, decided against the "Maximes des Saints" in March, 1699. Fénelon submitted with dignity, and publicly expressed his acquiescence in this decision. He might perhaps have been restored to favour at court, if a book, which he wrote to amuse the Duke of Burgundy, had not been made public, in 1699, through the infidelity of a servant whom he employed to transcribe the manuscript. This was "Les Aventures de Télémaque," his most celebrated production, and one of the most popular works in the French language. Louis XIV. suspected that this was a covert satire against his despotic régime, and endeavoured to suppress it. While Fénelon was thus proscribed at the French court, he was so highly honoured for his Christian virtues and wisdom among the nations of Europe, that, when adjacent parts of France were ravaged by hostile armies, the diocese of Cambray was protected from spoliation by the orders of the Duke of Marlborough and Prince Eugene. His eloquence and wisdom in conversation are highly extolled by Saint-Simon and other contemporaries. "We feel the power and ascendency of his rare genius," says La Bruyère, "whether he preaches without preparation, or pronounces a studied discourse, or explains his thoughts in conversation." He died on the 7th of January, 1715. Besides the above-named works, he wrote "Dialogues on the Eloquence of the Pulpit," a "Demonstration of the Existence of God," "On the Temporal Power of the Mediæval Popes," an excellent "Treatise on the Education of Girls," and a number of political treatises. He ranks among the most excellent masters of graceful and eloquent diction that France has produced.

"He had all the qualities," says Sir James Mackintosh, "which fit a man to be the preceptor of a prince, and which most disable him to get or to keep office. Even birth and urbanity and accomplishments and vivacity were an insufficient atonement for his genius and virtue." The same writer remarks, in another place, "Fénelon in his writings exhibits more of the qualities which predispose to religious feelings than any other equally conspicuous person : a mind so pure as steadily to contemplate supreme excellence; a heart capable of being touched and affected by the contemplation; a gentle and modest spirit, not elated by the privilege, but seeing its own want of worth as it came nearer to such brightness, and disposed to treat with compassionate forbearance those errors in others of which it felt a humbling consciousness." "There was indeed," says Macaulay, "one Frenchman who has discovered those principles which it now seems impossible to miss,—that the many are not made for the use of one ; that the truly good government is not that which concentrates magnificence in a court, but that which diffuses happiness among a people. These were the doctrines which Fénelon taught." (See review of Dumont's "Recollections of Mirabeau," in Macaulay's "Essays.")

See, also, RAMSAY, "Vie de Fénelon ;" CARDINAL DE BAUSSET, "Histoire de Fénelon," 4 vols., 1808 ; GOSSELIN, "Histoire littéraire de Fénelon," 1843 ; MACKINTOSH, "View of the Progress of Ethical Philosophy ;" CHARLES BUTLER, "Life of Fénelon," 1810 ; ALPHONSE DE LAMARTINE, "Fénelon," Paris, 1854 ; HENRI LEMAIRE, "Vie de Fénelon," 1826 ; THOMAS C. UPHAM, "Life of Fénelon ;" J. F. DE LAHARPE, "Éloge de F. Salignac de Lamotte-Fénelon," 1771 ; JEAN SIFFREIN MAURY, "Éloge de Fénelon," 1771 ; ROY, "Histoire de Fénelon," 1842 ; ALBERT WERFER, "Leben des F. Fénelon," etc., 1852 ; A. CÉLARIER, "Histoire de Fénelon," 1844 ; "Nouvelle Biographie Générale ;" "Biographie Universelle," by M. VILLEMAIN ; "Lives of the Most Eminent French Writers," by MRS. SHELLEY, vol. i.

Fénelon, de, (BERTRAND dẹh fȧ'nẹh-lôn' or făn'lôn', **de Salignac**—dẹh săʹlĕn'yăk',) MARQUIS, a distinguished French soldier, writer, and ambassador of Charles IX. at the court of England. His master having charged him to apologize to Queen Elizabeth for the Massacre of Saint Bartholomew, he answered, "Sire, address yourself to those who have advised you to it." He was the author of several diplomatic works. Died in 1589.

Fénelon, de, (GABRIEL JACQUES DE SALIGNAC,) MARQUIS, nephew of the illustrious Archbishop of Cambray, was lieutenant-general of the French armies, and ambassador from Louis XV. to the States of Holland. He wrote several diplomatic memoirs. He was killed by a cannon-ball at the battle of Rocour in October, 1746.

Fénelon, de, (J. B. A. SALIGNAC,) a French ecclesiastic and philanthropist, born in Périgord, was appointed almoner to the queen of Louis XV. The young Savoyards of Paris interested him so much that he received the title of "Bishop of the Savoyards." During the Revolution he was arrested as a suspected person, and, although his innocence was proved, he was beheaded in July, 1794.

Fen-es-tel'la, (LUCIUS,) a Roman historian, born 49 B.C., was the author of "Annals" which were esteemed by his contemporaries and are often quoted by Pliny and others. Few fragments only are extant. Died in 21 A.D.

Fénin, fȧ'năN', (PIERRE,) a French chronicler, born in Artois, wrote a history of the civil war between the houses of Burgundy and Orléans, which was printed in 1837. Died in 1506.

Fenn, (Lady ELEANOR,) an English writer of educational works, whose assumed name was MRS. LOVECHILD, was born about 1744 ; died in 1813.

Fenn, (Sir JOHN,) an English antiquary, born in Norwich in 1739, published a work entitled "Original Letters written under the Reigns of Henry VI., Edward IV., and Richard III.," which were the productions of different persons of distinction, and contained many curious and interesting anecdotes. Died in 1794.

Fen′ner, (WILLIAM,) an English Puritan divine, born in 1560. He became rector of Rochford, Essex, in 1629. Died in 1640. A volume of his sermons and other works was published in 1657.

Fenner von Fenneberg, fen′ner fon fen′neh-bĕRG′, leader of the insurrection in the Palatinate in 1848, was a native of the Tyrol. After the failure of his projects, he went to America, where, in 1851, he founded in New York a journal called the "Atlantis."

Fenoillet, feh-nwä′yà′, or **Fenouillet,** feh-noo′yà′, (PIERRE,) a French prelate, born at Annecy, was chaplain to Henry IV., and Bishop of Montpellier. He wrote, among other treatises, "Remonstrances to the King against Duels." Died in 1652.

Fenollar, fä-nol-yàR′, (BERNARDO,) a Spanish poet, born at Valencia in the thirteenth century.

See N. ANTONIO, "Bibliotheca Hispana Vetus."

Fenouillot. See FENOILLET and FALBAIRE.

Fen′rir or **Fen′ris,** called also **Fenrisulfr** or **Fenrisulf,** (fĕn′ris-ōōlf′,) in the mythology of the Northmen, the name of a monster, regarded as the most terrible enemy of the Æsir. He was the offspring of Loki, the god of evil, and the female Jötun Angurboda, (Angrboða, the "anguish-boding.") When he was young, the gods with great difficulty succeeded in binding him, (for an account of this, see TYR;) but at the approach of Ragnarök or Ragnaröck (the twilight of the gods) he will at length break loose. He will then rush forth with gaping mouth, his upper jaw touching heaven and his nether jaw the earth, and if there were room he would gape even more widely. He will first devour the sun, causing a severe loss, as may well be supposed, to mankind. Immediately afterwards, in the great battle with the gods, he will swallow Odin, but will the next moment be slain by Vidar. Some writers suppose that by the wolf Fenrir is typified volcanic fire. The name is probably derived from the same root as fen, a "marsh" or low place. Fenrir may signify the inhabitant of the lower world or the abyss. The monsters of the deep destined to destroy the beneficent gods (Æsir) may denote the blind and terrible powers which reside in the elements, and which, when they once break loose, are so destructive to the products of human intellect and industry; "because," says Schiller, "the elements hate the creations of the human hand."*

See the account of Ragnarök in THORPE's "Northern Mythology," vol. i. pp. 80, 81, 82; also p. 181 *et seq.*; MALLET's "Northern Antiquities," vol. ii., fable xxxii.; KEYSER's "Religion of the Northmen;" PETERSEN's "Nordisk Mythologi."

Fen′ton, (EDWARD,) an English navigator, born about 1550. In 1577 he accompanied Sir Martin Frobisher on his second voyage to the North Seas, as the commander of a small vessel. After making two voyages in the unsuccessful attempt to discover a passage by the northwest to the South Seas, he was given the command of four vessels to continue his explorations. He sailed first towards Africa, and then towards the Strait of Magellan. He fell in with three Spanish ships, one of which he succeeded in sinking, after a severe engagement. He then returned to England, and obtained the command of a vessel in the armament sent against the famous Armada in 1588, on which occasion he distinguished himself by his skill and bravery. Died in 1603.

See FULLER, "Worthies of England;" J. BARROW, "Memoirs of the Naval Worthies of Queen Elizabeth's Reign."

Fenton, (ELIJAH,) a distinguished English poet, born near Newcastle, Staffordshire, in 1683. He graduated at Oxford about 1704. He was secretary to the Earl of Orrery, who appointed him preceptor to his only son. He assisted Pope, whose esteem and friendship he possessed, in the translation of the "Odyssey," his portion being the first, fourth, nineteenth, and twentieth books. Among his other works were the tragedy of "Mariamne," (1723,) which was successful, and brought

* "Denn die Elemente hassen
    Das Gebild′ der Menschenhand."
        Das Lied von der Glocke.

him about £1000, a "Life of Milton," (1727,) which is highly praised by Johnson, and several poems. Died in Berkshire in July, 1730.

See JOHNSON, "Lives of the English Poets."

Fenton, (Sir GEOFFREY,) an able statesman and translator, was a brother of Edward, noticed above. He produced "Golden Epistles from Guevara and other Authors," (1575,) and an English version of Guicciardini's "History of the Italian Wars," (1579.) He was for many years secretary of state in Ireland in the reigns of Queen Elizabeth and James I. Died in 1608.

See WARTON, "History of English Poetry."

Fen′ton, (REUBEN E.,) an American lawyer and legislator, born at Carroll, Chautauqua county, New York, in July, 1819. He represented the thirty-third district of New York in Congress for four successive terms, from December, 1857, to March, 1865, and acted with the Republican party. He distinguished himself by his talents for business. In November, 1864, he was elected Governor of New York for two years. He was re-elected in 1866, and was chosen a Senator of the United States in 1869.

Fen′wick, (GEORGE,) the proprietor of a plantation near Saybrook, Connecticut, came to America in 1636. Having returned to England, he was appointed one of the judges in the trial of Charles I. Died in 1657.

Fenwick, (GEORGE,) an English theologian of the Hutchinsonian school, was rector of Hallaton, Leicestershire. He published "Thoughts on the Hebrew Titles of the Psalms," (1749.) Died in 1760.

Fenwick, (Sir JOHN,) a Roman Catholic agitator and conspirator during the reign of William III., was born in England near the middle of the seventeenth century. He was highly connected, having married a sister of the Earl of Carlisle. In 1696 he was arrested for high treason; but the government failed to convict him, in consequence of one of the chief witnesses having been prevailed upon by Fenwick's friends to hide himself on the continent. Thereupon he was tried under a bill of attainder, which, after an extraordinary excitement and conflict, passed both Houses of Parliament and received the royal assent. He was executed the 28th of January, 1697. He was the last person who suffered death in England by an act of attainder. For an extremely interesting account of his trial, see Macaulay's "History of England," vol. iv. chap. xxii.

Fen′wicke, (JOHN,) an Englishman, born in 1618, noted as the founder of a colony in New Jersey, was a member of the Society of Friends. He obtained in 1673 a grant of land in West Jersey, emigrated in 1675, and settled in Salem. His claim to the proprietorship was disputed by Governor E. Andros, who arrested him in 1678 and confined him in prison for two years. He died poor in 1683, after he had conveyed or transferred his claim to William Penn.

See L. Q. C. ELMER, "History of the Early Settlement of Cumberland County, New Jersey," 1869.

Fenyes, fĕn-yĕsh, (ALEXIUS,) a Hungarian geographer, born in the county of Bihar in 1807. He published two valuable works, entitled "Present Condition of Hungary and the Adjacent Countries in their Geographical and Statistical Relations," (6 vols., 1839,) and "Statistics of Hungary," (1849.)

Feo, fā′o, (FRANCESCO,) an Italian composer, born at Naples about 1699. He produced a number of masses, litanies, etc., and a successful opera, entitled "Ipermnestra."

Feodor, fā′o-dor, sometimes written **Fëdor, I.,** (IVAN-OVITCH,) Czar of Russia, the last of the dynasty of Rurik, was born in 1557, and ascended the throne in 1584. Under his reign the Church of Russia was declared independent of the Patriarch of Constantinople; and from that time it had a separate patriarch. Died in 1598.

See KARAMZIN, "Histoire de l'Empire de Russie."

Feodor or **Fëdor II.,** (ALEXIEVITCH,) elder brother of Peter the Great, became Czar of Russia in 1676, and distinguished his reign by passing some important laws of a reformatory character. Died in 1682.

Feodor or **Fëdor,** fā′o-dor, (IVANOVITCH,) a Russian or Kalmuck painter and engraver, born about 1765, near the frontier between Russia and China. He studied at

ā, ē, ī, ō, ū, ȳ, *long;* ă, ĕ, ĭ, ŏ, ŭ, ў, *short;* ą, ę, į, ǫ, *obscure;* fär, fàll, fät; mêt; nŏt; gōōd; mōōn;

Rome, became a skilful draughtsman, and accompanied Lord Elgin to Athens about 1800. He made drawings of the bas-reliefs and other antique monuments of Athens, called the Elgin Marbles. Died in 1821.

Feofan or **Feophan,** fā-o-fān', an eminent Russian prelate and writer, born at Kiev in 1681. He became Bishop of Pleskov and Narva about 1716, and Archbishop of Novogorod in 1721. He co-operated with Peter the Great in his projects of improvement and civilization. Died in 1736.

Fer, de, dęh faiR, (NICOLAS,) a French geographer, born in 1646; died in 1720.

Fer de la Nouerre, de, dęh fêR dęh lă noo'aiR', a French captain of artillery, and the author of "Science of Navigable Canals." Died about 1790.

Ferabosco, fâ-râ-bos'ko, (ALFONSO,) a composer, born at Greenwich about 1550, was a son of an Italian musician. He composed madrigals, and acquired a high reputation.

Feraldo. See FÉRAUD, (RAIMOND.)

Féraud, fâ'rō', (JEAN FRANÇOIS,) a French grammarian, born at Marseilles in 1725, published a valuable "Grammatical Dictionary of the French Language." Died in 1807.

Féraud or **Feraudi,** fâ'rō'de', sometimes written **Feraldo** or **Ferrando,** (RAIMOND,) a Provençal poet, who died about 1324.

Ferber, fêR'bȩr, (JOHAN JAKOB,) a distinguished Swedish mineralogist, born at Carlscrona in 1743. He studied under Linnæus, Wallerius, and Cronstadt, explored the mines of Germany, France, etc., and was appointed professor of natural history and philosophy at Mittau in 1774. He removed to Saint Petersburg in 1783, and entered the service of the King of Prussia in 1786. Among his numerous works are his "Descriptions of the Quicksilver-Mines of Idria," (1774,) and "Mineralogical History of Bohemia," (1774.) Died in 1790.

See MEUSEL, "Lexikon der vom Jahre 1750–1800 verstorbenen Deutschen Schriftsteller."

Ferchault de Réaumur. See RÉAUMUR.

Fȩr'dĭ-nand [Ger. pron. fêR'de-nänt'] **I.,** (KARL LEOPOLD FRANZ,) Emperor of Austria, born at Vienna in 1793, was the eldest son of Francis I., and uncle of Franz Joseph, the present emperor. He married, in 1831, Maria Anna Carolina, a daughter of Victor Emmanuel of Sardinia. He ascended the throne on the 2d of March, 1835. As he was subject to a chronic disorder by which his mind was impaired, the government was directed chiefly by Metternich as prime minister. In consequence of the revolutionary agitations which prevailed in 1848, he abdicated in favour of his nephew, Franz Joseph, in December of that year.

Ferdinand I., Emperor of Germany, and younger brother of Charles V., was born at Alcalá, in Spain, in 1503. His mother was a daughter of Ferdinand and Isabella of Spain. Having married Anne, sister and heiress of Louis, King of Hungary and Bohemia, upon the death of that monarch, in 1526, he laid claim to both crowns, and was recognized by the Bohemians; but in Hungary he met with opposition. John Zápolya, Vayvode of Transylvania, having been elected king by some of the Hungarian lords, called in the Turks to assist him, and defeated Ferdinand, who had marched against him. After this a compromise was effected, each retaining part of the kingdom. He obtained in 1521 the sovereignty of the German provinces of Austria by the consent of Charles V. Ferdinand was elected King of the Romans in 1531, and succeeded Charles V., who abdicated the imperial throne in August, 1556. His title was confirmed by the Diet in 1558. As a monarch, he was distinguished for his moderation and justice, and was a liberal patron of learning. Died in Vienna in July, 1564. He was succeeded by his son, Maximilian.

See ERSCH und GRUBER, "Allgemeine Encyklopaedie;" ALFONSO DE ULLOA, "Vita del Imperatore Ferdinando I.," 1565; F. B. BUCHHOLTZ, "Geschichte der Regierung Ferdinand's I.," 10 vols., 1830–41.

Ferdinand II., Emperor of Germany, son of Charles, Duke of Styria, and grandson of Ferdinand I., was born in July, 1578. Through the influence of his cousin, the emperor Matthias, he was crowned King of Bohemia in 1617, after having promised religious liberty to the Bohemian Protestants. Frederick, Elector Palatine, resolved to oppose him; and, as Ferdinand had refused to protect his Protestant subjects against the Catholics, the Bohemians declared that he had broken his oath and that the throne was vacant. This led to the famous Thirty Years' war. At the time that Ferdinand lost the crown of Bohemia, he was recognized King of Hungary, and, upon the death of Matthias, was elected emperor, in 1619. Frederick, after some hesitation, accepted the crown of Bohemia, which had been offered to him by the States, and leagued himself with all the enemies of the house of Austria. At the battle of Prague, which was fought in 1620, the Palatine was defeated by the army of Ferdinand under Maximilian of Bavaria, and he lost both his new and his old dominions; and in 1623 the emperor gave Maximilian full power in the Palatinate. In 1624 another Protestant league was formed against Ferdinand, with the King of Denmark at its head; but the latter was defeated by the imperialist general Wallenstein, and was forced to accept peace on humiliating terms. Ferdinand, thinking that the time had now arrived to extinguish Protestantism in his empire, as he could command an army of 150,000 men, while the league could muster only 30,000, was preparing to execute this design, when a new league was formed, about 1630, by Sweden, France, and Venice, with Gustavus Adolphus at its head, who gained many brilliant and important victories over the emperor. But at the battle of Lutzen, (1632,) where the Protestant arms were crowned with the most splendid success, the Swedish monarch was killed. The league was then directed by Chancellor Oxenstiern; and Ferdinand, more fortunate with his arms, succeeded in making peace with some of the allies, and procured the election of his son, Ferdinand Ernest, as King of the Romans. As a monarch, Ferdinand possessed great ability, but was tyrannical and bigoted. Died in February, 1637.

See SCHILLER, "History of the Thirty Years' War;" ERSCH und GRUBER, "Allgemeine Encyklopaedie;" J. P. SILBERT, "Ferdinand II., Römischer Kaiser," 1836; FRIEDRICH HURTER, "Geschichte Kaiser Ferdinand's II.," 4 vols., 1850–53.

Ferdinand III., born in 1608, succeeded his father, Ferdinand II., in 1637, on the imperial throne of Germany. The crowns of Bohemia and Hungary having been secured to him, he was elected emperor with little opposition; but during the first years of his reign he met with continual reverses. The Swedes, led on by their general, Bernhard of Saxe-Weimar, and assisted by the French, were scarcely less successful than they had been under Gustavus Adolphus; but the Duke of Saxe-Weimar died in the midst of his victories, — as some suppose, by poison. The war was still urged with such vigour by Louis XIII. and Cardinal Richelieu that the Austrians were beaten in nearly every battle until October, 1648, when, after the death of the French monarch and his prime minister, the emperor signed the treaty known as the Peace of Westphalia, which secured religious liberty to the Protestants. Ferdinand died in 1657, deeply regretted by his subjects, and was succeeded by his son, Leopold I.

See ERSCH und GRUBER, "Allgemeine Encyklopaedie."

Ferdinand [Sp. FERNANDO, fêR-nän'do] **I.,** King of Aragon and Sicily, surnamed THE JUST, born in 1373, was the second son of Juan I. of Castile. He became King of Aragon in 1412, and died in 1416, leaving the throne to his son, Alfonso V.

Ferdinand II. of Aragon. See FERDINAND V. of Castile.

Ferdinand (Fernando) I., King of Castile, a son of Sancho III., was crowned in 1035. In 1038 his brother-in-law, Bermudo, King of Leon, having invaded Castile, Ferdinand defeated him in a battle, in which Bermudo was slain. Ferdinand thus became King of Leon and the most powerful monarch in Spain. He afterwards carried on a successful war against the Moors, and forced the Kings of Saragossa and Toledo to become his tributaries. Historians speak in high terms of the ability and virtues of this prince. Died in 1065. He left Castile to his son Sancho, and Leon to his second son, Alfonso.

See FERRERAS, "Historia general de España."

Ferdinand (Fernando) II. of Leon, a son of Alfonso VII., mounted the throne of Leon in 1157, at the same time that his brother, Sancho III., became King of Castile. It was under the reign of this monarch that the famous order of the Christian knights of Saint James was founded. Ferdinand carried on successful wars against the Moors, in which he displayed great generalship and intrepidity. Died in 1187. He was particularly noted for his generosity.

Ferdinand (Fernando) III., called THE SAINT, a son of Alfonso IX., King of Leon, and Berengaria, Queen of Castile. He became King of Castile in 1217, and succeeded his father in 1230. In his Moorish wars he conquered the kingdom of Baeza, took Córdova, Seville, and several other rich and important places, and made the Kings of Granada and Murcia his tributaries. He died in 1252, and was succeeded by his son, Alfonso X.

See MIGUEL DE HERRERA, "Cronica del Rey Fernando III.," 1554; H. FLOREZ, "Elogio del S. Rey Fernando III.," 1754.

Ferdinand (Fernando) IV., King of Castile and Leon, born at Seville in 1285, was the son of Sancho IV., whom he succeeded in 1295. Like the preceding, he gained many victories over the Moors. He was vindictive, passionate, and unjust. He died in 1312, and left the throne to his son, Alfonso XI.

Ferdinand (Fernando) V., King of Castile and Aragon, surnamed THE CATHOLIC, was born at Sos on the 10th of March, 1452. He was the son of Juan II., King of Aragon. At this time Juan's son Carlos, Prince of Viana, was the presumptive heir to the throne of Aragon and Navarre. In 1461 the Prince of Viana died, and soon after the Aragonese tendered the oaths of allegiance to Ferdinand, as heir-apparent to that monarchy. In very early life he was trained to the use of arms, and was schooled in all the military science of that age, and, while yet a boy, exhibited great discretion and superior prowess on the field of battle. In 1469 he married the infanta Isabella, on whom had been fixed the succession to the throne of Castile. The glory of their reign and the commencement of the highest prosperity and grandeur of the Spanish monarchy are chiefly to be attributed to the eminent qualities of this princess. Spain at this period was divided into the kingdoms of Castile, Aragon, Navarre, and Granada, the latter of which was still possessed by the Moors; but Ferdinand and Isabella, before the close of their reign, by energetic and politic measures united the four sovereignties under their sway. In 1474 Henry IV. of Castile died, and Isabella was proclaimed queen at Segovia. Her title, however, was disputed by the princess Joanna, whom Henry had acknowledged to be his legitimate daughter. Joanna received assistance from several of the Castilian grandees and her uncle, Alfonso of Portugal, who invaded Spain to defend her cause. Ferdinand soon placed himself at the head of an army, and gained a decisive victory over the Portuguese at Toro, which caused Alfonso to withdraw to his own dominions. In a short time the entire kingdom of Castile submitted to Isabella, and finally, in 1479, a treaty of peace was ratified at Lisbon. The same year Ferdinand was crowned King of Aragon at the death of Juan II. The two sovereigns immediately commenced a course of salutary reforms, especially in Castile, where during the reign of Henry oppression and rapine had been carried to great excesses by the nobility. Various courts of justice were also formed, over which the king and queen frequently presided in person. A successful attempt was likewise made for reducing the power of the great feudal lords, who had frequently held the authority of their sovereigns in contempt. In 1480 an indelible stain was fastened on the otherwise unsullied fame of Isabella by the establishment of the Inquisition. Ferdinand subsequently gave his consent for its introduction into Aragon. After the king and queen had fully established their authority at home, they turned their attention towards the conquest of Granada, the most fertile portion of Spain. The invasion of that kingdom was, however, anticipated by the Moorish sovereign, who in 1481 surprised and captured the fortress of Zahara, in Andalusia. Soon after the Castilians took the strongly-fortified city of Alhama, in the heart of the Moorish dominions. This exploit struck the Moslems with terror, while it greatly inspirited the Christians. The war was now vigorously urged forward by Ferdinand, who commanded in person, and by Isabella, who was untiring in her efforts to encourage the nation and to keep in the field an efficient army. She imparted to the people her own zeal and heroic enterprise, which wavered not until the capitulation of the royal city of Granada, in November, 1491. In 1486 Columbus visited the court of Spain, to solicit from the sovereigns the assistance which would enable him to prosecute a voyage of discovery. At this time their treasury was drained, and the Moorish war engrossed their entire attention: so that they were unable either to fit out the armament which he wished, or to decide on the policy of the adventure. However, when the war was finished, Isabella made those arrangements with the illustrious Genoese which opened to the Castilians a far greater empire than the one just obtained. In 1492 an edict was issued for the expulsion of all Jews from the kingdom. In 1493 Columbus returned from his successful voyage to the New World. The same year they obtained a papal bull by which their titles were confirmed to all territories which they should discover in the Western hemisphere. Ferdinand and Isabella next turned their attention to the education of the Spanish youth. They invited learned men to settle in their dominions, and founded universities throughout the kingdom. In 1495 Charles VIII. of France invaded Italy and took possession of Naples. The proximity of so powerful an army to his Sicilian possessions filled the mind of Ferdinand with apprehension. He fitted out an army to assist the Neapolitan king, the command of which he gave to Gonsalvo de Córdova, known in history as the "Great Captain," who landed in Italy in May, and, after a series of brilliant victories gained over much larger forces, expelled the French and firmly established the King of Naples on his throne. Subsequently treaties of marriage were formed by the Spanish monarchs for their only son, Prince Juan, with Margaret, the daughter of the emperor Maximilian, and for the princess Joanna with the emperor's son Philip; and, to cement their friendship with England, their youngest daughter, known as Catherine of Aragon, was married to Arthur, Prince of Wales.

In 1497 the nation sustained a great calamity in the death of Prince Juan. Two years later, his sister, the Princess of Portugal, died. In 1501, the Moors having revolted, Ferdinand compelled them all either to be baptized or to leave the kingdom. The majority chose the former alternative. In 1500 Ferdinand concluded a treaty with Louis XII. of France, by which they divided the kingdom of Naples equally between them. The Great Captain had previously sailed for Italy with a powerful army, and in a short time the division was made. Disputes, however, soon arose between the invaders, which, after a war of four years, resulted in the complete overthrow of the French in Italy, and the firm establishment of the authority of Ferdinand over all the kingdom of Naples. In November, 1504, Queen Isabella died, and Ferdinand was appointed Regent of Castile, on account of the insanity of his daughter Joanna, the heir-apparent to that throne. In 1505 Ferdinand married Germaine de Foix, niece of Louis XII. In 1508 the treaty of Cambray was signed by the Emperor of Germany, the King of Aragon, the King of France, and the pope, for the division of the Venetian republic. After a decisive battle gained by the allies, the Spanish monarch received several cities as his share, which were incorporated into the kingdom of Naples. In 1511 a treaty was formed by the Spanish king and the Emperor of Germany for driving the French from Italy, which was accomplished after the battle of Ravenna. Jean d'Albret, King of Navarre, having leagued himself, offensively and defensively, with Louis of France, the King of Aragon invaded his dominions, drove him from the throne, and in 1513 completed the entire subjugation of that kingdom. Ferdinand died in January, 1516. As a sovereign, he was brave, affable, indefatigable in business, temperate in his habits, and strongly attached to the Catholic religion; but he was bigoted, cruel, selfish in the extreme, and ungenerous to those to whom he was greatly indebted. For shrewdness and policy he excelled every other monarch of his age. He was succeeded by Prince Carlos, celebrated as Charles V. of Germany, son of Philip of Austria and Joanna.

See PRESCOTT, " History of Ferdinand and Isabella," 3 vols., 1838; MARIANA, " Historia de Rebus Hispaniæ;" HERNANDO DEL PULGAR, " Crónica de los Señores Reyes Católicos," 1545; BALTHASAR GRACIAN, " El politico D. Fernando el Católico," 1641.

Ferdinand (Fernando) VI. of Spain, surnamed THE WISE, son of Philip V. and Mary of Savoy, was born at Madrid in 1713, and ascended the throne in 1746. The early part of his reign was distinguished by the many wise and just laws which he enacted, by the encouragement that he gave to commerce, manufactures, and the arts, and by the successful efforts he made to promote literature and science in Spain. Ferdinand was subject to long fits of melancholy, which materially interfered with his various plans for the welfare of his subjects. He died, without issue, in 1759, and was succeeded by his brother, Charles III.

Ferdinand (Fernando) VII., son of Charles IV., King of Spain, and Maria Louisa of Parma, was born in 1784. When he was six years of age, he was proclaimed Prince of Asturias and heir-apparent to the Spanish crown. He was kept in servile subjection by the queen and Godoy, the court favourite, but was provided with competent instructors. In 1802 Ferdinand married Maria Antoinette, daughter of Ferdinand IV., King of the Two Sicilies. This princess, possessing much talent and energy, attempted to raise her husband to his proper station at court; but, being unsuccessful, they were both obliged to go into retirement. She died in 1806, under circumstances which created a belief that Godoy had caused her to be poisoned. The favourite afterwards accused Ferdinand of plotting against the life of the king, and caused him to be thrown into prison; but he was liberated not long after. In 1808 Charles IV., alarmed by the French invasion, abdicated in Ferdinand's favour; but Napoleon succeeded by intrigue in drawing them to France, where he detained them for several years and caused them both to resign their authority. In 1813, when Joseph Bonaparte had been repeatedly driven from his capital, Napoleon restored Ferdinand to power. His reign was subsequently disturbed by the disputes of the two parties called the Liberals, or those who favoured the Constitution of 1812, and the Absolutists, or Apostolical party, the monarch favouring the latter. Ferdinand had two daughters by his fourth wife, Maria Christina, daughter of Francis, King of the Two Sicilies. The eldest of these, Maria Isabella, became Queen of Spain upon her father's death in 1833.

See SOUTHEY, "History of the Peninsular War;" DE PRADT, "Mémoires sur la Révolution d'Espagne," 1816; GENERAL FOY, "Guerre de la Péninsule," 4 vols.; GODOY, "Memoirs," 4 vols.

Ferdinand I., II., and **III.** of Bohemia. See FERDINAND I., II., and III., Emperors of Germany and Austria.

Ferdinand [It. FERDINANDO, fĕʀ-de-nân'do] **I.,** King of Naples, natural and only son of Alfonso, King of Aragon, was born in 1423, legitimized by Pope Eugene IV., and crowned King of Naples in 1458. The false and cruel character of Ferdinand soon caused a general revolt of his subjects, who invited John of Anjou to take possession of the throne. At first Ferdinand met with some severe losses; but, assisted by Pope Pius II. and the Duke of Milan, he gained, in August, 1462, at Troia, a decisive victory over the French, by which success his power was completely restored. In 1485 the barons, assisted by Pope Innocent VIII., revolted against Ferdinand, who obtained peace only on granting their demands; but as soon as they disarmed he caused the barons to be arrested and put to death. For this treacherous proceeding he was excommunicated by the pope. Ferdinand died in 1494, detested by his subjects, and was succeeded by his son, Alfonso II.

See MARIANA, "Historia de Rebus Hispaniæ;" SISMONDI, "Histoire des Républiques Italiennes;" GUICCIARDINI, "Istoria d'Italia;" PONTANO, "Historia Neapolitana ab Anno 1458 ad Annum 1494," 1617.

Ferdinand (Ferdinando) II., grandson of the preceding, and son of Alfonso II., was born about 1468, and ascended the throne of Naples in January, 1495. The Neapolitans, having a long time conceived a hatred for

the house of Aragon, now revolted, and Ferdinand was obliged to leave Naples, which was shortly afterwards invested by the French under Charles VIII. But, on obtaining assistance from the King of Aragon, who sent him troops commanded by the great captain Gonsalvo de Córdova, Ferdinand succeeded in driving the French from Naples. He died, without issue, in 1496.

See GUICCIARDINI, " Istoria d'Italia;" PHILIPPE DE COMINES, " Chronique."

Ferdinand (Ferdinando) III. of Naples. See FERDINAND V. of Spain.

Ferdinand (Ferdinando) IV., King of Naples, afterwards called **Ferdinand I.** of the United Kingdoms of the Two Sicilies, was born in 1751. He was a younger son of Charles III. of Spain. He began to reign when he was but eight years old. The Marquis Tanucci, who possessed much ability as a minister, was appointed regent. He, however, totally neglected the education of the young prince. In 1768 Ferdinand married Maria Carolina of Austria, daughter of Maria Theresa, who, being a princess of great ambition, cruelty, and energy, misgoverned Naples under her husband's name. In 1777, Tanucci, who had been created prime minister, was dismissed, and John Acton, an Englishman, came into power. His administration was even far less beneficial than Tanucci's. In 1792 the court of Naples joined the allies against France, but four years later purchased a peace from the French Directory. In 1798 it formed a secret alliance with Russia, Austria, and England, and the Neapolitan army marched against the French, by whom they were defeated about the end of 1798. The queen, becoming alarmed, fled to Sicily, whither she was followed by the king in 1799. The successes of the allies in 1799 restored to power Ferdinand and his queen, who, by the aid of Lord Nelson, inflicted a treacherous and bloody revenge on the republicans. Many of the best and noblest citizens of Naples were then executed. Ferdinand formed a treaty of peace with France in 1801, but in 1805 entered another secret alliance. Napoleon I. then declared that the Bourbon dynasty had ceased to reign at Naples, and created Murat sovereign of that kingdom. Ferdinand retired to Sicily, where he was protected by the British until the overthrow of the French emperor. In 1812 he was induced to resign his authority into the hands of his son Francis. On the fall of Napoleon, in 1814, he was restored to the throne of Naples. In 1816 he united the kingdoms of Naples and Sicily under the same form of government. He died, generally detested, in 1825, and was succeeded by his son, Francis I.

See BOTTA, "Storia d'Italia dal 1789 al 1814;" THIERS, "History of the French Revolution," and his "History of the Consulate and of the Empire."

Ferdinand (Ferdinando) II., King of the Two Sicilies, born in 1810, was a son of Francis I. He began to reign in November, 1830, and married Maria Theresa, an Austrian princess, in 1837. His oppressive and despotic reign provoked a series of conspiracies and insurrections, which were suppressed with great cruelty. He was nicknamed "Bomba." He died in 1859, and was succeeded by his son, Francis II.

See GLADSTONE, "Letters to Lord Aberdeen," 1851; FARINI, "Il Stato Romano," and English version of the same, by W. E. GLADSTONE, 1851.

Ferdinand (or Fernando) I., King of Portugal, son of Peter the Cruel and Constance of Castile, born at Coimbra in 1345, ascended the throne in 1367. He engaged in a war with Henry II. of Castile, who invaded Portugal, and, after gaining two victories, compelled Ferdinand to sue for peace, the articles of which were signed in 1371. Died in 1383. Ferdinand left behind him the reputation of a just and beneficent prince.

Ferdinand (or Fernando) II., King of Portugal, a younger son of Queen Maria II., was born about 1838. He succeeded his brother, Don Pedro V., in November, 1861.

His father, FERDINAND AUGUSTUS of Saxe-Coburg, had married the Portuguese queen Maria II., after whose death, in 1853, he was for a short time regent of the kingdom.

Ferdinand [It. FERDINANDO, fĕʀ-de-nân'do] **I. de' Medici**, Grand Duke of Tuscany, born in 1549, was a younger son of Cosimo I. He succeeded his brother, Francesco, in 1587. Died in 1609.

Ferdinand (Ferdinando) II., Grand Duke of Tuscany, born in 1610, was a son of Cosimo II., whom he succeeded in 1620. He was a liberal patron of literature and art. He died in 1670, and was succeeded by his son, Cosimo III.

Ferdinand (Ferdinando) III. of Tuscany, born in 1769, was a son of Pietro Leopoldo, and a brother of Francis II., Emperor of Germany. He began to reign in 1791, was expelled by the French about 1800, and restored in 1814. He was more liberal and mild than the other Italian princes of that period. Died in 1824, and was succeeded by his son, Leopold II.

See GONNELLI, "Elogio di Ferdinando III.," 1824; ZELLER, "Histoire d'Italie."

Ferdinand, (Ferdinando,) Duke of Parma, born in 1757, was a son of Philip of Bourbon. His mother was Elizabeth, a daughter of Louis XV. of France. He began to reign in 1765, and left the direction of affairs to the Marquis de Felino. Died in 1802.

Ferdinand, (Fernando,) son of James II., King of Aragon, born at Valencia in 1228. James had divided the kingdom among his sons, which produced a war between Don Ferdinand and his brother, Don Pedro, in which the former was defeated and taken prisoner. Don Pedro ordered him to be thrown into the river Cinga. This occurred in 1275.

Ferdinand, or Fernando, Infante of Portugal, born in 1402, was a younger son of John I. He accompanied a Portuguese army which invaded Barbary in 1437 and was defeated. He remained as a hostage in the power of the Moors, and died at Fez in 1443.

Ferdinand, (AUGUST FRANZ ANTON,) Duke of Saxe-Coburg-Gotha, and prince-consort of Portugal, was born in 1816. He married Maria, Queen of Portugal, in 1836. His son became king in 1855, with the title of Pedro V.

Ferdinand (Fernando) of Aragon, Archbishop of Saragossa, and grandson of Ferdinand the Catholic, was born at Madrid in 1514. He wrote, besides other works, a valuable history of the kings and prelates of Aragon. Died in 1575.

Ferdinand of Bavaria, Archbishop of Cologne, and Prince-Bishop of Liege and Münster, was born in 1577. He commanded a body of troops which fought against the Protestants in the Thirty Years' war. During his reign there were a series of bloody revolts at Liege. Died in 1650.

Ferdinand, or Fernando, Duke of Braganza, a Portuguese general, born in 1403, was a son of Alfonso, the first Duke of Braganza. Died in 1478.

Ferdinand (Fernando) of Córdova, celebrated for his universal knowledge, was born about 1420. He signalized his bravery under John II. of Castile in the war against the Moors; but, preferring the pen to the sword, he retired from the army, and occupied the chair of professor in several Spanish universities. He stood high in the favour of Ferdinand and Isabella, who granted him a pension. He was the author of several works on theology, etc. He is supposed to have died about 1480.

See N. ANTONIO, "Bibliotheca Hispana Nova."

Ferdinand (CHARLES JOSEPH) OF ESTE, Archduke of Austria, born in 1781, was a son of Ferdinand Charles Anton Joseph, and a nephew of the emperor Leopold. He commanded an army against the French, and afterwards against the Poles, in both instances unsuccessfully. Died in 1850.

Ferdinand (Fernando) OF SPAIN, CARDINAL, born in 1609, was the third son of Philip III. of Spain. He became Governor of the Low Countries in 1633, and invaded France in 1636. Died in 1641.

See SCHILLER, "History of the Thirty Years' War;" COXE, "History of the House of Austria," 3 vols., 1807.

Ferdinand (Fernando) de Jesus—dà Hà-soos', a Spanish Carmelite and ecclesiastical writer, born at Jaen in 1570. He wrote, besides other works, "Commentaries on Aristotle." Died at Granada in 1644.

Ferdinand de Talavera—dà tä-lä-vä'rä, a Spanish monk, and confessor to Queen Isabella of Castile, was born at Talavera de la Reyna in 1445. He was appointed

Archbishop of Granada by Ferdinand and Isabella. Died in 1507.

Ferdinandi, fĕR-de-nân'dee, (EPIFANIO,) a distinguished Italian philosopher and physician, born at Misagna, in the kingdom of Naples, in 1569. He was the author of numerous philosophical and medical works, among which is "Centum Historiæ, seu Observations et Casus Medici," (1621, often reprinted.) Died in 1638.

Ferdinandi, fĕR-de-nân'dee, or Fernandi, fĕR-nân'-dee, (FRANCESCO,) called IMPERIALI, a painter of the Roman school, who worked at Rome in 1730.

Ferdoucy or Ferdousi. See FIRDOUSEE.

Ferdusi. See FIRDOUSEE.

Fereedoon, Feridoun, or Ferîdûn, fĕr'ee-dōōn', a king of ancient Persia, of the Peshdadian dynasty, was a son of the famous Jemsheed, (or Jamshîd.) He is regarded by the Persians as a model of every virtue.

See ATKINSON'S "Abridgment of the Shâh-Nâmeh of Firdausî," London, 1832; and "A Short History of Persia," in vol. v. of SIR WILLIAM JONES'S Works.

Feretrius, a surname of JUPITER, which see.

Ferg, fĕRG, (PAUL FRANZ,) an excellent German landscape-painter, born at Vienna in 1689; died about 1740.

See DESCAMPS, "Vies des Peintres Flamands," etc.

Fer'gus I., King of Scotland, was engaged in wars with the Romans and Britons. Died about 450 A.D.

Fergus II. succeeded Eugene VII. in 764. He was killed in 767.

Fer'gus-on, (ADAM,) a distinguished Scottish writer and metaphysician, born in Perthshire in 1724, studied at the University of Saint Andrew's and at that of Edinburgh. He filled for some years the office of chaplain in a Highland regiment. In 1759 he was appointed to the chair of natural philosophy in the University of Edinburgh, where in 1764 he became professor of moral philosophy. In 1767 he published his first work, an "Essay on the History of Civil Society," which was translated into several languages. In 1778 he was appointed secretary to the five commissioners sent to the United States to effect a reconciliation. Of his numerous works the most important is his "History of the Progress and Termination of the Roman Republic," (3 vols., 1783.) Died in 1816.

See CHAMBERS, "Biographical Dictionary of Eminent Scotsmen;" "Edinburgh Review" for January, 1867.

Ferguson, (JAMES,) an eminent self-taught astronomer and mechanician, born near Keith, in the north of Scotland, in 1710. His father, though a day-labourer, succeeded in teaching all his children to read and write. Ferguson's mechanical genius was first developed when he was but seven or eight years old. The roof of their cottage had partly fallen in, and his father, in order to raise it, used a lever and fulcrum. It appeared almost incredible to young Ferguson that one man could raise such a great weight. He began to experiment with levers of different sizes. To these he added the wheel and axle, and drew up a short treatise on the subject. His father having placed him with a farmer to take charge of sheep, he began to study the stars at night, and to construct models of mills, spinning-wheels, etc. in the daytime. He afterwards went to live with a farmer named Glashan, who treated him with great kindness and allowed him leisure for his studies. He also made the acquaintance of Mr. Grant, a gentleman who soon took Ferguson into his service and placed him under the instruction of his butler, Robert Cautley, an ingenious and well-informed man, from whom he acquired some knowledge of arithmetic, algebra, and geometry. In order to amuse himself during an illness, he constructed a wooden clock, which was a good time-keeper. He also formed a wooden watch with a whalebone spring, and began to earn small sums by repairing and cleaning clocks. He turned his attention to drawing patterns for needle-work, copying pictures, and taking portraits in India-ink. In the last employment he was so successful that he was induced to go to Edinburgh, where, through the patronage of the Marchioness of Douglas, he gained a sufficient sum to support himself and to assist his parents. He followed this profession, as a means of obtaining a livelihood, for about twenty-six years. He invented an orrery on a less intricate plan than those formerly constructed. In 1743 he removed to London. In 1747 he published a "Dissertation on the Phenomena of the Harvest Moon," and in 1748 commenced lecturing on astronomy and mechanics. He was patronized by the Prince of Wales, afterwards George III., who, after he ascended the throne, granted Ferguson a pension of fifty pounds a year from his privy purse. Ferguson said that the best machine he ever invented was the Eclipsareon, which showed the time, quantity, duration, and progress of solar eclipses in all parts of the earth. Among his most important works we may mention "Astronomy explained upon Sir Isaac Newton's Principles, and made easy to those who have not studied Mathematics," (2 vols., 1821,) and "Lectures on Subjects in Mechanics, Hydrostatics, Pneumatics, Optics," etc. Died in 1776.

See his "Autobiography;" CHAMBERS, "Biographical Dictionary of Eminent Scotsmen;" C. HENDERSON, "Life of James Ferguson," Edinburgh, 1867; "Pursuit of Knowledge under Difficulties," vol. i., 1839; C. L. BRIGHTWELL, "Annals of Industry and Genius."

Ferguson or **Fergusson**, (ROBERT,) a Scottish poet, born in Edinburgh in 1750. He published a volume of poems in 1773. His habits were very dissipated. He became insane and died in 1774.

See D. IRVING, "Life of R. Ferguson," 1810; A. PETERKIN, "Life of R. Ferguson."

Ferguson, (ROBERT,) M.D., a British medical writer, born in 1799. He published a work "On Puerperal Fever." Died in 1865.

Ferguson, (ROBERT,) a British poet and prose writer, born at Carlisle about 1820. He published a collection of poems, entitled "The Shadow of the Pyramid," (1847,) and "The Pipe of Repose; or, Recollections of Eastern Travel," (1848.)

Ferguson, (WILLIAM,) a Scottish painter of still life. Died in 1690.

Fer′gus-son, (JAMES,) a celebrated architect, born at Ayr, in Scotland, in 1808. After spending ten years in India and China, he returned to England and employed his time in literary and scientific studies. In 1849 he brought forward a new theory in regard to fortifications, in which he advocated the superiority of round forts to those formed of angles, and the use of earth-work for masonry, and of terraces. His plan was at first ridiculed; but after the siege of Sebastopol, where Mr. Fergusson's suggestions had produced important results, it was received far more favourably. He is the author of numerous works upon architecture and fortifications, among which we may cite "An Essay on the Ancient Topography of Jerusalem," (1847,) "Picturesque Illustrations of Ancient Architecture in Hindostan," (1848,) "The Palaces of Nineveh and Persepolis Restored," (1851,) "Illustrated Hand-Book of Architecture," (1855,) and the "Peril of Portsmouth, or French Fleets and English Forts."

See "Edinburgh Review" for January, 1857, and July, 1863; "London Quarterly Review" for October, 1859.

Ferhâd- (fer-hâd′) **Pasha**, a Turk, who became grand vizier of Amurath III. in 1581. He was defeated near Nicopolis, for which he was put to death in 1596.

Ferichtah. See FERISHTA.

Ferid-eddin-Attâr, (or -Athar.) See ATTÂR-FE-REED-ED-DEEN.

Feridoun or **Ferîdûn.** See FEREEDOON.

Fériol or **Ferriol.** See PONT-DE-VEYLE.

Ferishta, **Ferischtah**, or **Ferichtah**, fĕr′ish-tah, (**Mohammed-Kâsim**, mo-hâm′med kâ′sim,) an eminent Persian historian, born at Astrabâd about 1550, or, according to some accounts, 1570. His great work was a "History of India," commencing about the close of the tenth century; though in the introduction he gives a short account of Indian history previous to the invasion of the Mohammedans. It was translated into English by Alexander Dow, (2 vols., 1768.) A better English version was published by General Briggs, "History of the Rise of the Mahomedan Power in India," (London, 4 vols. 8vo, 1829.) He is supposed to have died about 1625.

See VON HAMMER, article in the "Wiener Jahrbücher," vol. li.; BRIGGS, Preface to Translation of the "History of the Mahomedan Power in India."

Ferloni, fĕR-lo′nee, (SEVERINO ANTONIO,) a learned Italian ecclesiastic, born in the Papal States in 1740, was a partisan of Napoleon. Died in 1813.

Fermanel, fĕR′mä′nêl′, a French traveller, visited Palestine and other parts of Asia Minor in 1630, and published, after his return, a "Voyage to Italy and the Levant."

Fermat, de, dĕh fĕR′mä′, (PIERRE,) a celebrated French mathematician and lawyer. According to several biographers, he was born at Toulouse in 1595; but Dr. Hoefer states that he was born near Montauban in 1601. He was one of the counsellors of the parliament of Toulouse, and cultivated mathematics as a recreation. He corresponded with Descartes, Roberval, Mersenne, and others. The French savants claim that he is entitled to a great part of the honour of the discovery of the differential calculus, which is generally awarded to Newton. He made important discoveries in the theory of numbers, and invented a method of finding maxima and minima. According to La Place, Fermat shares with Pascal the honour of the invention of the calculus of probabilities. He died at Toulouse in January, 1665, leaving several works, which were published by his son Samuel, under the title of "Varia Opera," (1679.) He had married Louise du Long about 1631. "The geometer next in genius to Descartes," says Hallam, "and perhaps nearer to him than to any third, was Fermat, a man of various acquirements, of high rank in the parliament of Toulouse, and of a mind incapable of envy, forgiving of detraction, and delighting in truth, with almost too much indifference to praise." ("Introduction to the Literature of Europe.")

See MONTUCLA, "Histoire des Mathématiques;" GENTY, "De l'Influence de Fermat sur son Siècle," 1784; "Revue des Deux Mondes" for May, 1845; "Nouvelle Biographie Générale."

Fermat, de, (SAMUEL,) a French lawyer and poet, a son of the preceding, born at Toulouse in 1632, was a counsellor to the parliament. He wrote several treatises on law and other subjects. Died in 1690.

Ferme, fĕrm, (CHARLES,) a Scottish divine, born in Edinburgh, became minister at Fraserburgh about 1600. He wrote a Latin Commentary on the Epistle to the Romans, (1651.) Died about 1618.

Fermin, fĕR′min or fĕR′mân′, (PHILIPPUS,) a Dutch physician and traveller, born at Maestricht. He visited Surinam in 1754, resided there nearly ten years, and published several works relating to the geography and natural history of that colony.

Fermo, da, dä fĕR′mo, (LORENZINO,) an able Italian painter, born at Fermo, flourished about 1660.

Fermor, fĕR′mor, (WILHELM,) COUNT OF, a Russian general, born at Pleskov in 1704, served with distinction in the Seven Years' war and against the Turks, and was subsequently created a count. He commanded the Russian army which Frederick the Great defeated at Zorndorf in 1761. Died in 1771.

Fern, (FANNY.) See PARTON.

Fernand, fĕR′nôN′, [Lat. PHERNAN′DUS,] **Ferrand**, fȧ′rôN′, or **Frenand**, frĕh′nôN′, (CHARLES,) a teacher of theology and philosophy in the University of Paris, was born at Bruges about 1450. He became blind in childhood. He was the author of several ecclesiastical works. Died in 1496.

See VALÈRE ANDRÉ, "Bibliotheca Belgica."

Fernand, fĕR′nând′, or **Fernan**, fĕr-nân′, (GONZALEZ,) a famous Castilian hero or cavalier, born about 910 A.D., was the first Count of Castile. He gained several victories over the Moors. His adventures were favourite subjects of Spanish writers of romance. Died after 950.

Fernand Nuñez, (or **Nuñes**,) de, dä fĕR-nând′ noon′-yĕth, (or noon′yĕs,) COUNT, a Spanish noble, born in Madrid in 1778. As a partisan of Ferdinand VII., he was declared a traitor to France and Spain by Napoleon I. He escaped, however, the vengeance of the emperor; and when Ferdinand returned to his kingdom, in 1814, Fernand Nuñez was sent as ambassador to England, and subsequently to Paris. Died in 1821.

Fernandes, fĕR-nân′dĕs, (ALVARO, âl′vä-ro,) a distinguished Portuguese navigator, explored the west coast of Africa about 1448.

Fernandes, fĕR-nân′dĕs, or **Ferdinand**, fĕR′de-nânt, (VALENTIN,) a German printer and translator, lived at Lisbon about 1500. He translated part of Marco Polo's Travels into Portuguese, (1502.)

€ as k; ç as s; ḡ hard; ĝ as j; G, H, K, *guttural*; N, *nasal*; R, *trilled*; š as z; ŧh as in *this*.　(☞See Explanations, p. 23.)

Fernandes or **Fernandez**, (VASCO,) an eminent Portuguese painter, born at Viseu in 1552. Little is known of his life.

Fernandez. See HERNANDEZ.

Fernandez, fĕr-nȧn'dĕth,(ALFONZO,) a Spanish monk and historian, born at Palencia in 1572; died in 1640.

Fernandez, (ANTONIO de Arias—dȧ ä'rc-äs,) a celebrated Spanish painter, born at Madrid. His pictures had once a high reputation. Died in 1684.

Fernandez, (DIEGO,) a Spanish historian and soldier, born at Palencia. He embarked for Peru in 1545, and entered the service of the viceroy Hurtado de Mendoza, as historiographer, in 1555. He wrote a "History of Peru," (1571,) which is said to be the best contemporary work on that subject.

See N. ANTONIO, " Bibliotheca Hispana Nova."

Fernandez, fĕR-nȧn'dĕz, (DINIZ,) a Portuguese navigator, born in Lisbon, sailed about 1446 on an exploring expedition to Africa, and discovered the mouth of the Senegal, and the promontory at the extreme western part of Africa, to which he gave the name of Cape Verd.

Fernandez, (FRANCISCO,) a celebrated Spanish painter, born in Madrid in 1605; died in 1646.

See QUILLIET, " Vies des Peintres Espagnols."

Fernandez, (JOÃO,) a Portuguese traveller, who about 1446 visited the west coast of Africa. He is supposed to have been the first European who penetrated into the interior of that continent, which he entered at the mouth of the Rio do Ouro.

Fernandez, (JUAN,) a Spanish captain and navigator, entered in 1533 the service of Alvarado in South America. He accompanied Antonio de Sedeno in an expedition to Venezuela. Died in 1538.

Fernandez, (JUAN,) a Spanish pilot and navigator, discovered in 1563 the two islands which bear his name, and planted a colony on the larger island, which is eighteen miles long. The adventures of Alexander Selkirk on this island are supposed to have formed the basis of De Foe's story of "Robinson Crusoe." Other discoveries in the Southern Ocean are ascribed to him. Died in 1576.

See ANSON, " Voyage round the World," etc.

Fernandez, (LUIS,) a Spanish painter and disciple of Eugenio Caxes, was born in Madrid about 1594; died in 1654.

Fernandez de Córdova. See GONZALVO.

Fernandez de Laredo, fĕR-nȧn'dĕth dȧ lȧ-rä'DO, (JUAN,) a Spanish painter in fresco, born at Madrid in 1632; died in 1692.

Fernandez Navarrete. See MUDO, EL.

Fernandez Villareal, fĕR-nȧn'dĕz vil-lȧ-rä'ȧl, (MA-NOEL,) a Portuguese writer, born in Lisbon, published a curious work on the imprisonment of the Portuguese prince Duarte in Germany, "El Principe vendido," etc., (1643.) He was accused of observing the Mosaic law, and was strangled in Lisbon in 1652.

Fernandi. See FERDINANDI.

Fernau, fĕr'nŏw, (KARL,) originally SEBASTIAN FRANCIS DAXENBERGER, a German *littérateur*, born at Munich in 1809, wrote "Mythical Poems," and several dramas, among which is one called "Bianca Capello."

Ferne, fẽrn or farn, (HENRY,) a learned English prelate, born at York in 1602, was one of the first who openly defended by his writings the cause of Charles I. After the restoration he was made Bishop of Chester, in 1660. Died in 1661.

Ferne, (Sir JOHN,) an English antiquary, father of the preceding, born in Lincolnshire; died about 1610. He published "The Blazon of the Gentry," (1586.)

Ferneham, farn'hȧm, ? (NICHOLAS,) an English physician and naturalist, gave much attention to botany. He became physician to Henry III., and afterwards Bishop of Durham. Died in 1241.

Fernel, fĕR'nĕl', [Lat. FERNE'LIUS,] (JEAN,) an eminent French physician, surnamed THE MODERN GALEN, was born at Clermont in Beauvoisis in 1497. He practised in Paris, and acquired a high reputation as a practitioner, a professor, and an elegant writer. About 1547 he received the title of first physician to Henry II. He was the teacher of Vesalius. He wrote numerous works on anatomy, pathology, therapeutics, etc., among which

are " De abditis Rerum Causis," (1548,) and " J. Fernelii Medicina," (1554,) often reprinted. Died in April, 1558.

See G. PLANTIUS, "Vita Fernelii;" DE THOU, "Historia sui Temporis;" BAYLE, "Historical and Critical Dictionary."

Fernow, fĕR'no, (KARL LUDWIG,) a German author and critic, born at Blumenhagen, in Prussia, in 1763. He studied the theory and history of art at Rome under the direction of his friend Carstens, whose life he wrote, (1806.) Among his works are " Roman Studies," (" Römische Studien," 1806–08,) " Ariosto's Lebenslauf," (1809,) and " Francesco Petrarca," (1818.) Died in 1808.

See J. SCHOPENHAUER, "C. L. Fernow's Leben," 1810.

Féron, fâ'rôn', (FIRMIN ÉLOI,) a painter of history, born in Paris in 1802, gained the grand prize in 1825.

Fe-ro'nĭ-a, [Fr. FÉRONIE, fâ'ro'ne',] an ancient Italian divinity, whose worship originated with the Sabines. Her character is not well understood.

Feroze or **Ferose**. See FYROZ.

Ferracino, fĕr-rä-chee'no, (BARTOLOMMEO,) a celebrated Italian mechanician and engineer, was born near Bassano in 1692. Among his inventions were a saw driven by the wind, a hydraulic engine which raised water to the height of thirty-five feet, and a bridge over the Brenta at Bassano, which won for him a high reputation. The inhabitants of Bassano raised a monument to his memory. Died in 1777.

See F. MEMMO, "Vita di Bartolommeo Ferracino."

Ferracuti, fĕr-rä-koo'tee, (GIOVANNI DOMENICO,) an Italian landscape-painter, born at Macerata, flourished about 1700. He was a pupil of Claude Lorrain.

Ferraiuoli or **Ferrajuoli**, fĕr-rä-yoo-o'lee, (NUNZIO,) a Neapolitan landscape-painter, born in Nocera, near Salerno, in 1661; died in 1735.

Ferramola, fĕr-rä-mo'lä, (FIORAVANTE,) an Italian painter, born at Brescia; died in 1528.

Ferrand, fȧ'rôn', a French traveller and physician, born about 1670. He became medical adviser to the Khan of the Tartars of Crimea, and wrote several works relating to that country.

Ferrand, (ANTOINE,) a distinguished French writer of epigrams, born in Paris in 1678; died in that city in 1719.

Ferrand, (ANTOINE FRANÇOIS CLAUDE,) COUNT, a French writer on politics, history, etc., was born in Paris in 1751. He emigrated as a royalist in 1789. In 1814 he became director-general of the post-office. He was chosen a member of the French Academy by the king in 1816. Among his works is " The Spirit of History," (" L'Esprit de l'Histoire," 1802; 6th edition, 4 vols., 1826.) Died in 1825.

See CASIMIR DELAVIGNE, "Discours de Réception" at the French Academy.

Ferrand, (JACQUES,) a French physician and writer, born at Agen, lived about 1620.

Ferrand, (JACQUES,) a distinguished French general, born in 1746; died in 1804.

Ferrand, (JACQUES PHILIPPE,) a French painter, born in Joigny about 1653, was a member of the Royal Academy of Painting, and the author of a work entitled "Art of the Fire, or Manner of Enamelling." Died in 1732.

Ferrand, (LOUIS,) a French advocate and writer on theology, born in Toulon in 1645, was versed in Hebrew and other Oriental languages. He was the author of numerous works, among which is "Reflections on the Christian Religion," (1679.) Died in 1699.

Ferrand, (MARIE LOUIS,) a French general, born in Besançon in 1753, accompanied Leclerc in his expedition against Hayti in 1802, and, on the death of that general, succeeded to the chief command. Having failed in an attempt to suppress a revolt in Saint Domingo, he shot himself in 1808.

Ferrand de la Caussade, fȧ'rôn' dĕh lä kō'sȧd', (JEAN HENRI Bécays—bȧ'kȧ',) a French general, born in Mont-Flanquin, in Agenois, in 1736, served under Dumouriez at the defence of Valenciennes, where he greatly distinguished himself. Died in Paris in 1805.

Ferrando, fĕr-rȧn'do, (GONSALVO,) a Spaniard, born at Oviedo in the fifteenth century, introduced *lignum Guaiacum* into Europe, and wrote a tract on it.

Ferrandus, (FULGEN′TIUS,) [Fr. FULGENCE FER-
RAND, fül′zhŏNss′ fȧ′rŏN′,] a Christian writer, born in
Africa, was a deacon of the Church of Carthage. Among
his works is "Breviatio Canonum." Died about 550 A.D.

Ferrantini, fĕr-rȧn-tee′nee, (GABRIELE,) an Italian
painter, born at Bologna about 1580, was called GA-
BRIELE DEGLI OCCHIALI, (dȧl′yee ok-ke-ȧ′lee.) He excelled in frescos. Among his pupils was Guido Reni.

See LANZI, "History of Painting in Italy."

Fer′rar, (NICHOLAS,) a learned English gentleman,
born in London in 1592, had a high reputation for piety.
He formed at Little Gidding a community called "the
English nunnery," the inmates of which were his relatives.
The whole book of Psalms was repeated by them every
day, and this devotion was practised by them every hour
of the-night. Died in 1637.

See P. PECKARD, "Life of N. Ferrar," 1790.

Ferrar, (ROBERT,) an English divine, born in Yorkshire, was appointed Bishop of Saint David's by Edward
VI. in 1548. On the accession of Mary he was condemned as a heretic, and burnt, in 1555.

Ferrara, fĕr-rä′rä, (ALFEO,) a distinguished physician,
born in Sicily in 1777, was the author of a "Memoir
upon the Waters of Sicily," and other works. Died at
Paris in 1829.

Ferrara, (ANDREA,) an Italian, celebrated as a sword-
smith, lived about 1520-50. He worked in Spain.

Ferrara, (FRANCESCO,) an Italian economist and writer
on statistics, born at Palermo in 1810. He published,
besides other works, "The Importance of Political Economy," (1849.)

Ferrara, (MICHELE,) an Italian chemist and writer on
pharmacy, born in Terra di Lavoro in 1763; died in 1817.

Ferrara, (RENÉE,) DUCHESS OF. See RENÉE OF
FRANCE.

Ferrara, da, dä fĕr-rä′rä, (ANTONIO,) an Italian painter
of the school of Ferrara, flourished about 1450.

See VASARI, "Lives of the Painters."

Ferrara, da, (ERCOLE.) See GRANDI.

Ferrari, fĕr-rä′ree, (ANTONIO,) surnamed GALATEO,
[Lat. GALATE′US LECCEN′SIS,] an Italian physician and
antiquary, born in Galatina, in the kingdom of Naples,
in 1444, was the author of several philosophical and
historical works. He passed the latter part of his life
at Lecce, where he died in 1516.

Ferrari, (ANTONIO FELICE,) an Italian painter of the
school of Ferrara, born in 1668; died in 1719.

Ferrari, (BARTOLOMMEO,) an Italian religionist, born
at Milan in 1497. He founded the religious order or
institution of Barnabites. Died in 1544.

Ferrari, (BARTOLOMMEO,) a Venetian sculptor, born
in 1780. He executed a number of superior works in
marble, bronze, and wood, and completed the restoration of the bronze winged lion which adorns the Piazzetta
at Venice. Died in 1844.

Ferrari, [Lat. FERRA′RIUS,] (FRANCESCO BERNAR-
DINO,) a learned Italian, born at Milan in 1577, became
librarian of the Ambrosian Library about 1609. He
wrote several ecclesiastical and antiquarian works,
among which is "De Ritu sacrarum Ecclesiæ Catholicæ
Concionum," (1612.) Died in 1669. He collected the
manuscripts and books which formed the commencement
of the Ambrosian Library.

Ferrari, (GAUDENZIO,) an eminent painter and sculptor of the Milanese school of Leonardo da Vinci, was
born at Valduggia in 1484. He studied under B. Luini.
In 1516 he aided Raphael in painting frescos in the Vatican at Rome. He worked mostly at Varallo. His style
is somewhat Raphaelesque; but he is deficient in taste
and harmony of colour. He is regarded as the greatest
painter of the Milanese school after Leonardo da Vinci.
His subjects are all religious. Died at Milan in 1550.

See VASARI, "Lives of the Painters;" G. BORDIGA, "Vita di
Gaudenzio Ferrari," 1821; LOMAZZO, "Idea del Tempio della Pittura;" LANZI, "History of Painting in Italy."

Ferrari, (GIOVANNI BATTISTA,) an Italian Orientalist
and naturalist, born at Sienna in 1584, wrote "Nomenclator Syriacus," (1622,) and other works. Died in 1655.

Ferrari, (GIOVANNI MATTEO,) an Italian physician
and medical writer, born near Milan; died in 1472.

Ferrari, (GIUSEPPE,) an Italian philosopher, born at
Milan in 1811, became a resident in France. He was
appointed professor of philosophy at Strasbourg in 1841.
Among his works are "Vico and Italy," (1839,) and an
"Essay on the Principle and Limits of the Philosophy
of History," (1847.) Both are in French.

Ferrari, (GREGORIO,) a skilful painter of the Genoese
school, born in 1644; died in 1726. His son LORENZO,
called ABBÉ FERRARI, was also a painter. He was born
in 1680, and died in 1744.

Ferrari, (GUIDO,) an Italian scholar and Jesuit, born
at Novara in 1717. He wrote several antiquarian and
historical works. Died in 1791.

Ferrari, (LUCA,) an Italian painter, born at Reggio in
1605, studied under Guido Reni, and imitated his style
successfully. Died in 1654.

Ferrari, (LUDOVICO,) an Italian mathematician, born
at Bologna in 1522, was a pupil of the celebrated Cardan. He discovered the mode of resolving equations
of the fourth degree which is called by his name. Died
in 1565.

See MONTUCLA, "Histoire des Mathématiques."

Ferrari, (LUIGI,) son of the sculptor Bartolommeo
Ferrari, born at Venice in 1810, is ranked among the
most distinguished sculptors of the present time. His
figures of "Melancholy" and "The Lotos-gathering
Nymph" are esteemed master-pieces.

Ferrari, (LUIGI MARIA BARTOLOMMEO,) an Italian
ecclesiastic, and professor of mathematics and natural
philosophy at Bologna, born at Milan in 1747. He was
the author of various works upon religious subjects and
upon hydraulics. Died in 1820.

Ferrari, (ORAZIO,) a Genoese painter, born at Voltri
in 1606; died in 1657.

Ferrari, (OTTAVIANO,) an Italian scholar, born at
Milan in 1518, published a treatise "On the Origin of
the Romans," (1607,) and other critical and antiquarian
works. Died in 1586.

Ferrari, (OTTAVIO,) an Italian antiquary, nephew of
Francesco Bernardino, noticed above, was born at Milan
in 1607. He became professor of philosophy and Greek
literature at Padua in 1634. Among his chief works
is "Sources (or Elements) of the Italian Language,"
("Origines Linguæ Italicæ," 1676.) Died in 1682.

See J. FABRICIUS, "Vita Ferrarii," 1710.

Ferrari, de′, dä fĕr-rä′ree, (GIOVANNI ANDREA,) a
Genoese painter of history, landscapes, and animals, was
born about 1600; died in 1669.

See LANZI, "History of Painting in Italy."

Ferraris, fĕr-rä′ris, (JOSEPH,) COUNT OF, a celebrated
commander, born at Lunéville in 1726. He served in
the war of the Austrian succession, and afterwards in the
Seven Years' war. About 1777 he published the twenty-
five-sheet map of the Netherlands which is called by his
name. He was appointed vice-president of the imperial
council of war in 1798, and in 1801 field-marshal. Died
in 1807.

Fer′rars, (EDWARD,) an English writer, born in Warwickshire, was the author of several dramas, which have
been lost. Died in 1564.

Ferrars or **Ferrers,** (GEORGE,) an English lawyer,
poet, and historian, born near Saint Alban's about 1512.
He became a favourite courtier of Henry VIII., and
wrote a "History of the Reign of Queen Mary." He
contributed to "The Mirror for Magistrates" six tragedies or poems, among which are "The Fall of Robert
Tressilian" and "The Tragedy of King Richard II."
Died in 1579.

See "Biographia Britannica;" WARTON, "History of English
Poetry."

Ferrars, (HENRY,) a relative of Edward, noticed
above, born about 1560, was the author of several treatises
on antiquities and heraldry. He was a friend of the
celebrated Camden. Died in 1633.

Ferrata, fĕr-rä′tä, (ERCOLE,) an eminent Italian
sculptor, born near Como about 1610; died in 1685.

Ferrato Sasso. See SALVI.

Ferraud, fȧ′rō′, or **Féraud,** fȧ′rō′, a French deputy to
the National Convention, born in Armagnac in 1764, was
an adherent of the Girondists, and voted for the death
of the king. While resisting the populace, who were

endeavouring to force the doors of the Convention, in May, 1795, he was killed by a pistol-shot.

See THIERS, "History of the French Revolution;" "Nouvelle Biographie Générale."

Ferrein, fa͞'rǎN', (ANTOINE,) a distinguished French anatomist and physician, born near Agen in 1693; died in 1769. He was author of several anatomical works.

Ferreira, fĕr-rā'e-rä, (ALEXANDRE,) a Portuguese historian, born in Oporto. He wrote a "History of the Knights Templars," which is highly esteemed. Died in 1737.

Ferreira, fĕr-rā'e-rä, (ALEXANDRE RODRIGUES,) a Brazilian naturalist and traveller, born at Bahia in 1756. He spent nine years in exploring Brazil, from 1784 to 1793. Died in 1815.

Ferreira, (ANTONIO,) a celebrated poet, sometimes called "the Portuguese Horace," was born at Lisbon in 1528. He became a professor at the University of Coimbra, and wrote, besides numerous sonnets, odes, epistles, and epigrams, a tragedy of "Inez de Castro," which ranks among the most beautiful productions in the Portuguese language. He was one of the principal promoters of classical taste in Portuguese poetry. His epistles (*Cartas*) are regarded by some critics as his best works. Died in 1569.

See F. DENIS, "Résumé de l'Histoire littéraire du Portugal;" LONGFELLOW, "Poets and Poetry of Europe;" BARBOSA MACHADO, "Bibliotheca Lusitana;" J. M. DA COSTA E SYLVA, "Ensaio sobre os melhores Poetas Portuguezes," 1852.

Ferreira, (CHRISTOVÃO,) a Portuguese Jesuit, born about 1580 at Torres-Vedras, went as a missionary to Japan, where he remained twenty-four years, and suffered martyrdom at Nagasaki about 1652.

Ferrer, fĕr-rair', (BARTOLOMÉ,) a Spanish navigator, was chief pilot of an expedition which, under Cabrillo, explored the coast of California in 1542. He succeeded to the command on the death of Cabrillo, January, 1543.

Ferrer, (JAYME,) a Spanish cosmographer, was summoned to court in 1496, and employed to fix a line of demarcation which should separate the Spanish from the Portuguese possessions in the New World.

Ferreri, fĕr-rā'ree, (ANDREA,) an Italian sculptor and painter, born at Milan in 1673; died in 1744.

Ferreri, (ZACCARIA,) a Latin poet, born in 1479 in Vicenza, Italy, was appointed by Pope Leo X., in 1519, Bishop of Guardia, in the kingdom of Naples. Died about 1530.

Ferreras, de, dä fĕr-rā'räs, (JUAN,) a learned Spanish ecclesiastic and historian, born near Astorga in 1652. He assisted in compiling the great Spanish Dictionary; but his principal work is his "Historical and Chronological Synopsis of Spain," (16 vols. 4to.) It comes down to 1588, and is highly esteemed for its accuracy. Died in 1735.

Ferrero, fĕr-rā'ro, (EDWARD,) a general, born in Spain about 1832, came to the United States in his childhood. As colonel, he served with distinction in the Union army at Newbern, and at Antietam, September, 1862, and was not long after appointed a brigadier-general. He commanded a division of the army which besieged Petersburg in June, 1864.

Ferrers, (GEORGE.) See FERRARS.

Ferreti, fĕr-rā'tee, or **Ferreto,** fĕr-rā'to, [Lat. FER-RE'TUS,] an Italian historian and poet, born at Vicenza about 1296, wrote a History of Italy from 1230 to 1318.

Ferreti, (EMILIO,) a distinguished Italian jurist and legal writer, born in Tuscany in 1489, was secretary to Pope Leo X. He afterwards became counsellor to the Parliament of Paris, and French ambassador to Charles V. of Germany, whom he afterwards accompanied on his African expedition. Died in 1552.

See BAYLE, "Historical and Critical Dictionary."

Ferreti, (GIOVANNI BATTISTA,) an Italian antiquary, born at Vicenza in 1639. He wrote "Musæ Lapidariæ Antiquorum in Marmoribus Carmina," (1672.) Died in 1682.

Ferreti, (GIOVANNI DOMENICO,) a skilful Italian painter, born at Florence in 1692. His design is correct, and his colouring vivid. Died after 1750.

See LANZI, "History of Painting in Italy;" TICOZZI, "Dizionario;" "Nouvelle Biographie Générale."

Ferreti, (GIULIO,) an Italian jurist and writer on law, born in Ravenna in 1480; died in 1547.

Fĕr'rey, (BENJAMIN,) an English architect, born at Christ Church, in Hampshire, in 1810, was a pupil of A. Pugin. Among his principal structures are churches at Taunton and Eton, and Saint Stephen's Church, Westminster. He is the author of a treatise "On the Antiquities of the Priory of Christ Church," (1834.) His works are mostly in the Gothic style.

Ferri, fĕr'ree, or **Ferro,** fĕr'ro, [Lat. FER'RIUS,] (ALPHONSO,) an Italian physician, was first surgeon to Pope Paul III., and the author of several medical and surgical works. Died about 1580.

Ferri, (CIRO,) a distinguished Italian painter and architect, born in Rome in 1634, was a pupil of Pietro da Cortona, whose style he imitated successfully. He excelled as a fresco-painter, and assisted Pietro da Cortona in many of his great works. He is said to have been an almost universal artist. Died in 1689.

See WINCKELMANN, "Neues Mahler-Lexikon;" LANZI, "History of Painting in Italy;" TICOZZI, "Dizionario."

Ferri, (GERONIMO,) a learned Italian writer, born in Romagna in 1713. He was appointed professor of rhetoric in the University of Ferrara by Pope Clement XIV. He was the author of various works. Died in 1766.

Ferri, (PAUL.) See FERRY.

Fer'ri-ar, (JOHN,) an English physician, born at Chester in 1764, wrote "Medical Histories and Reflections," (3 vols., 1792–98,) and "Illustrations of Sterne," (1798.) Died in 1815.

Ferrier, fa͞'re-à', (AUGER,) a French physician and medical writer, born near Toulouse in 1513; died in 1588.

Fĕr'rĭ-er, (JAMES F.,) a British writer on moral philosophy, born in Edinburgh about 1808, was a son-in-law of Professor John Wilson. He was appointed professor of moral philosophy and political economy in the University of Saint Andrew's in 1845. His most important work is "Institutes of Metaphyics, the Theory of Knowing and Being," (1854,) which was favourably received. Died in 1864.

See "Blackwood's Magazine" for February, 1855, and March, 1867; "Edinburgh Review" for July, 1867.

Ferrier, (JEAN,) a French Jesuit, born at Rodez in 1619, wrote against the Jansenists. He became confessor to Louis XIV. in 1670. Died in 1670 or 1674.

Ferrier, (JÉRÉMIE,) a French professor of theology, born about 1560. He was a Protestant minister at Nîmes, and argued in 1602 that the pope was Antichrist. About 1612 he became a Roman Catholic. He was regarded as a traitor by the Protestants before his public avowal of his conversion. Died in 1626.

Ferrier, sometimes called erroneously **Ferrière,** (LOUIS,) a French poet, born in Arles in 1652; died in 1721.

Ferrier, (Miss MARY,) a Scottish novelist, born in Edinburgh about 1782. She produced a number of successful novels, among which are "Marriage," (1818,) "The Inheritance," (1824,) and "Destiny, or the Chief's Daughter," (1831.) She was intimate with Sir Walter Scott, who described her as a "gifted personage, having, besides her great talents, conversation the least *exigeante* of any author—female, at least—whom he had ever seen." Died in 1854.

See "Edinburgh Review" for January, 1842.

Ferrier, du, dü fa͞'re-à', (ARNAUD,) a French jurist, born at Toulouse about 1506. He represented Henry II. of France at the Council of Trent, where he gave offence by his liberal sentiments. He afterwards avowed himself a Protestant, and became chancellor of Henry of Navarre. Died in 1585.

See DE THOU, "Historia sui Temporis;" BAYLE, "Historical and Critical Dictionary."

Ferrière. See LA FERRIÈRE.

Ferrières or **Ferrière, de,** deh fa͞'re-air', (CLAUDE,) a distinguished French lawyer, born in Paris in 1639, was the author of numerous legal works. Died in 1714.

Ferro, del, dĕl fĕr'ro, (SCIPIONE,) an Italian mathematician, born at Bologna about 1465. He discovered a method to resolve equations of the third degree. Died about 1525, or after that date.

Ferron, Le, lẹh fȧ'ròN', (ARNOUL,) a French jurist and historian, born at Bordeaux in 1515. He wrote, in elegant Latin, a continuation of Paolo Emilio's "History of France," (1554.) Died in 1563.

Ferroni, fȇr-ro'nee, (GIROLAMO,) an Italian painter and engraver, born at Milan in 1687.

Ferrucci, fȇr-root'chee, (ANDREA,) an Italian sculptor, born at Fiesole. He died at an advanced age in 1522.

Ferrucci, (FRANCESCO,) surnamed DEL TADDA, a Florentine sculptor, who worked in porphyry. Died in 1585.

Ferrucci, (NICODEMO,) a skilful painter of the Florentine school, born at Fiesole ; died in 1650.

Ferrucci, (POMPEO,) an Italian sculptor, born at Fiesole, lived at Rome. Died about 1625.

Ferry, fȧ're', (CLAUDE JOSEPH,) a French statesman and savant, born near Saint-Dié in 1756. He was a republican member of the Convention of 1792, and succeeded Malus as examiner in the Polytechnic School in 1812, but was deprived of that place in 1814. Died in 1845.

Fĕr'rȳ, (ORRIS S.,) an American Senator, born at Bethel, Connecticut, in 1823, became a lawyer, and settled at Norwalk. He was elected a member of Congress for the fourth district of Connecticut in 1859. Having entered the army as colonel in 1861, he was appointed a brigadier-general about March, 1862. He was elected to the Senate of the United States by the legislature of Connecticut for six years, March, 1867-73.

Ferry or **Ferri,** [Lat. FER'RIUS,] (PAUL,) an eloquent French Protestant minister, born at Metz in 1591. He preached in his native place more than fifty years, and acquired great influence. He wrote many theological works, among which is "Scholastici Orthodoxi Specimen," (1616.) Died in 1669.

See BAYLE, "Historical and Critical Dictionary;" HAAG, "La France protestante."

Fersen, von, fon fȇr'sẹn, (AXEL,) a Swedish general and senator, born about 1715. He was an active and prominent member of the Diet, and opposed the policy of Gustavus III. Died in 1794.

See GEYER, "Histoire de la Suède."

Fersen, von, (AXEL,) COUNT, marshal of Sweden, a son of the preceding, born at Stockholm in 1750. He entered the French service, and fought for the United States, 1778-82. In the disguise of a coachman, he conducted Louis XVI. and his family out of Paris in his flight to Varennes, 1791. He returned to Sweden, and was appointed marshal of the kingdom about 1801. He was murdered in 1810 by a mob, who suspected him of complicity in the death of Prince Christian.

See LAMARTINE, "History of the Girondists;" "Nouvelle Biographie Générale."

Ferté-Imbaut, de la, dẹh lȧ fȇr'tȧ' ŏN'bō', MARQUISE, a celebrated French lady, was a daughter of Madame Geoffrin. She was married in 1733 to the Marquis de la Ferté-Imbaut.

Ferté, La. See LA FERTÉ.

Fertiault, fȇr'te'ō', (FRANÇOIS,) a French poet and *littérateur*, born at Verdun in 1814.

Ferus, fȧ'rŭs, (JOHANN,) a learned German ecclesiastic, whose original name was WILD, (wȋlt,) born at Metz in 1494. He wrote commentaries on the books of the Old and New Testaments, which are commended by Dupin and Bayle. Died in 1554.

Férussac, de, dẹh fȧ'rü'såk', (ANDRÉ ÉTIENNE JUST PASCAL JOSEPH FRANÇOIS d'Audebard—dōd'bȧR',) BARON, a French naturalist, the son of Jean Baptiste Férussac, noticed below, was born in 1786 or 1784. He published an important work, entitled "Natural History of Terrestrial and Fluviatile Mollusca," (1817,) and other treatises on natural history. He founded and edited a valuable scientific journal, called "Bulletin universel des Sciences," (1823-30.) Died in Paris in 1836.

Férussac, de, (JEAN BAPTISTE LOUIS D'AUDEBARD,) BARON, a French naturalist, born at Clérac, in Languedoc, in 1745. He was a captain in the navy before the Revolution. He wrote a work on fresh-water mollusca, (1807.) Died in 1815.

Fesca, fĕs'kȧ, (FRIEDRICH ERNST,) a German musician and composer, born at Magdeburg in 1789. He produced a number of symphonies, overtures, etc., and

two operas, entitled "Cantemira," and "Omar and Leila." Died in 1826.

Fesch, fĕsh, (JOSEPH,) born in Corsica in 1763, was half-brother to the mother of Napoleon. Soon after the concordat concluded by Bonaparte with Pius VII. in 1801, Fesch was created Archbishop of Lyons, and in 1803 was made a cardinal. In 1805 he was appointed grand almoner, and senator of the empire. When offered the archbishopric of Paris, in 1809, Cardinal Fesch, offended by Bonaparte's unkindness to the pope, refused the promotion, and in the Council of Paris, in 1810, boldly condemned the conduct of the emperor. For this he was banished to Lyons, where he remained until 1814. After the battle of Waterloo he took refuge at Rome, and died there in 1839. His celebrated collection of pictures, medals, etc. was sold at auction.

See "Le Cardinal Fesch, Fragments biographiques," Lyons, 1841; THIERS, "Histoire du Consulat et de l'Empire."

Fessard, fȧ'såR', (PIERRE ALPHONSE,) a French statuary, born in Paris in 1798 ; died in 1844.

Fes'sen-dẹn, (THOMAS GREEN,) an American satirical poet, born in Walpole, New Hampshire, in 1771, graduated at Dartmouth College in 1796, and studied law. He produced a poem called "The Country Lovers," which was very popular, went to England in 1801, and there published, in 1803, his humorous poem "Terrible Tractoration," (on the Metallic Tractors of Dr. Perkins.) He settled in Boston about 1804, and became the editor of the "New England Farmer." Died in 1837.

See DUYCKINCK's "Cyclopædia of American Literature," vol. i.

Fessenden, (WILLIAM PITT,) an American Senator, a son of the Hon. Samuel Fessenden, was born at Boscawen, New Hampshire, on the 16th of October, 1806. He graduated at Bowdoin College in 1823, studied law, and began to practise at Portland, Maine, about 1828. In 1840 he was elected a member of Congress by the Whigs of Maine. He served in the legislature of that State in 1845 and 1846, after which he passed several years in the practice of his profession. He was elected a Senator of the United States by the legislature of Maine in 1853 or 1854, and about that time joined the Republican party. He acquired a high reputation as a debater, was re-elected a member of the United States Senate in 1859, and was appointed chairman of the committee on finance. In July, 1864, he was appointed to the office of secretary of the treasury, rendered vacant by the resignation of Mr. Chase. He resigned this post about February, 1865, and in March of that year resumed his seat in the Senate, to which he had again been elected for a term of six years. He was one of the seven Republican Senators who decided that President Johnson was not guilty of high crimes or misdemeanours, May 16, 1868. Died in September, 1869.

Fess'lẹr, (IGNAZ AURELIUS,) a historian and novelist, born in Lower Hungary in 1756, was professor of Oriental languages at Lemberg about 1784. His principal work is a "History of Hungary," (10 vols., 1812-25.) He also wrote several historical romances, and an interesting autobiography, (1826.) Died at Saint Petersburg in 1839.

Festa, fĕs'tȧ, (CONSTANTINO,) an Italian musician and composer of madrigals, became a singer in the pontifical chapel at Rome in 1517. Died in 1545.

Fes'tus, (PORCIUS,) a Roman officer, who in 62 A.D. succeeded Felix as Governor of Judea. He gained an honourable and durable distinction by his conduct in the case of the Apostle Paul, who was arraigned before him by the Jews. (See Acts xxiv. 27, xxv. and xxvi.)

Festus, (SEXTUS POMPEIUS,) a Latin grammarian, supposed to have lived in the third or fourth century. His name is attached to a glossary entitled "De Significatione Verborum," ("On the Signification of Words,") which, though not preserved entire, is very important for the explanation of Latin grammar and Roman antiquities. It is an epitome of a work by M. Verrius Flaccus, which is lost. The epitome, however, contains valuable notes and criticisms added by Festus.

See FABRICIUS, "Bibliotheca Latina."

Feth-Ali-Schah. See FATEH-ALEE- (or ALI-) SHAH.

Feti, fȧ'tee, (DOMENICO,) sometimes called IL MANTUANO, an eminent Italian painter, born at Rome in

ẹ as k; ç as s; ḡ hard; ġ as j; G, H, K, guttural; N, nasal; R, trilled; s̄ as z; th as in this. (☞See Explanations, p. 23.)

58

1589, was a pupil of Cigoli. He worked at Mantua and Venice, injured his health by dissipation, and died in 1624. His works are chiefly oil-pictures of religious subjects.

See LANZI, "History of Painting in Italy;" "Nouvelle Biographie Générale."

Fétis, fä'tèss', (FRANÇOIS JOSEPH,) a Belgian composer, critic, and biographer, born at Mons in 1784. He became professor of composition in Paris in 1821, and founded in 1827 the "Revue Musicale," which was regarded as high authority. He composed several operas and pieces of sacred music. In 1833 he was appointed director of the Conservatory of Brussels. He published, besides several treatises on music, a "Universal Biography of Musicians," (8 vols. 8vo, 1834–44,) which is the most complete work on the subject. He also published, in 1869, a "General History of Music from the Earliest Times down to the Present," in 8 vols.

See a notice of M. FÉTIS, in his "Biographie Universelle des Musiciens;" GOLLMICK, "Herr Fétis als Mensch, Kritiker, etc.," 1852.

Feuchère, fuh'shair', (JEAN JACQUES,) a French sculptor, born in Paris in 1807 ; died in 1852.

Feuchères, de, deh fuh'shair', (SOPHIE,) BÁRONNE, born in the Isle of Wight in 1795. Her maiden name was DAWES. She was the mistress of the Duc de Bourbon, who was found dead in his chamber in 1830. She was suspected of being accessory to his death, but after trial was acquitted. Died in 1841.

See "Nouvelle Biographie Générale."

Feuchtersleben, von, fon foik'ters-lä'ben, (EDUARD or ERNST,) a German philosopher and physician, born in Vienna in 1806. He published, besides other works, "Zur Diätetik der Seele," (1838.) Died in 1849.

Feuerbach, foi'er-bâk', (ANSELM,) eldest son of the eminent jurist Paul Johann Alselm, noticed below, was born in 1798. He was the author of a work entitled "The Apollo of the Vatican," and other archæological treatises. Died in 1851.

Feuerbach, (FRIEDRICH HEINRICH,) an Orientalist, brother of the preceding, was born in 1806. He wrote "Religion of the Future," (1843–47.)

Feuerbach, (LUDWIG ANDREAS,) a speculative philosopher and skeptic, a son of the celebrated jurist, was born at Anspach in 1804. He published, besides other works, a "History of Modern Philosophy from Lord Bacon to Spinoza," (1833,) and "The Essence of Christianity," (" Das Wesen des Christenthums," 1841.) He is a disciple of Hegel.

See BROCKHAUS, "Conversations-Lexikon."

Feuerbach, (PAUL JOHANN ANSELM,) an eminent German jurist and reformer of criminal law, born at Jena in 1775. His first important work was entitled "Anti-Hobbes, or on the Limits of Civil Power, and the Compulsory Right of Subjects against their Sovereigns," (1798 ;) and the same year he published his "Examination of the Crime of High Treason." In his "Review of the Fundamental Principles and Ideas of Penal Law," (2 vols., 1799,) and the "Library of Penal Law," he entirely remodelled the science of criminal jurisprudence, and introduced into it most important and salutary reforms. In 1804 he brought out his "Critique of a Project of a Penal Code for Bavaria," in consequence of which he was soon after commissioned to draw up a criminal code for that kingdom, which also formed the basis of a reform in the penal codes of other German states. In 1812 he published "Considerations on the Jury," in which he censures the defects of French legislation, and in 1828 his "Exposition of Remarkable Crimes," one of his most celebrated works. Feuerbach was appointed about 1817 first president of the court of appeal at Anspach. In 1832 appeared his treatise entitled "Kaspar Hauser : an Instance of a Crime against a Soul," *(Verbrechens am Seelenleben,)* in which he gives the result of his investigations in that remarkable case. He was a firm opposer of all civil and ecclesiastical aggressions, and especially deserves the gratitude of mankind for the humanity he has infused into legislation. Died at Frankfort in 1833.

See "Leben und Wirken Anselm von Feuerbach," by his son, 1852; "Nouvelle Biographie Générale."

Feuerlein, foi'er-lïn', (GEORG CHRISTOPH,) a German physician and writer, born at Nuremberg in 1694 or 1695; died in 1756.

Feuerlein, (JAKOB WILHELM,) a German theologian, born at Nuremberg in 1689 ; died in 1776.

Feuerlein, (JOHANN CONRAD,) a German jurist, born at Wöhrd in 1725 ; died at Nuremberg in 1788.

Feugère, fuh'zhair', (LÉON JACQUES,) a French *littérateur,* born at Villeneuve-sur-Yonne in 1810 ; died in 1858.

Feuillade, de la, deh lä fuh'yäd', (FRANÇOIS d'Aubusson**—**dō'bü'sòn',) VICOMTE, chevalier of the order of Saint Louis, distinguished himself in the wars against the Spaniards and the Turks, and in 1675 was created by Louis XIV. marshal of France. Died in 1691.

Feuillade, de la, (LOUIS,) DUC, son of the preceding, was created marshal of France in 1724. Died in 1725.

Feuillet, fuh'yà', sometimes written **Feuillée,**(LOUIS,) a French botanist and astronomer, born near Forcalquier, in Provence, in 1660. He was the companion of J. Cassini in a geographical and hydrographical voyage to the Levant. Between 1703 and 1712 he travelled in South America. He published a "History of the Medicinal Plants of Peru and Chili," (3 vols.,) and a "Journal of Observations, Mathematical and Botanical, made on the Eastern Coasts of South America and in the West Indies," (2 vols., 1714.) Died at Marseilles in 1732.

See LELONG, "Bibliothèque historique de France;" "Nouvelle Biographie Générale."

Feuillet, (NICOLAS,) a noted French preacher and moralist, born in 1622 ; died in Paris in 1693.

Feuillet, (OCTAVE,) a French novelist and dramatist, born at Saint-Lo (Manche) in 1822. Among his works are comedies called "The Crisis," ("La Crise," 1848,) and "Dalila," (1857.) He was elected to the French Academy in 1862.

Feuquières, de, deh fuh'ke-air', (ANTOINE de Pas **—**deh pâ,) MARQUIS, a distinguished French general, grandson of the following, was born in Paris in 1648. He served with eminent ability from 1667 until 1697. He wrote an able work on military tactics, entitled "Mémoires sur la Guerre," (4 vols., 1731.) Died in 1711.

Feuquières, de, or **Feuquière,** (MANASSES DE PAS,) MARQUIS, a French general and diplomatist, born at Saumur in 1590. Having been sent on a mission to Germany after the death of Gustavus Adolphus, he formed an alliance with that country against Austria. He was killed at the siege of Thionville in 1640.

His son ISAAC, also a general and ambassador, was appointed Viceroy of America in 1660. Died in 1688.

Feutry, fuh'tRe', (AIMÉ AMBROISE JOSEPH,) a French *littérateur,* born at Lille in 1720 ; died in 1789.

Féval, fä'vàl', (PAUL,) a popular French novelist, born at Rennes in November, 1817. He began his literary career as a writer for several journals of Paris. In 1844 he produced, under the assumed name of Sir Francis Trolopp, "The Mysteries of London," (11 vols.) Among his works are "Captain Spartacus," (1845,) and "The Iron Man," ("L'Homme de Fer," 1856.)

See C. ROBIN, "Biographie de P. Féval," 1848.

Feversham, EARL OF. See DURFORT, (LOUIS.)

Fèvre, Le, (ANNE.) See DACIER, MADAME.

Fèvre, Le, leh fàvr or leh fêvr, (CLAUDE,) a French portrait-painter and engraver, born at Fontainebleau in 1633, was patronized by Louis XIV. He painted some subjects of sacred history. Died in London in 1675.

Fèvre, Le, (JACQUES,) a French polemical writer on theology, born at Lisieux. He wrote against the Protestant doctrines. Died in 1716.

Fèvre, Le, (JEAN BAPTISTE,) or **Lefebvre de Villebrune,** a French philologist, born at Senlis in 1732. He was master of many ancient and modern languages. Among his chief works is a translation of Athenæus. He became professor of Hebrew and Syriac in the College of France in 1792. Died in 1809.

Fèvre, Le, (NICOLAS,) [Lat. NICOLA'US FA'BER,] a French scholar, born in Paris in 1544, published a valuable edition of Seneca, with notes. As a critic he is highly commended by Lipsius and Scaliger. Died in 1611.

ā, ē, ī, ō, ū, ȳ, *long;* ă, ĕ, ĭ, ŏ, same, less prolonged; ă, ĕ, ĭ, ŏ, ŭ, ȳ, *short;* a, e, i, o, *obscure;* fär, fàll, fàt; mêt; nŏt; gŏŏd; mōōn ;

Fèvre, Le, (ROLAND,) a French portrait-painter, born about 1605, worked in England, where he died in 1677.

Fevret, feh-vRả', (CHARLES,) a learned and distinguished French jurist, born in 1583 at Semur-en-Auxois. He wrote several works on canon law, one of which is entitled "Traité de l'Abus," (1653.) Died in 1661.

His son PIERRE, born in 1625, founded the public library of Dijon. Died in 1706.

Fevret de Fontette, feh-vRả' deh fôN'tĕt', (CHARLES MARIE,) a learned French lawyer, a great-grandson of Charles Fevret, noticed above, was born at Dijon in 1710. He commenced a new edition of Lelong's "Bibliothèque historique de la France," and published one volume of that important work. Died in 1772.

See BARBEAU DE LA BRUYÈRE, "Vie de Fevret de Fontette," 2 vols., 1775.

Few, (WILLIAM,) COLONEL, an American patriot, born in Maryland in 1748, removed to Georgia about 1776. He was elected a member of Congress in 1780, and was a member of the Convention which framed the Federal Constitution in 1787. He served with distinction in several battles with the British and Indians. He was United States Senator from 1789 to 1793. Died in 1828.

Feydeau, fả'dō', (MATHIEU,) a zealous French Jansenist, born in Paris in 1616, was one of the ecclesiastics expelled by the faculty of the Sorbonne for refusing to condemn Arnauld. He was the author of "Reflections on the History and Harmony of the Gospels," (2 vols., 1673.) Died at Annonay in 1694.

Feyerabend, fi'er-ả'bĕnt, (SIGISMOND,) a German painter, engraver, and bookseller, born at Frankfort about 1526; died after 1585.

Feyjoo (or **Feijoo**) **y Montenegro,** fả-e-Hō' e montả-nả'gRo, (FRANCISCO BENITO JERONIMO,) a learned Spanish moralist and critic, sometimes called "the Spanish Addison," was born at Cardamiro in 1676, or, as others say, in 1701. He became a Benedictine monk, and abbot of the monastery of Oviedo. He attacked prevailing errors and prejudices in a series of essays, entitled "Teatro critico sobre los Errores comunes," (16 vols. 8vo, 1738-46.) He also published "Cartas eruditas y curiosas," (8 vols. 8vo, 1746-48.) His works contributed much to the diffusion of science and good morals. Died at Oviedo in 1764.

See TICKNOR, "History of Spanish Literature;" CAMPOMANES, "Vida de Feyjoo," prefixed to an edition of the works of Feyjoo, 33 vols., 1780.

Feynes, de, deh fản, (HENRI,) a French traveller, born in Provence in the sixteenth century. He spent nearly eighteen years in Asia, and on his return published an account of his travels.

Fezensac, de, deh feh-zôN'zăk', (RAYMOND ÉMERY PHILIPPE JOSEPH de Montesquiou — deh môN'tĕs'-ke-oo',) DUC, a French general of division, born in 1784, wrote "Souvenirs militaires de 1804 à 1814," (Paris, 1863,) which has a high reputation. Died in 1867.

See VAPEREAU, "Dictionnaire universel des Contemporains,' 1858; "Edinburgh Review" for January, 1868.

Fiacchi, fe-åk'kee, (LUIGI,) an able Italian critic and poet, born at Scarperi, in Tuscany, in 1754, was sometimes called CLASIO. Died in 1825.

See TIPALDO, "Biografia degli Italiani illustri."

Fiacco, fe-åk'ko, or **Flacco,** flåk'ko, (ORLANDO,) a painter of the Venetian school, born at Verona, lived about 1550.

Fialetti, fe-ả-let'tee, (ODOARDO,) an Italian painter and engraver, born at Bologna in 1573, was a pupil of the celebrated Tintoretto. Died in 1638.

Fialho, fe-ål'yo, (MANOEL,) a Portuguese historian, born at Evora in 1659. He wrote a history of Evora, entitled "Evora gloriosa," (1728.) Died in 1718.

See BARBOSA MACHADO, "Bibliotheca Lusitana."

Fialho-Ferreira, fe-ål'yo fĕR-rā'e-rả, (ANTONIO,) a Portuguese traveller and captain, was born at Macao. He commanded a fleet in 1633, after which he travelled by land from India to Lisbon, and returned by sea. He published a narrative of his travels in 1643.

Fiamma, fe-åm'mả, (GALVANEO,) an Italian historian, born at Milan in 1283, wrote a "History of Milan from the Origin of the City until the Year 1336." Died in 1344.

Fiammingo, fe-åm-min'go, (ARRIGO,) a Flemish painter, whose name is not known. He worked in Rome for Pope Gregory XIII. Died about 1600.

Fiammingo, Il, èl fe-åm-min'go, (or **Fiamingo,**) ("the Fleming,") the name given by the Italians to several artists of the Netherlands. See CALVAERT, (DENIS,) and DUQUESNOY, (FRANÇOIS.)

Fiasella, fe-ả-sel'lả, (DOMENICO,) a painter of the Genoese school, born at Sarzana in 1589; died in 1669.

Fibonacci. See LEONARDO DA PISA.

Fichard, fe'shằR' or fiK'åRt, (JOHANN,) a German jurist, born at Frankfort in 1512; died in 1591.

Ficherelli, fe-kả-rel'lee, or **Ficarelli,** fe-kả-rel'lee, (FELICE,) a skilful Florentine painter, born at San Gemigiano about 1605, was surnamed RIPOSO. Died in 1660.

Fichet, fe'shả, (ALEXANDRE,) a French Jesuit and scholar, born in Savoy in 1588; died in 1659.

Fichet, (GUILLAUME,) a French theologian and rhetorician, born at Aunay, near Paris. He became rector of the University of Paris in 1467, and was employed in diplomacy by Louis XI. About 1470 he established in the Sorbonne a printing-press,—probably the first used in Paris.

Fichte, fiK'teh, (IMMANUEL HERMANN,) son of the eminent philosopher Johann Gottlieb, was born at Jena in 1797. He studied at Berlin, and became in 1842 professor of philosophy in the University of Tübingen. He is the chief of a school which affects, it has been said, a *juste milieu* between mysticism and materialism. He has written numerous works relating to metaphysics, theology, etc., in some of which he has sought to defend and explain the views of his father. His "Speculative Theology," in 3 vols., appeared in 1847.

Fichte, (JOHANN GOTTLIEB,) the second in order of the four great teachers* of intellectual and moral philosophy in Germany, was born near Bischofswerda, in Upper Lusatia, in 1762. He studied at the Universities of Jena, Leipsic, and Wittenberg. He afterwards spent several years as private teacher in Zurich, where he formed a friendship with the celebrated Pestalozzi. Leaving Switzerland, he visited Leipsic, Warsaw, and lastly Königsberg, where he became acquainted with Kant, and published anonymously his first important work, entitled an "Attempt at a Criticism of all Revelation," ("Versuch einer Kritik aller Offenbarung,") which attracted much attention and was at first generally attributed to Kant himself. The fame of this work procured Fichte a call to the chair of philosophy at Jena, where he developed his system of metaphysics, to which he gave the name of "Wissenschaftslehre," ("Doctrine or Principles of Science.") Having been accused of holding atheistical opinions, he resigned his professorship about 1799, and soon after made to the public an "Appeal against the Charge of Atheism," ("Appellation gegen die Anklage des Atheismus.") This, however, was considered by many not to be a successful refutation of the objections which had been made to his doctrines. He appears to have held that God was not a Being, properly so called, but a supreme Law, or rather a system of laws, intellectual, moral, and spiritual, without what we call "personality," or personal consciousness; although there are passages in his works which seem to indicate that sometimes, at least, his views approximated those of the Theists. He was afterwards for a few months professor of philosophy at Erlangen; but when Germany became the theatre of war he withdrew for a time to Königsberg. In 1810 he was made professor of philosophy in the new University at Berlin.

Fichte took a deep interest in the cause of German independence, and employed all his influence and eloquence to stir up the patriotism of his countrymen against the domination of the French, during the contest which terminated in the fall of Napoleon in 1813. He died in January, 1814. Besides the different publications expounding his peculiar system of philosophy, his most important works are "On the Destination of Man," ("Ueber die Bestimmung des Menschen,") "Foundation of Natural Right," ("Grundlage des Naturrechts,") and his "System of Ethics," ("System der Sittenlehre."),

* Kant, Fichte, Schelling, and Hegel.

His "Addresses to the German Nation" ("Reden an die Deutsche Nation") are replete with eloquence and fervid patriotism. His collected works were published in 8 vols., (Berlin, 1845–46.)

"Among the illustrious four whose names are most intimately associated with the recent movement in German philosophy," says Professor Hedge, "his [Fichte's] function is that of moralist; a preacher of righteousness. ... Few philosophers have so honoured their theories with personal illustrations. He carried his philosophy into life and his life into philosophy, acting as he spoke, from an eminence above the level of the world." ("Prose Writers of Germany.")

See, also, IMMANUEL HERMANN FICHTE, "J. G. Fichte's Leben," etc., 2 vols., 1830; CARL BEYER, "Zu Fichte's Gedächtniss," 1835; WILLIAM SMITH, "Memoir of J. G. Fichte," 1846; WILHELM BUSSE, "J. G. Fichte und seine Beziehung zur Gegenwart des Deutschen Volkes," 2 vols., 1848–49; "Leben des Philosophen und Professors J. G. Fichte," Bautzen, 1851; ERSCH und GRUBER, "Allgemeine Encyklopaedie;" RITTER, "History of Philosophy;" G. H. LEWES, "Biographical History of Philosophy;" DE RÉMUSAT, "De la Philosophie Allemande;" "Nouvelle Biographie Générale;" "Foreign Quarterly Review" for October, 1845.

Fichtel, fĭk'tĕl, (JOHANN EHRENREICH,) a distinguished mineralogist, born at Presburg, in Hungary, in 1732. He wrote, besides other works, "Memoirs upon the Mineralogy of Transylvania." Died in 1795.

Ficino, fe-chee'no, (MARSILIO, maR-see'le-o,) [Lat. MARSIL'IUS FICI'NUS; Fr. MARSILE FICIN, mǎR'sèl' fe'săN',] a celebrated Italian philosopher and scholar, born at Florence on the 19th of October, 1433. He was educated by Cosimo de' Medici, studied Greek, and became an admirer of the Platonic philosophy. He was the president of the Platonic Academy founded at Florence by Cosimo de' Medici about 1450, and produced a Latin translation of the works of Plato about 1484. "This version," says Hallam, "has the rare merit of being at once literal, perspicuous, and in good Latin." ("Introduction to the Literature of Europe.") He wrote, besides other works, a "Life of Plato," "Theologia Platonica de Immortalitate," (1488,) and "On the Christian Religion," ("De Religione Christiana," 1510.) Died in 1499.

See GIOVANNI CORSI, "Vita Ficini," written in 1506, published in 1772; SCHELHORN, "Commentarius de Vita et Scriptis M. Ficini;" NICÉRON, "Mémoires;" ERSCH und GRUBER, "Allgemeine Encyklopaedie;" BRUCKER, "History of Philosophy;" A. M. BANDINI, "Commentarius de Vita M. Ficini," 1771.

Ficoroni, fe-ko-ro'nee, (FRANCESCO,) an Italian scholar and antiquary, born near Rome in 1664. He was the author of numerous works, chiefly on Roman antiquities. Died in 1747.

Ficquelmont, fe'kĕl'môN', (KARL LUDWIG,) a distinguished general and diplomatist, born in Lorraine in 1777. He served in the Austrian army in the principal campaigns against the French, and became lieutenant-field-marshal in 1830. Died in 1859.

Ficquet, fe'kå', (ÉTIENNE,) a distinguished French engraver, born in Paris in 1731; died in 1794.

Fidani, fe-dä'nee, (ORAZIO,) a Florentine painter, born about 1610; died after 1642.

Fidanza, fe-dän'zå, (FRANCESCO,) a skilful painter of landscapes and marine views, born in 1747, belonged to the Roman school. Died in Milan in 1819.

His brother GREGORIO was also a landscape-painter. Died about 1821.

Fiddes, fĭdz or fĭd'dĕs, (RICHARD,) an English writer, and a priest of the Anglican Church, born near Scarborough in 1671. He became rector of Halsham about 1694. He published a "System of Divinity," (2 vols., 1718–20,) and a "Life of Cardinal Wolsey," (1724,) in which he showed himself so unjust to the Reformers that he was suspected of being a Roman Catholic. Died in 1725.

Fidelis, fe-dä'lĕss, (FORTUNIO,) an Italian physician, born in Sicily about 1550, wrote a work on legal medicine, (1602.) Died in 1630.

Fidenza or **Fidanza,** (JOHN.) See BONAVENTURE, SAINT.

Field, (BARRON,) an English lawyer and botanist, born probably in London about 1786. He published "An Analysis of Blackstone's Commentaries," (1811,) and "Memoirs of New South Wales," (1826.) Died in 1846.

Field, (CYRUS W.,) an American merchant, distinguished by his successful efforts to open telegraphic communication between Europe and America, was born at Stockbridge, Massachusetts, in 1819. He acquired a fortune by trade in the city of New York, whither he had removed before he was of age. About 1854 he procured a charter for a telegraph from the American continent to Newfoundland, designing to connect it with a submarine Atlantic cable. To this arduous enterprise he devoted his time and fortune during many years. He organized the "Atlantic Telegraph Company" in 1856, and accompanied the expeditions sent out from England to lay the cable in 1857 and 1858. After two failures, Mr. Field and his coadjutors succeeded, and began to operate with the Atlantic telegraph, in August, 1866.

Field, (DAVID DUDLEY,) an American jurist, a brother of the preceding, born at Haddam, Connecticut, in 1805, was educated at Williams College. He was admitted to the bar in 1828, and commenced the practice of law in New York City. He gained distinction by his writings on law reform, and was appointed a commissioner on practice and pleadings by the legislature in 1847. He was appointed in 1857 president of a commission to digest a political code, a penal code, and a civil code.

Field, (GEORGE,) an English chemist and writer on various subjects, born about 1777. He published "Chromatics, or Harmony of Colours," (new edition, 1845,) "Outlines of Analytical Philosophy," (2 vols., 1839,) and other works. Died in 1854.

Field, (JOHN,) an English astronomer, said to have been the first in England that adopted the Copernican system. Died about 1587.

Field, (JOHN,) a skilful musician and composer for the piano, born at Dublin in 1782. He visited successively France, Germany, and Russia, where his performances were greatly admired. Died at Moscow in 1837.

Field, (NATHANIEL,) an English actor, born about 1570. While still very young, he appeared on the stage, and at length became a member of Shakspeare's company of players. He was the author of two spirited comedies, entitled "A Woman is a Weathercock," and "Amends for the Ladies."

Field, (RICHARD,) a learned and liberal English divine, born at Hempstead, in Hertfordshire, in 1561. He had a high reputation as a preacher. He became rector of Burghclere, canon of Windsor in 1604, and chaplain to James I. He wrote an important work, entitled "Of the Church," (1606,) which is highly praised by Coleridge. Died in 1616.

See "Memorials of the Life of R. Field," by his son, NATHANIEL, 1716.

Field, (STEPHEN J.,) an American jurist, a brother of David Dudley, noticed above, was chief justice of the supreme court of California from 1859 to 1863. He was appointed an associate justice of the supreme court of the United States in 1863 or 1864.

Field'ing, (COPLEY VANDYKE,) a celebrated English landscape-painter, born about 1787. He was one of the first to distinguish himself in water-colour paintings, of which he produced a great number. He held for a long time the office of president of the Society of Painters in Water-Colours. He represented British mountain- and lake-scenery and the downs of Southern England with a success which has perhaps not been equalled by any other artist. Died in 1855.

Fielding, (HENRY,) a celebrated English novelist, born at Sharpham Park, Somersetshire, on the 22d of April, 1707. He was the son of Edmund Fielding, who served as lieutenant-general under the Duke of Marlborough, and great-grandson of William, third Earl of Denbigh. At the age of eighteen he commenced the study of law at Leyden; but, owing to financial difficulties, he returned to London at the expiration of two years, where he abandoned himself to the wildest dissipation. At this period he published the comedy entitled "Love in Several Masques," which met with some success and was followed by numerous other plays. In 1734 he married a lady of great beauty and accomplishments, by whom he obtained £1500. Continuing his excesses, in a short time he was reduced to poverty. He now recommenced the study of law with great assiduity,

ā, ē, ī, ō, ū, ȳ, *long;* à, ė, ö, same, less prolonged; ă, ĕ, ĭ, ŏ, ŭ, ў, *short;* ạ, ẹ, ị, ọ, *obscure;* fär, fȧll, fȧt; mēt; nŏt; gŏŏd; mōōn;

and would doubtless have succeeded well in that profession had not violent attacks of the gout prevented him from attending the circuits. He therefore applied himself to literature as a means of support, and soon after became the editor of a paper called "The Champion." In 1742 he published the novel "Joseph Andrews," which was intended as a satire on Richardson's "Pamela." In 1749 appeared "Tom Jones," the greatest of his works, and in 1751 "Amelia" was issued, of which Dr. Johnson has observed that it "was perhaps the only book of which, being printed off betimes one morning, a new edition was called for before night." In 1750 he was appointed justice of the peace for the county of Middlesex, in which position he distinguished himself by his ability and activity. He was successful in extirpating numerous gangs of robbers which had previously been a terror to the inhabitants of the metropolis. The best-known of his works are "Joseph Andrews," "Tom Jones," and "Amelia," which have justly placed him in the highest rank of British novelists. His greatest strength appears to have been in portraying characters of those in the lower orders of society. His works display much wit and vigour, and his delineations are remarkable for their fidelity to nature. Though it is claimed that his writings have a moral tendency, the coarseness and vulgarity of many of his characters render their utility extremely problematical. Fielding was the author of numerous works in addition to those mentioned above. Among these were a "History of Jonathan Wild the Great," "The Journey from this World to the Next," and some important legal treatises. It is stated that all his works have been translated into the French language. Fielding died at Lisbon in 1754, whither he had gone in the hope of benefiting his health. A monument was erected to his memory in that city through the influence of the French consul, Chevalier Meyronnet. Lady Mary Montagu, who was a kinswoman of Fielding, in speaking of him, observes, "There was a great similitude between his character and that of Sir Richard Steele. Fielding had the advantage both in learning and, in my opinion, in genius; they both agreed in wanting money in spite of all their friends, and would have wanted it if their hereditary lands had been as extensive as their imagination." Sir James Mackintosh remarks, "Fielding will forever remain the delight of his country, and will always retain his place in the libraries of Europe, notwithstanding the unfortunate grossness, the mark of an uncultivated taste."

See MURPHY, "Life and Genius of Fielding;" LAWRENCE, "Life of Fielding," 1855; SIR W. SCOTT, Miscellaneous Prose Works; DISRAELI, "Quarrels of Authors;" WILLIAM WATSON, "Life of H. Fielding," London, 1808; "London Quarterly Review" for January, 1856; E. P. WHIPPLE, critique in the "North American Review" for January, 1849; "North British Review" for November, 1855.

Fielding, (Sir JOHN,) a half-brother of the great novelist, whom he succeeded as justice of the county of Middlesex. Although blind for many years, he fulfilled the duties of his office with much ability; and he received the order of knighthood in 1761. He was the author of three works, viz., "Extracts from the Penal Laws," (1761,) "Universal Mentor," (1762,) and "Description of the Cities of London and Westminster," (1777.) Died in 1780.

Fielding, (SARAH,) an English authoress of great learning, sister of the novelist, was born in 1714. Her principal works were a novel, entitled "The Adventures of David Simple," and an excellent translation of Xenophon's "Memoirs of Socrates, with the Defence of Socrates before his Judges." Died at Bath in 1768.

Fields, (JAMES T.,) an American poet, born in Portsmouth, New Hampshire, in 1820. He became a partner of the publishing-house of Ticknor & Fields, Boston. Among his poems are "Commerce," (1838,) "The Post of Honour," (1848,) and "The Fair Wind." "The poems Mr. Fields has given us," says R. W. Griswold, "are evidently the careless products of a singularly sensitive and fertile mind,—indications rather than exponents of its powers." ("Poets and Poetry of America.")

Fiennes, fenz, (NATHANIEL,) a son of William, Lord Saye, born at Broughton, Oxfordshire, in 1608. Having joined the army of Parliament in the civil war, he was appointed governor of Bristol, which he surrendered to Prince Rupert in 1643. For this act he was sentenced to death, but was pardoned. He afterwards became a prominent member of Parliament, and a partisan of Cromwell, who in 1654 or 1655 appointed him lord keeper of the great seal. He was one of the lords of the Upper House convened in 1658. Died in 1669.

See "Biographia Britannica;" NOBLE, "Memoirs of Cromwell."

Fiennes, (WILLIAM,) Lord Saye and Sele, an English statesman, born in Oxfordshire in 1582, was created a viscount in 1624. He co-operated with Hampden and Pym in opposition to the arbitrary government of Charles I. At the commencement of the rebellion (1642) he took sides with the Parliament. About 1650 he left the Presbyterians and joined the Independents. Lord Saye exerted a great influence in public affairs, and was an intimate friend of Cromwell. At the restoration he was appointed lord privy seal and chamberlain of the royal household by Charles II. Died in 1662. "He was," says Whitelocke, "a person of great parts, wisdom, and integrity."

See LLOYD, "State Worthies;" WOOD, "Athenæ Oxonienses."

Fiennes, de, dĕh fe'ĕn', (JEAN BAPTISTE,) an Oriental scholar, born at Saint-Germain, near Paris, in 1669, became professor of Arabic in the College of France in 1714. He was also interpreter to the king. Died in 1744.

Fiennes, de, (JEAN BAPTISTE HÉLIN,) an Orientalist and diplomatist, son of the preceding, was born at Saint-Germain-en-Laye in 1710. He became interpreter to the king for Oriental languages in 1746, and professor of Arabic at the College of France in 1748. Died in 1767.

Fiennes, de, (MAXIMILIEN FRANÇOIS,) a French general, born in 1669, took part in many battles in Flanders, and commanded an army about 1712–14. Died in 1716.

Fiennes, de, (ROBERT,) a French commander, rendered important services to King John and Charles V., and was rewarded with the office of Constable of France in 1356. Died about 1382.

Fieschi. See INNOCENT IV.

Fieschi, fe-ĕs'kee, singular **Fiesco,** fe-ĕs'ko, [Fr. FIESQUE, fe'ĕsk',] Counts of Lavagna, the name of one of the four principal families of Genoa or Liguria. The Fieschi in the twelfth century aspired to supreme power, and resisted the republic of Genoa without success. Among the eminent members of this family were Popes Innocent IV. and Adrian V. The Fieschi were attached to the Guelph party.

Fieschi, (JOSEPH MARCO,) born in Corsica in 1790, was the inventor of the so-called infernal machine, and the principal agent in the attempt on the life of the French king, Louis Philippe. His machine, consisting of twenty-four musket-barrels, was discharged in July, 1835, while the king, at the head of a military procession, was going to a review. Louis Philippe was very slightly injured; but ten others, including Marshal Mortier, were instantly killed. Fieschi, with his accomplices, was executed in February, 1836.

See LOUIS BLANC, "Histoire de dix Ans."

Fiesco, fe-ĕs'ko, (GIOVANNI LUIGI,) sometimes written **Fieschi,** Count of Lavagna, born in 1525. He was the chief of one of the most powerful families of Genoa, and aspired to supreme power. In this he was prevented by the more influential house of Doria, against which he formed a powerful conspiracy. He received assistance in this enterprise from Pope Paul III., the court of France, and Pietro Luigi Farnese, Duke of Parma and Piacenza. Fieschi endeavoured to procure the assassination of Andrew Doria, the chief of that family, and his nephew Giovannino, while they were at a banquet. In this, however, he was unsuccessful. Having resolved on another attempt, the arrangements were made with so great caution that no suspicions were aroused against the conspirators. On the night of the 2d of January, 1547, after the city had become quiet, Fieschi sent part of his followers to seize the palace of the Doria. He proceeded to the harbour to capture his enemy's galleys. As he was passing from one ship to another, the plank broke under him, and, encumbered by his armour, he was unable to save himself. His companions did not perceive the accident until too late to rescue him. In the attack on the palace, Giovannino Doria was killed, but his uncle escaped. As a consequence of this conspiracy, most of the family of Fieschi were put to death. Schiller wrote a tragedy on the conspiracy of Fiesco.

See E. VINCENS, "Histoire de la République de Gènes;" SISMONDI, "Histoire des Républiques Italiennes;" A. MASCARDI, "Congiura del Conte G. L. de Fieschi," 1627, (translated into English by HUGH HARE, 1693.)

Fiesole, da, dä fe-ā'ṡo-lä or fe-ês'o-lä, (FRA GIOVANNI,) an Italian painter, whose original name was SANTI TOSINI, or, according to Vasari, GIOVANNI GUIDO, was born at Mugello, in Tuscany, in 1387. He was surnamed FRA ANGELICO or BEATO ANGELICO, and was one of the most eminent among the restorers of painting in Italy. He is highly praised by Ruskin, who says, "In Angelico you have the entirely spiritual mind, incapable of conceiving any wickedness or vileness whatever." ("Modern Painters," vol. v. p. 300.) He was employed by Pope Nicholas V. to paint his private chapel in the Vatican, and the chapel of Saint Lorenzo. His easel-picture representing the "Coronation of Mary," which is considered a master-piece, now adorns the entrance-hall of the Louvre at Paris. He devoted himself exclusively to sacred subjects; and the purity and deep religious feeling which characterize all his works are a faithful reflection of his own life and character. Among his chief works are an "Annunciation," and the "Last Judgment." Died about 1455.

See VASARI, "Lives of the Painters;" LANZI, "History of Painting in Italy;" MRS. JAMESON, "Memoirs of Early Italian Painters;" TICOZZI, "Dizionario."

Fiévée, fe'ā'vā', (JOSEPH,) a French *littérateur* and politician, born in Paris in 1767. He wrote for the "Journal des Débats" and other journals, published several successful novels and political treatises, and was appointed censor in 1805. About 1808 he became master of requests. Died in Paris in 1839.

See SAINTE-BEUVE, "Causeries du Lundi," tome v.

Figino, fe-jee'no, or **Figine,** fe-jee'nä, (AMBROGIO,) an Italian painter, born at Milan about 1550, excelled in portraits. Died after 1595.

Figliucci, fêl-yoot'chee, (FELICE,) an Italian philosopher and voluminous writer, born at Sienna, made translations from Plato and Aristotle, and wrote several commentaries on the works of the latter. Died about 1590.

Figrelius, fe-gRā'le-ûs, called also **Griepenhielm** or **Greifenhelm,** (EDMUND,) a Swedish antiquary, and professor of history in the University of Upsal. He was preceptor of Charles XI., by whom he was created baron, senator, and chancellor of the court. Died in 1676.

Figueiras. See FIGUIEIRA.

Figueiredo, de, (ANTONIO PEREIRA.) See PEREIRA.

Figueiredo, de, dä fe-gà-e-rā'do, (MANOEL,) a Portuguese savant and scientific writer, born near Lisbon in 1568; died about 1630.

Figueroa, de, dä fe-gà-ro'ä, (BARTOLOMÉ CAYRASCO,) a Spanish poet, born at Logroño about 1540. He was the first to introduce into Spanish poetry the measure termed *esdruxolos,* or the *sdruccioli* of the Italians.

Figueroa, de, (CRISTOVAL SUAREZ,) a distinguished Spanish poet and miscellaneous writer, born at Valladolid about 1586. He translated into Spanish the "Pastor Fido" of Guarini, and was the author of a pastoral entitled "La constante Amarilis." Died in 1650.

Figueroa, de, (FRANCISCO,) a celebrated Spanish poet, surnamed THE DIVINE, born at Alcalá de Henares about 1540. He entered the army young, and served in Italy and Flanders. He wrote pastorals in imitation of the Italians. He caused most of his poems to be burnt a short time before his death; but the few that remain attest the superiority of his poetical genius. Died about 1620.

See TICKNOR, "History of Spanish Literature;" LONGFELLOW, "Poets and Poetry of Europe."

Figueroa, de, (GARCIAS Y SILVA, gaR-thee'äs e sêl'vä,) a Spanish diplomatist, born at Badajos in 1574. In 1618 he was ambassador at the court of Shah Abbâs, in Persia. On his return he published an interesting account of his travels in India and Persia. Died about 1625.

See N. ANTONIO, "Bibliotheca Hispana Nova."

Figueroa, de, (Don LOPEZ,) a Spanish officer under Philip II., born at Valladolid about 1520. He was conspicuous for his bravery in the war against the Moors,

and at the naval battle of Lepanto, where he served under Don John of Austria. Died in 1595.

Figuieira, fe-ge-ā'rä, or **Figueiras,** fe-gā'räs, (GUILLEM,) a celebrated Provençal troubadour, was born at Toulouse about 1190.

Figuier, fe'ge-ā', (LOUIS GUILLAUME,) a French chemist, was born at Montpellier in 1819. He became professor in the School of Pharmacy in Paris in 1853. Among his numerous and valuable works may be named his "Exposition and History of the Principal Modern Scientific Discoveries," (3 vols., 1855,) and "Vies des Savants illustres," (1866.)

Fig'u-lus, (P. NIGID'IUS,) a Roman Pythagorean philosopher, born about 100 B.C., was celebrated for his learning. He was a friend of Cicero, and was one of the senators appointed in 63 to receive testimony in the case of Catiline. He became prætor in 59 B.C., and was a partisan of Pompey in the civil war. Died in 44 B.C.

Filamondo, fe-lä-mon'do, (RAFAEL MARIA,) Bishop of Suessa, born at Naples about 1650; died in 1716.

Filangieri, fe-län-je-ā'ree, (CARLO,) an Italian general, son of Gaetano, noticed below, was born at Naples in 1785. He commanded the army which took Messina in 1848 and Palermo in 1849, after which he was Governor of Sicily. He was created Duke of Taormina.

Filangieri, (GAETANO,) an Italian writer on political economy, and one of the most celebrated publicists of his time, was born at Naples in 1752. In 1771 he commenced two works, one upon private and public education, and the other entitled "Morality for Princes," neither of which was finished. He rendered important services to humanity and legislative reform by his great work entitled "Scienza della Legislazione," the first volume of which appeared in 1780 and gave him an enviable reputation throughout Europe. In 1787 he was appointed by Ferdinand IV. a member of the board of finance. He died in 1788. His "Science of Legislation," which was not quite finished at his death, passed through numerous editions, and was translated into German, French, English, and Spanish. At the request of Dr. Franklin, the author sent a number of copies to America.

See SALFI, "Life of Filangieri," in a French translation of his works published in Paris in 1822; TIPALDO, "Biografia degli Italiani illustri;" "Nouvelle Biographie Générale;" DONATO TOMMASI, "Elogio storico del Cavaliere G. Filangieri," 1788; CARNEVALI, "Vita del Cavaliere G. Filangieri;" G. BIANCHETTI, "Elogio di G. Filangieri," 1819.

Filarete, fe-lä-rā'tä, (ANTONIO,) a Florentine architect and sculptor, flourished about 1450. Among his works was the grand hospital of Milan, built in 1456.

See VASARI, "Lives of the Painters and Sculptors."

Filastre or **Fillastre,** fe'lästR', (GUILLAUME,) a French prelate and Greek scholar, born in Maine about 1347. He translated some works of Plato, and wrote commentaries on Ptolemy. Died at Rome in 1428.

Filelfo, fe-lel'fo, [Lat. PHILEL'PHUS; Fr. PHILELPHE, fe'lêlf',] (FRANCESCO,) a celebrated Italian philologist and poet, born at Tolentino in 1398. He became an eminent Greek scholar, and obtained the chair of belles-lettres at Florence in 1429. Having written satires against the Medici and made many enemies among the literati, he was obliged to quit Florence in 1434. He became professor at Milan in 1440. About 1466 he removed to Rome, where he taught philosophy. His habits are said to have been very licentious. He wrote a poem, "La Sforziade;" "Epistles," ("Epistolarum Libri XVI.," 1485;) Latin Odes, (1497,) and other works. Died at Florence in 1481.

See C. ROSMINI, "Vita di Filelfo," 3 vols., 1808; MEUCCI, "Philelphi Vita," 1741; LANCELOT, "Vie de Philelphe;" PAOLO GIOVIO, "Elogia;" NICÉRON, "Mémoires."

Filesac, fêl'säk', (JEAN,) a learned French theologian, born in Paris about 1550. He was chosen rector of the University of Paris in 1586. His chief work is a "Treatise on the Authority of Bishops," (1606.) Died in 1638.

Filhol, fêl'yol', (MICHEL ANTOINE,) a French engraver, born in 1759, published "Complete Gallery of the Napoleon Museum," ("Galerie complète du Musée Napoléon," 10 vols., 1804–14.) Died in 1812.

Filiassi, fe-le-âs'see, (GIACOMO,) COUNT, an Italian physician, born at Venice in 1750, published a "Treatise upon the Prevailing Winds in the Venetian Marshes," and other works. Died in 1829.

Filicaia or **Filicaja, da,** dä fe-le-kä'yä, (VINCENZO or VINCENZIO,) a celebrated Italian lyric poet, and senator of Florence, was born in that city in 1642. He published numerous poems in Latin and Italian, which were remarkable for their spirit and elegance. His "Ode on the Victory over the Turks" gained for him the reputation of the first Italian poet of his time. He married Anna Capponi in 1673, and was patronized by Queen Christina of Sweden. Among his most admirable compositions are sonnets entitled "La Providenza" and "L'Italia," which are sublime in thought, imagery, and style. His moral character is represented as excellent. He died at Florence in September, 1707. "At Paris," says Macaulay, "Addison eagerly sought an introduction to Boileau; but he seems not to have been at all aware that at Florence he was in the vicinity of a poet with whom Boileau could not sustain a comparison,—of the greatest lyric poet of modern times, of Vincenzio Filicaja. This is the more remarkable because Filicaja was the favourite poet of the all-accomplished Somers, under whose protection Addison travelled." ("Review of the Life and Writings of Addison," in Macaulay's "Essays.")

See NEGRI, "Istoria dei Fiorentini Scrittori;" FABRONI, "Vitæ Italorum doctrina excellentium;" TIRABOSCHI, "Storia della Letteratura Italiana;" LONGFELLOW, "Poets and Poetry of Europe;" "Lives of the Italian Poets," by REV. HENRY STEBBING, London, 1831; "Retrospective Review," vol. x., 1824.

Filippi, fe-lèp'pee, (CAMILLO,) an Italian painter, born at Ferrara about 1510; died in 1574.

Filippi, de, dä fe-lèp'pee, (FILIPPO,) a naturalist, son of Giuseppe, noticed below, was born at Milan in 1814. He published "The Three Kingdoms of Nature," ("I tre Regni della Natura," 1852,) and other works.

Filippi, de, (GIUSEPPE,) an Italian medical writer, born in Piedmont in 1781. He was chief physician of the Italian army in 1814. Died in 1856.

Filippini, fe-lèp-pee'nee, (ANTONIO PIETRO,) an ecclesiastic, born in the island of Corsica in 1529, wrote a "History of Corsica."

Fil'lanš, (JAMES,) a Scottish sculptor, born in Lanarkshire in 1808, was apprenticed to a weaver, and afterwards to a stone-mason. About 1836 he settled in London as a sculptor. Among his best works are a bust of John Wilson, "The Blind Teaching the Blind," and a "Boy and Fawn." Died in Glasgow in 1852.

See PATERSON, "Life of James Fillans," 1854.

Filleau, fe'yō', (JEAN,) a French lawyer, noted as an adversary of the Jansenists, was born at Poitiers in 1600. He wrote an "Account of the Proceedings and Doctrines of the Jansenists." Died in 1682.

Filleul, fe'yul', or **Filleuil,** (NICOLAS,) a French poet and dramatist, born at Rouen about 1530.

Fill'more, (MIL'LARD,) the thirteenth President of the United States, was born in Cayuga county, New York, on the 7th of January, 1800. He was not liberally educated; but, after learning the trade of a fuller, he studied law, and supported himself for several years by teaching school. In 1821 he removed to Erie county, New York, where he practised law with success. He married Abigail Powers in 1826, and was elected to Congress in 1832 by the Anti-Jackson party. He was re-elected as a Whig in 1836, 1838, and 1840, and distinguished himself by his talents for business and diligent attention to it. In the session of 1841–42 he was chairman of the committee of ways and means, and was the chief author of the tariff of 1842. He was nominated for the office of Governor of New York in 1844, but was not elected. In 1847 he was elected comptroller of that State. Having been nominated as the Whig candidate for Vice-President, he was elected in November, 1848, when General Taylor was chosen President. He was raised to the office of President by the death of President Taylor on the 9th of July, 1850. He appointed Daniel Webster secretary of state, and approved Mr. Clay's Compromise Bill of 1850. Many of the Northern Whigs were offended by his signature of the act for the rendition of fugitive slaves. During his administration his opponents had a majority in both Houses of Congress. On the expiration of his term, in March, 1853, he returned to Buffalo, his former residence. He was

nominated as a candidate for the Presidency by the American party in 1856, but received no electoral votes except those of Maryland.

Fil'mer, (Sir ROBERT,) an English political writer, born in the county of Kent. He was a staunch advocate of absolute monarchy, and endeavoured to prove that this was the true and natural form of government. Locke wrote two treatises to refute this theory. Filmer wrote, among other works, "The Anarchy of a Limited and Mixed Monarchy," and "Patriarcha." Died in 1688.

Filon, fe'lòn', (CHARLES AUGUSTE DÉSIRÉ,) a French historian, born in Paris in 1800. He was professor of history in several colleges, and published, besides other works, a "History of Europe in the Sixteenth Century," (2 vols., 1838,) and a "History of the Roman Senate," (1850.)

Fim'brĭ-ą, (CAIUS FLAVIUS,) a Roman general, who was a violent partisan of Marius. Having been chosen lieutenant *(legatus)* to the consul Valerius Flaccus, who was sent to Asia to replace Sulla, Fimbria corrupted the soldiers, caused the consul to be assassinated, and took the command of the army, in which he was sanctioned by the Roman senate. After committing great outrages, he was surrounded by the army of Sulla. Fimbria, perceiving that it would be impossible to resist, as his soldiers were deserting him, put an end to his own life, in 85 B.C.

Finæus. See FINE.

Finch, (ANNE,) Countess of Winchelsea, an English poetess, born in the seventeenth century. Of her poems we may cite "The Spleen" and the tragedy of "Aristomenes." Died in 1720.

Finch, (DANIEL,) second Earl of Nottingham, born in 1647, was a son of Heneage Finch. He was one of the privy councillors who upon the death of Charles II. proclaimed the Duke of York king. Upon the accession of William and Mary (1689) he refused the office of lord high chancellor, but was appointed secretary of state. He rendered so much service to William that James II., in making a declaration in regard to his intended invasion, excluded Finch from the general pardon. He resigned office in 1694, and again became secretary in 1702. He wrote a work on the Trinity, (1721,) for which he was thanked by the University of Oxford. Died in 1730.

See WALPOLE, "Royal and Noble Authors;" MACAULAY, "History of England."

Finch, (HENEAGE.) See NOTTINGHAM.

Finch, (HENRY,) an English jurist, born in Kent about 1550; died in 1625.

Finch, (ROBERT,) a distinguished English antiquary and traveller, born in London in 1783. He died at Rome in 1830, leaving his valuable library and collection of antiquities to the Ashmolean Museum of Oxford.

Finch, (WILLIAM,) an English traveller, who lived about 1610, visited India and Africa, where he obtained much valuable geographical information, which was published after his return.

Finck, (THOMAS,) a Danish mathematician, physician, and first professor of rhetoric and medicine at Copenhagen, born in South Jutland in 1561. He was the author of various scientific and medical works. Died in 1656.

Fin'den, (WILLIAM,) a skilful English line-engraver, born in 1787. He engraved illustrations for numerous books, among which is "Don Quixote." He also published many illustrated works, entitled "The Byron Gallery," "The Gallery of the Graces," "The Gallery of British Art," etc. Died in 1852.

Find'lay, (ROBERT,) a Scottish divine, born in 1721, published a "Vindication of the Sacred Books and of Josephus against Voltaire," (1770,) and other works. Died in 1814.

Fine, fên, sometimes written **Finé,** (ORONCE, o'rònss',) [Lat. ORON'TIUS FINÆ'US,] a celebrated French mathematician, born at Briançon in 1494. In 1530 he was appointed professor of mathematics in the Royal College. Among his mechanical inventions was a clock of peculiar construction. He was the author of numerous scientific works. Died in 1555.

See NICÉRON, "Mémoires;" DELAMBRE, "Histoire de l'Astronomie au Moyen-Age."

Finelli, fe-nel'lee, (CARLO,) an able Italian statuary, born at Carrara in 1780, was a pupil of Canova. Among his master-pieces are statues of Raphael and of the archangel Michael. Died in 1854.

Finelli, (GIULIANO,) an Italian sculptor and architect, born at Carrara in 1602; died about 1658.

Finet, fe-net' or fe'nắ', (Sir JOHN,) an English author and wit, born near Dover in 1571. His principal work was "Fineti Philoxenus," which treated of the etiquette of the English court. Died in 1641.

Fingal, fing'gạl or fing'gaul, King of Morven, a province of ancient Caledonia, and father of the poet Ossian, by whom he was celebrated for his heroic exploits, was born in 282. A great part of his time was devoted to the wars against the Romans, who then held sway over a large portion of Britain.

Finiguerra, fe-ne-gwĕR'rä, (TOMMASO or MASO,) an Italian sculptor and goldsmith, who is believed to have been the inventor of the art of taking engravings from metallic plates on paper. Died in 1475.

See STRUTT, "Dictionary of Engravers;" VASARI, "Lives of the Painters," etc.

Fink, fĭnk, (GOTTFRIED WILHELM,) a German writer, born at Sulza in 1783, published several works on theology and music, and in 1827 was editor of the "Universal Musical Gazette." Died in 1846.

Fink, von, fon fĭnk, (FRIEDRICH AUGUST,) a Prussian general, born in Mecklenburg in 1718. In 1759 he was sent by the king, Frederick II., to oppose Marshal Daun, by whose greatly superior force he was defeated at Maxen. For this he was imprisoned and dismissed from the army. Died at Copenhagen in 1766.

• Finkenstein, von, fon fĭnk'ẹn-stīn',(CARL WILHELM FINCK,) COUNT, a Prussian minister of state, born in 1714. He was minister of foreign affairs for many years between 1750 and his death. Died in 1800.

Fin'lay, (fin'le,) (GEORGE,) a British historian, born in Scotland about 1800, resided some years at Athens. Among his principal works are "Greece under the Romans," (1843,) "History of the Byzantine and Greek Empires from 1057 to 1453," (1854,) and "Greece under the Othman and Venetian Dominion from 1453 to 1821." These productions are highly commended.

See "Fraser's Magazine" for October, 1844; "North British Review" for February, 1855.

Finlay, (JOHN,) a Scottish poet and prose writer, born at Glasgow in 1782. Among his works are "Wallace, or the Vale of Ellerslie," (1802,) a "Life of Cervantes," and a "Collection of Scottish Ballads, Historical and Romantic," (1808.) Died in 1810.

Fin'lay-son, (GEORGE,) a Scottish surgeon, born at Thurso about 1790, accompanied an embassy to Siam and Hue in 1822. He published "The Mission from Bengal to Siam and Hue," (1822.) Died in 1823.

Finlayson, (JAMES,) a Scottish Presbyterian minister, born about 1750. He was appointed professor of logic in the University of Edinburgh about 1788, and afterwards became, as minister, the colleague of Dr. Blair. He had great influence in the affairs of the church. Died in 1808.

See a notice of his life prefixed to a volume of his sermons, 1809; CHAMBERS, "Biographical Dictionary of Eminent Scotsmen."

Fin'ley, (JAMES BRADLEY,) a Methodist minister and author, born in North Carolina in 1781. He became chaplain of the Ohio penitentiary in 1845. Died in 1857. His "Prison Life," "Autobiography," and several of his other works have had an extensive circulation.

Finley, (ROBERT,) born at Princeton, New Jersey, in 1772, was for many years a tutor in Princeton College. He is regarded as the founder of the American Colonization Society. He was pastor at Baskingridge, New Jersey, from 1795 to 1817. Died in 1817.

Finley, (SAMUEL,) a Presbyterian minister, born in Armagh, Ireland, in 1715, came to America in 1734. He was chosen president of the College of New Jersey in 1761. Died in 1766.

Finn, (HENRY J.,) a popular American comic actor, born at Sydney, Cape Breton, about 1784. He performed in London and New York, and wrote several humorous works. He was lost in the steamer Lexington, which was burned in 1840.

Fin'ney, (CHARLES G.,) an American theologian and popular preacher, born in Litchfield county, Connecticut,

in 1792. He published, besides other works, "Lectures on Revivals," (1835; 13th edition, 1840,) and "Lectures on Systematic Theology," (1847.) He became president of Oberlin College, Ohio, in 1852.

See BARTLETT, "Modern Agitators."

Fino, fee'no, (ALEMANIO,) an Italian historian and elegant writer, born at Bergamo. Among his works are "The History of Crema," (1566,) and "The War of Attila, the Scourge of God," (1569.) Died about 1586.

See TIRABOSCHI, "Storia della Letteratura Italiana."

Fino Fini, fee'no fee'nee, surnamed ADRIANO, an eminent Italian scholar and Orientalist, born in the diocese of Adria in 1431; died in 1517.

Finoglia, fe-nòl'yä, (PAOLO DOMENICO,) an able Italian painter, born at Orta, (Naples;) died in 1656.

Fioravanti, fe-o-rä-vån'tee, (LEONARDO,) an Italian physician and surgeon, was a native of Bologna. He wrote, among other works, "The Mirror of Universal Science." Died in 1588.

Fioravanti, (VALENTINO,) an Italian composer, born at Rome about 1765, produced successful operas, among which were "I Virtuosi ambulanti" and "Il Furbo contra Furbo." Died in 1837.

See FÉTIS, "Biographie Universelle des Musiciens."

Fiore, del, dĕl fe-o'rä, (JACOBELLO,) a painter of the Venetian school, flourished from 1400 to 1436. He was a son of a painter named FRANCESCO DEL FIORE. The beauty and grace of his figures are praised. His master-piece is a "Coronation of the Virgin."

See VASARI, "Lives of the Painters;" LANZI, "History of Painting in Italy."

Fiore, del, (NICCOLÒ ANTONIO,) often called COLANTONIO DEL FIORE, a Neapolitan painter, born at Naples in 1352. He painted in distemper. Died in 1444.

Fiorentini, fe-o-rĕn-tee'nee, (FRANCESCO MARIA,) an Italian historian, born at Lucca about 1610; died in 1673.

Fiorentino, fe-o-rĕn-tee'no, (AGOSTINO,) a Florentine sculptor, flourished from 1442 to 1461.

Fiorentino, (PIETRO ANGELO,) an Italian *littérateur*, born in Naples in 1810. He became a resident of Paris about 1835, and contributed to the "Moniteur" and other journals. Among his works are several dramas.

Fiorentino, (STEFANO,) called STEFANO DA PONTE-VECCHIO, and, also, LO SCIMMIA, ("The Ape,") a Florentine painter, born in 1301, was a pupil of Giotto. He is highly praised by Vasari. Only one of his works is extant,—a fresco of Christ at Florence. Died in 1350.

See VASARI, "Lives of the Painters."

Fiörgyn, Fiörgvin, or **Fiörgynn.** See HLODYN.

Fiori, (FEDERIGO.) See BAROCCI.

Fiori, fe-o'ree, (GIORGIO,) a noted Italian lawyer, born at Milan about 1450. He wrote a history, in Latin, of the Italian and German wars of his time. Died about 1512.

Fiori, (GIUSEPPE,) a Sicilian poet. Died in 1646.

Fiori, de', dà fe-o'ree, (MARIO,) an Italian flower-painter, born in 1603; died in 1673.

Fiorillo, fe-o-rèl'lo, (JOHANN DOMINICUS,) a German artist and writer upon art, born at Hamburg in 1748. He produced several good pictures, but is chiefly known as the author of two excellent works, entitled "History of the Arts of Design from their Revival to the Most Recent Times," (5 vols., 1798–1808,) and "History of the Arts of Design in Germany and the Netherlands," (4 vols., 1815–20.) He was for many years professor of art in the University of Göttingen. Died in 1821.

Fiorini, fe-o-ree'nee, (GIOVANNI BATTISTA,) a Bolognese painter, flourished about 1560–90. He worked in partnership with Cesare Aretusi, who coloured the works which were designed by Fiorini.

His son GABRIELLO was a sculptor.

Fiorini, (PIETRO,) an able Italian architect, a son of Gabriello, began to work in 1581. He designed several churches of Bologna. Died in 1622.

Firdousee or **Firdausî,** fĭr-dŏw'see or fĕr-dŏw'see, written also, but less correctly, **Firdûsî, Firdousi,** and **Ferdoucy,** fir-doo'see, the surname by which the greatest of the Persian poets, **Abool-Kâsim-Mansoor,** (**Abûl-Kâsim-Mansûr,** or **Abou'l-Casim-Mansoor,** ä'bŏŏl kâ'sim mắn-sŏŏr',) is generally known. He was born at or near Toos, (Tûs,) in Khorassân, about 940 A.D. His surname FIRDOUSEE is supposed by some to have been given him because his father was a gardener, from the Persian *firdous* or *firdaus*, signifying a "garden," also "paradise;" according to others, the name implied a lofty eulogium on his poetry, as being worthy to be sung in Paradise, or because when it was recited at the court of Mahmood the hearers imagined themselves to be in Paradise. Firdousee had made himself intimately acquainted with the early history of Persia as it was known through the ancient chronicles and traditions. With these as a basis, he composed his great poem the "Shah-Namah" or "Shah-Nameh," (shäh nä′mah,) or "Book of Kings." As originally written, it is said to have contained 60,000 distichs or couplets ; but none of the existing manuscripts have more, it is stated, than about 56,000 distichs. When the fame of Firdousee became known, the Sultan Mahmood invited him to his court at Ghiznee, (Gazna ;) and he is said to have been charmed with the wit and genius of the poet. While the latter was writing the "Shah-Namah," Mahmood directed that he should be paid out of the royal treasury a thousand pieces of gold for every thousand couplets that he should compose ; but, through the envy or jealousy of influential courtiers, he received but a very small part of what was due to him. When at last, after a labour of thirty years, his immortal poem was completed, Mahmood, in an impulse of generous admiration, ordered, it is said, that an elephant-load of gold should be given to the poet. But afterwards, either repenting of his too great liberality, or else influenced by the representations of Firdousee's enemies, he revoked the order, and sent him 60,000 dirhems (small silver coins) instead. The money arrived while the poet was in one of the public baths. Enraged and rendered utterly reckless by this illiberal treatment, he gave one-third of the coins to the man who brought them, another third to a seller of refreshments, and the remainder to the keeper of the bath. When Mahmood learned how his gift had been received, he was filled with wrath, and ordered that the poet should be trampled to death under the feet of an elephant. Firdousee, in the greatest consternation, hastened into the king's presence, and, falling at his feet, implored his forgiveness, at the same time reciting a poem in which he spoke in terms of the most glowing eulogy of the glories of Mahmood's reign. The king pardoned him, and, according to some accounts, sought to make reparation for his former unworthy treatment. But the wound inflicted upon the mind of the poet was too deep to be forgiven. With a truly Oriental duplicity, he obtained from the royal librarian the copy of the "Shah-Namah" which he had presented to the king, ostensibly for the purpose of making some correction, and wrote in it a most scathing satire on Mahmood; he then fled from Ghiznee and sought refuge in Bagdâd. When the caliph learned that Firdousee was residing in his capital, he invited him to his court, and treated him with the greatest honour and liberality. Firdousee added to his great poem 1000 distichs in praise of the caliph, who gave the poet 60,000 pieces of gold. Some authors say that Firdousee sent the satire to Mahmood by the hand of a friend, who supposed it to be a petition of some sort.

The events of his life, however, are very differently related by different authors. According to one story, Mahmood after a time not only repented of his injustice and permitted the poet to return to Toos, his native city, but severely punished those courtiers by whose counsel he had been misled, and finally, as a tardy reparation for his wrongs, sent Firdousee 100,000 pieces of gold. Meanwhile, the days of the immortal bard were drawing to their close. He one day heard a child singing in the streets of Toos some of his own verses, which so vividly recalled his bitter wrongs and sufferings that he was seized with faintness, and, having been carried to his house, he soon after expired. It is said that while the mortal remains of the poet were passing through one of the gates of Toos to the cemetery without the city, the train of camels bearing the munificent but tardy present of the sultan was entering by another. One of the daughters of the deceased, to whom the gold was offered, rejected it with indignant disdain ; but her sister consented to accept it in order to construct a work of public utility

which her father had long had at heart : this was the erection of a stone dike to prevent the overflow of the river near his native town. Thus his wish was at last fulfilled, though not until after his death. When Firdousee died, he was eighty, or, as some authorities say, eighty-two years of age. Although to a European mind many of the incidents related in the "Shah-Namah" would appear extravagant, it is, nevertheless, of all the great Mohammedan poems that which corresponds most nearly to the taste of the Western nations and to the principles of European criticism. Sir William Jones styles the "Shah-Namah" "a glorious monument of Eastern genius and learning, which, if it should ever be generally understood in its original language, will contest the merit of invention with Homer himself." (See article "Firdousi" in the "Nouvelle Biographie Générale," and the bibliographic references subjoined. Of these, perhaps the most valuable for the English reader are the preface to Julius von Mohl's translation and commentary of the "Shah-Namah," Sir W. Gore Ouseley's "Biographical Notices of the Persian Poets," and the biographical notice prefixed to the "Abridgment of the Shah-Nameh," by J. Atkinson, London, 1832.)

See, also, J. VAN WALLENBURG, "Notice sur le Schâh Nâmeh de Ferdoussi," 1810 ; DE SACY, article in the "Magasin Encyclopédique," 1813 ; VON HAMMER, "Geschichte der schönen Redekünste Persiens," and an article in the "Wiener Jahrbücher," vol. ix. ; ALEXANDER ROSS, "Essay on the Life and Genius of Firdousi," in the "Annals of Oriental Literature," 1820 ; ROBINSON, "Sketch of the Life and Writings of Ferdoosee," in "Memoirs of the Literary and Philosophical Society of Manchester," 2d series, 1824 ; DE STARKENFELS, "Vie de Firdousi ;" E. NAZARIANZ, article on the "Life and Writings of Firdousee," (in Russian,) 1851 ; "Retrospective Review," vol. iv., 1821.

Firenzuola, fe-ren-zoo-o′lä, (AGNOLO,) a celebrated Italian writer, born at Florence in 1493. He was the author of satirical poems, sonnets, prose essays, novels, and dramas. His two comedies entitled "I Lucidi" and "La Trinuzia" are greatly admired, and both his prose writings and poems are ranked among the Italian classics. Died about 1545.

See NICÉRON, "Mémoires ;" TIRABOSCHI, "Storia della Letteratura Italiana ;" LONGFELLOW, "Poets and Poetry of Europe ;" G. NEGRI, "Istoria de' Fiorentini Scrittori."

Fir-mā′nus, (TARUTIUS,) a Roman astronomer, was a contemporary and friend of Cicero.

Firmenich, fĕr′mẹh-nik′, (JOHANNES MATTHIAS,) a German poet and dramatist, born at Cologne in 1808.

Firmian, von, fon fĕĕr′me-än, (KARL JOSEPH,) COUNT, an Austrian statesman, born in the Tyrol in 1716. He was a member of the aulic council at Vienna in the reign of Charles VI., after whose death he was Governor of Austrian Lombardy, to which he rendered important services. He founded libraries, and liberally patronized artists and men of letters. Died in 1782.

See PAOLO FRISI, "Elogio di T. Pomponio Attico," 1780 ; ANGELO TEODORO VILLA, "C. Comitis Firmiani Vita," 1783.

Fir′mĭ-cus Mạ-ter′nus, (JULIUS or VILLIUS,) an ecclesiastic of the fourth century. By some he is supposed to have been Bishop of Milan. The work by which he is chiefly known was addressed to the Roman emperors Constantius and Constans, entitled "De Errore Profanarum Religionum." His treatise is a forcible and striking exposition of the excellence and purity of the Christian religion as contrasted with the immoralities and absurdities of paganism. It was printed by Matthias Flaccius in 1562. There is also extant a work on astronomy, called "Mathesis," by Firmicus Maternus.

See HERTZ, "Dissertatio de J. Firmico Materno," 1817.

Fir-mil′ĭ-ạn, [Fr. FIRMILIEN, fĕr′me′le-än′,] SAINT, Bishop of Cesarea. He was successful in quelling the Novatian doctrines, and united with Saint Cyprian against Pope Stephen in the dispute in relation to the re-baptism of heretics. Firmilian was the intimate friend of Origen, and was distinguished even among the Christian Fathers for his exemplary piety. He presided at the Council of Antioch in the trial of Paul of Samosata. Died at Tarsus in 269 A.D.

See EUSEBIUS, "Historia Ecclesiastica ;" BAILLET, "Vies des Saints."

Fir′min, (GILES,) an English physician and nonconformist minister, born in Suffolk in 1617, wrote a work entitled "The Real Christian." Died in 1697.

Fir′min, (THOMAS,) a distinguished English philanthropist, born at Ipswich in 1632. Though a Socinian, he was held in high estimation by many of the ecclesiastics of the Established Church, especially by Archbishop Tillotson. He founded two houses to supply the poor with work, and liberally contributed to many of the benevolent institutions of his time. He published a work entitled "Proposals for the Employing of the Poor, and for the Prevention of Beggary." Died in 1697.

See CORNISH, "Life of T. Firmin," 1780; "Retrospective Review," vol. xii., 1825.

Fir′mŏnt, de, [Fr. pron. dẹh fĕr′mòn′,] (HENRY ESSEX EDGEWORTH,) a Catholic priest, vicar-general of the church of Paris, born at Edgeworthstown, in Ireland, in 1745, removed to France when quite young. He performed the office of confessor to Louis XVI., and accompanied that unfortunate monarch to the scaffold. Firmont died in 1807, greatly lamented by the royal family. Louis XVIII. composed his epitaph.

Fir′mus or **Fir′mĭ-us,** a native of Seleucia, in Syria. Having obtained great wealth and power, he seized Alexandria, was proclaimed Augustus, and formed an alliance with Zenobia. The emperor Aurelian, having defeated and taken him prisoner, ordered him to be crucified.

Fischart, fish′ärt, (JOHANN,) surnamed MENTZER, a celebrated German satirist, was born at Mentz or Strasburg about 1545. His satires in prose and verse are distinguished for their moral tone as well as caustic wit, and give a faithful picture of the manners of his time. He wrote a descriptive poem, called "Glückhafft Schiff," (1576,) which was much admired. Died in 1614.

See ERSCH und GRUBER, "Allgemeine Encyklopaedie."

Fischer, fish′ẹr, (CHRISTIAN AUGUST,) a German littérateur, born at Leipsic in 1771, was the author of "Mountain Travels," "Picture of Madrid," (1802,) "Picture of Brazil," (1819,) and other works. Died in 1829.

Fischer, (EDMUND RUDOLF,) a German writer, born at Hasen-Preppach in 1687, became in 1758 general superintendent, or Protestant archbishop. Died in 1776.

See ERSCH und GRUBER, "Allgemeine Encyklopaedie."

Fischer, (FRIEDRICH CHRISTOPH JONATHAN,) a German jurist and historian, born at Stuttgart in 1750. His chief work is a "History of German Commerce," (1791.)

Fischer, (GOTTHELF,) a German naturalist and chemist, born at Waldheim in 1771 or 1775, became professor of natural history at Moscow about 1804. He wrote on anatomy, natural history, etc.

Fischer, (GOTTHELF AUGUST,) a German mathematician and scientific writer, born in 1763; died in 1832.

See ERSCH und GRUBER, "Allgemeine Encyklopaedie."

Fischer, (JOHANN ANDREAS,) a German physician, born at Erfurt in 1667. He wrote "Iliad in a Nutshell, or Synoptic Medicine," ("Ilias in Nuce, seu Medicina synoptica," 1716,) and other works. Died in 1729.

Fischer, (JOHANN EBERHARD,) a German historian and antiquary, born at Essling in 1697; died at Saint Petersburg in 1771.

Fischer, (JOHANN FRIEDRICH,) an eminent German philologist, born at Coburg in 1726, resided chiefly at Leipsic. He edited Anacreon, Justin, Ovid, and other classics, and wrote works on biblical criticism. Died in 1799.

Fischer, (JOSEPH EMANUEL,) an architect, born about 1680, was a son of J. B. Fischer von Erlach, noticed below. He is said to have constructed in 1727 a steam-engine for carrying water in the garden of Schwarzenberg.

Fischer, (KUNO, koo′no,) a German writer of great merit, chiefly known as a philosophical critic and historian, was born at Sondewalde, in Silesia, in 1824. In 1856 he was appointed professor of philosophy at Jena. He has written "Diotima; or, The Idea of the Beautiful," (1849,) "History of Modern Philosophy," (2 vols., 1852–55,) "Bacon of Verulam," (1856,) and other works. As a lecturer on philosophy he is eminently popular.

Fischer, von, fon fish′ẹr, (KARL,) a noted German architect, born at Manheim in 1782, became professor of architecture at Munich about 1809. Died in 1820.

Fischer von Erlach, fish′ẹr fon ĕr′läk, (JOHANN BERNHARD,) BARON, a celebrated German architect, born at Prague (or, according to some authorities, at Vienna) in 1650. He built the Schönbrunn palace and the church

of San Carlo Borromeo at Vienna, and other public edifices. He was court architect to Joseph I. and to his successor, Charles VI. Died about 1730.

See NAGLER, "Neues Allgemeines Künstler-Lexikon."

Fisen, fee′zẹn or fe′zŏn′, (BARTHÉLEMY,) a Belgian Jesuit and historian, born at Liege in 1591; died in 1649.

Fish, (HAMILTON,) an American statesman, born in the city of New York in 1809, graduated at Columbia College. He studied law, was admitted to the bar in 1830, and was elected a member of Congress in 1843. In 1848 he was chosen Governor of New York by the Whig party. He was a United States Senator from 1851 to 1857, opposed the repeal of the Missouri Compromise in 1854, and joined the Republican party about that time. He was appointed secretary of state by President Grant in the spring of 1869.

Fish, (SIMON,) an English lawyer and author, born in Kent about 1520, wrote "The Supplication of Beggars," a satire on the Roman Catholic clergy. Died about 1534.

Fish′er, (ALVAN,) an American painter, born in Needham, Massachusetts, in 1792. His rural and domestic scenes are much admired. He also painted many portraits.

Fish′er, (EDWARD,) a Calvinistic writer, born in Gloucestershire, England, was distinguished for his knowledge of the Greek and Hebrew languages and ecclesiastical history. His principal work was entitled the "Marrow of Modern Divinity," (1646.)

Fisher, (JOHN,) [called in Latin ROFFEN′SIS, (from Roffa, the Latin name of Rochester,)] a learned English prelate, born at Beverley, in Yorkshire, England, in 1459. Margaret, Countess of Richmond and mother of Henry VII., chose him for her confessor. In 1501 he was appointed chancellor of the University of Cambridge. In 1504 he became Bishop of Rochester, and the year following accepted the presidency of Queen's College. While in this position, he invited Erasmus to Cambridge and had him appointed professor of Greek. Fisher took an active part against the Lutheran doctrines, writing several treatises upon the subject. When Henry VIII. attempted to procure a divorce from Catherine of Aragon, Fisher sided with the queen, thus incurring the king's displeasure. He was soon deprived of his bishopric, and, after the king's marriage with Anne Boleyn, refusing to take the oath of allegiance, he was thrown into the Tower. The king was still further exasperated, by Pope Paul III. having conferred the title of cardinal upon Fisher, and resolved to put him to death. He was soon after brought to trial, and executed in June, 1535.

See DR. BAILEY, "Life of Bishop Fisher," 1655; RICHARD HALL, "Life of J. Fisher," 1739; J. LEWIS, "Life of John Fisher," 1855; BURNET, "History of the Reformation;" HARTLEY COLERIDGE, "Lives of Distinguished Northerns."

Fisher, (JOHN,) an English Jesuit, whose proper name was PIERCY, was born in Yorkshire. He held public disputes with several Protestant divines, and wrote a "Treatise on Faith," (1600.) Died after 1641.

Fisher, (JOHN,) born in Middlesex, England, in 1748, became successively Bishop of Exeter and of Salisbury about 1804. He was appointed to superintend the education of the princess Charlotte of Wales. Died in 1825.

Fisher, (PAYNE,) [Lat. PAGA′NUS PISCA′TOR,] an English poet, born in Dorsetshire in 1614. During the protectorate of Cromwell he was regarded as the poet-laureate. He served as a major in the army of Charles I. Died in 1693.

Fisher, (THOMAS,) an English antiquary and writer, born at Rochester in 1772. He contributed for many years to the "Gentleman's Magazine." Died in 1836.

Fisk, (PLINY,) an American missionary in Palestine, born at Shelburne, Massachusetts, in 1792, graduated at Middlebury College in 1814, and in 1819 embarked for Palestine. On reaching Smyrna, he applied himself to the study of the Eastern languages, which he afterwards pursued at the college of Scio. Died at Beyroot in 1825.

Fisk, (WILBUR,) D.D., a distinguished Methodist divine, born in Brattleborough, Vermont, in 1792. He was for several years principal of the Wesleyan Academy in Wilbraham, Massachusetts, and in 1831 was chosen the first president of the Wesleyan University, Middletown, Connecticut, which, under his direction, became perhaps the most influential educational institution of the Methodist denomination in America. He was instrumental in 1832 in establishing the Indian mission in Oregon. In 1835–36 he visited Europe, and on his return published a volume of travels. Died in 1839.

Fisquet, fês'kȧ', (HONORÉ JEAN PIERRE,) a French biographer, born at Montpellier in 1818. He wrote, besides other works, a "History of Algeria," (1842,) and "Pontifical France, or a History of the Bishops who have governed the Dioceses of France," (4 vols.)

Fitch, (EBENEZER,) D.D., an American divine, first president of Williams College, Massachusetts, was born in Norwich, Connecticut, in 1756; died in 1833.

Fitch, (JOHN,) an American inventor, born in Windsor, Connecticut, in 1743. He became a brass-founder, and afterwards a silversmith. About 1780 he removed to Kentucky, where he was appointed deputy-surveyor, and was captured by the Indians, who took him to Detroit and detained him until he was exchanged. In 1785 he began to devote himself to the application of steam to navigation, and constructed a model of a steamboat. Having petitioned the legislatures of Pennsylvania, New Jersey, and Virginia for aid, without success, he formed in 1786 a private company for navigation by steam. In August, 1787, he made with a small steamboat an experiment on the Delaware River, with partial success. He built another boat, which, in 1790, plied as a passenger-boat on the Delaware at the rate of about seven miles an hour. Fitch, however, gained no profit from his enterprise, and afterwards wandered about in poverty, and was regarded by some as an insane projector. He died in Kentucky in 1798.

See a life of John Fitch in SPARKS's "American Biography;" THOMPSON WESTCOTT, "Life of John Fitch," 1857; "Lives of Eminent American Mechanics," etc., by HENRY HOWE.

Fitch, (RALPH,) an English traveller, left England in 1583, and spent eight years in the East Indies. On his return an interesting account of his travels was published.

See HAKLUYT, "Voyages."

Fitz-ğĕr'ald, (EDWARD,) LORD, an Irish revolutionist, born in 1763, was a younger son of the Duke of Leinster. From 1773 to 1779 he resided in France, where in learning the language he became partially assimilated to the tastes and manners of the French. Having entered the British army, he served with distinction in the battle of Charleston, South Carolina, in 1781. In 1784 he returned home and obtained a seat in the Irish Parliament. The sufferings of Ireland, added perhaps to the neglect with which he conceived himself to be treated, rendered him disaffected to the English government. He took his seat with the opposition, and aspired to rival Grattan and Curran in eloquence. In 1788 we find him at Halifax, America, with the fifty-fourth regiment, whence he travelled through the United States to New Orleans. He visited Paris in 1791 to consult and fraternize with the republicans. In 1792 he married the beautiful and accomplished Pamela, the protégée and supposed daughter of Madame de Genlis. The latter being employed by the Duke of Orléans as governess of his children, (one of whom, Louis Philippe, became King of France,) Pamela was educated with them. In 1796 he joined the United Irishmen, who sent him as their agent to the continent to procure French aid in liberating Ireland. A few months before the time set for the insurrection in 1798, the secret was divulged to the English ministry. He resisted the officers who arrested him, was wounded, and died in prison in 1798.

See THOMAS MOORE, "Life of Edward Fitzgerald," 1831; ERSCH und GRUBER, "Allgemeine Encyklopaedie."

Fitzgerald, (PAMELA,) a French lady, supposed to have been a daughter of the Duke of Orléans and Madame de Genlis. She was educated by the latter, and was married about 1792 to Lord Edward Fitzgerald. After his death she became the wife of a man named Pitcairn. Died in Paris in 1831.

See ERSCH und GRUBER, "Allgemeine Encyklopaedie."

Fitzgerald, (THOMAS.) See KILDARE, EARL OF.

Fitz-ğib'bọn, (JOHN,) Earl of Clare, an Irish nobleman, born in 1749. He rose to be lord high chancellor of Ireland in 1789, and was afterwards appointed vice-

chancellor of the University of Dublin. He was a zealous advocate for the Union. Died in 1802.

Fitzharris. See MALMESBURY, (EARL,) and HARRIS, (JAMES.)

Fitz-hẹr'bẹrt, (Sir ANTHONY,) a distinguished English lawyer under the reign of Henry VIII. In 1523 he became one of the justices of the court of common pleas. He wrote several able works, among which are "The Grand Abridgment," (1514,) and the "Office and Authority of Justices of the Peace," (1538.) Died in 1538.

Fitzherbert, (MARIA,) born in 1756, was the daughter of Waller Smythe, of Hampshire. Having become a widow the second time, she was privately married in 1785 to the Prince of Wales, afterwards George IV. After the king's separation from the princess Caroline, Mrs. Fitzherbert lived with him for a time, but at length retired to Brighton, where she died in 1837.

See CHARLES LANGDALE, "Memoirs of Mrs. Fitzherbert."

Fitzherbert, (NICHOLAS,) grandson of Sir Anthony, mentioned above, was born about 1550. He wrote, among other works, a "Treatise on the Antiquity and Duration of the Catholic Religion in England," (1608.) Died in 1621.

Fitzherbert, (THOMAS,) an English Jesuit, born in Staffordshire in 1552, was appointed rector of the English College at Rome. Among other works, he wrote a "Treatise concerning Polity and Religion," (1606–10,) and a "Refutation of some of the Principles of Machiavel." Died in 1640.

Fitzherbert, (Sir WILLIAM,) an English jurist, a relative of the preceding, born in Derbyshire in 1748, wrote a "Dialogue on the Revenue Laws." Died in 1791.

Fitzjames, (JAMES.) See BERWICK, DUKE OF.

Fitzjames, de, dĕh fêts'zhăm' or fe'zhăm', (CHARLES,) DUKE, Marshal of France, and grandson of James II., King of England, born in 1712. He served chiefly in the wars in Germany. Died in 1787.

Fitz-James, de, (ÉDOUARD,) COMTE, a French general, born in 1715, was a son of the Duke of Berwick. Died at Cologne in 1758.

Fitz-James, de, (ÉDOUARD,) DUC, a French peer and politician, born in 1776, was a grandson of Marshal Fitz-James. He was a partisan of the Bourbons. Died in 1838.

Fitz-pat'rick, (BENJAMIN,) a lawyer, born in Green county, Georgia, in 1802, removed to Alabama, of which he was Governor from 1841 to 1845. He became a Senator of the United States in 1848, and was re-elected in 1853.

Fitz-roy', (ROBERT,) an English navigator, meteorologist, and rear-admiral, born in 1805, was a son of General Lord Charles Fitzroy. As captain of the Beagle, he was employed in the survey of the west coast of South America in 1828–30. He also commanded the Beagle in a voyage round the world performed between 1831 and 1836, which expedition Charles Darwin accompanied as naturalist. The results of this expedition appeared in a "Narrative of the Surveying Voyages of H.M.S Adventure and Beagle between 1826 and 1836, etc.," (1839,) written by Captain Fitzroy and Captain King. In 1855 he was appointed chief of the meteorological department of the Board of Trade. Died in 1865.

Fitz-si'mons or **Fitz-si'mon,** (HENRY,) an Irish Jesuit, noted as a polemical writer, born in Dublin in 1569. He took an active part in the rebellion of 1641. Died in 1644.

Fitz-ste'phen, (WILLIAM,) a learned English monk and historian of the twelfth century. He was an intimate friend of Thomas à Becket, of whose murder he was an eye-witness. He wrote the "Life and Passion of Archbishop Becket," in Latin, to which was prefixed his "Description of the City of London," one of the earliest and most valuable accounts of that capital. Died about 1191.

Fitz-wil'liam, (CHARLES WILLIAM WENTWORTH,) EARL OF, a Liberal peer, born in London in 1786, was the eldest son of William Wentworth, noticed below. Before the death of his father, in 1833, he was styled Lord Milton. He was a warm friend of the Reform bill. Died in 1857.

Fitzwilliam, (WILLIAM,) Earl of Southampton, a celebrated naval commander, born about 1490. He served against the French in 1513 and in 1523, and was raised to the rank of admiral. In 1537 he received the title of Earl of Southampton, and was made lord privy seal in 1539. Died in 1542.

Fitzwilliam, (WILLIAM WENTWORTH,) EARL OF, an English statesman, nephew of the Marquis of Rockingham, was born in 1748. He began his public life as a friend of Fox, but separated from him on the issue of the French Revolution, and became president of the council under Mr. Pitt in July, 1794. In 1795 he was for a short time Viceroy of Ireland. He was again appointed president of the council in 1806, and retired from office in 1807. Died in 1833.

Fiurelli, fe-oo-rel'lee, (TIBERIO,) a famous Italian comedian, surnamed SCARAMOUCHE, was born at Naples in 1808. In early life he removed to Paris, where he died in 1694.

Fix, fiks or fĕks, (THÉOBALD,) a Swiss philologist, brother of Théodor, noticed below, was born at Soleure in 1802. He contributed to the new edition of Stephens's "Thesaurus Linguæ Græcæ," and published several editions of Greek classics.

Fix, (THÉODOR,) a Swiss writer on political economy, born at Soleure in 1800. He made contributions to several journals of Paris, and was a member of the Academy of Moral and Political Science. Died in 1846.

See THÉOBALD FIX, "Notice sur M. T. Fix," 1846.

Fixlmillner, fiks'l-mil'nẹr, or **Fixmillner,** fiks-mil'-nẹr, (PLACIDUS,) an eminent German astronomer, born at Achlenthen, near Linz, in 1721. His principal work is "Decennium Astronomicum," (1776,) which is the record of his observations for ten years. He was a monk of the monastery of Kremsmünster. Died in 1791.

Fizeau, fe'zō', (HIPPOLYTE LOUIS,) a French natural philosopher, born in Paris in 1819. He distinguished himself by his researches into the properties and motion of light, and received in 1856 the grand prize of the Institute, 10,000 francs. He married a daughter of Adrien de Jussieu.

Fizes, fĕz, (ANTOINE,) a French physician, and professor of medicine and mathematics at Montpellier, was born in that city in 1690. He published "Opera Medica," a "Treatise on Fevers," (1749,) a "Treatise on Physiology," and other works. Died in 1765.

See ESTÈVE, "La Vie et les Principes de M. de Fizes," 1765; DESGENETTES, article in the "Biographie Médicale."

Flac-çil'la, (ÆLIA,) wife of the Roman emperor Theodosius I., and mother of Arcadius and Honorius, was born in Spain, and became empress in 379 A.D. She left a high reputation for piety, virtue, and moderation. Died about 386.

Flac'cus, (CAIUS VALERIUS,) a Roman poet, born probably at Padua. He wrote a poem on the Argonautic expedition, ("Argonautica,") which is a free imitation of Apollonius of Rhodes, and contains beautiful passages and descriptions. The style is rather obscure and artificial. It is supposed that several of the last books of this poem are lost, or else it was left unfinished. Eight books are extant. He died about 88 or 90 A.D. Quintilian referred to his death in terms like these : "We have recently lost much in Valerius Flaccus." The critics are far from being agreed as to the merits of his poem.

See the Preface of BURMANN's edition of the "Argonautica," 1724; "Nouvelle Biographie Générale."

Flaccus, (CALPURNIUS.) See CALPURNIUS.

Flaccus, (HORATIUS.) See HORACE.

Flaccus, (L. VALERIUS,) a Roman general, was a partisan of Marius, and commanded an army in Asia. He was killed by Fimbria about 86 B.C.

Flaccus, (M. FULVIUS,) a Roman officer, who was consul in 125 B.C., and a political friend of the Gracchi. Carbo, Caius Gracchus, and Flaccus were the triumviri for the division of lands. Having taken arms for Caius Gracchus, he was put to death by Opimius in 121 B.C.

Flaccus, (PERSIUS.) See PERSIUS.

Flaccus, (Q. FULVIUS,) a Roman general, who was elected consul in 237 B.C. Having been re-elected in

212, he obtained command of an army, and defeated Hanno at Beneventum. Died about 200 B.C.

See LIVY, "History of Rome."

Flaccus, (Q. FULVIUS,) a son of the preceding, commanded with success in Spain in 181 B.C.

Flaccus, (VERRIUS,) a Roman grammarian, lived in the reign of Augustus. He wrote many and various works, which are not extant.

Flaccus Illyricus. See FRANCOWITZ.

Flach, (MATTHIAS.) See FRANCOWITZ.

Flachat, flȧ'shȧ', (JEAN CLAUDE,) a French merchant, who lived and traded many years in Constantinople, and published "Observations on the Commerce and Arts of Europe, Asia," etc., (2 vols., 1766.) Died in 1775.

Flacius. See FRANCOWITZ.

Flacourt, de, dẹh flȧ'kooR', (ÉTIENNE,) born at Orléans, in France, in 1607, was nominated commander of Madagascar in 1648. He returned to France in 1655, and published in 1658 a "History of Madagascar," which was written with much care and accuracy and contained the first general description of that island. Died in 1660.

Flagg, (EDMUND,) an American writer, born at Wiscassett, Maine, in 1815, became a lawyer, and edited several journals. He published a few novels, and "Venice, the City of the Sea, 1749–1849," (2 vols., 1853.)

Flahault de la Billarderie, flȧ'ō' dẹh lȧ bèl'yȧrd're', (AUGUSTE CHARLES JOSEPH,) COUNT, a French general, born in Paris in 1785. He became colonel in 1809, distinguished himself in the campaign of Russia, and was aide-de-camp to Napoleon in 1813. For his conduct at the battle of Leipsic (1813) he was made a general of division, and a count. He fought for Napoleon at Waterloo. The revolution of 1830 restored him to his rank as a peer and general. He was ambassador to Vienna from 1841 to 1848, and became a senator in 1853.

Flahaut, COUNTESS. See SOUZA, ADÈLE DE.

Flajani, flä-yä'nee, (GIUSEPPE,) an Italian surgeon, born near Ascoli in 1741, studied at Rome. Pope Pius VI. chose him for his surgeon-in-ordinary. Died in 1808.

Flamael. See FLÉMALLE.

Flam'bard, (RALPH,) an English prelate, who was chief minister of William Rufus. He became Bishop of Durham in 1099. Died in 1128.

Flameel. See FLÉMALLE.

Flamel, flȧ'mĕl', (NICOLAS,) a scribe, a dealer in manuscripts, and a famous alchemist, who lived in Paris about 1350, was the subject of many marvellous stories which have exercised the public credulity. He is supposed to have acquired by some means great wealth, which he spent partly in the erection of churches and in works of charity. There are several treatises on alchemy which are ascribed to him. Died in 1418.

See "Histoire critique de N. Flamel," anonymous, 1761.

Flamen, flȧ'mẹn, (ALBERT,) a Flemish painter and engraver, born at Bruges, lived in the seventeenth century.

Flamen, flȧ'mȯN', or **Flamin,** flȧ'mȧN', (ANSELME,) a French sculptor, born at Saint-Omer in 1647, worked in Paris. Died in 1717.

Flam-ĭ-nī'nus, (LUCIUS QUINTIUS,) a Roman admiral, born about 240 B.C., was a brother of Titus. He commanded a fleet sent against Philip of Macedon in 198 B.C. Died in 170.

Flamininus, (TITUS QUINTIUS,) sometimes called **Fla-min'ĭ-us,** a distinguished Roman general, was chosen consul 198 B.C., and obtained the province of Macedonia, then the seat of war with Philip of Macedon. He defeated the army of Philip in Epirus, and recovered possession of Thessaly. After the year of his consulship had expired, he was continued in the command of that province by the senate. All attempts to negotiate a peace having failed, the two armies again met at Cynocephalæ, in Thessaly. The phalanx of Philip having been broken by the elephants of the Romans, a panic seized his whole army, of whom 8000 were killed. After this victory, in a general concourse of Greeks assembled at the Isthmian Games, 196 B.C., Flamininus proclaimed liberty and independence to the people of Corinth, Phocis, Locris, Thessaly, etc. In 183 he performed a mis-

ā, ē, ī, ō, ū, ȳ, *long;* à, è, ò, same, less prolonged; ă, ĕ, ĭ, ŏ, ŭ, ў, *short;* ạ, ẹ, ị, ọ, *obscure;* fär, fàll, fàt; mĕt; nŏt; gŏŏd; mōŏn;

sion to Prusias, King of Bithynia, to demand the surrender of Hannibal, who frustrated that design by suicide.

See PLUTARCH, "Life of Flamininus;" LIVY, "History of Rome," books xxxi.-xxxix. ; NIEBUHR, "Roman History."

Flaminio, flä-mee'ne-o, (GIOVANNI ANTONIO,) an Italian writer, born at Imola about 1464. He was professor of belles-lettres at Seravalla and Bologna, and wrote Latin poetry with moderate success. He also wrote, in prose, a Dialogue on Education, and a treatise "On the Origin of Philosophy," which are better than his poems. Died in 1536.

Flaminio, (MARCANTONIO,) an eminent Latin poet, son of the preceding, was born at Seravalla in 1498. He was patronized by Cardinal Pole, with whom he lived for many years, and whom he accompanied to the Council of Trent in 1545. He translated thirty Psalms into Latin verse, (1558,) and wrote hymns and other Latin poems, "which," says Ginguené, "join to a rare elegance something sweet and amiable, like his own character." Died in Rome in 1550.

See AUGUST NEANDER, "Erinnerung an M. A. Flaminio," Berlin, 1837; BAYLE, "Historical and Critical Dictionary;" TIRABOSCHI, "Storia della Letteratura Italiana."

Fla-min'ï-us, (CAIUS,) a Roman general, noted for his valour, became tribune of the people in 232 B.C., and procured the passage of an agrarian law which was violently opposed by the Optimates. In 225 or 223 he was elected consul, and led an army against the Gauls. Having been chosen consul a second time, he commanded at the battle of Lake Thrasymene, where, after a brave and desperate resistance, the Romans were defeated by Hannibal, and Flaminius was slain, in 217 B.C. During this battle an earthquake destroyed the greater part of several cities of Italy; but it is said the armies were entirely unconscious of its shock. The "Via Flaminia," a great highway, was made during his censorship, and named in his honour.

His son CAIUS was consul in 185 B.C., and defeated the Ligurians.

See NIEBUHR, "Lectures on Roman History;" LIVY, "History of Rome," books xxi. and xxii.

Fla-min'ï-us, (NOBILIUS,) an Italian critic and theologian, born at Lucca in 1532; died in 1590.

Flam'ma, (CALPURNIUS,) a Roman officer, noted for one heroic or daring action in the first Punic war.

Flamma, (L. VOLUMNIUS,) a Roman general, who commanded in the Samnite war, 296 B.C.

Flam'steed, (JOHN,) an eminent English astronomer, and the first astronomer royal, was born at Denby, near Derby, on the 19th of August, 1646, and began the study of the stars at an early age. He was ordained, and obtained the living of Burstow, in 1684. He appears to have been the first modern astronomer who understood the theory of the equation of time, on which subject he published a practical demonstration about 1667. He made observations at Denby from 1668 to 1674, soon after which he went to London and associated with Newton, Halley, and Hook. About 1675 Charles II. appointed him astronomer royal, and gave him the direction of the new observatory of Greenwich, which was finished in 1676. Here he passed the remainder of his life in patient observation, and determined the position of 2884 stars. The results of his labours were published in 1725, with the title of "Celestial History," ("Historia Cœlestis.") This work surpassed all previous performances of the kind, contained the first accurate catalogue of the stars, and is one of the richest contributions ever made to practical astronomy. An imperfect edition was published, without his consent, in 1712. He died in December, 1719.

See "An Account of the Rev. John Flamsteed," 1835, derived from his own manuscripts, which details a celebrated quarrel between Newton and Flamsteed; BREWSTER, "Life of Sir Isaac Newton;" J. B. BIOT, "Notice sur Flamsteed," Paris, 1827; WHEWELL, "Newton and Flamsteed," 1836; "London Quarterly Review" for December, 1835; "Edinburgh Review" for January, 1836.

Flandin, flôn'dåN', (CHARLES,) a French physician, born at Aubues (Nièvre) in 1803. He wrote several treatises on arsenic, and became a member of the Conseil de Salubrité, in Paris, in 1845. His most important work is a "Complete Treatise on Poisons," (3 vols., 1846-53.)

Flandin, (EUGÈNE NAPOLÉON,) a French painter and antiquary, born at Naples in 1809. He visited Italy and Algeria, and witnessed the attack on Constantine, which he painted in 1838. Under the auspices of the Academy, he was attached to the Persian embassy, and explored the antiquities of Persia, 1839-41. The results of this mission were "Studies on Persian Sculpture," (3 vols.,) "Studies on Modern Persia," (100 plates,) and a "Narrative of a Journey to Persia," (2 vols., 1843.) In 1844 he was sent to the supposed site of Nineveh, where he made many designs, which were published by the government, (1845-54.)

Flandrin, flôn'drån', (AUGUSTE,) a French painter, born in Lyons in 1804; died in 1842.

Flandrin, (JEAN HIPPOLYTE,) a French historical painter, brother of the preceding, was born at Lyons in 1809, and was one of the best pupils of Ingres. He studied in Rome from 1833 to 1838, and settled in Paris. Among his works are "Euripides writing Tragedies," "Dante conducted by Virgil," (1836,) "Mater Dolorosa," (1845,) and "Napoléon Législateur," (1847,) ordered for the Council of State. His composition and design are highly praised. He excelled also in portraits. He was admitted into the Institute in 1853. Died in 1864.

See "Nouvelle Biographie Générale."

Flandrin, (JEAN PAUL,) a skilful landscape-painter, brother of the preceding, with whom he studied in Rome, was born at Lyons in 1811. He is called one of the representatives of classic landscape in France. Among his works are "The Campagna of Rome," "The Promenade of Poussin on the Tiber," (1843,) a "View of Rivoli," (1844,) and "The Rhone near Avignon," (1846.)

Flandrin, (PIERRE,) a French veterinary writer, born at Lyons in 1752; died in 1796.

Fiangini, flän-jee'nee, (LUIGI,) an Italian writer, born in Venice in 1733, was made cardinal in 1789. In 1801 the Austrian emperor conferred on him the titles of Patriarch of Venice, count of the empire, and councillor of state. He translated from the Greek the "Apology of Socrates" by Plato, and the "Argonautica" of Apollonius Rhodius into verse, (2 vols., 1791-94.) Died in 1804.

See TIPALDO, "Biografia degli Italiani illustri."

Flassans. See RAXIS.

Flat'man, (THOMAS,) a lawyer, poet, and a skilful painter, born in London in 1633. He wrote songs, Pindaric odes, and other small poems, which procured for him a temporary popularity. Died in 1688.

Flatters, flät'têrs, a German sculptor, born at Crevelt in 1784; died in 1845.

Flaugergues, flō'zhårg', (HONORÉ,) a French astronomer, born at Viviers in 1755. In 1815 the Academy of Nîmes awarded him a prize for a treatise on the tails of comets. Died in 1835.

Flaugergues, (PIERRE FRANÇOIS,) a French lawyer, born at Rodez about 1760. He was an active member of the legislative body in 1813, and was one of the committee of three who prepared the address on the state of the nation to Napoleon in December of that year. Died in 1836.

Flav'el, (JOHN,) an eminent English nonconformist and Calvinist divine, born in Worcestershire about 1627. He became rector of Dartmouth in 1656, and was ejected for nonconformity in 1662; after which he preached in private houses. His character is represented as excellent. Among his works, which are highly esteemed, are "Husbandry Spiritualized," (1669,) "Divine Conduct," (1678,) and "Method of Grace," (1698.) His "Token for Mourners," says Dr. Doddridge, "is inimitable." Died at Exeter in 1691. An edition of his works, in six volumes, was published in 1820.

See a "Life of Flavel," in an edition of his select works, 1833.

Flā'vǐ-an, [Lat. FLAVIA'NUS; Fr. FLAVIEN, flå've-åN',] Bishop of Antioch, is called a saint by the Roman Catholics. He was an adversary of Arianism, and was elected in 381 A.D. to the see of Antioch. The pope and the Western bishops recognized Paulinus, who had been chosen Bishop of Antioch by another party. Died in 404 A.D.

Flā'vǐ-an or **Flā-vǐ-ā'nus,** Patriarch of Constantinople, was chosen Pontiff of the Greek Church in A.D. 447. By his influence Eutyches was condemned as a heretic in a council held in 448. At another council, assembled at Ephesus in 449, the Eutychian party prevailed, and deposed or condemned Flavian. He died in 449, in consequence, it is said, of personal violence received from the hostile sect.

See Socrates, "Historia Ecclesiastica;" Sozomen, "Historia Ecclesiastica;" Fabricius, "Bibliotheca Græca."

Flavigny, flȧ'vĕn'ye', (Valérien,) a French Hebraist, born near Laon, was a doctor of the Sorbonne. He became professor of Hebrew in the Collége de France in 1630. He was chiefly occupied with philological discussions respecting the Hebrew text of the Bible, and was involved in a long dispute with Abraham Echellensis. Died in 1674.

Flavio, flȧ've-o, (Biondo,) or **Biondo Flavio**, [Lat. Fla'vius Blon'dus,] an Italian historian and antiquary, born at Forlì in 1388. He was secretary to Pope Eugenius IV. and to three succeeding pontiffs. He illustrated the antiquities of Italy and Rome in three works, viz., "Italia Illustrata," (1474,) "Ten Books of Rome Triumphant," ("Romæ Triumphantis Libri X.," 1482,) and "Three Books of Rome Restored," ("Romæ Instauratæ Libri III.," 1482.) These works were excellent for the time, and are still consulted. Died in 1463.

See Vossius, "De Historicis Latinis;" Tiraboschi, "Storia della Letteratura Italiana."

Flā'vĭ-us, (Caius or Cneius,) a Roman senator, of plebeian birth, who held the office of ædile about 303 B.C. He acquired great popularity by publishing legal formulas and technicalities, the knowledge of which the patricians and pontiffs wished to be confined to themselves. His collection of legal rules was called "Jus Flavianum."

Flavius, (Clemens.) See Clemens.

Flavius, (Josephus.) See Josephus.

Flā'vus, (Titus Lartius,) the first Roman dictator, appointed to that office in 498 B.C.

Flavy, de, deh flȧ've', (Guillaume,) a famous and powerful French captain, born at Compiègne about 1398. He had command of Compiègne when Joan of Arc was captured there, (1430,) and was suspected of treachery in that affair. He was notorious for his audacity and crimes, and was assassinated in 1449.

Flax'man, (John,) an English sculptor of great eminence, was born at York in 1755. His father, who was a moulder of figures, brought him to London in infancy. About the year 1770 he became a student in the Royal Academy, where he distinguished himself by his industry and received a silver medal. In 1782 he married Miss Denman, with whom he lived happily until her death in 1820. In 1787 he removed to Rome, where he executed his admirable and sublime compositions (in outline) illustrative of the prominent events of the "Iliad" and "Odyssey" and of the great poems of Æschylus and Dante. His success in these subjects was such as to acquire for him a very high celebrity, especially for invention and composition. After remaining in Rome about seven years, he returned home, and in 1797 was unanimously elected an associate of the Royal Academy. About this time he executed monuments of Lord Mansfield and Lord Nelson, which are much admired, and numerous marble groups of scriptural subjects, for which he was peculiarly qualified by his genius and his piety. In 1810 he became professor of sculpture in the Royal Academy. Among his latest productions are the "Shield of Achilles," his "Psyche," and the group of the "Archangel Michael and Satan." He died in 1826. Canova and other competent judges have pronounced him the greatest sculptor of modern times. "There was Flaxman," says Ruskin, "another naturally great man, with as true an eye for nature as Raphael;—he stumbles over the blocks of the antique statues, wanders in the dark valley of their ruins to the end of his days." ("Modern Painters.")

See Cunningham, "Lives of the Most Eminent British Painters, Sculptors, and Architects;" "Nouvelle Biographie Générale."

Flechère or **Flechière**. See Fletcher, (John William.)

F.échier, flȧ'she-ȧ', (Esprit,) an excellent French pulpit orator, born at Pernes, (Vaucluse,) June 10, 1632. Having gained distinction by his Latin verses, eloquent

conversation, and funeral orations, he was chosen a member of the French Academy in 1673. He was appointed Bishop of Lavaur in 1685, and Bishop of Nîmes in 1687. As an orator, he was admired for his graceful style, noble thoughts, and harmonious periods. He was considered by his contemporaries as equal or only second to Bossuet; but his reputation has since declined. Among his best works are an "Oration on Turenne," (1676,) and a "Life of Theodosius the Great," (1679.) Died at Montpellier in February, 1710.

See Labitte, "La Jeunesse de Fléchier," in the "Revue des Deux Mondes," May, 1845; D'Alembert, "Histoire des Membres de l'Académie," tomes i. and ii.; Fabre de Narbonne, "Discours sur la Vie de Fléchier," prefixed to an edition of his works, 10 vols., 1825.

Fleck, flĕk, (Johann Friedrich Ferdinand,) a celebrated German actor, born at Breslau in 1757, was especially admired for his personation of the prominent characters in Shakspeare. Died in 1801.

Fleck'noe, (Richard,) an English poet and dramatist, who lived in the reign of Charles II. He was poet-laureate in the time of Dryden, whose ridicule, and that of Pope, seem to have preserved Flecknoe's name from oblivion more than his own writings. He wrote "Fashionable Young Ladies," ("Damoiselles à la Mode," 1667,) and other plays, which were not successful. Died about 1680.

See Malone, "Life of Dryden;" Allibone, "Dictionary of Authors."

Fleet'wood, (Charles,) an English general, born in Lancashire, is commonly described as a fanatic or enthusiast of small capacity. He was returned to Parliament in 1645, and became a zealous republican and Puritan. As lieutenant-general, he distinguished himself at Dunbar and at the battle of Worcester, September, 1651. After the death of Ireton, (1651,) Fleetwood married his widow, Bridget, a daughter of Cromwell, and was appointed commander-in-chief of the army in Ireland. He was also lord deputy of Ireland in 1654 and 1655. The Protector afterwards gave him the first place among the major-generals whom he appointed in 1656. After the restoration he lived in obscurity until his death, about 1692. His promotion is ascribed to his remarkable gift for praying and preaching extempore.

See Hume, "History of England;" Guizot, "Histoire de la Révolution d'Angleterre."

Fleetwood, (John,) an English writer on theology, published "The Christian Dictionary," (1773,) and "The Life of Christ, and Lives of the Apostles," etc., (1813.)

Fleetwood, (William,) D.D., an eminent English divine, born in London on the 1st of January, 1656. After graduating at Cambridge, he became chaplain of King William III. He was chosen Bishop of Saint Asaph in 1708, and was promoted to the Bishopric of Ely in 1714. His sermons, of which a large number were published, were greatly admired, and he was probably the most eminent preacher in the Anglican Church of his time. Among his works are an "Essay on Miracles," (1701,) and "Chronicon Preciosum: an Account of English Money, the Price of Corn, Wages, etc., for the Last Six Hundred Years," (1707.) He published in 1712 four sermons, with a preface which, though condemned by the House of Commons to be burnt, was inserted in the "Spectator," No. 384, with commendatory remarks by the editor. He advocated Whig principles in this preface. Died in August, 1723.

See Powell, "Life of Fleetwood" prefixed to his Works; "Biographia Britannica;" Nicéron, "Mémoires."

Fleetwood, (William,) an English lawyer, became recorder of London about 1569. He wrote some legal and historical works. Died in 1593.

Fleischer, flī'sher, (Heinrich Leberecht,) an eminent German Orientalist, born at Schandau, in Saxony, in 1801. In 1835 he succeeded Rosenmüller as professor of Oriental languages at Leipsic. He published an edition of Abulfeda's "Anteislamica," with a Latin translation, (1831,) and a valuable commentary on the "Koran of Beidhawi," (1844.)

Flémalle, flȧ'mȧl', written also **Flamael**, flȧ-mȧl', **Flemael**, and **Flameel**, (Bertholet, bĕr'to'lȧ',) a Flemish painter, born at Liege in 1614. He worked in Paris some years. Died in 1675.

Flem'ing, (ABRAHAM,) an English classical scholar and translator, born in London, lived about 1580. He translated Virgil's "Bucolics," (1575,) Ælian's "History," (1576,) Virgil's "Georgics," (1589,) and other classic works.

Fleming, (CALEB,) an English Socinian minister, born in 1698, succeeded the eloquent James Foster at Pinners' Hall, London, in 1752. He published many theological writings. Died in 1779.

Fleming, (CHARLES,) a philologist, born at Perth, Scotland, in 1806. He became professor of English at the Collége Louis-le-Grand, Paris, in 1829, and at the Polytechnic School in 1844. With M. Tibbins he published an "English-French and French-English Dictionary," (Paris, 2 vols., 1840,) which is considered one of the best dictionaries of the two languages extant.

Fleming or **Flemming,** flêm'ming, (CLAUDIUS,) Constable of Sweden, born in Finland, commanded in that province when Sigismond inherited the throne at the death of his father, John III., in 1591. In the civil war that followed, Fleming supported Sigismond with fidelity, and defeated the insurgents. Died in 1597.

See ERSCH und GRUBER, "Allgemeine Encyklopaedie;" GEYER, "Histoire de la Suède."

Flem'ing, (JOHN,) an eminent Scottish naturalist, born near Bathgate, in Linlithgowshire, in 1785, became a minister of the Church of Scotland. He preached at Flisk, in Fifeshire. He produced, about 1822, the "Philosophy of Zoology," which was highly esteemed, and obtained the chair of natural philosophy at King's College, Aberdeen, in 1828 or 1832. His "History of British Animals" is a work of high authority. He was author of a work on "Molluscous Animals, including Shell-Fish," (1837,) and of many minor scientific treatises. Having identified himself with the Free Church, organized about 1843, he resigned his chair at Aberdeen. He became professor of natural history or natural science in the Free Church College of Edinburgh about 1845. Died in November, 1857.

Flem'ing, (PATRICK,) an Irish monk, born in the county of Louth in 1599, received at baptism the name of CHRISTOPHER. He taught philosophy at Rome and Louvain, and theology at Prague, and wrote "Lives of Irish Saints." He was murdered near Prague by some fanatical peasants in 1631.

Fleming, (ROBERT,) a Scottish theologian, born at Yester in 1630. He wrote the "Fulfilling of Scripture," (1681,) and other works. He preached many years at Rotterdam after 1676. Died in 1694.

Fleming, (ROBERT,) Jr., a learned Scottish author and clergyman, son of the preceding, preached in Holland and London, and published sermons, poems, and discourses on the prophecies of Scripture, which are highly esteemed. In 1701 he issued a "Discourse on the Rise and Fall of the Papacy," containing predictions which it is thought have been remarkably verified. He expected that 1848 would be an important era in the subversion of the papal power. Died in 1716.

See CHAMBERS, "Biographical Dictionary of Eminent Scotsmen."

Flemming, flêm'ming, (HANS HEINRICH,) COUNT, born in Pomerania in 1632, distinguished himself at the siege of Vienna in 1683, and was made count of the empire. He obtained the rank of field-marshal about 1688. Died in 1706.

Flemming, (JAKOB HEINRICH,) an able general, born in Pomerania in 1667. He entered the service of Augustus of Saxony, who became King of Poland. He had a high command in the war against Charles XII. of Sweden, and was appointed field-marshal and chief minister of Augustus about 1712. He defeated the Swedes under Steinbock in Pomerania, and was afterward victorious over the revolted Poles in 1715. Died in 1728.

See ERSCH und GRUBER, "Allgemeine Encyklopaedie;" M. RANFT, "Leben und Thaten des General J. H. Grafen von Flemming," 1752.

Flemming, (PAUL,) one of the most celebrated German poets of his time, was born at Hartenstein, in Saxony, in 1609. His "Spiritual and Secular Poems" (1642) are greatly admired for their melody of versification, and his sonnets display merit of a high order. He went with an embassy sent by the Duke of Holstein to Persia in 1636. Died at Hamburg in 1640.

See VARNHAGEN VON ENSE, "Biographische Denkmale," vol. iv.; KARL SCHMITT, "P. Flemming nach seiner literargeschichtlichen Bedeutung dargestellt," 1851.

Flemming or **Flemmynge,** (RICHARD,) born at Crofton, was appointed in 1420, by Henry V., Bishop of Lincoln. Having zealously opposed the opinions of Wycliffe, he received from the pope the appointment to the Archbishopric of York; but Henry did not permit him to occupy it. He founded Lincoln College, Oxford. Died in 1430.

Flemming, (ROBERT,) a nephew of the preceding, became Dean of Lincoln in 1451. He published a Greek and Latin Dictionary, and a Latin poem in praise of Pope Sixtus IV. Died in 1483.

Flers, flair, (CAMILLE,) a French landscape-painter, born at Paris in 1802. He revolted against academical traditions, and aimed to paint nature in its simplicity. His subjects are mostly taken from French scenery.

Flers, de, deh flair, (CHARLES,) a French general, born in 1756. In 1793 he commanded the army of the Eastern Pyrenees, and had several engagements with the Spaniards. Being accused of treason, he was arrested by order of the Convention and condemned to death in 1794.

Flesselle, de, deh flậ'sêl', (PHILIPPE,) a French physician, who graduated in 1528. He was employed professionally by Francis I., Henry II., Francis II., and Charles IX. Died in 1562.

Flesselles, de, deh flậ'sêl', (JACQUES,) a French civil officer, one of the first victims of the Revolution, was born about 1724. He held the office of provost of the merchants of Paris, the functions of which are similar to those of mayor. On the day the Bastille was stormed, July 14, 1789, he was charged with hostility to the popular cause and shot by one of the mob.

Fletch'er, (ABRAHAM,) a self-taught English mathematician and physician, born at Little Broughton in 1714, wrote the "Universal Measurer and Mechanic," (1762.) Died in 1793.

Fletcher, (ALEXANDER,) a British divine, born about 1787, was minister of Finsbury Chapel, London. He published a "Guide to Family Devotion, containing 730 Hymns, 730 Prayers," etc., which passed through many editions, "Addresses to the Young," (1851,) and other works. Died in 1860.

Fletch'er, (ANDREW,) an able Scottish republican writer and orator, often called FLETCHER OF SALTOUN, was born at Saltoun in 1653. He was elected to the Scottish Parliament, in which he opposed the arbitrary measures of the court. Having been outlawed about 1680, he retired to the continent, and fought against the Turks. At the revolution of 1688 he returned home, and again became a member of Parliament. "He was by far the most nervous and correct speaker in the Parliament of Scotland," says the Earl of Buchan; "for he drew his style from the pure models of antiquity." He published several political treatises, among which are "Two Discourses concerning the Affairs of Scotland," (1698.) Lockhart praises the "undaunted courage and pathetic eloquence" with which he exposed the oppression to which Scotland was subjected. Died in London in 1716. Although a determined foe to despotism, Fletcher appears to have had little confidence in the capacity of the common people for self-government. Macaulay goes so far as to accuse him of being "the author of a plan for reducing a large part of the working-classes of Scotland to slavery." ("History," vol. i. p. 501.)

See EARL OF BUCHAN, "Life and Writings of Andrew Fletcher," 1792; "Retrospective Review," vol. iv., 1821.

Fletcher, (ANDREW,) Lord Milton, a Scottish judge, nephew of the preceding, was born in 1692. He became a lord of session in 1724, and keeper of the signet in 1748. He was the confidential agent of the Duke of Argyll when the latter had the chief management of Scottish affairs. He is commended for his services in the promotion of commerce, manufactures, and agriculture. Died in 1766.

See CHAMBERS, "Biographical Dictionary of Eminent Scotsmen."

Fletcher, (GILES,) born in Kent, was the brother of Bishop Fletcher, and father of the poets Giles and Phineas. In 1588 he was ambassador to Russia, of which nation he wrote a curious account, (1590.) This was suppressed by government, lest it should give offence to the Russian court. Died in 1610.

Fletcher, (GILES,) a son of the preceding, born about 1588, was educated at Cambridge, and obtained the living of Alderton, in Suffolk. He wrote an admired and picturesque poem, "Christ's Victory and Triumph in Heaven and Earth over and after Death," (1610.) "Giles seems," says Hallam, "to have more vigour than his elder brother, [Phineas,] but less sweetness and smoothness. . . . They both bear much resemblance to Spenser. . . . They were endowed with minds eminently poetical, and not inferior in imagination to any of their contemporaries." ("Introduction to the Literature of Europe.") Died in 1623.

See CAMPBELL, "Specimens of the British Poets," vol. ii.

Fletcher, (JAMES,) an English writer and schoolteacher, born in 1811, lived in London. He published "The Siege of Damascus," "The Gem, and other Poems," and a "History of Poland," (1831.) In a fit of insanity, he committed suicide in 1832.

Fletcher, (JOHN,) an eminent English dramatic author, born in Northamptonshire in 1576, was a son of Richard, Bishop of Bristol and London. He was educated at Cambridge, and became the friend of Francis Beaumont, with whom his name is inseparably associated as a partner in authorship. The unity of feeling and identity of genius between them were such that critics are unable to assign their respective shares in their works. Among the dramas of Beaumont and Fletcher, which had immense success, are "The Maid's Tragedy," (before 1611,) "Philaster," (1611,) and "The Loyal Subject," (1618.) Fletcher was sole author of "The Faithful Shepherdess," "The Scornful Lady," (1616,) "The Spanish Curate," comedy, (1622,) "Rule a Wife and Have a Wife," a comedy, (1624,) and many other comedies, or tragi-comedies, in verse. Dryden informs us that in his time the plays of Beaumont and Fletcher were performed oftener than those of Shakspeare. "Fletcher," remarks Hallam, "is as much superior to Shakspeare in his knowledge of the stage, as he falls below him in that of human nature. . . . His sentiments and style, where not concealed by obscurity, are very dramatic. His thoughts are noble, and tinged with the ideality of romance; his metaphors vivid, though sometimes too forced. . . . Yet we are seldom arrested by striking beauties: good lines occur in every page, fine ones but rarely." ("Introduction to the Literature of Europe.") The same critic censures the "protracted indecency" of these authors. (See BEAUMONT, FRANCIS.) Died in 1625.

See LANGBAINE, "Account of the English Dramatic Poets," 1691.

Fletcher or **Fléchère,** (JOHN WILLIAM,) a divine, born at Nyon, in Switzerland, in 1729. He removed to England in his youth, became a priest of the Anglican Church, and obtained the living of Madeley, in Salop, in 1760. He was a religious associate of John Wesley, and author of several works, some of which were directed against Calvinism. His works were published in 8 vols., (1803.) He died in Shropshire in 1785. "No Church," says R. Southey, "has ever possessed a more apostolic minister."

See J. BENSON, "Life of J. W. Fletcher."

Fletcher, (PHINEAS,) an English poet, born in 1584, was the son of Giles Fletcher the ambassador. He was educated for the church, and obtained in 1621 the living of Hilgay. He wrote "The Locustæ, or Apollyonists," "Sicelides, a Drama," and other poems. His reputation as a poet rests on "The Purple Island, or the Isle of Man," (1633,) an allegorical description of the human body, faculties, and passions. Milton is said to have admired and imitated him. "He is entitled," says Headley, "to a very high rank among our old English classics." Hallam thinks him deserving of praise, but that his poem "from its very nature is insufferably wearisome." (See FLETCHER, GILES.) Died about 1650.

See JOHNSON and CHALMERS, "Lives of the English Poets;" "Biographia Britannica;" "Retrospective Review," vol. ii., 1820.

Fletcher, (RICHARD,) an English prelate, born in Kent, was the father of John the dramatist. He became

chaplain to Queen Elizabeth, who directed him in 1586 to attend Mary Stuart at her execution; but she declined to listen to his exhortations. He was appointed Bishop of Bristol in 1589, of Worcester in 1592, and of London in 1594. Died in 1596.

Fleuranges, de, deh fluh´rŏNzh´, (ROBERT **de la Marck**—deh lä mǎRk,) SEIGNEUR, a brave French officer, born of a noble family at Sedan in 1491, offered his services to Louis XII. at an early age, and became the companion of the Count of Angoulême, afterwards Francis I. At the battle of Novara, or Asti, he is said to have received forty-six wounds. In 1525 he was taken prisoner with Francis I. at the battle of Pavia. A few years after this he was promoted to the rank of marshal of France. He wrote a "History of Memorable Events which occurred from 1499 to 1521." Died in 1537.

Fleuriau, fluh´re-ō´, (JÉRÔME CHARLEMAGNE,) Marquis de Langle, (deh lŏNgl,) a French writer, born in Brittany about 1742; died in 1807.

Fleurieu, de, deh fluh´re-uh´, (CHARLES PIERRE **Claret**—klā´rǎ´,) COUNT, a skilful French hydrographer and statesman, born in Lyons in 1738. He entered the navy in his youth, acquired skill in naval tactics, and became director-general of the ports and arsenals in 1776. He was minister of marine from October, 1790, until May, 1791, after which he was chosen a member of the Institute. He planned the naval operations of the war against the British, 1778 to 1783, in which he displayed great strategical skill. He published, besides other writings, a valuable work, entitled a "Voyage around the World, made by Étienne Marchand," (4 vols., 1798,) with notes and many charts. He became councillor of state in 1799, and intendant-general of the emperor's household, and a senator, in 1805. Died in 1810.

See DELAMBRE, "Notice sur la Vie, etc. de M. le Comte de Fleurieu;" "Nouvelle Biographie Générale."

Fleuriot-Lescot, fluh´re-o´ lês´ko´, (J. A. C.,) born in Brussels about 1760, was a violent Jacobin, and acted for a short time as mayor of Paris, until the fall of Robespierre, his patron, with whom he was executed in 1794.

Fleury, fluh´re´, (ABRAHAM JOSEPH **Bénard**—bà´nǎR´,) a French comedian, born at Chartres in 1751. He performed in Paris with success from 1778 to 1818. Died in 1822.

See "Mémoires de Fleury," by J. B. LAFITTE, 1835.

Fleury, (CLAUDE,) ABBÉ, a pious and learned ecclesiastic, born in Paris in 1640, practised law several years before he entered the priesthood. In 1672 Louis XIV. chose him for tutor to the Princes de Conti. He was associated with Fénelon about sixteen years (1689-1705) as sub-preceptor of the Dukes of Burgundy, Anjou, and Berry. After their education was finished, the king gave him the rich priory of Argenteuil. In 1696 Abbé Fleury was elected a member of the French Academy in the place of La Bruyère. Contemporary writers agree in extolling his moral qualities, his profound learning, and his literary merit. He published a work on the "Morality of Christians," another on "Ecclesiastical Law," and a "Historical Catechism," (1683,) which had great success. His greatest work is his "Ecclesiastical History," ("Histoire ecclésiastique," 20 vols., 1691-1723,) comprising a period of about four centuries. His style is pure, clear, and concise, and his spirit liberal and candid. He was confessor to Louis XV. from 1716 to 1722. Voltaire said, "His history of the Church is the best that has been written." Died in July, 1723.

See RONDET, "Notice sur Abbé Fleury" prefixed to an edition of his "Opuscules," 5 vols., 1780; C. E. SIMONETTI, "Der Charakter eines Geschichtsschreibers in dem Leben und aus den Schriften des Abbts C. Fleury," 1746; JAEGER, "Notice sur C. Fleury considéré comme Historien de l'Église," 1847; A. MARTIN, "Essai sur la Vie et les Ouvrages de Fleury," 1837.

Fleury, (ÉMILE FÉLIX,) a French general, born in Paris in 1815. He served in Algeria, became a senator in 1865, and was sent as ambassador to Russia in 1869.

Fleury, (JULIEN,) a French philologist, born about 1650. He edited Apuleius "ad usum Delphini," (1688.) Died in 1725.

Fleury, de, deh fluh´re´, (AIMÉE de Coigny—deh kwân´ye´,) DUCHESSE, a literary French lady, born in

Paris about 1776. In 1794 she was confined in the same prison with André Chénier, and was the subject of his ode "La jeune Captive." She wrote a novel entitled "Alvar," (1818.) Died in 1820.

Fleury, de, (ANDRÉ HERCULE,) CARDINAL, an eminent French statesman, born at Lodève, in Languedoc, on the 22d of June, 1653, was educated at Paris. To superior mental faculties and wit he added high literary attainments and persuasive eloquence. In 1677 he was chosen almoner to the queen, and after her death, in 1683, he served in the same capacity Louis XIV., who in 1698 nominated him Bishop of Fréjus. Just before the death of Louis XIV., by a codicil to his will, he appointed Fleury preceptor to the heir-apparent, aged about six years, who in 1715 succeeded as Louis XV. He performed the duties of this office in such a manner that he gained the affection and respect of the young king, who in 1726 raised him to the dignity of prime minister,—an event which occasioned ample demonstrations of popular joy. In the same year he received from the pope a cardinal's hat. Adopting a pacific and economical policy, he exercised his power with wisdom and fidelity until his death. He maintained peace with Spain and England until 1740, when France, in spite of his efforts, was involved in the general war. He was a member of the French Academy. Died in Paris in January, 1743.

See SAINT-SIMON, "Mémoires;" VOLTAIRE, "Siècle de Louis XIV ;" F. J. BATAILLE, "Éloge historique de M. le Cardinal A. H. de Fleury," 1737; "Leben des Cardinals A. H. Fleury," Freiburg, 1743.

Fleury, de, (GUILLAUME FRANÇOIS **Joly.**) See JOLY.

Fleury de Chaboulon, fluh're' deh shä'boo'lôn', (PIERRE ALEXANDRE ÉDOUARD,) a Frenchman, born in 1779. He became private secretary of Napoleon on his return from Elba, and wrote "Memoirs of the Private Life and Reign of Napoleon in 1815," (2 vols., 1819,) which had a great success. Died in 1835.

Flex'man, (ROGER,) D.D., an English dissenting minister, born in Devonshire in 1708. He wrote several biographies, and made an index to "The Rambler," which provoked Dr. Johnson's indignation and disgust by entering Milton's name thus :—"Milton, Mr. John." He preached in London many years. Died in 1795.

Flin'deṛs, (MATTHEW,) an English navigator, born in Lincolnshire about 1760. He made a voyage to New Holland in 1795, and, in company with George Bass, discovered, in 1798, the strait since called Bass's Strait. As captain of the Investigator, he explored the southern coast of Australia, and discovered the Gulfs of Spencer and Saint Vincent. On a homeward-bound voyage, being compelled to put in to the Isle of France, he was detained a prisoner by the French about six years, 1803-10. He died in England in 1814, just after he had published his "Voyage to Terra Australis," (2 vols., 1814.)

See "London Quarterly Review" for October, 1814.

Flink or **Flinck,** flink, (GOVAERT, go'vȧrt,) a skilful Dutch painter of portraits and history, born at Cleves in 1616, was a pupil of Rembrandt, whose style he imitated with success. He worked at Amsterdam, and was patronized by the Elector of Brandenburg. Among his works are "Solomon praying for Wisdom," and a "Virgin and Child." Died in 1660.

See DESCAMPS, "Vies des Peintres Flamands, Hollandais," etc.

Flins des Oliviers, de, deh flȧn dȧ'zo'le've-ȧ', (CLAUDE MARIE LOUIS **Carbon**—kȧr'bôn',) a French poet, born at Rheims in 1757. He wrote "The Awaking of Epimenides," ("Le Reveil d'Epiménide,") a drama, and many other poems. Died in 1806.

Flint, (AUSTIN,) a distinguished American physician and medical writer, born in Petersham, Massachusetts, in 1812, graduated as M.D. at Harvard in 1833. He was one of the founders of the Buffalo Medical College in 1847. After having been a professor in several medical colleges in the United States, he was appointed in 1861 professor of the principles and practice of medicine in the Bellevue College Hospital, New York, and of pathology and practical medicine in the Long Island College Hospital. He has published, besides other valuable works, "Practical Treatise on the Pathology, Diagnosis, and Treatment of Diseases of the Heart," (1859,) and

an excellent work on the "Practice of Medicine," (1866; 3d edition, 1868.)

Flint, (AUSTIN,) a son of the preceding, born in Northampton, Massachusetts, in 1836, studied at Harvard, and graduated at Jefferson Medical College in 1857. He became professor of physiology in the University of Buffalo in 1858, and was afterwards professor of the same branch in the Long Island College Hospital. His essay on the Excretory Function of the Liver, translated into French, received from the Institute of France a prize of 1500 francs. He has made several valuable contributions to the "American Journal of Medical Sciences," and other periodicals.

Flint, (TIMOTHY,) an American author and traveller, born at North Reading, Massachusetts, in 1780. In 1815 he went as a missionary to the Valley of the Mississippi. In 1826 he published "Recollections of Ten Years passed in the Valley of the Mississippi." He also wrote "Geography of the Mississippi Valley," (2 vols., 1828,) "Arthur Clenning" (1828) and other novels, and made contributions to several periodicals. He died in Massachusetts in 1840.

See GRISWOLD, "Prose Writers of America."

Flin'toff, (OWEN,) a British legal writer of the present century. He published an excellent work on "The Law of Real Property," (1839,) also "The Rise and Progress of the Laws of England and Wales," and an "Introduction to Conveyancing," (1840.)

Flipart, fle'pȧr', (JEAN JACQUES,) a skilful French engraver and designer, born in Paris in 1723, was an associate of the Royal Academy. He engraved a "Holy Family," after Giulio Romano, and some works of Greuze and Vernet. Died in 1782.

Flocco, flok'ko, or **Floke,** a Norwegian or Swedish pirate, who acquired reputation by his enterprise in navigation. In 865 A.D. he visited Iceland, and gave it the name which it now bears.

Flocon, flo'kôn', (FERDINAND,) a French journalist, born in Paris about 1800. He became in 1845 chief editor of the "Réforme," the organ of the radical democracy, and in February, 1848, secretary of the provisional government formed by the revolutionists. His official career ended in June of that year.

Flodoard, flo'do'ȧr', a French historian and priest, born at Épernay in 894 A.D., wrote a history of the Church of Rheims, and a chronicle of events that occurred in France from 919 to 966. He was canon of Rheims when he died, in 966.

Floerke. See FLÖRKE.

Flögel or **Floegel,** flö'gel, (KARL FRIEDRICH,) a German writer, born in Silesia in 1729, became professor of philosophy at Liegnitz in 1774. He wrote a "History of the Human Intellect," (1776,) a curious work, of great research, "The History of Comic Literature," (4 vols., 1784-86,) which is commended, and a few other works. Died in 1788.

Floke. See FLOCCO.

Flood, flŭd, (Rt. Hon. HENRY,) an eloquent Irish orator, born in 1732. He was elected in 1759 to the Irish Parliament, where he became one of the chiefs of the opposition, and a rival of Grattan, with whom he was formerly intimate. They had a personal dispute in the House in 1783, which was a remarkable display of the power of invective on both sides. Flood challenged his opponent; but the meeting was prevented by the authorities. About that date Flood became a member of the English Parliament, in which he sat until 1790. Mr. Phillips, the biographer of Curran, informs us that the latter once said, "Flood was immeasurably the greatest man of his time in Ireland ;" but this opinion is not generally concurred in. He died in 1791. His speeches and poetical pieces have been published.

See W. FLOOD, "Life and Correspondence of Henry Flood," 1838.

Flood, (ROBERT.) See FLUDD.

Floquet, flo'kȧ', (ÉTIENNE JOSEPH,) a French composer, born at Aix in 1750 ; died in 1785.

Floquet, (PIERRE AMABLE,) a French historical writer and advocate, born at Rouen in 1797. His principal works are a "Eulogy on Bossuet," (1827,) and a "History of the Parliament of Normandy," (7 vols., 1840-43,) which gained a prize of the Institute.

e as k; ç as s; ḡ hard; ġ as j; G, H, K, guttural; N, nasal; R, trilled; ṡ as z; ᵗh as in this. (☞ See Explanations, p. 23.)

59

Flor, de, dẹh floR, (ROGER,) a famous military adventurer, born about 1264. In his youth he fought with the crusaders against the Saracens. About 1303 he entered the service of the emperor Andronicus, for whom he gained several victories over the Turks. He was assassinated, by order of the emperor, in 1306 or 1307.

See LE BEAU, "Histoire du Bas-Empire."

Flo′ra, [Fr. FLORE, floR,] an ancient Italian divinity, the goddess of flowers, appears to have been worshipped in the time of Numa, or earlier. Her annual festival (*Floralia*) was celebrated from April 28 to May 1. The Flora of the Romans corresponded to the Greek Chloris.

Flore, (FRANC.) See FLORIS, (FRANS.)

Flor′ence OF WORCESTER, (wŏŏs′tẹr,) a learned monk, was the first chronicler who wrote in England after the Norman Conquest. His chronicle (in Latin) was printed in 1592. Died in 1118.

Florencourt, von, fon flo′rŏn′kooR′, (FRANZ Chassot—shȧ′so′,) a German journalist and political writer, of aristocratic principles, was born at Brunswick in 1803. Since 1851 he has lived in Vienna.

Florencourt, von, (WILHELM CHASSOT,) a German antiquary and writer on numismatics; born about 1800.

Florent, flo′rĕnt, or **Floris,** flo′ris, **I.,** Count of Friesland, was killed in battle by the men of Brabant in 1061.

Florent II., Count of Friesland and Holland, succeeded his father, Thierry V., in 1091, at the age of ten. Died in 1122.

Florent III., Count of Holland, was a son of Thierry VI., whom he succeeded in 1157. He waged war against the Count of Flanders, and in 1189 followed the emperor Frederick I. in a crusade. He died at Antioch in 1190.

Florent IV. of Holland, born in 1210, began to reign in 1223. In his reign a great storm and inundation of the sea covered a populous district now occupied by the Zuyder Zee, which was then first formed. He was assassinated in 1235.

Florent V., a grandson of the preceding, was about two years old at the death of his father, in 1254. He waged a long war against the revolted West Frisians and against the Flemings. He was assassinated in 1296.

Florent-Chrétien. See CHRÉTIEN.

Florentino. See FIORENTINO.

Flo-ren-ti′nus, a Roman jurist, who had a high reputation, but of whom little is known. He is supposed to have lived in the time of Ulpian, (who died in 228 A.D.,) or later. He wrote many books of "Institutiones."

Flores, flo′rĕs, (ANDRES,) a minor Spanish poet, born at Segovia in 1484, wrote lyric poems. Died about 1560.

Flores, flo′rĕs or floR, (LOUIS,) born at Ghent in 1570, became a monk, and went as a missionary to the Philippine Isles. The Dutch imprisoned him, and then delivered him to the Japanese, who put him to death in 1622. He wrote an "Account of the State of Christianity."

Flores, de, dȧ flo′rĕs, (JUAN,) a Spanish novelist, who flourished about 1510. He wrote "The History of Cerisel and Mirabella," ("La Historia de Cerisel y Mirabella," 1524,) which was very popular.

Florez, flo′rĕth, (ENRIQUE,) a Spanish monk, and an excellent historian and numismatist, born at Valladolid in 1701, devoted his life to the investigation of history, especially that of Spain. His first essay, entitled "Key to History," ("Clave historical," 1743,) was very successful. He wrote a voluminous work on the Ecclesiastical History of Spain, ("España sagrada," in 29 vols., 1747-70.) After his death it was continued and completed, in forty-six volumes. This work has a high character for veracity and literary merit. He was also author of a learned antiquarian treatise on medals. Died in 1773.

See BOUTERWEK, "Histoire de la Littérature Espagnole;" FRANCISCO MENDEZ, "Noticias de la Vida y Escritos del P. H. Florez," Madrid, 1780.

Florian, (DOCAMPO.) See DOCAMPO.

Flo′rĭ-an, (in Latin, **Mar′cus** (or **An′nius) Floria′nus,**) a Roman emperor, who was a half-brother of the emperor Tacitus. At the death of the latter, Florian was proclaimed his successor by a part of the army, while the legions of the East supported the claims of Probus. A few months after this event, Florian was killed by his own soldiers, in 276 A.D.

Florian, de, dẹh flo′re′ŏN′, (JEAN PIERRE Claris—klȧ′rèss′,) a French novelist and poet, was born at the château de Florian, in the department of Gard, in March, 1755. In youth or childhood he often visited the house of Voltaire, who encouraged his literary aspirations. He became gentleman-in-ordinary to the Duc de Penthièvre, who treated him with much favour and confidence. In 1783 he published the romance of "Galatea," which was very popular, and was followed by "Numa Pompilius," (1786,) "Estelle," (1788,) and several comedies and fables, which obtained the public favour. He translated "Don Quixote" into French. He was admitted into the French Academy in 1788. During the reign of terror he was imprisoned several months, but was released by the *coup d'état* of 9th Thermidor. Among French fabulists he is considered next to La Fontaine. Died near Paris in 1794.

See ROSNY, "Vie de Florian," 1798; LACRETELLE, "Éloge de Florian," 1812; "Jeunesse de Florian, ou Mémoires d'un jeune Espagnol," 1807; VIANCIN, "Éloge de Florian," 1833.

Floriani, flo-re-ȧ′nee, (FRANCESCO,) a painter of the Venetian school, born at Udine, flourished about 1570.

Florida, de la, dȧ lȧ flo-ree′DȦ, (MARQUIS,) a Spanish general, born in Madrid about the year 1646. He distinguished himself by his military talents in the reigns of Charles II. and Philip V., defended Milan in 1706 against Prince Eugene, and commanded under the Duke of Vendôme at the important battle of Almanza, in 1707, where the French and Spaniards defeated the English and their allies. Died in 1714.

Florida Blanca, flo-ree′DȦ blȧn′kȧ, (JOSÉ Moñino—mŏn-yee′no,) COUNT OF, an eminent Spanish statesman, born at Helin, in Murcia, in 1728, belonged by birth to the middle class. After studying law at Salamanca, he practised several years with increasing reputation, and filled the office of fiscal of the Council of Castile. About 1770 he was appointed ambassador to Rome, where he displayed great diplomatic ability, and remained until the resignation of the prime minister Grimaldi, who, having the privilege of naming his successor, selected Moñino, who had recently been created Count of Florida Blanca. He entered the office in February, 1777, soon after which Charles III. of Spain formed an alliance with France against England. Moñino carried on the war with vigour, ability, and credit; and, though his efforts to recover Gibraltar were frustrated, the Spaniards captured Florida, Minorca, the Bahamas, and a fleet of fifty-five merchant-vessels. Peace having been made with England in January, 1783, he promoted the cause of popular education, patronized arts and sciences, and made several wise reforms in the domestic policy of Spain. Just before the death of Charles III., in 1788, he testified his confidence in his minister by commending him to the favour of his successor, Charles IV., who retained him in his service until the intrigues of the queen and the notorious Godoy effected his dismissal in 1792. His disposition is said to have been amiable, and his moral character high. Died in 1808.

See COXE, "Memoirs of the Kings of Spain of the House of Bourbon," 5 vols., 1815.

Floridor, flo′re′doR′, (JOSIAS de Soulas—dẹh soo′-lȧs′,) Sieur de Prinefosse, a popular French comedian, was born of a noble family in Brie in 1608. Floridor was a fancy name which he assumed when he became an actor. He performed the principal *rôles* in tragedy and high comedy, and was a great favourite with the public. Died about 1671.

Floridus, flo-ree′dŏŏce, (FRANCESCO,) an Italian philologist, born about 1500. He removed to Paris at the request of Francis I., who gave him a pension. He made a translation into Latin verse of eight books of the "Odyssey," (1545,) which had a great success. His death prevented the completion of it. He wrote an "Apology for the Latin Language," (1537,) and other works. Died in 1547.

Florigerio, flo-re-jä′re-o, or **Florigorio,** flo-re-go′-re-o, (SEBASTIANO,) an Italian painter of the Venetian school, born at Udine, lived about 1535.

Florimond de Remond, flo′re′môN′ dẹh rẹh-môN′, a French Roman Catholic theologian, born at Agen; died in 1602.

ă, ē, ĭ, ō, ū, ȳ, *long;* ȧ, ė, ȯ, same, less prolonged; ä, ĕ, ĭ, ŏ, ŭ, ў, *short;* ạ, ẹ, į, ọ, *obscure;* fär, fåll, fât; mĕt; nŏt; gŏŏd; mŏŏn;

Florio, flo're-o, (DANIELE,) COUNT, an Italian poet, born at Udine in 1710; died in 1789.

Florio, flo're-o, (JOHN,) surnamed THE RESOLUTE, a philologist and grammarian, born in London, of Italian parents, about 1545. He was professor of French and Italian in the University of Oxford, and in the reign of James I. was appointed to teach those languages to Prince Henry. He married a sister of Samuel Daniel the poet. He published an "Italian and English Dictionary," (1597,) the most copious then extant, a translation of Montaigne's "Essays," (1603,) and several other works. Shakspeare, it is supposed, ridiculed him in the character of Holofernes in "Love's Labour Lost." Died in 1625.

See WOOD, "Athenæ Oxonienses."

Floriot, flo're-o', (PIERRE,) a French moralist, born in 1604, became confessor to the recluses of Port-Royal. He wrote a pious work entitled "La Morale du Pater," or "La Morale chrétienne," ("Christian Morality," 5 vols., 1672,) which was much esteemed. Died in 1691.

Floris, flo'ris, (FRANS,) [Fr. FRANC-FLORE, frôNk flor,] an excellent Flemish painter, born at Antwerp in 1520, was surnamed THE RAPHAEL OF FLANDERS. His proper name was FRANS DE VRIEND, (vreend.) He studied the works of Michael Angelo in Rome, and returned to Antwerp. He was eminent for boldness of design, richness of invention, and facility of execution. Among his master-pieces are a "Nativity," a "Cruci-fixion," and "The Last Judgment." He is said to have been very intemperate. Died in 1570.

His son and pupil, FRANS FLORIS, was a skilful painter, especially of small pictures.

See DESCAMPS, "Vies des Peintres Flamands," etc.

Floris, flo'ris, (PIETER WILLEMSZOON,) a navigator, born at Dantzic. He sailed to the East Indies as factor of the English Company in 1610, before which he had visited those regions in the service of the Dutch. He returned in 1615, and wrote, in Dutch, an interesting journal of his voyage, a version of which was published by Purchas. Died in 1615.

Flörke or **Floerke,** flör'keh, (JOHANN ERNST,) a German author, born at Altenkalden in 1767; died in 1830.

Flo'rus, (DREPA'NIUS,) a theologian and poet, who probably wrote about 850 A.D., and was a canon or deacon of the church of Lyons. He composed, besides Latin poems, a commentary on the Epistles of Saint Paul, and a refutation of Erigena on predestination.

Flo'rus, (GESSIUS,) a Roman officer, who became governor of Judea in 64 A.D. His cruelty and rapacity provoked the last revolt of the Jews, which resulted in the destruction of Jerusalem, 70 A.D.

Florus, (JULIUS,) a celebrated orator of Gaul, born about 20 B.C., practised at the Roman bar, and after-wards in his native country. Quintilian speaks highly of his eloquence. Died about 55 A.D.

Florus, (LUCIUS ANNÆUS,) a Latin historian, who lived in the reigns of Trajan and Hadrian, and, accord-ing to some authors, was a native of Spain. He wrote an "Epitome of Roman History," ("Epitome de Gestis Romanorum,") from the origin of Rome to the time of Augustus, compiled probably from historians whose works are lost. Critics observe that he deals rather largely in panegyric, but give him credit for being an agreeable writer and generally exact. His style is ele-gant, but somewhat declamatory.

See VOSSIUS, "De Historicis Latinis;" J. M. HEINZE, "Com-mentatio de Floro non historico sed rhetore," 1787.

Flotow, von, fon flo'to, (FRIEDRICH,) a German composer, born at Teutendorf in 1811. He composed operas entitled "Martha," "Linda," "Albin," etc.

Flotte, flot, (PIERRE,) a French lawyer, who performed an important part in the quarrel between King Philip the Fair and Pope Boniface about 1300. He was sent to Rome with an answer to the pope's bull, and is said to have used insulting language to Boniface. He was killed at the battle of Courtray, in 1302.

Flotte, de, deh flot, (ÉTIENNE **Gaston**—gås'tôN',) BARON, a French *littérateur*, nephew of Lantier the poet, was born near Marseilles in 1805. He has written, besides other poems, the "Exile of Dante," (1833,) and "La Vendée," (1845.)

Flottes, flot, (JEAN BAPTISTE MARCEL,) ABBÉ, a French writer and professor of philosophy, born at Montpellier in 1789.

Flottwell, flot'wĕl, (EDUARD HEINRICH,) a Prussian statesman, born at Insterburg in 1786, was appointed minister of state in 1844.

Flourens, floo'rôN', (MARIE JEAN PIERRE,) an emi-nent French physiologist and author, born near Béziers in 1794. He took his degree in medicine in 1813, and became a resident of Paris in 1814. In 1822 he pro-duced "Researches on Irritability and Sensibility." He was admitted into the Academy of Sciences in 1828, after he had published an able work called "Researches on the Properties and Functions of the Nervous System in Vertebrate Animals," (1824.) He became professor of comparative anatomy in the museum in 1832, and perpetual secretary of the Academy of Sciences in 1833. Among his chief works are "Analysis of the Labours of Cuvier," ("Analyse raisonnée des Travaux de G. Cuvier," 1841,) "Buffon, Histoire de ses Idées et de ses Tra-vaux," (1844,) "Theory of the Formation of the Bones," (1847,) "Course of Comparative Physiology," (3 vols., 1854,) and "Human Longevity and the Quantity of Life on the Globe," (1854,) a very popular book. He was elected to the French Academy in 1840.

See QUÉRARD, "La France Littéraire;" "Nouvelle Biographie Générale."

Floyd, (JOHN,) an English writer on theology, born in Cambridgeshire, became a Jesuit about 1593. He was banished after that date.

Floyd, (JOHN,) an American officer, born in Virginia in 1769. He removed to Georgia in 1791, and became a major-general in the second war with Great Britain. From 1827 to 1829 he was a member of Congress. Died in 1839.

Floyd, (JOHN B.,) an American lawyer and general, born in Pulaski county, Virginia, in 1805. He was ap-pointed secretary of war by President Buchanan in March, 1857. To aid the cause of disunion, he trans-ferred more than one hundred thousand muskets and rifles, besides a great number of cannon, from Northern armories to the South, in 1860. He resigned about De-cember 25, 1860, after which he was accused of being a defaulter, but was not brought to trial. Having joined the army of the Confederates, he commanded at Fort Donelson when it was attacked by General Grant, Feb-ruary, 1862. When the capture of the fort became in-evitable, he turned the command over to Pillow, and escaped by flight. Died in 1863.

Floyd, (WILLIAM,) an American patriot, born in Suffolk county, New York, in 1734. He was chosen in 1774 a delegate to the first Continental Congress, in which he continued to serve about eight years, and signed the Declaration of Independence. Died in 1821.

See GOODRICH, "Lives of the Signers to the Declaration of Inde-pendence."

Floy'er, (Sir JOHN,) a skilful English physician, born at Hinters in 1649. He published several professional treatises, and translated the "Sibylline Oracles" from the Greek. His learning and piety were commended by Dr. Johnson, who had been under his medical care. He was a strenuous advocate of cold baths. Died in 1734.

Fludd, [Lat. DE FLUC'TIBUS,] (ROBERT,) an English physician and writer, born at Milgate in 1574, was re-puted a man of great learning, especially in occult sciences, and was an adept in the Rosicrucian philoso-phy. He published treatises on various subjects, abound-ing in abstruse philosophy and visionary theories, with some original ideas. Kepler and Gassendi did him the honour to write refutations of his system. Thomas Fuller says, "His works are for the English to slight or admire, for the French and other foreigners to under-stand or use." ("Worthies of England.") Died in 1637.

See BRUCKER, "History of Philosophy."

Flüe, de, deh flü'eh, (NICOLAS,) a Swiss patriot and hermit, born at the village of Saxeln in 1417, was revered by his countrymen for his piety and wisdom. When the confederacy was in great peril from civil dissension, he restored harmony on the basis of the Covenant of Stantz formed in 1481. Died in 1487.

Fluegel. See FLÜGEL.

Flügel, flü′g̣el, (GUSTAV LEBRECHT,) a German Oriental scholar, born at Bautzen in 1802. His most important work is the edition of the large encyclopædic-bibliographical Dictionary of Haji (Hadschi) Khalfa, with a Latin translation and commentary, six volumes of which were completed in 1852. He was professor at Meissen from 1832 to 1850.

Flügel, (JOHANN GOTTFRIED,) a distinguished German lexicographer, born at Barby, on the Elbe, in 1788. He brought out in 1830 his "Complete English-German and German-English Dictionary," (2 vols.,) and in 1840 his "Triglotte, or Merchant's Dictionary, in German, English, and French," (3 vols.) He lived at Leipsic. Died in 1855.

Flus′ser, (CHARLES W.,) an American naval officer, born in Maryland about 1832. He gained the rank of lieutenant in 1855. He commanded the gunboat Miami, and was killed in a battle against the iron-clad Albemarle, in Roanoke River, April, 1864.

Flygare-Carlén. See CARLÉN.

Foa, fo′ä′, (EUGÉNIE,) originally named GRADIS, a French authoress, born at Bordeaux about the end of the eighteenth century. She wrote "Le Petit Robinson de Paris," (1840,) and other moral tales for youth. Died in Paris in 1853.

Fodéré, fo′dȧ′rȧ′, (FRANÇOIS EMANUEL,) an eminent physician, born in Savoy in 1764. About 1814 he was elected professor of legal medicine in Strasbourg, and physician of the Royal College of that place, where he passed the rest of his life. He wrote numerous valuable professional works, among which are a "Treatise on Legal Medicine and Public Hygiene," (3 vols., 1798,) and a "Natural History of the County of Nice," (2 vols., 1812.) Died in 1835.

See DUCROS, "Notice sur la Vie et les Travaux du Dr. Fodéré," 1845; A. MOTTARD, "Notice historique sur la Vie du Professeur Fodéré," 1843.

Fodhail, fo-dīl′ or fo-dāl′, (**Aboo-Alee** or **Abû-Alî,** ä′boo ä′lee,) a Mussulman saint, born at Samarcand or in Khorassân. He was a highway-robber in his youth. Many of his sententious sayings have been preserved. Died in 803 A.D.

See IBN-KHALLIKÂN, "Biographical Dictionary;" ABOOLFEDA, "Annales."

Foe, De. See DE FOE.

Foelix, fä′lĕks′, (JEAN JACQUES GASPARD,) a French jurist, born at Oberstein in 1791. He published a "Treatise on Private International Law," ("Traité du Droit international privé," 1843.) Died in 1853.

Foerster. See FÖRSTER.

Foës, fo′ĕs′, (ANUCE,) [Lat. ANU′TIUS FOE′SIUS,] an eminent French physician, born at Metz in 1528, studied in Paris, and became an excellent Greek scholar. About 1556 he began to practise medicine in Metz, of which city he was chosen public physician. He received offers of patronage from several foreign princes, but declined them. He acquired a wide reputation by his excellent edition of Hippocrates, with a Latin translation, (1595,) and by another valuable work, entitled "Œconomia Hippocratis," (1588,) which explains obscure terms used by that writer. Died in 1595.

See WILLAUME, "Notice sur A. Foës," 1823.

Fogarasy, fo′gŏh-rŏsh-e, (JÁNOS,) a Hungarian jurist, born at Kásmark in 1801. He wrote, besides other important works, a "Hungarian-German Dictionary," (1836,) "Principles of the Civil Law of Hungary," (1839,) and "The Spirit of the Magyar Language," (1845.)

Fogelberg, fo′g̣el-bĕrg′, (BENGT,) a Swedish sculptor, born at Gothenburg in 1787. He went in 1820 to Italy, which became his adopted country. He produced admired statues of Odin, Thor, and Balder. A statue of Psyche is called his master-piece. Died at Trieste in 1854.

See "Nouvelle Biographie Générale."

Foggia, fod′jä, (FRANCESCO,) an eminent Italian musician, born in Rome in 1604. He was chapel-master of San Giovanni Laterano, Rome, from 1636 to 1661, and composed motets, masses, and other sacred music. He was the first Italian that wrote the tonal fugue. Died at Rome in 1688.

See FÉTIS, "Biographie Universelle des Musiciens."

Foggini, fod-jee′nee, (PIETRO FRANCESCO,) an Italian scholar and priest, born at Florence in 1713. He held high offices at Rome in the gift of the popes, and became keeper of the Vatican Library in 1775. He wrote several theological treatises, and published a famous manuscript of Virgil, (1741,) which is or was preserved in the Medicean Library, Florence. Died in 1783.

See "Elogio di P. F. Foggini," Florence, 1784.

Fogliani, fōl-yä′nee, or **Fogliano,** fōl-yä′no, [Lat. FOLIA′NUS,] (LUIGI,) an Italian writer on music, born at Módena; died about 1540.

Foglietta, fol-yĕt′tä, or **Foglieta,** fol-yä′tä, (UBERTO,) an admired Italian historian, born of a noble family in Genoa in 1518. In 1559 he issued at Rome a historical essay on the Republic of Genoa, which gave so much offence to the aristocracy that they condemned him to exile and confiscated his property. He found a liberal patron in Cardinal Este, who received him as an inmate of his house in Rome. Here he composed, in pure and elegant Latin, his most important work, a "History of Genoa from the Earliest Times to 1527," (1585,) on which he was employed at his death. He also wrote portions of the history of the emperor Charles V., and other works. Among the Italian writers of that age he is esteemed one of the most classical. Died in 1581.

See NICÉRON, "Mémoires;" TIRABOSCHI, "Storia della Letteratura Italiana."

Fogolino, fo-go-lee′no, (MARCELLO,) an excellent painter of the Venetian school, born at Vicenza, was living in 1530. He painted history and landscapes with equal skill. "The Adoration of the Magi" is called his master-piece.

Fo-Hi. See FOO-HEE.

Fohr, fōR, (KARL PHILIPP,) a German landscape-painter, born at Heidelberg in 1795, studied at Rome under Koch. Among his works are two pictures of rare excellence, one of which represents a rocky landscape with a waterfall. He was drowned in the Tiber in 1818.

See J. P. DIEFFENBACH, "Leben des Malers C. Fohr," 1823.

Foinard, fwä′nȧR′, (FRÉDÉRIC MAURICE,) a learned French priest, born at Conches about 1685, published a translation of Genesis with critical notes, and a few other works. Died in 1743.

Foisset, fwä′sȧ′, (JEAN LOUIS SÉVERIN,) a French author, born at Bligny-sous-Beaune in 1796. In 1820 he was engaged as assistant editor of the "Biographie Universelle," for which he wrote a great number of articles, including those on Mirabeau and Petrarch. Died in 1822.

Foix, de, deh fwä, (CATHERINE,) Queen of Navarre, born in 1470, was the daughter and heiress of Gaston de Foix, Prince de Viane, and Madeleine of France. She was married in 1484 to Jean d'Albret, to whom she brought Navarre as her dowry. She was a great-grandmother of the famous Henry of Navarre. Died in 1517.

Foix, de, (GASTON II.,) COMTE, succeeded his father in 1315. He rendered important services to the French king in the war against the English, (1337.) Died in 1343.

Foix, de, (GASTON III.,) COMTE, Vicomte de Béarn, born in 1331, was a son of Gaston II., and was surnamed PHŒBUS. He married Agnes, a daughter of the King of Navarre and a sister of Charles the Bad. During the revolt of La Jacquerie, 1358, he assisted in the rescue of the dauphin. He afterwards waged with success a war against Count d'Armagnac. His ruling passion was the love of the chase, on which he wrote a treatise, called "Miroir de Phébus des desduicts de la Chasse." According to Froissart, he was a brave, violent, and magnificent representative of the age of chivalry. He died, without an heir, in 1391, and left his domain to the King of France.

Foix, de, (GASTON IV.,) succeeded his father, Jean de Grailly, in 1436. He married a daughter of Juan II. of Aragon and Navarre, who in 1455 appointed him successor to the throne of Navarre. He was a minister of Charles VII. of France, and an ally of Louis XI. Died in 1472.

His son GASTON, Prince de Viane, married Madeleine, a daughter of Charles VII. of France, and died in 1470.

Foix, de, (GASTON,) Duc de Nemours, a brave French prince, born in 1489, was a son of Jean de Foix, Viscount of Narbonne, and the nephew of Louis XII. of France, who in 1505 created him Duc de Nemours. In 1512 he commanded the army of Italy with brilliant success against the Spaniards, and in the same year, after he had won the great victory of Ravenna, he was killed in the pursuit. Louis XII., on hearing of his loss, said he would gladly give up every inch of Italian ground if he could thus restore his nephew to life.

See BRANTÔME, "Vies des grands Capitaines."

Foix, de, (GERMAINE,) Queen of Aragon, born about 1488, was a niece of Louis XII. of France. She was married in 1506 to Ferdinand V. of Castile and Aragon, her grand-uncle. She had one son, who died in infancy. Died in 1538.

Foix, de, (LOUIS,) a French architect and engineer, born in Paris, was employed by Philip II. of Spain; and it is supposed he was one of the architects of the Escurial. He erected the remarkable tower of Cordouan, at the mouth of the Garonne, used as a light-house, which was commenced in 1584 and finished in 1610. It is one hundred and eighty feet high, and is regarded as the most magnificent light-house erected in modern times.

Foix, de, (MARC ANTOINE,) a French Jesuit, born at the château de Fabas in 1627, was noted as a preacher and wrote a few learned treatises, one of which is entitled the "Art of Preaching the Word of God." Died in 1687.

Foix, de, (ODET.) See LAUTREC.

Foix, de, (PAUL,) an eminent French jurist and statesman, born in 1528, was descended from the noble family of Foix. After a profound study of law, he was appointed a judge in the Parliament of Paris. By counselling moderation towards the Protestants in 1559, he rendered himself obnoxious to some persons in power, and in 1561 resigned his office. He became a councillor of state about 1565, was employed by Charles IX. as ambassador to England, Venice, etc., and was considered one of the ablest negotiators of his time. In 1576 he was made Archbishop of Toulouse. Died in 1584.

See DE THOU, "Historia sui Temporis;" SISMONDI, "Histoire des Français;" MONTAIGNE, "Essais;" MARC ANTOINE MURET, "Oratio in funere P. Foxii," 1584.

Foix, de, (RAIMOND ROGER,) COMTE, an able French captain, succeeded his father in 1188. In 1191 he led his vassals in a crusade against the infidels in Palestine. After his return he took arms in defence of the Albigenses, but without success. He died in 1222, and left his domain to his son, Roger Bernard.

Foix, de, (ROGER,) COMTE, a French nobleman, inherited his title and estate in 1070. He joined the crusade and went to Palestine in 1095. Died in 1125.

Foix, de, (ROGER BERNARD II.,) COMTE, surnamed THE GREAT, was an ally of Raymond, Count of Toulouse. He waged war against the crusaders who, under De Montfort, invaded the county of Foix, and was excommunicated by the pope. Died in 1241.

Foix, de, (ROGER BERNARD III.,) COMTE, a grandson of the preceding, was distinguished as a poet. He became Comte de Foix in 1265. Died in 1302.

Folard, de, deh fo'lȧr', (JEAN CHARLES,) a French officer and tactician, born at Avignon in 1669, entered the army at an early age, and made himself proficient in tactics and engineering. He served as aide-de-camp to the Duc de Vendôme in Italy in 1702, and was wounded at the battle of Cassano in 1705. The freedom with which he offered advice sometimes gave offence to his superiors ; but the court twice recognized the value of his services by granting him a pension. In 1709 he was severely wounded at Malplaquet. He accompanied Charles XII. of Sweden in his last campaign, (1718.) Folard acquired reputation by his version of the History of Polybius, with Commentaries, (6 vols., 1727–30,) which illustrate the tactics of the ancients. Died in 1752.

See "Mémoires pour servir à l'Histoire de la Vie de Folard," Paris, 1753; "Nouvelle Biographie Générale."

Folengo, fo-len'go, (GIAMBATTISTA,) an Italian monk and scholar, born at Mantua about 1500. He wrote a few Commentaries on Scripture, which were approved by the Protestants. Died in 1559.

Folengo, (TEOFILO,) (better known by the name MERLINO COCAJO or COCCAI,) a whimsical Italian poet, a brother of the preceding, was born of a noble family near Mantua in 1491. He entered a Benedictine convent at the age of sixteen, but soon exchanged that for a dissolute life. He was gifted with vivacity and great facility in versification, and published licentious and burlesque poems, in a style which he called Macaronic, the language being a mixture of Latin and Italian. He returned to the convent in 1526. Died in 1544.

See NICÉRON, "Mémoires;" GINGUENÉ, "Histoire littéraire d'Italie;" A. DALMISTRO, "Elogio di T. Folengo," 1803.

Fo'ley, (JOHN HENRY,) an eminent sculptor, born in Dublin in 1818, studied in the Royal Academy of London. His "Ino and Bacchus" (1840) placed him in the first rank of modern British sculptors. Among his works are "Lear and Cordelia," "Venus rescuing Æneas," (1842,) "Egeria," (1856,) a statue of Selden, a statue of John Hampden at the new palace of Westminster, and a bronze statue of Viscount Sir H. Hardinge at Calcutta.

Foley, (Sir THOMAS,) an English admiral, born in Pembrokeshire in 1757. He distinguished himself as captain at the battle of Cape Saint Vincent in 1797, and had the honour of leading the fleet of Nelson into action at the battle of the Nile, in August, 1798. He took a prominent part in the battle of Copenhagen, (1801,) and became a vice-admiral in 1812. At this battle Sir Hyde Parker signalled to Lord Nelson to discontinue the action ; but Nelson, putting the glass to his blind eye, said to Foley, "You know, Foley, I have only one eye, and have a right to be blind sometimes. I really do not see the signal." Died in 1833.

Folianus. See FOGLIANI.

Folieta. See FOGLIETTA.

Foligno. See FREZZI, (FEDERIGO.)

Folkema, fol'keh-mȧ,(JACOB,) an able Dutch engraver, born at Dokkum in 1692. He engraved plates for books after the designs of Picart, and portraits of eminent men. Died in 1767.

Folkes, fōlks, (MARTIN,) F.R.S., an eminent English antiquary, born in London in 1690, excelled in mathematics and philosophy, was chosen Fellow of the Royal Society in 1713, and succeeded Sir Hans Sloane as president of the same in 1741. He wrote several excellent treatises on ancient monuments and coins, and rendered important services to science. In 1750 he became president of the Society of Antiquaries. In 1742 he was chosen a member of the Academy of Sciences at Paris. Among his works is a "Dissertation on the Weights and Values of Ancient Coins," (1736.) Died in 1754.

Follen, fol'len, (ADOLF LUDWIG,) a German poet and scholar, brother of Charles Follen, noticed in the next article, was born at Giessen in 1794. He published in 1819 his "Free Voices of Fresh Youth," and in 1827 his "Picture-Gallery of German Poetry," both of which enjoy great popularity. He also made several excellent translations from the Latin, Greek, and Italian. Died in 1855.

See LONGFELLOW's "Poets and Poetry of Europe."

Fol'len, (CHARLES THEODORE CHRISTIAN,) born at Romrod, in Germany, in 1795, was educated at Giessen. His youthful zeal for liberty having subjected him to persecution from the government, he left his native land in 1820, and, after a visit to Paris, he found a home in Switzerland, where he was chosen, about 1821, professor of law in the University of Bâle. In 1824 the Holy Alliance demanded that he should be delivered up, and he escaped only by a sudden departure to Paris and by emigrating to the United States. Here he applied himself with success to the study of the English language. By the favour of La Fayette, he obtained influential friends, and was employed as German tutor at Harvard. He studied divinity with Dr. Channing in 1827, was admitted to the ministry in 1828, and officiated as teacher in the divinity school at Cambridge. From 1831 to 1834 he was professor of German literature at Harvard. In 1836 and 1837 he had charge of the First Unitarian Church in New York, where he gave offence by speaking against slavery. In 1839 he accepted a call from the church of East Lexington, Massachusetts. In the passage from New York to his home, in January, 1840, he lost his life by the burning of the steamer Lexington.

See a Memoir of his life, by his wife, ELIZA LEE FOLLEN, 1841.

e as k; ç as s; ḡ hard; ġ as j; G, H, K, guttural; N, nasal; R, trilled; s as z; ŧh as in this.   ($\mathbb{KF}$ See Explanations, p. 23.)

Follen, (ELIZA LEE,) wife of the preceding, born at Boston in 1787, was originally named Cabot. She was the author of "Twilight Stories," "Little Songs," and other popular works for children, and was for several years editor of the "Child's Friend." Died in 1859.

See GRISWOLD's "Female Poets of America."

Fol′lett, (Sir WILLIAM WEBB,) an able English lawyer, born at Topsham in 1798, began to practise law about 1823, and rapidly rose to eminence. He was returned to Parliament for Exeter by the Conservatives in 1835, acted a short time as solicitor-general under Sir Robert Peel, (1834–35,) and was twice re-elected to Parliament, in 1837 and in 1841. He was again appointed solicitor-general in 1841, and became attorney-general in 1844. Died in London in 1845.

See a notice of Sir W. Follett in "Blackwood's Magazine" for January, 1846.

Folleville, de, deh fol′vèl′, (GUYOT, ḡe′o′,) ABBÉ, a French priest, who in 1793 appeared in the royalist army of La Vendée and gave out that he was the Bishop of Agra, sent by the pope as apostolic vicar. He was received without distrust, and his presence excited great enthusiasm among the army ; but before long a brief from the pope informed the generals that he was an impostor. However, they kept the secret from the soldiers, and he continued to act his part until the republicans captured him and put him to death, in 1794.

Folli, fol′lee, or **Fuoli,** foo-o′lee, (CECILIO,) born at Fanano in 1615, was for many years professor of anatomy at Venice.

Folli, (FRANCESCO,) an Italian physician and writer, born in 1624 ; died in 1685.

Folo, fo′lo, (GIOVANNI,) an eminent Italian engraver, born at Bassano in 1764, worked at Rome, and imitated the style of Raphael Morghen. He engraved works of several Italian masters. Died at Rome in 1836.

Folquet, fol′kà′, or **Foulques,** fook, a French troubadour and prelate, born at Marseilles about 1160. He was appointed Bishop of Toulouse in 1205, and became a cruel persecutor of the Albigenses. Dante has, however, given him a place in his "Paradiso." Died in 1231.

See LONGFELLOW's "Poets and Poetry of Europe."

Foltz, folts, (PHILIPP,) a German painter, and professor in the Academy of Arts at Munich, born at Bingen, on the Rhine, in 1805. He painted in fresco, in the royal palace at Munich, a number of illustrations from Bürger's poems and Schiller's ballads. Among his works is a large oil-picture of "Otho of Bavaria departing from his Father's Palace for the Throne of Greece."

Folz, or **Volz,** folts, written also **Folcz,** (HANS,) a celebrated German poet and Protestant Reformer, born at Worms in 1479. He wrote lyrics, Carnival pieces, (*Fastnachtspiele*) and tales in rhyme.

Fonblanque, fon-blank′, (ALBANY W.,) an eminent English journalist and political writer, a son of the following, was born in London in 1797. He studied law, but never practised it. About 1822 he succeeded Leigh Hunt as editor of the "Examiner," a Liberal weekly journal, the previous high character of which was maintained by the caustic wit and literary abilities of Mr. Fonblanque. A selection of his editorial articles appeared under the title of "England under Seven Administrations," (3 vols., 1837.) He ceased to edit that journal in 1846, and was chosen director of the statistical department of the Board of Trade in 1852.

See R. H. HORNE, "New Spirit of the Age," 1844.

Fonblanque, (JOHN DE GRENIER,) an eminent English lawyer, born in 1759, descended from a French Protestant family, became senior king's counsel and senior bencher of the Society of the Middle Temple. He wrote an able and learned "Treatise on Equity," (1793,) which had a wide circulation and was considered as authoritative by the English courts. Died in 1837.

Fonblanque, (JOHN SAMUEL MARTIN,) a son of the preceding, born about 1787, became commissioner of bankrupts. He published, in 1825, "Bankrupt Statutes," and, with J. A. Paris, M.D., "Medical Jurisprudence," (1823.) Died in 1865 or 1866.

Foncemagne, de, deh fôNss′mäN′, (ÉTIENNE Lauréault—lō′rà′o′,) a French savant, born at Orléans in 1694. He was received in the Academy of Inscriptions in 1722, and chosen a member of the French Academy in 1737. He was eminent for learning, virtue, and talents, and distinguished himself in a literary war with Voltaire in relation to the "Testament politique" of Richelieu, which Voltaire thought was a fabrication. He wrote many able dissertations, inserted in the Memoirs of the Academy of Inscriptions. Died in 1779.

See SABATIER, "Les trois Siècles de la Littérature Française ;" DE CHABANON, "Éloge de M. de Foncemagne," 1780.

Fondolo, fon′do-lo, (GABRINO,) an Italian, who by treachery obtained the sovereignty of Cremona in 1406. He was executed by the Duke of Milan in 1420.

Fonfrède, fôN′îRàd′, (HENRI,) a French journalist, a son of the following, was born at Bordeaux in 1788. He founded at Bordeaux, in 1820, a journal called "La Tribune," which was soon suppressed by the government. He wrote spirited political articles for other journals, and supported liberal conservative principles. His works were published in 10 vols., 1844. Died in 1841.

See E. FERBOS, "Éloge de Henri Fonfrède ;" CHARLES CAMPAN, "Éloge historique de H. Fonfrède," 1845.

Fonfrède, (JEAN BAPTISTE **Boyer**—bwä′yà′,) an eloquent French Girondist, born at Bordeaux in 1766, was a brother-in-law of Ducos. He was elected to the Convention in 1792, and was president of that body in May, 1793. His career was short and memorable. In talents he was ranked next to Vergniaud, Guadet, and Gensonné. He was imprisoned in October, and declined to escape when an opportunity was offered, saying he would share the fate of Ducos. He was executed in October, 1793.

See LAMARTINE's "History of the Girondists," books xxxi. and xlvii.

Fonk, fonk, (PETER ANTON,) a German merchant, born near Cleves in 1781. He was convicted of murder at Treves in 1822, but was pardoned by the king, because his guilt was not clearly proved. Died in 1832.

Fons. See LA FONS.

Fonseca, da, dä fon-sä′kä, (ANTONIO,) a Portuguese theologian, born in Lisbon in 1517, obtained in 1544 the chair of theology in Coimbra. Having gained distinction as a pulpit orator, he became preacher to the king, John III. Died in 1588.

Fonseca, da, (GABRIEL,) a Portuguese physician, born at Lamego, was chief physician of Pope Innocent X. Died in 1668.

Fonseca, da, (PEDRO,) a Portuguese Jesuit and writer, born at Cortizada in 1528, was eminent as a professor of philosophy in the University of Evora, and was surnamed THE PORTUGUESE ARISTOTLE. He was employed in important affairs by Pope Gregory XIII. His principal works are "Institutes of Dialectics," (1564,) and a "Commentary on the Metaphysics of Aristotle," (4 vols., 1572–94.) He is reputed the inventor of the "Sciencia Media," a mode of reconciling free will with predestination. Died in 1599.

See BARBOSA MACHADO, "Bibliotheca Lusitana."

Fonseca, da, (PEDRO JOZÉ,) a Portuguese philologist, was the principal author or editor of the "Dictionary of the Portuguese Language" published by the Academy of Lisbon in 1793. Died in 1816.

Fonseca, da, fon-sä′kä, (ELEANORA **Pimentel**—pe-mên-têl′,) MARCHIONESS, a beautiful and gifted Italian lady, born in Naples in 1768, became the wife of the Marquis of Fonseca in 1784. She sympathized with the French republicans, and was an active adherent of the popular party in Naples. While the latter was in the ascendant, she edited a public journal. In 1799 the royalists again prevailed, and condemned her to a felon's death. She was hung in 1799.

Fonseca, de, dä fon-sä′kä, (JUAN RODRIGUEZ,) a bigoted Spanish prelate, born at Toro about 1452, became Bishop of Palencia and of Burgos, and a councillor of Queen Isabella. He patronized Torquemada, and opposed the enterprise of Columbus, whom he called a visionary and treated with persistent malignity. Died in 1524.

See CHARLEVOIX, "Histoire de Saint-Domingue ;" HERRERA, "Historia."

Fonseca Figueiredo y Sousa, de, dä fon-sä′kä fe-gà-rà′e-do e sō′sä, (JOZÉ MARIA,) a Portuguese writer,

---

ā, ē, ī, ō, ū, ȳ, *long;* à, è, ò, same, less prolonged; ă, ĕ, ĭ, ŏ, ŭ, ў, *short;* a, e, i, o, *obscure;* fär, fàll, fàt; mêt; nŏt; gōōd; mōōn;

born at Evora in 1690, was eminent as a theologian and diplomatist. He was aulic councillor of the emperor Charles VI. Died in 1760.

See BARBOSA MACHADO, "Bibliotheca Lusitana."

Fonseca Soares, de, dà fon-sā'kä so-ā'rēs, (AN-TONIO,) or **Antonio das Chagas,** (däs shä'gas,) a Portuguese theologian and poet, born at Vidigueira in 1631. He was noted for his ascetic piety, and wrote several devotional works. Died in 1682.

See BARBOSA MACHADO, "Bibliotheca Lusitana ;" M. GODINHO, "Vida de F. A. das Chagas," 1687.

Fontaine, or **Fontaine des Bertins,** fôn'tăn' dà bĕR'tăn', (ALEXIS,) an eminent French geometer, born at Claveison, in Dauphiny, about 1705, came to Paris at an early age, where he became intimate with Clairaut and Maupertuis. In 1733 the Academy of Sciences was opened to him, and in 1734 he published his famous memoir on the problem of "Tautochrones," which had been resolved by Huyghens and Newton by different methods, and in which he was afterwards surpassed by Lagrange. He made several important discoveries in mathematics and dynamics. Hearing Nollet read in the Academy a long essay on the value of various commodities, Fontaine said, "This man knows the value of everything except time." Died in 1771.

See CONDORCET, "Éloge de Fontaine ;" QUÉRARD, "La France Littéraire."

Fontaine, fôn'tăn', (CHARLES,) a French poet, born in Paris in 1515, translated Ovid's "Epistles" into verse, and wrote mediocre odes, epigrams, etc. Died about 1590.

Fontaine, (NICOLAS,) a pious Jansenist writer, born in Paris in 1625. He joined the recluses of Port-Royal in 1645, and shared the labours and persecutions of Arnauld, Nicole, and Sacy, with whom he was confined in the Bastille. He left interesting "Memoirs of Port-Royal," (2 vols., 1736.) Died in 1709.

Fontaine, (PIERRE FRANÇOIS LÉONARD,) a distinguished French architect, born at Pontoise on the 20th of September, 1762. He studied in Rome, and became in his youth the friend and associate of Charles Percier, and formed with him a partnership which was only dissolved by death. About 1801 he was appointed architect of the Tuileries. He was afterwards employed in the extension or restoration of the palaces of the Louvre, Saint-Cloud, and Fontainebleau. He erected the triumphal arch of the Carrousel, (1807,) and united the Tuileries with the Louvre. He was admitted into the Institute in 1812, and received the title of first architect of Napoleon in 1813. With Percier he published "Palaces and other Modern Edifices designed at Rome," (1798,) and a successful work "On Interior Decorations," (1812.) He retained the place of chief architect under Louis XVIII. and his successors until 1848. Died in 1853.

See "Journal des Beaux-Arts," 1842; "Nouvelle Biographie Générale."

Fontaine, La. See LA FONTAINE.

Fontaine-Malherbe, fôn'tăn' mǎl'ǎRb', (JEAN,) a French poet, born near Coutances about 1740, wrote two poems which were crowned by the French Academy, viz., "The Rapidity of Life," (1766,) and an "Epistle to the Poor," (1768.) Died in 1780.

Fontaines. See DESFONTAINES.

Fontana, fon-tā'nä, (ANNIBAL,) an Italian engraver on precious stones, born in Milan in 1540, acquired a high reputation in his art. Died in 1587.

Fontana, (CARLO,) a celebrated Italian architect, born at Bruciato, near Como, in 1634, was a pupil of Bernini. He passed nearly all his life in Rome, and was patronized by several popes. Under Clement X. he constructed the grand fountain in front of Saint Peter's. Among his numerous works are the Grimani palace, the Bolognetti palace, the theatre Tordinona, and the portal of Santa Maria in Trastevere. He wrote ample and valuable descriptions of the Church of Saint Peter, (1694,) and of the Coliseum, (1725.) Died at Rome in 1714.

See QUATREMÈRE DE QUINCY, "Dictionnaire d'Architecture ;" FONTENAI, "Dictionnaire des Artistes."

Fontana, (DOMENICO,) an Italian architect and engineer of celebrity, was born at Mili, near Lake Como, in 1543, and went to Rome at the age of twenty. His patron, Pope Sixtus V., employed him as chief architect

in several great works, the most memorable of which was the erection of the Egyptian obelisk in front of Saint Peter's Church. About five hundred engineers having offered their respective plans, that of Fontana was preferred. This great triumph of mechanical skill, which was accomplished in 1586 amidst the applause of the populace, was rewarded by a title of nobility and a large pension. Fontana afterwards raised large obelisks in the Piazza del Popolo and in front of San Giovanni Laterano. He built the palace of the Lateran, the Vatican Library, and the Quirinal Palace, Rome. In 1592 he went to Naples, where he designed the grand royal palace. Died at Naples in 1607.

See TICOZZI, "Dizionario ;" QUATREMÈRE DE QUINCY, "Dictionnaire d'Architecture ;" "Nouvelle Biographie Générale."

Fontana, (FELICE,) a learned Italian philosopher and naturalist, born at Pomarolo, in the Tyrol, in April, 1730, was a brother of Gregorio, noticed below, and was educated in the best schools of Italy. He was for some time professor of philosophy in Pisa, and afterwards lived in Florence, where he was patronized by the grand duke Leopold. By the order of this prince, he prepared anatomical models in wax, and a fine cabinet or museum of natural history and philosophy, which is one of the ornaments of Florence. He wrote many ingenious treatises on chemistry, physics, and physiology. He died in 1805, and was buried in Florence by the side of Galileo.

See MANGILI, "Elogio di F. Fontana," 1813; "Nouvelle Biographie Générale."

Fontana, (FRANCESCO,) a Neapolitan astronomer, published "New Observations on Celestial and Earthly Things," (1646.) Died in 1656.

Fontana, (FRANCESCO,) an Italian architect, a descendant of Domenico Fontana, was employed in 1705 in the erection of the column of Antoninus Pius on Monte Citorio, in Rome.

Fontana, (FRANCESCO LUIGI,) a learned Italian cardinal and writer, born in 1750, accompanied the captive pope to Paris in 1804. Died in 1822.

Fontana, (GAETANO,) an Italian priest and astronomer, born at Módena in 1645. He cultivated astronomy with success, corresponded with Cassini, and published "Institutio Physico-Astronomica," ("Physical and Astronomical Institutes," 1695.) Cassini said the observations of Fontana were the most exact of all that were sent to him. Died in 1719.

Fontana, (GIOVANNI,) an able Italian architect, born at Mili in 1540, was the brother of Domenico, above named. He was at one time architect of Saint Peter's Church, Rome, and was especially eminent as a hydraulic engineer. Died in 1614.

Fontana, (GIULIO CESARE,) a son of Domenico, was an architect, and a native of Rome. Among his best works is the Museo Borbonico at Naples. He flourished about 1600.

Fontana, (GREGORIO,) an eminent Italian mathematician, brother of Felice, noticed above, was born near Roveredo in 1735. In 1763 he became professor of logic and metaphysics in the University of Pavia, in which, a few years later, he obtained the chair of high mathematics. Though he attempted no large work, he left numerous treatises on the latter science, and translated several scientific works from the English. Died in 1803.

See G. B. SAVIOLI, "Elogio di G. Fontana," 1804.

Fontana, (LAVINIA,) an excellent painter, born at Bologna in 1552, was a daughter of Prospero Fontana, noticed below. She was married to an artist named Zappi, and worked in Rome with great success, especially in portraits. She was appointed painter to Gregory XIII. Some of her portraits were attributed to Guido. Among her works are a "Madonna," "The Miracle of the Loaves," and a "Holy Family." Died in 1614.

See LANZI, "History of Painting in Italy."

Fontana, (PROSPERO,) an Italian painter of high reputation, born in Bologna in 1512, was a pupil of Imola and Vasari. He was presented as an excellent portrait-painter by Michael Angelo to Pope Julius III. He also painted historical subjects in fresco, with which he adorned several churches in Rome and Bologna. He excelled in design and composition. Among his pupils were his daughter Lavinia and the Caracci. Died at Rome in 1597.

See LANZI, "History of Painting in Italy."

Fontana, (PUBLIO,) an Italian poet, born at Paluccio, in the diocese of Brescia, in 1548. He wrote the "Apotheosis of Tasso," a poem which extended his reputation through all Italy. His most popular work is "Delphinis," a Latin poem, (1582.) "Fontana is one of the modern poets," says J. Victor Rossi, "who have approached nearest to Virgil in beauty of imagery and harmony of diction." Died in 1609.

See TIRABOSCHI, "Storia della Letteratura Italiana."

Fontanella, fon-tä-nel'lä, (FRANCESCO,) an Italian philologist and classical scholar, born in Venice in 1768. He published, besides other works, "Universal Orthography of the Italian Language," ("Ortografia enciclopedica universale della Lingua Italiana," 1826.) He became professor of Greek and Hebrew in Venice. Died in 1827.

See his Autobiography, entitled "Vita di F. Fontanella, scritta da lui medesimo," 1825.

Fontanelle, (JEAN GASPARD DUBOIS.) See DUBOIS.

Fontanelli, fon-tä-nel'lee, (ALFONSO VINCENZO,) MARQUIS OF, an eminent Italian scholar and linguist, born at Reggio in 1706. He was employed as ambassador by the Duke of Módena. Died in 1777.

Fontanes, de, dęh fôn'tĕn', (JEAN PIERRE MARCELLIN,) born at Geneva in 1721. His ancestors had been exiled from France as Protestants. He was employed as inspector of manufactures in Poitou, and wrote treatises on agriculture. Died in 1774.

Fontanes, de, (LOUIS,) COUNT, a French statesman and author, son of the preceding, was born at Niort (Poitou) in 1757, and came to Paris at an early age. In 1778 he began his career as a poet by the "Forest of Navarre," a descriptive poem, which was favourably received, and was followed by "Le Verger," ("The Orchard,") and an "Essay on Astronomy," (1789.) The Directory having proscribed him and expelled him from the Institute, he took refuge in England in 1797. In January or February, 1800, by the order and under the auspices of the First Consul Bonaparte, he pronounced a funeral eulogy on Washington, which gained for the orator an exalted reputation, and opened to him a second time the doors of the Institute, (Académie Française,) in 1803. It is worthy of remark that the author of this noble and eloquent tribute, in analyzing a character so heroic and so admirably balanced as that of Washington, gives the moderation and good sense the pre-eminence over all his other virtues. He became a member of the corps législatif in 1802, and president of that body in January, 1804. In this position he maintained his reputation by his elegant addresses in reply to the annual speeches from the throne. During the empire he was raised to the rank of a peer of France, and chosen grand master of the Imperial University in 1808. He was appointed a senator in 1810. It appears that he had great influence with Bonaparte, who frequently admitted him to private interviews and invited him to his table. One day, as they were conversing on literature, Bonaparte said, "You like Voltaire : you are wrong : he is a busybody, an incendiary, a scoffer. He has sapped by ridicule the foundations of all authority, divine and human ; he has caused the revolution that has *dishonoured and ruined us.* You laugh, monsieur ; but will you laugh when I tell you that among twenty of my young officers nineteen had each a volume of this demon in his valise ?" He was admitted to the Chamber of Peers at the restoration. "He was," says Châteaubriand, "my guide in the world of letters, and his friendship was one of the honours of my life. The school founded by Boileau, Racine, and Fénelon ended in him." Died in Paris in March, 1821.

See VILLEMAIN, "Éloge de Fontanes," 1821 ; SAINTE-BEUVE, "Portraits littéraires ;" CHÂTEAUBRIAND, "Mémoires d'Outre-Tombe ;" "Nouvelle Biographie Générale."

Fontaney, de, dęh fôn'tä'nậ', (JEAN,) a French Jesuit and astronomer, who in 1685 was sent by Colbert to China on a mission partly scientific and partly religious. He and his companions were the pioneers of the French missionary enterprise in China. After he had laboured

at Nankin and other places, he returned to France in 1699. He was living in 1720.

Fontanges, de, dęh fôn'tônzh', (MARIE ANGÉLIQUE **Scoraille de Roussille**—sko'rä'yę dęh roo'sĕl',) DUCHESSE, a beautiful French lady, born in 1661, was the mistress of Louis XIV., over whom she possessed great influence for a few years. Died in 1681.

Fontanieu, fôn'tä'ne-ŭh',(GASPARD MOÏSE,) a French writer, born about 1700, was author of a "History of Charles VII.," (still in manuscript.) Died in 1767.

Fontanini, fon-tä-nee'nee, (GIUSTO,) a learned Italian critic and antiquary, born at Saint Daniel, in Friuli, in 1666, was educated for the church, and lived mostly in Rome. Clement XI. appointed him professor of eloquence in the Roman University. In 1706 he published his famous "Treatise on Italian Eloquence," which contains in the third part a Catalogue *(Bibliotheca)* of classic Italian works, with notes. He gave an improved and enlarged edition in 1736. Apostolo Zeno wrote an excellent critique on this work. Fontanini wrote also other treatises on various subjects, and left unfinished a "Literary History of Friuli." Clement XI. gave him several rich benefices, and Benedict XIII. made him titular Archbishop of Ancyra. Died in 1736.

See D. FONTANINI, "Vita di Fontanini," Venice, 1755 ; FABRONI, "Vitæ Italorum doctrina excellentium ;" TIPALDO, "Biografia degli Italiani illustri."

Fonte, fon'tå, (MODERATA,) an Italian lady, distinguished for talent, born at Venice in 1555. She married Filippo Giorgi, a lawyer, about 1572. Her memory is said to have been extraordinary. She wrote "Il Floridoro," and other poems. Her original name was MODESTA POZZO, (pot'so.) Died in 1592.

Fontanon, fôn'tä'nôn', (ANTOINE,) a French advocate and jurist, born in Auvergne, lived about 1580.

Fontanus or **Fonteyn,** fon'tìn', (NICOLAAS,) a Dutch physician and writer, lived at Amsterdam about 1620-40.

Fontenai, (JULIEN DE.) See COLDORÉ.

Fontenay. See COLDORÉ.

Fontenay, fônt'nậ', (LOUIS ABEL DE Bonafons—bo'nä'fôn',) usually called ABBÉ DE FONTENAY, a French Jesuit, born near Castres in 1737. He published a "Dictionary of Artists," (2 vols., 1777,) and several other works. Died in 1806.

Fontenay, MADAME. See CHIMAY.

Fontenay, (PIERRE CLAUDE,) a French Jesuit, born in Paris in 1663. On the death of Longueval he succeeded him as compiler of the "History of the Gallican Church," of which he finished the ninth and tenth volumes. Died in 1742.

Fontenay, de, dęh fônt'nậ', (J. B. Blain—blän,) an excellent French painter of flowers and fruits, born at Caen in 1654, was a pupil and son-in-law of Baptiste Monnoyer. He worked in Paris, and was much employed by Louis XIV. at Versailles, Marly, etc. He is said to have had no rival except Van Huysum and Monnoyer, the latter of whom he equalled. Died in 1715.

See D'ARGENVILLE, "Vies des Peintres Français."

Fontenelle, de, dęh fôn'tęh-nĕl', [Fr. pron. fônt'nĕl',] (BERNARD le **Bovier**—lęh bo've-à',) a celebrated French author, born at Rouen, February 11, 1657, was a nephew of the famous poet Corneille. In the interval of one hundred years which elapsed from his birth to his death, the greatest French authors began or ended their career. And though many of these illustrious men surpassed Fontenelle, either by the force, the originality, or the elevation of their genius, no one, perhaps, has been more admired or more influential. He owed this eminence chiefly to the variety of his talents, to the popular and congenial subjects on which he exercised them, to his matchless social qualities, and to an uncommon share of those graceful endowments for which the French are distinguished. His writings and principles were in harmony with his conduct, which was remarkable for moderation and self-control.

The dramas and pastorals with which he opened his literary career were not very successful. His "Dialogues of the Dead," published in 1683, formed the beginning of his celebrity, which was greatly increased by his "Discourse on the Plurality of Worlds," (1686.) In the latter he displays his peculiar talent for rendering science at-

ā, ē, ī, ō, ū, ÿ, *long;* à, ê, ò, same, less prolonged; ă, ĕ, ĭ, ŏ, ŭ, ÿ, *short;* ą, ę, į, ǫ, *obscure;* fär, fåll, fåt; mĕt; nŏt; gŏŏd; mŏŏn;

tractive, by blending useful instruction with ingenious amusement and by conducting the reader through easy paths to extensive, luminous, and profound views of the beautiful and sublime. With great spirit and vivacity he maintains the "fascinating paradox" that the planets and fixed stars are populous worlds. He also wrote a popular "History of Oracles," for which Van Dale's work supplied the crude materials. In 1691 he became a member of the French Academy, and in 1699 he was chosen perpetual secretary of the Academy of Sciences. His "Essay on the Geometry of the Infinite" (1727) is among his most admired productions. On presenting it to the Regent of France, Fontenelle said, "*There* is a book which only eight men in Europe are capable of understanding; and the author is *not* one of that number!" Died in January, 1757.

The mind of Fontenelle was characterized by a philosophic spirit and a union of judgment with subtilty of intellect, to which was often joined a strange fondness for paradox. He professed to adopt these two axioms,— "that everything is possible, and that everybody is right." In the opinion of Voltaire, Fontenelle was the most universal genius of his age. He once said, "If I had my hand full of truths, I should take good care not to open it." During a period of forty years, he composed eulogies on about seventy members of the Academy of Sciences. This collection of "Éloges" is esteemed one of the best books in the language.

See CHARMA, "Biographie de Fontenelle," 1846; TRUBLET, "Mémoires de Fontenelle;" FLOURENS, "Fontenelle, Histoire de ses Travaux et de sa Vie;" GARAT, "Éloge de Fontenelle;" SAINTE-BEUVE, "Causeries du Lundi," tome iii.; "Nouvelle Biographie Générale;" "Biographie Universelle."

Fontenu, de, deh fôNt′nü′, (LOUIS FRANÇOIS,) a French abbé, born of a noble family in 1667, visited Rome in 1700. He lived mostly in Paris, and was a member of the Academy of Inscriptions and Belles-Lettres, which he enriched with learned memoirs on antiquarian subjects. Died in 1759.

Fontette. See FEVRET DE FONTETTE.

Fonteyn. See FONTANUS.

Fonteyraud, fôN′tạ′rō′, (ALCIDE,) a French writer on political economy, born in the island of Mauritius in 1822; died in Paris in 1849.

Fonti, fon′tee, [Lat. FON′TIUS,] (BARTOLOMMEO,) an Italian philologist, born in 1445; died in 1513.

Fontrailles, de, deh fôN′trȧl′ or fôN′trȧ′ye, (LOUIS d'Astarac—dȧs′tȧ′rȧk′,) Marquis de Marestang, a French gentleman, remarkable for his factious intrigues and talents. He was an enemy of Richelieu and a friend of Cinq-Mars, whose fate he would have shared if he had not fled to England. He died in 1677.

Fonvielle, fôN′ve-êl′, (BERNARD FRANÇOIS ANNE,) a French royalist and writer on politics, etc., was born at Toulouse in 1759. He was a secret agent of the Bourbons in 1794. Died in 1837.

See his Autobiography, entitled "Mes Mémoires historiques sur la Révolution," 4 vols., 1824.

Foot, (SOLOMON,) an American Senator and lawyer, born in Addison county, Vermont, in 1802. He was elected to Congress in 1842, and again in 1844, by the Whigs. In 1850 he was chosen a Senator of the United States. Having joined the Republican party in 1854, he was re-elected a Senator in 1856. Died in 1866.

Foote, foot, (ANDREW HULL,) a distinguished American rear-admiral, born at New Haven, Connecticut, in September, 1806. He entered the navy about 1822, became a lieutenant in 1830, and a commander in 1852. In 1856 he was sent to China, and captured by storm a fort near Canton, the garrison of which had fired on one of his boats. He was appointed flag-officer of the flotilla in the Mississippi River in September, 1861. He rendered important assistance to General Grant in the capture of Fort Henry and Fort Donelson in February, 1862, with seven gunboats which he commanded : he was disabled in the latter action by a wound in the ankle. In July, 1862, he was raised to the rank of rear-admiral. He succeeded Dupont in June, 1863, as commander of the South Atlantic squadron, employed in operations against Charleston, but died in New York in the same month. Admiral Foote was distinguished for his high moral worth as well as for his ardent patriotism. By his ex-

ample and precept he promoted total abstinence from spirituous liquors in the navy.

See HEADLEY, "Farragut and our Naval Commanders," 1867.

Foote, foot, (Sir EDWARD JAMES,) a British admiral, born in Kent in 1767. He commanded the fleet which blockaded Naples in 1799. Died in 1833.

Foote, (HENRY S.,) an American politician, born in Fauquier county, Virginia, in 1800. He studied law, and removed about 1826 to Mississippi, where he was elected to the Senate of the United States in 1847. In 1851 he was chosen Governor of Mississippi by the Union party, when Jefferson Davis was his competitor. He was a member of the Confederate Congress during the civil war.

Foote, (JESSE,) an English surgeon, born in 1744, wrote the "Life of John Hunter," professional treatises, and other works. Died in 1827.

Foote, (SAMUEL,) a witty English comedian, was born at Truro, in Cornwall, about 1720, and educated at Oxford. Having spent his estate in gaming and other vices, he was induced by necessity to resort to the stage in 1744. In 1747 he opened the Haymarket Theatre on his own account, being at the same time director, author, and actor. Here he represented with great success a series of satirical pieces and farces, among which were "Diversions of the Morning," "The Auction of Pictures," "The Minor," "The Englishman in Paris," (1753,) and "The Mayor of Garratt," (1764.) He possessed great talents for ridicule and mimicry, and excelled in colloquial wit, which he used at the expense of others. "For loud, obstreperous, broad-faced mirth," said Johnson, "I know not his equal." Died in 1777.

See WILLIAM COOKE, "Memoirs of Samuel Foote, with some of his Writings," 3 vols., 1805; JOHN FORSTER, "Historical and Biographical Essays;" "Quarterly Review" for October, 1854.

Foppa, fop′pȧ, (VINCENZO,) an Italian painter, born at Brescia about 1420, founded a flourishing school at Milan, which preceded that of Leonardo da Vinci. He excelled in perspective, and was a good master of design. Died in 1492.

See VASARI, "Lives of the Painters."

Foppens, fop′pens, (JOHANNES FRANS,) a bibliographer, born at Brussels in 1689, was professor of theology at Louvain. He wrote several works on Belgian history, also the "Bibliotheca Belgica," (2 vols., 1739,) treating of Belgian authors and their works. Died in 1761.

Forabosco, fo-rȧ-bos′ko, (GIROLAMO,) a Venetian portrait-painter, born about 1600; died after 1659.

Forbes, for′bes, (ALEXANDER,) Lord Forbes of Pitsligo, a Scottish Jacobite, born about 1678, was supposed to be the original of the Baron of Bradwardine in Scott's "Waverley." He fought for the Pretender at Culloden in 1746, after which he fled to France. Died in 1749.

Forbes, (ALEXANDER,) a British writer of the present era. He published in 1839 an esteemed "History of Upper and Lower California," which he had explored.

Forbes, (DUNCAN,) an eminent Scottish judge and patriot, born at Culloden in 1686, acquired a high reputation at the bar, and was for many years a member of the British Parliament, which he entered in 1722. After filling other high stations, he was appointed in 1737 lord president of the court of sessions, and rendered important services to the crown in the rebellion of 1745. He published "Thoughts on Religion, Natural and Revealed," (1735,) and other religious works. Warburton thought him one of the greatest men that Scotland had produced, "both as a judge, a patriot, and a Christian." Died in 1747.

See JOHN HILL BURTON, "Life of Duncan Forbes," 1847; CHAMBERS, "Biographical Dictionary of Eminent Scotsmen;" "Edinburgh Review" for February, 1816; "North British Review" for May, 1847.

Forbes, forbz, (EDWARD,) an eminent English naturalist, born in the Isle of Man in February, 1815. In 1832 he went to Edinburgh, where he studied zoology and botany. He made scientific excursions through various parts of Europe, and published his valuable discoveries in several treatises on Mollusca and other marine animals. He accepted in 1844 the professorship of botany in King's College, London, and distinguished himself by contributions to various departments of natural history. In 1854

€ as *k*; ç as *s*; g̃ *hard*; g̃ as *j*; G, H, K, *guttural*; N, *nasal*; R, *trilled*; s̃ as *z*; th as in *this*. (☞See Explanations, p. 23.)

he was chosen president of the Geological Society, and professor of natural history in the University of Edinburgh. Professor Forbes and S. Hanley published a "History of British Mollusca," (4 vols. 8vo, 1853.) Among his works are a "History of British Star-Fishes," (1841,) "Travels in Lycia," (1846,) and "Zoology of the Voyage of H. M. Ship Herald," (3 vols. 4to.) He made an extensive use of the dredge as an instrument of research. He was profoundly versed in botany, zoology, and geology. He died near Edinburgh in November, 1854.

See "Memoir of Edward Forbes, F.R.S.," by the late Dr. George Wilson and Archibald Geikie, F.R.S.E. and F.G.S., London, 1861; "Encyclopædia Britannica;" William Jerdan, "Men I have known," London, 1866; "Blackwood's Magazine" for February, 1855; "Fraser's Magazine" for January, 1855.

Forbes, (James,) an English author, born in London in 1749. He was employed in the civil service of the East India Company, and returned from India about 1784. He published an interesting work entitled "Oriental Memoirs, a Narrative of Seventeen Years' Residence in India, embellished with ninety-five Fine Engravings and Coloured Plates," (4 vols., 1813–15,) which was received with great favour. Died in 1819.

See "London Quarterly Review" for October, 1814.

Forbes, (James David,) F.R.S., an eminent British physical philosopher, a grandson of Sir William Forbes, noticed below, was born at Colinton, near Edinburgh, in 1809. He succeeded Sir John Leslie as professor of natural philosophy in the University of Edinburgh in 1833. In 1843 he published "Travels in the Alps." He made discoveries in the laws of the motion of glaciers, and in the phenomena of radiant heat and light in relation to polarization. He received the Rumford medal, and the royal medal of the Royal Society of London. In 1860 he became principal of the United College in the University of Saint Andrew's. Among his works are "Norway and its Glaciers visited in 1851," (1853,) and the "Sixth Dissertation" prefixed to the "Encyclopædia Britannica."

See "Edinburgh Review" for January, 1861; "North British Review" for May, 1854.

Forbes, (Sir John,) F.R.S., an eminent British physician and medical writer, born in Banffshire, Scotland, about 1787, graduated in Edinburgh in 1817. He acquired distinction by translations of the works of Auenbrugger and Laennec "On Auscultation," (1824,) and practised successively at Penzance, Chichester, and London. He was one of the editors of the "Cyclopædia of Practical Medicine." In 1835 he published a "Manual of Select Medical Bibliography," and afterwards edited the "British and Foreign Medical Review." About 1840 he became physician-in-ordinary to the queen's household, and physician-extraordinary to Prince Albert. He published, besides other works, a "Physician's Holiday, or a Month in Switzerland in 1848," (1849.) Died in 1861.

Forbes, (John,) an English botanist and traveller, born in 1799. He attempted to ascend the river Zambezi, in Africa, but died during the journey, in 1824.

Forbes, (John,) of Corse, a Scottish divine, born in 1593, was the son of Bishop Patrick Forbes, noticed below. From 1619 to 1640 he was professor of divinity in King's College, Aberdeen, from which he was ejected for refusing to sign the Covenant. He published several admired religious works, among which is "Institutiones Historico-Theologicæ," (1645.) Died in 1648.

See Chambers, "Biographical Dictionary of Eminent Scotsmen."

Forbes, (Patrick,) Lord of Corse and Baron of O'Neil, a Scottish divine, born in Aberdeenshire in 1564. Having embraced Episcopacy, he was made Bishop of Aberdeen in 1618. He wrote a "Commentary on the Revelation of Saint John," and other religious works. Died in 1635.

See Chambers, "Biographical Dictionary of Eminent Scotsmen."

Forbes, [Lat. Forbe′sius,] (William,) a Scottish bishop, eminent for learning and eloquence, born at Aberdeen about 1580. He became principal of Marischal College about 1618, and minister in Edinburgh a few years later. He was the first Bishop of Edinburgh, but died about three months after his consecration, in 1634.

Forbes, (Sir William,) Baronet of Pitsligo, an eminent banker, was born in Edinburgh in 1739. With Sir James H. Blair, he founded the principal banking estab-

lishment of Edinburgh. He wrote a "Memoir of the Life and Writings of James Beattie" the poet, (2 vols., 1806,) which, says Lord Jeffrey, "is a great deal longer and a great deal duller than we are bound to tolerate." Scott lamented the loss of Forbes in the introduction to one of the cantos of "Marmion." Sir William Forbes was a member, with Johnson, Burke, and Reynolds, of the famous Literary Club of London. Died in 1806.

See Chambers, "Biographical Dictionary of Eminent Scotsmen."

Forbin, foR′bǎN′,(Claude,) a brave and skilful French naval officer, born at Gardanne, near Aix, in 1656. When Chaumont was sent as ambassador to Siam, in 1685, Forbin went with him as major. In 1686–87 he served as admiral and general-in-chief of the King of Siam. (See Constance, Faulcon.) Having accepted these offices with reluctance, he resigned them at the end of two years. From 1702 to 1710, in the war of the Spanish succession, as *chef-d'escadre,* he performed many bold and successful exploits against the English and Dutch, for which he was rewarded by Louis XIV. with the title of count. He retired from service in 1710, and wrote entertaining "Memoirs of his Life and Adventures," (2 vols., 1730.) He is esteemed one of the greatest naval commanders that France has produced. Died in 1733.

See Richer, "Vie de Forbin;" "Nouvelle Biographie Générale."

Forbin, de, dęh foR′bǎN′, (Louis Nicolas Philippe Auguste,) Comte, a French antiquary and painter, born on the Durance (department of Bouches-du-Rhône) in August, 1777. He was very accomplished, and was admired for his personal qualities. In 1804 he became chamberlain to Pauline Bonaparte. He served several campaigns as an officer in the army. At the restoration (1815) he was appointed director of the royal museums. The museum or gallery of the Luxembourg was originated by him. He painted history, genre, and landscape with success, and was a brilliant colorist. He wrote a "Voyage in the Levant," with plates, (1819.) Among his works of art are "Ines de Castro," (1819,) "The Ruins of Palmyra," (1824,) and "The Via Appia." Died in 1841.

See Quérard, "La France Littéraire."

Forbisserus. See Frobisher.

Forbonnais, de, dęh foR′bo′nả′, (François Véron—vả′ròN′,) an eminent French financier and writer, born at Mans in 1722, removed to Paris in 1752, and became a member of the Institute. In 1754 he published an able and important work, entitled "The Elements of Commerce," which was often reprinted and was translated into many languages. In 1756 he was chosen inspector-general of the mint, and in 1759 chief clerk in the office of the controller-general. The flourishing condition of the finances for several ensuing years is ascribed to his skill. He wrote a work on the Finances of France, ("Recherches et Considérations," etc., 2 vols., 1758,) which was highly esteemed, and several other treatises on political economy. Died in 1800.

See Delisle de Sales, "Vie littéraire de V. Forbonnais," 1801.

Forcade, foR′kǎd′, (Eugène,) a French journalist, born at Marseilles in 1820. He was a regular contributor to the "Revue des Deux Mondes," and edited several Liberal journals in Paris. Among his works is "Historical Studies," (1853.)

Forcade-Laroquette, de, dęh foR′kǎd′ lả′ro′kĕt′, (Jean Louis Victor Adolphe,) a French politician and lawyer, a half-brother of Marshal Saint-Arnaud, was born in Paris about 1820. He was appointed director-general of the customs, etc. In 1859, and minister of finance in November, 1860. Having been removed in November, 1861, he was then appointed a senator, and in 1869 minister of the interior.

Forcadel, foR′kǎ′dĕl′, (Étienne,) a French jurist and legal writer, born at Béziers in 1534, is chiefly noted as having been a competitor of the famous Cujas for the chair of law at Toulouse in 1554. As Cujas absented himself before the decision of the question, Forcadel gained the place. Died in 1573.

See Taisand, "Vies des plus célèbres Jurisconsultes."

Force, (Peter,) an American historian and compiler, born in New Jersey in 1790. He became president of the National Institute at Washington, District of Columbia. He expended many years in compiling a "Documentary History of the American Revolution," of which nine volumes have been published, under the title of "American Archives," (1837–53.) Died in January, 1868.

Force, de la, dẹh lä forss, (ARMAND **de Caumont—** dẹh kō'mòn',) a French general and marquis, born in 1615. He became maréchal-de-camp in 1651, and fought with Condé against the court. He was made a lieutenant-general in 1655, and served under Turenne. Having become a Protestant exile in 1685, he entered the army of the Dutch Republic as a general. Died in 1701.

Force, de la, (ARMAND **Nompar de Caumont—** nòn'pär' dẹh kō'mòn',) DUC, a French general, born about 1585, was a son of Jacques, noticed below. He distinguished himself in the wars of Italy and Germany, and obtained the rank of marshal of France in 1652. Died in 1675.

Force, de la, (CHARLOTTE ROSE DE CAUMONT,) a French authoress, born in Bazadois in 1650, was granddaughter of Marshal Force, noticed below. She was married to M. de Briou in 1687. She wrote several admired poems and historical romances, among which are "Secret History of Navarre," (2 vols., 1696,) and "Gustavus Vasa," (2 vols., 1698.) Died in 1724.

Force, de la, (HENRI NOMPAR DE CAUMONT,) DUC, a French general and Protestant, born in 1582, was a son of Jacques, noticed below. He presided over the political assembly of the Protestants at Sainte-Foy in 1613, after which he fought against the royal troops, and killed the Duke of Mayenne in battle. He served under his father in many campaigns. Died in 1678.

Force, de la, (JACQUES NOMPAR DE CAUMONT,) DUC, a French general, born about 1558, was a son of a Huguenot who was killed in the Massacre of Saint Bartholomew. He fought against the League for Henry IV., whose confidence he enjoyed. He was in the carriage with the king when the latter was assassinated in 1610. In the civil war that ensued, he commanded the Protestants, and defended Montauban in 1621, soon after which he accepted overtures of peace from Louis XIII., who gave him a marshal's bâton in 1622. He commanded with success in several campaigns against the Spaniards and Austrians between 1630 and 1638. He died in 1652, leaving Memoirs, which were published in 1843, (4 vols.)

Forcellini, for-chĕl-lee'nee, (EGIDIO,) [Lat. ÆGID'-IUS FORCELLI'NUS,] an eminent Italian lexicographer, born near Padua, August 26, 1688. In 1731 he received an appointment in the Seminary of Padua, with the free disposal of his time. He devoted about forty years to the great task of compiling a Latin Dictionary, in which he was assisted by Facciolati, and which was published in 1771. This enduring monument of his learning and industry, entitled "Lexicon of all Latinity," ("Totius Latinitatis Lexicon," 4 vols.,) is regarded as the most complete Latin lexicon that has ever been compiled, and entitles him to the honour of having performed one of the most important services ever rendered to the study of antiquity. Died at Fener in April, 1768.

See FERRARI, "Vita Ægidii Forcellini," Padua, 1792; "Nouvelle Biographie Générale;" "Biographie Universelle."

Forcellini, (MARCO,) an Italian poet, brother of the preceding, born at Campo in 1711; died in 1794.

Forchhammer, fork'häm'mẹr, (JOHAN GEORG,) a chemist and writer, born at Husum, in Denmark, in 1794. About 1850 he was elected titular professor at Copenhagen, and succeeded Oersted as secretary of the Academy of Sciences.

Forchhammer, fork'häm'mẹr, (PAUL WILHELM,) an antiquary, born at Husum in 1803. Having travelled in Italy and Greece, he visited Asia Minor in 1838, in order to ascertain the site of Troy, being assisted in this enterprise by the British Admiralty. His chart of Troy, with an English text, appeared subsequently in the publications of the Royal Geographical Society. Among his treatises is the "Topography of Athens," (1841.)

Förd, (JOHN,) an eminent English dramatic author, born at Ilsington in 1586, was contemporary with Shakspeare. He became a member of the Middle Temple in 1602, and appears to have practised law with success; but the details of his life are not well known. He wrote about sixteen plays, (most of which were performed between 1628 and 1639,) among which are the tragedies

of "Love's Sacrifice," "The Broken Heart," and **"The Lover's Melancholy."** He is admired for elegance, harmony, and pathos, but gives offence by bad taste and licentiousness. Hallam thinks "he does not display one particle of comic ability." "With none of the moral beauty and elevation of Massinger, he has in a much higher degree the power over tears." Suckling thus describes him in the "Sessions of the Poets:"

"In the dumps John Ford alone by himself sat,
With folded arms and melancholy hat."

See HAZLITT, "Lectures on Dramatic Literature;" BAKER, "Biographia Dramatica;" HALLAM, "Introduction to the Literature of Europe;" LORD JEFFREY, critique in the "Edinburgh Review" for August, 1811, vol. xviii.; "Lives of the British Dramatists," by CAMPBELL, LEIGH HUNT, etc.; "London Quarterly Review" for December, 1811.

Ford, (Sir JOHN,) an English engineer, born in Sussex in 1605, was knighted by Charles I., and served as colonel in the royalist army. In 1656, under the auspices of Cromwell, he invented a machine to raise water from the Thames. He was a great virtuoso, says Anthony Wood. Died in 1670.

Ford, (RICHARD,) an English descriptive writer, born in London in 1796. About 1830 he visited Spain, where he remained some years. After his return to England he became a contributor to the "Quarterly Review," and published an excellent "Hand-Book for Travellers in Spain and Readers at Home," describing the country and cities, the natives and their manners, etc., (2 vols., 1845,) which was praised by Irving, Lockhart, and other critics. His "Gatherings from Spain" (1846) consists chiefly of extracts from the preceding work, and "is the best English book," says the "London Quarterly Review," "that has ever appeared for the illustration of the topography, curiosities, and the national character and manners of Spain." Died in September, 1858.

See "Fraser's Magazine" for October, 1858.

Ford, (Rev. SIMON,) an English poet, born at East Ogwell in 1619, became vicar of Reading in 1651, and of All-Saints, Northampton, in 1659. He published sermons and Latin poems. Died in 1699.

Fordun, de, dẹh for-dun', (JOHN,) the earliest Scottish historian, lived about 1350. He is supposed to have been a priest in the church of Fordun, or a canon of Aberdeen. He wrote a Latin chronicle of Scottish affairs from the creation to 1053, entitled "Scoti Chronicon."

See CHAMBERS, "Biographical Dictionary of Eminent Scotsmen."

For-dȳce', (DAVID,) a Scottish moralist, born at Aberdeen in 1711, was a brother of Sir William, noticed below. He was appointed professor of moral philosophy in Marischal College in 1742, and published "Dialogues concerning Education," (2 vols., 1745–48,) a work of considerable merit. Returning from a continental tour, he was drowned at sea in 1751. He left "Theodorus, a Dialogue on the Art of Preaching," (1752,) and "Elements of Moral Philosophy," (1754.)

See CHAMBERS, "Biographical Dictionary of Eminent Scotsmen."

Fordyce, (GEORGE,) an eminent Scottish physician, born near Aberdeen in 1736, was a nephew of the preceding. About the year 1760 he settled in London, where he acquired reputation by his lectures on chemistry, etc. He was chosen physician of Saint Thomas's Hospital in 1770, and a Fellow of the Royal Society in 1776. He is the author of able medical treatises, and of "Elements of Agriculture and Vegetation," (1765.) Died in 1802.

See CHAMBERS, "Biographical Dictionary of Eminent Scotsmen."

Fordyce, (JAMES,) D.D., a Scottish author and divine, born at Aberdeen in 1720. In 1760 he came to London, where he became minister of a congregation of dissenters, and was distinguished for eloquence as a preacher. He published, besides other works, "Sermons to Young Women," (2 vols., 1765; 9th edition, 1778,) and a small volume of poems. Died in 1796. He was a brother of Sir William Fordyce, noticed below.

Fordyce, (Sir WILLIAM,) brother of David Fordyce, noticed above, was born at Aberdeen in 1724, and was educated at Marischal College, of which he became lord rector in the latter part of his life. He practised medicine and surgery in London with great success, and published several medical treatises, among which are "On

Putrid and Inflammatory Fevers," (1773,) and "Fragmenta Chirurgica et Medica," (1784.) Died in 1792.

See CHAMBERS, "Biographical Dictionary of Eminent Scotsmen."

Foreiro, fo-rā′e-ro, (FRANCISCO,) an eminent Portuguese ecclesiastic, born in Lisbon, entered the Dominican order. He was well versed in languages and theology, which he began to teach in 1540. He was reckoned the most eloquent preacher of his time in Portugal, and often preached before the court. He was a prominent member of the Council of Trent, (1561,) where he was selected with two others to compile a catechism, which was printed in 1565. He published a Latin version of the book of Isaiah, with notes, (1563.) Died in 1587.

See QUÉTIF ET ÉCHARD, "Scriptores ordinis Predicatorum."

Forest, fo′rạ′, (JEAN,) a French landscape-painter, born in Paris in 1636; died in 1712.

For′est or **Foreest, van,** vän for-āst′, [Lat. FORES′-TUS,] (PIETER,) a skilful Dutch physician, born at Alkmaar in 1522, studied in Italy and Paris. He practised with success about forty years at Delft, and published medical works which display much learning and judgment. Died in 1597.

See ÉLOY, "Dictionnaire historique de la Médecine."

Foresti, fo-rês′tee, (ANTONIO,) an Italian Jesuit, born at Carpi, published a "Universal History," (6 vols., 1690,) a work of some merit, which after his death was continued by Apostolo Zeno. Its title is "Mappamondo historico," etc. Died about 1700.

Foresti, (E. FELICE,) an Italian patriot, born near Ferrara about 1793. He was confined for a political offence in the prison of Spielberg, Moravia, from 1822 to 1835, and was then exiled to America. He became professor of Italian in Columbia College, New York, where he taught for many years. Died at Genoa in 1858.

See the "Atlantic Monthly" for November, 1859.

Foresti, (JACOPO FILIPPO,) (better known as JACOPO FILIPPO of Bergamo,) an Italian monk and historian, born at Soldio, near Bergamo, in 1434. He published in 1483 a valuable and successful work, entitled "Supplementum Chronicorum Orbis," etc., (a "Supplement of Universal History from the Beginning of the World to 1482.") Died in 1520.

Forestier, fo′rạ′te-ā′, (HENRI,) a French general, born at Pommeraye in 1775. In 1793 he joined the royalist army of Vendeans, and, after many successful battles, was made general-in-chief of the cavalry. The Vendeans were defeated and dispersed, and Forestier fled to England. Died in 1806.

See T. MURET, "Histoire de la Vendée."

Forestus. See FOREST.

Forey, fo′rạ′, (ÉLIE FRÉDÉRIC,) a French general, born in Paris in 1804. He served several campaigns in Africa, was a prominent actor in the *coup d'état* of December, 1851, and became general of division in 1852. He took part in the siege of Sevastopol in 1854, and commanded the division which defeated the Austrians at Montebello, May 20, 1859. In the summer of 1862 he was appointed general-in-chief of an expedition against Mexico. He captured the city of Mexico in 1863, and was made marshal of France.

Forfait, foR′fạ′, (PIERRE ALEXANDRE LAURENT,) a French engineer, was born at Rouen in 1752. He was appointed by Bonaparte minister of the marine in November, 1799, and afterwards councillor of state, maritime prefect at Havre, and inspector-general of the flotilla destined for the invasion of England. He wrote a "Memoir on Navigable Canals, and a Treatise on the Masting of Vessels," (1788.) Died in 1807.

Forgeot, foR′zho′, (NICOLAS JULIEN,) a French lawyer and comic writer, born in Paris in 1758; died in 1798.

Forget, foR′zhạ′, (PIERRE,) Sieur de Beauvais et de la Picardière, a French poet and diplomatist; died in 1638.

Forget, (PIERRE,) Sieur de Fresnes, a French statesman, was made secretary of state in 1589, and was employed by Henry IV. after that date. He drew up the famous edict of Nantes, (which granted to the Protestants the free exercise of their religion,) and acted as counsellor in the Treasury office. Died in 1610.

Forgues, foRg, (ÉMILE **Dauran**—dō′rôN′,) a French *littérateur*, who has written in several journals under the name of "Old Nick." Among his works is "The Minor

Miseries of Human Life," (1841.) He translated "Uncle Tom's Cabin" into French.

Forkel, foR′kĕl, (JOHANN NIKOLAUS,) a German composer and writer on music, born at Meeder, near Coburg, in 1749. He graduated at the University of Göttingen, and became director of music in that institution about 1778. He published, besides other works, a "General History of Music," (2 vols., 1788–1801, unfinished,) "General Literature of Music," (1792,) and a "Life of Sebastian Bach," (1803.) The first-named is a work of great erudition and research. He died at Göttingen in 1818.

See FÉTIS, "Biographie Universelle des Musiciens."

Forlenze, foR-lên′zà, (GIUSEPPE NICCOLÒ BLASIO,) a Neapolitan surgeon and skilful oculist, born at Picerno in 1769. He practised in Paris, where he was appointed oculist to the Hôtel-Dieu and the Hôtel des Invalides. Died in 1833.

Forli, foR-lee′, (JACOPO **della Torre**—del′lä tor′rä,) (better known as JACOPO FORLI,) an eminent Italian physician, born at Forli about 1350, was professor of medicine at Bologna and Padua. His medical writings were once in great vogue. Died in 1414.

Forli, da, dä foR-lee′, (ANSOVINO,) an Italian painter, born at Forli, lived about 1500.

Forli, da, (MELOZZO.) See MELOZZO DA FORLI.

Formaleoni, foR-mä-là-o′nee, (VINCENZO,) an Italian historical writer, born at Venice in 1752. He wrote two important works, entitled "Essay on the Ancient Navigation of the Venetians," ("Saggio sulla Nautica dei Veneziani,") and a "Philosophical History of the Navigation of the Black Sea," (2 vols., 1788;) also several tragedies. Died in 1797.

See TIPALDO, "Biografia degli Italiani illustri."

For′man, (SIMON,) a notorious English astrologer and physician, born near Wilton in 1552, studied at Oxford. He practised medicine and fortune-telling in London with success, and wrote on magic. Died in 1611.

See WOOD, "Athenæ Oxonienses."

Formey, foR′mī, (JOHANN HEINRICH SAMUEL,) a learned German writer, of French extraction, born at Berlin in 1711. He was appointed in 1748 perpetual secretary of the Academy of Sciences, on the members of which he wrote many eulogies. He made valuable contributions to the "New German Library," ("Nouvelle Bibliothèque Germanique,") and was the author of several theological and philosophical treatises, among which was a "Compendium of the Philosophy of Wolff," in French, (6 vols., 1741–53.) Died in 1797.

See J. H. S. FORMEY, "Souvenirs d'un Citoyen," 2 vols., 1789.

Formey, (JOHANN LUDWIG,) a Prussian physician, son of the preceding, was born in Berlin in 1766. He became in 1796 physician to Frederick William II. He wrote, besides other works, one "On the Actual State of Medicine," (1809.) Died in 1823.

Formi, foR′me′, (PIERRE,) a French physician, born at Nîmes, accompanied Gustavus Adolphus in his journey in France in 1631, and wrote verses in his honour. Died in 1679.

Formose. See FORMOSUS.

For-mo′sus, [Fr. FORMOSE, foR′moz′,] elected pope in 891 A.D. as successor to Stephen V., had previously been Bishop of Porto. He crowned Arnulph of Germany as Emperor or King of Italy in 895. He is said to have been the first pope who was transferred from another see to that of Rome. Died in 896.

Fornarina, La, foR-nä-ree′nä, the name of a beautiful Roman maiden, whom Raphael admired or loved, and in whose form he found the model of his ideal figures. He painted her in the "Transfiguration," in the fresco of "Parnassus," and in other compositions.

Fornaris, foR-nä′rèss, (FABRICIO,) an Italian comic author, born at Naples, lived about 1600. He wrote "Angelica," from which Molière borrowed some parts of his "Étourdi."

Forner, for-naiR′, (JUAN PABLO,) a Spanish author and critic, born at Merida in 1756. He endeavoured to reform the style of Spanish literature by satirical criticisms against prevalent affectation. Among his works is an "Apology for Spain and her Literary Merit," (1786.) Died at Seville in 1797.

ā, ē, ī, ō, ū, ȳ, *long;* ă, ĕ, ĭ, ŏ, ŭ, y̆, *short;* ạ, ẹ, ị, ọ, *obscure;* fär, fâll, fät; mĕt; nŏt; gōōd; mōōn;

Forner, (Don PABLO,) a Spanish lawyer and poet, born at Palma, in the island of Majorca, in 1750, practised law in Madrid, and obtained the office of attorney-general. He gained distinction by his eloquence and poetical talent. Besides odes and short poems, he wrote a successful comedy, called the "Enamoured Philosopher," ("Filosofo enamorado," 1798.) Died in 1799.

See TICKNOR, "History of Spanish Literature."

Fornerod, forn'rod', (CONSTANT,) a Swiss statesman, born in the Canton de Vaud in 1820. He studied law, became a leader of the Liberal party, and gained distinction as an orator. He was chosen president of the council of state in 1855, and president of the federal council (*i.e.* the highest officer in the republic) in 1857, and was again elected to the same office in 1867.

For'ney, (JOHN W.,) an American politician and journalist, born at Lancaster, Pennsylvania, in 1817. He began to edit a newspaper at Lancaster about 1838, and was originally a Democrat. In 1845 he removed to Philadelphia, where he became editor of the "Pennsylvanian," a daily journal, which was for many years the chief organ of the Democratic party in Pennsylvania. He was clerk of the national House of Representatives, 1852–55. He supported James Buchanan for the Presidency in 1856. In August, 1857, he established "The Press" in Philadelphia, which became an organ of the Douglas Democracy. He was chosen clerk of the House of Representatives in December, 1859. About the end of 1860 he left the Democratic party and joined the Republicans. He became secretary of the Senate of the United States in 1861, and held that office until 1868.

For'rest, (EDWIN,) a popular American actor, born in Philadelphia in 1806. He performed the rôles of Othello, Macbeth, Richard III., Spartacus, etc. with great applause. He visited England several times between 1834 and 1844. Mr. Forrest has been one of the most successful of American actors.

For'rest, (THOMAS,) a British navigator, was a captain in the service of the East India Company. He was author of two valuable works, viz., "A Voyage to New Guinea and the Moluccas," (made in 1774–76,) and a "Voyage from Calcutta to the Mergui Archipelago," (1792.)

For'res-ter, (ALFRED HENRY,) an English artist and comic writer, was born in London in 1806. About 1828 he co-operated with Hook and others in the production of the "Humourist Papers" in "Colburn's Magazine," writing under the name of "Alfred Crowquill." He was the first illustrator of "Punch." He has published "Comic Arithmetic," "Railway Raillery," etc.

Forsell, Af, åf foR'sĕl, (CARL,) a Swedish statistician, distinguished for his philanthropy, was born at Sköttorp in March, 1783. He attended Bernadotte as adjutant in the war in Germany in 1813, after which he was a member of the Diet of Sweden. About 1820 he applied steam-power to the navigation of Swedish waters. He was made director-general of the department for the survey of land in 1824, and published an important work, entitled "Statistics of Sweden," (1834.) Died in 1848.

See BROCKHAUS, "Conversations-Lexikon."

Forseti, for-sĕt'e, written also **Forsete,** [equivalent to the Latin PRÆSES, "seated before," and hence "presiding," or "president,"] in the Norse mythology, the god who presides over justice and settles quarrels. He is regarded as the son of Balder, (*i.e.* of spotless innocence.) His dwelling is called Glitnir, (the "shining,") because full light is necessary for the operations of justice.

See THORPE, "Northern Mythology," vol. i.; KEYSER, "Religion of the Northmen."

For'shall, (Rev. JOSIAH,) an English biblical critic, born about 1795. He was secretary of the British Museum from 1828 to 1851. Died in 1863.

Forskål, foR'skôl, written also **Forskahl** and **Forskael.** (PEHR,) a Swedish naturalist, born at Kalmar in 1736. Being well versed in Oriental languages and natural sciences, he was recommended by Linnæus to the King of Denmark, who chose him in 1761 to accompany Niebuhr and others in a scientific expedition to Egypt and Arabia. While engaged in this enterprise, he died at Yerim, (Jerim,) in Arabia, in July, 1763. The results of his labours, edited and published by Niebuhr, are a

"Fauna Orientalis," (1775,) and a "Flora Ægyptiaco-Arabica," (1775,) which acquired for him a high reputation as a naturalist. "Forskål is one of my best disciples," said Linnæus : "he excels in the knowledge of insects, and is but little inferior in other branches of natural history."

See ERSCH und GRUBER, "Allgemeine Encyklopaedie."

Förster, förs'ter, (ERNST JOACHIM,) a German painter and writer on art, born near Munich in 1800, executed a number of frescos in the Glyptothek and Arcade at Munich. Among his publications may be named his "History of German Art," (3 vols., 1851,) and "Truth from Jean Paul's Life," ("Wahrheit aus Jean Paul's Leben," 8 vols., 1827–33.) He edited the last five volumes of the latter.

Fors'ter, [Fr. pron. foRs'taiR',] (FRANÇOIS,) a Swiss engraver on copper, born at Locle in 1790. He became a citizen of Paris, where he gained the first grand prize in 1814, after which he went to Rome. He engraved in Paris many plates for the Musée Napoléon and Musée Royal, and was elected to the Institute in 1844. Among his best works are the "Vierge de la Légende," and "The Three Graces," both after Raphael, and a portrait of Raphael by himself.

See "Journal des Beaux-Arts" for October 10, 1842.

Fors'ter, (FRANK,) an English civil engineer, born at or near Newcastle about 1800. He was employed by Robert Stephenson on the London and Birmingham Railway, and afterwards became chief engineer of the metropolitan sewers. He had resigned this office a few weeks when he died, in 1852.

Förster, (FRIEDRICH,) a German *littérateur*, brother of Ernst Joachim, noticed above, was born in 1792, and became a resident of Berlin. His works include lyric poems, romances, and biographical and historical treatises, among which are "Albrecht von Wallenstein," (1834,) "Prussian Heroes," (4th edition, 1855,) and "Modern History of Prussia," (1st vol., 1850.)

Fors'ter, (FROBEN,) a German philosopher and monk, born at Königsfeld in 1709; died in 1791. He published several works on philosophy.

See ERSCH und GRUBER, "Allgemeine Encyklopaedie."

Forster, (GEORGE,) an English traveller, was an employee in the civil service of the East India Company. He performed in 1783–84 a perilous journey alone from India to Europe through Cashmere, Cabool, Candahar, and Herât, and published an interesting narrative, entitled "Journey from Bengal to England," etc., (2 vols., 1790–98.) He was afterwards envoy to the court of Nagpore, in the Deccan, where he died in 1792.

Forster, (JOHANN,) a learned German divine, born at Augsburg in 1495, was a favourite disciple of Melanchthon. He filled the chair of Hebrew at Wittenberg for many years with distinction, and published an esteemed Hebrew Dictionary, (1552.) Died in 1556.

Forster, (JOHANN,) a German theologian, born in the Palatinate in 1576; died in 1613.

Forster, (JOHANN GEORG,) son of the celebrated naturalist noticed below, was born near Dantzic in 1754. He accompanied his father on his various expeditions, and in 1777 published a work entitled "A Voyage around the World in 1772, 1773, 1775." He became professor of natural history at Wilna in 1784, and soon after married Theresa, daughter of the philologist Heyne. Among his principal works are his "History and Description of the Bread-Fruit," (1784,) "Views of the Lower Rhine, Brabant, Flanders, etc.," (3 vols., 1791,) etc. Forster is ranked among the classic prose writers of Germany. Died in Paris in 1794. He was a friend of Alexander von Humboldt. A collection of his Letters was published by his widow, (2 vols., 1828.)

See MOLESCHOTT, "Georg Forster der Naturforscher des Volks," 1854; GERVINUS, "J. G. Forster," 1843; ERSCH und GRUBER, "Allgemeine Encyklopaedie ;" "Westminster Review" for October, 1856.

Forster, (JOHANN REINHOLD,) a celebrated German traveller, and one of the first naturalists of his time, born near Dantzic, October 22, 1729. In 1765 he was commissioned by the Russian government to visit the colonies in Asiatic Russia, of which he gave an accurate account on his return. Having spent several years in England as a teacher, he accompanied Captain Cook in

1772 on his second voyage to the South Sea; but, being prohibited from giving a narrative of this voyage, it was published in 1777 by his son, who took part in the expedition. After his return to Germany, Forster became professor of natural history at Halle in 1780. Among his works, which display profound learning, may be named "On the Linen of the Ancients," ("De Bysso Antiquorum,") "Observations made during a Voyage round the World on Physical Geography, Natural History, and Ethic Philosophy," (1778,) and "Zoologia Indica," (1781.) Forster possessed a very retentive memory, and spoke and wrote seventeen languages. He was hasty in his temper and unpolished in his manners. It is related that on being presented to Frederick the Great he said, "I have seen seven kings, four wild and three tame ones, but none to be compared to your majesty." Died in 1798.

See J. G. FORSTER, "Voyage round the World in the Resolution, etc.;" ERSCH und GRUBER, "Allgemeine Encyklopaedie."

Fors'ter, (JOHN,) of the Inner Temple, an eloquent English author and editor, born at Newcastle in 1812. He was educated in the London University, studied law, and was called to the bar. About 1834 he began to write for "The Examiner," (see FONBLANQUE, ALBANY,) of which he has been chief editor since 1846. He published in 1840 "Lives of the Statesmen of the Commonwealth," (7 vols.,) which has obtained much popularity. "We regard these biographies," says the "London Morning Chronicle," "as additions of the very highest value to what we may term our political literature." His "Life and Adventures of Oliver Goldsmith" (1848) is greatly admired. "It is executed," says Irving, "with a spirit, a feeling, a grace, and an elegance that leave nothing to be desired." He was appointed secretary to the commissioners in lunacy in 1856. He also published "Historical and Biographical Essays," (2 vols., 1858,) many of which first appeared in the Edinburgh and Quarterly Reviews, "Life of Sir John Eliot," (1864,) and "Walter Savage Landor: a Biography," (2 vols., 1869.)

Förster or **Foerster,** (KARL,) a German scholar, born at Naumburg in 1784, published translations of Dante's "Vita Nuova" and Tasso's "Select Lyrics," and finished in 1838 the "Library of German Poets of the Seventeenth Century," begun by Müller. Died in 1841.

See L. FÖRSTER, "Biographische und literarische Skizzen."

Forster, (NATHANIEL,) a learned English divine, born at Stadscombe, in Devonshire, in 1717, became prebendary of Bristol and vicar of Rochdale in 1754. He edited Plato's "Dialogues," (1745,) and wrote an essay "On the Antiquity of Government, Arts, etc. in Egypt," (1743,) besides other works. Died in 1757.

See "Biographia Britannica."

Forster, (THOMAS IGNATIUS MARIA,) a naturalist and meteorologist, born in London in 1789. He published a "Natural History of the Swallow," (1808; 6th edition, 1817,) edited Catullus in 1816, and wrote essays on meteorology for "The Philosophic Magazine." He discovered a comet in 1819. Among his various works is a "Perpetual Calendar, illustrating the Events of every Day in the Year," etc., (1824.) Died about 1850.

Forster, (VALENTIN,) a German jurist, born at Wittenberg in 1530. Among his works is "Historia Juris civilis Romani," (1565.) Died in 1608.

See ERSCH und GRUBER, "Allgemeine Encyklopaedie."

Forster, (WILLIAM,) an English philanthropist, born at Tottenham, near London, in 1784. He became a minister of the Society of Friends in 1803, and married Anna, a sister of Thomas Fowell Buxton, in 1816. In 1820 he visited the United States. He settled near Norwich in 1838. In 1844–45 he laboured as a minister of the gospel in France. He took active measures to relieve the people of Ireland during the famine of 1846, and visited various parts of the island for this purpose. In 1849 he was commissioned by the Yearly Meeting of London to present an address on slavery and the slave-trade to the sovereigns and rulers of Christendom. After he had obtained interviews with many European monarchs, he proceeded to the United States in 1853, and presented the address to the President and also to the Governors of several Southern States. His mission was nearly fulfilled, when he died on the Holston River, in Blount county, Tennessee, in 1854. He left one son, William, noticed below.

See "Memoirs of William Forster," edited by BENJ. SEEBOHM, 2 vols., 1865.

Forster, (WILLIAM,) an English Liberal statesman and orator, a son of the preceding, and nephew of T. Fowell Buxton, was born in 1818. He married Jane, daughter of Dr. Arnold of Rugby. He was elected to Parliament for Bradford in 1861. About February, 1866, he became a member of the Russell ministry, and under-secretary for the colonies. He retired from office in July, 1866. He was appointed vice-president of the committee of council on education by Mr. Gladstone in December, 1868. "Few politicians in the country," says the "British Quarterly Review" for July, 1869, "are more deeply respected by men of all degrees and shades of opinion than Mr. Forster."

Forstner, forst'ner, (CHRISTOPH,) a German diplomatist, born in 1598; died in 1667.

Forsyth, for-sīth', (JOHN,) an American statesman, was born in Fredericksburg, Virginia, in 1780. After graduating at Princeton, he removed to Augusta, Georgia, where he studied law. He served with distinction as a member of Congress many years between 1813 and 1827, also as United States Senator from Georgia in 1818 and 1819. From 1819 to 1822 he was employed on a mission to Spain. He was elected Governor of the State in 1827, and was chosen Senator for a second term, commencing in 1829. He was secretary of state in the cabinet of General Jackson from 1834 to 1837, and also in that of Van Buren, from 1837 to 1841. Died in 1841.

Forsyth, for-sīth', (JOSEPH,) born at Elgin, in Scotland, in 1763, was a classical teacher near London. While making a tour on the continent, he was detained a prisoner by the French for several years. He published interesting "Remarks on Antiquities, Arts, and Letters during an Excursion in Italy." Died in 1815. Lord Byron called him "an accomplished traveller, of extraordinary capacity, extensive erudition, and refined taste."

Forsyth, (WILLIAM,) born in Scotland in 1737, was appointed in 1784 superintendent of the Royal Gardens at Kensington, and wrote a work on the "Culture and Management of Fruit-Trees," (1802.) Died in 1804.

Forsyth, (WILLIAM,) a British barrister, born about 1812, published a "Dictionary of the Statute Laws of Scotland," (1842,) a "History of the Trial by Jury," (1852,) and other legal works; also an interesting "Life of Cicero," (2 vols., 1864.)

See "Edinburgh Review" for January, 1864; "London Quarterly Review" for January, 1864.

Fort, Le. See LEFORT.

Forteguerri, foR-tà-gwĕr'ree, or **Fortiguerra,** foR-te-gwĕr'rà, (NICCOLÒ,) an Italian poet and priest, born at Pistoia in 1674. He became a resident of Rome, where he obtained the offices of chamberlain to the pope and prelate-referendary. In 1715 he was spending the autumn in the country, where he amused his friends by reading the verses of Berni, of Pulci, and of Ariosto. One of the company expressed his admiration at the art with which these poets had overcome the difficulties of the octave rhyme. Forteguerri maintained that the difficulty was imaginary, and engaged to produce on the ensuing evening the first canto of a poem which should imitate them all. He fulfilled his promise with such success that his friends persuaded him to continue the story. Such was the origin of the amusing and popular poem of "Ricciardetto," (1738,) in which the exuberance and extravagance of the author's fancy are equal to the facility, elegance, and freedom of his style. He also made an Italian version of Terence in blank verse. Died in 1735.

See TIRALDO, "Biografia degli Italiani illustri;" SEBASTIANO CIAMPI, "Memorie di N. Forteguerri," 1813; "Narrative and Romantic Poetry of the Italians," in the "London Quarterly Review" for April, 1819; and "Italian Narrative Poetry," in the "North American Review" for October, 1824, (by W. H. PRESCOTT.)

Forteguerri or **Fortiguerra,** (SCIPIONE,) called also **Carteromaco,** an Italian scholar, born at Pistoia in 1466. When Aldus Manutius instituted his Academy at Venice, (the chief object of which was to perfect editions of classic authors,) about 1495, he chose Forteguerri as secretary of this institution. Here he wrote his famous discourse in praise of Greek learning, "Oratio de Laudibus Literarum Græcarum," (1504,) and was appointed professor of Greek about 1500. Died in 1515.

See TIRABOSCHI, "Storia della Letteratura Italiana;" S. CIAMPI, "Memorie di S. Carteromaco," 1811.

For'tes-cue, (CHICHESTER SAMUEL PARKINSON,) an English statesman, born in 1823, was educated at Oxford, where he graduated in 1844. He was under-secretary of state for the colonies from 1859 to 1865, and was chief secretary for Ireland from November, 1865, to June, 1866. In December, 1868, he was reappointed to that office by Mr. Gladstone.

Fortescue, (Sir JOHN,) an eminent English lawyer, was the son of Sir Henry Fortescue. The date and place of his birth are unknown. He was made lord chief justice in 1442, and grand chancellor in the reign of Henry VI., whose adverse fortunes he shared in the war of the Roses. He wrote, in Latin, a work "On the Praises of British Laws," ("De Laudibus Legum Angliæ,") which is highly esteemed. Fuller, in his "Worthies," says, "His learned 'Commentaries on the Law' make him famous to all posterity." He died, it is supposed, about 1485.

See BRIDGMAN, "Legal Biography;" LORD CAMPBELL, "Lives of the Lord Chancellors;" FOSS, "The Judges of England," vol. iv.

For'tes-cue-A'land, (Sir JOHN,) first Baron Fortescue, an English judge and writer, a descendant of the preceding, was born in 1670. He was appointed a judge of the king's bench in 1718, and gained distinction by his literary merits. A collection of his reports was published in 1748. Died in 1746.

See FOSS, "The Judges of England," vol. viii.

Forti. See FORTIS.

Fortia, foR'te-ȧ', (AGRICOLE JOSEPH FRANÇOIS XAVIER PIERRE ESPRIT SIMON PAUL ANTOINE,) Marquis of Fortia-d'Urban, a French savant and writer, was born at Avignon in 1756. He wrote many and various works, among which are "Mélanges of Geography and History," (1795,) a "Life of Petrarch," (1804,) "Historical View of the World from its Origin to the Age of Alexander," (4 vols., 1810,) and an "Essay on the Origin of Writing," (1832.) Died in 1843.

See RIPERT-MONTCLAR, "Essai sur la Vie, etc. de Fortia-d'Urban," 1840.

Fortin, foR'tăN', (AUGUSTIN FÉLIX,) a French sculptor, born about 1760; died in 1832.

Fortis, foR'tèss, or **Forti,** foR'tee, (GIOVANNI BATTISTA,) ABBATE, an Italian writer, sometimes called ALBERT, born at Padua or Vicenza in 1741. He was noted for versatility of talent, and was by turns poet, naturalist, journalist, and biographer. He is chiefly remembered for his "Travels in Dalmatia," (1774.) Died in 1803.

See TIPALDO, "Biografia degli Italiani illustri."

Fortoul, foR'tool', (HIPPOLYTE NICOLAS HONORÉ,) a French writer and minister of state, born at Digne (Basses-Alpes) in 1811. In early life he professed republican principles, and gained literary distinction by writing for the "Revue de Paris" and other periodicals. He wrote, besides other works, "The Grandeur of Private Life," (1838,) a novel. He obtained the chair of literature in the University of Toulouse about 1840, and was chosen a member of the French Institute in 1854. Soon after the revolution of 1848 he was elected to the National Assembly, and in December, 1851, was appointed by Louis Napoleon minister of public instruction. He adopted an important innovation in education, called the system of *bifurcation*, by which sciences and belles-lettres were separated. Died in 1856.

See LOUANDRE et BOURQUELOT, "La Littérature Française contemporaine;" F. LACOINTA, "Notice sur M. H. Fortoul," 1853; "Nouvelle Biographie Générale."

For-tu'na, [Fr. FORTUNE, foR'tün',] the Roman name of the goddess of chance, fortune, and good luck, called Τύχη by the Greeks. Several temples of Fortune were erected at Rome and other cities of Italy.

Fortunat. See FORTUNATUS.

For-tu-na'tus, [Fr. FORTUNAT, foR'tü'nȧ',] (VENAN'TIUS HONO'RIUS CLEMENTIA'NUS,) SAINT, a Latin poet, born at Ceneda in 530 A.D., became Bishop of Poitiers.

Fortune. See FORTUNA.

For'tune, (ROBERT,) a British traveller and horticulturist, born at Berwick in 1813. He went to China in 1843 to collect botanical specimens for the London Horticultural Society. Having returned in 1846, he published "Three Years' Wanderings in the Northern Provinces of China." In 1848 he again visited China, to procure tea-plants for the East India Directors. The narratives of his various journeys were published together in 1853, under the title of "Two Visits to the Tea Countries of China, etc., with a Description of the Culture of the Tea-Plant and the Botany of China." He afterwards produced a "Residence among the Chinese : a Narrative of a Third Visit to China from 1853 to 1856," (1857.) "The value and interest of these books are very great." ("London Quarterly Review," article on "Fortune and Huc," July, 1857 ; see, also, "Edinburgh Review" for October, 1848.)

For'ward, (WALTER,) an American lawyer, born in Connecticut in 1786, removed in 1803 to Pittsburg, where he practised law with success. He was a member of Congress from 1822 to 1825, and in September, 1841, was appointed secretary of the treasury by President Tyler. Died in 1852.

Forzate, foRd-zȧ'tȧ, or **Forzati,** foRd-zȧ'tee, (CLAUDIO,) an Italian poet, born at Padua, lived about 1560–90. He wrote "Recinda," a tragedy.

Fosbroke, fos'brŏŏk, or **Fosbrooke,** (THOMAS DUDLEY,) an English antiquary and clergyman, born in London in 1770, obtained the living of Walford. He wrote, among other learned works, "British Monachism," (1802,) and an "Encyclopædia of Antiquities and Elements of Archæology," (2 vols., 1823–25.) Died in 1842.

Foscarari, fos-kȧ-rȧ'ree, (EGIDIO,) an Italian ecclesiastic, born at Bologna in 1512, became Bishop of Módena in 1550. He was one of three members of the Council of Trent appointed to compile a catechism about 1561. Died in 1564.

Foscari, fos'kȧ-ree, (FRANCESCO,) a celebrated doge of Venice, was born about 1372, and elected doge in 1423. He waged war for many years against the Duke of Milan and other Italian princes. The Venetians, though sometimes defeated, obtained possession of the provinces of Crema, Bergamo, and Brescia. "The ambition of Foscari," says Sismondi, "was advantageous to the republic, but fatal to his own happiness." His old age was rendered unhappy by the ruin of his son, unjustly condemned and tortured by the Council of Ten. He was deposed in 1457, and died about three days after that event. The sufferings of this doge and of his son form the subject of Byron's tragedy entitled "The Two Foscari."

See DARU, "Histoire de Venise ;" MARINO SANUTO, "Vite de' Duchi di Venezia;" SISMONDI, "Histoire des Républiques Italiennes."

Foscarini, fos-kȧ-ree'nee, (MARCO,) an eminent Italian statesman and author, born in Venice about 1696. After having gained distinction by his learning, talents, and eloquence, he was chosen procurator of Saint Mark, and employed successively in diplomatic missions to various courts of Europe. Before he departed on his first embassy, he had been selected by the Council of Ten to write a continuation of Venetian history. As this could not be performed without the examination of the archives of Venice, he undertook instead another national work, a "History of Venetian Literature." Of this he published in 1752 the first volume, "Della Letteratura Veneziana," which contains critical dissertations on the rise and progress of law, history, astronomy, and other sciences in Venice, and was highly appreciated. The pressure of various public duties prevented him from writing the second part of his projected work. In 1762 he was elected doge. Died in March, 1763.

See DARU, "Histoire de Venise;" TIPALDO, "Biografia degli Italiani illustri;" L. ARNALDI, "Orazione in Onore del Doge M. Foscarini," 1765.

Foscarini, (MICHELE,) a Venetian senator and historiographer, eminent for talents and eloquence, was born in 1632. The Council of Ten in 1678 selected him to continue the history of Venice, begun by Cardinal Bembo. He had composed seven books when his death occurred, in 1692. This work is esteemed authentic, being derived from the archives of the republic.

See NICÉRON, "Mémoires."

Foschini, fos-kee'nee, (ANTONIO,) an Italian architect, born about 1740, erected at Ferrara a number of buildings, the most remarkable of which was the theatre, considered one of the finest in Italy. Died about 1802.

Fosco, fos'ko, [Lat. FUS'CUS,] (PLACIDO,) a skilful Italian physician, born in 1509; died in 1574.

Foscolo, fos'ko-lo, (UGO,) an eloquent Italian poet and prose writer, born at Zante or at sea near Zante about 1776, was educated in Italy. In the political movements which followed the French Revolution he took a conspicuous part as a friend of national independence. About 1800 he produced a political romance, entitled "Letters of Jacopo Ortis," ("Lettere di Jacopo Ortis,") which had immense popularity. He was an officer in the army which Napoleon assembled for the invasion of England in 1805, but did not remain long in the service. He is praised for the lofty spirit of independence which refused to join in the general homage or adulation to Napoleon in Italy. His admirable lyric poem "The Monuments" ("I Sepolcri," 1807) is called his capital work. He was professor of eloquence at Pavía for a short time in 1808, and emigrated to England in 1816. He lectured on Italian literature in London in 1823. Among his works are "Ricciarda," a tragedy; an able "Discourse on the Text of Dante," (1826;) and an "Essay on Petrarch." Died near London in 1827.

See "Vita di Ugo Foscolo, scritta da G. Pecchio," 1830; G. CALEFFI, "Cenni sulla Vita, il Carattere, etc. di Ugo Foscolo," 1835; MAFFEI, "Storia della Letteratura Italiana, Secolo XIX.;" LUIGI CARRER, "Vita di Ugo Foscolo," Venice, 1842; LONGFELLOW, "Poets and Poetry of Europe;" "Nouvelle Biographie Générale;" "Foreign Quarterly Review" for May, 1832.

Foss, (EDWARD,) an English lawyer and writer of biography, born about 1788, published "The Grandeur of the Law, or the Legal Peers of England," (1843,) also a highly esteemed work on legal history, entitled "The Judges of England," (9 vols., 1848–64.)

See "London Quarterly Review" for April, 1866.

Fossati, fos-sä'tee, (DAVIDE ANTONIO,) an Italian painter and engraver, brother of Giorgio, noticed below, was born about 1714. He worked in Venice, where he painted frescos in the Contarini palace. He etched "The Family of Darius with Alexander," after Paul Veronese, and many views of Venice. Died about 1780.

See TICOZZI, "Dizionario."

Fossati, (DOMENICO,) an eminent Italian scene-painter, born in Venice in 1743, was the son of Giorgio, noticed below. He was employed in decorating theatres and palaces in Venice and Milan. He was killed by a fall in 1784.

Fossati, (GIORGIO,) an Italian architect and engraver, born at Morco, near Lugano, about 1705, engraved plates for the works of Palladio.

Fossati, (GIOVANNI ANTONIO LORENZO,) an Italian writer on medicine and phrenology, was born at Novara in 1786. He became a resident of Paris about 1824. Among his works is a "Manual of Phrenology, or Physiology of the Brain," (1845.)

See "Nouvelle Biographie Générale."

Fossati, (GIOVANNI FRANCESCO,) an Italian historian, born at Milan; died in 1653.

Fosse. See LAFOSSE.

Fossé, du, dü fo'sä', (PIERRE **Thomas,**) a learned French writer, born at Rouen in 1634. He became at an early age one of the recluses of Port-Royal, learned Hebrew and other languages, and acquired a high reputation for virtue and erudition. He published, besides other biographies, a "Life of Thomas à Becket," (1674,) and a "History of Tertullian and Origen," (1675,) both in French. Died in 1698.

See MORÉRI, "Dictionnaire Historique;" SAINTE-BEUVE, "Histoire de Port-Royal;" "Mémoires de P. Thomas Seigneur du Fossé," 1739.

Fossombroni, fos-som-bRo'nee, (VITTORIO,) an eminent Italian statesman and writer, born at Arezzo, in Tuscany, in 1754, excelled in mathematics and philosophy. In 1796 he became minister of foreign affairs of the Grand Duke of Tuscany, and he held several offices

under the new government which Bonaparte established in 1799. After the restoration of the grand duke (1814) Fossombroni was again appointed minister of foreign affairs, and chancellor of state. He published, in the course of his long life, many treatises on hydraulics and mathematics. Died in 1844.

See SAINT-MAURICE CABANY, "Le Comte V. Fossombroni," Paris, 1845.

Fos'ter, (BIRKET,) a skilful English engraver on wood, born at North Shields about 1825. He has illustrated the works of several English poets with wood-cuts. He published "Christmas with the Poets," (1850,) and "Cowper's Task, with Illustrations," (1855,) "which," says the "London Quarterly Review," "is one of the most beautiful gift-books that has ever appeared." He has also illustrated several other works.

Foster, (HENRY,) an English navigator, born in Lancashire in 1797. Under the auspices of the Royal Society, he was selected to command an expedition sent in 1828 to make observations in the Antarctic Ocean. In January, 1829, he had reached a portion of land in 63° 26' south latitude, which was within the circle of perpetual congelation. During the homeward voyage he was drowned in the river Chagres in February, 1831.

Foster, (JAMES,) a very popular English dissenting minister, born at Exeter in 1697. He began to preach at the Barbican, London, in 1724, and was eminent for eloquence and fervour of spirit. He was an Independent in his youth, and afterwards was baptized by immersion. In 1744 he became minister at Pinners' Hall. He published an "Essay on Fundamentals, especially the Trinity," (1720,) several volumes of sermons, and other works. Died in 1753. Foster is the subject of the following couplet of Pope :

"Let modest Foster, if he will, excel
Ten metropolitans in preaching well."
See POPE's "Satires," preface.

Foster, (JOHN,) an English philologist, born at Windsor in 1731. He became master of Eton School in 1765. He has left a memorial of his scholarship and critical sagacity in his "Essay on the Different Nature of Accent and Quantity," (1762; 3d edition, 1820.) Died in 1773.

Foster, (JOHN,) an English essayist and moralist of great merit, born at or near Halifax on the 17th of September, 1770. He worked at the trade of a weaver in his youth, and was educated for the ministry at the Baptist College of Bristol, which he entered in 1791. He became a Baptist minister at Chichester about 1797, but did not remain there long. He afterwards preached at Downend, near Bristol, and at Frome for a short time. As a minister he does not appear to have been very popular. He was the principal contributor to the "Eclectic Review," for which he began to write in 1806. His reputation is founded on Essays in a Series of Letters to a Friend, (1805 :) 1. "On a Man's Writing Memoirs of Himself;" 2. "On Decision of Character ;" 3. "On the Application of the Epithet Romantic ;" 4. "On some of the Causes by which Evangelical Religion has been rendered unacceptable to Persons of Cultivated Taste." These essays are the productions of a profound and original thinker. His morality is high-toned and his principles are liberal. "I have read with the greatest admiration the Essays of Mr. Foster," says Sir James Mackintosh. "He is one of the most profound and eloquent writers that England has produced." He married Maria Snooke, of Downend, about 1808, and relinquished the labours of the ministry. The last eighteen years of his life were passed at Stapleton, where he died in October, 1843. Among his principal works is an "Essay on the Evils of Popular Ignorance," (1819.)

See "Life and Correspondence of John Foster," by J. E. RYLAND, with Notices of Mr. Foster as a preacher and companion, by JOHN SHEPPARD, 2 vols., 1846; DE QUINCEY, "Essays."

Foster, (JOHN,) an English architect of Liverpool, born about 1786, studied the models of antiquity in Greece. In 1824 he was chosen corporation-architect and surveyor of the city of Liverpool, where he constructed several churches and other public edifices, among which is the custom-house, a sandstone building. It is the largest structure in Liverpool, but has a very heavy and dull appearance. Died in 1846.

ā, ē, ī, ō, ū, ȳ, *long;* ȧ, ė, ȯ, same, less prolonged; ă, ĕ, ĭ, ŏ, ŭ, ў, *short;* ạ, ẹ, ị, ọ, *obscure;* fär, fȧll, fȧt; mĕt; nŏt; gōōd; mōōn;

Fos'ter, (JOHN G.,) an American general, born in New Hampshire about 1824, graduated at West Point in 1846. He became a captain in 1860, and was one of the garrison of Fort Sumter when it was bombarded in April, 1861. He commanded a brigade under Burnside at Roanoke Island in February, and at Newbern in March, 1862. About August, 1862, he was appointed a major-general of volunteers, and commander of the department of Virginia and North Carolina. He succeeded General Burnside in East Tennessee in December, 1863, and commanded the department of the South in 1864.

Foster, (Sir MICHAEL,) an English lawyer, born at Marlborough in 1689. In 1745 he was knighted and appointed judge of the court of king's bench. He wrote a "Discourse on the Crown Law," which was much esteemed. Blackstone called him "a very great master of the crown law." Died in 1763.

See FOSS, "Judges of England;" BRIDGMAN, "Legal Biography;" M. DODSON, "Life of Sir M. Foster," 1811.

Foster, (RANDOLPH S.,) D.D., a Methodist divine and author, president of the Northwestern University at Evanston, Illinois, was born in Williamsburg, Ohio, in 1820. His principal works are "Christian Purity," and "Ministry for the Times."

Foster, (SAMUEL,) an English mathematician, born in Northamptonshire, was noted as an inventor of mathematical instruments. He published a treatise on the "Quadrant," (1624,) and other works. In 1636 he became professor of astronomy in Gresham College, London. Died in 1652.

Foster, (STEPHEN C.,) an American musical composer and writer of songs, was born in Pittsburg, Pennsylvania, in 1826. He produced many popular songs or ballads, among which are "My Old Kentucky Home," "Susannah," "Old Folks at Home," and "Willie. we have missed you." He died in New York in 1864.

See "Atlantic Monthly" for November, 1867.

Fotherby, foth'er-bỹ, (MARTIN,) an English theologian, born in Lincolnshire in 1559; died in 1619.

Fotherby, (ROBERT,) an English navigator, who was sent with Baffin, in 1614, to explore the Northern Ocean. Their progress being arrested by ice about the eightieth degree of latitude, they returned home.

Fothergill, foth'er-gill, (GEORGE,) an English divine, born in Westmoreland in 1705, became Vicar of Bramley in 1751, after having been tutor in Queen's College, Oxford. He published several volumes of approved sermons. Died in 1760.

Fothergill, (JOHN,) an English physician, highly distinguished for benevolence and professional skill, was born at Carr-End, near Richmond, in Yorkshire, in 1712, and was a member of the Society of Friends. After graduating in Edinburgh in 1737, he made the tour of Europe, and settled in London, where he obtained a large practice. Being deeply interested in natural history and rural economy, he laid out at Upton a large garden, in which he collected and acclimated such exotic plants as are useful in medicine and the arts. Dr. Fothergill wrote numerous treatises on therapeutics, pharmacy, etc. He was a coadjutor of Howard in his efforts to reform the management of prisons. Dr. Franklin once said of him, "I can hardly conceive that a better man ever existed." Died in December, 1780.

See a Memoir of Dr. Fothergill, prefixed to his works, by JOHN ELLIOT, M.D., 1781; J. C. LETTSOM, "Account of the Life of John Fothergill;" W. HIRD, "Tribute to the Memory of Dr. John Fothergill;" GILBERT THOMPSON, "Memoirs of the Life of J. Fothergill," 1782.

Fothergill, (SAMUEL,) an eminent and eloquent minister of the Society of Friends, a brother of the preceding, was born at Carr-End, England, in 1716. Having been converted from a life of dissipation or libertinism about the age of twenty-one, he soon appeared as a minister of the gospel, in the service of which he travelled extensively in Great Britain, Ireland, and North America. He resided in Warrington, and acquired a competence by trade. Many of his letters and some of his sermons have been published. Died in 1773.

See "Memoirs of the Life of Samuel Fothergill."

Fo-Thoo-Chhing or **Fo-Thou-Tchhing,** fo-t'hoo-ch'hing, a fabulous or semi-fabulous personage, who is

said to have been born in Hindostan, and to have greatly contributed, by his proficiency in magic or occult science, to the establishment of the religion of Buddha in China, about the year 310 A.D.

Foucaud, foo'kō', (JEAN,) a French fabulist, born at Limoges in 1747, was a zealous revolutionist about 1790. He imitated or translated into *patois* the fables of La Fontaine, (1809.) Died in 1818.

See O. PECONNET, "Foucaud, sa Politique et ses Fables,"1854.

Foucauld, foo'kō', (LOUIS,) Marquis de Lardimalie, born in Périgord, in France, in 1755, was a royalist member of the States-General in 1789-90. Died in 1805.

Foucault, foo'kō', (LÉON,) a French natural philosopher, born in Paris on the 18th of September, 1819. The invention of Daguerre turned his attention to optics, which he studied with great success. He invented in 1844 an apparatus by which electric light is used in optical experiments, microscopic researches, &c. He was associated with M. Fizeau in some improvements in photography and the theory of light, and proved that the velocity of light is not the same in a vacuum as in the air. His demonstration of the rotary motion of the earth by the pendulum and gyroscope attracted general attention. He became *physicien* to the Imperial Observatory, (1854,) and was a member of the Institute. About 1855 he obtained the Copley medal of the Royal Society for his measurement of the velocity of light. Died in 1868.

See "Nouvelle Biographie Générale."

Foucault, (NICOLAS JOSEPH,) a French antiquary and administrator, born in Paris in 1643; died in 1721.

Fouché, foo'shā', (JOSEPH,) Duke of Otranto, a French Jacobin, born at Nantes in 1763, received a liberal education, and adopted the profession of advocate. As a member of the National Convention, (1792-95,) he acted with the Jacobins, and voted for the death of the king. In 1794 he was chosen president of the Jacobin club, as a reward for his share in the massacre of Lyons, and in the same year, with Tallien and others, he plotted the ruin of Robespierre. He was appointed minister of the general police by the Directory in July, 1799. He filled this office many years, displaying great genius for intrigue and artifice ; and it seems he exerted himself to moderate the violence of party and to repair the evils which he and his accomplices had brought upon France. Under the consulate and the empire he rendered important services to Bonaparte, who in 1806 gave him the title of Duke of Otranto. On one occasion Napoleon blamed Fouché for the cold reception which he met with in Paris. The minister reminded him that he had previously directed that nothing should be done to produce a forced or feigned enthusiasm, and added, "In spite of the fusion of the Gauls with the Franks, we are still the same people,—unable to tolerate either liberty or oppression." Having lost the favour of Napoleon, he was dismissed from the police department in 1810, and appointed governor of Rome. After the return of Napoleon from Elba, Fouché served him as minister of police ; and he was retained in the same office by Louis XVIII. for a short period. He was banished in 1816, and died at Trieste in 1820.

See "Sketch of the Life of the Duke of Otranto," London, 1816; A. SERIEYS, "Fouché de Nantes, sa Vie privée," etc., 1816; "Vie de Fouché," Paris, 1821; "Mémoires de la Vie publique de M. Fouché," 1819; "Mémoires de Fouché," 2 vols., 1824, (said to have been written by ALPHONSE DE BEAUCHAMP, though it purports to be an autobiography;) "Nouvelle Biographie Générale."

Foucher, foo'shā', (PAUL,) a French scholar, born at Tours in 1704. He was admitted into the Academy of Inscriptions in 1753. He left a "Historical Treatise on the Religion of the Persians," and another on the "Religion of the Greeks," which were printed in the Memoirs of the above-named Academy. Died in 1778.

Foucher, (SIMON,) a French philosophical writer, born at Dijon in 1644, became a priest. He was an admirer of the philosophy of Plato, on which he wrote a treatise, entitled "Dissertation sur la Philosophie des Académiciens," (1692.) He also wrote "On the Wisdom of the Ancients," (1682.) Died in Paris in 1696.

Foucher, (VICTOR ADRIEN,) a French jurist and magistrate, born in Paris in 1803. He became director-general of civil affairs in Algeria, procureur at the tribunal of the Seine, and in 1850 a member of the court of

€ as *k*; ç as *s*; g̃ *hard*; g̃ as *j*; G, H, K, *guttural*; N, *nasal*; R, *trilled*; s̃ as *z*; ₺h as in *this*. (☞See Explanations, p. 23.)

60

cassation. He wrote several legal works, and edited a "Collection of the Civil and Criminal Laws of Modern States," (10 vols., 1833–58.) He rendered important services to the cause of order in 1848.

See "Nouvelle Biographie Générale."

Foucher d'Obsonville, foo'shả' dob'sŏn'vèl', a French traveller and naturalist, born at Montargis in 1734. He went to India by land about 1753, and remained there until 1771. He published "Essays on the Habits of Divers Animals, with Observations on the Morals and Customs of Several Nations," (1783.) Died in 1802.

Fouchier, foo'she-ả', (BERTRAND,) a Dutch portrait-painter, born at Berg-op-Zoom in 1609, was a pupil of A. Van Dyck. He also studied the works of Tintoret in Italy. Died in 1674.

Fouchy, de, dẹh foo'she', (JEAN PAUL **Grand-Jean** —grŏn'zhŏn',) a French savant, born in Paris in 1707, was elected perpetual secretary of the Academy of Sciences in 1743, and performed the duties of that office for thirty years with much ability. Died in 1788.

See CONDORCET, "Éloge de M. de Fouchy," 1788.

Foucquet. See FOUQUET.

Fougeret de Monbron. See MONBRON.

Fougeroux de Bondaroy, foozh'roo' dẹh bŏn'dả'-rwả', (AUGUSTE DENIS,) a French savant, born in Paris in 1732, was a nephew of the famous Duhamel, (Henri Louis.) He wrote, besides other works, "Researches among the Ruins of Herculaneum," (1769,) and "The Art of the Cutler," (1772.) Died in 1789.

Foo-hee or **Fou-hi,** foo-hee, supposed to have been the first Emperor of China, born in the province of Shansee, began to reign about 2950 B.C. He is said to have instituted matrimony, and to have invented music and writing.

Fouillou, foo'yoo', (JACQUES,) a French Jansenist polemical writer, born at La Rochelle in 1670; died in 1736.

Fouilloux, du, dü foo'yoo', (JACQUES,) a French gentleman, who wrote a popular treatise on "Hunting, and on the Habits of Animals," (1560.) Died in 1580.

Fouinet, foo'e'nả', (ERNEST,) a French poet and novelist, born at Nantes in 1799; died in Paris in 1845.

Foulcher (or **Foucher**) **de Chartres,** foo'shả' dẹh shaRtR, [Lat. FULCHE'RIUS CARNOTEN'SIS,] a French historian, born about 1050, joined the crusade for the conquest of the Holy Land. He was chaplain to Baldwin, King of Jerusalem, and wrote a history of the first crusade. Died about 1127.

Foulcoie, foo'kwả', [Lat. FULCO'IUS,] born at Beauvais, in France, about 1020, was one of the most popular poets of his time. The subjects of his poems are legends, lives of saints, etc. Died about 1083.

Fould, foo, (ACHILLE,) a French financier, born in Paris in 1800, was a son of a Jewish banker. He was elected to the Chamber of Deputies in 1842, and again in 1846. In the Constituent Assembly of 1848 he acted with the party of order, and distinguished himself by financial ability. He was appointed minister of finance three times between October, 1849, and January, 1852, during which period the public credit was improved or restored. He resigned in January, 1852, soon after which he was raised to the dignity of senator and appointed minister of state and of the household of the emperor. A large deficit having induced Napoleon to renounce the prerogative to raise money on credit without the assent of the legislative body, M. Fould was persuaded to resume the portfolio of finance in November, 1861. He was removed in February, 1867, and died the same year.

See "Biographie des Membres du Sénat."

Foulis, fŏw'lis, (ROBERT and ANDREW,) two learned and noted Scottish printers, were brothers and residents of Glasgow, where they followed their profession about thirty years, and printed editions of Greek and Latin classics remarkable for accuracy and elegance. Their famous Horace (1743) was reputed to be faultless, and a reward was offered to any person who should detect an error in it. After making handsome fortunes, they were ruined by the expense incurred in founding an academy of painting and sculpture at Glasgow. Their collection

of paintings was sold at auction in 1776. Andrew died in 1774, and Robert in 1776.

See CHAMBERS, "Biographical Dictionary of Eminent Scotsmen ;" LEMOINE, "History of Printing."

Foulkes, (MARTIN.) See FOLKES.

Foullon, foo'lŏn', (ABEL,) a French poet and mechanician, born in Maine in 1513, made a metrical version of the Satires of Persius,—the first that appeared in French. Died in 1563.

Foullon or **Foulon,** (JOSEPH FRANÇOIS,) a French administrator, born at Saumur in 1715. In 1771 he was intendant or controller of finance, and in July, 1789, was appointed controller-general in place of Necker, or (according to one account) administrator of the army. A few days after his appointment, before he had entered upon the office, he fell a victim to the violence of the Parisian mob. He proposed the repudiation of the public debt.

See MADAME CAMPAN, "Mémoires."

Foulon or **Foullon,** foo'lŏn', (JOHANN ÉRARD,) a Flemish historian and Jesuit, born at Liege in 1608 or 1609 ; died in 1668.

Foulon, foo'lŏn' or fŏw'lon, [Lat. FULLO'NIUS,] (WILLEM,) a Dutch poet and Protestant, born at the Hague in 1493. He became rector of the College of Elbing about 1536. Among his works are "Acolastus," a Latin drama on the subject of the Prodigal Son, (1540,) and the "Triumph of Eloquence," a Latin poem. Died in 1568.

Foulques, foolk or fook, [Lat. FUL'CO,] an eminent French prelate, born about 850 A.D. He became Archbishop of Rheims in 883, and acquired great influence both in the church and state. He promoted education and morality. He was killed by order of Baldwin, Count of Flanders, in 900.

See BARONIUS, "Annales."

Foulques I., Count of Anjou, surnamed LE ROUX, was the son of Ingelger and Alinde. Died in 938 A.D.

Foulques II., surnamed THE GOOD, Count of Anjou, son of the preceding, was a patron of learning. He died at Tours in 958 A.D.

Foulques III., Count of Anjou, grandson of the preceding, waged war against the Duke of Bretagne and the Count of Blois, founded monasteries, and visited the Holy Land. Died in 1040.

Foulques IV., grandson of Foulques III., born at Châteaulandon in 1043, inherited Saintonge, and conquered Anjou and Touraine from his brother Geoffroi. He married a daughter of Simon de Montfort. Died in 1109.

Foulques V., a son of the preceding, born about 1090, went twice to Palestine in the crusades, married a daughter of Baldwin II. in 1129, and succeeded him, in 1131, on the throne of Jerusalem. He was renowned for courage and other virtues. Died in 1142. He left his crown to his sons, Baldwin III. and Amaury.

Foulques, (GUI.) See CLEMENT IV.

Foulques de Marseille. See FOLQUET.

Foulques de Neuilly, fook dẹh nuh'ye', a French priest, celebrated for his zeal and eloquence and his promotion of the fourth crusade. He directed his efforts especially to the conversion of courtesans, and obtained from Pope Innocent III. a plenary indulgence for those who should marry them. He persuaded many nobles to join the crusade in 1198. Died in 1201.

See VILLEHARDOUIN, "Histoire de la Conquête de Constantinople."

Foulston, fŏls'tọn, (JOHN,) an English architect, was born about 1772. He worked for many years at Plymouth, was architect of nearly all the public buildings erected there in that period, and attempted various styles, including Grecian, Ionic, Doric, and Hindoo. Among his works are the Royal Hotel and Theatre, the Exchange, and the Town Hall, at Devonport. Died in 1842.

Fountaine, fŏwn'tin, (Sir ANDREW,) an English antiquary, born about 1680, was tutor of Prince William, and keeper of the mint from 1727 to 1753. He wrote a treatise on ancient coins. Died in 1753.

Fouqué, (FRIEDRICH HEINRICH KARL.) See LA-MOTHE-FOUQUÉ.

Fouqué, foo'kȧ', (HENRI AUGUSTE,) Baron de la Mothe, (dẹh lȧ mot,) a general, born at the Hague, of a French family, in 1698, entered the Prussian service in 1715. He acquired the friendship of the prince royal, (afterwards Frederick the Great,) who, on his accession in 1740, gave him a command in the army and decorated him with the order of merit. He served with credit in all the wars of that prince, and rose to the rank of general. In 1760 he commanded a corps-d'armée at Landshut, was wounded and taken prisoner. His correspondence with Frederick has been published with the works of that royal author. Lamotte-Fouqué, the author of "Undine," was his grandson. Died in 1774.

See FRIEDRICH DE LA MOTTE-FOUQUÉ, "Lebensbeschreibung des Generals H. A. Baron de la Motte-Fouqué," 1824.

Fouquet, foo'kȧ', (GUILLAUME,) Marquis de la Varenne, a French diplomatist, born in 1560, was a favourite of Henry IV. Died in 1616.

Fouquet, (HENRI,) an eminent French physician, born at Montpellier in 1727, graduated in 1759, and practised at Marseilles. In 1766 he settled in his native city, and published medical treatises which had a high reputation. He was chosen professor of medicine in the University of Montpellier about 1792. Died in 1806.

See "Biographie Médicale;" DUMAS, "Éloge de Fouquet," 1807.

Fouquet or **Foucquet,** foo'kȧ', (NICOLAS,) Marquis of Belle-Isle, a noted French minister of finance, born in Paris in 1615, was the son of Francis Fouquet, Vicomte de Vaux. At the age of thirty-five he became attorney-general of the Parliament of Paris. In 1652 he was appointed superintendent of the finances, which were then not in a flourishing state, and did not improve under his direction. Louis XIV. once demanded some money of Fouquet, who answered, "Sire, there is none in your majesty's coffers; but Cardinal Mazarin will lend you some." Fouquet expended about eighteen million francs on his palace of Vaux, which surpassed even the royal residence of Fontainebleau. "Never," says Voltaire, "was a dissipator of the royal finances more noble and generous." The king lost confidence in his integrity and financial skill, and it is thought Colbert promoted his disgrace. Fouquet was arrested in 1661, and, after a trial of three years' duration, sentenced to imprisonment for life. La Fontaine wrote verses in his defence during the trial. He died in 1680.

See VOLTAIRE, "Siècle de Louis XIV;" MADAME DE SÉVIGNÉ, "Lettres;" D'AUVIGNY, "Vies des Hommes illustres de la France;" SAINTE-BEUVE, "Causeries du Lundi."

Fouquet, de, dẹh foo'kȧ', (CHARLES LOUIS ARMAND,) Comte de Belle-Isle, a French general, born in 1693, was a brother of Marshal Fouquet, Duke of Belle-Isle. He was killed in battle in Piedmont in 1747.

Fouquet, de, (CHARLES LOUIS AUGUSTE,) Duc de Belle-Isle, a French general and diplomatist, born at Villefranche de Rouergue in 1684, was a grandson of the financier Nicolas Fouquet. He became maréchal-de-camp in 1718, and lieutenant-general in 1731. It appears that his influence with the king involved France in the general war which began in 1741. He was made a marshal of France in 1741, and gained some advantages over the Austrians in Bohemia. In 1745 he defeated the enemy at Vintimiglia and Montauban. He was appointed minister of state in 1756, and secretary of war in 1758. He is said to have been a diplomatist of great ability. "His whole life," says Macaulay, "was one wild day-dream of conquest and spoliation." ("Essay on Frederick the Great.") Died in 1761.

See VOLTAIRE, "Siècle de Louis XV;" DE COURCELLES, "Dictionnaire des Généraux Français."

Fouquier, foo'ke-ȧ', (PIERRE ÉLOY,) a French physician, born in Picardy in 1776. He practised and lectured in Paris, and became one of the consulting physicians of Charles X. He succeeded Dr. Marc as first physician to Louis Philippe. Died in 1850.

Fouquier-Tinville or **-Tainville,** foo'ke-ȧ' tăN'vèl', (ANTOINE QUENTIN,) born near Saint-Quentin in 1747. Among the French Jacobins he was one of the most atrocious. Under the auspices of Robespierre, he acted as public accuser before the bloody tribunal of the Revolution. When informed of the fall of Robespierre, he exclaimed, "No change for us! justice must take its course." However, after he had exercised his functions by sending his former patron to the guillotine, he was himself condemned to death, and executed in 1795.

See LAMARTINE, "History of the Girondists."

Fouquières, foo'ke-aiR', (JACQUES,) an eminent Flemish landscape-painter, was born at Antwerp in 1580, and studied with Rubens. In 1621 he went to France, by invitation of Louis XIII., who gave him a commission to paint the chief towns of the kingdom. Died in 1659.

See FÉLIBIEN, "Entretiens sur les Ouvrages des Peintres."

Four. See DUFOUR and LONGUERUE.

Fourcroy, de, dẹh fooR'kRwȧ', (ANTOINE FRANÇOIS,) COMTE, an eminent French chemist, born of poor parents in Paris in 1755, was a pupil of Macquer and Bucquet. He graduated as M.D. in 1780, and was appointed by Buffon, in 1784, professor of chemistry in the Jardin du Roi, the name of which was changed about 1794 to the Museum of Natural History. He lectured there for twenty-five years with great success. "The facility and elegance of his language," says Cuvier, "his copiousness, enthusiasm, and clearness, enchanted his auditors, and contributed greatly to diffuse a taste for chemistry in all parts of the world." In 1793 he became a member of the National Convention, in which he promoted the cause of education and did not partake in the excesses of the dominant party. He saved the life of Darcet in the reign of terror. He was one of the first members of the Institute. He was nominated a councillor of state in December, 1799, and director-general of public instruction in 1801. The schools flourished under his wise direction. He published in 1801 a "System of Chemistry," ("Système des Connaissances chimiques," 11 vols. 8vo,) a work of great merit. Among his best works is "The Philosophy of Chemistry," ("La Philosophie chimique," 1792.) He died suddenly in December, 1809, and left one son, who was killed at the battle of Lutzen.

See CUVIER, "Éloge de Fourcroy," 1811; PALISSOT DE BEAUVOIS, "Éloge historique de Fourcroy," 1810; PARISET, "Éloge de Fourcroy;" A. CATTANEO, "Cenni sulla Vita di A. F. Fourcroy," 1839; "Encyclopædia Britannica;" "Nouvelle Biographie Générale."

Fourcroy de Ramecourt, fooR'kRwȧ' dẹh răm'kooR', (CHARLES RENÉ,) a French military engineer, born in Paris in 1715. He served as engineer in the Seven Years' war, and obtained the rank of maréchal-de-camp. The Academy of Sciences rewarded his scientific services by admitting him as a "free associate." He wrote a treatise on "Fortification," (1786,) and other esteemed works. Died in 1791.

See CONDORCET, "Éloge de Charles René Fourcroy."

Fourier, foo're-ȧ', (FRANÇOIS CHARLES MARIE,) named "the Phalansterian," the founder of the famous system of "Fourierism," a form of socialism, born at Besançon, in France, in 1772, was the son of a merchant. After he had received his education in his native town, he was employed a few years in a counting-house in Lyons. During the Revolution he was compelled, in 1793, to take arms, and served one or two campaigns on the Rhine. He employed his leisure time while in the army, and in other situations, in study and reflection upon the social and political theories which then abounded in France. He also acquired proficiency in the exact sciences, not neglecting political economy. After leaving the army, he passed several years as a commercial traveller for mercantile houses of Marseilles and Lyons, diligently engaged in the problem the solution of which should remedy the miseries of the present social system. In 1803 he published, in a journal at Lyons, an article on European policy which attracted the favourable notice of Bonaparte. At length, having, as he thought, made the important discovery of which he was in search, he published, in 1808, his "Theory of Four Movements and General Destinies," designed as the prospectus of a more complete work, which appeared in 1822, entitled a "Treatise on Domestic and Agricultural Association." A later edition was entitled "Theory of Universal Unity," (4 vols., 1841.) These works were coldly received by the public and by the reviewers. Numerous experiments of his system of attractive industry and social harmony have been made in Europe and America; but they have not been successful. Fourier lived in Paris from 1830 until his death, which occurred in 1837.

See L. DE LOMÉNIE, "Galerie des Contemporains;" V. CONSIDÉRANT, "Exposition du Système de Fourier;" LECHEVALIER, "Études sur la Science sociale;" C. PELLERIN, "Charles Fourier, sa Vie et sa Théorie," 1838; VICTOR HENNEQUIN, "Théorie de C. Fourier," 1847.

Fourier, (JEAN BAPTISTE JOSEPH,) BARON, a celebrated French mathematician, born at Auxerre on the 21st of March, 1768. He espoused with ardour the popular cause in the Revolution; but, not keeping pace with the violent demagogues, he was twice imprisoned by the dominant faction. When the Polytechnic School was opened, about 1795, Fourier was appointed by Lagrange and Monge assistant professor. For his profound and varied acquirements he was selected as one of the savants who accompanied Bonaparte to Egypt in 1798, after which he was secretary of the Institute of Egypt. Here he distinguished himself by his industry in scientific excursions, and was employed with credit in negotiations with the natives. He was prefect of Isère at Grenoble from 1801 to 1815, and was admitted into the Academy of Sciences in 1817. He was elected a member of the Académie Française in 1827. Besides several minor treatises, Fourier published a great work on the theory of heat, "Théorie analytique de la Chaleur," (1822,) of which M. Cousin observes, "The grandeur of its results has no more been contested than their certainty, and, in the judgment of scientific Europe, the novelty of the analysis on which they rest is equal to its perfection. M. Fourier presents himself, then, with the evident mark of true genius: he is an inventor." He left an "Analysis of Determinate Equations," (1831.) Died in May, 1830.

See V. COUSIN, "Éloge de Fourier;" M. ARAGO, "Éloge historique de J. Fourier;" CHAMPOLLION-FIGEAC, "Fourier et Napoléon, l'Égypte et les Cent Jours;" "Foreign Quarterly Review" for October, 1831 ; see, also, an English version of ARAGO's "Éloge de Fourier," Boston, 1859.

Fourmont, foor'môN', (CLAUDE LOUIS,) an Orientalist, a nephew of Étienne, noticed below, was born at Cormeilles in 1708. About 1733 he acted as interpreter in the Royal Library. He visited Egypt in 1746, and published a "Historical and Geographical Description of the Plains of Heliopolis and Memphis," (1755.) Died in 1780.

Fourmont, (ÉTIENNE,) a French savant and distinguished Orientalist, born near Paris in June, 1683, was educated in various colleges of the capital. He possessed a powerful memory, and became eminent for his immense erudition, especially in Oriental languages. In 1715 he obtained the chair of Arabic in the Royal College, and became a member of the Academy of Inscriptions. About this time he was employed to assist a certain Chinese, named Hoang-Ji, in the compilation of a Chinese grammar and dictionary. This person having died in 1716, Fourmont pursued the task alone, and after twenty years' labour finished his "Grammatica Sinica," (1742,) one of the best Chinese grammars that have been published in Europe. In 1738 he was elected a Fellow of the Royal Society of London. He wrote "Critical Reflections on the History of Ancient Nations," (2 vols., 1735,) and numerous other works. Died in 1745.

See "Vie d'Étienne Fourmont," etc., prefixed to his "Réflexions sur l'Origine des anciens Peuples," Paris, 1747 ; FRÉRET, "Éloge de Fourmont ;" "Nouvelle Biographie Générale."

Fourmont, (MICHEL,) an accomplished linguist, a brother of the preceding, was born near Paris in 1690. In 1720 he became professor of Syriac in the Royal College, and in 1724 a member of the Academy of Inscriptions. He assisted his brother in his labours on the Chinese language. Louis XV. sent Fourmont with Abbé Sévin to Greece and other parts of the Levant in 1728, to purchase manuscripts and to copy inscriptions. They returned, with abundant success, in 1732. Died in 1746. Fourmont has been censured for the unnecessary destruction of ancient monuments in Greece.

See "Histoire et Mémoires de l'Académie des Inscriptions ;" "Nouvelle Biographie Générale."

Fournel, foor'nêl', (JEAN FRANÇOIS,) a learned jurist, born in Paris in 1745. He published a number of legal treatises, and a work on "The State of Gaul at the Epoch of the Conquest of the Franks." Died in 1820.

Fournet, foor'nâ', (VICTOR,) a French geologist, born in Paris in 1801, became professor of mineralogy at Lyons about 1834. He has laid the base of a new theory on the distribution of coal-fields in France, and is said to have rendered important services to science.

Fourneyron, foor'nâ'rôN', a French engineer and inventor, born at Saint-Étienne (Loire) in 1802. He invented or improved a turbine, which obtained in 1836 a prize of 6000 francs offered by the Academy of Sciences.

Fournier, foor'ne-â', (ÉDOUARD,) a learned French writer, born at Orléans in 1819, was the author of a "History of Printing and Publishing," (1854,) a Review of Wise and Witty Sayings of Eminent Men, ("L'Esprit dans l'Histoire,") and other works.

Fournier, (GEORGES,) a French Jesuit, born at Caen in 1595. As chaplain in the navy, he visited the coasts of Asia, and, after his return, published useful treatises on geography, hydrography, etc. Died in 1652.

Fournier, (MARC JEAN LOUIS,) a Swiss dramatist, born at Geneva in 1820, became a resident of Paris in his youth. His drama the "Clown," ("Paillasse," 1850,) in which he was assisted by Dennery, had great success.

Fournier, (PIERRE SIMON,) a skilful French engraver and founder of types, born in Paris in 1712. He wrote an "Essay on the Origin and Progress of the Art of Engraving on Wood," (1758,) and a useful work called "Manuel typographique," (2 vols., 1764.) Died in 1768.

Fournier, (RAOUL,) Sieur du Rondeau, a learned French author, born at Orléans in 1562, wrote approved works on law, morality, philosophy, religion, etc., also a Latin poem called "Cento Christianus." Died in 1627.

Fournier de la Contamine, foor'ne-â' dĕh lä kôN'tă'mèn', (MARIE NICOLAS,) a French bishop, born at Gex in 1760. By the influence of Cardinal Fesch, he was appointed chaplain, and then almoner, to Bonaparte, who, in 1806, made him Bishop of Montpellier. Died in 1834.

Fournier des Ormes, foor'ne-â' dâ'zorm', (CHARLES,) a French poet and landscape-painter, born in Paris in 1778, was a grandson of Pierre Simon, noticed above. He wrote a poem entitled "The Art of Painting," ("La Peinture," 1837,) and translated Lucretius's "De Rerum Natura" into French verse, (1848.) His landscapes are commended. Died in 1853.

See QUÉRARD, "La France Littéraire."

Fournier de Pescay, foor'ne-â' dĕh pês'kâ', (FRANÇOIS,) born at Bordeaux in 1771, became physician to Ferdinand VII. at Valençay. He wrote several treatises on medicine. Died about 1833.

Fournival, de, dĕh foor'ne-vâl', **Fournivaux,** foor'ne-vō', or **Furnival,** fûr'ne-vâl', (RICHARD,) one of the most noted novelists (*romanciers*) of his time, was a canon of the church of Amiens. He wrote several works about 1250, one of which is styled the "Power of Love."

See "Nouvelle Biographie Générale."

Fourquevaux, de, dĕh foork'vō', (FRANÇOIS de Pavie—dĕh pä've',) BARON, son of the following, was born near Toulouse in 1561. After making a tour in Europe and Asia, he was gentleman-ordinary and steward in the court of Henry of Navarre. He wrote the "Lives of Great French Captains," (1643.) Died in 1611.

Fourquevaux, de, (RAIMOND de Beccarie de Pavie—dĕh bă'kâ're' dĕh pä've',) BARON, a French general, born at Toulouse in 1509, served in several campaigns in Italy. In 1557 he became Governor of Narbonne. He wrote a treatise on military discipline. Died in 1574.

Foville, fo'vèl', (ACHILLE LOUIS,) a French medical writer, born at Pontoise in 1799. He wrote on the brain and cerebral diseases.

Fowler, (CHARLES,) an English architect, born in Devonshire in 1792. He gained the first premium for his design of London Bridge. Among his works are the Hungerford Market, the Devon Lunatic Asylum, and the Court of Bankruptcy, London.

Fowler, (CHRISTOPHER,) an English clergyman, born in 1611, left the Established Church in 1641, and joined the Presbyterians, among whom he became a prominent and zealous preacher. Died in 1676.

ă, ē, ī, ō, ū, ȳ, *long;* ă, ĕ, ĭ, ŏ, ŭ, ў, *short;* ą, ę, į, ǫ, *obscure;* fär, fåll, fåt; mět; nŏt; gōōd; mōōn;

Fowler, (EDWARD,) an English divine, born at Westerleigh in 1632, was appointed in 1691 Bishop of Gloucester. He wrote "The Design of Christianity," (1671,) which was attacked by Bunyan; also, a "Discourse on Christian Liberty," (1680.) Died in 1714.

See "Biographia Britannica."

Fowler, (JOHN,) a learned English printer, born at Bristol, was a zealous opponent of the Protestant Reformation, and a good classical scholar. He removed his press to Antwerp, to serve the Catholics more efficiently. Died in 1579.

See FULLER, "Worthies."

Fŏw'lẹr, (ORSON SQUIRE,) an American phrenologist, born in Cohocton, New York, in 1809. He has published a large number of works on phrenological and kindred subjects. In connection with his brother, Lorenzo N. Fowler, he has conducted the "Phrenological Journal" for many years.

Fŏw'lẹr, (THOMAS,) born at York, in England, in 1736, was a successful practitioner of medicine in that city, and wrote several medical treatises. Died in 1801.

Fownes, fŏwnz, (GEORGE,) an English chemist, born about 1815, was professor of practical chemistry in University College, London. He wrote a prize essay on "Chemistry as exemplifying the Wisdom and Beneficence of God," (1844,) and a "Manual of Elementary Chemistry," (1844,) which is a popular text-book and has been reprinted in Philadelphia, (1855.) Died in 1849.

Fox, (Sir CHARLES,) an English civil engineer, born at Derby in 1810. Among his works are several railways in England, and bridges and railway-stations. He constructed the building for the Great Exhibition of 1851, according to the plan of Sir Joseph Paxton, and was the architect of the Crystal Palace at Sydenham.

Fox, (CHARLES JAMES,) a celebrated English orator and statesman, born in London on the 24th of January, 1749, was the third son of Henry Fox, the first Lord Holland, and of Lady Georgiana Caroline Lennox, a daughter of the Duke of Richmond. His indulgent father was not slow to appreciate his splendid promise and hereditary genius, and bestowed particular attention on his education, although it is said that he permitted him to follow his own inclinations without restraint. About the age of nine he was sent to Eton, where he manifested a rare aptitude for all departments of learning, and an eager relish for the sports of youth and for all physical and intellectual pleasures. In the autumn of 1764 Fox went to Oxford, and entered Hertford College, where he appears to have been a hard student. He learned to read the Latin and Greek classics with facility, and in after-life he continued to delight in classic studies, to which he added an accurate knowledge of modern languages and history. About this period he began to indulge an insane passion for gaming and other modes of dissipation, which continued through his life to obscure the noble qualities that nature had given him. Leaving college in 1766, he went abroad, and passed two years on the continent. In May, 1768, he was returned to Parliament for Midhurst, though he had not yet attained the age of twenty.

He entered Parliament as a supporter of the ministerial or Tory party, and when Lord North became premier, in 1770, Fox was appointed junior lord of the admiralty. In 1773 he held for a few weeks the place of one of the lords of the treasury; but, being dismissed for his insubordination to the court, he joined the opposition, and found more congenial company with Burke and other Whig leaders. He strenuously opposed Lord North's policy in regard to American taxation. In March, 1774, he made a speech against the Boston Port Bill; and he continued to defend the cause of the colonies against the insane policy of the British ministry. Fox was returned for Westminster in 1780; and when the American war ended, in 1782, he had become the recognized leader of the Whigs in the House of Commons, the champion of freedom, and a "consummate master of the art of debate." On the formation of the new ministry under Rockingham, in 1782, he accepted the office of foreign secretary, but resigned in a few months, in consequence of the death of that premier. By a coalition between Fox and Lord North, the ministry of Lord Shelburne was

outvoted and compelled to resign, and in April, 1783, Fox became secretary of state in a cabinet of which the Duke of Portland was the premier. This ministry was weakened by the hostility of the king; and Fox, having been defeated on his India Bill, was dismissed from power in December, 1783, when Mr. Pitt became prime minister. Fox had lost popularity by his coalition with Lord North, and in the next election his rival obtained a large majority in Parliament. He was again elected for Westminster, after a warm contest, in 1784, and made a memorable speech on the scrutiny which was demanded by his opponent.

He powerfully seconded Burke in the impeachment of Warren Hastings in 1788 and the ensuing years. The warm political and personal friendship which had long existed between him and Burke was broken by the French Revolution, which Fox cordially approved in its first stages. Fox having expressed his admiration of the new French constitution in 1791, Burke spoke on the other side, and declared, "Our friendship is at an end." Mr. Fox continued to be the leader of the Whigs, and constantly opposed the long aggressive war which Pitt waged against the French republic. He supported Wilberforce's motion for the abolition of the slave-trade in 1791, and Mr. Grey's effort for parliamentary reform in 1793. His party having been reduced to a small minority, he resolved, in 1797, to take no part in legislation, and absented himself from Parliament for five years, which he passed in literary pursuits. In 1802 he visited Paris, and was treated with marked attention by Bonaparte. In consequence of the death of Pitt, in January, 1806, the Whigs, under Lord Grenville, came into power, and Fox became foreign secretary, and the master-spirit of the government. He was negotiating for peace with France when he died, on the 13th of September, 1806, leaving the reputation of an honest statesman and a real philanthropist. Brougham pronounced him "the most accomplished debater that ever appeared on the theatre of public affairs." "He possessed above all moderns," says Mackintosh, "that union of reason, simplicity, and vehemence which formed the prince of orators." He left an unfinished history of the reign of James II., which, says Lord Jeffrey, "we think is an invaluable work, not only as a memorial of the high principles and gentle dispositions of its illustrious author, but as a record of those sentiments of true English constitutional independence which seem to have been nearly forgotten in the bitterness and hazards of our recent contentions. . . . We do not think it has any great value as a history, nor is it very admirable as a piece of composition."

See LORD JOHN RUSSELL, "Life of Charles James Fox," 3 vols., 1867; SYDNEY SMITH, in the "Edinburgh Review," vol. xiv., (July, 1809,) "Quarterly Review," vol. ii., (November, 1809,) and "Edinburgh Review," vol. xviii.; SAMUEL PARR, "Character of the Late C. J. Fox," 2 vols., 1809; "Memorials of Charles James Fox," by LORD HOLLAND; BROUGHAM, "Statesmen of the Time of George III.;" TROTTER, "Memoirs of C. J. Fox," 1811; "Recollections of C. J. Fox," by B. C. WALPOLE, 1806; "Edinburgh Review" for July, 1808, and January, 1854; "London Quarterly Review" for November, 1809, December, 1811, and April, 1859.

Fox, (EDWARD,) an English bishop, born in Gloucestershire, was a strenuous promoter of the Protestant Reformation. He was sent by Wolsey, with Gardiner, to Rome, in 1528, to procure the divorce of Queen Catherine. In 1535 he became Bishop of Hereford, and was sent on a mission to the Protestant league of Schmalkalden. He was distinguished for his dexterity as a negotiator. He wrote "On the True Difference between Regal and Ecclesiastical Power," ("De vera Differentia Regiæ Potestatis et Ecclesiasticæ," 1534.) Died in 1538.

See "Biographia Britannica."

Fox, (FRANCIS,) an English clergyman, was vicar of Pottern and prebendary of Salisbury. He published the "New Testament Explained," (1722,) and a few other works. Died in 1738.

Fox, (GEORGE,) the founder of the Society of Friends, or Quakers, was born at Drayton-in-the-Clay, (now called Fenny Drayton,) Leicestershire, England, in July, 1624. His father, Christopher Fox, was a weaver, so distinguished for the uprightness of his character that he was called, among his neighbours, "righteous Christer." His mother, whose maiden name was Mary Lago, was eminent for her piety, and by her sympathy and encouragement doubtless did much to promote that religious thoughtfulness for which her son George was remarkable even from his childhood. At an early age he was placed with a man who was a shoemaker and dealt in wool. He was for some time employed as a shepherd, an occupation well suited to his cast of mind, and "a fit emblem," says William Penn, "of his future service in the Church of Christ." The parents of George Fox were members of the Church of England, and they endeavoured to educate their children in its doctrines and mode of worship. When he was in his nineteenth year, being on business at a fair, he was invited by his cousin and another person, both professors of religion, to join them in drinking a jug of beer, and he, being thirsty, consented. When they had drunk a glass apiece, they began to drink healths, and, calling for more beer, they said, "he that would not drink should pay all." Then George Fox, taking out a groat, laid it on the table, saying, "If it be so, I will leave you." He returned home much distressed. That night he did not go to bed, but spent the time in walking up and down and in earnest prayer. "The Lord said unto me," (we quote the words of his journal,) "Thou seest how young people go together into vanity, and old people into the earth : thou must forsake all, young and old, keep out of all, and be a stranger to all." "I fasted much," he says, "walked abroad in solitary places many days, and often took my Bible and sat in hollow trees and lonesome places till night came on ; and frequently in the night walked mournfully about by myself." As a remedy for his distress of mind, some of his relations advised him to marry; but he "told them he was but a lad, and must get wisdom." He went to different priests for consolation, but found them all "miserable comforters." One "ancient priest" bade him take tobacco and sing psalms. But tobacco he did not like, and psalms he was not in a state to sing. To sing belongs rather to the joyful ;[*] but George Fox suffered what few, we may hope, among the children of men are required to suffer. So great was his mental distress that, he says, "I could have wished I had never been born, or that I had been born blind, that I might never have seen wickedness nor vanity, and deaf, that I might never have heard vain and wicked words, and the Lord's name blasphemed." At times he was reduced almost to despair. On one occasion "a great cloud came over him," and there arose in his mind doubts even of the existence of a God ; but the temptation soon passed, and a divine voice within him said, "There is a living God, who made all things." He afterwards "saw that it was good that he had gone through that exercise ;" for, meeting with some who had embraced atheism, he was enabled to speak with convincing power to their minds, and forced them to confess that there is a living God. Amid all his trials he had moments of great rejoicing. He was filled with admiration of God's infinite love, and "saw through all these troubles and temptations," and that they were "good for him," being designed for the perfection of his faith. When all his hopes of obtaining comfort from any human source were gone, "I heard," he says, "a voice which said, 'There is one, even Christ Jesus, that can speak to thy condition.' When I heard it, my heart did leap for joy. Then the Lord let me see why there was none upon the earth that could speak to my condition, namely, that I might give him all the glory."

Some of his relations, observing the seriousness of his character, had wished that he should be educated for a priest ; but one morning, as he was walking in the field, it was shown to him "that being bred at Oxford or Cambridge was not enough to qualify men to be ministers of Christ ;" at which he wondered, because it was contrary to what the people were commonly taught to believe. At the same time he saw that it was the anointing of the Spirit which qualified one to be a true preacher of the gospel. At another time it was shown to him "that God, who made the world, did not dwell in temples made with hands." This also surprised him, because it was so different from the prevailing belief. He perceived that many read the Scriptures without a right understanding

of their meaning ; it was then shown to him that none could read them aright without a measure of the same Divine Spirit that gave them forth. He saw everywhere around him men attaching the greatest importance to the letter, while very few regarded the spirit, of the Bible ; many Christian professors who had an outward form of godliness showed too plainly by their conduct that they were without its life-giving power. George Fox believed that he was called by Heaven to awaken men from their lifeless forms and dogmas to a sense of the vital importance of an inward, living, spiritual religion. The field was already waiting for the labourers. He saw the harvest white and the heavenly seed lying thick on the ground, and none to gather it ; for this he mourned with tears. A report having gone forth that he had a "discerning spirit," people came from far and near to hear him. "I had," he says, "great openings and prophecies, and spoke unto them of the things of God." On a subsequent occasion he says, "We had great meetings : the Lord's power wrought mightily and gathered many." He was about twenty-three years old when he first began to preach, after which he travelled much in the ministry.

As, on the one hand, George Fox believed that he was required to do many things which in that age were generally considered to form no part of Christian duty, so, on the other, he was forbidden to do many things which other religious professors permitted or enjoined. However small or apparently trivial the requirement, he felt that he must yield an absolute obedience to the Divine voice within his soul. It was then deemed necessary, as a mark of honour, to address one's superiors or equals always with the plural pronoun : to "thou" a person was generally regarded as an expression of disrespect, or at least of familiarity. But Fox considered that to address a single person with a form of speech which could only in strictness be applied to two or more, was inconsistent with that simplicity and perfect truthfulness which the pure spirit of Christianity requires. He regarded also the custom of taking off the hat, as a mark of respect to our fellow-men, as improper, and thought that men ought not to demand such formal honours of one another, but should rather seek "the honour that cometh from God only." One of the principal reasons alleged by Fox for not taking off one's hat to men was, that this was an act of homage due only to the Creator, and that it appears from the words of the Apostle Paul, (see I. Cor. xi. 4,) and from the practice of the primitive Christians, to have been regarded as an especial mark of reverence to God. He seems to have considered complimentary forms and ceremonies as not only opposed to Christian simplicity and truthfulness, but as tending to foster a spirit of pride and vainglory incompatible with the humility which belongs to a true follower of the Redeemer, and unfavourable to that Christian equality and freedom which are necessary to the most perfect society.

Although the rise of the Society of Friends was primarily a religious movement, it has unquestionably exerted an important influence upon the political as well as the social condition of England and the United States. "It was," says Bancroft, "the consequence of the moral warfare against corruption,—the aspiration of the human mind after a perfect emancipation from the long reign of bigotry and superstition." "It marks," observes the same writer, in another place, "the moment when intellectual freedom was claimed unconditionally by the people as an inalienable birthright." (See "History of the United States," vol. i. p. 451, and vol. ii. p. 337.)

As Fox believed it to be required of him that he should not doff his hat "to any, high or low," and that he should, when addressing an individual, use invariably the singular pronoun, "without any respect to rich or poor, great or small," he gave great offence, and excited the rage of some who, he says, were "great professors of Christianity." He was thus furnished with an answer to those who thought this too trifling a matter to be so scrupulous about ; for what concerned so nearly the pride and passions of men was not so trivial as to be beneath the command of God.

Having, in 1648, at Nottingham, boldly opposed a

---

* See James v. 13.

priest respecting a point of doctrine in the presence of his congregation, he was arrested and sent to prison. He was again imprisoned in 1650 at Derby, upon a false accusation of blasphemy. On that occasion Justice Bennet, of Derby, called him and his friends "Quakers," because he bade the magistrates "tremble at the word of the Lord." During his imprisonment at Derby there was in the same jail a young woman who was to be tried for her life for stealing. "I wrote," says Fox, "to the judge and jury, showing them how contrary it was to the law of God in old time to put people to death for stealing; and moving them to show mercy." Throughout his life he appears never to have hesitated to rebuke falsehood, injustice, and cruelty, in whatever form they exhibited themselves, and without respect to persons. He felt also called upon to bear his testimony against all war, whether offensive or defensive, alleging the commands of our Saviour, "Love your enemies," "Resist not evil," etc. He cited the same Divine authority to prove not merely the unlawfulness of profane swearing, but of oaths of every kind. Their faithful adherence to their convictions, on these and other points, subjected Fox and his followers to much bitter persecution. He had in 1655 been imprisoned at Launceston. During his confinement in that place, one of his friends went to Oliver Cromwell and desired that he might be imprisoned in Fox's stead. This disinterested conduct appears to have greatly surprised the Protector. Turning to his councillors, he asked, "Which of you would do as much for me if I were in the same condition?" On the accession of Charles II., many hundred Quakers, who had been imprisoned under the governments of Oliver and Richard Cromwell, were set at liberty. But soon after the persecution against these unoffending people raged more fiercely than ever. In 1663 Fox was again arrested; but, when he was brought to be tried at the assizes, the judge declared that, in consequence of the errors in the indictment, he was free from all the charges made against him. But, as the scruples of the Quakers against swearing were well known, the judge, in order to find a pretext against him, required him to take the oath of allegiance and supremacy. On his refusing to do so, he was put into a filthy prison, in which there was, a part of the time, scarcely any ventilation, and yet the rain came in upon his bed, and he was exposed, without any fire, to the cold and wet during a long and severe winter. His confinement on this occasion lasted altogether, in different prisons, nearly three years. He was at length, in 1666, set at liberty. In 1669 he was married to Margaret Fell, the widow of Judge Fell, a man who was highly esteemed for his moderation and good sense, as well as for his piety. He had befriended George Fox in the early period of his ministry; and his wife and daughters had been convinced by Fox's preaching and led to embrace the principles of the Quakers. On behalf of these principles she had suffered long imprisonment and other persecution.

In 1671 Fox set sail for Barbadoes, where many were convinced by his ministry. While in this island, in company with some other Friends, he drew up an important paper setting forth the belief of the Society in regard to the fundamental doctrines of Christianity, and showing that the charges which had been made against them of denying the Divinity and Atonement of Christ and the divine inspiration of the Scriptures, were unfounded calumnies. He afterwards visited the colonies of Maryland, New Jersey, New England, etc. He embarked for England in March, 1673, and arrived at Bristol about the end of April. Some months afterwards he was again imprisoned, for refusing to swear, in Worcester jail. While here he had a severe illness, so that his life was almost despaired of. The king would freely have pardoned him, but Fox would not accept a release from prison on these terms; for to accept a pardon implied that he had committed something to be forgiven. After remaining in jail for more than a year, he was at last set at liberty, chiefly through the influence of Sir Matthew Hale. Subsequently, his health having been greatly impaired by his imprisonment, he spent, for the first time since his early youth, nearly two years in comparative repose at Swarthmore, in Lancashire. This place

had belonged to Margaret Fell, and was his ordinary residence during the latter period of his life. In 1677, accompanied by Penn, Barclay, and several others, he visited the "Friends" in Holland, and established Monthly and Quarterly Meetings and a Yearly Meeting in that country. After an absence of several months, he returned to England the same year. He died in London in 1690, in the sixty-seventh year of his age.

In the religious history of modern times there is perhaps no more remarkable character than that of George Fox. He presents a rare example of the greatest gentleness and meekness joined with a courage which no dangers could appall and a zeal which no obloquy nor suffering could abate, much less subdue. From early manhood until the very end of his life, in spite of ridicule, reproach, and the bitterest persecution, he pursued with an unfaltering faith, and a resolution that never wavered even for a moment, the path which had, as he believed, been divinely appointed him. Many men, deemed brave and virtuous, have, under the pressure of affliction or necessity, been led to reconsider and modify their principles, and, in order to gain what they considered a great good, have sometimes been willing to sacrifice a minute point of conscience; but George Fox never changed or qualified his views in the slightest degree, however great the emergency, and what he felt to be right in the beginning of his course he maintained unswervingly to the end of his life. If it be thought that he sometimes erred through excess of zeal, it should be borne in mind that, in those times of religious excitement and political commotion, many things were considered allowable, not by the Quakers only, but by a large proportion of the religious community, which would be universally condemned by the spirit of a later and more lukewarm age.

In person, George Fox was above the common stature. He was of a pleasing countenance, and, though grave, of easy and modest manners. "He was," says Penn, "civil beyond all forms of breeding." "A most merciful man, as ready to forgive as inapt to take offence." As a speaker, he was clear, forcible, and convincing. "But above all," says Penn, "he excelled in prayer. The inwardness and weight of his spirit, the reverence and solemnity of his address and behaviour, the fewness and fullness of his words, have often struck even strangers with admiration."

The popular but erroneous idea that Fox was opposed to all learning, has arisen doubtless from his having maintained not merely that human learning was insufficient of itself to qualify one to be a preacher of the gospel, but also that a man might be a true gospel minister without any such learning at all as is given at the universities. Nevertheless, he clearly showed the high value which he set upon education, both by his earnest recommendation that schools should be established among "Friends" for the proper instruction of their children, and still more by his applying himself, even after he had entered upon his ministry, to the study of the Hebrew tongue, of which he appears to have acquired a respectable knowledge; for we are assured, on the authority of his intimate friend, George Whitehead,* that "he was able to understand, read, and write Hebrew."

It would be a mistake, however, to regard Fox as a man of learning, in the ordinary acceptation of the phrase, although he well understood the use and value of learning. He was, to adopt the words of Coleridge, "an uneducated man of genius." "There exist folios," remarks the same great critic, "on the human understanding and the nature of man, which would have a far juster claim to their high rank and celebrity, if in the whole huge volume there could be found as much fulness of heart and intellect as burst forth in many a simple page of George Fox." ("Biographia Literaria," chap. ix.)

Fox wrote many epistles of advice and exhortation to the various meetings of the Society; and he has left us a journal of his life, of which Sir James Mackintosh says,

* See his pamphlet in reply to the charges of ignorance made against George Fox.

"It is one of the most extraordinary and instructive documents in the world, which no reader of competent judgment can peruse without revering the virtue of the writer."*

See GEORGE FOX's "Journal;" also the Preface to it, by WILLIAM PENN; MARSH's "Life of George Fox," 1 vol. 8vo; JANNEY's "Life of George Fox," 1 vol. 8vo; "George Fox," an Address to the Society of Friends, by C. H. SPURGEON, London, 1866; also, "George Fox, the Friends, and the Early Baptists," by WILLIAM TALLACK, London, 1868; and HERMANN WEINGARTEN's masterly work entitled "Revolutionskirchen Englands," Leipsic, 1868.

For the doctrinal views of George Fox and the early Quakers, see BARCLAY's "Apology;" also "Dissertation" appended to JANNEY's "Life of Fox;" and T. EVANS's "Exposition of the Faith of the Religious Society of Friends," Philadelphia, 1828.

For a full account of the various writings and publications of George Fox, see JOSEPH SMITH's "Catalogue of Friends' Books," vol. i. pp. 644–697.

Fox, (HENRY,) the first Lord Holland, was a son of Sir Stephen, and the father of the great orator Charles J. Fox. He was secretary at war in the reign of George II. about 1750. In 1755 he became secretary of state, and Whig leader of the House of Commons when the elder Pitt was leader of the opposition. Fox had parliamentary talents of a very high order, but was inferior to Pitt in declamation. According to Macaulay, Fox resembled his more celebrated son in disposition as well as talents. He had the same sweetness of temper, the same openness and impetuosity. Upon the dissolution of Newcastle's ministry, the king sent for Fox, and directed him to arrange a new cabinet in concert with Pitt; but the latter declined the coalition with his rival. In 1762 he accepted office in the ministry of Lord Bute, and became ministerial leader in the House; but in the next year Bute resigned, and Fox was raised to the peerage, as Lord Holland. According to the essayist above named, "he was the most unpopular statesman of his time, not because he sinned more, but because he canted less." Died in 1774, leaving his title to his son Stephen.

See MACAULAY, review of Thackeray's "History of the Earl of Chatham."

Fox, (JOHN,) an English author, born at Boston, in Lincolnshire, in 1517, adopted the principles of the Reformation. He was tutor in the family of Sir Thomas Lucy, and at a later period instructed the sons of the Earl of Surrey, then confined in the Tower. In 1545 he was accused of heresy and expelled from Magdalene College, of which he was a Fellow. To escape persecution, he retired to Bâle, and after the death of Queen Mary returned to England and received a prebend in the church of Salisbury. He is the author of "The Acts and Monuments of the Church," (1563,) commonly called the "Book of Martyrs," a work which obtained great and deserved popularity. Died in 1587.

See a Life of J. Fox, by his son Samuel; FULLER, "Worthies of England;" "Biographia Britannica."

Fox, (LUKE,) an English navigator, who commanded a vessel sent out in 1631 to explore the Northwest passage. After making discoveries in Hudson Bay, he returned home, and published an account of the same, dated 1635.

See PURCHAS, "Pilgrimages."

Fox, (MARGARET.) See FOX, (GEORGE.)

Fox, [Sp. pron. foH,] (MORZILLO SEBASTIAN,) a Spanish writer, born at Seville in 1528, wrote about the age of twenty a commentary on the "Topics of Cicero," and in 1554 he published a treatise on the "Analogy of the Philosophical Views of Plato and Aristotle," which was applauded by some critics. Philip II. appointed him preceptor of his son Carlos; but as he was on his way to this new scene of labour he perished by shipwreck, in 1560.

Fox, (RICHARD,) an English bishop and statesman, born at Ropesley, in Lincolnshire, in 1466. In the reign of Henry VII. he officiated as keeper of the privy seal, secretary of state, and ambassador to various courts. He was appointed Bishop of Winchester in 1500, having previously occupied the see of Durham and others. In 1516 he founded at Oxford the College of Corpus Christi, with a chair of Greek and Latin. He retained the favour and confidence of Henry VII. throughout his reign, and

* See MACKINTOSH's "History of the Revolution in 1688."

was supplanted by Wolsey in the councils of Henry VIII. Died in 1528.

See WOOD, "Athenæ Oxonienses."

Fox, (Sir STEPHEN,) an English politician, born at Farley, Wilts, in 1627, was the father of the first Lord Holland. He was "clerk of the green cloth" in the reign of Charles II., and held other offices. He built several almshouses, and was the first who projected Chelsea College as a military hospital. Died in 1716.

Fox, (WILLIAM JOHNSON,) an English politician and writer, was born near Wrentham, Suffolk, in 1786. He was once a Unitarian minister at Finsbury, and was a frequent and able contributor to the "Westminster Review." In 1847 he was returned to Parliament for Oldham, and became a prominent member of the advanced Liberal party. He published "Lectures to the Working Classes," and other works. Died in 1864.

Foy, fwâ, (MAXIMILIAN SÉBASTIEN,) a French general and eminent orator, born at Ham, in Picardy, in February, 1775. He served his first campaign in 1792 as lieutenant of artillery. In 1794, having expressed his abhorrence of the atrocities of the Convention, he was sent to prison, and would probably have been executed had not the crisis of the 9th Thermidor and the death of Robespierre subverted that bloody régime. He made the campaigns of 1796 and 1797 as commander of cavalry under Moreau. Foy was one of those republicans who opposed the assumption of imperial power by Napoleon, and thus retarded his own promotion. From 1807 to 1813 he served in Portugal and Spain, where he obtained the rank of general of division about 1810, and distinguished himself by his bravery, capacity, and colloquial talents. He was often wounded in battle. After Bonaparte landed from Elba, in 1815, General Foy did not long hesitate to join his standard in defending the soil of France from invasion, and he led a division at Waterloo, where he was again wounded. In 1819 he was elected by the department of Aisne to the Chamber of Deputies, where he speedily took his place in the first rank of orators. His past life, his noble character, added to his persuasive manner, gave him great influence, which he employed in favour of a liberal and constitutional government. Died in Paris in November, 1825. About one million francs were raised by national subscription for his family. He left (unfinished) a "History of the Peninsular War," (4 vols., 1827.)

See CUISIN, "Vie militaire, politique, etc. du Général Foy;" PAUL LACROIX, "Éloge historique du Général Foy;" RENÉ PERRIN, "Notice sur la Vie militaire de Foy," prefixed to "Pensées de Général Foy," 1821; F. VIDAL, "Vie du Général Foy," 1826.

Foyatier, fwâ'yǎ'te-à', (DENIS,) a French sculptor, born at Beson, near Feurs, (Loire,) in 1793. He became a student of art in Paris in 1816, and went to Rome in 1822. His reputation was established by a statue of Spartacus, (1830,) which was purchased by the king. Among his works are a statue of "Prudence," and an equestrian statue of Joan of Arc, inaugurated at Orléans in 1855.

Fra Angelico. See FIESOLE.

Fra Bartolommeo. See BACCIO DELLA PORTA.

Fracanzani, frä-kän-zä'nee, or **Fracanzano,** frä-kän-zä'no, (FRANCESCO,) an able Italian painter, worked in Naples, and was the master of Salvator Rosa, whose sister he married. His colouring is brilliant and vigorous. Died about 1657.

Fracastoro, frä-käs-to'ro, or **Fracastor,** (GIROLAMO,) an eminent Italian author, born at Verona in 1483, was one of the most learned men of his time, and excelled in philosophy, medicine, mathematics, and poetry. Before the age of twenty he was professor of logic at Padua. His reputation is derived chiefly from a Latin poem on the venereal disease, called "Syphilis, sive Morbus Gallicus," (1530,) which has been translated into several languages. Scaliger had so high an opinion of Fracastor's talents that he composed a poem in honour of him. Hallam gives him credit for "having delivered the rules of practical art in all the graces of the most delicious poetry, without inflation, without obscurity, and without affectation." ("Introduction to the Literature of Europe.") He was in his latter years chief physician to Pope Paul III. and to the Council of Trent, held in 1547. Died near Verona in August, 1553. He wrote a few scientific treatises.

See F. O. MENCKEN, "De Vita, Moribus, etc. Fracastorii Commentatio," 1731; NICÉRON, "Mémoires;" LONGFELLOW, "Poets and Poetry of Europe."

Fraccaroli, fRåk-kå-ro'lee, (INNOCENZO,) an able Italian sculptor, born at Castel-Rotto, near Verona, about 1804. He studied in Rome, and became professor of sculpture at Florence about 1842. His "Eve after the Fall" gained a medal of the first class at Paris, and is called a master-piece of grace. Among his other works is a statue of Achilles.

Frachetta, fRå-ket'tå, (GIROLAMO,) an Italian publicist and critic, born at Rovigo about 1560. In his youth he was secretary of Cardinal Este. He wrote a paraphrase of Lucretius, (1589,) with notes, a volume entitled "On Reasons of State," ("Della Ragione di Stato," 1623,) which is commended, and a few other works. Died at Naples in 1620.

See BAYLE, "Historical and Critical Dictionary."

Fra Diavolo, fRå de-å'vo-lo, an Italian chief of brigands, whose proper name was MICHEL POZZA, (pot'så,) was born at Itri. He fought in the army of Cardinal Ruffo against the French in 1799. In 1806 he became the chief of a band of insurgents in Calabria. He was arrested and hung at Naples in that year.

Fraehn. See FRÄHN.

Fragonard, fRå'go'nåR', (ALEXANDRE ÉVARISTE,) a French painter and sculptor, born at Grasse in 1780, was a pupil of David. Among his works are "Maria Theresa presenting her Infant Son to the Hungarians," (1822,) and "The Entrance of Joan of Arc into Orléans." Died in 1850.

Fragonard, (JEAN HONORÉ,) a French historical painter, born at Grasse in 1732. After gaining the first prize for painting in Paris, he went to Rome with a pension. He returned to Paris, was received in the Royal Academy, and became a fashionable artist. He is blamed for the sensual and licentious tendency of his productions. Died in 1806.

Fraguier, fRå'ge-å', (CLAUDE FRANÇOIS,) a French savant and elegant writer, born in Paris in 1666, became a good classical scholar, and one of the editors of the "Journal des Savants." He was admitted into the Academy of Inscriptions in 1705, and into the French Academy in 1708. He wrote an admired Latin poem, called "Platonic School on the Perfection of Man," ("Mopsus, seu Schola Platonica de Hominis Perfectione," 1721;) also dissertations on ancient history, literature, etc. Died in 1728.

See D'OLIVET, "Éloge de Fraguier;" NICÉRON, "Mémoires;" "Nouvelle Biographie Générale."

Frähn, fRån, or **Fraehn,** (CHRISTIAN MARTIN,) a German antiquary and Orientalist, born at Rostock in 1782. He became in 1815 director of the Asiatic Museum and member of the Imperial Academy of Sciences at Saint Petersburg. He published "Recension of Mahometan Coins in the Academy of Sciences at Petersburg," (1826,) and other similar works. Died in 1851.

See DORN, "Vie de Frähn," prefixed to a supplement of the work just noticed, 1855.

Fraikin, fRĪ'kin or fRẵ'kåN', (CHARLES AUGUSTE,) a successful Belgian sculptor, born near Antwerp in 1816. Among his works are "L'Amour captif," "Venus," (1848,) and "Le Sommeil," ("Sleep," 1856.)

Frain, fRån, (SÉBASTIEN,) an eminent French advocate, born at Rennes; died in 1645.

Framery, fRåm're', (NICOLAS ÉTIENNE,) a mediocre French writer, born at Rouen in 1745; died in 1810.

Franc, Le, leh fRôN, (MARTIN,) a French poet, born at Arras or Aumale. His chief work is "Ladies' Champion," ("Champion des Dames.") Died about 1460.

Français, fRôN'så', (FRANÇOIS LOUIS,) a French landscape-painter, born at Plombières in 1814, obtained a first medal in 1848, and a medal of the first class in 1855.

Français de Nantes, fRôN'så' deh nôNt, (ANTOINE,) born at Beaurepaire, in France, in 1756, was a warm partisan of the Revolution. He was elected to the Legislative Assembly in 1791, and to the Council of Five Hundred in 1797 or 1798. Under the consulate and the empire he enjoyed the favour of Bonaparte, who made him count, councillor of state, grand officer of the legion of honour, and director-general of the *Octrois.* He represented Isère in the Chamber of Deputies from 1819 to 1822, and voted with the opposition. Died in 1836.

See "Nouvelle Biographie Générale."

Francavilla. See FRANCHEVILLE, (PIERRE.)

Fran'ces, SAINT, an Italian lady, born in Rome in 1384, was noted for piety and benevolence. She died in 1440, and was canonized by Paul V. in 1608.

See BAILLET, "Vies des Saints."

Francesca, della, del'lå fRån-chês'kå, (PIETRO,) an eminent Italian painter, born at Borgo San Sepolcro, in Tuscany, about 1400, was often called **Pietro Borghese.** By invitation of Pope Nicholas V., he went to Rome and painted frescos in the Vatican. He excelled in foreshortening, perspective, and geometry. "The Dream of Constantine," at Arezzo, is one of the few works of this artist that have been preserved. He wrote treatises on perspective and geometry. Died about 1490.

See VASARI, "Lives of the Painters;" LANZI, "History of Painting in Italy."

Franceschetti, fRån-chês-ket'tee, (DOMENICO CESARE,) a Corsican general, born at Bastia in 1776. He entered the service of Murat, King of Naples, rose to the rank of general, and distinguished himself at Tolentino. He attended Murat in his last desperate expedition of 1815, and was taken prisoner. Died in 1835.

Franceschini, fRån-chês-kee'nee, (BALDASSARE,) a painter of the Florentine school, surnamed VOLTERRANO, was born at Volterra in 1611, and was a pupil of Matteo Rosselli. He worked in Florence, where he painted the translation of Elijah, and other frescos, also many oil-paintings. He excelled in perspective, colour, and composition. Died in 1689.

See LANZI, "History of Painting in Italy;" TICOZZI, "Dizionario."

Franceschini, (MARCANTONIO,) an excellent Italian historical painter, born at Bologna in 1648, was a pupil of Carlo Cignani. He was eminent for his rapidity of execution, fine taste, fertility of invention, and skill in colouring. He painted frescos in Bologna, Genoa, and Rome, and declined invitations from several princes of Europe. The Pope gave him the title of Knight of the Golden Spur. Among his chief works are an "Annunciation" and "Saint John in the Isle of Patmos." He also left many oil-paintings. Died in 1729.

See LANZI, "History of Painting in Italy;" ZANOTTI, "Storia dell'Accademia Clementina;" MALVASIA, "Felsina pittrice."

Francesquito, fRån-thês-kee'to, written also **Franceschitto,** fRån-thês-kee'to, a Spanish painter, born at Valladolid in 1681. He was a pupil of Giordano, who predicted that he would equal the best painters of Italy; but he died at the age of twenty-four, in Naples, whither he had accompanied Giordano.

Franc-Flore. See FLORIS, (FRANS.)

Francheville, fRÔNsh'vêl', or **Francavilla,** fRån-kå-vêl'lå, written also **Francqueville,** (PIERRE,) a skilful French sculptor, born at Cambrai in 1548. After he had worked in Italy with success, he was invited to Paris by Henry IV., who patronized him, and he was afterwards sculptor to Louis XIII. about 1614. Among his works is a group of "Time bearing away Truth," ("Le Temps enlevant la Vérité,") and a statue of Goliath. Died about 1620.

See CICOGNARA, "Storia della Scultura;" DUTILLEUL, "Notice sur P. de Francqueville," 1821.

Francheville, de, deh fRÔNsh'vêl', (JOSEPH Du Fresne—dü frẽn,) a French writer and accomplished scholar, born at Doullens in 1704. He published a "History of the Finances," (3 vols., 1738–40.) Having accepted the invitation of Frederick II. of Prussia, about 1742, he passed the rest of his life at Berlin. He wrote a poem called "Bombyx, or the Silk-Worm," (1755.) He was a member of the Academy of Berlin, which he enriched with treatises on history, antiquities, etc., and he edited the "Literary Gazette" of Berlin from 1764 to his death. Died in 1781.

See FORMEY, "Eloge de Francheville."

Franchi, fRån'kee, (ANTONIO,) an Italian painter, of the Florentine school, born at Villa Basilica, near Lucca, in 1634. Died in 1709.

See BARTOLOZZI, "Vita di A. Franchi Lucchese," 1754.

ɛ as *k;* ç as *s;* ğ *hard;* ğ as *j;* G, H, K, *guttural;* N, *nasal;* R, *trilled;* š as *z;* ŧh as in *this.* (☞See Explanations, p. 23.)

Franchi, (AUSONIO,) the assumed name of an Italian rationalistic philosopher, whose family name was BONAVINC, (bo-nä-vee′no.) He was born at Pegli, near Genoa, in 1820. He was a priest in his youth, but renounced that profession. His principal work, "The Philosophy of the Italian Schools," (1852,) is written with much ability. About 1854 he founded at Turin a journal called "La Ragione."

Franchi, (GIUSEPPE,) an Italian sculptor, born at Carrara in 1730; died at Milan in 1806.

Franchini, frän-kee′nee, (FRANCESCO,) an Italian poet, born at Cosenza in 1495; died in 1554.

Franchini, (NICCOLÒ,) an Italian painter, born at Sienna in 1704; died in 1783.

Francia, frän′chä, (DOMENICO,) an Italian painter, born at Bologna in 1702, visited Vienna in 1723, where he painted for the court. From 1736 to 1744 he was employed by the Swedish court. Died in 1758.

Francia, (FRANCESCO,) a celebrated Italian painter, whose proper name was FRANCESCO RAIBOLINI, (rī-bo-lee′nee,) was born at Bologna about 1450. He was a goldsmith in his youth. His style was a medium between the styles of Perugino and Bellini. He was a friend of Raphael, who praised his Madonnas, saying he had seen none "more handsome or more devout." Among his works is a Saint Sebastian, which was used for a long time as a model. He was an excellent colorist. The date of his death is variously given from 1518 to 1533.

See VASARI, "Lives of the Painters;" CALVI, "Memorie di F. Raibolini detto il Francia;" MALVASIA, "Felsina pittrice;" MRS. JAMESON, "Memoirs of Early Italian Painters."

Francia, (GIACOMO,) a skilful Italian painter of Bologna, was a son and pupil of the preceding, whom he imitated with success. He painted a Saint George, (1526,) and other saints and Madonnas, which were engraved by Agostino Caracci. Died in 1557.

See LANZI, "History of Painting in Italy."

Francia, (GIULIO,) a painter of the Bolognese school, was a relative of Raibolini. Died in 1540.

Francia, frän′se-ä or frän′the-ä, (Dr. JOSÉ GASPAR RODRIGUEZ,) Dictator of Paraguay, was born near Assumption about 1758. He studied law, and practised with success in Assumption, until the formation of a republic in Paraguay in 1811, when he became secretary of state. In 1813 he was chosen joint consul with Fulgencio. The republic having fallen into anarchy, he was made dictator for three years in 1814, and perpetual dictator in 1817. His reign was arbitrary and severe; but he appears to have repressed disorders with vigour. A system of non-intercourse with foreign countries was adopted by him, and a "rigorous sanitary line was drawn round all Paraguay." "We might define him," says Carlyle, "as the born enemy of quacks. So far as lay in Francia, no public or private man in Paraguay was allowed to slur his work." (See "Essays," vol. iv.) Among the most notorious of his arbitrary acts was the detention of Bonpland, a French botanist, who was arrested in 1821 and released in 1831. Dr. Francia died in September, 1840, when the power passed to a junta or directory of three.

See ROBERTSON, "Life of Dr. Francia;" BENGGER, "Essai historique sur la Révolution du Paraguay," etc., Paris, 1827; "Foreign Quarterly Review" for July, 1843.

Franciabigio, frän-chä-bee′jo, (MARCANTONIO,) a skilful Italian fresco-painter, born at Florence in 1483, was a pupil and friend of Andrea del Sarto. He painted the "Marriage of the Virgin," at Florence, in company with Andrea del Sarto. He excelled in perspective and in colouring. Died in 1524.

See VASARI, "Lives of the Painters;" FRIGERIO, "Vita di Marcantonio Franciabigio."

Francini, frän-chee′nee, (ANTONIO,) an Italian poet of patrician rank. He lived in Florence when Milton visited that city in 1638, and was one of seven Florentines specially mentioned by that poet as his friends. He complimented Milton in an Italian ode, the last stanza of which is praised by Dr. Johnson as "natural and beautiful." He is said to have left many poems in manuscript.

Francis I. OF AUSTRIA. See FRANCIS II. OF GERMANY.

Francis [Ger. FRANZ, fRänts] **I.,** Emperor of Germany, born at Nancy in 1708, was the eldest son of Leopold, Duke of Lorraine, and a French princess, Elizabeth Charlotte of Orléans. In accordance with a treaty made in 1735, Francis received Tuscany in exchange for Lorraine, which was ceded to Stanislas Leczinski, on the condition that at his death it should revert to the crown of France. He married Maria Theresa, the daughter and heiress of the emperor Charles VI., in 1736, (see MARIA THERESA,) and thus became the founder of the reigning dynasty of Habsburg-Lorraine. He was elected Emperor of Germany, as successor to Charles VII., in September, 1745, and was commander-in-chief of the army of Austria, which was then at war with France, until peace was restored in 1748. He is represented as a prince of good disposition and moderate capacity. He died in August, 1765, and was succeeded by his son, Joseph II.

See J. F. SEYFART, "Lebens- und Regierungsgeschichte Kaiser Franz I.," 1766; COXE, "History of the House of Austria;" VOLTAIRE, "Siècle de Louis XV."

Francis (Franz) II., (JOSEPH KARL,) Emperor of Germany, and **Francis I.** of Austria, was the eldest son of Leopold II. and of Maria Louisa of Spain. He was born at Florence in February, 1768, and at an early age went to reside at the court of Vienna. He married Maria Theresa of Naples in 1790 or 1791, and began to reign over the hereditary states of Austria in March, 1792. In the same year he was elected Emperor of Germany, and was involved in a war with the French, which was suspended by the treaty of Campo Formio, 1797. (See BONAPARTE.) In 1799 he entered into a coalition with Russia and England against the French. After gaining and losing many battles, the allies signed a treaty of peace at Lunéville in 1801. He assumed the title of hereditary Emperor of Austria in December, 1804, and, in alliance with England and Russia, again defied the power of Napoleon. This war was ended by the battle of Austerlitz, December, 1805, and the treaty of Presburg, by which Tyrol and Venetia were annexed to France. The German empire having been disorganized or subverted, Francis renounced the throne of the Cæsars in August, 1806, after which he was styled Francis I. of Austria. In March, 1809, he again declared war against Napoleon, who, after the capture of Vienna and the victory of Wagram, dictated terms of peace in October, 1809. He joined in 1813 the coalition which resulted in the final defeat of Napoleon, after which he recovered Venice and Lombardy, and reigned in peace until his death, in March, 1835. He was succeeded by his son, Ferdinand I. Francis was popular with his German subjects.

See J. VON HORMAYER, "Kaiser Franz I. und Metternich," 1848; H. MEYNERT, "Franz II. und sein Zeitalter," 1834.

Francis [Fr. FRANÇOIS, fRôn′swä′] **I.,** King of France, born at Cognac September 12, 1494, was the son of Charles, Count of Angoulême, (a cousin-german of King Louis XII.,) and Louise, daughter of Philippe, Duke of Savoy. As Francis had lost his father in infancy, Louis XII. took charge of his education, created him Duke of Valois, and gave him his daughter Claude in marriage in 1514. The king dying without any son to survive him, Francis succeeded to the throne on the 1st of January, 1515. In the same year he despatched an army under Constable Bourbon to conquer the Milanese, defended by a Swiss army, which the French engaged and defeated at Marignano. In 1519 Francis was an unsuccessful candidate for the empire of Germany, which was obtained by his rival, Charles V. of Spain. About two years later, a league was formed against the French king by Charles V., Henry VIII. of England, and the pope, Leo X., the first result of which was the expulsion of the French from the Milanese. The French were defeated in 1524 at the battle of Sesia, in which the famous Chevalier Bayard fell, and in 1525 at the decisive battle of Pavia, where Francis commanded in person and was taken prisoner, after receiving two wounds. It is commonly stated that he wrote a report of the event to his mother in these terms: "Madame, all is lost except our honour," ("tout est perdu fors l'honneur.") He was sent to Madrid, and closely confined until he consented to the conditions exacted by Charles V.,—namely, the cession of Burgundy, the renunciation of his claim to Flanders, and the restoration of Constable Bourbon to his estate and rank. After he obtained his liberation, in 1526, he refused to fulfil these conditions, and, forming an alliance with Henry VIII. and Pope Clement, continued the war until 1529, when the treaty of Cambrai was signed, by which Francis abandoned his claim to Italy, and married Eleonore, the sister of Charles. He afterwards devoted several years to the promotion of commerce, science, literature, and industry. He founded the Royal College of three languages in Paris in 1531, and obtained the title of "the Father of French literature." In 1539 the emperor surprised the European public by asking permission of his rival to pass through France on his way from Spain to the Low Countries. Francis granted the request, and entertained Charles, who, it seems, gave him the promise of the duchy of Milan. In 1542 war was again declared, and prosecuted in Piedmont and Picardy without important results, until the French gained a decisive victory at Ceresole, in April, 1544, and a treaty of peace was signed at Crespi in September of that year. Francis died in March, 1547, and was succeeded by his son, Henry II. He left a great reputation for gallantry, generosity, and royal accomplishments, but is justly censured for the persecution which the Protestants suffered during his reign.

See BRANTÔME, "Mémoires;" CAPEFIGUE, "François I et la Renaissance," 4 vols., 1844; MICHELET, "Renaissance;" A. VARILLAS, "Histoire de François I," 1684; GAILLARD, "Histoire de François I," 8 vols., 1768; MIGNET, "Rivalité de Charles Quint et de François I," 1854–66; MISS PARDOE, "Court and Reign of Francis I.," 1849; "Nouvelle Biographie Générale."

Francis II., King of France, born at Fontainebleau in January, 1543, was the eldest son of Henry II. and of Catherine de Médicis. In 1558 he married the beautiful Mary Stuart, Queen of Scots, and on the 10th of July, 1559, he succeeded to the throne of his father. In consequence of his youth and feeble character, he relinquished the power of the state into the hands of the Duc de Guise and Cardinal Lorraine, who were uncles of Mary Stuart, and zealous Catholics. Antoine de Bourbon, King of Navarre, the Prince of Condé, and other nobles, jealous of the influence and impatient of the domination of the Guises, formed a coalition with the Protestants, who were then objects of a violent persecution. In 1560 a conspiracy was discovered by the Guises, which was the prelude of the civil wars that afterwards raged in the kingdom. The States-General were assembled at Orléans, and the Prince of Condé was condemned to death; but he escaped this penalty in consequence of the death of the king, December 5, 1560. Francis was succeeded by his brother, Charles IX.

See HENAULT, "François II, Roi de France," 1748; VARILLAS, "Histoire de François II," 1693; DAVILA, "History of the Civil Wars of France;" W. ANDERSON, "History of France during the Reigns of Francis II. and Charles IX.," 5 vols., 1769–82.

Francis I., (GENNARO GIUSEPPE,) King of the Two Sicilies, born in Naples in 1777, was the son of Ferdinand I. of Naples and of Caroline of Austria. In 1797 he married Maria Clementina, daughter of the emperor Leopold II. While he was heir-presumptive he favoured the party of reform; but he afterwards became subservient to the Austrian policy. In 1814, when, by the fall of Murat, Ferdinand recovered Naples, Francis became Governor of Sicily. He succeeded to the throne in January, 1825. His reign was neither prosperous nor popular. He died in 1830, and was succeeded by his son, Ferdinand II.

Francis II., (MARIA LEOPOLDO,) King of the Two Sicilies, a son of Ferdinand II., was born in January, 1836. He succeeded his father on the 22d of May, 1859, and married the princess Maria Sophia Amelia of Bavaria in the same year. He persisted in the arbitrary policy which had rendered his father odious. His subjects revolted in 1860, and were led to victory by Garibaldi. After a siege of several months, Francis surrendered Gaeta in February, 1861, and his dominions have since been united to the new kingdom of Italy.

Francis (or François) I., Duke of Bretagne, born at Vannes in 1414, was the eldest son of Jean VI., and a nephew of Charles VII. of France. He began to reign in 1442, and formed an alliance with Charles VII. against the English. His memory is deeply stained by his cruelty to his brother Giles. Died in 1450.

Francis II., the last Duke of Bretagne, born in 1435, succeeded his uncle, Arthur III., in 1459. The principal events of his reign were a series of wars against Louis XI. of France, of whom Francis was a feudatory, and who desired to annex Bretagne to his kingdom. The duke formed an alliance with the King of England and the Duke of Burgundy. He was defeated in a decisive battle by the army of Charles VIII. of France in 1488, and died the same year. His daughter Anne became the wife of the French king.

Francis I., Duke of Lorraine, born in 1517, succeeded his father, Antoine, in 1544. He died in 1545, and left the dukedom to his son, Charles III.

Francis II. of Lorraine, a son of Charles III., born in 1571, became duke in 1624. He abdicated in favour of his son, Charles IV., the same year. Died in 1632.

Francis IV., Duke of Módena and Reggio, born in 1779, was a son of Ferdinand, Archduke of Austria, and Maria Beatrice of Este. He began to reign in 1814, and, by his despotic policy, acquired the surname of "the Tiberius of Italy." Died in 1846.

Francis V., Archduke of Austria, and last Duke of Módena, born in 1819, was a son of Francis IV., whom he succeeded in January, 1846. His reign was very unpopular. In the spring of 1859 his subjects revolted, drove him into exile, and decided by their votes that Módena should be annexed to the kingdom of Sardinia.

Francis, DUKE OF TUSCANY. See MEDICIS.

Fran'cis, (CONVERS,) an American writer, born at West Cambridge, Massachusetts, about 1796. He was pastor of a Unitarian church at Watertown, Massachusetts, from 1819 to 1842, and then became professor of pulpit eloquence at Harvard College. He wrote several biographies, etc. Died in 1863.

Francis, (JEAN CHARLES.) See FRANÇOIS.

Francis, (JOHN WAKEFIELD,) an eminent American physician, born in New York in November, 1789. He graduated at Columbia College in 1809, and took the degree of M.D. at the College of Physicians and Surgeons in 1811. Having entered into partnership with Dr. Hosack, he aided the latter in editing the "American Medical and Philosophical Register," (1810–14.) He became professor of materia medica in Columbia College about 1814, after which he visited the principal schools of medicine in Europe. On his return he was appointed professor of the institutes of medicine, and in 1817 obtained the chair of medical jurisprudence. In 1826 Dr. Francis, Dr. Hosack, and other professors resigned their chairs and organized the Rutgers Medical School, in which the former was professor of obstetrics and forensic medicine for four years. He was one of the editors of the "New York Medical and Physical Journal," (1822–24.) After 1830 he devoted his time chiefly to the practice of his profession and to literary pursuits. Among his numerous productions are "Cases of Morbid Anatomy,"(1814,) "Febrile Contagion,"(1816,) "Denman's Practice of Midwifery," with notes, (1825,) and "Old New York, or Reminiscences of the Past Sixty Years," (1857.) He was one of the founders of the New York Academy of Medicine, of which he was chosen president in 1847. He was prominently identified with the interests of New York, especially with its literary and scientific institutions. Died in 1861.

See H. T. TUCKERMAN, "Life of John W. Francis," 1855; "National Portrait-Gallery of Distinguished Americans," vol. iv.; DUYCKINCK, "Cyclopædia of American Literature," vol. ii.

Francis, (LUKE,) a Flemish painter of history and portraits, born at Mechlin in 1574. He was patronized at the courts of France and Spain. Died in 1643.

His son LUKE, born at Mechlin in 1606, gained a high reputation in the same branches of art. He worked several years in Paris, and then returned to Flanders. Died in 1654.

Francis, (Rev. PHILIP,) an eminent translator, born in Dublin, was the father of Sir Philip Francis. He lived many years in England, to which he removed about 1750. He became chaplain to Lord Holland, and a preceptor of his son, the celebrated Charles James Fox. He produced a poetical translation of Horace, which was successful, and has often been reprinted, (8th edition, 1778,) a translation of Demosthenes' Orations, (1753–55,) and several tragedies. Dr. Johnson considered his version of Horace the best that had been made. Died in 1773.

See BAKER, "Biographia Dramatica."

Francis, (Sir PHILIP,) an eminent British statesman, the son of the preceding, was born in Dublin in 1740, and removed to London about the age of ten. He was a clerk in the war office from 1763 to 1772, and was appointed in 1773 a member of the Supreme Council of Bengal, of which Warren Hastings was president. He was the leader of the party which opposed the measures of Hastings. While in this position he fought a duel with Hastings, (who asserted that Francis was void of truth and honour,) was severely wounded, and returned to England about December, 1780. In 1784 he was chosen a member of Parliament, in which he took a prominent part in the trial of Hastings, voted with Fox during the French Revolution, and zealously advocated the abolition of the slave-trade. The Grenville ministry conferred on Francis the title of Knight of the Bath in 1806, soon after which he retired from Parliament. He died in London in December, 1818. He was a writer and speaker of decided ability. He is generally believed to have been the author of the famous "Letters of Junius," though he always denied such responsibility. Brougham and Macaulay are among those who were convinced that Francis was the author of Junius. To account for his persistence in concealing his authorship of those letters, Lord Brougham remarks, "He has long, in his proper person, possessed the admiration of all who have a due regard for unblemished public virtue, great talents and accomplishments. He might well afford to forego the applause of the multitude, which could only be purchased by a sacrifice of the tranquillity so invaluable in the decline of life." "His style," says the same critic, "was admirable, excelling in clearness, abounding in happy idiomatic terms, not overloaded with words or figures, but not rejecting either beautiful phrases or appropriate ornament."

See J. TAYLOR, "Junius identified with a Distinguished Living Character;" HERMAN MERIVALE, "Memoirs of the Life of Sir Philip Francis," 2 vols., 1867; MACAULAY, "Essay on Warren Hastings;" "Edinburgh Review" for January, 1868.

Francis, SAINT, [It. SAN FRANCESCO, sän fränchĕs'ko; Fr. SAINT-FRANÇOIS, săN'fRŏN'swä',] the celebrated founder of an order of mendicant friars, called Franciscans, was born at Assisi, in Italy, in 1182. In his youth, prompted by enthusiasm and ascetic devotion, he renounced his inheritance, and resolved to live on public charity. Large numbers being attracted by his preaching and example to follow the same course, he composed rules for their organization, which Pope Innocent III. sanctioned about 1210, and by which they were forbidden to have any private property, and were bound to preach and labour without salaries, depending on alms for their simple subsistence. They were named Minor Friars, and sometimes also Cordeliers, from the cord with which their coarse tunic was girded. About the year 1220 he visited Palestine during one of the crusades, and attempted to convert Sultan Meledin, but without success. In 1223 Pope Honorius published a bull confirming the verbal sanction which the order had received from Innocent III. This fraternity became very numerous and influential. He died near Assisi in 1226, and was canonized by Pope Gregory in 1230.

See CHALIPPE, "Vie de Saint-François," 1728; CHAVIN DE MALAN, "Vie de Saint-François," 1841; N. PAPINI, "Storia di S. Francesco di Assisi," 2 vols., 1825-27; E. VOGT, "Der heilige Franciscus von Assisi," 1840; F. MORIN, "S. François d'Assise," 1853.

Francis de Pau'lo, (or **Pau'la,**) [It. FRANCESCO DI PAOLO, (or PAULA,) fränchĕs'ko de pow'lo, (or pŏw'lä;) Fr. FRANÇOIS DE PAULE, fRŏN'swä' dĕh pōl,] SAINT, founder of an order of monks called Minimi, was born at Paulo, in Calabria, in 1416. In early life he became a hermit, and by his asceticism acquired a great reputation for sanctity. In 1436 a monastery was built for him and his imitators, who were organized with the name of Eremites, or Hermits of Saint Francis, which was afterwards changed to Minimi. He went to Paris about 1483, at the invitation of the king, Louis XI., who was old and sick and hoped his life would be miraculously prolonged. He lived to see the order multiply rapidly and

become very numerous throughout Europe. The rules of this order were approved by a bull of Pope Sixtus VI. in 1474. Died in 1507.

See C. DUVIVIER, "Vie et Miracles de S. François de Paule," 1622; F. VICTONS, "Vita S. Francisci de Paula," Rome, 1625; I. TOSCANI, "Della Vita ed Miracoli di S. Francesco de Paolo," Rome, 1648; BAILLET, "Vies des Saints."

Francis de Sales. See SALES, SAINT FRANCIS DE.

Francis Joseph Charles, [Ger. FRANZ JOSEPH KARL, fränts yo'zĕf kärl,] usually called simply FRANCIS JOSEPH, Emperor of Austria, the eldest son of the Archduke Francis Charles Joseph, and a grandson of Francis I., was born on the 18th of August, 1830. His mother was Sophia, a daughter of the King of Bavaria. The stability of the throne having been imperilled by the insurrections in Vienna, Hungary, and Italy, the emperor Ferdinand, a feeble prince, abdicated in favour of his nephew, the subject of this article, December 2, 1848. With the aid of Russia, his armies subjugated the Hungarians in 1849. Many of the Hungarian generals were executed after they had surrendered. His army also defeated Charles Albert of Sardinia at Novara in 1849. He hastened to seize again the prerogatives which Ferdinand had given up, and to perfect a system of absolutism. In 1854 he married Elizabeth Amelia Eugenia, a daughter of the Duke of Bavaria. The Austrian court in the spring of 1859 demanded a disarmament on the part of Sardinia, which, supported by Napoleon III., refused to comply. Francis Joseph invaded Sardinia about the end of April, with a large army under Gyulai, who was soon forced to retire across the Ticino, and was defeated at Magenta on the 4th of June by the French and Sardinians. On the 24th of June, 1859, the Austrian army of 150,000 men or more, commanded by Francis Joseph in person, was defeated with great loss at Solferino by the allies, under the command of the emperor Napoleon. The war was ended by the treaty of Villafranca, (July, 1859,) and Lombardy was released from Austrian domination. (See VICTOR EMANUEL.) In 1864 he co-operated with Prussia in the conquest of Sleswick-Holstein and the spoliation of Denmark. About the 18th of June, 1866, war was declared between the Emperor of Austria and the King of Prussia, each of whom aspired to be the head of the German Bund. In this war Italy was an ally of Prussia, and the federal army of Germany fought on the side of Austria. The Prussians, with wonderful promptitude and rapidity, occupied Hanover, Saxony, Hesse, etc., and the main Prussian army entered Bohemia about the 25th of June. On the 3d of July, 1866, they gained a decisive victory over the grand Austrian army at Sadowa. In this short campaign of about ten days the Austrians lost nearly 100,000 men. Francis Joseph ceded Venetia to Louis Napoleon, and, after soliciting in vain the intervention of France, made overtures for peace to Prussia about July 25, 1866. The result of this war was a great humiliation of the house of Hapsburg, and the exclusion of Austria from the German Confederation and from Italy. In 1867 the constitutional autonomy of Hungary was restored, and the subjects of Francis Joseph acquired an increase of civil and religious liberty.

See EDMOND TEXIER, "Les Hommes de la Guerre d'Orient: François Joseph I," Paris, 1854.

Francis Xavier. See XAVIER.

Francisci, frän-sis'se, (JOHN,) a Danish poet and physician, born at Ripen in 1532, was chosen professor of medicine in Copenhagen in 1561. He wrote Latin poems, which were received with favour. Died in 1584.

Francisco de Borgia, fran-sis'ko (or frän-thĕs'ko) dä bor'jä, [Fr. FRANÇOIS DE BORGIA, fRŏN'swä' dĕh bor'zhe-ä',] SAINT, Duke of Gandia, born at Gandia, in Spain, in 1510, was inclined in early youth to the monastic life. To divert him from this, his parents placed him at the court of Charles V., who received him into his favour and made him Viceroy of Catalonia. In 1546 he joined the society of Jesuits, then recently founded by Ignatius Loyola, became a zealous preacher, and in 1565 was elected general of the order. He died in 1572, and was canonized in 1671 by Pope Clement X.

See RIBADENEIRA, "Vida de Francisco de Borgia," 1605; MIGNET, "Charles V au Monastère de Yuste;" "Ignatius Loyola and his Associates," in the "Edinburgh Review" for July, 1842.

ā, ē, ī, ō, ū, ȳ, *long;* à, ė, ò, same, less prolonged; ă, ĕ, ĭ, ŏ, ŭ, ў, *short;* ą, ę, į, ǫ, *obscure;* fär, fàll, fät; mêt; nŏt; gŏŏd; mŏŏn;

Francisco (or **Francis**) **de Jesu Maria,** frän-thĕs'-ko dȧ Hȧ-soo' mä-ree'ä, a Spanish Carmelite monk and writer on theology, born at Burgos ; died in 1677.

Fran-cis'co de Vi-to'rĭ-a, [Sp. pron. frän-thĕs'ko dȧ ve-to're-ä,] a Spanish Dominican monk, born at Vitoria. He published "Theologicæ Prælectiones." Died in 1549.

Fran'cĭ-us or **Fransz,** fränss, (PETER,) an excellent modern Latin poet, born at Amsterdam in 1645, studied under Gronovius at Leyden. He became, about 1675, professor of history, eloquence, and Greek in his native city. "He is justly reckoned," says the "Biographie Universelle," "among those moderns who have cultivated Latin poetry with most success." His "Poemata," consisting of elegies, epigrams, etc., were published in 1672. He also produced Dutch verses and Latin orations, (1692.) Died in 1703.

See NICÉRON, "Mémoires ;" "Nouvelle Biographie Générale."

Franck, frŏnk, (ADOLPHE,) a French philosopher, born in Meurthe in 1809. He wrote, besides other works, "The Religious Philosophy of the Hebrews," (1843,) and was editor of the "Dictionary of Philosophic Sciences," (6 vols., 1844–52,) for which he wrote many articles. He became one of the keepers of the Imperial Library in 1854, and professor of natural and public law in the College of France in 1856.

Franck, Frank, frȧnk, or **Francken,** frȧnk'kĕn, (AMBROSE,) a Flemish painter of history, born at Antwerp about 1545, was a pupil of Frans Floris. Among his works is the "Martyrdom of Saint Crépin and Saint Crépinien." Died in 1619.

Franck, (CONSTANTINE,) a Flemish painter, born at Antwerp in 1660. He excelled in battle-scenes. His master-piece is the "Siege of Namur by William III." Died about 1708.

Franck or **Francken,** (FRANCIS,) surnamed THE ELDER, a skilful painter, born at or near Antwerp about 1544, was a brother of Ambrose, noticed above. He painted, besides other historical works, "The Holy Family," and "Christ in the midst of the Doctors," which is called his master-piece. Died at Antwerp in 1616.

See DESCAMPS, "Vies des Peintres Flamands," etc.

Franck, (FRANCIS,) called THE YOUNGER, a son of the preceding, born at Antwerp in 1580, studied with his father. After travelling in Italy, he returned to his native place, and was received in the Academy in 1605. He is regarded by some as the most skilful artist of this family. Among his works, which are chiefly historical, are "The Prodigal Son," and "Laban Seeking his Idols." Died in 1642.

See DESCAMPS, "Vies des Peintres Flamands," etc.

Franck, (GABRIEL,) a Flemish painter, was director of the Academy of Antwerp in 1634.

Franck, (JEAN BAPTISTE,) grandson of Francis the Elder, was born at Antwerp in 1600. He excelled in the representation of picture-galleries, imitating the manner of various artists with skill. His master-piece is "Rubens and Van Dyck Playing Backgammon." Died in 1653.

See DESCAMPS, "Vies des Peintres Flamands," etc.

Franck, (JEROME,) a Flemish painter, born at Herenthals about 1542, was a brother of Ambrose, and a pupil of Frans Floris. He acquired a high reputation as a painter of portraits, and was appointed first painter to Henry III. of France. He also painted history with success in Paris and Antwerp. Among his works is a "Nativity," (Paris, 1585.) He was living in 1607.

See DESCAMPS, "Vies des Peintres Flamands," etc.

Franck, (SEBASTIAN,) son of Francis the Elder, above named, born about 1575, lived at Antwerp, and painted landscapes and battles with success. Died about 1636.

Franck von Franckenau. See FRANK.

Francke. See FRANKE.

Francke, frȧnk'kĕh, written also **Franke,** (AUGUST HERMANN,) a German Protestant divine and eminent philanthropist, born at Lubeck in 1663. He became professor of Oriental languages at Halle in 1692, and about the same time founded in that town an orphan-asylum

and a college for the poor, which received the name of Francke's Institutions. He was for many years professor of divinity at Halle. Died in 1727. Francke belonged to the Evangelical school of theology, and wrote "Methodus Studii Theologiæ," (1723,) besides other works.

See HIRSCHING, "Historisch-literarisches Handbuch ;" M. ALBERTI, "Monumentum A. H. Franckio positum," 1727 ; NIEMEYER, "Uebersicht von A. H. Francken's Leben," etc., 1788 ; GUERICKE, "Ueber A. H. Francke," Halle, 1827 ; G. E. LEO, "Leben A. H. Francke's," 1848.

Francke, frȧnk'kĕh, (JOHAN VALENTIN,) a Danish critic and philologist, was born at Husum about 1792. He became professor in the University of Dorpat, and wrote several works, the principal of which is his "Latin and Greek Inscriptions." Died in 1830.

See ERSCH und GRUBER, "Allgemeine Encyklopaedie."

Francke or **Franke,** (THEOPHILUS AUGUST,) a theologian, born at Halle in 1696, was a son of August Hermann, whom he succeeded, in 1727, as director of the institution at Halle. Died in 1769.

Francken. See FRANCK, (AMBROSE.)

Franckenstein, frȧnk'ĕn-stīn', (CHRISTIAN GOTTFRIED,) a German lawyer and historical writer, born at Leipsic in 1661 ; died in 1717.

His son JAKOB, born at Leipsic in 1689, was a jurist ; died in 1733.

Franck'lin, (THOMAS,) an English writer, born in London in 1721, became Greek professor at Cambridge in 1750, and was presented to the livings of Ware and Thundrich in 1758. In 1776 he became rector of Brasted, in Kent. He wrote several dramas, and other works in prose and verse, and published translations of Sophocles (2 vols., 1759) and of Lucian, (2 vols., 1780.) Died in London in 1784.

Fran'co [Fr. FRANCON or FRANKON, frôn'kôN'] of Cologne, a celebrated scholar and writer on music, flourished about Liege about 1050. He is supposed to have been born at Cologne. "He is the author," says Denne-Baron, "of the most ancient treatises which are extant on measured music and regular harmony," namely, "Ars Cantus Mensurabilis," and "Compendium de Discantu." ("Nouvelle Biographie Générale.")

See FÉTIS, "Biographie Universelle des Musiciens."

Franco, frȧn'ko, (BATTISTA,) called SEMOLEI, an eminent Venetian painter and engraver, born in 1498, studied at Rome, and imitated Michael Angelo. He practised his art in several cities of Italy with success, and engraved many subjects after Raphael. He was a skilful designer. Among his paintings is "Hannibal assailed by a Storm under the Walls of Rome." Died in Venice in 1561.

See VASARI, "Lives of the Painters ;" LANZI, "History of Painting in Italy."

Franco, (NICCOLÒ,) a satirical and licentious Italian poet, born at Benevento about 1510. He published, besides other works, "The Temple of Love," "La Priapea," (1541,) and "Dialogues on Beauty," (1542.) He was hung by order of Pope Pius V. in 1569, either for the immoral tendency of his books or for a personal satire on the pontiff.

See TIRABOSCHI, "Storia della Letteratura Italiana."

Franco, (VERONICA,) an Italian poetess, born at Venice in 1554 ; died about 1595.

Franco-Barreto, frȧn'ko bär-rä'to, (JOÃO,) a classic Portuguese poet, born in Lisbon about 1600. After serving in the armament sent to Brazil in 1646, he took orders, and became vicar of Barreiro in 1648. He published numerous works in verse and prose, among which is a poetical translation of the "Æneid," which is commended for its fidelity and other merits, (1664–70.) Died about 1668.

See BARBOSA MACHADO, "Bibliotheca Lusitana."

Francœur, frôN'kur', (LOUIS BENJAMIN,) a French geometer, born in Paris in 1773. He became professor of mathematics at the Faculty of Sciences in 1809. He wrote many good school-books, among which are a "Complete Course of Pure Mathematics," (2 vols., 1809,) and "Elements of Statics," (1810.) Died in 1849.

See FRANCŒUR FILS, "Notice sur la Vie de L. B. Francœur," 1854.

François, frŏn´swâ´, (JEAN CHARLES,) a French engraver, born at Nancy in 1717. He was the inventor of engraving in imitation of crayon or pencil. Died in 1769.

See BASAN, "Dictionnaire des Graveurs."

François, (LAURENT,) a French priest, born at Arinthod in 1698, was a defender of revealed religion against Voltaire and other skeptics. Among his works is a "Defence of the Christian Religion against the Objections of Infidels," (2 vols., 1755.) Died in 1782.

François, (LUC,) a Flemish painter. See FRANCIS, (LUKE.)

François, (SIMON,) a French portrait-painter, called LE VALENTIN, born at Tours in 1606; died in 1671.

François de Bourbon. See ENGHIEN, BOURBON, and MONTPENSIER.

François de Neufchâteau, frŏn´swâ´ deh nuh´-shâ´tō´, (NICOLAS LOUIS,) COMTE, a French statesman and poet, born in Lorraine in 1750. In his youth he was for a short time secretary to Voltaire. He favoured the Revolution, and was elected to the Legislative Assembly in 1791. In October, 1792, he was appointed minister of justice, but declined. His comedy "Pamela" was performed with success in 1793. He was a member of the executive Directory from September, 1797, until May, 1798, and became minister of the interior in July of that year. He was appointed a senator about the end of 1799, and was president of the senate two years, 1804-06. In this capacity he pronounced several eloquent addresses to the emperor. He was admitted into the French Academy in 1816, after which he retired from public life. Died in 1828.

See A. F. DE SILVESTRE, "Notice biographique sur M. le Comte François de Neufchâteau," 1828; H. BONNELIER, "Mémoires sur François de Neufchâteau," 1829; QUÉRARD, "La France Littéraire;" "Nouvelle Biographie Générale."

Francowitz, frăn´ko-wĭts´, (MATTHIAS **Flach**—flăk,) an eminent Protestant theologian and biblical critic, born in Istria in 1521, assumed the name of FLACCUS (or FLACIUS) ILLYRICUS. He was a pupil of Luther at Wittenberg, where he became a professor of Hebrew in 1544. He was chosen professor of theology at Jena in 1557. To superior talents he joined extensive learning. His character is represented as turbulent, impetuous, and disputatious. He wrote many controversial works, (partly against Melanchthon,) an excellent Ecclesiastical History, entitled "Centuries of Magdeburg," published in 3 volumes at Magdeburg, (1559-74,) which Mosheim calls "an immortal work," and "Key of the Holy Scriptures," ("Clavis Scripturæ Sacræ," 1567.) Died in 1575.

See TWESTEN, "Matthias Flacius Illyricus," Berlin, 1844; J. B. RITTER, "Beschreibung des Lebens Flaccii," 1723; M. ADAM, "Vitæ Germanorum Theologorum;" NICÉRON, "Mémoires;" "Nouvelle Biographie Générale."

Francucci, frăn-koot´chee, (INNOCENZIO,) called also INNOCENZIO DA IMOLA, an Italian painter, born at Imola about 1490, was a pupil of Francia. He lived in Bologna, and adorned the churches of that city with frescos which were greatly admired. The latest date on his works is 1549. A picture of the "Archangel Michael and Satan" is esteemed his master-piece.

See VASARI, "Lives of the Painters;" LANZI, "History of Painting in Italy;" PAPOTTI, "Elogio di I. Francucci, Imitatore glorioso del divino Raffaello," 1840.

Frangipani, frăn-je-pâ´nee, a powerful family of Rome in the eleventh and twelfth centuries, who derived their name from the distribution of bread in time of famine. They held the first rank among the nobility until the Colonna family and the Orsini gained the ascendant. Cenzio Frangipani produced a schism in the Church in 1118 by the election of the Antipope Burdino, who assumed the title of Gregory VIII.

Frangipani, (CLAUDIO CORNELIO,) a jurist, born in Venice in 1533, professed civil law with great credit in his native city, and wrote several legal treatises. Died in 1630.

See ERSCH und GRUBER, "Allgemeine Encyklopaedie."

Frangipani, (CORNELIO,) a Venetian of noble descent, born in Friuli, was the father of the preceding. He practised law in Venice, was distinguished as an orator, and translated three of Cicero's orations. Died in 1581.

Frank. See FRANCK.

Frank, or **Francke von Franckenau,** frănk´keh fon frănk´keh-nŏw´, (GEORG,) a learned German physician and elegant writer, was born in Naumburg, in Misnia, in 1643. He wrote agreeable verses in German, Latin, and Greek. After he had taught medicine at Wittenberg, he became chief physician and aulic councillor to Christian V. of Denmark. He published, besides other works, a "Flora Francica," (1685,) and "Twenty Medical Satires," ("Satyræ Medicæ Viginti," 1722.) He was created count by the emperor in 1691. Died in 1704.

See MORÉRI, "Dictionnaire Historique;" "Biographie Médicale."

Frank, or **Francke von Franckenau,** (GEORG FRIEDRICH,) a son of the preceding, born about 1670, was also a physician. He became professor at Copenhagen, and wrote several medical works. Died in 1732.

Frank, (JACOB,) a Polish Jew, born in 1712, was the founder of a sect called Frankists or Zoharites. He acquired a great reputation as a Cabalist, and made many disciples in Podolia about 1750. They rejected the Talmud, and professed faith in a book called "Zohar." Died in 1791.

Frank, (JOHANN PETER,) a celebrated German physician, born in the duchy of Baden in 1745, graduated at Heidelberg, succeeded Tissot in 1785 in the chair of clinics at Pavia, and in 1804 was appointed professor of medicine at Wilna, and soon after physician to the emperor Alexander of Russia. Among his principal works are his "System of a Perfect Medical Police," (1784,) and "Special Pathology and Therapeutics." Died in 1821. His son, JOSEPH, born in 1771, was a skilful physician, and the author of several valuable medical treatises. Died in 1842.

See "Biographie des J. P. Frank," Vienna, 1802; ERSCH und GRUBER, "Allgemeine Encyklopaedie."

Frank, (SEBASTIAN,) an excellent German prose writer, also noted as a visionary theologian, was born at Donauwörth, in Suabia, about 1500. He was a zealous Reformer, but by his mystical opinions and writings was involved in a quarrel with Luther. Among his numerous works were a Chronicle of Germany. Died about 1545.

See CHRISTIAN KARL AM ENDE, "Kleine Nachlese zu den vielen unvollständigen Nachrichten von S. Frank's Leben," 1796-99; S. G. WALD, "De Vita et Systemate mystico S. Franki," 1793.

Franke. See FRANCKE, (AUGUST H.)

Frankel, frăn´kel, (ZACHARIAS,) a learned Jewish writer, born at Prague in 1801. He became chief rabbi at Dresden about 1836. His works are said to be pervaded by the spirit of progress.

Frankl, frănkl, (LUDWIG AUGUST,) a German poet, of a Jewish family, born in Bohemia in 1810. His heroic poem of "Don Juan of Austria," (1846,) and an epic entitled "Christopher Columbus," (1836,) are among his best works.

Frankland, (Rev. THOMAS,) an English physician, born in 1633. He produced, besides other works, "The Annals of King James I. and Charles I.," (1681,) which are said to be impartial. Died in 1690.

Franklin, (ANNA ELEANOR PORDEN,) an English poetess, born in 1795, was a daughter of Mr. Porden, architect of Eton Hall. She learned several ancient and modern languages, and wrote poems entitled "The Veils, or the Triumph of Constancy," (1815,) "The Arctic Expedition," (1818,) and "Cœur-de-Lion, or the Third Crusade," an epic poem, (1824.) In 1823 she was married to the great navigator Sir John Franklin. Died in 1825.

Franklin, (BENJAMIN,) an eminent American philosopher and statesman, born at Boston, in Massachusetts, the 17th of January, 1706. He was the youngest son and fifteenth child of a family of seventeen children. His father, Josiah Franklin, emigrated from England to America in 1682: he followed the business of tallow-chandler and soap-boiler. Benjamin, when only ten years old, was employed in his father's shop, in cutting wicks, going errands, etc. ; but soon, becoming disgusted with the monotonous routine of his duties, he conceived a strong desire to go to sea. To prevent this, his father bound him apprentice to his brother James, who was a printer. Young Franklin had now free access to books, for which he had evinced a fondness even from infancy. He himself says he could not remember the time when he did not know how to read. To gratify his thirst for reading, he would often sit up the greater part of the night. During his apprenticeship, he made occasional anonymous contributions to a paper published by his brother, and once had the gratification to hear his articles warmly commended by some gentlemen who called at the office, and who little imagined him to be the author. He did not, however, neglect his duties as a printer; and he became in a few years well skilled in his trade. But the two brothers could not agree. The elder appears to have been of a severe and passionate temper, which the younger (as he himself intimates) may have sometimes provoked by his impertinence. At length, when seventeen years of age, young Franklin left Boston without the knowledge of his relations, embarking in a vessel bound for New York, whence he proceeded, partly by water and partly on foot, to Philadelphia. Here he obtained employment as a journeyman printer. In the following year, encouraged by the promise of assistance from a gentleman in Philadelphia, he resolved to set up business for himself. With this view he went to England in order to purchase type and other materials necessary for carrying on his trade. But, failing to receive the aid which he had expected from his pretended friend, he was obliged to work as a journeyman in London, where he remained more than a year. He returned in 1726 to Philadelphia, and in 1729, with the assistance of some friends, he established himself in business. The next year he married Miss Deborah Read, with whom he had become acquainted in Philadelphia before he went to England. In 1729 he became the editor and proprietor of a newspaper, (the "Pennsylvania Gazette,") which his talent for writing soon rendered very popular and very profitable. In 1732 he commenced the publication of an almanac purporting to be by "Richard Saunders." He sought to make this, as well as his paper, the vehicle of useful information for the people, especially inculcating the virtues of frugality, industry, etc. It was commonly called "Poor Richard's Almanac," under which name it acquired a wide celebrity. He soon won for himself a high reputation for public spirit as well as for wisdom and foresight. He warmly supported, both by his personal efforts and by his pen, every enterprise which in his judgment was calculated to promote the public good. To him is due the credit of founding the Philadelphia Library, which was commenced in 1731 and is now one of the largest in the United States. By his talents, prudence, and integrity, he continued to rise in the estimation of the community in which he lived, until he was deemed worthy of the highest honours which his country could bestow. He was made successively clerk of the General Assembly of Pennsylvania, (1736,) postmaster of Philadelphia, (1737,) and deputy postmaster-general for the British colonies, (1753.) A dispute having arisen between the Assembly and the proprietary governors, in consequence of the latter claiming exemption from taxation, Franklin was sent in 1757 to England to plead the cause of the people before the privy council. His representations and arguments prevailed; and it was decided that the estates of the proprietaries should bear their due proportion of the public burdens. On his return in 1762, he received the thanks of the Assembly for the able and faithful fulfilment of his mission.

Franklin had already become distinguished in the scientific world by his successful experiments on the nature of electricity. In 1752 he had made the important and brilliant discovery of the identity of lightning with the electric fluid, by means of a kite. Some letters, giving an account of his first experiments, were sent to England to his friend Mr. Collinson, who had them read before the Royal Society; but they attracted little attention. "One paper," says Franklin in his Autobiography, "which I wrote for Mr. Kinnersley, on the sameness of lightning with electricity, . . . was laughed at by the connoisseurs." These papers were not even thought worthy to be printed in the "Transactions" of the society. At the suggestion of Dr. Fothergill, they were published in a pamphlet by themselves. A copy having fallen under the notice of the celebrated Count de Buffon, it was, at his instance, translated into French, and excited great attention on the continent. The subject was brought again before the notice of the Royal Society; and "they soon made me," says Franklin, "more than amends for the slight with which they had before treated me." Without waiting for any application to be made on his behalf, they chose him a member of their body, and voted that he should be excused from the customary payments on admission, (amounting to twenty-five guineas;) they also bestowed upon him the Copley gold medal, (dated 1753,) and afterwards furnished him with their "Transactions" without charge. Alluding to Franklin's account of his electrical experiments, Sir Humphry Davy observes, "A singular felicity of induction guided all his researches, and by very small means he established very grand truths: the style and manner of his publication are almost as worthy of admiration as the doctrines it contains. . . . He has written equally for the uninitiated and for the philosopher." Before he left England, in 1762, the degree of Doctor of Laws was conferred upon him by the Universities of Edinburgh and Oxford.

In 1764, Franklin was again sent by the Assembly as agent to England.* The policy of taxing the colonies had already been agitated; and he was instructed by the Assembly to use his efforts against such a measure. But the ministry had formed their plans, and the Stamp Act was passed early in 1765. In the examination before the House of Commons in 1766, Franklin's talents, skill, and varied information were shown to great advantage, and the repeal of the obnoxious Stamp Act was the result. But other laws, deemed equally objectionable, remained in force. In the dispute between the American colonies and the mother-country, Franklin had sought sincerely and earnestly to prevent a disruption: when, however, he became convinced that a separation was inevitable, he returned home and took an active part in promoting the cause of independence. He arrived at Philadelphia on the 5th of May, 1775, after an absence of rather more than ten years. The day after his arrival he was unanimously elected by the Assembly of Pennsylvania a delegate to the second Continental Congress, then about to assemble. He was one of the committee of five chosen by Congress to prepare the "Declaration of Independence," which, having been agreed to on the 4th of July, 1776, he afterwards signed with the other leading patriots. Towards the close of 1776 he was sent as ambassador to the court of France: he arrived in Paris on the 21st of December. To Franklin is due the principal, if not the sole, credit of effecting between France and the United States the Treaty of Alliance, the stipulations of which were so eminently favourable to the latter country. This treaty, signed at Paris the 6th of February, 1778, may be said to have secured the independence of the American colonies. Franklin took an important part in the negotiation of peace with England, and signed the preliminary articles of a treaty of peace at Paris on the 30th of November, 1782. The definitive treaty of peace was signed at Paris by Franklin, Adams, and Jay, September 3, 1783. Franklin afterwards negotiated with Prussia a treaty, in which he inserted an article against privateering. "This treaty," said Washington, "marks a new era in negotiation. It is the most liberal treaty which has ever been entered into between independent powers." He returned home in September, 1785, and in the next month was chosen President of Pennsylvania for one year. He was re-elected in 1786 and 1787. He was a delegate to the convention which met at Philadelphia in May, 1787, to form a Constitution of the United States. It deserves to be mentioned that he introduced a motion for daily prayers in this convention, on which occasion he said, "I have lived a long time, and the longer I live the more convincing proofs I see of this truth, that God governs in the affairs of men. And if a sparrow cannot fall to the ground without his notice, is it probable that an empire can rise without his aid?"

At the close of the convention he made a speech, in which he said, "I consent to this Constitution, because I expect no better, and because I am not sure that it is not the best." His last public act was the signature of a memorial addressed to Congress by the Abolition Society, of which he was president.

* He was afterwards appointed agent by several of the other colonies.

He died in Philadelphia on the 17th of April, 1790, aged eighty-four years, leaving a son, William, who was Governor of New Jersey, and a daughter, Sarah Bache. His remains are entombed in the cemetery of Christ Church, at the southeastern angle of Fifth and Arch Streets, Philadelphia.

In person Franklin was of a medium stature, well formed and strongly built, with a light complexion and gray eyes. As a philosopher he was remarkable for simplicity of character and for practical common sense. He deemed nothing which concerned the interest or happiness of mankind unworthy of his attention; and he rarely, if ever, bestowed attention on any subject without permanently useful results. His services to science and liberty were expressed in this famous line by Turgot:

"Eripuit cœlo fulmen, sceptrumque tyrannis."*

"He never pretended to the accomplishments of an orator or debater. He seldom spoke in a deliberative assembly except for some special object, and then briefly and with great simplicity of manner and language." (Sparks's "Life of Franklin.")

Franklin left an interesting and highly-instructive autobiography of the earlier part of his life, (up to his fifty-second year.) A continuation has been added by Jared Sparks, prefixed to an edition of Franklin's entire works,—the whole being comprised in 10 vols. 8vo, (Boston, 1850.)

"Antiquity," says Mirabeau, "would have raised altars to this mighty genius, who, to the advantage of mankind, compassing in his mind the heavens and the earth, was able to restrain alike thunderbolts and tyrants." Lord Chatham, in a public speech made in 1775, characterized Franklin as "one whom all Europe held in high estimation for his knowledge and wisdom, and ranked with our Boyles and Newtons; who was an honour not to the English nation only, but to human nature." "His style," says Lord Jeffrey, "has all the vigour and even conciseness of Swift, without any of his harshness. It is in no degree more flowery, yet both elegant and lively. . . . The peculiar charm of his writings, and his great merit also in action, consisted in the clearness with which he saw his object, and the bold and steady pursuit of it by the surest and the shortest road."

See LORD JEFFREY's articles in the "Edinburgh Review," July, 1806, and August, 1817; CONDORCET, "Éloge de Franklin," 1790; BANCROFT, "History of the United States," vol. ix. chap. xxix.; A. NORTON, article in the "North American Review," vol. vii.; MIGNET, "Vie de Franklin;" BAUER, "Washington und Franklin," Berlin, 1803–06; C. SCHMALTZ, "Leben Benj. Franklins," 1840. In 1868 a corrected edition of his Autobiography was published by JOHN BIGELOW, who obtained the original MS. in Paris. See, also, LORD BROUGHAM, "Statesmen of the Time of George III.," vol. ii.; PARTON, "Life and Times of B. Franklin," 2 vols. 8vo, 1864.

Franklin, (JANE GRIFFIN,) LADY, the second wife of Sir John Franklin, was born about 1802. She was married about 1828, and went with her husband to Van Diemen's Land in 1836. Her name has been rendered memorable by her persevering efforts to ascertain the fate of Sir John Franklin. In 1850 she sent out a ship for that purpose at her own expense. Other expeditions were sent by the British government, without success, until 1857, when she fitted out the steamer Fox. See FRANKLIN, (SIR JOHN.)

Franklin, (Sir JOHN,) a distinguished English navigator and Arctic explorer, was born at Spilsby, in Lincolnshire, in April, 1786. He entered the navy as a midshipman about 1800, and in 1801 accompanied Captain Flinders in a voyage of exploration to Australia. He served with distinction at the battle of Trafalgar, October 21, 1805, and was slightly wounded in the attack on New Orleans, January, 1815. Having obtained the rank of lieutenant, he was appointed commander of the Trent in the Arctic expedition which, under Captain Buchan, sailed in 1818. The ship of Captain Buchan was disabled soon after their departure, and the expedition consequently failed. In 1819 he conducted an overland expedition sent to trace the coast-line of North America, in which service he and his party walked about fifty-five hundred and fifty miles. On his return to England he published a narrative of his expedition, and

was raised to the rank of captain. He was elected a Fellow of the Royal Society in 1823, and married Miss Eleanor Porden about that date. In 1825 he renewed the enterprise of exploration by land, and traced the coast of North America from the mouth of the Copper-mine River to the 150th meridian, for which service he was knighted. He afterwards commanded the Rainbow in the Mediterranean for several years. Having lost his first wife, he married Jane Griffin in 1828. He was Governor of Van Diemen's Land from 1836 to 1842.

The government having ordered a new expedition to discover a Northwest passage, and given the command of it to Sir John Franklin, he sailed with the Erebus and Terror in May, 1845, and never returned. Several expeditions were sent in search of him by the English and the Americans, without success; but Dr. Rae found, in 1854, some relics of the lost navigators. Lady Franklin sent out, in 1857, the steamer Fox, under Captain McClintock, who, in the summer of 1859, discovered on the shore of King William's Land a record deposited in a cairn by the survivors of Franklin's company. This document, dated April 25, 1848, stated that Sir John Franklin died June 11, 1847, that the Erebus and Terror were abandoned April 22, 1848, when the survivors, one hundred and five in number, started for the Great Fish River. Many relics were found of this party, who perished on their journey, probably soon after they left the vessels. It appears that Sir John is entitled to the honour of being the first to discover a Northwest passage.

See P. L. SIMMONDS, "Sir John Franklin and the Arctic Regions," 1852; "London Quarterly Review" for January, 1823; "North American Review" for July, 1850, (vol. lxxi.)

Franklin, (WILLIAM,) the last royal Governor of New Jersey, an illegitimate son of the celebrated Dr. Franklin, was born in Philadelphia about 1731. He served as an officer in the French war before he was of age. In 1757 he went with his father to London, where he studied law and was admitted to the bar. He was appointed Governor of New Jersey in 1762, became a Tory in the Revolution, and was confined in prison for two years, 1776–78. In 1782 he removed to England, where he remained until his death, in 1813. He left a son, William Temple Franklin.

Franklin, (WILLIAM B.,) an American general, born at York, Pennsylvania, in 1823, graduated at West Point in 1843, in the same class with Ulysses S. Grant. He served in the Mexican war, became a captain in 1857, and colonel in the regular army in 1861. He served as a general under McClellan in several battles near Richmond in June, 1862, commanded a corps at Malvern Hill, July 1, and at Antietam, September 17. He was appointed a major-general of volunteers about July, 1862. In December, 1862, he led a grand division of Burnside's army at Fredericksburg. He commanded a division of General Banks's army in the Red River campaign of 1864.

Franquelin, frŏNk'lăN', (JEAN AUGUSTE,) a French painter of genre, born in Paris in 1798; died in 1839.

Franscini, frän-shee'nee, (STEFANO,) a Swiss statesman of the Liberal party, born in the canton of Tessin (Ticino) in 1796. He was secretary of state from 1830 to 1837, after which he was a member of the Federal Council. In 1849 or 1850 he became minister of the interior and of public instruction. He published, besides other works, "Statistics of Switzerland," ("Statistica della Suizzera," 3 vols., 1828–51.) Died in 1857.

Fransoni, frän-so'nee, or **Franzoni,** frän-zo'nee, (LUIGI,) an Italian prelate, born at Genoa in 1789. He became Archbishop of Turin about 1831, and displayed a great zeal for ultramontane doctrines and absolutism. He was banished about 1853.

Fransz, (PETER.) See FRANCIUS.

Frantz, frănts, or **Frantzius,** frănt'se-ŭs, (WOLFGANG,) a German Protestant theologian, born at Plauen, in Saxony, in 1564, was professor of theology at Wittenberg. Among his works is "A Treatise on the Interpretation of the Sacred Scriptures," ("Tractatus de Interpretatione Sacræ Scripturæ.") Died in 1628.

See J. G. NEUMANN, "Programma de Vita W. Frantzii," 1709.

Franz, frănts, (AGNES,) born in Silesia in 1794, wrote a number of excellent and attractive works for children,

* "He wrested the thunderbolt from heaven and the sceptre from tyrants."

among which are "My Legacy to Youth," and the "Book of Childhood and Youth." Died in 1843.

Franz, (JOHANN MICHAEL,) a German geographer, born at Oehringen in 1700; died in 1761.

Franz, (JOHANNES,) a German scholar, born at Nuremberg in 1804. In 1832 he accompanied King Otho to Greece, where he was appointed chief interpreter. He published a "German-Greek Dictionary," (1838,) "Elements of Greek Epigraphy," and other works. Died in 1851.

Franz, (KARL JOSEPH,) Prince and Archduke of Austria, born in 1802, was a son of Francis I., and the father of the present emperor, Francis Joseph, in whose favour he resigned his own right to the throne in 1848.

Franzén, frȧnt-slīn', (FRANS MICHAEL,) a popular Swedish poet, born at Uleåborg, Finland, in 1772, was for some time pastor of a church in Stockholm, and about 1832 was made Bishop of Hernosand. From 1824 to 1834 he acted as secretary of the Swedish Academy. He wrote biographical memoirs of several persons, assisted in an authorized and excellent version of the Psalms, and published several volumes of songs and other poems, which are highly appreciated and have acquired for him the reputation of one of the most eminent Swedish poets of his age. Died in 1847. Among his poems is "Columbus, or the Discovery of America," ("Columbus, eller Amerikas Upptäckt," 1831.)

See G. H. MELLIN, "Minnes-Tal öfver F. M. Franzén," 1848; "Nouvelle Biographie Générale."

Fra Paolo. See SARPI.

Frā'ṣer, (ALEXANDER,) a Scottish painter, born about 1792. He painted domestic and familiar scenes with success. Among his works are the "Interior of a Highland Cottage," and "The Last Moments of Mary Queen of Scots." Died in 1865.

Fraser, (ALEXANDER CAMPBELL,) a Scottish metaphysician, born in Argyleshire about 1818. He studied under Sir William Hamilton, and became professor of logic in the New College, Edinburgh, in 1846, and editor of the "North British Review" about 1850. In 1856 he succeeded Sir William Hamilton as professor of logic and metaphysics in the University of Edinburgh. He published a work entitled "Rational Philosophy in History and in System."

Frā'ṣer, (CHARLES,) an American painter and writer, born in Charleston, South Carolina, in 1782, was a lawyer for many years. His portraits include La Fayette, and a great number of eminent persons of South Carolina. Died in 1860.

See DUNLAP, "History of the Rise and Progress of the Arts of Design in America."

Fraser, (JAMES BAILLIE,) a popular Scottish writer of travels, born in 1783, resided on his estate of Reelig, Inverness-shire. He spent many years in travelling in Asia, and published numerous entertaining works, among which are "Journal of a Tour through part of the Himalaya Mountains," (1820;) "Journey into Khorasan," (1825;) "The Persian Adventurer," a romance, (1828;) "History of Persia, Ancient and Modern," (1847;) and "Travels through Various Parts of Persia," (1838,) which, says the "London Athenæum," "can hardly be surpassed in lively delineations and rapid but graphic sketches." Died in 1856.

Fraser, (SIMON.) See LOVAT.

Fraser, (SIMON,) a British general of high reputation, was second in command of the army which, under Burgoyne, invaded New York in 1777. He was killed at the battle of Stillwater, in October of that year.

Frassen, frȧs'sŏN', (CLAUDE,) a French monk, born near Péronne in 1620. He published a "Course of Theology," (4 vols., 1672,) and other works. Died in 1711.

Fratellini, frȧ-têl-lee'nee, (GIOVANNA,) an Italian painter, born at Florence in 1666, was adopted in infancy by the grand duchess Vittoria. She excelled in portraits. Died in 1731.

Fratellini, (LORENZO,) a Florentine portrait-painter, a son of the preceding, born about 1690; died in 1729.

Fratta, frȧt'tä, (DOMENICO MARIA,) a skilful Italian painter, born at Bologna in 1696; died in 1763.

Frauenlob, frŏw'ĕn-lōp', originally **Heinrich von Meissen,** a famous German poet, was born in the thir-

teenth century. He composed "Songs," ("Lieder,") and witty or sententious sayings, ("Sprüche,") and invented many varieties of metre. His works are partly satirical. Died at Mentz in 1318.

See ERSCH und GRUBER, "Allgemeine Encyklopaedie;" K. GÖDEKE, "Das Mittelalter;" "Nouvelle Biographie Générale;" N. VOGT, "Heinrich Frauenlob," 1792.

Fraunce, (ABRAHAM,) an English poet, lived in the reign of Elizabeth, and was educated at Cambridge. He was author of "Lawyers' Logic," of "Arcadian Rhetoric," a mixture of prose and verse, and of several small poems in English hexameter, published between 1587 and 1591.

Fraunhofer, von, fon frŏwn'ho'fĕr, (JOSEPH,) an eminent German optician, born at Straubing, in Bavaria, in March, 1787. He was an apprentice to a manufacturer of mirrors, and afterwards became an assistant of Reichenbach in the fabrication of mathematical instruments, near Munich. He invented or perfected a heliometer and micrometer, and constructed the great parallactic telescope of Dorpat. Among his discoveries was the fact that the solar spectrum is crossed by about five hundred and ninety black lines. Died in 1826. We owe to him the art of making the finest glass for achromatic telescopes.

See UTZSCHNEIDER, "Umriss der Lebensgeschichte des J. von Fraunhofer;" ERSCH und GRUBER, "Allgemeine Encyklopaedie;" "Nouvelle Biographie Générale."

Frayssinous, frȧ̀'se'noo', (DENIS LUC,) a French prelate and eminent pulpit orator, born at Curières in 1765, became chaplain to Louis XVIII. He was appointed Bishop of Hermopolis in 1822, and grand master of the university in 1823. He was minister of public instruction from 1824 to 1828. Among his writings is a "Defence of Christianity," (1823.) Died in 1841.

See M. HENRION, "Vie de M. Frayssinous," 1842; "Nouvelle Biographie Générale."

Fra-zee', (JOHN,) an American sculptor, born at Rahway, New Jersey, in 1790. Among his works are busts of Marshall, Jackson, and Webster.

See DUNLAP, "Rise and Progress of the Arts of Design in America;" TUCKERMAN, "Book of the Artists."

Frea. See FRIGGA.

Fréard, (ROLAND.) See CHAMBRAY.

Fred-e-gā'rī-us, [Fr. FRÉDÉGAIRE, frȧ'dȧ'gȧR',] surnamed SCHOLASTICUS, a chronicler who lived (probably in France) in the seventh century. His work treats of the history of the Franks, ending about 640 A.D.

Fredegonda or **Frédégonde.** See FREDEGUNDA.

Fred-e-gun'da, [Fr. FRÉDÉGONDE, frȧ'dȧ'gȯnd',] a queen of the Franks, notorious for her crimes, was born about 545 A.D. She became the wife of Chilpéric I. about 565, after which she procured the assassination of his sons by a former marriage, and of Sigebert, King of Austrasia. After the death of Chilpéric (584) she was regent during the minority of her son Clotaire, and gained victories in a war against several kings. Died in 596 A.D.

See SISMONDI, "Histoire des Français."

Frédéric. See FREDERICK and FRIEDRICH.

Fred-er-ic'a̤ So-phi'a̤ Wil-hel-mi'na, (wil-hêl-mee'nȧ,) Margravine of Baireuth, daughter of Frederick William I. of Prussia, and favourite sister of Frederick the Great, was born at Potsdam in 1709. She was married in 1731 to the hereditary prince of Baireuth, and died in 1758, on the day of her brother's defeat at Hochkirchen. She left interesting "Memoirs" of her times, which see; also "Edinburgh Review" for November, 1812.

Fred'er-ick [Ger. FRIEDRICH, freed'rĭk; It. FEDERIGO, fȧ-dȧ-ree'go] I., Emperor of Germany, surnamed BARBAROSSA, born in 1121, was a son of Frederick, Duke of Suabia. He was elected emperor on the death of his uncle, Conrad III., in March, 1152. In 1155 he passed into Italy with an army, and was crowned by Pope Adrian IV. at Rome. He married Beatrice, heiress of Burgundy, about 1156, and reduced the King or Duke of Poland to become his vassal. He led in 1158 a large army into Italy, and subjected the revolted city of Milan, which was punished with rigour. Two rival popes, Victor IV. and Alexander III., having been elected in 1159, Frederick recognized the former and was excommunicated by the latter. His reign was disturbed by disputes with the pope, and wars with the cities of Lombardy. His

ɛ as k; ç as s; ḡ hard; g as j; G, H, K, guttural; N, nasal; R, trilled; ŝ as z; ʧh as in this. (✪See Explanations, p. 23.)

61

army was defeated with great loss by the Lombards near Legnano in 1176. He then made peace with Pope Alexander, and a truce with his other enemies in Italy. In 1183 the celebrated peace of Constance was concluded between Frederick and the Lombards. He joined the third crusade with an army of about 150,000 men in 1189, and, having marched by land as far as Asia Minor, defeated the Turks near Iconium. He was drowned in the river Calycadnus in 1190. Frederick was ambitious, but rather liberal, and passes for one of the greatest men of his time. He was succeeded by his son, Henry VI.

See RAUMER, "Geschichte der Hohenstaufen;" SISMONDI, "Histoire des Républiques Italiennes;" WILKEN, "Geschichte der Kreuzzüge;" COSMO BARTOLI, "Vita di Federigo Barbarossa," Florence, 1556; H. F. MASSMANN, "Kaiser Friedrich im Kyffhäuser," 1850.

Frederick II., Emperor of Germany, was a son of Henry VI., and was born at Iesi, in Italy, in 1194. His mother was Constance of Sicily. His education was directed by his guardian, Innocent III. He had superior talents, and was master of the Greek, Italian, French, and Arabic languages. He was crowned as emperor at Aix-la-Chapelle in 1214 or 1215, after the defeat of his rival, Otho, at Bovines, and was supported by the Ghibeline party in an attempt to unite Italy and Germany in one empire. This project was resisted by the pope and the Guelphs in a long contest. In 1220 he removed his court to Naples, which belonged to him by inheritance, and in which he founded a university. In accordance with a vow extorted from him in his youth by the pope, he undertook a crusade against the infidels in 1227, but turned back before he had reached Palestine, for which cause he was excommunicated by Gregory IX. He renewed the enterprise in 1228, obtained possession of Jerusalem, and made peace with the pope in 1230. He suppressed a rebellion raised in Germany by his son Henry, gained in 1237 a great victory over the Guelphs at Cortenuova, and waged war against Gregory IX. In 1245 Innocent IV. renewed the papal anathema against him, and absolved his subjects from their allegiance. In the midst of the contest Frederick died, in 1250. He was succeeded by his son, Conrad IV. Frederick was eminent for courage, generosity, and other royal qualities.

See RAUMER, "Geschichte der Hohenstaufen;" LUDEN, "Histoire d'Allemagne;" HOEFLER, "Kaiser Friedrich II.," 1844; T. L. KINGTON, "History of Frederick II., Emperor of the Romans;" CARL W. F. FUNK, "Geschichte Kaiser Friedrichs II.," 1790.

Frederick III., Emperor of Germany, surnamed THE PACIFIC, the son of Ernest, Duke of Austria, was born at Innspruck in 1415. He was elected emperor in 1440, on the death of Albert II. In 1452 he went to Rome, where he received from the pope the imperial crown and that of Lombardy. He is censured for supineness in defending Christendom against the Turks, and was incapable of ruling his large empire with success. In 1485 he was involved in war with Matthias Corvinus of Hungary, who conquered Vienna and Lower Austria. Died in 1493, and was succeeded by his son, Maximilian.

See LUDEN, "Histoire d'Allemagne;" J. CHMEL, "Geschichte Kaiser Friedrich's III.," 1840.

Frederick [Dan. FREDERIK, frā'dęh-rěk] **I.**, King of Denmark and Norway, born in 1471, was a son of Christian I., who founded the dynasty of Oldenburg. In 1522 he succeeded his nephew, Christian II., who was deposed. The latter raised an army and invaded Norway in 1532, but was forced to surrender and was confined in prison. Frederick favoured the propagation of Lutheranism in his kingdom. He died in 1533, and was succeeded by his son, Christian III.

Frederick II., King of Denmark and Norway, son of Christian III., was born in 1534, and ascended the throne in 1559. In 1561 he was involved in a war with Eric, King of Sweden, in which the Danes were victorious. Peace was restored in 1570. Frederick married Sophia of Mecklenburg, and had several children. He promoted commerce, and patronized men of science, especially Tycho Brahe, the eminent astronomer, for whom he built the Observatory of Oranienburg. He died in 1588, and was succeeded by his son, Christian IV.

See P. H. RESEN, "Frederik II. Krönike," 1680; PONTANUS, "Vita Friderici II., Regis Daniæ," 1735.

Frederick III., King of Denmark and Norway, a son of Christian IV., was born in 1609, and succeeded to the crown by inheritance and election in 1648. In 1657 Frederick and his senate declared war against Charles Gustavus of Sweden, who was so well prepared that he crossed the ice and suddenly besieged Copenhagen. The Danish king was compelled to sign a peace, by which he gave up several provinces, in 1658. Before the end of that year Charles Gustavus again besieged his capital, which was relieved by a Dutch fleet, and peace was concluded in 1660. At a diet held in 1660–61 a great change was effected in the constitution by a coalition of the clergy with the bourgeoisie against the nobles, so that the monarchy (which had been elective and limited) was made hereditary and absolute. He died in 1670, and was succeeded by his son, Christian V.

See R. MANLEY, "History of the Wars in Denmark," London, 1670; R. NYERUP, "Efterretninger om Kong Frederik III.," 1817; P. W. BECKER, "Samlinger til Danmarks Historie under Frederik III.," 1847.

Frederick IV., King of Denmark, son of Christian V., was born in 1671. After he had married Louisa of Mecklenburg-Güstrow, he ascended the throne in 1699. In 1700 he formed an alliance with Peter the Great and Augustus, King of Poland, against Charles XII. of Sweden, who soon besieged Copenhagen and dictated the terms of peace. During the reverses that befell Charles XII. in 1709, Frederick again declared war, and captured the fortress of Tönningen, Stralsund, and other places. In 1718 Charles invaded Norway and besieged Frederickshall, where he was killed by a cannon-ball. Frederick died in 1730, regretted by his subjects, whom he governed with ability, and was succeeded by his son, Christian VI.

See A. HOIER, "König Friedrich's IV. glorwürdigstes Leben," 1829; RIEGELS, "Udkast til Fjerde Frederiks Historie," 1799.

Frederick V., King of Denmark, son of Christian VI., was born in 1723. He succeeded his father in 1746, having previously married Louisa, daughter of George II. of England. His reign was remarkable for many institutions and enterprises for the promotion of commerce, industry, science, and arts. The emancipation of serfs was tried with success in some districts; a hospital and an academy of fine arts were founded in the capital. In 1761 Frederick sent Niebuhr and others on a scientific expedition to Egypt and Arabia. He died in January, 1766, after a prosperous and pacific reign, and was succeeded by his son, Christian VII.

See J. K. HOEST, "Märkvärdigheder i Kong Frederiks Levnet og Regjering," 1820; G. L. BADEN, "Frederiks Regjerings Aarbog," 1832; M. S. ARENTZ, "Ligpraediken over Kong Frederik V.," 1767.

Frederick VI., King of Denmark and Norway, born in 1768, was the only son of Christian VII. and Caroline Matilda. He became regent in 1784, (in consequence of the mental alienation of his father,) and king in 1808. Between these two dates he made many reforms. He formed an alliance with Napoleon in 1808, his capital having been previously bombarded by the British. In 1813 he refused to join the coalition against the French emperor. Russia and Sweden having entered into a convention to annex Norway to the latter, Bernadotte attacked the dominions of Frederick, who was compelled to cede Norway in 1814. He died in 1839, and was succeeded by his cousin, Christian VIII.

See O. L. BANG, "Mindetale over Kong Frederik VI.," 1840; H. P. GIESSING, "Kong Frederik VI. Regjerings Historie," 2 vols., 1850.

Frederick VII., King of Denmark, and Duke of Sleswick and Holstein, born in 1808, is the only son of Christian VIII., whom he succeeded in January, 1848. The German party in Holstein and Sleswick revolted in March of the same year. After several indecisive battles, the insurgents were defeated at Idsted in July, 1850, and the rebellion was suppressed in January, 1851. He contracted a morganatic marriage with the Countess Danner in 1850. In 1864 Austria and Prussia united in an aggressive war against Denmark, and conquered the duchies of Sleswick and Holstein.

Frederick [Ger. FRIEDRICH, freed'rik] **I.**, King of Prussia, born at Königsberg in 1657, was a son of Frederick William, Elector of Brandenburg. He succeeded his father in 1688, and was styled Frederick III. of Brandenburg. His wife was Sophia Charlotte, a sister of George I. of England. He joined the coalition against Louis XIV. of France in 1691. In 1700 the dukedom of

---

ā, ē, ᷔ, ō, ū, ȳ, *long;* ă, ĕ, ĭ, ŏ, ŭ, ў, *short;* ą, ę, į, ǫ, *obscure;* fär, fäll, fât; mêt; nôt; gŏŏd; mōōn;

Prussia was erected into a kingdom, with the assent of the emperor, and Frederick gained the great object of his life, the title of king, on condition that he would aid Austria in the war of the Spanish succession, and vote with Austria in the Diet. He died in 1713, and left the throne to his son, Frederick William I.

See STENZEL, "Geschichte des Preussischen Staats;" FRANZ HORN, "Friedrich III., erster König in Preussen," 1816; J. G. MITTAG, "Geschichte Friedrich's I. König's von Preussen," 1734; WERNER HAHN, "Friedrich I. König in Preussen," etc., 1851.

Frederick II., surnamed THE GREAT, [Ger. FRIED-RICH DER GROSSE, freed'riK dĕR grōs'seh; Fr. FRÉDÉRIC LE GRAND, frȧ'dȧ'rĕk' leh grŏN; It. FEDERIGO IL GRANDE, fȧ-dȧ-ree'go ĕl grȧn'dȧ; Sp. FEDERICO EL GRANDE, fȧ-Dȧ-ree'ko ĕl grȧn'dȧ,] King of Prussia, was the son of Frederick William I. and Sophia Dorothea, who was a daughter of George I. of England. He was born at Berlin on the 24th of January, 1712. He received from nature a strong and acute intellect, with a rare firmness of temper and intensity of will. The discipline and training to which he was subjected by his father were extremely rigid, perverse, and illiberal; the study of Latin was positively forbidden to him. "Oliver Twist in the parish workhouse, Smike at Dotheboys Hall," says Macaulay, "were petted children when compared with this wretched heir-apparent of a crown." It appears that the prince would have been put to death by his father for desertion, or running away from the army, if he had not been saved by the intercession of the Emperor of Germany. The penalty was commuted into close confinement. Frederick married (by compulsion) Elizabeth Christina of Brunswick, in 1733. His favourite study or resource in his youth was French literature. He wrote and read nothing but French.

He ascended the throne about June 1, 1740, and quickly displayed a political ability and an unscrupulous energy which surprised his courtiers and former companions. He seized the opportunity presented by the accession of Maria Theresa in October, 1740, and gave the first signal of the war of spoliation, called the war of the Austrian succession, by the sudden invasion of Silesia, which he occupied without much resistance. In April, 1741, he defeated the Austrians at the battle of Molwitz; after which Bavaria and France took arms as allies of Frederick. A separate peace was concluded in 1742 between him and Maria Theresa, who ceded Silesia to the victor. He renewed hostilities in 1744, and took Prague, but was forced to retreat about the end of that year. He commanded at Hohenfriedberg and at Sorr, where the Austrians were defeated, in 1745, and made peace with Austria in December of the same year. In the civil administration he was his own prime minister, or, rather, sole minister. "A love of labour for its own sake, an insatiable longing to dictate, to intermeddle, to make his power felt, a profound scorn and distrust of his fellow-creatures, indisposed him to ask counsel, to confide important secrets, to delegate ample powers." (Macaulay.) He was so parsimonious that in his household "not a-bottle of champagne was uncorked without his express order." He encouraged commerce, manufactures, and the fine arts. Every form of religion and of irreligion was tolerated by him. In 1750 he attracted to his court Voltaire, whom he treated with great favour. This eccentric friendship, however, soon ended in a violent quarrel. (See VOLTAIRE.)

A powerful coalition having been formed against Frederick by Maria Theresa, the Empress of Russia, the King of France, and other powers, he was thus involved in the Seven Years' war, with no ally but the English. He began the war by the invasion of Saxony, in August, 1756, and, having defeated the Austrians at Lowositz, made himself master of that country. He opened the next campaign by a march into Bohemia, and gained the great battle of Prague, (May, 1757,) where he lost about 18,000 men; but on the 18th of June he was defeated at Kolin by Marshal Daun, and driven out of Bohemia. His position now seemed desperate; but his passion for writing verses did not fail even in this gloomy crisis. "We hardly know," says Macaulay, "any instance of the strength and weakness of human nature so striking and so grotesque as the character of this haughty, vigilant,

resolute, sagacious blue-stocking, . . . bearing up against a world in arms, with an ounce of poison in one pocket and a quire of bad verses in the other."

Frederick defeated a French army twice as numerous as his own, at Rossbach, in November, and gained a complete victory over the Austrians at Leuthen on the 5th of December, 1757, when 27,000 of the enemy were killed, wounded, or taken. "That battle," said Napoleon, "was a master-piece. Of itself it is sufficient to entitle Frederick to a place in the first rank of generals." His fame was increased by a victory over the Russians at Zorndorf, near the Oder, in 1758. The principal event of the campaign of 1759 was the battle of Kunnersdorf, where the Prussians were routed by the allies and Frederick's coat was pierced with balls. After the enemy had taken Berlin and reduced him to desperation, the tide of fortune turned in 1760, at the battles of Liegnitz and Torgau. The campaign of 1761 was, on the whole, disastrous to Frederick; but, in consequence of the death of the empress Elizabeth, January, 1762, the policy of Russia was changed, and Maria Theresa, deserted by her allies, was obliged to make peace in February, 1763. The result of the war was that Frederick kept Silesia and ceded nothing.

He has been praised for the diligence and liberality with which he repaired the ruinous state to which the war had reduced his kingdom. On the partition of Poland, in 1772, he acquired Polish Prussia and a part of Great Poland. By the formation of the league called *Fürstenbund*, ("Princes' League,") in 1785, he frustrated the design of the emperor to acquire Bavaria in exchange for the Low Countries. He died, without issue, at his palace of Sans-Souci, on the 17th of August, 1786, and was succeeded by his nephew, Frederick William II. He left many and various works, which were published in 23 vols., 1790. His poem "On the Art of War," "History of My Time," and "History of the Seven Years' War," are reckoned among his best productions. Of his voluminous "Memoirs" Macaulay remarks, "The narrative is distinguished by clearness, conciseness, good sense, and a certain air of truth and simplicity, which is singularly graceful in a man who, having done great things, sits down to relate them."

See LORD DOVER, "Life of Frederick II.," 2 vols., 1840; "Frederick the Great and his Times," by THOMAS CAMPBELL, 4 vols., 1843; CARLYLE, "Life of Frederick the Great," 6 vols., 1858-65; BROUGHAM, "Statesmen of the Time of George III.," first series; MACAULAY, "Essays;" MIRABEAU, "De la Monarchie Prussienne sous Frédéric le Grand," 1788; THIEBAULT, "Souvenirs;" JOMINI, "Histoire critique et militaire des Guerres de Frédéric II;" PAGA-NEL, "Histoire de Frédéric le Grand;" PREUSS, "Friedrich der Grosse," 9 vols., 1832-34; J. C. ADELUNG, "Denkwürdigkeiten Friedrich's des Grossen," 9 vols., 1757-66; FISCHER, "Geschichte Friedrich's VI.," 2 vols., 1787; J. F. SEYFART, "Lebens- und Regierungs-geschichte Friedrich's des Andern," 9 vols., 1759-70; Buc-QUOY, "Leben und Ende Friedrich's des Einzigen," 4 vols., 1787-91; CHARLES JOSEPH DE LIGNE, "Mémoires sur le Roi de Prusse," 1788; CARLO DENINA, "Essai sur la Vie et le Règne de Frédéric II," 1788; CALZADA, "Vida de Federico II., Rey de Prusia," 4 vols., 1788. For further bibliographical information respecting Frederick II., the reader is referred to OETTINGER's "Bibliographie biographique universelle," 2 vols., 1854.

Frederick, (OF ARAGON,) King of Naples, son of Ferdinand I., succeeded his nephew, Ferdinand II., who died, without issue, in September, 1496. In 1501, Louis XII. of France and Ferdinand of Spain agreed to depose the King of Naples and partition his kingdom between them, and each sent an army to take possession of his share. Frederick, after a feeble resistance, surrendered himself to the French, received from Louis the duchy of Anjou, and died in 1504. His son having died without issue in 1550, the family became extinct.

Frederick I., (OF ARAGON,) King of Sicily, was the third son of Peter (Pedro) of Aragon and of Constance of Suabia. He is called Frederick II. by some writers. He was crowned in 1296, and soon found himself engaged in war against Charles II. of Naples and the pope; but, being zealously supported by his subjects, he made a successful defence, and obtained peace in 1302. He renewed the war in 1312 against Robert, the successor of Charles II., and waged it for many years. He died in 1337, and was succeeded by his son, Pietro II. Frederick is regarded as the founder of Sicilian nationality.

See BURIGNY, "Histoire générale de Sicile," 2 vols., 1745; MU-RATORI, "Annali d'Italia."

Frederick II. or **III.**, King of Sicily, born about 1340, was a son of Peter (Pietro) II., and succeeded his elder brother Louis in 1355. He found the kingdom in disorder, and at war with Joanna I. of Naples, who captured Messina and Palermo. In 1372 he obtained peace, and recovered those towns, by paying tribute. He died in 1377, leaving a daughter, Maria, who married Martin II. of Aragon.

See VILLANI, "Istoria ;" BURIGNY, " Histoire générale de Sicile."

Frederick, [Sw. FRED'RICK,] King of Sweden, a son of the Landgrave of Hesse-Cassel, was born at Cassel in 1676. He married Ulrica Eleonora, a sister of Charles XII. of Sweden, in 1715. She succeeded to the throne at the death of Charles, and in 1720 the Diet, at her request, elected Frederick king. He made peace before the end of 1721 with Russia and the other enemies whom the ambition of Charles XII. had armed against Sweden, by giving up Livonia, Ingria, etc. His reign was pacific, except a war with Russia in 1741 and 1742, in which the Swedes were defeated. He died in 1751, and was succeeded by Adolph Frederick of Holstein.

See GEYER, " Histoire de la Suède ;" J. ARKENHOLTZ, " Leben Friedrich's I. Königs von Schweden," 1752.

Frederick I., Duke of Austria, born in 1174, was a son of Leopold I. He led an army of crusaders to Palestine in 1197, and besieged Toron without success. Died in 1198.

See ERSCH und GRUBER, " Allgemeine Encyklopaedie."

Frederick III., Archduke of Austria, born in 1286, was the eldest son of the emperor Albert I. After the death of Albert the throne was claimed by Frederick and by Louis of Bavaria. The former was supported by the Guelphs, and his rival by the Ghibelines. In 1322 Frederick was defeated in battle and taken prisoner by Louis, who treated him generously. Died in 1330.

See ERSCH und GRUBER, " Allgemeine Encyklopaedie."

Frederick V., Duke of Austria, was a younger son of Leopold of Austria. He was an adherent of Pope John XXIII., and offended the emperor Sigismund in 1415 by aiding that pontiff to abscond from Constance, where the Council was then in session. Frederick was placed under the ban of the empire, and saved himself from ruin only by a humble submission. Died in 1436.

See ERSCH und GRUBER, " Allgemeine Encyklopaedie."

Frederick I., Elector Palatine, [Ger. FRIEDRICH CURFÜRST VON DER PFALZ,] surnamed THE VICTORIOUS, born in 1425, was a son of Louis III. He became regent at the death of his elder brother, in 1449. A league was formed against him by several princes, whom he defeated in 1460. Died in 1476.

See TRITHÈME, " Res gestæ Friderici Palatini," 1602; ERSCH und GRUBER, " Allgemeine Encyklopaedie."

Frederick II., Elector Palatine, surnamed THE WISE, a son of Philip, was born in 1482. He succeeded his brother Louis in 1544, and embraced the doctrines of Luther in 1545. He afterwards joined the league of Schmalkalden, and signed the formulary called the " Interim" in 1548. He died in 1556, and was succeeded by his nephew, Otho Henry.

See ERSCH und GRUBER, " Allgemeine Encyklopaedie."

Frederick III., Elector Palatine, surnamed THE PIOUS, born in 1515, was a son of John II., Duke of Simmern. He became a zealous Protestant. He obtained the dignity of Elector in 1559, and sent troops to aid the French Huguenots in 1568. He died in 1576, and was succeeded by his son, Louis VI.

See ERSCH und GRUBER, "Allgemeine Encyklopaedie."

Frederick IV., Elector Palatine, surnamed THE JUST, born in 1574, was a son of Louis VI. He began to reign in 1592. He founded Mannheim about 1606. Died in 1610.

Frederick V., Elector Palatine, and King of Bohemia, born in 1596, was a son of Frederick IV., and father of Prince Rupert, famous in English history. He married in 1613 Elizabeth, a daughter of James I. of England, and became the chief of the German Protestant Union. In 1619 he was elected King of Bohemia by the people of that country, who had revolted against the emperor. He was completely defeated in battle at Prague in 1620, lost his hereditary dominions, and was obliged to go into

exile. His electoral dignity was transferred to the Duke of Bavaria. Died in 1632.

See ERSCH und GRUBER, "Allgemeine Encyklopaedie ;" LIPOWSKI, " Friedrich V., Curfürst von der Pfalz und König von Böhmen."

Frederick III., surnamed THE SAGE, Elector of Saxony, born about 1463, was a son of Ernest, whom he succeeded in 1486. He magnanimously refused the imperial crown in 1519, and voted for Charles V. He promoted the Reformation, and was a faithful patron of Luther. When Luther was returning from the Diet of Worms, where he had been proscribed, in 1521, he was seized by order of Frederick, and secreted in the castle of Wartburg. Frederick died in 1525, and was succeeded by his brother John.

See PHILIP MELANCHTHON, "Oratio de Friderico duce Saxoniæ," 1551; H. O. MENCKE, "Dissertatio de Friderico III. Sapiente," 1712; P. EKERMAN, "Dissertatio de Friderico Sapiente," Upsal, 1761.

Frederick, Prince of Wales, the eldest son of George II., was born in 1707. He was estranged from his father and became the leader of the Opposition, who opposed Walpole.) "The royal family," says Macaulay, "was rather strengthened than weakened by the disagreement of its two most distinguished members." In 1736 he married Augusta, Princess of Saxe-Gotha. The fall of Walpole, in 1742, caused the dissension between the king and the prince to abate for a time ; but the latter soon resumed his opposition. He died in 1751, leaving a number of children ; one of his sons became King George III.

Frederick, Landgrave of Thuringia, born in 1256, was a son and rightful heir of Albert of Thuringia. His mother was a daughter of the emperor Frederick II. He waged war against his father, (who wished to exclude him from the succession,) and obtained possession of Thuringia and Misnia about 1308. Died in 1324.

Frederick, COLONEL, a Corsican officer, born about 1730, was supposed to be the son of Theodore, who was styled King of Corsica. He entered the service of the Duke of Würtemberg, who sent him to England as his agent. He wrote a "Description of Corsica," (1798.) He committed suicide in London in 1797.

Frederick Augustus I. and **II.**, Kings of Poland. See AUGUSTUS.

Frederick Augustus [Ger. FRIEDRICH AUGUST, freed′riK ŏw′gŏost] **I.**, King of Saxony, born at Dresden in 1750, was the eldest son of the Elector Frederick Christian, whom he succeeded in 1763. He is said to have uniformly consulted the happiness of his subjects. He abolished torture, (1770,) and made other reforms in legislation. In 1791 he refused the crown of Poland. He maintained neutrality in the war between the French and the allied powers until 1806, when he united his army with that of Prussia. In December, 1806, he assumed the title of king, joined the Confederation of the Rhine, and became an ally of Napoleon. He was deprived by the allied powers of a large part of his kingdom about 1815. He died in May, 1827, and was succeeded by his brother Antony.

See HERMANN, "Friedrich Augusts Leben," 1827; POELITZ, "Friedrich Augusts Leben," 2 vols., 1830.

Frederick Augustus II., King of Saxony, born in May, 1797, was a nephew of the preceding, and a son of Prince Maximilian. He married the archduchess Caroline of Austria in 1819. In July, 1830, he was appointed general-in-chief of the army. He began to reign in June, 1836, his father having renounced his right to the throne. He was so interested in botany that he made several botanical excursions to foreign countries after his accession. He died in August, 1854, and was succeeded by his brother John.

Frederick Charles, (or **Friedrich Karl,**) Prince of Prussia, a nephew of the king, Wilhelm I., and a son of Friedrich Karl Alexander, was born in 1828. He commanded the first Prussian army which defeated the Austrians at Sadowa, (Königgratz,) July 3, 1866. Another army, under the crown-prince, arrived some hours after the battle began, and contributed to the victory. The Austrians, commanded by Benedek, lost about one hundred and twenty pieces of cannon and 14,000 unwounded prisoners. About 200,000 men were engaged on each side.

ā, ē, ī, ō, ū, ȳ, *long;* ȧ, ė, ȯ, *same, less prolonged;* ă, ĕ, ĭ, ŏ, ŭ, ў, *short;* ą, ę, į, ǫ, *obscure;* fär, fȧll, fȧt; mēt; nŏt; gŏŏd; mōon;

Frederick Henry OF ORANGE. See ORANGE.

Frederick William, [Ger. FRIEDRICH WILHELM, freed′rik ẅil′hĕlm,] Elector of Brandenburg, surnamed THE GREAT ELECTOR, born in 1620, was the son of the Elector George William, the prince to whose policy the house of Hohenzollern owes its greatness. He succeeded his father in 1640, soon after which he obtained from the King of Poland the sovereignty of the duchy of Prussia. By the treaty of Westphalia (1648) he acquired Magdeburg, Minden, and part of Pomerania. In 1655 he joined Charles Gustavus of Sweden in a successful invasion of Poland. As the ally of Holland and the emperor, he took the field against Louis XIV. in 1672. The Swedes, having invaded his dominions, were totally defeated by him at Fehrbellin in 1675. In 1679 he made peace with Sweden and France, receiving from the latter 300,000 crowns. His first wife was Louisa Henrietta, Princess of Orange, author of a popular hymn, "Jesus mein Zuversicht." He possessed great political abilities, and his reign was very beneficial to Prussia. He died in 1688, and was succeeded by his son, Frederick I.

See SAMUEL VON PUFENDORF, "De Rebus gestis Friderici Wilhelmi," 1695; FRANZ HORN, "Leben Friedrich Wilhelms des Grossen," 1814; VON RAUMER, "Fried. Wilhelm's des grossen Kurfürsten Kinderjahre," 1850; S. HIRSCH, "Erinnerungen an den grossen Kurfürsten Friedrich Wilhelm, und an seine Gemahlin Louise," 1852.

Frederick William (or Friedrich Wilhelm) I., King of Prussia, a son of Frederick I., was born in 1688. He ascended the throne in February, 1713, having married Sophia Dorothea of Hanover. He was very parsimonious, eccentric, and arbitrary. "His eccentricities," says Macaulay, "were such as had never been seen out of a mad-house. . . . His taste for military pomp and order became a mania, like that of a Dutch burgomaster for tulips. . . . Every country was ransacked by his agents for men above the ordinary stature," for his army. Although he formed a large and highly-disciplined army, he was a pacific prince, and was not engaged in any important wars. He founded a medical college and other useful institutions at Berlin, but was hostile to literature, art, and metaphysics. He died in 1740, leaving the throne to his son, Frederick the Great.

See MORGENSTERN, "Ueber Friedrich Wilhelm I.," 1793; FÖRSTER, "Geschichte Friedrich Wilhelms I.," 1835; ERSCH und GRUBER, "Allgemeine Encyklopaedie;" E. MAUVILLON, "Histoire de Frédéric Guillaume I," 1741, (translated into English by W. PHELPS, 1750;) F. CRAMER, "Zur Geschichte Friedrich Wilhelm's I. und Friedrichs II.," 1829; "Foreign Quarterly Review" for October, 1835.

Frederick William II., King of Prussia, born in September, 1744, was a son of Augustus William, who was a brother of Frederick the Great. He was declared crown-prince, or heir to the throne, in 1758, and began to reign in August, 1786. His first wife, Elizabeth Christina Ulrica of Brunswick, having been divorced in 1769, he married the princess Louisa of Hesse-Darmstadt. In August, 1791, occurred a famous interview at Pilnitz between Frederick William and the Emperor of Austria, who agreed to intervene for the defence of Louis XVI. of France against his subjects. He invaded France with a large army in July, 1792, but retreated to the Rhine, without important results, in the autumn of that year. The dilatory movements of the Prussians in this and the ensuing campaign are ascribed to secret negotiations or intrigues. (See DUMOURIEZ, and BRUNSWICK, DUKE OF.) Frederick William united with Russia in the second partition of Poland, (1793,) by which he obtained Dantzic and Thorn, with about 1100 German square miles of territory. He made a separate peace with the French republic at Bâle in April, 1795. Died in November, 1797, leaving his throne to his son, Frederick William III.

See ERSCH und GRUBER, "Allgemeine Encyklopaedie;" MIRABEAU, "Histoire secrète de la Cour de Berlin."

Frederick William III., King of Prussia, the eldest son of the preceding, was born in August, 1770. His mother was Louisa of Hesse-Darmstadt. He married the Princess of Mecklenburg-Strelitz, and succeeded his father on the 16th of November, 1797. For the neutrality which he observed between the French and the coalition he was rewarded at the peace of Lunéville, 1801, with the bishoprics of Hildesheim and Paderborn, besides some other territories. The population of Prussia was then about ten millions.

He refused to join the third coalition against the French in 1805 until the French army had violated the neutral territory of Anspach. In November, 1805, he formed a secret alliance with Russia and the other powers; but a few days after the battle of Austerlitz he concluded with Napoleon a treaty of peace, by which Hanover was annexed to Prussia in exchange for Anspach, Cleves, and Neufchâtel. This transaction provoked England to declare war against Prussia. His alliance with France was broken by the aggressions of Napoleon, or by the offer of the latter to restore Hanover to England. He demanded as his ultimatum that the French troops should evacuate Germany; but before this demand reached Paris Napoleon had advanced far on his way to the seat of war. The Prussians were routed at Jena and Auerstadt on the 14th of October, 1806, a few days after which Napoleon entered Berlin. The war was ended in July, 1807, by the treaty of Tilsit, which deprived Frederick William of about half of his kingdom,—viz., the Polish provinces, and all that part which lies west of the Elbe.

He applied himself with success to repair the desolations caused by the war, made reforms in the government, and abolished serfdom. In 1812 he was compelled to furnish a large force to aid the French in the invasion of Russia ; but in March, 1813, he summoned his subjects to the war of liberation, for which they evinced the utmost enthusiasm. He gave proof of personal courage in several battles in 1813, and entered Paris in triumph in March, 1814. At the Congress of Vienna, 1814-15, he recovered nearly all the provinces he had lost, and acquired half of Saxony. He failed to give his people a free constitution, as he had promised. Frederick William was a ruler of moderate capacity. He died in June, 1840, and was succeeded by his son, Frederick William IV.

See LEUTSCH, "Geschichte des Preussischen Staats unter Wilhelm III.;" ERSCH und GRUBER, "Allgemeine Encyklopaedie;" THIERS, "History of the French Revolution ;" HENSE, "Friedrich Wilhelm III.," 1840; F. R. EYLERT, "Charakterzüge und historische Fragmente aus dem Leben Friedrich Wilhelm's III.," 3 vols., 1842-44, (translated into English by J. BIRCH, London, 1844.)

Frederick William IV., King of Prussia, was born on the 15th of October, 1795. He married in 1823 Elizabeth Louisa, a daughter of Maximilian, King of Bavaria. In consequence of the marriage of his sister to Nicholas of Russia, he became an intimate friend of the latter. He began his reign, June 7, 1840, with measures of indulgence and moderation, and excited hopes of reforms which were never realized. He refused to restrict his absolute power by a constitution, saying, "I would not have a piece of parchment interposed between me and my people." Excited by the triumph of the French revolutionists, the citizens of Berlin revolted in March, 1848. After several days of severe fighting, the king withdrew his troops from the city, changed his ministry, and made concessions to the Liberal party. He granted in December, 1848, a constitution which has since been modified or nullified, and professed a great zeal for German unity, until the National Assembly at Frankfort elected the Archduke John of Austria as lieutenant-general. He was censured for his irresolution and neutrality in the Crimean war. He was rendered incompetent to reign by a serious malady in 1858, after which his brother acted as regent. He died, without issue, in January, 1861, and was succeeded by his brother, styled William (Wilhelm) I.

Frederick William I., the last Elector of Hesse, born in 1802, was the son of William II., whom he succeeded in 1847. He became very unpopular. In 1866 he took side with Austria in the war against the King of Prussia, who deposed him and annexed Hesse to his own kingdom.

Frederick William, Prince Royal or Crown-Prince of Prussia, born on the 18th of October, 1831, is the eldest son of the regent Frederick William Lewis, afterwards William (Wilhelm) I. He commanded the second army which in June, 1866, entered Bohemia from Silesia, and, after several successful actions at Nachod, Trautenau, etc., effected a junction with the other Prussian army at Sadowa, July 3. He married Victoria Adelaide, a daughter of the Queen of England, in 1858.

Frederick William, Duke of Brunswick. See BRUNSWICK.

Frederick William Charles, King of Würtemberg, born at Treptow in 1754, received from nature superior abilities. In 1797 he married Charlotte Augusta Matilda, a princess of England, and succeeded his father, Frederick Eugene, as Duke of Würtemberg. He obtained the dignity of Elector in 1803. Having formed an alliance with Napoleon, (1805,) he gained a large accession of territory and the title of king. He joined the Confederation of the Rhine in 1806. His army fought for Napoleon in 1809, 1812, and 1813, but joined the allies in November, 1813. Died in October, 1816.

See Thiers, "Histoire du Consulat et de l'Empire;" Ersch und Gruber, "Allgemeine Encyklopaedie."

Frederick William Charles, Prince of the Low Countries, second son of William I., was born in 1797. He married a daughter of the King of Prussia in 1825, took a prominent part in the war of the Belgian revolution in 1830, and commanded in battle at Brussels, from which he was compelled to retreat in September of that year.

Fredro, frā'dro, (Maximilian,) Palatine of Podolia, a popular Polish author, noted for civil and military services. He published several able works on political and military affairs, which acquired a high reputation. One of these is entitled "Proverbs and Advice, Moral, Political, and Military." He died in 1676.

Free'ling, (Sir Francis,) born at Bristol, England, in 1764, entered the General Post-Office in 1787. For a long period he filled the office of secretary of that department with eminent ability and fidelity. His services were rewarded with the rank of baronet in 1828. Died in 1836.

Free'man, (Edward A.,) an English historian, born at Harborne, Staffordshire, in 1823. He studied at Trinity College, Oxford, of which he was elected a Fellow in 1845. He published, besides other works, "The History and Conquests of the Saracens," (1856,) "The History of Federal Government," (1st vol., 1863,) and a valuable "History of the Norman Conquest of England," of which the first volume appeared in 1867 and the third in 1869.

See "Edinburgh Review" for July, 1869.

Free'man, (James,) an American Unitarian minister, born in Charlestown, Massachusetts, in 1759, graduated at Harvard in 1777. He became about 1782 reader at the King's Chapel, Boston, and soon after separated from the Episcopal Church. He was the first minister in the United States that openly professed to be a Unitarian; and he continued to preach in Boston for fifty years. Died in 1835.

Freeman, (Thomas,) an English poet, born in Gloucestershire about 1590, was educated at Oxford. He wrote numerous epigrams.

Freeman, (William Peere Williams,) an English admiral, born in 1742, entered the navy about 1757, and gained distinction in the American war, 1776–82. He was made an admiral about 1830. Died in 1832.

Fregoso, frà-go'so, or **Fregose,** frà-go'sà, (in the plural, **Fregosi,** frà-go'see,) a Genoese family, which in the fourteenth century gained distinction among the popular party and by their rivalry with the Adorni occasioned frequent civil wars. Fregoso, (Domenico,) became Doge of Genoa in 1370. He conquered the isle of Cyprus, and was deposed in 1378. Pietro was a brother of the preceding. He commanded the armament which conquered Cyprus in 1373, and in 1393 was elected doge. Thomas was elected doge in 1415. Being attacked by Alfonso of Aragon and the Duke of Milan, he made a brave resistance, but was forced to retire from Genoa in 1421. In 1436 he was again elected, and held the office until 1443. Janus, a nephew of Thomas, was elected doge in 1447, and died the next year. Pietro, nephew of Thomas, was elected in 1450, and for eight years maintained his power against Alfonso of Aragon and the Adorni. In 1458 he ceded the seigniory of Genoa to Charles VII. of France. He was killed in an attempt to expel the French from Genoa in 1459. Paul, brother of Pietro, and Archbishop of Genoa, was an ambitious and unscrupulous priest. In 1461 he drove Prosper Adorno out of the city, and placed his own cousin, Spinetta Fregoso, in the office of doge. He caused himself to be elected in 1462, but was expelled from office

in 1464 by Sforza, Duke of Milan. He was again in power from 1483 to 1488. Died in 1498. Battista, a son of Pietro, was born at Genoa about 1440, elected doge in 1479, and deposed by a conspiracy in 1483. He wrote a "Life of Martin V.," and a treatise on love, "Anteros, sive De Amore." Octavian was elected doge in 1513, after having expelled the French. He was compelled in 1515 to cede the sovereignty of Genoa to Francis I. of France, in whose name he governed the same until 1522. In 1528 the success of Andrea Doria terminated the rivalry between the Adorno and Fregoso families. Frederico, a brother of Octavian, was born in Genoa about 1480. He was versed in Hebrew and other languages, and wrote, besides other works, a "Paraphrase on the Paternoster," in *terza rima*, and a "Treatise on Prayer," (1542.) He became a cardinal in 1539. Died in 1541.

See E. Vincens, "Histoire de Gênes;" Sismondi, "Histoire des Républiques Italiennes."

Fregoso, (Antonio Fileremo,) an Italian poet, born in Genoa, of the same family as the preceding, lived at the court of Milan about 1500, and enjoyed a high reputation as a poet. His principal poems are "The Laughter of Democritus and the Weeping of Heraclitus," (1506, often reprinted,) "Contest of Plutus and Irus," ("Contenzione di Pluto ed Iro,") and "La Cerva bianca," ("The White Deer," 1510.) Died about 1515.

See Ginguené, "Histoire Littéraire d'Italie;" Tiraboschi, "Storia della Letteratura Italiana."

Freher, frā'er, [Lat. Frehe'rus,] (Marquard,) a German historian, and a native of Augsburg, published "Ancient Bohemian Historians," "History of the Ancient Franks," and other works, which enjoy a high reputation. Died in 1614.

See Melchior Adam, "Vitæ Jurisconsultorum;" Nicéron, "Mémoires."

Freher, (Paul,) a German biographer, born at Nuremberg in 1611. He practised medicine in that city, and compiled a mediocre work, called "Theatre of Men eminent for Learning," ("Theatrum Virorum Eruditione clarorum," 1688,) containing notices of about 2850 eminent authors and other persons. Died in 1682.

Freherus. See Freher.

Freig, frĪG, or **Freige,** frĪ'geh, [Lat. Frei'gius,] (Johann Thomas,) a learned German writer, born at Friburg, in Brisgau, in 1543. He became rector of the college of Altorf in 1575. He wrote, besides other works in Latin, a "Life of Peter Ramus," (about 1580,) and "Rhetorica, Poetica, Logica," (1582,) and published Cicero's Orations with notes, (3 vols., 1581,) often reprinted. Died in 1583.

Freigius. See Freig.

Freiligrath, frĪ'lig-rȧt', (Ferdinand,) a celebrated German lyric and patriotic poet, born at Detmold in 1810. In 1833 he published some poems in the "Almanac of the Muses," which were so successful that he renounced his previous employment in a banking-house at Amsterdam, and devoted himself to literature. After the revolution of 1848 he brought out his spirited poem entitled "The Dead to the Living," for which he was tried by the government, but was acquitted. Owing to renewed political accusations, he left Germany in 1849, and settled in London. Among his best productions are his "Political and Social Poems," and "Confession of Faith," ("Glaubensbekenntniss,") which enjoy the greatest popularity among the Liberal party in Germany. Freiligrath's poetry, apart from the fervent patriotism it displays, possesses merits of a high order; and he has made several excellent translations from the English and French.

See Longfellow's "Poets and Poetry of Europe;" "Foreign Quarterly Review" for January, 1845.

Freind, frênd, or **Friend,** (John,) F.R.S., an English physician, born in Northamptonshire in 1675, was an excellent classical scholar, and eminent in his profession. He served as army physician under the Earl of Peterborough, in Spain, in 1705–07. He was chosen Fellow of the Royal Society in 1712, and member of Parliament in 1722. In 1727 he was appointed first physician to the queen of George II. He wrote many able medical works, of which the most important is his "History of

Physic from the Time of Galen to the Beginning of the Sixteenth Century," (2 vols., 1726–27.) Died in 1728.

See " Biographia Britannica."

Freind, (ROBERT,) D.D., an English divine, a brother of the preceding, was born in 1667. He resided in Westminster, wrote verses in Latin and English, edited "Cicero de Oratore," (1724,) and was an opponent of Bentley in the controversy respecting the Epistles of Phalaris. He was head-master of Westminster School. Died in 1751.

Freinsheim, frīns'hīm', [Lat. FREINSHE'MIUS,] (JOHANN,) a German scholar, born at Ulm in 1608. In 1642 he was appointed professor of eloquence and political economy at Upsal, and in 1647 was created by Queen Christina her librarian and historiographer. He was honorary professor at Heidelberg when he died in 1660. He published several editions of the classics, and wrote a valuable supplement to Livy and to Quintus Curtius, with a view of restoring the lost books of those authors.

See A. FREINSHEIM, "Laudatio posthuma J. Freinshemii," 1661.

Freinshemius. See FREINSHEIM.

Freire, frā'e-rà, (FRANCISCO JOZÉ,) a Portuguese philologist and historian, born at Lisbon in 1713. As a member of the Academy of Arcades, he was called "Candido Lusitano." He wrote "Maxims on the Art of Oratory," and a "Life of Prince Henry of Portugal," (1758.) Died in 1773. "He contributed much," says Ferdinand Denis, "to the restoration of literature by the purity of his style." ("Nouvelle Biographie Générale.")

Freire de Andrada, frā'e-rà dà ân-drä'dà, (BERNARDIM,) a Portuguese general, born in Lisbon in 1764. He had risen to the rank of lieutenant-general when the war against Bonaparte began. In 1808 he put himself at the head of the national army which co-operated with Wellington. He was accused of treason by some factious persons, and was killed by his own soldiers at Braga in 1809.

Freire de Andrada, (HYACINTH.) See ANDRADA, (JACINTO.)

Freire de Andrade, (or **Andrada,**) frā'e-rà dà ân-drä'dà, (or ân-drä'dà,) (GOMEZ,) a Portuguese general, and an able administrator, born about 1685. He was governor of Rio Janeiro for many years, beginning in 1733. He was the hero of the poem of Basileo da Gama entitled "O Uruguay." In 1756 he defeated the Spaniards in the war of the Seven Missions. Died in 1763.

See SOUTHEY'S " History of Brazil."

Freire de Andrade, (GOMEZ,) a Portuguese general, was born in Vienna in 1752. He obtained a command in the French army under Junot in 1808, served in Russia in 1812, and was governor of Dresden in 1813. Having returned to Lisbon, he was executed, on a charge of conspiracy against Marshal Beresford, in 1817. His innocence was recognized several years later.

See "Nouvelle Biographie Générale;" "Histoire de Jean VI, Roi de Portugal," etc., Paris, 1827.

Freire de Carvalho, frā'e-rà dà kaR-vâl'yo, (FRANCISCO,) a Portuguese critic, who became professor of eloquence in Lisbon about 1846. He published a good edition of the "Lusiad," (1843,) and an "Essay on the Literary History of Portugal," (1845.)

Freitag. See FREYTAG.

Frelinghuysen, free'ling-hī'zẹn, (FREDERICK,) an American statesman, born in New Jersey in 1753. He graduated at Princeton in 1770, and served with distinction as captain at the battles of Trenton and Monmouth. He was a member of the Continental Congress of 1775, and from 1793 to 1796 was a United States Senator. Died in 1804.

Frelinghuysen, (THEODORE,) an American statesman, a son of the preceding, was born in Somerset county, New Jersey, in 1787. He graduated at Princeton College in 1804, studied law, and was admitted to the bar in 1808. In 1829 he was elected to the Senate of the United States, in which he acted with the Whig party and took a prominent part in the debates until 1835. He became chancellor of the University of New York in 1838. In 1844 he was nominated as candidate for the Vice-Presidency of the United States by the Whig party, which also nominated Henry Clay for the Presidency; but they were not elected. He was chosen

president of Rutgers College, New Brunswick, in 1850. Died in 1862.

See T. W. CHAMBERS, " Memoir of the Life of T. Frelinghuysen," 1863, with portrait.

Frellon, frà'lôn', (JEAN and FRANÇOIS,) printers of Lyons, France, who acquired distinction by the perfection of their editions of the New Testament and other books, printed between 1530 and 1570.

Fre'mantle, (Sir THOMAS FRANCIS,) an English politician, born in 1798. He represented Buckingham in Parliament from 1827 to 1846, and acted with the Conservatives. He was secretary of war in 1844-45, and was appointed chairman of the board of customs in 1846.

Frémin, frà'mǎn', (RENÉ,) a French sculptor, born in Paris in 1673. In 1722 Philip V. of Spain employed him to embellish with statuary his gardens and palace of the Granja. Died in 1745.

Fréminet, frà'me'nà', (MARTIN,) an eminent French painter, born in Paris in 1567, studied many years in Italy with such success that Henry IV. of France chose him in 1603 as his first painter, and employed him in decorating the chapel of Fontainebleau, which contains his master-pieces. He imitated the style of Michael Angelo, and excelled in composition and perspective. Died in 1619.

See A. FÉLIBIEN, "Entretiens sur les Vies des plus célèbres Peintres."

Fre'mŏnt', (JOHN CHARLES,) the "Pathfinder" of the Rocky Mountains, an American explorer and general, born at Savannah, Georgia, January 21, 1813, was the son of a Frenchman and a Virginian mother. He graduated at Charleston College, South Carolina, and became a professor of mathematics in the navy about 1835; but he soon resigned that position. In 1838 and 1839 he assisted Nicollet in the exploration of the upper portion of the Valley of the Mississippi. He was appointed a second lieutenant of the topographical engineers in 1838, and was ordered in 1841 to explore and survey the river Des Moines. In October of that year he married Jessie, a daughter of Senator Benton, of Missouri. Having formed a project to explore the Rocky Mountains and to open an overland route to the Pacific Ocean, he began the arduous enterprise, under the authority of the government, in May, 1842. He examined the South Pass of the Rocky Mountains, and ascended, in August, the highest peak of the Wind River Mountains, (13,570 feet above the sea,) which is now called Fremont's Peak. In the autumn of 1842 he returned to Washington, and published a report of his discoveries, which was commended by Humboldt in his "Aspects of Nature."

In the summer of 1843 he conducted another expedition up the valley of the Platte and through the South Pass, explored Great Salt Lake, and made important discoveries in geography. He arrived in November at Fort Vancouver, near the mouth of the Columbia River, and in the ensuing winter attempted to return by a more southern route; but his progress was arrested by deep snows, and his party suffered severely from hunger and cold. Having changed his course, he reached the Sacramento River in March, 1844, and, returning through the Great Basin and the South Pass, arrived at Kansas in July of that year. The daring and fortitude exhibited in this expedition among hostile savages and inhospitable deserts have hardly been surpassed in the records of human adventure. Soon after his return he was promoted to the rank of captain, and prepared a report of his second expedition. In the spring of 1845 he conducted a third expedition, to explore the Sierra Nevada, California, &c. He was attacked by Mexicans near Monterey in March, 1846, defended himself with success, was raised to the rank of lieutenant-colonel in May, and was appointed Governor of California by Commodore Stockton, whose authority was disputed by General Kearney. Fremont, however, continued to recognize Commodore Stockton as his superior, and was arrested by General Kearney, who ordered him to report to the adjutant-general at Washington. He was tried by a court-martial, and found guilty of mutiny and disobedience, for which he was pardoned by the President; but he declined the pardon, and resigned his commission.

In 1848 Fremont attempted, at his own expense, another expedition across the continent, through the northern part of Mexico; but, the guide having lost his way, the party, after undergoing incredible sufferings, in which about one-third of their number perished, were compelled to return to Santa Fe, whence they had started.

In 1849 he settled in California, where he had purchased a large auriferous tract called the Mariposa estate. He exerted his influence to make California a free State, and was one of the Senators chosen to represent that State in the Federal Senate in 1850. His term in the Senate expired in March, 1851. For his services as an explorer he received, in 1850, a gold medal from the King of Prussia, and another from the Royal Geographical Society of London. In 1853 he conducted, at his own expense, an exploring party to the Pacific, and succeeded in finding a new route about latitude 38° north. He was nominated as candidate for the Presidency by the Republican National Convention in June, 1856, as the competitor of the Democratic candidate, James Buchanan. Colonel Fremont received one hundred and fourteen electoral votes, cast by eleven States, against one hundred and seventy-four votes given to his opponent.

In May, 1861, he was appointed a major-general of the regular army, and commander of the department of Missouri, or Western district. In August he issued an order for the emancipation of the slaves of those who should take arms against the United States; but this act was disapproved and annulled by the President, who considered it premature. Moving his army from the Missouri River, he pursued the enemy, who retired southwestward. He had just overtaken the army of insurgents at Springfield, when he was removed from the command, November 2, 1861. In March, 1862, he was appointed to the command of the Mountain department, including parts of Virginia, Kentucky, and Tennessee. About the 1st of June he began to pursue General Jackson, (Stonewall,) who, after chasing General Banks down the Shenandoah Valley to the Potomac, was retiring towards Harrisonburg. General Fremont attacked the enemy on the 8th of June, 1862, at Cross Keys, where he fought an indecisive battle. He was then recalled from the pursuit of General Jackson, and he resigned his command about the end of June, because he was not willing to serve under General Pope, his junior or inferior in rank.

See JOHN BIGELOW, "Life of John C. Frémont," 1856; C. W. UPHAM, "Life and Explorations of J. C. Frémont," 1856; "Frémont's Explorations," 2 vols., 1859.

Frémont d'Ablancourt, frȧ'môN' dä'blôN'kooR', (NICOLAS,) a French Protestant, born in Paris about 1625, was a nephew of Perrot d'Ablancourt. By the influence of Turenne he was appointed ambassador to Portugal in 1663. When the edict of Nantes was revoked, in 1685, he was obliged to leave France, and retired to Holland, where the Prince of Orange appointed him historiographer. He wrote, besides a few other works, "Memoirs in relation to the History of Portugal," (from 1659 to 1668, published in 1701.) Died in 1693.

See HAAG, "La France protestante."

Frémy, frȧ'me', (ARNOULD,) a French littérateur, born in 1809, has written some works of fiction.

Frémy, (EDMOND,) a French chemist, born in Paris in 1814. He was a favourite pupil of M. Pelouze, whom he aided as assistant professor in the Polytechnic School. He afterwards succeeded M. Pelouze as professor, and succeeded Gay-Lussac in the Museum of Natural History. In conjunction with Pelouze, he produced successful works, entitled "General Treatise on Chemistry," (6 vols., 1844-57,) and an "Abridgment (Abrégé) of Chemistry."

See "Nouvelle Biographie Générale."

French, (JOHN,) an English physician, born in 1616, attended professionally the parliamentary army under Fairfax. He wrote the "Art of Distillation," and the "Yorkshire Spaw." Died in 1657.

French, (NICHOLAS,) an Irish Roman Catholic bishop, born at Wexford in 1604. He was appointed Bishop of Ferns in 1643, soon after which date he went as an exile to the continent. He published, besides other works, "The Unkind Deserter of Loyal Men," (1676,) directed against Ormond. Died in 1678.

French, (SAMUEL G.,) an American officer in the Confederate army, born in New Jersey, was made a brigadier-general in 1861.

French, (WILLIAM HENRY,) an American officer, born in Maryland about 1818, served in the Mexican war, and in 1861 became a brigadier-general of volunteers in the Union army.

Frend, (WILLIAM,) an English writer on astronomy, political economy, etc., born at Canterbury in 1757. He was rector of Madingley, but, having adopted Socinian opinions, he resigned that living in 1787. Among his works is "Evening Amusements on the Beauties of the Heavens," issued annually, (1804-22.) Died in 1841.

Freneau, fre'nō', (PHILIP,) an American poet and journalist, of French descent, born at New York in 1752. He wrote, during the Revolution, many satirical and burlesque poems against the Tories. Some of these were very popular. He performed many voyages as a captain of a merchant-vessel between 1784 and 1789, and again after 1798. About 1790 he became translating clerk to Jefferson, (then secretary of state,) and editor of the "National Gazette," published at Philadelphia and notorious for virulent articles against the administration of Washington. Died near Freehold, New Jersey, in December, 1832.

See GRISWOLD, "Poets and Poetry of America;" DUYCKINCK, "Cyclopædia of American Literature," vol. i.

Frénicle, frȧ'nĕk'l', (NICOLAS,) a minor French poet, born in Paris in 1600, wrote "Niobe, a Tragedy," and other poems. Died in 1661.

Frénicle de Bessy, frȧ'nĕk'l' deh bȧ'se', (BERNARD,) a skilful French mathematician, brother of the preceding. He excelled in solving difficult questions without the use of algebra, so that Fermat, Descartes, and others confessed his superiority. His modus operandi was kept secret until his death, when it was ascertained by his papers to be the "method of exclusion." He was admitted to the Academy of Sciences in 1666. He wrote a "Treatise on Right-Angled Triangles in Numbers," and other works. Died in 1675.

See BAILLET, "Vie de Descartes;" CONDORCET, "Éloge de Frénicle de Bessy."

Frenzel or **Frentzel,** frĕnt'sĕl, (JOHANN,) a German poet, born at Annaberg in 1609. He was professor of poetry at Leipsic. Died in 1674.

Frère, frāir, (GEORGES,) a French general of division, born in Languedoc in 1764. He distinguished himself in the Austrian campaign of 1809. Died in 1826.

Frere, freer, (Right Hon. JOHN HOOKHAM,) of Norfolk, England, was born in 1769, and entered Parliament in 1796. He was ambassador to Spain in 1808, and performed other diplomatic services. He was one of the founders of the "London Quarterly Review," and acquired distinction as a poet by a humorous work, entitled "Prospectus and Specimen of an Intended National Work by William and Robert Whistlecraft, etc., relating to King Arthur and his Round Table." His translation of a Saxon poem on the victory of Athelstan at Brunnenburgh was much admired. Died at Malta in 1846.

See LOCKHART, "Life of Scott;" "London Quarterly Review" for September, 1843; "Gentleman's Magazine" for March and April, 1846.

Frère, (PIERRE ÉDOUARD,) a French painter, a pupil of Paul Delaroche, was born in Paris in 1819. His subjects are familiar domestic scenes.

Freres, frȧ-rȧ'? (THEODORE,) a Dutch painter, born at Enckhuysen in 1643, studied at Rome. He worked for some time at Amsterdam. Died at sea in 1693.

See DESCAMPS, "Vies des Peintres Flamands," etc.

Fréret, frȧ'rȧ', (NICOLAS,) an eminent French historical critic and savant, born in Paris, February 15, 1688, was early distinguished for his devotion to learning and his extraordinary attainments in ancient history, philosophy, and chronology. The Academy of Inscriptions was opened to him in 1714, about which time he wrote a "Discourse on the Origin of the French," which was much admired. The novel or candid opinions uttered in this work procured him a short confinement in the Bastille. He was versed in many ancient and modern languages. He appears to have been free from selfish ambition, and actuated by a disinterested zeal for

ā, ē, ī, ō, ū, ȳ, long; ȧ, ė, ȯ, same, less prolonged; ă, ĕ, ĭ, ŏ, ŭ, y̆, short; ą, ę, į, ǫ, obscure; fär, fȧll, fȧt; mĕt; nŏt; gōōd; mōōn;

the honour of the Academy, for which he wrote a multitude of profound dissertations on ancient history and chronology, in one of which he explodes the fabulous antiquity of the Chinese. Among his principal works are a "Treatise on the Origin of the Greeks," "Observations on the Cyropædia of Xenophon," and "Historical Researches respecting the Ancient Peoples of Asia." He was perpetual secretary of the Academy of Inscriptions and Belles-Lettres. Died in Paris in March, 1749. He is considered the greatest of French historical critics.

See BOUGAINVILLE, "Éloge de Fréret;" CHAMPOLLION-FIGEAC, "Vie de Fréret," prefixed to a new edition of his works. The first volume of this edition was published in 1825. See, also, "Nouvelle Biographie Générale."

Frerichs, frā′riks, (FRIEDRICH THEODOR,) a German physician, born at Aurich, in Hanover, in 1819. He became professor of pathology and therapeutics at Breslau about 1852. He wrote, besides other able works, a "Treatise on Diseases of the Liver," (1859.)

Fréron, frȧ′rôN′, (ÉLIE CATHERINE,) a distinguished French critic and *littérateur*, born at Quimper in 1719, assisted Desfontaines for several years in his critical reviews. From 1749 to 1754 he issued a spirited literary periodical, styled "Letters on Certain Contemporary Writings." From 1754 until his death he edited the "Literary Year," and acquired much notoriety by his attacks on Voltaire and the Encyclopedists, who retorted with great asperity. His ode on the battle of Fontenoy (1745) was admired. He wrote many other works. Died in 1776.

See GRIMM, "Correspondance littéraire;" C. NISARD, "Les Ennemis de Voltaire," 1853. ′

Fréron, (LOUIS STANISLAS,) son of the preceding, was born in Paris in 1765. He was a violent Jacobin, edited a paper called the "Orator of the People," voted for the death of the king in the Convention, and took an official and prominent part in the massacres at Marseilles and Toulon. He promoted the fall of Robespierre in 1794, and was appointed sub-prefect in Saint Domingo, where he died, soon after his arrival, in 1802.

See LAMARTINE's "History of the Girondists."

Frescobaldi, frĕs-ko-bȧl′dee, (GIROLAMO,) a renowned Italian organist and composer, born at Ferrara, probably about 1588. He became organist of St. Peter's in Rome. He displayed a rich imagination as a composer of canzoni, toccatas, etc. He is regarded as the father of that style of organ-music which the English call "voluntaries." Died about 1654.

See HAWKINS, "History of Music;" FÉTIS, "Biographie Universelle des Musiciens."

Fresenius, frȧ-zā′ne-ùs, (JOHANN FRIEDRICH,) a German theologian, born in 1717; died in 1783.

See F. A. FRESENIUS, "Lebenslauf, etc. J. F. Fresenii," 1789.

Fresia, frā′se-ȧ, or frȧ′ze′ȧ′, (MAURICE IGNACE,) BARON, a general in the French army, was born at Saluzzo, in Piedmont, in 1746. He was appointed Governor of Venice, and commandant of the Illyrian provinces, about 1810. Died in Paris in 1827.

Fresnaye, de la, dĕh lä frȧ′nȧ′, (JEAN **Vauquelin** —vōk′lȧN′,) a mediocre French poet, father of Desyveteaux, born in Normandy in 1536; died in 1606.

Fresne. See DUFRESNE and DU CANGE.

Fresne, frĕn, (FRANÇOIS **Ébaudy**—ȧ′bō′de′,) a French economist, born at Langres in 1743, published a "Treatise on Agriculture," (3 vols., 1788,) and proposed the saving-fund for servants, and other means of economy which have since been adopted. Died in 1815.

Fresnel, frȧ′nĕl′, (AUGUSTIN JEAN,) a celebrated French geometer and optician, born at Broglie (Eure) on the 10th of May, 1788, was the son of an architect. He studied in the École Polytechnique, and passed thence into the École des Ponts et Chaussées, which he quitted with the title of engineer. He began to experiment on the theory of light about 1815, and received a prize from the Academy of Sciences for his treatise "On the Diffraction of Light" in 1819. In 1823 he was elected a member of the Academy of Sciences. He wrote several memoirs on polarization and double refraction, which were inserted in the "Annales de Physique et Chimie," (1816-25.) He performed for physical optics what Newton did for astronomy. His experiments tend to prove

the truth of the theory that light consists in the vibrations of an elastic medium. His theory of double refraction and polarization is called one of the finest efforts of genius. He made the first successful application of lenses to the lamps of light-houses, and invented the illuminating apparatus which is used throughout the civilized world. He was chosen in 1825 a Fellow of the Royal Society of London, which in 1827 awarded to him the Rumford medal. When on his death-bed, this medal was presented to him by his friend Arago, to whom he said, "I thank you for performing this mission, which must have been a painful duty; for the brightest badge of honour appears dim and insignificant to him who must lay it down on the grave of a friend." Died in 1827.

See ARAGO's "Éloge de Fresnel," in the "Œuvres complètes" (of Arago,) tome i.; "Nouvelle Biographie Générale;" "Biographie Universelle," (Supplément.)

Fresnel, (FULGENCE,) a French Orientalist, born at Mathieu (Calvados) in 1795; died at Bagdâd in 1855.

Fresnoy. See DUFRESNOY, (CHARLES ALPHONSE.)

Fresnoy, (LENGLET DU.) See LENGLET.

Fresny. See DUFRESNY.

Fresse-Montval, frĕs′môN′vȧl′, (HENRI FRANÇOIS ALPHONSE,) a French *littérateur*, born at Perpignan in 1795, wrote a "Manual of Latin Composition," and made a translation of Pindar's works into French verse, which gained a prize of the French Academy in 1851.

Fressinet, frȧ′se′nȧ′, (PHILIBERT,) a French general, born in Burgundy in 1769. In 1813, for his conduct at the battle of Lutzen, he obtained the rank of general of division. Died in 1821.

Fréteau de Saint-Just, frȧ′tō′ dĕh sȧN′zhüst′, (EMMANUEL MARIE MICHEL PHILIPPE,) a French lawyer, born in 1745. He was elected in 1789 to the States-General, and was a moderate partisan of the Revolution. He was one of the presidents of the Constituent Assembly, and a judge of one of the courts in Paris. He was executed by the terrorists in 1794.

Freudenberger, froi′den-bĕR′ger, (SIGISMOND,) a Swiss painter and engraver, born in 1745; died in 1801.

Freudweiler, froid′wī′ler, (DANIEL,) a Swiss painter, born in 1793; died in 1827.

Freund, froint, (WILHELM,) a German lexicographer, of Jewish extraction, born at Kempen, in the province of Posen, in 1806. His "Dictionary of the Latin Language" (4 vols., 1834) enjoys a high reputation. He also published a Latin-German, Latin-Greek Dictionary for Schools, (1848.)

Freundsberg. See FRONDSBERG.

Freundweiler, froint′wī′ler, or **Freudweiler,** froit′-wī′ler, (HENRI,) a skilful Swiss painter of history, genre, and portraits, was born at Zurich in 1755; died in 1795.

Freux, de, dĕh fruh, [Lat. FRU′SIUS,] (ANDRÉ,) a French Jesuit and writer, born at Chartres about 1500, became secretary to Loyola at Rome. Died in 1556.

Frey, frī, or **Freyr,** frīr, [sometimes written in Latin FRIC′CO; etymology the same as that of FREYIA, which see,*] the son of Njörd, and the brother of Freyia. He presides over rain and sunshine and the fruits of the earth. His attributes correspond to those both of Frigga and Freyia. As the god of fertility, he resembles the former;† as the god of pleasure and love, he is the counterpart of the latter. We are told that he was (like Freyia) beloved by all, both gods and men. He had two remarkable gifts presented to him by Loki,—the ship Skidbladnir, which would always have a fair wind whenever the sails were set, and was so capacious that it could contain all the gods, with their weapons and armour, and yet could be folded up like a cloth and carried in one's pocket; and the boar named Gullinbursti, ("golden bristles,") which he could drive on the air and sea and which could travel

* Supposing the etymology given under FREYIA to be the true one, *Frey* is simply the masculine form of *Freyia*,—the masculine of *priyâ* being *priyǎ*, or (as the final *short a* is often dropped) simply *priy'*,—and signifies, like Freyia, "beloved," "dear." The Latin name *Fricco* goes to establish Frey's relationship with Frigga, and to confirm the view that Freyia and Frigga were originally one name, since nothing is more common than for *g* and *y* to interchange, as shown in such examples as "Day," Anglo-Saxon *Dag*, German *Tag ;* "Way," Anglo-Saxon and German *Weg*, etc.

† As Frigga was the goddess of marriage, so Frey was the god of marriage; for on such occasions, as Adam of Bremen tells us, the old Danes used to sacrifice to Frey.

far more swiftly than any horse. The wife of Frey was Gerda, (gĕr′dă,) or Gerd, (gĕrd,) the daughter of a giant named Gymir. It is related that one day Frey ascended Odin's throne Hlidskialf, whence he could view all the regions of the world. Towards the north he saw a magnificent palace, out of which came a woman whose beauty was so resplendent that it illumined the whole world. As a just punishment for his presumption in ascending the seat of the father of the gods, Frey was so deeply smitten with love that he could neither drink, speak, nor sleep. Thereupon Njörd sent Skirmir, Frey's attendant, to inquire the cause of his distress. When Skirmir learned it, he promised that if his master would give him his sword he would obtain for him the beautiful maiden, whose name was Gerda. In this undertaking he encountered great difficulties, but was at last successful. But Frey had parted with his good sword, which will prove a very serious loss at Ragnaröck, when the great battle will be fought between the Æsir and their enemies.

See THORPE'S "Northern Mythology," vol. i.; KEYSER'S "Religion of the Northmen;" MALLET'S "Northern Antiquities," vol. ii., Fable XIX.; PETERSEN'S "Nordisk Mythologi."

Frey, frī, (JEAN CÉCILE,) a Swiss philologist and physician, born at Kaiserstühl about 1580, taught philosophy in a college of Paris. He wrote, besides other works in Latin, "The Philosophy of the Druids," (1625.) Died in 1631.

See NICÉRON, "Mémoires."

Frey, (JEAN LOUIS,) a Swiss philologist and Orientalist, born at Bâle in 1682. He was appointed professor of history and theology in the Academy of Berne in 1711. He also distinguished himself by great knowledge and critical sagacity in theology, history, and philosophy, and wrote several works. Died in 1759.

See J. C. BECK, "De Vita et Meritis Philologi J. L. Frey," 1760.

Frey, (JOHANN JAKOB,) an excellent Swiss engraver, born at Lucerne in 1681, studied under Carlo Maratta, and worked mostly in Rome. He engraved a large number of the master-pieces of the Italian painters, reproducing with great fidelity the characteristic style of each master, and was perhaps the most excellent engraver of his time. Died in 1752. Among his works are "Bacchus and Ariadne" and "The Chariot of Aurora," after Guido; and "The Holy Family," after Raphael.

See STRUTT, "Dictionary of Engravers."

Freya. See FREYIA.

Freyberg, frī′bĕRG, (MAXIMILIAN PROKOP,) BARON, born at Freising in 1789, was appointed by Louis I. of Bavaria keeper of the archives at Munich. Besides legal treatises, he published several works relating to Bavarian history. Died in 1851.

Freycinet, de, dĕh frȧ′se′nȧ′, (LOUIS CLAUDE Desaulses—dĕh-sōl′,) a French navigator, born at Montélimart in 1779. He sailed with Baudin in a scientific expedition to Australia, and assisted in composing an account of the same. He obtained the rank of captain of a frigate in 1811, and commanded the expedition sent in the Uranie in 1817 to ascertain the figure of the earth and the elements of terrestrial magnetism. The result of this enterprise was a "Voyage around the World," etc., (13 vols., 1824-44,) of which the parts on navigation, hydrography, and magnetism were written by Freycinet. Died in 1842.

His brother HENRI, born in 1777, also distinguished as a navigator, was associated with him in nearly all his expeditions. Died in 1840.

See ROQUETTE, "Notices historiques sur MM. Henri et Louis de Freycinet," 1840; F. GRILLE, "L. de Freycinet, sa Vie de Savant et de Marin," etc., 1853; "Nouvelle Biographie Générale."

Freyia or **Freyja,** frī′yă, written also **Freya,** [probably allied to the Sanscrit *priyā,* signifying "dear," "beloved," and, as a substantive, a "wife:" compare the Swedish *fria* or *frija,* to "make love," to "seek in marriage,"] the goddess of love, the Venus of the Norse mythology. She is also called VAN′ADIS, or the "Vanir goddess." She is said to be the daughter of Njörd, the god of the air. (See VANIR.) She was married to Oder, (or Odur,) who afterwards left her and wandered far away. During his absence she weeps for him, shed-

ding golden tears. Matthew Arnold, in his beautiful poem entitled "Balder Dead," speaks thus of Freya:

"And Freya next came nigh, with golden tears,
The loveliest goddess she in heaven, by all
Most honoured after Frea, Odin's wife:
Her long ago the wandering Oder took
To mate, but left her to roam in distant lands;
Since then she seeks him, and weeps tears of gold:
Names hath she many; Vanadis on earth
They call her; Freya is her name in heaven."

One-half of the heroes who fell in battle belonged, it is said, to Freyia: hence she was sometimes called Valfreyia, (*i.e.* the "Freyia of the fallen,") in the same manner that Odin was styled Valföðr, (or Valfaðir,) or the "father of the slain." This is thus explained by some writers: Many warriors are impelled chiefly by their own fiery courage; these, falling in battle, belong to Odin, the god of courage: others, like the knights of the middle ages, seek to obtain by their prowess the admiration and favour of the other sex; these are the votaries of Freyia, the goddess of love and gallantry, and, when they fall in battle, belong especially to her.

Most etymologists agree that Freyia and Frigga were originally the same name. We may conjecture that among a simple and comparatively virtuous people the same power would preside over love and marriage, but that in a later and more corrupt age those offices which originally belonged to one became divided, as among the Greeks and Romans, between two distinct and independent deities. (See FREY.) There can scarcely be a reasonable question but that *Friday* signifies "Freyia's day;" though some suppose it to be "Frigga's day:" it was called in the Latin of the middle ages *Veneris dies,* ("Venus's day,") whence the French *Vendredi.*

See THORPE'S "Northern Mythology," vol. i.; "Religion of the Northmen," by RUDOLPH KEYSER, translated by BARCLAY PENNOCK; MALLET'S "Northern Antiquities," vol. ii., Fable XVIII.

Freylinghausen, frī′ling-hŏw′zĕn, (JOHANN ANASTAS or ANASTASIUS,) a German theologian and writer, born at Gandersheim in 1670. He became the colleague of the philanthropist A. H. Francke at Halle. Died in 1738.

Freyre. See FREIRE.

Freyre, frā′e-rȧ, (Don MANOEL,) a Spanish general, born at Osuna, in Andalusia, in 1765. He commanded the cavalry at Ocaña, where the Spaniards were defeated by the French, in 1809, and obtained the chief command of a corps in Murcia and Granada in 1810 or 1811. In 1813 he succeeded Castaños as general of the Spanish forces under Wellington. He was selected to command the royal army at the beginning of the revolution of 1820. After the king had, in March, 1820, sworn to restore the constitution of 1812, Freyre was deprived of the command. Died in 1834.

See "Defensa del General Manoel Freyre."

Freytag, frī′tȧG, (FRIEDRICH GOTTHILF,) a German professor and classical scholar, born in 1687; died in 1761.

Freytag, (FRIEDRICH GOTTHILF,) a German bibliographer, son of the preceding, was born at Pforta in 1723. He was a lawyer and burgomaster of Naumburg, and published several works, among which is "Analecta literaria de Libris rarioribus," (1751.) Died in 1776.

See ERSCH und GRUBER, "Allgemeine Encyklopaedie."

Freytag, (GEORG WILHELM FRIEDRICH,) a distinguished German philologist, born at Lüneburg in 1788, devoted himself to the study of the Arabic, Persian, and Turkish languages in Paris. Among his principal works are a "Lexicon Arabico-Latinum," (1830,) and "Arabum Proverbia," ("Proverbs of the Arabs.") He became professor of Oriental literature at Bonn in 1819. Died in November, 1861.

Freytag, (GUSTAV,) a popular German dramatist and novelist, born at Kreuzburg, in Silesia, in 1816. He produced, besides other dramas, "Count Waldemar," (1847,) and the "Journalists," (1854,) a comedy, which is commended. His novel entitled "Soll und Haben" (3 vols., 1855) was very successful.

Freytag, (JOHANN,) a German physician, born at Wesel in 1581. He was for many years first physician to the Prince-Bishop of Osnabrück, and became professor at Groningen in 1631. He wrote, besides other medical works, "Noctes Medicæ," (1616.) Died in 1641.

ā, ē, ī, ō, ū, ȳ, *long;* ȧ, ė, ȯ, same, less prolonged; ă, ĕ, ĭ, ŏ, ŭ, ў, *short;* ạ, ẹ, ị, ọ, *obscure;* fär, fäll, fȧt; mēt; nŏt; gōōd; mōōn;

Frézier, frȧ′ze-ȧ′, (AMÉDÉE FRANÇOIS,) a French military engineer, was born at Chambéry in 1682. He published, in 1706, a "Treatise on Fire-Works," which was much esteemed. Having been sent on a mission to Peru and Chili in 1712, he wrote a "Voyage to the South Sea and the Coasts of Chili and Peru," (1716,) which was often reprinted. He was chief engineer of the fortifications constructed in Brittany after 1740, and wrote several other works. Died in 1773.

See "Nouvelle Biographie Générale."

Frezzi da Foligno, frĕt′see dȧ fo-lèn′yo, (FEDERIGO,) an Italian poet, born in Umbria, became Bishop of Foligno in 1403. He wrote, in imitation of Dante, an allegorical poem called "Il Quadriregio," or poem of four kingdoms, which had great temporary success. It was first printed in 1481. Died in 1416.

Frezzolini, frĕt-so-lee′nee, (ERMINIA **Nencini**—nĕn-chee′nee,) a popular Italian vocalist, distinguished for dramatic power and a soprano voice of great compass, was born at Viterbo in 1820. After she had performed in London and Paris, she visited the United States in 1857.

Friant, fRe′ȯN′, (LOUIS,) a French general, born in Picardy in 1758. He became a brigadier-general in 1794. After he had served several campaigns on the Rhine and in Italy, he accompanied Bonaparte in 1798 to Egypt, where he signalized his courage and was promoted to the rank of a general of division. He succeeded Desaix when the latter departed from Upper Egypt. He was wounded at Austerlitz, (1805,) and contributed to the victories of Jena and Wagram. In 1812 he made the campaign of Russia as commander of the grenadiers of the Imperial guard. After Napoleon's return from Elba, Friant was made a peer, and was severely wounded at Waterloo. Died in 1829.

See THIERS, "Histoire du Consulat et de l'Empire;" "Nouvelle Biographie Générale."

Frias, de, dȧ fRee′ȧs, (DAMAS?) a Spanish poet, supposed to have lived about 1500, left a poem called the "Retreat of Silvia," and a few songs. Spanish critics rank him as one of the most agreeable lyric poets of his time.

Friche. See DUFRISCHE.

Frick, frîk, (ALBRECHT,) a learned German professor, born at Ulm in 1714; died in 1776.

Friedemann, free′deh-mân′, (FRIEDRICH TRAUGOTT,) a German teacher, philologist, and writer of educational works, was born at Stolpen, in Saxony, in 1793; died after 1852.

Friederich, free′deh-rik′, or **Frédéric,** frȧ′dȧ′rĕk′, (ANDRÉ,) a skilful French sculptor, born at Ribeauvillé (Haut-Rhin) in 1798. He studied at Dresden, Paris, and Rome, and settled at Strasbourg about 1826. Among his works are a granite monument to Turenne at Sulzbach, (1828,) and a bas-relief of the baptism of Clovis.

See "Nouvelle Biographie Générale."

Friedland, DUKE OF. See WALLENSTEIN.

Friedland, freet′lȧnt, (VALENTIN,) a learned German teacher, born in 1490, was surnamed TROTZENDORFF, from his birthplace in Upper Lusatia. Having visited Wittenberg in 1518, he acquired the friendship of Luther and Melanchthon. In 1531 he became rector of the academy at Goldberg, which, under his care, obtained the highest popularity and success. Died in 1556.

Friedrich, freed′riK, (KASPAR DAVID,) a German painter, born at Greifswalde in 1774; died in 1840.

Friedrich OF GERMANY. See FREDERICK.

Fries, freess, (BERNHARD,) a German painter, born at Heidelberg in 1820, studied in Rome. He worked at his native place after 1852, and painted landscapes with success. Among his works are "The Rocks of Nemi," and the "Valley of the Neckar."

Fries, freess, (ELIAS,) an eminent Swedish botanist and orator, born in Wexiö in 1794. He became professor of practical economy at Upsal in 1834, and introduced the natural system of botany into Sweden. He represented the University of Upsal in the Diet several years, and gained distinction as an orator. In 1851 he was chosen professor of botany at Upsal. Among his numerous and able works are a "Flora of Holland,"

(1817,) "Systema Mycologicum," (3 vols., 1821–29,) "Systema Orbis Vegetabilis," (a System of Botany according to the natural method, 1825,) and "Flora Scanica," (1835.) He is one of the eighteen members of the Academy of Stockholm.

See BROCKHAUS, "Conversations-Lexikon."

Fries, (ERNST,) a German landscape-painter, born at Heidelberg in 1801, was appointed in 1831 court painter at Carlsruhe, where he died in 1833. His productions are of great merit, and resemble the landscapes of Poussin. He was a brother of Bernhard, noticed above.

See NAGLER, "Neues Allgemeines Künstler-Lexikon."

Fries, frees, [Lat. FRI′SIUS,] (HENRY,) a Swiss professor of eloquence, lived at Zurich. He wrote "On the Seat of the Rational Soul," ("De Sede Animæ rationalis.") Died in 1718.

Fries, (JAKOB FRIEDRICH,) a German philosopher, born at Barby in 1773. He became in 1805 professor of philosophy and elementary mathematics at Heidelberg. He was the author of a "System of Logic," (1811,) "System of Philosophy as an Evident Science," (1804,) and other works, in which he favours the doctrines of Kant. He was professor of physics at Jena from 1816 to 1843. Died in 1843.

See KLOPFLEISCH, "Rede am Grabe des Herrn J. F. Fries," 1843; "Nouvelle Biographie Générale."

Fries, [Lat. FRI′SIUS,] (JOHN,) an eminent Swiss philologist, born at Gryffensee in 1505, was an intimate friend of Conrad Gesner. He was chosen professor of languages at Zurich about 1537, and gave a great impulse to the study of Oriental languages. His most important work is a "Latin-German Dictionary," (1541.) He also produced a Latin translation of Hesiod, (1548,) and several original works. Died in 1565.

His son JOHN JAMES, born at Zurich in 1547, was professor of theology in that city. He published "Chronological Library of the Classic Philosophers," (" Bibliotheca Philosophorum Classicorum Chronologica," 1592,) a work of some value. · Died in 1611.

See ERSCH und GRUBER, "Allgemeine Encyklopaedie," which contains notices of both the father and the son.

Friese, free′zeh, (MARTIN,) a Danish theological writer, born at Ripen in 1688; died in 1750.

Frig′ga or **Frigg,** written also **Friga, Frea,** and **Friia,** (probably of the same etymology as FREYIA and FREY, which see,) the daughter of Fjörgyn, and wife of Odin. She is called "the Mother of the Gods," (Æsir,) and the chief goddess, in the Norse mythology. Like Juno, she was the goddess of marriage. Her habitation is called Fensalir, (or Fensaler; pronounced fĕn-sä′ler.) She is generally regarded as a personification of the earth or of the productive power of the earth, and in this respect nearly corresponding to the Ceres of the Romans and the Demeter (i.e. "Mother Earth") of the Greeks.

See MALLET, "Northern Antiquities," vol. ii. chap. vi.; THORPE, "Northern Mythology," vol. i.; PETERSEN, "Nordisk Mythologi."

Frigimelica, fRe-je-mĕl′e-kȧ, (FRANCESCO,) a distinguished Italian physician, born at Padua in 1491. He became physician to Pope Julius III. in 1555. Died in 1559.

Friis, frees, (JOHAN,) a Danish statesman, born in 1494, became a disciple of Luther, whom he met at Wittenberg. He was chancellor under Christian III. Died in 1570.

Frimont, de, deh free′mȯN′, (JOHANN PHILIPP,) COUNT, an Austrian general, and Prince of Antrodocco, was born in Lorraine or Belgium about 1756. He commanded a corps which invaded France in 1814. He conducted a successful campaign in Italy in 1815, and forced the French to evacuate Savoy. Charged with the execution of the decrees of the Congress of Laybach in 1821, he marched to Naples and quelled an insurrection of the Liberal party. He was appointed president of the council of war at Vienna a short time before his death, which occurred in December, 1831.

See "Nouvelle Biographie Générale."

Fririon, fRe′re′ȯN′, (FRANÇOIS NICOLAS,) BARON, a French general, born in Lorraine in 1766. He distinguished himself in 1809 at Wagram, as chief of the staff of Massena's corps. Died in 1840.

---

e as k; ç as s; g̃ hard; g as j; G, H, K, guttural; N, nasal; R, trilled; s̃ as z; th as in this. (☞ See Explanations, p. 23.

Frisch, frĭsh, (Jodocus (or Josse) Leopold,) a naturalist and theologian, son of Johann L. Frisch, noticed below, was born in Berlin in 1714. He published several treatises on zoology, etc. Died in 1787.

See Ersch und Gruber, "Allgemeine Encyklopaedie."

Frisch, (Johann Leonhard,) a German philologist and naturalist, born at Sulzbach in 1666. He settled in Berlin about 1700, and was admitted into the Academy of Sciences in 1706. He was afterwards rector of a gymnasium in Berlin, and displayed great erudition in numerous works. His "German-Latin Dictionary" (1741) was the most complete and learned that had appeared in Germany. He wrote a good "Description of all the Insects of Germany," (13 parts, 1720–38,) and a work on German Ornithology, (1735–65.) Died in 1743.

See J. J. Wippel, "Das Leben, etc. Johann Leonhard Frisch," 1744; Ersch und Gruber, "Allgemeine Encyklopaedie;" "Nouvelle Biographie Générale."

Frisch, (Johann Leonhard,) a German philosopher, born in Berlin in 1737; died in 1795.

Frische, du, dü frĕsh, (Jacques,) a learned French Benedictine, born in Normandy in 1640. He published, with Lenourry, an excellent edition of Saint Ambrose's works, (1686–90.) Died in 1693.

Frischlin, frĭsh-leen', (Nicodemus,) a Latin poet and satirist, born at Balingen, in Würtemberg, in 1547. Having offended the Duke of Würtemberg, he was imprisoned in a fortress, and, after a confinement of several months, was killed in attempting to escape, in 1590. He was the author of satires, epigrams, and elegies, written in elegant Latin, and paraphrases on Virgil's "Bucolics" and "Georgics." For his comedy entitled "Rebecca" he was created by Maximilian II. poet-laureate and count palatine.

See "Nicodemus Frischlinus redivivus," by his brother, 1590; Lange, "Frischlinus Vita fama et Scriptis memorabilis," 1727; D. F. Strauss, "Leben und Schriften des N. Frischlin," 1856; Melchior Adam, "Vitæ Philosophorum."

Frischmuth, frĭsh'moot, (Johann,) a German Orientalist and theologian, born in Franconia in 1619, became professor of Hebrew and Greek at Jena in 1654. He wrote many philologico-theological treatises, among which are "On Tithes," ("De Decimis,") and "On Sacrifices." Died in 1687.

See Jöcher, "Allgemeines Gelehrten-Lexikon."

Frisi, free'see, (Paolo,) a celebrated Italian mathematician and philosopher, born at Milan in April, 1728. He entered at the age of fifteen the monastery of the Barnabites, where, with little or no aid except that of books, he made great progress in geometry. In 1750 he wrote an able treatise "On the Figure of the Earth," which established his reputation and procured for him a chair of philosophy at Milan. From 1756 to 1764 he was professor in the University of Pisa. During this period he published a treatise on "Electricity," and a prize essay "On the Diurnal Motion of the Earth." About 1757 he was chosen a Fellow of the Royal Society of London, and afterwards a member of the Academies of Saint Petersburg, Paris, and Berlin. In 1764 he accepted a chair of mathematics in Milan, and received a pension of one hundred sequins from Maria Theresa of Austria. He published (in Latin) in 1774 his greatest work, "Physical and Mathematical Cosmography," (2 vols. 4to.) He wrote also on "Universal Gravity," Mechanics, Architecture, Analytic Geometry, etc. Died in 1784. His brother Philip was Podesta of Ravenna, and author of an able work on public law.

See Count Verri, "Memorie appartenenti alla Vita, etc. del Paolo Frisi," Milan, 1787; F. Jacquier, "Elogio academico del Signor Abate Frisi."

Frisius. See Fries, (John and Henry.)

Frith or **Friyth,** frĭth, (John,) an English Reformer, born at Sevenoaks, in Kent. He had a controversy with Sir Thomas More, and was imprisoned in the Tower for his religion. Having refused to renounce his principles, he was burnt at Smithfield in 1553. He left several works on theology.

See Fox, "Acts and Monuments."

Frith, (William Powell,) a skilful English historical painter, born at Harrogate, in Yorkshire, in 1819 or 1820, was a student of the Royal Academy. He painted scenes from Shakspeare, Scott, Goldsmith, and Molière with

success, and was elected Royal Academician in 1853. His colour is brilliant, and his style adapted to the general taste of the people, if not to that of critics and artists. Among his works are "The Village Pastor," (1845,) "Coming of Age," (1849,) and "Life at the Sea-Side," (1854.)

Frit'ĭ-ğern, King of the Visigoths, crossed the Danube and established himself in Mœsia. He defeated the emperor Valens at Adrianople in 378 A.D. Died about 392.

See Gibbon, "History of the Decline and Fall of the Roman Empire."

Fritz, frĭts, (Samuel,) a Jesuit missionary, born in Bohemia in 1650. He laboured about forty years on the Upper Amazon, where he is said to have converted many thousand natives. He was skilful in several useful arts, and made a valuable chart of the river Amazon. Died in South America in 1730.

Fritzsche, frĭt'sheh, (Christian Friedrich,) a German theologian, born at Naundorf in 1776. He became in 1830 professor of theology at Halle. He wrote "Lectures on the Communion," and other religious treatises. Died in 1850.

Fritzsche, (Franz Volkmar—folk'mȧr,) a German scholar and critic, a son of the preceding, was born at Steinbach in 1806. He wrote a treatise "On the Monodies of Euripides," ("De Monodiis Euripideis,") and published editions of Lucian's "Alexander," "Demonax," etc., and "Questiones Lucianæ."

Fritzsche, (Karl Friedrich August,) a learned theologian and biblical critic, born at Steinbach in 1801, was a brother of the preceding. He published a number of commentaries on the New Testament, the most important of which is that on the Epistle to the Romans. Died in 1846.

His brother, Otto Fridolin, also distinguished himself as a biblical critic and philologist.

Friuli, Duke of. See Duroc.

Frizon, fre'zôn', (Pierre,) a French Jesuit, born in the diocese of Rheims. He wrote a history of the French cardinals and popes, entitled "Gallia Purpurata," (1629.) Died about 1650.

Frizzi, frĭt'see, (Antonio,) an Italian writer and lawyer, born at Ferrara in 1736. He wrote a History of Ferrara, (5 vols., 1791–1809.) Died in 1800.

Fröbel or **Froebel,** frö'bel, (Carl Poppo,) a German linguist and printer, born at Oberweissbach in 1786. He translated Sallust into German, (1821.) Died in 1824.

See Ersch und Gruber, "Allgemeine Encyklopaedie."

Fröbel or **Froebel,** (Friedrich,) a German teacher, a brother of the preceding, was born near Rudolstadt in 1782. He published in 1826 a work on education, ("Die Menschenerziehung,") and founded in 1837, at Blankenburg, a school called "Kindergarten," in which he pursued a new system of education. Died in 1852.

See Kuehne, "Fröbel's Tod und der Fortbestand seiner Lehre," 1852.

Fröbel or **Froebel,** (Julius,) a German writer and democrat, a nephew of the preceding, was born at Griesheim in 1806. He was professor of history and natural history at Zurich from 1833 to 1844, and published a "System of Crystalology," (1843.) He became a leader of the democratic party in Germany about 1848, and a member of the Parliament of Frankfort. He was united with Blum in a deputation to Vienna, and was arrested there, but acquitted. Among his works is "Experiences, Travels, Studies, etc. in America," ("Aus Amerika Erfahrungen, Reisen und Studien," 2 vols., 1858.)

Froben, fro'ben, [Lat. Frobe'nius,] (Johann,) a learned German printer, born in Franconia in 1460. He opened an office at Bâle in 1491, from which he issued a Latin Bible; and he was one of the first who introduced into Germany the Roman letters. He printed all the works of Erasmus, who resided many years in Bâle and was his warm personal friend. Died in 1527.

See Ersch und Gruber, "Allgemeine Encyklopaedie."

Frobenius. See Froben.

Frob'ish-ẽr, [Lat. Forbisse'rus,] (Sir Martin,) an English navigator, born at Doncaster, was the first of his countrymen who sought to discover the Northwest passage. In June, 1576, he sailed from Deptford with three small barks, explored the coast of Greenland, discovered the strait which bears his name, near 63° north latitude, and brought home a black mineral in which gold was found. He renewed his explorations in 1577 and 1578, without any great results. The chief object of his second expedition was to find gold. In 1588, as captain of the Triumph,—a large ship,—he signalized his bravery in the contest with the Spanish Armada, for which he was knighted. He commanded a small fleet sent to aid Henry IV. of France, and in the attack of a fort near Brest he received a wound of which he died in 1594.

See FREIGIUS, "Historia Navigationis Martini Forbisseri," 1675; CAMPBELL, "Lives of British Admirals;" J. BARROW, "Memoirs of the Naval Worthies of Queen Elizabeth's Reign," 1845.

Frochot, fRo'sho', (NICOLAS THÉRÈSE BENOÎT,) COUNT, a French administrator, born about 1760. In 1800 he was appointed, by the First Consul, prefect of the department of the Seine, in which position he directed with ability the municipal affairs of Paris until 1812, when he was dismissed from office because he had been in some measure the dupe of the conspirator Mallet. (See MALLET.) Died in 1828.

Froebel. See FRÖBEL.

Froeben. See FRÖBEN.

Froehlich. See FRÖHLICH.

Froelich. See FRÖLICH.

Fröhlich or **Froehlich,** frö'liK, (ABRAHAM EMMANUEL,) a Swiss poet, born at Brugg in 1796. He became pastor at Aarau in 1835, and produced epic poems, elegies, and fables, which were received with favour.

Froidmond, Froidmont, frwä'môn', or **Fromont,** fRo'môn', [Lat. FROMUN'DUS,] (LIBERT,) an eminent Catholic divine and scholar, born at Haccourt, in Belgium, in 1587. He was the friend of Jansen, whom he succeeded, about 1635, as professor of divinity in the University of Louvain. He wrote many works on theology, of which his "Commentary on St. Paul's Epistles" is among the best. Died in 1653.

Froila (fRo'e-lä or froi'lä) **I.,** King of Spain, was the son of Alfonso I., and began to reign in A.D. 757. His realm included Oviedo, the Asturias, and Leon, the Moors having possession of the rest of Spain. About 760 he gained a decisive victory over Omar, a Saracen prince. He was dethroned and killed by his brother Aurelio in 768.

Froila (written also **Fruela**) **II.** of Spain, born about the year 845 A.D., was Count of Galicia, and son of King Veremond. He was killed in 875 by Alfonso III., from whom he had usurped the throne of Leon.

Froila III., King of Leon, succeeded his brother Ordoño in 923 A.D. His cruelty and injustice impelled his subjects to drive him from the throne and to change the kingdom into a republic. He died in 924.

Froissart, frois'särt, [Fr. pron. fRwä'säR',] (JEAN,) a French historian and poet, born at Valenciennes in 1337. He was educated for the church; but his love of festive pleasure and romantic gallantry directed him into other pursuits. At the age of twenty he began to write chronicles of the wars of his time, and to obtain the requisite information he travelled much, and associated with the nobles and principal actors in public affairs. In the year 1361 he visited the court of Edward III. of England, where he remained five or six years and was treated with great favour, especially by the queen Philippa, who employed him as her clerk or secretary. He attended Lionel, Duke of Clarence, when he went to Italy to marry the daughter of the Duke of Milan. After the death of Philippa, in 1369, he officiated a short time as curate of Lestines, in France. About the year 1385, Guy, Count of Blois, employed Froissart as clerk, and the latter soon afterwards, in quest of historical materials, visited Gaston, Count of Foix. His active curiosity, even in his declining years, led him to frequent courts, festivals, and tournaments, and his Chronicles present a "faithful mirror" of the age of chivalry, with its beauties and deformities. He is esteemed for his veracity, and admired for picturesque description and a charming simplicity of expression. The period comprised in his history extends from 1326 to 1400; he probably died

soon after the latter date. He gives a brilliant but superficial picture of his times, and seems not to recognize the existence of any class except the noblesse.

See WALTER SCOTT, "Froissart," in the "Edinburgh Review" for January, 1805; VILLEMAIN, "Cours de Littérature Française au Moyen-Age;" HENRI LUCAS, "Notice sur la Vie et les Ouvrages de J. Froissart," Berlin, 1849; "Nouvelle Biographie Générale."

Frölich or **Froelich,** frö'liK, (ERASMUS,) an eminent German numismatist, born at Grätz, in Styria, in 1700. He became professor of history and antiquities at Vienna, and published many works (in Latin) on numismatics, among which are "The Utility of Numismatics," (1733,) and "The Annals of the Kings of Syria illustrated by Medals," (1744.) Died in 1758.

See HIRSCHING, "Historisch-literarisches Handbuch;" OETTER, "Lebensgeschichte des berühmten E. Froelich," 1773.

Fromage, fRo'mäzh', (PIERRE,) a French missionary, born at Laon in 1678; died in Syria in 1740.

Fromaget, fRo'mä'zhἀ', a French dramatic writer, published "Kara Mustapha," "Mirima," "The Magazine of Lost Things," etc. Died in 1759.

Froment or **Fromment,** fRo'môN', (ANTOINE,) a Protestant Reformer, born near Grenoble, France, about 1510, was a disciple of Farel. He began to preach against popery at Geneva in 1533, and settled as pastor in that city in 1537. He was deposed from the ministry (for some misconduct on the part of his wife) about 1552, and died about 1585, leaving a "History of the Reformation at Geneva," which was published in 1854.

See MM. HAAG, "La France protestante;" SENEBIER, "Histoire littéraire de Genève."

Froment, (FRANÇOIS MARIE,) a French pamphleteer and politician, born at Nîmes in 1756. He emigrated about 1790, after which he engaged in many intrigues for the restoration of the Bourbons. Died in 1825.

Froment, (PAUL GUSTAVE,) a French optician, noted as a skilful maker of instruments, was born in 1815. He produced some remarkable electro-magnetic apparatus.

Fromond, fRo-mônd', (GIOVANNI CLAUDIO,) an eminent natural philosopher, born at Cremona, Italy, in 1703. He was for twenty years professor of logic and philosophy at Pisa, and acquired a wide reputation. In 1758 he was chosen a correspondent of the Academy of Sciences of Paris. He has the credit of determining the characters of mechanical and physical forces. Among his chief works is a "General Introduction to Philosophy," (1748.) Died at Pisa in 1765.

See BIANCHI, "Elogio storico del G. C. Fromond," Cremona, 1781; TIPALDO, "Biografia degli Italiani illustri."

Fromundus. See FROIDMOND.

Frondeville, de, deh fRôNd'vèl', (THOMAS LOUIS CÉSAR,) MARQUIS, a French royalist, born at Lisieux in 1756. He was a member of the National Assembly, 1790–91. Died in 1816.

Frondsberg, fRonds'bĕRG, **Fronsperg,** fRons'pĕRG, or **Frundsberg,** fRoonds'bĕRG, (GEORG,) a German general, born at Mindelheim in 1475. He distinguished himself as colonel in the army of Charles V. in several campaigns, and contributed to the victory of Pavia in 1525. He reinforced with about 12,000 Germans, recruited by himself, the army with which Constable Bourbon took Rome in 1527. Died in 1528.

Fronteau, fRôN'to', (JEAN,) a learned French Jesuit and antiquary, born at Angers in 1614. He became a professor of philosophy, and in 1648 chancellor of the University of Paris. He wrote, besides other works, "Thomas à Kempis vindicatus," (1641,) an essay to prove that T. à Kempis was the author of "The Imitation of Christ," and "A Contrast between Augustine and Calvin," ("Antitheses Augustini et Calvini," 1651.) Died in 1662.

See LALLEMANT, "Vie de Fronteau," 1663.

Frontenac, fRôN'tĕh-näk', (LOUIS,) COUNT, a French officer, born in 1621, was appointed Governor-General of Canada in 1678. He built Fort Frontenac, on Lake Ontario, and was recalled to France in 1682. Died in 1698.

Frontin. See FRONTINUS.

Fron-ti'nus, [Fr. FRONTIN, fRôN'tăN',] (SEXTUS JULIUS,) a Roman general and author, of patrician rank, became prætor in 70 A.D., and was several times consul.

About the year 75 he was sent to Britain as proconsul, commanded the army which conquered the Silures, and returned to Rome in 78. In the reign of Nerva he superintended the operations which supplied Rome with water. He is the author of two well-written extant works,—viz. : "Military Stratagems," ("Stratagematica,") and a treatise on the Aqueducts of Rome. Died in 106 A.D.

See TACITUS, "History," book iv. ; SCHOELL, "Histoire de la Littérature Romaine ;" "Nouvelle Biographie Générale ;" NIEBUHR, "Roman History."

Fron'to, [Fr. FRONTON, frôn'tôn',] (MARCUS CORNELIUS,) an eminent Roman orator, was a native of Cirta, in Africa. He was preceptor of Lucius Verus and Marcus Aurelius, who made him consul in 143 A.D. and treated him with great favour. All of his works are lost, except small fragments and letters. In 1814 or 1815 a palimpsest was found by Angelo Mai in the Ambrosian Library at Milan, containing interesting letters from Fronto to Marcus Aurelius and Lucius Verus. Their answers were also discovered by Mai at Rome.

See "Nouvelle Biographie Générale ;" ROTH, "Bemerkungen über den Schriften des M. C. Fronton," etc., 1817.

Fronton. See FRONTO.

Fronton du Duc. See DUC.

Froriep, fro'reep, (JUSTUS FRIEDRICH,) a German Orientalist, born at Lubeck in 1745 ; died in 1800.

Froriep, von, fon fro'reep, (FRIEDRICH LUDWIG,) a German physician and writer, born at Erfurt about 1780 ; died in 1847.

Froriep, von, (ROBERT,) a physician, son of the preceding, was born at Jena in 1804. He became professor of medicine at Berlin in 1833, and published several anatomical works with plates, among which is "Atlas Anatomicus," (1850.) Died in 1861.

Frossard, fro'săr', (BENJAMIN SIGISMOND,) a Swiss Protestant divine, born at Nyon in 1754. He published "The Slave-Trade tried before the Tribunal of Reason, Policy, and Religion," (1789.) From 1815 to 1830 he was professor of theology at Montauban. Died in 1830.

Frost, (WILLIAM EDWARD,) an English painter, born at Wandsworth, Surrey, in 1810, studied in the Royal Academy. He gained a gold medal for his "Prometheus Bound," (1839.) His picture of "Una and the Wood-Nymphs" (1847) was purchased by the queen. Among his other works are "Nymphs Dancing," "Diana surprised by Actæon," (1846,) and "The Graces," (1856.) His pictures are admired for correct design and refined taste.

Frothingham, froth'ing-ạm,(NATHANIEL LANGDON,) D.D., an eminent Unitarian divine, born in Boston in 1793. He graduated at Harvard in 1811, and the next year, when only nineteen years of age, was appointed instructor in rhetoric and oratory in that institution. In 1815 he was ordained pastor of the First Church in Boston. Besides numerous sermons and addresses, he has written many short poems and hymns of great beauty, and made various translations from the German. A collection of these, entitled "Metrical Pieces, Original and Translated," was published in 1855.

Frothingham, (OCTAVIUS B.,) a Unitarian divine and rationalistic theologian, a son of the preceding, was born in Boston in 1822. He was educated at Harvard, where he also studied divinity. He was ordained in 1847. About 1859 he removed to New York ; and since February, 1860, he has been pastor of the Third Unitarian Society of that city. Mr. Frothingham possesses superior intellectual powers, with a high and broad literary culture. He is remarkable as representing the most radical phase of rationalistic Unitarianism as it exists at the present time in the United States : in this respect, indeed, he may be regarded as the successor of Theodore Parker, although differing widely from that writer in his mental characteristics, and also (it would seem) in many of his theological or philosophical views.

For some interesting remarks on Mr. Frothingham's position as a philosopher and a theologian, see an article contributed by one of his congregation to the New York "World," about the end of June, 1868.

Frothingham, (RICHARD,) Jr., an American journalist and historical writer, born in Charlestown, Massachusetts, in 1812, became associate editor of the "Boston Post," the leading Democratic paper in New England.

His "History of the Siege of Boston" (1849) has been warmly praised by Everett and Bancroft.

Frotté, de, dẹh fro'tă', (LOUIS,) COUNT, a French royalist chief, born in Normandy about 1755. He raised a revolt in Normandy in 1795, but was defeated and retired to England in 1796. In 1799 he again appeared in Normandy as general-in-chief of the royalist army. He resisted all efforts for pacification ; but, having lost several battles, he surrendered, and was executed, in 1800.

Froude, frood, (JAMES ANTHONY,) an eminent English historian, born at Totness, in Devonshire, about 1818. He was educated at Oxford, and became a Fellow of Exeter College. He published in 1847 "The Shadows of the Clouds," a novel, and in 1849 "The Nemesis of Faith," both of which have decided literary merit. The latter is charged with being heterodoxical. His principal work is a "History of England from the Fall of Wolsey to the Death of Elizabeth," (10 vols. 8vo, 1856-67.) As a historian, Mr. Froude's merits are of a high order. The work just named embraces a period equal, if not superior, in interest and importance to any other period of the same length in English history, and one which had not been adequately treated by any previous historian.

"The peculiar merit of Mr. Froude's work," says the "Edinburgh Review" for September, 1866, "is its wealth of unpublished manuscripts ; and the reign of Elizabeth is remarkably illustrated by the correspondence of the Spanish ambassadors and other agents of the court of Spain, which have been preserved in the Archives at Simancas. The extraordinary interest of such illustrations is apparent in every page of these volumes : they give novelty to the narrative and variety to the well-known incidents of the time ; and they bring in aid of historical evidence the contemporary opinions of society upon current events."

See "Edinburgh Review" for July, 1858, and January, 1864; "London Quarterly Review" for October, 1863 ; "British Quarterly" for January and April, 1864 ; "North British Review" for November, 1856 ; "Fraser's Magazine" for May, 1849, July, 1856, July and September, 1858, and July, 1860.

Froude, (RICHARD HUR'RELL,) an English clergyman, a brother of the preceding, was born in 1803. He graduated at Oriel College, Oxford, of which he became Fellow in 1826 and tutor in 1827. Several volumes of his writings (of the Oxford Tract School) have been published. Died in 1836.

Froumenteau, froo'môn'tō', (NICOLAS,) the assumed name of an unknown French Protestant author, who published in 1581 a remarkable work, entitled "The Secret of the Finances of France Discovered."

Frowde, frŏwd, (PHILIP,) an English dramatic poet, born about 1680, was intimate with Addison. He wrote some Latin verses which appeared in "Musæ Anglicanæ," and two tragedies. Died in 1738.

Frugoni, froo-go'nee, (CARLO INNOCENZIO,) one of the most popular Italian poets of the eighteenth century, born in Genoa in 1692, entered a monastery in 1708. Having gained the reputation of an elegant writer in Latin and Italian, he became professor of rhetoric at Brescia in 1716. In 1725 he found an asylum at the court of Parma, where he passed the greater part of his life and was liberally patronized by several successive dukes. In 1733 he was released from the monastic rules, which had become intolerable to him. His ode on the occasion of the capture of Oran was greatly admired. He wrote a multitude of sonnets, odes, eclogues, epistles, and other verses, which display a graceful style and a rich imagination. An edition of his works appeared in 9 vols., 1779. Died at Parma in December, 1768.

See CERATI, "Elogio de C. I. Frigoni," 1782 ; FABRONI, "Elogj d'illustri Italiani," 1786 ; TIPALDO, "Biografia degli Italiani illustri ;" "Lives of the Italian Poets," by REV. HENRY STEBBING, London, 1831 ; "Biographie Universelle ;" "Nouvelle Biographie Générale."

Fruitiers or **Fruytiers,** frü-e'te-ậ', (PHILIP,) a Flemish portrait-painter, born in Antwerp about 1625. He was employed by Rubens to execute a portrait of himself and family. This picture is highly praised by Weyermans. As a miniature-painter he was probably inferior to no artist of his time. He was living in 1650.

See DESCAMPS, "Vies des Peintres Flamands," etc.

Frumence. See FRUMENTIUS.

Frumentius, fru-mĕn'shĕ-us, [Fr. FRUMENCE, froo'-mŏnss',] SAINT, born at Tyre, is usually called "the Apostle of Ethiopia." He was employed in evangelizing Abyssinia. Having returned to Egypt, he was appointed a bishop in 331 by Athanasius, who sent him to propagate the faith in Ethiopia. Died about 360 A.D.

Frundsberg. See FRONDSBERG.

Frusius. See FREUX.

Fruytiers. See FRUITIERS.

Fry, (CAROLINE.) See WILSON, (MRS. C.)

Fry, (ELIZABETH,) an eminent philanthropist, daughter of John Gurney, of Earlham Hall, and sister of Joseph John Gurney, was born in Norwich, England, in 1780. Her father was an opulent banker, and a member of the Society of Friends. About the age of eighteen she became a serious professor of religion, and renounced the gay amusements in which she had before participated. In 1800 she was married to Joseph Fry, of London, and some years later she appeared as minister in the meetings of the Friends. About the year 1813 she began to make systematic efforts for the reformation of the female prisoners in Newgate and other prisons of London, in which she laboured for many years with great zeal and success, manifesting a true Christian sympathy for those unfortunate persons, and administering both to their spiritual and their physical necessities. Died in 1845.

See a Memoir of her life, containing her Journal and Letters, by her daughters, 2 vols., 1847; Rev. T. TIMPSON, "Memoirs of Elizabeth Fry," 1846; REV. E. NEALE, "Christianity and Infidelity Contrasted;" "London Quarterly Review" for December, 1847.

Fry, (JOHN,) an English Socinian writer, published, besides other works, "The Clergy in their Colours," (1650.) Died about 1650.

Fry, (Rev. JOHN,) an English author, a brother of Caroline Fry, was rector of Desford. He published several esteemed religious works, among which are "Lectures on Romans," (1816,) "The Second Advent," (1822,) and "A Short History of the Christian Church," (1825.)

Fry, (SPEED S.,) an American officer in the Union service, became brigadier-general of volunteers in 1862.

Fry, (WILLIAM HENRY,) an American composer and journalist, born in Philadelphia in 1815. He composed operas, symphonies, etc., and was assistant editor of several daily journals. Died in 1864.

Frye, (THOMAS,) a skilful portrait-painter, born in Ireland in 1710, lived in London. He is reputed to have been the first who manufactured English porcelain. Died in 1762.

See "Gentleman's Magazine," vol. xxxiv.

Fryxell, frŭks'ĕl, (ANDERS,) a Swedish historian, born in Dalsland in 1795. He published in 1824 a work on education, "Svensk Spraklæra," which was often reprinted. He became professor in Stockholm about 1833. His chief work, consisting of essays on the history of Sweden, "Berättelser ur Svenska Historien," ("Corrections of Swedish History,") is very popular. Of this publication about twenty volumes have already appeared. The first volume was issued in 1823.

Fuad-Effendi, foo'ăd ĕf-fĕn'dee, (MEHEMET,) a Turkish minister of state, distinguished as a linguist and diplomatist, was born at Constantinople about 1815. He was appointed minister of foreign affairs several times after 1852. He published an Ottoman Grammar, (1852.)

Fuca, de, dă foo'kă, (JUAN,) a Greek navigator, whose proper name was APOSTOLOS VALERIANOS, was a native of Cephalonia. He served about forty years as Spanish pilot in the East Indies. In 1596 he offered his services to the English, stating that he had discovered on the west coast of America, near latitude 48° north, a strait leading to the Atlantic, which he wished to explore further. He died about 1602. His name has been given to the strait which connects the Pacific with the Gulf of Georgia.

Fuchs. See FUX, (JOHANN JOSEPH.)

Fuchs, fŏoks, (GOTTLIEB,) a German poet, born in Upper Saxony in 1720, became a minister at Taubenheim. Among his poems, which are mostly lyrical, is "The Contented Peasant." Died about 1800.

Fuchs, (JOHANN CHRISTOPH,) a German naturalist, born at Gross-Germersleben in 1726. He was master of pages at the court of Frederick the Great from 1754 to 1766. Died in 1795.

See ERSCH und GRUBER, "Allgemeine Encyklopaedie."

Fuchs, (KONRAD HEINRICH,) a German physician, and professor of medicine at Göttingen, born at Bamberg in 1803. He published, among other treatises, a "Manual of Special Nosology and Therapeutics," (4 vols., 1845–48.) Died about 1855.

Fuchs, (LEONHARD,) a distinguished German botanist and physician, born at Wemdingen, (or Wemding,) in Bavaria, in 1501. He was professor of medicine at Tübingen from 1535 until his death, and contributed largely to the restoration of that school. He wrote many able medical works, among which is "Method of Curing," ("Medendi Methodus," 1541,) and acquired a high reputation by his botanical work "On the History of Plants," ("De Historia Stirpium Commentarii insignes," 1542,) with many figures well designed. This work was often reprinted and translated. The *Fuchsia* was named in his honour. Died in 1565.

See HIZLER, "Oratio de Vita, etc. L. Fuchsii," Tübingen, 1566; NICÉRON, "Mémoires;" M. ADAM, "Vitæ Eruditorum;" CARL LORENZ, "Dissertatio inauguralis medica de L. Fuchs," Berlin, 1846; "Nouvelle Biographie Générale."

Fuehrich. See FÜHRIG, (JOSEPH.)

Fuente. See LA FUENTE.

Fuente, la, lă fwĕn'tă, (JUAN LEANDRO,) a skilful Spanish historical painter, born at Granada in 1600, excelled in design and colouring, and in *clair-obscur*. Died in 1654.

Fuentes, fwĕn'tĕs, or **Fonte, de,** dă fon'tă, (BARTOLOMÉ,) a Spanish or Portuguese navigator, whose real or pretended voyages have been the subject of learned speculation. He is reported to have made discoveries on the west coast of North America about 1640.

See FOSTER, "Northern Voyages and Discoveries."

Fuentes, de, dă fwĕn'tĕs, (PEDRO HENRIQUEZ d'Azevedo—dă-thă-vă'Do,) COUNT, an eminent Spanish general, born at Valladolid in 1560. He made his first campaign in Portugal, under the Duke of Alva, about 1580. He performed with ability several important diplomatic missions. In 1606 he distinguished himself at the siege of Ostend, and was raised to the rank of general. He commanded the infantry in the war with France which began in 1635, and was killed, in 1643, at the battle of Rocroy, where he was defeated by the Prince of Condé.

See SISMONDI, "Histoire des Français."

Fuerst. See FÜRST.

Fuerstenberg. See FÜRSTENBERG.

Fuessli. See FÜSSLI.

Fuga, foo'gă, (FERDINANDO,) a skilful Italian architect, born at Florence in 1699. He was appointed about 1730 architect of the pontifical palaces by Clement XII. Among his works in Rome are the palace of the Consulta, a very fine edifice, and the palace Corsini. He was afterwards employed by the King of Naples in the embellishment of his capital, and was architect of the Albergo Reale dei Poveri, ("Royal Hotel for the Poor,") said to be the largest hospital of Europe. It was commenced in 1751. Died about 1780.

See QUATREMÈRE DE QUINCY, "Dictionnaire d'Architecture;" MILIZIA, "Vite degli Architetti;" TICOZZI, "Dizionario;" "Nouvelle Biographie Générale."

Füger, fü'ger, (FRIEDRICH HEINRICH,) a German painter, born at Heilbronn in 1751. He was patronized by the empress Maria Theresa. Died in 1818.

Fugger, fŏog'ger, the name of a German family in Suabia, who were originally linen-weavers and gradually amassed immense wealth by commerce. The brothers Ulric, George, and Jacob Fugger were ennobled by the emperor Maximilian in the latter part of the fifteenth century. Raimond and Antony, the founders of the two principal lines of the house of Fugger, were raised to the rank of count, in 1530, by Charles V., to whom they had lent money, and who also gave them the privilege of striking gold and silver coin. It is related that Charles V. on his return from Algiers was entertained by Antony Fugger, who made a fire of cinnamon-wood and kindled it with the emperor's bonds due to the Fuggers for the money they had lent him. Several members of this family were patrons of learning, and active in founding charitable institutions, of which we may name the Fuggerei at Augsburg.

See ERSCH und GRUBER, "Allgemeine Encyklopaedie."

Führig or **Fuehrig**, fü′riG, **Führich** or **Fuehrich**, fü′riK, (JOSEPH,) a German historical painter and engraver, born in Bohemia in 1800. He became professor of painting in the Academy of Vienna. He painted a number of subjects of sacred history, among which is "The Triumph of Christ."

Fuhrmann, fōōR′mån, (MATTHIAS,) a German historian, who wrote on Austrian history. Died at Vienna in 1773.

Ful′beck or **Ful′becke**, (WILLIAM,) an English jurist, born in Lincoln in 1560, published several legal works, which were esteemed, viz., "Preparative to the Study of the Law," (1600,) "Pandects of the Law of Nations," etc.

Fulbert, fül′baiR′, a French prelate and writer, was eminent for piety and learning, and was considered as one of the greatest ornaments of the Gallican Church in his time. He was chosen Bishop of Chartres in 1007, after he had been the master of a celebrated school at that place. "The writings of Fulbert," says the "Nouvelle Biographie Générale," "are almost the only historical monuments of France for his time." His sermons, hymns, and letters, of which about one hundred have been preserved, are esteemed precious for the light they throw upon that age. Died in 1028 or 1029.

See "Gallia Christiana;" "Nouvelle Biographie Générale."

Fulcherius Carnotensis. See FOULCHER DE CHARTRES.

Fulco. See FOULQUES.

Fulcodi Guido. See CLEMENT IV.

Fulcoius. See FOULCOIE.

Fulda, fōōl′då, (FRIEDRICH KARL,) a German philologist, born at Wimpfen, Suabia, in 1724, was noted for his mechanical ingenuity. He became minister of the Lutheran church at Mühlhausen-on-the-Enz. He gave much attention to the general theory of language, or what the Germans call "linguistik." He wrote, besides other works, a "Collection of German Idioms," (1788,) and a "Natural History of the German People," (1794.) Died at Enzingen in 1788.

See HIRSCHING, "Historisch-literarisches Handbuch."

Fulgence. See FULGENTIUS.

Fulgentius, [Fr. FULGENCE, fül′zhŏNss′,] (FABIUS CLAUDIUS GORDIANUS,) an eminent African bishop, was born at Leptis about 478 A.D. At an early age he resolved to renounce the world, and, entering a monastery, became noted for ascetic devotion. After visiting Rome in 500 and returning home, he was chosen Bishop of Ruspina, or Ruspa, by the Catholics, in 508. Soon after this date he was exiled to Sardinia by Thrasimund, King of the Vandals, who was an Arian and a persecutor of the orthodox. He was restored at the death of that king, and died about 533. He wrote, in Latin, treatises on the Trinity, Predestination, Faith, and Arianism, which are highly esteemed. His opinions and style resemble those of Augustine.

See FERRANDUS, "Vita Fulgentii."

Fulgentius, [Fr. FULGENCE,] (FABIUS PLANCI′ADES,) a Latin writer, who lived probably about the sixth century, is supposed by some to have been a bishop of Carthage. He wrote a work on Mythology, and a glossary of antiquated words, ("Expositio Sermonum antiquorum," etc.,) which are extant.

Fulgosio, fool-go′se-o, (RAPHAEL,) an Italian jurist, born at Placentia; died in 1427.

Fulke, fōōlk, (WILLIAM,) D.D., an eminent English Puritan divine, born in London, became rector of Warley in 1571, and afterwards Margaret professor of divinity at Cambridge. He published, in 1580, "The Text of the New Testament, etc.," said to be an invaluable assistant to the Protestant divine, treating of the relative merits of the Catholic and Protestant versions. Died in 1589.

See FULLER, "Worthies;" BROOK, "Lives of the Puritans," 1813.

Fulla, fōōl′lå, (*i.e.* "full,") in the Norse mythology, an attendant of Frigga, whose treasure-casket and slippers she is said to carry. She is also acquainted with the secret counsels of the mother of the gods. As Frigga represents the earth's fertility, Fulla would seem to typify the abundance which follows it. (See FRIGGA.)

Fülleborn, fül′leh-boRn′, (GEORG GUSTAV,) a German scholar and writer, born at Glogau in 1769; died in 1803.

Fuller, fōōl′ler, (ANDREW,) an eminent English Baptist minister, born at Wicken, in Cambridgeshire, in 1754. His education was defective or very limited. He preached a few years at Soham, and removed in 1782 to Kettering, Northamptonshire, where he remained until his death. He was the first secretary of the Baptist Missionary Society, formed about 1792, and acquired a high reputation by his writings, among which are "The Gospel its own Witness," (1800,) "Expository Discourses on Genesis," (2 vols., 1806,) "Dialogues, Letters, and Essays on Various Subjects," (1806,) "Sermons," (1 vol., 1814,) and "The Harmony of Scripture, or an Attempt to reconcile various Passages," (1817.) Died in 1815. Fuller has been styled the "Franklin of Theology." His writings are characterized by vigour, logical acumen, and deep insight into human nature. "He was a man," says Robert Hall, "whose sagacity enabled him to penetrate to the depths of every subject he explored; whose conceptions were so powerful and luminous that what was recondite and original appeared familiar, what was intricate, easy and perspicuous, in his hands."

See Memoirs of his Life, by J. W. MORRIS, 1815, and a Memoir, prefixed to an edition of his Works, (5 vols., 1832,) by his son, ANDREW GUNTON FULLER.

Fuller, (ISAAC,) an English painter of history and portraits. He painted for a church of Oxford an altar-piece which was praised by Addison in a Latin poem, and was very successful in portraits. Died in 1672.

Fuller, (MARGARET.) See OSSOLI.

Fuller, (NICHOLAS,) an eminent Oriental scholar, born at Southampton, England, in 1557. He became rector of Bishop Waltham, and published "Miscellanea Theologica," (1612.) Died in 1622.

See FULLER, "Worthies."

Fuller, (NICHOLAS,) an English lawyer and member of Parliament, who distinguished himself in the early part of the reign of James I. by his resolute opposition to the oppressive measures of the court of high commission. Died in 1620.

See GARDINER, "History of England from 1603 to 1616," vol. i. chap. viii., pp. 443-446.

Full′er, (RICHARD,) a Baptist minister and writer, born in Beaufort, South Carolina, in 1808. He became pastor of a Baptist church in Baltimore in 1847.

Fuller, (THOMAS,) an eminent English divine and author, born at Aldwinckle, in Northamptonshire, in 1608. Having graduated at Cambridge in 1628, he obtained the prebend of Salisbury, and was rector of Broad Windsor. About 1641 he removed to London and became minister of the Savoy. He favoured the cause of Charles I. in the civil war, and served as chaplain in the royal army, 1644-46. He was rector of Waltham, in Essex, from 1648 to 1658, and at the restoration, 1660, was appointed chaplain-extraordinary to Charles II. Died in 1661. His writings abound with quaint humour and conceits, and are much admired for originality, wit, and liberality. Among his principal works are a "History of the Holy War," (1639;) "The Holy and Profane State: a Collection of Characters, Moral Essays, and Lives, Ancient, Foreign, and Domestic," (1642;) "Good Thoughts in Bad Times," (1645;) "Good Thoughts in Worse Times," (1647;) "The Church History of Britain from the Birth of Christ to 1648," (1655;) and a "History of the Worthies of England," (1662.) "Fuller was," says S. T. Coleridge, "incomparably the most sensible, the least prejudiced, great man of an age that boasted of a galaxy of great men."

See ARTHUR T. RUSSELL, "Memorials of the Life and Writings of Thomas Fuller," 1844; HENRY ROGERS, "Essay on the Life and Writings of Thomas Fuller," vol. i.; "Retrospective Review," vol. iii., 1821, and vol. i., 2d series.

Fullerton, fōōl′ler-tọn, (Lady GEORGIANA Leveson Gower—commonly pronounced lew′sọn gōr,) a popular

English novelist, a daughter of Earl Granville, was born about 1814. She wrote "Ellen Middleton," (3 vols., 1844,) and "Grantley Manor," (1847.) She was married to Captain Alexander Fullerton in 1833.

Fullonius. See FOULON.

Fulton, fōol'tọn, (ROBERT,) a celebrated American engineer and inventor, was born in Little Britain, Lancaster county, Pennsylvania, in 1765. About the age of seventeen he went to Philadelphia, and began to cultivate a talent for drawing and portrait-painting, which he practised with skill and profit for three or four years. In 1786 he visited London, where he devoted several years to the same profession, under the tuition of Benjamin West, who received him as an inmate into his own house. He next resided for two years in Devonshire, and became acquainted with the Duke of Bridgewater and Lord Stanhope. About this time his mechanical genius impelled him to abandon painting and to follow the profession of civil engineer. In 1793 he was engaged in a project to improve inland navigation, having already conceived the idea of using steam as a motive power. He invented a machine for spinning flax, and another for making ropes, for which he obtained patents in England. In 1796 he published in London a "Treatise on Canal Navigation." From 1797 to 1804 he resided in Paris, in the family of Joel Barlow, where he displayed his characteristic enterprise and ingenuity in various projects and inventions and in the study of the sciences and modern languages. He was the proprietor of the first panorama exhibited in Paris. He invented a submarine or plunging boat, called a torpedo, designed to be used in naval warfare, and induced Bonaparte to appoint Volney, La Place, and Monge as a commission to examine it. In 1801 he made an experiment in the harbour of Brest, when he succeeded in remaining under water for an hour and in guiding the boat with ease. Other trials were made, with partial success, at the expense of the French government; but, as they at last declined to patronize the project, Fulton accepted, in 1804, an invitation from the English ministry, who also appointed a commission and made trials of his torpedo. It appears, however, that the English did not give him much encouragement; for in 1806 he returned to New York. Here, in co-operation with Robert Livingston, Esq., he succeeded, in 1807, in perfecting the great discovery of steam navigation. Though others had previously conceived the idea of steam navigation, Fulton is admitted to have been the first who successfully realized it. In 1807 his first boat, the Clermont, was launched at New York, and the trial was so successful that it excited great admiration, and steamboats were rapidly multiplied on the American rivers. The Clermont made regular passages between New York and Albany, at the rate of five miles an hour; but this rate was soon increased by improved machinery. Several other larger boats were built under the direction of Fulton, who expended large sums of money in this way, though he received nothing for his patent. In 1806 he married Harriet, daughter of Walter Livingston, by whom he had four children. He possessed great personal dignity, agreeable manners, and noble qualities of heart. In the midst of his triumph, and in the height of prosperity, he died in New York, in February, 1815.

See RENWICK, "Life of Fulton," in SPARKS'S "American Biography," vol. x.; also COLDEN, "Life of Fulton," 1817; MONT-GÉRY, "Notice sur la Vie et les Travaux de R. Fulton," 1825; "Encyclopædia Americana;" "Life of Robert Fulton," by J. F. REIGART, 1856; "National Portrait-Gallery of Distinguished Americans," vol. iii.

Ful'vi-a, [Fr. FULVIE, fül've',] a Roman lady, noted for intrigue and ambition, was the wife of Clodius the demagogue, who was killed by Milo. She afterwards became the wife of Mark Antony, the famous triumvir, and showed a vindictive spirit in the proscription of those whom she disliked. During the civil war that followed the death of Julius Cæsar she had great power in Rome, and instigated an unsuccessful revolt against Octavius, her son-in-law. Died in 40 B.C.

Fulvie. See FULVIA.

Ful'vi-us, (MARCUS NOBILIOR,) a Roman general, was prætor in Spain in 193 B.C., and defeated the Tectones and Celtiberians near Toletum, (Toledo.) Having been elected consul in 189 B.C., he obtained command in

Greece, where he captured Ambracia and dictated terms of peace to the Ætolians. In 179 B.C. he was chosen censor, and, from patriotic motives, was reconciled to Æmilius Lepidus, his enemy and colleague. He was a patron of Ennius the poet.

Fulvius Flaccus. See FLACCUS, (M. FULVIUS.)

Fulwell, fōol'wel, (ULPIAN,) an English writer, born in 1556, became rector of Naunton. He wrote the "Flower of Fame," a historical work, (1575,) and the "Art of Flattery," (1579.)

Fumagalli, foo-mä-gâl'lee, (ANGELO,) an Italian historian and monk, born in Milan in 1728, became superior of the monastery of Saint Ambrose, and was noted for his various erudition and the elegance and purity of his style. He wrote a work called "Diplomatic Institutes," ("Delle Istituzioni diplomatiche," 1802,) which was highly esteemed, and treatises "On the Antiquities of Milan," and "The Origin of Idolatry." He was one of the first members of the Italian Institute. Died in 1804.

See TIRABOSCHI, "Storia della Letteratura Italiana;" "Nouvelle Biographie Générale."

Fumani, foo-mä'nee, (ADAMO,) an Italian poet, born at Verona, became a canon in the cathedral of that city. He was chosen secretary of the Council of Trent about 1546. He wrote, in Latin, "Logices Libri quinque," a poetical treatise on logic, in which the rules of that art are explained with admirable clearness and elegance, besides other short poems. Died in 1587.

See TIRABOSCHI, "Storia della Letteratura Italiana."

Fumée, fü'mâ', (ADAM,) born in Touraine, in France, about 1430, was physician to Charles VII., and afterwards to Louis XI. Died in 1494.

Fumiani, foo-me-ä'nee, (GIOVANNI ANTONIO,) an Italian painter, born at Venice in 1633; died in 1710.

Fumicelli, foo-me-chel'lee, or **Fiumicelli,** fe-oo-me-chel'lee, (LUDOVICO,) a painter of the Venetian school, born at Treviso, flourished in 1536.

Funccius. See FUNCK.

Funck, fŏonk, or **Funch,** fŏonk, [Lat. FUNC'CIUS,] (JOHANN,) a German theologian, born near Nuremberg in 1518, was a son-in-law of Osiander, whose doctrines he adopted. He became chaplain to Duke Albert of Prussia, and wrote, besides other works, a Chronology from the Creation to 1560. He was executed at Königsberg in 1566, on a charge of treason or sedition.

Funck or **Funk,** [Lat. FUNC'CIUS,] (JOHANN NICOLAS,) a German philologist, born at Marburg in 1693. He became professor of eloquence and history at Rinteln about 1730, and wrote, in Latin, seven able treatises on the origin, growth, and decadence of the Latin language, among which are "On the Childhood of the Latin Language," ("De Pueritia Latinæ Linguæ," 1720,) and "On the Maturity of the Latin Language," ("De Virili Ætate Latinæ Linguæ," 1727.) Died in 1777.

See HIRSCHING, "Historisch-literarisches Handbuch."

Funck, (KARL WILHELM FERDINAND,) a German writer and officer, born at Brunswick in 1761, served against the French on the Rhine, and in 1810 became lieutenant-general. He published in 1820 "Pictures from the Age of the Crusades." He was also a contributor with Schiller and Goethe to the "Horen." Died in 1828.

Funes, foo'nĕs, (GREGORIO,) a historian, born at Córdova, in South America. He became dean of the church of Córdova, and wrote a "History of Paraguay, Buenos Ayres, and Tucuman," (3 vols., 1816 et seq.,) which is commended. Died about 1820.

Funke, fŏon'keh, (KARL PHILIPP,) a German naturalist, born in 1752. He wrote "Natural History and Technology," (3 vols., 1791,) and other works. Died in 1807.

Furetière, für'te-air', (ANTOINE,) a French writer, born in Paris in 1620, became Abbé of Chalivoy. He was chosen a member of the French Academy in 1662. In his "Bourgeois Romance" ("Roman bourgeois," 1666) he satirized the manners of the middle or inferior class; he also wrote "The Voyage of Mercury," a satire in verse, (1673.) Having undertaken to compile a Dictionary of the French language while that of the Academy

ε as k; ç as s; g hard; g as j; G, H, K, guttural; N, nasal; R, trilled; s as z; th as in this. (☞See Explanations, p. 23.)

62

was in progress, he was accused of plagiarism, and expelled from the Academy, in 1685. He died in 1688. His Dictionary was published in 1690, and was received with favour.

See "Fureteriana," 1696; MADAME DE SÉVIGNÉ, "Lettres," and "Ménagiana."

Furgault, für'gō', (NICOLAS,) a French professor, born in 1706, published a "Dictionary of Greek and Roman Antiquities," (1768.) Died in 1795.

Furgole, für'gol',(JEAN BAPTISTE,)an eminent French jurist, born at Castelferrus in 1690, practised at Toulouse with success. He published "Ordonnance de Louis XV pour fixer la Jurisprudence sur les Donations," (1733,) and a "Treatise on Wills, Codicils, and Donations," (4 vols., 1745,) which was one of the most complete works on that subject. Died in 1761.

See BERNADEAU, "Vies, Portraits et Parallèles des Jurisconsultes Domat, Furgole et Pothier," 1798.

Furies, [Lat. FURIÆ.] See EUMENIDES.

Furietti, foo-re-et'tee, (GIUSEPPE ALESSANDRO,) an Italian antiquary, born at Bérgamo in 1685. After making great progress in the study of law and theology, he removed to Rome, where he obtained preferment, and at the age of seventy-four was made a cardinal. He wrote an able treatise on the "History of the Mosaic Art," ("De Pictoriæ Mosaicæ Artis Origine," 1752,) and a few other works. Died about 1762.

Furini, foo-ree'nee, (FRANCESCO,) an Italian painter, born at Florence in 1600. His works are highly commended. Died in 1649.

See LANZI, "History of Painting in Italy."

Fu'rĭ-us, [Sp. pron. foo're-ooss,] (FEDERICO,) surnamed SERIOLANUS, a moralist, born in Valencia, Spain, about 1510. Charles V. appointed him historian to his son Philip II., by whom he was employed in the public affairs of the Low Countries. Furius published a treatise on Rhetoric, (1544;) also "The Counsel and Counsellor," ("Del Consejo y Consejero," 1559.) He is favourably noticed by De Thou, who ranks him with Montaigne. Died in 1592.

See DE THOU, "Historia sui Temporis;" N. ANTONIO, "Bibliotheca Hispana Nova."

Fu'rĭ-us, (MARCUS,) surnamed BIBAC'ULUS, a Latin satirical poet, born at Cremona about 102 B.C. He began a poem on the Gallic War by a line which represents Jupiter as spitting snow upon the Alps,—which Horace parodied in his fifth satire (book ii.) by substituting the name of Furius for Jupiter :

"Furius hybernas cana nive conspuet Alpes."[*]

Small fragments of his works are all that now remain.

Furlanetto, foor-lå-net'to, (BONAVENTURA,) distinguished as a composer of sacred music, was born at Venice in 1738. He composed "The Vow of Jephthah," "The Spouse of the Canticles," and other oratorios. Died in 1817.

Für'long, (THOMAS,) an Irish poet and satirist, born about 1792, was the son of a farmer. In his early youth he was employed in the shop of a merchant of Dublin. He published in 1819 or 1820 "The Misanthrope," a poem. Among his best works is "The Plagues of Ireland," (1824.) Died in 1827.

Furneaux, für'nō', (PHILIP,) an English dissenting minister, born at Totness, in Devonshire, in 1726. He was lecturer at Clapham, in Surrey, for twenty-three years, (1753-76.) He wrote "Letters to Judge Blackstone on his Exposition of the Toleration Act," (1793.) Died in 1783.

Für'ness, (WILLIAM HENRY,) D.D., a Unitarian divine and author, born in Boston in 1802. He graduated at Harvard in 1820, and afterwards studied for the ministry in the theological school of that institution. In 1825 he became pastor of the First Unitarian Congregational Church in Philadelphia. As a public preacher, he early distinguished himself by his zealous and unwavering opposition to the iniquities of slavery. Among his religious publications the most important are his "Remarks on the Four Gospels," (1836,) "Jesus and his Biographers," (1838,) "History of Jesus," (1850,) and "Thoughts on the Life and Character of Jesus of Nazareth," (1859.) For a critique on Dr. Furness's pe-

culiar views respecting the character of Christ, etc., see "North American Review" for October, 1850, (vol. lxxi.).

Dr. Furness is distinguished for his fine taste and high literary culture. He has made some admirable translations from the German, among which that of Schiller's "Das Lied der Glocke" ("The Song of the Bell") deserves particular mention, as being the best English version that has ever appeared of that exquisite poem.

His son, WILLIAM H. FURNESS, born in 1827, acquired a high reputation as a portrait-painter. Died in 1867.

See TUCKERMAN, "Book of the Artists."

Furrer, foor'rer, (JONAS,) a Swiss statesman, born at Winterthur in 1805.

Fürst, fürst, (JULIUS,) a German Orientalist, born of a Jewish family, in the duchy of Posen, in 1805, studied theology at Halle. He published, besides other works, a "History of the Jews in Asia," (1849,) and a "Hebrew-Chaldee Dictionary," (1851.)

Fürst, fürst, (WALTER,) a Swiss patriot, born at Altorf, lived about 1300. He co-operated with William Tell in the liberation of his country.

Fürstemberg, fürst'em-bĕrG', or **Fuerstenberg,** fürst'en-bĕrG', (FERDINAND,) a German prelate, born at Bilstein, Westphalia, in 1626, was distinguished for liberality and other virtues. He became Bishop of Paderborn in 1661, and Bishop of Münster in 1678. He published Latin poems, which are commended, and "Monuments of Paderborn," ("Monumenta Paderbornensia," 1669.) Died in 1683.

See ERSCH und GRUBER, "Allgemeine Encyklopaedie."

Furstenau, foor'stęh-now', (JOHANN HERMANN,) a German physician, born at Herford, in Westphalia, in 1688. He obtained the chair of medicine at Rinteln about 1720. He wrote many valuable medical works, among which is "Desiderata Medica," (1727.) Died in 1756.

See JÖCHER, "Allgemeines Gelehrten-Lexikon."

Fürstenberg, fürst'en-bĕrG', (FRIEDRICH WILHELM FRANZ,) BARON, a German statesman, born in 1729, was minister to Maximilian Frederick, Elector of Cologne. He founded the University of Münster, and introduced important reforms into the government. Died in 1810.

Furtado, foor-tå'do, (FRANCISCO,) a Portuguese poet, born in 1740; died in Italy after 1816.

Fuscus. See FOSCO.

Fus'cus, (AREL'LIUS,) a Latin rhetorician, flourished in the reign of Augustus.

Fuscus, (ARIS'TIUS,) a Latin poet, lived about 30 B.C. He was a friend of Horace, who addressed to him an epistle and an ode.

Fuseli, fū'sęh-le, or **Fuessli,** (JOHN HENRY,) a celebrated historical painter, born at Zurich about 1742, was the son of Johann Caspar Füssli, noticed below. His family name was changed to Fuseli by the subject of this article. Having gained distinction by his classic acquirements and by his poetical genius, he visited England in 1763. Sir Joshua Reynolds, on seeing some drawings of Fuseli, persuaded him to prefer the profession of painter to that of author. Between 1770 and 1778 he studied art in Italy, choosing Michael Angelo for his model, and in the latter year returned to London, where he speedily rose to the first rank of British painters. He was partial to the romantic style, and found congenial subjects in the most imaginative dramas of Shakspeare. In 1788 he married Sophia Rawlins, and was chosen an associate of the Royal Academy. He assisted Cowper in translating Homer. He was chosen professor of painting in the Royal Academy in 1799. His Lectures on Art are much admired, and have been published. Among his master-pieces are eight pictures of the "Shakspeare Gallery," and illustrations of Dante and Milton. His imagination was lofty and rich, but rather extravagant. "Of all the painters whom this country has encouraged," says Allan Cunningham, "no one had either the reach of thought or the poetic feeling of Fuseli." He published "Aphorisms on Art," and other works, which are highly prized. Died in London in 1825.

See "Life and Works of Fuseli," by JOHN KNOWLES, 3 vols., 1831; CUNNINGHAM, "Lives of Painters and Sculptors;" "Edinburgh Review" for July, 1803, and September, 1831.

---

[*] Furius will bespit the wintry Alps with white snow."

ā, ē, ī, ō, ū, ȳ, *long;* à, è, ò, same, less prolonged; ă, ĕ, ĭ, ŏ, ŭ, ў, *short;* ą, ę, į, ǫ, *obscure;* fär, fåll, fät; mĕt; nŏt; gōōd; mōōn;

Fusi, fü′ze′, (ANTOINE,) a Frenchman, born in Lorraine about 1565. He became a doctor of the Sorbonne, in Paris. Having been charged with sorcery and heresy, and persecuted, he retired to Geneva about 1618, adopted the Protestant religion, and became a minister. He wrote a book against the Jesuits, called "Le franc Archier de la vraie Église contre la A'bus de la fausse," (1619.) Died about 1635.

See NICÉRON, "Mémoires."

Fusina, foo-see′nä, (ANDREA,) an excellent Italian sculptor, of the Milanese school, flourished about 1490. He adorned the cathedral of Milan with bas-reliefs.

See TICOZZI, "Dizionario."

Fuss, von, fon fööss, (NIKOLAUS,) a Swiss mathematician, born at Bâle in 1755. He removed to Saint Petersburg in his youth, and was appointed adjunct professor in the Academy of Sciences in 1776. He obtained the dignity of councillor of state in 1800. He wrote many mathematical treatises. Died in 1826.

Füssli or **Fuessli,** füs′lee, (HANS HEINRICH,) a Swiss writer on art, born at Zurich in 1745, was a son of Johann Rudolph. He was distinguished for learning and eloquence. In 1802 he was chosen senator. He published, among other works, "The Life and Works of Raphael Sanzio," (1815.) Died in 1832.

See BROCKHAUS, "Conversations-Lexikon."

Füssli or **Fuessli,** (JOHANN CASPAR,) a Swiss artist and author, born at Zurich in 1707, excelled in landscapes and portraits. He wrote two esteemed works, viz., a "History of the Best Painters of Switzerland," (4 vols., 1769–79,) and a "Descriptive Catalogue (or Catalogue Raisonné) of the Best Engravers and of their Works," (1771.) He was the father of the celebrated John Henry Fuseli. Died in 1781.

Füssli or **Fuessli,** (JOHANN CASPAR,) a Swiss naturalist, son of the preceding, born at Zurich in 1745. He published a "Catalogue of Swiss Insects," (1775,) "Archives of the History of Insects," (1781–86,) and several other works. Died in 1786.

Füssli or **Fuessli,** (JOHANN CONRAD,) a Swiss author, born at Zurich or Wetzlar about 1705, spent many years in teaching school. He published several esteemed works, among which are "Historical Memoirs of the Reformation in Switzerland," (5 vols., 1741–53,) a "Description of Switzerland," (4 vols., 1770,) and a "History of the Mediæval Church," (3 vols., 1770–74.) Died in 1775.

See MEUSEL, "Gelehrtes Deutschland."

Füssli or **Fuessli,** (JOHANN RUDOLF,) a Swiss artist, born at Zurich in 1709, finished his studies in Paris. His reputation is founded chiefly on his "General Dictionary of Artists," in German, (1763–77.) This vast and excellent work was continued by his son, Hans Heinrich, and formed the basis of Nagler's "Allgemeines Künstler-Lexikon." Died in 1793.

Füssli or **Fuessli,** (JOHANN RUDOLF,) a painter and engraver, the eldest son of Johann Caspar, noticed above, was born at Zurich in 1737. He wrote an excellent work, entitled a "Catalogue (Raisonné) of Engravings executed after the Most Famous Artists of each School," (4 vols., 1806; unfinished.) Died in 1806.

Füssli or **Fuessli,** (MATTHIAS,) a skilful Swiss painter and engraver, born at Zurich in 1598, excelled in the representation of battles, conflagrations, and other terrible scenes. He also executed miniatures and frescos. Died in 1664.

Füssli or **Fuessli,** (MATTHIAS,) a Swiss portrait-painter, born in 1671; died in 1739.

Fust, (JOHANN.) See FAUST.

Futteh-Aly-Shah. See FATEH-ALEE-SHAH.

Fux or **Fuchs,** fööks, (JOHANN JOSEPH,) a German composer, born in Styria in 1660. He was successively chapel-master to the emperors Leopold I., Joseph I., and Charles VI. He composed operas and sacred music, and a treatise on music, entitled "Gradus ad Parnassum," (1725,) which is called a classic work. He was living in 1732.

See FÉTIS, "Biographie Universelle des Musiciens."

Fuzelier, füz′le-à′, (LOUIS,) a French dramatist, born in Paris about 1672, wrote numerous operas and plays of little merit. His "Momus fabuliste" is called his best piece. Died in 1752.

Fyens, fi′ēns, (THOMAS,) a Flemish physician, born in Antwerp in 1567. He became professor of medicine in Louvain in 1593. His chief work is a critical essay on eminent surgeons and their discoveries, "De Artis Chirurgicæ Controversis," (1649.) Died in 1631.

Fyot de la Marche, fe′o′ deh lä märsh, (CLAUDE,) a French priest, born at Dijon in 1630, was appointed in 1651 almoner of Louis XIV. In 1661 he became abbot of Saint-Étienne-de-Dijon, of which he wrote a history, (1696.) Died in 1721.

Fyrouz. See FYROZ.

Fyroz or **Feroze,** fee′rōz′, (written also **Ferose, Firoz, Fyrouz, Feyrouz,** and **Firuz,**) a Persian word, signifying "victorious," and forming the name of several kings ruling in Persia and Hindostan.

Fyroz I., King of Persia, son of Valas, is supposed to have been the same as the Pacorus mentioned by certain Greek and Latin authors. He succeeded his father in 83 A.D. As he was preparing to resist a Roman army which invaded his kingdom, he died, about 107, and was succeeded by his brother, Chosroes I.

Fyroz (Feroze, Fyrouz, or **Firuz) II.,** King of Persia, of the Sassanide dynasty, was the son of Yezdejerd II. He began to reign about 457, having put to death his brother Hormooz, who had reigned a short time. He made war on the Huns, by whom he was defeated and killed in battle about 488 A.D.

See FIRDOUSEE, "Shah-Namah;" MALCOLM, "History of Persia."

Fyroz (Feroze or **Firouz) Shah I.,** surnamed RŌŌKN-ED-DEEN (or ROKN-EDDÎN or -EDDYN,) (the "Support of the Faith,") a Moslem sovereign of India, began to reign in 1236 at Delhi. He abandoned himself to indolent pleasures, and in the same year was deposed, and succeeded by his sister. Fyroz died or was killed shortly after his disgrace.

Fyroz (Feroze or **Fyrouz) Shah II.,** Mohammedan King of Delhi, usurped the throne in 1289, after assassinating the late king, Kai Kobâd. His cruelty provoked a conspiracy, which deprived him of his throne and life about 1295.

Fyroz Shah III., Mohammedan King of Delhi or Hindostan, succeeded his uncle, Mohammed III., in 1351. He adopted a pacific policy, built the city of Fyroz-âbâd, and made several canals, and many other internal improvements, including mosques and schools. He abdicated in favour of his son in 1387, and died the next year, aged ninety.

See BRIGGS's translation of FERISHTA's "History of India."

Fyt or **Feydt,** fît, (JAN,) a Flemish painter of still life, born at Antwerp in 1625. He excelled in the representation of animals, flowers, fruits, etc. His design is correct, his colouring true, and his touch light. He is supposed to have died in 1671.

See DESCAMPS, "Vie des Peintres Flamands," etc.

G.

Gaab, gåp, (JOHANN FRIEDRICH,) a German Protestant theologian, born at Göppingen in 1761. He became professor at Tübingen in 1798, and afterwards general superintendent, or bishop. He wrote commentaries on the Scriptures. Died in 1832.

See ERSCH und GRUBER, "Allgemeine Encyklopaedie."

Gaal, gål, (BAREND,) a Dutch painter of landscapes and battle-pieces, born at Haarlem, was a pupil of Wouwerman. Died about 1670.

Gaal, gål, (JOSEPH,) a Hungarian comic poet and novelist, born at Nagy Karoly in 1811. He represents with fidelity the manners and language of the peasants.

Gabaret, gȧ'bȧ'rȧ', (——,) a brave French naval officer, who served many years in the reign of Louis XIV., and obtained the rank of commodore. He commanded the rear-guard at La Hogue, (1692,) and repulsed the English force which attacked Martinique in 1693. Died in 1693.

Gabbema, gåb'beh-må, (SIMON ABBAS,) a Dutch philologist, born at Leeuwarden about 1620, wrote a "History of Friesland," (1703,) and edited several Latin classics. Died about 1700.

Gabbiani, gåb-be-ȧ'nee, (ANTONIO DOMENICO,) an eminent historical painter and engraver, born in Florence in 1652. He studied in Rome and Venice, excelled in design, and was employed to decorate the churches and palaces of Florence, in which he opened a school and had many pupils. Among his works, which are much praised, is "The Dance of the Genii." Died in 1726.

See HUGFORD, "Vita di Antonio Domenico Gabbiani," 1762; LANZI, "History of Painting in Italy."

Gabelchover, gå'bel-ko'ver, (OSWALD,) a German physician and historical writer, born at Tübingen in 1538; died in 1616.

Gabelentz, von der, fon der gå'beh-lĕnts', (HANS CONON,) a German philologist, born at Altenburg in 1807. He published "Éléments de la Grammaire Mandschoue," (1833,) and "Philological Contributions," ("Beiträge zur Sprachenkunde," 1852.)

Gabelsberger, gå'bels-bĕR'ger, (FRANZ XAVER,) a German, who produced an improved method of stenography, was born at Munich in 1789. He published, besides other works, an "Introduction to Stenography," (1834.) Died in 1849.

Ga-bin'I-us, (AULUS,) a profligate Roman politician, was elected tribune in 66 B.C., (685 A.U.C.) He was the author of the famous Gabinian law, which gave Pompey the conduct of the war against the pirates. Having become consul in 58 B.C., he promoted the banishment of Cicero, and, at the end of his consulship, obtained command in Syria. About the year 56 he invaded Egypt, against the will of the senate, and restored Ptolemy to the throne. He was tried for treason, and acquitted, but was condemned to perpetual banishment for extortion, (de repetundis,) although Cicero made an oration in his defence. He died in 48 or 47 B.C.

See DION CASSIUS, books xxxix. and xliii.; DRUMANN, "Geschichte Roms."

Gabio, gå'be-o, or **Gabia, gå'be-å,** (GIOVANNI BATTISTA,) an Italian Hellenist, born at Verona, became professor of Greek in Rome. He translated into Latin the works of Sophocles, (1543,) and other Greek classics. Died in Rome about 1590.

Gabiot, gå'be'o', (JEAN LOUIS,) a French dramatist, born at Salins in 1759, lived chiefly in Paris, and wrote numerous comedies. Died in 1811.

Gabler, gåp'ler, (GEORG ANDREAS,) born at Altdorf in 1786, succeeded Hegel as professor of philosophy at Berlin. He published a "System of Theoretical Philosophy," (1827,) and a work entitled "The Philosophy of Hegel," (1843.)

Gabler, (JOHANN PHILIPP,) a learned German theologian, father of the preceding, was born at Frankfort-on-the-Main in 1753. He became professor of philosophy at Altdorf in 1785, and first professor of theology at Jena

in 1812. He wrote, besides other works, an "Essay on the Hermeneutics of the New Testament," (1788,) and an "Essay on the Mosaic History of the Creation," (1795.) Died in 1826.

See SCHROETER, "Erinnerungen an Gabler," 1827.

Gabotto. See CABOT.

Gå'brĭ-el, a Syrian physician, who practised at Bagdâd. He became chief physician to the Caliph Haroun-al-Raschid, with whom he had much influence, and to his successor, Alameen, (Alamîn.) He wrote several medical treatises. Died in 829 A.D.

Gabriel, gå'bRe'ĕl', (JACQUES,) a French architect, born in Paris in 1667. He erected the Hôtels-de-Ville of Rennes and Dijon, and designed the great sewer of Paris. He became architect to the king, chief engineer of bridges, etc. Died in 1742.

Gabriel, (JACQUES ANGE,) an eminent French architect, son of the preceding, born in Paris about 1710. He was employed by Louis XV. on the principal public works of his reign, among which was the restoration or completion of the Louvre. He designed the two colonnades which border the Place de la Concorde, and which were finished about 1772. The Military School of Paris is called his master-piece. Died in 1782.

See FONTENAY, "Dictionnaire des Artistes."

Gå'brĭ-el SIONI'TA or "THE SIONITE," a learned Maronite, born at Edden, on Mount Lebanon, was educated at Rome. In 1614 he removed to Paris, where he was chosen professor of Arabic in the College of France. He published an Arabic Grammar, and edited or translated into Latin the Arabic and Syrian texts of the Polyglot Bible of Le Jay. Died in 1648.

See ZENKER, "Bibliotheca Orientalis."

Gabriel de Chinon, gå'bRe'ĕl' deh she'nŏN', a French monk, went as a missionary, about 1640, to Ispahân. He died at Malabar in 1670, leaving a "Treatise on the Religion, Customs, etc. of the Persians and Armenians," (1671.)

Gabrielli, gå-bRe-el'lee, (CANTE,) an Italian condottiere and chief of the Guelph party. He served under Charles de Valois, and became Podesta of Florence about 1300. He banished Dante and others.

Gabrielli, (CATARINA,) a famous Italian singer, born in Rome in 1730. In 1747 she made her début as prima donna in the opera with complete success. She also performed with great applause at Naples, Vienna, and Saint Petersburg, and made a fortune rapidly. Having accepted an invitation from Catherine II. of Russia, she asked a salary of ten thousand roubles; but the empress objected that she did not pay her field-marshals so much. "Very well," replied Gabrielli: "your majesty may employ the field-marshals to sing." She had a voice of prodigious compass. Died in 1796.

See FÉTIS, "Biographie Universelle des Musiciens."

Gabrielli, (GIACOMO,) a son of Cante, noticed above, obtained the dictatorship or chief power at Florence in 1336. He was a tyrannical ruler. In 1338 he was appointed a senator of Rome by the pope. He received the title of captain (capitano) in 1352, and became governor of Florence in 1357. His son CANTE was Podesta or Captain of Florence about 1380.

Gabrielli, (GIULIO,) a cardinal, born in Rome in 1748. In 1808 Pope Pius VII. appointed him secretary of state. A few months later, he was arrested by the French and banished. Died in 1822.

Gabriello, gå-bRe-el'lo, (ONOFRIO,) an Italian painter of high reputation, born at Messina in 1616, painted portraits and easel-pictures at Venice and Messina. Died in 1706.

Gabrini or **Gabrino,** (NICCOLÒ.) See RIENZI.

Gabrini, gå-bRee'nee, (TOMMASO MARIA,) an Italian mathematician, born at Rome in 1726; died in 1807.

Gacé, de, deh gå'så', (CHARLES AUGUSTE de Matignon—deh mȧ'tèn'yŏN',) COUNT, a French general, born in Paris in 1646, distinguished himself at the sieges of Mons and Namur, and was made lieutenant-general in 1693. In 1708 he obtained the rank of marshal of France, and commanded an army which made an abortive attempt to aid the Pretender in obtaining the British crown. Died in 1729.

Gace Brulez, gȧss brü′là′, sometimes called **Gaste Blé,** a French poet of superior merit, flourished about 1220–50.

See LONGFELLOW's "Poets and Poetry of Europe."

Gachart or **Gachard,** gȧ′shȧR′, (LOUIS PROSPER,) archivist of Belgium, was born in Paris about 1800. He was naturalized as a Belgian citizen in 1831, and was appointed keeper of the Belgian archives. He published the "Correspondence of William the Silent," (4 vols., 1847–51,) and other documents for the history of the Netherlands.

See PRESCOTT, "History of Philip II.," vol. ii. book iii.; "Edinburgh Review" for January, 1868.

Gaches, gȧsh, (JACQUES,) a French advocate, born at Castres in 1558. He wrote Memoirs of events which occurred between 1555 and 1610. Died in 1612.

Gaches, (RAYMOND,) a French Protestant and eloquent preacher, grandson of the preceding, was born at Castres about 1619; died at Paris in 1668.

Gacon, gȧ′kôN′, (FRANÇOIS,) a French satirical poet, born at Lyons in 1667. He made a disgraceful use of his talents, and attacked the most eminent authors,—among others, Boileau and Bossuet. He produced a French version of Anacreon, (2 vols., 1712,) besides satires, odes, and other poems. Died in 1725.

Gacon-Dufour, gȧ′kôN′ dü′fooR′, (MARIE ARMANDE JEANNE,) a French authoress, born in Paris in 1753, was first known as Madame d'Humière. Dufour was the name of her second husband. Died in 1835.

Gadd, gȧd, (PETER ANTON,) a Swedish chemist and botanist, lived about 1760. He wrote, besides other works, one "On the Diseases of Plants," ("De Morbis Plantarum," 1748.)

Gaddesden, gȧdz′den, (JOHN OF,) an English physician of the fourteenth century, attended Edward II., and was the first native physician employed at the English court.

Gaddi, gȧd′dee, (ANGELO or AGNOLO,) a famous painter, born at Florence about 1324, was a son and pupil of Taddeo, noticed below. He painted in fresco and oil, and was a good colorist, but not equal to his father in expression. His chief work in fresco is a "History of the True Cross," in the church of Santa Croce, Florence. His Madonna in the church of Saint Ambrose is called his best work. He removed to Venice, and enriched himself by commerce. Died in 1387.

See VASARI, "Lives of the Painters."

Gaddi, (GADDO,) an Italian painter, born in Florence about 1240, was a pupil of Cimabue. He excelled in design and in mosaics. He was employed by Pope Clement V. to adorn the basilica of Saint Peter's and the church of Santa Maria Maggiore. Died in 1312.

See VASARI, "Lives of the Painters."

Gaddi, (TADDEO,) a Florentine painter and architect, son of the preceding, was born at Florence in 1300. He surpassed his father, and was the most eminent pupil of Giotto. His first works were frescos painted in the church of Santa Croce of Florence, the subjects of which were taken from the New Testament. He excelled in expression, and was probably the best painter of his time. Among his chief works is "The Virgin surrounded by Saints." He built a bridge over the Arno, called Ponte Vecchio. Died about 1360.

See VASARI, "Lives of the Painters;" LANZI, "History of Painting in Italy."

Gade, gȧ′deh, (NIELS WILHELM,) a Danish musician, born at Copenhagen in 1817. He composed symphonies, overtures, sonatas, etc., succeeded Mendelssohn as director of the concerts at Leipsic, and was appointed master of the royal chapel at Copenhagen about 1850.

Gadebusch, gȧ′deh-bōōsh′, (FRIEDRICH KONRAD,) a German writer, born in the island of Rügen in 1719, published several valuable works on the history and literature of Livonia and the adjacent provinces. He lived many years at Dorpat, where he died in 1788.

See ERSCH und GRUBER, "Allgemeine Encyklopaedie."

Ga-de′lĭ-us, [Sw. pron. gȧ-dĭl′le-ùs,] (ERIK,) a Swedish physician, born at Stockholm in 1778, was chosen in 1823 president of the Academy of Sciences. He gained a prize offered in 1802 for a treatise on medical jurisprudence. Died in 1827.

Gads′den, (CHRISTOPHER,) an American patriot, born at Charleston, South Carolina, in 1724. He was a resolute and early advocate of the popular cause before the Revolution, and was a delegate to the first Continental Congress, which met in 1774. He served as an officer in the army in 1776, resigned his commission in 1779, and was taken prisoner at Charleston in August, 1780. Died in 1805.

Gadsden, (CHRISTOPHER EDWARDS,) an American bishop, a grandson of the preceding, was born in Charleston, South Carolina, in 1785. He became a bishop of the Episcopal Church in 1840. Died in 1852.

Gadsden, (JAMES,) an American politician, born in Charleston, South Carolina, in 1788, was a brother of the preceding. He served under General Jackson in the war against the Indians of Florida about 1818. He was sent on a mission to Mexico in 1853, and negotiated a treaty or convention which defined the boundary between the United States and Mexico. In accordance with this treaty, the United States paid Mexico ten million dollars for Arizona. Died in 1858.

Gaede, gȧ′deh, (HENDRIK MORITZ,) a Danish naturalist, born at Kiel in 1796. He wrote, besides other works, a "Treatise on the Anatomy of Insects," (1815.) Died in 1834.

Gaelen, van, vȧn gȧ′len, (ALEXANDER,) a Dutch painter, born in 1670, visited many courts of Germany, and finally settled in London. He distinguished himself by pictures of battles and of animals. Died in 1728.

See ERSCH und GRUBER, "Allgemeine Encyklopaedie;" DESCAMPS, "Vies des Peintres Flamands," etc.

Gaertner. See GÄRTNER.

Gaeta, DUKE OF. See GAUDIN.

Gaëtan, gȧ-à-tȧn′, or **Gaëtano,** gȧ-à-tȧ′no, (GIOVANNI,) an Italian pilot, who in 1542 made a voyage in the service of Spain to the Moluccas, and wrote a narrative of the discoveries made in that region.

Gaetano. See CAJETAN, (CARDINAL.)

Gaetano, (BENEDETTO.) See BONIFACE VIII.

Gaëtano, gȧ-à-tȧ′no, or **Gaëtani,** gȧ-à-tȧ′nee, (CESARE,) Count della Torre, an Italian poet and antiquary, born at Syracuse in 1718, was professor of moral philosophy in that city. He wrote a work on the "Antiquities of Syracuse," a poem called "The Duties of Man," ("I Doveri dell'Uomo," 1790,) and other works. Died in 1808.

Gaëtano, [Lat. CAIETA′NUS; Fr. GAËTAN, gȧ′à′tôN′,] SAINT, often called **Gaetano di Tiene** — gȧ-à-tȧ′no de te-ȧ′nà, an Italian priest, born at Vicenza in 1480. His father's name was Thieni or Tiene. With a view to reform the priests, he undertook, in 1524, to found a new order of monks, and obtained the sanction of Pope Clement VII. His friend Caraffa was chosen superior of the order, which took the name of Theatines and became numerous in Italy, Spain, and the Levant. One of the rules of this order forbade them to have private property or receive salaries, or to resort to begging for support. He died in 1547, and was canonized by the pope in 1675.

See CASTALDI, "Vita di S. Gaëtano," 1612; B. DESTUTT DE TRACY, "Vie de S. Gaëtan de Thienne," 1774; S. PEPE, "Vita del B. Gaëtano Tiene," 1656.

Gaffarel, gȧ′fȧ′rěl′, (JACQUES,) a French Orientalist and priest, born at Mannes in 1601. He became librarian to Cardinal Richelieu, and chaplain to the king. He wrote, besides other works, "Curiosities of the Talismanic Sculpture of the Persians," (1630,) and a "History of the Subterranean World," containing a "Description of Caves, Grottoes, Caverns," etc., (1666.) Died in 1681.

See ERSCH und GRUBER, "Allgemeine Encyklopaedie."

Gaffarelli, gȧf-fȧ-rel′lee, or **Caffarelli,** kȧf-fȧ-rel′lee. (GAETANO,) a celebrated Italian singer, born at Bari in 1703, was the son of a peasant named MAJORANO. He began his career in a Roman theatre as soprano. He

e as k; ç as s; ğ hard; ğ as j; G, H, K, guttural; N, nasal; R, trilled; ś as z; th as in this. (☞ See Explanations, p. 23.)

performed with success in the other cities of Italy and in London, which he visited in 1730. Having amassed a large fortune, he bought the dukedom of Santo Dorato. He had the reputation of being one of the most admirable vocalists of his time. Died in 1783.

Gaforio, gä-fo're-o, **Gafforio,** gäf-fo're-o, or **Gafori,** gä-fo'ree, sometimes written **Gafuri** or **Gafurio,** [Lat. GAFO′RIUS,] (FRANCHINO,) an eminent writer on music, born at Lodi, Italy, in 1451. He taught music at Naples, and was appointed chapel-master of Milan Cathedral in 1484. He wrote, besides other works on music, " Practice of Music," etc., (" Practica Musicæ, sive Musicæ Actiones," 1496.) His writings had much influence, and were cited by later writers as a high authority. Died about 1522.

See BURNEY, " History of Music;" FÉTIS, " Biographie Universelle des Musiciens."

Gaforius. See GAFORIO.

Gage, (THOMAS,) a missionary, born in Ireland or England. He studied with the Jesuits, became a monk, and spent many years as a missionary in Mexico between 1625 and 1637. After many adventures, he returned to London, abjured Catholicism, and published a "New Survey of the West Indies," (1648,) which had great success. He became rector of Deal, in Kent. Died in Jamaica in 1655.

Gage, (THOMAS,) a British general, who succeeded General Amherst in 1763 as commander of the British army in America. In 1774 he was appointed Governor of Massachusetts colony, and general-in-chief for the continent. In April, 1775, he sent an expedition to Concord to seize the colony's stores, and thus provoked the battle of Lexington, the first explosion of the Revolution. In the following May the Provincial Congress resolved that "no obedience was in future due to Gage, and that he ought to be guarded against as an inveterate enemy." According to Bancroft, "Gage was neither fit to reconcile nor subdue. By his mild temper and love of society he escaped personal enmities, but in earnest business he inspired neither confidence nor fear." He was recalled in 1775, and died in 1787.

Gä′ger, (WILLIAM,) an English poet and civilian, who entered Oxford University in 1574, was reputed the best dramatist of his time. He wrote "Ulysses Redux," and other tragedies.

Gagern, von, fon gä′gĕrn, (FRIEDRICH BALDUIN,) a general, born at Weilburg, in Nassau, in 1794, was a son of the following. He fought against the French in 1813 –15, and became a general in the Dutch army. Having taken command of the army of Baden in 1848, he was killed by the insurgents in April of that year.

See "Leben des General Gagern," by his brother HEINRICH WILHELM, 3 vols., 1856.

Gagern, von, (HANS CHRISTOPH ERNST,) BARON, a German statesman, born near Worms in 1766, was employed in several missions by the Prince of Orange, who appointed him prime minister in 1814. He represented the King of Holland at the Congress of Vienna in 1815. He was the author of a number of historical and political works. Died in 1852.

Gagern, von, (HEINRICH WILHELM AUGUST,)BARON, son of the preceding, was born at Baireuth in 1799. He studied at Jena, and afterwards filled several offices under the Grand Duke of Hesse-Darmstadt. He was elected in May, 1848, president of the Parliament or National Assembly which met at Frankfort. He was a very popular leader of the Liberal or constitutional party, and favoured the union of the German States on the basis of the exclusion of Austria. He became president of the council of ministers, or prime minister of the empire, in December, 1848. He resigned office in March, 1849, probably because his project to effect the unity of Germany was defeated by the refusal of the King of Prussia to accept the imperial crown. He has a high reputation for probity and patriotism.

See MAX DUNCKER, "H. von Gagern; biographische Skizze," 1850.

Gagern, von, (MAXIMILIAN,) a brother of the preceding, born at Weilburg in 1810, was in his youth a councillor of the Duke of Nassau. In 1848 he was a Liberal member of the Parliament of Frankfort.

Gages, de, deh gäzh, ? (JEAN BONAVENTURE DU-MONT,) COUNT, a Spanish general, born at Mons, in Hainault, in 1682. He fought for Philip V. of Spain in the war of the Spanish succession, 1701–12. Having obtained command of the Spanish army in Italy in 1742, he defeated the Austrians at Campo-Santo in 1743. His skilful manœuvres in the ensuing campaigns (1744–46) were highly applauded. He was appointed Viceroy of Navarre in 1748. His retreat from Campo-Freddo in 1746 was called by Rousseau the most brilliant manœuvre of that century. Died in 1753.

See LAVALLÉE, " Histoire d'Espagne."

Gagliardi, gäl-yaR′dee, (BERNARDINO,) an Italian painter, born at Città-di-Castello in 1609, was an imitator of Guido and the Caracci. Died in 1660.

See LANZI, " History of Painting in Italy."

Gagliardo, gäl-yaR′do, (ACHILLE,) an Italian Jesuit and writer, born at Padua about 1537; died in 1607.

Gagliuffi, gäl-yoof′fee, (MARCO FAUSTINO,) an improvisator, born at Ragusa in 1764; died in 1834.

Gagnæus or **Gagnée.** See GAGNI.

Gagni, gän′ye', or **Gagnée, de,** deh gän′yà', [Lat. GAGNÆ′US,] (JEAN,) a French theologian, born in or near Paris. He became rector of the University of Paris in 1531, and afterwards chief almoner and preacher to Francis I., who employed him to read and expound books to him during his repasts. Having obtained from the king an order which opened to him all the libraries of France, he examined and published many manuscripts, and by this means promoted the revival of learning. He wrote several learned works on theology, and "Commentaries on the Four Gospels," (1552.) Died in 1549.

Gagnier, gän′ye-à', (JEAN,) a French priest and eminent Orientalist, was born in Paris about 1670. He emigrated to England about 1700, and, having renounced the Roman Catholic religion, became professor of Hebrew and Arabic at Oxford. He published, besides other works, a Latin version of Abulfeda's " Life of Mahomet," (1723,) and a "Life of Mahomet," in French, (2 vols., 1732.) Died in 1740.

See QUÉRARD, " La France Littéraire."

Gaguin, gä′gǎn', (ROBERT,) a French historian, orator, and monk, was born near Béthune about 1425. He was chosen professor of rhetoric in the University of Paris in 1463, and was employed with credit in diplomatic missions by Louis XI., Charles VIII., and Louis XII. He wrote, besides other works, in Latin, " A History of the French (or Franks) from Pharamond to the Year 1499," which was praised by Erasmus for fidelity and other merits. Died in 1501.

See NICÉRON, " Mémoires."

Ga-hä′gan, ? (USHER,) an Irish scholar, translated into Latin verse Pope's " Essay on Criticism" and " Temple of Fame." He was executed at Tyburn, for clipping coin, in 1749.

Gahn, gän, (JOSEPH GOTTLIEB,) a Swedish mineralogist and chemist, born in 1745, was a pupil of Bergmann. He discovered that phosphorus is a component of bones, and made some improvements in the arts of mining and metallurgy. He was the first who obtained manganese in the metallic state, and discovered the primitive form of calcareous spar. Died in 1818.

See H. JAERTA, "Åminnelse-Tal öfver J. G. Gahn," 1832.

Gaichiés, gä′she-à', (JEAN,) a French priest, born at Condom in 1647, wrote " Maxims for the Ministry of the Pulpit," (1710.) Died in 1731.

Gail, gäl or gä′ye, (EDME SOPHIE **Garre**—gäR,) the wife of the following, was born at Melun in 1776. She was an admirable musical genius, and composed several operas, one of which, called "The Jealous Couple," was performed in Paris, in 1813, with brilliant success. She also produced several charming ballads. She separated from M. Gail soon after their marriage, (1794.) Died in 1819.

See FÉTIS, " Biographie Universelle des Musiciens."

Gail, (JEAN BAPTISTE,) a French Hellenist, born in Paris in 1755. In 1791 he obtained the chair of Greek literature in the College of France, where he taught with success about twenty years. He became a member of the Institute in 1809, and keeper of the Greek and Latin manuscripts in the Royal Library in 1815. He published, besides a Latin version of Thucydides, (5 vols., 1807,) a great number of editions and translations of the Greek authors, and a Greek grammar, (1798.) Died in 1829.

See "Nouvelle Biographie Générale."

Gail, (JEAN FRANÇOIS,) a French Hellenist, a son of the preceding, was born in Paris in 1795. He was a substitute of his father as professor in the College of France. He published an excellent edition of Hudson's "Geographi Græci Minores," (3 vols., 1826–31,) and other successful works. Died in 1845.

See QUÉRARD, "La France Littéraire."

Gail Hamilton. See DODGE, (MARY ABIGAIL.)

Gailhabaud, gå'lȧ'bō', (JULES,) a French archæologist, born at Lille in 1810. He published a valuable work entitled "Ancient and Modern Monuments," ("Monuments anciens et modernes," 4 vols., 1840–49,) and "Architecture of the Period from the Fifth to the Sixteenth Century," (1857.)

Gaillard, gȧ'yȧR', (GABRIEL HENRI,) a popular French historian, born at Ostel, in Picardy, in 1726. He was admitted into the Academy of Inscriptions in 1760, and published in 1766 a "History of Francis I.," (7 vols.) His capital work is a "History of the Rivalry between France and England," ("Histoire de la Rivalité de la France et de l'Angleterre," 11 vols., 1771–77,) which opened to him the doors of the French Academy in 1771. Among his numerous other works are a "History of the Rivalry between France and Spain," (8 vols., 1801 ;) a "Historical Dictionary," (6 vols., 1789–1804,) which forms part of the "Encyclopédie Méthodique ;" and a "Life of Malesherbes," (1805,) who was his friend. His principal merits as a writer are clearness, elegance, facility, and truthfulness. Died near Chantilly in 1806.

See QUÉRARD, "La France Littéraire ;" "Nouvelle Biographie Générale."

Gaillard, gȧ'yȧR', ? (JOHN ERNEST,) a musical composer, born at Zell about 1686, lived in London, and composed for the stage. Died in 1749.

Gaillard, de, deh gȧ'yȧR', (HONORÉ REYNAUD,) a French Jesuit, born at Aix in 1641, gained distinction as a pulpit orator. He became rector of the College of Paris, and confessor to the queen of James II. of England. Died in 1727.

See MORÉRI, "Dictionnaire Historique."

Gaillard de Lonjumeau, gȧ'yȧR' deh lòN'zhü'mō', a French ecclesiastic, became Bishop of Apt in 1673. He conceived the project of a great historical dictionary, for which he collected copious materials. The work was edited by his chaplain, Moréri, and published in 1674. Died in 1695.

Gaillardot, gȧ'yȧR'do', (CLAUDE ANTOINE,) a French naturalist and physician, born at Lunéville in 1774. He found in the vicinity of that town fossils of many huge reptiles. He wrote a "Memoir on the Fossils of the Mottled Sandstone," (1806,) and other works. Died in 1833.

Gaï'nas, a Goth, who became a Roman general and served under Stilicho in 395 A.D. Soon after that date he obtained the chief command of an army which Arcadius sent against Tribigild, another Gothic chief ; but, instead of fighting him, he formed a coalition with him and marched against Constantinople. Arcadius was alarmed, and negotiated with Gainas, who was admitted into the capital with his army and received the title of "master-general." His demand of liberty of worship for the Goths (who were Arians) provoked the Catholics, who massacred many of his army. Gainas retreated into Thrace, and was killed near the Danube by the Huns in 400 A.D.

See GIBBON, "History of the Decline and Fall of the Roman Empire."

Gaines, gänz, (EDMUND PENDLETON,) an American general, born in Culpepper county, Virginia, in 1777. He served as captain at Chrystler's Field, in November, 1813, and, having become brigadier-general, defended Fort Erie with success in 1814. Died in 1849.

See "National Portrait-Gallery of Distinguished Americans," vol. iv.

Gainsborough, gänz'bŭr-ẹh, (THOMAS,) an excellent English landscape-painter, born at Sudbury in 1727. He became a student of art in London about the age of fifteen, and painted portraits chiefly in the early part of his career. Having worked some years at Ipswich, he removed to Bath about 1760. Among his works are several good portraits of the royal family. He settled in London about 1775, after which he devoted himself to landscapes. He was one of the first members of the Royal Academy. His works are admired for simplicity and fidelity to nature. His early style differed from his later, and exhibited more attention to minute details. He excels in richness of colour and in the distribution of light and shade, and is considered superior to any English landscape-painter who had appeared before his time. Among his works are "The Woodman in the Storm," "The Cottage Door," and "The Shepherd Boy." "Gainsborough's hand," says Ruskin, "is as light as the sweep of a cloud,—as swift as the flash of a sunbeam. His forms are grand, simple, and ideal. . . . The greatest colorist since Rubens, and the last, I think, of legitimate colorists,—that is to say, of those who were fully acquainted with the power of their material,—pure in his English feeling, profound in his seriousness, graceful in his gaiety, there are nevertheless certain deductions to be made from his worthiness," etc. ("Modern Painters.") Died in London, August, 1788.

See THICKNESS, "Sketch of the Life of Gainsborough ;" CUNNINGHAM, "Lives of British Painters."

Gaisʹford, (THOMAS,) D.D., a distinguished English scholar, born in Wiltshire in 1780. He became regius professor of Greek at Oxford about 1811, and afterwards Dean of Christ Church. He published, besides other works, "Poetæ Græci Minores," (3 vols., 1814–16,) an edition of Herodotus, (1824,) and one of Suidas, (1834.) He had a high reputation as a critic. Died in 1855.

Gāʹius (or **Gajus**) or **Cāʹius,** a Roman jurist of high authority, is supposed to have flourished in the reign of Antoninus Pius, 138–161 A.D. Little or nothing is positively known of his personal history. His writings were recognized as a standard by the Roman jurists until the compilation of the Code of Justinian, which was based upon the "Institutes" of Gaius. In 1816 Niebuhr discovered at Verona, on a palimpsest, a treatise on Roman law, which was ascertained to be the Institutes of Gaius and was published in 1820–21. This discovery was regarded as an important contribution to the history of law.

See ERSCH und GRUBER, "Allgemeine Encyklopaedie ;" "Nouvelle Biographie Générale ;" VAN YSSELMONDE, "Dissertatio de Gaji Legis Actionibus," 1840.

Gaj, gī, (LEWIS,) a Croatian journalist, born at Krapina in 1810. He founded, in 1835, the "Croatian Gazette," which became afterwards the "National Illyrian Gazette." This journal acquired extensive influence, and is said to have effected a great literary and political improvement among the Slavonians.

Galaccini, gä-lȧt-chee'nee, or **Gallaccini,** gäl-lȧt-chee'nee, (TEOFILO,) an Italian geometer, born at Sienna in 1564. He wrote an able work "On the Errors of Architects," (1767.) Died in 1641.

Galand. See GALLAND.

Galanino, gä-lä-nee'no, an Italian painter, whose proper name was BALDASSARE ALOISI, was born at Bologna in 1578. He was a pupil of the Caracci, and worked in Rome with success, especially in portraits. He also painted history. Died in 1638.

Galanti, gä-län'tee, (GIUSEPPE MARIA,) an Italian publicist, born at Campobasso in 1743. He published a "Geographical and Political Description of the Two Sicilies," (4 vols., 1786–93,) and other works. Died at Naples in 1806.

Galateo. See FERRARI, (ANTONIO.)

Galatin. See GALLATIN.

Galatin, (PETER,) a Franciscan monk, who flourished about 1520. He wrote "On the Mysteries of the Catholic Truth," ("De Arcanis catholicæ Veritatis," 1518.)

Galaup. See PÉROUSE, LA.

Galaup de Chasteuil, gȧ'lō' deh shä'tuI' or shä'-tuh'ye, (FRANÇOIS,) a French Orientalist, born at Aix in 1588. He passed his latter years as an anchorite on Mount Lebanon, where he died in 1644.

His nephew, PIERRE GALAUP DE CHASTEUIL, born in 1643, was a poet, and a friend of Boileau. His ode on the capture of Maestricht (1673) is admired. Died in 1727.

Galba, (PUB'LIUS SULPIÇ'IUS,) a Roman general, who was elected consul for 211 B.C. He commanded in the war against Philip of Macedon from 211 to 204, but performed nothing of much importance. In 200 B.C. he was re-elected consul, and renewed the war in Macedonia. He defeated Philip near Eordea in 199, and returned to Rome the next year.

Galba, (SERGIUS or SERVIUS SULPICIUS,) a Roman general and orator, who commanded in Spain in 150 B.C. and perfidiously massacred many thousand Lusitanians. Viriathus was one of those who escaped from this massacre. Galba was elected consul 144 B.C. His eloquence is highly praised by Cicero.

Galba, (SERVIUS SULPICIUS,) a Roman emperor, born in 3 or 4 B.C., of a noble family. He was consul under Tiberius in 33 A.D., and in the reign of Caligula commanded the army in Germany, where he acquired reputation for military skill. Claudius, having succeeded to the throne, appointed Galba Governor of Africa, in which post he obtained successes. He commanded an army in Spain at the death of Nero, 68 A.D. He was then proclaimed emperor by his own troops and the Prætorian guards, whose choice was confirmed by the senate. But he speedily lost the popular favour by his severity, parsimony, and impolitic measures. The army declared for Otho, and Galba was slain, after a reign of seven months, in 69 A.D. According to Tacitus, he would have been universally considered worthy to reign if he had never been emperor.

See PLUTARCH, "Life of Galba;" SUETONIUS, "Galba;" TACITUS, "Annales;" NIEBUHR, "History of Rome;" FRANZ HORN, "Historische Gemälde: Galba, Otho und Vitellius," 1812.

Gale, (JOHN,) an eminent Baptist minister, born in London in 1680. He studied at Leyden, and on his return became one of the ministers of Paul's Alley, near Barbican, London. His principal work is "Reflections on Wall's Defence (or History) of Infant Baptism," (1711,) which is called one of the best works on that subject. Died in 1721.

See "Life of John Gale," prefixed to his Works.

Gale, (ROGER,) son of Thomas Gale, of Scruton, born in 1672, was member of Parliament, Fellow of the Royal Society, and treasurer of the Antiquarian Society, and wrote several antiquarian treatises. Died in 1744.

Gale, (SAMUEL,) an English antiquary, a brother of the preceding, was born in London in 1682. He published a "History of Winchester Cathedral," (1715.) Died in 1754.

Gale, (THEOPHILUS,) a learned English nonconformist divine, born at Kings-Teignton, Devonshire, in 1628. He became a Fellow of Magdalene College, and a popular preacher at Winchester, from which he was ejected for nonconformity in 1661. His reputation is founded on a great work, called "The Court of the Gentiles; or, A Discourse touching the Original of Human Literature from the Scriptures," (5 vols., 1669-77,) in which he argues that the heathen theology and philosophy were derived from the Scriptures and the Jewish Church. He became assistant to John Rowe at Holborn, and succeeded him in 1677. Died in 1678.

Gale, (THOMAS,) an eminent English surgeon, born in 1507. He served in the army of Henry VIII. in France in 1544, and in that of Philip II. in 1557. He afterwards practised in London, and wrote several professional treatises, (1563-86.)

See ERSCH und GRUBER, "Allgemeine Encyklopaedie."

Gale, (THOMAS,) D.D., an eminent English classical scholar and critic, born at Scruton, Yorkshire, in 1636. He became professor of Greek in Cambridge University in 1666, and was master of Saint Paul's School, London, from 1672 to 1697. In the latter year he was appointed Dean of York. He was also a Fellow of the Royal Society. He published, besides other works, "Mythological, Ethical, and Physical Works or Treatises," ("Opuscula mythologica, ethica, et physica," 1671,) an edition of Herodotus's History, (1679,) and an edition of Cicero's Works, (1681.) Died in 1702.

See "Biographia Britannica."

Galeano, gä-lä-ä'no, (GIUSEPPE,) an eminent Italian physician, born at Palermo about 1605. He practised in that city, where he also taught medicine for twenty-five years with great success. He had a high reputation as a philosopher, and was regarded as a second Galen by his contemporaries. Among his works are "Hippocrates Revived," (1650,) a Treatise on the Use of Brandy, (1667,) and several poems. Died in 1675.

Galeazzo. See VISCONTI.

Galen, [Lat. CLAU'DIUS GALE'NUS; Gr. Κλαύδιος Γαληνός; Fr. GALIEN, gä'le-ân'; It. GALIENO, gä-le-ä'no,] a celebrated Greek medical writer and pagan philosopher, born at Pergamus, (or Pergamum,) in Mysia, in 131 A.D. He studied the Platonic and the Peripatetic philosophies, and was instructed in anatomy by Satyrus. In his youth he visited several foreign countries, to perfect his education at the best schools. At the age of thirty-four he removed to Rome, where he acquired great celebrity as a practitioner of medicine and surgery. He obtained the confidence of Marcus Aurelius, who appointed him physician to Commodus, the heir of the empire. He also lectured on anatomy in Rome. Towards the end of his life he returned to his native city. His death is variously dated from 200 to 210 A.D. He rendered important services to the science of medicine, and left a great number of works in Greek, many of which are lost. Of some others, only Latin versions have come down to us. "Galen had not," says the "Nouvelle Biographie Générale," "the noble simplicity of Hippocrates. . . . He impairs the purity of his principles by fanciful explanations and by subtilities. He is, nevertheless, the only one among all the ancients who has given us a complete system (corps) of medicine."

Galen rejected the various medical systems which were in vogue in his time, and formed a new eclectic system, which maintained its authority for thirteen centuries. He was regarded as an oracle by the Arabs and Europeans until the fifteenth century. Among his extant works (above eighty in number) are a treatise on anatomy, (Περὶ ἀνατομικῶν ἐγχειρήσεων,) a capital work on physiology, called "On the Uses of the Parts of the Human Body," Ὑγιεινά, "On Preserving Health," ("De Sanitate Tuenda,") and "De Locis affectis," a treatise on pathology, which Haller regarded as one of Galen's best productions. He wrote many able works on ethics, logic, and philosophy, in one of which he praises the temperance and self-denial of the Christians.

See SUIDAS, Γαληνός; ABOOLFARAJ, "Historia Dynastiarum;" FABRICIUS, "Bibliotheca Græca;" DANIEL LE CLERC, "Histoire de la Médecine;" SPRENGEL, "History of Medicine;" HALLER, "Bibliotheca Medicinæ;" DAREMBERG, "Exposé des Connaissances de Galien," 1841; ERSCH und GRUBER, "Allgemeine Encyklopaedie;" A. FUMANELLI, "De Vita et Moribus Galeni," 1577; A. WERNER, "Oratio de Vita Galeni," 1570; SMITH, "Greek and Roman Biography and Mythology;" "Nouvelle Biographie Générale."

Galen, van, vän gä'len, (JAN,) a brave naval officer, born at Essen, in Westphalia, about 1600. He entered the Dutch navy, distinguished himself in battles against the Spaniards, and rose to the rank of commodore. In 1653 he defeated the English fleet near Leghorn, and at the same time received a mortal wound.

See OOSTKAMP, "Leven, Daden en Lotgevallen van den Kommandeur J. van Galen," 1830.

Galen, von, fon gä'len, (CHRISTOPH BERNHARD,) a warlike German prelate, born in Westphalia about 1605. He was elected Prince-Bishop of Münster in 1650. In 1665 he joined Charles II. of England in a war against the Dutch, from whom he took some fortified places. He waged other aggressive wars, and is called by Sismondi a "mitred brigand." Died in 1678.

See LE LORRAIN, "Vie de C. B. de Galen, etc.," Rouen, 1679; JOHANN VON ALPHEN, "De Vita et Rebus gestis C. Bernardi Episcopi, etc.," 1694; E. WIENS, "Sammlung fragmentarischer Nachrichten über C. B. von Galen," 1834.

Galenus, (CLAUDIUS.) See GALEN.

Galeotti, gä-lä-ot'tee, (ALBERTO,) an eminent Italian jurist, born at Parma; died about 1285.

See TIRABOSCHI, "Storia della Letteratura Italiana."

Galeotti, (MARZIO,) an Italian writer, born at Narni about 1440. He was professor of belles-lettres at Bologna, from which he was expelled for his religious opinions. He afterwards was preceptor of the son of Matthias Corvinus, King of Hungary. Among his works

ā, ē, ī, ō, ū, ȳ, long; ă, ĕ, ĭ, ŏ, ŭ, y̆, short; a, e, i, o, obscure; fär, fâll, fât; mêt; nôt; good; moon;

is one entitled "On Man and his Parts," (" De Homine et ejus Partibus," 1490.) Died about 1494.

Galeotti, (SEBASTIANO,) an Italian painter, born at Florence about 1676. His chief works are his frescos in the church of La Madalena in Genoa. Died in 1746.

Galère. See GALERIUS.

Ga-le'rĭ-us, [Fr. GALÈRE, gǎ'laiR',] (CAI'US VALE'-RIUS MAXIMIA'NUS,) a Roman emperor, was a native of Dacia, and of humble origin. From the rank of private soldier he rose to the highest commands in the army. In the year 292 A.D. he was adopted as son or heir, with the title of Cæsar, by Diocletian, whose daughter he married; and a few years later he commanded the army which defeated the Persian king Narses. The violent persecution of the Christians by Diocletian is ascribed to the instigation of Galerius. When Diocletian and Maximian abdicated, in 305, Galerius and Constantius Chlorus succeeded as colleagues in the empire, and the former took for his share Illyria, Thrace, Macedonia, Greece, and the Eastern provinces. His colleague having died in 306, Galerius wished to choose Severus in his place; but Constantine and Maxentius opposed him, and Severus was slain. After he had failed in an attempt to capture Rome, he retired to one of his provinces, and died in 311 A.D.

See GIBBON, " Decline and Fall of the Roman Empire ;" TILLE-MONT, " Histoire des Empereurs."

Gales, gǎlz, (JOSEPH,) a distinguished journalist, born in England about 1760. He established and edited " The Sheffield Register," which, on coming to the United States in 1793, he sold to Montgomery the poet, who had been brought up in his family. After editing for some time "The Independent Gazetteer," in Philadelphia, a Republican journal, in which he introduced short-hand reports of debates in Congress, he founded, in 1799, "The Raleigh (N.C.) Register." Died in 1841.

Gales, (JOSEPH,) a son of the preceding, was born near Sheffield, England, in 1786. He removed to Washington in 1807, and became in 1810 the proprietor and editor of the "National Intelligencer," which after 1813 was issued daily. It became a very able and influential organ of the Whig party. Died in 1860.

Galestruzzi, gä-lĕs-troot'see, or **Gallestruzzi,** gäl-lĕs-troot'see, (GIOVANNI BATTISTA,) an Italian engraver and painter, born at Florence about 1618. He settled in Rome, and was received into the Academy of Saint Luke in 1652. Died in Rome about 1670.

Galfrid (or Geoffroy) de Beaulieu, gǎl'fre' deh bō'-le-uh', a French monk, confessor to Saint Louis, who was attended by him in his two crusades. Died in 1274.

Galfridus de Vinosalvo. See GEOFFROI DE VIN-SAUF.

Galhegos, de, dä gǎl-yā'gòs, (MANOEL, or MANUEL,) a popular Portuguese poet, born in Lisbon in 1597, was a friend of Lope de Vega. He produced a poem on the "Wars of the Giants against Jupiter," (1628,) which was admired for its brilliant imagery and elegant style, and a poem named "The Temple of Memory," (1635,) which increased his celebrity. He also wrote several dramas, which were performed with applause. Died in 1665.

Galiani, gä-le-ä'nee, (FERDINANDO,) ABBÉ, an Italian political economist, born at Chieti, in the Abruzzi, in 1728. He wrote (1750) an able treatise "On Currency," or Money, (" Della Moneta,") which acquired a European reputation and influenced the legislation of his own country, then disturbed by a surplus of precious metals and the consequent enormous rise in the price of commodities. In 1759 he was appointed secretary of legation at Paris, where he remained many years and attracted much notice by his wit and convivial powers. While in Paris, he argued against the free exportation of corn, in his "Dialogues on the Corn Trade," in French, (1770,) which obtained great success, and of which Voltaire said, "This work seems like the joint production of Plato and Molière." "No one," said Turgot, "could maintain a bad cause with more wit, grace, finesse, and reasonableness in details." Having returned to Naples in 1769, he was appointed one of the ministers of the junta of royal domains in 1777, and first assessor or minister of the council of finance in 1782. He wrote an able treatise "On the Reciprocal Duties of Neutrals

and Belligerents," (1782.) Died at Naples in 1787. He left in manuscript a Life of Horace and a Commentary on that poet, which, says Ginguené, are learned and original, like all his works. His "Letters to Madame d'Epinay" were published in 1818.

See MARMONTEL, "Mémoires ;" GRIMM, "Correspondance ;" SAINTE-BEUVE, "Causeries du Lundi."

Galiano, gä'le-ä'no, (ANTONIO ALCALA,) a distinguished Spanish political writer and orator, was born at Cadiz about 1790. He promoted with zeal the revolution of 1820, and was elected in 1821 to the Cortes, in which he highly distinguished himself as an orator and leader of the Liberal party. Having been driven into exile in 1823, he went to England, and became professor of Spanish in the London University about 1828. He wrote a "History of Spanish Literature in the Nineteenth Century," which was published in the "Athenæum" (1834) and is highly commended. He returned to Spain in 1834, and joined the Conservative party about 1836, after which he was again exiled, for political reasons.

Galien, the French for GALEN, which see.

Galien, gä'le-ÂN', (JOSEPH,) a French natural philosopher, born near Le Puy in 1699. He is said to have been one of the first who conceived the practicability of ascending by means of an apparatus lighter than air. He published "The Art of Aerial Navigation," and a treatise "On the Formation of Hail." Died in 1782.

Galieno, the Italian for GALEN, which see.

Galigai. See ANCRE, (MARSHAL D'.)

Galilæus or **Galilée.** See GALILEI.

Galilei, gä-le-lā'ee, (ALESSANDRO,) an Italian architect, born at Florence in 1691. He worked at Florence and Rome, where he was employed by Pope Clement XII., and where he built the façade of the church of Saint John of the Florentines, and the chapel Corsini, which is called his master-piece. Died in 1737.

Galilei, gä-le-lā'ee, [Fr. GALILÉE, gä'le'lÂ' ; Lat. GALILÆ'US or GALILE'US,] (GALILEO,) commonly called simply **Galileo,** gäl-e-lee'o, [It. pron. gä-le-lā'o,] an illustrious Italian mathematician and natural philosopher, was born of a noble family at Pisa, the 15th of February, 1564. From early childhood he showed a rare aptitude for mechanical invention. After having studied, at Florence, the classics, music, and painting, he went to Pisa in 1582 to study medicine. But the impulse of his genius and destiny caused him to prefer geometry and physical philosophy, in which he made rapid progress. He discovered about 1584 the isochronism of the vibrations of a pendulum. Like his contemporary, Bacon, he asserted his independence against the authority of Aristotle, (whose system was then followed with blind and servile submission,) and appealed to the impartial evidence and umpirage of experiment. In 1589 he was chosen professor of mathematics in the University of Pisa, where he demonstrated the fallacy of the received theory that bodies of unequal weights will fall with proportionate velocities, by dropping metallic balls of different sizes from the top of the Leaning Tower. He was also the first who discovered the law by which the velocity of falling bodies is accelerated. In 1592 the senate of Venice appointed him professor of mathematics in Padua for the term of six years, which term was renewed in 1598. During this period he invented a thermometer, and, after examining the rival theories of astronomy, he adopted the Copernican system, which was then regarded as heretical by the schoolmen and clergy of Italy. In 1609 his celebrity was greatly increased by the construction of his telescope (the honour of inventing which is generally conceded to him) and by the sublime results which he realized in its application to astronomy and the "structure of the universe." He saw with rapt and devout admiration the mountains and valleys of the moon, and the phases of Venus ; he discovered the satellites of Jupiter, and resolved into myriads of stars or flaming orbs the luminous nebulæ of the Milky Way. He hastened to impart these glorious revelations in his "Sidereal Messenger," (" Sidereus Nuncius,") published in 1610. About the year 1611 he accepted an invitation to Florence, where he was liberally patronized by Cosimo de' Medici.

While Galileo was thus employed in consolidating the

ϵ as *k*; ç as *s*; ḡ *hard*; ġ as *j*; G, H, K, *guttural*; N, *nasal*; R, *trilled*; s̄ as *z*; th as in *this*. (☞ See Explanations, p. 23.)

Copernican system by sensible evidence, and unfolding to the human mind the grandeur of the universe, the Jesuits and other enemies denounced him to the Inquisition as a heretic. In 1616 he was summoned to Rome, and had an interview with the pope, Paul V., who positively forbade him to teach the doctrine of the motion of the earth, and, on his giving a promise to that effect, permitted him to return to Florence. For a number of years he enjoyed a truce from persecution, and even received some kindness from the next pope, Urban VIII. In 1632 he published his great work, the "Dialogues on the Ptolemaic and Copernican Systems," in which, with graceful felicity of style, he employs all the resources of wit, fancy, reason, and eloquence to render the truth attractive. The dialogue is carried on by Salviati, Sagredo, and Simplicius, the last of whom (a fictitious person) maintains the theory of Ptolemy. The appearance of this work occasioned a great outcry at Rome. The pope was persuaded that the author had exposed him to ridicule, in the character of Simplicius; and Galileo was again cited before the Inquisition, in his seventieth year. After a confinement of several months, he was induced to sign a document abjuring the obnoxious theory, (that the earth had a diurnal motion, as well as a motion round the sun,) and promised to refrain from teaching it; but even this did not procure his liberation. It is said that, as he rose from the kneeling posture in which he signed his name, he whispered to a friend, "E pur se muove," ("It moves nevertheless.") His confinement was continued a few years, though not in the severest form, and it appears that he pursued his studies and observations until he became blind. He was visited by Milton in 1638. He died at or near Florence in January, 1642, within a year of the birth of Newton. He was never married. His temper was cheerful and sociable, his features comely, and his person of medium stature. Among his principal disciples were Torricelli and Viviani. In regard to the invention of the telescope, to which allusion has been made above, we may here remark that although Jens or Jansen, a Dutch optician, first invented a small spy-glass, intended for a plaything, yet Galileo was the first who constructed an astronomical telescope and applied it to its noblest use. Galileo himself says that he had heard of the invention in Holland of an instrument which enlarged the size of distant objects, but was not informed how it was constructed, and that the one he used was the result of his own study and experiments. The most important discovery of Galileo was that of Jupiter's satellites, the eclipses of which afforded the first good method of determining longitudes. His "Scienza mechanica" was written in 1592, but not printed until 1634. About 1582 he obtained the idea of the pendulum from the oscillations of a lamp suspended in a church; and Biot says he constructed a clock in 1633 in which the pendulum was used. Hume ranks Galileo above Lord Bacon as an author and philosopher. ("History of England," vol. iv.) A good edition of Galileo's complete works was published at Florence by Alberi, 20 vols., 1842–58.

See Viviani, "Vita del Galilei;" L. Brenna, "Vita Galilei," in Fabroni's "Vitæ Italorum;" Drinkwater Bethune, "Life of Galileo," in the "Library of Useful Knowledge;" Sir David Brewster, "Martyrs of Science," 1841; Nelli, "Vita di Galilei," 2 vols., 1793: Philarète Chasles, "Galileo; sa Vie, son Procès et ses Contemporains," 1862; G. Libri, "Histoire de la Vie et des Œuvres de G. Galilei," 1841: Campanella, "Apologia pro Galileo," 1622; Frisi, "Elogio del Galileo," 1775; A. Cattaneo, "Cenni su la Vita di G. Galilei," 1843; "North British Review" for November, 1860; Biot, article on Galileo in the "Biographie Universelle;" "Nouvelle Biographie Générale."

Galilei, (Vincentio,) the father of the great astronomer, resided in Florence, and was married in 1562 to Julia Venturi. He excelled in the theory and practice of music, and wrote a learned treatise entitled a "Dialogue on Ancient and Modern Music." He died about 1600.

Galileo, (the celebrated philosopher.) See Galilei, (Galileo.)

Galileo, (Vincentio,) a son of the great astronomer, was born about 1600. He aided his father in experiments, cultivated literature, and gave special attention to the application of the pendulum to clocks. Died in 1649.

Galileus. See Galilei.

Galimard, gȧ'le'mȧR', (Nicolas Auguste,) a French historical painter, born in Paris in 1813, was a pupil of

Ingres. Among his works are "Nausicaa and her Companions," and "The Evangelists."

Galin, gȧ'lȧN', (Pierre,) a French musician, born at Samatan in 1786, invented a new method of teaching music, named the "Method of the Méloplaste." Died in 1822.

Galindes de Caravajal, gȧ-lèn'dês dȧ kȧ-rȧ-vȧ-Hȧl', (Lorenzo,) a Spanish lawyer and historian, born at Placencia in 1472. Ferdinand the Catholic chose him as president of his council of state. He wrote a history of John II. of Castile, and other works. Died in 1532.

See Prescott, "History of Ferdinand and Isabella," vol. iii. part ii.

Galindo, gȧ-lèn'do, (Beatriz,) a Spanish lady, born at Salamanca in 1475, excelled in the use of the Latin language, and was regarded as a prodigy of learning. She became a lady of honour to Isabella of Castile. Died in 1535.

Galiot (or Galliot) de Genouillac, gȧ'le'o' deh zheh'noo'yȧk', Seigneur d'Acier, (dȧ'se-ȧ',) a French officer, born in Quercy about 1466, was made grand master of artillery in 1512, and afterwards grand equerry to Francis I. He displayed skill at the battles of Marignano and of Pavia, (1525.) Died in 1546.

See Brantôme, "Vie de Galliot," vol. ii.

Galisonnière. See Gallissonière.

Galitzin or Galitsin. See Gallitsin.

Gall, gȧl, (Ferdinand,) Baron, a German author, born at Battenberg, in Hesse, in 1809. He wrote, besides other works, "Travels in Sweden in the Summer of 1836," (2 vols., 1838,) and "Paris and its Salons," (2 vols., 1845,) which had a great success. In 1846 he became intendant of the royal theatre at Stuttgart.

Gall, gaul, [Ger. pron. gȧl,] (Franz Joseph,) a German physician, distinguished as the founder of the system of phrenology, was born at Tiefenbrunn, in Baden, on the 9th of March, 1758. He studied natural sciences at Strasburg, and passed thence to Vienna about 1781. He graduated as M.D. at Vienna in 1785, and practised in that city for many years. In 1791 he published a medical work entitled "Medical and Philosophical Researches on Nature and Art," ("Philosophisch-medicinische Untersuchungen über Natur und Kunst,") etc. He devoted much time to the study of the brain and to the external signs connected with the different functions and faculties of the human mind, and began in 1796 to lecture on these subjects in Vienna. Among his principal doctrines are the following: that the brain is the organ of all the faculties, propensities, and sentiments; that different parts of the brain are appropriated to particular mental faculties or moral affections; and that the capacity and character of a person are indicated by the external form of his skull. About 1805 he began, with his pupil and coadjutor, Dr. Spurzheim, to propagate their system by lectures in Paris, Berlin, and other cities of Europe. Dr. Gall became a permanent resident of Paris in 1807. He presented to the Institute in 1808 his "Researches into the Nervous System in General and the Brain in Particular," which was unfavourably criticised by a committee of the Institute, in their report. His principal work is entitled "The Anatomy and Physiology of the Nervous System in General, and of the Brain in Particular," (4 vols., 1810–19, in French.) He was assisted in this work by Dr. Spurzheim. (See Spurzheim.) Died in Paris in 1828.

See "Edinburgh Review" for June, 1815; "Quarterly Review" for April, 1815; "Nouvelle Biographie Générale."

Gall, (Richard,) a Scottish poet, born in 1776, was a printer of Edinburgh. He acquired distinction as the author of a poem called "Arthur's Seat," and of several popular songs, among which are "The Farewell to Ayrshire," and "The Braes o' Drumlie." Died in 1801.

See Chambers, "Biographical Dictionary of Eminent Scotsmen."

Gall, gaul, or Gal'lus, Saint, called "the Apostle of the Swiss," was born in Ireland about 550 A.D. He was a disciple of Saint Columban, whom he accompanied to Gaul in 585. He founded the monastery of Saint Gall, in the Swiss canton of that name. Died in 646 A.D.

See Karl Greith, "Der heilige Gallus der Apostel Allemanniens," 1845.

Gallæus. See Gallé.

ā, ē, ī, ō, ū, ȳ, long; ȧ, ė, ȯ, same, less prolonged; ă, ĕ, ĭ, ŏ, ŭ, ў, short; a, e, i, o, obscure; fär, fâll, fât; mĕt; nŏt; gōōd; mōōn;

Găl'la-ğhẹr, (WILLIAM D.,) an American poet and journalist, born in Philadelphia in 1808. He edited several literary journals in Ohio, and was associate editor of the "Cincinnati Gazette," 1840–50. He removed to Louisville, Kentucky, about 1853. Among his works are three volumes of poems entitled "Erato," (1835–37.)

See GRISWOLD, "Poets and Poetry of America."

Gallais, gȧ'lȧ', (JEAN PIERRE,) a French historical and political writer, born at Doué (Anjou) in 1756. In the Revolution he was a zealous royalist. He wrote many mediocre works, among which is a "History of France from the Death of Louis XVI. to the Peace of 1815," (2 vols., 1820.) Died in 1820.

Gallait, gȧ'lȧ', (LOUIS,) an eminent Belgian historical painter, born at Tournay in 1810, studied in Paris. Among his works are "Job and his Friends," "The Abdication of Charles V.," (1841,) and "The Last Moments of Egmont," (1853.)

Galland, gȧ'lôN', (ANTOINE,) a distinguished French Orientalist and antiquary, born at Rollot, in Picardy, in 1646. He made several journeys to the Levant to collect medals and copy inscriptions. About 1680 he had a commission from Colbert to make antiquarian researches in the East. He was admitted into the Academy of Inscriptions in 1701, and became professor of Arabic in the Royal College in 1709. His reputation is chiefly founded on his French version of the Arabian tales called "The Thousand and One Nights," (12 vols., 1704–17.) The style of this version is natural and simple. He translated other works from the Arabic and Persian, and wrote treatises on medals and antiquities. Died in 1715.

See ZENKER, "Bibliotheca Orientalis;" "Nouvelle Biographie Générale."

Galland, (AUGUSTE,) a French historical writer, born about 1570. He was a member of Henry the Fourth's council of state, and wrote, besides other works, "Memoirs to illustrate the History of Navarre and Flanders," (1648,) and a "History of the Reformation in France." Died before 1645.

Galland, (PIERRE,) a French scholar, born at Aire in 1510. He became professor of eloquence in the Royal College in 1545, and was a friend of Budé, (Budæus.) His argument "On Behalf of the Parisian School against the New Academy of P. Ramus" ("Pro Schola Parisiensi contra novam Academiam Petri Rami," 1551) was the signal for the persecutions which that author suffered. Died in 1559.

Gallas, gȧl'lȧs, (MATTHIAS,) an Austrian general, born at or near Trent in 1589. He was a major-general of the army which took Mantua in 1629, and became a general of cavalry, or field-marshal, in 1631. He commanded a corps under Wallenstein, in Bohemia, and distinguished himself in battles against the Swedes at Nuremberg and Lutzen in 1632. Gallas appears to have been the chief agent in the intrigues which resulted in the ruin of Wallenstein, whom he succeeded as general-in-chief in 1634. He gained a decisive victory at Nordlingen in 1634, but was outgeneralled and defeated near Magdeburg by Torstenson in 1644. Died in 1647.

See SCHILLER, "History of the Thirty Years' War;" ERSCH and GRUBER, "Allgemeine Encyklopaedie."

Găl'la-tin, [Fr. pron. gȧ'lȧ'tăN',] (ALBERT,) an eminent statesman, and a great oracle and leader of the Republican party in America, was born at Geneva in January, 1761. After graduating at the university of his native place, he emigrated to the United States in 1780. He acted as French tutor in Harvard University in 1782, and spent the two or three ensuing years in Virginia, where he purchased a large tract of land. In 1786 he fixed his home in Fayette county, Pennsylvania, and in 1790 was elected a member of the legislature of that State, in which he served several years, and acquired great influence with both parties, although he acted with the Republicans. In 1793 the legislature, in which the Federal party had a majority, paid him a high compliment by electing him to the Senate of the United States, in which, however, he served only two months, as that body decided, by a party vote, that he was not eligible, because he had not been naturalized nine years before the election. From 1795 to 1801 he represented a district of Pennsylvania in the Federal Congress, in which

he became one of the ablest debaters and was recognized as the leader of the Republicans, at least after Madison had retired from that arena in 1797. He spoke often, and was distinguished for his cool and ready dexterity, as well as his knowledge of political economy and finance. The first formation of the committee of ways and means was due to his suggestion. In 1801 President Jefferson appointed Gallatin secretary of the treasury, which he managed with eminent ability until 1813, having been continued in the office by Madison in 1809. He succeeded in effecting a great reduction of the public debt, and opposed the second war with England. In 1813 he retired from the cabinet, to take an active part in negotiating a peace with England; and, as the colleague of Adams, Clay, and others, he signed the treaty of Ghent in 1814. On this occasion, and in his subsequent career of diplomacy, he enjoyed a very high reputation as a negotiator, for which he was so well fitted by his extensive and exact information, his honourable character, his courteous address, and his logical ability. He was resident minister of the United States at Paris from 1816 to 1823, and in 1826 accepted a mission to England, where he settled a question of the boundary between the United States and British America, and regulated the subject of fisheries. Returning in 1827, he withdrew from political employment, and took up his residence in New York City. He subsequently wrote two able pamphlets on Currency, and in 1840 an essay on the Northeastern Boundary. In 1843 he was chosen president of the New York Historical Society. John Randolph, who witnessed his career in Congress, once remarked that Gallatin was unrivalled for readiness and dexterity in debate; and Judge Story pronounced him a truly great statesman, ranking him side by side with Hamilton. Died in 1849.

See DUYCKINCK, "Cyclopædia of American Literature," vol. i.

Gallatin, gȧ'lȧ'tăN', (JEAN LOUIS,) a Swiss physician, born at Geneva in 1751, was physician to the hospital founded in Paris by Madame Necker. He wrote a treatise on acute fevers, (1781.) Died in 1783.

Gal'lau-det', (Rev. THOMAS H.,) born in Philadelphia in 1787, rendered himself widely and favourably known by his successful efforts for the instruction of the deaf and dumb. After studying for the ministry at Andover, he took charge of a church in Portsmouth, New Hampshire. About 1815 he formed an association for the relief of the deaf and dumb, and was induced to undertake a mission to Europe to qualify himself for their tuition. At Paris he was kindly received by the Abbé Sicard, who gave him full facilities for learning the system followed in the institution under his charge. Having returned to the United States, he was chosen principal of the Asylum for the Deaf and Dumb at Hartford, which was opened in April, 1817, and which was the first institution that had been founded for that purpose in America. He continued to labour here with zeal and success until 1830, when he resigned on account of ill health. He published, besides other works, "The Child's Book of the Soul," (3d edition, 1850.) Died in 1851.

See HENRY BARNARD, "Discourse on the Life and Character of T. H. Gallaudet," 1852; "Life of T. H. Gallaudet," by H. HUMPHREY; "North American Review" for October, 1858.

Galle, gȧl, (ANDRÉ,) a French medallist and engraver, born at Saint-Étienne in 1761, settled in Paris. He engraved many portraits and medals in commemoration of the events of Napoleon's reign. Died in 1844.

Galle, gȧl'lẹh, (CORNELIS,) an excellent Flemish engraver, born at Antwerp in 1570, was a son and pupil of Philip Galle, (1537–1612.) He studied in Rome, and returned to Antwerp, where he engraved history after various masters, and portraits after Van Dyck. Among his works are a "Virgin and Child," after Raphael; a "Virgin crowned with Flowers," after Rubens; and some original designs. He was the most famous artist of the family.

See GANDELLINI, "Notizie degli Intagliatori."

Galle, (CORNELIS,) THE YOUNGER, a son of the preceding, born at Antwerp in 1600, was an engraver and designer. He engraved history and portraits, the latter of which are his best productions.

See BRYAN, "Dictionary of Painters and Engravers."

Galle, gâl′lẹh, (Dr. J. G.,) a German astronomer, born in Prussian Saxony about 1812, became director of the Observatory at Berlin, and was the first who observed with a telescope the planet Neptune, whose existence Leverrier had previously demonstrated. (See LEVER-RIER.) He announced this fact to Leverrier in a letter dated September 25, 1846. A few years later he obtained the chair of astronomy at Breslau.

Galle, (PHILIP,) a Flemish engraver, born at Haarlem in 1537, was a correct designer. He was a dealer in prints at Antwerp, and produced many engravings after his own designs and after those of other artists. Among his works are "Portraits of the Eminent Men of the Fifteenth and Sixteenth Centuries." Died in 1612.

His son THEODORE, born at Antwerp in 1560, was an engraver. He engraved some works of Rubens and other Flemish masters, besides his own designs.

See DESCAMPS, "Vies des Peintres Flamands," etc.

Gallé, gā′lȧ′, [Lat. GALLÆ′US,] (SERVAIS,) a Dutch writer, born at Rotterdam about 1628, published an edition of Lactantius, (1660,) and "Dissertations on the Sibyls and their Oracles," (1688.) Died in 1709.

Gallego, gâl-yā′go, (Don JUAN NICASIO,) a Spanish poet and priest, born at Zamora in 1777, became chaplain to the king in 1805, and, after the French invasion, was elected to the Cortes of Cadiz. He wrote, besides other fine poems, an "Elegy to the Second of May," ("Al Dos de Mayo," 1808,) and an "Ode on the Influence of Public Enthusiasm on the Arts," (1832.)

Gallegos, gâl-yā′gòs, (FERNANDO,) a renowned Spanish painter, born at Salamanca in 1461. He distinguished himself by accuracy of design and beauty of colouring. His subjects are chiefly Scriptural. His works are said to have been often mistaken for those of Albert Dürer. Died in 1550.

See BERMUDEZ, "Diccionario Historico."

Gallegos, (MANUEL.) See GALHEGOS.

Gallestruzzi. See GALESTRUZZI.

Galletti, gâl-let′tee, (FILIPPO MARIA,) a fresco-painter, born at Florence in 1636, adorned several churches of that city and of Parma. Died in 1714.

Galletti, gâl-let′tee, (JOHANN GEORG AUGUST,) a German historian, born at Altenburg in 1750, became historiographer to the Duke of Gotha in 1816. He wrote a number of educational treatises and historical works, among which is a "History of Germany," (10 vols., 1787-1819.) Died in 1828.

See ERSCH und GRUBER, "Allgemeine Encyklopaedie."

Galletti, (PIETRO LUIGI,) an Italian antiquary and monk, born in Rome in 1724. He published, besides other works, "Mediæval Inscriptions of Venice, Rome," etc., (7 vols., 1757-66.) Died in 1790.

Galli, gâl′lee, (FRANCESCO,) surnamed BIBBIENA, a painter and architect, born at Bologna in 1656, was a brother of Ferdinando, noticed below. He was gifted with a fine imagination. He practised the art of decoration at Naples, Verona, Vienna, and Rome, and became first architect to Philip V. of Spain. Among his greatest works was the theatre of Verona. Died in 1739.

His son GIOVANNI, or JEAN, was born at Nancy about 1710. He wrote, in French, several novels, and a comedy entitled "New Italy," ("La nouvelle Italie," 1762.) Died about 1779.

See MALVASIA, "Pittura, Scoltura ed Architettura di Bologna."

Galli, (GIOVANNI ANTONIO,) born at Bologna in 1708, was a skilful surgeon, and a professor of midwifery, which he taught by an improved method. Died in 1784.

Galli da Bibbiena, gâl′lee dâ bêb-be-ā′nâ, (or Bibiena, be-be-ā′nâ,) (FERDINANDO,) an able Italian painter and architect, born at Bologna in 1657, was a pupil of C. Cignani. He excelled in perspective and theatrical decorations. He became first painter and architect to Charles III. at Vienna. He published a "Treatise on Architecture and Perspective," (2 vols., 1711.) Died about 1745.

See LANZI, "History of Painting in Italy."

Galliani. See GALIANI.

Galliccioli, gâl-lèt-cho′lee, (GIOVANNI BATTISTA,) ABBÉ, an Italian Orientalist, born in Venice in 1733,

published, besides other works, one on "Ancient Venetian Memoirs." Died in 1806.

Gāl-lĭ-e′nus, [Fr. GALLIEN, gā′le-ân′,] (PUBLIUS LICINIUS VALERIUS,) a Roman emperor, born about 233 A.D., was a son of the emperor Valerian, who admitted him to a share in the empire in 253. Valerian having been defeated and taken prisoner by the Persians in 260 A.D., Gallienus succeeded to the throne. He made no effort to liberate his father from captivity, and disgraced himself by his cruelty and profligacy. His frontiers were invaded by barbarian armies, while Ingenuus, Aureolus, and other Roman generals revolted in different parts of the empire. After he had defeated Aureolus in battle, a conspiracy was formed against Gallienus by his own officers. During the siege of Milan, 268 A.D., "he received a mortal dart from an uncertain hand," says Gibbon, who thus describes him: "He was master of several curious but useless sciences, a ready orator, an elegant poet, a skilful gardener, an excellent cook, and a most contemptible prince." He was succeeded by Claudius II.

See GIBBON, "Decline and Fall of the Roman Empire;" TILLE-MONT, "Histoire des Empereurs;" ECKHEL, "Doctrina Nummorum."

Galligai. See ANCRE.

Gallinari, gâl-le-nâ′ree, (PIETRO,) an Italian painter, born at Brescia about 1629, was a favourite pupil of Guido. He was an artist of high promise, but died prematurely in 1664.

Gal′lĭ-o, (JUNIUS,) a Roman judicial officer, was an adopted son of the rhetorician Junius Gallio, and a brother of Seneca the philosopher. His original name was M. ANNÆUS NOVATUS. He is supposed by some persons to be the Gallio who was deputy or proconsul of Achaia, before whom Saint Paul was arraigned by the Jews. (See Acts xviii. 12-17.) Died in 65 A.D.

Galliot. See GALIOT.

Gallissonière, de la, deh lă gā′le′so′ne-aiR′, (ROLAND MICHEL Barrin—bä′rĂn′,) MARQUIS, a naval officer, born at Rochefort, in France, in 1693. He became a captain about 1738, and acted as Governor of Canada from 1745 to 1749. In 1756 his fleet defeated the English under Admiral Byng, near Minorca. Died in 1756.

Gallitsin, Gallitzin, or **Galitzin,** gâ-lit′sin or gâ-lèt′sèn, (ALEXANDER MIKHAILOVITCH,) a Russian general and prince, born in 1718, was a son of Mikhail, (1674-1730.) He distinguished himself in the Seven Years' war, (1756-63,) about the end of which he became general-in-chief. He afterwards obtained great favour with Catherine II., and defeated the Turks at Choczim in 1769. Died in 1783.

See "Nouvelle Biographie Générale."

Gallitsin, Gallitzin, or **Galitzin,** (DMITRI I.,) PRINCE OF, uncle of the preceding, was one of the Russian nobles who, after the death of Peter II., placed Anne on the throne, on the condition that she should sign a charter as a guarantee against despotic power. But, when she thought her authority established, she tore the charter in pieces and imprisoned its authors. Died in 1738.

Gallitsin or **Gallitzin,** (DMITRI ALEXIEVITCH,) PRINCE, a Russian author and diplomatist, was born about 1738. In 1763 he was appointed ambassador to France, where he remained several years, and corresponded with Voltaire, who praised his good qualities. In 1773 he became resident minister at the Hague. He wrote, besides other works, a "Physical Description of the Crimea," (1788,) and a "Treatise on Mineralogy," (1792.) Died in 1803.

Gallitsin or **Gallitzin,** written also **Galyzin,** (DMITRI AUGUSTINE,) a Russian missionary, a son of the preceding, was born at the Hague in 1770. He became a Roman Catholic priest, and went to the United States about 1792. He founded Loretto, in Cambria county, Pennsylvania, where he died in 1840.

Gallitsin, (DMITRI MIKHAILOVITCH,) PRINCE, was born in 1721. He was Russian ambassador at the court of Vienna from 1762 to 1792, and had a high reputation as a negotiator. He founded a hospital in Moscow. Died in 1793.

Gallitsin, (EMANUEL,) PRINCE, a Russian *littérateur*, born in Paris in 1804. He fought with distinction at the capture of Varna, soon after which he retired from the army. He translated several works from Russian into French, and wrote "Travels in Finland," (1852.) Died in Paris in 1853.

Gallitsin, (MIKHAIL,) PRINCE, a Russian admiral, born about 1685. During the reign of Catherine I. or Peter II. he became a senator and privy councillor. After the death of the empress Anne (1740) he obtained the rank of admiral. He was appointed grand admiral and president of the admiralty in 1756. Died in 1764.

Gallitsin, (MIKHAIL MIKHAILOVITCH,) PRINCE, a Russian nobleman, born in 1674. He entered the army as a private, became a general about 1708, and led a division at Pultowa (Poltava) in 1709. In 1711 he commanded an army against the Tartars and Poles. He had the chief command in Finland from 1713 to 1721, defeated the Swedes in a naval fight in 1720, and was made field-marshal in 1724. In 1730 he was appointed a senator, and president of the College of War. He was reputed to be the best general that Russia had then produced. Died in 1730.

See "Nouvelle Biographie Générale."

Gallitsin, Galitzin, Gallitzin, Galyzin, or **Gallitzine,** (VASILI, or BASIL,) an able and liberal Russian statesman, born about 1633. He was the minister or influential adviser of Feodor, (1676-82,) and promoted reform and civilization. He retained power or favour during the minority of Ivan and Peter and the regency of Sophia. In 1686 he concluded with Poland a treaty that was very advantageous to Russia. He commanded an expedition against the Crimean Tartars in 1687. For his alleged complicity in the conspiracy of Sophia against Peter the Great, he was exiled in 1689. Died in 1713.

See "Nouvelle Biographie Générale."

Gallizin or **Gallitzin.** See GALLITSIN.

Gallo, gäl′lo, (AGOSTINO,) born at Brescia, in Italy, in 1499, wrote a useful treatise called "Twenty Days of Agriculture," ("Vinti Giornate dell' Agricoltura," 1550,) and other similar works. He was regarded as the restorer of agriculture in Italy. Died in 1570.

Gallo, (ANDREA,) a Sicilian antiquary, born at Messina in 1732. He wrote an account of the earthquake which nearly ruined Messina in 1783. Died in 1814.

Gallo, (THOMAS.) See GALLUS, (THOMAS.)

Gallo, da, dä gäl′lo, (MARZIO **Mastrizzi**—mäs-trèt′see,) DUKE, a Neapolitan minister of state and able negotiator, was born at Palermo in 1753. He was sent as ambassador to Vienna in 1795, and performed a prominent part in the treaty of Campo Formio, (1797.) During the consulate of Bonaparte he was ambassador to Paris. He was minister of foreign affairs at Naples from the accession of Joseph Bonaparte, in 1806, until 1815. The revolution of 1820 restored him to the same office for a brief term. He retired when the government again became absolute, in 1821. Died in 1833.

See ERSCH und GRUBER, "Allgemeine Encyklopaedie."

Galloche, gä′losh′, (LOUIS,) a French painter, born in Paris in 1670, painted subjects from Scripture with success. He received a pension from the king, and was rector of the Academy in Paris when he died, in 1761. Lemoyne was one of his pupils. Among his best works is "The Removal of the Reliques of Saint Augustine."

Gallois, gä′lwä′, (CHARLES ANDRÉ GUSTAVE LÉO-NARD,) a French political and historical writer, born at Monaco in 1789. He removed to Paris in 1818, became an editor of the "Constitutionnel," and advocated democracy in several popular pamphlets. He also wrote a "Pictorial History of the French Revolution," (4 vols., 1830,) and a "History of the National Convention," (8 vols., 1835.) Died in 1851.

See "Nouvelle Biographie Générale."

Gallois, (JEAN,) a French editor and critic of much merit, born in Paris in 1632, was one of the founders of the "Journal des Savants," which he edited with ability from 1666 to 1674. He was admitted into the French Academy, on the same day as Racine and Fléchier, in 1673. He was a favourite protégé of Colbert. After the death of Colbert he became keeper of the Royal Library, and professor of Greek in the Collége Royal. Died in 1707.

See MORÉRI, "Dictionnaire Historique;" SABATIER, "Les trois Siècles de la Littérature;" "Biographie Universelle."

Gallois, (JEAN ANTOINE **Gauvain**—gō′văn′,) a politician, born in Paris in 1755. In 1802 he was president of the Tribunate, after the dissolution of which he passed into the legislative body. In 1813 he was a member of the commission to which the negotiations with the allied powers were referred. He translated from the Italian a treatise on the "Science of Legislation," by Filangieri, (1786-91,) and wrote some fugitive poems. Died in 1828.

Gallois, (JULIAN JEAN CÉSAR.) See LEGALLOIS.

Gallois, (LÉONARD JOSEPH URBAIN NAPOLÉON,) a son of Charles André Gustave Léonard, was born at Foix in 1815. He edited several political journals, and wrote a "Life of Ledru Rollin," (1849.)

Gallois, (PIERRE,) a French bibliographer, born in Paris, published "Academic Conversations," (2 vols., 1674.)

Galloni, gäl-lo′nee, or **Gallonio,** gäl-lo′ne-o, (AN-TONIO,) a learned Italian priest, born in Rome, published a "Treatise on Instruments of Torture or Martyrdom," ("De Martyrum Cruciatibus," 1594,) and a "Life of Saint Philip de Neri," (1602.) Died in 1605.

Galloway, EARL OF. See GALWAY.

Gäl′lo-way, (JOSEPH,) an American lawyer, born in Maryland about 1730, practised with distinction in Philadelphia. He became in 1774 a delegate to the Continental Congress, in which he took a prominent part and opposed the independence of the colonies. He removed to England in 1778. Died in 1803.

Gallucci, gäl-loot′chee, (GIOVANNI PAOLO,) an Italian astronomer, born at Salo, near Brescia, about 1550. He was one of the first members of the Academy founded at Venice in 1593. He published, besides other works, a "Theatre of the World and Time," ("Theatrum Mundi et Temporis," 1589,) which treats partly of astrology, and a "Speculum Uranicum," (1593.)

Gallucci, (TARQUINIO.) See GALLUZZI.

Galluccio, gäl-loot′cho, (ANGELO,) an Italian Jesuit, born at Macerata in 1593, was professor of rhetoric at Rome, and published "De Bello Belgico," a History of the War in the Low Countries from 1593 to 1609, (2 vols., 1671.) Died in 1674.

Gäl′lup, (JOSEPH ADAM,) an American physician and author, born in Stonington, Connecticut, in 1769. In 1827 he established at Woodstock a clinical school of medicine, which in 1835 was incorporated as the Vermont Medical College. He published "Outlines of the Institutes of Medicine," (1839.) Died in 1849.

Galluppi, (BALDASSARE.) See GALUPPI.

Galluppi, gäl-loop′pee, or **Galuppi,** gä-loop′pee, (PASQUALE,) an Italian metaphysical philosopher, born at Tropea, Calabria, in 1770, was professor of philosophy at Naples, and an adversary of skepticism. His "Elements of Philosophy" (4 vols., 1832) passed through many editions. He also wrote "The Philosophy of the Will," (4 vols., 1835-42,) and other works. Died in 1846.

See CARLO MARIA CURCI, "Elogio di P. Galluppi," 1847.

Gäl′lus, (ÆLIUS,) an eminent Roman jurist, who was a contemporary of Cicero. He wrote a treatise "On the Signification of Terms which pertain to the Civil Law," an extract from which is found in the "Digest." According to Lachmann, he was the same person that was prefect of Egypt in 25 B.C.

Gallus, (ÆLIUS,) a Roman general, who was prefect of Egypt in 25 and 24 B.C., and was the first who penetrated Arabia with a Roman army, (23 B.C.) The expedition failed, in consequence, partly, of the treachery of Syl-læus, an Arabian who was the guide of the Roman army. Strabo obtained from him new information in geography, and wrote an account of the expedition.

Gallus, (CAIUS AQUILIUS,) an eminent Roman lawyer and judge, noted for learning and integrity, became prætor in 66 B.C. He was a friend of Cicero, who esteemed him highly and paid him a handsome compliment in his oration for Cæcina. He was the author of a formula "De Dolo Malo," and effected some important legal reforms. His works have not come down to us.

Gallus, (CAIUS ASINIUS,) a Roman politician, was a son of C. Asinius Pollio. He became consul in 8 B.C., and married Vipsania, the repudiated wife of Tiberius, who hated him for that reason and for his freedom in expressing his mind. He was committed to prison by Tiberius in 30 A.D., and died in confinement about the year 33. He wrote a book called a "Comparison between my Father and Cicero," which is not extant.

See J. G. HEINECCIUS, "Oratio de C. A. Gallo," (about 1730.)

Gallus, (CAIUS CORNELIUS,) an eminent Roman poet and courtier, was born at Forum Julii (Fréjus) about 66 B.C. He served in the army under Octavius, who received him into his favour and confidence and gave him a high command in the war against Antony. After the death of Antony, about 30 B.C., Augustus appointed Gallus Governor of Egypt, which he ruled at first with success. But afterwards, being accused of oppression and peculation, he was condemned to perpetual banishment, and killed himself in 25 or 26 B.C. His Elegies, which were much admired, are all lost. Like his friend Mæcenas, he patronized literary men, especially Virgil, who was his intimate friend, and who has gracefully commemorated his name and merit in his sixth and tenth eclogues.

See DION CASSIUS, books l., liii.; QUINTILIAN, books i., x.; SUETONIUS, "De illustribus Grammaticis;" VÖLKER, "Commentatio de C. C. Galli Vita et Scriptis," 1840-44; "Nouvelle Biographie Générale."

Gallus, (CAIUS SULPICIUS,) a Roman astronomer and orator, was chosen consul for 166 B.C. He was eminent as an orator and a Greek scholar, and appears to have been one of the most remarkable men of his time. He is regarded as the earliest of Roman astronomers. The occurrence of an eclipse of the moon, at the hour which he predicted, on the eve of the battle of Pydna, 168 B.C., excited the admiration and raised the spirits of the army in which he then served as tribune. He is highly eulogized by Cicero.

See LIVY, "History of Rome," books xliii., xliv., and xlv.; CICERO, "Brutus," "De Republica," "De Senectute," and "De Officiis."

Gallus, (CAIUS VIBIUS TREBONIANUS,) a Roman emperor, born, it is supposed, in the isle of Gerba, on the coast of Africa, about 205 A.D. He succeeded Decius in 251, with Hostilian as his colleague, and purchased a disgraceful peace with the Goths by an annual tribute. The empire was soon invaded by other hordes of barbarians, who were defeated by Æmilian. The victor having been proclaimed emperor by his army, Gallus marched against him; but, before the armies met, he was killed by his own troops, in 253 A.D. He was generally unpopular and despised.

See TILLEMONT, "Histoire des Empereurs."

Gallus, (CESTIUS,) a Roman general, became Governor of Syria in 64 A.D. The Jews having rebelled in the year 65, he besieged Jerusalem, but failed to take it.

Gallus, (FLAVIUS CLAUDIUS CONSTANTIUS,) a nephew of Constantine the Great, was born about 325 A.D. In 351 the Roman emperor Constantius gave to him his sister Constantina in marriage, and raised him to the rank of Cæsar, with the command of the Eastern provinces. But he soon disgraced himself by his cruelty and tyranny, for which he was recalled and executed in 354 A.D. He was a half-brother of the emperor Julian.

Gallus, (SERVATIUS.) See GALLÉ.

Gallus or Gallo, (THOMAS,) a French monk, was one of the most eminent theologians of his time, and became abbé of Vercelli, where he founded a famous school. He translated from the Greek a work on mystic theology ascribed to Dionysius Areopagita. Died in 1246.

Galluzzi, gäl-loot'see, or Gallucci, gäl-loot'chee, (TARQUINIO,) an Italian Jesuit and poet, born in 1574, professed rhetoric and morality at Rome, and was eminent as a pulpit orator. He published a volume of poems, "Carmina," (1611,) another of Latin orations, (1617,) and "Vindications of Virgil," ("Virgilianæ Vindicationes," 1621.) Died in 1649.

Gäl'lȳ, (HENRY,) an English divine, born at Beckenham, in Kent, in 1696. He translated from the Greek the "Characters" of Theophrastus, (1725,) and wrote, besides other works, an "Essay on Clandestine Marriages," (1750.) In 1735 he became chaplain-in-ordinary to the king. Died in 1769.

Gâlt, (JOHN,) a Scottish author, born at Irvine in May, 1779. He became a resident of London about 1803, engaged in trade, and failed. He travelled in the south of Europe in 1809-11, after which he published "Letters from the Levant," (1813,) several biographies, and a volume of tragedies, which were not successful. In 1820 his "Ayrshire Legatees" appeared in "Blackwood's Magazine." This was more popular than his previous efforts, and was followed by "Annals of the Parish," (1821,) and other tales illustrative of Scottish life. Between 1826 and 1829 he spent two or three years in Canada, as agent of a land-company; but, though not deficient in energy and integrity, he did not succeed in pecuniary affairs, and returned to England insolvent. Among his numerous works are a "Life of Lord Byron," (1830,) "Lawrie Todd," (1830,) "The Provost," (1822,) and other novels. Many of his tales are entertaining, and characterized by rough good sense and a quaintness of expression. He also wrote his Autobiography, (2 vols., 1833.) He died at Greenock in 1839.

See CHAMBERS, "Biographical Dictionary of Eminent Scotsmen;" W. JERDAN, "Men I have known," London, 1866.

Galuppi, gä-loop'pee, (BALDASSARE,) a famous Italian composer, was born in 1703, in Burano, (whence he was called BURANELLO,) an island near Venice. He composed many operas, and some sacred music, and has been called the father of the Italian comic opera. Died at Venice in 1785.

See FÉTIS, "Biographie Universelle des Musiciens."

Galuppi, (PASQUALE.) See GALLUPPI.

Galuzzi, gä-loot'see, (RIGUCCIO, re-goot'cho,) an Italian historian and priest, born at Volterra in 1730, published a "History of Tuscany under the Rule of the House of Medici," from 1569 to 1737. Died in 1801.

Galvam or Galvão, gäl-vöwn', (ANTONIO,) an eminent Portuguese captain, son of Duarte, noticed below, was born about 1502. He was appointed Governor of the Moluccas in 1538. He subdued several chiefs by arms, and governed that region with ability. It is stated that he converted many natives to the Catholic faith, and refused the offer of sovereignty in the Moluccas. He was recalled about 1545, and died in 1557, leaving a valuable work "On the Discoveries, Ancient and Modern, in India," (1563.) His exploits are highly extolled by the Portuguese historians.

See JOÃO BARROS, "Asia, Decada IV;" FARIA Y SOUZA, "Asia Portugueza;" LA CLÈDE, "Histoire de Portugal."

Galvam or Galvão, (DUARTE,) a learned Portuguese historian, born at Evora about 1435, became secretary to John II., and ambassador to Rome, France, etc. He edited, revised, or continued the "Chronicles of Portugal" written by Lopez. Died in 1517.

See N. ANTONIO, "Bibliotheca Hispana Nova."

Galvani, gäl-vä'nee, (ALOISIO,) an eminent Italian, physician, and physiologist, born in 1737 at Bologna, where he became professor of anatomy in 1762. He composed valuable treatises "On the Kidneys and Ureters of Birds," ("De Renibus atque Ureteribus Volatilium,") and "On the Organs of Hearing in Birds," ("De Aure Volatilium.") His durable reputation is founded on the accidental discovery of the phenomena since called from his name Galvanism, which he announced in his "Commentary on the Power (or Effect) of Electricity on Muscular Motion," ("De Viribus Electricitatis in Motu musculari Commentarius," 1791.) These phenomena were first observed in some dead frogs, which had been procured as aliment for his invalid wife. While they were lying on the table near the conductor of an electrical machine, their muscles were convulsed by accidental contact with a scalpel. Galvani explained this fact by the theory that all animals have electricity inherent in their economy, especially in the nerves and muscles. (See VOLTA.) Having refused to take an oath of allegiance to the Cisalpine republic, 1797, he lost his chair at Bologna, but was restored a short time before his death, which occurred in December, 1798.

See ALIBERT, "Éloge de Galvani," Paris, 1806; "Nouvelle Biographie Générale."

Galvez, gäl'vĕth, (Don BERNARDO,) COUNT, a nephew of José, noticed below, was born at Malaga in 1756. About 1780 he was appointed Governor of Louisiana, made a successful campaign against the English in Florida, and took Pensacola in 1781. Soon after this he became Viceroy of Mexico, which he governed with credit until his death, in 1794.

Galvez, (Don José,) a Spanish statesman and lawyer, born at Velez-Malaga in 1729. After gaining some distinction by his eloquence, he was employed as confidential secretary by Grimaldi, the prime minister. In 1764 Charles III. appointed him a member of the Council of the Indies, and in 1771 sent him to Mexico to settle a difficulty between the viceroy and the Audiencia or supreme tribunal. Upon his return, about 1775, he obtained the place of minister of the Indies, the most important office in the kingdom, next to that of prime minister. He directed the affairs of the colonies with ability, and received the title of Marquis of Sonora. Died in 1786.

See COXE, "Memoirs of the Kings of Spain of the House of Bourbon," 1813.

Galvez de Montalvo, gål'vĕth då mon-tål'vo, (LUIS,) a popular Spanish poet, born at Guadalaxara in 1549, was a friend of Cervantes. In 1582 he published a pastoral romance called the "Pastor de Filida," in prose and verse, which was admired for its richness of imagery and purity of style. He wrote also "The Tears of Saint Peter," (1587.) He is praised by Lope de Vega in his "Laurel of Apollo." He took the monastic vows in the latter part of his life. Died at Palermo in 1610.

See TICKNOR, "History of Spanish Literature;" N. ANTONIO, "Bibliotheca Hispana Nova."

Gål'way or **Gål'lo-way,** (HENRY,) LORD, Marquis de Ruvigny, (rü'vèn'ye',) was born in France in 1647. Proscribed as a Protestant, he retired to England about 1685, and was made Earl of Galway for his services in Ireland in 1691. In the war of the Spanish succession, he commanded the English and allies, who captured Madrid in June, 1706. Having been appointed general-in-chief in place of Lord Peterborough, he joined battle with the French at Almanza, (1707,) where he was wounded and defeated with great loss. He was again defeated at Gudina in 1709, and soon after recalled from the command for his ill success. In 1715 he acted as lord justiciary of Ireland. Died in 1720.

Gama, gå'må, (ANTONIO de Leon y—då là'ōn' e,) an astronomer and geographer, born at Mexico about 1735. Without the aid of teachers, he made great progress in astronomy. He published "Memoirs on the Satellites of Jupiter," "On the Almanac and Chronology of the Ancient Mexicans," and on the "Climate of New Spain," which are commended by Humboldt and Prescott. Died about 1800.

See PRESCOTT, "History of the Conquest of Mexico," vol. i. book i.

Gama, (JOANNA,) a Portuguese poetess, born in 1515, wrote religious poems, sonnets, etc. Died in 1586.

Gama, da, då gå'må, (CHRISTOVÃO,) a Portuguese captain, was the son of Vasco, the admiral. He served under his brother Estevão in the East Indies in 1540, and commanded a small army sent to aid the King of Abyssinia, where he was taken prisoner and killed by the Moors in 1542.

Gama, da, (ESTEVÃO,) the son of Vasco, was also noted as a naval commander. In 1536 he was appointed Governor of Malacca, and in 1540 Viceroy of India, which he ruled with ability. In the course of a war with the Turks, he explored the Red Sea, of which one of his officers wrote a description, the first that had been made by a European. Gama returned to Portugal in 1542.

Another ESTEVÃO, brother of Vasco, commanded a division of five ships in the expedition of 1502.

Gama, da, (FILIPPO JOZÉ,) a Portuguese poet and scholar, born in Lisbon in 1713; died in 1742.

Gama, da, (JOZÉ BASILIO,) a Brazilian poet, born in Minas Geraes in 1740. He became a resident of Lisbon, and was patronized by the minister Pombal. His principal poem, entitled "Ó Uruguay," (1769,) has been often reprinted. Died in Lisbon in 1795.

Gama, da, (VASCO,) (commonly, but less correctly, called **Vasco de Gama**—då gå'må,) a celebrated Portuguese navigator, born at Sines. The date of his birth and the details of his private life are unknown. He ac-

quired celebrity as commander of the fleet which in 1497 Emanuel of Portugal sent to India, being the first that performed the voyage from Europe to that remote region by doubling the Cape of Good Hope. He sailed from Lisbon on the 8th of July, with three small vessels and one hundred and sixty men. After doubling the cape, he sailed along the eastern coast, landed at Mozambique and Melinda, at the latter of which he procured a skilful pilot, and arrived at Calicut on the 20th of May, 1498. He went on shore with a few men, had an interview with the native prince, but failed to negotiate a treaty, in consequence of the jealousy of the Moors, and returned to Lisbon in September, 1499. The discovery of this route was an important era in commercial history, diverting into a new channel the Indian trade, which had before passed through the Red Sea and the Mediterranean. This enterprise of Gama forms the subject of Camoens's "Lusiad." In 1502, Vasco was sent out to India with a larger fleet, and, having cannonaded Calicut in retaliation for some injuries, established a factory at Cochin. Returning home in December, 1503, he was received with great honour, and rewarded with the title of count. In 1524, after a repose of twenty years, he was appointed Viceroy of India. He died in Cochin in 1524.

See BARROS, "Decadas;" LAFITAU, "Histoire des Découvertes des Portugais," etc.; FARIA Y SOUZA, "Asia Portugueza;" FERNÃO LOPEZ DE CASTANHEDA, "Historia do Descobrimento e Conquista da India," 1551; FERDINAND DENIS, "Portugal."

Gama, de, (VASCO.) See GAMA, DA.

Gamaches, gȧ'mȧsh', (ÉTIENNE,) an agreeable French writer, born at Meulan in 1672, was a canon regular. He published, under the name of Clarigny, a metaphysical work, called "System of the Heart," ("Système du Cœur," 1704,) which is commended. He wrote other works, among which are "The Elegancies of Language reduced to their Principles," (1718,) and "Physical Astronomy," (1740.) Died in 1756.

See SABATIER, "Les trois Siècles de la Littérature."

Gamaches, de, dẹh gȧ'mȧsh', (JOACHIM Rouault—roo'ō',) a French officer, born in Poitou, fought against the English about 1450. In 1461 Louis XI. made him a marshal of France. Died in 1478.

Gamaches, de, (PHILIPPE,) a doctor of the Sorbonne, and one of the best French Catholic theologians of his time, was born in 1568. He became professor of theology in Paris in 1598, and wrote an excellent commentary on Saint Thomas, called "Theologia scholastica speculativa practica," (1627.) Died in 1625.

See BAYLE, "Historical and Critical Dictionary."

Ga-mā'lĭ-el, [Heb. נכליאל,] a Pharisee and eminent Jewish doctor, lived at Jerusalem in the first century. He was a member of the Sanhedrim, the preceptor of Saint Paul, (see Acts xxii. 3,) and, according to the Talmud, was a grandson of the celebrated Hillel. His moderation and prudence are shown by a brief speech recorded in Acts v. 34–39. Died about 88 A.D.

Gamba, gâm'bả, (BARTOLOMMEO,) an Italian biographer, born at Bassano in 1766. He became a member of the Academy of Florence. He published, besides other works, "Narrazione de' Bassanesi illustri," (1807,) a "Gallery of the Literati and Artists of the Venetian Provinces in the Eighteenth Century," (1824,) and a "Life of Dante," (1825,) a work of recognized merit. Died in 1841.

See BARTOLOMMEO GAMBA, "Narrazione della Vita e delle Opere di lui," 1841; ANTONIO NEYMAYR, "Memoria di B. Gamba," Venice, 1846; TIPALDO, "Biografia degli Italiani illustri."

Gamba, gŏn'bȧ', (JACQUES FRANÇOIS,) a French traveller, born at Dunkirk in 1763, published "Travels in Southern Russia, Georgia," etc., (1824.) Died in 1833.

Gamba, (PIETRO,) COUNT, brother of the countess Guiccioli, was born at Ravenna, in Italy, in 1801. He accompanied Lord Byron to Greece, and fought with distinction for the liberty of the Greeks. He published a "Narrative of Lord Byron's Last Journey to Greece," (1825.) Died in Greece in 1826.

Gambacorti, gâm-bȧ-koR'tee, the name of an Italian family who held the chief power in Pisa between 1348 and 1406. ANDREA became chief magistrate in 1348, and died about 1354. FRANCESCO, his successor, was beheaded by the emperor Charles IV. in 1355, when the other members of the family were exiled. PIETRO, the nephew of Francesco, directed the republic with wisdom, moderation, and ability from 1369 to 1392, and waged war against the pope, (1376.) He was assassinated in 1392. GIOVANNI, a nephew of Pietro, and the last of the family, surrendered Pisa, after a long siege, to the Florentines in 1406. This was regarded by the citizens of Pisa as an act of treachery.

See SISMONDI, "Histoire des Républiques Italiennes."

Gambara, găm-bä'rä, (GIOVANNI FRANCESCO,) COUNT, an Italian writer, born near Piacenza in 1771. He served in the French armies as a colonel about 1805–08. He wrote "The League of Cambray," a poem, (1825,) and several dramas. Died in 1848.

Gambara, (LATTANZIO,) an eminent Italian painter, born at Brescia in 1541, adorned the churches of Cremona, Brescia, and Parma with frescos. He was killed by a fall in 1574.

Gambara, (LORENZO,) a Latin poet, born at Brescia about 1500. He was attached to Cardinal Farnese, in whose house he lived for a long time in Rome. Among his principal Latin poems, which were praised by Paul Manutius and Justus Lipsius, is "Columbus, or the Discovery of the New World." The first edition of his works appeared in 1555. Died in 1596.

See BAYLE, "Historical and Critical Dictionary."

Gambara, (VERONICA,) a noble Italian lady, born at Pralboino, near Brescia, in 1485, was the daughter of Count Gambara, and was eminent for her poetical talents and her attainments in Latin and philosophy. In 1508 she was married to Giberto, Lord of Correggio. She wrote admired sonnets and letters. Died in 1550.

See RIZZARDI, "Rime, Lettere e Vita di F. Gambara," 1769; TIRABOSCHI, "Storia della Letteratura Italiana;" ZAMBONI, "Vita di V. Gambara," 1759.

Gambart, gŏN'bǎr', (JEAN FÉLIX ADOLPHE,) a French astronomer, born in Cette in 1800. He became director of the Observatory of Marseilles in 1822, and discovered many comets. Died in 1836.

See F. D. ARAGO, "Notice sur M. Gambart," 1836.

Gamberelli, găm-bä-rel'lee, (BERNARDO,) an able Florentine architect and sculptor, born about 1410. He was patronized by Pope Nicholas V., and restored, besides other churches of Rome, San Pietro-in-Vincoli and San Giovanni Laterano. Died in 1490.

Gambey, gŏN'bằ', (HENRI PRUDENCE,) a skilful French mechanician, who excelled in the fabrication of astronomical instruments, was born at Troyes in 1787. He invented a heliostat. In 1837 he was admitted into the Academy of Sciences. Died in Paris in 1847.

See ARAGO, "Notice de Gambey," in the "Annuaire du Bureau des Longitudes," 1850.

Gambier, gam'beer, (JAMES,) BARON, an English admiral, born in one of the Bahama Isles in 1756, entered the navy when young, and served in the American war at the capture of Charleston, South Carolina, and other places. In 1793 he contributed to Lord Howe's victory over the French. He was made a rear-admiral in 1795, and vice-admiral in 1799. In 1802 he was appointed Governor of Newfoundland. Having been raised to the rank of admiral, he commanded the fleet which bombarded Copenhagen in 1807 and captured the Danish fleet. For this exploit he was raised to the peerage as a baron. In 1808 he quitted the admiralty, to take command of the Channel fleet against the French, from whom he took several ships. He was one of the commissioners who negotiated a treaty of peace between England and the United States, at Ghent, in 1814. He obtained the rank of admiral of the fleet in 1830. Died in 1833.

See VAN TENAC, "Histoire générale de la Marine."

Gam'bold, (JOHN,) a learned English Moravian divine, born in South Wales about 1710. He was for many years minister of the Moravian church in London, and was chosen a bishop in 1754. He published an edition of the Greek Testament, (1742,) "Hymns for the Use of the Brethren," (1748,) a "Short Summary of Christian Doctrine," (1767,) and other works. He had a high reputation for piety and talents. Died at Haverford West in 1771.

See NICHOLS, "Literary Anecdotes of the Eighteenth Century."

Gamelia, a surname of JUNO, which see.

Gamelin, găm'lâN', (JACQUES,) a French historical painter, born at Carcassonne in 1739; died in 1803.

Gamelius, a surname of JUPITER, which see.

Gam'mel, (WILLIAM,) an American writer, born at Medfield, Massachusetts, in 1812. He graduated at Brown University in 1831, and was appointed professor of rhetoric in that institution in 1836, and of history and political economy in 1850. He also made numerous contributions to reviews, and wrote the Life of Roger Williams, and that of Governor Samuel Ward, in Sparks's "American Biography," and other works.

Gamon, gɛ'môN', (CHRISTOPHE,) a French poet, born at Annonay about 1575, wrote "The Week, or Creation of the World," (1609,) a poem, in which he explains and maintains the Copernican system. Died in 1621.

Gamon, (FRANÇOIS JOSEPH,) a French poet, born about 1763. In 1792 he was a Girondist member of the Convention. Died in 1832.

Gamperlin. See GRAF.

Gand, (or **Ghent,**) HENRY OF. See GOETHALS.

Gănd-hăr'vă, [Hindoo pron. gŭnd-hŭr'vŭ,] sometimes written **Gandharba.** In the Hindoo mythology, the Gandharvas are celestial musicians, who live in Swerga, (the heaven of Indra,) or else attend on the superior gods, as Siva, Krishna, (Vishnu,) etc.

Gandini, gân-dee'nee, (ANTONIO,) an Italian painter, born at Brescia about 1550; died in 1630.

Gandini, (GIORGIO, or GIORGIO DEL GRANO, an Italian painter, born at Parma, was a pupil of Correggio. Died about 1538.

Gando, gŏN'do', (NICOLAS,) a skilful type-founder, was born at Geneva, and lived in Paris. He made improvements in the printing of music. Died about 1767.

Gandolfi, gân-dol'fee, (BARTOLOMMEO,) born at Torria, in Italy, in 1753, was professor of natural philosophy in the College di Sapienza at Rome from 1792 to 1824. He published, besides other useful works, a treatise on Earthquakes, (1787.) Died in 1824.

Gandolfi, (GAETANO,) an able Italian historical painter and engraver, born in the province of Bologna in 1734, was professor in the school of Bologna. The Italians regarded him as one of the first artists of his time. His works are admired for correctness of design, gracefulness of expression, and harmony of clair-obscur. Died in 1802.

See GRILLI, "Elogio di Gandolfi;" MALVASIA, "Felsina pittrice;" LANZI, "History of Painting in Italy."

Gandolfi, (MAURO,) a skilful engraver and painter, a son of the preceding, died in 1834.

Gandolfi, (UBALDO,) a painter, brother of Gaetano, noticed above, was born in 1728; died in 1781.

Gandolfo, gân-dol'fo, (DOMENICO ANTONIO,) an Augustine monk, born at Vintimiglia about 1645, wrote memoirs of eminent writers who belonged to the order of Augustines, (1704.) Died in 1707.

Gan'don, (JAMES,) an English architect, born about 1742. He studied under Sir William Chambers, and won the first gold medal for architecture ever awarded by the Royal Academy. He acquired a high reputation by erecting public buildings in Dublin, among which is the Custom-House, (finished in 1791,) one of the finest structures of its class in the world. He edited the "Vitruvius Britannicus," (3 vols., 1767–71.) Died in 1824.

Gan'dy, (JAMES,) an English portrait-painter, born in 1619, was an imitator of Van Dyck. Died in 1689.

Gănêsă, gɛ-nä'sɛ, written also **Ganéça** and **Ganêsha,** in the Hindoo mythology, the god of prudence and policy, is said to be the eldest son of Siva and Pârvatî. He is represented with an elephant's head and trunk, a symbol of sagacity. He is identified by some writers with the Roman JANUS, (which see.) He is sometimes called POLLEÂR.

See MOOR, "Hindu Pantheon."

Ganga. See PÂRVATÎ.

Ganganelli. See CLEMENT XIV.

Ganilh, gɛ'nêl' or gɛ'ne'ye, (CHARLES,) a French writer and lawyer, was born at Allanche (Cantal) in 1758. He was a member of the Chamber of Deputies from 1815 to 1823. He wrote "The Theory of Political Economy founded on Facts," (2 vols., 1815–22,) and other works. Died in 1836.

ā, ē, ī, ō, ū, ȳ, *long;* â, ê, ò, same, less prolonged; ă, ĕ, ĭ, ŏ, ŭ, ў, *short;* ạ, ẹ, ị, ọ, *obscure;* fär, fàll, fàt; mêt; nŏt; gōōd; mōōn;

Gannal, gȧ'nȧl', (JEAN NICOLAS,) a French chemist and inventor, born at Sarre-Louis in 1791. He became about 1816 assistant of Thénard in his lectures in Paris. He invented a process for refining borax, an elastic roller for printing-presses, and a process for embalming dead bodies by injection, for which he received the Montyon prize of the Institute, about 1835. Died in 1852.

See "Nouvelle Biographie Générale."

Gan'nett, (EZRA STILES,) an American Unitarian divine, born at Cambridge, Massachusetts, in 1801. He graduated at Harvard College in 1820, was ordained in 1824, and subsequently became the colleague of Dr. Channing, after whose death he succeeded to the pastoral charge of the Federal Street Church in Boston. He was for some years associate editor of the "Christian Examiner." Mr. Gannett holds a prominent place among the conservative Unitarians of New England.

Gans, gänss, (EDUARD,) an eminent German jurist, of Jewish extraction, born in Berlin in 1798. He studied under Hegel and Thibaut at Heidelberg, and became an earnest advocate of the philosophical, as opposed to the historical, school of jurisprudence. In 1820 he published his "Scholia on Gaius," ("Scholien zum Gajus,") in which his views are ably set forth, and which caused much excitement among his opponents. He brought out in 1824 his "Law of Succession in its Historical Development," esteemed one of the most admirable works of the kind. Soon after this he was appointed professor of law at Berlin, where he obtained the highest reputation and success as a lecturer. His "Lectures on the History of Modern Times" were afterwards published, and are regarded as models of eloquence, wit, and erudition. Among his other works we may name "Retrospect on Persons and Conditions," (1836,) and "The Basis of Possession," (1839.) Died in Berlin in 1839.

See MARHEINEKE, "Rede am Grabe des Professor Dr. Gans," 1839; SAINT-MARC GIRARDIN, "Édouard Gans," in the "Revue des Deux Mondes" for December 1, 1839; "Nouvelle Biographie Générale."

Gansevoort, gänss'voort, (PETER,) an American officer, born at Albany, New York, in 1749. He defended Fort Stanwix with success in 1777 during a siege of twenty days, for which important service he received the thanks of Congress. In 1809 he became a brigadier-general in the United States army. Died in 1812.

Ganteaume, gôN'tōm', (HONORÉ JOSEPH,) COUNT, a French naval officer, born at La Ciotat in 1755. After serving in the American war (1779) and in the East Indies, he obtained the rank of captain in 1794. In 1798 he was wounded at the battle of Aboukir, and became a rear-admiral, with the command of the fleet employed on the coast of Egypt. He escorted Bonaparte from Egypt to France with two frigates in 1799, and was appointed a councillor of state. In 1804 he was raised to the grade of vice-admiral. Louis XVIII. made him a peer in 1815. Died in 1818.

See "Nouvelle Biographie Générale."

Gan-ȳ-me'dēs, in English **Gan'ȳ-mede,** [Gr. Γανυμήδης; Fr. GANYMÈDE, gȧ'ne'mȧd',] a personage of classic mythology, represented as the son of Tros and the cup-bearer of Jupiter, who selected him for that office on account of his extraordinary beauty.

Gaoutama, the French of GAUTAMA, which see.

Garamond, gȧ'rä'môN', (CLAUDE,) a celebrated engraver and type-founder, born in Paris. He surpassed all his predecessors in the fabrication of types. Francis I. employed him to engrave for editions of ancient authors the Greek characters since known by the name of Garamond. Died in 1561.

Garampi, gä-räm'pee, (GIUSEPPE,) an Italian antiquary and writer, born at Rimini in 1725, was made a cardinal by Pope Pius VI. Died in 1792.

Garasse, gȧ'rȧss', (FRANÇOIS,) a French Jesuit and popular preacher, born at Angoulême in 1585, noted for his scurrility and buffoonery, wrote many violent controversial works, among which was "La Doctrine curieuse des Beaux-Esprits de ce Temps," (1623.) Died in 1631.

Garat, gȧ'rȧ', (DOMINIQUE JOSEPH,) a French revolutionist and popular writer, was born near Bayonne in 1749. He gained literary distinction by his eulogies on Fontenelle and others, and took four prizes of elo-quence awarded by the French Academy between 1779 and 1784. In 1790 he became a member of the Constituent Assembly, of which he reported the proceedings in the "Journal de Paris." He succeeded Danton in 1792 as minister of justice, in which capacity it devolved on him to notify Louis XVI. that the Convention had sentenced him to death. He expressed his repugnance to this "frightful commission." He was minister of the interior for a short time in 1793, and was admitted into the Institute in 1795. Under the régime of Napoleon he became a senator, a count, and president of the Institute. Garat was excluded from office and from the Academy on the restoration of 1815. Besides many political treatises, he wrote "Memoirs of the Life of M. Suard," (1820.) Died in 1833.

See THIERS, "History of the French Revolution;" ARMAND MARRAST, "Notice sur D. J. Garat," 1838; VILLENAVE, "Notice sur la Vie de D. J. Garat;" "Nouvelle Biographie Générale."

Garat, (PIERRE JEAN,) a celebrated vocalist, nephew of the preceding, born at Ustarits in 1764. He was styled "the Modern Orpheus," "the Musical Proteus," etc. Died in 1823.

Garavaglia, gä-rä-väl'yä, (GIOVITA,) a skilful Italian engraver, born at Pavia in 1790. He engraved "The Holy Family," after Raphael, (1817,) "Beatrice Cenci," after Guido Reni, "The Infant Jesus with John," after C. Maratta, and other works. He became a professor in the Academy of Florence in 1833. Died in 1835.

See NAGLER, "Neues Allgemeines Künstler-Lexikon."

Garay. See LAGARAYE.

Garay, [Hun. pron. gŏr'oi,] (JÁNOS,) a popular Hungarian poet, born at Szekszard in 1812. He wrote "Csatár," (1834,) a heroic poem, "Elizabeth Báthory," a drama, (1840,) a volume of lyric verses called "The Pearls of Balaton Lake," (1843,) which were received with favour, and several popular ballads. · Died in 1853.

Garay, de, dȧ gä-ri', (JUAN,) a Spanish general, born at Badajos in 1541. He went to South America in his youth, fought with distinction against the natives, explored a vast region on the Paraná, and was appointed a lieutenant-general about 1576. He founded Buenos Ayres in 1580, soon after which he was killed by some savages who surprised him at night.

See FUNES, "Ensayo del Historia civil del Paraguay," etc., Buenos Ayres, 1816.

Garay, de, (DON MARTIN,) a Spanish financier, born in Aragon in 1760, was called the Necker of Spain. He became minister of finance about 1814, and proposed a plan of financial reform which gave much offence to the nobles and clergy. Died in 1822.

Gar'bett, (JAMES,) an English theologian, born about 1773, was archdeacon of Chichester, and professor of poetry at Oxford. Among his works are "Christ as Prophet, Priest, and King; Eight Lectures at Bampton Lecture," (1842,) and "The Beatitudes of the Mount, in Seventeen Sermons," (1853.) Died in 1857.

Garbieri, gaR-be-ā'ree, (LORENZO,) an Italian painter, born at Bologna in 1580, was a pupil of L. Caracci, of whom he is called one of the best imitators. He preferred for his subjects scenes of carnage or sorrow. Among his works is "The Plague at Milan." Died in 1654.

See LANZI, "History of Painting in Italy;" MALVASIA, "Felsina pittrice."

Garbo, del, dĕl gaR'bo, (DINO,) a Florentine physician, was professor in the University of Bologna. He was physician to the pope John XXII., and wrote treatises on medicine. Died in 1327.

Garbo, del, (RAFFAELINO,) an Italian painter, born at Florence in 1466. Among his best works is "The Resurrection of Christ." Died in 1524.

Garção or **Garcam,** gaR-sŏwN', (PEDRO ANTONIO Correa—kor-rā'ä,) a Portuguese lyric poet, called "the Portuguese Horace," was born in Lisbon in 1724, or, as some say, 1735. He wrote sonnets, satires, and odes, which are admired for good sense and elegant taste, and is reputed the best lyric poet that Portugal produced in the eighteenth century. He also wrote "Theatro Novo," a drama. His complete works were published in 1778. He died in 1772, in prison, where he was confined by Pombal for a reason which is not explained.

See "Nouvelle Biographie Générale."

€ as k; ç as s; ğ hard; ġ as j; G, H, K, guttural; N, nasal; R, trilled; ŝ as z; ₥h as in this. (☞See Explanations, p. 23.)

Garção-Stockler, gaR-sŏwn' stok'ler, ? (FRANCISCO DE BORJA,) a Portuguese mathematician, a nephew of the preceding, was born at Lisbon in 1759. He published an "Account of the True Principles of the Method of Fluxions," ("Memoria sobre os verdadeiros Principios do Methodo dos Fluxões," 1797,) "Historical Essay on the Origin and Progress of Mathematics in Portugal," (1819,) and other able works. He was chosen Captain-General of the Azores in 1820. Died in 1829.

Garces, gaR'thĕs, (JULIAN,) a Spanish bishop and pulpit orator, born in Aragon about 1460, was appointed chaplain to Charles V. and preacher to his court. In 1527 he was ordained Bishop of Tlascala, in Mexico. He wrote an "Epistle to the Pope in Favour of the Indians." Died about 1547.

Garcia or **Garzia,** gaR-see'ą or gaR-thee'ä, I., Count of Castile, born at Burgos in 938 A.D., succeeded his father, Fernando Gonzales, in 970. He defeated the redoubtable Almansor at Osma in 984. The latter having again invaded Castile in 990, Garcia gave him battle, and received a mortal wound. He was reputed a wise and just prince.

Garcia (or **Garzia**) **II.,** Count of Castile, grandson of the preceding, succeeded his father, Don Sancho, in 1022, at the age of fourteen. His virtues and talents gave promise of a prosperous reign ; but he was assassinated by the Counts of Vela, in the prime of life, about 1030.

Garcia or **Garzia,** gaR-thee'ä, or **Garcias,** gaR-thee'äs, King of Navarre, born at Tudela in 958 A.D., began to reign in 994. He was called "the Trembler," because his frame was agitated just before battle, and was the author of the saying, "My body trembles at the dangers to which my courage is about to expose it." In 998 Garcia and his allies defeated Almansor the Saracen in the great battle of Calacanaçor or Caltañazor. Died in 1001.

Garcia, (JOSÉ HIDALGO.) See GARZIA.

Garcia, (or **Garzia,**) (MANUEL,) an eminent teacher of music, was born at Madrid in 1805. He became professor of music in Paris and London, and wrote, besides other musical treatises, "School of Garcia : Complete Treatise on the Art of Singing," ("École de Garcia : Traité complet de l'Art du Chant," 1841.) The famous actress and singer Pauline Viardot is his sister.

Garcia, (or **Garzia,**) (MANUEL **de Populo Vicente** —dä po'poo-lo ve-thĕn'tä,) a Spanish composer and singer, born at Seville in 1775, was the father of the preceding and of Madame Malibran. He lived many years in Paris and London, where he taught music and performed with great success on the stage. He composed several successful operas, among which is "The Caliph of Bagdad," (1812.) About 1825 he visited the United States. Died in Paris in 1832.

Garcia, (PAULINE.) See VIARDOT.

Garcia de Mascarenhas, gaR-see'ä dä mäs-kä-rĕn'yäs, (BRAZ, or BLAISE,) a Portuguese poet, born at Avo in 1596. He enlisted in the army in 1614, went to Brazil, and fought against the Dutch. He returned to Lisbon in 1640, and was appointed Governor of Alfayates, which he defended against the Spaniards. Having been imprisoned on a false charge of conspiracy or treason, he wrote a poetical letter to John IV., escaped from prison, and obtained an interview with the king, who was satisfied of his innocence and restored him to office. His principal work is "Viriato," a national epic poem, (1699,) which, says the "Biographie Universelle," "entitles him to rank among the best epic poets of Portugal after Camoëns." Died in 1656.

See BARBOSA MACHADO, "Bibliotheca Lusitana ;" J. M. DA COSTA E SYLVA, "Ensaio biografico-critico sobre os melhores Poetas Portuguezes," 1854, vol. vii.

Garcia (or **Garzia**) **de Paredes,** gaR-thee'ä dä pä-rä'dĕs, (Don DIEGO,) a brave Spanish officer, born at Truxillo in 1466, served in the war against the Moors which resulted in the conquest of Granada, and afterwards, under Gonsalvo de Córdova, against the French. Like the Chevalier Bayard, to whom he is compared in loyalty and honour, he never held very high positions, though he had captured eight fortified places, besides

taking part in thirty-two battles and sieges. He distinguished himself at Pavía in 1525. Died in 1530.

See SISMONDI, "Histoire des Républiques Italiennes ;" GUICCIARDINI, "Historia Bellorum Italiæ ;" "Nouvelle Biographie Générale ;" DE VARGAS, "Vida de D. Garzia de Paredes," 1621.

Garcias Laso. See GARCILASO.

Garcias y Matamoros, gaR-thee'äs e mä-tä-mo'ròs, (ALPHONSO,) a learned priest, born at Córdova, in Spain, in 1490, left a single Latin work, "On the Academies and Learned Men of Spain," (1553.) Died about 1550.

Garcilaso (or **Garcilasso**) **de la Vega,** gaR-the-lä'so dä lä vä'gä, (or **Garcias Laso,** gaR-thee'äs lä'so,) a Spanish poet of superior merit, born at Toledo in 1503. His name is sometimes written **Garsias Lasso.** He entered in early youth the army of Charles V., under whom he made several campaigns, and distinguished himself at the battle of Pavía, (1525.) He commanded thirty companies of the Imperial army that invaded France in 1536, and was mortally wounded in the retreat from Marseilles. Died at Nice in November of that year. He acquired a durable and wide reputation by his pastoral and lyrical poems, and his successful efforts, in concert with his friend Boscan, to reform Spanish poetry by the introduction of the Italian measure, which forms an epoch in the literary history of Spain. Garcilaso excels in tenderness and pathos, and has been styled "the Spanish Petrarch." His works, which are comprised in one small volume, (1553,) consist of above thirty sonnets, three eclogues, and a number of odes and elegies. His first eclogue, which many poets have imitated but none has equalled, would alone suffice to immortalize his name as that of one of the best poets of Spain.

See SISMONDI, "Literature of the South of Europe ;" TICKNOR, "History of Spanish Literature ;" E. F. DE NAVARRETE, "Vida del celebre Poeta Garcilaso de la Vega," 1850 ; BOUTERWEK, "Histoire de la Littérature Espagnole ;" NICÉRON, "Mémoires ;" "Lyric Poetry of Spain," in the "Edinburgh Review" for July, 1824.

Garcilaso de la Vega, surnamed THE INCA, a Spanish historian, born at Cuzco, in Peru, about 1530. He derived his surname from his mother, who was a native princess, a descendant of the Incas. After collecting materials for the history of Peru, he went to Spain in 1560, and obtained a pension from Philip II. His history of Peru, entitled "Comentarios reales que tratan del Orígen de los Incas," (1609,) is esteemed for its fidelity and accuracy. He also wrote an account of the conquest of Florida by De Soto, (1605.) His death is variously dated from 1568 to 1616.

See TICKNOR, "History of Spanish Literature ;" PRESCOTT, "History of the Conquest of Peru," vol. i. book ii.

Garcilasso (or **Garcias Lasso**) **de la Vega y Vargas,** gaR-the-läs'so dä lä vä'gä e vaR'gäs, (SEBASTIAN,) a Spanish officer, was the father of the preceding. He went to Mexico with Alvarado, whom he aided in the conquest of Guatemala. He served with distinction under Pizarro in Peru, which he entered in 1534, and fought against Almagro in 1542. He became Governor of Cuzco in 1548. Died in 1559.

Garcin de Tassy, gǎr'sǎn' deh tä'se', (JOSEPH HÉLIODORE,) a French Orientalist, born at Marseilles in 1794, was chosen a member of the Academy of Inscriptions, in place of Talleyrand, in 1838. He became professor of Hindostanee at the "École de Langues orientales vivantes," in Paris. He published, among other works, a "History of Hindostanee Literature," (2 vols., 1837.)

Garczynski, gaR-chin'skee, (STEPHEN,) a Polish statesman, who was appointed vaïvode of Kalisch and palatine of Posen. He wrote the "Anatomy of the Kingdom of Poland," (1751.) Died in 1755.

Gardane, gǎr'dǎn', (ANTOINE,) a French general, born in Provence about 1760, became general of division about 1798, won distinction by his conduct at Marengo in 1800, and took part in the campaigns against Austria and Prussia in 1805 and 1806. Died in 1807.

Gardane, (JOSEPH JACQUES,) a French physician and medical writer, born in Provence, practised in Paris about 1770. He wrote several treatises on syphilis.

Gardane, de, deh gǎr'dǎn', (MATHIEU CLAUDE,) COMTE, a French officer, born in Marseilles in 1766, acted as aide-de-camp to Napoleon in 1804, and distinguished himself at Austerlitz, Jena, and Eylau. In 1807 he was sent as ambassador to Persia. Died in 1818.

Gar'dẹn, (ALEXANDER,) F.R.S., a British botanist, born in Edinburgh about 1730. He practised medicine for many years in Charleston, South Carolina, and corresponded with Linnæus, to whom he furnished information on the natural history of Carolina. He contributed to the "Philosophical Transactions" of London. Died in England in 1791. The genus *Gardenia* was named in honour of him by Linnæus.

Gar'dẹn, (ALEXANDER,) an American officer, who served in the war of the Revolution as aide-de-camp to General Greene. He wrote "Anecdotes of the Revolutionary War in America, with Sketches of Character," etc., (1822.) Died about 1825.

Garden, (FRANCIS,) called also LORD GARDENSTONE, a Scottish judge, born in Edinburgh in 1721. After he had practised at the bar with credit, he was chosen solicitor of the king in 1764, and judge of the court of sessions. He published a work entitled "Travelling Memoranda," (3 vols., 1792-95,) the result of his travels on the continent. Died in 1793.

See CHAMBERS, "Biographical Dictionary of Eminent Scotsmen."

Gardenstone, LORD. See GARDEN, (FRANCIS.)

Gardie, de la, dẹh lẳ gảr'de', (JAKOB,) COUNT, a skilful Swedish general, son of Pontus, noticed below, was born in 1583. He commanded the Swedish army against the Russians in the reign of Charles IX., subjected a large part of Muscovy, and advanced with his victorious army to Moscow, where a truce was negotiated. Gustavus Adolphus, having ascended the throne, renewed the war, and made his first campaign under the tuition of Count de la Gardie. After the peace of 1617 he became senator and minister of war. Died in 1652.

See J. SCHEFFER, "Oratio in obitum J. de la Gardie," 1652.

Gardie, de la, (MAGNUS GABRIEL,) an able Swedish statesman, son of the preceding, was born in 1622. In the reign of Charles X. (whose sister La Gardie married) he commanded one of the armies. Under Charles XI. he was grand chancellor, and for about twenty years principal minister of state. Died in 1686.

Gardie, de la, dẹh lẳ gảr'de', (PONTUS, pôn'tüss',) an able general, born at La Gardie, in France, about 1530. He entered the service of the King of Sweden about 1565, and commanded the army of Duke John in the war which resulted in the dethronement of Eric XIV., (1568.) He became a baron, field-marshal, and senator. About 1583 he was commander-in-chief of the Swedish army, and gained advantages over the Russians in Livonia. He was drowned near Narva in 1585.

See DE THOU, "Histoire universelle;" BAYLE, "Historical and Critical Dictionary;" C. OERNHIELM, "Vita illustrissimi Herois P. de la Gardie," 1690; "Svensk Plutarch," vol. ii.; "Nouvelle Biographie Générale."

Gardin-Dumesnil, gảr'dăn' dü'mẳ'nèl', (JEAN BAPTISTE,) an eminent French professor and scholar, born at Saint-Cyr in 1720. In 1758 he became professor of rhetoric in the College of Harcourt, Paris, where he lectured many years. He wrote a work entitled "Latin Synonyms," (1777.) Died in 1802.

Gardiner, gard'nẹr, (ALLAN,) LORD, an English admiral, born at Uttoxeter in 1742, entered the navy in 1755. He served against the Americans and French, and commanded the Duke in the battle of April 12, 1782. Having been for several years a member of the admiralty, he obtained the rank of rear-admiral in 1793, with command of the fleet stationed near the Leeward Islands. He distinguished himself in the battle of June 1, 1794. In 1800 he was promoted to the rank of admiral. He sat in several Parliaments, and was raised to the English peerage, as Baron Uttoxeter. Died in 1809.

Gardiner, (Captain ALLEN F.,) an English naval officer, born in 1794. He went as a missionary to Patagonia, and published "Voice from South America," (1847.) Died in 1851.

Gardiner, gard'nẹr, (JAMES,) a Scottish officer, eminent for his piety and courage, was born at Carriden in 1688. He was wounded at Ramillies, (1706,) and afterwards rose to the rank of colonel. He commanded a regiment of dragoons against the Pretender at Preston-

pans, where he was killed, in 1745. The circumstances of his death are minutely described by Scott in "Waverley."

See "Some Remarkable Passages in the Life of Colonel James Gardiner," by REV. PHILIP DODDRIDGE, 1796; CHAMBERS, "Biographical Dictionary of Eminent Scotsmen."

Gardiner, gard'nẹr, (JOHN,) an American lawyer, born in Boston in 1731. As a member of the legislature of Massachusetts, he procured the abolition of the law of primogeniture, and promoted several legal reforms. Died in 1793.

Gardiner, (JOHN SYLVESTER JOHN,) an Episcopal clergyman, a son of the preceding, was born in South Wales in 1775. He became rector of Trinity Church, Boston, in 1805. He was distinguished as a scholar and a writer. Died in 1830.

See DUYCKINCK, "Cyclopædia of American Literature," vol. i.

Gardiner, (RICHARD,) an English divine, born at Hereford in 1591. He became a canon of Christ Church in 1629, and chaplain to Charles I. in 1630. He wrote, besides other works, "Model of Oratory," ("Specimen Oratorium," 1653,) and a volume of sixteen Sermons, (1659.) Died in 1670.

Gardiner, (STEPHEN,) Bishop of Winchester, an English prelate and statesman, was born at Bury Saint Edmund's in 1483. At Cambridge he made himself master of Greek and Latin and of civil and canon law. While employed as secretary by Cardinal Wolsey, he attracted the notice and favour of Henry VIII., who in 1527 chose him as a commissioner to negotiate with the pope the divorce of Queen Catherine. Soon after his return he was made secretary of state, and in 1531 Bishop of Winchester. He strenuously opposed the Protestant Reformers, and urged the king to punish them with severity. He courted the favour of Henry VIII. by aiding him to procure divorces, but gave offence to him by being too officious in preparing the impeachment of Catherine Parr. Gardiner was an enemy of Cranmer, whom he attempted to convict of heresy, but without success. In the reign of Edward VI. he was committed to the Tower in 1548, and confined about five years. Queen Mary, having ascended the throne, hastened to reward him by the office of chancellor of England and the principal direction of affairs in church and state. The sanguinary persecutions of that reign are attributed to his influence by Hume, who says, "The severe manners of Gardiner inclined him to support by persecution that religion which at the bottom he regarded with great indifference." Died in 1555. "There was," says Froude, "something in Gardiner's character which was not wholly execrable. For thirty years he worked unweariedly in the service of the public; his judgment as member of the council was generally excellent. . . . He was vindictive, ruthless, treacherous; but his courage was indomitable."

See FROUDE'S "History of England," vol. vi. chap. xxxiii.; also HUME'S and LINGARD'S Histories of England; BURNET'S "History of the Reformation."

Gardiner, (SYLVESTER,) an American physician, father of John Gardiner, noticed above, was born in Kingston, Rhode Island, in 1717, and practised in Boston. Died in 1786.

Gardiner, (WILLIAM,) a skilful engraver, born in Dublin in 1766. He was a pupil or assistant of Bartolozzi. Among his works are "Illustrations of Shakspeare" and of other English authors. He committed suicide in 1814.

Gardiner, (WILLIAM,) an English writer on music, born in 1770. He published "Music of Nature," "Sights in Italy," and other works. Died in 1853.

Gardner, (GEORGE,) M.D., a Scottish botanist, born at Glasgow about 1812. He explored Brazil and other parts of South America, in which he passed several years, 1836-41. Having returned to England, he published "Travels in the Interior of Brazil," (1846.) He died in Ceylon in 1849.

See CHAMBERS, "Biographical Dictionary of Eminent Scotsmen," (Supplement.)

Garelli, gả-rel'lee, (PIO NICCOLÒ,) born at Bologna in 1670, became first physician to the Emperor of Germany. He wrote a treatise on "Viviparous Generation." Died in 1739.

€ as *k*; ç as *s*; g̃ *hard*; g̃ as *j*; G, H, K, *guttural*; N, *nasal*; R, *trilled*; ŝ as *z*; th as in *this*. (☞See Explanations, p. 23.)

Garengeot, de, dẹh gȧ′rŏn′zho′, (RENÉ JACQUES Croissant—krwȧ′sŏn′,) a French surgeon, born at Vitré in 1688. He began to lecture on anatomy in Paris in 1725, and was chosen Fellow of the Royal Society of London in 1728. He became surgeon-major of the king's regiment in 1742, and wrote several treatises, among which is "Traité des Opérations de Chirurgie," (2 vols., 1720.) Died in 1759.

Garet, gȧ′rȧ′, (JEAN,) a French scholar and Benedictine, born at Havre in 1627. He published an edition of Cassiodorus, (2 vols., 1676.) Died in 1694.

Gar′field, (JAMES A.,) an American general, born in Cuyahoga county, Ohio, in 1831. He was a teacher and a lawyer before the civil war, and became a brigadier-general early in 1862. He was elected a member of Congress from the nineteenth district of Ohio in October, 1862, served as chief of staff of General Rosecrans in 1863, and was raised to the rank of major-general for his services at Chickamauga in September of that year. He was elected to Congress by the Republicans in 1866 and 1868. He was appointed in 1867 chairman of the committee on military affairs.

Garibaldi, gȧr-e-bȧl′de, [It. pron. gȧ-re-bȧl′dee,] (GIUSEPPE,) a celebrated Italian patriot and general, born at Nice, July 4, 1807. He entered the navy in early youth. Having become an active friend of liberty, he was banished in 1834. About 1836 he took arms for the republic of Uruguay, and fought against Brazil for several years. Before the end of this war he married a South American lady, named Anita, who afterwards shared with him in Italy the dangers of his military career. In 1844 he volunteered to defend Montevideo against Rosas, and led his Italian legion to victory at San Antonio in 1846. He quitted South America in the spring of 1848, and joined the Italian patriots in the war against Austria. He offered his services to King Charles Albert, but was treated by him with coldness and distrust. After the flight of the pope, he took an active part in founding the Roman Republic and in the defence of Rome against the French army in April and May, 1849. During the siege of Rome he displayed great heroism, and gained several victories over the Neapolitans, who threatened that city. When the French captured Rome in July, 1849, Garibaldi escaped with several hundred men, and, after passing through many desperate adventures and conflicts with the Austrians, was again driven into exile, and became in 1850 a resident of New York. He worked for some time in a manufactory of candles near that city, and afterwards made several voyages in the Pacific.

Early in 1859 he offered his services to the King of Sardinia, and, having formed a detached corps, called "Hunters of the Alps," he gained several victories over the Austrians, at Varese, Como, etc. Having raised a small army for the liberation of Southern Italy from the domination of the Bourbon King of Naples, he landed at Marsala, in Sicily, in May, 1860. He speedily took Palermo and Messina, and, crossing over to the mainland in August, occupied the city of Naples about the 8th of September. His army, reinforced by many Liberals of Southern Italy, defeated the troops of King Francis in October, 1860, and expelled him from the country, which was soon after annexed to the kingdom of Italy. Garibaldi afterwards retired to his home in the island of Caprera. In April, 1862, he was appointed general-in-chief of the Italian national guard. He engaged in the summer of 1862 in an enterprise which was disapproved by the Italian government, and came into collision with the royal troops at Aspromonte, where he was wounded in the foot and taken prisoner.

In 1864 he visited England, where he was received with great enthusiasm. He fought against the Austrians in the short war of 1866, at the head of a corps of volunteers; but the hostilities were ended by a truce before he came to any decisive action. On several occasions he inflamed the patriotism of his countrymen by eloquent addresses. Acting without the authority of the Italian government, he raised, in the summer of 1867, an army for the liberation of Rome, which he wished to annex to the kingdom of Italy. In an address to the people of Rome, dated September 16, he said, "Break the rings of your chains on the necks of your oppressors, and henceforth you will share your glory with the Italians." He was arrested, by the order of the king, at Sinalunga, September 23, and confined, but soon escaped, and invaded the Papal States with a body of troops, who were defeated at Mentana by the papal forces and their French allies in November, 1867.

See his "Autobiography," edited by ALEXANDRE DUMAS, and translated into English by W. ROBSON, 1860; "Garibaldi at Caprera," by COLONEL VECCHJ, with a Preface by MRS. GASKELL, London, 1862; "Westminster Review" for October, 1859.

Garibay y Zamalloa, gȧ-re-bī′ e thȧ-mȧl-yo′ȧ, (ESTEBAN,) a Spanish historian, born at Mondragon in 1525. He was appointed in 1563 historiographer by Philip II., and published a "Compendium of the Chronicles and History of Spain," (4 vols., 1571.) Died in 1593.

Garidel, gȧ′re′dĕl′, (PIERRE,) a French physician and botanist, born at Manosque in 1659; died in 1737.

Gariel, gȧ′re-ĕl′, (PIERRE,) a French historian, born at Montpellier about 1582, wrote a "History of Montpellier," and other works. Died in 1670.

Garissoles, gȧ′re′sol′, (ANTOINE,) a French poet and Protestant divine, born at Montauban in 1587. He became pastor of the Calvinist church and professor of theology in his native town in 1627. He wrote Latin with purity and remarkable facility. Besides several approved works on theology, he wrote (1649) a Latin poem on the exploits of Gustavus Adolphus, entitled "Adolphis," and a few other poems. Died in 1651.

See BAYLE, "Historical and Critical Dictionary;" "Nouvelle Biographie Générale."

Gar′land, (HUGH A.,) an American lawyer and writer, born in Virginia in 1805. He was chosen clerk of the House of Representatives by the Democrats in 1838. He wrote a "Life of John Randolph," (2 vols., 1850.) Died in 1854.

Garland, (ROBERT R.,) an American officer in the Confederate army, became a brigadier-general, and was killed in the battle of South Mountain in 1862.

Garlande, de, dẹh gȧr′lŏnd′, ? (JEAN,) a poet of the eleventh century. The English and French both claim him as a native of their respective countries. Little is known of his history. Among the numerous works that bear his name are Latin poems on the "Mysteries of the Church," and on "Contempt of the World," "Facetus," a poem on the "Duties of Man," and "Floretus," or "Liber Floreti." Died after 1080.

Garnaud, gȧr′no′, (ANTOINE MARTIN,) a French architect, born in Paris in 1796; died in 1861.

Garneray, gȧrn′rȧ′, (AMBROISE LOUIS,) a French painter of marine views, born in Paris in 1783. He served several years in the navy. He painted naval battles with success, and designed and engraved many views of French ports. He was employed for about ten years in the porcelain-manufactory of Sèvres.

Garneray, (AUGUSTE SIMÉON,) a painter, brother of the preceding, was born in Paris in 1785. He was patronized by the empress Josephine and Queen Hortense. Died in 1823 or 1824.

Garneray, (JEAN FRANÇOIS,) a French painter of history and portraits, father of the preceding, was born in Paris in 1755. Among his works are a portrait of Charlotte Corday, and a picture of "Louis XVI. in the Temple." Died in 1837.

Garnerin, gȧrn′rȧn′, (ANDRÉ JACQUES,) a noted French aeronaut, born in Paris in 1769, was the first who descended from a balloon by a parachute, (1797.) At the coronation of Napoleon, in 1804, he was employed to celebrate the event by sending up a large balloon, which, it is said, was wafted by the wind to Rome, and, after soaring over the Vatican, struck against the monument of Nero, the next day after its ascent. Died in 1823.

See "Nouvelle Biographie Générale."

Garnerin, (JEAN BAPTISTE OLIVIER,) an aeronaut, a brother of the preceding, was born in Paris in 1766; died in 1849.

Gar′net, (HENRY,) an English Jesuit, born at Nottingham about 1555. Having become a Roman Catholic, he visited Rome and joined the Society of Jesus in 1575. He was appointed superior of the English Jesuits in 1586, and resided in or near London at the time of the Gunpowder Plot. For complicity in this affair he

ā, ē, ī, ō, ū, ȳ, *long;* ȧ, ė, ȯ, same, less prolonged; ă, ĕ, ĭ, ŏ, ŭ, ў, *short;* ạ, ẹ, ị, ọ, *obscure;* fär, fȧll, fȧt; mėt; nŏt; gŏŏd; mōŏn;

was tried, convicted, and hung in May, 1606. (See FAWKES, GUY.) He was regarded as a martyr by the Catholics, who admit that the plot had been revealed to him as a confessor, but assert that he discouraged it.

See HUME, "History of England," chap. xlvi.; GARDINER, "History of England from 1603 to 1616," chap. v.

Gar'nett, (JAMES MERCER,) an American agriculturist, born in Essex county, Virginia, in 1770. He was one of the principal founders, and the first president, of the United States Agricultural Society, and wrote many able papers on agriculture and other subjects. Died in 1843.

Garnett, (RICHARD B.,) an American general, born in Virginia, graduated at West Point in 1841. He commanded a brigade of General Lee's army, and was killed at Gettysburg, July 3, 1863, aged about forty-four years.

Garnett, (ROBERT SELDEN,) an American general, born in Virginia about 1821, graduated at West Point in 1841. He was aide-de-camp to General Taylor in the Mexican war, and became a captain in 1851. Having taken arms against the Union in 1861, he obtained a command in Western Virginia. He was defeated and killed at Carrick's Ford in July, 1861.

Garnett, (THOMAS,) an English physician, born at Casterton in 1766. He obtained in 1796 the chair founded by Anderson at Glasgow, and lectured on chemistry at the Royal Institution of London in 1799–1800. He published, besides other works, "Observations on a Tour through the Highlands," (2 vols., 1800,) and "Lectures on Chemistry," (1801.) Died in 1802.

Garnier, gȧr′ne-ȧ′, (ADOLPHE,) a French philosophical writer, was born in Paris in 1801. He became in 1838, at the Sorbonne, assistant, or substitute, of M. Jouffroy, to whose chair he afterwards succeeded. Among his works are a "Treatise on Social Morals," ("Traité de Morale sociale," 1850,) and a "Treatise on the Faculties of the Soul," ("Traité des Facultés de l'Ame," 3 vols., 1852,) which was crowned by the Academy in 1853.

Garnier, (CHARLES GEORGES THOMAS,) a French *littérateur* and advocate, born at Auxerre in 1746, published "Dramatic Proverbs," (1784,) "The Cabinet of the Fairies," (41 vols., 1785,) and other fanciful productions. Died in 1795. He was a brother of Germain Garnier, noticed below.

Garnier, (CLÉMENT JOSEPH,) a French political economist, born in the county of Nice in 1813. He was professor of political economy in the École des Ponts et Chaussées, Paris, from 1846 to 1856, and edited the "Journal des Économistes" about ten years, ending in 1855. Among his works is one called "Elements of Political Economy," (1846.) He belongs to the advanced Liberal school.

Garnier, (ÉTIENNE BARTHÉLEMY,) a French historical painter, born in Paris in 1759, studied in Rome, where he painted "Diogenes asking Alms of a Statue." He returned to Paris in 1793. His "Desolation of the Family of Priam" (1800) was admired," says the "Nouvelle Biographie Générale," "as one of the grandest pages of French painting." Among his master-pieces is "The Miracle performed on the Deaf-Mute," (1831.) Died in 1849.

See "Nouvelle Biographie Générale."

Garnier, (FRANÇOIS XAVIER PAUL,) a French jurist, born at Brest in 1793. He published works of high authority, among which is "Régime des Eaux," or a Treatise on the Waters of the Sea, Rivers, etc., (5 vols., 1839–51.)

Garnier, (GERMAIN,) a French economist, born at Auxerre in 1754, was a brother of Charles Georges Thomas, noticed above. He emigrated with the royalists in 1793, and returned in 1795. He was appointed prefect of the department of Seine-et-Oise in 1800, a senator in 1804, and president of the senate in 1809. At the restoration of 1814 he became a member of the Chamber of Peers. He was afterwards appointed a minister of state by Louis XVIII. He made a translation of Adam Smith's "Wealth of Nations," (5 vols., 1805,) which is the best in the French language, and published several treatises on currency, statistics, and political economy. Died in 1821.

See "Nouvelle Biographie Générale."

Garnier, (JEAN,) a French Jacobin, born at Saintes in 1754, was a member of the Convention, 1792–94, and passed into the Council of Five Hundred in 1795. Having been exiled in 1815, he went to the United States, and was drowned in the Ohio in 1820.

Garnier, (JEAN,) a learned French Jesuit and casuist, born in Paris in 1612, professed rhetoric, philosophy, and theology in Paris for many years. He wrote, in Latin, "Theses of Moral Philosophy," (1651,) "Journal of the Roman Pontiffs," ("Liber diurnus Romanorum Pontificum cum Notis," 1680,) and other works. Died in 1681.

See "Nouvelle Biographie Générale."

Garnier, (JEAN GUILLAUME,) a French mathematician, born near Guise, Picardy, in 1766, was professor of astronomy at Ghent from 1817 to 1830. He published, besides many other works, "Lessons on the Integral Calculus," (3d edition, 1812.) Died in 1840.

See QUETELET, "Notice sur J. G. Garnier," 1841.

Garnier, (JEAN JACQUES,) a French historian, born at Gorron, near Mayenne, in 1729. He went to Paris about 1747, and obtained a place as tutor in the College of Harcourt. He afterwards became professor of Hebrew in the College of France, to which he rendered eminent services as inspector. In 1761 his essay "On the Origin of the French Government" gained the prize of the Academy of Inscriptions, and opened to him the doors of that institution. He published in 1764 the "Man of Letters," and a "Treatise on Civil Education." He succeeded Villaret as historiographer, and published a continuation of Velly and Villaret's "History of France," (1765–85.) Died in 1805. "He is cold, prolix, and monotonous," says Walckenaer.

See DACIER, "Notice sur la Vie de Garnier," 1806; "Nouvelle Biographie Générale."

Garnier, (ROBERT,) a French tragic poet, born at La Ferté-Bernard (Maine) in 1534, published in 1568 the tragedy of "Porcie," which was very successful, and was followed by "Cornelia," "Mark Antony," "Antigone," "Les Juives," and several others. They were highly esteemed and often reprinted. Henry IV. made him councillor of state. Died in 1590.

See "Nouvelle Biographie Générale."

Garnier de l'Aube, gȧr′ne-ȧ′ dĕh lōb, a French revolutionist, born about 1760, was a partisan of Danton in the Convention. Died about 1812.

Garnier-Deschênes, gȧr′ne-ȧ′ dā′shĕn′, (EDME HILAIRE,) a French jurist and writer, born at Montpellier in 1732, lived in Paris. Died in 1812.

Garnier-Pagès, gȧr′ne-ȧ′ pä′zhĕs′, (ÉTIENNE JOSEPH LOUIS,) a French political orator, born at Marseilles in 1801. He studied law, joined the Liberal party in politics, and was elected to the Chamber of Deputies in 1831. He professed the republican faith, but was prudent and practical, and acquired distinction as a speaker on financial questions. He was re-elected in 1834 and in 1837. Died in 1841. "This orator," says Lamartine, "whose renown increased at each discourse, was with respect to the tribune what Carrel was in journalism,—a movement towards the future." ("History of the Restoration.")

See L. DE LOMÉNIE, "M. Garnier-Pagès," 1840; "Histoire populaire de Garnier-Pagès," 1841; M. DE CORMENIN, "Livre des Orateurs."

Garnier-Pagès, (LOUIS ANTOINE,) a republican financier, half-brother of the preceding, was born at Marseilles in 1805. He was elected to the Chamber of Deputies in 1842. He spoke with ability on financial affairs, was re-elected in 1846, and was a member of the provisional government formed by the revolutionists of February, 1848. Having become minister of finance on the 5th of March, he provided for the public exigencies by a land-tax, the forced circulation of bank or treasury notes, *(billets de banque,)* and other measures. His management of the finances is highly praised by Lamartine. In May, 1848, Garnier-Pagès was chosen by the Assembly a member of the executive committee of five. He has since been elected to the Corps Législatif.

See L. DE LOMÉNIE, "Galerie des Contemporains;" "Nouvelle Biographie Générale."

Garofalo, gȧ-ro′fȧ-lo, or **Garofano,** gȧ-ro′fȧ-no, the surname of an excellent painter of the Roman school, who was born at Garófalo, near Ferrara, in 1481. His proper name was BENVENUTO TISIO. He went to Rome about 1500, and was a pupil of G. Baldini. He afterwards studied or worked with Raphael, of whom he was an enthusiastic admirer and excellent imitator. After he parted from Raphael he worked mostly in Ferrara, where he painted in fresco and oil. Among his works are a copy of the "Transfiguration," (in oil,) " The Massacre of the Innocents," and "The Resurrection of Lazarus." He was an admirable colorist. Died in 1559.

See VASARI, "Lives of the Painters;" LANZI, "History of Painting in Italy;" DOMENICO C. MORA, "Vite di B. Tisio da Garofalo e di G. F. Barbieri," 1842.

Garofalo, [Lat. CARYOPH'ILUS,] (BIAGIO,) a learned priest and antiquary, born in Naples in 1677, wrote a "Dissertation on Ancient Marbles," (1738.) Died in 1762.

Garouda. See GARUDA.

Garran de Coulon, gȁ'rǒN' dęh koo'lôN', (JEAN PHILIPPE,) a French lawyer, born in 1749. He was a moderate member of the Convention of 1792, voting against the death of the king. He became a senator, a member of the Institute, and a count. Died in 1816.

Garrard, gȁr'rard', written also Geerards or Geeraerts, (MARK,) a Flemish painter, was born at Bruges about 1526. He worked some years in England, where he died about 1588.

His son MARK, born in 1561, was a portrait-painter in England. He had a high reputation. Died in 1635.

Gȁr'rett-sǫn, (FREEBORN,) a popular Methodist preacher, born in Maryland in 1752; died in 1827.

Gȁr'rick, (DAVID,) a famous English actor, born at Hereford in 1716. His father's family was of French descent. In 1735 he was a pupil of Dr. Johnson, (at Lichfield,) whom in the next year he accompanied to London. Here Garrick studied law in Lincoln's Inn for a short period. Having for several years cherished a growing inclination for the stage, he made his début at Ipswich in 1741, with complete success, and in the autumn of that year acted in the theatre of Goodman's Fields, in London, with a rapidly-growing popularity. He made his appearance in Drury Lane for the first time in May, 1742. His performance of "Richard III." was thought to excel all the efforts of former actors, and drew from Pope the prediction that Garrick would never have a rival. In 1745 he visited Dublin and performed for one season in the Royal Theatre. In 1747 he purchased, in partnership with Lacy, Drury Lane Theatre, of which he continued to be manager until he retired from the stage in 1776. In 1749 he married a danseuse of Vienna, Eva Maria Violette, who is said to have been an exceedingly estimable woman. He possessed in a preeminent degree the art of imitating the physiognomy of others and the expression of various emotions, and was equally at home in tragedy and comedy. His voice was sonorous and melodious, and even in a whisper it filled the whole house. His character, accomplishments, and matchless colloquial powers rendered him welcome in what is styled the best society. He also exercised his talents with success in writing numerous comedies, prologues, etc., among which are "The Lying Valet," "High Life below-stairs," "The Clandestine Marriage," and "Miss in her Teens." He receives credit for reforming the English theatre by rejecting the more licentious dramas and expurgating others, so that Dr. Johnson declared he had augmented the stock of innocent pleasures. He was intimate with Lord Chatham, the Duke of Devonshire, Lord Lyttleton, and Dr. Johnson, whose friendship he retained to the end of his life. In 1777 he was invited by the king and queen to read a drama to them in their palace, and selected for this occasion his own farce of "Lethe." Though he was rewarded by the expression of their satisfaction, he described its effect as like a "wet blanket," compared with the thunder of applause he usually received. He amassed, it is said, a fortune of £140,000. He died in February, 1779, and was buried with great pomp, beside the tomb of Shakspeare, in Westminster Abbey.

See "Garrick's Private Correspondence with the Most Celebrated Persons of his Time, with a Biographical Memoir," 2 vols., 1831-32; T. DAVIES, "Memoirs of the Life of D. Garrick," 2 vols., 1780; C. BLASIS, "Biografia di D. Garrick," Milan, 1840; P. FITZGERALD, "Life of David Garrick," 2 vols., 1868; ARTHUR MURPHY, "Life of Garrick," 2 vols., 1801; "Quarterly Review" for July, 1868.

Gȁr'rĭ-sǫn, (WILLIAM LLOYD,) an American philanthropist, the great leader of the advocates of immediate emancipation in the United States, was born in Newburyport, Massachusetts, December 12, 1804, (not in 1805, as stated in some publications.) When about fourteen, he was apprenticed to a cabinet-maker; but, being strongly averse to this occupation, he prevailed upon his master to release him. Shortly after, he was placed with Mr. E. W. Allen, editor of the "Newburyport Herald," to learn the art of printing. He soon became expert in the mechanical part of the business. About this time he began to write (at first anonymously) for the "Herald" and other papers. He once had the satisfaction of receiving from Mr. Allen, through the post-office, a letter in which the editor expressed his thanks to his unknown correspondent for his communications and hoped that he would still continue to write for the "Herald." Before he was twenty years old, he contributed to the "Salem Gazette" a series of ably-written articles, which attracted much attention. About this time the struggle of the Greeks for freedom awakened the interest of the friends of liberty in every part of the civilized world: young Garrison's sympathy was so strongly excited for the cause, that he seriously contemplated, it is said, entering the Academy at West Point, that he might fit himself for a military career. On the expiration of his apprenticeship, in 1826, he became the conductor of a paper of his own, called the "Free Press," which was published at Newburyport. It proved, however, unsuccessful, and was soon discontinued. In 1827 he became the editor of the "National Philanthropist," published in Boston, and the first paper in America devoted to the advocacy of the cause of "total abstinence." Towards the end of 1829 he accepted an invitation from Benjamin Lundy to assist in the editorship of the "Genius of Universal Emancipation," published in Baltimore. This journal had previously advocated the gradual abolition of slavery; but in the very first number that was issued after Garrison became associated with it, he distinctly avowed the doctrine that immediate emancipation was the right of the slave and the duty of the master. Not long after, he denounced with great severity certain persons engaged in the domestic slave-trade, and declared his purpose to "cover with thick infamy" all who were implicated therein. He was in consequence tried and convicted for a libel. Being unable to pay the costs, he was committed to prison, where he remained nearly two months. At length Mr. Arthur Tappan, a merchant of New York, paid his fine and released him.

On the 1st of January, 1831, he began, in Boston, the publication of "The Liberator," a weekly journal, devoted to the advocacy of the most decided and uncompromising anti-slavery views. He took for his motto "My country is the world, my countrymen are all mankind." His unsparing denunciation of slavery and of all those connected with it, met with sympathy in some portions of the country; but it excited in the Southern States, as was naturally to be expected, the most intense exasperation. Almost every mail brought letters from the South filled with threats of violence and even of assassination. The legislature of Georgia went so far as to offer a reward of five thousand dollars to any one who should arrest, bring to trial, and prosecute him to conviction under the laws of that State. So great was the excitement produced by the "Liberator," in even many parts of the North, that his life was more than once in the utmost peril in the capital of Massachusetts itself. Many of his friends, believing him to be in danger of assassination, entreated him to go armed in self-defence; but his non-resistent principles prevented him from complying with their request. In 1840 he was sent as a delegate to the World's Anti-Slavery Convention held in London; but he refused to take his seat, because the female delegates from the United States were excluded. After many years of long and earnest labour in the cause of emancipation, Mr. Garrison lived to see at first a great though gradual change in the public sentiment of the North in regard to slavery, and at last the fetters of the slave broken, according to a view which he had entertained for some years,—that *slavery could be abolished only by a dissolution of the Union;* but not, as he had once hoped, through the influence of moral suasion alone, and without fighting or bloodshed. In May, 1865, he resigned the presidency of the Anti-Slavery Society,—an office which he had held uninterruptedly for twenty-two years, (having been first elected in 1843;) and in December of the same year the "Liberator" was discontinued, the great object for which it had been established having, in his view, been fully accomplished.

Not long afterwards his friends set on foot a subscription designed as a national testimonial for his long and faithful labours in the anti-slavery cause. About thirty thousand dollars were raised, and presented to him in March, 1868.

See MRS. STOWE, "Men of our Times," Hartford, 1868.

Garsault, de, dĕh gȁr'sō', (FRANÇOIS ALEXANDRE,) a French author, born about 1692, was a member of the Academy of Sciences, and captain of the royal stud. He wrote useful treatises on the treatment of the horse and on certain mechanic arts, among which are "The Perfect Farrier," (1741,) and "The Horseman's Guide," (1759.) Died in 1778.

Garth, (Sir SAMUEL,) an English physician and poet, born in Yorkshire. He settled in London about 1691, acquired a large practice, and was noted for his wit and colloquial powers. He was interested in the subject of Dispensaries, which originated in his time and were opposed by the apothecaries; and for the purpose of ridiculing the latter he wrote the "Dispensary," a mock-heroic poem, (1699,) which ran through many editions, each of which was corrected by the author and, as Pope thought, improved by the change. Garth wrote also several prologues, epigrams, and other small poems, and translated a part of Ovid's "Metamorphoses." About 1714 he was knighted by George I., who appointed him royal physician and physician to the army. He enjoyed the friendship of Pope, Addison, and other literary men. Died in 1718.

See JOHNSON, "Lives of the Poets;" SPENCE, "Anecdotes;" "Biographia Britannica;" CIBBER, "Lives of the English Poets."

Gärtner or **Gaertner,** gěrt'nẹr, (BERNHARD AUGUST,) a German jurist, born at Cassel in 1719; died in 1793.

Gärtner or **Gaertner,** (JOHANN ANDREAS,) a German architect, born at Dresden about 1742, was the father of Friedrich von Gärtner, noticed below. He worked in Vienna, Coblentz, Würzburg, and Munich. In the last city he was employed by the king as *Hofbauintendant.* Died in 1826.

Gärtner, (JOSEPH,) an eminent German botanist, born at Calw, in Würtemberg, in 1732. He became professor of botany at Saint Petersburg in 1768; but, because the climate did not suit him, he returned to Germany in 1770. He devoted many years to the study of fruits and seeds as a basis of classification, and published the results in an important work entitled "Carpology; or, Treatise on the Fruits and Seeds of Plants," (Carpologia, seu De Fructibus et Seminibus Plantarum," 2 vols., 1789–91,) which is regarded as a classic work. Died in 1791.

See ERSCH und GRUBER, "Allgemeine Encyklopaedie;" DELEUZE, "Éloge de J. Gärtner," and German translation of the same, Stuttgart, 1805; "Nouvelle Biographie Générale."

Gärtner, (KARL CHRISTIAN,) a meritorious German critic and writer, born at Freiburg, in Saxony, in 1712, was a friend of Gellert and Ramler. He was professor of eloquence at the Carolinum College of Brunswick from 1747 until his death. He rendered useful services to German literature as editor of a journal called "Bremische Beiträge." He wrote a popular comedy called "Fidelity Proved," ("Die geprüfte Treue," 1768,) and other works, in prose and verse. Died in 1791.

See MEUSEL, "Lexikon der vom Jahre 1750–1800 verstorbenen Deutschen Schriftsteller."

Gärtner or **Gaertner, von,** fon gěrt'nẹr, (FRIEDRICH,) a German architect, born at Coblentz in 1792. He studied in Paris in 1812, and subsequently spent several years in Rome. He was appointed professor of architecture at Munich in 1820, and was soon after employed by the prince, afterwards king, Louis, to co-operate in the improvements he had projected. Among his principal edifices are the Ludwigskirche, the University, the Befreiungshalle, all at Munich, and an arched hall in the style of the Loggia di Lanzi at Florence. About 1840 he built at Athens a splendid palace for King Otho. Died in April, 1847.

Gär'u-dä, [common Hindoo pron. gŭr'ȯȯ-dạ or gŭr'ȯȯd; called in the popular dialect Gŭr'ȯȯr,] in the Hindoo mythology, the vāhän* or vehicle of Vishnu, a creature half man and half eagle, whose office it is to bear the preserving deity in all his journeys through the air, which is the appropriate element of Vishnu. Garuda is commonly said to be the son of Kâsyapa and Vinata, (whence he is sometimes called VINATEYA, vin-ạ-tā'yạ;) although some legends make him the offspring of Kâsyapa and Diti. As the eagle of Jupiter is often represented as holding in his talons the thunderbolt, so Garuda is sometimes pictured as bearing a bow and arrows. He is usually painted with green or blue wings. Garuda is supposed to be a personification of the sky, which apparently supports the sun, one of the symbols of Vishnu. (See VISHNU.)

See MOOR's "Hindu Pantheon;" COLEMAN's "Mythology of the Hindus."

Garuffi, gâ-roof'fee, (GIUSEPPE MALATESTA,) an Italian poet and antiquary, born at Rimini in 1655. He wrote "Il Rodrigo," a musical drama, (1677,) said to be the first example in Italy of a drama performed by a single person. Died about 1710.

Garve, gaR'vẹh, (CHRISTIAN,) a German philosopher and moralist, born at Breslau in 1742. He studied at Leipsic, and in 1769 succeeded Gellert as professor of philosophy in that city. He resigned this chair, on account of ill health, about 1772. He translated Burke's "Essay on the Sublime and Beautiful," and Ferguson's "Moral Philosophy," and wrote, besides several essays on moral philosophy, a treatise "On the Connection of Morals with Politics," (1788,) and "On Society and Solitude," (1792.) He was called by Kant a philosopher in the best sense of the word. Died in 1798.

See MANSO, "Garve nach seinem schriftstellerischen Character," 1799; S. G. DITTMAR, "Erinnerungen aus meinem Umgange mit Garve," etc., 1801; "Nouvelle Biographie Générale."

Garzi, gaRd'zee, (LUIGI,) an eminent Italian painter, born at Pistoia in 1638, was a pupil of Andrea Sacchi, and was successful in various branches of his art, which he practised in Naples and Rome. His style resembles that of Carlo Maratta. His drawing was true, and his touch easy and mellow. He excelled in the representation of Madonnas and infants. Died in 1721.

See LANZI, "History of Painting in Italy;" TICOZZI, "Dizionario;" PASCOLI, "Vite de' Pittori," etc.

Garzia. See GARCIA.

Garzia de Miranda, gaR-thee'ä dä me-rän'dä, surnamed EL MANCO because he had lost his right hand, was born in 1677. He was painter to Philip V., and an excellent artist. Died in Madrid in 1749.

Garzia (or **Garcia**) **Hidalgo,** gaR-thee'ä e-dãl'go, (JOSÉ,) a skilful Spanish painter of history, born at Murcia about 1656, became court painter to Philip V. of Spain. Died in 1712.

See QUILLIET, "Dictionnaire des Peintres Espagnols."

Garzoni, gaR-zo'nee, (GIOVANNI,) a learned Italian physician and *littérateur*, born at Bologna in 1419, wrote a Latin "History of Saxony," (1518.) Died in 1506.

Garzoni, (PIETRO,) a Venetian historian and senator, wrote a continuation of Foscarini's "History of Venice," ("Istoria della Repubblica di Venezia," 3 vols., 1705–16.) The last part relates the events of the war of the Spanish succession, (1701–13.) Died probably about 1720.

Garzoni, (TOMMASO,) an Italian author and monk, born at Bagnacavallo in 1549. He published several works remarkable for their oddity and erudition, among which are "La Piazza universale di tutte le Professioni del Mondo," (1585,) "The Hospital of Lunatics," (1586,) and "The Synagogue of the Ignorant," (1589.) The first of these was once a popular performance. It

* Etymologically related to the German *Wagen*, (a "carriage" or "vehicle,") to which it corresponds so nearly in sound. It is derived from the Sanscrit verb *vāh*, (or *vẹh*,) to "carry," which is cognate with the Latin verb *vẹh-o*, having the same signification.

treats at great length of all the professions, pursuits, trades, and occupations of man. Died in 1589.

See GHILINI, "Teatro d'Uomini letterati;" NICÉRON, "Mémoires;" "Nouvelle Biographie Générale."

Gasca, de la, dä lä gȧs'kä, (PEDRO,) a Spanish bishop, born at or near Plasencia in 1485, was eminent for his skill in negotiation, and was employed by Charles V. in several delicate and difficult missions. Having been sent to England with secret instructions in 1542, he was successful in forming a coalition with Henry VIII. against Francis I. In 1546 he was made president of the Royal Audiencia of Lima, and sent with vice-regal power to Peru, where he adroitly suppressed, without much fighting, the rebellion of Gonzales Pizarro. He returned in 1549, and became Bishop of Palencia. Died in 1560.

See PRESCOTT, "History of the Conquest of Peru," vol. i.; CIECA DE LEON, "La Cronica del Peru," 1554; "Nouvelle Biographie Générale."

Gascoigne, gas-koin', (GEORGE,) an English poet, born in Essex about 1535. He served in Holland under the Prince of Orange, and was afterwards a courtier and an attendant of Queen Elizabeth on one of her stately journeys. He wrote, besides other poems, the "Steel Glass," a satire, (1576,) "Jocasta," a tragedy, and the "Comedy of Supposes." Died in 1577. "His minor poems," says Hallam, "especially one called 'The Arraignment of a Lover,' have much spirit and gaiety." "He has much exceeded all the poets of his age," says Warton, "in smoothness and harmony of versification."

See WOOD, "Athenæ Oxonienses."

Gascoigne, [Lat. GASCO'NIUS,] (Sir WILLIAM,) an English judge, noted for his moral courage, was born in Yorkshire about 1350. He was appointed chief justice of the king's bench by Henry IV. in 1401. During the trial of a riotous person who was a companion of Prince Henry, the latter struck or insulted Gascoigne, who vindicated the majesty of the law by committing the prince to prison. (See Shakspeare's "Henry IV.") On the accession of the prince as Henry V., (1413,) Gascoigne, says Hume, "met with praises, instead of reproaches, for his past conduct." Died about 1420.

See LORD CAMPBELL, "Lives of the Chief Justices;" Foss, "The Judges of England."

Gasconius, the Latin of GASCOIGNE, which see.

Gascoygne or **Gascoigne,** (WILLIAM,) an English astronomer, born in Yorkshire about 1621. He invented the micrometer about 1641. He fought for Charles I., and was killed at Marston Moor, July, 1644.

Gas'kell, (Mrs. ELIZABETH C.,) an English authoress, born about 1822, was the wife of a Unitarian clergyman of Manchester. Her maiden name was STEVENSON. She produced, in 1848, a popular novel, entitled "Mary Barton, a Tale of Manchester Life," and maintained her literary reputation by other works of fiction, among which are "The Moorland Cottage," (1850,) and "Ruth," (1853.) She was a friend of Charlotte Brontë, of whom she published a very interesting Life, (2 vols., 1857.) She was for several years a regular contributor to "Household Words." Her other principal works are the novels of "North and South," "Cranford," "Sylvia's Lovers," and "Wives and Daughters:" she left the last unfinished at her death, in 1866. "Mrs. Gaskell," says George Sand, "has done what neither I nor other female writers in France can accomplish: she has written novels which excite the deepest interest in men of the world, and which every girl will be the better for reading."

For an interesting and admirable article on Mrs. Gaskell's writings, see the "British Quarterly" for April, 1867; from it we extract the following : "It is hardly possible to read a page of her writing without getting some good from it. The style is clear and forcible, the tone pure, the matter wholesome. . . . Other novel-writers of her generation [may] have more poetry, more scholarship, more grace, eloquence, and passion; but in the art of telling a story she has no superior, perhaps no equal." Of her unfinished "Wives and Daughters" the reviewer says, "We do not hesitate to pronounce it the finest of Mrs. Gaskell's productions,—that in which her

true womanly nature is most adequately reflected, that which will keep her name longest in remembrance."

See, also, "Edinburgh Review" for April, 1849; "Westminster Review" for April, 1849; "North British Review" for May, 1853; "Gentleman's Magazine" for February, 1866.

Gasnevides. See GAZNEVIDES.

Gasparin, de, deh gȧs'pȧ'raṅ', (ADRIEN ÉTIENNE PIERRE,) COMTE, a distinguished French rural economist and minister of state, born at Orange (Vaucluse) in 1783, was a son of T. A. Gasparin, noticed below. He gave special attention to agriculture, on which he wrote many able treatises. After the revolution of 1830 he was successively prefect of La Loire, of Isère, and of the Rhône. He was minister of the interior from September, 1836, to April, 1837, during which period he made a reform in the treatment of convicts. He filled the same office in the brief ministry formed in March, 1839, and was admitted into the Academy of Sciences in 1840. Among his works is an excellent "Course of Agriculture," (5 vols., 1843-49.) Died in September, 1862.

See "Nouvelle Biographie Générale."

Gasparin, de, (AGÉNOR ÉTIENNE,) COMTE, a son of the preceding, a Protestant by birth and conviction, and an eminent publicist and friend of liberty and order, was born at Orange in 1810. In early youth he was secretary to M. Guizot, minister of public instruction. He became auditor to the council of state, and was secretary to his father in 1836 and 1839. In 1842 he was elected by the voters of Bastia to the Chamber of Deputies, in which he advocated religious liberty for Protestants and the liberation of slaves. He wrote, besides other works, "Slavery and the Slave-Trade," (1838,) "Christianity and Paganism," (2 vols., 1850,) "The Schools of Doubt and the School of Faith : an Essay on Authority in Religion," (1853.) In 1846 he retired from political life. The great rebellion in the United States afforded him the subject of two remarkable and successful works, called "The Uprising of a Great Nation," ("Un grand Peuple qui se relève," 1861,) and "America in the Presence of Europe," ("L'Amérique devant l'Europe," 1862.)

Gasparin, de, MADAME, the wife of the preceding, and known as an authoress and moralist of a high order, was born about 1815. Among her works are "Marriage from the Christian Point of View," (3 vols., 1843,) which received the Montyon prize of the French Academy, "Some Defects of Christians at the Present Day," "Monastic Corporations in the Heart of Protestantism," (2 vols., 1855,) and three volumes of tales, entitled "Near Horizons," ("Les Horizons prochains,") "Heavenly Horizons," ("Les Horizons célestes,") and "Vesper," (1862.)

See "Nouvelle Biographie Générale."

Gasparin, de, (THOMAS AUGUSTIN,) a French revolutionist, born of a Protestant family at Orange in 1740 or 1750, was the father of Count Adrien, noticed above. He was elected in 1792 to the Convention, in which he acted with the Jacobins. He was on a mission to the army of the north when the defection of Dumouriez transpired, and confirmed the loyalty of the troops. In 1793 he was one of the commissioners who directed the siege of Toulon. It is stated that his influence induced the general to adopt in this siege the plan of Bonaparte, who in his will expressed his gratitude by a legacy of one hundred thousand francs to the heirs of M. de Gasparin. Died in November, 1793.

See LAMARTINE, "History of the Girondists;" "Nouvelle Biographie Générale."

Gasparini, gȧs-pä-ree'nee, (FRANCESCO,) an Italian composer, born at Lucca about 1655, was a professor of music in Venice. He composed many operas and cantatas, which were admired, and a work called "L'Armonico prattico al Cembalo," (1683.) Died in 1727.

Gasparino, gȧs-pä-ree'no, surnamed BARZIZZA or BARZIZZIO, (from the place of his birth,) an Italian scholar, born near Bérgamo about 1370, was professor of belles-lettres in Padua and Milan from 1407 to 1431. He is regarded as one of the restorers of sound literature and pure Latinity. Among his works is a treatise on Composition. By the diligent study of Cicero, he acquired an elegant style, and was reputed the best writer

ā, ē, ī, ō, ū, ȳ, *long;* ă, ĕ, ĭ, ŏ, ŭ, y̆, same, less prolonged; ä, ĕ, ï, ŏ, ŭ, y̆, *short;* a, ẹ, ị, ọ, *obscure;* fär, fȧll, fȧt; mĕt; nŏt; gōŏd; mōŏn;

of that generation. Several of his orations are extant, and are the earliest models of classical declamation in modern times. A volume of his epistles was the first book ever printed at Paris, (in 1471.) Died in 1431.

See FURIETTI, "Vita Gasparini," prefixed to Gasparini's Works, Rome, 1723; FABRICIUS, "Bibliotheca Latina mediæ et infimæ Ætatis."

Gaspre, Le. See DUGHET.

Gasse, gâs'să, (STEFANO and LUIGI,) two able Italian architects, born at Naples in 1778, were twin brothers, and partners in their profession. They studied in Rome, and were employed in the construction of palaces and public buildings in Naples, among which are the Observatory, the Dogana, (custom-house,) and the Palazzo Montemiletto. Luigi died in 1833, and Stefano in 1840.

Gassendi, gä'sŏN'de', (JEAN JACQUES BASILIEN,) born at Digne, in France, in 1748. He obtained the rank of a general of brigade in 1800. The First Consul gave him command of the artillery just before the battle of Marengo, in which he took part. Gassendi became a general of division in 1805, a councillor of state in 1806, and a senator in 1813. He published a volume of poems. Died in 1828.

See QUÉRARD, "La France Littéraire."

Gassendi, gas-sĕn'dee, [Fr. pron. gä'sŏN'de'; Lat. GASSEN'DUS,] written also **Gassend,** (PIERRE,) born at Champtercier, near Digne, in Provence, January 22, 1592, was one of the most eminent philosophers and savants of France, and one who added lustre to almost every branch of learning, being at the same time historian, naturalist, mathematician, astronomer, logician, Hellenist, metaphysician, and critic; and all this at a period when the sciences had scarcely emerged from their infancy. He is regarded as the most universal genius of that age. The first disciple of Bacon in France, he was also the correspondent and friend of Galileo and Kepler. Destined for the church, he studied at Aix and Avignon, and, at the age of twenty-one, obtained the chairs of philosophy and theology in the University of Aix. Though required to conform in his lectures to the doctrines of Aristotle, he early perceived the fallacy of that system, and by his studies prepared himself to become one of the leaders in that great controversy which resulted in depriving the philosopher of Stagira of the prestige of infallibility which he had so long enjoyed. Having obtained a benefice in the cathedral of Digne, and the office of provost, he resigned in 1623 the place of professor, and next year published the first volume of his "Paradoxical Essays against Aristotle," which made a great impression on the public mind, and was followed a few years later by a second volume with the same title. About this period he devoted most of his leisure to the study of the classics and to researches in anatomy and astronomy.

In 1642 he attacked the philosophy and bold innovations of his friend Descartes, with whom he became involved in controversy, refuting, with modest doubts, the dogmatism of his opponent. He was appointed in 1645 professor of mathematics in the Collège Royal of Paris, where his lectures on Astronomy were admired and largely attended by the *élite* of the capital. In 1647 appeared one of his best-known works, "The Life, Opinions, and Morals of Epicurus," ("De Vita, Moribus et Placitis Epicuri,") whose memory he defends against the accusations of the Stoics, at the same time exposing and combating those parts of his system which are at variance with Christianity. His admiration for Epicurus furnished some narrow-minded or envious persons with a pretext to accuse him of skepticism; but this charge is refuted by the tenor of his entire life. In 1654 he published the "Lives of Tycho Brahe, Copernicus, and other Astronomers," with a preface, in which he reviewed, in a luminous manner, the history of astronomy. Gassendi was the first to observe the transit of Mercury, (in 1631.) The parhelia, the eclipses of Jupiter's satellites, and the magnetic needle afforded him subjects for careful and profound research.

The mind of Gassendi was penetrating and refined, his style elegant and clear, his manners simple and full of amenity. In his efforts to subvert the inveterate prejudices of the Schoolmen with respect to Aristotle and Epicurus, he has displayed a union of vast erudition,

sound criticism, and mental independence. **Marivat,** having freely conversed with him while passing from Grenoble to Paris, without knowing his name, desired on their arrival to be presented to the celebrated Gassendi, and was agreeably surprised to recognize his identity with the modest companion of his journey. Besides the works already referred to, he wrote, in Latin, treatises on the laws of motion, a "System of Epicurean Philosophy," (1649,) and "The Philosophical System of Gassendi," ("Syntagma Philosophicum," etc., 1658.) The last is rather an eclectic than an original system, a selection and combination of the doctrines taught in the various schools of antiquity. It may be observed that in that age nearly all the philosophers of France were ranged under the two parties of Cartesians and Gassendists. Died in 1655.

See BERNIER, "Abrégé de la Philosophie de Gassendi," 1674; BOUGEREL, "Vie de Gassendi," 1737; SORBIÈRE, "De Vita et Moribus P. Gassendi," 1679; MENC, "Éloge de Gassendi," 1767; CAMBURAT, "Abrégé de la Vie et du Système de P. Gassendi," 1770; A. MARTIN, "Histoire de la Vie et des Ecrits de P. Gassendi," Paris, 1853; BRUCKER, "History of Philosophy;" "Nouvelle Biographie Générale."

Gassendus. See GASSENDI.

Gasser, gâs'ser, (JOHANN MICHAEL,) a learned German writer, born at Schweinfurt in 1700; died in 1754.

Gasser, (SIMON PETER,) a German jurist and economist, born at Colberg in 1676. He was professor of law and of political economy at Halle, and is said to have been the first German who conceived the idea of treating political economy as a science. His chief work is an "Introduction to Economical and Political Sciences," (1729.) Died in 1745.

See F. WIDEBURG, "Elogium S. P. Gasseri," 1746; ADELUNG, Supplement to JÖCHER's "Allgemeines Gelehrten-Lexikon."

Gassicourt, de, (CHARLES LOUIS CADET.) See CADET.

Gassies, gä'se', (JEAN BAPTISTE,) a French painter of history, marine views, and genre, born at Bordeaux in 1786. Among his works is "Virgil reading the Æneid to Augustus," (1814.) Died in 1832.

Gassies, (JEAN BAPTISTE,) a French naturalist, born at Agen in 1816. He published a "Description of the Terrestrial and Fresh-Water Mollusks of the Agenais," (1849,) and other works.

Gassion, de, dĕh gä'se'ŏN', (JEAN,) a French general, born at Pau in 1609, was attached to the Protestant cause, and served with distinction under Gustavus Adolphus as captain in 1631 and 1632. After the death of that prince he returned to the French army, in which he soon obtained the rank of maréchal-de-camp. In 1643 he commanded the right wing at the battle of Rocroy, under the famous Condé, who ascribed to him the honour of the day, saying, on the field of battle, as he embraced Gassion, "It is to you I am indebted for the victory." For this service he was rewarded with a marshal's bâton. He took part in several campaigns against the Spaniards in Flanders, and was killed at the siege of Lens in 1647. He was one of the most able and successful generals of his time. In reply to an officer who thought a certain enterprise impracticable, he said, "I have in my head, and at my side, all that is requisite for victory."

See RENAUDOT, "La Vie du Maréchal J. de Gassion," 1647; MICHEL DE PURE, "Vie de J. Gassion," 4 vols., 1673; "Nouvelle Biographie Générale."

Gassner, gâs'ner, (JOHANN JOSEPH,) a German exorcist, or thaumaturgus, and Catholic priest, born at Bratz in 1727. He practised the imposition of hands for the cure of diseases. Died in 1779.

Gast, (Rev. JOHN,) the son of a French Protestant exile, was born in Dublin in 1716, and became Archdeacon of Glandclogh. He published "Rudiments of Greek History," (1754,) which is commended for style and other merits, and a "History of Greece from Alexander of Macedon until its Subjection by the Romans," (1782.) Died in 1788.

Gastaldi, gâs-tâl'dee, (GIROLAMO,) an Italian prelate, born at Genoa. He was made Archbishop of Benevento, and cardinal, about 1658. Died in 1685.

Gastaldi, gâs'tâl'de', (JEAN BAPTISTE,) a French medical writer, born at Sisteron in 1674. He practised for many years at Avignon. Died in 1747.

ɇ as k; ç as s; g̃ hard; g̣ as j; G, H, K, guttural; N, nasal; R, trilled; s̃ as z; th as in this. (☞See Explanations, p. 23.)

Gastaud, gȧs′tō′, (FRANÇOIS,) a French Jansenist and controversialist, born at Aix about 1660; died in 1732.

Gastelier, gȧt′le-ȧ′, (RENÉ GEORGES,) a French physician and medical writer, born at Ferrières in 1741, practised in Paris with success. As a member of the Legislative Assembly, he gave offence to the Jacobins, by whom he was arrested in 1793, but was saved from death by the fall of Robespierre. Died in 1821.

Gaston, gȧs′tȯN′, Viscount of Béarn, was one of the French lords who distinguished themselves in the first crusade in company with Raimond of Toulouse. He commanded a part of the army at the victory near Antioch in 1098, and was present at the capture of Jerusalem, after which he returned home, (1101.) He was killed in fighting against the infidels in Spain, about 1130.

Gas′ton, (WILLIAM,) an eminent American jurist, born at Newbern, North Carolina, in 1778, was chosen in 1813 a member of the national House of Representatives, in which he sat four years and acquired a high reputation as a speaker. He was an influential leader of the Federal party. In 1834 he was appointed a judge of the supreme court of North Carolina. Died in 1844.

See "National Portrait-Gallery of Distinguished Americans," vol. ii.

Gaston de Foix. See FOIX, (GASTON DE.)

Gas′trell, (FRANCIS,) an English theologian, born at Slapton (Northampton) in 1662. He became canon of Christ Church, Oxford, in 1702, and Bishop of Chester in 1714. He published many approved religious treatises, one of which, entitled "The Christian Institutes; or, Sincere Word of God," (1707,) has been often reprinted. He also wrote "The Certainty of the Christian Revelation," (1699.) Died in 1725.

Gat′a-ker, (CHARLES,) an English clergyman, born at Rotherhithe about 1614, was rector of Hoggeston for about thirty years. He wrote treatises against popery, and other religious works, among which is "The Way of Truth and Peace," (1669.) Died in 1680.

See WOOD, "Athenæ Oxonienses."

Gataker, (THOMAS,) an English divine and critic of great learning, the father of the preceding, was born in London in 1574. He became rector of Rotherhithe, Surrey, in 1611, and published in 1616 "Of the Nature and Use of Lots: a Treatise historical and theological." He subscribed the Covenant, and during the Commonwealth was in fellowship with the Presbyterians. Among his works are excellent commentaries on Isaiah and Jeremiah, published, with other "Annotations on the Bible," by the Assembly of Divines at Westminster; "Cinnus, seu Animadversiones Variæ," 1651; and a commentary on Marcus Aurelius's "Meditations," with a Latin version. Died in 1654.

See a "Life of T. Gataker," London, 1655: "Biographia Britannica;" "Memoir of T. Gataker," prefixed to his "Adversaria miscellanea posthuma," published by his son Charles in 1659; NICÉRON, "Mémoires."

Gates, gāts, (HORATIO,) a general, born in England in 1728, entered the British army at an early age. He served as captain in the army of General Braddock when that general was defeated and mortally wounded, near Pittsburg, in 1755. Retiring then from service, he bought an estate in Virginia, where he resided when the war of the Revolution broke out. Having espoused the popular cause, his military talents and experience procured for him a rapid promotion. In 1776 he was made major-general, and appointed to the command of the Northern army, which had recently returned from the invasion of Canada and was in the vicinity of Ticonderoga. General Schuyler was then in command of that district. In order to prevent a collision, Congress declared that in appointing Gates they had no intention to supersede the former, but wished these two officers to act in concert. The English general Carleton, with a large force on Lake Champlain, advanced as far as Crown Point, which he captured; but, thinking the season too late to besiege the Americans, he retired into winter quarters. At the return of spring, Schuyler had the sole command. After the capture of Ticonderoga by Burgoyne in July, 1777, all the Northern generals were recalled by Congress, in a fit of disgust and vexa-

tion, and the choice of a new commander fell upon Gates, who assumed about the 22d of August the command of an army of 6000 men, besides detached parties of militia. On the 19th of September was fought the battle of Bemus Heights, which was terminated by the approach of night without decisive results. About this time a party of militia had made a successful attack on the British posts on Lake George, cut off Burgoyne's communications, and rendered his position very critical. The army of Gates was increased, September 22, by the arrival of militia under General Lincoln, who received command of the right wing. On the 7th of October, 1777, near the village of Stillwater, commenced another battle, in which the Americans had gained decisive advantages when darkness suspended the contest. The British lost a large part of their artillery and ammunition, and during the night retired to higher ground, where in the morning they appeared in order of battle. After slight skirmishes on the 8th, Burgoyne abandoned his position on the 9th, and retreated six miles to Saratoga, whither he was followed by General Gates and blockaded. Being reduced to great distress, he opened a treaty of capitulation, and surrendered, with the conditions that his army (amounting then to 5642 men) should give up their arms, artillery, and baggage, and be conveyed to England under a pledge not to serve against the United States. The capture of this army produced great exultation among the Americans, and was one of the most important events of the war. Burgoyne and other British officers bore testimony to the humanity of the victor in that campaign. In 1777 Gates was made president of the board of war. In 1780 he was appointed to command the Southern army, consisting of 6000 men, chiefly militia. On August 6 he was totally defeated at Camden, in South Carolina, by Cornwallis, with a loss of 900 killed and of many prisoners. On account of this disaster, Congress, on October 5, ordered inquiry to be made into the conduct of Gates, who was in consequence superseded in the command, and retired to his estate in Virginia. The inquiry resulted in an honourable acquittal; but it appears he took no further part in the war. In 1800 he removed to New York. Died in 1806.

See BANCROFT, "History of the United States;" HILDRETH, "History of the United States," vol. iii., chaps. xxxiii., xxxvii., and xl.

Gat′lin, (RICHARD CASWELL,) born in North Carolina about 1813, served in Mexico in 1845-46, and was made a brigadier-general of volunteers in the Confederate army in 1861.

Gatta, della, del′lä gȧt′tä, (BARTOLOMMEO,) an Italian painter and architect, born about 1420, worked at Arezzo and Rome. Died about 1500.

Gatta-Melata, gȧt′tä mä-lä′tä, (STEFANO GIOVANNI,) an able Italian condottiere, born at Narni. As a general in the service of Venice, he defeated the Marquis of Mantua in 1438. Died in 1443.

Gatteaux, gȧ′tō′, (JACQUES ÉDOUARD,) a French artist, born in Paris in 1788, engraved medals of Montaigne, Corneille, Racine, La Fayette, etc. Among his works are statues of Michael Angelo for the Louvre, and "Minerva," (1836,) which was purchased by the state.

Gatteaux, (NICOLAS MARIE,) a French engraver of medals, father of the preceding, was born in Paris in 1751. He engraved in 1798 the prize medal for the École de Médecine of Paris, which is regarded as his master-piece. He illustrated many historical events by medals, and made improvements in the mechanism of the art of engraving. Died in 1832.

Gattel, gȧ′tĕl′, (CLAUDE MARIE,) a lexicographer, born in Lyons, France, in 1743, published a French-Spanish Dictionary, (3 vols., 1790,) and a Portable French Dictionary, (1797.) Died in 1812.

Gatterer, gȧt′ter-er, (JOHANN CHRISTOPH,) a German historian, born near Nuremberg in 1727. He became professor of history at Göttingen in 1759, and wrote numerous works relating to history, chronology, and genealogy, among which are "The Complete History of the World," (2 vols., 1785-87,) "Universal Historical Library," (16 vols., 1767,) and "Elements of the Diplomatic Art." He founded, in 1764, the Historical Institute at Göttingen. Died in 1799.

See HEYNE, "Elogium J. C. Gattereri," Göttingen, 1800; J. G. EICHHORN, "J. C. Gatterer; biographische Skizze," 1800.

Gatterer, (MAGDALENE PHILIPPINE,) daughter of the preceding, born at Göttingen or at Nuremberg in 1756, published a volume of poems, "Neue Gedichte," (1821,) which were favourably received. Died in 1831.

Gattey, gȧ'tȧ', (FRANÇOIS,) a French mathematician, born at Dijon in 1753, published "Elements of the New Metrical System," (1801,) and other works. Died in 1819.

Gatti, gȧt'tee, (BERNARDINO,) an eminent Italian painter, surnamed IL SOGARO or SOGLIARO, (sȯl-yȧ'ro,) was born about 1495. Cremona, Pavía, and Vercelli dispute the honour of having given him birth. He was a pupil and successful imitator of Correggio, and worked in Cremona and Parma. Vasari speaks in praise of his skill. Among his master-pieces are frescos of "The Miracle of the Loaves," at Cremona, and "The Ascension," near Cremona. Died about 1575.

See LANZI, "History of Painting in Italy;" BRYAN, "Dictionary of Painters."

Gatti, (GERVASIO,) an Italian painter, born at Cremona about 1555, was a nephew and pupil of the preceding. His last works are dated in 1631.

Gatti, (GIOVANNI,) an Italian Dominican friar, born at Messina about 1420, professed theology at Florence and Bologna, and in 1472 was made Bishop of Cefalù. He possessed an extraordinary memory, and was distinguished for his attainments in languages, philosophy, mathematics, etc. Died in 1484.

Gatti, (GIROLAMO,) an Italian painter, born at Bologna in 1662, was a pupil of Franceschini, of many of whose works he made good copies. Died in 1726.

Gatti, (OLIVIERO,) an Italian engraver, born at Parma about 1570. He worked at Bologna for many years.

Gattinara. See ARBORIO.

Gau, gȯw or gȯ, (FRANZ CHRISTIAN,) an architect, born at Cologne in 1790. Having made a journey to Egypt and Nubia and designed many ruins, he published in 1823 "Antiquities of Nubia," with text by Niebuhr and Letronne. He added two volumes to the work on the "Ruins of Pompeii" which Mazois left unfinished. He was naturalized as a Frenchman in 1825, and designed several public buildings in Paris, by which he gained a high reputation. His chief work is the church of Saint Clotilde, commenced in 1846, the style of which is pointed, or *ogivale.* Died in 1853.

See "Nouvelle Biographie Générale."

Gaub, gȯwp, or **Gaube,** gȯw'beh, [Lat. GAU'BIUS,] (HIERONYMUS DAVID,) a German physician, born at Heidelberg in 1705, was a favourite pupil of Boerhaave, who procured him the succession to his chair of chemistry at Leyden about 1731. In 1733 he obtained in addition the chair of medicine, which he filled until his death. He published several valuable works, among which are "On the Government of the Mind which is within the Province of Medicine," ("De Regimine Mentis quod medicorum est," 1747,) and "Institutes of Pathology," ("Institutiones Pathologiæ," 1758.) Died in 1780.

See ERSCH und GRUBER, "Allgemeine Encyklopaedie;" J. BLEULAND, "Oratio qua Memoria H. D. Gaubii commendatur," 1792; "Biographie Médicale."

Gaubert, gȯ'baiR', (PAUL LÉON MARIE,) a French physician, born at Ermenonville in 1805, wrote, besides other works, "The Hygiene of Digestion," (1845,) which was very successful.

Gaubil, gȯ'bēl', (ANTOINE,) an eminent French missionary and Jesuit, who did much to promote a knowledge of the literature of Eastern Asia, was born at Gaillac in 1689. He went to China in 1723, and attained such proficiency in the Chinese language and learning that the native doctors confessed his superiority. He was also well versed in the exact sciences and astronomy. The Chinese emperor employed him for thirty years as interpreter of the diplomatic correspondence with Russia, and in other important offices. Gaubil's learning was displayed in several profound works, the most remarkable of which is his translation of the "Shoo-King," (1771,) a canonical treasury of Chinese history and

tradition. He published a "History of Jengis Khan and the Mongol Dynasty," 1739. Died in Pekin in 1759.

See A. DE RÉMUSAT, "Nouveaux Mélanges Asiatiques;" G. PAUTHIER, "La Chine;" "Nouvelle Biographie Générale."

Gaubius. See GAUB.

Gaucher, gȯ'shȧ', (CHARLES ÉTIENNE,) a French engraver, born in Paris in 1740. He wrote "Iconologie," a treatise on Allegories and Emblems, (4 vols., 1796,) and other essays on art. Died in 1804.

Gaucher de Chastillon. See CHASTILLON.

Gaucourt, gȯ'kooR', (RAOUL,) a French commander, who fought for Charles VII. against the English. He was appointed grand master of France in 1450, and again in 1456.

Gau'den, (JOHN,) an English bishop and author, born at Mayland, Essex, in 1605. In 1640, being then favourable to the popular party, he preached a sermon before the House of Commons, in consequence of which he obtained the deanery of Bocking. During the civil war and under the Commonwealth he kept his preferments, but ultimately joined the royalist party and wrote several tracts in its support. At the restoration he became, in 1660, chaplain to Charles II., and Bishop of Exeter ; but, as this did not satisfy him, he was, in 1662, transferred to the see of Worcester. His death, which occurred in 1662, was thought to have been hastened by the refusal of the king to reward him with the rich bishopric of Winchester. In soliciting preferment and royal favour, he claimed to be the real author of the famous "Eikon Basilike," or "Portrait of his Sacred Majesty in his Solitude and Sufferings," which was published a few days after the death of Charles I. and was generally supposed to have been written by that king. This book ran through many editions, and made so great an impression that the potent voice of Milton was invoked to counteract it. This question of authorship has been discussed at much length ; and the majority of critics seem to be agreed that Gauden was the author of the above-named work, or at least had a share in its composition.

See WOOD, "Athenæ Oxonienses;" NICHOLS, "Literary Anecdotes;" "Biographia Britannica;" "Edinburgh Review" for June, 1826, (vol. xliv.)

Gaudentius. See GAUDENZIO.

Gaudentius, gaw-dĕn'she-us, SAINT, was chosen Bishop of Brescia about 387 A.D. He wrote the life of his friend Saint Philaster, and several discourses and sermons, which are still extant. Died about 420.

See CAVE, "Historia Literaria."

Gaudenzi, gȯw-dĕn'zee, (PELLEGRINO,) an Italian poet, born at Forlì in 1749, removed to Padua in 1775. He wrote in 1781 "The Birth of Christ," ("La Nascita di Cristo,") which produced a vivid sensation and was much admired, and "La Campagna." He was endued with fine sensibility. Died in 1784.

See TIPALDO, "Biografia degli Italiani illustri;" MENEGHELLI, "Elogio storico di P. Gaudenzi," 1811.

Gaudenzio, gȯw-dĕn'ze-o, [Lat. GAUDEN'TIUS,] (PAGANINI,) an eminent savant and writer, born at Poschiavo, in Switzerland, in 1596, exchanged in youth Calvinism for the Catholic faith. From 1628 to 1648 he taught belles-lettres in the University of Pisa, then the most flourishing in Italy. He wrote, in Latin, many orations, and dissertations on philosophy and antiquities, among which his "Rise and Progress of Philosophy among the Romans" (1643) is esteemed the best. Died in 1648.

See FABRONI, "Vitæ Italorum doctrina excellentium;" NICÉRON, "Mémoires."

Gaudichaud-Beaupré, gȯ'de'shȯ' bȯ'prȧ', (CHARLES,) a French botanist, born at Angoulême in 1780. He served as botanist of Freycinet's scientific expedition of 1816-20, and wrote the botanical part of the work which was the result of that voyage. In 1836-37 he made a voyage around the world in the Bonite. Among his works are "Researches on Organography, Physiology, and Organogeny," (1841,) and "The Botany of the Voyage around the World in the Bonite." Died in Paris in 1854.

See LOUANDRE et BOURQUELOT, "La Littérature Française;" "Nouvelle Biographie Générale;" E. PASCALLET, "Notice biographique sur M. Gaudichaud-Beaupré," 1844.

Gaudin, gō′dăṅ′, (JEAN,) a French grammarian and Jesuit, born in Poitou in 1617, published a "Latin Grammar," and a "Dictionary of the Latin, Greek, and French Languages," (1680.) Died about 1690.

Gaudin, gŏw-dèn′, (LUIS PASCAL,) a Spanish painter of history, born at Villa-Franca in 1556; died in 1621.

Gaudin, (MARC ANTOINE AUGUSTIN,) a French chemist, born at Saintes in 1804. He invented in 1827 an air-pump which compresses air or reverses that process at will, and discovered a method to convert beef into a substance like milk. Among his works are a "Practical Treatise on Photography," (1845,) and one on the "Grouping of Atoms," etc., (1847.)

Gaudin, (MARTIN MICHEL CHARLES,) Duke of Gaeta, an able French minister of finance, born at Saint-Denis, near Paris, in 1756. He was one of six commissioners of the treasury appointed by the Assembly in 1791, and was minister of finance from November 10, 1799, until April, 1814. This protracted official career was almost without example among French financiers. He was created Duke of Gaeta in 1809. The restoration of the national credit is ascribed to him. He was governor of the Bank of France from 1820 to 1834. He published several treatises on finance. Died in 1844.

See his "Mémoires, Souvenirs," etc., 2 vols., 1826; A. PORTALIS, "Essai sur la Vie et l'Administration du Duc de Gaëte," 1842; "Nouvelle Biographie Générale."

Gaudy, gŏw′dee, (FRANZ BERNHARD HEINRICH WILHELM,) BARON OF, a German poet and *littérateur*, of Scottish extraction, born at Frankfort-on-the-Oder in 1800. He published a number of popular lyrics and tales, and made translations from the Polish writers Mickiewicz and Niemcewicz. Died in 1840.

Gauermann, gŏw′er-mân′, (FRIEDRICH,) a German landscape-painter, born near Guttenstein, in Austria, in 1807. He exhibited in 1834, at Vienna, "The Labourer," which was very successful. He was also a skilful painter of animals. Died in 1862.

Gauermann, (JAKOB,) a German landscape-painter and engraver, the father of the preceding, was born near Stuttgart in 1772. His best works represent scenes in the Tyrol, which are greatly admired.

Gauffier, gō′fe-à′, (LOUIS,) a French painter, born at Rochelle in 1761. He gained the first prize at Paris in 1784, and went with a royal pension to Rome, where he painted "Achilles recognized by Ulysses," and "The Roman Ladies offering their Jewels to the Senate." Died at Florence in 1801.

Gauli or **Gaulli.** See BACICCIO.

Gaullyer, gōl′yà′, (DENIS,) born at Cléry, in France, in 1688, was a professor in the University of Paris. He published "Poetical Rules drawn from Aristotle and others," (1728.) Died in 1736.

Gaulmin, gōl′măṅ′, (GILBERT,) a French philologist and linguist of great learning, was born at Moulins in 1585. He became a councillor of state, and a partisan of Mazarin. He wrote Latin epigrams, odes, and elegies, and published an edition of the romance of "Ismene and Ismenias," with a Latin version, (1618.) He is highly praised by Baillet and Colomiès. Died in 1665.

See BAILLET, "Jugements des Savants," tomes ii. and iv.

Gault, gō, (JEAN BAPTISTE,) a French priest, born at Tours in 1595. He was appointed Bishop of Marseilles about 1640. Died in 1643.

See SENAULT, "Vie de J. B. Gault," 1647.

Gaulthier, gō′te-à′, [Lat. WALTE′RIUS,] an able French theologian and statesman, born at Orléans, was bishop of that place in 876. Died in 892 A.D.

Gaultier, gō′te-à′, (ALOYSIUS ÉDOUARD CAMILLE,) ABBÉ, born of French parents in Italy in 1744, was noted for his benevolence and his zealous efforts to improve the method of education. For this purpose he invented games for children and wrote many popular school-books. During the Revolution he took refuge in England, whence he returned to Paris about 1802. Died in 1818.

Gaultier, (CHARLES,) a French advocate, noted for his eloquence and powerful sarcasm, was born in Paris in 1590; died in 1666. Boileau, in his Ninth Satire, says,

"Dans vos discours chagrins plus aigre et plus mordant
Qu'une femme en furie ou Gaultier en plaidant."

See TAISAND, "Vies des Jurisconsultes."

Gaultier, gŏwl′teer, (LEONARD,) a German engraver, born at Mentz in 1552. His master-piece is "The Last Judgment," after Michael Angelo.

Gaultier or **Gaultier de Lille,** gō′te-à′ dĕh lèl, (PHILIPPE,) born at Lille, in Flanders. He wrote a Latin heroic poem, entitled "Alexandreis," on the exploits of Alexander the Great, which was once in great vogue. Died about 1200. One of his verses has become proverbial :

"Instabile est regnum quod non clementia firmat."[*]

Gaultier (or **Gautier**) **de Coutances,** gō′te-à′ dĕh koo′tôṅss′, [Lat. GUALTE′RUS DE CONSTAN′TIIS,] an English or Norman prelate and statesman, acted an important part in the affairs of his time, and became Archbishop of Rouen in 1184. Under Richard I. he enjoyed great credit as a minister of state. Died in 1207.

Gaupp, gŏwp, (ERNST THEODOR,) a German jurist, and professor of law at Breslau, born in Lower Silesia in 1796.

Gaurico, gŏw-ree′ko, (LUCA,) [Fr. LUC GAURIC, lük gō′rèk′,] an Italian astrologer, born at Gifoni in 1476. He obtained eminence as a fortune-teller, and professed mathematics at Ferrara in 1531. In 1545 he was chosen Bishop of Civitata. He wrote treatises on astronomy, astrology, and geometry. Died in 1558.

Gaurico, [Fr. GAURIC, gō′rèk′,] (POMPONIO,) an Italian poet, brother of the preceding, was born at Gifoni. He wrote a treatise on sculpture, and one on the Poetic Art, (1541;) also epigrams, elegies, songs, and other verses. He was supposed to have been murdered about 1530, as he disappeared and was never found.

Gauss, gŏwss, (KARL FRIEDRICH,) a profound German mathematician, born at Brunswick on the 30th of April, 1777, was educated at Göttingen. He published in 1801 a remarkable work on transcendental arithmetic, entitled "Arithmetical Disquisitions," ("Disquisitiones Arithmeticæ,") which made an epoch in the history of the science. He increased his reputation by his calculations of the elements of the planets Ceres and Pallas, for which the French Institute awarded him a medal in 1810. In 1807 he was appointed professor of astronomy and director of the Observatory at Göttingen. He published in 1809 his celebrated work, "Theory of the Motion of the Celestial Bodies," ("Theoria Motus Corporum Cœlestium,") in which he developed an improved method for calculating the orbits of planets and comets. He invented the heliotrope, which he used in a triangulation between Göttingen and Altona about 1822. About 1832 he associated himself with Weber in researches in terrestrial magnetism. They contributed greatly to perfect this science, and published "Results of the Observations of the Magnetic Society, (*Verein,*) 1837-40." Gauss was author of other works. He had a remarkable facility in learning languages. Laplace is reported to have called him "the greatest mathematician of Europe." Died at Göttingen in February, 1855.

See WALTERSHAUSEN, "Memoir of Gauss," (in German :) "Nouvelle Biographie Générale."

Gaussen, gō′sôṅ′, (ÉTIENNE,) a French Protestant theologian, born at Nîmes, became professor of philosophy at Saumur in 1651, and of theology in 1655. He wrote several Latin works, that were highly esteemed, among which is "De Ratione Studii theologici," (1670.) Died at Saumur in 1675.

Gaussin, gō′săṅ′, (JEANNE CATHERINE,) a celebrated French actress, born about 1713, made her début in Paris in 1731 with unanimous applause. Voltaire confided to her the rôle of "Zaïre" in his tragedy of that name, the success of which was ascribed to her by the public, and even by the author. She was most successful in parts characterized by fine and artless sensibility. She retired from the stage in 1763, and died in 1767. Her father's name was GAUSSEM.

See VOLTAIRE, "Correspondance ;" ARSÈNE HOUSSAYE, "Philosophers and Actresses."

Gau′ta-ma [Hindoo pron. gŏw′ta-ma] or **Gō′ta-ma,** called also **Gautama Booddha** or **Buddha,**† (bŏŏd′da,) *i.e.* "Gautama the Sage," **Sâkya Muni,** (sắk′ya mŏŏ′nI,) "Sâkya the Sage," and **Sâkya Sinha,** "Sâkya the Lion,"

---

[*] "That kingdom which clemency does not establish is unstable."
† Booddha (Gautama) is called Fo by the Chinese, and BOODSDO by the Japanese.—The name, in French, is GAOUTAMA BOUDDHA.

---

the name of a celebrated Hindoo reformer, commonly supposed to have been the founder of Bŏŏddhism. Respecting the time that he lived, the greatest diversity prevails among the different Bŏŏddhistic authorities, several maintaining that he was born more than a thousand, and some not less than two thousand, years before the Christian era. Recent European writers, however, appear to have adopted approximatively the date given by the Ceylonese Bŏŏddhists, from whom we have the fullest and, on the whole, the most satisfactory account, both of Gautama and his doctrines, that can anywhere be found. According to the Ceylonese writers, Gautama was born in 624 and died in 543 B.C.* He was of the Kshatria or warrior caste, of the Sâkya† family or tribe, and the son of Sudhôdănă,‡ King of Mâghada, of which the chief city was Kapilavastu, supposed to have been ₊situated near the modern Bahar. In early life he was commonly called Siddhârtă, (sĭd-hãr′tạ.§)

The Bŏŏddhistic legends surpass in extravagance everything that can elsewhere be found in the records of human invention. Yet not only is some knowledge of these legends indispensable to a just appreciation of the spirit and genius of Bŏŏddhism, but it is through them alone that we can reach the few scattered germs of historic truth existing in the various accounts of Gautama which have come down to us.‖

According to the legends respecting Gautama, his birth was attended with great wonders : the earth quaked, the sun, moon, and stars stood still, the blind saw, the lame walked, etc. When he reached the age of sixteen, his father, fearing lest he might become a priest, was anxious to have him married. The young Siddhârta made out a long list of qualities, personal and moral, which he considered it necessary that his wife should possess. With this list the court priest went from house to house through Kapilavastu, and at length found a maiden fulfilling all the requisitions; but her father insisted that Siddhârta, before marrying her, should give proof that he was skilled in all knightly accomplishments, as well as in learning and wisdom. At a public trial he came off victorious over all competitors. We are told that he was examined in botany and zoology as well as in mathematics and philosophy. According to another legend, of which the boundless extravagance suggests a much later date, Sudhôdana sent to certain of the neighbouring kings to obtain their daughters as wives for his son ; they refused, on the ground that the young prince was inexperienced, and especially that he was unacquainted with the arts of war, and could not, therefore, defend himself against the powerful enemies by whom he was surrounded. Piqued at this answer, Siddhârta resolved to give public proof of his strength and skill. A day having been fixed for that purpose, in the presence of a vast concourse of kings and warriors, he carelessly took up a bow requiring the strength of a thousand men to bend it. By merely thrumming the string he produced a sound louder than the loudest thunder, filling the inhabitants of distant provinces with terror. He then placed four plantain-leaves at each corner of a square, and with a single flight of his arrow pierced them all. Even in the dark he could send an arrow with an aim so unerring as to divide a hair. By his ready answers to the most difficult and abstruse questions, he showed that his wisdom was not inferior

* Köppen, after a careful and thorough examination of the subject, comes to the conclusion that the death of Sâkya Muni should be placed, in round numbers, about two centuries before Asoka, (Açôka,) and that he (Sâkya) was very probably the contemporary of Darius Hystaspes, or Xerxes.

† Written Sâkja and Çâkja in German.

‡ Written also Çudhôdana and Çoudhodana.

§ Siddhârta or Siddhârtha (written also Sidhartta) is an abbreviation or corruption of SARVÂRTHASIDDHA, i.e. the "fulfilment of every wish."

‖ The intelligent reader need scarcely be informed that nothing deserving the name of history, as this word is understood among the nations of the West, is to be found in the literature of any portion of India, excepting only the little kingdom of Cashmere. The Hindoo mind, indeed, though gifted with extraordinary intelligence and rare sagacity in some departments of thought, would seem to be wholly incapable of appreciating the value of historic truth. It is not the probability or truth, but the grandeur, of a statement, which carries conviction to the minds of the people of India ; and their religious teachers are too wise or too sympathetic not to meet the popular demand.

to his strength or skill. The neighbouring kings were abundantly satisfied ; and not long after, no fewer than forty thousand princesses were sent to be the inmates of Siddhârta's palace.* Later accounts give the young prince eighty-four thousand concubines, besides two or three lawful wives. For a time the son of Sudhôdana lived in the enjoyment of every pleasure that youth and power could bestow.

At length a feeling of the utter vanity of all earthly things took possession of his mind ; a divine influence brought to him some dim remembrance of the innumerable sacrifices he had made in previous transmigrations in order to attain the Bŏŏddhaship and to free all living beings from the pains of existence. (See BOODDHA.) His father, warned by dreams and prophecies, tried to keep Siddhârta confined in his seraglio and in total ignorance of the world around him. But once, as the young prince happened to walk out, he saw an old man, with bent body, wrinkled face, bald head, and trembling limbs. Astonished at the sight, he asked his attendant what it was. The latter simply answered, "It is an old man." But when, on further inquiries, Siddhârta learned that decrepitude and misery were the lot of all in advanced age, he returned to his home full of sorrow. "What," thought he," can pleasure or power avail me if at last I must come to this ?" On another occasion he saw one afflicted with incurable leprosy and covered with sores, without a guide or helper. He exclaimed, "Alas ! for youth which is destroyed by age, and for health which is undermined by every form of disease !" At length he met a beggar, who was a religious devotee, and whose whole appearance betokened inward composure and peace. Siddhârta at last decides to renounce the world ; he now remembers that he is a Bôdhisattva, or Bôdhisat, (an aspirant to the Bŏŏddhaship,) and, in spite of the most determined opposition from his father, he resolves to devote his life to teaching mortals how to escape from the miseries of their changeful existence. According to the doctrine of the Bŏŏddhists, Siddhârta did not owe his wonderful gifts or his spirit of self-sacrifice to the mere accident of his having been born with a happy intellectual and physical constitution ; but the merit which he had acquired in innumerable previous existences caused him, by an unerring, inevitable law, to be thus wonderfully endowed in his last and most perfect birth. (See BOODDHA.) That power or principle which causes any being to be born in a condition corresponding to the merit or demerit acquired in previous transmigrations, is termed Kărmă, (or Kŭrma,) a Sanscrit term signifying "work" or "action." It may be regarded as the combined result of all one's previous acts, whether good or evil. "Destiny (Schicksal) in its Bŏŏddhistic acceptation," says Köppen, "is the product of the merit and the guilt of living (beseelten) creatures. . . . Every deed, whether good or evil, operates through endless periods, on and on, and bears, even after a hundred thousand kalpas,† its inevitable fruit, until its effect is destroyed through perfect sinlessness." (See "Religion des Buddha," p. 285.)

Siddhârta having, by his perseverance in acts of benevolence and self-sacrifice performed through innumerable previous transmigrations, accomplished everything necessary to make him a supreme Bŏŏddha, he acquired, at last, unlimited intelligence and power. But, after resigning the pleasures and splendours of royalty, it was necessary for him to pass through various trials and to overcome the opposition of powerful enemies—among others, that of Mârâ, a mighty dêva (or deity)—before he could attain to complete deification.

We are told, in true Oriental style, that, in his great contest with Mârâ, the latter, accompanied by all the powers of evil, came to the conflict riding on an elephant one hundred and fifty miles high. Mountains of immeasurable size are hurled at the Bôdhisattva ; but the moment they touch him they are changed into wreaths and

* It would appear that both in ancient and modern times it has been customary in the East to measure the splendour and dignity of a sovereign by the number of his wives. Akbâr, the greatest of the Mogul emperors, is said to have had more than five thousand, each lady having a separate apartment for herself.

† Kâlpâ (a day and night of Brahma) is a period of 4320 millions of our years.

festoons of flowers; at the same time the poison, which is spit upon him by his demoniac foes, becomes a halo of glory round his head. Having at last come off victorious over all his enemies, he becomes possessor of boundless wisdom and knowledge, and not only remembers with perfect distinctness all his experiences in his innumerable previous existences, but he also knows the exact circumstances of all the beings who have ever existed in the infinite worlds, and receives that divine vision which enables him to see the remotest parts of the universe as distinctly as if they were close at hand. "Then the beings of all the infinite sakwalas (or worlds) who had not before enjoyed that privilege, saw a supreme Booddha, and rejoiced in the rays of many-coloured light which proceeded from his person." Among the characteristics of beauty belonging to Booddha are mentioned curly locks and a golden-coloured complexion: accordingly, we always see his statues represented with curly hair; and generally, if not invariably, they are of a yellow colour.* The person of Booddha, it is said, was ordinarily only twelve cubits in height; but, when he willed to do so, he could enlarge himself beyond the limits of the highest heaven.

The followers of Gautama believe that throughout myriads of ages he voluntarily endured the severest privations, and often the most dreadful sufferings, in order that he might at last save the inhabitants of the different worlds from the miseries of existence. Millions of centuries ago he had acquired sufficient merit to enter Nirvâna or Nirwâna, (the supreme beatitude of the Booddhists;) but he preferred to suffer through countless ages, that he might become the benefactor of all beings. The Booddhists believe that in the universe the worlds (sakwalas) are beyond all computation. Each sakwala includes an earth, with its continents, islands, and oceans, as well as a number of heavens and hells, and is inhabited in its different parts by various beings, such as animals, men, demons, dêvas, and brahmas. The dêvas (dā'vas) are a sort of inferior deities. The brahmas are an order of godlike beings, who hold the highest rank among all the inhabitants of the universe, a Booddha alone excepted. Their state of passionless repose strongly reminds us of Lucretius's description of the gods of Epicurus, from whom they differ, however, in not possessing absolute immortality :

"Omnis enim per se Divôm natura necesse est
Immortali ævo summâ cum pace fruatur,
Semota ab nostris rebus sejunctaque longè;
Nam privata dolore omni, privata periclis,
Ipsa suis pollens opibus, nihil indiga nostri,
Nec bene promeritis capitur, nec tangitur irâ."†
           De Rerum Naturâ, lib. i.

One of the abodes of the dêvas is termed a dêvalôka, and an abode of the brahmas is called a brahmalôka. The ages of the different inhabitants of the universe vary according to the lôka which they occupy. The most short-lived of the dêvas live nine millions of our years; while those who enjoy the greatest longevity live more than nine thousand million years. The life-term of the brahmas also varies greatly; but it would be almost impossible to express in figures the age even of those whose lives are the briefest. Some of the Booddhistic writers, however, have endeavoured to convey an idea of those immeasurable periods in the following manner. There is fabricated in India a species of cotton cloth unequalled in the delicacy of its texture; it is sometimes called "woven wind," (in Latin, "ventus textilis.") Now, were

---

* See Moor's "Hindu Pantheon," p. 229. It appears that before Gautama's appearance as supreme Booddha, the putting on of a yellow garment was an indication that the wearer had renounced the world and become an ascetic. (See Köppen, pp. 83 and 85.) Whether Booddha's golden complexion may have been given to him in commemoration of his former character as an ascetic, we are unable to say: but it is still a prevailing, if not universal, custom, among the Booddhist priesthood, in many parts of the world, to wear a yellow dress.

† The following, by Dr. Good, though very imperfect, is perhaps the best poetical translation into English that has been made of the above passage:
"Far, far from mortals and their vain concerns,
In peace perpetual, dwell the immortal gods,
Each self-dependent and from human wants
Estranged forever. There nor pain pervades,
Nor danger threatens: every passion sleeps;
Vice no revenge, no rapture virtue prompts."

---

one to touch with this material, ever so lightly, once in a hundred years, a mountain of solid rock sixteen miles high and as many broad, the mountain would at length be completely worn to dust. But the time required for this would not amount to the thousandth part of the life-term of the greater number of the brahmas.

There is also an endless variety of beings of a less exalted order, and of various forms. Some of these, called Nâgas, appear as serpents, but are in fact demi-gods. The Garundas are like immense birds, and are represented as the mortal enemies of the Nâgas. The Asuras, (or Asurs,) who hold so prominent a place in the Brahmanical mythology, are too important to be omitted from a system of exaggeration designed to throw all the fictions of the Brahmans into the shade. Accordingly, we have them in all their glory. Râhu, (râ'hŏŏ,) one of the Asur chiefs, is expressly stated to be 76,800 miles high, and 19,200 miles across the shoulders. The Prêtas (prā'tas) are unhappy beings, of immense size, but so wasted and thin as to resemble a dry leaf.

Respecting the doctrines taught by Gautama himself, we cannot safely affirm anything positively. There seems, however, to be no reason to doubt that the primitive Booddhists were atheists. Those of Ceylon, (who have confessedly departed the least from the primitive doctrines of Booddhism,) as well as the most ancient sect of Nepaul, (the Swâbhâvîkâs,) are, strictly speaking, atheists, since they do not recognize any infinite self-existent Spirit who is the original source of all forms of being. They teach that an infinite multitude of separate finite souls have always existed. Some sects maintain that nothing exists in the universe except matter, which is endowed with certain inherent, inseparable properties, causing it to arrange itself in forms of beauty and order, and, consequently, that the souls of living beings are material. While thus teaching that existence had no beginning, they maintain not only that under every form it is an evil, but that, except where it is voluntarily endured, as in the case of the aspirants to the Booddhaship, it is invariably associated with demerit. If any being, whether man, dêva, or brahma, had sufficient merit, he would at once enter Nirvâna and cease to have any separate existence.

We have already spoken of the *Karma* (that power or destiny that determines the condition in which any being is to be born) as the combined influence or result of all one's previous actions, whether good or evil. In assigning to any one a place or condition according to the aggregate of the actions of his past existence, the Karma is held to be absolutely unerring, and irresistible as the decrees of fate. (To this, however, there is one exception: a candidate for the Booddhaship may voluntarily relinquish a superior condition for one far inferior, in order to gain more merit.) Nothing except severe penance and blameless conduct, continued through immeasurable periods, can suffice to change an evil Karma for a good one. The very shortest period that any of the inhabitants of Naraka (or hell) remain in torment is nine millions of our years. The great object for which a supreme Booddha is manifested is not only to encourage the various beings burdened with existence to enter the paths which lead to Nirvâna, but also to facilitate their progress therein. The Booddhists do not hold that a supreme Booddha is able to deliver any being from the evils of existence by his own direct power; but in various ways he can afford them opportunities of acquiring merit. Through his divine knowledge he can point out to them the true "paths," and by his divine eloquence he can often prevail upon the most reluctant to enter the way leading to Nirvâna. The preaching (*bana*, or "word") of Gautama is said to have exerted an astonishing influence upon the minds of his hearers. "It was," to adopt the language of his enthusiastic votaries, "as a divine charm to cure the poison of evil desire; a sovereign medicine to heal the disease of anger; a lamp in the midst of the darkness of ignorance; an all-consuming fire to destroy the evils of repeated existence; a meridian sun to dry up the mud of covetousness; a great rain to quench the flame of sensuality," etc. etc.

There are five great commandments, called "pǔn'cha seel," (or *pancha sîl*,) *i.e.* the "five duties or ordinances,"

ā, ē, ī, ō, ū, ȳ, *long;* ă, ĕ, ŏ, same, less prolonged; ă, ĕ, ĭ, ŏ, ŭ, ў, *short;* ạ, ẹ, ị, ọ, *obscure;* fär, fȧll, fȧt; mēt; nŏt; gŏŏd; mŏŏn;

which are especially binding on all the followers of Booddha, laymen as well as priests, viz.: 1. Do not kill; 2. Do not violate the law of chastity; 3. Do not steal; 4. Do not lie; 5. Do not drink intoxicating liquors. The transgressor of any one of the above commands is liable —unless there be important extenuating circumstances— to suffer in Naraka for myriads of ages. It may be observed that the Booddhistic idea as to what constitutes a lie differs materially from that entertained by European nations : according to the former, there must not only be an intentional misstatement with a purpose to deceive, but there must also be the *discovery by the person deceived* that what has been told him is untrue. (Hardy's "Manual of Budhism," p. 469.)

In regard to all classes of transgression, the degree of sin depends greatly upon the attending circumstances, and especially upon the character or condition of the person sinned against. Thus, to steal from a skeptic is a comparatively small offence ; to steal from a priest is a grievous sin ; but to steal from the associated priesthood is a crime of the blackest dye.

The Booddhist priesthood are required to observe not merely the five great precepts above mentioned, but a multitude of other ordinances, of the most stringent character, among which are the following. The priest must live on alms, and, if in good health, must himself carry the alms-bowl from house to house. He must not only observe the strictest celibacy, but he must (unless in company with other men) avoid as far as possible the presence of women : he must not sit on the same seat with one in any private place, nor may he accompany a woman on a journey even from one end of a village to the other. He must eat his food "meditatively," not for the pleasure it gives him, but merely for the purpose of warding off untimely death. He must in no case eat food after mid-day. A priest who has entered one of the paths leading to Nirvâna is called a Rahat (răh'hăt) or Ar'hat, (written also Archat.) The common term for the system of doctrines and precepts of Gautama is Dharmma, (or, as it is more usually written, Dharma,) (pronounced dŭr'mą,) that is, the "law," "virtue," "duty." The followers of Booddha are commonly called, in India, BAUDDHAS, (bŏwd'hąs.)

The Booddhists believe that all living creatures are homogeneous in their essence, the only difference being accidental and caused solely by a difference of merit, Hence a worm or insect may be as truly our brother, according to the profoundest and most essential laws of relationship, as a human being. Booddhism cannot, therefore, properly be said to teach the brotherhood of mankind, but rather the brotherhood of all creatures. It teaches that not merely all animals, including the vilest insects, have souls, but that the seeds of plants have souls also. And this may furnish the reason why a priest is required to live on alms, since in no other way could he escape the responsibility of taking life. If he caused grain to be ground, he would disembody the souls of innumerable beings ; but by living on offal he merely uses for his sustenance that which would otherwise be thrown aside and wasted. In regard to the relationship subsisting between different creatures, "with the exception," says Hardy, "of those beings who have entered one of the four paths leading to Nirvâna, there may be an interchange of condition between the highest and the lowest. He who is now the most degraded of demons may one day rule the highest of the heavens ; he who is at present seated upon the most honourable of the celestial thrones may one day writhe amid the agonies of a place of torment ; and the worm which we crush under our feet may in the course of ages become a Supreme Budha." ("Manual of Budhism," p. 36.)

The highest element of Booddhism was a feeling of benevolence and sympathy for other men or other creatures,—unquestionably the highest and noblest of human impulses. It was called into action by what was probably the most oppressive and fearful tyranny under which any great people ever suffered. It was not the tyranny of one or of a few tyrants, from which there might be some hope of escape by flight or concealment, but the tyranny of a multitudinous class,—of a class generally believed to be necessary to the very existence not merely of the state, but of the separate individuals composing the nation, (see "Institutes of Manu," i. 101 ; see, also, ix. 313–319,) and penetrating with its terrible and all-but omnipotent arms every ramification of society. As the vapours in the interior of the earth, exasperated by volcanic fires, will sometimes force aside or burst asunder the superincumbent mountains, so at length the masses of the Hindoo nation, maddened by their sufferings and rendered irresistible by their very despair, shook off the frightful incubus which pressed upon them. In this, as in all other cases of religious tyranny, the deliverance came through skepticism and denial of the prevailing dogmas. And, as was to be expected, the power and extent of the reaction were in proportion to the power of the tyranny under which the masses of the people had suffered. The revolution which accompanied the rise of Booddhism appears to have closely resembled, in its more important features, the French Revolution ; but, as it was a reaction against a more terrible oppression, it was followed by more extensive and more permanent results. As the oppression had been chiefly if not wholly religious in its origin, so the reaction, we have every reason to suppose, was accompanied and followed by a deeper spirit of denial and by a more universal unbelief. The reformers began with repudiating the authority of the Brahmans, and ended with not merely rejecting the sacred books of the priesthood, (the Vedas,) but in denying the very existence of those Higher Powers from which the Brahmans claimed to derive their authority. The reformation took a humanitarian direction, and at the same time carried the levelling principle to its utmost possible limits. It rejected absolutely all prescriptive claims, whether human or divine. It assumed that all beings in the universe stood exactly on the same ground, the only difference being made by the difference of conduct. But, as the religious sentiment found in all nations demanded something to satisfy it, men, deified by their merits, were made use of to supply this demand.

It will thus be seen (if, as there seems every reason to believe, the foregoing views are correct) that Booddhism originated in almost total unbelief, and owed its influence principally, if not wholly, to a great political revolution. The corner-stone of the building is atheism, the copestone (Nirvâna, or annihilation) is absolute despair. But between these terrible extremes there is a kindly human element, which is the only redeeming feature of the system, and to which is doubtless due whatever of vitality it possesses. But the influence of this humanity is greatly impaired and, indeed, rendered all-but nugatory by its impracticable and extravagant character. By teaching that we must not only spare the lives of vermin, (these being really our brethren,) but the lives of the seeds of plants, which form the sustenance of so large a portion of the human race, there is nothing left for the truly devout votary of Booddhism, as we have already seen, but thriftless indolence and helpless beggary.

As it is impossible for any people wholly to change their previous habits of thought, we need not be surprised to discover many points of resemblance between Booddhism and the Brahmanical system which it for a time displaced. First, as the basis of both, we find the doctrine of Metempsychosis, or the continued existence of the same being under various outward forms ; secondly, both teach alike a belief in accumulative merit, by which the meanest creature may, by a course of penance continued through successive ages, rise to the possession of godlike intelligence and power ; thirdly, they agree substantially in regarding Nirvâna, or the cessation of a distinct and separate existence, as the greatest blessing to which any being can attain,*—not to mention other points of less importance. (See BRAHMANISM.)

* With the primitive or orthodox Booddhists, Nirvâna is simply annihilation, while with the Brahmans it is absorption into the essence of Brahma, the supreme, self-existent Spirit. The etymology of Nirvâna is very obscure. It is supposed by some to be derived from the Sanscrit *nir*, "without," "not," and *van*, to "sound," to "blow as a flute." It may possibly have allusion to the exceedingly transitory character of every form of being, comparing it to the breath or sound of a musical instrument, which passes away we know not whither, Nirvâna would then imply the absence or cessation of that fitful, changeful existence which, with us, has been compared to a **passing** vapour.

e as *k;* ç as *s;* ḡ *hard;* ġ as *j;* G, H, K, *guttural;* N, *nasal;* R, *trilled;* ṣ as *z;* ŧh as in *this.*   (☞See Explanations, p. 23.)

They differ, on the other hand, with respect to caste, which the Brahmans make the corner-stone of their system, but which Gautama totally rejected.* Among the votaries of Brahmanism the priests could be chosen from the highest caste only, and it is regarded as a serious offence even to teach the Vedas (sacred books) to a Soodra (a person of the lowest of the pure castes) or to a woman. Among the Booddhists, on the contrary, all classes, including women and even the lowest outcasts, are freely admitted to the priesthood; none are rejected, except the deformed, or diseased, or those who are servants. It is considered that a servant cannot give himself to the priesthood, because he cannot give what is the property of another. They differ, also, totally with respect to the Vedas, which the Booddhists entirely reject, while the Brahmans regard them as the most sacred and excellent of all writings.

Again, the principal deities of the Brahmans are incarnations from Brahm, the supreme, eternal, self-existing Spirit. The principal deity of the Booddhists (strictly so called) is always a mortal, and may have begun his career as the most pitiful insect, though he always ends it as a deified man, in which form, however, he has but a brief existence, and soon dies, leaving the universe without even the semblance of a ruler.

The remarkable success of Gautama as a reformer was doubtless owing chiefly, if not entirely, to the democratic character of his doctrines; and we should probably not err in considering him to have been far more a political than a religious reformer. His doctrine of the impartial equality of all classes, dignified and rendered sacred by his twofold character of saint and sage, and promulgated at a time when the irksome and oppressive restrictions of caste, joined to the arrogance of the Brahmans, had become intolerable to a large majority of the people, was, we may confidently conjecture, eagerly, passionately welcomed by all, the dominant class alone excepted. So rapid was the spread of the new doctrines that only about two centuries after the death of Gautama we find Chandragupta, (the Sandracottus of the Greek historians,) a man of low caste, raised to the most powerful throne in Northern India. This event is the more remarkable because he does not appear to have been a believer in or a supporter of Booddhism, showing that it was a political rather than a religious revolution which placed him on the throne; although, as already intimated, the doctrines of the new religion may have powerfully co-operated with the new political principles in bringing about that result. His grandson, however, Asôka, (Açôka or Ashoka,) became a devoted follower of Gautama, and succeeded, it would appear, in establishing the new religion in every part of his widely-extended dominions. He is said—with Oriental hyperbole, no doubt—to have erected eighty-four thousand monasteries (vihârs) in honour of the eighty-four thousand discourses of Booddha. (See the "Bhilsa Topes," by Cunningham, p. 99.) His son Mahendra (or Mahindo) introduced Booddhism into Ceylon, which is still one of its principal seats. The persecutions to which the new religion was subjected in India in the early centuries of our era contributed undoubtedly to its diffusion among the neighbouring nations, but resulted at last in its almost total extirpation from the land wherein it had its origin.

Booddhism appears to have been first introduced into China in the latter part of the third century before Christ. From Ceylon it extended to Farther India and Cochin China. It is supposed to have been permanently established in Japan in the sixth century. Nepaul has long been one of its principal seats, whence it extended to Thibet and the country of the Mongols, receiving greater or less modifications from the peculiar genius of the various nations by whom it was adopted.

It would, perhaps, be difficult to explain satisfactorily how Booddhism, after it had once obtained such an ascendency among the people of India, could be so soon and so completely displaced by the old religion. But, if we regard the movement which for a time overthrew

the Brahmanical domination to have been due in a great measure to political causes, among which the tyranny of caste was probably the chief, we may suppose that when the pressure of those causes was removed the popular mind came gradually to look with less and less aversion, and perhaps at last with affectionate reverence, on the religion of their ancestors, a change of feeling which was probably much accelerated by the austere ordinances and comfortless, despairing doctrines of the new faith,—a faith which makes annihilation the final and highest reward for ages of self-denial, privation, and suffering. We may well believe that these doctrines never had any place in the popular affections, and that they were only accepted at all because they were accompanied by great ameliorations in the political and social condition of the people. We may conjecture that the Brahmans, taught by past experience, were very careful, at least for a time, not to repress, by any undue rigour or offensive assertions of superiority, the returning affections of the people.

There are some general and obvious points of resemblance between Booddhism and Christianity which can scarcely fail to strike one at first sight; such, for example, as the importance which each attaches to the practice of self-denial, and that regard for the welfare of others, however humble their condition, which forms so essential a feature in the ethical system of both. But, if we examine them more closely, and consider their deeper relations, we shall find that the difference between them is not only great, but absolutely immeasurable. It would, we feel assured, be a grave error to suppose (as some recent writers appear to do) that this difference is a mere divergence, though a very wide one, from a common principle or starting-point; for they are essentially and wholly different in their very origin. We need only allude to the remarkable difference between the accounts of the two systems that have come down to us,—the one filled with the wildest fables, which, from their very nature, must destroy, in every truth-loving mind, all confidence and everything deserving the name of belief; the other characterized by an unpretending and touching simplicity, which furnishes the strongest internal evidence of the entire sincerity and truthfulness of the writers.* But we refer more particularly to the character of the systems themselves,—the one owing its origin, as there is every reason to suppose, to an utter and almost universal unbelief, and being, like the worship of the goddess of Reason in France, a mere device to appease rather than satisfy the cravings of the religious instinct of the people; the other having for its foundation the highest and fullest belief ever presented to the world,—the belief in a Being, infinite in power and love, whose paternal care extends to the very humblest of his creatures. The one system, built upon atheism, has for its final scope annihilation: in other words, it is the religion of despair. The other, based upon a belief in God's infinite perfections and his boundless love to man, (see John iii. 16,) becomes the unfailing source of an infinite hope,—a hope not only of endless happiness, but of eternal progress towards perfection.

See KÖPPEN, "Religion des Buddha," Berlin, 1857; R. SPENCE HARDY, "Manual of Budhism," London, 1853; B. H. HODGSON, "Literature and Religion of the Buddhists," 1841; J. BARTHÉLEMY SAINT-HILAIRE, "Le Bouddha et sa Religion," Paris, 1862; GUIGNIAUT, "Religions de l'Antiquité," Paris, 1825; MOOR, "Hindu Pantheon;" STANISLAS JULIEN, "Histoire de la Vie de Hiouen-Thsang," etc., 1853; and the continuation of the same, under the name of "Mémoires sur les Contrées occidenta'es," 1857-58.

Gautherot, gō'tro', (CLAUDE,) an eminent French painter, born in Paris in 1769, was a pupil of David. Among his chief works are "Marius at Minturnæ," and "The Funeral of Atala," (1800.) Died in 1825.

Gauthey, gō'tā', (EMILAND MARIE,) an eminent French civil engineer, born at Châlons-sur-Saône in 1732, was employed from 1783 to 1791 in constructing the Canal du Centre. In 1791 he was appointed inspector-general. He wrote a "Treatise on the Construction of Bridges and Navigable Canals," (3 vols., 1809.) Died in 1806.

See "Nouvelle Biographie Générale."

---

* "There is caste," observes Hardy, "among the Budhists of Ceylon; but this is contrary to the tenets of the founder of their religion." ("Manual of Budhism," p. 78.)

* This internal evidence alone is such as not only to command the assent of multitudes of intelligent readers, but even sometimes to overcome the skepticism of the most gifted and critical minds. (See Niebuhr's "Letters," vol. i., Letter 148.)

ā, ē, ī, ō, ū, ȳ, *long;* ă, ĕ, ĭ, ŏ, ŭ, ў, same, less prolonged; ă, ĕ, ĭ, ŏ, ŭ, ў, *short;* ạ, ẹ, ị, ọ, *obscure;* fär, fäll, fät; mêt; nôt; gŏŏd; mŏŏn;

Gauthey, gō'tā', (LOUIS FRANÇOIS FRÉDÉRIC,) a Swiss Protestant teacher, born in the canton of Vaud in 1795. He published, besides other works, a treatise on education, "De l'Éducation," etc., (1854.)

Gauthier, gō'te-à', surnamed SANS-AVOIR, (sŏN-zå'vwÂR',) a Norman knight, who took a prominent part in the first crusade. He was killed in battle by the Turks near Nicea, in Asia, in 1097.

Gauthier, (FRANÇOIS,) ABBÉ, a French priest and able negotiator, born near Falaise. He lived many years in London, and was employed in secret negotiations, which resulted in the peace of Utrecht, 1713. Died in 1720.

Gauthier, (JEAN BAPTISTE,) a French theologian, born at Louviers in 1685. He published several works against the Jesuits and infidels. Died in 1755.

Gauthier, (PIERRE,) a French architect, born at Troyes in 1790. Among his works is a monument to Fénelon at Cambrai. Died in 1855.

Gautier. See GAULTIER, GAUTHIER, and WALTER.

Gautier, gō'te-à' (AMBROISE GEORGES JOSEPH,) a French jurist, born at Chevreuse in 1776, wrote "Studies on Commercial Jurisprudence," (1829.) Died in 1829.

See ANDRÉ MARIE JEAN JACQUES DUPIN, "Notice sur la Vie de Gauthier," 1829.

Gautier, (ARNAUD ÉLOY,) a French artist, son of J. Gautier-Dagoty, noticed below. He began to issue in 1752 "Periodical Observations on Natural History and the Arts, with Coloured Plates," which, after his death, was continued by Rozier, (1771-85.)

Gautier, (JOSEPH,) a French abbé and *littérateur*, born in Lorraine about 1714. He wrote, besides other works, a refutation of Rousseau's Essay on the question, "Do Sciences and Arts contribute to the Promotion of Morality?" (1751.) Died in 1776.

Gautier, (THÉOPHILE,) a French *littérateur* and critic, born at Tarbes about 1810. He produced "Albertus," and other poems, and an immoral romance called "Mlle. Maupin," (1835.) About 1836 he became assistant editor of the "Presse," for which he wrote criticisms on the drama and fine arts until 1854. After that date he had charge of the same department of the "Moniteur." Among his works is a book of travels in Spain, etc., entitled "Tras los Montes," (1843.) He has been extolled as an original and brilliant writer.

See LOUANDRE et BOURQUELOT, "La France Littéraire;" "Nouvelle Biographie Générale;" "Atlantic Monthly" for June, 1868.

Gautier - Dagoty, gō'te-à' dả'go'te', (ÉDOUARD,) a grandson of the following, was an engraver of Paris, where he published, about 1780, coloured engravings of twelve paintings in the Royal Gallery. Died in 1784.

Gautier- (or **Gauthier-**) **Dagoty,** (JACQUES,) a French anatomist and engraver, born at Marseilles, was remarkable for mental activity. He claimed to be the inventor of the art of producing coloured engravings, in which he used four colours. He published several works on anatomy, with coloured plates, and "Observations on Physics, Natural History, and Painting," (6 vols., 1752-55,) which was the origin of the "Journal de Physique," the first French journal of physical sciences. Died in 1758.

His son, JEAN BAPTISTE, was an engraver in colours. He published the "Galerie Française," a series of twelve portraits, (1770, unfinished.) Died in 1786.

Gautier de Metz, gō'te-à' deh mẳs, a French poet, who lived about 1230, is supposed to have written a didactic poem called "The Image of the World," ("L'Image du Monde.")

Gautieri, gŏw-te-ā'ree, (GIUSEPPE,) an Italian physician and naturalist, was born at Novara in 1769. He was appointed in 1808 inspector-general of woods and forests under the then kingdom of Italy. He retained this position twenty-two years. He wrote interesting works on forests and natural history, among which is a "General Treatise on the Science and Administration of Forests." Died in 1833.

Gautruche or **Gaultruche,** gō'trüsh', (PIERRE,) a French priest, born at Orléans in 1602, published a "Poetic History," ("Histoire poétique," 1658,) and a "Sacred History," (1672.) Died in 1681.

Gauzlin, gō'lån', a French prelate, reputed one of the most learned men of his time, was the natural son of Hugh Capet. He was made Archbishop of Bourges in 1013. Died in 1029.

Gavanti, gä-vän'tee, (BARTOLOMMEO,) an Italian friar, born at Monza about 1570, was general of the Barnabites. He wrote, besides other works, "Thesaurus Sacrorum Rituum," a commentary on the rubrics of the missal and the breviary of the Roman Church. Died in 1638.

Gavard, gä'vâr', (HYACINTHE,) an eminent French anatomist, born at Montmélian in 1753, was a successful teacher of surgery in Paris. He published several treatises on anatomy. His "Splanchnologie" (1800) is said to be superior to anything before printed on that subject. Died in 1802.

See "Biographie Médicale."

Gavarni, gä-vår'nee, the pseudonym of PAUL CHEVALIER, a very popular French caricaturist, born in Paris in 1801. In 1835 he began to issue a satirical journal called "Les Gens du Monde," in which he presented spirited pictures of Parisian society. Many of these designs were reproduced in the "Charivari," which owed to Gavarni a great part of its success. His works are remarkable for variety and fidelity to nature.

Gavarret, gä'vä'rà', (LOUIS DENIS JULES,) a French physician, born in 1809. He graduated in 1843, and in the same year became professor of medical physics. He published, besides other works, an excellent "Treatise on Electricity," (1857.)

Gavazzi, gä-vät'see, (Padre ALESSANDRO,) an Italian priest and political agitator, born at Bologna in 1809. He became professor of rhetoric in Naples, where he distinguished himself by his eloquence and liberal principles. He was chaplain of the army of volunteers which Pius IX. sent against the Austrians in 1848, and excited the enthusiasm of the people by his harangues. He continued to support the popular cause after the pope had recalled his army and changed his policy. In 1849, as chaplain-general of the republican army, he distinguished himself by his zeal in the siege of Rome. After Rome had been captured by the French, (1849,) he became an exile, and lectured against popery in England and the United States.

See a "Life of Father Gavazzi," London, 1851.

Gaveaux, gä'vō', (PIERRE,) a French composer and singer, born at Béziers in 1761. His "Léonore" (1798) furnished to Beethoven the subject of his opera "Fidelio." Died in 1825.

Găv'es-ton, de, [Fr. pron. gä'vĕs'tôN',] (PIERS, or PIERRE,) the favourite of Edward II. of England, was descended from a Gascon family. He appears to have acquired influence over the young prince by his vices, wit, and personal accomplishments. In 1300 he was banished by Edward I. Edward II., having come to the throne, recalled Gaveston, and made him Earl of Cornwall, and chief minister. His pride and insolence excited a conspiracy of the nobles, who attacked him in his castle and put him to death in 1312.

See "Life and Death of Piers Gaveston," 1740; HUME, "History of England."

Gaviniès, gä've'ne-ĕs', (PIERRE,) a French musician, born at Bordeaux in 1726. He is regarded as the chief of the French school of violinists. He composed "Matinées" for the violin, (1794.) Died in 1800.

See FAYOLLE, "Notices sur Corelli, Tartini, Gaviniès," etc., 1810.

Gavirol, gä-ve-rol', (SOLIMAN BEN,) a noted Rabbi, born in Málaga, Spain, excelled in grammar, philosophy, and other sciences. He wrote, in Arabic, two admired works on morality. Died about 1070.

Gay, gä, (CLAUDE,) a French botanist and traveller, born at Draguignan in 1800. He spent about twelve years in the exploration of the botany and zoology of Chili between 1828 and 1841, during which he received aid from the Chilian government. Having returned to Paris, he published, in Spanish, his excellent "Physical and Political History of Chili," ("Historia fisica y politica de Chile," 24 vols., 1843-51.) Eight volumes of this treat on botany. He was admitted into the Institute in 1856. Died in 1864.

See "Nouvelle Biographie Générale."

Gay, (DELPHINE.) See GIRARDIN.

ᵉ as *k*; ç as *s*; g̃ *hard*; g̃ as *j*; G, H, K, *guttural*: N, *nasal*; R, *trilled*; s̃ as *z*; ᵗh as in *this*. (☞See Explanations, p. 23.)

64

Gay, (EBENEZER,) D.D., an American divine, born in Dedham, Massachusetts, in 1696, graduated at Harvard in 1714, and from 1718 till his death, in 1787, was pastor in Hingham. He published numerous sermons, one of which, delivered on his eighty-fifth birthday, was entitled "The Old Man's Calendar."

Gay, (JOHN,) an English poet, born at Barnstaple in 1688. He became secretary to the Duchess of Monmouth in 1712. His first production, called "Rural Sports," (1711,) was dedicated to Pope, who became his constant friend. By his amiable disposition, his wit and poetic talents, he made many friends among literary men and the higher classes. He wrote comedies, farces, fables, ballads, etc., which were received with favour. "The Beggar's Opera," (1728,) and the farce "What d'ye call It?" were especially popular; though but little can be said in favour of their moral tendency. His fables are admired for ingenious reflections and for a graceful sprightly style. In "The Shepherd's Week," (1714,) a series of pastoral poems, he successfully describes the manners of English peasants. He wrote, also, "Trivia, or the Art of Walking the Streets of London," (1715.) In the latter part of his life the Duke of Queensberry received him into his house, and treated him kindly. He died in 1732, and was buried in Westminster Abbey. Dr. Johnson remarks that "he had not in any degree the *mens divinior*, the dignity of genius." Hazlitt thought his pastorals pleasing and poetical, and that his fables possess "great merit, both as to the quantity of invention implied, and the elegance and facility of the execution."

See JOHNSON, "Lives of the Poets;" SPENCE, "Anecdotes;" "Biographia Britannica;" CAMPBELL, "Specimens of the British Poets."

Gay, (JOSEPH JEAN PAUL,) born at Lyons, in France, in 1775, obtained the title of architect to his native city. Died in 1832.

Gay, (MARIE FRANÇOISE SOPHIE **Nichault de Lavalette**—ne'shō' dęh lä'vä'lĕt',) a popular French novelist, born in Paris in 1776, was the mother of Delphine Gay Girardin. She was married to M. Gay about 1800, after which she was intimate with Pauline Bonaparte. Among her numerous works are "Laure d'Estell," (1802,) "Léonie de Montbreuse," (1813,) "Celebrated Saloons," ("Les Salons célèbres," 2 vols., 1837,) and "Ellénore," (4 vols., 1846.) Her style is commended for its elegance. Died in 1852.

Gay, (WICKWORTH ALLAN,) an American landscape-painter, noted for his skill in mountain and coast scenery, was born in Hingham, Massachusetts, in 1821.

See TUCKERMAN'S "Book of the Artists."

Gay de Vernon, (gȧ dęh vêR'nòN', (LÉONARD,) a French revolutionist and priest, born in Limousin in 1748. He was chosen constitutional Bishop of Haute-Vienne about 1790, and a member of the Convention in 1792. He acted with the Jacobins, and was one of the Council of Five Hundred, 1795-98. Died in 1822.

Gay de Vernon, (SIMON FRANÇOIS,) a French engineer, and professor in the Polytechnic School, brother of the preceding, was born in 1760. He wrote an "Elementary Treatise on the Art of War and Fortification," (2 vols., 1805,) which was adopted in many military schools of Europe. Died in 1822.

Gay-Lussac, (gȧ'lü'sȧk', (JOSEPH LOUIS,) an eminent French chemist and natural philosopher, born at Saint-Léonard (Haute-Vienne) on the 6th of December, 1778, was educated in the school afterwards called L'École Polytechnique. He was a pupil and protégé of Berthollet. In August, 1804, under the auspices of the Institute, MM. Biot and Gay-Lussac made a memorable ascent in a balloon, in order to ascertain the intensity of the magnetic force, and reached a height of thirteen thousand feet. This was the first ascent ever made for scientific objects. Gay-Lussac ascended alone in the ensuing month to the height of 7016 metres,—23,040 feet,—or about four and one-third miles above the level of the sea, and there made observations which tend to prove that the magnetic force diminishes very little with the elevation. He ascertained that the air of that region is identical in composition with that found near the surface of the earth. The temperature at the height of 7016 metres was 14°.9 above zero of Fahrenheit, while that of the surface was 82° of Fahrenheit. He wrote in 1804 a memoir which announced that in the composition of water one hundred volumes of oxygen unite with two hundred volumes of hydrogen. He was elected a member of the Academy of Sciences about 1806, soon after which he discovered the law by which air and gases are expanded uniformly by increase of temperature. In 1808 Gay-Lussac and Thénard were directed to make experiments with a colossal voltaic pile constructed by order of Bonaparte. The important results of their labours were published in the "Recherches physico-chimiques," (2 vols., 1811,) and in several memoirs on boracic acid and fluoric acid read at the Institute, 1808-09. He was appointed professor of practical chemistry at the Polytechnic School in 1809, and professor of physics at the Sorbonne. Among his most remarkable discoveries is that of cyanogen, in 1815. He made important contributions to nearly every branch of chemical and physical science. He wrote many valuable memoirs, which appeared in the "Mémoires" of the Society of Arcueil, and in the "Annales de Chimie," of which he was an editor. In 1831 he was elected to the Chamber of Deputies, became professor of chemistry at the Jardin des Plantes in 1832, and was made a peer of France in 1839. Died in Paris in May, 1850.

See ARAGO, "Éloge de Gay-Lussac," in his "Notices biographiques," tome iii.; GARDEUR LE BRUN, "Notice sur M. Gay-Lussac," 1851; DR. F. HOEFER, in the "Nouvelle Biographie Générale;" L. DE LOMÉNIE, "M. Gay-Lussac, par un Homme de Rien," 1841.

Gayangos, de, dȧ gī-äng'gòs, (PASCUAL,) an eminent Spanish Orientalist, born at Seville in 1809, studied in Paris under Silvestre de Sacy. He resided some years in England, where he published (in English) a "History of the Mohammedan Dynasties of Spain," from the Arabic of Al-Makkari, with notes, (2 vols., 1840-43.) He wrote articles for several English Reviews. In 1843 he became professor of Arabic at Madrid, and produced, with Vedia, a Spanish version of Ticknor's "History of Spanish Literature," (1851-56.) He gave important aid to Prescott in the collection of materials for his "History of Philip II."

Gayarré, gī'ȧ'rȧ', (CHARLES ARTHUR,) an American historian and lawyer, born in Louisiana in 1805. He was appointed secretary of state by Governor Johnson, of Louisiana, and filled that office about seven years. He published, besides other works, a "Histoire de la Louisiane," (2 vols., 1847,) and "Louisiana: its History as a French Colony," (2 vols., 1851-52.)

Gayot de Pitaval, gȧ'yo' dęh pe'tȧ'vȧl', (FRANÇOIS,) a mediocre French compiler, was born at Lyons in 1673. He worked for the booksellers of Paris, and published "Sallies of Wit for Conversation," (2 vols., 1732,) and "Celebrated Trials," ("Causes célèbres," 20 vols., 1734-43.) Died in 1743.

Gayrard, gȧ'rȧr', (RAYMOND,) a French sculptor and engraver of medals, born at Rodez in 1777, gained distinction by two medallions engraved on the occasion of the marriage of Napoleon, 1810.

Gay'ton, [Lat. DE SPECIOSA VILLA,] (EDMUND,) an English humorous writer, born in 1609. According to Anthony Wood, "he lived in London, and wrote trite things merely to get bread to sustain him and his wife." His best-known work is "Festivious Notes on Don Quixote," (1654.) Died in 1666.

Gay'wood, (ROBERT,) an eminent English engraver, who lived about 1650, was a pupil and imitator of Hollar.

Gaza, gȧ'zȧ, written also **Gazis,** (THEODORE,) an eminent Greek scholar, born at Thessalonica about 1400. He emigrated to Italy soon after the capture of that city by the Turks, (1429,) and taught Greek for some time at Ferrara. About 1450 he removed to Rome, where he was patronized by Pope Nicholas V. He wrote an excellent Greek Grammar, (printed in 1495,) and translated into Latin many Greek works, among which are Aristotle's "History of Animals," (1476,) and Theophrastus's "History of Plants," (1483.) He was an excellent Latin scholar, and contributed much to the revival of classical learning. Died in Italy about 1478.

See FABRICIUS, "Bibliotheca Græca;" HODY, "De Græcis illustribus;" "Nouvelle Biographie Générale."

ā, ē, ī, ō, ū, ȳ, *long;* ȧ, ė, ȯ, same, less prolonged; ă, ĕ, ĭ, ŏ, ŭ, ў, *short;* ạ, ẹ, į, ọ, *obscure;* fär, fȧll, fȧt; mėt; nŏt; gōōd; mōōn·

Gazæus. See GAZET.

Gazan de la Peyrière, gȧ'zȯn' dęh lȧ pȧ're-air', (HONORÉ THÉOPHILE MAXIME,) COUNT, a French general, born at Grasse, in Provence, in 1765. He became a general of division in 1799, after which he gained successes over the Austrians at Marcello, and other places in Italy. He distinguished himself at Jena, (1806,) Saragossa, (1809,) and Albuera, (1811.) Died in 1844.
See " Nouvelle Biographie Générale."

Gazan Khan. See GHAZAN KHAN.

Gazee- (or **Gazi-**) **Hassan,** gȧ'zee hȧs'sąn, grand admiral and prime minister of the Ottoman Empire, raised himself from the lowest rank. He went to Constantinople in 1760, and entered the navy. In 1769, in the war between Russia and the Porte, Hassan was a vice-admiral. In 1771 he forced the Russians to raise the siege of Lemnos, and was promoted to the rank of capudan-pasha, (grand admiral.) Sultan Selim in 1789 appointed him grand vizier; but, as he failed to secure either peace or victory, he was deprived of office and of life in 1790.

Gazet, gȧ'zạ', [Lat. GAZÆ'US,] (GUILLAUME,) a French historian and priest, born at Arras in 1554. He wrote, besides other superficial works, an " Ecclesiastical History of the Low Countries," (1614.) He is considered an injudicious and credulous writer. Died in 1611.

Gazi, gȧd'zee, [Lat. GA'ZIUS,] (ANTONIO,) an Italian physician, born about 1450. His treatise on hygiene, entitled " Florida Corona Medicinæ," (1491,) was often reprinted. Died in 1530.

Gazis. See GAZA.

Gazius. See GAZI.

Gaznevides, (or **Ghaznevides,**) gaz'nę-vidz, (sing. **Gaznevide,** gaz'nę-vid,) written also **Ghasnevides** and **Gasnevides,** [Fr. pron. gȧz'nȧ'vèd'; Ger. GHASNE-WIDEN, gȧz-nęh-wee'dęn; Lat. GAZNEV'IDÆ and GAZ-NEVI'TÆ,] the name of the first Mohammedan dynasty which ruled in India. It was founded by Sebaktegeen about 980, and named from Gaza or Ghiznee, the seat of his empire. His son Mahmood, by far the most powerful and most famous of all the Gaznevide sultans, overran a large part of Northern India, whence he returned with untold riches, the fruit of his vast conquests, to Gazna. (See MAHMOOD.) Khosroo-Malek, (or -Melek,) the last sovereign of this dynasty, was taken and put to death by the Ghaurian conqueror in 1186.

Gazola, gȧd'zo-lȧ, (GIUSEPPE,) an Italian physician, born at Verona in 1661. In 1692 the emperor Leopold employed him as one of his medical attendants. In 1697 he returned to Verona, where he practised with success till his death. He wrote a popular work, called " Il Mondo ingannato da falsi Medici," (" The World deceived by False Physicians," 1716.) Died in 1715.

Gazon-Dourxigné, gȧ'zȯn'dooR'zèn'yȧ',(SÉBASTIEN MARIE MATHURIN,) a French *littérateur*, born at Quimper-Corentin, wrote a poem entitled "Antenor, or the Republic of Venice," (1748,) a Critique on Voltaire's Dramas, (1767,) " The Gardens," a poem, (1772,) and several other works. Died in 1784.

Gazzaniga, gȧt-sȧ-nee'gȧ, (GIUSEPPE,) an Italian composer of operas, born at Verona about 1745; died about 1815.

Geary, gȧ're, commonly called gee're, (JOHN W.,) an American general, born in Westmoreland county, Pennsylvania, about 1820. He commanded a regiment in the Mexican war, (1846-47,) and was appointed Governor of Kansas in July, 1856, which position he resigned about March, 1857. He became a brigadier-general early in 1862, fought at the battle of Gettysburg in July, 1863, and commanded a division of the army of General Sherman in the campaign against Atlanta in the summer of 1864. He was elected Governor of Pennsylvania by the Republicans in October, 1866, and again in 1869.

Gebauer, gȧ-bȯw'ęr, (GEORG CHRISTIAN,) a German jurist, born at Breslau in 1690. He became first professor of law at Göttingen in 1734, wrote many valuable legal works, and published an edition of the " Corpus Juris." Died at Göttingen in January, 1773.
See C. G. HEYNE," Programma de Vita et Meritis G. C. Gebauer," 1774; GOESCHEN, " Vita G. C. Gebaueri," 1837.

Gebelin. See COURT DE GEBELIN.

Geber, ḡêb'ęr or gȧ'bęr, sometimes written **Giaber,** a distinguished Arabian chemist and alchemist, lived in Mesopotamia in the eighth century. His real name was ABOO-MOOSSAH-JAAFAR-AL-SOFEE. Some writers have erroneously attributed to him the invention of algebra. He was the author of several works on alchemy and kindred subjects. He was classed by Cardan among the twelve most subtle intellects of the world. According to Dr. F. Hoefer, " he deserves to be placed in the first rank among the chemists or alchemists anterior to Van Helmont. Geber is for the history of chemistry what Hippocrates is for the history of medicine." (See " Histoire de la Chimie.")
See, also, BOREL, "Bibliotheca Chimica;" ABULFEDA, ii.

Gebhard Truchsess, ḡêp'hȧRt tRo͞ok'sĕss, Elector and Archbishop of Cologne, was born near Waldburg in 1547. Having become a Protestant and married the Countess Agnes of Mansfeld about 1582, he was involved in a contest with the Catholic party, which resulted in his being compelled to surrender his electorate to the Archbishop of Bavaria. Died in 1601.
See J. D. KOELER, " Dissertatio de Actis et Fatis Gebhardii Truchsessii," 1745; JÖCHER, " Supplementum Historiæ Gebhardi Truchsessii.

Gebhardi, ḡêp-haR'dee, (JOHANN LUDWIG LEVIN,) a German historian, born at Brunswick in 1699. He was professor of theology, logic, and mathematics at Lüneburg for many years. He published an important " Historical and Genealogical Account of the Royal and Imperial Houses of Europe," (1731,) and other works. Died in 1764.
See MEUSEL, "Lexikon der vom Jahre 1750-1800 verstorbenen Deutschen Schriftsteller."

Gebhardt, ḡêp'hȧrt, or **Geb-har'dus,** (JANUS,) a Dutch scholar, of German extraction. He wrote notes on Tibullus, Catullus, and Propertius. Died in 1632.

Gebler, ḡêb'lęr, (TOBIAS PHILIPP,) a German poet and dramatist, born in 1726, was a councillor of state in the reign of Maria Theresa, and became a member of the privy council in 1782. Died in 1786.

Gechter, zhĕsh'taiR', (JEAN FRANÇOIS THÉODORE,) a French sculptor, born in Paris in 1796. Among his works are colossal statues of the Rhine and Rhone, which adorn the Place de la Concorde, Paris. Died in 1844.

Ged, ḡĕd, (WILLIAM,) a Scottish goldsmith and artist, born probably in Edinburgh about 1690. He invented, about 1725, a method of printing by a plate cast in a mould of plaster. He published an edition of Sallust thus printed in 1744. The term " stereotype" was first applied to this process by Firmin Didot. Died in 1749.
See NICHOLS, " Literary Anecdotes;" CHAMBERS, " Biographical Dictionary of Eminent Scotsmen."

Ged'dęš, (ALEXANDER,) a learned Roman Catholic biblical critic and translator, was born in the county of Banff, Scotland, in 1737. He removed to London about 1780, and undertook a translation of the Bible, (for the use of Roman Catholics,) of which he published two volumes, (1792-97.) These contain the books from Genesis to Chronicles inclusive, with notes and critical remarks which gave offence to Christians generally. He was deposed from his priestly functions by the apostolic vicar for his attack on the divine authority of the Scriptures, and his version remained unfinished. He doubted or denied the miracles ascribed to Moses. Died in 1802.
See " Life of A. Geddes," by JOHN MASON GOOD, 1803.

Geddes, (ANDREW,) a Scottish painter, born in Edinburgh about 1789. He painted portraits of Dr. Chalmers and David Wilkie, and historical pictures, among which was " Christ and the Woman of Samaria." Died in 1844.

Geddes, (JAMES,) a Scottish advocate and writer, born in 1710. He published an " Essay on the Composition and Manner of Writing of the Ancients, particularly Plato," (1748.) Died in 1749.
See CHAMBERS, " Biographical Dictionary of Eminent Scotsmen."

Geddes, (MICHAEL,) a theologian, born in Scotland about 1640. He was chancellor of the diocese of Sarum, and published, besides other works, a " History of the Church of Ethiopia," (1696,) " Miscellaneous Tracts," (3 vols., 1702-06,) and " Tracts against Popery," (1715.)

His works were admired by Southey. Died about 1715.

See CHAMBERS, "Biographical Dictionary of Eminent Scotsmen;" WOOD, "Athenæ Oxonienses."

Gedike, gä'de-kẹh, or **Gedicke,** (FRIEDRICH,) a German teacher and educational writer, born in the province of Brandenburg in 1755. He became in 1779 director of the Friedrichswerder Gymnasium at Berlin, and in 1795 of the Berlin Gymnasium, both of which institutions he raised to the highest prosperity by his excellent system of instruction. Died in 1803.

See FRANZ HORN, "F. Gedicke's Biographie," 1808; DANIEL JENISCH, "Einige Worte zum Andenken des F. Gedicke," 1803.

Gedoyn, zhẹh-dwăN', (NICOLAS,) a French translator and abbé, born at Orléans in 1677. He became intimate with Ninon de Lenclos, who was his relative. In 1701 he obtained a canonicate in Paris. He produced in 1718 an elegant but rather free translation of Quintilian, which opened to him the French Academy. His other chief work is a version of Pausanias, (1731.) Died in 1744.

See D'ALEMBERT, "Éloge de Gedoyn;" "Nouvelle Biographie Générale."

Gee, (JOSHUA,) a distinguished London merchant, published in 1729 a work entitled "The Trade and Navigation of Great Britain Considered," which was once popular.

Geefs, gāfs or Hāfs, (JAN JOSEPH,) a distinguished Belgian sculptor, born at Antwerp in 1811. Among his best works are "Adonis departing 'to the Chase," and "Metabus, King of the Volsci." Died in 1860.

Geefs, (WILLEM,) a celebrated Belgian sculptor, a brother of the preceding, was born at Antwerp in September, 1806, and studied under Ramey in Paris. Among his master-pieces are statues of Rubens and of Malibran, the monument to Count Frederick de Merode, the "Lion in Love," a group in marble, and "Francesca da Rimini." He obtained the title of first sculptor to the king. His wife, FANNY, is a skilful painter of genre and portraits.

Geel, Hāl, or **Gell,** gēl, (JAKOB,) an eminent Dutch classical scholar, born at Amsterdam in 1789. He became chief librarian at the University of Leyden in 1833, and was one of the founders of the "Bibliotheca Critica Nova," commenced in 1825. Among his chief works is a "Critical History of the Greek Sophists," in Latin, (1823.) He edited Theocritus, (1820,) the "Phœnissæ" of Euripides, and other Greek works.

Geel, van, văn Hāl, (LOUIS,) a Belgian sculptor, born at Malines in 1789. He executed the colossal figure of a lion erected on the field of Waterloo. Among his master-pieces is a shepherd playing on a flute. Died in 1852.

Geer, de, dẹh Hār or gār, (LODEWIJCK,) a Dutch or Swedish manufacturer, born in 1587. He was employed by Gustavus Adolphus of Sweden in the fabrication of arms, and in the reign of Queen Christina distinguished himself by the construction of a fleet. He rendered other important services to Sweden. Died in 1652.

See BURÉN, "Åreminne öfver L. de Geer," 1790; ERSCH und GRUBER, "Allgemeine Encyklopaedie," 1852; FRANZÉN, "Aminnelse-Tal öfver L. de Geer."

Geer, von, fon yär, (CARL,) BARON, a distinguished Swedish naturalist, born in 1720, was the owner of a large fortune. He was a pupil or friend of Linnæus, and attained the dignity of marshal of the court. His favourite study was entomology, on which he published an excellent work, "Memoirs to illustrate the History of Insects," ("Mémoires pour servir à l'Histoire des Insectes," 8 vols., 1752–78, with good figures.) He was author of other scientific works. Died in 1778.

See T. BERGMANN, "Åminnelse-Tal öfver C. de Geer," 1779; ERSCH und GRUBER, "Allgemeine Encyklopaedie;" GEZELIUS, "Biographiskt-Lexicon."

Geeraerts. See GARRARD, (MARK.)

Geerts, Hārts, (CHARLES HENRI,) a Belgian sculptor, born at Antwerp about 1808; died in 1855.

Geffrard, zhă'fkăr', (FABRE,) a native of Saint Domingo, born in 1806, entered the army at an early age, and was made a lieutenant-general in 1845. After the deposition of Soulouque, in 1859, Geffrard became president of the republic of Hayti.

Gefion, gā'fe-on or gēf'e-on, or **Gefione,** [etymology unknown,] in the Northern mythology, a virgin goddess, who takes into her service all those who die virgins. For a fuller account of Gefion and the offices she is supposed to fulfil, see Petersen's "Nordisk Mythologi."

Gehema, von, fon gă-hā'mä, (JOHN ABRAHAM,) a Polish medical writer, born about 1660. He was physician to the Elector of Brandenburg and to the King of Poland.

Gehlen, gā'lẹn, (ADOLPH FERDINAND,) a German chemist, born at Bütow in 1775, became a professor at Munich about 1807. He was editor of a "Journal of Chemistry," (5 vols., 1803–05,) and published several chemical memoirs. He died at Munich, a victim to an experiment with arsenical hydrogen gas, in 1815.

Gehler, gā'lẹr, (JOHANN KARL,) a German physician and writer, born at Görlitz in 1732, was professor of botany, anatomy, and chemistry at Leipsic. He wrote able treatises on obstetrics, and other works. Died in 1796.

See ERSCH und GRUBER, "Allgemeine Encyklopaedie;" "Biographie Médicale."

Gehler, (JOHANN SAMUEL TRAUGOTT,) a German jurist and savant, born at Görlitz in 1751. He published in 1787 a valuable "Dictionary of Physical Science," in 5 vols. Died in 1795.

Gehren, gā'rẹn, (KARL CHRISTIAN,) a German preacher and writer on theology, born at Marburg in 1763; died in 1832.

See his "Selbstbiographie."

Geibel, gī'bẹl, (EMANUEL,) a celebrated German poet, born at Lubeck in 1815. Having accompanied the Russian ambassador Katakazi, as a family tutor, to Athens in 1838, he visited the most interesting parts of Greece and perfected himself in his classical studies. After his return to Germany he published, in 1840, a volume of poems, which were very well received; and in 1852 he became professor of æsthetics at Munich. He brought out in 1841 his "Voices of the Time," ("Zeitstimmen,") which was followed by "King Sigurd's Bridal Excursion," and the "Twelve Sonnets for Sleswick-Holstein," (1846.) His poetry is characterized by rich fancy, melodious versification, and deep religious feeling, and· he ranks among the most popular German poets of the age.

Geier, gī'ẹr, (MARTIN,) a German Lutheran divine, born at Leipsic in 1614, was professor of Hebrew. He wrote Commentaries on Scripture. Died in 1681.

Geiger, gī'gẹr, (ABRAHAM,) a Jewish rabbi and Oriental scholar, born at Frankfort-on-the-Main in 1810. Among his principal works is a treatise entitled "What has Mohammed borrowed from Judaism?" (1833,) and "Studies on Moses ben Maimon," (1850.)

Geiger, gī'gẹr, (JOHANN CONRAD,) a distinguished painter on glass, born in Zurich in 1597; died in 1674.

Geijer or **Geyer,** yī'ẹr, (ERIK GUSTAF,) an eminent Swedish historian and poet, born in the province of Wärmeland on the 12th of January, 1783. He studied at Upsal, where he became professor of history in 1817, and acquired great popularity by his lectures. In 1811 he had begun the great publication of a journal entitled "The Iduna," in which his finest poems—"The Viking," "The Last Skald," etc.—appeared, and soon established his reputation. He represented the University of Upsal in the Diets of 1828 and 1840, and was twice offered a bishopric, which he refused. In 1822 he was appointed royal historiographer, and subsequently president of the Royal Academy. His "History of the Swedish Nation," ("Svenska Folkets Historia," 3 vols.,) esteemed his most important work, came out in 1832, and was soon after translated into English, French, and German. Among his other productions may be named his "Sketch of the Condition of Sweden from the Death of Charles XII. to the Reign of Gustavus III.," (1839,) "Life of Charles XIV., Jean," (Bernadotte,) (1844,) and "Reminiscences," ("Minnen," 1834,) left unfinished, containing an account of his early life and of his visit to England and Germany. Geyer was a member of numerous learned institutions, both of his own and other countries, and was in 1840 created Commander of the Polar Star. He was from his·youth very intimate with the poet Tegnér, and numbered among his friends Frederika Bremer and other celebrated Swedish writers. He also possessed

ā, ē, ī, ō, ū, ȳ, *long;* å, ė, ȯ, *same, less prolonged;* ă, ĕ, ĭ, ŏ, ŭ, ў, *short;* ạ, ẹ, ị, ọ, *obscure;* fär, fåll, fåt; mėt; nȯt; gōōd; mōōn;

superior musical talent, and composed several pieces for Jenny Lind. Died April 13, 1847.

See Howitt, "Literature and Romance of Northern Europe," 1852; X. Marmier, "Histoire de la Littérature Scandinave;" Geijer, "Autobiographic Souvenirs," ("Minnen,") 1834; Stenberg, "Minnestal öfver E. G. Geijer," 1848; A. Cronholm, "Minnestal öfver E. G. Geijer," 1847; Carl Ploug, "E. G. Geijer's Minnesteckning," 1848; "Biographiskt-Lexicon öfver namnkunnige Svenska Män;" "Foreign Quarterly Review" for July, 1833, and April, 1844.

Geiler. See Geyler, (John.)

Geinitz, gī′nits, (Johann Bruno,) a German geologist, born at Altenburg in 1814, became professor of mineralogy and geology at Dresden in 1850. He was author of many works, among which is a "Geological Description of Saxony," (1843.)

Geinoz, zhä′no′, (François,) a Swiss scholar and critic, born at Bulle in 1696. He became a resident of Paris in 1730, and a member of the Academy of Inscriptions in 1735. He was afterwards chief editor of the "Journal des Savants," and was distinguished as a Hellenist. Among his works are "Observations on the Text and Version of the First Book of Herodotus." Died in Paris in 1752.

Geladas. See Ageladas.

Gélase. See Gelasius.

Gelasius, je-lā′she-us, [Gr. Γελάσιος; Fr. Gélase, zhä′läz′,] became Bishop of Cæsarea about the year 367. He was a member of the General Council of Constantinople. He wrote several works, among which is an "Ecclesiastical History." Died about 395.

Gelasius of Cyzicus [Fr. Gélase de Cyzique, zhä′läz′ deh se′zèk′] lived during the time of the emperors Basiliscus and Zeno, about 475 A.D. He wrote a "History of the Council of Nice," and some other works.

See Dupin, "Histoire des Auteurs ecclésiastiques."

Gelasius I., Saint, a native of Africa, was elected pope in 492. He died in 496, leaving several works, which are extant. The canonical books of Scripture were separated from the apocryphal in his pontificate.

Gelasius II., (originally Giovanni di Gaeta,) born at Gaeta about 1050, was elected pope in January, 1118. He was maltreated by some partisans of the emperor Henry V., who was his enemy, and who elected an antipope, Gregory VIII. Gelasius fled from Rome, and died at Cluny in 1119.

See Platina, "Vitæ Pontificum."

Geldenhauer, gĕl′den-hŏw′er or Hĕl′den-hŏw′er, or **Geldenhaur,** (Gerard,) a Dutch writer and Latin poet, born at Nymwegen about 1480, was sometimes called Gerard of Nymwegen. He was in early life a friend of Erasmus and reader to Charles V. His talent for Latin poetry procured for him the crown of poet-laureate in 1517. He was converted to the Protestant faith about 1526. Among his works are "Satires," (1515,) and a "History of Lower Germany," ("Germaniæ Inferioris Historia," 1532.) Died at Wittenberg in 1542.

See Bayle, "Historical and Critical Dictionary."

Gelder, van, vän gĕl′der or Hĕl′der, (Arnold,) a Dutch painter, born at Dort in 1645, was a pupil of Rembrandt. He distinguished himself in several branches of painting, designed correctly, and was a good colorist. Among his best works are "Christ before Pilate," a portrait of Peter the Great, and "The Toilet of the Jewish Bride." Died at Dort in 1727.

See Siret, "Dictionnaire des Peintres."

Gelée, (Claude.) See Claude Lorrain.

Gelée, zheh-lā′, (François Antoine,) a French engraver, born in Paris in 1796, gained the grand prize in 1824, and a first medal at the *Salon* in 1842.

Ge-le′nI-us, [Ger. pron. gä-lā′ne-ùs,] or **Ghelen,** gä′len, (Sigismund,) a philologist and translator, born at Prague in 1477. He was a friend of Erasmus, who procured for him the place of corrector of the press under Froben at Bâle. He translated into Latin the works of Josephus, Appian, Philo, and Justin Martyr, and published a dictionary of the Greek, Latin, German, and Slavonian languages, ("Lexicon Symphonum quatuor Linguarum," 1537.) Died in 1554.

Gelimer, gĕl′e-mer or jĕl′e-mer, written also **Gil′imer,** [Gr. Γελίμερ,] the last king of the Vandals in Africa, succeeded Hilderic in 530 A.D. He was defeated and taken

prisoner by Belisarius in 534, and then ceased to reign. The date of his death is unknown.

See Gibbon, "Decline and Fall of the Roman Empire."

Gelinek, gà-lee′něk, (Joseph,) a Bohemian composer, born at Selez in 1757, was a friend or associate of Mozart. He acquired a wide but temporary reputation. Died at Vienna in 1825.

Gell, (Jakob.) See Geel.

Gell, (Sir William,) an English scholar and antiquary, born in 1777, was a son of Philip Gell, of Hopton, Derbyshire. Being appointed one of the chamberlains to the Princess of Wales, he accompanied her to Italy in 1814. He published, among other works, the "Itinerary of Greece," (1810,) "Topography of Troy and its Vicinity," "Pompeiana," being a description of Pompeii, (1817,) and the excellent "Topography of Rome," (3 vols., 1834.) He resided some years at Rome and Naples. Died at Naples in 1836.

Gellert, gĕl′lert, (Christian Furchtegott,) a German poet and miscellaneous writer, born at Hainichen, in Saxony, on the 4th of July, 1715. Having been educated in the University of Leipsic, he was appointed professor of philosophy there in 1751. His "Tales" and "Fables" obtained a popularity in Germany not surpassed perhaps by any other works of the kind, and, by their pure morality, exercised the most salutary influence on society. His "Sacred Songs" are also highly esteemed, and his romance entitled "The Swedish Countess" is a superior production. As a man, Gellert was eminently virtuous and amiable. He was loved and reverenced by all classes, and received signal marks of favour from Frederick II. and the princes royal. "Such," says Guizot, "are the literary titles of a man who will always possess the merit of having powerfully contributed to form the language and improve the minds of his countrymen." ("Biographie Universelle.") Died in December, 1769.

See Lessing's Critique on Gellert; Johann August Ernesti, "Elogium C. F. Gellerti," 1770; Johann Andreas Cramer, "C. F. Gellert's Leben und Briefe," 2 vols., 1774, (translated into English by Mrs. Douglas, 1805;) Heinrich Döring, "Leben C. F. Gellerts," 2 vols., 1833; Ersch and Gruber, "Allgemeine Encyklopaedie;" Bouterwek, "Geschichte der poetischen National-Literatur der Deutschen;" Longfellow, "Poets and Poetry of Europe;" G. E. Leo, "Das fromme Leben C. F. Gellerts," 1845.

Gelli, jel′lee, (Giovanni Battista,) a celebrated Italian author and moralist, born at Florence in 1498, was a tailor by trade. He was one of the founders of the Florentine Academy, of which he was chosen president in 1548. He published in 1546 a collection of moral dialogues, entitled "I Capricci del Bottajo," ("The Whims of the Cooper,") and in 1549 a fable, or moral fiction, called "La Circe," which Ginguené commends as original and piquant. Among his works are "The Basket," ("La Sporta," a comedy, 1543,) and lectures on the "Divina Commedia" of Dante, (1551.) His writings are recognized as authorities in language by the Academy della Crusca. Died in 1563.

See Negri, "Scrittori Fiorentini;" Nicéron, "Mémoires;" Michele Capri, "Orazione nella Morte di G. B. Gelli," 1563; Ginguené, "Histoire littéraire d'Italie."

Gel′lI-brand, (Henry,) an English mathematician, born in London in 1597. He became professor of astronomy at Gresham College, London, in 1627, and wrote an "Epitome of Navigation," and several mathematical works. He completed Briggs's "Trigonometria Britannica," (1633,) at the request of the dying author. Died in 1636.

See Wood, "Athenæ Oxonienses."

Gel′lI-us, (Au′lus,) [Fr. Aulu-Gelle, ō′lü′ zhĕl,] a Roman writer and grammarian, born at Rome in the early part of the second century. He became a resident of Athens, but returned to Rome and obtained the office of judge. He wrote a work called "Attic Nights," ("Noctes Atticæ,") which consists of a curious collection of anecdotes, arguments, and observations on a variety of subjects. It contains fragments of several lost works, and is highly prized. He informs the reader that he wrote the "Noctes Atticæ" to amuse his children. It was translated into English by Beloe, (1795.) He died in the reign of Marcus Aurelius.

See Bähr, "Geschichte der Römischen Literatur."

Gellius, (CNEIUS,) a Roman historian, who lived about 150 B.C. He wrote a "History of Rome from the Earliest Times," which is not extant.

Ge'lon [Gr. Γέλων] **I.** succeeded Hippocrates as King of Syracuse in 485 B.C. He had distinguished himself in fighting under Hippocrates, and was appointed by him general of the cavalry. About 480 B.C. the Carthaginians, under Hamilcar, made an attempt to recover their possessions held by Gelon, but were defeated at Himera with immense loss, estimated at 150,000 men. After this the Carthaginians sued for peace, which was granted on condition of their abolishing human sacrifices and on the payment of two thousand talents. He died in 478 B.C., deeply regretted by all his subjects.

See NIEBUHR, "Roman History ;" GROTE, "History of Greece."

Gelon II., a son of Hieron II., King of Syracuse, was born about 266 B.C. He was a patron of Archimedes. It is said that he was about to abandon the alliance of the Romans, defeated at Cannæ, when he died in 216 B.C., leaving a son Hieronymus. It appears that Gelon was associated as king with his father, who survived him.

Gemberlein. See GRAF.

Gémeau, zhȧ'mō', (AUGUSTE PIERRE **Walbourg**— vȧl'booR',) a French general, born in Paris in 1790, became a general of division in 1845, and commander-in-chief of the army of occupation at Rome in 1850.

Gemelli, jȧ-mel'lee, (LODOVICO,) an Italian educational writer, born in Calabria in 1757 ; died in 1835.

Gemelli-Carreri. See CARRERI.

Gemignano. See GIMIGNANO.

Gemignano, di San, de sȧn jȧ-mên-yȧ'no, (VINCENZIO,) an Italian painter, born in Tuscany in 1490, was a pupil of Raphael. He was employed in the Vatican, at Rome. Died in 1530.

Geminiani, jȧ-me-ne-ȧ'nee, (FRANCESCO,) an eminent composer and violinist, born at Lucca about 1680, or, as some say, about 1666. He studied under A. Scarlatti, Lunati, and Corelli. In 1714 he removed to London, where he performed with great success. He composed beautiful concertos and sonatas, which display much skill in harmony, and published a "Guide to Harmony," ("Guida armonica," 1742,) which was received with favour. His expensive habits kept him always on the verge of poverty. He lost a valuable manuscript treatise on music, through the treachery of a servant, about 1761. Died in Dublin in 1762.

See BURNEY, "History of Music ;" FÉTIS, "Biographie Universelle des Musiciens."

Ge-mi'nus, [Γεμῖνος,] a Greek astronomer, who lived in the first century B.C. He quotes Hipparchus in his works, some of which are lost. It is supposed he was a native of Rhodes. He wrote an elementary work on astronomy, "Εἰσαγωγὴ εἰς τὰ Φαινόμενα," which is extant. "This work," says Delambre, "is rather superficial, but simple and luminous, and the best of those which have come down to us from the Greeks."

See DELAMBRE, "Histoire de l'Astronomie ancienne."

Ge-mis'tus, (GEORGE,) [Gr. Γεώργιος ὁ Γεμιστός ; Fr. GÉMISTE, zhȧ'mèst',] surnamed PLETHO, a Platonic philosopher, famous for his learning, was born at Constantinople. He was a deputy from the Greek Church to the Council of Florence in 1438. He was a zealous partisan of the philosophy of Plato, and an opponent of Aristotle. The prevalence of Platonism in Italy in the fifteenth century is ascribed to his efforts. He wrote many works on philosophy, history, etc., among which are a "History of Greece after the Battle of Mantinea," and "On the Difference between the Philosophy of Plato and that of Aristotle." He is said to have attained the age of one hundred years.

See FABRICIUS, "Bibliotheca Græca ;" Appendix to CAVE, "Historia Literaria ;" WILHELM GASS, "Gennadius und Pletho," Breslau, 1844 ; C. F. BOERNER, "De doctis Hominibus Græcis," Leipsic, 1754 ; "Nouvelle Biographie Générale."

Gem'ma, [Dutch pron. hěm'mȧ,] (CORNELIS,) a son of Reinier, noticed below, was born at Louvain in 1535. He became professor of medicine there about 1570. He wrote a learned work, "De Arte Cyclognomica," (1569,) and a Latin poem entitled "Menti rerum architectrici," etc. Died in 1577.

See CASTELLAN, "Vitæ illustrium Medicorum."

Gemma, [or **Gemma Frisius,** *i.e.* "Gemma the Frisian,"] (REINIER,) a Dutch physician and eminent astronomer, born at Dokkum in 1508. He was appointed professor of medicine at Louvain in 1541, and modestly declined the offer of Charles V., who invited him to his court. He published, besides other works, "The Principles of Astronomy and Cosmography," (1547.) Died at Louvain in 1555.

See DE THOU, "Historia sui Temporis ;" FOPPENS, "Bibliotheca Belgica ;" VOSSIUS, "De Scientiis Mathematicis."

Gemmingen-Hornberg, von, fon gĕm'ming-ẹn-horn'bĕRG, (OTTO HEINRICH,) BARON, born at Heilbronn in 1753, wrote several popular dramas, one of which was entitled "Der Deutsche Hausvater," on the model of Diderot's "Père de Famille." Died in 1836.

Gemusæus, gȧ-moo-zā'ŭs, or **Geschmauss,** gȧ'-shmŏwss', (HIERONYMUS,) a German philologist, born at Mülhausen, in Alsace, in 1505. He published a good edition of Paulus Ægineta, (1538,) and wrote, in Latin, a Life of Galen. Died in 1543.

Gence, zhŏNss, (JEAN BAPTISTE MODESTE,) a French writer, born at Amiens in 1755. He obtained the office of archivist at the Dépôt des Chartes before the Revolution. He published a Latin edition of the "Imitation of Christ," (1826,) and wrote several treatises to prove that Gerson was the author of that work. This subject was his hobby during nearly all his life. Died in 1840.

See "Biographie littéraire de J. B. M. Gence," by himself ; VILLENAVE, "Éloge de M. Gence," 1840.

Gendebien, zhŏN'dẹh'be-ȧN', (ALEXANDRE JOSEPH SÉBASTIEN,) a Belgian politician and eloquent advocate, born at Mons in 1789. He was a member of the provisional government in 1830, and opposed the election of Leopold in 1831. As a member of the Chamber of Deputies, he supported liberal principles until he retired from public service in 1839.

Gendebien, (JEAN FRANÇOIS,) a Belgian legislator, father of the preceding, was born in 1753. He promoted the liberation of Belgium from Austria in 1789, and was a member of the French legislative body from 1802 to 1813. In 1830 he was president of the Congress of Belgium. Died in 1838.

Gendre. See LEGENDRE.

Gendrin, zhŏN'dRȧN', (AUGUSTE NICOLAS,) a French physician, born at Châteaudun in 1796. He received the Montyon prize of the Institute for his "Anatomical History of Inflammations," (1826.) Among his other works is a "Philosophical Treatise on Practical Medicine," (3 vols., 1838–41.)

Gendron, zhŏN'dRŏN', (CLAUDE **Deshais**—dȧ'zȧ',) born at Beauce about 1663, was physician to the Duke of Orléans, Regent of France. Died in 1750.

Génébrard, zhȧ'nȧ'bRȧR',(GILBERT,)a learned French prelate, born at Riom in 1537. He became professor of Hebrew at Paris in 1563. He was a partisan of the League against Henry IV. In 1592 he was appointed Archbishop of Aix by the pope. He published an edition of Origen's works, (1574,) a commentary on the Psalms of David, (1577,) and other works. Died in 1597.

See NICÉRON, "Mémoires ;" POSSEVIN, "Apparatus Sacer."

Genelli, gȧ-nel'lee, ? (BONAVENTURA,) a German designer, born at Berlin in 1803, settled at Munich, where he produced, among other works, "Hercules playing on the Lyre," and "Jason and Medea."

Generali, jȧ-nȧ-rȧ'lee, (PIETRO,) an able Italian composer, born near Vercelli in 1783. His proper name was MERCANDETTI. He composed many operas, among which is "I Baccanali di Roma." Died in 1832.

See FÉTIS, "Biographie Universelle des Musiciens."

Genès, zhẹh'nèss', (written also **Genest**,) SAINT, sometimes called GENÈS OF ROME, was originally a comedian. It is said that as he was playing, in the presence of the emperor, a piece in derision of the Christians, he was miraculously converted to the new faith, for which he was beheaded by order of Diocletian.

Ge-ne'sĭ-us, (JOSEPH,) a Byzantine historian, flourished about 950 A.D. He wrote, in Greek, a history of Leo the Armenian, Michael II., Theophilus, and Michael III., (or, as some say, Basil I.)

Genest. See CAMPAN, (MADAME,) and GENÈS.

ā, ē, ī, ō, ū, ȳ, *long;* ȧ, ė, ȯ, same, less prolonged; ă, ĕ, ĭ, ŏ, ŭ, ў, *short;* ạ, ẹ, ị, ọ, *obscure;* fär, fȧll, fȧt; mēt; nŏt; gŏŏd; mŏŏn;

Genest, zhẹh-nà́, or **Genêt,** (Abbé CHARLES CLAUDE,) a French poet and dramatist, born in Paris in 1639. He gained in 1673 the prize of poetry offered by the French Academy, into which he was admitted in 1698. He expounded the Cartesian philosophy in a poem called "Principles of Philosophy," ("Principes de Philosophie," 1716,) which, says Voltaire, "demonstrated his patience rather than his genius." He wrote a mediocre drama entitled "Pénélope." Died in 1719.

See VOLTAIRE, "Catalogue des Écrivains du Siècle de Louis XIV;" "Nouvelle Biographie Générale."

Genest or **Genêt,** (EDMOND CHARLES,) a French diplomatist, born at Versailles about 1765, was a brother of Madame Campan. He was sent as ambassador to the United States in December, 1792, and on his arrival was received with enthusiasm by the people. He used his influence to involve the United States in war against the British, and denounced Washington for his neutrality. At the request of Washington, he was superseded; but he remained in the United States. Died at Schodac, New York, in 1834.

Genêt, (EDMOND CHARLES.) See GENEST.

Genet, zhẹh-nà́, (FRANÇOIS,) a French theologian and casuist, born at Avignon in 1640, became Bishop of Vaison in 1685. He wrote "Moral Theology; or, A Solution of Cases of Conscience," (3d edition, 7 vols., 1682,) which was approved by many bishops. Died in 1707.

Geneva, (ROBERT DE.) See ROBERT OF GENEVA.

Geneviève, jẹn'ẹh-veev', [Fr. pron. zhẹn-ve'àv',] Patron Saint of Paris, was born at Nanterre, in France, in 423 A.D., and took the veil when she was fifteen. It is said that when Attila, King of the Huns, menaced Paris, Geneviève assured the inhabitants of their safety, upon which they scoffed at her as a pretended prophetess; but, as the prediction was verified, they ever afterwards held her in great esteem. When Paris was besieged, she afforded the city great relief by the abundance of provisions which she procured. It has also been stated that she performed many miracles, and was the means of converting King Clovis. Died in 512.

See BAILLET, "Vies des Saints," etc.; MÉZERAY, "Histoire de France;" MRS. JAMESON, "Sacred and Legendary Art;" LE NAIN DE TILLEMONT, "Vie de S. Geneviève, Patronne de Paris," 1823; J. BARTHÉLEMY, "Vie de S. Geneviève," 1852.

Geneviève OF BRABANT, wife of the palatine Siegfried, is supposed to have lived in the eighth century. Being falsely accused of adultery, she was condemned to death; but the penalty was commuted to exposure in a forest. After five years, her husband hunting, and her innocence acknowledged.

See "Vie admirable de Geneviève de Brabant," Paris, 1842; GÖRRES, "Deutsche Volks-Bücher."

Genga, jẹn'gà, (BARTOLOMMEO,) an Italian architect, born at Cesena in 1518, was a son of Girolamo, noticed below. He was appointed intendant of public buildings by the Duke of Urbino. Among his works was the church of San Pietro de Mondovì. Shortly before his death he went to Malta to put that island in a state of defence. He traced the plan of Valetta, and designed several churches there, but died before they were finished, in 1558.

See VASARI, "Lives of the Painters," etc.; QUATREMÈRE DE QUINCY, "Dictionnaire d'Architecture."

Genga, (BERNARDINO,) an Italian anatomist, born in the duchy of Urbino about 1650. He wrote "Surgical Anatomy," (1672,) and other works. Died in 1734.

Genga, (GIROLAMO,) an eminent painter and architect, born at Urbino about 1476, was a pupil of Perugino and a friend of Raphael. He worked at Sienna, Rome, and Urbino. He excelled in perspective, and in the distribution of the effects of light. Among his masterpieces is an oil-painting of the "Resurrection of Christ" at Sienna. He was the architect of a ducal palace near Pésaro, and restored the archiepiscopal palace at Mantua. He wrote several treatises on the fine arts. Died in 1551. Pope Leo XII. is said to have been his descendant.

See VASARI, "Lives of the Painters, Sculptors," etc.; QUATRE-MÈRE DE QUINCY, "Dictionnaire d'Architecture;" LANZI, "History of Painting in Italy."

Genga, della, (ANNIBAL.) See LEO XII.

Genghis Khan. See JENGIS KHAN.

Génin, zhà́'nà̀N', (FRANÇOIS,) a French *littérateur* and philologist, born at Amiens in 1803. He became one of the editors of "The National," a daily paper of Paris, about 1837, and wrote for it spirited articles against the Jesuits. In 1845 the French Academy awarded a prize to his "Lexicon of the Language of Molière." He made successful researches in the origin of the French language and literature. Among his works are "The Variations of the French Language since the Twelfth Century," (1845,) and "Letters on French Philology," (1846.) Died in 1856.

See "Nouvelle Biographie Générale."

Génissieux, zhà́'ne'se-ụh', (J. J. V.,) a French advocate and revolutionist, born in Dauphiné about 1740. As a member of the Convention in 1792, he voted for the death of the king. He was minister of justice for the first three months of 1796. Died in 1804.

Genlis, zhòN'lèss', (STÉPHANIE FÉLICITÉ Ducrest de Saint-Aubin—dü'krà̀' dẹh sà̀Nt'ō'bà̀N',) COUNTESS OF, a celebrated French writer, born near Autun, in Burgundy, in 1746. Her talents, beauty, and skill in music introduced her at an early age into Parisian society. In her sixteenth year she was married to the Count de Genlis, who, having accidentally seen one of her letters, was so charmed with its style that he sought her acquaintance. Being appointed soon after governess to the children of the Duke of Orléans, one of whom, Louis Philippe, was afterwards king, she wrote a series of works for their instruction, the principal of which are "Les Annales de la Vertu," "Théâtre de l'Éducation," "Les Veillées du Château," and "Adèle et Théodore." She sympathized with the principles of the French Revolution, but was compelled in 1791—probably on account of her intimacy with the Duke of Orléans—to take refuge in England. She afterwards spent some time on the continent, and while in Belgium brought about a marriage between her adopted daughter Pamela and Lord Edward Fitzgerald. When Bonaparte became consul, Madame de Genlis returned to Paris, where she brought out many works in rapid succession. In her treatises entitled "On the Influence of Women on Literature," "Critical Observations towards the Literary History of the Nineteenth Century," and "The Dinners of Baron d'Holbach," she attacked a number of the most prominent French philosophers, as well as Madame de Staël and Madame Cottin. Her productions, which amount in all to more than eighty volumes, are written with great elegance, and display considerable talent; but their morality is not of a high order. When past eighty years of age, she wrote "Memoirs of the Eighteenth Century and the French Revolution," which, though containing much that is interesting, are disfigured by petty scandal and excessive and ludicrous vanity. In the words of a witty French writer, Madame de Genlis has in this work confessed everybody's sins but her own. Died in 1830.

See GRIMM, "Correspondance littéraire;" L. DE SEVELINGES, "Madame de Genlis en Miniature," etc., 1826; BACHAUMONT, "Mémoires secrets;" COUSIN D'AVALLON, "Genlisiana," 1820; SAINTE-BEUVE, "Causeries du Lundi," tome iii.

Gennade. See GENNADIUS.

Ģen-nā'dĭ-us [Gr. Γεννάδιος] was elected Bishop and Patriarch of Constantinople in 458. He wrote some ecclesiastical works. Died in 471 A.D.

Ģen-nā'dĭ-us, an ecclesiastic, whose original name was GEORGE SCHOLARIUS, advocated the union of the Greek and Latin Churches at the Council of Florence in 1438, but afterwards strenuously opposed that measure. He was chosen Patriarch of Constantinople in 1453, after the capture of that city by the Turks, and abdicated about 1458. He left many theological works.

Ģen-nā'dĭ-us [Fr. GENNADE, zhà̀-nǎd'] OF MAR-SEILLES, a priest or presbyter, who lived about 470-500 A.D. He wrote a book "On Illustrious Men," ("De Viris illustribus,") which is regarded as a continuation of Saint Jerome's work of similar title, and a treatise on "Doctrines," ("De Dogmatibus,") both of which are extant. He has been charged with Semi-Pelagianism.

See CAVE, "Historia Literaria;" WILHELM GASS, "Gennadius und Pletho, oder Aristotelismus und Platonismus in der Griechischen Kirche," 1844.

Gennari, jẹn-nä'ree, (BENEDETTO,) an Italian painter, born at Cento, near Bologna, about 1550. Among his chief works are "Saint Peter and Saint Paul," and "The

Repast of the Saviour with the Disciples at Emmaus." "His composition is simple and noble," says E. Breton, "his touch is easy, and his colour true." ("Nouvelle Biographie Générale.") Died in 1610.

See LANZI, "History of Painting in Italy."

Gennari, (BENEDETTO,) THE YOUNGER, a grandson of the preceding, was born at Cento in 1633. He was a pupil and nephew of Guercino, whom he imitated with success. Having visited England, he received the title of first painter to Charles II. and James II. His copies of certain works of Guercino can hardly be distinguished from the originals. Among his master-pieces are "Venus and Adonis," and "Saint Jerome." Died in 1715.

See LANZI, "History of Painting in Italy."

Gennari, (CESARE,) a brother of the preceding, born in 1641, was a pupil of Guercino, and was a skilful painter of landscapes and history. He worked at Bologna, where he died in 1688.

Gennari, (ERCOLE,) a son of Benedetto the elder, was born at Cento in 1597. He married a sister of Guercino, and copied many works of that master. Died at Bologna in 1658.

Gennari, (GIUSEPPE,) an Italian *littérateur*, born at Padua in 1721; died in 1800.

Gennaro, jĕn-nä′ro, (GIUSEPPE AURELIO,) an Italian jurisconsult and ingenious writer, born at Naples in 1701. He published in 1731 "Republic of Jurists," ("Republica Jurisconsultorum,") a history of law under a fictitious form, which was much admired and often reprinted. In 1748 he became a councillor of the king. He wrote "On the Vicious Manner of Defending Causes in Court," (1744.) Died in 1761.

See SPIRITI, "Elogio storico di G. A. Gennaro," 1762; TIPALDO, "Biografia degli Italiani illustri."

Genneté, zhĕn′tă′, (CLAUDE LÉOPOLD,) a French mechanician, born near Nancy in 1706. He wrote a work "On the Construction of Chimneys warranted not to Smoke," (1760.) Died in 1782.

Genod, zheh-no′, (MICHEL PHILIBERT,) a French painter of history and genre, born at Lyons in 1795.

Genoels, ga-nools′, [Dutch pron. Ha-nools′,] (ABRAHAM,) an eminent Flemish landscape-painter, born at Antwerp in 1640. He worked in Paris and Rome, whither he went about 1674. He painted the backgrounds of Lebrun's "Battles of Alexander," and several views in the vicinity of Rome. Died about 1722.

See BRYAN's "Dictionary of Painters."

Genoude, zheh-nood′, (ANTOINE EUGÈNE,) a noted French journalist, born at Montélimart in 1792. He became editor in 1821 of the "Gazette de France," a legitimist journal of Paris, in which post he displayed considerable ability, but, owing to his fondness for polemics, was involved in numerous difficulties. He wrote "Considerations on the Greeks and Turks," "The Life of Jesus Christ and the Apostles, drawn from the Gospels," (1836,) a "History of France," (16 vols., 1844–47,) and other works. Abbé Genoude took holy orders in 1835, after the death of his wife. Died in 1849.

See CRÉTINEAU-JOLY, "Histoire de M. de Genoude et de la Gazette de France," 1843; "Biographie de M. de Genoude," anonymous, Paris, 1844; "Nouvelle Biographie Générale."

Genoux, zheh-noo′, (CLAUDE,) a Savoyard writer and traveller, born in 1811, made the tour of the world twice, and published "Memoirs of a Savoyard Boy," (1844.) He wrote a "History of Savoy," (1852,) and other works.

Genovesi, jà-no-vā′see, (ANTONIO,) an eminent Italian philosopher and political economist, born near Salerno in 1712. He was ordained a priest in 1736, and became professor of metaphysics at Naples in 1741. He published "Elements of Metaphysics," (in Latin, 1st vol., 1743,) and a treatise on logic, "Elements of Logico-Critical Art," ("Elementa Artis logico-criticæ," 1745.) In these two works he combined the principles of Bacon, Descartes, Leibnitz, and Locke. He was the first occupant of the chair of political economy founded in 1754 at Naples. His lectures on that subject were very popular, and gave a great impulse to the study of the same. They were published by him under the title of "Lectures on Commerce or Civil Economy," ("Lezioni di Commercio o di Economia civile," 2 vols.) His "Logic for

Youth" ("Logica per i Giovannetti," 1766) is highly commended. Died at Naples in 1769.

See "Life of Genovesi," prefixed to his Works; G. M. GALANTI, "Elogio storico del Signor Abate A. Genovesi," 1772; TIPALDO, "Biografia degli Italiani illustri."

Ǥen′ser-ic, [Gr. Γιζέρικος; Lat. GENSERI′CUS or GIZERI′CUS,] a famous king of the Vandals, born at Seville about 406 A.D., was a son of King Godigisdus or Modigisdus. In 429 he crossed from Spain into Africa with a large army, was joined by many Donatists, and gained victories over the Roman general Bonifacius. His army committed great atrocities and devastation. He captured Carthage in 439, made himself master of Northern Africa, and, according to some writers, formed an alliance with Attila the Hun. He had a powerful fleet, which was a great scourge to the Romans. In 455 he was invited by the empress Eudocia, or Eudoxia, to fight against the usurper Maximus. He accordingly marched against Rome, which he sacked, and carried Eudoxia with many other Romans as captives to Carthage. His fleet defeated that of the emperor Majorian in 457. In religion Genseric was an Arian. Died in 477 A.D.

See PROCOPIUS, "Bellum Vandalicum;" GIBBON, "Decline and Fall of the Roman Empire;" LE BEAU, "Histoire du Bas-Empire."

Gensonné, zhôN′so′nà′, (ARMAND,) a French lawyer, and one of the leaders of the Girondists, born at Bordeaux in 1758, was one of the most energetic promoters of the Revolution. He was elected to the Legislative Assembly in 1791, and to the Convention in 1792. He opposed the execution of the king, and exerted himself for the welfare of the dauphin and his sister. In the struggle that followed between the Girondists and Jacobins, Gensonné was one of the most prominent and eloquent champions of his party. One day, in the tribunal, as he was picturing the horrible excesses that had been committed, and was in bold terms denouncing the perpetrators, some one cried, "But they have saved the country." "Yes," answered Gensonné; "as the geese saved the Capitol." When the Jacobins had obtained full power, he was arrested, and condemned to death, with twenty-one of his colleagues, in October, 1793.

See LAMARTINE, "History of the Girondists," book xlvii.; THIERS, "History of the French Revolution;" "Nouvelle Biographie Générale."

Gent, jĕnt, ? (THOMAS,) an English printer and antiquary, born in York in 1691. He wrote several works, among which is "An Ancient and Modern History of the Famous City of York." Died in 1778.

See the "Life of Thomas Gent," by himself.

Gentil. See LEGENTIL.

Gentil, zhôN′tĕl′ or zhôN′te′ye, (ANDRÉ ANTOINE PIERRE,) a French writer on agriculture, was born in Franche-Comté about 1728. He produced an "Essay on Agronomy," ("Essai d'Agronomie," 1777.) Buffon expressed a high opinion of his talents and character. Died in Paris in 1800.

Gentil, (JEAN BAPTISTE JOSEPH,) a French officer and historical writer, born at Bagnols in 1726. He went to India in 1752, fought several campaigns against the British, and entered the service of Sujah Dowlah. He made a rich collection of medals, manuscripts, etc., which he presented to the Royal Library and Museum of Paris. He returned to France in 1778, and died in 1799, leaving in manuscript a "History of the Mogul Empire," and other works. In 1822 M. Didot published his "Mémoires d'Indostan."

See "Précis sur J. B. J. Gentil," etc., Paris, 1814; MILL, "History of British India."

Gentile, jĕn-tee′là, (LUIGI PRIMO,) a Flemish portrait-painter, born at Brussels about 1606. He worked many years at Rome, and painted some historical pictures. He is called an excellent colorist. Died about 1670.

Gentile da Fabriano. See FABRIANO.

Gentile Gentili, jĕn-tee′là jĕn-tee′lee, [Lat. GENTI′LIS DE GENTIL′IBUS,] surnamed FULGINAS, a celebrated Italian physician, was born at Foligno. He was the author of several medical works. Died in 1348.

See G. GIROLAMI, "Discorso storico-critico sopra Gentile da Foligno," 1844.

Gentileschi. See LOMI, (ORAZIO.)

Gentilis. See GENTILE.

Ģen-tī′lis, (or jĕn-tee′lèss,) (ALBERICO,) an Italian jurist of high reputation, born in the March of Ancona in 1551. Having become a Protestant, he emigrated to England, found a patron in the Earl of Leicester, and obtained in 1587 the chair of civil law at Oxford. Among his numerous works the most important is "Three Books on the Law of War," ("De Jure Belli Libri tres," 1589,) which is said to contain sound principles on the law of nations. He died at Oxford in 1611.

See WOOD, "Athenæ Oxonienses;" TAISAND, "Vies des Jurisconsultes."

Gentilis, (GIOVANNI VALENTINO,) a Socinian theologian, born at Cosenza, in Italy, about 1520. He fled, to avoid persecution, to Geneva, and thence to Poland. Having been banished from Poland, he was tried at Berne for heresy, and beheaded, in 1566.

See ARETIUS, "Valentini Gentilis Historia."

Ģen-tī′lis, (ROBERT,) an English littérateur, born in London in 1590, was a son of Alberico Gentilis, noticed above. He translated "The History of the Inquisition" from the Italian of Fra Paolo, and made other translations from the Italian and Spanish. Died about 1654.

See WOOD, "Athenæ Oxonienses."

Gentilis, (SCIPIO,) a Protestant and jurist, born in the March of Ancona in 1563, was a brother of Alberico, noticed above. He became eminent as professor of law at Altorf, and wrote several legal works. Died in 1616.

See G. KÖNIG, "Leichpredigt auf S. Gentilis," 1617; G. MONTE-CHIARI, "Elogio storico di S. Gentili," 1816.

Gentillet, zhŏN′te′yȧ′, (INNOCENT,) a French jurist and Protestant, born at Vienne. He wrote, in Latin, "Anti-Machiavel," (1576,) an "Apology for the French Christians of the Reformed Religion," (1578,) and other works. Died at Geneva about 1595.

Gentilotti, jĕn-te-lot′tee, (GIOVANNI BENEDETTO,) a learned ecclesiastic, born in the Tyrol in 1672, was keeper of the Imperial Library of Vienna from 1707 to 1723. He became Bishop of Trent in 1725, and died the same year.

Gentius, gĕn′te-ùs, (GEORG,) a German Orientalist, born at Dahme in 1618. He published a Latin version of Saadi's "Gulistan," (1651.) Died in 1687.

See A. BEVER, "Historia Vitæ, etc. Georgii Gentii," 1733.

Ģen′tleman, (FRANCIS,) a dramatic writer and actor, born in Dublin in 1728. He wrote, besides dramas, "Royal Fables," in verse, (1766.) His best work is the "Dramatic Censor," (2 vols., 1770,) in which he criticised the dramas and actors of his time. Died in 1784.

See "Biographia Dramatica."

Gentz, von, fon gĕnts, (FRIEDRICH,) a distinguished German publicist, born at Breslau in 1764, became in 1802 imperial councillor in the state chancery at Vienna. He was an ardent opponent of the French Revolution. As head secretary, he was present at the Congress of Vienna, and at the conference of ministers at Paris in 1815. He was the principal contributor to the "Historical Journal," (1799,) and wrote a treatise "On the Political Condition of Europe before and after the French Revolution." He also translated Burke's "Reflections on the French Revolution." Died in 1832.

See VARNHAGEN, "Biographische Skizze über Gentz;" SCHLESIER, "Schriften von F. von Gentz," 1838; "Nouvelle Biographie Générale;" "Edinburgh Review" for January, 1807, and January, 1863.

Geoffrey, jĕf′re, (GAIMAR,) an English poet of the twelfth century, wrote a "History of England" in Anglo-Norman verse.

Geoffrey OF MON′MOUTH, surnamed ARTU′RUS, or ARTHUR, an English historian, was Bishop of Saint Asaph. His principal work is a "History of the Britons," which is generally believed to contain more romance and fable than true history. He also translated Merlin's "Prophecies" into Latin prose. Died in 1154.

Geoffrin, zho′frăN′, (MARIE THÉRÈSE Rodet—ro′dȧ′,) MADAME, a French lady, distinguished as a patroness of learning and the fine arts, born in Paris in 1699. She was on intimate terms with many celebrated characters, among whom were Montesquieu and Count Stanislas Poniatowski. The latter, on ascending the throne of Poland, invited her to visit Warsaw, where she was received with great honours. Died in Paris in 1777.

See MARMONTEL, "Mémoires;" GRIMM and DIDEROT, "Correspondance;" A. MORELLET, "Portrait de Madame Geoffrin," 1777.

Geoffroi, zho′fRwâ′, surnamed LE BEL, Duke of Anjou, called afterwards PLANTAGENET, (because he wore the plant named genêt, or genista,—a species of broom,—on his helmet,) was born in 1113. He married Matilda, a daughter of Henry I. of England, in 1129. He waged war against Stephen of Blois for the possession of Normandy. His son became Henry II. of England. Died in 1150.

See "Nouvelle Biographie Générale."

Geoffroi II., Duke of Bretagne, surnamed THE BEAUTIFUL, the third son of Henry II. of England, was born in 1158. He married Constance, daughter of Conan IV., and thus became the Duke of Brittany. He was the father of the unfortunate Prince Arthur who was assassinated by order of his uncle, John, King of England. In early youth he distinguished himself in the wars of Philippe Auguste against the dukes of Burgundy and others. Died in 1186.

See "Nouvelle Biographie Générale."

Geoffroi, [Lat. GEOFFRI′DUS,] Abbé de Vendôme, a powerful French cardinal, born at Angers; died in 1132.

Geoffroi de Beaulieu. See GALFRID DE BEAULIEU.

Geoffroy, zho′fRwâ′, (CLAUDE JOSEPH,) a chemist and pharmaceutist, a brother of Étienne François, noticed below, was born in Paris in 1685. He wrote, besides other works, "Observations on the Essential Oils," (1707.) Died in 1752.

See F. HOEFER, "Histoire de la Chimie;" QUÉRARD, "La France Littéraire."

Geoffroy, (ÉTIENNE FRANÇOIS,) a distinguished French physician, born in Paris in 1672. In 1709 he became professor of medicine and pharmacy in the College of France. He was a Fellow of the Royal Society of London, and a member of the Academy of Sciences in Paris. Among his works is a "Treatise on Materia Medica," ("Tractatus de Materia Medica," 1741,) which was translated into English, French, German, and Italian, and had a European reputation. Died in 1731.

See FONTENELLE, "Éloge de Geoffroy," prefixed to his "Traité de Matière médicale;" F. HOEFER, "Histoire de la Chimie;" "Nouvelle Biographie Générale."

Geoffroy, (ÉTIENNE LOUIS,) a French physician and entomologist, a son of the preceding, was born in Paris in 1725. Among his works are a valuable "Abridged History of the Insects which are found near Paris," (1762,) "Dissertations upon the Organ of Hearing in Man, in Reptiles, and in Fishes," (1778,) and "Hygiene sive Ars Sanitatem conservandi ; Poema," (1771.) This poem is commended by several French critics for its elegance and other merits. He died in 1810.

See F. HOEFER, "Histoire de la Chimie."

Geoffroy, (JULIEN LOUIS,) ABBÉ, a celebrated French critic and editor, born at Rennes in 1743. He became, in 1776, professor of rhetoric in the College of Navarre, Paris, and editor of the "Année littéraire," founded by Fréron. He wrote able critical articles for this periodical during fifteen years. In 1790–92 he edited a royalist journal. In 1800 he became an assistant editor of the "Journal des Débats," for which he wrote dramatical criticisms with great success. He indulged in bitter sarcasm and virulence against Voltaire and other authors. Died in 1814. His critiques in the "Journal des Débats" were published in 5 vols., (1819–20.)

See PASSERON, "Observations sur le Caractère et le Talent de feu Geoffroy," 1826; SAINTE-BEUVE, "Causeries du Lundi;" "Nouvelle Biographie Générale."

Geoffroy (or Geoffroi) d'Auxerre, zho′fRwâ′ dŏ′saiR′, a French abbot, was a disciple of Abelard, and afterwards of Saint Bernard. He wrote numerous ecclesiastical works, one of which was an "Epistle on Transubstantiation." Died about 1180.

Geoffroy (or Geoffroi) de Vinsauf—vȧN′sŏf′, [Lat. GALFRI′DUS DE VINOSAL′VO,] a Latin poet of the twelfth century, was a native of England. He wrote a treatise on the Art of Poetry, entitled "Nova Poetria."

Geoffroy-Château, zho′fRwâ′ shâ′tō′, (MARC ANTOINE,) a brother of Geoffroy-Saint-Hilaire, was born at Étampes in 1774. He served with distinction in Egypt as an officer, and in the campaign against Austria in 1805. Died in 1806.

Geoffroy-Martel, zho′fRwä′ mäR′tĕl′, Count of Anjou and Poitou, was born in 1006. For the great energy and bravery that he displayed in the feudal wars, and for his victories over the Saracens, he received the surname of MARTEL, ("hammer," or "mallet.") Died in 1061.

Geoffroy-Saint-Hilaire, zho′fRwä′ săN te′laiR′, (ÉTIENNE,) a distinguished French naturalist, born at Étampes (Seine-et-Oise) on the 15th of April, 1772. He was educated in the College of Navarre, Paris, and became a favourite pupil of Haüy. In 1793 he was appointed professor of zoology in the Museum of Natural History. He was one of the savants who accompanied Bonaparte's expedition to Egypt in 1798, and returned about the end of 1801 with a rich collection of animals, of which he wrote descriptions. He propounded his celebrated theory of the unity of organic composition (which may be said to have laid the foundation of philosophical anatomy) in several memoirs, which opened to him the doors of the Institute in 1807. In 1809 he was appointed professor of zoology (or anatomy) at the Faculty of Sciences. He published an important work, entitled "Anatomical Philosophy," ("Philosophie anatomique," 2 vols., 1818–22,) which excited a great controversy between the author and Cuvier. They differed in regard to the doctrine of final causes and the immutability of species, both of which were maintained by Cuvier. "We have a powerful ally in Geoffroy-Saint-Hilaire," said Goethe, (1830.) "The synthetic method of looking at nature, initiated by him in France, can no more retrograde." Among his numerous works are one "On the Principle of the Unity of Organic Composition," (1828,) a "Natural History of the Fishes of the Nile and Reptiles of Egypt," published in the great work of the Egyptian Commission, (1808–29,) and a "Natural History of Mammiferæ," (with F. Cuvier, 4 vols., 1820–42.) Died June 19, 1844.

See I. GEOFFROY-SAINT-HILAIRE, "Vie, Travaux, etc. d'Étienne Geoffroy-Saint-Hilaire," 1847; FLOURENS, "Mémoire de Geoffroy-Saint-Hilaire," (and English translation of the same, in the Smithsonian Report for 1861;) MERSSEMAN, "Geoffroy-Saint-Hilaire, son Caractère, ses Découvertes," 1844; "Nouvelle Biographie Générale;" "Westminster Review" for January, 1854.

Geoffroy-Saint-Hilaire, (ISIDORE,) a distinguished French zoologist, son of the preceding, was born in Paris, December 16, 1805. He was elected to the Academy of Sciences in 1833, and afterwards became successively inspector-general of the University, member of the council of public instruction, (1845,) and professor of zoology, (1850.) Among his principal works are "Essays on General Zoology," (1840,) "Natural History of Insects and Molluscs," (1841,) and "General Natural History of the Organic Kingdoms," (1852.) Died in November, 1861.

See DE QUATREFAGES, "Mémoire d'Isidore Geoffroy-Saint-Hilaire," (and English version of the same, in the Smithsonian Report for 1862.)

George, [Ger. GEORG, gā′ORG,] Duke of Saxony, surnamed THE BEARDED, was born in 1471. He began to reign in 1500, and opposed the Reformation initiated by Luther. Died in 1530.

George, a learned Eastern physician and Nestorian of the eighth century, was the confidential friend and medical adviser of Al-Mansoor, the Caliph of Bagdâd. He wrote a "Treatise on Medicine," in Syriac.

George (LEWIS) **I,** King of Great Britain, was the son of Ernest Augustus, Elector of Hanover, and Sophia, the youngest daughter of Elizabeth Stuart, Queen of Bohemia, who was a sister of Charles I. of England. He was born at Osnaburg in May, 1660, and married his cousin, Sophia Dorothea, the daughter of the Duke of Zell, in 1682. In 1698 he succeeded his father (originally Duke of Brunswick and Lüneburg) as Elector of Hanover. In 1701 the English Parliament passed the Act of Settlement, excluding the son of James II. and her Catholic claimants, and entailing the crown on the Electress Sophia of Hanover, as the nearest Protestant heir, in case neither the reigning king nor the princess Anne should leave issue. Sophia died in May, 1714, and on the death of Queen Anne, August 1 of the same year, the son of Sophia was proclaimed as George I. He selected his cabinet almost exclusively from the Whig party, giving his chief confidence to Lord Townshend, who was secretary of state. The Tories were re-

garded by him with strong suspicion and dislike. In 1715 the partisans of the Pretender, headed by the Earl of Mar, raised a rebellion in Scotland, and were defeated at Sheriffmuir. Another army of Jacobites surrendered at Preston, and the rebellion was suppressed early in 1716. In 1717 Townshend was dismissed from power, and Mr. Stanhope and the Earl of Sunderland became the principal ministers. War was declared against Spain in 1718, and, after a few battles, was ended by a peace in the next year. In 1720 the ministry received an important accession in Robert Walpole, who ingratiated himself with the Prince of Wales and effected a reconciliation between him and the king. (See next article.) About this time the famous South Sea scheme exploded, and thousands of families were reduced to beggary in a moment. Stanhope having died in 1721, Walpole became prime minister, with Townshend as his principal colleague. In 1725 a treaty of defensive alliance was signed between England, France, and Prussia, and the former was involved in a war against Spain; but no important battles were fought by these powers. George I. died at Osnaburg in June, 1727, and was succeeded by his son, George II. George I. was ignorant of the English language, and was deficient in popular qualities. He was steady in his friendships, and is said to have had more virtues than accomplishments.

See E. PUFENDORF, "Vita et Res gestæ Georgii I. Regis Magnæ Britanniæ," 1728; P. H. LIMIERS, "Mémoires du Règne de George I," 5 vols., 1729–31; LINGARD, "History of England."

George (AUGUSTUS) **II.,** King of Great Britain, was the only son of George I. and Sophia Dorothea, and was born at Hanover in 1683. In 1705 he married the princess Caroline of Brandenburg-Anspach. He displayed courage at the battle of Oudenarde, (1708,) where he fought against the French. On his father's accession to the throne, he accompanied him to England, and was created Prince of Wales in September, 1714. The king was jealous of his heir-apparent, who was a rather undutiful son. In 1718 the latter assumed the attitude of open opposition, and kept his own court. They were reconciled in 1720, by the mediation of Walpole.

George II. ascended the throne in June, 1727. By the influence of Queen Caroline, Walpole was retained in office as prime minister, and but little change was made in the cabinet, which was composed of Whigs and supported by a large majority in Parliament. A treaty of peace was concluded with Spain in November, 1729. The ascendency of Walpole was confirmed by a general peace, which lasted ten years, and by the growing prosperity of the country. About 1736, Frederick, Prince of Wales, quarrelled with his father, and became the chief of the opposition, which included William Pitt and other Whigs. In 1739 public opinion or popular clamour compelled Walpole to renew the war against Spain on the question of maritime right. The question of the Austrian succession produced in 1740 a general European war, in which the English ministry became an ally of Maria Theresa of Austria against Prussia, Spain, etc. In January, 1742, Walpole was forced to resign by an adverse majority in the House, (though he still retained the favour of the king,) and was succeeded by Lord Wilmington as first lord of the treasury. Lord Carteret, however, soon became, through royal favour and his own merit, the most influential minister. George II. gained a victory over the French at Dettingen, (1743,) the last battle in which a king of England appeared at the head of his troops.

About the end of 1743, Henry Pelham was appointed first lord of the treasury, or premier. In the summer of 1745 the Pretender Charles Edward Stuart landed in Scotland, and raised a formidable rebellion. His army took Edinburgh, and defeated the royal troops at Prestonpans. He pursued his victorious march towards London as far as Derby, whence he retreated to Scotland, followed by the royal army. In April, 1746, the Duke of Cumberland gained a decisive victory over the insurgents at Culloden, after which they were unable to renew the contest. By the treaty of Aix-la-Chapelle, in 1748, the European war was terminated, or rather suspended. In 1755 the English and French were again embroiled by the question of the American Boundary,

ā, ē, ī, ō, ū, ȳ, *long;* à, ė, ò, same, less prolonged; ă, ĕ, ĭ, ŏ, ŭ, ў, *short;* ą, ę, į, ǫ, *obscure;* fär, fäll, fät; mĕt; nŏt; gōōd; mōōn;

and the former became the ally of Frederick the Great in the Seven Years' war, 1756–62. Mr. Pitt (afterwards Lord Chatham) in June, 1757, became the master-spirit of an administration perhaps the most glorious that had presided over the destinies of the nation. (See PITT, WILLIAM.) A series of brilliant victories over the French, in Canada, India, and at sea, illustrated the last years of George the Second's reign. He died on the 25th of October, 1760, and was succeeded by his grandson, George III. "He had scarcely one kingly quality," says Lord Mahon, "except personal courage and justice. Of acquired knowledge he had little, professing great contempt for literature."

See LORD MAHON, "History of England;" LORD HERVEY, "Memoirs of the Reign of George II.," 1848; HORACE WALPOLE, "Memoirs of the Last Ten Years of the Reign of George II.," 4 vols., 1822; "Edinburgh Review" for June, 1822; "Blackwood's Magazine" for April, 1868; THACKERAY's "Lectures on the Georges."

George (WILLIAM FREDERICK) **III.**, King of Great Britain, born on the 4th of June, 1738, was the eldest son of Frederick Lewis, Prince of Wales, and a grandson of George II. His mother was Augusta, daughter of Frederick, Duke of Saxe-Gotha. His education was directed by Lord Harcourt as governor, and the Bishop of Norwich as preceptor, until 1752. He was brought up in strict seclusion by his mother. In 1751 he was created Prince of Wales. Before his accession his groom of the stole, Lord Bute, acquired an almost unbounded influence over him, and instilled Tory principles into his mind. He ascended the throne on the 25th of October, 1760, being the first sovereign of the house of Hanover who was a native of Great Britain. He had received from nature a strong will and mental capacities which qualified him to become a good man of business. His age, his appearance, and his moral character prepossessed the nation warmly in his favour. Lord Bute, who still retained his ascendency over the king, was appointed secretary of state, and several of his partisans were introduced into the cabinet. Pitt, who was then prime minister, finding himself overruled, resigned in October, 1761, and was succeeded by Bute. For the first time since the accession of the house of Hanover, the Tory party came into power. In 1761 George III. married the princess Charlotte, a daughter of the Duke of Mecklenburg-Strelitz. War was declared against Spain in January, 1762. The treaty of Paris, in February, 1763, restored the peace of Europe and recognized the right of England to Canada and Florida. In April of the same year the nation was amazed by the sudden resignation of Bute, and George Grenville became first lord of the treasury. "We are inclined to think," says Macaulay, "that the worst administration which has governed England since the Revolution was that of Grenville. His public acts may be classed under two heads,—outrages on the liberty of the people, and outrages on the dignity of the crown." He offended the king by insisting that no secret adviser (alluding to Bute) should have access to the royal ear; but he was kept in office, because the king had no choice except between him and the Whigs. In 1765 Grenville proposed and enacted a bill for imposing stamp-duties on the North American colonies,—"the effects of which," says Macaulay, "will long be felt by the whole human race." The ministers became so intolerable to George III. that he sent for Pitt and solicited him to form a ministry; but Pitt was impracticable, and at last the king reluctantly called the Whigs into his council. The Marquis of Rockingham became prime minister in July, 1765, and the Stamp Act was repealed in the next session. But the new ministry was not cordially supported by the king, and was assailed and obstructed by the king's friends at every turn. The court having secured the services of Pitt by lavish promises and caresses, Rockingham was dismissed in 1766, and Pitt, now created Earl of Chatham, was appointed prime minister. But diseases of body and mind soon rendered him unable to attend to business. New taxes imposed on the Americans in 1767 provoked violent opposition. Lord Chatham resigned in October, 1768. Lord North was prime minister from January, 1770, until March, 1782, during which period the revolted colonies resisted with success the British armies, and

were finally separated from the empire. (See WASHINGTON.) In 1778 England was involved in war with France, which had become the ally of the United States.

The resignation of Lord North was followed by the brief ministries of Rockingham, Shelburne, and Portland. Peace was concluded between England on one hand, and the United States, France, and Spain on the other, by the treaty of Paris, in 1783. In December, 1783, William Pitt commenced his long and eventful Tory administration. "With more power than any minister ever possessed," says Lord Brougham,—"with a friendly court, an obsequious Parliament, a confiding people,—he held the supreme place in the public councils for twenty years, and, except the Union with Ireland, (1800,) he has not left a single measure behind him for which the community whose destinies he so long swayed has any reason to respect his memory. (See PITT, WILLIAM.) The most important event of his administration was the war against the French republic and Bonaparte, which began in 1793. Naval victories were gained by Lord Howe in 1794, and by Nelson, at the battle of the Nile, in 1798. In March, 1801, Pitt resigned, and Addington became premier. The war was suspended by the treaty of Amiens, in March, 1802, and renewed in May, 1803. Mr. Pitt was restored to power in 1804, and died in January, 1806, when a Whig ministry was formed by Fox and Lord Grenville. After the death of Fox, in 1807, Mr. Percival and Lord Liverpool were successively the prime ministers. George III. having become insane in 1810, his son George was appointed regent. Among the important events of this reign were the victory of Trafalgar, 1805, the American war, 1812–14, and the battle of Waterloo, 1815. The mental malady of the king continued until his death, in January, 1820, when he was succeeded by his son, George IV. George III. was the father of nine sons and six daughters. His reign of sixty years' duration was the longest and one of the most eventful in the annals of Britain. "Few princes," says Lord Brougham, "have been more exemplary in their domestic habits or in the offices of private friendship. But the instant that his prerogative was concerned, or his bigotry interfered with, or his will thwarted, the most bitter animosity, the most calculating coldness of heart, the most unforgiving resentment, took possession of his whole breast, and swayed it by turns."

See ADOLPHUS, "History of England from the Accession of George III. to 1783;" MACFARLANE, "History of the Reign of George III.," 2 vols., 1770–96; "George the Third, his Court and Family," 1820; BROWN, "Memoirs of George III.;" JOHN AIKIN, "Annals of the Reign of King George III.," 2 vols., 1820; LORD BROUGHAM, "Historical Sketch of the Statesmen of the Time of George III.;" LINGARD, "History of England;" "Georgiana, or Anecdotes of George III.," 1820; "Correspondence of King George III. with Lord North from 1768 to 1783," London, 1867; "Memoirs of the Life and Reign of George III.," by J. HENEAGE JESSE, London, 1867.

George (AUGUSTUS FREDERICK) **IV.**, King of Great Britain, the eldest son of George III. and Queen Charlotte, was born on the 12th of August, 1762. His education was confided in 1771 to Lord Holderness as governor, and Markham, Bishop of Chester, as preceptor, who both resigned in 1776. Their places were supplied by the Duke of Montague and Dr. Hurd. His natural abilities were above mediocrity, but were not diligently or wisely improved. In his youth he became an object of his father's invincible aversion, and by a natural consequence attached himself to the Whig party, who were also treated as enemies by the king. He exhausted prematurely the resources of sensual indulgence, and was deeply involved in debt by gaming and extravagance. About 1786 he married privately Mrs. Fitzherbert, a Roman Catholic lady, who was the object of his most lasting attachment. This marriage was illegal, and, when the subject was broached in Parliament, was publicly disowned by the Prince of Wales. The pressure of pecuniary difficulties rendered a regular marriage necessary, as the king refused to supply his extravagant wants except on condition that he should marry. In 1795 he married his cousin, Caroline Amelia Elizabeth, a daughter of the Duke of Brunswick, who became the mother of the princess Charlotte in 1796, and whom he treated with studied neglect, if not contempt. A final separation

---

took place in 1796, and scandalous reports against her honour were circulated.

The king having become, through insanity, incompetent for the duties of royalty, the Prince of Wales was appointed regent in February, 1811. He retained in office the Tory ministry of Mr. Percival, abandoning his former political friends, who accused him of ingratitude. The foreign policy of the prince regent was the same as that of George III. The war against the French was prosecuted with vigour and success in the Peninsula. In June, 1812, war was declared against the United States, with which a treaty of peace was concluded in December, 1814. Lord Liverpool succeeded Percival as prime minister in 1812. The only child of the prince regent, the princess Charlotte, died in 1817. On the death of his father, George IV. ascended the throne, on the 29th of January, 1820. Great excitement was produced by the process instituted by the ministry in 1820 against Queen Caroline, for alleged infidelity to her husband. The majority for the ministers on this question in the House was so small that they abandoned the case. (See CAROLINE AMELIA ELIZABETH.) The prime minister, Lord Liverpool, having been prostrated by apoplexy, was succeeded by Mr. Canning in April, 1827. On the death of Canning, in August of the same year, Viscount Goderich became premier. In January, 1828, a new ministry was formed, under the Duke of Wellington. A bill for the relief of Roman Catholics from political disabilities was passed, after a long contest, in April, 1829. George IV. died in June, 1830, and was succeeded by his brother, the Duke of Clarence, as William IV. George IV. had no public virtues, and took little interest in the affairs of government.

See WALLACE, "Memoirs of the Life and Reign of George IV.;" COBBETT, "History of George IV.;" MACKINTOSH, "History of England;" LLOYD, "George IV.: Memoirs of his Life," 1830; REV. GEORGE CROLY, "Life and Times of George IV."

George I., King of Georgia, of the dynasty of Pagratides, ascended the throne in 1015. He reigned over a great extent of territory besides that included in Georgia, and was one of the most powerful Christian monarchs of his time. He revolted against Basil II., Emperor of Constantinople, who ravaged Georgia with fire and sword and compelled George to sue for peace. Died in 1027.

See LE BEAU, "Histoire du Bas-Empire."

George II., grandson of the preceding, was crowned King of Georgia in 1072. He carried on an unsuccessful and disastrous war against the Sultan of Persia, to whom he was forced to become a tributary. Died in 1089.

George III. usurped the throne of Georgia in 1156, when the true heir to the crown was his nephew Temna. George waged several long and successful wars against the Persian and Turkish Moslems. Died in 1180.

George IV. ascended the Georgian throne in 1198, and added fresh glory to the arms of the Georgians by his brilliant victories over his Mohammedan neighbours. In 1220 the Moguls invaded and laid waste a great part of Georgia. George attacked them, and was defeated; but one of his generals soon after succeeded in driving the invaders from the country. Died in 1223.

George VI. succeeded his cousin George V. For the ability that he exhibited in quelling the civil disturbances in Georgia, and the successful efforts he made to repair the effects of long and fierce wars, he received the title of "Most Illustrious." Died in 1346.

George VII. ascended the throne of Georgia in 1394. His father, Bagrat V., had been compelled to submit to Tamerlane and embrace the Moslem faith; but George determined to yield neither his freedom nor his religion to the conqueror. Tamerlane invaded Georgia twice for the purpose of subduing the Georgian monarch and spreading the Mohammedan religion; but he did not succeed. After the second invasion, George collected all his forces, recaptured the fortresses that had fallen into the hands of the enemy, and compelled all Mussulmans to leave Georgia. Died in 1407.

See VON HAMMER, "Histoire de l'Empire Ottoman."

George I., VLADIMIROVITCH, written also **Juri** or **Jouri,** Grand Duke of Russia, ascended the throne in 1149. He was the son of Vladimir Monomachos, who

married Gyda, daughter of Harold, the last Saxon king of England. On account of his ambitious and grasping character, George received the surname of DOLGOROOKI, (Long-Handed.) He founded the city of Moscow, and in various ways promoted the civilization of his country. Died in 1157, and was succeeded by his son Andrew.

See ERSCH und GRUBER, "Allgemeine Encyklopaedie."

George II., USEVOLODOVITCH, grandson of George I., became Archduke of Russia in 1212. He was soon after compelled to abdicate by his brother Constantine, who, however, on his death-bed, 1219, named George as his successor. In 1224 Russia was invaded by the troops of Jengis Khan, who defeated an army of one hundred thousand Russians, and ravaged the country as far as the Dnieper, and then suddenly retired. In 1237 the Moguls reappeared, with three hundred thousand men, and took and destroyed Moscow, and the capital Vladimir. George was killed in 1238, while bravely resisting the invaders.

See KARAMZIN, "Histoire de l'Empire de Russie," translated by DIVOFF; ERSCH und GRUBER, "Allgemeine Encyklopaedie."

George, Duke of Clarence, a younger brother of Edward IV. of England, was born in 1449. He married Isabella, a daughter of the Earl of Warwick, "the Kingmaker," and aided the latter to dethrone Edward IV. about 1470. Soon after that date he deserted Warwick and joined the army of Edward; but, having again offended his royal brother, he was accused of treason, and was found dead in the Tower in 1478. (See Shakspeare's "Henry VI., Part III.")

George OF CYPRUS, a learned writer, who became Patriarch of Constantinople in 1283 and abdicated in 1289. He wrote, besides other works, an autobiography, "Vita Georgii Cypri," (Venice, 1763.) Died in 1290.

See FABRICIUS, "Bibliotheca Græca."

George OF DENMARK, PRINCE, a younger son of Frederick III., was born in 1653. He married Anne, daughter of James II. of England, in 1683, and was a privy councillor in the reign of his father-in-law. In November, 1688, in company with the Duke of Ormond, he deserted James II. at Andover, and joined the party of the Prince of Orange. "The impenetrable stupidity of Prince George," says Macaulay, "served his turn on this occasion better than cunning would have done. It was his habit, when any news was told him, to exclaim, in French, 'Est-il possible?' 'Is it possible?' This catchword was now of great use to him. 'Est-il possible?' he cried, when he had been made to understand that Churchill and Grafton were missing." He was created Duke of Cumberland in 1689, and, on the accession of his wife as queen, received nominally the chief command of the army. Died in 1708.

See MACAULAY, "History of England;" BURNET, "History of his Own Time."

George DANIELOVITCH, Grand Duke of Russia, was a rival of his uncle Michael, against whom he waged war. He was assassinated by a son of Michael in 1328.

George OF TREBIZONDE, [Gr. Γεώργιος Τραπεζούντιος,] a celebrated scholar, born in the isle of Crete in 1396. About 1430 he became professor of Greek at Venice, and was afterwards appointed secretary to Pope Eugenius. He wrote, besides many other works, a "Commentary on the Philippics and other Orations of Cicero," and a "Comparison between Plato and Aristotle," (in Latin.) He also translated many Greek books into Latin, among which were Aristotle's "Rhetoric and Problems." Died in 1486.

See FABRICIUS, "Bibliotheca Græca;" PAOLO GIOVIO, "Elogia Virorum illustrium;" NICÉRON, "Mémoires;" CAVE, "Historia Literaria."

George, [Γεώργιος,] SAINT, OF CAPPADOCIA, a celebrated ecclesiastic of the fourth century, rose, through the influence of the Arians, whose doctrines he professed, to be Archbishop of Alexandria in 354. Having, by his rapacity and his persecutions of both orthodox and pagans, incurred the hatred of the people, he was imprisoned, and, while awaiting his trial, taken away by force and murdered by the mob. He was canonized by Pope Gelasius about 494. During the first crusade he was chosen by the English soldiers as their patron, and about the time of Edward III. was generally regarded as the guardian saint of England. He was designated among the Greeks by the name of "Tropæophoros," (the "Trophy-bearer," or the "Victorious,") and was famed for having destroyed a terrible dragon, (supposed to be that mentioned in the book of Revelation.) Some writers have conjectured that there was another person of the same name to whom this achievement should be attributed.

See Mrs. Jameson, "Sacred and Legendary Art;" Gibbon, "Decline and Fall of the Roman Empire," chap. xxi. ; T. Lowick, "History of the Life and Martyrdom of Saint George;" Peter Heylin, "Historie of that famous Saint and Soldier of Jesus Christ, Saint George," 1631 ; John Milner, "Historical and Critical Inquiry into the Existence and Character of Saint George," 1795.

George Acropolita. See ACROPOLITA.
George Chrysococces. See CHRYSOCOCCES.
George Codinus. See CODINUS.
George Czerni. See CZERNI.
George David. See DAVID, (GEORGE.)
George Pachymeres. See PACHYMERES.
George Pis'i-dēs, [Gr. Γεώργιος Πισίδης,] a Greek writer, lived in Constantinople in the seventh century. He was the author of a poem of three thousand verses on the Creation, and several works of a historical and ecclesiastical character.

See CAVE, "Historia Literaria."

George Sand. See SAND.
George Scholarius. See GENNADIUS.
Georgel, zhor'zhêl', (JEAN FRANÇOIS,) a French ecclesiastic, born in Lorraine in 1731. He was secretary of embassy at Vienna in 1772, and soon after became grand vicar of Cardinal Prince Rohan, whose defence he managed in the affair of the diamond necklace. He died in 1813, leaving historical memoirs, which were published in 1817, (6 vols.)

See "Edinburgh Review" for September, 1818.

Georges, gà-or'gès, (KARL ERNST,) a German lexicographer, born at Gotha in 1806. He published, in 1834, a "German-Latin Hand-Lexicon."

Georges-Weymer, zhorzh vǎ'maiʀ', (MARGUERITE,) one of the most celebrated French actresses of recent times, born at Bayeux about 1787, performed in Paris (1802) and other cities of Europe with brilliant success.

Georgi. See GIORGI.

Georgi, gà-or'gee, (CHRISTIAN SIGISMUND,) a German biblical critic, born at Luckau in 1702, became professor of theology at Wittenberg in 1743. He published many dissertations on the sacred text. Died in 1771.

Geppert, gĕp'pert, (KARL EDUARD,) a meritorious German philologist and critic, born at Stettin in 1811. He published, besides other works, "De Versu Glyconeo," ("On the Glyconian Verse," 1833,) a "Chronicle of Berlin," (3 vols., 1837-42,) and "On the Origin of the Homeric Poems," (2 vols., 1840.)

Geraldini, jà-rål-dee'nee, (ALESSANDRO,) an Italian prelate, born in 1455, entered the service of Isabella of Spain, was appointed preceptor of the Infantas, and was afterwards ambassador to several European courts. He exerted his influence to promote the great enterprise of Columbus. He became Bishop of San Domingo in 1520. Died in 1525.

See B. DE LAS CASAS, "Historia general de las Indias."

Geramb, zhęh-rôɴ', (FERDINAND,) BARON, a noted adventurer, of Hungarian extraction, born at Lyons in 1770. After fighting against the French in Austria and in Spain, he fell into the power of Napoleon, by whom he was imprisoned in 1812. On his release, in 1816, he became a monk of La Trappe, and rose to be procureur-général of the order. In 1831 he made a pilgrimage to Palestine, of which he published an account, written in French, (1844, 3 vols.) It has been translated into German, Italian, and Spanish. Died in 1848.

See "Nouvelle Biographie Générale."

Gerando, de, often written **Degerando,** dęh zhęh-rôɴ'do', (JOSEPH MARIE,) a distinguished French metaphysical philosopher, born at Lyons in 1772. He entered the army about 1798, and in 1799 gained the prize of the Institute for an essay on the question, "What is the Influence of Signs on the Formation of Ideas?" He published this essay, with additions, with the title of "Des Signes et de l'Art de Penser," (1803,) and an im-

portant work, called "A Complete History of Systems of Philosophy considered in Relation to the Principles of Human Knowledge," (3 vols., 1803,) which opened to him the Academy of Inscriptions. He was appointed secretary-general of the ministry of the interior in 1804, master of requests in 1808, and member of the council of state in 1811. Under the restoration he retained the last-named office. He gained a high reputation for philanthropy by his labours and writings, one of which is entitled "On Public Beneficence," ("De la Bienfaisance publique," 4 vols., 1839.) He was called to the Chamber of Peers in 1837. Died in Paris in 1842.

See E. F. Jomard, "Discours sur la Vie et les Travaux du Baron Degerando," 1843 ; "Nouvelle Biographie Générale;" Octavie Morel, "Essai sur la Vie de J. M. Baron Degerando," 1846 ; "North American Review," April, 1861.

Gerard. See GIRARD.

Ge-rard', (ALEXANDER,) a Scottish author and divine, born in the county of Aberdeen in 1728. In 1760 he became professor of theology in Marischal College, and in 1771 was appointed to fill the same chair in the University of King's College. Among his various works we may cite an "Essay on Taste," (1759,) for which a gold medal was awarded him by the Philosophical Society of Edinburgh, and "Dissertations on the Genius and Evidences of Christianity," (1766.) Died at Aberdeen in 1795.

See CHAMBERS, "Biographical Dictionary of Eminent Scotsmen."

Gerard, (Captain ALEXANDER,) son of Gilbert Gerard, noticed below, was born at Aberdeen about 1795. He spent many years in scientific explorations among the Himalayas. He died in 1840, leaving an "Account of Koonawur in the Himalaya," which was published in 1841.

Gérard, zhà'ʀăʀ', (BALTHASAR,) a Catholic fanatic, and a native of Franche-Comté, in France, is notorious as the assassin of William of Nassau, Prince of Orange. He was executed in July, 1584, a short time after he committed the deed; and Philip II. of Spain ennobled his family.

Gérard, (FRANÇOIS,) an eminent painter of the French school, was born at Rome in 1770. He studied in Paris under David, and about 1795 produced his picture of "Belisarius." His "Battle of Austerlitz," painted at the request of Napoleon, is of immense size, (thirty feet wide by sixteen high,) and an admirable work of its kind. Among his other productions are "The Entrance of Henry IV. into Paris," "Saint Theresa," "Corinna at the Cape of Miseno," and "Thetis with the Armour of Achilles." Gérard was created by Napoleon an officer of the legion of honour, chevalier of Saint Michael, and a member of the Institute, and was afterwards made a baron by Louis XVIII. Besides the works above mentioned, he painted a great number of portraits, including those of the Bonaparte family and other distinguished persons. As a painter of history and portraits, he ranks among the greatest European artists of recent times. Died in Paris in 1836.

See CHARLES LENORMANT, "F. Gérard, Peintre d'Histoire; Essai de Biographie et de Critique," 1846 ; "Nouvelle Biographie Générale."

Gérard, (FRANÇOIS ANTOINE,) a French general, born at Nancy in 1786, served with distinction in the campaign of 1814, and rendered important services to the Greek cause in 1829. In 1848 he became general of division. Died in 1856.

Gerard, (GILBERT,) a distinguished scholar and theologian, son of Dr. Alexander Gerard, was born at Aberdeen. He was the author of "Institutes of Biblical Criticism." Died in 1815.

Gerard, (JAMES,) a surgeon and traveller, son of the preceding, was born at Aberdeen in 1795. He explored Hindostan, Thibet, and the Himalayas, in company with his brother Alexander, between 1818 and 1835. He died in Bengal in 1835.

Gérard, (JEAN IGNACE ISIDORE,) an eminent French artist and caricaturist, who assumed the name of GRANDVILLE, was born at Nancy in 1803. He brought out in 1828 the first of a series of humorous sketches, entitled "Metamorphoses of the Day," which were exceedingly admired and at once established his reputation. After the passage of the law prohibiting political caricatures, he made illustrations for La Fontaine's and Florian's Fables, Béranger's Poems, "Gulliver's Travels," and other popular works. His "Speaking Animals," ("Animaux parlants,") in which he has represented animals with human physiognomies, is unsurpassed in its comic power and keen and delicate satire. His works are very numerous, and rank among the most perfect of their kind, both in conception and execution. He died in 1847, of grief caused by the sudden death of a favourite child.

See "Dictionnaire de la Conversation."

Gerard or **Gerarde,** (JOHN,) an English surgeon and botanist, born at Nantwich in 1545. He had a large botanical garden in London, and was one of the first who introduced exotics. He wrote a general "History of Plants," (1597,) which was highly esteemed. Died about 1607.

Gérard, (JULES,) a French officer, surnamed "the Lion-Killer," born at Pignans in 1817. Having entered the army, he went to Africa in 1842, and became distinguished as a hunter. It is stated that he killed his twentyninth lion in 1855. He published an account of his exploits, "The Lion-Hunt," ("La Chasse au Lion," 1855.) Died in 1864.

Gérard, (LOUIS,) a French botanist, born at Cotignac in 1733. He published in 1761 his "Flora Gallo-Provincialis," said to be the first work in which plants are arranged according to a natural system. Died in 1819.

Gérard, (MAURICE ÉTIENNE,) COUNT, marshal and peer of France, born at Danvilliers in 1773. For his bravery at Austerlitz he was made a commander of the legion of honour on the field of battle, and was afterwards intrusted by Bernadotte with the command of the Saxon cavalry at Wagram. In the Russian campaign of 1812 he displayed signal courage at the taking of Smolensk and the passage of the Berezina. He had a principal share in the victory of Bautzen in 1813. Being severely wounded at Leipsic, he was obliged for a time to quit the army. On the return of Bonaparte from Elba, Gérard obtained the command of the army of the Moselle. When the battle of Waterloo was taking place, on the 18th of June, he urged Marshal Grouchy to advance towards the scene of action. After the accession of Louis Philippe, he was created marshal and peer of France, and minister of war, but, owing to infirm health, soon resigned this post to Marshal Soult. In 1835 he was made grand chancellor of the legion of honour. He died, according to the "Nouvelle Biographie Générale," in 1855.

See "Victoires et Conquêtes des Français," etc.; J. NOLLET-FABERT, "Notice sur le Maréchal Gérard," 1852; "Nouvelle Biographie Générale;" L. DE LOMÉNIE, "Galerie des Contemporains."

Gérard, (PHILIPPE LOUIS,) a French ecclesiastic, born in Paris in 1737, wrote a moral fiction called "The Count of Valmont, or the Wanderings of the Reason," (1774,) and "Study of the French Language, Rhetoric, and Philosophy." Died in 1813.

Gérard de Nerval. See NERVAL.

Gérard de Nimeguen. See GELDENHAUR.

Gérard de Rayneval. See RAYNEVAL.

Gerard Groot. See GROOT.

Gerard of Cre-mo'na, [Lat. GHERAR'DUS CREMONEN'SIS; It. GHERARDO CREMONESE, gȧ-raR'do krȧ-mo-nā'sȧ; Fr. GÉRARD DE CRÉMONE, zhȧ'rȧR' deh krȧ'mon',] an Italian translator, was born at Cremona, in Lombardy, about 1114. He translated, it is said, seventy-six different works from the Arabic into Latin, chiefly relating to mathematics and medicine. Of these we may mention "Theory of the Planets," and the "Ars Parva" of Galen. Died in 1187.

See BONCOMPAGNI, "Della Vita, etc. di Gherardo Cremonese," etc.

Gérard Thom, zhȧ'rȧR' tôn, or **Tenque,** tôNk, the founder and first grand master of the knights of the order of Saint John of Jerusalem, was born about 1040, on an island near the coast of Provence. He went to Jerusalem when quite young, and was appointed superior of a hospital built for the benefit of pilgrims. Here he was held in great esteem, even by the Saracens, before the crusades began. The Moslems, suspecting Gerard of aiding the crusaders, put him in prison; but he was liberated by Godfrey of Bouillon. In 1100 he founded that

order of warrior monks which afterwards became so celebrated. Died in 1121.

See MICHAUD, "Histoire des Croisades;" BOSIO, "Histoire de l'Ordre de Saint-Jean-de-Jérusalem;" D. ARBAUD, "Dissertation historique sur le B. Gérard Tenque," 1851.

Gerardi. See GHERARDI.

Gerbais, zhěR'bȧ', (JEAN,) a French ecclesiastical writer, born near Rheims in 1629; died in 1699.

Gerbel, gĕR'bel, [Lat. GERBE'LIUS,] (NIKOLAUS,) a German jurist, professor at Strasburg, born at Pforzheim, wrote "The Rise and Progress of the Anabaptists," and other works. Died in 1560.

Gerber, gĕR'ber, (ERNST LUDWIG,) a German organist and writer on music, born at Sondershausen in 1746. He published a valuable "Historical and Biographical Lexicon of Musicians," (2 vols., 1790–92, and a more complete work, entitled "Neues historisch-biographisches Lexikon der Tonkünstler," (4 vols., 1810–14.) Died in 1819.

See FÉTIS, "Biographie Universelle des Musiciens."

Gerberon, zhěRb'rôN', (GABRIEL,) a French Benedictine monk, born at Saint-Calais (Maine) in 1628. He became a zealous Jansenist, and was imprisoned for his opinions at Vincennes from 1706 to 1710. He wrote, besides many other works, a "History of Jansenism," (3 vols., 1700.) Died in 1711.

See "Nouvelle Biographie Générale."

Gerbert. See SYLVESTER II.

Gerbert, gĕR'bĕRt, (MARTIN,) Baron von Hornau, (hor'nöw,) a learned German priest and writer on music, who became Prince-Abbot of Saint-Blaise, was born at Horb, in Würtemberg, in 1720. His principal works are a history of church music, entitled "De Cantu et Musica sacra," (1774,) and "Ecclesiastical Writers on Sacred Music," ("Scriptores ecclesiastici de Musica sacra," etc., 3 vols., 1784,) which are highly esteemed. Died in 1793.

See J. B. WEISS, "Trauerrede auf den Fürst-Abbt M. Gerbert," 1793; FÉTIS, "Biographie Universelle des Musiciens."

Gerbet; zhěR'bȧ', (OLYMPE PHILIPPE,) a French ecclesiastic, born in 1798. He wrote, among other works, a "Sketch of Christian Rome," ("Esquisse de Rome chrétienne," 1844–50.) In 1853 he became Bishop of Perpignan.

Gerbier, zhěR'be-ȧ', (PIERRE JEAN BAPTISTE,) a French lawyer and orator, born at Rennes in 1725, was advocate to the Parliament of Paris. Died in 1788.

Gerbier d'Ouvilly, zhěR'be-ȧ' doo'vȧ'ye', (Sir BALTHASAR,) a Flemish architect and painter, born at Antwerp about 1592, visited England at an early age, and was successively patronized by James I., Charles I., and Charles II. He was employed by James to negotiate the marriage of Prince Charles with the Spanish Infanta. Among his best works is a portrait of the Duke of Buckingham on horseback. Gerbier designed the triumphal arches for the reception of Charles II. Died in 1667.

See "Nouvelle Biographie Générale."

Gerbillon, zhěR'be'yôN', (JEAN FRANÇOIS,) a French Jesuit, born in 1634. In 1686 he went as a missionary to China, where, on account of his medical skill, he was received with great favour by the emperor. He wrote a "Relation" of eight journeys into Grand Tartary, the "Elements of Geometry," and "Geometry, Practical and Speculative." The last two were written in Chinese. Died at Pekin in 1707.

See MICHAULT, "Mélanges historiques et philologiques."

Gerbo, zhěR'bo', (LOUIS,) a Flemish painter, born at Bruges in 1761, worked some years in Paris, where he died in 1818.

Gerd, Gerda, or **Gerde.** See FREY.

Gerdes, gĕR'dĕs, (DANIEL,) a meritorious German Protestant minister, born at Bremen in 1698. He became professor of theology at Groningen (one account says at Utrecht) in 1735. His chief work is a "History of the Reformation," (in Latin, 4 vols., 1744–52.) Died in 1767.

See HIRSCHING, "Historisch-literarisches Handbuch."

Gerdil, jěR-dĕl' or jěR-dȇl', (GIACINTO SIGISMONDO,) a learned Italian cardinal, born in Savoy in 1718. He became professor of philosophy at Turin, (1749,) and preceptor to the Prince of Piedmont, afterwards Charles

Emanuel IV. He was made a cardinal in 1777, and, soon after, prefect of the Propaganda. He wrote, besides other works in Latin, French, and Italian, "The Immateriality of the Soul demonstrated against Locke," etc., (1747,) and "Anti-Émile, or Reflections on the Theory and Practice of Education, against the Principles of J. J. Rousseau," (1763.) Died in 1802.

See FONTANA, "Elogio letterario del C. G. S. Gerdil," 1802; TIPALDO, "Biografia degli Italiani illustri."

Gerdy, zhĕr'de', (PIERRE NICOLAS,) a French physician and surgeon, born at Loches (Aube) in 1797. Among his works are "Physiology of the Sensations and Intelligence," (1846,) and "Practical Surgery," (3 vols., 1850–55.) Died in 1856.

Geree, ge-ree', ? (JOHN,) an English Puritan minister, born in Yorkshire in 1600. He preached at Saint Alban's and in London. Died in 1649.

Gerhard, gĕr'hărt, (EDUARD,) a German archæologist, born at Posen in 1795. In 1822 he visited Rome, where he resided many years, and had a share in Platner's "Description of Rome," which was conducted by Baron Bunsen. In conjunction with the latter and other savants, he founded at Rome the Institute for Archæological Correspondence. After his return, about 1837, he was appointed professor in the University of Berlin, and archæologist at the Royal Museum. Among his numerous treatises on ancient works of art, we may name "Greek and Etruscan Drinking-Cups," (1843,) "Vases of Apulia," and "Antique Sculpture," (1827–44.)

See BROCKHAUS, "Conversations-Lexikon."

Gerhard, (EPHRAIM,) a German philosopher, born in Silesia in 1682. He wrote, in Latin, "Delineation of Rational Philosophy." Died in 1718.

Gerhard, (JOHANN,) a learned Lutheran theologian, born at Quedlinburg in 1582, became professor of divinity at Jena in 1616, and was employed in missions by several princes. His "Meditationes Sacræ" (1627) were often reprinted, and translated into several languages. He wrote other works, and was chief editor of the Bible of Weimar. Died at Jena in 1637.

See E. R. FISCHER, "Vita J. Gerhardi," 1723; ARNOLD, "Kirchen-und Ketzer-Historie."

Gerhard, (JOHANN ERNST,) a son of the preceding, born at Jena in 1621, was an Orientalist, and professor of history in his native city. He wrote "Harmony of Oriental Languages," and other treatises. Died in 1688.

See ERSCH und GRUBER, "Allgemeine Encyklopaedie."

Gerhard, (KARL ABRAHAM,) a German mineralogist, born in 1738, wrote an "Essay of a History of the Mineral Kingdom," (Berlin, 2 vols., 1781.) Died in 1821.

Gerhard Groot. See GROOT.

Gerhard, zhȧ'răr' or gĕr'hărt, (CHARLES FRÉDÉRIC,) a French chemist, born at Strasbourg in 1816. He was professor of chemistry from 1844–48 at Montpellier, and removed thence to Paris, where he devoted himself to experiments on homologous series, the theory of types, and anhydrous acids. He proposed an improved classification of organic chemistry, and published an important "Treatise on Organic Chemistry," (4 vols., 1854–56.) In 1855 he became professor of chemistry at Strasbourg. Died in August, 1856.

See "Nouvelle Biographie Générale."

Gerhardt or **Gerhard,** (PAUL,) a German Protestant divine and poet, born in Saxony about 1606. He was the author of a collection of hymns, which are greatly esteemed. He preached in Berlin and at Lübben. Died at Lübben in 1675.

See ERSCH und GRUBER, "Allgemeine Encyklopaedie;" ERNST G. ROTH, "P. Gerhard nach seinem Leben und Wirken," 1829; LANGBECKER, "P. Gerhard's Leben und Lieder," Berlin, 1841; WILDENHAHN, "P. Gerhard: kirchengeschichtliches Lebensbild," etc., 2 vols., 1845, (translated into English by MRS. STANLEY CARR, London, 1846.)

Géricault, zhȧ're'kō', (JEAN LOUIS THÉODORE ANDRÉ,) a French painter, born at Rouen in 1790, studied under Vernet and Guérin, and about 1819 produced his master-piece, "The Shipwreck of the Medusa." His pictures of horses are greatly admired. Died in 1824.

See ÉMILE COQUATRIX, "Géricault, Prose et Vers," 1846; C. BLANC, "Géricault," Paris.

Gericke, gā'rĭk-keh, (PETER,) a German physician and writer, born at Stendal in 1683; died in 1750.

Gering, gā'ring, (ULRIC,) a Swiss printer, who, with his associates, Crantz and Friburger, introduced the art of printing into France in 1469. The first work which they printed was the "Epistles of Gasparini Barzizza," Paris, (1470.) Died in Paris in 1510.

See GRESWELL, "Parisian Typography;" LACAILLE, "Histoire de l'Imprimerie," etc.; "Nouvelle Biographie Générale," (by A. F. DIDOT.)

Gerini, jà-ree'nee, (GERINO, jà-ree'no,) an Italian painter, born at Pistoia, lived about 1530. He was a pupil of Perugino, whose manner he adopted. Among his works is "The Miracle of the Loaves."

See VASARI, "Lives of the Painters," etc.

Gerlach, gĕr'lăk, (BENJAMIN GOTTLIEB,) a German philologist, born at Liegnitz in 1698, wrote an essay "On the Portable Chinese Temple," ("De Templo Sinensi portatili," 1739.) Died in 1756.

Gerlach, (FRANZ DOROTHEUS,) a German philologist, born in Gotha in 1793, published editions of Sallust, and of the "Germania" of Tacitus, and wrote several historical treatises. He became professor of Greek at the University of Bâle in 1820.

Gerlach, (STEPHEN,) a German Protestant divine, born in Würtemberg in 1546, was chaplain to the imperial embassy at Constantinople for five years, (1573–78.) He left a "Journal of the Embassy," (published in 1674,) and several theological works. Died in 1612.

See ERSCH und GRUBER, "Allgemeine Encyklopaedie."

Gerlache, de, deh zhĕr'läsh', (ÉTIENNE CONSTANTIN,) BARON, a Belgian historian and statesman, born in Luxembourg in 1785. He became a member of the Belgian Congress in 1830, president of the Chamber of Representatives in 1831, and president of the court of cassation in 1832 or 1833. He wrote several historical works, the most popular of which is a "History of the Kingdom of the Netherlands from 1814 to 1830," (2 vols., 1839.) He belonged to the Catholic conservative party.

See GERMANUS.

Gerle, zhȧrl, (Dom CHRISTOPHE ANTOINE,) a French ecclesiastic, born in Auvergne in 1740, became an adherent of the fanatic Catherine Théot. Died about 1805.

Germain. See GERMANUS.

Germain, zhĕr'mâN', (CHARLES ANTOINE,) a French political orator, born at Narbonne about 1770. He was an ultra-republican in the Revolution, and became a strenuous opponent of the Directory, by whom he was banished in 1797. Died in 1835.

Germain, (MICHEL,) a French antiquary, born at Péronne in 1645; died in 1694.

Germain, (PIERRE,) a distinguished carver on metals, born in Paris in 1647, was patronized by Louis XIV. Died in 1682.

Germain, [Lat. GERMA'NUS,] SAINT, OF AUXERRE, was born at Auxerre, France, about 380 A.D. He was of illustrious birth, and was created duke of several French provinces by the emperor Honorius. He afterwards embraced an ecclesiastical life, and, on the death of Saint Amator, became Bishop of Auxerre. In 428, Germain was sent to Britain, where, meeting with great success in suppressing Pelagianism and promoting education, he remained nearly eighteen years. Died at Ravenna in 448.

See BAILLET, "Vies des Saints."

Germain, (SOPHIE,) a French lady, distinguished for her knowledge of mathematics, was born in Paris in 1776. In 1815 she obtained the prize offered by the Institute for the best essay on the vibration of elastic plates. She wrote, besides other works, "Researches on the Theory of Elastic Surfaces," (1821.) Died in 1831.

See "Nouvelle Biographie Générale."

Germain, (THOMAS,) an architect and sculptor, a son of Pierre, noticed above, was born in Paris in 1673. He studied under the painter Boullongne, and subsequently at Rome, where he was principally employed in executing ornamental work in gold for different European monarchs. Died in 1748.

Germain de Paris, zhĕr'mâN' deh pä're', SAINT, born in Paris, of which city he became bishop in 554. He was distinguished for his great zeal for religion, and wrote some ecclesiastical works. Died in 576 A.D.

See DUPLESSY, "Histoire de Saint-Germain," 1841; GAILLET, "Vies des Saints."

Ģer-man′ĭ-cus, (Cæsar,) a celebrated Roman general, born in 14 B.C., was the oldest son of Drusus Nero Germanicus, and brother of Claudius, who afterwards became emperor. At the request of Augustus Cæsar, Germanicus was adopted by his uncle Tiberius. When he was twenty years of age, he fought in Dalmatia and Pannonia with such distinction that he obtained a triumph on his return to Rome. In 12 A.D. he became consul, and soon after received from Augustus the command of the legions on the Rhine. The news of the death of this emperor caused several of the legions of the Lower Rhine to break out in a dangerous mutiny while Germanicus was absent. On his return the soldiers desired to raise him to the imperial power; but he refused to accede to their wishes, and succeeded in restoring discipline. He immediately marched against the Germans, whom he defeated in several battles, repulsed the great German leader Arminius, and penetrated to the place where the legions of Varus had been destroyed. The next year he was victorious in two important battles fought against Arminius. Germanicus wished to remain in Germany another year, in order to complete its subjugation; but Tiberius, who was very jealous of the popularity of the conqueror, ordered him to return to Rome, where he was honoured with a brilliant triumph in 17 A.D. He was again chosen consul for the year 18, with Tiberius as his colleague, and was sent to quell some serious disturbances which had broken out in the East. Having brought this expedition to a successful issue, he died at Antioch in the year 19, it is supposed from the effects of poison administered to him by the orders of the emperor and of Cneius Piso, Governor of Syria. Germanicus was greatly beloved by the Romans; and even the nations whom he vanquished regarded him as a noble and generous foe. He left, by his wife Agrippina, granddaughter of Augustus, several children, one of whom was the notorious Caligula. His daughter Agrippina became the mother of Nero.

See Tacitus, "Annales;" Louis de Beaufort, "Histoire de C. Germanicus," 1741; Lagerloef, "Vita C. Germanici," Upsal, 1698; J. Hillebrand, "Germanicus," 2 vols., Frankfort, 1817.

Germanus. See Germain.

Ģer-mā′nus [Fr. Germain, zhĕʀ′mǎN′] I., Patriarch of Constantinople, was an enemy of the Iconoclasts, and had a contest respecting the worship of images with the emperor Leo, by whom he was deposed in 730 A.D. Died about 740.

See Cave, "Historia Literaria."

Germanus II. was elected Patriarch of Constantinople about 1224. He left numerous writings. Died about 1250.

Germanus III. became Patriarch of Constantinople about 1265. He resigned in 1266 or 1267.

German y Llorente, hĕʀ-mȧn′ e lo-rĕn′tä, (Bernardo,) a distinguished Spanish painter, born at Seville in 1685. His chief work was a picture of the Virgin represented as a shepherdess. After this work, Murillo gave him the surname of "the Painter of Shepherdesses." Died in 1757.

See Quilliet, "Dictionnaire des Peintres Espagnols."

Germar, gĕʀ′mȧʀ, (Ernst Friedrich,) a German naturalist, born at Glauchau, in Saxony, in 1786, was appointed chief councillor of mines at Halle in 1844. He wrote a treatise "On the Petrifactions of the Coal Formation of Wettin," etc.

Germon, zhĕʀ′mòN′, (Barthélemi,) a French Jesuit, born at Orléans in 1663, distinguished himself in a controversy with Mabillon, and other Benedictines, in regard to ecclesiastical diplomatics. He wrote several works on this subject. Died in 1718.

See Moréri, "Dictionnaire Historique."

Germonio, jĕʀ-mo′ne-o, (Anastasio,) an Italian canonist, born near Parma in 1551. In 1608 he was appointed Archbishop of Tarantaise. He was the author of numerous ecclesiastical works. Died in 1627.

See Taisand, "Vies des Jurisconsultes anciens et modernes."

Germyn, hĕʀ-mīn′, (Simon,) a Dutch landscape-painter, born at Dort about 1650; died in 1719.

Gerner, gĕʀ′nẹr, (Hendrik,) a Danish author, born at Copenhagen in 1629, became Bishop of Viborg in

1693. He published a "Translation from Hesiod into Danish Verse," and an "Epitome of Danish Philology." Died in 1700.

Gerner, (Hendrik,) a naval architect, born at Copenhagen in 1742, wrote "Songs for the Amusement of Danish Sailors." Died about 1800.

Gerning, (Johann Christian,) a German naturalist, born at Frankfort in 1746; died in 1802.

Gérôme, zhä′rōm′, (Jean Léon,) a French painter, born at Vesoul (Haute-Saône) in 1824, was a pupil of Delaroche. He received a medal of the second class at the Paris Exposition of 1855. Among his works are "The Augustan Age," (1855,) "La Sortie du Bal masqué," and "The Gladiators."

Gerrard, gĕʀ′rȧʀt or hĕʀ′rȧʀt, of Haarlem, a Dutch oil-painter, born at Haarlem in 1460; died in 1488.

Gerrards, van, vȧn gĕʀ′rȧʀts,(G. P.,) a Dutch painter, born at Amsterdam in 1607. He imitated Van Dyck, who was his friend. Died in 1667.

Gerritsz, gĕʀ′rits, (Dirck or Dirk,) a famous Dutch navigator, born at Enkhuisen about 1555. He made a voyage to China, the coasts of which he is said to have explored. He commanded one of the five vessels which in 1598 sailed to the South Sea and discovered land about 64° south latitude. Died about 1602.

Ģer′rȳ, (Elbridge,) an American statesman, born in Marblehead, Massachusetts, in 1744, graduated at Harvard in 1762. He was elected to the legislature of Massachusetts in 1772, and soon became a prominent political leader. Having been chosen a member of the Continental Congress in 1776, he signed the Declaration of Independence, and was placed on several important committees. He became chairman of the treasury board in 1780, and was a member of the convention which, in 1787, formed the Federal Constitution. About 1790 he was again elected to Congress, from which he retired in 1795, and was sent on a mission to France in 1797 with General Pinckney and Mr. Marshall. He was invited to remain when his colleagues were ordered to leave France; and he did remain. He joined the Democratic party, by which he was elected Governor of Massachusetts in 1810. He was elected Vice-President of the United States in 1812, when Madison was chosen President. Died in November, 1814.

See J. T. Austin, "Life of Elbridge Gerry;" Goodrich, "Lives of the Signers to the Declaration of Independence."

Gersdorf, gĕʀs′dorf, (Johann,) a German physician and surgeon, practised at Strasburg about 1520-40. He published a "Manual of Surgery," (1517.)

Gersdorf, (Karl Friedrich Wilhelm,) a German general, born at Lobau in 1765. After the alliance of Saxony with France, he fought for Napoleon in the campaigns of 1809, 1810, and 1812. Died in 1829.

Gerson, de, deh zhĕʀ′sòN′, (Jean Charlier—shȧʀ′-le-ȧ′,) surnamed the Most Christian Doctor, was born at the village of Gerson, near Rheims, in 1363. Soon after completing his studies he became chancellor of the University of Paris and canon of Notre-Dame. Having boldly denounced the assassins of the Duke of Orléans, he was persecuted by the Duke of Burgundy, his house was pillaged by a mob, and he saved his life only by concealing himself. He was one of the most energetic members of the Council of Pisa, which deposed the rival popes Benedict XIII. and Gregory XII. and elected Alexander V. He afterwards exerted a great influence at the Council of Constance, which deposed Pope John XXIII. Gerson sat in this council as the ambassador of the French king and the representative of the Church of France and of the University. While at this place, he had a fierce disputation with John Huss. Gerson always maintained that the Church had the right to make any reforms, even without the consent of the pope. Owing to the enmity of the party of the Duke of Burgundy, he went from Constance to Bavaria disguised as a pilgrim. After remaining in Germany several years, he returned to France, and entered a convent at Lyons, where he died in 1429. He wrote a treatise "On the Consolation of Theology," ("De Consolatione Theologiæ,") and is supposed by some to have been the author of the "Imitation of Jesus Christ," which has generally been attributed to Thomas a Kempis.

See LÉCUY, "Essai sur la Vie de J. Gerson," 1832; VON DER HARDT, "Gersoniana;" THOMASSY, "Jean Gerson," 1843; C. SCHMIDT, "Essai sur Gerson," 1839; "Nouvelle Biographie Générale."

Gerstäcker or **Gerstaecker**, ğĕR'stĕk'kĕr, (FRIEDRICH,) a German traveller and writer, born at Hamburg in 1816. In 1837 he visited the United States, where he spent six years, and after his return published "Streif- und Jagdzügen durch die Vereinigten Staaten Nord-amerikas," ("Wanderings and Hunting Excursions through the United States of North America,") "The River-Pirates of the Mississippi," and several other fictitious works.

Gersten, ğĕR'stĕn, or **Gerstein**, ğĕR'stīn, (CHRIS-TIAN LUDWIG,) a German mathematician, born in 1701 at Giessen, where he became professor of mathematics in 1733. He was imprisoned twelve years (1748–60) for writing an offensive letter to the Landgrave of Hesse-Darmstadt. Died in 1762.

Gerstenberg, ğĕR'stĕn-bĕRG',(HEINRICH WILHELM,) a German littérateur, born at Tondern in 1737. He wrote a successful tragedy, entitled "Ugolino," and a number of poems. Died in 1823.

Gerstner, von, fon ğĕRst'nĕr, (FRANZ ANTON,) a German engineer, born at Prague in 1795, was appointed in 1818 professor of geometry in Vienna. For the pur-pose of examining the railroads, he several times visited England, and in 1834 laid the foundation of the railway from Saint Petersburg to Tsarkoe-Selo, the first made in Russia. During a visit to the United States, he died, in 1840.

Gerstner, von, (FRANZ JOSEPH,) an eminent German astronomer and mechanician, the father of the preceding, was born in Bohemia in 1756. He was professor of mathematics at Prague, and published, besides other works, a "Hand-Book of Mechanics," (3 vols., 1838–41.) Died in 1832.

See BOLZANO, "Leben des F. J. Ritter von Gerstner," 1837.

Gertrude, jĕr'trood, SAINT, Abbess of Nivelle, was born in Brabant about 626 A.D.; died in 659.

Gérusez or **Géruzez**, zhā'rü'zĕ', (EUGÈNE,) a French littérateur, born at Rheims in 1799. He was the substi-tute (suppléant) of Villemain in the chair of literature at Paris from 1833 to 1852. He published a "Course of Philosophy," (1833,) which is commended, and "Es-says on Literary History," (2 vols., 1853.)

Gervaise. See GERVASE.

Gervaise, zhĕr'vâz', (FRANÇOIS ARMAND,) a French writer, and abbot of the order of La Trappe, born in Paris about 1660. Among his works are the "Lives of many of the Christian Fathers," a "Life of Abelard and Hé-loise," (2 vols., 1720,) and a "Life of Saint Paul," (3 vols., 1734.) Died in 1751.

See SAINT-SIMON, "Mémoires;" MARSOLLIER, "Vie de l'Abbé de Rancé."

Gervaise, (NICOLAS,) a French ecclesiastic, brother of the preceding, was born in Paris about 1662. When quite young, he went as a missionary to Siam, where he remained four years. In 1724 the pope appointed him Bishop of Horren, and soon after sent him to America, where in 1729 he and all his companions were massa-cred by the Caribs. Gervaise wrote a "Natural and Political History of the Kingdom of Siam," (1688.)

See MORÉRI, "Dictionnaire Historique."

Gervase, jer'vas or jer-vāz', [Lat. GERVA'SIUS,] OF CANTERBURY, an English monk and historian of the thirteenth century, wrote a "Chronicle of the Kings of England," and a "History of the Archbishops of Can-terbury."

Gervase [Fr. GERVAIS, zhĕR'vȧ' ; Ger. GERVA'SIUS] OF TILBURY, a historian of the thirteenth century, and marshal of the kingdom of Arles, in France, was born at Tilbury, in Essex. He is said to have been the nephew of King Henry II. of England. Among his works are a "History of Britain," and a history of the kings of England and France, entitled "Otia Imperialia."

See T. WRIGHT, "Biographia Britannica Literaria."

Gerville, de, deh zhĕR'vĕl', (CHARLES ALEXIS ADRIEN du Hérissier—dü hā're'se-à',) a French anti-

quary, born at Gerville, near Coutances, in 1769. He wrote treatises on French antiquities. Died in 1853.

Gervinus, ğĕR-vee'nŭs, (GEORG GOTTFRIED,) an eminent German historian and critic, born at Darmstadt in May, 1805. He became professor of history and literature at Göttingen in 1836, but was removed in 1837 because he signed a protest against the abolition of the constitution of Hanover. He published an important work, called "History of the National Poetic Literature of the Germans," (3 vols., 1835–38,) and, as a continua-tion or complement of the same, "Neuere Geschichte der poetischen National-Literatur der Deutschen," (2 vols., 1840–42.) He was chosen professor at Heidelberg in 1844. Among his works is an excellent critical essay on "Goethe's Correspondence," (1836,) a "Study of Shakspeare," (4 vols., 1850,) and a "History of the Nineteenth Century," (3 vols., 1858.) He was a leader of the Liberal party and member of the National As-sembly at Frankfort in 1848. He afterwards advocated republican principles.

See SAINT-RENÉ TAILLANDIER, in the "Revue des Deux Mondes," 1856; and his "Études sur l'Allemagne;" "Nouvelle Biographie Générale."

Ge'ry-on or **Ge-ry'o-nēs**, [Gr. Γηρυόνης,] a monster of classic mythology, represented as having three heads, or the bodies of three men united. One of the labours imposed on Hercules was to bring the oxen of Geryon from an island on which they were kept. Hercules accomplished the task, and slew Geryon.

Geselschap, Hā'sĕl-sKăp', (EDUARD,) a Dutch painter of history and genre, born at Amsterdam in 1814. Among his earlier productions are "The Adoration of the Magi," and "Gustavus Adolphus at Lützen." His later works represent scenes of German life, and display much ima-gination.

Gesenius, ğe-see'ne-ŭs or gȧ-zā'ne-ŭs, (FRIEDRICH HEINRICH WILHELM,) an eminent German Orientalist and biblical critic, was born at Nordhausen on the 3d of February, 1785. He studied at Göttingen, and became professor of theology at Halle in 1811. He published a "Hebrew Grammar," "Hebrew and Chaldee Hand-Lexicon for the Old Testament," (1810–12,) which has been translated into English and Latin, "On the Origin, Nature, and Authority of the Samaritan Penta-teuch," ("De Pentateuchi Samaritani Origine, Indole," etc., 1815,) "Critical History of the Hebrew Language and Writing," (1815,) and a translation of the prophet Isaiah, with a historical, critical, and philological com-mentary. He was also a contributor to Ersch and Gruber's "Encyclopaedie." As a theologian, Gese-nius belonged to the philosophical and critical school. Died at Halle in October, 1842.

See "Gesenius, eine Erinnerung an seine Freunde," 1843; "Nou-velle Biographie Générale."

Gesenius, (WILHELM,) a German medical writer, born in the duchy of Brunswick in 1760. He practised at Nordhausen. Died in 1801.

Ges'ner, (ABRAHAM,) M.D., a geologist of the present age, born at Cornwallis, Nova Scotia. He published a treatise "On the Mineralogy and Geology of Nova Scotia," (1847.) He is said to have discovered kero-seal gas.

Gesner, ğĕs'nĕr, (ANDREAS SAMUEL,) a German teacher, born at Roth (Anspach) in 1690, was a brother of Johann Matthias, whom he aided in the "Thesaurus Linguæ Latinæ," ("Treasury of the Latin Tongue.") Died in 1778.

Gesner, (CONRAD,) a celebrated Swiss naturalist and scholar, whom Cuvier calls a "prodigy of application, learning, and sagacity," was born at Zurich on the 26th of March, 1516. He studied languages and sciences at Zurich, Bourges, Bâle, etc., and, after teaching Greek three years at Lausanne, took the degree of doctor of medicine at Bâle about 1540. He practised medicine at Zurich. In 1545 he published the first volume of his famous "Bibliotheca Universalis," the first great work on bibliography which the moderns have produced. The second volume, called "Pandectes," appeared in 1548. From his youth he had conceived the plan of an ex-tensive work on natural history, in prosecution of which he travelled in Germany and other countries. His "His-

ɛ as k; ç as s; ğ hard; ğ as j; G, H, K, guttural; N, nasal; R, trilled; ŝ as z; ŧh as in this. (☞See Explanations, p. 23.)

65

tory of Animals" ("Historiæ Animalium") is perhaps the work by which he has gained the most durable reputation. The first part of it was published in 1551. "This work," says Cuvier, "may be considered as the basis of all modern zoology; copied almost literally by Aldrovandus, abridged by Johnston, it has become the foundation of much more recent works; and more than one famous author has borrowed from it nearly all of his learning. He deserved their confidence by his accuracy, his clearness, his good faith, and sometimes by the sagacity of his views."

Gesner also acquired celebrity as a botanist. He formed a botanic garden at Zurich, and designed or painted with his own hand more than fifteen hundred plants for a History of Plants which he projected and left unfinished. His engravings were used in the "Epitome Mathioli de Plantis," published by Camerarius in 1586. His botanical manuscripts were published by Schmiedel in 1754. "He has the credit," says Hallam, "of having discovered the true system of classifying plants according to the organs of fructification, which, however, he does not seem to have made known, nor were his botanical writings published till the last century. Gesner was the first who mentions the Indian sugar-cane and the tobacco." ("Introduction to the Literature of Europe.") In 1556 he published a valuable translation of the works of Ælian into Latin. His "Mithridates sive de Differentiis Linguarum" ("On the Differences of Languages") is an effort on a great scale to arrange the various languages of mankind by their origin and analogies. He died at Zurich in December, 1565, leaving a good reputation for piety and virtue.

See SIMLER, "Vita C. Gesneri," 1566; Life by SCHMIEDEL, prefixed to Gesner's botanical works; HALLER, "Bibliotheca Botanica;" NICÉRON, "Mémoires;" J. HANHART, "C. Gesner, Beitrag zur Geschichte des wissenschaftlichen Strebens," etc., 1824.

Gesner, (JEAN,) a Swiss botanist, born at Zurich in 1709. At the University of Leyden he formed a lifelong friendship with the great Haller. He taught mathematics and physics about forty years in the Academy of Zurich. Haller's "Description of Swiss Plants," says the "Biographie Universelle," was in great part the work of Gesner, who, through modesty, declined to attach his name to the work. He wrote another botanical work, the "Tabulæ Phytographiæ," which was published after his death, and is highly commended. Died in 1790.

See "Biographie Médicale;" H. C. HIRZEL, "Denkrede auf J. Gesner," 1790; RUDOLPH WOLF, "J. Gesner, Freund von Haller," etc., 1846.

Gesner, (JEAN JACQUES,) a Swiss antiquary, brother of the preceding, born at Zurich in 1707. He was professor of Hebrew at Zurich from 1740 until his death. His favourite study was numismatology. He wrote a work entitled "All Ancient Coins of Nations and Cities," ("Numismata antiqua Populorum et Urbium omnia,") in which he attempted to present all Greek and Roman medals. It contains many errors. Died in 1787.

Gesner, (JOHANN MATTHIAS,) an eminent German scholar, born near Nuremberg in 1691, became professor of eloquence at Göttingen, (1734.) He published excellent editions of Horace, Quintilian, Claudian, and the "Scriptores de Re Rustica," ("Writers on Agriculture,") also a compilation entitled "New Treasure of the Roman Language," etc., ("Novus Linguæ et Eruditionis Romanæ Thesaurus," 4 vols., 1749.) Died in 1761.

See J. D. MICHAELIS, "Memoria J. M. Gesneri," 1761; JOHANN AUGUST ERNESTI, "Narratio de J. M. Gesnero," 1762.

Gessi, jès'see, (GIOVANNI FRANCESCO,) an Italian painter, called the "Second Guido," ("Guido Secondo,") was born at Bologna in 1588. He was a pupil of Guido, whose manner he imitated with success. He is said to have equalled that master in freedom and firmness of touch and in mellowness of colour. Among his works are a "Virgin and Child," and a "Repose in Egypt." He died in 1625, or, according to some writers, in 1649.

See LANZI, "History of Painting in Italy."

Gessner, gĕs'ner, or **Gesner,** (SALOMON,) a Swiss poet and artist, born at Zurich in 1730. In 1754 he brought out his poem of "Daphnis," which was followed by "Inkle and Yarico," and a volume of "Idyls," all of which were very favourably received, both in Germany

and France. His "Death of Abel," a kind of prose poem, appeared in 1758. As a landscape-painter, Gessner holds a high rank, and his engravings after his own pictures are of superior merit. His poetry, though distinguished for elegance of language and fine versification, gives unreal delineations of life, and no longer enjoys its former popularity. He died at Zurich in 1787.

See HOTTINGER, "S. Gessner," Zurich, 1796; LONGFELLOW, "Poets and Poetry of Europe;" FILIPPO MORDANI, "Elogio storico di S. Gessner," 1840; MEYER, "Denkmal S. Gesner's in Zurich," 1790; BERTOLA, "Elogio di S. Gesner," 1789.

Gestrin, yĕs-treen', (JOHN,) a Swedish mathematician, who lived under the reign of Gustavus Adolphus.

Gesualdo, jà-soo-âl'do, (CARLO,) Prince of Venosa, an Italian amateur musician, lived about 1580. He composed madrigals, which were published in 1595. He excelled in pathos.

Ge'ta, (SEPTIMUS ANTONINUS,) Emperor of Rome, colleague and younger brother of Caracalla, and son of Septimus Severus, was born in Milan about 190 A.D. His disposition appears to have been as open and generous as that of his brother was treacherous and cruel. Caracalla, envious of the great popularity of his brother, and also being determined to reign alone, made several attempts to assassinate him. He accomplished this in 212, by concealing some centurions in the apartments of Julia, the mother of the emperors. Geta was holding a conference with his mother when the assassins killed him and wounded her while she endeavoured to shield him.

See GIBBON, "Decline and Fall of the Roman Empire;" TILLEMONT, "Histoire des Empereurs Romains;" WM. MUSGRAVE, "Geta Britannicus, avec des Notes par Isaac Casaubon, Janus Gruter et Claude Saumaise," London, 1716.

Geth'in, (Lady GRACE,) born in Somerset, England, in 1676, wrote a book entitled "Reliquiæ Gethinianæ," containing essays on love, friendship, death, courage, and several other subjects. Congreve has highly eulogized this work in one of his poems. She died in 1697. A beautiful monument was erected to her memory in Westminster Abbey.

See BALLARD, "Memoirs of Several Ladies of Great Britain."

Geulincx, HUH'links or zhuh'lânks', (ARNOLD,) a learned Flemish Protestant theologian and Cartesian philosopher at Louvain, born at Antwerp about 1625. He wrote several philosophical and metaphysical works, one of which is called "Metaphysica vera," (1691.) Died in 1669.

See MORÉRI, "Dictionnaire Historique."

Geuns, van, vän HUns, (STEPHEN JAN,) a Flemish physician and naturalist, born at Groningen in 1767. He wrote several botanical and medical works, and enriched Gorter's "Flora of Holland" with two hundred species of plants. Died in 1795.

Geusau, von, fon goi'zŏw, (LEVIN,) a Prussian general, born near Eisenach in 1734, served with distinction in the Seven Years' war. Died in 1808.

Gevaerts. See GEVARTIUS.

Ge-var'ti-us or **Gevaerts,** gà-vârts', (JAN KASPAR,) a celebrated Belgian philologist, born at Antwerp in 1593. In 1611 he was created councillor of state, and historiographer, by the emperor Ferdinand III. of Germany. He wrote Latin poems, and other works. Died in 1666.

Geyer. See GEIJER, (ERIC GUSTAF.)

Geyer, gī'er, (HENRY SHEFFIE,) an American jurist, born at Fredericktown, Maryland, in 1790, settled at Saint Louis, Missouri, about 1812. He was elected to the legislature of Missouri several times, and took an important part in revising the statutes of that State in 1825. In 1851 he was chosen a Senator of the United States. Died in 1859.

Geyger. See GEIGER.

Geyler or **Geiler,** gī'ler, (JOHANN,) a Swiss preacher, born at Schaffhausen in 1445; died at Strasburg in 1510.

Geyser, gī'zer, (CHRISTIAN THEOPHILUS,) a skilful German engraver, born at Görlitz in 1742. Among his most admired productions are landscapes after Wouwerman and Pynaker, and the vignettes of Heyne's edition of Virgil. Died about 1806.

Ge-ze'li-us, [Sw. pron. yà-zīī'le-us,] (GEORG,) a learned Swedish ecclesiastic, born in 1736. He pub-

---

ā, ē, ī, ō, ū, ȳ, *long;* ă, ĕ, ŏ, same, less prolonged; ă, ĕ, ĭ, ŏ, ŭ, ў, *short;* ą, ę, į, ǫ, *obscure;* fär, fåll, fåt; mĕt; nŏt; gŏŏd; mōōn;

lished a "Biographical Dictionary of the Illustrious Men of Sweden," (3 or 4 vols., 1776–78.) Died in 1789.

See "Biographiskt-Lexicon öfver namnkunnige Svenska Män."

Gezelius, (JOHAN,) a prelate of Finland, born in 1615. He became professor of theology and Greek at Dorpat, in Livonia, and in 1664 was ordained Bishop of Åbo. He wrote a valuable "Commentary on the Bible" in the Swedish language, and several works in Latin. Died in 1690.

See ACHRELIUS, "Oratio in exequias J. Gezelii," 1690; J. J. TENGSTROEM, "Biskopen i Åbo Stift J. Gezelii den äldres Minne," 1825.

Gezelius, (JOHAN,) a son of the preceding, born in 1647. He became Bishop of Åbo in 1690, and finished his father's commentary or translation of the Bible. He also wrote "Nomenclator Adami." Died in 1718.

Gfrörer, gfrö'rer, (AUGUST FRIEDRICH,) a German historian, born at Calw, in Würtemberg, in 1803, became in 1846 professor at the Catholic University of Freiburg. He published, among other works, a "Universal Church History," and "Gustavus Adolphus of Sweden and his Times," (1835.)

Ghasnevides. See GAZNEVIDES.

Ghasnewiden. See GAZNEVIDES.

Ghâzân, gâ'zǎn', (written also **Kâzân,**) **Khan,** a Mongol sovereign of Persia, born about 1270, was a son of Argoon (Argoun) Khan. He began to reign while still very young, but met at first with much opposition. In 1294 he renounced Booddhism, after which many of the Mohammedan chiefs, who had previously opposed him, joined his cause. He extended his empire by conquest from the river Jihon to the Persian Gulf on the south and Syria on the west. He died in 1304. He was a man of great talents and rare acquirements. Few, if any, among his numerous subjects, were more thoroughly acquainted than he with the history of the ancient Mongols. His government, though severe, appears to have been, on the whole, just and enlightened. For a particular account of his reign, see the "Nouvelle Biographie Générale."

Ghaznevides. See GAZNEVIDES.

Ghazzâlee, (or **Ghazzali,**) **Al.** See ABOO-HAMID-MOHAMMED.

Ghedini, gâ-dee'nee, (FERDINANDO ANTONIO,) an Italian naturalist and poet, born at Bologna in 1684; died in 1767.

Ghelen. See GELENIUS.

Gherardesca, gâ-rÄR-dês'kÄ, a celebrated noble family of Tuscany, of the thirteenth century. They were opposed to the other families of nobles, and placed themselves at the head of the popular party.

Gherardesca, (FAZIO or BONIFACIO,) appointed chief of the republic of Pisa in 1329, threw off the yoke of the emperor Louis of Bavaria, and concluded an honourable peace with the Guelphs. Died in 1340.

Gherardesca, (FILIPPO,) a distinguished Italian composer, born at Pistoia in 1730; died in 1808.

Gherardesca, (UGOLINO,) COUNT OF, an Italian soldier, who endeavoured to usurp the government of Pisa, but failed and was banished from that city. He then joined the army of Florence, which enabled him to succeed in his projects in 1284. He afterwards governed so despotically that a conspiracy was formed against him, with Ubaldini, the Archbishop of Pisa, at its head. Ugolino was attacked in his palace, where, after a brave defence, he was captured, with three sons and one grandson. By the archbishop's orders, they were all imprisoned in the tower, where they were starved to death, (1288.) This is the Gherardesca of Dante's "Inferno."

See SISMONDI, "Histoire des Républiques Italiennes;" "Nouvelle Biographie Générale."

Gherardi, gâ-rÄR'dee, (ANTONIO,) a painter of the Roman school, born in Umbria in 1644; died in 1702.

Gherardi, (CHRISTOFANO,) called DOCENO, (do-châ'-no,) a painter of the Florentine school, born at Borgo San Sepolcro in 1500. He assisted Vasari in his works. Died in 1556.

Gherardi, (FILIPPO,) an Italian painter, born at Lucca in 1643, was a pupil of Pietro da Cortona. Among his works is the "Battle of Lepanto." Died in 1704.

Gherardi del Testa, gâ-rÄR'dee dêl tês'tÄ, (TOMMASO,) COUNT, an Italian dramatist, born near Pisa in 1818. He produced in 1845 a successful comedy, called "Mad Ambition," (" Una folle Ambizione.") He composed about forty dramas, and a popular poem, entitled "The Creator and his World," (" Il Creatore ed il suo Mondo,") with other poetical works.

Gherardini, gâ-rÄR-dee'nee,(ALESSANDRO,) a painter, born at Florence in 1655. A picture of the "Crucifixion" is called his master-piece. Died in 1723.

Gherardo da Sabbionetta, gâ-rÄR'do dÄ sÄb-be-o-net'tÄ, a celebrated Italian physician and astrologer, born near Cremona between 1200 and 1250. He translated into Latin the works of Avicenna and Almansor.

See BONCOMPAGNI, "Della Vita e delle Opere di Gherardo da Sabbionetta;" "Nouvelle Biographie Générale."

Ghesquière, de, dęh gês'ke-air', (JOSEPH,) a Jesuit and antiquarian writer, born at Courtrai, in Belgium, in 1736; died in 1802.

Gheyn, de, dęh gin or hin, (JACOB,) THE ELDER, a noted Flemish painter and engraver, born at Antwerp in 1565; died in 1615.

See DESCAMPS, "Vies des Peintres Flamands," etc.

Gheyn, de, (JACOB,) THE YOUNGER, an engraver, born at Antwerp about 1610; died about 1660.

Ghezzi, gêt'see, (GIUSEPPE,) an Italian painter, born in 1634. He adorned several churches of Rome. Died in 1721.

Ghezzi, (PIETRO LEONE,) a painter and engraver, son of the preceding, was born at Rome in 1674, and excelled in enamel-work and engraving on stones. He was employed by Pope Clement XI. His prophet Micah, in the church of San Giovanni Laterano, is commended. Died in 1755.

See LANZI, "History of Painting in Italy."

Ghezzi, (SEBASTIANO,) an Italian painter and architect, the father of Giuseppe, noticed above, was born near Ascoli about 1600; died about 1650.

Ghiberti, ge-bêR'tee, (LORENZO,) the greatest sculptor of his time, born at Florence in 1378, was also a painter. He received lessons in design from Bartoluccio, a goldsmith, and opened a new era in the art of sculpture by a restoration of the antique style. In 1400 he produced a design for a bronze gate of the baptistery of Saint John at Florence, which was preferred to those of his competitors, among whom was Brunelleschi. He spent twenty years on this bronze gate, which represents scenes from the New Testament. He afterwards executed for the same building another gate, superior to the first. Michael Angelo extolled one or both of these works as worthy to adorn the entrance to Paradise. Among his master-pieces were a statue of Saint Matthew, and the bas-reliefs of the shrine of San Zenobi. "These works," says the "Biographie Universelle," referring to the second gate of the baptistery and the shrine of San Zenobi, "are remarkable for the propriety of the composition, the truth of the attitudes, the accuracy and firmness of the outlines, and the vivacity and dignity of the expression." He was chosen a colleague of Brunelleschi in the erection of the Duomo of Florence. Died about 1455.

See AUGUST HAGEN, "Chronik seiner Vaterstadt von Lorenz Ghiberti," 1833; CICOGNARA, "Storia della Scultura;" LANZI, "History of Painting in Italy;" VASARI, "Lives of the Painters and Sculptors;" GONELLI, "Elogio di L. Ghiberti," etc., 8vo, 1822.

Ghica or **Ghicca.** See GHIKA.

Ghika, gee'kÄ, **Ghica,** or **Ghicca,** (GREGORY,) became Hospodar of Moldavia in 1662. He was deposed by the grand vizier Kuprili in 1673, and died about 1680.

Ghika or **Ghica,** (GREGORY,) a dragoman at the Ottoman Porte. Having been taken prisoner by the Russians, he was sent to Saint Petersburg. Through the influence of the empress Catherine II., he was appointed in 1774 Prince of Moldavia. He was assassinated in 1777, by order of the Sultan.

Ghika, (GREGORY,) was Hospodar of Moldavia and ruler of Wallachia for many years in the first half of the eighteenth century.

Ghika, (GREGORY,) Hospodar of Moldavia, born in Moldavia in 1807. He became hospodar in 1849, and adopted several liberal measures. He was removed by the Turkish Sultan in 1856. Died in 1857.

Ghilini, ğe-lee′nee, (GIROLAMO,) a learned Italian priest, born at Monza in 1589, published a work entitled "Theatre of Literary Men," ("Teatro d'Uomini letterati," (1633.) Died about 1670.

Ghingi, ğĕn′jee, (FRANCESCO,) a celebrated Italian gem-engraver, born at Florence in 1689. He executed a "Venus de Medici" carved from a piece of amethyst weighing eighteen pounds. This master-piece afterwards came into the possession of Augustus III. of Poland. His works are by some esteemed equal to the finest antiques. Died in 1766.

Ghini, ğee′nee, (LUCA,) an Italian botanist, born near Imola in 1500. He taught botany at Pisa, where he planted a botanic garden. Died in 1556.

Ghirlandaio, ğeer-lân-dī′o or ğĕR-lân-dâ′yo, a celebrated painter, whose proper name was DOMENICO CORRADI or CURRADI, was born at Florence about 1450. He excelled in invention, and was the first Florentine who attained skill in aerial perspective. He painted many scenes from the life of the Virgin Mary and John the Baptist. Among his chief works are "The Massacre of the Innocents," "The Death of Saint Francis," and "The Calling of Saint Peter and Andrew," which is still preserved in the Sistine Chapel, Rome. Michael Angelo was one of his pupils. Died in 1495. His brothers BENEDETTO and DAVID were painters of inferior ability.

See VASARI, "Lives of the Painters," etc.; LANZI, "History of Painting in Italy;" MRS. JAMESON, "Memoirs of Early Italian Painters."

Ghirlandaio, (RIDOLFO,) a skilful painter, son of the preceding, born at Florence in 1482. He was the master of a numerous school. "The Coronation of the Virgin" is one of his most admired works. His genius is said to have resembled that of Raphael, whose friendship he enjoyed. He had a talent for the imitation of nature, with the addition of ideal charms. Died in 1560.

See VASARI, "Lives of the Painters," etc.

Ghisi, (ADAMO.) See MANTUANO.

Ghisi, (DIANA.) See MANTUANO.

Ghisi, ğee′see, (TEODORO,) an Italian painter of the Mantuan school, was a brother of Giorgio Ghisi, surnamed MANTUANO, and lived about 1530–80. He was a pupil of Giulio Romano, some of whose works he finished.

See VASARI, "Lives of the Painters," etc.

Ghisleri. See PIUS V.

Ghisolfi, ğe-šol′fee, (GIOVANNI,) an Italian painter, born at Milan in 1624. He worked with success at Rome, Genoa, Milan, and Naples. Died in 1683.

See LANZI, "History of Painting in Italy."

Giaber. See GEBER.

Giacobbi, jâ kob′bee, or **Giacobi,** jâ-ko′bee, (GIROLAMO,) an Italian composer, born at Bologna in 1575. He excelled in sacred music, and composed several operas, said to have been the first performed in Europe. Died in 1650.

Giacomelli, jâ-ko-mel′lee, (MICHELANGELO,) an Italian translator, born at Pistoia in 1695, became Archbishop of Chalcedon in 1761. He translated into Italian the "Electra" of Sophocles, (1754,) and other Greek works. His versions were highly esteemed. Died in 1774.

See A. M. MATANI, "Elogio storico di M. A. Giacomelli," 1775.

Giacunto or **Giacquinto,** jâ-kwĕn′to, (CORRADO, kor-râ′do,) an Italian painter, born at Molfetta about 1695. He went to Madrid, and became first painter to the king about 1752. Died in 1765.

Giafar. See JAAFAR.

Giambelli. See GIANIBELLI.

Giamberti. See SAN GALLO.

Giambullari, jâm-bool-lâ′ree, (BERNARDO,) an Italian poet, born at Florence about 1450.

Giambullari, (PIETRO FRANCESCO,) a son of the preceding, was born at Florence about 1495. He wrote, besides other works, "Rules for Writing and Speaking the Tuscan Language," (1549.) Died in 1564.

Giampaolo, jâm-pŏw′lo or jâm-pâ′o-lo, (PAOLO NICCOLÒ,) an Italian writer, born in the kingdom of Naples in 1757. He became a member of Joseph Bonaparte's council of state in 1807. His chief work is "Dialogues on Religion," (4 vols., 1815–28.) Died in 1832.

Gianibelli, jâ-ne-bel′lee, or **Giambelli,** jâm-bel′lee, (FEDERIGO,) an Italian mechanician and pyrotechnist, who lived about 1570–90. He was the projector of the "infernal machines" which did such fearful execution against the troops of Parma, near Antwerp, April, 1585.

See MOTLEY, "United Netherlands," vol. i. p. 189.

Giannettasio, jân-nĕt-tâ′se-o, (NICCOLÒ **Partenio**—paR-tâ′ne-o,) a Latin poet and Jesuit, born at Naples in 1648. He published in 1685 a didactic poem on navigation, entitled "Piscatoria et Nautica." The nobleness, facility, and harmony of his poetry are praised by Ginguené. He wrote other poems. Died in 1715.

Giannetti, jân-net′tee, (FILIPPO,) an able landscape-painter, born at Messina. He worked at Naples, where he died in 1702.

Gianni, jân′nee, (FRANCESCO,) an Italian poet and improvisator, born at Rome in 1759. He went to Paris about 1800, and obtained a pension from Bonaparte, whose victories he had celebrated. Died in Paris in 1822.

Giannini, jân-nee′nee, (GIUSEPPE,) an Italian physician, born near Milan in 1773, published several valuable medical works. He practised at Milan. Died in 1818.

Giannone, jân-no′nà, (PIETRO,) an eminent Italian historian, born at Ischitella, in the kingdom of Naples, in 1676. He studied law, and practised as an advocate at Naples. He devoted many years to the composition of a "History of the Kingdom of Naples," ("Storia civile del Regno di Napoli," 4 vols., 1723,) in which he attacked the temporal power of the pope and censured the abuses of the Roman Catholic Church. He was excommunicated by the Archbishop of Naples, and, to escape the violence of the clerical party, he retired to Vienna about 1723. He received from the emperor Charles VI. an annual pension of one thousand florins. Having in a subsequent work avowed opinions which were considered heterodox, he was deprived of his pension about 1734, and removed to Geneva in 1735. He wrote a work entitled "Il Triregno, ossia del Regno del Cielo, della Terra e del Papa," ("The Triple Kingdom, or the Kingdom of Heaven, of the Earth, and of the Pope,") which was never printed. In this work he opposed the Catholic dogmas of purgatory, the eucharist, etc. Having been enticed into Savoy by Joseph Guastaldi in 1736, he was arrested by the order of the King of Sardinia, and confined in prison until his death. He died at Turin in March, 1748.

See F. PANZINI, "Vita di P. Giannone," 1765; A. FABRONI, "Vitæ Italorum doctrina excellentium;" CORNIANI, "Secoli della Letteratura Italiana;" TIPALDO, "Biografia degli Italiani illustri."

Giannotti, jân-not′tee, (DONATO,) an Italian historian, born at Florence in 1494, was elected secretary of the republic. His chief work is a history of Venice, called "Republica di Venezia," (1540,) which is commended for accuracy and elegance. Died in 1563.

Giannotti, (SILVESTRO DOMENICO,) an Italian sculptor in wood, born at Lucca in 1680; died in 1750.

See CRESPI, "Vita di S. Giannotti," 1770.

Giants. See GIGANTES and JÖTUNS.

Giardini, jaR-dee′nee, (FELICE,) a celebrated Italian violinist and composer, born at Turin in 1716. Having performed with brilliant success in Germany, he visited London, where he was received with equal favour. He subsequently became one of the managers of the King's Theatre, which post he was forced to resign, after suffering a heavy pecuniary loss. He died, in great poverty, at Saint Petersburg, Russia, in 1796. He was esteemed one of the best musicians of his time, and his compositions for the violin are also of great merit.

See FÉTIS, "Biographie Universelle des Musiciens."

Giattini, jât-tee′nee, (GIOVANNI BATTISTA,) an Italian Jesuit and Latin writer, born at Palermo about 1600; died in 1672.

Gib, (ADAM,) a Scottish theologian, born in Perthshire in 1713, was one of the founders of the Secession Church in Scotland. On the division of this church (1746) he became the leader of the Anti-burghers. He wrote "Sacred Contemplations," (1786.) Died in 1788.

See CHAMBERS, "Biographical Dictionary of Eminent Scotsmen."

Gibault, zhe′bō′, (HIÉRÔME BONAVENTURE,) a French jurist, born at Poitiers; died about 1832.

Gibbes, g̃ibz, (JAMES ALBAN,) a physician and medical writer, born of English parents at Rouen about 1616. He practised in Rome. Died in 1677.

Gibbes, g̃ibz, (ROBERT WILSON,) an American physician, born at Charleston, South Carolina, in 1809. He wrote, besides several medical and scientific treatises, a "Documentary History of the American Revolution," etc., (3 vols., 1853 *et seq.*)

Gib'bon, (EDWARD,) one of the most distinguished of English historians, was born at Putney in 1737. At the age of twelve he was sent to Westminster School, where his feeble health prevented his making much progress in classical studies. When nearly fifteen, however, he became more robust, and entered Magdalene College; but the picture he has drawn of the Oxford professors and their discipline gives us anything but a favourable impression, and he speaks of the fourteen months he spent there as "the most idle and unprofitable of his whole life." About this time he was converted to the Catholic faith, in consequence of which his father sent him to Lausanne, in Switzerland, to reside with M. Pavillard, a Calvinistic divine, under whose teachings he was brought back to Protestantism. Here he lived five years in retirement, preparing himself by study and reflection for future eminence. He regarded his "banishment" as a fortunate circumstance, but for which "those important years so liberally improved in the studies and conversation of Lausanne would have been steeped in port and prejudice among the monks of Oxford." In 1758 he returned to England, and in 1761 published his first work, entitled "Essay on the Study of Literature," written in French, with which at that time he was better acquainted, as he himself states in his Autobiography, than with his native tongue. Soon after this he became a captain in the Hampshire militia, and engaged with much ardour in the study of military tactics; but, becoming weary of this pursuit, he gave it up, and in 1763 went to Paris. Leaving Paris, he repaired to Lausanne, and in a short time set out for Rome, where, he tells us, "as he sat musing amidst the ruins of the Capitol, while the bare-footed friars were singing vespers in the temple of Jupiter, the idea of writing the decline and fall of the city first started to his mind." He did not, however, begin it until several years later. On his return to England he wrote a history of the Swiss Revolution; but this work was never published. In 1767 he began to publish, conjointly with his Swiss friend Deyverdun, a work called "Literary Memoirs of Great Britain." In 1770 appeared his first work written in English, "Critical Observations on the Sixth Book of the Æneid." In 1774 he obtained a seat in Parliament, where he supported Lord North's administration, in return for which he was made a commissioner of trade, with a salary of £800 a year. On Lord North's resignation, Gibbon gave up his place in Parliament and his "convenient salary." In 1776 the first volume of the "Decline and Fall of the Roman Empire" appeared, and proved a brilliant success. "The first impression was exhausted in a few days; a second and third edition were scarcely adequate to the demand." He was especially gratified by the praise of Hume and Robertson, and he says, in his Autobiography, "a letter from Mr. Hume overpaid the labour of ten years." The hostility of this work to the Christian religion, however, gave great offence to many, and it was severely attacked by several English divines, to only one of whom—Mr. Davis—he replied, "because he assailed not the faith, but the fidelity, of the historian." This charge, however, is generally thought to have been fully refuted. The second and third volumes were published in 1781; and in 1783 he again retired to Lausanne, where he gave himself up to literary pursuits and repose. Here he finished the three remaining volumes of his history, which appeared in 1788. He returned to England in 1793, and died in London, January, 1794. His great work has by common consent been placed in the very highest rank of the English classics. As a historian and man of learning, he merits, perhaps, all the praises he has received. As a man, though possessing many amiable traits, he had too little moral elevation and religious sentiment to appreciate the sublime courage of Christian martyrs;

and his political course shows far more regard for his personal interest than devotion to principle.

Mr. Prescott, after some excellent remarks on the qualifications demanded for a perfect historian, speaks of Gibbon as one of the most accomplished writers in this department of literature. He observes, however, that the author of the "Decline and Fall" is wanting in good faith: "his most elaborate efforts exhibit too often the perversion of learning and ingenuity to the vindication of preconceived hypotheses. He cannot, indeed, be convicted of ignorance or literal inaccuracy; but his disingenuous mode of conducting the argument leads precisely to the same unfair result. Thus, in his celebrated chapters on the 'Progress of Christianity' . . . he has often slurred over in the text such particulars as might reflect most credit on the character of the religion, or shuffled them into a note at the bottom of the page, while all that admits of a doubtful complexion in its early propagation is ostentatiously blazoned and set in contrast to the most amiable features of paganism. At the same time, by a style of innuendo that conveys 'more than meets the ear,' he has contrived, with Iago-like duplicity, to breathe a taint of suspicion on the purity which he dares not openly assail." (See "Biographical and Critical Miscellanies.") Porson, alluding to the "Decline and Fall," observes, "An impartial judge must, I think, allow that Mr. Gibbon's history is one of the ablest performances of the kind that has ever appeared. His industry is indefatigable; his accuracy scrupulous; his reading, which indeed is sometimes ostentatiously displayed, immense; . . . his style emphatic and expressive; his periods harmonious." The same able and impartial critic admits that Gibbon's bitter hostility to Christianity is a great blemish on his character as a historian, and adds, "He often makes, when he cannot readily find, an occasion to insult our religion, which he hates so cordially that he might seem to revenge some personal injury." Porson also justly stigmatizes "that rage for indecency which pervades the whole work, but especially the last volumes." (Preface to his "Letters to Travis.") "The 'History of the Decline and Fall,'" says Professor Smyth, "must always be considered as one of the most extraordinary monuments that have appeared in the literary powers of a single mind; and its fame can perish only with the civilization of the world." ("Lectures on Modern History.") Alison, the historian, calls the "Decline and Fall" "the greatest historical work in existence." For a fuller presentation of various critical opinions respecting Gibbon, the reader is referred to Allibone's "Dictionary of Authors."

See GIBBON's autobiographic "Memoirs of his Life and Writings," 1799; HENRY HART MILMAN, "Life of E. Gibbon," 1839; GUIZOT, "Notice sur Gibbon;" SAINTE-BEUVE, "Causeries du Lundi," tome viii.: J. B. CHRISTOPHE, "Étude sur l'Historien Gibbon," 1852; VILLEMAIN, "Tableau de la Littérature au dix-huitième Siècle;" "Quarterly Review" for January, 1815, (vol. xii.,) and January, 1834, (vol. l.)

Gib'bon, (JOHN,) an American general, born in Pennsylvania about 1826, graduated at West Point in 1847. He obtained the rank of captain in 1859. He commanded a brigade at Antietam, September, 1862, and at Gettysburg, July, 1863. Having been appointed a major-general, he took part in the battles of the Wilderness, Spottsylvania Court-House, and Cold Harbour, May-June, 1864.

Gib'bons, (CHRISTOPHER,) a son of Orlando, noticed below, was a skilful musician and composer. He was organist of Westminster Abbey. Died about 1675.

Gibbons, (GRINLING,) a distinguished sculptor, of Dutch extraction, born in London (or, as some writers state, in Rotterdam) about 1650. He was appointed by Charles II. one of the directors of public works, and commissioned by him to ornament Windsor Castle with sculpture in wood and marble. Among the most exquisite specimens of his skill in wood-carving are the decorations of a room at Petworth. "There is no instance," says Horace Walpole, "of a man before Gibbons who gave to wood the loose and airy lightness of flowers." He is said to have carved feathers which could not be distinguished from real ones. Died in 1721. See CHALMERS, "Biographical Dictionary;" WALPOLE, "Anecdotes of Painting."

Gibbons, (ORLANDO,) an eminent English composer and musician, born at Cambridge in 1583. His anthems are regarded as master-pieces of the kind; and he also composed madrigals of great beauty. He was created Doctor in Music in 1622. Died in 1625.

See BURNEY, "History of Music."

Gibbons, (THOMAS,) an English Calvinistic divine, born near Newmarket in 1720. He published a work entitled "Female Worthies; or, The Lives of Pious Women." Died in 1785.

Gibbs, (GEORGE,) an American mineralogist, born in Rhode Island about 1780. He collected the valuable cabinet of minerals now owned by Yale College and purchased of him by that institution in 1825. Died in 1833.

Gibbs, (JAMES,) a Scottish architect, born at Aberdeen about 1680. He studied in Holland and in Italy, and after his return built Saint Martin's Church and Saint Bartholomew's Hospital in London, and the Radcliffe Library at Oxford. Died in 1754.

See CHAMBERS, "Biographical Dictionary of Eminent Scotsmen."

Gibbs, (JOSIAH WILLARD,) LL.D., an American philologist, born in Salem, Massachusetts, in 1790. He graduated at Yale College, where he became in 1824 professor of sacred literature. He published, besides other works, a "Manual Hebrew and English Lexicon," abridged from Gesenius, (1828,) and "Philological Studies," (1857.) Died in 1861.

Gibbs, (Sir VICARY,) an English judge, born at Exeter in 1752. He distinguished himself in the trials of Hardy, Horne Tooke, and others, for treason, in 1794. He became solicitor-general in 1805, and attorney-general in 1807. He was appointed chief justice of the court of common pleas in 1813. Died in 1820.

See FOSS, "The Judges of England."

Gibelin, zheb'làN', (ESPRIT (ês'pRe') ANTOINE,) a French painter of history, born at Aix in 1739. He worked in Paris, chiefly in fresco, and wrote several antiquarian treatises. Died in 1814.

Gibelin, (JACQUES,) a physician and naturalist, brother of the preceding, was born at Aix in 1744; died in 1828.

Gibert, zhe'baiR', (BALTHASAR,) a French critic, of high reputation, born at Aix in 1662. He was professor of rhetoric at the Collége Mazarin, Paris, for more than fifty years, during which he instructed many who became eminent. His principal work is "The Judgment of Savants on the Authors who have treated on Rhetoric," (3 vols., 1713-19,) which is remarkable for power of analysis and judicious reflections. Died in 1741.

See MORÉRI, "Dictionnaire Historique."

Gibert, (CAMILLE MELCHIOR,) a French physician, born in Paris in 1797. He wrote, besides other works, "Manual of Diseases pertaining to the Skin," ("Manuel des Maladies spéciales de la Peau," 1834.)

Gibert, (JEAN PIERRE,) a writer on canon law, born at Aix, Provence, in 1660, was a cousin of Balthasar, noticed above. His "Institutions ecclésiastiques et bénéficiales" (1720) is called his best work. Died in 1730.

See GOUJET, "Éloge de J. P. Gibert," 1736.

Gibert, (JOSEPH BALTHASAR,) a historical writer and antiquary, born at Aix in 1711, was a nephew of Balthasar. In 1746 he was admitted into the Academy of Inscriptions. Died in 1771.

Gibert de Montreuil, zhe'baiR' deh môN'tRuI' or môN'tRuh'ye, a French *trouvère* of the twelfth century, was the author of a romance in verse, entitled "La Violette," which ranks among the best productions of the kind in the middle ages. It is supposed to have furnished to Boccaccio the subject of one of his novels, "Novella IX., Giornata seconda," from which Shakspeare has taken the plot of "Cymbeline." "La Violette" was first printed in the original text at Paris in 1834.

Giberti, je-bêR'tee, (GIAMMATTEO,) a Sicilian bishop, eminent for learning and piety, born at Palermo in 1495. He was appointed to the see of Verona in 1524. He was a generous patron of literature; and several excellent editions of the Greek Fathers were published at his charge. Died in 1543.

See P. F. ZINI, "Boni Pastoris Exemplum."

Gibieuf, zhe'be-uf', (GUILLAUME,) a French doctor of the Sorbonne, born at Bourges, was appointed vicar-

general of the order of the Carmelites. He wrote a work entitled "De Libertate Dei et Creaturæ." Died in 1650.

Gibson, (EDMUND,) an English prelate, distinguished for his attainments in the Northern tongues, was born in Westmoreland in 1669. Among his principal publications may be named an edition of the "Chronicon Saxonicum," a translation of Camden's "Britannia," and his "Body of English Ecclesiastical Law," ("Codex Juris Ecclesiastici Anglicani.") As chaplain to Tennison, Archbishop of Canterbury, he maintained the rights of the clergy during the contest between the two Houses concerning the extent of their respective powers. He was appointed Bishop of Lincoln in 1715, and in 1723 removed to the see of London. He was a zealous defender of the claims of the Church, and opposed the efforts of Protestant dissenters to remove the disability under which they suffered. He is said to have incurred the displeasure of the king by his denunciation of masquerades and other court amusements. Died in 1748.

See COXE, "Life of Walpole;" "Biographia Britannica."

Gibson, (JOHN,) one of the most eminent sculptors of recent times, born at Conway, Wales, in 1791, removed at an early age to Liverpool. His talents soon attracted the notice of Roscoe, through whose influence he was enabled in 1817 to visit Rome. He studied under Canova, and afterwards under Thorwaldsen. Among his principal works are the groups of "Mars and Cupid" and "Psyche borne by Zephyrs," a "Narcissus," a "Wounded Amazon," and other productions of a poetical character, which are regarded as models of classic elegance. His statues of Queen Victoria, Huskisson, Sir Robert Peel, and others, are less admired, owing in part to their being represented in antique costume. Gibson also favoured the practice of painting statues, which was opposed by his brother artists. Died in 1866.

See "Life of John Gibson," edited by LADY EASTLAKE, 1869; "Gentleman's Magazine" for March, 1866.

Gibson, (JOHN BANNISTER,) an eminent American jurist, born in Pennsylvania in 1780. His father, Lieutenant-Colonel Gibson, was killed in Saint Clair's expedition against the Indians in 1791. He was admitted to the bar in 1803. He was repeatedly re-elected to the State legislature by the then Republican party, and was appointed presiding judge of one of the judicial districts in 1813. He became in 1816 associate justice of the supreme court of Pennsylvania, and succeeded Judge Tilghman as chief justice in 1827. In consequence of a change in the constitution of the State, making the offices of judges elective, he was deprived of his seat in 1851, but was elected an associate justice the same year. He died in Philadelphia in 1853, having occupied a prominent position as a judge for about forty years.

For some excellent and discriminating, though eulogistic, remarks on his character, by CHIEF-JUSTICE BLACK, see Harris's "Pennsylvania State Reports," vol. vii. pp. 10-14; see, also, a biographical sketch of Chief-Justice Gibson, by W. A. PORTER, Esq., 1855.

Gibson, (RICHARD,) an English painter and dwarf, born in 1615, excelled particularly in water-colours. He was three feet ten inches high; and his wife was of exactly the same stature. Of five children who grew to maturity, all were of usual size. Gibson was appointed preceptor to the princesses Mary and Anne, daughters of James II. Died in 1690.

Gibson, (THOMAS,) an English naturalist and Protestant divine, was distinguished for his learning. He wrote works on various subjects. Died in 1562.

Gibson, (THOMAS MILNER,) a Liberal English legislator, born at Trinidad in 1807. He entered Parliament in 1837 as member for Ipswich, and became an effective orator of the Anti-Corn-Law League. In 1841 he was returned to Parliament for Manchester. He was appointed a privy councillor and vice-president of the board of trade in 1846, but resigned in 1848. His opposition to the Russian war rendered him so unpopular that he was defeated at the general election of 1857. About the end of that year he was elected a member of Parliament by the voters of Ashton-under-Lyne. He was appointed president of the board of trade (with a seat in the cabinet) by Palmerston in 1859. He is identified with the "Manchester school" in politics. In June, 1866, he retired from office.

Gibson, (WILLIAM,) a self-taught English mathematician, born near Appleby in 1720. He became a school-teacher and land-surveyor. Died in 1791.

Gibson, (WILLIAM,) an eminent American surgeon, born in Baltimore, Maryland, in 1788, graduated at the University of Edinburgh in 1809, and succeeded Dr. Physick as professor of surgery in the University of Pennsylvania in 1819. He resigned this position in 1855. Died at Savannah, in Georgia, in 1868. He was one of the first American surgeons who performed the Cæsarian operation with complete success. (See "American Journal of Medical Sciences" for May, 1838.)

See DR. CARSON's "History of the Medical Department of the University of Pennsylvania," 1869.

Gichtel, gĭK'tĕl, (JOHANN GEORG,) a German mystic, born at Ratisbon in 1638, professed doctrines similar to those of Jacob Boehme. His disciples obtained the name of Gichtelians, or Angelic Brothers. He published a work entitled "Practical Theosophy." Died in 1710.

See REINBECK, "Sur la Vie et les Doctrines de Gichtel," Berlin, 1732.

Gid'dings, (JOSHUA REED,) a distinguished leader in the anti-slavery movement in the United States, was born in Athens, Pennsylvania, in 1795. In 1805 his parents were among the first settlers in Ashtabula county, Ohio, (Western Reserve.) He commenced the practice of law in 1820, and in 1838 was elected a representative to Congress, which position he held by subsequent re-elections for twenty-one years. He united with Mr. Adams in his memorable struggle for the overthrow of the obnoxious "gag-law," enacted for the purpose of preventing the agitation of the slavery question. In 1842 Mr. Giddings was censured by a Congressional vote of 125 to 69 for his agitation of slavery. He instantly resigned his seat, but was soon after re-elected by a large majority. He acted for the most part with the Whig party, voting for Harrison in 1840 and for Clay in 1844, but he supported Van Buren in 1848. While in Congress he took a conspicuous part in all the debates on the slavery question, including the fugitive-slave law of 1850, the repeal of the Missouri Compromise in 1854, etc. In March, 1861, he was appointed consul-general for the British North American provinces. Died at Montreal, May 27, 1864. He published two volumes of essays and speeches, a work entitled "The Exiles of Florida," (1858,) and "The Rebellion, its Authors and Causes," (New York, 1864.)

Giddings, (SALMON,) a pioneer missionary in the Mississippi Valley, was born at Hartford, Connecticut, in 1782. He organized eleven churches in Missouri and Illinois, and visited many of the Indian tribes in what are now Kansas and Nebraska. Died in 1828.

Gid'e-on, [Heb. גִּדְעוֹן; Fr. GÉDÉON, zhǎ'dǎ'ôN',] an Israelite of the tribe of Manasseh, and son of Joash, became judge of Israel. His nation had been suffering seven years under the tyranny of the Midianites, when a heavenly messenger was sent to Gideon, commanding him to take arms in defence of his country. With three hundred men he totally defeated the Midianites. Gideon was judge of Israel forty years. Died about 1236 B.C.

See Judges vi., vii., and viii.

Gié, de, dĕh zhe'ǎ', (PIERRE de Rohan—dĕh ro'ôN',) a French marshal, born in Brittany about 1450. He enjoyed the favour and confidence of Louis XI. and his successor Charles VIII., whom he accompanied in his Italian expedition. He was appointed by Louis XII. preceptor to the young prince, afterwards Francis I. He was subsequently deprived of his dignities, on a charge of having abused his authority. Died in 1513.

See BRANTÔME, "Histoire des grands Capitaines."

Giedroyc, ge-â'dROits, (R. THADDEUS,) PRINCE, a Polish general, born in Lithuania in 1750. He served with distinction against the Russians in the campaigns of 1792 and 1794, and rose to the rank of lieutenant-general. Died in 1824.

Gierig, ğee'riG, (GOTTLIEB ERDMANN,) a German philologist, born at Wehrau, Lusatia, in 1753. He published good editions of Ovid (1784) and of Pliny the Younger, and several original treatises. Died in 1814.

Giesecke. See GISEKE.

Gieseler, ğee'zĕh-lĕr, (JOHANN KARL LUDWIG,) a German Protestant theologian, distinguished as an ecclesiastical historian, was born at Petershagen, near Minden, about 1792. He published in 1818 an able "Historical and Critical Essay on the Origin of the Gospels," and was appointed professor of theology at Bonn in 1819. He obtained the chair of theology at Göttingen in 1831. His principal work is his "Manual of Ecclesiastical History," which was not completed until after his death. Died in 1854.

See "Nouvelle Biographie Générale."

Giffen, van, vän ğif'fĕn, [Lat. GIPHA'NIUS,] (HUBERT,) a Flemish philologist and eminent jurist, born in 1534. The emperor Rudolph II. made him councillor and referendary of the empire. His treatises on law and philology are greatly esteemed. Died in 1604.

Gif'ford, (ANDREW,) an English Baptist minister and noted antiquary, born in 1700. He preached in London, and became assistant librarian of the British Museum in 1757. He published a new edition of Folkes's "Tables of English Coins," (1763.) Died in 1784.

Gifford, (JOHN,) the assumed name of JOHN RICHARD GREENE, an English journalist, born in 1758. He was one of the founders of the "British Critic" and "The Anti-Jacobin Review," and wrote, among other works, a "Life of the Right Hon. William Pitt." Died in 1818.

Gifford, (RICHARD,) an English divine, born in 1725, became rector of North Okendon in 1772. He wrote "Contemplation," a poem, and "Answer to Dr. Priestley's Disquisition on Matter and Spirit." Died in 1807.

Gifford, jif'ford, (ROBERT,) Baron Saint Leonard's, an able English lawyer, born at Exeter in 1779. He was appointed solicitor-general in 1817, and attorney-general in 1819. In this capacity he conducted the prosecution of Queen Caroline in 1820, after which he received the title of baron. He became master of the rolls and chief justice of the common pleas in 1824. Died in 1826.

See FOSS, "The Judges of England," vol. ix.

Gif'ford, (SANFORD R.,) a distinguished American landscape-painter, born in Saratoga county, New York. He resided in early life at Hudson, in the vicinity of the Catskill Mountains. Among his works, which are highly praised by Tuckerman, are the "Coming Storm," "Waves Breaking on the Beach at Early Dawn," and "Morning in the Mountains."

See TUCKERMAN's "Book of the Artists."

Gifford, (WILLIAM,) an eminent English critic and author, and principal founder of the "Quarterly Review," was born at Ashburton, Devonshire, in April, 1757. He was a shoemaker's apprentice for about five years, and afterwards studied at Oxford. He began his literary career by "The Baviad," a poetical satire, (1794,) which was highly successful. His satire "The Mæviad" (1795) was also much admired. In 1797 Gifford was editor of "The Anti-Jacobin." In 1802 he produced a poetical version of Juvenal, which is highly commended. He was editor of the "Quarterly Review" from 1809 until 1824, during which period he showed himself a bitter partisan of Toryism and a severe critic of authors, whom "he regarded," says Southey, "as a fishmonger regards eels, or as Izaak Walton did worms, slugs, and frogs." He was a powerful master of sarcasm, and unsparing in the use of it. Died in December, 1826.

"William Gifford," says Mr. Whipple, "seems to have united in himself all the bad qualities of the criticism of his time. He was fierce, dogmatic, bigoted, libellous, and unsympathizing. Whatever may have been his talents, they were exquisitely unfitted for his position,—his literary judgments being contemptible, where any sense of beauty was required." ("North American Review" for October, 1845, vol. lxi.)

See "Autobiography" prefixed to his translation of Juvenal, and "Autobiography of William Jerdan," vol. iv. chap. vii.

Gī-gan'tēs, [Gr. Γίγαντες; Fr. GÉANTS, zhǎ'ôN',] gigantic beings of classic mythology, supposed to be the sons of Terra or Tartarus, and to have waged war against the gods. Some ancient poets confounded them with the Titans. They were conquered by the gods, but not until the latter obtained the aid of Hercules.

See SMITH's "Dictionary of Greek and Roman Biography and Mythology."

Giggei, jĕd-jā'ee, or **Giggeo,** jĕd-jā'o, [Lat. GIGGE'IUS,] (ANTONIO,) an Italian ecclesiastic and Orientalist, was patronized by Pope Urban VIII. He published a "Thesaurus Linguæ Arabicæ," which had a high reputation at that time. Giggei was an intimate friend of Cardinal Federigo Borromeo. Died in 1632.

Gigli, jĕl'yee, (GIROLAMO,) an Italian dramatist and satirist, born at Sienna in 1660. His original name was NENCI, (nĕn'chee.) He wrote successful comedies and tragedies, among which were a translation of Molière's "Tartuffe," entitled "Don Pilone," (1711,) and "The Sister of Don Pilone," (1721,) in which he burlesqued himself and his wife. He attacked the Academy della Crusca in his "Vocabulary of the Works of Saint Catherine," ("Vocabolario delle Opere di Santa Caterina," 1717.) He is called an original genius by Ginguené. Died at Rome in 1722.

See F. CORSETTI, "Vita di G. Gigli," 1746; TIPALDO, "Biografia degli Italiani illustri."

Gignoux, zhên'yoo', (FRANCISQUE **Régis**—rà'zhĕss',) a French landscape-painter, born in Lyons about 1816. He emigrated to New York about 1840, and produced pictures of American scenery, among which is "Niagara Falls by Moonlight."

See TUCKERMAN, "Book of the Artists."

Gigot, zhe'go', (PHILIPPE FRANÇOIS MATHIEU,) a Belgian writer, born at Brussels in 1793. He wrote an "Abridged History of Holland," (1820.) Died in 1819.

Gigot d'Elbée. See.ELBÉE.

Gigoux, zhe'goo', (JEAN FRANÇOIS,) a French painter, born at Besançon in 1806, obtained a medal of the first class at Paris in 1848. Among his works are a "Magdalene," "The Death of Cleopatra," "The Baptism of Clovis," and a portrait of Lamartine.

Gil, Heel or Hĕl, a Spanish friar, distinguished as a preacher, born in Andalusia about 1745 ; died in 1815.

Gil'bart, (JAMES WILLIAM,) an English writer on banking, born in London about 1794, was manager of the London and Westminster Bank. He published a "Practical Treatise on Banking," (1827 ; 6th edition, 1855,) and other esteemed works. Died in 1863.

Gil'bert, called THE UNIVERSAL, an English prelate, who received his surname on account of his great learning. He was created Bishop of London in 1128. Died in 1134.

See B. HAURÉAU, "De la Philosophie scolastique."

Gilbert, zhĕl'bair', (ANTOINE PIERRE MARIE,) a French antiquary, born in Paris in 1785. He published historical descriptions of the cathedrals of Rouen, Chartres, and Amiens. Died in 1858.

Gilbert, (CHARLES C.,) an American officer, born in Ohio in 1827, became brigadier-general of volunteers in the United States army in 1862.

Gilbert, (DAVIES,) a distinguished English savant, whose original name was GIDDY, born in Cornwall in 1767. He was president of the Royal Society, and was noted for his generous patronage of literary and scientific men. He was one of the first to recognize the genius of Sir Humphry Davy, whom he materially assisted in early life and introduced to the notice of the managers of the Royal Institution. He published "A Plain Statement of the Bullion Question," and other learned treatises. In 1827 he succeeded Sir Humphry Davy as president of the Royal Society ; he resigned this position in 1830. Died in 1839.

Gilbert, (GABRIEL,) a French dramatic poet, born about 1610. His works are numerous, but have little merit. It is evident, however, that some of the best French writers—Racine, for example—have sometimes borrowed from him. He was patronized by Christina, Queen of Sweden, who invited him, after her abdication, to her court in France, and made him her secretary. Died about 1680.

See MM. HAAG, "La France protestante."

Gilbert, (Sir GEOFFREY or JEFFREY,) an English jurist, born in 1674, became chief baron of the exchequer in Ireland, (1716,) and in England, (1725.) He wrote the "Forum Romanum," (1756,) "History and Practice of Chancery," (1758,) and other legal works. Died in 1726.

Gilbert, (Sir HUMPHREY,) a celebrated English navigator, born of an ancient family in Devonshire in 1539. By the marriage of his mother, after becoming a widow,

with Mr. Raleigh, he was half-brother to the famous Sir Walter Raleigh. After leaving Oxford, he distinguished himself in several military enterprises. As commander-in-chief in the province of Munster, he assisted in quelling the insurrection in Ireland. He published in 1576 a "Discourse to Prove a Passage by the Northwest to Cathaia," etc. He obtained letters-patent from the queen in 1578, with permission to make discoveries in North America and take possession of any part yet unoccupied. His first expedition to Newfoundland was unsuccessful ; but in 1583 he again set sail. "The commander," says Bancroft, "on the eve of his departure received from Elizabeth a golden anchor guided by a lady, a token of the queen's regard." When he arrived in the Bay of Saint John, he took possession in the queen's name of the surrounding country, and granted leases to those of his company who desired them. It having been represented to him that there were silver-mines in Newfoundland, he sailed, with his little fleet of three vessels, along that coast. They had not gone far, however, when, owing to the negligence of the crew, their largest ship was wrecked and nearly all on board perished. Gilbert now set sail for England in the Squirrel, a vessel of only ten tons. He was requested to go on board the larger vessel, called the Hind ; but he refused to leave the little company who had shared with him so many dangers. They encountered very rough seas, and the little bark was in the greatest danger. "The general, sitting abaft, with a book in his hand, cried out to those in the Hind, 'We are as near to heaven by sea as by land.' That same night, about twelve o'clock, the lights of the Squirrel suddenly disappeared, and neither the vessel nor any of its crew was ever again seen."

See BANCROFT, "History of the United States," vol. i. chap. iii. ; PRINCE, "Worthies of Devon ;" F. DENIS, "Génie de la Navigation ;" HILDRETH, "History of the United States," vol. i. chap. iii. ; J. BARROW, "Memoirs of the Naval Worthies of Queen Elizabeth's Reign," 1845.

Gilbert, (JOHN,) an English historical painter, born in Kent in 1817. Among his works are "The Murder of Thomas à Becket," and "Don Quixote giving Advice to Sancho Panza."

Gilbert, (JOHN GRAHAM,) a painter of history and portraits, was born at Glasgow in 1794.

Gilbert, (L. T.,) a French dramatist and novelist, born in Paris in 1780 ; died in 1827.

Gilbert, gil'bĕrt, (LUDWIG WILHELM,) a German physician, born in Berlin in 1769. He founded in 1799 "The Annals of Physics and Chemistry," ("Annalen der Physik und Chymie," 150 vols.) Died in 1824.

See L. CHOULANT, "L. W. Gilberts Leben und Wirken," 1825.

Gilbert, (NICOLAS JOSEPH LAURENT,) an excellent French satiric and lyric poet, born near Remiremont, in Lorraine, in 1751. He became a resident of Paris in 1774, with no resources but his talents. In 1775 he produced a satire against the skeptical philosophers, called "The Eighteenth Century." His odes "On the Jubilee," (1776,) "On the Present War," (1778,) and his poem entitled "At the Banquet of Life" ("Au Banquet de la Vie") contain passages of great beauty. According to the "Biographie Universelle," he became insane, swallowed a key, and died in November, 1780. His death is attributed to a fall from a horse by the "Nouvelle Biographie Générale," which calls him "the most eminent satirist of the eighteenth century."

See "Nouvelle Biographie Générale ;" PINARD, "Gilbert, ou le Poëte malheureux," 1840 ; "Mémoires de la Marquise de Créquy."

Gilbert, (NICOLAS PIERRE,) a French physician and medical writer, born at Brest in 1751. He became professor at Val-de-Grace, Paris, in 1796, and physician-in-chief to the grand army in 1806. Died in 1814.

See "Biographie Médicale."

Gilbert, (PIERRE JULIEN,) a French painter of marine views, born at Brest in 1783.

Gilbert, SAINT, a French ecclesiastic, accompanied the second crusade to the Holy Land. Died in 1152.

Gilbert, (THOMAS,) an English nonconformist minister, born about 1612 ; died in 1694.

Gilbert or Gilberd, (WILLIAM,) an eminent English physician and scientific writer, born at Colchester in 1540. Having taken his degree in a foreign university, he was, after his return to England, chosen a Fellow of the College of Physicians, in London. He acquired a high reputation in his profession, and became physician-in-ordinary to Queen Elizabeth. His great work entitled "On the Magnet, the Magnetic Bodies," etc. (" De Magnete, Magneticisque Corporibus," etc.) came out in 1600. His reputation was at once established by this production, which presents many original and striking views. "It contains," says Whewell, "all the fundamental facts of the science, so fully examined, indeed, that even at this day we have little to add to them." It was eulogized by Erasmus, Galileo, and other eminent men of the time. Died in 1603.

See WOOD, "Athenæ Oxonienses;" HUMBOLDT, "Cosmos."

Gilbert [Lat. GILBER'TUS] OF-SEMPRINGHAM, SAINT, an English ecclesiastic, born in Lincolnshire in 1083, was the founder of the order of Gilbertines. He established thirteen monasteries and a number of hospitals. Died in 1189.

Gilbert de la Porré, zhĕl'baiR' dĕh lắ po'rắ', [Lat. GISLEBER'TUS PORRETA'NUS,] a French theologian and scholastic philosopher, born at Poitiers about 1070. He became Bishop of Poitiers, and wrote a celebrated work called " Book of Six Principles," (" Liber sex Principiorum.") He was a realist in philosophy. Died in 1154.

See B. HAURÉAU, "De la Philosophie scolastique."

Gilbert de Voisins, zhĕl'baiR' dĕh vwä'zăN',(PIERRE PAUL ALEXANDRE,) COMTE, a French judge, born near Paris in 1779. He was appointed first president of the imperial court under Napoleon, and in 1830 became a member of the court of cassation. Died in 1843.

Gil'christ, (ALEXANDER,) a British writer on art, born about 1827. He wrote a "Life of William Etty," (2 vols., 1855.) Died in 1861.

Gilchrist, (EBENEZER,) a Scottish physician, born at Dumfries in 1707. He practised at his native place with success, and wrote "On the Use of Sea-Voyages in Medicine," (1756.) Died in 1774.

Gil'christ, (JOHN BORTHWICK,) an English Orientalist, born in 1759. He published several valuable works on the Hindostanee language. Died in 1841.

Gilchrist, (OCTAVIUS,) an English dramatic critic, born at Twickenham in 1779. He wrote a "Letter to W. Gifford on a Late Edition of Ford's Plays," (1811,) and other works. Died in 1823.

Gil'das, SAINT, surnamed SAPIENS, (the "Wise,") an eminent ecclesiastic, supposed to have been a native of Wales, was born about 511 A.D. Having spent several years in France in his studies, he founded after his return a church and school in Pembrokeshire. On the invitation of Saint Bridget, he visited Ireland, where he effected a great reformation in the Church. He afterwards founded the monastery of Saint Gildas de Ruys in Brittany. The work entitled "De Excidio Britanniæ" has been ascribed to this writer.

See LOBINEAU, "Vies des Saints de Bretagne."

Gil'do or **Gil'don,** a Mauritanian chief, son of Nabal, was raised by the emperor Theodosius to the chief command in Africa. In the quarrel between Arcadius and Honorius he sided with the former, for which he was declared a public enemy by the Romans. His army was soon after defeated by the Roman forces under Mascezel, and Gildo, being imprisoned, destroyed himself, (398 A.D.)

See GIBBON, "Decline and Fall of the Roman Empire."

Gil'don, (CHARLES,) an English writer and actor, born in Dorsetshire in 1665. He published "The Deist's Manual," (1705,) "The Complete Art of Poetry," and several dramas. "His memory is still preserved," says Macaulay, "not by his own voluminous works, but by two or three lines in which his stupidity and venality have been contemptuously mentioned by Pope." Died in 1723.

See LELAND, "Deistical Writers;" CIBBER, "Lives of the Poets."

Giles. See ÆGIDIUS.

Gileš, jīlš, (HENRY,) a Unitarian minister and writer, born in Wexford county, Ireland, in 1809, emigrated to the United States about 1840. Among his works are "Lectures and Essays," (2 vols., 1845,) and "Christian Thoughts on Life," (1850.) He has lectured extensively in the United States.

Giles, jīlz, (Rev. JOHN A.,) an English editor and historian, born about 1802. He published a number of valuable works, among which are a "Greek-and-English Lexicon," (1846,) a "History of the Ancient Britons," (2 vols., 1847,) and "The Life and Times of Alfred the Great," (2d edition, 1854.) He edited the "Entire Works of the Venerable Bede," (12 vols., 1843–44.)

Giles, (WILLIAM BRANCH,) an American statesman and orator, born in Amelia county, Virginia, in 1762. He was educated at Hampden-Sidney College and at Princeton. In 1790 he was elected a representative to Congress by the Federal party, but soon became a Democrat. He made in 1793 a violent attack on Hamilton, then secretary of the treasury, and offered resolutions censuring him for an undue assumption of power; but these were not adopted by the House. He vigorously opposed Jay's treaty with England in 1796. Having retired from Congress in 1798 to accept a seat in the Virginia legislature, he co-operated with Madison in procuring the passage of the celebrated resolutions of 1798 against the alien and sedition laws. He was again a representative in Congress in 1801–2, and in 1804 was elected to the United States Senate. In this body he continued to be one of the ablest supporters of the administrations of Jefferson and Madison until 1811 or 1812, when he took sides with the opposition. He retired from the Senate in 1815. In 1825 he was again a candidate for re-election, but was defeated by John Randolph. He was chosen Governor of Virginia in 1827. In 1829 the famous Constitutional Convention met; and, though Governor of the State, he served as a delegate, and took a conspicuous part in its deliberations. Died in 1830.

"Mr. Giles," says Senator Benton, "was considered by Mr. Randolph to be in our House of Representatives what Charles Fox was admitted to be in the British House of Commons,—the most accomplished debater that his country had ever seen. But their acquired advantages were very different: Fox was a ripe scholar, Giles neither read nor studied; Fox perfected himself in the House, speaking on every subject, Giles out of the House, talking to everybody."

See BENTON's "Thirty Years' View," etc.

Giles de Corbeil. See ÆGIDIUS CORBOLIENSIS.

Giles of Viterbo. See ÆGIDIUS OF VITERBO.

Gil-fil'lan, (Rev. GEORGE,) a Scottish writer, born in Perthshire in 1813. He published in 1845 his "Gallery of Literary Portraits," which was favourably received, and was followed by a second and a third series in 1849 and 1855. Among his other works are "The Book of British Poesy, Ancient and Modern," "The Martyrs, Heroes, and Bards of the Scottish Covenant," and "The Bards of the Bible." "Gilfillan is sometimes happy in his metaphors and apt in his allusions, but is more likely to be extravagant in the one and grotesque in the other." (Allibone's "Dictionary of Authors.")

Gilfillan, (ROBERT,) a Scottish poet, born at Dunfermline about 1798. He wrote songs and other poems, (4th edition, 1851.) Died in 1850.

See a "Memoir of the Author," prefixed to the edition of his poems, 1851; CHAMBERS, "Biographical Dictionary of Eminent Scotsmen."

Gilianez, zhe-le-ä'nĕz, or **Gilles-Anès,** a Portuguese navigator, who made discoveries on the west coast of Africa about 1435.

Gilibert, zhe'le'baiR', (JEAN IMMANUEL,) a French physician and naturalist, born at Lyons in 1741. He planted a botanic garden at Grodno about 1775, and returned to Lyons in 1783. He published, besides other works, "Medical Anarchy," (" L'Anarchie médicinale," 3 vols., 1772,) which was commended by Haller, "Flora Lithuanica," (1781,) a "History of the Plants of Europe, or Elements of Practical Botany," (2 vols., 1798,) and an "Abridgment of the Natural System of Linnæus," (1802.) Died in 1814.

See J. MOLLET, "Éloge historique de J. E. Gilibert," 1816; QUÉRARD, "La France Littéraire."

Gilimer. See GELIMER.

Gilj or **Gili,** jee'lee-ee or jĕl'yee, (FILIPPO LUIGI,) an Italian astronomer and botanist, born at Corneto in 1756, was director of the observatory founded by Gregory XIII. Died at Rome in 1821.

Gilkens, hĭl′kĕns, (PETER,) a jurist and legal writer, born at Ruremond, Netherlands, about 1558.

Gill, (Rev. ALEXANDER,) an English scholar and theologian, born in Lincolnshire in 1564. He was the author of "Sacred Philosophy of the Holy Scriptures," and of several educational works. Died in 1635.

See WOOD, "Athenæ Oxonienses."

Gill, (ALEXANDER,) a son of the preceding, was born in London in 1597. He became usher, and afterwards head-master, of Saint Paul's School. Among his pupils was the poet Milton, who in some of his letters has expressed much esteem for him. Died in 1642.

Gill, (JOHN,) an English Baptist divine, of great learning, born at Kettering, Northamptonshire, in 1697. He was well versed in Hebrew, Greek, and Latin. In 1719 he settled in London, as pastor of a congregation at Horsleydown, where he preached for fifty years. He published an "Exposition of the New Testament," (3 vols., 1746-48,) and an "Exposition of the Old Testament," (6 vols., 1748-63,) which are highly esteemed by the Baptists. Among his numerous other works is "A Body of Doctrinal and Practical Divinity," (3 vols., 1769 -70.) Died in 1771.

See "Life of Gill," prefixed to his "Exposition of the Bible," 1809.

Gille, zhĕl, (CHARLES EUGÈNE,) a French lyric poet and dramatist, born in Paris in 1820, published "The Barber of Pézénas," a comedy, and a number of popular songs. He committed suicide in 1856.

Gilles, zhĕl, (JEAN,) a French musical composer, born at Tarascon in 1669; died in 1705.

Gilles, (NICOLE,) a French historian, who was *sécrétaire-contrôleur* of the treasury in the reign of Charles VIII. He wrote "Annals of France," a work of some merit, often reprinted. Died in 1503.

Gilles, (PIERRE,) a French naturalist, born at Albi in 1490. He travelled in the Levant for scientific purposes. "He was one of the first in France," says Weiss, "who cultivated natural history with success." ("Biographie Universelle.") He published, in Latin, a work "On the Nature of Animals," (1533,) consisting chiefly of translations from Ælian, a "Treatise on the Antiquities of Constantinople," (1561,) and other works. Died at Rome in 1555.

See NICÉRON, "Mémoires ;" MORÉRI, "Dictionnaire Historique."

Gilles, zhĕl, (PIERRE,) a Swiss Protestant minister, born about 1570, wrote a "History of the Church of the Vaudois," (1644.)

Gilles de Colonne. See COLONNA, (EGIDIO.)

Gilles de Delft. See DELPHUS.

Gil-lĕs′pie, (GEORGE,) a Scottish Presbyterian theologian, who was one of the commissioners sent to the Assembly of Westminster in 1643. He published "Treatises of Miscellaneous Questions," (1649,) "The Ark of the Testament Opened," (2 vols., 1661-77,) and other works. Died in 1648.

See CHAMBERS, "Biographical Dictionary of Eminent Scotsmen."

Gillespie, (THOMAS,) a Scottish Presbyterian minister, born near Edinburgh about 1708. He founded, about 1750, a sect called the "Synod of Relief." Died in 1774.

Gil-lĕs′pie, (WILLIAM MITCHELL,) LL.D., an American engineer and writer, born in New York in 1816. He graduated at Columbia College in 1834, and became professor of civil engineering in Union College at Schenectady in 1845. His principal work is "Roads and Railroads: a Manual for Road-Making," (1845,) said to be one of the best treatises on the subject in the English language, (7th edition, 1854.) Died in 1868.

Gillet, zhe′lā′, (NICOLAS FRANÇOIS,) a French sculptor, born in 1709. He worked in Saint Petersburg, returned to France about 1778, and died in 1791.

Gilli, jĕl′lee, or **Gilj,** (FILIPPO SALVATOR,) an Italian Jesuit and missionary, born near Spoleto in 1721. He spent twenty-five years in South America, and published after his return "The Natural, Civil, and Sacred History of the Spanish Provinces in South America," which was esteemed one of the best works that had been written on those countries until Humboldt's Travels appeared. Died in 1789.

Gil′lieŝ, (JOHN,) a Scottish historian, born at Brechin, in Forfarshire, in January, 1747. He published in 1778 his translation of the Orations of Lysias and Isocrates. The first part of his principal work, "The History of Ancient Greece and its Colonies," (2 vols. 4to,) came out in 1786, and in 1793 he succeeded Dr. Robertson as royal historiographer of Scotland. He afterwards published his "History of the World from the Reign of Alexander to that of Augustus," (2 vols., 1807-10,) which is a continuation of his History of Greece. He died at Clapham, near London, in 1836.

See CHAMBERS, "Biographical Dictionary of Eminent Scotsmen," (Supplement ;) "Nouvelle Biographie Générale."

Gillies, (ROBERT PIERCE,) a Scottish writer, favourably known by his translations from the German. He lived near Edinburgh, and was a friend of Sir Walter Scott and of Wordsworth the poet. He was the first editor of the "Foreign Quarterly Review," and author of various works, among which are "Childe Alarique," a poem, and autobiographic "Memoirs of a Literary Veteran," (3 vols., 1851.)

See PRESCOTT's "Miscellanies," p. 180.

Gill′more, (QUINCY ADAMS,) an American general, born in Lorain county, Ohio, about 1825, graduated at West Point in 1849. He gained the rank of captain in 1861, and that of brigadier-general of volunteers early in 1862. He displayed skill as an engineer by the capture of Fort Pulaski in April, 1862, and was appointed commander of the department of the South in June, 1863. He made a successful attack on the enemy's fortified position on Morris Island in July, began to bombard Fort Sumter and Charleston in August, and took Fort Wagner in September, 1863. Fort Sumter was reduced to a ruinous condition; but its garrison continued to hold it until February 17, 1865. He also damaged Charleston by batteries about four and a half miles distant from that city. He commanded the tenth corps in the operations against Petersburg and Richmond in the summer of 1864. He was appointed a brevet major-general of the regular army in March, 1865.

See REID, "Ohio in the War," 1868; GREELEY, "American Conflict."

Gillot, zhe′yo′, (CLAUDE,) a French designer and engraver, born at Langres in 1673, was the master of Watteau. He was most successful in etching. His compositions are chiefly burlesque. Died in Paris in 1722.

See BASAN, "Dictionnaire des Graveurs."

Gillot, (JACQUES,) a French scholar, born at Langres about 1550. He was a friend of Scaliger and Casaubon, and one of the authors of the celebrated "Satire Ménippée," which contributed greatly to the success of Henry IV. against the League. He wrote "Letters to Joseph Scaliger," which were printed. Died in 1619.

See MAIMBOURG, "Histoire de la Ligue," vol. iii.

Gill′ray, (JAMES,) a celebrated English caricaturist, born about 1750, excelled both in drawing and engraving. The satire of his caricatures was directed against social and political abuses; but he was frequently extravagant, and indulged in too great personalities. Died in 1815.

See "Retrospective Review," vol. i., second series, 1853.

Gilly, zhe′ye′, (JACQUES LAURENT,) a French general of division, born in Languedoc in 1769; died in 1829.

Gil′lỹ, (WILLIAM STEPHEN,) an English writer, born about 1790, was canon of Durham and vicar of Norham. He published "The Spirit of the Gospel," (1818,) "Excursion to the Mountains of Piedmont and Researches among the Vaudois," (1824,) "Second Visit, or Waldensian Researches," (1831,) and other works. Died in 1855.

Gil′man, (CAROLINE,) an American authoress, wife of the Rev. Samuel Gilman, was born in Boston in 1794. Among her most popular works are "Recollections of a New England Housekeeper," and "Recollections of a Southern Matron." She has also published "Oracles for Youth," (1854,) "Sibyl, or New Oracles from the Poets," (1854,) and "Jairus's Daughter."

See GRISWOLD's "Female Poets of America."

Gilman, (JOHN TAYLOR,) an American Governor, born at Exeter, New Hampshire, in 1759. He was a member of the Continental Congress in 1782 and 1783, and became treasurer of his State in the latter year. In 1797 he was elected Governor of New Hampshire by the Federalists. He was re-elected annually until

1807, was a very popular Governor, and filled the same office in 1813, 1814, and 1815. Died in 1828.

Gilman, (SAMUEL,) D.D., an American divine and author, born in Gloucester, Massachusetts, in 1791, graduated at Harvard in 1811. He was pastor of a Unitarian church in Charleston, South Carolina, from 1819 until his death. Among his works are "Memoirs of a New England Village Choir," (1829,) and a poem called "The History of a Ray of Light." Died in 1858.

Gil'mer, (THOMAS W.,) a Virginian politician and member of Congress. He was appointed secretary of the navy by President Tyler, and was killed by the explosion of a large gun on the steamer Princeton in February, 1844.

Gil'pin, (BERNARD,) an excellent English divine, born in Westmoreland in 1517. He was appointed one of the first professors of Christ Church College soon after it was founded by Henry VIII. He was educated in the Catholic faith; but he was subsequently converted to Protestantism, and, soon after the accession of Queen Mary, visited France and Holland. Returning to England in 1556, he was appointed Archdeacon of Durham and rector of Houghton-le-Spring, in the county of Durham, during the reign of Mary. The reformation he effected among the lawless borderers of this region, and his bold denunciations of the wickedness of the times, obtained for him the name of "the Apostle of the North." He refused the bishopric of Carlisle, offered him by Queen Elizabeth, preferring to remain at Houghton, where he thought his labours were most needed. Died in 1583.

See WM. GILPIN, "Life of Bernard Gilpin," 1753; G. CARLETON, "Vita Bern. Gilpini," 1628.

Gil'pin, (HENRY D.,) an American lawyer and classical scholar, born in Philadelphia in 1801. He graduated at the University of Pennsylvania in 1819, was admitted to the bar in 1822, and soon became distinguished as an able lawyer. In 1840 he was made attorney-general of the United States. He edited the papers of James Madison, (3 vols. 8vo, 1840.) Died in 1860.

See "Memorial of Henry D. Gilpin," 1860; ALLIBONE, "Dictionary of Authors."

Gilpin, (RICHARD,) an English nonconformist minister, born in Cumberland about 1625. He published a "Treatise of Satan's Temptations," (1677.) Died in 1699.

Gilpin, (SAWREY,) an English painter, brother of William Gilpin, noticed below, was born at Carlisle in 1733. His favourite subjects were horses and other animals, which he painted with extraordinary fidelity. Among his master-pieces are a "Group of Tigers," and the "Horses of Diomede." Died in 1807.

See BRYAN, "Dictionary of Painters."

Gilpin, (Rev. WILLIAM,) a distinguished English author, born at Carlisle in 1724. He taught a school at Cheam, in Surrey, until one of his pupils—Colonel Mitford, the historian—procured for him the living of Boldre, in Hampshire. He was the author of many valuable and well-written works, among which are a "Life of Bernard Gilpin," (1753,) a "Life of Wickliff," (1765,) a "Life of Cranmer," (1784,) and "Essays on Picturesque Beauty," etc. He described and illustrated the picturesque scenery of England in a series of works, with plates finely engraved by himself. Died in 1804.

Gil Vicente, zheel or zhèl ve-sěn'tà, an eminent Portuguese dramatist, born at Barcellos in 1485. He was patronized by King John III., who, it is said, often performed parts in his comedies. He was himself an actor, and his daughter Paula was esteemed the first Portuguese actress of her time. Gil Vicente's works enjoyed a European reputation, and Erasmus is said to have learned Portuguese for the sole purpose of reading his comedies. He wrote nearly a century before Lope de Vega and Shakspeare, and probably did more than any other to build up the modern drama. His compositions include tragedies, comedies, and farces; also autos, or religious pieces for Christmas festivals. Among his best comedies are "The Judge of Beyra," and the "Portuguese Fidalgo." Died in 1557.

See LONGFELLOW, "Poets and Poetry of Europe;" BARBOSA MACHADO, "Bibliotheca Lusitana;" BOUTERWEK, "Littérature Espagnole et Portugaise;" "Nouvelle Biographie Générale," (under VICENTE.)

Gil y Zarate, hèl e thâ-râ'tà, (Don ANTONIO,) a Spanish dramatist, born in 1793 at the Escurial, where his parents resided as court actors. He brought out in 1835 his tragedy of "Doña Blanca de Borbon," which was favourably received, and was soon followed by another, entitled "Carlos II. el Hechizado," which established his reputation. Among his other dramas we may name "Rosamunda," and "Guzman el Bueno:" the latter is esteemed his best piece. Zarate filled several offices under the government, and was appointed professor of history at Madrid, and a member of the Spanish Academy.

Gimignano, je-mèn-yâ'no, or **Geminiani,** jà-me-ne-â'nee, (GIACINTO,) an Italian painter, born at Pistoia in 1611, studied under Pietro da Cortona. His principal works are frescos in the Lateran at Rome and the Niccolini palace at Florence. Died in 1681. His son LODOVICO (1644-97) was a painter of some merit.

See LANZI, "History of Painting in Italy."

Gimma, jèm'mà, (GIACINTO,) an Italian writer, born at Bari in 1668; died in 1735.

Ginani, je-nâ'nee, or **Zinani,** dze-nâ'nee, (GABRIEL,) an Italian poet, born at Reggio about 1560. Among his works is "Amerigo," (1590,) which Tiraboschi ranked with the best Italian tragedies of the sixteenth century. Died about 1635.

Ginani, (GIUSEPPE,) COUNT, an Italian naturalist, born at Ravenna in 1692. He made a valuable collection of plants, shells, and other objects of natural history, on which he wrote several treatises. Died in 1753.

Gines or **Ginez.** See SEPULVEDA.

Ginguené, zhăn'gēh-nà', (PIERRE LOUIS,) an eminent French critic and *littérateur*, born at Rennes in 1748. He became a resident of Paris in 1772. On the breaking out of the Revolution he favoured the republican cause, but always showed himself a friend to moderation. He was appointed in 1795 director-general of the commission of public instruction, and in 1798 was ambassador to the King of Sardinia. On his return he obtained, in 1799 or 1800, a seat in the Tribunat, from which, however, he was soon dismissed, on account of his opposition to the acts of Bonaparte. He now abandoned politics, and became a contributor to the "Literary History of France," which had been begun by the Benedictines. His greatest work, the "Literary History of Italy," (9 vols., 1810-24,) was left by him incomplete, and was continued by Salfi. Ginguené was the author of a poem of great merit, entitled "The Confession of Zulmé," and contributed numerous notices of Italian writers to the "Biographie Universelle." Died in Paris in November, 1816.

See "Notice sur Ginguené," by SALFI, appended to the "Histoire littéraire d'Italie," tome x.; DACIER, "Éloge de Ginguené;" D. J. GARAT, "Notice sur la Vie et les Ouvrages de P. L. Ginguené," 1817; "Nouvelle Biographie Générale;" "London Quarterly Review" for April, 1814.

Gin'kel or **Ginkell, van,** (GODARD or GODART,) sometimes written **Ginkle,** Earl of Athlone, a Dutch general of great ability, born at Utrecht, or in Gelderland, about 1630. He had attained the rank of general when he accompanied the Prince of Orange to England, (1688.) He served at the battle of the Boyne, (1690,) and was appointed commander-in-chief in Ireland in 1691. He took Athlone, gained a decisive victory over the Irish at Aghrim in July, 1691, and completed the subjection of the island before the end of that year. He was rewarded with the title of the Earl of Athlone in 1692. He commanded the Dutch cavalry in Flanders in 1695 and 1696. "Ginkel was one of the bravest and ablest officers of the Dutch army," says Macaulay. In 1702 he obtained command of the Dutch troops under Marlborough. He died at Utrecht in 1703, leaving two sons.

See MACAULAY's "History of England," vol. iv.

Giobert, jo-bàrt', (GIOVANNI ANTONIO,) an Italian chemist, born near Asti in 1761. He was the first in Italy to propagate the doctrines of Lavoisier, and he made some reforms or innovations in agriculture. In 1800 he became professor of rural economy at Turin. He published "Annals of Rural Economy," (3 vols., 1793,) and other works. Died in 1834.

See "Nouvelle Biographie Générale."

Gioberti, jo-bĕR'tee, (VINCENZO,) an eminent Italian philosopher and patriotic statesman, born at Turin in April, 1801. He graduated at the University of Turin, where in 1825 he was appointed professor of theology. In 1831 he became chaplain to the king, Charles Albert; but, being soon after accused of favouring the liberal party, he was first imprisoned, and subsequently exiled. He resided more than ten years in Brussels, where he wrote his "Theory of the Supernatural," ("Teoria del Sopranaturale," 1838,) and "Introduction to the Study of Philosophy," ("Introduzione allo Studio della Filosofia," 1839.) In 1843 he published his "Civil and Moral Supremacy of the Italians," ("Il Primato civile e morale degli Italiani,") in which he advocates the restoration of the greatness of Italy, through a reformed papacy, a constitutional monarchy, and moderate freedom of the press. This work was received with enthusiasm by his countrymen, with the exception of the Jesuits, several of whom replied to it. His "Modern Jesuit," ("Gesuita moderno,") which appeared in 1847, caused a great sensation, and the expulsion of the Jesuits from Italy was soon after decreed by the pope. Gioberti's return to Turin in 1848 was celebrated by the Italians with the liveliest demonstrations of joy, and he was chosen soon after president of the Chamber of Deputies. The same year he was appointed minister of public instruction, and afterwards placed at the head of the ministry as president of the council. Owing to disagreement with his colleagues, he resigned this post in February, 1849. He died in Paris in October, 1851 or 1852, having previously published a treatise "On the Civil Renovation of Italy," (1851,) which was very favourably received. He was an eloquent and powerful writer and orator.

See CRUGER, "Esquisses Italiennes;" G. MASSARI, "Vita di V. Gioberti," 1848, (translated into French, Brussels, 1853;) CERISE, "V. Gioberti," Paris, 1853; "Nouvelle Biographie Générale."

Giocondo, jo-kon'do, [Lat. JOCUN'DUS,] (Fra GIOVANNI,) a celebrated architect and antiquary, born at Verona about 1435. He became in 1494 professor of the ancient languages in his native city, and numbered among his pupils J. C. Scaliger. Being invited to Paris by Louis XII. in 1499, he built the bridge of Notre-Dame, which is regarded as one of the finest of that time. He was afterwards employed by the Venetians to superintend the turning off the waters of the Brenta from the lagunes of Venice. He was subsequently commissioned by Pope Leo X. to assist Raphael and San Gallo in the building of Saint Peter's Church. Giocondo had made a very large and valuable collection of ancient inscriptions, which he presented to Lorenzo the Magnificent. Died about 1537.

See VASARI, "Lives of the Painters," etc.; QUATREMÈRE DE QUINCY, "Dictionnaire d'Architecture."

Gioeni, jo-ā'nee, (GIUSEPPE,) an Italian naturalist, born at Catana in 1747. He published in 1790 a "Treatise on the Lithology of Vesuvius," ("Saggio di Litologia Vesuviana.") Died in 1822.

Gioffredo, jof-frā'do, (MARIO GAETANO,) an able architect, born at Naples in 1718. He was employed by the government at Naples, and received the title of chief architect. Among his works are the church of Spirito Santo, and the Palazzo Campolieto. He published a "Treatise on Architecture," (1768.) Died in 1785.

See N. A. CARLINI, "Elogium M. G. Gioffredi," 1785.

Gioffredo, (PIETRO,) an Italian historian, born at Nice in 1629. He wrote "A History of Nice," in Latin, (1658,) and a "Description of the Maritime Alps." Died in 1692.

Gioja, jo'yā, (FLAVIO,) an Italian navigator, born near Amalfi about 1300. The invention of the mariner's compass has been erroneously ascribed to him.

See KLAPROTH, "Lettre sur l'Invention de la Boussole," Paris, 1834.

Gioja, (MELCHIORRE,) an eminent Italian political economist, born at Piacenza in 1767. He advocated the republican form of government in an essay which obtained a prize in 1796, and was appointed director of the bureau of statistics at Milan about 1803. He expressed his preference of the French régime in his work entitled "The French, Germans, and Russians in Lombardy,"

("I Francesci, i Tedeschi, i Russi in Lombardia," 1805.) He published an important work on political economy, called "New View of the Economic Sciences," ("Nuovo Prospetto delle Scienze economiche," 6 vols., 1815–19.) Among his other remarkable works are a "Treatise on Merit and Rewards," (1819,) and "The Philosophy of Statistics," (2 vols., 1826.) "M. Gioja," says Silvio Pellico, "was the most eminent thinker that the economical sciences have had in Italy in modern times." Died at Milan in 1829.

See TIPALDO, "Biografia degli Italiani illustri;" GIUSEPPE SACCHI, "Memoria sulla Vita di M. Gioja," 1829; F. BETTINI, "Cenni intorno alla Vita ed alle Opere di M. Gioja," 1843.

Giolfino, jol-fee'no, or **Golfino,** gol-fee'no, (NICCOLÒ,) an Italian painter, born at Verona, lived about 1475.

Giolito de' Ferrari, jo-lee'to dà fĕr-rä'ree, (GABRIELE,) a distinguished Venetian printer, whose works are remarkable for the beauty of their typography. He was ennobled by the emperor Charles V. Died in 1581.

Giordani, joR-dä'nee, (VITALE,) a Neapolitan mathematician, born at Bitonto in 1633. He became professor of mathematics in the College di Sapienza, at Rome. Died in 1711.

Giordano, joR-dä'no, (LUCA,) surnamed FA PRESTO, an eminent Italian painter, born at Naples in 1632, was a pupil of Ribera, (Spagnoletto.) He afterwards studied under Pietro da Cortona at Rome, and was distinguished for the skill and rapidity with which he copied the works of the great masters. His father, who was very covetous, was constantly urging him to haste, from which he obtained the sobriquet of Fa Presto, ("Make Haste.") An anecdote is often told of him, that, when painting a picture of the Saviour and the Apostles, his father called him to dinner: "Luke, come down instantly: the soup is getting cold." "I am at your service," he replied: "I have only to make the twelve Apostles." He has been called "the Proteus of Painting," from his admirable imitations of the works of other artists. Being invited to Spain in 1679 by Charles II., he adorned the Escurial with frescos, which rank among his master-pieces. His other principal works are the grand altar-piece in the church of the Ascension at Naples, and a number of frescos at Rome and Florence. Critics, while admitting the wonderful versatility of his genius, deny to him the highest rank in his art, since he never reaches the sublime. Died in 1705.

See STIRLING, "Annals of the Artists of Spain;" LANZI, "History of Painting in Italy;" BELLORI, "Vite de' Pittori;" NAGLER, "Neues Allgemeines Künstler-Lexikon;" "Nouvelle Biographie Générale."

Giordano, (SOFIA,) an Italian portrait-painter, born at Turin in 1779; died in 1829.

Giorgi, joR'jee, (ALESSANDRO,) an Italian scholar and Latin poet, born at Venice in 1747; died in 1779.

Giorgi, (ANTONIO AGOSTINO,) an Italian monk and linguist, born near Rimini in 1711. He wrote a work on the grammar, religion, and history of Thibet, entitled "Alphabetum Thibetanum," (1762.) "His erudition," says the "Biographie Universelle," "is confused, vain, and mendacious." Died in 1797.

See FONTANI, "Elogio del P. Giorgi," 1798.

Giorgi, (DOMENICO,) an Italian antiquary and bibliographer, born in 1690, lived in Rome. Died in 1747.

Giorgini, joR-jee'nee, (GIOVANNI,) an Italian chemist, born at Carpi in 1821. He wrote several able chemical works.

Giorgione, joR-jo'nà, (GIORGIO Barbarelli—bar-bä-rel'lee,) called IL GIORGIONE DI CASTELFRANCO, a celebrated painter, was born at Castelfranco, near Treviso, in 1477. He is considered the founder of the Venetian school. He was a pupil of Giovanni Bellini, and a fellow-student of Titian, who became his rival. Before him no one had possessed so free and firm a touch, so true and rich a colouring. He continued to ennoble his manner, and to present more ample outlines, more animated figures, and bolder foreshortenings. He was an excellent portrait-painter. His pictures are rare, many of his frescos having been injured by the air of Venice. Among his oil-paintings are "The Concert," at Florence, "Christ Allaying the Storm," at Venice, and "Moses Saved from the Water," at Milan. He died at Venice in 1511, aged thirty-four. As a colorist he was equalled only by Titian and perhaps a few artists of a later period. "There have been only seven supreme colorists," says Ruskin, "among the true painters whose works exist, —namely, Giorgione, Titian, Veronese, Tintoret, Correggio, Reynolds, and Turner; but the names of great designers are multitudinous."

See Vasari, "Lives of the Painters," etc.; Lanzi, "History of Painting in Italy;" Mrs. Jameson, "Memoirs of Early Italian Painters;" Carlo Ridolfi, "Vite degli illustri Pittori Veneti," etc., 2 vols., 1648; Ruskin, "Modern Painters."

Gioseffo, the Italian of Josephus, which see.

Giottino, jot-tee'no, (Tommaso **di Stefano** — de stêf'â-no,) or Tommaso di Lappo, an Italian painter, born at Florence in 1324. He was surnamed Giottino because he imitated the manner of Giotto. He painted frescos and oil-pictures, some of which are extant. Died in 1356.

See Vasari, "Lives of the Painters," etc.

Giotto Angiolotto, jot'to ân-jo-lot'to, or **Ambrogiotto,** âm-bro-jot'to, [Lat. Joctus,] (Bondone,) an eminent Florentine painter, born in 1276. He studied under Cimabue, whom he far surpassed in the grace of his figures, harmony of colouring, and the easy flow of his draperies. He is regarded as one of the principal reformers of painting in Italy, and his portraits are characterized by a spirit and fidelity hitherto unknown since the revival of arts. He was also an architect and sculptor, and excelled in mosaics, one of which, called the Navicella, in the church of Saint Peter, is esteemed his master-piece. He numbered among his friends the illustrious Dante, and adorned with paintings the church of Saint Francis, where the great Italian poet was buried. He executed a number of historical pictures in fresco, nearly all of which have been lost. His portraits of Dante and Brunetto Latini are among his best works in that department. Died in 1336.

See Vasari, "Lives of the Painters;" Lanzi, "History of Painting in Italy;" Mrs. Jameson, "Memoirs of Early Italian Painters."

Giovanelli, jo-vä-nel'lee, (Ruggiero,) an Italian composer, born at Velletri about 1560. He succeeded Palestrina as chapel-master at Saint Peter's, Rome, in 1594. He composed masses, motets, etc. He was living in 1615.

Giovanetti, jo-vä-net'tee, (Francesco,) an Italian jurist, born at Bologna; died in 1586.

Giovanetti, (Giacomo,) an eminent Italian jurist and economist, born at Orta (province of Novara) in 1787. He wrote "On the Civil State," ("Sullo Stato civile," 1809,) and "On the Statutes of Novara," ("Degli Statuti Novaresi," 1830,) and other works. Died in 1849.

Giovanni, jo-vân'nee, (or **John,**) an Italian painter, was patronized by the emperor Otho III., whose palace at Aix-la-Chapelle he ornamented with paintings about 1000 A.D.

Giovanni, jo-vân'nee, (or **John,**) of Udine, (oo'de-nä,) an Italian painter, born in 1494, was a student of Raphael. He was particularly known for his pictures of animals and flowers. Died in 1564.

Giovanni da Fiesole. See Fiesole.

Giovanni da San Giovanni. See Manozzi.

Giovanni Pisano, jo-vân'nee pe-sâ'no, an Italian sculptor and architect, erected the Campo Santo at Pisa and the Castello del Novo at Naples. He also designed and executed the monuments of three of the popes, and various other works. Died in 1320.

Giovannini, jo-vân-nee'nee, (Giacomo Maria,) an able engraver, born at Bologna in 1667. He engraved several works of Correggio. Died in 1717.

Giove, the Italian of Jupiter, which see.

Giovenazzi, jo-vä-nât'see, (Vito Maria,) an Italian poet, born in Apulia in 1727; died in Rome in 1805.

Giovene, jo'vä-nà, (Giuseppe Maria,) an Italian naturalist, born at Molfetta in 1753; died in 1837.

Giovini, jo-vee'nee, (Angelo Aurelio Bianchi,) an able Italian historian and journalist, born at Como in 1799. He published a "History of the Hebrews," (1844,) a "History of the Longobards," (1848,) and other works. He became editor of "L'Opinione," a Liberal journal of Turin, in 1848, and of the "Unione" in 1853. In 1852 he began the publication of a "History of the

Popes," of which ten or more volumes have appeared. He was hostile to the papal supremacy. Died in 1862.

See "Nouvelle Biographie Générale."

Giovio, jo've-o, (Benedetto,) a historian and Latin poet, brother of Paolo, noticed below, was born at Como in 1471; died in 1544.

Giovio, (Giovanni Battista,) Count, an Italian writer, born at Como in 1748; died in 1814.

Giovio, [Lat. Jo'vius; Fr. Jove, zhov,] (Paolo,) a celebrated Italian historian, of an ancient family, born at Como in 1483. He was patronized by Leo X. and his successor, Clement VII., who made Giovio Bishop of Nocera and conferred upon him other distinctions. He was also distinguished by the favour of Francis I. and Charles V., and, having amassed a large fortune, built an elegant villa on Lake Como. His principal works are his "Lives of Illustrious Men," ("Elogia Virorum illustrium," (1546,) and "History of his Own Times," (1550,) both written in Latin and remarkable for grace and purity of style. As a historian, he cannot be relied on, since he himself admits in his letters that he wrote to please his patrons, and he was accustomed to say he had two pens,—one of gold, the other of iron. Died at Florence in 1552.

See Vossius, "De Arte historica;" Bayle, "Historical and Critical Dictionary," under Jove; De Thou, "Histoire universelle;" "Nouvelle Biographie Générale."

Giovio, (Paolo,) [Fr. Paul Jove, pôl zhov,] the Younger, a Latin poet and bishop, born at Como about 1530, was a grandson of Benedetto, noticed above. He became Bishop of Nocera in 1560, and was a member of the Council of Trent. He wrote short Latin poems of superior merit. Died about 1585.

Giraldi, je-râl'dee, (Cinzio Giambattista,) an Italian dramatist and littérateur, born at Ferrara in 1504, was for many years professor of medicine and philosophy in his native city. He wrote numerous tragedies, one of which, entitled "Orbecche," is esteemed one of the best dramas of that time. He also published "Gli Hecatomiti," or "The Hundred Novels," which acquired a wide popularity. Died in 1573.

See Tiraboschi, "Storia della Letteratura Italiana."

Giraldi,[Lat. Giral'dus,](Lilio Gregorio,) a learned Italian poet and antiquary, born at Ferrara in 1479. He lived some years in Rome, and was appointed apostolic prothonotary. His chief works are a "History of the Heathen Gods," ("De Diis Gentium,") a "History of Greek and Latin Poets," (1545,) and critical "Dialogues on the Poets of our Times," (1551.) Died in 1552.

See Tiraboschi, "Storia della Letteratura Italiana;" Frizzoli, "De Vita et Operibus L. G. Giraldi," Venice, 1553; De Thou, "Histoire universelle;" Nicéron, "Hommes illustres."

Giraldus. See Giraldi.

GI-räl'dus Cam-bren'sis, sometimes called **Giraldus de Barry,** and **Sylvester Giraldus,** a learned ecclesiastic and historian, born in Pembrokeshire, Wales, about 1146. He studied at the University of Paris, where he became a proficient in rhetoric and civil and canon law. After his return he was appointed one of the chaplains to Henry II., and preceptor to Prince John. Among his principal works are two on the geography of Ireland and of Wales, viz.: "Topographia Hiberniæ" and "Descriptio Cambriæ." As a historian, he shows great learning and research, mingled, however, with superstition. Died about 1220.

See "Edinburgh Review" for July, 1806.

Girard, je-rard' or He-rart', (Albert,) a Dutch mathematician, wrote a "New Invention in Algebra," (1629,) which Montucla called a remarkable work. Died in 1634.

Girard, zhe'râr', (Alexis François,) a French engraver, born at Vincennes in 1789. Among his best works is "The Three Marys at the Tomb," after Ary Scheffer.

Girard, (Balthasar.) See Gerard.

Girard, Baron, a French general, born at Geneva in 1750, served with distinction under Moreau on the Rhine in 1796. For his services at Essling and Wagram, in 1809, he received the title of baron. Died in 1811.

Girard, je-rard', [Fr. pron. zhe'râr',] (Charles,) a naturalist, born at Mülhausen, France, about 1822, was a pupil and assistant of Agassiz. He became about 1850

a resident of Washington, United States, and wrote numerous treatises on fishes, reptiles, etc. He described the reptiles collected by the United States Exploring Expedition.

Girard, (GABRIEL,) one of the most distinguished of French grammarians, born at Clermont-en-Auvergne about 1677. He was appointed royal interpreter for the Russian and Sclavonic languages. His work entitled "French Synonyms" (1736) was received with great favour, and has taken its place among the French classics. Voltaire said, "It will subsist as long as the language, and will even serve to make it subsist." Girard was elected to the French Academy in 1744. Died in 1748.

See D'ALEMBERT, "Éloges des Académiciens."

Girard, (GRÉGOIRE,) called PÈRE GIRARD, a Swiss teacher, born at Freyburg in 1765. He wrote several treatises on education, one of which, called "Educational Course of the Mother-Tongue," ("Cours éducatif de la Langue maternelle," 1840,) obtained the Montyon prize of the French Academy. Died in 1850.

See E. NAVILLE, "Notice biographique sur le Père Girard," 1850; SEVERUS, "G. Girard; ein Character- und Lebensbild," 1853.

Girard, (JEAN,) a French jurist and Latin poet, born at Dijon in 1518; died in 1586.

Girard, (JEAN,) a French veterinary physician, born near Clermont-en-Auvergne in 1770. He wrote the "Anatomy of Domestic Animals," (2 vols., 1807,) and other valuable works. Died in 1852.

Girard, (JEAN BAPTISTE,) a French Jesuit and popular preacher, born at Dole about 1680. His name obtained a scandalous publicity by a charge of sorcery and other crimes, for which he was tried and acquitted in 1731. Died in 1733.

See "Détails historiques sur le Père Girard," etc., Paris, 1845.

Girard, (JEAN BAPTISTE,) a French general, born at Aulps (Var) in 1775, distinguished himself at Austerlitz in 1805, became general of division in 1809, and was killed at Ligny in 1815. "He was one of the most intrepid soldiers of the army," said Napoleon : "he had evidently the sacred fire."

Girard, (JEAN **de Villethierri**—deh vèl'te'ậ're',) a French ecclesiastic, born in Paris in 1641, wrote many excellent treatises on morals and religion. Died in 1709.

See DUPIN, "Bibliothèque des Auteurs ecclésiastiques."

Girard, (PIERRE SIMON,) an eminent French engineer, born at Caen in 1765. He was attached to the expedition to Egypt in 1798, and there obtained data for his valuable treatise "On the Agriculture, Commerce, and Industry of Egypt." He was appointed director of waters at Paris by Napoleon, and admitted into the Institute in 1813. He wrote many treatises on navigable canals. Died in 1836.

See CHARLES DUPIN, "Discours aux Funerailles de Girard;" BOISSARD, "Les Hommes illustres de Calvados;" QUÉRARD, "La France Littéraire."

Gi-rard', (STEPHEN,) a famous merchant and banker, born near Bordeaux, in France, May 24, 1750, was not liberally educated. He became a cabin-boy, a mate, and afterwards master, of a coasting-vessel. About 1776 he settled in Philadelphia as a trader. He eventually owned a fleet of merchant-vessels. When the yellow fever raged in that city in 1793, he distinguished himself by his humane attentions to the sick, whom he nursed in the hospitals. Having purchased the building of the United States Bank, he established in 1812 a private bank, with a capital of $1,200,000, which was increased to $4,000,000. His bank prospered, and his notes were at par when all other paper money was depreciated. "It was the war of 1812," says Parton, "which suspended commerce, that made this merchant so enormously rich. . . . He was the very sheet-anchor of the government credit during the whole of that disastrous war." Although he could sometimes act the part of a benefactor to the community, it is said that he never had a friend. He died, without issue, in 1831, leaving property valued at about $9,000,000, and directed that two millions should be applied to found a college for orphan boys, which was commenced in 1833 and opened in 1848. The main building of this college is considered the most admirable specimen of Grecian

architecture in America. It is one hundred and sixty-nine feet long, by one hundred and eleven feet wide, and is surrounded by a portico of thirty-four columns, each fifty-five feet high and six feet in diameter.

See PARTON, "Famous Americans of Recent Times," 1867, "North American Review" for January, 1865; FREEMAN HUNT, "Lives of American Merchants," vol. i.

Girard, de, deh zhe'rȧr', (PHILIPPE HENRI,) a French engineer and inventor, born in Vaucluse in 1775. He made some improvements in the steam-engine, and, according to a French biographer, produced rotary motion without a working-beam, (1806.) In 1810 he invented a useful machine for spinning flax, for which the jury of the Exposition of National Industry awarded him a gold medal in 1844. His friends claim for him the invention of the steam-gun, which is also ascribed to Perkins. He invented other machines, and owned or directed extensive manufactories of flax in France, Austria, and Poland. Died in Paris in 1845.

See ÉMILE DESCHAMPS, "Notice biographique sur P. de Girard Inventeur, etc.," 1853; CHAPSAL, "P. de Girard," 1853; "Nouvelle Biographie Générale."

Girardet, zhe'rȧr'dā', (ABRAHAM,) a Swiss engraver, born at Locle in 1764. He engraved the "Transfiguration," after Raphael, and the "Rape of the Sabine Women," after Poussin. Died in Paris in 1823.

Girardet, (CHARLES,) a Swiss painter, of high reputation, born at Locle about 1808. He called himself KARL to distinguish himself from his father, Charles, who was an engraver. He produced a capital picture of "Protestants surprised at Meeting," (1842,) and some Swiss and Italian landscapes.

See "Nouvelle Biographie Générale."

Girardet, (ÉDOUARD,) a Swiss painter of genre, and engraver, a brother of the preceding, was born at Neufchâtel in 1819. He travelled in Egypt with his brother Karl, and worked in Paris. He represents Swiss scenery, manners, and costumes with success.

His brother PAUL, an engraver, was born in 1821. His master-piece is "Washington Crossing the Delaware," after Leutze.

Girardet, zhe'rȧr'dā', (JEAN,) a French historical painter, born at Lunéville in 1709, received the title of first painter to Stanislas, ex-King of Poland. Died in 1778.

See NAGLER, "Neues Allgemeines Künstler-Lexikon."

Girardi, je-raR'dee, (MICHELE,) an Italian anatomist, born at Limone, on Lake Garda, in 1731. He was professor of anatomy at Padua and Parma. He edited a magnificent edition of the "Plates of Santorini," (1775.) Died in 1797.

Girardin. See SAINT-MARC GIRARDIN.

Girardin, zhe'rȧr'dȧn', (JEAN PIERRE LOUIS,) an eminent French chemist, born in Paris in 1803, was a pupil of Thénard. He became in 1828 professor of chemistry applied to the arts, at Rouen. He published, besides other works, "Lectures on Elementary Chemistry," (1835,) which obtained two medals at Paris, "Memoirs of Applied Chemistry," and a "Treatise on Agriculture," (2 vols., 1852.) About 1858 he accepted a chair at Lille.

Girardin, de, deh zhe'rȧr'dȧn',(ALEXANDRE,)COMTE, a son of René Louis, noticed below, born in 1776, distinguished himself at Austerlitz, in Spain, Russia, etc., and became a general of division in 1814. Died in 1855.

Girardin, de, (DELPHINE GAY,) a popular authoress, born at Aix-la-Chapelle in January, 1804, was a daughter of Sophie Gay, noticed in this work. Her verses entitled "The Sisters of Saint Camille" (1822) gained a prize of the French Academy. She produced in 1824 a volume of "Essais poétiques." Her beauty and esprit rendered her a popular favourite. She was married to Émile de Girardin in 1831, after which she wrote "The Quiz," ("Le Lorgnon," 1832,) and other romances, among which is "The Cane of M. de Balzac," ("La Canne de M. de Balzac," 1836.) Her reputation was increased by the sparkling and charming prattle of her "Lettres Parisiennes," which appeared in "La Presse" from 1836 to 1848. Died in Paris in 1855.

See SAINTE-BEUVE, "Causeries du Lundi," February, 1851; LAMARTINE, "Cours familier de Littérature;" "Foreign Quarterly Review" for January, 1844.

Girardin, de, (ÉMILE,) an enterprising French journalist, a natural son of Count Alexandre de Girardin, was born in Paris about 1804. He founded in 1831 the "Journal des Connaissances utiles," and made some efforts for the diffusion of cheap literature among the masses. In 1836 he founded "La Presse," a daily paper, (at forty francs per annum, about half the usual price,) which he conducted with great ability and success until 1856. He killed Armand Carrel in a duel in 1836. He was elected a deputy several times, and supported nearly all parties in turn. The abdication of Louis Philippe is ascribed to the influence of Girardin, who attempted to secure the succession for the Comte de Paris. He opposed Napoleon III. after his usurpation of imperial power, December, 1851. He afterwards became editor of the paper "La Liberté."

See LARCHER, "Emile de Girardin, son Enfance," etc., 1849; P. FOREST, "Biographie d'É. de Girardin," 1842; "Nouvelle Biographie Générale."

Girardin, de, (ERNEST STANISLAS,) a son of the following, was born in Paris in 1803. He became in 1848 a moderate member of the Legislative Assembly. In 1852 he was made a senator.

Girardin, de, (LOUIS STANISLAS CÉCILE XAVIER,) COMTE, a French officer, born at Lunéville in 1762, was a son of René Louis, noticed below. He was educated partly by J. J. Rousseau. As a deputy to the Legislative Assembly, 1791-92, he acted with the Constitutional party. He became a member of the Tribunat in 1800, and a general of brigade in the army of Joseph Bonaparte in Spain about 1808. After the restoration he was a Liberal member of the Chamber of Deputies. He left, besides political tracts, "Journal and Souvenirs, Speeches and Opinions," (2 vols., 1828.) Died in 1827.

See VATOUT, "Hommage à la Mémoire de S. Girardin," 1827; "Nouvelle Biographie Générale."

Girardin, de, (RENÉ LOUIS,) MARQUIS, born in Paris in 1735, was a friend of the celebrated Rousseau, to whom he gave a retreat on his beautiful domain of Ermenonville. He wrote, besides other works, a treatise "On the Composition of Landscapes," (1777,) which was translated into several languages. Died in 1808.

See QUÉRARD, "La France Littéraire."

Girardon, zhe'rǎr'dòn', (FRANÇOIS,) an eminent French sculptor, born at Troyes in 1630. He studied at Rome, and after his return was distinguished by the favour of Louis XIV., being successively appointed professor, rector, and chancellor of the Academy of Painting and Sculpture. Among his master-pieces may be named the sculptures of the "Fountain of Pyramids" and the four principal figures of the "Bath of Apollo" at Versailles, the "Mausoleum of Cardinal Richelieu," and the "Rape of Proserpine." He enjoyed the friendship and patronage of the great painter Le Brun. Died in 1715.

See "Nouvelle Biographie Générale."

Giraud, zhe'rō', (CHARLES JOSEPH BARTHÉLEMY,) a French jurist, born at Pernes in 1802. He was minister of public instruction in 1851, soon after which he became professor of Roman law in the Faculty of Paris.

Giraud, (GIOVANNI,) COUNT, a celebrated Italian dramatist, of French extraction, born at Rome in 1776. He produced a number of successful comedies, (4 vols., 1808.) The most popular of these is entitled "The Tutor in a Quandary," ("L'Ajo nell' Imbarazzo," 1807.) He excels in comic power and vivacity. Died in 1834.

See TIPALDO, "Biografia degli Italiani illustri;" "Nouvelle Biographie Générale."

Giraud, (PIERRE,) a French cardinal, born at Montferrand in 1791. He became Archbishop of Cambrai in 1841, and a cardinal in 1847. Died in 1850.

See J. P. FABER, "Biographie du Cardinal Giraud," 1850.

Giraud, (PIERRE FRANÇOIS,) a French sculptor, born at Luc, in Provence, in 1783, gained the grand prize in 1806 for his "Wounded Philoctetus." Died in 1836.

Giraud, (PIERRE FRANÇOIS EUGÈNE,) a French painter and engraver, born in Paris in 1806.

Girault de Saint-Fargeau, zhe'rō' deh sǎN'fǎR'zhō', (EUSÈBE,) a French *littérateur*, born in Yonne in 1799. He published a "Geographical and Historical Dictionary of all the Communes of France," (3 vols., 1846-47,) and other works.

Girault-Duvivier, zhe'rō' dü've've-à', (CHARLES PIERRE,) a French grammarian, born in Paris in 1765. He published an "Analysis of the Best Treatises on French Grammar," (2 vols., 1811,) which was approved by the French Academy in 1814. Died in 1832.

Girey-Dupré, zhe'rǎ' dü'prǎ', (JOSEPH MARIE,) a French Girondist, born in Paris in 1769, assisted Brissot in the "Patriote Français." He was executed in November, 1793.

Girod-Chantrans, zhe'rō' shòN'tRòN', (JUSTIN,) a French naturalist, born at Besançon in 1750; died in 1841. He wrote several scientific works.

Girod de l'Ain, (AMÉDÉE,) BARON, an able French advocate and legislator, born at Gex (Ain) in 1781. He was elected president of the Chamber of Deputies in 1831, and was president of the council of state from 1832 until 1847. Died in 1847.

Girodet-Trioson, zhe'rō'dǎ' tRe'o'zòN', (ANNE LOUIS,) a celebrated French painter, born at Montargis in 1767. He studied for a time under David, and subsequently at Rome, where he produced his "Dream of Endymion," and several other pictures. Among his master-pieces we may name "Pygmalion and Galatea," a "Scene from the Deluge," and "The Revolt of Cairo." His works are characterized by great excellence of design, but they are frequently disfigured by extravagance and are deficient in animation. Girodet was an officer of the legion of honour, and a member of the Academy of Painting. Died in 1824.

See P. A. COUPIN, "Notice nécrologique sur la Vie, etc. de Girodet," 1825; QUATREMÈRE DE QUINCY, "Éloge de Girodet," 1825; "Nouvelle Biographie Générale."

Giron. See OSUNA.

Giron de Loaysa, He-ròn' dà lo-i'sà, (GARCIAS,) a learned Spanish prelate, born at Talavera in 1542. He became almoner to Philip II. of Spain in 1585, and Archbishop of Toledo in 1598. Died in 1599.

Gironi, je-ro'nee, (ROBUSTIANO,) an Italian antiquary, born near Milan in 1769; died in 1838.

Girou de Buzareingues, zhe'roo' deh bü'zà'rǎng', (LOUIS FRANÇOIS CHARLES,) a French physiologist and writer on agriculture, born in 1773; died in 1856.

Giroust, zhe'roo', (JACQUES,) a French Jesuit and pulpit orator, born at Beaufort, in Anjou, in 1624; died in 1689.

Girs, yĕĕrs ?(GILES, or ÆGIDIUS,) a Swedish chronicler, born in Södermannland about 1580, wrote a work entitled "Chronicles of Gustavus I. and Eric XIV.," ("Gustaf I. och Eric XIV. Chrönicor," 1670.) Died in 1639.

Girtanner, gĕĕR'tǎn'ner, (CHRISTOPH,) a Swiss physician, born at Saint Gall in 1760. Among his works is a "Treatise on Venereal Diseases," (1794.) Died in 1800.

Gir'tin, (THOMAS,) an English artist, born in 1773. Among his works are a collection of "Views in Paris." Died in 1802.

Giry, zhe're', (FRANÇOIS,) a learned French ecclesiastic and philanthropist, son of Louis, noticed below, was born in Paris in 1635. He was the author of a number of religious works. Died in 1688.

See RAFFRON, "Vie du P. Giry," 1691.

Giry, (LOUIS,) a French translator, born in Paris in 1595. He was a member of the French Academy. Among his versions, which were received with favour, were those of Plato's "Crito," Plato's "Apology for Socrates," and ten books of Saint Augustine's "Civitas Dei." Died in 1665.

See PELLISSON, "Histoire de l'Académie Française."

Gisbert, zhĕs'baiR', (BLAISE,) a French Jesuit and pulpit orator, born at Cahors in 1657. He was the author of "Christian Eloquence in Theory and Practice," and other works. Died in 1731.

Gisbert, (JEAN,) a French Jesuit, born at Cahors in 1639, became professor of theology and principal of the Jesuits' College at Toulouse. He was the author of a work entitled "Antiprobabilismus," etc., which is eulogized by Dupin. Died in 1711.

See DUPIN, "Bibliothèque des Auteurs ecclésiastiques," etc.

Gis'borne, (THOMAS,) an English divine and poet, born at Derby in 1758. He became perpetual curate of Barton-under-Needwood, Staffordshire, in 1783, and prebendary of Durham in 1826. His principal works are

---

ₑ as *k; ç* as *s; ḡ hard; ġ* as *j;* G, H, K, *guttural;* N, *nasal;* R, *trilled;* ŝ as *z;* ᵺh as in *this.* (☞See Explanations, p. 23.)

" Principles of Moral Philosophy," (1789,) " Walks in a Forest, or Poems," (1794,) " Duties of the Female Sex," (14th edition, 1847,) and sermons, which were commended by Robert Hall. Died in 1846.

See "Gentleman's Magazine" for June, 1846.

Gis′co, [Gr. Γίσκων or Γέσκων; Fr. GISCON, zhĕs′kŏN′,] a Carthaginian general, who commanded in Sicily in 338 B.C.

Gisco, a Carthaginian general, who at the end of the first Punic war, 241 B.C., took command of the army in Sicily. On their arrival in Africa his troops mutinied and commenced the civil war called "the Inexpiable." Gisco, having been sent to negotiate with the rebels, was seized by them and put to death about 239 B.C.

Giseke, ḡee′zeh-keh, or **Giesecke,** (NIKOLAUS DIETRICH,) a German poet, born in Hungary in 1724. He became court preacher at Quedlinburg, and superintendent at Sondershausen. He wrote religious and lyric poems, which were favourably received. Died in 1765.

Giseke, (PAUL DIETRICH,) a German botanist and physician, born at Hamburg in 1745 ; died in 1796.

Gismondi, jès-mon′dee, (CARLO GIUSEPPE,) an Italian mineralogist, born at Mentone in 1762 ; died in 1824.

Gisors, zhe′zor′, (ALPHONSE HENRI,) born in Paris in 1796, was appointed architect of the Palais du Luxembourg in 1834. Among his works are the Normal School, Paris, (1842,) and the chamber of the senate. He became a member of the Institute.

Gī-tī′a-das, [Gr. Γιτιάδας,] a Lacedæmonian architect, statuary, and poet, flourished about 520 B.C. He completed the temple of Athena Poliouchos at Sparta, and adorned it with a bronze statue of the goddess.

Giudici, joo′de-chee, (CARLO MARIA,) an Italian painter and sculptor, born in the province of Milan in 1723, was the master of Andrea Appiani. Among his works is a bas-relief of " Adam and Eve expelled from Eden." Died in 1804.

Giulay. See GYULAI.

Giuliano, (MAJANO DI.) See MAJANO.

Giulini, joo-lee′nee, (GIORGIO,) an Italian historical writer, born at Milan in 1714. He displayed great erudition and good judgment in a work on the mediæval history of Milan and the Milanese, " Memorie spettanti alla Storia, al Governo ed alla Descrizione della Citta e della Campagna di Milano ne' Secoli bassi," (9 vols., 1760–75.) Died in 1780.

See FABRONI, "Vitæ Italorum doctrina excellentium."

Giulio Romano, joo′le-o ro-mä′no, sometimes also written **Julio Romano,** [Fr. JULES ROMAIN, zhül ro′mäN′,] or **Giulio Pipi,** joo′le-o pee′pee, a celebrated Italian painter and architect, born in Rome in 1492. He was a student and intimate friend of Raphael, of whom he became the principal heir. After the death of his preceptor he completed several works which that great artist had left unfinished. He was also employed by Pope Clement VII. as architect of a palace. He was liberally patronized by the Duke of Mantua, in whose saloon he painted his greatest work, a representation of the Giants struck by the Thunderbolts of Jupiter. The designs of Giulio display great powers of invention and uncommon sublimity of thought ; but his colouring is dry and defective. As an architect, he stood so high that upon the death of San Gallo he was appointed to superintend the construction of Saint Peter's at Rome ; but he died in 1546, before reaching that city. About two hundred and fifty of Giulio's best designs have been engraved, one of which is the " Triumph of Titus and Vespasian."

See VASARI, "Lives of the Painters," etc. ; LANZI, "History of Painting in Italy ;" " Nouvelle Biographie Générale," under PIPPI.

Giunone. See JUNO.

Giunta, joon′tä, sometimes called **Zonta,** dzon′tä, (FILIPPO,) an Italian printer, born in Florence in 1450. In company with his son Bernardo, he established presses in Florence, Geneva, and Venice. Their editions of the Greek authors were highly valued. Filippo died in 1519, Bernardo in 1551.

Giunta da Pisa, joon′tä dä pee′sä, a painter of the Florentine school, flourished between 1210 and 1240.

He painted frescos at Pisa and Assisi. He was perhaps the best artist of his epoch.

See VASARI, "Lives of the Painters," etc.

Giuntino, joon-tee′no, or **Giuntini,** joon-tee′nee, (FRANCESCO,) an Italian astronomer, born at Florence in 1523. He became a Protestant, and settled at Lyons, where he died in 1590.

Giusti, joos′tee, (ANTONIO,) an Italian painter of the Florentine school, born in 1624. He painted landscapes and animals with success. Died in 1705.

Giusti, (GIUSEPPE,) an eminent Italian satiric poet, born near Pescia in 1809. He published in 1835 a poem "On the Death of Francis I.," which caused a great sensation. This was succeeded by the " Dies Iræ," " Health-Drinking to the Weathercock," (" Il Brindisi di Girella,") " The Humanitarians," (" Gli Umanitari,") and other caustic satires on the political and social vices of the day. An adherent of moderate liberalism, he was equally severe on the oppressors of his country and on the so-called party of Young Italy. He became a member of the Tuscan Chamber of Deputies in 1848. Giusti numbered among his friends Capponi, Manzoni, and D'Azeglio. Died in 1850.

See "Giuseppe Giusti and his Times," 1864, by SUSAN HORNER; "North British Review" for November, 1864.

Giustiniani, joos-te-ne-ä′nee, written also **Justiniani,** (AGOSTINO,) a learned ecclesiastic, born at Genoa in 1470. He was profoundly versed in biblical literature and the Oriental tongues, and published an edition of the Psalter in Hebrew, Greek, Arabic, and Chaldee, with three Latin interpretations and glosses, being the first polyglot edition of the Scriptures. He was invited to Paris by Francis I., who conferred on him a pension and appointed him professor of Oriental languages in the university of that city. He was made Bishop of Nebbio, in Corsica, in 1514. He was lost at sea in 1536, while going from Genoa to Corsica.

See TIRABOSCHI, "Storia della Letteratura Italiana ;" BAYLE, "Historical and Critical Dictionary ;" P. GIOVIO, " Elogia Virorum illustrium."

Giustiniani or **Justiniani,** (BERNARDO,) a Venetian statesman and historian, of a noble family, born in 1408. He was employed on several important embassies, and rose through various preferments to be a member of the Council of Ten, and procurator of Saint Mark, the highest office in the republic next to that of doge. He wrote a " History of Venice," (in Latin,) which is highly valued for its accuracy. It was left unfinished. Died in 1489.

See STELLA, "Vita di Bernardo Giustiniani," 1553.

Giustiniani or **Justiniani,** (FABIAN,) Bishop of Ajaccio, born in Genoa about 1578 ; died in 1627. He wrote a Biblical concordance.

Giustiniani or **Justiniani,** (GERONIMO,) a poet, born at Genoa about 1560. He wrote "Jephthah," a tragedy, (1583,) and translated the "Ajax Furiosus" of Sophocles into Italian, (1603.)

Giustiniani or **Justiniani,** (LORENZO,) [Lat. LAUREN′TIUS JUSTINIA′NUS ; Fr. LAURENT JUSTINIEN, lŏ′rŏN′ zhüs′te′ne′äN′,] SAINT, first Patriarch of Venice, was born at Venice in 1380. He became patriarch in 1451, and died in 1465, leaving many sermons and letters.

See BERNARDO GIUSTINIANI, "Sancti L. Justiniani Vita," 1475; JOHANN PETER SILBERT, " Leben des heiligen L. Justiniani," 1836.

Giustiniani, (LORENZO,) an Italian bibliographer, born in 1761. He became keeper of the Royal Library at Naples in 1815. Among his works are a "Geographical Dictionary of the Kingdom of Naples," (13 vols., 1797 –1816,) and " Historical and Critical Memoirs of the Royal Library (Borbonica) of Naples," (1818.) Died in 1824.

Giustiniani or **Justiniani,** (MARCANTONIO,) was Doge of Venice from 1684 until 1688, during which time the Venetians conquered the Morea from the Turks. Died in 1688.

Giustiniani or **Justiniani,** (MICHELE,) born at Genoa in 1612, wrote "Memorable Letters," (" Lettere memorabili," 3 vols., 1675.) Died about 1680.

Giustiniani or **Justiniani,** (ORSATTO,) a Venetian poet and nobleman, born in 1538. He produced, besides other poems, a poetical version of the " Œdipus Tyrannus" of Sophocles, (1585.) Died in 1603.

ā, ē, ī, ō, ū, ȳ, *long;* ă, ĕ, ĭ, ŏ, ŭ, ў, *short;* ạ, ẹ, ị, ọ, *obscure;* fär, fâll, fåt; mĕt; nŏt; gŏŏd; mōōn;

Giustiniani or **Justiniani**, (PIETRO,) a Venetian senator and historian. He published, in 1576, a Latin "History of Venice."

Giustiniani or **Justiniani**, (POMPEIO,) an Italian general, born in Corsica in 1569, was appointed governor or commandant of Candia by the Venetians. He was killed in 1616.

Givry, de, dẹh zhèv're', (ANNE d'Anglure—dǒn'-glür',) a celebrated French captain, born about 1560, was a faithful adherent of Henry IV., for whom he fought against the League. He was killed at the siege of Laon in 1594.

Gjallar-horn. See HEIMDALL.

Gjöranson, jö'rän-son, (JOHAN,) a Swedish divine and antiquary, born about 1712; died in 1769.

Gjörwell, jör'well, (KARL KRISTOFER,) a Swedish editor, born at Landscrona in 1731. He founded the "Swedish Mercury," (1755,) and was the first who edited literary and critical journals in Sweden. Died in 1811.

See "Biographiskt-Lexicon öfver namnkunnige Svenska Män."

Glaber, glȧ'bẹr, (RODULPHE,) a French chronicler of the eleventh century. He wrote a chronicle of events from 900 A.D. to 1046, which is of some value.

Glabrio. See ACILIUS.

Gladbach, glȧt'bȧk, (GEORG JAKOB,) a German naturalist, born at Frankfort-on-the-Main in 1736, wrote a "Treatise on Butterflies," (1777.) Died in 1796.

Glad'den, (A. H.,) an American general, born in South Carolina. He served as an officer in the Mexican war, (1846–47.) Having taken arms against the Union, he was killed at Shiloh in April, 1862.

Gladstone, glad'stọn, (Sir JOHN,) a British merchant, born in Scotland about 1764. He became an eminent citizen and successful merchant of Liverpool, which he represented in Parliament. Died in 1852.

Gladstone, (The Right Hon. WILLIAM EW'ART,) an eminent English statesman, financier, orator, and author, a younger son of the preceding, was born in Liverpool, December 29, 1809. In 1831 he graduated at Christ Church, Oxford, as a double first-class,—that is, with the highest excellence in classics and mathematics. He was elected to Parliament by the Conservatives of Newark in 1832, and appointed a lord of the treasury by Sir Robert Peel in December, 1834. On the accession of the Whigs, in April, 1835, he retired from office. In 1838 he published "The State in its Relations with the Church," an argument in favour of the union of church and state, which, says Macaulay, "though not a good book, shows more talent than many good books. It contains some eloquent and ingenious passages. It bears the signs of much patient thought." ("Edinburgh Review" for April, 1839.) He married a daughter of Sir Stephen R. Glynne in 1839.

On the formation of a new ministry by Sir Robert Peel in 1841, Mr. Gladstone became vice-president of the board of trade, and master of the mint. He distinguished himself in this position by his financial skill and knowledge of commercial affairs, and was made president of the board of trade in May, 1843. He was appointed secretary for the colonies in 1845, and supported Sir Robert Peel in the repeal of the corn-laws in 1846.

In 1847 he was elected as representative of Oxford University in Parliament. Having differed from his party on several important questions, and having become identified with the Conservative Liberals, or Peelites, he entered the coalition ministry of Lord Aberdeen, as chancellor of the exchequer, in December, 1852. A short time after the accession of Palmerston as premier, in February, 1855, Mr. Gladstone resigned, with several other Peelites. He co-operated with Cobden and others in 1855 in their efforts to terminate the Crimean war; and he strenuously opposed the Chinese war in 1857. He declined to take office in the ministry of Lord Derby in 1858, but accepted an embassy as commissioner to the Ionian Isles in that year. In June, 1859, he was appointed chancellor of the exchequer in the cabinet of Palmerston. His humane aversion to war and his partiality for free trade and frugality inclined him to act with the Liberal party and the Manchester school. He is considered the greatest of British financiers, and as an orator has probably no equal in the House of Commons except John Bright. His speech of four hours on the Budget of 1860 was a wonderful union of reasoning and declamation. Commenting on this speech, the "London Quarterly Review" for April, 1860, declares, "We find ourselves in the enchanted region of pure Gladstonism,—that terrible combination of relentless logic and dauntless imagination. We soar into the empyrean of finance. Everything is on a colossal scale of grandeur,—all-embracing free-trade, abysses of deficit, and mountains of income-tax."

He continued to represent Oxford University until 1865, when he was defeated by the Tory candidate. After the death of Lord Palmerston he became the leader of the House of Commons, and retained the office of chancellor of the exchequer under Earl Russell. Russell and Gladstone introduced a bill for electoral reform, on which the latter made a great speech, April 28, 1866. This bill having been defeated, the ministers resigned in June, 1866. He advocated the disestablishment and disendowment of the Episcopal Church of Ireland, which was opposed by Disraeli and the Tories. After a long debate on this measure, Gladstone's resolution was passed, by a majority of sixty-five, on the 1st of May, 1868; but Disraeli, though defeated, would not resign, and the question became the chief issue in the next election. The Liberal party having gained a large majority in the general election of November, Mr. Gladstone became prime minister, December 4, 1868. He appointed Sir William Page Wood lord chancellor; Robert Lowe, chancellor of the exchequer; Lord Clarendon, secretary for foreign affairs; and John Bright, president of the board of trade. He brought in a bill to disestablish the Irish Church, which passed the House of Commons by a majority of one hundred and fourteen about May 31, but was mutilated in the House of Lords by important amendments, which the Commons rejected after Mr. Gladstone had made a great speech on the subject. This resistance of the peers to the will of the majority of the nation caused great excitement, and a dangerous crisis seemed to be imminent; but in July, 1869, a compromise was effected, and the bill of Mr. Gladstone, slightly modified, was adopted by the House of Lords. This compromise did not affect the principle of the bill, which the London "Times" calls "the greatest and boldest act of legislation of modern times."

Among his important publications is "Studies on Homer and the Homeric Age," (3 vols., 1858.) "A more attractive composition, on the one hand, so far as taste and feeling are concerned,—one more unsatisfactory, on the other, as a critical essay, the product of accurate learning,—it is scarcely possible to imagine. Under the first point of view, the volumes well deserve the great admiration, not to say enthusiasm, which they have excited, especially among younger and fresher readers." ("Edinburgh Review," October, 1858.) In 1869 appeared his "Juventus Mundi: the Gods and Men of the Heroic Age." As prime minister, Mr. Gladstone may be said to be one of the most popular and influential that ever ruled England.

See "The Four Reform Orators," in the "London Quarterly Review" for April, 1867; J. McGILCHRIST, "Life of W. E. Gladstone," 1869; SAMUEL SMILES, "Brief Biographies;" "London Quarterly Review" for December, 1839; "Edinburgh Review" for October, 1858; "Blackwood's Magazine" for August, 1858; "British Quarterly" for July, 1869.

Glafey, glȧ'fī, (ADAM FRIEDRICH,) a German publicist, born at Reichenbach in 1692, became archivist at the court of Dresden in 1726. Among his works are "The Kernel (Kern) of the History of Saxony," (1722,) and a "History of the Law of Nature," (1739.) Died in 1753.

See HIRSCHING, "Historisch-literarisches Handbuch."

Glaire, glâR, (JEAN BAPTISTE,) a French theologian and Orientalist, born at Bordeaux in 1798. He became professor of Hebrew at the Sorbonne in 1841, and in 1845 councillor of the University. He published a "Hebrew and Chaldee Hand-Lexicon," (1830,) an "Arabic Concordance of the Koran," and other valuable works.

Glaize, glẹz, (AUGUSTE BARTHÉLEMY,) a French painter, born at Montpellier about 1812. He worked in Paris, and gained a first medal in 1854.

Glandorp, glân'dorp, (JOHANN,) a German philologist, born at Münster, learned languages under Melanch-

e as k; ç as s; ğ hard; ġ as j; G, H, K, guttural; N, nasal; R, trilled; ŝ as z; th as in this. (☞ See Explanations, p. 23.)

66

thon. He became professor of history at Marburg in 1560, and published "Onomasticon Historiæ Romanæ," (1589,) and other works. Died in 1564.

See REINECCIUS, "Vita Glandorpii."

Glanvil, (BARTHOLOMEW.) See BARTHOLOMÆUS DE GLANVILLE.

Glan'vil, (Sir JOHN,) an able English lawyer, born about 1590, was speaker of Parliament in 1640. Having become a partisan of Charles I., he was imprisoned by the dominant party from 1645 to 1648. He died in 1661, and left "Reports of Cases of Controverted Elections."

See PRINCE'S "Worthies of Devon."

Glanvil, (JOHN,) an English poet, grandson of the preceding, born in 1664. He made the first English translation of Fontenelle's "Plurality of Worlds," and published a number of poems. Died in 1735.

Glan'vil or **Glan'vill,** (JOSEPH,) an eminent English divine, born at Plymouth in 1636. Having taken his degree at Oxford University, he published in 1661 a work entitled "The Vanity of Dogmatizing," in which he assails the system of Aristotle. In 1665 he published his "Scepsis Scientifica," etc., a remodelling of the former treatise, which is commended by Hallam. About the same time he was elected a Fellow of the Royal Society. He was a believer in witchcraft, and published, among other works, "Philosophic Considerations touching the Being of Witches," etc. Died at Bath in 1680.

See WOOD, "Athenæ Oxonienses;" "Retrospective Review," vol. i., 1853; "Biographia Britannica."

Glan'ville, de, (RANULPHUS or RALPH,) an eminent English lawyer, became chief justiciary of the kingdom under Henry II. He is supposed to have been the author of one of the earliest legal treatises that appeared in England. Having accompanied Richard I. to Palestine, he lost his life at the siege of Acre in 1190.

See FOSS, "The Judges of England," vol. i.

Glaph'ў-ra, [Gr. Γλαφύρα,] daughter of Archelaus, King of Cappadocia, was successively married to Alexander, son of Herod and Mariamne, Juba, King of Libya, and Archelaus, son of Herod. Died 7 A.D.

Glap'thorne or **Glap'thorn,** (HENRY,) an English dramatic poet of the time of Charles I. He was the author of "Albertus Wallenstein," a tragedy, "The Hollander," a comedy, and other plays, which were popular in their time.

See BAKER, "Biographia Dramatica;" "Retrospective Review," vol. x., 1824.

Glareanus, glä-re-ä'nûs, (HENRICUS LORITUS,) a Swiss poet, musician, and scholar, born at Glarus in 1488, was a friend of Erasmus. In 1512 he was crowned as poet-laureate by the emperor Maximilian. He founded a school for belles-lettres at Friburg, in Brisgau, and acquired a high reputation by his vast erudition. Among his chief works are "Annotations in Titum Livium," (1540,) and a valuable treatise on music, entitled "Dodecachordon," (1547.) Died at Friburg in 1563.

See H. SCHREIBER, "H. L. Glareanus, gekrönter Dichter," etc., 1837; ERASMUS, "Epistolæ XVIII.;" M. ADAM, "Vitæ Philosophorum Germanorum;" G. VOSSIUS, "De Scientiis Mathematicis."

Glaser, glä'zer, (CHRISTOPH,) a Swiss chemist, born at Bâle, was apothecary to Louis XIV. of France. He published a "Treatise on Chemistry," (1663,) which was often reprinted.

See F. HOEFER, "Histoire de la Chimie."

Glaser, glä'zer, (JOHANN FRIEDRICH,) a German physician and chemist, born in 1707; died in 1789.

Glass or **Glas,** (JOHN,) a Scottish clergyman, born in Fifeshire in 1695, is noted as the founder of a sect called Glassites. For his opposition to some of the principles of the Church of Scotland, he was deprived of his benefice in 1728. His sect were afterwards called Sandemanians. Died in 1773. He left works published in 4 vols., 1762.

See CHAMBERS, "Biographical Dictionary of Eminent Scotsmen."

Glass, (JOHN,) a son of the preceding, born at Dundee in 1725. He became captain of a merchant-ship, and on a voyage from Brazil to London was murdered by his crew, in 1765. He left a "Description of Teneriffe."

Glass, gläs, [Lat. GLAS'SIUS,] (SOLOMON,) a German Lutheran divine, eminent as a biblical critic, was born at

Sondershausen in 1593. He became professor of theology at Jena, and superintendent of the churches and schools of Saxe-Gotha. His principal work is "Sacred Philology, in which the Style, Literature, and Signification of the Holy Scriptures are unfolded," ("Philologia Sacra qua S. Scripturæ Stylus Litteratura et Sensus expanditur," 1623,) which was highly esteemed and often reprinted. Died in 1656.

See "Nouvelle Biographie Générale."

Glassbrenner, glâs'bRĕn-nẹr, (ADOLF,) a German satirist, born at Berlin in 1810. He wrote, among other humorous works, "Berlin as it Eats and Drinks," (1832,) and "Pictures and Dreams from Vienna," (1836.)

Glassius. See GLASS, (SOLOMON.)

Glauber, glŏw'bẹr, (JOHANN,) a distinguished landscape-painter, sometimes called POLYDORE, was born at Utrecht in 1646. His pictures are chiefly representations of Italian and Alpine scenery. Died in 1726.

Glauber, (JOHANN GOTTLIEB,) a landscape-painter, surnamed MYRTILL, born in 1656, was a brother of the preceding. Died in Breslau in 1703.

Glauber, glau'bẹr or glŏw'bẹr, (JOHANN RUDOLPH,) a German chemist, born at Karlstadt about 1604, was a professor of alchemy. He lived at Frankfort, Cologne, and Amsterdam. He made several useful discoveries, among which was the salt that bears his name, and made improvements in chemical apparatus. Between 1646 and 1668 he published numerous Latin and German works, among which is "Miraculum Mundi," (1653.) Died in Amsterdam in 1668.

See F. HOEFER, "Histoire de la Chimie."

Glaucia, glau'she-ạ, (CAIUS SERVIL'IUS,) a Roman demagogue, contemporary with L. Apuleius Saturninus, whose fate he shared about 99 B.C. (See SATURNINUS.)

Glau'çi-as, [Γλαυκίας,] a Greek sculptor of Egina, flourished about 480 B.C.

Glaucias, a king of the Illyrians in the time of Alexander the Great.

Glau'con, [Γλαύκων,] a Greek philosopher, a brother of Plato, lived about 400 B.C. He was one of the interlocutors in the "Republic" of Plato, and in the "Parmenides."

Glaucus, [Gr. Γλαύκος,] a prophetic marine deity of Greek mythology. According to one tradition, he was originally a fisherman, who obtained immortality by eating a certain herb. He built the ship Argo, and accompanied the Argonautæ to Colchis.

See KEIGHTLEY'S "Mythology."

Glaucus, a Greek statuary, born at Chios, (Scio,) lived in the sixth century B.C. He is said to have invented the art of soldering metals.

See MEYER, "Kunstgeschichte."

Glaucus, a son of Minos, while a child fell into a vessel of honey and was smothered. The poets feigned that he was restored to life by Polyidus, a soothsayer.

Gleditsch, glä'ditsh, (JOHANN GOTTLIEB,) an eminent German botanist, born at Leipsic in 1714. He was appointed professor of anatomy, and director of the botanic garden at Berlin, in 1740. His chief merit was that he applied botany to rural economy. He published, besides other works, a "System of Plants founded on the Position of the Stamens," (in Latin, 1764,) "Essays on Physics, Botany, and Economy," (3 vols., 1767,) and an "Introduction to Forest Science," (1774.) Died in 1786.

See WILLDENOW and USTERI, "Biographie des Hofrath und Professor Gleditsch," 1790; "Biographie Médicale;" "Nouvelle Biographie Générale."

Gleichen, von, fon glī'kẹn, (FRIEDRICH WILHELM,) a German naturalist, called RUSSWORM, was born at Baireuth in 1717. He gave special attention to infusoria and spermatic animalcula, and was a skilful microscopic observer. Among his works is "Microscopic Discoveries in Plants, Insects," etc., (1777.) Died in 1783.

See WEIKARD, "Biographie des Herren von Gleichen," 1783.

Gleig, glĕg, (GEORGE,) a Scottish theologian, born in 1753. He became Bishop of Brechin about 1810, and published several works on theology. Died in 1839.

Gleig, (Rev. GEORGE ROBERT,) a Scottish divine and voluminous writer, born in 1795. Having served in the Peninsular war and in America, he was subsequently appointed chaplain-general to the forces, (1846.) Among his principal works are the romances of "The Hussar," "Chelsea Pensioners," and "The Subaltern," (1825,) "The Campaign of New Orleans," "The Story of the Peninsular War," "Life of Lord Clive," and "Memoirs of Warren Hastings," which Lord Macaulay has characterized as "three big, bad volumes, full of undigested correspondence and undiscerning panegyric." "Mr. Gleig's Life of Hastings," says Mr. Allibone, "forms a proper companion to Abbott's 'Life of Napoleon.' We can say nothing more condemnatory of both."

Gleim, glīm, (JOHANN WILHELM LUDWIG,) a popular German poet, sometimes called "Father Gleim," born near Ermsleben in 1719. He was the author of fables, romances, anacreontic poems, a didactic poem entitled "Halladat," etc.; but he is chiefly celebrated for his "War-Songs," (" Kriegslieder.") Died in 1803.

See LONGFELLOW, "Poets and Poetry of Europe;" WILHELM KÖRTE, "J. W. L. Gleim's Leben," 1811; MEUSEL, "Gelehrtes Deutschland."

Gleizes, glāz, (JEAN ANTOINE,) a French vegetarian and philosophical writer, born at Dourgne in 1773; died in 1843.

Glemona, da, dä glā-mo'nä, (BASILE,) a missionary and Chinese scholar. He resided many years in China, and produced a Chinese lexicon.

Glen, de, dĕh glĕn, (JOHN,) a Flemish engraver on wood, born at Liege. He published in 1601 a curious work, called "On Dress, Manners, Ceremonies," etc., (" Des Habits, Mœurs, Cérémonies et Façons de faire.")

Glenbervie. See DOUGLAS, (SYLVESTER.)

Glen'dŏw-ẹr or **Glendwr**, (OWEN,) a celebrated Welsh chieftain, born in Merionethshire about 1350, was descended from Llewelyn, Prince of Wales. He was early patronized by King Richard II., to whom he faithfully adhered until the deposition of that monarch. Being roused to resistance by the oppression exercised against his countrymen by Henry IV., he laid claim, about 1400, to the crown of Wales. The king soon after marched with an army against Glendower, who, without coming to an engagement, led them through the mountainous tracts until, worn with fatigue and famine, they were forced to retreat. A second expedition undertaken by King Henry was likewise unsuccessful; and in 1402 Glendower gained a signal victory over the English near Knighton. Having assembled a large army, the king marched for the third time into Wales; and Glendower, unwilling to risk an encounter with so superior a force, retired to the mountains. With Mortimer and Henry Percy, surnamed Hotspur, he formed a conspiracy against the English king, who defeated their army near Shrewsbury in 1403. Having made a treaty with Charles VI. of France, Glendower again invaded the enemy's country, capturing a number of fortresses; but in 1405 he was defeated by Henry, the young Prince of Wales. After several unsuccessful attempts at negotiation, Glendower died in 1415.

See HUME, "History of England;" SHAKSPEARE, "Henry IV.;" "Retrospective Review," vol. xiii., 1826.

Glenelg, LORD. See GRANT, (CHARLES.)

Glen'ie or **Glen'nie**, (JAMES,) F.R.S., a Scottish mathematician and artillery officer, born in 1750. He published some mathematical works, and a "History of Gunnery," (1776.) Died in 1817.

See CHAMBERS, "Biographical Dictionary of Eminent Scotsmen."

Glent'worth, (GEORGE,) an American physician, born in Philadelphia in 1735, was appointed senior surgeon in the army during the Revolution. Died in 1792.

Gley, glâ, (GÉRARD,) a French linguist and writer, born in Lorraine in 1761. Among his numerous works is a "French-German Dictionary," (1795.) Died in 1830.

Gleyre, glār, (CHARLES,) a Swiss painter of high reputation, born in the canton de Vaud in 1807. His picture of "Evening," or "Illusions perdues," (1843,) is called one of the most poetical compositions of the modern school. He produced a picture of the "Separation of the Apostles," which is much admired.

Glichezare or **Glichesære.** See HEINRICH DER GLICHEZARE.

Glid'don, (GEORGE R.,) was born in Devonshire, England, about 1808. He went to Egypt, where he passed

many years. He published "Ancient Egypt," etc., (1850,) and, with Dr. J. C. Nott, of Mobile, the "Types of Mankind," etc., (1854.) Died at Panama in 1857.

Gliemann, glee'măn, (JOHANN GEORG THEODOR,) a geographer, born at Oldenburg in 1793; died in 1828.

Glinka, glink'kä, (FEODOR NIKOLAEVITCH,) a Russian officer and poet, born in the government of Smolensk in 1788, served in the campaigns of 1805 and 1815. Among his military writings, which are highly esteemed, are "Letters of a Russian Officer on the Campaigns of 1805," etc. His war-lyrics also enjoy a wide popularity; and he has made poetical versions of the Psalms and other sacred books.

Glinka, (GREGOR ANDREEVITCH,) a Russian writer, born in the government of Smolensk in 1774, became in 1802 professor of Russian literature at Dorpat. He was afterwards appointed tutor to the grand duke Nicholas, whom he accompanied on his travels. Among his principal works is a treatise "On the Ancient Religion of the Slavonians." Died about 1818.

Glinka, (MICHAEL,) a Russian composer, produced in 1837 an opera entitled "Tsarskaya Zheezn," (or "Zarkaja Shisn,") which was very successful, and is regarded as the first national work of the kind.

Glinka, (SERGEI NIKOLAEVITCH,) a Russian *littérateur*, born in the government of Smolensk in 1774. He has published poems, dramas, operas, and historical works: among these we may name a "History of the Migration of the Armenians of Azerbaïjân from Turkey to Russia," and "Russian History for Youth." He also translated Young's "Night Thoughts" into Russian.

Glinski, glins'kee, (MICHAEL,) a Polish nobleman, who, having lost the favour of King Sigismund, offered his services to the Czar of Russia, then at war with his country. He captured Smolensk in 1514; but the Czar soon after, suspecting him of treachery, caused him to be put in prison, where he died in 1534.

Gliscenti, gle-shĕn'tee, (FABIO,) an Italian physician and moralist, born near Brescia about 1550, wrote "The Market," (" Il Mercato," 1620,) a moral fable. Died about 1620.

Glis'son, (FRANCIS,) a celebrated English physician and anatomist, born in Dorsetshire in 1597. Having taken his degree at Cambridge, he became professor of physic in that university, and in 1634 was chosen a Fellow of the College of Physicians, London. He wrote a "Treatise on the Rickets," (1650,) and "Anatomy of the Liver." The latter work is highly esteemed; and a part of the liver which he has minutely described has been called the "Capsule of Glisson." He was the first who attributed to simple fibre the innate principle of irritability, which he distinguishes from sensibility. Dr. Glisson was eulogized by Harvey; and the celebrated Boerhaave pronounced him "the most accurate of all anatomists that ever lived." Died in 1677.

See BIRCH, "History of the Royal Society;" AIKIN, "Biographical Memoirs of Medicine."

Glitner. See FORSETI.

Glocker, glok'kẹr, (ERNST FRIEDRICH,) professor of mineralogy at Breslau, was born at Stuttgart in 1793. He wrote a "Manual of Mineralogy," (1829,) and other works on that science.

Gloucester, DUKE OF, was a title of Richard III. of England, before his accession to the throne.

Gloucester, glos'tẹr, (HUMPHREY,) DUKE OF, was a brother of Henry V. of England, by whose last will he was appointed Regent of England in 1422. He was invested by Parliament with the office of "protector" during the absence of his brother, the Duke of Bedford. The affairs of the nation were thrown into confusion by a long contest for supremacy between Gloucester and Cardinal Beaufort. Having been arrested on a charge of treason, he was murdered in prison, by the order, it is supposed, of Cardinal Beaufort, in 1447.

See HUME, "History of England;" SHAKSPEARE, "Henry VI., Part II."

Gloucester, (ROBERT OF,) an early English writer, who flourished in the thirteenth century, is supposed to have been a monk of Gloucester Abbey. He was the author of a History of England from the earliest times down to the reign of Henry III., written in verse, and furnishing a valuable monument of the language of that time.

Gloucester, (WILLIAM FREDERICK,) DUKE OF, born at Rome in 1776, was a nephew of George III. of England, and a son of Prince William Henry. He obtained the rank of general in 1808, and was afterwards a field-marshal. He married Princess Mary, a daughter of George III. Died in 1834.

Glover, glŭv'ẹr, MRS., an Irish actress, born in 1781. She performed a great variety of characters with success. Died in 1850.

Glover, glŭv'ẹr, (RICHARD,) an English poet and scholar, born in London in 1712, was a merchant in his youth. He published in 1737 "Leonidas, an Epic Poem on the Persian War," which had great temporary success and was extravagantly praised by Lord Lyttleton, Fieldin᷈, and other prominent members of the Whig party. It has not retained its popularity, which was owing more to the peculiar circumstances of the times than its own intrinsic merit. His ballad of "Hosier's Ghost" (1739) caused a great sensation, and is still a popular national song. He was also the author of two tragedies, entitled "Medea" and "Boadicea." He was elected a member of Parliament for Weymouth in 1761, and was several times re-elected. Glover is styled by Warton one of the best Greek scholars of his time. Died in 1785.

See "Memoirs of a Distinguished Literary and Political Character," 1813; CAMPBELL, "Specimens of the British Poets;" "Retrospective Review," vol. ii., 1820.

Glover, (ROBERT,) an English heraldic writer, born at Ashford in 1543. He wrote "On Political or Civil Nobility," (" De Nobilitate politica vel civili," 1608.) Died in 1588.

See FULLER's "Worthies."

Glück, glŭk, (CHRISTIAN FRIEDRICH,) a learned German jurist, born at Halle, on the Saale, in 1755. He became professor of law at Erlangen in 1784. His "Complete Explanation of the Pandects" (1796) was esteemed a standard work. Died in 1831.

Gluck, von, fon glŏŏk, (JOHANN CHRISTOPH,) an eminent German composer, born near Neumarkt in 1714. He visited Italy in 1738, and studied composition under Martini. His first operas, "Artaxerxes" and "Demetrius," and a third, entitled "The Fall of the Giants," brought out in London, met with no decided success. Having made the acquaintance of the Florentine poet Calzabigi, they resolved to effect a reform in the Italian Opera, which resulted in the production of "Alceste," "Orfeo," and "Helena and Paris," (1762–69.) These operas were received with general applause both in Germany and Italy. In 1774 he brought out at Paris his "Iphigenia in Aulis," which, in spite of the opposition of the French composers, met with an enthusiastic reception. In the musical contest which was now carried on with great violence between the partisans of Gluck and those of Piccini, who had been invited to Paris, the queen, Marie Antoinette, actively supported the former, who had been her teacher in music. His "Iphigenia in Tauris," which came out in 1779, is ranked among his master-pieces. Died in Vienna in November, 1787.

See BURNEY, "General History of Music;" A. SCHMID, "Christoph, Ritter von Gluck dessen Leben," etc., 1854; FÉTIS, "Biographie Universelle des Musiciens;" MIEL, "Notice sur Gluck," 1840.

Gly'cas, (MICHAEL,) [Gr. Μιχαὴλ ὁ Γλυκᾶς,] a learned Byzantine historian, supposed to have lived about 1150–80. He was the author of "Annales," being a history of the world from the creation to the birth of Christ, and that of the Byzantine emperors down to the death of Alexius I. Comnenus.

See CAVE, "Historia Literaria."

Glȳ'con, [Γλύκων,] a Greek sculptor of uncertain period and of high reputation. He is only known as the sculptor of a famous colossal statue called the "Farnese Hercules," which is in the Royal Museum at Naples. No ancient writer mentions Glycon; but ΓΛΥΚΩΝ ΑΘΗΝΑΙΟΣ ΕΠΟΙΕΙ ("Glycon the Athenian made it") is engraved on the rock which supported the statue.

Glȳnn, (ROBERT,) M.D., an English poet, born at Cambridge, was a Fellow of Queen's College. He wrote

"The Day of Judgment," a poetical essay, which obtained the Seatonian prize in 1757. Died in 1800.

Gmelin, gmä'lin, (FRIEDRICH WILHELM,) a skilful German engraver, born at Badenweiler in 1745. He worked many years at Rome, where he died in 1821.

Gmelin, (JOHANN FRIEDRICH,) a German naturalist, born at Tübingen in 1748, was a son of Philipp Friedrich, noticed below. He was professor of medical sciences in the University of Göttingen for about thirty years, ending in 1804, and acquired an extensive reputation by his lectures and his numerous and voluminous works on botany, chemistry, and other natural sciences. Among these are a "Dictionary of Botany," (9 vols.,) and a "History of Natural Sciences," (1799.) He also edited the thirteenth edition of Linnæus's "Systema Naturæ," (1788–93,) in which work he has shown himself defective in critical judgment. Died in 1804.

See "Biographie médicale ;" "Nouvelle Biographie Générale."

Gmelin, (JOHANN GEORG,) an eminent German botanist and naturalist, an uncle of the preceding, was born at Tübingen in June, 1709. Having taken his degree in medicine, he went to Saint Petersburg, and obtained, about 1731, the chair of chemistry and natural history. In 1733 he was sent by the empress, in company with G. F. Müller and others, on an exploring expedition to Siberia. In this arduous enterprise he spent about ten years, and, having returned to Saint Petersburg in 1743, published his "Flora of Siberia," ("Flora Sibirica," 1747,) which is praised by Haller. He became professor of botany and chemistry at Tübingen in 1749, and published (in German) "Travels in Siberia," (1752,) a work of considerable merit. Died at Tübingen in 1755.

See HIRSCHING, "Historisch-literarisches Handbuch;" "Nouvelle Biographie Générale."

Gmelin, (LEOPOLD,) a chemist, son of Johann Friedrich, noticed above, was born in 1788. He became professor of chemistry at Heidelberg in 1817. His principal works are a "Manual of Theoretical Chemistry," (5 vols., 1841,) and a "Text-Book of Chemistry," (1844.) He retired from the chair at Heidelberg in 1851. Died in 1853.

Gmelin, (PHILIPP FRIEDRICH,) a German physician and botanist, a brother of Johann Georg, noticed above, was born at Tübingen in 1721. He wrote treatises on medicine, botany, etc. Died in 1768.

Gmelin, (SAMUEL GOTTLIEB,) M.D., an eminent botanist and traveller, born at Tübingen in 1744, was a nephew of the preceding. He obtained a chair of botany in Saint Petersburg about 1766, and published a "Treatise on Sea-Weeds," ("Historia Fucorum," 1768.) In 1768, Gmelin and his friend Pallas were associated in a scientific exploration of Russia in the service of the empress Catherine. The former directed his researches to the regions of the Don and the Volga, and explored the western and eastern coasts of the Caspian. He was seized on his homeward route by the Kaïtaks, was imprisoned in Caucasus, and died, in consequence of ill treatment, in 1774. Soon after that date his "Travels through Russia, with a View to Investigate the Three Kingdoms of Nature," (in German,) was published.

See HIRSCHING, "Historisch-literarisches Handbuch."

Gnäditsch, gnä'ditch, written also **Gnieditsch,** (NIKOLAI IVANOVITCH,) a Russian poet, born at Poltava in 1784. He is chiefly known from his excellent translation of the "Iliad" into Russian hexameter verse. He also made translations from Byron and several French poets, and published, among other original poems, "The Fishers," and "Popular Songs of the Modern Greeks." Died in 1833.

Gneisenau, gnī'zẹh-nŏw', (AUGUST **Neidhardt**—nīt'haRt,) COUNT, a celebrated Prussian field-marshal, born at Schilda, in Saxony, in 1760. He served with great distinction in the principal campaigns from 1807 to 1809, when he was sent on embassies to London and Saint Petersburg. In 1813 he was appointed quartermaster-general of Blücher's army; and to his counsel and strategic skill are chiefly to be attributed the advantages gained by the Prussian army at that time. He was made a general in 1814, and received the title of count. After the defeat at Ligny he made a skilful retreat, and collected the remains of the army that by its timely arrival at Waterloo decided the event of that day. He was appointed governor of Berlin and councillor of state in 1818, and in 1825 field-marshal. Died in 1831.

See C. G. Lischke, "A. Gneisenau's Urne," 8vo, 1832; "Nouvelle Biographie Générale."

Gnieditsch. See Gnäditsch.

Gni'pho, (Marcus Antonius,) a Roman rhetorician, born in Gaul in 114 B.C. He taught rhetoric, at Rome, to Cicero and other eminent men, and wrote several works, which are not extant. Died 63 B.C.

Gōad, (John,) a classical teacher, born in London in 1615, was head-master of the Merchant Taylors' School for about twenty years. Among his works is "Astro-Meteorologia," (1686.) Died in 1689.

See Wilson, "History of Merchant Taylors' School."

Gōad'bў, (Robert,) an English printer and writer, of Sherborne, in Dorsetshire, wrote "Illustration of the Scriptures by Notes," (3 vols., 1759–64.) Died in 1778.

Goar, go'ǎr', (Jacques,) a French Dominican monk, born in Paris about 1606. He published a work on the ritual of the Greek Church, "Eukologion sive Rituale Græcorum," (1647.) Died in 1653.

Goar, van. See Graf.

Gobbo, gob'bo, (Andrea,) a painter, distinguished as a colorist, born at Milan about 1470; died in 1527.

Gobbo da Cortona, gob'bo dǎ koR-to'nǎ, an Italian painter, whose proper name was Paolo Bonzi, was born at Cortona about 1580. He excelled in painting fruits. Died about 1640.

Gobel, go'běl', (Jean Baptiste,) a French revolutionist, born in Alsace in 1727, was a deputy of the clergy to the States-General in 1789. When the oath to the civil constitution was offered to the clergy, he attached to it some restrictions; but he subsequently withdrew them. As a reward for his compliance, he obtained the bishoprics of the Upper Rhine, the Upper Maine, and of Paris. He renounced his ecclesiastical functions about the end of 1793. Having incurred the displeasure of the Jacobins, he was guillotined in 1794.

See Lamartine, "History of the Girondists;" "Nouvelle Biographie Générale;" "Biographie Universelle."

Göbel or **Goebel,** gö'běl, (Johann Heinrich Ertmann,) a German writer, born at Lauban in 1732; died in 1795.

Göbel or **Goebel,** (Traugott Friedemann,) a German chemist and traveller, born in Thuringia in 1794, became professor of chemistry at Dorpat in 1828. He published "Travels in Southern Russia," (1838,) "Elements of Pharmacy," ("Grundlehren der Pharmacie," 4 vols., 1843–47,) and other works. Died in 1851.

Göbel or **Goebel, von,** fon gö'běl, (Johann Wilhelm,) a German jurist and publicist, born in Westphalia in 1683. His works on public law were much esteemed. Died in 1745.

Gobelin, gob'lǎn', (Gilles and Jean,) brothers, and celebrated French dyers, who about 1450 established dye-houses on the Bièvre, (Faubourg Saint-Marcel, Paris.) A manufactory of tapestry was afterwards founded, and, under the supervision of the celebrated Le Brun, were produced those superb pieces of tapestry which have excited the admiration of the world.

See Lacordaire, "Notice historique sur la Manufacture des Gobelins."

Gobet, go'bà', (Nicolas,) a French savant, born about 1735, wrote "The Ancient Mineralogists of France," (2 vols., 1779,) and other works. Died about 1781.

Gobien. See Legobien.

Gobinet, go'be'nà', (Charles,) a French religious writer, born at Saint-Quentin in 1613; died in 1690.

Göbler or **Goebler,** gö'běr, (Justin,) a German historian, born in Hesse. He wrote a "History of the Emperor Maximilian I.," (1566.) Died in 1567.

Goblet, go'blà', (Albert Joseph,) Count of Alviella, a Belgian officer, born at Tournay in 1790. In 1835 he obtained the rank of lieutenant-general.

Go'brў-as, one of the seven Persian noblemen who conspired against Smerdis, 521 B.C. He married a sister of King Darius, and was the father of Mardonius.

Gockel, gok'kěl, (Eberhard,) born at Ulm in 1646, was physician to the Duke of Würtemberg. His writings were highly esteemed.

Göckingk or **Goeckingk,** gök'kink, (Leopold Friedrich Gunther—goon'ter,) a German poet, born near Halberstadt in 1748, was appointed to several high offices in the Prussian government. He wrote epigrams, satiric fables, and "The Songs of Two Lovers," ("Lieder zweier Liebenden," 1777.) The last-named are especially admired. Died in 1828.

Goclenius, go-klā'ne-ús, (Conrad,) a German philologist, born in Westphalia in 1455. He was a friend and correspondent of Erasmus. He wrote "Scholia in Tullii Officia," and edited Lucian. Died about 1535.

Goclenius, (Rudolph,) a German philosopher, born at Corbach in 1547, was professor of logic at Marburg. He wrote, besides other works, "Miscellanea philosophico-theologica," (3 vols., 1607–09.) Died in 1628.

Goclenius, (Rudolph,) a physician, son of the preceding, was born at Wittenberg in 1572. He became professor of physics at Marburg, and wrote various works. Died in 1621.

Godard, go'dǎr', (Jean,) a French poet, born in Paris in 1564, wrote odes, dramas, etc., which were once popular. Died about 1630.

Godart, go'dǎr', (Jean Baptiste,) a French naturalist, born in Picardy in 1775. He published four volumes of a "History of the Lepidoptera of France," (1822–25,) which, after his death, was finished by Duponchel. It is a work of much merit. Died in 1823.

God'dạrd, (Arabella,) a popular pianist, born of English parents in Brittany, France, in 1836, was a pupil of Thalberg. She made her first appearance in public in London in 1850, since which time she has been constantly increasing in popular favour. In 1860 she was married to Mr. Davison, but still retains her maiden name.

See "Men of the Time," 1868.

Goddard, (Jonathan,) a distinguished English physician and chemist, born at Greenwich in 1617. Being appointed head-physician in the army in 1649, he accompanied Cromwell to Ireland and Scotland, and in 1653 became a member of the council of state. On the formation of the Royal Society, in 1663, Dr. Goddard was chosen one of its council. He published, among other works, a "Discourse concerning Physic, and the many Abuses thereof by Apothecaries," (1668.) He was also noted for his scientific attainments, and made great improvements in optical instruments. Died in 1674.

See "Biographie médicale;" Chalmers, "Biographical Dictionary."

Goddard, (William Stanley,) an English clergyman, born in 1757, was master of Winchester School, and rector of Repton, Derby. He gave large sums of money for charity. Died in 1845.

Godde, god, (Étienne Hippolyte,) a French architect, born at Breteuil in 1781, was appointed chief architect of the city of Paris in 1813. His chief work is the addition to the Hôtel de Ville.

Godeau, go'dō', (Antoine,) a French writer, born at Dreux in 1605, was one of the founders and first members of the French Academy. He was distinguished for his wit and social accomplishments, and was one of the coterie of the Hôtel de Rambouillet. He was created Bishop of Grasse by Cardinal Richelieu in 1636, and was afterwards Bishop of Vence. He wrote a "History of the Church from the Creation to the End of the Eighth Century," (5 vols., 1653–78,) "Christian Morals," and various other works. Died in 1672.

See Dupin, "Bibliothèque des Auteurs ecclésiastiques;" Nicéron, "Mémoires;" Speroni degli Alvarotti, "Vita di A. Godeau Vescovo di Vence," 1761.

God'e-bẹrt, [Lat. Godeber'tus,] written also **Gundepert,** King of the Lombards, succeeded his father in 661 A.D. He was killed by Grimoald in 662.

Godefroi. See Godfrey.

Godefroi, god'frwà', [Lat. Gothofre'dus,] (Denis,) the Elder, an eminent French jurist, born in Paris in 1549. He studied successively at Louvain, Heidelberg, and Cologne, and, after his return, was made a councillor in the Parliament of Paris. He became professor of law at Geneva in 1580. On the invitation of Frederick, the Elector-palatine, he repaired to Heidelberg, where, owing to the troubles of war, he did not remain long. He died at Strasburg in 1622. He published a "Body of Civil

Law," ("Corpus Juris civilis," 1583,) and other valuable legal works, and enjoyed the reputation of one of the first jurists of his time.

See NICÉRON, "Mémoires."

Godefroi, (DENIS,) THE YOUNGER, a French historian, born in Paris in 1615, was a grandson of the preceding. He was made historiographer of France in 1640, and wrote a "History of the Constables, Chancellors, etc. of France," (1658.) Died in 1681.

Godefroi, (JACQUES,) son of Denis the Elder, born at Geneva in 1587, became professor of law in his native town. He was afterwards appointed secretary of state and syndic of the republic. His edition of the "Codex Theodosianus" (1665) is highly esteemed. Died in 1652.

Godefroi, (JEAN,) Sieur d'Aumont, son of Denis the Younger, born in Paris in 1656. He filled several important offices under the government, and published editions of the "Mémoires de Comines," and other works. Died in 1732.

Godefroi, (THÉODORE,) a French jurist and historical writer, born at Geneva in 1580, was a son of Denis the Elder, noticed above. He was appointed historiographer of the kingdom in 1632. He published, among other works, "Le Cérémonial de France," (1619,) and one "On the True Origin of the House of Austria," (1624.) Died in 1649.

Godefroid (or **Godefroi**) **de Bouillon.** See GODFREY OF BOUILLON.

Godefroidus Boloniensis, (or **Bulloniensis.**) See GODFREY OF BOUILLON.

Gödeke or **Goedeke,** gö'deh-keh, (KARL,) a German littérateur, born at Celle in 1814. He published, besides other works, "The Poets of Germany from 1813 to 1843," (1844,) and "The Middle Ages and their Literature," (1852–54.)

Goderich. See RIPON, EARL OF.

Godescalch or **Godeschalcus.** See GOTTSCHALK.

Godescard, go'dĕs'kȧr', (JEAN FRANÇOIS,) a French ecclesiastical writer, born near Rouen in 1728, published, besides other works, "Lives of the Fathers, Martyrs," etc., (12 vols. 8vo.) Died in 1800.

God'frey, (Sir EDMUNDBURY,) an English magistrate, who took the evidence of Oates in relation to a suspected popish plot. His dead body was found, after he had been missing some days, at Primrose Hill, in October, 1678. A great excitement was caused by his murder.

See "Memoirs of the Life and Death of Sir E. Godfrey," London, 1682.

God'frey, (THOMAS,) an American mechanician and inventor, born in Philadelphia. About 1730 he made an improvement in the quadrant, which was communicated to the Royal Society. A similar improvement was made nearly at the same time by Mr. Hadley in England; and a reward was given to both by the society. Died in 1749.

God'frey of Bouillon, (boo'yòN',) [Fr. GODEFROID (or GODEFROI) DE BOUILLON, go'deh-frwȧ' deh boo'-yòN'; Ger. GOTTFRIED VON BOUILLON, got'freet fon boo'yòN'; It. GOFFREDO DI BUGLIONE, gof-frȧ'do de bool-yo'nȧ; Lat. GODEFROI'DUS (or GOTHOFRE'DUS) BOLONIEN'SIS,] the illustrious leader of the first crusade, son of Eustace II., Count of Boulogne, was born near Nivelle, in France, about 1058. He early distinguished himself while fighting for Henry IV. of Germany, by whom he was created Duke of Bouillon. He was one of the first to engage in the crusade for the recovery of the Holy Sepulchre, and to him was intrusted the command of the principal army. In 1096 he set out for Constantinople, accompanied by the most distinguished of the nobility. Being informed that Hugh, Count of Vermandois, brother of the King of France, was detained there as a prisoner, Godfrey demanded his release of the emperor Alexius, and on his refusal threatened to besiege the capital, in consequence of which the captive was liberated. After much difficulty, a treaty was concluded between Alexius and the crusaders, by which the latter agreed to do homage to the emperor on condition of his assistance. The army next advanced to Nice, which surrendered after a protracted siege. In June, 1098, Antioch was taken, after great suffering had been endured from famine and disease. With the remnant of his army Godfrey now marched to Jerusalem, the siege

of which was begun in June, 1099, and ended the July following by the capture of the city. By the unanimous wish of the crusaders, he was chosen King of Jerusalem; but he refused the title of royalty, saying "he would never accept a crown of gold in a city where his Saviour had worn a crown of thorns." Soon after this he obtained another victory over the Saracens, at Ascalon. Godfrey gave to the city a set of laws, called the "Assize of Jerusalem," resembling the feudal system of Europe. He survived but a year after the taking of Jerusalem, dying in July, 1100. Godfrey is the hero of Tasso's "Jerusalem Delivered ;" and the poet appears not to have exaggerated the merits of a character which was a rare combination of wisdom and heroism with Christian virtues of a high order.

See MICHAUD, "Histoire des Croisades ;" C. DE PLANCY, "Godefroid de Bouillon," 1842; WILKEN, "Geschichte der Kreuzzüge," 1839; R. PICO, "Vita di G. Duca di Buglione," 1626; H. PRÉVAULT, "Histoire de G. de Bouillon," 2 vols., 1833; J. B. D'EXAUVILLEZ, "Histoire de G. de Bouillon," 1842; GIBBON, "Decline and Fall," etc.; H. VON SYBEL, "Geschichte des ersten Kreuzzugs," 1841.

Godfrey of Viterbo, a historian of the twelfth century. He was employed as secretary and chaplain by the emperors Conrad III., Frederick I., and Henry IV. of Germany. His principal work is entitled "Pantheon," being a history of the world from the creation to the year 1186. It is written in Latin, and displays great learning ; but the style is somewhat barbarous.

See VOSSIUS, "De Historicis Latinis."

Godin, go'dȧN', (LOUIS,) an eminent French mathematician and astronomer, born in Paris in 1704. In 1725 he was admitted into the Academy of Sciences. When, in 1735, the Academy sent some of its members to measure a degree of the meridian, Godin was appointed to conduct the enterprise. He was for a time professor of mathematics at Lima, and after his return to Europe became director of the Naval Academy at Cadiz. He wrote, besides other works, a "History of the Academy of Sciences from 1680 to 1699," (11 vols.) Died in 1760.

See GRAND-JEAN DE FOUCHY, "Éloge de Godin."

Godinot, go'de'no', (JEAN,) a French ecclesiastic and philanthropist, born at Rheims in 1661. He devoted his large fortune to benevolent purposes, founded free schools, and conferred numerous other benefits upon his native city. Died in 1749.

Go-di'va, [Fr. GODIVE, go'dèv',] a celebrated English lady, who lived in the time of Edward the Confessor and was the wife of Leofric, Earl of Leicester. According to tradition, she procured the exemption of Coventry from a tax by riding naked through that city on horseback. Tennyson has written a poem on this subject.

Godive. See GODIVA.

God'ley, (JOHN ROBERT,) an English politician and writer. He published "Letters from Canada and the United States," (2 vols., 1844.) Died in 1862.

God'man, (JOHN D.,) an eminent American naturalist and physician, born at Annapolis, Maryland, in December, 1794. He enlisted in the navy in 1814, and served at the defence of Fort McHenry, but left the service in 1815. He then began to study medicine, and graduated in the University of Maryland in 1818. In 1821 he was chosen professor of surgery in the Medical College of Ohio at Cincinnati ; but he removed to Philadelphia in 1822, after which he lectured on anatomy to a private class. He became in 1824 one of the editors of the "Philadelphia Journal of the Medical Sciences," and was appointed professor of anatomy in Rutgers College, New York, in 1826. About the end of 1827 he resigned his chair, on account of ill health. He died at Germantown, near Philadelphia, in April, 1830. As a lecturer on anatomy and as a naturalist, Professor Godman had few, if any, superiors among his contemporaries in the United States. He was also well versed in the Latin, French, and German languages. His work on "American Natural History" (3 vols. 8vo, 1823–28) the "North American Review" pronounces "undoubtedly superior to any previous publication on the same subject," and adds, "We consider Dr. Godman in some respects among the most extraordinary men that have adorned the medical profession in our country." Among his other publications may be mentioned his "Anatomical Investigations,"

ā, ē, ī, ō, ū, ȳ, long; ă, ĕ, ĭ, ŏ, ŭ, ȳ, same, less prolonged; ä, ĕ, ĭ, ŏ, ŭ, ȳ, short; ą, ę, į, ǫ, obscure; fär, fȧll, fȧt; mĕt; nŏt; gōōd; mōōn;

"Rambles of a Naturalist," and an edition of Bell's "Anatomy," with notes. Dr. Godman had adopted the materialistic views of the French naturalists; but, on being called, in 1827, to witness the death of a medical student, who died a Christian, he was led to embrace Christianity, and was ever after a devoutly religious man. A "Memoir of his Life," by Dr. Sewall, has been published by the Tract Society.

See, also, GROSS, "American Medical Biography;" "North American Review" for January, 1835.

Godoi. See GODOY.

Go-dol′phin, (JOHN,) an eminent civilian, born at Godolphin, in the island of Scilly, in 1617. He was appointed a judge of the admiralty in 1653, and king's advocate after the restoration of 1660. He published "The Holy Harbour, a Body of Divinity," (1651,) and "Admiralty Jurisdiction," (1661.) Died in 1678.

See WOOD, "Athenæ Oxonienses."

Godolphin, (SIDNEY GODOLPHIN,) EARL OF, an eminent English statesman, of a distinguished family in Cornwall. The year of his birth is not known; but he entered early into the service of Charles II., and on the restoration was appointed by that prince one of the grooms of the bed-chamber. In 1678 he was intrusted with the management of a confidential correspondence between the Prince of Orange and the Duke of York, and the following year he became one of the lords of the treasury. When the Duke of Monmouth and Lord Salisbury were dismissed, in 1679, he shared with Viscount Hyde and the Earl of Sunderland the chief management of affairs. In 1683 he was one of those ministers employed in secret negotiations with Louis XIV. to renew the dependency of Charles on the French king. He was made first commissioner of the treasury in 1684, and was created Baron Godolphin of Rialton. Although he had voted to exclude James II. from the crown, he was retained in office when that sovereign succeeded to the throne, (1685,) but in a subordinate place at the treasury board. On the arrival of the Prince of Orange, Godolphin was one of the noblemen employed to negotiate with him on the part of the king. On the accession of the Prince of Orange he retained his office as one of the lords of the treasury, and in 1690 was made first lord in that department. He was dismissed from office in 1697. When Queen Anne succeeded to the throne, (1702,) he became lord high treasurer. This office he had refused until the Duke of Marlborough declared he could not command the armies on the continent unless the treasury was in Godolphin's hands. In 1704 he was made knight of the Garter, and in 1706 Earl of Godolphin. He was removed from his post of lord high treasurer in 1710, when the Duke and Duchess of Marlborough, with whom he had been connected, had lost the favour of the queen. Bishop Burnet says of Godolphin, "He was the silentest and modestest man who was perhaps ever bred in a court. He had true principles of religion and virtue, and never heaped up wealth." During the greater part of his political course he acted with the Tories; but about 1705 he attached himself to the Whig party. Died in 1712.

See MACAULAY, "History of England," vol. iv.; BURNET, "History of his Own Times."

Godolphin, (SYDNEY,) an English poet, born in Cornwall in 1610. He fought for Charles I., and was killed at Chagford in 1643. He translated "The Loves of Dido and Æneas" from Virgil, and wrote several original poems. His judgment and fancy are praised by Hobbes, who was his friend.

Godoonof, Godounof, or **Godunow,** go′doo-nof′, sometimes written **Gudenow,** (BORIS,) Czar of Moscow, born in 1552, was of Tartar origin, and was made a member of the supreme council of state by Ivan the Terrible in 1582. When the imbecile Feodor succeeded Ivan, Godoonof became his chief favourite, and obtained from him the highest honours. In 1591 Demetrius, the half-brother of Feodor, was said to have been murdered by the orders of Godoonof. In 1598 Feodor died, leaving the throne to his widow Irene, the sister of Godoonof, and, on her refusal to accept the crown, the latter was proclaimed Czar by the unanimous wish of the people. About this time he defeated the Khan of the Crimea, and brought

Siberia to subjection. He displayed great ability and energy in his administration, and his policy was generally marked by clemency. He manifested great zeal in the cause of education, and invited to his country distinguished foreigners whom he thought likely to promote its civilization. During the terrible famine of 1601 he showed himself a benefactor to his people by his exertions in their behalf. In 1604 a report was raised that Prince Demetrius, who was supposed to have been murdered, was still alive and was preparing to enter Russia. As he was approaching Moscow, Godoonof died suddenly, in April, 1605; and it is supposed he took poison.

See P. MÉRIMÉE, "Un Épisode de l'Histoire de Russie; les faux Démétrius;" MARGARET, "L'Estat de la Russie," etc., 1607.

Godounof or **Godunow.** See GODOONOF.

Go-doy′, de, [Sp. pron. då go-DO′ee,] (Don MANUEL,) (ALVAREZ de Faria Rios Sanchez y Zarsoa—då få-ree′å ree′ôs sån′chêth e thaR-so′å,) Duke of Alcudia, a Spanish courtier, surnamed THE PRINCE OF PEACE, was born at Badajoz in 1767. He became the chief favourite of Charles IV. and of his queen, and was appointed prime minister in 1792. He received the title of "Prince of Peace" because he made peace with France in 1795. His influence over the feeble king and the queen was unbounded; but he became very unpopular. Ferdinand, the heir of the throne, was among his enemies. Godoy's administration was very corrupt. His palace was attacked in March, 1808, by a mob, who were appeased by the abdication of Charles IV. and the disgrace of the favourite. He took refuge in France, and died in Paris in 1851.

See OVILO Y OTERO, "Vida política y militar de Don Manuel Godoy," etc., 1844; TORENO, "Guerra, Revolucion, etc. de España;" "Westminster Review" for April, 1836; "Nouvelle Biographie Générale."

Godron, go′dRòn′, (DOMINIQUE ALEXANDRE,) a French naturalist of the present age. He was professor of natural history at Nancy, and published a "Flora of France," (6 vols., 1848–56.)

God′win, EARL, a celebrated Saxon baron, was the son of Ulnoth, or Wolfnoth, Earl of Sussex. In 1017 he accompanied Canute in an expedition against Sweden, and so distinguished himself by his bravery that the king bestowed upon him his daughter in marriage. On the death of Canute, Godwin espoused the cause of Hardicanute in opposition to Harold Harefoot, but, soon changing his course, supported the claims of Harold, and, in concert with him, planned the murder of the young princes Alfred and Edward, sons of Ethelred and Emma. When Hardicanute came to the throne, Prince Edward accused Godwin of the murder of his brother; but a magnificent present from the guilty earl induced the king to pardon him. In 1041, on the death of Hardicanute, Godwin was reconciled to Edward, and promoted his succession on condition of his marrying his daughter Editha. About this time the counties of Kent and Sussex were added to his domain. Having openly disobeyed the king, the latter summoned a council of his nobles at London, and passed judgment on the rebellion. Godwin, with three of his sons, took refuge in Flanders. Their estates were confiscated. Having gained adherents in Flanders, Godwin equipped a fleet, and, with his son Harold, entered the Thames and appeared before London. The king now entered into negotiations with him, and Godwin, with his sons, after giving hostages to preserve the peace, were reinstated in their possessions. Died in 1053.

See LINGARD's "History of England."

Godwin, (FRANCIS,) an English antiquary, born in Northamptonshire in 1561, was appointed Bishop of Llandaff. He was the author of a "Catalogue of the Bishops of England," etc., also a work entitled "The Man in the Moon, by Domingo Gonsales." He became Bishop of Hereford in 1617. Died in 1633.

Godwin, (GEORGE,) F.R.S., an English architect, born in Middlesex in 1815. He wrote a descriptive work called "The Churches of London," (1838,) a collection of tales entitled "Facts and Fancies," (1844,) "History in Ruins," and other works. He became editor of the "Builder" in 1844, since which he has contributed many articles to that valuable weekly journal. He was afterwards employed on the restoration of the church of Saint Mary Redcliff.

Godwin, (MARY.) See WOLLSTONECRAFT.

Godwin, (PARKE,) an American author and editor, born at Paterson, New Jersey, in February, 1816, graduated at Princeton College in 1834. He married a daughter of William C. Bryant, the poet, whom he assisted as associate editor of the New York "Evening Post" from 1837 to 1853. He published a periodical, called "The Pathfinder," for several months in 1843, contributed to the "Democratic Review" many political, literary, and biographical articles, and was editor of "Putnam's Magazine." He translated into English Goethe's "Autobiography," Lamotte-Fouqué's "Undine" and "Sintram and his Companions," and has been engaged, it is said, for several years in writing a "History of France," (1860.) He is a member of the Republican party.

Godwin, (THOMAS,) an English prelate, born in Berkshire in 1517. He became a Protestant at an early age, and was appointed Dean of Christ Church in 1565. He was made Bishop of Bath and Wells in 1584. Died in 1590.

See WOOD, "Athenæ Oxonienses."

Godwin, (THOMAS,) a learned English divine, born in Somersetshire in 1587, was master of Royse's free school, in Abingdon, for the use of which he wrote his "Anthology of Roman History." In 1616 he published a "Synopsis of Hebrew Antiquities." Died in 1643.

Godwin, (WILLIAM,) a celebrated English novelist, was born in Cambridgeshire in 1756. He studied at the Independent Theological College at Hoxton. After having filled the clerical office for five years, he visited London, where he began his career as an author. His first work, entitled "Political Justice," appeared in 1793. It made a great sensation, and brought much opprobrium on the author, who was thought to sympathize with the principles of the French Revolution. The next year he published "Caleb Williams," a novel, which was very successful. In 1794, when several of Godwin's friends were tried for high treason, he wrote "Cursory Strictures" on the charge delivered by Judge Eyre to the jury, and in this way rendered essential service to the accused. In 1796 he married Mary Wollstonecraft, and after her death, in 1797, he edited her posthumous works and published a memoir of her. He produced "Saint Leon," a novel, in 1799, and engaged in business as a bookseller about 1804. In 1808 he wrote an "Essay on Sepulchres ; or, Proposal for Erecting some Memorial of the Illustrious Dead on the Spot where their Remains have been interred." In 1816 his novel "Mandeville" appeared. He next wrote a "Treatise on Population," and in 1828 published his "History of the Commonwealth of England." His last novel, "Cloudesley," was brought out in 1830, when the author was seventy-four years of age. His last work, entitled "Lives of the Necromancers," appeared in 1834. When Lord Grey came into power, he bestowed on Godwin the office of yeoman usher of the exchequer. Though distinguished as a political writer, he has displayed his greatest talent in his novels, of which "Caleb Williams" and "Mandeville" are considered the best. Died in 1836.

See the critique on Godwin in HAZLITT's Miscellaneous Works, vol. v.; "Edinburgh Review" for April, 1830; DE QUINCEY, "Literary Reminiscences," vol. i.

Goebel. See GÖBEL.

Goeckingk. See GÖCKINGK.

Goedeke. See GÖDEKE.

Goelike. See GÖLIKE.

Goenner. See GÖNNER.

Goeppert. See GÖPPERT.

Goeree, HOO′RÀ, (JAN,) a Dutch painter, son of Willem, noticed below, was born at Middelburg in 1670. He adorned with his pictures the Burghers' Hall at Amsterdam. Died in 1731.

Goeree, (WILLEM,) a Dutch writer and bookseller of extensive learning, born at Middelburg in 1635. He published a "History of the Jewish Church," etc., and other works on various subjects. Died in 1711.

Goerenz. See GÖRENZ.

Goergei or **Goergey.** See GÖRGEY.

Goerres. See GÖRRES.

Goertz. See GÖRTZ, (JOHANN EUSTACH.)

Goertz or **Görtz,** görts, (GEORG HENRIK,) BARON, a Swedish statesman, who became minister of finance under Charles XII. Soon after the death of that sovereign he was arrested and executed at Stockholm (1719) on a charge of having prolonged the war and brought pecuniary distress upon the nation.

See VOLTAIRE, "Histoire de Charles XII."

Goertze. See GÖRTZE.

Goes or **Goez, de,** då go′ĕz, (DAMIÃO,) a Portuguese historian and statesman, born near Lisbon in 1501. He was sent on important missions to Poland, Denmark, and Sweden, and afterwards appointed historiographer of the kingdom and keeper of the archives. He wrote a "History of the Prince Don Juan," a "Chronicle of Don Emanuel," (1567,) and other valuable works. He was also an accomplished musician. Died in 1560.

See BARBOSA MACHADO, "Bibliotheca Lusitana;" "Nouvelle Biographie Générale."

Goes, de, (PERO,) brother of the preceding, was one of the first colonists of Brazil, where he settled about 1535 and introduced the culture of the sugar-cane.

Goes, van der, vän dẹr HOOS, (HUGO,) a celebrated Flemish painter, born at Bruges about 1420, studied under Van Eyck. He is especially admired for the elegance of his female heads. Among his best works we may mention "David and Abigail," and the "Crucifixion between the Two Thieves." During the general destruction of pictures and images in 1566, the latter piece was preserved by being coated with black and inscribed with the ten commandments. It was afterwards restored.

See DESCAMPS, "Vies des Peintres Flamands," etc.

Goes, van der, vän dẹr HOOS, (WILLEM,) a Dutch jurist and philologist, born at Leyden in 1611, was councillor of the supreme court of justice at the Hague. His principal work is called "Pilatus Judex," wherein he attempts to throw light upon circumstances attending the Passion of our Saviour. Died in 1686.

Goeschel. See GÖSCHEL.

Goeschen. See GÖSCHEN.

Goethals, HOO′tâls, (FELIX VICTOR,) a Belgian littérateur, born at Ghent in 1799, became librarian of the public library at Brussels in 1830. Among his works is a "History of Letters and Arts in Belgium and Adjoining Countries," (4 vols., 1840-44.)

Goethals, (HENDRIK,) called also **Gredals** or **Crodals,** a Flemish diplomatist, born at Ghent in 1359. He was successively ambassador to Constantinople, Paris, London, and Rome, and filled, among other offices, that of private secretary to Philip the Bold. Died in 1433.

Goethals, van, vän HOO′tâls, [Lat. MUDA′NUS,] (HENDRIK,) a noted Dutch theologian, born at Muda, near Ghent, (Gand,) about 1218, became Archdeacon of Tournay. He was author of several popular works on theology, one of which is entitled "Summa Theologiæ." Died in 1293.

Goethe or **Göthe, von,** fon gö′tẹh, (JOHANN WOLFGANG,) the most illustrious name in German literature, and one of the greatest poets of any age or country, was born at Frankfort-on-the-Main, August 28, 1749. His father, Johann Caspar Goethe, imperial councillor, was of a stern, obstinate, and somewhat pedantic character, though on the whole an upright and worthy man. His maternal grandfather, Johann Wolfgang Textor, was a person of note and the chief magistrate *(Schultheiss)* of the city of Frankfort. His mother was genial, warmhearted, and of a singularly bright and happy disposition. She says of herself, "I always seek out the good that is in people, and leave what is bad to Him who made mankind and knows how to round off the corners." Goethe says in one of his poems that from his father he derives his earnestness of purpose, and from his mother his happy disposition and his love of story-telling. The circumstances with which the poet was surrounded in early life were eminently favourable to the development of his great and varied powers, and undoubtedly contributed in no small degree to cultivate that "many-sidedness" for which he was afterwards so distinguished. In his autobiography, entitled "Poetry and Truth from my own Life," ("Aus meinem Leben Dichtung und Wahrheit," published in 1811,) he describes, with graceful *naïveté*, the influence exerted on his mind by the various events and experiences of childhood. The young Goethe exhibited a wonderful precocity of intellect. Early in his seventh year (November 1, 1755) the great earthquake which destroyed a large part of Lisbon occurred, and filled his mind with perplexity and doubt. He found it impossible to reconcile that terrible phenomenon with what he had been taught respecting the goodness of Providence. "It was in vain," he says, "that my young mind strove to recover itself from these impressions; the more so as the wise and learned in Scripture themselves could not agree upon the view which should be taken of the event." His religious perplexities, however, seem gradually to have passed away. In his eighth year we find him, wholly self-prompted, erecting to the Deity an altar in the form of a pyramid, on the sides of which were arranged a variety of substances representing the natural productions of the earth. At the apex was placed the incense, which he kindled by means of a burning-glass just as the sun was rising above the neighbouring house-tops. Before he was nine years of age he could write several different languages, including French, Latin, and Greek.

He had scarcely reached his tenth year when the French troops occupied the city of Frankfort: this occurred during the Seven Years' war. The Comte de Thorane, the king's lieutenant, was quartered in the house of the poet's father. Young Goethe was thus brought into contact with new characters: he also became acquainted with the French theatre. He had several years before amused himself and his mother with inventing romantic stories; he now began to write French plays. A French boy, near his own age, with whom he had become acquainted, took him to the theatre and introduced him behind the scenes. This same lad sought to instruct him in the proper mode of writing plays, and criticised the dramatic efforts of our poet somewhat unmercifully. This led him to inform himself more particularly respecting the principles of criticism. The result was that he rejected with contempt the canons of the French school; and it is not improbable that the occurrences just related may have exerted an important influence upon the productions of his maturer years. In 1761 the French troops quitted Frankfort, and his regular studies were resumed. About this time he learned to read English, and commenced the study of Hebrew, which led him to a more intimate acquaintance with the Bible. He composed a poem on the subject of Joseph and his brethren. The education of Goethe, until he was sixteen, was carried on at home, under the superintendence of his father. It was his rare happiness to find in his only sister, Cornelia, not merely an object of his tenderest affection, but one who shared his tastes and cordially sympathized with his poetic aspirations. In October, 1765, he commenced his collegiate studies at Leipsic. It was a practice which he adopted in early life, that he always sought, whenever any subject interested him deeply, to give his thoughts and feelings expression in writing. He himself says that all his works are but fragments of the grand confession of his life. While at Leipsic, he composed the first of his poems which have been preserved, "The Humours of a Lover," ("Die Laune des Verliebten;") "The Fellow-Sinners" ("Die Mitschuldigen") followed soon after. He left Leipsic for Frankfort in 1768. After having been some time detained at home by ill health, he repaired to Strasburg University, in 1770, for the purpose of completing his law studies. At Strasburg he became acquainted with Herder, who was already distinguished among the great men of Germany. The friendship thus formed was not without important influence upon the mind of Goethe. By Herder his attention was directed to the Hebrew poets, to Ossian, and to Shakspeare. During his stay at Strasburg he also became acquainted with Frederica, with whom he fell passionately in love. She was the daughter of Herr Brion, pastor of Sesenheim. This little place could be seen from the lofty gallery of Strasburg Cathedral, whence the young lover and poet sometimes pointed out to his

friends the home of his beloved. Goethe pleased himself with likening Herr Brion to the Vicar of Wakefield, Frederica to Sophia, and the elder sister to Olivia.

On his return to Strasburg it was understood that he was the accepted lover of Frederica; although it is probable that they were not formally betrothed. He afterwards left her, because, as his friends suggest, his love was not strong enough to justify marriage. Alluding to some of his earlier love-passages, he says, "Gretchen had been taken from me, Annchen had left me; but now [in the case of Frederica] for the first time I was guilty: I had wounded to its very depths one of the most beautiful and tender of hearts. And that period of gloomy repentance, deprived of the love which had so strengthened me, was agonizing, insupportable."

Goethe took the degree of Doctor in 1771. But although, in accordance with his father's wishes, he had studied law, his inclinations led him to other pursuits; he seems indeed, even in youth, never to have lost sight of that universal self-culture which was one of the great aims of his life. Not only poetry, but art, science, the languages, philosophy, and criticism,—all were studied by him with an impartiality and success of which the history of the human mind probably furnishes no other example.

In 1771 he composed one of his most celebrated works, "Götz von Berlichingen." He had been deeply interested in the life of Gottfried (or Götz) von Berlichingen, of the sixteenth century, written by Götz himself. Goethe undertook to dramatize it. "I had," he says, "talked the matter over with my sister, who was interested heart and soul in such subjects; and I so often renewed this conversation, without taking any step towards beginning the work, that at last she impatiently and urgently entreated me not to be always talking, but at once to set down on paper what was so distinctly present to my mind. I wrote the first scenes, and in the evening read them aloud to Cornelia. She warmly applauded them, but doubted whether I should go on so; she even expressed a decided disbelief in my perseverance. This only excited me the more. I wrote on the next day, and also the third. Thus I kept on, without interruption, looking neither backwards nor forwards, neither to the right nor the left; and in about six weeks I had the pleasure of seeing the manuscript finished." "Götz von Berlichingen," as first written by Goethe, was a dramatized history; but in this form it was not published until many years later. Having been revised and adapted to the stage, it appeared in 1773 as a drama, *(Schauspiel,)* the form by which it is popularly known. It produced a great sensation in the literary circles of Germany. "It is a piece," says one of the critics of that day, "in which the three unities are shamefully violated, and which is neither a tragedy nor a comedy, and is, notwithstanding, the most beautiful, the most captivating, monstrosity." In 1774 appeared another work, "Sorrows of Young Werther," ("Leiden des jungen Werther,") which excited a still greater and more universal admiration than "Götz" had done. It seemed to fascinate alike men of every class and every nation, and through it Goethe first acquired a European renown. During his Egyptian campaigns, Napoleon is said to have read it through several times; and its fame, it is asserted, extended even to China. "Werther," says Carlyle, "is but the cry of that dim-rooted pain under which all thoughtful men of a certain age were languishing: it paints the misery, it passionately utters the complaint; and heart and voice, all over Europe, loudly and at once respond to it. True, it prescribes no remedy; for that was a far different, far harder enterprise, to which other years and a higher culture were required; but even this utterance of pain, even this little, for the present, is grasped at, and with eager sympathy appropriated in every bosom."

In 1775, attracted by the fame of Goethe, Charles Augustus, (Karl August,) Grand Duke of Saxe-Weimar, invited him to spend some time at his court. The acquaintance thus begun ripened afterwards into a life-long friendship. Weimar was at that time the residence of several distinguished persons, among whom were Wieland, Herder, Musæus, Knebel, and Seckendorf. Wieland, who repeatedly calls Goethe a "godlike creature," was captivated by him at first sight. In a letter written soon after their first interview, he says, "How I loved the magnificent youth as I sat beside him at table! All I can say is this: since that morning my soul is as full of Goethe as a dew-drop of the morning sun." Knebel says, "He rose like a star in the heavens: everybody worshipped him, especially the women." For several months after his arrival at Weimar, he appears to have abandoned himself wholly to the excitements of his new life. The duke and the poet were constant companions, and plunged together for a time into the most insane frolics and wildest dissipation. "Goethe will never," says Wieland, "leave this place again; Karl August can no longer either swim or wade without him." It is almost needless to say that such a life could not long satisfy such a mind. "The want to be once more among simple people and lovely scenes drove him away from Weimar to Waldeck. Amid the crowded tumult of life he ever kept his soul sequestered; and from the hot air of society he broke impatiently away to the serenity of solitude." (Lewes's "Life of Goethe," vol. i. p. 355.) He was called back to Weimar by the grand duke, and in June, 1776, created *Geheimer-Legationsrath*, ("Privy Councillor of Legation,") with a salary of twelve hundred thalers. The duke, writing to Goethe's father, said that the appointment was a mere formality; adding, "Goethe can have but one position, —that of my friend: all others are beneath him."

The first great production of our poet, after he had seriously resumed his studies, was "Iphigenia auf Tauris," ("Iphigenía at Tauris.") This piece was first written in prose; Goethe afterwards turned it into verse, producing what many critics have declared to be the finest modern specimen of the Greek tragedy. In 1786 Goethe visited Italy. In order that he might pursue his studies undisturbed, he travelled *incognito*. He spent some time in Venice, with which city he seems to have been enchanted. He passed through Ferrara, Bologna, and Florence, on his way to Rome, where he arrived about the end of October. He remained there four months. "All the dreams of my youth," he says, "I now see living before me. Everywhere I go I find an old familiar face. Everything is just what I thought it, and yet everything is new." He subsequently visited Naples, Pompeii, and the ruins of Pæstum, carrying with him everywhere a soul intensely susceptible to the beauties both of nature and of art. An account of what he saw and felt while in Italy is given in his "Italiänische Reise," ("Italian Journey.") He returned to Weimar in June, 1788. In the autumn of that year he first became acquainted with Christiane Vulpius, a young woman in humble life, whom he afterwards married. She had presented him a petition entreating him to procure some position for her brother, a young author, then living at Jena. Goethe was greatly smitten with her beauty, *naïveté*, and sprightliness. His *liaison* with her gave rise to much scandal, on account of the disparity of station; and the scandal was not lessened when, many years later, (1806,) he performed an act of tardy justice in marrying her. She had, in 1789, borne him a son, August von Goethe, to whom the Duke of Saxe-Weimar stood godfather. After this event Goethe took Christiane, with her mother and sister, to live with him in his own house; and he appears always to have regarded the connection as a marriage. His conduct in relation to this affair was, however, a source of mortification and deep regret to many of his admirers. "The nation," says Schäfer, "has never forgiven its greatest poet for this rupture with law and custom; nothing has stood so much in the way of a right appreciation of his moral character, nothing has created more false judgments on the tendency of his writings, than this half-marriage." His friends urge two considerations in extenuation of his conduct, which certainly ought not to be lost sight of: first, the general laxity of morals then prevailing among the upper classes in Germany; secondly, the disparity of position between the humble Christiane and the illustrious Goethe, the world-renowned poet, and the councillor and intimate friend of the Grand Duke of Weimar. It is said that she rejected his offers of marriage on this very ground, and

that she herself had declared that it was her own fault that the marriage ceremony had been so long delayed.

In 1792, with the duke, Charles Augustus, Goethe accompanied the Prussian army in the invasion of France. In that campaign he showed that he was not wanting in courage of the most reckless kind; but he returned to Weimar thoroughly disgusted with the war and with military life. He published soon after a scientific work, entitled "Theory or Doctrine of Colours," ("Farbenlehre,") in which he called in question the correctness of the Newtonian theory. It is proper to state that his views have not been adopted by the scientific world.

The poet Schiller had in 1789, partly through Goethe's influence, been appointed to the chair of history in the University of Jena. In 1794 these two illustrious men —"twin sons of Jove," (*Dioscúri*,) as the Germans delighted to call them—were brought frequently together; and, although their characters were so different that they seemed to have scarcely anything in common excepting literary taste and transcendent genius, their acquaintance gradually ripened into a noble and enduring friendship, which exerted an important and most beneficial influence on the minds of both. The correspondence of Schiller and Goethe is of rare interest and value to all the lovers of literature.

To return to Goethe's works. "Egmont," a tragedy, which had been completed in Italy, was published in 1788, soon after his return to Weimar. His "Tasso" appeared in 1790. In 1795, "Wilhelm Meister's Lehrjahre" ("Apprenticeship") was given to the world; this was long after (1821) followed by his "Wanderjahre," ("Travelling Years.") In 1806 appeared the first part of "Faust," the great work of Goethe's life. He had revolved the subject in his mind for more than thirty years. This long delay was not without its fruits. The great poet has, indeed, embodied in this work the results of his mature and infinitely varied experience, with his ripest, richest, and profoundest thoughts; the whole being wrought out with admirable skill, and everywhere illumined, so to speak, with passages of the most exquisite poetry, touching in turn every chord of the human heart. Without indorsing the enthusiastic praise of some of Goethe's admirers, who have pronounced "Faust" to be unqualifiedly "the greatest poem of modern times," we may safely say that it is one of the most wonderful productions of genius to be found in the whole compass of literature. The tale, or novel, entitled "Wahlverwandtschaften," ("Elective Affinities,") appeared in 1809. Considered simply as a piece of creative art, this is one of the most admirable of all of Goethe's productions. In none of his other works are the characters drawn with more vividness and power. The illusion produced by the poet-artist is perfect; so that each of the persons represented is to the reader an absolute and living reality. The moral tendency, however, of the story is more than questionable. The aim of the author, it would seem, is to teach that the attachments between the sexes are governed, like chemical affinities, by fixed, inevitable laws, which it is as impossible to oppose successfully as to resist the decrees of fate.

Besides those already noticed, we may mention among Goethe's works "Clavigo," (published in 1774,) "Hermann and Dorothea," (1796-97,) "Eugenie," (1804,) and "West-Oestliche Divan," (1819,) in which Oriental images and scenes are described with Western feelings and colouring; hence the epithet "West-Oestliche" ("West-Eastern") which the author has applied to this work. The second part of "Faust" was not finished until 1830. It has enjoyed far less popularity than the first part, and by the great majority of critics is considered to be decidedly inferior to it. Goethe's mind was active to the last. He continued to study and to write till within a few days of his death, which took place at Weimar on the 22d of March, 1832.

In person Goethe was eminently handsome,—tall, graceful, and well proportioned. "That accordance of personal appearance with genius," says Heine, "which we ever desire to see in distinguished men, was found in perfection in Goethe. His outward appearance was just as imposing as the word that lives in his writings. Even his form was symmetrical, expressive of joy, nobly

---

ā, ē, ī, ō, ū, ȳ, *long;* ă, ĕ, ŏ, same, less prolonged; ă, ĕ, ĭ, ŏ, ŭ, ў, *short;* a, ẹ, ị, ọ, *obscure;* fär, fȧll, fât; mêt; nŏt; gōōd; mōōn;

proportioned; and one might study the Grecian art upon it as well as upon an antique." The same writer continues, in a more extravagant strain, "His eyes were calm as those of a god. It is the peculiar characteristic of the gods that their gaze is ever steady, and their eyes roll not to and fro in uncertainty. . . . The eye of Goethe remained in his latest age just as divine as in his youth." (Heine's "Letters," translated by G. W. Haven, Boston, 1836.)'

Never, perhaps, was there a human character about which more varying and contradictory opinions have been entertained than about that of Goethe. This is to be chiefly attributed,—first, to the wonderful depth and originality of his mind, and, secondly, to its many-, or rather myriad-, sidedness. It has been said that, in spite of the beautiful sentiments and admirable characters with which his works abound, he himself was cold, calculating, and thoroughly selfish. But this charge is contradicted by his whole life. He appears, indeed, to have always felt for every form of actual suffering a true and ready sympathy, which he manifested rather by acts than by words.* Another charge, more frequently urged, and perhaps better founded, than the preceding, is that he was utterly destitute of any real sympathy with the rights and interests of the common people. It was one of his marked peculiarities that he entertained a distrust and dislike of all abstractions, and he had little or no sympathy with mere ideas or ideal systems. He felt no interest in democracy, because to him democracy was an abstraction. He did not sympathize with his countrymen in their struggle for German independence, because they aimed, as he thought, at what was impracticable. However mistaken this opinion proved to be, it was beyond all doubt perfectly sincere. He disliked politics, for which, indeed, he appears to have felt he had no vocation. His genius lay in a totally different direction.

His aversion to abstractions and his love of the concrete may be said to have given form to all his views, religious, moral, and social. He refused to recognize a Deity that was above and distinct from the world; for he considered every part of nature—the entire universe, in short—to be divine. He did not hold, with the Platonists or Christians, that mankind have fallen from an ideal or divine perfection, after which they must continually strive if they would be restored.

He was a worshipper of Nature; and his moral creed, if not distinctly avowed, may be readily gathered from many expressions in his works or his recorded conversations: it may be thus briefly summed up, "Everything that is natural is right;" in other words, "Nothing is really wrong except what is unnatural." We accordingly find him quoting with apparent approbation the saying of Thraseas, "He who hates faults or vices hates men," ("Qui vitia odit homines odit,") which, says Mr. Lewes, "was just the sort of passage to captivate him." It may readily be conceded that, whatever evils might result from the general adoption of so loose a system of morals, these evils would be much mitigated in one whose perception of moral as well as æsthetic beauty was so vivid and intense. But it was not without an injurious influence even upon him. It was the great defect of Goethe's character that his virtues, like his faults, were too often the offspring of mere feeling or impulse uncontrolled by any fixed principles of duty or right. It is thus, indeed, we are to explain the fact that so many of his writings are destitute of anything like a moral purpose. This charge has been made particularly against his "Wilhelm Meister." It is not enough to reply that the author did not set himself up as a preacher of morality. His admirers will not deny that he aimed to give a picture of human life, or a narrative of human events: in either case there should have been at least so much of moral teaching as we find everywhere interwoven with the tissue of human affairs. If Goethe had possessed a just and true appreciation of the importance of moral principles, such a conviction could not fail to make itself felt in his works. The moral need not, to use the language of Miss Edgeworth, be "sewed on in purple

* For a remarkable instance of this, see Lewes's "Life of Goethe," book iv. chapter viii.

patches," but be "interwoven with the very texture of the stuff." In the dramas of Shakspeare we perceive a moral element constantly pervading the story, yet without being in the least obtruded upon the reader. So in history we behold a "divinity that shapes our ends, rough hew them how we will."* Many of Goethe's sincerest admirers have felt and acknowledged the faults in his character to which we have adverted. While giving him credit for a rare sincerity and for many generous and noble qualities, they cannot help regretting the absence of a fixed and lofty moral purpose which might serve as a keystone to his other attributes. (Respecting Goethe's character and moral influence, see an excellent article in the "Edinburgh Review" for July, 1857, vol. cvi.) With regard to Goethe's rank as a man of genius, if we cannot concede all that Carlyle and some of his other devoted admirers claim for him, still less can we agree with De Quincey, that, owing to a rare combination of external circumstances, it has been his fortune to take a far higher rank in European literature than his actual merits would justify. But these are questions which the reader must examine and settle for himself.

See Lewes, "Life of Goethe," 2 vols., 1855; Goethe, Autobiography, "Aus meinem Leben Dichtung und Wahrheit," 5 vols., 1811–12, (translated into English by Parke Godwin, 2 vols., 1847;) Viehoff, "Göthe's Leben," 4 vols., 1847; Eckermann, "Conversations with Göthe," ("Gespräche mit Göthe;") "Characteristics of Göthe," by Sarah Austin, 3 vols., London, 1833; Carlyle, "Essays;" De Quincey, "Biographical Essays," article "Goethe;" Emerson, "Representative Men;" Longfellow, "Poets and Poetry of Europe," 1855; Heinrich Döring, "Goethe's Leben," 1828; Varnhagen von Ense, "Goethe in den Zeugnissen der Mitlebenden," 1823; Rosenkranz, "Goethe und seine Werke," 1856; Carl Morgenstern, "J. W. Goethe," 1833; Marmier, "Études sur Goethe," 1835; F. Pfeiffer, "Goethe und Klopstock," 1840; J. W. Schaefer, "J. W. Goethe's Leben," 1851; F. Riemer, "Mittheilungen über Goethe," 2 vols., 1841; A. Nicolovius, "Ueber Goethe," etc., 1828; Düntzer, "Göthe als Dramatiker," 1837.

Goettling. See Göttling.

Goetz. See Götz.

Goetze. See Götze.

Goetzinger. See Götzinger.

Goez. See Göz.

Goffe or **Gough**, gof, (Thomas,) an English divine and dramatist, born in Essex about 1592. He was the author of tragedies entitled "The Raging Turk," and "Orestes;" also of several comedies. Died in 1629.

Goffe, gof, (William,) an English Puritan and regicide, was one of the judges of Charles I., and a general in Cromwell's army. In company with Whalley, another outlaw, he retired to New England in 1660, and lived in concealment. During an attack of the savages on Hadley, (1675,) Goffe, it is said, suddenly appeared, rallied the whites, and repulsed the enemy.

See Neal's "History of New England."

Goffredo di Buglione. See Godfrey of Bouillon.

Gogol, go'gol, (Nikolai Vassilievitch,) a celebrated Russian writer, born about 1810. Having visited Saint Petersburg about 1830, he published soon after a series of tales entitled "Evenings at a Farm-House," containing admirable delineations of rural life in Russia. They immediately obtained great popularity, and were translated into French by M. Viardot. His next publication was the comedy of the "Revisor," which also met with brilliant success, and is perhaps the most popular work of the kind in the language. "The Dead Souls," (1842,) a comic satire on ignorance and prejudice, was received with equal enthusiasm. Gogol, who had previously been appointed professor of history in the University of Saint Petersburg, soon after visited Rome, where he wrote a series of letters (published at Saint Petersburg in 1847) which gave great offence to his liberal friends in Russia. In these he appears as the defender of tyranny, both in church and state, instead of the advocate of serf-emancipation and popular progress, as he had shown himself in

* One of the ablest and most thorough historians of the present age, and one who will scarcely be accused of a disposition to accept popular theories without examination, tells us that, amid all the hard truths and uncertainties of history, one lesson is distinctly taught,— that "THE MORAL LAW IS WRITTEN ON THE TABLETS OF ETERNITY. For every false word or unrighteous deed, for cruelty and oppression, for lust or vanity, the price has to be paid at last." (Lecture on "Science of History," in Froude's "Short Studies on Great Subjects.")

ɇ as k; ç as s; g̃ hard; g̃ as j; G, H, K, guttural; N, nasal; R, trilled; s̃ as z; ŧh as in this. (☞See Explanations, p. 23.)

his novel of "The Dead Souls." He returned to Russia in 1848, and died at Moscow in February, 1852. An excellent French translation of the "Revisor" has been made by M. Mérimée, and an imperfect English version of "The Dead Souls" came out in 1854, entitled "Home-Life in Russia."

See "Nouvelle Biographie Générale;" "British Quarterly Review" for April, 1868.

Goguet, go'gȧ', (ANTOINE YVES,) a French jurist, born in Paris in 1716. He wrote an important work "On the Origin of Laws, Arts, and Sciences, and their Progress among the Ancients," (3 vols., 1758,) "the success of which," says M. Weiss, "was brilliant and merited." ("Biographie Universelle.") Died in 1758.

Gohier, go'e-ȧ', (LOUIS JÉRÔME,) a director of the French republic, was born at Semblançay in 1746. He was elected to the Legislative Assembly in 1791, and succeeded Garat as minister of justice in March, 1793. Having been removed in April, 1794, he was elected a member of the Directory in June, 1799. He was president of the Directory when Bonaparte returned from Egypt, and, in concert with Moulins, opposed the *coup d'état* of the 18th Brumaire, even after their colleagues had resigned. "He was an honest citizen," says Thiers, "and devoted to the republic." ("History of the French Revolution.") Died in Paris in 1830.

See LOUIS JÉRÔME GOHIER, "Mémoires," 2 vols., 1824; "Nouvelle Biographie Générale."

Gohl. See GOLIUS.

Gohory or **Gohorry,** go'o're', (JACQUES,) a French *littérateur*, born in Paris, translated into French Machiavel's "Prince," and other works, and wrote a treatise "On the Knowledge of the Virtues of the Herb called Petum, [Tobacco,]" (1572.) Died in 1576.

Gois, gwâ, (EDME ÉTIENNE FRANÇOIS,) a French sculptor, born in Paris in 1765, executed statues of Charlemagne, Joan of Arc, and Bonaparte. Died in 1836.

Golbéry, de, dĕh gol'bȧ're', (MARIE PHILIPPE AIMÉ,) a French lawyer and antiquary, born at Colmar in 1786, wrote many antiquarian treatises, and translated into French Niebuhr's "History of Rome." Died in 1854.

See QUÉRARD, "La France Littéraire."

Golbéry, de, (SYLVAIN MEINRAD XAVIER,) a French officer, born at Colmar in 1742, explored the western coast of Africa in 1785–87, and wrote a "Fragment of a Journey in Africa," (2 vols., 1802.) Died in 1822.

Goldast von Heimingsfeld, gol'dȧst fon hī'mings-fĕlt', (MELCHIOR,) a learned historian and jurist, born near Bischofszell, in Switzerland, in 1576. Among his most important works we may cite "Scriptores Rerum Suevicarum," (1605,) and "Collectio Constitutionum Imperialium," (1607.) Died in 1635.

See FRORIEP, "Beiträge zu der Lebensgeschichte des Publicisten Goldast," 1789; BAYLE, "Historical and Critical Dictionary;" NICÉRON, "Mémoires."

Goldfuss, golt'fㅎㅎss, (GEORG AUGUST,) a German naturalist, and professor of zoology and mineralogy at Bonn, was born near Baireuth in 1782. He published "Representations and Descriptions of the Petrifactions of Germany," and other works. Died in 1848.

Goldhagen, golt'hä'ḡen, (HERMANN,) a German philologist, born at Mentz in 1718, published, besides other works, a "Greek-Latin Lexicon,"(1753.) Died in 1794.

Goldhagen, (JOHANN EUSTACE,) a German philologist, born at Nordhausen in 1701, was rector of the gymnasium of Magdeburg. He translated Herodotus, Xenophon, and Pausanias into German. Died in 1772.

Gȯld'ing, (ARTHUR,) an English writer and able translator, born in London, lived about 1560–90. He finished the translation of Philippe de Mornay's treatise "Sur la Vérité du Christianisme," commenced by Sir Philip Sidney, and published versions of the theological works of Calvin and Grosteste, also of Cæsar, Seneca, and other Latin classics. He also translated Ovid's "Metamorphoses" into English verse.

See WARTON, "History of English Poetry."

Goldmann. See CHRYSANDER.

Goldmayer, golt'mī'er, (ANDREAS,) a German astronomer and astrologer, born at Günzenhausen in 1603; died in 1664.

Goldoni, gol-dō'nee, (CARLO,) a celebrated Italian comic author, born in Venice in 1707. He manifested a passion for theatrical performances in early childhood, and wrote a comedy at the age of eight. He was liberally educated, studied law, and graduated at Padua in 1731, after which he practised as an advocate in Venice for a short time. In 1734 he produced a drama called "Belisario." He married a Genoese lady in 1736. Having renounced the profession of advocate, he composed in rapid succession numerous comedies, which were performed with applause, and effected an important reform of the Italian theatre. He became a resident of Paris in 1761, and received a pension from the king, who also appointed him Italian teacher to the princesses. He wrote several comedies in French, one of which, "Le Bourru bienfaisant," (1771,) met with brilliant success. Among his other comedies are "The Flatterer,"(" L'Adulatore,") "La Donna di Garbo," "Il Bugiardo," and "Il Vecchio bizarro." Goldoni was one of the best comic writers that Italy has produced. He died in Paris in 1793, leaving Memoirs of his Life, (3 vols., 1787, in French,) which are said to be very interesting, and were pronounced by Gibbon "more comic than the best comedies of their author."

See, also, G. GIOVANNI, "Vita di Carlo Goldoni," 1821; MENEGHEZZI, "Memorie della Vita di Carlo Goldoni," 1827; LUIGI CARRER, "Saggio su la Vita e su le Opere di C. Goldoni," 3 vols., 1824; LONGFELLOW, "Poets and Poetry of Europe."

Goldsborough, gōlz'bŭr-reh, (LEWIS M.,) an American rear-admiral, born in Washington, District of Columbia, in 1805. He became a lieutenant in 1825, married a daughter of William Wirt, and gained the rank of commander in 1841. In 1855 he was raised to the rank of captain, and in September, 1861, took command of the North Atlantic Blockading Squadron. He commanded the fleet which co-operated with General Burnside in the capture of Roanoke Island in February, 1862.

Goldschmidt, golt'shmit, (HERMANN,) a German painter and astronomer, born at Frankfort-on-the-Main in 1802. He settled in Paris about 1836. Among the works which have procured him a high reputation are the "Cumæan Sibyl," (1845,) "The Offering to Venus," (1846,) and "Cleopatra." He has acquired celebrity by astronomical observations which have resulted in the discovery of the following asteroids : Lutetia, (1852,) Pomona, (1854,) Atalanta, (1855,) Harmonia and Daphne, (1856,) Nysa, (1857,) etc.

See "Nouvelle Biographie Générale."

Goldschmidt, MADAME. See LIND, (JENNY.)

Goldschmidt, golt'shmit, (MEYER AARON,) a Danish novelist, born in Jutland in 1819. Among his works is "The Homeless Man," (5 vols., 1853–57.)

Gȯld'smith, (OLIVER,) an eminent poet and miscellaneous writer, was born in Ireland, at Pallas, in the county of Longford, in 1728. Having early manifested a talent for making rhymes, his uncle, the Rev. Thomas Contarine, offered to send him at his own expense to the University of Dublin. He entered Trinity College as a sizar in 1745. Here he was more remarkable for idleness and love of dissipation than for his devotion to his studies. He took his degree of B.A. in 1749, two years after the regular time. Yielding to the wishes of his uncle, he now prepared to enter the church ; but he was rejected by the bishop when he applied for orders. His uncle next sent him to London to study law ; but on his way he spent in gambling the money furnished for his travelling expenses, and returned home with empty pockets. His generous relative, however, forgave all his offences, and soon after sent him to study medicine at Edinburgh, where he spent two years ; after which he visited Leyden, where he remained about a year, and then set out, "with only one clean shirt, and no money in his pocket," to make the tour of Europe on foot. The following passage in the "Vicar of Wakefield," which probably has reference to himself, may explain to us how he supported himself while travelling. "I had some knowledge of music, and now turned what was once my amusement into a present means of subsistence. Whenever I approached a peasant's house towards nightfall, I played one of my most merry tunes ; and that procured me not only a lodging, but subsistence for the next day."

ā, ē, ī, ō, ū, ȳ, *long;* à, ė, ò, same, less prolonged; ă, ĕ, ĭ, ŏ, ŭ, ў, *short;* a, e, i, o, *obscure;* fär, fȧll, fȧt; mĕt; nŏt; gㅎㅎd; mㅎㅎn;

He sojourned six months at Padua, in Italy, and is supposed to have taken his medical degree either at that place or Louvain. Having heard, while in Italy, of the death of his uncle, he immediately set out for England, where he landed in 1756.

On his arrival in London he was first employed as an usher in a school at Peckham, and afterwards became an apothecary's assistant. In 1758 he was appointed physician to one of the factories in India, but he declined the offer, and turned his attention to the study of letters. In 1759 he published his "Present State of Literature in Europe." In the same year he wrote several essays for a periodical called "The Bee," of which only eight numbers appeared. He next published some contributions to Smollett's "British Magazine," and the "Chinese Letter." In 1762 he wrote "The Vicar of Wakefield," while under arrest for debt, from which he was released by Dr. Johnson, who obtained from a bookseller £60 for the work. It was not published, however, till 1766. "The Traveller," a part of which had been written in Switzerland, came out in 1764. It was received with great favour, and at once established the reputation of its author. About this time he wrote "Letters from a Nobleman to his Son," "Life of Beau Nash," and several compilations. In the early part of 1768 the comedy of "The Good-natured Man" was brought out at Covent-Garden Theatre, but was not very well received. "The Deserted Village" appeared in 1770. Soon after this he began his Histories of Rome, Greece, and England, and in also engaged, with several of his literary friends, in a periodical called "The Gentleman's Journal," which, however, had a very brief existence, dying, as Goldsmith said, "of too many doctors." His next comedy, "She Stoops to Conquer," came out in 1773, and met with complete success. Dr. Johnson said that "he knew of no comedy for many years that had answered so much the great end of comedy,—making an audience merry." His "History of the Earth and Animated Nature" was published in 1774. Shortly after the appearance of this work, Goldsmith was attacked by a fever, which, being aggravated by improper treatment, and also by pecuniary troubles, caused his death, on the 4th of April, 1774. Though Goldsmith's fame rests chiefly on his poems, he merits little less admiration as a prose-writer. The rich yet delicate humour of some of his essays has perhaps never been excelled. He possessed great benevolence and warmth of feeling, but he wanted steadiness of principle, and was at all times the creature of impulse. He also manifested on many occasions a considerable degree of vanity and feelings of petty jealousy.

"Of all romances in miniature," says Schlegel, "the 'Vicar of Wakefield' is the most exquisite;" and this may be said to be the judgment of nearly all competent critics. Perhaps no English prose work of fiction is so generally admired in Germany as that above named.

See JOHN FORSTER, "Life and Adventures of O. Goldsmith," 1848; W. IRVING, "Goldsmith; a Biography," 1850; JAMES PRIOR, "Life of O. Goldsmith," 2 vols., 1837; JOHNSON'S and CHALMERS'S "Lives of the English Poets;" PERCY, "Life of Goldsmith," 1801; JOHN MITFORD, "Life of O. Goldsmith;" SIR W. SCOTT'S Miscellaneous Prose Works; "London Quarterly Review," vol. lvii.; "Edinburgh Review" for April, 1837; MACAULAY'S notice of Goldsmith in the "Encyclopædia Britannica."

Go-li′ath, [Heb. נָּלְיַת,] a giant leader of the Philistines, is supposed to have flourished in the eleventh century B.C. Having challenged the Israelites to single combat, no one was found willing to meet him except David, who slew him with a stone from his sling. (See 1st Book of Samuel.)

Go′li-us, (JAKOB,) an eminent Dutch Orientalist, born at the Hague in 1596. He distinguished himself at the University of Leyden by his attainments in the classics, mathematics, and philosophy, and subsequently studied Arabic under Erpenius. In 1622 he accompanied the Dutch embassy to Morocco as interpreter, and presented a memorial in Arabic to the emperor. Erpenius having died in 1624, Golius succeeded him as professor of Arabic at Leyden. He soon after obtained permission to visit the East, and, having spent four years in Asia Minor and Arabia, returned in 1629, bringing with him a very large and choice collection of manuscripts. He

had been appointed during his absence professor of mathematics. His principal work is his "Lexicon Arabico-Latinum," (1653,) which is still highly esteemed; he also finished the translation of Elmacin's "History of the Saracens," which was begun by Erpenius, and published other learned works. Died in 1667.

See J. F. GRONOVIUS, "Laudatio funebris J. Golii," 1668; BAYLE, "Historical and Critical Dictionary;" "Nouvelle Biographie Générale."

Golius, (PIETER,) brother of the preceding, born at Leyden, was also distinguished as an Oriental scholar. He became professor of Arabic in the Carmelite Seminary at Rome, and was afterwards a missionary to Asia, where he founded a monastery of his order on Mount Lebanon. He translated into Arabic the "Imitation of Jesus Christ," and published other works. Died in 1673.

Gollut, go′lü′, (LOUIS,) a French historian, born in Burgundy, wrote "Historical Memoirs of the Republic and the Princes of Burgundy." Died in 1595.

Golovin, go-lo-veen′, (FEODOR ALEXIEVITCH,) a distinguished Russian, who became high-chancellor under Peter the Great. In 1689 he was commissioned to sign a treaty of perpetual peace between Russia and China. Died in 1706. His son NICHOLAS, born in 1694, was sent as Russian minister to the court of Sweden, and became afterwards president of the College of the Admiralty. Died in 1745.

See BANTICH-KAMENSKI, "Histoire des Hommes illustres du Règne de Pierre le Grand."

Golovin or **Golowin,** (IVAN,) a Russian senator and admiral, distinguished for integrity, lived in the reign of Peter the Great, who ordered a medal to be struck in his honour. He was made a vice-admiral in 1725.

See BERCH, "Histoire d'Ivan Golovin."

Golovin, Golovine, or **Golowin,** (IVAN,) a Russian littérateur, born about 1816, travelled in England, France, and Germany, and in 1855 visited the United States. He published "Russian Types and Characters," (1847,) "Russia under Nicholas I.," (in French,) and "Stars and Stripes; or, American Impressions."

Golovin, Golovine, or **Golowin,** (SEMEN VASSILIEVITCH,) a Russian general and statesman, born in 1560. Having supported the claims of Michael Feodorovitch to the throne, he was rewarded with a title of nobility, and appointed Governor-General of Kazan. Died in 1634.

Golovine. See GOLOVIN.

Golovkin, go-lov-kèn′, (GABRIEL,) COUNT, a Russian statesman, born in 1660, was a favourite of Peter the Great, whom he accompanied in several of his campaigns. He was created chancellor of the empire in 1709. He was also patronized by Catherine I. and Peter II. Died in 1734.

Golovnin, Golovnine, or **Golownin,** go-lov-neen′, (VASILII,) a Russian navigator, who sailed in 1809 to make a survey of the coasts of the Russian empire. After an absence of two years, during which he was imprisoned for a time in Japan, he returned to Russia, where he published in 1816 an account of his voyage and captivity, which was translated into several languages. Died in 1832.

See "Nouvelle Biographie Générale;" "London Quarterly Review" for November, 1820.

Golowin. See GOLOVIN.

Golowkin. See GOLOVKIN

Golownin. See GOLOVNIN.

Goltz, golts, (AUGUST FRIEDRICH FERDINAND,) COUNT, a Prussian statesman, born at Dresden in 1765. In conjunction with Kalckreuth, he concluded the peace of Tilsit, and in 1812 he negotiated the treaty between France and Prussia. He was subsequently appointed grand marshal of the court. Died in 1832.

Goltz, von, fon golts, (GEORG CONRAD,) BARON, an able Prussian general, born in Pomerania in 1704. He was appointed adjutant-general by Frederick the Great in 1740. Died in 1747.

Goltzius, golt′se-us, (HEINRICH,) a celebrated Dutch engraver and painter, born near Venloo in 1558. He studied under Leonhard at Haarlem, and afterwards at Rome. He executed a number of good pictures; but his reputation rests chiefly on his engravings, which are of great excellence and very numerous. Among these we may name the "Annunciation," after Raphael, the "Adoration of the Shepherds," after Bassano, and an "Adoration of the Kings." Died at Haarlem in 1617.

See DESCAMPS, "Les Peintres Flamands;" NAGLER, "Neues Allgemeines Künstler-Lexikon."

Goltzius, (HUBERT,) a Dutch antiquary, artist, and numismatist, born at Venloo in 1526. He was appointed royal historjographer and painter by Philip II. of Spain, to whom he dedicated one of his works. He published "Roman Fasti from Antique Coins," etc., ("Fasti Magistratum et Triumphorum Romanorum," etc.,) and other similar treatises. Died at Bruges in 1583.

See NICÉRON, "Mémoires;" FOPPENS, "Bibliotheca Belgica;" "Nouvelle Biographie Générale;" FÉLIX VAN HULST, "H. Goltzius."

Gomar, go'mar, (FRANCIS,) a celebrated Protestant theologian and controversialist, born at Bruges in 1563. He completed his studies at Oxford and Cambridge in England, and in 1594 was appointed professor of theology at Leyden. He filled the same chair at Saumur in 1614, and subsequently became professor of Hebrew and divinity at Groningen, (1618.) He is chiefly known from his controversy with Arminius; and the Calvinistic party in Holland received from him the name of Gomarists. Died at Groningen in 1641.

See R. SIMON, "Histoire critique des principaux Commentateurs du Nouveau Testament," chap. xl.; BAYLE, "Historical and Critical Dictionary;" "Nouvelle Biographie Générale."

Gomara, de, dà go-mä'rä, (FRANCISCO LOPEZ,) a Spanish historian, born at Seville in 1510, was the author of a "Crónica de la Nueva España," published in 1553. It is written in a concise and elegant style, and was translated into several languages. Died about 1560.

See PRESCOTT, "History of the Conquest of Mexico," vol. ii. book v.

Gombauld, de, dĕh gòN'bō', (JEAN Ogier—o'zhe-â',) a French poet and epigrammatist, one of the founders of the French Academy, was born at Saintonge in 1567. He was celebrated for his wit, and was one of the circle who frequented the Hôtel de Rambouillet. His works include romances, dramas, and sonnets, and epigrams which were particularly admired. It is related of him that he once read one of his poems to Cardinal Richelieu, who remarked, "Here are some things I do not understand." "That is not my fault," replied Gombauld. Among his principal works may be named "Endymion," a prose romance, and "Amaranthe," a pastoral. Died in 1666.

See PELLISSON, "Histoire de l'Académie Française;" BAYLE, "Historical and Critical Dictionary;" MORÉRI, "Dictionnaire Historique;" "Nouvelle Biographie Générale."

Gomberville, Le Roi de, lĕh Rwä dĕh gòN'bĕR'vĕl', (MARIN,) a French *littérateur*, born in Paris in 1600, wrote many poems and romances, and was one of the first members of the French Academy. Died in 1674.

See PELLISSON, "Histoire de l'Académie Française."

Gomera, de. See GOMARA.

Go'mer-sall, (ROBERT,) an English divine and poet, born in London in 1600. He published a tragedy entitled "Ludovic Sforza," "The Levite's Revenge," a poem, and a number of sermons. Died in 1646.

See WOOD, "Athenæ Oxonienses."

Gomes or **Gomez,** go'mĕz, (FRANCISCO DIAS,) a Portuguese poet and critic, born at Lisbon. He wrote "The Seasons," and other poems, also a critical essay on the styles of Sá de Miranda, Ferreira, and Camoens, (1790.) Died in 1795.

See "Nouvelle Biographie Générale."

Gomes or **Gomez,** (JOÃO BAPTISTA,) a distinguished Portuguese dramatist, wrote a very popular tragedy entitled "Iñez de Castro," (published about 1806.) It has been translated into French and German. Died about 1812.

See LONGFELLOW, "Poets and Poetry of Europe."

Gomez, go'mĕth, (FERNANDO,) a Spanish soldier, born at Toledo in 1138, distinguished himself by his skill and bravery in the wars against the Moors. He is said to have been the original founder of the order of Alcántara. Died in 1182.

Gomez, (JUAN,) a Spanish painter, born about 1550, became court painter to Philip II. Died in 1597.

Gomez, (SEBASTIANO,) a celebrated Spanish painter, called "the Mulatto of Murillo," born at Seville about 1616. He was originally a slave of Murillo, but, on account of the genius he displayed, was liberated by his master and received among his pupils. Among his master-pieces is a "Virgin and Child." Died about 1690.

See QUILLIET, "Dictionnaire des Peintres Espagnols."

Gomez, de, dĕh go'mĕz', (MADELÈNE ANGÉLIQUE Poisson—pwä'sòN',) MADAME, a French novelist, born in Paris in 1684. Among her best works are "Les Cent Nouvelles" and her "Persian Anecdotes." Died in 1770.

Gomez de Becerra, de, dà go'mĕth dà bà-thĕr'rä, (ALVARO,) a Spanish jurist and statesman, born in Estremadura in 1771, became a senator and president of the chamber of the Cortes.

Gomez de Castro, (ALVAREZ.) See CASTRO.

Gomez de Ciudad Real, go'mĕth dà the-oo-DâD' rà-âl', (ALVAREZ,) a Spanish Latin poet, born at Guadalaxara in 1488. He wrote several Latin poems, among which is "Thaliachristia," (1522.) Died in 1538.

Gomez de Ciudad Real, (FERDINANDO,) born at Ciudad Real in 1388, became physician to John II., King of Castile. Died in 1457.

Gomez (or **Gomes**) **de Oliviera,** go'mĕz dà o-le-ve-ä'rä, (ANTONIO,) a Portuguese poet, who lived about 1620. He wrote "Idyls of the Sea," ("Idylios maritimos,") and numerous sonnets.

Gomez de Silva. See SILVA.

Gomez de Vasconcelle, de, dĕh go'mĕz' dĕh väs'kòN'sĕl', (LOUISE GENEVIÈVE,) a literary lady, of Portuguese extraction, published an abridged translation of the "Orlando Furioso" into French; also several romances. Died in 1718.

Gomez-Ferreira, go'mĕz fĕr-rā'e-rä, (LUIS,) a learned Portuguese physician, born in 1680. He wrote a valuable work, entitled "Mineral Treasury." Died in 1741.

Gomm, (Sir WILLIAM MAY'NARD,) a British general, born in 1784. He served in the Peninsula, 1808–14, and at Waterloo. He became commander-in-chief in India in 1850 or 1851, and was relieved in 1855.

Gonçalo de Cordova. See GONSALVO.

Gonçalves, gon-sâl'vĕz, (JOAQUIM AFFONSO,) a learned Portuguese missionary and Chinese scholar, born in 1780. In 1812 he visited Brazil, the Philippine Islands, and Macao. He published a Portuguese-Chinese Grammar, entitled "Arte China," (1829,) and a "Diccionario Portuguez-China," which are highly esteemed. Died in 1841.

Gondebaud, gòN'dĕh-bō', or **Gun'do-bâld,** second son of Gondioc, King of Burgundy. Having slain his brother Chilpéric, and defeated his army, he ascended the throne in 491 A.D. In 499 he made an unsuccessful attempt to reconcile the Catholics and Arians. He was defeated near Dijon, in 500 A.D., by Clovis, King of the Franks, to whom he became tributary. He drew up a system of laws for his subjects, since called the "Burgundian Code." In religion he was an Arian. Died in 516.

See SISMONDI, "Histoire des Français."

Gondebaud or **Gon'do-vâld,** King of Aquitaine, surnamed BALLOMER, was a natural son of Clotaire I. On the death of Chilpéric, King of Austrasia, he succeeded to the throne, (584.) He was afterwards betrayed into the hands of Gontran, King of Burgundy, and put to death, 585.

See SISMONDI, "Histoire des Français."

Gondebald-Ballomer. See preceding article.

Gondegisile, gòN'dĕh-zhe'zĕl', [Lat.GONDEGISI'LUS,] a younger son of Gondioc, King of Burgundy, was born about 470 A.D. He ruled over the territory between the Rhone and the Doubs, and was an ally of Clovis. He was killed by his brother Gondebaud in 501.

Gon'de-mar, or **God'o-mar,** King of Burgundy, was a son of Gondebaud. He reigned from 523 to 534 A.D., and defeated Clodomir, King of Orléans, in battle.

Gon'de-mar, (FLAVIUS,) was elected king of the Visigoths in Spain in 610 A.D. Died in 612.

Gonderic. See GONDIOC.

Gondi. See RETZ, CARDINAL DE.

Gondi, de, dĕh gòN'de', (PHILIPPE EMANUEL,) a French naval officer, born at Limoges in 1584. In 1622

ā, ē, ī, ō, ū, ȳ, *long;* à, ė, ò, same, less prolonged; ă, ĕ, ĭ, ŏ, ŭ, y̆, *short;* ą, ę, į, ǫ, *obscure;* fär, fàll, fât; mĕt; nŏt; gōōd; mōōn;

he assisted the Duke of Guise in the blockade of La Rochelle. He was a patron of the celebrated Vincent de Paul. Died in 1662.

Gondicaire, gôN'de'kǎR', [Lat. GUNDICA'RIUS,] or **Gundahaire,** first King of Burgundy, born about 385 A.D. Having invaded Germany about 413, he established himself with his subjects on the Rhine, whence the Romans vainly endeavoured to expel them. His army was defeated by the Huns under Attila in 436, and he himself slain.

See SISMONDI, "Histoire des Français."

Gon'dī-oc or **Gon'der-ic,** [Lat. GUNDERI'CUS,] son of Gondicaire, noticed above, was the second King of Burgundy, and ascended the throne in 436 A.D. He greatly extended, both by conquest and by treaties, the territory left him by his father. Died about 473.

See AUG. THIERRY, "Lettres sur l'Histoire de France."

Gondola, gon'do-lä, (GIOVANNI DI FRANCESCO,) a distinguished poet, born at Ragusa, in Illyria, in 1588. He wrote an epic poem entitled the "Osmanide," in which he celebrates the deeds and misfortunes of Osman I. He also translated into Illyrian Tasso's "Gerusalemme Liberata," and wrote other works. Died in 1638. His son SIGISMUND was an accomplished poet, and became rector of the republic of Ragusa.

See F. M. APPENDINI, "Memoria sulla Vita e su gli Scritti di G. F. Gondola," 1837.

Gondouin, gôN'doo-ǎN', (JACQUES,) a French architect, born at Saint-Ouen-sur-Seine in 1737. He designed the École de Chirurgie, since called École de Médecine, in Paris, which, says Quatremère de Quincy, "is the most classic work of the eighteenth century." Died in 1818.

See QUATREMÈRE DE QUINCY, "Vies des plus célèbres Architectes."

Gondrin, de, deh gôN'dRǎN', (LOUIS ANTOINE **de Pardaillan**—deh pǎR'dǎ'yôN',) Duc d'Antin, (dôN'tǎN',) a French courtier, born in 1665, was a son of Madame de Montespan. He won the favour of Louis XIV., and of his son, the dauphin. Died in 1736.

See "Nouvelle Biographie Générale."

Gondrin, de, (LOUIS HENRI **de Pardaillan,**) a French Jansenist, born in the diocese of Auch in 1620. He was made Archbishop of Sens in 1646. Died in 1674.

Gon'dulf or **Gun'dulf,** a French prelate, born in the diocese of Rouen in 1023, became Abbot of Saint Stephen's at Caen, and in 1076 was made Bishop of Rochester, in England. Died in 1108.

Gonelli, go-nel'lee, or **Gonnelli,** gon-nel'lee, (GIOVANNI,) an Italian sculptor, surnamed "the Blind Man of Cambassi," born in Tuscany in 1610. He became blind at the age of twenty, but continued the practice of his art, and, it is said, modelled portraits in clay by the touch alone. Died in 1664.

Gonet, go'nǎ', (JEAN BAPTISTE,) a learned French Dominican, born at Béziers in 1616, became professor of theology at Bordeaux. He published a work entitled "Shield of the Theology of the Thomists," ("Clypeus Theologiæ Thomisticæ," 18 vols. 12mo,) of which Bayle remarks, "The Spaniards call it a very pretty compendium of divinity." Died in 1681.

Gongora y Argote, gon-go'rä e aR-go'tä, (LUIS,) a Spanish poet, born at Córdova in 1561. He took holy orders at the age of forty-five, before which he had composed elegant sonnets, satires, and ballads. He became chaplain to Philip III. about 1616. In the latter part of his life he adopted a fantastic, affected, and obscure style, which he called *estilo culto,* and which was imitated by many of his contemporaries and is sometimes called *Gongorism.* Died in 1627.

See TICKNOR, "History of Spanish Literature;" LONGFELLOW, "Poets and Poetry of Europe;" N. ANTONIO, "Bibliotheca Hispana Nova."

Gonnelieu, de, deh gon'le-uh', (JÉRÔME,) a French Jesuit, pulpit orator, and theologian, born at Soissons in 1640; died in 1715.

Gönner or **Goenner,** gön'ner, (NIKOLAUS THADDÄUS,) a German jurist, born at Bamberg in 1764. He published, among other works, a treatise "On German Public Law," (1804,) and a "Manual of Common Pro-

cess," ("Handbuch des gemeinen Processes," 4 vols., 1805.) Died in 1827.

See H. J. JÄCK, "N. T. von Gönner's Biographie," 1813.

Gonsalo, gon-sä'lo, (FERNANDO,) Count of Castile, a Spanish military commander, who gained a victory over Sancho, King of Navarre, in 924, and afterwards defeated the Moors in several engagements.

Gonsalvo, gon-säl'vo, **Gonzalo,** gon-thä'lo, or **Gonçalo de Córdova,** (HERNANDEZ or FERNANDEZ,) [Fr. GONSALVE DE CORDOUE, gôN'sǎlv' deh koR'doo',] a celebrated Spanish commander, surnamed THE GREAT CAPTAIN, was born at Montilla, near Córdova, in 1443, (or, according to some writers, in 1453.) He was a brother of Don Alonzo de Aguilar. He distinguished himself in the long war of Granada which ended in 1492. In 1495 he was selected by Queen Isabella to command the army sent to aid the King of Naples against Charles VIII. of France. He expelled the French by a rapid succession of victories, succoured the pope by capturing Ostia from a piratical horde, and returned to Spain in 1498. A secret treaty for the partition of the kingdom of Naples having been made by Ferdinand of Spain and Louis XII. of France in 1500, Gonsalvo was appointed lieutenant-general of Calabria and Apulia. The French and Spaniards were involved in a war with each other in 1502. "The Great Captain" gained decisive victories at Cerignola and Garigliano in 1503, and drove the French out of the kingdom of Naples. In 1506 he was recalled to Spain by Ferdinand, who was jealous of his glory or suspicious of his loyalty. He was received with enthusiasm by the people, but was treated with coldness at court. Died at Granada in 1515. "His splendid military successes," says Prescott, "have made the name of Gonsalvo as familiar to his countrymen as that of the Cid, which, floating down the stream of popular melody, has been treasured up as a part of the national history. . . . His characteristics were prudence, coolness, steadiness of purpose, and intimate knowledge of man. He betrayed none of the cruelty and licentiousness which disgrace the age of chivalry." (See Prescott's "Ferdinand and Isabella," vol. ii. Part II., chap. ii.; and vol. iii. chaps. xii., xiv., and xxiv.)

See PAOLO GIOVIO, "De Vita et Rebus gestis G. F. Cordubæ;" BRANTÔME, "Vies des grands Capitaines;" M. J. QUINTANA, "Vida de G. F. de Córdova," 1827; FERNANDEZ DE PULGAR, "Coronica del gran Capitan G. F. de Córdova," 1580.

Gonthier, gon'teer, one of the best poets of the thirteenth century, was born in Germany. His chief work is entitled "Ligurinus sive de Rebus a Friderico I. gestis," ("On the Achievements of Frederick I.")

Gonthier, [Fr. pron. gôN'te-à',] (JOHANN,) a German physician and Hellenist, was born at Andernach in 1487. He became physician to Francis I. of France in 1535, and lectured on anatomy at Paris, where Vesalius was among his pupils. Having been persecuted as a Protestant, he retired to Strasburg, where he was chosen professor of Greek. Among his works, which were highly esteemed, are "Anatomical Institutes according to the Views of Galen," ("Anatomicæ Institutiones secundum Galeni Sententiam," 1536,) and "On Ancient and Modern Medicine," ("De Medicina veteri et nova," 1571.) Died in 1574.

See HÉRISSANT, "Éloge de Gonthier d'Andernach," 1765; NICÉRON, "Hommes illustres;" ÉLOY, "Dictionnaire de la Médecine;" M. ADAM, "Vitæ Medicorum."

Gontran, gôN'tRôN', a son of Clotaire I., inherited the kingdom of Burgundy in 561 A.D. Died in 593.

Gonzaga, gon-zä'gä, (THOMAS ANTONIO,) a popular Portuguese lyric poet, born at Oporto in 1747, was surnamed DIRCEO. He was banished for a political offence to Mozambique in 1793, and died there in the same year.

See F. DENIS, "Résumé de l'Histoire littéraire du Brésil;" "Nouvelle Biographie Générale."

Gonzaga, de,* deh gon-zä'gä, [Fr. GONZAGUE, gôN'zǎg',] (ANNE,) Princess-Palatine, born about 1616, was a daughter of Charles, Duke of Mantua and Nevers. She was married in 1645 to Edward, a son of Frederick V., Prince-Palatine and King of Bohemia. She passed much

* Some authorities give these names without the particles, (*de,* or *di;*) in inserting them we have followed the "Nouvelle Biographie Générale."

time at the French court, and was distinguished for her political talents and influence in the war of the Fronde. Died in 1684. Bossuet pronounced her funeral oration.

See CARDINAL DE RETZ, "Mémoires;" SENAC DE MEILHAN, "Mémoires d'Anne de Gonzague," 1786.

Gonzaga, de,* dà gon-zä'ga, (MARIA LOUISA,) Queen of Poland, born about 1612, was a sister of Anne Gonzaga, noticed above, and was eminent for beauty. Her mother was Catherine of Lorraine. She was married in 1645 to Sigismond Ladislas, King of Poland, who died in 1648. Soon after that event she became the wife of his brother and successor, John Casimir. Died in 1667.

See "Nouvelle Biographie Générale;" BASSOMPIERRE, "Mémoires."

Gonzaga, di,*(CARLO,) Duke of Mantua, Montferrato, and Nevers, was a grandson of Federico, noticed below, and heir of his cousin Vincenzo, who died in 1627. His claim was disputed by the emperor Ferdinand II., whose army took and pillaged Mantua in 1630. Gonzaga recovered Mantua about a year later. Died in 1637.

Gonzaga, di* or **de,** (CURTIUS,) an Italian poet, who lived about 1580. He wrote an epic poem called " Fido Amante," (1582.)

Gonzaga, di,* (ERCOLE,) an Italian cardinal, son of Francis II., Duke of Mantua, born in 1505. He was made successively Bishop of Mantua, Cardinal, and Archbishop of Tarragona. He was intimate with Cardinal Bembo and other eminent scholars of the time. Died in 1563.

See UGHELLI, "Italia Sacra."

Gonzaga, di,* (FEDERICO,) Duke of Mantua, succeeded his father, Giovanni Francesco, in 1519. He became an ally of Charles V. in 1521, and fought with distinction against the French. He was created Duke of Mantua by the emperor, and obtained the marquisate of Montferrato in 1536. Died in 1540.

Gonzaga, di,*[Fr. GONZAGUE, gǒN'zǎg',](FERDINAND or FERRANTE,) Duke of Molfetta and Guastalla, born in 1506, was a younger son of the Duke of Mantua. He acquired a high reputation as a general in the service of Charles V., who appointed him Viceroy of Sicily in 1536, and Governor of the Milanese in 1546. Died at Brussels in 1557.

See ALFONSO DE ULLOA, "Vita del gran Capitano F. Gonzaga," 1563; GOSELLINI, "Vita del Principe F. Gonzaga," 1574.

Gonzaga, di,* (FERDINANDO CARLO,) last Duke of Mantua, succeeded his father in 1665. He was extremely dissolute. In the war of the Spanish succession he was the ally of France. The Austrians took Mantua in 1707 and annexed it to the Milanese. He died in 1708.

Gonzaga, di,* (GIOVANNI FRANCESCÒ,) first Marquis of Mantua, began to reign in 1407. He waged war against Visconti, Duke of Milan, and became general-in-chief of the Venetian army in 1432. He entered the service of the Duke of Milan in 1438, after which he defeated the Venetians and their allies under F. Sforza, one of the ablest generals of that time. He died in 1444, aged about fifty, and was succeeded by his son Luigi, who was distinguished as a general and patron of poets and artists.

See MORÉRI, "Dictionnaire Historique;" POSSEVIN, "Historia Gonzagarum," etc.

Gonzaga, di,* (GIOVANNI FRANCESCO,) a grandson of Luigi, became Marquis of Mantua in 1466. He commanded the army which the Italian allies raised in 1495 to resist Charles VIII. of France. He was general of the League of Cambrai in 1509. Died in 1519.

Gonzaga, di,*(LUCREZIA,) a learned Italian lady, was married to Gian Paolo Manfroni, afterwards imprisoned for conspiracy against the life of the Duke of Ferrara. Her letters were greatly admired by her contemporaries. Died in 1576.

Gonzaga, di,* [Fr. GONZAGUE,] (LUIGI,) Lord of Mantua, was the founder of a sovereign house which reigned at Mantua from 1328 to 1707. They belonged to the Ghibeline party. He died in 1361.

Gonzaga, di,* (SCIPIONE,) an Italian writer and cardinal, born in 1542, was an intimate friend of Tasso. He

wrote verses and Latin Memoirs of his own Life, (1791.) Died in 1593.

See POSSEVIN, "Historia Gonzagarum," etc.

Gonzaga, di,* (VESPASIANO,) Duke of Sabbionetta, an Italian military commander, born in 1531, served with distinction in the wars of Charles V. and Philip II. of Spain. He was also a generous patron of learning and the arts. Died in 1591.

Gonzague, the French of GONZAGA, which see.

Gonzales, gon-thä'lês, (BARTOLOMÉ,) a Spanish painter, born at Valladolid in 1564. He was patronized by Philip III., who employed him to restore the Escurial and other palaces. Died in 1627.

Gonzalès, gǒN'zǎ'lês', (LOUIS JEAN EMMANUEL,) a French *littérateur*, born at Saintes in 1815, became assistant editor of the "Siècle." He wrote a successful novel, entitled "The Pearl-Diver," or "Les Frères de la Côte," ("Filibusters," or "Buccaneers.")

Gonzales-Velasquez, gon-thä'lês và-läs'kêth, (ALEJANDRO,) a Spanish painter and architect, born at Madrid in 1719. He adorned with paintings the royal palace of San Ildefonso. Died in 1772.

Gonzales-Velasquez, (ANTONIO,) a Spanish painter, brother of the preceding, born in Madrid in 1729. He excelled in frescos, and became court painter in 1757. Died in 1793. His brother LUIS, born in 1715, was also a painter. Died in 1764.

Gonzalez, gon-thä'lêth, or **Gonzales,** (DIEGO,) a Spanish poet, born at Ciudad Rodrigo in 1733; died in 1794.

Gonzalez, (TIRSO,) a Spanish Jesuit, who was chosen general of his order about 1685. He wrote a work against the doctrine of probability, entitled "Fundamentum Theologiæ Moralis," etc., (1689.) Died in 1705.

See DUPIN, "Bibliothèque des Auteurs ecclésiastiques du dix-septième Siècle."

Gonzalez-Cabrera-Bueno, gon-thä'lêth kâ-brä'rä bwä'no, (Don JOZÉ,) a distinguished admiral, born in the island of Teneriffe about 1670, was sent in 1701, by Pedro II., King of Portugal, as commander of a fleet, to the Philippines. He published a valuable treatise on navigation.

Gonzalez de Andrada. See ANDRADA, (PAOLO.)

Gonzalez de Berceo, gon-thä'lêth dà bêR-thä'o, (JUAN,) the earliest Spanish poet of whom anything is known, was born in Castile in 1196. He was a Benedictine monk, and wrote in verse the lives of San Domingo de Silos and San Millan. Died in 1266.

See TICKNOR, "History of Spanish Literature;" SISMONDI, "Littératures du Midi de l'Europe;" LONGFELLOW, "Poets and Poetry of Europe."

Gonzalez-Velasquez. See GONZALES-VELASQUEZ.

Gonzalo or **Gonzalvo.** See GONSALVO.

Gonzalvo. See GONSALVO.

Gooch, (ROBERT,) an English physician, born at Yarmouth in 1784. He practised in London, whither he removed in 1811. He published an excellent work on "Diseases Peculiar to Women," (1829.) Died in 1830.

Good, (JOHN MASON,) an eminent English physician and author, born at Epping in May, 1764. He was apprenticed to a surgeon at Gosport in 1779, and, having studied at Guy's Hospital for a short time, began to practise at Sudbury in 1784. In 1793 he removed to London, where he devoted much attention to literature and contributed to several reviews. He was versed in many ancient and modern languages, which he learned with uncommon facility. In 1805 he produced a translation in verse of Lucretius "De Rerum Naturâ." Among his chief medical works are a "Physiological System of Nosology," (1817,) and "The Study of Medicine," (4 vols., 1822; 2d edition, with notes by Dr. Samuel Cooper, 5 vols., 1828,) one of the most complete and learned works on that subject that ever appeared in the language. He also published "The Book of Nature," (3 vols., 1826,) a "Translation of the Book of Psalms," and several original poems. In 1820 he took the degree of M.D. at Marischal College, Aberdeen. Died in January, 1827.

Commenting on his translation of Lucretius, Lord Jeffrey says, "Upon the whole, this book is very dull, and as a translation very flat and unpoetical; yet it is

* See note on preceding page.

ā, ē, ī, ō, ū, ȳ, *long;* à, ê, ò, same, less prolonged; ă, ĕ, ĭ, ŏ, ŭ, ў, *short;* a, ę, į, ǫ, *oöscure;* fär, fàll, fât; mêt; nôt; gŏŏd; mōōn;

evidently the work of a man of no ordinary vigour or intelligence : it contains a very correct edition of Lucretius, with more information on the subject of his poem than could be gathered from all his other commentators put together." (" Edinburgh Review" for April, 1807.)

See OLINTHUS GREGORY, "Memoirs of the Life of J. M. Good," 1828; "Gentleman's Magazine" for March, 1827.

Goodall, gŏŏd′al, (EDWARD,) an English artist, chiefly known as an engraver, born at Leeds in 1795. His vignette landscapes, after Turner, are esteemed master-pieces. Among his works are the illustrations of Rogers's "Italy" and other poems, and the plates in Turner's "South Coast." He reproduces the manner of Turner with exquisite tact.

Goodall, (FREDERICK,) an eminent painter of history and genre, a son of the preceding, was born in London in 1822. He obtained a silver medal from the Society of Arts at the age of fifteen. His early works represent the life of the peasants of Normandy and Brittany. He produced "The Departure of the Émigrant-Ship," and other scenes of Irish life, and afterwards devoted himself chiefly to English subjects. Among his later works are "The Village Festival," (1847,) "Raising the May-Pole," (1851,) and "Cranmer at the Traitors' Gate," (1856.) He was chosen an associate of the Royal Academy in 1852.

Good′all or **Good′al,** (WALTER,) a Scottish antiquary, born in Banffshire in 1706. He published an "Examination of the Letters said to be written by Mary to James, Earl of Bothwell;" also an edition of the "Scoti-Chronicon" of Fordun. Died in 1766.

Goode, gŏŏd, (FRANCIS,) an English divine, born about 1797. He wrote "The Better Covenant," (5th edition, 1848,) which is highly commended. Died in 1842.

Goode, (WILLIAM,) an English theologian, born about 1800. Among his works is "The Divine Rule of Faith and Practice," (2 vols., 1842,) and treatises against the doctrines of the Puseyites. He became Dean of Ripon in 1860.

Good′man, (CHRISTOPHER,) an English Puritan, born at Chester about 1520. He retired to the continent in the reign of Mary, and became pastor of an English church at Geneva. About 1560 he was appointed minister at Saint Andrew's, Scotland. He wrote a "Commentary on Amos." Died in 1602.

See WOOD, "Athenæ Oxonienses."

Goodman, (GODFREY,) an English writer, born in Denbighshire in 1583. He became Bishop of Gloucester in 1625, and joined the Church of Rome about 1640. He wrote, besides other works, a "History of his Own Times," which was published in 1839. Died in 1655.

See FULLER, "Church History."

Good′rich, (CHARLES A.,) of Hartford, Connecticut, a historian and clergyman, born in 1790. He wrote, besides other works, a "History of the United States of America." Died in 1862.

Goodrich, (CHAUNCEY,) an American Senator, born at Durham, Connecticut, in 1759, was a son of Elizur, noticed below. He was a member of Congress from 1795 to 1801, and represented Connecticut in the Senate of the United States from 1807 to 1813. Died in 1815.

Goodrich, (CHAUNCEY ALLEN,) an American scholar and divine, born at New Haven in October, 1790, was a son of Elizur, noticed below, (1761–1849.) He graduated at Yale College in 1810, and afterwards studied theology. He was professor of rhetoric and oratory in Yale College from 1817 to 1839, and in the latter year obtained the chair of theology in that institution. In 1847 he produced an enlarged edition of Webster's Dictionary. He also edited Webster's Unabridged Dictionary, with an Appendix and Vocabulary of Proper Names, (1859,) and published "Select British Eloquence," (1852.) Died in 1860.

See ALLIBONE's "Dictionary of Authors."

Goodrich, (ELIZUR,) an American divine and scholar, born in Wethersfield, Connecticut, in 1734; died in 1797.

Goodrich, (ELIZUR,) an American lawyer, son of the preceding, was born in Durham, Connecticut, in 1761. He was professor of law in Yale College from 1801 to 1810, and was a judge of probate for many years. Died in 1849.

Goodrich, (FRANK B.,) an American writer, son of Samuel G. Goodrich, noticed below, was born in Boston in 1826. He published, besides several other works, "The Court of Napoleon, or Society under the First Empire, with Portraits of its Beauties," etc., (1857.)

Goodrich, (SAMUEL GRISWOLD,) an American writer, known under the assumed name of PETER PARLEY, was born at Ridgefield, Connecticut, in 1793. He was a nephew of Chauncey A. Goodrich. He became proprietor of a publishing-house in Boston about 1825, soon after which he began to write a series of juvenile books under the name of "Peter Parley." These works, the subjects of which were history, geography, travels, etc., enjoyed an extensive popularity. Some of them were translated into French. He edited a periodical called "Parley's Magazine," (1841–54.) He was consul of the United States in Paris for several years, (1848–52.) Among his numerous works are "Recollections of a Lifetime," (2 vols., 1857,) "Illustrated Natural History of the Animal Kingdom," (2 vols., 1859,) and "Peter Parley's Own Story," etc., (1864.) Died in 1863.

For a particular account of his various publications, see ALLIBONE's "Dictionary of Authors."

Goodrich, (THOMAS,) an English prelate, born in Lincolnshire about 1480. He rose through various preferments to be Bishop of Ely in 1534. He was also a member of the privy council under Henry VIII. and Edward VI., and in 1551 was made lord chancellor. He assisted in the compilation of the Bishops' Book and the Book of Common Prayer of 1548. Died in 1554.

Good′win, (FRANCIS,) an English architect, among whose principal works are the Manchester Town Hall and Lissadell Court. Died in 1835.

Goodwin, (JOHN,) an English Puritan divine, born in 1593, resided many years in London, where he was distinguished for his pulpit eloquence. He was a zealous republican, and defended the execution of the king. By his writings and in his pulpit he maintained the Arminian doctrines. He was the author of "The Divine Authority of Scripture Asserted," "Right and Might Well Met," "Redemption Redeemed," etc. The first-named is considered a master-piece of polemic theology. Died in 1665.

See "Life of John Goodwin," by THOMAS JACKSON.

Goodwin, (THOMAS,) an English nonconformist divine and writer, born in Norfolk in 1600. He took his degree at Cambridge, and in 1632 became vicar of Trinity Church, in that town. This post he soon after resigned, on account of a change in his religious opinions. After a short residence in Holland, he was, on his return to England, elected as one of the ablest and most active leaders of the Independent party. His zeal in this cause procured for him the favour of Cromwell, who in 1649 appointed him president of Magdalene College, Oxford. He wrote numerous theological and controversial works, which enjoy a high reputation. Died in 1679.

See NEAL, "History of the Puritans;" WOOD, "Athenæ Oxonienses."

Good′year, (CHARLES,) an eminent American inventor, born at New Haven, Connecticut, in 1800. His early education was very defective. He removed in 1826 to Philadelphia, where he opened a small store. About 1834 he became deeply interested in the manufacture of India-rubber. The cloth, shoes, and other articles made from this substance had proved failures on account of the effect produced upon it by heat and cold. After five years spent in constant experiments, during which time he and his family lived in extreme destitution, Mr. Goodyear succeeded in producing, by means of sulphur, the vulcanized India-rubber now so extensively used in manufactures. In 1851 he visited London, and exhibited at the Crystal Palace a great variety of useful and ornamental articles of the new material. He obtained on this occasion the Grand Council medal. He also attended the Paris Exposition of 1855, and received from the French emperor the grand medal of honour and the cross of the legion of honour. He returned to America in 1858, and devoted himself with untiring energy

ē as k; ç as s; ḡ hard; ġ as j; G, H, K, guttural; N, nasal; R, trilled; s̄ as z; th as in this. (☞See Explanations, p. 23.)

67

to the perfection of his discoveries, although suffering from chronic disease. Died in July, 1860. "He lived," says Parton, "to see his material applied to nearly five hundred uses, and to give employment, in England, France, Germany, and the United States, to sixty thousand persons. But we should greatly undervalue the labours of Charles Goodyear if we regarded them only as opening a new source of wealth. . . . Art, science, and humanity are indebted to him for a material which serves the purposes of them all, and serves them as no other known material could."

See REV. BRADFORD K. PEIRCE, "Trials of an Inventor," New York, 1866; PARTON, "Famous Americans of Recent Times," 1867.

Googe, gooj, (BARNABY,) an English translator of the sixteenth century, published versions of the "Zodiake of Life," by Paiingenius Stellatus, the "Spanish Proverbs" of Lope de Mendoza, and Aristotle's "Categories;" he was also the author of a collection of sonnets and other poems.

See WARTON, "History of English Poetry."

Gook'in, (DANIEL,) a writer, born in Kent, England, about 1612, removed to Massachusetts in 1644. He became a major-general in 1681. He wrote "Historical Collections of the Indians of Massachusetts," (published in 1792.) Died in 1687.

Gool, van, vän gōl or hōl, (JAN,) a Dutch painter, born at the Hague in 1685, painted admired landscapes, and wrote a mediocre "Biography of Flemish and Dutch Painters," (1751.) Died in 1757.

Gôpâla, one of the names of KRISHNA, which see.

Göppert or **Goeppert,** göp'pĕrt, (HEINRICH ROBERT,) professor of medicine and botany at Breslau, was born in Silesia in 1800. He published a treatise "On the Anatomical Structure of the Coniferæ," "On the Fossil Ferns," and other similar works.

Gor'dĭ-an, [Fr. GORDIEN, goR'de-âN'; Lat. GORDIA'-NUS, (MAR'CUS ANTO'NIUS AFRICA'NUS,)] a Roman emperor, born about 160 A.D., of an illustrious family. He was appointed proconsul of Africa in 237, and was declared emperor by the insurgents who rebelled against Maximinus. His son Gordian was associated with him in the empire, and their election was confirmed by the Roman senate. Soon after this, Capellianus, Governor of Mauritania, assembled an army in favour of Maximinus, and attacked Carthage. In the combat that ensued, the younger Gordian was slain; and his aged father, on hearing of his fate, strangled himself, in 238 A.D. Gordian was distinguished for his love of letters, and was the author of several poems. He spent a great part of his immense wealth in procuring games and amusements for the people. His reign lasted but six weeks.

See GIBBON, "Decline and Fall of the Roman Empire."

Gordian, [Lat. GORDIANUS, (MARCUS ANTONIUS PIUS,)] grandson of the elder Gordian, was born about 225, and was proclaimed Cæsar by the Roman people when news arrived of the death of the two Gordians in Africa. He was made colleague of the new emperors Maximus and Balbinus, and after their death became emperor, in July, 238 A.D. Gordian, accompanied by his father-in-law, Misitheus, repelled an invasion of Sapor, King of Persia, in 242. He afterwards attacked the Persians, and defeated their army on the banks of the Chaboras. Meanwhile, Philippus, an officer in the Roman army, availing himself of his popularity, caused himself to be proclaimed a colleague of the emperor, and soon after had Gordian put to death, in 244 A.D.

See TILLEMONT, "Histoire des Empereurs;" MONTESQUIEU, "Grandeur et Décadence des Romains;" GISBERT CUPER, "Historia trium Gordianorum," 1697; CAPITOLINUS, "Gordiani tres."

Gordianus, the Latin of GORDIAN, which see.

Gordien, the French of GORDIAN, which see.

Gor'dĭ-us, a Phrygian peasant who was raised to the throne, was the father of Midas. His name is associated with the famous "Gordian Knot," which Alexander the Great, unable to untie, cut with his sword.

Gor'don, (ALEXANDER,) of Achintoul, a relative of Patrick, noticed below, visited Russia in 1693. He was patronized by the Czar, to whom he rendered important services in his wars against Sweden and Poland. He wrote a valuable "History of Peter the Great," (1755.) Died in 1752.

Gordon, (ALEXANDER,) a distinguished Scottish antiquary, wrote "Itinerarium Septentrionale," or travels in Scotland and the North of England, (1726,) and a "Complete History of Ancient Amphitheatres," (1730.) Died in 1750.

See CHAMBERS, "Biographical Dictionary of Eminent Scotsmen."

Gordon, (ANDREW,) a distinguished scholar, born near Aberdeen in 1712, became professor of philosophy at Erfurt, in Germany. He published a work entitled "Phenomena of Electricity Exposed," (1744.) He made important discoveries in that science; and he is said to have been the first who used a cylinder instead of a globe in electrical apparatus. Died in 1751.

See PRIESTLEY, "History of Electricity."

Gordon, goR'dŏN', [Lat. GORDO'NUS,] (BERNARD,) a French physician, became professor of medicine at Montpellier in 1285. He wrote "Lilium Medicinæ," and other professional works, which were highly esteemed. Died about 1320.

Gordon, (GEORGE,) Earl of Huntley, an ambitious and powerful Scottish nobleman, was a Roman Catholic. He became lord chancellor of Scotland about 1546. Having taken arms against Queen Mary and Regent Murray, he was defeated and killed in 1562. His son GEORGE, the fifth Earl, was accessory to the death of Lord Darnley, after which he was an adherent of Queen Mary.

Gordon, (GEORGE,) sixth Earl of Huntley, a son of the fifth Earl, was a turbulent and powerful nobleman. He engaged in treasonable intrigues with the King of Spain in order to restore the Romish Church in Scotland. He rebelled openly in 1594, was defeated, and fled to the continent, but soon returned. Died in 1635.

Gordon, (GEORGE,) the son of Cosmo George, Duke of Gordon, was born in London in 1750. On taking his seat in Parliament, he distinguished himself by his violent opposition to the Act of Toleration, passed in 1778 in favour of the Catholics. In 1780, at the head of a mob estimated at one hundred thousand persons, Gordon presented a petition to Parliament for the repeal of the Bill of Toleration; and, on the refusal of that body to take it into immediate consideration, his followers spread themselves over the city and plundered and burned several Roman Catholic chapels. These outrages being feebly repressed, the mob broke out a few days after with greater violence. A great number of private houses as well as churches were destroyed, and the prisons forced open. At length the king commanded the military to disperse the mob, and order was restored. Gordon was tried for high treason, but was acquitted, because it could not be proved that he had assembled the populace with bad intentions. He afterwards was condemned to five years' imprisonment for contempt of court. He died in prison in 1793.

See ROBERT WATSON, "Life of Lord George Gordon," 1795; LINGARD, "History of England;" CHAMBERS, "Biographical Dictionary of Eminent Scotsmen."

Gor'don, (GEORGE H.,) an American general, born in Charlestown, Massachusetts, about 1826. He was a lawyer before the civil war. He commanded a brigade of the army of General Banks in May, 1862, and took part in the battle of Antietam, September 17 of that year.

Gordon, (GEORGE HAMILTON.) See ABERDEEN, EARL OF.

Gordon, (JAMES HUNTLEY,) a learned Jesuit, from a noble Scottish family, born in Paris in 1543. He became successively professor of theology and of the learned languages at Rome, Paris, and Bordeaux, and was also employed on several apostolic missions. Died in 1620.

See CHAMBERS, "Biographical Dictionary of Eminent Scotsmen."

Gordon, (Sir JOHN WATSON,) an eminent Scottish portrait-painter, born in Edinburgh about 1790. He painted portraits of nearly all the eminent Scotsmen of his time, including Sir Walter Scott, the Duke of Argyle, Dr. Chalmers, (1837,) and Professor Wilson, (1851.) He was chosen president of the Royal Scottish Academy in 1850, and received the title of painter-limner to the queen. Died in 1864.

Gordon, (Lady LUCY DUFF,) daughter of the celebrated Mrs. Austin, and wife of Sir Alexander Duff Gordon, published a number of excellent translations from the German and French. Among these are Von Feuerbach's "Remarkable Crimes and Trials," Meinhold's "Amber Witch," and the "Celebrated Crimes" of Dumas. She wrote "Letters from Egypt," (1865.) Died in Egypt in 1869.

Gordon, (PATRICK,) a Scottish officer, born in 1635, entered the service of Peter the Great of Russia, whose favour he won, and who made him commander-in-chief of his army. Died in 1699.

See BECKMANN, "Peter der Grosse als Mensch und Regent," 1830; "London Quarterly Review" for April, 1852; "Edinburgh Review" for July, 1856; "Blackwood's Magazine" for April, 1861.

Gordon, (ROBERT,) a Scottish geographer, born in Aberdeenshire about 1580, was appointed by Charles I. to complete the "Theatrum Scotiæ," which forms a part of the geographical work projected by Blaeu of Amsterdam. Died about 1660.

See CHAMBERS, "Biographical Dictionary of Eminent Scotsmen."

Gordon, (Sir ROBERT,) a brother of the Earl of Aberdeen, born in 1791, was sent as ambassador to Constantinople in 1829, and was minister at Vienna from 1841 to 1846. He died at Balmoral in 1847.

Gordon, (THOMAS,) a Scottish writer, born at Kirkcudbright about 1685. He was the author, in conjunction with his friend Trenchard, of "Cato's Letters," and "The Independent Whig," (2 vols., 1732.) His translation of Tacitus is esteemed the best in the English language. Died in 1750.

See CHAMBERS, "Biographical Dictionary of Eminent Scotsmen."

Gordon, (THOMAS F.,) an American historian, published a "History of Pennsylvania," (1823,) a "Digest of the Laws of the United States," (1827,) a "History of New Jersey," (1831,) a "Gazetteer of New Jersey," (1834,) and other works.

Gordon, (WILLIAM,) an English historian, born at Hitchin in 1729, became pastor of an Independent church at Ipswich. He removed to America in 1770, preached for some years at Roxbury, Massachusetts, favoured the popular party in the Revolution, and returned to England in 1786. He published a "History of the Rise, Progress, and Establishment of the Independence of the United States of America," (4 vols., 1788.) He states that General Washington furnished material for this work. Died in 1807.

Gordon, (WILLIAM,) an English physician and philanthropist, born near Ripon in 1801, practised in Hull. He wrote a "Critical Inquiry concerning a New Membrane of the Eye," (1832,) and other works. Died in 1849.

See NEWMAN HALL, "The Christian Philosopher Triumphing over Death," etc.

Gordonus. See GORDON, (BERNARD.)

Gore, (CATHERINE GRACE,) originally named FRANCIS, a distinguished English authoress, born in Nottinghamshire in 1799. Among her most popular novels, which are principally delineations of fashionable life, are "Cecil ; or, The Adventures of a Coxcomb," (1841,) "Peers and Parvenus," "The Hamiltons," and "The Ambassador's Wife." She also published a comedy entitled "The School for Coquettes," and other dramatic works. Mrs. Gore's productions display superior talent, and a number of her novels have been translated into German. Died in 1861.

See R. H. HORNE, "New Spirit of the Age," 1844; "Edinburgh Review" for July, 1830.

Gore, (CHRISTOPHER,) an American Governor, born in Boston in 1758. He was elected Governor of Massachusetts in 1809, and a Senator of the United States in 1814. Died in 1827. He left nearly $100,000 to Harvard College.

Gore, (Sir JOHN,) a British naval officer, who became a vice-admiral in 1825. Died in 1836.

Gore, (THOMAS,) an English writer, born in Wiltshire in 1631, was the author of several genealogical works. Died in 1684.

See WOOD, "Athenæ Oxonienses."

Görenz or **Goerenz,** gö'rĕnts, (JOHANN AUGUST,) a German philologist and Latin scholar, born in Saxony in 1765. He published a good edition of Cicero's philosophical works, viz., "De Legibus," "De Finibus," and "Academica," (3 vols., 1809–12.) Died in 1836.

Görgei. See GÖRGEY.

Gor'gĕs, (Sir FERDINANDO,) an Englishman, born in Somersetshire. He planted a colony in Maine, and spent a large sum of money in attempts to explore and settle that province. About 1637 he obtained a large grant of land, and was appointed lord proprietary of Maine. His colony did not prosper. Died in 1647.

Görgey or **Goergey,** gör'gī, (ARTHUR,) a famous Hungarian general, born at Toporcz in 1818. He entered the army in 1837, but retired from it in 1845 and became a student in the University of Prague. In the spring of 1848 he joined the army which took the field against Austria, and received a captain's commission. Having given proofs of superior military talents, he was appointed commander-in-chief by Kossuth on the 1st of November, 1848. He issued in January, 1849, a proclamation against the separation of Hungary from Austria, and in the next month was superseded by Dembinski, whom he refused to obey. He was soon restored to the command, and defeated the Austrians at Nagy Sarlo in April, after which he became minister of war. Having been defeated near Komorn in July, he made a skilful retreat to Arad. On the 11th of August, 1849, he was appointed dictator, and a few days later he capitulated without conditions to the Russian general. He was pardoned by the emperor, and incurred the suspicion of treason to the cause of Hungary. In 1852 he published "My Life and Acts in Hungary in 1848 and 1849."

Gor'gĭ-as [Gr. Γοργίας] OF LEONTINI, a celebrated orator and sophist, was born at Leontini, (or Leontium,) in Sicily, and was a contemporary of Socrates. He was sent by his fellow-citizens to Athens on a political mission about 426 B.C., soon after which he became a resident of Athens. He taught rhetoric with great éclat, and wrote a philosophical work entitled " Of the Non-Being, or of Nature," in which he argued that nothing was existence or reality. Some extracts from this are extant. His mind was eminently subtle and brilliant. He appears to have promoted the advancement of philosophy by demonstrating the distinction between the conception and its object. But he was more remarkable for the graces of language than for earnestness of feeling. "Like a great man of modern times," says Fournier, "he propagated doubt with finesse, and suggested or generated ideas with an art of which Socrates alone furnished a model." Plato gave the name of Gorgias to one of his dialogues which is extant. Gorgias survived Socrates, and reached the age of one hundred years.

See PHILOSTRATUS, "Vitæ Sophistarum ;" H. E. Foss, "Commentatio de Gorgia Leontino," 1828; LUIGI GAROFALO, "Discorsi intorno Gorgia Leontino," 1831; "Nouvelle Biographie Générale ;" ARISTOTLE, "De Xenophane, Gorgia," etc.; SEXTUS EMPIRICUS, "Adversus Mathematicos ;" GROTE, "History of Greece," vol. viii. chap. lxvii.

Gor'gon, [Lat. GOR'GON ; Gr. Γοργώ, (plural Γόργονες;) Fr. GORGONE, gor'gon'.] The Gorgons of the classic mythology were three sisters, named Stheno, (or Stheino,) Eury'ale, and Medusa. By the later poets they were represented as having on their heads serpents instead of hair, or serpents entwined among their hair. According to the popular legend, all persons who looked at them were changed into stone.

See KEIGHTLEY, "Mythology ;" "Biographie Universelle," (Partie mythologique.)

Gorgonia, a surname of MINERVA, which see.

Gori, go'ree, (ANTONIO FRANCESCO,) an Italian antiquary, born in 1691 at Florence, where he became professor of history. Among his numerous and valuable works we may name "Inscriptiones antiquæ Græcæ et Romanæ," etc., an account of ancient inscriptions found in Tuscany, and a superb work entitled "Museum Florentinum," (6 vols. fol., 1731–43.) In 1735 he founded the Academia Columbaria. Died in 1757.

See "Nouvelle Biographie Générale ;" GOETHE, "Winckelmann und sein Jahrhundert."

Gorini, da, dâ go-ree'nee, (GIUSEPPE CORIO,) MARQUIS, an Italian dramatic poet, born at Milan. He composed many tragedies and comedies, some of which were very successful. His tragedy of "Jezebel" is called his master-piece. He died after 1761.

Go-rī-on'ĭ-dēs, or **Joseph Ben Gorion,** a Jewish compiler, who is supposed to have lived in France in the ninth century. He was the reputed author of a "History of the Jews."

Gorlæus, gor-lā′us, (ABRAHAM,) a distinguished antiquary and numismatist, born at Antwerp in 1549. He collected a valuable cabinet of medals, which was sold after his death to James I. of England. His principal works are his "Dactyliotheca, etc.," and "Thesaurus Numismatum," ("Treasury of Coins," 1608.) Died in 1609.

Gorm or **Gor′mon**, surnamed THE OLD, a king of Denmark, who united the whole of that country into one kingdom. He was hostile to Christianity, and resisted all the efforts of the missionaries to convert his people. Died in 935.

Gor′man, (WILLIS A.,) an American general, born in Kentucky about 1814. He represented a district of Indiana in Congress from 1849 to 1853, and was Governor of Minnesota Territory from 1853 to 1857. He commanded a brigade of the Union army at the battles of Fair Oaks, June 1, and Antietam, September 17, 1862.

Gornicius. See GORNICKI.

Gornicki, goR-nèts′kee, [Lat. GORNI′CIUS,] (LUKE,) a Polish historian, born in 1530, became secretary to Sigismund Augustus, King of Poland. He wrote a "History of the Kingdom of Poland." Died in 1600.

Gor′on-wȳ, (OWEN,) a Welsh poet, born in 1722, wrote poems in his own language and in Latin.

Goropius or **Gorophius.** See BECAN, (JOHN.)

Gorostiza, go-ros-tee′så, (Don MANUEL EDUARDO,) a distinguished diplomatist and dramatic writer, born at Vera Cruz, in Mexico, in 1790. He was employed by his countrymen in several important missions to London and Paris, and was on his return appointed councillor of state. His comedies entitled "Bread and Onion with Thee!" ("Contigo Pan y Cebolla,") and "Indulgence towards All," ("Indulgencia para Todos,") enjoy great popularity.

Gorræus. See GORRIS.

Gorran, de, dĕh go′rŏṉ′, (NICOLAS,) a French theologian, born in Maine about 1230. He wrote commentaries on Scripture. Died in 1295.

Görres or **Goerres**, gör′rĕs, (JAKOB JOSEPH,) an able German writer and publicist, was born at Coblentz in 1776. He edited in 1814 the "Rheinisches Mercur," an organ of the Liberal party in Germany, and was appointed professor of history at Munich in 1827. He wrote on a great variety of subjects. Among his principal works are "Aphorisms on Art," (1802,) "Faith and Science," ("Glauben und Wissen," 1805,) "Mythological History of the Asiatic World," (1810,) "Christian Mystic," ("Christliche Mystik," 4 vols., 1836–42,) and a number of contributions to the "Historico-Political Journal." Died at Munich in 1848.

See SEPP, "J. von Görres; eine Skizze seines Leben," 1848; S. BRUNNER, "Einige Stunden bei Goerres," 1848; "Nouvelle Biographie Générale," (where he is called JEAN JOSEPH DE GOERRES.)

Gorresio, gor-rā′se-o, (GASPARD,) an Italian Orientalist, born in Piedmont in 1808, became professor of Sanscrit at Turin. He produced a good Italian version of the Sanscrit poem "Râmâyäna," (Paris, 9 vols., 1843–56.)

Gorris, de, dĕh go′rĕss′, [Lat. GORRÆ′US,] (JEAN,) a French physician, born in Paris in 1505 ; died in 1577.

Gorsas, goR′så′, (ANTOINE JOSEPH,) a French politician and revolutionist, born at Limoges in 1752. As editor of the "Courrier de Versailles," he contributed greatly to excite the populace to the outrages of the 20th of June and the 10th of August. He was a deputy to the National Convention in 1792. In 1793 he was arrested by the Revolutionary Tribunal, and executed.

See LAMARTINE, "History of the Girondists."

Gorski, goRs′skee, or **Gors′kĭ-us**, (JAMES,) a Polish writer, born in Masovia about 1525. He wrote on rhetoric, theology, etc. Died about 1584.

Gortchakof or **Gortschakow**, goR′chå-kof′, written also **Gortchakov** or **Gortchakoff**, (ALEXANDER,) a Russian general, born in 1764. He obtained the rank of general about 1798, served in several campaigns against the French, and defeated Marshal Lannes at Heilsberg in 1807. He acted as minister of war in 1812. Died in 1825.

Gortchakof or **Gortschakow**, (ALEXANDER,) PRINCE, a Russian statesman, born about 1800. He was appointed secretary of legation to London in 1824, and in 1832 councillor of the embassy in Vienna. In 1841 he negotiated the marriage of the grand duchess Olga with the crown-prince of Würtemberg. He represented Russia at the court of Vienna in 1854 and 1855, and became minister of foreign affairs about 1857.

Gortchakof or **Gortschakow**, (DMITRI,) a Russian poet, born in 1756. He wrote odes, satires, etc., and was considered one of the best Russian poets of his time. Died in 1824.

Gortchakof or **Gortschakow**, (MICHAEL,) PRINCE, an able general, brother of Prince Alexander, was born in 1795. He served in the Polish campaign of 1831, and distinguished himself at Ostrolenka and Warsaw. He was made general of artillery in 1843, and in 1846 military governor of Warsaw. He commanded the army which entered the Danubian principalities in 1853, and succeeded Prince Mentchikof as commander of the army in the Crimea in March, 1855. The skill with which he defended Sevastopol and conducted the retreat of his army is highly extolled. He was Governor of Poland when he died, about June, 1861.

See "Gentleman's Magazine" for July, 1861.

Gortchakof or **Gortschakow**, (PETER,) PRINCE, eldest brother of the preceding, born about 1790, served against the French in 1813–14, and subsequently in the Caucasus under Yermolof. In 1839 he became Governor-General of Western Siberia, and in 1843 general of infantry. According to Vapereau, he commanded a wing of the army at Alma and the Inkerman, (1854.)

Gortchakov or **Gortschakow.** See GORTCHAKOF.

Gorter, van, vȧn goR′ter, (DAVID,) a Dutch physician and botanist, son of Jan, noticed below. He succeeded his father as physician to the Empress of Russia, and published "Flora Ingrica," and other botanical works. Died in 1783.

Gorter, van, (JAN,) a celebrated Dutch physician, born in West Friesland in 1689. He studied at Leyden under Boerhaave, and in 1754 was invited to Russia by the empress Elizabeth, who made him her first physician. Among his principal works are a "Compendium of Medicine," and a treatise "On Insensible Perspiration," (in Latin.) Died in Holland in 1762.

Gor′ton, (JOHN,) an English editor, of whom we have little information. He published a valuable "General Biographical Dictionary," (2 vols., 1828–30.) A new edition, with a supplement, appeared, in 4 vols., in 1851.

Gorton, (SAMUEL,) a religionist or enthusiast, born in England about 1600, emigrated to Boston in 1636. He was whipped for a contemptuous speech against the magistrates, and about 1642 was accused of heresy and found guilty. For this offence he was imprisoned until 1644. Died in 1677.

See "Life of S. Gorton," in SPARKS's "American Biography."

Görtz, (GEORG HENRIK.) See GOERTZ.

Görtz or **Goertz**, görts, (JOHANN EUSTACH,) Count of Schlitz, a Prussian statesman, born in the grand duchy of Hesse in 1737. He was created by Frederick II. minister of state and grand master of the wardrobe. He died in 1821, leaving, among other works, "Authentic Memoirs relative to the Negotiations which preceded the Partition of Poland," (1810.)

See "Historische und politische Denkwürdigkeiten des Grafen von Goertz," 2 vols., 1827; "Nouvelle Biographie Générale."

Göschel or **Goeschel**, gö′shĕl, (KARL FRIEDRICH,) a German jurist and philosopher, born at Langensalza in 1784. He graduated at Bonn in 1835, and was appointed in 1845 first president of the Consistory for the province of Saxony. He published in 1828 "Cæcilius and Octavius, or a Conversation on the Principal Objections to Christian Truth," and in 1829 "Aphorisms on Ignorance and Absolute Knowledge in Relation to the Christian Confession of Faith," in which he advocates Hegel's philosophy and seeks to prove its harmony with the Christian faith. He also wrote an answer to Strauss's "Life of Jesus."

See "Nouvelle Biographie Générale;" BROCKHAUS, "Conversations-Lexikon."

ā, ē, ī, ō, ū, ȳ, *long;* ȧ, ė, ȯ, same, less prolonged; ä, ĕ, ĭ, ŏ, ŭ, ў, *short;* ą, ę, į, ǫ, *obscure;* fär, fåll, fåt; mĕt; nŏt; gŏŏd; mōōn;

Göschen, go'shẹn or gosh'en, (GEORGE JOACHIM,) an English financier, of German extraction, born in London in 1831, was educated at Oxford. He wrote, besides several treatises on financial subjects, "The Theory of Foreign Exchanges." Since 1863 he has represented the city of London in Parliament. As chancellor of the duchy of Lancaster, he was a member of the Liberal ministry from January to June, 1866. He became a member of Mr. Gladstone's cabinet, as president of the poor-law board, in December, 1868.

Göschen or **Goeschen,** gö'shẹn, (JOHANN FRIEDRICH LUDWIG,) an able German jurist, born at Königsberg in 1778. He studied Roman law at Berlin under Savigny and Niebuhr, and in 1813 was appointed professor at the Berlin University. He published an edition of the "Institutes of Gaius," and "Lectures on Common Civil Law." Died in 1837.

Goselini, go-sà-lee'nee, (GIULIANO,) an Italian poet and historical writer, born at Rome in 1525. He became secretary to Ferdinand Gonzaga, Viceroy of Sicily, of whom he wrote a biography. He also published a work entitled "Tre Congiure," etc., and a number of poems. Died in 1587.

See TIRABOSCHI, "Storia della Letteratura Italiana."

Goslicki, gos-lĕt'skee, (LAURENTIUS GRIMALIUS,) a Polish prelate and diplomatist, born in 1535, was secretary to Sigismund III. He was successively Bishop of Kamieniec and Posen. His chief work is entitled "The Accomplished Senator," ("De Optimo Senatore.")

Gosse, goss, (ÉTIENNE,) a French dramatist, born at Bordeaux in 1773. He wrote many comedies, and "Dramatic Proverbs," (2 vols., 1819.) Died in 1834.

Gosse, goss, (HENRI **Albertet**—ål'bĕR'tà',) a Swiss chemist and apothecary, born at Geneva in 1753, made improvements in the fabrication of potters' ware and of leather, and in other arts. He is said to have been the inventor of artificial mineral waters. Died in 1816.

Gosse, (LOUIS FRANÇOIS NICOLAS,) a French historical painter, born in Paris in 1787. Among his works are "The Adoration of the Magi," (1828,) "The Creation," and a "Visit of Napoleon III. to the Louvre," which was ordered for the Salle du Trône in the Senate-house.

Gosse, goss, (PHILIP HENRY,) an English naturalist, born at Worcester in 1810. He made a scientific tour through Canada, the United States, and Jamaica, and published, after his return, "The Canadian Naturalist," (1840,) "The Birds of Jamaica," (1845,) and "A Naturalist's Sojourn in Jamaica." His "Rambles of a Naturalist on the Devonshire Coast" appeared in 1853, and his "Aquarium" in 1854. These works were received with general favour, and have contributed greatly to excite an interest in those departments of natural history which he has so well illustrated. In 1850 Mr. Gosse was chosen a Fellow of the Royal Society. He produced in 1860 a "History of British Sea-Anemones and Corals."

See "Westminster Review" for July, 1847.

Gossec, go'sĕk', (FRANÇOIS JOSEPH,) an eminent musical composer, born in Hainault in 1733. He studied in Paris under Rameau, and subsequently became professor in the Conservatory of Music. His compositions are various; among his master-pieces are "The Mass for the Dead," "The Nativity," an oratorio, the opera of "Sabinus," the music for the funeral of Mirabeau, and the apotheosis of Voltaire. Died in 1829.

See P. HÉDOUIN, "Gossec, sa Vie et ses Ouvrages," 1852; CHORON et FAVOLLE, "Dictionnaire des Musiciens;" "Nouvelle Biographie Générale."

Gosselin, goss'lȧn', (ANTOINE,) a French ecclesiastic, born near Amiens about 1580, became professor of rhetoric at Caen. His principal work is a "History of the Old Gauls," (in Latin.) Died in 1645.

Gosselin, (JEAN,) a French writer, born at Vire, in Normandy. He was patronized by Margaret of Navarre, and was appointed keeper of the Royal Library in Paris. He published "Signification of the Ancient Game of Pythagorean Cards," and other works. Died in 1604.

Gosselin or **Gossellin,** (PIERRE FRANÇOIS JOSEPH,) a celebrated French geographer, born at Lille in 1751. He was a deputy to the National Assembly in 1789, and

in 1791 became a member of the central administration of commerce. He was elected to the French Institute soon after its formation, and in 1799 succeeded Barthélemy as keeper of the medals in the National Library. His geographical works are numerous and valuable; among the most important may be named his "Geography of the Greeks Analyzed," (4to, with ten maps, 1790,) and "Inquiries into the Positive and Systematic Geography of the Ancients," (4 vols. 4to, fifty-four maps, 1798.) Gosselin was employed by Napoleon to assist in the translation of Strabo. Died in 1830.

See "Nouvelle Biographie Générale."

Gossin, go'sån', (PIERRE FRANÇOIS,) a French revolutionist, born near Verdun in 1744. He was elected to the States-General in 1789, and was chairman of the committee which divided France into departments. He was guillotined in July, 1794.

Gos'son, (STEPHEN,) an English divine and dramatist, born in Kent in 1554, was the author of a tragedy entitled "Catiline's Conspiracies," and "Captain Mario," a comedy. He afterwards wrote with great severity against the stage. Died in 1623.

Goszczynski, gosh-chĭn'skee, (SEVERIN,) a Polish poet, born in the Ukraine in 1806. His principal works are "The Castle of Kaniow," an epic poem, and a number of lyrics.

Got, de, (BERTRAND.) See CLEMENT V.

Gotama. See GAUTAMA.

Go'ter or **Go'ther,** (JOHN,) an English Catholic theologian, born in Hampshire about 1640, wrote many theological and controversial works. Died in 1704.

Gotescalc. See GOTTSCHALK.

Goth. See CLEMENT V.

Göthe. See GOETHE.

Gothofredus. See GODEFROI, (DENIS.)

Gothofredus Boloniensis. See GODFREY OF BOUILLON.

Gotter, got'tẹr, (FRIEDRICH WILHELM,) a German poet and dramatist, born at Gotha in 1746, was one of the founders of the "Musen-Almanach" in that city. Besides a number of tragedies, comedies, and farces, he wrote admired songs, elegies, etc. Died in 1797.

Gottfried von Nifen, got'fReet fon nee'fẹn, a German minnesinger, flourished about 1230.

See LONGFELLOW, "Poets and Poetry of Europe."

Gottfried (or **Godefroi**) **von Strasburg,** got'fReet fon stRås'booRg, a celebrated German poet, who lived about 1200, was the author of an epic poem entitled "Tristan and Isolde," which ranks among the finest productions of the kind in the middle ages. Editions of it have been published by Massmann and others.

Gotti, got'tee, (VINCENZO LUIGI,) a learned Italian cardinal, born at Bologna in 1664, became professor of philosophy in his native city in 1688. He was the author of a treatise "On the True Church of Christ," (in Italian,) and other religious works, in Latin. Died in 1742.

Gottigniez, go'těn'ye-à', (GILLES FRANÇOIS,) a mathematician, was born at Brussels in 1630. He taught mathematics at Rome, and wrote, besides other works, "Elements of Geometry," (Rome, 1669.) Died in 1689.

Gottleber, got'là'bẹr, (JOHANN CHRISTOPH,) a German philologist, born at Chemnitz in 1733. Among his works are "Observations on Plato's Phædon and Alcibiades," ("Animadversiones ad Platonis Phædonem et Alcibiadem," 1771.) Died in 1785.

Göttling or **Goettling,** göt'ling,(JOHANN FRIEDRICH AUGUST,) a German chemist, born at Bernburg in 1755. He taught chemistry and philosophy at Jena, and wrote many useful works, among which is a "Chemical and Philosophical Encyclopædia," (3 vols., 1805–07.) Died in 1809.

See HIRSCHING, "Historisch-literarisches Handbuch."

Göttling or **Goettling,** (KARL WILHELM,) a German scholar, born at Jena in 1793, was professor of ancient literature in that city, and in 1826 librarian of the university. He published a treatise "On the Historical Part of the Nibelungenlied," and several other critical and antiquarian works.

Gottschalk or **Gotschalk,** got'shålk, written also **Gotescalc,** [Lat. GODESCHAL'CUS or GOTHESCHAL'-

cus,] a German monk, born about 808 A.D. His exposition of Saint Augustine's doctrine of predestination subjected him to the charge of heresy. By the influence of Hincmar, he was condemned as a heretic in 849 A.D., and punished with imprisonment for life. Died about 860.

See "Nouvelle Biographie Générale."

Gottschall, got'shâl, (RUDOLPH,) a Prussian poet, born at Breslau in 1823. He displayed a rich imagination in his poems, among which are "Songs of the Present Time," ("Lieder der Gegenwart," 2d edition, 1842,) "Madonna and Magdalene," (1843,) "The Goddess," ("Die Göttinn," 1852,) and a drama called "Lambertine de Méricourt," (1851.)

Gottsched, got'shĕt, [Lat. GOTTSCHE'DIUS,] (JOHANN CHRISTOPH,) a German critic and littérateur, born near Königsberg in 1700. He published "The German Theatre according to the Rules and Examples of the Ancients," "Essay on a Critical Art of Poetry," (1730,) and Poems, (1736.) His writings contributed much to refine the German language and to introduce a purer taste into its literature. He was for many years professor of philosophy, etc. at Leipsic, and edited several journals, among which was "Die vernünftige Tadlerinnen." Died in 1766.

See JOHANN AUGUST ERNESTI, "Memoria J. C. Gottschedii," 1767; T. W. DANZEL, "Gottsched und seine Zeit," 1848; GERVINUS, "Geschichte der National-Literatur der Deutschen;" "Nouvelle Biographie Générale."

Gottsche, (LUISE ADELGUNDE VICTORIE,) originally CULMUS, a learned authoress, born at Dantzic in 1713, was the wife of the preceding. She translated Addison's "Cato" and "Spectator" into German, and wrote "Letters," (1771,) which are much admired. "She surpassed her husband," says Bernhard, "in taste, wit, and purity of style." Died in 1762.

See J. H. S. FORMEY, "Éloge de Madame Gottsched," 1767.

Gottschedius. See GOTTSCHED, (JOHANN CHRISTOPH.)

Gottwald, got'wält, (CHRISTOPH,) a German naturalist, born at Dantzic in 1636. He made a rich collection of specimens, which was purchased by Peter the Great, and wrote a few treatises. Died in 1700.

Götz. See BERLICHINGEN.

Götz, göts, (JOHANN NIKOLAUS,) a German poet, born at Worms in 1721, wrote lyrics, epigrams, etc., and made translations from Anacreon and Sappho. Died in 1781.

Götze or **Goetze,** göt'seh, (GEORG HEINRICH,) a learned Lutheran divine, born at Leipsic in 1667. He was chosen superintendent of the churches of Lubeck in 1702. His works are numerous and curious, but mostly short or unimportant. Two of them are entitled "On the Relics of Luther," (1703,) and "On Learned Merchants," (1708.) Died in 1728.

See SEELEN, "Memoria G. H. Goetzii," 1728; NICÉRON, "Mémoires."

Götze or **Goetze,** (JOHANN AUGUST EPHRAIM,) a distinguished German naturalist, born at Halberstadt in 1731. He was minister at Quedlinburg from 1756 to 1787. He is said to have been one of the first entomologists of his time. Among his numerous works are "Entomological Memoirs," (4 vols., 1777-81,) a "Natural History of Intestinal Worms," (1782,) and "Nature, Human Life, and Providence," (6 vols., 1789-92.) Died in 1793.

See CRAMER, "Zum Andenken des Pastors Goetze," 1793; "Biographie Universelle."

Götze or **Goetze,** (JOHANN MELCHIOR,) a German theologian and scholar, a brother of the preceding, born at Halberstadt in 1717, was pastor of Saint Catherine's Church at Hamburg. His passion for controversy involved him in disputes with Goethe, Lessing, and other eminent men of the time; and his intolerance obtained for him the name of "The Inquisitor of Hamburg." He died in 1786, leaving a number of learned treatises.

See LESSING, "Mendelssohn, Risbeck und Götze," 1787; J. L. SCHLOSSER, "Nachricht an das Publikum J. M. Goetze betreffend," 1770; C. F. BAHRDT, "Standrede am Grabe J. M. Goetzens," 1786.

Götzinger or **Goetzinger,** göt'sing-ẹr, (MAX WILHELM,) a German grammarian and littérateur, born near

Stolpen in 1799, published "Elements of German Grammar," (1825,) "Commentaries on the German Poets," (1831,) and other works.

Gouan, goo-ôN', (ANTOINE,) a French botanist, born in 1733 at Montpellier, where he became professor of botany in 1767. He published, besides other works, "The Botanic Garden of Montpellier," ("Hortus Monspeliensis," 1762,) and "Flora Monspeliaca," (1765.) He corresponded with Linnæus and Haller. Died in 1821.

See PIERRE JOSEPH AMOREUX, "Notice historique sur A. Gouan," 1822; HALLER, "Bibliotheca Botanica;" "Nouvelle Biographie Générale."

Gouaz, le, lẹh goo'äz', (YVES,) a French engraver, born at Brest in 1742. He executed, from designs by Ozanne, more than sixty views of French sea-ports and scenes in the Antilles. Died in 1816.

Gouchtasp. See GUSHTÂSP.

Gouda, van, vän gŏw'dä or hŏw'dä, (CORNELIS,) a skilful Dutch painter, born at Gouda, lived about 1550.

Goudar, goo'däR', (ANGE,) a French writer, born at Montpellier about 1720. He published, among other works, "The Chinese Spy; or, Secret Envoy from the Court of Pekin," (6 vols., 1768.) Died in 1791.

Goudchaux, goo'shō', (MICHEL,) a French financier, of a Jewish family, was born at Nancy in 1801. He was chosen minister of finance in February, 1848, under the new régime, but resigned about the 6th of March. He had the portfolio of finance in the administration of Cavaignac from June to October, 1848.

Goudelin. See GOUDOULI.

Goudelin, hŏw'dẹh-lin, [Fr. pron. good'lâN'; Lat. GUDELI'NUS,] (PIETER,) a learned jurist, born in Hainault in 1550, was professor of law at Louvain, and published, among other works, a treatise "On the Law of Peace," (in Latin.) Died in 1619.

Goudimel, goo'de'mĕl', (CLAUDE,) a French musical composer and Protestant, born at Besançon about 1510. He set to music the Psalms of Beza and Marot. He was condemned and put to death by the Catholics soon after the Massacre of Saint Bartholomew, (1572.)

See BURNEY, "History of Music;" FÉTIS, "Biographie Universelle des Musiciens."

Goudin, goo'däN', (MATHIEU BERNARD,) a French geometer, born in Paris in 1734; died in 1817.

Goudouli, goo'doo'le', or **Goudelin,** good'lâN', (PIERRE,) a French poet, born at Toulouse in 1579. Among his works is a "Chant royal," composed on the death of Henry IV. Died in 1649.

Goudt, gŏwt or hŏwt, (HENDRIK,) COUNT, a distinguished Dutch painter and engraver, born at Utrecht in 1585. Among his master-pieces are the engravings of "Tobias and the Angels," "The Flight into Egypt," and "Philemon and Baucis." Died about 1630.

Gouffé, goo'fä', (ARMAND,) a French song-writer, born in Paris in 1775. Among his most remarkable songs are "The Praise of Water," and "Saint Denis." He also wrote many vaudevilles. Died in 1845.

Gouffier. See CHOISEUL-GOUFFIER.

Gouffier, (GUILLAUME.) See BONNIVET.

Gouge, gooj, ? (THOMAS,) an English nonconformist divine, a son of William, noticed below, was born near Stratford in 1605. He studied at Cambridge, and in 1638 obtained the living of Saint Sepulchre, London, where he resided more than twenty years. He resigned this post when the Act of Uniformity was passed. Having formed a plan for the moral and religious improvement of Wales, he visited that country about 1671, founded between three and four hundred schools, and printed eight thousand Bibles in the Welsh language. He died in 1681, and his funeral sermon was preached by Dr. Tillotson. He was the author of "Principles of Religion Explained," and other similar works.

Gouge, (WILLIAM,) an English Puritan divine, distinguished for his learning and piety, born at Stratford-le-Bow, in Middlesex, in 1575. He became rector of Saint Anne's, Blackfriars, London, in 1608, and was afterwards nominated one of the Assembly of Divines. He opposed in 1648 the execution of the king. He published a "Commentary on the Epistle to the Hebrews," and other works. Died in 1653.

See MIDDLETON, "Evangelical Biography."

ā, ē, ī, ō, ū, ȳ, long; ă, ĕ, ĭ, ŏ, ŭ, ў, short; ạ, ẹ, ị, ọ, obscure; fär, fâll, fât; mĕt; nŏt; gōōd; mōōn;

Gouges, de, dẹh goozh, (MARIE OLYMPE,) a French dramatic writer, born at Montauban in 1755. She was at first a zealous partisan of the Revolution, but, alarmed by its excesses, changed her views, and opposed the execution of the king. She was condemned to death, and executed in November, 1792.

See MICHELET, " Les Femmes de la Révolution," etc.

Gough, gof, (HUGH,) VISCOUNT, a distinguished British general, born at Woodstown, Ireland, in November, 1779. He served as colonel in the Peninsular war, 1808–14, and became a major-general in 1830. He commanded a corps of the army operating against the Chinese in 1841, and took Canton. Having obtained the chief command in India, he defeated the Mahrattas at Maharajpore in December, 1843. For his victories over the Sikhs in 1845 and 1846 he was raised to the peerage, as viscount. He also commanded the army which fought against the Sikhs in 1849 and gained a decisive victory at Goojerat, (Guzerat.) He became a field-marshal about 1862. Died in March, 1869.

Gough, gof, (JOHN B.,) a celebrated lecturer on temperance, born in Kent, England, in 1817. He came to America in 1829, and, while learning the bookbinding business in New York, fell into habits of intemperance, and finally sunk to the lowest depths of poverty and wretchedness. Having been induced about 1840 to sign the total-abstinence pledge, he became deeply interested in the temperance reform, and soon distinguished himself as one of the most eloquent and most successful advocates of the cause. Since 1843 he has devoted himself almost without interruption to lecturing on temperance in the United States, Canada, and the British Islands. He has spoken, it is said, nearly one hundred times on the subject of temperance in Exeter Hall, London. Mr. Gough combines in an eminent degree the qualities of an actor with those of a great orator. His autobiography was published in 1846, and a volume of his orations in 1854.

Gough, (RICHARD,) a celebrated English antiquary, born in London in 1735. He studied at Cambridge, was elected to the Society of Antiquaries in 1767, and in 1775 a Fellow of the Royal Society. His principal works are his "Anecdotes of British Topography," (1768,) and "Sepulchral Monuments of Great Britain," (3 vols., 1799.) He also edited Camden's "Britannia," (3 vols. fol., 1789,) Martin's "History of Thetford," and other antiquarian works. Died in 1809.

See NICHOLS, " Literary Anecdotes."

Goujet, goo'zhǎ', (CLAUDE PIERRE,) a French writer and Jansenist, born in Paris in 1697. He published a "Life of Nicole," and a number of biographical and historical works, and wrote a supplement to Moréri's "Historical Dictionary." Died in 1767.

See BARRAL, "Mémoires historiques, etc. de l'Abbé Goujet," 1767.

Goujon or **Gougeon,** goo'zhòN', (JEAN,) an eminent sculptor and architect, regarded as the restorer of sculpture in France, was born in Paris about 1515. He was patronized by Henry II., who employed him in the decoration of the Louvre. Among his best works are the bas-reliefs of the Naiads of the Fountain of the Innocents, and the colossal Caryatides which adorn the Salle des Cent-Suisses in the Louvre. He excelled in bas-relief. He was sometimes called "the Correggio of sculpture." He was a Protestant, and was killed at Paris during the Massacre of Saint Bartholomew, in 1572.

See F. MILIZIA, "Memorie degli Architetti antichi e moderni," 1781; AUDOT et POTTIER, "Essai sur la Vie de Goujon," prefixed to Réveil's engravings of Goujon's works, 1827–44; M. FÉLIBIEN, "Recueil historique de la Vie des plus célèbres Architectes;" "Nouvelle Biographie Générale."

Goujon, (JEAN JACQUES ÉMILE,) an astronomer, born in Paris in 1823. He entered the Observatory of Paris, as a student or assistant, in 1841, and made many thousand observations. He and Mauvais were selected to observe the total eclipse of the sun at Dantzic in 1851. He was appointed adjunct astronomer to the Observatory in 1854. Died in 1856.

Goujon, (JEAN MARIE CLAUDE,) a French revolutionist, born at Bourg-en-Bresse in 1766. He obtained a seat in the Convention in April, 1794, and acted with the party of the Mountain. Having been sentenced to death for alleged complicity in the bloody sedition of May 20, 1795, he killed himself.

Goulard, goo'lard', [Fr. pron. goo'lăr',] (THOMAS,) a French surgeon, who has given his name to the preparations known as "Goulard's Cerate," "Goulard's Lotion," etc. Died about 1790.

Goulart, goo'lăr', (SIMON,) a learned French Protestant divine and compiler, born at Senlis in 1543. He became pastor of a church at Geneva about 1570, and was elected in 1607 to succeed Beza as president of the company of pastors. He published a great number of works, some of which were translations, and was regarded as one of the best prose-writers of the sixteenth century. Among his original works are "Discourses touching the State of the World and the Church," (1591,) and "Treasury of Admirable and Memorable Histories of our Time," (2 vols., 1600.) Died at Geneva in 1628.

See BAYLE, "Historical and Critical Dictionary;" SENEBIER, "Histoire littéraire de Genève;" NICÉRON, "Mémoires;" HAAG, "La France protestante."

Goulart, (SIMON,) son of the preceding, born at Geneva about 1575, was pastor of the French Protestant church at Wesel, and subsequently of the Walloon church at Amsterdam. Having refused to subscribe to the Synod of Dort, he was banished, and died in Sleswick in 1628.

See BAYLE, "Historical and Critical Dictionary;" NICÉRON, "Mémoires."

Goulburn, gool'bŭrn, (HENRY,) an English politician, born in London in 1784. He was appointed chief secretary for Ireland about 1822, was chancellor of the exchequer in the ministry of Wellington from 1828 to 1830, and was chosen to represent the University of Cambridge in Parliament in 1831. He was a Conservative, and opposed the Reform Bill. In the cabinet of Sir Robert Peel he was home-secretary from December, 1834, to April, 1835, and chancellor of the exchequer from September, 1841, to June, 1846. Died in 1856.

Gould, goold, (AUGUSTUS ADDISON,) M.D., an American physician and eminent naturalist, born at New Ipswich, New Hampshire, in 1805. He graduated at Harvard in 1825, and was afterwards for some time instructor in botany and zoology in that institution. Having taken the degree of M.D. in 1830, he began to practise in Boston. In the department of conchology Dr. Gould has few superiors. His chief works are a "System of Natural History," (1833,) "The Mollusca and Shells of the United States Exploring Expedition under Wilkes, with an Atlas of Plates," (1852,) and "The Mollusca of the North Pacific Expedition under Ringgold and Rodgers," (1860.) In connection with Professor Agassiz, he published in 1848 a work entitled "Principles of Zoology." Dr. Gould made many valuable contributions to scientific journals, etc. Died in 1866.

Gould, (HANNAH FLAGG,) an American poetess, born in Lancaster, Massachusetts. She published in 1832 a volume of poems, which were favourably received; also two other volumes of poems in 1836 and 1841, and "Hymns and Poems for Children," (1854.) Died in 1865.

See GRISWOLD, "Poets and Poetry of America," and "Female Poets of America;" CLEVELAND, "Compendium of American Literature;" "North American Review" for October, 1835.

Gould, (JAMES,) an American jurist, born in Connecticut about 1770. He was a justice of the supreme court of that State, and published a "Treatise on the Principles of Pleading in Civil Actions." Died in 1838.

Gould, (JOHN,) an eminent English naturalist, born in Dorsetshire in 1804. He published in 1831 an admirable work, entitled "A Century of Birds from the Himalaya Mountains," in folio, with coloured plates, and in 1837 "The Birds of Europe." He visited Australia in 1838, and spent two years in collecting materials for his "Birds of Australia," which came out in 1848, in 7 vols. folio, and contains six hundred species. The figures in this superb work, as well as in the preceding, were exquisitely coloured by his wife. He also published monographs of the "Trochilidæ," the "Rhamphastidæ," and the "Trogonidæ."

See "Westminster Review" for April, 1841.

Gould, (ROBERT,) a British poet, published in 1689 "Poems, chiefly consisting of Satires." Died in 1708.

Goulin, goo'lân', (JEAN,) a learned French physician, born at Rheims in 1728, was professor of the history of medicine in the Medical School of Paris. Died in 1799.

Gŏul'ston or **Gōul'son,** written also **Gulson,** (THEODORE,) a learned English physician, born in Northamptonshire about 1576, was the founder of the Goulstonian Lectureship of Pathology. He translated several works from the Greek into Latin. Died in 1632.

Goulu, goo'lü', (JEAN,) a French ecclesiastic, born in Paris in 1576, wrote a "Life of Saint Francis de Sales," and made several translations from the Latin and Greek. He is chiefly known through his violent controversy with Balzac. (See BALZAC, JEAN LOUIS GUEZ.) Died in 1629.

Gounod, goo'no', (CHARLES or FÉLIX CHARLES,) a popular French composer and musician, born in Paris in 1818. He gained the grand prize for composition in 1839, after which he pursued his studies in Rome. In 1851 he produced the opera of "Sappho." He was appointed director of the Orphéon of Paris in 1852. His opera of "Faust" (about 1859) was performed with brilliant success. Among his other works are symphonies, and operas entitled "La Nonne sanglante" and "La Colombe."

Goupil or **Goupyl,** goo'pe', (JACQUES,) a French physician, born in Poitou, became professor of medicine at Paris in 1555. He edited Aretæus and other Greek medical works, and translated Dioscorides "De Materia Medica" into Latin. Died in 1564.

Gourdan, goor'dôn', (SIMON,) a French monk, born in Paris in 1646. He composed hymns which were sung in churches, and "The Sacrifice of Faith and Love at the Holy Sacrament," (1714,) which was often reprinted. Died in 1729.

Gourgaud, goor'gō', (GASPARD,) BARON, a French general and military writer, born at Versailles in 1783. Having entered the army in 1803, he served in the principal campaigns from 1805 to 1814, and was made a general by Napoleon after the battle of Fleurus, (1815.) He accompanied the emperor to Saint Helena, where, owing to a disagreement with Montholon, he did not remain long. After the revolution of July, 1830, Gourgaud was created a lieutenant-general, and a peer of France in 1841. He published, conjointly with Montholon, "Memoirs to illustrate the History of France under Napoleon," etc., (8 vols., 1822,) "Refutation of the Life of Napoleon by Sir Walter Scott," and several other works. Died in 1852.

See SARRUT and SAINT-EDME, "Biographie des Hommes du Jour;" QUÉRARD, "La France Littéraire;" "Nouvelle Biographie Générale."

Gourgues, de, dĕh goorḡ, (DOMINIQUE,) a celebrated French seaman, born at Mont-de-Marsan about 1530. Having heard of the atrocious massacre by the Spaniards of the French colonists in Florida, he with some assistance equipped a small fleet, and with upwards of two hundred followers sailed, in 1567, for that country. In conjunction with his Indian allies, he totally defeated the Spaniards, and took a number of prisoners, whom he hanged. The head of Gourgues was demanded by the Spanish king, and having lived for some time concealed in France, he was invited by Queen Elizabeth to take command of an English fleet. He died on the journey to London, in 1593.

See BAZANIER, "Voyage du Capitaine de Gourgues dans la Floride;" HILDRETH, "History of the United States," vol. i. chap. iii.

Gouriet, goo're-à', (JEAN BAPTISTE,) a French littérateur, born in Paris in 1774. He published tales, verses, etc. Died in 1855.

Gourlier, goor'le-à', (CHARLES PIERRE,) an architect, born in Paris in 1786. He published a useful work on the public buildings erected in France in the nineteenth century, "Choix d'Édifices publics," etc., (3 vols., 1825-50.) Died in 1857.

Gourmelen, goorm'lôn', (ÉTIENNE,) an eminent French surgeon, born in Finistère, became professor of surgery in the College of France in 1578. He published, besides other works, "Synopsis Chirurgiæ," (1566,) which was for a long time the basis of surgical instruction in the Faculty of Paris. Died at Melun in 1593.

Gournay, de, dĕh goor'nà', (MARIE le Jars—lĕh zhằr,) a literary French lady, born in Paris in 1566, was an intimate friend and admirer of Montaigne, who called her his daughter, (fille d'alliance.) She published two editions of his "Essays," (1595 and 1635.) She gained a high reputation by her writings, among which were a treatise "On the Equality of Men and Women," several moral essays, and verses, some of which Grotius translated. Died in 1645.

See MLLE. DE GOURNAY, "Sa Vie, par elle-même;" L. FEUGÈRE, "Mlle. de Gournay," 8vo, 1853; BAYLE, "Historical and Critical Dictionary;" NICÉRON, "Mémoires."

Gourné, de, dĕh goor'nà', (PIERRE MATHIAS,) ABBÉ, a French geographer, born at Dieppe in 1702. Among his principal works are his "Methodical Geography," etc., (1741,) and "Geographical Description of the Kingdoms of Spain and Portugal," (1743.) Died about 1770.

Gourville, de, dĕh goor'vèl', (JEAN Hérault—hà'rō',) SIEUR, a celebrated French financier, born at La Rochefoucauld in 1625. He was patronized by the Prince of Condé, to whom he rendered many important services, and was afterwards employed by Cardinal Mazarin in various negotiations. He was subsequently ambassador from Louis XIV. to the court of Brunswick. He died in 1703, leaving memoirs of his life, etc., which are highly commended by Madame de Sévigné.

See "Mémoire de Gourville;" "Lettres de Madame de Sévigné."

Gousset, goo'sà', [Lat. GUSSE'TIUS,] (JACQUES,) a learned French Protestant divine, born at Blois in 1635. His principal work is his "Commentaries on the Hebrew Language," ("Commentarii Linguæ Ebraicæ," etc.) He was for many years professor of Greek and theology at Groningen. Died in 1704.

Gousset, (THOMAS MARIE JOSEPH,) a French prelate, born in Haute-Saône in 1792. He became Archbishop of Rheims in 1840, and a cardinal in 1850 or 1851. Among his works is a treatise on "Moral Theology," (1836,) which is highly esteemed.

Goustasp. See GUSHTÂSP.

Gouthières or **Goutières,** goo'te-aiR', written also **Guthier,** [Lat. GUTHE'RIUS,] (JACQUES,) a French jurist and antiquary, born at Chaumont in 1568, published, among other works, a treatise "On the Old Pontifical Law of Rome." Died in 1638.

Gouttes, goot, (JEAN LOUIS,) a French ecclesiastic, born at Tulle in 1740, was a deputy to the States-General in 1789. In 1791 he succeeded Talleyrand as Bishop of Autun. He was arrested by the committee of public safety, and executed, in 1794.

Gouvea, gō-vā'ä, or **Govea, de,** dà go-vā'ä, [Lat. GOVEA'NUS,] (ANTONIO,) an eminent Portuguese jurist and writer, born at Beja in 1505. He became a member of the privy council of Emanuel Philibert, Duke of Savoy, having previously filled the chair of jurisprudence at Cahors and Valence, in France. He wrote a number of legal works in Latin, also Latin poems of great elegance. He died at Turin in 1565, leaving the reputation of one of the first jurists of his time.

Gouvea, de, (ANTONIO,) a Portuguese historian and monk, born at Beja about 1570. He was sent as an ambassador to Persia in 1602, and wrote an account of the war between Shah Abbâs of Persia and the Turks, (1611.) Died in 1628.

Gouvest. See MAUBERT.

Gouvion Saint-Cyr, goo've-ôN' sằn'sèR', (LAURENT,) a French marshal, was born at Toul in 1764. He served in the army of the Rhine in 1796, and in 1797 succeeded Massena as commander of the army of Rome. He took a prominent part in the Austrian and Prussian campaigns of 1805-06, and in 1812 obtained a signal victory over the Russian prince Wittgenstein at Polotsk, for which he received a marshal's bâton. After the accession of Louis XVIII. he was created successively a peer and a marquis, and in 1817 became minister of war. He died in 1830, leaving "Memoirs towards a Military History under the Directory, the Consulate, and the Empire," (1831,) which is regarded as a standard work and has been translated into several languages.

See GAY DE VERNON, "Vie de Gouvion Saint-Cyr;" NOLLET-FABERT, "Le Maréchal Gouvion Saint-Cyr," 1853.

Gouye, goo-e', (THOMAS,) a French Jesuit and mathematician, born at Dieppe in 1650, wrote "Physical and Mathematical Observations," etc. Died in 1725.

Gouye de Longuemarre, goo-e' dẹh lŏng'mǎR', (N.,) a French advocate and historical writer, born at Dieppe in 1715. He published several dissertations relative to the early history of France. Died in 1763.

Gouz or **Goux,** goo, (FRANÇOIS de la Boullaye le —dẹh lǎ boo'lǎ' lẹh,) a French traveller and diplomatist, born in Anjou about 1610, was sent in 1688 on an embassy to the Great Mogul. He died in Persia in 1689.

See "Retrospective Review," vol. i., (new series,) 1853.

Govea. See GOUVEA.

Govinda, a name of KRISHNA, (which see.)

Go-vin'dạ Singh, (sing,) a famous chief of the Sikhs, born at Patna in 1661, was the last Guru (or Gŏŏ'rŏŏ) or religious head of that sect. He was a son of the ninth Gooroo, who was put to death by Aurung-Zeb. He reformed or reorganized the Sikhs, whom he converted into a tribe of formidable warriors and taught that it was meritorious to exterminate the Mongols, over whom he gained several victories. Having been abandoned by nearly all his partisans, he escaped in disguise to the desert. Died in 1708.

See J. MALCOLM, "Sketch of the Sikhs," in the "Asiatic Researches," vol. xi.

Govona, go-vo'nä, (ROSA,) was born at Mondovì, in Italy, in 1716. Left an orphan at an early age, she not only supported herself by her industry, but formed an association of destitute young girls, whom she instructed in various kinds of labour. In 1755, assisted by several of the nobility, she founded at Turin an industrial institution, which was patronized by King Charles Emanuel III. Similar establishments were formed in other Italian towns, and called Rosines in honour of their foundress. Died in 1776.

See "Nouvelle Biographie Générale."

Gŏw'er, (JOHN,) one of the earliest English poets, born about 1320, is supposed to have been a native of Yorkshire. He studied law in London, where he formed an intimate friendship with Chaucer, who is said to have been his fellow-student. His principal works are his "Speculum Meditantis," ("Mirror of Meditation,") "Vox Clamantis," ("Voice of One Crying,") and "Confessio Amantis," ("Lover's Confession.") The last-named only has been printed, and was one of the first works issued from Caxton's press, (1483.) Gower was in opulent circumstances, and contributed largely to the rebuilding of the conventual church of Saint Mary Overy, now Saint Saviour's Church. His learning was profound and varied, but his merits as a poet are not of a high order. His sonnets, in French, are pronounced by Warton superior to his other compositions. He died in 1402, and was interred in Saint Saviour's Church.

See WARTON, "History of English Poetry;" DISRAELI, "Amenities of Literature;" "Retrospective Review," vol. ii., 2d series; H. J. TODD, "Illustrations of the Lives, etc. of Gower and Chaucer."

Gower, (LEVESON.) See GRANVILLE, LORD, and EGERTON, (FRANCIS.)

Gŏw'rie, (JOHN RUTHVEN,) EARL OF, born about 1578, was a son of William Ruthven, noticed below. He and his brother Alexander were the chief actors in the mysterious affair called the Gowrie conspiracy. In 1600 King James was induced to visit the earl in his castle at Perth, and an attempt was made against his liberty or life by the Ruthvens, who were both killed by the king's attendants.

See ROBERTSON, "History of Scotland;" HUME, "History of England;" JAMES SCOTT, "History of the Life and Death of John, Earl of Gowrie," 1818.

Gowrie, (WILLIAM RUTHVEN,) EARL OF, was a son of the Lord Ruthven who took a prominent part in the murder of David Rizzio. He was the leader of the conspirators who seized James VI. at Ruthven Castle in 1582 and detained him as a captive about ten months. This seizure of the king was called the "Raid of Ruthven." He was convicted of treason, and executed in 1584.

Goya y Lucientes, go'yä e loo-the-ĕn'tĕs, (FRANCISCO,) a skilful Spanish painter, born in Aragon in 1746. He received the title of painter to Charles IV. in 1799. He painted religious subjects, portraits, caricatures, etc.

with success. He also engraved a series of caricatures and moral scenes called "Caprichos." Died at Bordeaux in 1828.

See VIARDOT, "Notices sur les Peintres d'Espagne."

Goyen, van, vän goi'ẹn,? (JAN,) a celebrated Dutch painter of landscapes and marine views, born at Leyden in 1596. His pictures are admirably executed; but the colours, not being well chosen, are injured by time. Died in 1656.

Göz or **Goez,** göts, (JOSEPH FRANZ,) BARON, a German painter, born at Hermannstadt in 1754. He published about 1784 a series of plates entitled "Exercises of Imagination on Different Human Characters and Forms," which are regarded as little inferior to the designs of Hogarth. Among his best pictures are the portrait of Kosciusko, and "The Madness of King Lear." Died in 1815.

See NAGLER, "Neues Allgemeines Künstler-Lexikon."

Gozlan, goz'lŏn', (LÉON,) a witty French dramatist and novelist, born at Marseilles in 1806. He displayed great talent for observation in his works, among which are "The Notary of Chantilly," (1836,) "Céleste," (1839,) "The Châteaus of France," (4 vols., 1844,) "Le Gâteau des Reines," (1855,) and "Il faut que Jeunesse se paye," (1858.) Died in 1866.

Gozon, de, dẹh go'zŏn', (DEODATUS or DIEUDONNÉ,) a celebrated French chevalier, who, according to tradition, delivered the island of Rhodes from a monstrous serpent which infested it. This achievement has been immortalized by Schiller in his poem entitled "The Combat with the Dragon," (" Der Kampf mit dem Drachen.") Gozon was afterwards elected grand master of the order of Saint John of Jerusalem. Died in 1353.

See VERTOT, "Histoire des Chevaliers de Malte."

Gozzi, got'see, (CARLO,) COUNT, a celebrated Italian dramatist, was born at Venice about 1720. He published in 1761 his drama entitled "The Loves of the Three Oranges," ("Amore delle tre Melarance,") which met with brilliant success. It was followed by "Mrs. Serpent," ("Donna Serpente,") "King Stag," ("Il Re Cervo,") "Turandot," and other fairy-pieces, (Fiabe,) of a similar nature, which are characterized by wonderful and striking incidents, drawn from Oriental fables. They were received with general admiration, more especially in Germany, where they have been imitated by several eminent writers. Gozzi's "Turandot, Princess of China," has been translated and re-wrought by Schiller. Died in 1806.

See FR. HORN, "Ueber K. Gozzi's dramatische Poesie;" TIPALDO, "Biografia degli Italiani illustri;" LONGFELLOW, "Poets and Poetry of Europe;" also Gozzi's Autobiography, entitled "Memorie inutili di Carlo Gozzi," 3 vols., 1788, and the French version of the same, by PAUL DE MUSSET, 1848; "Nouvelle Biographie Générale."

Gozzi, (GASPARO,) COUNT, a distinguished Italian writer, brother of the preceding, was born at Venice in 1713. He was the author of the "Venetian Observer," ("Osservatore Veneto," 12 vols., 1768,) on the model of Addison's "Spectator," which it resembles in its graceful style and delicate satire; and of "Epistles," in verse, ("Sermoni,") which are greatly admired for their elegance. He also made several excellent translations from the Latin, French, and English, and published a "Defence of Dante," which is esteemed a standard work. Died at Padua in 1786.

See GHERARDINI, "Vita di G. Gozzi," 1821; PINDEMONTE, "Elogio del Conte G. Gozzi," 1787; "Nouvelle Biographie Générale;" F. FANZAGO, "Delle Lodi del Conte G. Gozzi," 1788.

Gozzoli, got'so-lee, (BENOZZO,) a distinguished Italian painter, born at Florence about 1405, was a pupil of Fra Angelico. He worked at Florence, Rome, Orvieto, and Pisa. Among his best works are his frescos, which cover an entire side of the Campo Santo at Pisa. The subjects of these are taken from the Bible. "These marvellous frescos," says the "Nouvelle Biographie Générale," "display in the highest degree the genius for invention and the talent for execution." Some of his frescos at Pisa and Florence are still well preserved. Died about 1485.

See MRS. JAMESON, "Memoirs of Early Italian Painters;" VASARI, "Lives of the Painters;" LANZI, "History of Painting in Italy;" "Nouvelle Biographie Générale."

ɛ as k; ç as s; ğ hard; ġ as j; G, H, K, guttural; N, nasal; R, trilled; s as z; th as in this. (☞See Explanations, p. 23.)

Graaf or **Graef, de**, dęh grȧf, (REINHART,) a Dutch physician and anatomist, born at Schoonhoven in 1641. He studied at Leyden, and afterwards settled at Delft, where he died in 1673. He published, among other works, in Latin, a treatise "On the Nature and Use of the Pancreatic Juice."

See NICÉRON, "Mémoires."

Graaso. See GRAUW, (HENDRIK.)

Graat, grȧt, (BERNARD or BARENT,) a skilful Dutch painter of landscapes and animals, born at Amsterdam in 1628. His colouring is vigorous and harmonious, and his design correct. He excelled in animated landscapes, and painted some historical pieces with success. Among his best works is a "David and Bathsheba." He worked mostly at Amsterdam, where he died in 1709.

Grabbe, grȧb'bęh, (CHRISTIAN DIETRICH,) a German dramatic poet, born at Detmold in 1801. Among his best productions are the tragedies of "The Duke of Gothland," "Hannibal," "The Battle of Hermann," (1838,) and a comedy entitled "Jest, Satire, Irony," etc. ("Scherz, Satire, Ironie," etc.,) which is esteemed a master-piece of wit and humour. Died in 1836.

See E. DULLER, "C. Grabbe's Leben," 1838; LONGFELLOW, "Poets and Poetry of Europe;" KARL ZIEGLER, "Biographie C. Grabbe's," 1848.

Grabe, grȧ'bęh, (JOHANN ERNST,) a German theologian, born at Königsberg in 1666. About 1705 he settled in England, where he obtained the degree of D.D. He published several religious works, the principal of which was an edition of the Septuagint, (8 vols. 8vo, 1707–20.) Died in 1711.

See NICÉRON, "Mémoires."

Grabener, grȧ'bęh-nęr, (GOTTLIEB,) a German philologist and writer, born in 1685; died in 1750.

See "Vita Grabeneri," by his son, C. G. GRABENER, 1751.

Gråberg (grȯ'bĕRg) **von Hemso,** (JAKOB,) a learned Swedish geographer, born in the island of Gottland in 1776, was appointed by his government, in 1823, consul in Tripoli. Among his most important works, which are composed in several languages, are a "Historical Essay on the Skalds," (1811,) a "Geographico-Statistical Essay on the Regency of Algiers," (1830,) and a good work on the "Geography of Morocco," (1834, in Italian.) He possessed a choice collection of antique coins and Oriental manuscripts. Died at Florence in 1847.

See his "Autobiography ;" "Nouvelle Biographie Générale."

Grabowski, grȧ-bov'skee, (AMBROSIUS,) a Polish archæologist, born near Cracow in 1782, published "The Historic Antiquities of Poland," (1840.)

Grac'chus, (CAIUS SEMPRONIUS,) a celebrated Roman statesman and orator, born in 159 (or, as some say, 154) B.C., was a brother of Tiberius. He was carefully educated by his mother, the wise and virtuous Cornelia. He was elected quæstor in 126 B.C., and in that capacity served in Sardinia, where he acquired much popularity, and, according to Plutarch, exhibited "a noble specimen of every virtue." As he was endowed with great talents and excelled in eloquence, the aristocratic party always regarded him with a jealous eye. He was elected tribune of the people in 123 B.C., and was the author of several laws tending to improve the condition of the poor and to moderate the power of the senate. By one of his laws the judiciary power was transferred from the senate to the equestrian order. He promoted commerce by opening good public roads. "They who hated and feared him," says Plutarch, "were struck with his amazing industry and the celerity of his operations." He was re-elected tribune for the year 122. During his second term he proposed to give the Roman franchise, or right of citizenship, to all the Latins. To counteract his influence, the senate resorted to a trick or stratagem. They induced the tribune M. Livius Drusus to act the part of a demagogue, and to propose measures more radical or democratic than those of Gracchus, who was thus supplanted in the popular favour. Caius conducted a colony to Carthage, and after an absence of seventy days returned to Rome. Opimius, an enemy of Gracchus, was chosen consul for the year 121, and the adherents of the senate began to repeal the laws of the latter, who was now a private citizen. Fulvius Flaccus, a rash partisan of Gracchus, and many others,

took arms in his defence; but Gracchus himself was averse to violent resistance. He perished in a general massacre, ordered by Opimius, in 121 B.C.

See PLUTARCH, "Life of Caius Gracchus;" LIVY, "Epitome ;" DION CASSIUS, "Fragmenta;" F. D. GERLACH, "Tiberius und Caius Gracchus; historischer Vortrag," 1843.

Gracchus, (TIBERIUS SEMPRONIUS,) a Roman general of the second Punic war. He was elected consul for 215 B.C., and defeated Hanno near Beneventum in 214. In the next year he was the colleague of Fabius Maximus in the consulship. He was killed in an ambuscade in 212 B.C.

Gracchus, (TIBERIUS SEMPRONIUS,) a Roman general, who married Cornelia, a daughter of Scipio Africanus, and was the father of the famous Gracchi. He became consul in 178 B.C., (or 576 A.U.C.,) and again in 163 B.C. He gained a victory over the Sardinians. His character is extolled by Cicero. Died about 158 B.C.

Gracchus, (TIBERIUS SEMPRONIUS,) a popular and eminent Roman statesman, born about 168 B.C. His mother was the celebrated Cornelia, a daughter of the greatest Scipio. He served at the capture and destruction of Carthage under Scipio Africanus the Younger, who had married a sister of Gracchus. In 137 B.C. he was elected quæstor, and was employed in the Numantian war, in which he greatly distinguished himself by his courage and capacity. About 134 B.C. he was elected tribune of the people, and proposed an important reform in the disposition of the public lands. His first effort was to restore or enforce (with some modifications) the Licinian law, which prohibited any man from occupying more than five hundred acres of public land, and which had never been formally repealed, but was generally neglected and violated. "There never was," says Plutarch, "a milder law made against so much injustice and oppression. For they who deserved to have been punished for their infringement on the rights of the community were to have a consideration for giving up their groundless claims. . . . In this just and glorious cause Tiberius exerted an eloquence which might have adorned a worse subject, and which nothing could resist." He was violently opposed by the aristocracy and the tribune M. Octavius, whose veto retarded the passage of the bill. At length Octavius was deposed, and the agrarian law was adopted. Gracchus again offered himself as a candidate for the office of tribune. During the election, which occurred in June, when many of his friends were engaged in harvesting, the partisans of the aristocracy, led by Scipio Nasica, appealed to force, and killed Gracchus, with about three hundred of his supporters, in 133 B.C.

See PLUTARCH, "Life of Tiberius Gracchus;" LIVY, "History of Rome;" CRELL, "Elogium et Character T. et C. Gracchorum," 1727; NIEBUHR, "History of Rome;" HEEREN, "Tiberius und Caius Gracchus;" F. D. GERLACH, "Tiberius und Caius Gracchus; historischer Vortrag," 1843.

Gracian, grȧ-the-ȧn', (BALTASAR,) a Spanish ecclesiastic, born at Calatayud in 1584, was rector of the Jesuits' College at Tarragona. He wrote "Reflections on the Political Conduct of Ferdinand the Catholic," a work entitled "The Hero," (1637,) which was translated into several languages, and "Criticon," an allegory, (1650–53.) Died in 1658.

See TICKNOR, "History of Spanish Literature;" BOUTERWEK, "Histoire de la Littérature Espagnole."

Gradenigo, grȧ-dà-nee'go, (GIOVANNI AGOSTINO,) an Italian antiquary and writer, born at Venice about 1722. He became Bishop of Chioggia and Ceneda. Died in 1774.

See L. DOGLIONI, "Elogio storico di G. A. Gradenigo," 1774.

Gradenigo, (GIOVANNI GIROLAMO,) an Italian prelate, born at Venice in 1708, became Archbishop of Udine in 1766. Died in 1786.

Gradenigo, (PIETRO,) born in 1249, was Doge of Venice from 1289 to 1311. He originated the revolution that deprived the people of their privileges and made the aristocracy hereditary. During the war with Genoa in 1297, he passed the decree called the Closing of the Grand Council, which took from the people the right of electing the members of that council. Died in 1311.

See MARINO SANUTO, "Vite dei Duchi di Venezia, P. Gradenigo; DARU, "Histoire de Venise."

ā, ē, ī, ō, ū, ȳ, *long;* ȧ, ė, ȯ, same, less prolonged; ă, ĕ, ĭ, ŏ, ŭ, ў, *short;* ą, ę, į, ǫ, *obscure;* fär, fȧll, fȧt; mĕt; nŏt; gōŏd; mōŏn;

Gradi, grȧ'de', [Lat. DE GRAD'IBUS,] (JEAN,) a French jurist and legal writer, who lived about 1490–1520.

Gradivus, a surname of MARS, which see.

Græcinus, grē-sī'nus, (JULIUS,) a Roman senator, who refused to appear as the accuser of Marcus Silanus, and was in consequence put to death by order of Caligula. "He was," says Seneca, "too good a man to be permitted to live under a tyrant."

Graefe. See GRÄFE, and GRÄVIUS, (JOHANN G.)

Graeffe. See GRÄFFE.

Græme, grām, (JOHN,) a Scottish poet, born at Carnwath, Lanarkshire, in 1748. His elegies and other poems were published in 1773. Died in 1772.

Graesse. See GRÄSSE.

Graeter. See GRÄTER.

Graevel. See GRÄVEL.

Grævius. See GRÄVIUS.

Graf, grȧf, (called also **Urs, Ours, Ursus, Gamperlin, Gemberlein,** and **Van Goar,**) a noted Swiss engraver, born at Bâle about 1485.

Gräfe. See GRÄVIUS.

Gräfe, grä'feh, (HEINRICH,) born at Buttstädt, in Germany, in 1802, wrote "Universal Science of Education," ("Allgemeine Pädagogik," 1845.)

Gräfe or **Graefe,** fon grä'feh, (KARL FERDINAND,) a celebrated surgeon and oculist, born at Warsaw in 1787. He became, about 1811, professor of surgery and director of the ophthalmo-surgical clinic at Berlin, and wrote, besides other works, one on the rhinoplastic art, which he greatly improved. Died in 1840.

ALBRECHT VON GRÄFE, a son of the preceding, born at Berlin in 1828, became professor of ophthalmic surgery in his native city in 1857. He was regarded as the greatest oculist in Europe. Died in 1870.

Graff, grȧf, (ANTOINE,) an eminent Swiss portrait-painter, born at Winterthur in 1736. He was appointed in 1766 court painter at Dresden. His works are numerous and highly esteemed. Died in 1813.

Graff, grȧf, (EBERHARD GOTTLIEB,) a German philologist, born at Elbing in 1780, was profoundly versed in the old German language and literature. His principal work is the "Treasure of the Old German Language," which, after his death, was completed by Massmann. Died in Berlin in 1841.

Gräffe or **Graeffe,** grêf'feh, (JOHANN FRIEDRICH CHRISTOPH,) a German philosopher and writer, born in 1754 at Göttingen, where he became professor of philosophy. Died in 1816.

Grafigni, grȧ-fèn'yee, (AGOSTINO,) a Genoese merchant, residing at Antwerp and London about 1590, was a principal agent in the secret negotiations between Queen Elizabeth and Alexander of Parma.

See MOTLEY'S "History of the United Netherlands," chap. viii.

Grafigny or **Graffigny,** grȧ'fèn'ye', (FRANÇOISE d'Issembourg d'Happoncourt—de'sŏN'boor' dȧ'-pŏN'koor',) a French writer, born at Nancy in 1695. Her principal works are the comedy of "Cenia," and "Lettres d'une Péruvienne," a romance. Died in 1758.

See VOLTAIRE, "Correspondance générale."

Grafstrœm or **Grafström,** grȧf'strŏm, (ANDERS ABRAHAM,) a Swedish poet and clergyman, born at Sundsvall in 1790. He married a daughter of the poet Franzén. Among his works are "Sånger från Norrland," (1841.)

Graf'ton, (AUGUSTUS HENRY FITZROY,) DUKE OF, a British minister of state, was born in 1736. He became one of the two secretaries of state in the Whig cabinet in 1765, and was appointed first lord of the treasury in a ministry which Lord Chatham formed of very discordant materials in 1766. In consequence of Lord Chatham's ill health, the functions of prime minister devolved on the Duke of Grafton, whose character and measures were assailed with violent invective by Junius. Lord Chatham resigned about October, 1768, and the duke resigned in 1770. He was lord privy seal from 1771 to 1775, after which he opposed the American war and the measures of Lord North. Died in 1811.

See LORD MAHON'S "History of England."

Grafton, (RICHARD,) an English printer and historical writer, published in 1569 "Chronicles at Large and Meere History of the Affayres of England."

Grafunder, grȧ'foon-der, (DAVID,) a German Orientalist, published a "Chaldaic Grammar," and other works. Died in 1680.

Graham, (CATHERINE.) See MACAULAY.

Graham, grä'am, (GEORGE,) F.R.S., a distinguished English mechanician and astronomer, born in Cumberland in 1675. He was commissioned to furnish instruments for the French Academicians who were sent to the North to ascertain the figure of the earth, (1735.) He also constructed the mural arch in the Observatory at Greenwich, and the sector by which Dr. Bradley made discoveries relating to the fixed stars. He was esteemed one of the best watchmakers of his time. Died in 1751.

See THIOUT, "Traité d'Horlogerie."

Graham, grä'am, (ISABELLA,) a Scottish philanthropist, born at Lanark in 1742. She emigrated to New York City in 1789, after she had been married to Dr. John Graham, (1765.) She took a prominent part in founding several benevolent institutions in New York, and abounded in works of charity. Died in 1814.

See DR. MASON, "Memoirs of Mrs. Graham."

Graham, (Sir JAMES ROBERT GEORGE,) a British statesman, born at Netherby in 1792. He was elected to Parliament for Hull as a Liberal in 1818. In 1830 he became first lord of the admiralty under Earl Grey, and managed that department with rigid economy. He promoted the passage of the Reform Bill in 1831, and resigned office in 1834. On the accession of Sir Robert Peel, in 1841, he entered the cabinet as home-secretary. He rendered efficient aid to Peel in the repeal of the corn-laws, and retired from office with the same chief in 1846. He gave a general support to the Whig administration which followed, and about the end of 1852 was appointed first lord of the admiralty in the ministry of Lord Aberdeen. His opposition to the Russian war appears to have been the cause which induced him to resign, about February, 1855. The ill success of the Baltic fleet in the Russian war was attributed, by Sir C. Napier and others, to his parsimony and mismanagement. He represented Carlisle in Parliament for many years. Died in October, 1861.

See "Blackwood's Magazine" for April, 1863; "Westminster Review" for June, 1844.

Graham, (JOHN,) Viscount Dundee, called **Claverhouse**—klav'er-üs, a Scottish officer, distinguished for his military talents and for his merciless severity towards the Covenanters, was born about 1650. He served in the Dutch army under the Prince of Orange, and returned to Scotland in 1677. Soon after this date he became a captain in a troop of dragoons which was ordered to enforce the penal laws against the Scottish Covenanters. Though defeated by them at Drumclog in 1679, he was afterwards more successful, and rendered his name forever odious by his atrocities. In 1689 he raised a body of Highlanders to fight for James II. He was killed in June, 1689, at Killiecrankie, where his army was victorious. "During the last three months of his life," says Macaulay, "he had proved himself a great warrior and politician; and his name is therefore mentioned with respect by that large class of persons who think that there is no excess of wickedness for which courage and ability do not atone."

See MACAULAY, "History of England," vol. i. chap. iv., and vol. iii. chap. xiii.; CHAMBERS, "Biographical Dictionary of Eminent Scotsmen;" J. PAGET, "New Examen," 1861; "Edinburgh Review" for July, 1863; "North British Review" for May, 1850; SIR WALTER SCOTT, "Old Mortality."

Graham, grä'am, (JOHN ANDREW,) born in Connecticut in 1764, wrote a "Descriptive Sketch of the Present State of Vermont," (1797,) and "Memoirs of John Horne Tooke," (1828.) Died in 1841.

Graham, (JOSEPH,) an officer of the American Revolution, was born in Chester, Pennsylvania, in 1759. He emigrated to North Carolina. He served with distinction under General Lincoln, and was afterwards made a brigadier-general. Died in 1836.

Graham, (MARIA.) See CALLCOTT, (LADY.)

Graham, (MARY JANE,) a literary Englishwoman, born in London in 1803, was acquainted with Greek and other languages. She published "The Test of Truth," (7th edition, 1852.) Died in 1830.

Graham, (ROBERT,) a Scottish physician and botanist, born at Stirling in 1786, became professor of botany at Glasgow about 1818. He was a contributor to the "Botanical Magazine" and other scientific journals. In 1820 he obtained a chair of botany in the University of Edinburgh. Died in 1845.

Graham, (SYLVESTER,) a noted American reformer and writer on dietetics, was born in Suffield, Connecticut, in 1794. He studied at Amherst College, officiated for a time as a Presbyterian minister, and about 1830 was employed by the Pennsylvania Temperance Society as a lecturer. His experience in this vocation led him to the conviction that the prevention and cure of intemperance were chiefly to be found in the adoption of a purely vegetable diet, which he supposed would take away the desire for stimulants. He subsequently applied this theory to all cases of disease. He published in 1839 "Lectures on the Science of Human Life," (in 2 vols.) Died in 1851.

Graham, (THOMAS,) F.R.S., an eminent British chemist, born at Glasgow in 1805. He became professor of chemistry in the Andersonian University in 1830, and in the London University in 1837. He published in 1842 a valuable work, entitled "Elements of Chemistry." Among his important discoveries is the law of the diffusion of gases. He was the first president of the Chemical Society of London. He succeeded Sir John Herschel as Master of the Mint in 1855. Died in 1869.

Graham, (Sir THOMAS.) See LYNEDOCH.

Graham, (WILLIAM A.,) an American politician, born in North Carolina in 1800. He represented North Carolina in the Senate of the United States in 1841-43, was elected Governor of that State by the Whigs in 1844, and re-elected in 1846. He became secretary of the navy in July, 1850, and retired from that office in 1852. In the latter year he was the candidate of the Whig party for the Vice-Presidency.

Grahame, grā'am, (JAMES,) a Scottish poet and divine, born at Glasgow in 1765. He studied in the university of his native city, and subsequently practised law for a time. He entered holy orders in 1809, and was appointed curate of Shipton, in Gloucestershire. His principal poem, "The Sabbath," is esteemed one of the finest compositions of the kind. He also published "British Georgics," "The Birds of Scotland," etc. Died in 1811.

See CHAMBERS, "Biographical Dictionary of Eminent Scotsmen;" "Edinburgh Review" for April, 1810; "London Quarterly Review" for May, 1810.

Grahame, (JAMES,) a British historian, published a "History of the Rise and Progress of the United States of North America till the British Revolution of 1688." It is styled by Prescott "the most thorough work, and incomparably the best on the subject, previous to Mr. Bancroft's." Died in 1842.

Grain. See LE GRAIN.

Graindorge, grăn'dorzh', (ANDRÉ,) a French physician and naturalist, born at Caen in 1616, wrote a treatise "On the Nature of Fire, Light, and Colours," and other works, in Latin. Died in 1676.

Graindorge, (ANDRÉ,) a French weaver, born at Caen, lived about 1600. He was the first artisan who wove diaper in flowers and squares. His son RICHARD perfected the art by representing animals and other figures.

Grain'ger, (JAMES,) a Scottish physician and poet, born at Dunse in 1723. He was the author of a mediocre poem entitled "Sugar-Cane," (1764,) and an "Ode on Solitude," which Dr. Johnson admired. He also translated the "Elegies" of Tibullus. Died in 1767.

See JOHNSON and CHALMERS, "Lives of the English Poets;" CHAMBERS, "Biographical Dictionary of Eminent Scotsmen."

Grain'ger, (RICHARD,) an English architect, born at Newcastle-upon-Tyne in 1798. He acquired wealth by his enterprise, and made extensive improvements in Newcastle, among which were new streets, an exchange, market-house, and other public buildings. Died in 1861.

Grainville, grăn'vèl', (JEAN BAPTISTE CHRISTOPHE,) a French littérateur, born at Lisieux in 1760, made several translations from the Spanish and the Italian, and published a number of original poems. Died in 1805.

Grainville, de, dęh grăn'vèl', (JEAN BAPTISTE FRANÇOIS XAVIER Cousin—koo'zăn',) a French ecclesiastic and distinguished pulpit orator, born at Havre in 1746. He published a poem entitled "The Last Man," "The Judgment of Paris," (a drama,) and several other works. Died in 1805.

Gram, grăm, (JOHAN or HANS,) a Danish philologist, born in Jutland in 1685, became successively professor of Greek at Copenhagen, (1714,) historiographer, royal librarian, and archivist, (1731.) In 1745 he was made a councillor of state. He published, in Latin, a "History of the Gods, from Xenophon," and other critical and historical works, which enjoy a high reputation. He was the founder of the Scientific Society of Copenhagen. Died in 1748.

See JENS MOELLER, "H. Grams Levnet," 1810; KRAFT cg NYERUP, "Litteraturlexicon."

Gramaye, grā'mā', (JEAN BAPTISTE,) a Flemish antiquary and historical writer, born at Antwerp about 1580. He became professor of law and rhetoric at Louvain, and was afterwards appointed historiographer to the Netherlands. He wrote a "History of Brabant," "Antiquities of Flanders," and other works, in Latin. Died in 1635.

Grammatica, grăm-mā'te-kä, (ANTIVEDUTO, ăn-te-vă-doo'to,) an Italian painter, born near Rome in 1571. He was a skilful imitator and counterfeiter of the works of great masters. Died in 1626.

See LANZI, "History of Painting in Italy."

Grammatico, grăm-mā'te-ko, (NICAISO,) an Italian Jesuit, born at Trent; died in 1736.

Gramond or **Grammont,** grā'môn', [Lat. GRAMUN'DUS,] (GABRIEL BARTHÉLEMY,) a French writer, born at Toulouse about 1590, published a "History of the Reign of Louis XIII.," etc., (in Latin.) Died in 1654.

Gramont or **Grammont, de,** dęh grā'môn', (ANTOINE,) DUC, born in 1604, became lieutenant-general in 1641, and soon after a marshal of France. Died in 1678.

Gramont, de, (ANTOINE,) DUC, a grandson of the preceding, was born in 1672, and was first called COMTE DE GUICHE. He served in many battles in Flanders, and was made lieutenant-general in 1704, and marshal in 1724. Died in 1725.

Gramont, de, (ANTOINE LOUIS MARIE,) DUC, a French general, born in 1755. He emigrated in 1789. Died in 1836.

Gramont, de, (ARMAND.) See GUICHE.

Gramont, de, (GABRIEL,) a French prelate, became Archbishop of Bordeaux in 1529, and in 1530 was made a cardinal. Died in 1534.

Gramont or **Grammont, de,** (PHILIBERT,) COMTE, a French courtier, celebrated for his wit, frivolity, and gallantry, was born in 1621. He distinguished himself in several campaigns under Condé and Turenne, and obtained the rank of general. He passed some time at the court of Charles II. of England. Died in 1707. His brother-in-law, Anthony Hamilton, published "Memoirs of Grammont," which is much admired. (See HAMILTON, ANTHONY.)

Gramont, de, (SCIPION,) a French poet, born in Provence, was secretary to Louis XIII. Died about 1638.

Granacci, grä-nät'chee, (FRANCESCO,) a Florentine painter, born about 1475, was a pupil of Ghirlandaio, and afterwards of Michael Angelo, whose style he adopted. Among his master-pieces we may name "The Virgin giving her Girdle to Saint Thomas." Died in 1544.

See VASARI, "Lives of the Painters," etc.

Granada, de, dä grä-nä'Dä, (Fray LUIS,) [Fr. LOUIS DE GRENADE, loo'e' dęh gręh'năd',] a celebrated Spanish ecclesiastic, and one of the first pulpit orators of his time, born at Granada in 1504, was educated in the family of the Count of Tendilla. He refused the archbishopric of Braga, which was offered him, and devoted himself in Lisbon to preaching and religious compositions. Free from the persecuting spirit of his time, he won the hearts of his hearers by his mild persuasive eloquence and the shining example of his own life. Among his principal works are "The Sinner's Guide," a "Memorial of the Christian Life," (1566,) "Symbol of the Faith," and "Rhetorica Ecclesiastica." His "Guide to Sinners,"

ā, ē, ī, ō, ū, ȳ, *long;* ă, ĕ, ĭ, ŏ, ŭ, ў, *short;* ą, ę, į, ǫ, *obscure;* fär, fäll, fät; mĕt; nŏt; gōōd; mōōn;

says Ticknor, "was translated into nearly all the languages of Europe, including Greek and Polish." Died in 1588.

See TICKNOR, "History of Spanish Literature;" LUIS MUÑOZ, "La Vida de Luis de Granada," 1639.

Granberg, gRan′bĕRg, (PEHR ADOLF,) a Swedish historian, born at Gottenburg in 1770, published a "History of the Union of Calmar," (3 vols., 1807–11,) and a "History of the Wars in Scandinavia from the Rupture of the Union of Calmar to the Death of Charles XII.," (1821.) Died in 1841.

See "Biographiskt-Lexicon öfver namnkunnige Svenska Män."

Gran′bў, (JOHN MANNERS,) MARQUIS OF, an English general, born in 1721, was the eldest son of the Duke of Rutland. He obtained the rank of lieutenant-general about 1758, and contributed to the victory of Minden, (1759.) In the ensuing campaigns of the Seven Years' war he commanded the British troops at Warburg and Homburg, (1762.) He was appointed master-general of the ordnance in 1763, and commander-in-chief of the British armies in 1766. He died in 1770, leaving several sons, one of whom, Charles, became Duke of Rutland. "Granby, honest, generous, and brave as a lion, had neither science nor genius." (Macaulay's "Essays.")

Grancolas, gRŏn′ko′lä′, (JEAN,) a French theologian and doctor of the Sorbonne, born near Châteaudun about 1660. He wrote a "Treatise on Liturgies," and other works, on the traditions, rites, and usages of the Church. Died in 1732.

Grand. See LEGRAND.

Grandami, gRŏn′dä′me′, (JACQUES,) a French Jesuit and astronomer, born at Nantes in 1588, published a treatise on eclipses, and another on chronology, (1668.) Died in 1672.

Grandet, gRŏn′dä′, (JOSEPH,) a French priest and biographer, born at Angers in 1646. Among his works is a "Life of an unknown Recluse, supposed to be the Count of Moret," (1699.) Died in 1724.

Grandi, gRän′dee, (ERCOLE,) an Italian painter, born in Ferrara in 1491. Among his works is "The Conversion of Saint Paul," now in London. Died in 1531.

Grandi, [Lat. GRAN′DIUS,] (GUIDO,) an Italian mathematician, born at Cremona in 1671, became professor of philosophy at Pisa in 1700. He published a treatise "On Series and Infinitesimals," and another "On Sound," which caused his election to the Royal Society of London. His works are numerous, and chiefly written in Latin. He was a friend of Newton, Leibnitz, and other eminent philosophers of the time. Died in 1742.

See G. M. ORTES, "Vita del Padre G. Grandi," 1744; FABRONI, "Vitæ Italorum doctrina excellentium;" TIPALDO, "Biografia degli Italiani illustri;" A. M. BANDINI, "G. Grandi Elogium," 1745.

Grandi, (JACOPO,) an Italian physician and naturalist, born in the duchy of Módena in 1646; died in 1691.

Grandidier, gRŏn′de′de-à′, (PHILIPPE ANDRÉ,) a French historian, was born at Strasburg in 1752. He wrote a "History of the Bishopric and Bishops of Strasburg," (2 vols., 1778.) Died in 1787.

See LOUIS SPACH, "Éloge de Grandidier," 1851.

Grandier, gRŏn′de-à′, (URBAIN,) a French ecclesiastic, and canon of Loudun, born near Sablé. Having been accused of sorcery by some monks who were his enemies, he was condemned to death, and burnt at the stake in 1634.

See BAZIN, "Histoire de Louis XIII," vol. iii.; "Nouvelle Biographie Générale."

Grandin, gRŏn′dân′, (MARTIN,) a French theologian and doctor of the Sorbonne, born at Saint-Quentin in 1604. He was appointed professor of philosophy and divinity in Le Moine College, and was the author of "Theological Institutes," (in Latin.) Died in 1691.

Grandjean de Fouchy. See FOUCHY.

Grandmesnil or **Grandménil, de**, deh gRŏn′mä′-nèl′, (JEAN BAPTISTE **Fauchard**—fō′shäR′,) a popular French actor and dramatic writer, born in Paris in 1737; died in 1816.

Grandpré, gRŏn′pRà′, (LOUIS MARIE JOSEPH **Ohier** —o′e-à′,) a French voyager, born at Saint-Malo in 1761. He published a "Voyage to India and Bengal, made in 1789–90," (1801,) a "Universal Dictionary of Maritime

Geography," (3 vols., 1803,) and other works. Died in Paris in 1846.

Grandval, de, deh gRŏn′vâl′, (FRANÇOIS CHARLES **Racot**—rä′ko′,) a French actor and *littérateur*, born in Paris in 1710, published a number of poems and dramas. Died in 1784.

Grandville. See GÉRARD, (JEAN IGNACE ISIDORE.)

Granelli, gRä-nel′lee, (GIOVANNI,) an Italian Jesuit and dramatic poet, born at Genoa in 1703, was also celebrated as a pulpit orator. He was the author of several popular tragedies and other works. Died in 1770.

Granet, gRä′nà′, (FRANÇOIS,) a French *littérateur*, born at Brignoles in 1692, contributed to the "Bibliothèque Française," and to the "Nouvelliste du Parnasse" of Desfontaines, and wrote other works. Died in 1741.

Granet, (FRANÇOIS MARIUS,) an eminent French painter of history and genre, born at Aix in 1775, was a friend of Comte de Forbin. He studied and worked for many years in Rome. Among his master-pieces are "Stella in the Prison of the Capitol," (1810,) and "The Choir of the Capuchins," which he repeated several times. He was a good colorist, and represented the effects of light with great success. Died in 1849.

See RAOUL ROCHETTE, "Notice sur la Vie de M. Granet," 1851; "Nouvelle Biographie Générale."

Grange, (JOSEPH DE CHANCEL DE LA.) See LA GRANGE.

Grangeneuve, gRŏnzh′nuv′, (JACQUES ANTOINE,) a French Girondist, born at Bordeaux in 1750. As a member of the National Convention, he was conspicuous for his severity towards the royal family, the clergy, and the emigrants; though he did not vote for the death of the king. He was executed at Bordeaux in 1793.

Grān′gẹr, (FRANCIS,) an American politician, born in Hartford county, Connecticut, in 1787. He removed to the State of New York, and was elected to Congress as a Whig in 1834. He was re-elected in 1838, and was postmaster-general from March to September, 1841. Died in August, 1868.

Granger, (GIDEON,) an American lawyer, born in Suffield, Connecticut, in 1767, was the father of the preceding. He was appointed postmaster-general by President Jefferson in 1801, and was re-appointed by President Madison in 1809. He retired from that office in 1814, and was elected a member of the Senate of New York in 1819. Died in 1822.

Granger, (GORDON,) an American general, born in New York about 1825, graduated at West Point in 1845. He became a captain in the regular army in 1861, and commanded a brigade of cavalry in Mississippi in the summer of 1862. Having been appointed a major-general, he served at Chickamauga in September, 1863. He commanded the army which, aided by Admiral Farragut, took Fort Morgan in August, 1864. In 1866 he became a colonel in the regular army.

Grān′gẹr, (JAMES,) an English writer, born in Berkshire about 1715. Having studied at Oxford and taken orders, he became vicar of Shiplake, in Oxfordshire. His principal work is a "Biographical History of England from Egbert the Great to the Revolution," (2 vols., 1769, with portraits.) Died in 1776.

Granger, gRŏn′zhà′, (JEAN PERRIN,) a French historical painter, born in 1779, was a pupil of David. He gained the first prize in Paris in 1801. Died in 1840.

Granger - Tournechot, gRŏn′zhà′ toorn′sho′, a French traveller, born at Dijon in the seventeenth century, visited Asia and the northern part of Africa, and died at Bassora in 1734. His travels were published after his death.

Grangier, gRŏn′zhe-à′, (BALTHASAR,) a French translator, almoner to Henry IV., produced in 1596 the first French translation of Dante, (in verse.) He aimed to render verse for verse, and by this extreme fidelity became often obscure.

Granier de Cassagnac, gRä′ne-à′ deh kä′sän′yäk′, (BERNARD ADOLPHE,) a French journalist and historian, born in the department of Gers about 1805. He became in 1850 chief editor of "Le Pouvoir," and a partisan of Louis Napoleon. In 1852 he was elected to the legislative body. Since that date he has been an editor or frequent contributor to the "Constitutionnel." Among his works are a "Voyage to the Antilles and United States," (1842–44,) a "History of the Causes of the French Revolution of 1789," (4 vols., 1850,) and a "History of the Fall of Louis Philippe and the Revolution of 1848," etc., (2 vols., 1855–57.) He was a zealous advocate of slavery.

See "Nouvelle Biographie Générale."

Grant (Mrs. ANNE) OF LAGGAN, an accomplished Scottish writer, born at Glasgow in 1755, was the daughter of Duncan McVicar, an officer who went with his regiment to America about 1758. Having resided nearly ten years in that country, the family returned to Scotland, and in 1779 Miss McVicar was married to the Rev. James Grant, subsequently minister of Laggan, in Inverness-shire. Having lost her husband in 1801, Mrs. Grant applied to authorship for the maintenance of her family. "The Highlanders, and other Poems," came out in 1803, and was well received; it was followed by her "Letters from the Mountains," (1806,) which established her reputation and immediately obtained a wide popularity. She afterwards published "Memoirs of an American Lady," (1808,) and "Essays on the Superstitions of the Highlands," (1811,) both of which are highly esteemed. "She has," says Lord Jeffrey, "great powers of description both of character and scenery, much force of conception, acuteness, and reach of mind in reasoning, great occasional brightness and perpetual activity of fancy, and a fine enthusiasm for virtue, simplicity, and the Highlands." Died in 1838.

See CHAMBERS, "Biographical Dictionary of Eminent Scotsmen," (Supplement;) "Memoirs of the Literary Ladies of England," etc., by MRS. ELWOOD; DE QUINCEY, "Literary Reminiscences," vol. i.; "Edinburgh Review" for August, 1811.

Grant, (CHARLES,) an East India proprietor, born in Scotland in 1746. At an early age he went to India, where in 1772 he became secretary to the board of trade, and on his return to England in 1790 was appointed one of the East India directors. In 1802 he was elected to the House of Commons. He was vice-president of the Bible Society, and contributed greatly to the extension of Christianity in India. He published a treatise entitled "Observations on the State of Society among the Asiatic Subjects of Great Britain." Died in 1823.

Grant, (CHARLES,) Lord Glenelg, a son of the preceding, was born in Bengal about 1782. He became president of the board of trade in 1828, and president of the board of control in 1830. He retired from office with his party (the Whigs) in 1834, and was created Baron Glenelg. He was colonial secretary from 1834 to 1839.

Grant, (EDWARD.) See GRAUNT.

Grant, (FRANCIS,) Lord Cullen, a celebrated Scottish lawyer, born about 1660. He was the author of a treatise entitled "Law, Religion, and Education Considered," (1715,) and other legal works. Died in 1726.

Grant, (FRANCIS,) a distinguished Scottish artist, born in Perthshire about 1804. He enjoyed a high reputation as a portrait-painter, and was extensively patronized by the nobility. Among his portraits may be named those of Disraeli, Macaulay, and Lady Howard. He also produced several hunting-scenes. He was elected to the Royal Academy in 1851, and became president of the same in 1866.

Grant, (JAMES,) one of the most eminent Scottish lawyers of his time, born about 1742. He published "Essays on the Origin of Society, Languages," etc., and "Thoughts on the Origin and Descent of the Gael," (1813.) Died in 1835.

Grant, (JAMES,) editor of the "London Morning Advertiser," born in Scotland about 1806. He wrote "Random Recollections of the House of Lords," (1830,) "The Great Metropolis," (1836,) and other popular works.

Grant, (JAMES,) a popular writer, born at Edinburgh in 1822. Among his principal works are the "Adventures of an Aide-de-Camp," (1848,) "Memoirs of Kirkaldy of Grange," (1849,) "Memorials of Edinburgh Castle," and "Walter Fenton," (1850.)

Grant, (Sir JAMES HOPE,) a British general, a brother of Francis Grant the artist, was born in 1808. He served in India during the mutiny of 1857, and commanded the British army which, aided by the French, defeated the Chinese in September, 1860, and captured Pekin.

Grant, (PATRICK,) Lord Preston-Grange, a Scottish judge, born in 1698; died in 1762.

Grant, (ROBERT,) born at Grantoun, in Scotland, in 1814, wrote a "History of Physical Astronomy," (1852,) which has a high reputation.

Grant, (ROBERT EDMUND,) a British physician, distinguished as a comparative anatomist, was born in Edinburgh in 1793. He graduated in 1814, and began to practise in his native city about 1820. He wrote several able treatises on "The Structure and Functions of the Sponge," and made other contributions to comparative anatomy. In 1828 he was chosen professor of comparative anatomy and zoology in the London University, where he lectured about thirty years. He published in 1835 the first volume of an important work, entitled "Outlines of Comparative Anatomy."

Grant, (ULYSSES SIMPSON,) a distinguished American general, and the eighteenth President of the United States, was born at Point Pleasant, Clermont county, Ohio, April 27, 1822. He is the eldest son of Jesse R. and Hannah Simpson Grant, both natives of Pennsylvania. Having acquired the rudiments of education at a common school, he entered the Military Academy at West Point in 1839. He was a diligent student, but graduated without special distinction in 1843, standing twenty-first in a class of thirty-nine. He left West Point as brevet second lieutenant of the Fourth Infantry, with which he went to Mexico, and served with distinction at Palo Alto and Resaca de la Palma in May, 1846. For meritorious conduct at Molino del Rey and Chapultepec, September, 1847, he was made first lieutenant. In 1848 he married Miss Julia T. Dent, of Saint Louis. He was raised to the rank of captain in 1853, but resigned his commission in July, 1854. In 1859 or 1860 he entered into business with his father, as a dealer in leather and saddlery, at Galena, Illinois.

Immediately after the breaking out of the rebellion in 1861, he raised a company and marched with it to Springfield. Having been appointed colonel of the twenty-first regiment of volunteers in June, he was first employed in Missouri, and became a brigadier-general in August, 1861. About this time he was ordered to Cairo, and took command of the important district of Cairo, or "Southeast Missouri," including both sides of the Mississippi River. He occupied Paducah on the 6th of September. His first battle was fought at Belmont, Missouri, nearly opposite Columbus, which latter place was occupied by a large force of the enemy. On the 7th of November he captured the camp of the insurgents at Belmont, and in the act of retiring was attacked by troops which had crossed the river from Columbus. Both parties claimed the victory in this affair. In December, 1861, the district commanded by Grant was enlarged so as to include Southeastern Missouri and all that part of Kentucky which lies west of the Cumberland River.

The famous Prince Eugene observed that the greatest generals have commonly been those who have been at once raised to the command of an army, without spending much time in the petty calculations and manœuvres of an inferior officer. It may at least be said that Grant was no exception to this rule. In January, 1862, he opened the campaign by a flank movement against a large rebel force which was strongly fortified at Columbus, on the Mississippi River. Ascending the Tennessee River with the aid of iron-clad gun-boats, he took Fort Henry on the 6th of February, thus breaking the chain of defences which extended from Columbus eastward. The navigation of the Cumberland was obstructed by Fort Donelson, a very important position, which was held by a garrison of 20,000 men. Grant attacked this fort on the 14th of February, and fought a severe battle on the 15th with the garrison, which made a sortie from their works. On the 16th, General Buckner made overtures, in reply to which Grant wrote, "No terms other than unconditional and immediate surrender can be accepted. I propose to move immediately upon your works." The fort was accordingly surrendered to him, with about 13,500 prisoners. Among the results of this

ă, ĕ, ĭ, ŏ, ŭ, ў, *long;* à, è, ò, same, less prolonged; ă, ĕ, ĭ, ŏ, ŭ, ў, *short;* ạ, ẹ, į, ọ, *obscure;* fär, fâll, fât; mĕt; nŏt; gŏŏd; mŏŏn;

victory was the speedy evacuation of Columbus and Nashville by the insurgents. Grant was appointed a major-general in February, 1862.

The rebel general A. S. Johnston, forced to retire from Tennessee, had occupied a strong position at Corinth, in Mississippi, with a large army. To operate against this force, General Grant advanced to Pittsburg Landing, on the Tennessee River, where he awaited the arrival of General Buell, who was ordered to join him with the army of the Ohio. General Johnston attacked the Union army at Shiloh on the morning of the 6th of April, and took several thousand prisoners. The battle was renewed on the 7th, when Grant, having been reinforced by the army of Buell, attacked and defeated the enemy. The Union army lost here about 1600 killed and 7200 wounded, and the enemy lost as many or more. In July, Grant became commander of a newly-formed department, comprising Northern Mississippi, West Tennessee, and Western Kentucky. His great object was to open the Mississippi River by the capture of Vicksburg,—a very difficult enterprise. A part of his army, under Rosecrans, gained a decisive victory at Corinth on the 4th and 5th of October. Generals Grant and Sherman made several unsuccessful attempts to take Vicksburg in the winter of 1862–63. Having adopted a new plan of approach, he moved his army by land on the west bank of the river to a point below Vicksburg. Co-operating with him, the gun-boats under Captain Porter, and transports loaded with supplies, passed the batteries of Vicksburg safely on the night of April 16. Grant's army crossed the river about the 30th of April, defeated the enemy at Raymond, at Jackson, May 14, at Champion's Hill, (or Baker's Creek,) May 16, and at the Big Black. Having prevented General J. E. Johnston from effecting a junction with Pemberton, who commanded at Vicksburg, he commenced the siege of that important place about the 18th of May. The capture of Vicksburg, which, with about 30,000 prisoners, was surrendered on the 4th of July, 1863, caused great exultation among the friends of the Union. General Grant was rewarded for this service by promotion to the rank of major-general in the regular army.

In October, 1863, he obtained command of the Military Division of the Mississippi, comprising the departments of the Ohio, of the Cumberland, and of the Tennessee. Among General Grant's important characteristics as a great commander is the rare sagacity which he uniformly displayed in the choice of his subordinate officers. On this occasion he selected Generals Sherman and Thomas as his principal lieutenants, and concentrated his armies for the defence of Chattanooga, which was partly invested by General Bragg. His design was promoted by the imprudence of Bragg, who sent Longstreet with about 20,000 men to besiege Knoxville. The army of Bragg, holding strong positions on the Missionary Ridge and Lookout Mountain, was attacked on the 24th and retreated on the 25th of November. A part of this great battle, it is said, was fought above the clouds. It is stated that from the beginning of the war to December 7, 1863, the armies under Grant's command had captured 472 pieces of cannon and 90,000 prisoners. In the mean time, the Federal armies in the East had failed disastrously in successive campaigns against Richmond; and the eyes of the nation turned to Grant as the general most competent to direct all the armies of the Union. The grade of lieutenant-general was revived for him by Congress, and he was appointed commander of all the armies by the President on the 12th of March, 1864,—the most important appointment ever made by an American President. He was thus summoned to a new scene of action and a position of immense responsibility. The forces of the enemy were mostly concentrated in two large armies,—one in Virginia, commanded by Robert E. Lee, and the other in Northern Georgia, led by J. E. Johnston. General Grant selected General Sherman to oppose the latter, and himself directed in person the army of the Potomac, which opened the campaign by crossing the Rapidan on the 4th of May and moving towards Richmond by a route which was naturally strong for purposes of defence and was well fortified at various points. Before he began this movement, he appointed

General Sheridan commander of all the cavalry of his army. Hancock, Warren, Sedgwick, and Burnside, subject to the orders of General Meade, commanded the several corps of the army of the Potomac, which probably amounted to 150,000 men.

On the 5th of May, Grant's army met the enemy near Mine Run; and then began the great and indecisive battle of the Wilderness, so named because it was fought in an extensive forest. The battle was renewed about five A.M. on the 6th, and continued with unabated fury until darkness interposed. In the ensuing night Lee's army retired behind their intrenched lines. Grant then moved his army by the enemy's right flank, intending to put his whole force between Lee and Richmond; but Lee, moving on a shorter line, again checked his progress at Spottsylvania Court-House, where the 9th, 10th, and 11th were spent in fighting and manœuvring without decisive results. A dispatch of Grant, dated May 11, concludes with this famous sentence: "I propose to fight it out on this line, if it takes all summer." On the 12th Hancock's corps attacked the enemy and captured nearly 4000 prisoners. In the mean time, another army, directed by General Butler and operating against Richmond from the east, took City Point and Bermuda Hundred on the 5th of May. In consequence of another flank movement made by Grant about May 21, Lee marched southward across the North Anna River, and again confronted the Federal army. Finding Lee's position on the North Anna very strong, Grant again turned it by moving round the enemy's right, and crossed the Pamunkey River on the 28th, at a point about fifteen miles from Richmond.

On the 3d of June, Grant attacked the enemy's works at Cold Harbour, but was repulsed with heavy loss. The army of the Potomac crossed the James River, June 14 and 15, formed a junction with the army of Butler, and commenced the siege of Petersburg. Having made a breach in the works by exploding a mine, the Union army assaulted Petersburg on the 30th of July, but failed to take it. In September and October, General Sheridan gained several decisive victories in the Shenandoah Valley. (See SHERIDAN, PHILIP H.) The army of Grant remained nearly inactive before Petersburg during the winter of 1864–65; but Sherman continued to operate in Georgia and Carolina with signal success, and moved rapidly towards Virginia. Savannah, Charleston, and Wilmington were taken in quick succession by General Sherman.

The armies operating against Richmond and Petersburg commenced a movement on the 31st of March to cut the Danville and Southside Railroads, by which Lee's army was supplied. On the 1st of April, Sheridan and Warren assaulted the works at Five Forks, and took about 5000 prisoners. On the morning of the 2d a combined assault was made on the lines of Petersburg, with great success. Having been driven from their main line of defence, and having lost several thousand prisoners in this attack, Lee's army evacuated Petersburg and Richmond in the night of April 2, and retreated towards Danville, closely pursued. The Federals attacked a part of Lee's force near Sailor's Creek on the 6th, and captured about 6000 prisoners. On the 7th, General Grant opened a correspondence with General Lee, who surrendered his army at Appomattox Court-House on the 9th of April, 1865, after which the insurgents everywhere gave up the contest.

To reward the services of Grant, Congress passed in July, 1866, a bill to "revive the grade of General of the Army of the United States," and he was appointed to that position. He became secretary of war *ad interim* about the 1st of August, 1867. When President Johnson ordered the removal of General Sheridan, General Grant, departing from his habitual reticence, defended the latter with spirit, and objected to his removal in a letter which convinced the public that the writer was not an admirer of Johnson's policy. He ceased to be secretary *ad interim* on the 14th of January, 1868, when he gave up the war department to Mr. Stanton against the will of the President, who vainly tempted General Grant to violate the law of Congress. In a letter of General Grant, dated February 3, 1868, and addressed to President Johnson, he writes, "I cannot but regard this whole matter as an attempt to involve me in the resistance of law for which you hesitated to assume the responsibility, in order thus to destroy my character before the country." At the National Republican Convention, May 21, 1868, he was unanimously nominated a candidate for the Presidency of the United States on the first ballot, receiving the votes of six hundred and fifty delegates.

His Democratic competitor was Horatio Seymour, of New York. General Grant accepted the nomination by a letter ending with this sentence, " Let us have peace !" which became the watchword of the campaign. After a very exciting canvass, Grant and Colfax were elected by a large majority, receiving two hundred and fourteen electoral votes, cast by twenty-six States,—viz., the six States of New England, Pennsylvania, Ohio, North Carolina, South Carolina, West Virginia, Florida, Alabama, Tennessee, Arkansas, Missouri, and all the Western States except Oregon. Mr. Seymour received eighty electoral votes. This result proved that the name of General Grant was a tower of strength to the Republican party, whose ascendency had been seriously menaced by the reaction of 1867. During the first half-year of his administration the public debt was reduced over fifty million dollars, and order and prosperity were rapidly restored, especially in the Southern States. After his election to the Presidency, he declared himself in favour of the fifteenth Amendment to the Constitution, which ordains that no person shall be disfranchised on account of colour, race, etc. Having resigned his supreme rank in the army, he conferred the same on his friend and companion-in-arms, General W. T. Sherman.

See A. BADEAU, "Military History of U. S. Grant," 2 vols.; C. A. PHELPS, "Life of U. S. Grant," 1868; J. T. HEADLEY, "Life of U. S. Grant;" A. D. RICHARDSON, "Personal History of U. S. Grant," 1868; HARRIET BEECHER STOWE, "Men of our Times," Hartford, 1868; H. COPPÉE, "Grant and his Campaigns," 1866; E. HOWLAND, "Grant as a Soldier and Statesman," London, 1868; "Edinburgh Review" for January, 1869.

Grant, (Sir WILLIAM,) an eminent orator and judge, born in the county of Moray, Scotland, in 1754. He entered Parliament about 1790, and supported Pitt. He became solicitor-general in 1799, and was master of the rolls from 1801 to 1817. Died in 1832. His forensic eloquence is highly praised.

See LORD BROUGHAM, "Statesmen of the Time of George III.;" FOSS, "The Judges of England," vol. viii.

Granucci, grä-noot′chee, (NICCOLÒ,) an Italian writer, born at Lucca about 1534, published lives of Tamerlane and Scanderbeg, and a number of tales and novels.

Granvelle, de, gran′vêl, [Fr. pron. dęh grŏn′vêl′,] (ANTOINE de Perrenot—dęh på′ręh-no′ or pêR′no′,) CARDINAL, an eminent French statesman, was born at Besançon in 1517. He was early distinguished by the favour of Charles V. of Germany, who employed him in several important embassies, and, at the time of his abdication, recommended him to his son, Philip II. He was successively created Bishop of Arras, Archbishop of Mechlin, councillor of state and keeper of the seals, (1550,) and a cardinal, (1561.) His business talent was extraordinary; and he is said to have dictated to five secretaries at once in different languages. When Margaret of Austria became the ruler of the Netherlands, Granvelle was made her chief counsellor. In this post the severity of his measures against the Protestants roused the people to such resistance that Philip was compelled to remove him in 1563. He was subsequently created Archbishop of Besançon, and Viceroy of Naples about 1571. Died at Madrid in 1586. Nine volumes or more of his letters, state papers, etc. have been published since 1841.

See MOTLEY, "Rise of the Dutch Republic," vol. i. p. 248, and vol. iii. p. 492; PRESCOTT, "History of Philip II.," vols. i. and ii.; COURCHETET, "Histoire du Cardinal de Granvelle," 1761; E. C. DE GERLACHE, "Philippe II et Granvelle," 1842.

Granvelle, de, (NICOLAS PERRENOT,) a distinguished French diplomatist, father of the preceding, was born at Ornans in 1486. Having filled several high offices in France, he entered the service of Charles V. of Germany, who honoured him with his confidence, and made him a chancellor in 1530. He was also employed in various important negotiations. Died in 1550.

Gran′ville, Green′ville, or **Gren′ville,** (GEORGE,) Viscount Lansdowne, an English statesman and poet, born in 1667. He studied at Trinity College, Cambridge, and in 1696 published his tragedy of "Heroic Love." It was followed by "The British Enchanters," (1706,) a drama, which was very successful. Soon after the accession of Queen Anne, he was elected to Parliament for Fowey, and acted with the Tory party. On the change of the ministry in 1710, he succeeded Walpole as secretary of war. He was made a peer of Great Britain, with the title of Lord Lansdowne, in 1711, and in 1712 was appointed one of the privy council, and treasurer of the household. On the accession of George I. he was deprived of his place, and, being suspected of promoting the cause of the Pretender, was imprisoned for a time in the Tower. In 1722 he visited Paris, where he resided ten years. Granville was a generous patron of literary men, and was one of the first to encourage the rising genius of Pope, who dedicated to him his "Windsor Forest." Died in 1735.

See "Biographia Dramatica;" JOHNSON and CHALMERS, "Lives of the English Poets;" WALPOLE, "Royal and Noble Authors."

Granville, (GRANVILLE GEORGE LEVESON GOWER,) EARL, an English statesman, son of Earl Granville, noticed below, was born in 1815. He was twice elected member of Parliament for Morpeth, and represented Lichfield from 1841 to 1846, when he succeeded his father in the House of Lords. During the Universal Exhibition of 1851 at the Crystal Palace in London, Lord Granville was chairman of the executive committee. In December, 1851, he succeeded Lord Palmerston as minister of foreign affairs in Lord Russell's cabinet, and in 1855 was appointed president of the council. He resigned in 1858. He was again president of the council in the cabinet of Palmerston, and leader of the House of Lords, from 1859 to June, 1866. In December, 1868, he became secretary of state for the colonies in the new cabinet formed by Mr. Gladstone. He is distinguished as a skilful debater, and is called the leader of the House of Lords.

Granville, (GRANVILLE LEVESON GOWER,) EARL, an English statesman, a son of the Marquis of Stafford, was born in 1773. He was appointed lord of the treasury under Pitt in 1800, and was afterwards employed on important missions to Russia, the Netherlands, and France. He was created Baron Leveson and Earl Granville in 1833, having previously obtained the grand cross of the order of the Bath. Died in 1846.

Granville, LORD. See CARTERET, (JOHN.)

Granville, (MARY.) See DELANY, (MARY.)

Grapaldi, grä-pâl′dee, (FRANCESCO MARIO,) a learned Italian writer, born at Parma about 1465; died in 1515.

Grapius, grä′pe-ůs, or **Grappius,** (ZACHARIAS,) a German philologist, born at Rostock in 1671, wrote, besides other works, a "Literary History of the Talmud," (1696.) Died in 1713.

Grappin, grä′pǎN′, (PIERRE PHILIPPE,) a French Benedictine and historical writer, born in Franche-Comté in 1738; died in 1833.

See CHARLES WEISS, "Notice sur Dom Grappin."

Graser, grä′zer, (JOHANN BAPTIST,) a German divine and educational writer, born in Lower Franconia in 1766. He published "Divinity, or the Principle of True Education," (1810,) and other works. Died in 1841.

Graslin, grä′lăN′, (JEAN JOSEPH LOUIS,) a French political economist, born at Tours in 1727; died in 1790.

Grässe or **Graesse,** grĕs′seh, (JOHANN GEORG THEODOR,) a German bibliographer and antiquary, born at Grimma in 1814. He wrote a "Manual of the General History of Literature," (1837,) a "Manual of Ancient Numismatics," and other works.

Grasse, de, COMTE. See GRASSE-TILLY.

Grasser, grås′ser, (JOHANN JAKOB,) a Swiss theologian and historical writer, born at Bâle in 1579, wrote a history of the Waldenses, ("Chronicon der Waldenser.") Died in 1627.

Grasse-Tilly, de, dęh grås′te′ye′, (FRANÇOIS JOSEPH PAUL,) COMTE, commonly known as COUNT DE GRASSE, a French naval officer, born at Valette in 1723. He served in the American war, and in 1781 assisted Washington, La Fayette, and Rochambeau in the capture of

Cornwallis. He was afterwards sent to the West Indies, where he was defeated and taken prisoner by the English admiral Rodney in April, 1782. Died in 1788.

See GÉRARD, "Vies des plus illustres Marins Français."

Grassi, grȧs'see, (GIUSEPPE,) one of the best Italian portrait-painters of his time, born in Friuli in 1756. He became professor in the Academy of Arts at Dresden in 1799. Died in 1838.

Grassi, (GIUSEPPE,) an Italian writer, born at Turin in 1779. Among his works is an "Essay on the Synonyms of the Italian Language," (1821 ; 3d edition, 1824.) Died in 1831.

Grassi, (ORAZIO,) an Italian astronomer and mathematician, born at Savona in 1582. He was chiefly noted for his controversy with Galileo about the nature of comets. Grassi affirmed that comets revolve around the sun in definite orbits. Died in 1654.

Grassis, de, dȧ grȧs'sèss, (PARIS,) an Italian historical writer, born at Bologna. He became Bishop of Pesaro in 1513. Died in 1528.

Graswinkel, grȧs'win'kel, (THEODORUS,) an eminent Dutch jurist, born at Delft in 1600. He was appointed to several important offices under the government, and was made a knight of Saint Mark by the Venetians for having defended their republic in a dispute with the Duke of Savoy. He was the author of a treatise "On the Sovereignty of the States of Holland," (in Dutch,) and "Vindication of the Freedom of the Sea," ("Maris Liberi Vindiciæ," 1652,) and other works in Latin. He was a relative of the celebrated Grotius. Died in 1666.

See BAYLE, "Historical and Critical Dictionary;" FOPPENS, "Bibliotheca Belgica."

Grataroli, grȧ-tȧ-ro'lee, (GUGLIELMO,) an Italian physician and medical writer, born at Bérgamo in 1516. To avoid persecution for religion, he removed to Bâle, where he died in 1568.

See NICÉRON, "Mémoires."

Gratella, grȧ-tel'lȧ, or **Gratello**, grȧ-tel'lo, the surname of FILIPPO SEBASTIANO BASTIANINO, an eminent Italian painter, born at Ferrara about 1530, was a pupil and one of the most successful imitators of Michael Angelo. He excelled in the science of design and in energy of composition. His fresco of "The Last Judgment," in the cathedral of Ferrara, is esteemed his master-piece. Died in 1602.

See LANZI, "History of Painting in Italy;" TICOZZI, "Dizionario."

Gräter or **Graeter**, grȧ'ter, (FRIEDRICH DAVID,) a German antiquary, born in 1768. His "Nordische Blumen" (1789) had great success. Died in 1830.

Gratiæ, the Latin name of the GRACES. See CHARITES.

Gratian, grȧ'she-an, [Lat. GRATIA'NUS ; Fr. GRATIEN, grȧ'se-ȧN',] a Roman emperor, who in 375 A.D. succeeded his father, Valentinian I., and became joint ruler of the Western Empire with his brother, Valentinian II. His uncle, Valens, who ruled the Eastern Empire, having fallen in battle in 378, Gratian appointed Theodosius in his place. In 383 a revolt broke out in Britain, and a certain Maximus proclaimed himself emperor and invaded Gaul. Gratian advanced to meet him, but, being forsaken by the greater part of his army, was seized and put to death at Lyons. He was distinguished for his justice and clemency, and his zeal in promoting Christianity.

See GIBBON, "Decline and Fall of the Roman Empire," books xxvii., xxviii., xxix., and xxx. ; AMMIANUS MARCELLINUS ; SOCRATES, "Historia Ecclesiastica;" TILLEMONT, "Histoire des Empereurs."

Gratian or **Gratia'nus**, [Fr. GRATIEN,] an Italian Benedictine monk, a native of Tuscany, lived about 1125–50, and was the author of a work entitled "Decretum," being a collection of the canons of the Church. It was received with great favour by the pope, and has been generally adopted by the Catholic colleges.

Gratiani. See GRAZIANI.

Gratien, the French for GRATIAN, which see.

Gratien, grȧ'se-aN', (JEAN BAPTISTE,) a French theologian and writer, born in 1747, was appointed Bishop of the Lower Seine in 1792. Died in 1799.

Gratiolet, grȧ'te'o'lȧ', (LOUIS PIERRE,) a French naturalist and anatomist, born at Sainte-Foy (Gironde)

in 1815. He wrote treatises on anatomy, and became in 1854 an assistant naturalist in the Museum of Natural History, Paris. Died in 1865.

Gra'tius, (grȧ'she-us,) a Latin poet, and friend of Ovid, surnamed FALIS'CUS from the place of his birth. His only extant poem is entitled "Cynegeticon."

Gratius, grȧt'se-ùs, or **Graes**, grês, (ORTWIN,) a German Roman Catholic theologian, born in the diocese of Münster, became professor at Cologne in 1509. He was ridiculed by Hutten and Reuchlin in the "Letters of Obscure Men," ("Epistolæ Obscurorum Virorum,") which were addressed to Gratius. Died in 1541.

Grat'tan, (HENRY,) an eminent Irish statesman and orator, born at Dublin in 1750. He was educated at Trinity College, and subsequently studied law in London. In 1775 he was chosen to represent the borough of Charlemont in the Irish Parliament, where he acted with the opposition or Whig party and distinguished himself by his zeal and eloquence, and acquired great popularity. In 1780 he procured the passage of the resolution "that the king's most excellent Majesty, and the Lords and Commons of Ireland, are the only power competent to make laws to bind Ireland." About this time he received from the Irish Parliament the sum of fifty thousand pounds, "as a testimonial of the national gratitude for his great national services." In 1785 he opposed the propositions relating to the trade between Great Britain and Ireland, known as Orde's Propositions, and, in consequence chiefly of his efforts, they were abandoned. He was returned to Parliament in 1790 for Dublin, and advocated the cause of Catholic emancipation. On the recall of Lord Fitzwilliam from Ireland, Grattan retired temporarily from the public service. When the union with Great Britain was proposed, he took his seat again, in order to oppose it, and after the measure was carried, in 1805, entered the Imperial Parliament, first as member for Malton, and the following year for Dublin. In 1806 he was offered by Mr. Fox the office of chancellor of the exchequer, which he declined. Having been requested by the Catholics of Ireland to present a petition to the British Parliament, he complied, although in declining health. He grew worse after his arrival in London, and died there in May, 1820. Sir James Mackintosh, in his eulogium on Grattan, says, "The purity of his life was the brightness of his glory. Among all the men of genius I have known, I have never found so much native grandeur of soul accompanying all the wisdom of age and all the simplicity of genius."

See H. GRATTAN, JR., "Life and Times of Henry Grattan," 1839 ; T. DAVIS, "Life of J. P. Curran and H. Grattan," 1846 ; "Edinburgh Review" for February, 1823 ; "Blackwood's Magazine" for September and October, 1839.

Grattan, (THOMAS COLLEY,) a popular Irish novelist, born in Dublin in 1796, passed some years on the continent of Europe. Among his principal works are "Philibert, a Poetical Romance," (Bordeaux, 1819,) "High-Ways and By-Ways," (2 vols., 1823,) "The Heiress of Bruges," (4 vols., 1830,) "Men and Cities ; or, Tales of Travel," (3 vols.,) and "Agnes de Mansfelt," (1847.) He was British consul at Boston from 1839 to 1853. Died in 1864.

Graumann, grow'mȧn, (JOHANN PHILIPP,) a German financier, who is called the reformer of the monetary system in Germany, published several works on currency and exchange. He became director of the mint at Berlin about 1750. Died in 1762.

Graun, grown, (KARL HEINRICH,) a celebrated German composer, born in Saxony in 1701. The fame of his early performances having reached the crown-prince, afterwards Frederick the Great, he was taken into his service, and in 1740 appointed his chapel-master. His oratorio of "The Death of Jesus" and his "Te Deum" are esteemed master-pieces ; his operas had but a transient reputation. Died in Berlin in 1759.

See FÉTIS, "Biographie Universelle des Musiciens."

Graunt or **Grant**, (EDWARD,) an eminent English scholar and teacher, born about 1550, was for twenty years head-master of Westminster School. In 1598 he was appointed rector of Toppersfield, in Essex. He published elegant Latin poems, and a "Spicilegium of the Greek

Language," ("Græcæ Linguæ Spicilegium," 1575.) He was a friend of Camden and of Roger Ascham, whose works he edited, with a eulogy, (1577.) Died in 1601.

Graunt, (JOHN,) an English merchant, born in London in 1620, wrote "Observations on the Bills of Mortality." He was elected a Fellow of the Royal Society in 1662. Died in 1674.

Grauw, grŏw or HRŏw, or **Graaso,** grä'so, (HENDRIK,) a Dutch painter, born at Horn or Hoorn in 1627, was a pupil of Van Kampen. He studied in Rome, and settled at Alkmaar, where he died in 1681. "His manner of composition," says Descamps, "is noble, his draperies are flowing, and his colour good."

See DESCAMPS, "Vies des Peintres Flamands, Hollandais," etc.

Gravander, grä-vän'dẹr, (LARS FREDERIC,) a Swedish poet and physician, born in 1778, was active in his efforts to introduce vaccination into his country. Died in 1815.

Grave, de, dẹh grä'vẹh, (CHARLES JOSEPH,) a Flemish jurist, born at Ursel in 1736. He wrote a curious work, entitled "The Republic of the Elysian Fields, or the Ancient World," (3 vols., 1806.) Died in 1805.

Grävel or **Graevell,** grä'vẹl, (MAXIMILIAN KARL FRIEDRICH WILHELM,) a German jurist, born at Belgard in 1781, published, among other treatises, "The Anti-Platonic State," (1808,) and "General Theory of Compacts according to Prussian Law."

Gravelot, grăv'lo', (HUBERT FRANÇOIS **Bourguignon**—booR-gên'yôN',) a celebrated French designer and engraver, born in Paris in 1699, was a brother of the great geographer D'Anville. He studied under Restout, and subsequently resided many years in London, where he acquired great skill in design and composition and was patronized by booksellers and publishers. Among his best works are the etchings for Theobald's "Shakspere," and illustrations for the works of Racine and Voltaire. Died in 1773.

See BASAN, "Supplément au Dictionnaire des Graveurs."

Gravenberg, von, fon grä'vẹn-bêRG', (WIRNT,) a German poet, who flourished about 1210. His chief work is entitled "Wigalois."

Graverol, grăv'rol', (FRANÇOIS,) a French Protestant, born at Nîmes in 1635, was eminent as a jurist and scholar. He was the author of "Sorberiana, etc.," "Observations on the Decisions of the Parliament of Toulouse," and numerous antiquarian treatises, chiefly in French. He was well versed in ancient and modern languages and numismatics, and was perpetual secretary of the Academy of Nîmes. Died in 1694.

See MORÉRI, "Dictionnaire Historique;" MM. HAAG, "La France protestante."

Graverol, (JEAN,) a brother of the preceding, born at Nîmes in 1636, (or according to some, in 1647,) became successively minister of the Calvinistic churches at Lyons, Amsterdam, and London, and wrote several esteemed theological works. Died about 1720.

Graves, (RICHARD,) an English divine, born in Gloucestershire in 1715, was an intimate friend of the poet Shenstone. He studied at Pembroke College, Oxford, and became rector of Claverton, near Bath, in 1750. His principal work is a satirical novel, entitled "The Spiritual Quixote." He also wrote "Recollections, etc. of the Life of William Shenstone." Died in 1804.

Graves, (RICHARD,) a divine, born in the county of Limerick, Ireland, in 1763. He became Dean of Ardagh in 1813, and professor of divinity in the University of Dublin. He published, besides other works, "Lectures on the Four Last Books of the Pentateuch," (2 vols., 1807,) which are highly esteemed. Horne pronounces them "indispensably necessary to the biblical student." ("Biblical Bibliography.") Died in 1829.

See a "Life of Richard Graves," by his son, R. H. GRAVES, 1840.

Graves, (ROBERT J.,) an Irish physician, son of the preceding, born in Dublin about 1797. He was professor of medicine in the school of physic, Trinity College, Dublin. His "Clinical Lectures on the Practice of Medicine" (1843) have been reprinted in the United States. Died in 1853.

Gravesande, 's, ('s Gravesande,) van, vän sgrä'vẹh-sän'dẹh, (WILLEM JACOB,) an eminent Dutch philosopher and mathematician, born at Bois-le-Duc in 1688. He studied at Leyden, and began to practise law at the

Hague about 1707. In 1715 he accompanied as secretary the embassy sent to England by the States-General to congratulate George I. on his accession to the throne. While in London, he became intimate with Sir Isaac Newton, and was chosen a Fellow of the Royal Society. Having been appointed, on his return in 1717, professor of mathematics and astronomy at the University of Leyden, he introduced the Newtonian philosophy into that institution. He published, among other scientific works, "Institutes of the Newtonian Philosophy." Died in 1742.

See C. MALLET, "Mémoire sur la Vie, etc. de 's Gravesande," 1858; "Nouvelle Biographie Générale."

Gravina, grä-vee'nä, (GIOVANNI VINCENZO,) an eminent Italian jurist and writer, born at Roggiano, in Calabria, in 1664. He studied at Naples, and in 1689 repaired to Rome, where he was appointed in 1699 professor of civil law in the college di Sapienza, and, in 1703, of canon law in the same institution. He was one of the founders of the Academy of the Arcadi, and was the author of a treatise entitled "Origin of Civil Law," ("Origines Juris civilis," 1713,) which obtained great celebrity, "Canonical Institutes," (in Latin,) and a "Treatise on the Art (or Principles) of Poetry," ("Della Ragione poetica,") also a number of poems and orations. Gravina was the preceptor of the celebrated poet Metastasio, whom he adopted as his son and to whom he bequeathed his property. Died in Rome in 1718.

See FABRONI, "Vitæ Italorum;" ANDREA SERRAO, "De Vita e Scriptis Gravinæ Commentarius," 1758; F. VALDRIGI, "Elogio storico di G. V. Gravina," 1816; "Nouvelle Biographie Générale."

Gravina, (PIETRO,) a Sicilian poet and ecclesiastic, born at Palermo in 1453. He was patronized by Gonsalvo de Córdova, who appointed him in 1500 a canon of Naples. His poems in Latin and Italian were highly esteemed at the time. Died in 1527.

See ROSCOE, "Life of Leo X.;" PAOLO GIOVIO, "Elogia Virorum illustrium;" "Vita Gravinæ," in an edition of his poems.

Gravina, da, dä grä-vee'nä, (DOMENICO,) an Italian historian, born in the kingdom of Naples. He was the author of a "History of Naples from 1332 to 1350," (in Latin.) Died about 1350.

Gravina, de, dä grä-vee'nä, (FEDERICO,) DUKE, an admiral in the Spanish service, was born at Naples about 1750. For his services against the French he obtained the rank of rear-admiral in 1794. Having been raised to the highest rank—*capitan-general*—in 1805, he combined his fleet with that of the French admiral Villeneuve. They were defeated by Nelson at Trafalgar, (October 21, 1805,) where Gravina was wounded. He died of the wound, at Cadiz, in February, 1806.

See VAN TENAC, "Histoire générale de la Marine;" "Nouvelle Biographie Générale."

Gravius. See GREAVES, (JOHN.)

Grävius or **Graevius,** grä've-ûs, (JOHANN GEORG,) an eminent German scholar and critic, whose original name was GRÄFE, (or GRAEFE,) was born at Naumburg in January, 1632. He became professor of history at Utrecht, (1661.) He received distinguished marks of favour from Louis XIV. of France and other sovereigns of Europe, and was created by William III. of England his historiographer. Among his numerous and excellent editions of the classics we may name those of Hesiod, Suetonius, Cicero, Propertius, Catullus, and Cæsar. He also wrote "Treasury of Roman Antiquities," ("Thesaurus Antiquitatum Romanarum," 12 vols., 1694,) and "Treasury of Italian Antiquities and Histories," ("Thesaurus Antiquitatum et Historiarum Italiæ.") The latter was continued by Peter Burmann. Died at Utrecht in 1703.

See NICÉRON, "Mémoires;" C. BURMANN, "Trajectum eruditum;" P. BURMANN, "Oratio funebris in Grævii Obitum," 1703; "Nouvelle Biographie Générale."

Gray. See GREY.

Gray, (ASA,) an eminent American botanist, born at Paris, Oneida county, New York, in November, 1810. He graduated as M.D. at Fairfield College in 1831, but preferred the study of botany to the practice of medicine. In 1842 he was appointed Fisher professor of natural history at Harvard College. He published excellent works entitled "Elements of Botany," (1836,) "Botanical Text-Book," (1842,) "Genera of Plants of the United States," (1849,) "Lessons in Botany," "Manual of the Botany of the Northern United States," (1848,) "Structural and Systematic Botany," (1858,) and "How Plants Grow," (1858.) Professor Gray and Dr. Torrey were joint authors of a "Flora of North America," (1st vol., 1838.) "As an accurate analyst," says the "North American Review" for October, 1858, "Professor Gray has received a just meed of praise from all foreign botanists. Standing as he does at the head of the science in our own country, and scarcely inferior to any botanist of the Old World, we consider it a subject of congratulation that he has found time, amidst his multifarious avocations of a high order, to write two books expressly for the young." His "Botanical Text-Book" was used for several years in the University of Edinburgh.

See "North American Review" for January, 1843.

Gray, (DAVID,) a Scottish poet, born not far from Glasgow in 1838; died in 1861. A volume of his poems, with an introductory notice by R. Monckton Milnes, and memoirs of his life, was published in 1865.

Gray, (FRANCIS CALLEY,) an American lawyer and scholar, born at Salem, Massachusetts, in 1790. He was private secretary to John Quincy Adams during his mission to Russia. He contributed many articles to the "North American Review," and published other works, in prose and verse. Died in 1856.

Gray, (GEORGE ROBERT,) an eminent English naturalist, and senior assistant in the zoological department of the British Museum, was born at Chelsea in 1808. He published "The Genera of Birds," illustrated by D. W. Mitchell, (3 vols. 4to, with 371 plates, 1837-49,) a splendid and valuable work. He also wrote many memoirs on birds and insects for scientific journals, etc.

Gray, (HENRY PETERS,) an American painter, born in New York in 1819. He studied in Europe, and on his return, in 1846, established himself in his native city. Among his numerous works we may mention "Cupid Begging his Arrows," "The Wages of War," "Apple of Discord," "Blessed are the Pure in Heart," and "Hagar and the Angel."

Gray, (JOHN EDWARD,) F.R.S., an eminent English naturalist, brother of George Robert, noticed above, was born at Walsall in 1800. He was for many years the head of the department of natural history in the British Museum, the completeness and excellent order of which are to be ascribed, it is said, chiefly to his efforts. He prepared several catalogues of that museum, and between 1825 and 1860 wrote several hundred memoirs on zoology, which have been published in various journals.

Gray, (ROBERT,) an English divine, born in London in 1762, became, in 1827, Bishop of Bristol. He was the author of a "Key to the Old Testament and Apocrypha," (1790,) "Connexion between the Sacred Writings and the Literature of Jewish and Heathen Authors," (1819,) and other valuable religious works. Died in 1834.

Gray, (STEPHEN,) an English experimental philosopher, made several valuable discoveries with regard to electricity, and was the inventor of an electric planetarium. Died in 1736.

See PRIESTLEY'S "History of Electricity."

Gray, (THOMAS,) an eminent English poet, born in London in 1716. He was sent at an early age to Eton, where he formed an intimacy with Horace Walpole and Richard West, son of the Chancellor of Ireland. He studied at Peter-House College, Cambridge, and in 1739 visited France and Italy in company with Horace Walpole. After they had spent some time together at Rome and Florence, the difference in their tastes caused a disagreement between them, and they separated. "Gray," says Walpole, "was too serious a companion. He was for antiquities, etc., whilst I was for perpetual balls and plays: the fault was mine." Gray returned to England in 1741, and in 1742 took his degree of bachelor of civil law at Cambridge, where he continued to reside, on account of the facilities for study which the place afforded. About this time he wrote his "Ode to Spring," "Hymn to Adversity," and "Ode on a Distant Prospect of Éton College," which were published some years after. His "Elegy written in a Country Church-Yard" (1749) received with the greatest favour, and soon ran through eleven editions. No poem, perhaps, was ever more universally admired: it has been translated into the prin-

cipal modern languages of Europe, a dozen different versions having, it is said, appeared in French. In 1743 Gray lost his most intimate friend, West, whom he has lamented in an English sonnet and in the apostrophe to his unfinished poem "De Principiis Cogitandi." This bereavement was followed in 1753 by the death of the poet's mother, a woman of great excellence, to whom he had been devotedly attached. He published in 1757 his "Ode on the Progress of Poesy," and "The Bard," which, being less adapted to the popular taste, were less generally appreciated. On the death of Cibber, in the same year, the vacant laureateship was offered to Gray; but it was declined. He was appointed in 1769 professor of modern history at Cambridge. In 1770 his health, which had been some time declining, became much worse, and he died in July, 1771, of an attack of gout in the stomach. Gray occupies a very high rank in English literature, not only as a poet, but as an elegant prose-writer and an accomplished scholar. He delighted in knowledge for its own sake, and his profound and varied learning embraced, in addition to classical and scientific studies, those of antiquities and the fine arts.

See MASON, "Life of T. Gray," 1778; MITFORD, "Life of T. Gray," prefixed to his Works, 1816; JOHNSON, "Lives of the English Poets;" HAZLITT, "Lectures on the English Poets;" HENRY REED, "Memoir of T. Gray," prefixed to an edition of his poems, 1850; ALLIBONE, "Dictionary of Authors."

Gray'don, (ALEXANDER,) a writer, born at Bristol, Pennsylvania, in 1752, was a soldier in the American Revolution. He published "Memoirs of a Life chiefly passed in Pennsylvania," etc., (1811.) Died in 1818.

See DUYCKINCK, "Cyclopædia of American Literature," vol. i.

Gray'son, (WILLIAM J.,) an American politician and poet, born in Beaufort, South Carolina, in 1788. He represented a district of that State in Congress from 1833 to 1837. Among his works are "The Hireling and the Slave," a poem, (1854,) and "Chicora," an Indian tale.

Graziani, grät-se-ä'nee, an Italian sculptor, whose proper name was BATTISTA BALLANTI, was born at Faenza in 1762; died in 1835.

Graziani, (ANTONIO MARIA,) an Italian prelate and historical writer, born in Tuscany in 1537. He became secretary to Pope Sixtus V. in 1584, and in 1592 was created Bishop of Amelia by Clement VIII., in whose election he had a prominent part. He wrote a "History of the War of Cyprus," (in Latin,) and a work "On the Fortunes of Illustrious Men," ("De Casibus Virorum illustrium," 1680,) also a life (in Latin) of his friend and patron Cardinal Commendone. Died in 1611.

See TIRABOSCHI, "Storia della Letteratura Italiana;" GRAZIANI, "De Scriptis invitâ Minervâ," 1725, which contains his autobiography.

Graziani, (GIOVANNI,) an Italian historian, born at Bérgamo about 1670, wrote a "History of Venice from 1615 to 1700," (2 vols., 1728.) Died about 1730.

Graziani or **Gratiani,** (GIROLAMO,) an Italian poet, once popular, was born at Pérgola in 1604. His chief works are "Cleopatra," (1626,) "The Conquest of Granada," (1650,) and "Cromwell," ("Il Cromvello," a tragedy, 1671.) Died in 1675.

Grazzini, (ANTONIO FRANCESCO.) See LASCA.

Grazzini, grät-see'nee, (GIOVANNI PAOLO,) an Italian painter, of the school of Ferrara. He began to paint when he was about fifty years old. Died in 1632.

Greathead. See GROSSETESTE.

Great'heed, (BERTIE,) an English *littérateur*, born in Warwickshire in 1759. He wrote a tragedy entitled "The Regent." Died in 1826.

See "Biographia Dramatica."

Great'o-rex, (THOMAS,) an English musician and savant, born in Derbyshire in 1758. He became professor of music in London in 1788, and in 1819 organist of Westminster Abbey. He was a Fellow of the Royal Society, and contributed to the "Philosophical Transactions" a treatise on measuring mountains by the barometer. Died in 1831.

Great'rakes, (VALENTINE,) a celebrated empiric, born in the county of Waterford, Ireland, in 1628, professed to be able to heal diseases by his touch. Having visited England, he was invited to Whitehall, and was patronized by Dr. Henry More and other learned men.

He enjoyed a high reputation for integrity and benevolence, and several eminent physicians bore witness to the efficacy of his cures. Died about 1700.

See J. GLANVIL, "Scepsis Scientifica;" DELEUZE, "Histoire critique du Magnétisme animal."

Greaves, greevz, (Sir EDWARD,) an English physician, was born in Surrey about 1615. In 1643 he became first professor of medicine at Merton College, and was appointed, after the restoration, physician-in-ordinary to Charles II. Died in 1680.

Greaves, [Lat. GRA'VIUS,] (JOHN,) an eminent English mathematician and antiquary, was born in Hampshire in 1602. He became professor of geometry at Gresham College, London, in 1630, and in 1637 visited Egypt and the Levant. He took a survey of the Pyramids, of which he published the first accurate description. After his return he was appointed, in 1643, Savilian professor of astronomy, which post he was compelled to resign in 1648 because he was a royalist. He published, among other works, a "Discourse on the Roman Foot and Denarius," etc. Died in 1652.

See "Life of Greaves," by BIRCH, prefixed to his Miscellaneous Works; WARD, "Lives of the Gresham Professors;" NICÉRON, "Mémoires;" THOMAS SMITH, "Vita J. Gravii," 1699.

Greaves, (THOMAS,) an English Orientalist of high reputation, born about 1610, was a brother of the preceding, and a friend of Selden. He rose through several preferments to be a prebendary of Peterborough. He wrote some valuable philological treatises. Died in 1676.

See WOOD, "Athenæ Oxonienses."

Grechetto. See CASTIGLIONE, (GIOVANNI BENEDETTO.)

Grécourt, de, deh grà'koor', (JEAN BAPTISTE JOSEPH **Willart**—ve'lǎr',) a French poet, of Scottish extraction, born at Tours in 1684. He was the author of songs, epigrams, and fables of a licentious character. Died in 1743.

See VOLTAIRE, "Age of Louis XIV."

Gree'ley, (HORACE,) an American journalist, distinguished as an opponent of slavery, born at Amherst, New Hampshire, in February, 1811, was the son of a poor farmer, who removed to Vermont in 1821. He learned the art of printing at East Poultney, Vermont, where he worked about four years, (1826-30,) and became at an early age well versed in party politics. He adopted the Universalist creed before he was of age, and supported the Anti-Masonic party. After he had worked a few months in a printing-office in Erie, Pennsylvania, he sought employment in the city of New York in August, 1831, having only ten dollars in his pocket. As he had no friends or acquaintances in New York, and his dress was very odd and shabby, he met with many repulses; but at last he obtained work. He was employed as a journeyman printer for fourteen months, and in January, 1833, became a partner of Francis Story, and began to print the "Morning Post," the first daily penny paper ever published. It was discontinued in a few weeks. The firm of Greeley & Co. founded in March, 1834, "The New-Yorker," a weekly literary journal, (neutral in politics,) of which Mr. Greeley wrote the editorial articles. The "New-Yorker" was issued for seven years, and became an influential paper, but was not profitable to the publishers. He married Miss Cheney, of North Carolina, in 1836. From March, 1838, to March, 1839, he edited "The Jeffersonian," a weekly Whig paper, published under the direction of the Whig Central Committee of the State of New York. About May, 1840, he began to publish "The Log Cabin," a weekly paper, which supported General Harrison for President, and had a large circulation, (over 80,000.) "The Log Cabin," says Parton, "gave him an immense reputation in all parts of the country as an able writer and a zealous politician."

In April, 1841, he founded "The Daily Tribune," price one cent, of which Henry J. Raymond (afterwards editor of the New York "Times") was assistant editor. Since that date the size and the price of the "Tribune" have been much increased. Mr. Greeley advocated the election of Henry Clay to the Presidency in 1844, and, after his defeat, assumed an attitude of more decided hostility to slavery. In 1848 he was elected member of Congress to fill a vacancy for a term which expired in

March, 1849. He published in 1850 "Hints towards Reforms," composed partly of lectures which he had delivered at various places on temperance, popular education, the organization of labour, etc. "His subject," says Parton, "is ever the same; the object of his public life is single. It is the 'EMANCIPATION OF LABOR;' its emancipation from ignorance, vice, servitude, poverty." Having visited Europe in 1851, he published "Glances at Europe." He supported, in successive Presidential elections, General Scott in 1852, J. C. Fremont in 1856, and Abraham Lincoln in 1860, having exerted his influence against the nomination of W. H. Seward at the Chicago Convention of that year. In 1864 he published the first volume of "The American Conflict," (2 vols.) He favoured the plan of universal amnesty and universal suffrage at the end of the civil war, and offered himself as bail for Jefferson Davis in May, 1867, for which he was censured by many of his own party.

See PARTON, "Life of Horace Greeley," 1855; D. W. BARTLETT, "Modern Agitators;" BUNGAY, "Off-Hand Takings," 1854; H. GREELEY, "Recollections of a Busy Life," 1868.

Green, (ASHBEL,) an American theologian, born in Hanover, New Jersey, in 1762, graduated at Princeton in 1782. He became pastor of the Second Presbyterian Church in Philadelphia in 1787, and officiated as chaplain to Congress from 1792 till 1800. He was a principal founder of the Philadelphia Bible Society, formed in 1809. In 1812 he was appointed president of Princeton College. He resigned that position in 1822, and returned to Philadelphia, where he edited the "Christian Advocate." He published Sermons, Discourses, etc. Died in 1848.

See JOSEPH H. JONES, "Life of Ashbel Green, begun to be written by himself," etc., 1849.

Green, (EDWARD BURNABY,) an English scholar, a brother of Admiral Burnaby, made translations from Anacreon, Pindar, and Apollonius Rhodius. Died in 1788.

Green, (HORACE,) an American physician, born in Chittenden, Vermont, in 1802, graduated at Middlebury College in 1824. He took a prominent part in founding the New York Medical College in 1850, and has since been president of its faculty, and emeritus professor of the theory and practice of medicine. Dr. Green is distinguished for his novel treatment of diseases of the air-tubes which had very generally been deemed incurable. In 1846 he published a "Treatise on Diseases of the Air-Passages." Among his other works are his "Pathology and Treatment of the Croup," (1849,) and "Surgical Treatment of the Polypi of the Larynx and the Œdema of the Glottis," (1852.)

Green, (JACOB,) M.D., professor of chemistry in Jefferson Medical College, born in Philadelphia in 1790. Among his works may be mentioned his "Chemical Philosophy," "Astronomical Recreations," "Botany of the United States," "Trilobites of North America," and "Travels in Europe," (1828.) Died in 1841.

Green, (JAMES S.,) an American politician, born in Fauquier county, Virginia, in 1817. He settled in Missouri, and was elected a member of Congress in 1846. He represented Missouri in the Senate of the United States from 1857 to 1861. He was a disunionist Democrat.

Green, (JOHN,) an English prelate, born in Yorkshire about 1706. He studied at Saint John's College, Cambridge, where he became regius professor of theology in 1748, and vice-chancellor about 1750. In 1756 he was created Bishop of Salisbury. Died in 1779.

Green, (JOHN RICHARD.) See GIFFORD, (JOHN.)

Green, (JOSEPH HENRY,) an English surgeon, born in 1791. He became professor of surgery in King's College, London, about 1830. He published "Vital Dynamics" and "Mental Dynamics." Died in 1863.

Green, (MARY ANNE **Everett,**) an English authoress, a daughter of Rev. Robert Wood, was born at Sheffield about 1818. She married a Mr. Green in 1845. She published "Letters of Royal and Illustrious Ladies of Great Britain," (3 vols., 1846,) "Lives of the Princesses of England," (6 vols., 1849-55,) which is highly esteemed, and the "Letters of Henrietta Maria, Queen-Consort of Charles I.," (1857,) with other important works.

ā, ē, ī, ō, ū, ȳ, *long;* ă, ĕ, ŏ, same, less prolonged; ă, ĕ, ī, ŏ, ŭ, ў, *short;* ạ, ẹ, ị, ọ, *obscure;* fär, fåll, fåt; mët; nŏt; gōōd; mōōn;

Green, (MATTHEW,) an English poet, born in London in 1696, wrote a poem, "The Spleen," which was commended by Pope and other critics. Died in 1737.

See JOHNSON and CHALMERS, "Lives of the English Poets;" CAMPBELL, "Specimens of the British Poets."

Green, (THOMAS,) an English writer, born at Ipswich in 1769. He published a work on the "Theory of Morals," and "Extracts from the Diary of a Lover of Literature," (1810.) Died in 1825.

Green, (THOMAS,) an American general, born in Virginia about 1816. He took arms against the Union in 1861, became a commander of cavalry, and distinguished himself in several actions in Louisiana in 1863. He was raised to the rank of major-general, and was killed on Red River in April, 1864.

Green, (VALENTINE,) a celebrated English engraver, born in Warwickshire in 1739, settled in London, where he acquired great skill in mezzotint engraving. In 1774 he became associate engraver of the Royal Academy. Among his master-pieces are his prints after West's picture of the "Return of Regulus to Carthage," and portraits after Sir Joshua Reynolds. Died in 1813.

See BRYAN's "Dictionary of Painters."

Greene, (CHARLES GORDON,) an American journalist, born in Boscawen, New Hampshire, in 1804. He became proprietor of the "Boston Statesman," and in 1831 established in Boston the "Morning Post," a Democratic paper, which was successful.

Greene, (CHRISTOPHER,) COLONEL, an American officer, born in Warwick, Rhode Island, in 1737. He commanded Fort Mercer, at Red Bank, on the Delaware River, in 1777, and was repulsed a body of Hessians who attacked that fort. He was killed near the Croton River in May, 1781.

Greene, (GEORGE S.,) an American general, born in Rhode Island about 1801, graduated at West Point in 1823. He became a brigadier-general in 1862, and served at the battle of Antietam in September of that year, at Gettysburg, July 2 and 3, 1863, and in other actions.

Greene, (GEORGE WASHINGTON,) an American author, a grandson of General Nathaniel Greene, was born at East Greenwich, Kent county, Rhode Island, in 1811. He was consul of the United States at Rome from 1837 to 1845. He contributed a "Life of General Nathaniel Greene" to Sparks's "American Biography," edited Addison's Complete Works, (1854,) and wrote, besides other works, "Historical Studies, chiefly on Italian History and Literature," (1850,) and a "Life of General Nathaniel Greene," (of which the first volume appeared in 1867.)

Greene, (MAURICE,) an eminent English composer of church music, born in London about 1696. He was appointed in 1726 organist and composer to the chapels royal, and became professor of music in the University of Cambridge. His "Forty Anthems" (2 vols. fol.) are esteemed his master-pieces; he also composed songs and cantatas of great beauty. Died in 1755.

See HAWKINS, "History of Music."

Greene, (NATHANIEL,) a distinguished American general, born in Warwick, Rhode Island, on the 27th of May, 1742. His father was a member of the Society of Friends, and owner of an iron-forge, in which Nathaniel worked for many years. In 1770 he was elected to the General Assembly of the colony. Anticipating the impending appeal to arms, he began to study the art of war. He married Miss Littlefield in July, 1774. In May, 1775, he was chosen a brigadier-general of the militia of Rhode Island, and joined the army near Boston. He soon gained the confidence of General Washington, who selected him to command the army sent to defend Long Island; but a violent attack of fever prevented him from taking part in the battle of Long Island, August, 1776. He commanded the division with which Washington marched in person at the battle of Trenton, December, 1776. In September, 1777, he distinguished himself at the battle of the Brandywine, and in October commanded the left wing at the battle of Germantown. At the request of General Washington, he accepted in March, 1778, the position of quartermaster-general, the duties of which he performed with great ability until August, 1780. He commanded the right wing at Monmouth, June, 1778, and defeated Sir Henry Clinton at Springfield,

New Jersey, on the 23d of June, 1780. In the October ensuing he was appointed to the command of the Southern army, then greatly disorganized and nearly destitute of supplies. A part of his army gained a victory at Cowpens in January, 1781, soon after which he moved his army to the Catawba River. Pursued by a superior force under Lord Cornwallis, he retreated in good order through North Carolina to the Dan River in February. On this occasion General Washington wrote to him, "Your retreat before Cornwallis is highly applauded by all ranks." Having been reinforced, he marched to Guilford Court-House, where he encountered the enemy on the 15th of March, 1781. Here was fought an indecisive battle, and the British remained masters of the field; but their loss had been so severe that Cornwallis immediately retreated towards the sea. In April, 1781, General Greene adopted the bold resolution to march into South Carolina, and was defeated at Hobkirk's Hill, near Camden. The British, however, were unable to follow up this victory, and in May General Greene marched to the siege of Ninety-Six, a fortified post near the Saluda River. The siege was raised about the end of June by the approach of Lord Rawdon; but the place was soon after evacuated by the British, who, retiring southeastward, were pursued to Orangeburg by General Greene. The next important event of the campaign was the severe battle of Eutaw Springs, (September, 1781,) where Greene lost 555 killed and wounded, but remained master of the field. So great was his energy and skill that before the end of the year the enemy were driven from all parts of South Carolina, except the vicinity of Charleston. A medal was presented to him by Congress for his victory at Eutaw Springs. In 1782 his operations were greatly retarded by the want of ammunition, money, and other resources. He proposed to enlist several regiments of negro soldiers; but this proposal was rejected by the civil authorities of the State. After the end of the war he resolved to settle with his family in Georgia, and in 1785 he removed to an estate which had been presented to him by the State of Georgia, and which was situated near Savannah. He died of a sunstroke, June 19, 1786. He is generally considered to have been superior in military skill and in force of character to all the generals of the Revolution, Washington only excepted.

See a "Life of General Greene," by his grandson, GEORGE W. GREENE, 3 vols., 1867 et seq.; SPARKS'S "American Biography," vol. xx., (or x. of second series;) BANCROFT, "History of the United States;" WILLIAM JOHNSON, "Life and Correspondence of Nathaniel Greene," 2 vols., 1822; "National Portrait-Gallery of Distinguished Americans," vol. i.

Greene, (NATHANIEL,) a journalist, a brother of Charles Gordon, noticed above, was born in Boscawen, New Hampshire, in 1797. He founded in 1821 the "Boston Statesman," a Democratic paper. In 1829 he was appointed postmaster of Boston. He translated "Tales from the German," (2 vols., 1837,) and other works.

Greene, (ROBERT,) one of the principal English dramatists who preceded Shakspeare, was born at Ipswich about 1560. He began to write for the stage about 1584, and from that time gave himself up to a course of dissipation, varied by occasional fits of remorse. Among the works known to be his are the "History of Orlando Furioso," and the "Comical History of Alphonsus, King of Aragon," also a prose treatise entitled "Greene's Groatsworth of Wit bought with a Million of Repentance." His novel of "Pandosto" is said to have been the original of Shakspeare's "Winter's Tale." He died in great poverty in 1592.

See COLLIER, "History of English Dramatic Poetry;" DRAKE, "Shakespeare and his Times;" DISRAELI, "Calamities of Authors."

Greene, (THOMAS,) an English divine, born at Norwich in 1658. On the accession of George I. he was appointed one of his chaplains, and in 1721 became Bishop of Norwich. He was the author of "Principles of Religion Explained," and other works. Died in 1738.

Green'field, (WILLIAM,) an English Orientalist and profound scholar, published a "Comprehensive Bible," (1827,) "Novum Testamentum," (1829,) and other works. Died in 1832.

Greenham, green'am, (RICHARD,) an English Puritan divine, born about 1630, was rector of Dry-Drayton for many years. He left Sermons and other religious works. "He excelled in experimental divinity," says Bishop Hall. Died in 1591.

Green'hill, (JOHN,) an English painter, born in 1649, was a pupil of Sir Peter Lely. He copied some works of Van Dyck. Died in 1676.

Greenhill, (WILLIAM,) an English divine and commentator, became rector of Stepney about 1656. He was ejected in 1662 for nonconformity. He wrote "Expositions of Ezekiel," (5 vols., 1645–62.) Died about 1675.

Green'hŏw, (ROBERT,) M.D., an American writer, born in Richmond, Virginia, in 1800, graduated at the College of Physicians and Surgeons in New York in 1821. He published a "History of Oregon and California," (1846.) Died at San Francisco in 1854.

Green'leaf, (SIMON,) an American jurist, born in Newburyport, Massachusetts, in 1783, became Royall professor of law at Harvard in 1833, and Dane professor in 1846. His chief work is a "Treatise on the Law of Evidence," (3 vols., 1842–53.) Died in 1853.

Greenough, green'ō, (GEORGE BELLAS,) an English geologist, born about 1777; died in 1854.

Greenough, green'ō, (HORATIO,) an eminent American sculptor, born in Boston in 1805. He was educated at Harvard, where he enjoyed the friendship of Allston. Before graduating, he went to Rome, to prosecute his artistic studies; and, with the exception of a brief visit to his native city in 1826, he resided in Italy, chiefly at Florence, until 1851, when he returned to the United States. Died near Boston in December, 1852. Of his numerous works we may mention his "Chaunting Cherubs," the first group in marble ever executed by an American sculptor, (ordered by his devoted friend and patron, J. Fenimore Cooper,) "The Angel and Child," "Venus contending for the Golden Apple," (greatly admired in Florence,) a colossal statue of Washington in front of the national Capitol, for which Congress paid twenty thousand dollars, and a group entitled "The Rescue," (1851,) representing a scene in the early settlement of the American colonies, executed by order of Congress. A volume of Greenough's Essays, with a Memoir of his Life by H. T. Tuckerman, was published in 1853.

See, also, TUCKERMAN, "Book of the Artists."

Greenville. See GRANVILLE.

Green'ville, (Sir BEVIL,) an English officer, born in 1596, was a grandson of Sir Richard, noticed below. He represented the county of Cornwall in the Long Parliament in 1640, and supported the royalist party. He had a prominent share in the victory gained by the royal army at Stratton in 1643; but he was mortally wounded at the battle of Lansdowne the same year. Lord Clarendon says of Sir Bevil, "A brighter courage and gentler disposition were never married together."

See CLARENDON, "History of the Rebellion."

Greenville, (DENIS,) a son of the preceding, was born about 1630. He was created Dean of Durham in 1684; but he was deprived of his office in 1690 for refusing to take the oath of allegiance to William III. He died in Paris in 1703.

See WOOD, "Athenæ Oxonienses."

Greenville, (RICHARD.) See TEMPLE, EARL.

Greenville, (Sir RICHARD,) a brave English officer, born in the West of England about 1540, was a relative of Sir Walter Raleigh. He was elected to Parliament for Cornwall in 1571. As vice-admiral of a squadron, he sailed in 1591 to intercept some Spanish merchant-vessels. These being strongly escorted, an obstinate struggle took place, which resulted in the defeat of the English. Sir Richard, though severely wounded, refused to surrender until his men accepted the offers of quarter. He was taken on board a Spanish ship, but, though kindly treated, soon after died of his wounds, (1588.)

See HAKLUYT, "Voyages," vol. iii.; "Biographia Britannica;" CAMPBELL, "Lives of British Admirals."

Green'wood, (FRANCIS WILLIAM PITT,) an American Unitarian minister, born in Boston in 1797, graduated at Harvard in 1814. He became pastor of King's Chapel, in Boston, in 1824. He contributed to the "North American Review," and published sermons, essays, etc. Died in 1843.

Greenwood, (GRACE.) See LIPPINCOTT, (SARAH J.)

Grĕg'an, (JOHN EDGAR,) a noted Scottish architect, born in 1813. His principal works are in Manchester and its vicinity, and include the bank of Sir Benjamin Heywood, a number of churches, warehouses, and private dwellings. Gregan was a Fellow of the Institute of British Architects. Died in 1855.

Gregg, (DAVID M.,) an American general of cavalry, born in Pennsylvania, graduated at West Point in 1855. He commanded a division of cavalry under General Sheridan in a raid around Lee's army in May, 1864, and at the battles of Meadow Bridge and Trevilian Station, in June of that year. He directed the cavalry of the army of the Potomac from August, 1864, to February, 1865.

Gregg, (JOHN,) an American general, born about 1828. He became a brigadier-general of the Confederate army, and was killed at Petersburg, Virginia, in October, 1864.

Gregg, (MAX'CY,) an American general, born in South Carolina about 1814, was a lawyer before the civil war. He was killed at Fredericksburg, fighting against the Union, in December, 1862.

Grégoire, the French of GREGORY, which see.

Grégoire, grà'gwȧr', (HENRI,) a French ecclesiastic and eminent writer, born near Lunéville in 1750. He was elected by the clergy to the States-General in 1789. In 1792 he was chosen Bishop of Blois under the civil constitution, and a member of the Convention, in which he took a prominent part in the abolition of royalty and negro slavery, (1794.) The Jacobins accused him of a design to "Christianize the Revolution." He was chosen one of the legislative body about the end of 1799, and a senator in 1801. He was one of the founders and members of the Institute, and corresponded with many savants among foreign nations. His election as deputy in 1819 caused great excitement, and was nullified by the royalist majority. Among his principal works is a "History of Religious Sects," (1810.) Died in 1831.

See CARNOT, "Notice historique," prefixed to the "Mémoires ecclésiastiques, politiques," etc. of Grégoire, 2 vols., 1837; J. LAVAUD, "Notice sur H. Grégoire," 1819; "Nouvelle Biographie Générale;" G. KRUEGER, "H. Grégoire, Bischof von Blois," 1838; "London Quarterly Review" for October, 1822.

Grégoire, (PIERRE,) [Lat. GREGO'RIUS TOLOSA'NUS,] a French jurist, born at Toulouse about 1540, became professor of civil law at Pont-à-Mousson. He published several legal works in Latin. Died about 1597.

See BAYLE, "Historical and Critical Dictionary."

Grégoire de Nazianze. See GREGORY NAZIANZEN.

Grégoire de Nysse. See GREGORY OF NYSSA.

Grégoire le Grand. See GREGORY (POPE) I.

Gregor, the German for GREGORY, which see.

Greg'o-ras Ni-ceph'o-rus, [Gr. Νικηφόρος ὁ Γρηγόρας,] a Byzantine historian and mathematician, born about 1295, was the author of a "History of Constantinople from 1204 to 1359." The principal part of it was published, with a Latin translation, in 1562. He wrote many other works. He proposed a method for reforming the calendar, which was adopted about three hundred years later by Gregory XIII. Died about 1360.

See FABRICIUS, "Bibliotheca Græca;" BOIVIN, "Vita Nicephori Gregoræ," in an edition of his History, Paris, 2 vols., 1702.

Gregorio, grà-go're-o, sometimes written **Gregori,** (CARLO,) an Italian engraver, born at Florence in 1719; died in 1759.

His son FERDINANDO (1740–1800) was a skilful engraver, and worked at Florence.

Gregorio, (MAURISIO,) a Sicilian theologian and writer, born at Camerata in 1575; died in 1651.

Gregorio, (ROSARIO,) an Italian antiquary and historian, born in 1753, became canon of a church at Palermo, and professor of law. Among his works are an "Introduction to the Study of the Public Law of Sicily," (1794,) and "Discourses on the History of Sicily." Died in 1809.

Gregorio il Grande. See GREGORY (POPE) I.

Gregorius, the Latin of GREGORY, which see.

Gre-go'rĭ-us, (PUBLIUS,) an Italian scholar, surnamed TIPHER'NUS, born in Umbria, translated into Latin the last seven books of Strabo. Died in 1469.

Gregorius Ariminensis. See GREGORY OF RIMINI.

Gregorius Florentius. See GREGORY OF TOURS.

Gregorius Magnus. See GREGORY (POPE) I.

Gregorius Nazianzenus. See GREGORY NAZIANZEN.

Gregorius Nyssenus. See GREGORY OF NYSSA.

Gre-go'rĭ-us Par'dus, called also **Gregory of Corinth,** an Archbishop of Corinth in the twelfth century, was the author of a work on Dialects.

See "Biographie Universelle."

Gregorius Tolosanus. See GRÉGOIRE, (PIERRE.)

Gregorj or **Gregorii,** grà-go're-ee, (GIOVANNI GASPARO,) an Italian writer, born in 1769, became president of the imperial court in Rome in 1811. Died in 1846.

Greg'o-rŷ I., POPE, surnamed THE GREAT, [Lat. GRE-GO'RIUS MAG'NUS; Fr. GRÉGOIRE LE GRAND, grȧ'gwȧr' lĕh grŏN; It. GREGORIO IL GRANDE, grȧ-go're-o èl grän'dä,] was born about 550, of an illustrious Roman family. He became prefect of Rome in 573. On the death of Pelagius, in 590, he was elected pope, and in this station showed great zeal in reforming the Church and propagating Christianity. Previous to his becoming pope, he had induced Pelagius II. to send missionaries to England. His character was distinguished by many eminent virtues, much alloyed, however, by superstitious weakness. Among other inconsistencies, he is charged with having flattered infamous rulers to secure their protection to the Church. His principal works are a treatise "On the Sacerdotal Office," ("De Cura sacerdotali,") "Books of Morals," ("Moralium Libri,") and "Letters and Dialogues." Died in 604.

See MAIMBOURG, "Histoire du Pontificat de Grégoire le Grand," 1686; BAYLE, "Historical and Critical Dictionary;" GEORG PFAHLER, "Gregor der Grosse und seine Zeit," 2 vols., 1853; FLEURY, "Histoire ecclésiastique;" G. GRADENIGO, "S. Gregorius Magnus, etc. vindicatus," 1753; DENIS DE SAINTE-MARTHE, "Histoire de S. Grégoire le Grand," 1697.

Gregory II., POPE, was born in Rome, and succeeded Constantine in 715 A.D. When in 726 the emperor Leo forbade the worship of images, Gregory attempted to dissuade him from it. He convoked a council against the Iconoclasts, and one to forbid marriage to monks. It was during his rule that Boniface preached Christianity in Germany. Died in 731.

See UGHELLI, "Italia Sacra."

Gregory III., a native of Syria, was the successor of Gregory II. In 732 he passed a decree establishing the worship of images. In 740 he was involved in a dispute with Luitprand, King of the Lombards. Died in 741.

See ALLETZ, "Histoire des Papes," 1776.

Gregory IV., born at Rome, became pope on the death of Valentinus, in 827. Being called upon to adjust the quarrel between Louis le Débonnaire and his sons, he offended both parties and also the French bishops. He built a new town near Ostia as a defence against the Saracens, which he named Gregoriopolis. Died in 844.

See ARTAUD DE MONTOR, "Histoire des souverains Pontifes."

Gregory V. was a native of Germany and a relative of Otho III. Through the influence of that emperor he became pope in 997. Soon after this, Crescentius, a man of wealth, assumed the title of consul, and drove the new pope from the city. He raised John, Bishop of Piacenza, to the tiara; but the next year Otho and Gregory returned with an army, imprisoned John, and executed Crescentius. Died in 999.

See PLATINA, "Vitæ Summorum Pontificum."

Gregory VI. was a native of Rome, and succeeded Benedict IX. in 1044. In 1046 the emperor Henry III., in a council at Sutri, deposed the three popes Benedict, Sylvester III., and Gregory, and elected Clement II., upon which Gregory retired to a monastery, where he died in 1047.

Gregory VII. (or **Hil'de-brand**) was born near Soana, in Tuscany, about 1015. On the death of Alexander II., in 1073, he was elected his successor. He now set about reforming the Church, especially with regard to simony, which was very prevalent. He resolved to take away from secular princes the right of disposing of sees within their dominions. With this view, he sent legates to Henry IV. of Germany, one of the most guilty in this respect. His admonitions having no effect, he next assembled a council at Rome in 1074, in which persons guilty of simony were anathematized, and it was decreed that no one should be admitted to holy orders unless

he had taken a vow of celibacy. He summoned another council in 1075, in which kings were forbidden, under pain of excommunication, to give the investiture of sees and abbeys. Henry IV., without regarding Gregory's decrees, and indignant at his assumptions, assembled a diet at Worms and deposed him; whereupon Gregory solemnly excommunicated the emperor in a council at the Lateran palace, and declared his subjects released from their allegiance. This act of Gregory was the boldest assumption of power hitherto exercised by any pontiff. After Henry had endured a most humiliating penance, a reconciliation was effected between them, which, however, was not lasting. Gregory at length retired to Salerno, where he died in 1085. He appears to have been sincere in his efforts to reform the Church, but to have allowed his ambition to get the mastery of him, and aimed to make all powers subordinate to the papal see.

See SPITTLER, "Geschichte der Hierarchie von Gregor VII.;" GRIESLEY, "Life and Pontificate of Gregory VII.," 1829; RANKE, "History of the Popes;" PLATINA, "Vitæ Summorum Pontificum;" J. VOIGT, "Hildebrand als Papst Gregor VII.," 2 vols., 1813; French version of the same, Paris, 1837; JOHN W. BOWDEN, "Life and Pontificate of Gregory VII.," 2 vols., 1840; G. CASSANDER, "Das Zeitalter Hildebrands für und gegen ihn," 1842; "Fraser's Magazine" for November, 1866.

Gregory VIII., (ALBERTO DI MORA,) born at Benevento, succeeded Urban III. in 1187. He survived but two months, and was followed by Clement III. He must be distinguished from the anti-pope of the name of Bourdin, who also assumed the name of Gregory VIII.

Gregory IX. (Cardinal UGOLINO) was Bishop of Ostia, and a native of Anagni. He succeeded Honorius III. in 1227. Soon after his election, he insisted on Frederick II. of Germany engaging in a crusade, and, on his delay, immediately excommunicated him. The whole of this pontiff's rule was signalized by a struggle for supremacy between Frederick and the Ghibelines on the one side, and the Guelphs, with the pope, on the other. Died in 1241.

See G. VOSSIUS, "Gregorii Papæ Noni Gesta," 1686.

Gregory X., (TEBALDO **Visconti,**) born at Piacenza, succeeded Clement IV. in 1271. In 1274 he convoked a general council at Lyons, and effected a transient reconciliation between the Greek and Latin Churches. Among other reforms, the mode of electing popes by conclave was adopted. Died in 1276.

See P. M. CAMPI, "Vita Gregorii X.," Rome, 1665; BONUCCI, "Istoria del Pontefice B. Gregorio X.," 1711.

Gregory XI., (PIERRE ROGER **de Montroux**—dĕh mŏN'troo',) a native of France, and son of the Count of Beaufort, was born about 1330. He succeeded Urban V. in 1370. In 1377 he transferred the papal see from Avignon, where it had been for nearly seventy years, back to Rome. Gregory was the first pope who condemned the doctrines of Wicliff. He was a man of great learning, and highly esteemed for his unblemished character. Died in 1378.

See ALLETZ, "Histoire des Papes," 1776.

Gregory XII., (ANGELO **Cornaro,**) a native of Venice, born about 1325, was chosen successor to Innocent VII. in 1406. Owing to the schism which had divided the Western Church since 1379, he had a rival in the anti-pope Benedict XIII. In a council at Pisa in 1409, the sovereigns of Europe deposed both Gregory and Benedict, and elected Peter Philargi, a Greek. The other two, however, persisted in their claims, and the Western Church had three popes instead of one. The great Council of Constance again deposed them in 1415, and Gregory was appointed legate to the Marches of Ancona. Died in 1417.

See ALLETZ, "Histoire des Papes," 1776.

Gregory XIII., (UGO **Buoncompagni,**) a native of Bologna, born in 1502, succeeded Pius V. in 1572. He was distinguished for his knowledge of civil and canon law, and his zeal in the cause of education. He endowed several colleges at Rome, one of which was called the Gregorian College. He reformed the Julian Calendar; and the "New Style," (as it is called,) which he introduced, has been generally adopted. Died in 1585.

See RANKE, "History of the Popes;" G. P. MAFFEI, "Annali di Gregorio XIII.," 2 vols., 1742; A. DE VIDAILLAN, "Vie de Grégoire XIII.," 1840.

Gregory XIV., (NICCOLÒ **Sfondrato,**) a native of Cremona, succeeded Urban VII. in 1590. He did much to promote the French league against Henry IV. of France, whom he excommunicated. Died in 1591.

Gregory XV., (ALESSANDRO **Ludovisio,**) a native of Bologna, born in 1554, succeeded Paul V. in 1621. He was of a mild and humane character, and exerted himself to put an end to the persecution of the Protestants in Valtellina. He founded the college De Propaganda Fide. He was the author of a "Letter to Shah Abbâs, King of the Persians." Died in 1623.

See RANKE, "History of the Popes;" ALLETZ, "Histoire des Papes."

Gregory XVI., (MAURO **Capellari,**) born at Belluno in 1765. He was made a cardinal by Leo XII. in 1825, and soon after became prefect of the college De Propaganda Fide. He conducted the negotiation with the kingdom of Prussia under Pius VIII., and was elected pope in 1831. Died in 1846. He was succeeded by Pius IX.

See A. MANAVIT, "Notice historique sur Grégoire XVI," 1846; B. WAGNER, "Papst Gregor XVI., sein Leben und sein Pontificat," 1846; FARINI, "Lo Stato Romano," translated into English by the HON. W. E. GLADSTONE; WISEMAN, "Recollections of the Last Four Popes."

Gregory OF AGRIGENTUM, a Greek theologian, born about 524. He visited Antioch, Constantinople, and Rome, and was appointed by the pope Bishop of Agrigentum, in Sicily. Died about 565.

Gregory OF ANTIOCH, a Greek ecclesiastic, who became Patriarch of Antioch about 570 A.D. Died about 594.

Gregory OF CORINTH. See GREGORIUS PARDUS.

Gregory OF NYSSA, [Lat. GREGO'RIUS NYSSE'NUS; Fr. GRÉGOIRE DE NYSSE, grà'gwȧr' deh nèss,] Bishop of Nyssa, an eminent Greek Father, was born at Cæsarea, in Cappadocia, about 332 A.D., and was a brother of Basil the Great. He became bishop about 372, opposed Arianism, and was banished at the instigation of the Arians by Valens in 375 A.D. On the death of Valens (378 A.D.) he was restored to his see. He had a high reputation for learning and eloquence. He died about 398 A.D., and left many sermons, doctrinal treatises, orations, letters, etc., which have often been printed.

See DUPIN, "Histoire des Auteurs ecclésiastiques;" J. RUPP, "Gregor's des Bischofs von Nyssa Leben," etc., 1834; VILLEMAIN, "Tableau de l'Éloquence chrétienne au quatrième Siècle;" FABRICIUS, "Bibliotheca Græca;" S. P. HEYNS, "Disputatio historico-theologica de Gregorio Nysseno," 1835.

Gregory OF RIMINI, [Lat. GREGO'RIUS ARIMINEN'SIS,] an Italian ecclesiastic, born at Rimini, became general of the order of Augustines at Montpellier. He wrote several theological works. Died in 1358.

Gregory, [Lat. GREGO'RIUS,] SAINT, first Patriarch of Armenia, born in 257 A.D., was of the royal Persian family of the Arsacidæ, and was surnamed THE ILLUMINATOR, from his having converted Armenia to Christianity.

See GRAVINA, "Vita e Miracoli di San Gregorio."

Gregory OF SAINT VINCENT. See SAINT VINCENT.

Gregory THE THAUMATURGIST, [Lat. GREGO'RIUS THAUMATUR'GUS; Gr. Γρηγόριος ὁ Θαυματουργός; Fr. GRÉGOIRE THAUMATURGE, grà'gwȧr' tō'mȧ'türzh',] one of the early Christian theologians, born in Cappadocia in the third century, was a disciple of Origen. He owed his surname to his reputation for working miracles. He became Bishop of Neo-Cæsarea in 240 A.D. He was the author of a "Eulogy on Origen," "Symbol of the Faith," and other works. Died about 270.

See PALLAVICINI, "Vita Gregorii Thaumaturgi," Rome, 1644; FLEURY, "Histoire ecclésiastique;" "Nouvelle Biographie Générale."

Gregory OF TOURS, [Lat. GEOR'GIUS FLOREN'TIUS GREGO'RIUS,] one of the earliest French historians, born at Auvergne in 544 A.D., was appointed Bishop of Tours. His principal work, entitled "Historia Francorum," is a history of France from the establishment of Christianity till 595 A.D. Being persecuted for denouncing the crimes of the French sovereigns Chilpéric and Frédégonde, he retired to Rome, where he died in 595.

See DUPIN, "Bibliothèque des Auteurs ecclésiastiques;" J. W. LOEBELL, "Gregor von Tours und seine Zeit," 1839; "Gallia Christiana," tome xiv.; "Nouvelle Biographie Générale."

Greg'o-rȳ, (DAVID,) a Scottish philosopher, born about 1627, was the brother of James, who invented the reflecting telescope, and was the ancestor of several great mathematicians. He was himself remarkable for his skill in medicine, philosophy, etc. His three sons, David, James, and Charles, were at the same time mathematical professors in three universities.

Gregory, (DAVID,) son of the preceding, born at Aberdeen in 1661, was a skilful mathematician, and one of the most eminent members of this remarkable family. At the age of twenty-three he succeeded his uncle James as professor of mathematics in the University of Edinburgh. He has the credit of being one of the first who taught the Newtonian philosophy in his public lectures. He published, from 1684 to 1703, several works on astronomy and geometry. In 1691 he obtained the Savilian professorship of astronomy at Oxford. He afterwards wrote "Elements of Spherical Dioptrics and Catoptrics," and "Elements of Physical and Geometrical Astronomy," (1702,) the latter of which is his most important work. Professor Hutton says, "It was esteemed by Newton himself as a most excellent explanation and defence of his philosophy." Died in 1708. His brother James was chosen professor of mathematics in Edinburgh in 1791. Another brother, Charles, occupied the chair of mathematics at Saint Andrew's from 1707 to 1739, when he was succeeded by his son David.

See HUTTON, "Mathematical Dictionary;" CHAMBERS, "Biographical Dictionary of Eminent Scotsmen."

Gregory, (DUNCAN FARQUHARSON,) a British mathematician, born in 1814, was the son of James Gregory, M.D., (1753-1821,) and a descendant of the first James, noticed below. He was a Fellow and sub-lecturer of Trinity College, Cambridge, and principal contributor to the Cambridge "Mathematical Journal." In 1841 he published an excellent work on the "Differential and Integral Calculus." Died in 1844.

Gregory, (EDMUND,) an English writer, published a "Historical Anatomy of Christian Melancholy," (1646.) Died in 1650.

Gregory, (GEORGE,) D.D., an English author, born in 1754, was curate of Saint Giles, London, from 1782 to 1804. He published a "History of the Christian Church," (2 vols., 1794,) a "Dictionary of Arts and Sciences," and other works on various subjects. Died in 1808.

Gregory, (JAMES,) a celebrated Scottish geometer, born at Aberdeen in 1638, was the most eminent individual in a family which during several successive generations has been distinguished for profound attainments in the exact sciences. After leaving the university he devoted his talents to optics, and, at the age of twenty-four, invented the reflecting telescope which bears his name, and which he described in a treatise entitled "Optica Promota." About 1665 he visited Italy, where he passed several years and published a work on the "Quadrature of the Circle and Hyperbola," (1667.) These works procured for him the friendship of Newton, Huyghens, and other eminent philosophers. On his return to England, in 1668, he was elected a Fellow of the Royal Society, and professor of mathematics at Saint Andrew's. In 1674 he obtained the same chair in the University of Edinburgh, where he died suddenly in October, 1675, at the age of thirty-six. Charles Hutton expressed the opinion that "his mathematical genius as an inventor was of the first order." The list of his inventions comprises, besides the Gregorian telescope, burning mirrors, the solution of the Keplerian problem, a method for the transformation of curves, a converging series for making logarithms, etc. He wrote, besides the works above named, a "Part of Universal Geometry," and "Geometrical Essays." He left one son, James, born in 1674, who became professor of medicine at Aberdeen and was the father of John Gregory, M.D., noticed below. It is said that sixteen members of this family have held professorships in British colleges and schools.

See MONTUCLA, "Histoire des Mathématiques;" "Biographia Britannica;" HUTTON, "Mathematical Dictionary;" CHAMBERS, "Biographical Dictionary of Eminent Scotsmen."

Gregory, (JAMES,) M.D., a Scottish physician, born at Aberdeen in 1753, was the son of John Gregory, M.D., noticed below. He attained eminence as a professor of medicine in Edinburgh, and published a "General View of Theoretical Medicine," ("Conspectus Medicinæ Theoreticæ,") and other professional works. Died in 1821.

See CHAMBERS, "Biographical Dictionary of Eminent Scotsmen."

Gregory, (JOHN,) an English minister and historical writer, born in Buckinghamshire in 1607. His various works were published under the title of "Gregorii Posthuma," with a Life of the author by John Gurgany, (1st part, 1649.) Died in 1646.

Gregory, (JOHN,) M.D., a grandson of James Gregory the eminent geometer, was born at Aberdeen in 1724. He became successively professor of philosophy and medicine at Aberdeen, and in 1766 was appointed professor of the practice of physic in Edinburgh. His principal works are "Elements of the Practice of Physic," "A Comparative View of the State and Faculties of Man with those of the Animal World," and "A Father's Legacy to his Daughters." Died in 1773.

See CHAMBERS, "Biographical Dictionary of Eminent Scotsmen."

Gregory, (OLINTHUS GILBERT,) LL.D., a distinguished mathematician and philosopher, born in Huntingdonshire, England, in 1774. His "Treatise on the Use of the Sliding Rule" procured for him the notice of Dr. Hutton, to whom in 1800 he dedicated his "Treatise on Astronomy." Soon after this he became editor of the "Gentleman's Diary" and the "Pantalogia." He was appointed a mathematical master in the Royal Military Academy, Woolwich, in 1802, and, on the resignation of Dr. Hutton, succeeded him as professor of mathematics in that institution. Among his other writings are "A Treatise on Mechanics," "Plane and Spherical Trigonometry," "Lessons Astronomical and Philosophical," a "Memoir of John Mason Good," a "Dissertation on Weights and Measures," and "Evidences of Christianity," (1815.) Dr. Gregory was one of the twelve founders of the Royal Astronomical Society. As a man, he was greatly beloved and esteemed for his goodness of heart and eminent Christian virtues. Died in 1841.

Gregory, (WILLIAM,) a Scottish chemist and physician of high reputation, born in Edinburgh about 1803, was the author of "Outlines of Chemistry," (1848,) and "Letters to a Candid Enquirer on Animal Magnetism," (1853.) He also translated Von Reichenbach's "Researches on Magnetism," and edited several of Liebig's works. He became professor of chemistry in the University of Edinburgh about 1844. Died in 1858.

Gregory the Great. See GREGORY (POPE) I.

Greg'o-rȳ Naz-ĭ-an'zen, [Lat. GREGO'RIUS NAZIANZE'NUS; Gr. Γρηγόριος Ναζιανζηνός; Fr. GRÉGOIRE DE NAZIANZE, grȧ'gwȧR' deh nȧ'ze'ôNz'; Ger. GREGOR (or GREGORIUS, grȧ-go're-ûs) VON NAZIANZ, grȧ-gōR' fon nat-se-ânts',] a celebrated Greek Father, surnamed THE THEOLOGIAN, was born near Nazianzus about 328 A.D. He studied successively at Cæsarea, Alexandria, and Athens, where he formed an intimacy with Saint Basil. He was afterwards associated with his father in the bishopric of Nazianzus, where he was distinguished for his pulpit eloquence and by the poetical graces and the mild conciliatory spirit of his compositions. During the Arian persecution under Valens, he repaired to Constantinople, where he took charge of a private chapel; but, having incurred the enmity of zealots and courtiers by his mildness and his simple style of living, he resigned his office. His farewell sermon on this occasion is an admirable specimen of pulpit eloquence, full of dignity and pathos. Having previously visited Cæsarea and delivered the funeral oration of his friend Basil, he retired to his native place, where he devoted himself for the remainder of his life to his religious duties and the composition of his poems. A collection of these was published at Venice in 1504. He also wrote numerous orations and epistles, which have gone through several editions. "Gregorius," says Dupin, "deserves to be classed with the most perfect orators of Greece," excelling his contemporaries "in the nobleness of his expressions, the beauty of his reasonings, and the sublimity of his thoughts." Died in 389 A.D.

See VILLEMAIN, "Tableau de l'Éloquence chrétienne au quatrième Siècle;" ULLMANN, "Gregorius von Nazianz," 1825; GODEFROY HERMANT, "Vie de S. Grégoire de Nazianze," 1675; FABRICIUS, "Bibliotheca Græca;" SOCRATES, "Historia Ecclesiastica;" CAVE, "Scriptorum Ecclesiasticorum Historia Literaria;" "Westminster Review" for October, 1851.

Greif. See GRYPHIUS.

Greiff, grīf, (FRIEDRICH,) a German chemist, born at Tübingen in 1601; died in 1668.

Greig, grēg, (SAMUEL CARLOVITCH,) a Scottish admiral, who entered the Russian service in 1764 and accompanied Count Orlof in his expedition against the Turks. He was made commandant of Cronstadt in 1775, and admiral in 1782. Died in 1788. A monument was erected to him at Revel by the empress Catherine.

See Count SÉGUR, "Mémoires;" CHAMBERS, "Biographical Dictionary of Eminent Scotsmen."

Grel-let', (STEPHEN,) a minister of the Society of Friends or Quakers, born in France in 1773, was originally a Roman Catholic. He entered the body-guard of Louis XVI. about 1790, and emigrated to New York in 1795. He was converted to the principles of the Friends about 1796, and became a preacher, in which capacity he travelled extensively. He resided in the latter part of his life at Burlington, New Jersey, where he died in 1855.

See "Memoirs of the Life of Stephen Grellet," edited by B. SEEBOHM, 2 vols., 1860.

Gren, grên, (FRIEDRICH ALBRECHT KARL,) a German chemist and writer, born at Bernburg in 1760; died at Halle in 1798.

Grenade, de, (LOUIS.) See GRANADA.

Grenan, grȩh-nôN', (BÉNIGNE,) a Latin poet, born at Noyers, in Burgundy, about 1680, was professor of rhetoric at Paris. His style is said to be pure and animated. He translated Boileau's tenth and eleventh Satires into Latin. Died in 1723.

See MORÉRI, "Dictionnaire Historique."

Gren'fell, (PAS'COE,) M.P., an English opponent of the slave-trade, born in 1762. He was a coadjutor of Wilberforce, and spoke in the House of Commons against the slave-trade. Died in 1838.

Grenier, grȩh-ne-ȧ', (JACQUES RAYMOND,) a French hydrographer and naval officer, born in 1736, sailed in 1767 to explore the seas bordering on the coast of Coromandel and the adjacent islands. He published, after his return, a number of valuable charts, and "The Art of Naval Warfare," etc., (1787.) Died in 1803.

See "Archives de la Marine," etc.

Grenier, (JEAN,) BARON, a French jurist, born in Auvergne in 1753, published a "Treatise on Donations and Wills," (1807,) and other works. Died in 1841.

Grenier, (PAUL,) COUNT, a French general of division, born at Sarre-Louis in 1768; died in 1827.

Gren'ville, (Hon. GEORGE,) a distinguished English statesman, born in 1712, was a younger brother of Richard, Earl Temple, and brother-in-law of William Pitt the elder. He became ministerial leader of the Commons in 1762, having been treasurer of the navy for some years previous. He had mostly acted with the Whigs. While advocating a tax on cider, he called on his opponents to say where they would have a tax laid : "Let them tell me where; I repeat it, sir, tell me where." Pitt, who was then in the Opposition, raised a general laugh against him by murmuring the line of a well-known song,

"Gentle shepherd, tell me where."

In 1763 the prime minister, Lord Bute, resigned, and Grenville succeeded him as first lord of the treasury and chancellor of the exchequer. "We are inclined to think," says Macaulay, "that the worst administration which has governed England since the Revolution was that of George Grenville. His public acts may be classed under two heads,—outrages on the liberty of the people, and outrages on the dignity of the crown." Among the former was the famous Stamp Act of 1765. The king hated Grenville, and at last got rid of him in July, 1765, when the Marquis of Rockingham became premier. He died in 1770, leaving three sons, one of whom was Thomas, Lord Grenville.

See SMITH, "Grenville Papers;" LORD MAHON, "History of England;" MACAULAY, article on the "Earl of Chatham," in the "Edinburgh Review" for October, 1844.

Grenville, (GEORGE NUGENT.) See NUGENT.

Grenville, (RICHARD.) See TEMPLE, (EARL.)

Grenville, (THOMAS,) born in 1755, was a son of George Grenville, noticed above. He was employed in important missions to the United States, France, and Prussia, and after the death of Fox became first lord of the admiralty. This post he resigned in 1807, because the new ministry was hostile to Catholic emancipation. He died in 1846, having bequeathed to the British Museum his magnificent library, consisting of more than 20,000 volumes.

Grenville, (WILLIAM WYNDHAM GRENVILLE,)LORD, an able English statesman and orator, born in 1759, was the third son of George Grenville, noticed above. He was elected to Parliament in 1782, was appointed paymaster-general of the army in 1783, and was chosen Speaker of the Commons under 1789. In 1790 he was created Baron Grenville, and in 1791 became secretary for foreign affairs in the ministry of Pitt. He retired from office with Pitt in 1801. In the Whig ministry formed by himself and Fox about February, 1806, he was first lord of the treasury (premier) for about one year. During several years after 1808, Lords Grenville and Grey were the leaders of the opposition ; but the former did not support the Reform bills of Lord Grey. He wrote Latin poems, entitled "Nugæ Metricæ," ("Metrical Trifles," 1824.) For many years he was chancellor of the University of Oxford. His wife was Anne Pitt, daughter of Lord Camelford. He died, without issue, in 1834.

See J. SMITH, "Grenville Papers," 1852; "Edinburgh Review" for January, 1820; ALISON, "History of Europe."

Greppi, GREP′pee, (GIOVANNI,) an Italian dramatist, born at Bologna in 1751. His works are numerous, and were popular at the time. Died in 1811.

See TIPALDO, "Biografia degli Italiani illustri," vol. viii.

Gresh′am, (Sir THOMAS,) a wealthy English merchant, born in London in 1519. He was employed by Queen Elizabeth as her agent at Antwerp, and was also sent on several diplomatic missions. About 1566 he built at his own expense the Royal Exchange, London, the first edifice of the kind in England. He founded in London, in 1575, the college called by his name. Died in 1579.

See "Life of Sir Thomas Gresham," London, 1845; WARD, "Lives of the Gresham Professors."

Gresley, grà′le′, (GABRIEL,) a French painter, born .at L'Isle-sur-le-Doubs about 1710. He excelled especially in domestic scenes. Died in 1756.

Grēs′ley, (WILLIAM,) a popular English writer, born about 1800. Among his works (published 1835–51) are "Bernard Leslie," a novel, "Coniston Hall," "Forest of Arden," and "Help to Prayer."

Greslon, grà′lôn′, (ADRIEN,) a French Jesuit, born at Périgueux in 1618. He visited China in 1657, and published, after his return, a "History of China under the Rule of the Tartars," (1661.) Died in 1697.

Gresset, grà′sà′, (JEAN BAPTISTE LOUIS,) a celebrated French poet and dramatist, born at Amiens in 1709. He entered the order of Jesuits, and, at the age of twenty-four, produced a comic poem called "Vert-Vert," which had great success, and is one of the most witty and ingenious specimens of persiflage in the language. It has been translated into English by T. G. Cooper. About 1735 he ceased to be a Jesuit, and removed to Paris. His "Epistle to my Sister on my Convalescence" is greatly admired. He wrote a very successful comedy, called "Le Méchant," (1747,) and several tragedies. In 1748 he was admitted into the French Academy. Died in 1777. "After the lapse of a century," says De Pongerville, "Gresset has lost nothing of his high renown. He is considered one of the ornaments of our poetical firmament." ("Nouvelle Biographie Générale.")

See BAILLY, "Éloge de Gresset," 1785; SAINTE-BEUVE, in the "Revue des Deux Mondes," September, 1845; LONGFELLOW, "Poets and Poetry of Europe;" DE CAYROL, "Essai historique sur la Vie de Gresset," 2 vols., 1845.

Gressly, grĕss′lee, (ARMAND,) a Swiss geologist, born near Laufen about 1813. He gained distinction by his researches in the geology of the Jura Mountains. Died near Berne in 1865.

Gres′wĕll, (EDWARD,) a learned English theologian, born at Manchester in 1797. He became a Fellow of Corpus Christi College, Oxford. He published, besides other works, "Harmonia Evangelica," (1830,) and

"An Exposition of the Parables and other Parts of the Gospels," (5 vols., 1834–35.)

Gretch or **Gretsch,** grĕtch, (NIKOLAI IVANOVITCH,) a Russian *littérateur* and critic, born at Saint Petersburg in 1787. He was for a time editor of a political and patriotic journal, entitled "The Son of the Fatherland," and was afterwards associated with Boolgarin (Bulgarin) in editing "The Northern Bee." His principal work is a "History of Russian Literature," (1819–22.) He also published a valuable Russian Grammar, and a "Military Lexicon," in which he was assisted by his friend Baron von Seddeler.

See KÖNIG, "N. Gretch und die Russische Literatur," 1846.

Grétry, grà′tre′, (ANDRÉ ERNEST MODESTE,) a celebrated opera-composer, born at Liege in 1741. He visited Rome in 1759, having previously given proof of his genius by the composition of six symphonies and a mass. He became a pupil of the famous Martini. He afterwards repaired to Paris, where he brought out his comic opera of "Huron," (1769,) which met with brilliant success; it was followed in rapid succession by "The Speaking Picture," ("Le Tableau parlant,") "Sylvain," "Zémoire et Azor," "The Rose-Tree of Salency," ("La Rosière de Salency,") "Richard Cœur de Lion," and other comic operas, which raised his reputation to the highest point. Grétry was a member of the French Institute, and of the Academy of Music at Stockholm, and obtained various other distinctions. He died in 1813, and a monument, by Geefs, was erected to him at Liege.

See LE BRETON, "Notice sur la Vie et les Ouvrages de Grétry," 1814; "Grétry en Famille," etc., by A. J. GRÉTRY, his nephew, 1815; E. C. DE GERLACHE, "Essai sur Grétry," 1844; FÉTIS, "Biographie Universelle des Musiciens;" F. VAN HULST, "Grétry," 1842.

Gretser, grĕt′ser, (JAKOB,) a distinguished German Jesuit and philologist, born at Markdorf, in Suabia, in 1561. He wrote numerous works, among which is a treatise "On the Holy Cross," ("De Sancta Cruce," 1600.) Died at Ingolstadt in 1625.

See his Life prefixed to an edition of his Works, 17 vols. fol., 1734 –41; BAYLE, "Historical and Critical Dictionary;" NICÉRON, "Mémoires."

Greuze, gRUZ, (JEAN BAPTISTE,) a distinguished French painter, born in Burgundy in 1726. He excelled in delineating domestic scenes of a touching and impressive character. Among his master-pieces may be named a "Father explaining the Bible to his Children," "Saint Mary in Egypt," ("Sainte-Marie Égyptienne,") "The Good Mother," a "Young Girl holding a Dove," and "The Paternal Blessing." Died in 1805.

See MÉRIMÉE, "De la Peinture à l'Huile;" "Nouvelle Biographie Générale."

Greve or **Greeve,** grā′veh or HRĀ′veh, (EGBERT JAN,) a Dutch theologian and Orientalist, born at Deventer in 1754, wrote a treatise "On the Last Chapters of the Book of Job," (in Latin.) Died in 1811.

Greve, van, vän grā′veh, (JAN,) a Dutch Arminian theologian, born about 1580. He wrote "Tribunal Reformatum."

Greve, van, (PIETER,) a Dutch jurist, born at Deventer in 1641 ; died in 1677.

Grev′ille or **Grev′ile,** (Sir FULKE,) Lord Brooke, an English poet and miscellaneous writer, born in Warwickshire in 1554, was distinguished by the favour of Queen Elizabeth, who made him a knight. He was appointed by King James I. under-treasurer and chancellor of the exchequer in 1615, and obtained from that monarch the castle of Warwick, (then in a ruinous condition,) which he repaired at vast expense. He was created a peer, with the title of Baron Brooke, in 1620. He was mortally wounded, in a quarrel with an old servant, in 1628. Lord Brooke was the intimate friend of Sir Philip Sidney, of whom he published a biography. He also wrote a number of poems and tragedies.

See HORACE WALPOLE, "Royal and Noble Authors;" "Biographia Britannica."

Greville, (ROBERT,) born in 1608, was a cousin of the preceding, whose title he inherited. He fought in the Parliamentary army, and was killed at the battle of Lichfield in 1643. Among his principal works are a "Discourse opening the Nature of the Episcopacy exercised in England," (1641,) and "The Nature of Truth."

See LODGE's "Portraits."

ā, ē, ī, ō, ū, ȳ, *long;* ȧ, ė, ȯ, same, less prolonged; ă, ĕ, ĭ, ŏ, ŭ, y̆, *short;* ạ, ẹ, ị, ọ, *obscure;* fär, fȧll, fȧt; mĕt; nŏt; gŏŏd; mōōn;

Greville, (ROBERT KAYE,) a British botanist, born in the county of Durham about 1794. He published, besides other works, "Flora Edinensis : Plants of Edinburgh," (1824,) and "The Scottish Cryptogamic Flora," (6 vols., 1822-28,) which was called by Loudon "a truly admirable work." Died in 1866.

Grévin, grĕ'vȧN', (JACQUES,) a French poet, born at Clermont-en-Beauvoisis about 1540, was a Calvinist. He wrote dramas which had great success, and became physician to the Duchess of Savoy. Died in 1570.

See LA HARPE, "Cours de Littérature."

Grew, (NEHEMIAH,) an English naturalist, son of Obadiah, noticed below, was born at Coventry about 1628. He was a Fellow of the Royal Society and of the College of Physicians, and published, among other works, "The Anatomy of Vegetables," (1682,) and "Idea of a Philosophical History of Plants." The former treatise was translated into French. Died in 1711.

See REES, "Cyclopædia;" "Biographia Britannica."

Grew, (OBADIAH,) an English Puritan divine, born in Warwickshire in 1607. He joined the party of the Parliament on the breaking out of the civil war, but he opposed the execution of the king. Died in 1698.

Grey, grā, (CHARLES,) second EARL, an eminent English statesman and champion of Parliamentary reform, was the eldest son of the first Earl Grey. He was born at Fallowden, near Alnwick, in March, 1764, and educated at Cambridge. Entering Parliament in 1786, as member for Northumberland, he became a constant supporter of the Whig party and a warm personal friend of Fox. He had won a prominent position by his splendid talents and eloquence, when he was appointed by the House a member of the committee to manage the impeachment of Warren Hastings, in 1788. "At twenty-three," says Macaulay, "he had been thought worthy to be ranked with the veteran statesmen who appeared as the delegates of the British Commons at the bar of the British nobility."

When the Whig party was disorganized by hostility to the French Revolution, Fox and Grey remained constant to their principles, and were the leaders of the opposition. Mr. Grey was one of the founders of the "Society of the Friends of the People," a political association formed in 1792 to promote reform in Parliament. In the stormy and critical times which followed, when the more timid Whigs deserted to the dominant party, when liberal principles were stigmatized as Jacobinical, when the coercive policy of Pitt was supported by large majorities, Mr. Grey did not falter in his devotion to the popular cause. In 1793 he presented a petition for a change in the system of representation, and advocated it in an impressive speech. In 1797 he again made an unsuccessful effort for reform in the House of Commons. On the formation of the Whig ministry of Fox and Grenville, in 1806, Mr. Grey, who had recently received the title of Lord Howick, was appointed first lord of the admiralty. At the death of Fox, September, 1806, Lord Howick succeeded him as secretary of foreign affairs and leader in the House of Commons. The most memorable act of this brief ministry was the abolition of the slave-trade, which he cordially supported. The Whig cabinet was dissolved in March, 1807. In the same year, Lord Howick, at the death of his father, became Earl Grey, and a member of the House of Lords. In 1812 the prince-regent solicited Lords Grey and Grenville to accept places in his Tory cabinet ; but they declined thus to sacrifice their consistency and principles, and continued to be the opposition leaders in the House of Lords. In 1829 Lord Grey concurred in the passage of the Catholic Emancipation Bill, which had long been a fundamental point in his political creed.

The cause of Reform in 1830 received a new impulse by the accession of William IV., and the second French revolution. Wellington was compelled to resign, and Earl Grey became premier, adopting for his policy peace, retrenchment, and reform. The first Reform bill having been defeated in 1831, the ministers dissolved Parliament and appealed to the people, who returned to the new House a large majority of Liberals. A second bill passed the House of Commons, but was lost in the Upper House. The measure finally triumphed in June, 1832. The Reformed Parliament, which met in 1833, abolished colonial slavery and the monopoly of the East India Company. In consequence of dissensions in the cabinet, Lord Grey resigned in July, 1833. He died in 1845. He had married in 1784 Mary E. Ponsonby, and left eight sons, the eldest of whom is the third Earl Grey.

See ROEBUCK, "History of the Whig Party of 1830;" HARRIET MARTINEAU, "History of Thirty Years' Peace."

Grey, (Sir GEORGE,) born in Ireland, travelled in Australia in 1837, and published, after his return to England, "Journals of Two Expeditions in Northwest and Western Australia." He was successively appointed Lieutenant-Governor of Southern Australia, Governor of New Zealand, (1846,) and Governor of the Cape of Good Hope, (1854.) He wrote a treatise "On Polynesian Mythology, and the Traditional History of the New Zealand Race," (1855.)

Grey, (Right Hon. Sir GEORGE,) G.C.B., a British statesman, born at Gibraltar in 1799, was a nephew of the second Earl Grey. He graduated with honour as a classical scholar at Oxford, and was called to the bar about 1826. In 1832 he was elected to Parliament by the Whigs of Devonport. He was appointed judge-advocate general in 1839, and entered the cabinet of Lord John Russell as home secretary in 1846. Having retired with his party in 1852, he was appointed to the same office by Palmerston in 1855, and resigned in 1858 when Lord Derby became premier. In July, 1861, he again obtained the office of home secretary, which he resigned in June, 1866.

Grey, (HENRY GEORGE,) third EARL, the eldest son of Charles, the second Earl Grey, was born in December, 1802. He was appointed under-secretary of state for the colonies in 1830, and resigned in 1833. From May, 1835, to August, 1841, he was secretary at war under Lord Melbourne. He became an able parliamentary debater. He succeeded to the earldom in 1845, before which he was styled Lord Howick. In 1846 he was appointed colonial secretary by Lord John Russell. He retired from office on the defeat of the Whig ministry in 1852.

Grey, (Lady JANE,) daughter of Henry Grey, Marquis of Dorset, and Frances Brandon, granddaughter of Henry VII., was born in 1537. She early manifested extraordinary talents and a passionate love of learning, and, according to her tutor, Roger Ascham, spoke and wrote Latin, Greek, French, and Italian with the greatest ease. At the early age of sixteen she wrote excellent Latin ; "but the matter of her letters," says Froude, "is more striking than the language, and speaks more for her than the most elaborate panegyrics of admiring courtiers." (See "History of England," vol. vi. chap. xxx.) She was married in 1553 to Lord Guilford Dudley, son of the Duke of Northumberland. The latter, in concert with Lady Jane's father, then Duke of Suffolk, prevailed upon Edward VI. to settle the crown upon Lady Jane Grey, to the exclusion of his sisters Mary and Elizabeth. The crown being offered to her after the death of Edward, she at first refused, but at length yielded to the authority of her father and the solicitations of her husband. Ten days later, the people having declared for Mary, Lady Jane and her husband were sent to the Tower, and, after an imprisonment of several months, were executed in February, 1554.

See HUME, "History of England :" SIR N. H. NICOLAS, "Memoirs and Literary Remains of Lady Jane Grey," 1825; D. W. BARTLETT, "Life of Lady Jane Grey," 1853; GEORGE HOWARD, "Lady Jane Grey and her Times."

Grey or **Gray,** (NICHOLAS,) born in London in 1590, became head-master of Eton in 1631. He was the author of a Latin-and-English Dictionary. Died in 1660.

Grey, (RICHARD,) an English clergyman, born at Newcastle in 1694, became rector of Kincote and prebendary of Saint Paul's. He published, besides other works, "The Art of Memory," ("Memoria Technica," 1730.) Died in 1771.

Grey, (ZACHARY,) an English divine, born in Yorkshire in 1687, became vicar of Saint Peter's, Cambridge. He edited Butler's "Hudibras," (1744,) and published several theological and controversial works. Died in 1766.

e as k; ç as s; g hard; g̣ as j; G, H, K, guttural; N, nasal; R, trilled; s̄ as z; th as in this. (☞See Explanations, p. 23.)

Grey, de. See DE GREY AND RIPON.

Gribaldi, gre-bȧl′dee, (MATTEO,) a learned Italian jurist and legal writer, born in Piedmont, was successively professor of law at Pisa, Toulouse, and Padua. About 1550 he became a Protestant. Died in 1564.

See BAYLE, "Historical and Critical Dictionary;" TIRABOSCHI, "Storia della Letteratura Italiana."

Gribeauval, gre′bŏ′vȧl′, (JEAN BAPTISTE **Vaquette** —vȧ′kĕt′,) a distinguished French general and military engineer, was born at Amiens in 1715. He entered the Austrian army in 1757, and rendered very important services to Maria Theresa during the Seven Years' war. Among these the defence of Schweidnitz, in 1762, against Frederick the Great, deserves especial mention. He was made lieutenant-general in 1765. Died in 1789.

See GAUCHER DE PASSAC, "Précis sur M. de Gribeauval." 1816.

Griboyedof, Griboyedov, or **Gribojedow,** grebo-yä′dof, (ALEXANDER SERGIEVITCH,) a celebrated Russian poet and dramatist, born at Moscow about 1795. Having served for a time in the army, he was sent as minister plenipotentiary to Persia in 1828. In February, 1829, the populace of Teherân, incensed against the Russian embassy, attacked their house and assassinated the minister, together with the Russians who were his companions. His principal work, entitled "The Misfortunes of Genius," ("Gore ot Uma,") is the most popular comedy in the language, and is so universally admired that many of its sentences have become proverbs.

See E. MESTCHERSKI, "Les Poëtes Russes."

Grid′ley, (JEREMIAH,) an eminent American lawyer, born about 1705, became attorney-general of Massachusetts. He defended in 1761 the writs of assistance, which were obnoxious to the popular party. Died in 1767.

Gridley, (PHILO,) an American jurist, born in Paris, Oneida county, New York, in 1796, was elected a judge of the supreme court of New York in 1846. Died in 1864.

Gridley, (RICHARD,) GENERAL, a brother of Jeremiah, noticed above, was born in Boston in 1711. He served as engineer in the war against the French, and became chief engineer of the American army in 1775. He was wounded at Bunker Hill in June of that year. Died in 1796.

Griebner, gReep′ner, or **Gribner,** grip′ner,(MICHAEL HEINRICH,) a German jurist, born at Leipsic in 1682, was professor of law at Wittenberg. Died in 1734.

Griepenhielm. See FIGRELIUS.

Griepenkerl, gree′pen-kêrl′, (ROBERT,) a Swiss littérateur, born at Hofwyl in 1810, wrote, besides other works, two tragedies, "The Girondists," and "Maximilian Robespierre."

Grier, greer, (ROBERT COOP′ER,) a distinguished American jurist, born in Cumberland county, Pennsylvania, in 1794. He graduated at Dickinson College, in which institution he is said to have acted as principal before he had reached the age of twenty-one. He afterwards studied law, and rose to be a justice of the supreme court of the United States, (1846.) He resigned in February, 1870, and died in September of the same year.

See LIVINGSTON'S "Portraits of Eminent Americans."

Grier′son, (CONSTANTIA,) an Irish lady, eminent for her talents and learning, born in the county of Kilkenny in 1706. She was an accomplished classical scholar, and was also well versed in philosophy and the exact sciences. She published valuable editions of Tacitus and Terence, and was the author of a number of poems. Died in 1733.

See CIBBER'S "Lives of the Poets."

Gries, greess, (JOHANN DIETRICH,) a German poet and littérateur, born at Hamburg in 1775. His "Phaeton," a poem, published about 1798, led to his acquaintance with Schiller, who inserted it in the "Musenalmanach." He translated Tasso's "Jerusalem Delivered," and the "Orlando Furioso" of Ariosto, from the Italian, and Calderon's dramas from the Spanish. Died in 1842.

Griesbach, greess′bȧk, (JOHANN JAKOB,) a German theologian and celebrated biblical critic, born at Butzbach, Hesse-Dai nstadt, in 1745. Having studied at Tübingen, Halle, and Leipsic, he devoted himself chiefly to the revision of the Greek text of the New Testament. He became professor of theology at Halle in 1773. In 1775 he published his excellent edition of the Greek

New Testament. The text established by him has been generally adopted. He was chosen professor of divinity in Jena in 1776. He published, in Latin, many critical works, among which is "Symbolæ Criticæ," etc., (1785–93;) and in German, an "Introduction to the Study of the Popular Christian Dogmas," ("Populäre Dogmatik,") (1779,) which is his most celebrated work. Died in 1812.

See J. C. W. AUGUSTI, "Ueber J. J. Griesbach's Verdienste," 1812; F. A. KÖTHE, "Gedächtnissrede auf J. J. Griesbach nebst einer Skizze seines Lebens," 1812; "Nouvelle Biographie Générale."

Griesheim, von, fon greess′hīm, (KARL GUSTAV JULIUS,) a Prussian general, born at Berlin in 1798. He published several military works.

Grif′fen-feld or **Griffenfeldt,** (PETER SCHUHMACHER,) COUNT OF, a Danish statesman, born at Copenhagen in 1635, rose, through various offices, to be president of the supreme tribunal and chancellor of the University of Copenhagen. His haughtiness and abuse of power having made him many enemies, he was charged in 1676 with treasonable negotiations with foreign courts, and was imprisoned twenty-seven years. Died in 1699.

See C. P. ROTHE, "Griffenfelds Liv og Levnet," 1745; GIESSING, "Griffenfeld; en historisk Fremstilling," 1846.

Griffet, gre′fȧ′, (HENRI,) a learned French Jesuit, born at Moulins in 1698, wrote numerous theological and historical works. Died in 1771.

Griffet de la Beaume, gre′fȧ′ deh lȧ bōm, (ANTOINE GILBERT,) a nephew of the preceding, born at Moulins in 1756, wrote, among other works, a comedy entitled "Galatea." Died in 1805.

Griffier, grif′feer, (JOHN,) THE ELDER, an eminent Dutch painter, born at Rotterdam in 1656. He resided for a time in London, where he died in 1718.' Among his master-pieces are several views on the Rhine, and a "View of the Seven Castles," in Germany. His landscapes rival in beauty those of Teniers and Ruysdael.

Griffier, (ROBERT,) THE YOUNGER, son of the preceding, was born in England in 1688. He was distinguished, like his father, for his exquisite landscapes and river-views. Died about 1750.

See DESCAMPS, "Vies des Peintres Flamands, Hollandais," etc.

Griffin or **Griffon.** See GRYPHON.

Grif′fin, (CHARLES,) an American general, born in Ohio about 1826, graduated at West Point in 1847. He became a captain in the regular army early in 1861, and a brigadier-general of volunteers about April, 1862. He commanded a division at the battles of Gaines' Mill and Malvern Hill, July 1, 1862, and served under General Grant in his operations against Richmond in the summer of 1864. He commanded a corps at Five Forks, April 1, 1865. Died at Galveston in September, 1867.

Griffin, (Rev. EDMUND DORR,) an American Episcopalian divine, born at Wyoming, Pennsylvania, in 1804. He died in 1830, leaving "Literary Remains," which were published in 2 vols., with a Memoir by the Rev. John McVickar, (1831.)

See "North American Review" for January, 1832.

Griffin, (EDWARD DORR,) D.D., an American Presbyterian divine and eminent pulpit orator, born in East Haddam, Connecticut, in 1770, graduated at Yale in 1790. He was for some time professor of sacred rhetoric in the Theological Seminary at Andover, and in 1811 became pastor of the Park Street Church, Boston. It was here that he delivered his well-known "Park Street Lectures" on the doctrines of Calvinism. In 1815 he accepted the presidency of Williams College. Died in 1837.

See SPRAGUE, "Life of E. D. Griffin," 1839.

Grif′fin, (GERALD,) an Irish novelist, born at Limerick in 1803. He was the author of "Holland Tide, or Munster Popular Tales," (1827,) "The Collegians," and other works. Died in 1840.

Grif′fith, (ELIZABETH,) a writer of fiction, born in Wales in 1750, published conjointly with her husband, Richard Griffith, a popular work, entitled "Letters of Henry and Francis," (1756.) Mrs. Griffith also wrote a number of novels and comedies, and "The Morality of Shakespeare's Dramas Illustrated." Died in 1793.

Grif′fith, (Sir RICHARD JOHN,) a geologist, born in Dublin in 1784. He was a civil engineer in early life, and became professor of geology in Dublin. About 1850 he was appointed chairman of the board of public works of Ireland. He published a Geological Map of Ireland.

Grif'fith, (WILLIAM,) M.D., an English naturalist, born in 1810. He went to India as a surgeon about 1832, and spent much time in exploring the botany of that region. He wrote several treatises for scientific journals, and made large collections of plants and animals. Died in Malacca in 1845.

Grif'fiths, (RALPH,) an English journalist, born in Shropshire about 1720, founded in 1749 the "Monthly Review" in London. Died in 1803.

Griffon. See GRYPHON.

Grignan, de, dęh grĕn'yôN', (FRANÇOISE MARGUE-RITE de Sévigné—dęh să'vĕn'yà',) COMTESSE, a French lady, distinguished for talents and beauty, born in 1648. She was a daughter of the celebrated Madame de Sévigné, who addressed to her the "Letters" so widely known and so generally admired. Madame de Grignan was the author of a "Summary of the System of Fénelon on the Love of God." Died in 1705.

See SAINT-SIMON, "Mémoires;" "Nouvelle Biographie Générale."

Grigoletti, gre-go-let'tee, (MICHELANGELO,) an Italian painter, born at Pordenone in 1801, became professor in the Academy of Venice in 1839. Among his works is a celebrated picture of "The Last Interview between the Foscari," (1838.)

Grijalva, de, dà gre-hâl'và, (JUAN,) a Spanish navigator, and the discoverer of Mexico, born at Cuellar. He sailed on a voyage of discovery in 1518, and arrived first at the island of Cozumel, (called by him Santa Cruz,) in the Bay of Yucatan. He gave to Mexico the name of New Spain.

See PRESCOTT, "History of the Conquest of Mexico;" A. DE SOLIS, "Historia de la Conquista de Mexico."

Grill, gRil, (CLAUDIUS,) a learned Swede, born at Stockholm in 1705, was one of the first members of the Academy of Sciences in his native city. Died in 1767.

Grillet, gRe'yà', (JEAN,) a French Jesuit, born about 1630, was one of the first missionaries to Guiana. He published, after his return, an account of Guiana, which is still esteemed. Died about 1675.

Grillet, gRe'yà', (JEAN LOUIS,) a historical writer, born in Savoy in 1756. He was one of the founders of the College of Carouge, near Geneva, which admitted Catholics, Protestants, and Jews without distinction. Died in 1812.

Grillo, gRèl'lo, (Don ANGELO,) a learned Genoese nobleman, born about 1550, was a friend of the poet Tasso, and was patronized by the popes Urban VIII. and Alexander VII. Died in 1629.

Grillparzer, gRil'pàRt-sęr, (FRANZ,) a German dramatist, born in 1790 at Vienna, where he appears to have since resided. Among his best productions are "The Waves of the Sea and of Love," a tragedy founded on the story of Hero and Leander, and another, called "Sappho," which was translated into Italian.

See "Fraser's Magazine" for August, 1852.

Grimaldi, gre-mâl'dee, (ANTONIO,) a Genoese admiral, of a noble family, captured several vessels from the Catalonians in 1332, but was defeated in 1353 by the Spanish and Venetian fleet under Niccolò Pisani.

Grimaldi, (CARLO,) surnamed THE GREAT, Prince of Monaco, was commander of the Genoese fleet against the Flemings in 1338. He was mortally wounded at the battle of Crécy, in 1346.

Grimaldi, (CONSTANTINO,) a Neapolitan jurist and philosopher, born in 1667. He is chiefly known from his controversy with Benedictis on the doctrine of Aristotle, and published an able defence of the Cartesian philosophy. Died in 1750.

Grimaldi, (DOMENICO,) a Genoese prelate, who, being appointed by the pope commissary-general of the galleys of the Church, took an active part in the battle of Lepanto in 1571. He afterwards became Archbishop and Vice-Legate of Avignon. Died in 1592.

Grimaldi, (DOMENICO,) MARQUIS, an Italian writer on rural and political economy, born at Seminara in 1735; died in 1805.

Grimaldi, (FRANCESCO,) an Italian architect, born in the kingdom of Naples about 1550. Among his best works are the church of Santa Maria degli Angeli, and the chapel of San Januario, at Naples.

Grimaldi, (FRANCESCO,) a Neapolitan Jesuit and Latin poet, born about 1678; died in 1738.

Grimaldi, (FRANCESCO ANTONIO,) an Italian jurist and historian, born in Calabria in 1740, wrote "Annals of the Kingdom of Naples." Died in 1784.

Grimaldi, (FRANCESCO MARIA,) an Italian Jesuit and natural philosopher, born at Bologna in 1618 or 1619. He wrote a valuable work entitled "Physico-Mathesis de Lumine, Coloribus," etc., (1665,) being an account of his experiments and discoveries relating to the interference of rays of light. He is said to have been the discoverer of the diffraction of light. Died in 1663.

See FABRONI, "Vitæ Italorum doctrina excellentium;" MONTUCLA, "Histoire des Mathématiques."

Grimaldi, (GIOVANNI,) Prince of Monaco, a Genoese admiral, who signally defeated the Venetians in 1431. Died in 1454.

Grimaldi, (GIOVANNI FRANCESCO,) a celebrated Italian painter of landscapes and architectural pieces, surnamed IL BOLOGNESE, born at Bologna in 1606, was a pupil of the Caracci. He was employed by Louis XIV. and Cardinal Mazarin to paint in the Louvre, and was patronized by Pope Innocent X. Died in 1680.

See LANZI, "History of Painting in Italy."

Grimaldi, gre-mâl'dee, (JOSEPH,) a celebrated comic actor, born in England in 1779. He performed the part of a clown with success in London. Died in 1837.

See "Memoirs of Joseph Grimaldi," edited by Boz.

Grimaldi, (ONORIO,) Prince of Monaco, born in 1597, was created Duke of Valentinois by Louis XIII. of France, and obtained many other distinctions. He wrote "Genealogica et historica Grimaldiæ Gentis Arbor," being a history of the Grimaldi family. Died in 1662.

Grimaldi, (RANIERI,) Prince of Monaco, a leader of the Guelph faction, entered the service of Philippe le Bel in 1302, and rose to be admiral of France. He gained a victory over the Flemish fleet in 1304, and took prisoner Guy de Namur, son of the Count of Flanders.

Grimaldo, de, dà gre-mâl'do, (Don JOSÉ **Gutie-rez de Solorzano**—goo-te-à'rĕth dà so-loR-thà'no,) MARQUIS, a Spanish minister of state, born in Biscay in 1664. He was secretary of the marine and of war, and afterwards chief minister, of Philip V. Died in 1733.

Grimani, gre-mä'nee, (ANTONIO,) a Venetian nobleman, born in 1436. He was appointed in 1499 procurator of Saint Mark, and captain-general of the fleet sent against the Sultan Bayazeed, (Bajazet.) He was elected Doge of Venice in 1521. He died in 1523.

See DARU, "Histoire de Venise."

Grimani, gre-mä'nee, (HUBERT,) a Dutch painter, sometimes called JACOBS, was born at Delft in 1599. He studied in Venice, and was a good colorist. Died in 1629.

Grimani, (MARINO,) became Doge of Venice in 1595. Under his rule an expedition was fitted out against the pirates of the Adriatic Sea. Died in 1605.

Grimani, (PIETRO,) succeeded Ludovico Pisani as Doge of Venice in 1741. He died in 1752, and was succeeded by Francesco Loredano.

Grimarest, de, dęh gre-mä'rà', (JEAN LÉONOR le **Gallois**—lęh gà'lwà',) SIEUR, a French littérateur, born in Paris, was noted for witticisms and anecdotes. He wrote, besides other works, a "Life of Molière," (1705.) Died in 1720.

Grimaud, de, dęh gre'mō', (JEAN CHARLES MARGUE-RITE GUILLAUME,) a French physician, born at Nantes in 1750, became professor in the Medical University of Montpellier. He wrote an "Essay on Irritability," and other valuable works. Died in 1789.

Grimauld. See URBAN V.

Grim'bäld, written also **Grimbold** and **Grimoald,** (NICHOLAS,) an English poet, was one of the first among his countrymen who wrote in blank verse. "As a writer of verses in rhyme," says Warton, "he yields to none of his contemporaries for a masterly choice of chaste expression and the concise elegancies of didactic versification." He was also the author of a Latin tragedy, entitled "John the Baptist," and made several translations from the Greek and Latin. Died about 1563.

See WARTON, "History of English Poetry."

Grimké, grim'ke, (FREDERICK,) an American judge, of Huguenot descent, born in Charleston, South Carolina, in 1791, removed to Ohio. He wrote "The Nature and Tendency of Free Institutions," (1848.)

Grimké, (THOMAS SMITH,) LL.D., an American jurist and philanthropist, a brother of the preceding, was born in Charleston, South Carolina, in 1786. He graduated at Yale in 1807. He was widely known for his efforts in behalf of peace, religion, and education. A volume of his Addresses on these and other subjects was published at New Haven in 1831. Died in 1834.

Grimm, grĭm, (FRIEDRICH MELCHIOR,) BARON, a witty German writer, born at Ratisbon on the 25th of December, 1723. Having accompanied Count Schönberg to Paris, he became acquainted with Rousseau, Baron Holbach, and other celebrated persons, and attracted general admiration by his elegant accomplishments and conversational talent. When the war broke out in the musical world between the partisans of the French composer Rameau and the Italian musicians, Grimm espoused the cause of the latter. He was the head of the queen's party, called "Coin de la Reine" from their assembling in the pit under the queen's box, while the "Coin du Roi," the French party, took their station under the box of the king. About this time he published a spirited and witty satire, entitled "Le petit Prophète de Boemischbroda," (1753,) and soon after his "Lettres sur la Musique Française," in which he gained a complete victory over his antagonists. After becoming secretary to the Duke of Orléans, he wrote, in conjunction with Diderot and the Abbé Raynal, his literary bulletins, containing acute criticisms on French literature. Catherine of Russia appointed him her minister at Hamburg in 1795. He died at Gotha in December, 1807, leaving "Correspondance littéraire, philosophique et critique," which was published by J. Taschereau, (15 vols., 1829-31.)

See TASCHEREAU, "Notice sur Grimm," prefixed to this edition; MADAME D'ÉPINAY, "Mémoires;" ROUSSEAU, "Confessions;" SAINTE-BEUVE, "Causeries du Lundi;" SAINTE-BEUVE et LIMAYRAC, "Gazette littéraire de Grimm: Histoire, Littérature, Philosophie, 1753-99. Études sur Grimm," Paris, 8vo, 1854; "Nouvelle Biographie Générale;" "London Quarterly Review" for March and October, 1813, and July, 1814; "Edinburgh Review" for July, 1813.

Grimm, (JAKOB LUDWIG,) an eminent German jurist and philologist, born at Hanau on the 4th of January, 1785. He studied law at Marburg, under Savigny. He was secretary of legation to the Congress of Vienna in 1814, and shortly after was sent to Paris to reclaim the manuscripts which had been taken away from Prussia by the French under Napoleon. In 1830 he obtained a professorship at Göttingen, and was also made librarian. He was deprived of that chair in 1837 for his liberal political principles. In 1841 he was invited to Berlin, where he was elected to the Academy of Sciences. He wrote "Legal Antiquities of Germany," (1828,) "History of the German Language," (1848,) and "German Mythology," all of which are esteemed standard works. He also published a German Grammar, and editions of "Reinhart Fuchs" and other fables of the middle ages. The "Kinder- und Hausmährchen," written conjointly with his brother Wilhelm Karl, enjoy great popularity, and have been frequently translated. Died in Berlin in September, 1863.

See J. SCHMIDT, "Geschichte der Deutschen National-literatur im neunzehnten Jahrhundert;" "Nouvelle Biographie Générale;" "Foreign Quarterly Review" for January, 1832, and July, 1838; "Blackwood's Magazine" for February, 1840.

Grimm, (LUDWIG EMIL,) a German painter and engraver, younger brother of the preceding, was born at Hanau in 1790. He became, in 1832, professor in the Academy of Painting at Cassel. Died in 1863.

Grimm, (WILHELM KARL,) an eminent linguist, a brother of the preceding, was born at Hanau in 1786. He was associated in the literary labours of his brother Jakob Ludwig, whom he accompanied to Göttingen in 1830, and subsequently to Berlin, where he became a member of the Academy of Sciences. He published editions of the "Hildebrandslied," "Grave Ruodolf," "Rolands-

lied," and other German poems of the middle ages; also a translation of "Old Danish Hero-Ballads," a treatise "On German Runic Inscriptions," and one "On German Traditions." He was engaged with his brother Jakob Ludwig on a large and very complete German Dictionary, of which two volumes appeared in 1859. Died in 1859.

Grimmelshausen, von, fon grĭm'mĕls-hŏw'zĕn, (CHRISTOFFEL,) a German writer, born in Hesse-Cassel about 1625, produced a romance entitled "Simplicissimus," (1669,) a work of superior merit. Died in 1676.

Grimmer, grĭm'mĕr, or **Grimaar,** gree'mär, (JACOB,) a Flemish landscape-painter, born at Antwerp in 1510; died in 1546.

See DESCAMPS, "Vies des Peintres Flamands," etc.

Grim'o-ald, son of Pepin the Elder, mayor of the Austrasian palace, succeeded his father in that office in 642 A.D. King Sigebert died in 656, leaving a son, Dagobert, whom Grimoald sent to a monastery, and attempted to make his own son king. He was soon after arrested and put to death by order of Clovis.

Grimoald III., Duke of Benevento, succeeded his father on the throne of Lombardy in 787 A.D. He was at first tributary to Charlemagne; but he soon renounced his allegiance, and carried on a vigorous and successful warfare against that monarch and his successor Pepin.

See SISMONDI, "Histoire des Français."

Grimoard, de, dĕh gre'mo'är', (PHILIPPE HENRI,) COMTE, a French general and historical writer, born at Verdun about 1750. He published a "Theoretic Essay on Battles," (1775,) "Life and Reign of Frederick the Great," (1788,) and other works. Died in 1815.

Grimod de la Reynière, gre'mo' dĕh lä rȧ'ne-air', (ALEXANDRE BALTHASAR LAURENT,) a witty and eccentric French writer, born in Paris in 1758. His "Almanach des Gourmands" (8 vols., 1803-12) made a great sensation throughout Europe. His zeal to promote what Montaigne styled "the science of the palate" induced him to establish a jury, which held monthly sessions, to decide on the merits of particular dishes. Died in 1838.

Grimoud, Grimou, or **Grimoux,** gre'moo', (ALEXIS,) a Swiss painter, born in the canton of Fribourg about 1688. His works are chiefly portraits and domestic scenes, and are highly esteemed. Died about 1740.

See FUESSLI, "Geschichte der besten Künstler in der Schweiz."

Grim'shawe, (Rev. THOMAS SHUTTLEWORTH,) an English clergyman, born at Preston in 1777. He published a "Life of the Rev. Legh Richmond," and "Life and Works of Cowper," (1836.) Died in 1850.

Grim'stone or **Grim'ston,** (Sir HARBOTTLE,) a noted English lawyer, born in Essex about 1596. He favoured the cause of the Parliament, but opposed the execution of the king. He was one of the commissioners who waited upon Charles II. at Breda; and he was afterwards appointed master of the rolls. Died in 1683.

See CLARENDON, "History of the Rebellion;" BURNET, "History of his Own Time."

Grin'dal, (EDMUND,) an English prelate, born in Cumberland in 1519, rose to be Archbishop of Canterbury in 1575. He was distinguished for learning and piety, and was a contributor to Fox's "Acts and Monuments," ("Book of Martyrs.") Died in 1583.

See STRYPE'S "Life of Grindal."

Grin'field, (EDWARD W.,) an English clergyman and biblical critic, born about 1784. He published, under the title of "Novum Testamentum Græcum," (4 vols., 1843-48,) a work designed to show the close connection of the Greek Testament with the Septuagint; also other works on theology. Died in 1864.

Gringore, grăn'goR', or **Gringoire,** grăn'gwäR', (PIERRE,) one of the early French dramatists, born in Lorraine about 1475, produced a play entitled "The Prince of Fools and the Foolish Mother," said to have been written, at the instigation of Louis XII., to ridicule Pope Julius II. Died about 1544.

See "Retrospective Review," vol. i., 1853.

Grin-nell', (JOSEPH,) an American merchant, born at New Bedford, Massachusetts, in 1788. He acquired a large fortune by trade in New York city, and became a resident of New Bedford about 1830. He was elected a member of Congress about 1843, and re-elected several times.

Grinnell, (MOSES,) an American merchant, a brother of the preceding, was born at New Bedford in 1803. He became the head of the firm of Grinnell, Minturn & Co., New York. He represented a district of New York in Congress for one term, (1839–1841.) He was one of the most liberal contributors to Dr. Kane's Arctic expedition, (1853–55.) In 1869 he was appointed collector of the port of New York.

Gripenhielm. See FIGRELIUS.

Gris-aunt', (WILLIAM,) a learned English astronomer and physician, lived about 1350. Being accused of magic, he took refuge in France, where he acquired a high reputation in his profession. He wrote "Speculum Astrologiæ," and other scientific works.

Gris'com, (JOHN,) LL.D., an American educationist, a member of the Society of Friends, was born in Salem county, New Jersey, in 1774. He was for more than a quarter of a century an eminent teacher in New York, whither he removed in 1807. Among other things, he was chiefly instrumental in organizing the Society for the Prevention of Pauperism and Crime, which was the parent of many important reform movements. He was one of the first to introduce lectures on philosophy, chemistry, geology, etc., and, with Dr. Mott, Dr. Francis, and others, organized Rutgers Medical College, (New York,) in which he was made professor of chemistry and natural philosophy. "For thirty years," says Dr. Francis, "Dr. Griscom was the acknowledged head of all other teachers of chemistry among us." Died in 1852. He was author of "A Year in Europe," (2 vols., 1823.)

See a "Memoir of John Griscom," by his son, JOHN H. GRISCOM.

Griscom, (JOHN HOS'KINS,) a physician, a son of the preceding, was born in New York in 1809. He became professor of chemistry in the New York College of Pharmacy in 1836. He wrote, besides other works, "The Sanitary Condition of the Labouring Classes of New York," and "The Uses and Abuses of Air," etc., (1850.)

Grisebach, gREE'zeh-bȧk, (AUGUST HEINRICH RUDOLPH,) a German botanist, born at Hanover in 1814, became professor at Göttingen about 1847. Among his works are a "Journey through Roumelia," (1841,) and "Outlines (*Grundriss*) of Systematic Botany," (1854.)

Griselda, gRe-zĕl'dä, **Griseldis,** gRe-zel'dis, or **Gris'la,** the heroine of a popular romance of the middle ages, was, according to Italian tradition, the wife of Walter, Marquis of Saluzzo, who, in order to test her virtues, treated her for a time with great unkindness. Her patience and constancy triumphed over all; and her story has formed the subject of several works by celebrated writers, including Chaucer, who introduced it into his "Canterbury Tales," and Boccaccio, who has remodelled it in his "Decameron." It was also translated into Latin by Petrarch, and dramatized by Hans Sachs.

Grisi, gREE'see, (GIULIA,) (Madame MELCY,) a celebrated Italian vocalist, born at Milan in 1810, performed with distinguished success in the principal cities of Europe, and visited the United States in 1854. She had been married in 1836 to M. Girard de Melcy. Died at Berlin in 1869.

See FÉTIS, "Biographie Universelle des Musiciens."

Grisoni, gRe-so'nee, (GIUSEPPE,) a Florentine painter of history, landscapes, and portraits. Died in 1769.

Gris'wold, (ALEXANDER VIETS,) D.D., was born in Simsbury, Connecticut, in 1766. He was ordained as a pastor in the Episcopal Church in 1795. Upon the formation of the new diocese comprising the States of Massachusetts, Vermont, New Hampshire, and Rhode Island, in 1810, Dr. Griswold was elected the first bishop. He succeeded Bishop White as presiding bishop in 1836. Died in 1843.

See J. S. STONE, "Life of Bishop Griswold."

Griswold, (ROGER,) an American statesman, born in Lyme, Connecticut, in 1762, graduated at Yale College in 1780. Elected to Congress in 1794, he was for many years a leader of the Federalists. In 1807 he became judge of the supreme court of Connecticut, and in 1811 was elected Governor of the State. Died in 1812.

Griswold, (RUFUS WILMOT,) an American critic and editor, born at Benson, Rutland county, Vermont, in February, 1815. He became in early life a Baptist minister, and successively associate editor of "The New Yorker," "Brother Jonathan," and "The New World." He published a volume of Poems in 1841. He contributed to the history of American literature several valuable works, entitled "Poets and Poetry of America," (1842; 16th edition, 1855,) "The Prose Writers of America," (1846,) and "The Female Poets of America," (1848.) These contain short biographies and critical remarks. "His 'Prose Writers of America,'" says W. H. Prescott, "will be an important contribution to our national literature. The range of authors is very wide; the biographical notices full and interesting. . . . The selections appear to me to be made with discrimination, and the criticism shows a sound taste, and a correct appreciation of the qualities of the writers, as well as I can judge." "In these sketches," says the "North American Review" for January, 1856, "we find reason to admire the author's impartiality and kindness. We have been unable to find a single instance in which he has suffered any of the usual grounds of prejudice to warp his judgment or to scant his eulogy." Among his other works is "The Republican Court; or, American Society in the Days of Washington," with twenty-one portraits of distinguished women, (1854.) He edited "The International Magazine," (New York, 1850–52.) Died in the city of New York in August, 1857.

See HORACE BINNEY WALLACE, "Literary Criticisms and Literary Portraits."

Gritti, gRèt'tee, (ANDREA,) born at Venice in 1454, acquired a high reputation as a general in the war carried on by the Venetians against the League of Cambrai, and reconquered the towns of Brescia and Bérgamo from the French in 1512. Being afterwards made prisoner, he signed a treaty of alliance between Louis XII. and the Venetian republic. He was elected Doge in 1523. Died in 1538.

See N. BARBARIGO, "A. Gritti Principis Venetiarum Vita," 1793; DARU, "Histoire de Venise."

Gro'cyn, (WILLIAM,) an English philologist, born at Bristol in 1442. About 1489 he visited Rome, where he studied the Greek language, at that time little cultivated in England. He was appointed after his return professor of Greek at Oxford. He was an intimate friend of Erasmus, by whom he was highly esteemed. Died in 1519.

See WOOD, "Athenæ Oxonienses;" KNIGHT, "Life of Erasmus."

Groddeck, grod'dĕk, (ERNST GOTTFRIED,) a German philologist, born at Dantzic in 1762, became a professor at Wilna about 1804. He published "Elements of the Literary History of the Greeks," (in Latin, 1811,) and other similar works. Died in 1824.

See MALINOWSKI, "Biographie de Groddeck," 1825.

Groddeck, (GABRIEL,) a German philologist, born at Dantzic in 1672; died in 1709.

Groen van Prinsterer, groon vȧn pRin'steh-rer, a Belgian writer of the present age, published the "Archives of the House of Orange-Nassau," ("Archives de la Maison d'Orange-Nassau.")

See PRESCOTT, "History of Philip II.," vol. ii. book iii.

Groening. See GRÖNING.

Grohmann, gRo'mȧn, (JOHANN GOTTFRIED,) a German compiler, born in Upper Lusatia in 1763. He published a "Dictionary of the Fine Arts," (2 vols., 1795,) a "Biographical Dictionary," (7 vols., 1796–99,) and other works, which were favourably received. Died in 1805.

Grolier or **Grollier de Servier,** gRo'le-ȧ' dẹh sĕR'-ve-ȧ', (JEAN,) Vicomte d'Aguisy, a French scholar and patron of literature, born at Lyons in 1479, numbered among his friends Erasmus and Budæus. Died in 1565.

See DIBDIN's "Bibliomania."

Grolman, von, fon gRol'mȧn, (HEINRICH DIETRICH,) an eminent Prussian jurist, born at Bochum in 1740, filled several important posts under Frederick the Great, and became a member of the state council in 1817. He died in 1840, at the age of nearly a hundred years.

Grolman, von, (KARL LUDWIG WILHELM,) a German statesman and jurist, born at Giessen in 1775. He was created chancellor of the university in 1815, minister of state about 1819, and in 1821 president of the united ministry, (*Vereinten Ministerien.*) He published "Principles of Criminal Jurisprudence," (1798,) and other works. Died in 1829.

See "Nouvelle Biographie Générale."

Grolman, von, (KARL WILHELM GEORG,) a brother of the preceding, was born at Berlin in 1777. He served as a general in the principal campaigns against the French from 1806 till 1815. Died in 1843.

Gröning or **Groening,** grö′ning, (JOHANN,) an able German publicist and jurist, born at Wismar in 1669. He wrote valuable treatises on the law of nature and of nations. Died after 1700.

Gronov. See GRONOVIUS.

Gro-no′vĭ-us, or **Gro′nov,** (ABRAHAM,) son of Jakob Gronovius, noticed below, was born at Leyden in 1694. He was librarian of the university in that city, and published editions of Pomponius Mela, Justin, and Tacitus. Died in 1775.

Gronovius, or **Gronov,** (JAKOB,) an eminent philologist, son of Johann Friedrich, noticed below, was born at Deventer in October, 1645. He was appointed in 1679 professor of belles-lettres at Leyden. He published in 1697 his "Dictionary of Greek Antiquities," (" Thesaurus Antiquitatum Græcarum," 13 vols.,) which ranks very high among works of the kind. He also edited Polybius, Aulus Gellius, Macrobius, and other classics. Died at Leyden in 1716.

See NICÉRON, "Mémoires;" CREUZER, "Zur Geschichte der classischen Philologie;" "Nouvelle Biographie Générale."

Gronovius, or **Gronov,** (JOHANN FRIEDRICH,) a celebrated German scholar and antiquary, born at Hamburg in 1611. In 1658 he became professor of history and eloquence in the University of Leyden. He published valuable editions of Statius, Tacitus, Livy, Seneca, and other Latin classics. He also wrote a work entitled "De Sestertiis," (1643,) respecting ancient Greek and Roman coins, which is much esteemed. Died at Leyden in 1671. He was distinguished for his critical sagacity, and was one of the most profound Latin scholars of modern times.

See "Daventria illustrata," Leyden, 1651; WILKENS, "Leben des berühmten J. F. Gronovii," 1723; FOPPENS, "Bibliotheca Belgica;" CREUZER, "Zur Geschichte der classischen Philologie;" "Nouvelle Biographie Générale."

Gronovius, (JOHANN FRIEDRICH,) an eminent naturalist, a son of Jakob, noticed above, was born about 1690. He studied law, and became a magistrate of Leyden. He published "Flora Virginica," (1743,) Rauwolf's "Flora Orientalis," (1755,) and other works. He was a friend of Linnæus. Died in 1760.

Gronovius, (LAURENTIUS THEODORUS,) a son of the preceding, was a naturalist and a lawyer of Leyden. He published "Library of the Animal and Mineral Kingdoms," ("Bibliotheca Regni Animalis et Lapidei," 1740,) and Clayton's "Flora Virginica." Died in 1777.

Gronovius, (LAURENTIUS THEODORUS,) a Dutch antiquary and jurist, brother of Jakob, was born about 1660. He wrote "Emendationes Pandectarum," ("Emendations of the Pandects," 1688,) and notes on Vibius Sequester.

Gro′now, (REES HOWELL,) CAPTAIN, a British writer and officer, born in 1794. He served in the Peninsular war, (1808-14,) and wrote "Recollections and Reminiscences," (2 vols., 1863.) Died in 1865.

Groot, grōt, (GERARD,) or **GERARD THE GREAT,** a celebrated theologian, reformer, and founder of religious orders, was born at Deventer, Holland, in 1340. He was a popular preacher, and formed associations of friars, whom he employed in transcribing the Scriptures. They were called " Brethren of the Common Life." Died in 1384.

See HODGSON's "Reformers and Martyrs," Philadelphia, 1867.

Groot, (HUGO.) See GROTIUS.

Gropper, grop′per, (JOHANN,) a Roman Catholic theologian, born in Westphalia in 1501. He wrote a "Manual of the Christian Religion," (1546,) and several works against the Protestants. Died at Rome in 1558.

Gros, grō, (ANTOINE JEAN,) an eminent French painter, born in Paris in March, 1771, was a pupil of David. He worked several years in Italy, and returned home about 1802, after which he produced "The Plague

of Jaffa," "The Battle of Aboukir," (1806,) "The Battle of Eylau," (1808,) "The Capture of Madrid by Napoleon," (1810,) "The Battle of Wagram," and numerous good portraits. About 1824 he completed a large oil-painting in the cupola of Sainte-Geneviève. This is considered by some critics his master-piece. He was found dead in the Seine, near Meudon, in June, 1835.

See "Nouvelle Biographie Générale;" J. B. DELESTRE, "Gros et ses Ouvrages, ou Mémoires historiques," etc., 1845.

Gros, (ÉTIENNE,) a French philologist, born at Carcassonne in 1797. He translated the works of Ovid, (5 vols., 1836,) part of Dion Cassius, (4 vols., 1845-55,) and other classics. Died in 1856.

Gros de Boze. See BOZE, DE, (CLAUDE GROS.)

Gros, Le. See LEGROS, (NICOLAS and PIERRE.)

Grose, (FRANCIS,) an English antiquary, born in Middlesex in 1731. He was the author of "Views of Antiquities in England and Wales," (8 vols., 1787,) "Military Antiquities," (2 vols., 1788,) a "Treatise on Ancient Armour," etc., (1789,) "Antiquities of Scotland," (2 vols., 1790,) "Antiquities of Ireland," (2 vols., 1794,) and other works finely illustrated with his own designs. Captain Grose was noted for his wit, good humour, and conviviality, and was an intimate friend of the poet Burns, who has mentioned him in his poems. Died in 1791.

Grosier, gro′ze-à′, (JEAN BAPTISTE GABRIEL ALEXANDRE,) ABBÉ, a French critic, born at Saint-Omer in 1743. He was assistant editor of Fréron's "Année littéraire." He published, with Le Roux des Hauterayes, a "General History of China," (12 vols., 1777-84.) Died in 1823.

Grosley, gro′lā′, (PIERRE JEAN,) a French lawyer and facetious writer, born at Troyes in 1718. Among his works is a "Life of Pithou." Died in 1785.

See "Vie de Grosley," partly by himself, 1787; E. T. SIMON, "Notice sur la Vie de Grosley," 1826.

Gross, grōs, (JOHANN GOTTFRIED,) a German publicist, born in Baireuth in 1703, was for twenty-eight years editor of the able "Gazette" of Erlangen, (1741-68.) Died in 1768.

Gröss, (SAMUEL D.,) M.D., an American surgeon, born near Easton, Pennsylvania, in 1805. In 1856 he was appointed professor of surgery in the Jefferson Medical College in Philadelphia. Among his publications we may specify his "Elements of Pathological Anatomy," (2 vols., 1839; 3d edition, 1857,) and his "System of Surgery," (2 vols. 8vo, 1859.) He edited "American Medical Biography," (1861.)

Grosser, gros′ser, (SAMUEL,) a German philologist, born in Silesia in 1664. He wrote a work on logic, entitled "Light-House of the Intellect," ("Pharus Intellectus," 1697,) and other works. Died in 1736.

Grosseteste, gros′test, or **Grost′head,** [Lat. CAP′ITO,] (ROBERT,) an eminent English prelate, was the author of "Compendium Spheræ Mundi," and several other scientific treatises. He was made Bishop of Lincoln in 1235.

See S. PEGGE, "Life of Robert Grosseteste," 1793; MILNER, "Church History."

Grossi, gros′see, (TOMMASO,) an Italian poet, born at Bellano (province of Como) in 1791. Among his works are "Ildegonda," (1820,) "G. Maria Visconti," a tragedy, "The Lombards in the First Crusade," (1826,) and "Marco Visconti," a historical romance, which has been translated into English. "He is full of grace and elegance," says the "Nouvelle Biographie Générale;" "and these qualities do not exclude force, passion, and elevation." Died at Milan in 1853.

See CHERUBINI, "I Poeti vernacoli."

Grossmann, grōss′mån, (CHRISTIAN GOTTLOB LEBRECHT,) a learned German theologian, born at Priessnitz in 1783, became professor of theology at Leipsic. He founded in that city the Evangelical Union, called the Gustavus Adolphus Institution. He published a treatise "On the Reformation of the Constitution of the Protestant Church," etc., and other works.

Grossmann, (GUSTAV FRIEDRICH WILHELM,) a German dramatist and actor, born at Berlin in 1744. He wrote, among other popular comedies, "Wilhelmine von Blondheim," and "Only Six Plates." Died in 1796.

See GRÄSSE, "Geschichte der Deutschen Literatur."

ā, ē, ī, ō, ū, ȳ, *long;* à, è, ò, same, less prolonged; ă, ĕ, ĭ, ŏ, ŭ, ȳ, *short;* a, e, i, o, *obscure;* fàr, fàll, fàt; mĕt; nŏt; gŏŏd; mŏŏn;

Grostête or Grosteste, gro'têt', (CLAUDE,) a French Protestant theologian and writer, born at Orléans in 1647; died in London in 1713.

Grosvenor, gro'ven-or or grov'en-or, or Grovenor, (BENJAMIN,) born in London in 1675, was a popular preacher among the Independents. He was one of the lecturers at Salters' Hall, London. Died in 1758.

Grote, (GEORGE,) an eminent English historian, of German extraction, born near Beckenham, in Kent, in 1794. He was educated for the employment of a banker by his father, one of the firm of Prescott, Grote & Co. in London. His earliest literary productions were contributions to the Westminster and Edinburgh Reviews, and a treatise on "On the Essentials of Parliamentary Reform." In 1832 he represented London in Parliament, where he distinguished himself by the liberality of his views. He was twice re-elected, but in 1841 retired from public life. In 1846 he published the first two volumes of his "History of Greece." The remaining volumes, amounting in all to twelve, and ending at the death of Alexander, appeared successively between 1847 and 1856. Mr. Grote, in the words of a critic in the "London Quarterly," "unites the practical knowledge of the British statesman with the erudition of a German professor;" and the same writer pronounces his "History of Greece" "the most important contribution to historical literature in modern times." He has also published "Plato and the other Companions of Socrates," (3 vols., 1865,) and a review of Stuart Mill's "Examination of Sir William Hamilton's Philosophy," (1868.) His wife (originally Mrs. HARRIET LEWIN) has written a Life of Ary Scheffer, and other works.

See "London Quarterly" for June, 1846, April, 1850, July, 1856, and January, 1866; "Edinburgh Review" for October, 1846, January, 1850, July, 1851, July and October, 1853, and April, 1866; MÉRIMÉE, "Mélanges historiques et littéraires."

Grotefend, gro'teh-fênt', (FRIEDRICH AUGUST,) a German philologist, nephew of Georg Friedrich, noticed below, was born at Ilfeld in 1798; died in 1836.

Grotefend, (GEORG FRIEDRICH,) a German scholar and antiquary, born at Münden in 1775. He was director of the lyceum or gymnasium of Hanover for twenty-eight years, (1821-49.) He published several valuable treatises on the cuneiform writings of Persepolis and Babylon, and made contributions to Ersch and Gruber's "Encyclopædia." He also wrote a work "On the Geography and History of Ancient Italy," (1840-42.) He is said to have been the first who deciphered the cuneiform inscriptions. Died in December, 1853.

Grothusen, von, fon grōt'hoo'zen, (CHRISTIAN ALBRECHT,) BARON, a general, born probably in Germany. He entered the service of Charles XII. of Sweden, of whom he became a favoured companion, and treasurer. He accompanied that king in his retreat into Turkey in 1709. He was killed in battle in the island of Rügen in 1714.

Grotius, gro'she-us, or De Groot, deh grōt, (HUGO,) an eminent Dutch jurist and theologian, and one of the most celebrated scholars of his time, was born at Delft, April 10, 1583. As a child he was remarkable for precocity of intellect, and is said to have written Latin verses when but eight years of age. He studied at Leyden under Joseph Scaliger and the theologian Junius, and devoted himself to divinity, law, and mathematics. In 1598 he accompanied a Dutch embassy to Paris, on which occasion Henry IV. presented him with a golden chain. Soon after his return, in 1599, he published editions of several classics, and wrote a Latin poem entitled "Prosopopœia," which was greatly admired and translated into French and Greek. In 1613 he obtained the important post of pensionary of Rotterdam, which gave him a seat in the Assembly of the States of Holland and in that of the States-General. Being sent to England in 1615 on some public business, he formed the acquaintance of Isaac Casaubon. In 1618 he was involved in the defeat and misfortune of the Liberal or Arminian party, of which his friend Barneveldt was the leader. He was tried for treason, and unjustly condemned to perpetual imprisonment, and his property was confiscated. In June, 1619, he was sent to the fortress of Loevestein. He here devoted himself to study, and wrote, during his captivity, several works, among which was his celebrated treatise "On the Truth of the Christian Religion," ("De Veritate Religionis Christianæ," 1627.) At the end of eighteen months, Grotius escaped from his prison by means of a stratagem devised by his wife, who had been permitted to share his confinement. He went immediately to France, where he was well received by Louis XIII., who granted him a pension of three thousand livres. On the death of the stadtholder Maurice, Grotius was persuaded by his friends to return to Holland in 1631, but was again compelled to leave it. In 1634 he was appointed councillor to the Queen of Sweden by Chancellor Oxenstiern, and her ambassador to the court of France. In 1645 he repaired to Stockholm, where he was received with the greatest favour by Queen Christina; but, soon becoming weary of court life, he embarked for Lubeck in August. After a stormy passage, he arrived at Rostock, very ill from exposure and fatigue, and died on the 28th of August, 1645. Grotius left numerous works on jurisprudence, divinity, history, and poetry. Referring to his theological works, Leibnitz said that he preferred Grotius to all other commentators. His treatise on International Law, ("De Jure Belli et Pacis,") a work of the greatest merit, has been translated into the principal European languages. Among his historical productions we may mention "The History of the Goths, Vandals, and Lombards," "Belgian History and Annals," and "On the Origin of the American Tribes." These were all written in excellent Latin. His Latin poems comprise three tragedies and numerous lyrical and elegiac compositions. Grotius was distinguished for sincere piety, and his character combined mildness with remarkable energy.

See BUTLER, "Life of H. Grotius;" LUDEN, "H. Grotius nach seinen Schicksalen und Schriften dargestellt," 1806; LÉVESQUE DE BURIGNY, "Vie de H. Grotius," 1750, (and English version of the same, London, 1754;) BAYLE, "Historical and Critical Dictionary;" CASPAR BRANDT, "Historie van het Leven des Heeren H. de Groot," 2 vols., 1727; G. F. CREUZER, "Luther und Grotius, oder Glaube und Wissenschaft," 1846; NICÉRON, "Mémoires;" "Nouvelle Biographie Générale;" LONGFELLOW, "Poets and Poetry of Europe;" "Edinburgh Review" for October, 1860.

Grotius, (PIETER,) a son of the preceding, was born in 1610. He was appointed in 1660 pensionary at Amsterdam, and was afterwards ambassador to Denmark, Sweden, and France. Died in 1680.

Grotius, (WILLEM,) a Dutch jurist, born at Delft in 1597, was a brother of the celebrated Hugo Grotius. He was appointed advocate of the India Company in 1639. He published several legal works in Latin. Died in 1662.

Gro'to or Grot'to, (LUDOVICO,) an Italian poet, called "Il Cieco d'Adria," ("The Blind Man of Adria,") was born at Adria in 1541. He wrote numerous plays and poems, which had a temporary popularity. Died in 1585.

See GINGUENÉ, "Histoire Littéraire d'Italie."

Grouchy, groo'she', or Grouché, groo'shà', [Lat. GRU'CHIUS,] (NICOLAS,) a French scholar and Protestant, born about 1520. He published, besides other works, "De Comitiis Romanorum Libri tres," (1555,) and "The Logic of Aristotle," (1558.) Died at La Rochelle in 1572.

Grouchy, (SOPHIA.) See CONDORCET.

Grouchy, de, deh groo'she', (EMMANUEL,) MARQUIS, a celebrated French general, born in Paris in 1766. He entered the republican army about 1790, and as major-general commanded the cavalry in the campaign against Savoy, (1792.) He was soon after sent against the Vendeans, whom he defeated in several engagements. He served under Moreau in the campaign of Piedmont, (1798,) and was severely wounded at the battle of Novi and made prisoner by the Austrians. He was released after a year's captivity, and, having joined the army of Moreau, assisted in gaining the victory of Hohenlinden. He was conspicuous for his skill and courage in the battles of Jena and Eylau, and at Friedland, where he commanded the cavalry. His services on this occasion were mentioned by Napoleon with high commendation. He was appointed governor of Madrid in 1808. In the campaign of 1812, Napoleon gave a signal proof of his confidence in Grouchy by placing him at the head of

ε as k; ç as s; ğ hard; ġ as j; G, H, K, guttural; N, nasal; R, trilled; š as z; ᵗh as in this. (☞See Explanations, p. 23.)

69

his "Sacred Battalion." His conduct in the engagements of Brienne, La Rothière, and Vauchamps won for him the applause of the nation, and he was soon after made a marshal, (1814.) On the 18th of June, 1815, while the battle of Waterloo was in progress, General Grouchy, who was stationed near Wavre, was urged by his officers to march in that direction; but he refused to disobey the orders he had received from the emperor. He became an exile in 1815, and was restored to the rank of marshal in 1830. Died in 1847.

See THIERS, "Histoire du Consulat et de l'Empire;" JOMINI, "Précis politique et militaire de la Campagne de 1815;" "Opinions et Jugements de Napoléon;" NORVINS, "Histoire de Napoléon;" "Nouvelle Biographie Générale." ☞ Respecting the question of Grouchy's responsibility for the defeat of Waterloo, see LIEUT.-COL. J. B. A. CHARRAS, "Histoire de la Campagne de 1815—Waterloo," Brussels, 2 vols. 8vo, 1858, 5th edition, 1863, (which ably and unanswerably refutes the falsehoods of Napoleon and his admirers against Grouchy and Ney;) E. QUIRET, "Histoire de la Campagne de 1815," 1862; LIEUT.-COL. CHARLES C. CHESNEY, "Waterloo Lectures," 1868; PIÉRART, "Le Drame de Waterloo," 1868.

Grouvelle, groo'vĕl', (PHILIPPE ANTOINE,) a French revolutionist and writer, born in Paris in 1758. As secretary of the provisional executive council in 1792, he read to Louis XVI. the decree of the Convention which condemned him to death. He was sent as minister to Denmark in 1793, and in 1800 was elected to the legislative body. He published a "Historical Memoir of the Templars," etc., and other works. Died in 1806.

Grōve, (HENRY,) an English dissenting divine, born in Somersetshire in 1683, wrote a treatise "On the Immortality of the Soul," (1718,) and other religious works, which are highly commended by Doddridge. He was director of an academy at Taunton. Died in 1738.

Grove, (JOSEPH,) an English writer, was an attorney of Richmond. He was the author of the "Life and Times of Cardinal Wolsey," (4 vols., 1742–44,) and other works. Died in 1764.

Grove, (WILLIAM ROBERT,) F.R.S., an eminent English electrician and natural philosopher, born at Swansea in July, 1811. He graduated at Oxford in 1835, studied law, and became a successful barrister. He devoted much attention to physical science, in which he has made important discoveries. He invented, about 1839, the nitric-acid battery which bears his name, and effected the recomposition of water by the battery. In a lecture delivered in 1842 he maintained or suggested the doctrine that heat, light, and electricity are mutually convertible, and that heat is a mode of motion. This theory was more fully developed in his "Correlation of Physical Forces," (4th edition, 1862.) He received the medal of the Royal Society in 1847, and was chosen vice-president of that institution. He contributed to the "Philosophical Transactions" numerous treatises on electricity, etc.

See DR. F. HOEFER, article in the "Nouvelle Biographie Générale."

Grovenor. See GROSVENOR.

Grō'ver, (CUVIER,) an American general, born at Bethel, Maine, about 1830, graduated at West Point in 1850. He commanded a division of General Banks's army at the capture of Port Hudson, July, 1863, and a division under General Sheridan at the battle of Cedar Creek, October 19, 1864.

Grōw, (GALUSHA A.,) an American politician, born in Windham county, Connecticut, in 1823. He studied law, was admitted to the bar in 1847, and settled in Susquehanna county, Pennsylvania. He represented the fourteenth district of Pennsylvania in Congress from December, 1859, to March, 1863, and was chosen Speaker of the House of Representatives by the Republicans in December, 1861.

Grozelier, groz'le-à', (NICOLAS,) born at Beaune, in France, in 1692, published, besides other works, a "Collection of Fables in Verse." Died in 1778.

Grubenmann, groo'ben-mȧn', or **Grubemann,** groo'beh-mȧn', (JOHANN ULRICH,) a Swiss architect of the eighteenth century, born at Teufen. He built a noble bridge over the Rhine at Schaffhausen, and another at Reichenau. These were burned by the French in 1799.

Gruber, groo'ber, (GREGOR MAXIMILIAN,) a German antiquary, born at Horn, in Austria, in 1739, was professor of history at Vienna. He wrote, besides other works, a

"System of Diplomatics for Austria and Germany," (1783.) Died in 1799.

Gruber, (JOHANN DANIEL,) a German jurist and historian, born in Franconia, wrote a work on the early history of Livonia, ("Origines Liviniæ," 1740.) Died in 1748.

Gruber, (JOHANN GOTTFRIED,) a distinguished German scholar and miscellaneous writer, born at Naumburg in 1774. His essays "On the Literature of Romance," and his "Comparison of the Philosophy of many Nations," won for him the regard of Wieland, who chose him for his biographer. In 1815 he was appointed professor of philosophy at Halle. He soon after became engaged with Ersch in the publication of the "Universal Encyclopædia of Sciences and Arts," ("Allgemeine Encyklopaedie," etc.,) extending to more than one hundred volumes 4to. In 1818 he published a complete edition of Wieland's works, accompanied by a biography. He was also a contributor to the "Conversations-Lexikon" and to the "Universal Literary Gazette." Died in 1851.

Gruchius. See GROUCHY, (NICOLAS.)

Grudius. See EVERARD.

Grueneisen. See GRÜNEISEN.

Gruenewald. See GRÜNEWALD.

Gruithuisen, groit'hoi'zen, or HROIT'hoi'zen, (FRANZ VON PAULA,) an astronomer, surgeon, and scientific writer, born in 1774. He was the inventor of a surgical instrument for performing lithotrity, for which he received from the French Academy a prize of one thousand francs. Died in 1852.

See "Nouvelle Biographie Générale."

Grumbach, von, fon grōōm'bȧk', (WILHELM,) a German adventurer, born in 1503, was the leader of an insurrection against the government, commonly called "Grumbach's Rebellion." Having captured and plundered the city of Würzburg in 1563, he was put under the ban of the empire, and in 1566 was taken and executed.

Grün, (ANASTASIUS.) See AUERSPERG.

Grunæus. See GRYNÆUS.

Grund, grōōnt, (JOHANN JAKOB NORBERT,) a German miniature-painter, born at Günzenhausen in 1755, became professor in the Academy of Florence. He wrote "Painting among the Greeks, or the Rise, Progress, and Decadence of Painting," (2 vols., 1811.) Died in 1815.

Grundtvig, grōōnt'vig, (NICOLAI FREDERIK SEVERIN,) a distinguished Danish theologian, poet, and historian, was born at Udby, in Seeland, in September, 1783. He published in 1808 "Mythology of the North," ("Nordens Mythologie," revised edition, 1832,) which treats the subject in a poetical and philosophical spirit. He preached for some time at Copenhagen, and acquired great influence as a theologian. In 1820 he was appointed pastor of Prästöe. He produced several poetical and historical works, which, according to P. L. Moller, are characterized by sublime inspirations and mystical tendencies. He became minister of a church of Copenhagen in 1839. Since 1848 he has been an active member of the Diet and a leader of the Anti-German party.

See HOWITT'S "Literature and Romance of Northern Europe;" "Nouvelle Biographie Générale."

Grundtvig, (SVEN HERSLEB,) a Danish writer, a son of the preceding, was born at Christianshavn in 1824. His favourite subjects are the songs and popular traditions of his country. Among his publications is "The Ancient Popular Songs of Denmark," (2 vols., 1853–56.)

See ERSLEW, "Almindeligt Forfatter-Lexicon."

Grün'dȳ, (FELIX,) an American lawyer and Senator, born in Berkeley county, Virginia, in 1777. He removed to Nashville, Tennessee, about 1808, and in 1811 was elected a member of Congress, in which he supported Mr. Madison's administration. He was chosen a Senator of the United States in 1829, as a political friend of General Jackson, and was re-elected in 1833. In 1838 he was appointed attorney-general of the United States. Having resigned in 1840, he was again elected a Senator. Died in December, 1840.

See "National Portrait-Gallery of Distinguished Americans," vol. iii.

Grüneisen or **Grueneisen,** grün'ī'zen, (KARL,) a German writer and divine, born at Stuttgart in 1802.

He published a collection of popular songs, (" Lieder," 1823,) and other works.

Gruner, groo′nẹr, (CHRISTIAN GOTTFRIED,) a German physician, born at Sagan, in Silesia, in 1744, became professor of botany at Jena. He published " Library of Ancient Physicians," (2 vols., 1782,) and other medical works. Died in 1815.

See MEUSEL, "Gelehrtes Deutschland."

Gruner, groo′nẹr, (GOTTLIEB SIEGMUND,) a Swiss naturalist, born at Berne in 1717. He published a " Description of the Swiss Glaciers," (3 vols., 1762,) and other works. Died in 1778.

Gruner, (JOHANN FRIEDRICH,) a German philologist, born at Coburg in 1723. He became professor of theology at Halle, and wrote some theological works. He published good editions of Eutropius, (1752,) Aurelius Victor, (1757,) and Velleius Paterculus, (1762.) Died in 1778.

See HARLESIUS, "Vitæ Philologorum;" HIRSCHING, "Historisch-literarisches Handbuch."

Gruner, (JOHANN GERHARD,) a German historical writer, born at Coburg in 1734 ; died in 1790.

Gruner, (WILHELM HEINRICH LUDWIG,) an eminent German engraver, born at Dresden in 1801. He published two splendid works, entitled " Fresco Decorations and Studies," (1844,) and " The Decorations of the Garden Pavilion in the Grounds of Buckingham Palace," with text by Mrs. Jameson, (1846.) In 1851 he was employed in the decorations of the Crystal Palace in London. Among his finest prints are " Christ on the Mount of Olives," and several Madonnas, after Raphael.

Gruner, von, fon groo′nẹr, (KARL JUSTUS,) a German diplomatist, born at Osnabrück in 1777, entered the Prussian civil service. About 1814 he was one of the important agents of the allies. Died in 1820.

Grunert, groo′nẹrt, (JOHANN AUGUST,) an able German mathematician, born at Halle in 1797. He published " Spheroidal Trigonometry," (1833,) and " Contributions to Meteorological Optics and its Auxiliary Sciences," (1850.)

Grünewald or **Gruenewald,** grü′nẹh-wȁlt′, (MATTHÄUS,) a German painter, supposed to have been a native of Aschaffenburg. Among his works is a "Crucifixion," which displays great power. He was contemporary with Albert Dürer, whom, in the opinion of many critics, he nearly equalled.

Gru-pel′lo, de, (GABRIEL,) a Belgian sculptor, born at Grammont in 1644 ; died in 1730.

Grupen, groo′pẹn, (CHRISTIAN ULRICH,) a German antiquary and jurist, born at Harburg in 1692, wrote treatises on mediæval antiquities, etc. Died in 1767.

Gruppe, grŏŏp′pẹh, (OTTO FRIEDRICH,) a German philosophical and critical writer, born at Dantzic in 1804, became professor-extraordinary of philosophy in Berlin in 1844. In his works entitled "Antæus" and "The Crisis of Philosophy in the Nineteenth Century" (1834) he has assailed the system of Hegel. He wrote "Alboin," an epic, (1830,) and other poems.

Gruter, grü′tẹr, or HRÜ′tẹr, or **Gruytère,** grü-e′taiR′, [Lat. GRUTE′RUS,] (JAN,) an eminent scholar, was born at Antwerp in 1560. He studied at Cambridge and Leyden, and subsequently filled various professorships in Germany, at Wittenberg and Heidelberg. His greatest work is entitled "Ancient Inscriptions of the Whole World known to the Romans," (" Inscriptiones antiquæ totius Orbis Romanorum," about 1602.) He also published numerous editions of the classics, and " Lampas, sive Fax Artium liberalium," being a collection of the best critical and antiquarian treatises of the sixteenth century. Died at Heidelberg in 1627.

See F. H. FLAYDER, "Vita Gruteri," 1628 ; BAYLE, "Historical and Critical Dictionary;" NICÉRON, "Mémoires;" FÉLIX VAN HULST, "Jean Gruytère," 1847 ; "Nouvelle Biographie Générale."

Gruter, (PIETER,) a Dutch physician and writer, born about 1555. He published many Latin epistles, "Epistolarum Centuria," (1609.) Died at Amsterdam in 1634.

Grÿl′lus, [Gr. Γρύλλος,] a son of Xenophon, was killed at the battle of Mantinea, 362 B.C. According to tradition, he killed Epaminondas in this battle.

Grynæus, gRe-nā′ŭs, (JOHANN JAKOB,) a theologian, born at Bâle in 1540, was a grand-nephew of Simon, noticed below. He was professor of theology at Bâle,

and wrote commentaries on Scripture, and other works. Died in 1618.

See NICÉRON, "Mémoires;" J. J. BRUNN, " Vir sanctus et incomparabilis, hoc est Vita J. J. Grynæi," 1618.

Grynæus, (SAMUEL,) a Swiss jurist, son of the following, was born at Bâle in 1539 ; died in 1599.

Grynæus, (SIMON,) a distinguished Protestant theologian, born at Veringen, in Suabia, in 1493, was a friend of Melanchthon and Erasmus. He became professor of Greek at Heidelberg in 1523, removed to Bâle in 1536, and attended the conference at Worms in 1540. He discovered the last five books of Livy, published the "Almagest" of Ptolemy in Greek, (1538,) wrote several works, and translated Plato into Latin. He published in 1532 a curious work, entitled "The New World of Regions and Islands unknown to the Ancients," which contains the narratives of Marco Polo and many other travellers. Died at Bâle in 1541.

See MELCHIOR ADAM, "Vitæ Theologorum;" BRUCKER, "History of Philosophy."

Gryph. See GRYPHIUS.

Gryphius, gRee′fe-ŭs or grif′e-ŭs, or **Gryph,** gRĬf, originally **Greif,** gRĬf, (ANDREAS,) a celebrated German poet and dramatist, born in Silesia in 1616. Among his principal works are the tragedies of "Leo Armenius," "Cardenio and Celinda," and "Carolus Stuartus," and a very popular comedy, entitled " Peter Squenz." He is regarded as the greatest dramatic poet of the seventeenth century in Germany. His epigrams, lyrics, and spiritual odes also possess great merit. He was an accomplished linguist, and was well versed in mathematics and physical science. Died in 1664.

See J. HERMANN, " Ueber A. Gryphius ; literar-historischer Versuch," 1851 ; CASPAR KNORR, "Gedächtniss A. Gryphii," 1665.

Gryphius, (CHRISTIAN,) a son of the preceding, was born at Fraustadt in 1649. His "History of the Orders of Knighthood" (1697) is his best work. Died in 1706.

Gryphius, (SEBASTIAN,) a learned and celebrated printer, born in Suabia in 1493, settled at Lyons. Among his publications was a Latin Bible, (1550.) Died at Lyons in 1556.

See BAYLE, "Historical and Critical Dictionary."

Grÿph′on or **Grif′fon,** [Lat. GRY′PHUS or GRYPS, (plural GRY′PHES;) Gr. Γρύψ; Fr. GRIFFON, gRe′fôN′,] a monster of the classic mythology, having the body of a lion with the head and wings of an eagle. (See SEEMOORGH.)

Guadagni, goo-ä-dän′yee, (LEOPOLDO ANDREA,) an Italian jurist, born at Florence in 1705 ; died in 1785.

Guadagnini, goo-ä-dän-yee′nee, (GIAMBATTISTA,) an Italian ecclesiastic and controversial writer, born at Piacenza about 1720 ; died in 1806.

Guadagnoli, goo-ä-dän-yo′lee, (FILIPPO,) an Italian Orientalist, born at Magliano about 1596. He became professor of Arabic in the college di Sapienza at Rome. He published " Institutiones Linguæ Arabicæ," and an "Apology for Christianity," etc., (in Latin,) which is esteemed a standard work. Died in 1656.

See NICÉRON, "Mémoires."

Gua de Malves, de, dẹh gä dẹh mälv′, (JEAN PAUL,) a French mathematician, born at Carcassonne in 1713, became professor of philosophy in the College of France. He was a member of the Academy of Sciences, and published several scientific treatises. Died in 1788.

See DESESSARTS, "Siècles littéraires de la France."

Guadet, gä′dạ′, (MARGUERITE ÉLIE,) a French statesman, and one of the principal leaders of the Girondist party, was born near Bordeaux in 1758. He was a deputy in 1791 to the Legislative Assembly, where, says Lamartine, "he formed with Vergniaud and Gensonné a triumvirate of talent, opinion, and eloquence." One of his first acts was to accuse the French emigrants in conspiracy against the government ; and in 1792 he supported the decree of accusation against the brothers of the king, which was passed. He was soon after a deputy from Bordeaux to the National Convention, where he was conspicuous for his bold and vehement eloquence. In common with his colleagues, he at last yielded to the rage of the populace, and voted for the death of the king, after having appealed in vain to the people to sustain them in their efforts to preserve his life. On the downfall of his party, Guadet took refuge with his friends, near Bordeaux, where he was discovered, and was executed in that city in July, 1794.

See LAMARTINE, "History of the Girondists;" THIERS, "History of the French Revolution;" "Nouvelle Biographie Générale."

Guagnino, goo-ân-yee′no, (ALESSANDRO,) a historian, was born at Verona in 1548. He served in the Polish army against the Russians, and wrote a "History of Poland," ("Rerum Polonicarum Libri tres," 1574,) which is praised for accuracy and elegance. Died in 1614.

See ADELUNG, "Uebersicht der Reisenden in Russland bis 1700."

Gualandi, goo-â-lân′dee, (MICHELANGELO,) an Italian antiquary, born at Bologna in 1793. He published a valuable work on the fine arts, entitled "Memorie originali Italiani risguardanti le belle Arti," (3 vols., 1840–45.)

Gualdim-Paes, gwâl-deen′ pâ-ês′, a Portuguese ecclesiastic, born at Braga, founded, about 1160, the magnificent monastery of Thomar. Died in 1195.

Gualdo-Priorato, goo-âl′do pRe-o-râ′to,(GALEAZZO,) Count of Comazzo, an Italian soldier, diplomatist, and historian, born at Vicenza in 1606. He served successively under Maurice, Prince of Orange, Count Mansfeld, and Wallenstein, and was afterwards sent on various important missions. He wrote a "History of the Wars of Ferdinand II. and Ferdinand III.," a "History of Wallenstein," (1643,) and other works. Died in 1678.

See M. A. ZORZI, "Vita di Gualdo-Priorato," in the "Opuscoli scientifici," Venice, 1728 ; "Nouvelle Biographie Générale."

Gualterus, gwâl-tā′rŭs, sometimes written **Gualther,** (RUDOLF,) a Swiss divine, born at Zurich in 1518, was a son-in-law of Zwingle. He became first minister of Zurich, and wrote several popular works. Died in 1586.

Gualtieri, (GIOVANNI.) See CIMABUE.

Gualtieri, goo-âl-te-â′ree, (NICCOLÒ,) an Italian physician and naturalist, born in Tuscany in 1688, was professor of medicine at Pisa. Died in 1744.

Guarco, goo-aR′ko, (ANTONIOTTO,) a son of Niccolò, noticed below, became Doge of Genoa in 1394. He was assassinated in Parma about 1404.

Guarco, (NICCOLÒ,) was elected Doge of Genoa in 1378. Under his rule a war was carried on between the Genoese and the Venetians. Died in 1383.

Guardi, goo-aR′dee, (FRANCESCO,) a painter, born at Venice in 1712, was a pupil and successful imitator of Canaletto. He painted Venetian scenery and architecture. Died in 1793.

See LANZI, "History of Painting in Italy."

Guarienti, goo-â-re-ên′tee, **Guariento,** goo-â-re-ên′to, or **Guariero,** goo-â-re-â′ro, written also **Guarente,** an Italian painter, who lived about 1360–90. He painted the hall of the Grand Council at Venice, which in 1508 was renewed by Tintoretto.

See VASARI, "Lives of the Painters."

Guarin, gâ′rân′, (PIERRE,) a French ecclesiastic and distinguished Orientalist, born in Normandy in 1678. He published "Grammatica Hebraica et Chaldaica," and other valuable works. Died in Paris in 1729.

Guarini, goo-â-ree′nee, (CAMILLO Guarino—goo-â-ree′no,) an Italian architect, born at Módena in 1624. Among his works are the Chapel Royal at Turin, and the Convent of the Theatines at Módena. Died in 1683.

See QUATREMÈRE DE QUINCY, "Vies des plus célèbres Architectes."

Guarini, (GIAMBATTISTA,) son of Guarini da Verona, noticed below, became professor of Greek at Ferrara, and numbered among his pupils Aldus Manutius and Giraldus. He wrote a treatise "On the Sect of Epicurus," ("De Secta Epicuri,") and other works in Latin, and made translations from Demosthenes, Dion Chrysostom, and Saint Gregory Nazianzen. Died in 1513.

See TIRABOSCHI, "Storia della Letteratura Italiana."

Guarini, (GIAMBATTISTA,) a celebrated Italian poet, born at Ferrara December 10, 1537. He became professor of rhetoric in his native city about 1560, and was afterwards patronized by Alfonso, Duke of Ferrara, who made him a chevalier and employed him in various diplomatic missions. For these services he received little except empty honours. He published in 1590 his "Pastor Fido," a pastoral tragi-comedy, in verse, which met with brilliant success and was translated into the

principal languages of Europe. Guarini was the author of other dramas, and of a number of sonnets and madrigals. He was a friend of the poet Tasso. Died in Venice in 1612.

See TIRABOSCHI, "Storia della Letteratura Italiana ;" GINGUENÉ, "Histoire Littéraire d'Italie ;" APOSTOLO ZENO, "Vita del Guarini," in the "Galleria di Minerva ;" LONGFELLOW, "Poets and Poetry of Europe ;" NICÉRON, "Mémoires ;" "Lives of the Italian Poets," by REV. HENRY STEBBING, London, 1831.

Guarini da Verona, goo-â-ree′nee dâ vâ-ro′nâ, [Lat. VARI′NUS,] one of the restorers of classical literature in Italy, born at Verona in 1370. He studied Greek at Constantinople under Chrysoloras, and brought with him on his return a valuable collection of manuscripts. He afterwards became professor of Greek at Florence or Verona, being, it is said, the first Italian who publicly taught that language. He made a Latin translation of the first ten books of Strabo, and of portions of Plutarch Died in 1460.

See ROSMINI, "Vita e Disciplina di Guarini Veronese," etc., 3 vols., 1805 ; BAYLE, "Historical and Critical Dictionary ;" NICÉRON, "Mémoires ;" PAOLO GIOVIO, "Elogia Virorum illustrium."

Guarino. See FAVORINUS.

Guarnacci, goo-aR-nât′chee, (MARIO,) an Italian prelate and antiquary, born at Volterra in 1701, published, among other works, a "Dissertation on the Twelve Tables." Died in 1785.

Guarnieri-Ottoni, goo-aR-ne-â′ree ot-to′nee, (AURELIO,) an Italian antiquary, born at Osimo in 1748, wrote a work on the Claudian Way, etc. Died in 1788.

Guasco, da, dâ goo-âs′ko, (OTTAVIANO,) a writer, born at Pinerolo, in Piedmont, in 1712, published a work entitled "Satires of Prince Cantemir," etc., also an "Essay on the State of Sciences in France under Charles VI.," etc. Guasco was an intimate friend of Montesquieu. Died in 1781.

Guaspre, Le. See DUGHET.

Guatemozin, gwâ-te-mo′zin, or **Quah-te-mot′zin,** son-in-law and successor of Montezuma, Emperor of Mexico, was the last prince of the Aztec dynasty. After a brave defence of his capital against the Spaniards, he was forced to capitulate, and was taken prisoner. He was then cruelly tortured, by order of Cortez, to compel him to reveal where the treasures of the empire were concealed. Being afterwards unjustly accused of exciting his subjects to rebellion, he was put to death without any form of trial, in 1522. "Among all the names of barbarian princes, there are few entitled to a higher place on the roll of fame than Guatemozin. He was called to the throne in the convulsed and expiring hours of the monarchy, when the banded nations of Anahuac and the fierce European were thundering at the gates of the capital. No one can refuse his admiration to the intrepid spirit which could prolong a defence of his city while one stone was left upon another ; and our sympathies for the time are inevitably thrown more into the scale of the rude chieftain thus battling for his country's freedom, than into that of his civilized and successful antagonist." (Prescott's "Conquest of Mexico," vols. ii. and iii.)

Guay, gâ, (JACQUES,) a French gem-engraver, born at Marseilles in 1715 ; died in 1787.

Guay-Trouin. See DUGUAY-TROUIN.

Guazzesi, goo-ât-sâ′see, (LORENZO,) an Italian littérateur, born at Arezzo in 1708. He published several historical works. Died in 1764.

Guazzo, goo-ât′so, (MARCO,) an Italian poet and littérateur, born at Padua about 1496 ; died in 1556.

Guazzo, (STEFANO,) an Italian poet and essayist, born at Casali in 1530 ; died in 1593.

Gubbio, da, dâ goob′be-o, (ODERIGI,) an Italian painter, born at Gubbio, near Perugia, was a friend of Dante, who mentions him with honour in his great poem. He worked at Bologna, and was distinguished as a painter of missals and miniatures. Died about 1300.

See VASARI, "Lives of the Painters," etc.

Gubitz, goo′bits, (FRIEDRICH WILHELM,) a German engraver and littérateur, born at Leipsic in 1786. He wrote several dramas, and other works.

Gude. See GUDIUS.

Gudelinus. See GOUDELIN.

Gudenof. See GODOONOF.

ā, ē, ī, ō, ū, ȳ, *long;* à, ė, ò, same, less prolonged; ă, ĕ, ĭ, ŏ, ŭ, ў, *short;* ạ, ẹ, ị, ọ, *obscure;* fär, fàll, fât; mèt; nŏt; gŏŏd; mŏŏn;

Gudin, gü′dǎN′, (JEAN ANTOINE THÉODORE,) a celebrated marine painter, born in Paris in 1802, was a pupil of Girodet. Among his best works are "The Storm in the Bay of Algiers," a "View of Constantinople," "The Shipwreck," and a "View of Gibraltar."

Gudin de la Brenellerie, gü′dǎN′ dęh lǎ bRęh-nêl′re′, (PAUL PHILIPPE,) a French dramatic poet, born in Paris in 1738. He published a number of tragedies, and a mock-heroic poem entitled "The Conquest of Naples by Charles VIII." Died in 1812.

See "Notice sur Gudin de la Brenellerie," Paris, 1812.

Gudin de la Sablonnière, gü′dǎN′ dęh lǎ sǎ′blo′-ne-aiR′, (CÉSAR CHARLES ÉTIENNE,) COUNT, a French general, born at Montargis in 1768. He distinguished himself at Eylau, (1807,) Eckmühl, and Wagram, (1809,) and was killed at Volutina-Gora, in Russia, in 1812.

Gudius, goo′de-ůs, or **Gude**, goo′dęh, (GOTTLOB FRIEDRICH,) a German minister and writer, born at Lauban in 1701; died in 1756.

See MEISSNER, "Gedächtnissrede auf Gude," 1756.

Gudius or **Gude**, (MARQUARD,) a German philologist and antiquary, born at Rensburg in 1635, became councillor to the King of Denmark. He collected many manuscripts and Greek and Latin inscriptions, which were published in 1731. Died in 1689.

Gudmundsson, gōōd′mōōnd′son, (THORGEIR,) a distinguished scholar and antiquary of Iceland, born in 1794, was one of the founders of the Society of Northern Antiquaries at Copenhagen in 1845.

Gudmundus, gōōd-mōōn′důs, (ANDREAS,) a learned Icelander, wrote several antiquarian works, and a "Lexicon Islandico-Latinum." Died in 1654.

Guébriant, de, dęh gà′bRe′öN′, (JEAN BAPTISTE Budes—büd,) COMTE, a French marshal, born in Brittany in 1602. He served with great distinction in Germany during several campaigns of the Thirty Years' war, and in 1641 gained a signal victory over the Imperial troops at Wolfenbüttel. He was made a marshal in 1642. He was mortally wounded at Rothweil in 1643.

See LE LABOUREUR, "Histoire du Maréchal de Guébriant," 1657.

Guébriant, de, (RENÉE du Bec-Crispin—dü bĕk′-kRês′pǎN′,) wife of the preceding, was appointed in 1643 ambassadress-extraordinary to the King of Poland, being, it is said, the first woman who ever acted in that capacity independently of her husband. Died in 1659.

See "Lettres de Madame de Guébriant à la Princesse-Palatine Anne de Gonzague."

Guédier de Saint-Aubin, gà′de-ą′ dęh sǎN′tö′bǎN′, (HENRI MICHEL,) a French theologian, born at Gournay-en-Bray in 1695. He wrote "The Sacred History of the Two Covenants," (7 vols., 1741.) Died in 1742.

Gueel y Rente, hāl e rěn′tà, (Don JOSÉ,) a Spanish writer and statesman, born at Havana about 1820. He studied in Spain, became a deputy to the Cortes about 1854, and was re-elected in 1857. He had married in 1848 the Infanta Josefa, sister of the King of Spain. He has published poems entitled "Tears of the Heart" ("Lagrimas del Corazon") and "Sorrows of the Heart," ("Amarguras del Corazon,") and "Thoughts Moral and Political."

Guelf, **Guelph**, gwělf, or **Welf**, wělf, the name of a noble family in Germany, the founder of which lived in the time of Charlemagne.

Guelfo, gwěl′fo, **Welfo**, or **Guelf II.** flourished in the eleventh century. He was engaged in a contest with the emperor Conrad II., which was the beginning of the long strife between the Dukes of Bavaria and the German emperors.

Guelfo III. was created Duke of Carinthia by the emperor Henry III. as a reward for his services in the war with the Hungarians. Died about 1055.

Guelfo IV., called THE GREAT, was made Duke of Bavaria by Henry IV., but subsequently took up arms against him. After alternate victories and defeats, a peace was concluded in 1097. Died about 1120.

Guelfo V. succeeded his father, Guelfo IV., as Duke of Bavaria. He married Matilda, the heiress of Tuscany, and widow of Godfrey, Duke of Lorraine. After she had made a donation of her domains to the Church of Rome, Guelfo returned to Germany, where he took part

with Henry V. in his quarrel with his father, Henry IV. Died about 1120.

Guelfo VI., nephew of Guelfo V., and son of Henry the Black, was born in 1115. Having embraced the cause of his nephew, Henry the Lion, in his contest with the emperor Conrad III., he was defeated by that sovereign at Weinsberg in 1140. It was on this occasion that the war-cry of Guelphs (or Welfs) and Ghibelines was first used, the latter name being derived from Waiblingen, the seat of the Hohenstaufen family at Würtemberg. Died in 1191. The popes having taken sides with the Guelphs, the names of Guelph and Ghibeline were used to designate the parties of the emperor and the pope.

See EICHHORN, "Urgeschichte des Hauses der Welfen;" SISMONDI, "Histoire des Républiques Italiennes."

Guénard, gà′nǎR′, (ÉLISABETH,) Baronne de Méré, a romance-writer, born in Paris in 1751; died in 1829.

Guéneau de Montbéliard, gà′no′dęh mǒN′bà′le-ǎR′, (PHILIBERT,) an eminent French naturalist, born at Semur-en-Auxois in 1720. He was an intimate friend of Buffon, and prepared the ornithological department for his great work; he was also a contributor to the "Encyclopédie," and wrote an "Abridgment of the History and the Memoirs of the Academy of Sciences," (4 vols., 1770.) Died in 1785.

See QUÉRARD, "La France Littéraire."

Guénée, gà′nà′, (ANTOINE,) an eminent French ecclesiastic and controversial writer, born at Étampes in 1717, was for many years professor of rhetoric in the college Du Plessis in Paris. In 1785 he obtained the abbey of Loroy, in the diocese of Bourges. He wrote a very able work, entitled "Letters of some Portuguese, German, and Polish Jews to Voltaire," etc., in which he defends the Old Testament against Voltaire, clearly convicting him of contradictions and of ignorance. Died in 1803.

See QUÉRARD, "La France Littéraire."

Guenzi, goo-ên′zee, (GIOVANNI FRANCESCO,) an Italian poet and translator, born in 1713; died in 1753.

Guépin, gà′pǎN′, (AUGUSTE,) a French writer and physician, born at Pontivy about 1805. His chief work is "The Philosophy of Socialism," (1850.)

Guérard, gà′rǎR′, (BENJAMIN EDME CHARLES,) a French antiquary, born at Montbard in 1797. He was an assistant librarian in the Royal Library of Paris, and published treatises on the social state of France in the middle ages. Died in 1854.

Guérard, (ROBERT,) a French Benedictine monk, born at Rouen about 1641. He published an "Abridgment of the Bible," (1707.) Died in 1715.

Guerazzi, goo-à-ràt′see or goo-êr-àt′see, or **Guerrazzi**, (FRANCESCO DOMENICO,) an Italian writer and Liberal statesman, born at Leghorn in 1805. In 1848 he was appointed president of the cabinet and minister of the interior by the grand duke Leopold II. He was the author of the "Siege of Florence," ("Assedio di Firenze,") and other historical romances, and an "Apology for the Political Life of F. D. Guerazzi," (1851.)

See "Memorie di F. D. Guerrazzi," 1848, written by himself.

Guerchin. See GUERCINO.

Guerchois, le, lęh gěR′shwä′, (MADELÈNE,) a French lady, eminent for her talents and piety, born in Paris in 1679, was a sister of Chancellor D'Aguesseau. She wrote "Christian Reflections on the Historical Books of the Old Testament." Died in 1740.

Guerchy, de, dęh gěR′she′, (CLAUDE FRANÇOIS LOUIS RÉGNIER,) COMTE, a French general, born in 1715, served in Flanders under Marshal Saxe, and particularly distinguished himself at Fontenoy and Hastenbeck, (1757.) He was afterwards ambassador to London. Died in 1767.

See "Lettres et Mémoires du Maréchal de Saxe."

Guercino, gwêR-chee′no or goo-êR-chee′no, [Fr. GUERCHIN, gěR′shǎN′,] (GIOVANNI FRANCESCO Barbieri—baR-be-ā′ree,) called GUERCINO DA CENTO, a celebrated Italian painter, born at Cento, near Bologna, in 1590. He at first painted in the style of the Caracci, but he afterwards adopted that of Caravaggio. Among his master-pieces are "The Death of Dido," "Santa Petronilla," in the Capitol at Rome, "Aurora," a fresco in the Villa Ludovisi, a "Saint William," and "Angels weeping over the Dead Body of Christ." Guercino was an intimate friend of Guido Reni. He worked many years at Cento, from which he removed to Bologna in 1642. His works are mostly oil-paintings, and include about a hundred altar-pieces. Died at Bologna in 1666.

See LANZI, "History of Painting in Italy;" CALVI, "Notizie della Vita e delle Opere di G. F. Barbieri," 1808; DOMENICO C. MORA, "Vite di Benvenuto Tisio e di G. F. Barbieri," 1842; CHARLES BLANC, "Histoire des Peintres;" BRYAN, "Dictionary of Painters."

Gueret, gĕh-rȧ́', (GABRIEL,) a French lawyer and miscellaneous writer, born in Paris in 1641. Among his principal works are his "Conversations on the Eloquence of the Pulpit and the Bar," "Parnassus Reformed," and "War of the Authors." Died in 1688.

See QUÉRARD, "La France Littéraire."

Guericke, gĕr'rik-kĕh, (HEINRICH ERNST FERDINAND,) a German theologian, born at Wettin, in Prussian Saxony, in 1803, published a "Manual of Church History," (1833,) and other works.

Guericke, von, fon gĕr'ik-kĕh or gä'rik-kĕh, (OTTO,) a celebrated German savant and experimental philosopher, born at Magdeburg in 1602. Having studied mathematics and mechanics at Leyden, he visited France and England. After his return, he was made in 1646 burgomaster of Magdeburg. In 1650 he invented the air-pump, of which he made the first public experiment before the Diet at Ratisbon in 1651. Having fitted together two large hollow hemispheres made of copper and brass, with strong rings attached to them, to which horses were harnessed, he exhausted the air from the globe; and it was only after the number of horses was increased to upwards of thirty that the parts were separated. He was also the inventor of the instrument called Guericke's Weather Mannikin, which was used, before the invention of the barometer, to denote the changes of the weather. He published in 1672 a work entitled "New Magdeburgian Experiments, as they are called, relating to a Vacuum," ("Experimenta Nova, ut vocant, Magdeburgica, de vacuo Spatio.") Died in 1686.

See FONTENELLE, "Éloges historiques des Académiciens;" JÖCHER, "Allgemeines Gelehrten-Lexikon."

Guérin, gȧ'rȧn', (ADOLPHE CLAUDE,) COLONEL, a French officer, born at Mortagne in 1805, served in several campaigns in Algeria as chief of engineers. He subsequently distinguished himself in the Crimean war, and was killed in June, 1855, at the siege of Sebastopol, where he had rendered important services as chief of the staff of engineers.

See "Nouvelle Biographie Générale."

Guérin, (FRANÇOIS,) a French scholar, born in Touraine in 1681, translated Livy and Tacitus into French. Died in 1751.

Guérin, (GILLES,) an able French sculptor, born in Paris in 1606. He was employed in the decoration of the Louvre. Among his chief works is a statue of Louis XIV. Died in 1678.

Guérin, (JEAN BAPTISTE PAULIN,) a French painter, born at Toulon in 1783, worked at Paris. Among his productions are "Adam and Eve driven from Eden," (1827,) and a "Holy Family," (1829.) Died in 1855.

Guérin, (JOSEPH XAVIER,) a French physician and naturalist, born at Avignon in 1775. Among his works are a "Panorama of Avignon and Vaucluse," (1829,) and "Meteorologic Observations," (1839.) Died in 1850.

Guérin, (JULES,) a French physician, born at Boussu (Belgium) in 1801. He studied and afterwards resided at Paris. He gave special attention to malformations of the feet, and wrote an able treatise on Orthopedy, (16 vols., 1837,) which gained the prize of the Academy of Paris.

Guérin, (NICOLAS FRANÇOIS,) a French scholar and writer, born at Nancy in 1711; died in 1782.

Guérin, (PIERRE NARCISSE,) BARON, an eminent French painter, born in Paris in 1774, was a pupil of Regnault. He produced about 1800 "Marcus Sextus" and "Phèdre et Hippolyte," which had great popularity. His subjects are mostly antique, and his style is classic. His chief merits are purity of contour, good taste in details, and harmony of colour. He was director of the French Academy at Rome from 1822 to 1828. Among

his works are "Aurora and Cephalus," (1810,) "Dido listening to Æneas," (1817,) and a "Clytemnestra." He died at Rome in 1833.

See QUATREMÈRE DE QUINCY, "Notice sur la Vie de P. Guérin," 1833; "Nouvelle Biographie Générale."

Guérin, de, dĕh gȧ'rȧn', (EUGÉNIE,) a French writer, born at the château Du Cayla, in Languedoc, in 1805. She was endowed with rare intelligence, and was an example of deep and fervent piety. Her life may be said to have been absorbed in her brother Maurice, to whom she was intensely devoted. She died in May, 1848, leaving a Journal and Letters, which were published in 1863. "Her Journal," says the "Edinburgh Review" for July, 1864, "is the outpouring of one of the purest and most saintly minds that ever existed upon earth. The style is exquisitely beautiful, and it lingers in the memory like the dying tones of an Æolian harp, full of ineffable sweetness. Amidst the impurity which has so long flooded French literature, it is delightful to come upon the streams of thought that flowed in limpid clearness from the fountain of her mind, and to find in a young French girl a combination of piety and genius with so much felicity and force of expression that her countrymen have not scrupled to compare her style to that of Pascal himself."

Guérin, de, (MAURICE du Cayla—dü kȧ'lä',) a French poet, brother of the preceding, was born near Albi, in Languedoc, in 1810. He died prematurely in 1839, leaving several poetical fragments, among which is "Le Centaure." "This revealed," says Sainte-Beuve, "a nature of talent so new, so powerful, so vast, that the word genius seems appropriate to it." His Letters, Poems, etc. were published in 1860, under the title of "Maurice de Guérin: Reliquiæ," (2 vols.,) preceded by a biographical notice of the author by Sainte-Beuve.

See SAINTE-BEUVE, "Causeries du Lundi;" "Nouvelle Biographie Générale;" "Fraser's Magazine" for January, 1863.

Guérin du Rocher, gȧ'rȧn' dü ro'shȧ', (PIERRE,) a learned French Jesuit, born at Falaise in 1731, wrote "The True History of Fabulous Times," (3 vols., 1776.) He was massacred in September, 1792.

Guérin-Méneville, gȧ'rȧn' mȧn'vĕl', (FÉLIX ÉDOUARD,) a French naturalist, born at Toulon in 1799, published a "Magazine of Zoology, Comparative Anatomy, and Palæontology," (33 vols., 1831-44,) and other works.

Guerle. See DEGUERLE.

Guernier. See DUGUERNIER.

Gueronnière. See LA GUERONNIÈRE.

Guéroult, gȧ'roo', (ADOLPHE,) a French journalist, born at Radepont (Eure) in 1810. He became chief editor of the "Presse," a daily paper of Paris, in 1857.

Gueroult, gĕh-roo', (PIERRE CLAUDE BERNARD,) a French classical scholar, born at Rouen in 1744. He was director of the Normal School at Paris under the empire. He translated Pliny's "Natural History," (3 vols., 1803,) and some works of Cicero. Died in 1821.

Guerra, goo-ĕr'rä or gwĕr'rä, (GIOVANNI,) an Italian architect and painter, born at Módena in 1544. He was employed by Sixtus V. to adorn the Vatican and Quirinal palace. Died in 1618.

See LANZI, "History of Painting in Italy."

Guerre, de la, dĕh lä gair, (ÉLISABETH CLAUDE Jacquet—zhä'kȧ',) a French lady, celebrated for her musical talents, was born in Paris about 1659. Among her compositions are a Te Deum and a number of cantatas. Died in 1729.

Guerre-Dumolard, gair dü'mo'lȧr',(JEAN,) a French jurist, born at Allevard (Dauphiné) in 1761; died in 1845.

Guerrero, gĕr-rä'ro, (VINCENTE,) a Mexican partisan leader, who became President of Mexico in April, 1829. He was supplanted or overpowered about the end of that year by Bustamente. Having afterwards appealed to arms, he was defeated, taken prisoner, and executed in February, 1831.

Guerrini, gwĕr-ree'nee, (GIACOMO,) an Italian painter, born at Cremona in 1718; died in 1793.

Guesclin. See DU GUESCLIN.

Guess, gĕss, or **Se-quoy'ah,** (GEORGE,) a half-breed Cherokee Indian, born about 1770, was noted as the inventor of the Cherokee syllabic alphabet, consisting of eighty-five characters, representing the syllables in

ā, ē, ī, ō, ū, ȳ, *long;* ȧ, ė, ȯ, same, less prolonged; ă, ĕ, ĭ, ŏ, ŭ, ў, *short;* ą, ę, į, ǫ, *obscure;* fär, fȧll, fȧt; mĕt; nŏt; gŏŏd; mōōn;

use among the Cherokees. It has proved a great success, having been employed both in writing and printing. He lived in Georgia, from which he removed with his tribe beyond the Mississippi. Died in 1843.

Guettard, gå′tăr′, (JEAN ÉTIENNE,) a celebrated French naturalist and physician, born at Étampes in 1715. He studied natural science under Réaumur in Paris, and in 1743 was elected a member of the Academy of Sciences. He was afterwards appointed by the Duke of Orléans keeper of his cabinet of natural history. He first ascertained the volcanic nature of the mountains of Auvergne, and determined the true character of organic remains which had been only partially recognized before. He was the author of "Memoirs on some Mountains of France formerly Volcanoes," (1752,) a treatise "On the Granites of France compared with those of Egypt," (1755,) and other valuable works. Died in Paris in 1786.

See CONDORCET, "Éloge de Guettard;" "Nouvelle Biographie Générale."

Gueulette, guh′lĕt′, (THOMAS SIMON,) a popular writer, born in Paris in 1683, published numerous tales in the Oriental style, and several comedies. Died in 1766.

See QUÉRARD, "La France Littéraire."

Guevara, gå-vå′rå, (Don FELIPE **Ladron y**—lå-dRŏn′ e,) a Spanish painter, born about 1510, was a pupil or friend of Titian. He distinguished himself at the siege of Tunis under Charles V. in 1535. Died in 1563.

Guevara, (LUIS **Velez de las Dueñas y**—vå′lĕth då lås doo-ĕn′yås e,) a celebrated Spanish dramatist, born in Andalusia in 1574. His works are principally comedies, which were highly popular at the time, and were commended by Lope de Vega. He also published a witty satirical romance, entitled "El Diablo cojuelo," ("The Lame Devil,") said to have been the original of Le Sage's "Diable boiteux." Died in 1646.

See TICKNOR, "History of Spanish Literature."

Guevara, (SEBASTIAN **Velez**—vå′lĕth,) a Spanish poet, born at Valladolid in 1558, published a continuation of the "Romancero," or collection of Spanish romances, (1594.) Died in 1610.

See TICKNOR, "History of Spanish Literature."

Guevara, de, då gå-♦å′rå, (ANTONIO,) a Spanish prelate and historian, born in the province of Alava about 1490, was preacher and historiographer to Charles V. of Germany. He was afterwards created Bishop of Mondonedo. His "History of Marcus Aurelius," published in 1529, is said to contain less truth than fiction. He also began a "History of Charles V.," which was never published. His "Golden Epistles" were translated into French and English. Died in 1544.

See TICKNOR, "History of Spanish Literature."

Guevara, de, (ANTONIO,) a relative of the preceding, was appointed almoner to Philip II. of Spain. He wrote several commentaries on the Scriptures.

Guevara, de, (JUAN N.,) a Spanish painter and brilliant colorist, born at Malaga in 1631, was a pupil of Alonzo Cano. Died in 1698.

Guez de Balzac. See BALZAC.

Guffroy, gü′frwä′, (ARMAND BENOÎT JOSEPH,) a French journalist and politician of the Jacobin faction, born at Arras in 1740. He was elected to the National Convention in 1792, and in 1793 became a member of the committee of public safety. He voted for the death of the king. Died in 1800.

Guglielmi, gool-yĕl′mee, (PIETRO,) one of the most celebrated Italian composers of his time, born at Massa-Carrara in 1727. He studied at Naples under Durante, and subsequently visited Venice, Dresden, and London. He was appointed chapel-master at the Vatican in 1793. Among his operas, which amount to more than two hundred, we may name "Iphigenia in Aulide," "Clemenza di Tito," "Didone," "Tamerlano," and "Don Ambrogio." Died in 1804.

See FÉTIS, "Biographie Universelle des Musiciens."

Guglielmini, gool-yĕl-mee′nee, (DOMENICO,) an eminent Italian physician, astronomer, and natural philosopher, born at Bologna in 1655, became professor of mathematics in his native city in 1686, and of theoretic medicine at Padua in 1702. He published a "Dissertation on the Nature and Origin of Comets," "The Measure of Running Waters," "Hydrostatic Epistles," "Phy-

sico-Mathematical Treatise on the Nature of Rivers," (1697,) and other valuable works. He had been appointed in 1686 intendant of water-works, and gained distinction as a hydraulic engineer. Died in 1710.

See MORGAGNI, "Vita di Guglielmini," prefixed to his Works, 1719; FONTENELLE, "Éloge de Guglielmini," 1710; NICÉRON, "Mémoires."

Guglielmo d'Apulia, gool-yĕl′mo då-poo′le-å, [Fr. GUILLAUME DE POUILLE, ge′yŏm′ deh pool or poo′ye,] an Italian writer of the eleventh century, was the author of a historical poem, in Latin, "On the Deeds of the Normans in Sicily," etc., first published in 1582.

Guhr, gooR, (KARL WILHELM FERDINAND,) a German composer, born in Silesia in 1787. Among his operas is "Aladdin, or the Wonderful Lamp." Died in 1848.

Guhrauer, goo′rŏw′er, (GOTTSCHALK (got′shålk) EDUARD,) a German littérateur, born in Posen in 1809, published a "Biography of Leibnitz," (2 vols., 1842,) which is commended, "Goethe's Correspondence with Knebel," (2 vols., 1852,) and other works. Died in 1854.

Guhyăkă or **Guhyaca,** gŏŏh′ya-ka. In the Hindoo mythology, the Guhyakas, the servants of Kuvêra, (the deformed god of riches,) are a kind of demons into which transmigrate the souls of men particularly addicted to covetousness and selfishness.

Gui d'Arezzo. See GUIDO D'AREZZO.

Gui da Ravenna, goo-ee′ då rå-vĕn′nå, an Italian historian of the ninth century, wrote a "History of the Roman Pontiffs," and a "History of the Gothic War," (in Latin,) neither of which is extant.

Gui de Crema. See PASCHAL III.

Gui de Doucié, ge deh doo′se-å′, a French poet of the fourteenth century, of whose writings only fragments are extant. He translated into French the "Consolation of Philosophy" by Boethius.

Gui de Lusignan. See GUY DE LUSIGNAN.

Guibal, ge′bål′, (BARTHÉLEMY,) a French sculptor and architect, born at Nîmes in 1699; died in 1757.

Guibal, (NICOLAS,) a French painter, son of the preceding, born at Lunéville in 1725; died in 1784.

Guibaud, ge′bo′, (EUSTACHE,) a French Jansenist, born at Hières in 1711. He wrote "Groans of a Penitent Soul," and other devotional works. Died in 1794.

Guibert, ge′baiR′, Archbishop of Ravenna, was a native of Parma. He was made anti-pope by Henry IV. of Germany, with the name of Clement III., and in opposition to Hildebrand, (Gregory VII.) Guibert, having crowned Henry emperor, was enabled by his protection to resist successively three legitimate popes. Died in 1100.

Guibert, MADAME, a French writer, born at Versailles in 1725, published a number of poems and dramas, which were popular at the time. Died in 1788.

Guibert, de, deh ge-baiR′, (CHARLES BENOÎT,) COMTE, a French general, born at Montauban in 1715, served with distinction in Italy and Flanders, and subsequently against the Prussians in the Seven Years' war. Died in 1786.

Guibert, de, (JACQUES ANTOINE HIPPOLYTE,) COMTE, a popular and witty French author, born at Montauban in 1743, was the son of the preceding. He accompanied his father in the Seven Years' war, (1756–62,) and studied military tactics with great success. In 1773 he published a "General Essay on Tactics," which obtained a European celebrity and was read with avidity even by the ladies. Voltaire complimented the author in a short poem entitled "La Tactique." His tragedy of "Constable Bourbon" excited in the salons of Paris a temporary admiration scarcely equalled by that accorded to the productions of the greatest tragic poets; but this is not justified by the intrinsic merit of the work. In 1786 he was chosen a member of the French Academy. He died in 1790. Madame de Staël in the same year composed a eulogy on him. He was the object of an unhappy passion on the part of Mademoiselle L'Espinasse, whose letters to him were much admired.

See MADAME DE STAËL, "Éloge de Guibert;" TOULONGEON, "Notice historique sur Guibert," 1802; FORESTIÉ, "Biographie du Comte de Guibert," 1855; E. A. BARDIN, "Notice sur J. A. H. Guibert," 1836.

Guibert de Nogent, ge′baiR′ deh no′zhŏN′, a learned French ecclesiastic, born near Clermont-en-Beauvoisis in 1053, wrote a history of the first crusade, entitled "Gesta Dei per Francos," published in Paris in 1651. Died in 1124.

Guicciardini, gwe-char-dee′nee or goo-èt-châr-dee′-nee, [Lat. GUICCIARDI′NUS; Fr. GUICHARDIN, ge′shär′-dăn′,] (FRANCESCO,) an eminent Italian historian and diplomatist, born at Florence in 1482. At the early age of twenty-three he became professor of jurisprudence in his native city. He was appointed by Pope Leo X. Governor of Módena and Reggio in 1518, and he also enjoyed the favour of Adrian VI. and Clement VII. The latter, having become the ally of France, intrusted Guicciardini with the command of the pontifical troops, with the title of lieutenant-general of the Holy See. On the surrender of Florence to the Imperial army in 1530, he became the agent of the Medici in that city, and one of the commission of twelve called "the reformers of the state." Having greatly contributed to establish the tyranny of the Medici at Florence, he retired from public life about 1536, and devoted himself to the composition of his "History of Italy from 1494 to 1532," (1564.) It is esteemed a standard work, though somewhat prolix: it has been translated into Latin and French. Died in 1540.

His "History of Italy" "is well known," says Hallam, "for the solidity of the reflections, the gravity and impartiality with which it is written, and the prolixity of the narrative. . . . Guicciardini has generally held the first place among Italian historians, though he is by no means equal in literary merit to Machiavel." ("Introduction to the Literature of Europe.")

See R. FIGRENTINI, "Vita di F. Guicciardini," 1560; F. SANSOVINO, "Vita di Guicciardini," 1665; G. ROSINI, "Saggio sulle Azioni e sulle Opere di F. Guicciardini," 1822; NICÉRON, "Mémoires;" GINGUENÉ, "Histoire littéraire d'Italie;" "Nouvelle Biographie Générale;" "Edinburgh Review" for July, 1869.

Guicciardini, (LUIGI,) a nephew of the preceding, was born at Florence in 1523. He resided many years in Antwerp, where he published a "Description of the Low Countries," and several other works. Died in 1589.

Guicciardinus. See GUICCIARDINI.

Guiccioli, gwèt′cho-lee, (TERESA **Gamba,**) COUNTESS, a beautiful Italian lady, born in Romagna in 1801. She was married about 1817 to Count Guiccioli, a wealthy nobleman of Ravenna. She owes her celebrity to her *liaison* with Lord Byron, who appears to have loved her with as true and tender an affection as it was possible for a man of his character to do. In 1851 she was married to the Marquis de Boissy, a French senator and peer, (who was born at Paris in 1798; died in 1866.) Left a second time a widow, she has recently given to the world a book which has attracted much attention,— "My Recollections of Lord Byron and those of Eye-Witnesses of his Life," (London and Philadelphia, 1869;)—for, although she does not put her own name to the work, there appears to be no doubt as to its authorship.

See MOORE, "Life of Byron," vol. ii.; VAPEREAU, "Dictionnaire des Contemporains," under the head of BOISSY, (HILAIRE-ÉTIENNE-OCTAVE ROUILLÉ, Marquis de.)

Guichard, ge′shär′, (CLAUDE,) a French antiquary of the sixteenth century, born at Saint-Rambert-en-Bugey, was historiographer to Charles Emanuel, Duke of Savoy. He published a work entitled "The Funerals and Various Methods of Burial among the Romans, Greeks," etc., (1581.) Died in 1607.

Guichard, (JEAN FRANÇOIS,) a French poet and dramatist, born near Melun in 1731; died in 1811.

Guichard, (LOUIS **Anastase**—ä′nä′stăz′,) a French ecclesiastic, wrote a "History of Socinianism," and other works. Died in 1737.

Guichardin. See GUICCIARDINI.

Guiche, (PHILIBERT DE LA.) See LA GUICHE.

Guiche, de, deh gèsh, (ARMAND DE GRAMONT,) COMTE, a distinguished French general, born in 1638. He served against the English in the campaign of 1666, and subsequently in Holland under Condé. He died in 1674, leaving "Memoirs concerning the United Provinces," etc.

See "Mémoires du Maréchal de Gramont."

Guichen, ge′shŏN′, (LUC URBAIN **du Bouexic**—dü boo′ĕks′ĕk′,) a French naval officer, born at Fougères in

1712. He was made a lieutenant-general in 1779, and commander of the marine of Brest. In 1780 he gained a victory over the English fleet under Admiral Rodney at Dominique, and sunk one of their ships. In 1781 De Guichen was in turn defeated by Admiral Kempenfeld, who took fifteen of his vessels. Died in 1790.

See GÉRARD, "Vies des plus célèbres Marins Français."

Guichenon, gèsh′nòN′, (SAMUEL,) a French historian, born at Mâcon in 1607, was appointed historiographer of France and Savoy by Louis XIV., and created a count-palatine by Ferdinand III., Emperor of Germany. He published a "Genealogical History of the House of Savoy," and other similar works. Died in 1664.

See NICÉRON, "Mémoires."

Guidal, ge′däl′, (MAXIMILIEN JOSEPH,) a French officer, born at Grasse about 1760. Having joined the conspiracy of Mallet in 1812, he was executed by order of Napoleon.

Guidalotti, goo-e-dä-lot′tee, (DIOMEDE,) an Italian scholar and poet, born at Bologna about 1482; died in 1526.

Guide, Le. See GUIDO RENI.

Guidi, goo-ee′dee, or **Guido,** goo-ee′do, (CARLO ALESSANDRO,) an Italian poet, born at Pavía in 1650. Having visited Rome in 1683, he obtained the patronage of Christina, Queen of Sweden, who made him a member of her Academy. He was the author of "Amalasunta in Italia," "Endimione," a pastoral, and a number of sonnets and lyric poems of superior merit. He is ranked among the principal reformers of Italian poetry. Died in 1712.

See FABRONI, "Vitæ Italorum," etc., vol. xi.; CRESCIMBENI, "Vita di Guidi," prefixed to his poems; "Lives of the Italian Poets," by REV. HENRY STEBBING; NICÉRON, "Mémoires;" G. TURRONI, "Elogio storico di C. A. Guidi," 1827.

Guidi, (TOMMASO.) See MASACCIO.

Guidi da San Giovanni. See MASACCIO.

Guidiccioni, goo-e-dèt-cho′nee, (CRISTOFORO,) an Italian poet, born at Lucca about 1530, became Bishop of Ajaccio. He translated from the Greek the "Electra" of Sophocles and the "Bacchantes," the "Andromache," and the "Trojans" of Euripides. Died in 1582.

Guidiccioni, (GIOVANNI,) an Italian writer, born at Lucca about 1500. In 1534 he was appointed Governor of Rome by Pope Paul III., and the same year made Bishop of Fossombrone. He was soon after sent as nuncio to the emperor Charles V., whom he accompanied to Tunis. He was the author of a number of poems, letters, and orations. Died in 1541.

See LONGFELLOW's "Poets and Poetry of Europe."

Guido, gwee′do or goo-ee′do, [Fr. LE GUIDE, lĕh gèd,] or, more properly, **Guido Reni,** (goo-ee′do rä′-nee,) an eminent Italian painter, born at or near Bologna about 1575. He first studied under Denis Calvart, at Bologna, and was afterwards a pupil of the Çaracci. Having resided many years at Rome, where he was liberally patronized by Pope Paul V., he returned to his native city and devoted himself to painting and to the instruction of young artists. His pictures are very numerous, both in oil and fresco. His first works are painted in the style of the Caracci; but he subsequently adopted in some degree that of Caravaggio. His pictures are models of grace, delicacy, and beauty of expression. He succeeded especially in pathetic and devotional subjects. Among his master-pieces are "The Martyrdom of Saint Peter," (in the Vatican,) "Aurora," a fresco in Rome, "The Assumption," a picture of Saint Peter and Saint Paul, "Fortune," and "The Massacre of the Innocents." Died at Bologna in 1642.

See VASARI, "Lives of the Painters," etc.; LANZI, "History of Painting in Italy;" MALVASIA, "Felsina pittrice;" CRISPI, "Vite de' Pittori Bolognesi," 1769; BRYAN, "Dictionary of Painters," under RENI; "Nouvelle Biographie Générale."

Guido, (ALESSANDRO.) See GUIDI.

Guido, goo-ee′do, (GUERRA,) an Italian soldier, was one of the principal leaders of the Guelph faction in Florence. He commanded the Florentine forces in the victorious campaign of 1254, and upon the arrival of Charles of Anjou in Naples joined him with four hundred men, and had a prominent part in gaining the victory of Grandella, (1266.) Dante has assigned to

Guido a place in his "Inferno," at the same time highly commending his abilities.

See SISMONDI, "Histoire des Républiques Italiennes," vol. iii.

Guido, (NOVELLO,) a Florentine general of the Ghibeline faction. He assisted in gaining the victory of Arbia, in 1260.

Guido, (UBALDO,) MARQUIS, an Italian mathematician, born at Urbino about 1540, wrote the "Theory of Universal Planispheres," (in Latin,) and other works, which are commended by Montucla. Died about 1600.

See MONTUCLA, "Histoire des Mathématiques."

Guido (or **Gui,** goo-ee') **d'Arezzo,** goo-ee'do dã-rĕt'so, an eminent Italian musician and ecclesiastic, born about 990. He was the inventor of the modern system of notation in music, and founded a school at Pomposa, in which he taught the new method with great success.

See BURNEY, "General History of Music;" FÉTIS, "Biographie Universelle des Musiciens."

Guido Canlassi, goo-ee'do kân-lâs'see, called also **Cagnacci,** (kân-yât'chee,) an Italian historical painter, born near Rimini in 1601, was a pupil of Guido Reni. He worked many years for the emperor Leopold I. Died in Vienna in 1681.

See LANZI, "History of Painting in Italy."

Guido da Siena, goo-ee'do dã se-ā'nã, or **Guidone da Ghezzo,** goo-e-do'nã dã ğet'so, an Italian painter of the early part of the thirteenth century. His "Madonna and Child," in the church of the Dominicans at Sienna, is esteemed one of the finest works of the time.

See VASARI, "Lives of the Painters," etc.

Guido delle Colonne, goo-ee'do del'lã ko-lon'nã, [Lat. DE COLUM'NIS,] a Sicilian historian and poet of the thirteenth century, wrote a "History of the Trojan War," ("Historia Trojana,") which enjoyed a great reputation in its time and has been translated into nearly all the languages of Europe. It is said to have been the original of Boccaccio's "Filostrato," and, consequently, of Shakspeare's "Troilus and Cressida."

See TIRABOSCHI, "Storia della Letteratura Italiana."

Guidobono, goo-e-do-bo'no, (BARTOLOMMEO,) an Italian painter, called "the Priest of Savona," born at that town in 1654; died in 1709.

Guidonis, ğe'do'nèss', (BERNARD,) a French Dominican monk, born near Limoges about 1260. He was created Bishop of Lodève in 1324. He wrote "Annals of the Pontiffs," and other works. Died in 1331.

Guidotti-Borghese, goo-e-dot'tee boR-gā'sã, (PAO-LO,) an Italian painter, sculptor, and architect, born at Lucca about 1565, was patronized by Pope Sixtus V., who employed him to paint the Vatican. He was afterwards appointed by Paul V. conservator of the Museum of the Capitol. Died in 1629.

See LANZI, "History of Painting in Italy."

Guienne,(ÉLÉONORE DE.) See ELEANOR OF GUIENNE.

Guienne, de, dĕh ğe'ĕn', (N.,) a French lawyer of the Parliament of Paris, born at Orléans; died in 1767.

Guignard, ğĕn'yåR', (JEAN,) a French Jesuit, surnamed BRIQUAREL, (bRe'kã'rĕl',) was executed for high treason in 1595 for having openly justified the attempted assassination of Henry IV. by Châtel.

See SISMONDI, "Histoire des Français," vol. xxi.

Guignes, de, dĕh ğĕñ, (CHRÉTIEN LOUIS JOSEPH,) a French Orientalist, born in Paris in 1759, was a son of Joseph, noticed below. He was appointed French resident in China in 1784, and returned to France about 1800. He published "Voyages to Peking and Manilla," (3 vols., 1808,) and a "Chinese-French-Latin Dictionary," (1813.) Died in 1845.

See QUÉRARD, "La France Littéraire;" "London Quarterly Review" for November, 1809.

Guignes, de, (JOSEPH,) an eminent French Orientalist, born at Pontoise in 1721. He became professor of Syriac in the Collége Royale in 1757, having previously been elected a Fellow of the Royal Society in London, and a member of the Academy of Inscriptions in Paris. He was afterwards appointed royal censor, and keeper of the antiques of the Louvre. He was the author of a "General History of the Huns, Turks, Mongols, and other Western Tartars," etc., (1756,) "Historical Memoir on the Origin of the Huns and Turks," "History

of China," and other works, which enjoy a high reputation for learning and accuracy. Died in Paris in 1800.

See QUÉRARD, "La France Littéraire;" "London Quarterly Review" for April, 1815.

Guigniaut, ğĕn'ye-ō', (JOSEPH DANIEL,) an eminent French scholar and antiquary, born at Paray-le-Monial in May, 1794. He became a director of the Normal School, a member of the Institute in 1837, and professor of history in the Collége de France in 1854. His chief work is "The Religions of Antiquity, considered principally in their Symbolical and Mythological Forms," (3 tomes, in 10 vols., 1825–51,) which is a translation of Creuzer's "Symbolik," with additions.

See "Nouvelle Biographie Générale."

Guignon, ğĕn'yòN', (JEAN,) a distinguished violinist, born at Turin in 1702, was appointed musician to the royal chapel in Paris. He composed a number of sonatas and concertos. Died in 1774.

See FÉTIS, "Biographie Universelle des Musiciens."

Guijon, ğe'zhòN', (JEAN,) a French scholar and naturalist, born in 1544, became professor of rhetoric and languages in the College of Navarre. He published several scientific works, and a number of Latin poems. Died in 1605.

Guilandinus, gwe-lân-dee'nûs, or **Guilandini,** gwe-lân-dee'nee, (MELCHIOR,) a German naturalist, whose proper name was WIELAND, was born at Königsberg. He became professor of botany at Padua on the death of Fallopius, and wrote, in Latin, "Papyrus; or, A Commentary on the Three Chapters of Pliny the Elder concerning Papyrus," (1572.) Died in 1589.

See DE THOU, "Histoire;" MORÉRI, "Dictionnaire Historique."

Guilbert, ğèl'baiR', (PIERRE,) a French writer, born in Paris in 1697, was the author of "Chronological and Historical Memoirs of Port-Royal." Died in 1759.

Guilbert de Pixérécourt, ğèl'baiR' dĕh pèk'så'rã'-kooR', (RENÉ CHARLES,) a French dramatist, born at Nancy in 1773. He wrote many vaudevilles and melodramas. Died in 1844.

Guild, ğîld, (WILLIAM,) a Scottish divine, born at Aberdeen in 1586. He became one of the ministers of Aberdeen in 1631, and principal of King's College in 1640. For devotion to the royal cause he was deposed in 1651. He wrote, besides other works, "The Harmony of all the Prophets concerning Christ's Coming," (1619,) and "Moses Unveiled," (1620.) Died in 1657.

See CHAMBERS, "Biographical Dictionary of Eminent Scotsmen."

Guildford, EARL OF. See NORTH.

Guilhelmus Pictavensis. See GUILLAUME DE POITIERS.

Guilhem de Castro. See CASTRO.

Guilhem de Clermont-Lodève. See SAINTE-CROIX, (GUILLAUME EMANUEL JOSEPH.)

Guillain, ğe'yåN', (SIMON,) a French sculptor, born in Paris in 1581. Among his best works are the statues in the church of the Sorbonne, and those of the Virgin and Saint Francis de Paulo in the convent of Minims. Guillain was one of the founders of the Academy of Painting and Sculpture, and one of its first rectors. Died in 1658.

See LENOIR, "Musée des Monuments Français," vol. v.

Guillard, ğèl'yåR' or ğe'yåR', (NICOLAS FRANÇOIS,) a French dramatist and lyric poet, born at Chartres in 1752. He brought out "Iphigenia in Tauris," a lyric tragedy, (1779,) and "Œdipus at Colona," which were greatly admired. Died in 1814.

Guillaume, ğe'yòm', sometimes called **Frère Guillaume,** a French artist, skilled in painting on glass, was born at Marseilles in 1475. He was patronized by Pope Julius II., who employed him in various works at Rome. His paintings on the windows of the Vatican and in the church of the Madonna del Popolo are ranked among the finest productions of the kind. He also excelled as an architect and painter in fresco. Died in 1537.

See VASARI, "Lives of the Painters," etc.

Guillaume, surnamed LONGUE-ÉPÉE, (lòNğ'å'pã',) (LONG-SWORD,) son of Rollo, Duke of Normandy, succeeded his father about 927. He became one of the most powerful vassals of the crown of France. He was treacherously killed by Arnould, Count of Flanders, in 943.

ē as *k;* ç as *s;* ğ *hard;* ğ as *j;* G, H, K, *guttural;* N, *nasal;* R, *trilled;* s̄ as *z;* th as in *this.* (☞ See Explanations, p. 23.)

Guillaume, SAINT, surnamed THE GREAT, a French ecclesiastic and military commander, served under Charlemagne against the Saracens, and received from him the title of Duke of Aquitaine. In 808 he founded in the valley of Gellone a monastery, since called that of Saint Guillaume in the Desert. His deeds were celebrated in a metrical romance of the ninth century. Died in 812.

See BAILLET, "Vies des Saints."

Guillaume, SAINT, a French theologian, became Archbishop of Bourges. He died in 1209, and was canonized by Pope Honorius III. in 1218.

Guillaume d'Auvergne, ge'yŏm' dō'vȧRñ', or **Guillaume de Paris,** a celebrated French theologian and philosopher, born at Aurillac, was created Bishop of Paris in 1228. He was one of the most learned men of his time, and wrote several Latin works distinguished for the purity and elegance of the style. Died in 1249.

See "Histoire littéraire de la France."

Guillaume de Chartres, ge'yŏm' deh shȧRtR, a French ecclesiastic and historian, born at Chartres about 1225. He was chaplain to Louis IX., whom he accompanied on his expeditions to Palestine, and was present at his death in 1270. He wrote a supplement to the "Vita Sancti Ludovici" ("Life of Saint Louis") begun by Geoffroy (or Galfrid) de Beaulieu. Died about 1280.

See "Histoire littéraire de la France," vol. ix.; BOLLANDUS, "Acta Sanctorum."

Guillaume de Jumiéges, ge'yŏm' deh zhü'me-àzh', a French historian and ecclesiastic, who lived about 1070, wrote a "History of the Normans," (" Historiæ Normannorum Libri VII.,") which he dedicated to William the Conqueror. It has been published in Camden's "Angliæ Scriptores" and Duchesne's "Normannorum Antiqui Scriptores," (1619.)

Guillaume de Poitiers, ge'yŏm' deh pwȧ'te-ȧ', [Lat. GUILHEL'MUS PICTAVEN'SIS,] a French or Norman chronicler, born in Normandy in 1020, was chaplain to the Duke William afterwards King of England. His principal work is a "History of William the Conqueror," (in Latin,) which is not all extant.

Guillaume de Pouille. See GUGLIELMO D'APULIA.

Guillaume le Breton, ge'yŏm' leh bReh-tŏN', or **Bri'to-Ar-mo'rĭ-cus,** a French chronicler and poet, born in Brittany about 1165, was chaplain to Philip Augustus. He was the author of "Historia de Vita et Gestis Philippi Augusti," ("Life and Deeds of Philip Augustus,") and a poem entitled the "Philippide."

See NICÉRON, "Mémoires."

Guillaumet, ge'yō'mȧ', (TANNEGUY (tȧn'ge') or THÉVENIN, tȧv'nȧN',) born at Nîmes about 1560, became surgeon to Henry IV., and published several medical works. Died in 1630.

Guillaumot, ge'yō'mo', (CHARLES AXEL,) a Swedish architect, of French extraction, born at Stockholm in 1730. Having visited Paris in 1754, he was appointed, on the death of Sauflot, intendant-general of the royal buildings, gardens, etc. Died in 1807.

Guillem or **Guilhem de Castro.** See CASTRO.

Guillemain, ge'ye-mȧN' or gèl'mȧN', (CHARLES JACOB,) a French dramatist, born in Paris in 1750. His comedies are very numerous, and enjoyed a temporary popularity. Died in 1799.

Guillemeau, ge'ye-mo' or gèl'mo', (JACQUES,) an eminent French surgeon, born at Orléans about 1530, was a pupil of Ambrose Paré. He became successively surgeon-in-ordinary to Charles IX., Henry III., and Henry IV. He published, among other works, a treatise "On Diseases of the Eye." Died in 1613.

Guillemeau, (JEAN LOUIS MARIE,) a French naturalist and physician, born at Niort in 1766, wrote many works on botany, ornithology, etc. Died about 1850.

Guillemin, ge'ye-mȧN' or gèl'mȧN', (JEAN ANTOINE,) a French botanist, born at Pouilly-sur-Saône in 1796. He made a scientific voyage to Brazil in 1838. Died at Montpellier in 1842.

Guilleminot, de, deh ge'ye-me'no' or gèl'me'no', (ARMAND CHARLES,) COMTE, a French general and diplomatist, born at Dunkirk in 1774. He served under General Moreau in Italy and on the Rhine, made the Russian campaign of 1812, and became general of divi-

sion in 1813. He was sent as ambassador to Constantinople in 1824. Died in 1840.

Guilleragues, ge'ye-rȧg' or gèl'rȧg', (GABRIEL JOSEPH,) Comte de Lavergne, a French littérateur and diplomatist, born at Bordeaux. He was sent as ambassador to the Ottoman court in 1679, and died at Constantinople in 1684. His work entitled "Embassies of Count de Guilleragues and M. de Girardin to the Grand Seigneur" was published in 1687. He was an intimate friend of Boileau, who dedicated to him his fifth Epistle.

See "Lettres de Madame de Sévigné;" SAINT-SIMON, "Mémoires."

Guillet de Saint-Georges, ge'yȧ' deh sȧN'zhoRzh', (GEORGES,) a French writer, born in Auvergne about 1625. He was a member, and the first historiographer, of the Academy of Painting and Sculpture. He was the author of "Athens, Ancient and Modern, and the Present State of the Turkish Empire," and several other works. Died in 1705.

Guillim, gwil'lim,? (JOHN,) an English writer on heraldry, was born in Herefordshire about 1565. He wrote "The Display of Heraldry," (1610.) Died in 1621.

Guillon, ge'yŏN', (L. GABRIEL,) a French surgeon, born near Tours in 1798. He invented several instruments and methods of surgery.

Guillon, (MARIE NICOLAS SILVESTRE,) ABBÉ, a French ecclesiastic, born in Paris in 1760. He was professor of rhetoric and theology in Paris, and was appointed Bishop of Morocco in 1833. Among his numerous works is a "History of Ancient and Modern Philosophy," (1835.) Died in 1847.

See QUÉRARD, "La France Littéraire."

Guillon de Montléon, ge'yŏN' deh mŏN'lȧ'ŏN', (AIMÉ,) a French historical and theological writer, born at Lyons in 1758. He became keeper of the Mazarin Library, Paris, in 1816. Among his works is "Historical Memoirs of Lyons," (3 vols., 1824.) Died in 1842.

Guillotine, gil-lo-teen', [Fr. pron. ge'yo'tèn',] (JOSEPH IGNACE,) a French physician, born at Saintes in 1738. He was a deputy in 1789 to the States-General, where he proposed, as a humane measure, to substitute decapitation for other modes of punishment. He was not, however, the inventor of the machine called by his name. He was one of the founders of the Academy of Medicine in Paris. Died in 1814.

See "Éloge funèbre de Guillotine," 1814; CROKER, "The Guillotine: an Historical Essay."

Guillou, ge'yoo', (JEAN RENÉ,) a French ecclesiastic, born at Châteaudun in 1730, was the author of a "Funeral Oration for the Dauphin," which was greatly admired. Died in 1776.

Guimet, ge'mȧ', (JEAN BAPTISTE,) a French chemist, born at Voiron in 1795, discovered the art of making artificial ultramarine in 1826.

Guinand, ge'nŏN', a Swiss optician, born about 1745. He discovered the art of fabricating large flint-glass discs for telescopes, and became a partner or assistant of Fraunhofer. Died in 1824 or 1825.

Guinet, ge'nȧ', (FRANÇOIS,) a French jurist and legal writer, born at Nancy in 1604; died in 1681.

Guinicelli, goo-e-ne-chel'lee, (GUIDO,) an Italian poet, born at Bologna, is eulogized by Dante in his "Purgatorio," canto xxvi. Died in 1276.

Guiniforte, goo-e-ne-foR'tȧ, an Italian scholar and orator, born at Pavia in 1406, was surnamed BARZIZZA or BARZIZZIO. Died about 1460.

Guinigi, goo-e-nee'jee, (PAOLO,) an Italian nobleman of the Guelph faction, who in 1400 made himself master of the city of Lucca. After a rule of thirty years, he was dispossessed of his power by the Duke of Milan, and died, after two years' imprisonment, in 1431.

Guiot, ge'o', (JOSEPH ANDRÉ,) a French ecclesiastic and Latin poet, born at Rouen in 1739; died in 1807.

Guiran, ge'rôN', (GAILLARD,-gȧ'yȧR',) a French jurist and antiquary, born at Nîmes in 1600; died in 1680.

Guiraud, ge'rō', (PIERRE MARIE THÉRÈSE ALEXANDRE,) BARON, a French poet and dramatist, born at Limoux in 1788. He wrote two successful tragedies, in verse, entitled "Les Machabées," (1822,) and "Count Julien," (1822,) and other works. He was elected to the French Academy in 1826. Died in 1847.

ă, ē, ī, ō, ū, ȳ, long; ȧ, ė, ò, same, less prolonged; ă, ĕ, ĭ, ŏ, ŭ, ȳ, short; a, ę, į, o, obscure; fär, fȧll, fȧt; mėt; nŏt; gōōd; mōōn;

Guiraudet, ḡe′rō′dȧ′,(Charles Philippe **Toussaint** —too′säN′,) a French statesman and writer, born at Alais in 1754, became secretary-general of the ministry of foreign affairs under the Directory. Died in 1804.

Guiscard, ḡês′kȧR′, [Lat. Guiscar′dus,] (Robert,) a celebrated military commander, born in Normandy, was one of the sons of Tancred de Hauteville. He assisted his brother Humphrey in the conquest of Calabria, and on his death (1057) proclaimed himself Count of Apulia. Pope Nicholas II., who had previously excommunicated him, now created him Duke of Apulia, Calabria, and Sicily. In 1081 he marched against the Greek emperor Alexius, whom he defeated at Durazzo in 1084. He soon after liberated Pope Gregory VII., who had been imprisoned at Saint Angelo. Died in 1085.

See Mala-Terra, "De Gestis Roberti Guiscardi," 1578 ; " Nouvelle Biographie Générale."

Guiscardus. See Guiscard, (Robert.)

Guischard, ḡe′shȧR′, (Karl Gottlieb,) a Prussian officer, born at Magdeburg in 1724, was a favourite of Frederick the Great, who gave him the name of Quintus Icilius. He served in the Seven Years' war, and rose to the rank of colonel. He wrote, in French, an interesting work entitled "Military Memoirs of the Greeks and Romans," in which he has exposed the errors of Folard. Died in 1775.

Guise, gīz,? (William,) an English divine and Orientalist, born near Gloucester in 1653 ; died in 1683.

Guise, de, dẹh gweez, (or gü-èz′,) (Antoinette de Bourbon—dẹh boor′bôN′,) Duchesse, a French lady, eminent for her piety and benevolence, born in 1493, was the daughter of Francis de Bourbon, Count of Vendôme, and the wife of Claude de Lorraine, Duke of Guise. Died in 1583.

See Hilarion de Coste, "Vies des Dames illustres."

Guise, de, (Catherine de **Clèves**—dẹh klȧv,) Duchesse, born in 1547, was a daughter of the Duke of Nevers, and was married to Henry, first Duke of Guise, in 1570. She was chiefly instrumental in procuring the submission of the Guises to Henry IV. Died in 1633.

See Varillas, "Histoire de Henri III."

Guise, de, (Charles,) Cardinal de Lorraine, born at Joinville in 1525, was a son of Claude, first Duke of Guise. He became Archbishop of Rheims in 1538, and cardinal in 1547, and was subsequently minister of finance under Francis II. and Charles IX. In 1569 he negotiated the marriage of the latter with Elizabeth of Austria. He was conspicuous, even in that age of persecution, for his intolerance and bitter hostility to the Protestants, and was one of the chief promoters of the civil wars of the time. He made several attempts to introduce the Inquisition into France, and he is believed to have approved of the Massacre of Saint Bartholomew, although absent at the time. Cardinal Lorraine is represented by Brantôme and other contemporary writers as possessed of eminent abilities, but false, cruel, and ambitious. They admit, however, that he was a liberal patron of learning, and that he did a great deal to check the usurpations of the Papal See. Died in 1574.

See Bayle, " Historical and Critical Dictionary ;" Brantôme, " Vies des grands Capitaines ;" " Mémoires de Condé," 1743.

Guise, de, (Charles de Lorraine,) Duc, eldest son of Henry of Guise and Catherine of Cleves, noticed above, was born in 1571. On the assassination of his father, in 1588, he was imprisoned at Tours. Having made his escape in 1591, he entered the service of Henry IV., and in 1596 besieged and recaptured the city of Marseilles. In 1631 he was obliged by Richelieu to leave the kingdom. Died in 1640.

Guise, de, dẹh gweez, [Fr. pron. gü-èz′,] (Claude de Lorraine,) first Duke, born in 1496, was the younger son of René II., Duke of Lorraine. He became a citizen of France, and married Antoinette de Bourbon, about 1514. He served in the army with distinction at Marignano and other places, and was created Duke of Guise by Francis I. He died about 1550, leaving many children, among whom were Francis, Duke of Guise, Charles, (the Cardinal de Lorraine,) and a daughter, Mary, who became queen of James V. of Scotland.

See Bayle, "Historical and Critical Dictionary."

Guise, de, (François de Lorraine,) Duke, a prominent leader of the Catholic party in France, and one of the greatest commanders of his time, was born in 1519. He was a son of Claude, first Duke of Guise, and Antoinette de Bourbon, and a brother of the cardinal, noticed above. Having previously gained important victories at Landrecies and other places, he raised his reputation to the highest point by his defence of Metz in 1553 against Charles V., who was forced to retire with the loss of 30,000 men. Soon after the battle of Saint-Quentin, in 1557, he was appointed by Henry II. lieutenant-general of the kingdom and invested with almost absolute power. The capture of Calais from the English in 1558, and the subsequent victories at Guines and Thionville, justified the confidence reposed in him, and made him more than ever the idol of the nation. In conjunction with his brother the cardinal, he defeated the conspiracy of Amboise, formed by the Prince of Condé and other Protestant leaders. He had a prominent share in the victory at Dreux, where he took the Prince of Condé prisoner. At the siege of Orléans, soon after, he was assassinated by a Calvinist, named Poltrot de Mérey, in 1563. He was the author of "Mémoires," which are valuable and interesting records of his time.

See Davila, " History of the Civil Wars of France ;" Brantôme, " Vies des grands Capitaines ;" Du Trousset de Valincourt, " Vie de François de Lorraine," 1668 ; Bayle, " Historical and Critical Dictionary ;" L'Estoile, " Journal de Henri III ;" " Nouvelle Biographie Générale."

Guise, de, (François Joseph de Lorraine,) seventh and last Duke, was born in 1670 ; died in 1675. The family of Guise became extinct in 1688.

Guise, de, (Henry I. of **Lorraine**,) Duke, eldest son of Francis, Duke of Guise, born in 1550, was a cousin of Mary, Queen of Scots. He inherited in a great degree the talents and accomplishments of his father, and even surpassed him in his bitter opposition to the Protestants. When less than nineteen years of age, he defended Poitiers against Coligny, and soon after had a share in the victory of Moncontour, (1569.) At the battle of Dormans he received a wound on the cheek, from which he was surnamed Balafré, or the " Scarred." He was one of the instigators of the Massacre of Saint Bartholomew in 1572, and was concerned in the murder of Coligny. In 1576, Henry of Guise, with his brother, the Cardinal de Guise, headed the faction called the League, ostensibly formed for the defence of the Catholic religion and the king, but really designed to assist the family of Guise in usurping the royal power. On the accession of Henry III. the Duke of Guise prevailed upon him to adopt more severe measures against the Protestants. The king, however, becoming weary of the arrogance of the Guises, forbade the duke to appear at court, whereupon he openly revolted, and in May, 1588, on the " day of the Barricades," entered Paris with his troops, disarmed the Swiss guard, and obliged the king to abandon his capital. Henry III. soon after summoned the States-General at Blois, where the Duke of Guise demanded to be appointed constable and lieutenant-general of the kingdom. The king now, in conjunction with several of his courtiers, resolved to take the life of the duke ; and, as the latter entered the king's apartment, he was dispatched by the daggers of the assassins, in December, 1588.

See L'Estoile, " Journal de Henri III ;" Brantôme, " Vie de l'Admiral de Chastillon ;" Enrico Caterino Davila, " La Sera di S. Bartolommeo e la Morte del Duca di Guisa," 1828 ; Davila, " History of the Civil Wars in France ;" " Nouvelle Biographie Générale."

Guise, de, (Henry II. of **Lorraine**,) Duke, and Prince de Joinville, born at Blois in 1614, was the son of Charles IV., Duke of Guise. He joined the conspiracy of the Count of Soissons against the French government in 1641, and was condemned to death, but escaped. In 1647 he went to the assistance of the Neapolitans, who had revolted against Spain. Being made generalissimo of their army, he took Naples, which, however, was soon recovered by the Spaniards, and the Duke of Guise taken prisoner. After his release he was appointed, in 1655, high chamberlain of France. He died in 1664, leaving " Memoirs," which were published in 1668.

See Tallemant de Réaux, " Historiettes ;" " Nouvelle Biographie Générale."

Guise, de, (JEAN de **Lorraine**,) CARDINAL, brother of Claude, noticed above, was born in 1498. He was sent on an embassy to the emperor Charles V. in 1536. He obtained the archbishoprics of Lyons, Rheims, and Narbonne, and various other preferments, and was distinguished for his munificence and extensive charities. Died in 1550.

See DE THOU, "Histoire universelle," vol. i., 1734; SISMONDI, "Histoire des Français."

Guise, de, (LOUIS I. de **Lorraine**,) CARDINAL, brother of Francis and of the cardinal Charles de Lorraine, was born in 1527. He was successively appointed Bishop of Troyes and of Alby, and Archbishop of Sens, being made a cardinal in 1553. Died in 1578.

Guise, de, (LOUIS II. de **Lorraine**,) CARDINAL, son of Francis, Duke of Guise, born at Dampierre in 1555. He succeeded his uncle as Archbishop of Rheims, and in 1578 was made a cardinal. Having been associated with his brother Henry I., Duke of Guise, as one of the chiefs of the League, he was, on the death of the latter, imprisoned, and a few days after assassinated, (1588.)

See L'ESTOILE, "Journal de Henri III."

Guise, de, (LOUIS III. de **Lorraine**,) CARDINAL, son of Henry I. de Lorraine, was born about 1580. He obtained numerous benefices in the Church, and was created a cardinal by Paul V. in 1615. Died in 1621.

Guiton, ḡe′tŏN′, (JEAN,) a French Huguenot, who was admiral and mayor of Rochelle in 1627, when that city was besieged by the royalists. He surrendered in 1628. Died in 1654, aged about seventy years.

Guittone d'Arezzo, goo-ĕt-to′nȧ dä-rĕt′so, an Italian poet, born at Arezzo about 1230, was one of the chief reformers of Italian literature in that age. Died in 1294.

See LONGFELLOW, "Poets and Poetry of Europe."

Guizot, gü-e′zo′ or ḡe′zo′, (ÉLISABETH CHARLOTTE PAULINE **de Meulan**—dĕh muh′lôN′,) a French authoress, born in Paris in 1773, was left by the death of her father with no resources but her talents. She produced in 1800 an ingenious and sprightly work of fiction, entitled "The Contradictions," and, by her contributions to Suard's literary journal "Le Publiciste," gained distinction as a critic and a moralist. She was married to M. Guizot in 1812. Among her works are "Domestic Education," (2 vols., 1826,) and "A Family," ("Une Famille," 1828.) Died in 1827.

See SAINTE-BEUVE, "Portraits of Celebrated Women;" "Nouvelle Biographie Générale."

Guizot, gwe′zo′ or gü-e′zo′,* (FRANÇOIS PIERRE GUILLAUME,) a distinguished French statesman and historian, born at Nîmes on the 4th of October, 1787, was a son of an able advocate who fell a victim to the reign of terror in 1794. Having been educated as a Protestant at Geneva, he went to Paris in 1805, and published an edition of Gibbon's History, in French, about 1810. He married Pauline de Meulan, noticed above, and was appointed professor of modern history at the Sorbonne by Fontanes, in 1812. He defended constitutional principles in a pamphlet "On Representative Government and the Present State of France," (1816,) became a leader of the party called Doctrinaires, and councillor of state in 1817. In 1822 he was suspended from his functions as professor, because his principles were offensive to the ministry. In 1828 he founded the "Revue Française," and was reinstated in the chair of history. He acquired much celebrity as a lecturer, and formed with Cousin and Villemain a triumvirate of professors. His lectures were published with the title of a "History of Civilization," (5th edition, 5 vols., 1845.)

He was elected to the Chamber of Deputies from Lisieux in January, 1830, and promoted the accession of Louis Philippe, who appointed him minister of the interior on the 1st of August. His ministry (the policy

* So pronounced by M. Guizot himself, as stated in a letter from him, now before us. He says, "Dans mon pays natal, la ville de Nîmes, on prononce mon nom *ghi-zo.* A Paris on dit en général *gwi-zo;* et je crois cette prononciation plus correcte." A near relative, however, of the great French historian and statesman takes a different view of the question. He says the name of his family is always pronounced *ghi-zo* in the south of France, where the name originated; and he maintains, with great appearance of reason, that the invariable usage of the people of Nîmes ought to be decisive as to the pronunciation of *un nom Nîmois.*

of which was styled *juste milieu*) was dissolved in November, 1830. In October, 1832, Guizot became minister of public instruction in the cabinet of Marshal Soult. While in this office, he rendered an important service to the public by organizing a system of primary schools. He was compelled to resign in February, 1836, when his rival Thiers obtained power for a brief term. He was elected to the French Academy in 1836. In 1838 Guizot and Thiers (who had been superseded by Count Molé) formed a coalition, which was regarded by many as discreditable to the former. He was sent as ambassador to London in February, 1840. On the 29th of October, 1840, he became minister of foreign affairs, and really prime minister, in a cabinet of which Soult was nominally president. He maintained himself in power until the revolution of February, 1848, which was provoked partly by his inflexible resistance to electoral reform.

He escaped in disguise to England, wrote a pamphlet on "Democracy in France," and returned to his native country in 1849; after which, it is said, he favoured a fusion between the two parties of Legitimists and Orléanists. Among his principal works are an excellent "History of the Revolution in England, from the Accession of Charles I. to that of Charles II.," ("Histoire de la Révolution d'Angleterre," etc., 6 vols., 1827-56,) and "Memoirs to illustrate the History of my Time," ("Mémoires pour servir à l'Histoire de mon Temps,") of which four or more volumes have appeared. These have been translated into English. He is generally considered to be more successful as a historian than he was as a statesman. He has also shown himself to be an effective and imposing parliamentary orator.

"Among this band of great and honourable men," says the "Edinburgh Review" for October, 1858, "we think that M. Guizot will retain in history, as he has occupied in life, the first and highest place. Other writers, gifted with livelier powers of imagination and appealing more directly to the sentiment of their contemporaries, may, like Châteaubriand, have exercised for a time a more powerful influence on the literature of France. . . . Other statesmen have enjoyed far more of popular sympathy in their day. But in the depth and variety of his literary labours, which have enlarged the philosophy of history, in the force and precision of his oratory, which at one swoop could bend an assembly or crush a foe, and in the systematic consistency of his whole political life, . . . M. Guizot has had no equal, either in his own country or, as far as we know, in any other." Comparing him with Burke and Pitt, the same critic adds, "In M. Guizot the speculative genius of the one was united to the practical authority of the other; and, though each of these great Englishmen may have possessed his own peculiar qualification in a still higher degree, Guizot stands before them both in the rare union of the contemplative and active faculties."

See LOUIS DE LOMÉNIE, "M. Guizot, par un Homme de Rien," 1844; THOMAS DESCHÈRRES, "Biographie de M. Guizot," 1843; VICTOR VERNEUIL, "M. Guizot, par un Homme du Peuple," 1846; GAINET, "Études critiques sur les Travaux historiques de M. Guizot," 1851; "Nouvelle Biographie Générale;" "London Quarterly Review" for December, 1848, January, 1854, July, 1856, and January, 1868; "Edinburgh Review" for April, 1849; "Blackwood's Magazine" for December, 1837; "Foreign Quarterly Review" for April, 1845; "Fraser's Magazine" for December, 1844.

Guldberg, gŏŏld′bĕRG, (FREDERIK HÖEGH,) son of the following, was born at Copenhagen in 1771. He wrote a number of lyric and elegiac poems, and made good metrical translations of Plautus, Tibullus, and Terence. He lived many years at Kiel. Died in 1852.

See ERSLEW, "Forfatter-Lexicon."

Guldberg, (OVE HÖEGH, o′veh hö′ĕg,) an eminent Danish historian, statesman, and theologian, born at Horsen in 1731. He was the author of a "History of the World," (1768,) "Determination of the Dates of the Books of the New Testament," (1785,) and "Translation of the New Testament, with Notes." He was minister of state from 1775 to 1784. Died in 1808.

See H. P. GIESSING, "Struensee og Guldberg, etc.; historisk Skildring," 1848; KRAFT og NYERUP, "Litteraturlexicon."

Güldenstädt or **Gueldenstædt,** gül′dẹn-stĕt′, (ANTON JOHANN,) a Russian physician and naturalist, of

---

ā, ē, ī, ō, ū, ȳ, *long;* ȧ, ė, ȯ, same, less prolonged; ă, ĕ, ĭ, ŏ, ŭ, ў, *short;* ạ, ẹ, ị, ọ, *obscure;* fär, fåll, fåt; mĕt; nŏt; gŏŏd; mōōn;

German extraction, was born at Riga in 1745. He accompanied in 1768 a scientific expedition sent out by Catherine II. to explore the different parts of Russia and the Caucasus. He died in 1781, and his "Travels in Russia and the Mountains of the Caucasus" was published in 1791, (2 vols., in German.)

See BERNOULLI, "Reisen."

Guldin, gōōl-deen', [Lat. GULDI'NUS,] (PAUL,) a Swiss mathematician, born at Saint Gall in 1577. He wrote a treatise "On the Centre of Gravity," in which he is thought to have borrowed from Pappus. He opposed the method of indivisibles invented by Cavalieri. Died in 1643.

See MONTUCLA, "Histoire des Mathématiques."

Guldinus. See GULDIN.

Gŭl'lȳ, (JAMES MANBY,) an English physician, born at Kingston, Jamaica, in 1808. He removed about 1842 to Malvern, in England, where he practised hydropathy. He published several medical works.

Gŭm'mer-e, (JOHN,) a mathematician, born at Willow Grove, Pennsylvania, in 1784, published a valuable treatise on Surveying, (1814,) and became professor of mathematics at Haverford College in 1833. Died in 1845.

See "Memorials of J. Gummere," by WILLIAM J. ALLINSON, Burlington, 1845.

Gundegisilus. See GONDÉGISILE.

Gundericus. See GONDIOC.

Günderode or **Guenderode, von,** fon gün'deh-ro'-deh, (CAROLINE,) a German poetess, born at Carlsruhe in 1780. Her works are distinguished for great powers of fancy, but are frequently tinctured with melancholy. A disappointment in love caused her to commit suicide in 1806. Her friend Bettina Brentano published, in 1840, "The Günderode Letters," consisting of the correspondence which passed between herself and Mademoiselle Günderode.

Gundicarius. See GONDICAIRE.

Gundling, gōōnt'ling, (NIKOLAUS HIERONYMUS,) a German jurist and *littérateur,* born near Nuremberg in 1671. He became professor of the law of nature and of nations at Halle, and was afterwards made privy councillor. Among his works are "The Way to Truth," ("Via ad Veritatem," 3 vols., 1713,) a collection of essays, entitled "Gundlingiana," (1715–32,) and a "History of Erudition," (5 vols., 1734–36.) Died in 1729.

See WIDEBURG, "Memoria Gundlingii," 1729; C. F. HEMPEL, "N. H. Gundling's umständliches Leben und Schriften," 1736; NICÉRON, "Mémoires;" RAMBACH, "Leichenpredigt auf N. H. Gundling," 1729.

Gundling, von, fon gōōnt'ling, (JACOB PAUL,) BARON, a German historian and court fool, born near Nuremberg in 1673. He received from the King of Prussia the titles of baron, privy councillor, councillor of war, etc. He amused the court at Berlin by his oddities and vanity. He wrote a "History of the Emperors Frederick I., Henry VII., and Conrad IV.," (4 vols., 1715–19,) and other works. Died in 1731.

See A. B. KOENIG. "Leben J. P. von Gundlings," etc., 1795.

Gundobald. See GONDEBAUD.

Gun'dulf, a Norman ecclesiastic, who was appointed Bishop of Rochester by William the Conqueror. He was the architect of Rochester Castle, and is said to have built the Tower of London. Died about 1108.

Gundulitsch, goon'dōō-litch', (IVAN,) a distinguished poet, born at Ragusa, in Servia, in 1588. He wrote an epic poem, entitled "The Osmanide," celebrating the war between Osmân III. and the Poles; also several admired dramas. He was the earliest dramatic poet among the Slavonians. Died in 1638.

Gunês. See GANÊSA.

Gunnerus, gōōn-nā'rŭs, (JOHN ERNEST,) a Norwegian prelate and naturalist, born at Christiania in 1718, was one of the founders of the Scientific Society of Norway. He was the author of a "Flora Norvegica," and other works, and was a friend of Linnæus, who gave the name of Gunnera to a South American plant. He was created Bishop of Drontheim in 1758. Died in 1773.

Gŭn'ning, (PETER,) an English pulpit orator, born in Kent in 1613, rose to be Bishop of Ely under Charles II. He published several controversial works. Died in 1684.

Gunst, van, vän gŭnst or hŭnst, (PIETER,) a skilful Dutch engraver of portraits, born at Amsterdam about 1566. Among his works are engravings of portraits after Van Dyck, dated about 1715 or later.

Gŭn'ter, (EDMUND,) an eminent English mathematician, born in Hertfordshire in 1581. About 1606 he invented the sector, of which he wrote a description in Latin; and in 1619 he became professor of astronomy at Gresham College. He also invented the Logarithmic Rule for the use of draughtsmen, called "Gunter's Scale," the cross-staff, and other instruments, and the "Canon Triangulorum," ("Law of Triangles.") Gunter is said to have been the first to discover the variation of the compass. Died in 1626.

See MONTUCLA, "Histoire des Mathématiques."

Günther, gün'ter, (ANTON,) a German Catholic theologian, born at Lindenau in 1785. He published "Preparatory School of Speculative Theology," "The Juste-Milieu in the German Philosophy of the Present," and other treatises in opposition to Hegel's philosophy.

Günther, (JOHANN CHRISTIAN,) a German poet, born in Lower Silesia in 1695, wrote poetical epistles, satires, songs, and odes, which display uncommon power and were eulogized by Goethe. He fell into dissipated habits, and died in extreme poverty in 1723.

See his Autobiography, "Lebens- und Reisebeschreibung," etc., 1732; M. W. DÖRING, "J. C. Günther: Beitrag zur Deutschen Literatur-Geschichte," 1831; HOFFMANN VON FALLERSLEBEN, "J. C. Günther; literar-historischer Versuch," 1832.

Günther von Schwarzburg, gün'ter fon shwÄrts'-bōŌRG, a warlike German prince, born in 1304. He was elected King of the Germans in 1343, and Emperor of Germany in January, 1349. His title to the imperial throne was disputed by Charles IV. Gunther died in June, 1349.

See F. L. HOFFMANN, "Günther von Schwarzburg," 1819; WEBER, "Kurzgefasstes Memoire vom Leben Güntheri Bellicosi," 1720.

Gurlitt, gōōr'lit, (JOHANN GOTTFRIED,) a German archæologist, born at Halle in 1754, wrote "On the Science of Gems," and other works. Died in 1827.

Gŭr'nall, (WILLIAM,) an English divine, born in 1617. He became rector of Lavenham in 1644, and remained there thirty-five years. He published "The Christian in Complete Armour," (3 vols., 1656–62.) Died in 1679.

Gŭr'ney, (HUDSON,) M.P., an English antiquary and poet, born about 1774. He produced a good translation of the "Golden Ass" of Apuleius, entitled "Cupid and Psyche," (1799.) Died in 1864.

Gurney, (Rev. JOHN HAMPDEN,) an English divine of the present age. He published several volumes of sermons, (1845–57,) and "Historical Sketches, 1400–1546," (1852, second series, 1855, and third series, 1858.) He died in 1862, aged about sixty years.

Gurney, (JOSEPH JOHN,) an English philanthropist and minister of the Society of Friends, born near Norwich in 1788. He studied at Oxford, where he was distinguished for his attainments in mathematics and the ancient languages. In 1841, in company with his sister, the celebrated Mrs. Fry, he set out on a tour on the continent, with the view of introducing improvements into prison-discipline and of inducing the French government to abolish slavery in their colonies. He was the author of "Notes and Dissertations on the Bible," "Observations on the Distinguishing Views, etc. of the Society of Friends," "Hints on the Portable Evidence of Christianity," and other valuable works. He possessed great wealth, of which he made a most liberal use, both in public and private charities. In 1837–39 he visited the United States and the West Indies, and wrote "A Winter in the West Indies," giving an interesting account of the results of emancipation in those islands. Died in 1847.

See BERNARD BARTON, "Memorial of J. J. Gurney," 1847; "The British Friend" for 1st month, 1847; "Memoirs of J. J. Gurney, with Selections from his Journal," etc.

Gurowski, goo-rov'skee, (ADAM,) COUNT, a Polish writer and patriot, born in the government of Kalisz about 1810. After the revolution of 1830 he repaired to Paris, where he employed himself for a time as a journalist, and in 1849 visited America. He published, in French, "Thoughts on the Future of Poland," (1841,) "Russia and Civilization," (1841,) (in German,) and various other works. Died in 1866.

See "Atlantic Monthly" for November, 1866.

Gurtler, goōRt'lẹr, (NICHOLAS,) a Swiss Protestant divine, born at Bâle in 1654; died in 1711.

See NICÉRON, "Mémoires."

Gur'wood, (JOHN,) a brave English officér, born in 1791, served in the Peninsular war, and was leader of the forlorn hope at the storming of Ciudad Rodrigo in 1812. He became private secretary to the Duke of Wellington, and in 1841 was made a colonel. He published in 1838 "The Despatches of the Duke of Wellington during his Various Campaigns," etc., (13 vols. 8vo,) a very popular and valuable work. Died in 1845.

Gushtâsp, goōsh-tâsp', or **Gustâsp,** goōs-tâsp', written also **Goshtasp, Histasp,** and **Kishtasp,** a famous Persian hero and king, who has been by some writers identified with Darius I., (surnamed Hystaspis,) by others with Hystaspes, the father of Darius. There is so much that is fabulous in the Persian accounts that have come down to us, that it seems impossible, in most cases, to settle in any satisfactory manner the question of identity between the kings of the Persian writers and those of the Greek historians. Firdousee, (Firdausî,) who is generally believed to have taken the facts of Persian history for the basis of his great poem, (the "Shâh Nâmah,") represents Gushtâsp as having ruled over Persia many years as an absolute sovereign, and as having under his command "a thousand thousand warriors armed with shining steel,"—which could not very well refer to Hystaspes, who was but a satrap or inferior prince under Cambyses, but would answer exactly to the circumstances of Darius Hystaspis. As "Darius" (in Persian, "Dârâ" or "Dârâb") was not originally a proper name, but a title, signifying "lord," "prince," or "king," it seems probable that he should have been generally known among the Persians by his patronymic *Hystaspes,* (in Persian, *Gushtâsp.*) Darius Hystaspis would then signify, according to the Greek mode of speaking, the "Prince [son] of Hystaspes." According to Firdousee, Gushtâsp was the first Persian king who openly professed the religion of Zoroaster, who (if we may trust the poet-historian) was the contemporary of Gushtâsp and his most influential counsellor. (See DARIUS I., and HYSTASPES.)

See J. ATKINSON, "Abridgment of the Shâh Nameh of Firdausi," London, 1832; SMITH, "Greek and Roman Biography and Mythology."

Gusman, (BARTHOLOMEU LOURENÇO.) See GUZMAN.

Gussetius. See GOUSSET.

Gustaf, the Swedish of GUSTAVUS, which see.

Gustafsköld or **Gustafskoeld,** goōs'tâfs-chöld', originally named ABRAHAM **Hellichius,** a Swedish general, born in 1723. Having rendered a very important service to the king, Gustavus III., he was made a general by him, and received a title of nobility, with the surname of GUSTAFSKOELD, ("Shield of Gustavus.") Died in 1792.

Gustav or **Gustave.** See GUSTAVUS.

Gustavus, gŭs-tā'vus or gŭs-tā'vus, [Lat. GUSTA'VUS; Sw. GUSTAF, goōs'tâf; Ger. GUSTAV, goōs'tâf; Fr. GUSTAVE, gŭs'tȧv'; It. GUSTAVO, goos-tâ'vo,] **I.,** commonly called **Gustavus Vasa,** (or **Wasa,** vä'sa,) King of Sweden, was born near Stockholm in 1496. Christiern II. of Denmark, having usurped the crown of Sweden in 1519, caused Gustavus to be imprisoned. Within three days after his coronation, Christiern violated his solemn promise of protection to the Swedish nation, and ordered the execution of the heads of the first Swedish families. Among the eighty-four persons who perished was Eric Vasa, the father of Gustavus. The latter, having escaped from prison, fled to the mountains of Dalecarlia. After enduring great hardships, he at length succeeded in attaching to himself a powerful party, with which he marched towards Stockholm. In 1521, at the head of fifteen thousand men, he took the town and fortress of Westerås, and finally obtained possession of Stockholm, after an obstinate defence. The crown was now offered to Gustavus, which he refused, and chose rather to govern under the title of stadtholder. But, as the nation was still molested by the King of Denmark and his allies the Catholic party, they again solicited Gustavus to become their sovereign; and in June, 1527, he was crowned King of Sweden. He died in 1559, after a reign of thirty-three years, during which he had gained

the love of his people by his wise and beneficent administration. He was succeeded by his son, Eric XIV.

See HOLBERG, "Histoire du Danemarck;" GEYER, "Histoire de la Suède;" VERTOT, "Histoire des Révolutions de la Suède;" OLAF CELSIUS, "Konung Gustafs I. Historia," 2 vols., 1746-53; J. W. ARCHENHOLZ, "Geschichte Gustav Wasa's Konigs von Schweden," 2 vols., 1801, (and French version of the same, Paris, 1803.)

Gustavus II. See GUSTAVUS ADOLPHUS.

Gustavus III., King of Sweden, eldest son of Adolphus Frederick, born in 1746, succeeded to the throne in 1771. Soon after his accession he formed the project of diminishing the power of the nobles, at this time so great as to be dangerous to the crown, while their oppressions made them hated by the people. Having by his favours secured the co-operation of the army, he offered his plan for a new constitution to all the military officers of the capital, who received it with applause. After exacting an oath of obedience from the soldiers, he next arrested the chief members of the States-General, and made a public declaration of his project. The following day, the house in which the States-General were assembled was surrounded by soldiers and cannon, and the king, with his military staff, entered, and proposed to them the new constitution. It was accepted, and confirmed by signatures. Those who had been arrested were released, and the revolution was effected without bloodshed. In 1788, however, the nobles showed their hostility to the king by refusing to grant him supplies during his wars with Denmark and Russia. In 1789 Gustavus caused a law to be passed which greatly increased the royal prerogatives, and at the same time he arrested the leaders of the opposition in the Diet. About 1792 several Swedish noblemen conspired against the king's life; and at a masked ball given at Stockholm he was assassinated by one of their number, named Ankarström, in March, 1792. In addition to his talents as a statesman, Gustavus was distinguished as a poet and a dramatist.

See GEISLER, "Leben des Königs von Schweden, Gustavs III.;" GEYER, "Histoire de la Suède;" E. L. POSSELT, "Geschichte Gustav's III. Königs der Schweden," 1792; F. BECCATINI, "Storia del Regno e della Vita di Gustavo III.," 4 vols., 1792.

Gustavus IV., born in 1778, succeeded his father, Gustavus III., in 1792. From his childhood he had manifested a singular obstinacy of disposition, which in after-life resembled monomania. A zealous advocate of the divine right of kings, he made it the principal object of his life to restore the Bourbon family to the throne of France. He travelled through Germany in 1803 in order to unite the princes of the Empire against Napoleon I. He would have no intercourse with the nations of Europe who were in the least degree friendly to the French emperor. By these follies he alienated the affections of his people and brought them into innumerable difficulties. The Swedes, in order to rescue their country from the ruin which his conduct was likely to bring upon it, formed a plan for deposing him. Gustavus, suspecting their designs, attempted to obtain possession of the money in the Bank of Sweden, but was prevented by force, and soon after imprisoned as a traitor, (1809.) The king and his direct descendants were declared by the Diet to have forfeited their right to the crown, and his uncle, Duke Charles, was proclaimed king, under the title of Charles XIII. The deposed king, after travelling over Europe, fixed his residence in the town of Saint Gall, in Switzerland, where he assumed the name of Colonel Gustavson, and supported himself by his writings, together with a small pension. His son Gustavus obtained the title of Prince of Wasa. Died in 1837.

See LE BAS, "Suède et Norvège;" "London Quarterly Review" for December, 1812.

Gus-ta'vus A-dol'phus, [Fr. GUSTAVE ADOLPHE, gŭs'tȧv' ȧ'dolf'; Ger. GUSTAF ADOLF, goōs'tâf ä'dolf; It. GUSTAVO ADOLFO, goos-tâ'vo ä-dol'fo,] or **Gustavus II.,** King of Sweden, the most illustrious hero of his time, born at Stockholm on the 9th of December, 1594, was the son of Charles IX., and grandson of Gustavus Vasa. He ascended the throne in his seventeenth year, and soon gave proof of his extraordinary abilities. Sweden having been invaded by Sigismund, King of Poland, and his ally the Czar of Russia, Gustavus defeated them, and in 1629 concluded a peace by which he gained a great part of Livonia and the town of Riga. Soon after this he was invited by the Protestants of Germany, suffering under the persecutions of Ferdinand II., to be the champion of their cause. Their solicitations, combined with the interest which he as a zealous Protestant felt in the success of their arms, induced him to comply. Before setting out, he published a declaration to the effect that he did not take this step from the love of conquest, but for the defence of his religion and to avenge the injuries he had received from the Emperor of Austria. In June, 1630, Gustavus landed in Pomerania, at the head of 8000 men. His army was soon after reinforced by six Scottish regiments under the Duke of Hamilton, and took the fortress of Wolgast, which supplied them with arms and ammunition. Having advanced into Mecklenburg, Gustavus received proposals of peace from the emperor, offering him, among other things, the possession of Pomerania. These proposals were rejected, and Gustavus, with his army increased by large numbers of German Protestants, continued his march through Pomerania and Mecklenburg, taking one town and fortress after another in rapid succession. He was soon after opposed by Field-Marshal Tilly, whom, after several indecisive engagements, he signally defeated at Leipsic in September, 1631. In a second encounter with Tilly, on the banks of the Lech, in April, 1632, that general lost his life. Ferdinand, now becoming alarmed at the victories of Gustavus, summoned Wallenstein, whom he had shortly before dismissed, to oppose him. On the 16th of November, 1632, these commanders, the most eminent of their time, and both hitherto unconquered, met on the plain of Lützen. In the early part of the action Gustavus was mortally wounded; and the Swedes, exasperated in the highest degree by the loss of their king, whom they idolized, fought with irresistible fury, and compelled the enemy to retreat. The Duke of Saxe-Lauenburg, a cousin of Gustavus, who was near him when he fell, and who soon afterwards entered the service of Austria, was strongly suspected of having assassinated him. The military talents of Gustavus were of the highest order; but they were surpassed by his admirable qualities as a man and his virtues as a ruler. He was succeeded by his daughter and only child, Christina. "Gustavus was," says Schiller, "incontestably the first commander of his century, and the bravest soldier in the army which he had created. His eye watched over the morals of his soldiers as strictly as over their bravery. In everything their law-giver was also their example. In the intoxication of his fortune he was still a man and a Christian, and in his devotion still a hero and a king."

See SCHILLER, "History of the Thirty Years' War;" R. DE PRADE, "Histoire de Gustave Adolphe dit le Grand," 1686; GEYER, "Histoire de la Suède;" WALTER HARTE, "History of the Life of Gustavus Adolphus," 2 vols., 1759; N. VOGT, "Gustav Adolph König von Schweden," 2 vols., 1790; JONAS HALLENBERG, "Svea Rikes Historia under Konung Gustaf Adolfs Regering," 5 vols., 1790-96; AXEL OXENSTIERNA, "Histoire de la Jeunesse de Gustave Adolph;" ANDERS FRYXELL, "Gustaf II. Adolph," 1833; J. F. HOLLINGS, "Life of Gustavus Adolphus," 1838; GFRÖRER, "Geschichte Gustav Adolph's," 2 vols., 1837; "Gustav Adolf," von C. DROYSEN, 1869.

Gustavus Eriksson. See GUSTAVUS I.

Gustavus Vasa, (or **Wasa.**) See GUSTAVUS I.

Gutberleth, goot'ber-lêt', (HEINRICH,) a German professor of philosophy at Deventer, born at Hirschfeld in 1592, wrote a treatise (in Latin) "On Human Affections Physically and Morally considered." Died in 1635.

Gutberleth, gŭt'ber-lêt', (TOBIAS,) a Dutch antiquary, born in Friesland about 1674, was the author of a treatise "On the Mysteries of the Cabiri Gods," (in Latin,) and other works. Died in 1703.

Gŭtch, (JOHN,) an English antiquary, born in 1745, was registrar of the University of Oxford. He published "The History and Antiquities of the University of Oxford, from the Manuscripts of Anthony Wood, with a Continuation," (1786.) Died in 1831.

Gutch, (JOHN MATTHEW,) an English antiquary, son of the preceding, born about 1777, wrote "A Lytell Geste of Robin Hode," (2 vols., 1847.) Died in 1858.

Gutenberg, goo'ten-bêRG', (JOHANN or HENNE,) the inventor of printing, was born at Mentz, in Germany, about 1400. His original name was GÄNSFLEISCH, (gênss'-flîsh;) but he afterwards assumed his mother's family name of Gutenberg. In 1450 he entered into partnership with John Faust, a citizen of Mentz, in conjunction with whom he printed a vocabulary, called a "Catholi-

con," by means of letters cut on blocks of wood. Types of copper or tin were soon after substituted for wood; and with these a Latin Bible was printed, with great difficulty and expense. In 1455, owing to some disagreement in pecuniary matters, Gutenberg and Faust separated, after having had a law-suit. The former, being unable to pay the sum awarded to Faust by the judge, was obliged to give up to him his printing-materials and his invention. Gutenberg subsequently practised his art at Mentz. He was appointed by the archbishop elector of that city and one of the nobles of his court, and obtained other preferments. A bronze monument, by Thorwaldsen, was erected to his memory at Mentz in 1837. Died in 1468.

See DUPONT, "Histoire de l'Imprimerie;" FALKENSTEIN, "Geschichte der Buchdruckerkunst," 1840; OTTLEY, "Inquiry into the Origin, etc. of Engraving on Copper and Wood," 1816; MEERMANN, "Origines Typographicæ," 1765; SOTHEBY, "The Typography of the Fifteenth Century," 1845; ALPHONSE DE LAMARTINE, "Gutenberg, Inventeur de l'Imprimerie," 1853; CHARLES SCHMIDT, "Nouveaux Détails sur la Vie de Gutenberg," 1841; DOMENICO TACCIO, "Notizie storico-critico-tipografico-bibliografiche di Gutenberg," etc., 1844; "Memoirs of Celebrated Characters," by LAMARTINE, 1856.

Gutenberg or **Guttemberg,** gŏōt'tem-bêRG', (KARL GOTTLIEB,) a German engraver, born near Nuremberg about 1742. He worked in Paris, where he died in 1792. Among his works were engravings after Rembrandt and Mieris.

Gutherius. See GOUTHIÈRES.

Guthier. See GOUTHIÈRES.

Gŭth'rie, (GEORGE JAMES,) an English surgeon, born in London in 1785. He lectured on surgery in London for many years, and wrote several professional works. Died in 1856.

Gŭth'rie, (JAMES,) an American statesman and jurist, born in Nelson county, Kentucky, in 1793. He began to practise law at Louisville about 1820, and was for several years a member of the State legislature for that city. In 1850 he was president of the convention which framed the new constitution of Kentucky. He was appointed by President Pierce secretary of the United States treasury in 1853, and was elected to the Senate of the United States in 1865. Died in 1869.

See LIVINGSTON's "Portraits of Eminent Americans."

Gŭth'rie, (THOMAS,) D.D., a Scottish divine, born at Brechin about 1800. He became an eloquent preacher, and minister of Free Saint John's, Edinburgh, in 1840. As an associate of Dr. Chalmers, he took a prominent part in the institution of the Free Church in 1843. He published "The Gospel in Ezekiel." He was the chief founder of the original Ragged or Industrial School of Edinburgh.

Guthrie, (WILLIAM,) a Scottish littérateur, born in the county of Angus about 1708. He published a "General History of England from the Invasion of the Romans under Julius Cæsar to the Revolution of 1688," a "History of the English Peerage," a "History of Scotland," and other compilations. Died in 1770.

See DISRAELI, "Calamities of Authors;" CHAMBERS, "Biographical Dictionary of Eminent Scotsmen."

Gŭth'rȳ or **Guthrie,** (HENRY,) a Scottish divine, was one of the adherents of Charles I. in his contest with the Parliament. He became Bishop of Dunkeld in 1665. He died in 1676, leaving a "History of his Own Time," published in 1748.

See CHAMBERS, "Biographical Dictionary of Eminent Scotsmen."

Gutierrez, goo-te-êr'rêth, or **Gutierres,** goo-te-êr'-rês, (ANTONIO **Garcia**—gaR-thee'â,) a popular Spanish dramatist, born near Cadiz about 1814. He produced about 1834 "El Trovador," a drama. Among his works are "El Page," and "Magdalena."

Gutsmuths, gŏōts'mŏōts, (JOHANN CHRISTOPH FRIEDRICH,) a German teacher and educational writer, born at Quedlinburg in 1759. He published "Plays for the Exercise and Recreation of Body and Mind," (1796,) and other similar treatises. Died in 1839.

Gutzkow, gŏōts'ko, (KARL FERDINAND,) a popular German novelist and dramatist, born in Berlin in 1811. He became about 1830 one of the chiefs of the school called "Young Germany." He published, besides many other works, successful tragedies entitled "Patkul" (1841) and "Uriel Acosta," (1847,) a comedy called "Das Urbild des Tartuffe," a collection of critical essays entitled "Gods, Heroes, and Don Quixote," (1838,) and "Die Ritter vom Geist," a political and social romance, (1850–52,) which was very popular. He became a resident of Dresden in 1847.

See HEINRICH HOFF, "G. Gutzkow und die Gutzkowgraphie," 1839; "Nouvelle Biographie Générale."

Gützlaff, gŭts'laf or gŭts'lâf, (KARL,) a celebrated German missionary and Chinese scholar, born at Pyritz, in Pomerania, in 1803. He repaired to Siam in 1828, and, in conjunction with Tomlin, translated the New Testament into Siamese. With a view of introducing the gospel into China, he settled at Macao, where he formed an intimate friendship with Dr. Morrison, after whose death Gützlaff became, in 1835, first interpreter for the superintendence of British commerce. He visited England in 1849, and died at Hong-Kong, shortly after his return, in 1851. Among his various works (which are mostly written in English) we may name his "China Opened," (1838,) and "History of the Chinese Empire." He also had a share in a new translation of the Bible into Chinese.

Guy. See GUI and GUIDO.

Guy, gī, (THOMAS,) the founder of Guy's Hospital, London, was born in that city in 1643. Having acquired a large fortune, principally by the sale of South Sea stock, he built additions to Saint Thomas's Hospital in Southwark in 1707, and subsequently founded the hospital near Saint Thomas's which bears his name. He is said to have made more munificent donations for charitable purposes than any other private man in the kingdom. Died in 1724.

Guy, gī or ge, (or **Guido,** gwee'do) **de Lusignan,** (deh lü'sèn'yŏN',) King of Jerusalem, was of French origin. He married Sibylla, daughter of Amaury, King of Jerusalem. In 1186, Baldwin V., the son of Sibylla by a former husband, the Marquis of Montferrat, became heir to the throne, but died in the same year. Guy de Lusignan then obtained the title of king. His capital was taken by Saladin in 1187, and his title was disputed by Isabella, a sister of Sibylla. Guy applied for aid to Richard I. of England, who gave him the kingdom of Cyprus (1192) on condition that he would renounce his claim to Jerusalem. He was succeeded by his brother Amaury about 1194.

See MICHAUD, "History of the Crusades."

Guyard, ge'ăr', (BERNARD,) a French friar, born at Craon in 1601, had the title of preacher (*prédicateur*) to the king, and wrote several works. Died in 1674.

Guyard, (LAURENT,) a French sculptor, born at Chaumont-en-Bassigni in 1723, was a pupil of Bouchardon the Younger. Died in 1788.

See J. B. VARNEY, "Notice sur L. Guyard," 1806.

Guyard de Berville, ge'ăr' deh bĕR'vèl', a French biographer, born in Paris in 1697. He wrote a "Life of Chevalier Bayard," (1760,) and a "Life of Bertrand Du Guesclin," (1767.) Died in a hospital in 1770.

Guyet, ge'ā', (FRANÇOIS,) a French scholar, born at Angers in 1575. He wrote annotations on various Greek and Latin classics, and some Latin poems. He was a friend of De Thou, Ménage, and Balzac. Died in 1655.

Guyétand, ge'ā'tôN', (CLAUDE MARIE,) a French poet and satirist, born in 1748, wrote "Genius Avenged," and other poems. Died in 1811.

Guyon, ge'ôN', (CLAUDE MARIE,) a French historian, born in Franche-Comté in 1699. He published a continuation of Echard's "Roman History," (10 vols., 1736,) a "History of the Amazons, Ancient and Modern," (1740,) a "History of the Indies," (3 vols., 1744,) and other works. Died in 1771.

See DESESSARTS, "Les Siècles littéraires de la France."

Guyon, gī'ǫn, [Fr. pron. ge'ôN',] (JEANNE **Bouvier de la Motte**—boo've-a' deh lă mot,) MADAME, a French lady, celebrated for her talents and piety, born at Montargis in 1648. In her sixteenth year, in compliance with her parents' wishes, she married M. Guyon, whom she had never seen till a few days previous. On becoming a widow, in 1676, she devoted herself to the service of the Church, and a few years later retired to a religious establishment at Gex. She soon after wrote "The Song of Songs of Solomon, interpreted according to the Mystic

Sense," and a "Short and Easy Method of Prayer," two very popular works, which, however, gave offence to some of the clergy. In consequence of their persecutions, she was imprisoned nearly eight months. On her release she became intimately acquainted with Fénelon, who had considerable sympathy with her peculiar religious views and continued to be one of her truest friends. About this time she put her writings into the hands of Bossuet, Bishop of Meaux, who expurgated them from what he regarded as the heresy of Quietism. Notwithstanding the submission of Madame Guyon to the censure of Bossuet, she was involved in the persecutions of Fénelon, and about 1695 was imprisoned in the Bastille. On her release, in 1700, she devoted herself to writing; and her works, it is said, form 39 octavo volumes. Her Autobiography has been translated by Cowper, who had a great esteem for her character and her writings.

See UPHAM, "Life of Madame Guyon," 1851; DE BAUSSET, "Histoire de Fénelon ;" VOLTAIRE, "Siècle de Louis XIV ;" PHÉLIPEAUX, "Lettres sur l'Histoire du Quiétisme ;" HODGSON, "Reformers and Martyrs," Philadelphia, 1867.

Guyon, gī'ǫn, (RICHARD DEBAUFRE,) a distinguished general, born near Bath, in England, in 1813. He entered the Austrian service in 1832, and rose in a few years to be aide-de-camp of the Hungarian field-marshal Splenyi, whose daughter he married. He fought with great distinction against the Austrians in the principal battles of the revolution of 1848, and was created a general. After Görgey's surrender, (August, 1849,) Guyon escaped with Kossuth to Turkey, where he obtained a high command in the Sultan's army. He organized the army which defended Kars, (1854.) Died at Constantinople in 1856.

See A. KINGLAKE, "Gen. Guyon on the Battle-Fields of Hungary."

Guyot. See DESFONTAINES, ABBÉ.

Guyot, ge'o', (ARNOLD HENRY,) Ph.D., LL.D., a meritorious writer on physical geography, was born near Neufchâtel, in Switzerland, in 1807. He was a fellow-student and friend of Agassiz, graduated at Berlin in 1835, and spent several years in the study of glaciers, in which he made important discoveries. He came to the United States in 1848, and in the ensuing winter delivered in Boston a course of lectures on physical geography, which were published under the title of "The Earth and Man," (1849.) He is author of a series of text-books on geography. He has been for some years professor of geology and physical geography at Princeton College, New Jersey.

Guyot, ge'o', (CLAUDE ÉTIENNE,) a French general, born near Lons-le-Saulnier in 1768, served as general of division in Russia in 1812. Died in 1837.

Guyot, (GERMAIN ANTOINE,) a French jurist, born in Paris in 1694; died in 1750.

Guyot, (JOSEPH NICOLAS,) a French jurist, born in Lorraine in 1728, published, besides other works, a useful compilation called a "Universal and Descriptive (*raisonné*) Repertory of Civil, Criminal, and Canonical Jurisprudence," (64 vols., 1775–86.) Died in 1816.

Guyot de Fère, ge'o' deh faiR, (FRANÇOIS FORTUNÉ,) a French journalist and *litté rateur,* born in Paris in 1791. In 1826 he founded the "Journal of Arts and Trades," ("Journal des Arts et Métiers.") He published, among other works, a "History of Prince Eugene Beauharnais," (1821.)

Guyot de Folleville. See FOLLEVILLE.

Guyot des Herbiers, ge'o' dà zêR'be-ā', (CLAUDE ANTOINE,) a French poet, born at Joinville in 1745 ; died in 1828.

Guys, ge, (PIERRE ALPHONSE,) a French *littérateur,* son of Pierre Augustin, noticed below, was born at Marseilles in 1755. He was the author of a comedy entitled "The House of Molière," a "Eulogy on Antoninus Pius," and several other works. Died in 1812.

Guys, (PIERRE AUGUSTIN,) a French merchant and traveller, born at Marseilles in 1721, visited Asia and Greece, and published in 1776 a "Literary Journey in Greece," which was eulogized by Voltaire in some verses. Died in 1799.

Guyse. See GUISE.

Guyse, gīz, ? (JOHN,) an eminent English Calvinist and Independent minister, born at Hertford in 1680. He preached for some years in London. His principal work, "An Exposition of the New Testament in the Form of a Paraphrase," (3 vols., 1739-42,) has been often reprinted. Died in 1761.

Guyton de Morveau, ge'tòn' dęh moR'vō', (LOUIS BERNARD,) an eminent French chemist, born at Dijon in January, 1737, was educated for the law, and in 1755 became advocate-general in Parliament. Without relinquishing the law, he pursued the study of chemistry with success, and in 1772 published a work on the subject, entitled "Academic Digressions." In 1773 he made the important discovery of the power of certain fumigations against infectious effluvia, and checked a fatal disease at Dijon by chlorine gas. In 1782 he proposed a methodical nomenclature for chemistry, and afterwards united with Lavoisier in forming that system of nomenclature which has since been generally adopted with such extensive utility. He displayed great erudition and judgment in his "Chemical Dictionary" for the "Encyclopédie Méthodique," (1786.) As a member of the Convention in 1792, he participated in the excesses of the popular party. About 1795 he took a prominent part in the establishment of the Polytechnic School, in which he occupied a chair for eleven years. He contributed many articles to the Institute, of which he was a member, and to the "Annales de Chimie," of which he was editor. He was a Fellow of the Royal Society of London. During the empire of Napoleon he received the title of baron, and was an officer of the legion of honour. Died in 1816.

See BERTHOLLET, "Éloge historique de Guyton de Morveau;" HOEFER, "Histoire de la Chimie;" "Encyclopædia Britannica;" "Nouvelle Biographie Générale."

Guzman, gooth-mân', (ALEJANDRO,) a Spanish politician, born in Granada in 1752, entered the republican army soon after the breaking out of the French Revolution, and became one of the most violent members of the Jacobin faction. He was guillotined in Paris in 1794.

Guzman, de, då gooth-mân', (ALFONSO PEREZ,) surnamed THE GOOD, a celebrated Spanish commander, born at Valladolid in 1258. Having been appointed by King Sancho IV. governor of Tarifa, he defended that fortress against the Infant Don Juan, brother of the king. Don Juan, having failed in his efforts to take the place, threatened to put to death a son of Guzman who had fallen into his hands, if the fortress was not instantly surrendered. To this menace Guzman replied "that, sooner than be guilty of such infamous treachery, he would lend him a poniard to kill his son," at the same time throwing his dagger from the ramparts. The atrocious threat was executed; and the wife of Guzman died soon after, of grief. This incident has been celebrated in one of Lope de Vega's dramas. Guzman afterwards distinguished himself in several engagements with the Moors, and fell in battle in 1309. He was the ancestor of the Dukes of Medina-Sidonia.

See QUINTANA, "Lives of Celebrated Spaniards."

Guzman or **Guzmão, de,** då goos-mŏwn', (BARTHOLOMEU LOURENÇO,) a Portuguese mechanician and ecclesiastic, born at Santos about 1680, is called the original inventor of the balloon. He made the first experiment with his machine near Lisbon in 1709; but he was deterred from prosecuting his labours by the fear of the Inquisition. Died about 1725.

See "Encyclopædia Americana," edited by FRANCIS LIEBER; "Encyclopædia Britannica."

Guzman, de, (ENRIQUE,) Duke of Medina-Sidonia, a Spanish grandee, acted a prominent part in the conquest of Granada. Died in 1492.

Guzman, de, (Don FERNANDO PEREZ,) a Spanish poet and chronicler, born in 1405, left a "Chronicle of John II. of Castile." Died in 1470.

Guzman, de, (Donna LUISA,) a daughter of Juan Perez, Duke of Medina-Sidonia, became the queen of John of Braganza, King of Portugal. On his death, in 1656, she was appointed regent, and distinguished herself by the wisdom and firmness of her administration. Having concluded a treaty with Charles I. of England, she gave her daughter in marriage to his son, afterwards Charles II. Soon after the accession of her son, Alfonso VI., she retired to a convent, where she died in 1666. Under her rule the independence of Portugal was secured.

Guzman, de, (OLIVAREZ.) See OLIVAREZ.

Guzman, de, (PEDRO,) a Spanish painter, surnamed EL COXO, ("the Lame,") born about 1557, was patronized by Philip III., who made him his painter in 1601.

See QUILLIET, "Dictionnaire des Peintres Espagnols."

Gwilt, (GEORGE,) an English architect and antiquary, was born in London in 1775. Among his principal works are the warehouses of the West India Docks. Being employed in repairing Bow Church in 1820, he identified the Norman remains of the original building, which he described in a treatise entitled "Observations on the Church of Saint Mary-le-Bow," etc. He also restored the church of Saint Mary Overy, and other edifices in London. Died in 1856.

Gwilt, (JOSEPH,) a brother of the preceding, born in 1784, was distinguished as a writer on architecture. He designed Markree Castle, near Sligo. Among his works are "Rudiments of Architecture, Practical and Theoretical," (1826,) and an "Encyclopædia of Architecture, Historical, Theoretical, and Practical," (1842,) which is commended as a standard work.

Gwilym, gwĭl'im, (DAVID AP,) a Welsh bard, born in Cardiganshire in 1340; died about 1400. His poems, in Welsh, were published in 1792.

Gwin, (WILLIAM M.,) a Democratic politician, born in Sumner county, Tennessee, in 1805. He was elected to the Senate of the United States for California in 1850, and was re-elected in 1857. He acted with the pro-slavery party.

Gwinn, (WILLIAM,) an American naval officer, born at Columbus, Indiana, in 1831. He became a lieutenant in 1856, and commanded a gunboat at the battles of Fort Donelson and Shiloh, February and April, 1862. He was killed in the attack on Haines' Bluff, near Vicksburg, in January, 1863.

Gwinne, gwĭn, (MATTHEW,) an English physician, born in London about 1554, was appointed in 1582 regent of Saint John's College, Oxford, and in 1596 first professor of medicine in Gresham College. He was also a Fellow of the College of Physicians. Died in 1627.

See WARD's "Lives of the Gresham Professors."

Gwin-nett', (BUTTON,) born in England about 1732, emigrated to Georgia about 1772. In 1776 he was elected to Congress, in which he signed the Declaration of Independence. He became president of the provincial council of Georgia in 1777, and was killed in a duel by General McIntosh in May of that year.

See GOODRICH's "Lives of the Signers to the Declaration of Independence."

Gwynn or **Gwynne,** gwĭn, (ELEANOR,) an English actress and celebrated beauty, was born in London about 1650. After she had achieved success as an actress, she became a mistress of Charles II. Died about 1690.

See P. CUNNINGHAM, "The Story of Nell Gwynn," 1852; W. H. D. ADAMS, "Famous Beauties and Historic Women," vol. i., London, 1865.

Gy'ḡēs, [Gr. Γύγης,] first Lydian king of the dynasty of the Mermnadæ, was minister of King Candaules, whose throne he usurped after having put him to death. He is said to have possessed a magic ring which made the wearer invisible. He reigned about thirty-eight years. Died about 680 B.C.

Gylippe. See GYLIPPUS.

Gy-lip'pus, [Gr. Γύλιππος; Fr. GYLIPPE, zhe'lėp',] a skilful Spartan general in the Peloponnesian war. In 414 B.C. he was sent to command the army at Syracuse, which was then besieged by the Athenians. He defeated the enemy in several actions, and captured their whole army, commanded by Nicias and Demosthenes, in 413. After the capture of Athens by Lysander, Gylippus was commissioned to convey to Sparta the treasure there obtained. He was convicted of stealing a large part of it, and was condemned to death, but escaped, and died in exile.

See THUCYDIDES, books vi., vii., viii.; PLUTARCH, "Nicias" and "Lysander;" MÜLLER, "The Dorians."

Gyllembourg-Ehrensvärd, gül'lęm-bŏŏRG' ā'ręn-svērd', (THOMASINE CHRISTINE BUNTZEN,) MADAME, a celebrated Danish novelist, born in 1773, was married in 1790 to the dramatist Peter Andreas Heiberg. She was subsequently divorced, and in 1801 became the wife of Count Gyllembourg-Ehrensvärd. Her "Novels, Old

e as k; ç as s; ḡ hard; ġ as j; G, H, K, guttural; N, nasal; R, trilled; s as z; th as in this. (☞See Explanations, p. 23.)

70

and New, by the Author of a Story of Every Day," ("Gamle og Nye Noveller af Forfatteren til en Hverdags Historie,") appeared in 1834. They acquired a wide popularity, and were translated into French and German. Died in 1856.

See ERSLEW, "Forfatter-Lexicon."

Gyllenborg, yül′lẹn-borg′, (CHARLES,) COUNT, a Swedish nobleman and diplomatist, born at Upsal in 1679. He was employed by Charles XII. as resident minister in London from 1703 to 1717, and subsequently rose to be a councillor of state and chancellor of the University of Upsal. He was the author of "Disputatio de Regno Ostro-Gothorum in Italia," ("Dissertation on the Ostro-Gothic Kingdom in Italy.") Died in 1746.

See JOHAN IHRE, "Oratio in Memoriam C. Gyllenborg," 1747.

Gyllenborg, (GUSTAVUS FREDERIC,) COUNT, a cousin of the preceding, born in 1731, was one of the first members of the Academy of Stockholm. He published a number of odes, satires, fables, and poems of various kinds, among which may be named "The Passage of the Belts." Died in 1809.

Gyllenhaal, yül′lẹn-hâl, (LEONHARD,) a Swedish entomologist, born in West Gothland in 1752, was a pupil of Linnæus. He wrote an able work on the insects of Sweden, ("Insecta Suecica," 4 vols., 1808–27.) Died in 1840.

Gyllenhielm, yül′lẹn-hyêlm′, (CARL CARLSSON,) BARON, a natural son of Charles IX. of Sweden, was born in 1574. He served with distinction in France in the army of Henry IV., and afterwards was made a senator, high admiral of Sweden, and one of the preceptors of the princess Christina. Died in 1650.

Gyöngyösy, dyön′dyö-se, (STEPHEN,) one of the earliest Hungarian poets, born in 1620. His works are still popular among his countrymen, and have passed through numerous editions. Died in 1704.

Gyrowetz, gĭr′o-wêts′, (ADALBERT,) a distinguished musical composer, born at Budweis, in Bohemia, in 1763. After visiting Paris and London, where he was received with great favour, he settled at Vienna, and became chapel-master at the Imperial Theatre. Among his best operas are "The Oculist," and "Felix and Adele." He also composed masses, sonatas, and symphonies : the last-named are particularly admired. Died in 1850.

See his Autobiography, "Biographie von ihm selbst geschrieben," 1848 ; FÉTIS, "Biographie Universelle des Musiciens."

Gyulai or **Gyulay,** dyoo′lī, (FRANZ,) COUNT, a Hungarian general in the Austrian service, was born at Pesth in 1799. He became colonel about 1830, and lieutenant-field-marshal in 1846. He was minister of war a short time in 1850, after which he was commandant at Milan. In 1857 he succeeded Radetzky as commander-in-chief of the army of Italy. He had the chief command in the war which began in May, 1859, and was defeated by the Franco-Sardinian army at the great battle of Magenta in June. Before the end of this month he was deprived of the command. Died in 1862.

Gyulai or **Gyulay,** (IGNATIUS,) COUNT, an Austrian commander, the father of the preceding, born at Hermannstadt in 1763, served against the Turks and in the principal campaigns against the French. In 1805 he concluded the peace of Presburg, in conjunction with Prince Liechtenstein, and was soon after made Ban of Croatia, Dalmatia, and Slavonia. He was appointed field-marshal-general in 1813, and in 1830 president of the aulic council. Died in 1831.

Gyzen, gī′zẹn or hī′zẹn,(PETER,) a Flemish landscape-painter, born at Antwerp in 1636. His works are rare, and are prized for their high finish. Died about 1700.

H.

Haag, hÃg, (EUGÈNE and ÉMILE,) brothers, and French Protestants, born at Montbéliard in 1808 and 1810. They published "Protestant France, or the Lives of French Protestants who have made for themselves a Name in History," ("La France protestante," etc., 9 vols. 8vo, 1847–59.)

Haak, hÃk, (THEODOR,) a German divine, born near Worms in 1605. He translated the Dutch annotations on the Bible into English, and was one of the founders of the Royal Society of London. He passed many years in England. Died in 1690.

Haansbergen, van, vÃn hÃns′bêR′gẹn, (JAN,) a Dutch painter, born at Utrecht in 1642, was one of the best pupils of Poelemburg, whom he imitated. He settled at the Hague in 1669, and painted portraits, nymphs, etc. Died in 1705.

Haaren, van, (WILLEM.) See HAREN.

Haas, hÃss, (GUILLAUME,) a Swiss engraver and type-founder, born at Bâle in 1741 ; died in 1800.

See ERSCH und GRUBER, "Allgemeine Encyklopaedie."

Haas, hÃss, or **Hasius,** hÃ′ze-ùs, (JOHANN MATTHIAS,) a German historian and geographer of great merit, born at Augsburg in 1684. He taught mathematics at Wittenberg, and wrote "Phosphorus Historiarum," etc., (1743.) Died in 1742.

Haas, de, dẹh hÃs, (F. H.,) a skilful marine painter, born at Rotterdam about 1830. He opened, a few years since, a studio in New York, where he now resides.

See TUCKERMAN, "Book of the Artists."

Haas, de, dẹh hÃs, (JOHN PHILIP,) born in Holland about 1735, distinguished himself in the war of the Revolution, and was made a brigadier-general by Congress in 1777. Died in Philadelphia about 1795.

Haase, hÃ′zẹh, (HEINRICH GOTTLOB FRIEDRICH CHRISTIAN,) an eminent German philologist, born at Magdeburg in 1808. He became titular professor of philology at Breslau in 1846. He published good editions of Thucydides, (1842,) of Seneca, (1852,) and other classics ; also "The Past and Future of Philology," (1835.)

Hab′ak-kuk, (or ha-bak′kuk,) [Heb. קוקבח; Fr. at Issoudun about 1520. He produced, besides many

Habacuc, hÃ′bÃ′kük′,] one of the minor Hebrew prophets, and author of a canonical book of the Bible. He is supposed to have prophesied about 600 B.C. His language is highly poetical and imaginative. A passage of his book is quoted by Saint Paul, Acts xiii. 41.

Habeneck, hÃb′nêk′, (ANTOINE FRANÇOIS,) a French musician, born at Mézières in 1781 ; died in 1849.

Häberlin or **Haeberlin,** hÃ′bẹr-leen′, (FRANZ DOMINICUS,) an eminent German historian, born near Ulm, on the Danube, in 1720. He became professor of history at Helmstedt in 1746, and professor of public law there in 1751. Soon after that date he was privy councillor of the Duke of Brunswick. He published a "Universal History," ("Allgemeine Weltgeschichte," 12 vols., 1767 –73,) a "Modern History of the German Empire since the Beginning of the War of Schmalkalden," (20 vols., 1774–86,) which is praised as a classic work, and other histories. His chief merits are exactitude and thorough research. Died in 1787.

See MEUSEL, "Lexikon der vom Jahre 1750–1800 verstorbenen Deutschen Schriftsteller."

Häberlin, (KARL FRIEDRICH,) a German publicist, son of the preceding, born in 1756 at Helmstedt, where he became professor of public law about 1786. He published a "Repertory of German Public Law and Feudal Law," (1781–95,) and other works. Died in 1808.

Häberlin, (KARL LUDWIG,) a novelist, a son of the preceding, was born at Erlangen in 1784. He published many historical novels, among which are "The Exile," ("Der Heimathlose,") and "The Prime Minister," (4 vols., 1835.)

Habermann. See AVENARIUS.

Hab′er-sham, (JOSEPH,) born at Savannah, Georgia, in 1750. He took part in the war of the Revolution, and obtained the rank of lieutenant-colonel. In 1785 he was chosen a member of Congress. From 1795 to 1800 he was postmaster-general. Died in 1815.

See "National Portrait-Gallery of Distinguished Americans."

Habert, hÃ′baiR′, (FRANÇOIS,) a French poet, born

ā, ē, ī, ō, ū, ȳ, *long;* â, ê, ô, same, less prolonged; ă, ĕ, ĭ, ŏ, ŭ, ў, *short;* a, ẹ, ị, ọ, *obscure;* fär, fàll, fât; mêt; nŏt; gōōd; mōōn;

original poems, a version of Ovid's "Metamorphoses," which was often reprinted. Died about 1568.

Habert, (ISAAC,) a French poet, nephew of the preceding, born in Paris about 1560, wrote a poem "On Meteors," ("Des Météores," 1585.)

Habert, (ISAAC,) a French theologian and writer, son of Germain, (de Cérisy,) noticed below, was born in Paris. He became preacher to the king, and in 1645 Bishop of Vabres. Died in 1668.

Habert, (LOUIS,) a French theological writer, born near Blois in 1636; died in 1718.

Habert, (PHILIPPE,) a French poet, born in Paris about 1605, was one of the first members of the French Academy, and author of a poem called the "Temple of Death." He was killed at a siege in Flanders in 1637.

Habert, (PIERRE JOSEPH,) BARON, a French general, born at Avallon in 1773. He distinguished himself at Heliopolis, (1798,) Jena, (1806,) and Eylau, (1807,) and subsequently in the Spanish campaign of 1814. In 1815 he obtained command of a division, and was severely wounded at Waterloo. Died in 1825.

Habert de Cérisy, *hȧ'*bair'* dĕh sȧ're'se', (GERMAIN,) a brother of Philippe Habert, noticed above, was a member of the French Academy, and wrote poems which were once admired. Died in 1655.

Habicht, *hȧ'*bikt, (CHRISTIAN MAXIMILIAN,) a German Orientalist, born at Breslau in 1775. He published an edition of "The Arabian Nights," ("Tausend und eine Nächte," 8 vols., 1825-39,) and, with the aid of Schall and Von der Hagen, made a German version of the same, (15 vols., 1825.) Died in 1839.

Habicot, *hȧ'*be'ko', * (NICOLAS,) a French anatomist, born at Bonny about 1550, studied in Paris, and became surgeon to the Hôtel-Dieu and to the army. He was one of the most skilful anatomists of his time, and wrote several professional treatises. Died in 1624.

Hab'ing-ton, (WILLIAM,) an English poet, born at Hendlip in 1605. His father, Thomas, was implicated in the Gunpowder Plot, but was pardoned. William wrote "The Queen of Aragon," a tragi-comedy, and a collection of small poems, entitled "Castara," (1635.) Died in 1645.

See JOHNSON, "Lives of the English Poets;" SIR S. E. BRYDGES, "Censura Literaria;" HALLAM, "Introduction to the Literature of Europe;" "Retrospective Review," vol. xi., 1825.

Habsburg or **Hapsburg,** haps'bŭrg, [Ger. pron. hȧps'bōōrg,] HOUSE OF, an ancient sovereign family of Austria, which derives its name from the castle of Habsburg, or Hapsburg, in Switzerland. The first member of the family who acquired great celebrity was Rudolf of Habsburg, born in 1218 and elected Emperor of Germany in 1273. He obtained Austria and other provinces by conquest, and founded the dynasty which now reigns over the Austrian empire, and which since 1736 has been styled the house of Habsburg-Lorraine. (See RUDOLF OF HABSBURG.)

See, also, E. M. VON LICHNOWSKY, "Geschichte des Hauses Habsburg," 2 vols., 1836-37.

Hachette, *hȧ'*shĕt', * the surname of JEANNE FOURQUET, (fooR'kȧ',) a French heroine, born at Beauvais in 1454. She acted a prominent part in the defence of Beauvais against Charles the Bold in 1472. She used a small axe (*hachette*) as a weapon: hence her surname.

Hachette, (JEAN NICOLAS PIERRE,) an able French mathematician, born at Mézières in 1769, was educated at the University of Rheims. By the influence of Monge, he was appointed assistant professor in the Polytechnic School in 1794, and in 1797 he obtained the chair of descriptive geometry, which he retained until 1816. In 1830 he became a member of the Institute. He published a "Supplement to the Descriptive Geometry of Monge," (1811,) "Elements of Geometry of Solids," (1817,) "Applications of Descriptive Geometry," (1821,) a "Treatise on Machines," etc. He rendered a great service by applying geometry to the construction of machinery. Among his pupils was Arago. Died in 1834.

See QUÉRARD, "La France Littéraire."

Hachette, (LOUIS CHRISTOPHE FRANÇOIS,) born at Rethel, in France, in 1800, was the proprietor of a great publishing-house in Paris. Died in 1864.

* On the pronunciation of the initial French *h*, see p. 1215, *note*.

Hackaert. See HAKKERT.

Hackelmann, hȧk'kĕl-mȧn', (LEOPOLD,) a German jurist and legal writer, born near Bremen in 1563; died in 1619.

Hackert. See HAKKERT.

Hackert, hȧk'kĕrt, (GEORG,) an engraver, a brother of Philipp, noticed below, was born in Prussia in 1755. He engraved the "View of Rome" and other works of his brother Philipp. Died at Florence in 1805. His brother JOHANN, born in 1744, was a landscape-painter. Died at Bath, in England, in 1773. Another brother, WILHELM, born in 1748, was a painter of history and portraits. He was professor of design in the Academy of Saint Petersburg when he died, about 1786.

See NAGLER, "Neues Allgemeines Künstler-Lexikon."

Hackert, (PHILIPP,) an excellent German landscape-painter, was born at Prenzlau, in Prussia, in 1737. He visited Rome about 1768, and passed the rest of his life mostly in Italy. He painted for the empress Catherine of Russia six pictures of the naval victory over the Turks at Tchesme in 1770. He painted a "View of Rome," "Views in the Vicinity of the Villa Horace," and many Italian sea-ports. About 1786 he was appointed first painter to the King of Naples. He left Naples in 1799, and settled at Florence, where he died in 1807. His merit consisted in a close imitation of nature. Goethe wrote a memoir of his life, ("P. Hackert ; biographische Skizze," 1811.)

See, also, ERSCH und GRUBER, "Allgemeine Encyklopaedie."

Hack'et, (JOHN,) born in London in 1592, was educated at Cambridge, and made Bishop of Lichfield and Coventry in 1661. He published a volume of sermons, and a "Life of Archbishop Williams." Died in 1670.

See THOMAS PLUME, "Life of Bishop Hacket," 1675.

Hack'ett, (HORATIO BALCH,) an American biblical scholar, born in Salisbury, Massachusetts, in 1808. He graduated at Amherst College in 1830, studied theology at Andover, and afterwards at Halle, in Germany. He obtained the chair of Hebrew and biblical interpretation in the Newton (Baptist) Theological Seminary of Massachusetts about 1840. Among his works are a Chaldee Grammar, translated, with additions, from the German of Winer, and a "Commentary on the Original Text of the Acts of the Apostles," (1853 ; same edition, greatly enlarged, 1858.)

Hackett, (JAMES HENRY,) an American actor, born in New York in 1800. He performed comedy in the United States and in England.

Hackländer, hȧk'lĕn'dĕr, (FRIEDRICH WILHELM,) a popular German novelist, born near Aix-la-Chapelle about 1816. He served in the Prussian army for several of his early years. In 1841 he published "Scenes of Military Life during Peace," which had a great success. He became secretary to the prince-royal of Würtemberg in 1843. He wrote numerous popular works, among which are "Military Life in Time of War," (1849,) "Scenes from Life," ("Bilder aus dem Leben," 1850,) "Nameless Histories," ("Namenlose Geschichten," 3 vols., 1851,) and "Eugene Stillfried," (1852.) He has been called "the Charles Dickens of Germany."

Hack'ley, (CHARLES W.,) a mathematician and Episcopal clergyman, born at Herkimer, New York, in 1808, became professor of mathematics in Columbia College, New York, in 1843. He published, besides other works, a "Treatise on Algebra," (1846.) Died in 1861.

Hackluyt. See HAKLUYT.

Hackspann or **Hackspan,** hȧk'spän, (THEODOR or THEODORIC,) a learned German theologian and philologist, born at Weimar in 1607. He was a pupil of Calixtus, whose liberal opinions he adopted, was well versed in Oriental languages, and became professor of Hebrew at Altorf. He published, besides other works, in Latin, "Philological Disputations," (1643,) "The Faith and Laws of Mohammed," (1646,) and "Miscellanea Sacra," (1660.) Died in 1659.

See ERSCH und GRUBER, "Allgemeine Encyklopaedie."

Hacquet, *hȧ'*kȧ', (BALTHASAR,) a naturalist, born at Conquet, in Bretagne, in 1740, was chosen professor of natural history in Lemberg, Austria, in 1788. He published, in German, several accounts of his travels among the Alps and Carpathian Mountains, which furnish valuable information on geography and other sciences. One of his works is "Physico-Political Journeys among the Alps," (4 vols., 1785-87.) Died in Vienna in 1815.

See ERSCH und GRUBER, "Allgemeine Encyklopaedie."

Haddik, håd'dik, (ANDREAS,) COUNT OF, an able Austrian general, born at Futak, in Hungary, in 1710, gained distinction in the war against the Turks. In the Seven Years' war, as lieutenant-field-marshal, he fought against the Prussians near Görlitz, and took Berlin by surprise in 1757. In 1765 he was chosen Governor of Galicia, and in 1774 he became president of the war department, or council of war, with the title of field-marshal. Died in 1790.

Had'dock, (Sir RICHARD,) an English admiral, born in Essex about 1630. He was wounded at Solebay in 1667. Died in 1715.

Had'don, (WALTER,) an English scholar, born in Buckinghamshire in 1516, contributed to the revival of classical learning. In 1550 he became professor of civil law in Cambridge, and in 1552 president of Magdalene College, Oxford. He enjoyed favour at the court of Elizabeth, who praised his skill in Latin composition by saying, "Haddonum nemini postpono," ("I rank Haddon behind none.") Died in 1572.

See "Biographia Britannica."

Hâdee-Moosa, Hady-Moussa, or **Hadi-Mûssa, Al,** ål hå'dee mōō'så, a caliph of the family of Abbassides, born about 760 A.D., succeeded his father Al-Mahdee (or -Mahdî) on the throne of Bagdâd in 785. He was a brother of Haroun-al-Raschid. After a reign of fifteen months, he died, in 786.

See ABOOLFEDA, "Annales."

Hā'dēs, [Gr. Ἀιδης or Ἄδης,] a name applied by the Greeks to Pluto and to his dominions. (See PLUTO.)

Hadji-Khalfa. See HAJI-KHALFA.

Had'ley, (JAMES,) an American scholar, was born in Fairfield, Herkimer county, New York, the 30th of March, 1821. He is the son of Dr. James Hadley, who was for many years professor of chemistry in the Medical College at Fairfield and afterwards held the same chair in the Medical College at Geneva, New York. He entered in September, 1840, the junior class of Yale College, and graduated in 1842. In 1848 he became assistant professor of Greek at Yale, and in 1851 professor in full, in place of President Woolsey, who had retained until then his charge of that department. In August, 1851, he married a daughter of Stephen Twining, Esq., of New Haven. In 1860 he published an excellent "Greek Grammar for Schools and Colleges," founded on a similar work by Professor Georg Curtius in Germany. An abridgment appeared in 1869, under the name "Elements of the Greek Language." He has contributed articles to various scientific and literary periodicals, especially the "New-Englander," and has been an active member of the American Oriental Society.

Had'ley, (JOHN,) an English astronomer, became a Fellow of the Royal Society in 1717, of which he was afterwards vice-president. In 1731 he presented to that society a sextant, of which he claimed to be the inventor, and which has since been generally used in nautical astronomy. It is commonly known as "Hadley's Sextant." Many, however, give Sir Isaac Newton credit for this invention. Died in 1744.

Hadlub, håt'loop, or **Hadloub,** (JOHANN,) a German poet or minnesinger, lived at Zurich about 1300. His poems present agreeable pictures of rustic life and interesting details about the manners of the peasantry of that age.

See ETTMÜLLER, "J. Hadlouber, Gedichte," 1840; LONGFELLOW, "Poets and Poetry of Europe."

Hadorph, hå'dorf, (JOHAN,) a Swedish antiquary, born near Linköping in 1630; died in 1693.

Hā'drĭ-an or **A'drĭ-an,** [Lat. HADRIA'NUS; Fr. ADRIEN, ä'dRe-åN'; It. ADRIANO, ä-dRe-ä'no,] or, more fully, **Hadria'nus Pub'lius Æl'lius,** a Roman emperor, born at Rome in January, 76 A.D., was a son of Ælius Hadrianus Afer, and a cousin of Trajan. His favourite study was the Greek language and literature. He won the favour of Trajan, and accompanied him in his campaign against the Dacians. He was chosen tribune of the people in 105 A.D., and prætor in 107. When Trajan was forced

by illness to retire from the army which he had conducted against the Parthians, he gave the chief command to Hadrian. On the death of Trajan, Hadrian was proclaimed emperor (at Antioch) by the army in August, 117 A.D.; and their choice was confirmed by the senate. The question whether Trajan had adopted Hadrian as his heir appears to remain undetermined. The new emperor hastened to make peace with the Parthians by abandoning all the provinces which Trajan had conquered beyond the Euphrates, and rendered himself popular by the remission of taxes and other acts of liberality. The greater portion of his reign was spent in journeys through the provinces of his vast empire, in which he displayed durable evidences of his liberality, political wisdom, and love of the fine arts. He commenced these journeys in 119 A.D. He built a famous wall across the island of Britain from Solway Frith to the German Ocean, to protect the Roman province from the incursions of the Picts and Scots. He founded cities in other provinces, completed the temple of Jupiter Olympius at Athens, and erected many great architectural works, among which were a magnificent villa at Tibur, and his mausoleum at Rome, now called the Castle of Saint Angelo. In 131 A.D. he promulgated the "Edictum Perpetuum," a fixed code of laws drawn up by Salvius Julianus. This event forms an important epoch in the history of Roman law. His reign was peaceful, and tended to consolidate the empire as well as to civilize the people. He patronized literary men, artists, and philosophers, and composed a number of works, in prose and verse, which are not extant. He aspired to distinction as an architect and painter, and indulged a petty vanity and jealousy towards artists, which sometimes prompted him to acts of cruelty. A short time before his death, he adopted as his successor Arrius Antoninus, surnamed "the Pious," and composed the following verses addressed to his own soul:

> "Animula, vagula, blandula,
> Hospes comesque corporis,
> Quæ nunc abibis in loca,
> Pallidula, rigida, nudula,
> Nec, ut soles, dabis jocos?"*

Died in July, 138 A.D. Many statues and medals of Hadrian are extant.

See SPARTIANUS, "Vita Hadriani;" NIEBUHR, "Lectures on Roman History;" TILLEMONT, "Histoire des Empereurs;" GIBBON, "History of the Decline and Fall of the Roman Empire."

Hadschi-Chalfa, (or **-Khalfa.**) See HAJI-KHALFA.

Hady-Moussa. See HÂDEE-MOOSA.

Haeberlin. See HÄBERLIN.

Haedo, de, dà ä-ä'DO, (DIEGO,) a Spanish monk and historian, lived about 1600. He wrote an account of Algiers, ("Topographia e Historia de Argel," 1612.)

Haeffner. See HÄFFNER.

Haehnel. See HÄHNEL.

Haellstroem. See HÄLLSTRÖM.

Haelwig. See HÁLVIG.

Haen or **Haan, van,** vån hån, (ANTOON,) an eminent Dutch physician, born at the Hague in 1704, was a pupil of Boerhaave. He practised twenty years in his native place, and was chosen first professor of medicine in Vienna in 1754. He succeeded Van Swieten as chief physician to the empress Maria Theresa. He published many medical works, of which the most important is the "Method of Treatment (or Curing) in Hospitals," ("Ratio Medendi in Nosocomio practico," 1757-74,) often reprinted. Died in Vienna in 1776. Desgenettes calls him "one of the most illustrious practitioners of the eighteenth century."

See F. G. BOISSEAU, "Biographie Médicale;" "Nouvelle Biographie Générale."

Haendel. See HANDEL.

Haenel. See HÄNEL.

Haenke. See HÄNKE.

Haering. See HÄRING, (WILHELM.)

---

* "Ah, fleeting spirit! wandering fire,
  That long hast warmed my tender breast,
  Must thou no more this frame inspire,
  No more a pleasing, cheerful guest?
  Whither, ah, whither art thou flying?
  To what dark, undiscovered shore?
  Thou seem'st all trembling, shivering, dying,
  And wit and humour are no more."—POPE.

ā, ē, ī, ō, ū, ȳ, *long;* à, ė, ò, same, less prolonged; ă, ĕ, ĭ, ŏ, ŭ, ȳ, *short;* a, e, i, o, *obscure;* fär, fåll, fåt; mêt; nŏt; gōōd; mōōn;

Haerlem or **Haarlem, van,** văn hăr'lĕm, (DIRCK,) a Dutch painter, born at Haarlem about 1410; died in 1470.

Haeser. See HÄSER.

Haeusser. See HÄUSSER.

Haffner, hăf'nĕr, (ANTON,) a painter of perspective, of Swiss extraction, was born at Bologna in 1654. He lived many years at Genoa, where he painted admirable frescos in the church of Saint Luke and other churches. He was also employed by the grand duke at Florence. Died in 1732. His brother HENRY, born in 1640, painted decorations in several palaces at Rome and in churches of Bologna. Died in 1702.

Häffner or **Haeffner,** hĕf'nĕr, (JOHANN CHRISTIAN FRIEDRICH,) a German composer, born in Thuringia in 1759; died at Upsal in 1833.

Hafis, the German spelling of HAFIZ, which see.

Hâfiz, hä'fiz, written also **Hafitz** and **Hafis,** (**Mohammed Shems-ed-Deen,** mo-hăm'med shĕms ed-deen',) a celebrated Persian poet, born at Shirâz about 1300. Love and wine are the favourite subjects of his poems, which are condemned as licentious by strict Mussulmans. He is regarded as the greatest lyric poet of Persia. His poems, which collectively are entitled the "Divan," are praised for purity of style, harmony of versification, and brilliant imagination. Among the recorded events of his life is an interview with Tamerlane in 1387. Died about 1390. His poems were published in Persian at Calcutta in 1791. Some portions of them have been translated into English by J. Richardson, (1774,) J. H. Hindley, (1800,) and other Oriental scholars.

See SIR W. GORE OUSELEY, "Biographical Notices of Persian Poets," London, 1846; "Nouvelle Biographie Générale;" "Fraser's Magazine" for January. 1846, and September, 1854.

Hā'gar or **A'gar,** [Heb. הגר,] an Egyptian woman, was the second wife of the patriarch Abraham, and the mother of Ishmael. (See Genesis xvi. and xxi.)

Hageau, hȧ'zho', (AMABLE,) a French engineer, born in 1756, was appointed divisionary inspector of bridges and roads beyond the Alps. Died in 1836.

Hagedorn, hä'gĕh-doRn', (CHRISTIAN LUDWIG,) an eminent critic of art, a brother of Friedrich, the poet, was born at Hamburg in 1713. He served the Elector of Saxony many years as secretary of legation to various courts. In 1764 he was appointed director-general of the Academies of Fine Arts at Dresden and Leipsic. He produced in 1762, in German, "Reflections on Painting," (2 vols.,) which is considered a classic work by artists. Died at Dresden in 1780.

See ERSCH und GRUBER, "Allgemeine Encyklopaedie."

Hagedorn, von, fon hä'gĕh-doRn', (FRIEDRICH,) an elegant German poet, born at Hamburg in April, 1708. In 1733 he became secretary to a company of merchants, called "The English Court," at Hamburg. He published in 1738 a volume of fables and tales in verse, and afterwards a volume of "Moral Poems." Among his masterpieces are "The Savant," a satire, (1740,) "The Sage," (1741,) and "Ode on Happiness," (1743.) The merit of restoring good taste in German poetry is ascribed to Hagedorn and Haller. Wieland called him "the German Horace." Died in 1754.

See ESCHENBURG, "F. von Hagedorn's Werke," 5 vols., 1800, the 4th vol. of which contains a memoir of Hagedorn; LONGFELLOW, "Poets and Poetry of Europe;" C. H. SCHMID, "Biographie der Dichter;" GERVINUS, "Geschichte der Deutschen Dichtung."

Hagemann, hä'gĕh-mân', (THEODOR,) a German jurist, born at Stiege, Brunswick, in 1761, became aulic councillor and judge of the court of appeal at Zelle. He published a valuable work, entitled "Practical Explanations of All Sorts of Juridical Subjects," (6 vols., 1798-1818.) Died in 1827.

Hagen, hä'gĕn, (ERNST AUGUST,) an ingenious German novelist and writer on art, was born at Königsberg in 1797. He became professor of æsthetics in Königsberg about 1830. Among his works are "Olfrid and Lisena," a poem, (1820,) and "Leonardo da Vinci at Milan," (1840.)

Hagen, (KARL GOTTFRIED,) a German chemist and writer, born at Königsberg in 1749; died in 1829.

Hagen, van, văn hä'gĕn or hä'Hĕn, (JAN,) a Dutch landscape-painter, who lived about 1650.

Hagen, van der, văn dĕr hä'gĕn or hä'Hĕn, (STEVEN,) a Dutch admiral, born about 1560, commanded an expedition which explored the Chinese Sea and the Sunda Isles in 1600. In 1604 he defeated the Portuguese in several actions, and expelled them from the Moluccas. Died about 1610.

Hagen, von, fon hä'gĕn, (JOHANN GEORG FRIEDRICH,) a German antiquary, born at Baireuth in 1723. He formed a rich cabinet of medals, pictures, etc., and was a liberal patron of artists. He wrote a "Description of the Silver Coins of Nuremberg," (1766,) and other valuable works. Died in 1783.

See ERSCH und GRUBER, "Allgemeine Encyklopaedie."

Hagen, von der, fon dĕR hä'gĕn, (FRIEDRICH HEINRICH,) an eminent German critic and philologist, born at Schmiedeberg, in Prussia, in February, 1780. He became professor of German literature at Berlin in 1810, and devoted his attention to the mediæval German literature. He published, besides other works, "Heroic Romances of the North," (5 vols., 1814-28,) "Monuments of the Middle Ages," (1824,) and "The Minnesinger," (5 vols., 1838-56,) a poetical collection, which is called his chief work. Died in Berlin in 1856.

See BROCKHAUS, "Conversations-Lexikon;" "Nouvelle Biographie Générale."

Hagenbach, hä'gĕn-bȧk', (KARL RUDOLF,) a Swiss Protestant theologian, was born at Bâle in 1801. He became professor of theology at Bâle about 1828, and was author of lectures on the "Essence and History of the Reformation," (6 vols., 1834-43,) "Ecclesiastic History of the Eighteenth and Nineteenth Centuries," (2 vols.; 3d edition, 1856,) and other esteemed works, (in German.)

Hagenbuch, hä'gĕn-bōōk', (JOHANN CASPAR,) a Swiss antiquary, born at Zurich in 1700. Among his writings is a curious treatise on certain Greek and Latin inscriptions, entitled "Epistolæ Epigraphicæ," etc., (1747.) Died in 1763.

See ERSCH und GRUBER, "Allgemeine Encyklopaedie."

Hager, hä'gĕr, (JOHANN GEORG,) a German geographer, born in the district of Baireuth in 1709. He published an edition of Homer's "Iliad," (1745-67,) and a "System of Geography," ("Ausführliche Geographie," 3 vols., 1746-51,) which had great success. Died in 1777.

See ERSCH und GRUBER, "Allgemeine Encyklopaedie."

Hager, (JOSEPH,) an Orientalist, of German extraction, born at Milan in 1757. He published a treatise on Chinese worship, called "Panthéon Chinois," (1802,) and "Elements of the Chinese Language," (London, 1806.) In 1809 he became professor of Oriental languages at Pavia. Died in 1819.

See ERSCH und GRUBER, "Allgemeine Encyklopaedie."

Hăg'ga-ī, [Heb. חגי; Fr. AGGÉE, ăg'zhă',] one of the twelve minor Hebrew prophets, lived about 520 B.C., during the erection of the second temple, the glory of which he predicted should transcend that of the first. (Haggai ii. 9.) His mission was chiefly to urge the Jews to greater diligence in the erection of the temple. His language is quoted in Hebrews xii. 26.

Haghe, häg, (LOUIS,) a skilful painter and lithographer, born in Belgium in 1802. He removed in his youth to London, where he has since resided. He published many fine lithographs of Flemish monuments designed by himself, and painted in water-colours the interiors of Flemish town-halls and churches. Among his most admired works are paintings of the Palais de Courtray and the Audience-Chamber of Bruges.

Hagström or **Hagstroem,** häg'stRöm, (JOHAN OTTO,) a Swedish naturalist and writer, born at Fröson in 1716; died in 1792.

Hague, häg, (CHARLES,) an English composer, born in Tadcaster in 1769. He became professor of music at Cambridge about 1796. Died in 1821.

Hague, häg, (WILLIAM,) an American Baptist minister, born in New York about 1805, graduated at Hamilton College in 1826. He published, besides other works, "Christianity and Statesmanship," (1855.)

Haguenot, hăg'no', (HENRI,) a French physician, born at Montpellier in 1687. He wrote a "Treatise on Small-Pox," (1734.) Died in 1775.

Hahn, hän, (AUGUST,) a German theologian, one of the leaders of the orthodox Protestant party, was born near Querfurt, in Prussia, in 1792. He became professor of theology at Leipsic in 1826, and general superintendent of Silesia in 1844. He published, besides other works, a "Text-Book of the Christian Faith," (1828,) and "On the Present State of Christianity, and the Relations which exist between Theology and Science," (1832.)

Hahn, (CARL AUGUST,) a German philologist, born at Heidelberg in 1807 ; died in 1857.

Hahn, (JOHANN DAVID,) a German natural philosopher, born at Heidelberg in 1729, published a treatise "On the Mutual Subservience of Mathematics and Chemistry," and other works. Died in 1784.

See ERSCH und GRUBER, "Allgemeine Encyklopaedie."

Hahn, (LUDWIG PHILIPP,) a German dramatic poet, born at Trippstadt in 1746. He wrote tragedies entitled "The Rebellion of Pisa," (1776,) and "Robert von Hohenecken," (1778,) which are admired for energy of style and elevation of thought. Died in 1787.

Hahn, (PHILIPP MATTHÄUS,) a German, noted for inventive mechanical genius, was born near Stuttgart in 1739. He settled as pastor at Onsmettingen in 1764, before which he had made astronomical and optical instruments. He invented a machine which represented the motions of the celestial bodies, and another which performed operations in arithmetic. He published several treatises on theology, sermons, etc. Died in 1790.

See ERSCH und GRUBER, "Allgemeine Encyklopaedie ;" "Annals of Industry and Genius," by C. L. BRIGHTWELL, London, 1863.

Hahn, (SIMON FRIEDRICH,) a German historian and publicist, born at Klosterbergen, in Prussia, in 1692. He is said to have understood Greek, Latin, and French at the age of ten. At the age of twenty-four he became professor of history and public law at Helmstedt. He published an excellent "History of the Constitution of the Empire and German Emperors," ("Teutsche Staats-Reichs- und Keyser Historie," (4 vols., 1721–24,) and other historical works. Died at Hanover in 1729.

See J. F. C. HAHN, "Schediasma de Vita Hahnii," 1729; ERSCH und GRUBER, "Allgemeine Encyklopaedie."

Hähnel or Haehnel, hä'nel, (ERNST JULIUS,) a German contemporary sculptor, studied under Reitschel and Schwanthaler. Among his master-pieces is the statue of Beethoven at Bonn, completed in 1845.

Hahnemann, hä'neh-män, (SAMUEL CHRISTIAN FRIEDRICH,) a celebrated German physician, born in Meissen, in Saxony, in 1755, was the founder of the system of medicine known as homœopathy. He graduated at Erlangen in 1779, and practised for some years at Dresden. About 1796 he announced his new system, founded on the principle that in order to cure any diseased affection we should employ a medicine having power to produce a similar affection in the body of a healthy person : an artificial affection (caused by the medicine) displaces the original disease, and on the discontinuance of the medicine this secondary disease ceases of itself. Hence the motto adopted by the homœopathists, "Similia similibus curantur," (" Like cures like.") Hahnemann afterwards settled in Leipsic. He developed his system in a work called "Organon of Rational Medicine," (Dresden, 1810.) Died in Paris in 1843.

See "Nouvelle Biographie Générale."

Hahn-Hahn, von, fon hän-hän, (IDA MARIE LUISE SOPHIE,) COUNTESS, a poetess and novelist, called "the German George Sand," was born at Tressow, Mecklenburg-Schwerin, in 1805. About 1826 she was married to Count von Hahn-Hahn, from whom she was divorced in 1829, after which she visited France, Italy, Spain, and the Levant. She produced in 1835 "Poems," ("Gedichte,") and in 1836 "Venetian Nights," which had great success. Among her most popular novels is "Faustine," (1841.) She has published several narratives of travel, and "Oriental Letters," (1845.) About 1850 she avowed her conversion to Roman Catholicism.

See LISCH, "Geschichte und Urkunden des Geschlechtes Hahn," 1844; "Edinburgh Review" for January, 1844; "Foreign Quarterly Review" for January, 1843; "North British Review" for August, 1847.

Haid, hīt or hīd, (JOHANN GOTTFRIED,) a German engraver, born at Augsburg in 1710, worked in England.

Died in 1770. His brother, JOHANN LORENZ, born in 1702, was an engraver in mezzotint. Died in 1750.

Haid, (JOHANN JAKOB,) a German engraver of portraits, born near Ulm in 1704 ; died in 1767. His son, JOHANN ELIAS, (1739–1809,) was also an engraver.

Haïder Ali. See HYDER ALI.

Haidinger, hī'ding'er, (WILHELM,) a German geologist, born in Vienna in 1795. He was appointed councillor of mines at Vienna in 1840, and director-in-chief of the Geological Institute of Austria in 1849. He published a "Treatise on Mineralogy," ("Handbuch der bestimmenden Mineralogie," (1845,) a "Geognostic Chart of the Austrian Empire," (1847,) and other works. His father, KARL, born in Vienna in 1756, was a mineralogist of merit. He was author of an "Essay towards a Systematic Division of the Different Kinds of Rocks," (1786.) Died in 1797.

Hailes, LORD. See DALRYMPLE, (Sir DAVID.)

Haillan, du, dü hä'yôN', (BERNARD de Girard—deh zhe'răR',) SEIGNEUR, a French historian, born at Bordeaux in 1535. He wrote a history of France, ("De l'État et Succès des Affaires de France," 1570,) which passed through many editions and was approved by Charles IX., who rewarded him with the title of historiographer. Died in 1610.

See BAYLE, "Historical and Critical Dictionary."

Haimävätä, hī'ma-va-ta, or Haimavat, hī'ma-vat, [i.e. "snowy" or "snow-clad," from the Sanscrit *hīmă* or *haimă*, "cold," "frost," "snow,"] called the "king of mountains," was, according to the Hindoo mythology, the father of Ganga, (Ganges,) or PÂRVATÎ, which see.

Haimo. See HAYMO.

Haizinger, hīts'ing'er, (AMALIE,) a popular German actress, born at Carlsruhe in 1800.

Haji- (or Hadji-) Khalfa, häj'ee kāl'fa, written also Hadschi-Chalfa, (or -Khalfah,) a celebrated Turkish historian and bibliographer, born in Constantinople. His proper name was MUSTAFA-BEN-ABDAL-LAH. He was minister of finances under Amurath IV. He wrote a "History of Constantinople," and an excellent work on bibliography, which contains notices of 18,550 Arabic, Persian, and Turkish books, with memoirs of the authors. It served as the basis of Herbelot's "Bibliothèque Orientale." Died in 1658.

See VON HAMMER, "Histoire de l'Empire Ottoman."

Hakem. See ALHAKEM.

Hakem-Biamrillah, hä'kem be-äm-ril'lah, (Aboo-Alee-Mansoor, or Abu-Ali-Mansûr, ä'boō ä'lee män-soōR',) third Fatimite caliph of Egypt, succeeded his father, Azeez-Billah, in 996 A.D. A capricious despot, he was noted for his cruelty and extravagance. After subjecting the Christians to numerous vexations, he banished them from Egypt, and thus furnished one of the chief motives of the crusades. He died, or was killed, in 1021.

Hakewill, häk'wil, (GEORGE,) D.D., born at Exeter, in England, in 1579, became Archdeacon of Surrey in 1616. He published several sermons, and "An Apology or Declaration of the Power and Providence of God in the Government of the World," (1627,) which is commended for piety and learning. It is designed to refute the doctrine of modern degeneracy, and to prove that the powers of nature are not doomed to a progressive decline. Died in 1649.

See PRINCE, "Worthies of Devon."

Hakewill, (JAMES,) an English writer and architect, published a "History of Windsor," (1813,) and a "Picturesque Tour of Italy," (1817.) Died in 1843.

Hakkert, häk'keRt, or Hackaert, häk'käRt, (JAN,) a skilful Dutch landscape-painter, born at Amsterdam about 1540. He painted chiefly wild and mountainous scenery, and was intimate with Adrian van der Velde, who furnished the figures of many of Hakkert's landscapes. Died about 1635.

Hakluyt, häk'loot, (RICHARD,) prebendary of Westminster, an English historian, born at Yatton in 1553. He became greatly interested in geography and navigation, and was appointed professor of these branches at Oxford. In 1589 he published his celebrated work on the voyages and discoveries of the English, dedicated to Walsingham, his patron, which was afterwards enlarged and published in 1600, with the following title: "Principal Navigations, Voyages, Traffics, and Discoveries of the English Nation, by Sea or Overland, to the Most Remote and Distant Quarters of the Earth, at any Time within the Compass of 1500 Years." This work contains official documents relative to each voyage, as patents, letters of ministers, charters, etc., and has preserved from oblivion many precious monuments of Anglo-Saxon enterprise. He died in 1616.

See WOOD, "Athenæ Oxonienses;" "Retrospective Review," vol. xi., 1825.

Hal, van, vän häl, a Flemish painter, born at Antwerp in 1668. His early historical pieces are admired.

Halb Suter, hälp soo'ter, a Swiss poet, born at Lucerne about 1370, was the author of a popular song entitled "The Battle of Sempach."

See LONGFELLOW, "Poets and Poetry of Europe."

Halcyone. See ALCYONE.

Haldane, häl'dàn, (JAMES ALEXANDER,) a Scottish Independent clergyman, born at Dundee in 1768, was the brother of Robert Haldane, noticed below. In 1785 he entered the naval service of the East India Company, and in 1793 was appointed captain of the Melville Castle. The next year he retired from the sea, in order to devote himself to the ministry of the gospel. He became pastor of the Tabernacle, Edinburgh, in 1799, and continued to preach in that city until his death, in 1851. He published several religious works.

See ALEXANDER HALDANE, "Memoirs of Robert and James A. Haldane," 1852; CHAMBERS, "Biographical Dictionary of Eminent Scotsmen," (Supplement.)

Haldane, (ROBERT,) was born of Scottish parents in London in 1764, and was educated at Edinburgh. He served in the navy from 1780 to 1783, and afterwards became an Independent minister, noted for his zeal and liberality in the diffusion of religious instruction. It is stated that he expended £30,000 in the erection of churches. In 1816 he published his "Evidence and Authority of Divine Revelation." In 1817 and 1818 he was successful at Geneva and Montauban in promoting a revival of religion and in forming the evangelical school, which has done so much to propagate Protestantism in France. His "Exposition of the Epistle to the Romans" (1835) is esteemed an excellent standard work, especially by Calvinists. Died in 1842.

See ALEXANDER HALDANE, "Memoirs of Robert and James A. Haldane;" CHAMBERS, "Biographical Dictionary of Eminent Scotsmen," (Supplement;) "London Quarterly Review" for April, 1856.

Haldat du Lys, häl'dä' dü le, (CHARLES NICOLAS ALEXANDRE,) M.D., a French physicist, born at Bourmont, in Lorraine, in 1770. He wrote several treatises on magnetism, biographies, and other works. Died in 1832 or 1852.

Halde, Du. See DUHALDE.

Hâl'de-man, (S. S.,) an American naturalist and philologist, born in Lancaster county, Pennsylvania, in 1812. He was appointed an assistant in the geological survey of Pennsylvania in 1837. He published "Freshwater Univalve Mollusca of the United States," (1840–44,) "Zoological Contributions," (1843,) "Analytic Orthography," (the Trevelyan Prize Essay,) and other works. In 1851 he became professor of natural history in the University of Pennsylvania, and about 1855 he obtained a similar office in Delaware College, at Newark.

Haldenwang, häl'den-wäng', (CHRISTIAN,) an eminent German engraver, was born at Durlach in 1770. He engraved many landscapes after Poussin, Claude Lorrain, and Ruysdael, and executed some prints for the "Musée Napoléon." Died in 1831.

Haldorsen, häl'dor'sen, (BJÖRN,) an Icelandic lexicographer, born in 1724. He published a "Lexicon Islandico-Latino-Danicum," (2 vols., 1814.) Died in 1794.

See KRAFT og NYERUP, "Litteraturlexicon."

Hâle, (Rev. BENJAMIN,) an American educator, born at Newburyport, Massachusetts, in 1797, graduated at Bowdoin College in 1818. He became professor of chemistry at Dartmouth College in 1827, and president of Geneva College (now Hobart Free College) in 1836. Died in 1863.

Hale, (DAVID,) an American journalist, born in Lisbon, Connecticut, in 1791. In 1827 he established, in

connection with Gerard Hallock, the New York "Journal of Commerce." He was a distinguished advocate of the sub-treasury, free trade, and other leading measures of the Democratic party. Died in 1849.

Hale, (HORATIO,) an American lawyer and philologist, a son of Mrs. Sarah J. Hale, was born in New Hampshire about 1817. He graduated at Harvard in 1837. He produced a work entitled "Ethnology and Philology," which, says Dr. Latham, "contains the greatest mass of philological data ever accumulated by a single inquirer." The "North American Review," in a notice of the volume in July, 1846, says, "Mr. Hale has succeeded in giving a certain classical completeness to his work which makes it a model for future labourers in the same or similar fields of research."

Hale, (JOHN P.,) an American statesman, born at Rochester, Strafford county, New Hampshire, in March, 1806. He graduated at Bowdoin College in 1827, studied law, and was admitted to the bar in 1830. He was appointed district attorney for New Hampshire by President Jackson in 1834, and reappointed by Van Buren. In 1843 he was elected a member of Congress by the Democrats of a district in New Hampshire. He became in Congress a decided opponent of slavery, for which reason his party opposed his election in 1845. About this date he resided at Dover, New Hampshire. He was Speaker of the House of Representatives of his native State in 1846. By a combination of anti-slavery Democrats and Whigs, he was elected Senator of the United States for New Hampshire in 1847. For several years he stood almost alone in the Senate on the question of slavery, and maintained a position independent of party. He was an easy and ready speaker, and by his wit or humour was often successful in turning aside the attacks of the pro-slavery Senators or in mitigating the bitterness of party animosity. He was nominated as candidate for the Presidency by the Liberty party in 1852, and received about 155,800 votes. On the expiration of his senatorial term in 1853, a Democrat was chosen to fill his place. Mr. Hale was again elected a member of the national Senate in 1855, to fill a vacancy. Having joined the Republican party, he was re-elected a Senator by the legislature of New Hampshire for a term of six years, 1859–65. He was appointed minister to Spain in 1865, and recalled in 1869.

Hâle, (Sir MATTHEW,) an eminent English judge, born at Alderley on the 1st of November, 1609, was educated at Oxford. About the age of twenty he entered Lincoln's Inn, where he pursued the study of law with great assiduity, and reformed his habits of dissipation. He was admitted to the bar a few years before the commencement of the civil war, during which he maintained a neutral position, and acted as counsel for royalists in several important trials, among which were the cases of Strafford and Archbishop Laud. After the execution of Charles I., he recognized the Commonwealth, and accepted from Cromwell, in 1653, the post of judge of the common bench, the duties of which he performed with great fidelity, ability, and honour. He was twice elected to Parliament,—in 1658 and in 1660. Charles II. appointed him chief baron of the exchequer in 1660, and lord chief justice of England in 1671. He is regarded as one of the greatest, wisest, and best judges that ever attained this dignity. His "History of the Common Law" and "Pleas of the Crown" are esteemed as very high authority. He wrote also several religious and moral treatises, among which we may notice his "Contemplations" and "Primitive Origination of Mankind." He was twice married, and had a numerous offspring. Died in December, 1676.

See GILBERT BURNET, "Life of Sir Matthew Hale," 1682; DR. WILLIAMS, "Life of Sir Matthew Hale," 1835; ROSCOE, "Life of Sir Matthew Hale;" LORD CAMPBELL, "Lives of the Chief Justices;" FOSS, "The Judges of England."

Hale, (NATHAN,) CAPTAIN, an American patriot, born at Coventry, Connecticut, in 1755, graduated at Yale College in 1773, and entered the army in 1775. In 1776 he took part in the battle of Long Island. He was sent by General Washington to penetrate the enemy's lines and procure intelligence in September, 1776. Having been seized as a spy, he was executed the next day.

See STUART, "Life of Nathan Hale," 1856.

e as k; ç as s; g hard; g as j; G, H, K, guttural; N, nasal; R, trilled; ş as z; th as in this. (☞See Explanations, p. 23.)

Hale, (NATHAN,) a journalist and lawyer, a nephew of the preceding, was born in Westhampton, Massachusetts, in 1784. He became in 1814 owner and editor of the "Boston Daily Advertiser," the first daily paper issued in New England, which he conducted for many years with ability. It was an influential organ successively of the Federalist, Whig, and Republican parties. In 1816 he married a sister of Edward Everett. He rendered important services in both branches of the legislature of Massachusetts, and was one of the founders of the "North American Review." He published a good map of New England in 1825. Died in 1863.

Hale, (SARAH JOSEPHA,) an American authoress, daughter of Mr. Buell, of Saybrook, Connecticut, born in 1795 at Newport, New Hampshire, was married in 1814 to Mr. David Hale. She published in 1823 "The Genius of Oblivion, and other Poems," followed by "Northwood," a novel, (1827.) In 1828 she became editor of the "Ladies' Magazine," Boston, which in 1837 she merged into the "Lady's Book" of Philadelphia. Among her poetic productions may be mentioned "Ormond Grosvenor," a tragedy, "Three Hours, or, The Vigil of Love ; and other Poems," issued in 1848, and "Harry Guy, a Story of the Sea."

See GRISWOLD's "Female Poets of America."

Halem, hä′lem, (BERNHARD JAKOB FRIEDRICH,) a German *littérateur,* born at Oldenburg in 1768. He translated from the English Hallam's "Middle Ages," and several of the romances of Sir Walter Scott. Died in 1823.

See ERSCH und GRUBER, "Allgemeine Encyklopaedie."

Halem, von, fon hä′lem, (GERHARD ANTON,) a German historian, born at Oldenburg in 1752. Among his works are a "History of the Duchy of Oldenburg," (3 vols., 1796,) and a "Life of Peter the Great," (1805.) Died in 1819.

See his "Selbstbiographie," 1840; ERSCH und GRUBER, "Allgemeine Encyklopaedie."

Halen, van, vän ä′lěn, ? (Don JUAN,) Count of Peracampos, a Spanish general, of Belgian extraction, was born in the isle of Leon in 1790. He fought as officer for the Constitutional party in 1821, and went into exile about 1823. In 1830 he obtained command of the Belgian insurgents, and drove the Dutch army from Brussels. He returned to Spain in 1836, and, as general of division, defeated the Carlists in Navarre. He was president of the council of war sometime between 1852 and 1856. Died in November, 1864.

See JUAN VAN HALEN, "Relacion de su Cautividad en los Calabozos de la Inquisicion," 2 vols., 1827, and English translation, London, 1827.

Hales or Hayles, hälz, (JOHN,) an English scholar and writer, born in Kent ; died in 1572.

Hales, (JOHN,) THE EVER-MEMORABLE, a noted English scholar and Arminian divine, born at Bath in 1584, was educated at Oxford, and was a Fellow of Merton College. In 1618 he took part in the Synod of Dort, and in 1639 he became canon of Windsor. He wrote sermons, letters, and treatises on theology, which were highly commended for learning, subtlety, and wit. Clarendon called him one of the greatest scholars in Europe ; and many writers agree in praising both his character and acquirements. Died in 1656.

See "Biographia Britannica ;" "Account of the Life and Writings of John Hales," 1719.

Hales, (STEPHEN,) D.D., an eminent English philosopher, born at Beckesbourn in 1677, resided for the greater part of his life at Teddington, of which he was curate. He made important discoveries in vegetable physiology, of which he published an account in a work entitled "Vegetable Statics," (1727.) In 1717 he was elected a Fellow of the Royal Society. He wrote treatises on anatomy, temperance, the circulation of the blood, and other subjects, and invented an improved plan for ventilating prisons. Died in 1761.

See FOUCHY, "Éloge de Hales."

Hales, (THOMAS.) See HELE, D'.

Hales, (WILLIAM,) an Irish clergyman and scientific author, wrote, besides works on mathematics and theology, a "New Analysis of Chronology," (3 vols., 1809–

14,) which is highly commended by Horne and Orme. Died at Kildare in 1821.

Hales, de, (ALEXANDER.) See ALEXANDER DE HALES.

Halévy, hä′lä′ve′, (JACQUES FRANÇOIS FROMENTAL ÉLIE,) an excellent French composer, born in Paris, of Jewish parents, in 1799, was a favourite pupil of Cherubini. He produced in 1829 "Claria," an opera, which was successful. His reputation was greatly increased by "The Jewess," ("La Juive," 1835,) which is called his capital work. The text of this was written by E. Scribe. He was chosen professor in the Conservatory in 1833. Among his later works are the operas of "The Queen of Cyprus," (1841,) "La Fée aux Roses," (1849,) and "Valentine d'Aubigné," (1856,) which display beauties of the first order. Died in March, 1862.

See FÉTIS, "Biographie Universelle des Musiciens ;" "Nouvelle Biographie Générale ;" EBERS, "Spohr und Halévy und die neueste Kirchen- und Opern-Musik," 1837.

Halévy, (LÉON,) a French poet, brother of the preceding, was born in Paris in 1802. He produced about 1830 an excellent version of the Odes of Horace, and afterwards imitations of many great foreign poets, entitled "Poésies Européennes." His original drama of "Luther" is commended. Among his other works are a "History of the Jews," (1828,) versions of several tragedies of Æschylus, Sophocles, and Euripides, and a version of "Macbeth," (1853.) He was a clerk in the ministry of public instruction many years.

Hälford, (Sir HENRY,) an eminent English physician, born on the 2d of October, 1766, was the son of Dr. James Vaughan, of Leicester. After graduating at Oxford, he practised in London with success, and, having given proof of his consummate skill, was chosen as medical attendant by George III., by whom he was knighted in 1809. Having inherited a large fortune from a relative named Halford, he adopted the name of his benefactor in 1815. Sir Henry continued to be royal physician during the reigns of George IV., William IV., and Victoria. He was for many years president of the College of Physicians, before which he delivered several elegant Latin orations ; and he wrote numerous essays on professional subjects, some of which are interesting and attractive even to the general reader. His professional income at one period amounted to £10,000 a year. Died in 1844.

See "Gentleman's Magazine" for May, 1844.

Halgan, hǎl′gôN′, (EMMANUEL,) a French admiral, born in Bretagne in 1771. He became captain of a ship about 1805, and by his skilful seamanship escaped in the disastrous affair of the fire-ships at the isle of Aix in 1809. He was made a vice-admiral in 1829, and Governor of Martinique in 1834. Died in 1852.

Häl′hed, (NATHANIEL BRASSEY,) M.P., an English author, born in 1751, published a "Grammar of the Bengal Language," and a "Code of Gentoo Laws," translated from the Persian. Died in 1830.

Häl′i-bur-ton, (THOMAS CHANDLER,) a humorous and popular English author, was born in Nova Scotia about 1802. In early life he practised law. About 1837 he obtained celebrity by his "Clockmaker, or the Sayings and Doings of Sam Slick of Slickville," an amusing personation of Yankee character. A second series of these Sayings and Doings appeared in 1838, and a third in 1840. He was appointed a judge about 1841, and removed to England in 1850. He also wrote "Sam Slick in England," (1843,) and "Nature and Human Nature," (1855.) Died in 1865.

Halifax. See HALLIFAX, (SAMUEL.)

Häl′I-fax, (CHARLES MONTAGU,) EARL OF, an English statesman, born at Horton in April, 1661, was the younger son of George Montagu, and a grandson of the Earl of Manchester. He was educated at Cambridge, where he formed an acquaintance with Sir Isaac Newton. He acquired distinction by his verses on the death of Charles II. in 1685, for which he was patronized by the Earl of Dorset. Being the youngest son of a younger brother, and consequently without fortune, he chose the profession of a politician, and obtained in 1690 a seat in the House of Commons, where he speedily distinguished himself by his talents for debate and for other duties of a statesman. His efforts on the question of trials for treason in 1692 raised him to the first rank of parliamentary orators, and in the same year he became one of the lords of the treasury. About this time Montagu and Somers were the leaders of the Whig party in the House of Commons; and when Somers retired from that arena the former remained without an equal. In 1695 he was appointed chancellor of the exchequer, and projected the general fund. He became first lord of the treasury in 1697, and was raised to the peerage, as Baron Halifax, in 1700.

In 1701 he was impeached by the House of Commons, in which the Tories had gained the ascendency, but was acquitted by the House of Lords. At the death of Queen Anne, in 1714, he acted as one of the regents until the arrival of George I., who created him Earl of Halifax and appointed him first lord of the treasury. He died in 1715, and, leaving no issue, his earldom became extinct; but his nephew and heir, George Montagu, was soon after made Earl of Halifax. He receives credit for consistency as a statesman, but is censured for inordinate vanity. He ceased to be a versifier soon after he entered Parliament, but was noted as a patron of literary men, among whom were Addison and Steele. By these and other writers he was, as Pope remarked, "fed with dedications." His chief production as a poet is his "Epistle to the Earl of Dorset on the Battle of the Boyne." The Earl of Halifax originated the project for the formation of a public library and the purchase of the Cotton manuscripts, which were the commencement of the British Museum. He is called the author or originator of the national debt and of the Bank of England.

See MACAULAY's "Essay on Addison," and his "History of England;" "Biographia Britannica."

Halifax, (GEORGE SAVILE or SAVILLE,) MARQUIS OF, an English statesman, born in 1630, was the son of Sir William Savile, of Yorkshire, and grandfather of Lord Chesterfield. In 1668 his loyalty to the Stuart family was rewarded by a peerage, with the title of Viscount Halifax. In the reign of Charles II. he was the rival of Shaftesbury. He was a man of eminent abilities and accomplishments, and acquired great influence in Parliament by his readiness in debate, his copious eloquence, and his extensive knowledge. In 1679 he was appointed member of the Council of Thirty, and in 1682 was made a marquis. He opposed the bill for the exclusion of the Duke of York from the throne, and was Speaker of the Lords in the Convention or Parliament which settled the succession in the revolution of 1688. At the accession of William III., Halifax was appointed lord privy seal, but resigned that office in 1690, and joined the opposition. He was called "the trimmer of trimmers" in politics, and censured for inconstancy. Macaulay, however, represents him as "the most accomplished, the most enlightened, and, in spite of great faults, the most estimable" of the statesmen who were formed in the corrupt court of Charles II. He wrote two political tracts,—"The Character of a Trimmer," and "Anatomy of an Equivalent,"—which entitle him to a place among English classical authors. He left an only son, at whose death, about 1700, the title became extinct. Died in 1695.

See MACAULAY's "History of England," vol. i. chaps. ii. and iv.; vol. iii. chaps. vi., vii., ix., and x.: vol. iii. chaps. xi., xiv., and xv.; vol. iv. chap. xxi.

Halirsch, hä′lĕĕrsh, (FRIEDRICH LUDWIG,) a German poet, born in Vienna in 1802; died at Milan in 1832.

Hăl′ket, (Lady ANNE,) originally named MURRAY, a learned lady, born in London in 1632. She left in manuscript many volumes, a portion of which was published under the title of "Meditations," (1702.) Died in 1699.

Hăl′kett, (Sir PETER,) a British naval officer, born in 1766, became vice-admiral in 1821, and admiral in 1837. Died in 1840.

Hall, (ANNA MARIA.) See HALL, (Mrs. S. C.)

Hăll, (Rev. ANTHONY,) born in Cumberland in 1679, edited Leland "De Scriptoribus," (1709,) and other works. Died in 1723.

Hall, (Captain BASIL,) born in Edinburgh in 1788, entered the royal navy about the age of fifteen, and became a post-captain in 1817. About 1816 he accompa-

nied Lord Amherst on the embassy to China, and after his return published "A Voyage of Discovery to Corea and Great Loo-Choo Island," which was well received. He published in 1823 "Extracts from a Journal written on the Coasts of Chili, Peru, and Mexico;" and in 1829 appeared his "Travels in North America," which was followed by "A Winter in Lower Styria," "Travels in South America," etc. Captain Hall was a Fellow of the Royal Society, to the "Transactions" of which he contributed several scientific treatises. His books of travel obtained a liberal share of popularity. "Blackwood's Magazine," reviewing his "Travels in North America," gives him credit for "striking talent and many just and profound observations." He died in an asylum for the insane, in 1844.

See CHAMBERS, "Biographical Dictionary of Eminent Scotsmen, (Supplement.)

Hall, (Rt. Hon. Sir BENJAMIN,) a liberal British legislator, born probably in Wales in 1802. He was elected to Parliament in 1831, after which he represented Marylebone for many years. He favoured the extension of the right of suffrage, and other reforms, and acted a prominent part in the often-repeated effort to abolish church rates. In 1854 he became president of the board of health, and privy councillor. He was raised to the peerage, with the title of Baron Llanover, about 1859.

Hall, hâl, (CARL CHRISTIAN,) a Danish orator of the Liberal party, born at Copenhagen about 1812. In 1854 he was appointed minister of worship and public instruction, and president of the council in 1856.

Hâll, (DOMINICK AUGUSTINE,) an American magistrate, born in South Carolina in 1765, became United States judge for Louisiana in 1812. He is chiefly known from his controversy with General Jackson at New Orleans in 1815. (See JACKSON, ANDREW.) Died in 1820.

Hall or **Halle,** (EDWARD,) an English historian, born in London. In 1540 he was appointed a judge of the sheriff's court. He wrote a chronicle, entitled "The Union of the Two Noble and Illustrate Families of Lancaster and York," (1542.) Died in 1547.

Hall, (GEORGE,) a son of the Bishop of Norwich, was born at Waltham Holy Cross in 1612. He became Bishop of Chester in 1662, and published some sermons, (1655-66.) Died in 1668.

Hăll, (GORDON,) the first American missionary to Bombay, was born in West Granville, (now Tolland,) Massachusetts, in 1782. He graduated at Williams College in 1808, was ordained in February, 1812, and the same month sailed for the East under the auspices of the American Board for Foreign Missions. After his arrival at Bombay he continued to labour with great zeal and success till his death, (of cholera,) in 1826, just after completing the publication of the New Testament in the Mahratta language.

Hall, (Sir JAMES,) Baronet of Dunglass, a Scottish gentleman, born in 1761, was the father of Captain Basil Hall. He wrote an "Essay on the Origin, Principles, and History of Gothic Architecture," said to be the most popular and valuable work on the subject. He was president of the Royal Society of Edinburgh. By experiments on the fusion of mineral substances he contributed greatly to the progress of geological science. Died in 1832.

See CHAMBERS, "Biographical Dictionary of Eminent Scotsmen."

Hall, (JAMES,) an eminent American author and judge, born in Philadelphia in 1793. He joined the army and served with distinction against the British in the war of 1812-15. In 1820 he removed to Shawneetown, Illinois, where he practised law and held several civil offices, including that of judge. After 1833 he resided in Cincinnati. He established at Vandalia about 1830 "The Illinois Monthly Magazine," which he conducted for several years with much ability. He published, besides other works, "Legends of the West," (1832,) "Sketches of the West," (1835,) "Tales of the Border," (1835,) "Notes on the Western States," (1838,) and "The Wilderness and the War-Path," (1845.) Judge Hall and T. L. McKenney were joint authors of a splendidly-illustrated work, "The History of the Indian Tribes of North America," (3 vols., 1838-44.) A new edition of his Works, revised by himself, was published about 1856, in 4 vols. Died in July, 1868.

See GRISWOLD, "Prose Writers of America;" DUYCKINCK, "Cyclopædia of American Literature," vol. ii.; ALLIBONE, "Dictionary of Authors."

Hall, (JAMES,) an American geologist, born at Hingham, Massachusetts, in 1811. He was educated at the Rensselaer School, Troy, where he was a pupil of Amos Eaton. About 1837 he was appointed one of the geologists of the State of New York, and commenced the survey of the western part of that State. His "Report on the Geology of New York, Fourth District," was published by the government in 1843. He acquired distinction by his researches in the fossils of the lower and middle Silurian rocks, which he described in his excellent work on "The Palæontology of New York," (3 vols., 1847–59.) He was appointed geologist of the State of Iowa in 1855.

Hall, (JOHN,) an English author, born at Durham in 1627, was educated for the law. He wrote a volume of poems, treatises on Emblems and on Paradoxes, and a translation of Longinus "On the Sublime." Died in 1656.

Hall, (JOHN,) an English engraver, born near Colchester in 1739. He was historical engraver to George III. Died in 1797.

Hall, (JOHN E.,) an American lawyer and editor, a brother of Judge James Hall, noticed above, was born in 1783. He began to practise law in Baltimore about 1805, and there edited the "American Law Journal," (6 vols., 1808–16.) In 1816 he became editor of the "Port-Folio," (published in Philadelphia,) to which he contributed "Memoirs of Anacreon." Died in 1829.

Hall, (JOSEPH,) an English bishop and author, born at Ashby-de-la-Zouch, July 1, 1574. After graduating at Cambridge, he was ordained, and became chaplain to James I. and Dean of Worcester in 1617. He was a deputy to the Synod of Dort in 1618. In 1627 he was appointed Bishop of Exeter, from which he was transferred to the see of Norwich in 1641. His earnest piety subjected him to the charge of Puritanism. Having united with other bishops in protesting against the validity of acts of Parliament passed in their compulsory absence, he was committed to the Tower in 1641, and confined a few months. The revenues of his bishopric having been sequestered about 1642, he passed the remainder of his life in poverty, at Higham. Died in 1656. Bishop Hall was a man of excellent character, and author of many learned and eloquent productions in prose and verse, among which may be noticed "Virgidemiarum," (Poetical Satires, 1598,) "Epistles," "Christian Meditations," (1640,) "Enochismus; or, Treatise on the Mode of Walking with God," and "Contemplations upon the Principal Historical Passages of the New Testament," (1612–15.) The last, in the opinion of Doddridge, is "incomparably valuable for language, criticism, and devotion." "Both Taylor and Hall," says Hallam, "were full of learning and fertile of illustration; both may be said to have had strong imagination and poetical genius, though Taylor let his predominate a little more."

See REV. JOHN JONES, "Memoirs of the Life and Writings of Joseph Hall;" "Autobiography," in his "Specialities;" PRATT, "Life of Joseph Hall;" WARTON, "History of English Poetry;" "Biographia Britannica."

Hall, (LOUISA JANE,) an American poetess, born at Newburyport, Massachusetts, in 1802. She wrote, besides other works, a dramatic poem, entitled "Miriam," (1837,) and a "Life of Elizabeth Carter."

See GRISWOLD's "Female Poets of America."

Hall, (LYMAN,) a physician, born in Connecticut, graduated at Yale College in 1747, and settled at Sudbury, Georgia. Having joined the popular cause, he was chosen a member of the Congress of 1775, and signed the Declaration of Independence. He retired from Congress in 1780, and was elected Governor of Georgia in 1783. Died in 1791.

See GOODRICH, "Lives of the Signers to the Declaration of Independence."

Hall, (MARSHALL,) an English medical writer, born near Nottingham in 1790. He published, besides other works, "Principles of the Theory and Practice of Medi-

cine," (1837;) reprinted by Drs. J. Bigelow and O. W. Holmes, (Boston, 1839.) Died in 1857.

See "Memoirs of Marshall Hall," by his widow, London, 1861.

Hall, (NEWMAN,) an English dissenting minister, born in 1816. He graduated at the London University, and preached to the Congregational church of Hull from 1842 to 1854. In the latter year he became minister of Surrey Chapel, London. He wrote a work called "Come to Jesus," which had a large circulation. Among his other works is "Italy, the Land of the Forum and the Vatican," (1853.) He distinguished himself as an advocate of American liberty during the civil war of 1861–65. He visited the United States in 1867.

Hall, (PETER,) an English theologian, born in 1803, became rector of Milston, Wiltshire. He edited the works of his ancestor, Bishop Joseph Hall, and wrote "Reliquiæ Liturgiæ," (5 vols., 1847,) and "Fragmenta Liturgica," (7 vols., 1848.) Died in 1849.

Hall, hâl, (PETER ADOLF,) an eminent Swedish miniature-painter, born at Borås in 1739, worked in Paris. Died at Liege in 1794.

Hall, (RICHARD,) an English Catholic theologian, professor of theology at Douay, in France, wrote a "Life of Fisher, Bishop of Rochester," (1653,) which goes under the name of its editor, Bailey. Died in 1604.

Hall, (ROBERT,) an eloquent English Baptist minister, born at Arnsby, in Leicestershire, on the 2d of May, 1764. He was a remarkable instance of early mental development. It is said that before the age of nine years he perused with interest Jonathan Edwards's treatises on the "Affections" and the "Will." After graduating at King's College, Aberdeen, where he formed a friendship with Sir James Mackintosh, he became, in 1783, assistant pastor in the church of Broadmead, near Bristol, to which a crowded audience was attracted by his wonderful eloquence. From 1791 to 1804 he was minister of a Baptist congregation in Cambridge. In consequence of excessive application to study and habitual privation of social recreation, he suffered an attack of insanity in November, 1804, from which he was restored in about two years. But it was thought expedient for him to resign his ministerial charge, and to abstain from mental exertion for a year or two. In 1807 or 1808, having improved in health, he accepted a call from the church of Harvey Lane, Leicester, where he was married in 1808. Here he continued to labour for a period of twenty years, and maintained his high reputation as a pulpit orator. In 1826 he left Leicester and returned to the scene of his early labours at Bristol, where he died in 1831. His published sermons are ranked among the most perfect specimens of pulpit eloquence. "In his highest flights, what he said of Burke might, with the slightest deduction, be applied to himself,—'that his imperial fancy laid all nature under tribute,' and collected riches from every scene of the creation and every walk of art." (Dr. Gregory.) In the excitement occasioned by the French Revolution, he published an "Apology for the Freedom of the Press," and other political treatises.

See OLINTHUS GREGORY, "Brief Memoir of the Life of Robert Hall;" J. W. MORRIS, "Life of Robert Hall," 1846; JOHN GREENE, "Reminiscences of Robert Hall;" "Quarterly Review," vol. xlviii., 1832; "Encyclopædia Britannica."

Hall, (ROBERT PLEASANTS,) an American lawyer and poet, born in Chester district, South Carolina, in 1825. He removed with his parents to Georgia during his minority. He published a volume of poems about 1848. Died in 1854.

Hall, (SAMUEL CARTER,) an English editor and critic, was born at Topsham, Devon, in 1800. He was successively editor of the "New Monthly Magazine," "The Book of Gems," "The Baronial Halls of England," and other illustrated annuals. In co-operation with his wife, (see next article,) he published a successful work entitled "Ireland: its Scenery, Character," etc., (3 vols., 1841–43.) He has been for about twenty years editor of the London "Art Journal," an illustrated monthly periodical of high character. It was founded chiefly by him, and has contributed greatly to the advancement of the arts in Great Britain.

Hall, (Mrs. S. C.,) (ANNA MARIA FIELDING,) a popular Irish authoress, born at Dublin about 1804. At

ā, ē, ī, ō, ū, ȳ, *long;* à, è, ò, same, less prolonged; ă, ĕ, ĭ, ŏ, ŭ, ў, *short;* ą, ę, į, ǫ, *obscure;* fär, fåll, fåt; mët; nŏt; gōōd; mōōn;

fifteen she removed to London, and was married to S. C. Hall, noticed above, in 1824. She produced in 1829 "Sketches of Irish Character," which was favourably received, and in 1834 "Tales of Woman's Trials." Her reputation was maintained by "Lights and Shadows of Irish Life," (1838, 3 vols.,) "Tales of the Irish Peasantry," (1840,) and other graphic descriptions of the same people. She also wrote two successful dramas, entitled "The French Refugee," (1837,) and "The Groves of Blarney." Her talents have been enlisted in the temperance cause and other benevolent enterprises.

See "Autobiography of William Jerdan," vol. iv. chap. xvii.

Hall, (SAMUEL READ,) an American teacher, born at Croydon, New Hampshire, in 1795. He opened a school for the training of teachers at Concord, Vermont, about 1823, and published "The Instructor's Manual."

Hăl'lam, (ARTHUR HENRY,) a critic and essayist, born in London on the 1st of February, 1811, was a son of Henry Hallam the historian. He was educated at Eton and at Trinity College, Cambridge, where he graduated in 1832. He gained a prize at Cambridge for an English essay on the Philosophical Writings of Cicero. After he left college, he visited the continent in company with his father. He died in Vienna in September, 1833, leaving a number of short poems and essays, since published under the title of "Remains in Prose and Verse," to which a Memoir by his father is prefixed. His intimate friend Tennyson has raised an immortal monument to his name in his "In Memoriam." One of his fellow-students, in a letter to Henry Hallam, writes, "I have met with no man his superior in metaphysical subtlety; no man his equal as a philosophical critic on works of taste." See an article on "Precocity" in the "Saturday Review" of April 4, 1863, from which we quote the following : "No matter how often his prose Remains are read and pondered, our admiration continues as fresh as ever. We say prose Remains, because his poems . . . are wanting in those astounding evidences of matured thought which meet us in every page of his three great prose essays."

See the "North British Review" for February, 1851 ; "Atlantic Monthly" for December, 1860.

Hallam, (HENRY,) an English historian and critic of great merit, born at Windsor in 1777, was educated at Eton and Oxford. Soon after he left college he became a resident of London, where he passed the greater part of his life, engaged in literary studies and in the labours of authorship. He married a daughter of Sir Abraham Elton. He was one of the earliest contributors to the "Edinburgh Review." His political affinities associated him with the Whigs ; but he was remarkably free from a partisan spirit. He was a prominent coadjutor of Wilberforce in the abolition of the slave-trade. He published in 1818 an important and valuable work, a "View of the State of Europe during the Middle Ages," which has run through eleven editions. "It is written throughout," says the "Edinburgh Review," (vol. xxx., June, 1818,) "with a spirit of freedom and liberality that do credit to the author. A firm but temperate love of liberty, an enlightened but cautious philosophy, form its distinguished excellence."

His next great work was "The Constitutional History of England from the Accession of Henry VII. to the Death of George II.," (1827.) "Mr. Hallam," says Macaulay, "is, on the whole, far better qualified than any other writer of our time for the office which he has undertaken. He has great industry and great acuteness. His knowledge is extensive, various, and profound. His mind is equally distinguished by the amplitude of its grasp and the delicacy of its tact. . . . His work is eminently judicial. He sums up with a calm, steady impartiality. On a general survey, we do not scruple to pronounce the 'Constitutional History' the most impartial book that we ever read." In 1830 he received one of the two gold medals instituted by George IV. for excellence in historical composition. He published in 1837-39 an "Introduction to the Literature of Europe in the Fifteenth, Sixteenth, and Seventeenth Centuries," (4 vols.,) a work of immense research, which was received with great favour and which placed the author in the highest rank as a critic. A writer in the "Edinburgh

Review" for October, 1840, pronounced it "the most important contribution to literary history which English libraries have received for many years." Hallam was a Fellow of the Royal Society, and a corresponding member of the French Institute. He died in January, 1859.

See a Sketch of his Life in the "Proceedings of the Royal Society," vol. x. No. 40 ; MACAULAY, "Essay on Hallam's Constitutional History of England ;" WM. JERDAN, "Men I have known," London, 1866 ; "Biographical Sketches," by HARRIET MARTINEAU, London, 1869 ; critique on "Hallam's Constitutional History," in the "Quarterly Review" for January, 1828, (by SOUTHEY,) also the same Review for February, 1837, and March, 1840 ; and articles in the "Edinburgh Review" for June, 1818, and October, 1840 ; and "Blackwood's Magazine" for May, 1837 ; ALLIBONE, "Dict. of Authors."

Hallam, (HENRY FITZMAURICE,) a son of the preceding, was born in August, 1824. He studied at Eton, became a good classical scholar, and entered Trinity College, Cambridge, in 1842. Having gained the first prize for English declamation in 1845, he quitted Cambridge in 1846, and commenced the study of law. He had been called to the bar a few months, when he died, at Sienna, Italy, in October, 1850. An American student who knew him at Cambridge says, "He was the neatest extempore speaker I ever heard." (See Memoir prefixed to "Arthur Henry Hallam's Remains.")

Hallberg-Broich, von, fon hăl'berG' bro'ik, (THEODOR HUBERT,) BARON, an eccentric German traveller, born near Dusseldorf about 1775. He published a "Tour in Scandinavia," (1818,) "Travels in Italy," (1829,) and a "Journey to the East," ("Reise nach dem Orient," 1839.)

Hallé, (ANTOINE.) See HALLEY, (ANTOINE.)

Hallé, hȧ'lă', (CLAUDE GUI,) a French painter, born in Paris in 1652. He gained many prizes at the Academy, and was employed to decorate the royal residences and several churches of Paris. Died in 1736.

Hallé, (JEAN NOËL,) an eminent French physician, son of Noël Hallé the painter, was born in Paris in 1754. After he had acquired skill in the art of design at Rome, he returned to Paris to study medicine. In 1794 he was appointed professor of hygiene and medicine in the Ecole de Santé, where his lectures were very popular. Hallé was admitted to the Academy of Sciences at the first formation of the Institute, (1796.) In 1804 he obtained the chair of medicine in the College of France ; and about the same period Napoleon chose him as his first physician. After the restoration he was employed professionally by the king's brother, (afterwards Charles X.) His vast erudition was displayed by his professional works and by various scientific treatises, which form part of the Memoirs of the Institute and of the "Encyclopédie Méthodique." In his character were united many estimable qualities. Died in 1822.

See CUVIER, "Éloge de Hallé ;" DESGENETTES, "Éloge de Hallé," 1823 ; F. DUBOIS D'AMIENS, "Éloge de J. N. Halle," 1852.

Hallé, (NOËL,) the son of Claude Gui, noticed above, was born in Paris in 1711, and gained distinction as a historical painter. Having obtained several prizes, he was sent to Rome at the public expense. In 1771 he was made superintendent of the tapestries of the crown, and afterwards director of the Academy of France which the king instituted at Rome. Died in 1781.

Hallé, (PIERRE,) a French poet and orator, born at Bayeux in 1611. He wrote on canon law. Died in 1689.

Hăl'leck, (FITZ-GREENE,) a distinguished American poet, born in Guilford, Connecticut, July 8, 1790. He was descended on his mother's side from John Eliot, the "Apostle of the Indians." He appears to have enjoyed but few advantages for education. About the age of eighteen he became, in the city of New York, a clerk in the banking-house of Jacob Barker, in whose employ he continued for a number of years. Mr. Halleck's mind was not remarkable for precocity, and his earliest productions show, but slight traces of that genius which charmed and dazzled in his maturer years. The first of his poems that attracted much attention appeared (1818-19) in the New York "Evening Post," under the signature of "Croaker & Co.," a literary partnership consisting of himself and his gifted friend Joseph Rodman Drake. The early death of the latter (in 1820) was commemorated by his brother poet in some beautiful and touching lines. About the beginning of 1820 he published "Fanny," his longest poem,—a satire upon the fashionable and political follies of the day,—which had a great success and passed through numerous editions. In 1822 he visited Europe, and after his return published in the "New York Review" his "Marco Bozzaris," one of the finest martial lyrics in the language, and in the "United States Review" his beautiful poem to the memory of Burns, concerning which Mr. Bryant remarks, "I am not sure that the verses are not the finest in which one poet ever celebrated another." A volume of his poems, including the two last named, appeared in 1827. Among his other productions we may particularly name "Alnwick Castle," "Connecticut," and "Red Jacket." Although Mr. Halleck's most ardent admirers would hardly claim for him the name of a "great" poet, all competent critics must, we think, admit that there are in the productions of his happier moments a facility, sweetness, and grace scarcely surpassed by any of the most gifted poets of the present age. In none of his poems, perhaps, are these qualities exhibited to better advantage than in his charming lines on "Woman," written in the album of an unknown lady.

For many years Mr. Halleck was employed as a clerk by John Jacob Astor, the celebrated millionnaire. Some time after he had given up this position, he received from J. J. Astor a small legacy, to which a liberal addition was made by Mr. W. B. Astor. During the latter years of his life he resided chiefly in Connecticut, in his native town. He died November 19, 1867. A complete edition of Halleck's poems appeared in 1858. The "Croaker Papers," including portraits of Halleck and Drake, were published by the Bradford Club in a handsome octavo volume, (New York, 1860,) the typography of which has probably never been surpassed by that of any other work issued in this country. It is said to be the first complete edition of the "Croaker Papers" that has appeared.

See JAMES GRANT WILSON, "Life and Letters of Fitz-Greene Halleck," 1869; W. C. BRYANT, "Address on Fitz-Greene Halleck," delivered before the New York Historical Society, February 2, 1869; DUYCKINCK, "Cyclopædia of American Literature," vol. ii. ; GRISWOLD, "Poets and Poetry of America;" CLEVELAND, "Compendium of American Literature."

Halleck, (HENRY WAGER,) an American general, born near Utica, in New York, in 1814. He graduated at West Point in 1839. He published "Elements of Military Art and Science," (1846.) As first lieutenant, he served in the Mexican war in 1846–47, after which he filled several civil offices in California. He became a captain of engineers, but resigned his commission in 1854, and practised law at San Francisco from that time until 1861. In August, 1861, he was appointed a majorgeneral of the United States army. He obtained the command of the department of Missouri in November, 1861, and of the department of the Mississippi in March, 1862. He commanded in person at the siege of Corinth, which the enemy evacuated about the end of May, 1862. He was general-in-chief of the armies of the United States from July 11, 1862, till March, 1864, during which period he remained at Washington, directing the movements of the generals in the field. He was superseded March 12, 1864, by General Grant, and was appointed chief of staff of the United States army. He took command of the military division of the Pacific in August, 1865.

Hallenberg, hâl'len-bĕrg', (JONAS,) a learned Swedish historian and antiquary, born in Småland in 1748. He was appointed in 1784 historian of the kingdom, and ordered to write the history of the reign of Gustavus Adolphus, which was published, in 1790, in 5 vols., and is considered an accurate work. In 1818 he received a title of nobility. Died in 1834.

See J. H. SCHROEDER, "Minne af J. Hallenberg," 1838; "Biographiskt-Lexicon öfver namnkunnige Svenska Män."

Haller, hâl'ler, (BERTHOLD,) a Swiss Reformer, born in Suabia in 1492, was a coadjutor of Zwingle. He was the principal agent in the conversion of the people of Berne to the Protestant religion. Died in 1536.

Haller, (JOHANN,) a German sculptor, born at Innspruck in 1792. He worked in Munich, was patronized by King Ludwig, and adorned the Glyptothek with statues of ancient heroes. Among his works are many busts of eminent moderns. Died in 1826.

Haller, von, fon hâl'ler, (ALBERT,) a distinguished Swiss physiologist, botanist, and poet, was born at Berne on the 16th of October, 1708. His intellectual powers developed themselves very early. At the age of nine or ten, it is said, he wrote a composition in Greek, and compiled Hebrew and Chaldee grammars. In 1725 he studied medicine and anatomy under Boerhaave and Albinus at Leyden, where he graduated in 1727. At Paris he pursued his studies under Winslow and Ledran, and, after taking lessons in mathematics from Bernoulli at Bâle, he returned to practise medicine at Berne. Here he cultivated botany and poetry with ardour, and had charge of the public library. In 1736 he accepted the chair of medicine, anatomy, and botany in the University of Göttingen, in which during seventeen years he officiated with great zeal and distinction. Amidst his multifarious official duties he found time for careful researches and important discoveries in science, and for the collection of materials for his projected publications.

At Göttingen he published his "Anatomical Plates," the first volume of his "Swiss Flora," his "Experiments on Sensibility and Irritability," and his "First Outlines of Physiology," besides a great multitude of memoirs contributed to learned societies and recorded in their "Transactions." When the Royal Society of Göttingen was founded, in 1751, Haller was chosen perpetual president. Some years previously he was elected Fellow of the Royal Society of London, and was named physician to the King of England. His renown was such that the Universities of Oxford and Leyden were eager to engage his services as professor, and Frederick the Great invited him to his court.

The delicate state of his health rendering repose needful, he resigned his professorship at Göttingen in 1753, and returned to Berne, the citizens of which in his absence had chosen him a member of the Supreme Council, and now added other dignities. Still he maintained his prodigious mental activity as an author and a student of nature, which, aided by a powerful memory, rendered him profoundly versed not only in natural sciences, but also in languages, history, geography, and antiquities. Among his numerous and voluminous writings may be specially mentioned "Icones Anatomicæ," ("Anatomical Plates," 1743–56,) esteemed one of his best works, and "Elementa Physiologiæ Corporis Humani," ("Elements of the Physiology of the Human Body," 8 vols., 1757–66.) This work opened a new era in physiology, and is highly praised for its admirable arrangement and the elegance of its style, as well as for the multitude of its scientific facts and its thorough discussion of the theories of others. The principal idea developed in it is the irritability of the muscular fibre considered as a motive power, and distinguished from sensibility elsewhere diffused. He published, also, "Opera Minora," a collection of forty treatises on "Anatomy and Physiology," (3 vols. 4to, 1762–68,) and a "Flora of Switzerland," (1768.) In botany Haller may be called a rival of his contemporary Linnæus, whose artificial system he laboured to supplant by the system founded on natural affinities, now generally adopted.

His poetical works were written in German, and were published when he was about twenty years of age. The most extensive among them is a poem on the Alps, which ran through twenty-two editions. His elegiac odes, his verses on "Eternity," and his didactic poems on "Reason" and "Superstition," are admired for their sensibility and elevated thought. Haller was thrice married, and had a large family of children. His religious views were evangelical, as was shown by his defence of revelation in answer to Voltaire. Died in 1777.

See "Life of Haller," (in German,) by J. G. ZIMMERMANN, 1755; THOMAS HENRY, "Memoirs of Albert de Haller," 1783; CONDORCET, "Éloge de Haller;" SENEBIER, "Éloge historique de Albert von Haller," 1778; LONGFELLOW, "Poets and Poetry of Europe;" CUVIER, "Histoire des Sciences naturelles;" ERSCH und GRUBER, "Allgemeine Encyklopaedie;" ISIDORE BOURDON, "Illustres Médecins et Naturalistes des Temps modernes," 1844; "Biographie de Albert de Haller," 2d edition, 1846.

Haller, von, (ALBERT,) a son of the preceding, born at Berne in 1758, was an excellent botanist, and left several works in manuscript. He performed several diplomatic missions with honour. Died at Berne in 1823.

ă, ē, ī, ō, ū, ȳ, *long;* ă, ĕ, ĭ, ŏ, same, less prolonged; ă, ĕ, ĭ, ŏ, ŭ, ў, *short;* ą, ę, į, ǫ, *obscure;* fâr, fâll, fât; mĕt; nŏt; gŏŏd; mōōn;

Haller, von, (CHARLES LOUIS,) a Swiss publicist, born at Berne in 1768, was a grandson of the great Haller. He was chosen a member of the Grand Council in 1814. He asserted the divine right of kings in his "Restoration of Political Science," (in German, 6 vols., 1816-22.) About 1820 he avowed his conversion to Roman Catholicism, and obtained an office in the ministry of foreign affairs in Paris. He returned to Switzerland in 1830. Died in 1854.

See QUÉRARD, "La France Littéraire."

Haller, von, (GOTTLIEB IMMANUEL,) a Swiss antiquary and bibliographer, the eldest son of the celebrated physiologist, was born at Berne in 1735. He studied jurisprudence, and served the state in several offices, among which was that of magistrate *(bailli)* of Noyon. He published a "Cabinet of Swiss Coins and Medals," (1780,) and a bibliography of Swiss historians, "Bibliothek der Schweizer-Geschichte systematisch-chronologisch geordnet," (6 vols., 1785-87,) which is called an excellent work. Died in 1786.

See MEUSEL, "Lexikon der vom Jahre 1750-1800 verstorbenen Deutschen Schriftsteller."

Hallerstein. See ALLERSTEIN.

Häl'let, (JOSEPH,) an English dissenting minister, born at Exeter in 1692. He wrote "A Free and Impartial Study of the Holy Scriptures Recommended," (1729-36.) Died in 1744.

Hallette, *hä'lĕt',* (A.,) a French engineer, born in 1788. He invented a hydraulic press for the production of olive oil, and applied atmospheric pressure as a motive power on railways. Died at Arras in 1846.

Halley, *hä'lä',* or **Hallé,** *hä'lä',* (ANTOINE,) a French writer of Latin poetry, born in 1595; died in 1675.

Häl'ley, (EDMUND,) an eminent English astronomer and mathematician, was born in a suburb of London on the 26th of October, 1656, and educated at Oxford. He began to cultivate astronomy with ardour, and before the age of twenty he had made observations of the planets and had written a memoir on the problem of Kepler. Perceiving that the advancement of astronomy depended on an accurate knowledge of the position of the stars, and that the catalogues of Ptolemy and Tycho were no longer adequate to the requirements of the science, he resolved, while Flamsteed and Hevelius were engaged in a survey of the Northern latitudes, to apply his own energies and observations on a catalogue of the Southern hemisphere. Having received aid and patronage from the king, he embarked in 1676 for Saint Helena, where he remained about two years, and prepared his "Catalogue of Southern Stars," ("Catalogus Stellarum Australium,") published in 1679, which contains three hundred and fifty stars. He also discovered a method of obtaining the sun's parallax by means of the transits of Mercury or Venus.

In 1678 he was elected a Fellow of the Royal Society. Two years later he made observations on a remarkable comet, since designated "Halley's comet," and in 1683 published his theory of the variation of the magnet. Having become intimate with Newton, he persuaded him to publish his "Principia," in 1686. In 1698, under the auspices of William III., Halley commanded a successful scientific expedition to the South Atlantic Ocean, one object of which was to observe the variation of the magnet. At his return, in 1700, he published his "Chart of the Variations of the Magnetic Needle." After performing other public services of a scientific character, he obtained in 1703 the Savilian chair of geometry at Oxford. Still pursuing the study of astronomy with unabated activity, he was the first who successfully predicted the return of a comet, having ascertained that the comet of 1680 revolved in a period of about seventy-six years. The Royal Society elected him their secretary in 1713.

In 1720 he was appointed astronomer royal, in place of Flamsteed, deceased, and then undertook a task which would require nineteen years to perform, namely, to observe the moon throughout an entire revolution of her nodes. He lived to finish this task, in which he arrived at an important discovery in the theory of the moon,—the acceleration of her mean motion,—and also made some corrections in the lunar tables. Having turned his attention to the distance and parallax of the

fixed stars, he advanced the opinion that their parallax and diameter were insensible, or at least too small to be measured by any means which astronomers then possessed. He appears to have been one of the first who conceived or discovered the sublime doctrine of the proper motion of the fixed stars in universal space. Besides the works already named, he published a translation of Apollonius's "Conic Sections," treatises on the Trade Winds, on Logarithms, on the Use of the Barometer, etc. Of his success in poetry we have an instance in the well-known Latin verses prefixed to Newton's "Principia." He had married in 1682 a daughter of Mr. Tooke, auditor of the exchequer. Died in January, 1742.

See MACAULAY, "History of England," vol. i.; "Biographia Britannica;" THOMPSON, "History of the Royal Society."

Häl'lĭ-day, (Sir ANDREW,) an eminent British physician and historical writer. He served as physician in the army in the Peninsular war, and at Waterloo, (1815,) after which he attended the Duke of Clarence, then travelling for his health. He wrote, among other works, a "Memoir of the Campaign of 1815," "Annals of the House of Brunswick," (2 vols., 1826,) and "Annals of the House of Hanover," (2 vols., 1826.) Died in 1840.

Hallier, *hä'le-à',* (FRANÇOIS,) a doctor of the Sorbonne, was born at Chartres, in France, in 1595. He officiated as *promoteur* of the assembly of the clergy in 1645. In 1652 he went to Rome and obtained against the Jansenists the bull *cum ascensione.* In 1656 he was appointed Bishop of Cavaillon. He wrote "On Elections and Ordinations," (1636,) and other works, in Latin. Died in 1658.

Häl'lĭ-fax, (SAMUEL,) D.D., LL.D., an English scholar, born at Mansfield in 1733, was appointed professor of Arabic in the University of Cambridge in 1768. He became chaplain-in-ordinary to George III. in 1774, Bishop of Gloucester in 1781, and Bishop of Saint Asaph in 1787. He published an "Analysis of the Roman Civil Law compared with the Laws of England," (1774.) Died in 1790.

Häl'lĭ-well, (JAMES ORCHARD,) a learned British archæologist, born at Chelsea in 1821. He has distinguished himself by his researches into the literary history of Great Britain, and by his services as a Shakspearian critic. He edited numerous old writings, and published several original works, among which are a "History of Free-Masonry in England," (2d edition, 1844,) and a "Life of William Shakespeare," (1848.) For many years he was engaged on a costly illustrated edition of Shakspeare's Works, (16 vols., 1855-65.)

Hallman, *häl'män,* (CARL ISRAEL,) a Swedish dramatic writer, born in 1732. He obtained an obscure position in the College of Mines, and produced successful comedies and parodies, among which are "Skeppar Rolf," (1778,) and "Petis och Telee," (1779.) Died in 1800.

See "Biographiskt-Lexicon öfver namnkunnige Svenska Män."

Hallman, (JOHAN GUSTAF,) a Swedish writer of prose and verse, born in Södermannland, was the father of the preceding. Died about 1758.

Häl'lŏck, (GERARD,) a journalist, a son of Moses, noticed below, born in Plainfield, Massachusetts, in 1800, became in 1828 one of the two owners of the New York "Journal of Commerce," which he and David Hale conducted for over twenty years. Died in 1866.

Hallock, (JEREMIAH,) an American clergyman, born in Brookhaven, Long Island, in 1758. He preached for many years at West Simsbury, Connecticut, where he settled in 1785. Died in 1826.

Hallock, (MOSES,) a clergyman, a brother of the preceding, was born in Long Island in 1760. He became pastor at Plainfield, Massachusetts, in 1792, and educated many young men for the ministry. Died in 1837.

Halloran. See O'HALLORAN.

Hällström or **Haellstroem,** *hĕl'ström,* (CARL PETER,) a Swedish geographer and engineer, was born at Ilmola in 1774. He rendered important services to the geography of Sweden by surveys, triangulations, etc., and published many geographical works. Died in 1836.

Halm, (FRIEDRICH.) See MUNCH-BELLINGHAUSEN.

Halma, *häl'mä',* (NICOLAS,) ABBÉ, a French mathematician and linguist, born at Sedan in 1755, removed to Paris in 1797. He published, besides other works, a French translation of the "Almagest" of Ptolemy, (2 vols., 1813-16.) Died in 1828.

See "Nouvelle Biographie Générale."

Haloander, hä′lo-än′der, (GREGOR,) a German jurist and Hellenist, born at Zwickau, published "Digestorum seu Pandectarum Libri L.," (1529,) and translated Justinian's "Novellæ" into Latin, (1530.) Died in 1532.

Hals, häls, (FRANS,) an excellent Flemish portrait-painter, born at Mechlin in 1584. He was reputed to be second only to Van Dyck among the portrait-painters of his time. He worked in Delft, Haarlem, and other places. Died in 1666 or 1656.

His brother DIRCK, born in 1589, painted interiors of buildings, and animals, with success. Died in 1656.

See DESCAMPS, "Vies des Peintres Flamands," etc.

Halthaus, hält′höwss, or **Haltaus,** häl′töwss, (CHRISTIAN GOTTLOB,) a German antiquary and philologist, born at Leipsic in 1702, excelled in the study of mediæval history. He was successively con-rector, and rector, of a school in Leipsic. He published a "Calendarium Medii Ævi," (1729,) and an important work, in Latin, called a "Glossary of Mediæval German Words," (1758.) Died in 1758.

See ERSCH und GRUBER, "Allgemeine Encyklopaedie."

Hälvig or **Haelwig,** hêl′vig, (ALBRECHT,) of Copenhagen, a Danish engraver, flourished about 1650.

Haly-Abbâs. See ALEE-IBNOOL-ABBÂS.

Haly-Rodoan. See ALEE-IBN-RODHWÂN.

Hal′y̆-bur′ton, (THOMAS,) a Scottish divine, born at Duplin, near Perth, in 1674. He became professor of divinity at Saint Andrew's about 1710. He wrote "Natural Religion insufficient and Revealed necessary to Happiness," (1714,) "The Great Concern of Salvation," (1722,) and other works, which were highly esteemed. Died in 1712.

See "Memoirs of Thomas Halyburton," by himself.

Ham, [Heb. חם; Gr. Χάμ; Fr. CHAM, käm,] the second son of Noah, is supposed to have lived about 2400 B.C.

See Genesis vi., vii., and ix.

Hamadânee or **Hamadâni,** hä-mä-dä′nee, the surname of **Abool-Fadhl-Ibn-Hosein,** (ä′bool fäd′l ib′n ho′sĭn,) an Arabian writer and improvisatore, born at Hamadân about 968 A.D. ; died in 1007.

See HAJI-KHALFA, "Lexicon Bibliographicum ;" ABOOLFEDA, "Annales Moslemici."

Hamaker, hä′mä′ker, (HENDRIK ARENS,) an eminent Dutch Orientalist, born at Amsterdam in 1789. He became in 1815 professor of Oriental languages at Franeker. In 1817 he was invited to Leyden to teach those languages in the university, first as assistant, and in 1822 as titular professor. In 1820 he published a catalogue of the Oriental manuscripts in the library of the university, accompanied with Arabic texts, biographies, and notes, which form one of the best modern compendiums of Oriental literature. His oral lectures and conversations gave a better idea of his immense attainments in the language, history, and geography of the Orientals, than many of his works, which bear marks of haste and negligence. He had a prodigious memory, and he is said (with some hyperbole, no doubt) to have known nearly all the languages of Europe and Asia. His health failed under his excessive application, and he died at Leyden in 1835.

See BERGMAN, "Levensschets van H. A. Hamaker," 1836 ; JUYNBOLL, "Oratio de H. A. Hamaker," 1837 ; "Nouvelle Biographie Générale."

Hamal, hä′mäl′, (JEAN NOËL,) a distinguished musical composer, born at Liege in 1709, studied music at Rome in 1728. In 1738 he became maître de chapelle in the cathedral of Liege. His oratorios of "Jonathan" and "Judith," and his opera of "The Journey of Chaufontaine," were much admired. His "In Exitu Israël" is accounted by some his master-piece. Died in 1778.

See FÉTIS, "Biographie Universelle des Musiciens."

Hamann, hä′män, (JOHANN GEORG,) (styled by himself "the Magus of the North,") a German thinker and writer of a very peculiar stamp, born at Königsberg in 1730. He studied theology in the university of his native city; but an impediment in his speech, and a decided taste for general literature, caused him to turn his attention to other pursuits. He supported himself for a time as a private tutor. As a student, he devoted himself especially to ancient literature and the Oriental languages. In 1764, in order to recruit his health, he made a journey through Germany and Switzerland. Some years later he received an appointment connected with the customs-department at Königsberg. He died in 1788. "Hamann," says Dr. Hedge, "is indebted for his reputation to the testimony of a few names of the highest mark, such as Herder, Jacobi, Goethe, and Jean Paul, rather than to any great popularity which his works have had with the German public. He belonged to that class of writers who repel, by the uncouth shapes in which their thoughts are disguised, more readers than they attract by the rarity of the thoughts themselves. He is a humourist, but of a sombre complexion, with a strong dash of cynicism. At the same time, a deep religious sentiment pervades his writings." "The great Hamann," observes Jean Paul, "is a deep sky full of telescopic stars, with many a nebula which no eye can resolve." His best-known works are perhaps "Sibylline Leaves, by the Magus of the North," and the "Memorabilia of Socrates." A collection of all his writings was published at Berlin, in 8 vols., 1821-43.

See F. H. HEDGE, "Prose Writers of Germany."

Hamarskiold. See HAMMARSKÖLD.

Hamazani. See HAMADÂNEE.

Hamberger, häm′bĕR′ger, (GEORG ALBRECHT,) a German mathematician and writer, born in Franconia in 1662, was professor of physics at Jena. Died in 1716.

Hamberger, (GEORG CHRISTOPH,) a German bibliographer, born at Feuchtwang, in Anspach, in 1726. He became professor of philosophy and literary history at Göttingen in 1755. He wrote "Literary Germany," ("Gelehrtes Deutschland,") a dictionary of living German authors, (5 vols., 1768.) Died in 1773.

Hamberger, (GEORG ERHARD,) a German physician, born at Jena in 1697. He was professor of physics and medicine at Jena for many years, and was the first German professor who in his lectures applied mathematics to the physical sciences and medicine. He wrote, besides other works, "Elements of Physics," etc., ("Elementa Physices Methodo mathematica," 1727,) which was regarded as a standard work. Died in 1755.

See J. C. BLASCH, "Das Leben G. E. Hambergers," 1758 ; ERSCH und GRUBER, "Allgemeine Encyklopaedie."

Hambræus, häm-brä′us, (JONAS,) a Swedish Orientalist, born in Helsingland in 1588, became professor of Hebrew in Paris, where he died in 1671.

See EKERMAN, "Dissertatio de Meritis ac Fatis J. Hambræi," 1749.

Hamel, hä′mel, (JOSEPH,) a natural philosopher, born at Sarepta, on the Volga, about 1788. He invented an electrical machine in 1807, ascended Mont Blanc in 1820, and wrote a "History of the Steam-Engine." Died in London in 1862.

Hamel, du. See DUHAMEL.

Hamel, du, dü hä′mel′, (VICTOR AUGUSTE,) VICOMTE, a French writer, born in Paris in 1810, published a "Constitutional History of the Spanish Monarchy from 411 to 1833," (2 vols., 1845.)

Hamel du Monceau. See DUHAMEL DU MONCEAU.

Hamelin, hȧm′lăn′, (FERDINAND ALPHONSE,) a French admiral, born at Pont-l'Évêque (Calvados) in 1796. He became captain of a frigate in 1828, and distinguished himself by his nautical skill in the Pacific Ocean. In 1842 he was raised to the rank of rear-admiral. He commanded the naval station of Oceanica from 1843 to 1846, and became a vice-admiral in 1848. He commanded the fleet which in 1854 co-operated with the English fleet in the bombardment of Odessa, and he directed with ability the debarkation of troops in the Crimea. He became a full admiral and senator in 1854, and minister of the marine in April, 1855. Died in 1864. His uncle, JACQUES FÉLIX ÉMANUEL HAMELIN, was also an admiral. Died in 1839.

See EDMOND TEXIER, "Les Hommes de la Guerre d'Orient : le Vice-Amiral Baron Hamelin," 1854.

Hamelmann, hä′mel-män′, (HERMANN,) a German Protestant historian, born at Osnabrück in 1525. He had a high reputation as an eloquent preacher, and became intendant-general of the churches of Oldenburg. He wrote, in Latin, besides theological works, a "Chronicle of Oldenburg," (3 vols., 1599,) and a "History of Westphalia in the Sixteenth Century." Died in 1595.

See LEUCKFELD, "Historia Hamelmanni," etc., 1720.

Hamelsveld, van, văn hä′mels-vĕlt′, (YSBRAND,) a Dutch divine, born in 1743 at Utrecht, where he became professor of theology. He produced a good Dutch version of the Bible, (1802,) a "General History of the Christian Church," (22 vols., 1800–12,) and other works. Died in 1812.

Hamerani, hä-mä-rä′nee, (ALBERTO,) a German engraver of medals, worked at Rome. He engraved fine medals of several popes, among whom were Clement IX. and Clement X.

Hamerani, (ERMENGILD,) a medallist, son of Giovanni, noticed below, was born at Rome in 1683; died in 1744.

Hamerani, (GIOVANNI,) a son of Alberto, noticed above, was medallist to Pope Innocent XI. and his successors. Died in 1705.

Hamerken, (THOMAS.) See KEMPIS.

Ha-mil′car, [Gr. Ἀμίλκας or Ἀμίλχαρ,] a Carthaginian general, who commanded a large army sent against Sicily in 480 B.C. He was defeated at Himera, and killed by the army of Gelon, in that year.

Hamilcar, son of Gisco, a Carthaginian general, was commander of a large fleet which was sent against Sicily in 311 B.C. He defeated Agathocles and reduced a large part of the island. Having attacked Syracuse, he was made prisoner, and put to death, in 309 B.C.

Hamilcar, a Carthaginian general, who was distinguished in the first Punic war. He obtained command of the army in Sicily in 262 B.C., and defeated the Romans near Therma. He was associated with Hanno in the command of the fleet in 256. They were defeated with great loss in the same year by Regulus, near the coast of Sicily.

Hamilcar, [Gr. Ἀμίλκας or Ἀμίλχαρ,] surnamed BARCA or BARCAS, a famous Carthaginian general, was the father of Hannibal, and the leader of the popular party at Carthage. The date of his birth is unknown. During the first Punic war, in 247 B.C., he obtained command of the army in Sicily, where for five years he defended himself against the Romans, with whom he fought many indecisive battles. In 241 a treaty of peace was made, and Hamilcar led the army back to Africa. Soon after this he was successfully employed against a formidable revolt of the mercenary troops of Carthage. In the year 238 he led an army into Spain, where he passed nine years in war with the natives, and had made extensive conquests, when he was killed in battle in 229 B.C. It is said he caused Hannibal in his childhood to swear eternal hostility to Rome. His sons Hasdrubal and Mago were distinguished in the second Punic war. Hamilcar was perhaps nearly equal to Hannibal in military talents.

Hamilcar, son of Bomilcar, a Carthaginian general, was defeated by the two Scipios in Spain at the siege of Illiturgi, in 215 B.C.

Ham′il-ton, (ALEXANDER,) an English Orientalist, born about 1765. He resided many years in India, and learned the Sanscrit. After his return to England, he was chosen professor of Sanscrit at Haileybury College. He published a "Catalogue of the Sanscrit Manuscripts of the Imperial Library, Paris, with Notes," (1809,) a "Sanscrit Grammar," (1815,) and other works. Died in 1824.

Ham′il-ton, (ALEXANDER,) an illustrious American statesman, orator, and general, born in the West Indian island of Nevis on the 11th of January, 1757. He was the son of James Hamilton, a Scottish merchant, and a grandson of Alexander Hamilton, of Grange, in Ayrshire. His mother, whose name was Faucette, was a daughter of a French Huguenot. He entered in 1769 the counting-house of a merchant in Saint Croix, where he acquired habits of order and methodical industry. The literary talents displayed in his early essays induced his friends to give him a liberal education. He was sent to New York in 1772, and entered King's College in 1773. In July, 1774, he addressed the citizens of New

York in a public speech, which was inspired by the spirit of freedom, and was highly applauded. He also promoted the popular cause by pamphlets so remarkable for sagacity and logical ability that the public were greatly surprised to learn that they were written by a youth only about eighteen years of age.

He applied himself to the study of military tactics, and was appointed captain of a company of artillery in March, 1776. He served with distinction at the battles of Long Island, White Plains, Trenton, and Princeton, and was appointed aide-de-camp to General Washington, with the rank of lieutenant-colonel, in March, 1777. He gained the special favour and confidence of Washington, who employed him as secretary. "Hamilton became," says Renwick, "the depositary of the most secret thoughts of his chief, and the organ of their promulgation." He also assisted in planning campaigns and in devising means to support the army. In November, 1777, he was sent to Albany to urge General Gates to send reinforcements to the army of Washington.* Referring to this mission, his son and biographer says, "This deportment of a lad of twenty, negotiating with an officer buoyed up with his recent successes, already placed before the popular eye as the rival of Washington, sustained by a majority of Congress, and hoping soon to supplant him, will be regarded as not the least remarkable nor the least interesting incident of his life: by Washington it was never forgotten." Hamilton took an active part in the battle of Monmouth, June, 1778, and was highly commended for his conduct in that affair. In 1780 he married Eliza, a daughter of General Schuyler, of Albany, and in February, 1781, he retired from the staff and military family of Washington.

Before this date he had turned with "eager aptitude" to the financial affairs of the country, and had written on that subject several letters admirable for maturity of judgment and perspicuity of style. In the spring of 1780 he wrote to James Duane a celebrated letter on the state of the nation, in which he urged the necessity of a new constitution, and expressed the opinion that "Congress should have complete sovereignty in all that relates to war, peace, trade, finance, and to the management of foreign affairs," etc. He also recommended a national bank. In July, 1781, he obtained command of a battalion of the army of Washington. He led this body at the siege of Yorktown, and took a redoubt by assault on the 14th of October, 1781. On the capture of the British army at Yorktown, which virtually ended the war, he applied himself to the study of law, retaining his rank in the army, but declining to receive any pay. In 1782 he was elected a member of the Continental Congress by the legislature of New York. He was often the chairman of the committees which had charge of the subjects of the greatest importance. According to one of his biographers, "his modes of thinking imparted to the proceedings of this body a new tone and character, and his winning eloquence was the delight and wonder of friend and foe." Washington expressed the opinion that "no one exceeded him in probity and sterling virtue."

About August, 1783, he resigned his seat in Congress, and commenced the practice of law in the city of New York. Although the course of his legal studies had been brief, having a mind peculiarly adapted to the analysis of first principles, he soon rose to the first rank in his profession. He exerted his talents and influence to protect the Tories from persecution at a time when the popular sentiment of New York was too vindictive towards that party. His qualifications for the bar are thus described by Chancellor Kent: "Hamilton, by means of his fine melodious voice and dignified deportment, his reasoning powers and persuasive address, soared above all competition; his pre-eminence was at once universally conceded."

He was an active member of an anti-slavery society formed in New York, and offered, about 1784, a resolution that every member of that society should liberate his own slaves. In 1786 he was elected to the legisla-

---

* Gates had previously been ordered to send troops to Washington, but preferred to keep them, although he had no especial need of them after the capture of Burgoyne.

---

ture of New York, which met in January, 1787. Hamilton and two other citizens of New York were chosen as delegates to the convention which met in Philadelphia in May, 1787, to form a Federal Constitution for the country, which for several years had suffered greatly from the want of an efficient government and from the prostration of trade and the loss of public credit.* It appears that Hamilton was the principal author of this movement towards a firm and durable union of the States. "He was lauded by some," says Renwick, "and decried by others,' according to their feelings on the question, as the founder of the Union which superseded the Confederacy." ("Life of Hamilton.") His two colleagues from New York were partisans of Clinton, and adverse to the proposed Union or Constitution. "The policy of Clinton," says J. C. Hamilton, "had placed him there to become a cipher and a sacrifice."

On the 18th of June, Hamilton addressed the Convention in a long speech, of which no report has been preserved, but which was pronounced by Gouverneur Morris to be "the most able and impressive he had ever heard." In the course of this speech, he read his plan of government, an outline of which is given in J. C. Hamilton's "History of the Republic of the United States," vol. iii. pp. 286–301. Although the plan adopted differed from that of Hamilton, he signed the new Constitution in September, 1787, and warmly urged the people of New York to ratify it. With the co-operation of Madison and Jay, he advocated the adoption of the Constitution in a series of essays which first appeared, under the signature of "Publius," in the "New York Gazette," and were afterwards published in several volumes, entitled "The Federalist." Hamilton wrote more than half of these profound and luminous political treatises, which are recognized by all parties as the best commentary on the Constitution. This instrument was strenuously opposed by a powerful party, misled by the *ignis-fatuus* of State sovereignty. "Hamilton must be classed," says Guizot, "among the men who have best known the vital principles and fundamental conditions of government. . . . There is not in the Constitution of the United States an element of order, strength, or durability which he did not powerfully contribute to introduce into it." ("Character and Influence of Washington.") He proposed to give the right of suffrage to all freemen, without distinction of colour.

Hamilton was appointed secretary of the treasury in September, 1789, a few days after Congress had enacted a bill to organize a treasury department, and at a time when the nation was burdened with a heavy debt and almost destitute of credit. In January, 1790, he presented to Congress a report on public credit, and a plan for the support of the same, which became the basis of the financial system of the nation. Among the measures which he proposed were the funding system and a national bank. A bill to establish a national bank was passed by Congress in February, 1791, and, though denounced as unconstitutional by Jefferson, was approved by the President. The results of Hamilton's financial policy were the restoration of public credit and a rapid revival of trade and industry. He advocated the encouragement of domestic manufactures by a protective tariff.

Hamilton and Jefferson, who became the respective leaders of the Federal and Republican parties, differed widely on financial questions and in regard to their foreign policy. The former advised the President to maintain neutrality in the war between the French and British. Having failed in his efforts to defeat Hamilton and eject him from the cabinet, Jefferson resigned, about January 1, 1794. Hamilton, whose salary was scarcely sufficient for the support of his family, and who was unwilling to neglect longer his private interests, resigned his office, January 31, 1795. He declined the position of chief justice of the supreme court of the United States. In a series of able essays, signed "Camillus," he defended Jay's treaty with Great Britain. Washington testified his great esteem for Hamilton by consulting him in the

preparation of his "Farewell Address," which, says Renwick, "would have been less perfect as a composition had it not passed through the hands of Hamilton."

In the Presidential election of 1796 he supported Adams and Pinckney; but it appears that he wished the latter to obtain the office of President. He had offended Mr. Adams in a previous election by his efforts to secure a larger vote for Washington than for Adams. The French Directory having provoked the American people by acts of hostility, the army was reorganized in the summer of 1798. Washington then accepted the chief command of the army, on condition that Hamilton should be the second in command. He was accordingly made inspector-general, with the rank of major-general, after the general-in-chief had overcome the repugnance of the President to Hamilton's appointment by a menace of resignation. On the death of General Washington, December, 1799, he succeeded him as commander-in-chief; but the army was soon disbanded, and he resumed the practice of law.

Hamilton and many other leading Federalists censured President Adams for appointing an embassy to France, about September, 1799. This affair caused a breach in the Federal party, which was defeated in the Presidential election of 1800. When the duty devolved on the House of Representatives to decide whether Jefferson or Burr should be President, Hamilton advised his friends to prefer the former. In 1804 Aaron Burr presented himself as a candidate for the office of Governor of New York, and hoped to receive the votes of many Federalists; but Hamilton opposed the election of Burr, expressing his opinion that he was a dangerous man and unfit to be trusted with power. The election of General Lewis blasted the ambitious projects of Burr, who insolently demanded an explanation of Hamilton, and finally challenged him. Hamilton accepted the challenge, was mortally wounded at Weehawken, and died July 12, 1804. His death was profoundly and generally lamented. His eldest son had been killed in a duel by a political adversary about 1802.

In person, Hamilton was not above the middle size. He had blue eyes and a fair complexion. "Virtue so rare, so pure, so bold," says Fisher Ames, "by its very purity and excellence inspired suspicion as a prodigy. His enemies judged of him by themselves: so splendid and arduous were his services, they could not find it in their hearts to believe that they were disinterested." Talleyrand once said to Mr. George Ticknor, of Boston, "he had known nearly all the marked men of his time, but had never known one, on the whole, equal to Hamilton." Hamilton's Works were edited by his son, John C. Hamilton, (7 vols. 8vo, 1851.)

See JAMES RENWICK, "Life of A. Hamilton," 1841; "Life of A. Hamilton," by his son, JOHN C. HAMILTON, 2 vols., 1834–40; JOHN C. HAMILTON, "History of the Republic of the United States as traced in the Writings of Alexander Hamilton and of his Contemporaries," 6 vols., 1858–60; "Reminiscences of James A. Hamilton," etc., New York, 1869; REV. J. M. MASON, "Eulogy on Hamilton;" WILLIAM COLEMAN, "Collection of the Facts and Documents relative to the Death of Major-General A. Hamilton," New York, 1804; R. W. GRISWOLD, "Prose Writers of America;" DUYCKINCK, "Cyclopædia of American Literature;" "North American Review" for April, 1858.

Hamilton, (ANDREW J.,) an American politician, born in Madison county, Alabama, in 1815, became a lawyer. He removed to Texas about 1846, and was elected a member of Congress from that State in 1858 or 1859. He was loyal to the Union in the crisis of 1861, and was appointed military Governor of Texas in 1862, and provisional Governor in June, 1865. He retired from that office in 1866.

Ham'il-ton, (ANTHONY,) COUNT, born in Ireland about 1646, was of Scottish descent. His mother was a sister of the Duke of Ormond. His wit and elegant accomplishments rendered him a favourite at the courts of Charles II. and James II. He was brother-in-law of the famous Count de Grammont, and had the principal share in producing the "Memoirs of Grammont," (1713,) which is greatly admired as a highly-finished picture of the voluptuous court of Charles II. La Harpe said, "Of all frivolous books, it is the most agreeable and most ingenious." He wrote, also, several fairy-tales. Died at Saint-Germain in 1720.

See CHAMBERS, "Biographical Dictionary of Eminent Scotsmen."

---

* The impotence of Congress is shown by the following incident: In June, 1783, Congress had been driven from Philadelphia by the insults and menaces of a small body of mutinous soldiers, and had adjourned to Princeton.

Hamilton, (Captain CHARLES,) an officer in the service of the East India Company, was born at Belfast in 1753. He wrote a "History of the Rohilla Afghans," (1787,) and translated the "Hedaya," (or "Guide,") a commentary on Mussulman law, (1791.) Died in 1792. He was a brother of Elizabeth Hamilton, the authoress, noticed below.

Hamilton, (CHARLES S.,) an American general, born in New York about 1824, graduated at West Point in 1843. He lived in Wisconsin when the civil war began. He served as brigadier-general in the army of the Potomac, 1862, and distinguished himself at the battle of Corinth, October 3 and 4 of that year. He was commended by General Grant for his conduct at Iuka, September, 1862, and was promoted to be a major-general in March, 1863. He resigned in the ensuing month.

Hamilton, (Lord CLAUDE,) was a son of James, second Earl of Arran. He commanded the forces of Queen Mary at Langside about 1568; but it appears that he conspired secretly against her life. The assassination of Regent Lenox was instigated by him. His brother, Lord JOHN, was an accomplice in the plot against Queen Mary. Having been banished in 1577, Lord John returned in 1585 at the head of an army, and seized the king, who created him Marquis of Hamilton in 1599. He was grandfather of the first Duke of Hamilton. Died in 1604.

Hamilton, (DAVID,) a Scottish architect, born in Glasgow in 1768. He gained distinction by the erection of the Glasgow Exchange, about 1840, and of several banks and castles in Scotland. He was one of the successful competitors who obtained premiums of £500 for their designs for the New Houses of Parliament. Died in 1843.

Hamilton, (ELIZABETH,) a meritorious writer, born at Belfast, Ireland, in 1758. She resided some time in Scotland, as governess of the daughters of a nobleman. She published "Memoirs of Modern Philosophers," (3 vols., 1800,) "Letters on the Elementary Principles of Education," (2 vols., 1801,) and a tale called "The Cottagers of Glenburnie," (1808.) The last work is called by Sir Walter Scott "a picture of the rural habits of Scotland of striking and impressive fidelity." Died in 1816, at Harrowgate.

See MISS BENGER, "Memoirs of Elizabeth Hamilton;" MRS. ELWOOD, "Memoirs of the Literary Ladies of England," etc., vol. ii., 1843; "Edinburgh Review" for July, 1808.

Hamilton, (Lady EMMA,) a fascinating and profligate woman, whose name was originally LYON born at Preston, or in Cheshire, about 1764. She was married in 1791 to Sir William Hamilton, and accompanied him to Naples. She acquired great influence over the Queen of Naples, and captivated Lord Nelson. She died in poverty at Calais in 1815.

See "Memoirs of Lady Hamilton," 1816; "Blackwood's Magazine" for April, 1860.

Hamilton, (GAVIN,) a Scottish historical painter, born at Lanark about 1730, passed the greater part of his life at Rome. He displayed skill and good taste rather than inventive genius. His illustrations of Homer's "Iliad" are among his best productions. He rendered service to art by his discoveries of statues, bas-reliefs, and other buried monuments, many of which adorn the Museo Clementino, and published "The Italian School of Painting," illustrated with splendid plates, (1773.) Died at Rome in 1797.

See CHAMBERS, "Biographical Dictionary of Eminent Scotsmen."

Hamilton, (GEORGE,) Earl of Orkney, a Scottish general, and a younger son of William Douglas, Earl of Selkirk, was born in 1666. He distinguished himself at the battle of the Boyne in 1690, and in 1696 was made Earl of Orkney. In 1704, as lieutenant-general, he took part in the battle of Blenheim. In 1707 he became a member of the British House of Peers. Died in 1737.

See MACAULAY, "History of England," vol. v.

Hamilton, (HUGH,) an Irish bishop and mathematician, born in the county of Dublin in 1729, became Bishop of Ossory in 1799. He published theological and mathematical works, among which was a "Treatise on Conic Sections." Died in 1805.

Hamilton, (JAMES,) second Earl of Arran, was a son of James Hamilton, Earl of Arran, who died in 1529. At the death of James V., in 1542, he was appointed Regent of Scotland. He obtained in 1549, from Henry II. of France, the duchy of Châtellerault. The queen-mother extorted from Regent Arran (who was a man of feeble character) a resignation of his office about 1554. After Mary Stuart became a captive in England, he was the chief of a party which adhered to her cause and took arms against Regent Lennox. Died in 1575.

See BURTON, "History of Scotland," vol. iii. chaps. xxxiv.–xxxvi.; ROBERTSON, "History of Scotland."

Hamilton, (JAMES,) of Bothwellhaugh, a notorious desperado, who lived about 1570. He was the murderer of the regent Murray, and afterwards offered his services to the agents of Philip II. for the purpose of assassinating the Prince of Orange.

See FROUDE, "History of England," vol. ix.

Hamilton, (JAMES,) first DUKE OF, a Scottish nobleman, born in 1606, was the son of the Marquis of Hamilton. In the civil war he was an adherent of Charles I., who gave him the title of duke. By the influence of his rival Montrose, he was imprisoned in 1645. In 1648 he raised an army of about 20,000 men in Scotland, with which he marched south to Preston, where he was defeated by Cromwell and taken prisoner. He was tried for treason, condemned, and executed, in 1649.

See NEEDHAM, "Life of the Duke of Hamilton," 1649; CHAMBERS, "Biographical Dictionary of Eminent Scotsmen."

Hamilton, (JAMES,) fourth DUKE OF, (previously Earl of Arran,) son of William Douglas, Earl of Selkirk, born in 1657, succeeded to the title in 1694. He was a Jacobite, and in 1711 he was made a peer, with the title of Duke of Brandon; but the House of Lords refused to admit him. Queen Anne appointed him ambassador to France; but before his departure he was killed (1712) in a duel with Lord Mohun, who also was mortally wounded.

See "Memoirs of James, Duke of Hamilton," London, 1742; CHAMBERS, "Biographical Dictionary of Eminent Scotsmen."

Hamilton, (JAMES,) born in London about 1775, is known as the author of the Hamiltonian system of teaching languages by the use of a literal interlinear translation before learning the rules of grammar. Died in 1829.

Hamilton, (JAMES,) a politician and lawyer, born at Charleston, South Carolina, in 1786. In 1830 he became Governor of South Carolina, and was a zealous promoter of nullification. He represented Texas as minister to England in 1841. He was drowned at sea in 1857.

Hamilton, (JAMES,) D.D., a popular British author and Presbyterian divine, born at Paisley in 1814. He became about 1840 minister of the National Scottish Church, Regent Square, London. He was an eloquent preacher, and author of numerous works. Among these are "Life in Earnest," (which has had a very extensive circulation,) "The Mount of Olives," and "The Happy Home," (new edition, 1855.) Died in November, 1867.

Hamilton, (JAMES,) a distinguished painter of marine views, born in Ireland about 1820, came to the United States in infancy. He practised his art in Philadelphia, and acquired much distinction by his illustrations of Dr. Kane's "Arctic Explorations," (1856.) His "Capture of the Serapis" and "Old Ironsides" have been greatly admired. Hamilton is particularly successful in the representation of all water-scenes, whether he attempts to bring before us the rush and tumult of Niagara or the infinitely diversified appearances of the mighty ocean.

See TUCKERMAN'S "Book of the Artists."

Hamilton, (JOHN,) Archbishop of Saint Andrew's, an ambitious Scottish prelate, was a brother of the Earl of Arran, the regent. He was a persecutor of the Protestants, and took an active part in the political contests of the reign of Mary Stuart. He was tried for treason, convicted, and hung, in 1571.

See CHAMBERS, "Biographical Dictionary of Eminent Scotsmen."

Hamilton, (JOHN,) a Scottish priest, born in the sixteenth century. He wrote a "Treatise on Theology" about 1581.

See LORD HAILES, "Life of John Hamilton."

Hamilton, (Sir JOHN,) a British general, born in 1755. He served in several campaigns in India, and

ε as *k*; ç as *s*; ḡ *hard*; ǧ as *j*; G, H, K, *guttural*; N, *nasal*; R, *trilled*; š as z; th as in *this*. (☞ See Explanations, p. 23.)

71

became a brigadier-general in 1805. He distinguished himself in the Peninsular war. Died in 1835.

Hamilton, (JOHN C.,) an American writer, a son of Alexander Hamilton, was born in Philadelphia in 1792. He served in the army in the war against Great Britain, 1812–14. He published "Memoirs of the Life of Alexander Hamilton," (2 vols., 1834–40,) and a "History of the Republic of the United States as traced in the Writings of Alexander Hamilton and his Contemporaries," (6 vols., 1858.)

Hamilton, (PATRICK,) commonly regarded as the first Scottish Reformer, was born in 1503. He adopted the principles of Luther, whom he had heard preach in Germany, and on his return to Scotland he openly attacked the errors of the Roman Church. He was condemned as a heretic, and suffered martyrdom with constancy at the age of twenty-three.

See CHAMBERS, "Biographical Dictionary of Eminent Scotsmen;" J. G. LORIMER, "Patrick Hamilton: a Historical Biography," 1857; REV. ROBERT STEEL, "Burning and Shining Lights," London, 1864.

Hamilton, (RICHARD WINTER,) an English preacher, born in London in 1794. He became pastor of an Independent church, Albion Chapel, Leeds, in 1815. He was eminent as a platform orator, and wrote a series of essays entitled "Nugæ Literariæ," ("Literary Trifles," 1841.) Several volumes of his sermons have been published. Died in 1848.

See W. H. STOWELL, "Memoir of R. W. Hamilton," 1850.

Hamilton, (ROBERT,) a Scottish physician, born at Edinburgh in 1721; died at Lynn in 1793.

Hamilton, (ROBERT,) a Scottish political economist, born in Edinburgh about 1742. He was professor of natural philosophy and mathematics in Marischal College, Aberdeen, from 1782 to 1829. His chief work is an "Inquiry concerning the Rise and Progress, the Redemption and the Present State, and the Management, of the National Debt of Great Britain," (1813.) "This important work," says McCulloch, "opened the eyes of the public to the delusive nature of the sinking fund." Among his other works is "The Progress of Society," (1830.) Died in 1829.

Hamilton, (SCHUYLER,) an American general, a son of John C. Hamilton, and a grandson of Hamilton the great statesman, was born in New York in 1822. He graduated at West Point in 1841, served as aide-de-camp to General Scott in the Mexican war, (1846–47,) and resigned his commission in 1855. In 1861 he became a brigadier-general of volunteers. He rendered important services in Missouri, and suggested the canal which was cut near New Madrid in March and April, 1862. He was made a major-general in September, 1862, and resigned, on account of ill health, in February, 1863.

Hamilton, (THOMAS,) a captain of the British army, born in 1789. He served in the Peninsular war, and in the second war between the United States and Great Britain. He contributed many articles to "Blackwood's Magazine," and published several able works, namely, "Annals of the Peninsular Campaign," "The Youth and Manhood of Cyril Thornton," a novel, (1827,) and "Men and Manners in America," (1833.) These books were favourably noticed by British critics. Died in 1842.

Hamilton, (WALTER,) a British geographer, published "The East India Gazetteer," (London, 1814,) and a "Geographical, Statistical, and Historical Description of Hindostan," (2 vols., 1820,) which the "London Quarterly Review" pronounced "an inestimable work, containing a more full, detailed, and faithful picture of India than any former work on the subject."

Hamilton, (WILLIAM,) second DUKE OF, born in 1616, was brother of James, the first Duke of Hamilton, whose title he inherited. He officiated as secretary of state in Scotland, and, after serving in the army of Charles II., died in 1651, of wounds received at the battle of Worcester. The duchy devolved on his niece, Anne Hamilton, who was married to William Douglas.

Hamilton, (WILLIAM,) of Bangour, a Scottish poet, born in Ayrshire in 1704, joined the party of the Pretender in 1745. He wrote a volume of poems, among which is "The Braes of Yarrow." Died in 1754.

See CHAMBERS, "Biographical Dictionary of Eminent Scotsmen."

Hamilton, (Sir WILLIAM,) a diplomatist, antiquary, and connoisseur, born in Scotland in 1730. He was appointed ambassador to Naples in 1764, and retained that post until 1800. In 1766 he was admitted a Fellow of the Royal Society, and in 1772 was made Knight of the Bath. During his residence at Naples he contributed much to the advancement of art and science by collecting Etruscan and Greek vases and other antiquities (now in the British Museum) and by observing the volcanic phenomena of Vesuvius. He published, in 1772, "Observations on Mount Vesuvius, Mount Etna," etc., and in 1776 another work on the same subject, entitled "Campi Phlegræi." In 1766 appeared an elegant work, in French and English, named "Etruscan, Greek, and Roman Antiquities, drawn from the Cabinet of Mr. Hamilton," by D'Hancarville. Died in 1803. His second wife, EMMA, gained notoriety by her disgraceful connection with Lord Nelson.

See CHAMBERS, "Biographical Dictionary of Eminent Scotsmen."

Hamilton, (Sir WILLIAM,) one of the greatest metaphysicians of modern times, was born at Glasgow on the 8th of March, 1788. He was descended from the ancient Scottish family of the Hamiltons of Preston, and was educated at Balliol College, Oxford, where he obtained first-class honours. In 1821 he was appointed professor of universal history in the University of Edinburgh, where he had much leisure for the pursuit of his favourite metaphysical studies. He commenced in 1829 to write for the "Edinburgh Review" on mental philosophy, logic, and other subjects. Among the titles of these essays or reviews are the "Philosophy of the Absolute: Cousin-Schelling," (1829,) "Philosophy of Perception: Reid and Brown," (1830,) and "Logic: the Recent English Treatises on that Science," (1833.) He combated the system of Schelling and Hegel in the essay first named. From 1836 until his death he was professor of logic and metaphysics in the University of Edinburgh. Before the former date he had acquired a European reputation by his vast erudition and extraordinary acuteness of intellect. His influence and success as a professor were augmented by a noble person, a sonorous voice, and perfect dignity of manner. He published in 1846 an edition of Reid's Works, with notes and supplementary dissertations; and in 1852, "Discussions on Philosophy and Literature, Education and University Reform, chiefly from the 'Edinburgh Review,' enlarged, with Notes and other Additions," (1 vol. 8vo.) In 1845 he was partially disabled by paralysis, which, however, did not impair his mental activity. His last publication was an edition of the Works of Dugald Stewart, (9 vols., 1854–56.) He died in Edinburgh on the 6th of May, 1856. He combined the power of analysis and generalization in a degree perhaps unequalled since the time of Aristotle. In a thorough acquaintance with the history of philosophy he has never been surpassed by any writer.

"Sir William Hamilton," says the "Edinburgh Review," "has attained to the very highest distinction as a philosopher, and in some respects he is decidedly superior to any of his illustrious predecessors,—Reid, Stewart, or Brown. With a remarkable power of analysis and discrimination, he combines great decision and elegance of style, and a degree of erudition that is almost without a parallel." "Hamilton never deviates," says M. Cousin, "from the *grande route* of common sense; and at the same time he has much *esprit* and sagacity. I assure you (as I know by experience) that his dialectic is very inconvenient to an adversary. . . . His independence is equal to his knowledge; and he is especially great in logic. I now address you professionally, *(en homme de métier.)* Know then, that M. Hamilton, among all your compatriots, understands Aristotle the best; and if there is a chair of logic vacant in the three kingdoms, give it to him, by all means, without delay." (Letter to Mr. Pillans, of Edinburgh, 1836.)

See JOHN VEITCH, "Memoir of Sir William Hamilton, Bart.," (with portrait,) 1869; E. P. WHIPPLE, "Essays and Reviews," 1851; "North American Review" for January, 1853, vol. lxxvi.; "Nouvelle Biographie Générale;" "Blackwood's Magazine" for October, 1859; "North British Review" for May, 1859, September, 1865, and July, 1868. See, also, J. S. MILL's "Examination of Sir William Hamilton's Philosophy," 1865, and the Introduction to DR. JAMES McCOSH's "Examination of Mr. J. S. Mill's Philosophy," 1866.

ă, ē, ī, ō, ū, ȳ, *long;* ă, ĕ, ĭ, ŏ, ŭ, ў, *short;* ạ, ẹ, ị, ọ, *obscure;* fär, fåll, fåt; mēt; nŏt; gŏŏd; mōŏn;

Hamilton, (WILLIAM,) R.A., a British painter, born about 1750, was a pupil of Zucchi, in Rome. He was successful as a painter of ornaments, and was elected a Royal Academician in 1789. He worked mostly in England, and was one of the artists employed on the "Shakspeare Gallery." Died in 1801.

Hamilton, (WILLIAM DOUGLAS,) Earl of Selkirk, was created Duke of Hamilton in 1660. He married Anne, Duchess of Hamilton, with the condition that their children should take her family name. William III. appointed him lord high commissioner of Scotland in 1689, and again in 1693. Died in 1694.

See MACAULAY, "History of England," vol. ii. chap. vi.; also vol. iii. chaps. xiii. and xvi.

Hamilton, (WILLIAM GERARD,) often called "Single-Speech Hamilton," was born in London in 1729. Having been educated at Oxford, he obtained a seat in Parliament in 1754, and made his first speech in November, 1755, which was received with great applause. It is said that no maiden speech at that House ever made such a sensation. In 1756 he was appointed one of the lords of trade. He wrote a treatise on "Parliamentary Logic," and was conjectured, without evidence or probability, to be the author of "Junius." From 1765 to 1784 he was chancellor of the exchequer in Ireland, and made several eloquent speeches in the Irish Parliament. He was one of Dr. Johnson's most valued friends. Died in 1796.

See "Edinburgh Review," vol. xv.

Hamilton, (WILLIAM RICHARD,) an English antiquary and diplomatist, born in London in 1777. He was private secretary of Lord Elgin in the embassy to Constantinople, and aided in the removal of the Elgin Marbles from Athens. After a visit to Egypt, he published a work on the antiquities of that country, called "Ægyptiaca," (1810.) He procured for the British Museum the famous Rosetta Stone. He was under-secretary of state for foreign affairs between 1810 and 1822. Died in 1859.

Hamilton, (Sir WILLIAM ROWAN,) an eminent Irish astronomer and geometer, born in Dublin in 1805. He learned, or at least studied, thirteen languages before he had completed his thirteenth year, and about the age of fifteen became versed in the higher mathematics. In 1823 he began to apply algebraic geometry to optics, and entered the University of Dublin, where he "uniformly obtained the chief honour in both science and classics." He was appointed Andrews professor of astronomy and astronomer royal for Ireland at the age of twenty-one, and produced in 1828 his important "Theory of Systems of Rays," in which he developed the application of algebra to optics, and announced two new laws of light,—the *internal* and *external conical refraction* of biaxial crystals. He received a gold medal from the Royal Society of London for this discovery, in reference to which Professor Plücker, of Bonn, declared, "No experiment in physics has made such an impression on my mind." He was chosen president of the Royal Irish Academy in 1837. Among his chief works is "Elements of Quaternions," (1866.) Died in 1865. "There can be but one opinion," says the "North British Review" for September, 1866, "of the extraordinary genius and untiring energy of him who, unaided, composed in so short a time two such enormous treatises as the 'Lectures,' (1853,) and the 'Elements of Quaternions,' (1866.) As a repertory of mathematical facts and a triumph of analytical and geometrical power, they can be compared only with such imperishable works as the 'Principia' and the 'Mécanique Analytique.'"

See "Gentleman's Magazine" for 1866.

Ham'ley, (Lieutenant-Colonel EDWARD BRUCE,) R.A., a contemporary British writer of fiction, published "Lady Lee's Widowhood," (2 vols., 1854,) and "The Story of a Campaign: a Narrative of the War in Southern Russia, written in the Crimea," (1855.) These works first appeared in "Blackwood's Magazine."

Ham'lin, (HANNIBAL,) an American Senator, born at Paris, Oxford county, Maine, in August, 1809. He practised law from 1833 to 1848. He was Speaker of the House of Representatives of Maine in 1837, 1839, and 1840, and represented a district of that State in Congress from 1843 to 1847. In May, 1848, he was elected a Senator of the United States for four years, to fill a vacancy. He was re-elected a Senator for six years by the legislature of Maine in 1851. He was originally a Democrat, but differed from his party on the question of slavery, and joined the Republicans about 1855. In 1857 he was Governor of Maine for a short time, but, having been again elected to the Federal Senate, he resigned the office of Governor. He was elected Vice-President of the United States by the Republicans in 1860. In January, 1869, he was again elected a Senator of the United States.

Hammarsköld or Hammarskoeld, håm'mars-chöld', (LARS,) an able Swedish critic and author, born at Tuna, in Calmar, in 1785. He published a volume of poems, "Poetiska Studier," (1813,) "Hellvin och Elvina," a tale, (1817,) "Swedish Literature," ("Svenska Vitterheten," 1818,) which is highly commended, and an excellent work entitled "Historical Remarks on the Progress and Development of Philosophic Studies in Sweden," (1821.) Died in 1827.

See "Minnen af L. Hammarskoeld," 1827.

Hammer, håm'mer, (JULIUS,) a German writer, born at Dresden in 1810, published "Life and Dreaming," ("Leben und Traum," 1839,) and other novels. A volume of his poems, entitled "Look around thee and Look within thee," ("Schau' um Dich und schau' in Dich," 1851,) was often reprinted.

Hammerer, håm'meh-rer, (JOHANN,) an Alsatian architect and sculptor, superintended the erection of the Strasburg Cathedral from 1510 to 1520.

Hammerich, håm'meh-rik, (FREDERIK PEDER ADOLF,) a Danish author and divine, born at Copenhagen in 1809. He produced popular national songs in a work entitled "Skandinaviske Reiseminder," (1840,) "Heroic Songs," ("Heltesange," 1841,) "The Awakening of Denmark," (1848,) and other admired poems. In 1845 he became pastor of a church in Copenhagen. He published several well-written works on Danish history, among which is "Denmark under the Union of Calmar," ("Denmark under de Nordiske Rigers Forening 1375–1523," 1849.)

See ERSLEW, "Forfatter-Lexicon."

Hammerlein, håm'mer-līn', [Lat. MALLE'OLUS,] (FELIX,) a Swiss theologian, born in Zurich in 1389. He distinguished himself at the Council of Bâle by his zeal for the maintenance of discipline. He wrote many religious treatises, which exposed him to persecution, and was condemned to perpetual detention in a convent, where he died about 1460.

See ERSCH und GRUBER, "Allgemeine Encyklopaedie."

Hammer-Purgstall, von, fon håm'mer pōōRG'stâl', (JOSEPH,) BARON, an eminent German Orientalist and historian, was born at Grätz, in Styria, in 1774. He was a friend of Goethe, Herder, and Wieland in his youth. In 1802 he went to Constantinople as secretary of legation, and in 1807 he returned to Vienna, where he chiefly resided. He was appointed interpreter to the imperial court about 1815, and aulic councillor in 1817. He spoke and wrote ten foreign languages, among which were the Persian, Arabic, Greek, and Turkish. His literary career was long and prosperous. He was elected president of the Academy of Vienna in 1847, and was an associate of the French Institute. Probably no other European has been so successful in the illustration of the manners, history, and literature of the Mussulmans. His histories are the most complete that we have on the subjects of which he treats. One of his chief works is a "History of the Ottoman Empire," ("Geschichte des Osmanischen Reichs," 10 vols., 1827–35.) He was author of numerous other works, among which are a "History of Ottoman Poetry," (4 vols., 1836–38,) and a "History of Arabic Literature," ("Literaturgeschichte der Araber," 7 vols. 4to, 1850–56.) He also translated poems from the Persian, Arabic, etc. His original name was JOSEPH HAMMER; but, having in 1837 inherited certain estates of the Counts of Purgstall, he added their name to his own, and was created a baron. Died in 1856.

See his Autobiography, "Denkwürdigkeiten aus meinem Leben;" K. SCHLOTTMANN, "Joseph von Hammer-Purgstall;" "Foreign Quarterly" for November, 1827; "Nouvelle Biographie Générale."

Ham'mond, (ANTHONY,) M.P., born at Somersham Place, England, in 1668, gained distinction in literature and parliamentary eloquence. In 1720 he edited a "New Miscellany of Original Poems," some of which were his own productions. Died in 1738.

Hammond, (HENRY,) an English divine and author, born at Chertsey in 1605, was appointed Archdeacon of Chichester in 1643, and canon of Christ Church, Oxford, in 1645. Being a zealous royalist, he attended Charles I. as chaplain while he was a prisoner in 1646-47. He was an excellent orator, and an author of superior merit. Among his works are "A Practical Catechism," (1644,) "Paraphrase and Annotations on the New Testament," (1653,) "Paraphrase and Annotations on the Book of Psalms," (1659,) and "A Pacific Discourse on God's Grace and Decrees," (1660.) "I would recommend," says Dr. Johnson, "Lowth and Patrick on the Old Testament, and Hammond on the New." Died in 1660.

See BISHOP FELL, "Life of H. Hammond," 1661; R. FULMAN, "Life of H. Hammond," 1684.

Hammond, (JABEZ D..) an American lawyer and writer. He represented a district of New York in Congress in 1815-17, and was elected regent of the University of New York in 1845. He wrote a "Political History of New York," (2 vols., 1843,) and a "Life of Silas Wright." Died at Cherry Valley in 1855.

Ham'mond, (JAMES,) M.P., an English poet, son of Anthony, noticed above, was born about 1710. He was equerry to the Prince of Wales, and sat in Parliament in 1741. He wrote "Love Elegies," (partly translated or imitated from Tibullus.) Died in 1742.

Hammond, (JAMES HAMILTON,) a politician, born in Newberry district, South Carolina, in 1807. He was a nullifier about 1832, was elected to Congress in 1835, and was chosen Governor of South Carolina in 1842. In 1857 he became a United States Senator. Died in 1861.

Hammond, (LE ROY,) COLONEL, an American officer, born in Richmond county, Virginia, about 1740. He removed to South Carolina, where he fought against the British in 1776-82 and distinguished himself as a leader in guerilla warfare. Died about 1800.

Hammond, (MARCUS C. M.,) a military writer, a brother of James H. Hammond, noticed above, was born in Newberry district, South Carolina, in 1814, and graduated at West Point in 1836. He wrote for the "Southern Quarterly" a series of essays on the Mexican war.

Hammond, (SAMUEL,) an able American officer, born in Richmond county, Virginia, in 1757. He served with distinction at King's Mountain, Cowpens, Eutaw, and other battles in South Carolina and Georgia. He was appointed civil and military commandant of Upper Louisiana about 1805. In 1831 he became secretary of state of South Carolina. Died in 1842.

Hammond, (WILLIAM A.,) an American surgeon and distinguished medical writer, born in Annapolis, Maryland, August 28, 1828, graduated as M.D. at the University of New York in 1848. In October, 1860, he was appointed professor of anatomy and physiology in the University of Maryland. In 1861 he entered the army as an assistant surgeon, was appointed surgeon-general in April, 1862, and was dismissed in August, 1864. He has published, besides other valuable works, "Military Hygiene," (1863,) and "Sleep and its Derangements," (1869.)

Hamon, hä'môn', (JEAN,) a distinguished Jansenist writer, was born at Cherbourg in 1618. He entered the monastery of Port-Royal about 1650, before which he had acquired distinction by his talents. He was extremely abstemious or ascetic in his way of life. He wrote treatises on prayer and on solitude, and other devotional works, the morality and unction of which entitle him to rank with the best writers of Port-Royal. He practised medicine before and after his retirement from the world. Died in 1687.

"Tout brillant de savoir, d'esprit et d'éloquence,
Il courut au désert chercher l'obscurité."—BOILEAU.

See THOMAS DUFOSSÉ, "Histoire de Port-Royal;" "Nouvelle Biographie Générale."

Hamon, (JEAN LOUIS,) a French painter of genre, born at Plouha (Côtes-du-Nord) in 1821. His works are admired for grace, finesse, and subtlety of idea and execution. Among his master-pieces are "My Sister is not here," (1853,) "Cupid and his Flock," (1855,)

and "The Butterfly Chained," ("Le Papillon enchaîné," (1857.)

Hamp'den, (JOHN,) an illustrious English patriot and statesman, born in London in 1594, was the eldest son of William Hampden of Hampden and Elizabeth Cromwell, who was aunt of the Protector, Oliver Cromwell. He inherited at an early age the ample estate of his ancestors, in the county of Bucks. Having been educated at Oxford, he became in 1613 a student in the Inner Temple, and attained proficiency both in literature and law. While a student, he was chosen to write an epithalamium on the marriage of the princess Elizabeth, sister of Charles I. In 1619 he married Elizabeth Symeon, and in the next year was returned to Parliament by the borough of Grampound. Of his private life not many particulars have been recorded. It appears that party spirit and detraction failed to find any vice in his morals or any vulnerable point in his character. Clarendon mentions a change which occurred in his habits, probably, about the age of twenty-five. "On a sudden," he says, "from a life of great pleasure and license, he retired to extraordinary sobriety and strictness." But even after this change "he preserved his natural cheerfulness and vivacity, and, above all, a flowing courtesy to all men." Hampden represented Wendover in the House of Commons in 1625, and also in the next Parliament, which met in 1626 and denied the right of the king to levy tonnage and poundage without their consent. When the king resorted to a forced loan, Hampden, with many others, refused to pay his portion, and was imprisoned. Having been restored to liberty, he entered Parliament in 1628, and distinguished himself by his industry and capacity for business. The king having resolved to dispense with Parliaments, Hampden retired to his estate in 1629, and passed many years in rural occupations. In 1636 he obtained great credit and popularity by his firm resistance to the arbitrary measures of the court in reference to ship-money. The sum required of him was only a few shillings; but, as he considered the demand despotic in principle and tendency, he thought it his duty to abide by the constitution, and refused to pay a farthing. Towards the end of 1636 this great cause was tried in the Exchequer Chamber before all the (twelve) judges of England. The arguments of the counsel occupied about twelve days. Four of the judges decided in Hampden's favour, and seven or eight against him.

Many Puritans now sought a refuge from persecution and oppression by emigration to America under the auspices of Lord Say and Lord Brooke. Hampden, perceiving that neither his person nor his property was safe, determined to follow their example. In 1638, in company with his cousin, Oliver Cromwell, he took passage in a ship on the point of sailing to America, when the voyage was arrested by an order of Council, and the two friends remained, to teach despotic power an ever-memorable lesson. In 1640 the king called the famous Long Parliament, in which Hampden sat as a member for Bucks, being regarded as the leader of the opposition and the most popular man in England. "He was," says Macaulay, "a greater master of parliamentary tactics than any man of his time. . . . His speaking was ready, weighty, perspicuous, condensed. He seldom rose till late in a debate." In 1641 the court proposed to form a popular administration, under the direction of the Earl of Bedford, and to select Hampden as tutor of the Prince of Wales; but the death of the earl prevented this desirable consummation. During the stormy debate which attended the passage of the Grand Remonstrance, when the excited disputants were near coming to blows, they were pacified, as an eye-witness states, "by the sagacity and great calmness of Mr. Hampden."

On the 3d of January, 1642, the king sent the attorney-general to impeach Hampden, Pym, Hollis, and two other members of the House, on a charge of high treason. As the Commons refused to surrender these members, Charles went in person, with his guards, to arrest them in their seats; but the five members had retired a few minutes before, and escaped from his grasp. This desperate attempt against the privilege of Parliament excited the greatest indignation. The city of London rose in arms. In a few days the Commons openly defied the court, and the citizens escorted the accused members in triumph back to their seats in Westminster. When the news reached Buckinghamshire, four thousand freeholders rode to London to defend their representative.

When all attempts to negotiate had failed between the two parties, Hampden received a commission as colonel, and raised a regiment in his own county. They wore the device "Vestigia nulla retrorsum," a fitting motto for one whose character was so straightforward and determined. As a member of the committee of public safety, he was incessantly employed in a variety of labours. Had he lived a few years longer, it is probable he would have been commander-in-chief. He took part in the battle of Edgehill, and in several skirmishes, exposing his person with a bravery bordering on rashness. In June, 1643, Prince Rupert, returning from a marauding expedition, encountered Hampden, with a small troop, on Chalgrove field. In the first charge Hampden received a fatal shot in the shoulder; and a few days after the great Commoner expired.

He left three sons and six daughters, whose mother died in 1634. Clarendon, though a political opponent, renders the following tribute to his memory: "He was indeed a very wise man, and possessed with the most absolute spirit of popularity, and the most absolute faculties to govern the people, of any man I ever knew. ... His reputation of honesty was universal. ... The eyes of all men were fixed upon him as their patriæ pater, and the pilot that must steer the vessel through the tempests that threatened it."

See LORD NUGENT, "Memorials of Hampden," 1832; MACAULAY'S review of the same, in his "Essays;" CLARENDON, "History of the Rebellion;" JOHN FORSTER, "Lives of Eminent British Statesmen;" HUME, "History of England," chap. lvi.; GUIZOT, "Histoire de la Révolution d'Angleterre;" HALLAM, "Constitutional History of England;" ISAAC DISRAELI, "Eliot, Hampden, and Pym," 1832.

Hampden, (Rev. RENN DICKSON,) an English divine and scholar, born in Barbadoes about 1794. He became a Fellow of Oriel College, Oxford, where he was also a tutor. He published, among other works, "Philosophical Evidence of Christianity," (1827,) and "The Scholastic Philosophy in its Relation to Christian Theology," (1832.) In 1836 he was appointed by the Whig ministry regius professor of divinity at Oxford. This appointment gave rise to a fierce controversy. It was condemned by the high-church party, who charged Hampden with unsoundness of doctrine; and it was stigmatized by Southey as "an insult to the University." He became Bishop of Hereford in 1847. He contributed able articles on Socrates, Plato, and Aristotle to the "Encyclopædia Britannica." Died in 1868.

Hampden, (RICHARD,) a son of the great John Hampden, was a Whig member of the House of Commons in 1689, also a commissioner of the treasury, and member of the privy council. In 1690 he was made chancellor of the exchequer,—"probably to reward him for the moderation of his conduct," says Macaulay.

See MACAULAY'S "History of England," vol. ii. chap. x.; vol. iii. chaps. xi. and xv.

Ham'per, (WILLIAM,) an English biographer and antiquary, born at Birmingham in 1776. He served as magistrate in Warwickshire. Among his works were several antiquarian treatises in the "Gentleman's Magazine," and "The Life, Diary, and Correspondence of Sir William Dugdale," (1837,) which contains valuable historical information. Died in 1831.

Hamp'ton, (Rev. JAMES,) an English translator, who published a version of the "General History" of Polybius, (2 vols. 4to, 1756–72,) with a preface by Dr. Johnson. "The English translator," says Gibbon, "has preserved the admirable sense and improved the coarse original." Died in 1778.

Hamp'ton, (WADE,) an American general, born in South Carolina in 1755. He served in the Revolutionary war, and gained the rank of brigadier-general in 1809. He commanded an army which made an unsuccessful invasion of Canada in October, 1813. Died in 1835.

Hampton, (WADE,) a grandson of the preceding, was born at Columbia or Charleston, South Carolina, about 1828, or, as others say, in 1818. He took arms against the Union in 1861, served as a brigadier-general at the

battle of Antietam, September, 1862, and was wounded at Gettysburg, July, 1863. Having been raised to the rank of major-general, he commanded all the cavalry of Lee's army in Virginia in the summer of 1864. He served in South Carolina in February, 1865, and, according to the report of General Sherman, "ordered that all cotton, public and private, should be moved into the streets [of Columbia] and fired." Generals Hampton and Sherman mutually accused each other of burning Columbia.

See "Southern Generals," anonymous, 1865; GREELEY, "American Conflict," vol. ii. pp. 699–701.

Hamsfort, hâms'fort, (CORNELIUS,) a Danish historian, who published in 1585 a succession of Kings of Denmark from Dan to Frederick II. He also wrote a "Chronology of Danish History." Died in 1627.

Hamza, hâm'zâ, surnamed AL-HÂDEĆ, (or AL-HÂDÎ,) i.e. "the Director," called by some authorities the founder of the sect of the Druses, flourished in Cairo about the year 1000. He wrote the "Book of Testimonies to the Mysteries of the Unity," thought by some to rival the Koran.

Hamza, or **Hamzah,** was also the name of one of Mohammed's foster-brothers. He fell at Bedr, 622 A.D.

Hanbal. See IBN-HANBAL.

Hancarville, d', dôN'kăR'vèl', the title of an ingenious French antiquary, whose proper name was PIERRE FRANçOIS **Hugues,** (hüg,) born at Nancy in 1719. He lived many years in Italy, and attained some skill in design. He published a splendid work entitled "Etruscan, Greek, and Roman Antiquities, drawn from the Cabinet of Sir William Hamilton," (4 vols., Naples, 1766,) and "Researches into the Origin, Spirit, and Progress of the Arts in Greece," (1785.) Died in Padua in 1805.

Hanckius, hânk'e-ûs, or **Hanke,** hânk'ĕh, (MARTIN,) a German philologist, born near Breslau in 1633. He became professor of history in Breslau in 1661, and afterwards inspector of the Lutheran schools. He wrote a useful work on Roman historians, entitled "De Romanarum Rerum Scriptoribus," (1669–75,) and several interesting works on the civil and literary history of Silesia, among which is a work on learned Silesians, "De Silesiis Indigenis eruditis ab Anno 1165 ad Annum 1550," (1707.) Died in 1709.

See ERSCH und GRUBER, "Allgemeine Encyklopaedie;" CASPAR NAUMANN, "Martinalia Christiana, seu Concio funebris in Obitum M. Hanckii," 1710.

Han'cock, (JOHN,) an American statesman, born in Quincy, Massachusetts, January 12, 1737, graduated at Harvard in 1754. He became a merchant of Boston, and heir to a large fortune. His wife was a daughter of Edmund Quincy. He was chosen a member of the House of Representatives of Massachusetts in 1766, became a bold assertor of liberty, and was president of the Provincial Congress in 1774. In June, 1775, Governor Gage offered a pardon to all the rebels except Samuel Adams and John Hancock. He was chosen president of the Continental Congress in 1775, and signed the Declaration of Independence in 1776. Having resigned his seat in Congress, on account of ill health, in October, 1777, he was elected Governor of Massachusetts in 1780. He was a very popular Governor, and was annually re-elected, except for the years 1785 and 1786, until his death. His eloquence, his affable disposition, and his polished manners rendered him a general favourite. As a presiding officer, he was dignified and very successful. He made a generous use of his fortune, and was a liberal benefactor to Harvard College. Died in October, 1793.

See GOODRICH, "Lives of the Signers to the Declaration of Independence;" BANCROFT, "History of the United States."

Hancock, (WINFIELD SCOTT,) a distinguished American general, born in Montgomery county, Pennsylvania, in 1824. He graduated at West Point in 1844, and served as lieutenant in the Mexican war, (1846–47,) after which he was employed for several years in Missouri. In 1855 he obtained the rank of captain. He was appointed a brigadier-general of volunteers in 1861, and served with distinction in the army of the Potomac in the spring of 1862. He took part in the battle of Antietam, September, 1862, and when General Richardson was killed there, succeeded him as commander of a division, which he directed at Fredericksburg in December of that year. He commanded a corps at the battle of Gettysburg, July 1–3, 1863, where he was wounded. In the spring of 1864 he obtained command of the second corps of the army of General Grant. His corps captured nearly 4000 prisoners, and twenty pieces of cannon, in the battle fought near Spottsylvania Court-House on the 12th of May, 1864. He was promoted to the rank of brigadier-general of the regular army in August of that year. In August, 1867, he was appointed commander of the fifth military district, comprising Louisiana and Texas. He resigned that position in March, 1868. He received at the National Democratic Convention of July, 1868, one hundred and forty-four and a half votes as a candidate for the Presidency.

Hand, hânt, (FERDINAND GOTTHELF,) a German philologist, born at Plauen, in Saxony, in 1786. He was professor of Greek literature in the University of Jena from 1817 until 1851. Among his principal works are a "Treatise on Latin Style," ("Lehrbuch des Lateinischen Stil," 1833,) and "Æsthetics of the Musical Art," (2 vols., 1837–41.) Died in 1851.

See GUSTAV QUECK, "F. G. Hand nach seinem Leben und Wirken dargestellt," 1852.

Hän'del, [Ger. HÄNDEL or HAENDEL, hěn'děl,] (GEORGE FREDERICK,) one of the most excellent, profound, and original of musical composers, was born at Halle, in Prussian Saxony, on the 24th of February, 1684. He manifested in childhood a ruling passion for music, which he studied first under Zachau of Halle, and composed sonatas at the age of ten. In 1703 he became connected with the Opera of Hamburg, where in the next year he produced his "Almeria" with great success. He visited Italy in 1708, and composed his first Italian opera, "Rodrigo," which was performed at Florence. Having produced other operas, etc. at Venice and Rome, he went to England in 1710, and composed the music for the opera "Rinaldo," which was greatly admired. In 1712 he settled in England, and in 1714 became chapel-master of George I.

About 1720 he was engaged as manager of the new Academy of Music founded by the English nobility, and composed the opera "Radamista," which was received with great enthusiasm. After he had produced many other operas, he retired from the direction of the Academy in 1728. He lost nearly all his fortune, £10,000, in an unsuccessful attempt to support another opera-house between 1728 and 1740. Thenceforth devoting himself to sacred music, which is the chief foundation of his celebrity, he composed the oratorio of "Saul," (1740,) and in 1741 his sublime master-piece, the "Messiah," which was received with immense applause. Among his other oratorios (the words of all of which are English) are "Samson," "Moses in Egypt," "Joshua," (1747,) and "Jephthah," (1751.)

He became blind in 1751, but continued for several years to conduct his oratorios in public concerts. He died in April, 1759, and was buried in Westminster Abbey. Handel is regarded by some critics as the greatest composer that ever lived. He was chiefly preeminent in majesty and sublimity of conception. The centennial anniversary of his birth was celebrated in London, in 1784, with great *éclat.*

See "Life of Handel" in BURNEY's "History of Music;" ESCHENBURG, "Life of Handel," (in German,) 1785; MATHESON, "Life of Handel," (in German;) 1761; FÉTIS, "Biographie Universelle des Musiciens;" J. M. WEISSBECK, "Der grosse Musikus G. F. Händel im Universalruhme," 1805; "Edinburgh Review" for July, 1857; "Fraser's Magazine" for September, 1857; "British Quarterly Review" for January, 1862.

Handjeri. See HANJERI.

Handmann, hânt'mân, (EMANUEL,) a Swiss painter of history and portraits, born at Bâle in 1718; died in 1781.

Haneefah or **Hanîfa,** hâ-nee'fâ, **Aboo-al-Nomân-Ibn-Tâbet,** (**Abû-al-Nomân-Ibn-** (or **Ebn-**) **Thâbet—**â'boo âl no-mân' Ib'n tâ'bet,) the founder of the sect of Haneefites, the first of the four orthodox sects among Mohammedans, was born at Cufâ about 700 A.D. This sect prevails chiefly among the Turks and Tartars. They are called by an Arabian writer followers of reason, while the other three sects are called followers of tradition, as

being more tenacious of the traditions of the prophet. Haneefa died in prison at Bagdâd in 767. He was imprisoned because he refused to act as kâdi, or judge, alleging that he was unfit for the office. It is said that while in prison he read the Koran through seven thousand times.

See SALE's "Koran," Preliminary Discourse.

Hänel or **Haenel,** hä'něl, (ERNST JULIUS,) a German sculptor, born at Dresden about 1810, executed a statue of Beethoven, which was erected at Bonn in 1845.

Hänel or **Haenel,** (GUSTAV FRIEDRICH,) an eminent German jurist, born in 1792 at Leipsic, where he became professor of law about 1838. He edited "Ulpianus de Edendo," (1838,) "Codex Theodosianus," (1839–42,) and other works.

Hänel, Haenel, or **Handl,** hândl, (JAKOB,) surnamed GALLUS, a German composer, born in Carniola about 1550, was imperial chapel-master at Vienna. His "Media in Vita" is esteemed a master-piece. Died in 1590.

Hanfstängel or **Hanfstaengel,** hânf'stěng'ěl, (FRANZ,) a German lithographer, born in Upper Bavaria in 1804. His chief work is "The Principal Pictures in the Royal Gallery of Dresden," (1836–52.)

Hang'er, (Colonel GEORGE,) a whimsical English writer, born in 1760, was a younger son of Lord Coleraine. Among his works is his "Life, Adventures, and Opinions," (1801.) Died in 1824.

Hangest, de, děh hôN'zhěst', (JÉRÔME,) a French theologian, born at Compiègne, wrote against Luther. Died in 1538.

Hanîfa. See HANEEFAH.

Hanjeri or **Handjeri,** hân'jeh-ree, (ALEXANDER,) PRINCE, a noted linguist, born at Constantinople in 1760, was appointed Hospodar of Moldavia by the Sultan in 1807. He removed to Moscow about 1821. He compiled a "Dictionary of the French, Arabic, Persian, and Turkish Languages," (3 vols., 1844.) Died at Moscow in 1854.

Hanka, hânk'â, (WENCESLAUS,) a distinguished Bohemian antiquary and critic, born at Horenowes in 1791. He was liberally educated at Prague, and about 1820 became librarian of the Bohemian Museum of that city. He discovered in 1817, at Kralodvor, a precious manuscript of old Bohemian poems, which are greatly admired, and of which he published an edition, called "Kralodvorsky Rukopis," (1817.) He published a "Collection of Bohemian Poems of the Thirteenth and Fourteenth Centuries," (5 vols., 1817–25,) and other works.

Hanke. See HANCKIUS, (MARTIN.)

Hanke, hânk'eh, (HENRIETTE WILHELMINE,) a successful German novelist, originally named ARNDT, was born at Jauer, in Silesia, in 1785. She produced about one hundred volumes of novels, among which we may name "Claudia," (1825,) "The Pearls," (1836,) and "My Winter Garden," (1854.)

Hänke or **Haenke,** hěnk'eh, (THADDEUS,) a Bohemian naturalist and traveller, born at Kreibitz in 1761, visited Mexico and the islands of the South Sea. Died in Peru in 1817. A description of the plants which he collected was published in 1825.

See ERSCH und GRUBER, "Allgemeine Encyklopaedie."

Han'mer, (JONATHAN,) an English nonconformist minister, born at Barnstaple; died in 1687.

Hanmer, (MEREDITH,) an English scholar and divine, born in 1543. He produced a translation of the "Ecclesiastic Histories of Eusebius, Socrates, and Evagrius," (1577.) Died in 1604.

Hanmer, (Sir THOMAS,) an English legislator, born about 1676, was for thirty years a member of the House of Commons, of which he was chosen Speaker in 1713. He published an edition of Shakspeare on which much time and labour were expended, (1744.) Died in 1746.

See Sir H. BUNBURY, "Life of Sir Thomas Hanmer," 1838.

Hann, (JAMES,) an English mathematician, born about 1799; died in London in 1856.

Han'na, (Rev. WILLIAM,) LL.D., a British clergyman, a son-in-law of the eminent Dr. Chalmers, was born at Belfast in 1808. He became editor of the "North British Review" about 1846, and afterwards edited the "Memoirs of the Life and Writings of Dr. Chalmers," (4 vols.,

1849–52.) In 1850 he became colleague of Dr. Guthrie in Saint John's Church, Edinburgh. He published about 1868 a "Life of Christ," (6 vols.)

Han'nah, [Heb. חַנָּה,] a Hebrew matron, was the wife of Elkanah, and the mother of the prophet Samuel.

See I. Samuel i. and ii.

Han'nay, (JAMES,) a successful British writer of fiction, was born at Dumfries in 1827. He served about five years in the royal navy, from which he retired in 1845. He contributed to several periodicals and journals, and gained distinction by his novel "Singleton Fontenoy," (3 vols., 1850.) Among his other works are "Satire and Satirists," (1853,) and "Eustace Conyers," (1855.)

Hanneken or **Hannecken,** hän'neh-ken, (MEMNON,) a German Lutheran minister, born at Blaxen, in Oldenburg, in 1595 ; died in 1671.

His son, PHILIPP LUDWIG, born at Marburg in 1637, was a writer on theology. Died in 1706.

Hanneman, hän'neh-män', (ADRIAN,) a Dutch portrait-painter, born at the Hague about 1610. He worked in his native place with a high reputation, and was patronized by the princes of the house of Nassau. He also painted allegorical subjects. Died after 1666.

Hannetaire, hän'tär', (JEAN NICOLAS **Servandoni**—sĕR'vŏN'do'ne',) a French comedian, born at Grenoble in 1718, excelled in the personation of Molière's characters. He wrote "Observations on the Art of a Comedian," (1764,) which was often reprinted. "This work," says Marmontel, "is one of the few whose fault is too great brevity." Died in 1780.

Han'nĭ-bạl, a grandson of that Hamilcar who was killed in 480 B.C. He invaded Sicily with a large army in 409 B.C., and defeated the Syracusans at Himera. He died at Agrigentum in 406.

Hannibal, a son of Gisco, a general of the first Punic war. He ravaged the coast of Italy with a large fleet in 261 B.C., and was defeated in a great naval battle by Duilius in 260. He was killed by his mutinous troops about 258 B.C.

Han'nĭ-bạl or **An'nĭ-bạl,** [Gr. Ἀννίβας; Fr. ANNIBAL, ắ'ne'bằl'; It. ANNIBALE, än-ne-bä'lâ, or ANNIBAL, än-ne-bâl',] one of the greatest generals that ever lived, was born about 247 B.C. He was the son of the Carthaginian commander Hamilcar Barca, who was killed in battle in 229 B.C. When he was but nine years old, he was taken to Spain by his father, who then caused him solemnly to swear on the altar of the gods an eternal hostility to the Romans,—an oath which he appears never to have forgotten. This anecdote was related by Hannibal himself, many years later, to Antiochus the Great, King of Syria. Hannibal was present at the battle in which his father fell, and had already given proof of superior military genius in several campaigns in Spain. On the death of Hasdrubal, Hamilcar's son-in-law, (221 B.C.,) Hannibal became commander-in-chief of the army, then engaged in the subjugation of some Spanish tribes, which he completed in two campaigns, 221 and 220 B.C.

Early in the year 219 he attacked Saguntum, which was situated on the Iberus (Ebro) and was an ally of the Romans. The Saguntines defended their city with desperate courage, but it was taken after a siege of eight months. This was the beginning of the second Punic war, which Hannibal did not wish to avert or postpone. Having resolved upon the invasion of Italy, he crossed the Ebro in the spring of 218 B.C. with about 100,000 men ; but his army was greatly reduced in number before he reached the Rhone. In his march across the Alps, which was one of the most remarkable military achievements of antiquity, he was opposed by the Gaulish mountaineers, and lost about 30,000 men. Great diversity of opinion has prevailed among the learned in respect to the route by which he crossed the Alps. According to some ancient authors, he removed the rocks which obstructed his passage by means of vinegar :

"Diducit scopulos et montem rumpit aceto."*
JUVENAL, Satire X.

---

* Literally, "He separates the rocks and breaks the mountain with vinegar."—Respecting this much-vexed question, the reader is referred to the works named at the close of this article.

When he entered the plains of Piedmont, he had about 26,000 men, of whom 6000 were cavalry and all were veterans. He met a Roman army, commanded by Publius Scipio, near the Ticinus, (now Ticino,) and gained a victory in a battle between the cavalry of the two armies. Scipio retreated to Placentia, and was joined by another army, under the consul T. Sempronius, who, confiding in the superior numbers of the Romans, eagerly offered battle on the banks of the Trebia. Hannibal gained here a complete victory about the end of 218, and in the ensuing winter increased his army by numerous recruits obtained among the friendly tribes of Gauls. In the spring of 217 he entered Etruria, and encountered a Roman army under the consul Flaminius, whom he defeated in a great battle at Lake Thrasymene. Hannibal took in this action about 15,000 prisoners, many of whom were Italian allies of the Romans. The victorious general liberated without ransom these Italians, in the hope that by this course he might detach some states of Italy from the alliance with Rome. He next marched into Apulia, where he passed a great part of the summer, during which the dictator Fabius took command of the Roman army and adopted a defensive policy. Hannibal entered and devastated the fertile plains of Campania, but could not induce Fabius to risk a general battle. The Carthaginian army remained in winter-quarters at Geronium until late in the spring of 216 B.C.

The Romans raised an army of about 90,000 men, commanded by the consuls L. Æmilius Paulus and C. Terentius Varro, who gave battle to Hannibal on the banks of the Aufidus, near Cannæ, in Apulia, in the summer of 216 B.C. The army of Hannibal was probably much inferior in number to that of the Romans. The battle of Cannæ, which was one of the most memorable and decisive in universal history, resulted in the rout and almost total destruction of the Roman army. It is estimated by Livy and others that more than 40,000 Romans, including eighty senators, fell on this day ; and many thousands were taken prisoners. Hannibal lost at Cannæ about 4500 men.

According to some military critics, Hannibal failed to improve and follow up this victory with due vigour and celerity by an advance against the Roman capital. The Apulians, Lucanians, and Bruttians declared in favour of Carthage soon after the victory at Cannæ ; but the Romans maintained the contest with a resolute and unfaltering spirit, and resorted to the extreme measure of arming their slaves.

Hannibal took about the end of 216 the large and opulent city of Capua, the second city of Italy, and there passed the ensuing winter, which is considered as the turning-point in the fortune of the war. According to ancient rhetoricians, his soldiers were enervated by their luxurious life in Capua ; but Hannibal continued to gain victories wherever he commanded in person. The Romans, however, changed their plan of operations, and adhered to a defensive and Fabian policy, instead of opposing a large army to the enemy. No decisive battles were fought in the campaigns of 215 and 214 B.C. Hannibal formed an alliance with Philip of Macedon in 215, and made himself master of Tarentum in 213. In the year 212 Hasdrubal gained a victory over the two Scipios in Spain, and Hannibal defeated Cneius Fulvius at Herdonea ; but he lost Capua, which was taken in 211. His principal adversaries at this period were Fabius Cunctator and M. Marcellus, who had recently returned from the conquest of Syracuse. The latter was led into an ambush by Hannibal and was killed in 208 B.C. Hannibal expected to be reinforced by his brother Hasdrubal, who crossed the Alps with an army and entered Cisalpine Gaul ; but before he could effect a junction with Hannibal he was defeated and killed by the Romans, on the Metaurus, in 207 B.C. This was an irreparable disaster to the Carthaginians, who after that defeat ceased to act on the offensive. Having concentrated his forces in the peninsula of Bruttium, Hannibal defended himself against superior numbers for nearly four years, during which he displayed great fertility of resources and mastery of defensive tactics. He erected near Crotona a column, on which he inscribed the principal events of his great expedition.

ɛ as k; ç as s; ğ hard; ġ as j; G, H, K, guttural; N, nasal; R, trilled; š as z; ʇh as in this. (☞See Explanations, p. 23.)

In the mean time, Scipio Africanus had passed with a victorious army from Spain into Africa, and had gained several victories over the Carthaginians, who urged Hannibal to return to the defence of his native country. About the end of 203 he evacuated Italy and moved his army by sea to Leptis, in Africa. The statement that an interview occurred between Hannibal and Scipio is discredited by some historians. In 202 B.C. they fought the decisive battle of Zama, in which Hannibal was defeated and about 20,000 Carthaginians were slain. The Carthaginians sued for peace, and in 201 B.C. concluded a treaty of which the Romans dictated the terms. Thus ended the second Punic war, in which Hannibal had received little aid from the government of Carthage, and had won a long series of victories by his own personal influence, resources, and military genius.

He next turned his attention to political affairs, effected some reforms in the administration, and was chosen chief magistrate of the republic. He also made constitutional changes which reduced the power of the judges and the aristocracy. By these reforms he incurred the enmity of a powerful faction, which excited the suspicion of the Roman senate by a charge that Hannibal was instigating Antiochus of Syria to wage war against Rome. The Romans having demanded the expulsion of Hannibal, he retired to the court of Antiochus about 194 B.C., and was received with great honour. The King of Syria soon after commenced hostilities against the Romans, and employed Hannibal as a commander, but would not follow his advice in the conduct of the war. When peace was restored between Antiochus and the Romans, in 190 B.C., Hannibal took refuge at the court of Prusias, King of Bithynia. The Romans sent an embassy to demand the surrender of the fugitive, which Prusias did not refuse; but Hannibal killed himself by poison, and thus escaped the power of his enemies, in 183 B.C.

Plutarch mentions a report that Hannibal and Scipio once met at Ephesus after the battle of Zama, and fell into conversation about great generals. Hannibal asserted that Alexander was the greatest general the world had ever seen, that Pyrrhus was the second, and himself the third. Scipio smiled at this, and said, "But what rank would you have placed yourself in if I had not conquered you?" "O Scipio," said he, "then I would not have placed myself the third, but the first." ("Life of T. Q. Flaminius.") His temperance and fortitude are extolled by several ancient writers. Polybius expresses his admiration of the wonderful management by which for a series of years he maintained his authority over an army composed of many different nations.

See POLYBIUS, "History;" CORNELIUS NEPOS, "Life of Hannibal;" BERNEWITZ, "Leben Hannibals," 1802; PLUTARCH, "Life of Fabius Maximus;" ARNOLD, "History of Rome," vol. iii.; NIEBUHR, "Lectures on Roman History," vol. i.; VAUDONCOURT, "Histoire des Campagnes d'Annibal en Italie," 3 vols., 1812; BECKER, "History of the Second Punic War," (in German;) ROLLIN, "Ancient History;" A. GÉRARD, "Résumé des Campagnes d'Annibal," 1844; H. L. LONG, "March of Hannibal from the Rhone to the Alps," 1831; JOHN WHITAKER, "Course of Hannibal over the Alps ascertained," 2 vols., 1794.

Han'no, [Gr. Ἄννων,] a famous Carthaginian navigator, supposed to have lived about 500 B.C. He commanded an expedition sent to explore the coast of Africa beyond the pillars of Hercules. A Greek version of the account of his voyage (Περίπλους) has come down to us. Geographers and critics have discussed at great length the questions of the date and extent of his voyage, which remain undetermined.

Hanno, a Carthaginian general, who commanded in the war against Agathocles, King of Sicily. He was killed in a battle near Carthage about 309 B.C.

Hanno, a Carthaginian general, who commanded in Sicily in the first Punic war. He was defeated by the Romans in a great battle near Agrigentum in 262 B.C. and recalled to Carthage. Hanno and Hamilcar commanded jointly at the naval battle of Ecnomus, where the Romans gained the victory in 256 B.C.

Hanno, a Carthaginian admiral, commanded in a great naval battle near Sicily in the year 241 B.C., in which he was defeated by the Roman consul Lutatius Catulus. This action terminated the first Punic war, and secured to Rome the empire of the sea. He was punished with death for this disaster by the senate of Carthage.

Hanno, a son of Bomilcar, a Carthaginian general who, in the second Punic war, followed Hannibal in his invasion of Italy. He commanded the right wing at the battle of Cannæ, 216 B.C., after which, at the head of a separate force, he took Crotona. He was defeated near Beneventum by Tiberius Gracchus in 214, but he routed the army of L. Pomponius in the next year. Having returned to Carthage after Scipio had invaded Africa, he commanded the army for a short time until the arrival of Hannibal, in 202 B.C.

See LIVY, "History of Rome," books xxi., xxiii., xxv., and xxvii.; APPIAN, "Punica."

Hanno, surnamed THE GREAT, (a title which his actions apparently did not justify,) was the leader of the aristocratic party of Carthage, and a political rival of Hamilcar Barca. Having acquired distinction in Africa during the first Punic war, he was appointed in 240 B.C. to command the army against the revolted mercenaries. After the enemy had surprised his camp, his incompetence became so apparent that the senate gave the command to Hamilcar Barca, or perhaps divided it between him and Hanno. He maintained in the councils of Carthage a persistent hostility to the influence and policy of Hamilcar and his son Hannibal, and opposed the prosecution of the second Punic war, (217–201 B.C.)

See LIVY, "History of Rome," books xxi., xxiii., and xxx.

Hanouman or **Hanooman.** See HANUMÂN.
Hanriot. See HENRIOT.
Han'sard, (LUKE,) an English printer, born at Norwich in 1752. He became printer to the House of Commons, and published "Hansard's Parliamentary Debates." Died in 1828.

Hansemann, hân'seh-mân', (DAVID JUSTUS LUDWIG,) an eminent Prussian financier and statesman, born near Hamburg in 1790. In early life he was a successful merchant of Aix-la-Chapelle. About 1830 he began to advocate the adoption of the constitutional system of government in Prussia, and published a treatise "On the Constitutions of Prussia and Germany." He was afterwards one of the chief representatives of the Liberal party. In March, 1848, he became minister of finance, and in the ensuing June succeeded Camphausen as the head of a new cabinet. He lost his popularity, and resigned office in September of the same year. His policy accorded neither with that of the conservatives nor that of the advanced democrats.

See BROCKHAUS, "Conversations-Lexikon."

Hansen, hân'sen, (CHRISTIAN FREDRIK,) a Danish architect, born at Copenhagen in 1756, designed the Raad-hus (Council-house) of Copenhagen. Died in 1645.

Hansen, hân'sen, (MORITZ CHRISTOFFER,) a popular Norwegian novelist and poet, born at Modum in 1794, published novels entitled "Morgana," (1820,) "The Journal of Theodore," (1820,) and "Tone," (1843;) also, a "Garland of Norwegian Idyls," ("Norsk Idylkrands," 1831.) Died in 1842.

See M. NISSEN, "Norsk Bog Fortegnelse."

Hansen, hân'sen, (PETER ANDREAS,) a German astronomer, born at Tondern, in the duchy of Sleswick, in 1795. He was chosen in 1825 director of the Observatory of Seeberg, near Gotha. He wrote "Researches on the Mutual Perturbations of Jupiter and Saturn," (1831,) a Latin treatise on "The Moon's Orbit," (1838,) and able memoirs on the higher mathematics.

Hans-Sachs, hâns sâks, written also **Hans-Sachse,** a popular German poet, born at Nuremberg in 1494. He was a shoemaker, and became afterwards *meister-sänger* and a schoolmaster in his native city. He versified the Psalms and Proverbs of Scripture, and composed a great number of sacred and other comedies and tragedies, by which he acquired much celebrity. In theology he was a zealous disciple of Luther. Died in 1576.

See "Retrospective Review," vol. x., 1824.

Hansteen, hân'stân, (CHRISTOFFER,) a Norwegian astronomer, born at Christiania in 1784. He obtained a chair of mathematics in that town in 1814, and published in 1819 "Researches on Terrestrial Magnetism," which attracted much attention. In 1828, 1829, and 1830 he performed an excursion to Siberia to promote the science of magnetism. About 1837 he was chosen to direct the triangulation of Norway. He wrote a "Manual of Geometry," (1835,) and other works, and became director of the Observatory of Christiania.

See KRAFT og NYERUP, "Litteraturlexicon."

Hanstein, hân'stĭn, (GOTTFRIED AUGUST LUDWIG,) a German Protestant theologian and pulpit orator, born at Magdeburg in 1761 ; died about 1820.

Hănumân, hăn-ōō-mân', common Hindoo pron. hŭn-ōō-mân', [*i.e.* "having large jaws or cheeks," from the Sanscrit *hânu*, a "jaw" or "cheek,"] the name of the King of the Monkeys, in the Hindoo mythology. He is sometimes called the son of Pavana, the regent or god of the winds, perhaps in allusion to his extraordinary fleetness. He was the friend and prime minister of the god RÂMA, (which see.) He is represented as having been of such strength as to fly through the air a thousand miles, carrying a huge mountain in his arms. He is always represented in pictures with a tail, and sometimes with two and sometimes with ten arms.

See MOOR, "Hindu Pantheon."

Hanusch, hâ'nōōsh, (IGNAZ JOHANN,) a Bohemian philosopher, born at Prague in 1812. He published a "History of Philosophy from its Origin to the Suspension of the Philosophic Schools by Justinian," (1849,) and other works of merit. In 1849 he became professor of philosophy at Prague.

Hanvill. See HAUTEVILLE.

Han'way, (JONAS,) a benevolent English merchant, born at Portsmouth in 1712, lived some years in Saint Petersburg. Having travelled on business in Persia, he published in 1753 an interesting "Journal of Travels through Russia into Persia," etc., and a "Historical Account of the British Trade over the Caspian Sea." He wrote many other works, and was chiefly instrumental in the formation of the Marine Society and the Magdalen Charity. Died in 1786.

See JOHN PUGH, "Remarkable Occurrences in the Life of Jonas Hanway."

Han-Yu, hân yoo, called also **Han-Wăn-Kung,** (*i.e.* "duke or prince of literature,") a famous Chinese scholar and philosopher, who lived in the eighth century of our era. He wrote an "Examination into the Nature of Man," in which he criticises the doctrine of Mencius, who held that man's nature is good, and that of Seun, who maintained that it is evil. (See SEUN-KING.) Han-Yu taught that in the nature of man there are three grades, of which the highest is purely good ; the middle is not so good, but is capable of being led ; the lowest grade is purely evil: it may be restrained, but not changed. Besides the essay referred to above, Han-Yu has left some other critical writings.

See LEGGE, "Chinese Classics," vol. ii. ; also "Review of The Ethics of the Chinese," by the REV. GRIFFITH JOHN, read before the North China Branch of the Royal Asiatic Society, November, 1859.

Haoucal. See HAUKÂL.

Hapsburg. See HABSBURG.

Haquin, hâ'kwin, **I.,** King of Norway, born in 915 A.D., was the fifth son of Harold Harfager. He was educated as a Christian at the court of Athelstan of England, and succeeded his father in 935. On account of his mildness and justice, he was surnamed THE GOOD. His attempt to introduce Christianity into Norway was met by violent resistance. In repelling an invasion by the sons of Eric, he was killed in 961.

See SAXO GRAMMATICUS, "Historia Danica."

Hara, a name of SIVA, which see.

Harambure, d', dä'rôN'bür',(LOUIS FRANÇOIS ALEXANDRE,) BARON, a French general, born at Preuilly, in Touraine, in 1742. As a member of the National Assembly, in 1789, he favoured the Revolution. He became general of division in March, 1792, and after the removal of Luckner was general-in-chief of the army of the Rhine for a short time. Died in 1828.

Harbaugh, har'baw, (HENRY,) an American theologian, born in Franklin county, Pennsylvania, in 1817. He became pastor of a German Reformed church at Lancaster in 1850. Among his works are "The Heavenly Home, or the Employments and Enjoyments of the Saints in Heaven," (1853,) and "The Fathers of the German Reformed Church in Europe and America," (3 vols., 1857–58.) Died in 1867.

Har'bȳ, (ISAAC,) an American writer, born in Charleston, South Carolina, in 1788. He produced, besides other works, dramas entitled "The Gordian Knot ; or, Causes and Effects," (1807,) and "Alberti," (1819.) Died in 1828.

Har'cōurt, (HARRIET EUSEBIA,) a learned English lady, born near Richmond in 1705. She collected a company of cultivated women, who lived in a sort of monastic seclusion on her estate. Died in 1745.

Harcourt, (WILLIAM,) EARL OF, an English officer, born in 1743, entered the army in 1759. In the American Revolution he distinguished himself by the capture of General Lee in 1777. On his return to England he was appointed aide-de-camp to the king, and commanded the queen's regiment of dragoons. In 1809 he inherited his father's title and estate. Died in 1830.

Harcourt, d', dăR'koor', (FRANÇOIS EUGÈNE GABRIEL,) DUC, a French diplomatist, born in 1786.

Harcourt, d', (FRANÇOIS HENRI,) DUC, born in 1726, was appointed governor of the dauphin about 1787, and elected to the French Academy in 1789. He died in England about 1802.

Harcourt, d', (HENRI,) DUC, a French general and diplomatist, born in 1654, was a son of François, Marquis de Beuvron et de Thury-Harcourt. He was a fine specimen of the old French nobility. He distinguished himself at the sieges of Cambrai and Fribourg, in 1677, and for a victory over the Germans at /Courteville was made a lieutenant-general in 1692. He was ambassador to Madrid from 1697 to 1700, and managed the negotiations relating to the Spanish succession with skill and success. He received the title of duke in 1700, and became a marshal of France in 1703. Died in 1718.

His son FRANÇOIS, second Duke of Harcourt, born in 1689, was a general. He was severely wounded at Dettingen, (1743,) and obtained a marshal's bâton in 1746. Died in 1750. Another son, ANNE PIERRE, (1701–83,) the father of François Henri, noticed above, became a marshal of France.

See LAROQUE, "Histoire de la Maison de Harcourt," 4 vols.; "Nouvelle Biographie Générale."

Harcourt, d', (HENRI de Lorraine,) COMTE, an able French general, born in 1601, was a younger son of Charles de Lorraine, Duc d'Elbœuf. He commanded in Piedmont in 1639, defeated the Spaniards at Quiers, and captured Turin. In 1643 he was sent to mediate between Charles I. of England and his Parliament. He defeated the Spaniards at Valenciennes and Condé in 1649. In the war of the Fronde, about 1650, he fought on both sides. Died in 1666.

See LAROQUE, "Histoire de la Maison de Harcourt."

Har'cōurt, de, [Fr. pron. dăR'koor',] (GODEFROI or GEOFFREY,) was a Norman knight, who rebelled against Philip VI. of France in 1345, and commanded the army of Edward III. of England in the war against the French. After the battle of Crécy, he asked and received pardon of Philip, but again revolted, and was killed in battle in 1356.

Hardeby, hard'be, (GEOFFREY,) an English monk and writer, confessor to King Henry II., wrote a "History of the Order of Saint Augustine." Died in 1360.

Har'dee, (WILLIAM J.,) an American general, born at Savannah, Georgia, about 1818, graduated at West Point in 1838. He became a captain in 1844, and published a work on Tactics, (1855.) He served as major-general at the battle of Shiloh, April, 1862. About October, 1862, he was appointed a lieutenant-general in the Confederate army. He commanded a corps at the battle of Stone River, December 31, 1862–January 2, 1863, and in several battles fought between Dalton and Atlanta, May–September, 1864. He commanded an army which defended Savannah without success against General Sherman in December, 1864.

See "Southern Generals," anonymous, 1865.

Hardenberg, haR'den-bĕRg', (ALBERT,) a Dutch Protestant divine, born in Overyssel in 1510. He preached at Bremen from 1547 to 1561, and became pastor primarius at Emden in 1567. Died in 1574.

Hardenberg, (FRIEDRICH LUDWIG.) See NOVALIS.

Hardenberg, von, fon haR'den-bĕRg', (KARL AUGUST,) PRINCE, an able Prussian statesman, born at

Essenroda, in Hanover, in May, 1750. He obtained in 1778 an office in the administration of Hanover, with the title of count. About 1785 he entered the service of the Duke of Brunswick, in whose hands the will of Frederick II. of Prussia was deposited. Hardenberg was chosen in 1786 to transmit that important document to the heir, Frederick William, who in 1791 appointed him a minister of state. He was the negotiator on the part of Prussia at the Conference of Bâle, where he concluded a peace with France in 1795. In August, 1804, he was appointed prime minister, and in 1805 formed an alliance with Russia against Napoleon. Soon after the battle of Austerlitz, (1805,) he was driven from power by his rival Haugwitz.

Hardenberg was minister of foreign affairs for a few months in 1806–07, after which he passed several years in exile. Having become chancellor of state in 1810, he equalized taxation, and made reforms which contributed materially to improve the condition of the peasants. In 1814 he signed, on the part of Prussia, the peace of Paris, and was created a prince. He was the Prussian plenipotentiary at the Congress of Vienna in 1815, and became in 1817 president of the council, or prime minister. His administration was favourable to education, trade, and other important interests. He died at Genoa in 1822, leaving Memoirs in manuscript.

See W. HENNINGS, "Biographie des Fürsten und Staats-Kanzlers Von Hardenberg," 1824; WOLF, "Geschichte des Geschlechts Von Hardenberg," 1824; KARL LUDWIG KLOSE, "Leben C. A. Fürsten Von Hardenberg," Halle, 1851; "Nouvelle Biographie Générale."

Harder, haR′der or hăR′daiR′, (JOHANN JAKOB,) a Swiss physician and scientific writer, born at Bâle in 1656. He practised with success in his native town, and obtained the chairs of philosophy, anatomy, botany, etc. The emperor Leopold made him a count-palatine. Died in 1711.

See ERSCH und GRUBER, "Allgemeine Encyklopaedie."

Hardi, (ALEXANDRE.) See HARDY.

Har′di-ca-nūte′, written also **Harthacanute** and **Hardy-Canute,** King of England and Denmark, was the eldest son of Canute the Great and Emma, daughter of Richard I., Duke of Normandy. At the death of Canute, in 1035, Hardicanute succeeded to the throne of Denmark; but his claim to England was contested by his half-brother Harold, who was in actual possession. An agreement was made by these two that Harold should retain the country north of the Thames and his rival should possess the remainder. At the death of Harold, in 1040, Hardicanute became King of all England. He died, without issue, in 1042, and was succeeded by his half-brother, Edward the Confessor.

Hardime, hăR′dĕm′, (PIERRE, or PETER,) a Flemish painter of flowers and fruit, born at Antwerp or the Hague about 1675. His master-piece is "The Four Seasons." Died in 1748.

Hardime, (SIMON,) a Flemish painter, brother of the preceding, born in 1672; died in 1737.

Hard′ing, (CHESTER,) an American portrait-painter, born in Conway, Massachusetts, in 1792. He became successively a soldier, a cabinet-maker, and a house-painter. Having resolved to be an artist, he visited England in 1823, and returned about 1826. Among his works are portraits of Henry Clay, Daniel Webster, J. Q. Adams, and James Monroe.

See DUNLAP, "Rise and Progress of the Arts of Design in America;" "Atlantic Monthly" for April, 1867.

Hard′ing, (JAMES DUFFIELD,) an eminent English landscape-painter and popular writer on art, was born at Deptford in 1798. He was one of the first to employ lithography with success in teaching the art of design, and excelled in the representation of trees and foliage. In 1836 he published "Sketches at Home and Abroad," 60 tinted drawings of scenes in Italy, Germany, France, etc. He painted a great number of landscapes in oil and in water-colours. His works are remarkable for variety, fidelity to nature, and facility of execution. "J. D. Harding is, I think," says Ruskin, "nearly unequalled in the drawing of running water. . . . His foregrounds and the rocks of his middle distances are also thoroughly admirable. His work in near passages of fresh-broken, sharp-edged rock is absolute perfection. Let us refresh

ourselves by looking at the truth. We need not go to Turner; we will go to the man who next to him is unquestionably the greatest master of foliage in Europe,— J. D. Harding." He wrote several valuable works for the use of students, among which is "The Principles and Practice of Art," (1850.) Died in 1863.

Harding or **Hardyng,** (JOHN,) an English chronicler, born in 1378, was a member of the household of Sir Henry Percy, (Hotspur,) whom he attended in several battles. After the death of Percy he served under Sir Robert Umfraville. In the reign of Henry V. he was sent to Scotland to search for deeds of homage, or documents to prove that the Scottish kings owed fealty to the English. He wrote a "Metrical Chronicle of England" from the earliest times to the reign of Henry VI. Died about 1465.

Harding, haR′ding, (KARL LUDWIG,) a German astronomer, born at Lauenburg in 1765. He became in 1796 assistant of Schröter in the Observatory of Lilienthal, and in 1803 gained distinction by the discovery of the telescopic planet Juno. He was chosen a member of the Royal Society of London, and of the French Institute. In 1805 he obtained a chair of astronomy at Göttingen. He published a "Celestial Atlas," (1822.) Died in 1834.

See "Nouvelle Biographie Générale."

Harding, (THOMAS,) an English theologian, born in Devonshire in 1512. He became professor of Hebrew at Oxford in 1542, and tutor of Lady Jane Grey. On the accession of Queen Mary he turned Roman Catholic, and was appointed prebendary of Winchester in 1554. He wrote some polemical works in answer to Bishop Jewel. Died in 1572.

Harding, hard′ing, (GEORGE,) an English lawyer, born in 1744, became attorney-general to the queen in 1789. He wrote "The Essence of Malone," (1800,) "Letters to Burke on the Impeachment of Hastings," and other works, in prose and verse. Died in 1816.

Hardinge, (HENRY,) VISCOUNT, an English general, born at Wrotham, Kent, in March, 1785, was the third son of the Rev. Henry Hardinge. Having entered the army in 1798, he became captain in 1804. In the Peninsular war he served with credit, under Wellington, as staff-officer and quartermaster-general, and was wounded at Vimiera and Vitoria. In 1815, being then brigadier-general, he received a wound two days before the battle of Waterloo, which disabled him for a short time, so that he could not be present at that action. Soon after this event he was knighted, and in 1820 he was elected to Parliament. Hardinge was appointed secretary of war, and member of the privy council in the ministry of Wellington, in 1828. He officiated as secretary for Ireland during the brief ministry of Sir Robert Peel in 1834–35. In 1841 he accepted the office of secretary at war in the cabinet of Sir Robert Peel. In 1844 he succeeded Lord Ellenborough as Governor-General of India, which he governed with ability. About the end of 1845 the British territory was invaded by the Sikhs, whom he defeated at Moodkee and Aliwal and compelled to sue for peace. For these services he received a pension of three thousand pounds, and was raised to the peerage, as Viscount Hardinge of Lahore. In 1848 he was superseded by Lord Dalhousie as Governor-General. On the death of the Duke of Wellington, in 1852, he succeeded him as commander-in-chief, and in 1855 was made a field-marshal. He died in 1856, and left his title to his son, Charles Stewart Hardinge.

See "Nouvelle Biographie Générale."

Hardinge, (NICHOLAS,) an English antiquary, born in 1700, was the father of George, noticed above. He was a good classical scholar, and wrote short poems in Latin, Greek, and English. He was clerk of the House of Commons from 1731 to 1752. Died in 1758.

Hardion, hȧR′de′ôN′, (JACQUES,) a French historian and scholar, born at Tours in 1686, resided in Paris. He was admitted to the Academy of Inscriptions and Belles-Lettres in 1715, and to the French Academy in 1730. In 1748 he was chosen to give lessons in history to the princesses of the royal family. He published "Essays on the Origin and Progress of Eloquence in Greece," and a "Universal History," (20 vols., 1754–69,) which

ā, ē, ī, ō, ū, ȳ, *long;* à, ė, ò, same, less prolonged; ă, ĕ, ĭ, ŏ, ŭ, ў, *short;* a, e, i, o, *obscure;* fär, fåll, fåt; mêt; nôt; gōōd; mōōn;

had much success and was translated into several languages. Died in 1766.

Hardouin, *hăr'doo-ăn'*, (HENRI,) a French musician and composer of sacred music, born about 1724; died in 1808.

Hardouin, (JEAN,) a French Jesuit, born at Quimper in 1646, was deeply versed in history, languages, and numismatology, but addicted to fancies and to paradox. He maintained that ancient history and many other classic writings were forged by the monks of the thirteenth century,—that the works of Cicero, Horace, Pliny, and Virgil's "Georgics" were the only genuine classics extant. For this odd conceit he was reprimanded by his superiors, and in 1708 he retracted publicly. He produced several treatises on coins and medals, and for the use of the dauphin an excellent edition of Pliny's "Natural History," (5 vols., 1685.) Died in 1729.

See MORÉRI, "Dictionnaire Historique."

Hardt, von der, fon děr haRt, (HERMANN,) an eminent German philologist, born at Melle, in Prussia, in 1660. He was chosen professor of Oriental languages at Helmstedt in 1690, and was more noted for learning than judgment. Among his numerous works (in Latin) are "Elements of Universal Exegesis," (1691,) a "Literary History of the Reformation," (5 vols., 1717,) and "Ænigmata Prisci Orbis," ("Enigmas of the Primeval World," 1723.) Died in 1746.

See ERSCH und GRUBER, "Allgemeine Encyklopaedie."

Harduin, *hăr'dü-ăn',*(ALEXANDRE XAVIER,)a French author, born at Arras in 1718. He wrote agreeable verses, among which were an "Ode to Health," and "Pan et Glycère," a lyric pastoral; also several treatises on grammar. Died in 1785.

Hard'wick, (CHARLES,) an English theologian, born about 1820, became a Fellow of Saint Catherine's Hall, Cambridge. He published, besides other works, a "History of the Thirty-Nine Articles," (1851,) and a "History of the Christian Church from the Seventh Century to the Reformation," (1853,) which is highly commended by British reviewers. He was appointed Archdeacon of Ely a short time before his death, in 1859.

Hardwick, (PHILIP,) an English architect, born in London in 1792. He erected the hall of the Goldsmiths' Company about 1832, and afterwards many public buildings in London, among which was the hall and library of Lincoln's Inn. He was elected Royal Academician about 1841. His son, PHILIP CHARLES, also an architect, worked in conjunction with his father in several edifices, and was chief architect of the Great Western Hotel in London.

Hard'wicke, (CHARLES PHILIP YORKE,) fourth EARL OF, a son of Admiral J. S. Yorke, and a nephew of the third Earl, born about 1800, was elected to the House of Commons in 1831, and inherited the title of earl in 1834. He obtained the rank of rear-admiral on the reserve list in 1854, and was lord privy seal in the cabinet of Lord Derby in 1858 and 1859.

Hardwicke, (PHILIP YORKE,) first EARL OF, an eminent English jurist, born at Dover in 1690, was the son of an attorney. He never attended any school except a private one at Bethnal Green. He was entered as a student in the Middle Temple in 1708, and soon after was introduced to Lord Macclesfield, who recognized his merit and employed him as the tutor of his sons. In 1712 he wrote a letter, signed Philip Homebred, which was inserted in the "Spectator," No. 364. Admitted to the bar in 1715, he rapidly acquired an extensive practice. In 1719, by the favour of Macclesfield, then lord chancellor, Mr. Yorke obtained a seat in the House of Commons. He was appointed solicitor-general in 1720, and attorney-general in 1724. In 1733 he became lord chief justice of the king's bench, and was raised to the peerage, as Baron Hardwicke. In 1737 he was promoted to the dignity of lord chancellor, which he retained nearly twenty years, discharging the functions of that office with such wisdom and justice as to obtain universal approbation. None of his decrees was ever reversed. He was made Earl of Hardwicke and Viscount Royston in 1754. In 1756 he resigned the great seal and retired to private life. "He is deservedly considered," says Lord Campbell, "the most consummate

judge who ever sat in the court of chancery." As a statesman he was consistent and upright, and a supporter of Sir Robert Walpole. Died in 1764. His second son, CHARLES, became lord chancellor of England.

See GEORGE HARRIS, "Life of Lord Chancellor Hardwicke," 1847; LORD CAMPBELL, "Lives of the Lord Chancellors;" Foss, "The Judges of England;" "Blackwood's Magazine" for April, 1848.

Hardwicke, (PHILIP YORKE,) second EARL OF, eldest son of the preceding, was born in 1720. He made a respectable figure in literature and politics, and was attached to the Whig party. He was returned to Parliament in 1741, in 1747, and again in 1754. In 1765 he was a member of council during the short administration of Lord Rockingham. He also officiated as high-steward of the University of Cambridge. He published "Miscellaneous State Papers," and was one of the authors of the celebrated "Athenian Letters," (1741.) (See YORKE, CHARLES.) Died in 1796.

Hardwicke, (PHILIP YORKE,) third EARL OF, born in 1757, was the eldest son of Charles Yorke, lord chancellor of England. He succeeded to the earldom at the death of his uncle, in 1796. From 1801 to 1805 he governed Ireland with wisdom and justice as lord lieutenant. He was a Fellow of the Royal Society. He died, without male issue, in 1834, and the title passed to his nephew.

Hardy, *hăr'de'*, (ALEXANDRE,) a French dramatic author and actor, born in Paris, lived in the reigns of Henry IV. and Louis XIII. He was reputed the first French tragic writer of his time; but his works are not highly appreciated at present. "'Mariamne' is the most tolerable of his tragedies," says Hallam. Died about 1630. He left about six hundred dramas, some of which are comedies.

Hardy, (ANTOINE FRANÇOIS,) a French revolutionist, born at Rouen in 1756. In the National Convention he acted with the Girondists in 1793. Died in 1823.

Hardy, (CLAUDE,) a French linguist and geometer, born at Mans about 1600, published a Greek edition of the "Data" of Euclid, (1625,) with a Latin version. He was a friend of Descartes, who esteemed him highly. Died in 1678.

Har'dy̆, (GATHORNE,) an English Conservative politician, born in Yorkshire in 1814. He became a member of the cabinet, as president of the poor-law board, in July, 1866, and resigned with his colleagues in December, 1868. He represents (1869) Oxford University in Parliament.

Hardy, (J.,) a French general, born at Pont-à-Mousson, Lorraine, in 1763; died in 1802.

Hardy, (PETER,) an English mathematician and actuary, born in Jamaica about 1812. He distinguished himself in the practical application of mathematics and in the compilation of tables for life-assurance companies.

Hardy, (THOMAS DUFFUS,) an English writer, born in Jamaica in 1804, edited several ancient manuscripts in the Rolls collection, and published a "Life of Lord Langdale," (2 vols., 1852.)

Hardy, (Sir THOMAS MASTERMAN,) an English naval officer, born near Dorchester in 1769. For his brave conduct at the battle of Saint Vincent he was made commander in 1797. In 1803 he became flag-captain to Admiral Nelson; and at the battle of Trafalgar, in 1805, Captain Hardy was one of the officers of Nelson's flag-ship, the Victory. When Nelson was dying, he sent for Hardy, to whom he was warmly attached, and said, "Don't throw me overboard: kiss me, Hardy." From 1820 to 1824 he commanded the South American squadron. In 1830 he was appointed a lord of the admiralty, and in 1834 governor of Greenwich Hospital. Died in 1839.

Hardy-Canute. See HARDICANUTE.

Hardyng. See HARDING, (JOHN.)

Hăre, (AUGUSTUS WILLIAM,) an English divine, born at Rome in 1792. He became rector of Alton-Barnes in 1829, after he had produced, in conjunction with his brother, Julius Charles, "Guesses at Truth." He composed two volumes of Sermons, (1837,) which have been often reprinted, and which, says the "London Quarterly Review," vol. lix., "are compositions of very rare merit in their kind." Died in Rome in 1834.

Hare, (FRANCIS,) an English bishop, born in London. He obtained the deanery of Worcester in 1708, and that

---

e as k; ç as s; ğ hard; ġ as j; G, H, K, *guttural;* N, *nasal;* R, *trilled;* ŝ as z; ʇh as in *this.* (☞See Explanations, p. 23.)

of Saint Paul's in 1726. In 1731 he became Bishop of Chichester. He wrote an "Essay on the Difficulties and Discouragements that attend the Study of Scripture," and other learned works. His essay just named was censured by the convocation of divines as tending to skepticism. Died in 1740.

Hare, (HENRY,) Lord Coleraine, an English antiquary and linguist, born in Surrey in 1693 ; died in 1749.

Hare, (JOHN INNES CLARK,) son of Robert Hare, the distinguished chemist, was born in Philadelphia in 1817. He studied law, and, in conjunction with the late Horace Binney Wallace, published about 1852 "American Leading Cases in Law," (2 vols.,) Smith's "Leading Cases," (fourth American from third London edition, 2 vols.,) and White and Tudor's "Leading Cases in Equity," (3 vols.) The American notes to these works are thorough and exhaustive, and are highly esteemed by legal critics. In 1851 Mr. Hare was elected associate judge of the district court of Philadelphia, and became afterwards presiding judge in the same court.

Hare, (JULIUS CHARLES,) an eminent English divine, born in 1796, was grandson of Bishop Francis Hare. Having graduated at Cambridge in 1819, he took holy orders. In 1827 he acquired distinction by the publication of "Guesses at Truth," in which he was assisted by his brother, Rev. Augustus William Hare. He became rector of Hurstmonceaux in 1832, Archdeacon of Lewes in 1840, canon of Chichester in 1851, and chaplain to the queen in 1853. His character and literary talents rendered his influence extensive. In the church he was considered one of the leaders of the "broad party" with liberal and moderate principles. He published numerous sermons and controversial works. In conjunction with C. Thirlwall, he translated Niebuhr's "History of Rome." Died in 1855.

See "Gentleman's Magazine" for April, 1855.

Hare, (ROBERT,) a distinguished American chemist, born in Philadelphia January 17, 1781. He discovered, about the age of twenty-one, a mode of producing the most intense heat by the combustion of hydrogen with oxygen, and invented the compound blow-pipe, for which the Rumford medal was awarded him by the American Academy at Boston. In 1818 he was appointed professor of chemistry in the medical department of the University of Pennsylvania. He occupied this chair nearly thirty years, during which he made several useful discoveries in chemistry. In 1816 he invented a galvanic apparatus which he called a Calorimotor, capable of producing intense heat. With an improved form of this apparatus, named a Deflagrator, Professor Silliman succeeded in not merely fusing but in volatilizing carbon. Dr. Hare contributed many treatises to the "American Journal of Science," and other periodicals. Among his other works is "Chemical Apparatus and Manipulations," (1836.) Died in 1858.

See "Lives of Eminent Philadelphians," 1859.

Ha-ree'ree or **Harîrî,** (**Al Kâsem,** ăl kâ'sem,) a popular Arabian author, born at Bassorah about 1055 A.D. He received a liberal education, and at an early age was employed in political affairs. His principal work is his "Macamat," (or "Assemblies,") composed of alternate portions of verse and prose. The author has availed himself of this plan to display by turns the most elegant expressions of the Arabic language, and the most familiar proverbial phrases. The Arabs use the "Macamat" as a dictionary of synonyms, and regard it as the best subject of study in order to penetrate the genius of their language. The character of the "Macamat" is chiefly imaginative and dramatic. It has exercised an immense influence over the nations of Islam, from Bengal to the Atlantic Ocean. The durable popularity of this work may be attributed partly to the knowledge of human nature which it exhibits. Hareeree also composed two treatises on philology, which have come down to us, and are entitled "Molhat-al-Irab" and "Dorrat-al-Gauas," or the "Pearl of the Diver." He was accustomed to read his productions aloud in the portico of the grand mosque of Bassorah, and thus expose them to the ordeal of public opinion. He died in 1122. A complete edition of the "Macamat" was published in Calcutta, (3 vols., 1809-14.) Silvestre de Sacy wrote a commentary on the

"Macamat," (1821.) The same work was translated into Latin by Peiper in 1832, and into German by F. Rückert, 1826. In 1850, Theodore Preston published in London "Macamat, or Rhetorical Anecdotes of Al-Hariri of Basra, translated from the Original Arabic." An excellent translation of the Macamat, by T. Chenery, M.A., appeared in London in 1867.

See LOUIS DELATRE, "Hariri, sa Vie et ses Écrits," in the "Revue Orientale," 1857.

Harel, hă'rĕl', (F. A.,) a French littérateur, born at Rouen in 1790, was a nephew of Luce de Lancival. His "Eulogy on Voltaire" obtained the prize of the French Academy in 1844. Died in 1846.

Harembure. See HARAMBURE.

Haren, van, văn hă'ren, (ONNO ZWIER,) a Dutch poet and statesman of merit, born at Leeuwarden in 1713, was a brother of Willem, noticed below. He was employed as a diplomatist at Aix-la-Chapelle. He was the author of a popular patriotic poem, entitled "The Beggars," ("Les Gueux," 1769.) This derisive appellation was given by their enemies to those who liberated Holland from the power of Spain in the sixteenth century ; and that liberation is the subject of the poem. He also wrote many odes, among which are an "Ode to Liberty," and an "Ode to Commerce." His tragedy of "Agon, Sultan of Bantam," is highly praised by the "Biographie Universelle." Died in 1779.

Haren, van, (WILLEM,) a Dutch diplomatist, born at Leeuwarden in 1626. In 1665 Van Haren and De Witt were associated in the direction of a fleet sent against England. He displayed ability as a negotiator at the treaty of Nymwegen in 1678, and at the peace of Ryswick in 1697. Died in 1708.

Haren, van, (WILLEM,) a Dutch poet, grandson of the preceding, born at Leeuwarden in 1713. He was of a noble family, and filled several public offices with distinction. His reputation is founded chiefly on his poem entitled "The Adventures of Friso," (1741,) of which De Vries remarks that "it is perhaps the only true epic poem which we possess in our language." It is commended for beautiful descriptions, harmony, and pure morality. Van Haren also succeeded in lyric poetry. Voltaire complimented him in verses which begin thus :

"Démosthène au conseil et Pindare au Parnasse,
L'auguste liberté marche devant tes pas."

Died in 1768.

See DE VRIES, "Histoire de la Poésie Hollandaise."

Harenberg, hă'ren-bĕRG', (JOHANN CHRISTOPH,) a German historian and Protestant theologian of great learning, was born at Langenholtzen in 1696. He became professor of ecclesiastic history in the Carolinum of Brunswick. Among his works (in Latin) are "Laws of the Jews in Palestine," (1724,) a "History of the Church of Gandersheim," (1734,) and a "History of the Order of Jesuits," (in German, 1760.) Died in 1774.

See HIRSCHING, "Historisch-literarisches Handbuch."

Har'ford, (JOHN S.,) an English biographer and connoisseur in art, was born near Bristol about 1785. He wrote a "Life of Thomas Burgess, Bishop of Salisbury," and a "Life of Michael Angelo."

Har'grāve, (FRANCIS,) an eminent English lawyer, born in 1741, published an "Argument in Defence of Literary Property," and a "Collection of State Trials." In 1772 he was counsel in the case of Somerset, a fugitive slave, and procured a decision that every slave became free as soon as he touched the soil of Britain. He was afterwards recorder of Liverpool. His legal attainments and ability were highly commended by Lord Lyndhurst. Died in 1821.

Har'grāves, (EDMUND HAMMOND,) an Englishman, noted as the discoverer of gold in Australia, was born at Gosport about 1816. He settled in Australia in his youth, and in 1849 went to California, where he acquired some practical skill in digging gold. Having observed that the gold-region of California resembled a part of New South Wales, he began to explore the latter in February, 1851, and soon discovered rich deposits of gold near the Macquarie River. For this service the colonial government voted him a reward of £10,000. He returned to England in 1854, and published "Australia and its Gold-Fields."

ā, ē, ī, ō, ū, ȳ, *long;* ă, ĕ, ŏ, same, less prolonged; ä, ē, ī, ŏ, ŭ, ȳ, *short;* a, e, i, o, *obscure;* fär, fäll, fät; mēt; nŏt; gōōd; mōōn;

Hargreaves, har′greevz, (JAMES,) an English operative, who invented the spinning-jenny about 1768.

See HENRY HOWE, "Lives of Eminent American and European Mechanics."

Hăr′ĭ or **Hĕr′ĭ**, [modern Hindoo pron. hŭr′ee,] a Sanscrit word signifying "green," and forming one of the many names of VISHNU, which see.

Haring, hä′ring, (DAVID,) a Dutch portrait-painter, born in 1636, worked at the Hague with great success, and was director of the Academy there. Died in 1706.

Häring or **Haering,** hä′ring, (WILHELM,) a popular German novelist, born at Breslau in 1798, is widely known under the assumed name of WILIBALD ALEXIS. He produced in 1823 "Walladmor," a novel, which he announced as a translation from Sir Walter Scott, and which had great success. He published a book of travels, called "Excursions in the South," (1828,) and numerous historical novels. His novel "Cabanis" (6 vols., 1832) is called his best work. Among his later productions are "Roland of Berlin," (1840,) and "Dorothee," (1855.)

See BROCKHAUS, "Conversations-Lexikon."

Harington. See HARRINGTON.
Hariot. See HARRIOT, (THOMAS.)
Harîrî. See HAREEREE.

Harispe, hȧ′rèsp′, (JEAN ISIDORE,) COUNT, a French general, born in Basse-Pyrénées in 1768. He distinguished himself in many actions in the Peninsula, and was made a general of division in 1810. During the Hundred Days he took the field for Napoleon. He became a peer of France in 1835, and was raised to the rank of marshal in 1851. Died in 1855.

Har′ker, (CHARLES G.,) an American general, born in New Jersey about 1836. He graduated at West Point in 1858. He served as colonel at Stone River, December 31, 1862–January 2, 1863, distinguished himself at the battle of Chickamauga, September 19–20, 1863, and was killed at Kenesaw in June, 1864.

Har′lan, (RICHARD,) an American naturalist, born in Philadelphia in 1796, graduated as M.D. at the University of Pennsylvania in 1817. Among his principal works is "Fauna Americana," (1825.) Died at New Orleans in 1843.

See "Encyclopædia Americana," (Supplement.)

Harlay, de, dęh hȧR′lạ′, (ACHILLE,) a French judge, noted for his learning, integrity, and loyalty, was born in Paris in 1536, and was son-in-law of De Thou. He became first president of the Parliament of Paris in 1582, and firmly opposed the factious designs of the League a few years later. After the death of Henry III., in 1589, he promoted the cause of Henry IV., and opposed ultramontane doctrines. He is called one of the greatest men who have illustrated the French magistracy. Died in 1616.

See DE LA VALLÉE, "Éloge de M. de Harlay," 1624; DE THOU, "Histoire;" "Nouvelle Biographie Générale."

Harlay, de, (ACHILLE,) a French judge, noted for his learning and caustic wit, was born in Paris in 1639, and was chosen first president of the Parliament of Paris in 1689. Died in 1712.

See SAINT-SIMON, "Mémoires."

Harlay de Chanvalon, hȧR′lạ′ dęh shŏn′vȧ′lôn′, (FRANÇOIS,) a French courtier and prelate, born in Paris in 1625, became Archbishop of Paris in 1670. He obtained the favour of Louis XIV., was hostile to the Jansenists, and persecuted the Protestants. He was a member of the French Academy. Died in 1695.

See LEGENDRE, "Vie de Harlay," 1720; SAINT-SIMON, "Mémoires."

Hårleman. See HORLEMAN.

Harless or **Harles,** haR′lĕss, (CHRISTIAN FRIEDRICH,) a German physician, son of Gottlieb C. Harless, was born at Erlangen in 1773. He was professor of medicine at Bonn from 1818 until 1853. He wrote, besides other works, a "History of Cephalology and Neurology in Antiquity," (1801.) Died in 1853.

Harless or **Harles,** (GOTTLIEB CHRISTOPH,) a learned German philologist, born at Culmbach in 1740. He became professor of eloquence at Erlangen in 1770, and wrote numerous Latin works, the most important of which are "The Lives of Philologists of the Present Age," (4 vols., 1764–72,) an "Introduction to the History of the Greek Language," (1778,) and a new edition of the "Bibliotheca Græca" of Fabricius, (12 vols., 1790–1810.) Died in 1815.

See C. F. HARLES, "Vita Viri amplissimi T. C. Harles," Erlangen, 1818.

Harless, (GOTTLIEB CHRISTOPH ADOLF,) an influential German Protestant theologian, born at Nuremberg in 1806. He was professor of theology at Erlangen from 1836 to 1845, and acquired eminence as a pulpit orator and an author. Among his works are a "Commentary on the Epistle to the Ephesians," (1834,) a volume of sermons entitled "Christi Reich und Christi Kraft," (1840,) and "Christian Ethics," (1842,) which has been often reprinted. In 1852 he became president of the Consistory of Munich. Died in 1862.

Harleville, (COLLIN D'.) See COLLIN-HARLEVILLE.

Har′ley, (ROBERT,) Earl of Oxford, born in London in 1661, was the son and heir of Sir Edward Harley, a Puritan officer, who fought against Charles I. in the civil war. At the Revolution Sir Edward and his son raised a troop of horse for the Prince of Orange. In 1689 Robert obtained a seat in Parliament, where at first he acted with the Whigs. However, he often voted with the opposition, and by degrees became identified with the Tories. He acquired great influence in the House by his industry, gravity, and political artifice, and after a few years was recognized as one of the leaders of his party. He was chosen Speaker of the House of Commons in 1701, and again in 1702.

In 1704 this wily politician became secretary of state, probably through the influence of his cousin, Mrs. Masham, who was the favourite of Queen Anne. Harley, with his ally Bolingbroke, resigned in 1708, in consequence of the enmity of Marlborough and Godolphin, whom he attempted to supplant and who insisted on his dismissal. In 1710, a change of the ministry having occurred, Harley was appointed chancellor of the exchequer. In 1711 a French emissary named Guiscard, while being examined before the privy council, stabbed Harley with a pen-knife and wounded him slightly. This affair rendered him more popular; and soon after he was made Earl of Oxford and of Mortimer and lord high treasurer. The most important event of his administration is the peace of Utrecht, in 1713. The rivalry which had existed between the premier and his colleague Bolingbroke resulted in the dismissal of the former in July, 1714; and the death of Queen Anne, a few days after, ruined his political prospects. In 1715 he was impeached by the Commons, and sent to the Tower, in which he was confined nearly two years. While in prison he maintained a treasonable correspondence with the Stuart family. In 1717 he was acquitted and released. Died in 1724. "His influence in Parliament," says Macaulay, "was altogether out of proportion to his abilities. His intellect was both small and slow." He was the patron of Pope and Swift. His valuable collection of manuscripts was purchased by Parliament, and now forms part of the British Museum, with the name of the Harleian Collection. His private character is said to have been strictly moral; but he was justly distrusted by both parties for his duplicity. Pope said, "Oxford was not a very capable minister, and had a good deal of negligence into the bargain."

See MACAULAY, "History of England," vol. iv.; LORD MAHON, "History of England;" DUCHESS OF MARLBOROUGH, "Account of her own Life."

Har′lŏw, (GEORGE HENRY,) an English historical and portrait painter, born in London in 1787, studied with Sir Thomas Lawrence. He acquired great executive facility, and was very successful in portraits. In 1818 he visited Rome, where in the short space of eighteen days he produced a copy of Raphael's "Transfiguration." Among his chief works is "The Trial of Queen Catherine," the prominent characters of which are portraits of the Kemble family. He died in 1819.

Harmand, hȧR′mŏN′, (JEAN BAPTISTE,) a French revolutionist, of the moderate party, a member of the Convention, 1792–94, born at Souilly (Meuse) in 1751; died in 1816.

ᴇ as k; ç as s; ḡ hard; ġ as j; G, H, K, guttural; N, nasal; R, trilled; s as z; ᴛh as in this. (☞See Explanations, p. 23.)

Harmansen, haʀ'män-sẹn, (WOLPHART,) born about 1550, commanded a Dutch commercial expedition sent to the East Indies in 1601. Died about 1610.

Har'mạr, (JOHN,) a learned English divine, born in 1594, was chosen professor of Greek at Oxford in 1650. He published "Lexicon Etymologicon Græcum," (1637,) and other works. Died in 1670.

Harmenopule. See HARMENOPULUS.

Har-men-o-pū'lus, [Fr. HARMENOPULE, hǎʀ'mẹh-no'pül',] (CONSTANTIN,) a noted Greek jurist, born in Constantinople about 1320. He held the high offices of councillor, curopalate, and grand chancellor under the emperor John Palæologus. He wrote a "Manual of Laws," (Πρόχειρον τῶν νόμων,) a work of high authority among the Greeks, and a treatise on canon law. Died in 1383.

Har'mẹr, (THOMAS,) a learned English dissenting minister, born at Norwich in 1715. He had charge of the Independent church in Wattesfield, in Suffolk, from 1735 to 1788. He published, besides other works, "Observations on Various Passages of Scripture, placing them in a New Light, compiled from Relations incidentally mentioned in Books of Travels in the East," (1764,) which is esteemed an able and useful work. An enlarged edition of it was published in 4 vols. (1816) by Dr. Adam Clarke. Died in 1788.

Har-mo'dĭ-us, [Gr. Ἁρμόδιος,] a young Athenian, who, with his friend Aristogi'ton, acquired celebrity by a conspiracy against the Pisistratidæ, Hippias and Hipparchus, who held the chief power in Athens about 525 B.C. Harmodius having received a personal affront from Hipparchus, the two friends conspired to revenge this by the death of both the brothers, and chose the occasion of a public festival for the execution of their design. They first attacked and killed Hipparchus, whose guards then slew Harmodius and arrested Aristogiton, who was afterwards put to death by the order of Hippias. The latter, having become tyrannical and unpopular, was expelled from the state about three years after that event, 511 B.C. Statues were erected at the public expense to the memory of the conspirators, who were regarded as heroes and martyrs of liberty. It is said that when the tyrant Dionysius asked Antipho which was the finest kind of brass, he replied, "That of which the statues of Harmodius and Aristogiton are formed."

Har-mo'nĭ-ạ, [Gr. Ἁρμονία; Fr. HARMONIE, ǎʀ'-mo'ne',] in classic mythology, a personification of the order or harmony of the universe, said to be a daughter of Mars and Venus, (or, according to some authorities, of Jupiter and Electra,) and a wife of Cadmus. She received on her wedding-day, from some of the gods, a rich necklace, which proved fatal to every person who successively possessed it.

See SMITH, "Greek and Roman Biography and Mythology."

Harmonie. See HARMONIA.

Harms, härmz, (CLAUDE,) a Danish theologian, born at Fahrstedt (Holstein) in 1778. He was an adversary of rationalism, and became principal pastor of Kiel in 1835. Among his most important works are "Pastoral Theology," (3 vols., 1834,) and "The Augsburg Confession," (1847.) Died in 1855.

Har'ness, (WILLIAM,) an English theologian and dramatist, born in Hampshire in 1790.

Har'nett, (CORNELIUS,) an American statesman, born in England in 1723. He became a citizen of North Carolina before the Revolution, in which he took a prominent part against the British government. He was elected to the Congress at Halifax in 1776, after which he was a member of the Continental Congress. Died in 1781.

Har'ney, (WILLIAM SELBY,) an American general, born in Tennessee in 1800. He became a captain in 1825, served in the Florida war, and obtained the rank of colonel in 1846. He took part in several battles in Mexico, (1846–47,) and was raised to the rank of brigadier-general in 1858. As military commandant of Oregon, in 1859, he occupied the island of San Juan, (on the west coast of North America,) which was claimed by the British. He was soon after removed from his command.

Harnisch, haʀ'nish, (WILHELM,) a meritorious German teacher and educational reformer, born at Wilsnach,

near Potsdam, in 1787. He was preceptor to the princess Charlotte, afterwards Empress of Russia. Among his chief works are a "Manual of Popular Instruction," (1820,) and "Cosmology," ("Die Weltkunde," 4th edition, 1827, 3 vols.)

Haro, de, dä ä'ro, (JUAN,) a Spanish historical painter, born in Castile. He was living at Madrid in 1604.

Haro, de, (Don LUIS,) a Spanish minister of state, born at Valladolid in 1598. He was the son of the Marquis of Carpio, and a nephew of the famous Duke of Olivares, whom in 1644 he succeeded as prime minister and favourite of Philip IV. He carried on a disastrous war against France, Portugal, and the Dutch for many years, and in 1659 signed, with the French minister Mazarin, the treaty of the Pyrenees. The king rewarded him for his services by erecting the marquisate of Carpio into a dukedom. He is represented to have directed the arduous affairs of state with prudence and ability. Died in 1661.

See ERSCH und GRUBER, "Allgemeine Encyklopaedie."

Hǎr'ọld I., surnamed HAREFOOT, King of England, was the second son of Canute the Great by Algiva, daughter of the Earl of Northampton. At the death of Canute, in 1035, Harold and Hardicanute (son of Queen Emma) were the chief competitors for the throne of England, which their father, on his marriage with Emma, had agreed to leave to her issue. But Harold had the advantage of possession, and was recognized by the Danes and people of Mercia. (See HARDICANUTE.) In 1037, Alfred, the younger son of Emma, having invaded the country and been defeated and killed, Harold became King of all England. He died in 1040, and was succeeded by Hardicanute.

Harold II., King of England, was a son of Godwin, Earl of Kent, a powerful Saxon nobleman. On the death of Godwin, in 1053, he inherited with his father's talents the earldom of Kent. Having been appointed commander of the army of the king, Edward the Confessor, he gained victories over the Welsh about 1062. He was thrown by a storm on the coast of France about 1065, and became the prisoner of William, Duke of Normandy, who, as a condition of his liberation, required Harold to swear that on the death of Edward the Confessor he would aid William to obtain the throne of England. Edward died in January, 1066, and Harold was proclaimed king by the assembly of thanes and the citizens of London, without opposition from any native competitor except his own brother, Tostig. The Norman duke demanded that Harold should surrender to him the crown; but he refused to be bound by an oath which was extorted from him by force. In September, 1066, Harold gained a complete victory over Tostig and the King of Norway, who had invaded England. Three days after this battle, the Duke of Normandy landed in Sussex with an army of about 60,000 men, which Harold encountered at Senlac, (now Battle,) near Hastings, on the 14th of October, 1066. After a long and obstinate combat, in which Harold and his two brothers were killed, William gained a decisive victory, which rendered him master of England.

See FREEMAN, "History of the Norman Conquest of England;" HUME, "History of England;" AUGUSTIN THIERRY, "Histoire de la Conquête de l'Angleterre;" WILLIAM OF MALMESBURY, "History of the Kings of England."

Hǎr'ọld (or Harald) Harfager, (har'fä'gẹr, almost har'fä'hẹr,) a king of Norway, whose reign is considered to mark the commencement of authentic Norwegian history. About 895 he subdued the jarls, or petty chieftains, and united the various sections of Norway into one kingdom. He reigned above thirty years, and left his crown to his son, Haco (or Haquin) the Good, who first introduced Christianity into Norway.

Haroun-al-Raschid,[*] hä-rōōn' äl räsh'id, or, more correctly, **Haroon-ar-Rasheed,** (or **Harûn-ar-Rashîd,**) hä-rōōn' ạr-rä-sheed', the most celebrated of the Eastern caliphs, and the most powerful sovereign of the dynasty of the Abbassides, was born about 766 A.D. He was a son of the caliph Mahdee, (Mahdî,) and succeeded

[*] In this instance we have departed from our general rule of spelling according to the sound of Oriental names. The spelling *Haroun* seems to have become, indeed, a part of the English language.

his elder brother Hadee (Hadi) in 786. In the early part of his reign the Barmecides Yahia and Jaafar were his favourite ministers. About 804 A.D. he waged a successful war against the Byzantine emperor Nicephorus, whom he compelled to pay tribute. Haroun was a liberal patron of poets and scholars; but he scarcely merited the surname of Ar-Rasheed, ("the Just.") (See JAAFAR.) He is chiefly renowned as the principal hero of the "Arabian Nights' Entertainments." Died in 809 A.D.

See ABOOLFEDA, "Annales Moslemici;" ABOOLFARAJ, (ABUL-PHARAGIUS,) "Historia Dynastiarum;" WEIL, "Geschichte der Chalifen;" ELMACIN, "Historia Saracenica."

Har'pa-gus, [Gr. Ἅρπαγος,] a noble Mede, said to have saved the life of Cyrus the Great. Afterwards, under Cyrus, he reduced several Greek cities of Ionia.

Har'pa-lus, [Gr. Ἅρπαλος,] a Macedonian whom Alexander the Great made satrap of Babylon and intrusted with the care of his accumulated treasures on his departure for India. Harpalus abused his trust, and, when he heard that his master was returning, fled to Athens with a large sum of money. The Athenians being unable or unwilling to protect him against Antipater, Alexander's lieutenant, who demanded that he should be given up, he retired to Crete, where he was killed in 324 B.C. Demosthenes, having advocated his cause, was tried on a charge of bribery and fined.

See THIRLWALL, "History of Greece."

Har-păl'ў-çe, [Gr. Ἁρπαλύκη,] daughter of Harpal'ycus, King of Thrace, was distinguished for her courageous defence of her father's kingdom against Neoptolemus, the son of Achilles.

Harpe, La. See LA HARPE.

Har'pẹr, (JAMES,) an American publisher, born at Newton, Long Island, in 1795. He and several of his brothers founded in New York the great publishing house of Harper & Brothers about 1825. He was elected mayor of New York in 1844. Died in 1869.

Harper, (ROBERT GOODLOE,) an eminent lawyer and Senator of the United States, born near Fredericksburg, Virginia, in 1765. After graduating at Princeton, New Jersey, in 1785, he studied law in Charleston, South Carolina, and settled in the interior of that State. From 1795 to 1800 he represented one of the districts of South Carolina in the National Congress, of which he was one of the most prominent members and one of the ablest debaters. In the latter part of this period he was the principal leader of the Federal party in the House of Representatives. In 1801 he retired from office, married the daughter of Charles Carroll, and settled in Baltimore, where he resumed the practice of law. He was employed as counsel for the defence in the impeachment of Judge Chase, of the supreme court of the United States, who was acquitted. In 1815 he was elected a Senator of the United States by the legislature of Maryland. A volume of his speeches, arguments, and letters was published in 1814. John Neal, in "Blackwood's Magazine," says, "His writings are energetic, manly, profound. We hold him to be one of the ablest men that North America has produced." Died in 1825.

Harper, (WILLIAM,) an American lawyer and politician, born in the island of Antigua in 1790. He settled in Missouri in 1818, removed to South Carolina in 1823, and became a Senator of the United States in 1826. He was appointed a judge of the court of appeals in 1831, and elected chancellor in 1834. Died in 1847.

Harphius, haR'fe-ŭs, (HENRY,) an eminent Flemish mystic theologian, born at Erp or Herp, was superior of a Franciscan abbey at Malines, where he died in 1478. He wrote the "Eden of the Contemplative," "The Mirror of Perfection," and other religious works.

Har'pies, [Gr. Ἅρπυιαι; Lat. HAR'PYIÆ; Fr. HAR-PYES, äR'pe',] winged monsters of classic mythology, regarded as the daughters of Neptune, and supposed by some to be personified storm-winds. They polluted all that they touched.

See VIRGIL's "Æneid," book iii. 212-262.

Har-poc'ra-tēs or **Har'po-krat,** a divinity of the ancient Egyptians, sometimes identified with Horus, and called the god of silence or secrecy. He was represented as holding a finger on his mouth.

Har-po-crā'tǐ-on, [Gr. Ἁρποκρατίων,] (VALERIUS,) a Greek rhetorician of Alexandria, of whose life scarcely anything is known. He appears to have lived in or after the second century. He wrote a very important work, called "Lexicon for the Ten Orators," (Λεξικὸν τῶν δέκα ῥητόρων,) which is extant. He explains in this the political and other terms used by the Athenian orators, and affords much valuable information on the public and civil law and history of Athens.

Harps'field or **Harps'feld,** (NICHOLAS,) an English Catholic, born in London, was chosen professor of Greek in Oxford in 1546, and Archdeacon of Canterbury in 1554. He wrote an "English Ecclesiastical History." He was imprisoned about twenty years during the reign of Elizabeth. Died about 1582.

Harpyes. See HARPIES.

Harpyiæ. See HARPIES.

Harring, hăr'ring, (HARRO PAUL,) a writer, born near Husum, Denmark, in 1798. He travelled in many countries, and was several times arrested as a conspirator and revolutionist. He wrote several dramas and other works of fiction, and "Memoirs of Poland under Russian Domination," (in French, 1831.)

Här'ring-ton, (CHARLES STANHOPE,) EARL OF, born in England in 1753, was previously styled LORD PETERS-HAM. He entered the army in 1769, and was returned to Parliament in 1776. At the death of his father, about 1778, he became a member of the House of Lords. He served in several campaigns in America and in the West Indies, and was aide-de-camp to General Burgoyne at the capitulation of Saratoga. After his return he became aide-de-camp to the king, George III., in 1792 a colonel of the life-guards, and in 1798 lieutenant-general. About 1802 he was envoy-extraordinary to Berlin. From 1807 to 1812 he commanded the army in Ireland. Died in 1829.

Harrington, (HENRY,) an English physician and poet, born at Kelston in 1729, resided at Bath. He published "An Ode to Harmony," "An Ode to Discord," and a few other works. Died in 1816.

Harrington, (JAMES,) an English author, born at Upton in 1611, was educated at Oxford under Dr. Chillingworth. In youth he made the tour of the continent. In 1646 he officiated as groom of the bed-chamber to Charles I., then a prisoner, whom he attended at his execution. In 1656 he published his principal work, entitled "Oceana," which attracted much attention and was greatly admired. It is a political allegory, exhibiting, in imitation of Plato's "Atlantis," the plan or model of an ideal republic, named Oce'ana, which is supposed to represent England. His project was generally considered visionary, impracticable, and Utopian. Hume said, "It is justly admired as a work of genius and invention;" while Hallam thinks that the author "is in general prolix, dull, pedantic, yet seldom profound." He was arrested in 1661 on a charge of treason, and (though the case was never brought to trial) closely confined until he became deranged. The cause of his arrest was probably his avowed republican principles. Died in 1677.

See TOLAND, "Life of James Harrington," prefixed to his Works, 1700; "Biographia Britannica;" WOOD, "Athenæ Oxonienses."

Harrington, (JAMES,) an English lawyer, born in 1664, contributed some Latin verses to the "Musæ Anglicanæ," and wrote the preface to the first volume of Wood's "Athenæ." Died in 1693.

Harrington or **Harington,** (JOHN,) of Stepney, an English poet, born in 1534. He wrote elegant "Verses on Isabella Markham," dated about 1564. "If these are genuine," says Hallam, "they are as polished as any written at the close of the queen's reign." Died in 1582.

Harrington, (SIR JOHN,) an English poet and courtier, a son of the preceding, was born at or near Bath in 1561. He became a favourite of Queen Elizabeth. He was the author of an admired English version of Ariosto's "Orlando Furioso," (1591.) He wrote numerous epigrams, which were published in 1615, a "Brief View of the State of the Church," and other works. About 1600 he served under the Earl of Essex as commander of the horse. Died in 1612.

See "Life of Sir J. Harrington," prefixed to his "Nugæ Antiquæ," 2 vols., 1804.

€ as k; ç as s; g̃ hard; g̃ as j; G, H, K, guttural; N, nasal; R, trilled; ŝ as z; ᵺh as in this.   (☞ See Explanations, p. 23.)

Här'rĭ-ǫtt or **Harriot,** (THOMAS,) an eminent English mathematician, born at Oxford in 1560. He visited Virginia in the service of Sir Walter Raleigh (who had been his pupil) in 1584, and published an Account of that province in 1588. He was liberally patronized by the Earl of Northumberland, in whose house he spent the latter part of his life. Harriott was noted for skill in algebra, his treatise on which, entitled "Artis Analyticæ Praxis," was published in 1631. It is said that he observed the satellites of Jupiter in 1610, a few days after Galileo first discovered them, and that he was the first who detected the spots on the sun, December 8, 1610. "Harriott was destined," says Hallam, " to make the last great discovery in the pure science of algebra. He arrived at a complete theory of the genesis of equations, which Cardan and Vieta had but partially conceived." ("Introduction to the Literature of Europe.") Died in 1621.

See MONTUCLA, "Histoire des Mathématiques;" "Biographia Britannica;" ERSCH und GRUBER, "Allgemeine Encyklopaedie."

Här'ris, (GEORGE,) a son of the Bishop of Llandaff, published an English version of Justinian's "Institutiones," (1756.) Died in 1796.

Harris, (GEORGE,) LORD, an English general, born at Brasted in 1746, entered the army in 1759. As captain, he took part in the battle of Bunker Hill in 1775, where he was severely wounded, and in that of Long Island, (1776.) In 1790–91 he served in India against Tippoo Sultan, and in 1794 was promoted to the rank of major-general. About four years later he was appointed Governor of the Madras Presidency, and commanded the army which was sent against Tippoo and which captured Seringapatam. For his services he was rewarded by a peerage, as Lord Harris of Seringapatam and Mysore. Died in 1829.

See S. R. LUSHINGTON, "Life of General Lord Harris."

Harris, (JAMES,) an English author, born at Salisbury in 1709, was the son of James Harris and of Lady Cooper, who was sister of Lord Shaftesbury. He was an excellent classical scholar. In 1761 he obtained a seat in Parliament, and in 1763 became a lord of the treasury, and in 1774 secretary and controller to the queen. In 1751 he published his "Hermes; or, A Philosophical Inquiry concerning Language and Universal Grammar," which, according to Coleridge, is "written with the precision of Aristotle and the elegance of Quintilian." He wrote three treatises, viz., on "Art," on "Music, Painting, and Poetry," and on "Happiness." Died in 1780.

See " Life of James Harris," by LORD MALMESBURY, 1801.

Harris, (JAMES,) first Earl of Malmesbury, an able diplomatist, born at Salisbury in 1746, was the only son of the preceding. He was educated at Oxford and Leyden, and in 1767 was appointed secretary of embassy at Madrid. A few years after, being left as chargé-d'affaires in the same court, he acquitted himself so well in an important affair that he received in 1772 the mission to Prussia, and in 1777 that to Saint Petersburg, from which he returned home in 1784. Although he was a political friend of Fox, he received from Pitt, then premier, the appointment of minister to the Hague, where he negotiated, in 1788, a treaty with Holland and Prussia. The same year he was created Baron Malmesbury. In 1793 he joined the Tory or Conservative party. He was subsequently employed on missions to Berlin and the French republic, in which he maintained his reputation as a skilful diplomatist. In 1800 he was raised to the rank of Earl of Malmesbury and Viscount Fitzharris. He died in 1820, leaving one son and several daughters. The present earl is his grandson. Since his death his " Diaries and Correspondence" has been published.

See " London Quarterly Review" for October, 1844, and March, 1845.

Harris, (JAMES HOWARD.) See MALMESBURY, EARL OF.

Harris, (JOHN,) D.D., an English divine, born about 1667, became prebendary of Rochester. He was secretary and vice-president of the Royal Society. Besides a variety of scientific works, he published a valuable "Collection of Voyages and Travels." His "Dictionary of Arts and Sciences," (1704,) explaining both the terms of art and the arts themselves, was the prototype, it is said, of all the cyclopædias which have since appeared. Died in 1719.

Harris, (JOHN,) D.D., an English dissenting minister, born at Ugborough in 1804. After preaching for the Independent Church at Epsom, he became in 1837 professor of theology in Cheshunt College. About 1850 he was appointed principal of New College, the chief theological seminary of the Independents. Dr. Harris was a popular preacher, and acquired a wide reputation as an author. Among his chief works are "The Great Teacher," (1835,) "Covetousness the Sin of the Christian Church," of which ninety thousand copies had been sold in 1856, "The Great Commission," (1842,) "The Pre-Adamite Earth," (1847,) and "Man Primeval." Died in 1856.

Harris, (JOSEPH,) an astronomer, and assay-master of the English mint, wrote an "Essay on Money and Coins," (1757,) a "Treatise on Optics," etc. Died in 1764.

Harris, (MOSES,) an English naturalist and artist, published in 1766 "The Aurelian; or, Natural History of English Moths and Butterflies," and an "Exposition of English Insects," (1776.)

Harris, (ROBERT,) D.D., an eminent English Puritan divine, born in Gloucestershire in 1578. He was president of Trinity College, Oxford, from 1648 to 1658. He was a popular preacher, and a man of excellent gifts and graces. He published a volume of Sermons, Letters, etc. Died in 1658.

See DURHAM, "Life of Robert Harris," 1660.

Här'ris, (THADDEUS MASON,) born at Charlestown, Massachusetts, in 1768, was pastor of a Congregational church in Dorchester from 1793 until his death in 1842. He published, besides many sermons and other works, a "Natural History of the Bible."

Harris, (THADDEUS WILLIAM,) M.D., an eminent entomologist, a son of the preceding, was born in 1795. He graduated at Harvard College in 1815, and was librarian at that institution from 1831 until his death. I⸗ 1837 he was employed in the Zoological and Botanic⸗ Survey of Massachusetts. He wrote, besides other work⸗, an official "Report on the Insects of Massachusetts Injurious to Vegetation," (1841.) Died in 1856.

Harris, (THOMAS L.,) a spiritualistic poet and preacher, born in England, emigrated in early life to the United States. Among his works is an "Épic of the Starry Heavens," (1854.)

Harris or **Harries,** (WALTER,) an English physician, born at Gloucester in 1647, began to practise in London in 1676, and was chosen physician to William III. about 1689. He wrote several professional treatises. Died in 1725.

Harris, (WILLIAM,) D.D., an English divine, born in 1675, was minister of a dissenting church in London. He published "Practical Discourses on the Principal Representatives of the Messiah," (1724,) and assisted in the continuation of Matthew Henry's "Commentary on the Bible." "He was reckoned," says Doddridge, " the greatest master of the English tongue among the dissenters." Died in 1740.

Harris, (WILLIAM,) D.D., an English dissenting minister and biographer, born at Salisbury in 1720. He was successively pastor at Wells and Honiton. He published valuable biographies of Hugh Peters, (1751,) of James I., (1753,) of Charles I., (1758,) of Oliver Cromwell, (1762,) and of Charles II., (1766.) His positions and statements are confirmed by copious notes and original documents. He is commended for his fidelity to the truth by several critics. Died in 1770.

Harris, (Sir WILLIAM CORNWALLIS,) a British officer and writer of travels. He published, in 1839, "Wild Sports in Southern Africa," and afterwards "The Highlands of Ethiopia," (3 vols., 2d edition, 1844.)

Harris, (WILLIAM SNOW,) an English surgeon, distinguished by his researches in physical sciences and by his inventions, was born at Plymouth about 1792. He gave special attention to electricity, magnetism, and meteorology. In 1831 he was chosen a Fellow of the Royal Society, which awarded him the Copley medal in 1835. He invented a new steering-compass, and made important improvements in the construction of conductors of the electric fluid. By a system of metallic conductors applied to the masts and hulls of ships, he greatly diminished the ruinous effects of lightning in the navy. He published "The Nature of Thunder-Storms," (1843,) and "Rudiments of Electricity," (1849.) Died in January, 1867.

Här'rĭ-son, (BENJAMIN,) born at Berkeley, on the James River, Virginia, about 1740, was the father of President William H. Harrison. In 1764 he was a member of the Virginia legislature, and in 1774 was elected to the national Congress, in which he was distinguished for his patriotic services and signed the Declaration of Independence. From 1782 to 1784 he was Governor of Virginia. He was also a member of the convention which framed the Constitution of the United States in 1788. Died in 1791.

See C. A. GOODRICH, "Lives of the Signers to the Declaration of Independence."

Här'rĭ-son, (JOHN,) an English republican general, served in the parliamentary army in the civil war, and was one of the judges of the court in which Charles I. was tried in 1649. He had obtained the rank of major-general, when he became a member of the council of state, in 1653. Cromwell, when Protector, endeavoured to gain his support by the offer of an exalted position; but he refused to co-operate with the "usurper," as he called him. In 1657 he was deprived of his commission and confined. In 1660 he was executed for his share in the death of Charles I. Before the judges who tried him, he spoke with courage and complacency of the act for which he was about to suffer.

Harrison, (JOHN,) an English mechanician, born at Faulby, in Yorkshire, in 1693, learned the trade of a carpenter. He became interested in the mechanism of clocks, in which he made several improvements, the greatest of which was the compound pendulum. In this, the variation of temperature is compensated by the unequal expansibility of different metals. Large rewards having been offered to any one who would ascertain the longitude within sixty miles or less, Harrison, in 1735, exhibited his chronometer to the Royal Society, and a man-of-war was put at his disposal, in which he made a voyage to Lisbon and corrected the reckoning a degree and a half. After repeated trials, he perfected in 1761 a chronometer which determined the longitude within eighteen miles, by which he became entitled to the reward of £20,000 offered by government. After it had been tested in several voyages, and it was found that other persons could construct the instrument, the above premium was paid to Harrison in 1765-67. Died in 1776.

Harrison, (THOMAS,) an English architect, often called HARRISON OF CHESTER, was born at Richmond, Yorkshire, in 1744. He studied at Rome several years, and received there a gold and a silver medal for certain designs. After his return home he resided in Chester, where he built the county courts, and a fine bridge over the Dee. He was also the architect of the Athenæum in Liverpool, of the Exchange and Theatre in Manchester, and of other public buildings. Died in 1829.

Harrison, (WILLIAM,) born in London, became canon of Windsor. He wrote a "Historical Description of the Island of Britain," which contains valuable information respecting manners, customs, etc. Died about 1592.

Harrison, (WILLIAM,) an English scholar and poet, was a Fellow of New College, Oxford. He was a favourite of Swift, who described him as a "pretty fellow, with a great deal of wit, good sense, and good nature." Swift procured for him the office of secretary of embassy to the Hague. Harrison edited the fifth volume of the "Tatler." Died in 1713.

Harrison, (WILLIAM HENRY,) the ninth President of the United States, was born in Charles City county, Virginia, on the 9th of February, 1773. He was a son of Benjamin Harrison, noticed above, and was educated at Hampden-Sidney College. He entered the army in 1791, served as aide-de-camp to General Wayne in the Indian war, and became a captain in 1794. In 1797 he resigned his commission, and in 1799 he was chosen a delegate to Congress for the Northwest Territory. He was appointed Governor of the Territory of Indiana in 1801, and, having been reappointed by several successive Presidents, held that office until 1813, and made many treaties

with the Indians. On the 7th of November, 1811, he defeated the Indians at Tippecanoe. He was appointed a brigadier-general in 1812, and a major-general in the regular army in 1813. In October of that year he gained a complete victory over the British at the battle of the Thames. He represented Cincinnati in Congress in 1817 and 1818, and was elected to the Senate of the United States in 1824. President Adams sent him in 1828 as minister to the republic of Colombia; but he was recalled by General Jackson in the spring of 1829. He passed many subsequent years on his farm at North Bend, on the Ohio River. In 1836 he was the Whig candidate for the Presidency of the United States, and received seventy-three electoral votes, but was defeated by Mr. Van Buren. Having been again nominated by the Whigs, he was elected in 1840 by a large majority over Van Buren, who received only sixty electoral votes out of two hundred and ninety-four, which was the whole number. This political campaign was remarkable for its immense mass-meetings, processions, and novel modes of exciting the people. He entered upon the office March 4, and died April 4, 1841.

See M. DAWSON, "Life of General W. H. Harrison," 1824; JAMES HALL, "Memoir of the Public Services of W. H. Harrison," 1836; S. J. BURR, "Life and Times of W. H. Harrison," 1840; "Life of William Henry Harrison," by ISAAC R. JACKSON; "National Portrait-Gallery of Distinguished Americans," vol. iii.

Här'row-bў, (DUDLEY RYDER,) EARL OF, an English peer and philanthropist, born about 1798. He inherited the earldom at the death of his father in 1847, and was lord privy seal in 1856 and 1857.

Här'rў, BLIND, or **Henry the Minstrel,** a Scottish bard of the fifteenth century, who was blind from his birth, and wrote a heroic poem on the "Adventures of Sir William Wallace." But little is known of the events of his life. It appears that he made a poetical version of the popular traditions in relation to his hero, in which he followed in a humble degree the example of Homer. Some of his statements are confirmed by recent researches into the monuments and records of history. "The work, therefore," says Tytler, "cannot be treated as an entire romance."

See CHAMBERS, "Biographical Dictionary of Eminent Scotsmen."

Harsdörfer or **Harsdoerfer,** haRs'dör'fer, (GEORG PHILIPP,) a German poet, born at Nuremberg in 1607, wrote in German and Latin. Among his works, which are nearly forgotten, are "The Poetical Filter," ("Poetischer Trichter," 3 vols., 1653,) and "Gesprächspiele." Died in 1658.

See ERSCH und GRUBER, "Allgemeine Encyklopaedie;" A. G WIDMANN, "Vitæ Curriculum G. P. Harsdorferi," 1707.

Hars'net, (SAMUEL,) born at Colchester, England, in 1561, became Bishop of Chichester in 1609, and Archbishop of York in 1628. He published a volume of Sermons, and a "Declaration of Popish Impostures," etc. Died in 1631.

Hart, (GEORGE VAUGHAN,) a British general, born in 1752; died in 1832.

Hart, (JAMES M.,) a landscape-painter, born at Kilmarnock, in Scotland, in 1828. He studied at Dusseldorf, and afterwards settled in New York. His "Woods in Autumn," and "Moonrise in the Adirondacks," are among his master-pieces. His brother WILLIAM, also a landscape-painter, born at Paisley about 1820, removed to the United States in 1831. Among his best works are "Peace and Plenty," a harvest scene, and "October's Golden Hours."

See TUCKERMAN, "Book of the Artists."

Hart, (JOEL T.,) an American sculptor, born in Clark county, Kentucky, in 1810. He was a mason or stone-cutter in his youth. In 1849 he visited Italy, where he executed a marble statue of Henry Clay. Among his other works is "Angelina."

See TUCKERMAN, "Book of the Artists."

Hart, (JOHN,) one of the signers of the Declaration of Independence, was the son of Edward Hart, of Hopewell, New Jersey. He was elected to Congress in 1774 by the people of New Jersey. Died in 1780.

Hart, (SOLOMON,) an eminent English historical painter, born at Plymouth in 1806. He produced in 1830 "The Elevation of the Law," (in the Jewish wor-

---

ᵉ as k; ç as s; g̃ hard; g̃ as j; G, H, K, guttural; N, nasal; R, trilled; s̃ as z; ŧh as in this.   (☞See Explanations, p. 23.)

72

ship,) and was elected Royal Academician in 1840. He afterwards exhibited several pictures annually at the Academy, and treated a great variety of subjects with success. Among his works are "Richard and Saladin," (1835,) "The Interior of a Synagogue," "Milton visiting Galileo in Prison," (1847,) and "The Student preparing for Honours," (at Oxford,) (1852.)

Harte, hart, (WALTER,) an English poet and priest, born about 1700, was educated at Oxford, took orders, and became canon of Windsor in 1751. He wrote a poem named an "Essay on Reason," in imitation of Pope, who assisted him in its composition. He wrote also an "Essay on Painting," (in verse,) and "The History of Gustavus Adolphus," (1759.) Dr. Johnson commended him as a scholar and a man of the most companionable talents, and said, "The defects of his History [*i.e.* in respect to the style] proceeded not from imbecility, but from foppery." (Boswell.) His poems were once much admired. His History of Gustavus is prized in respect to the matter. Died in 1774.

See CAMPBELL, "Specimens of the British Poets."

Hartenkeil, haR'ten-kīl', (JOHANN JAKOB,) a German medical writer, born at Mentz in 1761, settled at Salzburg. He published "The Medico-Surgical Gazette," (72 vols., 1790-1808.) Died in 1808.

Hartenstein, haR'ten-stīn', (GUSTAV,) a German philosopher, born at Plauen, Saxony, in 1808. He wrote "The Problems and Principles of General Metaphysics," (1836,) and other treatises, and published an edition of the "Complete Works of Kant," (10 vols., 1839.)

Harthacanute. See HARDICANUTE.

Hartig, haR'tiG, (FRANZ ANTON,) COUNT, a *littérateur*, born at Prague in 1758, wrote, in French, "Letters on France, England, and Italy," (1785,) and "Mélanges of Verse and Prose," (1788.) Died in 1797.

Hartig, haR'tiG, (GEORG LUDWIG,) a German writer on the culture of forests, born near Marburg in 1764. He was appointed grand master of the forests of Prussia in 1811, and published, besides other works, "The Science or Economy of Forests in all its Extent," ("Die Forstwissenschaft nach ihrem ganzen Umfange," 1831,) and a "Manual or Text-Book for Foresters," ("Lehrbuch für Förster," (3 vols., 9th edition, 1851.) Died in 1836.

See "Nouvelle Biographie Générale."

Hartig, (THEODOR,) a German botanist and writer on the culture of forests, was a son of the preceding. He published a "Treatise on Botany and its Application to the Science of Forests," (1840-51,) and other works.

Har'ting-ton, (SPENCER COMPTON CAVENDISH,) MARQUIS OF, an English minister of state, and the eldest son of the Duke of Devonshire, was born in 1833. He graduated at Trinity College, Cambridge, in 1854, was elected to Parliament as a Liberal in 1857, and became under-secretary of war in April, 1863. He was secretary of war from February to July, 1866, and was appointed postmaster-general by Mr. Gladstone in December, 1868.

Hartleben, haRt'lā-ben, (FRANZ JOSEPH,) a German jurist, born at Dusseldorf in 1740; died in 1808.

Hartleben, (THEODOR KONRAD,) a German jurist, a son of the preceding, was born in 1770. From 1816 to 1827 he published a valuable legal review, "Deutsche Justiz- und Polizeifama." Among his works is a "Method or System of German Public Law," (1800.) Died in 1827.

See ERSCH und GRUBER, "Allgemeine Encyklopaedie."

Hart'ley, (DAVID,) an eminent English physician and philosopher, born at Armley, in Yorkshire, in 1705, was educated at Cambridge University. He practised medicine at Newark, London, and Bath. His reputation as an author is founded on an excellent metaphysical work, entitled "Observations on Man : his Frame, his Duty, and his Expectations," (1748.) The design of this work is to investigate the principles of association in application to the phenomena of mind. "Hartley," says Dr. Parr, "has explained the principle of association more accurately and applied it more usefully than even his great predecessor Locke." Dr. Priestley said "he had learned more from Hartley than from any book he had ever read, except the Bible." Died in 1757.

See "Life of D. Hartley," by his son.

Hartley, (DAVID,) a son of the preceding, born in England about 1730, was educated at Oxford. He represented Hull in Parliament for many years, and distinguished himself by his opposition to the American war and to the slave-trade. About 1782 he was appointed plenipotentiary to negotiate with Dr. Franklin, at Paris, a treaty of peace between England and the United States. He wrote "Letters on the American War." Died in 1813.

Hartlib, haRt'lip, (SAMUEL,) a native of Poland, came to England about 1640. He was interested in the practical application of science, was noted for public spirit, and published a treatise on agriculture, for which Cromwell granted him a pension. About the year 1646 Milton addressed a "Treatise on Education" to Hartlib, who had recently founded an academy on a new system.

See CHALMERS's "Biographical Dictionary."

Hartman, haRt'mân, (GEORG,) a German mathematician of Nuremberg, born in 1489, invented the bombarding staff. Died in 1564.

Hartmann, haRt'mân, (ANTON THEODOR,) a German Orientalist, born at Dusseldorf in 1774. He was appointed professor of theology at Rostock in 1811. He was author of several works on the antiquities and literature of the Hebrews, among which is "Historical and Critical Researches on the Formation, Epoch, and Plan of the Five Books of Moses," (1831.) Died in 1838.

Hartmann, haRt'mân, (CARL JOHAN,) a Swedish naturalist and physician, born at Gefle in 1790. He published a "Description of the Plants of Sweden and Norway," ("Handbok i Skandinaviens Flora," 1830 ; 6th edition, 1854.) Died in 1849.

Hartmann, (FERDINAND,) a German historical painter, born at Stuttgart in 1770.

Hartmann, (JOHANN,) a German chemist, born at Amberg, in Bavaria, in 1568. His chief work is "Praxis Chymiatrica," ("Chemico-Medical Practice," 1633,) often reprinted. Died at Cassel in 1631.

Hartmann, (JOHANN ADOLF,) a German historian, born at Münster in 1680, published a Latin "History of Hesse," (3 vols., 1741-46.) Died in 1744.

Hartmann, (JOHANN MELCHIOR,) a German Orientalist, born at Nordlingen in 1764. He published a good "Geographical and Historical Description of Egypt," (1799,) and other works. Died in 1827.

Hartmann, haRt'mân, (JOHANN PETER EMIL,) a Danish composer, born at Copenhagen in 1805, furnished the music for two of Andersen's operas and for several of Oehlenschläger's dramas.

Hartmann, (MORITZ,) a popular German poet, born at Duschnik, in Bohemia, in 1821. He produced in 1845 a volume of lyrical poems, called the "Cup and Sword," ("Kelch und Schwert,") which had great success. Having been prosecuted for his liberal political opinions, he took refuge in Paris in 1846. In 1847 he published "New Poems," ("Neuere Gedichte,") and in 1848 was a prominent democratic member of the Parliament at Frankfort. He fought for the insurgents under Bem, in or near Vienna, in 1849, after which he was driven into exile and passed some years in Paris. Among his other works are "The Rhyming Chronicle of the Clerk Mauritius," a witty political satire, (1849,) "The War about the Forest," ("Der Krieg um den Wald," 1850,) and "Shadows," ("Schatten," 1851.)

See BROCKHAUS, "Conversations-Lexikon."

Hartmann, (PHILIPP JAKOB,) a German physician, born at Stralsund in 1648, published able treatises on amber, anatomy, and physiology. Died in 1707.

Hartmann von Aue, haRt'mân fon ŏw'ĕh, a celebrated German minnesinger, born about 1170. Editions of his principal works have been published by Müller, Lachmann, and others.

See GERVINUS, "Deutsche National-Literatur."

Harts'horne, (Rev. CHARLES HENRY,) an English antiquary, born about 1802, became rector of Holdenby, in Northamptonshire. He published "The Book Rarities in the University of Cambridge," (1829,) "Salopia Antiqua," (1841,) and other works. Died in 1865.

Harts'horne, (JOSEPH,) M.D., an eminent physician of Philadelphia, was born at Alexandria, Virginia, December 12, 1779. His father was a native of New Jersey,

ā, ē, ī, ō, ū, ȳ, *long;* à, ĕ, ò, same, less prolonged; ă, ĕ, ĭ, ŏ, ŭ, ў, *short;* a, ę, į, ǫ, *obscure;* fär, fâll, fât; mĕt; nŏt; gōōd; mōōn;

his mother of Philadelphia. When only five years old, he was, while under the influence of calomel, exposed to cold, which resulted in incurable lameness. His inability to engage in the sports of boyhood led him at an early age to seek the companionship of books, and to cultivate his mind, which was endowed with powers of no common order. While attending lectures at the University of Pennsylvania, he performed the duties of apothecary and resident surgeon in the Pennsylvania Hospital, where he enjoyed the rare advantage of the practical instructions of Rush, Wistar, and Physick, who were at the same time physicians and surgeons at the hospital and lecturers in the university. A little before the expiration of his term of five years at the hospital, he accepted the position of surgeon and supercargo on an East India merchantman. In the two trips to India which he made in this capacity, he acquired a practical acquaintance with many of the diseases of tropical climates. On his return from the East he devoted himself assiduously and faithfully to the duties of his profession, in which he gradually rose to the very highest rank. Among the many distinguished physicians and surgeons that Philadelphia has produced, in sagacity and sound judgment, as well as in a thorough acquaintance with all the resources of his art, he has had few equals, and probably no superior. During the latter period of his life he was very extensively employed as a consulting physician. He died the 20th of August, 1850. Dr. Hartshorne was a firm and devout believer in the great truths of Christianity, and his moral and religious convictions went hand in hand. One who knew him well said of him, "He was the most scrupulously truthful man I ever knew. On whatever subject he spoke, it never occurred to his auditor that an idea or word could be at variance with his real opinion or inconsistent with the fact as he understood it."—Of his sons, Dr. EDWARD HARTSHORNE has attained a high and just reputation both as physician and surgeon, and has written ably on medical jurisprudence, surgery, and other subjects. HENRY, another son, formerly a successful practitioner and medical writer, is now professor of hygiene in the University of Pennsylvania, and of organic science and philosophy at Haverford College.

See S. D. GROSS, "American Medical Biography;" "Biographical Notice of Dr. Joseph Hartshorne," by DR. CHARLES EVANS, 1851; 'Lives of Eminent Philadelphians," 1859.

Hartsoeker, haR̄t'soo'kĕr, (NIKLAAS,) a Dutch natural philosopher and optician, born at Gouda in March, 1656. In his childhood he was interested in astronomy, which he studied furtively at night in his own apartment. Having observed the spherical form produced accidentally by fusing a glass filament in a flame, he obtained in this way a powerful microscope, and discovered animalcules in animal fluids. While a student at Leyden, about 1676, he was encouraged in his favourite inquiries by Huyghens, who introduced him to Cassini in Paris. There he constructed a telescope equal or superior to any then in use. In 1694 he published in Paris his "Essay on Dioptrics," ("Essai de Dioptrique,") which contains, besides the principles of that science, novel and ingenious theories on the properties of bodies. He developed his system more fully in "Principles of Physics," ("Principes de Physique," 1696.) He lived in Holland from 1696 to 1704. About 1700 he taught mathematics to Peter the Great, who invited him to Russia; but he did not accept the invitation. In 1704 he was chosen professor of mathematics and philosophy in Dusseldorf. Prompted by a love of controversy, he published in 1722 an attack on the system of Newton and another on the theories of Leibnitz. Died in 1725.

See FONTENELLE, "Éloge de Hartsoeker;" NICÉRON, "Mémoires."

Hart'stēne, (HENRY J.,) an American naval officer, born in South Carolina, was sent by the United States government in 1855 to the Arctic regions in search of Dr. E. K. Kane and his party, whom he rescued. (See KANE.) Died in 1868.

Hart'suff, (GEORGE L.,) an American general, born in the State of New York about 1830, graduated at West Point in 1852. He was appointed a brigadier-general in the spring of 1862, and was wounded at the battle of

Antietam, September 17 of that year. This wound disabled him for active service.

Hartzenbusch, haRts'en-boosh', (JUAN EUGENIO,) a Spanish dramatic poet, of German extraction, born in Madrid in 1806. In 1836 he produced "The Lovers of Teruel," a successful drama. Among his works, which are admired for a vivid imagination and an energetic style, are "The Visionary," a comedy, (1840,) "Honoria," (1842,) and "Primero Yo," a drama, (1842.)

Hartzheim, haRts'hīm, (JOSEPH,) a learned German Jesuit and historian, born at Cologne in 1694, was professor of philosophy and theology in his native city. He wrote a valuable collection entitled "Bibliotheca Coloniensis," (1747,) containing notices of the lives and writings of authors who lived in the diocese of Cologne, and edited five volumes of the "Councils of Germany," ("Concilia Germaniæ," 1759–63.) Died in 1763.

See MEUSEL, "Gelehrtes Deutschland."

Hartzoeker, haRt'soo'kĕr, (THEODORUS,) a skilful Dutch painter, born at Utrecht in 1696; died in 1740.

Harun-al-Raschid, (or **-ar-Rashîd.**) See HAROUN-AL-RASCHID.

Har'vard, (JOHN,) an English nonconformist divine, born in 1608, graduated at Cambridge University in 1631. After having been ordained, he emigrated to Massachusetts, and officiated a short time at Charlestown. At his death he left a legacy of £779 to endow a school at Cambridge, and thus became memorable as the founder of the university which bears his name. Died in 1638. One hundred and ninety years after his death, a granite monument was erected over his grave in Charlestown.

Har'vey, (Sir ELIAB,) an English admiral, a descendant of the celebrated Dr. William Harvey, born in 1759, entered the navy in 1771. During the French Revolution he served as captain in the West Indies and in the Channel fleet. In 1805 he distinguished himself at Trafalgar, and was raised to the rank of rear-admiral the same year. He became vice-admiral in 1810, and full admiral in 1819. In 1825 he was made a G.C.B. He was elected to Parliament in 1780, and again in 1806. Died in 1830, aged about seventy.

Harvey, (GABRIEL,) LL.D., an English lawyer and poet, born about 1545, was a Fellow of Trinity College, Cambridge, and practised law in London. He was an intimate friend of the poet Spenser, and author of an admired poem entitled "Hobbinol," prefixed to the "Fairy Queen." He published several letters and orations in English and Latin. Died about 1630.

Har'vey, (GEORGE,) a popular Scottish painter, born near Stirling in 1806. He became a member of the Scottish Academy about 1828, and devoted his talents to the illustration of the national character, scenery, and history of Scotland. Among his works are "Covenanters Preaching," (1830,) "The Battle of Drumclog," (1836,) "A Highland Funeral," (1844,) "Glen Enterkin," (1846,) "The Past and Present," (1848,) and "The Bowlers," (1850.) He is regarded as one of the most original and earnest masters of the Scottish school.

Harvey, (GIDEON,) an English physician and writer, born in Surrey, was the medical attendant of Charles II. in his exile, and was subsequently physician to William III., and to the Tower of London. Died in 1700.

Harvey, (WILLIAM,) an English anatomist, celebrated for his discovery of the circulation of the blood, was born at Folkestone, Kent, in April, 1578. He entered Caius College, Cambridge, in 1593, and graduated in 1597, after which he studied medicine and anatomy under Fabricius ab Acquapendente at Padua. He returned home about 1602, married a lady named Browne, and commenced the practice of medicine in London. In 1609 he was appointed physician to Saint Bartholomew's Hospital. He was chosen by the College of Physicians in 1615 to deliver lectures on anatomy and surgery, and soon after that date made the important discovery of the circulation of the blood, which he taught in London in 1619, but which was not published until 1628. In this year he produced "Essays on the Motion of the Heart and the Blood," ("Exercitationes de Motu Cordis et Sanguinis.") His new theory was generally rejected by the physicians of his time, and was so unpopular that he complained that his practice declined after the publication of the treatise above mentioned. Parisanus, Riolanus, and others wrote against Dr. Harvey on this subject; but, after the truth of his doctrine was generally recognized, attempts were made to deprive him of the honour of the discovery. He became physician to Charles I. about 1630, and attended him during the civil war which began about 1642. This service caused him to neglect his duties at Saint Bartholomew's Hospital. In the latter part of the civil war a party of soldiers plundered his house and burned some valuable manuscripts. He gave much attention to the subject of generation, and published a work "De Generatione Animalium," (1651,) in which he maintained that every animal is produced from an egg. He was elected president of the College of Physicians in 1654; but he declined, on account of his advanced age. He died in June, 1657. An edition of his Works was published by the College of Physicians, in 2 vols., 1666.

"Harvey is entitled," says Hume, "to the glory of having made, by reasoning alone, without any mixture of accident, a capital discovery in one of the most important branches of science. He had also the happiness of establishing at once this theory on the most solid and convincing proofs." ("History of England," chap. lxii.) "It is manifest," says Hallam, "that several anatomists of the sixteenth century were on the verge of completely detecting the law by which the motion of the blood is governed. . . . It may, indeed, be thought wonderful that Servetus, Columbus, or Cæsalpin should not have more distinctly apprehended the consequences of what they maintained; . . . but the defectiveness of their views is not to be alleged as a counter-balance to the more steady sagacity of Harvey." ("Introduction to the Literature of Europe," vol. ii.)

See DR. LAWRENCE, "Life of William Harvey," prefixed to the edition of his Works above mentioned, 1666; "Lives of British Physicians," London, 1857.

Harvey, (WILLIAM,) an English artist, born at Newcastle-on-Tyne about 1796, was a pupil of the famous engraver Bewick. He settled in London at an early age, and became distinguished as a designer for engravings on wood. His skill was displayed in the illustration of various works, among which are "The Zoological Gardens," "The Pilgrim's Progress," and "The Arabian Nights' Entertainments."

Harvey, (WILLIAM HENRY,) professor of botany in the University of Dublin, was born at Limerick in 1811. He published a "History of British Sea-Weeds," (3 vols., 1846-51,) a work of high character, "Nereis Australis; or, Illustrations of the Algæ of the Southern Ocean," (1848,) "The Sea-Side Book," (3d edition, 1854,) and "Flora Capensis," (3 vols., 1865.) He explored the coasts of Australia and the South Sea islands in 1853-55, and obtained the chair of botany in Dublin in 1856. Died in May, 1866.

See ASA GRAY, "Notice of W. H. Harvey," in "Silliman's Journal," republished in the "Report of the Smithsonian Institution" for 1867.

Har'wood, (Sir BUSIC,) an English anatomist, born at Newmarket about 1745. He became professor of anatomy at Cambridge in 1785, and published lectures on that science. Died in 1814.

Harwood, (EDWARD,) an English Unitarian minister, born in Lancashire in 1729. He had charge of a congregation in Bristol from 1765 to 1770, after which he lived in London. He excelled as a classical and biblical scholar, and published numerous able works, of which the most important are "An Introduction to the Study of the New Testament," (1767,) a "View of the Various Editions of the Greek and Roman Classics," (1775,) "An Edition of the Greek Testament, with English Notes," (1776,) and "Biographia Classica," (new edition, 2 vols., 1778.) Died in 1794.

Hǎs'dru-bal or **As'dru-bal,** [Gr. Ἀσδρούβας,] a distinguished Carthaginian general and a popular leader of the democratic party, was a son-in-law of Hamilcar Barca, with whom he went to Spain in 238 B.C. After the death of Hamilcar Barca, 229 B.C., he obtained the chief command in Spain. He founded the city of New Carthage, (Carthagena,) which became one of the richest in the world, and greatly extended the power of Carthage in Spain, partly by his victories in battle and partly by his political talents. He made a treaty with the Romans, stipulating that the river Ebro should be the boundary between the two nations. He was assassinated by a slave in Spain in 221 B.C.

Hasdrubal or **Asdrubal,** a son of Gisco, was a general of the second Punic war. He entered Spain with an army in 214 B.C., and shared with Mago the chief command in that country after the other Hasdrubal marched to Italy, 207 B.C. They were defeated in a decisive battle at Silpia or Elinga, by Scipio, in 206. In 204 he was general-in-chief of a large army raised to oppose Scipio, who had invaded Africa. His camp near Utica was fired by the Romans, and nearly all his army, it is said, perished in the flames or by the sword.

Hasdrubal or **Asdrubal,** an able Carthaginian general, and brother of the great Hannibal, commanded in Spain in the second Punic war, in 218 B.C., while Hannibal crossed the Alps and invaded Italy. He maintained the war against the Romans under Publius and Cneius Scipio with various success until 212, when he gained a complete victory, in which both the Scipios were killed. Five years later, he marched across the Alps to reinforce his brother in Italy; but before he could effect this design he was attacked by the Romans at the river Metaurus, defeated, and killed, in 207 B.C. His head was cut off and thrown into the camp of Hannibal. The Roman writers represent him as a very able commander.

Hasdrubal or **Asdrubal,** a Carthaginian officer, who served under Hannibal in Italy. He contributed greatly to the victory of Cannæ, (216 B.C.,) where he commanded the left wing and completed the rout of the enemy by a cavalry charge on their rear.

Hasdrubal or **Asdrubal,** an able Carthaginian general, who had the chief command in the third Punic war. He defeated the consul Manilius at Nepheris about 148 B.C., and obstinately defended Carthage against the besieging army of Scipio Africanus in 146 B.C., and assumed despotic power in that city. He finally surrendered to Scipio, who spared his life, the remainder of which he passed in captivity.

Hase, hä'zeh, (HEINRICH,) a German antiquary, born at Altenburg in 1789, published a "Treatise on Greek Antiquities," (1828,) and other works. Died in 1842.

Hase, (KARL AUGUST,) an eminent German theologian, born at Steinbach, Saxony, in 1800. He became professor of theology at Jena about 1830. He endeavoured to reconcile the Lutheran faith with the progress of modern science, in his "Evangelical Dogmatics," (1823,) and his work called "Gnosis," (3 vols., 1828.) He wrote other able works, among which is a "History of the Church," (Kirchengeschichte," 1834; 6th edition, 1848,) which, by avoiding all sectarian partiality, has obtained general favour.

Hase, (KARL BENEDICT,) an eminent Hellenist, born near Naumburg, in Prussian Saxony, in 1780. He became professor of Greek palæography and modern Greek in Paris in 1816. He was admitted into the Academy of Inscriptions about 1824. He published, besides other works, an edition of Leo Diaconus, (1819.)

See "Nouvelle Biographie Générale."

Hase, von, fon hä'zeh, (THEODOR,) a German Lutheran divine, born at Bremen in 1682. He wrote "Critical Dissertations." Died in 1731.

Hasenclever, hä'zen-klä'ver, (JOHANN PETER,) an excellent German painter of genre, born at Remscheid, Prussia, in 1810, was a pupil of Schadow, of Dusseldorf. He worked at the latter city, and gained much popularity by his humorous productions, among which are "The Return of Job from College," and other pictures, the subjects of which are derived from the "Jobsiad," a comic poem. He was a member of the Academy of Fine Arts, Berlin. Died in 1853.

Hasenclever, (PETER,) a German merchant and manufacturer, distinguished by the magnitude of his operations and his influence on the commerce and industry of two continents, was born at Remscheid, Prussia, in 1716. He made improvements in the fabrication of iron and of woollen stuffs. About 1763 he formed in London a company, and became director of a great industrial enterprise in New York and New Jersey, where they worked mines of iron and prepared that metal for use. He settled at Landshut, in Silesia, in 1775, where he carried on an extensive linen-trade. Died in 1793.

See ERSCH und GRUBER, "Allgemeine Encyklopaedie."

Hasenmüller or **Hasenmueller**, hä'zęn-mül'ler, (DANIEL,) a German Orientalist, born at Eutin (Holstein) in 1651, was professor of Oriental languages at Kiel, and published a Hebrew Grammar and Dictionary, (1691.) Died in 1691.

Häser or **Haeser**, hä'zer, (HEINRICH,) a German physician and medical writer, born at Rome in 1811.

Hasius. See HAAS, (JOHANN.)

Has'lam, (JOHN,) a British physician, born in 1764, published in 1798 "Observations on Insanity." He afterwards practised in London. Died in 1844.

Haslewood, hä'z'l-wŏŏd, (JOSEPH,) an English bibliographer, born in London in 1769 ; died in 1833.

Has'sall, (ARTHUR HILL,) a British physician, microscopist, and naturalist, a nephew of Sir James Murray, was born in Middlesex in 1817. He wrote, among other works, a "History of British Fresh-Water Algæ,"(1845,) and "Food and its Adulterations," (London, 1855.) The latter, digested from the reports of a sanitary commission, produced considerable sensation.

Hassan, hâs'sạn, a caliph, born in 625 A.D., was a son of Alee, and grandson of Mohammed. He succeeded his father in 660 ; but a few months later he resigned the throne to his rival Moaweeyah. He had a high reputation for piety. Died in 669 A.D.

See ELMACIN, "Historia Saracenica;" WEIL, "Geschichte der Chalifen."

Hassan-Pasha, (or **-Pacha**.) See GAZEE-HASSAN.

Hasse, hâs'sęh, (FRIEDRICH CHRISTIAN AUGUST,) a German historical writer, born at Rehfeld, near Herzberg, in 1773. He became professor in the Cadettenhaus of Dresden in 1798, and obtained a chair of history at Leipsic in 1828. He wrote a "History of Lombardy," (4 vols., 1828,) and other works, and was one of the editors of the "Conversations-Lexikon" published by Brockhaus. Died in 1848.

Hasse, (JOHANN ADOLF,) a celebrated German composer, born at Bergedorf, near Hamburg, in March, 1699. He was called by the Italians IL SASSONE, ("the Saxon.") He went to Italy about 1724, and became a pupil of A. Scarlatti at Naples. There he produced in 1726 the opera "Il Sesostrate," by which he gained a high reputation. His "Miserere" (1727) is called a master-piece of sacred music. He afterwards lived in Venice, Dresden, London, and Vienna, and composed the operas of "Artaserse," "Arminio," (1745,) etc. Died in 1783. The words of his operas were composed by Metastasio.

See BURNEY, "History of Music;" KANDLER, "Cenni storicocritici intorno alla Vita ed alle Opere di G. A. Hasse," Venice, 1820; "Nouvelle Biographie Générale."

Hasse, (KARL EWALD,) a physician, and a son of Friedrich Christian August, noticed above, was born at Dresden in 1810. He published "A Description of the Diseases of the Organs of Circulation and Respiration," (1841,) which he announced as the first volume of a large work on pathological anatomy. He was chosen professor of pathology at Heidelberg in 1852, and professor of the same at Göttingen in 1856.

Hassel, hâs'sęl, (JOHANN GEORG HEINRICH,) a German statistician, born at Wolfenbüttel in 1770. He became director of the bureau of statistics of Westphalia in 1809. He published, besides other works, "Text-Book (Lehrbuch) of the Statistics of the European States," (1812,) a "Complete Manual of Modern Geography and Statistics," (1816-20,) and a "General Geographical Dictionary," (2 vols., 1818.) He lived mostly at Weimar after 1814, and was one of the editors of Ersch and Gruber's "Encyclopædia." Died in 1829.

See BROCKHAUS, "Conversations-Lexikon."

Hasselquist, hâs'sęl-kwist', (FREDRIK,) a Swedish naturalist, born at Törnvalla in 1722, was one of the most eminent pupils of Linnæus, under whom he studied at Upsal. In 1747 he wrote an able thesis on the "Virtues of Plants." Having heard Linnæus express a wish that some naturalist would explore Palestine, in order to develop its natural history, then but little known, he prepared himself for the journey, and embarked in 1749.

He explored Egypt, Arabia, and Palestine, and was about to return, with a rich collection of plants, minerals, fishes, insects, etc., when he died at Smyrna in 1752. His valuable journal, observations, and descriptions were published by Linnæus in Swedish, with the title of "Iter Palæstinum ; or, A Tour through Palestine, with Memoirs and Remarks on Objects of Natural History," (2 vols., 1757,) which is an excellent scientific work.

See "Biographiskt-Lexicon öfver namnkunnige Svenska Män," 23 vols.; HIRSCHING, "Historisch-literarisches Handbuch," 1797; A. BAECK, "Aminnelse-Tal öfver F. Hasselquist," 1758.

Hassencamp, hâs'sęn-kâmp', (JOHANN MATTHÄUS,) a German Orientalist, born at Marburg in 1743, published a "Commentary on the Pentateuch," (1765,) and "Annals of Theological Literature," (1789-96.) Died in 1797.

Hassenfratz, hä'sŏN'fRäts', (JEAN HENRI,) a French chemist, born in Paris in 1755. He was director or foreman of Lavoisier's laboratory about 1785, and was an active Jacobin in the Revolution. In 1797 he became tutor of physics in the École Polytechnique. He wrote, besides other works, "Cours de Physique céleste," (1803,) and "The Art of Smelting Iron-Ore," (4 vols., 1812.) Died in 1827.

See "Nouvelle Biographie Générale."

Hassenpflug, hâs'sęn-pflŏŏG', (HANS DANIEL LUDWIG FRIEDRICH,) a German politician, born at Hanau in 1793. Having shown himself a partisan of absolutism, he was appointed minister of justice and the interior at the court of Hesse-Cassel in 1832. He became very unpopular, and in 1837 went into exile. In 1841 he obtained a seat in the superior court (Obertribunal) of Berlin. He was recalled to Cassel in 1850 as prime minister, and renewed his arbitrary acts, which provoked a popular revolt in 1855. The Elector was forced to fly from his capital, and his minister resigned. Died in October, 1862.

See BROCKHAUS, "Conversations-Lexikon."

Hassenstein, hâs'sęn-stīn', (BOGISLAUS,) Baron von Lobkowitz, (lop-ko'wits',) a Bohemian poet and nobleman, was a liberal patron of letters. He wrote a volume of Latin poems, called "Farrago Poematum," (1570.) He was secretary of state of Hungary. Died in 1510.

See IGNAZ CORNOVA, "Der grosse Böhme B. von Lobkowitz nach seinen eigenen Schriften geschildert," 1808; J. C. COLER, "Dissertatio de Vita B. Hassensteinii," 1719.

Hassler, hâss'ler, (FERDINAND R.,) a Swiss mathematician, born at Geneva in 1769. He was appointed superintendent of the United States Coast Survey in 1815 or 1816. The operation was discontinued about 1818, but he was again employed in that service from 1832 until his death in 1843.

Has'tęd, (EDWARD,) an English antiquary, born at Hawley, Kent, in 1732. He published a valuable "History and Topographical Survey of the County of Kent," (4 vols., 1788-99.) Died in 1812.

Hās'ting or **Hās'tings**, a daring and successful adventurer or sea-king, is supposed to have been a Dane or Norman by birth. In the reign of Charles the Bald he ravaged the western coast of France with his piratical crew. He ascended the Loire in 867, attacked Anjou and Poitou, and captured Angers. In 894, with a large fleet and an army of Northmen, he invaded England, and, after many fierce conflicts, he was defeated by Alfred, and driven out of the island, in 896 A.D.

See DEPPING, "Histoire des Expéditions maritimes des Normands."

Hās'tings, (Lady ELIZABETH,) born in England in 1682, was the daughter of Theophilus Hastings, Earl of Huntingdon, and sister-in-law of the well-known Lady Huntingdon. She built churches, established schools, and was eminent for piety and benevolence. Died in 1739.

See THOMAS BERNARD, "Life of Lady E. Hastings."

Hastings, (Lady FLORA,) daughter of the Marquis of Hastings, was born in 1806, and became lady of the bed-chamber to the Duchess of Kent. She was an excellent scholar, and author of a number of graceful poetical effusions, among which are "The Rainbow" and "The Cross of Constantine." Died in 1839.

Hastings, (FRANCIS RAWDON,) Marquis of Hastings, the eldest son of the Earl of Moira, was born in 1754. He took part in the battle of Bunker Hill in 1775, and became adjutant-general in 1778. In 1781 he defeated the Americans at Camden, South Carolina. In 1783 he was raised to the peerage, as Baron Rawdon, and in 1793 succeeded his father as Earl of Moira. He fought as major-general against the French in Flanders in 1794. On the formation of a Whig ministry in 1806, he was named master-general of the ordnance. From 1813 to 1823 he held the office of Governor-General of India, and maintained war against the Mahrattas and Goorkas. His administration, on the whole, was accounted prosperous, and his policy liberal. In 1816 he was created Viscount Loudoun, Earl of Rawdon, and Marquis of Hastings. In 1824 he was appointed Governor of Malta. Died in 1826.

Hastings, (HANS FRANCIS.) See HUNTINGDON, EARL.

Hastings, (SELINA.) See HUNTINGDON, COUNTESS OF.

Hastings, (WARREN,) the first Governor-General of British India, was born in Worcestershire in 1732. His father, Pynaston, was the son of the rector of Daylesford, who belonged to a noble and once wealthy family. Warren was educated at Westminster, where he formed an intimacy with the poet Cowper, his fellow-student. In 1750 he obtained a clerkship at Calcutta in the service of the East India Company. A few years afterwards, he was selected to negotiate with the native princes, because, in addition to his other qualifications, he was master of the Persian and Hindostanee languages, which few Englishmen at that time could speak. He served as a member of the Council of Bengal from 1761 to 1764, after which he returned to England, having realized a moderate fortune, which was soon dissipated by his liberality or imprudence.

After a repose of four years, he again offered his services to the directors, who appointed him a member of the Council at Madras, where he managed affairs with such ability and success that in 1772 he was made president of the Council of Bengal. In 1773, by an act of Parliament, the control of all British India was given to the Council of Bengal, consisting of four members besides the president, who now obtained the title of governor-general and a large accession of power, except in the contingency that a majority of the council should oppose his measures,—which presently occurred. Sir Philip Francis, combining with two other members, obtained for about two years the chief control, and thwarted the policy of the governor. When the account of Hastings's cruelty and ambition in respect to the Rohilla war, etc. reached England, the directors condemned his conduct; and, as his agent in London had presented to them a conditional resignation received from Hastings, they gladly accepted it, and appointed Mr. Wheler to succeed him. But in the mean time one of his opponents in the council had died, and the governor, having the casting vote, was again absolute. He asserted that he had not resigned; and, with the sanction of the supreme court, (who pronounced his resignation invalid,) and with the popular feeling in his favour, he was able to keep the office. In 1780, Hastings having said in the council that the conduct of Francis was void of truth and honour, the latter challenged him, and in the exchange of shots was severely wounded. Soon after this, the governor had to contend against Hyder Ali, the King of Mysore, who invaded the Carnatic with 90,000 men, (led by French officers,) defeated several detachments of English, captured their forts, and threatened to subvert their empire. By the prompt, energetic, and politic measures of Hastings the government passed safely through this crisis, and the ambitious designs of Hyder Ali were blasted by the British victory at Porto Novo.

To supply the deficit in the treasury occasioned by this war, he resorted to those violent and unscrupulous measures which provoked his impeachment and have left a stain on his character that even his great talents and services cannot efface. He resolved to plunder Cheyte Sing, the rich Rajah of Benares. By repeated extortions he provoked him to resist, and then punished that resistance by expelling him from his dominions and confiscating his revenue. The spoliation of the Begums of Oude, under circumstances of peculiar atrocity, was an-

other crime laid to his charge. In 1785 he resigned his office and returned to England. After two sessions had been spent in preparation for his impeachment, the case was formally opened in 1788, by Burke, Fox, and others, and terminated in his acquittal in 1795. For a full account of his trial, see Macaulay's "Essay on Warren Hastings." The company rewarded Hastings with an annuity of £4000, and lent him £50,000 without interest for eighteen years. He purchased the manor of Daylesford, the home of his ancestors, and retired from public life. A few years before his death he was admitted into the privy council, and stood high in the royal favour. Died in 1818.

See MACAULAY, "Essays;" GLEIG, "Life of Warren Hastings," 3 vols., 1841; JAMES MILL, "History of British India;" WILHELM HAERING, "W. Hastings; Vortrag," etc., Berlin, 1844.

Haszkarl, hâs'kaʀl, (JUSTUS KARL,) a German botanist, born at Cassel in 1811, made in 1836 a voyage to Java, which he explored for six years. He published a treatise "On the Utility of the Plants of Java," (1844,) and (in Latin) "The Rare Plants of Java," (1847.)

Hatch, (JOHN P.,) an American general, born in the State of New York, graduated at West Point in 1845. He commanded a division at South Mountain, where he was severely wounded, September, 1862, and was employed in South Carolina in 1864 as commander of several districts.

Ha-tee'fee or **Hatîfî,** (**Moolana Abdalla,** mōō-lä'nä äb-däl'lä,) a Persian poet, was a nephew of Jâmee. Died in 520.

See HAJI-KHALFAH, "Lexicon Bibliographicum;" SIR W. G. OUSELEY, "Biographical Notices of Persian Poets."

Hat'field, (THOMAS,) an English divine, became Bishop of Durham in 1345. He founded Trinity College, Oxford. Died in 1381.

Hatherley, LORD. See WOOD, (WILLIAM PAGE.)

Hatîfî. See HATEEFEE.

Hat'sell, (JOHN,) an Englishman, born at Cambridge in 1742. He was clerk of the House of Commons many years, ending about 1796. He published an important work called "Precedents of Proceedings in the House of Commons, with Observations," (1781; 4th edition, 4 vols., 1818.) Died in 1820.

Hat'ton, (Sir CHRISTOPHER,) an English statesman and favourite courtier of Queen Elizabeth, born in 1540 at Holdenby. He was appointed lord chancellor in 1587, and, though not a lawyer by profession, he performed the duties of that office with credit. His character and capacity were represented to have been excellent. The public were much astonished when it was announced that the queen had selected for this dignity one whom Lord Campbell describes as "a gay young cavalier, never called to the bar, and chiefly famed for his handsome person, his taste in dress, and his skill in dancing." Some persons ascribe to Hatton the fourth act of "Tancred and Gismund," and several legal treatises. Died in 1591.

See SIR N. HARRIS NICOLAS, "Life and Times of Sir Christopher Hatton," 1847; LORD CAMPBELL, "Lives of the Lord Chancellors;" FOSS, "The Judges of England."

Hatzfeldt, von, fon hâts'fêlt', (FRANZ LUDWIG,) PRINCE, a Prussian general, born in 1756. He was governor of Berlin when that city was taken by the French in 1806. Died in 1827.

Hauber, hŏw'bĕr, (EBERHARD DAVID,) a German theologian, born in Würtemberg in 1695. He wrote a work against magic, entitled "Bibliotheca Acta et Scripta Magica continens," (3 vols., 1741.) Died in 1765.

Haubold, hŏw'bolt, (CHRISTIAN GOTTLIEB,) an eminent German jurist and writer, born at Dresden in 1766. He began to give, as *privat-docent*, a course of lectures on the history of Roman law at the University of Leipsic in 1786. In 1796 he obtained there a chair of Saxon law. Among his works are a "History of Roman Law," ("Historia Juris Romani," 1790,) and "Institutiones Juris Romani Literariæ," (1809.) Died in 1824.

See OTTO, "Necrolog Haubolds," 1824; ERSCH und GRUBER, "Allgemeine Encyklopaedie;" FRIEDERICI, "Lebensbeschreibung des Dr. Haubold," 1826.

Haucal. See HAUKÂL.

Hauch, von, fon hŏwk, (JOHANNES CARSTEN,) a popular Danish poet, born at Frederikshald in 1791.

He became professor of natural science at Soröe. About 1828 he published two volumes of dramas, including "Tiberius," "Bajazet," and "Hamadryaden," a dramatic epic. His "Lyric Poems" ("Lyriske Digte," 1842) had great success. He also wrote several romances, among which are "The Alchemist," and "Robert Fulton," (1853.) In 1850 he was chosen professor of belles-lettres at Copenhagen.

See ERSLEW, "Forfatter-Lexicon;" P. L. MÖLLER, article in the "Dansk Pantheon;" "North British Review" for September, 1867.

Haudebourt, *hŏd'booR',* (ANTOINETTE CÉCILE HORTENSE **Lescot**—lĕs'ko',) a skilful French painter of genre, born in Paris in 1784; died in 1845.

Hauenschild, von, fon *hŏw'ẹn-shĭlt',* (RICHARD GEORG SPILLER,) a German poet, whose *nom de plume* is MAX WALDAU, was born at Breslau in 1822. He published a volume of lyric poems, called "Leaves in the Wind," ("Blätter im Winde," 1848,) a novel, entitled "After Nature," ("Nach der Natur," 3 vols., 1850,) and other works. Died in 1855.

Hauff, *hŏwf,* (WILHELM,) a German novelist, born at Stuttgart in 1802. He was educated at the University of Tübingen, and produced in 1826 "Lichtenstein," a historical novel, which is greatly admired. He afterwards published "The Man in the Moon," a satire, a number of popular tales, among which is "The Portrait of the Emperor," ("Das Bild des Kaisers,") and a humorous, fantastic work, called "Phantasien im Bremer Rathskellêr," (1827.) He died prematurely, and much regretted, in November, 1827. Hauff belonged to the school of Hoffmann, but was inferior to him, perhaps, in richness of imagination.

See "Hauff's Leben," by G. SCHWAB, prefixed to an edition of his Works, 36 vols., 1830, and 10 vols., 1837.

Haug, *hŏwG,* (JOHANN CHRISTIAN FRIEDRICH,) a German poet, born in Würtemberg in 1761; died in 1829.

Haug, (JOHANN CHRISTOPH FRIEDRICH,) a celebrated German epigrammatist, born in the duchy of Würtemberg in 1761. His works are distinguished for elegant versification, and brilliant wit without causticity. In conjunction with Weisser, he published in 1807 an "Epigrammatic Anthology," in 10 vols. Died in 1829.

See BROCKHAUS, "Conversations-Lexikon."

Haughton, haw'tọn, (Sir GRAVES CHAMPNEY,) an English author, born in 1787. He was professor at the East India College, Haileybury, from 1817 to 1827. He published, besides other works, a "Bengali, Sanscrit, and English Dictionary," and "An Inquiry into the First Principles of Reasoning," (1839.) Died near Paris in 1849.

Haughton, (WILLIAM,) an English dramatist in the reign of Queen Elizabeth, wrote a comedy called "Englishmen for my Money," (1616,) and was one of the authors of the comedy of "Patient Grissill," printed in 1603.

Haugwitz, von, fon *hŏwG'ŵits,* (CHRISTIAN HEINRICH KARL,) COUNT, a Prussian statesman, born near Oels, in Silesia, in 1752. He was sent as ambassador to the court of Vienna in 1790, and became minister of foreign affairs in 1792. He favoured an alliance with France, and was superseded by Hardenberg in 1804. After the success of Napoleon at Ulm, Haugwitz was recalled and sent to Vienna to treat with the victor, in November, 1805. In the ensuing December he signed a treaty of alliance with France, by which Hanover was ceded to Prussia. He was prime minister in 1806 until the battle of Jena, before which he had made efforts to preserve peace with France. His administration was unpopular. After the disastrous campaign of 1806 he was excluded from all political employment. Died in 1832.

See MINUTOLI, "Der Graf von Haugwitz und Job von Witzleben," 1844.

Haukâl, (**Haucal** or **Haoucâl**,) **Ibn**, Ib'n *hŏw-kâl',* (**Abool-** (or **Abûl-**) **Kâsem -Mohammed,** â'bōōl kâ'sem mo-hâm'med,) called also simply **Haukâl,** a distinguished Arabian traveller and geographer, was born probably at Bagdâd. Departing from that city in 943 A.D., he traversed for many years the countries which lie between the Indus and the Atlantic. He wrote about 975 A.D. an important work, entitled "A Book of Roads and Kingdoms," which is furnished with maps and is considered reliable.

See UIJLENBROEK, "Dissertatio de Ibn-Haukalo Geographo," 1822; "Nouvelle Biographie Générale."

Hauks'bee or **Hawks'bee,** (FRANCIS,) an English philosopher, who was made a Fellow of the Royal Society in 1705, and was one of the earliest experimenters and discoverers in electricity, which he perceived was excited by the friction of glass. In 1709 he published his "Experiments on Various Subjects, touching Light and Electricity," which was translated into Italian and French.

Haupt, *hŏwpt,* (HERMAN,) an American engineer, born in Philadelphia in 1817, graduated at West Point in 1835. He published a "General Theory of Bridge-Construction," (1853,) and before the war of 1861–65 was distinguished as a civil engineer. He was appointed a brigadier-general about August, 1862.

Haupt, *hŏwpt,* (MORITZ,) an eminent German philologist, born at Zittau, in Saxony, in 1808. He was appointed professor of German literature at Leipsic in 1843, but was removed in 1850 because he had taken part in the political movements of 1849. He edited several old German poets, and published a number of works on classical philology, among which is "Observationes criticæ," (1841.) A "Review of German Antiquities," founded and edited by him, (1841–60,) is called an excellent work.

Hauptmann, *hŏwpt'mân,* (MORITZ,) a German composer, born at Dresden in 1792. He was employed in the chapel of the Elector of Hesse-Cassel from 1822 to 1842. He composed masses, sonatas for the piano and violin, an opera named "Matilda," and other works, which are admired for purity of style. He also wrote a treatise on music, "Harmonik und Metrik," (1855.)

Hauréau, *hŏ'rȧ'ō',* (BARTHÉLEMY,) an eminent French author, born in Paris in 1812. He was keeper of the manuscripts of the National Library from 1848 to 1852. Among his works, which have a high reputation, are a "Literary History of Maine," (4 vols., 1843–47,) an "Essay on the Scholastic Philosophy," (2 vols., 1850, crowned by the Institute,) and "Francis I. and his Court," (1853.) He wrote articles for Didot's "Biographie Générale," which see.

Hauser, *hŏw'zẹr,* (KASPAR,) the celebrated Nuremberg foundling, whose mysterious history excited intense interest throughout Europe, was first observed on the 26th of May, 1828, at Nuremberg, by a citizen of that place. He was apparently about sixteen years of age, walked with difficulty, and manifested childish ignorance on the most common affairs of life. When interrogated, he replied in a few broken sentences, and presented a letter purporting to be from a Bavarian peasant, who stated that the boy had been left at his door and had been secretly maintained by him. Having been received into the house of the burgomaster Binder, it was gradually ascertained that Kaspar Hauser, as he called himself, had been kept from infancy in a dark, subterranean prison, provided with bread and water, and otherwise cared for, during his sleep, by an unknown keeper. A short time previous to his escape, however, a man had appeared who, after teaching him to write and to walk, had put him on the road to Nuremberg. He was next taken into the family of Professor Daumer, of Nuremberg, where he showed an eager desire for knowledge, and a surprising memory. While near his patron's house, he was wounded one day by a person who suddenly disappeared and evaded all search. He was soon after this taken under the protection of Lord Stanhope, who sent him to Anspach to be educated. In December, 1833, he was invited to a rendezvous with a person who promised him information of his origin, but who, while Hauser was reading a paper presented to him, inflicted upon him a wound of which he died in three days.

See MERKER, "Kaspar Hauser," 1830; DAUMER, "Mittheilungen über Kaspar Hauser," 1832; SINGER, "Leben Kaspar Hauser's," 1834; LORD STANHOPE, "Materialien zur Geschichte Kaspar Hauser's," 1835; A. VON FEUERBACH, "Account of an Individual kept in a Dungeon."

Hausmann, *hŏwss'mân,* (JOHANN FRIEDRICH LUDWIG,) a German geologist, born at Hanover in 1782. He obtained in 1811 the chair of geology and mineralogy at Göttingen. .He published a "Manual of Mineralogy," (3 vols., 1813,) which is highly esteemed, a "Journey through Scandinavia," (5 vols., 1818,) and a work "On the Formation of the Hartz Mountains," (1842.)

Häusser or **Haeusser**, hois'ser, (LUDWIG,) a German historian, born in Alsace in 1818. Among his works, which are highly esteemed, is a "History of Germany from the Death of Frederick the Great to the Formation of the Germanic Confederation," (4 vols., 1855.)

Haussez, d', dō'så', (CHARLES Lemercher de Longpré—leh-mĕR'shå' deh lôN'pRå',) BARON, a French minister of state, born in Normandy in 1778. He was minister of marine from August, 1829, to July, 1830. Died in 1854.

Haussmann, hōss'mŏN',(GEORGES EUGÈNE,) BARON, a French administrator, a grandson of Nicolas, noticed below, was born in Paris in 1809. He obtained in 1853 the important office of prefect of La Seine, (at Paris.) By a lavish expenditure of the public treasure he adorned Paris with new boulevards and other costly public works. He was made a senator in 1857.

Haussmann, (JEAN MICHEL,) a French chemist and manufacturer, born at Colmar in 1749, made improvements in the art of dyeing or printing calico. Died in 1824.

Haussmann, (NICOLAS,) brother of the preceding, born in 1761, was an active member of the Convention, (1792–95.) Died in 1846.

Haussonville, d', do'sôN'vèl', (JOSEPH OTHENIN BERNARD de Cléron—deh klà'rôN',) COMTE, a French *littérateur*, born in 1809, was elected to the Chamber of Deputies in 1842 and in 1846. He published a "History of the Foreign Policy of the French Government from 1830 to 1848," (2 vols., 1850,) and other works.

Hautefeuille, hōt'fuI' or hōt'fuh'ye, (LAURENT BASILE,) a French jurist, distinguished as a writer on maritime law, was born in Paris in 1805. His principal works are "Législation criminelle maritime," (1839,) "Code of Maritime Fishery," (1844,) and "The Rights and Duties of Neutral Nations in Time of Maritime War," (4 vols., 1848–49.) His works have a high reputation on both sides of the Channel.

Hautefeuille, de, deh hōt'fuI' or hōt'fuh'ye, (JEAN,) a French ecclesiastic and mechanician, born at Orléans in 1647. The Duchess of Bouillon patronized him and gave him a pension. Among his inventions was the spiral spring which moderates the movements of the balance of a watch, (1674.) This invention was also claimed by Huyghens. He wrote an "Essay on the Cause of the Echo," (1718,) and many treatises on mechanics, etc. Died in 1724.

Hautefort, d', dōt'foR', (MARIE,) Duchesse de Schomberg, a favourite of Louis XIII. of France, was born in 1616. She gained the favour of the king about 1630, and became a maid of honour to the queen, Anne of Austria, with whom she maintained confidential relations. Richelieu induced the king to dismiss her from court in 1640. Died in 1691.

See "Vie de Madame d'Hautefort," anonymous; VICTOR COUSIN, "Madame d'Hautefort."

Hautemer, d', dōt'maiR', (GUILLAUME,) Comte de Grancey and Seigneur de Fervaques, (fěR'våk',) a French general, born in 1538. He fought with distinction against the Spaniards at Saint-Quentin and Gravelines, (1558,) and entered the service of Henry IV., who made him a marshal of France in 1595. Died in 1613.

Hauterive, d', dōt'rèv', (ALEXANDRE MAURICE Blanc de Lanautte—blôN deh lă'nŏt',) COMTE, an able French diplomatist, born at Aspres (Hautes-Alpes) in 1754. Having been ordered by Bonaparte to compose a manifesto to foreign powers, he produced in 1800 "On the State of France at the End of the Year VIII." He became the confidential secretary of the First Consul, and in 1803 was made a councillor of state. In 1807 he was appointed keeper of the archives of France. He was often consulted by the emperor on foreign affairs, and acted as minister *ad interim* while Champagny and Caulaincourt followed the army. Died in 1830.

See ARTAUD DE MONTOR, "Histoire de la Vie et des Travaux politiques du Comte d'Hauterive," 1839; "Nouvelle Biographie Générale."

Hauteroche. See ALLIER, (LOUIS.)

Hauteroche, d', dōt'rosh', (NOËL LE BRETON,) SIEUR, a French dramatist and actor, born in Paris about 1617. He produced several popular comedies, among which is "Crispin Médecin," (1670.) Died in 1707.

Haute-Serre, d', dōt'saiR', (ANTOINE Dadin—dă'dăN',) a French jurisconsult, born in the diocese of Cahors, became in 1644 professor of law in Toulouse. He published learned works on the law and on the early history of France. Died in 1682.

Hautesrayes. See DESHAUTESRAYES.

Hauteville, hōt'vèl', or **Hanvill, de**, deh hŏN'vèl', (JEAN,) a French poet, who lived about 1150–90. He left a Latin poem, called "Archithrenius," which was once popular.

Hautpoul, d', dō'pool', (ALPHONSE HENRI,) MARQUIS, a French general, born at Versailles in 1789. He became maréchal-de-camp in 1823, and obtained the rank of lieutenant-general in 1841. In 1849 he was appointed commander-in-chief of the army of Rome, and showed himself hostile to the republican régime. He was minister of war for several months in 1849 and 1850, and was made a senator in 1852.

Hautpoul, d', (ANNE MARIE de Montgeroult—deh môN'zheh'roo',) COMTESSE, a French authoress, born in Paris in 1763, published "Sappho to Phaon," a poem, (1790,) and several novels. Died in 1837.

Hautpoul-Salette, d', dō'pool' să'lět', (JEAN JOSEPH,) a French general, born in 1754 of a noble family in Languedoc. He became general of division under Moreau, and in 1805 distinguished himself at the battle of Austerlitz, soon after which he was made a senator. He contributed to the victory at Jena in 1806, and was killed at Eylau in February, 1807.

Haüy, hā'we' or hā'ü-e', (RENÉ JUST,) ABBÉ, a distinguished French mineralogist, born at Saint-Just, Picardy, on the 28th of February, 1743. He was educated at the College of Navarre, Paris, in which he was appointed professor of Latin in 1764. His interest in mineralogy was first excited by hearing a lecture from Daubenton, after which he became a diligent student under that professor. By a happy accident, he made an important discovery in crystallography in 1781. As he was examining a prism of calcareous spar in the cabinet of a friend, it fell into and was broken into fragments, which presented crystalline faces different from those of the prism, and revealed to him the germ of a new science. Continuing his observations, he demonstrated that the structure of crystals is conformed to invariable laws, that the same mineral contains uniformly the same primary form as the basis of its crystallization, and that they may be cloven in such directions as to lay bare their peculiar primitive forms which lie concealed within them. These discoveries opened a new era in mineralogy, and, when modestly announced to the Academy of Sciences, made a profound sensation. In 1783 Haüy was chosen a member of that Academy. In 1792 he was imprisoned a short time by the revolutionists for refusing to take the required oath. In 1794 the Convention intrusted to him the charge of the cabinet of the School of Mines, and in 1802 he became professor of mineralogy in the Museum of Natural History. Napoleon granted him a pension, and named him canon of Notre-Dame and a member of the legion of honour. At the formation of the University he obtained the chair of the faculty of sciences. Amidst the homage of the great world he preserved the modest simplicity of his manners which had distinguished his early life. He published a "Treatise on Mineralogy," (1801,) a standard work of great merit; an "Elementary Treatise on Physics," (1803;) and a "Treatise on Crystallography," (1822.) He refused an offer of 600,000 francs for his collection of minerals. Cuvier has observed that the discoveries of Haüy, like those of Newton, far from losing in generality with the lapse of time, will continually gain in that respect. Died in 1822.

"From the moment that the genius of Haüy discovered the general fact that they could be *cloven* or split in such directions as to lay bare their peculiar primitive or fundamental forms, (which lay concealed within them as the statue might be conceived encrusted in its marble envelope,) from that moment mineralogy ceased to be an unmeaning list of names, a mere laborious cataloguing of stones and rubbish." (Sir John Herschel, "Preliminary Discourse on the Study of Natural Philosophy.")

See CUVIER'S "Memoir on R. J. Haüy," and translation of the same in "Smithsonian Report" for 1860; LUIGI CONFIGLIACHI, "Memorie intorno alla Vita ed alle Opere dei due Naturalisti Werner e Haüy," 1827; QUÉRARD, "La France Littéraire;" "Nouvelle Biographie Générale."

Haüy, (VALENTIN,) brother of the preceding, was born at Saint-Just, in France, in 1745. He was noted for his zeal and success in the education of the blind, a branch of instruction which had been entirely neglected before he, with the aid of the Philanthropic Society, opened a school in Paris in 1784. His success having attracted the attention of the public, Haüy received the title of interpreter and secretary to the king, who took his school under the protection of the state. He published an "Essay on the Education of the Blind," (1786.) About 1800 he ceased to be director of the institution, and his services were acknowledged by the grant of a pension of two thousand francs. A few years later, he founded an institution for the blind in Saint Petersburg. Died in Paris in 1822.

Hav'e-lock, (Sir HENRY,) a distinguished British general, born at Bishop's Wearmouth, Durham, on the 5th of April, 1795. He entered the army in 1815, as lieutenant, and was ordered to India in 1823. He distinguished himself by his attention to the religious instruction of the men under his command, and was a strict disciplinarian. About 1828 he married Hannah, a daughter of the Rev. Mr. Marshman, a missionary. In consequence of his earnest and zealous religious character he was stigmatized as a fanatic by many of his fellow-officers. His promotion was slow. He obtained the rank of captain in 1838, and served on the staff of Sir W. Cotton in the Afghan war. He came to England on sick-leave in 1849, and remained there about two years. In the spring of 1854 he was appointed quartermaster-general. He became adjutant-general in the ensuing winter, and commanded a division in the war against Persia which began in 1856. He returned to India about the beginning of the great Sepoy mutiny which broke out in February, 1857. In July he defeated the Sepoys at Futtehpore, Arny, and Cawnpore. Having driven Nana Sahib out of Cawnpore, he advanced with about 1500 men to the relief of Lucknow, in which a small garrison was besieged by a large army of Sepoys; but his army was so reduced by disease and the casualties of battle that he was compelled to fall back and await reinforcements. In the mean time General Outram, superior in rank to Havelock, arrived; but he generously waived his rank, and offered to serve as a volunteer, declaring that Havelock was entitled to the honour of relieving Lucknow. He entered that place about the 25th of September, and defended it until the arrival of Sir Colin Campbell. He was promoted to the rank of major-general in September, 1857, and died in India in November of the same year.

See J. T. HEADLEY, "Life of General H. Havelock," 1859; JOHN MARSHMAN, "Life of Sir H. Havelock," 1860; "British Quarterly Review" for July, 1860.

Havemann, hä'veh-mân', (WILHELM,) a German historian, born at Lüneburg in 1800, became professor of history at Göttingen in 1838. Among his works is a "History of Brunswick and Lüneburg," (2 vols., 1838.)

Hä'ven, (ALICE,) originally EMILY BRADLEY, an authoress, born at Hudson, New York, about 1825. Her first husband was Joseph C. Neal, of Philadelphia, editor of Neal's "Saturday Gazette." She produced juvenile stories, among which are "Helen Morton," and "No such Word as Fail."

Haven, (ERASTUS OTIS,) D.D., an American Methodist divine, born in Boston in 1820. He graduated at the Wesleyan University, Middletown, Connecticut, in 1842, and subsequently became professor of Latin and Greek in the University of Michigan. In 1856 he was appointed editor of "Zion's Herald and Wesleyan Journal," published in Boston.

Haven, (NATHANIEL APPLETON,) an American journalist, born at Portsmouth, New Hampshire, in 1790. He graduated at Harvard in 1807, and from 1821 to 1825 was editor of the "Portsmouth Journal." Died in 1826. A volume of his writings, consisting chiefly of

poems and orations, with a memoir of the author's life, by George Ticknor, was published in 1827.

See "North American Review" for July, 1828.

Havercamp, hâv'er-kâmp', (SIGEBERT,) a celebrated Dutch critic and author, born at Utrecht in 1683. He succeeded Gronovius in 1721 as professor of Greek at Leyden, where he afterwards obtained the chair of history and eloquence. Among his most important works are "Dissertations on the Coins of Alexander the Great," (1722,) "Universal History explained by Medals," (in Dutch, 1736,) "Introduction to Roman Antiquities," (in Latin, 1740,) several treatises on Medals, and good editions of Lucretius, (1725,) Josephus, (1726,) and Sallust, (1742.) Died at Leyden in 1742.

See ERSCH und GRUBER, "Allgemeine Encyklopaedie;" MORÉRI, "Dictionnaire Historique."

Haverman, hä'ver-mân', (MARGARET,) a skilful painter of flowers and fruits, born at Amsterdam in 1720. She worked in Paris. Died about 1795.

Hävernick or **Haevernick,** hä'ver-nik', (HEINRICH,) a German theologian and critic, was professor at Rostock and at Königsberg. He published an "Introduction to the Old Testament," (1836–44,) and other works. Died in the prime of life in 1846.

Hav'ers, (CLOPTON,) an English anatomist, who lived about 1690, wrote "Osteologia Nova," (1691.)

Havet, hä'vä', (ARMAND ERNEST MAURICE,) a French physician and botanist, born at Rouen in 1795; died in Madagascar in 1820.

Hav'i-land, (JOHN,) an architect, born near Taunton, in England, in 1792, emigrated to the United States in his youth. He designed the United States Mint, Philadelphia, the Hospital for the Insane, at Harrisburg, Pennsylvania, the Eastern State Penitentiary, at Philadelphia, and other public edifices. Died in 1852.

Haweis, hau'wis,? (THOMAS,) an English theologian, born at Truro in 1734, was chaplain to the Countess of Huntingdon. He published, besides other works, "The Communicant's Spiritual Companion," (1763,) and a "History of the Church of Christ," (3 vols., 1800.) Died in 1820.

Hawes, hauz, (JOEL,) an American writer and Congregational minister, born in Medway, Massachusetts, in 1789. He graduated at Brown University in 1813, and preached many years at Hartford, Connecticut. Among his works are "Lectures to Young Men," (1828,) and "The Religion of the East," (1845.) Died in 1867.

Hawes, hauz, (STEPHEN,) an English poet, who lived about 1500, was a native of Suffolk, and became groom of the privy chamber to Henry VII. He published in 1517 "The Pastime of Pleasure," an allegorical poem, which displays much learning and reflection. Warton says, "If the poems of Rowley are not genuine, the 'Pastime of Pleasure' is almost the only effort of imagination and invention which had appeared in our poetry since Chaucer."

Hawes, (WILLIAM,) an English physician, born at Islington in 1736, practised in London the most of his life. He distinguished himself by his zealous efforts in behalf of the Humane Society, instituted in 1774. He published several medical works, and an "Account of Dr. Goldsmith's Last Illness." Died in 1808.

Hawke, hauk, (EDWARD,) LORD, an English admiral, born in 1715, became a captain in 1734, rear-admiral in 1747, and vice-admiral of the blue in 1748. He commanded the fleet which in 1759 defeated the French near Belleisle. In 1765 he was named first lord of the admiralty, and in 1776 was raised to the peerage. Died in 1781.

See CAMPBELL, "Lives of British Admirals."

Haw'ker, (ROBERT,) an English Calvinistic divine, born at Exeter in 1753. He was for fifty years vicar of a church in Plymouth. He published a valuable "Commentary on the Old and New Testament," (9 vols., 1816,) and other religious works. Died in 1827.

Hawkesworth, hauks'worth, (JOHN,) an English essayist, born in London between 1715 and 1719. He began his literary career as a contributor to the "Gentleman's Magazine" about 1740. In 1752, 1753, and 1754 he gained distinction as the editor of the "Adventurer," a series of essays, in which he was assisted by

Dr. Johnson and others. About half of these were his own composition. In 1761 he published an edition of Swift's Works, with a life of that author, which is highly commended. He received from government £6000 for writing an account of Captain Cook's First Voyage, (1773.) Hawkesworth is accounted one of the most elegant essayists of his time. Dr. Johnson, in his "Life of Swift," represents him as one "capable of dignifying his narrations with elegance of language and force of sentiment." Died in 1773.

See DRAKE, "Essays;" W. H. PRESCOTT, "Miscellanies."

Haw′kins, (BENJAMIN WATERHOUSE,) an English naturalist, artist, and geologist, born in London in 1807. He published several educational works, among which is "Elements of Form," (1842.) He lectured in New York in 1868. He is eminently skilful in delineating the forms of animals and in restoring fossil remains.

Hawkins, (Sir JOHN,) M.P., (called by the Italian and Spanish writers of that day **Achines** or **Aquines,**) an able English naval officer, born at Plymouth about 1520. After following the slave-trade several years, he was defeated by the Spanish in 1567 near San Juan de Ulloa. As rear-admiral, in 1588, he served with distinction against the Spanish Armada, and was rewarded with the honour of knighthood. In 1595 Hawkins and Drake commanded a large fleet sent against the Spanish colonies in the West Indies; but they were unsuccessful. He is said to have been the first Englishman who was engaged in the slave-trade. Died in 1595.

See CAMPBELL, "Lives of British Admirals;" FROUDE, "History of England," vol. vii.; J. BARROW, "Memoirs of the Naval Worthies of Queen Elizabeth's Reign," 1845.

Hawkins, (Sir JOHN,) a descendant of the preceding, born in London in 1719, was educated for the law. In 1749 he was admitted a member of Johnson's literary club that met in Ivy Lane. In the early part of his life he contributed to the "Gentleman's Magazine." Having married in 1753 a wealthy lady named Storer, he retired from the practice of law. In 1763 he was elected a member of the celebrated literary club to which Burke, Johnson, and Goldsmith belonged, and in 1772 he was knighted for his active services in the magistracy. His principal productions are a "History of Music," (in 5 vols., 1776,) (which was coldly received, but is now more esteemed,) and a "Life of Dr. Johnson," (1787.) He was an intimate friend of Johnson, who chose him as one of his executors. He died in 1789, and was buried in Westminster Abbey.

Hawkins, (JOHN SIDNEY,) eldest son of the preceding, was born about 1757. He wrote a "Life of Da Vinci," and essays on various subjects. Died in 1842.

Hawkins, (LÆTITIA MATILDA,) a sister of the preceding, wrote "The Countess and Gertrude," a novel, (4 vols., 1811,) "Memoirs, Biographical Sketches, and Anecdotes," (2 vols., 1824,) and other works.

Hawkins, (Sir RICHARD,) an English mariner, son of the rear-admiral, noticed above, was born about 1555. He commanded one of the ships which encountered the "Invincible Armada" in 1588. In 1593 he led an expedition of three ships to the South Sea, and was captured by the Spaniards near Peru. After his release he published "Observations" on the voyage. Died in 1622.

See J. BARROW, "Memoirs of the Naval Worthies of Queen Elizabeth's Reign," 1845.

Hawkins, (Sir THOMAS,) an English translator, lived in the reign of Charles I. He produced a version of the Odes of Horace, (1631.)

Hawks, hauks, (FRANCIS LISTER,) D.D., an American clergyman and author, born at Newbern, North Carolina, in 1798. He studied law and was admitted to the bar; but his religious convictions induced him in 1821 to enter the ministry of the Episcopal Church. In 1829 he became pastor of a church in Philadelphia. In 1830 he assumed the pastoral charge of Saint Stephen's Church in New York, and afterwards of Saint Thomas's. In 1837 he and Dr. C. S. Henry commenced the "New York Review," which they continued to publish until 1841. He preached in New Orleans for five years, (1844–49,) and became rector of Calvary Church, New York, about 1850. Among his various works are "Egypt and its Monuments," (1849,) and a "History of North Carolina,"

(1857 *et seq.*) He edited the "Romance of Biography," and other juvenile works. Died at New York in 1866.

Hawks′moor,(NICHOLAS,) an eminent English architect, born in 1666, was a pupil of Sir Christopher Wren. He was employed on several churches of London, and made additions to All-Souls College, Oxford. It is said that he was associated with Vanbrugh on the palace of Blenheim and Castle Howard. One of his most admired and original works is Saint George's Church, Bloomsbury, which Walpole criticised as "a master-stroke of absurdity." Died in 1736.

Hawk′wood, (Sir JOHN,) an English military adventurer, was the leader of a band of outlaws who entered Italy about 1360. He rendered himself famous by his skill, audacity, and success, and was hired to fight by the Florentines and the Visconti of Milan. He died at Florence in 1394.

Haw′ley, (GIDEON,) a missionary, who laboured among the American Indians, was born in Connecticut in 1727. He became pastor at Marshpee, Massachusetts, in 1758, and remained there until his death in 1807.

Hawley, (JOSEPH,) an American patriot, born at Northampton, Massachusetts, in 1724, graduated at Yale in 1742. He practised law in his native place, and attained eminence in his profession. In the contest between the colonies and the mother-country he gained distinction by his political wisdom, eloquence, and patriotism. He was chosen a member of the Massachusetts legislature in 1764. In 1776 ill health induced him to retire from public life. Died in 1788.

Hâ′worth, (ADRIAN,) an English naturalist of Cottenham, Yorkshire. He wrote, among other treatises, "Lepidoptera Britannica," (4 parts, 1803–28,) which is called a work of great value. Died in 1833.

Haw′thorne,(NATHANIEL,) a distinguished American author, was born at Salem, Massachusetts, on the 4th of July, 1804. His father, a ship-captain, died at Havana about 1810. Nathaniel graduated at Bowdoin College in 1825, Longfellow the poet being one of his classmates. He was endowed by nature with an acute and subtle intellect, and with imaginative powers of no common order; but these were associated with an extreme and almost morbid sensibility. While at college, his health was delicate, and he is said to have suffered from excessive diffidence and from occasional fits of gloom and deep dejection. Under these circumstances he made the acquaintance of Franklin Pierce, (afterwards President of the United States,) who did much to cheer and encourage him in his moments of despondency. The friendship thus begun lasted through life. After leaving college, Hawthorne spent several years mostly in seclusion and study, writing occasional tales for the papers and periodicals. In 1837 he issued a volume entitled "Twice-told Tales," so named because they had previously been published in another form. This book attracted the notice of Mr. Longfellow, who spoke of it in terms of high praise in the "North American Review." In 1843 Mr. Hawthorne removed to Concord, and resided for some time in an old manse, from the windows of which, it is said, the minister of the parish looked out upon the battle fought between his fellow-townsmen and the British troops on the memorable 19th of April, 1775. In 1846 appeared a volume entitled "Mosses from an Old Manse," a collection of sketches and tales written by him while occupying the manse at Concord. In 1846, under Mr. Polk's administration, he was appointed surveyor of the port of Salem, a position which he held for three years. He published in 1850 his celebrated "Scarlet Letter," a romance of extraordinary power, which raised its author at once to the first rank among American prose writers of fiction. In 1851 appeared his "House of the Seven Gables," in 1852 his "Blithedale Romance," and in 1860 his "Marble Faun," regarded by some as the best of all his works. He had published in 1852 a life of his friend Franklin Pierce, (the Democratic candidate for the Presidency,) who, after his inauguration, appointed his biographer United States consul for Liverpool, perhaps the most lucrative position within the gift of a President. He held this office for four years, after which he spent some time in travelling on the continent of Europe. Soon after his

ā, ē, ī, ō, ū, ȳ, *long;* ă, ĕ, ŏ, same, less prolonged; ă, ĕ, ĭ, ŏ, ŭ, ў, *short;* ą, ę, į, ǫ, *obscure;* fâr, fâll, fât; mĕt; nŏt; gŏŏd; mōͅon;

return to the United States, Mr. Hawthorne published "Our Old Home," containing sketches of English life and character. He died in 1864. Since his death a very attractive work, entitled "Hawthorne's Notes," has been published, (2 vols., 1869,) consisting of his observations on a great variety of subjects.

Mr. Hawthorne's merits as an author are of a peculiar and very high order. As a novelist, all critics acknowledge his power to awaken a deep, intense, and sustained interest; but some of the reviewers object that the tone of his works is not healthful. "The Scarlet Letter," says "Blackwood" for May, 1855, "glows with the fire of a suppressed, secret, feverish excitement: it is not the glow of natural life, but the hectic of disease, which burns upon the cheek of its actors." "The House of the Seven Gables," observes the same writer, "is not less remarkable nor less unwholesome than its predecessor." But, whatever may be thought of the tone of his works, all must concede to him not only great power and originality, but a subtle and exquisite humour, as well as a marvellous felicity in the use of language. His style, indeed, may be said to combine almost every excellence,—elegance, dignity, simplicity, grace, clearness, and force.

See GRISWOLD, "Prose Writers of America;" DUYCKINCK, "Cyclopædia of American Literature," vol. ii.; "Blackwood's Magazine" for November, 1863; "North American Review" for July, 1837, July, 1850, and January, 1853; "Atlantic Monthly" for May, 1860, (by E. P. WHIPPLE,) and September, 1868.

Haw'trey, (EDWARD CRAVEN,) D.D., an English scholar, born in 1789, became head-master of Eton about 1834, and afterwards provost of the same. Died in 1862.

Haxo, /häk'so', (FRANÇOIS NICOLAS BENOÎT,) an able military engineer, born at Lunéville in 1774. He directed the operations at the siege of Saragossa, (1809.) In 1812 he held a high command in the Russian campaign, and was made general of division. He commanded the corps of engineers during the Hundred Days, and was at Waterloo. In 1832 he conducted the siege of Antwerp as commander-in-chief of the engineers. Died in 1838.

See MENGIN, "Notice sur Général Baron Haxo," 1838.

Haxo, (NICOLAS,) a French general, uncle of the preceding, was born at Lunéville about 1750. He distinguished himself at the battle of Chollet, and gained a victory at Noirmoutiers. He was killed in 1794.

Hāy, (DAVID RAMSAY,) a British artist and eminent writer on the principles of form and colour, was born in Edinburgh in 1798. He learned the trade of house-painter, and was employed by Sir Walter Scott in the decoration of Abbotsford. In 1828 he published "The Laws of Harmonious Colouring," (6th edition, 1847.) He wrote, among other works, "Proportion, or the Geometric Principle of Beauty Analyzed," (1843,) "Science of Proportions of the Human Head and Countenance," (1849,) and "The Science of Beauty as Developed in Nature and Applied in Art," (1856.)

Hāy, (JAMES,) a Scottish diplomatist, employed by James I. He was raised to the English peerage as Earl of Carlisle. Died in 1636.

Hay, (WILLIAM,) born in Sussex, England, about 1700, represented Seaford in Parliament from 1734 to 1755. He published an "Essay on Civil Government," (1728,) and a few other works. Died in 1755.

Haydn, hä'd'n, [Ger. pron. hīd'n,] (JOSEPH,) a celebrated and original composer, was born at Rohrau, on the frontier of Austria and Hungary, March 31, 1732. His father was a poor mechanic. When he was about eight years old, his voice attracted the notice of Reuter, chapel-master of the cathedral in Vienna, under whom he passed eight years as chorister. Afterwards, being left to his own resources, he endured extreme poverty for several years, during which he became acquainted with the poet Metastasio, from whom he learned Italian. He received some lessons in composition from Porpora, and between the ages of nineteen and twenty-six composed many sonatas, concertos, and symphonies, which were admired. In 1760 he was appointed chapel-master to Prince Esterhazy at Eisenstadt. With this patron and his heir he passed about thirty years, and enjoyed prosperity, excepting the troubles of an ill-assorted marriage, from which he was relieved by a divorce. Having composed a great number of works and acquired a wide reputation, he produced in London in 1791 six grand symphonies, which were received with great enthusiasm. His noble master-piece the oratorio of "The Creation" was performed in Vienna in 1798, and procured his admission into the French Institute. He surpassed his predecessors in symphonies, and displayed extraordinary fertility of invention. Among his last works is a piece of church music called "The Seasons," (1801.) Died at Vienna, May 31, 1809. Haydn appears to have been exempt from the spirit of rivalry and envy. On one occasion he designated Mozart as the first composer of the world. His happy and genial temperament is reflected in his compositions.

See C. A. GRIESENGER, "Biographische Notizen über Joseph Haydn," 1810; "Letters on the Life and Works of Haydn," in Italian, by CARPANI, ("Le Haydine," etc.,) 1812; FRAMERY, "Notice sur Joseph Haydn," 1810; LE BRETON, "Vie de Joseph Haydn," 1810; FÉTIS, "Biographie Universelle des Musiciens;" A. C. DIES, "J. Haydn's Biographie," 1810; L. A. C. DE BEYLE, (under the pseudonym of BOMBET,) "Vie de Haydn, Mozart et Métastase," Paris, 1817; English version of the same, 1817, and Boston, 1839; "London Quarterly Review" for October, 1817.

Haydn, hä'd'n, (JOSEPH,) an English author, who published a "Dictionary of Dates and Universal Reference," which is highly commended; also a "Hand-Book of Dignities." Died in London in 1856.

Haydn, (MICHAEL,) a brother of Joseph Haydn the musician, was born at Rohrau in 1737. He was an excellent organist and composer, and became chapel-master in the cathedral of Salzburg. He composed numerous oratorios, masses, Te Deums, and other works. His brother Joseph considered him the greatest composer of sacred music of his time except Mozart. Died in 1808.

See FÉTIS, "Biographie Universelle des Musiciens."

Hāy'don, (BENJAMIN ROBERT,) an eminent English painter, born at Plymouth in 1786. He went to London in 1804, and was admitted as a student at the Royal Academy. In 1807 he exhibited a painting of the Holy Family resting during their flight to Egypt. In 1809 his "Dentatus" gained the first prize in the exhibition of the British Institution. His "Judgment of Solomon" was purchased for seven hundred guineas. In the early part of his career he quarrelled with the Academy, and when he applied for admission as an associate he was refused. In 1815 he opened a school of painting, in which several eminent artists were formed; but in pecuniary matters he was not successful. While confined in prison for debt in 1827, he painted the "Mock Election," for which George IV. paid him five hundred guineas. "Napoleon Musing at Saint Helena" was one of his most admired productions. In 1837-38-39 he gave lectures on Painting, which were very popular, and were published in 1844. The last years of his life were rendered unhappy by pecuniary difficulties, and his mind became so disordered that he committed suicide in June, 1846. His merit as a painter is variously estimated. The Landseers were his pupils.

See his Life, by THOMAS TAYLOR, 1853, 3 vols.; "London Quarterly Review" for October, 1853; "Edinburgh Review" for October, 1853; "Blackwood's Magazine" for November, 1853.

Haye, La. See CORMENIN and DELAHAYE.

Hayer, hä'yà', (JEAN NICOLAS HUBERT,) a French monk, born at Sarre-Louis about 1708. He defended revealed religion against infidels in several works. Died in 1780.

Hayer du Perron, le, lĕh hä'yà' dü pä'rôn', (PIERRE,) a French poet, born at Alençon in 1603; died after 1678.

Hayes, hāz, (AUGUSTUS ALLEN,) an American chemist, born at Windsor, Vermont, in 1806. He made several important discoveries, and contributed to Silliman's "Journal of Science," and other scientific publications.

Hayes, hāz, (CATHERINE,) a popular vocalist, born at Limerick, Ireland, about 1820. She performed with success in the theatres of Italy, Vienna, and London. In 1851 she visited the United States, and sang in the principal cities. Died in 1861.

See "Gentleman's Magazine" for September, 1861.

Hayes, (CHARLES,) an English mathematician, born in 1678, wrote learned and ingenious works, among which are treatises on "Fluxions and Conic Sections," on "Longitude," and "Chronology of the Septuagint." Died in 1760.

€ as k; ç as s; g hard; ġ as j; G, H, K, guttural; N, nasal; R, trilled; s as z; th as in this. (☞See Explanations, p. 23.)

Hayes, (ISAAC I.,) an American explorer, born in Chester county, Pennsylvania, in 1832, graduated as M.D. at the University of Pennsylvania in 1853. The same year he accompanied Dr. Kane on an exploring expedition to the North Pole. After passing two winters in the northern regions, blocked up in the ice, and suffering incredible hardships, they returned in the autumn of 1855. (See KANE, ELISHA K.) Dr. Hayes published an interesting account of his share in this expedition, entitled "An Arctic Boat Journey," (Boston, 1860.) In 1860 he conducted a second expedition to the Arctic regions, and returned in the autumn of 1861. He has since written a tale, entitled "Cast away in the Cold," first published in the pages of "Our Young Folks."

Hayes, (WILLIAM,) an English musical composer, born in 1708; died in 1777.

Hayez, ä'yä', ? (FRANCESCO,) an Italian historical painter and excellent colorist, born at Venice in 1792. Among his works are "Laocoon," and "The Two Foscari."

See "Westminster Review" for April, 1841.

Hay'ley, (WILLIAM,) an English author, born at Chichester in 1745, resided at Eartham, and enjoyed an easy fortune in literary pursuits. In 1792 he became acquainted with the poet Cowper, whose life he afterwards wrote, (1804.) He published a variety of works in prose and verse, which once were very popular, but are not now ranked above mediocrity. His chief poems are "An Essay on History," (1780,) "Triumphs of Temper," (1781,) "An Essay on Painting," and "An Essay on Epic Poetry," (1782.) He was not without taste, and possessed some skill in versification; but his poetry is feeble and infected with mawkish sentiment. Southey once remarked, "Every thing about that man is good except his poetry." Died in 1820.

See "Memoirs of W. Hayley," by himself, 1823; CAREY, "Lives of English Poets from Johnson to Kirke White;" "London Quarterly Review" for December, 1824.

Haym, hīm, (NICCOLÒ FRANCESCO,) a musician and bibliographer, born in Rome about 1680. He composed several admired sonatas, and published a valuable work on Italian bibliography, called "Notices of Rare Books in the Italian Language," (1726.) Died in London in 1730.

Hay'man, (FRANCIS,) an English historical painter, born at Exeter in 1708, lived chiefly in London. He was one of the earliest members of the Royal Academy. Among his principal productions are his illustrations of Shakspeare and Milton. Died in 1776.

Haymo or **Haimo,** hī'mo, or **Aimo,** ī'mo, a German ecclesiastic, whose writings had a high reputation, became Bishop of Halberstadt in 841 A.D. He wrote "Commentaries on the Scriptures." Died in 853.

Haynau, von, fon hī'nŏw, (JULIUS JAKOB,) BARON, an Austrian general, born at Cassel in 1786, was a natural son of the Elector of Hesse-Cassel. He entered the Austrian service in 1801, became colonel in 1830, and field-marshal-lieutenant in 1844. In the suppression of a revolt in Italy in 1848 and 1849, he displayed some military skill and became notorious for his cruelty. He obtained in May, 1849, the chief command of the Austrian army in Hungary, and defeated the Hungarians in several actions. The execution of the vanquished chiefs and patriots by his orders excited general indignation. He was deprived of his command in 1850. During a visit to London in 1850, he was assaulted and roughly treated by the draymen of Barclay & Perkins's brewery. Died in 1853.

See "Nouvelle Biographie Générale."

Hayne, (ARTHUR P.,) a brother of Robert Y. Hayne, noticed below, was born at Charleston, South Carolina, in 1790. He entered the army in 1807, served during the war of 1812, distinguished himself at the battle of New Orleans, January, 1815, and obtained the rank of adjutant-general. He resigned his commission in 1820, and became a lawyer. In 1858 he was chosen a United States Senator.

Hayne, hī'neh, (FRIEDRICH GOTTLOB,) a German botanist, born in 1763, became professor of botany at Berlin. He published, besides other works, an excellent "Description and Representation of Plants used in Medi-

cine," (11 vols., 1802-31, with 600 plates designed by himself.) Died in 1832.

See CALLISEN, "Medicinisches Schriftsteller-Lexikon."

Hayne, (ISAAC,) an officer, born in South Carolina in 1745, became a wealthy planter. He served against the British at the siege of Charleston in 1780, was taken prisoner and paroled. The British by threats induced him to subscribe a declaration of allegiance, and afterwards required him to take arms for the king. To avoid this necessity, he joined the American army, was taken prisoner, and hung in August, 1781.

Hayne, (JULIA DEAN,) a popular American actress, born at Pleasant Valley, New York, in 1830, has performed with success in the United States and England.

Hayne, (PAUL H.,) a poet, and nephew of Robert Y. Hayne, noticed below, was born at Charleston, South Carolina, in 1831. He published a volume of Poems in 1854.

Hayne, (ROBERT YOUNG,) a distinguished American orator, born in the parish of Saint Paul, South Carolina, in 1791, was a grand-nephew of Isaac Hayne, who was executed by the British in 1781. He studied law with Langdon Cheves, and became eminent in his profession. In 1818 he was chosen Speaker of the legislature of South Carolina, which he represented in the national Senate from 1823 to 1832. In January, 1830, he made an eloquent speech in the Senate, to which Webster replied in one of his most successful and memorable efforts. He was Governor of his native State from 1832 to 1834, and advocated nullification. Died in 1840.

See "National Portrait-Gallery of Distinguished Americans," vol. ii.

Hayne, (Rev. THOMAS,) an English critic and teacher, born in Leicestershire in 1581, was a graduate of Oxford, and an excellent linguist. He published a "Latin Grammar," a "Life of Luther," a "General View of the Holy Scripture," and other works. Died in 1645.

Haynes, hānz, (HOPTON,) born in 1672, was assay-master of the English mint, and a friend of Sir Isaac Newton. He wrote zealously in defence of Unitarian doctrines. Died in 1749.

Haynes, (JOHN,) an Anglo-American governor, was born in Essex, England, and removed to Boston in 1633. In 1635 he was chosen Governor of Massachusetts. In 1636 he became one of the chief founders of Connecticut, of which he was chosen the first Governor in 1639, and was afterwards several times re-elected. Died in 1654.

Haynes, hānz, (LEMUEL,) an eminent coloured minister, born in West Hartford, Connecticut, in 1753. He early displayed a remarkable thirst for knowledge, and, by devoting all his leisure to study, became in a few years a good Latin and Greek scholar. In 1775 he joined the American army, and the next year served in the expedition to Ticonderoga. Licensed to preach in 1780, he was thirty years pastor in West Rutland, Vermont. From 1822 until his death, in 1833, he preached to a congregation in Granville, New York. His famous sermon against Universalism, in reply to Hosea Ballou, has been widely read. A memoir of his life was published by the Rev. Dr. Cooley.

Hays, hāz, (ALEXANDER,) an American general, born in Pittsburg, Pennsylvania, about 1824, graduated at West Point in 1844. He became a brigadier-general of volunteers in September, 1862, commanded a division at Gettysburg, July, 1863, and was killed at the battle of the Wilderness in May, 1864.

Hays, (WILLIAM JACOB,) a painter of animals, was born in the city of New York in 1830. He produced many pictures of dogs and game.

Hay'ter, (Sir GEORGE,) an English painter of history and portraits, was born in London about 1792. He studied for several years in Italy, and after his return obtained the title of first painter to the queen, by whom he was knighted in 1842. Among his finest productions are "Victoria taking the Oath at the Coronation," and "The Trial of Lord Russell."

Hayter, (Rev. JOHN,) an Englishman, who was employed to superintend the process of unrolling the Greek manuscripts found at Herculaneum. He published a "Report on the Herculaneum Manuscripts," (1811.) Died in 1818.

Hāy'ward, (Sir JOHN,) an English historian, who published in 1599 "The First Part of the Reign of Henry IV." He was knighted in 1619. He also wrote the lives of William I., William II., and Henry I. Died in 1627.

Haywood, (ELIZA.) See HEYWOOD.

Hāy'wood, (ELIZABETH,) an English authoress, born in London in 1693, wrote "The Female Spectator," and other works. Died in 1756.

Haz'ard, (EBENEZER,) born in Philadelphia about 1744, was postmaster-general of the United States from 1782 to 1789. He published "Historical Collection of State Papers," etc., (1792.) Died in 1817.

Hazard, (SAMUEL,) a son of the preceding, was born in Philadelphia in 1784. He published in 1828–36 the "Register of Pennsylvania," containing historical documents, etc. He also wrote the "Annals of Pennsylvania from 1609 to 1682."

Hā'zen, (WILLIAM B.,) an American general, born in Vermont in 1830, graduated at West Point in 1855. He served as colonel at the battle of Shiloh, April 7, 1862, and as brigadier-general at the battles of Stone River, which ended in January, 1863, and Chickamauga, September 19 and 20 of the same year. He commanded a division of the army of General Sherman in the campaign against Atlanta, and in the march from that place to the sea, in 1864; and he was made a major-general of volunteers in December of that year.

Hā'zle-rig, written also **Heselrige,** (Sir ARTHUR,) an English Puritan, who took a prominent part in the opposition to Charles I., was born about 1612. He represented Leicestershire in the Long Parliament, and was one of the five members whom the king attempted to arrest in 1642 on a charge of treason. During the civil war he served in the army of Parliament as colonel. In 1649 he was chosen a member of the council of state, and in 1658 was created a peer by Cromwell, but preferred to retain his seat in the House of Commons. Died in 1660.

Hāz'litt, (WILLIAM,) an eminent English critic and miscellaneous author, born at Maidstone, April 10, 1778, was the son of a Unitarian minister. After making creditable essays in the art of painting, he adopted literature as a profession, and in 1803 obtained employment as a reporter for the London newspapers. In 1805 he published his first work, "An Essay on the Principles of Human Action," followed by "The Eloquence of the British Senate," (1808,) with critical notes. In 1808 he married Miss Stoddart. Between 1813 and 1818 he delivered lectures on philosophy and English poetry, some of which were published and favourably received. Of his very numerous and various works the following are perhaps the principal: "Characters of Shakspeare's Plays," (1817,) "Original Essays," (1821,) "The Spirit of the Age," (1824,) "The Plain Speaker," "Political Essays," "Table-Talk," (1824,) and "The Life of Napoleon," (4 vols., 1828.) In the latter part of his life he contributed to the "Edinburgh Review." He enjoyed a high reputation as a critic; but allowance must be made for his prejudice against living authors. Sir Archibald Alison expressed the opinion that "in critical disquisitions on the leading characters and works of the drama, he is not surpassed in the whole range of English literature." Died in 1830.

See "Literary Remains of W. Hazlitt, with a Notice of his Life, by his Son," etc., 2 vols., 1836. For a full account of Hazlitt's Works, see "List of the Writings of William Hazlitt and Leigh Hunt, chronologically arranged," etc., by ALEXANDER IRELAND, London, 1868; WILLIAM CAREW HAZLITT, "Memoirs of William Hazlitt," London, 1867; see also the "Edinburgh Review" for August, 1817, and January, 1837; "Monthly Review" for 1826.

Hazlitt, (WILLIAM,) JR., a lawyer, a son of the preceding, was born about 1810. He has distinguished himself as the translator of various works, among which are a "Life of Luther," (1846,) Guizot's "History of the English Revolution," (1846,) and Thierry's "History of the Conquest of England by the Normans," (1847.) He has edited the Works of De Foe, (1840,) and those of his father.

His son, WILLIAM CAREW H., born in 1834, published a "History of the Republic of Venice," (4 vols., 1860.)

Head, hed, (Sir EDMUND WALKER,) an English colonial governor, born near Maidstone, Kent, in 1805. He was appointed Lieutenant-Governor of New Brunswick in 1847, and succeeded Lord Elgin as Governor-General of Canada in 1854. He wrote a "Hand-Book of the History of the Spanish and French Schools of Painting," (1848,) a work of merit. Died in January, 1868.

Head, (Sir FRANCIS BOND,) a popular English writer, born near Rochester, Kent, in 1793. He was a captain in the army when, in 1825, he went to South America as agent of a mining association, and in 1826 published "Rough Notes of a Journey across the Pampas," etc., which was received with much favour. In 1833 he produced a successful humorous book, called "Bubbles from the Brunnen of Nassau." He became in 1836 Lieutenant-Governor of Upper Canada, in which an insurrection broke out in 1837. After the suppression of this he resigned, and returned to England in 1838. He wrote "The Emigrant," (6th edition, 1852,) and other works.

See "Sir F. Head; a Narrative;" "Edinburgh Review" for April, 1847; "London Magazine" for October, 1826.

Head, (Sir GEORGE,) a brother of the preceding, was born near Rochester in 1782. He served in the army in the Peninsula from 1809 to 1814, when he was ordered to Canada and Nova Scotia. After his return to England he published "Forest Scenes and Incidents in the Wilds of North America," (1829,) and several other books of travel. In 1849 appeared his "Rome: a Tour of Many Days," said to be a standard work. He was made a knight in 1831. Died in 1855.

Head, (RICHARD,) an Irish dramatist, wrote comedies. He was drowned at sea in 1678.

Headley, hĕd'le, (HENRY,) an English author, born at Norwich in 1766, was educated at Oxford. In 1786 he published a volume of poems, and wrote several articles for the "Gentleman's Magazine," and No. 16 in "Olla Podrida." In 1787 he published "Select Beauties of Ancient English Poets, with Remarks." His biographer, Rev. H. Kett, says, "His principles of criticism are sound, and his remarks pertinent. . . . His biographical sketches of the old English poets may be considered as a rich cabinet of exquisite portraits." Died in 1788.

See H. KETT, "Sketch of H. Headley," prefixed to his "Select Beauties of Ancient English Poets," 1810.

Headley, hĕd'le, (JOEL TYLER,) an American writer, born in Delaware county, New York, in 1814, graduated at Union College in 1839. Among his numerous works are "Napoleon and his Marshals," (2 vols., 1846,) a "Life of Oliver Cromwell," (1848,) and a "History of the Second War between England and the United States," (2 vols., 1853.) In 1855 he was elected secretary of state for New York.

See GRISWOLD, "Prose Writers of America."

Hēa'lŷ, (GEORGE PETER ALEXANDER,) an American portrait-painter, born in Boston in 1808. He worked for some years in Paris, and obtained a medal of the second class there in 1855. Among his works are "Webster's Reply to Hayne," and "Dr. Franklin before Louis XVI. of France."

See TUCKERMAN, "Book of the Artists," 1867.

Hēa'pŷ, written also **Heaphy,** (THOMAS,) an English portrait-painter, born about 1775; died in 1835.

Hearne, hern, (SAMUEL,) an English traveller, born in London in 1745, was for several years a midshipman in the royal navy. Having entered the service of the Hudson Bay Company, he was sent in 1769 on an expedition to discover a Northwest passage, and was the first European who penetrated to the ocean north of America. Of this journey an account was published in 1795. Died in 1792.

Hearne, (THOMAS,) an eminent English antiquary and collater of manuscripts, was born at White Waltham, Berkshire, in 1678. He became assistant librarian of the Bodleian Library, Oxford, in 1712; but, being a zealous Jacobite, he refused to take the oath to George I., and lost his office. He published accurate editions, with annotations, of many old works, among which are Livy's "History," (1708,) Spelman's "Life of Alfred the Great," (1710,) Leland's "Itinerary," (9 vols., 1710,) and Camden's "Annals," (3 vols., 1717.) He is introduced in Pope's "Dunciad" under the name of "Wormius." Died in 1735.

See HUDDESFORD, "Life of Thomas Hearne," 1772.

Hearne, (THOMAS,) an English artist, born at Marshfield in 1744, was a landscape-painter in water-colours, and a topographical designer. Died in 1817.

Hēath, (BENJAMIN,) an English lawyer and scholar, who published in 1740 an "Essay on the Divine Existence, Unity, and Attributes," and in 1765 a "Revisal of Shakspeare's Text." Died in 1766.

Heath, (CHARLES,) an English editor and engraver, born in 1784, gained distinction by the publication of the "Shakspeare Gallery," "Waverley Gallery," "Book of Beauty," and other annuals. Died in 1848.

Heath, (JAMES,) a historical writer, born in London in 1629. He wrote a "Chronicle of the Late Intestine War in the Three Kingdoms," (1661,) "The Glories of Charles II.'s Restoration," (1662,) and other works. Died in 1664.

Heath, (JAMES,) an eminent English engraver, born about 1760. Among his principal works are "The Death of Lord Nelson," after West, and a portrait of Washington, after Stuart. He was the father of Charles Heath, noticed above. Died in 1834.

Heath, (NICHOLAS,) born in London about 1500, became Archbishop of York and lord chancellor in 1556, in the reign of Queen Mary. Having refused to take the oath of supremacy, he was deprived of his office by Queen Elizabeth in 1558, and confined in the Tower. Died in 1579.

See FOSS, "The Judges of England."

Hēath, (WILLIAM,) an American general, born at Roxbury, Massachusetts, in 1737, was a farmer when the Revolution began. In 1775 he was appointed a brigadier-general, and in August, 1776, a major-general. He commanded near King's Bridge, New York, in 1776, and in the next year was transferred to the Eastern army, stationed near Boston, where he had temporary charge of the troops of Burgoyne who had surrendered at Saratoga. He returned to the main army in 1779, and was employed in the Highlands of the Hudson until the end of the war. In 1798 he published a volume of military "Memoirs." Died in 1814.

Hēath'cōat, (JOHN,) an English mechanical genius, born in Leicestershire in 1784. He settled at Nottingham as a "setter-up" of hosiery and warp frames, and invented a machine for making lace. Died in 1861.

Hēath'cote, (RALPH,) an English clergyman and author, born in Leicestershire in 1721. He became vicar of Barkby in 1748, and prebendary of Southwell in 1768. He wrote a "History of Astronomy," and a "Sketch of Lord Bolingbroke's Philosophy," besides other works on various subjects. Died in 1795.

Heathfield, LORD. See ELLIOT, (GEORGE AUGUSTUS.)

Hebbel, hĕb'bĕl, (FRIEDRICH,) a lyric poet and dramatist, born in Ditmarsch, in Holstein, in 1813, lived many years in Vienna. He wrote tragedies entitled "Genoveva" and "Maria Magdalena," and poems which were well received.

See EMIL KUH, "F. Hebbel; eine Characteristik," 1854.

He'be, [Gr. Ἥβη; Fr. HÉBÉ, à'bà',] a goddess of the Greek mythology, and the personification of youth, was represented as a daughter of Jupiter and Juno, (Hera.) According to Homer, she was a minister of the gods, and it was one of the duties of her office to fill their cups with nectar. She became the wife of Hercules after his apotheosis.

Hebel, hā'bĕl, (JOHANN PETER,) a distinguished German poet, born at Bâle in 1760, became in 1808 rector of the Academy of Carlsruhe, and in 1819 provost of the ecclesiastic chapter, (*Kirchen-Commission.*) His poems in the Suabian dialect ("Allemannische Gedichte," 1803) rendered his name popular throughout Germany. He describes nature in a simple and effective style. He published "Bible Histories for Youth," and several other works. Died in 1826.

See LONGFELLOW, "Poets and Poetry of Europe;" J. G. SCHULTHEISS, "Lebensbeschreibung von J. P. Hebel," 1831; ERSCH und GRUBER, "Allgemeine Encyklopaedie;" GERVINUS, "Geschichte der Deutschen Dichtung;" and the article entitled "The German Burns" in the "Atlantic Monthly" for April, 1862, (by BAYARD TAYLOR.)

Hebenstreit, hā'bĕn-strīt', (JOHANN CHRISTIAN,) a German theologian, born in 1686; died in 1756.

Hebenstreit, (JOHANN ERNST,) a German naturalist and physician, born at Neustadt on the Orla, Saxony, in 1703, was professor of medicine at Leipsic. He wrote an admired Latin poem on Man, "De Homine Sano et Ægroto," (1758,) "Palæologia Therapiæ," (1779,) and an interesting account of a "Journey to Algiers, Tunis, etc.," which he made in 1732. Died in 1757.

See ERSCH und GRUBER, "Allgemeine Encyklopaedie;" JOHANN AUGUST ERNESTI, "Memoria J. E. Hebenstreitii," 1759.

He'ber, (REGINALD,) an excellent English poet and prelate, born at Malpas, in Cheshire, on the 21st of April, 1783. He was the second son of Reginald Heber, rector of Hodnet. In 1800 he entered Brazennose College, Oxford, where he produced in 1803 his beautiful prize poem "Palestine." He made a tour on the continent in 1805 and 1806, obtained the living of Hodnet in 1807, and married Amelia Shipley in 1809. In 1812 he published a volume of poems, containing translations from Pindar, and a poem entitled "Europe: Lines on the Present War." He afterwards composed more than fifty "Hymns adapted to the Weekly Church Service." "These hymns," says D. M. Moir, "have been by far the most popular of his productions, and deservedly so; for in purity and elevation of sentiment, in simple pathos and eloquent earnestness, it would be difficult to find anything superior to them in the range of lyric poetry." He was elected preacher to Lincoln's Inn in 1822, and appointed Bishop of Calcutta in January, 1823. After visiting many remote parts of his very extensive diocese, he died of apoplexy, at Trichinopoli, on the 3d of April, 1826, leaving a high reputation for genius, piety, and liberality. His journal of a "Journey through India from Calcutta to Bombay, with Notes on Ceylon," (2 vols., 1828,) is called by the "London Quarterly Review" "one of the most delightful books in the language." "Independently of its moral attraction," says Lord Jeffrey, "we are induced to think it the most instructive and important publication that has ever been given to the world on the actual state and condition of our Indian empire." The same critic pays this high tribute to his character: "Learned, polished, and dignified he was undoubtedly; yet far more conspicuously kind, humble, tolerant, and laborious;—zealous for his church, too, and not forgetful of his station; but remembering it more for the duties than for the honours that were attached to it, and infinitely more zealous for the religious improvement and for the happiness of his fellow-creatures of every tongue, faith, and complexion; indulgent to all errors and infirmities; liberal in the best and truest sense of the word; humbly and conscientiously diffident of his own excellent judgment and never-failing charity."

See "Life of Reginald Heber," by his widow, 4 vols., 1830; REV. GEORGE BONNER, "Memoir of R. Heber;" KROHN, "Hebers Leben," Berlin, 2 vols., 1831; THOMAS TAYLOR, "Memoirs of the Life and Writings of the Rev. Reginald Heber;" "Edinburgh Review" for December, 1828.

Heber, (RICHARD,) a bibliomaniac and an excellent classical scholar, a half-brother of the preceding, was born in Westminster in 1773. He was educated at Oxford. In 1804 he inherited his father's estate at Hodnet, and represented the University of Oxford in Parliament from 1821 to 1826. He indulged an extravagant passion for collecting books, on which he is said to have spent about £180,000. He owned large libraries in London, Oxford, Paris, Antwerp, Ghent, Hodnet, and other places. He edited Silius Italicus and Claudian in 1792. Died in 1833. Sir Walter Scott dedicated to him the sixth canto of "Marmion."

Hĕb'er-dĕn, (WILLIAM,) an eminent physician, born in London in 1710, was educated at Cambridge. In 1748 he began the practice of medicine in London, in which he acquired a high reputation. In 1750 he became a Fellow of the Royal Society, to whose "Transactions" he contributed. He was reputed one of the best classical scholars of his time. His greatest work, "Medical Commentaries," (1802,) was written in elegant Latin. His moral character was excellent. Died in 1801. His son, WILLIAM HEBERDEN, M.D., wrote a "Treatise on the Increase and Decrease of Different Diseases," (1801.)

ā, ē, ī, ō, ū, ȳ, *long;* ă, ĕ, ĭ, ŏ, ŭ, ў, *short;* a, e, i, o, *obscure;* fär, fåll, fåt; mët; nŏt; gŏŏd; mŏŏn;

Heberer, hā′bĕh-rẹr, (MICHAEL,) a German traveller, born in Baden about 1550. He passed about three years as a captive and slave in Egypt and Turkey, and published a Narrative of his adventures. Died in 1610.

Hébert, hā′baiR′, (ANTOINE AUGUSTE ERNEST,) a French historical painter, born at Grenoble in 1817, was a pupil of David of Angers. He gained the first grand prize in 1839 for his picture of "The Cup found in the Sack of Benjamin." Among his works, which are admired for vigour of expression, are "Tasso in Prison," "The Malaria," (1850,) and "Les Filles d'Alvito," (1855.)

See "Nouvelle Biographie Générale."

Hébert, (JACQUES RENÉ,) a French demagogue, born at Alençon in 1755, came to Paris when quite young, and was a desperate adventurer when the Revolution began. He gained notoriety by editing a scurrilous Jacobin paper named "Père Duchêne." Hébert and Chaumette were the authors of the atheistical festivals of Reason. Having been proscribed by Robespierre and Danton and charged with a conspiracy to massacre the Convention, he was executed in March, 1794.

Hébert, (MICHEL PIERRE ALEXIS,) a French advocate, born at Granville (Manche) in 1799.

Hébert, (PAUL O.,) an American general in the Confederate service, born in Louisiana. He served in Mexico in 1847, became Governor of Louisiana in 1854, and was made a brigadier-general in 1861.

Hébrail, hā′bRāl′ or hā′bRă′yẹ, (JACQUES,) a French bibliographer, born at Castelnaudary in 1716. He published "La France littéraire," (2 vols., 1769,) which is praised for accuracy. Died about 1800.

Hécart, hā′kăR′, (GABRIEL ANTOINE JOSEPH,) a French littérateur, born at Valenciennes in 1755 ; died in 1838.

Hecatæus, hĕk-ạ-tee′us, [Gr. Ἑκαταῖος ; Fr. HÉCATÉE, hā′kā′tā′,] OF ABDE′RA, a Greek historian, who lived about 330 B.C. He wrote a work on the Hyperboreans, and another on Egypt. Fragments of these are extant.

Hecatæus OF MI-LE′TUS, son of Hegesander, lived about 500 B.C. He was an eminent geographer, and one of the earliest Greek historians. Like Herodotus, he travelled in Egypt and other countries to obtain materials for history. His works were highly esteemed by the ancients.

See KLAUSEN, "De Vita et Scriptis Hecatæi ;" C. MÜLLER, "De Vita et Scriptis Hecatæi."

Hecate, hĕk′ạ-te or hĕk′ạt, [Ἑκάτη,] in Greek mythology, was the daughter of Perses and Asteria. She is first mentioned by Hesiod, and appears to have been unknown in the age of Homer. Her attributes were various and apparently contradictory: she was said to dispense blessings and avert misfortunes, and was also described as a cruel infernal deity, presiding over magic and nocturnal incantations. She was represented with a hideous aspect, having her head surrounded with serpents, and infernal dogs howling around her.

Hec′a-ton, [Gr. Ἑκάτων,] a Greek Stoic philosopher, born at Rhodes, lived in the first century after Christ.

Hecht, hĕkt, (CHRISTIAN,) a German philologist and Lutheran divine, born at Halle in 1696 ; died in 1748.

Heck, van, vän hĕk, (JAN,) an excellent Flemish painter of landscapes, flowers, and fruit, born near Oudenarde about 1625. He worked in Rome and Antwerp. Died after 1660.

Heck, van der, vän dẹr hĕk, (NIKLAAS,) a Dutch painter of Alkmaar, was born about 1580. He excelled in landscape and history, was a good colorist, and skilful in chiaroscuro. Died in 1638.

Heck, von. See HEGIUS.

Heckel, hĕk′ẹl, (JOHANN FRIEDRICH,) a German philologist, born at Gera about 1640 ; died in 1715.

Hecker, hĕk′kẹr, (AUGUST FRIEDRICH,) a German physician and medical writer, born near Halle in 1763 ; died in 1811.

Hecker, (FRIEDRICH KARL FRANZ,) a German radical politician and lawyer, born in Baden in 1811. After the revolution of 1848–49 he emigrated to the United States, and settled at Belleville, Illinois.

Heck′ẹr, (ISAAC THOMAS,) an American theologian, born in New York in 1819. He became a Roman

Catholic priest about 1848. He published "Questions of the Soul," (1855,) and other works.

Hecker, (JUSTUS FRIEDRICH KARL,) son of August Friedrich, noticed above, was born at Erfurt in 1795. He published "The Black Death in the Fourteenth Century," and other valuable medical treatises. Died in 1850.

Heckewelder, hĕk′ẹh-wĕl′dẹr, (Rev. JOHN,) a Moravian missionary, born in Bedford, England, in 1743, was employed many years among the Delaware Indians. He wrote an interesting, but rather flattering, account of the "History, Manners, and Customs of the Indian Nations," (1819.) "His account," according to General Cass, "is pure unmixed panegyric." His death is variously dated 1810, 1823, and 1826.

See E. RONDTHALER, "Life of J. Heckewelder," Philadelphia, 1847.

Heckscher, hĕk′shẹr, (JOHANN GUSTAV MORITZ,) a German politician, born at Hamburg in 1797. As a member of the Parliament of Frankfort, he voted for the Archduke John as vicar of the empire, and was appointed by him minister of justice and of foreign affairs in 1848. He was removed from office before 1849.

Hecquet, hā′kā′, (PHILIPPE,) an eminent French physician, born ạt Abbeville in 1661. In 1688 he began to practise at Port-Royal, where he adopted habits of rigid abstinence and other austerities, to which he adhered to the end of his life. In 1697 he became a member of the Faculty of Paris, who employed him as professor of materia medica. He advocated the free use of the lancet, and wrote numerous professional treatises, one of which is called "Novus Medicinæ Conspectus," (1722.) It is said that Hecquet was the prototype of "Doctor Sangrado" in "Gil Blas." He was sometimes called "the French Hippocrates." Died in 1737.

See SAINT-MARC, "Vie de P. Hecquet ;" "Biographie Médicale."

Hec′tọr, [Gr. Ἕκτωρ ; It. ETTORE, êt-to′rà,] a famous Trojan hero, the eldest son of Priam and Hecuba, was the most valiant defender of Troy when that city was besieged by the Greeks. His character is one of the most admirable conceptions of Homer's genius. After performing prodigies of valour, fighting single combats with Ajax and Diomed, and slaying Patroclus, he was killed by Achilles.

See HOMER's "Iliad," passim.

Hec′u-bạ or **Hek′ạ-be,** [Gr. Ἑκάβη ; Fr. HÉCUBE, ā′küb′,] was the second wife of Priam, King of Troy. She was the mother of nineteen children, among the most celebrated of whom were Hector, Paris, Cassandra, and Helenus. Having, after the fall of Troy, been enslaved by the Greeks, she threw herself into the sea. Other accounts state that she was stoned by the Greeks and was metamorphosed into a dog.

Hécube. See HECUBA.

Hed′ding, (ELIJAH,) an American Methodist bishop, born in the State of New York in 1780. He was elected a bishop about 1824. Died at Poughkeepsie in 1852.

Hédelin. See AUBIGNAC, D'.

Hedenborg, hā′dẹn-boRg′, (JOHAN,) a Swedish physician and traveller, born at Heda in 1787, visited the Levant in 1825. He published "The Manners and Customs of the Turks," (1839–42,) and "Travels in Egypt and the Interior of Africa," (1843.)

Hederich, hā′dẹh-riK′, or **Hed′ẹr-ic,** (BENJAMIN,) an eminent German lexicographer, was born at Geithain, in Saxony, in 1675. He was rector of the College of Grossenhain for forty-two years, and published many useful school-books, among which are a "Lexicon Manuale Græcum," (1722,) and a "Dictionary of Mythology," (1724.) The former was extensively used in Germany and England. An improved edition was published by Ernesti in 1766. Died in 1748.

See ERSCH und GRUBER, "Allgemeine Encyklopaedie ;" "Nouvelle Biographie Générale."

Hedge, (FREDERICK HENRY,) D.D., a distinguished scholar and Unitarian divine, born at Cambridge, Massachusetts, December 12, 1805. He studied in Germany ; after his return he graduated, in 1825, at Harvard, where also he was a student in divinity. He officiated for some years in West Cambridge ; and in 1835 he removed to Bangor, Maine. In 1847 he visited Europe ạ second time, and on his return was settled for a few years in

Providence, Rhode Island. He was invited in 1856 to take the pastoral charge of the Unitarian church at Brookline, Massachusetts, where he still resides. In 1857 he was chosen professor of ecclesiastical history at the divinity school of Harvard. The same year he became editor of the "Christian Examiner," to which he has made many valuable contributions. Of his numerous publications the most important are " The Prose Writers of Germany," (1848,) "Reason in Religion," (1865,) and "The Primeval World of Hebrew Tradition," (1870.) Dr. Hedge is distinguished for his varied learning and high literary culture, as well as for strength, originality, and acuteness of intellect ; and his writings are destined, we doubt not, to take a permanent place in his country's literature.

See "North American Review" for ——, 1848.

Hedge, (LEVI,) the father of the preceding, born at Warwick, Massachusetts, in 1767, was for many years professor of logic and metaphysics at Harvard. His "System of Logic" (1818) had a great success, and was translated into German. Died in 1843.

Hedg'eš, (Sir CHARLES,) an English politician, graduated at Oxford in 1675. In 1700 he was appointed one of the chief secretaries of state. About the same time he was returned to Parliament, in which· he sat many years. The Whigs dismissed him from the office of secretary in 1706. Died in 1714.

Hedin, hå-deen', (SVEN ANDERS,) a Swedish medical writer, born in Småland in 1750, was a pupil of Linnæus. He became first physician to the King of Sweden in 1798. He wrote, besides other works, a "Eulogy on Linnæus," (1808.) Died in 1821.

Hedio, hā'de-o, (KASPAR,) a German Protestant divine, born at Ettlingen, in Baden, in 1494. He became about 1520 court preacher at Mentz, whence he removed to Strasburg in 1523. He preached in the cathedral of this city, and made many converts. He wrote a work on the history of his times, called "Chronicon Germanicum," (1530,) and other works. Died in 1552.

See MELCHIOR ADAM, "Vitæ Germanorum Philosophorum;" MM. HAAG, "La France protestante."

Hedlinger, hĕt'ling-ẹr, (JOHANN KARL,) an eminent Swiss engraver of medals, born at Schwitz in 1691, learned his art with Saint-Urbain, of Nancy. He went to Paris in 1717, after which Charles XII. of Sweden appointed him director of the mint. In 1735 he accepted an invitation from the Russian court, which rewarded him with large presents. He also engraved for other European courts. He is thought to approach the perfection of the ancients more closely than any other modern artist. Died in 1771.

See NAGLER, "Neues Allgemeines Künstler-Lexikon."

Hédouin, hå'doo-ăN', (CHARLES FRANÇOIS,) a French naturalist, born in Paris in 1761 ; died in 1826.

Hédouin, (EDMOND,) a French painter of landscapes and genre, born at Boulogne-sur-Mer in 1819.

Hédouin, (PIERRE,) a French *littérateur* and musician, born at Boulogne-sur-Mer in 1789.

Hédouin de Pons-Ludon, hå'doo-ăN' dẹh pòN lü'-dòN', (JOSEPH ANTOINE,) a French poet and *littérateur,* born at Rheims in 1739 ; died in 1817.

Hédouville, hå'doo'vèl', (GABRIEL THÉODORE JOSEPH,) COUNT, a French general, born at Laon in 1755. He succeeded Hoche in 1797 as general-in-chief of the army of the West, where the royalists were in arms. He served as chief of the staff of Jerome Bonaparte in the campaign of 1806. Died in 1825.

Hed'wig, written also **Hedwige** and **Jadwiga,** Queen of Poland, born in 1371, was a daughter of Louis of Hungary, and was chosen by the Polish nobles to succeed him on the throne in 1384. She was married to Jagellon, Duke of Lithuania. Historians represent her as beautiful and wise. Died in 1399.

Hedwig, hĕd'ẇig, (JOHANN,) a celebrated German botanist, born at Cronstadt, in Transylvania, in 1730. He made several important discoveries with the microscope, which he used with great skill. He published in 1795 his "Analytic Description and Designs of New and Doubtful Cryptogamous Plants," (4 vols. fol.,) which is esteemed a standard work ; also, "Observations on

the True Parts of Generation in Mosses," which he was the first to discover. Died in 1799.

See ERSCH und GRUBER, "Allgemeine Encyklopaedie ;" "Edinburgh Encyclopædia."

Heede, van, văn hā'dẹh, (VIGOR,) a Flemish painter, born at Furnes in 1659. He worked in France and Italy, and his native place. Died in 1718.

Heede, van, (WILLEM,) a skilful painter, a brother of the preceding, was born in 1660. He worked at Rome, Venice, and Vienna, where he was patronized by the emperor. His colouring, design, and composition are praised. Died in 1728.

Heem, van, văn hām, (JAN DAVID,) an excellent Dutch painter of fruit, flowers, and still life, born at Utrecht in 1600. He is regarded as one of the greatest painters in his department of art. His works have an exquisite finish without the appearance of effort, and were sold for very high prices. Died in 1674.

His son, CORNELIS, was a painter of similar subjects.

See DESCAMPS, "Vies des Peintres Flamands, Hollandais," etc.

Heemskerk, van, văn hāms'kĕrk, written also **Hemskerk,** (JACOB,) a brave and skilful naval officer, born at Amsterdam. He commanded an expedition sent in 1595 to explore a northeast passage to China, but was not successful, his progress being obstructed by ice. Having obtained the rank of admiral, and the command of a fleet of twenty-six vessels, he signally defeated the Spaniards near Gibraltar in 1607. Heemskerk and the Spanish admiral were both killed in this action.

See ENGELBERTS GERRITS, "Leven en Daden der Zeehelden J. van Heemskerk en P. P. Hein," 1825; MOTLEY, "United Netherlands," vol. iv. chaps. xl.-xlvii.

Heemskerk, van, (MARTIN,) an eminent Dutch historical painter, born at Heemskerk in 1498. His family name was VAN VEEN. He studied with J. Schoorel, and produced at Haarlem a fine picture of "Saint Luke Painting the Virgin Mary." About 1532 he visited Rome, where he consulted and imitated Michael Angelo. He afterwards returned to Haarlem. His design is correct rather than elegant. Among his works is "Mars and Venus surprised by Vulcan." Died in 1574.

See DESCAMPS, "Vies des Peintres Flamands, Hollandais," etc.

Heerbrand, hāR'bRănt, (JAKOB,) a German Lutheran divine, born at Giengen, in Suabia, about 1520, studied under Luther at Wittenberg. He was professor of theology at Tübingen for about forty years, and wrote "Compendium Theologiæ," (1573.) Died in 1600.

Heere, de, dẹh hā'rẹh, (LUCAS,) a skilful Flemish painter and poet, born at Ghent in 1534, was the son of John de Heere, a noted sculptor. He was patronized by the court of France, and worked some years in England, where he painted portraits of Queen Elizabeth and of some of the nobility. Among his works are "The Pentecost," and a "Resurrection." He wrote, in Flemish, "The Garden of Poetry," (a poem.) Died in 1584.

See HOUBRAKEN, "Vies des Peintres ;" DESCAMPS, "Vies des Peintres Flamands," etc. ; P. BLOMMAERT, "Levensschets van L. de Heere," 1853.

Heeren, hā'rẹn, (ARNOLD HERMANN LUDWIG,) an eminent German historian, born near Bremen in October, 1760. Having studied philology at Göttingen under Heyne, he visited Italy, Paris, and the Netherlands. He published in 1801 an edition of the "Eclogæ Physicæ et Ethicæ" of Stobæus, and about the same time became professor of history at Göttingen, having previously married a daughter of Heyne. His "Ancient History" ("Geschichte der Staaten des Alterthums") appeared in 1799, and his "History of the Political Systems and Colonies of Europe" in 1809. His greatest work, "Ideas on the Politics, Commerce, and Trade of the Principal Nations of Antiquity," ("Ideen über die Politik, den Verkehr, und den Handel der vornehmsten Völker," etc., in 5 vols.,) was completed in 1824, and is generally allowed to possess merits of the highest order. Heeren was editor for a time of the "Gelehrten Anzeigen" at Göttingen, and also had a share in the publication of the "Library of Ancient Literature and Art." He was a member of the principal learned societies of Europe. Died at Göttingen in 1842.

See C. HOECK, "A. H. L. Heeren: Gedächtnissrede," 1843; JACOB GEEL, "Levensschets van A. H. L. Heeren," Delft, 1822; "Nouvelle Biographie Générale;" "Foreign Quarterly Review" for January, 1838; "North American Review" for January, 1829.

ā, ē, ī, ō, ū, y̆, *long;* à, è, ò, same, less prolonged; ă, ĕ, ĭ, ŏ, ŭ, ў, *short;* ạ, ẹ, ị, ọ, *obscure;* fär, fàll, fàt; mêt; nŏt; gŏŏd; mŏŏn;

Heerkens, hār′kẹns, (GERARD NIKLAAS,) a Dutch physician, and writer of Latin verse, born at Groningen in 1728. He owed his reputation chiefly to his discovery of the country-house of Horace in Italy. He composed, besides other Latin poems, " Iter Venetum," (" A Venetian Tour," 1760,) and gave an interesting account of his travels in Italy in a book called " Notabilia," (1765.) Died in 1801.

Heermann, hār′mǎn, (JOHANNES,) a German divine and poet, born in Silesia in 1585. His sacred songs, entitled " Music of the House (or Home) and Heart," (1644,) are highly esteemed, and many of them are still used in the churches. Died in 1647.

See ERSCH und GRUBER, " Allgemeine Encyklopaedie."

Heers, van, vằn hārs, (HENDRIK,) of Liege, a Flemish medical writer, born about 1570 ; died about 1636.

Heffter, hěf′tẹr, (AUGUST WILHELM,) a German jurist and legal writer, born at Schweidnitz in 1796.

Heffter, (MORITZ WILHELM,) a brother of the preceding, was the author of a treatise " On the Religion of the Greeks, Romans, Ancient Egyptians, and Indians," (2d edition, 1848,) and other works.

Hegel, hā′ğel, (GEORG WILHELM FRIEDRICH,) one of the most eminent philosophers of the German school of metaphysics, was born at Stuttgart in 1770. At the age of eighteen he entered the University of Tübingen as student of theology. Here he formed an intimate acquaintance and friendship with Schelling, although the two friends became subsequently rival candidates for the leadership of German philosophy. On leaving the university he engaged as a private teacher, first at Berne and afterwards at Frankfort-on-the-Main. He became in 1801 a lecturer in the University of Jena. In the same year appeared his first important work, " On the Difference between the Philosophical Systems of Fichte and Schelling." In 1806 he became professor-extraordinary of philosophy at Jena ; but, that town having soon after been taken by the French, he was thrown out of employment. For some time he edited a political paper at Bamberg. Here was published (1807) his " Phænomenology," the first part of his " System of Knowledge." In 1808 he was appointed rector of the gymnasium at Nuremberg, where he finished his " Science of Logic," (" Wissenschaft der Logik," in 3 vols., 1812–16.) In 1811 he married Marie von Tucher, a lady of strong religious convictions and rare moral virtues. He was devotedly attached to her, and their union was eminently a happy one. He was called in 1816 to the chair of philosophy at Heidelberg, and while here published his " Encyclopædia of the Philosophical Sciences," in which his whole scheme of philosophy is comprised. In 1818 he succeeded at Berlin to the professorship of philosophy left vacant by the death of Fichte. He died of cholera in 1831. Soon after his death his works were collected and published at Berlin, in 18 vols., (1832–41.)

The philosophy of Hegel is regarded by his followers as by far the most logical, complete, and comprehensive of all the pantheistic systems. With our narrow limits it would be impossible to give even a satisfactory outline of his scheme. Suffice it to say that it is generally regarded as the completion of the great philosophic edifice of which Kant had laid the foundations, and to which Fichte and Schelling had contributed important materials. One of the most striking peculiarities of Hegel's philosophic system is the complete identification of logic with metaphysics. The Hegelians have been divided into three classes, (according to the nomenclature of the French legislative assemblies,) namely, the right, the centre, and the left. The right maintain that the Hegelian philosophy is perfectly harmonious with orthodox Christianity : in other words, it is Christianity viewed in its philosophic aspects. The left, represented by such writers as Strauss, Michelet, Ruge, etc., for the most part deny the personality of God, as well as the truths of Christian revelation, though they differ as to whether the universe is purely material or spiritual in its essence. The centre (it is scarcely necessary to say) occupy middle ground : here belong Rosenkrantz, Vatke, Gans, etc.

" Hegel's system, [of philosophy,]" says Dr. Hedge, "has produced a profound impression upon the German mind. The theological and philosophical controversies of the day rage around it. It is reputed to be the most comprehensive and analytic of pantheistic schemes. Its author and some of his disciples have asserted that it is the same system, in the form of philosophy, which Christianity gives us in the form of faith. But its present position is that of hostility to Christianity." (" Prose Writers of Germany.")

For a full account of Hegel's system, see J. M. STERLING, " Secret of Hegel," 2 vols. 8vo, London, 1865 ; F. ADOLF TRENDELENBURG, " Logische Untersuchungen," 2 vols., 2d edition, 1862 ; J. WILLM, " Histoire de la Philosophie Allemande depuis Kant jusqu'à Hegel," (Paris, 4 vols., 1846,) vol. iii. See, also, K. F. GOESCHEL, " Hegel und seine Zeit," Berlin, 1832 ; ROSENKRANTZ, " G. W. F. Hegel's Leben," 1844 ; PREVOST, " Hegel, Exposition de sa Doctrine," 1844 ; C. DE RÉMUSAT, " De la Philosophie Allemande," 1845 ; HAYM, " Hegel und seine Zeit," 1857 ; COUSIN, " Souvenirs d'un Voyage en Allemagne," 1857.

He-ġe′mon [‛Ηγήμων] of Thasos, an Athenian comic poet, flourished about 450 B.C. Aristotle attributes the invention of parody to him.

Hegemon, an Athenian orator, who favoured the Macedonian party. Died in 317 B.C.

Hegendorf, hā′ğen-dorf′, (CHRISTOPH,) a German philologist, and friend of Luther, born at Leipsic in 1500 ; died in 1540.

He-ġe′sĭ-as, [‛Ηγησίας,] a Greek orator and historian, was born at Magnesia, and lived about 300 or 250 B.C. He wrote a " History of Alexander the Great," which appears to have had little merit. Several ancient critics censure the inflated style of his oratory, which was one of the first examples of the " Asiatic" style.

See VOSSIUS, " De Historicis Græcis."

Hegesias, a Cyrenaic philosopher, who is supposed to have lived about 300 B.C., was a disciple of Aristippus. He founded a new sect, called Hegesiacs, maintained that happiness is impossible, and that death is preferable to life. His doctrines induced so many to commit suicide that Ptolemy closed his school.

Hegesias the sculptor. See HEGIAS.

Hégésippe. See HEGESIPPUS.

Heġ-e-sip′pus, [Gr. ‛Ηγήσιππος ; Fr. HÉGÉSIPPE, ā′-zhā′zěp′,] an Athenian orator, who lived about 340 B.C. He advocated a declaration of war against Philip of Macedon, and was a colleague of Demosthenes in an embassy to the Peloponnesians.

Hegesippus, an ecclesiastical historian, was a Jew by birth, and lived at Rome in his later years. Having been converted to Christianity, he wrote a " History of the Church," which was the first essay ever made in that department. A few fragments of his work have been preserved by Eusebius. Died about 180 A.D.

See ALLEMAND-LAVIGERIE, " De Hegesippo Disquisitio historica," 1850.

Hegetschweiler, hā′ğet-shwī′lẹr, (JOHANN,) a Swiss botanist, born at Richerschweil in 1789, produced a " Flora" of Switzerland. Died in 1839.

Hegewisch, hā′ğeh-ŵish′, (DIETRICH HERMANN,) a German historian, born near Osnabrück in 1740. He wrote a " History of Charlemagne," (1772,) and a " History of the Emperor Frederick II.," (1792.) Died in 1812.

He′ġĭ-as, [‛Ηγίας,] a famous Greek sculptor, who lived about 450 B.C. and was a contemporary of Phidias. Among his works was a statue of Minerva mentioned by Pliny. By some writers he is regarded as identical with Hegesias, an eminent sculptor of the same period.

Hegira, (Hejra.) See MOHAMMED.

Hegius, hā′ğe-ùs, or **von Heck,** fon hěk, (ALEXANDER,) a German scholar, born at Heck, in Westphalia, about 1440, was a pupil of Thomas à Kempis. He taught the classics for thirty years in the College of Deventer, where Erasmus and other eminent men were his pupils, and was the first who introduced the study of Greek into Holland. He wrote Latin verses, and dialogues " De Scientia," etc., and " De Rhetorica." Erasmus classes Hegius among the restorers of classic learning. Died in 1498.

See SAX, " Onomasticon Literarium."

Heiberg, hī′běRG, (JOHAN LUDWIG,) a popular Danish dramatist and poet, born at Copenhagen in 1791. He produced in 1811 a drama called " Tycho Brahe's Prediction," and passed several years in France, from which he introduced the vaudeville into Denmark. Among his successful dramas of that kind are " Solomon

e as k; ç as s; ğ hard; ġ as j; G, H, K, guttural; N, nasal; R, trilled; s as z; ᵗh as in this. (☞See Explanations, p. 23.)

73

and the Hatter," (1826,) and "The Danes in Paris," (1833.) He received in 1829 the title of royal dramatic poet and translator. He published several metaphysical works, among which is "The Significance of the Philosophy of the Present Day," ("Ueber die Bedeutung der Philosophie der Gegenwart," 1833.) His poetical works were published in 9 vols., (1833–41.) Died in Paris in 1860.

See BROCKHAUS, "Conversations-Lexikon;" HOWITT, "Literature and Romance of Northern Europe," vol. ii.

Heiberg, (JOHANNE LOUISE,) whose maiden name was JOHANNE LOUISE PÄTGES, born at Copenhagen in 1812, was the wife of the preceding, and was the favourite actress of that capital. She was successful in comedy, tragedy, and the opera.

Heiberg, (PEDER ANDREAS,) a distinguished Danish dramatic poet, born at Vordingborg in 1758, was the father of Johan Ludwig Heiberg. Having been banished, on a charge of seditious writing, in 1799, he went to Paris, where he was employed until 1814 by Napoleon and Talleyrand as translator in the department of foreign affairs. He wrote, in Danish, "Heckingborn," a comedy, "The Voyager to China," and other dramas; also a "Historical and Critical Summary of the Danish Monarchy," (1820,) and various other works. Died in Paris in 1841. His wife, THOMASINA CHRISTINA BUNTSEN, an authoress, is noticed in this work under GYLLEMBOURG, which see.

See Memoirs of Heiberg's Life in France, by himself, entitled "Erindringer af min politiske og literaire Vandel i Frankrige," 1830; LONGFELLOW, "Poets and Poetry of Europe;" PEDER ANDREAS HEIBERG, "Tre Aar i Bergen; autobiografisk Episode," 1829.

Heidanus, hī-dä′nŭs, (ABRAHAM,) a theologian and Cartesian philosopher, born in the Palatinate in 1597, became professor of theology at Leyden about 1647. Died in 1678.

Heideck. See HEIDEGGER, (KARL WILHELM.)

Heidegger, hī′dĕk′er, (JOHANN HEINRICH,) a Swiss author and Protestant divine, born in the canton of Zurich in 1633. He became professor of Hebrew at Heidelberg in 1656, and of theology at Zurich in 1666. He wrote, in Latin, a "Biblical Manual," (1680,) a "History of the Papacy," (1684,) "Anatome Concilii Tridentini," (1672,) and other works on theology. Died in 1698.

See his Autobiography, "Historia Vitæ J. H. Heideggeri," 1698.

Heidegger, (JOHANN JAKOB,) a Swiss adventurer, born at Zurich in 1659 or 1660, was called the "Swiss Count." He was patronized by George II. of England as master of revels, manager of operas, etc. Died in 1749.

Heidegger, von, fon hī′dĕk′er, or **Heideck,** hī′dĕk, (KARL WILHELM,) a German general and artist, born at Saaralben, Lorraine, in 1788, was Baron von Heideck. He fought as an officer for the liberation of Greece about 1826. In 1830 he settled at Munich as an artist, and produced many remarkable pictures, the subjects of which are taken from Grecian history or scenery. He painted in the Glyptothek a fresco of the "Four-Horse Chariot of the Sun." About 1832 he went to Greece with King Otho, whom he served as chamberlain. He afterwards obtained the rank of general in the Bavarian army. Died in February, 1861.

See "Nouvelle Biographie Générale."

Heideloff, hī′deh-lof′, (KARL ALEXANDER,) a German architect, son of Victor Peter, noticed below, was born at Stuttgart in 1788. He built the castles of Landsberg and Altenstein, restored the cathedral of Bamberg, and designed many fine structures at Nuremberg. Among his writings is a "Treatise on the Orders of Architecture," (1827.)

Heideloff, (VICTOR PETER,) a German painter, born at Stuttgart in 1757; died in 1818.

Heidenstein, hī′den-stīn′, (REINHOLD,) a German historian, born in 1555, wrote, in Latin, a "History of Poland," (1672.) Died in 1620.

Heil, van, vān hīl, (DANIEL,) a Flemish painter, born at Brussels in 1604, had a high reputation as a painter of landscapes and conflagrations. Among his masterpieces is "The Burning of Troy."

Heil, van, (JEAN BAPTISTE,) a good painter of history and portraits, brother of the preceding, was born at Brussels in 1609. He died after 1661. His brother LEO painted insects and flowers with success.

Heilbronner, hīl′bRon′ner, (JOHANN CHRISTOPH,) a German mathematician, born at Ulm about 1700, published "Historia Matheseos universæ," (1742.) Died about 1747.

Heilmann, hīl′mân, [Lat. HEILMAN′NUS,] (JOHANN DAVID,) an eminent German Hellenist, born at Osnabrück in 1727, obtained the chair of theology at Göttingen in 1758. Among his works are a good German translation of Thucydides, (1760,) and, in Latin, a "Compendium of Dogmatic Theology," (1761,) which is remarkable for elegance of style. Died in 1764.

See G. G. HEYNE, "Heilmanni Memoria," 1764.

Heilmann, hīl′mân, (JOHANN KASPAR,) a historical painter, born at Mülhausen, (Mulhouse,) in Alsace, in 1718. He studied at Rome, and removed in 1742 to Paris, where his portraits were in great request. He also employed his talent with success on paintings for churches and on landscapes. Died in 1760.

See NAGLER, "Neues Allgemeines Künstler-Lexikon."

Heilmannus. See HEILMANN.

Heim, hīm, (ERNST LUDWIG,) a German physician and medical writer, born in 1747, practised in Berlin. Died in 1834.

Heim, ăN, (FRANÇOIS JOSEPH,) a French historical painter, born at Belfort (Haut-Rhin) in 1787. He gained the grand prize in 1807, went to Rome, with a pension, afterwards worked in Paris, and was chosen a member of the Institute in 1829. Among his works are "The Clemency of Titus," (1819,) "The Defeat of the Cimbri by Marius," (1853,) and portraits of many eminent men.

See T. GAUTIER, "Les Beaux-Arts en Europe."

Heim, (GEORG CHRISTOPH,) a naturalist, brother of Ernst Ludwig, noticed above, was born at Solz in 1743. He published a "German Flora," ("Deutsche Flora," 2 vols., 1799–1800.) Died in 1807.

Heim, (JOHANN LUDWIG,) a German geologist, brother of the preceding, was born at Solz in 1741. He wrote a "Treatise on the Geology of the Mountains of Thuringia," (6 vols., 1796–1812.) Died in 1819.

Heimbach, hīm′bÂK, (CARL WILHELM ERNST,) a German jurist, born at Merseburg in 1803.

Heimburg, hīm′bŏŏRG, [Lat. HEIMBUR′GIUS,] (GREGOR,) an eminent German jurist, was born at Würzburg. At the Council of Bâle he opposed the pretensions of the pope, and in 1431 settled at Nuremberg. He died in 1472, and left several legal works, which exhibit an acute intellect and a noble spirit of freedom.

See J. A. BALLENSTADIUS, "Vita Heimburgii," 1737.

Heimburgius. See HEIMBURG.

Heimdall, hīm′dâl, or **Heimdallr,** [etymology uncertain,] a god in the Northern mythology, regarded as the watchman of the Æsir, and the warder of heaven, is called a son of Odin, but on the maternal side is descended from the Jötun race. He drinks mead in his bright hall, called Himinbjörg, ("Heaven's Castle,") at the bridge-head where the rainbow (Bifröst*) reaches heaven. He sleeps less than a bird, and sees by night, as well as by day, more than a hundred leagues around him. His hearing is so acute that he can hear the grass grow in the meadows of the earth, and the wool on the back of the sheep. When he blows upon his trumpet, called Gjallar-horn, (or Gjaller-horn,) it is heard through all the worlds. His teeth are said to be of gold, and he has a horse with a golden mane. It is not improbable that the name of this god may be some change or corruption of Heimdelling, ("home of dawn,") as the dawn seems to keep still watch in heaven for the approach of day, and may well be said to ride on a horse with a golden mane. The original fable of Heimdall, if it ever had any distinct allegorical significance, would seem to have been not a little confused by incongruous additions, made probably at a later period.

See MALLET, "Northern Antiquities," vol. ii. Fable XV.; THORPE, "Northern Mythology," vol. i. p. 200 et seq.; KEYSER, "Religion of the Northmen;" PETERSEN, "Nordisk Mythologi."

* The name Bifröst, from bifa, to "tremble," and röst, a "road" or "way," signifying the "trembling or swinging way," was applied to the rainbow, perhaps on account of its apparent want of stability, or its inconstancy. Its curved form may have suggested the idea of Heimdall's great horn, (the Gjallar-horn, i.e. the "yelling or loud-sounding horn,") which he blows on the approach of any extraordinary danger. It was actually believed that at the "end of the rainbow" a golden treasure was hidden, and that golden money fell from the bow.

ā, ē, ī, ō, ū, ȳ, long; ă, ĕ, ĭ, ŏ, ŭ, ў, short; ạ, ẹ,ị, ọ, obscure; fär, fàll, fât; mĕt; nŏt; gōŏd; mōon;

Hein or **Heyn**, hīn, (PIETER,) a brave Dutch admiral, born at Delftshaven in 1570, was the son of a common sailor. In 1628 he captured in the Bay of Matanzas a Spanish fleet, with a rich cargo of silver. For this exploit he was made a vice-admiral. In 1629 he defeated the French near Dunkirk, and lost his life in the action.

See ENGELBERTS GERRITS, "Leven en Daden der Zeehelden J. van Heemskerk en P. P. Hein," 1825; SOUTHEY, "History of Brazil;" "Nouvelle Biographie Générale."

Heine, (CHRISTIAN GOTTLOB.) See HEYNE.

Heine, hī'neh, (HEINRICH,) a celebrated German poet and author, of Jewish extraction, born at Dusseldorf in 1800. He studied law at Bonn, Berlin, and Göttingen, and took his degree at the Göttingen university. His first poems appeared in 1822, and were followed by the tragedies of "Almansor" and "Radcliff," (1823.) In 1825 he renounced the Jewish faith, and professed Christianity; but he subsequently became an avowed unbeliever. His "Pictures of Travel" ("Reisebilder," 4 vols., 1831) were received with great favour, and were afterwards translated by him into French, under the title of "Tableaux de Voyages." His other principal works are the "Book of Songs," ("Buch der Lieder," 1827,) "Contributions to the History of Recent Belles-Lettres in Germany," ("Beiträge zur Geschichte der neuern schönen Literatur in Deutschland," 2 vols., 1833,) "Der Salon," (4 vols., 1835,) "The Romantic School," ("Die Romantische Schule," 1836,) and the poem of "Atta Troll, a Summer Night's Dream," (1847.) Heine had removed in 1831 to Paris, where he married a French lady, and where he resided till his death. About 1848 his health became very much impaired, and he lost his sight; but he still employed himself in literary composition, with the assistance of an amanuensis. Among the works he produced at this period are the "Romanzero," (1851,) "Doctor Faust," (1851,) "Das Buch des Lazarus," (1854,) and the "New Spring," ("Neuer Frühling," 1855.) After an illness of eight years, a great part of which time had been passed in extreme suffering, he died in February, 1856. Several years before his death he had renounced infidelity. The spirit of satire seems to have been innate in Heine; but it is not in satire alone that he excels. For a certain simplicity and grace of style, as well as for an exquisite vein of humour, which is occasionally lighted up with flashes of the most brilliant wit, Heine has no superior among the poets or prose writers of Germany. His prose is remarkable for its transparent beauty, and is perhaps unequalled by that of any other German author except Goethe.

"Heine," says a critic in the "Westminster Review" for January, 1856, "adds to Teutonic imagination, sensibility, and humour, an amount of *esprit* that would make him brilliant among the most brilliant Frenchmen. He is a surpassing lyric poet, who has uttered our feelings for us in delicious songs; an artist in prose literature, who has shown even more completely than Göthe the possibilities of German prose."

See "Heinrich Heine," in MATTHEW ARNOLD'S "Essays;" "London Quarterly Review" for December, 1835; "Edinburgh Review" for July, 1856; "North British Review" for May, 1860; "Fraser's Magazine" for November, 1866.

Heine, (SALOMON,) an opulent German banker and philanthropist, born at Hanover in 1766, was a Jew, and uncle of Heine the poet. He lived at Hamburg, and gave large sums of money for charitable institutions. Died in 1844.

See J. MENDELSSOHN, "S. Heine, Blätter der Würdigung und Erinnerung," 1845.

Heinecius, hi-nĕk'se-ŭs, or **Heinecke**, hī'nĕk-keh, (JOHANN GOTTLIEB,) an eminent German jurist, born at Eisenberg in September, 1681. He became professor of philosophy at Halle in 1713, obtained a chair of law there in 1720, and removed to Franeker in 1723. He afterwards lectured a few years at Frankfort-on-the-Oder, was appointed professor of law at Halle in 1733, and published numerous works, which were esteemed as high authority. He invented a new method of teaching jurisprudence, called "the axiomatic." Among his principal works are "Elements of Civil Law according to the Order of the Institutes," ("Elementa Juris civilis secundum Ordinem Institutionum," 1725,) "Elements of Civil Law according to the Order of the Pandects," ("Ele-

menta Juris civilis secundum Ordinem Pandectarum," 1728,) "Elements of the Law of Nature and Nations," ("Elementa Juris Naturæ et Gentium," 1730,) and a "History of Roman and German Law," (in Latin, 1733.) Died in 1741.

See "Commentarius de Vita et Scriptis J. G. Heineccii," by his son, JOHANN CHRISTIAN GOTTLIEB, 1765; HIRSCHING, "Historisch-literarisches Handbuch," 17 vols., 1794-1815; ERSCH und GRUBER, "Allgemeine Encyklopaedie."

Heineccius or **Heinecke**, (JOHANN MICHAEL,) a writer and eloquent preacher, brother of the preceding, was born at Eisenberg in 1674. He became pastor at Halle about 1710. He published several antiquarian works. Died in 1722.

Heinecke. See HEINECCIUS.

Heinecken, hī'nĕk-ken, (CHRISTIAN HEINRICH,) known as "the Boy of Lubeck," born in that city in 1721, was a brother of Karl Heinrich von Heinecken, noticed below. He was one of the most remarkable instances of mental precocity on record. At the age of two years he was well versed in the history of the Bible, in his third year learned French and Latin, and in his fourth studied ecclesiastical history. He died in 1725.

See C. VON SCHÖNEICH, "Leben, Thaten, etc. des Knaben von Lübeck," Lubeck, 1726.

Heinecken, von, fon hī'nĕk-ken, or **Heinecke**, (KARL HEINRICH,) a German writer on art, born at Lubeck in 1706. He published in 1755 a splendid work entitled "Collection of Prints from the Most Celebrated Pictures of the Royal Gallery at Dresden," and "Dictionnaire des Artistes, etc. dont nous avons des Estampes," (4 vols., 1778-90, unfinished.) Died in 1791.

See ERSCH und GRUBER, "Allgemeine Encyklopaedie."

Heinicke, hī'nik-keh, (SAMUEL,) born at Weissenfels in 1729, was the founder of a system of instruction for deaf-mutes. About 1778 he established at Leipsic the first institution for the education of the deaf and dumb in Germany, of which he continued director till his death, in 1790. He published a treatise "On the Dispositions of Deaf-Mutes," and other works.

See ERSCH und GRUBER, "Allgemeine Encyklopaedie."

Heinlein, hīn'līn', (HEINRICH,) a distinguished German landscape-painter, born at Nassau-Weilburg in 1803, worked for many years in Munich. Among his favourite subjects are sombre forests and Alpine glaciers.

Heinrich, (Emperors or Princes of Germany.) See HENRY.

Heinrich, hīn'rik, (KARL FRIEDRICH,) a learned German critic, born in the duchy of Saxe-Gotha in 1774. He was successively professor of Greek and of eloquence at the Universities of Kiel and Bonn. He edited the works of Juvenal and Persius, and Cicero's "De Re Publica," and was the author of "Epimenides aus Creta," an essay on Epimenides and his works, which is highly esteemed. Died in 1838.

Heinrich der Glichezare, hīn'rik dĕR glik'ĕt-sä'reh, a German poet, supposed to have been the author of "Reineke (or Reinhart) Fuchs," lived about 1150-90.

See J. GRIMM, "Reinhart Fuchs;" GERVINUS, "Geschichte der Deutschen Literatur."

Heinrich der Grosse. See HENRY IV., (of France.)
Heinrich der Löwe. See HENRY THE LION.
Heinrich der Stolze. See HENRY THE PROUD.

Heinrich von Anhalt, hīn'rik fon än'hält, a German poet, of noble birth, lived in the thirteenth century.

See LONGFELLOW, "Poets and Poetry of Europe."

Heinrich von Breslau, hīn'rik fon brĕs'low, a German poet, and Duke of Breslau, lived about 1280.

See LONGFELLOW, "Poets and Poetry of Europe."

Heinrich von Morung, hīn'rik fon mo'roong, a German minnesinger of the early part of the thirteenth century.

See LONGFELLOW, "Poets and Poetry of Europe."

Heinrich von Rispach, hīn'rik fon ris'päk, a German minnesinger, surnamed THE VIRTUOUS CLERK, lived about 1170-90.

See LONGFELLOW, "Poets and Poetry of Europe."

Heinroth, hīn'rōt, (JOHANN CHRISTIAN FRIEDRICH AUGUST,) a German physiologist, was born at Leipsic in 1773. He became professor of medicine at Leipsic in 1812, and published, besides other works, a "Treatise on Nosology," (1810,) a "Manual of Anthropology," (1822,) and a work on psychology, (1827.) Died in 1843.

Heinse, hīn'sęh, (JOHANN JAKOB WILHELM,) a German *littérateur,* born in Thuringia about 1748. He visited Italy in 1780–83, and became secretary to the Elector of Mentz in 1787. He published translations of Tasso's "Jerusalem Delivered," (1781,) and of Ariosto's "Orlando," and several immoral fictitious works, the style of which is admired. His romance "Ardinghello" (1787) contains eloquent criticisms on painting. Died in 1803.

See ERSCH und GRUBER, "Allgemeine Encyklopaedie."

Heinsius, hīn'se-ŭs, (ANTOON,) an eminent Dutch statesman, born in 1641, was elected in 1689 grand pensionary of Holland, and re-elected at the end of each successive term of five years until his death. He performed an important part in the political affairs of his time, especially in the coalition against Louis XIV. of France. Heinsius, Prince Eugene, and Marlborough formed a triumvirate which directed the affairs of the allied powers. He enjoyed in a high degree the confidence of William III. of England, to whom he rendered great services. Among the allies he was the last to assent to the peace with Louis XIV. He was an accomplished negotiator, reserved but polite in manner, simple and moderate in his way of life. Died in 1720.

See VAN DER HEIM, "Dissertatio historico-politica de A. Heinsio," 1834; VOLTAIRE, "Siècle de Louis XIV ;" RAPIN, "History of England ;" SISMONDI, "Histoire des Français ;" SAINT SIMON, "Mémoires ;" MACAULAY, "History of England," vol. iii. chap. xi.

Heinsius, (DANIEL,) a distinguished Dutch scholar and linguist, born at Ghent in 1580, studied at the Hague and at Leyden, where he became the pupil and friend of Scaliger. About 1600 he was appointed Latin and Greek tutor, and in 1606 professor of history and politics, in the University of Leyden. His reputation for learning was such that several sovereigns invited him to their courts ; but he declined to leave his native land. Gustavus Adolphus conferred on him the dignity of privy councillor, and the States of Holland appointed him their historiographer. In 1618 he officiated as secretary of the Synod of Dort. His Latin poems, published in 1602, were admired by his contemporaries ; but his reputation now rests chiefly on his editions of Aristotle, Horace, Livy, Ovid, and other Greek and Latin classics. He wrote also Latin orations, Dutch verses, and Greek verses. "Grotius," says Hallam, "had the reputation of writing with spirit and elegance ; but he is excelled by Heinsius, whose elegies may be ranked high in modern Latin." ("Introduction to the Literature of Europe.") Died in 1655.

See ERSCH und GRUBER, "Allgemeine Encyklopaedie ;" FOPPENS, "Bibliotheca Belgica ;" T. CREUZER, "Zur Geschichte der classischen Philologie."

Heinsius, (NIKLAAS,) an eminent philologist, a son of the preceding, was born at Leyden in July, 1620. After he had visited the principal seats of learning in Europe, and had become distinguished as a scholar and critic, he accepted in 1649 an invitation from Christina, Queen of Sweden, and remained in her service about five years. In 1654 he was appointed minister of the United Provinces at the court of Sweden. His leisure hours were passed in the cultivation of poetry and in classic studies. In 1667 he was sent on an embassy to the court of Russia, from which he returned in 1671. He published editions of Claudian, (1650,) Ovid, (1652,) Virgil, (1664,) and Valerius Flaccus, (1680.) He also wrote several Latin poems, (1666,) which are commended for purity and elegance. Died in 1681.

See BURMANN, "N. Heinsii Vita," prefixed to the "Adversaria" of Heinsius, 1742 ; ERSCH und GRUBER, "Allgemeine Encyklopaedie ;" FOPPENS, "Bibliotheca Belgica."

Heinsius, hīn'se-ŭs, (OTTO FRIEDRICH THEODOR,) a German philologist, born in Berlin in 1770. He became director of the College of Graue-Kloster. Among his works, which are much esteemed, are a "History of German Literature," (1810; 6th edition, 1843,) and a "Popular German Dictionary," (4 vols., 1818–32.) Died in 1849.

Heintzelman, hīnt'sęl-man', (SAMUEL P.,) an American general, born in Pennsylvania about 1807, graduated at West Point in 1826. He served as colonel at Bull

Run, July, 1861, soon after which he became a brigadier-general. He commanded a corps in the battles near Richmond in June, 1862, and took part in the second battle of Bull Run, August, 1862.

Heinz or **Heintz,** hīnts, (JOSEPH,) a distinguished Swiss painter, born at Berne about 1555. He was employed by the emperor Rudolph at Prague, and afterwards in Italy, where he copied the works of the best masters. Among his works is "The Rape of Proserpine." He died at Prague about 1600.

Heinz, (JOSEPH,) a son of the preceding, was a painter of high reputation. He adorned the churches and palaces of Venice. Died in 1660.

Heinze, hīnt'sęh, (VALENTIN AUGUST,) a German historian, born at Lüneburg in 1758. He published, besides other works, a "History of Humanity," (5 vols., 1780–85.) Died in 1801.

Heinzman, hīnts'mǎn, (KARL FRIEDRICH,) an eminent German landscape-painter, born at Stuttgart in 1795. He worked at Munich.

Heiss, von, fon hīss, (JOHANN,) a historian, born in Germany, wrote, in French, a "History of the Empire, containing its Origin, Progress, etc.," (3 vols., 1685.) Died in Paris in 1688.

Heister, hīs'tęr, (LORENZ,) an eminent German surgeon, born at Frankfort-on-the-Main in 1683, was professor of surgery at Helmstedt from 1719 to 1758. He published a treatise "On Surgery," (1719,) and an "Anatomico-Surgical Lexicon," (1753.) The former is a standard work of its kind, and has been translated into the principal European languages. Died in 1758.

See ERSCH und GRUBER, "Allgemeine Encyklopaedie ;" HIRSCHING, "Historisch-literarisches Handbuch," 17 vols. ; MEELBAUM, "Leichenpredigt auf Dr. L. Heister," 1758.

Hejra or **Hejrah.** See MOHAMMED.

Hekabe. See HECUBA.

Hĕl or **He'la,** [Icelandic pron. hā'la ; from *hilan,* to "conceal,"] in the Norse mythology, the goddess of death, and the queen of the world of shades. She is represented as the offspring of Loki and the giantess Angurboda. Soon after her birth, the Æsir, fearing her growing power, cast her down into Niflheim,* (the "home or habitation of fogs or mist,") and gave her the rule over nine realms or worlds, to the nine entrances of which Gray makes allusion in the following lines :

"Down the yawning steep he rode
That leads to Hela's drear abode,
Till full before his fearless eyes
The portals nine of Hell arise."

Her hall is called Eliudnir, said to signify the "wide place of clouds or storms ;" her dish is Hunger, and her knife Starvation, *(Sult.)* Under one of the three roots of the great life-tree Yggdrasil, in Niflheim, is the fountain Hvergelmir, from which flow the streams of Hell. In this fountain dwells the malignant serpent or monster Nidhögg, who constantly gnaws at the root of the tree of life. (See NIDHÖGG.) As, on the one hand, all those men who fell bravely in battle belonged either to Odin or Freyia and were brought by the Valkyries to Valhalla, so, on the other, all those who died of sickness or old age belonged to Hela, and were inexorably doomed to dwell in some one of her gloomy realms.

The following lines descriptive of "Hela's drear abode" are from Matthew Arnold's poem entitled "Balder Dead :"

"And he beheld spread round him Hela's realm,
The plains of Niflheim, where dwell the dead,
And heard the thunder of the streams of Hell.
For near the wall the river of Roaring flows,
Outmost ; the others near the centre run,—
The Storm, the Abyss, the Howling, and the Pain ;
*   *   *   *   *   *
And from the dark flocked up the shadowy tribes,
Women, and infants, and young men who died
Too soon for fame, with white ungraven shields ;
And old men known to glory, but their star
Betrayed them, and of wasting age they died,
Not wounds ; yet dying they their armour wore,
And now have chief regard in Hela's realm."

The aspect of Hela herself is usually represented as peculiarly grim and horrid, the upper part of her body being livid, as from congealed blood. In one of the fables

* *Nifl* is related etymologically to the Greek νεφέλη, Latin *nebula,* (German *Nebel,*) a "cloud" or "mist."

ā, ē, ī, ō, ū, ȳ, *long;* ȧ, ė, ȯ, same, less prolonged; ă, ĕ, ĭ, ŏ, ŭ, ȳ, *short;* ą, ę, į, ǫ, *obscure;* fär, fȧll, fȧt; mêt; nŏt; gŏŏd; mōŏn;

of the Edda, however, she makes her appearance as a toothless old woman. (See THOR.)

See THORPE, "Northern Mythology," vol. i.; KEYSER, "Religion of the Northmen;" MALLET, "Northern Antiquities," vol. ii. Fables XVI., XXV., and XXVI.; PETERSEN, "Nordisk Mythologi."

Held, hĕlt, (WILLIBALD,) a German writer on law, born at Erolzheim in 1726 ; died in 1789.

Hele, hāl, or **Hāles,** sometimes written **D'Héle,** (THOMAS,) an English dramatic writer, born in Gloucestershire in 1740. He settled in Paris about 1770, and learned to write in French with ease and elegance. He produced, in French, several successful comedies, among which are "The Judgment of Midas," (1778,) and "The Jealous Lover." Died about 1780.

Hĕl'en, [Gr. Ἑλένη; Lat. HEL'ENA ; Fr. HÉLÈNE, à'lȧn'; It. ĔLENA, à-lā'nä,] a Grecian princess, celebrated for her transcendent beauty, was the daughter of Leda and the Spartan king Tyndarus, or, according to other authorities, of Leda and Jupiter. At an early age her hand was sought by some of the most renowned princes of Greece, among whom were Ulysses, Ajax, Diomedes, and Menelaus. At the suggestion of Ulysses, Tyndarus bound the suitors by an oath to submit to the choice which Helen should make, and to unite in her defence if any attempt should be made to carry her away from her husband. She selected Menelaus, from whom, after a short union, she was abducted by Paris, son of Priam, upon which the Greek kings declared war against Troy. After the death of Paris, Helen married his brother Deiphobus, whom, after she became reconciled to Menelaus, she betrayed into the hands of the latter. The accounts of her death are various : the most probable is that she was put to death by Polyxo, Queen of Rhodes, whose husband had been killed at Troy.

Helena, the Latin of HELEN, which see.

Hel'e-na, SAINT, [Fr. SAINTE-HÉLÈNE, sȧnt'à'lȧn'; It. SANT' ELENA, sȧnt-à-lā'nä,] mother of the emperor Constantine, was born of a humble family at Drepanum, in Bithynia, about 250 A.D. She became the wife of Constantius Chlorus, who, having been raised to the rank of Cæsar in 292 A.D., divorced her in order to marry Theodora. The accession of Constantine to the throne restored her to prosperity and honour. About 325 she made a pilgrimage to Palestine, where she built the church of the Holy Sepulchre and that of the Nativity. Died in 327.

Helena, daughter of Constantine the Great, was married at Milan in 355 A.D. to her first-cousin Julian, who had just become a Cæsar and was afterwards Emperor of Rome. She died at Vienne, in Gaul, in 359.

Hel'e-nus, [Gr. Ἕλενος; Fr. HÉLÉNUS, à'là'nüs',] a son of Priam and Hecuba, was celebrated as a soothsayer. Having been captured by the Greeks, he declared that Troy could not be taken unless Philoctetes would repair to the siege. After the fall of Troy he fell to the share of Pyrrhus, who gave him Andromache in marriage and left him at his death a portion of his kingdom.

Heli, a Sanscrit name of the sun. See SÛRYA.

Héli, the French for ELI, which see.

Heliade, hĕl'e-âd, (JOHN,) a celebrated poet, born at Turgowiste, (Tergovist,) in Rumania, about 1800. He founded in 1831 a journal called "The Wallachian Courier." Among his poems are "Mircea," a drama, (1844,) and a national poem, "Michael the Brave," (1846.)

Hel-ĭ-co-nī'a-dĕs, a name given to the Muses, because they lived on Mount Helicon. (See MUSÆ.)

Hélie, hȧ'le', (FAUSTIN,) a French jurist, born at Nantes about 1798, published "Traité de l'Instruction criminelle," (8 vols., 1845–58.) He was elected a member of the Institute in 1855.

Hélinand, hȧ'le'nôn', (DAN,) a French poet, who had a high reputation in his time. Died about 1225.

Héliodore. See HELIODORUS.

He-lĭ-o-dō'rus, [Gr. Ἡλιόδωρος; Fr. HÉLIODORE, à'le'o'doR',] a Greek statuary of an uncertain epoch, is favourably mentioned by Pliny. His master-piece was a marble group called "Symplegma," which was at Rome in the time of Pliny.

Heliodorus, a Greek surgeon, lived at Rome, and was a contemporary of Juvenal, who mentions him in his Tenth Satire.

Heliodorus, born at Emessa, in Syria, in the fourth century, became Bishop of Tricca, in Thessaly. He wrote in his youth a celebrated Greek romance entitled "Æthiopica," which narrates the adventures of two lovers, named Theagenes and Chariclea. It was first printed in 1534, and has been translated into many languages. The style is pure and polished, the incidents are novel and natural, and the characters are admirably sustained.

See FABRICIUS, "Bibliotheca Græca;" BAYLE, "Historical and Critical Dictionary;" DUNLOP, "History of Fiction;" ERSCH und GRUBER, "Allgemeine Encyklopaedie;" VILLEMAIN, "Notice sur les Romans Grecs."

Heliodorus OF LARISSA, a Greek mathematician of an uncertain epoch, wrote a short treatise on Optics, which is extant.

Héliogabale and **Heliogabalus.** See ELAGABALUS.

He-lī'os, [Gr. Ἥλιος; Lat. HE'LIUS,] the god of the sun in the Greek mythology, represented as the son of Hyperion. He was partially identified with Apollo by the Romans; but, in the poems of Homer, Helios and Apollo were distinct persons. (See APOLLO.)

Hell, hĕl, (MAXIMILIAN,) an able Hungarian astronomer, born at Schemnitz in 1720, became a Jesuit about 1738. From 1756 to 1792 he held the official position of astronomer and director of the Observatory at Vienna. He distinguished himself by a successful observation of the transit of Venus which he made in Lapland in June, 1769, and of which he published an account, "De Transitu Veneris," etc., (1770.) He published annually from 1757 to 1786 "Ephemerides," which were esteemed. Among his works (in Latin) are a "Treatise on the Parallax of the Sun," (1773,) and "Methodus Astronomica sine Usu Quadrantis vel Sectoris," (1774.) Died in 1792.

See MEUSEL, "Gelehrtes Deutschland."

Hell, (THEODOR.) See WINKLER, (KARL GOTTFRIED.)

Hel-lā'dĭ-us, a Greek grammarian, born in Egypt, lived about 325 A.D. He composed, in Iambic verse, a "Chrestomathie," of which some fragments are preserved.

Helladius, a Greek grammarian, born at Alexandria, lived in the fifth century after Christ.

Helladius, (ALEXANDER,) a Greek of Thessaly, who lived about 1700. He wrote a curious Latin work, entitled "The Present State of the Greek Church," published in 1714 at Altorf, Germany, where he then resided.

Hel-la-nī'cus [Ἑλλάνικος] OF MITYLENE, an early Greek prose writer and historian, was born probably about 495 B.C. He was the best or most distinguished writer of the class called logographers. Among his works were a "History of Argos," a "History of Attica," and a "History of Persia." Only small fragments of his writings are extant. He died about 410 B.C.

See PRELLER, "Dissertatio de Hellanico Lesbio Historico," 1840; C. MÜLLER, "De Hellanico."

Hel'le, [Gr. Ἕλλη,] a daughter of Athamas and Nephele. The poets relate that she was persecuted by her step-mother Ino, and was rescued by a golden-fleeced ram, on the back of which she rode through the air; but she fell into the sea, (since called Hellespont, or "sea of Helle,") and was drowned.

Hel'len, [Gr. Ἕλλην,] the mythical ancestor of the Helle'nes, or Greeks, was supposed to be a son of Deucalion and Pyrrha, and the father of Æolus, Dorus, and Xuthus. The name Hellenes was afterwards applied to the whole Greek nation.

Heller, hel'ler, (JOSEPH,) a German writer on art, born at Bamberg in 1798. He published a "Manual for Amateurs of Engravings," (3 vols., 1823–36,) "Documents *(Beitrag)* for the History of Art," (1828,) "The Life and Works of Albert Dürer," (1827–31,) and other works. Died in 1849.

Heller, hel'ler, (STEPHEN,) a Hungarian composer, born at Pesth in 1813, became a resident of Paris. His compositions for the piano are much admired in Germany, and are regarded by some critics as equal to those of Mendelssohn.

Hellichius, (ABRAHAM.) See GUSTAFSKÖLD.

Hellot, hȧ'lo', (JEAN,) a French chemist, born in Paris in 1685. He was a Fellow of the Royal Society of London and of the Academy of Sciences of Paris. He edited the "Gazette de France" from 1718 to 1732, and wrote a valuable treatise On the Art of Dyeing Woollen Stuffs." Died in 1766.

Hellvig or **Helwig, von,** fon hĕl'viG, (AMALIE,) a German poetess, born at Weimar in 1776; died in 1831.

Helm, (BENJAMIN HARDIN,) an American general, son of Governor John L. Helm, was born in Kentucky in 1831. He graduated at West Point in 1851, took arms against the Union in 1861, and was killed at the battle of Chickamauga, September 20, 1863.

Helman, hĕl'mŏN', (ISIDORE STANISLAS,) a French engraver, born at Lille in 1743; died about 1806.

Helmbreeker, hĕlm'brā'ker, (DIEDERIK,) a skilful Dutch painter, born at Haarlem in 1624, worked mostly in Rome, and painted history and landscapes. Among his works are a "Mater Dolorosa" and a "Nativity." Died in 1694.

See ERSCH und GRUBER, "Allgemeine Encyklopaedie."

Helmers, hĕl'mers, (JAN FREDERIK,) a popular Dutch epic and lyric poet, born in Amsterdam in 1767. He produced an ode entitled "Night," (1787,) a poem on Socrates, (1790,) and an epic poem, called "The Dutch Nation," ("De Hollandsche Natie," 1812,) the style and versification of which are admired. He published his minor poems in 2 vols., 1810. Died in 1813.

See ERSCH und GRUBER, "Allgemeine Encyklopaedie;" H. H. KLIJN, "J. F. Helmers, geschetst in eene Redevoering," 1815.

Helmersen, von, fon hĕl'mer-sĕn', (GREGOR,) a Russian geologist and traveller, born near Dorpat in 1803. Having explored Russia, Sweden, etc., he published, in 1831, "Observations on the Geology of the Southern Ural."

Helmfeldt, hĕlm'fĕlt, (SIMON GRUNDEL,) BARON OF, a Swedish field-marshal, born at Stockholm in 1617, distinguished himself in the campaigns of Poland under Charles X. He was killed at the battle of Landscrona, in 1677.

Helmholtz, hĕlm'holts, (HERMANN LUDWIG FERDINAND,) an eminent German physiologist, mathematician, and natural philosopher, born at Potsdam in 1821. He became professor of physiology at Heidelberg in 1858, and wrote some able treatises on the relations of physical forces. One of these has been translated into English by Professor John Tyndall, under the title of "Essay on the Interaction of Natural Forces." Helmholtz stands in the foremost rank among the living physiologists and natural philosophers of Europe. He is a member of the Royal Societies of London and Edinburgh, and of the learned societies of the other principal capitals of Europe.

Helmich, hĕl'mik, (WERNER,) a Dutch Protestant minister, born at Utrecht about 1550, preached at Utrecht and Amsterdam, and promoted the Reformation in Holland. Died in 1608.

Helmold, hĕl'molt, [Lat. HELMOL'DUS,] a German historian and ecclesiastic, born near Lubeck, travelled as a missionary among the Slavonians. He was the author of a "Chronicon Slavorum," which, though rude in style, is valuable for its accuracy. Died about 1177.

See VOSSIUS, "De Historicis Latinis;" J. MOLLER, "Diatriba de Helmoldo," 1782.

Helmoldus. See HELMOLD.

Helmont, van, vän hĕl'mont, (FRANCIS MERCURIUS,) a physician, son of the following, born in Belgium in 1618, inherited his father's taste for the occult sciences, on which he wrote several treatises. He professed to believe in a universal remedy and the philosopher's stone, and pretended that he had discovered the original language. Died in 1699.

Helmont, van, (JAN BAPTISTA,) a famous chemist, physiologist, and visionary, was born at Brussels in 1577. He studied medicine, which he practised gratis, and had numerous disciples, though he was hostile to the doctrines of the Galenists. He seems to have been an honest enthusiast, infected with the delusions of alchemy, and to have spent much time and money in chemical experiments, by which he made important discoveries. "Van Helmont," says Dr. Hoefer, "is much superior to Paracelsus, whom he took in some measure as his model. He had the durable glory of revealing scientifically the existence of invisible, impalpable substances,—namely,

gases." He was the first who used the word gas as the name of all elastic fluids except common air. He contributed to the progress of physiology by an experiment on a willow-tree, which he found to gain one hundred and sixty-four pounds, while the soil in which it grew lost only a few ounces. Among his works are one on the magnetic cure of wounds, ("De magnetica Vulnerum naturali Curatione," 1621,) and one on "The Origin of Medicine," etc., ("Ortus Medicinæ, id est Initia Physicæ inaudita," 1648.) He died near Vilvorde in 1644.

See LOOS, "Biographie des J. B. van Helmont," 1807; CAILLAU, "Mémoire sur Van Helmont," 1819; FRAENKEL, "Dissertatio, Vita et Opiniones Helmontii," 1837; CUVIER, "Histoire des Sciences naturelles;" HOEFER, "Histoire de la Chimie;" RIXNER und SIBER, "J. B. Helmont," 1826.

Helmont, van, (LUCAS GASSEL,) an able Flemish landscape-painter, who lived about 1595.

Helmont, van, (MATTHEW,) a Flemish painter of Antwerp, born in 1653, painted markets, shops, etc. with success. Died in 1726.

Helmont, van, (SEGRES JACOB,) an eminent Flemish painter of history, born at Antwerp in 1683, was a pupil of his father, Matthew. He worked at Brussels, and derived his subjects mostly from sacred history. Among his chief works are "The Sacrifice of Elijah," "Joseph Recognized by his Brethren," and "The Triumph of David." His manner is noble, his colour good, and his design correct. He was ranked among the greatest Flemish painters of his time. Died in 1726.

See DESCAMPS, "Vies des Peintres Flamands," etc.

Helmsdorf, hĕlms'dorf, (FRIEDRICH,) an able German landscape-painter, born at Magdeburg in 1784.

Héloise, ā'lo'ĕz', Eloise, or Louise, a beautiful and renowned Frenchwoman, born at Paris about 1100, was a niece of Fulbert, canon of Notre-Dame. She was distinguished for her attainments in languages and philosophy, and became successively the pupil, mistress, and wife of Abelard. Soon after their marriage she entered the convent of Argenteuil, of which she became prioress. She afterwards acquired a high reputation for piety and devotion. Her letters, written in elegant Latin, and printed with those of Abelard, are the expressions of a noble and fervent spirit. Died in 1164. (See ABELARD.)

See LAMARTINE, "Celebrated Characters."

Helps, (ARTHUR,) a popular English essayist and historian, born about 1818. He graduated at Cambridge in 1835, and produced in 1843 "Catherine Douglas, a Tragedy," in verse, which was received with favour. In 1847 he published, anonymously, a volume of dialogues on moral questions, entitled "Friends in Council: a Series of Readings and Discourses thereon," which was generally admired for graceful style and original insight. His next work was "Companions of my Solitude," (1851,) which a critic in "Blackwood's Magazine" considers "far the most interesting of all Mr. Helps's essays." Among his later works are "The Conquerors of the New World, and their Bondsmen," (2 vols., 1848–52,) a "History of the Spanish Conquest of America, and its Relations to the History of Slavery," (3 vols., 1855–57,) "Realmah, a Tale," and a "Life of Columbus," (1869.) "A true thinker, who has practical purpose in his thinking," says Ruskin, "and is sincere, as Plato, or Carlyle, or Helps, becomes in some sort a seer, and must be always of infinite use to his generation." He held for many years an office in the civil service, and became clerk or secretary of the privy council about 1860.

See "Edinburgh Review" for January, 1859; "Blackwood's Magazine" for October, 1851; "Fraser's Magazine" for September, 1857.

Hel'sham, (RICHARD,) professor of physic and natural philosophy in the University of Dublin. He was an intimate friend of Dean Swift. Died in 1738. His lectures on philosophy were published in 1739, and have been often reprinted.

Helst, van der, vän der hĕlst, (BARTHOLOMEW,) an excellent Dutch portrait-painter, born at Haarlem in 1613. He painted landscapes in his youth, but he afterwards confined himself mostly to portraits, and settled in Amsterdam. Among his works is a picture of the militia or trained bands, which is in the Stadt-House of Amsterdam, and which Sir Joshua Reynolds is said to have pronounced "the best picture of portraits in the world." Died about 1670.

See Bryan, "Dictionary of Painters;" Descamps, "Vies des Peintres Flamands, Hollandais," etc.

Helvetius, hĕl-vee′she-us, [Fr. pron. ĕl′vă′se′üs′,] (Claude Adrien,) a celebrated French author and philosopher, born in Paris in 1715, was the son of Jean Claude Adrien, noticed below, who destined him for financial pursuits. At the age of twenty-three he obtained, through the influence of the queen, a place as farmer-general, which was worth one hundred thousand crowns per annum. In 1751 he resigned this office, and married an accomplished lady named De Ligniville or Ligneville. He published in 1758 an ingenious metaphysical work, entitled "On the Mind," ("De l'Esprit,") which was condemned by the court, the Jesuits, and the bishops as the summary of the creed of the Encyclopædists, and was burned by order of Parliament, thus acquiring additional celebrity and a wider circulation. The author publicly apologized, and disclaimed any purpose to assail the Christian doctrines. He is admitted to have been generous, and his life and character appear to have been. better than his writings, which, deriving all virtue from self-interest, and condemning as folly all actions proceeding from any higher motive, are in the highest degree demoralizing. He wrote a poem "On Happiness," and a treatise on "Man, his Faculties and his Education," (1772.) In 1765 he was an invited and honoured guest in the palace of Frederick the Great. Died in 1771.

See Saint-Lambert, "Essai sur la Vie et les Ouvrages d'Helvetius;" Lemontey, "Notice sur C. A. Helvetius," 1823; William Mudford, "Life of Helvetius," London, 1807; Voltaire, "Correspondance;" Marmontel, "Mémoires;" Damiron, "Mémoire sur Helvetius," 1853.

Anne Catherine de Ligniville, (lĕn′ye′vĕl′,) Madame **Helvetius,** the wife of the preceding, was born in Lorraine in 1719. After the death of her husband her house at Auteuil was the rendezvous of celebrated men, among whom were Dr. Franklin, Turgot, and Thomas Jefferson. Died in 1800.

See Dr. Roussel, "Notice sur Madame Helvetius."

Helvetius, hĕl-vee′she-us, (Jan,) a classical scholar and Latin poet of the eighteenth century, was born in Amsterdam. He described in elegant verses his travels in England, "Iter Britannicum," and wrote other works.

Helvetius, (Jean Adrien,) a Dutch physician, born about 1660. He was present in Paris on a visit during the prevalence of dysentery, which he treated with such success that Louis XIV. urged him to divulge the remedy. He said it was ipecacuanha, and received from the king a present of one thousand louisd'ors. He settled in Paris, and became physician to the regent of the kingdom, the Duke of Orléans. He wrote several treatises on medicine. Died in 1727.

See "Biographie Médicale;" Moréri,"Dictionnaire Historique."

Helvetius, (Jean Claude Adrien,) son of the preceding, born in Paris in 1685, graduated as physician in 1708. Having given proof of his professional skill, he was in 1719 called to attend Louis XV., then an infant, whom he cured of a dangerous illness. After this he enjoyed the confidence of the royal family, and was made councillor of state, and first physician to the queen, Marie Leczinski. He was a member of the Academies of Sciences of Paris, Berlin, and London, and wrote several professional treatises, among which is a "Method of Curing the Principal Diseases," (1737.) Died in 1765.

See "Biographie Médicale;" Quérard, "La France Littéraire."

Helvicus, hĕl-vee′kŭs, or. **Helwig,** hĕl′ŵig, (Christoph,) an eminent German philologist, born near Frankfort in 1581. He could speak Latin, Greek, and Hebrew at the age of fourteen, and became professor of Greek at Giessen in 1605. Among his works are a "System of Chronology," ("Theatrum Chronologicum," 1609,) and a "General Grammar." Died in 1617.

Helwig, hĕl′ŵig, or **Helwing,** hĕl′ŵing, (Georg Andreas,) a Prussian naturalist, born at Angerburg in 1666, became minister of the church at that town in 1705. He wrote, besides other works, "Flora Quasimodogenita," (1712,) a description of the indigenous plants of Prussia. Died in 1748.

Helwig, (Johann Otto,) a German physician and alchemist, born in Thuringia in 1654. He became first physician to the Elector-palatine, who appointed him professor at Heidelberg. He wrote a curious work, entitled "Introitus in veram et inauditam Physicam," (1678,) and several treatises on alchemy. Died in 1698.

See Ersch und Gruber, "Allgemeine Encyklopaedie."

Hélyot, hă′le-o′, (Pierre,) called also **Père Hippolyte,** a French monk, born in Paris in 1660. He wrote a "History of Military and Religious Monastic Orders," said to be the most complete work on that subject. Died in 1716.

Hem′ans, (Felicia Dorothea,) an amiable and excellent English poetess, born in Liverpool on the 25th of September, 1794, was the daughter of a merchant named Browne. About the year 1800 he removed with his family to Grwych, in North Wales. Her first volume of poems was published in 1808. In 1812 she was married to Captain Hemans, of the British army; but the union was not a happy one, and after the lapse of six years they finally separated, their five children remaining with the mother. In 1825 she removed to Rhyllon, in Wales, and in 1828 resided at Wavertree, near Liverpool. She cherished a passionate love of poetry and of natural scenery, and became the most popular of English poetesses. Lord Jeffrey pronounced her poetry "infinitely sweet, elegant, and tender, touching, perhaps, and contemplative, rather than vehement or overpowering. ... We do not hesitate to say that she is the most touching and accomplished writer of occasional verses that our literature has yet to boast of." "In her poetry," says Moir, "religious truth, moral purity, and intellectual beauty ever meet together." The following are the titles of some of her poems: "Domestic Affections," (1812,) "Modern Greece," (1817,) "Vespers of Palermo," (1823,) "The Forest Sanctuary," (1826,) "Records of Woman," (1828,) "National Lyrics," (1834,) and "Scenes and Hymns of Life." Her character may be said to be truly portrayed in her writings. She resided in Dublin from 1831 until her death, which occurred in 1835.

See H. F. Chorley, "Memoirs of Mrs. Hemans," 1837; "Memoir of Mrs. Hemans," by her sister, 1839; Sainte-Beuve, "Causeries du Lundi," tome iii.; Mrs. Elwood, "Memoirs of the Literary Ladies of England from the Commencement of the Last Century;" "Edinburgh Review" for October, 1829.

Hemelar, hā′meh-lâr′, (Jan,) a Dutch medallist and poet, born at the Hague, wrote a commentary on Roman medals. Died in 1640.

Hemert, van, văn hā′mĕrt, (Paul,) a Dutch philosopher, born at Amsterdam in 1756. He published "Elements of the Philosophy of Kant," (4 vols., 1795,) and other works. Died in 1825.

He-mi′na, ? (L. Cassius,) a Roman historian, who flourished between 200 and 150 B.C. He wrote a history or annals of Rome from the origin of the city to his own time, which has not come down to us. This work is often cited by Pliny, Nonius, and Aulus Gellius.

Hemingford, de, dĕh hem′ing-ford, (Walter,) was a canon of Gisborough Abbey, and wrote a "History of England from 1066 to 1308." Died in 1347.

Hemling. See Memling, (Hans.)

Hemmerlein. See Hammerlein.

Hemminga, hĕm-ming′gä or hĕm-ming′Hä, (Sixtus,) a Dutch mathematician, born in 1533; died in 1570.

Hem′pel, (Charles Julius,) a medical writer, born at Solingen, Prussia, in 1811, emigrated to the United States about 1835. He produced, besides other works, a "System of Homœopathic Materia Medica and Therapeutics," (1859.)

Hemprich, hĕm′pʀiK, (Friedrich Wilhelm,) a German naturalist, was born at Glatz in 1796. He accompanied Ehrenberg in the exploration of Egypt and Arabia, and died at Massowah in 1825. He left "Rudiments (Grundriss) of Natural History," (1820.)

Hemskerck, hĕms′kĕrk′, (Egbert,) called the Old, an able Dutch painter, born at Haarlem about 1610, was an attentive student of nature. His favourite subjects were fairs, feasts, and familiar scenes among the lower classes. Died about 1680.

Hemskerck, (Egbert,) the Young, born at Haarlem in 1645, was probably a son of the preceding. He painted rural sports and wild, fanciful, or humorous scenes. Died in London in 1704.

Hemskerk. See HEEMSKERK, VAN.

Hemsterhuys, hĕm'stẹr-hois', [Lat. HEMSTERHU'-SIUS,] (FRANS,) a meritorious philosopher, writer, and moralist, born at Groningen in 1720, was a son of Tiberius, noticed below. He passed the greater part of his mature life at the Hague, where he was assistant secretary or first clerk of the council of state. Among his characteristic traits were simplicity, modesty, and liberality of spirit. Like Plato, of whom he was an admirer, he directed towards the ideal the intellectual and moral activity of man. His favourite topics were the theory of beauty in the arts, and questions of practical philosophy. He wrote, in French, a "Letter on Sculpture," (1769,) a "Letter on the Desires," (1770,) a "Letter on Man and his Relations," (1772,) and two dialogues, entitled "Sophyle, or on Philosophy," and "Aristée, or on the Divinity," ("Aristée, ou de la Divinité," 1779.) Died in 1790.

See MEYBOOM, "Comment. de Hemsterhusii Meritis," 1840; VAN DE WEYER, "Notice sur Hemsterhuys," 1827; TIJDEMAN, "Proeve eener Lofrede op F. Hemsterhuys," 1834; "Nouvelle Biographie Générale."

Hemsterhuys, (TIBERIUS,) a Dutch philologist, and one of the most learned Hellenists of his time, was born at Groningen in 1685. He became professor of philosophy and mathematics at Amsterdam in 1704, and continued the study of Greek until he had read all the authors in that language. He was chosen professor of Greek at Franeker in 1720, and obtained the same chair at Leyden in 1740. In consequence of his efforts, the study of Greek, which had been neglected, again became popular in Holland. He published Lucian's "Dialogues," (1708,) the "Plutus" of Aristophanes, (1744,) "Notes on Xenophon of Ephesus," (1784,) "Latin Orations," (1784,) and other works. Died in 1766.

See RINCK, "T. Hemsterhuys und David Ruhnken," 1801; DAVID RUHNKEN, "Elogium T. Hemsterhusii," 1768; ERSCH und GRUBER, "Allgemeine Encyklopaedie;" "Nouvelle Biographie Générale."

Henao, à-nä'o, (GABRIEL,) a Spanish Jesuit, born at Valladolid in 1611, was for fifty years professor of positive theology at the University of Salamanca, of which he was also rector. He gained a high reputation as a casuist, and wrote numerous theological works. Died in 1704.

Hénault, hả'nō', (CHARLES JEAN FRANÇOIS,) a French historian, born in Paris in 1685. In youth he cultivated literature and obtained a prize in the French Academy, of which he became a member in 1723. His wit, amenity, and politeness rendered him a favourite in fashionable society, for which he composed ingenious verses and songs. He became president of the first Chambre aux Enquêtes in 1710, and, a few years later, superintendent of the queen's household. He gained a conspicuous position among French authors by his "Compendium of the History of France," ("Abrégé chronologique de l'Histoire de France," 2 vols., 1744,) a work of great merit, which was often reprinted. Hénault wrote, besides other dramas, "Marius," a tragedy, (1715,) and the "Awaking of Epimenides," a comedy, (1757,) both of which were performed with success. Died in 1770.

See "Mémoires du Président Hénault, écrites par lui-même," 1854; SAINTE-BEUVE, "Causeries du Lundi," tome xii.

Hénault, (JEAN.) See HESNAULT.

Henckel. See HENKEL.

Hen'der-sọn, (ALEXANDER,) an able Scottish divine, born in Fife in 1583, was a leader among the Covenanters. He was repeatedly appointed a commissioner to treat with Charles I., and was an adherent of Parliament in the civil war. He contributed much to effect a union between the Covenanters and the English Parliament. Died in 1646.

See AITON, "Life and Times of A. Henderson;" CHAMBERS, "Biographical Dictionary of Eminent Scotsmen."

Hen'der-sọn, (EBENEZER,) an eminent British biblical critic, born at Dunfermline in 1784. He was employed by the Bible Society to supply the people of Iceland with a version of the Scriptures in 1814. He published a "Journal of a Residence in Iceland," (2 vols., 1818,) and "Biblical Researches and Travels in Russia," (1826.)

His commentary on Isaiah (of which he made a new version, 1840) is highly commended. He was professor of theology and minister of the Independents at Highbury, near London. Died in May, 1858.

See ERSLEW, "Almindeligt Forfatter-Lexicon."

Henderson, (JOHN,) a celebrated English actor, born in London in 1746. In 1772 he performed at Bath, under the name of Courtney, and in 1777 came to London, where he attracted crowded houses in Drury Lane and Covent Garden. He performed with great applause the parts of "Falstaff," "Shylock," "Richard III.," etc. Died in 1785.

Henderson, (JOHN,) born in Ireland in 1757, was distinguished for his genius and eccentricity. After teaching Latin at the age of eight, and Greek four years later, he was sent to Oxford University, where he was regarded as a prodigy in learning and mental capacity. A fellow-student, being vanquished by him in an argument, threw a glass of wine into the face of Henderson, who calmly remarked, "This is only a digression, sir: let us now examine your argument." He wrote a few small poems and essays. Died in 1788.

Henderson, (THOMAS,) a Scottish astronomer, born at Dundee in 1798, pursued for some years the profession of an attorney. About 1830 he was employed as secretary by Lord Jeffrey. Having devoted his leisure time to astronomy, he was appointed in 1832 director of the observatory at the Cape of Good Hope. He obtained in 1834 the charge of the Edinburgh Observatory, as first astronomer-royal for Scotland, and performed the duties of this post with credit until his death, in 1844. Many of his astronomical treatises and observations have been published, and are highly esteemed. About 1840 he ascertained that the star α Centauri has a parallax of nearly one second, and is, consequently, about 18,918,000,000,000 miles from the sun. This was the first fixed star of which the parallax has been measured.

See CHAMBERS, "Biographical Dictionary of Eminent Scotsmen," (Supplement;) "Nouvelle Biographie Générale."

Hen'dricks, (THOMAS A.,) an American Senator, born in Muskingum county, Ohio, in 1819. He studied law, and settled in Indiana. He represented a district of Indiana in Congress from 1851 to 1855, was commissioner of the general land office from 1855 to 1859, and was elected a Senator of the United States for six years, 1863-69. In 1868 he was the Democratic candidate for Governor of Indiana, and was defeated.

Henel von Hennefeld, hā'nẹl fon hĕn'nẹh-fĕlt', (NIKOLAUS,) a German jurist and historian, born in Silesia in 1582. He was author of several legal and historical works. Died in 1656.

See ERSCH und GRUBER, "Allgemeine Encyklopaedie."

Hĕn'frey, (ARTHUR,) F.R.S., an eminent English botanist, born at Aberdeen on the 1st of November, 1819. He translated several botanical works from the German, and wrote "Outlines of Structural and Physiological Botany," (1847,) "The Vegetation of Europe," (1852,) and an "Elementary Course of Botany, Structural, Physiological, and Systematic," (1857.) The last is a work of high character. He co-operated with Dr. Griffith in a "Micrographic Dictionary," (1857,) which is highly prized. In 1854 he was chosen professor of botany in King's College, London. Died in 1859.

Hengist, hĕng'gĭst, a Saxon chief, who founded the kingdom of Kent, in England. About 450 A.D. the Britons solicited the aid of the Saxons to defend them against the Picts and Scots. Hengist and his brother Horsa, at the head of a small army, came over, and, after defeating the Picts and Scots, turned their arms against their British allies. After many battles, in one of which Horsa was slain, Hengist, aided by reinforcements from Saxony, obtained possession of Kent, where he reigned thirty years. Died in 488.

See TURNER, "History of the Anglo-Saxons."

Hengstenberg, hĕng'stẹn-bĕRg', (ERNST WILHELM,) an eminent German orthodox theologian, born at Fröndenberg, in Prussia, in 1802. He became professor of theology in the University of Berlin in 1829, and chief editor of an influential religious journal, "Evangelische Kirchenzeitung." He published several com-

ā, ē, ī, ō, ū, ȳ, *long;* à, ė, ȯ, same, less prolonged; ă, ĕ, ĭ, ŏ, ŭ, ў, *short;* ạ, ẹ, ị, ọ, *obscure;* fär, fåll, fåt; mēt; nŏt; gōōd; mōōn;

mentaries on the Holy Scriptures, and "Christologie des Alten Testaments," ("Christology of the Old Testament," 3 vols., 1829-35,) which has been translated into English. He was one of the principal leaders of the orthodox or Lutherans of Germany. Died in June, 1869.

Henisch, hā′nish, (GEORG,) a philologist, born in Hungary in 1549, published "Thesaurus Linguæ et Sapientiæ Germanicæ," (1616,) said to be the first good dictionary of the German language, (though not extending beyond the letter H.) Died in 1618.

Henkart, hĕnk′ȧrt, (PIERRE JOSEPH,) a Belgian poet and judge, born at Liege in 1761 ; died in 1815.

Henke, hĕnk′eh, (ADOLF CHRISTIAN HEINRICH,) a German physician, born at Brunswick in 1775, became professor at Erlangen in 1805. He published a valuable "Treatise on Legal Medicine," (1812 ; 12th edition, 1851.) Died in 1843.

Henke, (HEINRICH PHILIPP KONRAD,) an able German theologian, born in the duchy of Brunswick in 1752, became professor of theology at Helmstedt in 1780, and subsequently vice-president of the Consistory at Brunswick. He published, besides other works, an "Ecclesiastical History," (6 vols., 1788-1804,) a work displaying great learning and research, and "Lineamenta Institutionum Fidei Christianæ," (1783.) Died in 1809.

See F. A. LUDEWIG, "Abriss einer Lebensgeschichte Henkes ;" BOLLMANN und WOLFF, "H. P. C. Henke, Denkwürdigkeiten aus seinem Leben," 1816 ; ERSCH und GRUBER, "Allgemeine Encyklopaedie."

Henke, (HERMANN WILHELM EDUARD,) a jurist, brother of Adolf Christian Heinrich, noticed above, was born in 1783.

Henkel or **Henckel,** hĕnk′el, (JOACHIM FRIEDRICH,) a skilful Prussian surgeon, born in 1712. He practised and lectured in Berlin, and published, besides other works, "Medical and Surgical Observations," (1744.) Died in 1779.

Henkel, (JOHANN FRIEDRICH,) an able chemist and mineralogist, born at Freiberg, in Saxony, in 1679. He was appointed counsellor of mines by King Augustus II., and improved the porcelain fabrics of Meissen. He wrote "Flora Saturnizans," (1722,) "Principles of Mineralogy," (1747,) and other works. Died in 1744.

See ERSCH und GRUBER, "Allgemeine Encyklopaedie."

Henkle, hĕnk′el, (MOSES MONTGOMERY,) D.D., an American Methodist divine, born in Pendleton county, Virginia, in 1798. In 1860 he removed to Philadelphia. He wrote, besides other works, "Primary Platform of Methodism," (1851.)

Henle, hĕn′leh, (FRIEDRICH GUSTAV JAKOB,) a German physician, born in Franconia in 1809, became professor of anatomy and director of the Anatomical Institute at Göttingen in 1852. He published a "Manual of Rational Pathology," (1846-52,) and other medical works.

Hen′ley, (ANTHONY,) an English scholar and writer, born in Hampshire, was educated at Oxford. In 1698 he was elected to Parliament, where he acquired much influence. He was a person of distinguished wit, refinement, and accomplishments, possessed a large fortune, and was a liberal patron of literary men. He contributed to the "Tatler" and the "Medley," and wrote lyric verses. Died in 1711.

His son ROBERT became lord chancellor

Henley, (JOHN,) often called ORATOR HENLEY, was born at Melton-Mowbray in 1692, and educated at Cambridge. Before he had left the university, he wrote a letter inserted in the 396th number of the "Spectator." In 1719 he published a "Universal Grammar." Having taken holy orders, he came to London and opened a chapel, where large crowds were attracted by his elocution and by his questionable modes of courting popularity. Pope commemorates him in the "Dunciad" as "the Zany of his age." On Sundays he lectured on theology, and on Wednesdays on politics, fashions, and affairs in general. He edited a paper called the "Hyp Doctor,"—a farrago of nonsense,—by which, it is said, he made one hundred pounds a year. Died in 1756.

See "Retrospective Review," vol. xiv., 1826 ; DISRAELI, "Calamities of Authors."

Henley, (JOSEPH WARNER,) a British conservative legislator, born about 1794. He was elected to the

House of Commons for Oxfordshire in 1841. He was appointed president of the board of trade by Lord Derby in 1852, and again in 1858. On account of his hostility to the Reform Bill, he resigned in 1859.

Henley, (ROBERT,) Lord Northington, son of Anthony Henley, was born in 1708, and educated at Oxford. He was called to the bar in 1732, and began to practise in the Western Circuit, of which he afterwards became the leader. In 1747 he was returned to Parliament for Bath, and became an active debater. In 1756 he obtained the place of attorney-general. According to Lord Campbell, "Henley had not the most distant notion of the great seal being offered to him ; but his mediocrity was the real cause of his elevation ;" and in 1757 he was named lord keeper by Pitt, then one of the chiefs of the ministry. After the accession of George III., he received in 1761 the title of lord chancellor, and was created Earl of Northington. In 1766, after overturning the Rockingham ministry, with which as a Tory he could not agree, he resigned his office, and accepted that of president of the council. He acquitted himself respectably as a judge. Died in 1772.

See R. HENLEY, "Memoir of Robert Henley, Earl of Northington ;" LORD CAMPBELL, "Lives of the Lord Chancellors ;" FOSS, "The Judges of England."

Hen′ne-pin, [Fr. pron. ḣĕn′pȧN′ or ḣĕn′neh-pȧN′,] (LOUIS,) a missionary, was born in Flanders about 1640. Having a passion for exploring remote regions, he embarked for Canada, arriving at Quebec in 1675, and joined the party of La Salle in 1678. When they had reached the Illinois River, La Salle being forced to return, Hennepin proceeded without him, in 1680, and explored the Upper Mississippi as far as the falls, to which he gave the name of Saint Anthony, and which had not before been visited by any European. He returned to Quebec in 1680, and sailed to France, where he published in 1683-84 an account of his travels, under the title of a "Description of Louisiana." Thirteen years later, he published his "New Discovery of a Vast Country situated in America," etc., which contained the same matter as the former, with the addition of an account of his voyage down the Lower Mississippi, which, according to Professor Sparks, is a fabrication, copied from Le Clercq's narrative. (Sparks's "Life of La Salle.") Hennepin receives credit for courage and resolution, and for general accuracy in his descriptions of Indian life, etc.

See FÉLIX VAN HULST, "Notice sur le Père Hennepin d'Ath," 1845 ; "Nouvelle Biographie Générale."

Hennequin, ḣĕn′kȧN′, (AMÉDÉE,) an advocate and writer, a son of the following, born in Paris in 1817, wrote "The Conquest of Algeria," (1857,) and other works.

Hennequin, (ANTOINE LOUIS MARIE,) a distinguished French lawyer, born at Monceaux, near Paris, in 1786. He had a high rank as an eloquent pleader, and acted as counsel in many political trials. He defended Peyronnet, ex-minister, in 1830, and was elected to the Chamber of Deputies in 1834. In politics he was a legitimist. His principal work is a "Treatise on Legislation and Jurisprudence," (2 vols., 1838.) Died in 1840.

Hennequin, (PIERRE AUGUSTE,) a French historical painter, born at Lyons in 1763, was a pupil of David. He studied in Rome, and was a zealous partisan of the Revolution, after which he worked in Paris. Among his capital works is "Orestes pursued by the Furies." Died in 1833.

Hennet, ḣȧ′nȧ′, (ALBIN JOSEPH ULPIEN,) a French writer, born at Maubeuge in 1758. Among his works is a "History of the French Academy," (6 vols., in manuscript.) Died in 1828.

Henniges, von, fon hĕn′neh-gĕs′, (HEINRICH,) a Prussian publicist, born at Weissenburg in 1645. He represented Prussia at the Diet of Ratisbon in 1709, and at that of Frankfort in 1711. Among his works are "Observations on Grotius," (1673,) and "Reflections on the Treaty of Münster," (1706.) Died in 1711.

Hen′ni-ker, (Sir FREDERICK,) an English traveller, born in London in 1793. He published in 1824 an amusing narrative, entitled "Notes during a Visit to Egypt, Nubia," etc. Died in 1825.

---

e as k ; ç as s ; ğ hard ; ġ as j ; G, H, K, guttural ; N, nasal ; R, trilled ; š as z ; th as in this. (☞See Explanations, p. 23.)

Hennin, hå′nåN′, (PIERRE MICHEL,) a French linguist, who corresponded with Voltaire, and left "Diplomatic Correspondence," (1796.) Died in 1807.

Hen′ning, (JOHN,) a Scottish sculptor, born at Paisley in 1771, worked some years in Edinburgh, whence he removed to London in 1811. He executed reduced copies of the Panathenaic frieze. Died in 1851.

Henninges, hĕn′ning-ĕs, or **Henniges,** (HIERONYMUS,) a German genealogist, of great learning, born at Lüneburg about 1550, published "Theatrum Genealogicum," etc., (5 vols., 1598.) Died in 1597.

Hennings, hĕn′nings, (AUGUST ADOLF FRIEDRICH,) born in Holstein in 1746, wrote "Philosophic Essays," (2 vols., 1780,) and other works. Died in 1826.

Hennuyer, le, lĕh hĕn′nü-e′yå′, (JEAN,) born at Saint-Quentin, in France, in 1497, became Bishop of Lisieux in 1560. He held the office of first almoner to Henry II., Francis II., Charles IX., and Henry III. Died in 1578.

Henri, (Kings of France.) See HENRY.

Henri de Bourgogne, hŏN′re′ dĕh booR′goñ′, surnamed THE GREAT, was the first proprietary Duke of Burgundy. In 987 his brother, Hugh Capet, having become King of France, gave him the duchy of that province as his proper heritage. Died in 1002.

Henri de Bourgogne, ancestor of the first branch ′of the kings of Portugal, was born about 1035. He was nephew of Henry I., King of France. About 1060 he went to Spain, and fought against the Moors under Alphonso VI. of Castile, who made him count *souverain* of the country between the Douro and the Minho. In 1103 he took part in the crusade in Palestine. He died about 1112. His son ALFONSO was the first King of Portugal.

Henri de Lausanne, hŏN′re′ dĕh lō′zăn′, an eloquent monk and zealous reformer. He preached in various parts of France, attacked boldly the vices of the clergy, and made many converts. He was opposed by Saint Bernard, and was cast into a prison, where he died in 1148.

See HODGSON, "Reformers and Martyrs," Philadelphia, 1867.

Henri de Saint-Ignace, hŏN′re′ dĕh săN′tĕn′yăss′, a Flemish theologian, born at Ath; died about 1720.

Henri de Valois. See HENRY III., (of France.)

Henri le Grand. See HENRY IV.

Henri le Lion. See HENRY THE LION.

Henri le Superbe. See HENRY THE PROUD.

Henrici, hĕn-rit′see, (CHRISTIAN FRIEDRICH,) a German poet, whose assumed name was PICANDER, born at Stolpe, Saxony, in 1700; died in 1764.

Henriet, hŏN′re-å′, (ISRAEL,) an able French engraver, born at Nancy in 1608. He imitated the designs and engravings of his friend Callot with success, and was selected as master of design to Louis XIV. Died at Paris in 1661.

Henricus, the Latin for HENRY, which see.

Henricus Auceps. See HENRY THE FOWLER.

Henricus Leo. See HENRY THE LION.

Henricus Magnus. See HENRY IV., (of France.)

Henricus Superbus. See HENRY THE PROUD.

Henricus Valesius. See HENRY III., (of France.)

Hen-rĭ-et′ta Anne, a daughter of Charles I. of England and of Henrietta Maria, was born at Exeter in 1644, and was married in 1661 to the Duke of Orléans, brother of Louis XIV., of whose court she was regarded as one of the brightest ornaments. At her funeral, in 1670, Bossuet pronounced one of his most eloquent discourses.

See W. H. D. ADAMS, "Famous Beauties and Historic Women," London, 1865.

Hen-rĭ-et′ta Ma-ri′a, [Fr. HENRIETTE MARIE,] Queen of England, born in 1609, was a daughter of Henry IV. of France and Mary de Medici. She was married in 1625 to Prince Charles, afterwards Charles I. of England, and it was stipulated that she should enjoy liberty to use the Catholic forms of worship. "By her sense and spirit, as well as beauty, she justified the fondness of her husband." In 1645 she was compelled to retire to France. She died near Paris in 1669.

See HUME, "History of England;" VOLTAIRE, "Siècle de Louis XIV;" AGNES STRICKLAND, "Queens of England."

Henriette Marie. See HENRIETTA MARIA.

Henrion, hŏN′re′ôN′, (DENIS,) a French mathematician, who translated Euclid into French, (1632,) was the first Frenchman who published a table of logarithms. Died about 1640.

Henrion, (MATHIEU RICHARD AUGUSTE,) a French Catholic writer, born at Metz in 1805, published a "History of the Papacy," (3 vols., 1832,) and other works. Died in 1862,

Henrion, (NICOLAS,) a French numismatist, born at Troyes in 1663; died in 1720.

Henrion de Pansey, hŏN′re′ôN′ dĕh pôN′să′, (PIERRE PAUL NICOLAS,) a learned French judge and jurist, born near Ligny, in Lorraine, in 1742. He gained distinction by pleading the cause of a negro claimed as a slave, who obtained his liberty. About 1770 he opened an office for consultation, and in 1779 published an excellent "Dissertation on Feudal Law." In 1810 Napoleon appointed him a member of the council of state, saying, "You should have been in the council these last ten years: I have scolded Cambacérès for not speaking of you sooner." He became first president of the court of cassation in 1828. He wrote several able works on civil and public law. Died in 1829.

See LOUIS ROZET, "Notice sur la Vie et les Ouvrages de Henrion de Pansey," 1829; L. D. BERNARD, "Notice historique sur Henrion de Pansey," 1829; TAILLANDIER, "Notice sur Henrion de Pansey," 1829; "Nouvelle Biographie Générale."

Henriot or **Hanriot,** hŏN′re′o′, (FRANÇOIS,) born at Nanterre in 1761, was one of the miscreants who gained a bad eminence in the reign of terror by their atrocities. He was chosen by the Commune leader of the armed populace which in May, 1793, surrounded the Convention and extorted from that body by violence and terror the proscription of the Girondists. At the time of Robespierre's downfall, in 1794, Henriot made desperate efforts to rescue him, but failed, and was executed with him.

Henrique. See HENRY THE NAVIGATOR.

Henriquet-Dupont, hŏN′re′kå′ dü′pôN′, (LOUIS PIERRE,) an eminent French engraver, born in Paris in 1797, engraved portraits (after French artists) of Andrew Chénier, Mirabeau, and Montaigne; also, "The Virgin and Child," after Raphael.

Henriquez, ên-ree′kĕth, (CRISOSTOMO,) a Spanish author, born at Madrid in 1594, wrote biographies of saints, etc., and some historical works. Died in 1632.

Henry (Heinrich) I., surnamed THE FOWLER, [Lat. HENRI′CUS AU′CEPS; Fr. HENRI L'OISELEUR, hŏN′re′ lwȧz′luR′,] Emperor of Germany, born in 876 A.D., was the son of Otho, Duke of Saxony, and the first German emperor of the Saxon house. Though he had previously been engaged in a war with the emperor Conrad I., he was recommended by that sovereign on his death-bed for his successor, and he was elected in 919. After waging war for some time against the Hungarians without success, he gained a decisive victory over them near Merseburg in 933. Henry was the first German emperor who granted municipal privileges. He died in 936, and was succeeded by his son, Otho I.

See N. H. GUNDLING, "Liber de Henrico Aucupe," 1711; J. P. LUDEWIG, "Henricus Auceps, Historia anceps," 1713; E. BURCKHARDT, "Dissertatio de Henrico I. Germanorum Rege," 1831; ADELBOLD, "Vita Henrici Aucupis," in the "Scriptores Rerum Brunswicensium" of Leibnitz.

Henry (Heinrich) II., called THE SAINT, was the son of Henry, Duke of Bavaria, and great-grandson of Henry the Fowler. He was born in 972. Having accompanied the emperor Otho III. to Rome, where he died, Henry took possession of the crown jewels, and in 1002 caused himself to be crowned emperor at Mentz. He was engaged in numerous broils with his brother Bruno, Henry, (the Marquis of Schweinfurt,) and Harduin of Ivrea. He died in 1024, and was succeeded by Conrad II.

See A. CRAMMER, "Admiranda Vita S. Henrici," 1770; J. RION, "Das heilige Kaiserpaar, oder Leben und Thaten des heiligen Heinrichs," etc., 1832.

Henry (Heinrich) III., born in 1017, was the son of Conrad II., and was chosen emperor in 1039. He curbed the power of his principal nobles, carried on successful wars in Bohemia, Hungary, and Northern Italy, and in 1046 deposed successively the popes Benedict IX., Sylvester III., and Gregory IV., and raised Clement II. to the pontificate. He died in 1056, having previously caused his son Henry to be elected emperor. Henry III. was endowed with commanding talents and great energy of character, and ranks among the ablest of German rulers.

See NEU, "Themata quædam selectiora de Henrico III.," 1718.

Henry (Heinrich) IV., son of Henry III., born in 1050, was five years of age at his father's death. In 1065, in an assembly at Worms, he was declared of age, through the influence of his preceptor, Adalbert, Archbishop of Bremen, who assumed the chief power. About 1073 Henry became engaged in a contest with Magnus, Duke of Saxony, in the course of which he appealed to Pope Gregory VII. The latter, having in vain remonstrated with the emperor for selling sees and benefices in his dominions, now summoned him to Rome to answer the charges preferred against him. Upon this, Henry, in a Diet at Worms in 1076, deposed the pope, and was soon after excommunicated by him. The emperor, finding his subjects inclined to revolt, and fearing the loss of his crown, set out for Italy with his wife and child in the midst of winter, and, meeting the pope at the castle of Canossa, was required to stand barefoot for three days in an open court-yard before the ban was removed. A civil war now ensued, attended by new excommunications on the part of the pope and another deposition on that of the emperor, till at length the latter, whose son Henry had rebelled against him, took refuge at Liege, where he died in 1106. (See GREGORY VII.)

See J. MASCOV, "Commentarii de Rebus Imperii Romano Germanici sub Henrico IV. et Henrico V.," 1748; J. AVENTINUS, "Vita Henrici IV.," 1518; J. STUMPF, "Historie Kayser Heinrichs IV.," 1556.

Henry V., born in 1081, was the son of Henry IV., and the last emperor of the Salic line. During his father's lifetime he had, at the instigation of Pope Paschal II., been acknowledged as emperor in 1106. Though at first inclined to favour the pope, he soon showed his determination to maintain his right of investiture, and Paschal at length consented to crown him in 1111, at which time he married Matilda, daughter of Henry I. of England. After a contest with the papal party, he succeeded in deposing the pope, and set up Gregory VIII. in his stead. This measure was opposed by the cardinals, who chose Gelasius II., on whose death Calixtus II. succeeded to the tiara. With the latter Henry concluded a treaty in 1122, by which he gave up the right of investiture. He died in 1125, and was succeeded by Lothaire of Saxony.

See J. MASCOV, "Commentarii de Rebus Imperii Romano-Germanici," 1748; E. GERVAIS, "Geschichte Deutschlands unter der Regierung Kaiser Heinrichs V.," 1842.

Henry VI., born in 1165, was the son of Frederick Barbarossa, whom he succeeded as Emperor of Germany in 1190. With the view of subduing Sicily, which he claimed by right of his wife Constance, he invaded that country, but, being unsuccessful, was obliged to return to Germany. Here, with the ransom-money which he received for his prisoner Richard Cœur de Lion, he fitted out another expedition. After taking Naples and bringing Sicily into subjection, he caused himself to be crowned at Palermo. His conduct towards the Sicilians was marked by great tyranny and cruelty, and his death, which took place in 1197, is supposed to have been caused by poison. Henry VI. was the third emperor of the Hohenstaufen line. He was succeeded by Philip of Suabia and Otho IV., between whom the crown was contested for several years. (See OTHO IV.)

See W. JÄGER, "Geschichte Kaiser Heinrichs VI.," 1790.

Henry VII., born in 1262, was the son of Henry, Count of Luxemburg, and was chosen emperor in 1308. Soon after his accession he marched into Italy and sought to restore peace in that country, then distracted by the war of the Guelphs and Ghibelines. He was on the point of attacking Naples, when he died suddenly in 1313,—as is generally believed, by poison.

See F. H. BARTHOLD, "Der Römerzug König Heinrichs von Lutzelburg," 1830; JAKOB PAUL VON GUNDLING, "Geschichte Kayser Heinrichs VII.," 1719.

Henry I., King of England, surnamed BEAUCLERC, born at Selby, Yorkshire, in 1068, was the fourth son of William the Conqueror by Matilda of Flanders. As his surname indicates, he received a better scholastic education than was then usual even among princes. His father at his death left him a legacy of five thousand pounds. Henry was hunting with his brother William Rufus in the New Forest in August, 1100, when the latter was killed. The eldest brother, Robert, being absent in foreign travel, Henry usurped the throne. The people were the more disposed to acquiesce as he presently issued a charter in which their rights and liberties were reaffirmed. He married Maud, or Matilda, a Scottish princess, the niece of Edgar Atheling. In 1101 Robert entered England with an army; but the contest was settled without a battle, and Henry remained in quiet possession of the throne. A few years after, Henry required Robert to cede to him the duchy of Normandy for a sum of money, and, on his refusal, invaded Normandy in 1106, defeated Robert at Tenchebrai, and deprived him of his dominions and liberty. In 1113 Louis VI. of France attempted with an army to assert the right of Robert's son, but without success. Henry's only son William perished at sea in 1120, after which the father was never seen to smile. His daughter Matilda was declared his heir in 1126, and next year was married to Geoffrey Plantagenet, Earl of Anjou. The issue of this marriage became Henry II. Though the character of Henry was far from amiable, he possessed a large share of kingly qualities, including judgment, eloquence, and bravery. He died in 1135, and was succeeded by his nephew, Stephen of Blois.

See HUME, "History of England," chap. vi.: JOHN HAYWARD, "Lives of Three Norman Kings of England," 1613.

Henry II., King of England, founder of the Plantagenet dynasty, was born at Le Mans, France, in 1133. His father was Geoffrey Plantagenet, (so named from the broom-plant—in Latin, *planta genista*—which he wore in his cap,) and his mother was Matilda, daughter of Henry I. In the contest which followed the death of Henry I., Stephen obtained England, and the infant Henry was recognized as heir of Normandy, to which at the death of his father, in 1151, Anjou, Touraine, and Maine were added. The next year he married Eleanor, Duchess of Guienne, (whom Louis, King of France, had divorced,) whose dowry was Poitou and Guienne; and he thus became master of nearly half of France. In 1153 he invaded England; but, before much blood was spilled, a treaty was made, by which Stephen retained the crown during his lifetime, and Henry was recognized as his successor. Stephen died in 1154.

Henry began his reign by discharging the foreign troops, razing to the ground the castles of the rebellious barons, and by other energetic and politic measures. He was several times involved in war with the King of France, without important results. His reign was greatly disturbed by the usurpations of the pope and clergy, and by a contest with the haughty Thomas a Becket, whom he had made prime minister and Archbishop of Canterbury. In 1164 a council of nobles and prelates adopted the famous Constitutions of Clarendon, which recognized the supremacy of the crown over the church. Becket was murdered in 1170 by an over-officious servant of the king, who in 1174 performed severe penance at his tomb, and soon after the Constitutions above named were repealed. The conquest of Ireland was effected by Henry's arms between 1169 and 1175. His last years were rendered unhappy by the rebellion of his sons, who were instigated by Queen Eleanor and supported by Louis of France. "Henry was," says Hume, "the greatest prince of his time for wisdom, virtue, and abilities. His character in private as well as public life is almost without a blemish." But Michelet charges him with sensuality and other vices. He died at Chinon, in France, in 1189, and was succeeded by his son, Richard I.

See HUME, "History of England," chaps. viii. and ix.; MICHELET, "History of France;" E. BOLTON, "Life of Henry II.;" LORD LYTTELTON, "History of Henry II.," 1764-67; BERINGTON, "Life of Henry II.," 1790.

Henry III., King of England, surnamed OF WINCHESTER, from the place of his birth, was born in 1206, and was the eldest son of King John by his queen, Isabella of Angoulême. He was acknowledged king in

1216, and the Earl of Pembroke was appointed regent during the minority. In 1222 Henry was declared of age to exercise some of the functions of royalty. In 1230 he invaded France, with which he had been at war for several years, but returned without any important achievement. He married Eleanor, daughter of Raymond, Count of Provence, in 1236, and a few years afterwards renewed hostilities against Louis IX. of France, by whom he was defeated. His feeble character, misgovernment, and ill success rendered him an object of contempt among his people· and provoked many contests with his Parliaments. He confirmed the Magna Charta, but repeatedly violated it. In 1258 the barons, headed by the ambitious and popular Simon de Montfort, Earl of·Leicester, revolted against the king, who was forced to yield his power to a committee of twenty-four. For several years a civil war was waged between the king and the barons, with various success, until the latter, in 1264, obtained a decisive victory at Lewes, where the king and his son Edward were taken prisoners. The Earl of Leicester then became dictator of the country. In 1265 Prince Edward escaped, raised an army, and defeated the barons at Evesham, where De Montfort was slain, and the royal authority was restored. After a reign of fifty-six years,—the longest in the English annals, —Henry died in 1272, and was succeeded by his son, Edward I. This reign presents the first example of a Parliament constituted, as at present, of representatives from the counties, cities, and boroughs.

See HUME, "History of England," chap. xii.; R. COTTON, "Life of Henry III.," 1627; W. PRYNNE, "Life of Henry III.," 1670.

Henry IV., King of England, surnamed BOLINGBROKE, was·the eldest son of John of Gaunt, Duke of Lancaster, who was the fourth son of King Edward the Third. His mother was Blanche, daughter of Henry Plantagenet, a descendant of Henry II. He was born at Bolingbroke in 1366. In 1397 he married Mary de Bohun, daughter of the last Earl of Hereford, and was created Duke of Hereford. The next year he was banished for ten years by Richard II. By the death of his father, in 1399, he became Duke of Lancaster; but the king refused to give him possession of his estate. With the avowed purpose of vindicating his right, Henry returned to England, where he was joined by other nobles, and soon assembled an army of 60,000 men. The king, unable to resist, and deserted by his disaffected subjects, was deposed by Parliament in 1399, and Henry succeeded him, with the general consent of the nation, although the Earl of March was the more legitimate heir. In 1402 a Scottish army, which invaded England with the pretext of restoring Richard, was defeated at Homildon Hill. Soon afterwards his throne was menaced by the rebellion of the famous Henry Percy, surnamed Hotspur, in concert with the Welsh chieftain Owen Glendower and others. At the battle of Shrewsbury, where the king fought with desperate courage, the rebels were completely defeated, and Percy, their leader, was slain. Glendower maintained for several years an irregular warfare in the mountains of Wales; and the Percy family again revolted in 1408, but were finally defeated at Branham, where the Earl of Northumberland was killed. The popularity which Henry enjoyed at his accession was not retained in the latter part of his reign. Hume says, "His prudence, vigilance, and foresight in maintaining his power were admirable; and he possessed many qualities which fitted him for his high station, and which rendered his usurpation of it, though pernicious in aftertimes, rather salutary during his own reign to the English nation." He died in 1413, and was succeeded by his son, Henry IV. Henry IV. gives the name to one of Shakspeare's most popular dramas, in two parts.

See HUME, "History of England," chap. xviii.; SIR J. HAYWARD, "Life and Reign of Henry IV.," 1599; G. P. R. JAMES, "Life of Henry IV."

Henry V., King of England, born at Monmouth in 1388, was the eldest son of Henry IV. and of Mary de Bohun. In his father's reign he displayed courage at the battle of Shrewsbury, and gave proof of great military talents in the war with the Welsh. In 1413 Henry was proclaimed king, with abundant expression of the popular favour, and began his reign with several acts of gene-

rosity. He released the Earl of March (the lawful heir of the crown) from prison, and restored the heir of Percy to his title and estate. Having resolved to assert his claim to the throne of France, which was then a prey to civil dissensions, he embarked in 1415 with an army of 30,000 men. After taking Harfleur, and losing a large part of his army by disease, he was marching homeward, when his progress was opposed by D'Albret, Constable of France, with an army about four times more numerous than his own. On the 25th of October, 1415, was fought the memorable battle of Agincourt, in which the French were defeated, with a loss of about 24,000 men, including prisoners. The victor returned to England without delay.

In 1417, profiting by the imbecility of the French king and the feuds among the nobles, he renewed hostilities, captured Rouen, and threatened Paris. In 1420 a treaty of peace was made at Troyes, with the conditions that Henry should marry Catherine, the daughter of King Charles VI., and should inherit the crown at the death of the latter. One of the French factions, however, headed by the dauphin, did not consent to this disgraceful transaction, and made a brave stand for the national cause. Henry's brother, the Duke of Clarence, was defeated and slain at Baugé; but at other places the English were successful, and Henry seemed on the point of realizing his ambitious projects, when he died prematurely in 1422, (a few weeks before Charles VI.,) leaving an infant son, who afterwards reigned as Henry VI. After his death, his widow Catherine married Owen Tudor, a Welshman, whose posterity became the royal family of England. The frankness and energy of his character and the glory of his victories rendered Henry the idol of the English people; but his glory is obscured or stained by the injustice of the enterprise in which his life was chiefly spent. Henry V. gives the name to one of Shakspeare's historical dramas, and constitutes a prominent and interesting character in both parts of the twofold drama entitled "Henry IV."

See HUME, "History of England," chap. xix.; ELHAM, "Vita et Gesta Henrici V;" GOODWIN, "Life of Henry V.," 1604; P. F. TYTLER, "Memoirs of the Life and Character of Henry V.," 1830; "Henry of Monmouth: or, Memoirs of the Life, etc. of Henry V. of England," by J. ENDELL TYLER.

Henry VI., King of England, surnamed OF WINDSOR, from the place of his birth, was the only son of Henry V. and Catherine of France. He was born in 1421, and was only nine months old when he became king. His uncle, the Duke of Gloucester, was appointed Regent or Protector of England. At the death of Charles VI. of France, in 1422, Henry was proclaimed king at Paris; but a large party of the French openly sided with the dauphin, who was styled Charles VII. Henry's uncle, the Duke of Bedford, acted as regent and representative of the English power in France. In 1424 the English gained a victory at Verneuil, after which their power gradually declined. The city of Orléans in 1429 was delivered from siege by the enthusiasm with which the heroic Joan of Arc inspired her countrymen. In 1436 the English garrison of Paris was forced to surrender. In 1445 Henry married a French lady, Margaret of Anjou, daughter of René, titular King of Sicily. She was superior in ability and energy to her husband, over whom she easily acquired a permanent ascendant.

Victory continued to attend the French arms, and before the close of 1451 not a single province of France remained in the power of the English. And now England in her turn was destined to experience the evils of an imbecile ruler, a disputed title, and an intestine war between the houses of York and Lancaster. The Duke of York, who claimed the crown as a descendant of Edward the Third's second son, was supported by many powerful nobles, among whom was the Earl of Warwick, "the King-maker." The battle of Saint Alban's, (1455,) in which the partisans of York were victorious and Henry was taken prisoner, was the beginning of a war which lasted, with interruptions, for thirty years, and in which the English nobility were nearly annihilated. As a consequence of the victory of Saint Alban's, the Duke of York became Protector. After vain attempts to reconcile the contestants, in 1460 another battle was fought, at Northampton, where the royalists were defeated, and Henry was again made prisoner by the Earl of March, the son of the Duke of York. His queen, Margaret, escaped to Scotland, and continued the war several years with vigour and partial success. At the battle of Wakefield the Duke of York was defeated and killed; but his son was proclaimed king in 1461, with the title of Edward IV. Henry, after being several times liberated and recaptured, died in prison, or, as some suppose, was murdered, in 1471. He was remarkably gentle and inoffensive, and seemed to feel little interest in the quarrel maintained on his account. Henry VI. furnishes the name to one of Shakspeare's historical dramas, in three parts, in which are represented the principal events of his reign.

See HUME, "History of England," chaps. xx. and xxi.

Henry VII., King of England, the founder of the royal line of Tudor, was born at Pembroke Castle in 1456. By his father, Edmond Tudor, Earl of Richmond, he was descended from the royal family of France; by his mother, Margaret Beaufort, he derived a claim to the English crown, as one of her ancestors was John of Gaunt, the head of the house of Lancaster. His father dying in 1456, Henry became Earl of Richmond. He was confined as a prisoner by Edward IV. for several years, and when the Lancastrians were finally defeated, in 1471, he escaped with his uncle, the Earl of Pembroke, to Brittany, where he remained until the accession of Richard III., in 1483. As Henry was now recognized as the head of the Lancastrian party, many people looked to him as the most eligible person to deliver them from Richard, who was generally detested. The leaders of both the rival houses, therefore, invited Henry to assume the royal power. The first attempt to dethrone Richard, made in 1483, was a failure. Renewing his enterprise in 1485, he landed in Wales with about 2000 men, and, after receiving large accessions, encountered Richard at Bosworth, where the latter was defeated and slain, August 22, 1485.

In accordance with a plan previously formed to reconcile the rival parties of York and Lancaster, Henry, in 1486, married Elizabeth, daughter of Edward IV.,—an event which gave great satisfaction to the people. For several years his reign was disturbed by the seditious attempts of the impostors Lambert Simnel and Perkin Warbeck, the latter of whom pretended to be Richard, the younger brother of Edward V., and was supported by the court of France and by many English nobles. He was executed in 1499, after which the kingdom enjoyed internal tranquillity. Henry lost somewhat of the popular favour by his partiality for the Lancastrians and his severity towards the other party, as well as by his rapacity in raising money. Empson and Dudley became notorious as the agents of his exactions. In 1501 the king's eldest son, Arthur, was married to Catherine, a Spanish princess; and, though he died about six months after, the remote consequences of the match were very momentous. (See HENRY VIII.) In 1503 a treaty of peace with James IV. of Scotland was confirmed by the marriage of James with Margaret, daughter of Henry VII., which was one of the first steps towards a permanent union of the two kingdoms. The ministers and councillors who possessed the greatest favour and influence in this reign were Morton, Archbishop of Canterbury, and Fox, Bishop of Winchester. Henry possessed prudence, vigour, and an excellent capacity, but seems to have been deficient in the better qualities of the heart. Avarice was his ruling passion. His reign, though rather arbitrary, was accounted fortunate for the nation, and forms an important era in history, in which the discovery of America and the invention of printing gave a wonderful impetus to the human mind. He died in 1509, and was succeeded by his son, Henry VIII.

See HUME, "History of England," chaps. xxiv., xxv., and xxvi.; FRANCIS BACON, "Historia Regni Henrici VII.," 1642; ALEYN, "History of Henry VII.," in verse, 1638; MARSOLLIER, "Histoire de Henri VII." 1697.

Henry VIII., King of England, the second son of Henry VII. and of Elizabeth of York, was born at Greenwich in 1491. By the death of his brother Arthur, in 1502, he became heir-apparent of the crown, and assumed the title of Prince of Wales. The next year he was, against his will, obliged by his father to affiance

himself to his brother's widow, Catherine of Aragon. His accession at the death of his father, in 1509, was the occasion of great rejoicing among the people, who were prepossessed in his favour by his personal advantages and other popular qualities. He appears to have been in early life one of the most exemplary and most accomplished princes in Europe. (See Froude's "History of England," vol. i. chap. ii.) His marriage with Catherine, who was his senior by six years, was solemnized a few months after his accession. In 1512 he was induced to join the pope, the King of Spain, and the emperor in a league against the King of France, and sent 10,000 men to invade Guienne; but the expedition was a total failure. The next year he invaded France in person, and defeated the French at Guinegaste. In 1514 a treaty of peace was made, the chief condition of which was that Louis XII. should marry Henry's sister Mary. In 1513, James IV. of Scotland, the ally of France, having marched across the border, was defeated and slain, at the great battle of Flodden, by the English under the Earl of Surrey.

In the beginning of this reign the chief competitors for favour and influence at court were Thomas Howard, Earl of Surrey, who was treasurer, and Fox, Bishop of Winchester, who held the office of secretary. The latter introduced to the king Thomas Wolsey, who soon supplanted them both by his insinuating arts and became the prime favourite and sole minister. For about fifteen years he directed the affairs of state with almost absolute authority. In 1515 he was made Archbishop of York, and soon after a cardinal. In the long contest for supremacy between Charles V. and Francis I., Henry, whose friendship was courted by both, might have derived great advantage from his position; but, guided rather by impulse than policy, his actual influence was inconsiderable. Charles having secured Wolsey's influence by promising to concur in his election to the papacy, Henry in 1522 declared war against France, which was invaded by an English army the next year. But the cardinal had become estranged from Charles after the election of Pope Adrian, and in 1525 he concluded a treaty of peace with Francis. In 1526 Henry was declared protector of the "Holy League" formed by the pope against Charles V.; but after this period the foreign transactions of his reign are unimportant and overshadowed by the domestic events.

The impression made on the king by the beauty of Anne Boleyn, and the scruples which he felt or feigned respecting the lawfulness of his former marriage, induced him in 1527 to apply to the pope for a divorce. This question of divorce was rendered more exciting and momentous by its bearing on the Reformation, which about that time began to agitate the Church,—Anne Boleyn favouring the Protestants, and Catherine being a zealous Catholic. The pope gave him specious promises, but interposed the delay of a legal process for several years. In 1529 Wolsey was disgraced, and Cranmer, a Protestant, became Archbishop of Canterbury. Henry, whose passions and interest inclined him to favour the Reformers, as his quarrel with the pope increased both his power and revenue, was declared in 1531 supreme head of the Church. After the Convocations of York and Canterbury had pronounced the marriage with Catherine invalid, Henry, without the pope's permission, married Anne Boleyn, in 1533. Queen Catherine died in 1536. By acts of Parliament, the English church and people were declared independent of the court of Rome, and many innovations were made in religion. The monasteries, six hundred and forty-five in number, were gradually abolished, under the direction of Thomas Cromwell, secretary of state and vicar-general, and a new translation of the Bible was made by royal authority.

In 1536, Queen Anne, having lost the favour of the king, became the victim of his jealousy, which has generally been supposed to have had no other ground on her part than slight indiscretions and levity of manner. But Froude takes a different view, which he supports by many forcible arguments. (See "History of England," chap. xi.) But, whatever opinion we may form of the guilt or innocence of the queen, it is impossible to justify the conduct of Henry, who married his new favourite, the beautiful Jane Seymour, the next day after the execution of Anne. Queen Jane died in 1537, on giving birth to a son, afterwards Edward VI. In 1540 Henry married a Flemish princess, Anne of Cleves, who was divorced about six months afterwards. The same year he married, as his fifth wife, Catherine Howard. In 1538 the pope published a bull against Henry, and formally delivered his soul to the devil. The king, however, maintained several of the Catholic dogmas, (among which was that of the real presence,) and many Protestants, refusing to conform, fell victims to his arbitrary power. In 1542 Queen Catherine was beheaded, on a charge of infidelity to her marriage-vow, and the next year her place was supplied by Catherine Parr. Notwithstanding his cruelty and excesses, Henry seems to have retained the affection of his subjects in general to the close of his life. "He possessed," says Hume, "great vigour of mind, courage, vigilance, and inflexibility." But the catalogue of his vices, it must be confessed, includes some of the worst qualities of human nature. He, however, who would form a just estimate of Henry's character, should read the first four volumes of Froude's "History of England," which contain by far the most complete account of his reign that has yet been written. He died in 1547, and was succeeded by his son, Edward VI. Henry VIII. furnishes the title to one of Shakspeare's historic dramas.

See, besides FROUDE, GODWIN, "History of the Reign of Henry VIII.," 1616; LORD HERBERT of Cherbury, "Life and Reign of Henry VIII.," 1649; P. F. TYTLER, "Life of Henry VIII.;" HUME's and LINGARD's "Histories of England;" STRICKLAND, "Queens of England."

Henry I., King of Castile, born in 1204, was the son of Alfonso III. of Castile. After a reign of three years, he died in 1217.

Henry II., King of Castile, often called HENRY OF TRANSTAMARE, born at Seville in 1333, was the natural son of Alfonso XI. He received the title of Count of Transtamare from his brother, King Pedro the Cruel. After striving to supplant Pedro by intrigue, he joined the King of Aragon in a war against Castile, was defeated, and fled to France. There he raised an army, and again invaded Castile in 1366, but was beaten by Pedro's ally, the English Black Prince. In a third attempt, with a French army led by Du Guesclin, he was more successful. Pedro was defeated and killed in 1368, after which Henry reigned in such a manner as to secure the favour of his subjects. He died in 1379, and left the throne to his son, John I.

See FERRERAS, "Histoire générale d'Espagne," 16 vols., 1700; PUFFENDORF, "Histoire universelle," 10 vols., 1722; P. LOPEZ DE AYALA, "Crónicas de los Reyes de Castilla," 1495, and 4 vols., 1779.

Henry III., King of Castile, born in 1379, succeeded his father John in 1390, and married Catherine of Lancaster. The early part of his reign was disturbed by the rebellion of the Duke of Benavente and the Count of Gijon, whom he defeated. Having exercised his authority in certain points of church government, Pope Boniface declared him a schismatic, and absolved his subjects from allegiance to him. After this Henry recognized the rival pope, Benedict XIII., in 1403. He resisted successfully the aggressions of the Portuguese, and was engaged in a war against the Moors of Granada when he died in 1406, leaving the reputation of a wise and good king. He was succeeded by his son, John II.

See C. ROMEY, "Histoire d'Espagne," 12 vols.; GONZALES DA-VILA, "Historia de la Vida y Hechos del Rey Henrique III. de Castilla," 1638.

Henry IV., King of Castile, the son of John II., was born at Valladolid in 1423, and was surnamed THE IMPOTENT. Having wasted his youth in vice and dissipation, he succeeded his father in 1454. He married Joanna of Portugal, whose character was so depraved or doubtful that the Cortes would not acknowledge her child Joanna to be the legitimate heir. In 1465 several grandees, encouraged by the prevalent disaffection of the people, revolted, and proclaimed Henry's brother, Alfonso, king. Henry raised an army, and a civil war followed until 1468, when Alfonso died. A peace was then made, Henry consenting to disinherit Joanna and adopt as heiress his sister, the well-known Isabella of Castile, who was married to Ferdinand of Aragon in

1469. For many years Henry waged war against the Moors of Granada without any important advantage. He died in 1474. His reign was remarkable for anarchy, oppression, and misery.

See PRESCOTT, "Ferdinand and Isabella," vol. i. chaps. iii. and iv.; ENRIQUEZ DE CASTILLO, "Crónica del Rey D. Henrique el Quarto," 1787; ZURITA, "Histoire d'Aragon," 7 vols.

Henry [Fr. HENRI, hôN're'] **I.,** King of France, a son of Robert, and grandson of Hugh Capet, born about 1005, ascended the throne in 1031. He was soon involved in a civil war with his younger brother Robert, who was favoured by their mother, Constance. Aided by the Duke of Normandy, Henry maintained his throne, and ceded to Robert the duchy of Burgundy. At thirty-nine he married Anna, daughter of Yaroslaf, Duke of Russia. He was almost continually at war with his vassals or neighbours, among others with William, Duke of Normandy, who conquered England. He died in 1060, and was succeeded by his son, Philip I.

See SISMONDI, "Histoire des Français."

Henry II., King of France, second son of Francis I and of Queen Claude, was born at Saint-Germain-en-Laye in 1518, and came to the throne in 1547. He married Catherine de' Medici, (or de Médicis.) In 1550 he concluded a peace with England, by which Boulogne was restored to the French. In 1552 he formed an alliance with the Protestant princes of Germany against Charles V., and took Metz, Toul, and Verdun. The Germans having made a separate peace, Henry alone sustained the war against the Spaniards. A truce of five years was signed in 1556 between Henry and Charles; but the war was renewed the next year by Philip II. of Spain, whose army gained a great victory at Saint-Quentin. In 1558 Calais was taken by the French, after having been held by the English more than two hundred years. A treaty of peace was signed at Câteau-Cambresis in 1559, by which France retained Calais, Metz, and Verdun, and gave up Savoy. Among the results of this treaty was a marriage between Henry's daughter Elizabeth and Philip II. of Spain. At a tournament given on this occasion, Henry by accident received a mortal wound, in 1559, and was succeeded by his eldest son, Francis II.

See A. VARILLAS, "Histoire de Henri II," 1692; C. F. LAMBERT, "Histoire et Règne de Henri II," 1752; MICHELET, "Histoire de France."

Henry III., [often called in French HENRI DE VALOIS, hôN're' deh väl'wä', in Latin HENRI'CUS VALE'SIUS, i.e. "Henry of Valois,"] King of France, third son of Henry II. and of Catherine de Médicis, was born at Fontainebleau in 1551, and succeeded his brother, Charles IX., in 1574. Previously to this he was styled Duc d'Anjou, had defeated the Calvinists at Jarnac and Moncontour, and in 1573 was elected King of Poland, the people of which country made unavailing efforts to retain him. He found his French kingdom a prey to a civil or religious war between two factions, the Catholics under Henry of Guise, and the Huguenots under Henry of Navarre, the founder of the Bourbon dynasty. In 1575 he married a French lady, Louise, daughter of the Count of Vaudesmont. Henry having issued an edict of pacification favourable to the Protestants in 1576, the Catholics formed a general league, sworn to defend the interest of their Church even with the sacrifice of their loyalty to the king, who seems to have been justly distrusted by both parties, but thought it his policy to declare himself the head of the League. His court was disgraced by favouritism, intrigues, bigotry, and licentiousness; and his personal character was not such as to command the popular respect. Henry's brother, the Duke of Alençon, died in 1584, and, as the king had no children, the question of the succession assumed great importance; and it is thought that the Duke of Guise aspired to the throne. In 1587 Henri of Navarre gained the battle of Coutras; and soon after the Duke of Guise and his ligueurs took arms at Paris against the king, who was compelled to flee to Rouen. In 1588 the Duke of Guise was assassinated, probably by the order of Henry, who for this crime was excommunicated by the pope. The king then applied to Henry of Navarre for aid against the League, which was generously granted, and they were pressing the siege of Paris, when Henry III.

was assassinated by a monk named Jacques Clément, in 1589. He was the last king of the house of Valois.

See G. Sossius, "De Vita Henrici III. Libri IX.," 1628; VARILLAS, "Histoire de Henri III," 1694; ADRIEN DE VALOIS, "De Vita Henrici Valesii," 1677; SAUVIGNY, "Histoire de Henri III," 1788; L'ESTOILE, "Journal des Choses mémorables advenues durant le Règne de Henri III," 1621.

Henry IV., [often called in French HENRI LE GRAND, *hŏn're' leh grŏn*; Lat. HENRI'CUS MAG'NUS, *i.e.* "Henry the Great,"] King of France and of Navarre, and founder of the royal house of Bourbon, was born at Pau, December 14, 1553. His father was Antoine de Bourbon, Duc de Vendôme, a lineal descendant of Louis IX., and his mother was Jeanne d'Albret, only child and heiress of Henri d'Albret, King of Navarre. She was a woman of superior merit, ardently devoted to the Protestant faith, in which she educated her son. In 1569, the civil war being renewed, Henry, then styled Prince of Béarn, joined the Protestant army, led by his uncle, the Prince of Condé, (who recognized him as the chief of the party,) and was present at the battles of Jarnac and Moncontour. The Protestants having gained a victory at Arnay-le-Duc, a treacherous peace was offered by the court and accepted in 1570. To inspire the Huguenots with greater confidence, a marriage was negotiated between Henry and the king's sister Margaret. While the Queen of Navarre was making preparation at Paris for the marriage of her son, she died suddenly, in 1572, and he became King of Navarre. A few days after the marriage was celebrated occurred the Massacre of Saint Bartholomew. (See CHARLES IX.) Henry's life was spared on condition that he would adopt the Roman Catholic religion; but he was confined and strictly watched for several years. In 1576 he escaped to Rochelle, and assumed the command of his friends, then menaced by the Catholic League. He displayed great skill and bravery in several campaigns, the operations of which were, however, for the most part on a small scale. In 1587 the Huguenots gained a decisive victory at Coutras. The King of France died in 1589, and named for his successor the subject of this article, who, since the death of the king's brother, was presumptive heir of the crown. His claim was disputed by a large army under the Duc de Mayenne, and by the fanatical populace of Paris, who kindled bonfires to show their joy at the death of Henry III., and whose resistance was stimulated by Spanish gold. Baffled in his attempt to obtain possession of his capital, he marched towards Dieppe, where his army was increased by 5000 English sent by his ally Elizabeth. In 1590 he gained a decisive victory at Ivry over the Duke of Mayenne, after electrifying his army with this brief harangue: "Fellow-soldiers, you are Frenchmen; behold the enemy! If you lose sight of your ensigns, rally around my plume: you will always find it on the high road to honour!" In 1592 he defeated a Spanish army under Farnese, the celebrated Prince of Parma, near Yvetot.

His devotion to the interest of France (we may charitably suppose) now induced him to conciliate his enemies by a profession of the Roman Catholic religion in 1593,—the Protestants at the same time being assured of the continuance of his favour and protection. In 1594 he entered Paris without resistance, and granted a general pardon. After numerous battles and sieges, a treaty of peace was made at Vervins with Philip II. of Spain in 1598, and Henry was acknowledged by the whole kingdom. The same year he gave liberty of conscience to his subjects by the edict of Nantes. Directing his attention to the finances, agriculture, and industrial arts, in which he was seconded by his minister Sully, he proved himself a wise and able statesman, and rendered himself very popular by his sympathy with the lower classes and his generosity to all. His popularity was increased by the spirited and eloquent public addresses which he made on various occasions, and by the frank simplicity of his manners. In 1600 he married an Italian princess, Marie de' Medici, having obtained a divorce from his first wife. The last half of his reign was peaceful and prosperous. He founded a hospital, a college, and a public library in Paris, and encouraged learned men, among whom were Casaubon and Grotius. His memory is more cherished by the French than

that of any other of their kings, and his character is regarded by them as the beau-idéal of a Frenchman, a warrior, a monarch, and a statesman. On the 14th of May, 1610, while riding in his carriage, he was assassinated by a fanatic named Ravaillac. He left the crown to his son, Louis XIII.

See MOTLEY, "United Netherlands," vol. i. chap. ii. p. 45 *et seq.*, and vol. ii. chap. xvii. p. 340; P. HOOFT, "Het Leven van König Hendrik IV.," 1626; J. PELEUS, "Histoire de la Vie de Henri le Grand," 1613-16; G. SOSSIUS, "De Vita Henrici Magni Libri IV.," 1622; HARDOUIN DE PÉRÉFIXE, "Histoire du Roi Henri le Grand," 1661; DE BURY, "Histoire de la Vie de Henri IV.," 1765; MUSSET-PATHAY, "Vie militaire et privée de Henri IV.," 1803; POIRSON, "Histoire du Règne de Henri IV.," 3 vols., 1857; G. P. R. JAMES, "Life of Henry IV.," 3 vols., 1847; DAUBIGNÉ, "Histoire universelle;" MICHELET, "Histoire de France;" L'ESTOILE, "Journal du Règne de Henri IV;" DAVILA, "History of the Civil Wars in France;" F. A. MIGNET, "Histoire de la Ligue et du Règne de Henri IV.," 5 vols., 1829; also a review of the "Letters of Henry IV.," in the "Foreign Quarterly Review" for April, 1842.

Henry, PRINCE OF WALES, the eldest son of James I. of England, was born at Stirling in 1594. He is represented to have been unlike his father, brave, generous, and constant, was fond of maritime adventure, and earnestly opposed to popery. He befriended Sir Walter Raleigh, and used to say that no king but his father would keep such a bird in a cage. Died in 1612.

See T. BIRCH, "Life of Henry, Prince of Wales," 1760; GARDINER, "History of England from 1603 to 1616," chaps. viii. and x.; HARNEY, "History of England," chap. xlvii.; CORNWALLIS, "Life of Prince Henry," in the "Somers Tracts."

Henry, (Heinrich,) or Friedrich Heinrich Ludwig, a Prussian prince, distinguished for his skill in strategy, born in Berlin in 1726, was a brother of Frederick the Great. He commanded the right wing at the battle of Prague, 1757, and decided the fortune of the day. He outgeneralled the enemy in the campaign of 1758, and obtained some advantages in 1759. In 1760, with 35,000 men, he held in check a superior force of Russians by skilful marches, and prevented their junction with the Austrians. He gained a signal victory at Freyburg in October, 1762, which was the last important action of the Seven Years' war. He was less enterprising as a general than his brother, who in 1763 saluted him "as the only general that in this war has not committed a single fault." Died in 1802.

See "Schilderung des Privatlebens des Prinzen Heinrich von Preussen," 1784; "Anecdoten und Characterzüge aus dem Leben des Prinzen Heinrich von Preussen," 1804; GUYTON, "Vie privée d'un Homme célèbre, ou Détails des Loisirs du Prince Henri de Prusse," 1784; BOUILLÉ DU CHAROL, "Vie du Prince Henri de Prusse," 1809.

Henry OF ALKMAAR. See ALKMAR.

Henry OF CHAMPAGNE, (shŏn'păn',) born in 1180, was the nephew of Richard Cœur de Lion. In the third crusade he distinguished himself at the siege of Saint-Jean-d'Acre. By his marriage with Isabella, widow of Conrad of Tyre, and with the consent of the chiefs, he became King of Jerusalem. He died during the fourth crusade.

Henry OF HAINAULT, [Fr. HENRI DE HAINAULT, *hŏn're' deh hă'nŏ',*] born at Valenciennes in 1174, was a brother of Baldwin of Flanders. In 1202 he took part in the crusade against the Turks, and in 1206 succeeded his brother Baldwin as Emperor of Constantinople. He is represented as a brave and prudent prince. Died, without issue, in 1216.

Henry OF HUNTINGDON, an English historian, who lived about 1150, became Archdeacon of Huntingdon. He wrote a general history of England from the earliest accounts to the death of Stephen, (1154,) which was published by Sir Henry Savile in 1596. He also wrote Latin poetry, which is not without merit.

Henry (or **Henrique**) OF PORTUGAL. See HENRY OF BURGUNDY.

Henry [Port. HENRIQUE, en-ree'kă] OF PORTUGAL, [Fr. HENRI DE PORTUGAL, *hŏn're' deh por'tü'găl',*] a celebrated patron of science, sometimes called HENRY THE NAVIGATOR, was born at Oporto in 1394. He was a younger son of John I. of Portugal, and a nephew of Henry IV. of England. He was distinguished for his attainments in mathematics, geography, and navigation. About 1419 he founded an observatory and nautical school in Algarve, and enlisted the most skilful mariners in enterprises of maritime discovery. Under his auspices the west coast of Africa was explored as far as Sierra

Leone, and Madeira and the Azores were discovered. Died in 1463.

See FRANCISCO JOZÉ FREIRE, "Vida do Infante D. Henrique por Candido Lusitano," 1758; ABBÉ DE COURNAND, "Vie de Henri de Portugal," Paris, 2 vols., 1761; R. H. MAJOR, "Life of Prince Henry the Navigator," London, 1868.

Henry (or **Henrique**) OF PORTUGAL, third son of Emanuel, King of Portugal, was born in Lisbon in 1512. He was educated for the church, and became Archbishop of Ev'ora in 1540. He consented to the establishment of the Inquisition in his diocese. At the death of his nephew, King Sebastian, in 1578, he succeeded to the throne. He was urged to designate which of the claimants should succeed him, but delayed, and died, without a decision, in 1580. Philip II. of Spain was his successor.

Henry OF TRANSTAMARE. See HENRY II. OF CASTILE.

Hen'rỹ, (CALEB SPRAGUE,) an American author, born in Rutland, Massachusetts, in 1804, graduated at Dartmouth College in 1825. He took orders in the Protestant Episcopal Church about 1835, and became professor of philosophy and history in the New York University in 1839. He published, besides other works, "Cousin's Psychology," (1834,) and a "Compendium of Christian Antiquities," (1837.)

Hen'rỹ, (DAVID,) born at Aberdeen in 1710, removed to London at an early age, and was employed by Cave, (the publisher of the "Gentleman's Magazine,") whose sister he married in 1736. He was a frequent contributor to the above magazine, and at the death of E. Cave, in 1754, he became a partner in its management. He was the author of the "Complete English Farmer," and of a few other works. Died in 1792.

Henry, *hŏN're',* (ÉTIENNE OSSIAN,) a French chemist, born in Paris about 1798. He distinguished himself by researches into the action and composition of mineral waters, and gained the Montyon prize for a method of producing sulphate of quinia. He published, besides other chemical works, a "Manual of the Chemical Analysis of Mineral Waters," (1825,) in which his father assisted.

Henry, (JOSEPH,) an American savant and natural philosopher, born at Albany, New York, in 1797. He began a series of experiments in electricity about 1827, and is said to have invented the first machine moved by the agency of electro-magnetism. He wrote on electricity and magnetism several papers inserted in "Silliman's Journal." In 1832 he was appointed professor of natural philosophy in the College of New Jersey at Princeton. He published "Contributions to Electricity and Magnetism," (1839,) and became secretary of the Smithsonian Institute in 1846. He has contributed numerous valuable papers to the various scientific periodicals in the United States.

Henry, (MARIE JOSEPH,) a French historian, born in Basses-Alpes in 1778, published a History of Egypt, ("L'Égypte Pharaonique," 2 vols., 1846,) and other works. Died in 1850.

Hen'rỹ, (MATTHEW,) an eminent English divine, born in Iscoyd township, Flintshire, in October, 1662. After receiving a liberal education, he accepted in 1687 the charge of a dissenting church in Chester. In 1712 he removed to Hackney, where he preached until his death, in 1714. He published many sermons and theological works, of which the most important is his "Commentary on the Old and New Testament," (1710.) This is thought by some to be the best work of that kind ever published. It was highly commended by Robert Hall, Dr. Doddridge, and Adam Clarke. The latter, speaking of certain abridgments of the above work, says, "Every one of them, while professing to lop off his redundancies and supply his deficiencies, falls, by a semi-diameter of the immense orb of literature and religion, short of the author himself."

See TONG, "Life of Matthew Henry," 1716; WILLIAMS, "Memoirs of the Life, Character, and Writings of M. Henry," 1828.

Henry, (NOËL ÉTIENNE,) a French chemist, father of Étienne Ossian, noticed above, was born at Beauvais (Oise) in 1769. He wrote a "Treatise on Pharmacy, Practical and Theoretical," (1828.) Died at Paris in 1832.

See "Notice biographique sur Noël Étienne Henry," by BARON SILVESTRE.

Henry, (PATRICK,) a celebrated American orator and patriot, born at Studley, Hanover county, Virginia, May 29, 1736. His father, John Henry, was a native of Scotland, and a nephew of the eminent historian Robertson. His mother's maiden name was Sarah Winston. Under his father's tuition he learned the common English branches and acquired a smattering of Latin; but he had little inclination to book-learning. In his youth he was passionately addicted to dancing, hunting, and fishing. Finding him indisposed for literary and professional pursuits, his father set him up in mercantile business about 1753. His success in trade was hindered by his negligent and indolent habits. About the age of eighteen he married a Miss Shelton. Having become insolvent, he abandoned mercantile pursuits and began to cultivate a small farm; but after an experiment of two years he sold his land and returned to merchandise. He failed again in trade about 1760, and then resolved to try the profession of the law. After he was admitted to the bar, he passed several years in poverty and obscurity; but he gained sudden distinction in 1763 by his speech against the clergy, who undertook to enforce the payment of their salaries in tobacco.* This cause, called "the Parsons' Cause," which had produced much excitement in the country, was tried before a court over which Patrick Henry's father presided as judge. "On this occasion he rose very awkwardly," says Wirt, "and faltered much in his exordium." . . . But, "as his mind rolled along and began to glow from its own action, all the exuviæ of the clown seemed to shed themselves spontaneously." The result of this plea, the first he ever made in court, was a verdict for the people.

In 1765 he was elected a member of the House of Burgesses, and offered in that body a series of resolutions against the famous Stamp Act. He advocated these resolutions by a powerful speech, in which he exclaimed, "Cæsar had his Brutus, Charles the First his Cromwell, and George the Third"—here he was interrupted by loud cries of "Treason!" from all parts of the House—"may profit by their example. If this be treason, make the most of it." His resolutions passed the House by a small majority in May, 1765. "During the period between this date and the Revolution, Mr. Henry," says Alexander H. Everett, "was constantly in advance of the most ardent patriots. He suggested and carried into effect, by his immediate personal influence, measures that were opposed as premature and violent by all the other eminent supporters of the cause of liberty." In 1774 he was chosen a delegate to the Continental Congress. Among the greatest triumphs of his unrivalled eloquence was a speech in the Virginia Convention (March, 1775) for the passage of a resolution "that the colony be immediately put in a state of defence." He insisted on the necessity of fighting for independence, and closed with the words "Give me liberty, or give me death!"

He was elected Governor of Virginia in 1776, and, by successive re-elections, held that office until 1779. In this capacity he rendered important services to the popular cause. In 1784 and 1785 he was again chosen Governor. As a member of the Virginia Convention of 1788, he opposed the adoption of the Federal Constitution, against which he made several speeches of extraordinary eloquence. He said the Constitution had "an awful squinting towards monarchy." He died June 6, 1799, leaving the reputation of the greatest of American orators. He was a devout believer in Christianity, but was not a member of any religious denomination.

See WILLIAM WIRT, "Life and Character of Patrick Henry," 1817; A. H. EVERETT, "Life of Patrick Henry," in SPARKS's "American Biography," vol. xi. ; "Nouvelle Biographie Générale ;" "London Quarterly Review" for December, 1840.

Henry, (PHILIP,) an English dissenting minister, born in London in 1631, was father of Matthew Henry the commentator. He was ejected from his living for nonconformity at the restoration. In the latter part of his life he resided at Broad Oak, where his labours in the ministry were highly approved. Died in 1696.

See "Life of Philip Henry," by his son MATTHEW, 1696; WILLIAM BATES, "Life of Philip Henry," 1699.

* By virtue of an old statute, each clergyman was entitled to 16,000 pounds of tobacco per annum.

ā, ē, ī, ō, ū, ȳ, *long;* ă, ĕ, ĭ, ŏ, ŭ, ў, *short;* ą, ę, į, ǫ, *obscure;* fär, fȧll, fät; mēt; nŏt; gŏŏd; mŏŏn;

Henry, (PIERRE FRANÇOIS,) a French *littérateur*, born at Nancy in 1759, translated from the English Marshall's "Life of Washington," and many other works. He also wrote the article on Washington in the "Biographie Universelle." Died in 1833.

See QUÉRARD, "La France Littéraire."

Henry, (Rev. ROBERT,) a Scottish historian, born at Muirtown in 1718. He was licensed to preach in 1746, and officiated at Carlisle from 1748 to 1760. In 1768 he removed to Edinburgh, where he became minister of the New Grey-Friars' Church. From 1776 to 1790 he was colleague-minister of the Old Church. His reputation as an author is founded on his "History of Great Britain," (6 vols., 1771–93.) It embraces the period from the first invasion of the Romans to the death of Henry VIII., and is composed on an original plan, since adopted in the more popular history of Charles Knight. The plan is to treat the history of politics, of religion, of learning, of manners and customs, etc. in separate divisions. Henry's work is executed with great erudition and fidelity; but the style is not attractive. It was acrimoniously criticised by Gilbert Stuart when it first appeared, but was commended by Hume. Died in 1790.

See a "Life of R. Henry," in the sixth volume of his "History;" CHAMBERS, "Biographical Dictionary of Eminent Scotsmen."

Henry, (Rev. ROBERT,) born at Charleston, South Carolina, in 1792, graduated at the University of Edinburgh in 1814. He was chosen president of the College of South Carolina in 1842, resigned in 1845, and then became professor of Greek in that institution. He contributed to the "Southern Review." Died in 1856.

Henry, (WILLIAM,) an English chemist, born at Manchester in 1775. He graduated as M.D. at Edinburgh in 1807, and practised with success at Manchester. He had previously made valuable researches in chemistry, on which he contributed numerous memoirs to the "Philosophical Transactions" of the Royal Society. In 1803 he ascertained the law of the absorption of gases by water of different temperatures. In 1808 he was elected a Fellow of the Royal Society, which the next year awarded to him Sir G. Copley's donation, as a testimonial of his scientific merit. He is the author of well-written sketches of Davy, Priestley, and Wollaston; also of an excellent work, entitled "Elements of Experimental Chemistry," (1800,) which passed through many editions. His moral character is represented as excellent. Died in 1836.

See "Encyclopædia Britannica."

Henry the Lion, [Ger. HEINRICH DER LÖWE, hīn'-rĭk dĕR lö'wĕh,] born in 1129, was the son of Henry the Proud, Duke of Saxony, and grandson of the emperor Lothaire. On his succeeding his father, in 1146, he demanded the restoration of Bavaria, which had been wrested from his family, and which in 1154 was conceded to him. While on a crusade in Palestine, his dominions were invaded by his enemies, whereby he was involved in numerous contests after his return. He died in 1195, leaving the reputation of a wise ruler and a patron of learning and commerce. He married as his second wife Matilda, daughter of Henry II. of England.

See KARL WILHELM BÖTTIGER, "Heinrich der Löwe," 1819; RAUMER, "Geschichte der Hohenstaufen."

Henry the Minstrel. See HARRY, (BLIND.)

Henry the Proud, [Fr. HENRI LE SUPERBE, hŏN're' lĕh sü'pâRb'; Ger. HEINRICH DER STOLZE, hīn'rĭk dĕR stolt'seh; Lat. HENRI'CUS SUPER'BUS,] Duke of Bavaria and Saxony, born in 1102, was an able and warlike prince. Died in 1139. He was the father of Henry the Lion.

See ALBRICUS, "De Vita Henrici Superbi."

Henrys, hŏN're', (CLAUDE,) a French jurisconsult and legal writer, born at Montbrison in 1615. He co-operated with Chancellor Séguier in his effort to establish a uniform system of jurisprudence. Died in 1662.

Hen'rȳ-sọn, (ROBERT,) a schoolmaster of Dunfermline, lived about 1460–90, and was one of the best Scottish poets of his time. He wrote "Orpheus Kyng," "The Testament of Cressid," and "Robene and Makyne," thought to be the earliest of Scottish pastoral poems.

See "Memoir of Robert Henryson," by D. LAING, 1866; CHAMBERS, "Biographical Dictionary of Eminent Scotsmen."

Hens, van, vän hĕns, (ABRAHAM,) a Dutch painter of plants and insects, born at Utrecht about 1645; died after 1705.

Hensel, hĕn'sẹl, (WILHELM,) a German painter, born in the province of Brandenburg in 1794. Among his best pictures are "Christ before Pilate," and excellent portraits of the Duke of Brunswick and of the celebrated composer Mendelssohn. His wife, FANNY HENSEL, sister of Felix Mendelssohn, was distinguished for her skill and taste in music, and produced several admired compositions. Died in 1847.

See NAGLER, "Neues Allgemeines Künstler-Lexikon."

Hĕn'shaw, (JOHN PRENTICE KEWLEY,) D.D., Bishop of the Protestant Episcopal Church, was born in Middletown, Connecticut, in 1792. After graduating at Middlebury College, Vermont, in 1808, he embraced the tenets of the Episcopal Church. Through his zealous labours, several new churches were organized in Vermont. In 1817 he became pastor of Saint Peter's Church in Baltimore. He was elected Bishop of Rhode Island in 1843. Died in 1852.

Henshaw, (J. SIDNEY,) changed from J. HENSHAW BELCHER, an American lawyer and writer, born in Boston in 1814. He published, besides other works, "Philosophy of Human Progress," (1835,) and "Round the World," (2 vols., 1840.) Died in 1859.

Hensler, hĕns'lẹr, (PHILIP GABRIEL,) a Danish physician, born at Oldensworth in 1733, became physician to the King of Denmark in 1775. Died in 1805.

Hĕns'lōw, (Rev. JOHN STEVENS,) a distinguished English botanist, born in 1796. He took the degree of B.A. at Cambridge in 1818, and was appointed professor of botany in that university about 1825. In 1837 he became rector of Hitcham, in Suffolk, where he continued to reside until his death. He was a popular lecturer, and contributed memoirs on botany and other parts of natural history to the Transactions of several societies. His principal productions are "Principles of Descriptive and Physiological Botany," (1835,) a work of great merit, which has been extensively used as a text-book, and a "Catalogue of British Plants." Died in 1861.

See JENYNS, "Life of J. Henslow," 1862; "Gentleman's Magazine" for July, 1861.

Hentz, hĕnts, (CAROLINE LEE,) born at Lancaster, Massachusetts, about 1804, was the daughter of General John Whiting. In 1825 she was married to Professor N. M. Hentz. Her tragedy "De Lara, or the Moorish Bride," gained a prize of five hundred dollars; and several of her tales and novelettes had a wide circulation. She wrote, among other tales, "The Planter's Northern Bride," "Linda," and "Ernest Linwood." Died in 1856.

Hentzner, hĕnts'nẹr, (PAUL,) born in Silesia in 1558, was the author of a "Journey through Germany, France, Italy, etc.," written in elegant Latin. Part of it was translated into English. Died in 1623.

See L. BRIGHTWELL, "By-Paths of Biography;" MOTLEY, "History of the United Netherlands," vol. i. chap. vi.

Hepburn, (JAMES.) See BOTHWELL.

Hep'burn, (JAMES BONAVENTURA,) a Scottish philologist, born in 1573. After travelling in Europe and Asia, he entered a convent near Avignon. It is said that he knew seventy-two languages. He produced a Hebrew and Chaldean Dictionary, and an Arabic Grammar. Pope Paul V. appointed him keeper of the Oriental books and manuscripts of the Vatican. Died in 1621.

See CHAMBERS, "Biographical Dictionary of Eminent Scotsmen."

Hephæstus, he-fĕs'tus, [Gr. Ἥφαιστος; Fr. HÉPHESTE, à'fĕst', or HAPHESTE, ä'fĕst',] the Greek name of the god VULCAN, which see.

Hephestion or **Hephæstion,** he-fĕs'tĭ-on, [Gr. Ἡφαιστίων,] a Macedonian courtier, the son of Amyntor of Pella, became a favourite of Alexander the Great, whom he followed in the invasion of Persia and India. In the return of this expedition, Hephestion and Craterus commanded a separate part of the army. When Alexander married Roxana, daughter of Darius, he gave her sister, Drypetis, to Hephestion. He died soon after that event, in 325 B.C. The grief of Alexander for his loss was so profound that he tasted no food for three days.

See ARRIAN, "Anabasis;" THIRLWALL, "History of Greece."

ẹ as *k*; ç as *s*; ğ *hard*; ġ as *j*; G, H, K, *guttural*; N, *nasal*; R, *trilled*; š as *z*; ᵺ as in *this*. (☞ See Explanations, p. 23.)

74

Hephestion, a grammarian of Alexandria, lived about 150 A.D., and wrote a treatise entitled "Enchiridion de Metris."

He'ra, [Gr. Ἥρα or Ἥρη,] a goddess of the Greek mythology, was the daughter of Cronos, (Saturn,) and the wife of Jupiter, and was identical with the Juno of the Romans. The chief seats of her worship were Argos and Samos. (See JUNO.)

Heracleidæ. See HERACLIDÆ.

Heracleides. See HERACLIDES.

Heracleitus. See HERACLITUS.

He-rac'le-on, [Gr. Ἡρακλέων,] a Gnostic or heretic of the second century. He adopted the doctrines of Valentine, with modifications.

He-rac-le-o'nas, the son of the emperor Heraclius, was born in 626 A.D. At the death of his father, in 641, he succeeded to the throne in partnership with his half-brother Constantine. A few months later the latter was poisoned by Martina, the mother of Heracleonas. In consequence of this and other crimes, the guards of the palace revolted and seized Martina and her son, who were banished by the senate. He was succeeded by his nephew, Constans II.

See GIBBON, "Decline and Fall of the Roman Empire."

Hĕr'a-clēs, [Gr. Ἡρακλῆς,] the Greek form of the name of HERCULES, which see.

Heraclidæ or **Heracleidæ,** hĕr-a-klī'dee, [Gr. Ἡρα-κλεῖδαι ; Fr. HÉRACLIDES, ả'rả'klēd'; Ger. HERAKLIDEN, hȧ-rȧ-klee'den,] a name applied to a noble and powerful Grecian race, who were, or claimed to be, descendants of Hercules, (Heracles.) The sons of Hercules took refuge in Attica from the persecution of Eurystheus. In alliance with the Dorians, the Heraclidæ invaded Peloponnesus, parts of which they claimed as their heritage. This expedition was called the return of the Heraclidæ. After several failures, they conquered the Peloponnesus.

Héraclide. See HERACLIDES.

Hĕr-a-clī'dēs or **Hĕr-a-clei'dēs,** [Gr. Ἡρακλείδης ; Fr. HÉRACLIDE, ả'rả'klēd',] a Syracusan general, who aided Dion to dethrone Dionysius the Younger. Having become an enemy of Dion, he was put to death, by his order, in 354 B.C.

Heraclides, a Greek historian, born probably in Egypt, lived about 170 B.C.

Hĕr-a-clī'dēs OF PON'TUS, [Fr. HÉRACLIDE DU PONT, ả'rả'klēd' dü pôn,] a Greek philosopher, born at Heraclea, lived in the fourth century before Christ. He studied under Speusippus and Aristotle, and is classed among the Peripatetics by Diogenes Laertius. He wrote, on history, philosophy, politics, and other subjects, many works, which are lost, except fragments of his treatise on the constitutions of various states, Περὶ πολιτειῶν ὑπόμνημα.

See DIOGENES LAERTIUS; VOSSIUS, "De Historicis Græcis;" ROULEZ, "Commentatio de Vita et Scriptis Heraclidæ Pontici," 1828.

Heraclides OF TARENTUM, a Greek physician, lived in the second or third century before Christ. He is quoted and praised by Galen.

Héraclite. See HERACLITUS.

Heraclitus or **Heracleitus,** hĕr-a-klī'tus, [Gr. Ἡρά-κλειτος ; Fr. HÉRACLITE, ả'rả'klēt' ; It. ERACLITO, ả-rả-klee'to,] surnamed THE NATURALIST, a celebrated Greek philosopher, and the founder of a sect, was a native of Ephesus, and lived about 500 B.C. According to several accounts, he studied the Pythagorean philosophy under Hippasus and Xenophanes ; but he professed to be self-taught. His father was one of the principal citizens of Ephesus, the chief magistracy of which was offered to Heraclitus, but was refused. The current notion that he was addicted to habitual weeping on account of the vices and follies of men, appears to be unfounded ; but his gloomy and unsociable temper, or his love of study, caused him to decline intercourse with the world and to retire to the solitude of a mountain. When Darius of Persia invited him to his court, he rather rudely refused the intended honour. He founded a new school of philosophy, which did not, however, survive as a distinct school long after his own time.* His principal work

* Nevertheless, Heraclitus may be said to have anticipated some of the most "advanced" ideas of the most distinguished physicists of the present age. After observing that the "world (Kosmos or Uni-

was a "Treatise on Nature," of which fragments only are extant. Socrates, after reading it, said that so much of it as he could understand was good, but that he found it for the most part unintelligible. He affected an obscure and concise style, comparing himself to the Sibyl, who utters in mysterious language the austere oracles of inspiration, and received the epithet σκοτεινός, the "obscure." He taught that fire is the principle of all things ; that death is only a change of form ; that natural phenomena are produced by the antagonism of two opposite forces, namely, attraction and repulsion ; that motion is essential to matter, and, as a result of this incessant change, "no man has ever floated twice on the same stream." He attached little value to worldly wisdom or human lore, saying that the science of men is only ignorance ; their grandeur, meanness ; and their pleasure, pain. He represented contentment as the chief good. He died about the age of sixty.

See RITTER, "History of Philosophy;" G. H. LEWES, "Biographical History of Philosophy;" LASSALLE, "Die Philosophie des Heracleitos," Berlin, 2 vols., 1858 ; F. SCHLEIERMACHER, "Heraclitus of Ephesus," (in German,) 1808 ; F. MENZ, "Programma de Heraclito Ephesio," 1736 ; DIOGENES LAERTIUS.

Heraclitus, an elegiac poet, born at Halicarnassus, lived about 250 B.C., and was a friend of Callimachus.

Hĕr-a-clī'us [Gr. Ἡράκλειος] I., a Roman Emperor of the East, son of Heraclius, Governor of Africa, born about 575 A.D., was a native of Cappadocia. By the violent death of the tyrant Phocas, in 610, Heraclius, who had served in the army with credit, obtained the imperial power ; and soon after he married Eudoxia. In the early part of his reign the empire was ravaged by pestilence and the barbarian armies of Chosroës, (Khosroo,) King of Persia. In 622 he led an army against Persia, defeated Chosroës at Tauris, and fought several successful campaigns, in which he displayed great military talents and personal courage. Having made peace with Persia, he returned to Constantinople in 628, and abandoned himself to inglorious ease, sensual vices, and the subtleties of Monothelism, of which he became the supporter, while the victorious progress of the Mussulman arms threatened to subvert his empire. He died in 641. His character is a puzzle, and presents surprising contradictions.

See GIBBON, "History of the Decline and Fall of the Roman Empire ;" LE BEAU, "Histoire du Bas-Empire."

Heraclius II. See CONSTANTINE III., EMPEROR OF THE EAST.

Herakleides. See HERACLIDES.

Herakleitus or **Herakleitos.** See HERACLITUS.

Heraklides. See HERACLIDÆ.

Heraldu3. See HÉRAULD.

Hĕr'a-path, (JOHN,) an English mathematician and writer on physics, born at Bristol in 1793. He was the editor of "Herapath's Railway Journal." Besides several treatises on physics, he wrote two volumes on "Mathematical Physics," (1847.) Died in 1868.

Herapath, (WILLIAM,) an eminent English chemist, born at Bristol in 1796, was the son of a brewer, whom he succeeded in his business. He made important discoveries in toxicology, and was consulted as a chemist in the trials of persons suspected of causing death by poison. For many years he held the place of first teacher of chemistry in the Bristol Medical School. He wrote several chemical memoirs. He was a prominent Liberal in politics. Died in 1868.

His son, WILLIAM BIRD HERAPATH, is a physician, and author of several medical treatises.

Heraud, hȧ'rō', ? (JOHN A.,) an English poet and dramatic writer, born in London about 1800. He pro-

verse) was made neither by any of the gods, nor by any man, it was and is and ever shall be an ever-living fire, in due measure self-kindled, and in due measure self-extinguished," he goes on to say, "ALL IS CONVERTIBLE INTO FIRE, AND FIRE INTO ALL, just as gold is convertible into wares, and wares into gold." If we take the word fire to include heat, light, and electricity, (lightning,) a sense in which it was not unfrequently used by the ancients, we shall perceive a striking analogy between the thought of the preceding passage and that of the following from Herbert Spencer: "Those modes of the Unknowable which we call motion, heat, light, chemical affinity, etc. are alike transformable into each other, and into those modes of the Unknowable which we distinguish as sensation, emotion, thought: these in their turns being directly or indirectly re-transformable into the original shapes." ("First Principles," chap. ix. p. 280.)

duced "The Judgment of the Flood," a poem, (1834,) "Videna," a tragedy, (1854,) and other works.

Hérauld, /hā'rō', [Lat. HERAL'DUS,] (DIDIER,) a French Protestant lawyer and critic, born about 1579. In youth he obtained the chair of Greek at Sedan, and afterwards practised law with success at Paris. He gained distinction as a critical scholar, and was highly eulogized by Grotius. He published notes on Martial, Minutius Felix, and Tertullian, and several other works. Died in 1649.

See BAYLE, "Historical and Critical Dictionary;" MM. HAAG, "La France protestante."

Hérault de Séchelles, /hā'rō' deh sā'shēl', (MARIE JEAN,) a French revolutionist, born of an aristocratic family in Paris in 1760. He gained distinction as a lawyer and orator before the Revolution. Elected to the Legislative Assembly in 1791, he became a leader of the Jacobins, and was president of the Convention in June, 1793, when the Girondists were proscribed. He was the author or *rédacteur* of the document called the "Constitution of 1793," and was president and chief speaker at the national festival of August 10, 1793. In the same year he was a member of the sanguinary committee of public safety. Proscribed by Robespierre and accused of complicity in a conspiracy, he was executed with Danton in April, 1794. "He died," says Lamartine, "with the serenity of a just man who glories in being a martyr of liberty." He is described by Lord Brougham (in a sketch of Danton) as a man of unsullied character. He left a work entitled "Theory of Ambition," (1802.)

See LAMARTINE, "History of the Girondists;" THIERS, "History of the French Revolution;" "Nouvelle Biographie Générale."

Herbart, hĕr'bärt, (JOHANN FRIEDRICH,) an eminent German philosopher, born at Oldenburg in May, 1776. He was a pupil of Fichte in the University of Jena. In 1805 he published a treatise on Platonic philosophy, "De Platonici Systematis Fundamento," and became adjunct professor of philosophy at Göttingen. He produced in 1808 a "General Practical Philosophy," and "The Chief Points of Metaphysics," (" Hauptpunkte der Metaphysik.") He was professor at Königsberg from 1809 to 1833, during which period he published, besides other works, an "Introduction to Philosophy," (1814,) and "Psychology as a Science newly based on Experience, Metaphysics, and Mathematics," (" Psychologie als Wissenschaft neu gegründet auf Erfahrung, Metaphysik und Mathematik," 2 vols., 1825.) In 1833 he obtained the chair of philosophy at Göttingen. He originated a peculiar system of philosophy. Died at Göttingen in August, 1841.

See HARTENSTEIN, "Herbart's Leben," 1843: SCHILLING, "Lehrbuch der Psychologie," 1851; "Nouvelle Biographie Générale."

Herbel, hĕr'bĕl', (CHARLES,) a French painter and engraver, born at Nancy; died in 1703.

Herbelin, /hĕrb'lɛ̃N', (JEANNE MATHILDE,) an eminent French painter of miniatures, a daughter of Baron Habert, born at Brunoy about 1818. She won first-class medals at Paris in 1847 and 1855.

Herbelot, d', dĕr'blo', (BARTHÉLEMY,) an eminent French Orientalist, born in Paris in 1625. Having learned Arabic, Hebrew, Persian, etc., he was employed as Oriental secretary and interpreter by the king, who granted him a pension: he was also appointed professor of Syriac in the Collége Royal. He published a "Bibliothèque Orientale," or "Universal Dictionary," containing generally all that regards the Knowledge of the Eastern Nations," a work of great labour and erudition, which was not quite finished at his death in 1695. It was published in 1697.

See PERRAULT, "Hommes illustres;" "Nouvelle Biographie Générale."

Herberay, d', dĕrb'rā', (NICOLAS,) Seigneur des Essarts, a French officer, who, by order of Francis I., translated the first eight books of "Amadis de Gaule" into French, (1548.) Died about 1550.

Herberstein, von, fon hĕr'bĕr-stīn', (SIGISMUND,) BARON, a German historian, born in Carniola or Styria in 1486. He was employed in several important missions, and rose to be president of the college of finance. His "Commentaries on Russian History" (Rerum Mos-

coviticarum Commentarii," 1549) is esteemed the most valuable historical work on the early Russians.

See F. ADELUNG, "Siegmund Freiherr von Herberstein," etc., 1818.

Herbert, (Hon. ALGERNON,) an English author and lawyer, born in 1792, was the youngest son of Henry, Earl of Carnarvon. He wrote several learned works, among which are "Nimrod: a Discourse on Certain Passages of History and Fable," and "Britannia after the Romans." Died in 1855.

Herbert, (EDWARD,) Lord Herbert of Cherbury, an English author and courtier, was born at Montgomery, Wales, in 1581, and was a descendant of the Earl of Pembroke. About 1610 he served in the English army in the Netherlands, and received the title of knight from James I. In 1618 he was sent as ambassador to France, where he published in 1624 his first and principal work, a Latin treatise "On Truth as it is distinguished from Revelation, from Probability, from Possibility, and from Falsehood," which Hallam represents as a "monument of an original, independent thinker," although "justly deemed inimical to every positive religion." In 1631 he was raised to the peerage. He was also the author of a "History of the Life and Reign of Henry VIII.," (1649,) which Horace Walpole calls a "master-piece of historic biography," and "The Life of Lord Herbert, written by himself," (1764.) He was reputed one of the most eminent English statesmen and philosophers of the age in which he lived. Died in 1648.

See HALLAM, "Introduction to the Literature of Europe;" HORACE WALPOLE, Preface to Herbert's Autobiography; CH. DE RÉMUSAT, "Notice of Herbert," in the "Revue des Deux Mondes," 1854; "Retrospective Review," vol. vii., 1823.

Herbert, (GEORGE,) an English poet, a brother of the preceding, was born at Montgomery, Wales, in 1593. In 1619 he was chosen public orator of Cambridge University, of which he was a graduate. Having taken orders, he was made, in 1626, prebendary of Layton Ecclesia, and in 1630 was presented by the king to the living of Bemerton. His poetical writings were once very popular, and have been admired by such men as Cowper and Coleridge; but they are censured by modern critics for quaint and ludicrous conceits. His principal prose work is "The Country Parson." Coleridge remarks that "the quaintness of some of his thoughts—not of his diction, than which nothing can be more pure, manly, and unaffected—has blinded modern readers to the great general merits of his poems, which are for the most part exquisite in their kind." Died in 1632.

See IZAAK WALTON, "Life of Herbert;" WILLMOTT, "Lives of the English Sacred Poets;" "Retrospective Review," vol. iii., 1821; "British Quarterly Review" for July, 1867.

Herbert, (HENRY WILLIAM,) born in London in 1807, was the son of the Rev. William Herbert, noticed below, and a lineal descendant of the Earls of Pembroke. He emigrated to the United States in 1831. He displayed remarkable versatility of talents in his voluminous works, consisting of novels, fugitive poems, historical sketches, etc. Under the name of FRANK FORESTER, he wrote "The Field Sports of the United States," (1849,) "The Deer-Stalkers," (1849,) and other sporting works. Professor Felton represents him as "a poet of vivid imagination, a successful novelist, and an able and accomplished critic." He committed suicide in 1858.

See "North American Review," vol. lxix.

Herbert, (JOHN ROGERS,) an eminent English painter of history and portraits, was born at Malden, Essex, in 1810. He studied in the Royal Academy, and for some years painted portraits with success. Having become a Roman Catholic, he changed his style, and devoted himself to religious subjects. He produced "The First Introduction of Christianity into Britain," (1842,) and "John the Baptist reproving Herod," (1848.) He was elected a Royal Academician in 1848, and painted frescos illustrating "King Lear" in the new palace of Westminster, about 1849.

Herbert, (MARY,) *née* SIDNEY. See SIDNEY.

Herbert, (SIDNEY,) of Lea, BARON, an English statesman of eminent merit, born in 1810, was the second son of the Earl of Pembroke. He graduated at Oxford in 1831, and entered Parliament as a Conservative in 1832. In 1841 he was appointed secretary to the admiralty, and in 1845 became secretary at war in the cabinet of Sir Robert Peel. Having gradually adopted liberal principles, he favoured the repeal of the corn-laws in 1846, and retired from office with his political chief in the summer of that year. On the formation of the Aberdeen ministry, in December, 1852, he was again appointed secretary at war. He resigned, in company with other Peelites, about February, 1855. From June, 1859, until July, 1861, (when he resigned on account of ill health,) he filled the same office in the cabinet of Palmerston, with eminent ability. As a war minister he appears to have been universally popular. In January, 1861, he was raised to the peerage, as Baron Herbert of Lea. He married about 1846 a daughter of General A'Court. He erected on his estate at Wilton a church which is an admirable model of the Italian or Romanesque style. "He combines," says the "Spectator," "with the administrative ability which is the claim of the Peelites to power, great personal tact, and enough of oratorical ability to hold his own in the House of Commons." Died August 2, 1861.

Herbert, (Sir THOMAS,) an English writer, born at York about 1608, was related to the Earl of Pembroke, who procured him an office under the ambassador to Persia in 1626. In 1634 he published a "Relation of Travels in Africa and Asia," which contains a better account of Persia than any which had previously appeared. During the civil war he was chosen by Parliament one of the commissioners to treat with the king, and in 1647 was selected by Charles I. to wait on his person in his confinement. He wrote an account of the last two years of Charles I., under the title of "Threnodia Carolina," (1678.) Died in 1682.

See "Biographia Britannica;" WOOD, "Athenæ Oxonienses;" "Mémoires de Sir Thomas Herbert, Valet-de-Chambre de Charles I." Paris, 1823.

Herbert, (WILLIAM,) Earl of Pembroke, born at Wilton, England, in 1580, was lord-steward of the king's household about 1626. He wrote indifferent verses, and is supposed to be the person to whom Shakspeare's Sonnets were addressed. Pembroke College was named in honour of him. Died in 1630.

Herbert, (WILLIAM,) an English antiquary, born in 1718. After spending some years in London as a merchant, he went to the East Indies as purser's clerk. He is chiefly known as the editor of "Ames's Typographical Antiquities," published in 1785. Died in 1795.

Herbert, (Rev. WILLIAM,) an English author, born at Highclere Castle, Bucks, in 1778, was the third son of the Earl of Carnarvon. After distinguishing himself in the House of Commons, he took holy orders, became rector of Spofforth in 1814, and Dean of Manchester in 1840. He contributed to the "Edinburgh Review," and published a great variety of works in prose and verse, among which is an epic poem, called "Attila, King of the Huns; or, The Triumph of Christianity," (1838,) "a production," says Hallam, "displaying a union of acuteness and erudition with great poetical talents." Died in 1847.

See "Edinburgh Review" for June, 1815, and January, 1838; SIR WALTER SCOTT, critique on Herbert's Poems, in the "Edinburgh Review" for October, 1806, vol. ix.

Herbigny. See FAVART D'HERBIGNY.

Herbigny, d', dĕR'bēn'ye', (PIERRE FRANÇOIS XAVIER Bourguignon — booR'gēn'yôN',) a French political writer, born at Laon in 1772, was a partisan of the Bourbons. Died in 1846.

Herbin, hĕR'bǎN', (AUGUSTE FRANÇOIS JULIEN,) a French Orientalist, born in Paris in 1783. He excelled in the Oriental languages at a very early age. He published an Arabic Grammar, an Arabic-French Dictionary, a "History of Persian Poets," and other works. Died in 1806.

Herbinius, hĕr-bee'ne-ŭs, (JOHANN,) a learned Lutheran minister, born in Silesia in 1633. He preached at Stockholm, Wilna, etc., and published, besides other books, a curious work on cataracts and other aqueous phenomena, "De admirandis Mundi Cataractis, supra et subterraneis," etc., (1670.) Died in 1676.

See ERSCH und GRUBER, "Allgemeine Encyclopaedie."

Herbst, hĕRpst, (JOHANN ANDREAS,) a German musician and writer on music, born at Nuremberg in 1588; died in 1660.

Herbst, (JOHANN FRIEDRICH WILHELM,) a German pulpit orator and entomologist, born at Petershagen, in Prussia, in 1743, was pastor of several churches of Berlin. Among his works are an "Introduction to the Study of Insects," (3 vols., 1784-87,) and a "Natural System of Butterflies," (7 vols., 1783-95.) Died in 1807.

See ERSCH und GRUBER, "Allgemeine Encyclopaedie."

Herculano de Carvalho, êR-koo-lä'no dä kaR-väl'yo, (ALEXANDRE,) a Portuguese poet and historian, born at Guimaraens about 1809, was educated in Paris. He published in 1826 "A Voz de Propheta," ("The Voice of a Prophet,") a poem. His "History of Portugal" (6 vols., 1848-52) is commended.

Hercule. See HERCULES.

Hercules, [Gr. Ἡρακλῆς, (Hēraklēs;) Lat. HER'CULES; Fr. HERCULE, êR'kül'; It. ERCOLE, êR'ko-lȧ,] called also **Al-çī'dēs,** [Gr. Ἀλκείδης,] the most celebrated hero of antiquity, was, according to Homer, the son of Jupiter and Alcmena, the wife of Amphitryon. Thebes was generally supposed to have been his birthplace. His birth is said to have been delayed by Juno because it had been ordained that of the two, Hercules and Eurystheus, the younger should serve the other. While he was an infant in the cradle, he strangled two serpents which Juno sent to destroy him. According to a popular story, when he had arrived at the age of a young man, Virtue and Pleasure appeared to him, each offering to be his guide. He preferred the former, and soon became renowned for his heroic exploits, the first of which was his victory over the lion of Cithæron. He afterwards delivered Thebes from the annual tribute of a hundred oxen which that city was required to pay to Erginus. As a reward for this service, Creon, King of Thebes, gave him his daughter Megara in marriage.

Having consulted the oracle of Apollo, he was directed to serve Eurystheus for twelve years, after which he should become immortal. Eurystheus, who regarded him with jealousy and enmity, imposed on him a number of arduous enterprises, called the Twelve Labours of Hercules. The result of his first labour was the death of the Nemean lion, which he choked in his den. He afterwards wore the skin of this animal. His next task was to kill the Lernean hydra, which infested the vicinity of Argos, and had seven (or, according to some writers, nine) heads, the middle one of which was immortal. He cut off several of its heads, but two new heads grew in place of each one amputated, until he seared the wounded part by burning. He buried the immortal head under a rock, and dipped his arrows in the gall of the hydra, so that the wounds which they inflicted were incurable. The third labour was to bring to Eurystheus a certain stag which had golden horns and was exceedingly swift of foot. He pursued it for a whole year, and at length caught it, after he had wounded it with his arrow. He was next ordered to bring alive to Mycenæ a wild boar that ravaged the vicinity of Erymanthus. He chased this animal into a snow-drift, bound him with fetters, and carried him to Eurystheus. In this expedition he encountered and vanquished the Centaurs. (See CENTAURI.) The fifth labour was to cleanse in one day the stables of King Augeas, who kept many cattle, the dung from which had accumulated for years. He performed this task by turning the rivers Alpheus and Peneus into the Augean stables. Eurystheus objected to count this among the twelve labours, because Hercules had worked for hire. (See AUGEAS.) His sixth labour was the destruction of the Stymphalian birds, which had brazen claws and beaks, discharged their feathers as arrows, and infested Lake Stymphalus in vast numbers. His seventh exploit was the capture of a mad bull which ravaged the island of Crete. He carried the bull alive to the continent and let it loose. It afterwards did much mischief at Marathon. Eurystheus next ordered him to bring from Diomedes of Thrace his horses, which fed on human flesh. The hero killed Diomedes and performed the appointed task. The subject of the ninth labour was the girdle of Hippolyte, Queen of the Amazons, which he was required to bring. He was accompanied in this expedition by Theseus and other heroes, and obtained the girdle after he had defeated the Amazons in fight. He was next commanded to bring the oxen of the monster Geryon from the fabulous island of Erythea, situated in the far-distant west. In the course of this expedition he erected on the Strait of Gibraltar two pillars, called the pillars of Hercules, and performed several exploits besides the killing of Geryon. His eleventh labour was to bring some golden apples which were guarded by a dragon in the garden of the Hesperides. He did not know where this garden was; but he obtained information from Nereus. As he was passing through Egypt in his route, he killed Busiris, the king and tyrant of that country. By the advice of Prometheus, whom he delivered from penal suffering, he sent Atlas for the apples, and supported the heavens in his place until Atlas returned with the fruit.*

The last and most dangerous service was his descent to Hades to bring up the dog Cerberus. He obtained the consent of Pluto to take the monster, provided he would not use any weapon. He accordingly seized Cerberus, carried him alive to Eurystheus, and then returned him to Pluto.

Having been affected with insanity, he consulted an oracle, which advised him to sell himself as a slave for three years. He became a slave to Omphale, Queen of Lydia, in whose service he wore the dress of a woman and was employed in spinning. He afterwards conducted a successful expedition against Troy to punish Laomedon for a breach of his promise.

He married Dejanira, (daughter of the King of Calydon,) to whom the centaur Nessus once offered violence. Hercules, with a poisoned arrow, killed Nessus, who, as he was about to die, persuaded Dejanira to preserve his blood as a love-charm. She became jealous, and applied this blood to a tunic, which he put on. He was poisoned by this garment, which produced violent pain, and stuck to his flesh when he tried to pull it off. He was about to seek relief by voluntary death on Mount Œta, when he was conveyed by a cloud to Olympus and rewarded with immortality. He was afterwards worshipped as a divinity by all the Greeks. In the character of Hercules it is difficult or impossible to distinguish the purely mythical or allegorical from what may be considered as mere exaggerations built upon a historic basis.

See GUIGNIAUT, "Religions de l'Antiquité," Paris, 1825–29, vol. ii. book iv. chaps. v. and vi.

Herder, von, fon hĕr′dĕr, (JOHANN GOTTFRIED,) one of the most remarkable and gifted writers that Germany has produced, was born at Mohrungen, in East Prussia, in 1744. He commenced the study of surgery

---

* Several of the most remarkable exploits of Hercules are vividly described by Darwin:

" So mighty Hercules o'er many a clime
 Waved his vast mace in Virtue's cause sublime ;
 Unmeasured strength, with early art combined,
 Awed, served, protected, and amazed mankind.
 First, two dread snakes, at Juno's vengeful nod,
 Climbed round the cradle of the sleeping god :
 Waked by the shrilling hiss, and rustling sound,
 And shrieks of fair attendants trembling round,
 Their gasping throats with clenching hands he holds,
 And Death untwists their convoluted folds.
 Next in red torrents from her sevenfold heads
 Fell Hydra's blood on Lerna's lake he sheds ;
 Grasps Achelous with resistless force,
 And drags the roaring river to his course ;
 Binds, with loud bellowing and with hideous yell,
 The monster Bull, and threefold Dog of hell.
 Then, where Nemea's howling forests wave,
 He drives the Lion to his dusky cave,
 Seized by the throat, the growling fiend disarms,
 And tears his gaping jaws with sinewy arms ;
 Lifts proud Antæus from his mother-plains,
 And with strong grasp the struggling giant strains ;
 Back falls his fainting head, and clammy hair,
 Writhe his weak limbs, and flits his life in air ;—
 By steps reverted, o'er the blood-dropp'd fen
 He tracks huge Cacus to his murderous den,
 Where, breathing flames through brazen lips, he fled,
 And shakes the rock-roofed cavern o'er his head.
 Last, with wide arms the solid earth he tears,
 Piles rock on rock, on mountain mountain rears ;
 Heaves up huge Abyla on Afric's sand,
 Crowns with high Calpe Europe's salient strand,
 Crests with opposing towers the splendid scene,
 And pours from urns immense the sea between.
 Loud o'er her whirling floods Charybdis roars,
 Affrighted Scylla bellows round his shores,
 Vesuvio groans through all his echoing caves,
 And Etna thunders o'er the insurgent waves "
                                   Botanic Garden, Canto I.

---

in Königsberg, (1762 ;) but, having fainted at the first operation which he witnessed, he turned his attention to theology. His thirst for knowledge was boundless, and his acquisitions embraced an immense variety of subjects. While in Königsberg, he became acquainted with Kant, who permitted him to attend his lectures without any charge. Towards the close of 1764 he was appointed teacher, and afterwards preacher, at the cathedral school in Riga. While here, he became acquainted with an enthusiastic attachment and devotion. In 1770 he was invited to Bückeburg, where he became court preacher, and soon acquired great distinction as a divine, in consequence of which he received a call to the professorship of theology at Göttingen. While he was still hesitating whether or not to accept the invitation, he was offered the position of court preacher, general superintendent, and counsellor of the Upper Consistory at Weimar, whither he removed in October, 1776. As an eloquent preacher, a zealous friend of education, and an encourager of rising talent, he won the esteem and love of both prince and people. The remainder of his life was spent in Weimar. In 1793 he was made vice-president, and in 1801 president, of the Upper Consistory. Died in 1803.

Among his multifarious writings there is, perhaps, not one complete work : yet he is admitted to have exercised a most important influence upon German literature, criticism, and philosophy. His greatest work (unfinished) is entitled "Ideas on the Philosophy of the History of Mankind," ("Ideen zur Philosophie der Geschichte der Menschheit.") Among his other publications we may name his "Spirit of Hebrew Poetry," ("Geist der Hebräischen Poesie,") and his "Volkslieder," a collection of the popular songs of different nations. Alluding to the difficulty of understanding or describing Herder's many-sided intellect, Richter observes, "The starry heaven no star-map paints, although painting may represent a landscape." In another place he says, "It was Herder's fault that he was not a star of the first magnitude or any other magnitude, but a clump of stars out of which each one spells a constellation to please himself." A complete edition of Herder's works was issued at Stuttgart, in 45 vols., (1806–20,) and a pocket edition afterwards appeared, in 60 vols.

See KARL L. RING, "Herder's Leben," 1822; H. DÖRING, "Herder's Leben," 1824; EMIL G. VON HERDER, "J. G. von Herder's Lebensbild," etc., 3 vols., 1847; HEINSIUS, "Herder nach seinem Leben und Wirken," 1847; L. G. KOPP, "Études sur Herder," etc., 1852; F. H. HEDGE, "Prose Writers of Germany;" E. P. WHIPPLE, "Characteristics of Men of Genius," vol. i.; "Foreign Quarterly Review" for July, 1846.

Herder, von, (SIGMUND AUGUST WOLFGANG,) a mineralogist, born in 1766, was a son of the great Herder. Died in 1838. His brother, WILHELM GOTTFRIED, born in 1774, was a physician. Died in 1806.

See ERSCH and GRUBER, "Allgemeine Encyklopaedie."

Héreau, hå′rō′, (EDME JOACHIM,) a French littérateur, born in Paris in 1791. He killed himself in 1836.

Heredia, à-rà-dee′å, (JOSÉ MARIA,) a popular poet, born at Santiago de Cuba in 1803. He was appointed ministro de la audiencia by the President of Mexico in 1826. Among his most admired poems are "The Teocallis of Choluca," "Ode to the Ocean," "To the Greeks in 1821," ("A los Griegos en 1821,") and verses on Niagara, ("Al Niagara.") The most complete edition of his poems is that published recently in New York. Died at Toluca in 1839.

See LONGFELLOW, "Poets and Poetry of Europe ;" "Nouvelle Biographie Générale ;" FORNARIS Y LEON, "Cuba poetica ;" J. KENNEDY, "Modern Poets and Poetry of Spain," 1852.

Heredia, de, dà à-rà-dee′å, (PEDRO MIGUEL,) born at Valladolid in 1590, was first physician to Philip IV. Died in 1659.

Hereford, BISHOP OF. See HAMPDEN, (RENN DICKSON.)

Heresbach, hā′rĕs-bâk′, (CONRAD,) a German writer, born at Heresbach, in Cleves, about 1502. He wrote an esteemed work on agriculture, "Rei Rusticæ Libri quatuor," (1570.) Died in 1576.

See ERSCH und GRUBER, "Allgemeine Encyklopaedie ;" A. G. SCHWEITZER, "Dissertatio de C. Heresbachii Vita et Scriptis," 1849; NICÉRON, "Mémoires."

Hĕr′e-ward, an English captain, distinguished in the war of the Norman conquest. Died in 1072.

Heri. See HARI and HÉRY.

Héricart de Thury, hä´re´kȧr´ dęh tü´re´, (LOUIS ÉTIENNE FRANÇOIS,) VICOMTE, a French engineer and agriculturist, born in Paris in 1776. As engineer-in-chief, he directed the immense works of the catacombs of Paris for about twenty years, (1810–30.) He wrote a work on "Artesian Wells," (1823,) and many treatises on mines, ores, etc. Died in 1854.

See QUÉRARD, "La France Littéraire."

Héricourt, de, dęh hä´re´koor´, (LOUIS,) a learned French lawyer and canonist, born at Soissons in 1687. From 1714 to 1736 he contributed to the "Journal des Savants," the earliest of modern reviews. His principal work is "The Ecclesiastical Laws of France, placed in their Natural Order," (1719.) Tabaraud designates him "the most celebrated French canonist." Died in 1752.

See MORÉRI, "Dictionnaire Historique."

Hĕr´ĭ-ǫt, (GEORGE,) a Scottish goldsmith, born about 1563, founded a hospital in Edinburgh, which bears his name, and in which many boys are educated gratuitously. It was finished in 1659. Died in 1624.

See "Memoirs of George Heriot;" CHAMBERS, "Biographical Dictionary of Eminent Scotsmen;" SIR WALTER SCOTT, "Fortunes of Nigel."

Heriot, (JOHN,) a Scottish writer, born at Haddington in 1760. During the French Revolution he edited papers in London, called "The World" and "The True Briton," in support of the English ministry. Died in 1833.

Heriri. See HAREEREE.

Hérissant, hä´re´sŏn´, (FRANÇOIS DAVID,) a French medical writer, born at Rouen in 1714; died in 1773.

Hérissant, (LOUIS ANTOINE PROSPER,) a French writer and physician, born in Paris in 1745, wrote "Typography," a poem, and articles on natural history for the "Bibliothèque historique de France." Died in 1769.

See JEAN GOULIN, "Éloge de L. A. P. Hérissant," 1769.

Hérissant, (LOUIS THÉODORE,) a French littérateur, brother of the preceding, was born in Paris in 1743. He published "My Little Portfolio," (2 vols. 12mo, 1774,) and various other works, and compiled the last volume of the "Bibliothèque de Société," (begun by Chamfort, 4 vols., 1771.) Died in 1811.

Héritier. See L'HÉRITIER.

Héritier de Villandon. See L'HÉRITIER DE VILLANDON.

Hęr´kĭ-męr, a general of the New York militia. In 1777 he commanded the militia of Tryon county, who marched to relieve the garrison of Fort Stanwix, on the Mohawk, then besieged by the British. In an engagement a few miles from the fort, he was mortally wounded.

Herlicius, hĕR-lit´se-ŭs, (DAVID,) a German astrologer, born at Zeitz in 1558; died in 1636.

Herloszsohn, hĕR´los-sŏn´, (GEORG KARL,) a German romancer, born at Prague in 1802, published "The Hungarian," (" Der Ungar," 1832,) "The Venetian," (2d edition, 1837,) and "Forest Flowers," (" Waldblumen," 1847.) Died in 1849.

Her-mag´o-ras ['Ερμαγόρας] OF TEMNOS, a Greek rhetorician, lived about 50 B.C.

Her´mann or Her´man, (or hĕR´män,) [Lat. ARMIN´-IUS; Dutch, ARMIJN, ȧR-mīn´; Ger. ARMIN, ȧR-meen´,] a celebrated German hero, born 16 B.C., was the son of Sigimer, chief of the Cherusci. He is called Armenios by the Greek writers, and Arminius by the Romans. He entered the Roman army at an early age, and obtained the privileges of knighthood and of citizenship at Rome. Indignant at the oppression which his country was suffering under Quintilius Varus, then governor, he formed on his return a plan for its deliverance. By false pretences he induced the Roman commander to advance with his army beyond the Rhine, where, entangled in the forest and marshes near the Lippe, they suffered a signal defeat in 9 A.D. In 16 A.D., Germanicus, with a large army, invaded Germany, and completely defeated Hermann near Hameln, on the Weser. Nevertheless, Hermann not long after overthrew Maroboduus, (Marbod,) chief of the Suevi; but, being suspected of aiming at supreme dominion, he was assassinated by his own relatives, in the thirty-seventh year of his age. "Unlike other kings and commanders," says Tacitus, "he had the boldness to attack the Roman people, not in the beginning, but in the fulness, of their power; in battle not always victorious, but unconquered in war."

See TACITUS, "Annales;" FLORUS, "History;" ROTH, "Hermann und Marbod," 1817; VON LEDEBUR, "Das Land und Volk der Bructerer," 1827; MASSMANN, "Arminius Cheruscorum Dux et Decus," 1839; KÖNIG, "Armin der Cherusker; zum Denkmal im Teutoburger Wald," 1840.

Hermann, hĕR´män, (JAKOB,) a Swiss mathematician, born at Bâle in 1678. By the favour of Leibnitz, he obtained the chair of mathematics in the University of Padua. In 1724 he accepted an invitation from Peter the Great to teach the grand duke. His principal work is a Latin "Treatise on the Forces and Movements of Solid and Fluid Bodies," (1715.) Died in 1733.

See ERSCH und GRUBER, "Allgemeine Encyklopaedie."

Hermann, hĕR´mŏn´, (JEAN,) an able French naturalist, born at Barr, near Strasburg, in 1738. He obtained at Strasburg the chair of philosophy in 1778, and that of pathology in 1782. In 1784 he became professor of botany and chemistry. He wrote many short treatises on natural history, furnished materials for the large work of Buffon, and published a treatise on the affinities of animals, entitled "Tabula Affinitatum Animalium," (1783.) Died in 1800.

His son, JEAN FRÉDÉRIC, (1768–93,) wrote a thesis on Osteology, and a "Memoir on Wingless Insects," which Cuvier says "were excellent for the time."

See T. LAUTH, "Vie de Jean Hermann," 1801; "Nouvelle Biographie Générale."

Hermann, (JOHANN GOTTFRIED JAKOB,) an eminent German philologist and critic, born at Leipsic on the 28th of November, 1772. He became in 1809 professor of eloquence and poetry at Leipsic, where his lectures on archæology and the Greek classics attracted great numbers of students. Among his principal works are "Elements of Metrical Doctrine," (" Elementa Doctrinæ Metricæ," 1816,) "On the Metres of Pindar," (" De Metris Pindari," 1817,) and "Opuscula," (7 vols., 1827–30,) consisting of essays and odes written in elegant Latin. He also prepared editions of several Greek writers, of which those of Bion and Moschus were published in 1849. Died in December, 1848.

See JAHN, "J. G. Hermann: eine Gedächtnissrede," Leipsic, 1849; CARL F. AMEIS, "G. Hermann's pädagogischer Einfluss," 1850; ERSCH und GRUBER, "Allgemeine Encyklopaedie," under "Philologie;" "Nouvelle Biographie Générale."

Hermann, (KARL FRIEDRICH,) a German antiquary, born at Frankfort-on-the-Main in 1804, became in 1842 professor of eloquence at Göttingen. He published a "Manual of Greek Antiquities," (1841,) and other works. Died in 1855.

Hermann, (KARL HEINRICH,) a German historical painter, born at Dresden in 1802, was a pupil of Cornelius at Dusseldorf. Among his master-pieces are the frescos in the Königsbau and the Arcade of the Hofgarten at Munich.

Hermann, (MARTIAL JOSEPH ARMAND,) a French revolutionist and lawyer, born at Saint-Pol in 1750. In 1793, as a partisan of Robespierre, he became president of the Revolutionary Tribunal. He was executed in 1795.

See THIERS, "History of the French Revolution."

Hermann, (PAUL,) an eminent German botanist, born at Halle in 1646. He practised medicine about eight years in the East Indies, and became professor of botany at Leyden in 1679. Among his works, which are illustrated with fine engravings, are a "Catalogue of the Botanic Garden of Leyden," (1687,) and "Batavian Garden," (" Paradisus Batavus," 1698.) Died in 1695.

See ERSCH und GRUBER, "Allgemeine Encyklopaedie;" "Biographie Médicale."

Hermann, (PHILIPP,) an excellent painter on glass, adorned the cathedral of Metz, where he died in 1392.

Hęr´mann Con-trac´tus, one of the early German historians, born in 1013, was a monk in the cloister of Reichenau. He wrote a "Chronicon," which comes down to 1054 and bears some resemblance to that of the Venerable Bede. Died in 1054.

See ERSCH und GRUBER, "Allgemeine Encyklopaedie."

Hermant, hĕR´mŏn´, (GODEFROI,) a French biographer and Jansenist theologian, born at Beauvais in 1617, wrote, besides other works, a "Life of Saint John

Chrysostom," (1664,) a "Life of Athanasius," (1671,) and a "Life of Saint Ambrose," (1678.) Died in 1690.

See A. BAILLET, "Vie de M. G. Hermant," 1717; MORÉRI, "Dictionnaire Historique."

Hermant, (JEAN,) a French priest, born at Caen in 1650; died in 1725. He wrote a history of heresies.

Hermaphrodite. See HERMAPHRODITUS.

Her-maph-ro-di'tus, [Gr. Ἑρμαφρόδιτος; Fr. HERMAPHRODITE, ĕr'mȧ'fro'dĕt',] in classic mythology, the offspring of Mercury (Hermes) and Venus, (Aphrodite,) was said to combine both sexes.

See OVID, "Metamorphoses."

Her-mar'ehus, [Ἕρμαρχος,] a Greek philosopher, born in Mitylene, was a disciple of Epicurus, who bequeathed to him his garden. He succeeded Epicurus as the head of the school about 270 B.C. His works are lost.

Her'mas, a Christian writer of the first century, is supposed by some to be the person mentioned by Saint Paul in the Epistle to the Romans, chapter xvi. He lived in Italy, and wrote, in Greek, a book entitled "The Pastor, or Shepherd," composed of visions, precepts, and similitudes. It was frequently quoted and highly esteemed by the ancient Fathers of the Church. Origen, Irenæus, and Clement of Alexandria regarded it as divinely inspired. It is prized as a relic of the primitive Church, and as a medium of interesting traditions. The original is nearly all lost; but a Latin version is extant.

See NEANDER, "History of the Church;" CAVE, "Historia Literaria;" FABRICIUS, "Bibliotheca Græca."

Hermbstädt, hĕrmp'stĕt, (SIGISMUND FRIEDRICH,) a German chemist, born at Erfurt in 1760; died in 1833.

Hermelin, hĕr'me-leen', (SAMUEL GUSTAVUS,) a learned Swedish baron and mineralogist, born at Stockholm in 1744. He was a member of the council of mines, and spent many years in travel in order to explore and develop the mineral resources of Sweden. In 1782 he visited the United States, with credentials as an agent of the king, to obtain information on mineralogy and metallurgy. On these subjects he published several useful works, also on statistics and geography. A new and correct atlas of Sweden was the result of his labours. Died in 1820.

See C. P. HAELLSTROEM, "Biographi öfver Bergs-Rädet S. G. Hermelin," 1821; "Biographiskt-Lexicon öfver namnkunnige Svenska Män."

Hermengarde. See ERMENGARDE.

Hermenric. See ERMERIC.

Her'mēs, [Gr. Ἑρμῆς; Fr. HERMÈS, ĕR'mĕs',] the name which the Greeks gave to the herald of the gods, corresponding nearly with the Mercurius of the Roman mythology. (See MERCURY.) Hermes was identified with the Egyptian Thoth or Thot, the inventor of arts and sciences.

Hermes, hĕR'mĕs, (GEORG,) a celebrated Catholic theologian, born in Westphalia, in Germany, in 1775, was the founder of a philosophical school of Christian doctrine. In 1807, when appointed professor of theology in Münster, he distinguished himself by his opposition to the system of Kant and Fichte. He became in 1820 professor at the University of Bonn, where he was highly esteemed for his abilities as a lecturer and his amiable character. He had published in 1819 his "Introduction to Christian Catholic Theology," which, though not assailing any dogmas of the Church, was made the occasion of a charge of heresy. In 1835 a brief was issued by the pope, condemning the work, and a warm controversy was long carried on between the papal and the Hermesian party. Died in 1831.

See W. ESSER, "Denkschrift auf G. Hermes," 1832; ELVENICH, "Der Hermesianismus und Johannes Perrone," 1844.

Hermes, (JOHANN AUGUST,) a German Protestant writer on theology, born at Magdeburg in 1736. His "Manual of Religion" was translated into French, Swedish, and Dutch. Died in 1822.

See J. H. FRITSCH, "J. A. Hermes," 1827; ERSCH und GRUBER, "Allgemeine Encyklopaedie."

Hermes, (JOHANN TIMOTHEUS,) a German novelist, born in Pomerania in 1738, was the originator of the romances called psychological. His principal work is

"The Journey of Sophia from Memel to Saxony," (6 vols., 1770–78.) Died in 1821.

See ERSCH und GRUBER, "Allgemeine Encyklopaedie."

Hermes, (KARL HEINRICH,) a German historical writer, born at Kalisz, in Poland, in 1800, published a "History of the Last Twenty-Five Years," (1842; 6th edition, 3 vols., 1853.)

Her'mēs Tris-me-ĝis'tus, [Gr. Ἑρμῆς Τρισμέγιστος, Fr. HERMÈS TRISMÉGISTE, ĕR'mĕs' tRĕs'mȧ'zhĕst',] called by Milton the "thrice great Hermes," the reputed author of many Greek works which were probably written in Egypt in the first three centuries of the Christian era. Some of them are still extant. According to one opinion, Hermes was an Egyptian priest. The principal work which has come down to us under his name is "Poemander," which treats of "the nature of all things and of the creation of the world."

See J. H. URSINUS, "Exercitatio de Mercurio Trismegisto," 1661; FABRICIUS, "Bibliotheca Græca;" BAUMGARTEN-CRUSIUS, "De Librorum Hermeticorum Origine et Indole," 1827.

Her-mi'as, (or her-mi'as,) [Gr. Ἑρμείας or Ἑρμίας,] a friend and patron of Aristotle, was a slave in his youth. He became tyrant or ruler of Assos and Atarneus, in Mysia, and entertained Aristotle with honour at his court about three years, 348–345 B.C. Hermias was put to death by the King of Persia about 345 B.C. Aristotle afterwards married Pythias, the adopted daughter of Hermias, and celebrated his memory in a beautiful poem entitled a "Hymn to Virtue," which is extant.

See DIOGENES LAERTIUS; DIODORUS.

Hermias, a Christian philosopher, who lived in the second century A.D. He ridiculed the pagan philosophy in a small Greek book entitled Διασυρμὸς τῶν ἔξω φιλοσόφων, a work of merit, which is still extant.

Hermida, ĕR-mee'Dȧ, (BENITO y Porras-Bermudez-Maldonado—e por'rȧs bĕR-moo'Dĕth mȧl-do-nȧ'Do,) a Spanish minister of state, born at Santiago in 1736. He took a prominent part at the siege of Saragossa and in resistance to the French invasion. He was chosen by the central junta minister of grace and justice in 1808. He translated "Paradise Lost" into Spanish verse, (1814.) Died in 1814.

See "Nouvelle Biographie Générale."

Hermilly, d', dĕR'me'ye', (N. VAQUETTE,) a French littérateur, born in Paris about 1710. He translated from the Spanish Ferreras's "History of Spain," (1742,) and Camoëns's "Lusiad," (1776.) Died in 1778.

Her-min'I-us, a Roman warrior, was one of the three who defended the Sublician bridge against Porsena.

Her-mi'o-ne, [Ἑρμιόνη,] in classic mythology, was a daughter of Menelaus and Helen. She was promised to Orestes, her cousin, but was married to Pyrrhus, according to some authors. After the death of Pyrrhus she became the wife of Orestes.

Her-mip'pus, [Ἕρμιππος,] an Athenian poet of the old comedy, was a brother of the poet Myrtilus, and lived about 450 B.C. He inserted satires against Pericles in his plays. Plutarch says he prosecuted Aspasia for impiety.

Hermippus OF SMYRNA, an eminent Greek philosopher, of whom little is known, was surnamed THE CALLIMACHEIAN. Hence it is inferred that he was a disciple of Callimachus, and flourished about 250 or 225 B.C. He wrote the lives of Pythagoras and other philosophers, and was often quoted by ancient writers. None of his works have come down to us.

See VOSSIUS, "De Historicis Græcis."

Hermite. See ERMITE.

Hermite, ĕR'mĕt', (CHARLES,) a French mathematician, born at Dieuze (Meurthe) in 1822, was admitted into the Institute in 1856.

Hermocrate. See HERMOCRATES.

Her-moc'ra-tēs, [Gr. Ἑρμοκράτης; Fr. HERMOCRATE, ĕR'mo'kRȧt',] an eminent Syracusan general and statesman. He was one of the three generals to whom the people confided the defence of Syracuse against the Athenians in 414 B.C. Having been defeated in the first actions of the war, he and his colleagues were deprived of command. He held a high command at the naval battle of Cynossema, and was banished in 409 B.C. In

€ as k; ç as s; ğ hard; ğ as j; G, H, K, guttural; N, nasal; R, trilled; š as z; th as in this.   (See Explanations, p. 23.)

an attempt to reinstate himself, or make himself master of Syracuse, he was killed there about 406 B.C. He left a high character for patriotism, energy, and incorruptibility, though his later acts in inaugurating a civil war cannot be justified.

See GROTE, "History of Greece," vol. x. chap. lxxxi.

Her′mod or **Hermódr**, written also **Hermode**, [etymology uncertain,] the son and messenger of Odin, corresponding in several respects to the Hermes or Mercury of classic mythology.

See THORPE, "Northern Mythology," vol. i.; MALLET, "Northern Antiquities," vol. ii. Fable XXIX.

Hermodore. See HERMODORUS.

Her-mo-do′rus [Gr. Ἑρμόδωρος; Fr. HERMODORE, ĕR′mo′doR′] OF EPHESUS, a Greek philosopher, who lived about 450 B.C. According to Pomponius, he aided the Roman decemviri in compiling the Twelve Tables.

See GRATAMA, "De Hermodoro Ephesio vero XII. Tabularum Auctore," 1818.

Hermodorus OF SALAMIS, a Greek architect, lived about 150 B.C., and built a temple of Mars in Rome.

Hermogène. See HERMOGENES.

Her-mog′e-nēs, [Gr. Ἑρμογένης; Fr. HERMOGÈNE, ĕR′mo′zhăn′,] an Athenian philosopher, a son of Hipponicus, lived about 450 B.C. He was an interlocutor in the "Cratylus" of Plato.

Hermogenes surnamed XYSTER, [Ξυστήρ,] a celebrated Greek rhetorician, born at Tarsus, in Cilicia, lived in the reign of Marcus Aurelius, (161-180 A.D.) He was a remarkable instance of precocious genius. At the age of fifteen he was a professor of rhetoric at Rome, and had acquired fame by his eloquent discourses. About two years later he wrote a work on Rhetoric, (Τέχνη ῥητορική,) which was for a long time used as a text-book in the schools. He was author of other works on rhetoric. At the age of twenty-five he lost his memory and all capacity for usefulness, which he never recovered, though he survived many years. His works are extant.

See PHILOSTRATUS, "Vitæ Sophistarum;" FABRICIUS, "Bibliotheca Græca."

Hermogenes, a Greek architect, was a native of Alabanda, in Caria. It is not known when he lived. Vitruvius mentions him among the most eminent architects of antiquity, and as having contributed to the progress of the art by his improvements and discoveries. He invented the pseudo-dipterus, and built a temple to Diana in the city of Magnesia.

Hermogenes, a painter, lived about 170-200 A.D., and was accused of heresy by Tertullian, who wrote a book against him,—"Adversus Hermogenem." He was originally a pagan.

Her-mo-ġe-nī-ā′nus or **Her-moġ′e-nēs**, a Roman jurist, lived under Honorius, in the fourth century.

Her-mo-lā′us, [Gr. Ἑρμόλαος,] a page of Alexander the Great, who formed a conspiracy against his sovereign, and was put to death about 327 B.C.

Hermolaus Barbarus. See BARBARO.

Hermotime. See HERMOTIMUS.

Her-mo-tī′mus [Gr. Ἑρμότιμος; Fr. HERMOTIME, ĕR′mo′tēm′] OF CLAZOMENÆ, a Greek philosopher, lived about 500 B.C. According to Aristotle, he first advanced the doctrine that the νοῦς (mind, or spirit) is the cause of all things.

See ARISTOTLE, "Metaphysics;" DIOGENES LAERTIUS; DENZINGER, "De Hermotimo Clazomen. Commentatio," 1825.

Hernandes, ĕR nän′dĕth, (FRANCISCO,) a Spanish physician and naturalist, who was born at Toledo, and received from Philip II. a commission to visit North America and to describe the plants, animals, and minerals found therein. The result of his labours was a valuable work (in Spanish) entitled a "Natural History of Trees, Plants, and Animals of New Spain," etc., (1615.) He was the first European naturalist who explored this region for the benefit of science, and appears to have performed the task with creditable fidelity.

See N. ANTONIO, "Bibliotheca Hispana Nova;" "Biographie Médicale."

Hernandez-Velasco, ĕR-nän′dĕth và-lås′ko, (GREGORIO,) a Spanish priest and poet, born at Toledo about 1550, translated the "Æneid" of Virgil into Spanish verse,

(1585.) Though the style is rather inflated, the version is correct, and presents some elegant passages.

See N. ANTONIO, "Bibliotheca Hispana Nova."

Hernando de Soto. See DE SOTO.

Hern′don, (WILLIAM LEWIS,) an American naval officer and writer, born in Fredericksburg, Virginia, in 1813. He entered the navy in 1828, and served in the war with Mexico. In 1851 he commenced, under the direction of the United States government, his explorations of the Amazon River. Ascending the Andes from Lima, he struck the head-waters of the Huallaga, a tributary of the Amazon, and, after nearly seven hundred miles of canoe-navigation, he entered the main channel of the great river. Forty thousand copies of his "Exploration of the Valley of the Amazon," with maps and plates, were published by Congress in 1853. In 1857, Lieutenant Herndon sailed from Havana for New York, in command of the steamer Central America, with 475 passengers and about $2,000,000 in gold. While off the coast of Georgia, the steamer, in a violent gale, sprung a leak, and he was drowned, along with the greater number of the passengers.

Herne, hĕrn, (THOMAS,) a native of Suffolk, England, a Fellow of Merton College, Oxford. He wrote several controversial works on theology. Died young in 1722.

Hernquist, hĕRn′kwist, (PEHR,) a Swedish naturalist, born in the parish of Skara in 1726, studied under Linnæus at Upsal. He founded a veterinary school at Skara, and wrote "Anatomia Hippiatrica," and other works. Died in 1808.

See J. WALLIN, "Minne af P. Hernquist," 1818; L. TIDÉN, "Åreminne öfver P. Hernquist," 1818.

Hero. See HERON.

He′ro, [Gr. Ἡρώ,] a priestess of Venus at Sestos in Thrace, was loved by Leander, a youth of Abydos, who, it is said, swam across the Hellespont every night to visit her. He was at length drowned in a storm, and Hero, in despair, threw herself into the sea. This story has formed the subject of poems by Musæus, Schiller, and others.

Héroard, hà′ro′ăr′, (JEAN,) a French physician, born at Montpellier, graduated in 1575. He was patronized by Charles IX., and was afterwards first physician to Louis XIII. Died in 1627.

Hĕr′od, [Gr. Ἡρώδης; Lat. HERO′DES; Fr. HÉRODE, à′rod′; It. ERODE, à-ro′dà,] surnamed THE GREAT, King of Judea, born at Ascalon in 72 B.C., was the son of Antipater the Idumæan, who made him Governor of Galilee about the year 47. After the death of Julius Cæsar, he at first sided with Brutus and Cassius, but on their defeat made peace with Antony, by whose influence he was appointed King of Judea, 40 B.C. He married Mariamne, a granddaughter of the high-priest Hyrcanus. In the civil war between Octavius and Antony, Herod joined the latter, and fought for him against the Arabians, but was pardoned by the victorious Octavius. Among other acts of cruelty by which his reign was disgraced, was the execution of Hyrcanus and the brother of Mariamne, who herself at length became the victim of his jealousy. It is said he suffered great remorse for this act; but it did not restrain him from taking the life of her two sons, on which occasion Augustus remarked that he would rather be Herod's swine than his son. He erected several grand edifices in his capital, and rebuilt the Jewish temple on a magnificent scale. The birth of the Messiah, which occurred in his reign, became the signal for the indiscriminate massacre of infants recorded in Matthew, chap. ii. Herod died within a year after that event, and left the throne to his son Archelaus. His name has become proverbial for murderous violence and remorseless cruelty.

See JOSEPHUS, "History of the Jews;" DION CASSIUS, "History;" SCHLIPAL, "Dissertatio de Herode Magno," 1711; SCHLOSSER, "Geschichte der Familie des Herodes," 1818; MILMAN, "History of the Jews."

Hĕr′od A-grip′pa [Gr. Ἡρώδης Ἀγρίππας] **I.,** born about 1 A.D., was the son of Aristobu′lus by Berenice, the daughter of Herod the Great, and received a part of his education at Rome. At the accession of Caligula, in 37 A.D., he was released from prison, in which he had been confined by Tiberius, and was made ruler of several

ā, ē, ī, ō, ū, ȳ, *long;* à, ė, ȯ, same, less prolonged; ă, ĕ, ĭ, ŏ, ŭ, y̆, *short;* a, e, i, o, *obscure;* fär, fåll, fåt; mêt; nŏt; gōōd; mōōn;

tetrarchies, viz., Abilene, Auranitis, and Trachonitis, to which in 39 Galilee was added. Under the emperor Claudius his power was increased, and he became King of Judea and Samaria. To promote his popularity with the Jews, he persecuted the Christians, as is related in the twelfth chapter of the Acts. He died suddenly in 44 A.D., when, in the language of Scripture, "he was smitten by an angel, because he gave not God the glory."

Herod Agrippa II., a son of the preceding, was born about 27 A.D. Judea having been reduced to a Roman province, the emperor Claudius gave him in 48 the kingdom of Chalcis, which was afterwards exchanged for Gaulonitis, Trachonitis, Batanæa, and other districts. His dominions were subsequently extended by Nero. The subject of this article is the Agrippa of Scripture, before whom the Apostle Paul, in the year 60, made that sublime and noble argument which almost persuaded a king to be a Christian. (Acts xxvi.) When the Jews revolted against Vespasian, Herod Agrippa adhered to the Romans; and after the capture of Jerusalem he retired to Rome, where he died about 100 A.D.

See JOSEPHUS, "History of the Jews."

Hĕr'od An-ti'pas, [Gr. Ἡρώδης Ἀντίπας,] son of Herod the Great and Malthace, after his father's death obtained the office of Tetrarch of Galilee, with the consent of the emperor Augustus. Having married the daughter of an Arabian prince, (Aretas,) he divorced her in 33 A.D., and took in her place Herodias, the wife of his brother Philip, who was then living. For this sinful act John the Baptist reproved him, and was put to death. (Mark vi. 17-28.) His interview with the Saviour, who was sent to him by Pilate and treated with indignity, is related in the twenty-third chapter of Luke. Herod was banished in 39 A.D. by Caligula, and died in obscurity.

Hérode, the French for HEROD, which see.

Herodes, the Latin for HEROD, which see.

He-ro'dēs, (TIBERIUS CLAUDIUS ATTICUS,) [Fr. HÉRODE ATTICUS, à'rod' à'te'küs',] an Athenian orator and statesman, born at Marathon about 110 A.D., was the son of Julius Atticus, from whom he inherited a large fortune. Having gained distinction as a rhetorician, he gave public lectures on eloquence at Athens, which were attended and admired by the *élite* of that city, and was employed by the emperor Antoninus Pius as tutor of his adopted sons, M. Aurelius and Lucius Verus. He became a Roman consul in 143, married a Roman lady named Annia Regilla, and a few years after returned to Greece. He built a theatre or Odeon at Athens, and other costly edifices in different places of Greece and Asia. He is said to have been the greatest orator of his time. His speeches and writings are all lost, except one harangue printed in Gruter's collection in 1609. He died about 185 A.D.

See PHILOSTRATUS, "Vitæ Sophistarum;" BURIGNY, "Sur la Vie d'Hérode Atticus," in the "Mémoires de l'Académie des Inscriptions."

He-ro'dēs Phil-ip'pus, a son of Herod the Great and Mariamne, was the first husband of Herodias, the persecutor of John the Baptist. He is called simply Philip by the Evangelists. (See Matthew xiv. 3, Mark vi. 17, and Luke iii. 19.)

He-ro'dĭ-an, [Gr. Ἡρωδιανός; Lat. HERODIA'NUS; Fr. HÉRODIEN, à'ro'de'ăɴ',] a historian of the third century, is thought to have lived at Rome, and to have performed a respectable part in political affairs; but the time and place of his birth are not known. He wrote, in Greek, a history of the Roman emperors whose reigns he had witnessed, comprising the period from 180 A.D. to 238, in which no less than seventeen emperors assumed the purple. His work, which is extant, is commended for veracity, moderation, and elegance of diction, and is the more prized as it is almost the only contemporary account of that eventful period.

See VOSSIUS, "De Historicis Græcis;" WOLF, "Narratio de Herodiano," prefixed to his edition of Herodian's "History," Halle, 1792; LEISNER, "Prolusio de Herodiano Historico," 1761.

Herodian, (the Grammarian.) See HERODIANUS ÆLIUS.

Herodianus. See HERODIAN.

He-ro-dĭ-ā'nus (or Herodia'nos) Æ'lĭ-us, (ee'le-us,) [Gr. Αἴλιος Ἡρωδιανός; Fr. HÉRODIEN, à'ro'de'ăɴ',] a celebrated grammarian of the second century after Christ, was a son of Apollonius Dyscolus, and was born

at Alexandria. He became a resident of Rome, and enjoyed the favour of Marcus Aurelius. He wrote many works on grammar, which are not extant. Fragments of some of them have been preserved. His work on prosody (Μεγάλη Προσωδία) was highly prized.

See FABRICIUS, "Bibliotheca Græca;" AUGUST WETTIN, "Commentatio de Herodiano Grammatico," 1842; SMITH, "Dictionary of Greek and Roman Biography."

He-rod'ĭ-cus, [Ἡρόδικος,] a Greek physician, born at Selymbria, in Thrace, lived in the fifth century B.C., and was one of the masters of Hippocrates.

Hérodien. See HERODIAN.

Herodot or **Hérodote.** See HERODOTUS.

He-rod'o-tus, [Gr. Ἡρόδοτος; Fr. HÉRODOTE, à'ro'dot'; Ger. HERODOT, hà'ro-dot; It. ERODOTO, à-rod'-o-to,] a celebrated Greek historian, born at Halicarnassus, a Dorian colony in Caria, about 484 B.C. He was the son of Lyxus and Dryo, and the nephew of the poet Panyasis. He is the earliest of the Greek historians whose works have been preserved entire, and is frequently styled "the Father of History." Cicero mentions him as "the first who adorned this species of composition." Little is known of his life, except what may be collected from his writings. Before he attained the age of thirty he took a prominent part in the expulsion of Lygdamus, the tyrant of Halicarnassus. But, having failed to gain the popular favour, he soon left his native country, spent a few years in Athens, and settled in the Athenian colony of Thurium, in Italy, in 443, where he is said to have died. Before he wrote his great national work (one of the most precious memorials of antiquity) he prepared himself by travelling over the principal countries of the civilized world, viz., Egypt, Tyre, Babylon, Asia Minor, Greece, and Italy, and by studying their manners, customs, and institutions. Throughout his narrative, however, he maintains a modest reserve respecting the extent of his travels; and it is a doubtful question in what period of his life they were performed. The principal subject of his history is the war between the Greeks and Persians, comprised in a period of sixty-eight years, from the time of Cyrus the Great to the triumph of the Greeks in 478 B.C. By way of episode, he inserts sketches of the different nations which he had visited in person. His account of Egypt is the most abundant and reliable source from which we derive our knowledge of the ancient history of that country. He is more highly appreciated by the moderns than he was by his contemporaries. Some of his marvellous stories which once excited ridicule and incredulity have been confirmed by modern discoveries. His work is pervaded by a deep religious sentiment, and by a liberal spirit towards foreigners. He unites in a high degree accuracy of observation, rectitude of intention, and the faculty of graphic description. His style is easy, natural, and sometimes poetical. Plutarch and Eusebius state that Herodotus recited his history at a public festival of the Athenians, who rewarded him with a present of ten talents. "Of the romantic historians," says Macaulay, "Herodotus is the earliest and the best. His animation, his simple-hearted tenderness, his wonderful talent for description and dialogue, and the pure, sweet flow of his language, place him at the head of narrators. He reminds us of a delightful child. . . . But he has not written a good history. . . . The faults of Herodotus are the faults of a simple and imaginative mind. . . . He wrote as it was natural that he should write. He wrote for a nation susceptible, curious, lively, insatiably desirous of novelty and excitement; for a nation in which the fine arts had attained their highest excellence, but in which philosophy was still in its infancy." (See "Essay on History," in the "Edinburgh Review," 1828.)

See CREUZER, "Herodot und Thucydides," 1798; DAHLMANN, "Herodot aus seinem Buche sein Leben," 1823; HEYSE, "De Herodoti Vita et Itineribus," 1826; BLUM, "Herodot und Ktesias die frühesten Geschichtsforscher des Orients," 1836; SMITH, "Dictionary of Greek and Roman Biography;" ERSCH und GRUBER, "Allgemeine Encyklopaedie;" DE QUINCEY, "Historical and Critical Essays," vol. i.

Herodotus, a Greek physician, who practised at Rome probably about 100 A.D., left works which are often cited by Galen.

Héroet, hà'ro'à', (ANTOINE,) a French poet, born in Paris, became Bishop of Digne in 1552. Died in 1568.

Herold, hā'rolt, (JOHANN BASIL,) a German writer and Protestant minister, born at Hochstädt, on the Danube, in 1511, edited a good edition of the Latin works of Petrarch, (1581,) and several original treatises. Died about 1570.

See BAYLE, "Historical and Critical Dictionary."

Hérold, hā'rold', (LOUIS JOSEPH FERDINAND,) an eminent French composer, born in Paris in 1791. He produced, in 1826, "Marie," an opera, which was completely successful. His capital works are "Zampa," (1831,) and "Le Pré aux Clercs," (1832.) He is called one of the first among modern French composers. Died in 1833.

See FÉTIS, "Biographie Universelle des Musiciens."

He'ron or **He'ro,** [Gr. Ἥρων,] an eminent mathematician and writer, lived in Alexandria about 100 B.C. He obtained a high reputation by his skill in geometry, mechanics, pneumatics, etc., on which he wrote several treatises. One of these mentions a machine of which steam is the motive power. His name is rendered familiar by connection with the experiment in pneumatics called "Hero's fountain." Another philosopher of this name, who is supposed to have lived in the seventh century, was noted as a writer on warlike machines, on geometry, and on military tactics.

See FABRICIUS, "Bibliotheca Græca;" R. C. WAGNER, "Dissertatio de Heronis Alexandrini Vita, Scriptis et Inventis," 1714; MONTUCLA, "Histoire des Mathématiques."

Hĕr'on, (ROBERT,) a Scottish writer, born at New Galloway in 1764, wrote a "History of Scotland," a "Universal Geography," etc. He also translated several works, and contributed to periodicals. Died in 1807.

See CHAMBERS, "Biographical Dictionary of Eminent Scotsmen."

Héron de Villefosse, hā'rôN' dĕh vĕl'foss', (ANTOINE MARIE,) a French engineer, born in Paris in 1774, became inspector-general of mines in 1807, and published a useful work, entitled "On Mineral Riches," ("De la Richesse minérale," 3 vols., 1810-19.) Died in 1852.

Hérophile. See HEROPHILUS.

He-roph'I-lus, [Gr. Ἡρόφιλος; Fr. HÉROPHILE, à'ro'-fèl',] a celebrated physician of Chalcedon, in Bithynia, was born about 344 B.C., and lived in Alexandria in the reign of Ptolemy Lagus. He was contemporary with Erasistratus, and is accounted the greatest anatomist of antiquity, as well as the first who dissected human subjects. He enriched the science with many discoveries in the nervous system, the arterial pulsations, the lacteal vessels, and the structure of the eye. The term *retina* originated with him. His writings are all lost, except extracts made from them by Galen and Cœlius Aurelianus.

See HALLER, "Bibliotheca Anatomica;" SPRENGEL, "Geschichte der Medicin;" KARL F. H. MARX, "Commentatio de Herophili Vita, Scriptis," etc., 1840.

Hérostrate. See HEROSTRATUS.

He-ros'tra-tus or **E-ros'tra-tus,** [Gr. Ἡρόστρατος; Fr. HÉROSTRATE, à'ros'tRăt',] an incendiary, who, to immortalize his name, set fire to the temple of Diana at Ephesus, in 356 B.C. The authorities of Ephesus vainly attempted to frustrate his design by ordering that his name should never be mentioned.

Herpin, hĕR'păN', (JEAN CHARLES,) a French writer on rural economy, born at Metz in 1798.

Herregouts, hĕR'goo', (HENRI,) a Flemish historical painter, born at Malines in 1666, worked mostly at Antwerp. Lacaze praises his design, colour, and the expression of his figures. Among his works are "The Last Judgment," and a penitent Magdalene. He had a son, called HERREGOUTS LE JEUNE, ("the Younger,") who was a skilful painter.

See DESCAMPS, "Vies des Peintres Flamands," etc.

Herrenschwand, hĕR'ren-shwănt', (JEAN FRÉDÉRIC,) born at Morat, in Switzerland, in 1715, became physician to Stanislas, King of Poland. Died in 1796.

Herrera, êr-rā'rā, (ALONZO,) a Spanish painter of religious subjects, born at Segovia in 1559.

Herrera, de, dà êr-rā'rā, (FERNANDO,) an eminent Spanish poet, surnamed THE DIVINE, born at Seville about 1534. Very little is known of his history. He was one of the most popular lyric poets of his time,— which is accounted the golden age of Spanish poetry. He made bold innovations in poetical language. "Her-

rera was a poet," says Bouterwek, "of powerful talent. But amid traits of real beauty his poetry everywhere presents marks of affectation." According to Hallam, "his odes appear to possess a lyric elevation and richness of phrase derived in some measure from the study of Pindar. Those on the battle of Lepanto are the most celebrated ; they pour forth a torrent of resounding song in those rich tones which the Castilian language so abundantly supplies." ("Introduction to the Literature of Europe.") His poems were published collectively in 1582. He died about 1595, or, as others say, in 1589.

See LONGFELLOW, "Poets and Poetry of Europe;" TICKNOR, "History of Spanish Literature;" N. ANTONIO, "Bibliotheca Hispana Nova."

Herrera, de, (FRANCISCO,) surnamed EL VIEJO, ("the Elder,") a skilful Spanish painter, born at Seville in 1576. He studied under Luis Fernandez, and reformed the style of the Seville school. He excelled in design, colouring, and rapidity of execution. He founded a new school, in which the famous Diego Velasquez was his pupil. Among his works is the "Last Judgment," in the church of San Bernardo, Seville. Died in 1656.

See CEAN BERMUDEZ, "Diccionario historico;" QUILLIET, "Dictionnaire des Peintres Espagnols."

Herrera, de, (FRANCISCO,) surnamed EL MOZO, ("the Younger,") a son of the preceding, born at Seville in 1622, was a painter and architect. After studying at Rome, he worked at Seville, where he painted for the churches. In 1660 he was chosen vice-president of the Academy, of which Murillo was president. Impatient of the presence of a superior, he removed to Madrid, where he gained a high reputation in oil-painting and fresco. He was appointed principal painter to Philip IV. "The Ascension of the Virgin," a fresco at Madrid, is one of his most admired works. Died in 1685.

See RAPHAEL MENGS, "Las Obras;" QUILLIET, "Dictionnaire des Peintres Espagnols," 1826.

Herrera, de, dà êr-rā'rā, (JOSÉ JOAQUIN,) a Mexican, born in the eighteenth century, became President of Mexico about the end of 1844, was deposed in December, 1845, and re-elected in June, 1848. Died in 1851.

Herrera, de, (JUAN,) an eminent Spanish architect, who was employed on the Escurial after 1567. He built the royal pleasure-house at Aranjuez. According to Prescott, he was the pupil of Toledo, and completed the Escurial, begun by that architect. Died in 1597.

See PRESCOTT, "History of Philip II.," vol. iii.

Herrera-Barnuevo, êr-rā'rā baR-nwä'vo, (SEBASTIANO,) a Spanish painter and sculptor, born at Madrid in 1619, worked for the king in the Escurial. He excelled in design and colour. Died in 1671.

Herrera y Tordesillas, êr-rā'rā e toR-dà-sèl'yăs, (ANTONIO,) an eminent Spanish historian, born at Cuellar in 1549, was the son of a man named Tordesillas ; Herrera was the name of his mother. Philip II. gave him the title of first historiographer of the Indies and of Castile. He published in 1601 his "General History of the Acts of the Castilians on the Islands and Terra Firma of the Ocean from 1492 to 1554," (4 vols.) His work is praised by Dr. Robertson for its accuracy and candour, and has served as the guide of later historians who have treated of that period. He wrote several other historical works. Died in 1625.

See PRESCOTT, "Conquest of Mexico," vol. ii. book iii., and "History of Ferdinand and Isabella," vol. ii. part ii.; TICKNOR, "History of Spanish Literature;" N. ANTONIO, "Bibliotheca Hispana Nova."

Herreros, êr-rā'ròs, (MANUEL Breton de los—bRà-tòn' dà lòs,) a popular Spanish poet, born at Quel, in Logroño, about 1798. He produced in 1824 a successful comedy, "A la Vejez Viruelas," and in 1834 was chosen keeper of the National Library in Madrid. He composed and translated many dramas, remarkable for grace and energy of diction, for comic power, and for true portraiture of character. He also wrote successful satires, among which is "The Carnival," (1833.)

See JAMES KENNEDY, "Modern Poets and Poetry of Spain," 1852.

Herrgott, hĕR'got, (MARQUARD,) a monk and antiquary, born at Friburg, in Brisgau, in 1694. He acquired a great reputation by his writings, among which are a history of the House of Hapsburg, ("Genealogia diplomatica Gentis Habsburgicæ," 2 vols., 1738,) and "Monuments of the Imperial House of Austria," (3 vols., 1750–60,) with plates. Died in 1762.

See ERSCH und GRUBER, "Allgemeine Encyklopaedie."

Herrich Schäffer or **Schaeffer,** hĕr'riK shĕf'fẹr, (GOTTLIEB AUGUST,) a German entomologist, born at Ratisbon in 1799, has published, among other works, a continuation of Panzer's "Fauna Insectorum Germaniæ," and "Nomenclator Entomologicus," (unfinished.)

Hĕr'rick, (ROBERT,) an English poet and clergyman, born in London in 1591. For about twenty years he was vicar of Dean Prior, in Devonshire, from which he was ejected by Cromwell. In 1648 he published a volume of poems, entitled "Hesperides ; or, Poems Human and Divine." Of these, the "human" excel the divine in literary merit. The tenor of them is amorous, and in some parts licentious. "Herrick has," says Hallam, "as much variety as the poetry of kisses can well have. He has much of the lively grace that distinguishes Anacreon and Catullus." ("Introduction to the Literature of Europe.") He was restored to his living in 1660. Died about 1674.

See DRAKE, "Literary Hours," and the "Retrospective Review," vol. v., 1822; CAMPBELL, "Specimens of the British Poets."

Herries, hĕr'rĕz, (JOHN CHARLES,) a British financier, born about 1780. He became secretary of the treasury in 1823, and in 1827 chancellor of the exchequer in the ministry of Goderich, which was dissolved in 1828. He was secretary of war in a Tory cabinet for a few months in 1834 and 1835, and was afterwards a prominent member of the protectionist party. In 1852 he was appointed president of the India Board. Died in 1855.

Hĕr'ring, (JOHN FREDERICK,) an English painter of animals, was born in Surrey in 1795. He was a coach-driver in his youth. He excelled in the representation of horses, hounds, and other animals. For many years he painted the winners at the Doncaster races. Among his works are "The Country Bait," "The Roadside," "The Members of the Temperance Society," and "The Baron's Charger." Died in 1865.

Herring, (THOMAS,) an English prelate, born in Norfolk in 1691. He became Bishop of Bangor in 1737, Bishop of York in 1743, and Archbishop of Canterbury in 1747. His sermons and letters were published, 1763–77. Died in 1757.

Herrliberger, hĕr'le-bĕrg'ẹr, (DAVID,) an able Swiss engraver, born at Zurich in 1697. He published a "New Topographical Description of Switzerland," with plates. Died in 1777.

Hĕr'ron, (FRANCIS J.,) an American general. He served at the battle of Pea Ridge, March, 1862, and was appointed a brigadier-general in the same year. He commanded at the battle of Prairie Grove, Arkansas, in December, 1862.

Hersan, hĕr'sŏN', (MARC ANTOINE,) a French professor and Latin poet, born at Compiègne in 1652. His Latin verses were published under the title of "Selecta Carmina." Died in 1724.

Herschel, her'shẹl, (CAROLINE LUCRETIA,) born in Hanover in 1750, was sister of Sir William Herschel, whom she assisted in his astronomical observations and computations. She lived with him near Windsor, England, from 1772 until his death, sharing his daily labours and nightly vigils, and inscribed her name with indelible and luminous characters in the records of astronomy. She has the credit of discovering five new comets between 1786 and 1797. In 1798 she published a valuable "Catalogue of Five Hundred and Sixty-One Stars observed by Flamsteed." In 1828 the Astronomical Society awarded her a gold medal for her Catalogue of Nebulæ and Clusters of Stars. Died in 1848.

Herschel, (Sir JOHN FREDERICK WILLIAM,) an eminent astronomer and philosopher, the only son of Sir William Herschel, was born at Slough, near Windsor, in 1790. He was educated in Saint John's College, Cambridge, where he displayed superior talents for mathematics. Between 1825 and 1833 he spent eight years in reviewing the nebulæ discovered by his father, of which he published a "Catalogue arranged in the Order of Right Ascension," (1833.) He produced in 1830 an excellent "Preliminary Discourse on the Study of Natural Philosophy," which acquired a great popularity and is a standard work. "This discourse," says the "London Monthly Review," "as a collection of important facts interesting to every human being, is without a rival."

In 1834 he established, at his own expense, an observatory at Cape Town, Africa, where he passed four years in the survey of the heavens with a reflecting telescope of twenty feet focus and eighteen and one-quarter inches clear aperture. The Royal Society awarded him a gold medal in 1836. He published in 1847 "Results of Astronomical Observations made during 1834–38 at the Cape of Good Hope, being the Completion of a Telescopic Survey of the Whole Surface of the Visible Heavens," one of the most important astronomical works of the nineteenth century. His "Outlines of Astronomy" (1849) was received with favour, and has passed through five or more editions. He edited an important collection of treatises, entitled "Manual of Scientific Inquiry," (1849,) published by the government. Sir John was appointed master of the mint in 1850, but resigned his office in 1855. The same year he was chosen a foreign associate of the Institute of France. Among his recent works are "Essays from the Edinburgh and Quarterly Reviews," (1857,) the articles "Meteorology" and "Physical Geography" in the "Encyclopædia Britannica," (1857–59,) and "Familiar Lectures on Scientific Subjects," (1866.)

"Sir John Herschel," says the "London Journal of Science" for April, 1868, "combines in his own person the assiduous astronomical observer, the acute mathematician, the deep-thinking philosopher, and the graceful poet. It is not to many men that intellectual powers of so high order have been given ; it is not in many men that we find such perfect balancing of those varied powers ; it is in few men that we discover such profound humility and such a deep sense of reverence for the Creator of those works the study of which has been a life-labour of love. . . . Sir John Herschel has ever maintained the serene dignity of a true philosopher, and his utterances of truths which have inspired him with their divinity have ever been received with delight by those who have listened to his subdued but impressive eloquence."

See "Edinburgh Review" for July, 1833; "London Quarterly Review" for July, 1849; "Foreign Quarterly Review" for April, 1831; "North British Review" for February, 1848.

Herschel, (Sir WILLIAM,) one of the greatest astronomers that any age or nation has produced, was born at Hanover on the 15th of November, 1738. His father was Jacob Herschel, a skilful musician, who, having six sons, was not able to give them a very complete education. They all, however, became excellent musical performers, and William adopted the profession of musician. Before he left the paternal roof he took lessons in French and cultivated a taste for metaphysics. In 1759, in company with his brother Jacob, he went to England in search of employment ; but for two or three years he received no encouragement, and suffered great privation. About 1761 he was employed to instruct a military band at Durham, or in that vicinity, and in 1765 obtained the situation of organist at Halifax. Here, by intense study, he learned Latin and Italian and acquired a thorough knowledge of mathematics. The last science he studied as preliminary to the theory of music. In 1766 he became organist of the Octagon Chapel, Bath, where his skill was in great request at oratorios, public concerts, and reunions of fashion. It appears that he was about thirty years of age before he directed his attention to astronomy and optics, in which his talents found their most congenial arena and the basis of his permanent renown. A casual view of the starry heavens through a small telescope sufficed to rouse his enthusiasm and to kindle the latent ardour of genius. He must be an astronomer ; he must have a telescope of greater power ; and, as the price demanded by opticians exceeded his resources, he resolved to construct one with his own hands. After a multitude of trials and several years of persistent application, he completed in 1774 a reflecting telescope of five feet focal length, and, stimulated by this success, did not relax his efforts until he obtained one of dimensions four times greater, with which in 1779 he began a systematic survey of the sidereal universe.

His arduous vigils and well-directed labours were rewarded in March, 1781, by the discovery of a new primary planet, which was named by him Georgium Sidus, in honour of King George, and is since called Uranus. Besides the éclat thrown around his name by this signal success, he received from George III. a pension of £400, with the title of private astronomer to the king. He was elected a Fellow of the Royal Society, who awarded to him their annual gold medal. Herschel now fixed his residence at a village near Windsor, named Slough,— "a name," says Arago, "which the sciences will transmit to the remotest posterity; for there exists no spot on the earth which has been rendered memorable by more numerous and surprising discoveries." Continuing his observations with unremitting assiduity, he discovered two new satellites of Saturn and six satellites of Uranus. He measured the rotation of Saturn, and observed the volcanic structure of the lunar mountains and the surprising phenomena of Saturn's ring. After he had made several telescopes of twenty feet focal length, he completed, in 1789, with pecuniary aid from the king, his gigantic instrument of forty feet in length, which was far superior to any that had previously been made.

He was now enabled to penetrate farther into space than his predecessors, and by his sublime speculations on the constitution of the nebulæ he made some approach to a conception of the illimitable extent and variety of the celestial phenomena. In 1803 he ascertained the motion of the double stars around each other,—the grandest fact in sidereal astronomy,—attesting the universal influence of that attractive force which binds the members of the solar system. He soon after announced that the whole solar system is progressing in the direction of the constellation Hercules. Between 1780 and 1820 he contributed seventy-one memoirs to the "Philosophical Transactions." His discoveries were so far in advance of his time, they had so little relation or resemblance to those of his predecessors, that he may be said to have initiated a new era in astronomy, and almost to have founded a new science, by revealing the immensity of the scale on which the universe is constructed. He was married in 1788, and left one son, Sir John, who inherits his father's talents and virtues. Died in August, 1822.

See Arago, "Memoir of Herschel," (translated into English,) Boston, 1859; "Edinburgh Review," vol. i.: "Edinburgh Philosophical Journal" for April, 1823; Ersch and Gruber, "Allgemeine Encyklopaedie;" Dr. Hoefer, Notice in the "Nouvelle Biographie Générale;" Zach, "Monatliche Correspondenz," vol. v.

Hersent, *hěr'sŏn',* (Charles,) a French priest and pulpit orator, born in Paris about 1595, was made chancellor of the church of Metz in 1625. He published in 1640, as a warning against Cardinal Richelieu's alleged design to make a schism in the church, a book called "Optatus Gallus," which was burned by order of Parliament. He wrote other theological treatises. Died after 1660.

Hersent, (Louis,) an eminent French painter of history, born in Paris in 1777, was admitted into the Institute in 1822. His design is correct and elegant. Among his works is "Daphnis and Chloe."

Her-sil'ı̆-a, a Sabine woman, the wife of Romulus. One account makes her the wife of Hostus and mother of Tullus Hostilius.

Hersleb, *hěrs'lěb,* (Peter,) a Norwegian divine and writer, born at Stod in 1689, became Bishop of Copenhagen in 1737. Died in 1757.

Hert, *hěrt,* or **Hertius,** *hěrt'se-ŭs,* (Johann Nikolaus,) a German jurist, born near Giessen, in Hesse-Darmstadt, in 1651, became professor of public law in Giessen about 1690. He wrote, in Latin, several valuable works, among which is "Elementa Prudentiæ civilis," (1689.) Died in 1710.

See Ersch und Gruber, "Allgemeine Encyklopaedie."

Her'tha, Her'thus, or **Ner'thus,** [allied etymologically to the English Earth, Anglo-Saxon Eorðe, German Erde, Scandinavian Jord, Alemannic Ertha, Mœso-Gothic Airtha.] Hertha was the goddess Earth among the ancient Germans, regarded by some as the wife of Thor, by others as the wife of Odin, and hence

synonymous with Frigga. She may be considered as the personification of fertility. Herthus, or Nerthus, was a male deity, with the same or similar attributes.

See Grimm, "Deutsche Mythologie;" Rabus, "Dissertatio de Dea Hertha," Augsburg, 1842.

Hertz. See Herz.

Hertz, *hěrts,* (Heiman Adolph,) a Danish poet, son of Johan Michael, noticed below, was born in 1796. He wrote a historical poem called "Gustavus Vasa," (1856.)

Hertz, (Hendrik,) an eminent Danish poet and dramatist, born at Copenhagen in 1798. He produced many comedies, among which are "The Moving-Day," ("Flyttedagen," 1828,) "Cupid's Master-Strokes," ("Amors Geniestreger," 1830,) and "The Plumage of the Swan," ("Svanehammen," 1841.) A lyrical drama, entitled "King René's Daughter," (1845,) is considered his master-piece. He traces characters with much ability. He is author of a didactic poem "On Nature and Art," (1832,) a poem called "Tyrfing," (1840,) and a fiction of great merit, entitled "Svend Dyring's House," (1837.)

See P. L. Möller, "Notice of Hertz" in the "Dansk Pantheon," 1844; Erslew, "Almindeligt Forfatter-Lexicon;" "Nouvelle Biographie Générale."

Hertz, (Johan Michael,) a Danish poet, and Bishop of Ribe, born near Vordingborg in 1766. His principal work is "The Deliverance of Israel," ("Det befriede Israel," 1804,) a poem. Died in 1825.

Hertzberg. See Herzberg.

Hertzen or **Herzen,** *hěrt'sen,* (Alexander,) a Russian socialist, and an able republican writer, born in Moscow in 1812. He published "Dilettantism in Science," (1842,) "Letters on the Study of Nature," (1845,) and a romance called "Whose Fault is it ?" ("Kto Vinovat," 1847.) In 1847 he quitted Russia, to the government of which he vowed implacable hostility. He afterwards resided in England, where he founded a "Russian Free Press" and issued several works in Russian. Among his publications are "Letters from France and Italy," (1850,) and memoirs of his life, entitled "My Exile," (2 vols., 1855.) Died in Paris in 1870.

See "Nouvelle Biographie Générale."

Hervas, *ěr'vâs,* (José Martinez,) Marquis of Almanara, a Spanish diplomatist, born at Uxyar in 1760. In 1806 he was sent as minister to Constantinople. Returning to Spain in 1809, he became minister of the interior under Joseph Bonaparte. Died in 1830.

Hervas y Panduro, *ěr'vâs e pân-doo'ro,* (Lorenzo,) a Spanish Jesuit and philologist, born at Horcajo in 1735. He made extensive researches into the origin and affinity of languages, and published a "Catalogue of the Known Languages, with Remarks on their Affinity and Diversity," (1784,) "Polyglot Vocabulary of more than One Hundred and Fifty Tongues, with Introductory Observations," and a "Collection of the Versions of the Lord's Prayer in more than Three Hundred Tongues," (1787.) Died in 1809.

See Adelung, "Mithridates;" "Nouvelle Biographie Générale."

Hervé, *ěr'vâ',* born in Champagne, became Archbishop of Rheims in 900 a.d., and grand chancellor of France in 911. Died in 922.

Hervé-Fierabras, *ěr'vâ' fe'ĕh-rä'brä',* a French physician, born at Rouen, lived about 1550. He published an able treatise on Surgery, (1550.)

Hervet, *hěr'vȧ',* (Gentian,) a learned French theologian, born near Orléans in 1499, distinguished himself at the Council of Trent, (1545,) and wrote against Calvinism. He translated some works of the Greek Fathers into Latin. Died in 1584.

See Nicéron, "Mémoires;" De Thou, "Éloges," with additions of Teissier.

Her'vey, (Augustus John,) third Earl of Bristol, son of Lord John, noticed below, was born in 1724. He became a post-captain in 1747, and displayed courage in several battles in the Mediterranean and in the West Indies. In 1771 he was appointed one of the lords of the admiralty, and in 1775, by the death of an elder brother, became Earl of Bristol. Soon after this he was created an admiral. He died in 1779, and his title was inherited by his brother Frederick, Bishop of Derry.

Hervey, (Eleonora Louisa,) an authoress, whose maiden name was Montague, born at Liverpool in 1811.

ā, ē, ī, ō, ū, y̅, *long;* ă, ĕ, ŏ, same, less prolonged; ă, ĕ, ĭ, ŏ, ŭ, y̆, *short;* ạ, ẹ, į, ọ, *obscure;* fär, fäll, fät; mĕt; nŏt; gŏŏd; mōōn;

She began to write graceful verses for the periodicals at an early age, and published in 1839 "The Landgrave," a dramatic poem. In 1843 she was married to Thomas K. Hervey, noticed below. Among her works are tales in prose, entitled "Margaret Russell," (1849,) and "The Pathway of the Fawn," (1851.)

Hervey, (FREDERICK,) fourth Earl of Bristol, born in 1730, was a brother of Augustus John, noticed above. He became Bishop of Derry in 1768, and succeeded to the earldom on the death of his brother, in 1779. He was eccentric in habits, and was a liberal patron of the fine arts. Died at Albano, Italy, in 1803.

Hervey, (JAMES,) an English divine and author, born at Hardingstone, near Northampton, in 1714, was educated at Oxford University, and was a good classical scholar. Having taken orders, he became curate of Dummer in 1736, and of Bideford in 1738. From 1743 until 1750 he was curate of Weston Favell, of which his father was rector, and at the death of the latter, in 1752, the son obtained that living. He was noted for piety and benevolence. His "Meditations and Contemplations," published in 1746, were extensively popular, notwithstanding his faulty style, which is too flowery and sublimated to please the most correct taste. These very faults probably rendered him a greater favourite with the common people, as Southey represents the book as equally "laudable in purport and vicious in style, and therefore one of the most popular that ever was written." It is or was generally found on the shelves of English cottages by the side of the Bible and "Pilgrim's Progress." Hervey also wrote "Theron and Aspasia, a Series of Dialogues and Letters," and a few minor works. Died in 1758.

See COLE, "Herveiana; or, Graphic and Literary Sketches of James Hervey," 1822-26; JOHN BROWN, "Life and Character of J. Hervey," 1822.

Hervey, (Lord JOHN,) an English writer, born in 1696, was the eldest son of the first Earl of Bristol. He obtained a seat in Parliament soon after the accession of George I., and in 1730 became a privy councillor. In 1733 he was raised to the peerage, as Baron Hervey of Ickworth, and in 1740 was appointed lord privy seal in the cabinet of Walpole. He wrote able political pamphlets, verses, and an "Epistle from a Nobleman to a Doctor of Divinity," the last of which was an answer to Pope, who satirized him, in the character of Sporus, as "the mere white curd of asses' milk." He also wrote interesting "Memoirs of the Court of George II." Died in 1743.

See HORACE WALPOLE, "Royal and Noble Authors;" "Edinburgh Review" for October, 1848.

Hervey, (THOMAS KIBBLE,) an English poet and editor, born in Manchester in 1804. He studied at Cambridge and Oxford. In 1824 he published "Australia, and other Poems," which was received with favour. His "Poetical Sketch-Book" appeared in 1829. He afterwards produced "Illustrations of Modern Sculpture," (1832,) a work of merit, and "The Book of Christmas," (1836.) From 1846 to 1854 he was chief editor of the "Athenæum." Died in February, 1859.

Herwarth von Bittenfeld, hĕr'wart fon bit'tĕn-fĕlt', a Prussian general, commanded a corps of the army which entered Bohemia under the crown-prince and contributed to the victory of Sadowa, July 3, 1866.

Herwart von Hohenburg, hĕr'wart fon ho'ĕn-bōōrG', (JOHANN GEORG,) a German scholar, born at Augsburg in 1554; died in 1622.

See ERSCH und GRUBER, "Allgemeine Encyklopaedie."

Herwegh, hĕr'wĕG, (GEORG,) a popular German lyric poet, born at Stuttgart in 1817. He published at Zurich, in 1841, a volume of republican or liberal poems, entitled "Gedichte eines Lebendigen," ("Poems of a Living Man,") which had great success. He became a citizen of Bâle, and about 1845 joined the radicals of Paris. In the spring of 1848 he raised a legion and invaded Baden with a design to revolutionize it; but he failed, and took refuge in Switzerland.

See LONGFELLOW, "Poets and Poetry of Europe;" F. LIPP, "G. Herwegh's viertägige Irr- und Wanderfahrt mit der Pariser Deutschdemokratischen Legion," etc., 1850; "Foreign Quarterly Review" for April, 1843.

Héry, de, dĕh hã're', (THIERRY,) a skilful French surgeon, born in Paris about 1505. Having practised with success in Paris, he was employed by Francis I. in the army of Italy, and acquired a great reputation by the cure of syphilis, on which he wrote an original and able treatise,—the first ever written in French on that subject. Died in 1599.

See ÉLOI, "Dictionnaire de la Médecine."

Herz, hĕrts, (HEINRICH,) a celebrated pianist and composer, born at Vienna in 1806. He met with brilliant success in London, Edinburgh, and Paris, and afterwards resided several years in America. As a performer he is scarcely surpassed, and his pieces for the piano are general favourites.

Herz, (HENRIETTA,) a German lady, distinguished for her wit and beauty, born in Berlin in 1764. She married M. Herz about 1780. Her house in Berlin was frequented by many eminent men. Died in 1847.

Herz, (MARCUS,) a German physician, born at Berlin in 1747; died in 1803.

Herzberg or **Hertzberg, von,** fon hĕrts'bĕrG, (EWALD FRIEDRICH,) a celebrated Prussian statesman, born near Neustettin in 1725. He filled several important posts under Frederick the Great, and, after negotiating a treaty of peace with Russia and Sweden in 1762, was appointed second minister of state. He was made a count by Frederick's successor, and also curator of the Academy at Berlin. Died in 1795. He was a zealous patron of learning, particularly of German literature.

See POSSELT, "Ewald Friedrich Graf von Hertzberg," 1798; WEDDIGEN, "Fragmente aus dem Leben des Grafen von Hertzberg," 1796; "Nouvelle Biographie Générale."

Heselrige. See HAZLERIG.

Heshâm, (Heschâm,) hĕsh-âm', or **Hishâm,** hish-âm', (or, more fully, **Heshâm-Ibn-Abd-el-Malek,** hĕsh-âm' Ib'n âbd-el mâl'ek, i.e. "Heshâm the son of Abd-el-Malek,") the tenth caliph of the house of Omeyyah, succeeded his cousin, Omar II., in 724 A.D. During the reign of Heshâm, Abd-er-Rahman, one of his generals, invaded France, where he was defeated and slain by Charles Martel, October 25, 732. Heshâm died in 743, leaving the reputation of an eminently just and virtuous sovereign.

See WEIL, "Geschichte der Chalifen," vol. i. chap. xiv.

Heshâm (or Hishâm) I., (or, more fully, **Heshâm-Abool (-Aboul or -Abûl) -Waleed, (-Walîd,)** â'bōōl wâ-leed',) second Emir or King of Córdova of the Omeyyah dynasty, succeeded his father, Abd-er-Rahman, in 788 A.D. He waged a successful war against the Christians of Galicia, Astorga, etc., founded schools, and promoted the arts. Died in 796.

Heshâm (or Hishâm) II., (El- (or Al-, âl) Muyyed-Billah, el mōō'e-yed bil'lah,) sometimes corrupted into ISSAM or ISSEM by the Spanish historians, was born in 965, and succeeded his father, Hakem II., on the throne of Córdova, in 976 A.D. In his minority the kingdom enjoyed prosperity under the ministry of the famous Al-Mansoor, who gained victories over the Kings of Leon and Navarre. After the death of Al-Mansoor the reign was disturbed by rebellions and anarchy, and the feeble king became a prisoner of Soleimân, and died, or was killed, about 1012.

See AL-MAKKARI, "History of the Mohammedan Dynasties in Spain."

Heshâm (or Hishâm) III., (El-Mo'tad-Bil'lah, or **Al-Mutadd- (âl mōō'tâd) Billah,)** became King of Córdova in 1026, and was the last of the Omeyyah dynasty. Several nobles having refused allegiance to him, he attempted, without success, to subdue them by arms. In 1031 a sedition in the capital forced him to abdicate. Died in 1036.

Heshusius, hês-hoo'ze-ûs, (TILLEMANNUS,) a German Lutheran divine, born at Wesel in 1526, was an opponent of Calvinism. Died in 1588.

Hesiod, hee'she-od, [Gr. Ἡσίοδος; Lat. HE'SIODUS; Fr. HÉSIODE, â'ze'od'; Ger. HESIOD, hä'ze-ot; It. ESIODO, â-see'o-do,] an eminent Greek poet, born at Ascra, in Bœotia, at the foot of Mount Helicon, lived probably about 800 B.C. According to most modern critics, his period was posterior to that of Homer, with whom some writers have conjectured that he was contemporary.

From his own writings the fact is derived that he was a competitor in a poetical contest at Chalcis on the occasion of the funeral of Amphidamas, and that he gained the prize. It appears that he was employed in pastoral and rural pursuits, his knowledge of which is evinced by his most famous poem, entitled Ἔργα καὶ Ἡμέραι; ("Works and Days.") This work contains reflections and precepts on farming and rural economy, interspersed with maxims of morality and mythical fables. Aristotle, Plato, and Cicero eulogize this poem, and Virgil derived from it the idea of his "Georgics," in which he has surpassed his model. According to Pausanias, the Bœotians regarded this as the only genuine work of Hesiod. The other poems commonly ascribed to the Ascræan bard are entitled "Theogony" and "The Shield of Hercules." The former purports to be an account of the origin of the world and the birth of the gods, and is the most ancient composition we have on the subject of Greek mythology. It is characterized by a rude simplicity which sometimes rises into sublimity, and by that speculative tendency which was afterwards so largely developed in the Hellenic philosophy. "The Shield of Hercules" is a fragment or collection of fragments, supposed to be written by different authors. Quintilian says, apparently in reference to the "Works and Days," "He is distinguished by useful sentences of morality and a sweetness of expression, and he deserves the palm in the middle style of writing." According to Plutarch, Hesiod was murdered at Locris, in revenge for a crime of which he was erroneously suspected.

See PAUSANIAS, ix. and x.; LUCIAN, "Dialogue on Hesiod;" CREUZER und HERMANN, "Briefe über Homer und Hesiod," 1817; HEYNE, "De Theogonia ab Hesiodo Condita," 1779; HERMANN, "De Hesiodi Theogoniæ Forma antiquissima," 1844; ERSCH und GRUBER, "Allgemeine Encyklopaedie;" GIOVANNI LAMI, "Saggio delle delizie dei dotti e degli eruditi, risguardante le Vite e gli Scritti dei due primi grandi Uomini dell' Antichità, Esiodo ed Omero," 1775; "Quarterly Review" for March, 1832.

He-sī'o-ne, [Gr. Ἡσιόνη,] a daughter of Laomedon, King of Troy. The poets feigned that Hercules delivered her from a sea-monster after her father had promised to give him the horses he had received from Jupiter; but Laomedon failed to keep his word. She became the wife of Telamon and mother of Teucer.

Hesnault or **Hénault,** hȧ'nō', (JEAN,) a French poet, born in Paris, was educated by Gassendi. He appears to have been an Epicurean or materialist. In 1670 he published a volume of sonnets, letters, etc. He translated a large part of Lucretius. Died in 1682.

See BAYLE, "Historical and Critical Dictionary."

Hesperiden. See HESPERIDES.

Hes-pĕr'ĭ-dēs, [Gr. Ἑσπερίδες; Fr. HESPÉRIDES, ĕs'-pȧ'rĕd'; Ger. HESPERIDEN, hĕs-pȧ-ree'dĕn,] the "children of Hesperus," (or "of the evening,") the name of three or four celebrated nymphs of classic mythology, who guarded the golden apples growing in an enchanted garden in the western part of the world. According to some authors, they were the daughters of Atlas, and hence were called ATLAN'TIDES. A large dragon assisted them to guard the golden apples which were the subject of one of the twelve labours of Hercules.

Hes-pe'rĭ-us, a Roman civil officer, was a son of the poet Ausonius. He was proconsul of Africa about 376 A.D., and afterwards prætorian prefect of Rome.

Hes'pę-rus, [Gr. Ἓσπερος; Fr. HESPER, ĕs'pair', or HESPÉROS, ĕs'pȧ'ros',] a personage of classic mythology, said to be a son or brother of Atlas. According to one tradition, he ascended Mount Atlas to observe the stars, and disappeared. He received divine honours, and was identified with the evening star. One account says he came to Italy, which received from him the name of Hesperia.

Hĕss, (JOHANN JAKOB,) one of the most eminent of the Swiss Protestant theologians, was born in Zurich in 1741. He wrote, in German, "The Three Last Years of the Life of Jesus," (6 vols., 1768–73; 8th edition, 1828,) "On the Kingdom of God," (1774,) a "History of the Israelites before Jesus," (12 vols., 1776–88,) and other works. He became first minister of Zurich in 1795. Died in 1828.

See GEORG GESSNER, "J. J. Hess, voorgesteld in eenege Omtrekken van zijn Leven en Werkzamheid," 1830; ERSCH und GRUBER, "Allgemeine Encyklopaedie;" H. ESCHER, "J. J. Hess, Skizze seines Lebens," etc., 1837.

Hess, (KARL ADOLF HEINRICH,) a German artist, born at Dresden in 1769, acquired a high reputation as a painter of horses. Among his master-pieces we may cite "The March of the Cossacks through Bohemia in 1799." Died in 1849.

Hess, (KARL ERNST CHRISTOPH,) a German engraver, born at Darmstadt in 1755. He was appointed in 1782 professor in the Academy of Arts at Dusseldorf, where he was afterwards employed to engrave the pictures of the gallery. Among his best works are "The Ascension of Mary," after Guido, and a "Holy Family," after Raphael. About 1806 he settled at Munich, where he died in 1828.

See FUESSLI, "Schweizer Künstler."

Hess, (LUDWIG,) an excellent Swiss landscape-painter, born at Zurich in 1760. He painted many pictures of Alpine scenery. "His works," says the "Biographie Universelle," "surpass all that we know in their kind for correctness of design, for the taste displayed in the composition, for truth of colouring, and for the transparency of the water." He engraved some of his own designs. Died in 1800.

Hess, (PETER,) a brother of the painter Heinrich von Hess, noticed below, was born at Dusseldorf in 1792. In 1839 he was invited to Russia, where he painted eight large pictures representing the battles of 1812. He is regarded as one of the first battle-painters of recent times.

See NAGLER, "Neues Allgemeines Künstler-Lexikon."

Hess, von, fon hĕss, (HEINRICH,) BARON, an Austrian general, born in Vienna in 1788. He fought at Wagram, (1809,) and became colonel in 1829. In 1842 he was made a lieutenant field-marshal. As quartermaster-general, he rendered important services in Italy in 1848. The chief merit of this campaign is ascribed to him. He was appointed chief of the staff of the Austrian army, (*Chef des Generalstabs,*) and master of the ordnance, (*Feldzeugmeister,*) in 1849. He succeeded Gyulai soon after the battle of Magenta, formed the plan of the battle of Solferino, July, 1859, and, after the emperor left the army, was the commander-in-chief.

Hess, von, (HEINRICH,) a distinguished historical painter, a son of the engraver Karl Ernst Hess, noticed above, was born at Dusseldorf in 1798. He became professor in the Academy of Munich in 1826. The frescos in the Basilica of Saint Boniface and in the church of All Saints in Munich are among his master-pieces.

Hesse, hĕss, (JEAN BAPTISTE ALEXANDRE,) a French painter, a nephew of the following, was born in Paris in 1806. Among his best works is "The Funeral Honours rendered to Titian," (1833.)

Hesse, (NICOLAS AUGUSTE,) a French painter of history, born in Paris in 1795, won a medal of the first class in 1838.

Hesse, hĕs'sęh, (PHILIPP,) LANDGRAVE OF, surnamed THE MAGNANIMOUS, was born in 1504. He avowed himself a convert to the Reformed religion in 1526, signed the creed called the Confession of Augsburg in 1530, and entered into a league with the Protestant princes by the treaty of Schmalkalden in 1531. He distinguished himself in the war which the German Protestants waged against Charles V. in 1546, but was taken captive and imprisoned four years. He died in 1567.

See HARTMANN, "Historia Hessiaca," 1741; TURKHEIM, "Histoire de la Maison souveraine de Hesse," 2 vols., 1819-20.

Hesse, (WILHELM IV.,) LANDGRAVE OF, a son of the preceding, surnamed THE WISE, was born at Cassel about 1545. He reigned in peace, and was distinguished as a patron of sciences, especially astronomy, which he cultivated himself with diligence. He founded an observatory at Cassel in 1561, and made observations for many years. The results of these labours were published by W. Snellius, (1628.) Died in 1597.

Hesse-Philippsthal, von, fon hĕs'sęh fee'lips-tȧl', (LUDWIG,) a German general, born in 1766, was a son of the Landgrave of Hesse. Died in 1816.

Hesselbach, hĕs'sęl-bȧk', (FRANZ KASPAR,) a German anatomist, born near Fulda in 1759; died in 1816.

Hesselink, hĕs'sęh-link, sometimes written **Hesseling,** (GERARD,) a Dutch writer and Anabaptist preacher, born at Groningen in 1755. He published a "Hermeneutical Dictionary of the New Testament," and several other works. Died in 1811.

See KOOPMANS, "Hulde aan G. Hesselink," 1812.

Hes-se'lĭ-us, [Sw. pron. hĕs-sĭ'le-ùs,] (ANDERS,) a poet of Swedish extraction, born in North America, became a teacher of English at Upsal. He wrote "Eric IX.," (1739,) "The Twelve Charleses," (of Sweden,) ("De Tolf Caroler," 1748,) and other works. He was living in 1755.

Hesselius, hĕs-sā'le-us, (FRANS,) a Dutch philologist, born at Rotterdam in 1680; died in 1746.

Hesselius, (JOHAN,) a Swedish savant, born at Fahlun in 1687; died in 1752.

Hessels, hĕs'sęls, or **Hesselius** (JEAN,) born at Louvain in 1522, was noted as a theologian. He was a member of the Council of Trent, and author of many theological works, among which are a "Catechism," and "Commentaries on Scripture." Died in 1566.

Hessus. See EOBAN.

He'sus, a deity of the ancient Gauls, corresponding to the Mars of the Romans. See MARS.

He-sy̆ch'ĭ-us, [Gr. Ἡσύχιος,] the author of a valuable Greek Lexicon, (first printed by Aldus in 1514,) which explains technical terms, unusual words found in the works of poets, orators, and physicians, terms used in sacrifices, divinations, and such as depart from ordinary usage. It is supposed that the existing text is an abridgment or imperfect copy of the original. The time in which Hesychius lived is not known; but it was probably since the Christian era, as numerous scriptural glosses or phrases are found in his work.

See PEARSON, "Adversaria Hesychiana," 2 vols., 1844; ERSCH und GRUBER, "Allgemeine Encyklopaedie."

Hesychius OF MILETUS, [Lat. HESYCH'IUS MILE'-SIUS,] surnamed THE ILLUSTRIOUS, lived in the sixth century. He wrote (in Greek) a universal history from Belus to his own times, (about 520 A.D.,) of which some fragments only are now extant. He left also an abridgment of the "Lives of the Philosophers," derived chiefly from Diogenes Laertius. This was published by J. C. Orelli, Leipsic, 1820.

See THORSCHMID, "De Hesychio Milesio illustri Christiano Commentatio," in Orelli's edition just mentioned.

Hĕth, (HENRY,) born in Virginia, became a brigadier-general in the Confederate service in 1862.

Hetherington, heth'ę-rĭng-tǫn, (WILLIAM M.,) a Scottish theologian and historian of the present century, wrote a "History of the Church of Scotland," (1841,) and other works.

Hetsch, hĕtsh, (GUSTAV FRIEDRICH,) a German architect, born at Stuttgart in 1788, lived in Copenhagen.

Hetsch, von, fon hĕtsh, (PHILIPP FRIEDRICH,) a painter, father of the preceding, was born at Stuttgart in 1758. Among his works are "Paris and Helen," and "Marius among the Ruins of Carthage." Died in 1838.

Hettner, hĕt'nęr, (HERMANN JULIUS THEODOR,) a German archæologist, born in Silesia in 1821, wrote "The Plastic Arts among the Ancients," (1848.)

Hetzel or **Hezel,** hĕt'sęl, (JOHANN WILHELM,) a German Orientalist, born at Königsberg, in Franconia, in 1754, published grammars of the Hebrew, Arabic, and Syriac languages, and "The Old and New Testament, with Notes," (10 vols., 1780-91.) Died in 1829.

See ERSCH und GRUBER, "Allgemeine Encyklopaedie."

Hetzel, hĕt'sĕl', (PIERRE JULES,) a French *littérateur,* whose pseudonym is P. J. STAHL, born at Chartres in 1814. He has published "Scenes from Animal Life," "The Devil in Paris," "History of a Man with a Cold," "Beasts and People," and other attractive works. George Sand has compared him to Sterne.

Heugh, hū, (HUGH,) a Scottish divine, born in 1782. He published, besides other works, "The State of Religion in Geneva and Belgium," (1844.) Died in 1846.

See his "Life and Select Works," by H. MACGILL, 1850; CHAMBERS, "Biographical Dictionary of Eminent Scotsmen;" "North British Review" for November, 1850.

Heumann, hoi'mȧn, (CHRISTOPH AUGUST,) a German writer on various subjects, born in Saxe-Weimar in 1681. He became professor of theology at Göttingen in 1734. Among his works are "Acts of the Philosophers," ("Acta Philosophorum," 3 vols., 1715-27,) and

an "Exposition of the New Testament," (1750-63.) Died in 1764.

See HEYNE, "Memoria Heumanni," 1764; CASSIUS, "Lebensbeschreibung Heumanns," 1768; ERSCH und GRUBER, "Allgemeine Encyklopaedie."

Heumann von Teutschenbrunn, hoi'mȧn fon toitsh'ęn-bRōōn', (JOHANN,) a German jurist and writer, born in Bavaria in 1711; died in 1760.

Heun, hoin, (KARL GOTTLOB SAMUEL,) a German novelist, born in Lusatia in 1771. He wrote under the pseudonym of H. CLAUREN. Died in 1854.

Heures. See HORÆ.

Heurn, van. See HEURNIUS.

Heurnius, huR'ne-us, [in Dutch, VAN HEURN, vȧn huRn,] (JAN,) an eminent physician, born at Utrecht in 1543, was appointed in 1581 professor of medicine at Leyden, and physician to Maurice of Nassau. He wrote a good commentary on Hippocrates, (1609,) and other medical works. Died in 1601.

See ERSCH und GRUBER, "Allgemeine Encyklopaedie."

Heurteloup, huRt'loo', (CHARLES LOUIS,) a French surgeon, born in Paris in 1793, made improvements in lithotrity, which were generally adopted, and wrote several treatises on that subject.

Heurteloup, (NICOLAS,) an eminent French surgeon, father of the preceding, born at Tours in 1750. About 1800 he was appointed first surgeon of the French armies, and received the title of baron. Died in 1812.

Heus, hus, or hös, or **Heusch, van,** vȧn hush, (WILLEM,) a Dutch landscape-painter, born at Utrecht about 1630, was a pupil of John Both. His pictures of scenery on the Rhine are commended. Died at Utrecht about 1700. His nephew and pupil, JACOB, born at Utrecht in 1657, was a good landscape-painter. "His landscapes," says the "Nouvelle Biographie Générale," "are full of nature, his touch easy, and his colour true." Died in 1701.

See DESCAMPS, "Vies des Peintres Flamands, Hollandais," etc.

Heusch, van, vȧn husk or hösk, (ABRAHAM,) a Dutch painter of plants, insects, etc., was born at Utrecht in 1650; died in 1712.

Heuschling, husk'ling or hush'lȧn', (ÉTIENNE,) a Belgian philologist, born at Luxemburg in 1762, was professor of Hebrew at Louvain. Died in 1847.

Heuschling, (PHILIPPE FRANÇOIS XAVIER,) a Belgian economist, a nephew of the preceding, born at Luxemburg in 1802, published an "Essay on Universal Ethnographic Statistics," (1847-49.)

Heusde, hŭs'dęh, [Lat. HEUS'DIUS,] (PHILIPPUS WILLEM,) an eminent Dutch writer, born at Rotterdam in 1778, became professor of eloquence and history at Utrecht, where he lectured with great success. He published several works on philosophy, history, and education, among which is "The Socratic School," ("De Socratische School," 4 vols., 1834-39.) Died in 1839.

See KIST, "Memoria Heusdii," 1839; STÖCKFELD, "Andenken an den grossen Professor P. W. van Heusde," 1840; ROVERS, "Memoria Heusdii," 1841; ROULEZ, "Notice biographique sur P. G. van Heusde," 1841.

Heusdius. See HEUSDE.

Heusinger, hoi'zing'er, (JAKOB FRIEDRICH,) a German philologist and scholar, born at Useborn in 1719, was rector of the College of Wolfenbüttel. His edition of Cicero's "De Officiis" (1783) is called a master-piece in respect to criticism. Died in 1778.

Heusinger, (JOHANN MICHAEL,) an uncle of the preceding, was born near Gotha in 1690, and was an able philologist. He taught at Gotha and Eisenach, and published editions of Julian's "Emperors" and Æsop's "Fables," (1741.) Died in 1751.

See ERSCH und GRUBER, "Allgemeine Encyklopaedie;" F. A. TOEPFER, "Vita J. M. Heusingeri," 1751.

Heusinger, (KARL FRIEDRICH,) a physician, born near Eisenach in 1792, published, besides other works, "Outlines of an Encyclopædia and Methodology of Natural and Medical Sciences," (3 vols., 1844-53.)

Heuzet, hŭh'zȧ', (JEAN,) a French classical scholar, born at Saint-Quentin about 1660; died in 1728.

Hevel. See HEVELIUS.

He-ve'lĭ-us, [Ger. pron. hȧ-vā'le-ùs,] (**Joannes** or **John Hevel**—hā'vęl, written also **Hovel** and **He-**

welcke,) an eminent astronomer, born at Dantzic in 1611, was a pupil of Kruger. His parents were noble and wealthy. After studying at Leyden and making the tour of Europe, he devoted his uninterrupted attention to astronomy for nearly fifty years. In 1641 he built an observatory at his own residence, which he furnished with telescopes and other instruments made by his own hands. In 1647 he published "Selenographia," a description of the moon, with plates, followed by letters on the "Libration of the Moon," and on Eclipses, (1654.) His treatise on the phases of Saturn appeared in 1656, and his "Observations on the Transit of Mercury" in 1661. He wrote, also, "Cometographia," a general description of comets, (1668.) Hevelius was chosen a Fellow of the Royal Society of London in 1664. He was repeatedly elected consul and judge by his fellow-citizens, by whom he was highly esteemed. In 1673 he published the first part of his "Machina Cœlestis," a description of his observatory, instruments, and *modus operandi,* the second part of which appeared in 1679. In the latter year a fire consumed his observatory, library, and nearly all the copies of the book just named. After his death his widow published "Harbinger of Astronomy," ("Prodromus Astronomiæ,") and "Firmamentum Sobieskanum," dedicated to John Sobieski, King of Poland. In skill, accuracy, and diligence in observation, he was an astronomer of a very high, if not of the first, order. Died in 1687.

See H. WESTPHAL, "Leben, Studien und Schriften des J. Hevelius," 1820; HUTTON, "Mathematical and Philosophical Dictionary," article "Hevelius;" MONTUCLA, "Histoire des Mathématiques;" ERSCH und GRUBER, "Allgemeine Encyklopaedie."

Hévin, hǎ'vǎN', (PIERRE,) a French jurist, born at Rennes in 1621; died in 1692.

Hévin, (PRUDENT,) a French surgeon, born in Paris in 1715. Having distinguished himself as royal professor of therapeutics, he was employed by Louis XV. to attend the dauphiness. Some years later he became first surgeon to the dauphin. In 1780 he published a "Course of Pathology and Therapeutics." Died in 1789.

Hewelcke. See HEVELIUS.

Hewes, hūz, (JOSEPH,) an American patriot, born in New Jersey in 1730, settled at Edenton, North Carolina, about 1760. In 1774 he represented a district of North Carolina in Congress, and signed the Declaration of Independence in 1776. Having been re-elected to Congress, he died at his post, in Philadelphia, in 1779.

See GOODRICH, "Lives of the Signers to the Declaration of Independence."

Hew'itt, (MARY ELIZABETH,) originally Miss MOORE, an American poetess, born in Malden, Massachusetts. In 1829 she removed to New York. Her principal works are "Songs of Our Land, and other Poems," (1845,) and the "Heroines of History," (in prose, 1856.)

See GRISWOLD, "Female Poets of America."

Hew'son, (WILLIAM,) an English surgeon, born at Hexham in 1739. In 1759 he attended the lectures of John and William Hunter in London, with whom he was afterwards associated as a lecturer on anatomy. In 1771 he was chosen a Fellow of the Royal Society, which awarded him the Copley medal for his researches in the lymphatic system of birds and fishes. In 1772 he published "Experimental Inquiries into the Properties of the Blood." He was an eminent anatomist, and made valuable discoveries in the nature of blood. Died in 1774.

Hexham, (RICHARD OF.) See RICHARD OF HEXHAM.

Hey, hā, (JOHN,) a learned divine of the Anglican Church, born in England in 1734. From 1780 to 1795 he was first Norrisian professor of divinity at Cambridge. He wrote an "Essay on Redemption," (a prize poem,) "Lectures on Divinity," and other esteemed works. Died in 1815.

Hey, (WILLIAM,) F.R.S., an English surgeon of Leeds, born in 1736; died in 1819.

See his Life, by JOHN PEARSON.

Heyden, van der, vǎn der hī'den, or **Heyde,** hī'deh, an eminent Dutch painter, born at Gorcum about 1637. He exercised his talents with great success on architectural subjects and landscapes. He excelled in chiaroscuro. His pictures of cities, temples, palaces, and ruins are admired for their general effect, mellow tints, and

exquisite finish. The figures in some of his works are painted by A. van der Velde. Died at Amsterdam in 1712.

See J. C. WEYERMAN, "De Schilderkonst der Nederlanders;" DESCAMPS, "Vies des Peintres Flamands, Hollandais," etc.

Heyden, von, fon hī'den, COUNT, born in 1772, entered the Russian service, and became a rear-admiral in 1817. He commanded the Russian fleet at the battle of Navarino, in 1827. Died in 1850.

Heyden, von, fon hī'den, (FRIEDRICH AUGUST,) a German poet, born near Heilsberg, in East Prussia, in 1789. He was one of the governors of the prince-royal of Prussia, and in 1826 became royal councillor at Breslau. Among his chief works are "Conradin," and other successful dramas; "Reginald," a poem, (1831,) which is admired; and "The Shepherd of Ispahan," ("Der Schäfer von Ispahan," 1850,) an excellent romantic poem. Died in 1851.

See T. MUNDT, "Das Leben Heydens," 1852.

Heydenreich, hī'den-rīK', (KARL HEINRICH,) an ingenious philosophic writer, born at Stolpen, in Saxony, in 1764, was a disciple of Kant. He became professor of philosophy at Leipsic in 1789. He wrote verses on "Solitude," and other short poems, of some merit, which were published in 2 vols., 1792. Among his prose works are "Letters on Atheism," (1796,) "Psychological Development of Superstition," (1797,) and "Philosophy considered with Respect to the Sufferings of Humanity," (2 vols., 1798.) Died in 1801.

See SCHELLE, "Characteristik C. H. Heydenreich's," 1802; WOHLFAHRT, "Die letzten Lebensjahre C. H. Heidenreich's," 1802; EICHHORN, "Geschichte der Literatur," vol. iv.

Heydt, von der, fon dĕr hit, (AUGUST,) a Prussian statesman, born in Elberfeld in 1801. He was appointed minister of commerce, industry, and public works in December, 1848.

Heyking,von, fon hī'king,(HEINRICH KARL,) BARON, born in Koorland (Courland) in 1751, was appointed a senator by Paul I. of Russia. Died in 1809.

Heylin, hā'lIn, ? (PETER,) an English writer, born at Burford in 1600. In 1621 he wrote his "Microcosmos." In 1629 he became chaplain to Charles I., and obtained several benefices, from which in the civil war he was ejected as a partisan of Laud and the High Church. He wrote a "Life of Bishop Laud," a "Defence of the Church of England," (1658,) and other theological works. Died in 1662.

See GEORGE VERNON, "Life of P. Heylin," 1681; DR. BARNARD, "Life of P. Heylin," 1682.

Heym. See HEIM.

Heyn, (PIETER.) See HEIN.

Heyne, hī'neh, [Lat. HEY'NIUS,] (CHRISTIAN GOTTLOB,) an illustrious German scholar and critic, was born at Chemnitz, in Saxony, in 1729. Owing to the poverty of his family, he enjoyed few advantages of education; but, having by nature an irrepressible desire for knowledge, he improved to the utmost the opportunities which he possessed, so that in 1763 he succeeded Gesner as professor of eloquence at Göttingen. He was soon after made chief librarian of the university. His lectures, illustrating the history and mythology of the ancients in the most attractive manner, gained him a high reputation, which was increased by his numerous and excellent writings. Among the most important of these are editions of Tibullus, (1755,) Virgil, Epictetus, (1756,) Pindar, etc., with commentaries, and "Opuscula Academica," (6 vols., 1785-1812.) Died at Göttingen in July, 1812.

"Nothing," says Sir William Hamilton, "has contributed so decisively to maintain and promote the study of classical literature, as the combination which Heyne has effected of philosophy with erudition, both in his commentaries on the ancient authors and in those works in which he has illustrated various points of antiquity." ("Encyclopædia Britannica.")

See HEEREN, "C. G. Heyne, biographisch dargestellt," 1812; DACIER, "Éloge de Heyne;" VAN ASSEN, "Hulde aan C. G. Heyne," Amsterdam, 1816; BECHER, "Programma ad Memoriam C. G. Heynii," 1812; "Nouvelle Biographie Générale;" "Edinburgh Review" for July, 1803.

Heyne, (CHRISTIAN LEBRECHT,) a German *littérateur,* whose pseudonym was ANTON WALL, was born near Meissen in 1751; died in 1821.

Heynius. See HEYNE, (CHRISTIAN GOTTLOB.)

Heyrick, hā'rĭk, (ELIZABETH,) an English philanthropist, born about 1770, was originally named COLTMAN. She became a member of the Society of Friends, and was eminent for her active benevolence. She published in 1824 a treatise entitled "Immediate, not Gradual, Emancipation," which principle she was the first to advocate. Died in 1831.

Heyse, hī'zęh, (JOHANN CHRISTIAN AUGUST,) a German grammarian and writer, born at Nordhausen in 1764; died in 1829.

Heyse, (KARL WILHELM LUDWIG,) an able German philologist, born at Oldenburg in 1797, was a son of the preceding. He was chosen professor at Berlin in 1829. He published, besides other works, an excellent "Dictionary of the German Language," (3 vols., 1833–49.) Died in 1855.

Heyward, hā'wặrd, (THOMAS,) born at Saint Luke's, South Carolina, in 1746, studied in London, returned home and became a lawyer. In 1775 he was elected a member of Congress, and next year signed the Declaration of Independence. In 1778 he was appointed a judge. He was taken prisoner at Charleston by the British in 1780. He retired from the bench in 1798. Died in 1809.

See GOODRICH, "Lives of the Signers to the Declaration of Independence."

Heywood, hā'wŏŏd, (ELIZA,) an English novelist, born in London about 1695. Her maiden name was FOWLER. She resorted to authorship to gain a subsistence for herself and her children, and wrote several novels, which procured her a place in Pope's "Dunciad." She offended less against decorum in her subsequent works, viz., "The Female Spectator," "Husband and Wife," etc. Died in 1756.

Heywood, (JASPER,) an English poet and Jesuit, born in London in 1535, wrote "The Paradise of Dainty Devices," (1573.) Died in 1598.

Heywood, (JOHN,) one of the earliest English dramatists, lived in the reign of Henry VIII., at whose court he was received with favour as a jester. He was intimate with Sir Thomas More. He wrote numerous epigrams and indifferent plays or interludes. Died about 1565.

See CAMPBELL, "Specimens of the British Poets."

Heywood, (OLIVER,) an English nonconformist divine, born in Lancashire in 1629. His works, in 5 vols., were published in 1827. Died in 1702.

See his Life, by FAWCETT, 1798, and by JOSEPH HUNTER, 1842.

Heywood, (THOMAS,) an English actor and dramatic author, who lived in the reigns of Elizabeth, James I., and Charles I. He produced numerous dramas, in verse and prose, which were once popular and are still admired. "Heywood," says Charles Lamb, "is a sort of prose Shakspeare. His scenes are to the full as natural and affecting." Among his best dramas are "The English Traveller," "A Woman Killed with Kindness," and "A Challenge for Beauty." The second of these is commended by Hallam. He also wrote a "General History of Women," etc. The dates of his birth and death are not known.

See his Life, by J. P. COLLIER, 1850; "Retrospective Review," vol. xi., 1825.

Hez-e-ki'ah, [Heb. יְחִזְקִיָּהוּ or חִזְקִיָּה; Fr. EZÉCHIAS, à'zȧ'ke'ǎs',] King of Judah, a son of Ahaz, was born about 750 B.C., and began to reign in 726. He took prompt measures to restore the true religion, which had been forsaken by his father. He broke the images or statues, and the brazen serpent of Moses, to which the people had burnt incense. He rebelled against the King of Assyria, to whom his father had paid tribute. In the fourteenth year of his reign, Sennacherib, King of Assyria, invaded Judah and besieged the capital. In this crisis the divine favour was invoked by the king and Isaiah, the latter of whom prophesied the safety of Zion and the defeat of her proud invader. (Isaiah, chap. xxxvii.) The angel of the Lord smote the Assyrians, so that 185,000 died in one night. Hezekiah died after a reign of twenty-nine years.

See II. Kings, chaps. xviii., xix., xx.

Hezel. See HETZEL.

Hi-a-coo'mes, an American Indian, who is said to have been the first Indian convert to Christianity in New England, became pastor of an Indian church at Martha's Vineyard in 1670. Died about 1690.

Hiaerne. See HJÄRNE.

Hib'bard, (FREEBORN GARRETSON,) an American divine of the Methodist Episcopal Church, born at New Rochelle, New York, in 1811. He published several works on theology.

Hiç'ę-tas [Gr. Ἱκέτας or Ἱκέτης] OF SYRACUSE, an ancient Pythagorean philosopher, is noticed by Diogenes Laertius and Cicero. The latter informs us that he taught that the earth revolves on its axis, and that the heavenly bodies were stationary.

Hickes, hiks, (GEORGE,) D.D., an eminent English divine and philologist, born at Newsham in 1642. He took orders in 1666, and became Dean of Worcester in 1683. For refusing to take the oath to William III. he was deprived of his deanery in 1689, and in 1694 was consecrated Bishop of Thetford by the nonjuring Sancroft. He was a profound scholar, and author of many polemical and other works, among which the following are now most prized, viz., "Treasure of Ancient Northern Languages," and "Institutes of Anglo-Saxon and Mœso-Gothic Grammar," (1689.) "Of all the Englishmen of his time," says Macaulay, "he was the most versed in the old Teutonic languages." ("History of England," vol. iii. chap. xiv.) Died in 1715.

See, also, "Biographia Britannica."

Hick'ey, (Rev. WILLIAM,) an Irish clergyman and rural economist, born in the county of Cork in 1790. He published, under the assumed name of MARTIN DOYLE, a valuable work called "Hints to Small Farmers," and other works on farming.

Hick'man, (HENRY,) an English nonconformist divine, born in Worcestershire; died at Leyden in 1692.

Hick'ok, (LAURENS PERSEUS,) D.D., an American divine and metaphysician, born in Danbury, Connecticut, in 1798. He graduated in 1820 at Union College, in which he accepted (1852) the professorship of mental and moral science. His principal works are "Rational Psychology," (1848,) "Empirical Psychology," (1854,) and "Rational Cosmology," (1858.)

Hicks, (ELIAS,) a noted preacher of the Society of Friends, or Quakers, was born in Hempstead, Queen's county, Long Island, in 1748. He began to speak in public as a minister of the gospel in 1775. He was early convinced of the iniquity of slavery, and felt it to be his duty to abstain, as far as practicable, from all participation in the products of slave labour,—a duty which he appears to have scrupulously observed throughout the remainder of his life. For many years he was a zealous and approved minister in the Society of which he was a member; but early in the present century he began to promulgate religious views widely different from those held by a large majority of the Quakers. He advocated the most radical Unitarian doctrines, and asserted that Christ came as a Saviour to the Israelites only, his special mission being limited to that nation. He even went so far as to express the opinion that the Scriptures had been "the cause of fourfold more harm than good to Christendom since the apostles' days." In consequence of the expression of these and similar views, he was severely censured and denounced by many of those who were anxious to maintain unchanged the doctrines of the early Quakers. The result was a schism in the Society. The elders of the Philadelphia Yearly Meeting had taken a leading part in the opposition to Elias Hicks; and it was in that Yearly Meeting (in April, 1827) that the first separation took place, which was followed, in 1828, by divisions in the Yearly Meetings of New York, Baltimore, Ohio, and Indiana. The two parties were respectively known as the "Orthodox" and the "Hicksites." In the Philadelphia and Ohio Yearly Meetings the two sections were nearly equal; but those called "Hicksites" were greatly in the majority in the Yearly Meetings of New York and Baltimore, while in Indiana the "Orthodox" were numerically much superior to the other party.

It is proper to observe that among those who most admired the bold and stirring eloquence of Hicks there were probably but few, comparatively speaking, who fully endorsed his extreme views; yet, regarding him as the representative of liberal and progressive ideas, they

€ as k; ç as s; ğ hard; ġ as j; G, H, K, guttural; N, nasal; R, trilled; ṡ as z; th as in this. (☞ See Explanations, p. 23.)

75

warmly espoused his cause. On the other hand, many who strongly disapproved—and under other circumstances would perhaps have severely condemned—his innovating doctrines, yet believing that he had been unfairly and harshly dealt with by the "Orthodox" elders, made common cause with what they considered the persecuted party, and contributed greatly to swell the number of his adherents. It may be proper to add that the anti-orthodox division of the Society do not acknowledge the name of "Hicksites," alleging, not without reason, that as a large majority of their members had espoused the cause of Hicks in the interest of religious liberty, not because they approved of his peculiar views, it is unjust to apply to them as a religious society a name which would naturally give the impression that they were, strictly speaking, his followers, and that they accepted, if not all, at least the greater part, of his religious teachings. They claim, on the contrary, to be the followers of no man; and although they accept the doctrine of the inward light, and many other of the views of the early Friends, it is not because of the *authority* of Fox, Penn, or Barclay, but simply because those views commend themselves to that divinely given or intuitive perception of right which, as they maintain, has been bestowed in a measure upon every human being. Elias Hicks died on the 27th of February, 1830, having maintained through life a blameless and exemplary moral character.

See "Elias Hicks's Journal of his Life and Labours," Philadelphia, 1828; JANNEY, "History of the Society of Friends," vol. iv. chap. v., also the second part of the same volume, entitled "The Separation;" "Life of Stephen Grellet."

Hicks, (FRANCIS,) a Greek scholar, born in Worcestershire, England, in 1566. He produced a translation of Lucian, (1634.) Died in 1630.

Hicks, (THOMAS,) an American painter, born at Newtown, Bucks county, Pennsylvania, in 1823. He went to Europe in 1845, and passed several years at Rome, where he copied the works of old masters, and painted portraits. He has resided for many years in the city of New York.

See TUCKERMAN, "Book of the Artists," p. 465.

Hicks or **Hickes,** (WILLIAM,) was an English captain in the time of Charles I., and author of the first Jest-Book in the English language, published at Oxford, (1669.)

Hidalgo, (JOSÉ GARCIA.) See GARZIA.

Hidalgo y Costilla, e-DÄl'go e kos-tĕl'yä, (Don MIGUEL,) a Spanish priest, who was curate of Dolores, in Mexico. He acquired great influence among the natives, of whom he became the leader in the revolution of 1810. After losing several battles, he was taken by the Spaniards and executed in 1811.

Hi-emp'sal, a Numidian prince, a son of Micipsa, was murdered by Jugurtha, according to Sallust.

Hien-Fung, he-ĕn' fŭng, Emperor of China, born about 1830, was a younger son of Taoo-Kooang. He ascended the throne in 1850, and appointed ministers who wished to maintain an exclusive policy towards foreigners. In the same year began a great insurrection, raised and directed by Tien-Te or Tai-Ping-Wang. The insurgents were generally victorious, and captured Nankin in 1853. (See TAI-PING-WANG.) A war broke out between the Chinese and the British, who entered Pekin in triumph in 1860. Died in 1861.

Hiero. See HIERON.

Hi-ĕr'o-clēs, [Gr. Ἱεροκλῆς,] an eminent Platonic philosopher, who was the head of a flourishing school in Alexandria in the fifth century. He is the author of a "Commentary on the Golden Verses of Pythagoras," which has been preserved entire, and of a "Treatise on Providence (or Foreknowledge) and Fate," of which some fragments remain. The former is written in Greek, and is admired for the beauty of the thoughts and of the style.

See ANDRÉ DACIER, "Vie de Hiéroclès," 1706.

Hierocles, the author of a work on veterinary medicine, addressed to Cassianus Bassus, lived in the third or fourth century of our era.

Hierocles, a grammarian, who is supposed to have lived in the sixth century, wrote, in Greek, a "Hand-

Book for Travellers,"(Συνέκδημος,) which contains descriptions of the towns and provinces of the Eastern empire. There was also a Stoic philosopher named HIEROCLES, of whom we have little information. He is supposed to have lived in the second century. Another HIEROCLES compiled or wrote a collection of anecdotes and ridiculous sayings of pedants, students, etc., with the Latin title of "Facetiæ Hieroclis."

Hierocles OF ALABANDA, a Greek rhetorician, lived about 100 B.C. He composed orations in the style which Cicero calls the "Asiatic."

Hierocles OF BITHYNIA was the principal author of the persecution of the Christians in the reign of Diocletian, (about 300 A.D.) He wrote two books against Christianity, entitled "Sincere Discourses to the Christians," (Λόγοι φιλαλήθεις,) in which he maintains that the Scripture is full of contradictions. He was prefect of Bithynia and of Alexandria.

Hi'ę-ron or **Hi'ę-ro** [Gr. Ἱέρων] **I.,** King of Syracuse, succeeded his brother Gelon in 478 B.C. The first part of his reign was tyrannical. He expelled the citizens of Naxos and Catana, and colonized those towns with his own subjects. He is applauded for his patronage of literature and his appreciation of genius. His court was the resort of the most eminent poets and sages of his time, among whom were Pindar, Æschylus, Simonides, and Epicharmus. Pindar wrote several odes on the occasion of Hieron's victories at the Olympic games, and Simonides enjoyed his friendship and bounty. Died in 467 B.C.

See XENOPHON, "Hieron."

Hieron (or **Hiero**) **II.,** King of Syracuse, was the son of Hierocles, a private citizen. Having served in the army of Pyrrhus, who left Sicily in a state of anarchy, Hieron was chosen general by the soldiers in 275 B.C., and recognised as king about 270. At the beginning of the first Punic war he took side with the Carthaginians, and was defeated by the Romans about 264 B.C. He then made peace with the victors by the payment of tribute, and was ever after a faithful ally of Rome. Under his wise rule the kingdom for many years enjoyed peace and prosperity. Died in 216 B.C. Archimedes lived in Syracuse in this reign, and exercised his mechanical genius in constructing machines and ships of great size.

See LIVY, "History of Rome," books xxi.-xxiv.; DIODORUS SICULUS, books xxii.-xxvi.; DROYSEN, "Hellenismus," vol. ii.

Hi'ę-ron, (SAMUEL,) an English Puritan, born at Epping in 1572, was rector of Modbury, and published sermons and other works on theology. Died in 1617.

Hiéronyme. See HIERONYMUS.

Hi-e-ron'ў-mus, [Gr. Ἱερώνυμος; Fr. HIÉRONYME, e'á'ro'nèm',] King of Syracuse, was the grandson of Hieron II., whom he succeeded in 216 B.C., at the age of fifteen. He broke the alliance with the Romans, who had recently been defeated at Cannæ, and formed a league with the Carthaginians. He was on the point of taking an active part in the war, when he was killed by his own subjects about a year after his accession. He left no issue; and the Syracusans thenceforth dispensed with royalty.

Hieronymus was the Latin name of Saint Jerome, one of the Fathers of the Church.

Hieronymus OF CARDIA, [Fr. HIÉRONYME, e'á'ro'nèm', (or JÉRÔME, zhä'rom',) DE CARDIE, dẹh kăr'de',] a Greek historian, who flourished about 300 B.C. He entered the service of Eumenes, who employed him on a mission to Antipater in 320. He was afterwards an adherent of Demetrius, who appointed him Governor of Bœotia in 292 B.C. He wrote historical memoirs of the successors of Alexander the Great,—a work which is often cited by the ancients, but has not come down to us.

See VOSSIUS, "De Historicis Græcis;" SEVIN, "Recherches sur la Vie et les Ouvrages de Jérôme de Cardie."

Hieronymus OF RHODES, a Greek philosopher, and disciple of Aristotle, lived about 300 B.C.

Hif'fẹr-nan, (PAUL,) born in the county of Dublin, Ireland, in 1719, lived many years in London as a literary hack, and wrote several mediocre dramas, etc. His habits were eccentric. Died in 1777.

Hig'dẹn, (RANULPH or RALPH,) an English monk, connected with a Benedictine monastery at Chester,

wrote "Polychronicon," a Latin chronicle. He died, at a great age, about 1370.

Hig′gins, (GODFREY,) an English antiquary, born in Yorkshire in 1771, wrote "The Celtic Druids," and other works. Died in 1833.

Higgins or **Higins,** (JOHN,) an English writer, born about 1544, was a clergyman and school-teacher. He published the "Flosculi" of Terence, a popular school-book, and contributed to the "Mirror for Magistrates," of which he published a new edition.

Higgins, (MATTHEW JAMES,) an English journalist, born about 1815, wrote under the assumed name of JACOB OMNIUM. He contributed many articles to the London "Times," the "Pall Mall Gazette," and other journals. His writings were mostly devoted to the exposure of abuses in the social and military systems of England. Died in 1868.

Hig′gin-son, (FRANCIS,) a distinguished divine, born in England in 1588. He was educated at Cambridge University, and appointed rector of a church in Leicester, in which position he laboured with great zeal and success until removed for nonconformity. He came to Massachusetts in 1629, and the next month was ordained with Mr. Skelton, the first minister of Salem. Died in 1630. He was the author of "New England's Plantation," (1630.)

Higginson, (JOHN,) born in England in 1616, accompanied his father Francis to Massachusetts in 1629. He was minister of the church at Salem from 1660 until his death in 1708, and published sermons and other theological works. He was regarded as the most able and eloquent American author of his time. Among his works is his "Attestation to Cotton Mather's Magnalia."

Hig′gons, (Sir THOMAS,) was born in Shropshire, England, in 1624. He married the notorious Countess of Essex, (see CARR, ROBERT,) at whose funeral in 1656 he pronounced an oration, which was printed. He was sent as ambassador to Vienna in 1673. Died in 1691. His son, BEVIL, born in 1670, wrote, besides several poems, a "Short View of English History," (1723.) He was a zealous Jacobite, and went into exile with James II. Died in France in 1735.

High′more, (JOSEPH,) an English portrait-painter, born in London in 1692, was a pupil of Kneller. He executed portraits of the Knights of the Bath, and was employed by George I. to paint some members of the royal family. In 1742 he painted the portraits of the Prince and Princess of Wales. He wrote a treatise on Perspective. Died in 1780.

Highmore, (NATHANIEL,) an eminent English physician, born at Fordingbridge in 1613, practised with success at Sherborne. He wrote able treatises on anatomy. Died in 1684.

Hilaire. See GEOFFROY-SAINT-HILAIRE.

Hilaire. See HILARY.

Hi-lā′rī-on, SAINT, a noted ascetic or hermit of Palestine, and pioneer of monastic life, was born at Tabatha, near Gaza, about 292 A.D. At an early age he went to Alexandria as a student, and was converted to Christianity. Returning to Palestine, he retired from the world, passed many years in the desert, and gained a wide reputation by his austerities. Many monasteries were founded by him or by the influence of his example. Died about 372.

See SAINT JEROME, "Vita Hilarioni;" BAILLET, "Vies des Saints."

Hilarius. See HILARY.

Hi-lā′rī-us, surnamed DIAC′ONUS, a native of Sardinia, lived about 350 A.D., and became a deacon of the church in Rome. He was an adversary of Arianism.

Hil′a-rў, [Lat. HILA′RIUS; Fr. HILAIRE, e′lăr′,] a native of Sardinia, was chosen Bishop or Pope of Rome in 461 A.D., as successor to Leo I. In 449 he had officiated as legate at the Council of Ephesus, where he zealously opposed the Eutychians. The events of his pontificate were unimportant. It appears that he claimed the pre-eminence of the see of Rome. He died in 467, and was succeeded by Simplicius.

Hilary or **Hilarius,** [Fr. HILAIRE, e′lăr′,] SAINT, an orthodox theologian, was born at Poitiers, (Pictavi,)

in Gaul, of which place he became bishop about 350 A.D. He took a prominent part in defence of Athanasius against the Arians, for which he was banished to Phrygia in 356. In 359, at the Council of Seleucia, he defended the doctrine of the Trinity, and afterwards published a violent invective against the Arian emperor Constantius, whom he denounced as Antichrist. Having returned to Italy and Gaul, he laboured zealously to purge the churches of heresy. He wrote a "Treatise on Synods," a "Commentary on Saint Matthew," and a few other works. Died in 367 A.D.

See CAVE, "Scriptores Ecclesiastici;" TILLEMONT, "Mémoires."

Hilary or **Hilarius,** SAINT, was born about 400 A.D., probably in Gaul or Belgium. He became Bishop of Arles in 429, and was highly esteemed for piety and learning. His contest with Leo, Bishop of Rome, forms an important epoch in the history of the Gallic Church. Celidonius, a bishop, having been deposed by a council at which Hilarius presided, appealed to Leo, who reinstated him, and, supported by an edict of the emperor Valentinian III., deprived Hilarius of his bishopric because the latter refused to own the supremacy of Rome. This was one of the first efforts made to build up the papal power. Died in 449. His "Eulogy on Honoratus" is much admired.

See BELLARMIN, "De Scriptoribus Ecclesiasticis;" TILLEMONT, "Mémoires;" "Gallia Christiana."

Hil′da, SAINT, a grand-niece of Edwin, King of Northumbria, was converted to Christianity in her childhood, became abbess of the convent of Heorthen (afterwards Whitby) about 660, and died in 680 A.D.

Hil′de-bâld, [Lat. HILDEBAL′DUS,] King of the Ostrogoths in Lombardy. After Belisarius had conquered the Ostrogoths, they proclaimed Hildebald their king at Pavia in 540 A.D. The next year he gained a victory over the Romans, soon after which he was assassinated by one of his guards.

See JORNANDES, "De Regnorum Successione;" GIBBON, "History of the Decline and Fall of the Roman Empire."

Hil′de-bert, [Lat. HILDEBER′TUS,] a French prelate and poet, born at Lavardin in 1057, became Archbishop of Tours in 1125. He was eminent for his piety and learning, and was one of the best writers of his time. His works are written in Latin, and consist of epistles, sermons, and poems. Died in 1134.

See "Gallia Christiana;" "Vita Hildeberti," prefixed to his Works, published by BEAUGENDRE in 1708.

Hildebertus. See HILDEBERT.

Hildebrand. See GREGORY VII.

Hildebrandt, hîl′de-brȧnt′, (FERDINAND THEODOR,) a German historical painter, and one of the most eminent masters of the Dusseldorf school, was born at Stettin in 1804. He studied under W. Schadow at Berlin, and settled at Dusseldorf. Among his works are "King Lear and Cordelia," (1826,) "Tancred and Clorinda," (1828,) and "Othello relating his Adventures to Desdemona," (1848.)

Hildebrandt, (GEORG FRIEDRICH,) a German physician and naturalist, born at Hanover in 1764, wrote, besides other works, a "Manual of Human Anatomy," (4 vols., 1789–92.) Died in 1816.

Hil′de-gard′ or **Hildegarde,** SAINT, a German nun, born in 1098, became abbess of Saint Rupert's Mount, near Bingen, on the Rhine. Died in 1180.

See J. C. DAHL, "Die heilige Hildegardis; historische Abhandlung," 1832.

Hildenbrand, von, fon hîl′den-brȧnt′, (VALENTIN JOHANN,) a German medical writer, born in Vienna in 1763; died in 1818.

Hil′ders-hȧm, (ARTHUR,) an English Puritan divine, born in Cambridgeshire in 1563. He held the living of Ashby-de-la-Zouch from 1593 until his death. He was a grand-nephew of Cardinal Pole, and was related to the royal family. He wrote various theological works, and was esteemed a shining light among the Puritans. Died in 1631.

Hil′des-ley, (MARK,) an English theologian, born in Kent in 1698. He became Bishop of Sodor and Man in 1755, and caused the Bible to be translated into the Manx language. Died in 1772.

See WEEDON BUTLER, "Memoirs of M. Hildesley," 1799.

є as *k*; ç as *s*; ḡ *hard*; ġ as *j*; G, H, K, *guttural*; N, *nasal*; R, *trilled*; ŝ as *z*; ʈh as in *this*. (☞See Explanations, p. 23.)

Hil'dreth, (RICHARD,) an American journalist and historian, was born in Deerfield, Massachusetts, June 28, 1807. He graduated at Harvard in 1826, and, while studying law, contributed numerous articles to magazines. Admitted to the bar in Boston in 1830, he abandoned the legal profession at the expiration of two years, to accept the position of associate editor of the "Boston Atlas," which soon became one of the ablest Whig journals in New England. His health having failed, he spent the year 1835 in Florida, and while there wrote "Archy Moore," an anti-slavery novel. It was republished and favourably reviewed in England, and an enlarged edition, under the title of "The White Slave," was issued in the United States in 1852. In 1837 he furnished to the columns of the "Atlas" a series of articles which contributed powerfully towards defeating schemes then on foot for the annexation of Texas. He took a conspicuous part in the Presidential canvass which resulted in the nomination and election of General Harrison. He also gave to the public during this period his "Despotism in America," an able review of the social, political, and economical aspects of slavery in the United States, to which he added in 1854 a chapter on the "Legal Basis of Slavery." His health having again failed, he embarked in 1840 for British Guiana, and, during a residence of three years at Georgetown, the capital, wrote his "Theory of Morals," published in 1844, and "Theory of Politics, or an Inquiry into the Foundation of Governments and the Causes and Progress of Political Revolutions," issued in 1853. Mr. Hildreth is best known, however, by his "History of the United States of America," from the discovery of the continent to the close of the Sixteenth Congress in 1820, (6 vols. 8vo, 1849–52.) It was projected while the author was a student at Harvard. The work has been variously criticised; but all agree in classing it among the standard histories of our country. Died at Florence in July, 1865.

See DUYCKINCK, "Cyclopædia of American Literature," vol. ii. ; CLEVELAND, "Compendium of American Literature."

Hildreth, (SAMUEL PRESCOTT,) M.D., an American physician, born in Massachusetts in 1783. He settled in Ohio in 1806. His principal works are a "Pioneer History of the Ohio Valley," (1848,) and "Biographical and Historical Memoirs of the Early Settlers of Ohio," (1852.) Died at Marietta, Ohio, in 1863.

Hill, (AARON,) an English writer, born in London in 1685. About the age of sixteen he went to Constantinople, and by the aid of his kinsman, Lord Paget, visited several countries of the East. In 1709 he published a "History of the Ottoman Empire." Soon after he became manager of Drury Lane Theatre, and wrote "Elfrida," a tragedy, which was followed by several other dramas. The most successful of these are "Alzira" and "Zara," adapted from Voltaire. He wrote a satire on Pope, who had noticed him in the "Dunciad" in terms which some think rather complimentary. Died in 1750.

See "Biographia Britannica."

Hill, (ABRAHAM,) an English gentleman and scholar, born in 1632. He was a Fellow of the Royal Society. A volume of his "Letters" was published in 1767. Died in 1721.

Hill, (AMBROSE POWELL,) an American general, born in Culpepper county, Virginia, about 1825, graduated at West Point in 1847. He fought against the Union at Bull Run, July, 1861, and became a major-general about June, 1862. He commanded a division at the battles of Mechanicsville and Gaines's Mill in June, and at the second battle of Bull Run, August 29, 1862. In the next month he served at Harper's Ferry and Antietam. He commanded a division at the battle of Fredericksburg, December, 1862, and at Chancellorsville, May, 1863. For his services in the latter action he was promoted to the rank of lieutenant-general. He directed a corps at the battle of Gettysburg, July 1–3, 1863, and in the several battles fought by Generals Grant and Lee in 1864, at the Wilderness, Spottsylvania Court-House, Cold Harbour, etc. He was killed in a battle near Petersburg on the 2d of April, 1865.

See "Southern Generals," New York, 1865; TENNEY, "Military and Naval History of the Rebellion."

Hill, (DANIEL H.,) an American general, born in South Carolina about 1824, graduated at West Point in 1842.

He commanded a division at the battles of Mechanicsville and Malvern Hill, July 1, 1862, and South Mountain, September, 1862. He attempted to take Newbern, North Carolina, in March, 1863, but failed, and served under General Bragg at Chickamauga the same year. He commanded at Augusta, Georgia, in February, 1865.

Hill, (DAVID OCTAVIUS,) a Scottish landscape-painter, born at Perth in 1802. He has been for many years secretary to the Royal Scottish Academy. His subjects are chiefly Scottish scenes. He produced an illustrated work entitled "The Land of Burns."

Hill, (FREDERICK,) a brother of Sir Rowland Hill, noted for his efforts to reform prison-discipline and to prevent crime, was appointed about 1835 inspector of prisons in Scotland. He published an able work, entitled "National Education : its Present State and Prospects," and "Crime : its Amount, Causes, and Remedies," (1853.)

Hill, (GEORGE,) D.D., a Scottish divine, born at Saint Andrew's in 1750. He was principal of Saint Mary's College, in his native town, and succeeded Dr. Robertson as leader of the General Assembly. He published, besides other works, "Lectures on Divinity," which are commended by Dr. Chalmers, who said, "I am not sure if I can recommend a more complete manual of divinity." Died in 1819.

See GEORGE COOK, "Life of George Hill."

Hill, (GEORGE,) an American contemporary poet, born at Guilford, near New Haven. Among his principal poems are "The Ruins of Athens," and "Titania."

See GRISWOLD's "Poets and Poetry of America."

Hill, (ISAAC,) a journalist, born in Ashburnham, Massachusetts, in 1788. He was for many years editor of the "New Hampshire Patriot," a Democratic journal, was elected a United States Senator for New Hampshire in 1830, and Governor of that State in 1836. Died in 1851.

Hill, (Sir JOHN,) an English writer and literary quack, born at Spalding in 1716. He obtained skill as a botanist, made and sold quack medicines, and edited "The Inspector," a journal which owed its success to the scandal it contained. He was refused admission to the Royal Society on account of his doubtful character, and sought revenge by writing a review of their works. His "Vegetable System," in 26 vols., with splendid plates, sold at one hundred and sixty guineas per copy. He was knighted by the King of Sweden, to whom he had presented a copy of the last-named work. Died in 1775. Garrick has defined his merits in the following epigram:

"For physic and farces, his rival there scarce is ;
His farces are physic, his physic a farce is."

See DISRAELI, "Quarrels of Authors."

Hill, (JOSEPH,) an English scholar, born near Leeds in 1625, became minister of an English church at Middelburg, Holland. He published an improved edition of Schrevelius's "Greek Lexicon," (1676.) Died in 1707.

Hill, (MATTHEW DAVENPORT,) a brother of Frederick, noticed above, born in Birmingham about 1792, became a barrister. He was one of the active members of the Society for the Diffusion of Useful Knowledge, and laboured with zeal and success to procure amendments of the laws. He was one of the chief promoters of "juvenile reformatories."

Hill, (Sir RICHARD,) born in 1733, a brother of Rowland, was member of Parliament for Salop, and sometimes preached in the Calvinistic Methodist chapels. He wrote a few religious works. Died in 1808.

Hill, (ROBERT,) a self-taught English linguist, born at Miswell in 1699, was a tailor by trade. He was master of several ancient languages, and wrote "Criticisms on Job," and a few other works. Died in 1777.

See "Pursuit of Knowledge under Difficulties," vol. i., 1839.

Hill, (Rev. ROWLAND,) a popular preacher and disciple of Whitefield, was born at Hawkstone, England, in 1744. He was the son of Sir Rowland Hill, and uncle of General Lord Hill. After leaving college he was ordained a deacon of the Anglican Church, but soon became a zealous and eloquent preacher among the Calvinistic Methodists. Addressing the people in the streets, the open air, or wherever he could gain audience, he made many converts in various parts of the kingdom. In 1783 he built Surrey Chapel, London, in which he preached about fifty winters. He was the author of "Village Dialogues," and other works. Southey, in reference to a particular occasion, says, "His manner was animated and striking, sometimes dignified and impressive. The purport of his sermon was good,—nothing fanatical, nothing enthusiastic." Died in 1833.

See J. SHERMAN, "Memorial of the late Rev. R. Hill, chiefly consisting of Anecdotes," etc., London, 1851; E. SIDNEY, "Life of the Rev. Rowland Hill," 1834; WILLIAM JONES, "Memoirs of the Life of Rev. Rowland Hill."

Hill, (ROWLAND,) VISCOUNT, an English general, born at Prees, Shropshire, in 1772, was the second son of Sir John Hill, and nephew of the Rev. Rowland Hill. He entered the army as ensign in 1790, and obtained the rank of colonel in 1800. In 1806 he was made a major-general and appointed on the staff. In 1808 he served in Portugal, under Sir Arthur Wellesley and Sir John Moore, until the battle of Corunna. Promoted to the rank of lieutenant-general in 1809, he was employed several years in the Peninsular war, and gained a high reputation in his profession. In 1814 he was raised to the peerage, as Baron of Almarez and Hawkstone. He took part in the battle of Waterloo in 1815, and afterwards was second in command of the army of occupation in France. Lord Hill was commander-in-chief of the army from 1828 until 1842, when he resigned and was created a viscount. He died in 1842, and left the title to his nephew, Sir Rowland Hill.

See E. SIDNEY, "Life of Viscount Hill," 1850; NAPIER, "History of the Peninsular War."

Hill, (Sir ROWLAND,) an Englishman, known as the author of the cheap postage system, was born at Kidderminster in 1795. In 1837 he wrote a pamphlet on "Post-Office Reform, its Importance and Practicability." Through his persistent efforts, a bill was passed in the session of 1839-40 to reduce the rate of postage and render it uniform. The postage has since been further reduced, and letters are now carried for one penny each to any part of the United Kingdom. The people expressed their gratitude for this benefit by a present of £13,000 raised by subscription. He was appointed secretary to the postmaster-general in 1846, and sole secretary to the post-office in 1854.

Hill, (S. W.,) a recent American painter, of the Pre-Raphaelite school, has particularly distinguished himself by his landscapes and fruit-pieces.

Hill, (THOMAS,) a mathematician and Unitarian minister, born at New Brunswick, New Jersey, in 1818, graduated at Harvard in 1843. He published, besides other works, "Geometry and Faith," and contributed many articles to the "North American Review" and the "Atlantic Monthly." In 1859 he succeeded Horace Mann as president of Antioch College, Ohio. He investigated the properties of curves with success.

Hill, (THOMAS FORD,) an English antiquary and philologist, published "Ancient Erse Poems." Died in 1795.

Hill, (WILLIAM,) D.D., an American divine, born in Cumberland county, Virginia, in 1769. He graduated at Hampden-Sidney College in 1788. From 1800 to 1834 he was pastor of the Presbyterian church in Winchester, where he died in 1852.

Hil′lard, (GEORGE STILLMAN,) an eminent American writer, lawyer, and orator, born at Machias, Maine, in 1808. While pursuing his collegiate course at Harvard, (where he graduated in 1828,) he is said to have been especially distinguished in declamation and English composition. He was afterwards for some time associated with George Bancroft in his Round Hill Seminary at Northampton, Massachusetts, and in 1833 was admitted to the bar in Boston. Besides attending to an extensive professional business, he has since twice visited Europe, and has been a member of both branches of the Massachusetts legislature. He is author of a great number of orations, lectures before the Lowell Institute, and contributions to the "Christian Examiner," "North American Review," etc. In 1852 he was selected by the authorities of Boston to deliver the eulogy on the character of Daniel Webster. The next year appeared his "Six Months in Italy," (in 2 vols. 12mo,) which had reached the fifth edition in 1855. "Mr. Hillard's work," says the "London Quarterly Review" for April, 1858, "is that of a scholar and a gentleman, a man of sense as well as of taste and feeling. His style is pointed and

full of happy expressions and striking images." Among other literary labours, Mr. Hillard has edited the Poetical Works of Spenser, (in 5 vols. 8vo.) He was for some time associate editor of the "Jurist," and was for several years one of the principal editors of the "Boston Courier." He contributed several important articles to the "New American Cyclopædia," including those on Alexander and Edward Everett and Rufus Choate.

Hillebrand, hil′leh-brânt′, (JOSEPH,) a German philosophical writer, born near Hildesheim in 1788. He published, among other works, "The Philosophy of the Spirit," (2 vols., 1835,) and "The German National Literature since the Beginning of the Eighteenth Century," (2 vols., 1845.)

Hil′lel, a famous Jewish rabbi, born at Babylon about 110 B.C., was descended from King David. He went to Jerusalem at the age of forty, acquired a thorough knowledge of the law, and was chosen president of the Sanhedrim about 30 B.C. The origin of the Talmud or Mishna is ascribed to Hillel, who was the leader of a numerous school or party. He died at the age of one hundred and twenty years.

Hillel, a noted rabbi, supposed to have lived about 300 A.D., was a descendant of the preceding. He reformed the Jewish calendar by means of a cycle of nineteen years.

Hiller, hil′ler, (FERDINAND,) a celebrated German composer, born of Jewish parents at Frankfort, October 24, 1811. His oratorio of the "Destruction of Jerusalem" (1840) was received with great applause. In 1851 he was made director of the Italian Opera at Paris.

See BROCKHAUS, "Conversations-Lexikon."

Hiller, (MATTHÄUS,) a German Orientalist, born at Stuttgart in 1646, was professor of Oriental languages and theology at Tübingen. He wrote a "Latin-Hebrew Lexicon," (1685.) Died in 1725.

Hiller, von, fon hil′ler, (JOHANN,) BARON, an Austrian general, born at Neustadt, near Vienna, in 1754. In 1809 he obtained command of the sixth corps of the army of the archduke Charles. Although he was defeated by Napoleon at Landshut in April, he contributed greatly to the success of the Austrians at Aspern in the next month. Died in 1819.

See ERSCH und GRUBER, "Allgemeine Encyklopaedie."

Hillerup, hil′leh-rûp′, (FREDERIK CHRISTIAN,) a Danish poet, born at Vedelsborg in 1793, published a work called "Italica," (1829,) and "New Poems," ("Nye Digte,") in 1854.

Hill′house, (JAMES,) an American lawyer, born in Connecticut in 1754. He was a Senator of the United States from 1794 to 1810. Died in 1832.

Hillhouse, (JAMES A.,) an American poet, son of the preceding, born at New Haven in 1789. He removed to New York City, and married Cornelia Lawrence in 1824. His first poem, "The Judgment, a Vision," appeared in 1812. He also wrote the following admired dramas: "Percy's Masque," "Hadad," and "Demetria." Died in 1841.

See GRISWOLD, "Poets and Poetry of America;" DUYCKINCK, "Cyclopædia of American Literature," vol. ii.; CLEVELAND, "Compendium of American Literature;" "North American Review" for January, 1840.

Hilliard, hil′yard, (HENRY W.,) a lawyer and politician, born in Cumberland county, North Carolina, in 1808. He was a Whig, and represented a district of Alabama in Congress from 1845 to 1851. In 1857 he joined the Democratic party.

Hilliard, hil′yard, (NICHOLAS,) an English painter, born at Exeter in 1547, learned the trade of a jeweller, and afterwards became eminent as a miniature-painter. He executed an admired portrait of Mary Queen of Scots, and was patronized by Queen Elizabeth and James I. Died in 1619.

Hil′ton, (JOHN,) an English composer and musician, was admitted to the degree of bachelor of music at Cambridge in 1626. He composed anthems, songs, catches, etc. Died about 1656.

Hilton, (WALTER,) an English monk of the fifteenth century, lived at Sheen, and wrote "The Ladder of Perfection."

ᵉ as k; ç as s; ḡ hard; ġ as j; G, H, K, guttural; N, nasal; R, trilled; s as z; th as in this. (☞See Explanations, p. 23.)

Hilton, (WILLIAM,) a successful English historical painter, born at Lincoln in 1786. About 1800 he became a student in the Royal Academy, and in 1804 exhibited his "Hector reinspired by Apollo." In 1819 or 1820 he was elected a member of the Academy, and in 1825 succeeded Fuseli as keeper of that institution. He attained a high rank among the English artists of his time. Among his best works are "Nature blowing Bubbles," and "The Graces teaching Cupid to play on the Lyre." Died in 1839.

See PILKINGTON's "Dictionary of Painters."

Hi-me'rī-us, ['Ιμέριος,] an eminent Greek sophist of Prusa, Bithynia. He became master of a celebrated school in Athens, and afterwards secretary of the emperor Julian at Antioch about 362 A.D. He composed many orations, of which about twenty are extant. His style is rather bombastic. Among his pupils were Gregory Nazianzen and Saint Basil. He was always a pagan, but moderate or friendly to the Christians.

Hī-mil'co or **Hī-mil'çon,** a Carthaginian navigator, the date of whose adventures is unknown. Pliny states that he sailed northward from Gades on a voyage of discovery about the time that Hanno explored the western coast of Africa. R. Festus Avienus quotes him as his authority for an account of the islands of the Hiberni and Albioni.

Himilco or **Himilcon,** an able Carthaginian general, who was joined with Hannibal in the command of a large army in the war against Dionysius, tyrant of Syracuse. He took Agrigentum after a long siege, during which the death of Hannibal left him sole commander, (406 B.C.) He defeated Dionysius about 405, soon after which peace was concluded. The war having been renewed in 397 B.C., Himilco raised an army of 100,000 men, with which he marched victoriously to the gates of Syracuse. While he was besieging this city, his army was wasted by pestilence and defeated by the Syracusans. He escaped to Carthage and killed himself.

See DIODORUS SICULUS, books xiii., xiv., and xx.

Himilco or **Himilcon** was commander of the fleet of Carthage, on the coast of Sicily, in 214 B.C., while Marcellus commanded the Romans in that island. He landed an army in 213, gained some advantages, and, having failed in an attempt to relieve Syracuse, died of pestilence in 212 B.C.

Himly, him'lee, (KARL GUSTAV,) a German physician, born at Brunswick in 1772, was professor of medicine at Göttingen. He was distinguished for his skilful treatment of diseases of the eyes, on which he published a valuable work. Died in 1837.

Himmel, him'mel, (FRIEDRICH HEINRICH,) a German composer, born in the duchy of Brandenburg in 1765, was appointed chapel-master at Berlin about 1796. Among his best works are the operas of "Fanchon" and "The Sylphs." Died in 1814.

See FÉTIS, "Biographie Universelle des Musiciens."

Hinch'cliffe, (JOHN,) an English divine and orator, born at Westminster in 1731. He became head-master of Westminster School in 1764, and Bishop of Peterborough in 1769. Died in 1794.

Hinckeldey, hink'kel-dī, (KARL LUDWIG FRIEDRICH,) a Prussian administrator, born near Meiningen in 1803. He became minister or prefect of police in Berlin in 1848. He was killed in a duel in 1856.

Hinckelmann, hink'kel-män', (ABRAHAM,) a German Orientalist, born at Döbeln in 1652, published an edition of the Koran, (1694,) said to be the first ever printed in Arabic. Died in 1695.

Hinck'ley, (JOHN,) an English clergyman, born in 1617, was rector of Drayton. Died in 1695.

Hincmar, hink'mär, a learned French prelate, born in 806 A.D., entered the Abbey of Saint-Denis in childhood. He acquired much influence, and became a favourite at the court of Charles the Bald. In 845 he was elected Archbishop of Rheims. He distinguished himself by his firmness in defending the Church against the encroachments of the papal and royal power. He wrote, besides other works, two treatises on Predestination, in one of which he attempts to refute the famous Erigena. He is censured for his severity to Godeschalcus, who

was confined in a dungeon for his heretical opinions on the question of predestination. Died in 882 A.D.

See "Gallia Christiana;" W. F. GESS, "Merkwürdigkeiten aus dem Leben und den Schriften Hincmar's," 1806; "Nouvelle Biographie Générale."

Hincks, (Rev. EDWARD,) distinguished for his knowledge of Assyrian and Egyptian inscriptions, was born in Cork, Ireland, about 1791. Died about 1866.

Hind, (JOHN RUSSELL,) an eminent English astronomer, born at Nottingham in 1823. He obtained in 1840 a situation in the Royal Observatory at Greenwich. In 1845 he removed to another observatory in Regent's Park, London, where he has had remarkable success as an observer. He discovered, besides several comets, ten telescopic planets, namely, Iris, (1847,) Flora, (1847,) Victoria, (1850,) Irene, (1851,) Melpomene, Fortuna, Calliope, and Thalia, (all in 1852,) Euterpe, (1853,) and Urania, (1854.) He wrote several works, among which is "The Solar System : a Descriptive Treatise on the Sun, Moon, and Planets," (1852.)

Hind'man, (THOMAS C.,) an American general, born in Tennessee about 1818. He lived in Arkansas before the civil war, and was a member of Congress. He commanded the rebel forces at Prairie Grove, Arkansas, in December, 1862, and served as major-general at the battle of Chickamauga, September 19 and 20, 1863.

Hinojosa y Carbajal, e-no-Hō'sä e kaR-bä-Häl', (ALVARO DE,) a Spanish poet, who lived about 1620.

See LONGFELLOW, "Poets and Poetry of Europe."

Hinrichs, hin'riks, (HERMANN FRIEDRICH WILHELM,) a German philosopher, born in Oldenburg in 1794, published "The Genesis of Science," ("Genesis des Wissens," 1835,) and other works.

Hin'ton, (JOHN HOWARD,) an English writer on history and theology, was born probably about 1800. He became minister of a Baptist congregation in Devonshire Square, London. He published, besides other works, "The History and Topography of the United States of North America," (2 vols., 1832.)

Hiob, the German of JOB, which see.

Hiooen- or **Hiouen-Thsang** or **Youen-Thsang,** yoo'ĕn-tsang, a celebrated Chinese traveller and priest of Booddha, was born about 602 A.D. He travelled in Hindostan and other countries, of which he wrote descriptions. He translated into the Chinese many Hindoo works on the religion of Booddha. Died in 664 A.D.

See "Nouvelle Biographie Générale."

Hip-par'chus, [Gr. Ἵππαρχος; Fr. HIPPARQUE, e'pärk',] son of Pisistratus, an Athenian, who, in partnership with his brother Hippias, obtained the chief power in the state in 527 B.C. He was assassinated by Harmodius and Aristogiton in 514. Hippias survived; but, having rendered himself unpopular by cruelty and suspicious habits, (although it is said he was previously mild and affable,) he was expelled from Athens in 511. He afterwards passed many years at the court of the Persian king Darius, served as guide to the Persian army which invaded Greece, and was at the battle of Marathon, where, according to some writers, he was killed, 490 B.C.

See HERODOTUS, books ii., v., vi., and vii.; THIRLWALL, "History of Greece."

Hipparchus, [Gr. Ἵππαρχος; Fr. HIPPARQUE; It. IPPARCO, ĕp-paR'ko,] the founder of the science of astronomy, and the greatest astronomer of antiquity, was a native of Nicæa, in Bithynia. He was of Greek extraction, and flourished about 150 B.C. Many of his observations were made at Rhodes. His writings are all lost, except a "Commentary on Aratus," which is the least important ; but the knowledge of his discoveries has been preserved by Ptolemy in his "Syntaxis." The first who made systematic observations, he was also the first who discovered that fundamental fact in astronomy,—the precession of the equinoxes. A discovery so important would have sufficed to immortalize him ; but he also greatly enriched the science of mathematics, and was the first who understood trigonometry, both plane and spherical. He invented the planisphere and the stereographic projection, and gave rules for the calculation of eclipses, by means of which he determined the longitude. According to Pliny, who calls him the confidant and interpreter of nature, Hipparchus, having perceived a new star that suddenly appeared in his time, was stimulated by it to form his Catalogue of one thousand and eighty stars, which is preserved in the "Almagest" of Ptolemy. In this operation he used the astrolabe, which was probably invented by him. He originated a more complete system of geography, and the mode of determining the position of towns by circles drawn on the earth corresponding to those of the celestial sphere. Among his lost works were "On the Magnitudes and Distances of the Sun and Moon," "The Movement of the Moon in Latitude," and "On the Retrogradation of the Equinoctial and Solstitial Points."

See PLINY, "Natural History;" MONTUCLA, "Histoire des Mathématiques;" DELAMBRE, "Histoire de l'Astronomie ancienne;" DR. HOEFER's article in the "Nouvelle Biographie Générale;" J. A. SCHMIDT, "Dissertatio de Hipparcho," etc., 1689.

Hipparchus, an Athenian comic poet, who lived probably about 300 B.C.

Hipparque. See HIPPARCHUS.

Hip′pa-sus, [Gr. Ἵππασος,] a Pythagorean philosopher, born at Metapontum, held, it is said, the doctrine that fire was the origin of all things.

Hippeau, e′pō′, (CÉLESTIN,) a French *littérateur*, born at Niort in 1803, published, besides other works, a "History of Ancient and Modern Philosophy," (1833.)

Hippel, von, fon hip′pel, (THEODOR GOTTLIEB,) a German humorist and original thinker, born at Gerdauen, in Prussia, in 1741. He studied law, and became in 1780 burgomaster of Königsberg. He claimed for women admission to civil offices and a greater social equality. Among his works are a "Treatise on Marriage," ("Ueber die Ehe," 1774,) "Designs after Nature," (1790,) an Autobiography, (1800,) and "The Education of Women," (1801.) His character was eccentric. Died in 1796.

See GERVINUS, "Geschichte der Deutschen Dichtung," fourth edition, vol. v.; W. G. KEBER, "Nachrichten und Bemerkungen den geheimen Kriegsrath von Hippel betreffend," 1802; "Biographie T. G. von Hippel's zum Theil von ihm selbst verfasst," 1800.

Hippias. See HIPPARCHUS and HARMODIUS.

Hip′pĭ-as, [Ἱππίας,] a Greek sophist, born at Elis, was a contemporary of Socrates. His character is exhibited by Plato in his dialogue called "Hippias Major."

Hip′pis-ley or **Hippesley,** (Sir JOHN COXE,) an Englishman, born in Somersetshire in 1765, was returned to Parliament about 1790. He wrote a "Treatise on Prison Discipline," (1823.) Died in 1825.

Hip′po or **Hip′pon,** [Ἵππων,] a Greek philosopher, who is supposed to have lived in the fifth century B.C., and to have been a native of Samos, or of Rhegium. He held that moisture, or water, is the principle of all things, and derived much of his system from Thales.

See BRUCKER, "History of Philosophy."

Hippocrate. See HIPPOCRATES.

Hip-poc′ra-tēs, [Gr. Ἱπποκράτης; Fr. HIPPOCRATE, e′po′kRǎt′; It. IPPOCRATE, ėp-pok′Rǎ-tà,] the most eminent physician of antiquity, justly styled the "Father of Medicine," was born in the island of Cos in 460 B.C., and was contemporary with Socrates and Plato. He was the son of Heraclides, a descendant of Esculapius, from whom he derived his first lessons in medicine. His family, the Asclepiadæ, for many generations had practised the same art. The materials for writing his personal history are deficient. He is said to have studied medicine at Athens under Herodicus, after which he practised and taught in Cos, also in Thessaly, and at the court of Perdiccas, King of Macedonia, etc. Soranus relates that he acquired fame by checking the ravages of the plague in Athens, and was rewarded with the freedom of that city, and with other honours. The story that he refused the invitation and magnificent offers of Artaxerxes, is by some discredited.

His superior talents, his rare sagacity, his signal success, and his devoted humanity, inspired universal confidence and respect. He had a great number of pupils, from whom he exacted an oath that they would never abuse their trust by criminal practice, nor divulge professional secrets. He held that the body is composed of four primary elements, fire, air, earth, and water, which produce the four cardinal humours, blood, phlegm, bile, and black bile. He knew but little of anatomy.

He carried forward the reform begun by his ancestors, in substituting experiment and observation for speculative theories. He paid more attention than his predecessors to diet and changes of weather. Among the most remarkable of his discoveries is that of critical days in fevers. Of the numerous (Greek) works ascribed to him, it is probable that some were composed by other writers, as there were several noted physicians of the same name. He died at Larissa, at an age which is variously stated between eighty-five and one hundred and nine years. As an inventor he is unrivalled by any physician of ancient or modern times. Among his chief works are "Prognostics," "Epidemics," "Aphorisms," and "On Air, Water, and Locality."

See SORANUS, "Vita Hippocratis," in FABRICIUS, "Bibliotheca Græca;" BOERHAAVE, "De Studio Hippocratis," 1721; A. DE HALLER, "Bibliotheca Medico-practica," 1776; G. CRAMER, "Dissertation sur Hippocrate," 1748; HOUCLUROS, "Essai historique et critique sur la Vie et les Écrits d'Hippocrate," 1840; G. SPRENGEL, "Apologie des Hippocrates und seiner Grundsätze," 2 vols., 1789–92; C. P. GESNER, "De Divino Hippocrate," 1739; KARL F. MARCUS, "Dissertatio de Vita\ Hippocratis," 1838; A. OETTINGER, "Hippocratis Vita," 1836.

Hippocrates, a Syracusan, shared with his brother Epicydes the command of the army which defended Syracuse against Marcellus, 213 B.C. Died in 212 B.C.

Hippocrates OF CHIOS, a noted Greek geometer, who lived in the fifth century before Christ. He studied at Athens, where he opened a celebrated school. He first discovered the quadrature of the lune.

Hip-po-da-mi′a [Gr. Ἱπποδάμεια] or **Hip-pod′a-me,** a daughter of Œnomaus.

Hip-pod′a-mus [Ἱππόδαμος] OF MILETUS, an eminent Greek architect, lived about 440 B.C. He built the Piræus of Athens, under the order of Pericles, and planned the city of Rhodes, about 408 B.C.

Hippolyte. See HIPPOLYTUS.

Hip-pol′y̆-te, [Ἱππολύτη,] the Queen of the Amazons, was called a daughter of Mars. The poets feigned that she had a girdle coveted by Eurystheus, who ordered Hercules to bring it to him. She was killed by Hercules.

Hip-pol′y̆-tus, [Fr. HIPPOLYTE, e′po′lèt′; It. IPPOLITO, ėp-pol′e-to,] SAINT, a Christian martyr and ecclesiastical writer, who has recently attracted great attention on the part of scholars and theologians. He was Bishop of Portus Romanus, the harbour of Rome, and the author of numerous learned works, highly extolled by Eusebius, Jerome, and other Christian Fathers. After occupying the see of Portus Romanus eighteen years or more, he suffered martyrdom about 238 A.D.

In 1842 M. Minas found at Mount Athos a Greek manuscript on "Heresies," which, at first ascribed to Origen, was proved by Bunsen to be the lost work of Hippolytus, entitled a "Refutation of all the Heresies." This is a work of great interest and importance as a monument of the social state, intellectual improvement, and doctrinal belief of the Christians of the third century. Bunsen published in 1852, in English, "Hippolytus and his Age; or, The Doctrine and Practice of the Church of Rome under Commodus and A. Severus, and Ancient and Modern Christianity Compared," (in 4 vols.)

See EUSEBIUS, "Historia Ecclesiastica;" SAINT JEROME, "De Viribus illustribus;" BARONIUS, "Annales;" CAVE, "Historia Literaria;" C. WORDSWORTH, "Saint Hippolytus and the Church of Rome," etc., 1853; DÖLLINGER, "Hippolytus und Kaliistus," 1853; "Edinburgh Review" for January, 1853.

Hippolytus, [Ἱππόλυτος,] a son of Theseus and Hippolyte, or Antiope. The poets relate that his stepmother Phædra made to him amorous overtures which he rejected, that she then by calumny induced Theseus to curse him, and that, at the request of Theseus, Neptune caused the horses of Hippolytus to become unruly, and to drag him until he was dead.

Hip-pom′e̜-don, [Ἱππομέδων,] a Spartan warrior, was a son of Agesilaus, and a cousin of King Agis IV. He supported Agis in his efforts to reform the Spartan institutions. He was living in 220 B.C.

Hip-po′na, the name of a goddess who presided over horses. Her statues were placed in stables.

Hip′po-nax, [Ἱππώναξ,] a Greek poet, who lived about 540 B.C., was a native of Ephesus. Having been expelled from that city by its tyrants, he removed to Clazomene. He wrote satires, of which only a few fragments now remain. He was the first who employed the modification of the Iambic metre termed Choliambic.

Hi'ram, King of Tyre, began to reign about 1025 B.C. He was contemporary with David and Solomon, with whom he formed an alliance and always maintained friendly relations. He was a wise and successful ruler.

See I. Kings v., and I. Chronicles xiv.

Hiranyakasipu. See NARASINGHA.

Hire, de la. See LA HIRE.

Hirnheim, hĕĕRn'hīm, or **Hernhaym,** hĕRn'hīm, (HIERONYMUS,) a German monk and writer, born at Troppau in 1635; died in 1679.

Hirsch, hĕĕRsh, (JOHANN CHRISTOPH,) a German economist and numismatist, born in 1698; died in 1780.

Hirscher, hĕĕRsh'er, (JOHANN BAPTIST,) a Swiss Catholic theologian, born near Altorf in 1788. His principal work is "Christian Morality," ("Christliche Moral," 3 vols., 5th edition, 1851.)

Hirsching, hĕĕRsh'ing, (FRIEDRICH KARL GOTTLOB,) a German antiquary, born at Uffenheim in 1762, became professor of philosophy at Erlangen in 1792. He published several useful works, among which are a "Description of the Best Libraries of Germany," (4 vols., 1790,) and a "Historical and Literary Manual of Eminent Persons who died in the Eighteenth Century," ("Historisch-literarisches Handbuch berühmter Personen," etc., 1794-1815, 17 vols.) The last 12 volumes of this were edited by J. H. M. Ernesti. Died in 1800.

See ERSCH und GRUBER, "Allgemeine Encyklopaedie."

Hirschvogel, hĕĕRsh'fo'gel, (AUGUSTIN,) a German painter and engraver, born at Nuremberg in 1506; died in 1560.

Hirst, (HENRY B.,) an American poet, born in Philadelphia in 1813. He studied law, and was admitted to the bar in 1843. His first poems appeared in "Graham's Magazine," and were favourably received. He afterwards published "The Coming of the Mammoth, the Funeral of Time, and other Poems," (1845,) and "Endymion, a Tale of Greece, in four cantos," (1848.)

Hirt, hĕĕRt, (ALOYS,) a German antiquary and critic, born in Baden in 1759. He published "Architecture according to the Principles of the Ancients," (1809,) and other works. Died in 1836.

Hirt or **Hirth,** (JOHANN FRIEDRICH,) a German Orientalist and writer, born at Apolda in 1719, was professor of theology at Jena. Died in 1784.

Hirtius, hir'she-us, (AULUS,) a Roman consul and general, was a patrician by birth. Cicero, who was his intimate friend, speaks highly of his talents. He served under Cæsar in the Gallic war, and supported his party in the civil war. After the death of Cæsar, Hirtius joined Brutus against Antony, and was elected consul with C. Vibius Pansa. In 43 B.C. these consuls gained a victory over Antony at Mutina, (Módena;) but Hirtius was killed in the action. He is supposed to be the author of the continuation of "Cæsar's Commentaries" which forms the eighth book of the "Gallic War," and also of two other treatises on the campaigns of Cæsar, viz., the Alexandrian and the African.

See CICERO, "Philippics;" DION CASSIUS, books xliv., xlv., xlvi.; VOSSIUS, "De Historicis Latinis;" NIEBUHR, "Lectures on Roman History."

Hirzel, hĕĕRt'sel, (BERNHARD,) a Swiss Orientalist, born at Zurich in 1807, translated the "Sakuntala" of Kâlidâsa from the Sanscrit into German. Died in 1847.

Hirzel, (HANS CASPAR,) a Swiss physician and senator, born at Zurich in 1725, wrote a "Treatise on Rural Economy," and "The Rustic Socrates," (1761-74.) Died in 1803.

Hisely, hèz'le', (JEAN JOSEPH,) a Swiss historian, born in 1800, wrote, in French, "Researches on William Tell," (1843,) and other works on Swiss history.

Hisham. See HESHÂM.

Hisinger, hee'sing-er, or **Hising,** hee'sing, (WILHELM,) a Swedish mineralogist, born in 1766, published, besides other works, "Lethea Suecica, seu petrificata Sueciæ," (1837-40.) Died in 1852.

Histiæus, his-te-ee'us, [Gr. Ἱστιαῖος; Fr. HISTIÉE, ès'te'à',] an able and crafty ruler of Miletus, to whom Darius intrusted the duty of guarding a bridge over the Danube during his invasion of Scythia, about 512 B.C.

He refused to desert Darius at the instigation of Miltiades; but he afterwards revolted, and was put to death by the Persians about 494 B.C.

Histiée. See HISTIÆUS.

Hita, de, dà ee'tâ, (GINES PEREZ,) a Spanish chronicler, born in Murcia, lived between 1550 and 1600. He wrote an interesting work, entitled "The Civil Wars of Granada."

See TICKNOR, "History of Spanish Literature."

Hitch'cock, (EDWARD,) an eminent American geologist, born at Deerfield, Massachusetts, May 24, 1793. He became pastor of the Congregational church in Conway, Massachusetts, in 1821, and professor of chemistry and natural history in Amherst College in 1825. In 1840 he published his "Elementary Geology," a valuable work, which passed through twenty-five or more editions. From 1845 to 1854 he was president of Amherst College, the prosperity of which increased greatly under his direction. He became about 1845 professor of natural theology and geology in that institution. Having been appointed State geologist for Massachusetts, he made a geological survey of that State, and wrote "Reports on the Geology of Massachusetts," (1833-41.) Among his numerous works are "The Geology of the Connecticut Valley," (1823,) "The Religion of Geology and its Connected Sciences," (1851,) and "Illustrations of Surface-Geology," (1857.) By his exposition of the fossil footprints of the Connecticut valley he originated a new branch of science, called Ichnology. He published in 1848 "Fossil Footprints in the United States." He was the chief founder and first president of the American Geological Association. Died in 1864.

See "Silliman's Journal," vol. xli.; "North British Review" for February, 1860.

Hitchcock, (ETHAN ALLEN,) an American writer and military officer, a grandson of Ethan Allen, was born in Vergennes, Vermont, in 1798. He graduated at West Point in 1817, and served in the Seminole war in Florida. In the war with Mexico he was attached to the staff of General Scott, and in 1847 promoted to the rank of brigadier-general. He was subsequently sent to California, as commandant of the Pacific division, but he returned in 1854, and the next year resigned his commission. He wrote "Swedenborg a Hermetic Philosopher," (1858.)

Hitchcock, (PETER,) an American jurist, born in Cheshire, Connecticut, in 1780, graduated at Yale in 1801. He represented a district of Ohio in Congress from 1817 to 1819, and was subsequently judge of the supreme court of the State for twenty-eight years, for six years of which period he was chief justice. Died in 1853.

Hittorf, hit'toRf or he'toRf', (JACQUES IGNACE,) an eminent architect and antiquary, born at Cologne in 1793, was a pupil of Bélanger. He was appointed architect to the King of France in 1818, after which he visited Italy. He commenced about 1834 the church of Saint Vincent de Paul, (in the Italian style,) and designed the remarkable works of the Place de Concorde. Among his capital works are the Grand Circus, (1840,) the Panorama, the roof of which is supported by twelve iron cables, and the Cirque-Napoléon, (1851.) M. Hittorf acquired a European reputation by these structures, and by his writings on classical art, namely, "Polychromic Architecture of the Greeks," (1830.) "Modern Architecture of Sicily," (1837,) and "Ancient Architecture of Sicily." He was a member of the Institute. Died in 1867.

See "Nouvelle Biographie Générale."

Hitzig, hit'sıG, (FERDINAND,) a German biblical critic, born in Baden in 1807. He became professor of theology at Zurich in 1833. His principal works are a "Translation and Exposition of Isaiah," (1833,) and commentaries on the other greater prophets, (1841-50.)

Hjærne or **Hiærne,** he-ĕR'neh, (URBAN,) a Swedish physician and naturalist, born in 1641, became first physician to the king Carl XI., and vice-president of the Council of Mines. He wrote, besides other works, "Acta et Tentamina chimica," ("Chemical Experiments," 1712,) and "Oryctographia Suecana," (1716.) Died in 1724.

See "Biographiskt-Lexicon öfver namnkunnige Svenska Män."

ā, ē, ī, ō, ū, ȳ, *long;* à, è, ò, same, less prolonged; ă, ĕ, ĭ, ŏ, ŭ, ў, *short;* ą, ę, į, ǫ, *obscure;* fâr, fàll, fât; mĕt; nŏt; gōōd; mōōn;

Hjelm, he-êlm′, (PETER JACOB,) a Swedish mineralogist, born at Wexio in 1746, was president of the Academy of Sciences. Died in 1813.

Hjort, he-ORT′ or hyORT, (PEDER,) a Danish grammarian, born near Copenhagen in 1793. After an extensive tour in France and Italy, he became professor of German at Soröe. He wrote several successful works on grammar, among which are "Tydsk Grammatik for Dansktalende," ("German Grammar for the Use of Danes," 5th edition, 1851,) "Tydsk Läsebog for Dansktalende," ("German Reader for the Use of Danes," 3d edition, 1843,) and "Den Danske Börneven," ("The Danish Child's Friend," 6th edition, 1852.)

Hlin, hleen, **Hlina**, hlee′na̩, or **Lyna**, lee′na, [supposed to be derived from *hlyna*, to "warm" or "become warm,"] in the Northern mythology, a goddess, whose office it is to watch over those whom Frigga wishes to guard from peril. As Frigga represents the earth's fertility, so Hlin typifies the mild warmth which protects the tender plants from the breath of the Frost-giants.

Hlodyn, hlo′din, [in all probability the same as HLUDANA, the Latin name of a deity of the ancient Germans,] in the Norse mythology, the mother of Thor, and probably another name for Fiörgyn or Fiörgvin, (also called the mother of Thor,) the goddess of the earth. Thorpe derives it from *hlaða*, (allied to the English "lade" and "load,") to "heap up," to "load." Fiörgynn (as a masculine noun) was said to be the father of Frigga.

See THORPE's "Northern Mythology," vol. i. pp. 21 and 170.

Hlubek, hloo′běk, (FRANZ XAVER WILHELM,) a German writer on rural economy, born in Silesia in 1802. His principal works are "The Nutrition of Plants and Statics of Agriculture," (1841,) and a "Complete Treatise on Rural Economy," (2 vols., 1846.)

Hōad′ley or **Hoadly**, (BENJAMIN,) an English divine, born at Westerham in 1676, took orders about 1700. His zeal for religious liberty and opposition to the High-Church principles caused his promotion in 1715 to the see of Bangor. In 1717 he preached a sermon before the king, from which arose the great Bangorian controversy. This was maintained by Snape, Law, and other partisans of the High Church on one hand, and Hoadley on the other. He was made Bishop of Hereford in 1721, and of Winchester in 1734. He wrote a "Life of Dr. Samuel Clarke," and a few other works. Died in 1761.

See "Biographia Britannica."

Hoadley, (BENJAMIN,) M.D., eldest son of the preceding, was born in London in 1705, and graduated in 1729. In 1742 he was appointed physician to the king's household, and in 1746 to that of the Prince of Wales. He wrote "The Suspicious Husband," a comedy, which was successful, and assisted Hogarth in the "Analysis of Beauty." Died in 1757.

Hoadley, (Rev. JOHN,) LL.D., brother of the preceding, was born in 1711. He took orders in 1735, and obtained the livings of Wrington, Alresford, etc. He wrote several short poems and dramas. Died in 1776.

Hōar, (EBENEZER ROCKWOOD,) an able lawyer, the son of Samuel Hoar, noticed below, was born at Concord, Massachusetts, in 1816. His mother was a daughter of the celebrated Roger Sherman. He graduated at Harvard in 1835, studied law, was admitted to the bar about 1840, and practised in Boston. In 1859 he was appointed a justice of the supreme court of Massachusetts, and attorney-general of the United States in March, 1869.

Hoar, (SAMUEL,) a lawyer, born at Lincoln, Massachusetts, in 1778, was the father of the preceding. He was sent by the Governor of Massachusetts to South Carolina in 1844, to protect the rights of certain free negro sailors who had been imprisoned in Charleston; but he was driven from that city by a mob before he could perform his mission. Died in 1856.

Hōare, (PRINCE,) an English artist and dramatist, born at Bath in 1754, was the son of William Hoare, noticed below. He studied painting at Rome, and in 1799 was chosen foreign secretary of the Royal Academy. He is chiefly known as the author of dramas, as "No Song, No Supper," "Lock and Key," etc. Died in 1834.

Hoare, (Sir RICHARD COLT,) a noted English antiquary, born in 1758, married in 1783 the daughter of Lord Lyttleton, and inherited the title of baronet in 1787. He gained distinction as a topographer and antiquarian by his "Ancient and Modern History of Wiltshire," and wrote several other works. Died in 1838.

Hoare, (WILLIAM,) R.A., an English historical and portrait painter, born at Bath about 1706. He was one of the original members of the Royal Academy. After studying many years at Rome, he returned to Bath, and worked with great success, especially in portraits. Died in 1792.

Hō′bart, (Sir HENRY,) was lord chief justice of the court of common pleas in the reign of James I. "Hobart's Reports" (1641) have been often reprinted.

Hō′bart, (JOHN HENRY,) D.D., born in Philadelphia in 1775, was ordained in 1798. He was successively pastor at New Brunswick, Hempstead, and Trinity Church, New York, and was chosen Bishop of New York in 1816. He published numerous theological works. Died in 1830.

See DUYCKINCK, "Cyclopædia of American Literature," vol. i.

Hobbema or **Hobbima**, hob′be-mâ, (MINDERHOUT; Ger. MEINDERT; Fr. MINARD,) an excellent Flemish landscape-painter, was born probably at Coeverden about 1610. Little is known of his personal history. His favourite subjects were simple rural and sylvan scenes diversified by a winding stream, a ruined tower, or a distant village. He excelled in perspective and colouring. His works are rare, and command very high prices. About fifteen thousand dollars has been offered for one.

See PILKINGTON's "Dictionary of Painters."

Hobbes, hôbz, (THOMAS,) a famous English philosopher, born at Malmesbury in 1588. As tutor in the family of the Earl of Devonshire, he travelled several times on the continent with his pupils, and became acquainted with Gassendi, Descartes, etc. In 1628 he published a Latin translation of Thucydides, and in 1642 a treatise on government,—"Elementa Philosophica de Cive." He was a royalist in the civil war, and an advocate of unconditional obedience to the king. In 1647 he was mathematical tutor to the Prince of Wales, (Charles II.,) then in Paris. His treatise on "Human Nature" (1650) was followed by the "Leviathan," (a complete system of his philosophy, including his political, moral, and theological views,) which made a great sensation, and gave offence to theologians, and—though it was hostile to liberal principles—even to the royalists. In 1666 this work and his "De Cive" were censured by Parliament. Soon after the restoration, he received a pension of one hundred pounds. His paradoxical opinions were warmly controverted by Cudworth, Clarendon, and others. In 1675 he published a translation in verse of the "Iliad" and the "Odyssey," which drew from Pope the assertion that "his poetry is too mean for criticism." In his old age, which was passed at the seat of his patron, the Earl of Devonshire, he published a "History of the Civil War from 1640 to 1660," and other works. "A permanent foundation of his fame," says Mackintosh, "consists in his admirable style, which seems to be the very perfection of didactic language. Short, clear, precise, pithy, his language never has more than one meaning, which never requires a second thought to find. . . . His little tract on 'Human Nature' has scarcely an ambiguous or a needless word. . . . Perhaps no writer of any age or nation, on subjects so abstruse, has manifested an equal power of engraving his thoughts on the mind of his readers. . . . His style so stimulates attention that it never tires, and, to those who are acquainted with the subject, appears to have as much spirit as can be safely blended with reason." In another place he says, "Hobbes having thus struck affections out of his map of human nature, and having totally misunderstood (as will appear in a succeeding part of this dissertation) the nature even of the appetites, it is no wonder that we should find in it not a trace of the moral sentiments." "Hobbes," says Macaulay, "had, in language more precise and luminous than has ever been employed by any other metaphysical writer, maintained that the will of the prince was the standard of right and wrong. . . . Thousands eagerly welcomed a theory which, while it exalted the kingly office, relaxed the obligations of morality, and degraded religion into a mere affair of state." ("History of England," vol. i. chap. ii.)

"Hobbes's politics," says Hume, in his "History of England," "are fitted only to promote tyranny, and his ethics to encourage licentiousness. Though an enemy to religion, he partakes nothing of the spirit of skepticism, but is as positive and dogmatical as if human reason could attain a thorough conviction in these subjects." He lived, however, in formal communion with the Anglican Church. Died in 1679.

See "Vita Thomæ Hobbes," in Latin verse, by himself, 1679; "Life of Hobbes," by RICHARD BLACKBURNE, 1681; "Biographia Britannica;" Life prefixed to WOOD's "Annals;" BRUCKER, "History of Philosophy;" MACKINTOSH, "View of the Progress of Ethical Philosophy;" ALLIBONE, "Dictionary of Authors."

Hob'house, (Sir BENJAMIN,) M.P., an English statesman, born in 1757, was a prominent member of the House of Commons from 1797 to 1818, held several civil offices, and was attached to the party of Fox. He wrote a "Treatise on Heresy," and "Remarks on France and Italy." Died in 1831.

Hobhouse, (JOHN CAM,) Lord Broughton, an English statesman and writer, born in 1786, was a son of the preceding. He became intimate at college with Lord Byron, in company with whom he visited Spain, Greece, and Turkey in 1809. He published in 1812 "A Journey through Albania, and other Provinces of Turkey, with Lord Byron," which is the best account of that country, and, in 1816, "Letters on the Hundred Days, or Last Reign of Napoleon," (in 2 vols.) He was elected to Parliament by the Radicals or Liberals of Westminster in 1819, and obtained some success as a speaker. In 1831 he became secretary of war in the Whig ministry. He was appointed secretary of state for Ireland in 1833, and was president of the board of control from 1846 to 1851. Died in June, 1869.

See "London Quarterly Review" for October, 1813.

Hoc'cleve or **Oc'cleve,** (THOMAS,) an early English poet and lawyer, is supposed to have been born about 1370. He wrote "The Story of Jonathan," and other poems. "His poetry," says Hallam, "abounds with pedantry, and is destitute of all grace and spirit."

Hoche, hôsh or hosh, (LAZARE,) a French general, who rose from a very humble rank in society, was born at Montreuil, near Paris, in 1768, and entered the French guards at the age of sixteen. He favoured the Revolution of 1789, and was made a lieutenant in 1792. Having studied tactics, and served with credit at Thionville, Dunkirk, etc., he became in a short time successively general of brigade and general of division, and at the age of twenty-four commanded the army of the Moselle. In 1793 he defeated Wurmser and drove him out of Alsace, soon after which he was arrested by the Jacobin leader Saint-Just and imprisoned at Paris. The fall of Robespierre in 1794 restored him to liberty and command. Employed to subdue the royalists of La Vendée, he effected much by his address and moderation, and in 1795 defeated the enemy at Quiberon. In 1797, commanding the army of the Sambre and Meuse, he opened the campaign against the Austrians by a daring passage of the Rhine in their presence, and defeated them in several actions. In the contest between the Directory and the Legislative Councils, Hoche favoured the former, who invoked the aid of his army, but soon issued counter-orders and employed another in the service. He died, of poison, (as was suspected,) in 1797. He was one of the noblest spirits and ablest generals that the Revolution produced, and, if he had lived, might have been a formidable rival of Bonaparte.

See DAUNOU, "Éloge du Général Hoche," 1798; PRIVAT, "Notes historiques sur la Vie du Général Hoche," 1798; ROUSSELIN, "Vie de Lazare Hoche," 1798; "Vie et Pensées du Général Hoche," Berne; CHAMPROBERT, "Notice historique sur Lazare Hoche," 1840; DOURILLE, "Histoire de Lazare Hoche," 1844; J. J. ABEL, "Geschichte der Krankheit und des Todes des Obergenerals L. Hoche," 1798.

Hochstetter, hoK'stĕt'ter, (ANDREAS ADAM,) a German Protestant divine, born at Tübingen in 1688; died in 1717.

Hocquincourt, d', do'kåN'kooR', (CHARLES DE MONCHY,) born in Picardy in 1599, became marshal of

France in 1651, and commanded the royal army which was defeated by the Prince of Condé in 1652. He deserted to the Spaniards, and was killed at Dunkirk in 1658.

Hö'der, Hö'dur, (Höðr,) or **Höd,** written also **Hoder,** the blind god in the Norse mythology. Through the cunning malice of Loki, he became the slayer of his brother Balder, whose death Vali avenged by killing Höder. (See BALDER, and VALI.)

Hodge, (CHARLES,) D.D., an eminent American theologian, born in Philadelphia in 1797. He graduated at Princeton in 1815, and studied divinity at the Princeton Theological Seminary, in which he became professor of Oriental and Biblical literature in 1822. In 1840 he succeeded to the chair of didactic and exegetical theology, and in 1852 added to it the professorship of polemic theology. In 1825 Dr. Hodge established, and, with but one brief interruption, has since edited, the "Biblical Repertory and Princeton Review." It is now the oldest theological quarterly in America. It was the chief organ of the Old-School division of the Presbyterian Church. Two volumes of his contributions to this "Review," entitled "Princeton Theological Essays," were published in 1846-47, and a third volume, "Reviews and Essays," in 1857.

Hodges, hŏj'ez, (NATHANIEL,) an English physician, who practised in London, and gained distinction by his faithful services during the great plague of 1665, when the most of the doctors fled from the danger. He wrote, in Latin, an account of this calamity, (1672.) He died in prison for debt in 1684.

Hodges, (WILLIAM,) R.A., an English painter, born in London about 1744. He painted landscapes with moderate success, and was employed as draughtsman in Captain Cook's second voyage, (1772.) He afterwards visited India and painted some Indian views. He published "Select Views in India," (2 vols., 1788,) and "Travels in India in 1780-83," (1793.) Died in 1797.

Hödg'kin-son, (EATON,) born at Anderton, Cheshire, in 1789, is distinguished for his researches respecting the strength of iron pillars, rails, etc. He discovered that an iron rail in the form of an inverted letter T will support a greater pressure than any other. From numerous experiments he derived formulæ for solid and hollow iron pillars, which are generally adopted. He co-operated with Mr. Stephenson in the construction of the tubular Britannia bridge about 1845. He wrote several valuable treatises on the strength of iron and other materials used in building. Died in 1861.

Hödg'son, (FRANCIS,) an English poet, born in 1781, was a friend of Lord Byron, and provost of Eton College. He produced a version of Juvenal, (1808,) "Sacred Lyrics," (1842,) and other poems. Died in 1852.

Hodgson, (Rev. JOHN,) an English antiquary, published a "History of Northumberland," (vol. i., 1827; vol. iii., 1841.) Died in 1845.

Hodgson, (ROBERT,) an English divine, was a nephew of Bishop Porteus. He became Dean of Carlisle in 1820. He published, besides numerous sermons, a "Life of Bishop Porteus," (1811,) and edited the works of Porteus, (6 vols., 1816.) Died in 1844.

Hodierna, o-de-êR'nå, or **Adierna,** å-de-êR'nå, (GIAMBATTISTA,) a Sicilian astronomer and priest, born at Ragusa in 1597, verified the positions of the fixed stars, and discovered the motions of Jupiter's satellites. His "Mediceorum Ephemerides" (1656) is the first book, says Lalande, "in which we find observations on the eclipses of Jupiter's satellites." He wrote a treatise on the System of Saturn, (1657,) and other works. Died in 1660.

Hodius. See HODY.

Ho'dy̆, [Lat. HO'DIUS,] (HUMPHRY,) D.D., an English divine and eminent scholar, born at Oldcombe in 1659. About 1694 he became chaplain to Archbishop Tillotson. He was chosen professor of Greek at Oxford in 1698, and Archdeacon of Oxford in 1704. He published an excellent work "On the Original Texts of the Bible, and the Greek and Latin Versions," ("De Bibliorum Textis Originalibus," etc., 1705,) also, "On the Illustrious Greek Restorers of the Greek Language," (1742,) which is commended by Hallam. Died in 1706.

See DR. JEBB, "Notitia de Vita et Scriptis H. Hodii."

Hoe, (RICHARD MARCH,) born in New York City in 1812, is known as the inventor of Hoe's type-revolving printing-press, which makes the impression on both sides of the sheet at the same time. It is capable of striking off, it is said, fifteen thousand copies per hour, and is especially useful in large newspaper establishments.

Hoë, or **Hoë von Höenegg,** ho'ĕh fon ho'ĕh-nĕk', (MATTHIAS,) a German theologian and controversialist, born in 1580; died in 1645.

See TAUBNER, "Memoria M. Hoë ab Hoënegg," Dresden, 1792.

Hoeck. See ÆPINUS and HOEK.

Hoefer, hö'fĕr, |Fr. pron. ho'fair',| (JOHANN CHRISTIAN FERDINAND, a German writer, distinguished for his learning and versatility, was born at Doeschnitz, in Thuringia, in 1811. He became in 1834 secretary to Victor Cousin, whom he assisted in the translation of the works of Plato. He left Cousin in 1836, after which he studied medicine, and practised several years in Paris. In 1843 he was sent to Germany by M. Cousin to examine the German methods of medical instruction and practice. He published, besides other works, a "History of Chemistry from the Earliest Times to the Present," (2 vols., 1842.) In 1851 he was selected by MM. Didot to direct their great biographical dictionary, "Nouvelle Biographie Générale," for which he wrote able articles on Aristotle, Cæsar, Columbus, Descartes, Erasmus, and others.

Hoefken. See HÖFKEN.

Hoefnaeghel, hoof'nä'g̃el or hoof'nä'hĕl, (GEORGE,) a Flemish painter, born at Antwerp in 1545, was painter to the Elector of Bavaria. He excelled in water-colour painting. Died at Vienna in 1600.

Hoek or **Hoeck, van,** vän hook, also written **Houk,** (JAN,) a Flemish painter of history, born at Antwerp about 1600, was one of the most skilful pupils of Rubens. He worked for a long time in Germany, and was patronized by the emperor Ferdinand II. He passed his latter years in Antwerp. His design and colouring are highly praised He was very successful in portraits. Among his master-pieces are "Samson and Delilah," and "Christ on the Cross," (at Bruges.) Died in 1650.

See J. C. WEYERMAN, "De Schilderkonst der Nederlanders."

Hoek, (ROBERT,) a brother of the preceding, born in 1609, was a skilful painter. He painted miniatures which were admired for extreme fineness of touch and beauty of colour. His principal works are "The Twelve Apostles," an army, and a camp. Died in 1668.

See DESCAMPS, "Vies des Peintres Flamands, Hollandais," etc.

Hoelderlin. See HÖLDERLIN.

Hoelty. See HÖLTY.

Hoeltzlinus. See HÖLTZLINUS.

Hoenir or **Hönir,** hö'nir, [etymology unknown,] in the Norse mythology, a god who, with Lodur, assisted Odin in creating mankind. He is supposed to have contributed as his portion sense or perception, while Odin gave breath and vitality, and Lodur animal warmth and the flowing (or circulating) blood. (See ODIN.)

Hoepfner. See HÖPFNER.

Hoepken. See HÖPKEN.

Hoerberg. See HÖRBERG.

Hoeschel. See HÖSCHEL.

Hoest. See HÖST.

Hoet, hoot, (GERARD,) an eminent Dutch historical painter, born at Bommel in 1648. He worked mostly at Utrecht and the Hague. Among his chief works are the "Rape of the Sabines," and the "Sacrifice of Dido." "The talent of Hoet," says Descamps, "is known throughout Europe. He composed with much genius, and his works display vast erudition." Died in 1733.

See DESCAMPS, "Vies des Peintres Flamands, Hollandais," etc.

Hoeven, van der, vän der hoo'ven, (JAN,) an able Dutch naturalist, born at Rotterdam in 1801, became professor of zoology at Leyden in 1835. His principal work is an excellent "Manual of Zoology," ("Handboek der Dierkunde," 2 vols., 1827-33,) which has been translated into English, (London, 1854.) His brother ABRAHAM (1798-1855) was professor of theology at Amsterdam and Utrecht, and was considered one of the most eloquent orators of Holland.

Hoeyer. See HÖYER.

Hofacker, höf'äk'ĕr, (CARL CHRISTOPH,) a German jurist, born in Würtemberg in 1749; died in 1793.

Höfer. See HOEFER.

Hofer, ho'fĕr, (ANDREAS,) a celebrated Tyrolese patriot, born in the valley of the Passeyr in 1767. On the breaking out of the insurrection against the French and the Bavarian government, to which the Tyrol had been lately transferred, he entered into secret negotiations with the archduke John for the deliverance of the country. In April, 1809, with the assistance of an Austrian army, Hoefer, at the head of the Tyrolese peasantry, defeated the French and Bavarian troops at the Sterzinger Moose. In the May following, the Austrians, under General Chasteler, suffered a defeat from the superior numbers of the enemy near Wörgl. Soon after this the Tyrolese were again victorious in an engagement near Mount Isel; but, the Austrian army being withdrawn after the battle of Wagram, the country was once more invaded by Marshal Lefebvre. On the 13th of August, 1809, Hofer, with his army of Tyrolese peasants, signally defeated the French commander near Mount Isel, after a long and obstinate conflict; but, overpowered at last by the reinforcements sent from France, he took refuge in the mountains. Being soon after betrayed by a former friend, he was tried at Mantua, and was shot in February, 1810.

See "Andreas Hofer und die Tyroler Insurrection," Munich, 1811; HORMAYR, "Geschichte Andreas Hofer's Sandwirths," etc., 1809; BECKER, "Andreas Hofer und der Freiheitskampf in Tyrol," 3 vols., 1842; "Memoirs of Andrew Hofer," translated from the German by C. H. HALL; "London Quarterly Review" for July, 1817.

Hoff, von, fon hoff, (KARL ERNST ADOLF,) a German geologist, born at Gotha in 1771, wrote a "History of the Natural Changes of the Surface of the Globe," (5 vols., 1822-41,) and edited, from 1801 to 1816, "The Almanac of Gotha," a statistical publication of very high character. Died in 1837.

Hoffbauer, hof'bŏw'ĕr, (JOHANN CHRISTOPH,) a German writer, born at Bielefeld in 1766, published, besides other works, "Researches into the Diseases of the Soul," (3 vols., 1802-07.) Died in 1827.

Höff'man, (CHARLES FENNO,) a popular American poet and novelist, born in New York in 1806, graduated at Columbia College. He studied law, and was admitted to the bar about 1828. In 1835 he produced a successful descriptive work entitled "Winter in the West." He edited successively "The American Monthly Magazine" and "The New York Mirror." Among his works are "The Vigil of Faith, and other Poems," and a number of songs. "No American," says R. W. Griswold, "is comparable to him as a song-writer." He published in 1840 "Greyslaer," a novel. Since about 1850 he has been afflicted with a mental derangement.

See GRISWOLD, "Poets and Poetry of America," and "Prose Writers of America;" DUYCKINCK, "Cyclopædia of American Literature," vol. ii.

Hoffman, (DAVID,) an eminent American lawyer, born in Baltimore in 1784, was professor of law in the University of Maryland from 1817 to 1836. He afterwards resided in Philadelphia. He published a "Course of Legal Study," which has been highly commended. According to Judge Story, "it contains by far the most perfect system for the study of the law that has ever been offered to the public." He also wrote or compiled "Chronicles selected from the Originals of Cartaphilus the Wandering Jew," (2 vols., 1855.) Died in 1854.

See "North American Review" for January, 1830.

Hoffman, hof'môn', (FRANÇOIS BENOÎT,) an able French critic and dramatic poet, born at Nancy in 1760. He produced many successful operas and dramas, among which are "Phædra," (1786,) "Adrien," (1792,) and "Stratonice," a comedy, (1792.) He wrote literary critiques for the "Journal de l'Empire" and the "Journal des Débats" for many years. "He had," says Sainte-Beuve, "many qualities of a true critic,—conscience and independence. . . . He was learned with variety and without pedantry." Died in 1828.

See SAINTE-BEUVE, "Causeries du Lundi" for February 25, 1850; "Nouvelle Biographie Générale."

Hoffmann, hof'män, (ANDREAS GOTTLIEB,) a German theologian, born in the county of Mansfeld in 1796, became professor of theology at Jena in 1822. He published a "Treatise on Hebrew Antiquities," (1832,) and wrote many articles for the "Encyclopædia" of Ersch and Gruber.

Hoffmann, (AUGUST HEINRICH,) an eminent lyric poet and philologist, called also **Hoffmann von Fallersleben,** (fäl'lers-lä'ben,) was born at Fallersleben, in Hanover, in 1798. He studied at Göttingen and Bonn, and became in 1835 professor of the German language and literature at Breslau. He published "German Social Songs of the Sixteenth and Seventeenth Centuries," and "Mines for the History of the German Language and Literature;" also ballads, songs for children, war lyrics, and other poems, which are greatly admired for their simplicity, fervour, and pathos.

See LONGFELLOW, "Poets and Poetry of Europe;" "Levensschets van A. H. Hoffmann von Fallersleben."

Hoffmann, (CASPAR,) a German physician, born at Gotha in 1572, published numerous works on medicine. Died at Altdorf in 1648.

See ERSCH und GRUBER, "Allgemeine Encyklopaedie."

Hoffmann, hof'mån, (CHARLES ALEXANDER,) a Polish writer, born in Masovia in 1798, produced in 1827 a Polish translation of the works of Dr. Franklin. Having been identified with the insurrection of 1830, he was driven into exile in 1832. He was the husband of Clementina Hoffmanowa, noticed below.

Hoffmann, (CHRISTIAN GOTTFRIED,) a German jurisconsult, born at Lauban, in Lusatia, in 1692, became professor of law at Leipsic in 1718, and afterwards at Frankfort-on-the-Oder. He acquired a high reputation by his writings, (in Latin,) among which are a "History of the Roman Law of Justinian," (1720-24,) and "Library of German Public Law," ("Bibliotheca Juris publici Germanici," etc., 1734.) Died in 1735.

See ERSCH und GRUBER, "Allgemeine Encyklopaedie;" HIRSCHING, "Historisch-literarisches Handbuch."

Hoffmann, (CHRISTOPH LUDWIG,) an eminent medical writer, born at Rheda, in Westphalia, in 1721, was physician to the Electors of Cologne and Mentz. Among his principal works are treatises "On the Small-Pox," (2 vols., 1778,) and "On the Sensibility and Irritability of the Diseased Parts," (1779.) Died in 1807.

Hoffmann or **Hoffmanowa,** hof-må-no'vä, (CLEMENTINA,) a popular Polish authoress, whose maiden name was TANSKA, was born at Warsaw in 1798, and liberally educated. She produced about 1820, in Polish, her "Memorial of a Good Mother," which had a great popularity. She was married to Charles A. Hoffmann, with whom she removed to Paris about 1832. Among her works, which were published collectively in 1833, (in 10 vols.,) are letters, historical tales, essays, and biographies of eminent Poles. Died in 1845.

Hoffmann, (DANIEL,) a German Lutheran divine, born at Halle about 1538, was professor of theology at Helmstedt. He was censured for teaching that the truths of philosophy conflict with the truths of religion. Died in 1611.

Hoffmann, (ERNST THEODOR WOLFGANG; afterwards called ERNST THEODOR AMADEUS,) one of the most remarkable and original of German story-tellers, *(Erzähler,)* was born at Königsberg in 1776. He studied law, and subsequently received several minor appointments under the government. In 1816 he became counsellor of the royal court of judicature at Berlin. Died in 1822, his health having been previously undermined by dissipation. His gifted and versatile mind led him to the cultivation of music, poetry, and art. But he "is celebrated chiefly," says Dr. Hedge, "for his successful use of the magic and demoniac element in fiction. He does not seek to make the flesh creep and the hair bristle, but aims rather at the diaphragm. He views all these *infernalia* on the humorous side; and if any one trait is particularly prominent in his writings, it is irony." Menzel, after alluding to the strange combination which his mind exhibited of manliness, humour, poetry, and morbid sensibility, remarks, "From the devil down to a wry-faced child's doll, from the dissonance of life which rends the soul down to a dissonance in music which only rends the ear, the immeasurable kingdom of the ugly, the repulsive, the annoying, was gathered around him,

and his descriptions paint alternately these tormenting objects, and the torments which they prepare for a beautiful soul, with inimitable vividness and truth." Again, he says, "Hoffmann's innermost being was music; and the prayer of Saint Anthony is never wanting to his hellish caricatures, nor the Christmas bell to the witches' sabbath." Among his principal works are "Phantasiestücke in Callot's Manier," (4 vols., 1814,) and "Serapions Brüder," (4 vols., 1819-21.) His various other tales, etc. would fill several volumes.

See FUNCK, "Aus dem Leben zweier Dichter E. T. W. Hoffmann und F. G. Wetzel," 1836; J. E. HITZIG, "Aus E. T. W. Hoffmanns Leben," etc., 2 vols., 1823; GERVINUS, "Geschichte der Deutschen Dichtung," 1853; ERSCH und GRUBER, "Allgemeine Encyklopaedie;" "Nouvelle Biographie Générale;" "Foreign Quarterly Review" for July, 1827.

Hoffmann, [Lat. HOFFMAN'NUS,] (FRIEDRICH,) an illustrious German physician, was born at Halle in 1660. He studied at Jena, and, after travelling in England and Holland, settled as a physician at Halberstadt in 1688. On the establishment of the university at Halle he was appointed in 1693 its first professor of medicine by the Elector Frederick III. of Brandenburg. On the invitation of Frederick I. of Prussia, he removed in 1708 to Berlin, where he was made royal physician, but still retained his professorship. He returned in 1712 to Halle, where he died in 1742. Hoffmann rendered most important services to practical medicine by his experiments with various remedies: his "Elixirium Viscerale" and "Liquor Anodynus Mineralis," commonly called "Hoffmann's Anodyne," are still popular, and he was one of the first to bring mineral waters into more general use. He wrote, in Latin and German, numerous medical works, among which is "Medicina Rationalis systematica," (9 vols., 1718-40.) His complete works were published in 6 vols. quarto, (1740.)

See SCHULZE, "Vita F. Hoffmanni," prefixed to his Works, 1730; BALDINGER, "Programma de F. Hoffmanni et H. Boerhavii Meritis in Medicinam practicam," 1772; LOVEN, "Dissertatio de F. Hoffmanno ejusque Medicina Rationali systematica," 1846; "Nouvelle Biographie Générale."

Hoffmann, (JOHANN GOTTFRIED,) a German writer on political economy, born at Breslau in 1765. He became councillor of state in Berlin in 1808, and attended the Congress of Vienna in 1814. Among his works is "The Science of Money," ("Die Lehre vom Gelde," 1838.) Died in 1847.

Hoffmann, (JOHANN JAKOB,) a Swiss scholar, born at Bâle in 1635, obtained in 1667 the chair of Greek in his native city. His principal work is a "Universal Lexicon, Historical, Geographical, Political," etc., (in Latin, 1667.) Died in 1706.

See ERSCH und GRUBER, "Allgemeine Encyklopaedie."

Hoffmann, (MORITZ,) a German physician and botanist, born at Fürstenwalde in 1622, became professor of surgery at Altdorf, and published several medical and botanical works. Died in 1698.

His son, JOHANN MORITZ, born at Altdorf in 1653, was a physician and botanist. He practised at Anspach with success, and wrote on anatomy, etc. Died in 1727.

See ERSCH und GRUBER, "Allgemeine Encyklopaedie."

Hoffmann, hof'mån, (TYCHO,) a Danish writer, was keeper of the seals of Denmark. He wrote "Historical Portraits of Eminent Danes." Died in 1754.

Hoffmannsegg, von, fon hof'mån-sèg', (JOHANN CENTURIUS,) COUNT, a German botanist, born at Dresden in 1766. Having explored the botanical riches of Portugal for several years, he returned to Germany in 1804, and published with M. Link his magnificent "Portuguese Flora," (in French, 22 parts, 1809-33.) Died in 1849.

Hoffmannus. See HOFFMANN.

Höfken or **Hoefken,** höf'ken, (GUSTAV,) a German writer on national economy, born at Hattingen, in Prussia, in 1811. He published, besides other works, "The Condition, Policy, and Development of the Power of England," (2 vols., 1846.)

Hofland, (BARBARA,) a popular English writer, born at Sheffield in 1770, was the daughter of Robert Wreaks. She became the wife of Thomas Hofland, the painter, in 1808. She wrote numerous novels and moral tales, which had a wide circulation. The "Son of a Genius" (1813) is probably her most successful work. She was patronized by Queen Charlotte. The name of her first husband was Hoole. It is said that three hundred thousand copies of her books were sold in Great Britain. Among the titles of them are "Decision," "Fortitude," "Beatrice," and "Self-Denial." Died in 1844.

See T. RAMSAY, "Life of Barbara Hofland," 1849.

Hofland, (THOMAS CHRISTOPHER,) an eminent English landscape-painter, born at Worksop, in Nottinghamshire, in 1777. He married Mrs. Hoole, who, under the name of Hofland, became well known as a novelist, and resided mostly in or near London. His subjects were chosen from the river and lake scenery of the British Islands. He published a richly illustrated volume called "The British Angler's Manual," (1839.) Died in 1843.

Hofmann, hof'mån, (AUGUST WILHELM,) a German chemist, born at Giessen in April, 1818. He has made discoveries in organic chemistry, on which he has contributed several memoirs to the "Philosophical Transactions," and has attained eminence as a lecturer on chemistry at the Royal Institution. In 1855 he was appointed chemist to the mint. He edited Fownes's "Chemistry," (1858.)

Hofmann, (JOHANN CHRISTIAN KONRAD,) a Protestant German theologian, born at Nuremberg in 1810. Among his principal works is "Prophecy and Fulfilment," (2 vols., 1841–44.)

Hofmannswaldau, von, fon hof'måns-wål'döw, sometimes written **Hofmandswaldau,** (CHRISTIAN HOFMANN,) a German poet, born at Breslau in 1618. He published in 1673 a collection of poems, entitled "Sinnreiche Heldenbriefe." Died in 1679.

See GERVINUS, "Geschichte der Deutschen Nationalliteratur."

Ho'gan, (JOHN,) an Irish sculptor, born at Tallow, Waterford county, in 1800. He studied in Rome, 1823–29, and settled in Dublin. Among his chief works is "The Drunken Faun," for which he received a medal at the Exposition of Paris in 1851. Died about 1858.

Ho'garth, (GEORGE,) a Scottish writer on music, born about 1796, is the father-in-law of Charles Dickens, the novelist. He published "Musical History, Biography, and Criticism," (2 vols., 1836,) which is highly commended, and "Memoirs of the Musical Drama," (2 vols., 1838.) He became musical and dramatic critic for the London "Daily News" in 1846. Died in 1870.

Hogarth, (WILLIAM,) a celebrated satirical painter, born in London in 1697, was apprenticed to a silversmith, whom he left in 1718. He then earned a subsistence for some time by engraving, and studied drawing in the academy of Sir James Thornhill, whose daughter he married in 1730. He acquired skill in portraits, but soon exchanged that branch of art for one more suited to his original genius,—the dramatic or satirical species, in which he is unrivalled. In 1733 he published a series of engravings called the "Harlot's Progress," which had a large sale, and was followed by the "Rake's Progress," "Marriage à la Mode," "Industry and Idleness," "Beer Lane," and "The Enraged Musician." His pictures abound in comic humour, and display great skill in caricature, as well as great originality and fertility of invention. His works have also the merit of conveying useful lessons of morality. In 1753 he published his "Analysis of Beauty," in which he maintains that a waving line or curve is the essential element of beauty. In 1757 he became painter to the king. Died in 1764.

See CHARLES LAMB, "On the Genius of Hogarth;" "Anecdotes of Hogarth, by himself, with an Essay on his Life" by NICHOLS, 1833; "Encyclopædia Britannica;" JOHN IRELAND, "Hogarth Illustrated," 3 vols., 1791–98; "Historical Sketches of the Reign of George II.," in "Blackwood's Magazine" for August, 1869; "Foreign Quarterly Review" for January, 1836.

Hogendorp, van, vån ho'gen-dorp', (DYRK,) COUNT, a Dutch general, born at Rotterdam in 1761, was minister of war under King Louis in 1806. In 1811 he became general of division and aide-de-camp to Napoleon, whom he followed in the Russian campaign. After the battle of Waterloo he went to Brazil, where he died in 1830.

Hogendorp, van, (GIJSBERT KAREL,) COUNT, a Dutch statesman, brother of the preceding, born at Rotterdam in 1762. He united with several others to form a provisional government in 1813, and was president of the commission which framed a new constitution. He was

minister of foreign affairs, and vice-president of the council, until he resigned in 1816. He wrote "Considerations on the Political Economy of the Low Countries," (10 vols., 1818–23.) Died in 1834.

See VREEDE, "Jets bij de Dood van G. K. van Hogendorp," 1 34.

Hogg,(JAMES,)"the Ettrick Shepherd," born in Ettrick Forest, in Scotland, in 1772, was the son of a shepherd, and followed his father's employment until he was thirty years of age. In 1803 a collection of his poems was published, under the title of "The Mountain Bard," the proceeds of which (about £300) enabled him to take a farm. He failed, however, in this enterprise. After many struggles with adversity, he went to Edinburgh, to try his fortune in authorship, about 1810. Having issued a literary periodical called "The Spy," without success, he was encouraged by his friends to devote himself to poetry, and in 1813 gave to the public the "Queen's Wake," which procured him a high reputation as a poet. It is generally considered as his best work. His success stimulated him to the rapid production of many other poems, among which are "The Pilgrims of the Sun," (1815,) "Poetic Mirror," "Sacred Melodies," and "The Border Garland," (1819.) He wrote, in prose, "The Brownie of Bodsbeck, and other Tales," (1818,) "Winter Evening Tales," (1820,) "The Three Perils of Man," etc., and contributed to "Blackwood's Magazine." In 1820 he married Margaret Phillips, and resided afterwards on a farm at Altrive. Hogg is one of the principal actors and interlocutors in Christopher North's famous "Noctes Ambrosianæ." Died in 1835. "The Queen's Wake," says Professor Wilson, "is a garland of fair forest-flowers, bound with a band of rushes from the moor. Some of the ballads are very beautiful; one or two even splendid. 'Kilmeny' alone places our (ay, our) shepherd among the undying ones."

See WILSON, "Memoir of James Hogg," prefixed to an edition of Hogg's Works, Edinburgh, 5 vols., 1850; R. S. MACKENZIE, "Life of James Hogg," prefixed to an edition of "Noctes Ambrosianæ," New York, 1855; LORD JEFFREY's article in the "Edinburgh Review" for November, 1814, (vol. xxiv.;) CHAMBERS, "Biographical Dictionary of Eminent Scotsmen;" WILLIAM JERDAN, "Men I have known," London, 1866; "Edinburgh Review" for November, 1819; "Fraser's Magazine" for February, 1832.

Hohenhausen, von, fon ho'en-höw'zen, (ELIZABETH PHILIPPINE AMALIE,) BARONESS, a German poetess, born near Cassel in 1789, wrote lyric poems entitled "Spring Flowers," (1817,) and translated Byron's "Corsair," and some of the works of Sir Walter Scott.

Hohenlohe-Ingelfingen, ho'en-lo'eh ing'el-fing'en, (FRIEDRICH LUDWIG,) PRINCE, a Prussian general, born in 1746. He distinguished himself in the campaigns of 1792 and 1793, and obtained command of an army in 1795. He commanded the Prussian forces which were defeated by Napoleon at Jena on the 14th of October, 1806. On the 16th the king gave him command of all the troops that had escaped from Jena and Auerstadt. He was compelled to abandon Berlin to the enemy, and soon after was taken prisoner, with about 15,000 men, at Prentzlow. He retired to private life, and died in 1817 or 1818.

Hohenlohe-Waldenburg-Schillingsfürst, ho'-en-lo'eh wål'den-böörg' shil'lings-fürst', (ALEXANDER LEOPOLD FRANZ EMMERICH,) PRINCE of, a Hungarian prelate, born at Kupferzelle in 1794. He pretended to cure disease by prayer. Died in 1849.

Hohenstaufen, ho'en-stöw'fen, [from *hoch*, "high," and *Staufen*, "hill" or "eminence,"] in the singular, **Hohenstaufe,** ho'en-stöw'feh, a celebrated family of German princes, who reigned from 1138 to 1254. The first of the line, FRIEDRICH VON BÜREN, received the name on account of having removed his dwelling from a valley *auf den Staufen,* ("up the hill" or "mountain.") His son, FRIEDRICH VON STAUFEN, was rewarded by the emperor Henry IV. for his eminent services by the duchy of Suabia and the hand of his daughter Agnes. Henry also made him Regent of Germany while he fought against the pope in Italy. Friedrich died in 1105, leaving two sons, Friedrich and Conrad, the latter of whom was crowned King of Germany, with the title of CONRAD III. His nephew, FRIEDRICH BARBAROSSA, the most celebrated of the line, was chosen emperor in 1152. (See FREDERICK I. of Germany, and KYFFHÄUSER.) The Hohenstaufen line ended with CONRADIN in 1268.

e as k; ç as s; g hard; ġ as j; G, H, K, *guttural;* N, *nasal;* R, *trilled;* s as z; th as in *this.* (☞See Explanations, p. 23.)

Hohenzollern, ho′ęn-tsol′lĕRn, the name of an ancient princely German family, from which the Kings of Prussia are descended. The name is derived from the castle of Zollern, in Suabia, which is said to have been built by Tassillon or Thasilio about 800 A.D.

Höijer, hö′e-yer, (BENJAMIN CARL HENRIK,) an eminent Swedish philosopher, born in Dalecarlia in 1767. His promotion was hindered by the liberal political principles of his youth. He produced a treatise "On the Progress of Critical Philosophy," an "Outline of the History of the Fine Arts," and other works. In 1808 he became professor of philosophy at Upsal, where he gained a high reputation as a lecturer. Died in 1812.

Ho′kan-son, (OLOF,) a Swedish orator, originally a peasant, born in the province of Bleking in 1695, was elected in 1726 to the Diet, in which he acquired great influence by his prudence and eloquence. Died in 1769.

Holanda, de, dā o-làn′dȧ, (FRANCISCO,) a Portuguese painter, born in 1518, studied in Rome, and appears to have returned to Portugal. He painted portraits for Charles V. of Germany, and was skilful in miniature. Under the patronage of John III. he painted oil pictures for the palaces and churches of Lisbon. Dièd in 1584.

Holbach, d′, dol′bȧk or dol′bȧk′, (PAUL THIERRY or THYRY, also given as PAUL HEINRICH DIETRICH and PAUL FRIEDRICH,) BARON, a skeptical philosopher, born at Heidelsheim (Palatinate) in 1723. He inherited a fortune, and passed all his life, except childhood, in Paris, where he was the patron and associate of the Encyclopædists. Diderot, Helvetius, Grimm, Rousseau, and other authors often met at his table. He translated from the German several works on chemistry and mineralogy. His atheistic opinions were developed in his "System of Nature," (" Le Système de la Nature," 1770,) under the pseudonym of MIRABAUD, the morality of which book Voltaire stigmatized as execrable. It was also refuted by Frederick the Great. Holbach was the reputed author of other works, among which were "The Social System," (1773,) and "La Morale universelle," (1776.) Died in 1789.

See DIDEROT, "Mémoires," *passim;* ROUSSEAU, "Confessions;" DAMIRON, "Mémoire sur Thierry d′Holbach," 1851.

Holbein, hol′bīn, (FRANZ,) a popular German dramatist and actor, born near Vienna in 1779.

Holbein, (HANS,) THE ELDER, a German painter of Augsburg, born about 1450. Among his master-pieces are the scenes from the life of Saint Paul in the church of Saint Paul at Augsburg. He died in 1526, leaving three sons, AMBROSE, BRUNO, and HANS, who were artists; the last-named rose to great eminence.

Holbein, (HANS,) THE YOUNGER, one of the most celebrated German painters, born at Grünstadt in 1497. At an early age he removed to Bâle, where, after practising his art for a time, he was recommended by Erasmus to the English chancellor, Sir Thomas More. After residing in his family about three years, Holbein was introduced to King Henry VIII., who gave him abundant employment and bestowed upon him a large pension. He devoted himself, while in England, chiefly to portrait-painting; and his numerous productions in this department are esteemed master-pieces. His drawings, upwards of eighty in number, representing the principal personages of Henry′s court, are characterized by Walpole as "exceedingly fine, and possessing a strength and vivacity equal to the most perfect portraits." Holbein died in London, of the plague, in 1554, or, according to R. N. Wornum and others, in 1543. Among his greatest historical pictures are the celebrated "Dance of Death," the "Adoration of the Shepherds and Kings," and a "Last Supper." His portraits of Sir Thomas More and of Erasmus also deserve especial mention. "His works," observes Cunningham, "have sometimes an air of stiffness, but they have always the look of truth and life. He painted with great rapidity and ease, wrought with his left hand, and dashed off a portrait at a few sittings." Holbein was also a skilful architect and wood-engraver.

See HEGNER, "Leben Hans Holbein′s," Berlin, 1827; DESCAMPS, "Vies des Peintres Flamands, Allemands," etc.; R. N. WORNUM, "Life of Holbein;" NAGLER, "Allgemeines Künstler-Lexikon;" CUNNINGHAM, "Lives of Painters, Sculptors," etc.; KARL FRIEDRICH VON RUMOHR, "H. Holbein der Jüngere in seinem Verhältniss zum Deutschen Formschnittwesen," 1830; "Edinburgh Review" for April, 1867.

Holbein, (SIGISMUND,) a German painter and engraver, is supposed to have been an uncle of the preceding. Died after 1540.

Holberg, von, fon hol′bĕRG, (LUDWIG,) BARON, an eminent Danish author and comic poet, born of poor parents, at Bergen, Norway, in 1684. In youth he was employed as a private tutor, and learned French, Italian, and English. He studied philosophy at Oxford, England, for about two years. Impelled by a love of travelling, he visited many countries of Europe, and was afterwards professor of eloquence at Copenhagen. About 1720 he published his heroic-comic poem "Peder Paars," which was immensely popular. His celebrity was increased by numerous comedies which appeared between 1723 and 1746. One of his best comedies is "The Busy Idler; or, The Man who never has Time." His fertile mind enriched nearly every department of literature, and raised him to affluence. His talent for satire is displayed in "Niels Klim′s Subterranean Journey," in Latin, (1741,) the plan of which resembles "Gulliver′s Travels." He also wrote a "History of Denmark," (1735,) and a "Universal History." Frederick V. created him a baron in 1747. He is the founder of the Danish theatre, and the first Danish author who excelled in humorous and satirical composition. Died in 1754.

See his Autobiography, in Latin, 1727–44, (English translation, London, 1827;) and his Life, in German, by ROBERT PRUTZ, 1857; K. L. RAHBEK, "Om L. Holberg som Lystspildigter," etc., 2 vols., 1815–16; P. T. WANDAL, "Levensbeschrijving van L. Holberg," 1765; WERLAUFF, "Historiske Antegnelser til L. Holbergs Lystspil," 1838; HOWITT, "Literature and Romance of Northern Europe," chap. xxi.; "Nouvelle Biographie Générale;" C. L. BRIGHTWELL, "Annals of Industry and Genius," London, 1863; "North British Review" for July, 1869.

Hol′bourne, (Sir ROBERT,) M.D., an eminent English lawyer, was a member of Charles I.′s privy council during the civil war. He published several legal treatises. Died in 1647.

Hōl′brook, (JOHN EDWARDS,) M.D., a distinguished American naturalist, born in Beaufort, South Carolina, in 1795. He graduated at Brown University in 1815; and, having taken his medical diploma at Philadelphia, he prosecuted his professional studies for four years in Europe. He returned to the United States in 1822, and in 1824 succeeded to the chair of anatomy in the Medical College of South Carolina. In 1842 appeared his "American Herpetology, or a Description of the Reptiles inhabiting the United States," (5 vols. 4to,) which is said to have laid the foundation of that branch of science in this country.

Hol′croft, (THOMAS,) an English dramatist and translator, born in London in 1744. He was successively a groom, shoemaker, school-master, and actor. He wrote numerous dramas and several novels. His comedies "Duplicity," (1781,) and "The Road to Ruin," (1792,) were very successful. He made good translations of numerous French and German works, among which are Lavater′s "Essays on Physiognomy," "The Posthumous Works of Frederick the Great," (1789,) and "Tales of the Castle." He was indicted for treason with Hardy and Horne Tooke in 1794, but was discharged without a trial. Died in 1809.

See "Memoirs of his Life," by himself, 3 vols., 18·5; "Edinburgh Review" for April, 1804, and October, 1806.

Holda, hŏl′dȧ or hol′dȧ, written also **Holle,** [probably from the German *hold*, "kind," "propitious," "lovely,"] an ancient German goddess, corresponding in some respects to the Frigga of the Northmen. She presides over aerial phenomena, and imparts fertility to the earth.

See THORPE′S "Northern Mythology," vol. i. p. 277.

Hōl′den, (GEORGE,) an eminent English Hebraist, born near Lancaster in 1793, became perpetual curate of Mayhull, at Liverpool. Among his principal works are "An Attempt towards an Improved Translation of the Proverbs of Solomon," (1819,) and "The Scripture Testimonies to the Divinity of our Lord," (1820.)

See ALLIBONE′S "Dictionary of Authors."

Holden, (HENRY,) a learned Roman Catholic priest, born in Lancashire, England, in 1596, lived for many years in Paris. He wrote, in Latin, an "Analysis of Divine Faith," (1652,) which was commended by Dupin, and other works on theology. Died in 1662.

ā, ē, ī, ō, ū, ȳ, *long;* ȧ, ė, ȯ, same, less prolonged; ă, ĕ, ĭ, ŏ, ŭ, ȳ, *short;* ą, ę, į, ǫ, *obscure;* fär, fàll, fȧt; mēt; nŏt; gōōd; mōōn;

Hŏl'dẹr, (WILLIAM,) F.R.S., an English writer, born in Nottinghamshire in 1614, published, besides other works, "Elements of Speech," (1669,) and "Treatise on the Natural Grounds and Principles of Harmony," (1694,) which, says M. Fétis, "is one of the best works on that subject." It is said that he taught a deaf-mute to speak. Died in 1697.

Hölderlin or Hoelderlin, höl'dẹr-leen', (JOHANN CHRISTIAN FRIEDRICH,) a German poet, born at Lauffen in or about 1770. He wrote "Hyperion, or the Hermit in Greece," (2 vols., 1799,) a romance, which has some beautiful passages, and "Lyric Poems," (1826,) which are admired for fervour of fancy and depth of thought. Died in 1843.

See WAIBLINGER, "Notice sur Hölderlin;" A. JUNG, "F. Hoelderlin und seine Werke," 1848; F. HALLENSLEBEN, "Beiträge zur Characteristik Hoelderlin's," 1849.

Hŏl'dich, (JOSEPH,) a Methodist minister and writer, born in England about 1800, emigrated to the United States in his youth. He became secretary to the American Bible Society about 1850.

Hŏlds'worth, (EDWARD,) an English scholar, born in 1688, was educated at Oxford. He wrote a Latin poem, called "Muscipula," ("Mouse-trap.") Died in 1747.

Holdsworth, written also Holsworth, Oldsworth, and Oldisworth, (RICHARD,) an English divine, born at Newcastle-on-Tyne in 1590. He became professor of divinity at Gresham College in 1629, and master of Emanuel College in 1637. He left, besides other works, "Valley of Vision," in twenty-one sermons, (1651.) Died in 1649.

Hŏle, (MATTHEW,) an English religious writer, born about 1640, was vicar of Stoke Courcy, in Somersetshire. He wrote "Discourses on the Liturgy of the Church of England," (6 vols., 1714-16,) and other works. Died about 1730.

Hŏle, (RICHARD,) an English poet, born at Exeter. He produced a poetical version of Homer's "Hymn to Ceres," (1781,) "Arthur," a poetical romance, (1789,) and a few other works. He became rector of Farringdon in 1792. Died in 1803.

Hŏle, (WILLIAM,) an English engraver of little merit, flourished about 1613.

Hŏl'ĭnṡ-hed or Hŏl'ĭngṡ-hed, (RAPHAEL,) an English annalist, the date and place of whose birth are unknown. He published valuable chronicles of England, Scotland, and Ireland, (1577.) Modern historians have borrowed largely from him. Died about 1580.

Hŏl'kạr, (Jĕswunt Rao, jĕs'wŭnt rä'o,) a son of Tuckagee, noticed below, was an able warrior, and a formidable enemy of the British. He defeated Scindia in 1802, and raised a large army. In the spring of 1804 war broke out between him and the British. Holkar defeated Colonel Monson's division of 12,000 men in July, near the Chumbul and Bannas Rivers. In November of 1804 he was surprised and routed by Lord Lake at Furruckabad. He made a treaty of peace in January, 1806. Died in 1811.

See MILL, "History of British India;" GRANT DUFF, "History of the Mahrattas," 3 vols., 1826.

Holkar, (Mul'hạr Ra'o or Row,) a Mahratta chief, born at Hol, in the Deccan, in 1693. Having distinguished himself in war, he became ruler of a large part of Malwa. He died in 1766.

A daughter-in-law of the preceding, named AHALYA BAEE, (ä-hä'le-ä bä'ee,) or ALYA BHYE, (then a widow,) succeeded to the government on the death of Mulhar Rao Holkar, and during an administration of more than thirty years displayed extraordinary virtues both as a woman and a ruler. She was equally distinguished for her wisdom, her humanity and benevolence, and her moderation and sense of justice.

For a very interesting account of her character and administration, see SIR JOHN MALCOLM's "History of Central India."

Holkar, (Tuckagee,) supposed to be a nephew of Mulhar Rao Holkar, obtained possession of his dominions in 1767. He was the ally of Scindia against the Rajpoots. Died in 1797.

See GRANT DUFF, "History of the Mahrattas," 3 vols, 1826.

Holl, hol, (ELIAS,) an eminent German architect, born at Augsburg in 1573, studied his art in Venice. His capital work is the Rathhaus, or Town Hall, of Augsburg, (1618,) one of the finest structures for that purpose in Germany. He built also the arsenal, the church called "Mariahilf," and other public edifices of Augsburg. Died in 1636.

Holl, (FRANZ XAVER,) a German Jesuit, born in the Upper Palatinate in 1720; died in 1784.

Hol'lạnd, (EDWIN CLIFFORD,) an American poet and journalist, born in Charleston, South Carolina, about 1794. He edited for some time the "Charleston Times," and became noted as a satirist and controversialist. In 1814 he published a volume of "Odes, Naval Songs, and other Poems," originally contributed to Dennie's "Port-Folio." Died in 1824.

Hol'lạnd, (HENRY,) an eminent English architect, born about 1746. He was patronized by the Prince of Wales, (afterwards George IV.,) for whom he designed the Pavilion at Brighton, and Carlton House, the portico of which was much admired. He was architect of the old Drury Lane Theatre, begun about 1790, and afterwards burned. Died in 1806.

Holland, (Sir HENRY,) M.D., F.R.S., an eminent English physician, born at Knutsford, in Cheshire, in October, 1788. Having graduated at Edinburgh in 1811, he made the tour of Europe, and published, on his return, "Travels in the Ionian Isles, Albania, and Greece," (1815.) He settled in London, and gradually rose to great distinction in his profession. He became physician-in-ordinary to Prince Albert in 1840, and to Queen Victoria in 1852. In 1853 he was created a baronet. His principal work is "Medical Notes and Reflections," (1836.) He married in 1834 Saba, eldest daughter of the Rev. Sydney Smith. She wrote a "Memoir of the Rev. Sydney Smith," (2 vols., 1855.) She died in 1867.

Holland, (HENRY RICHARD VASSALL FOX,) LORD, an English peer, born in Wiltshire in 1773, was the only son of Stephen Fox, second Lord Holland, and Mary Fitzpatrick. By the death of his father he succeeded to the peerage in 1774, at the age of one year. He inherited a large share of the talents and noble dispositions of the family of Fox. He was educated at Oxford, and married Lady Webster in 1797. In the House of Lords he spoke frequently against the administration, and supported the measures of his uncle, the famous orator Charles James Fox. His powers as a speaker were of a very high order. In 1802 he visited Paris, in company with his uncle and Lady Holland. He held the office of privy seal a few months in 1806. Throughout his career he was constant to the Whig party; and when they came into power in 1830 he was appointed chancellor of the duchy of Lancaster. He published an excellent "Life de Lope de Vega," (1817,) and "Three Comedies from the Spanish," which are rendered with great poetical felicity. His "Foreign Reminiscences" appeared after his death, which occurred in 1840. In his time Holland House was the favourite resort, as Macaulay says, "of wits and beauties, of painters and poets, of scholars, philosophers, and statesmen."

See MACAULAY, "Essays;" "London Quarterly Review" for July, 1852, and April, 1854; "Edinburgh Review" for January, 1851; "Fraser's Magazine" for February, 1851.

Holland, (JOSIAH GILBERT,) M.D., a popular American author, born at Belchertown, Massachusetts, in 1819, has written under the assumed name of TIMOTHY TITCOMB. Among his works are "Letters to the Young," (1858,) "Bitter Sweet," a poem, (1858,) and a "Life of Abraham Lincoln," (1865.) He also published a "History of Western Massachusetts," (2 vols., 1855.)

Holland, LORD. See FOX, (HENRY.)

Holland, (NATHANIEL.) See DANCE.

Holland, (PHILEMON,) a physician and teacher, born at Chelmsford, England, in 1551, rendered valuable services to his country by translating Livy, Pliny, Plutarch's "Morals," Xenophon, etc., and received the title of translator-general. Died in 1636.

Hollanda. See HOLANDA.

Hollar, hol'lȧR, (WENZEL or WENCESLAUS,) a celebrated Bohemian engraver and designer, born at Prague in 1607. Having met with the Earl of Arundel in Cologne, he accompanied him on his return to London, and was employed to engrave some of the pictures of his gallery. In 1639 he brought out his "Ornatus Mulie-bris Anglicanus," an admirable work, illustrating the dress of Englishwomen of all classes at that time. Owing to the troubled state of the country, he was, notwithstanding his genius and industry, soon reduced to great poverty. Many of his works are etchings. Died in London in 1677.

See BRYAN, "Dictionary of Painters and Engravers;" NAGLER, "Allgemeines Künstler-Lexikon."

Hollerius. See HOULLIER.

Holles. See HOLLIS.

Hol'ley, (HORACE,) D.D., born at Salisbury, Connecticut, in 1781, graduated at Yale College in 1803. He became minister of the Hollis Street Unitarian Church, Boston, in 1809, and president of Transylvania University, Kentucky, in 1818. He published a volume of sermons. Died in 1827.

See a "Memoir of Dr. Holley," by his widow.

Hol'lins, (GEORGE N.,) an American naval officer, born in Baltimore about 1800. He became a commander in 1841, and bombarded Greytown, in Nicaragua, in 1852. He took arms against the Union in 1861, and commanded the naval forces which were defeated by Captain Farragut below New Orleans in April, 1862.

Hol'lins, (JOHN,) an English painter of genre and portraits, born at Birmingham in 1798; died in 1855.

Hol'lis or **Hol'les,** (DENZIL,) LORD, an English politician, second son of the Earl of Clare, and brother-in-law of the Earl of Strafford, was born at Haughton in 1597. In the reign of Charles I. he was one of the leaders of the opposition in Parliament, and in 1629 was condemned to imprisonment during the king's pleasure. He was one of the five members whom the king rashly attempted to arrest in the House of Commons on a charge of treason, (1642.) After the division between the Presbyterians and Independents occurred, Hollis was the leader of the former. He was expelled from Parliament at the time of Pride's Purge, and fled to France. He favoured the restoration, was created a peer by Charles II. in 1660, and was sent as ambassador to France in 1663. Died in 1680.

See "Memoirs of Denzil Holles," 1699; HUME, "History of England;" "Biographia Britannica;" GUIZOT, "Monk's Contemporaries," London, 1865.

Hollis, (THOMAS,) a munificent benefactor of Harvard College, born in England in 1659. He was for many years a successful merchant in London, where he died in 1731. He founded two professorships in Harvard, —the Hollis divinity professorship and the professorship of mathematics. Besides books and philosophical apparatus, his bequests to the college in money amounted to about £5000,—probably equal to more than five times as much as these figures would represent at the present time.

Hollis, (THOMAS,) F.R.S., an English gentleman and republican, born in London in 1720, was an ardent friend of civil and religious liberty, and noted for his public spirit. He possessed a large fortune, which he used liberally for charitable purposes and in the publication of books. He published good editions of Toland's "Life of Milton," (1761,) and Algernon Sidney's Works. Died in 1774.

See HOLLIS's "Memoirs," compiled by Rev. FRANCIS BLACKBURN, privately printed in 1780, 2 vols., with many fine portraits.

Hollis, (THOMAS BRAND,) an English gentleman, was a friend and the heir of Thomas Hollis, noticed above, (1720-74.) He contributed to Harvard College. Died in 1804.

See J. DISNEY, "Memoirs of Thomas B. Hollis," 1808.

Hollis, (THOMAS PELHAM.) See NEWCASTLE, DUKE OF.

Hollmann, hol'mån, (SAMUEL CHRISTIAN,) a German philosopher, born at Stettin about 1696, was professor of philosophy at Göttingen for about fifty years. He wrote, in Latin, several works on philosophy, metaphysics, and logic. Died in 1787.

Hol'lo-way, (THOMAS,) a skilful English engraver, born in London in 1748. He engraved the plates for Lavater's "Physiognomy," and the Cartoons of Raphael at Windsor. He spent several years on the latter, and had the title of engraver of history to the king. Died in 1827.

Hōl'man, (JAMES,) an Englishman, distinguished as "the Blind Traveller," was born about 1788. He served for some years in the royal navy, until he became blind, (about 1812.) He performed a journey through several countries of Europe, (1819-21,) of which he published a narrative in 1822. After that date he visited the other continents, and published "Travels through Russia, Siberia," etc., (1825,) and a "Voyage round the World," (4 vols., 1840.) He was arrested as a spy by the Russians. Died in 1857.

Holman, (JOSEPH GEORGE,) an actor and dramatist, born in London. After performing in London and Dublin, he emigrated to the United States in 1800, and was manager of the Charleston Theatre. He wrote a few comic operas. Died in 1817.

Holmes, hōmz, (ABIEL,) D.D., an American divine, born at Woodstock, Connecticut, in 1763, graduated at Yale in 1783. He was pastor of the First Congregational Church, Cambridge, Massachusetts, from 1792 to 1832. In 1805 he published "American Annals," the result of great industry and research. "We consider it," says Professor Sparks, "among the most valuable productions of the American press." He was the father of Dr. O. W. Holmes, noticed below. Died in 1837.

See "Quarterly Review" for November, 1809, (by SOUTHEY.)

Holmes, hōmz, (GEORGE,) an English antiquary, born in Yorkshire in 1662, was clerk to the keepers of the records in the Tower. Died in 1749.

Holmes, (ISAAC EDWARD,) a political leader in South Carolina, born in Charleston in 1796, rose to eminence at the bar of Charleston, took a conspicuous part in the nullification movement of South Carolina in 1832-33, and from 1839 to 1851 was a representative in Congress.

Holmes, (NATHANIEL.) See HOMES.

Holmes, (OLIVER WENDELL,) M.D., a distinguished American author, wit, and poet, was born in Cambridge, Massachusetts, August 29, 1809. He graduated at Harvard in 1829, and commenced the study of law, but soon abandoned it for medicine. Early in 1833 he visited Europe, where for nearly three years he pursued his medical studies, attending the hospitals of Paris and other large cities. He returned to his native country in 1835, and took the degree of doctor of medicine at Harvard in 1836. In 1838 he was elected professor of anatomy and physiology in Dartmouth College. About two years afterwards he resigned this position, and in 1847 was chosen to fill the same chair at Harvard University, as successor to Dr. Warren. Holmes had distinguished himself as a poet even before he left college. In 1836 he read before the Phi Beta Kappa Society, at Cambridge, "Poetry, a Metrical Essay," which was soon after published in a small volume, with a number of his other poems. In 1857-8 he contributed to the "Atlantic Monthly" a series of papers entitled "The Autocrat of the Breakfast-Table," which were followed in 1859 by another series, called "The Professor at the Breakfast-Table." These contributions abound in humour and wit, and exhibit at the same time a shrewd insight into human character. Dr. Holmes has more recently given to the world two prose works of fiction, which have proved a decided success,—"Elsie Venner," (1861,) and "The Guardian Angel," (1868.) Both of these works were first published in the columns of the "Atlantic Monthly." He has also written ably on various subjects connected with the medical profession.

As a poet, Dr. Holmes is especially distinguished for wit and humour joined with a remarkable felicity of expression. As a song-writer he has few, if any, superiors in America; but he more particularly excels in the playful vein. Among his effusions of this class we could not, perhaps, select an example which better exhibits his playful fancy or his wonderful facility and fertility of resources as a versifier, than his lines addressed to Agassiz when setting out on his scientific tour in South America.

See DUYCKINCK, "Cyclopædia of American Literature," vol. ii.; GRISWOLD, "Poets and Poetry of America;" CLEVELAND, "Compendium of American Literature;" "North American Review" for January, 1847; also an article on "American Humour" in the "North British Review" for November, 1860; "Littell's Living Age" for March, 1849, (by WHITTIER.)

Holmes, (ROBERT,) D.D., an English divine, born in Hampshire in 1749. In 1790 he was chosen professor of poetry at Oxford, and in 1804 Dean of Winchester. He wrote odes, tracts, and sermons, and commenced an edition of the Septuagint, which was finished by Parsons. Died in 1805.

Holmes, (THEOPHILUS H.,) an American general, born in North Carolina, graduated at West Point in 1829. He became a general in the Confederate army in 1861, and commanded in Arkansas in 1862–63. Died in August, 1863.

Holmskiold, holm'ske-old', (THEODOR,) a Danish physician and naturalist, born in 1732. He published a fine work on the Fungi in 1790. Died in 1793.

Holmström or **Holmstrœm**, holm'ström, (ISRAEL,) a popular Swedish poet, born at Stockholm, followed Charles XII. in his campaigns, with the title of councillor of war. Died in 1708.

Hol-o-fer′nēs, an Assyrian general, who lived at an uncertain epoch, and was killed by Judith, a patriotic Jewess.

See the Apocryphal Book of Judith.

Hol′royd, (JOHN BAKER,) Earl of Sheffield, an English political writer and military officer, born in Yorkshire in 1741. He edited some posthumous works of Gibbon. Died in 1821.

Holst, holst, (HANS PETER,) a Danish poet, born at Copenhagen in 1811. He published "National Romances," (1832,) "Poems," ("Digte," 1840,) and other works, written in an elegant style. His poem called "Adieu" ("Farvel," 1840) has been translated into many languages.

See P. L. MÖLLER, notice in the "Dansk Pantheon."

Holste. See HOLSTENIUS.

Holstein, hol′stīn, (JOHAN LUDWIG,) a worthy Danish statesman, born at Lübtz in 1694, became prime minister in 1735, and president of the Royal Academy of Sciences in 1742. Died in 1763.

See KOFOD ANCHER, "Cursus Vitæ Holsteinianæ."

Hol-ste′nǐ-us, [Ger. pron. hol-stā′ne-ŭs,] (LUCAS,) the Latin form of the name of LUCAS HOLSTE, (hol′stěh,) an eminent German scholar, born at Hamburg in 1596. He studied at Leyden, and went to Paris, where he joined the Roman Catholic Church in 1626. His friend Peiresc recommended him to Cardinal Barberini, whom he accompanied to Rome in 1627. He became librarian to Barberini in 1636, and librarian of the Vatican in the pontificate of Innocent X. He projected great literary works, some of which he left unfinished. In 1630 he published a Greek and Latin edition of Porphyry's "Life of Pythagoras," to which he added an excellent notice of Porphyry. Among his other published works is "Demophili, Democratis et Secundi Sententiæ Morales Græce et Latine," ("The Moral Maxims of Demophilus, Democrates, and Secundus, in Greek and Latin," with notes, 1638.) Died in 1661.

See WILKENS, "Leben des gelehrten Lucæ Holstenii." 1723; NICÉRON, "Mémoires," vol. xxxi.; MÖLLER, "Cimbria Literata;" "Nouvelle Biographie Générale."

Hōlt, (FRANCIS LUDLOW,) an English barrister, was queen's counsel and vice-chancellor of Lancashire from 1826 to 1844. For many years he was editor of Bell's "Weekly Messenger." Died in 1844.

Holt, (Sir JOHN,) an eminent English judge, born at Thame in December, 1642, was entered at Gray's Inn in 1658, and called to the bar in 1663. Having become eminent in his profession, he was chosen recorder of London ; but for his firm opposition to the despotic measures of James II. he was removed. He distinguished himself in the Convention Parliament of 1688, and at the accession of William III. was appointed lord chief justice of the king's bench in 1689. In 1700 he declined the office of lord chancellor. He performed the duties of chief justice with wisdom, honour, and courage, until the end of his life. "His name," says Mackintosh, "never can be pronounced without veneration as long as wisdom and integrity are revered among men." Died in 1709.

See LORD CAMPBELL, "Lives of the Chief Justices;" "Life of Sir John Holt," (anonymous,) 1764; FOSS, "The Judges of England."

Holt, (JOHN,) an English writer and teacher, born in Cheshire in 1742. He wrote, besides a few other works,

"Characters of the Kings and Queens of England," (3 vols., 1786–88.) Died in 1801.

Hōlt, (JOSEPH,) an American minister of state, born in Breckinridge county, Kentucky, about 1807. He practised law at Louisville. In March, 1859, he was appointed postmaster-general. He succeeded John B. Floyd as secretary of war in December, 1860, and by his energy and zeal for the Union rendered important services in the critical times which ensued. About September, 1862, he became judge-advocate-general of the army.

Holte, hōlt, (JOHN,) an English school-master, born in Sussex about 1470, wrote the first Latin grammar ever printed in England, which was dated about 1497.

Holtei, von, fon hol′tī′, (KARL,) a German poet and dramatist, born at Breslau in 1797. He produced many comedies and dramas, among which are "The Old General," and "Glory and Poverty," a volume of poems, ("Gedichte," 1826,) "German Songs," (1834,) and memoirs of his life, entitled "Forty Years," (8 vols., 1843–50.)

Hölty or **Hoelty**, höl′tee, (LUDWIG HEINRICH CHRISTOPH,) an excellent German lyric poet, born at Mariensee, near Hanover, in 1748. He studied at Göttingen, where he formed friendships with Voss, Stollberg, and others. He supported himself for a time by translating from the English, and giving lessons, until his health failed. His elegies, idyls, and odes are admired for tenderness of feeling, artless grace, and naïveté. He died prematurely in 1776. The first edition of his poems appeared in 1783.

See J. M. MILLER, "Etwas über Hölty's Character," 1776; BOUTERWEK, "Geschichte der Poesie," etc.; LONGFELLOW, "Poets and Poetry of Europe ;" notice of Hölty in an edition of his works published by Voss in 1804.

Höltzlinus, hölts-lee′nŭs, (JEREMIAS,) a German philologist, born at Nuremberg; died at Leyden in 1641.

Holtzmann, holts′män, (ADOLF,) a German philologist, born at Carlsruhe in 1810, wrote, among other works, "Indian Legends," ("Indische Sagen," 3 vols., 1845–47.)

Hol′well, (JOHN ZEPHANIAH,) born in Dublin in 1711. Having studied surgery, he went to India in 1732, and became a member of the council at Calcutta about 1755. He was one of those who survived the confinement in the "Black Hole," of which he published a narrative, (1757.) He succeeded Colonel Clive as Governor of Bengal in 1759. Holwell also published "Interesting Historical Events relative to Bengal and Hindostan, with the Mythology of the Gentoos," (3 vols., 1764–71.) Died in 1798.

Hol′y̆-dāy, (BARTEN,) D.D., an English divine, born at Oxford in 1593, was chaplain to Charles I. He wrote "Survey of the World," a poem, and translated Juvenal and Persius. Died in 1661.

Holyoak, hōl′yōk, (FRANCIS,) an English clergyman, born in Warwickshire about 1567, published a "Dictionary of Latin Words," (1606,) which was enlarged by his son Thomas. Died in 1653.

Holyoke, hōl′yōk, (EDWARD AUGUSTUS,) M.D., an American physician, was born in Marblehead, Massachusetts, in 1728. He graduated at Harvard in 1746, and for seventy-nine years followed his profession with eminent success in Salem, where he died, March 31, 1829. At the age of ninety-two he performed the operation of paracentesis, and on his hundredth anniversary partook of a public dinner given him by the physicians of Salem and Boston.

See "Memoirs of Edward A. Holyoke," Boston, 1829.

Hol′y̆-wood, **Hal′ĭ-fax**, or **Sac′ro Bos′co**, (JOHN,) a noted mathematician of the thirteenth century, was professor of mathematics in the University of Paris. The time and place of his birth are unknown. He wrote a work entitled "De Sphæra Mundi."

Holzbauer, holts′bŏw′er, (IGNAZ,) a German composer, born in Vienna in 1711, produced operas, symphonies, etc. "He has a good style," says Mozart, "and composes very fine fugues." Died in 1783.

Holzer, holt′ser, (JOHANN,) an eminent German fresco-painter and engraver, was born near Marienburg, in the Tyrol, in 1709. He painted numerous frescos in Augsburg of religious subjects, among which is "The

e as k; ç as s: ḡ hard; ġ as j; G, H, K, guttural; N, nasal; R, trilled: š as z: th as in this. (☞See Explanations, p. 23.)

76

Martyrdom of Saint Sebastian." He produced spirited etchings of "The Adoration of the Magi," after Berg-müller, of the "Ecce Homo," after his own design, and of other paintings. Died in 1740.

See ZAPF, "Holzers Leben," 1781, in MEUSEL's "Miscellanien Artistischen Inhalts."

Holzhauser, holts'hŏw'zer, (BARTHOLOMÄUS,) a German devotee, born at Langenau in 1613, founded a community called "Bartholomäer." Died in 1658.

Homann, ho'mån, (JOHANN BAPTIST,) a German geographer and engraver of maps, born at Kamlach, in Suabia, in 1664. He settled in Nuremberg, and published many maps, which were more than ordinarily accurate. He formed a large collection of the same, under the title of "Atlas," (1716.) His establishment, called "Officina Homanniana," was well known throughout Europe. Died in 1724.

Homberg, hom'bêRG, (WILHELM,) M.D., an excellent chemist, born of German parents at Batavia, in Java, in 1652, came to Europe at an early age. He studied chemistry and other natural sciences with Otto Guericke and Boyle, and visited the principal capitals of Europe in pursuit of knowledge. About 1685 he practised medicine at Rome with success, and in 1691 removed to Paris, where he was chosen a member of the Academy of Sciences, to which he contributed many memoirs. He was patronized by the Duke of Orléans, who chose him as his first physician. He discovered boracic acid and Homberg's pyrophorus. Died in Paris in 1715.

See FONTENELLE, "Éloge de Homberg;" NICÉRON, "Mémoires ;" F. HOEFER, "Histoire de la Chimie," tome ii. ; "Nouvelle Biographie Générale."

Home, (DAVID.) See HUME.

Hōme, (DAVID,) a Scottish Protestant minister, who lived in France during the reign of James I. of England. He wrote "Apologia Basilica," (1626.)

Home, (Sir EVERARD,) an eminent Scottish surgeon, born in the county of Berwick in 1756, studied medicine with his brother-in-law, the celebrated John Hunter. He practised in London with distinction, and was president of the Royal College of Surgeons. He published "Lectures on Comparative Anatomy," and other professional works. Died in 1832.

Home, (HENRY,) Lord Kames, a Scottish judge, born at Kames in 1696, was called to the Edinburgh bar in 1724. After publishing several legal treatises, which were well received, he was appointed in 1752 a judge of the court of sessions, and took the title of Lord Kames. In 1758 he wrote a valuable work, entitled "Historical Law Tracts." His greatest work, "Elements of Criticism," (1762,) was regarded by some as an admirable performance, and is highly commended by Dugald Stewart. Dr. Johnson said, "The Scotchman has taken the right method in his 'Elements of Criticism.'" He was appointed one of the lords of justiciary in 1763. Died in 1782.

See LORD WOODHOUSELEE, "Memoirs of the Life of Henry Home," 1807-10, 2 vols. ; WILLIAM SMELLIE, "Life of Lord Kames," 1800 ; CHAMBERS, "Biographical Dictionary of Eminent Scotsmen."

Home or **Hume,** (JOHN,) a popular Scottish dramatist, born at Ancrum in 1724. He was licensed to preach in 1747, and settled at Athelstaneford. In 1756 he became at once distinguished by the publication of his "Tragedy of Douglas," which was performed first at Edinburgh with unbounded applause, and is still very popular on the stage. "I think nobody can bestow too much praise on Douglas," says Professor Wilson. "There has been no English tragedy worthy of the name since it appeared." It rendered the author so obnoxious to the elders of the Kirk that he retired from the ministry. He was patronized by the Earl of Bute, who procured him a pension of £300. Home wrote several other dramas, much inferior to "Douglas," and a "History of the Rebellion in 1745." Mrs. Siddons once said "she never found any study [which, in the technical language of the stage, means the getting verses by heart] so easy as that of Douglas." Died in 1808.

See SIR WALTER SCOTT's critique on the "Life and Writings of John Home," in the "Quarterly Review" for June, 1827 ; HENRY MACKENZIE, "Life of John Home," prefixed to a collection of his works, 3 vols. 8vo, 1822 ; "Noctes Ambrosianæ" for April, 1822 ; CHAMBERS, "Biographical Dictionary of Eminent Scotsmen."

Ho'mer, [Gr. Ὅμηρος ; Lat. HOME'RUS ; Fr. HOMÈRE, o'maiR' ; Ger. HOMER, ho-mār' ;* It. OMERO, o-mā'ro,] the reputed author of the two great epics the "Iliad" and the "Odyssey," and the most celebrated poet that ever lived, is generally supposed to have been born at Smyrna, or Chios,† (Scio,) and to have flourished about one thousand years before the Christian era ; but both the place and the century of his birth are involved in the greatest uncertainty. The best ancient authorities, including Aristotle and Aristarchus, represent him as contemporary with the Ionian migration which occurred about one hundred and forty years after the Trojan war. Of the two great poems above named, the "Iliad" has been aptly called "the beginning of all literature." In the opinion, indeed, of the greatest critics of antiquity, it was not only the beginning, but the end ; it was not merely the first attempt at the production of a great poem, but the faultless model which excited alike the admiration and despair of all succeeding poets. In the words of Aristotle, Ὅμηρος . . . λέξει καὶ διανοίᾳ πάντας ὑπερβέβληκε.‡ "Hic omnes sine dubio," says Quintilian, "in omni genere eloquentiæ procul a se reliquit."§ Some other ancient writers speak in even stronger terms of praise.

Among the ancients, none appears ever to have doubted that Homer was a real personage, and that he was the author of the most wonderful poem of antiquity, (the "Iliad.") But before or about the time of the Christian era there was a class of critics who denied that the "Iliad" and "Odyssey" were the productions of the same author. They were called Χωρίζοντες, or "Separators." It cannot be denied that there is a remarkable difference between those works, not in one or two points only, but in several important respects. Perhaps the most striking difference is that which exists in respect to the character of the gods in the two poems. The gods of the "Iliad" are completely human in their character,—unless it be that they have more than human foibles or vices. They are capricious and selfish, and seldom, if ever, show much regard for justice. The deities of the "Odyssey" appear as the rewarders of merit and the avengers of sin or crime. There is, moreover, a marked difference in the spirit or tone of the two poems. To explain this difference, Longinus tells us that the "Iliad" was composed by Homer when he was in the vigour of life, while the "Odyssey" was the production of his old age.

Modern critics had seemed disposed to leave the question of Homer's age and the authorship of the Homeric poems very much where they had been left by the writers of antiquity, until a little before the close of the last century, when F. A. Wolf startled the world by announcing a new theory respecting the Homeric poems, (1795.) He maintained that, as writing was not in use among the Greeks until long after the time in which those poems must have been composed, it would have been wholly impossible for any poet, however great his genius, to compose and retain in memory even one such work as the "Iliad" or "Odyssey." For this and other reasons, he concludes that the two great epics which go under the name of Homer were really produced by a number of different authors, and that these separate productions were, after the introduction of the art of writing, thrown

* See principles of German pronunciation, in the Introduction.

† If the weight of authorities is in favour of Smyrna, the greater number would seem to be on the side of Chios. (See Smith's "Classical Dictionary.") Byron appears to give the preference to the latter ; for he calls Homer

"The blind old man of Scio's rocky isle."
Bride of Abydos, canto ii.

It has been suggested (and it seems highly probable) that Homer, though born at Smyrna, may have afterwards removed to Chios, where his family, or a branch of it, (the Homeridæ,) are said to have lived for several generations. Seven different cities are said to have disputed for the honour of having given birth to Homer, as expressed in the following couplet by Antipater of Sidon:

Ἑπτὰ πόλεις μάρναντο σοφὴν διὰ ῥίζαν Ὁμήρου,
Σμύρνα, Χίος, Κολοφών, Ἰθάκη, Πύλος, Ἄργος, Ἀθῆναι.

Literally, "Seven cities (or states) contended for the wise race of Homer, [i.e. the race or origin of the wise Homer,] Smyrna, Chios, Colophon, Ithaca, Pylos, Argos, and Athens." Some writers substitute Salamis for Ithaca.

‡ "Homer has surpassed all [other writers] in diction (or expression) and in thought."

§ "In every kind of eloquence he undoubtedly has left all [others far behind him."

ā, ē, ī, ō, ū, ȳ, *long;* ă, ĕ, ĭ, ŏ, ŭ, ў, *short;* ạ, ẹ, ị, ọ, *obscure;* fär, fãll, fät; mēt; nŏt; gōōd; mōōn;

together as they happened to fit, so as to form a continuous whole. The inconclusiveness, not to say absurdity, of such a train of reasoning must, we think, be obvious to every unbiassed mind. We meet, even now, with persons who by two or three perusals can commit to memory the whole of such a poem as the "Lady of the Lake." "Who can determine," says Müller, "how many thousand verses one thoroughly filled with his subject . . . might produce in a year and confide to the faithful memory of disciples devoted to their master and his art?" When we take into consideration the fact that the mental activity of the ancients, instead of being divided and diluted among an endless variety of studies or pursuits, was concentrated and constantly exercised on a comparatively few, the retaining of even two such works as the "Iliad" and "Odyssey" will not, perhaps, seem more incredible than many feats of memory which are known to have been performed in modern times. Nor must it be forgotten that the poetry of Homer, unlike that of many of our great modern poets, is, generally speaking, remarkable for the simplicity and directness of its language; and these qualities, added to the marvellous facility and animation of the narrative, render the verse extremely easy to be learned and retained in memory.

The consummate art with which the various parts of the "Iliad" (though sometimes seemingly disconnected) are arranged and adapted so as to delay the dénouement and yet to heighten the interest till near the very end, proves the poem to have been, beyond all reasonable doubt, the work of one master-mind. But this master-mind may very probably have used materials prepared for him by preceding poets, just as the consummate architect, when erecting an edifice designed to be the admiration of all coming time, may avail himself of the materials, and, for subordinate parts of the building, even of the designs, furnished by inferior workmen. There seem, indeed, to be strong reasons for believing that before the time of Homer there existed many poems treating of the events of the Trojan war, and that he, in selecting and combining the facts necessary to the plot of his great work, occasionally adopted some of the finest lines of his predecessors, at the same time changing or adapting others to suit his purpose, so as to give the whole poem the impress of his matchless skill and transcendent genius. This supposition will perhaps best explain the introduction into the poem of such a great variety of words or phrases differing in different parts of the work, as well as the marked diversity of dialects. It is well known that Shakspeare used freely, in some of his historic dramas, not only the ideas, but, in repeated instances, the very lines, of some of the poets that had gone before him. At other times he appears to have adopted some of the leading ideas, and perhaps many of the expressions, of previous dramatists, and yet to have so cast them into the mould of his own mind, and so coloured them with the hues of his wonderful imagination, that he may be said to have surpassed the fabled achievements of the alchemists, and transmuted his crude materials into something far more precious than gold.

But, while we claim it as a point established, that the "Iliad" is virtually and essentially the production of a single poet, we must admit that the question is still undecided whether the same Homer was also the author of the "Odyssey." "If," says the learned and accomplished critic already quoted, "the completion of the 'Iliad' and 'Odyssey' seems too vast a work for one man, we may perhaps have recourse to the supposition that Homer, after having sung the 'Iliad' in the vigour of his youthful years, in his old age communicated to some devoted disciple the plan of the 'Odyssey,' which had long been working in his mind, and left it to him for completion." (K. O. Müller's "History of Greek Literature.")

The prevailing belief that Homer was blind appears to have taken its origin from one of the so-called Homeric hymns addressed to the Delian Apollo, the author of which calls himself the blind poet who lived in rocky Chios. The hymn in question was considered by some of the most judicious of the ancient writers to be the production of Homer himself; but this view is not accepted by the best modern critics. The wonderful accuracy of many of the descriptions in the "Iliad" utterly

precludes the idea of their having been written by a poet who had not himself been an eye-witness of the scenes which he paints so admirably. But there is nothing unreasonable in the supposition that he might have described in his blind old age scenes which had been indelibly stamped upon his memory in youth or early manhood. (See, on the various questions connected with the Homeric poems, the very able article on "Homerus," in Smith's "Dictionary of Greek and Roman Biography," from the pen of Dr. Ihne, of Bonn.)

See, in addition to the works referred to in the article, OLOF CELSIUS, "Dissertatio de Homeri Vita et Scriptis," 1714; LUDOLPH KUESTER, "Historia critica Homeri," 1696; THOMAS BLACKWELL, "Enquiry into the Life and Writings of Homer," 1735; KÖPPEN, "Ueber Homer's Leben und Gesänge," 1788; CARL ERNST SCHUBARTH, "Ideen über Homer und sein Zeitalter," 1821; MATTHIAS ASP, "Disputationes de Homero," 1714; J. E. TURR, "Homerus en zijn Schriften," 1810; ALPHONSE DE LAMARTINE, "Homère," 1852; FORTIA D'URBAN, "Homère et ses Écrits," 1832; BERNARD THIERSCH, "Das Zeitalter des Homer," 1824; J. PASCHIUS, "Dissertatio de Poetarum Principe Homero," 1687; ÉDOUARD JUSTE, "Dissertation sur l'Origine des Poëmes attribués à Homère," 1849; "Homer and his Successors in Epic Poetry," in the "London Quarterly Review" for January, 1857; MATTHEW ARNOLD's admirable observations "On Translating Homer," in his "Essays," 1865.

Hŏ'mẹr, (Rev. HENRY,) an English scholar, born at Birdingbury in 1752, was educated at Cambridge. He edited several Latin authors, and, in partnership with Dr. Combe, published a complete edition of Horace. Died in 1791.

Homère. See HOMER.

Homeridæ, ho-mĕr'e-dee, (singular, **Ho-mĕr'ĭ-dēś,**) or **Ho'mer-ids,** the name applied to the family of the poet Homer. (See HOMER, note †.)

Homerus. See HOMER.

Homes or **Holmes,** hōmz, (NATHANIEL,) D.D., an English theologian, ejected for nonconformity in 1662, was a believer in the fifth monarchy. He wrote the "Resurrection Revealed," and other works. Died in 1678.

Ho-mil'ĭ-us, [Ger. pron. ho-mee'le-ûs,] (GOTTFRIED AUGUST,) an eminent German organist and composer of church music, born at Rosenthal, in Bohemia, in 1714. Among his best works are a cantata for Christmas, and a number of motets. He was organist and director of music at Dresden. Died in 1785.

Hommaire de Hell, ho'mǎR' dẹh hĕl, (IGNACE XAVIER MORAND,) a French geologist, born at Altkirch in 1812, explored the regions which border on the Black and Caspian Seas, and left an account of his travels, in 3 vols. Died at Ispahân in 1848.

Hommel, hom'mẹl, [Lat. HOMME'LIUS,] (KARL FERDINAND,) a learned jurist and ingenious writer, born at Leipsic in 1722. He became professor of feudal law at Leipsic in 1752, and of civil institutes in 1756. Among his works are "Literatura Juris," (1761,) a very piquant treatise on legal literature, "Rhapsodia Quæstionum in Foro quotidiè obvenientum," ("Questions occurring daily in the Forum," 5 vols., 1765-79; 4th edition, 7 vols., 1787,) and "Sceleton Juris civilis," ("Skeleton of Civil Law," 4th edition, 1767.) Died in 1781.

See ERNESTI, "Hommelii Memoria," 1783, and RÖSSIG, "Vita Hommelii," 1782, both of which may be found in the 7th vol. of Hommel's "Rhapsodia," 1787; "Nouvelle Biographie Générale."

Hommelius. See HOMMEL.

Hompesch, von, fon hom'pẹsh, (FERDINAND,) the last grand master of the Knights of Malta, was born at Dusseldorf in 1744; died in 1803.

Honain, (or **Honein,**) ho-nīn', (**Aboo-Yezeed** or **Abu- (Abou-) Yezĭd,** ă'b00 yeh-zeed',) otherwise called **Honain-Ben-Ishâk,** (bĕn is'hâk',) an Arabian physician, born at Heerah, (Hirah,) in Mesopotamia, lived mostly at Bagdâd. Died about 875 A.D. He translated into Arabic the works of Hippocrates, Galen, Euclid, etc.

See IBN-KHALLIKAN, "Biographical Dictionary;" HAJI-KHALFA, "Lexicon Bibliographicum."

Hondekoeter, hon'dẹh-koo'tẹr, (GILES,) a noted Dutch landscape-painter, born at Utrecht in 1583, was the son of the Marquis of Westerloo. He often added to his landscapes highly-finished figures of birds.

Hondekoeter, (GYSBRECHT,) a son of the preceding, and a painter of poultry, was born in 1613; died in 1653.

Hondekoeter, (MELCHIOR,) an excellent painter son of the preceding, was born at Utrecht in 1636. He studied with his father and his uncle, John B. Weenix.

He painted poultry, pea-fowls, and other birds, with a skill that has never been surpassed. The backgrounds of his pictures are adorned with beautiful landscapes. Among his works is "The Entrance of the Animals into the Ark." Died in 1695.

See JAKOB CAMPO WEYERMAN, "De Schilderkonst der Nederlanders."

Hondius, hon'de-us, or **Hondt,** hŏnt, (ABRAHAM,) a Dutch painter and engraver, born at Rotterdam in 1638. He painted hunting-scenes, animals, and landscapes with success. "He often equals the best masters," says Descamps. Among his works are "The Burning of Troy," and "The Animals entering the Ark." He worked some years in England, where he died about 1692.

Hondius, (HENDRIK,) an engraver of maps and portraits, born at Ghent in 1573. His principal work is a series of portraits of one hundred and forty-four artists, mostly Flemings. He also engraved some pictures by Albert Dürer and Holbein. Died at the Hague in 1610.

See BASAN, "Dictionnaire des Graveurs;" STRUTT, "Dictionary of Engravers."

Hondius or **De Hondt,** dĕh hŏnt, (HENRY,) called THE YOUNGER, born in London in 1580, was accounted the best engraver of the family. He engraved portraits, landscapes, and history after several Flemish painters. Among his works are portraits of Queen Elizabeth and James I. Died at Amsterdam about 1650.

See BASAN, "Dictionnaire des Graveurs."

Hondius or **De Hondt,** (JOSSE or JODO'CUS,) a skilful Flemish engraver and geographer, born at Wacken about 1550, was the father of the preceding. He had a high reputation as an engraver on copper. He worked in London, and afterwards settled in Amsterdam, where he engraved maps of superior quality, and published new editions of the "Grand Atlas" of Mercator. Died in 1611.

Hondt, hŏnt, (WILLEM,) a Flemish engraver, a brother of Henry the Younger, born at the Hague in 1601.

Hone, ho'nĕh, (GEORG PAUL,) a German lawyer, born at Nuremberg in 1662, wrote "Iter Juridicum," and other works. Died in 1747.

Hōne, (NATHANIEL,) a portrait-painter, born in Dublin about 1730; died in 1784.

Hōne, (WILLIAM,) an English writer, born at Bath in 1779, resided in London, and failed several times as a bookseller. He wrote "The Political House that Jack Built," a satire, which was illustrated by Cruikshank and ran through fifty editions. He was prosecuted for his Parody on the Liturgy in 1818, and, having ably defended himself, was acquitted. In 1826 he began to issue in weekly numbers his "Every-Day Book," which had a large sale, and was commended by Professor Wilson, Scott, Lamb, and Southey. It was followed by the "Table-Book" and the "Year-Book," which were well received, but did not save the author from insolvency. He was in prison for debt about three years. Died in 1842.

See "The Early Life and Conversion of William Hone," written by himself.

Honestis, (PETRUS DE.) See DAMIANI.

Honeywood, hŭn'ne-wŏŏd, (SAINT JOHN,) an American poet, born in Massachusetts in 1765; died in 1798.

See GRISWOLD, "Poets and Poetry of America."

Honoré de Sainte-Marie, o'no'rȧ' dĕh sȧnt'mȧ're', [Lat. HONORIUS DE SANCTA MARIA,] called, after he entered the cloister, BLAISE VAUXELLE, (vō-sĕl',) a learned monk, born at Limoges in 1651; died in 1729.

Ho-no'rĭ-us I., a native of Campania, was elected Pope or Bishop of Rome in 626 A.D. He is charged with assenting to the heresy of Monothelism. The Council of Constantinople, held in 680, condemned his doctrine on this point. Died in 638.

Honorius II., POPE, previously known as Cardinal Lamberto and Bishop of Ostia, succeeded Calixtus II. in 1124. Tebaldus was chosen pope at the same time by a number of bishops, but forbore to contest his claim. Honorius died in 1130.

Honorius III., elected Pope in 1216, was a Roman by birth. His proper name was CENCIO SAVELLI. He crowned Frederick II. Emperor of Germany in 1220, in the hope that he would lead a crusade against the Turks. He was more successful in instigating the King of France

to a crusade against the Albigenses. He died in 1227, and was succeeded by Gregory IX.

Honorius IV., POPE, (Cardinal GIACOMO Savelli,) a native of Rome, was elected in 1285 as successor to Martin IV. Died in 1287.

Ho-no'rĭ-us, (FLAVIUS,) a Roman emperor, the second son of Theodosius the Great, was born at Constantinople in 384 A.D. At the death of his father, in 395, he inherited the Western Empire, (his elder brother Arcadius having obtained the Eastern,) under the guardianship of Stilicho, a famous general, whose daughter he married. His court was held at Milan, and afterwards at Ravenna. About 402 Alaric the Goth invaded Italy, and was defeated by Stilicho at Pollentia. In 408 Stilicho was put to death by order of Honorius, who was a man of weak and vicious character. From this event may be dated the fall of the Roman power. Rome was taken and pillaged by Alaric in 410, and the empire went rapidly to ruin. He died, without issue, in 423, and was succeeded by Valentinian III.

See GIBBON, "History of the Decline and Fall of the Roman Empire;" SOZOMEN, "Historia Ecclesiastica;" JORNANDES, "De Rebus Geticis;" TILLEMONT, "Histoire des Empereurs."

Honorius de Sancta Maria. See HONORÉ DE SAINTE-MARIE.

Hontheim, von, fon hont'hīm, (JOHANN NIKOLAUS,) a German jurist and Catholic priest, born at Treves in 1701. He became Bishop *(in partibus)* of Myriophis in 1748, and suffragan of the see of Treves. He published under the pseudonym of JUSTINIUS FEBRONIUS a famous book against the usurpations of the popes, entitled "De Statu Ecclesiæ et legitima Potestate Romani Pontificis," (5 vols., 1763,) which was often reprinted. Died in 1790.

Honthorst, hŏnt'horst, or **Hundhorst,** hŭnt'horst, (GERARD,) a Flemish painter, called also by the Italians GERARDO DELLA NOTTE, ("Gerard of the Night,") because he excelled in nocturnal scenes. He was born at Utrecht in 1592, and was a pupil of A. Bloemaert. He worked in Rome and in England, where he painted portraits of the royal family and gained a high reputation. Among his works is "The Prodigal Son." He was a good colorist, and excelled in design. Died at the Hague in 1660. His brother WILLEM was a successful portrait-painter. Died at Berlin in 1683, aged about eighty.

See PILKINGTON, "Dictionary of Painters;" DESCAMPS, "Vies des Peintres Flamands," etc.

Hood, hŏŏd, (ALEXANDER,) Viscount Bridport, an English naval officer, was a younger brother of Lord Samuel Hood, noticed below. After having gained distinction in subordinate stations, he was made rear-admiral in 1780. In 1784 he was second in command under Lord Howe, in the Channel fleet. The next year he took three French ships, and in 1796 succeeded Lord Howe as commander of the fleet. In 1801 he was raised to the peerage, as Viscount Bridport. Died in 1814.

Hood, (EDWIN PAXTON,) an English dissenting minister, born at Weston about 1820. He wrote numerous works, among which are "Self-Formation," and "William Wordsworth," a biography, (1856.)

Hood, hŏŏd, (JOHN B.,) an American general, born in Bath county, Kentucky, in 1831, graduated at West Point in 1853. He commanded a division of Lee's army at Antietam, September, 1862, and at Gettysburg, July 1-3, 1863. He lost a leg at the battle of Chickamauga, September 20, 1863, soon after which he was promoted to be a lieutenant-general. In the spring of 1864 he commanded a corps of the army opposed to General Sherman in Northern Georgia. He succeeded General Johnston in July as commander-in-chief of that army, which was then near Atlanta. General Johnston was removed because he had adhered to a cautious and defensive policy. Hood assumed the offensive, and attacked General Sherman on the 22d of July, and again on the 28th, but was repulsed with heavy loss. He was compelled to abandon Atlanta on the 1st of September, 1864. (See SHERMAN, W. T.) After he had damaged the railroad by which Sherman's army was supplied, General Hood invaded Middle Tennessee, attacked General Schofield at Franklin, November 30, and besieged Nash-

---

ā, ē, ī, ō, ū, ȳ, *long;* ȧ, ė, ȯ, same, less prolonged; ă, ĕ, ĭ, ŏ, ŭ, ў, *short;* ą, ę, į, ǫ, *obscure;* fär, fȧll, fȧt; mĕt; nŏt; gŏŏd; mŏŏn;

ville. He was defeated on the 16th of December, 1864, by General Thomas, at the decisive battle of Nashville, where he lost fifty pieces of cannon, and was relieved of the command in January, 1865.

See "Southern Generals," New York, 1865.

Hood, (ROBIN,) a famous English outlaw, who is supposed to have lived in the reign of Richard I. Sherwood Forest was his head-quarters. His exploits are the subject of many popular ballads, which applaud his gallantry to the ladies and his generosity in sharing among the poor the spoils of the rich. He was the chief of a numerous band, who seem to have lived chiefly on the products of the chase.

See W. W. CAMPBELL, "Historical Sketch of Robin Hood and Captain Kidd," New York, 1853: "Edinburgh Review" for July, 1847: "North American Review" for January, 1857.

Hood, (SAMUEL,) VISCOUNT, an English admiral, born at Butley in 1724, entered the navy in 1740, and became captain in 1754. In 1780 he was made a rear-admiral, and was second in command in the West Indies. The next year he succeeded Rodney in command of the fleet, with which he fought De Grasse near the mouth of the Chesapeake, but failed to relieve the British army at Yorktown. He took part in the victory over De Grasse in April, 1782, and was rewarded with the title of Baron Hood of Catherington. In 1784, after a close contest with Fox, he was elected to Parliament, and in 1788 appointed a lord of the admiralty. In 1793 he commanded against the French in the Mediterranean and at the siege of Toulon. He was made, in 1796, Viscount Hood of Whitley, and afterwards an admiral. Died in 1816.

See CAMPBELL, "Lives of British Admirals."

Hood, (Sir SAMUEL,) cousin of the preceding, was a vice-admiral in the British navy, and a brave and skilful officer. He took part in the victory of Rodney over De Grasse in 1782, and in the battle of the Nile, (1798.) In 1806 he was returned to Parliament for Westminster, and captured three French ships near Rochefort. He was afterwards appointed to command in the East Indies, where he died in 1814.

Hood, (THOMAS,) a famous English humourist and popular author, born in London in 1798, was the son of a bookseller. He served an apprenticeship to an engraver, but soon exchanged that employment for literary pursuits. In 1821 he became sub-editor of the "London Magazine," by which he gained access to the society of many authors who have since risen to eminence. His "Whims and Oddities" (1826) displayed an abundant vein of inimitable wit and comic power. He issued the "Comic Annual" from 1830 to 1842, which was followed by his "Comic Album," "Whimsicalities," and "Hood's Own." His tales and novels were less successful than his humorous works. Among his most popular poems are the "Song of the Shirt," (which first appeared in "Punch,") the "Bridge of Sighs," and the "Dream of Eugene Aram." He was editor of "The Gem" for one year, and, in the latter years of his life, editor of the "New Monthly Magazine." Like poor Yorick, he was "a fellow of infinite jest, of most excellent fancy." As a punster he is unrivalled. Some of his serious poems are exquisitely tender and pathetic. In 1844 he began to issue "Hood's Magazine," for which he wrote until his last illness. A pension of £100 which had been granted to him was transferred to his widow. Died in 1845.

See "Life of Hood." by his children, 1860; E. P WHIPPLE, "Essays and Reviews;" R. H. HORNE, "New Spirit of the Age," 1844; "Edinburgh Review" for April, 1846; "Quarterly Review" for October, 1863; "Blackwood's Magazine" for January, 1827; "London Magazine" for December, 1826; "British Quarterly Review" for October, 1867.

Hooft, höft, (NIKLAAS,) a Dutch historical painter, born at the Hague in 1664; died in 1748.

Hooft or **Hoofft,** (PIETER CORNELIS,) an excellent Dutch poet and historian, born in Amsterdam in March, 1581. After leaving college he travelled in France and Italy, and filled several civil offices. He published about 1602 "Granida," a tragi-comedy, which is a master-piece. He wrote other dramas, and erotic poems of great merit, and translated Tacitus into Dutch. His chief prose works are a "Life of Henry IV. of France," (1626,) and a "History of the Netherlands,"("De Nederlandsche Historien," 2 vols., 1642–54,) which is esteemed a model

of grace, purity, and vigour, both in thought and style. He has the honour of rendering his vernacular language more polished and classical than it was before his time. He was a friend of Grotius. "Though deeply religious," says the "Biographie Universelle," "he never ranged himself under the banner of any outward communion." Died in 1647.

See ERSCH und GRUBER, "Allgemeine Encyklopaedie;" and VAN KAMPEN's article on "Holländische Sprache und Literatur," in the same work; also, "Nouvelle Biographie Générale;" JAN VAN KRUYFF, "Lofreden of P. C. Hooft," 1810; JACOB KONING, "Geschiedenis van het Slot te Muiden, en Hoofts Leven op het zelve," 1827; VAN HEUSDE, "Commentatio literaria de Hooftio cum Tacito comparato," 1838; LONGFELLOW, "Poets and Poetry of Europe;" "Fraser's Magazine" for March, 1854.

Hooge, de, dęh hō'ęh or hō'Hęh, written also **Hoogh,** (PIETER,) a Dutch painter of *genre*, born about 1644. Little is known of his history. His colour is good, his design correct, and his manner natural. He represents the effects of light with great skill. Among his works (which command high prices) are a "Supper," an "Interior," and a "Guard-Room." Died in 1708.

See DESCAMPS, "Vies des Peintres Flamands, Hollandais," etc.

Hooge or **Hooghe, de,** (ROMEYN,) an eminent Dutch designer and engraver, was born at the Hague about 1640, or, as others say, about 1650. He worked for a long time in Paris, and passed his latter years at the Hague. He had a rich imagination and great facility, but was deficient in correctness. Among his works are "The Entrance of Louis XIV. into Dunkirk," and "The Assassination of De Witt." Died in 1725.

See J. C. WEYERMAN, "De Schilderkonst der Nederlanders."

Hoogeveen, hō'ģeh-vān' or hō'Hęh-vān', sometimes written **Hoogeven,** (HENDRIK,) a Dutch Hellenist, born at Leyden in 1712, was successively rector of the gymnasiums of Breda, Dort, and Delft, and was an excellent grammarian. He is the author of a valuable treatise on "Greek Particles," ("Doctrina Particularum Linguæ Græcæ," 2 vols., 1769,) and "Dictionarium Analogicum Linguæ Græcæ," (Cambridge, 1800.) Died in 1791.

See ERSCH und GRUBER, "Allgemeine Encyklopaedie;" HARLESS, "Vitæ Philologorum."

Hoogstaad, van, văn hōG'stät', (GERART,) a Flemish painter of history and portraits, born at Brussels, was living in 1661.

Hoogstraaten, van, văn hōG'strä'tęn, (DAVID,) a Dutch scholar, a nephew of the following, was born at Rotterdam in 1658, and became a classical professor at Amsterdam. He compiled a Latin-Dutch Dictionary, (1704,) and wrote several elegant Latin poems, "Poemata," (1710.) Died in 1724.

Hoogstraaten, van, (SAMUEL,) a Dutch painter, born at Dort in 1627, was a pupil of Rembrandt, and the master of Houbraken. He painted portraits, landscapes, etc. with success, and wrote a good work on the theory of painting. Died in 1678.

His father, DIRCK, born at Antwerp in 1596, was also a skilful landscape-painter. Died in 1640.

See PILKINGTON's "Dictionary of Painters."

Hoogvliet, hōG'vleet or hoH'vleet, (ARNOLD,) a popular Dutch poet, born at Vlaardingen in 1687, was educated for a merchant, and held the position of cashier in his native place. His reputation is founded on an epic poem, called "Abraham the Patriarch," (1727,) which was received with extraordinary and durable favour. "No book in Dutch literature," says Marron, "has been honoured with a more decided national adoption." ("Biographie Universelle.") He afterwards published a collection of poems on various subjects, which are not unworthy of his name. Died in 1763.

See JAN VAN KRUYFF, "Leven van A. Hoogvliet," 1782; WILLEM TERPSTRA, "Oratio de A. Hoogvlietio Poeta," 1816.

Hoogzaat, hōG'zät, (JAN,) an able Dutch painter, born at Amsterdam in 1664. He decorated the château of Loo for William III. of England. Died in 1712.

Hook, hŏŏk, (JAMES,) an English composer and musician, born at Norwich in 1746. He was employed as organist at Vauxhall Garden, London, for many years, and composed numerous popular ballads, songs, concertos, etc. Died in 1827.

Hook, (JAMES,) LL.D., an English writer, brother of Theodore E. Hook, was born in London about 1771. He was educated for the church, and in 1825 was appointed

Dean of Worcester. His principal works are two novels, called "Pen Owen" and "Percy Mallory." Died in 1828.

Hook, (JAMES CLARKE,) an English historical painter, born about 1820. In the early part of his career he painted subjects from Italian history, among which are "Bianca Capello," and a "Dream of Venice." He afterwards produced "The Defeat of Shylock," (1851,) and other scenes from Shakspeare. He became a Royal Academician in 1859.

Hook, (THEODORE EDWARD,) born in London in 1788, was the son of James, the musical composer, noticed above. He was an excellent vocalist, an expert mimic, and a prodigy of colloquial power. In 1805 he wrote "The Soldier's Return," an operatic farce, which was very successful. He was addicted to punning, to extravagant dissipation, and to audacious practical jokes. His brilliant wit and marvellous faculty of improvisation rendered him an idol of the gay world, and commended him to the favour of the prince-regent, who procured his appointment in 1812 as treasurer to the colony of Mauritius, with a salary of about £2000. In 1818, a large deficit being found in his treasure-chest, he was sent home charged with peculation. The legal inquiry, however, proved nothing against him except a culpable negligence of his official duties. In 1820 he became editor of the "John Bull" newspaper, which was very successful in a pecuniary respect and obtained great notoriety. Among his most popular works are "Sayings and Doings," (of which he issued three series,) "Maxwell," a novel, and "Gilbert Gurney," a novel, which contains an autobiography of himself. In 1836 he was editor of the "New Monthly Magazine." Died in 1841.

See R. H. BARHAM, "Life and Writings of Theodore Hook," 1848; "Life of T. Hook," from the "Quarterly Review," London, 1852; R. H. HORNE, "New Spirit of the Age," 1844; "Quarterly Review" for May, 1843, (vol. lxxii.;) "Noctes Ambrosianæ;" MOIR, "Poetical Literature of the Past Half-Century;" SAMUEL SMILES, "Brief Biographies;" "Memories of Authors," in the "Atlantic Monthly" for April, 1865.

Hook, (WALTER FARQUHAR,) an English theologian, a nephew of the preceding, was born in London in 1798. He became vicar of Leeds in 1837, and Dean of Chichester in 1859. Among his works are "Hear the Church," (28th edition, 1838,) "Ecclesiastical Biography," (8 vols., 1845-52,) "Church Dictionary," (7th edition, 1854,) and "Lives of the Archbishops of Canterbury," (of which the first volume was published in 1860, and the seventh appeared in 1868,—not yet finished, 1869.) He is noted for his zeal and success in the cause of church extension.

See "London Quarterly Review" for July, 1862.

Hooke, ho͞ok, (NATHANIEL,) a Roman Catholic historian, born about 1690, was an intimate friend of Pope the poet. His principal work is "The Roman History from the Building of Rome to the End of the Commonwealth," (4 vols. 4to, 1733-71,) which was often reprinted, and is commended as a faithful compilation. He was employed by Sarah, Duchess of Marlborough, as editor of her Memoirs, (1742.) Died in 1764.

Hooke, (ROBERT,) M.D., an English philosopher, born at Freshwater, in the Isle of Wight, in 1635, and noted for his inventive faculty, mechanical genius, and scientific acquirements. In 1662 he was chosen curator of experiments to the Royal Society, of which he was a Fellow, and afterwards secretary. About 1666 he became professor of geometry in Gresham College, and city surveyor of London. Among his multifarious accomplishments was skill in architecture, which he exercised in drawing the plan of Bedlam and other public buildings in London. He wrote many memoirs on various branches of natural science. He had a dispute with Hevelius on the subject of the telescope, and attacked Newton's theory of light and colours. He claimed the invention of the barometer, quadrant, balance-spring for watches, etc. Died in 1702.

See "Biographia Britannica;" WALLER, "Life of R. Hooke;" WOOD, "Gresham Professors."

Hook'er, (HERMAN,) an American Episcopalian divine, born at Poultney, Rutland county, Vermont. He published, among other works, "The Portion of the Soul," etc., (1835,) "The Philosophy of Unbelief in Morals and Religion," and "Uses of Adversity," (1846.) Died in 1857.

See GRISWOLD, "Prose Writers of America."

Hook'er, (ho͞ok'er,) otherwise called **Vŏw'ell,** (JOHN,) M.P., an English historian, born at Exeter about 1524, was uncle of Richard Hooker, noticed below. He represented Exeter in Parliament in 1571. He compiled a large part of Holinshed's "Chronicles," (1586,) and wrote a treatise on the order and usage of Parliaments, and a few other works. Died in 1601.

Hook'er, (JOSEPH,) an American general, born in Hadley, Massachusetts, in 1819, graduated at West Point in 1837. He served as captain in the Mexican war, (1846-47,) and gained the brevet of lieutenant-colonel at Chapultepec. Having resigned his commission about 1853, he lived several years in California. He was appointed a brigadier-general of volunteers about May, 1861, served at the battle of Williamsburg, and in the "seven days' battles" near Richmond, June 26-July 1, 1862. He became a major-general in July, and commanded a corps at the battle of Antietam, September 17, 1862, a few days after which he was promoted to the rank of brigadier-general in the regular army. He commanded a grand division under General Burnside at Fredericksburg in December, 1862, and succeeded Burnside as commander of the army of the Potomac in January, 1863. This army, which probably amounted to 100,000 men or more, engaged the enemy at Chancellorsville, May 2 and 3, and was defeated, but was not pursued. During this battle he was stunned by a cannon-ball. He was relieved of the command on the 28th of June, 1863, and was sent to Tennessee with two corps in September of that year. He contributed to the victory gained by General Grant at Lookout Mountain, November 24 and 25, 1863, and commanded a corps of the army which General Sherman moved from Dalton to Atlanta, May-August, 1864. He had command of the Northern department from September, 1864, to July, 1865.

Hooker, (JOSEPH DALTON,) F.R.S., an eminent botanist and traveller, a son of Sir William Jackson Hooker, was born in 1817. He studied medicine, and in 1839 sailed as surgeon with the expedition of Sir James Ross to the Antarctic Ocean. On his return he published "Flora Antarctica," (2 vols., 1844-47,) the descriptions and illustrations of which are highly commended. Between 1848 and 1852 he explored the botanical productions of the Himalayas. The results of this arduous enterprise appeared in a very interesting work called "Himalayan Journals," (2 vols., 1854,) and in his "Flora Indica." Among his other works are "The Rhododendrons of Sikkim Himalaya," (1851,) a "Flora of New Zealand," (1852-54,) and "On the Vegetation of the Carboniferous Period."

Hooker, (RICHARD,) an eminent English divine and author, born at Heavytree, near Exeter, in 1553. After graduating at Oxford, he took orders in 1581, and in an unguarded hour married a scolding wife. By the favour of Sandys, Bishop of London, he became Master of the Temple in 1585. Here he was involved in a controversy with Mr. Travers, a Calvinist, who was also a lecturer in the Temple. One of the consequences of this dispute was the production of his great argument for the constitution and discipline of the Anglican Church, entitled "The Laws of Ecclesiastical Polity." After he began this work, desiring a more retired station than the Temple, he obtained in 1591 the rectory of Boscombe, to which the prebend of Salisbury was added. From 1595 until his death he was rector of Bishopsbourne. His work above-named was published from 1594 to 1597. It is regarded as a great bulwark of the Church, a monument of sound learning, and a noble model of literary excellence. According to Hallam, "the finest as well as the most philosophical writer of the Elizabethan period is Hooker. The first book of his 'Ecclesiastical Polity' is at this day one of the master-pieces of English eloquence. . . . So stately and graceful is the march of his periods, so various the fall of his musical cadences upon the ear, so rich in images, so condensed in sentences, so grave and noble his diction, that I know not whether any later writer has more admirably

ā, ē, ī, ō, ū, ȳ, *long;* ă, ĕ, ĭ, ŏ, ŭ, ȳ, *short;* a, e, i, o, *obscure;* fär, fâll, făt; mĕt; nŏt; gōōd; mo͞on;

displayed the capacities of our language, or produced p... sages more worthy of comparison with the splendid monuments of antiquity." ("Introduction to the Literature of Europe.") Died in 1600.

See IZAAK WALTON, "Life of Richard Hooker," 1666; "Biographia Britannica;" "Life of Hooker," in Gauden's edition of his works, 1662, and in Keble's edition, Oxford, 4 vols., 1836; "North British Review" for February, 1857.

Hooker, (REV. THOMAS,) one of the founders of Connecticut, was born at Marfield, England, in 1586. After preaching in Holland, he emigrated in 1633 to Boston, Massachusetts, and was the first pastor of Cambridge. In 1636, in company with Samuel Stone, he founded the city of Hartford, where he was minister until his death. He was a very influential man in the churches, and wrote many treatises, among which is the "Application of Redemption." Died in 1647.

See E. W. HOOKER, "Life of Thomas Hooker," 1849.

Hooker, (WILLIAM JACKSON,) F.R.S., a distinguished English botanist, born at Norwich in 1785. He published in 1811 "A Journal of a Tour in Iceland in 1809," and described, with Dr. Taylor, British mosses in "Muscologia Britannica," (1818.) His "Flora Scotica" appeared in 1821. He produced an excellent "Flora Exotica," (3 vols., 1823-27.) For many years he was professor of botany in the University of Glasgow. Among his greatest works are "Icones Filicum," or "Figures and Descriptions of Ferns," (with Dr. Greville, 2 vols., 1829-31,) "Flora Boreali-Americana," (2 vols., 1829-40,) and a "British Flora," (1830; 6th edition, 1850,) which gives a complete description of British plants, arranged after the natural method. He was appointed about 1840 director of the royal gardens at Kew, which have been greatly improved under his superintendence, and are said to surpass all other gardens in the world in the number and variety of the plants. He was the father of Dr. J. D. Hooker, noticed above. Died in 1865.

Hoolâkoo, Houlakou, Hûlâkû, hoo'lâ-koo', or **Hoolagoo,** hoo-lâ-goo', sometimes very improperly written **Hulakoo,** a grandson of Jengis Khan, born in 1217, was the first of the Eel-Khans, (Ilkhans or Ilchans,) or Mongol kings of Persia. He was commanded by his elder brother Mangoo (the father of Kooblai Khan) to complete the conquest of Persia, which he accomplished about the year 1255. He exterminated the Ismaeelians, or *Assassins*, and afterwards directed his forces against Bagdâd, which he took in February, 1258, and delivered up to pillage and massacre. If we may believe the statements of the Moslem historians, nearly 800,000 persons, including Motassem (the last of the Abbasside caliphs) and his eldest son, perished on that occasion. As a warrior, Hoolâkoo was distinguished for his sanguinary cruelty: he was nevertheless a patron of science, and the celebrated Eel-Khânee (or -Khannee) astronomical tables were prepared under his auspices, and derive their name from his title of Eel-Khân, signifying the prince or chief of the tribe. He died in 1265, and was succeeded by his son, Abâkâ Khan.

See MALCOLM, "History of Persia," vol. i. chap. x.; VON HAMMER, "Geschichte der Ilchane;" D'OHSSON, "Histoire des Mongols."

Hoole, hool, (REV. CHARLES,) born at Wakefield, England, in 1610, taught school with credit in London, etc., and was afterwards rector of Stock. He wrote a "Latin Grammar," and other school-books. Died in 1666.

Hoole, (ELIJAH,) an English Orientalist and Wesleyan minister, born at Manchester about 1798. He served as a missionary in India, and published "Madras, Mysore, and the South of India."

Hoole, (JOHN,) an English dramatist and translator, born in London in 1727, was educated in Grub Street. He was a friend of Dr. Johnson, and was a clerk in the East India House about forty years. He wrote several tragedies, and translated into bad or insipid verse the great poems of Tasso and Ariosto. In reference to his version of Tasso, (published in 1763,) Sir Walter Scott called Hoole a "noble transmuter of gold into lead." His "Orlando Furioso" appeared in 5 vols., 1773-83. Died in 1803.

See "Biographia Dramatica."

Hoole, MRS. See HOFLAND, (BARBARA.)

Hoomâyoon or **Humâyûn,** hoo'mâ'yoon', Emperor of Hindostan, of the dynasty of the Great Moguls, was the eldest son of Bâber. He was born at Cabool in 1508, and ascended the throne in 1530. Agra was his capital. He was defeated by the Afghans in 1540. His brothers having rebelled against him, he was driven out of his kingdom, and took refuge at the court of Persia. In 1545 he returned with an army and recovered his throne. He gained decisive victories over the Afghans, under Sekunder Shah, on the Sutlej, in 1554, and at Sirhind in 1555. He died in 1556, and was succeeded by his son, the celebrated Akbär. He was versed in astronomy, and wrote several poems.

See "Private Memoirs of Houmaioon," translated from the Persian by MAJOR C. STEWART; FERISHTA, "History of the Rise of the Mahomedan Power in India," translated by GENERAL BRIGGS; W. ERSKINE, "History of India under Baber and Humayun," 2 vols., 1854; ABOOL-FADHL, "Akbar-Nameh."

Hoop'er, (GEORGE,) D.D., an English prelate, born at Grimley in 1640, was educated at Oxford, and was an excellent classical and Oriental scholar. In 1677 he was almoner to Mary, Princess of Orange, and in 1691 became chaplain to William and Mary, and Dean of Canterbury. He obtained the bishopric of Saint Asaph in 1703, from which he was afterwards transferred to that of Bath and Wells. He published numerous religious works. Died in 1727.

See TODD, "Lives of the Deans of Canterbury."

Hooper or **Hoper,** (JOHN,) an English reformer and martyr, born in Somersetshire about 1495. While a student at Oxford, he was converted to the Protestant faith. In 1539, to escape the Bloody Statutes of Henry VIII., he retired from England and passed several years at Zurich. At the death of Henry he settled in London, where he became an eminent and eloquent preacher. In 1550 he was made Bishop of Gloucester, and in 1552 received the bishopric of Worcester *in commendam*. Soon after the accession of Mary he was condemned as a heretic, and, refusing to recant, was burned at the stake in 1553. He wrote numerous theological works.

See FOX, "Book of Martyrs;" BURNET, "History of the Reformation."

Hoop'er, (LUCY,) an American writer, born at Newburyport, Massachusetts, in 1816, wrote sketches entitled "Scenes from Real Life," (1840,) "The Poetry of Flowers," and other works. She died in 1841, and her "Literary Remains" were published in 1842, with a Memoir.

See GRISWOLD, "Female Poets of America;" "Democratic Review" for July, 1842.

Hooper, (ROBERT,) a British medical writer, born in the eighteenth century. Among his works are a "Medical Dictionary," (1798; 8th edition, by Dr. Grant, in 1839,) and "Surgeon's Vade-Mecum," (3d edition, enlarged by Dr. Dunglison, 1824.)

Hooper, (WILLIAM,) an American patriot, was born in Boston in 1742. He graduated at Harvard in 1760, studied law with James Otis, and rose to eminence in his profession in Wilmington, North Carolina. In 1774 he was chosen one of the delegates to the first Continental Congress. Soon after signing the Declaration of Independence, in 1776, he resigned his seat. Died in 1790.

Hoorn van Vlooswyck, hōrn vån vlòs'wĭk, (PIETER NIKLAAS,) BARON, a Dutch nobleman, born at Amsterdam in 1742, possessed an immense fortune. Having a taste for art, he formed a splendid collection of gems, cameos, mosaics, etc. Died in 1809.

Hoornbeek or **Hoornbeck,** hōrn'bāk, (JAN,) a Dutch writer on theology, born at Haarlem about 1616, was professor at Utrecht. Died in 1666.

Hoorne, COUNT. See HORN.

Hoorne, van, vån hōr'neh, or **Horne,** (JAN,) a Dutch anatomist, was born at Amsterdam in 1621. He became professor of surgery at Leyden about 1650, and gained a high reputation. He published, besides other works on anatomy, a "Brief Introduction to the History of the Human Body," ("Brevis Manuductio ad Historiam Corporis humani," 1660,) a work of much merit. Died in 1670.

See ERSCH und GRUBER, "Allgemeine Encyklopaedie;" CHARLES DRELINCOURT, "Oratio de J. van Horne," 1670.

Hope, (ALEXANDER JAMES BERESFORD,) M.P., an author and connoisseur, son of Thomas Hope, noticed below, was born in London in 1820. Among his works are an essay on "Newspapers and their Writers," (1858,) and "The English Cathedral of the Nineteenth Century," (1861.)

Hope, (Rev. FREDERICK WILLIAM,) F.R.S., an English entomologist, born about 1800, wrote "The Coleopterist's Manual." Died in 1862.

Hope, (Sir HENRY,) a British admiral, born in 1787; died in 1863.

Hope, (JAMES,) a British physician of the present century, was physician to Saint George's Hospital, London, and published "Principles and Illustrations of Morbid Anatomy," (1834,) and a "Treatise on Diseases of the Heart and Great Vessels," (1839.) Died about 1840.

Hope, (JOHN,) M.D., F.R.S., a Scottish botanist, born in 1725, was educated at Edinburgh and Paris, and practised in the former city. In 1761 he was appointed king's botanist in Scotland, and superintendent of the royal garden, and in 1786 regius professor of botany in the University of Edinburgh. He commenced a work on botany, which he did not live to finish. Died in 1786.

See ANDREW DUNCAN, "Life of John Hope," 1786.

Hope, (JOHN,) Earl of Hopetoun, a British general, born near Linlithgow in 1766, was a younger son of the second Earl of Hopetoun. After passing through the inferior grades, he was made a colonel in 1796, and returned to Parliament. In 1800 he served as adjutant-general under General Abercrombie in Egypt, and in 1802 obtained the rank of major-general. Having been made lieutenant-general in 1808, he took part in the battle of Corunna, in 1809, and at the death of Sir John Moore succeeded him in the command. He was commander-in-chief in Ireland about 1812. In 1814 he was raised to the peerage, as Baron of Niddry, and at the death of his elder brother, in 1816, inherited his title. Died in 1823.

See CHAMBERS, "Biographical Dictionary of Eminent Scotsmen."

Hope, (Sir THOMAS,) a Scottish lawyer, born in Edinburgh. He was knighted and appointed king's advocate in 1627, after gaining distinction at the bar. He wrote valuable legal treatises. His father, Henry Hope, was related to the wealthy family of Hope in Amsterdam. Died in 1646.

See CHAMBERS, "Biographical Dictionary of Eminent Scotsmen."

Hope, (THOMAS,) an English novelist and miscellaneous writer of rare merit, born about 1770, was a member of the wealthy family of Hope of Amsterdam. After traversing Europe, Asia, and Africa, to gratify his passion for architecture, and retiring from business with an immense fortune, he settled in London, and distinguished himself as a patron of the fine arts. He formed galleries of paintings and statues, and magnificent collections of rare works of art. In 1807 he published a work on "Household Furniture," which produced quite a revolution in upholstery and an improvement in the public taste. Soon after appeared "The Costume of the Ancients," and "Modern Costumes," which evince great antiquarian lore. In 1819 he published, anonymously, "Anastasius; or, Memoirs of a Modern Greek," which was attributed to Byron, and made a vivid sensation by its surprising combination of Oriental romance and classic learning. "Mr. Hope will excuse us," says Sydney Smith, "but we could not help exclaiming; in reading it, 'Is this Mr. Thomas Hope?—is this the man of chairs and tables?—the Œdipus of coal-boxes?—he who meditated on muffineers and planned pokers? Where has he hidden all this eloquence and poetry up to this hour?' The work before us places him in the highest list of eloquent writers and of superior men." Byron said he would have given his two most approved poems to have been the author of "Anastasius." Hope also wrote an "Essay on the Origin and Prospects of Man," and a "Historical Essay on Architecture," (1835,) which was received with favour. He married in 1807 Louisa Beresford, a daughter of W. Beresford, Archbishop of Tuam. Died in 1831.

See SYDNEY SMITH's article in the "Edinburgh Review" for March, 1821, (vol. xxxv.,) also for July, 1807; "Quarterly Review," vol. xxiv.

Hope, (THOMAS CHARLES,) an eminent teacher of chemistry, born in Edinburgh in 1766, was a son of John

Hope, the botanist, noticed above. He became professor of chemistry at Glasgow in 1787, and discovered a new earth, which he named "Strontites," about 1792. In 1798 he succeeded Dr. Black in the chair of chemistry in Edinburgh, where he lectured until 1843. He was reputed the most popular teacher of chemistry in Great Britain. He wrote several short treatises, one of which is "On the Point of Greatest Density of Water," (1805.) Died in 1844.

Hope, (Sir WILLIAM JOHNSTONE,) M.P., a British naval officer, born at Finchley in 1766. As post-captain, he served with distinction under Lord Howe against the French in 1794. In 1819 he was raised to the rank of vice-admiral, and the next year became a lord of the admiralty. He was knighted in 1825. He was a member of the House of Commons for thirty years. Died in 1831.

Hoper. See HOOPER, (JOHN.)

Höpfner or **Hoepfner,** höpf'ner, (JOHANN GEORG CHRISTIAN,) a German archæologist, born at Leipsic in 1765. He published, besides other works, a "Manual of Greek Mythology," (1795.) Died in 1827.

Hôpital. See L'HÔPITAL.

Höpken or **Hoepken,** höp'ken, (ANDERS JOHAN,) a Swedish statesman and writer of great merit, born in 1712, became a member of the senate in 1746. He was one of the first who formed the Swedish language on the models of Greece and Rome. His Eulogies on Count Tessin and Ekeblad are greatly admired. Died in 1789.

See E. M. FANT, "Åminnelse-Tal öfver A. J. von Höpken," 1789; GYLDENSTOLPE, "Åminnelse-Tal öfver A. J. von Höpken," 1789.

Hop'kins, (CHARLES,) born at Exeter in 1664, was the son of Bishop Ezekiel Hopkins. He was intimate with Dryden and Congreve, wrote several tragedies, and translated Ovid's "Art of Love." Died in 1699.

His brother JOHN, born in 1675, was the author of a collection of poems entitled "Amasia," (3 vols., 1700,) and other poems, among which is "The Triumphs of Peace, or the Glories of Nassau," (1698.) Died after 1700.

Hop'kins, (EDWARD,) Governor of Connecticut, born in London in 1600, emigrated to Boston, Massachusetts, in 1637. He was chosen Governor of Connecticut in 1640, and was re-elected every other year until 1654. Soon after this he returned to England, where he was appointed warden of the fleet and commissioner of the admiralty, and was elected to Parliament. Died in 1657.

Hopkins, (ESEK,) an American naval officer, born in Scituate, Rhode Island, in 1718. He was appointed commander-in-chief of the navy in 1775. He captured a British fort at New Providence, and several vessels of war, in 1775 or 1776. Died in 1802.

Hopkins, (EZEKIEL,) an English Calvinistic divine, born at Sandford, Devonshire, in 1633, was a popular preacher, and one of the standard theologians of England. He became Bishop of Raphoe in 1671, and Bishop of Londonderry in 1681. He was driven from this place by the Catholic insurgents in 1688. Among his works (which are admired even by many who are not Calvinists) are a "Treatise on the Vanity of the World," (1663,) "Sermons," (4 vols., 1691–96,) the "Doctrine of the Two Covenants," and "Exposition on the Lord's Prayer," (1692.) His style is remarkable for sententious brevity. Died in 1690.

Hopkins, (JOHN,) an English teacher, who graduated at Oxford in 1544, is chiefly noted for his share in the poetical version of David's Psalms by Sternhold and Hopkins. He is supposed to have been a clergyman.

Hopkins, (JOHN HENRY,) an Episcopal theologian, born in Dublin, Ireland, in 1792, came to the United States in 1800. He became rector of a church at Pittsburg in 1824, and was chosen Bishop of Vermont in 1832. Among his numerous works are "The Primitive Creed Examined and Explained," (1834,) a "Scriptural, Ecclesiastical, and Historical View of Slavery," (1864,) in which work he advocates the Southern view of slavery, and "The Law of Ritualism," (1866.) Died in 1868.

Hopkins, (LEMUEL,) M.D., born at Waterbury, Connecticut, in 1750. He practised medicine at Litchfield from 1776 to 1784, and at Hartford until 1801. He wrote "The Hypocrite's Hope," and other poems. He was

ā, ē, ī, ō, ū, y̆, *long;* ă, ĕ, ĭ, ŏ, *same, less prolonged;* ă, ĕ, ĭ, ŏ, ŭ, y̆, *short;* ą, ę, į, ǫ, *obscure;* fär, fàll, fàt; mêt; nôt; gōōd; mōōn;

associated with Barlow and Trumbull in writing "The Anarchiad," a poem. Died in 1801.

See Duyckinck, "Cyclopædia of American Literature," vol. i.

Hopkins, (Mark,) a Presbyterian minister and writer, born in Stockbridge, Massachusetts, in 1802, graduated at Williams College in 1824. He became professor of moral philosophy in that college in 1830, and president of the same in 1836. He published, besides other works, "Miscellaneous Essays and Discourses," (1847.)

Hopkins, (Samuel,) an American divine, born at Waterbury, Connecticut, in 1721, is called the founder of the Hopkinsian school. He studied theology under Jonathan Edwards, was ordained a minister in 1743, and began in that year to preach at Housatonnoc, now Great Barrington. In 1769 he removed from that place to Newport, Rhode Island. "Dr. Hopkins," says Allen, "was a very humble, pious, and benevolent man. . . . His life was spent chiefly in meditation; his preaching had but little effect." He published a "System of Doctrines contained in Divine Revelation Explained and Defended," (2 vols., 1793.) He also wrote a "Dialogue against Slavery," (1776,) and other works. He forms a prominent character in Mrs. Stowe's "Minister's Wooing." Died in 1803.

See a "Life of Dr. Hopkins," prefixed to his Works, 3 vols., 1853.

Hopkins, (Stephen,) an American statesman, born at Scituate, Rhode Island, in 1707, was a farmer in his youth, and afterwards a merchant. He was chief justice of the superior court from 1751 to 1754, and subsequently Governor of Rhode Island. In 1774 he was elected to Congress, and signed the Declaration of Independence in 1776. The unsteadiness of his hand indicated by his signature was occasioned not by fear, but by a nervous affection. He continued in Congress until 1779. Died in 1785.

See Goodrich, "Lives of the Signers to the Declaration of Independence."

Hopkins, (Rev. William,) a learned antiquary, born at Evesham, England, in 1647, was made prebendary of Worcester in 1675, and vicar of Lindridge in 1686. Died in 1700.

See Dr. Hicks, "Life of W. Hopkins."

Hopkins, (William,) an English Arian writer, born at Monmouth in 1706, became vicar of Bolney in 1731. He wrote a treatise in favour of Arianism, and translated the book of Exodus, (1784.) Died in 1786.

Hop'kin-son, (Francis,) an eminent author, wit, and patriot, born in Philadelphia in 1737. He graduated at the college of his native city, and chose the profession of the law. Having visited England in 1765, and passed two years there, he returned home, settled at Bordentown, and married Miss Ann Borden. From 1774 to 1777 he published "The Pretty Story," "The Prophecy," and the "Political Catechism," three humorous and popular essays, which contributed to foment the spirit of freedom and to prepare the people for national independence. He represented New Jersey in the Continental Congress of 1776, and signed the Declaration of Independence. He was appointed judge of the admiralty of Pennsylvania in 1779, and in 1790 judge of the district court of the United States. Besides the above essays, he wrote the "Battle of the Kegs," a ballad, and other works, in prose and verse. Died in 1791.

See Sanderson, "Biography of the Signers to the Declaration of Independence;" "National Portrait-Gallery of Distinguished Americans," vol. iii.

Hopkinson, (Joseph,) LL.D., an American jurist, author of "Hail Columbia," and son of the preceding, was born in Philadelphia in 1770. He was educated at the University of Pennsylvania, studied law, and rose to eminence in his profession in his native city. He was the leading counsel for Dr. Rush in his famous libel suit against William Cobbett in 1799, and was also employed in the trials under the alien and sedition laws before Judge Chase in 1800, and in the impeachment of the latter for alleged misdemeanour in office during these trials, before the United States Senate, in 1805. From 1815 to 1819 he was a representative in Congress, in which he distinguished himself as a speaker, particularly in opposition to the United States Bank, and on

the Seminole war. In 1828 he was appointed by President Adams judge of the United States court for the eastern district of Pennsylvania, which position he held till his death, in 1842.

See "Lives of Eminent Phi'adelphians," 1859.

Hop'per, (Isaac Tatem,) a distinguished philanthropist, a member of the Society of Friends, born near Woodbury, New Jersey, in 1771. He resided many years in Philadelphia, but passed the latter part of his life in New York. He was a man of great energy, courage, and intellectual acuteness, and distinguished for his life-long efforts to promote benevolent and humane objects,—especially negro emancipation. In the controversy which resulted in the separation of the Society of Friends in 1827, he was one of the most zealous adherents of the anti-orthodox party. Died in 1852.

See Lydia M. Child, "Life of I. T. Hopper," 1853; "Lives of Eminent Philadelphians," 1859.

Hop'per, (Thomas,) an English architect, born at Rochester about 1775. After being employed by the prince-regent on Carleton House, he erected many castles and mansions for the nobility, among which Penrhyn Castle is regarded as one of the best. He possessed superior conversational powers, and associated freely with people of distinction. Died in 1856.

Hoppers, hop'pers, or **Hopper,** hop'per, (Joachim,) [Lat. Hoppe'rus,] a Dutch jurist, born in Friesland in 1523. In 1566 he became privy councillor at Madrid, and chancellor for the affairs of the Netherlands. He was more moderate than the other ministers of Philip II. Among his works is one "On the Legal Art," ("De Juris Arte Libri tres," 1553.) Died in 1576.

See Motley, "Rise of the Dutch Republic," part ii. chap. v., and part iv. chap. iv.

Hop'pin, (Augustus,) an American artist, born in Providence, Rhode Island, in 1828. He pursued a collegiate course at Brown University, and entered upon the profession of law, but subsequently devoted himself to drawing on wood. He has illustrated "The Autocrat of the Breakfast-Table," the poem of "Nothing to Wear," and numerous other subjects.

Hoppin, (Thomas F.,) an American painter and designer, brother of the preceding, was born in Providence, Rhode Island, in 1816. Among the most important of his designs are the figures on the great window of Trinity Church, New York.

See Tuckerman, "Book of the Artists."

Hopp'ner, (John,) R.A., an excellent English portrait-painter, born in London in 1759. He studied in the Royal Academy, and was patronized by the Prince of Wales. For many years he was the most fashionable portrait-painter of London, except Sir Thomas Lawrence. Hoppner was very successful in portraits of women. His colouring is natural and powerful, and his tones are mellow and deep. His works have a charming air of facility and negligence. Died in 1810.

See Cunningham, "Lives of Painters," etc.

Hop'ton, (Arthur,) a learned English mathematician, born in Somersetshire in 1588, was intimate with Selden. He wrote "Speculum Topographicum," (1611,) and a few other works. Died in 1614.

Hopton, (Sir Ralph,) an English royalist officer, who fought for Charles I. in the civil war. He obtained some success in Cornwall in 1643. In 1646 he commanded about 8000 men at the battle of Torrington, where he was defeated by Fairfax. Died about 1652.

Hopton, (Susanna,) an English authoress, born in 1627, wrote "Hexameron, or Meditations on the Six Days of Creation." Died in 1709.

Horace, hŏr'ass, [Lat. Hora'tius; Fr. Horace, o'rȧss'; Ger. Horaz, ho-rȧts'; It. Orazio, o-rȧt'se-o,] or, more fully, **Quin'tus Hora'tius Flac'cus,** an excellent and popular Latin poet, born at Venusia, (now Venosa,) in Italy, in December, 65 B.C. His father was a freedman, who gained a competence as a *coactor,* (collector of indirect taxes or of the proceeds of auctions,) and purchased a farm near Venusia, on the bank of the Aufidus, (Ofanto.) At an early age he was sent to Rome, and became a pupil of the noted teacher Orbilius Pupillus, with whom he learned grammar and the Greek language.

About his eighteenth year, he went to prosecute his studies in the groves of the Academy at Athens,—then the principal seat of learning and philosophy,—where he remained until the death of Julius Cæsar (in 44 B.C.) involved the empire in a civil war. As Brutus passed through Athens, Horace, with patriotic ardour, joined his army, was made a military tribune, took command of a legion, and witnessed the fatal defeat of the cause at Philippi, where he threw away his shield. (Carmina, ii. 7.) His estate having been confiscated, he went to Rome, where he supported himself a short time by acting as clerk in the treasury. His early poems having excited the interest of Virgil and Varius, they recommended him to Mæcenas, in whom he found a liberal patron and intimate friend. Thenceforth his life was eminently prosperous, and serenely passed in congenial studies and patrician society. Preferring independence to the tempting prizes of ambition, he refused the office of private secretary to Augustus, who treated him with particular favour. He had a true relish for rural pleasures and the charms of nature, which he often enjoyed at his Sabine farm or his villa in Tibur. Died in November, 8 B.C. He was never married. He was of short stature, and had dark eyes and hair. His character, as deduced from his writings, is well balanced, and unites in a high degree good sense, good nature, urbanity, and elegant taste. His poems, consisting of odes, satires, and epistles, may all be contained in one small volume. His chief merits are a calm philosophy, a graceful diction, an admirable sense of propriety, and a keen insight into human nature, which have attracted an admiration growing from age to age, and have rendered him, next to Virgil, the most illustrious poet of ancient Rome. "It is mainly," says "Blackwood's Magazine" for April, 1868, "to this large and many-sided nature of the man himself that Horace owes his unrivalled popularity,—a popularity which has indeed both widened and deepened in its degree in proportion to the increase of modern civilization." His "Epistles" are among the few poems which represent the most perfect and original form of Latin verse. There is no very good English translation of Horace's entire works: that of Francis (4 vols., 1747) is perhaps the best. Lord Bulwer's translation of the Odes (1869) is highly praised.

See SUETONIUS, "Vita Horatii;" MASSON, "Vita Horatii," 1708; HENRY H. MILMAN, "Life of Q. Horatius Flaccus," 1854; VAN OMMERN, "Horaz als Mensch und Bürger von Rom," 1802; C. FRANCKE, "Fasti Horatiani," 1839; WALCKENAER, "Histoire de la Vie et des Poésies d'Horace," 2 vols., 1840; J. MURRAY, "Original Views of the Passages in the Life and Writings of Horace," 1851; J. (or F.) JACOB, "Horaz und seine Freunde," 1852; ERSCH und GRUBER, "Allgemeine Encyklopaedie;" see, also, the excellent article on Horatius in SMITH's "Dictionary of Greek and Roman Biography," by the late DEAN H. H. MILMAN, (author of the "Life of Q. Horatius Flaccus;") "Horace and his Translators," in the "London Quarterly Review" for October, 1858: "Horace and Tasso," in the "Edinburgh Review" for October, 1850.

Horæ, ho'ree, [Gr. Ὧραι; Fr. HEURES, ur, or HORES, OR,] the Hours or Seasons, which the ancients imagined to have charge of the gates of heaven or doors of Olympus. They appear to have been originally personifications of the order of nature and of the seasons. They were also regarded as goddesses of justice, peace, and order. Milton associates them with the Graces:

> "while universal Pan,
> Knit with the Graces and the Hours in dance,
> Led on the eternal Spring."
>
> *Paradise Lost,* book iv.

Ho-ra-pol'lo or **Ho'rus A-pol'lo,** [Gr. Ὡραπόλλων; Fr. HORAPOLLON, o'rä'po'lôn',] the celebrated author of a Greek treatise on the Egyptian hieroglyphics. His name and the epoch in which he lived have been the subject of much discussion. Recent critics favour the opinion that he lived at Alexandria about the fifth century.

See SMITH, "Dictionary of Greek and Roman Biography;" A. S. COREY, "The Hieroglyphics of Horapollo," 1840; GOULANIOF, "Essai sur les Hiéroglyphes d'Horapollon," 1827.

Horapollon. See HORAPOLLO.

Horatius. See HORACE.

Horatius, ho-rā'she-us, (in the plural, **Horatii,** ho-rā'she-ī,) a hero of the early Roman legends, who with his two brothers fought against the three Curiatii for the supremacy of Rome over Alba. His brothers fell in the first onset. By a feigned flight he separated his antagonists, and slew them one after the other.

Horatius Cocles. See COCLES.

Hörberg or **Hoerberg,** hör'bĕRG, (PEHR,) an eminent Swedish painter, born in Småland in 1746. He practised his art with success at Olstorp, chiefly on religious subjects, and received the title of historical painter to the king. Died in 1816.

See his "Autobiography," (in Swedish,) published in 1817, and translated into German by SCHILDENER, 1819; C. MOLBECH, "Leben und Kunst des Malers P. Hoerberg," 1819; "Biographiskt-Lexicon öfver namnkunnige Svenska Män."

Hor'be-ry, (MATTHEW,) D.D., an English divine, born in Lincolnshire in 1707, was educated at Oxford. He became canon of Lichfield, vicar of Hanbury, and rector of Standlake. His sermons were published in several volumes, (1745-74,) and were pronounced excellent by Dr. Johnson. Died in 1773.

Horebout, ho'reh-bōwt', (GÉRARD or GUÉRARD,) a Flemish painter of high reputation, was born at Ghent. He removed to England, and became first painter to Henry VIII.

Hores. See HORÆ.

Horfelin, de, dĕ or-fā-leen', (ANTONIO,) a Spanish painter of history and portraits, born at Saragossa in 1597; died in 1660.

Horleman or **Hårleman,** hoR'leh-mân', (CARL,) BARON, a Swedish architect, born at Stockholm in 1700, designed the cathedral of Calmar, and completed the royal palace at Stockholm. He was ranked among the greatest architects of Sweden. Died in 1753.

Hor'man, (WILLIAM,) of Eton College, an English botanist, born at Salisbury. He published "Herbarum Synonyma." Died in 1535.

Hormayr, von, fon hoR'mīR, (JOSEPH,) a German historian, born at Innspruck in 1781. He fomented a revolt in the Tyrol against the French in 1809, and was appointed historiographer of Austria in 1815. He became councillor for the foreign department of Bavaria in 1828, and minister from Bavaria to Hanover in 1832. Among his works are a "History of Tyrol," (1808,) "The Austrian Plutarch, or Lives of all the Austrian Princes," (20 vols., 1807-20,) "General History of Modern Times, 1787 to 1815," (1817-19, 3 vols.,) and "Vienna, its History and Curiosities," (9 vols., 1823-25.) Died in 1848.

See BROCKHAUS, "Conversations-Lexikon;" "Foreign Quarterly Review" for January, 1845.

Hor-mis'das [Persian, HORMOOZ] **I.,** King of Persia, son of Shahpoor (or Sapor) I., began to reign in 271 A.D. After an uneventful reign of fourteen months, he died in 272, and was succeeded by his son, Bahram I.

See FIRDOUSEE, "Shah Namah;" MIRKHOND, "Histoire des Sassanides."

Hormisdas II., King of Persia, of the Sassanide dynasty, was the son of Narses, whom he succeeded in 303 A.D. He died in 311, leaving the throne to his infant son, Shahpoor II.

Hormisdas III., a son of Yezdejerd III., became King of Persia in 457 A.D. He was defeated and deposed by his brother Fyrooz about 460.

Hormisdas IV., King of Persia, a son of Chosroes (Khosroo) I., began to reign in 579 A.D. He waged war against Tiberius, Emperor of the East, by whose army he was defeated in several battles. Provoked by his tyranny, his subjects revolted against him, and he was deposed and put to death in 591 A.D.

See ABOOLFARAJ, "Historia Dynastiarum;" MIRKHOND, "Histoire des Sassanides," 1793; GIBBON, "Decline and Fall of the Roman Empire."

Hor-mis'das, a native of Frusino, Italy, was elected pope in 514 A.D., as successor to Symmachus. He used his influence against the Eutychians and against Acacius, Patriarch of Constantinople. He died in 523.

Hormuzd. See ORMUZD.

Horn, hoRn, (ARVID BERNARD,) COUNT, a Swedish statesman, born in 1664. His influence secured the elevation of Frederick of Hesse-Cassel to the throne in 1720. He became the head of the party of "Bonnets," which was in power until 1738. Died in 1742.

See GUSTAV HORN, "A. B. Horn," 1852; THOMAEUS, "Svensk Plutarch."

Horn or **Horne,** (CHARLES EDWARD,) born in London in 1786, was noted as a composer of music. He was the author of "The Deep, Deep Sea," and other popular songs. He died in Boston, Massachusetts, in 1850.

Horn, horn, (Franz Christoph,) a German critic, born at Brunswick in 1781. He published several novels, a "Critical History of German Poetry and Eloquence," (4 vols., 1822–29,) and "The Dramatic Works of Shakspeare," ("Shakespeare's Schauspiele," 5 vols., 1823–31.) Died in 1837.

See "Franz Horn : biographisches Denkmal," Leipsic, 1839.

Horn, horn, (Fredrick,) Count of Aminne, a Swedish general in the French service, born at Husby in 1725. As aide-de-camp of Marshal D'Estrées, he had an important part in the victory of Hastenbeck, (1757.) He obtained the rank of lieutenant-general in the Swedish army in 1778. Died in 1796.

His son, Count Horn, was an accomplice in the assassination of Gustavus III. in 1792, for which he was banished for life. Died in 1823.

Horn, [Lat. Hor'nius,] (Georg,) a German historian, born at Greussen in 1620. He became professor of history at Leyden about 1648, and wrote, in Latin, works on history and geography, among which are an "Ecclesiastical and Political History," (1665,) and "Noah's Ark, or a History of the World," (1666.) Died in 1670.

See Johann Adam Flessa, "Dissertatio de Vita G. Hornii," 1738.

Horn, (Gustaf,) Count of, an able Swedish general, born in Upland in 1592. Having served with credit in Poland and Livonia, he was appointed a senator about 1624. At the battle of Leipsic, in 1631, he commanded the left wing, and contributed to the victory. After Gustavus Adolphus was killed at Lützen, Horn gained some advantages over the enemy, but was taken prisoner at Nordlingen in 1634. Restored to liberty in 1642, he was made commander-in-chief of the Swedish army in the war against Denmark, in which he was successful. The queen rewarded him (about 1652) with the office of Constable of Sweden and the title of count. Died in 1657.

See Emporagius, "Likpredikan öfver G. C. Horn," 1660; Florander, "Encomium Militiæ Hornianæ," 1648; J. F. af Lundblad, "Svensk Plutarch," 1823; "Biographiskt-Lexicon öfver namnkunnige Svenska Män."

Horn, (Uffo Daniel,) a German *littérateur*, born at Tratenau, in Bohemia, in 1817.

Horn or **Hoorn, de,** deh hōrn, also written **Hoorne** and **Hornes,** (Philippe de Montmorency-Nivelle,) Count, a Flemish noble, born in 1522, was the son of Joseph de Nivelle and Anne of Egmont. After the death of his father, his mother married Count de Horn, whose name and vast fortune he inherited. He distinguished himself at the battles of Saint-Quentin and Gravelines, and served Philip II. of Spain many years as admiral of the Low Countries, president of the council of state, governor of Gueldres, etc. Arrested by the Duke of Alva, with Count Egmont, on a charge of treason, he was unjustly condemned and executed in 1568.

See Motley, "Rise of the Dutch Republic;" Prescott, "History of Philip II.," vol. ii.

Horn'blōw-er, (Joseph C.,) an American jurist, born at Belleville, New Jersey, in 1777. He was chief justice of the supreme court of New Jersey from 1832 to 1846. He decided in 1856 that Congress had no right to pass a law for the rendition of fugitive slaves. Died at Newark in June, 1864.

Horne, horn, (George,) D.D., an English bishop and author, born at Otham, in Kent, in 1730, was a good Hebrew scholar. He was chosen vice-chancellor of Oxford in 1776, Dean of Canterbury in 1781, and Bishop of Norwich in 1790. He wrote against the philosophy of Newton, and published treatises in favour of John Hutchinson, and other works on theology. His "Commentary on the Book of Psalms" (2 vols., 1771) is esteemed an excellent performance, and has often been reprinted. He was a friend of Dr. Samuel Johnson. Died in 1792.

See William Jones, "Memoirs of the Life and Writings of the Rev. G. Horne," 1795.

Horne, (Richard Henry,) an English poet and dramatist, born in London about 1802. He produced, besides other dramas, a tragedy entitled "Gregory the Seventh," (1840.) His reputation is founded on "Orion, an Epic Poem," (1843,) which was announced at the price of one farthing, as a sarcasm upon the low estimation into which epic poetry had fallen. After three editions had been sold, the price was raised to one shilling, and finally to five shillings. This poem found many admirers. Among his other works are "The New Spirit of the Age," (2 vols., 1844,) and "Ballads and Romances," (1846.) In 1852 he removed to Australia.

Horne, (Thomas Hartwell,) D.D., an eminent English author, born in 1780, was educated in London. He passed eight years in the labour of a barrister's clerk, and acquired some knowledge of law, while his leisure was diligently improved in literary studies. In 1818 he published his principal work, the "Introduction to the Critical Study and Knowledge of the Holy Scriptures," (3 vols., 1818; 10th edition, enlarged, 1856,) which is considered the most complete and valuable work on that subject, and was soon adopted as a class-book in all the universities and colleges of England and in some of those in the United States. Having no sectarian tendency, it is appreciated by Christians generally, and has conduced greatly to the diffusion of sound biblical literature. In 1819 Horne was ordained by the Bishop of London, and obtained a prebend in Saint Paul's Cathedral, besides other livings. Among his other numerous publications are "Deism Refuted," (1819,) and a "Manual of Biblical Bibliography," (1839.) Died in January, 1862.

See "Reminiscences of Thomas H. Horne," London, 1862

Horne Tooke. See Tooke.

Horne, van, (Jan.) See Hoorne.

Horneck, hor'nĕk, (Anthony,) D.D., was born at Bacharach, in Germany, in 1641, removed to England about 1660, and became prebendary of Exeter, Westminster, and Wells. He wrote many devout religious works, among which are "The Great Law of Consideration," (1677; 11th edition, 1729,) and "The Happy Ascetic," (1681.) His writings were commended by Doddridge as "exceedingly pathetic and elegant." Died in 1696.

See his Life, by Bishop Kidder.

Horneck, von, hor'nĕk, (Ottokar,) called also Ottokar von Steiermark, (stī'er-mark',) one of the earliest who wrote in the German language, was the author of a "History of the Great Empires of the World to the Death of Frederick II.," (1280,) and a chronicle in rhyme. It has been published in Petz's "Austrian Historians," and is valued for its interesting account of the manners and customs of that age.

See T. Jacobi, "Dissertatio de Ottocari Chronico Austriaco," 1839.

Horneman, hor'nĕh-män', (Jens Wilken,) a Danish botanist, born at Marstal in 1770, became professor of botany at Copenhagen in 1808. He continued the "Flora Danica," a magnificent work, which other naturalists commenced, and which appeared in 14 vols. folio, (1806–40.) He wrote "Economical Botany for Denmark," (1798,) and other works. Died in 1841.

See his Autobiography; Erslew, "Forfatter-Lexicon."

Hornemann, hor'nĕh-män', (Friedrich Conrad,) a German traveller, born at Hildesheim in 1772, attempted in 1797 to explore Northern and Central Africa. He left Moorzook with a caravan bound for Bornoo in April, 1800, after which date he was never heard from.

Hor'ner, (Francis,) an eminent British statesman and lawyer, born in Edinburgh in 1778, was educated in the university of that city, and studied law with his friend Henry Brougham. Having removed to London in 1803, he was welcomed by the leading Whigs, such as Fox, Mackintosh, and Romilly, who hastened to enlist his eminent abilities in the public service. In 1806 he was returned to Parliament for Saint Ives. The death of Fox having produced a change of ministry and a dissolution of the House, Horner was returned for Wendover in 1807. He acquired great influence in Parliament by his integrity, wisdom, liberality, and knowledge of political economy. In 1810 he was a member of the Bullion committee and author of a part of the "Bullion Report," and made an able speech on that question. In 1813–14 he was recognized as one of the leaders of his party, and in 1816 he made a speech on Catholic claims, which was his last speech in the House. Compelled by ill health to retire from business, he set out on a journey to the south of Europe, and died, greatly lamented, at Pisa, in 1817. He was one of the originators of the "Edinburgh

Review," for which he wrote numerous articles. "He died at the age of thirty-eight," says Lord Cockburn, "possessed of greater public influence than any other private man." "No eminent speaker of Parliament," says Sir J. Mackintosh, "owed so much of his success to his moral character. His high place was therefore honourable to his audience and to his country."

See "Memoirs and Correspondence of F. Horner," published by his brother, LEONARD HORNER, in 1843; CHAMBERS, "Biographical Dictionary of Eminent Scotsmen;" "Edinburgh Review" for October, 1843; "London Quarterly Review" for May, 1843.

Horner, (LEONARD,) F.R.S., a British geologist, and younger brother of the preceding, took a prominent part in the organization of the London University, of which he was appointed warden in 1827. About 1833 he became inspector of factories, in which capacity he contributed largely to the moral and physical improvement of the operatives. He wrote articles on the "Mineral Kingdom" for the "Penny Magazine," "On the Employment of Children in Factories," (1840,) and other short works. Died in 1864.

Hor'ner, (WILLIAM E.,) an American anatomist, born in Virginia about 1790, became in 1816 demonstrator of anatomy to Dr. Wistar, of the University of Pennsylvania, and in 1831 succeeded Dr. Physick as professor of anatomy in that institution. Died in 1853. (See WISTAR, CASPAR.)

See GROSS, "American Medical Biography," 1861; CARSON, "History of the Medical Department of the University of Pennsylvania," 1869.

Hornius. See HORN, (GEORG.)

Horrebow or **Horreboe,** hoR'reh-bo, (CHRISTOFFER,) a Danish astronomer, born at Copenhagen in 1718. He succeeded his father as professor of astronomy about 1750, and published, besides other works, a Latin treatise "On the Annual Parallax of the Fixed Stars," (1747.) Died in 1776.

See KRAFT og NYERUP, "Litteraturlexicon."

Horrebow, (NIKOLAUS,) a Danish author, born at Copenhagen in 1712, became a judge of the supreme court. In 1750 he was sent by government to explore Iceland, of which he wrote a description, said to be very correct. Died in 1750.

See KRAFT og NYERUP, "Litteraturlexicon."

Horrebow or **Horreboe,** (PEDER,) an eminent Danish astronomer, the father of Christoffer, noticed above, was born in Jutland in 1679. He became professor of astronomy at Copenhagen in 1710. He determined the parallax of the sun more exactly in his "Clavis Astronomiæ," a treatise on physical astronomy, in which he favours the theory of Descartes. He wrote other works, among which is "Copernicus Triumphans, sive de Parallaxi Orbis Annui," (1727.) Died in 1764.

See KRAFT og NYERUP, "Litteraturlexicon;" NYERUP, "Universitaets Annalen."

Horrebow, (PEDER,) a son of the preceding, born in 1728, observed the transit of Venus in 1761, and wrote an account of it. Died in 1812.

Hor'rocks or **Hor'rox,** (JEREMIAH,) a distinguished English astronomer, born at Toxteth, near Liverpool, in 1619, was educated at Cambridge, took orders, and became curate of Hoole. He was the author of the true theory of lunar motion, and was the first who observed the transit of Venus, (in 1639,) which he had successfully foretold, and of which he wrote an account, entitled "Venus sub Sole visa." His other works on astronomy were published by Dr. Wallis in 1672. "His investigations," says the "Edinburgh Review" for October, 1843, "are all stamped with the clear indications of a genius of the first order; and he doubtless would have achieved far greater discoveries had not his privations and successes, his toils and triumphs, been together cut short by his premature death, in 1641."

See A. B. WHATTON, "Memoir of the Life and Labours of J. Horrox," 1859.

Horsburgh, hors'bŭr-ęh, or **Horsbury,** hors'bęr-e, (JAMES,) F.R.S., a Scottish hydrographer, born at Elie in 1762, was for some years captain of a merchant-ship navigating the East Indian seas. In 1809 he was appointed hydrographer of the East India Company. He was author of a valuable work entitled "Directions for

Sailing to and from the East Indies, China," etc., (1809.) Died in 1836.

See CHAMBERS, "Biographical Dictionary of Eminent Scotsmen," (Supplement;) "Nouvelle Biographie Générale."

Horse'field, (Rev. THOMAS W.,) an English antiquary, published the "History and Antiquities of Sussex." Died in 1837.

Hors'field or **Horsefield,** (THOMAS,) M.D., F.R.S., an eminent naturalist and traveller, born in Pennsylvania in 1773. He explored the natural history of Java for many years, and returned to England about 1820. He published "Zoological Researches in Java," etc., (1821-24.) The plants which he collected were described in an excellent work entitled "Plantæ Javanicæ Rariores," (1838-52, with fifty coloured engravings,) in which he was aided by Robert Brown and J. J. Bennett. He also wrote several smaller works. Died in London in 1859.

Hors'ley, (CHARLES,) an English composer, born at Kensington in 1821. He composed oratorios entitled "David" and "Joseph," (1852.)

Horsley, (JOHN,) F.R.S., an eminent British antiquary, born in Mid-Lothian in 1685, became pastor of a dissenting church at Morpeth. He wrote an excellent work entitled "The Roman Antiquities of Britain," ("Britannia Romana," 1732.) Died in 1731.

See REV. J. HODGSON, "Memoirs of the Life, etc. of John Horsley," London, 1831; CHAMBERS, "Biographical Dictionary of Eminent Scotsmen;" NICHOLS, "Literary Anecdotes."

Horsley, (JOHN CALLCOTT,) an English historical painter, born in London in 1817. His cartoon of "Saint Augustine Preaching" (1843) received one of the prizes of £200 from the Commission of Fine Arts. He was one of the artists commissioned to adorn the House of Lords, in which he painted a fresco of the "Spirit of Religion," (1845.) Among his master-pieces are "L'Allegro and Il Penseroso," (1851,) "Lady Jane Grey and Roger Ascham," (1853,) and a "Scene from Don Quixote," (1855.)

Horsley,(SAMUEL,) LL.D., an eminent English bishop and writer, born in London in 1733, was educated at Cambridge. In 1759 he obtained the rectory of Newington Butts, and, after receiving other preferments, became Bishop of Saint David's in 1788, of Rochester in 1793, and of Saint Asaph in 1802. To superior talents he joined profound learning, both classical and scientific. He was elected a Fellow of the Royal Society in 1767, and secretary of the same in 1773. In 1783 he gained distinction by a controversy with Dr. Priestley on Unitarianism, in which it is usually conceded that Horsley had the advantage. He published in 1796 an excellent treatise "On the Prosodies of the Greek and Latin Languages," and "Critical Disquisitions on the Eighteenth Chapter of Isaiah." Among his numerous publications are sermons, treatises on mathematics, and several admired performances in biblical criticism. Died in 1806.

See "Edinburgh Review" for February, 1811; "London Quarterly Review" for May, 1810, (vol. xvii.)

Hors'man, (EDWARD,) a British lawyer and politician, born in 1807. He represented Stroud in Parliament from 1853 to 1868. He is one of those who were called "Adullamites," who voted against the Reform bill in 1866, although elected as Liberals.

Horst, horst, [Lat. HOR'STIUS,] (GREGOR,) a German physician, was born at Torgau, in Saxony, in 1578. He became professor at Ulm in 1622, and was surnamed THE GERMAN ÆSCULAPIUS. Among his chief works are "On Diseases and their Causes," ("De Morbis eorumque Causis," 1612,) and "Anatomy of the Human Body," (1617.) Died in 1636.

See BAYLE, "Historical and Critical Dictionary;" ERSCH und GRUBER, "Allgemeine Encyklopaedie;" FREHER, "Theatrum Eruditorum."

Horst, van der, vän der horst, (NIKOLAAS,) a Flemish painter of history and portraits, born at Antwerp, was a pupil of Rubens. His works are highly prized. Died in 1646.

Horstius. See HORST.

Horstius. hoR'ste-ůs, (JACOBUS,) a Dutch religious writer, originally named MERLER, was born at Horst about 1597. He wrote, in elegant Latin, "Paradise of the Christian Soul," ("Paradisus Animæ Christianæ," 1630.) Died in 1644.

Horstius, hoR'ste-ùs, (JAKOB,) a German physician, born at Torgau in 1537; died in 1600.

Hort or **Horte,** (JOSIAH,) an English theologian, educated at a dissenting academy with Dr. Watts, who expressed a high opinion of him. He became Bishop of Kilmore and Ardagh in 1727, and Archbishop of Tuam in 1742. A collection of his sermons was published. He died at an advanced age in 1751.

Hortemels, hoR'teh-mĕls' or hoRt'mĕl', (FRÉDÉRIC,) a French engraver, born at Paris about 1688.

Hortemels, (MARIE MADELEINE,) an able engraver, born in Paris about 1688, was the wife of the celebrated engraver Nicolas Cochin. Died in 1777.

Hortense Eugénie de Beauharnais, oR'tŏNss' uh'zhä'ne' deh bō'ăR'nä', Queen of Holland, and mother of the emperor Napoleon III., was born in Paris in 1783. She was the daughter of Alexandre, Vicomte de Beauharnais, and Josephine Tascher, afterwards Empress of France. Her personal charms and amiable character rendered her a favourite with Napoleon and the ornament of his court. Against her own inclination, and through the influence of her mother, she became in 1802 the wife of Louis Bonaparte, with whom she did not live happily. It is said that she wept abundantly at the performance of the ceremony. In 1806 her consort Louis was made King of Holland. On this occasion Hortense said she would have preferred the throne of Naples. "I would have rekindled," said she, "the flame of the fine arts in Italy." She disliked the Dutch fogs, and deemed sunshine and Parisian society indispensable blessings.

Hortense was the mother of three sons, whom by the edicts of 1804 and 1805 the emperor had preferred as successors to his crown : 1. NAPOLEON LOUIS CHARLES, who died in 1807; 2. NAPOLEON LOUIS, who died at Pésaro in 1831; 3. CHARLES LOUIS NAPOLEON, the present Emperor of France. In 1810 Louis abdicated his throne, and was separated from his wife, who, with her sons, returned to Paris. At the restoration of 1814 she was created Duchess of Saint-Leu, through the favour of some of the allied powers. Louis XVIII., after an interview with her, declared he had never seen a woman who united so much grace and dignity. After sharing the brief and brilliant triumphs of the Hundred Days, she was compelled to fly from France. The authorities of Geneva refused her an asylum; but she received a hospitable offer from the canton of Thurgau, where she purchased the castle of Arenenberg in 1817. For many years she passed the summer at this place and the winter at Rome. When Louis Napoleon was exiled to the United States, in 1836, she wished to go with him, but had not sufficient strength to bear the voyage; and she died in 1837, in the arms of her son, who, learning her illness, had returned home. We should not omit to mention that she excelled in music, and composed the popular air of "Partant pour la Syrie," one of the favourite national songs of France.

See LASCELLES WRAXALL, "Memoirs of Queen Hortense;" COMTE DE LAGARDE, "Esquisse biographique sur la Reine Hortense," 1853; "Foreign Quarterly Review" for July, 1838.

Hortensius. See DESJARDINS.

Hor-tĕn'sĬ-us, (LAMBERT,) a Dutch philologist, born at Montfort about 1500. He wrote "On the German War," (" De Bello Germanico," 1560,) and annotations on Virgil's "Æneid," (1567.) Died about 1575.

Hortensius, hor-ten'she-us, (QUINTUS,) an eminent Roman orator, born of an equestrian family in 114 B.C. At an early age he acquired celebrity in the Forum, where, a few years afterwards, he maintained a spirited and generous rivalry with Cicero, who applauds his eloquence and calls him his friend. After serving in the army of Sulla in Asia, he became successively quæstor, ædile, prætor, and, in 69 B.C., consul. In the previous year he was counsel for Verres, when Cicero made his memorable speech for the prosecution. His orations and other works are all lost. His eloquence is said to have been ornate, flowery, Oriental in exuberance, and enlivened with sententious and brilliant passages. He had a retentive memory, a sonorous voice, and a graceful gesture. Died in 50 B.C.

See ONOMASTICON TULLIANUM; PLINY, "Natural History," books ix., x., xxxiv.; QUINTILIAN, books iv., x., xi., xii.; LINSÉN, "Dissertatio de Hortensio Oratore," Abo, 1822.

Horto, ab, ăb oR'to, or **de la Huerta,** dà lä wĕR'tä, (GARCIA,) called also **Garcia da Orta,** a Portuguese botanist, went to India as physician to the viceroy, and wrote "On the Plants and Drugs of India," (1563.)

See BARBOSA MACHADO, "Bibliotheca Lusitana."

Hor'ton, (THOMAS,) D.D., born in London about 1600, was professor of divinity in Gresham College, and published a number of sermons. Died in 1673.

Ho'rus, [Gr. Ὧρος, probably related etymologically to the Sanscrit Sûrya, Lat. Sol, and Sp. Sur,] the Egyptian god of the Sun, was regarded as the son of Isis and Osiris. (See OSIRIS and HARPOCRATES.) For the etymology of Horus, see SÛRYA.

Horus Apollo. See HORAPOLLO.

Horush. See BARBAROSSA.

Horváth, hoR'vät, (MICHAEL,) a Hungarian historian, born at Szentes in 1809. He became Bishop of Csanad in 1848, and minister of public instruction in 1849. After the defeat of the patriotic cause he went into exile in 1849. He wrote a valuable "History of the Magyars," (4 vols., 1842–46.)

Hos'ack, (DAVID,) LL.D., F.R.S., an eminent American physician, born in New York City in 1769. After graduating in Philadelphia in 1791, and prosecuting his studies in Edinburgh and London, he returned to New York, and became professor of botany and materia medica in Columbia College in 1795. He taught clinical medicine and obstetrics in the College of Physicians and Surgeons nearly twenty years, between 1807 and 1826. For many years he was one of the most successful practitioners and most influential citizens of New York. From 1820 to 1828 he was president of the New York Historical Society. His first wife was the sister of Thomas Eddy, and his second the widow of Henry A. Costar. He wrote a treatise on Vision, published by the Royal Society of London, (1794,) "Memoirs of De Witt Clinton," (1829,) a "System of Practical Nosology," (1829,) "Lectures on the Theory and Practice of Physic," (1838,) several volumes of medical essays, and other works. Died in 1835.

See J. W. FRANCIS, "Memoir of Dr. Hosack;" GROSS, "American Medical Biography," 1861; "National Portrait-Gallery of Distinguished Americans," vol. ii.

Höschel or **Hoeschel,** hö'shel, [Lat. HOESCHE'-LIUS,] (DAVID,) a distinguished German Hellenist, born at Augsburg in 1556. He was professor of Greek and keeper of the public library at Augsburg. He edited numerous Greek works, among which are the Homilies of Saint Basil and Saint Chrysostom, and the book of "Origen against Celsus," (1605.) His "Catalogue of the Greek Manuscripts in the Augsburg Library" (1595) is highly esteemed. Died in 1617.

See BRUCKER, "De Meritis in Rem literariam D. Hoeschelii," 1738; BAYLE, "Historical and Critical Dictionary;" NICÉRON, "Mémoires;" J. A. FABRICIUS, "Bibliotheca Græca."

Ho-se'a or **O-se'a,** [Heb. הושע; Fr. OSÉE, o'zà',] one of the twelve minor Hebrew prophets, of whom little is known, except that he lived in the "days of Uzziah, Jotham, Ahaz, and Hezekiah, Kings of Judah." It is inferred that his prophetic career extended from about 785 to 725 B.C. His language is remarkably obscure. "He is the most difficult and perplexed of all the prophets," says Lowth. He is quoted in Matthew ii. 15, ix. 13, Romans ix. 25, (where his name is written Osee,) and Revelation vi. 16.

Ho-she'a or **Ho-se'a,** [Heb. הושע,] the last King of Israel, began to reign about 730 B.C., after he had assassinated King Pekah. (See II. Kings xv. 30 and xvii. 1 to 7.) After a reign of nine years, his capital, Samaria, was taken by Shalmaneser, King of Assyria, who carried Hoshea with his subjects as captives to Halah, Habor, and the cities of the Medes. Since this event the fate of the ten tribes has been involved in mystery.

Ho'sĬ-us, (STANISLAS,) an eminent cardinal, born at Cracow, in Poland, in 1504. After holding responsible civil offices, he entered the Church, and was made successively Bishop of Culm and of Warmia. He was a violent opponent of heretics and Protestants. In 1561 he received a cardinal's hat from Pius IV., who sent him as legate to the Council of Trent. He wrote the "Confession of the Catholic Faith," (1551,) and other works. Died in 1579.

See RESCIUS, "Vita Hosii," Rome, 1587; BAYLE, "Historical and Critical Dictionary;" ERSCH und GRUBER, "Allgemeine Encyklopaedie."

Hos'king, (WILLIAM,) an English architect and writer on architecture, born in Devonshire in 1800. He became a resident of London in his youth, and acquired distinction by a "Treatise on Architecture and Building," republished from the "Encyclopædia Britannica," (1839.) About 1840 he was chosen professor of civil engineering and architecture at King's College, London. He wrote "Guide to the Regulation of Buildings as a Means of Securing the Health of Towns," (1848.)

Hos'kins or **Hos'kyns,** (JOHN,) Sr., an English writer and lawyer, born in Herefordshire in 1566. He was noted for skill in Latin and English poetry, and wrote epigrams, law treatises, etc. According to Wood, it was Hoskins who "polished Ben Jonson the poet," and revised Sir Walter Raleigh's History before it went to press. Died in 1638.

Hoskins, (JOHN,) an English portrait-painter, patronized by Charles I. Died in 1664.

Hos'mer, (HARRIET,) an American sculptor, born in Watertown, Massachusetts, in 1831, studied in Rome, where she fixed her residence. Among her works are "Medusa," "Beatrice Cenci," and an admired statue of "Zenobia in Chains," ("Zenobia Captiva.")

See TUCKERMAN, "Book of the Artists."

Hosmer, (WILLIAM,) an American divine of the Methodist Episcopal Church, born in Brimfield, Massachusetts, in 1810. He was editor of the "Northern Christian Advocate," published at Auburn, New York, and of the "Northern Independent," a religious anti-slavery journal. He wrote, besides other works, "Christian Beneficence," etc., (1855.)

Hosmer, (WILLIAM HENRY CUYLER,) an American poet, born at Avon, in the Genesee valley, New York, in 1814, studied in Geneva College, and practised law in his native town. He spent much time among the Indians. In 1854 he took up his residence in New York. He wrote, besides other works, "Indian Traditions and Legends of the Senecas," etc., (1850.) A complete edition of his Poetical Works, in 2 vols., was published in 1854.

See GRISWOLD, "Poets and Poetry of America."

Hos-pin'ī-ạn, [Ger. pron. hos-pe-ne-ân'; Fr. HOSPINIEN, hos'pe'ne-âN'; Lat. HOSPINIA'NUS,] (RUDOLF,) an eminent Swiss Protestant theologian, born at Altorf in 1547. He became the minister of a church near Zurich, and wrote a number of learned works, in Latin, among which are "On the Origin and Progress of Ceremonies, Rites, and Holydays (Festis) among Christians," (1585,) "History of Sacraments," ("Historia Sacramentaria," 1598,) and a "History of the Jesuits," (1619.) Died in 1626.

See JOHN H. HEIDEGGER, "Historia Vita Rodolphi Hospiniani," 1681; BAYLE, "Historical and Critical Dictionary."

Hospinianus. See HOSPINIAN.

Hospinien. See HOSPINIEN.

Hospital. See L'HÔPITAL.

Hossch. See HOSSCHIUS.

Hosschius, hos'ke-ûs, or **Hossch,** hosK, (SIDONIUS,) a Flemish Jesuit, born at Merckhem in 1596, published in 1635 a collection of Latin elegies, which were much admired. Died in 1653.

Höst or **Hoest,** höst, (GEORG,) a Danish traveller, born in Jutland in 1734, became secretary for foreign affairs, etc. He wrote an "Account of the Kingdoms of Morocco and Fez," (1779.)

Höst or **Hoest,** (JENS KRAGH,) a Danish historian, son of the preceding, was born at Saint Thomas, in the Antilles, in 1772. He was the author of "Politics and History," (5 vols., 1816,) "Johann Friedrich Struensee and his Ministry," (3 vols., 1824,) and other works. Died near Copenhagen in 1844.

See J. K. HOEST, "Erindringer;" ERSLEW, "Almindeligt Forfatter-Lexikon."

Host, host, (NIKOLAUS THOMAS,) an Austrian, born in 1763, was first physician to the Emperor of Austria, and published "Flora Austriaca," (2 vols., 1827.) Died in 1834.

Hoste, höt, (JEAN,) a French geometer, born at Nancy, became professor of mathematics at Pont-à-Mousson. He published several treatises on geometry. Died in 1631.

Hoste, L', lot, (PAUL,) a French Jesuit, born at Pont-de-Vesle in 1652, was professor of mathematics in Toulon. He wrote a treatise on the "Construction of Ships and Naval Tactics," (1697.) Died in 1700.

Hos-til'ĭ-an, [Fr. HOSTILIEN, os'te'le-âN',] or, more fully, **Cai'us Va'lens Mes'sius Quin'tius Hostilia'-nus,** second son of the Roman emperor Decius. At the death of his father, 251 A.D., he was acknowledged by some as a partner in the empire with Gallus; but he died a few months after, in 252.

Hostilien. See HOSTILIAN.

Hos-til'ī-us, (TULLUS,) the third King of Rome, and the successor of Numa, reigned about 650 B.C. Among the principal events of his reign, which is semi-fabulous, was the war against Alba, terminated in favour of Rome by the victory of Horatius over the Curiatii.

Hostrup, hos'trŭp, (CHRISTOFFER,) a Danish dramatist, born in 1819, produced many successful comedies, among which are "The Neighbours," ("Gjenboerne,") and "The Intrigues."

Hostus, hos'tŭs, (MATTHÄUS,) a German antiquary, born in 1509; died in 1587.

Ho'thạm, (HENRY,) an English vice-admiral, born in 1776. In 1815 he commanded the Channel fleet, was charged after the battle of Waterloo to blockade the west coast of France, and received Napoleon as a prisoner on board his flag-ship, the Bellerophon. He was appointed one of the commissioners of the admiralty in 1818. Died in 1833.

Hotho, ho'to, (HEINRICH GUSTAV,) a German writer on art, born in Berlin in 1802. He became professor of philosophy at the University of Berlin in 1829, and was considered one of the chief representatives of the school of Hegel. He wrote a "History of Painting in Germany and the Low Countries," (2 vols., 1840-43.)

Hotman, hot'môN', (ANTOINE,) a French jurist, a brother of François, noticed below, was born about 1525; died in 1596.

Hotman or **Hottoman,** [Lat. HOTOMAN'NUS and HOTTOMAN'NUS,] (FRANÇOIS,) an eminent French jurist and Protestant, born in Paris in 1524, was a friend of Calvin. He was deeply versed in jurisprudence, literature, and antiquities. He became professor of law at Strasburg about 1550, and at Valence in 1561. By concealment he escaped the Massacre of Saint Bartholomew, (1572,) after which he retired to Geneva and Bâle. He was appointed councillor of state by Henry IV. about 1580. He performed an important part in the scientific revolution which was produced in jurisprudence in the sixteenth century. His famous work on public French law, entitled "Treatise on the Government of the Kings of Gaul," ("Franco-Gallia, sive Tractatus de Regimine Regum Galliæ," 1573,) had an immense influence. He wrote, in elegant Latin, many other works, among which are a "Commentary on Legal Words," ("Commentarius de Verbis Juris," 1558,) and "Celebrated Questions," ("Quæstiones illustres," 1573.) Died at Bâle in 1590. His son JEAN (1552-1636) was a diplomatist and writer.

See BAYLE, "Historical and Critical Dictionary;" HAAG, "La France protestante;" NEVELET, "Vita Hottomanni," prefixed to Hotman's Works, about 1600; DARESTE, "Essai sur F. Hotman," 1850; "Nouvelle Biographie Générale."

Hotmann or **Hottomann.** See HOTMAN.

Hotmannus or **Hottomannus.** See HOTMAN.

Hottinger, hot'ting-ẹr, (JOHANN HEINRICH,) an eminent Swiss Orientalist and Protestant divine, born at Zurich in 1620. After studying in his native city, at Geneva, and Leyden, and becoming one of the best Oriental scholars of his time, he was chosen in 1648 professor of theology and Oriental languages at Zurich. In 1655 he accepted the chair of Oriental languages at Heidelberg, where he remained until 1661, when he was elected rector of the University of Zurich. The University of Leyden persuaded him to accept their chair of theology; but before he arrived at that scene of labour he was accidentally drowned, in 1667. Among the numerous monuments of his vast erudition, the following are, perhaps, the prin-

ā, ē, ī, ō, ū, ȳ, long; ă, ĕ, ĭ, ŏ, ŭ, ў, same, less prolonged; ä, ĕ, ĭ, ŏ, ŭ, ў, short; ạ, ẹ, ị, ọ, obscure; fär, fåll, fât; mêt; nôt; gōōd; mōōn;

cipal : "Oriental History," (" Historia Orientalis," 1651,) "Ecclesiastical History of the New Testament," (9 vols., 1651–67,) and " Etymologicum Orientale," a lexicon of seven languages, (1661.)

See J. H. HEIDEGGER, "Historia Vitæ J. H. Hottingeri," 1667; BAYLE, " Historical and Critical Dictionary;" G. H. HAHN, " Untersuchung ob des gelehrten Hottinger's wirkliche Lebensgefahr," etc., 1742; NICÉRON, " Mémoires."

Hottinger, (JOHANN JAKOB,) a Swiss theologian, a son of the preceding, was born at Zurich in 1652. From 1698 until his death he was professor of theology in his native city. He wrote, besides other works, an "Ecclesiastical History of Switzerland," in German, (4 vols., 1708–29.) Died in 1735.

Hottinger, (JOHANN JAKOB,) a Swiss professor and philologist, born at Zurich in 1750. He taught Greek and Latin in his native city, and published several good editions and translations of classic authors. Died in 1819.

Hottinger, (JOHANN JAKOB,) a Swiss writer, born in 1783 at Zurich, where he became professor of history, and published, besides other works, a "History of the Schism in the Swiss Church," in German, (2 vols., 1827.)

Hotze, von, fon hot'seh, (DAVID,) an Austrian general, born near Zurich about 1740. He commanded the army which was opposed to Massena in Switzerland in 1799. He was killed in a battle near Zurich, in September, 1799.

Houard, oo'ăR',* (DAVID,) a French jurist, born at Dieppe in 1725 ; died in 1802.

Houbigant, hoo'be'gŏN',* (CHARLES FRANÇOIS,) a French priest, born in Paris in 1686, was a member of the Oratory, and an excellent biblical scholar. After teaching rhetoric at Marseilles and philosophy at Soissons, he became deaf about 1722, and thenceforth devoted himself to study and writing. He gave especial attention to Hebrew, with a view to correct the text of the Bible. The principal fruit of his labours is an edition of the Hebrew Bible, with Critical Notes and a Latin Version, (4 vols., 1753,) which is highly commended. Died in Paris in 1783.

See J. F. ADRY, " Notice sur la Vie de C. F. Houbigant," 1806; " Nouvelle Biographie Générale."

Houbraken, hŏw'brä'ken, (ARNOLD,) a Dutch painter, engraver, and critic, born at Dort in 1660. He painted history and portraits with success at Amsterdam, and wrote (in Dutch) "The Lives of Dutch and Flemish Painters," with portraits, (3 vols., 1718,) a work of much merit. Died in 1719.

See JAKOB CAMPO WEYERMAN, "De Schilderkonst der Nederlanders."

Houbraken, (JACOB,) son of the preceding, was born at Dort in 1698. He worked many years at Amsterdam, was almost unrivalled as an engraver, and executed several hundred portraits, among which are a collection of "Illustrious Persons of Great Britain," (London, 1748.) He also engraved the "Sacrifice of Manoah," after Rembrandt, and the portraits in his father's "Lives of the Dutch and Flemish Painters." Died in 1780.

See BASAN, "Dictionnaire des Graveurs."

Houchard, oo'shăR',* (JEAN NICOLAS,) a French general, born at Forbach in 1740. He served in the army before the Revolution, in which he espoused the popular party. In 1792 he succeeded Custine in the command of the armies of the Moselle and of the North. In August, 1793, he gained a victory at Hondschoote, and forced the British to raise the siege of Dunkirk; but he was arrested by the dominant faction, and executed, in 1793, on the charge that he had permitted the enemy to escape after the battle just mentioned.

See THIERS, "History of the French Revolution."

Houdard. See MOTTE, LA.

Houdart de la Motte. See MOTTE, LA.

Houdetot, oo'deh-to',* (ÉLISABETH FRANÇOISE SOPHIE DE LA LIVE DE BELLEGARDE,) COUNTESS, a French lady, born about 1730, was the wife of General

Houdetot, the sister-in-law of Madame Épinay, and a favourite of Rousseau, to whose passion and indiscretion she chiefly owes the publicity of her name. Her *liaison* with M. Saint-Lambert was well known. Died in 1813.

Houdon, oo'dŏN',* (JEAN ANTOINE,) an eminent French sculptor, born at Versailles in 1741. About 1760 he won the grand prize for sculpture at the Academy, and went to Rome with a pension. After remaining there ten years, during which he executed an admired statue of Saint Bruno, he returned to Paris, and was admitted into the Royal Academy in 1775. About 1785 he received from Dr. Franklin a commission to execute the marble statue of Washington which adorns the State-House at Richmond, Virginia. He came to Philadelphia to obtain the model of this work. His reputation was increased by his statues of Voltaire and Cicero, and his busts of Rousseau, Buffon, Franklin, D'Alembert, Napoleon, Ney, etc. His heads of young girls are highly successful in the expression of modesty and innocence. Houdon was a member of the Institute. His personal character was amiable and estimable. Died in 1828.

See "Nouvelle Biographie Générale."

Houdry, oo'dRe',* (VINCENT,) a French Jesuit, born at Tours in 1631, was employed as preacher in the chief cities of France. He published sermons, and a compilation entitled "Bibliothèque des Prédicateurs," (23 vols., 1712 *et seq.*) Died in 1729.

Houel, hoo'êl',* (JEAN PIERRE LOUIS LAURENT,) a French landscape-painter and engraver, born at Rouen in 1735. In a journey through Italy, Sicily, etc., he collected materials for an interesting work, entitled "A Picturesque Tour through Sicily, Malta, and the Lipari Islands," (4 vols., 1782–87, with 264 engravings.) Died in 1813.

Hough, hŭf, (JOHN,) D.D., an English scholar, born in Middlesex in 1651, was elected president of Magdalene College, Oxford, in 1687, in opposition to the illegal dictation of James II. The king then sent a mandate to the Fellows to elect Parker, a Catholic. In this contest Hough firmly maintained his rights and those of the college, and the king's agents broke open the door in order to place Parker in the president's chair. In 1688 Hough was reinstated, and in 1690 was made Bishop of Oxford. Translated to the see of Lichfield and Coventry in 1699, he refused the Archbishopric of Canterbury in 1715, and became Bishop of Worcester in 1717. He was eminent for piety and learning. Died in 1743.

See JOHN WILMOT, " Life of Rev. John Hough," 1812; MACAULAY, " History of England," vol. ii. chap. viii.

Houghton, hō'ton, (DOUGLAS,) M.D., a naturalist, born at Troy, in New York, about 1810. He was appointed State geologist for Michigan in 1837, and was drowned in Eagle River in 1845.

Houghton, LORD. See MILNES, (RICHARD MONKTON.)

Houghton, hō'ton, MAJOR, an English traveller, who was sent by the African Company to explore the sources of the Niger. He started in 1790, ascended the Gambia many hundred miles, and afterwards proceeded by land. It is supposed that he died near Jarra, in 1791 ; but his papers were never recovered.

Houlakou or **Houlagou.** See HOOLÂKOO.

Houlières, des. See DESHOULIÈRES.

Houllier, hool'e-à', [Lat. HOLLE'RIUS,] (JACQUES,) an eminent French physician, born at Étampes, obtained a large practice in Paris, and was chosen Dean of the Faculty in 1546. He wrote able commentaries on Hippocrates, (1579,) and other works. Died in 1562.

Houmayoun or **Houmaioon.** See HOOMÂYOON.

Houseman, (C.) See HUYSMAN.

Houssaye. See AMELOT DE LA HOUSSAYE.

Houssaye, hoo'să', (ARSÈNE,) a successful French *littérateur* and poet, born near Laon in 1815. He produced "La Couronne des Bluets," (1836,) and many other novels. His "History of Flemish and Dutch Painting" (1846) was received with favour. In 1844 he

---

* There is perhaps no question in French pronunciation attended with more difficulty than that respecting the aspiration of the letter *h*. The best French authorities differ in regard to the initial *h* of many names. Some respectable authorities assert that the *h* should never / be sounded in any case ; others maintain that in certain words it should be slightly sounded, while in others it is entirely mute. Respecting this subject, see the remarks on French pronunciation in the Introduction.

---

e as *k*; ç as *s*; ğ *hard*; ğ as *j*; G, H, K, *guttural*; N, *nasal*; R, *trilled*; ş as *z*; ṯẖ as in *this*. (☞See Explanations, p. 23.)

published a "Gallery of Portraits of the Eighteenth Century," (1st series, 2 vols.,) which was completed in 5 vols. about 1850. From 1849 to 1856 he was director of the Théâtre Français. He also wrote able critiques on art, and published a volume of poems, "Poésies complètes," (1849,) and "Le Roi Voltaire," (1858.) He was chosen inspector-general of the works of art and *Musées* in 1856.

See BOURQUELOT, "La Littérature Française contemporaine;" CHARLES ROBIN, "Biographie d' A. Houssaye," 1848; CLÉMENT DE RIS, "Portraits à la Plume:" ALFRED DE MUSSET, "A. Houssaye," etc., 1853; "Nouvelle Biographie Générale;" "Blackwood's Magazine" for June, 1851.

Houston, hū′stǫn, ? (GEORGE SMITH,) an American Democratic politician, born in Tennessee in 1811. He studied law, which he practised at Huntsville, Alabama, and was elected a member of Congress in 1841. He was chairman of the committee of ways and means in the House of Representatives during two terms, 1851-55.

Houston, hū′stǫn, (SAM,*) an American general, born near Lexington, Virginia, in 1793, was taken to Tennessee in his childhood. He studied law, which he practised at Nashville, was elected a member of Congress in 1823, and Governor of Tennessee in 1827. In 1829 he resigned his office, and, renouncing civilized society, passed several years with the Cherokee Indians, who lived west of Arkansas. About the end of 1832 he emigrated to Texas, where he took an active part in the ensuing revolt against the Mexican government. Having been chosen commander-in-chief of the Texan army, he defeated and captured Santa Anna at San Jacinto, April 21, 1836. He was elected President of Texas in July, 1836, and re-elected for a term of three years in 1841. After the annexation of Texas to the Union, (1845,) he was chosen a United States Senator, and at the end of his term in 1853 was elected for a second term. He made an able speech against the Kansas-Nebraska bill in March, 1854, about which time he joined the American (Know-Nothing) party. He was chosen Governor of Texas in 1859. On the breaking out of the civil war he favoured the Union, but was overborne by a large majority of the people. Died in 1862.

See "Sam Houston and his Republic," by CHARLES E. LESTER, 1855.

Houstǫn, (WILLIAM,) F.R.S., an English surgeon and naturalist, born about 1695, studied under Boerhaave, at Leyden, in 1728-29, and made there, with Van Swieten, experiments respecting the respiration of animals. About 1732 he made a voyage for scientific purposes to the West Indies, where he died in 1733, after collecting and describing many rare plants. The results of his botanical labours were published by Sir Joseph Banks.

See "Biographie Médicale."

Houteville or **Houtteville,** hoot′vèl′, (CLAUDE FRANÇOIS,) a French priest of the Oratory, born in Paris in 1686. He published, in 1722, "The Truth of the Christian Religion proved by Facts," which attracted much attention and hostile criticism. In 1723 he was chosen a member of the French Academy. He was elected perpetual secretary of the Academy in 1742, and died in the same year.

See MORÉRI, "Dictionnaire Historique."

Houtman, hŏwt′mȧn, (CORNELIS,) a Dutch navigator, born at Gouda, was the pioneer or founder of the commerce between Holland and the East Indies. As agent of a company, he made the first voyage in 1595, and returned home in 1597. In 1598 he renewed the enterprise with two ships, and landed at Acheen, in Sumatra, where he was arrested with some of his men, and kept a prisoner several years, until his death. Died about 1605.

See RAYNAL, "Histoire philosophique des deux Indes;" "Nouvelle Biographie Générale."

Houtman, (FREDERIK,) a navigator, born about 1570, was a brother of the preceding, whom he accompanied in his voyage to the East Indies in 1598. He was afterwards Governor of Amboyna, and published a "Malay Dictionary," (1603.) Died about 1613.

Houtteville. See HOUTEVILLE.

Hove, van, vȧn ho′veh, (ANTOON,) a Dutch historian and Latin poet, born about 1505; died in 1568.

Hoveden, hŭv′dẹn or hōv′dẹn, **de,** (ROGER,) an English historian, born at York, lived about 1170-1200. He was professor of theology at Oxford, and filled responsible offices at the court of Henry II. He wrote, in Latin, a "History of England from 731 to 1202," which is commended by Leland, Selden, and others for its fidelity.

See VOSSIUS, "De Historicis Latinis."

Hovel. See HEVELIUS.

Hovey, hŭv′e, (ALVAH,) an American divine and author, born in Chenango county, New York, about 1820. He graduated at Dartmouth in 1843, and about 1850 became a professor in the Baptist Theological Seminary at Newton. His principal work is the "Life and Times of Backus," (1857.)

Hovey, (ALVAN P.,) an American officer, who entered the service as major of an Indiana regiment in 1861, and became a brigadier-general about April, 1862. He commanded a division and contributed to the victory at Champion's Hill, May 16, 1863.

Hovey, (CHARLES EDWARD,) an American officer, born at Hartford, Vermont, in 1827, removed to Illinois, and was made a brigadier-general of volunteers in 1862.

Hŏw, (WILLIAM,) M.D., born in London in 1619, became a captain in the royal army in the civil war, and afterwards practised medicine in his native city. He is said to have been the author of the first English Flora, ("Phytologia Britannica," 1650,) which contains twelve hundred and twenty plants. Died in 1656.

Hŏw′ȧrd, the name of an ancient and noble family of England, the head of which is the Duke of Norfolk and the premier peer of Great Britain. The Earls of Carlisle and Suffolk also belong to the Howard family.

Howard, (ANNE,) daughter of Charles, Earl of Carlisle, was married to Richard, Viscount Irwin. She wrote a "Poetical Essay on Pope's Characters of Women," and other poems. Died in 1760.

Howard, (CHARLES,) Lord Effingham, or Lord Howard of Effingham, an English admiral, born in 1536, was the son of William, Lord Effingham, and grandson of Thomas Howard, second Duke of Norfolk. After important civil and military services, he was appointed in 1585 lord high admiral by Queen Elizabeth, and successfully opposed the Invincible Armada in 1588. In 1596 he was associated with the Earl of Essex in the victorious expedition against Cadiz, and was rewarded with the title of Earl of Nottingham. About three years later, when another Spanish invasion was expected, the sole command of the army and navy for a short time was committed to him, with the title of lieutenant-general of England. He retained his honours and offices under James I. Died in 1624.

See CAMPBELL, "Lives of British Admirals;" J. BARROW, "Memoirs of the Naval Worthies of Queen Elizabeth's Reign," 1845.

Howard, (CHARLES,) Earl of Carlisle, born about 1630, was employed in the reign of Charles II. in diplomatic missions to Muscovy, Sweden, and Denmark, of which an account was published in 1669. Died in 1686.

Howard, (CHARLES,) tenth Duke of Norfolk, (previously Hon. CHARLES HOWARD, of Greystock Castle, Cumberland,) succeeded to the dukedom in 1777. He published "Thoughts, Essays, and Maxims, chiefly Religious and Political," (1768,) and "Historical Anecdotes of some of the Howard Family." Died in 1786.

Howard, (CHARLES,) eleventh Duke of Norfolk, an English nobleman, born in 1746, was the son of the tenth Duke. In 1780, being then styled the Earl of Surrey, he exchanged the Catholic faith for that of the Anglican Church. Representing Carlisle in Parliament, he acted with the opposition during the ministries of Lord North and Lord Shelburne. At the death of his father, in 1786, he became Duke of Norfolk. As a member of the House of Lords, he opposed the measures of Pitt. Died in 1815.

Howard, (Hon. EDWARD,) an English writer, a son of Thomas, Earl of Berkshire, lived about 1650. He wrote several unsuccessful dramas, and "The British Princes; a Heroic Poem," in which occur these lines, often quoted in ridicule:

"A painted vest Prince Vortigern had on,
Wh'ch from a naked Pict his grandsire won."

---

* So called by himself.

ā, ē, ī, ō, ū, ȳ, *long;* à, è, ò, same, less prolonged; ă, ĕ, ĭ, ŏ, ŭ, ў, *short;* a, ę, i, ǫ, *obscure;* fȧr, fàll, fȧt: mêt: nŏt; gōōd: mōōn;

Pope, in the "Dunciad," alludes to him in these terms :

"And high-born Howard, more majestic sire,
With fool of quality completes the choir."

Howard, (EDWARD,) a popular English novelist, was a lieutenant in the royal navy. He published "The Old Commodore," (1837,) "Ratlin the Reefer," (1838,) "Outward-Bound," etc. Died in 1842.

Howard, (FRANK,) an able English designer and writer on art, a son of Henry Howard the painter. He published "The Spirit of the Plays of Shakspeare, exhibited in Outline Plates," (5 vols., 1827-33,) and the "Science of Drawing," (1840.) Died in 1866.

Howard, (FREDERICK,) fifth Earl of Carlisle, an English poet and statesman, born in 1748, was the son of Henry, and grandson of the third Earl, noticed above. He succeeded to the family title in 1758. In 1778 he was one of the commissioners sent to persuade the people of the United States to submit to the British rule. He acted with the Whig party until the French Revolution, after which he supported the ministry. He published a volume of Poems, and several tragedies, one of which, called "The Father's Revenge," was commended by Dr. Johnson. His mother, Isabella Byron, daughter to the fifth Lord Byron, was first-cousin to the father of the poet Byron. Died in 1825.

Howard, (GEORGE EDMUND,) a British poet and architect, was educated at Trinity College, Dublin. He published in 1782 several volumes of miscellaneous works, the most important of which treat on the exchequer, revenue, and trade of Ireland. Died in 1786.

Howard, (GEORGE WILLIAM FREDERICK,) Earl of Carlisle and Viscount Morpeth, a statesman and author, born in 1802, was a grandson of Frederick, fifth Earl of Carlisle. He was styled Lord Morpeth before the death of his father, which occurred about 1848. Under the Whig ministry which was dissolved in 1841 he was secretary for Ireland. He visited the United States between 1842 and 1846, and, after his return, imparted to the public some observations on that country in a lecture. In 1854 he published a "Diary in Turkish and Greek Waters," which is a work of merit. He was lord-lieutenant of Ireland about three years, (1855-58,) and was reappointed to that office by Palmerston in June, 1859. He had the reputation of a liberal statesman and benevolent man. Died in 1864.

Howard, (HENRY,) Earl of Surrey, a celebrated English poet, born about 1516, was the son of Thomas, third Duke of Norfolk, and of Elizabeth Stafford. He excelled in the accomplishments of a scholar, courtier, and soldier, and cultivated as well as patronized the fine arts. About 1535 he married Lady Frances Vere. In 1544 he accompanied Henry VIII. in his invasion of France, was made a field-marshal, and was appointed governor of Boulogne after it was captured by the English. Soon after this he became the object of the king's suspicion. He was recalled in 1546, arrested with his father, condemned, and executed in 1547. He left two sons and three daughters. (With respect to Surrey's guilt or innocence, see Froude's "History of England," vol. iv. chap. xxiii.)

Surrey is the first who used blank verse in our language, and is considered the first English classical poet. He did much to improve the style of versification. One of his principal productions is a translation into blank verse of the second book of the "Æneid," which is admired for its fidelity and poetic diction. He also wrote numerous sonnets and songs. There is some doubt of the reality of his romantic passion for Geraldine, who is the subject of his most admired effusions. She was a child of thirteen, named Lady Elizabeth Fitzgerald, who afterwards became the wife of the Earl of Lincoln.

See HALLAM, "Introduction to the Literature of Europe;" WARTON, "History of English Poetry;" JOHNSON and CHALMERS, "Lives of the English Poets;" "Edinburgh Review," vol. xlii.

Howard, (HENRY,) Earl of Northampton, second son of the preceding, was born at Norfolk about 1539. He was a person of much learning, but of bad principles. He became a privy councillor at the accession of James I., who made him Earl of Northampton. In 1608 he was appointed lord privy seal. He was suspected of complicity in the murder of Sir Thomas Overbury, and in the disgraceful conduct of his relative, the Countess of Essex. Died in 1614.

See GARDINER's "History of England from 1603 to 1616," vol. i. chap. ii. pp. 63 and 64; also, chaps. x. and xii.

Howard, (HENRY,) born in 1757, was the son of Philip Howard of Corby Castle, England, and a descendant of the noble Earl of Surrey. He published "Indication of Memorials, etc. of the Howard Family," (1834,) and other works. Died in 1842.

Howard, (HENRY,) an English painter, born in 1769, entered the Royal Academy as a student in 1788. In 1790 he won two of the highest premiums,—a gold medal for the best historical painting, and a silver medal for the best drawing from life. After a visit to Rome he was chosen a member of the Royal Academy in 1808, and secretary of that body in 1811. His favourite subjects are classical and poetical, and are treated with elegant taste. Among his best works are "The Birth of Venus," "The Solar System," "The Circling Hours," and "The Story of Pandora." Died in 1847.

Howard, (Sir JOHN,) was a son of Sir Robert Howard and Margaret, a daughter of Thomas Mowbray, Duke of Norfolk. He was a partisan of the house of York during the wars of the Roses. He was created Duke of Norfolk in 1483, and was killed with Richard III. at Bosworth in 1485.

Howard, (JOHN,) F.R.S., a celebrated English philanthropist, born at Hackney, near London, in 1726. He was the son of a London tradesman, who died in his minority and left him an independent fortune. Having made a tour on the continent, he returned home and took lodgings with a widow named Loidore, by whom he was kindly nursed when his health required such attention, and whom he married out of mere gratitude in 1752, although she was more than twenty years his senior. After their marriage she lived only three or four years. In 1756 he embarked for Lisbon, in the desire to relieve the miseries caused by the great earthquake of 1755, but during the passage was taken by a French privateer, and detained in prison long enough to excite his lasting sympathy with prisoners and to impress him with the necessity of a reform in their treatment. After he was released he returned home, and married in 1758 Henrietta Leeds, with whom he lived happily at Cardington until her death in 1765. He had by this marriage one son, whose vicious habits produced first disease and then incurable insanity. Having been appointed sheriff of the county of Bedford in 1773, he witnessed with pain the abuses and cruelties to which prisoners were usually subjected. After visiting most of the county jails of England, and collecting much information respecting them, he induced the House of Commons in 1774 to begin a reform in prison discipline, to which his life thenceforth was constantly, heroically, and successfully devoted. In 1777 he published a valuable volume on "The State of the Prisons in England," etc. From 1778 until his death he was almost continually employed in traversing all parts of Europe, visiting prisons and hospitals, relieving the sick, and, as Burke expresses it, "taking the gauge and dimensions of misery, depression, and contempt." He died of fever in 1790, at Cherson, on the Black Sea. His habits were simple, temperate, and self-denying. Having been educated among Protestant dissenters, he continued in their fellowship through life.

See "Life of Howard," by W. HEPWORTH DIXON, 1849; another Life, by JOHN FIELD, 1850; AIKIN, "Life of John Howard," 1792; J. B. BROWN, "Memoirs of the Life of John Howard," 1818; "Encyclopædia Britannica;" "Blackwood's Magazine" for January, 1850.

Hŏw'ạrd, (JOHN EAGER,) an officer, born in Baltimore county, Maryland, in 1752. He commanded a regiment which distinguished itself by its brilliant bayonet-charge at Cowpens, January, 1781, and its gallantry at Guilford Court-House, March, 1781, and Eutaw Springs, in September of that year. He was chosen Governor of Maryland in 1788, and was a United States Senator from 1796 to 1803. Died in 1827.

See "National Portrait-Gallery of Distinguished Americans."

Howard, (LUKE,) an English meteorologist, born about 1770, published an "Essay on Clouds," (1802,) and other works on meteorology. Died in 1864.

ε as k; ç as s; ḡ hard; ġ as j; G, H, K, guttural; N, nasal; R, trilled; š as z; th as in this. (☞See Explanations, p. 23.)

77

Howard, (OLIVER OTIS,) an American general, born at Leeds, Kennebec county, Maine, in November, 1830. He was educated at Bowdoin College and at the Military Academy of West Point, where he graduated in 1854. He became first lieutenant of ordnance in 1857, and colonel of the Third Maine Volunteers in May, 1861. He commanded a brigade at Bull Run, July 21, and obtained the rank of brigadier-general in September, 1861. At the battle of Fair Oaks, May 31, 1862, he lost his right arm. He commanded a division at the battle of Antietam, September 17, and at Fredericksburg, December, 1862. In November, 1862, he was appointed a major-general of volunteers, and in April, 1863, obtained command of the eleventh army corps, which he led at Chancellorsville, and at Gettysburg, July 2 and 3, 1863. He served with distinction at the battle of Missionary Ridge and Chattanooga, November 25, 1863. In his report of this campaign General Sherman commends him as "exhibiting the highest and most chivalrous traits of the soldier." General Howard commanded the fourth corps of the army which, under General Sherman, fought its way from Chattanooga to Atlanta, May–September, 1864. He was appointed, July 27, commander of the army of the Tennessee in place of McPherson, who was killed near Atlanta. In the memorable march of Sherman's army from Atlanta to the sea, Howard led the right wing, and was the second or third in command. (See SHERMAN, WILLIAM T.) In May, 1865, he was appointed chief of the Freedmen's Bureau. He has the reputation of being a model Christian soldier. He is a brigadier-general of the regular army by a commission dated December, 1864.

Howard, (PHILIP,) of Corby Castle, England, was a descendant of the eminent poet the Earl of Surrey, and father of Henry, noticed above, (1757–1842.) He wrote the "Scriptural History of the Earth and of Mankind," (1797.) Died in 1810.

Howard, (Sir ROBERT,) M.P., an English poet, born in 1626, was a brother of the Hon. Edward Howard, noticed above. He was a royalist in the civil war, and, after the restoration, was appointed auditor of the exchequer. His most successful dramas were "The Committee" and "The Indian Queen." He was the original hero of "The Rehearsal," in which he is called Bilboa. "The poetry of the Berkshire Howards," says Macaulay, "was the jest of three generations of satirists." The poet Dryden married Howard's sister. Died in 1698.

See MACAULAY, "History of England," vol. iii. chap. xiv.; CIBBER, "Lives of the Poets."

Howard, (SAMUEL,) an English musical composer, who flourished about 1750, produced several popular ballads. Died in 1783.

Howard, (THOMAS,) second Duke of Norfolk, and Earl of Surrey, was a son of John, first Duke. He fought for Richard III. at Bosworth, where his father was killed, in 1485. He commanded the English army which gained a great victory over the Scotch at Flodden in 1513, and received the title of Duke of Norfolk for this service, before which he was styled Earl of Surrey. He died in 1524, aged about seventy, and was succeeded by his son Thomas.

Howard, (THOMAS,) third Duke of Norfolk, a son of the preceding, and an eminent English statesman and general, was born about 1473. In 1513 he was chosen high admiral of England, and, in co-operation with his father, defeated the Scotch at the battle of Flodden. For this service he was made Earl of Surrey, while his father was made Duke of Norfolk. In 1523 he became lord high treasurer, and in 1524, at the death of his father, inherited his title. His devotion to the Church of Rome made him hostile to Anne Boleyn, though she was his own niece. After Henry VIII. had married Catherine Howard, the duke, who was her uncle, had much influence in the royal councils, and used it for the persecution of the Protestants. In 1547 he was arrested on a charge of treason, and ordered for execution; but before the fatal day came the king died. Norfolk was released from prison in 1553, and died the next year. His son, the Earl of Surrey, was executed in 1547.

See FROUDE, "History of the Reign of Henry VIII.," particularly vols. iii. and iv.; HUME's and LINGARD's Histories of England.

Howard, (THOMAS,) fourth Duke of Norfolk, was a grandson of the preceding. He was the only peer who at that time possessed the highest title of nobility; and, as there were no princes of the blood, his rank, together with his great wealth and abilities, rendered him the first subject in England. He is represented as generous, prudent, and moderate, and sincerely attached to the Protestant religion. In 1559 Elizabeth appointed him her lieutenant in the northern counties. By aspiring to become the husband of Mary Queen of Scots, he gave offence to Elizabeth, and was committed to the Tower in 1569. Having been released, he renewed his suit, received a promise of marriage from the captive queen, and joined a conspiracy for her liberation. For this he was condemned and executed in 1572.

See HUME, "History of England;" FROUDE, "History of England," vols. ix. and x.

Howard, (THOMAS,) Earl of Arundel, a branch of the ancient and noble family of Howard, was employed in foreign embassies by Charles I. In 1639 he was appointed commander of an army raised to subdue the Scotch; but peace was made before any important action occurred. He formed an extensive collection of Grecian antiquities and productions of ancient artists, parts of which were presented by one of his heirs to the University of Oxford, under the name of the Arundelian marbles. His grandson Henry became sixth Duke of Norfolk. The earl wrote several relations of his embassies and voyages. Died in 1646.

How'den, (JOHN FRANCIS CARADOC,) BARON, a British general, born in 1762, was the son of John Cradock, Archbishop of Dublin. He entered the army in 1777. In 1801 he was one of Abercrombie's staff, and was engaged in several battles in Egypt. He afterwards commanded the British army in India, and in Portugal in 1808. In 1831 he was raised to the peerage, as Baron Howden. Died in 1839.

• **Howden,** (JOHN HOBART CARADOC,) BARON, an English diplomatist, a son of the preceding, was born in 1799. He served in the army, and gained the rank of major-general. He was sent as ambassador to Madrid in 1850.

Howe, (ALBION P.,) an American general, born in Maine about 1818, graduated at West Point in 1841. He became a brigadier-general in April, 1862, served at Antietam, September 17, and commanded a division at the battles of Fredericksburg, December 13, 1862, and Gettysburg, July 2 and 3, 1863.

Howe, (CHARLES,) born in Gloucestershire, England, in 1661, was employed as a diplomatist by James II. He wrote "Devout Meditations," of which the poet Young says, "A greater demonstration of a sound head and a sincere heart I never saw." Died in 1745.

Howe, (ELIAS,) an eminent American inventor, born at Spencer, Massachusetts, about 1819. While employed as a machinist he made many experiments for the invention of a sewing-machine, and about 1844 entered into a partnership with Mr. George Fisher, of Cambridge, who agreed to give him pecuniary assistance on condition of becoming proprietor of half the patent. In April, 1845, he finished a machine, which in essential points is esteemed by competent judges equal to any that have succeeded it. He obtained a patent in 1846. His invention not meeting in the United States with the success which he had anticipated, he resolved to visit England. He resided several years in London in great destitution, and returned in 1849, without having succeeded in making known the merits of his invention. Meanwhile the sewing-machine had been brought into general notice and favour, various improvements having been added by Mr. Singer, with whom, as an infringer of his patent, Mr. Howe had a law-suit, which was decided in his favour in 1854. Soon after the breaking out of the rebellion in 1861, Mr. Howe raised and equipped at his own expense a regiment, in which he served as a private until ill health obliged him to resign.

See the "History of the Sewing-Machine," in the "Atlantic Monthly" for May, 1867, by JAMES PARTON.

Howe, (JOHN,) an eminent English dissenting minister and author, born at Loughborough, May 17, 1630, was educated at Cambridge. Soon after he was ordained he was appointed domestic chaplain to Cromwell, then

Protector, at whose death he was retained in the same office by Richard Cromwell. After the latter was deposed, Howe preached at Great Torrington, until he was ejected for nonconformity, in 1662. In 1675 he became minister of a Puritan congregation in London, where he continued to labour (except during a few years of absence) until his death. He was eminent for piety, for wisdom, for profound learning, and for classical scholarship. As an author he is highly applauded for his originality, sublimity, and evangelical spirit. Among his principal works are "The Living Temple," (1674–1702,) "The Blessedness of the Righteous," "The Redeemer's Tears," (1684,) and "The Vanity of this Mortal Life." Robert Hall said, "I have learned more from John Howe than from any other author I ever read." "Nothing in the language," says William Jay, "can equal, as a whole, Howe's 'Living Temple.'" He is accounted the most philosophical thinker among the Puritan divines. Died in 1705. His complete works were published in 8 vols., 1810–22.

See EDMUND CALAMY, "Life of John Howe," 1724; H. ROGERS, "Life of John Howe," 1836; THOMAS TAYLOR, "Memoir of John Howe," 1835; SAMUEL DUNN, "Life of John Howe," 1836; "Biographia Britannica;" MACAULAY, "History of England," vol. ii. chaps. vii. and viii.; R. SOUTHEY, article on Howe, in "Quarterly Review" for October, 1813, (vol. x.;) "Encyclopædia Britannica."

Howe, (JOHN,) M.P., a noted English politician and versifier, was returned to the Convention Parliament for Cirencester in 1689, and was several times re-elected. He was conspicuous in the House for his volubility, asperity, and audacity of speech. Having turned Tory, he became in the reign of Anne a member of the privy council, and paymaster of the army. He wrote a "Panegyric on William III.," and several short poems. Died in 1721.

See MACAULAY, "History of England," vol. iii. chaps. xi. and xiv.

Howe, (JOSIAH,) an English poet and clergyman, became a Fellow of Trinity College, Oxford, in 1637, and preached before Charles I. at Oxford in 1644. He wrote some epigrammatic verses prefixed to the works of Beaumont and Fletcher. Died in 1701.

Howe, (JULIA WARD,) an American poetess, daughter of Samuel Ward, a banker in New York, was born in 1819. She was educated with great care, and in 1843 was married to Dr. Samuel G. Howe, of Boston, with whom she has twice visited Europe, making on each occasion an extensive tour. Some of her poems possess merit of a very high order. Among the principal are "Passion-Flowers," published in 1854, and "Words for the Hour." She is the author of the deservedly popular song entitled "Battle Hymn of the Republic."

See GRISWOLD, "Female Poets of America."

Howe, (RICHARD,) EARL, a distinguished English admiral, born in 1725, was the second son of Lord Emanuel Scrope Howe. He entered the navy about the age of fourteen, and obtained the rank of captain about 1747. He distinguished himself in the Seven Years' war against the French. At the death of his elder brother, in 1758, he inherited the title of viscount. In 1763 and 1764 he occupied a seat at the board of admiralty, and in 1770 he became a rear-admiral of the blue, and commanded the Mediterranean fleet. From 1776 to 1778 he commanded on the coast of the United States, where he maintained his credit by skilful operations against the French fleet under D'Estaing. He was promoted to the rank of admiral of the blue in 1782, and in the next year acted as first lord of the admiralty. In 1788 he was created Earl Howe. On June 1, 1794, he gained a decisive victory over the French fleet, of which he captured seven ships of the line. Died in 1799. He was regarded as the first sea-officer of his time.

See CAMPBELL, "Lives of British Admirals;" GEORGE MASON, "Life of Richard, Earl Howe;" JOHN BARROW, "Life of Lord Richard Howe," 1838.

Howe, (Dr. SAMUEL GRIDLEY,) an eminent American philanthropist, born in Boston in 1801. He graduated at Brown University in 1821, and entered upon the study of medicine in his native city. In 1824 he went to Greece, and fought valiantly in the war of independence. When famine threatened that country in 1827, he came to the United States and procured large contributions of provisions, clothing, and money, which he distributed

among the Greek patriots. On his return to his native city, in 1831, he entered with ardour into a plan for establishing in that city a school for the blind; and he visited Europe, to procure information, teachers, etc. The next year (1832) he opened the institution, (Perkins Institution for the Blind,) of which he became the principal. His success in the case of Laura Bridgeman, a deaf blind mute, whom he taught to read from raised letters and instructed in religion, morality, etc., attracted great attention. (See BRIDGEMAN, LAURA.) Dr. Howe has also devoted much attention to the education of idiots, for whom a school has been established in South Boston. Besides his other labours, he distinguished himself by the active part he took in the anti-slavery cause. He is the author of a "Historical Sketch of the Greek Revolution," (1828,) a "Reader for the Blind," and of various essays and reports on the education of the blind and the idiotic, and other subjects.

Howe, (Sir WILLIAM,) an English general, was a younger brother of Admiral Richard Howe, noticed above. In 1774 he was returned to Parliament for Nottingham, professing to disapprove the policy of the ministers in relation to the Americans. In 1775 he was appointed commander-in-chief of the army sent to subdue the colonies, though deficient in nearly all the qualities which constitute a great general. His constituents censured him for accepting the command. His first exploit after this promotion was the battle of Bunker Hill, (1775,) in which he lost one-third of his men present in the action. In August, 1776, he gained the battle of Long Island and took New York City. He obtained an advantage over the Americans at Brandywine in September, 1777, in consequence of which Philadelphia was occupied by his army. At his own request, he was recalled in 1778, and was succeeded by Sir Henry Clinton. Died in 1814.

See BANCROFT, "History of the United States," vol. ix. chaps. v., vi., x., xiv., xxiii., xxv.

Hŏw′el THE GOOD, or **Hy′wel Dda,** a Cambrian prince of the tenth century, noted as a legislator, succeeded his father Cadell as King of Wales. After visiting Rome about 926, he framed a code of laws, which continued in force a long time.

Hŏw′el or **Hŏw′ell,** (LAURENCE,) a learned English nonjuring divine, graduated at Cambridge in 1688. He wrote a "Synopsis of the Canons of the Latin Church," and other works on theology. For his pamphlet on the "Schism in the Church of England" he was convicted of sedition in 1716, and confined in Newgate until his death, in 1720.

Hŏw′ell, (JAMES,) a British author, born in Carmarthenshire about 1595. Soon after leaving college he went to London, and, as agent of a glass-manufactory, made a tour on the continent, where he learned several languages. He was returned to Parliament in 1627, and exercised his versatile talents in several civil offices until 1643, when he was imprisoned, for reasons not positively known. He was released about 1649, and at the restoration became historiographer-royal, being the first who had that honour. He wrote "Dodona's Grove, or the Vocal Forest," a poem, (1640,) and various prose works. His "Familiar Letters" (1645) are very entertaining, and passed through ten editions before 1750. Died in 1666.

See "Biographia Britannica."

Howell, (WILLIAM,) an English writer, of whose life little is known. He was at one time chancellor of the diocese of Lincoln. He wrote a "History of the World from the Earliest Times to the Ruin of the Roman Empire," a work of some merit. Died in 1683.

Hŏw′ellṡ, (WILLIAM,) a popular English preacher, born in 1778. He was minister of Long Acre Episcopal Chapel, and belonged to the Evangelical school. Several volumes of his sermons were published. Died in 1832.

See CHARLES BOWDLER, "Memoir of William Howells," prefixed to his Sermons, 2 vols., 1835.

Howick, LORD. See GREY, EARL OF.

Hŏw′itt, (ANNA MARY,) an artist and writer, a daughter of William and Mary Howitt, was born about 1830. She has produced a work of merit called "The Art-Student in Munich," (2 vols., 1853,) and "The School of Life," (Boston, 1855,) which is highly commended. She was recently married to a son of the poet Alaric Watts.

Howitt, (MARY,) a popular English authoress and moralist, born at Uttoxeter about 1804. Her maiden name was BOTHAM. She was educated as a member of the Society of Friends, and was married to William Howitt in 1823. They published jointly "The Forest Minstrel, and other Poems," (1823,) "The Desolation of Eyam, and other Poems," (1827,) "The Book of the Seasons," (1831,) and "The Literature and Romance of Northern Europe," (1852,) the most complete work on that subject in English. Mary Howitt is sole author of numerous instructive books, among which are "Hope on, Hope ever," (3d edition, 1844,) "Hymns and Fireside Verses," (1839,) "Sowing and Reaping," (1840,) and "Sketches of Natural History," (8th edition, 1853.) She has translated many works of Frederika Bremer, and several stories of Hans Christian Andersen. "Her language," says Professor Wilson, "is chaste and simple, her feelings tender and pure, and her observation of nature accurate and intense." ("Blackwood's Magazine," vol. xxiv.)

Howitt, (RICHARD,) a poet and physician, a brother of William Howitt. He published in 1830 "Antediluvian Sketches, and other Poems," which was noticed favourably by the reviewers. "Richard too," says Professor Wilson, "has a true poetical feeling and no small poetical power." He settled in Melbourne, Australia, and wrote "Impressions of Australia Felix," (1845.)

Howitt, (WILLIAM,) an eminent English author, born at Heanor, in Derbyshire, in 1795, was educated as a member of the Society of Friends. His first published work was "The Forest Minstrel, and other Poems," (1823,) partly written by his wife. Their other joint productions have been noticed in the article on MARY HOWITT. He wrote a "History of Priestcraft," (1834,) which was very successful, and often reprinted, "Rural Life of England," (1837,) and "Colonization and Christianity," (1839.) In 1840 William and Mary Howitt removed to Heidelberg, where they passed several years. His "Rural and Domestic Life in Germany" (1842) was received with favour both by the English and Germans. He published "Homes and Haunts of the Most Eminent British Poets Illustrated," (2 vols., 1847,) besides various other original works, and translations from the German, and edited "Howitt's Journal" (weekly) for about three years, (1847-49.) He described his adventures and labours in Australia (where he passed about two years) in his "Land, Labour, and Gold," (2 vols., 1855.) Among his important works are "Visits to Remarkable Places, Old Halls, Battle-Fields," etc., (2 vols., 1839-41,) and a "History of England," (6 vols., 1861.)

See PROFESSOR WILSON, "Noctes Ambrosianæ," in "Blackwood's Magazine" for April, 1831; "Nouvelle Biographie Générale;" "Fraser's Magazine" for February, 1847; "North American Review" for April, 1843, (by W. B. O. PEABODY.)

Hŏw′ley, (WILLIAM,) an English prelate, born at Ropley, in Hampshire, in 1765. He became Bishop of London in 1813, and Archbishop of Canterbury in 1828. He published several sermons. Died in 1848.

Hŏw′sọn, (JOHN,) an English theologian, born in London in 1556. After having occupied the see of Oxford, he became Bishop of Durham in 1628. He wrote and preached numerous discourses against the Roman Catholics, which were printed. Died in 1631.

Howson, (JOHN SAUL,) an English divine, born about 1815. He published, with W. J. Conybeare, "The Life and Epistles of Saint Paul," (2 vols., 1850-52.)

Höyer, (ANDREAS,) a Danish historian and jurist, born at Karlum, published a "Life of Frederick IV.," (1732,) and other works. Died in 1739.

Hoyer, ho′yẹr, (JOHANN GOTTFRIED,) a German military officer and writer, born at Dresden in 1767, published a "Dictionary of Artillery." Died in 1848.

Hoy′ẹr, [Fr. pron. hwȧ′yȧ′,] (MICHEL,) a Flemish priest and Latin poet, born in 1593; died in 1650.

Hoyle, hoil, (EDMUND,) an Englishman, born in 1672, wrote popular treatises on Whist and other games. Died in 1769.

Hoyt, (EPAPHRAS,) a historical and military writer, born in Deerfield, Massachusetts, in 1765. He published "Cavalry Discipline," (1797,) and "Antiquarian Researches," (1824.) He was a major-general of militia. Died in 1850.

Hoyt, (RALPH,) an American Episcopal clergyman and poet, born in New York in 1810. He published "The Chaunt of Life, and other Poems," (1844.)

Hoz, de la, dȧ lȧ ôth, (JUAN,) a Spanish dramatic poet, born at Madrid about 1620, wrote an admired comedy, "El Castigo de la Miseria." Died after 1689.

Hozier, d′. See D′HOZIER.

Hrimfaxi. See NÖRVI.

Hrotsvitha, hRots′vee′tȧ, also written **Hrosuitha, Hroswitha,** and **Roswitha,** a celebrated German poetess of the tenth century, born in Lower Saxony, was educated in the convent of Gandersheim. She wrote Latin poems, which are valuable monuments of the literature of that time, and six dramas, (in Latin,) that rank among the best productions of the kind in the middle ages. Among her poems was one in hexameters, containing the history of Otto I., only half of which is extant.

See GUSTAV FREYTAG, "Dissertatio de Hrosuitha," 1839; DAUBER, "Die Nonne von Gandersheim," 1858; "Nouvelle Biographie Générale."

Hrungnir, hrŭng′nịr, in the Norse mythology, a giant, who, on his horse Gullfaxi, ("Goldmane,") visited Asgard, and, having become intoxicated, defied the gods, and threatened to carry Valhalla to Jötunheim, (the "habitation of the giants.") He was slain by Thor, who gave Gullfaxi to his own son Jarnsaxa. Some explain the foregoing myth by supposing Hrungnir (whose name they derive from *hruga*, to "heap up") to be a lofty mountain piled up to the sky, thus appearing to menace heaven itself. Its summit being smitten and rent by the lightning, is compared by the Norse poets to the head of a giant whose skull Thor ("thunder") broke with his terrible hammer.

See THORPE'S "Northern Mythology," vol. i. pp. 69-71, 174.

Hrym, hreem, sometimes written **Rymer,** in the Northern mythology, the leader of the Frost-giants (Hrimthursar) in the great battle against the gods at Ragnarök. The name is clearly another form of *Hrim*, "frost," and cognate with the Latin *rima* ("hoarfrost") and the Sanscrit *hīmă*, (Gr. χεῖμα,) "frost," or "winter."

Hua, *hü′ȧ′*, (EUSTACHE ANTOINE,) a French lawyer, born at Mantes in 1759, was a moderate member of the Legislative Assembly in 1791. He became in 1818 attorney-general in the court of cassation. Died in 1836.

Huabalde. See HUBALD.

Huarte, oo-aR′tȧ, (JUAN DE DIOS,) a Spanish physician and philosopher, born in Navarre about 1535. He published about 1580 a remarkable book, entitled "Examen de Ingenios para las Scienzias," which was often reprinted and translated. The English version was called "Trial of Wits." It contains some new truths, with many bold paradoxes. Died about 1600.

See BAYLE, "Historical and Critical Dictionary;" TICKNOR, "History of Spanish Literature."

Huascar, hwȧs′kar, an Inca of Peru, a son of Huayna Capac, whom he succeeded in 1525, was defeated in battle and dethroned by his brother Atahualpa in 1532. (See ATAHUALPA.)

Huayna Capac, hwī′nȧ kȧ-pȧk′, Inca of Peru, ascended the throne in 1493. He extended his dominions by conquest, and enriched them by the arts of peace. Died in 1525.

Hu′bȧld, written also **Huabalde, Hucbald,** and **Hugbald,** [Lat. HUBAL′DUS,] a Flemish monk of Saint-Amand, born about 840 A.D., wrote a treatise on music, and Latin verses in praise of baldness, in which every word begins with C; for example,

"Carmina Clarisonæ Calvis Cantate Camœnæ."

Died in 930.

Hub′bạrd, (WILLIAM,) a historian, born in England in 1621, was ordained minister at Ipswich, Massachusetts, about 1656. He died in 1704, leaving in manuscript a "History of New England," which was published by the Massachusetts Historical Society in 1815.

Hube, hoo′bĕh, (R.,) a Polish jurist, born at Warsaw in 1803, published "Principles of Penal Law," (1830,) and other works. He was appointed councillor of state at Saint Petersburg in 1843, after which he was employed in the compilation of a new penal and civil code.

Huber, hoo′bẹr, (FRANCIS,) a Swiss naturalist, born at Geneva in 1750. The taste for nature and the habit of observation which he derived from his father were confirmed by the lectures of Saussure. At the age of fifteen his sight began to fail, and was before long quite lost. Soon after the occurrence of this privation he married Mdlle. Lullin, and was blessed with domestic happiness. Pursuing his researches into the economy and habits of bees, by the aid of his servant, he made many interesting discoveries, and in 1792 published "New Observations on Bees," which excited a great sensation. He was chosen a member of the Academy of Sciences at Paris, and of other similar institutions. He also wrote a "Memoir on the Origin of Wax," and a few other treatises. Died in 1830 or 1831.

See AUGUSTIN PYRAME DECANDOLLE, "Notice sur la Vie et les Écrits de F. Huber," 1832; "Monthly Review," in the Appendix of vol. lxxxii., 1817.

Huber, (JOHANN,) an artist, born in Geneva in 1722, was intimate with Voltaire, of whose domestic life he drew several pictures. He was noted for skill in cutting profiles in paper or parchment, and wrote "Observations on the Flight of Birds of Prey," (1784.) Died in 1790.

Huber, (JOHANN JAKOB,) an eminent Swiss anatomist, born at Bâle in 1707, was a pupil of Haller, whom he assisted in his "Swiss Flora." He was chosen professor of anatomy at Göttingen about 1737, and became professor and court physician at Cassel in 1742. He was a Fellow of the Royal Society of London, and a member of the Academy of Sciences at Berlin. His principal work is a "Treatise on the Spinal Marrow," (1739.) Died in 1778.

See ERSCH und GRUBER, "Allgemeine Encyklopaedie."

Huber, (JOHANN RUDOLF,) an eminent Swiss painter, born at Bâle in 1668, studied several years in Italy. He worked mostly in his native place. He painted portraits and history with rapidity and success. On account of his brilliant colouring, he was surnamed THE SWISS TINTORET. Died in 1748.

See NAGLER, "Allgemeines Künstler-Lexikon."

Huber, hü′bair′ or hoo′bẹr, (LOUIS FERDINAND,) a distinguished *littérateur*, son of Michael, noticed below, was born in Paris in 1764. In 1794 he married Theresa, the widow of John George Forster and daughter of the eminent philologist Heyne. He became in 1798 editor of the "Allgemeine Zeitung" at Stuttgart. He wrote several dramas, and a collection of popular tales. Died in 1804.

Huber, (MARIE,) a Swiss authoress and Protestant theologian, remarkable for her peculiar religious views, which appear to have been a mixture of rationalism and mysticism, was born at Geneva in 1695. She wrote, besides other religious and moral works, "Letters on the Religion essential to Man, as distinguished from that which is Conventional," *(accessoire,)* (1738,) in which she uses a very subtle dialectic, and "The Insane (or Foolish) World preferred to the Wise," ("Le Monde fol préféré au Monde sage," 2 vols., 1731–44.) Died at Lyons in 1753.

See "Nouvelle Biographie Générale."

Huber, (MICHAEL,) a German translator, born at Frontenhausen, in Bavaria, in 1727. He lived many years in Paris, and became professor of French at Leipsic in 1766. He made good French translations of many German works, among which were Gessner's poems and Winckelmann's "History of Ancient Art," (3 vols., 1781.) Died in 1804.

See QUÉRARD, "La France Littéraire."

Huber, (PETER, or PIERRE,) son of Francis, noticed above, published a "History of the Habits of Indigenous Ants," "Observations on Drones," and other zoological treatises. Died in 1841.

See "Edinburgh Review" for July, 1812, and October, 1815.

Huber, (THERESE,) a German novelist, born at Göttingen in 1764, was a daughter of C. G. Heyne, the philologist. She was married to John George Forster, an eminent author, in 1784, and to Ludwig F. Huber (noticed above) in 1794. Died at Augsburg in 1829.

Huber, (VICTOR AIMÉ,) a historian and critic, son of Louis Ferdinand, noticed above, was born at Stuttgart in 1800. He popularized Spanish literature in Germany by his "History of the Cid" (1829) and his "Sketches of Spain," (4 vols., 1828–35.) For many years he was professor of languages and history at Marburg and Berlin.

Huber, hü′bẹr, [Lat. HUBE′RUS,] (ULRICH,) a Dutch jurist, born at Dokkum in 1636. In 1665 he was chosen professor of law at Franeker. He published many able treatises on civil law, among which are "De Jure Civitatis," (1672,) and "Prælectiones ad Pandectas," (1686.) From the former Rousseau derived many of the ideas or principles of his "Contrat Social." Died in 1694.

See VITRINGA, "Oratio in Excessum U. Huberi," 1694; "Nouvelle Biographie Générale;" JÖCHER, "Allgemeines Gelehrten-Lexikon."

Hubert, hü′bair′, (FRANÇOIS,) a French engraver, born at Abbeville in 1744; died in 1809.

Hubert, (MATHIEU,) an eloquent French preacher, born near Mayenne in 1640. He taught belles-lettres in various colleges, preached in Paris and the provinces, and died in 1717. His Sermons were published in 5 vols., (1725.)

Huberus. See HUBER, (ULRICH.)

Hübner or **Huebner,** hüp′nẹr, (JOHANN,) a German geographer and teacher, born at or near Zittau in 1668. His "Questions on Ancient and Modern Geography" (1693) was often reprinted. Died in 1731.

Hübner or **Huebner,** (RUDOLF JULIUS BENNO,) a skilful German historical painter, born at Oels, in Silesia, in 1806, was a pupil of Schadow. He settled at Dresden in 1839, and became a professor in the Academy of Arts in that city in 1841. His works are admired for grace of expression and beauty of colour. Among his masterpieces are "Boaz and Ruth," "Christ and the Evangelists," "The Golden Age," and "Felicity and Sleep."

Hübner, von, fon hüp′nẹr, (JOSEPH ALEXANDER,) an Austrian diplomatist, born in Vienna in 1811, was ambassador to the French court, and signed the treaty of peace at the Congress of Paris in 1856.

Hübsch or **Huebsch,** hüpsh, (HEINRICH,) a German architect, born at Weinheim, Baden, in 1795.

Huc, hük, (Abbé ÉVARISTE RÉGIS,) a French Catholic missionary and traveller, born at Toulouse in 1813. He went to China in 1839, learned the Chinese language, and laboured as a missionary. About the end of 1845 he visited Lassa, the capital of Thibet, where he was permitted to remain only a few weeks. Having returned to France in 1852, he published his very curious and amusing "Travels in Tartary, Thibet, and China," ("Souvenirs d'un Voyage dans la Tartarie," etc., 2 vols., 1852,) which obtained a wide popularity, and was translated into English by W. Hazlitt, Jr. He afterwards published "The Chinese Empire," (2 vols., 1854,) and "Christianity in China, Tartary, and Thibet," (3 vols., 1857.) Died in 1860.

See "Nouvelle Biographie Générale;" "London Quarterly Review" for July, 1857; "Fraser's Magazine" for April, 1855.

Hucbald. See HUBALD.

Huch. See ÆPINUS.

Huchtenburgh, van, vän hük′tẹn-bŭRG′, written also **Hugtenburg,** (JAKOB,) a skilful Dutch landscape-painter, born at Haarlem in 1639, was a pupil of Berghem. He went in his youth to Rome, where he worked with success until his death, in 1669.

Huchtenburgh, Hugtenburg, oɽ **Huchtenburg, van,** (JAN,) an excellent Dutch painter, brother of the preceding, was born at Haarlem in 1646. He studied in Italy and Paris with Van der Meulen, acquired a high reputation for battle-pieces, and was employed by Prince Eugene to paint those actions in which he and Marlborough commanded. He was also a skilful engraver. Died in 1733.

See DESCAMPS, "Vie des Peintres Flamands, Hollandais," etc.

Hud′dart, (JOSEPH,) F.R.S., an English navigator and hydrographer, born at Allonby in 1741, was for many years a captain in the service of the East India Company. He was a skilful nautical surveyor, and published some valuable charts. Died in 1816.

Hudde, hŭd′dẹh, (JAN,) born at Amsterdam about 1636, was councillor, treasurer, and burgomaster of his native city. He was well versed in mathematics, on which he wrote some able treatises. Died in 1704.

See MONTUCLA, "Histoire des Mathématiques."

Hud'des-ford, (GEORGE,) a humorous English poet, who lived about 1800. He wrote several burlesque poems, which had some success, viz., "Topsy-Turvy," (1790,) "Salmagundi," (1793,) and "Imperial Mushrooms," (1805.)

Huddesford or **Hud'des-ford,** (WILLIAM,) D.D., an English antiquary, was principal of Trinity College, Oxford, and wrote the Lives of Leland, Hearne, and Anthony Wood. Died in 1772.

Huddleston, hud'dels-ton, (ROBERT,) a Scottish antiquary, born in 1776, published a new edition of Toland's "History of the Druids," (1814.) Died in 1826.

Hŭd'son, (HENRY or HENDRIK,) an eminent English navigator, of whose early life nothing is known. In 1607 he commanded a vessel sent by some London merchants to discover a direct route to India by way of the North pole or Northern Ocean. Having advanced beyond 80° north latitude, he was prevented by the ice from making farther progress, and returned. He made several other unsuccessful attempts in that direction. In the service of the Dutch East India Company, he discovered in 1609 the river of New York which bears his name. He renewed the enterprise in April, 1610, and discovered and explored Hudson Bay, in which he passed the winter and suffered much for want of provisions. As he was returning in 1611, his crew mutinied, and, forcing the captain with eight men into a small boat, abandoned them to their fate. They were never heard of afterwards. A few of the mutineers returned to Ireland.

See PRÉVOST, "Histoire générale des Voyages;" PURCHAS'S "Collection;" "Life of Henry Hudson," in SPARKS'S "American Biography," vol. x., (by H. R. CLEVELAND;) "Nouvelle Biographie Générale;" J. M. READ, "Historical Inquiries concerning Henry Hudson," 1866.

Hŭd'son, (HENRY NORMAN,) an Episcopal clergyman, born in Cornwall, Vermont, in 1814, published "Lectures on Shakspeare," (2 vols., 1848,) and edited the Works of Shakspeare, (11 vols., 1850–57.)

Hudson, (JOHN,) D.D., a learned English critic, born in Cumberland in 1662, was for many years a tutor in Oxford University, and from 1701 until his death librarian of the Bodleian Library. He published excellent editions of Thucydides, Longinus, Josephus, Æsop's Fables," etc. Died in 1719.

Hudson, (THOMAS,) an English portrait-painter, born in Devonshire in 1701. He was a pupil of Richardson, after whose death he was the most fashionable or successful artist in that line in London until he was surpassed by his own pupil, Joshua Reynolds, about 1754. Among his works is a portrait of Handel. Died in 1779.

Hudson, (WILLIAM,) F.R.S., an eminent English botanist, born in Westmoreland in 1730, resided in London as an apothecary. He was one of the first in England that adopted the Linnæan system, and in 1762 published an "English Flora," ("Flora Anglica,") which procured him admission into the Royal Society. Died in 1793.

Hue, hü, (FRANÇOIS,) born at Fontainebleau, France, in 1757, became a valet to the dauphin. In the reign of terror he served the royal family at the risk of his life, and was imprisoned. He wrote "The Last Years of the Reign and Life of Louis XVI.," (1806.) Died in 1819.

Huebner. See HÜBNER.

Huebsch. See HÜBSCH.

Huegel. See HÜGEL.

Huel, hü'êl', (JOSEPH NICOLAS,) a French philosopher, born at Mattaincourt in 1690; died in 1769.

Huellmann. See HÜLLMANN.

Huerta. See HORTO.

Huerta, de la, dả lã wĕr'tä, (VINCENTE GARCIA,) a popular Spanish poet, born at Zafra in 1729, was the leader of the national school of poetry, in opposition to the partisans of the French models. He produced in 1778 the tragedy of "Rachel," ("Raquel,") which was performed with great applause in Madrid and in Italy. He wrote other poems, ("Obras poeticas," 2 vols., 1778,) and was the editor of the "Spanish Theatre," ("Teatro Español,") a selection from the best Spanish dramatists, with notes, (17 vols., 1788.) Died in 1797.

See BOUTERWEK, "Histoire de la Littérature Espagnole."

Huet, hü'êt', (PAUL,) a French landscape-painter, born in Paris in 1804, gained medals of the first class in 1848 and 1855.

Huet, (PIERRE DANIEL,) an eminent French critic and scholar, born at Caen in February, 1630, was educated at Paris. In 1652, in company with Bochart, he visited the court of Christina of Sweden, which then offered rare attractions to the learned; but he soon returned to Caen, and passed many years in various studies. He was appointed in 1670 sub-preceptor of the dauphin, and was the principal editor of the well-known series of the Latin classics "ad usum Delphini," ("for the use of the dauphin.") In 1674 he became a member of the French Academy, and in 1685 Bishop of Avranches. He wrote numerous able critical and religious works, (in Latin and French,) among which the best-known is his "Demonstratio Evangelica," (1679.) This was for a long time a standard work on the Evidences of Christianity. Died in 1721.

See D'ALEMBERT, "Éloge de Huet;" SAINT-MAURICE, "Éloge de D. Huet," 1850; HUET's Autobiographic Memoirs, entitled "Commentarius de Rebus ad eum pertinentibus," 1718, (translated into English by JOHN AIKIN, 2 vols., 1810;) "Huetiana," Paris, 1722; BRUCKER, "History of Philosophy;" ABBÉ FLOTTES, "Étude sur Daniel Huet," 1857; "Nouvelle Biographie Générale;" "London Quarterly Review" for August, 1810.

Huet de Froberville, hü'å' deh fRo'bêr'vêl', (CLAUDE JEAN BAPTISTE,) a French writer, born at Romorantin in 1752; died in 1838.

Huette, hü'êt', (LOUIS,) a French optician, born at Rennes in 1756; died in 1805.

Hufeland, hoo'feh-lånt', (CHRISTOPH WILHELM,) an excellent German physician and medical writer, was born at Langensalza (Prussian Saxony) in 1762. He became professor at Jena in 1793, and afterwards physician to the King of Prussia. In 1809 he obtained the chair of special pathology and therapeutics at Berlin. He produced in 1796 a celebrated work on the "Art of Prolonging Life," ("Makrobiotik, oder die Kunst das menschliche Leben zu verlängern,") often reprinted and translated. Among his other works are a "System of Practical Medicine," (2 vols., 1800–05,) and "Enchiridion Medicum," (1836; 9th edition, 1851.) Died in 1836.

See F. L. AUGUSTIN, "Hufelands Leben und Wirken für Wissenschaft, Staat und Menschheit," 1837; STOURDJA, "Hufeland, Esquisse de sa Vie et de sa Mort," 1837.

Hufeland, (GOTTLIEB,) a German jurist, born at Dantzic in 1760, was professor of law at Halle, where he died in 1817. He wrote a "Manual of the Law of Nature."

Hüfnagel. See HÖFNAEGEL.

Hug, hoōg, (JOHANN LEONHARD,) a German Catholic theologian, born at Constance in 1763. His "Introduction to the Books of the New Testament" is highly esteemed, and has been translated into French and English. Died in 1846.

Hugbald. See HUBALD.

Hügel or **Huegel, von,** (KARL ALEXANDER ANSELM,) BARON, a German traveller and naturalist, was born at Ratisbon in 1796. He performed a scientific exploration of Greece, Egypt, India, and other parts of Asia, about 1831–36, and brought home large collections of objects of natural history, coins, etc. He published "Cashmere and the Dominion of the Sikhs," (4 vols., 1842,) "The Basin of Cabool," ("Das Becken von Kabul," 2 vols., 1852,) and other works. Died, 1870.

Hugenius. See HUYGENS.

Huger, ū'jee', (BENJAMIN,) an American general, born at Charleston, South Carolina, about 1806, graduated at West Point in 1825. He led a division of the army that fought against the Union at Fair Oaks, May 31, and at Malvern Hill, July 1, 1862.

Huger, (FRANCIS KINLOCK,) an officer, born in South Carolina in 1764. He joined Dr. Eric Bollman in an attempt to release La Fayette from the dungeon of Olmutz; but they failed, and were imprisoned. He served as a colonel in the war of 1812. Died in 1855.

Huger, (ISAAC,) an uncle of the preceding, was born about 1725. He served as a brigadier-general in the Revolution, and rendered distinguished service at the sieges of Savannah and Charleston. In the battle of Guilford Court-House he commanded the right wing of the American army. Died in 1782.

Hug'ford, (IGNAZIO,) an artist, born of English parents at Florence in 1703, was a noted connoisseur and a skilful painter. Died in 1778.

ā, ē, ī, ō, ū, ȳ, *long;* ă, ĕ, ĭ, ŏ, ŭ, ў, *short;* a, e, i, o, *obscure;* fâr, fåll, fât; mĕt; nŏt; gŏŏd; mŏŏn;

Hŭg′ḡinṣ, (WILLIAM,) F.R.S., an English astronomer of the present age, especially distinguished for his observations and discoveries made with the spectroscope on the sun and stars. He is secretary of the Royal Astronomical Society.

Hugh, hū, [Fr. HUGUES, hüg,] a French prelate, eminent for talents and piety, was chosen Archbishop of Besançon in 1031. Died in 1066.

Hugh (Hugues) I., Duke of Burgundy, was the son of Henry, and grandson of Duke Robert, whom he succeeded in 1075. In 1078 he retired into a convent, resigning his dukedom to his brother Eudes. Died in 1093.

Hugh (Hugues) II., Duke of Burgundy, nephew of the preceding, succeeded in 1102 his father Eudes, who went on a pilgrimage to the Holy Land. Died in 1142.

Hugh (Hugues) III., Duke of Burgundy, succeeded his father, Eudes II., in 1162. About 1190 he followed Philip Augustus of France in a crusade, and when that king turned back, Hugues took command of the French. He died at Tyre in 1192, and left his dukedom to his son, Eudes III.

Hugh (Hugues) IV., son of Eudes III., born in 1212, inherited the dukedom in 1218. He died in 1272, and was succeeded by his son Robert.

Hugh (Hugues) V., Duke of Burgundy, son of Robert II., inherited the title in 1308, and died prematurely in 1315, leaving the dukedom to his brother, Eudes IV.

Hugh (Hugues) DE CLUNY, (deh klü′ne′,) a French monk, born at Semur about 1024, became Abbot of Cluny in 1048. He was consulted on important questions by several kings and popes. Died in 1109.

Hugh (Hugues) D′AMIENS, (dä′me-ăN′,) a French prelate and writer, reputed one of the most learned theologians of his time, was chosen Archbishop of Rouen in 1130. Died in 1164.

See "Gallia Christiana," tome ii.

Hugh (Hugues) DE FLAVIGNY, (deh flȧ′vėn′ye′,) a French monk, born in 1065, was chosen Abbot of Flavigny in 1097. He wrote the "Chronicle of Verdun," which contains valuable historical data.

Hugh (Hugues) DE FLEURY (deh fluh′re′) or **DE SAINTE-MARIE, (deh sǎnt′mȧ′re′,)** a French monk, who was eminent for his knowledge. He asserted the divine right of kings in an able treatise "On Royal Power and Sacerdotal Dignity," and wrote a general History. Died about 1125.

Hugh OF PROVENCE, King of Italy, was a son of Theobald, (or Thibault,) Count of Provence. Favoured by the pope, John X., and by many Lombard chiefs, he obtained the crown of Italy in 926 A.D., but was expelled by Berenger in 947, and died the same year.

See ERSCH und GRUBER, "Allgemeine Encyklopaedie."

Hugh (Hugues) DE SAINT-CHER, (deh sȧN′shaiR′,) a learned French monk and cardinal, was born near Vienne. His most important work was a concordance of the Bible, said to be the first ever compiled. He used the Latin in this work. Died in 1263.

Hugh (Hugues) DE SAINT-VICTOR, (deh sȧN′vėk′toR′,) a monk, born near Ypres, entered the monastery of Saint-Victor, in Paris, in 1118. He wrote theological works which had a high reputation. Died in 1140.

Hugh Capet. See CAPET.

Hugh the Great, [Fr. HUGUES LE GRAND, hüg leh gRŏN,] Duke of France and Count of Paris, a powerful noble, was the son of Robert, Count of Paris, and the father of Hugh Capet. He married a sister of Otho, King of Germany, and waged war against Louis d'Outre-Mer. Died in 956.

Hugh the Great, Count of Vermandois, third son of Henry I., King of France, born in 1057, was noted for chivalrous courage. He departed in 1096 on a crusade, and distinguished himself at the siege of Antioch. He was killed in battle in 1102.

See MICHAUD, "History of the Crusades."

Hughes, hūz, (Rev. GRIFFITH,) an English minister of Saint Lacy's parish, Barbadoes, published in 1750 a "Natural History of Barbadoes."

Hughes, (JABEZ,) an English writer, born in 1685, was a brother of John Hughes, the poet, noticed below. He published translations from Claudian, Lucan, Suetonius, and Cervantes. Died in 1731.

Hughes, (JOHN,) an English poet and essayist, born at Marlborough in 1677, was educated in London, where he mostly resided. He filled, besides other civil posts, that of secretary to the commissioners of the peace. His character and talents secured him the friendship of Addison, Pope, and Congreve. He contributed numerous well-written essays to the "Spectator," "Tatler," and "Guardian," and once had a fair reputation as a poet. His best poem is "The Siege of Damascus," a tragedy, which was first performed on the last night of the author's life, and was very successful. He made good translations from Fontenelle and Vertot. Swift having classed him in the ranks of mediocrity, Pope answered, "What he wanted in genius he made up as an honest man." Addison had so good an opinion of his ability that he requested him to write the fifth act of "Cato," which, however, he declined. Died in 1720.

See JOHNSON, "Lives of the English Poets;" "Biographia Britannica."

Hughes, hūz, (JOHN,) an eminent Roman Catholic prelate, born in Ireland in 1798. He came to America in 1817, and preached several years in Philadelphia. He became Bishop of New York about 1840, and was raised to the rank of archbishop in 1850. He published several sermons and lectures. He was a man of great ability, and was particularly distinguished for his skill in dialectics. Died in 1864.

See JOHN R. G. HASSARD, "Life of John Hughes," 1866.

Hughes, (JOHN,) an English writer and artist, was the father of Thomas Hughes, M.P. He published in 1822 an "Itinerary of Provence and the Rhone," (with good etchings by himself,) which was praised by Sir Walter Scott. He also wrote some poetical pieces.

Hughes, (THOMAS,) an English author, social economist, and barrister, born in Berkshire in October, 1823. His father was John Hughes, noticed above, whom Christopher North calls "Bullar of Brazennose." He acquired celebrity by a work of fiction entitled "Tom Brown's School-Days," (1857,) which quickly passed through several editions. This story is continued in his "Tom Brown at Oxford." He is a warm friend of the working-classes, and represented Lambeth in Parliament, to which he was elected in 1865 by the Liberals. In 1868 he was returned as a member for Frome.

Hughes, (THOMAS SMART,) an English historian, graduated at Cambridge as M.A. in 1811. He became prebendary of Peterborough in 1827, and rector of Hardwick in 1832. He wrote, besides other works, a "History of England from the Accession of George III. to the Accession of Victoria, 1760–1837," (7 vols., 1836,) a continuation of Hume and Smollett. Died in 1847.

See a "Memoir of T. S. Hughes," prefixed to his "Essay on the Political System of Europe," 1855.

Hugi, hoo′gee, (FRANZ JOSEPH,) a Swiss naturalist, born at Grenchen in 1795. Among his works is a "Treatise on Glaciers," (1842.)

Hugo, hü′go′, (CHARLES LOUIS,) a French monk, born at Saint-Mihiel in 1667, became Abbé of Estival. He wrote, besides other works, a "Life of Saint Norbert," (1707,) and a "History of Moses," (1709.) Died in 1739.

Hugo, (FRANÇOIS VICTOR,) a son of Victor Marie, noticed below, was born in Paris in 1828. He produced a version of Shakspeare's Sonnets, (1857.)

Hugo, hoo′go, (GUSTAV,) a German jurist, distinguished for his profound knowledge of Roman law, was born at Lorrach, in Baden, in 1764. He studied at Göttingen, and became professor of law in that city in 1792. His principal work, a "Manual of a Course of Civil Law," consisting of seven volumes, with different titles, ranks among the standard productions of modern jurisprudence. Died at Göttingen in 1844.

See H. EYSSENHARDT, "Zur Erinnerung an G. Hugo," 1845.

Hu′go, (HERMAN,) a learned Jesuit, born at Brussels in 1588, became chaplain to General Spinola. He was the author of a treatise on the invention of letters, "De prima Scribendi Origine," (1617,) and a few other works. Died in 1629.

Hugo, (J. ABEL,) a French littérateur, brother of Victor Hugo, was born about 1798. Among his works are "Picturesque France," (3 vols., 1833,) and "Military

France," a history of the French armies from 1792 to 1833, (5 vols., 1834.) Died in 1855.

Hugo, (JOSEPH LÉOPOLD SIGISBERT,) a French general and count, born at Nancy in 1774. After serving Joseph Bonaparte as marshal of the palace at Naples, he fought for him in Spain as general of brigade from 1809 to 1813, gained several victories, and was raised to the rank of general of division. In 1823 he published "Memoirs of General Hugo." Died in 1828.

See JULES NOLLET-FABERT, "Le Général J. L. S. Hugo," 8vo, 1853; "Nouvelle Biographie Générale."

Hugo, hü'go', (VICTOR MARIE,) VICOMTE, a celebrated French lyric poet and novelist, a son of the preceding, was born at Besançon in 1802. His mother, Sophie Trébuchet, was a Vendean royalist, with whose political sentiments he sympathized in his youth. His first poem, "On the Advantages of Study," (1817,) obtained an honourable mention from the Académie Française. He received prizes for several royalist odes in 1818, and married Mdlle. Foucher in 1822. In the same year he published the first volume of his "Odes and Ballads," which quickly raised him to the first rank among the French poets of his time. He produced "Cromwell," a drama, (1827,) and a volume of odes, entitled "Les Orientales," (1828,) remarkable for richness of imagination. The literati of France having ranged themselves in two hostile schools, styled the Classic and the Romantic, Victor Hugo became the recognized chief of the latter, formed mostly of young men. Of his dramas, "Hernani" (first acted in 1830) and "Marion Delorme" (1831) proved brilliant successes. Among his most successful and popular works are "Notre Dame de Paris," a romance, (1831,) "Le Roi s'amuse," a drama, (1832,) "Les Misérables," a novel, (1862,) "The Toilers of the Sea," (1865,) and poems entitled "The Leaves of Autumn," ("Les Feuilles d'Automne,") which, says a French critic in the "Nouvelle Biographie Générale," "contain beauties of the first order." He was admitted into the French Academy in 1841, and raised to the rank of a peer in 1845. He gave his cordial adhesion to the republic of 1848, and was elected to the Constituent Assembly by the voters of Paris. He opposed Cavaignac, and in 1849 joined the party of advanced democrats, of whom he became a leader and distinguished orator. For his opposition to the *coup d'état* of December 2, 1851, he was banished. He retired to the island of Guernsey, where he has since resided. During his exile he published several works, including a historical work entitled "Napoléon le Petit," ("Napoleon the Little," 1852,) and poetical "Contemplations," (2 vols., 1856,) which are much admired. Of his more recent publications, "L'Homme qui rit" (1869) is perhaps the most important.

See DE LOMÉNIE, "Galerie des Contemporains illustres;" SAINTE-BEUVE, "Portraits contemporains," 1846; CHARLES ROBIN, "Biographie de V. Hugo," 1848; LONGFELLOW, "Poets and Poetry of Europe;" "Quarterly Review" for March, 1843. and October, 1862; "Edinburgh Review" for January, 1863; also "Fraser's Magazine" for March, 1863, and June, 1866; "Foreign Quarterly Review" for July, 1831; "British Quarterly Review" for July, 1860, and January, 1863; "Westminster Review" for April, 1855, and October and January, 1863; "North American Review" for July, 1836, (by MRS. F. A. KEMBLE.)

Hu-go-li'nus, (or hoo-go-le'nus,) an Italian jurist and legal writer, born at Bologna; died about 1233.

Hugtenburg. See HUCHTENBURG.

Hugues Capet. See CAPET.

Huijgens. See HUYGENS.

Huillard-Bréholles, ü-e'lȧR' brȧ'ol', (J. L. ALPHONSE,) a French antiquary, born in Paris in 1817, published, with M. E. Ruelle, a "History of the Middle Ages," (2 vols., 1843.)

Hulaku or **Hulakoo.** See HOOLAKOO.

Huldericus. See HULDRICH.

Huldrich, hōŏlt'riK, [Lat. HULDERI'CUS,] (JOHANN JACOB,) a Swiss divine, born at Zurich in 1683, was a professor of law in the university of that town. He published a few religious works, and "Miscellanea Tigurina," (3 vols., 1722.) Died in 1731.

See ZIMMERMANN, "Vita Hulderici," 1732.

Hulin or **Hullin,** hü'lȧN', (PIERRE AUGUSTIN,) a French general, born in Paris in 1758. He became general of brigade in 1804, commandant at Vienna in 1805, and in 1807 general of division. He had the chief

command at Paris when the conspirator Malet made his daring attempt in 1812, and was shot in the face by Malet. He was banished in 1815. Died in 1841.

See "Nouvelle Biographie Générale."

Hüll, (EDWARD,) an English geologist, born about 1810, published several works on the geology of Great Britain.

Hüll, (ISAAC,) an American commodore, born in Derby, Connecticut, in 1775. He distinguished himself in the war with Tripoli, (1804–5,) was promoted to the rank of captain in 1806, and at the commencement of the war of 1812 was in command of the frigate Constitution. In July of the same year, while cruising off New York, he fell in with a British squadron, which pursued him in hot chase for three days and nights, but which, by his skill in seamanship, he managed to escape. On August 19 following, he captured, after a close action of thirty minutes, the British frigate Guerriere, Captain Dacres, with the loss of only fourteen in killed and wounded, while that of the Guerriere was seventy-nine. This was the first naval action after the declaration of war; and in acknowledgment of Captain Hull's distinguished services Congress presented him with a gold medal. He subsequently commanded the United States squadron in the Pacific and in the Mediterranean. Died in Philadelphia in 1843.

Hull, (THOMAS,) an English actor and poet, born in London in 1728, composed and altered numerous plays. His most popular poem is "Richard Plantagenet," a legendary tale, (1774.) Died in 1808.

Hull, (WILLIAM,) an officer in the American Revolution, born in Derby, Connecticut, in 1753. He joined the Revolutionary army at Cambridge at the head of a company of volunteers in 1775. He took part in many of the battles of the war, and for his gallant services in conducting the expedition against Morrisiana he was honoured with a vote of thanks by Congress. After the war he became a major-general in the Massachusetts militia, and in 1805 was appointed by Jefferson Governor of the Territory of Michigan. On the breaking out of the second war with Great Britain, in 1812, he was appointed to the command of the Northwestern army; and in August of the same year he surrendered with 2000 troops to the British under General Brock, at Detroit. For this act he was tried by court-martial, in 1814, and sentenced to be shot. President Madison approved the sentence, but remitted its execution in consideration of General Hull's age and services in the Revolution. He published a defence of himself before the court-martial, (1814.) Died in 1825.

See, also, "Life and Services of General W. Hull," by his daughter, MARIA CAMPBELL, 1848.

Hul'lah, (JOHN PYKE,) an English composer and popular teacher of music, was born in 1812. He composed the music of Dickens's comic opera "The Village Coquettes," (1836.) About 1840 he introduced a new system of instruction in vocal music, which was very successful. He became professor of vocal music in King's College, London, in 1844.

Hullin. See HULIN.

Hüll'man'dęl, (CHARLES JOSEPH,) an excellent lithographer, born in London in 1789. He made several improvements in the art of lithography, and invented the process of lithotint. He published, in 1824, "The Art of Drawing on Stone." Died in 1850.

Hüllmann or **Huellmann,** hül'män, (KARL DIETRICH,) a German historian and antiquary, born at Erde-born in 1765, became a professor at Bonn. He published, besides other works, a "History of the Origin of Ranks or Orders *(Stände)* in Germany," (3 vols., 1808,) and a "History of the Commerce of the Greeks," (1839.) Died in 1846.

Hul'lock, (Sir JOHN,) an English lawyer, born in the county of Durham about 1764, practised in London with success, and was made one of the barons in the exchequer court in 1823. Died in 1829.

Hülls, (JONATHAN,) an English mechanician and inventor, obtained in 1736 a patent for a "machine for carrying ships out of, or into, any harbour against wind and tide." This machine was to be moved by steam-power, but failed because he did not use the proper means to transfer the motion from the piston to the axle.

ā, ē, ī, ō, ū, ȳ, *long;* ȧ, ė, ȯ, same, less prolonged; ă, ĕ, ĭ, ŏ, ŭ, ў, *short;* ą, ę, į, ǫ, *obscure;* fär, fȧll, fȧt; mȇt; nŏt; gōŏd; mōŏn;

Hulot, *hü'lo',* (HENRI,) a French lawyer, born in Paris in 1732, translated into French fifty books of Justinian's Pandects, (7 vols., 1803.) Died in 1775.

Hulse, hŭlss, (Rev. JOHN,) born at Middlewich, England, in 1708, founded the Hulsean Lecture of the University of Cambridge, in which he had graduated. Died in 1790.

Hulsemann, hōōl'seh-mȧn',(JOHANN,) a learned German Lutheran divine, born at Essen in 1602, was professor of divinity at Leipsic. Died in 1661.

Hulsius, hŭl'se-us, (ANTOON,) a Protestant scholar and theologian, born in 1615, became professor of divinity and Oriental languages at Leyden. Died in 1685.

Hulsius, (HENDRIK,) a theological writer, son of the preceding, was born at Breda in 1654; died in 1723.

Hulst, van der, vȧn der hŭlst, (PIETER,) a Dutch painter, born at Dort in 1652, was successful in painting flowers, fruits, etc. He studied or worked in Rome. Died in 1708.

Hulthem, van, vȧn hŭl'tem, (CHARLES JOSEPH EMANUEL,) a Belgian bibliomaniac, born at Ghent in 1764. He made a vast collection of books, manuscripts, etc., which were purchased by the Belgian government for 279,400 francs. Died in 1832. A catalogue of his library was published in 6 vols., 1836.

Hultz, hōōlts, (JOHANN,) a German architect, of whom little is known. The completion of the great tower of the cathedral of Cologne is ascribed to him. It was finished in the first half of the fifteenth century.

Humann, *hü'mȧn',* (JEAN GEORGES,) a French financier, born at Strasburg in 1780, became minister of finance in 1832; died in 1842.

Humayun. See HOOMÂYOON.

Humbert, *hüN'baiR',* a French Dominican monk and writer, born at Romans about 1200; died in 1277.

Hum'bert, CARDINAL, an eminent French Benedictine monk, born in Burgundy; died about 1063.

Humbert, *hüN'baiR',* (JEAN,) a Swiss Orientalist, born at Geneva in 1792, published, besides other works, an "Arabian Anthology," with French versions, (1819.) Died in 1851.

Humbert, (JOSEPH AMABLE,) a French general, born of humble parents at Rouvray, in Lorraine, about 1760. Having a fine figure, a pleasing address, and great audacity, he was rapidly promoted, and in 1795, as general of brigade, served under Hoche against the Vendean royalists. In 1798, as general of division, he commanded the army of about 1500 men which invaded Ireland, where, after gaining a victory over General Lake, he was forced to surrender to Lord Cornwallis. In 1802 he was employed in the expedition to Hayti under Leclerc, at whose death he returned to France in company with Pauline, the widow of Leclerc, and sister of Bonaparte. By aspiring to her hand he offended the First Consul. He consulted his safety by emigrating to the United States, where he lived in obscurity. Died at New Orleans in 1823.

See THIERS, "History of the French Revolution;" "Nouvelle Biographie Générale."

Humboldt, hŭm'bōlt, von, [Ger. pron. fon hōōm'-bolt,] (FRIEDRICH HEINRICH ALEXANDER,) BARON, an illustrious German savant and traveller, born in Berlin on the 14th of September, 1769. He was a son of Major von Humboldt, who served as adjutant or aide-de-camp to the Duke of Brunswick in the Seven Years' war. In 1786 he entered the University of Frankfort-on-the-Oder, where he studied natural science and political economy. He became a pupil of Heyne, Blumenbach, and Eichhorn, at Göttingen, in 1788. In 1790 he travelled in France, Holland, and England, and published a treatise "On the Basalts of the Rhine." He studied mineralogy under Werner at Freiberg in 1791, and was appointed director-general of the mines of Anspach and Baireuth in 1792. He published in 1792 a work on subterranean plants, "Specimen Floræ subterraneæ Fribergensis." At an early age he cherished a passion to visit far-distant and unexplored regions of the globe. With this view he resigned his office about 1796, and passed some time at Jena, where he formed friendships with Goethe and Schiller. His reputation was extended by a treatise "On the Irritability of Muscles and Nervous Fibres," (1797.) Several

of his projects for undertaking a voyage of discovery were frustrated by the wars that followed the French Revolution. At length, in June, 1799, he joined Aimé Bonpland in a voyage to South America. They spent about four years in the exploration of the northern part of South America, especially those portions which are drained by the Oronoco and the Rio Negro. They ascended the Magdalena as far as they could by water, and penetrated by land to Quito. In June, 1802, they ascended Chimborazo to a point nineteen thousand feet or more above the level of the sea, the highest point of the Andes ever reached by man. They passed nearly a year in the exploration of Mexico, visited the United States, and returned to Europe in July, 1804, with rich collections of plants, animals, and minerals. Humboldt became a resident of Paris, where he remained about twenty years, the greater part of which he spent in digesting and publishing the results of his observations. In this task he was assisted by Bonpland, Cuvier, Oltmanns, Arago, Kunth, and others. Between 1807 and 1817 they published, in French, a "Journey to the Equinoctial Regions of the New Continent," (3 vols.,) "Astronomical Observations and Measurements by the Barometer," (2 vols., 1808–10,) a "View of the Cordilleras, and Monuments of the Indigenous Peoples of America," (1810,) a "Collection of Observations on Zoology and Comparative Anatomy," (2 vols.,) a "Political Essay on the Kingdom of New Spain," (2 vols., 1811,) and "General Physics and Geology." He made an important contribution to botanical geography by his Latin work "On the Geographical Distribution of Plants according to the Temperature and Altitude," (1817.) His botanical collections were classed and described by S. Kunth in a work entitled "Nova Genera et Species Plantarum quas in Peregrinatione ad Plagam æquinoctialem Orbis novi collegerunt A. Bonpland et A. de Humboldt," (7 vols., 1815–25.) An English translation of his "Personal Narrative of Travels" was made by Helen Maria Williams, (5 vols., 1814–21.) In 1810 he was chosen a member of the French Institute in place of Cavendish. He removed to Berlin in 1826, and received, with the title of councillor, many marks of royal favour. At the request of Nicholas, Emperor of Russia, and at his expense, Humboldt, Ehrenberg, and Rose made in 1829 a scientific exploration of Asiatic Russia. Among the results of this extensive expedition was an excellent work by Humboldt, entitled "Central Asia : Researches on the Chains of Mountains and the Comparative Climatology," (3 vols., 1843.) He was sent to Paris on several political missions by the King of Prussia between 1830 and 1848. He published a "Critical Examination of the Geography of the New Continent," (5 vols., 1835–38.) When he was more than seventy-four years old, he composed his celebrated work entitled "Kosmos ; Entwurf einer physischen Weltbeschreibung," ("Cosmos ; Essay of a Physical Description of the Universe,") the first volume of which appeared in 1845, and the fourth in 1858. "The first volume," says the author, "contains a general view of nature, from the remotest nebulæ and revolving double stars to the terrestrial phenomena of the geographical distribution of plants, of animals, and of races of men,—preceded by some preliminary considerations on the different degrees of enjoyment offered by the study of nature and the knowledge of her laws, and on the limits and method of a scientific exposition of the physical description of the universe." "The author of the remarkable book before us," says the "Edinburgh Review" for January, 1848, "is assuredly the person in all Europe best fitted to undertake and accomplish such a work. Science has produced no man of more rich and varied attainments, more versatile in genius, more indefatigable in application to all kinds of learning, more energetic in action, or more ardent in inquiry, and, we may add, more entirely devoted to her cause in every period of a long life. At every epoch of that life, from a comparatively early age, he has been constantly before the public, realizing the ideal conception of a perfect traveller ; a character which calls for almost as great a variety of excellences as those which go to realize Cicero's idea of a perfect orator. . . . Above all things is necessary a genial and kindly temperament, which excites no enmities, but, on the contrary, finds or makes friends everywhere. No man in the ranks of science is more distinguished for this last characteristic than Baron von Humboldt. We believe that he has not an enemy. The "Kosmos" has been translated into French by H. Faye and Ch. Galusky, (1848–57,) and into English by Mrs. Sabine. He received from the French government the title of grand officer of the legion of honour, and was a member of all the principal Academies of the world. Among his other works is "Aspects of Nature," ("Ansichten der Natur," 1808; 3d edition, 2 vols., 1849.) He died in Berlin, May 6, 1859, in his ninetieth year.

See JULIETTE BAUER, "Lives of the Brothers Humboldt," London, 1852; H. KLENCKE or KLETKE, "A. von Humboldt; ein biographisches Denkmal," 1852; Review of the "Kosmos" in the "London Quarterly Review," vol. lxxvii.; R. H. STODDARD, "Life of Alexander von Humboldt," New York, 1859; AGASSIZ, "Eulogy on Humboldt" in the "Living Age" for October 2, 1869; PRUYS VAN DER HOEVEN, "A. von Humboldt, Interpres Naturæ," 1845; "London Quarterly Review" for January and July, 1816, October, 1817, April, 1819, July, 1821, December, 1845, and January, 1854; "Edinburgh Review" for June, 1815; "Fraser's Magazine" for February, 1848.

Humboldt, von, (KARL WILHELM,) BARON, a celebrated German philologist and statesman, born at Potsdam on the 22d of June, 1767, was a brother of the preceding. His early education was directed by Joachim Campe, a distinguished philanthropist. About 1788 he entered the University of Göttingen, where he studied philology under G. Heyne. Among the intimate friends of his youth was George Forster, the traveller. In July, 1789, he visited Paris, and hailed with enthusiasm the advent of the new régime. He afterwards studied at Jena, and there formed an intimate and lasting friendship with the poet Schiller, who encouraged and directed him in his literary pursuits. Humboldt became also the friend and literary counsellor of Goethe. About 1791 he married Caroline von Dachenröden. Among his early works was an excellent "Essay on the Greeks," (1792.) In 1799 he produced an admirable critical essay on Goethe's "Hermann and Dorothea," which established his reputation as a critic. He was appointed minister to Rome by the King of Prussia about 1802, and soon after that date produced a poem entitled "Rome," (" Rom.") He returned to Prussia in 1808, and was appointed minister of public instruction about the end of that year. He took a prominent part in the foundation of the University of Berlin. About 1810 he resigned his office, and was sent as ambassador to Vienna. While thus employed in the public service, he devoted his leisure time to the study of languages, in many of which he was profoundly versed. He acquired distinction as a diplomatist, and induced Austria to join the coalition against Napoleon in August, 1813. He represented Prussia at the Conference of Châtillon and the Congress of Vienna, 1814. Talleyrand's opinion of him is said to have been expressed in these words : " Europe does not possess three statesmen of such power," (" L'Europe n'a pas trois hommes d'état de cette force.") He was sent as ambassador to London about 1816, and was appointed minister and privy councillor at Berlin in 1819. He advocated a liberal constitution, and, when he found that the king was determined to adopt a reactionary policy, he resigned his office about the end of 1819, after which he took no part in political affairs. He composed numerous poems, the most of which remained in manuscript until his death, and many treatises on language, philology, etc. Among his principal works are an "Essay on the New French Constitution," (1792,) a metrical translation of the "Agamemnon" of Æschylus, (1816,) which is highly commended, "Researches on the Aborigines of Spain by Means of the Basque Language," (1821,) and a " Memoir on Comparative Linguistic." He was one of the greatest philosophers and critics of his time, and has been called the creator of comparative philology. The interesting correspondence between Schiller and Wilhelm von Humboldt was published in 1830. In the latter part of his life he devoted his attention to the study of the languages of barbarous tribes of America and Asia. He died at Tegel, near Berlin, April 8, 1835, leaving unfinished an extensive and excellent work, entitled " On the Kawi Language in the Island of Java," (" Ueber die Kawi Sprache auf der Insel Java,") which was published in

1836. His works were collected and edited by his brother Alexander, under the title of "Wilhelm von Humboldts Gesammelte Werke," (4 vols., 1841–52.)

See GUSTAV SCHLESIER, "Wilhelm von Humboldts Leben ;" KLENCKE, " W. von Humboldts Leben," (translated into English by JULIETTE BAUER in 1852;) SCHLESIER, " Erinnerungen an Wilhelm von Humboldt," 2 vols., 1843–45; ROBERT HAYM, "Wilhelm von Humboldt Lebensbild und Charakteristik," 1856; "Foreign Quarterly Review" for January, 1842 ; "London Quarterly Review" for April, 1868.

Hume, (Rev. ABRAHAM,) an English antiquary, born about 1815. He became incumbent of a parish in Liverpool about 1846, and distinguished himself as a promoter of education. He wrote, besides other works, "The Learned Societies and Printing-Clubs of the United Kingdom," (1847.)

Hume, (ALEXANDER,) a Scottish poet and minister, born about 1560, preached at Logie. He published a volume of "Hymns or Sacred Songs," which were admired, especially the "Day Estival." Died in 1609.

See CHAMBERS, " Biographical Dictionary of Eminent Scotsmen."

Hume or **Home,** (DAVID,) of Godscroft, a Scottish minister and writer, supposed to have been born about 1560. He preached some years in France. He wrote some Latin poems, "Apologia Basilica," (" Apology or Defence of the King," 1626,) and " The History of the House and Race of Douglas and Angus," (1644.)

See CHAMBERS, " Biographical Dictionary of Eminent Scotsmen."

Hume, (DAVID,) an eminent English historian and philosopher, born in Edinburgh on the 26th of April, 1711. He was a younger son of Joseph Hume or Home, who, though related to the Earl of Home, was not wealthy. In his Autobiography he says, " My studious disposition, my sobriety, and my industry gave my family a notion that the law was a proper profession for me ; but I found an insurmountable aversion to everything but the pursuits of philosophy and general learning ; and, while they fancied I was poring upon Voet and Vinnius, Cicero and Virgil were the authors which I was secretly devouring." For the sake of economy, he went to France in 1734 or 1735, and spent about two years at Rheims and La Flèche, where he wrote his "Treatise on Human Nature." This was published in London in 1738, but was treated with discouraging neglect. He says himself, " It fell from the press without reaching such distinction as even to excite a murmur among the zealots." Mackintosh calls this work "the first systematic attack on all the principles of knowledge and belief, and the most formidable, if universal skepticism could ever be more than a mere exercise of ingenuity." He passed several ensuing years in Scotland in his favourite studies, and issued in 1742 the first part of his " Essays, Moral, Political, and Literary," which was moderately successful. These contain new, ingenious, and suggestive ideas on commerce, political economy, and other subjects.

In 1746 he was appointed secretary to General Saint Clair, with whom he passed two years on the continent. Returning to his brother's residence in Scotland, he composed an " Enquiry concerning the Principles of Morals," and the second part of his Essays, which appeared in 1752, with the title of " Political Discourses." The latter of these was received with favour abroad and at home, while the other was scarcely noticed. About this time he commenced his most celebrated work, the " History of England," the first volume of which (comprising the reigns of James I. and Charles I.) was published in 1754. He describes its reception in these terms : " I was assailed by one cry of reproach, disapprobation, and even detestation : English, Scotch, and Irish, Whig and Tory, churchman and sectary, freethinker and religionist, patriot and courtier, united their rage against the man who had presumed to shed a generous tear for the fate of Charles I. and the Earl of Strafford ; and after the first ebullitions of their fury were over, what was still more mortifying, the book seemed to sink into oblivion. Mr. Millar told me that in a twelvemonth he sold only forty-five copies of it." The subsequent volumes, however, were better appreciated, and the whole work became very popular and raised the author to affluence. The last volume was published in 1761. His style is generally admired, as graceful, natural, and perspicuous. But the value of his history

ā, ē, ī, ō, ū, ȳ, *long;* ă, ĕ, ŏ, same, less prolonged; ă, ĕ, ĭ, ŏ, ŭ, ȳ, *short;* ą, ę, į, ǫ, *obscure;* fär, fåll, fåt; mêt; nŏt; gōōd; mōōn;

is materially lessened by his partiality and inaccuracy. He was, as a skeptic, prejudiced against religion, and in civil government was inclined to favour prerogative. He is not profoundly versed in the philosophy of history, or in the progressive development of the British constitution. "He was far too indolent," says Alison, "to acquire the vast stores of facts indispensable for correct generalization on the varied theatre of human affairs." Macaulay compares him to "an accomplished advocate, whose insidious candour only increases the effect of his vast mass of sophistry."

Respecting his merits as a political economist, Lord Brougham says, "Of the 'Political Discourses' it would be difficult to speak in terms of too great commendation. They combine almost every excellence which can belong to such a performance. The great merit, however, of these discourses is their originality." In 1763 Hume accepted the office of secretary to the Earl of Hertford, ambassador to Paris, and having returned in 1766, much delighted by the caresses of the Parisians, he was employed two years as under-secretary of state. In 1769 he retired from office, and, with an income of £1000 a year, took up his residence in Edinburgh, where he died in August, 1776. Besides the works above named, he wrote the "Natural History of Religion," (1755,) and "Dialogues concerning Natural Religion," (1783.) He was never married. His personal character appears to have been amiable and respectable on the score of morality. "The Life of Mr. Hume," says Mackintosh, "written by himself, is remarkable above most, if not all, writings of that sort for hitting the degree of interest between coldness and egotism which becomes a modest man in speaking of his private history. Few writers, whose opinions were so obnoxious, have more perfectly escaped every personal imputation."

See Hume's "Autobiography," 1777; David Dalrymple, "Life of D. Hume," 1787; John Hill Burton, "Life and Correspondence of D. Hume," 2 vols., 1846; T. E. Ritchie, "Account of the Life and Writings of D. Hume," 1807; Mackintosh, "Progress of Ethical Philosophy," 1 vol. 8vo; Brenner, "Das Genie des Herrn Hume," etc., 1774; Brougham, "Lives of Men of Letters of the Time of George III.;" R. Pratt, "Apology for the Life of D. Hume," 1777; Macaulay, "History of England," vol. iv. chap. xix.; "Edinburgh Review" for January, 1847; "Quarterly Review" for March, 1844, and June, 1846; "Historical Sketches of the Times of George II.," in "Blackwood's Magazine" for June, 1869; "Westminster Review" for September, 1846; also, an elaborate article on Hume in Allibone's "Dictionary of Authors;" Chambers, "Biographical Dictionary of Eminent Scotsmen."

Hume, (David,) an able Scottish lawyer, born in 1756, was a nephew of the preceding. He was professor of Scottish law in the University of Edinburgh, and a baron of the court of exchequer. He wrote a valuable legal text-book, entitled "Commentaries on the Law of Scotland respecting the Description and Punishment of Crimes," (1797.) Died in 1838.

Hume, (Grizel,) a Scottish heroine, born in 1665, was a daughter of Sir Patrick, noticed below. She endured much hardship in efforts to conceal her father from his pursuers, and attended him in exile. In 1690 she was married to Mr. Baillie. She wrote poetry which is admired. Died in 1746.

See a Memoir of her life, by her daughter, Lady Murray.

Hume, (Hugh Campbell,) third Earl of Marchmont, born in 1708, was a grandson of Patrick, the first Earl. He acted a prominent part in Parliament as an opponent of Walpole, and was keeper of the great seal of Scotland from 1764 to 1794. Died in 1794, without male issue.

See Chambers, "Biographical Dictionary of Eminent Scotsmen."

Hume, (James Deacon,) an English financier, born at Newington in 1774, obtained in 1790 a clerkship in the London custom-house. Having given proof of ability and energy in responsible positions, he was employed in 1823 in the arduous task of simplifying and reducing to order the multitude of discordant statutes by which the transactions of the custom-house were complicated and perplexed. For this important service he received from government a present of five thousand pounds, and in 1829 he was appointed assistant secretary of the board of trade. He resigned in 1840, and died in 1842.

See Badham, "Life of J. D. Hume."

Hume, (Joseph,) M.P., a British statesman of the Radical party, was born at Montrose, Scotland, in 1777.

Having studied surgery, he entered as surgeon the service of the East India Company in 1797. He learned the native languages of India, and, by combining the functions of interpreter and paymaster with those of army-surgeon, he acquired a handsome competence, and returned home in 1808. By a careful study of the national resources and the condition of the people, he prepared himself for the task of a legislator and reformer, and entered Parliament in 1812. From 1818 to 1830 he represented Montrose in Parliament, where he gained great distinction by his industry and independence and by his important services to the working-classes. He was for many years pre-eminent in the House as a financial reformer and a sturdy opponent of monopolies and high taxes. He declined political preferment on several occasions, and continued to serve in the House of Commons until his death, in 1855.

See Harriet Martineau, "History of Thirty Years' Peace;" "Biographical Sketches," by the same, London, 1869.

Hume, (Sir Patrick,) Earl of Marchmont, a Scottish patriot, was born in 1641. He was persecuted in the reign of Charles II., and escaped to Holland in 1684. Having returned in 1688, he was made lord chancellor in 1696, and Earl of Marchmont. Died in 1724.

See Macaulay, "History of England;" Chambers, "Biographical Dictionary of Eminent Scotsmen."

Hume, (Patrick,) a Scottish critic, who taught school in London. He published in 1695 "Annotations on Milton's Paradise Lost," which was the first attempt to illustrate that author, and was commended by Bishop Newton. His critical labours have been appropriated by later commentators. According to "Blackwood's Magazine," Hume is "the father of that style of comparative criticism which has been so much employed during these later days in illustrating the works of our great poet."

See Chambers, "Biographical Dictionary of Eminent Scotsmen."

Humières, d', dü'me-air', (Louis de Crevant—deh kReh-vŏN',) Duc, a French general and courtier of Louis XIV., was created marshal in 1668, and commanded the right wing at the victory of Cassel, in 1677. He commanded the army in Flanders which was defeated by Waldeck in 1689. Died in 1694.

See Voltaire, "Siècle de Louis XIV;" Sismondi, "Histoire des Français."

Hummel, hŏŏm'mel, (Johann Erdmann,) a German painter, born at Cassel about 1770. He worked in Berlin, and became in 1809 professor of perspective, etc. in the Royal Academy of that city. Died in 1827.

Hummel, hŏŏm'mel, (Johann Nepomuk,) an excellent composer and pianist, born at Presburg, Hungary, in 1778. About the age of eight he became a pupil of Mozart in Vienna, and at the age of sixteen he was accounted one of the most skilful performers in Germany. He entered the service of Prince Esterhazy in 1803, and became chapel-master to the King of Würtemberg in 1816. He was chapel-master to the Duke of Weimar from 1818 until his death, during which period he performed with applause in London, Paris, and Saint Petersburg. Among his best works are concertos and sonatas for the piano. Died in 1837.

See Fétis, "Biographie Universelle des Musiciens;" "Nouvelle Biographie Générale."

Hummelius, hŏŏm-mā'le-ùs, or **Hummel,** (Johann,) a German mathematician, born at Memmingen in 1518, was professor at Leipsic. Died in 1562.

Humphrey, hŭm'fre,* (Heman,) D.D., an American divine, born in Simsbury, Connecticut, in 1779. He graduated at Yale in 1805. He was six years minister in Pittsfield, Massachusetts. He became president of Amherst College in 1823, and was succeeded in that office by Dr. Edward Hitchcock in 1845, when he removed to Pittsfield. He wrote several valuable works, among which are a "Tour in France, Great Britain, and Belgium," (2 vols., 1838,) "Domestic Education," (1840,) and "Letters to a Son in the Ministry," (1845.) Died in 1859.

* This name is pronounced differently in different parts of the United States: some families writing their names Humphrey or Humphreys always omit the initial h in pronunciation.

ę as k; ç as s; ğ hard; ġ as j; G, H, K, guttural; N, nasal; R, trilled; ŝ as z; th as in this.   (☞ See Explanations, p. 23.)

Humphrey, hŭm'fre, (LAWRENCE,) an English Calvinistic divine, born at Newport-Pagnel about 1527. In 1555 he retired to Zurich to escape persecution, and returned after the death of Queen Mary. He became professor of divinity in Oxford in 1560, and Dean of Winchester in 1580. He published several able theological works. Died about 1590.

Humphrey or **Humphry,** (OZIAS,) R.A., an English portrait-painter, born at Honiton in 1743, settled in London in 1763. He painted a miniature for the queen, was received into the Royal Academy, and rose to eminence in his branch of art. Died in 1810.

Humphreys, hŭm'frĕz,* (ANDREW A.,) an American general, born in Pennsylvania about 1812. He became a brigadier-general about April, 1862, and commanded a division at Gettysburg, July 1-3, 1863. He commanded a corps in the battles near Petersburg, February–April, 1865.

Humphreys, (DAVID,) an American poet, born in Derby, Connecticut, in 1753. He entered the army about 1776, and became in 1780 a colonel and aide-de-camp to General Washington. In 1784 he went to Europe with Jefferson, as secretary of legation. He aided Barlow and other poets in "The Anarchiad," and wrote other works, among which are a "Poem on the Happiness of America," and an "Address to the Armies of the United States," (1772.) He was sent as minister to Portugal in 1790, and to Spain in 1797. Died in 1818.

See GRISWOLD, "Poets and Poetry of America;" DUYCKINCK, "Cyclopædia of American Literature," vol. i.; "National Portrait-Gallery of Distinguished Americans," vol. ii.

Humphreys, hŭm'frĕz, (HENRY NOEL,) a British antiquary and numismatist, born at Birmingham in 1810. He published "The Coins of England," (1847,) "Ten Centuries of Art," (1851,) and other works.

Humphreys, (JAMES,) an English lawyer, born in Montgomeryshire, published a valuable work on "English Laws of Real Property," (1820.) Died in 1830.

Humphreys or **Humphrey,** (PELHAM,) an English composer and musician, born in 1647. He composed anthems and songs. Died in 1674.

Humphry, OLD. See MOGRIDGE.

Hu'nald, [Lat. HUNAL'DUS,] Duke of Aquitaine, succeeded his father Eudes in 735 A.D., and defended his domain against Charles Martel and his sons. He was defeated by Charlemagne about 769, and was killed in 774, at the siege of Pavia, being the last prince of the Merovingian race.

Hunauld, hü'nō', (FRANÇOIS JOSEPH,) a learned French physician, born at Châteaubriant in 1701, resided in Paris. He was a member of the Academy of Sciences, and a Fellow of the Royal Society of London. In 1730 he became professor of anatomy in the Jardin des Plantes. He wrote dissertations on osteology, etc. Died in 1742.

See QUÉRARD, "La France Littéraire."

Hund, hŏont, (WIGULÆUS,) a German genealogist, born in 1514, became aulic councillor at Munich in 1540. Died in 1588.

See J. T. KÖHLER, "Leben und Schriften Hunds," 1750.

Hundeshagen, hŏon'dĕs-hä'g̣en, (JOHANN CHRISTIAN,) a German writer on forests, was born at Hanau in 1783. Among his works is an "Encyclopædia of the Science of Forests," (2 vols., 1821.) Died in 1834.

Hundeshagen, (KARL BERNHARD,) a theologian, son of the preceding, was born in Hesse-Cassel in 1810. He became professor at Heidelberg in 1847, and published "German Protestantism: its Past and Present," (1846.)

Hundhorst. See HONTHORST.

Hundt, hŏont, (MAGNUS,) a German naturalist and writer, born at Magdeburg in 1449. He taught physics in the University of Leipsic. Died in 1519.

Hun'e-ric or **Hun'ne-ric,** [Gr. Ὀνώριχος,] second King of the Vandals of Africa, was the eldest son of Genseric, whom he succeeded in 447 A.D.; but he did not inherit his father's abilities. He married the daughter of the emperor Valentinian III. His reign was extremely cruel and tyrannical. As an Arian, he persecuted the Catholics in particular. He died in 484, and left three sons, of whom Hilderic was the eldest; but

* See note on page 1227.

Gondamond, a nephew of Huneric, was proclaimed his successor.

See GIBBON, "Decline and Fall of the Roman Empire."

Hu-ni'a-dĕs or **Hun'ya-dĕs,** [Hun. HUNYADY, hoon'yŏd̄y; Fr. HUNIADE, hü'ne-ăd',] (JOAN'NES CORVI'NUS,) a brave Hungarian general, who about 1440 was chosen Vaivode of Transylvania. Soon after Ladislaus, King of Poland, was killed at the battle of Varna by the Turks, (1444,) Huniades was made captain-general of his army and Governor of Hungary. His chief exploit was the successful defence of Belgrade against Mahomet II., in 1456. He died of wounds received in this action. His son, Matthias Corvinus, was elected King of Hungary.

See MAJLÁTH, "History of the Magyars;" PRAY, "Annales Regum Hungariæ;" G. BESSENYEI, "Hunyadi János," etc., 1788; G. FEJER, "Genus, Incunabula et Virtus J. Corvini de Hunyad," etc., Buda, 1844.

Hun'nis, (WILLIAM,) chapel-master to Queen Elizabeth, wrote several volumes of psalms and hymns, (published from 1550 to 1588.)

Hunnius, hoon'ne-ûs, (ÆGIDIUS,) a Lutheran theologian, noted for intolerance, was born at Winnenden, in Würtemberg, in 1550. He was professor at Wittenberg, and wrote, besides other works, "Calvinus Judaizans," (1593.) Died in 1603.

See HUTTER, "Threnologia de Vita Hunnii," 1603; JOHANN GEORG NEUMANN, "Programma de Vita Hunnii," 1704; S. GESNER, "Leichenpredigt auf A. Hunnius nebst dessen Lebenslauf," 1603.

Hunnius, (NIKOLAUS,) an able Lutheran theologian, son of the preceding, was born at Marburg in 1585. He was superintendent of all the churches of Lubeck from 1623 to 1643. He wrote against Popery, Calvinism, and Socinianism. Died in 1643.

See L. HELLER, "N. Hunnius, sein Leben und Wirken," 1843.

Hunold, hoo'nolt, (CHRISTIAN FRIEDRICH,) a German littérateur, who wrote under the pseudonym of MENANTES, born near Arnstadt in 1680. His works include romances, tales, and poems. Died in 1721.

Hŭnt, (EDWARD B.,) an American military engineer, born in Livingston county, New York, in 1822. He graduated at West Point in 1845, was employed as engineer on several forts and light-houses, invented a submarine battery, and gained the rank of captain in 1859. Died in 1863.

Hŭnt, (FREDERICK KNIGHT,) an English editor, born in Buckinghamshire in 1814. After writing for the "Illustrated London News," etc., he was chief editor of the London "Daily News" from 1851 until his death. He wrote "The Book of Art," and "The Fourth Estate; or, Contributions to the History of Newspapers," etc., (1850.) Died in 1854.

Hunt, (FREEMAN,) an editor, born in Quincy, Massachusetts, in 1804. He became in 1839 the editor and owner of the "Merchants' Magazine," issued monthly in New York. He published, besides other works, "Lives of American Merchants," (2 vols., 1856.) Died in 1858.

Hunt, (GEORGE WARD,) an English politician, born in 1825. He was elected a member of Parliament for the county of Northampton in 1857, as a Conservative. He was re-elected, and gained distinction by a bill to counteract the cattle-plague of 1866. He became chancellor of the exchequer about March 1, 1868, and resigned in December of that year.

Hunt, (HENRY,) M.P., an English Radical, born in Wiltshire in 1773, acquired popularity with his party by his intrepid audacity and by his inflammatory harangues. He often presided at the meetings against the corn-laws. In 1820 he was arrested at Manchester, while addressing a political meeting, and punished with a fine and several years' imprisonment. He was returned to Parliament for Preston in 1831, defeating the Earl of Derby, his opponent, and witnessed the triumph of the Reform bill, for which he had toiled and suffered. Died in 1835.

Hunt, (ISAAC,) a native of the West Indies, was educated in Philadelphia. He took the royalist side in the Revolution, removed to England, and became a preacher at Paddington about 1780. He published "The Rights of Englishmen." He was the father of Leigh Hunt.

Hunt, (JAMES HENRY LEIGH,) a popular English poet and littérateur, born at Southgate, near London, in 1784, was the son of Isaac Hunt, noticed above, and

ā, ē, ī, ō, ū, ȳ, *long;* ă, ĕ, ŏ, same, less prolonged; ă, ĕ, ī, ŏ, ŭ, ȳ, *short;* a, e, i, o, *obscure;* fär, fâll, fât; mĕt; nŏt; gōōd; mōōn;

Mary Shewell, of Philadelphia. He left school at the age of fifteen, and acted as clerk in the War Office until 1808, when he formed a partnership with his brother John to issue "The Examiner," a journal of liberal politics, which attained under his editorship a high reputation for literary merit. In 1812 the brothers were condemned to pay each a fine of five hundred pounds, and to be imprisoned two years, for a satirical article in which the prince-regent was styled an "Adonis of fifty." While in prison, he wrote "Rimini," (1816,) one of his most admired poems, "The Descent of Liberty," and "The Feast of the Poets." At this period he was intimate with Byron, Moore, Shelley, and Keats. From 1818 to 1822 he edited "The Indicator," a series of periodical essays, admired for genial humour, easy style, and brilliant fancy. In 1822 he was associated with Byron and Shelley as an editor of "The Liberal," a political and literary journal; and for this object he resided with Byron in Pisa and Genoa. But Shelley was drowned, Byron and Hunt became estranged, and after the issue of four numbers "The Liberal" was discontinued. Hunt returned to England about 1824, and published "Recollections of Byron," (1828,) which gave great offence to Byron's friends. He was editor of "The Companion" and the "London Journal," and wrote for several periodicals. Among the multifarious productions of his versatile genius are a popular poem entitled "Captain Sword and Captain Pen," (1835,) "Stories from the Italian Poets," "Men, Women, and Books," (1847,) "Imagination and Fancy," and his "Autobiography," (3 vols., 1850.) A pension of two hundred pounds was granted him in 1847. Died August 28, 1859. Professor Wilson, of Edinburgh, speaks of Hunt as "the most vivid of poets and most cordial of critics." ("Recreations of Christopher North.")

See his "Autobiography," 1850; HAZLITT, "Spirit of the Age," and his "Table-Talk;" LORD JEFFREY, critique in the "Edinburgh Review" for June, 1816, (vol. xxvi.;) E. P. WHIPPLE, "Essays and Reviews;" W. GIFFORD, critique in the "Quarterly Review" for January, 1816, (vol. xiv.;) "Brief Biographies." by SAMUEL SMILES. For a full account of the writings of Leigh Hunt, see a "List of the Writings of William Hazlitt and Leigh Hunt," by ALEXANDER IRELAND, London, 1868; "North British Review" for November, 1850, and November, 1860; "London Quarterly Review" for January, 1816.

Hunt, (JEREMIAH,) an English dissenting minister, born in London in 1678, preached for many years at Pinners' Hall. Died in 1744.

Hunt, (LEIGH.) See HUNT, (JAMES HENRY LEIGH.)

Hunt, (RICHARD MORRIS,) a distinguished American architect, born in Brattleborough, Vermont, October 31, 1829. He was several years in the Boston High School. In 1842 he went to Europe, and studied architecture in Paris and Geneva. He subsequently visited various parts of Europe, and also Asia Minor and Egypt, for the purpose of becoming better acquainted with the architecture of different countries. After his return to Paris, he was appointed inspector at the Louvre; in 1867 he was a member of the jury on architecture at the Exposition Universelle. He has since resided in New York.

Hunt, (ROBERT,) an English author and philosopher, born at Devonport in 1807. His youth was passed in poverty, from which he was relieved by William Allen, the chemist, who procured him a situation in London. In 1832 he opened a druggist's shop in Penzance, having previously been a diligent student of chemistry and other sciences. He published his discoveries of the chemical action of the solar rays in an interesting work entitled "Researches on Light," (1844,) and in 1849 he gave to the world "The Poetry of Science." His "Panthea; or, The Spirit of Nature," (1849,) is designated by a writer in the "North British Review" as "a work of a very peculiar character, in which philosophy and poetry are finely blended, and where great truths and noble sentiments are expressed in language full of beauty and eloquence." Among his later productions are "Elementary Physics," (1851,) and "Memoirs of the Geological Survey of Great Britain," (1855.) He has a high reputation as a lecturer on science.

See "North British Review" for May, 1850; "Fraser's Magazine" for April, 1849.

Hunt, (THOMAS,) D.D., an English scholar, born in 1696, became in 1747 professor of Hebrew in Oxford University. He wrote "Observations on the Book of Proverbs." Died in 1774.

Hunt, (THOMAS STERRY,) a distinguished American chemist and geologist, born in Norwich, Connecticut, in 1826. He studied medicine for some time in his native town, and afterwards became assistant chemist to Professor Silliman at Yale College. About 1847 he became connected with the geological survey of Canada, and professor of chemistry at Quebec. Besides his contributions to the London "Philosophical Magazine" and the Transactions of the Royal Society, French Academy of Sciences, etc., he has published above seventy papers in the "American Journal of Science." While acting as a juror to the International Exhibition at Paris in 1855, Mr. Hunt had conferred on him the cross of the legion of honour by Napoleon III.; and in 1859 he was elected an honorary member of the Royal Society of London.

Hunt, (THORNTON,) an English journalist, the eldest son of Leigh Hunt, was born in 1810. He wrote, besides other works, "The Foster-Brother," a romance, (1845.)

Hunt, (WILLIAM HENRY,) an English painter in water-colours, born in London in 1790. His subjects are simple and homely, such as a "Peasant Boy" in various moods and phases, a "Farm-House Beauty," flowers, fruits, and other objects of still life. His works are admirable for colouring and perfection of finish. "I have seen," says Ruskin, "frequent instances of very grand ideality in treatment of the most commonplace still life by our own Hunt." ("Modern Painters.") Died in 1864.

See "Fraser's Magazine" for October, 1865.

Hunt, (WILLIAM HOLMAN,) an eminent historical painter, one of the chief founders of the pre-Raphaelite school of England, was born in London about 1827. He began to exhibit at the Royal Academy in 1846. About 1850 he and several other artists assumed the name of "Pre-Raphaelite Brethren," proposing to restore the art of painting from the degenerate style of Raphael and his coevals. His works are very minutely finished, and are close imitations of nature. Among his master-pieces are "Our English Coasts," (1853,) "The Awakening Conscience," (1854,) and "The Light of the World," (1854,) a symbolic figure of the Saviour. "Hunt's 'Light of the World,'" says Ruskin, "is, I believe, the most perfect instance of expressional purpose with technical power which the world has yet produced." ("Modern Painters.")

Hunt, (WILLIAM MORRIS,) an American artist, born at Brattleborough, Vermont, about 1825, studied at Dusseldorf and in Paris. His works are chiefly portraits and genre pictures.

See TUCKERMAN, "Book of the Artists."

Hunt′er, (ALEXANDER,) F.R.S., a Scottish physician, born in Edinburgh in 1729, practised at Beverley and York. He was the principal founder of a lunatic-asylum at York. He wrote, besides professional treatises, "Georgical Essays," (a work on rural economy,) and edited Evelyn's "Sylva." Died in 1809.

Hunter, (ANNE,) wife of the great surgeon John Hunter, and sister of Sir Everard Home, was born in Scotland in 1742. She wrote "My Mother bids me braid my Hair," and other songs, set to music by Haydn. Her poems, published in 1802, were praised by "Blackwood's Magazine." Died in 1821.

Hunter, (CHRISTOPHER,) an English physician and antiquary, born in Durham in 1675; died in 1757.

Hunt′er, (DAVID,) an American general, born in Washington, District of Columbia, in 1802, graduated at West Point in 1822. He became a colonel in May, 1861, served in the battle of Bull Run, July 21, was appointed a major-general of volunteers about August, and took command of the army and department of Missouri in November, 1861. About the 1st of April, 1862, he was appointed commander of the army at Port Royal, or Hilton Head. In May ensuing he issued an order that the "persons heretofore held as slaves in South Carolina, Georgia, and Florida are declared forever free." This order was annulled by the President as premature. He defeated General W. E. Jones at Piedmont, Virginia, June 5, 1864, after which he attacked Lynchburg (June 18) without success. He retreated westward by way of the Kanawha River, and was superseded by General Sheridan in August, 1864.

Hunter, (HENRY,) D.D., a Scottish divine and author, born at Culross in 1741, was a man of superior talents. From 1771 until his death he was pastor of a Scottish church in London. He was the author of a popular work styled "Sacred Biography," (1783-1802,) and translated Lavater's "Essays on Physiognomy," Saint-Pierre's "Studies of Nature," and other French works. His translation of Lavater, finely illustrated, sold for forty guineas a copy. Died in 1802.

See CHAMBERS, "Biographical Dictionary of Eminent Scotsmen."

Hunter, (HUMPHREY,) a patriot of the American Revolution, born in Ireland in 1755. About 1760 his widowed mother emigrated with her family to Mecklenburg, North Carolina. He entered the Revolutionary army in 1776, and rendered distinguished service at the battle of Eutaw Springs. He was ordained in 1789, and from 1805 till his death, in 1827, was pastor of the Presbyterian church at Steele Creek, North Carolina.

Hunter, (JOHN,) an eminent British anatomist and surgeon, born at Long Calderwood, near Glasgow, in 1728, was the youngest of ten children. After receiving a very defective education, he worked a few years with a cabinet-maker in Glasgow. In 1748 he went to London, where he was employed by his brother William as an assistant in the dissection-room. Having pursued the study of anatomy with ardour and remarkable success, he was received in 1754 as a partner in his brother's school, and lectured regularly for about five years. In 1760, for the sake of his health, he exchanged this employment for that of army-surgeon, and at the peace of 1763 returned to London. In 1767 he was elected a Fellow of the Royal Society, and soon after surgeon of Saint George's Hospital. He was eminent for surgical skill, and acquired greater celebrity by his researches in comparative anatomy, physiology, and natural history, on which he wrote several treatises. His museum is said to have cost £70,000. Died in 1793. He is admitted to be the greatest British anatomist of the eighteenth century, and was noted for originality, independence, and estimable moral qualities. Among his best works are a "Treatise on the Blood, Inflammation, and Gun-Shot Wounds," and another on "Certain Parts of the Animal Economy."

See EVERARD HOME, "Life of John Hunter;" JESSE FOOTE, "Life of J. Hunter," 1794; JOSEPH ADAMS, "Memoirs of the Life and Doctrines of J. Hunter," 1816; CHAMBERS, "Biographical Dictionary of Eminent Scotsmen;" "Nouvelle Biographie Générale."

Hunter, (JOHN,) a British naval officer, born at Leith in 1738, obtained the rank of vice-admiral. Died in 1821.

Hunter, (JOHN,) a Scottish critic, born at Closeburn in 1747, was for many years professor of humanity in Saint Andrew's, and published good editions of Horace, (1797,) Virgil, (1800,) and Juvenal, (1806.) Died in 1837.

Hunter, (Rev. JOSEPH,) an English antiquary, born at Sheffield in 1783. He was for many years minister of a congregation of dissenters at Bath. He published several valuable works, among which are a "History and Topography of the Deanery of Doncaster," (2 vols., 1828,) and "Illustrations of the Life and Studies of Shakspeare," (2 vols., 1845.) He was assistant keeper of the public records. Died in 1861.

Hunter, (ROBERT,) an English officer and writer, was appointed Governor of New York in 1710, and acted as Governor of Jamaica from 1728 until his death. He wrote a "Letter on Enthusiasm," ascribed to Swift and Shaftesbury. Died in 1734.

Hunter, (ROBERT MERCER TALIAFERRO,) an American statesman, born in Essex county, Virginia, April 21, 1809. He graduated at the University of Virginia, studied law, and commenced its practice in his native town in 1830. He voted for Jackson in 1832, and was elected to the legislature of Virginia in 1833. He was chosen a representative to Congress in 1837. His first speech in this body was in favour of the independent treasury and against a national bank. He also took strong grounds in opposition to the protective policy of Mr. Clay, and in all his subsequent career was an able advocate of free trade. In 1839 he was chosen Speaker of the House, and for his dignified and impartial discharge of its duties received, at the close of the term, in 1841, a unanimous vote of thanks. He favoured the election of James K. Polk, and supported his policy with regard to Texas and the tariff. The warehousing system, which was first incorporated in the tariff bill, was originated and drawn up by Mr. Hunter. He was elected in 1847 to the United States Senate, in which he served through two full terms, and was elected for a third term ending in 1865. He supported the Douglas Kansas-Nebraska bill in 1854, and the admission of Kansas under the Lecompton Constitution in 1858. He was secretary of state of the Southern Confederacy from July, 1861, to February, 1862, and was one of the two Senators who represented Virginia in the Senate at Richmond from February, 1862, to 1865.

Hunter, (WILLIAM,) a distinguished anatomist and physician, born at Long Calderwood, near Glasgow, in 1718, was a brother of John Hunter, noticed above. He received a liberal education in the University of Glasgow, and formed a professional connection with Dr. Cullen, who afterwards became so eminent as a medical writer. In 1741 he removed to London, where he acquired a high reputation as a lecturer on anatomy and a medical practitioner. He formed a partnership with his brother John in 1748. Having obtained a large and lucrative practice, he was appointed in 1764 physician-extraordinary to the queen. In 1767 he was chosen a Fellow of the Royal Society, to whose "Transactions" he contributed. About 1770 he founded in London an anatomical museum, to which were attached a classical library, and a cabinet of rare medals, which cost £20,000. The most important of his publications is the "Anatomy of the Gravid Uterus," (1774.) He died in 1783.

See S. F. SIMMONS, "Life and Writings of William Hunter," 1783; "Lives of British Physicians," London, 1857; CHAMBERS, "Biographical Dictionary of Eminent Scotsmen."

Hunter, (WILLIAM,) a British surgeon, born at Montrose, was employed in the service of the East India Company in Bengal. He published an "Account of Pegu," (1785,) "Caverns near Bombay," a "Hindostanee Dictionary," and several medical treatises. He was eminent as an Orientalist, and from 1794 to 1808 was secretary of the Asiatic Society. Died in 1815.

Hunt′ing-don, (SELINA,) COUNTESS OF, an English lady, eminent for her piety and munificence, was the daughter of the Earl of Ferrers. Her maiden name was SHIRLEY. She was born in 1707, and in 1728 was married to Theophilus Hastings, Earl of Huntingdon. After her husband's death, about 1746, she lived in fellowship with the Calvinistic Methodists, chose Whitefield for her chaplain, and was noted for her zeal and devotion. She founded at Trevecca a seminary for preachers, built chapels, and spent large sums for religious purposes. Her sect was known as the "Countess of Huntingdon's Connection." Died in 1791.

See "Life and Times of Selina, Countess of Huntingdon," 1839; "The Women of Methodism," by ABEL STEVENS.

Hunt′ing-ford, (GEORGE ISAAC,) D.D., an English theologian, born at Winchester in 1748. He was made Bishop of Gloucester in 1802, and of Hereford in 1815. He published several Greek and Latin school-books, "Thoughts on the Trinity," and sermons. Died in 1832.

Hunt′ing-ton, (DANIEL,) a distinguished American painter, born in New York in 1816. He became about 1835 a pupil of Professor Morse at New York, and in 1839 visited Florence and Rome, where he painted his "Sibyl" and "Shepherd Boy of the Campagna." Having returned to New York, he painted numerous portraits and historical subjects. He was elected president of the National Academy of Design in 1862. Among his works are "Lady Jane Grey and Feckenham in the Tower," and "Henry VIII. and Catherine Parr."

See TUCKERMAN, "Book of the Artists."

Huntington, (FREDERICK D.,) D.D., an American divine and author, born in Hadley, Massachusetts, in 1819. He graduated at Amherst in 1839, studied divinity at Cambridge, and from 1842 to 1855 was minister of the South Congregational Church in Boston. He became preacher and professor of Christian morals in Harvard University. Although formerly a Unitarian, he has recently embraced the faith of the Episcopal Church. He became Bishop of Central New York in April, 1869. He published "Sermons for the People," (6th edition, 1860.)

ă, ē. ī, ō, ū, ȳ, *long;* ă, ĕ, ĭ, ŏ, ŭ, ў, *short;* ą, ę, į, ǫ, *obscure;* fär, fåll, fåt; mêt; nŏt; gŏŏd; mōŏn

Huntington, (JEDEDIAH VINCENT,) an author, a brother of Daniel, noticed above, was born in New York in 1815. He became an Episcopalian priest about 1840, and afterwards joined the Roman Catholic Church. He wrote, besides other works, a volume of Poems, (1843,) and "Lady Alice, or the New Una," a novel, (1849.)

Huntington, (ROBERT,) D.D., an English Orientalist, born at Deerhurst in 1636. From 1670 to 1680 he was chaplain to a factory at Aleppo, and collected many valuable manuscripts in the Levant. He was chosen Bishop of Raphoe in 1701, and died in the same year. He wrote a "Letter on the Porphyry Pillars in Egypt," (published in the "Philosophical Transactions," No. 161.)

Huntington, (SAMUEL,) president of the American Congress, was born in Windham, Connecticut, in 1732. He distinguished himself in the Colonial Council of 1775 by his opposition to the aggressive policy of Great Britain, and in 1776 took his seat in Congress and signed the Declaration of Independence. In 1779 he succeeded John Jay as president of the Congress of the Confederation, and was again chosen to the same office in 1780. He again served in Congress in 1783, and was shortly after appointed chief justice of Connecticut. In 1786 he was elected Governor of the State, as the successor of Roger Griswold, and was annually re-elected to the same office till his death, in 1796.

See GOODRICH, "Lives of the Signers to the Declaration of Independence."

Huntington, (WILLIAM,) an English Methodist preacher, born in Kent in 1744, was originally a poor labourer. He became a popular preacher among the Calvinistic Methodists in London, and published many tracts and controversial works. Died in 1813.

See notice in the "Quarterly Review" for January, 1821, (by SOUTHEY.)

Hŭn'tọn, (PHILIP,) an English nonconformist divine, born in Hampshire, was appointed provost of Durham College in 1657. He wrote a "Treatise on Monarchy," (1644,) which gave great offence to the High-Church party. Died about 1682.

Hunts'mạn, (BENJAMIN,) an English artisan, born in Lincolnshire in 1704, is said to have been the inventor of cast steel. He lived in Sheffield. Died in 1776.

See SMILES, "Industrial Biography."

Hunyades. See HUNIADES.

Hunyady. See HUNIADES.

Huot, hü'o', (JEAN JACQUES NICOLAS,) a French naturalist, born in Paris in 1790, published a "Complete Manual of Mineralogy," (2 vols., 1841,) and revised and continued the "System of Universal Geography," which Malte-Brun left unfinished. The last two volumes of this were written by M. Huot. Died in 1845.

See "Vie de J. J. N. Huot," by his son, PAUL HUOT, 1846.

Hupfeld, hŏop'fĕlt, (HERMANN,) a German theologian and Orientalist, born at Marburg in 1796, became professor of theology at Halle in 1843. He published, besides other works, "De Vera Festorum apud Hebræos Ratione," (2 vols., 1852,) and a version of the Psalms, (1855.) He was an excellent Hebrew scholar. Died at Halle in April, 1866.

Huppazoli, oop-pâd-zo'lee, (FRANCESCO,) an Italian, noted for longevity, born at Casal in 1587, was at one time a merchant, and in 1669 was appointed Venetian consul at Smyrna. He was abstemious in his habits, and retained the use of his faculties to the last. Died in 1702.

Hurault. See CHIVERNY.

Hŭrd, (RICHARD,) D.D., an eminent English writer and critic, born at Congreve in 1720, was educated at Cambridge, and became a friend of Warburton. He was appointed Bishop of Lichfield and Coventry in 1775, and translated to the see of Worcester in 1781. The archbishopric of Canterbury was offered to him, but was declined. Among his works, which are very numerous and able, are "Dialogues, Moral and Political," "Letters on Chivalry," (1762,) "Commentary on Horace's Ars Poetica," "Lectures on the Prophecies," and a "Life of Warburton," (1794.) "Hurd has perhaps," says Hallam, "the merit of being the first who, in this country, aimed at philosophical criticism : he had great ingenuity, a good deal of reading, and a facility in applying it ; but

he did not feel very deeply, was somewhat of a coxcomb, and assumes a dogmatic arrogance which offends the reader." ("Introduction to the Literature of Europe.") Died in 1808.

See FRANCIS KILVERT, "Memoirs of Bishop Hurd," 1860; "Life of R. Hurd," by himself, in an edition of his Works, 8 vols., 1811; "North British Review" for May, 1861.

Hur'dis, (Rev. JAMES,) an English poet, born in Sussex in 1763, was a friend of the poet Cowper. In 1784 he became tutor to the Earl of Chichester's son, and in 1793 professor of poetry at Oxford. He wrote "The Village Curate," (1788,) "Sir Thomas More," a tragedy, and other poems. Died in 1801.

See "Retrospective Review," vol. i., 1820.

Huré, hü'Rȧ', (CHARLES,) a French Jansenist writer, born at Champigny-sur-Yonne in 1639, was for many years an eminent professor of languages in the University of Paris. He published an approved "Dictionary of the Bible." Died in 1717.

Huret, hü'rȧ', (GRÉGOIRE,) a French engraver, born at Lyons in 1610. His work is easy and mellow, and his heads expressive. Died in 1670.

Hurl'but, (STEPHEN A.,) an American general, born at Charleston, South Carolina, about 1815, commanded a division of General Grant's army at Shiloh, April.6–7, 1862. With the rank of major-general, he directed a corps of General Sherman's army in the raid to Meridian in February, 1864.

Hurl'stọne, (FREDERICK YEATES,) an English painter of history and portraits, was born in London in 1801. Soon after 1830 he joined the Society of British Artists, of which he became president. Among his works are "The Spanish Beauty" and "The Last Sigh of the Moor." His portraits are much admired. Died in 1869.

Hurtado de Mendoza. See MENDOZA.

Hurtault, hür'tō', (MAXIMILIEN JOSEPH,) a French architect, born at Huningue in 1765. He was appointed architect of the Fontainebleau Palace, in which he restored the gallery of Diana. Died in 1824.

Hurter, hŏŏr'tẹr, (FRIEDRICH EMANUEL,) a German historian, born at Schaffhausen in 1786, published a "History of Pope Innocent III.," (4 vols., 1834–42,) and a "History of the Emperor Ferdinand II. and his Family," (Eltern,) (9 vols., 1850–57.)

Hus'bạnds, (HERMAN,) a native of Pennsylvania, became a leader of the "Regulators" in North Carolina in 1768, and fought against Governor Tryon in 1771. Died about 1794.

Huschke, hōōsh'kẹh, (EMANUEL GOTTLIEB,) a German philologist, born in 1761, published a good edition of Tibullus, (1819,) and other works. Died in 1828.

Huschke, (GEORG PHILIPP EDUARD,) a German jurist, born at Münden in 1801, published "Studies on Roman Law," (1830,) and other works.

Hus'kis-sọn, (WILLIAM,) an English statesman and financier, born in Worcestershire in 1770, went to Paris in 1783, where he lived with one of his uncles and learned the French language. Sympathizing with the Revolution, he was present at the storming of the Bastille, and he became a prominent member of the "Société de 1789." In 1790 he was employed as secretary to Lord Gower, then ambassador at Paris, with whom he returned to England in 1792. Having attracted the favourable notice of Pitt, he was appointed in 1795 under-secretary in the department of war and the colonies, and the next year was returned to Parliament for Morpeth. He was secretary of the treasury from 1804 until the death of Pitt, and again from 1807 until 1809, when, as a friend of Canning, he resigned with him. In Parliament he represented successively Harwich, Chichester, (1812–23,) and Liverpool, (1823–30.) He gained distinction by his knowledge of finance and commerce, and by his methodical and luminous reports. In 1823, under the auspices of Canning, he became president of the board of trade, treasurer of the navy, and a member of the cabinet. From the death of Canning (1827) to 1829 he acted as colonial secretary. In the latter part of his life he inclined to the policy of the Liberal party in respect to electoral reform, the corn-laws, and other restrictions on commerce. He resigned in May, 1829, because he differed from the Tory ministry. At the opening of the

Liverpool and Manchester Railway he was killed by an engine, September 15, 1830.

See "Speeches and Biography," by WRIGHT, 3 vols., 1831; WM. JERDAN, "Men I have known," London, 1866; "Nouvelle Biographie Générale."

Hüss, (JOHN,) [Ger. JOHANN HUSS, yo'hän hõõss; Lat. JOHAN'NES HUSS,] a celebrated reformer of the Church, was born at Husinec, (or Hussinetz,) in Southern Bohemia, in 1373. Being appointed in 1402 preacher at the Bethlehem Chapel in Prague, he became a zealous advocate of the doctrines of Wickliffe, whereby he incurred the censure of the Catholic clergy. As rector of the University of Prague, he had the works of Wickliffe translated into Bohemian; but they were soon after burned by order of Archbishop Sbinko. In 1412 he denounced the papal bull issued by John XXIII. against Ladislaus, King of Naples, and with his coadjutor, Jerome of Prague, condemned the sale of indulgences. He was excommunicated the next year, upon which he wrote his work "On the Church," exposing the abuses of popery. Cited before the Council of Constance in 1414, and provided with a pass by the emperor Sigismund, he was arrested on his arrival, and, as he adhered firmly to his opinions, he was burned by order of the treacherous emperor.

See ÉMILE DE BONNECHOSE, "Les Réformateurs avant la Réforme," 2 vols., 1847; "J. Huss et Hieronymi Pragensis Historia et Monumenta," Nuremberg, 1558; J. COCHLÉE, "Historia Hussitarum," 1549; HODGSON, "Reformers and Martyrs," Philadelphia, 1867; AUGUST NEANDER, "Züge aus dem Leben des unvergesslichen J. Huss," Berlin, 1819; WM. GILPIN, "Lives of John Wickliffe and of the Most Eminent of his Disciples, Lord Cobham, J. Huss," etc., 1765; GEORG LOMMEL, "J. HUSS," 1847; HELFERT, "Huss und Hieronymus von Prag," 1853; "North American Review" for October, 1847, (by H. W. TORREY.)

Hussein Pasha, hoos'sīn' pä'shä', a famous Turkish admiral, born about 1750, was a favourite of Selim III., who in 1789 appointed him capudan-pasha. He possessed superior talents, and served his master with fidelity in reforming the discipline and management of the navy. He commanded the fleet which in 1801 co-operated with the English against the French on the coast of Egypt. Died in 1803.

Hussein Pasha, (or **Pacha,**) last Dey of Algiers, born at Smyrna about 1773. At the death of Ali Pasha, in 1818, he was proclaimed his successor. To avenge an insult received by the French consul, the French government sent in June, 1830, an army which, after several days' fighting, forced Hussein to capitulate. He was deposed, and died in 1838.

See A. NETTEMENT, "Histoire de la Conquête d'Alger," 1857.

Hüs'sey, (GILES,) an English painter, born in 1710, studied in Italy, and settled in London in 1742. He excelled in portraits, and attempted to apply to his art the hypothesis of harmonic proportions. Died in 1788.

Husson, hü'sôN', (JEAN HONORÉ ARISTIDE,) a skilful French sculptor, born in Paris in 1803. He gained the grand prize of Rome in 1830. Among his works are "Dante and Virgil," a bas relief, (1836,) a statue of Voltaire, (1839,) and a marble statue of "Haïdée," (1850.) Died in 1864.

Hu'ston, (LORENZO DOW,) a Methodist minister, born in Cincinnati, Ohio, in 1820, preached in Kentucky, and edited several papers.

Hutch'e-son, [Lat. HUTCHESO'NUS,] (FRANCIS,) a metaphysician, born in the north of Ireland in 1694, was educated at Glasgow, and was ordained as a Presbyterian minister. While employed as principal of an academy in Dublin, he published about 1725 an excellent work, entitled an "Inquiry into the Original of our Ideas of Beauty and Virtue," which was followed by an "Essay on the Passions and Affections," (1728.) In 1729 he was appointed professor of moral philosophy in the University of Glasgow. Died in 1747. His greatest work, "A System of Moral Philosophy," was published in 1755. Sir J. Mackintosh thinks Hutcheson "was the father of the modern school of philosophy in Scotland." He adopted the opinions of Lord Shaftesbury in moral philosophy, and maintained that disinterested affections and a distinct moral faculty are essential parts of human nature.

See WILLIAM LEECHMAN, "Life of F. Hutcheson," prefixed to his "System of Moral Philosophy," 1755; "Biographia Britannica," (Supplement;) SIR J. MACKINTOSH, "Preliminary Dissertation" in the "Encyclopædia Britannica;" JACOB BAART DE LA FAILLE, "Dissertatio de Vita et Scriptis F. Hutchesoni," 1812.

Hutchesonus. See HUTCHESON.

Hutch'ins, (Rev. JOHN,) born at Bradford-Peverel, in England, in 1698, wrote the "History and Antiquities of the County of Dorset." Died in 1773.

Hutch'ins, (THOMAS,) an American geographer, born in Monmouth county, New Jersey, about 1735. He was appointed geographer to the United States by Congress, and published, besides other works, a "Topographical Description of Virginia, Pennsylvania, Maryland, and North Carolina," (1778.) Died in 1789.

Hutch'in-son, (ANN,) a religious enthusiast, born in Lincolnshire, England, about 1600. She was the wife of William Hutchinson, whom she accompanied to Boston in 1636. She taught many doctrines which were condemned as heretical by the Synod of 1637. Mrs. Hutchinson herself was banished, and in 1642 removed to what is now Westchester county, New York. The next year her house was set on fire by the Indians, and she and all her family, consisting of sixteen persons, (except a child taken captive,) either perished in the flames or were killed by the savages.

See "Life of Anne Hutchinson," by GEORGE E. ELLIS, in SPARKS's "American Biography," vol. vi., 2d series; HILDRETH's "History of the United States," vol. i. chap. ix.

Hutchinson, (JOHN,) COLONEL, an English Puritan and regicide, born at Nottingham in 1616. In 1638 he married Lucy Apsley. (See HUTCHINSON, LUCY.) In 1642 he obtained the rank of lieutenant-colonel in the army of Parliament, and next year was appointed governor of the town and castle of Nottingham, which he bravely defended in a long siege against the royalists. He was one of the judges who condemned Charles I., and afterwards was a member of the council of state. He was hostile to the government of Cromwell. After the restoration he was included in the act of amnesty, but, on a groundless suspicion of a treasonable conspiracy, was confined in the Tower and Sandown Castle from 1662 to his death in 1664. His character was excellent, and free from the austere errors to which the Puritans were most inclined.

See "Memoirs of Colonel Hutchinson," by his wife, 1806.

Hutchinson, (JOHN,) an English writer, born at Spennithorne in 1674, was the founder of the Hutchinsonian or mystical school of biblical interpretation. He was employed as steward by the Duke of Somerset, and afterwards as his riding-purveyor. His first work, called "Moses' Principia," was designed to refute the arguments of Newton's "Principia." He published, also, a "Treatise on Power, Essential and Mechanical," "Glory or Gravity, Essential and Mechanical," "The Hebrew Writings Complete," "Moses sine Principio," and other works. His leading idea is that the Hebrew Scriptures contain the elements of natural philosophy as well as of religion. His views excited much controversy, and were adopted by Bishop Horne, Parkhurst, and other eminent divines. Died in 1737.

See JULIUS BATES, "Defence of John Hutchinson's Tenets," 1751; FLOYD, "Bibliotheca Biographica."

Hutchinson, (JOHN HELY,) an Irish statesman and lawyer, born in 1715, resided in Dublin, and became secretary of state. Died in 1794.

Hutchinson, (JOHN HELY,) a British general, born in 1757, was the second son of the preceding. He entered the army in 1774. Having gained distinction in the Irish rebellion, he was made major-general in 1796. In 1800 he went to Egypt as second in command under Sir Ralph Abercrombie. When the latter was killed, in March, 1801, Hutchinson succeeded to the command, and obliged the French army under Menou to capitulate at Alexandria in the same year. He was rewarded for these services by the title of Baron Hutchinson. In 1825, on the death of his brother, he inherited the title of Earl of Donoughmore. Died in 1832.

Hutchinson, (LUCY,) an English authoress of great merit, was the daughter of Sir Allan Apsley, lieutenant of the Tower of London, in which Tower she was born in 1620. She was married in 1638 to Colonel John Hutchinson, noticed above, after having received a liberal education. She shared the counsels and dangers of her husband in the civil war, attended him in prison, and wrote Memoirs of his life, (1806,) which are greatly admired. "We have not often met with anything," says

Lord Jeffrey, "more interesting and curious than this volume. . . . It challenges our attention as containing an accurate and luminous account of military and political affairs from the hand of a woman, and as exhibiting the most liberal and enlightened sentiments in the person of a Puritan. The views which it opens into the character of the writer and the manners of the age will be to many a still more powerful attraction."

See "Memoirs of Eminent Englishwomen," by LOUISA S. COSTELLO, London, 1844: "Edinburgh Review" for October, 1808, (vol. xiii. ;) "Monk's Contemporaries," by GUIZOT, London, 1865.

Hutchinson, (RICHARD HELY,) Earl of Donoughmore, born in Dublin in 1756, was the eldest son of John H. Hutchinson, noticed above. He served in the army during the Irish rebellion of 1798, and in 1800 was raised to the peerage, as Earl of Donoughmore. In 1805 he obtained the rank of major-general. In Parliament he advocated with zeal and constancy the claims of the Catholics. He was created a peer of the United Kingdom in 1821. Died in 1825.

Hutchinson, (ROGER,) an early English Reformer, became Fellow of Saint John's College, Cambridge, in 1543. He left theological works, which were published in 1842. Died in 1555.

Hutchinson, (THOMAS,) a royal governor of Massachusetts, was born in Boston in 1711. He became a judge of probate in 1752, and chief justice of Massachusetts in 1760. His course in relation to the Stamp Act rendered him very unpopular. He succeeded Bernard as governor in 1769, and pursued a policy which tended to provoke a revolt in the colonies. When the tea was brought to Boston in 1773, the inhabitants, in town-meeting, resolved that it should not be landed, but be returned to its owners. Hutchinson, however, refused to grant the ships a pass. The result was the destruction of the tea by citizens in the disguise of Indians. In 1772, Dr. Franklin, colonial agent in London, had sent over to Massachusetts confidential letters written by Hutchinson to England, which showed that his whole policy had been characterized by duplicity and evasion,—that, professing to be the friend of the colony, he had secretly advised the sending of troops to Boston, and other obnoxious measures. He retired to England in 1774. Died near London in 1780. His principal works are a "History of the Province of Massachusetts Bay from 1628 to 1749," (2 vols. 8vo, issued in 1764–67,) and a "Collection of Original Papers relative to the History of Massachusetts Bay," (1769.) The "North American Review" calls his work "a mine of wealth to all future historians and antiquaries." "It is written," says Bancroft, "with lively inquisitiveness and lawyer-like criticism, though without a glimpse of the great truths which were the mighty causes of the revolution he describes."

See ALLEN's "American Biographical Dictionary."

Huth, hōōt, (GEORG LEONHARD,) a German naturalist, born at Nuremberg in 1705 ; died in 1761.

Hutin, hü'täN', (CHARLES,) a French painter and sculptor, born in Paris in 1715, worked mostly at Dresden, where he died in 1776.

Hutten, von, fon hōōt'ten, [Lat. HUTTE'NUS,] (ULRICH,) a German poet, and one of the earliest Protestant Reformers, born near Fulda in 1488. He studied at Frankfort-on-the-Oder, and afterwards at Pavía, in Italy. About 1520 he repaired to Mentz, where he published a succession of severe attacks on the Roman clergy, and soon after became acquainted with Luther, whose cause he openly espoused. Owing to the persecution he now encountered, he was obliged to take refuge in Switzerland, where he died in 1523. He possessed rare talents, but lacked discretion. Among his works are "Epistolæ Obscurorum Virorum," satires on certain pedants, (1516.)

See SCHUBART, "Leben Ulrich von Hutten's," 1791; BURCKHARD, "Commentarius de Fatis et Meritis Ulrici Hutteni," 1717–23; STRAUSS, "Ulrich von Hutten," 1858; BAYLE, "Historical and Critical Dictionary;" WAGENSEIL, "U. von Hutten nach seinem Leben," etc., 1823; ZELLER, "U. de Hutten, sa Vie, ses Œuvres, son Temps," Paris, 1849; GERVINUS, "Geschichte der Deutschen National-Literatur;" "Nouvelle Biographie Générale;" "Fraser's Magazine" for August, 1849.

Huttenus. See HUTTER.

Hutter, hōōt'ter, (ELIAS,) a German linguist, born at Ulm about 1555. He published an edition of the Bible in Hebrew, and a Polyglot Bible. Died about 1602.

Hutter, [Lat. HUTTE'RUS,] (LEONHARD,) a German theologian, a brother of the preceding, was born at Ulm in 1563. He was noted for his rigour and excessive zeal for Lutheranism. He was professor of theology at Wittenberg from 1596 until 1616. Among his numerous works is a "Compendium of Theological Subjects," ("Compendium Locorum theologicorum," 1610.) Died in 1616.

See BAYLE, "Historical and Critical Dictionary ;" J. G. NEUMANN, "Programma de Vita L. Hutteri," 1706.

Hutterus. See HUTTER.

Hut'ton, (CHARLES,) LL.D., an eminent English mathematician, born at Newcastle-upon-Tyne in 1737, was employed for some years as a teacher in his native place. Here he published treatises on arithmetic and mensuration. From 1773 to 1806 he was professor of mathematics in the Military Academy at Woolwich. In 1774 he was chosen a Fellow of the Royal Society, which he also served as foreign secretary and enriched with able scientific memoirs. He acquired celebrity by numerous works, among which are "Mathematical Tables," (1785,) "Elements of Conic Sections," a "Mathematical and Philosophical Dictionary," (1795,) a "Course of Mathematics," (1798,) etc. From 1804 to 1809 he assisted Shaw and Pearson in abridging the "Philosophical Transactions." He was eminent for benevolence, modesty, and simplicity of character. In 1807 his services were rewarded by a pension of £500. Died in 1823.

See ERSCH und GRUBER, "Allgemeine Encyklopaedie ;" "Gentleman's Magazine" for 1823.

Hut'ton, (JAMES,) M.D., a philosopher and geologist, distinguished as the author of the Plutonian theory of geology, was born in Edinburgh in 1726. He graduated as M.D. at Leyden in 1749. About 1768 he became again a resident of Edinburgh, where he published, besides other works, a "Dissertation on the Philosophy of Light, Heat, and Fire," (1794,) and "Theory of the Earth," (1795.) His geological theory excited much discussion and opposition, being attacked by Kirwan and defended by Professor Playfair, who wrote "Illustrations of the Huttonian Theory of the Earth," (1802.) Died in 1797.

See CHAMBERS, "Biographical Dictionary of Eminent Scotsmen ;" "Edinburgh Review," vol. ii.

Hutton, (MATTHEW,) an English prelate, born in 1529, was made Bishop of Durham in 1589, and Archbishop of York in 1594. He wrote a work on Predestination. Died in 1605.

Hutton, (MATTHEW,) became Archbishop of York in 1747, and was translated to Canterbury in 1757. He published several sermons. Died in 1758.

Hutton, (WILLIAM,) an English antiquary and author, born of poor parents at Derby in 1723. He received a defective education. At the age of fifty-six he commenced his career as an author. His chief works are a "History of Birmingham," (1781,) a "History of Derby," (1790,) "Edgar and Elfrida," a poem, "The Roman Wall," (1801,) and an instructive volume of "Autobiography," (1816.) His daughter CATHERINE wrote "the Miser Married," a novel. He died in 1815.

See his "Autobiography ;" "Pursuit of Knowledge under Difficulties," vol. i.

Huvé, hü'vä', (JEAN JACQUES MARIE,) a French architect, born at Versailles in 1783. He succeeded Vignon as architect of the grand church La Madeleine, which he finished. He was admitted into the Institute in 1838. Died in 1852.

See CHARLES LENORMAND, "Notice sur J. J. M. Huvé," 1853.

Hux'ham, (JOHN,) an English physician, born at Halberton in 1694, studied under Boerhaave at Leyden, and practised with success at Plymouth. He wrote several popular books on medicine, one of which is an "Essay on Fevers," (1750.) Died in 1768.

Hux'ley, (THOMAS HENRY,) F.R.S., an eminent English physiologist and naturalist, born at Ealing, Middlesex, in 1825. He was in his youth a surgeon in the royal navy. About 1848 he produced a treatise "On the Anatomy and Affinities of the Family of the Medusæ." He succeeded E. Forbes as professor of palæontology in the School of Mines about 1854, and became professor of physiology at the Royal Institution. Among his principal works is a "History of the Oceanic

Hydrozoa," (1857,) "Man's Place in Nature," (1863,) "Lectures on the Elements of Comparative Anatomy," (1864,) and an essay entitled "Protoplasm; or, The Physical Basis of Life," (1869.) In 1869 he was chosen president of the British Association for 1870. He contributed numerous memoirs to the Transactions of the Royal Geological and Zoological Societies. He is a very popular lecturer on natural science, and stands in the foremost rank among British physiologists and naturalists. In natural science he favours the Darwinian theory.

See "Edinburgh Review" for April, 1863; "London Quarterly Review" for October, 1869.

Huydecoper, hoi′dĕh-ko′pĕr, (BALTHASAR,) a Dutch poet and excellent critic, born at Amsterdam in 1695. He produced "Arsaces," (1722,) and three other tragedies, a good metrical version of the Satires, Epistles, and "Ars Poetica" of Horace, (1737,) and other poems. His "Essays, Philological and Poetical, or Observations on Vondel's Dutch Version of Ovid's Metamorphoses," (1730,) are highly commended. "All that he has done in this department," says the "Biographie Universelle," "is classical." Died in 1778.

See ERSCH und GRUBER, "Allgemeine Encyklopaedie;" VAN EFFEN, "Hollandische Spectator," vol. iv.; SCHOTEL, "Commentatio de B. Huydecoperi in Linguam Literasque Belgicas Meritis," Leyden, 1830.

Huygens or **Huyghens**, hī′gĕns, [Dutch pron. almost hoi′Hĕns; Lat. HUGE′NIUS,] (CHRISTIAN,) a celebrated Dutch astronomer and geometer, born at the Hague, April 14, 1629. He inherited the title of Lord of Zuylichem. About the age of sixteen he went to Leyden, where he studied law and mathematics under Vinnius and Schooten. Soon after leaving the university, he began to distinguish himself by his admirable scientific discoveries and mechanical inventions. In 1651 he published his "Theorems on the Quadrature of the Hyperbola," etc., and in 1656 discovered a satellite of Saturn with a telescope of his own construction. In 1657 he rendered important service to science and society by improving the clock, being the first to apply the pendulum to the measurement of time. Two years later he published, in his "System of Saturn," a description of Saturn's ring, which he had discovered with a telescope of twenty-two feet focal length. These and other successes had rendered him pre-eminent among the contemporary savants and philosophers of all nations. Newton was then a young student preparing to rival or surpass him. The years 1660 and 1661 were passed by Huygens in France and England. In 1663 he was chosen a Fellow of the Royal Society of London. From 1665 to 1681 he resided in Paris, whither Colbert had invited him in order to add éclat to the newly-founded Academy of Sciences. In this period he demonstrated the law of the impact of bodies, (1669,) wrote an elegant treatise on Dioptrics, and published his great work entitled "Horologium Oscillatorium," (1673,) dedicated to Louis XIV. Besides the theory of the pendulum, this work contains several very important mechanical discoveries, among which are the fact that the cycloid is the curve all the arcs of which, measured from the lowest point, are synchronous, and the theory (without demonstration) of the centrifugal force in circular motion, by which he made a near approach to those laws of gravitation afterwards proved by Newton. He has the credit of inventing the spiral spring which is used to regulate the balance of watches, which invention was also claimed by Hautefeuille. In 1681 Huygens returned to Holland, where he spent some years in constructing a planetarium, and telescopes of enormous dimensions, one of which had a focal length of two hundred and ten feet. In 1690 appeared (in French) his "Treatise on the Cause of Gravity," and a "Treatise on Light," which is esteemed one of his greatest works. It contains arguments in favour of the undulatory theory, which was first proposed by him and is now generally adopted. He died in 1695. He left a work styled "Cosmotheoros," (printed in 1698,) in which he advances bold speculations or conjectures on the constitution of the planets, which he believed to be inhabited. Huygens was never married. He loved retirement, and maintained a good character as a man. He kept up a friendly correspondence with

Leibnitz and Newton, the latter of whom called him "Summus Hugenius."

See "Vita Hugenii," prefixed to his "Opera Varia," 1724; CONDORCET, "Éloge de Huygens;" ERSCH und GRUBER, "Allgemeine Encyklopaedie;" MONTUCLA, "Histoire des Mathématiques;" DELAMBRE, "Histoire de l'Astronomie moderne;" P. H. PEERLKAMP, "Annotatio in Vitam C. Hugenii," 1821; M. LEMANS, "Lebensbeschrijving van C. Huijgens;" DR. F. HOEꟾER, article in the "Nouvelle Biographie Générale."

Huygens or **Huijgens**, (CONSTANTIJN,) Seigneur of Zuylichem, (or Zulichem,) born at the Hague in 1596, was the father of the preceding. He acted with credit as secretary to three successive princes of Orange, the last of whom was William III. of England. He wrote Latin epigrams, and other poetical performances, which were received with favour. Died in 1687.

See his Autobiography, in verse, entitled "De Vita propria Sermones;" BAYLE, "Historical and Critical Dictionary," (in Z;) LONGFELLOW, "Poets and Poetry of Europe;" SCHINKEL, "Bijdrage tot de Kennis van het Karakter van C. Huijgens," 1842; "Fraser's Magazine" for May, 1854.

Huyghens, hoi′Hens, (GOMARUS,) a Dutch Roman Catholic theologian, born in Brabant in 1631; died in 1702.

Huyot, hü′yo′, (JEAN NICOLAS,) a French architect, born in Paris in 1780. He passed several years in the Levant, exploring the ruins of Ephesus, Thebes, Athens, and other cities. Died in 1840.

Huysman, hois′mån, sometimes written **Houseman**, (CORNELIS,) an eminent Flemish landscape-painter, born at Antwerp in 1648. He worked mostly at Malines, (Mechlin.) His colouring is praised by Descamps, who also observes that he had a great talent for painting mountains. Among his works is "The Disciples Going to Emmaus." Died in 1727.

See J. C. WEYERMAN, "De Schilderkonst der Nederlanders."

Huysman or **Houseman**, (JACOB,) a Flemish painter of history and portraits, born at Antwerp in 1656; died in London in 1696.

Huysum, van, vån hoi′sŭm, (JACOB,) brother of Jan, noticed below, was born at Amsterdam about 1680. He excelled in flower-painting, and copied several of his brother's works with accuracy. Died in London in 1740.

Another brother, JUSTUS, born in 1684, excelled in battle-pieces, but died prematurely in 1706.

Huysum, van, (JAN,) a celebrated Dutch painter, born in Amsterdam in 1682, was a pupil of his father, Justus. His favourite subjects were flowers and fruits, in which he is thought to be unrivalled. His works unite tasteful composition, richness and harmony of colour, freedom of touch, and exquisite finish. His pictures were often adorned with insects, dew-drops, birds' nests, etc. He had a peculiar art of preparing his colours, which he always kept secret. Died in 1749.

See PILKINGTON, "Dictionary of Painters."

Huysum, van, (JUSTUS,) THE OLD, a Dutch landscape-painter, born at Amsterdam in 1659, was the father of the preceding. Died in 1716.

Huzard, hü′zăR′, (JEAN BAPTISTE,) a noted French veterinary physician, born in Paris in 1755, was a member of the Institute. He wrote numerous able and popular works on the veterinary art and rural economy, and he had collected a library of forty thousand volumes pertaining to his speciality. Died in 1839.

See PARISET, "Éloge de Huzard;" BARON SILVESTRE, "Notice sur Huzard."

Hvergelmir. See NIDHÖGG.

Hvitfeld, hvit′fĕld, (ARILD,) a Danish historian, born in 1549. In 1586 he attained the dignity of senator, and afterwards was chancellor of the kingdom. He wrote a "Chronicle of the Kingdom of Denmark," which is considered authentic. Died in 1609.

See KRAFT og NYERUP, "Litteraturlexicon for Danemark."

Hwiid, hweed, (ANDREAS CHRISTIAN,) a Danish critic, born at Copenhagen in 1749, was educated for the church, and was skilled in Oriental languages. He published a "Life of Cyrus the Great and the Younger," and several commentaries on Scripture. Died in 1788.

Hyacinthe. See HYACINTHUS.

Hyacinthe, e′ȧ′sȧNt′, (CHARLES LOYSON,) PÈRE, an eminent French pulpit orator, born at Orléans about 1828. He became a Carmelite monk, preached for some time in Lyons, and removed about 1865 to Paris, where his conferences in the church of Notre-Dame attracted

ă, ē, ī, ō, ū, ȳ, *long;* ă, ĕ, ŏ, same, less prolonged; ă, ĕ, ĭ, ŏ, ŭ, ў, *short;* ą, ę, į, ǫ, *obscure;* fär, fåll, fåt; mĕt; nŏt; gōōd; mōōn;

much attention. In September, 1869, he published, in a letter to the general of his order, a protest against the ultramontane doctrines and practices of the Roman Church, called forth by the Encyclical letter by which the pope had convened a general council. This protest caused a great commotion in the religious world. "Since Luther," says Mr. Bigelow, "there has been no such signal revolt against the authority of the Romish hierarchy." About October, 1869, he visited the United States. It appears that he has not formally separated from the communion of the Catholic Church.

See notice of "Father Hyacinthe and his Church," in "Putnam's Monthly Magazine" for January, 1870, (by JOHN BIGELOW.)

Hy-ạ-cin'thus, [Gr. Ὑάκινθος; Fr. HYACINTHE, e'ȧ'-sȧNt',] a beautiful Spartan youth, beloved by Apollo, by whom he was accidentally killed in a game of discus. The poets feigned that Apollo changed him into the flower called Hyacinth.

Hỹ'ạ-dēṣ, [Gr. Ὑάδες,] Anglicised as HY'ADS, nymphs of classic mythology, and daughters of Atlas. According to the poetic legend, they were changed into stars, and now form part of the constellation of Taurus. When they rose and set with the sun, it was regarded as a sign of rainy weather.

Hỹ'ạtt, (JOHN,) a Calvinistic Methodist preacher, born in 1767, officiated in the Tabernacle, London. He published several volumes of sermons. Died in 1826.

Hỹb're-as, [Ὑβρέας,] an eminent Greek orator, a native of Caria, flourished about 40 B.C.

Hỹde, (ANNE,) a daughter of Lord Clarendon, was born in 1637. She was married about 1660 to the Duke of York, afterwards James II. She was the mother of Queen Mary and Queen Anne. Died in 1671.

See "Memoirs of Eminent Englishwomen," by LOUISA STUART COSTELLO.

Hyde, (EDWARD.) See CLARENDON, EARL OF.
Hyde, (HENRY.) See CLARENDON, EARL OF.
Hyde, (LAWRENCE,) M.P., son of Sir Nicholas Hyde, distinguished himself by his successful efforts in promoting the escape of Charles I. after the battle of Worcester. The king passed one night in the house of Lawrence Hyde's tenant, and thence was conducted by Hyde to the sea-shore. Died in 1682.

Hyde, (LAWRENCE,) first Earl of Rochester, was the second son of Edward, Earl of Clarendon. He was an ultra Tory, and was the leader of the High-Church party in the reign of Charles II. He became first commissioner of the treasury in 1679. At the accession of James II., in 1685, he was appointed lord treasurer, (prime minister.) Though extremely subservient to the policy of the king, he was removed from office in December, 1686, because he would not turn Roman Catholic. After the flight of James II., Hyde gave his adhesion to William III. Died in 1711.

See MACAULAY, "History of England," vol. i. chaps. ii. and iv., vol. ii. chaps. vi., ix., and x.

Hyde, (Sir NICHOLAS,) an English judge, born in 1572, was the father of Lawrence Hyde, and uncle of the first Earl of Clarendon. He was appointed chief justice of the king's bench in 1626, and presided when Sir John Eliot was unjustly condemned to prison. Died in 1631.

Hyde, (THOMAS,) D.D., a learned English divine, born in Shropshire in 1636, became Archdeacon of Gloucester in 1678, professor of Arabic at Oxford in 1691, and regius professor of Hebrew in 1697. He excelled in Oriental languages, and was interpreter of the same to Charles II., James II., and William III. From 1665 to 1701 he was principal librarian of the Bodleian Library. He published a treatise on Chinese weights and measures, (1688,) and one on "Oriental Games," (1694.) His principal work, a "History of the Religion of the Ancient Persians and Magi," in Latin, (1700,) displays a vast erudition, and for a long time had a great reputation. "The variety and novelty of its contents," says Hallam, "gave this book a credit which in some degree it preserves; but Hyde was ignorant of the ancient language of Persia, and is said to have been often misled by Mohammedan authorities." ("Introduction to the Literature of Europe.") He wrote other works, and compiled dictionaries of the Persian and Turkish languages. Died in 1703.

See "Biographia Britannica;" WOOD, "Athenæ Oxonienses."

Hyde de Neuville, hėd dẹh nuh'vėl', (JEAN GUILLAUME,) a French politician, born in the department of Nièvre in 1776. He was an active royalist during the republic and the empire. After the restoration he acted with the ultra royalists as a deputy in 1815, and was minister to the United States of North America from 1816 to 1821. He was minister of the marine in the Martignac cabinet for a short time in 1828. Died in 1857.

Hyder, the German of HYDRA, which see.

Hyder-Alee or **Hyder-Ali,** hī'dẹr ä'lee, [sometimes written, in French, HAÏDER-ALI,] a celebrated Hindoo prince, born about 1718, entered the army of the Rajah of Mysore. His military talents procured his promotion to the command of an army, with which he captured Bangalore and fought against the Mahrattas. About 1759, by a bold and successful coup d'état, he obtained the chief power in Mysore, leaving his former master the title of rajah and a pension. The English, alarmed by his encroachments, formed a league with the Mahrattas against him, (1766.) In the war that ensued, Hyder gained such advantages that the English sued for peace ·and entered into alliance with him, (1769.) In 1771 he was defeated by the piratical Mahrattas, the English having failed to aid him according to the treaty. Having made an alliance with the French and the Mahrattas against the English, he suddenly invaded the Carnatic in 1780, took several fortresses, defeated some detachments, and ravaged the country almost to the walls of Madras. In 1782 he was defeated by Sir Eyre Coote at Porto Novo, and died in the same year, leaving his throne to his son, Tippoo Sâhib. Hyder was a Mussulman. He is reputed the most able enemy the British have had to contend with in India.

See MEER HUSSEIN ALI KHAN KIRMAIN, "History of Hyder Ali," (translated into English by COLONEL W. MILES, 1842;) F. ROBSON, "Life of Hyder-Ali," 1786; M. CARPANI, "Memorie sopra la Vita d'Hyder Ali," 1784; JOSEPH MICHAUD, "Histoire du Progrès et de la Chute de l'Empire de Mysore," etc., 2 vols., 1801.

Hy'drạ, [Gr. Ὕδρα; Fr. HYDRE, ėdr; Ger. HYDER, hee'dẹr; It. IDRA, ee'DRȧ,] a monster which infested the Lernean marsh and was destroyed by Hercules. It was said to have had nine heads. (See HERCULES.)

Hydre. See HYDRA.

Hỹ-ģe'iạ or **Hỹ-ği-eï'ạ,** [Gr. Ὑγίεια; Fr. HYGIE, e'zhe', or HYGÉE, e'zhả',] written also **Hygea** or **Hygia,** the goddess of health, in Greek mythology, said to be the daughter of Asclepias. She was represented as holding a cup in one hand, and in the other a serpent, drinking from the cup.

Hygie or **Hygée.** See HYGEIA.

Hy-ģi'nus [Fr. HYGIN, e'zhăN'] became Bishop of Rome in 138 A.D., and died in 142. He is supposed to have been a Greek.

Hy-ģi'nus or **Higinus,** (CAIUS JULIUS,) a Romaı. grammarian, born in Spain or Alexandria. Originally a slave, he was set free by Augustus Cæsar, who gave him charge of the Palatine Library. He wrote a "Commentary on Virgil," and other esteemed works, which are lost. Other works bearing his name are extant, viz., "Mythological Fables," and "Poeticon Astronomicon," but are supposed to have been written by a Hyginus who lived at a later date.

See BUNTE, "Dissertatio de C. J. Hygini Vita et Scriptis," 1846.

Hylander, hü'lȧn'dẹr, (ANDERS,) a Swedish Orientalist, born at Tunhem in 1750; died in 1830.

Hylaret, he'lȧ'rả', (MAURICE,) a French monk and preacher, born at Angoulême in 1539, was a partisan of the League. Died in 1591.

See JEAN DU DOUET, "Vie de Hylaret."

Hỹ'lạs, [Gr. Ὕλας,] a favourite of Hercules, whom he accompanied in the Argonautic expedition. The Naiads, enamoured with his beauty, drew him into the water, so that he was lost to Hercules forever.

Hyll, hil, (?) (ALBAN,) an English physician, who practised in London with a high reputation. He wrote a "Commentary on Galen." Died in 1559.

Hỹl'lus, [Gr. Ὕλλος,] a son of Hercules and Dejanira, was persecuted by Eurystheus, and after the death of his father was the leader of the Heracli'dæ. Aided by the Athenians, he invaded Peloponnesus, and defeated Eurystheus, whom he killed with his own hand.

Hȳ'men or **Hymenæus,** him-e-nee'us, [Gr. 'Υμήν or 'Υμέναιος; Fr. HYMEN, e'mĕn', or HYMÉNÉE, e'mă'nà',] the god of marriage of the Greeks and Romans, was represented as a handsome youth, crowned with flowers, and holding a nuptial torch in his hand. According to one tradition, he was a son of Apollo and one of the Muses. Another account makes him the son of Bacchus and Venus.

Hymir, hī'mjr, written also **Eymer,** [supposed to be derived from *humr,* the "sea,"] the name of a great giant mentioned in the Norse mythology as the owner of a huge kettle, a mile deep, which Thor carried off, having first placed it over his head, so that he was entirely hidden by it. It was the same giant with whom Thor went a fishing and caught the World-serpent.

See THORPE, "Northern Mythology," vol. i.; MALLET, "Northern Antiquities," vol. ii. Fable XXVII

Hym'nĭ-a, [Gr. 'Υμνία; Fr. HYMNIE, èm'ne',] a surname of Diana, under which she was worshipped in Arcadia.

Hymnie. See HYMNIA.

Hynd'ford, (JOHN CARMICHAEL,) EARL OF, a Scottish diplomatist, born in 1701. In 1741 he was employed with credit as ambassador to the Prussian court, and in 1744 was sent in the same capacity to Russia. After successful efforts to terminate the war of the Austrian succession by a treaty of peace, he acted as envoy to Vienna in 1752. In 1764 he was appointed lord vice-admiral of Scotland. He died in 1767.

Hypatia, hī-pā'she-a, [Gr. 'Υπατία; Fr. HYPATIE, e'pă'te',] a celebrated female philosopher and mathematician, born at Alexandria in the latter part of the fourth century. She was the daughter of Theon, and displayed even greater talents than this famous mathematician in the study of philosophy and the sciences. She pursued her studies with great assiduity, often studying late in the night. After having improved herself by travelling and attending lectures at Athens of the most distinguished teachers of philosophy, she returned to Alexandria, where she was invited by the magistrates of the city to teach philosophy. She favoured the Neo-Platonic philosophy. She had many celebrated disciples, some of whom embraced Christianity and cherished through life feelings of friendship for her, although she continued to worship the heathen deities of Greece. She was noted for her virtue, her beauty, her simplicity of dress, her accomplishments, and her strength of mind. Orestes, the prefect of Alexandria, admired her wisdom, and often availed himself of her counsels. Cyril, the Christian patriarch, and his fanatical monks, appear to have regarded Hypatia as the principal supporter of the old religion; and at last their frenzy reached such a point that they tore her from her chariot as she was going to her school, and murdered her. This occurred in March, 415 A.D. The works of Hypatia were destroyed when the Mohammedans burned the library of Alexandria. Among these were a "Commentary on Diophantus," an "Astronomical Canon," and a "Commentary on the Conics of Apollonius of Perga." The titles of all her other works are lost.

See TILLEMONT, "Mémoires;" WERNSDORF, "Quatre Dissertations sur Hypatie;" CHARLES KINGSLEY's historical romance entitled "Hypatia."

Hypatie. See HYPATIA.

Hy-per'bo-lus, ['Υπέρβολος,] an Athenian demagogue, born about 450 B.C., was a leader of the democratic party after the death of Cleon. He was ostracised by a coalition of Nicias and Alcibiades in 415. Died about 410 B.C.

Hypéride. See HYPERIDES.

Hȳ-per-ĭ'dēs, [Gr. 'Υπερείδης or 'Υπερίδης; Fr. HYPÉRIDE, e'pă'rèd',] a famous Athenian orator, was the son of Glaucippus, and a pupil of Plato. He was identified with the party that opposed Philip of Macedon. After the battle of Chærone'a, (338 B.C.,) he proposed to recall the exiles, to liberate the slaves, and to take other vigorous measures, which were adopted, and procured peace on favourable terms. Having refused to touch the gold with which Harpalus corrupted other

orators of Athens, he was chosen to conduct the prosecution against Demosthenes for his share in that transaction. Hyperides was put to death by Antipater in 322. Cicero ranks him next to Demosthenes; and other ancient critics agree that his eloquence was of the highest order. He is the only one of the Ten Orators of Athens whose orations have all been lost.

See PLUTARCH, "Vitæ Decem Oratorum;" GROTE, "History of Greece;" CICERO, "Brutus," "De Oratore," and "Orator;" KIESSLING, "De Hyperide Oratore Attico," 1737; QUINTILIAN, book xii.; THIRLWALL, "History of Greece."

Hȳ-per-ĭ'on, (or hī-pee're-on,) [Gr. 'Υπερίων,] in Greek mythology, the name of a Titan, a son of Uranus and Ge, (or Terra,) and the father of Aurora and Helios. In Homer, Hyperion is a name of the sun.

Hy-pe'rĭ-us, [Dutch pron. he-pā're-ŭs,] (ANDRÉ GERARD,) an eminent Protestant theologian, born at Ypres in 1511. He was professor of theology at Marburg from 1542 to 1564. Among his works are "De Formandis Concionibus sacris," ("On the Composition of Sermons," 1555,) and "De Theologo seu de Ratione Studii theologici," ("On the Theologian, or on the Method of Theological Study," 1556.) Died in 1564.

See WILHELM WILLE, "Programma de A. Hyperio Hassorum Theologo," 1788; BAYLE, "Historical and Critical Dictionary."

Hy-perm-nes'tra, [Gr. 'Υπερμνήστρα; Fr. HYPERMNESTRE, e'pĕRm'nĕstR',] one of the DANAIDES, which see.

Hȳp'sĭ-clēs, ['Υψικλῆς,] a Greek mathematician of an uncertain epoch, is supposed to have lived at Alexandria in the second century. He wrote a treatise "On the Right Ascension of the Constellations of the Zodiac," which is extant. He is regarded by some as the author of the fourteenth and fifteenth books of the "Elements" of Euclid. According to Delambre, he lived about 146 B.C.

Hȳp-sip'ȳ-le, [Gr. 'Υψιπύλη,] a queen of Lemnos, who, according to tradition, saved the life of her father when the other women of the island killed their husbands and male relations. She was afterwards sold into slavery by the Lemnian women.

See LEMPRIERE's "Classical Dictionary."

Hyrcan. See HYRCANUS.

Hyr-cā'nus [Gr. 'Υρκανός; Fr. HYRCAN, èr'kôN'] I., (JOHN,) high-priest of the Jews, was the son of Simon Maccabeus, whom he succeeded in 135 B.C. After the death of Antiochus Sidetes, 130 B.C., he conquered the Idumeans and destroyed the city of Samaria. Though educated as a Pharisee, in the latter part of his life he favoured their rivals the Sadducees. He died in the year 103, leaving his office to his son Aristobu'lus.

See JOSEPHUS, "History of the Jews;" Apocryphal Book of Maccabees.

Hyrcanus II., high-priest of the Jews, succeeded his father, Alexander Jannæus, in 76 B.C. His brother Aristobu'lus having usurped the regal power, Hyrcanus, who was a weak prince, appealed to the Roman Pompey, who restored him to the throne and priesthood. Antigonus, son of Aristobulus, with the aid of the Parthians, deposed Hyrcanus about 38 B.C., and was soon after supplanted by Herod, who married Mariamne, the granddaughter of Hyrcanus, and put the latter to death, 30 B.C.

See JOSEPHUS, "History of the Jews."

Hyrtl, hĕR't'l, (JOSEPH,) an able anatomist, born at Eisenstadt, Hungary, in 1811. He became professor of anatomy in Vienna in 1845. He published, besides other works, a "Text-Book of Human Anatomy," ("Lehrbuch der Anatomie des Menschen," 2 vols., 1847,) which has been adopted by the German universities as a standard.

Hystaspe. See HYSTASPES.

Hys-tas'pēs, [Gr. 'Υστάσπης; Fr. HYSTASPE, ès'tăsp'; Persian, GUSHTÂSP,] a satrap of Persia, and the father of Darius I., lived about 550 B.C. He is said to have been the first who introduced into Persia the learning of the Indian Brahmans. According to one account, he was the chief of the Magians, which accords with the Persian tradition that Gushtâsp patronized the religion of Zoroaster. (See GUSHTÂSP.)

Hywell. See HOWELL THE GOOD.

ā, ē, ī, ō, ū, ȳ, *long;* à, ê, ò, *same, less prolonged;* ă, ĕ, ĭ, ŏ, ŭ, ȳ, *short;* a, e, i, o, *obscure;* fär, fâll, fât; mĕt; nŏt; gŏŏd; mōŏn;